Who's Who in the South and Southwest®

Who's Who in the South and Southwest®

2015

41st Edition

Including Alabama, Arkansas, Florida, Georgia, Kentucky, Louisiana, Mississippi, North Carolina, Oklahoma, South Carolina, Tennessee, Texas, Virginia, West Virginia, Puerto Rico, and the Virgin Islands

MARQUIS Who'sWho®

430 Mountain Avenue, Suite 400
New Providence, NJ 07974 U.S.A.
www.marquiswhoswho.com

Who'sWho in the South and Southwest®
Marquis Who's Who

Published by Marquis Who's Who LLC.

For information, contact: Marquis Who's Who
430 Mountain Avenue, Suite 400
New Providence, New Jersey 07974
1-800-473-7020; www.marquiswhoswho.com

WHO'S WHO IN THE SOUTH AND SOUTHWEST® is a registered trademark of Marquis Who's Who® LLC, used under license.
Library of Congress Catalog Card Number 50-58231
International Standard Book Number 978-0-8379-0846-5
International Standard Serial Number 0083-9809

Table of Contents

Preface

Marquis Who's Who is proud to present the 2015 Edition of *Who's Who in the South and Southwest,* our 41st compilation of biographical information on men and women of distinction whose influence is concentrated in the southern and southwestern sectors of North America, but may also be felt nationally and internationally.

This volume contains more than 17,900 biographies of people working in Alabama, Arkansas, Florida, Georgia, Kentucky, Louisiana, Mississippi, North Carolina, Oklahoma, South Carolina, Tennessee, Texas, Virginia, West Virginia, Puerto Rico, and the Virgin Islands. Some individuals listed are not residents of this region; however, the professional activities of these listees have been widely influential in the South and Southwest.

The individuals profiled in this volume represent virtually every important field of endeavor. Included are executives and officials in government, business, education, religion, broadcasting/media, entertainment, law, civic activities, and many other fields. Also included are leaders in the fields of science, healthcare, engineering, and notable people involved in the arts and cultural affairs.

Factors such as position, noteworthy accomplishments, visibility, and prominence in a field are all taken into account in making selections for the book. Final decisions concerning inclusion or exclusion are made following extensive discussion, evaluation, and deliberation.

Biographical information is gathered in a variety of manners. In most cases, we invite our biographees to submit their biographical details. In many cases, though, the information is collected independently by our editorial staff who use a wide assortment of tools to gather complete, accurate, and up-to-date information. Sketches researched by Marquis Who's Who will be followed by an asterisk (*).

While the Marquis Who's Who editors exercise the utmost care in preparing each biographical sketch for publication, in a publication involving so many profiles, occasional errors may appear. Users of this publication are urged to notify the publisher of any issues so that adjustments can be made.

All of the profiles featured in *Who's Who in the South and Southwest* are available on www.marquiswhoswho.com through a subscription. At the present time, subscribers to *Marquis Biographies Online* have access to all of the names included in all of the Marquis Who's Who publications, as well as many new biographies that will appear in upcoming publications.

We sincerely hope that this volume will be an indispensable reference tool for you. We are always looking for ways to better serve you and welcome your ideas for improvements. In addition, we continue to welcome your Marquis Who's Who nominations. *Who's Who in the South and Southwest* and all Marquis Who's Who publications pay tribute to those individuals who make significant contributions to our society. It is our honor and privilege to present their profiles to you.

Key to Information

[1] STEELE, FLETCHER DAVID, [2] mechanical engineer; [3] b. Normal, Ill., Jan. 20, 1960; [4] s. Thomas William and Susan (Shobe) S.; [5] m. Julie Ann Walsh, Sept. 8, 1985; [6] children: Elizabeth Carter, Michael Thomas. [7] BSME, Purdue U., 1981; MS, U. Ill., 1984. [8] Registered profl. engr., Fla. [9] Asst. engr. Kelly, Kitching, Berendes & Brault, Engrs., Chgo., 1987-89, engr., 1989-95; sr. engr. Kelly, Kitching, Berendes & Brault, Internat., Miami, 1995-2000, mgr. fluids divsn. 2001-07, v.p. R & D, 2007-09, exec. v.p. 2010—. [10] Lectr. Drake U., 2005-07. [11] Contbr. articles to Jour. Biomech. Engring., Jour. Fluids Engring. [12] Asst. troop leader Des Moines coun. Boy Scouts Am., 2014—. [13] Lt. US Army, 1985-86. [14] Recipient Nat. Engring. award, 2005; Fulbright scholar, 2009. [15] Mem. ASME, NSPE, Fla. Mech. Engrs. Assn., Big Sand Lake Club. [16] Republican. [17] Roman Catholic. [18] Achievements include design of L16500 Workhorse rotor; patent for internal piston lock for hydraulic cylinders; research in linear regression analysis for large-lot engine data comparisons. [19] Avocations: cooking, running. [20] Home: 733 N Ottawa Rd Miami FL 33176 [21] Office: 1245 34th St Miami FL 33176*

KEY

[1]	Name
[2]	Occupation
[3]	Vital statistics
[4]	Parents
[5]	Marriage
[6]	Children
[7]	Education
[8]	Professional certifications
[9]	Career
[10]	Career-related
[11]	Writings and creative works
[12]	Civic and political activities
[13]	Military
[14]	Awards and fellowships
[15]	Professional and association memberships, clubs and lodges
[16]	Political affiliation
[17]	Religion
[18]	Achievements information
[19]	Avocations
[20]	Home address
[21]	Office address
[*]	Researched by Marquis Who's Who

Table of Abbreviations

The following is a list of some frequently used Marquis abbreviations:

A

A Associate (used with academic degrees)
AA Associate in Arts
AAAL American Academy of Arts and Letters
AAAS American Association for the Advancement of Science
AACD American Association for Counseling and Development
AACN American Association of Critical Care Nurses
AAHA American Academy of Health Administrators
AAHP American Association of Hospital Planners
AAHPERD American Alliance for Health, Physical Education, Recreation, and Dance
AAS Associate of Applied Science
AASL American Association of School Librarians
AASPA American Association of School Personnel Administrators
AAU Amateur Athletic Union
AAUP American Association of University Professors
AAUW American Association of University Women
AB Arts, Bachelor of
AB Alberta
ABA American Bar Association
AC Air Corps
acad. academy
acct. accountant
acctg. accounting
ACDA Arms Control and Disarmament Agency
ACHA American College of Hospital Administrators
ACLS Advanced Cardiac Life Support
ACLU American Civil Liberties Union
ACOG American College of Ob-Gyn
ACP American College of Physicians
ACS American College of Surgeons
ADA American Dental Association
adj. adjunct, adjutant
adm. admiral
adminstr. administrator
adminstrn. administration
adminstrv. administrative
ADN Associate's Degree in Nursing
ADP Automatic Data Processing
adv. advocate, advisory
advt. advertising
AE Agricultural Engineer
AEC Atomic Energy Commission
aero. aeronautical, aeronautic
aerodyn. aerodynamic

AFB Air Force Base
AFTRA American Federation of Television and Radio Artists
agr. agriculture
agrl. agricultural
agt. agent
AGVA American Guild of Variety Artists
agy. agency
A&I Agricultural and Industrial
AIA American Institute of Architects
AIAA American Institute of Aeronautics and Astronautics
AIChE American Institute of Chemical Engineers
AICPA American Institute of Certified Public Accountants
AID Agency for International Development
AIDS Acquired Immune Deficiency Syndrome
AIEE American Institute of Electrical Engineers
AIME American Institute of Mining, Metallurgy, and Petroleum Engineers
AK Alaska
AL Alabama
ALA American Library Association
Ala. Alabama
alt. alternate
Alta. Alberta
A&M Agricultural and Mechanical
AM Arts, Master of
Am. American, America
AMA American Medical Association
amb. ambassador
AME African Methodist Episcopal
Amtrak National Railroad Passenger Corporation
AMVETS American Veterans
ANA American Nurses Association
anat. anatomical
ANCC American Nurses Credentialing Center
ann. annual
anthrop. anthropological
AP Associated Press
APA American Psychological Association
APHA American Public Health Association
APO Army Post Office
apptd. appointed
Apr. April
apt. apartment
AR Arkansas
ARC American Red Cross
arch. architect
archeol. archeological
archtl. architectural
Ariz. Arizona
Ark. Arkansas
ArtsD Arts, Doctor of

arty. artillery
AS Associate in Science, American Samoa
ASCAP American Society of Composers, Authors and Publishers
ASCD Association for Supervision and Curriculum Development
ASCE American Society of Civil Engineers
ASME American Society of Mechanical Engineers
ASPA American Society for Public Administration
ASPCA American Society for the Prevention of Cruelty to Animals
assn. association
assoc. associate
asst. assistant
ASTD American Society for Training and Development
ASTM American Society for Testing and Materials
astron. astronomical
astrophys. astrophysical
ATLA Association of Trial Lawyers of America
ATSC Air Technical Service Command
atty. attorney
Aug. August
aux. auxiliary
Ave. Avenue
AVMA American Veterinary Medical Association
AZ Arizona

B

B Bachelor
b. born
BA Bachelor of Arts
BAgr Bachelor of Agriculture
Balt. Baltimore
Bapt. Baptist
BArch Bachelor of Architecture
BAS Bachelor of Agricultural Science
BBA Bachelor of Business Administration
BBB Better Business Bureau
BC British Columbia
BCE Bachelor of Civil Engineering
BChir Bachelor of Surgery
BCL Bachelor of Civil Law
BCS Bachelor of Commercial Science
BD Bachelor of Divinity
bd. board
BE Bachelor of Education

BEE Bachelor of Electrical Engineering
BFA Bachelor of Fine Arts
bibl. biblical
bibliog. bibliographical
biog. biographical
biol. biological
BJ Bachelor of Journalism
Bklyn. Brooklyn
BL Bachelor of Letters
bldg. building
BLS Bachelor of Library Science
Blvd. Boulevard
BMI Broadcast Music, Inc.
bn. battalion
bot. botanical
BPE Bachelor of Physical Education
BPhil Bachelor of Philosophy
br. branch
BRE Bachelor of Religious Education
brig. gen. brigadier general
Brit. British
Bros. Brothers
BS Bachelor of Science
BSA Bachelor of Agricultural Science
BSBA Bachelor of Science in Business Administration
BSChemE Bachelor of Science in Chemical Engineering
BSD Bachelor of Didactic Science
BSEE Bachelor of Science in Electrical Engineering
BSN Bachelor of Science in Nursing
BST Bachelor of Sacred Theology
BTh Bachelor of Theology
bull. bulletin
bur. bureau
bus. business
BWI British West Indies

C

CA California
CAD-CAM Computer Aided Design– Computer Aided Model
Calif. California
Can. Canada, Canadian
CAP Civil Air Patrol
capt. captain
cardiol. cardiological
cardiovasc. cardiovascular
Cath. Catholic
cav. cavalry
CBI China, Burma, India Theatre of Operations
CC Community College
CCC Commodity Credit Corporation
CCNY City College of New York
CCRN Critical Care Registered Nurse
CCU Cardiac Care Unit
CD Civil Defense
CE Corps of Engineers, Civil Engineer

CEN Certified Emergency Nurse
CENTO Central Treaty Organization
CEO chief executive officer
CERN European Organization of Nuclear Research
cert. certificate, certification, certified
CETA Comprehensive Employment Training Act
CFA Chartered Financial Analyst
CFL Canadian Football League
CFO chief financial officer
CFP Certified Financial Planner
ch. church
ChD Doctor of Chemistry
chem. chemical
ChemE Chemical Engineer
ChFC Chartered Financial Consultant
Chgo. Chicago
chirurg., der surgeon
chmn. chairman
chpt. chapter
CIA Central Intelligence Agency
Cin. Cincinnati
cir. circle, circuit
CLE Continuing Legal Education
Cleve. Cleveland
climatol. climatological
clin. clinical
clk. clerk
CLU Chartered Life Underwriter
CM Master in Surgery
CM Northern Mariana Islands
cmty. community
CO Colorado
Co. Company
COF Catholic Order of Foresters
C. of C. Chamber of Commerce
col. colonel
coll. college
Colo. Colorado
com. committee
comd. commanded
comdg. commanding
comdr. commander
comdt. commandant
comm. communications
commd. commissioned
comml. commercial
commn. commission
commr. commissioner
compt. comptroller
condr. conductor
conf. Conference
Congl. Congregational, Congressional
Conglist. Congregationalist
Conn. Connecticut
cons. consultant, consulting
consol. consolidated
constl. constitutional
constn. constitution
constrn. construction
contbd. contributed
contbg. contributing

contbn. contribution
contbr. contributor
contr. controller
Conv. Convention
COO chief operating officer
coop. cooperative
coord. coordinator
corp. corporation, corporate
corr. correspondent, corresponding, correspondence
coun. council
CPA Certified Public Accountant
CPCU Chartered Property and Casualty Underwriter
CPH Certificate of Public Health
cpl. corporal
CPR Cardio-Pulmonary Resuscitation
CS Christian Science
CSB Bachelor of Christian Science
CT Connecticut
ct. court
ctr. center
ctrl. central

D

D Doctor
d. daughter of
DAgr Doctor of Agriculture
DAR Daughters of the American Revolution
dau. daughter
DAV Disabled American Veterans
DC District of Columbia
DCL Doctor of Civil Law
DCS Doctor of Commercial Science
DD Doctor of Divinity
DDS Doctor of Dental Surgery
DE Delaware
Dec. December
dec. deceased
def. defense
Del. Delaware
del. delegate, delegation
Dem. Democrat, Democratic
DEng Doctor of Engineering
denom. denomination, denominational
dep. deputy
dept. department
dermatol. dermatological
desc. descendant
devel. development, developmental
DFA Doctor of Fine Arts
DHL Doctor of Hebrew Literature
dir. director
dist. district
distbg. distributing
distbn. distribution
distbr. distributor
disting. distinguished
div. division, divinity, divorce
divsn. division
DLitt Doctor of Literature
DMD Doctor of Dental Medicine

DMS Doctor of Medical Science
DO Doctor of Osteopathy
docs. documents
DON Director of Nursing
DPH Diploma in Public Health
DPhil, Doctor of Philosophy
DR Daughters of the Revolution
Dr. Drive, Doctor
DRE Doctor of Religious Education
DrPH Doctor of Public Health
DSc Doctor of Science
DSChemE Doctor of Science in Chemical Engineering
DSM Distinguished Service Medal
DST Doctor of Sacred Theology
DTM Doctor of Tropical Medicine
DVM Doctor of Veterinary Medicine
DVS Doctor of Veterinary Surgery

E

E East
ea. eastern
Eccles. Ecclesiastical
ecol. ecological
econ. economic
ECOSOC UN Economic and Social Council
ED Doctor of Engineering
ed. educated
EdB Bachelor of Education
EdD Doctor of Education
edit. edition
editl. editorial
EdM Master of Education
edn. education
ednl. educational
EDP Electronic Data Processing
EdS Specialist in Education
EE Electrical Engineer
EEC European Economic Community
EEG Electroencephalogram
EEO Equal Employment Opportunity
EEOC Equal Employment Opportunity Commission
EKG electrocardiogram
elec. electrical
electrochem. electrochemical
electrophys. electrophysical
elem. elementary
EM Engineer of Mines
EMT Emergency Medical Technician
ency. encyclopedia
Eng. England
engr. engineer
engring. engineering
entomol. entomological
environ. environmental
EPA Environmental Protection Agency
epidemiol. epidemiological
Episc. Episcopalian
ERA Equal Rights Amendment
ERDA Energy Research and Development Administration

ESEA Elementary and Secondary Education Act
ESL English as Second Language
ESSA Environmental Science Services Administration
ethnol. ethnological
ETO European Theatre of Operations
EU European Union
Evang. Evangelical
exam. examination, examining
Exch. Exchange
exec. executive
exhbn. exhibition
expdn. expedition
expn. exposition
expt. experiment
exptl. experimental
Expy. Expressway
Ext. Extension

F

FAA Federal Aviation Administration
FAO UN Food and Agriculture Organization
FBA Federal Bar Association
FBI Federal Bureau of Investigation
FCA Farm Credit Administration
FCC Federal Communications Commission
FCDA Federal Civil Defense Administration
FDA Food and Drug Administration
FDIA Federal Deposit Insurance Administration
FDIC Federal Deposit Insurance Corporation
FEA Federal Energy Administration
Feb. February
fed. federal
fedn. federation
FERC Federal Energy Regulatory Commission
fgn. foreign
FHA Federal Housing Administration
fin. financial, finance
FL Florida
Fl. Floor
Fla. Florida
FMC Federal Maritime Commission
FNP Family Nurse Practitioner
FOA Foreign Operations Administration
found. foundation
FPC Federal Power Commission
FPO Fleet Post Office
frat. fraternity
FRS Federal Reserve System
FSA Federal Security Agency
Ft. Fort
FTC Federal Trade Commission
Fwy. Freeway

G

GA, Ga. Georgia
GAO General Accounting Office

gastroent. gastroenterological
GATT General Agreement on Tariffs and Trade
GE General Electric Company
gen. general
geneal. genealogical
geog. geographic, geographical
geol. geological
geophys. geophysical
geriat. geriatrics
gerontol. gerontological
GHQ General Headquarters
gov. governor
govt. government
govtl. governmental
GPO Government Printing Office
grad. graduate, graduated
GSA General Services Administration
Gt. Great
GU Guam
gynecol. gynecological

H

hdqs. headquarters
HEW Department of Health, Education and Welfare
HHD Doctor of Humanities
HHFA Housing and Home Finance Agency
HHS Department of Health and Human Services
HI Hawaii
hist. historical, historic
HM Master of Humanities
homeo. homeopathic
hon. honorary, honorable
House of Dels. House of Delegates
House of Reps. House of Representatives
hort. horticultural
hosp. hospital
HS High School
HUD Department of Housing and Urban Development
Hwy. Highway
hydrog. hydrographic

I

IA Iowa
IAEA International Atomic Energy Agency
IBRD International Bank for Reconstruction and Development
ICA International Cooperation Administration
ICCE International Council for Computers in Education
ICU Intensive Care Unit
ID Idaho
IEEE Institute of Electrical and Electronics Engineers
IFC International Finance Corporation

IL, Ill. Illinois
illus. illustrated
ILO International Labor Organization
IMF International Monetary Fund
IN Indiana
Inc. Incorporated
Ind. Indiana
ind. independent
Indpls. Indianapolis
indsl. industrial
inf. infantry
info. information
ins. insurance
insp. inspector
inst. institute
instl. institutional
instn. institution
instr. instructor
instrn. instruction
instrnl. instructional
internat. international
intro. introduction
IRE Institute of Radio Engineers
IRS Internal Revenue Service

J

JAG Judge Advocate General
JAGC Judge Advocate General Corps
Jan. January
Jaycees Junior Chamber of Commerce
JB Jurum Baccalaureus
JCB Juris Canoni Baccalaureus
JCD Juris Canonici Doctor, Juris Civilis Doctor
JCL Juris Canonici Licentiatus
JD Juris Doctor
jg. junior grade
jour. journal
jr. junior
JSD Juris Scientiae Doctor
JUD Juris Utriusque Doctor
jud. judicial

K

Kans. Kansas
KC Knights of Columbus
KS Kansas
KY, Ky. Kentucky

L

LA, La. Louisiana
LA Los Angeles
lab. laboratory
L.Am. Latin America
lang. language
laryngol. laryngological
LB Labrador
LDS Latter Day Saints
lectr. lecturer
legis. legislation, legislative
LHD Doctor of Humane Letters

LI Long Island
libr. librarian, library
lic. licensed, license
lit. literature
litig. litigation
LittB Bachelor of Letters
LittD Doctor of Letters
LLB Bachelor of Laws
LLD Doctor of Laws
LLM Master of Laws
Ln. Lane
LPGA Ladies Professional Golf Association
LPN Licensed Practical Nurse
lt. lieutenant
Ltd. Limited
Luth. Lutheran
LWV League of Women Voters

M

M Master
m. married
MA Master of Arts
MA Massachusetts
MADD Mothers Against Drunk Driving
mag. magazine
MAgr Master of Agriculture
maj. major
Man. Manitoba
Mar. March
MArch Master in Architecture
Mass. Massachusetts
math. mathematics, mathematical
MB Bachelor of Medicine, Manitoba
MBA Master of Business Administration
MC Medical Corps
MCE Master of Civil Engineering
mcht. merchant
mcpl. municipal
MCS Master of Commercial Science
MD Doctor of Medicine
MD, Md. Maryland
MDiv Master of Divinity
MDip Master in Diplomacy
mdse. merchandise
MDV Doctor of Veterinary Medicine
ME Mechanical Engineer
ME Maine
M.E.Ch. Methodist Episcopal Church
mech. mechanical
MEd. Master of Education
med. medical
MEE Master of Electrical Engineering
mem. member
meml. memorial
merc. mercantile
met. metropolitan
metall. metallurgical
MetE Metallurgical Engineer

meteorol. meteorological
Meth. Methodist
Mex. Mexico
MF Master of Forestry
MFA Master of Fine Arts
mfg. manufacturing
mfr. manufacturer
mgmt. management
mgr. manager
MHA Master of Hospital Administration
MI Military Intelligence, Michigan
Mich. Michigan
micros. microscopic
mid. middle
mil. military
Milw. Milwaukee
Min. Minister
mineral. mineralogical
Minn. Minnesota
MIS Management Information Systems
Miss. Mississippi
MIT Massachusetts Institute of Technology
mktg. marketing
ML Master of Laws
MLA Modern Language Association
MLitt Master of Literature, Master of Letters
MLS Master of Library Science
MME Master of Mechanical Engineering
MN Minnesota
mng. managing
MO, Mo. Missouri
moblzn. mobilization
Mont. Montana
MP Member of Parliament
MPA Master of Public Administration
MPE Master of Physical Education
MPH Master of Public Health
MPhil Master of Philosophy
MPL Master of Patent Law
Mpls. Minneapolis
MRE Master of Religious Education
MRI Magnetic Resonance Imaging
MS Master of Science
MS, Ms. Mississippi
MSc Master of Science
MSChemE Master of Science in Chemical Engineering
MSEE Master of Science in Electrical Engineering
MSF Master of Science of Forestry
MSN Master of Science in Nursing
MST Master of Sacred Theology
MSW Master of Social Work
MT Montana
Mt. Mount
mus. museum, musical
MusB Bachelor of Music
MusD Doctor of Music
MusM Master of Music

mut. mutual
MVP Most Valuable Player
mycol. mycological

N

N. North
NAACOG Nurses Association of the American College of Obstetricians and Gynecologists
NAACP National Association for the Advancement of Colored People
NACA National Advisory Committee for Aeronautics
NACDL National Association of Criminal Defense Lawyers
NACU National Association of Colleges and Universities
NAD National Academy of Design
NAE National Academy of Engineering, National Association of Educators
NAESP National Association of Elementary School Principals
NAFE National Association of Female Executives
N.Am. North America
NAM National Association of Manufacturers
NAMH National Association for Mental Health
NAPA National Association of Performing Artists
NARAS National Academy of Recording Arts and Sciences
NAREB National Association of Real Estate Boards
NARS National Archives and Record Service
NAS National Academy of Sciences
NASA National Aeronautics and Space Administration
NASP National Association of School Psychologists
NASW National Association of Social Workers
nat. national
NATAS National Academy of Television Arts and Sciences
NATO North Atlantic Treaty Organization
NBA National Basketball Association
NC North Carolina
NCAA National College Athletic Association
NCCJ National Conference of Christians and Jews
ND North Dakota
NDEA National Defense Education Act
NE Nebraska
NE Northeast
NEA National Education Association
Nebr. Nebraska

NEH National Endowment for Humanities
neurol. neurological
Nev. Nevada
NF Newfoundland
NFL National Football League
Nfld. Newfoundland
NG National Guard
NH New Hampshire
NHL National Hockey League
NIH National Institutes of Health
NIMH National Institute of Mental Health
NJ New Jersey
NLRB National Labor Relations Board
NM, N.Mex. New Mexico
No. Northern
NOAA National Oceanographic and Atmospheric Administration
NORAD North America Air Defense
Nov. November
NOW National Organization for Women
nr. near
NRA National Rifle Association
NRC National Research Council
NS Nova Scotia
NSC National Security Council
NSF National Science Foundation
NSTA National Science Teachers Association
NSW New South Wales
nuc. nuclear
numis. numismatic
NV Nevada
NW Northwest
NWT Northwest Territories
NY New York
NYC New York City
NYU New York University
NZ New Zealand

O

ob-gyn obstetrics-gynecology
obs. observatory
obstet. obstetrical
occupl. occupational
oceanog. oceanographic
Oct. October
OD Doctor of Optometry
OECD Organization for Economic Cooperation and Development
OEEC Organization of European Economic Cooperation
OEO Office of Economic Opportunity
ofcl. official
OH Ohio
OK, Okla. Oklahoma
ON, Ont. Ontario
oper. operating
ophthal. ophthalmological
ops. operations

OR Oregon
orch. orchestra
Oreg. Oregon
orgn. organization
orgnl. organizational
ornithol. ornithological
orthop. orthopedic
OSHA Occupational Safety and Health Administration
OSRD Office of Scientific Research and Development
OSS Office of Strategic Services
osteo. osteopathic
otol. otological
otolaryn. otolaryngological

P

PA, Pa. Pennsylvania
paleontol. paleontological
path. pathological
pediat. pediatrics
PEI Prince Edward Island
PEN Poets, Playwrights, Editors, Essayists and Novelists
penol. penological
pers. personnel
PGA Professional Golfers' Association of America
PHA Public Housing Administration
pharm. pharmaceutical
PharmD Doctor of Pharmacy
PharmM Master of Pharmacy
PhB Bachelor of Philosophy
PhD Doctor of Philosophy
PhDChemE Doctor of Science in Chemical Engineering
PhM Master of Philosophy
Phila. Philadelphia
philharm. philharmonic
philol. philological
philos. philosophical
photog. photographic
phys. physical
physiol. physiological
Pitts. Pittsburgh
Pk. Park
Pky. Parkway
Pl. Place
Plz. Plaza
PO Post Office
polit. political
poly. polytechnic, polytechnical
PQ Province of Quebec
PR Puerto Rico
prep. preparatory
pres. president
Presbyn. Presbyterian
presdl. presidential
prin. principal
procs. proceedings
prod. produced
prodn. production

prodr. producer
prof. professor
profl. professional
prog. progressive
propr. proprietor
pros. prosecuting
pro tem. pro tempore
psychiat. psychiatric
psychol. psychological
PTA Parent-Teachers Association
ptnr. partner
PTO Pacific Theatre of Operations,
Parent Teacher Organization
pub. publisher, publishing, published,
public
publ. publication
pvt. private

Q

quar. quarterly
qm. quartermaster
Que. Quebec

R

radiol. radiological
RAF Royal Air Force
RCA Radio Corporation of America
RCAF Royal Canadian Air Force
Rd. Road
R&D Research & Development
REA Rural Electrification Administration
rec. recording
ref. reformed
regt. regiment
regtl. regimental
rehab. rehabilitation
rels. relations
Rep. Republican
rep. representative
Res. Reserve
ret. retired
Rev. Reverend
rev. review, revised
RFC Reconstruction Finance Corporation
RI Rhode Island
Rlwy. Railway
Rm. Room
RN Registered Nurse
roentgenol. roentgenological
ROTC Reserve Officers Training Corps
RR rural route, railroad
rsch. research
rschr. researcher
Rt. Route

S

S. South
s. son of
SAC Strategic Air Command
SAG Screen Actors Guild

S.Am. South America
san. sanitary
SAR Sons of the American Revolution
Sask. Saskatchewan
savs. savings
S B Bachelor of Science
SBA Small Business Administration
SC South Carolina
ScB Bachelor of Science
SCD Doctor of Commercial Science
ScD Doctor of Science
sch. school
sci. science, scientific
SCV Sons of Confederate Veterans
S D South Dakota
SE Southeast
SEC Securities and Exchange Commission
sec. secretary
sect. section
seismol. seismological
sem. seminary
Sept. September
s.g. senior grade
sgt. sergeant
SI Staten Island
SJ Society of Jesus
SJD Scientiae Juridicae Doctor
SK Saskatchewan
S M Master of Science
SNP Society of Nursing Professionals
So. Southern
soc. society
sociol. sociological
spkr. speaker
spl. special
splty. specialty
Sq. Square
SR Sons of the Revolution
sr. senior
S S Steamship
St. Saint, Street
sta. station
stats. statistics
statis. statistical
STB Bachelor of Sacred Theology
stblzn. stabilization
STD Doctor of Sacred Theology
std. standard
Ste. Suite
subs. subsidiary
SUNY State University of New York
supr. supervisor
supt. superintendent
surg. surgical
svc. service
SW Southwest
sys. system

T

Tb. tuberculosis
tchg. teaching

tchr. teacher
tech. technical, technology
technol. technological
tel. telephone
telecom. telecommunications
temp. temporary
Tenn. Tennessee
TESOL Teachers of English to Speakers
of Other Languages
Tex. Texas
ThD Doctor of Theology
theol. theological
ThM Master of Theology
TN Tennessee
tng. training
topog. topographical
trans. transaction, transferred
transl. translation, translated
transp. transportation
treas. treasurer
TV television
twp. township
TX Texas
typog. typographical

U

U. University
UAW United Auto Workers
UCLA University of California at Los
Angeles
UK United Kingdom
UN United Nations
UNESCO United Nations Educational,
Scientific and Cultural Organization
UNICEF United Nations International
Children's Emergency Fund
univ. university
UNRRA United Nations Relief and
Rehabilitation Administration
UPI United Press International
urol. urological
US, USA United States of America
USAAF United States Army Air Force
USAF United States Air Force
USAFR United States Air Force Reserve
USAR United States Army Reserve
USCG United States Coast Guard
USCGR United States Coast Guard
Reserve
USES United States Employment
Service
USIA United States Information Agency
USMC United States Marine Corps
USMCR United States Marine Corps
Reserve
USN United States Navy
USNG United States National Guard
USNR United States Naval Reserve
USO United Service Organizations
USPHS United States Public Health
Service
USS United States Ship

USSR Union of the Soviet Socialist
Republics
USTA United States Tennis Association
UT Utah

V

VA Veterans Administration
VA, Va. Virginia
vet. veteran, veterinary
VFW Veterans of Foreign Wars
VI Virgin Islands
vis. visiting
VISTA Volunteers in Service to
America
vocat. vocational
vol. volunteer, volume
v.p. vice president

vs. versus
VT, Vt. Vermont

W

W West
WA, Wash. Washington (state)
WAC Women's Army Corps
WAVES Women's Reserve, US Naval
Reserve
WCTU Women's Christian
Temperance Union
we. western
WHO World Health Organization
WI Wisconsin, West Indies
Wis. Wisconsin
WV, W.Va. West Virginia
WY, Wyo. Wyoming

X, Y, Z

YK Yukon Territory
YMCA Young Men's Christian
Association
YMHA Young Men's Hebrew
Association
YM & YWHA Young Men's and Young
Women's Hebrew Association
yr. year
YT Yukon Territory
YWCA Young Women's Christian
Association

zool. zoological

Alphabetical Practices

Names are arranged alphabetically according to the surnames, and under identical surnames according to the first given name. If both surname and first given name are identical, names are arranged alphabetically according to the second given name.

Surnames beginning with De, Des, Du, however capitalized or spaced, are recorded with the prefix preceding the surname and arranged alphabetically under the letter D.

Surnames beginning with Mac and Mc are arranged alphabetically under M.

Surnames beginning with Saint or St. appear after names that begin Sains, and are arranged according to the second part of the name, e.g., St. Clair before Saint Dennis.

Surnames beginning with Van, Von, or von are arranged alphabetically under the letter V.

Compound surnames are arranged according to the first member of the compound.

Many hyphenated Arabic names begin Al-, El-, or al-. These names are alphabetized according to each biographee's designation of last name. Thus Al-Bahar, Neta may be listed either under Al- or under Bahar, depending on the preference of the listee.

Also, Arabic names have a variety of possible spellings when transposed to English. Spelling of these names is always based on the practice of the biographee. Some biographees use a Western form of word order, while others prefer the Arabic word sequence.

Similarly, Asian names may have no comma between family and given names, but some biographees have chosen to add the comma. In each case, punctuation follows the preference of the biographee.

Parentheses used in connection with a name indicate which part of the full name is usually omitted in common usage. Hence, Chambers, E(lizabeth) Anne indicates that the first name, Elizabeth, is generally recorded as an initial. In such a case, the parentheses are ignored in alphabetizing and the name would be arranged as Chambers, Elizabeth Anne.

However, if the entire first name appears in parentheses, for example, Chambers, (Elizabeth) Anne, the first name is not commonly used, and the alphabetizing is therefore arranged as though the name were Chambers, Anne.

If the entire middle name is in parentheses, it is still used in alphabetical sorting. Hence, Belamy, Katherine (Lucille) would sort as Belamy, Katherine Lucille. The same occurs if the entire last name is in parentheses, e.g., (Brandenberg), Howard Keith would sort as Brandenberg, Howard Keith.

For visual clarification:

Smith, H(enry) George: Sorts as Smith, Henry George
Smith, (Henry) George: Sorts as Smith, George
Smith, Henry (George): Sorts as Smith, Henry George
(Smith), Henry George: Sorts as Smith, Henry George

Who'sWho in the South and Southwest®

AABERG, THOMAS MARSHALL, SR., academic administrator; b. St. Paul, Sept. 5, 1936; m. Judith S. Young, June 17, 1961; children: Thomas M. Jr., Leigh, Sarah. BA, Dartmouth Coll., 1958, MS, 1959; MD, Harvard U., 1961; MSPH in Preventive Medicine, U. Okla., 1967. Diplomate Am. Bd. Ophthalmology. Asst. prof. ophthalmology Med. Coll. Wis., Milw., 1969-71, assoc. prof. ophthalmology, 1971-76, prof. ophthalmology, 1976-88; chmn. Emory U., Dept. Ophthalmology Sch. Medicine, Atlanta, 1988—2008, emeritus chmn., 2008—. Surgeon USPHS, 1966-68. Office: Emory Eye Ctr 2391 Parrots Pointe Rd Greensboro GA 30642 Business E-Mail: ophttma@emory.edu.

AAHOLM, SHERRY A., delivery service executive; Attended, U. Wis., Green Bay. Various info. tech. & transp. positions Schneider Nat./Schneider Logistics, Inc., Wis.; v.p., info. tech. GeoLogistics Americas Inc.; sr. v.p., express & freight solutions, sr. v.p., info. tech. FedEx Svcs., exec. v.p., info. tech.; v.p., CIO FedEx Logistics, 1999. Mem. Coun. of Logistics Mgmt.; bd. dirs. The Arc of the Mid-South. Named one of The Premier 100 IT Leaders, Computerworld, 2005. Office: FedEx Services 942 S Shady Grove Rd Memphis TN 38120 Office Phone: 901-818-7500. Office Fax: 901-395-2000. Business E-Mail: saaholm@fedex.com.

AARDSMA, DAVID A., waste management executive; Joined Waste Management, Inc., 1977, v.p. sales Western Group, v.p. sales, 2000—05, sr. v.p. sales and mktg. to chief sales & mktg. officer, 2005—. Office: Waste Mgmt Inc 1001 Fannin Ste 4000 Houston TX 77002 Office Phone: 713-512-6200.

AARON, HANK (HENRY LOUIS AARON), professional sports team executive, retired professional baseball player, entrepreneur; b. Mobile, Ala., Feb. 5, 1934; s. Herbert and Estella A. Aaron; m. Billye Suber Aaron, Nov. 1973; 1 child, Ceci; children: Gail, Hank, Lary, Gary(dec.). HHD (hon.), Princeton U., 2011. Former semi-pro baseball player; baseball player Milw. Braves, 1954—65, Atlanta Braves, 1966—75, Milw. Brewers, 1975—76; v.p. player devel. Atlanta Nat. League Baseball Club, Inc., 1976—89, sr. v.p., asst. to pres., 1989—; founder, chmn. 755 Restaurant Corp., Atlanta, 1995—; pres., CEO Hank Aaron Automotive Group, 1999—2007. Mem. Nat. League All-Star Team, 1955—74, American League All-Star Team, 1975; bd. dirs. Turner Broadcasting Sys., Inc., 1980—96, Retail Ventures, Inc., 2000—, Medallion Fin. Corp., 2004—. Author: (autobiography) I Had A Hammer: The Hank Aaron Story, 1991. Co-founder Hank Aaron Chasing the Dream Found.; organizer Hank Aaron Scholarship Fund; mem. bd. governors Boys & Girls Clubs America; bd. advisors Atlanta Falcons Football Club, Atlanta Tech. Inst. Recipient Nat. League Gold Glove award, 1958—60, Lou Gehrig Meml. award, 1970, Presdl. Citizens Medal, 2001, Presdl. Medal of Freedom, The White House, 2002; named Player of Yr., The Sporting News, 1956, 1963, The Nat. League's Most Valuable Player, 1957; named one of The 100 Greatest Baseball Players, The Sporting News, 1999; named to The Nat. Baseball Hall of Fame, 1982, Maj. League Baseball's All-Century Team, 1999. Achievements include leading the National League in: doubles, 1955, 1956, 1961, 1965; batting average, hits, 1956, 1959; runs, 1957, 1963, 1967; home runs, 1957, 1963, 1966, 1967; runs batted in, 1957, 1960, 1963, 1966; member of World Series championship winning Milwaukee Braves, 1957; holding Major League Baseball's all-time record for: total bases (6856); runs batted in (2297); extra base hits (1477); breaking Babe Ruth's career home run record hitting his 715th home run, April 8, 1974 (total career home runs: 755); held record for most career home runs until 2007. Office: 755 Restaurant Corp 5101 Buffington Rd Ste 34 Atlanta GA 30349-2922 Office Phone: 404-766-2727. Business E-Mail: haaron@retailventuresinc.com.

ABATE, VICTOR R. (VIC ABATE), manufacturing company executive; BS in Mech. Engring., Rensselaer Polytechnic Inst., MBA; M in Engring., Union Coll. Quality leader GE Power Sys., 1996—99, master black belt, 1996—99, fulfillment leader, turbine volume ramp (energy products), 1999, gen. mgr., steam turbine tech.; v.p., power generation tech. General Electric Energy, 2006—. Office: General Electric Co 4200 Wildwood Pkwy Atlanta GA 30339

ABAUNZA, DONALD RICHARD, lawyer; b. New Orleans, Oct. 25, 1945; s. Alfred E. and Virginia (White) A.; m. Carolyn Thompson; 1 child, Richard. BA, Vanderbilt U., 1966; JD, Tulane U., 1969. Bar: La. 1969, U.S. Dist. Ct. (ea. dist.) La. 1969, U.S. Dist. Ct. (we. dist.) La. 1980, U.S. Supreme Ct. 1986. Ptnr. Liskow & Lewis, New Orleans, 1977—, mng. ptnr., 1996—2003. Adj. faculty Tulane Sch. Law, 1981-89. Named one of Best Lawyers in Am., 2007. Fellow Am. Coll. Trial Lawyers; mem. La. Bar Assn. (Pres.'s award 1988). Office: Liskow & Lewis 1 Shell Sq 50th Fl 701 Poydras St New Orleans LA 70139-5099 Office Phone: 504-556-4110. Business E-Mail: drabaunza@liskow.com.

ABBITT, PATRICIA L., diagnostic radiologist, educator; MD, Tufts U., 1981. Diplomate Am. Bd. Radiology-diagnostic radiology, 1986. Resident diagnostic radiology Univ. Va. Med. Ctr., Charlottesville, 1983—86, fellow breast imaging, 1986—87; prof. radiology Coll. of Medicine Univ. of Fla.; hosp. affiliation includes Shands at the Univ. of Fla. Named one of the Top Doctor, US News, 2011. Office: Shands Healthcare Department of Radiology 1600 SW Archer Rd Gainesville FL 32610 Office Phone: 352-265-0291.

ABBOTT, GAY O., bank executive; BBA, Emory U., Atlanta, 1983. Comml. banking tng. assoc. SunTrust Banks, Inc., Atlanta, 1983, exec. v.p., retail banking line of bus. mgr. Ctrl. Group, corp. exec. v.p. comml. line of bus. Bd. trustees Agnes Scott Coll., 2006—. Office: SunTrust Banks Inc PO Box 4418 Atlanta GA 30302-4418 Office Phone: 404-588-7711. Office Fax: 404-827-6173.

ABBOTT, GREGORY W., state attorney general, former state supreme court justice; s. Calvin Roger and Doris Lacristia (Jacks) Abbott; m. Cecilia Therese Phalen, 1982; 1 child, Audrey. BBA in Fin., U. Tex., Austin, 1981; JD, Vanderbilt U. Law Sch., Nashville, 1984. Bar: Tex. 1985, US Dist. Ct. (southern dist.) Tex. 1985. Atty. Butler & Binion, Houston, 1984-92; trial judge 129th State Dist. Ct., Houston, 1992-96; justice Texas Supreme Ct., 1996—2001; atty. gen. State of Tex., 2002—. Mem. Gov.'s Com. Promote Adoption. Hon. state chmn. Big Brothers/Big Sisters Tex., 2004; bd. trustees Ctrl. Tex. Goodwill Industries; mem. adv. bd. Career & Recovery Resources Inc.; bd. dirs. Tex. Inst. Rehab. & Rsch. Found., Maywood Children & Family Services. Recipient American Jurisprudence award, 1983; named Outstanding Trial Judge, Tex. Assn. Civil Trial & Appellate Specialists, 1995, Jurist of Yr., Tex. Rev. Law & Politics, Appellate Judge of Yr., American Bd. Trial Advocates (Tex. chpt.); named an Outstanding Young Texan, Tex. Jaycees, 1995. Mem.: Tex. Assn. State Judges, Houston Young Lawyers Assn., Houston Bar Assn. (Outstanding Young Lawyer 1994), State Bar Tex. (Supreme Ct. liason com. on jud. ethics). Republican. Roman Catholic. Office: Office of the Attorney General PO Box 12548 Austin TX 78711-2548 Office Phone: 512-463-2100.*

ABBOTT, JAMES A., bank executive; b. Raleigh, NC, Oct. 27, 1939; s. Abbott. BA in Economics, U. NC, 1961; postgrad., Northwestern U., 1966. Br. mgr. Cameron-Brown Co., Greensboro and Charlotte, NC, 1964—70, adminstrv. v.p., 1970—74, residential div. head, sr. v.p. Raleigh, NC, 1974—80, pres., 1980; pres., CEO First Union Mortgage Corp., 1980—94; chmn., prin. American Security Mortgage Corp., 1999—. Bd. dirs. MGIC Investment Corp., 1989—. Bd. dirs. Children's Theatre, Charlotte, 1981; mem. exec. com. World Srs. Invitational Golf Tournament, Charlotte, 1984. Mem.: Mortgage Bankers of the Carolinas (pres. 1984—85, Young Mortgage Banker of Yr. 1979), Mortgage Bankers Am. (bd. govs. 1983—85). Presbyterian. Office: American Security Mortgage Corp 8600 Sam Furr Rd Huntersville NC 28078-6138 Office Phone: 704-237-1333. Business E-Mail: james_abbott@mgic.com.

ABDALIAN, SUE ELLEN (SUSAN ABDALIAN), internist, educator; MD, Tulane U., New Orleans, 1979. Diplomate Am. Bd. Internal Medicine, 1983, Am. Bd. Internal Medicine-adolescent medicine, 1994. Resident internal medicine Mayo Clinic, Rochester, 1980—82; fellow Univ. Minn. Hosp., Mpls., 1985—87; prof. medicine Tulane Univ.; physician Tulane Med. Ctr. Office: Tulane Medical Center 1415 Tulane Ave New Orleans LA 70112 Office Phone: 504-988-8000.

ABDEL-KHALIK, SAID IBRAHIM, nuclear and mechanical engineering educator; b. Alexandria, Egypt, Aug. 9, 1948; came to U.S., 1969; s. Ibrahim Saad and Esha Farag (Ahmad) A.-K.; m. Sharon Lora Duncan; 1 child, Faith Austen Khalik. BS summa cum laude, Alexandria U., 1967; MS in Mech. Engring., U. Wis.-Madison, 1971, PhD in Mech. Engring., 1973. Postdoctoral fellow in chem. engring. U. Wis., Madison, 1973-74, asst. prof. nuclear engring., 1976-78, assoc. prof., 1978-82, prof., 1982-87; Ga. Power disting. prof. nuclear engring. Ga. Inst. Tech., Atlanta, 1987-89, assoc. dir. sch. mech. engring., 1990-92, so. nuclear disting. prof., 1993—; instr. Alexandria U., 1967-69; sr. engr. Babcock & Wilcox, Lynchburg, Va., 1975. Guest rsch. scientist Nuclear Rsch. Ctr., Karlsruhe, Fed. Repub. Germany, 1979; vis. prof. EPFL, Inst. de Genie Atomique, Lausanne, Switzerland, 1982; cons. Kewaunee Nuclear Plant, Green Bay, Wis., 1983-93, So. Nuclear Vogtle, Hatch, & Farley Nuclear Plants, 1999-, numerous rsch. orgns. & govtl. agys.; adv. com. reactor safeguards U.S. Nuc. Regulatory Commn., mem. 2006-12; Chmn. 2010-11; Adv. Coun., Inst. Nuclear Power Ops., 2013-. Contbr. articles to profl. jours. Fellow Am. Nuclear Soc., ASME; chair Fusion Energy Divsn. Am. Nuclear Soc. 2005; mem. Am. Soc. Engring. Edn. (Glenn Murphy award 1999), Profl. Reactor Operators Soc., Am. Inst. Physics, Assn. Egyptian-Am. Scholars, Sigma Xi, Phi Kappa Phi. Achievements include patents in field. Avocations: sailing, chess. Home: 3579 Midvale Cove Tucker GA 30084-3210 Office: Sch Mech Engring Ga Inst Tech Atlanta GA 30332-0405 Office Phone: 404-894-3719. Business E-Mail: said.abdelkhalik@me.gatech.edu, sa8@mail.gatech.edu.

ABDEL-MOTTALEB, MOHAMED, electrical engineer, educator; s. Said Elsayed and Enayat Abdelaal; m. Laila Ibrahim; children: Noha, Mostafa. PhD, U. Md., College Park, 1993. Project leader Philips Rsch., Briarcliff Manor, NY, 1993—2001; prof. U. Miami, Coral Gables, 2001—. Bd. dirs. Nur Ul Islam Acad., Cooper City, Fla. Grantee, NSF, 2003—07. Mem.: IEEE. Achievements include patents in field. Office: Univ Miami 1251 Memorial Dr Coral Gables FL 33146

ABDUL-SALAAM, ROBERTA, state legislator; b. Sept. 7, 1955; 4 children. Attended, City Coll. Chgo., Mercer Univ., Univ. Md. Paralegal Golden & Associates, 2001—04; mem. Dist. 74 Ga. House Reps., 2005—. Service Award from Mrs. Coretta Scott King, and a citation from former Secretary of State, George Schultz. Founder, president, Grassroots Connection, Inc. Democrat. Baptist. Office: Rm 612 Legis Off Bldg Atlanta GA 30334 Mailing: PO Box 960941 Riverdale GA 30274 Office Phone: 404-656-0325, 678-489-2047. Business E-Mail: roberta.abdul-salaam@house.ga.gov.

ABE, VALENTIN, entrepreneur; b. Ivory Coast, 1963; BA, Auburn U. Sch. Agrl., Ala., MS, 1991; Ph.D, Auburn U. Sch. Agrl., 1995. Dir., COO Haiti Fish Devel. Project, Social Enterprise Fund, Inc. Named one of The 100 Most Influential People in the World, TIME mag., 2010. Achievements include introducing fish farming within poor Haitian communities, powering his entire operation with solar energy and involving local fish farmers whose incomes he's multiplied two or three times or more, providing jobs and lean proteins for malnourished people. Mailing: Social Enterprise Fund 819 Spinnakers Reach Ponte Vedra Beach FL 32082

ABELL, KELLEY, healthcare company executive; Attended, Am. U., Washington, DC; B in Comm., U. Louisville, Ky. Joined ResCare, Inc., 1997, chief govt. rels. officer. Office: Res-Care Inc 9901 Linn Station Rd Louisville KY 40223 Office Phone: 502-394-2100. Office Fax: 502-394-2206. Business E-Mail: kabell@capitolsolutions.net.

ABENDSCHEIN, ROBERT D., energy executive, petroleum engineer; BS in Petroleum Engring., Tex. A&M U. Registered profl. engr., Tex. Joined Anadarko Petroleum Corp., 1984, various positions including onshore reservoir engring. mgr., onshore ops. mgr. and v.p., worldwide deepwater ops., v.p., exploration and production services, 2008—. Mem. Soc. of Petroleum Engrs. Co-recipient Engring. Project of the yr., 2008. Office: Anadarko Petroleum Corp 1201 Lake Robbins Dr The Woodlands TX 77380 Office Phone: 832-636-1000. Office Fax: 832-636-8220. Business E-Mail: robert.abendschein@anadarko.com.

ABERNATHY, CAMMY R., engineering professor, dean; m. Steve Pearton; 1 child, Mark. BS, MIT, 1980; MS, Stanford U., 1982, PhD in Materials Sci., 1985. Rsch. asst. Dept. Materials Sci. and Engring. Stanford U., Calif., 1981—85; mem. tech. staff Bell Labs., Murray Hill, NJ, 1985—93; prof. materials sci. Coll. Engring., U. Fla., Gainesville, 1993—, assoc. dean academic affairs, 2004—09, dean, 2009—. Fellow: Electrochemical Soc. Office: University of Florida College of Engineering 300 Weil Hall PO Box 116550 Gainesville FL 32611 Office Phone: 352-392-6000. E-mail: caber@mse.ufl.edu.

ABERNATHY, ROBERT E., health products executive; b. San Marcos, Tex., 1954; m. Laura Abernathy; 2 children. BS in Chemistry, U. Ala., 1976; MS, Inst. Paper Chemistry, 1978. Rsch. scientist Kimberly-Clark Corp., 1982, v.p., North Am. Diaper ops., 1992—94, mng. dir., Kimberly-Clark Australia Pty. Ltd., 1994—96, group pres., 1996—98, group pres., bus.-to-bus. segment, 1998—2004, group pres., developing and emerging markets, 2004—08, group pres., North Atlantic Consumer Products, 2008—. Bd. dirs. Lubrizol Corp., 2006—. Office: Kimberly Clark Corp 351 Phelps Dr Irving TX 75038 Office Phone: 972-281-1200. Office Fax: 972-281-1490.

ABERSON, LESLIE DONALD, lawyer; b. St. Louis, May 30, 1936; s. Hillard and Adele (Wenneker) A.; m. Regene Jo Lowenstein, Oct. 16, 1960; children: Karen, Angie, Leslie. BS, U. Ky., 1957, JD, 1960. Bar: Ky. 1960, U.S. Dist. Ct. (we. dist.) Ky. 1964, U.S. Tax Ct. 1968, U.S. Supreme Ct. 1975. Dir. Bank of Louisville. Bd. dirs. Ky. Athletic Hall of Fame, 1965—2003, NCCJ; past bd. dirs. Jewish Hosp. Louisville, Louisville Med. Rsch. Found.; past pres. B'rith Sholom Temple; bd. dirs., past v.p. Jewish Cmty. Fedn. Louisville; bd. dirs. Louisville Free Pub. Libr. Found. Recipient Louis Cole Young Leadership award. Mem.: Louisville Bar Assn., Ky. Bar Assn., U. Ky. Law Sch. Alumni Assn. (bd. dirs.). Home: 5431 Harbortown Cir Prospect KY 40059-9257 Office: Ste 102 5940 Timber Ridge Dr Prospect KY 40059

ABLARD, CHARLES DAVID, administrative judge; b. Enid, Okla., Oct. 25, 1930; s. Charles Ross and Mary M. (Pattie) Ablard; m. Doris Maria Perl, Nov. 14, 1959; children— Jennifer, Jonathan, Catherine BA, U. Okla., 1952, JD, 1954; LLM, George Washington U., 1959. Bar: DC. Jud. officer US Post Office Dept., Washington, 1958-60; ptnr. Ablard and Harrison, Washington, 1960-63; v.p., counsel Mag. Pubs. Assn., Washington, 1963-69; gen. counsel USIA, Washington, 1969-72; assoc. dep. atty. gen. Dept. Justice, Washington, 1972-74; assoc. dean Vt. Law Sch., South Royalton, 1974; gen. counsel Dept. Army, Washington, 1975-77; ptnr. Gage and Tucker, Washington, 1979-92, Faegre and Benson, Washington and Mpls., 1992-97, Perkins, Smith, Cohen & Crowe, Washington and Boston, 1997—2003; adminstrv. judge Office Hearings and Appeals US Dept. Def., Arlington, Va., 2003—09; counsel Pub. Diplomacy Coun., 2008—. Adj. prof. Cath. U., Washington, 1984; mem. Fgn. Svc. Grievance Bd., 1998-2003. Contbr. articles to profl. jours. Bd. dirs. Hist. Alexandria Found., Pub. Diplomacy Coun.; commr. Alexandria Hist. Restoration and Preservation Commn.; mem. coun. Adminstrv. Conf. US, Washington, 1970-73; mem. Bd. Internat. Broadcasting, Washington, 1980-84; bd. dirs. Radio Free Europe/Radio Liberty, Washington, 1983-84. Col. USAF, 1954-56, ret. Fellow Ctr. Internat. Studies, Downing Coll., Cambridge U., Eng., 1974; recipient Profl. Achievement award George Washington U., 1976, Disting. Civilian Svc. award Dept. Army, 1975, 76 Fellow Am. Bar Found. (life); mem. ABA (chmn. adminstrv. law sect. 1984-85), English Speaking Union US (bd. dirs.). Clubs: Cosmos (Washington); Army-Navy Country (Arlington, Va.); Small Point (Maine). Republican. Episcopalian. Home Phone: 703-751-8590.

ABNEY, DAVID P., delivery service executive; m. Sherry Abney; children: Valerie, Matt. BBA in Mktg., Delta State U. Various positions United Parcel Service, Inc. (UPS), Atlanta, 1974—95, mgr. SonicAir, 1995—2000, Fritz cos. integration mgr., 2001—02, sr. v.p., pres. Internat., 2003—07, pres. UPS Airlines, 2007—08, COO, 2007—. Bd. mem. Air Courier Conf. Am. Trustee UPS Found.; bd. mem. U.S. Japan Bus. Council, Southern Ctr. for Internat. Studies, Coalition Svc. Industries, Delta State Univ. Alumni Found. Office: UPS 55 Glenlake Pky NE Atlanta GA 30328

ABOU-KHALIL, BASSEL WILLIAM, neurologist, epileptologist; s. William and Wafa Abou-Khalil; m. Rima Khallouf, Aug. 6, 1988; children: May Wafa, Lena Noor. BS, Am. U. Beirut, Lebanon, 1974, MD, 1978. Cert. Am. bd. Clin. Neurophysiol. Inc., 1986, in neurology Am. Bd. Psychiatry and Neurology, 1986, in clin. neurophysiol. Am. Bd. Psychiatry and Neurology, 1992. Epilepsy monitoring unit dir. Vanderbilt U., Nashville, 1988—, epilepsy program dir., 1988—, asst. prof. neurology, 1988—95, assoc. prof. neurology, 1995—2001, prof. neurology, 2001—, clin. neurophysiol. and epilepsy tng. program dir., 1990—. Fellow: Am. Clin. Neurophysiol. Soc., Am. Acad. Neurology; mem.: So. Clin. Neurol. Soc., So. Epilepsy and EEG Soc. (pres. 2000—01), Am. Clin. Neurophysiol. Soc., Am. Epilepsy Soc., Am. Neurol. Assn.

ABRAHAM, EDWARD, dean, medical educator; b. Chgo., Apr. 17, 1952; s. Willard and Dale Abraham; m. Norma-May Isakow, Nov. 22, 1989; children: Claire, Erin. BA, Stanford U., 1974, MD, 1978. Diplomate Am. Bd. Internal Medicine, Critical Care. Asst. prof. UCLA Sch. Medicine, LA, 1981—87, assoc. prof., 1987—93, U. Colo. Health Sciences Ctr., Denver, 1993—95, prof. medicine, 1995—2000, Roger Sherman Mitchell prof. pulmonary and critical care medicine, 2000—06, head divsn. pulmonary scis. and critical care medicine, 2000—06, vice chair dept. medicine, 2002—06; prof., chair dept. medicine U. Ala., Birmingham, 2006—11, Spencer chair in med. sci. leadership, 2006—11; dean Wake Forest U. Sch. Medicine, Winston-Salem, NC, 2011—. Editor: Textbook of Critical Care Medicine; editor: Am. Jour. Respiratory Critical Care Medicine, 2004-09; sect. editor assoc. editor Jour. Immunology, 2007-; contbr. articles to profl. jours.; chpts. to books. Area program com. Am. Friends Svc. Com., Denver, 2004—06. Recipient Pres.'s citation, Soc. Critical Care Medicine, 1999, 2002, 2004, Young Investigator award, Soc. of Critical Care Medicine, 1985, Winthrop Breon Young Scholar award, 1986; named Best Doctors in America, 2001—. Fellow Am. Coll. Critical Care Medicine; mem. Soc. Critical Care Medicine (Young Investigator award 1985), Am. Thoracic Soc., Shock Soc., Am. Soc. Clin. Investigation, Assn. Am. Physicians. Avocations: jogging, gardening. Office: Wake Forest Bapt Med Ctr Medical Center Blvd Winston Salem NC 27157*

ABRAHAM, HENRY JULIAN, retired political science professor; b. Offenbach am Main, Germany, Aug. 25, 1921; s. Frederick and Louise Kullmann Abraham; m. Mildred Kosches; children: Philip F., Peter D. AB summa cum laude, Kenyon Coll., 1948, LHD (hon.), 1972; MA, Columbia U., 1949; PhD, U. Pa., 1952; LLD (hon.), U. Hartford, 1982, Knox Coll., 1982; LittD (hon.), St. Joseph's U., 1987; LLD (hon.), Old Dominion U., 1996. Faculty U. Pa., 1949-72, prof.

polit. sci., 1962-72; Doherty prof. govt. and fgn. affairs U. Va., 1972—78, James Hart prof., 1978-97, James Hart prof. emeritus, 1997—. Vis. prof. Swarthmore Coll., CCNY, Colo. U., Columbia U., Richmond Law Sch., Copenhagen U., U. Stockhholm, Aarhus U., Lund U., Goteborg U., U. Oslo, U. Helsinki, U. Uppsala, U. Amsterdam, U. London, univs. in India and Iran, 1978, univs. in Peru, Bolivia, Brazil, Paraguay, Argentina, 1979, univs. in Japan, China, Taiwan, The Philippines, New Zealand, and Australia, 1982, univs. in Republic of Korea, 1982, 1984. Author: Compulsory Voting, 1955, Government as Entrepreneur, 1956, Courts and Judges, 1959, Elements of Democratic Government, 1964, Essentials of National Government, 1971, Justices & Presidents, 1992, American Democracy, 1990, The Judiciary, 1997, The Judicial Process, 1997, Freedom and the Court, 2003, Justices, Presidents and Senators, 2008. Mem. com. on non-discrimintion Phila. Bd. Edn., 1962; mem. vis. com. on govt. Lehigh U., 1967-71; trustee fedn. Jewish Agys. Greater Phila., 1970-72, Kenyon Coll., 1987-93; mem. Va. Commn. on Bicentennial of Constn. of US, 1985-92, Va. Coun. on Human Rights, 1999-2002, sr. statesman, Va. Recipient award excellence undergrad. teaching U. Pa., 1959, 67, Kite and Key Tchg. award, 1967, award excellence undergrad. teaching U. Va., 1978, Thomas Jefferson award U. Va., 1983, Alumni Tchg. award, 1986, Disting. Svc. award Va. Social Sci. Assn., 1982, Disting. Prof. award U. Va. Alumni Assn., 1986, First Lifetime Achievement award, org. sec. on law & courts, Am. polit., sci. Assn., 1993, Americanism award Daughter Am. Revolution, 2007, others; NEH, 1975-76, 78, 80-81, NSF fellow, 1965, fellow Am. Philos. Soc., 1961-67, 79, Rockefeller Found. fellow, 1978, Earhart fellow, 1984, Bradley Found., 1989-97; scholarships U. South Australia, 2004-05. Mem. Fellows in Am. Studies (pres. 1966), Am. Polit. Sci. Assn. (v.p. 1980-82), Raven Soc., Am. Soc. for Legal History, So. Polit. Sci. Ass. (rec. sec. 1980-81), Soc. of Fellows, English-Speaking Union, Met. Opera Guild, Nat. Trust, Golden Key, Greencroft Club (v.p. 1985-87, Charlottesville, Va.), Z Club, Imp Club, Yale Club (NYC), Capitol Hill Club (Washington), Oliver Turner Soc., Phi Beta Kappa (vis. scholar 1970-71), Pi Sigma Alpha, Pi Gamma Mu, Omicron Delta Kappa. Home: 250 Pantops Mountain Rd Apt 5311 Charlottesville VA 22911 Home Phone: 434-924-2482.

ABRAHAM, MAGID M., Internet company executive; PhD in Ops. Rsch., MIT, MBA; holds an engring. degree, Ecole Polytechnique. Founder Paragren Technologies, Inc. (now part of Siebel Systems), CEO, 1995—99; with Information Resources, Inc., 1985—95, pres., CEO, 1993—94; pres., CEO, co-founder comScore Networks, Inc., Reston, Va., 1999—. Spkr. in field; vice chmn. Info. Resources, Inc., 1994—95; mem. bd. dirs. ComScore, Inc., 1999—, Milo.com, 2008—. Author: (several articles) Harvard Business Review and Marketing Science. Co-recipient Paul Green award, Am. Mktg. Assn., 1996, William F. O'Dell award, 2000. Office: Comscore 11950 Democracy Dr Reston VA 20190-5624 Office Phone: 203-438-2000. Office Fax: 203-438-2051. Business E-Mail: mabraham@comscore.com.

ABRAMS, ELLIOTT, foreign policy analyst, former federal official; b. NYC, Jan. 24, 1948; s. Joseph and Mildred (Kauder) Abrams; m. Rachel Decter, Mar. 9, 1980 (dec. June 7, 2013); children: Jacob, Sarah, Joseph. BA, Harvard U., 1969, JD, 1973; MS in Internat. Rels., London Sch. Economics, 1970. Atty. Breed, Abbott & Morgan, NYC, 1973—75; asst. counsel US Senate Permanent Subcommittee Investigations, Washington, 1975; spl. counsel to Senator Henry M. Jackson US Senate, 1975-76, spl. counsel to Senator Daniel P. Moynihan, 1977-78, chief of staff to Senator Daniel P. Moynihan, 1978-79; atty. Verner, Liipfert, Bernhard & McPherson, Washington, 1979—81; asst. sec. for internat. orgn. affairs US Dept. State, Washington, 1981, asst. sec. for human rights & humanitarian affairs, 1981-85, asst. sec. for Inter-American affairs, 1985-89; sr. fellow Hudson Inst., Washington, 1989—96; pres. Ethics & Pub. Policy Ctr., Washington, 1996-2001; spl. asst. to Pres., sr. dir. democracy, human rights, & internat ops. NSC, Washington, 2001—02, spl. asst. to Pres., sr. dir. Near East & North African Affairs, 2002—05, dep. asst. to Pres., dep. nat. security adv. for global democracy strategy, 2005—09; sr. fellow for Middle Eastern studies Coun. Fgn. Rels., Washington, 2009—; adj. prof. Georgetown U. Sch. Fgn. svc., 2011—. Bd. dirs. Inter-American Found., 1985—90; mem. US Commn. on Internat. Religious Freedom, 1999—2001, 2012—, chmn., 2000—01; mem. US Holocaust Meml. Coun., 2009—. Author: Undue Process, 1992, Security and Sacrifice, 1995, Faith or Fear: How Jews Can Survive in a Christian America, 1997, Tested by Zion, 2013. Mem.: Coun. Fgn. Rels. Republican. Office: Council on Foreign Relations 1777 F St NW Washington DC 20006

ABRAMS, HAROLD EUGENE, lawyer; b. Pensacola, Fla., Jan. 18, 1933; s. Samuel Ralph and Sadie (Gerhardt) A.; m. Nancy Gray, June 22, 1958; children: Shari Abrams Marx, Eric Gray. BA, U. Mich., 1954; JD, Harvard U., 1957. Bar: Ga. 1958, D.C. 1976, U.S. Supreme Ct. 1970. Law clk. to presiding judge U.S. Ct. Appeals (5th cir.), Atlanta, 1957-58; assoc. Kilpatrick & Cody, Atlanta, 1958-63; ptnr. Kilpatrick Stockton, Atlanta, 1963—2007, Abrams, Davis, Mason & Long LLC, 2007. Pres. Atlanta Tax Forum, 1990-91, Atlanta Estate Planning Coun., 1991-92; bd. dirs. Randall Bros., Inc., Atlanta. Contbr. articles on tax and estate planning to profl. publs. Pres. Buckhead Little League, Atlanta, 1972-73; bd. dir. Atlanta chpt. Am. Jewish Com., 1987-2001, Atlanta Jewish Fedn., 1996-2006; sec. Ronald McDonald's Children's Charities, Atlanta, 1988. With U.S. Army, 1957-58. Recipient Greater Good award, Ga. Planned Giving Coun., 2011. Fellow Am. Coll. Tax Counsel; mem. State Bar of Ga. (chmn. tax sect. 1964-65), So. Fed. Tax Inst. (trustee 1964-2001, pres. 1970-71, treas. 1986-95), Atlanta Lawyers Club. Avocations: tennis, travel. Office: Abrams Davis Mason & Long LLC Ste 1600 1100 Peachtree St NE Ste Atlanta GA 30309-4530 Office Phone: 404-815-6600. Business E-Mail: habrams@abramsdavis.com.

ABRAMS, STACEY, state legislator; b. Madison, Wis., Dec. 9, 1973; BA, Spelman Coll., 1995; MPA, Univ. Tex., Austin, 1998; JD, Yale Univ., 1999. Georgia State Representative, District 84, 2007-; member, Defense and Veterans Affairs, Judiciary Non Civil and Code Revision Committees, 2007-, Georgia House Representatives.Atty, currently. Council on Foreign Relations, American Marshall Memorial Fellow, Georgia delegate to the 2004 Democratic National Convention . Democrat. Methodist. Office: 1912 Hosea Williams Dr Atlanta GA 30317 Office Phone: 404-378-9434. Fax: 404-378-3328. E-mail: stacey.abrams@house.ga.gov.

ABRAMSON, HYMAN NORMAN, engineering and science research executive; b. San Antonio, Mar. 4, 1926; s. Nathan and Pearl (Westerman) A.; m. Idelle Rebecca Ringel, Apr. 20, 1947; children: Phillip David, Mark Donald. BSME, Stanford U., 1950, MS in Engring. Mechanics, 1951; PhD in Engring. Mechanics (So. Fellowship Fund fellow), U. Tex., Austin, 1956. Engr. U.S. Naval Air Missile Test Center, Point Mugu, Calif., 1947—48; project engr. Chance Vought Aircraft Co., Dallas, 1951-52; assoc. prof. aero. engring. Tex. A&M U., 1952-55; sect. mgr., dept. dir. S.W. Research Inst., San Antonio, 1956-72, v.p. div. engring. scis., 1972-85, exec. v.p., 1985-91, also bd. dirs.; disting. engring. rsch. prof. U. Tex., San Antonio, 2008—. Mem. many research adv. coms. U.S. Govt.; bd. dirs. Broadway Nat. Bank. Author: An Intro to the Dynamics of Airplanes, 1958, reprinted, 1971; contbr. numerous articles to profl. publs.; editor: (with others) Applied Mechanics Surveys, 1966, The Dynamic Behavior of Liquids in Moving Containers, 1966; assoc. editor: (with others) Applied Mechanics Revs, 1954-85; editorial adv. bd.: (with others) Jour. Computers and Structures, 1970—, Aeros. and Astronautics, 1975-80. Mem. Greater San Antonio C. of C., and City of San Antonio Market Sq. Adv. Com., 1973-77; mem. U.S. Bicentennial Com. of San Antonio, 1975-76; mem. adv. bd. dirs. U.S. Alamo, Inc., 1985-90; mem. adv. bd. Karta Techs., 1991—. Served with USN, 1943-45. Fellow AIAA (Disting. Service award 1973, dir., Structures, Structural Dynamics and Materials medal 1991), ASME (v.p., gov., hon. mem. 1979, Gold medal 1999); mem. Nat. Acad. Engring., Soc. Naval Architects and Marine Engrs., Nat. Acad. Engring. Mexico, AAAS, Sigma Xi. Republican. Jewish. Home: 1511 Spanish Oaks San Antonio TX 78213-1635 Office: SW Research Inst PO Box 28510 San Antonio TX 78228-0510 Home Phone: 210-342-5764; Office Phone: 210-522-2207.

ABRAMSON, JERRY EDWIN, Lieutenant Governor of Kentucky, former mayor; b. Louisville, Sept. 12, 1946; s. Roy and Shirley (Botwick) A.; m. Madeline M. Abramson; 1 child, Sidney Robert. BS in Bus. Econ., Ind. Univ., 1968; JD with honors, Georgetown Univ., 1973; LLD (hon.), Ky. Wesleyan Coll., 1990, Spalding U., 1995. Atty. Frost Brown Todd LLC; ptnr. Greebaum Doll & McDonald, Attys., 1973—85; mem. bd. aldermen, chmn. fin. com. City of Louisville, 1975—79, mayor, 1986—99, 2003—11; gen. counsel to Gov. State of Ky., Frankfort, 1979—80, lt. gov., 2011—. Lectr. law U. Louisville, 1974-75; pres. Ky. League of Cities, 1989-90; bd. dirs. Ctr. Strategic Studies, 1991—; pres. U.S. Conf. Mayors, 1993-94, mem. exec. bd.; mem. adv. bd. Barnard-Columbia Ctr. Leadership in Urban Pub. Policy, 1994—; co-chair Task Force Excellence in State and Local Govt. through Labor Mgmt. Cooperation, 1994—; exec.-in-residence Bellarmine U. 2011. Mem. Mayors Against Illegal Guns Coalition; pres. United States Conference of Mayors, 1993—94. Served in US Army, 1969—71. Named Man of Yr. Jaycees, 1971, Ky. State Jaycees Man of the Yr., 1977, One of the Top 20 Mayors in America U.S. News & World Report, 1987, Mcpl. Leader of the Yr. Am. City & County Mag., 1990, One of the Top 25 Mayors Newsweek Mag., 1996; recipient Richard Strauss award NCCJ, 1989, Michael A. diNunzio Spl. award U.S. Conf. Mayors, 1993, Pub. Sector award Nat. Alliance to End Homelessness, 1996. Mem. ABA, Louisville Bar Assn., B'nai B'rith (Great American Traditions award 1987), Rotary, Zeta Beta Tau. Democrat. Jewish. Office: Office of Lieutenant Governor 700 Capitol Ave Ste 142 Frankfort KY 40601 Office Phone: 502-564-2611. Office Fax: 502-564-2849.*

ABRAMSON, NEIL C., state legislator; BA in Govt., Dartmouth Coll., Hanover, NH; JD, La. State U. Mem. Dist. 98 La. House of Reps., 2007—, vice chair judiciary com., mem. civil law and procedure com., health and welfare com., legis. audit adv. counc., chair select com. on hurricane recovery. Democrat. Mailing: 365 Canal St Ste 2740 New Orleans LA 70130 Office Phone: 504-275-8051. Office Fax: 504-568-3342. E-mail: abramson@legis.state.la.us.

ABREU, LUIS ALBERTO, lawyer; b. Pinar Del Rio, Cuba, Apr. 20, 1956; came to U.S., 1961; s. Arnaldo Jesus and Justa (Villar) A.; m. Sallie Brown Shadrick, Aug. 23, 1980; children: Sarah, Maria. BA, Davidson Coll., 1978; JD, U. Fla., 1981. Bar: Va. 1981, U.S. Bankruptcy Ct. 1981, U.S. Ct. Appeals (4th cir.) 1981. From assoc. to ptnr. Clement & Wheatley, Danville, Va., 1981—2003; prin. Carter Craig, Attys. at Law, Danville, Va., 2003—10, Luis A. Abreu PLLC, 2011—. Mng. mem. Sunset Ridge, LLC, 2005—; bd. mem. Danville Sci. Ctr., 2002—08. Chmn. Local Human Rights Com., Danville, Va., 1986—89; commr. Commn. Archtl. Rev.; mem. Am. Bankruptcy Inst., 1984—, bd. govs.; bd. dirs., pres. YMCA, 1992; mem. planning and budget com. United Way; bd. dirs. Danville Sci. Ctr., 2002—08. Recipient Bob Griese award Miami Touchdown Club, 1976; named one of Va.'s Legal Elite Bus. Mag., 2002-13, Va. Super Lawyers, 2013, 2014; Alex Hemby scholar Davidson Coll., 1974-78, 2008. Mem.: ABA, Mental Health Assn. (bd. dirs.), Va. Bar Assn., Danville Mus. Fine Arts, Hist. Soc., Lions (pres. 1984—85). Republican. Roman Catholic. Home: 453 Country CLub Dr Danville VA 24541 Office: Luis A Abreu PLLC 626 N Ridge St Danville VA 24541 Office Phone: 434-791-4677. Business E-Mail: labreu@luisabreulaw.com.

ABREU, MARIA T., gastroenterologist, educator; MD, U. Miami Sch. of Medicine, 1986. Diplomate Am. Bd. Internal Medicine-gastroenterology, 2005, Am. Bd. of Med. Examiners, Am. Bd. of Gastroenterology. Resident Brigham and Women's Hosp., Boston, 1990—92; fellow gastroenterology UCLA, 1992—95; postdoc. rsch. fellow Cedars-Sinai Med. Ctr., LA, 1993—96; dir. inflammatory bowel disease Mt. Sinai Sch. of Medicine, assoc. prof. medicine gastroenterology divsn.; chief gastroenterology divsn. Univ. of Miami Sch. of Medicine, prof. medicine, prof. microbiology and immunology. Author: (articles) Practical techniques for detection of Toll-like receptor-4 in the human intestine, 2009, A novel Toll-like receptor 4 antagonist antibody ameliorates inflammation but impairs mucosal healing in murine colitis, 2009, Innate Immune Signaling by Toll-like receptors-4 (TLR4) shapes the inflammatory microenvironment of colitis-associated tumors, 2009, and several others. Fellow: ACP; mem.: NIH Gastrointestinal Mucosal Pathobiology, Am. Gastroent. Assn. (com.), Am. Coll. of Gastroenterology (com.), Am. Soc. of Clin. Investigators. Office: University of Miami School of Medicine Rm 534 Gautier Medical Research Bldg 1011 N W 15th St Miami FL 33136 Office Phone: 305-243-8644.

ABRUZZO, JOSEPH, state legislator; b. Ill., Aug. 14, 1980; BA, Lynn U., 2003. Port security specialist US Coast Guard Dept. Homeland Security, 2005—; southern regional dir. mktg. Cataldo Interiors Group; v.p. bus. devel. Gateway Mktg. Internat.; mem. Dist. 85 Fla. House of Reps., 2008—, mem. econ. devel. and cmty. affairs policy coun., econ. devel. policy com., fin. and tax coun., govt. ops. appropriations com., mem. select com. on Seminole Indian compact rev. Mem. Boca Raton Edn. Adv. Bd., 2002—03, Palm Beach County Consumer Affairs Hearing Bd., 2008—; former mem. Palm Beach County Sports Commn.; trustee Palms West C. of C.; steering com. mem. Congressman John Conyers Universal Health Care Conf.; legis. com. mem. Palm Beach County Dem. Exec. Com. Decorated Nat. Defense Svc. medal, Global War on Terrorism Svc. medal, Good Conduct medal US Coast Guard; recipient Physical Fitness award, US Coast Guard Combat Veterans Assn. Mem.: Lynn U. Alumni Assn., Voters Coalition, United South County Dem. Club, Mid County Dem. Club, Lake Worth West Dem. Club, Greater Boynton Dem. Club. Democrat. Catholic. Office: 412 House Office Bldg 402 S Monroe St Tallahassee FL 32399-1300 also: 1035 S State Rd 7 Ste 315-27 Wellington FL 33414-6134 Office Phone: 850-488-4791, 561-791-4774. Business E-Mail: joseph.abruzzo@myfloridahouse.gov.

ABSTON, DUNBAR, JR., management consultant; b. Memphis, Jan. 26, 1931; s. Dunbar and Esther (Cook) A.; m. Constance Condon, Apr. 29, 1978; children— Lauri Abston Arnold, Dunbar III, Linda Abston Larsen, Frank Norfleet; stepchildren— Selden Early Popwell, Martha McKellar Early, William Cole Early III, Elizabeth Early Gore. AB, Princeton U., 1953; MBA, Harvard U., 1955; M.Phil., Oxford U., 1989. Joined Parts Inc., Memphis, 1959, chmn., 1979; pres. parent co. Parts Industries Corp., Memphis, 1981-83, pres., chief exec. officer, 1983-87; pres., proprieter Abston Mgmt. Co., Memphis, 1987—. Pres. Tract-O-Land Plantation, Lake Comorant, Miss., Abston-Norfleet Realty Co., Memphis. Past chmn. Memphis Symphony Orch., Memphis Plough Community Found.; trustee Rhodes Coll., Lawrenceville Sch. Baker scholar Harvard U., 1954. Mem. Automotive Warehouse Distbrs. Assn. (past chmn.), Memphis Econ. Club (past chmn.), Phi Beta Kappa. Republican. Presbyterian. Home: 4010 Dumaine Way Memphis TN 38117 Office: Abston Mgmt Co 4727 Spottswood Ave Memphis TN 38117-4818 Home (Winter): 1285 Gulf Shore Blvd N Naples FL 34102

ABUNAEMEH, MALEK AMIR, physics professor; b. Demasscuss, Syria, Aug. 20, 1977; s. Amir Mahmmoud Abunaemeh and Basemh Ahmad Hakki. BS in Elec. Engring., U. Ala., Tuscaloosa, 2001; MS in Physics, U. Ala., Huntsville, 2007; PhD in Physics, Ala. A&M U., Normal, 2011. Physics prof. Talladega Coll., Ala., 2011—13, Lehman Coll., Bronx, NY, 2013—. Office: 119 Sagebrook Dr Madison AL 35757 Business E-Mail: abunaem@uah.edu.*

ABUNASER, BASHAR, healthcare services company executive; CFO Chestatee Regional Hosp., Dahlonega, Ga., 2003—06, Mo. Southern Healthcare, Dexter, Mo., 2003—06; dir., fin. ops. SunLink Health Sys., Inc., 2006—07; CFO, Fla. market IASIS Healthcare, LLC, 2007—. Office: IASIS Healthcare LLC Bldg E 117 Seaboard Ln Franklin TN 37067 Office Phone: 615-844-2747. Office Fax: 615-846-3006.

ACABA, JOSEPH M., astronaut; b. Inglewood, Calif., 1967; s. Ralph and Elsie. BS in Geology, U. Calif., Santa Barbara, 1990; MS in Geology, U. Ariz., 1992. Hydro-geologist, LA; environ. edn. awareness promoter US Peace Corps, Dominican Republic; island mgr. Caribbean Marine Rsch. Ctr., Lee Stocking Island, Exumas; shoreline revegetation coord. Vero Beach, Fla.; with Melbourne HS, Fla.; math and sci. tchr. Dunnellon Middle Sch., Fla.; mission specialist, astronaut NASA, 2004—. Mission specialist STS-119 Discovery Mission, 2009. Mem.: Fla. Assn. Sci. Teachers, Internat. Tech. Edn. Assn. Avocations: bicycling, camping, mountain climbing, kayaking, scuba diving, reading. Office: NASA Johnson Space Ctr Astronauts Office 2101 NASA Parkway Houston TX 77058

ACEVEDO, ART, police chief; b. Havana, Cuba; US, 1968; m. Tanya Acevedo; children: Melissa, Matthew, Jake. AA in Comm., Rio Hondo Coll., 1986; BS in Pub. Adminstrn. with honors, U. La Verne. Joined Calif. Highway Patrol, 1986, divsn. chief; chief police Austin Police Dept., 2007—. Mem.: Nat. Latino Peace Officers Assn. (former Calif. state pres.). Office: Austin Police Department PO Box 689001 Austin TX 78768-9001 E-mail: Art.acevedo@ci.austin.tx.us.

ACEVEDO, WILLIAM, retail executive; Grad., Brown U. Exec. trainee, sr. v.p., regional dir., stores Macy's East, 1996—2002; v.p. Banana Republic, 2002—08; exec. v.p., chief stores officer Zale Corp., 2008—. Office: Zale Corp 901 W Walnut Hill Ln Irving TX 75038-1003 Office Phone: 972-580-5266. Office Fax: 972-580-5523.

ACHENBAUM, WILBERT ANDREW, historian, gerontologist; b. Phila., Mar. 2, 1947; s. Wilbert Andrew and Muriel Maine Achenbaum; children: Emily Achenbaum Harris, Laura Schieve. BA, Amherst Coll., Mass., 1968; MA, U. Pa., Phila., 1970; PhD, U. Mich., Ann Arbor, 1976. Asst. prof. history Canisius Coll., Buffalo, 1976—80; asst. to prof. of history Carnegie Mellon U., Pitts., 1980—87; prof. history U. Mich., Ann Arbor, 1987—99; prof. history and social work U. Houston, 2002—, Gerson & Sabina David prof. global aging, 2009—. Assoc. v.p. for academic affairs Carnegie Mellon U., Pitts., 1984—87; dep. dir., inst. of gerontology U. Mich., Ann Arbor, 1989—99; dean, coll. of liberal arts and social sciences U. Houston, 1999—2002; adj. prof., geriatrics & palliatric care U. Tex. Health Sci. Ctr., Houston, 2005—; faculty Inst. Spirituality & Health, McGovern Ctr. Ethics and Human Spirit, Inst. Aging Oxford U.; dep. dir. Consortium Aging, Tex. Med. Ctr., 2013—, U. Tex. Consortium Aging. Author: (books on hist. gerontology) Old Age in the New Land, 1978, Shades of Gray, 1983, Social Security, 1986, Crossing Frontiers: Gerontology Becomes a Science, 1995, Older Americans, Vital Communities, 2005, Robert N. Butler MD: Visionary of Healthy Aging, 2013; editor: Pub. Policy and Aging e-Newsletter, 2006—13. Cons. Interfaith Ministries, Houston, 2005—; mem. bd. Inst. Interfaith Dialog, 2006—, Alzheimer's Assn., Houston, 2007—10, interfaith care ptnrs., 2009—; bd. mem. Albert Schweitzer Found., Houston, 2009—; mem. Gerontology Coun., World Econ. Forum, 2008—10; former chair The Ctr. Christ Ch. Cathedral; bd. chair and leadership coun. Nat. Coun. on Aging, Washington, 1993—2011; sec., policy chair Gerontol. Soc. of Am., Washington, 2001—07; academic Holocaust Mus., Houston, 2001—07. Sgt. US Army, 1970—72. Recipient Kent award, Gerontological Soc., 2007; named Outstanding Educator of Yr., Mich., 1992, Gerontological Profl. Yr., Houston, 2006, Outstanding Faculty, U. Houston, 2009. Fellow: Assn. Gerontology in Higher Edn.; mem.: Gerontol. Soc. America, Phi Beta Kappa, Nat. Coun. Aging, Am. Soc. Aging, Houston Philosophical Soc. Democrat. Episcopalian. Home: 425 Westmoreland St Houston TX 77006 Office: Grad Coll Social Work Univ of Houston Houston TX 77204 Business E-Mail: achenbaum@uh.edu.

ACHESON, HUGH, chef; b. Canada; Stage Babbo, NYC; cook Henri Burger, Ottawa, Mecca, San Francisco; sous chef Gary Danko, San Francisco; chef, ptnr. Five & Ten, Athens, Ga., 2002—, The National, Athens, Ga., 2007—, Gosford Wine, Empire State South. Appeared on (TV series) Top Chef Masters, 2011, judge Top Chef, 2011; author: A New Turn in the South: The Cuisine of Hugh Acheson, 2011. Named one of America's Best New Chefs, Food & Wine mag., 2002, Atlanta's Rising Star Chefs, StarChefs.com, 2007; nominee Best Chef: Southeast, James Beard Found., 2007. Office: Five and Ten 1653 S Lumpkin St Athens GA 30606 Office Phone: 706-546-7300.

ACHORD, JAMES LEE, retired gastroenterologist; b. Dayton, Ohio, Sept. 24, 1931; s. Lonnie M. and Ethel E. (Collins) A.; m. Patsy Jane Moore, Dec. 18, 1954; children: J. Michael, Ann Elizabeth, Andrew P. DMD, Emory U., 1952, MD, 1956. Intern Emory Hosp., 1956-57; resident Emory U., Atlanta, 1959-62, instr., assoc. prof., 1962-71; med. dir. Med. Ctr. Cen. Ga., Macon, 1971-75; assoc. dean, prof. East Tenn. State Sch. Medicine, Johnson City, 1975-76; prof., dir. div. digestive diseases U. Miss. Med. Ctr., Jackson, 1976-98, prof. emeritus, 1998. Editor book revs. Am. Jour. Gastroenterology, 1985-91, Dig. Dis. Sci., 1994-96; mem. editl. bd. Am. Jour. Clin. Gastroenterology, 1999—08; contbr. numerous articles and editls. to profl. jours. and chpts. to books. Capt. U.S. Army, 1957-59. Master ACP (gov. Miss. chpt. 1993-97), Am. Coll. Gastroenterology (pres. 1983-84), Am. Soc. Gastroenterologic Endoscopy; fellow Am. Gastroent. Assn.; mem. Am. Assn. Study Liver Disease.

ACKART, JENNIFER C., corporate financial executive; Worked Price Waterhouse LLP; sr. v.p. Raymond James Financial, Inc., contr., chief acctg. officer, 1994—. Office: Raymond James Financial Inc 880 Carillon Pky Saint Petersburg FL 33716 Office Phone: 727-567-1000. Office Fax: 727-567-8915. Business E-Mail: jennifer.ackart@raymondjames.com.

ACKER, RODNEY, lawyer; b. Jacksonville, Tex., Sept. 29, 1949; s. Mike and Dorothy (Kennedy) Acker; m. Judy Bruyere, Sept. 2, 1972; children: Amy, Shelley, Rachel, Sam. BBA, U. Tex., Arlington, 1971; JD with honors, Tex. Tech, 1974. Bar: Tex. 1974, NY 2007, US Dist. Ct. No., So., Ea., We. Districts Tex., US Ct. Appeals 5th & 11th Circuits, US Supreme Ct.; cert. in civil trial law. Law clk. to Hon. Eldon Mahon, US Dist. Ct., Ft. Worth, 1974-76; assoc. Kendrick, Kendrick & Bradley, Dallas, 1976, Jenkens & Gilchrist, P.C., Dallas, 1976-79, ptnr., then shareholder, 1979—, mng. shareholder Dallas office; ptnr. Fulbright & Jaworski L.L.P., Dallas, 2007—08. Named a Texas Superlawyer; named one of Top 15 Defenders, Dallas Bus. Jour., 2007, 2008, Best Lawyers in Am., Best Lawyers in Dallas; named to Internat. Acad. Trial Lawyers. Fellow Am. Bar Found., Tex. Bar Found., Dallas Bar Found., Am. Coll. Trial Lawyers; mem. ABA, State Bar Tex., Dallas Bar Assn., Am. Bd. Trial Advocates, State Bar Coll., Patrick E. Higginbotham Am. Inns of Ct., Securities Industry Assn., Tex. Assn. Bank Counsel, Tex. Assn. Defense Counsel, Tex. Judicature Soc., Phi Delta Phi. Baptist. Office: Fulbright & Jaworski LLP 2200 Ross Ave Ste 2800 Dallas TX 75201 Office Phone: 214-855-7466. Office Fax: 214-855-8200. Business E-Mail: racker@fulbright.com.

ACKER, WILLIAM MARSH, JR., federal judge; b. Birmingham, Ala., Oct. 25, 1927; s. William Marsh and Estelle (Lampkin) A.; m. Martha Walters, 1957; children— William Marsh III, Stacey Reed. BA, Birmingham So. Coll., 1949; LLB, Yale U., 1952. Bar: Ala. 1952. Assoc. Graham, Bibb, Wingo & Foster, Birmingham, Ala., 1952-57, Smyer, White, Reid & Acker, 1957-72, Dominick, Fletcher, Yeilding, Acker, Wood & Lloyd, Birmingham, 1972-82; judge US Dist. Ct. (no. dist. Ala.), 1982—96, sr. judge, 1996—. Mem. Ala. Republican Exec. Com.; del. to Repub. Nat. Convention, 1972, 76, 80. Mem. Birmingham Bar Assn. Office: US Dist Ct No Dist Ala 481 Hugo L Black Courthouse 1729 5th Ave N Birmingham AL 35203-2000

ACKERMAN, DAVID P., lawyer; b. Wilmington, Del., Feb. 22, 1957; BA with honors, Bucknell Univ., 1979; JD, George Washington Univ., 1982. Bar: Fla. 1983, US Dist. Ct. (so., no., middle dist. Fla.), US Ct. Appeals (11th cir.). Law clk. Judge James C. Paine, US Dist. Ct.; ptnr. Gunster Yoakley & Stewart, 1984—96; founding ptnr., bus. litigation Ackerman Link & Sartory, West Palm Beach, Fla., 1996—. Past chmn. Judicial Nominating Commn. for 15th Judicial Cir., Palm Beach County, Fla.; trustee, past pres. Legal Aid Soc., Palm Beach County, Fla. Contbr. articles to CLE publ. Recipient Pro Bono Svc award, Legal Aid Soc. Palm Beach County; named one of Fla. Legal Elite, Fla. Trend mag., 2004. Fellow: Am. Coll. Trial Lawyers; mem.: ABA, Fla. Bar (mem. exec. council Bus. Law sect.), Palm Beach County Bar Assn. Office: Ackerman Link & Sartory LLP Suite 1250 Esperante 220 Lakeview Ave West Palm Beach FL 33401 Office Phone: 561-838-4100. Office Fax: 561-838-5305. Business E-Mail: dackerman@alslaw.com.

ACKERMAN, ROY ALAN, research and development company executive; b. Bklyn., Sept. 9, 1951; s. Jack A. and Estelle (Kuchlik) A.; m. Janet Sharon Ostrow, July 4, 1974 (div. 1984); children: Shanna Avrah, Shira Batya; m. Kathleen T. Smith, 1989 (div. 2000); 1 child, Daniel Jacob. BSChemE, Poly. Inst. of N.Y., 1972; MSChemE, MIT, 1974; PhD, U. Va./U. B.H., 1984. Chem. engr. Tri-Flo Rsch. Labs., Bellmore, NY, 1972-74; sr. project engr. Thetford Corp., Ann Arbor, Mich., 1975; dir. R & D Applied Sci. Through Rsch. and Engring. (now ASTRE), Ann Arbor, 1976-77, ASTRE Cons. Corp., Charlottesville, Va., 1978-81; tech. dir. ASTRE Corp. Group, Charlottesville, 1981-89, Alexandria, Va., 1989—, The Adjuvancy, Alexandria, 2005—. Bd. dirs. Indsl. Microgenics Ltd., Charlottesville, Automated Bus. Cons., Elifecare, LLC; chmn. Bicarbolyte Corp., Alexandria, Va. Author: Water Reuse and Recycle, 1981; patentee in field. Lay leader Congregation Beth Israel, Charlottesville, 1979-89. Scholar Samuel Ruben Found., 1968-72. Mem. Water Pollution Control Fedn., Am. Assn. Rsch. Cos., Sigma Xi, Tau Beta Pi. Avocations: reading, swimming, tennis, politics, dance. Personal E-mail: raackerman@hotmail.com.

ACKS, JUDY, furniture manufacturing company executive; V.p. mktg. & sales furniture & textiles Hickory Business Furniture; v.p., Barbara Barry Brand Henredon Furniture Industries, Inc., 2006—. Office: Henredon Furniture Industries Inc 400 Henredon Rd Morganton NC 28655 Office Phone: 828-437-5261. Office Fax: 828-437-5264.

ACOMB, ROBERT BAILEY, JR., lawyer, educator; b. New Orleans, July 28, 1930; s. Robert Bailey and Catherine (Ryan) Acomb; m. Greta LeBlanc, Apr. 25, 1953; children: Robert III, Dwight J., Greta, William Ryan, John. BBA, Tulane U., New Orleans, 1951, JD, 1953. Bar: La. 1953, US Dist. Ct. (ea. and mid. dist.) La. 1953, US Ct. Appeals (5th cir.) 1955, US Supreme Ct. 1967, US Ct. Appeals (7th cir.) 1976, US Ct. Appeals (11th cir.) 1981, US Dist. Ct. (we. dist.) La. 1989. Assoc. Jones, Walker, Waechter, Poitevent, Carrere & Denegre, New Orleans, 1953-56, ptnr., 1956, sr. ptnr., 1968—. Adj. prof. law Tulane U., New Orleans, 1969—; pres. bd. dirs. Christian Bros. Found., Inc., New Orleans, 1975—77; chmn. Christian Bros. Retirement Trust, 1989—. Author: Collision and Limitation of Liability, 1997, Transportation Contracts, Charter Parties, Towing Contracts and Affreightment Contracts, 2002, Maritime Personal Injury & Death, 4th edit., 2008, Martindale-Hubbell Bar Register of Preeminent Lawyers, 93rd edit., 2009; editor: Damages Recoverable in Maritime Matters, 1984; contbr. articles to profl. jours., chapters to books; chmn. adv. editors Tulane Maritime Law Jour., 1976—, mem. editl. bd. Benedicts Maritime Bull., 2003—. Chmn. Archbishop's Cmty. Appeal, New Orleans, 1993; pres. Tulane U. Assocs., New Orleans, 1990—92; mem. bd. adminstrs. Tulane Edn. Fund, 1996—2000. Decorated knight grand cross Equestrian Order of Holy Sepulchre of Jerusalem, Lt. of Southeastern Lieutency Cardinal Furno, knight of St. Gregory Pope Johna Paul II; recipient Boisfontaine Trial Advocacy award, La. Bar Assn., 2002; named Outstanding Alumnus, Emeritus Club U. Tulane, 2003, Order of St. Louis, Archbishop Shulte; named one of 50 Top Lawyers, New Orleans City Bus., 2005; named to Best Lawyers in America, 1952; nominee Preeminent Lawyers, Bartindale Hubbell Bar Register, 2009. Fellow: Am. Bar Found., Am. Coll. Trial Lawyers (state chair 1978—81); mem.: ABA (mem. standing com. admiralty, chmn. 1979—83), Found. Bethlehem U. (named Super Lawyers 1988), Assn. Average Adjusters US (chmn. 1992—93), Tulane Maritime Law Inst., Maritime Law Assn. US (proctor, meme. exec. com. 1981—84), Tulane Maritime Law Ctr. (chmn. 1982—), New Orleans Bar Assn. (Disting. Maritime Lawyer 1996, Pres. award 2002), Navy League US (pres. New Orleans chpt. 1987—88, state pres. 1990—94), Tulane U. Alumni Assn. (pres. 1989—90, Vol. or the Yr. 1992), Stratford Club, Pickwick Club, Cornell Club, Boston Club, New Orleans Country Club, Order of St. Louis, Mil. Order Fgn. Wars (comdr. La Commandery). Roman Catholic. Avocations: photography, travel, sports. Office: Jones Walker Waechter Poitevent Carrere & Denegre 201 Saint Charles Ave Fl 48 New Orleans LA 70170-1000 Home Phone: 504-866-0619; Office Phone: 504-582-8112. Office Fax: 504-582-8010. Business E-Mail: bacomb@joneswalker.com.

ACOSTA, ALEX (RENE ALEXANDER ACOSTA), dean, former prosecutor; b. Miami; BA, Harvard U., JD, 1994. Law clk. US Ct. Appeals (3rd cir.); assoc. Kirkland & Ellis, 1995—97; sr. fellow Ethics & Pub. Policy Ctr., 1997—2000; prin. dep. asst. atty. gen. civil rights divsn. US Dept. Justice, Washington, 2001—02, asst. atty. gen. civil rights divsn., 2003—05, interim US atty. (so. dist.) Fla. Miami, 2005—06, US atty. (so. dist.) Fla., 2006—09; dean Fla. Internat. U. Law Sch., Miami, 2009—. Mem. NLRB, 2002—03. Recipient Disting. Leadership award, Arab American Anti-Discrimination Com. Mich., 2004, Excellence in Govt. Svc. award, Mex.-American Legal Def. and Edn. Fund, 2003, Hugh A. Johnson, Jr. Meml. award, DC Hispanic Bar Assn., 2003, Friend in Govt. award, American-Arab Anti-Discrimination Com., 2005. Office: Florida International University Law School University Park Campus Rafael Diaz-Balart Hall Miami FL 33199 Office Phone: 305-348-1118. Office Fax: 305-348-1159. E-mail: acosta@fiu.edu.

ACOSTA, EFREN ALEJANDRO, lawyer; b. New Orleans; BA, U. Houston, 1997, JD magna cum laude, 2000. Bar: Tex. Assoc. Locke Liddell & Sapp LLP, Houston, 2000—06; sr. assoc. Fulbright & Jaworski LLP, Houston, 2006—09, ptnr., 2010—. Contbr. articles to profl. jours. Dir. Hispanic Bar Assn. Houston, 2002—08, mem. adv. bd., 2008—, The Entrepreneurship Inst., 2005, Youth About Bus., 2011. Named a Rising Star, Mergers & Acquisitions, Law & Politics, 2010, 2011; named one of Minority 40 Under 40, The Nat. Law Jour., 2011. Mem.: Internat. Bar Assn., State Bar Tex., Bus. Law Sect., Houston Bar Assn. Office: Fulbright & Jaworski LLP Fulbright Tower 1301 McKinney Ste 5100 Houston TX 77010-3095 Office Phone: 713-651-5373. Business E-Mail: eacosta@fulbright.com.

ACOSTA, LYDIA M., library director; AA, Brevard CC, 1968; BA, U. South Fla., Tampa, 1970, MA in Libr. Sci., 1973. Dir., libr. East Baton Rouge Parish Libr., 2003—08, sec. libr. bd. control; v.p. info. svcs., univ. libr. Nova Southeastern U., Ft. Lauderdale, Fla., 2008—. Mem. Children's Coalition, Vols. in Pub. Schs. Mem.: La. Libr. Assn., Baton Rouge Area Libr. Club (former pres.). Office: Nova Southeastern U Library 3301 College Ave Fort Lauderdale FL 33314 Office Phone: 225-231-3700. E-mail: lacosta@ebr.lib.la.us.

ACOSTA, RAYMOND LUIS, retired federal judge; b. NYC, May 31, 1925; s. Ramon J. and Carmen J. (Acha-Jimenez) Acosta-Colon; m. Marie Hatcher, Nov. 2, 1957; children: Regina, Gregory, Ann Marie. Student, Princeton U., 1948; JD, Rutgers U., 1951. Bar: N.J. 1953, U.S. Supreme Ct. 1956, P.R. 1959. Sole practice, Hackensack, NJ, 1953-54; spl. agt. FBI, San Diego, Washington, Miami, Fla., 1954-58; asst. U.S. atty. San Juan, 1958-61; sole practice, 1961-67; trust officer Banco Credito y Ahorro Ponceno, San Juan, 1967-80; U.S. atty. Dist. P.R., Hato Rey, 1980-82; judge US Dist. Ct. PR, San Juan, 1982—94, sr. judge, 1994—2010; ret., 2010. Alt. del. U.S.-P.R. Commn. on Status, 1962-63; mem. Gov.'s Spl. Com. to Study Structure and Orgn. Police Dept., P.R., 1969 Contbr. articles to profl. jours. Pres. United Fund, P.R., 1979. Served with USN, 1943-46, Normandy. Recipient Merit cert. Mayor of San Juan, 1973. Mem. Fed. Bar Assn. (pres., P.R. 1967), P.R. Bankers Assn. (chmn. trust div. 1971, 75, 77), P.R. Bar Assn., Soc. Former Spl. Agts. FBI. Office: US Courthouse & PO Bldg Ste 348 300 Recinto Sur St San Juan PR 00901

ACTON, ELIZABETH S., corporate financial executive; b. 1952; BA, U. Minn.; MBA, Ind. U. V.p., multinational banking group Continental Bank; asst. treas. Ford Motor Co., 1995—98; exec. v.p., fin., CFO Ford Motor Credit Co., Dearborn, Mich., 1998—2000; v.p., treas. Ford Motor Co., Dearborn, Mich., 2000—02; exec. v.p., CFO Comerica, Inc., 2002—, treas., 2004—05, Comerica Bank (subs. Comerica Inc.), 2004—05. Bd. dirs. Vista Maria, Ford Holdings, Inc. Office: Comerica Inc Comerica Bank Tower 1717 Main St Dallas TX 75201 Office Phone: 214-462-6831. Business E-Mail: beth_acton@comerica.com.

ADAIR, CHARLES E., information technology executive; b. Birmingham, Ala., Dec. 26, 1947; s. Charles Watkins and Martha Edd (Chisenball) A.; m. Alice Virginia Barker, Jan. 31, 1970; children: Charles Thomas, Emily Elizabeth. Student, Vanderbilt U., 1966; BS in Acctg., U. Ala.-Tuscaloosa, 1970. C.P.A. Sr. acct. Haskins & Sells, Birmingham, 1970—73; CFO Durr-Fillauer Medical, Inc., Montgomery, Ala., 1973—77, exec. v.p., 1977—81, pres., COO, 1981—92; ptnr. Cordova Ventures, Montgomery, Ala., 1993—. Bd. dirs. Tech Data Corp., 1995—, PSS World Med., Inc., 2002—, Torchmark Corp., 2003—. Served to sgt. U.S. Army, 1970. Mem. Fin. Execs. Inst., AICPA, Ala. Soc. CPAs. Home: 2436 Wildwood Dr Montgomery AL 36111-1626 Office: Cordova Ventures 3 NorthWinds Ctr 2500 North-Winds Pky Ste 475 Alpharetta GA 30004 Office Phone: 678-942-0300. Office Fax: 678-942-0301. Business E-Mail: ea@cordovaventures.com.

ADAMS, ALMA, state legislator; Adminstr., prof. arts; former state rep. Dist. 26 NC; state rep. Dist. 58 NC, 2003—. Mem. Aging com., Edn. com., Edn. Subcom. on Universities, Health com.; vice chmn. Commerce, Small Bus and Entrepreneurship com.; chmn. Appropriations com. Democrat. Office: North Carolina House of Representatives 300 N Salisbury St Rm 604 Raleigh NC 27603-5925 Office Phone: 919-733-5902. E-mail: Alma.Adams@ncleg.net.

ADAMS, BEN C., lawyer; BA in Economics, U. NC, Chapel Hill, 1978; JD, Vanderbilt U. Sch. Law, Nashville, 1981. Bar: Tenn. 1981. Shareholder Baker, Donelson, Bearman, Caldwell & Berkowitz, PC, Memphis, mng. ptnr. of firm, 1993—98, chmn., CEO of firm, 2003—. Former sr. warden Ch. of Holy Communion, 2003—04; chmn. Dixie Homes Boys & Girls Club, 1993—94, Memphis U. Sch., 1997—2004, Memphis Area Legal Services 2007 Access to Justice Campaign, Memphis Shelby Crime Commn., Boys & Girls Club Greater Memphis; mem. Vanderbilt Law Sch. Adv. Bd.; bd. dirs. Memphis Tomorrow; bd. trustees Elmwood Cemetery, pres., 2004—06. Named Memphis Corp. Lawyer of Yr., Best Lawyers, 2011; named one of Best 101 Lawyers in Tenn., Bus. Tenn., 2004, 2005, Best 150 Lawyers, 2007, The Best Lawyers in America, Corp. Law, Trusts and Estates, 2006—, Top 50 Attorneys in Memphis, Mid-South Super Lawyers, 2010, Top 100 Attorneys in Tenn., 2010; named to Mid-South Super Lawyers, 2006—. Fellow: Memphis Bar Found.; mem.: ABA, Tenn. Bar Assn., Memphis Bar Assn., Memphis Estate Planning Coun., Phoenix Club (pres. 1989—90), Phi Beta Kappa, Order of Coif. Office: Baker Donelson Bearman Caldwell & Berkowitz PC First Tennessee Bldg 165 Madison Ave Memphis TN 38103 Office Phone: 901-577-2307. Office Fax: 901-577-0714. Business E-Mail: badams@bakerdonelson.com.

ADAMS, BRYAN, state legislator; Fire truck salesman; fire chief Dist. 5 Terrytown Vol. Fire Dept., La.; mem. Dist. 85 La. House of Reps., Baton Rogue, 2012—. Republican. Office: PO Box 1158 Gretna LA 70054 also: La House of Reps 900 N 3rd St Baton Rouge LA 70804 Office Phone: 504-361-6013. Business E-Mail: adamsb@legis.la.gov.

ADAMS, C. DAN, diversified financial services company executive; Degree in Bus. Adminstrn., U. S.C., 1983; grad., La. State U., 1989. Cert. comml. investment mem. Pres., prin., Spartanburg Capital Corp. of America, Inc., 1991—, pres., prin., Greenville, 1991—; pres., owner Southeastern Capital Partners, LLC; chmn. First Nat. Bancshares Inc. Office: First National Bancshares Inc 215 N Pine St Spartanburg SC 29302 Office Phone: 864-948-9001. Office Fax: 864-281-0830.

ADAMS, CHARLES P., JR., lawyer; b. Jackson, Miss., Feb. 28, 1949; BSBA cum laude, Georgetown U., 1971; JD, Georgetown U. Law Ctr., 1974. Bar: Miss. 1975. Mng. ptnr. Adams and Reese, LLP, 2001—. Mem.: Miss. Bar, Hinds County Bar Assn. Office: Adams and Reese LLP 701 Poydras St Ste 4500 New Orleans LA 70139 Office Phone: 601-292-0720. Office Fax: 601-944-9020. Business E-Mail: charles.adams@arlaw.com.*

ADAMS, CHRISTINE BEATE LIEBER, psychiatrist, educator; b. Greensboro, NC, June 20, 1949; d. Paul Lieber Adams and Marjorie Pinckney (Quackenbos) Ould; 1 child, Justin McKendree Adams-Tucker. Student, Agnes Scott Coll., 1967-69; BA in English Lit. with honors, U. Fla., 1971, MD, 1976. Diplomate Am. Bd. Psychiatry and Neurology (examiner 1985), Am. Bd. Child Psychiatry (examiner 1984, 91), Nat. Bd. Med. Examiners. Resident in gen. psychiatry U. Louisville Sch. Medicine, 1976-78, fellow in child psychiatry, 1978-80, asst. clin. prof. dept. psychiatry and behavioral scis., 1981—2005, attending psychiatrist consultation-liaison svc., 1992, 93; pvt. practice, Louisville, 1980—. Med. advisor Social Security Adminstrn., HHS, Louisville, 1986—; child psychiatry cons. Seven Counties Svcs., Ky. Dept. Human Resources, 1989, 93; physician advisor Nat. Health Svcs., Louisville, 1993-2000, physician reviewer in child and adult psychiatry, 2000-01; physician advisor Magellan Behavioral Health Svcs., 2003—, ValueOptions, 2004—; reviewer Am. Jour. Psychiatry, 1983—; cons. So. Ind. Mental Health and Guidance Ctr., Jeffersonville, 1981-83, U. Fla., 1982; presenter in field. Contbr. articles to med. jours., chpts. to books. Mem dirs. Gainesville (Fla.) Women's Health Ctr., 1973-75, Discover Louisville Orch., 1999-2001; mem. Jefferson County (Ky.) Juvenile Justice Commn., 1982-86. Psychiatrist cons. Mil. Entrance Processing Sta. US Army, 2007—, Louisville, Ky. Recipient award Nat. Psychiat. Endowment Fund, 1980. Fellow Am. Acad. Child and Adolescent Psychiatry (com. on rights and legal matters 1984-92); mem. Am. Psychiat. Assn. (mem. com. family violence and child sexual abuse 1987-94), Ky. Acad. Child Psychiatry (sec.-treas. 1980-81, pres.-elect 1981-82, pres. 1982-83). E-mail: cbladams@bellsouth.net.

ADAMS, CHRISTOPHER STEVE, JR., retired electronics executive, military officer; b. Shreveport, La., July 8, 1930; s. Christopher Steve and Armenda Lee (Tanner) A.; m. Mary Alene Mitchell, Aug. 22, 1953; children: Cynthia, Charlotte, Cheri, Christopher III. AS, Tarleton State U., 1950; BS, Tex. A&M U., 1952; MS in Mil. Studies, Indsl. Coll. Armed Forces, Washington, 1973. Commd. U.S. Air Force, 1952, advanced through grades to maj. gen., 1979, B-36, B-52 pilot Ramey AFB, P.R.; dir. plans and policy J-5, Def. Nuclear Agy., Washington, 1970-73; comdr. 90th Strategic Missile Wing, 1973-75; comdr. 12th Air Div., 1975-78; chief of staff SAC, 1982-83; ret., 1983; assoc. dir. Los Alamos Nat. Lab., 1983—86; v.p. bus. devel. Andrew Corp., Dallas, 1987-94, ret., 1994. Author: The Cold War Series, 10 books, 1999—2010. Decorated D.S.M., Def. Superior Service medal, Legion of Merit (2), Air Force Commendation medal, Air medal (2); recipient Disting. Alumnus award Tarleton State U., 1990, Disting. Alumnus award Tex. A&M U., 1991, Medal of Honor, Nat. Soc. DAR, 2011. Presbyterian. Home: 9408 Gimmee Ct Granbury TX 76049 Personal E-mail: cadamsusaf@charter.net.

ADAMS, DANIEL FENTON, law educator; b. Reading, Pa., July 29, 1922; s. Daniel Snyder and Carrie Betsy (Vought) A.; m. Eloise Williams, Sept. 6, 1968. AB, Dickinson Coll., 1947; LL.B., Dickinson Sch. Law, 1949. Bar: Pa. 1951, Ark. 1984. Prof. law Dickinson Sch. Law, Carlisle, Pa., 1949-65, asst. to dean, 1952-54, 56-60, acting dean, 1954-56, asst. dean, 1960-65; prof. Sch. Law U. Ark., Little Rock, 1965-70, 77-93, prof. emeritus, 1993—; asst. dean U. Ark. Sch. Law, Little Rock, 1966-70, acting dean, 1981-82, interim dean, 1989-91; prof. U. Miss. Sch. Law, Oxford, 1970-77. Vis. prof. Stetson U. Sch. Law, St. Petersburg, Fla., 1976-77, 99-00, U. Tenn. Coll. Law, 1993. Contbr. articles to profl. jours. Served with U.S. Army, 1943-44 Mem. ABA, Pa. Bar Assn., Ark. Bar Assn. Personal E-mail: condodfa@aol.com.

ADAMS, DAVID HUNTINGTON, federal judge; b. Cleve., May 30, 1942; s. Donald Croxton and Nancy Adams; m. Mary Watson, Dec. 4, 1982; children from previous marriage: Ann Arendell, David Huntington, Susanna Camp. AB, Washington and Lee U., 1965, JD, 1968. Bar: Va. 1968, US Dist. Ct. (eastern dist.) Va. 1968, US Ct. Appeals (4th cir.) 1968, US Supreme Ct. 1973. Law clk. US Dist. Ct. (eastern dist.) VA., Norfolk, Va., 1968-69; assoc. Willcox, Savage, Norfolk, 1969-72; ptnr. Agelasto, Bernard & Adams, Norfolk, 1972-74, Taylor, Walker, Bernard & Adams, Norfolk, 1974-78, Taylor, Walker & Adams, Norfolk, 1974-87, Clark & Stant, P.C., 1987-93; judge US Bankruptcy Ct. (eastern dist.) Va., Newport News, Va., 1993—. Master of the bench James Kent American Inn of Ct., 1994-99, pres., 1995; lectr. bankruptcy practice joint com. on cont. legal edn. Va. Bar Found., 1981, 89, 93—; adminstrv. hearing officer Commonwealth of Va., 1974-89; mem. 4th Cir. Jud. Coun., 2003-2005, Adminstrv. Office Bankruptcy Judges Adv. Coun., 2001—04, Bankruptcy Judges Adv. Group, 2001—04, Adminstrv. Office Joint Adv. Com., 2003-2005 Author: Virginia Landlord/Tenant Law, 1980. Bd. dir. Heritage Mus., Norfolk, 1991-94, Virginia Beach Neptune Fest., 1997—, King Neptune XXVI; chmn. Neptune Found., 2002; pres. Bay Colony Civic League, Virginia Beach, 1978, Princess Anne Hills Civic League, Virginia Beach, 1988; mem. 4th Cir. Jud. Conf., 1974—; 4th Cir. Jud. Coun., 2002—; mem. 2d dist. ethics com. Va. State Bar, 1983-84. Recipient Superior Pub. Svc. award, Sec. of Navy, 2004. Mem.: ABA, Va. Bar Assn. (bd. dir. bankruptcy sect. 1990—93, mem. coun. jud. sect. 1995—, chmn. 1997), Virginia Beach Bar Assn., Norfolk-Portsmouth Bar Assn., Nat. Conf. Bankruptcy Judges (bd. govs. 1996—2000, sec. 2000, pres. 2004—05), Am. Bankruptcy Inst., Hampton Roads Naval Historical Found. (bd. dir. 2005—), Hampton Roads Coun. Navy League U.S. (life; pres. 2000—04, nat. dir. 2002—04), N.Y. Yacht Club, Cavalier Golf and Yacht Club (bd. dir. 1993—98, commodore 1994). Episcopalian. Avocations: yachting, swimming, bicycling. Office: US Bankruptcy Court 101 25th St Newport News VA 23606 Office Phone: 757-595-9805.*

ADAMS, FELICIA COLETTE, federal prosecutor; b. Holly Springs, Miss., 1960; BS, Jackson State U., Miss., 1981; JD, U. Miss. Sch. Law, 1984. Bar: Miss. 1984, US Dist Ct. (northern & southern districts) Miss. 1984, US Ct. Appeals (5th cir.) 1984. Law clk. to Hon. Odell Horton, Sr. US Dist. Ct. (western dist.) Tenn., Memphis, 1984—85; spl. asst. to atty. gen. State of Miss., Jackson, 1985—88, legal counsel to Gov., 1988—89; asst US atty. (northern dist.) Miss. US Dept. Justice, Oxford, Miss., 1989—2000, asst US atty. (southern dist.) Miss. Jackson, 2000—11, dep. civil chief, 2003—11, acting first asst. US atty. (northern dist.) Miss. Oxford, 2011, US atty. (northern dist.) Miss., 2011—. Guest lectr. Jackson State U., 1985—89. Recipient Daniel E. Lynn award for superior performance in civil litigation, Office US Atty. (southern dist.) Miss., 2003; James O. Eastland scholar, 1981—84. Mem.: Charles Clark American Inns of Ct., Magnolia Bar Assn., Nat. Bar Assn., Miss. State Bar, Phi Delta Phi. Office: US Attorney's Office 900 Jefferson Ave Oxford MS 38655 Office Phone: 662-234-3351.*

ADAMS, GARY LEE, systems engineer; s. William Ellsworth and Ethel Mae (Ling) A.; m. Rebecca Estelle Peppers, Dec. 29, 1967; children: William Matthew, Preston Lee. BSEE, Tulane U., 1969; Grad. of Theology, Bapt. Bible Coll., 1974. Cert. in sys. engring., U. Ala. at Huntsville. Assoc. engr. Westinghouse Electric Corp., Balt., 1969-71; asst. prin., dean edn. Hollywood (Fla.) Christian Sch., 1974-79; assoc. engr. Martin Marietta Corp., Orlando, Fla., 1979-80, engr., 1980-82, sr. engr., 1982-84, group engr., 1984-85; sr. lead engr. Harris Corp., Orlando, Fla., 1985, engring. sect. head, 1985-89; engring. br. mgr. PEI Electronics, Inc., Huntsville, Ala., 1989-98, lead sys. engr., 1998—2003; project engr. DRS Techs., Huntsville, Ala., 2003—05, sys. engr. sup., 2005—11; sr. tech. adv. SAIC, 2012—. Vice chmn. Nat. Indsl. Assn. MATE Users Group Test Program Set Com., Washington, 1986-88. Contbr. articles to profl. publs. Deaf interpreter First Bapt. Ch., Hollywood, 1974-79, Tabernacle Bapt. Ch., Orlando, 1979-89, Triana Village Bapt. Ch., Huntsville, 1989-93; deacon Granite Bapt. Ch., Glen Burnie, Md., 1970-71, Friendship Bapt. Ch., Huntsville, 1995-2009, Bible tchr. Friendship Bapt. Ch., Huntsville, 1990-. With Air Force ROTC, 1965—67. Recipient Jung scholarship Tulane U., 1965-68. Mem. IEEE, Assn. U.S. Army, Internat. Coun. Sys. Engring. Republican. Baptist. Avocations: coin collecting/numismatics, camping, home computing, metal detecting, travel. Home: 13436 Wendy Dr Madison AL 35757-6530 Office Phone: 256-971-6451. Personal E-mail: gladgladams@gmail.com.

ADAMS, HENRY LEE, JR., federal judge; b. Jacksonville, Fla., 1945; BS in Polit. Sci., Fla. A&M U., 1966; JD, Howard U., 1969. Staff atty. Duval County Legal Aid Assn., 1969-70; asst. pub. defender, pub. defender's office 4th Jud. Cir., 1970-72, judge, 1979-93; atty. Sheppard, Fletcher, Hand & Adams, Jacksonville, 1972-76, Marshall & Adams, Jacksonville, 1976-79; judge US Dist. Ct. (middle dist.) Fla., Jacksonville, 1993—2010, sr. judge, 2010—. Active Tots N' Teens; mem. adv. bd. Fla. Augustus Secure Care Unit; mem. Habijax Adv. Bd.; mem. local sch. adv. coun. Mid. W. Gilbert Mid. Sch. Mem. NAACP, Nat. Bar Assn., Fla. Bar Assn., Fla. Conf. Circuit Judges (mem. legis. com.), Jacksonville Bar Assn., D.W. Perkins Bar Assn., Kappa Alpha Psi. Office: US Dist Ct Simpson US Courthouse 300 N Hogan St Rm 11-200 Jacksonville FL 32202

ADAMS, J. GLEN, retail executive; Chmn., pres., CEO The Great Western Sugar Co., 1986—89, Southmark Corp., 1990—96. Bd. dirs. Zale Corp., 1993—. Office: Zale Corp 901 W Walnut Hill Ln Irving TX 75038-1003 Office Phone: 972-580-4000. Office Fax: 972-580-5547.

ADAMS, JIMMIE VICK, communications systems company executive, retired military officer; b. Prichard, Ala., May 1, 1936; s. Anthony J. and Verlie (Adams) Antonidis; m. Ouida Bumpers, Dec. 27, 1955; children: Vickie, Lisa Floyd. BS in Mech. Engring., Auburn U., Ala., 1957; MME, U. Tex., 1963; grad., Squadron Officer Sch., 1964, Indsl. Coll. Armed Forces, 1978, Joint Flag Officer Warfighting Course, 1987. Advanced through ranks to gen. USAF, 1957, commd., 1958, various flying and staff positions, 1958-85, dep. chief of staff Requirements HQTAC Langley AFB, Va., 1985-87, comdr. 1st Air Force, 1987-88, vice comdr. Tactical Air Command, 1988-89, dep. chief of staff Plans and Ops. Washington, 1989, comdr. in chief Pacific Air Forces Hickam AFB, Hawaii, 1993; positions up to v.p., officer Loral Corp., 1993—96; v.p. Washington ops. for C3I and Systems Integration Sector Lockheed Martin; sr. v.p. Washington ops. L-3 Comm. Holdings, Inc. Mem. AF Assn., Daedalians. Avocations: golf, fishing. Office: L-3 Comm Holdings Inc 1215 S Clark St Ste 1205 Arlington VA 22202 Office Phone: 703-412-7190.

ADAMS, JOHN C., JR., board member; b. Memphis; BA in Gov., U. Va., 1970. From mem. staff to pres., owner Gem Inc., Byhalia, Miss., 1973-78, pres., owner, 1978-82; 1pres. Miami divsn. Malone & Hyde, 1983-90; prin., owner NCC L.P., 1990—94; exec. v.p. AutoZone, 1994—97, chmn., CEO, 1997—2001. Bd. dirs. Keebler Foods Co.; WD-40 Co., 2001-; Tractor Supply Co., 2007-; Repco Corp. Ltd., 2008-. With USN, 1970-73; bd. trustees LeMoyne-Owen Coll., Memphis. Office: Tractor Supply Co Bd Directors 200 Powell Pl Brentwood TN 37027 Office Fax: 615-366-4686. Business E-Mail: jadams@tractorsupply.com.

ADAMS, JOHN LEWIS, board member, retired transportation executive; BBA in Fin, U. Tex., 1966, JD, 1969. Joined Tex. Commerce Bank, Houston, 1973, pres., 1983—87, chmn., CEO Dallas - Fort Worth, 1987—88; vice chmn. Tex. Commerce Bank NA, 1988—97; chmn., pres., CEO Chase Bank of Tex., 1997—98; exec. v.p. Trinity Industries, Inc., Dallas, 1999—2005, vice chmn., 2005—07; bd. dir. Group 1 Automotive, Inc., Houston, 1999—, non-exec. chmn., 2005—. Bd. dirs. Children's Med. Ctr., Dallas; bd. trustees American Heart Assn., Dallas; mem. bus. sch. adv. bd. U. Tex. Chancellor's Coun. Office: Group 1 Automotive Inc 800 Gessner Ste 500 Houston TX 77024 Office Phone: 713-647-5700.

ADAMS, JOHN W., former state legislator; b. Hopkinsville, Ky., June 29, 1936; m. Mary Helen Adams; children: John, William. BS, U. Ky., 1958, MS, 1960. Adv. U. Ky.; farmer, 1963—; bus. officer, registrar Ky. C.C., 1964—69; bus. mgr. Hopkinsville C. C., 1965—69; exec. dir. planning and devel. co. Pennyrile ADD, 1969—93; real estate property appraiser, 1997—2002; mem. Ky. Ho. of Reps., 1996—2004. Mem. Ky. Bd. Agr., 1983—87. Mem. Heart of Hopkinsville; deacon First Christian Ch.; bd. dirs. Hopkinsville C.C. 1st lt. USAF, 1960—63. Home: 6255 Huffman Rd 11 R6 Hopkinsville KY 42240

ADAMS, JULIE RAQUE, state legislator; b. Louisville, June 11, 1969; m. James Adams; 2 children. BA, St. Mary's Coll., U. Notre Dame; MA, George Wash. U. Former mem. Louisville Metro Coun.; founder, prin. Adams & Call, Inc.; mem. Dist. 32 Ky. House of Reps., Frankfort, 2011—. Republican. Roman Catholic. Office: Kentucky House of Reps Annex Rm 405 702 Capitol Ave Frankfort KY 40601

ADAMS, KENNETH FRANCIS, automotive executive; b. Danbury, Conn., Feb. 4, 1946; s. Donald and Evelyn Trocola (Mulvihill) Adams; m. Annette Talarico, Sept. 28, 1968; children: Amy, Ella Louise, Elizabeth. BS in Fin., Mt. St. Mary's U., 1968. CPA. Audit mgr. Price Waterhouse & Co., Bridgeport, Conn., 1968—74; v.p. fin. & adminstrn., treas. & bd. dirs. through CFO Saab Cars USA, Inc., Norcross, Ga., 1974—2005; CEO, CFO Saab Fin. Svcs. Corp., 1997. Bd. dirs. Telzuit Med. Technologies Inc. (formerly Taylor Madison Corp.), 2006—08, Telzuit Technologies Inc. (subs. Telzuit Med. Technologies Inc.), 2006—08, Gen. Automotive Corp., 2008—. With USAR, 1968—74. Mem.: AICPA, Inst. Mgmt. Accts., Fin. Exec. Inst., Conn. Soc. CPAs. Roman Cath. Office: General Automotive Corp Bd Directors 7803 Southland Blvd Ste 203 Orlando FL 32809-6978 Office Phone: 407-363-5633. Office Fax: 407-363-4574. Business E-Mail: kadams@generalautomotive.com.

ADAMS, LAVONNE MARILYN BECK, critical care nurse, educator; b. Bridgeport, Conn., Feb. 22, 1965; d. Adolf and Hazel B. (Henderson) Beck. ASN, Kettering Coll. Med. Arts, 1985; BSN, Wright State U., 1988; MSN, Andrews U., 1992, PhD, 2003. CCRN. Staff nurse Kettering Med. Ctr., Ohio, 1985-89, resource staff nurse, 1989-95, instr. in nursing, 1989-92; asst. prof. nursing Kettering Coll. Med. Arts, 1992—99, Southwestern Adventist U., Keene, Tex., 1999—2003, assoc. prof., 2003—04; asst. prof. nursing Harris Coll. Nursing and Health Scis. Tex. Christian U., Ft. Worth, 2004—10, assoc. prof., 2010—; PRN staff nurse Huguley Mem. Hosp., 2002—. Vol. Adventist Comty. Svcs.Disaster Response, 2004—, ARC, 2005—. Mem.: Am. Assn. Critical Care Nurses, Pi Lambda Theta, Sigma Theta Tau, Phi Kappa Phi. Avocations: music, travel. Home: 7000 Welch Ct Fort Worth TX 76133-6726 Office: Tex Christian U Harris Coll Nursing and Health Scis TCU Box 298620 Fort Worth TX 76129

ADAMS, LAWRENCE M., pediatric gastroenterologist; MD, St. George's U., 1981. Diplomate Am. Bd. Pediatrics, 1987, Am. Bd. Pediatrics-pediatric gastroenterolgy, 2005. Resident pediat. Univ. of Medicine and Dentistry NJ Children's Hosp., 1983—84, Schneider Children's Hosp., 1984—85, fellow pediatric gastroenterology, 1985—87; divsn. dir. pediat. St. Mary's Med. Ctr. Chmn. med. adv. com. Crohn's & Colitis Found. of America; pediatric med. advisor Celiac Disease Found. Fellow: Am. Acad. of Pediat.; mem.: North Am. Soc. for Pediatric Gastroenterology Hepatology and Nutrition. Office: St Mary's Medical Center 901 45th St West Palm Beach FL 33407-2495 Office Phone: 561-844-6300.*

ADAMS, MICHAEL FRED, academic administrator, political scientist, educator; b. Montgomery, Ala., Mar. 25, 1948; s. Hubert W. and Jean (Taylor) A.; m. Mary Lynn Ethridge, June 7, 1969; children: David Winston, Stephen Taylor. BA, Lipscomb U., 1970; MA, Ohio State U., 1971, PhD, 1973. Asst. prof. Ohio State U., 1973-74; chief of staff for Sen. Howard Baker, Washington, 1975-79; advisor to gov. State of Tenn., Nashville, 1981-82; v.p. Pepperdine U., Malibu, Calif., 1982-88; pres. Centre Coll., Danville, Ky., 1988-97, U. Ga., Athens, 1997—. Chmn. Nat. Assn. Ind. Colls. and Univs., 1995-96, Assoc. Colls. of South; mem. coun. for advancement and support of edn. NCAA Pres. Commn., 1992-94; chmn. Commn. on Colls. of So. Assn. Colls. and Schs.; vice chmn. task force that founded Coun. for Higher Edn. Accreditation; chair Am. Coun. on Edn., 2000. Author: Rhetorical Strategies of Howard Baker, 1973; contbr. articles to various publs. Pres. Circle K Internat., Chgo., 1970; nominee for U.S. Congress, Nashville, 1980; mem. site host com. 1984 Olympiad, L.A.; elder Christian Ch. Recipient Bronze Quill award Internat. Assn. Bus. Communicators, 1986, Excellence award Nat. Sch. Pub. Relations Soc., 1985; named one of 50 Most Influential People in Sports Bus., Street & Smith's SportsBus. Jour., 2009; Ohio State U. grad. fellow, 1970-73. Mem. Young Pres. Orgn., Speech Comm. Assn., Ctr. for Study of Presidency, Univ. Club (N.Y.C.), Coun. Fgn. Relations. Republican. Avocations: golf, reading, travel. Office: University of Georgia Office of President, Administration Bldg 220 S Jackson St Athens GA 30601-1661 Office Phone: 706-542-0024. E-mail: presuga@uga.edu.*

ADAMS, NELSON L., III, obstetrician, gynecologist; Cert. Obstetrician/Gynecologist. Founder Access IPA, 1993—; chmn. dept. OB/Gyn Parkway Regional Med. Ctr.; pres., chmn. Access Health Solutions, 2001—. Mem. bd. trustees Barry U., Meharry Med. Coll., Fla. Internat. U. Found. Named to Power 150, Ebony mag., 2008. Mem.: Nat. Med. Assn. (former pres., mem. bd. trustees), Dade County Med. Assn. (v.p.). Office: Access Health Solutions 1301 International Pkwy Ste 400 Sunrise FL 33323-2874

ADAMS, REX, investment company executive; m. Ellen Cates; 3 children. Studied, U. Oxford; BA in Polit. Sci. magna cum laude, Duke U., 1962. Govt. rels. trainee Mobil Internat., 1965-70; dir., employee and govt. rels. Mobil Oil, Libya, 1970-72, pers., dir. European ops., 1972-75; mgr., recruitment and placement Mobil Oil Corp., 1975-79, mgr., employee rels. exploration and producing divsn., 1979-84; v.p., employee rels. Mobil Corp., 1984-88; v.p., adminstrn. Mobil Oil Corp. and Mobil Corp., 1988-96; prof., bus. adminstrn., dean, Fuqua Sch. Bus. Duke University, 1996-2001, prof., bus. adminstrn., dean emeritus, 2001—; chmn. Invesco Ltd., 2006—. Past chmn. bd. dirs. PBS; bd. dirs. Vintage Pet., Alleghany Corp., Vera Inst. Justice; trustee Com. for Econ. Devel. and Woods Holes Oceanog. Instn.; former trustee Duke U. and Va. Union U. Rhodes scholar Merton Coll., Oxford U., 1962. Fellow Nat. Acad. Human Resources (disting.); mem. Phi Beta Kappa. Office: PO Box 47 Woods Hole MA 02543-0047 also: Invesco Ltd Two Peachtree Pointe 1555 Peachtree St NE Ste 1800 Atlanta GA 30309 Office Phone: 404-479-1095. Office Fax: 404-439-4911. Business E-Mail: rex.adams@invesco.com.

ADAMS, RICHARD LLOYD, lawyer; b. Cape Girardeau, Mo., Feb. 25, 1951; s. John Alexander and Opal Elizabeth Adams; m. Susan Hefley, Feb. 12, 1983 (div. May 11, 2000); children: Audrey Elizabeth, Adelaide Hefley, Wilson Joseph; m. Sheila Bellinger, Dec. 9, 2011. BA, S.E. Mo. State U., 1972; JD, U. Mo., 1974. Bar: Mo. 1975, Fla. 1975, Tex. 1978, US Ct. Appeals (8th cir.) 1975, US Ct. Appeals (5th and 11th cirs.) 1981, US Ct. Appeals (10th cir.) 1982, US Ct. Appeals (DC cir.) 1987, US Ct. Appeals (9th cir.) 1992, US Supreme Ct. 1982, US Ct. Appeals (fed. cir.) 1997. Assoc. Schafly, Griesedieck Ferrell & Toft, St. Louis, 1975—78; mng. ptnr. Worsham Forsythe Wooldridge LLP, Dallas, 1978—2001; ptnr. Hunton & Williams LLP, 2002—08, Vinson & Elkins LLP, 2008—. Mem. editl. bd. Missouri Law Rev. Mem. bd. dirs. Beringer Wine Estates, 1996—2000. Named Tex. Super Lawyer, Tex. Monthly Mag., 2012, Am. Leading Lawyers Bus. Energy Law, Chambers USA, 2014, Best Lawyers in America Energy Law Adminstr. Law, 2014. Mem.: ABA, Mo. Bar, Fla. Bar, State Bar Tex., Whispering Pines Golf Club, Preston Trail Golf Club. Republican. Methodist. Avocations: golf, travel, wine collecting, art. Home: 7202 Centenary Ave Dallas TX 75225 Office: Vinson & Elkins LLP 2001 Ross Ave 3700 Dallas TX 75201 Business E-Mail: radams@velaw.com.

ADAMS, ROBERT WAUGH, retired state agency administrator, economist, educator; b. Johnstown, Pa., Oct. 26, 1936; s. Robert Waugh and Mary Louise (Pyle) A.; m. Karen Day, June 13, 1964; children: Robert W. and Tara Anne Adams Mason. BS in Acctg., Pa. State U., 1958; MBA, U. Louisville, 1967. Acct., comptr., v.p. lending Citizens Fidelity Bank, Louisville, 1959-77; dir. fin., planning, and from dep. exec. dir. to exec. dir. Ky. Housing Corp., Frankfort, 1977-96; owner Adams Consulting Co., Louisville, 1996—2004, ret., 2004. Past pres. Bank Adminstrv. Inst., 1966, Planning Exec. Inst., 1970, Fin. Exec. Inst., 1974. Bd. dirs. Clifton Ctr. Capt. U.S. Army Infantry, 1958-62. Mem. Louisville Boat Club (past pres.). Republican. Roman Catholic. Home: 5210 Tamerlane Rd Louisville KY 40207-1160 Home Phone: 502-899-1621.

ADAMS, ROYCE W., state legislator; b. Sept. 29, 1938; married. Farmer; horse breeder; owner Royce Adams Oil Co.; mem. Dist. 61 Ky. House of Reps., 1993—. Served with US Army. Mem.: Nat. Fed. Ind. Businessmen, Am. Morgan Horse Assn., Bluegrass Morgan Horse Assn., Grant County C. of C. Democrat. Christian. Office: Ky Legislature Annex Rm 324C 702 Capitol Ave Frankfort KY 40601 Home: 45 Roselawn Dr Williamstown KY 41097-9765 Office Phone: 859-824-3387, 502-564-8100 ext. 627.

ADAMS, RUSSELL LEE, neuropsychologist; b. Jefferson, Tex., Mar. 2, 1941; s. Irby Ray and Verda Mae Adams; m. Carolyn Sue Pulley, Aug. 8, 1964; children: David Lee, Scott Russell. BBA, Tex. A&M U., College Station, 1962; PhD, U. Tex., Austin, 1967. Diplomate Am. Bd. Clin. Neuropsychology. Assoc. prof. dept. psychiatry U. Tex. Health Scis. Ctr., San Antonio, 1969—78; assoc. prof. U. Okla. Health Scis. Ctr., Oklahoma City, 1978—82, prof., 1978—, dir. psychology internship program, 1978—, dir. postdoctoral neuropsychology fellowship program, 1982—. Co-author: Neuropsychology In Clinical Practice; mem. editl. bd numerous profl. jours., 1980—2006; contbr. articles to profl. jours. Adminstr. Scott Russell Adams Meml. Scholarship Baylor U., Waco, Tex., 1990—2006. Capt. US Army, 1967—69. Recipient Gordon Deckert award for Sustained Excellence In Edn., U. Okla. Health Scis. Ctr., 1989, 2002. Fellow: APA (various positions 1980—2006), Nat. Acad. Neuropsychology (com. chair 1980—2006). Baptist. Avocations: travel, reading. Office: U Okla Health Scis Ctr 920 Stanton L Young Blvd Oklahoma City OK 73104 Office Phone: 405-271-8801. Office Fax: 405-271-8802. Business E-Mail: russell-adams@ouhsc.edu.

ADAMS, RYAN (DAVID RYAN ADAMS), musician; b. Jacksonville, NC, Nov. 5, 1974; m. Mandy Moore, Mar. 10, 2009. Founder The Patty Duke Syndrome, NC; co-founder Whiskeytown, 1994—99; solo career, 2000—; mem. The Cardinals, 2005—09. Singer: (albums) Heartbreaker, 2000, Gold, 2001, Demolition, 2002, Rock N Roll, 2003, Love is Hell, 2004, Cold Roses, 2005, Jacksonville City Nights, 2005, 29, 2006, Easy Tiger, 2007, Follow the Lights, 2007, Cardinology, 2008. Office: Lost Highway Records 401 Commerce St Ste 1100 Nashville TN 37219-2489 Office Phone: 310-865-5000.

ADAMS, SANDRA (SANDY ADAMS), former United States Representative from Florida, former state legislator; b. Wyandotte, Mich., Dec. 14, 1956; m. John H. Adams; children: John Jr., Sonya, Kathryn. BA in Criminal Justice Adminstrn., Columbia Coll., 2000. Investigator Orange County Sheriff's Office, 1985—2002; pres., Ctrl. Fla. chpt. Concerns of Police Survivors, Inc., 1992—2001; mem. Dist. 33 Fla. House of Reps., Tallahassee, 2002—10; mem. US Congress from 24th Fla. Dist., Washington, 2011—13, US House Judiciary Com., 2011—13, US House Science, Space & Tech. Com., 2011—13. Served in USAF, 1974—75. Recipient Recognition award, US Secret Svc., FBI, Concerns of Police Survivors, Inc., IRS Investigative Divsn., Seton award, Orange County Sheriff's Office. Republican. Episcopalian.

ADAMS, THOMAS C., JR., bank executive; Exec. v.p., dept. mgr. First Tennessee Bank, exec. v.p., treas., funds mgmt. mgr., 2007—08, exec. v.p., chief investment officer, treas., funds mgmt. mgr., 2008—, First Horizon National Corp., 2008—; exec. v.p., interim CFO First Tennessee Bank National Association, 2008—. Office: First Horizon National Corp 165 Madison Ave Memphis TN 38103 Office Phone: 901-523-4444. Office Fax: 901-523-4266. Business E-Mail: tadams@firsthorizon.com.

ADAMS, THOMAS L., medical association administrator; AB in History, Lenoir Rhyne Coll., 1973, DHL (hon.), 2002; cert., U. Del., 1986. Staff asst. Senator Robert Morgan U.S. Senate, Washington, 1973—76; exec. asst. Congressman Lamar Gudger U.S. Congress, Washington, 1976—77; spl. asst. to the fed. co-chmn. Appalachian Regional Commn., Washington, 1977—78; dir. dept. govtl. affairs N.C. Med. Soc., Raleigh, 1978—83; dir. Office Govtl. Affairs Am. Soc. Anesthesiologists, Washington, 1983—86; exec. v.p., CEO State Med. Soc. Wis., Madison, 1986—96; pres., CEO Med. Group Mgmt. Assn., Denver, 1996—98, Washington, 1996—98; exec. dir. Am. Soc. Plastic Surgeons, Arlington Heights, Ill., 1999—2001; CEO Assn. Clin. Rsch. Profls., Washington, 2001—. Mem. adv. com. AMA Exec. V.p., 1993—96; mem. adv. com. human resource protections U.S. Sec. Office HHS, 2004—. Contbr. articles to profl. jours. Active U.S. Trade Mission to Japan, 1978; chair State Coun. on Health Programs for the Uninsured, Wis., 1989—92; mem. capital campaign cabinet Salvation Army, Madison, Wis., 1994; divsn. chair United Way Dane County, 1994; mem. furnishings com. Monona Terr. Conv. Ctr., 1995; mem. adv. bd. Hawaii Conv. and Visitor Bur., 2001—. With N.C. Air Nat. Guard, 1977. Named one of 25 most influential people in Wis., Madison Mag., 1995. Mem.: Profl. Conv. Mgmt. Assn., Assn. Forum Chgo., Am. Soc. Assn. Execs. (cert. assn. exec.), Am. Assn. Med. Soc. Execs. Office: ACRP Ste 800 500 Montgomery St Alexandria VA 22314 Home: 151 Crest Rd Southern Pines NC 28387-3148

ADAMS, THOMAS R., tobacco company executive; B in Acctg., Duke U. Ptnr. Deloitte & Touche LLP, 1985—99; sr. v.p., controller R.J. Reynolds Tobacco Holdings, Inc., Winston Salem, NC, 1999—2004, sr. v.p., chief acctg. officer, 2004—05, sr. v.p., bus. process, 2005—06; sr. v.p., chief acctg. officer Reynolds American, Inc., Winston Salem, 2004—05, sr. v.p., bus. process, 2006—07, sr. v.p., chief acctg. officer, 2007—08, exec. v.p., CFO, 2008—. Bd. dirs. Tech. Concepts & Designs, Inc.; bd. commissioners City Housing Authority, Winston Salem. Mem. Old Hickory Coun. Boy Scouts of Am. Office: Reynolds Am Inc 401 N Main St Winston Salem NC 27101

ADAMS, TODD PORTER, financial and investment advisor; b. Nyack, NY, Oct. 11, 1955; s. Edmond Robert and Georgina (Porter) A.; m. Catherine Elizabeth Jarboe, Dec. 26, 1982 (div. Dec. 1985); 1 child, Danielle Elyce; m. Janine Marilyn Leduc, Jan. 29, 1994 (div. Jan. 2003). BS, St. Thomas Aquinas Coll., 1977; MBA, SUNY, Buffalo, 1981. CFP. Acct. trainee Allied Chem., Syracuse, N.Y., 1977-78, from acct. to supr. of acctg. Buffalo, 1978-80; pvt. practice fin. cons. Buffalo, 1980-81; account exec. Dean Witter Reynolds, Cape Coral, Fla., 1981-82, E.F. Hutton & Co., Cape Coral, 1982-85; v.p. investments Advest, Inc., Ft. Myers, Fla., 1985-90; rep. LPL Financial, Ft. Myers, 1990—; v.p. Mills-Price & Assoc., Inc., Ft. Myers, 1997-99, pres., 1999—. Investment and inf. commentator WINK-TV, 1989—94. Chmn. Jr. Olympic Torch Run, Lee County, Fla., 1990. Mem. Inst. CFPs, Nat. Assn. Investors Corp., Am. Assn. Ind. Investors, Assn. MBA Execs., Kiwanis (life, v.p. house South Ft. Myers chpt. 1984—, Kiwanian of Yr. award 1983, 95, 99). Republican. Presbyterian. Avocations: all sports, stamp and coin collecting. Office: Mills-Price & Assoc Inc 12444 Brantley Commons Ct Fort Myers FL 33907-5684 Office Phone: 239-433-1223. E-mail: jmpmpa@aol.com.

ADAMS, TOM P.H., foreign language services executive; b. Stockholm; BA in History with honors, Bristol U., England, 1993; MBA, INSEAD. Commodities merchant Trafigura, 1994—2000; CEO Fairfield & Sons Ltd., 2003, Rosetta Stone Inc., Arlington, Va., 2003—, pres., bd. dirs., 2006—. Named Ernst & Young Entrepreneur Of Yr., 2008, Exec of Yr., Am. Bus. Awards, 2009, CEO of the year, 2009. Office: Rosetta Stone Inc 1919 N Lynn St 7th Fl Arlington VA 22209 Business E-Mail: tadams@rosettastone.com.

ADAMS, W. ANDREW, healthcare executive; b. Woodbury, Tenn., Oct. 20, 1945; s. Carl E. and Jennie Mae (Mitchell) A.; m. Dorothy Jean Bryant, Sept. 7, 1966; children: Andrea, Andrew, Anthony. BS, Mid. Tenn. State U., 1968, MBA, 1971. Acctg. mgr., reimbursement mgr. Nat. HealthCare Corp., Murfreesboro, Tenn., 1972—74, pres., 1975—86, gen. ptnr., 1987, chmn; chmn., pres. & CEO Nat. Health Realty, Inc.; pres. National Health Investors, Inc., 1991—2009, chmn., CEO, 1991—. Bd. dirs. Nat. Health Corp., Murfreesboro; pres. Nat. Council Health Care Ctrs., 1979-80; served on various state and nat. health care coms. Mem. Ch. of Christ. Home: 1927 Lebanon Hwy Murfreesboro TN 37130 Office: National Health Investors Inc 222 Robert Rose Dr Murfreesboro TN 37129 Office Phone: 615-890-9100. Office Fax: 615-225-3030. Business E-Mail: wadams@nhinvestors.com.

ADAMS, WANDA, former city councilwoman; BS in Public Affairs, Tex. Southern U. Formerly with Houston Housing Authority; clin. coord. Harris County Mental Health & Mental Retardation Assn., Houston; sr. cmty. liaison Citizen's Assistance Divsn. Office of Mayor, Houston, 2000, cmty. rels. coord. Solid Waste Mgmt. Dept.; councilwoman, Dist. D Houston City Coun., 2008—14; bd. mem. Dist. 9 Houston Ind. Sch. Dist., 2014—. Vol. American Red Cross, Keep Houston Beautiful, YMCA, YWCA Meals on Wheels; Sunday sch. tchr. Fountain of Praise Ch. Mem.: Delta Sigma Theta. Office: Houston Independent School District (HISD) 4400 West 18th St Houston TX 77092 Office Phone: 713-556-6005.*

ADAMS, WILLIAM PETER, JR., plastic surgeon, educator; b. Feb. 14, 1965; BS with honors, Princeton U., NJ; MD, Vanderbilt U. Med. Sch., Nashville, 1991. Diplomate Am. Bd. Plastic Surgery. Intern gen. surgery U. Tex. Southwestern Med. Ctr., Dallas, 1991—92, resident gen. surgery, 1992—94, plastic surgery fellow, 1994—95, resident plastic surgery, 1995—97, asst. prof. dept. plastic surgery, 1997—2000, assoc. clin. prof. dept. plastic surgery, 2001—; pvt. practice Dallas, 2001—. Co-editor: (textbook) Dallas Rhinoplasty; editl. bd. Selected Readings in Plastic Surgery; contbr. articles to profl. jours., chapters to books. Recipient Excellence in Rsch. award, U. Tex. Southwestern Dept. Plastic Surgery, 1997, Excellence in Tchg. award, 1997, Faculty Excellence award, 2001, Faculty Tchg. award, 2005; named Clinician of Yr., 1998. Mem.: Dallas Soc. Plastic Surgeons, Tex. Soc. Plastic Surgery, Dallas County Med. Soc., Am. Soc. Aesthetic Plastic Surgery, Am. Soc. Plastic & Reconstructive Surgeons. Achievements include development of a new irrigant for use in clinical breast implant surgery that may make breast enlargement and breast reconstruction safer. Office: 2801 Lemmon Ave W Ste 300 Dallas TX 75204 also: 5600 W Lovers Ln Ste 212 Dallas TX 75209 Office Phone: 214-965-9885. E-mail: dr@dr-adams.com.

ADAN, JOSEPH I., child and adolescent psychiatrist; MD, U. Ctrl. Del Este, Dominican Republic, 1986. Diplomate Am. Bd. Psychiatry and Neurology, 2003. Resident psychiatry St. Vincents Med. Ctr., NYC, 1990—93; fellow child and adolescent psychiatry Mt. Sinai Med. Ctr., NYC, 1994—95; psychiatric cons.; med. dir. Charter facility Largo, Fla., 1997—2000; designated health authority Eckerd Camp Challenge; staff A&M Psychiatric Svcs. P.A. Office: A&M Psychiatric Services PA 1938 Soule Rd Clearwater FL 33759 Office Phone: 727-726-7442. Office Fax: 727-288-1111.

ADCOCK, DAVID FILMORE, radiologist, educator; b. Columbia, SC, Sept. 19, 1938; s. David Filmore and Eloise (Daniel) A. BS, U. S.C., 1958, MPH, 1986; MD, Med. Coll. S.C., 1962. Diplomate Am. Bd. Radiology, Am. Bd. Nuclear Medicine, Am. Bd. Preventive Medicine. Asst. prof. radiology U. N.C.-Chapel Hill, 1970-72, assoc. prof., 1972-73; dir. nuclear medicine Richard Meml. Hosp., Columbia, 1974-79; prof., chmn. dept. radiology U. S.C.-Columbia, 1979—. Cons. in field Contbr. articles to profl. jours. Served as capt. U.S. Army, 1963-66. Fellow Am. Coll. Preventive Medicine; mem. Radiol. Soc. N.Am., Assn. Univ. Radiologists, Soc. Chmn. Acad. Radiology Depts., Alpha Omega Alpha. Office: U SC Sch Medicine Dept Radiology Columbia SC 29208-0001 Office Phone: 803-733-3295. Business E-Mail: david.adcock@uscmed.sc.edu.

ADCOCK, SAMUEL DENTON, lobbyist, former legislative director; b. Baton Rouge, La., July 30, 1962; s. Lawrence Devon and Patsy Lynn (Pinter) Adcock. BA, Anderson Coll., 1984; MPA, U. Pitts., 1987. Presdl. mgmt. analyst Naval Sea Sys. Command, USN, 1987-89, bus. mgmt. analyst, 1990; legis. asst. for def. and nat. security US Senator Trent Lott, Washington, 1990-91, legis. dir., 1991; dir. defense and security policy for majority leader US Senate; v.p. govt. and bus. rels. Daimler-Benz; joined EADS N.Am. (European Aeronautic Defense and Space Co.), 2000, sr. v.p. govt. rels. Mem. Long Range Air Power Panel, 1997. Republican. Avocations: golf, skiing, basketball. Office: EADS North America Ste 1600 2550 Wasser Ter Herndon VA 20171-6177 Office Phone: 703-236-3300. Office Fax: 703-236-3301.

ADDIS, KAY TUCKER, newspaper editor; AB in English, Coll. William and Mary, 1970. Editor The Virginian-Pilot, Norfolk, 1996—. Office: Virginian Pilot P O Box 449 Norfolk VA 23501-0449

ADDISON, DAVID DUNHAM, lawyer; b. Richmond, Va., Aug. 23, 1941; s. Grafton Dulany and Anne (Withers) A.; m. Marion Lee Wood, Aug. 21, 1965; children: David Dunham Jr., Marion Lee, Elizabeth Townshend. BA, Hampden-Sydney Coll., 1964; LLB, U. Va., 1967. Bar: Va. 1967. Assoc. Browder, Russell, Morris & Butcher, Richmond, 1967—72; ptnr., dir. Browder & Russell, P.C., Richmond, 1972—90; mem. firm, shareholder Williams, Mullen, P.C., Richmond, 1990—. Contbr. articles to profl. jours. Fellow Am. Coll. Trust and Estate Counsel (state chmn. 1986-92); mem. ABA (com. chmn. 1987-94), SAR, Va. Bar Assn., Richmond Bar Assn., Estate Planning Coun. Richmond (pres. 1987-88), Richmond Trust Adminstrs. Coun. (pres. 1986-87), Kiwanis Club Richmond (pres. 1998-99), Country Club Va., Commonwealth Club. Episcopalian. Avocations: travel, golf. Office: Williams Mullen 200 S 10th St Richmond VA 23219-4000 Office Phone: 804-420-6483. Business E-Mail: daddison@williamsmullen.com.

ADDISON, JAMES (JIMMY) E., electric power industry executive; b. Lancaster, SC; BS in Acctg., U. SC, 1982, M in Accountancy. CPA SC. With Deloitte and Touche, Columbia, Charlotte; joined SCANA Corp., 1991; contr. SCE&G (subs. SCANA Corp.), 1991; v.p., fin. SCANA Corp., 2001—06, sr. v.p., CFO, 2006—. Mem. Oliver Gospel Mission, Saluda Shoals Found., Sexual Trauma Svcs., USC Acctg. Adv. Bd., EdVenture Children'''s Museum, SC Bd. Accountancy, AICPA, SC Assn. CPA; bd. dirs. SC Tax Realingment Commn., SC Higher Edn. Found., USC Moore Sch. Bus. Partnership Found., SC Bank & Trust; treas. Southeastern Electric Exch. Recipient Moore Sch. Bus. Disting. Young Alumni award, 2001. Office: SCANA Corp 220 Operation Way Cayce SC 29033-3701 Office Phone: 803-217-9668. Business E-Mail: jaddison@scana.com.

ADDISON, WINNIFRED ALLEN, gynecologist, educator; b. Toccoa, Ga., May 24, 1934; s. Allen Richard and Cordelia (McCurry) A.; m. Sally Bender, Aug. 28, 1959; children: Rebecca Dee, Cynthia Ann, Amy Sue. BA, Duke U., 1956, MD, 1960. Diplomate Am. Bd. Ob-Gyn (examiner). Prof., dir. div. gynecology, residency coord. Duke U., Durham, N.C., 1976—. Contbr. articles to scientific jours. Served to capt. U.S. Army, 1965-67. Fellow Am. Coll. Obstetricians and Gynecologists; mem. S. Atlantic Assn. Obstetricians and Gynecologists, Soc. Gynecologic Surgeons, Bayard Ctr. Assn. Obstetricians and Gynecologists, N.C. Soc. Obststricians-Gynecologists. Republican. Episcopalian. Avocation: horseback riding. Home: PO Box 727 Hillsborough NC 27278-0727 Office: Duke Univ Med Ctr PO Box 3296 Durham NC 27715-3296 Home Phone: 919-732-2206; Office Phone: 919-684-3866. E-mail: addisonsa@embergmail.com.

ADEGBOYEGA, PATRICK, physician, educator; MD, U. Ilorin, Nigeria, 1987. Diplomate American Bd. Pathology, 1996, Internat. Com. Dermatopathology, 2006. Prof. LSU Health Scis. Ctr.-Shreveport, La., 2006—, dir. tissue and serum repository, dir. histopathology rsch. lab. Office: LSU Health Sciences Center-Shreveport 1501 Kings Hwy Shreveport LA 71130*

ADELMAN, KENNETH LEE, journalist, former ambassador; b. Chgo., June 9, 1946; s. Harry and Corinne (Unger) Adelman; m. Carol Craigle, Aug. 29, 1971; children: Jessica, Jocelyn. BA, Grinnell Coll., Iowa, 1968; MA, Georgetown U., Washington, 1969, PhD, 1975. With US Dept. Commerce, Washington, 1968-70; asst. to sec. US Dept. Def., Washington, 1976-77; sr. polit. scientist Stanford Research Inst., Arlington, Va., 1977-81; amb., dep. permanent rep. to UN US Dept. State, NYC, 1981-83; dir. US Arms Control & Disarmament Agy., Washington, 1983-88; exec. dir. USA for Innovation, Washington; nat. editor Washingtonian mag., 1991—; sr. counsel Edelman Pub. Rels. Worldwide, 2001—. Former mem. Def. Policy Bd., Comm. on Present Danger, Project for New Am. Century; vice-chmn. Newmyer Assoc.; bd. dirs. IPAC; Shakespeare instr. Georgetown U., George Washington U. Author: African Realities, 1981, The Great Universal Embrace, 1989, Getting the Job Done, 1992; co-author: The Defense Revolution, 1990, Shakespeare in Charge: The Bard's Guide to Leading and Succeeding on the Business Stage, 1999; contbr. numerous articles to profl. jours., newspapers and mags. Jewish.

ADELMAN, MICHAEL D., academic administrator; m. Cheryl Adelman. DPM, Phila. Coll. Podiatric Medicine, 1977; DO, Coll. Osteo. Medicine and Surgery, 1981; postgrad., U. Toledo Coll. Law. Prof. Temple U., Phila., U. Toledo, Del. Valley Cmty. Coll., Doylestown, Pa.; assoc. dean for acad. affairs Ohio U. Coll. of Osteopathic Medicine, Athens, Ohio, 1998—2002; v.p. acad. affairs and dean W. Va. Sch. Osteo. Medicine, 2002—10, acting pres., 2010—11, pres., 2011—. Fellow: Am. Osteo. Coll. of Proctology (exec. dir. 1994—2000, Proctologist of the Year); mem.: W.Va. Soc. Osteo. Medicine (pres.). Avocations: magic, ventriloquism. Office: West Virginia School Osteopathic Medicine Office of President 400 N Lee St Lewisburg WV 24901 Office Phone: 304-647-6295. Office Fax: 304-645-4859. E-mail: madelman@osteo.wvsom.edu.

ADELMAN, ROBERT PAUL, retired construction executive, lawyer; b. NYC, Dec. 7, 1930; s. Saul and Eva (Ochs) A.; m. Renee Gratum, June 7, 1953 (dec. Apr. 1998); children: Michael, Susan, John; m. Judith A. Turner, Jan. 9, 1999. BA, Columbia U., 1952, JD, 1954. Bar: N.Y. 1954, U.S. Supreme Ct. 1960. Assoc. Winthrop, Stimson, Putnam & Roberts, NYC, 1956-64; with Celanese Corp., NYC, 1964-71; v.p., treas., gen. counsel Calina Industries, Inc., NYC, 1971-73; chief fin. officer Rockefeller Group, Inc., NYC, 1975-84; chmn., chief exec. officer, pres. Rogers Group, Inc., Nashville, 1984-88, chmn., 1988-92, vice chmn., 1992—2001, cons. to the pres. and CEO, 2001—04. Mem. Fin. Execs. Inst., 1973-84, Conf. Bd. Exec. Coun., 1985-90; trustee No. European Oil Royalty Trust, 1987—, chmn. audit com., 1995-2006, mng. trustee, 2006—; bd. dirs. CPRC Group LLC, 2004-. Treas. and chief fin. officer NY State Urban Devel. Corp., 1973-75; trustee The Jackson Lab., 1981—. Served with US Army, 1954-56, instr. Corps of Cadets US Mil. Acad., West Point, NY. Mem. University Club (N.Y.C.), Amelia Island Club. Avocations: sailing, golf. Home: 9 Fox Tail Rd Amelia Island FL 32034-6610

ADELSON, DAVID M., dermatologist, educator; MD, Emory U., 1985. Diplomate Am. Bd. Dermatology, 1989. Resident dermatology Emory Univ. Med. Ctr., Atlanta, 1986—89; intern Washinton Univ. Sch. of Medicine, St. Louis; assoc. prof. dermatology Coll. Medicine Univ. Okla.; hosp. affiliations include St. Francis Hosp., St. John Med. Ctr. Office: Tulsa Physicians & Surgeons Ste 502 1705 E 19th St Tulsa OK 74104 Office Phone: 918-619-4000, 918-619-4000. Office Fax: 918-619-4005.

ADELSON, TOM, state legislator; m. Julie Adelson; 4 children. BA, Stanford Univ.; JD cum laude, So. Methodist Univ. Practice law since, 1992; operated, now ptnr. oil and gas bus.; private law practice, 1998—; sec. Okla. Dept. Health; mem. Dist. 33 Okla. State Senate, 2004—. Founding bd. mem. Tulsa Coalition of Children's Health; past pres. & bd. mem. Tulsa Mental Health Assn.; mem. Cmty. Hosp. Authority, Tulsa, Okla. Univ. Health Care Task Force. Mem.: Tulsa Mental Health Assn. (former pres., bd. mem.). Democrat. Mailing: 2448 East 26th Pl Tulsa OK 74114 Office: 2300 N Lincoln Blvd Rm 527 Oklahoma City OK 73105 Office Phone: 405-521-5551. Business E-Mail: adelson@oksenate.gov.

ADERHOLT, ROBERT BROWN, United States Representative from Alabama, lawyer; b. Haleyville, Ala., July 22, 1965; s. Bobby Ray and Mary Frances Aderholt; m. Caroline McDonald; children: Mary Elliot, Robert Hayes. BA, Birmingham Southern U., 1987; JD, Samford U. Cumberland School of Law, 1990. City judge, Haleyville, Ala., 1992—96; asst. legal advisor to Gov. State of Ala., Montgomery, 1995—96; mem. US Congress from 4th Ala. Dist., Washington, 1997—. Mem. Helsinki Commn. on Security and Cooperation in Europe. Republican. Office: US House of Representatives 2369 Rayburn House Office Building Washington DC 20515 also: 247 Carl Elliott Bldg 1710 Alabama Ave Jasper AL 35501*

ADKINS, GREGORY D., higher education administrator; b. Charleston, W.Va., May 20, 1941; s. Wondel Lafayette and Corda Christenia (Carnes) A.; m. Dolores June Lowe, Sept. 9, 1961; children: Christenia Lea, Angela Dawn BS, U. Charleston, 1962; MEd, Fla. Atlantic U., 1966; M.C.S., U. Miss., 1968, EdD, 1970. Assoc. prof. edn. Palm Beach Atlantic Coll., West Palm Beach, Fla., 1972-74, chair dept. edn., 1972-73, chair div. profl. studies, dir. tchr. edn., 1973-74; assoc. dean career edn. W.Va. No. Community Coll., Wheeling, 1974-75, dean acad. affairs, 1975-79; coordinator instrn. and planning Colo. State Bd. C.C.s. and Occupational Edn., Denver, 1979-81; pres. So. W.Va. Community Coll., Logan, 1981-88, Bluefield (W.Va.) State Coll., 1988-93, Franklin County Schs., Frankfort, Ky., 1993-94, Jefferson Coll., Hillsboro, Mo., 1994—. Vice chmn. adv. coun. of pres. W.Va. Bd. Regents, 1986-87; chair legis. affairs com., 1986-87; bd. dirs. Missourians for Higher Edn., Mo. Coordinating Bd. for Higher Edn. Com. on Transfer and Articulation, 1997—, Jefferson Coll. Found. Inc. Mem. Gov.'s Labor/Mgmt. Coun., Charleston, 1986-93, W.Va. Enterprise Zone Authority, Charleston, 1987-93, Mercer County Econ. Devel. Authority, 1989-93; bd. dirs. Bluefield Regional Med. Ctr., 1988-89, W.Va. Joint Commn. for Vocat. and Occupational Edn., 1989-93, Missourians for Higher Edn., 1996—; mem. coms. on transfer and articulation Mo. Coordinating Bd. for Higher Edn., 1996—. Recipient Alumnus of Yr. award U. Charleston, 1984, award VFW, Chapmanville, 1987; NSF grad. fellow 1967-68, Richard Weaver fellow Intercollegiate Studies Inst., 1969-70. Mem. W.Va. Assn. Coll. and Univ. Pres. (pres. 1984-85), W.Va. C.C. Assn. (pres. 1985-86), Mo. C.C. Assn. (bd. dirs. 1995-97, adv. coun. of pres. 1994—), North Ctrl. Assn. (cons., evaluator 1984—, commr.-at-large 1984-90), Kiwanis, Rotary Internat., Chi Beta Phi (pres.). Mem. Ch. of Christ. Avocations: outdoor sports, gardening. Office: Jefferson Coll 1000 Viking Dr Hillsboro MO 63050-2440

ADKINS, JANET H., state legislator; b. Jacksonville, Fla., Oct. 9, 1965; m. Doug Adkins; children: Emily, Douglas. AA with honors, Fla. Cmty. Coll.; BA in Computer Info. Sci. magna cum laude, U. North Fla., 1987, MBA, 1990. Client ptnr. Info. Sys. of Fla. Inc., 1987—99; committeewoman Nassau County, 2000—; mem. Dist. 12 Fla. House of Reps., 2008—, mem. govt. accountability act coun., govt. ops. appropriations com., joint com. on pub. counsel oversight, mil. and local affairs policy com. Vice chmn. Rep. 4th Congl. Caucus, 2001—03, chmn., 2003—05. Mem. Nassau County Sch. Bd., 1998—2008, Nassau County Planning & Zoning Bd., 2002—05, Amelia Island Coun., 2004—, Citizen's Budget Policy Reform Com., 2005, Rep. Party Fla. Rules Com., 2007, Fernandina Beach Underground Utility Task Force, 2007—08; vol. Boys & Girls Club Brick Campaign, 2005, Southside Elem. Sch., 2005—06, Atlantic Elem. Sch., 2006—07, Girl Scout Gateway Coun., 2007; adv. bd. Micah's Place, 2002; sec. Nassau County Drug, Alcohol & Crime Coalition, 2006—; co-chmn. Bush & Cheney Campaign, 2003—04. Mem.: NRA, Nassau Federated Rep. Women (first v.p. 1999—2001), Nassau County Cmty. Alliance (chmn. 2006—), Daughters Am. Revolution Amelia Island Chpt., Rotary Internat., Fernandina Beach Rotary Club. Republican. Baptist. Office: 212 The Capitol 402 S Monroe St Tallahassee FL 32399-1300 also: 905 S 8th St Fernandina Beach FL 32034-3706 also: 945 N Temple Ave Starke FL 32091 Office Phone: 850-488-6920, 904-491-3664, 904-966-6215. Business E-Mail: janet.adkins@myfloridahouse.gov.

ADKINS, NORMAN, electric power industry executive; BS in Indsl. Engring., Va. Poly. Inst. and State U.; MBA in Fin., Internat. Bus., NY U. Mentor, new bus. venture program NY U.; with Pricing Society; v.p., sales and bus. devel, energy div. Southwire Co., dir., internat. sales and mfg., 1998, dir., mktg., energy div., 2001, sr. v.p., pres., Southwires OEM Div., 2005—. Mem. Va. Tech Alumni Assn., Am. Mgmt. Assn. Office: Southwire Co 1 Southwire Dr Carrollton GA 30119 Office Phone: 770-832-4242. Business E-Mail: norman_adkins@southwire.com.

ADKINS, ROCKY, state legislator, mining executive; b. Morehead, Ky., Nov. 4, 1959; m. Leah Adkins; children: Kristen, Brandon, Victoria Elise. BA, MA, Morehead State U. Coal firm exec.; mem. Dist. 99 Ky. House of Reps., Ky., 1987—; majority fl. leader, 2004—. Recipient Outstanding Leadership award, Morehead State U. Mem.: Plumbers & Pipefitters Union, Nat. Rifle Assn., Elliot County Sportsmen Club, Lions Club (Sand Hook). Democrat. Baptist. Mailing: PO Box 688 Sandy Hook KY 41171 Office: Ky Legislature Annex Rm 309 702 Capitol Ave Frankfort KY 40601 also: Ky Legislature Capitol Rm 304 700 Capitol Ave Frankfort KY 40601 Office Phone: 502-564-5565, 606-928-0407. Office Fax: 606-929-5213.

ADKINS, TRACE (TRACY DARRELL ADKINS), musician; b. Sarepta, La, Jan. 13, 1962; s. Aaron and Peggy (Carraway) Adkins; m. Rhonda Forlaw (separated Mar. 2014); children: Mackenzie, Brianna, Trinity;children from previous marriage: Tarah, Sarah. Attended, La Tech U. Singer, musician (albums) Dreamin' Out Loud, 1996, Big Time, 1997, More..., 1999, Chrome, 2001, Comin' On Strong, 2003, Greatest Hits Collection, Vol. 1, 2003, Songs About Me, 2005, Dangerous Man, 2006, American Man: Greatest Hits Volume II, 2007, X, 2008, Cowboy's Back in Town, 2010, The Definitive Greatest Hits: 'Til the Last Shot's Fired, 2010, Proud to Be Here, 2011, 10 Great Songs, 2012, Love Will..., 2013, The King's Gift, 2013, Icon, 2013, (songs) I Got My Game On, 2007 (Male Video of Yr., Country Music TV Awards, 2008), You're Gonna Miss This, 2008 (Single of Yr., Acad. Country Music Awards, 2009), (with Blake Shelton songs) Hillbilly Bone, 2009 (Vocal Event of Yr., Acad. Country Music Awards, 2010, Collaborative Video of Yr., Country Music TV Awards, 2010); actor: (TV series) Yes, Dear, 2004, The Young and the Restless, 2008; (films) An American Carol, 2008, The Lincoln Lawyer, 2011, The Between, 2012, Saving Santa, 2013; contestant Celebrity Apprentice, 2008; author: (autobiography) A Personal Stand: Observations and Opinions from a Freethinking Roughneck, 2007. Named Top New Male Vocalist, Acad. Country Music Awards, 1996; named to Grand Ole Opry, 2003. Office: c/o Show Dog-Universal Music 2303 21st Ave S Nashville TN 37212*

ADKISSON, PERRY LEE, university system chancellor; b. Hickman, Ark., Mar. 11, 1929; s. Robert Louis and Imogene (Perry) A.; m. Frances Rozelle, Dec. 29, 1956 (dec. 1995); m. Gloria Ray, May 16, 1998; 1 dau., Jean Amanda. BS, U. Ark., 1950, MS, 1954; PhD in Entomology, Kans. State U., 1956; DS (hon.), U. Ark., 1997; DHL, Tex. A&M U., 2001. Asst. prof. entomology U. Mo., 1956-58; assoc. prof. Tex. A&M U., 1958-63, prof., 1963-67, Disting. prof. entomology, 1967—, head dept. entomology, 1967-78, v.p. for agr. and renewable resources, 1978-80, dep. chancellor for agr., 1980-83, dep. chancellor, 1983-86, chancellor, 1986-91, regent's prof., 1991-95. Cons. Internat. AEC, Vienna, 1969-74; chmn. sci. adv. panel Gov. Tex. on Agrl. Chems., 1970-72; chmn. Tex. Pesticide Adv. Com., 1972; mem. panel experts on integrated pest control UN/FAO, Rome, 1971-78, chmn., 1992-96; mem. Structural Pest Control Bd., Tex., 1972-78, NRC World Food and Nutrition Study Team, 1977; chmn. com. biology pest species NRC, 1974; mem. environ. studies bd., study group problems pest control NAS-NRC, 1973-75; mem. U.S. directorate UNESCO Man and the Biosphere Program, 1975-77; mem. bd. on agr. NRC, 1985-87, mem. Nat. Sci. Bd., 1985-96; mem. governing bd. Internat. Crops Rsch. Inst. for Semi-Arid Tropics, 1982-88; mem. rsch. adv. com. Agr. for Internat. Devel., 1986; mem. com. on life scis. NRC, 1985-85; mem. Tex. Sci. and Tech. Coun., 1986-88; mem. Standing Com. for Internat. Plant Protection Congresses, 1984—, adv. dir. Export-Import Bank U.S., 1987. Mem. editorial com. Ann. Rev. Entomology, 1973-78; contbr. articles to profl. jours. Exec. dir. G.H.W. Bush Presdl. Libr. Ctr. and Bush Libr. Found., 1991-93. With M.C., U.S. Army, 1951-53. Recipient Faculty Disting. Achievement award for rsch. Tex. A&M U., 1965, Alexander Von Humboldt award, 1980; Disting. Svc. award Am. Registry Prof. Entomology, 1979, Disting. Scientist of Yr. award Tex. Acad. Scis., 1982, Disting. Alumnus Svc. award Kans. State U., 1980, Disting. Svc. award Am. Inst. Biol. Sci., 1987, Nat. 4-H Alumni award, 1988, Outstanding Alumnus award Coll. of Agr. and Home Econs., U. Ark., 1990, Disting. Alumni award U. Ark., 1990, Disting. Svc. award Am. Agrl. Editors Assn., 1992, Wolfe prize in agr., Wolf Found., Israel, 1994-95, World Food prize, 1997, medallion alumni award Kans. State U., 1999; USPHS postdoctoral fellow Harvard U., 1963-64; Tex. Heritage Hall of Honor, 1998. Fellow AAAS, Entomol. Soc. Am. (governing bd. 1971-75, pres. 1974, Bussart Meml. award 1967, Founders Meml. lectr. 1985); mem. Am. Acad. Arts and Scis., Kans. Entomol. Soc., Internat. Orgn. Biol. Control, Am. Registry Profl. Entomologists (governing council 1976-78, pres. 1977), Nat. Acad. Scis., Phi Kappa Phi, Sigma Xi. Office: Tex A&M U Dept Entomology College Station TX 77843-0001

ADKISSON, RANDALL LYNN, minister; b. Atlanta, May 28, 1957; s. John Earl and Mearl (Cox) A.; m. Salee Robin Smith, Nov. 7, 1981; children: Katheryn Lynsey, Keith Alan. BA in Journalism, U. Ga., 1979; MDiv, Southwestern Bapt. Theol. Sem., Ft. Worth, 1985; PhD, New Orleans Bapt. Theol. Sem., 1990. Ordained to ministry So. Bapt. Conv., 1979. Min. of youth Bethel Bapt. Ch., Good Hope, Ga., 1976-79; assoc. pastor Orange Hill Bapt. Ch., Austell, Ga., 1979-82; pastor Shifalo Bapt. Ch., Kiln, Miss., 1985-88, 1st Bapt. Ch., Foxworth, Miss., 1988-91, Monroeville, Ala., 1991-98, sr. pastor Cookeville, Tenn., 1998—; com. on bds. Tenn. Bapt. Conv., 2003—07. Tchg. fellow New Orleans Bapt. Theol. Sem., 1985-86. Bd. dirs. Judson Coll., 1994-98, Romanian-Am. Missions, 1998. Mem. Marion Bapt. Assn. (pastoral ministries dir. 1990-91, pres. min.'s conf. 1990-91), Nat. Assn. Bapt. Profs. Religion, Soc. Bibl. Lit., Alumni Assn. New Orleans Bapt. Theol. Seminary (v.p. to pres.-elect Ala. chpt., 1993, pres. 1994), Am. Assn. Christian Counselors, Tenn. Bapt. Conv. (mem. bd. com., chair-com. on bds., exec. com. mem., internat. commn. bd. dirs.). Office: 1st Bapt Ch 18 S Walnut Ave Cookeville TN 38501-3284

ADLER, FREDERICK RICHARD, lawyer, corporate financial executive; b. NYC, Apr. 4, 1925; s. Samuel and Rose (Axelrod) A.; m. Catherine R. George, Apr. 25, 1986; Christopher Wells, Frederick George Richard; children by previous marriage: Barbara Ilene, James Richard, Susan Ruth Chapman, Elizabeth Anne Wertheimer. BA, Bklyn. Coll., 1948; JD magna cum laude, Harvard U., 1951; Doctorate (hon.), Technion-Israel Inst. Tech., 1998. Bar: NY 1952. Assoc. Reavis & McGrath, NYC, 1951-58, ptnr., 1959-89, Fulbright, Jaworski, Reavis & McGrath, NYC, 1989-91; ret. sr. ptnr. Fulbright & Jaworski, NYC, 1991-95, of counsel, 1996—2009; dir., chmn. exec. com. Data Gen. Corp., Westbo, Mass., 1968-99; mng. ptnr. Adler & Co. Bd. dirs. Senti Search Corp., Fla., SIT Investment Assocs., Minn. Trustee Tchrs. Ins. and Annuity Assn., 1977-95; bd. mem. overseers Meml. Sloan-Kettering Cancer Ctr.; mem. dean's adv. bd. Harvard Law Sch; trustee Horace Mann School; With US Army, 1943-45. Mem. Harvard Club, Met. Club, Univ. Club (NY), Atlantic Golf Club (Southampton, NY), Palm Beach Country Club, NY Athletic Club. Office: 220 Sunrise Ave Palm Beach FL 33480-3869

ADLER, PETER HOLDRIDGE, entomologist, educator; b. South Charleston, W.Va., Oct. 16, 1954; BS, Washington and Lee U., 1976; MS, Pa. State U., 1979, PhD, 1983. Prof. entomology Clemson (S.C.) U., 1984—. Postdoc. U. Alta., 1984; grad. faculty, biology U. South Ala., 2000—. Author: The Black Flies (Simuliidae) of North America (Assn. of Am. Publishers Outstanding Achievement in Profl. & Scholarly Pub.: Best Single Vol. Reference in Sci., 2004); co-editor: (book) Insect Biodiversity: Science and Society; contbr. chapters to books, over 180 refereed sci. jour. articles. Recipient Faculty Rsch. Scientist award, Clemson U. Sigma Xi Chpt., 1993, Bd. Trustees Faculty of Excellence award, Clemson U., 2000, 2004, 2006—07, Godley-Snell award for Excellence in Agrl. Rsch., 2003, Alumni award for Outstanding Achievements in Rsch., 2005, Outstanding Alumnus award, Pa. State Coll. Agrl. Scis., 2008, Tchg. Merit award, North Am. Coll. and Tchrs. Agriculture, 2011, Tchg. Excellence award, Coll. Agrl., Forest & Environ. Scis., Clemson U., 2011, Whooping Crane Conservation award, Internat. Crane Found., 2013. Mem.: Lepidopterists' Soc., Soc. Freshwater Sci., Entomol. Soc. Washington, Entomol. Soc. Am. (J.H. Comstock award 1983, Thomas Say award 2005), S.C. Entomol. Soc. (pres. 1997—98, J.H. Cochran award for Excellence in Entomology 1999), Sigma Xi. Office: Clemson University E143 Poole Agricultural Ctr Clemson SC 29634-0310 Office Fax: 864-656-5069. Business E-Mail: padler@clemson.edu.*

ADLEY, ROBERT R., state legislator; b. Sept. 3, 1947; s. Roy and Peggy Adley; m. Claudia Henagan; children: Brice (dec.), Brandon. Former chmn. appropriations com. Bond Commerce & Interim Emergency Bd., former chmn. budget com.; mem. La. House Rep., Parish County Aging, 1977; pres. ABCO Petroleum Corp., 1974—99, Pelican Gas Mgmt. Inc., 1993—; city councilman-at-large Bossier, 1977—79; mem. Dist. 8 La. House of Reps., 1980—95; candidate gov., 1995; mem. Dist. 36 La. State Senate, 2003—, vice chair revenue and fiscal affairs com., select com. on consumer affairs and tech., chair select com. on vets. affairs, mem. judiciary C com., transp., hwys. and pub. works com., select com. on vocat. and tech. edn. Named Outstanding Young Bus., Bossier Parish, 1976, Outstanding Young Men, Bossier City, 1980. Mem.: VFW, Muscular Dystrophy Assn., Rotary, Jaycees, Exchange Club. Republican. Methodist. Mailing: 611 Jessie Jones Dr Benton LA 71006-4247 also: 716 Main St Minden LA 71055 Office: PO BOX 94183 Baton Rouge LA 70804 Office Phone: 318-371-2420. E-mail: adleyr@legis.state.la.us.

ADNANI, AMIR, mining executive; BS, U. BC. Officer Fort Sun Investments Inc., 2001—04; founder, pres. Blender Media Inc., 2004; pres., CEO, prin. exec. officer Uranium Energy Corp., 2005—. Former bd. dirs. Blender Media Inc., 2006, bd. dirs., 2004, Fort Sun Investments Inc., 2001—04, Uranium Energy Corp., 2005—. Office: Uranium Energy Corp Ste 230 PO Box 2955 Corpus Christi TX 78403-2955 Office Phone: 512-828-6980. Office Fax: 512-535-0832. Business E-Mail: aadnani@uraniumenergy.com.

ADREAN, LEE, corporate financial executive; BS in Acctg. summa cum laude & phi beta kappa, Bucknell U., 1974; MBA, Harvard U., 1976. Various sr. positions Bain & Co., Inc., Peat, Marwick, Mitchell & Co. (now KPMG), Providian Corp.; exec. v.p., CFO First Data Corp.; CFO, exec. v.p., fin. & adminstrn. EarthLink; exec. v.p., CFO NDCHealth Corp., 2004—06; corp. v.p., CFO Equifax, Inc., 2006—. Bd. trustees, chmn., investment com. & Long range planning com. Bucknell U. Mem. Fin. Execs. Inst., Ga. State CFO Roundtable. Office: Equifax Inc 1550 Peachtree St NW Atlanta GA 30309 Office Phone: 404-885-8000. Office Fax: 408-885-8988. Business E-Mail: lee.adrean@equifax.com.

ADUEN, JAVIER FRANCISCO, physician, researcher; b. Ovejas, Colombia, Mar. 28, 1959; s. Reginaldo Aduen and Bray Hellen; m. Diana Mattos, 1985; 1 child, Paula Andrea. Physician (hon.), Universidad del Norte, Colombia, 1983; Internal Medicine Residency (hon.), Universidad Nacional De Colombia, 1988, Critical Care Medicine Clin. fellowship (hon.), 1989; Critical Care Medicine Clin. Fellowship, Johns Hopkins U. Sch. of Medicine, Balt., 1994; Internal Medicine Residency, Maimonides Med. Ctr., Bklyn., 1997; Critical Care Medicine Fellowship, Mayo Clinic, Minn., 1999; Pulmonary Fellowship, Mayo Clinic, Jacksonville, 2001. Cert. Am. Bd. Internal Medicine, 1997, Critical Care Medicine Am. Bd. Internal Medicine, 1999, Pulmonary Am. Bd. Internal Medicine, 2002. Mandatory med. svc. Hosp. Monte Carmelo, El Carmen de Bolivar, Colombia, 1983—84; physician-in-chief ICU, Hosp. Universitario de Barranquilla, Barranquilla, Colombia, 1989—91, ICU, Clinica del Caribe, Barranquilla, Colombia, 1994—95; assoc. cons. Critical Care Medicine, Mayo Clinic, Jacksonville, 1999; asst. prof. medicine Divsn. of Pulmonary Medicine, Dept. Critical Care Medicine, Mayo Clinic, Jacksonville, 2001—, sr. assoc. cons., 2001—. Author: (book chpt.) Magnesium and calcium: Two keys to unlocking the dilemmas of cardiovascular diseases. In: Critical Care State of the Art. Society of Critical Carte Medicine, 1993, Adrenal disease in the critically ill patient. In: Critical Care Medicine, Principles of Diagnosis and Management, 1995, Lactic acidosis. In: Critical Care State of the Art. Society of Critical Care Medicine, 1995. Recipient Invited Prof., Universidad del Norte. Barranquilla, Colombia, 1990—, Best Resident of Yr. Internal Medicine Residency Program, Maimonides Med. Ctr., Bklyn., 1997, Am's. Top Physician award, Consumer's Rsch. Coun. of Am., 2003. Achievements include research in Predictive Biological Markers of Acute Lung Injury After Liver Transplantation; Predictive Biological Markers of Ischemia-Reperfusion-Induced Lung Injury After Lung Transplantation; Etiology of Leukocytosis in the Early Postoperative Period After Lung Transplantation; Lung Allograft Rejection Gene Expresion Observational (Largo) Study; The Impact of Standardizing Initial Sepsis Management in the Four Mayo Clinic Hospitals: A Quality Improvement Intervention. Avocations: soccer, movies.

AEBERSOLD, CAROL, writer; Taught music; co-owner CCA and B (Creatively Classic Activities and Books, LLC), 2005—. Co-author (with daughters Chandra Bell and Christa Pitts): The Elf on the Shelf-A Christmas Tradition, 2005; co-exec. prodr. with daughters The Elf on the Shelf: An Elf's Story, 2011, co-writer (songs) Each and Every Christmas, Extravaganzalorious. Achievements include The Elf on the Shelf brand going global by hosting readings and book signings throughout the world. Avocations: writing, motivational speaking, supporting community theatre groups. Office: CCA and B-The Elf on the Shelf 1174 Hayes Industrial Dr Marietta GA 30062 Office Phone: 877-919-4105. Office Fax: 678-990-1182.*

AEHLERT, BARBARA JUNE, health facility administrator; b. San Antonio, June 17, 1956; d. Bobby Ray and Ronella Su (Light) Mahoney; m. Dean A. Aehlert, Sept. 6, 1980; children: Andrea, Sherri. AA in Nursing, Glendale CC, Ariz., 1976; BS in Profl. Arts, St. Joseph's Coll., Windham, Maine, 1997. Cert. ACLS instr., BLS and PALS instr., emergency med. tng./paramedic instr. Gen. mgr. Hosp. Ambulance Svc., Phoenix, 1982-83; critical care nurse Samaritan Health Svcs., Phoenix, 1978-80, coord. patient transp., 1980-82, mgr. clin. programs, 1983-92; dir. emergency med. svcs. edn. EMS Edn. and Rsch., 1992-97; pres. S.W. EMS Edn. Inc., Glendale, Ariz., 1997—; dir. field tng. S.W. Ambulance, Mesa, Ariz., 2006—09. EMS coord., City of Mesa Fire Dept., 2001-04. Author: (book) Emergency Med. Technician: EMT in action, 2008, ACLS Study Guide, 3d edit., 2007, ACLS Quick Review Study Cards, 2003, PALS Study Guide, 3d edit., 2006, ECGs Made Easy, 4th edit., 2010, ECGs Made Easy Study Cards, 2003, Mosby's Comprehensive Pediatric Emergency Care, 2005, Paramedic Practice Today, 2009. Republican.

AEPPEL, GLYN FERGUSON, personal care industry executive; b. Pretoria, Republic of South Africa, Oct. 27, 1958; came to U.S., 1977; d. Raymond Clive and Sybil Gladys (Van Den Dool) Ferguson; m. Timothy Aeppel. BA, Principia Coll., 1981; MBA, Harvard U., Boston, 1985. Chief investment officer Andre Balazs Properties; Policy analyst US C. of C., 1981—83; assoc. fellow, fin. Harvard Business School, 1985—86; mgr., treasury dept. Marriott Corp., 1986—89; dir., planning and devel. Am. Trucking Assn. Inc., Alexandria, Va., 1989; dir., devel. Holiday Inn Worldwide, Wiesbaden, Germany, 1990—93; ptnr. Lodging Evaluation Group, 1993—95; sr. v.p., acquisitions and devel. FFC Hospitality, LLC, 1998—2001; v.p., devel. Interstate Hotels & Resorts, Inc., 1995—98, exec. v.p., bus. devel. & acquisitions, 2001—02; exec. v.p., bus. devel., Americas Le Meridien Hotels and Resorts, 2002—04; prin. Aeppel and Assocs., 2004—06; exec. v.p., acquisitions and devel. Loews Hotels, 2006—08. Bd. dirs. Sunrise Sr. Living Inc., 2008—. Sustaining mem. Republican Nat. Com., Washington, 1985—. Mem. Am. C. of C. in Germany, Am. Mgmt. Assn. Avocations: tennis, skiing, squash, piano playing, music composition. Office: Sunrise Senior Living Inc 7900 Westpark Dr Ste T900 Mc Lean VA 22102-4217 Office Phone: 703-273-7500. Office Fax: 703-744-1601. Business E-Mail: glyn.aeppel@sunrise-al.com.

AERTKER, GAYLE, real estate company executive; Attended Acctg., La. State U., 1976; BSBA, Northwestern State U., 1977. Mng. ptnr. Millennium Retail Ptnrs., LLC; v.p., real estate acquisitions Costco, Issaquah, Wash., 1989—92; v.p., real estate Toys R Us, Wayne, NJ, 1992—98; sr. v.p., real estate Office Depot, Inc., 1998—2000, exec. v.p., real estate & constrn. Delray Beach, Fla., 2000—06; sr. v.p., real estate & store devel. Dollar General Corp., 2006—. Office: Dollar General Corp 100 Mission Ridge Goodlettsville TN 37072 Office Phone: 615-855-4000. Office Fax: 615-855-5252. Business E-Mail: gayle.aertker@dollargeneral.com.

AFIELD, WALTER EDWARD, psychiatrist, health facility administrator, educator; b. NYC, Dec. 28, 1935; s. Walter Edward and Mollie Evelyn (MCGovern) A.; m. Nancy Browning, Dec. 27, 1973; children: Walter Edward, Neva Browning. AB, U. Pa., Phila., 1956; MD, Johns Hopkins U., Balt., 1960. Intern Grady Meml. Hosp., Atlanta, 1960-61; fellow in psychiatry Harvard U., Cambridge, Mass., 1961-64, 66-67; asst. prof. psychiatry Johns Hopkins U., Balt., 1967-70, dir. dept. child psychiatry, 1967-70; prof. U. South Fla. Coll. Medicine, 1970-74, chmn. dept. psychiatry, 1970-74; exec. dir. Tampa Bay Neuropsychiat. Inst., Tampa, Fla., 1970—; chmn., chief exec. officer The Mental Health Programs Corp., Tampa, 1985-92. Author: The Children of Resurrection City, 1970; contbr. articles to profl. jours. Pres. Fla. Lyric Opera, 1976—. Capt. USAF, 1964-66. Fellow Am. Coll. Psychiatrists; mem. AMA, Am. Acad. Neurology, Univ. Club, Tampa Yacht Club. Republican. Roman Catholic. Home: 4619 W Bay To Bay Blvd Tampa FL 33629-7610 Office: 4107 Spruce St Ste 100 Tampa FL 33607-1765 Personal E-mail: hogheavn@tampabay.rr.com.

AFRICK, LANCE M., federal judge; b. NYC, 1951; BA, U. NC, 1973, JD, 1975. With Normann & Normann, 1967-77; law clk. to Hon. James Gulotta La. Ct. Appeals (4th cir.), 1975-76; asst. dist. atty. Orleans Parish, 1977-80; assoc. Kierr, Gainsburgh, Banjamin, Fallon & Lewis, 1980-81, McDermott Inc., 1981-82; asst. US atty. US Dist. Ct. (ea. dist.) La., 1983-90, magistrate judge New Orleans, 1990—2002, judge, 2002—. Instr. U. New Orleans, 1986—. Office: US Dist Ct 500 Pydras St Rm C405 New Orleans LA 70130 Fax: (504) 589-3781.

AGAIAN, SOS SUIEN, electrical engineer, researcher; b. Yerevan, Armenia, Sept. 7, 1946; came to U.S., 1993; s. Suren and Granush (Gurdian) A.; m. Gayane Abrahamian, June 18, 1992; 1 child, Sarkis. BSc summa cum laude, yerevan U., 1966, MSc, 1968; PhD, Steklov Inst. Math., Moscow, 1974; DSc, Computer Ctr., Acad. Sci., Moscow, 1985. Dep. dir. Inst. Problems of Informatics and Automation, Nat. Acad. Sci., Yerevan, 1971-79; chmn. dept. computation and digital signal/image processing Nat. Acad. Sci. and Yerevan U., 1979-93; prof. Yerevan U. and U. Tech., 1971-88; vis. prof. Tufts U., Medford, Mass., 1993-97; sr. scientist Aware, Inc., Bedford, Mass., 1996-97; assoc. prof. U. Tex., San Antonio, 1997-2001; vis. prof. CUNY, 2001—. Author: Binary Polymonials, Transforms and digital Filtering, 1995, others; contbr. numerous articles to profl. jours. Recipient Best Ann. Rsch. awards Armenian Nat. Acad. Scis., 1983, 88, 97. Mem. IEEE, SPIE, N.Am. Fuzzy Info. Processing Soc. Achievements include some 11 Russian and Finnish patents. Office: U Tex San Antonio 6900 North Loop 1504 West San Antonio TX 78249*

AGAN, CAMI D., literature and language professor; BA, Okla. Christian U., Okla. City, 1991; M, Boston Coll., Chesnut Hill, 1993; PhD, Duqesne U., Pitts., 1997. Prof. English Okla. Christian U., 1997—, chair, dept. lang. & lit., 1998—. Exec. com. mem. Okla. Christian Faculty Assn.; campus coord. Okla. Scholar-Leadership, 1998—2007. Contbr. articles to profl. jour. Vol. UR Spl., Edmond, Okla., 1999—2007. Mem.: MLA (chpt. Frances Sherrilan tchg. vol., chpt. J.R.R. Tolkien vol.), Sigma Tau Delta (faculty sponsor).

AGARWAL, PANKAJ K., computer engineering educator; BS in Electronics and Comm., U. Roorkee, India, 1982; MS in Computer Sci., U. Calif., Santa Barbara, 1986; PhD in Computer Sci., Courant Inst. Math. Scis., NYC, 1989. Faculty Duke U., Durham, NC, 1989—, Earl D. McLean jr. prof. dept. computer sci., 2000—05, former chair dept. computer sci. Contbr. articles to numerous profl. jours. Recipient Nat. Young Investigator award, NSF, 1993; fellow Alfred P. Sloan Found., 1996. Fellow: Assn. Computing Machinery. Office: Duke U Dept Computer Sci Levine Sci Rsch Ctr D214A PO Box 90129 Durham NC 27708-0129 Office Phone: 919-660-6540. Office Fax: 919-660-6519. Business E-Mail: pankaj@cs.duke.edu.

AGATA, TETSUO, automotive executive; BA in Social Science, Hitotsubashi U., Tokyo, 1976. Joined Toyota Motor Corp., 1976, gen. mngr. various divsns., 2000, mng. officer, 2004—08, sr. mng. dir., 2008—; vp prodn. control and corp. strategy divsn. Toyota Motor Engring. and Mfg., 2000, pres., 2008—. Bd. dirs. Toyota Motor Corp., 2008—. Office: 25 Atlantic Avenue Erlanger KY 41018 Office Phone: 859-746-4000.

AGATSTON, ARTHUR STEPHEN, cardiologist, educator; b. NYC, Jan. 22, 1947; s. Howard James and Adell (Paymer) Agatston; m. Sari Agatston, Mar. 7, 1983; 1 child, Adam; 1 child, Evan. BA, U. Wis., 1969; MD, NYU, 1973. Diplomate Am. Bd. Internal Medicine, Am. Bd. Cardiovasc. Disease. Intern medicine Montefiore Hosp. Med. Ctr., Albert Einstein Coll. Medicine, NYC, 1973-74, resident, 1974-76; cardiology fellow NYU Med. Ctr., NYC, 1977-79; dir. noninvasive cardiology Mt. Sinai Med. Ctr., Miami Beach, Fla., 1980; assoc. prof. medicine U. Miami Miller Sch. Medicine; ptnr. pvt. practice South Fla. Cardiology Assocs., Miami. Pres. greater Miami chpt. Am. Heart Assn., 1992; bd. dirs. Am. Dietetic Assn. Found.; expert cons. Clin. Trials Com. NIH; founder Agatston Rsch. Found., Miami Beach, 2004—. Author: South Beach Diet: The Delicious, Doctor-Designed, Foolproof Plan for Fast & Healthy Weight Loss, 2003, South Beach Diet Cookbook, 2004, South Beach Diet Good Fats/Good Carbs Guide: The Complete & Easy Reference for All Your Favorite Foods, 2004, South Beach Diet Quick and Easy Cookbook: 200 Delicious Recipes Ready in 30 Minutes or Less, 2005, South Beach Diet Dining Guide, 2005, South Beach Diet Parties & Holidays Cookbook, 2006, South Beach Diet Taste of Summer Cookbook, 2007, South Beach Heart Health Revolution, 2007, The South Beach Diet Supercharged: Faster Weight Loss & Better Health for Life, 2008; contbr. articles to profl. jours., chapters to books. Fellow: Am. Coll. Cardiology; mem.: Soc. Atherosclerosis Imaging (founding mem. bd. dirs.), Am. Soc. Echocardiography. Achievements include development of (with others) the electron beam tomography scan (EBT), a screening method used to detect coronary artery disease and other diseases. Office: Agatston Rsch Found 1691 Michigan Ave Ste 500 Miami Beach FL 33139 Office Phone: 305-538-3828.

AGEE, BOB R., academic administrator, minister, educator; b. Brownsville, Tenn., Sept. 30, 1938; s. Edwin L. and Katie L. (Stewart) A.; m. Nelle Rose; children— Nancy Denise, Robyn Janelle BA, Union U., Tenn., 1960; M.Div., So. Bapt. Theol. Sem., 1964, D.Min., 1974; PhD, Vanderbilt U., 1986. Ordained to ministry Baptist Ch. Pastor Shively Heights Bapt. Ch., Louisville, 1964-70, Ardmore Bapt. Ch., Memphis, 1970-75; dean, v.p. religious affairs Union U., Jackson, Tenn., 1975-82, dir. Master's program in Christian Studies, prof. ednl. leadership, 2005—; pres. Okla. Bapt. U., Shawnee, 1982-98, pres. emeritus, 1998—. Mem. edn. commn. So. Bapt. Conv., 1985-93, chmn., 1987-90; bd. dirs. Co-op Svcs. Internat. Edn. Consortium, chmn., 1988-90; cons. evaluator North Ctrl. Assn. Colls. and Univs., 1987—; bd. dirs. Nat. Assn. Ind. Colls. and Univs., 1986-90, 93—. Author Bibl. study materials and articles Mem. human relations com. Memphis Bd. Edn., 1972-74; mem. Memphis Mayor's Crime Commn., 1973-75; mem. Okla. Ind. Coll. Found., 1982-98, chmn., 1985-87. Inducted into Okla. Higher Edn. Hall of Fame, 1999. Mem. Soc. Coll. and Univ. Planning, Shawnee C. of C. (bd. dirs. 1983-98), So. Bapt. Theol. Sem. Alumni Assn. (nat. pres. 1985-86), AAUP, Am. Assn. Univ. Adminstrs., Nat. Assn. Ind. Colls. and Univs. (bd. dirs. 1988-97), Coun. for Christian Colls. and Univs. (bd. dirs. 1997-2003), Assn. So. Bapt. Colls. and Schs. (exec. dir. 1998—, exec. dir. consortium global edn. 1998-2002). Republican. Avocations: racquetball, golf, fishing, writing. Office: PO Box 11655 Jackson TN 38308-0127

AGEE, G(EORGE) STEVEN, federal judge, former state supreme court justice; b. Roanoke, Va., Nov. 12, 1952; m. Nancy Howell; 1 child, Zachary S. BA, Bridgewater Coll., 1974; JD, U. Va., 1977; LLM in Taxation, NYU, 1978. Bar: Va. 1977, DC 1979. Assoc. Martin, Hopkins & Lemon, 1977—79, Rocovich, Dechow, Parvin & Wilson, P.C., 1979—80; shareholder, dir. Osterhoudt, Ferguson, Natt, Aheron, & Agee P.C., 1980—2001; mem. Va. Ho. Dels., 1982—94; judge Va. Ct. Appeals, Richmond, 2001—03; justice Va. Supreme Ct., Richmond, 2003—08; judge US Ct. Appeals (4th Cir.), 2008—. Mem. Va. Criminal Sentencing Commn., 1997—2000. Trustee Bridgewater Coll.; bd. mem. Bradley Free Clinic, Roanoke. Served in Judge Advocate General Corps USAR, 1985—97. Mem.: Roanoke County-Salem Bar Assn. (pres. 1990—91), Va. Bar Assn., DC Bar Assn., Salem Rotary Club. Office: US Ct Appeals 1100 E Main St Richmond VA 23219

AGGARWAL, JAGDISHKUMAR KESHORAM, electrical and computer engineering educator, administrator, researcher; came to US, 1960, naturalized; s. Keshoram J. and Harkaur A.; m. Shanti Seth, July 1965; children: Mala, Raj. BS, U. Bombay, 1957; B in Engring., U. Liverpool, Eng., 1960; MS, U. Ill., 1961, PhD, 1964. Registered profl. engr., Tex. Rsch. asst. Marconi's Rsch. Lab., Chelmsford, Eng., 1959; fellow U. Ill., Urbana, 1960-61, rsch. asst. coordinated sci. lab., 1961-64; asst. prof. elec. engring. U. Tex., Austin, 1964-68, assoc. prof. elec. engring., 1968-72, prof. elec. and computer engring., 1972—, John J. McKetta Energy prof., 1981-90, Cullen Trust for Higher Edn. Endowed prof. No. 2, 1990—. Dir. Computer and Vision Rsch. Ctr., Austin, 1985—; cons. IBM Corp., Shell Devel. Corp. Co-author: Deconvolution of Seismic Data, 1982, Motion Understanding, 1988; editor: Multisensor Fusion for Computer Vision, 1993. Recipient Outstanding Contbn. award Pattern Recognition Soc., 1985, 86, 2004, Disting. Alumnus award U. Ill., 1986, Alumni Honor award U. Ill. Coll. Engring., 1987, Am. Soc. Engring. Edn. Sr. Rsch. award, 1992, Kirchmayer Grad. Tchg. award IEEE 2005, Okawa prize Okawa Found. Japan, 2007, K S FU prize Internat. Assn. Pattern Recognition 2004 Fellow (life) IEEE (editor Expert jour. 1986-89, editor Trans. Parallel and Dist. Systems 1992-96), AAAS, Internat. Assn. Pattern Recognition (rep. 1985-2000, treas. 1989-92, pres. 1992-94, computer vision program chmn. 1990 conf.); mem. IEEE Computer Soc. (chmn. tech. com. on pattern recognition and machine intelligence 1987-89, gen. chmn. conf. on computer vision and pattern recognition 1993), Austin Yacht Club. Avocation: sailing. Office: University Tex Dept Elec and Computer Engring Computer and Vision Rsch Ctr Austin TX 78712-1084 Business E-Mail: aggarwaljk@mail.utexas.edu.*

AGLER, RICHARD DEAN, rabbi; b. NYC, May 11, 1952; s. Eugene and Sylvia (Spieler) A.; m. Mindy Steinberg, June 19, 1976; children: Jesse Allen, Talia Faith, Sarah Suzan. BA in Polit. Sci., NYU, 1973; MA in Hebrew Lit., Hebrew Union Coll.-Jewish Inst. Religion, 1976; DDiv (hon.), Hebrew U., 2003. Ordained rabbi, 1978. Rabbi Stephen Wise Free Synagogue, NYC, 1978-80, Temple Beth Shalom, Vero Beach, Fla., 1980-82, Temple Beth El, Boca Raton, Fla., 1982-84; founding rabbi Congregation Bnai Israel, Boca Raton, 1984—. Bd. dir. Anti Defamation League, Palm Beach County; mem. pres.'s rabbinic coun., Hebrew Union Coll., Jewish Inst. Religion, 2005. V.p. Handgun Control of Palm Beach County, Fla., Fla., 1983—93; co-founder Boca Raton Black-Jewish Fellowship, 1984—; founder Ctr. Justice, Boca Raton, 1989, Save Darfur Coalition South Palm Beach County, 2004. Named Outstanding Young Man Am., 1989. Mem. Ctr. Conf. Am. Rabbis, South Palm Beach County Rabbinical Assn. (pres. 1991-93), S.E. Assn. Ctrl. Conf. Am. Rabbis (spirituality chair 1984-2002), Assn. Reform Zionists of Am. (life, bd. dirs.), Palm Beach County Bd. Rabbis. Jewish. Avocations: literature, athletics, sailing.

AGNEW, CHRISTOPHER MACK, minister, historian; b. Santa Barbara, Calif., Aug. 7, 1944; s. Jack and Agnes Emma (Mack) A.; m. Suzanne Marie Souder, June 1, 1974 (div.); m. Elizabeth Lewis Lyddane, Apr. 25, 1998. AB, Bucknell U., Lewisburg, Pa., 1967; MA, U. Del., Newark, 1975, PhD, 1980; STM, Gen. Theol. Sem., NYC, 1991. Ordained to ministry as deacon Episcopal Ch., 1991, as priest Episcopal Ch., 1992. Reference libr. Dover (Del.) Pub. Libr., 1969—72; tchg. asst. dept. history U. Del., Newark, 1972—76; manuscript libr. Hist. Soc. Del., 1979—81; asst. prof. history and Can. studies SUNY, Plattsburgh, 1981—84; registrar Diocese of Del., Wilmington, 1985—89; assoc. ecumenical officer Episcopal Ch., NYC, 1989—94; deacon St. Thomas' Ch., Newark, 1991—92; priest-in-charge St. Marks, Teaneck, NJ, 1992; priest assoc. All Angels Ch., NYC, 1992—95; interim rector St. Martin's, Maywood, NJ, 1994—95, All Hallows, Wyncote, Pa., 1995, St. Michael's, Litchfield, Conn., 1995—97, Ch. of the Ascension, Norfolk, Va., 1997, St. Peter's in Great Valley, Paoli, Pa., 1997—99; priest in charge St. Paul's, Owens, Va., 2000—02; interim rector Vauter's Ch., Loretto, Va., 2002—03, priest in charge, 2003—09; vicar St. Paul's, Nomini Grove, Va., 2002—. Exec. bd. Episcopal Diocesan Ecumenical Officers, 1989—94, 2007—, v.p., 2010—; mem. Episcopal-Reformed Episcopal Dialogue, 1989—94, staff standing com. ecumenical rels., 1989—94; mem. NCC Christian-Muslim Rels. Commn., 1989—91, NCC Christian-Jewish Rels. Commn., 1989—99, chiar., 1991—99; mem. Anglican-Roman Cath. Consultation, U.S.A., 1989—94, NCC Interfaith Working Group, 1990—95; mem. planning com. Nat. Workshop on Christian Unity, 1990—94, 2007—10, nat. chair, 2008—09; mem. NCC Faith and Order Commn., 1991—95; chmn. NCC Christian-Jewish Rels. Commn., 1991—99; mem. Parliament of the Worlds Religions, 1993, Interfaith Rels. Commn., 1996—99, Episcopal-Reformed Episcopal-Anglican Province of Am. Dialogue, 2003—, Episc. Russian Orthodox Joint Coordinating Com., 1990—94; alt. dep. gen. Convention Episcopal Ch., 2010—. Editor: The Ecumenical Bull., 1989-94, Anglican Statements on the Church: Selected Documentary Sources for a Study of Anglican Ecclesiology, 1994; author: God With Us, 1986; contbr. articles to profl. jours. Mem. Ecumenical Interfaith Commn. Diocese Va., 2000—, co-chmn., 2004—; mem. faith and order commn. Va. Coun. Chs., 2002—, chair faith and order commn., 2004—; ecumenical officer Episcopal Diocese Va., 2009—. Recipient Faith Action award, Va. Coun. Chs., 2013. Mem. Nat. Episc. Historians Assn. (mem. exec. bd. 1995-99, 2006-13, pres. 2008-12), Hist. Soc. Episc. Ch. (bd. dirs. 2005—), Order Crown Charlemagne U.S. (asst. chaplain 1997-2005, chaplain 2005—), Assn. for Preservation Va. Antiquities (trustee No. Neck br. 2004-05, 13-), Orgn. Am. Historians, Am. Hist. Assn., N.Am. Acad. Ecumenists (mem. exec. bd. 2004—), Can. Hist. Assn., Assn. Can. Studies in U.S., Interim Ministry Network, Mil. Order of Loyal Legion of U.S. (chaplain-in-chief 1995—2009), Mil. Order of Stars and Bars, Soc. Colonial Wars, N.Am. Guild of Change Ringers. Home: 12433 Richards Ride King George VA 22485

AGNEW, PAUL L., state legislator; b. Anderson, SC, Dec. 23, 1960; BA, Erskine Coll., 1983; JD, U. SC, 1986. Law clk. for Judge James E. Moore, 1987; instr. govt. Erskine Coll., 1988, 1990, 1992, 1994, instr. bus., 1989; pub. defender Abbeville County, 1989—90; mem. Dist. 11 SC House of Reps., 2004—, mem. Agr., Natural Resources and Environ. Affairs Com. Democrat. Mailing: 436B Blatt Bldg Columbia SC 29201 Home: PO Box 382 Abbeville SC 29620 Office Phone: 803-734-2993. Business E-Mail: AgnewP@scstatehouse.net.

AGOSTA, JEFFREY A., corporate financial executive; B in Acctg., U. Okla. CPA; cert. insolvency and restructuring advisor. With D. R. Payne Assocs., KPMG, LLC (Audit & Consulting Groups); mgr., corp. planning & fin. Devon Energy Corp.; with Devon Energy Corp. (Corp. Devel. group), 1997; treas. Devon Energy Corp., 2003—10, sr. v.p., corp. fin., 2009—10, sr. v.p., CFO, 2010—. Office: Devon Energy Corp 333 W Sheridan Ave Oklahoma City OK 73102-5010 Office Phone: 405-235-3611. Office Fax: 405-552-4550. Business E-Mail: jeff.agosta@dvn.com.

AGRESTI, ALAN, statistics educator; b. Syracuse, NY, Feb. 6, 1947; m. Jacalyn Levine. BA, U. Rochester, 1968; PhD, U. Wis., 1972; doctorate (hon.), De Montfort U., 1999. Prof. U. Fla., Gainesville, 1972—. Author: Categorical Data Analysis, 2002, 3rd edit., 2012, Statistical Methods for the Social Sciences, 2008, Analysis of Ordinal Categorical Data, 2010, Introduction to Categorical Data Analysis, 2007, Statistics: The Art and Science of Learning From Data, 2008, 3rd edit., 2012. Fellow Am. Statis. Assn., Inst. Math. Stats.; mem. Royal Statis. Soc., Biometric Soc., Office: U Fla Griffin-Floyd Hall Gainesville FL 32611-8545

AGUERA, RALPH D., beverage company executive; m. Judy Aguera; children: Celeste, Ralph David. V.p. trade rels. Brown-Forman Corp., Louisville. Pres. Sky Ranch for Boys Found., 1994—; bd. dirs. Derby Festival Bd., Ctr. for Interfaith Rels., Share Our Strength, Gilda's Club. Recipient Hope Award, Am. Cancer Soc., WAABI Unity Award, Martin Luther King, Jr. Award, Top Shelf Award, Am. Beverage Licensees, 2009; named Nat. Hispanic Corp. Achiever of Yr., Man of Yr., Nat. Liquor Store Assn.; named to Sky Ranch Hall of Fame. Office: Brown-Forman Corp 850 Dixie Hwy Louisville KY 40210 Office Phone: 502-585-1100. Office Fax: 502-775-2483. Business E-Mail: ralph_aguera@b-f.com.

AGUILA, ALEX, computer company executive; Co-founder, pres., COO Alienware (acquired by Dell. Inc.), Miami, Fla., 1996—. Office: Alienware 14591 SW 120 St Miami FL 33186-8638 Office Phone: 305-251-9797. Office Fax: 305-259-9874.

AGUILAR, ARACELI, wholesale distribution executive; With Ingram Micro Mex., 2003—08; mng. dir. ScanSource de Mexico, 2008—. Office: ScanSource Inc 6 Logue Ct Greenville SC 29615 Office Phone: 864-288-2432. Office Fax: 864-288-1165.

AGUILAR, RODOLFO J., JR., lawyer; b. Baton Rouge; BA in Fin., La. State U., 1979; JD, La. State U. Paul M. Hebert Law Ctr., 1982. Bar: La. 1982, US Dist. Ct. (ea., we. and mid. dists.) La. Mng. mem. McGlinchey Stafford PLLC, Baton Rouge. Contbr. articles to profl. jours. Bd. dirs. Baton Rouge Cmty. Coll. Found. Named a La. Super Lawyer, Law & Politics Mag., 2007—11. Mem.: ABA, Internat. Lawyers Network, La. State Bar Assn., Baton Rouge Bar. Assn., Baton Rouge Rotary Club, Phi Kappa Phi, Order of the Coif. Office: McGlinchey Stafford PLLC 301 Main St One American Pl 14th Fl Baton Rouge LA 70825 Office Phone: 225-382-3625. Office Fax: 225-343-3076. E-mail: rudyaguilar@mcglinchey.com.

AGUILERA, SHINO BAY, dermatologist, educator, medical researcher; MD, Western U. of Health Sciences. Diplomate Am. Bd. of Dermatology, dermatologic surgeon. Internship Wellington Regional Med. Ctr., resident; fellow in osteopathic dermatology; asst. prof. dermatology NOVA Univ., L.E.C.O.M., Suncoast Univ., Universidad del Rosario; volunteer instr. dermatology Univ. Miami. Fellow: Am. Osteopathic Coll. of Dermatology; mem.: Broward Dermatol. Soc., Am. Soc. of Laser Medicine and Surgery, Am. Soc. for Dermatologic Surgery, Am. Acad. of Dermatology. Office: Shino Bay Cosmetic Dermatology and Laser Institute Ste 110 Ground Fl 350 Las Olas Blvd Fort Lauderdale FL 33301 Office Phone: 954-765-3005.

AGUIRRE, EDUARDO, JR., consulting firm executive, former ambassador; b. Cuba, July 30, 1946; m. Maria Theresa Aguirre; children: Eddy, Tessy. BS, La. State U.; D (hon.), U. Tecnologica Santiago, Dominican Republic, U. Conn., U. Houston. With Tex. Commerce Bank, 1969, Bank of America Corp., 1978—2000, pres. Internat. Pvt. Bank, 1999—2000; vice chmn., 1st v.p. Export-Import Bank of US, Washington, 2001—02; dir. Bur. Citizenship & Immigration Services US Dept. Homeland Security, Washington, 2003—05; US amb. to Spain and Andorra US Dept. State, Madrid, 2005—09; chmn., CEO Atlantic Partners Group, L.L.C., Houston, 2009—; prin. Command Consulting Group, LLC, Washington, 2009—. Hon. prof. Beijing Poly. U., Ctrl. U. Nationalities, Beijing; former chmn. bd. trustees Tex. Bar Found.; founding chmn. bd. dirs. Houston Livestock Show and Rodeo; former chmn. bd. dirs. Tex. Children's Hosp.; regent U. Houston Sys. Bd. Regents, 1995—2001, chmn., 1996—98; bd. dirs. BBVA Compass, 2009—. Bd. mem. Tex. Children Hosp., Houston Livestock Show & Radio. Recipient Order of José Matías Delgado, Grade of Grand Officer, Republic of El Salvador, Order of Christopher Columbus, Grade of Grand Officer, Dominican Republic, Americanism medal, Daughters of the American Revolution, 2004, Lifetime Achievement award, Delta Sigma Pi; named an Outstanding American By Choice, US Dept. Homeland Security, 2007; named to The La. State U. Hall of Distinction. Office: Command Consulting Group LLC 1501 M St NW Fifth Fl Washington DC 20005

AGWUNOBI, JOHN ODERAH, retail executive, former federal agency administrator; b. Dundee, Angus, Scotland, Oct. 4, 1964; arrived in US, 1989; MB, BChir, U. Jos, Plateau State, Nigeria, 1987; MBA, Georgetown U., Washington, DC, 2000; MPH, Johns Hopkins U., Balt., 2004. Diplomate Am. Bd. Pediat. Resident in pediat. Howard University, Washington, 1990-93; attending pediatrician Hosp. for Sick Children, Washington, 1993-2000, med. dir., 1998—99, v.p. med. affairs & patient services, 1999—2000; dep. sec. Fla. Dept. Health, 2000—01, sec., 2001—05; asst. sec. for health US Dept. Health & Human Svcs., Washington, 2005—07; admiral US Pub. Health Svc. Commd. Corps, 2006—07; sr. v.p., pres. health & wellness. divsn. Wal-Mart Stores, Inc., Bentonville, Ark., 2007—. Chmn. US African Devel. Found., Washington, 2008—. Bd. dirs. Ct. Apptd. Spl. Advs., Montgomery County, Md., 1996. Fellow: Am. Acad. Pediat.; mem.: AMA, Am. Coll. Physician Execs., Nat. Med. Assn. Office: Wal-Mart Stores Inc 702 SW 8th St MS0240 Bentonville AR 72716 also: US African Devel Found 1400 I St NW Ste 1000 Washington DC 20005

AHEARNE, JOHN FRANCIS, science society director, researcher; b. New Britain, Conn., June 14, 1934; s. Daniel Paul and Balbena Marian (Baloski) A.; m. Barbara Helen Drezek, June 19, 1956; children: Thomas, Paul, Mary Ann, Robert, Patricia. B of Engring. Physics, Cornell U., 1957, MS in Physics, 1958; MA, Princeton U., 1963, PhD, 1966. Nuc. weapons analyst USAF, 1959-61; assoc. prof. physics USAF Acad., 1964-69; from analyst to dir. tactical air Office Asst. Sec. Def. for Systems Analysis, 1969-72; dep. asst. sec. def. for gen. purpose programs, 1972-74; prin. dep. sec. def. manpower and res. affairs, 1974-76; staff White House Energy Office, 1977; dep. asst. sec. Dept. Energy, 1978; commr. U.S. Nuc. Regulatory Commn., 1978-83, chmn., 1980-81; mgmt. cons. Comptr. Gen of U.S., 1983-84; v.p., sr. fellow Resources for the Future, 1984-89; exec. dir. Sigma Xi, The Sci. Rsch. Soc., Research Triangle Park, NC, 1989-96; dir. Sigma Xi Ctr., 1995-99; dir. ethics program Sigma Xi, 1999—2007, exec. dir. emeritus, 2007—; lectr. pub. policy Duke U., Durham, NC, 1995—2006. Adj. fellow Resources for Future, 1992—; adj. prof. civil and environ. engring. Duke U., 1996-2002, 08-; adj. prof. U. Colo., 1966-69; adj. fellow Resources for the Future, 1992—; vice-chmn. Nat. Rsch. Coun. Bd. on Radioactive Waste Mgmt., 1997-99, chmn., 2000—04; chmn. adv. com. on nuc. facility safety U.S. Dept. Energy, 1988-91, environ. mgmt. adv. bd., 1994-2002, co-chmn. adv. com. on external regulation, 1995-96, nuc. energy adv. com., 1998—, vice chmn., 2002—; chmn. risk perception and comm. com. NAS, 1987-89, chmn. future nuc. power com., 1990-93, com. on tech. bases for Yucca Mountain Stds., 1993-96, com. on risk characterization, 1994-97, dual use techs. and export controls com., electrometallurg. tech. com., co-chmn. burning plasma experiment assessment com., 2002-04, co-chmn. forum on the environment, 1995-97, vice-chmn. com. risk assessment and mgmt. marine sys., 1996-98, com. on battlefield radiation exposure, 1996-99, chmn. com. to rev. rsch. under EPACT, 1997-99, co-chmn. com. on end points of U.S. and Russian nuc. waste, 2001—03, com. on indigenization of programs to prevent leakage, jt. acad. com. on counterterrorism challenges for Russia and the US, 2002—, chmn. com. on earth penetrator nuc. weapons, 2004-06; co-chair, joint US Nat. Acad. Studies/Russian Acad. Studies com. internat. fuel cycle, 2006-08, chair, chair com. Opportunities US-Russian Coop. Combating Radiological Terrorism, 2004-10; mem. pres.'s coun. for nat. labs. U. Calif., 1998-2007; vice-chmn. U.S. Commn. for IIASA, 1992-93, chmn., 1994-98; adv. com. Princeton Plasma Physics Nat. Lab., 1993-98; co-chmn. panel on opportunities in plasma sci. tech. NAS, 1992-96, reactor panel for disposition of weapons plutonium, 1992-96; bd. dirs. Wis. Energy Corp., 1994-2008; lectr. Colo. Coll., 1966-69; pres. com. adv. S&T Energy R&D panel, 1997-98; USGAO exec. coun. Info. Mgmt. and Tech., 1997-2004; mem. adv. coun. Jet Propulsion Lab., 2004—05; mem. Nat. Academic Com. Internat. Security and Arms Control, 2005-. Bd. dirs. Woodstock Theol. Ctr., chmn., 1980-85; past mem. Nat. Coun. for Radiation Protection and Measurement. Gen. Electric Coffin fellow, 1957-58; recipient Dept. Def. Disting. Civilian Svc. medal and bronze palm, Sec. Def. Meritorious Svc. medal; named Boss of Year D.C. chpt. Nat. Secs. Assn., 1976, award, Am. Phys. Soc. Szilard award, 2011, Richard Garwin award, FAS, 2012. Fellow AAAS, Am. Phys. Soc. (chmn. forum on physics and soc. 1996-97, chair panel on pub. affairs 2003—04, Szilard award 2011), Am. Acad. Arts and Scis., Soc. Risk Analysis; mem. NAE, Nat. Acads. (nat. assoc.), Am. Nuc. Soc., Soc. for Risk Analysis (past pres.), Sigma Xi. Democrat. Roman Catholic. Office Phone: 919-547-5213. Business E-Mail: ahearne@sigmaxi.org, jfahearne@earthlink.net.

AHERN, LAWRENCE T., state legislator; b. Detroit, Apr. 26, 1955; m. Maureen Ahern; children: Lauren, Lindsey Anderson, Sarah Byrne. V.p. Jack's Liquor Super Mart, 1978—81; pres. Tyrone Pool Supply Inc, 1981—2003, Ahern & Byrne Inc., 2004, Larry Ahern Pool Remodeling Inc., 2006; mem. Dist. 51 Fla. House of Representatives, 2011—. Republican. Office: 5511 Park St N Ste 101 Saint Petersburg FL 33709-6399 also: Fla House of Reps 1102 The Capitol 402 S Monroe St Tallahassee FL 32399-1300 Office Phone: 727-545-6421, 850-488-6197.

AHLERS, GLEN-PETER, SR., law library director, educator, consultant; b. NYC, Mar. 15, 1955; s. LeGrande Jacob and Joan (Stoltz) A.; m. Sondra Sue Wadley, May 17, 1987; children: Glen-Peter II, Sandia Marie, Gavin Patrick, Sierra Le Ann Rose, Stacia Camille, Sienna Catherine. BS, U. N.Mex., Albuquerque, 1979; MA, U. of South Fla., 1983; JD, Washburn U., 1987. Bar: Kans. 1987, U.S. Dist. Ct. Kans. 1987, U.S. Ct. Mil. Appeals 1988, D.C. 1990. Reference asst. U. N.Mex. Sch. Law, Albuquerque, 1979-83; asst. dir. Washburn Sch. Law Libr., Topeka, 1983-87; assoc. libr. dir. Wake Forest U., Winston-Salem, N.C., 1987-90; libr. dir., assoc. prof. D.C. Sch. Law, Washington, 1990-92, U. Ark., Fayetteville, 1992-2000, prof., 2001—02; assoc. dean info. services Barry U. Dwayne O. Andreas Sch. of Law, Orlando, Fla. Computer and libr. cons. Ctr. for R&D in Law-Related Edn., Winston-Salem, 1987-90; adj. prof. Sch. of Law Wake Forest U., Winston-Salem, N.C., 1987-90; Mid-Am. Law Sch. Libr. Consortium, 1992-2002, bd. dirs. Consortium of Southestern Law Librs., 1988-90, pres. 2000-02. Author: History of Law School Libraries in the United States, 2002, Election Laws of the United States, 1995; co-author: Notary Law and Practice, 1997; editor The Maall Newsletter, 1984-87, The Scrivener, 1992—2004; tech. editor Washburn Law Jour., 1985-86; contbr. articles to profl. jours. Mediator N.C. Neighborhood Justice Ctr., Winston-Salem, 1989-90. Mem. ABA, ALA, Fla. Bar Assn., Am. Assn. Law Librs., Southwestern Assn. Law Librs. (pres. 1995-97), Southeastern Assn. of Law Librs., Mid Am. Assn. Law Librs. (pres. 1999-2000), Scribes (exec. dir. 1997—), Phi Kappa Phi, Kappa Delta Pi, Beta Phi Mu. Avocation: writing. Office: Barry U Dwayne O Andreas Sch of Law 6441 E Colonial Dr Orlando FL 32807-3650 Home: 2050 Jessup Rd Oviedo FL 32765-7743 Business E-Mail: gahlers@mail.barry.edu.

AHMAD, RASHID M., thoracic surgeon; married. ScB, Brown U., Providence, 1988; MD, Columbia Med. Sch., NYC, 1992. Diplomate Am. Bd. Thoracic Surgery, 2005. Asst prof. Vanderbilt Heart and Vascular Inst., Nashville, 2002—14, chief informatics officer, 2007—. Mem.: Soc. Thoracic Surgeons. Office: 1215 21st Ave South Medical Center E Nashville TN 37232 Business E-Mail: rashid.ahmad@vanderbilt.edu.*

AHN, SHI HYUN, professional golfer; b. Inchon, Republic of Korea, Sept. 15, 1984; Profl. golfer Korea LPGA, 2002—, LPGA, 2002—. Mem. Korean Nat. Team, 2000—01. Recipient LPGA Rookie of Yr., 2004. Achievements include winning LPGA event: CJ Nine Bridges Classic, 2003; winning Korea LPGA event: MBC-Xcanvas Open, 2004. Avocation: quilting. Office: c/o LPGA 100 International Dr Daytona Beach FL 32124-1092

AHUJA, SANJIV, telecommunications industry executive; BS in Elec. Engring., Delhi Univ.; MS in Computer Sci., Columbia Univ., NYC, 1979. With IBM Corp.; CEO Comstellar Tech., Calif.; COO Orange Communications, 2003—04, CEO, 2004—07; chmn. Orange UK, 2007—08; founder, chmn. Augere, 2007—; chmn., CEO LightSquared Inc., Reston, Va., 2010—12, chmn., 2012—. Office: LightSquared Inc 10802 Parkridge Blvd Reston VA 20191 Office Phone: 877-678-2920.*

AIKEN, CLAY (CLAYTON HOLMES AIKEN), singer; b. Raleigh, NC, Nov. 30, 1978; s. Vernon Grissom and Faye (Parker) Aiken; 1 child, Parker Foster. Student, U. NC at Charlotte. Founder Bubel/Aiken Found. for children. Singer: (single) This is the Night, 2003, (albums) Measure of a Man, 2003 (triple platinum), Merry Christmas with Love, 2004, A Thousand Different Ways, 2006, On My Way Here, 2008, Tried and True, 2010, Steadfast, 2012; singer: (with various artists) American Idol Season 2: All Time, 2003; singer, runner up (TV series) American Idol: The Search for a Superstar, 2003; performer: Miss America Pageant, 2003, An American Idol Christmas, 2003, The Nick at Nite Holiday Special, 2003, Fromage, 2003, (Broadway plays) Spamalot, 2008; co-author (with Allison Glock): Learning to Sing: Hearing the Music in Your Life, 2004. Apptd. mem. President's Com. for People with Intellectual Disabilities.

AIKEN, VERNOY FRED, government agency administrator; b. Atlanta, Jan. 30, 1938; s. Vernoy Grady and Anne Whitehead Aiken; m. Sue Carol Camp, Aug. 1, 1959; 1 child, Susan Leigh Aiken Grier. Student, U. Ga., 1960; LLB, Atlanta Law Sch., 1965; banking cert., La. State U., 1969. V.p. Cobb Bank and Trust, Smyrna, Ga., 1973—79; owner Alfredo's Restaurant, Dallas, Ga., 1975—89; state rep. Ga. State Ho. Reps., Atlanta, 1980—92; dist. rep. U.S. Congressman Newt Gingrich, 1992—97; dist. dir., sr. dist. rep. U.S. Congressman Bob Barr, Marietta, Ga., 1997—2003; econ. devel. and devel. gov. rels. specialist Ga. Dept. Labor, Atlanta, 2003—. Bd. mem. SafePath Child Advocacy Ctr.; active No. Ga. Svcs. for Blind and IOW Vision, Cancer Crusade, March of Dimes; past pres. Smyrna Rotary, Marietta-Metro Rotary. Sgt. Ga. Air Nat. Guard. Named Outstanding Legislator, Ga. Mcpl. Assn., 1980. Mem.: Cobb County C. of C. (pres. 1976), Jaycees. Republican. Avocations: reading, golf, watching College football, Nascar auto racing. Home: 4020 Pineview Dr Smyrna GA 30080 Office: Ga Dept Labor Ste 650 148 International Blvd Atlanta GA 30303-1751 Office Phone: 404-232-3789.

AIKMAN, TROY KENNETH, sportscaster, retired professional football player; b. West Covina, Calif., Nov. 21, 1966; m. Rhonda Worthey, Apr. 8, 2000 (separated 2011); children: Jordan Ashley, Alexa Marie; 1 stepchild, Rachel. Student, U. Okla., Norman, 1984—86, UCLA, 1986—89, BA in Sociology, 2009. Quarterback Dallas Cowboys, 1989—2000; color commentator Fox Sports, 2001, mem. lead announcing crew, 2002—; limited ptnr. San Diego Padres, 2009—. Mem. Super Bowl Championship Team, 1992, 1993, 1995. Co-host (with Brad Sham) weekly radio show, 1989—2000, co-host (with Pat Summerall) TV program, co-host (with Bruce Murray) Troy Aikman Football Show, Sporting News Radio, 2003. Founder The Troy Aikman Found., 1992—. Recipient Davey O'Brien award, 1988, Walter Payton Man of Yr. award, 1997; named Super Bowl XXVII MVP, NFL, 1993, NFL All-Pro, 1993, 1994, 1995, TV's Top Newcomer, Sports Illus., 2001; named one of Top 25 Football Broadcasters, The Sporting News & SportsBusiness Jour., Daily, 2009; named to Sporting News Coll. All-Am. team, 1988, Nat. Football Conf. Pro Bowl team, NFL, 1991, 1992, 1993, 1994, 1996,

Sporting News NFL All-Pro team, 1993, Pro Football Hall of Fame, 2006, Coll. Football Hall of Fame, 2008. Mailing: The Troy Aikman Found PO Box 3427 Coppell TX 75019 Office: SPRINGboard Agency 3329 Boggett Ct Southlake TX 76092-3332

AILERU, AZEEZ A., physiologist, educator; s. Tajudeen M. and Mary Fagbemi Aileru; m. Grace Michele Garrett, May 20, 1987 (div. Jan. 13, 2001); children: Amanda Elizabeth, Julian Garrett. BS, NC Centeral U., Durham, 1986; MS, NC Centeral U., 1990; PhD, Howard U., DC, 1995. Postdoctoral fellow in neurophysiology and pharmacology, Balt., 1995—97; prof. neurophysiology, dept. life scis. Winston-Salem State U., NC, 1997—; adj. prof. physiology, dept. physiology and pharmacology Wake Forest U. Sch. Medicine, Winston-Salem, 2001—; dir. biomed. rsch. infrastructure ctr. Winston-Salem State U., 2002—. Mentor, advisor summer rsch. Nat. Heart, Lung and Blood Inst., Bethesda, Md., 1998—; mentor NC Alliance Minority Participation, Winston-Salem, 1999—; mem. peer rev. com. mem. Am. Heart Assn., Dallas, 2001—05; mentor post bachelorate program NIGMS, NIH, Bethesda, 2001—; editl. bd. rev., ad hoc com. mem. hypertension jour. Am. Heart Assn., 2002—; mem. minority programs rev. com. Nat. Inst. Gen. Med. Scis., Bethesda, 2003—04, mem. grant rev. panel, 2007—; mem. rsch. infrastructure in minority institutions NCMHD, NIH, 2003—, mem. loan repayment spl. emphasis rev. panel, 2006—; mem. export spl. emphasis panel program project rev. Nat. Ctr. Minority Health and Health Disparities, Bethesda, 2004—, mem. spl. emphasis panel program project rev. on establishing, 2006—; mem. rev. panel NSF, Arlington, Va., 2006—; program dir., prin. investigator minority access to rsch. careers, undergrad. student tng. in academic rsch. Winston-Salem State U., 2007—, program dir. excellence in partnerships for cmty. outreach, rsch. on health disparities and tng. grants, 2007—. Mem. Piedmont Triad Rsch. Pk. Cmty. Adv. Com., Winston-Salem, 2002—08, Piedmont Triad Rsch. Pk. Exec. Leadership Forum Com., Winston-Salem, 2004—08, Piedmont Triad Rsch. Pk. Tenant Adv. Coun., Winston-Salem, 2005—08. Recipient MARC Program Grant Writing award, NIH, 1999, Excellence in Cardiovasc. Rsch. for Minority Tng. award, 2001—08, Wilma Lassiter WSSU Master Tchr. award, Winston-Salem State U., 2002, Wilveria B. Atkinson Disting. Rsch. award, 2002, 2007, Disting. Faculty award, Thurgood Marshall Coll. Found., 2008; grantee Rsch. Infrastructure In Minority Instn. award, NIH, 1999—2002, Rsch. grant, 1999—2002, 2000—01, 2000—02, Post-Bachelorate Program Co-mentor grant, 2001—05, Mentored Minority Faculty Devel. award, 2001—06, Biomed. Rsch. Infrastructure Ctr. grant, 2002—08, USA-Brazil Consortia for Biomed. Scis. Exch. grant, Fund Improvement of Post-secondary Edn., 2007—, Minority Access grant, NIH, 2007—, Excellence in Partnerships for Cmty. Outreach and Rsch. on Disparities in Health and Tng. grant, 2007—; Porter Physiology Rsch. fellowship, APS, 1991—93, Travel fellowship, Nat. Inst. Diabetes and Digestive and Kidney Diseases, 1995. Mem.: NC Coun. Undergrad. Rsch. Com., Nat. Inst. Neurol. Disorders and Stroke, Assn. Ethnic Diversity in Neurosci., Soc. Neurosci., Am. Physiol. Soc. D-Liberal. Baptist. Avocations: travel, soccer, water sports. Office: Winston-Salem State Univ Biomed Rsch Ctr 115 S Chestnut St Winston Salem NC 27101

AINSWORTH, WILLIAM P., manufacturing executive; BS in Mktg., Auburn U., Ala., 1978. With Luria Bros., Atlanta, 1979, regional trader Erman Howell divsn. Birmingham, Ala.; founder, v.p. trading Amex Steel, Birmingham, 1981—83; founder, pres., CEO Steel Processing Svcs., 1983—93; pres., CEO Progress Rail Services Corp. (acquired by Caterpillar, Inc.), Albertville, Ala., 1993—; v.p. Caterpillar, Inc., 2006—. Office: Progress Rail Services Corp 1600 Progress Dr Albertville AL 35950 also: Caterpillar Inc 100 NE Adams St Peoria IL 61629 Office Phone: 256-593-1260. Office Fax: 256-593-1249. E-mail: bainsworth@progressrail.com.

AIOSA, CHARLOTTE NELSON, music educator; b. Detroit, Dec. 21, 1949; d. Theron Seth and Vera Charlotte Nelson; m. Angelo Aiosa, Dec. 18, 1993. BS in Music Edn., U. Md., 1972, MusM in Voice Performance, 1977; D of Musical Arts in Voice Performance, U. Mich., 1987. Prof. music Shenandoah Conservatory Music, Shenandoah U., Winchester, Va., 1979—. Chmn. voice divsn. Shenandoah Conservatory Music, Winchester, 1988—98. Recipient Wilkens Faculty Appreciation award, Shenandoah Conservatory Music, 1992; grantee Grad. Assistantship, U. Md., 1977, U. Mich., 1985—86; Regents fellow, Rackham Grad. Sch., U. Mich., 1984—86, Opera scholar Aspen Opera Program, Aspen Music Festival, 1985. Mem.: Mid Atlantic NATS Region (gov. 2009—11), Nat. Assn. Tchrs. Singing (v.p. Va. chpt. 2001—03, pres. Va. chpt. 2003—05, pres. emeritus Va. chpt. 2005—), Pi Kappa Lamda, Sigma Alpha Iota (life; pres. 1971—72, Svc. award 1972). Office: Shenandoah University 1460 University Dr Winchester VA 22601 Office Fax: 540-665-5402. Business E-Mail: caiosa@su.edu.

AIUTO, RUSSELL, science education consultant; b. Monroe, Mich., July 13, 1934; s. Crispino and Maria (d'Aiuto) A.; m. Nancy Jane Obenauf, Dec. 17, 1955 (dec. 1980); children: Mary T. Carroll, Susan M. Summa; m. Beverly Bradley, Jan. 3, 1981 BA, Ea. Mich. U., 1958, U. Mich., 1995; MA, U. N.C., 1963, PhD, 1971. Tchr. speech, drama Monroe High Sch., Mich., 1958-61; prof. biology Albion Coll., Mich., 1966-82, provost Mich., 1982-85; pres. Hiram Coll., Ohio, 1985-88; div. dir. tchr. preparation and enhancement NSF, Washington, 1988-90; program mgr. Nat. Sci. Tchrs. Assn., Washington, 1990-93, Coun. Ind. Colls., 1993-95. Cons. Gygi Found., Dundee, Mich., 1984—2001; adj. prof. Montgomery Coll., Md., 2005—09, Kennesaw St. U., Ga. Author: Mencken and Sara, 1980, Ring Lardner's America, 1984, Dorothy Parker, 1986; co-author: Science Interactions, 3 vols., 1993; contbr. articles to profl. jours. Vice chmn. Albion Improvement Com., 1983-85; v.p. Patton Ridge Homeowners Corp., 2001-. NSF grantee, 1968 Mem. Sigma Xi, Omicron Delta. Episcopalian. Avocation: collecting books. Home: 291 Wylstream Pl SW Marietta GA 30064-1569

AKA, EBENEZER OSITA, urban planner, educator, researcher, consultant; b. Onitsha, Anambra, Nigeria, Mar. 10, 1953; s. Ebenezer Uwabunkeonye and Rachael Nwannediya Aka; m. Victoria Uchenna Ezenwanne, July 18, 2002; m. Jessie Ifeoma Ezeokonkwo, May 21, 1983 (div. July 18, 1991); children: Nancy Uchechukwu, Jennifer Ifeoma, Valentine Afamuefuna, Noble Amamchukwu, Christian Ositadinma. MA, U. La., Lafayette, 1981; MCRP, Rutgers State U., NJ, NB, 1983; PhD, Tex. A & M U., College Station, Tex., 1987. H.s. instr. Bendel State Sch. Sys., Benin, Nigeria, 1973—77; prof. Morehouse Coll., Atlanta, 1987—, dir., urban studies program, 2001—, chmn., polit. sci. dept., 2013—. Author: (book) Regional Disparities in Nigeria's Development (U. Press Am., 2000); contbr. articles to profl. jour. Ch. elder Riverdale Presbyn. Ch., Ga., 1991—94. Recipient Excellence award, 2011, Internat. Peace prize, 2012; grantee Prudential award, United Negro Coll. Fund, 2003—04. Mem.: Environ. Justice Group (Atlanta), Am. Planning Assn. (APA). Conservative. Achievements include research in issues of regional disparities in Nigeria's development process: challenges and prospects; numerous awards on various jour. papers. Avocations: reading, travel, community organizations, gardening, volunteering. Home: 4343 Bramwell Drive Stone Mountain GA 30083 Office: Morehouse College 830 Westview Dr SW Atlanta GA 30314 Office Fax: 404-215-3485; Home Fax: 404-215-3485. Business E-Mail: eaka@morehouse.edu.

AKANBI, LINDA BARBARA, education educator; b. Richmond, Va., Nov. 27, 1944; d. George Woodrow Wilson Atkinson and Hula Atkinson Scott; m. David Kunle Akanbi, July 17, 1976; children: Hula Bolanle, Akintayo Oluwole. BS in Edn., W.Va. State U.; MEd in Reading; EdD, SUNY, Buffalo, 1972—78. Reading coord. SUNY, 1971—76; title I reading tchr. Newport News Pub. Schs., Va., 1966—68, Hampton City Schs., Va., 1968—70; instr. So. Ill. U., Carbondale, 1977—78; asst. prof. Norfolk State U., Va., 1978—79; lectr. Obafemi Awolowo U., Ile-Ife, Osun State, Nigeria, 1979—81; coord. grad. reading program, assoc. prof. Albany State U., Ga., 1982—92; prof. elem. & early childhood edn., dept. chair Kennesaw State U., Ga., 1992—99, dir. reading inst., 1999—2003, prof. emeritus reading edn., 2008—; owner Akanbi Reading Solutions, Aknabi Reading Solutions. Cons. chpt. I reading staff devel. workshops Colquitt County Sch. Dist., Moultrie, Ga., 1983—84; literacy vols. tng. cons. Project READ, Albany, 1988—88; writing across curriculum project cons. W.Town Elem. Sch., Albany, 1989—90; bd. mem. U. Sys. Ga. Reading Consortium, 1999—2004; project dir. minority future tchr. scholars program Kennesaw State U., 2003—05; tech. vol. Internat. Reading Assn., Nigeria Project, 2004; mem. literacy & reading educators del. People-to-People Amb. Programs, Nigeria Project, South Africa, 2004; presenter literacy workshop for parents King Springs Elem. Sch., Marietta, Ga., 2005; presenter Oxford Round Table, 2005, World Congress Reading, Costa Rica, 2008. Contbr. chapters to books, articles to profl. jours. Mem. edn. task force Albany C. of C., 1990—92, mem. equal opportunity task force, 1991; leadership mem. Cobb County C. of C., Marietta, 1993—94; v.p. Parent Student Tchr., Assn. Awtry Mid. Sch., Kennesaw, 1993—94; mem. N.Cobb HS Adv. Coun., Kennesaw, 1994—95; mem. adult steering com. youth leadership Cobb County C. of C., 2002—03; bd. mem. Ben Hill United Meth. Ch. Christian Acad., 2008—; mem. Cobb Democratic Women, 2009—. Recipient Outstanding Coll. Reading Tchr. of Yr. award, Albany Area Chpt. Internat. Reading Assn., 1992, Coll. Adminstr. of Yr. award, Cobb Edn. Enrichment Program, 1995, Partnership award for dedication to Children's Acad., Kennesaw State U., 2005; Minority Future Tchr.-Scholars Programg grant, Coca Cola Found., 2003—04. Mem.: Nat. Reading Conf., Oxford Round Table, Internat. Reading Assn. (pres. 1992), Ga. Assn.Tchr. Educators (gateways tchr. edn. editl. bd. mem. 1991—93), Nat. Assn. Multicultural Edn., Ga. Reading Assn. (chair history com. 1990—92), Internat. Reading Assn., Phi Delta Kappa, Alpha Kappa Alpha Sorority. Achievements include research in home influences on literacy acquisition across different ages, languages and cultures; the relationship between the reader's organizational schema and prose comprehension; development of diagnostic reading test; phonics program; preschool literacy curriculum for parents and childcare providers; training materials for the International Reading Association's pilot program in Nigeria, creating an active learning environment in multicultural classrooms. Avocations: travel, reading, music. Personal E-mail: akanbil@comcast.net.

AKBARI, HOMAYOON MOHAMMED, colon and rectal surgeon, educator; Attended, Johns Hopkins U.; grad., NYU; MD, U. Medicine and Dentistry of NJ, Newark. Diplomate Am. Bd. Surgery, 2003, Am. Bd. Colon and Rectal Surgery, 2004. Resident in surgery Georgetown Univ. Hosp., DC, 1998—99, Univ. Toronto Hosp., 1999—2002; fellow in colon and rectal surgery St. Lukes Roosevelt Hosp., NY, 2002—03; assoc. prof. surgery Va. Commonwealth Univ.; hosp. affiliation includes Va. Commonwealth Univ. Med. Ctr. Office: Virginia Commonwealth University Medical Center PO Box 980428 417 N 11th St Richmond VA 23298 Office Phone: 804-828-8000.

AKDAG, MENDERES, manufacturing executive; BSBA in Fin., U. Fla. With Lens Express, Inc., 1991—2000, CFO, 1991—92, CEO, 1992—96, pres., 1996—2000; CEO Internat. Cosmetics Mktg. Co., 2000—01, PetMed Express, Inc., 2001—, pres., 2005—; with Ernst & Young Entrepreneur, 2009. Bd. dirs. Integrity Tracking LLC, Lens Express, Inc., 1991—96, PetMed Express, Inc., 2002—. Office: PetMed Express Inc 1441 SW 29th Ave Pompano Beach FL 33069 Office Phone: 954-979-5995. Office Fax: 954-971-0544. Business E-Mail: makdag@petmeds.com.

AKEEL, HADI ABU, robotics executive; b. Cairo, Apr. 9, 1938; came to U.S., 1961; s. Kobaisi Aly Abu-Akeel and Zeinab Makhlouf; children: Shereef, Nezar; m. Naglaa Mostafa. BS in Mech. Engring., Cairo U., 1959; MS in Applied Mechanics, UCLA, 1963; PhD in Mech. Engring., U. Calif., Berkeley, 1966. Cert. mfg. engr. Acting instr. U. Calif., Berkeley, 1963-66; analytical specialist Bendix Corp., South Bend, Ind., 1966-69; assoc. prof. Ain Shams U., Cairo, 1969-74; sr. staff engr. GM Mfg., Warren, Mich., 1974-76; program mgr. GM Corp., Warren, 1976-78; dept. head mfg. staff GM, Warren, 1978-80, chief engr. flexible automation systems, 1980-82; v.p., chief engr. GMFanuc Robotics Corp., Auburn Hills, Mich., 1982-92; sr. v.p. Fanuc U.S.A., 1992-96, also bd. dirs., vice chmn., 1992-98; gen. mgr. Berkeley Lab. Fanuc Am. Corp., Union City, Calif., 1992—2001; sr. v.p. Fanuc Robotics Am., Inc., 1996—99. Tech. advisor FANUC Ltd., Japan, 1992—06; advisor Mgmt. of Tech. Program U. Calif., Berkeley, 1988-92; chmn. bd. dirs. Robotics Internat. of SME, Dearborn, Mich., 1992-93; pres. Amteng Corp., 1996—; independent cons. & expert witnes intellectual property, 2008-. Author: Machine Design, 1972; contbr. articles to profl. jours.; holds over 60 U.S. and fgn. patents. Soccer coach Am. Youth Soccer Orgn.; mem. bd. advisors Sch. Engring., U. Mich., Dearborn, 1991-2006; chmn. bd. visitors Sch. Engring., Oakland U., 1991-92. Recipient Joseph F. Engleberger award Robotic Industries Assn., 1989, Mich. Sci. Trailblazer award State Mich., 1989. Fellow ASME, Soc. Mfg. Engrs. (internat. dir. 1998-2003); mem. IEEE, Nat. Acad. Engring. Independent. Muslim. Avocations: tennis, swimming, camping, travel, machine shop. Office: Fanuc Robotics Corp 3900 W Hamlin Rd Rochester Hills MI 48309-3253 Home: 3000 Holiday Dr Apt 904 Fort Lauderdale FL 33316-2494 Personal E-mail: majesticet-who@yahoo.com.

AKERS, J. KEVIN, energy executive; b. Owensboro, Ky. BS in Petroleum Engring., U. Ala. Various positions, engring. and ops., various divsns. Atmos Energy Corp.; with Atmos Energy Corp. (Miss. Valley Gas Transition Team); v.p., Northern Region Ops. Atmos Energy Corp., La., sales engr., asst. dist. mgr. Ky., engr., 1991—97, v.p., Eastern Region Ops. Ky., 1997—2001, pres. Miss., 2002—07, Ky., 2007—, pres., Mid-States Divsn., 2007—; bd. dirs. Wachovia Corp. (now Wells Fargo & Co.), asst. v.p., team leader 2, 2005—. Sr. gas. engr. Ind. Utility Regulatory Commn., 1989-91. Office: Atmos Energy Corp 3 Lincoln Ctr Ste 1800 5430 LBJ Freeway Dallas TX 75240 Office Phone: 972-934-9227. Office Fax: 972-855-3040. Business E-Mail: kevin.akers@atmosenergy.com.

AKERS, WILLIAM WALTER, chemical engineering educator; b. Panola County, Tex., Dec. 31, 1922; s. Oscar Walter and Lela (Malone) A.; m. Nancy Tressel, Mar. 1, 1947; children— Susan Elaine, Carol Lorraine. BS, Tex. Tech Coll., 1943; MS, U. Tex., 1944; PhD, U. Mich., 1951. With Atlantic Refining Co., 1947; mem. faculty Rice U., 1947-93, prof. chem. engring., 1956—93, prof. emeritus, 1993—, chmn. dept., 1955-66; dir. Bio-Med. Engring., Lab., 1963-69, asst. to pres. univ., 1973-74, dir. univ. relations, 1974, v.p. for external affairs, 1975-80, v.p. adminstrn., 1980-89. Cons. chem. industries, 1947-65; mem. coun. Oak Ridge Inst. Nuclear Studies, 1958-63, vice chmn., 1962, bd. dirs., 1963-69; tech. adviser to Yugoslavia, 1962; mem. U.S.-Afghanistan Ednl. Consortium, 1963-70; rshc. project dir. Baylor Coll. Medicine, 1965-70; mem. biomed. engring. fellowship com. NIH, 1967-70; mem. Sec.'s Adv. Coun. for Coal Mine Health Rsch., 1970-71; mem. adv. coun. Nat. Inst. Occupational Safety and Health, 1971-73; mem. adv. com. on nuclear energy Tex. Energy and Natural Resources Adv. Coun., 1980-88. Author papers in field. Trustee St. Luke's Hosp., Houston, 1975-79; bd. dirs. South Main Center Assn., 1976-87, Houston Symphony Soc., 1983-85; mem. adv. bd. Salvation Army, 1998. Served with C.E., AUS, 1941-43. Recipient Disting. Engring. Alumnus award Tex. Tech U., 1967, Disting. Alumnus award, 1968 Mem. AAAS, Am. Chem. Soc., Am. Inst. Chem. Engrs. (Best Fundamental Paper award 1967, Distinguished lectr. 1969), Am. Soc. Artificial Organs, Council on Fgn. Relations, Houston Philos. Soc., Sigma Xi, Tau Beta Pi. Episcopalian. Home: 4718 Hallmark Dr Apt 1001 Houston TX 77056

AKIN, THOMAS B., mortgage company executive; BA, U. Calif., Santa Cruz; MBA in Fin., UCLA. Employee Salomon Bros., 1978—81; regional dir. LA & San Francisco, mng. dir. western US Merrill Lynch Instl. Svcs., 1981—94; mng. gen. ptnr. Talkot Capital, LLC, Sausalito, Calif., 1995—; chmn. Dynex Capital, Inc., 2003—, CEO, 2008—. Former bd. dirs. Advance Data Exch., Acacia Rsch. Inc.; bd. dirs. Centiv Services, Inc., eFax.com, Inc., 1996, CombiMatrix, 1998—, Dynex Capital, Inc., 2003—. Office: Dynex Capital Inc 4991 Lake Brook Dr Ste 100 Glen Allen VA 23060 Office Phone: 804-217-5800. Office Fax: 804-217-5860. Business E-Mail: akin@dynexcapital.com.

AKINS, ZANE VERNON, agricultural products executive; b. Bethel, Kans., Apr. 13, 1940; s. Gerald Vernon and Vesta Jean (Rutherford) A.; m. Kay Ellen Cowan, Aug. 17, 1963; children: Michael Scott, Deborah Lynn, Christine Sue. BS in Agr., U. Mo., 1962. Farmer, 1962-64; svc. technician No. Ohio Breeders Assn., Tiffin, 1964-66; program dir. Holstein Assn. Am., Brattleboro, Vt., 1966-73, mgr. sire devel. svc., 1973-77, adminstrv. asst., 1977-78, CEO, 1978-90; exec. v.p. Holstein-Friesian Svcs., Inc., Brattleboro, 1978-90; pres. Zane Akins and Assocs., West Brattleboro, 1991—. Pres., chmn. bd. dirs. Nat. Integrated Techs. Inc., 1996—; bd. dirs. Earthwide Assocs., Inc., pres. 1994—2000; pres. A&S Assocs., Ltd., 1995—; bd. dirs. Vt. Nat. Bank, 1987-2000, Earthwide Sys. Inc., v.p., 1995—2000; v.p. Earthwide Products Corp., 1996—2000; bd. dirs. Vt. Fin. Svcs., 1987-2000, chmn. exec. com., 1995-96, chmn. audit com., 1996-97, chmn. loan com., 1997-98; regional leader Primerica Fin. Svcs., 1991-2006; chmn. bd. dirs. Anitech Internat. Inc., Boulder, Colo., 1991-92; trustee N.E. Delta/Vt. Dental Soc., Inc., 1990-99, chmn., 1995-99; chmn. bd. NEDA, 1999-2004; pres. Vt. Natural Food Products Inc., 2001—; real estate agt., 2004—09; ptnr. Akins Fin. Group, 2005—. Bd. dirs. Windham County United Way, 1980-84; corporator Brattleboro Meml. Hosp., 1980-2009, chmn. pub. rels. com., 1982-83, bd. dirs., 1983-86; pres. Windham County Humane Soc., 1992-93; bd. dirs. Brattleboro Area Boys & Girls Club, 1998-2002, treas., 1999-2002. Sears & Roebuck scholar, Freshman Curators scholar, Borden's scholar, U. Mo., 1958-59, Sophomore Curators scholar, Campus Chest scholar, 1958-60; recognized as Man of the Yr. Tri-State Breeders Coop., 1984; recipient Citation of Merit U. Mo., 1986, Hon. Ky. Col., 2014. Mem. Purebred Dairy Cattle Assn. (bd. dirs. 1978-90, Recognition award 1991), Nat. Soc. Livestock Records Assn. (v.p. 1982-84), Nat. Pedigree Livestock Coun. (pres. 1984-86, sec., treas. 1989—, Disting. Svc. award 1993), Received Honorary Lifetime Membership, 2007; Nat. Coop. Dairy Herd Improvement Programs (policy bd. 1980-90), Geonomics Inst., Boston Dist. Export Coun., Brattleboro C. of C. (bd. dirs. 1979-81), Alpha Zeta (Centennial Honor Roll 1997, inductee Mo. HS Hall of Fame, Humensville, 1999), Alpha Gamma Rho (regional v.p. 1980-84, bd. dirs. 1984-90, grand pres. 1986-89, Man of Yr. award Chgo. Alumni chpt. 1991, Bro. of the Century 2004, inductee Hall of Fame 2006), U. Mo. Coleman Club (inductee AGR Hall of Fame 2008). Congregationalist. Home and Office: 177 Palermo Pl Lady Lake FL 32159-0094 Personal E-mail: zaneakins@gmail.com.

AKKARA, JOSEPH AUGUSTINE, chemist, educator, researcher; arrived in US, 1964, naturalized, 1980; s. Augustine Aippu Akkara and Theresa Anthony Kolapran; m. Mary Ann Malaickel, Aug. 18, 1969; children: Augustine Viju, Jeena Theresa. PhD in Biochemistry, U. Mo., 1969. Med. rschr. Med. Coll. Trivandrum, Kerala, India, 1959-61; tech. asst. Ctrl. Food Technol. Rsch. Inst., Mysore, India, 1961-64; grad. asst., rsch. assoc. Sch. Medicine U. Mo., Columbia, 1964-69; rsch. assoc. Rockefeller U., NYC, 1969-71, Brookdale Hosp. Med. Ctr., Bklyn., 1971-73, chief radioassay, 1973-80; sr. scientist Med. Rsch. Inst., Worcester, Mass., 1980-81; biochemist stat. Toxicology Svc. Boston, 1981-84; rsch. chemist U.S. Army Natick Rsch. and Engring. Ctr., 1984-99; program dir. NSF, 1999—. Adj. faculty Framingham State Coll., 1996-99; mem. biotechnology adv. bd. Mass. Bay Coll.; advisor NRC; bd. dirs. Invention Evaluation. Recipient R&D award U.S. Army, 1992, 96, Inventor of Yr. award U.S. Army Soldier Sys. commd., 1998. Mem. Materials Rsch. Soc., Am. Chem. Soc., Kerala Assn. New Eng. (pres. 1986-87), Indian Assn. Greater Boston (sec. 1986-88, 1st v.p. 1988-89), Lions Club, Nat. Press Club, Rotary (pres. Falls Church Club 2006-07, 10-11), Sigma Xi (pres. Natick chpt. 1998-99). Roman Catholic. Achievements include patents and publications in synthesis, modification, characterization, and applications of polymers and materials for electro-optic and high performance multifunctional applications; enzymology and research program management. Home: 7520 Walnut Hill Ln Falls Church VA 22042-3539

ALARIO, JOHN A., JR., state legislator; b. New Orleans, Sept. 15, 1943; m. Alba Ree Williamson, 1965; children: John W, Jan M, Christopher B, Kevin G. Mem. Dist. 83 La. House of Reps., 1972—2007, spkr., 1984—88, 1992; del. Dem. Nat.Conv., 1972, La State Constl. Conv, 1973; mem. Dist. 8 La. State Senate, 2008—, mem. commerce, consumer protection and internat. affairs com., fin. com., chair select com. on coastal restoration and flood control; acct. & teacher; owner John Alario, Jr, Income Tax Svc., 2009—. Recipient Hale Boggs Member Award, 1975—76, Outstanding Alumnus, S.E La Univ, 81. Democrat. Catholic. Office: Dist Off 1063 Muller Pkwy Westwego LA 70094 also: Capitol Off PO Box 94183 Baton Rouge LA 70804 Office Phone: 504-342-7263 504-342-7263. Fax: 504-342-0402. E-mail: alarioj@legis.state.la.us.

ALAUPOVIC, PETAR, biochemist, educator; b. Prague, Czech Republic, Aug. 3, 1923; arrived in US, 1957; married, 1947; 1 child. ChemE, U. Zagreb, 1948, PhD in Chemistry, 1956; DHC (hon.), U. Lille, France, 1987, U. Buenos Aires, 1994, U. Goteborg, 1999. Rschr. pharms. rsch. lab. Chem Corp, Prague, 1948-49; rschr. organic lab. Inst. Indsl. Rsch., Yugoslavia, 1949-50; asst. agrl. faculty U. Zagreb, 1951-54, asst. chem. inst. med. faculty, 1954-56; rsch. biochemist U. Ill., 1957-60; with cardiovascular sect. Okla. Med. Rsch. Found., Oklahoma City, 1960—, head lipoprotein lab., 1972-92, also head Lipid and Lipoprotein Lab. Prof. rsch. biochemistry, sch. med. U. Okla., 1960—. Assoc. editor Lipids, 1974-78. Named Disting. Career Scientist Okla. Med. Rsch. Fund, 1990; NIH grantee, 1961-95. Mem. AAAS, Am. Soc. Biol. Chemists, Am. Chem. Soc., Am. Heart Assn. (Spl. Recognition award 1994), Am. Oil Chemistry Soc. Achievements include research in chemistry of naturally occuring macromolecular lipid compounds such as serum and tissue lipoproteins and bacterial endotoxins, biochemistry of red cell membranes isolation and characterization of tissue lipases. Office: Okla Med Rsch Found Lipid and Lipoprotein Lab 825 NE 13th St Oklahoma City OK 73104-5005 Office Phone: 405-271-7703. Business E-Mail: alaupovicp@omrf.org.

ALBANESE, JAY SAMUEL, criminologist, educator; b. Mineola, NY, Feb. 10, 1953; s. Samuel S. and Doris (Mather) A.; m. Leslie Elizabeth King, July 12, 1980; children: Thomas, Kelsey. BA, Niagara U., 1974; MA, Rutgers U., 1976, PhD, 1981. Chief Internat. Ctr. Nat. Inst. Justice, 2002—06; prof. Niagara U., Niagara Falls, NY, 1981-96; prof. govt. and pub. policy Va. Commonwealth U., Richmond, 1996—. Vis. prof. Simon Fraser U., Vancouver, B.C., Can., 1988. Author: Dealing with Delinquency, 2d edit., 1993, Crime in America, 1993, White Collar Crime in America, 1995, Organized Crime in Our Times, 6th edit., 2011, Criminal Justice, 5th edit., 2013, Transnational Crime and The 21st Century, 2011, Professional Ethics in Criminal Justice, 3rd edit., 2012; co-author: Comparative Criminal Justice Systems, 2014; editor: Organized Crime: World Perspectives, 2003, Combating Piracy-Intellectual Property Theft and Fraud, 2009; contbr. articles to profl. jours. Recipient Sears Found. Tchg. Excellence award, 1989-90, Founder's award, Acad. Criminal Justice Sciences, 2000, Elske Smith Disting. Lectr. award Va. Commonwealth U. Coll. Humanities and Sciences, 2001, Disting. Tchr. award, 2013, Scholar award, Va. Social Sci. Assn., 2009, Gerhard Mueller award, Acad. Criminal Justice Sciences Internat. Sect., 2011, Outstanding Tchr. award VCU Wilder Sch. Govt. Pub. Affairs, 2012, Disting. Tchg. award VCU Coll. Humanities & Scis., 2013. Fellow Acad. Criminal Justice Sciences, 2002, Am. Soc. Criminology Divsn. Internat. Criminology (chair 2011-13); American Soc. Criminology (exec. bd. 2013-), Internat. Assn. Study Organized Crime (exec. dir. 2002—2006), Northeastern Assn. Criminal Justice Sciences (pres. 1988-89), Acad. Criminal Justice Sciences (pres. 1995-96), White Collar Crime Res. Consortium (pres. 2000-02), Phi Kappa Phi.

ALBANI, THOMAS J., investor; b. Hartford, Conn., May 3, 1942; s. Charles A. and Marie F. Albani; m. Suzanne Beardsley, Sept. 3, 1966; children: Karin, Steven. BA, Amherst Coll., 1964; MBA, Wharton Sch. U. Pa., 1967. Asst. product mgr. Gen. Mills, Inc., Mpls., 1967-69; dir. mktg. Am. Can Co., Greenwich, Conn., 1969-73; mgmt. cons. McKinsey and Co., Inc., NYC, 1973-78; gen. mgr. GE, Bridgeport, Conn., 1978-84; group v.p. Black & Decker, Inc., Bridgeport, 1984; pres. Sunbeam No. Am. Appliance Div. Allegheny Internat., Oak Brook, Ill., 1984-86; pres. appliance bus. Allegheny Internat. Inc., Pitts., 1986, exec. v.p., COO, 1986-89; prin. New Eng. Cons. Group, Westport, Conn., 1990-91; pres., CEO Electrolux Corp., Atlanta, 1991-98; pres. Canopache Cons., Siasconset, Mass., 1999—. Bd. dir. Select Comfort Corp., Barnes Group Inc., Doskocil Mfg. Co. Home: 31 Island Pl Orchid FL 32963-9505 Office: Canopache Cons PO Box 855 Siasconset MA 02564-0855 Personal E-mail: tjalbani@aol.com.

ALBERS, CHARLES EDGAR, retired investment company executive; b. Flushing, NY, Nov. 30, 1940; s. Edwin M. and Olive F. (Van Dyke) A.; m. Judy Mae Hite, Dec. 18, 1961 (dec. June 1998); children: Robert, Karin, Laura. AB in Econ., cum laude, Kenyon Coll., Gambier, Ohio, 1962; MBA, Columbia U., NYC, 1967. CFA. Portfolio mgr. Guardian Park Ave. Fund, Inc., NYC, 1972—98; sr. v.p. Oppenheimer Funds, NYC, 1998—2003; portfolio mgr. Oppenheimer Main St. Fund, NYC, 1998—2003; ret., 2003; dir. Atlas Economic Rsch. Found. Dir. Ivy League Club Sarasota, Instl. Investor Trust, Parents in Charge Found. Woodrow Wilson Fellow in Econ., 1962-1963. Named to Forbes Mag.'s Mutual Funds Honor Roll 9 times. Variable Annuity Mgr. of Yr. Morningstar, 1996 Mem.: Short Hills Club, Columbia Club. Avocations: public policy, economics, classical music. Personal E-mail: chuckalbers@aol.com.

ALBERS, JOHN, state legislator; b. Aug. 18; m. Kari Albers; children: Will, Ryan. Attended, U. Louisville. Corp. exec., ptnr. Nat. Fin. Svc. Co.; mem. Dist. 56 Ga. State Senate, 2011—. Vol. firefighter Alpharetta Fire Dept., Ga. Mem.: NRA, Ga. Firefighters Assn. Republican. Office: 885 Woodstock Rd #215 Ste 430 Roswell GA 30075 also: Georgia State Senate 324B Coverdell Legis Office Bldg Atlanta GA 30334 Office Phone: 678-667-3656, 404-463-8055. Business E-Mail: info@senatoralbers.com.

ALBERS, MARK W., oil industry executive; b. Calgary, Alta., Canada; B engring., Tex. A&M Univ. Mgmt. positions ExxonMobil Corp., 1979—91; tech. mgr., ops. mgr. Esso Australia, Melbourne, 1991; Alaska interests mgr. ExxonMobil Corp., prod. mgr. we. U.S.; v.p. Africa, Chad/Nigeria Exxon Mobil Develop. Co., Houston, 2001; exec. asst. to chmn. & pres. ExxonMobil Corp.; pres. Exxon Mobil Develop. Co., Houston, 2004—07; sr. v.p., mem. mgmt. com. ExxonMobil Corp., Irving, Tex., 2007—. Mem. engring. adv. council Tex. A&M Univ. Mem.: CEO Forum, Inst. Engineers Australia, Soc. Petroleum Engineers. Office: Exxon Mobil Corp 5959 Las Colinas Blvd Irving TX 75039

ALBERT, ALAN DALE, lawyer, writer; b. Christiansburg, Va., Feb. 6, 1956; s. Horace Wendell and Alma Juanita (Morris) A.; m. Charlotte Lynne Anders, Sept., 27, 2003; children: Amber Reed Sappington, Alexander, Caroline. AB magna cum laude, Harvard Coll., 1979; MPhil, Oxford U., 1981; JD cum laude, Harvard U., 1985. Bar: Va. 1985, US Dist. Ct. (ea. dist.) Va. 1989, US Ct. Appeals (4th cir.) 1989, US Bankruptcy Ct. (ea. dist.) Va. 1991, US Ct. Appeals (fed. cir.) 2003 US Supreme Ct. 2005, US Dist. Ct. (west dist.) Va., 2008, US Bankruptcy Ct. (west dist.) Va., 2008, US Ct. Appeals (11th cir.) 2012. Instr. in legal methods, teaching fellow in fed. litigation Harvard Law Sch., 1983-85; teaching fellow faculty arts and scis. Harvard U., 1984-85; law clk. Office of the Legal Adviser U.S. Dept. State, 1984; rsch. dir., speech writer Baliles for Gov., Richmond, Va., 1985; dir. policy devel. Gov.'s Transition Office Commonwealth of Va., Richmond, 1985-86, spl. asst. to Gov. of Va., 1986-89; assoc. Mays & Valentine, Norfolk and Richmond, 1989-93, ptnr., 1994—2000, Troutman Sanders LLP, Norfolk and Richmond, Va., 2001—04; shareholder, v.p. LeClair Ryan PC, 2004—; pres. Norfolk Law Libr., 2006—. Mem. Va. Bd. Conservation and Recreation, Richmond, 2002—13, chmn., 2002—06. Author books on environ. law, real estate and land use law, freedom of info. and pub. records access; editor Harvard Law Rev., 1983-85; contbr. articles to profl. jours., columns in newspapers. Vol. Dem. nat., state and local polit. campaigns and com. activities, 1976—; exec. dir. Va. Dems., 1988; bd. dir. Va. Opera, 1990—, pres., 1998-2000, chmn., 2011-; trustee Va. Symphony, 2008—13, librarian and mem. Va. Symphony Orchestra Chorus, 2002-; co-founder, chmn. Creative Resources Empowering Artists Telling Our Stories, Inc., 2011-; co-founder, gen. coun. Commonwealth Theatre Co.; co-founder; mem. Leadership Metro Richmond, 1987-88. Harvard Nat. scholar, 1974-79, George C. Marshall scholar, 1979-82, European Consortium Polit. Rsch. scholar, 1982, Pres.'s Disting. Svc. award Treas. Assn. of Va., 1995, 2003. Fellow Am. Bar Found., Va. Law Found.; mem. ABA, Fed. Bar Assn., Am. Intellectual Property Law Assn., Va. Bar Assn. (sect. bd. govs. 1991-94), Va. State Bar, Tidewater Legal Aid Soc. (bd. dir. 1990-93), Norfolk-Portsmouth Bar, Va. Beach Bar, Holdsworth Soc., Phi Beta Kappa. Office: LeClair Ryan PC 999 Waterside Dr Ste 2100 Norfolk VA 23510 Address: 951 E Byrd St Richmond VA 23219 Office Phone: 757-441-8914. Business E-Mail: alan.albert@leclairryan.com.

ALBERT, MATTHEW ROSS, colon and rectal surgeon, educator; BS in Ecol., Evolutionary, Organismal Biology, Tulane U., New Orleans, 1994; MD, Tufts U., Boston, 1998. Diplomate Am. Bd. Surgery, 2004, Am. Bd. Colon and Rectal Surgery, 2005, lic. Fla. Resident in gen. surgery Tufts-New England Med. Med. Ctr., Boston, 1998—2003; fellow in colon and rectal surgery Univ. Tex., Houston, 2003—04; started Ctr. for Colon and Rectal Surgery, 2004; faculty mem. gen. surgery resident Fla. Hosp., Altamonte Springs, 2005, asst. program dir. colon and rectal surgery fellowship program, 2010, process improvement chmn. outpatient mgmt. group Ambulatory Surgery Ctr., 2009; clin. asst. prof. Fla. State Univ., Tallahassee, 2008. Author: Vessel sealing in laparoscopic colonic surgery, 2009, Hand Assisted Laparoscopic Surgery In The Morbidly Obese Patient, 2009, Early Multi-Institution Experience with Single Incision Laparoscopic Colectomy (SILC), 2010, Results of Doppler Guided Hemorrhoidal Arterial Ligation with RectoAnal Repair in 175 patients, 2010, Transanal Minimally Invasive Surgery - A Giant Leap Forward, 2010, various others. Fellow: Am. Soc. of Colon and Rectal Surgeons, ACS; mem.: Fla. Outpatient Mgmt. Group. Office: Florida Hospital 661 E Altamonte Dr Ste 220 Altamonte Springs FL 32701 Office Phone: 407-303-5191. Office Fax: 407-303-5193.

ALBERT, MOSES K., dermatologist; B in Physics summa cum laude, Georgetown U.; MD, Wash. U., 1978. Diplomate Am. Bd. Dermatology, 1982. Resident dermatology George Washington Univ. Med. Ctr., Washington, 1979—82; established The Shalom Children's Fund; hosp. affiliation includes Inova Fairfax Hosp.; with Fairfax Dermatology. Mem.: Phi Beta Kappa. Office: Fairfax Dermatology Ste 504 3020 Hamaker Ct Fairfax VA 22031 Office Phone: 703-849-8036. Office Fax: 703-204-3448.

ALBERT, ROSS ALAN, lawyer; b. Boston, Nov. 22, 1958; s. Richmond G. and Mary (Day) A. AB, Harvard U., 1982, postgrad., 1985—86; JD, U. Calif., Berkeley, 1986. Bar: Mass. 1986, DC 1988, Ga. 2002, U.S. Dist. Ct. Md. 1987, U.S. Dist. Ct. (no. dist.) Ga. 2005, U.S. Ct. Appeals (4th cir.) 1987, U.S. Ct. Appeals (5th cir.) 1993, U.S. Ct. Appeals (DC cir.) 1994, U.S. Ct. Appeals (2d cir.) 1994, U.S. Ct. Appeals (6th cir.) 1994, U.S. Ct. Appeals (9th cir.) 1994, U.S. Ct. Appeals (11th cir.) 1994, U.S. Supreme Ct. 1994, U.S. Ct. Appeal (8th cir.) 1995, U.S. Ct. Appeals (3rd Cir.) 2007. Jud. law clk. U.S. Dist. Ct. Md., Balt., 1986-88; assoc. Wilmer, Cutler & Pickering, Washington, 1988-93; spl. counsel Office of Gen. Counsel-appellate group U.S. SEC, Washington, 1993-97, counsel to commr. Norman S. Johnson, 1997-2000, sr. spl. counsel Divsn. of Enforcement, 2000-01; ptnr. Morris, Manning & Martin LLP, Atlanta, 2001—. Assoc. editor Calif. Law Rev., 1985-86; contbr. chpts. to books. Alumni Assn. Securities & Exchange Commn.; mem. reunion com. Boalt Hall Class 1986; mem. scholarship com. U. Calif.-Berkley Alumni Club, Ga.; pres. U. Calif.-Berkley Club, 2008, 2012, v.p., pres.-elect Ga., 2007—11, bd. mem., 2006—; mem. sch. and scholarship com. Harvard Club, Ga. Mem.: ABA, Atlanta Bar Assn., Ga. Bar Assn. Office: Morris Manning & Martin LLP 1600 Atlanta Fin Ctr 3343 Peachtree Rd Atlanta GA 30326 Office Phone: 404-504-7768. Personal E-mail: ra81@post.harvard.edu. Business E-Mail: raa@mmmlaw.com.

ALBERTSON, CHRISTOPHER ADAM, librarian; b. Oak Park, Ill., Dec. 10, 1951; Student, U. New Orleans, 1969—70; BA with high honors, U. Tex.-Arlington, 1972; MLS, U. N. Tex., 1973. Cataloger Orange (Tex.) Pub. Libr., 1974-75, asst. libr., 1975-79, city libr., 1979-81, Tyler (Tex.) Libr., 1981—. Contbr. articles to profl. jours. Mem. ALA, ASPA, Am. Soc. Info. Sci., Tex. Libr. Assn. Presbyterian. Home: 3100 Pounds Ave Tyler TX 75701-8034 Office: Tyler Pub Library 201 S College Ave Tyler TX 75702-7381 Business E-Mail: citylibn@tylertexas.com.

ALBO, DAVID BARR, state legislator; b. Flushing, NY, Apr. 18, 1962; BA in Economics, U. Va., 1984; JD, U. Richmond, Va., 1988. Former asst. atty. Fairfax City Prosecutor's Office, Va.; mem. Dist. 42 Va. House of Delegates, 1994—; mem. Gen. Laws Com., Conservation & Natural Resources Com., Ct. Justice, Privileges & Elections Com., Legislature Com., Gov.'s Comn. Justice Reform. Mem.: Springfield Optimists, West Springfield Rotary. Republican. Episcopalian. Office: 6350 Rolling Mill Pl Ste 102 Springfield VA 22152 Office Phone: 703-451-3555. Business E-Mail: deldalbo@house.virginia.gov.

ALBRIGHT, JOSEPH WILLIAM, management consultant; b. Chillicothe, Ohio, Feb. 3, 1954; s. Herman LeRoy and Catherine Regina (Rieder) A.; m. Iris J. Evans; children: Andrea Lyn, Jason Michael, James Darrell Evans, Marie Elizabeth Evans. BME, U. Dayton, 1976; M in Strategic Studies, U.S. Army War Coll., 2000; MS in Indsl. Engring., U. Tenn., 2001. Commd. 2nd lt. Ordnance br. U.S. Army, 1976; advanced through grades to col. Ordnance br. U.S. Army, 1999; accountable officer 9th ordnance co. 9th Ordnance Co., Germany, 1977-79, ops. officer, 1979-80; rsch. engr., chief integrated logistic support office large caliber weapon sys. lab., 1980-82; material officer 3rd ordnance bn. 59th ordnance brigade 3d Ordnance Bn., 59th Ordnance Brigade, 1982-85; Dept. of Army coord. for ammunition logistics Dept. of Army, 1985-87; asst. exec. officer to dep. commanding gen. Material Readiness Army Material Commd., 1987-88; commdr. 96th ordnance co. 96th Ordnance Co., 1988-90; inspector gen. Tech. Insp. divsn. Army Material Command Tech. Insp. divsn. Army Materiel Command, 1990-93, chief program mgmt. divsn., 1993-94; comdr. Milan Army Ammunition Plant Milan Army Ammunition Plant, Tenn., 1994-96; dep. support ops. officer 3rd corps support command V U.S. Army Corps, 1996-98; depot maintenance project chief Hdqrs., Dept. of Army, 1998-99, indsl. ops. project chief, office dep. chief staff logistics, 2000—02; sr. logistics analyst Office of Dep. Undersec. of Army, Washington, 2002—04; ret., 2004. Sr logistician Office of Sec. Army, Washington, 2004—05; dir. situational awareness Office Deputy Under Sec. Army For Bus. Transformation., 2005—08; pres. Performance Based Solutions Inc., 2008—10, Managing Consult., 2010—11; divsn. v.p. for tech. support Sodexo Sch. Facility Mgmt., 2012—. Decorated Legion of Merit, Meritorious Svc. medal 6 awards, Army Commendation medal 2 awards, Army Achievement medal; named Disting. Mil. Grad., 1976, Disting. Grad. Ordnance Officer Advanced Course, 1980. Mem. ANSI, NFPA, ASME, SAR, US Army Ordanance Corps Assn. (life), Pi Sigma Tau, Orgn. Hope (chair, bd. dirs 2010-), Fellowship Christian Athletes West Tenn. (bd. leaders 2010-). Office Phone: 731-686-0403, 731-487-3770. Business E-Mail: joseph.albright@charter.net.

ALBRIGHT, MICHAEL, construction executive; BS in Acctg., Miss. State U., MBA. CPA. Audit mgr. Arthur Andersen; sr. v.p. Carlisle Property Co., Dallas; group v.p. Rollins, Inc., Atlanta; pres. Tex. Trust Savings Bank, FSB, 1994; contr. Centex Corp., 1987—89, v.p., 1989; chmn., CEO Centex Life Solutions (divsn. of Centex corp.), 1996—99; sr. v.p. adminstrn. Centex Corp., 1999—. Mem.: AICPA, Tex. Soc. CPAs. Office: Centex Corp 2728 N Harwood Dallas TX 75201 Office Phone: 214-981-5000. Office Fax: 214-981-6859. Business E-Mail: malbright@centexhomes.com.

ALBRINK, MARGARET JORALEMON, medical educator; b. Warren, Ariz., Jan. 6, 1920; d. Ira Beaman and Dorothy (Rieber) Joralemon; m. Wilhelm Stockman Albrink, Sept. 16, 1944 (dec. July 1991); children: Frederick Henry, Jonathan Wilhelm, Peter Varick (dec. March 2003). BA in Psychology cum laude, Radcliffe Coll., 1941; MS in Physiol. Chemistry, Yale U., 1943, MD, 1946, MPH, 1951. Cert. Diplomate Am. Bd. Med. Examiners, Diplomate Am. Bd. Nutrition, Diplomate Am. Bd. Physician Nutrition Specialists. Intern New Haven (Conn.) Hosp., 1946—47; NIH postdoctoral fellow Yale U., New Haven, 1947—49, fellow pub. health, 1950—51, instr. medicine, 1952—58, asst. prof. medicine, 1958—61; assoc. prof. W.Va. U., Morgantown, 1961—66, prof. medicine, 1966—90, prof. emerita, 1990—, mem. grad. faculty, 1977—92; mem. med. and dental staff W.Va. U. Hosp., Morgantown, 1961—2000. Vis. scientist Donner Lab., U. Calif., Berkeley, 1993-2009; assoc. physician Grace-New Haven Cmty. Hosp., 1952-61; cons. nutrition study sect. NIH; vis. scholar U. Calif., Berkeley, 1977-78; established investigator Am. Heart Assn., 1958-63. Guest editor: Clinics in Endocrinology and Metabolism, 1976; guest editor Am. Jour. Clin. Nutrition, 1968, mem. editorial bd., 1963-68; mem. editorial adv. bd. Jour. Am. Coll. Nutrition, 1988-89; reviewer jours.; contbr. articles, chpts. and abstracts to profl. jours. Recipient Rsch. Career award Nat. Heart, Lung and Blood Inst., 1963-90. Fellow: ACP, Am. Coll. Nutrition, Am. Heart Assn. (emeritus, fellow arteriosclerosis coun., fellow coun. epidemiology); mem.: LWV, Am. Diabetes Assn. (epidemiology coun.), Am. Soc. Clin. Nutrition, Am. Soc. Clin. Investigation, Am. Fedn. Clin. Rsch., Phi Beta Kappa, Alpha Omega Alpha. Democrat. Avocations: music, archaeology, computers, nature conservation. Office: WVa U Dept Medicine PO Box 9159 Morgantown WV 26506-9159 Home: 2117 Cherokee Pkwy Louisville KY 40204-2212 E-mail: mjalbrink@aol.com.

ALBRITTON, BEN, state legislator; b. Lakeland, Fla., Aug. 17, 1968; m. Missy Schrader; children: Rebecca, Joshua, Ryan. BS in Citrus & Bus., Fla. So. Coll., 1990. With Columbia U.; mng. ptnr. Albritton Companies; chmn. Fla. Citrus Commn., 2007—10; mem. Dist. 66 Fla. House of Representatives, 2011—. Republican. Office: 150 N Central Ave PO Box 1966 Bartow FL 33831-1966 also: Fla Houise of Reps 1301 The Capitol 402 S Monroe St Tallahassee FL 32399-1300 Office Phone: 863-534-0073, 850-488-9465.

ALBRITTON, BRIAN (A. BRIAN ALBRITTON), lawyer, former federal prosecutor; b. Tampa, May 14, 1957; BA, New Coll. of U. South Fla., 1979; MTS, Harvard U., 1982; JD cum laude, Boston Coll., 1988. Bar: Fla. 1988, US Supreme Ct., US Ct. Appeals (11th cir.), US Dist. Ct. (no., middle and so. dists.) Fla. Law clk. to Hon. William Terrell Hodges US Dist. Ct. (middle dist.) Fla., 1988—90; atty. Holland & Knight LLP, Tampa, 1990—2008; US atty. (middle dist) Fla. US Dept. Justice, 2008—10; ptnr. Phelps Dunbar LLP, Tampa, 2010—. Adj. prof. law Stetson U. Coll. Law, 1998—2004; spkr. in field. Contbr. articles to law jours. Mem.: Hillsborough County Bar Assn. (co-chair Criminal Law Sect. 2000, 2001), Hillsborough County Assn. Criminal Defense Lawyers, Fed. Bar Assn. (pres. Tampa Bay Chpt. 2007—08). Office: Phelps Dunbar LLP 100 S Ashley Dr Ste 1900 Tampa FL 33602 Office Phone: 813-472-7550. Office Fax: 813-472-7570.

ALBRITTON, WILLIAM HAROLD, III, federal judge; b. Andalusia, Ala., Dec. 19, 1936; s. Robert Bynum and Carrie (Veal) A.; m. Jane Rollins Howard, June 2, 1958; children: William Harold IV, Benjamin Howard, Thomas Bynum. AB, U. Ala., 1959, JD, 1960. Bar: Ala. 1960. Assoc. firm Albrittons & Rankin, Andalusia, 1962-66, ptnr., 1966-76; ptnr. firm Albrittons & Givhan, Andalusia, 1976-86; ptnr. Albrittons, Givhan & Clifton, Andalusia, 1986-91; judge US Dist. Ct. (mid. dist.) Ala., Montgomery, 1991—98, chief judge, 1998—2004, sr. judge, 2004—. Mem. 11th Circuit Jud. Coun., 1998—2004, com. on ct. adminstrn. and case mgmt. US Jud. Conf., 1999-2004. Pres. Ala. Law Sch. Found., 1988-91 Fellow Am. Coll. Trial Lawyers, Am. Bar Found.; mem. Fed. Judges Assn. (bd. dirs. 1999-2002), Ala. State Bar (commr. 1981-89, disciplinary commn. 1981-84, v.p. 1985-86, pres.-elect 1989-90, pres. 1990-91), Am. Judicature Soc., Am. Inns of Ct., Bluewater Bay Sailing Club, Phi Beta Kappa, Phi Delta Phi, Omicron Delta Kappa, Alpha Tau Omega.

ALCALDE, HECTOR, public relations executive; b. NYC; BA in Govt., U. Tampa; MA in Edn. & Adminstrn., Vanderbilt U. Former educator, Fla.; chief staff to former chmn., ways and means comm. U.S. House of Representatives, Washington, 1962—74; founder, chmn. Alcalde & Fay, Arlington, Va., 1973—. Bd. dirs. SAFLink, Inc. Fomer trustee Fairfax County Pub. Schs. Edn. Found. Office: Alcalde & Fay 2111 Wilson Blvd 8th Fl Arlington VA 22201 Office Phone: 703-841-0626. Office Fax: 703-243-2874.

ALDAG, EDWARD KARL, JR., investment company executive; b. Eufaula, Ala., Nov. 13, 1963; s. Edward Karl Aldag and Elizabeth (Earl) Aldag Godwin; m. Melinda Bishop, June 21, 1986. BS in Commerce & Bus., U. Ala., 1986. V.p. Guilford Co., Inc., Montgomery, Ala., 1986—89; pres., bd. dirs. Guilford Med. Properties, Inc., Montgomery, Ala., 1989—2001, Guilford Capital, 1990—2001; chmn., pres., CEO Medical Properties Trust, Inc., 2003—. V.p., COO Guilford Capital Corp., Montgomery, 1989—. Pres. arts action coun. Bus. Com. for Arts of Montgomery, 1989-90. Mem. Rotary. Episcopalian. Office: Medical Properties Trust Inc 1000 Urban Center Dr Ste 501 Birmingham AL 35242 Office Phone: 205-969-3755. Office Fax: 205-969-3756. Business E-Mail: Ealdag@medicalpropertiestrust.com.

ALDAY, GENE, state legislator; Attended, Northwest Jr. Coll., Elkins Inst. Small bus. owner; former mayor Town of Walls, Miss.; mem. Dist. 25 Miss. House of Reps., Jackson, 2012—. Republican. Methodist. Office: Miss House of Reps PO Box 1018 Jackson MS 39215 Business E-Mail: galday@house.ms.gov.

ALDEAN, JASON (JASON ALDEAN WILLIAMS), musician; b. Macon, Ga., Feb. 28, 1977; s. Barry and Debbie; m. Jessica Ussery, Aug. 4, 2001 (separated Apr. 2013); children: Keeley, Kendyl. Musician: (albums) Jason Aldean, 2005 (Top New Male Vocalist, Acad. Country Music Awards, 2006), Relentless, 2007, Wide Open, 2009, My Kinda Party, 2011 (Album of Yr., Country Music Assn. Awards, 2011, Album of Yr., Am. Country Awards, 2011, Top Country Album, Billboard Music Awards, 2012), Night Train, 2012, (songs) (with Kelly Clarkson) Don't You Wanna Stay, 2010 (Musical Event of Yr., Country Music Assn. Awards, 2011, Single of Yr.: Vocal Collaboration, Am. Country Awards, 2011, Music Video of Yr.: Group or Collaboration, Am. Country Awards, 2011, Vocal Event of Yr., Acad Country Music Awards, 2012, Single Record of Yr., Acad. Coiuntry Music Awards, 2012), My Kinda Party, 2010 (Single of Yr.: Male, Am. Country Awards, 2011), Dirt Road Anthem, 2011 (Top Country Song, Billboard Music Awards, 2012), Tattoos on This Town, 2011 (Performance of Yr., CMT Music Awards, 2012), The Only Way I Know (with Luke Bryan and Eric Church), 2012 (Vocal Event of Yr., Acad. Country Music Awards, 2013, Collaborative Video of Yr., CMT

Music Awards, 2013). Named Artist of Yr., Am. Country Awards, 2011, Touring Artist of Yr., 2011, Male Vocalist of Yr., Acad. Country Music Awards, 2013, 2014. Office: c/o Spalding Entertainment 54 Music Square East Suite 200 Nashville TN 37203*

ALDERMAN, CHARLES WAYNE, university dean; b. Mobile, Ala., Oct. 10, 1950; s. Charles B. and E. Mae (Henderson) A.; m. Mary Noel Perritt. BS, Auburn U., 1971, MBA, 1972; D in Bus. Adminstrn., U. Tenn., 1977. CPA, cert. internal auditor. Sr. auditor Ernst & Young, Birmingham, Ala., 1973-75; asst. prof. U. Tex., 1978-79, Auburn (Ala.) U., 1979-82, assoc. prof., 1982-87, Coopers & Lybrand prof., dir. Sch. Accountancy, 1987-89, assoc. dean Coll. Bus., 1990-93, dean bus., south trust endowed prof., 1993—, dean enrollment, 2006—. Bd. dirs. Auburn Bank, IntraMicron, Inc. Co-author: Accounting Information Systems, 1982, 86, 90, Auditing, 1987, 90, 93, 96, 99; contbr. articles to profl. jours. Ernst & Young grantee, 1976-77. Mem. AICPA (bd. examiners 1995-98), Ala. Soc. CPAs, Am. Acctg. Assn., Mortar Board, Omicron Delta Kappa, Phi Gamma Delta (faculty advisor 1982-99). Presbyterian. Office: Auburn U Quad Ctr Auburn AL 36849

ALDERMAN, JAMES F., pediatrician; MD, Med. U. SC, 1982. Diplomate American Bd. Pediatrics, 2009. Resident in pediat. Boston City Hosp., 1983—84, Med. Univ. SC, 1984—85; physician Carolinas Med. Ctr.; pvt. practice Charlotte Pediatric Clinic. Office: Charlotte Pediatric Clinic-Pineville 6235 Blakeney Park Dr Charlotte NC 28277-5658 Office Fax: 704-540-5873.*

ALDERSON, ROBERT E., retail executive; Sr. ptnr. Menzies, Rainey, Kizer & Alderson.; sr. v.p., chief adminstrv. officer Kirkland's, Inc., 1986—97, COO, 1997—2001, pres., 1997—2005, 2006, 2008—, CEO, 2001—05, 2006—, chmn., 2004—06. Bd. dirs. Kirkland's, Inc., 1986—. Office: Kirklands Inc 431 Smith Ln Jackson TN 38301 Office Phone: 731-988-3600.

ALDRICH, CLARENCE KNIGHT, physician, educator; b. Chgo, Apr. 12, 1914; s. L. Sherman and Bessie A. (Knight) A.; m. Julie H. Murphy, Feb. 4, 1942; children— Carol K., Michael S., Thomas K., Robert F. BA, Wesleyan U., 1935; MD, Northwestern U., 1940. Faculty U. Minn. Med. Sch., 1947-55, asst. prof., 1947-52, assoc. prof., 1952-55; prof. psychiatry U. Chgo. Sch. Medicine, 1955-70, chmn. dept. psychiatry, 1955-64; prof., chmn. dept. N.J. Med. Sch., Newark, 1970-73; prof. psychiatry Sch. Medicine, U. Va., Charlottesville, 1973-77, prof. psychiatry and family medicine, 1977-84, prof. emeritus, 1984—, mem. Ctr. Advanced Studies, 1981-84. Vis. prof. psychiatry U. Edinburgh, 1963-64; dir. Blue Ridge Mental Health Ctr., 1973-75; Mayne guest prof. U. Queensland, Australia, 1986. Author: Psychiatry for the Family Physician, 1955, Introduction to Dynamic Psychiatry, 1966, (with C. Nighswonger) A Casebook for Pastoral Counseling, 1968, The Medical Interview: Gateway to the Doctor-Patient Relationship, 1993, Quest for a Star, 2003. Served from asst. surgeon to surgeon USPHS, 1940-46. Fellow Am. Coll. Psychiatrists, Am. Orthopsychiat. Assn., Am. Psychiat. Assn.; mem. Group for Advancement Psychiatry. Home and Office: 250 Pantops Mountain Rd Apt 5115 Charlottesville VA 22911 Home Phone: 434-972-2414. Business E-Mail: cka3f@virginia.edu.

ALDRICH, JOHN HERBERT, political science professor; b. Pitts., Sept. 24, 1947; s. Herbert Canon and Ruth Eleanor (Taggart) A.; m. Cynthia Kay Aldrich, June 13, 1970; 1 child, David Shawn BA, Allegheny Coll., 1969; MA, U. Rochester, 1971, PhD, 1975. Asst. prof. polit. sci. Mich. State U., East Lansing, 1974-78, assoc. prof., 1978-81; assoc. prof. polit. sci. U. Minn., Mpls., 1981-83, prof., 1983-87, Duke U., Durham, NC, 1987—, chmn. dept. polit. sci., 1992—96, 1999—2000, Pfizer-Pratt univ. prof., 1997—. Vis. prof. Harvard U., 1996-97. Author: Before the Convention, 1980, Why Parties?, 1995; co-author: Change and Continuity in the 1980 Elections, 1982, rev. edit., 1983, Change and Continuity in the 1984 Elections, 1986, rev. edit., 1987, Change and Continuity in the 1988 elections, 1990, rev. edit., 1991, Change and Continuity in the 1992 Elections, 1994, rev. edit., 1995, Change and Continuing in the 1996 Elections, 1997, Change and Continuity in the 1996 and 1998 Elections, 1999, Change and Continuity in the 2000 and 2002 Elections; Change and Continuity in the 2004 Elections, 2006, Change and Continuity in the 2004 and 2006 Elections, 2007; co-editor: A Positive Change in Political Sic., 2007; co-editor: Am. Jour. Polit. Sci., 1985-87; contbr. articles to profl. jours. Served with U.S. Army, 1970-72, Vietnam Named Gold Citation, Allegheny Coll., 2008; ctr. for Advanced Study in Behavioral Scis. fellow, 1989-90; NSF rsch. grantee, 1977-79, 81-87; NEH teaching grantee, 1977-79; resident fellow Rockefeller Found., 2002. Fellow: Am. Acad. Arts and Scis.; mem.: Midwest Polit. Sci. Assn. (pres. 2004—05), So. Polit. Sci. Assn. (rec. sec. 1992—93, v.p. 1995—96, pres. 1998—99, Pi Sigma Alpha award 1997), Am. Polit. Sci. Assn. (sec. 1993—94, Eulau prize 1990, Kammerer prize 1996, CQ Press award 1996). Office: Duke U Dept Polit Sci Box 90204 Durham NC 27708 Business E-Mail: aldrich@duke.edu.*

ALDRICH, RICHARD W., biomedical researcher, neurobiology professor; BS in Biol. Scis. with high distinction, U. Ariz., 1975; PhD in Neuroscience, Stanford U., Calif., 1980. Postdoctoral in physiology Yale U., molecular neurobiology faculty, asst. prof.; neurobiology faculty mem. Stanford U., 1985, chair, dept. molecular and cellular physiology, 2001—04; mem. Howard Hughes Med. Inst., 1990—2006; prof., chair neurobiology, Sch. Biol. Scis., Karl Folkers Chair II in Interdisciplinary Biomedical Rsch. U. Tex., Austin, 2006—. Contbr. articles to profl. jours. Fellow: Biophysical Soc.; mem.: NAS, Soc. Gen. Physiologists (coun. mem., pres.). Office: Univ Tex Sch Biol Scis 1 University Station A6500 Austin TX 78712-0182 Office Phone: 512-475-9657.

ALDRIDGE, ADRIENNE YINGLING, accountant, writer; b. Hershey, Pa., June 10, 1959; d. Richard Terry Yingling and Dolores Jean (Ott) Brown. BA in Acctg. summa cum laude, N.C. State U., 1989. CPA; FLMI. Asst. mgr. Fast Fare, Raleigh, 1979—80; statis. analyst S.P.A.R., Elmsford, NY, 1980-81; relocation dir., sales assoc. Realty World, Cary, NC, 1981-83; product mgr. Southeastern Electronics, Raleigh, 1983-84; results acct. No. Telecom, Rsch. Triangle Park, NC, 1984-88; sr. auditor Deloitte & Touche, 1989-93; group contr. SPAR Mktg., Bloomington, Minn., 1994; pvt. practice, 1995; acctg. mgr. U. NC Physicians & Assocs., Chapel Hill, 1996-97, Progress Energy Svc. Co., Raleigh, NC, 1998—2007, ElectiCities, 2007—. Mem.: NCACPA, AICPA. Avocations: writing, physical fitness, travel, paleontology. Office Phone: 919-760-6252. Personal E-mail: yofreespirit@gmail.com.

ALDRIDGE, BRIAN, state legislator; b. Tupelo, Miss., May 6, 1977; Mem. Dist. 17 Miss. House of Reps., 2004—, mem. agr. com., conservation and water resources com., juvenile justice com., wildlife, fisheries and pks. com. Republican. Baptist. Mailing: PO Box 2611 Tupelo MS 38803 Home Phone: 662-842-0401; Office Phone: 662-841-5833. E-mail: baldridge@house.ms.gov.

ALDRIDGE, CLIFF A., state legislator; b. Wagonner, Okla., 1962; m. DeeAnn Swarb A. Aldridge; children: Cara, Courtney, Chloe. Attended, Okla. Christian Coll. Agt. owner Farmers Ins., 1984; mem. Dist. 42 Okla. State Senate, 2002—. Mem.: Midwest City C. of C., Choctaw Kiwanis. Republican. Avocations: golf, antiques, softball. Office: 2300 N Lincoln Blvd Rm 511 Oklahoma City OK 73105 Mailing: PO Box 10946 Oklahoma City OK 73140 Office Phone: 405-521-5584. Business E-Mail: aldridge@oksenate.gov.

ALDRIDGE, DAVID, sportscaster, journalist; b. Washington, Feb. 10, 1965; BA in Journalism, Am. U., 1987, BA in History, 1987. Sports reporter Washington Post, 1987-96; NBA reporter, analyst ESPN, 1996—2004; columnist Phila. Inquirer; reporter, studio analyst Turner Sports, 2004—. Recipient Sam Lacy Journalist of Yr. award, Rainbow/PUSH Coalition, 2002. Office: Turner Sports One CNN Ctr 13 S Tower Atlanta GA 30303

ALDRIDGE, MELVIN DAYNE, engineering educator; b. Crab Orchard, W.Va., July 20, 1941; s. William Bert and Gladys Revelle A.; m. Nancy L. Dickinson, June 6, 1963; children: Kenrick Lee, Randal Jay. BSEE with high honors, W.Va. U., 1963; MEE, U. Va., 1965, D of Elec. Engring., 1968. Registered profl. engr., W.Va. Electronic engr. NASA, 1963-68; from asst. prof. to assoc. prof. elec. engring. W.Va. U., Morgantown, 1968-76, prof., 1976-84; dir. Energy Rsch. Ctr., 1978-84; asst. dean for rsch. Auburn (Ala.) U., 1984-87, dir. engring. expt. sta., 1984-89, prof. elec. engring., 1984-89, acting dean coll. engring., 1987-88, assoc. dean for rsch., 1988-90, assoc. dean for cross-disciplinary programs, 1989-99, dir. ctr. for tech. mgmt., 1989-99; dean, prof. Mercer U., Macon, Ga., 1999—2008, Kaolin chair engring., 2004—08; adj. accreditation dir. engring. ABET Inc., 2002—. Chmn., officer Engring. Accreditation Commn.; cons. tp pvt. and govtl. orgns. Contbr. articles to profl. publs. Thomas Walter Eminent scholar Auburn U., 1994-99; recipient Rufus A. West award, 1963; named Outstanding Young Engr. W.Va., 1977-78. Fellow IEEE (sr.), ASEE, Accreditation Bd. for Engring. and Tech. (officer); mem. Indsl. Applications Soc. of IEEE (officer). Baptist. Home: 24 Honey Bear Ln Dillard GA 30537

ALESCHUS, JUSTINE LAWRENCE, retired real estate broker; b. New Brunswick, NJ, Aug. 13, 1925; d. Walter and Mildred Lawrence; m. John Aleschus, Jan. 23, 1949; children: Verdene Jan, Janine Kimberley, Joanna Lauren. Student, Rutgers U., New Brunswick, NJ. Dept. sec. Am. Bapt. Home Mission Soc., NYC, 1947-49; claims examiner Republic Ins. Co., Dallas, 1950-52; broker Damon Homes, LI, 1960-72; pres. Justine Aleschus Real Estate, Smithtown, NY, 1975—2002; ret. Exclusive broker estate of Kenneth H. Leeds, L.I., N.Y., 1980-90; past pres. S.C. Real Estate Bd. Past pres. Nassau-Suffolk Coun. of Hosp. Aux, 1981-82; hon. mem. aux. St. Catherine of Siena, Smithtown, N.Y., past pres., hosp. adv. bd.; past pres. L.I. Coalition for Sensible Growth, Inc.; past v.p. Suffolk County Boy Scouts Am.; grad. S.C. Citizen Police Acad., Suffolk Co., LI; Stephen min., 2011. Mem. Sky Island Club (gov.), Jacksonville Beach Citizens Police Acad. Alumni. Republican. Lutheran.

ALEWINE, JAMES WILLIAM, financial executive; b. Williamston, SC, Apr. 26, 1930; s. David Andrew and Ruby Mae (Moore) A.; children: David, Susan. BA, Carolina Sch. Commerce, 1961. Cert. internal auditor, S.C. With Daniel Internat. Corp., Greenville, S.C., 1947-92, mgr. internal audit, 1970-72, mgr. M & M divsn., 1972-73, fin. adminstr. Jenkinsville, S.C., 1973-77, mgr. acctg. M-E-T Group Greenville, S.C., 1977-78, asst. treas., 1978-92. With USN, 1952-55, lt. col. S.C. State Guard, 1993—2003. Named Ky. Col. Mem. Inst. Internal Auditors (pres. Palmetto chpt. 1975-76), Masons (past grand high priest, knight York grand cross of honour, 32d degree), Scottish Rite, York Rite, Elks. Baptist. Home: 2010 Edgewood Ave Anderson SC 29625-2843

ALEXANDER, CECIL ABRAHAM, academic administrator, consultant, retired architect; b. Atlanta, Mar. 14, 1918; s. Cecil Abraham and Julia (Moses) A.; m. Hermione Weil, Jan. 20, 1943 (dec. 1983); children: Therese, Judith, Douglas; m. Helen Eisemann, 1985. Student, Ga. Inst. Tech., 1936; AB, Yale, 1940; student, Mass. Inst. Tech., 1941; M. Arch., Harvard, 1947. Partner Alexander & Rothschild (architects), Atlanta, 1949-58; chmn. bd. Finch, Alexander, Barnes, Rothschild & Paschal, Architects and Engrs., Inc., Atlanta, 1958-86; archtl. cons. Atlanta, 1986-90; coord. continuing edn. Ga. Inst. Tech. Coll. Architecture, Atlanta, 1994-96; prin.-in-charge Leo A. Daley Archtl. Engrs., Atlanta, 1996-97; ptnr. Alexander-Weiner Baker Architects, Atlanta, 1997—, Alexander Weiner Architects, 00—. Coord., chmn. bd. A.S.D. Inc., interior design svc.; chmn. Atlanta Citizens Adv. Com. Urban Renewal, 1958-60; vice chmn. Atlanta Met. Planning Commn., 1962—; past chmn. Ga. Fgn. Trade Zone Corp. Prin. works include Ga. Power Bldg., Atlanta, 1st Nat. Bank, Atlanta, Cin. Riverfront Stadium, Coca-Cola Internat. Hdqs., Sci. Atlanta Hdqs., U.S. Pavilion Expo '82, So. Bell. Hdqs.; designer new Ga. flag, 2001. Past vice chmn. Cmty. Coun., Atlanta; mem. Mayor's Adv. Com. Race Rels., Nat. Citizens Com. Cmty. Rels.; chmn. Atlanta chpt. Am. Jewish Com., 1963; chmn. housing resources com. City of Atlanta; past chmn. coun. Yale Sch. Architecture; pres., founder Resurgens Atlanta; past v.p. Atlanta Symphony Orch.; mem. Yale Nat. Alumni Bd., 1963; bd. dirs. Atlanta U.; bd. dirs. emeritus Clark Atlanta U.; past bd. dirs. Marist High Sch., Atlanta; chmn. Com. to Combat Drugged and Drunken Driving; past pres. Atlanta's Clifton Corridor Biomed. Rsch. Coun. Served to lt. col. USMCR, World War II. Decorated Air medal, D.F.C.; (2) Recipient Brotherhood award NCCJ, 1973; Archdiocesan medal of St. Paul, 1980, Yale medal, 1980. Fellow AIA (pres. Ga. 1957, Ivan Allen award, Bernard B. Rothschild award, Ga. chpt.); mem. Atlanta C. of C. (dir., Whitney Young award, Nat Am. Inst. Architects). Home: 2677 Rivers Rd NW Atlanta GA 30305-3549 Office Phone: 404-261-9230. E-mail: cecilalexander@comcast.net.

ALEXANDER, CYNTHIA LOUISE, psychologist, educator; d. Glenn Elting and Flora Louise Alexander. BS in Psychology, summa cum laude, Tex. Christian U., 1994; MS in Clin. Psychology, Nova Southeastern U., 1995, D in Psychology, 1999. Intern Nova, Broward Gen. Hosp., Ft. Lauderdale, Fla.; clin. cons. U. Pavilion Hosp., Tamarac, Fla., coord. social svcs., 1999—2004; adj. prof. psychology Nova Southeastern U., Ft. Lauderdale, Fla., 2002—06; psychologist 17th Cir. Ct. Fla., Ft. Lauderdale, 2003—, Cleveland Clinic Fla., Weston, 2004—. Mem. editl. bd.: Bariatric Times, 2003—11; author: The Emotional First Aid Kit-A Guide to Life After Bariatric Surgery, 2nd Edit., 2009. Mem.: APA Sport & Exercise Psychology, Nat. Register Psychologist, Am. Soc. Bariatric and Metabolic Surgery, Psi Chi. Avocations: kayaking, travel, mountain climbing, Triathlon, scuba diving. Office: Cleveland Clinic Fla 3100 Cleveland Clinic Blvd Weston FL 33331 Office Phone: 954-689-5773. Business E-Mail: alexanc3@ccf.org.

ALEXANDER, EBEN, neurosurgeon; b. Charlotte, NC, Dec. 11, 1953; AB, U. NC, Chapel Hill, 1975; MD, Duke U. Med. Sch., Durham, NC, 1980. Research asst. neurosurgery U. Minn. Sch. Medicine, 1978; research asst. pathology Bowman Gray Sch. of Medicine, Wake Foresr U., 1980; research asst. neuroendocrinology Duke U. Med. Ctr., Durham, NC, 1978—79, intern gen. surgery, 1980—81, resident neurological surgery, 1981—83, 1985—87; research fellow neurosurgery Mass. Gen. Hosp., Harvard Med. Sch., Boston, 1983—85; acting resident neurology Mass. Gen. Hosp., Boston, 1985, clin. assoc. neurosurgery, 1998—2003; sr. registrar and cerebrovascular fellow, neurosurgical service Newcastle General Hosp., Newcastle-Upon-Tyne, England, 1987; research fellow neurosurgery Brigham & Women's Hosp., Harvard Med. Sch., Boston, 1987, instr. surgery, 1988—90, assoc. surgeon, 1988—2003; asst. prof. surgery (neurosurgery) Harvard Med. Sch., Boston, 1990—94, asst. prof. radiation therapy, Joint Ctr. for Radiation Therapy, 1990—2001, assoc. prof. surgery (neurosurgery), 1994—2001, U. Mass. Med. Sch., Worcester, 2001—03; asst. prof. research in neurological surgery U. Va. Med. Sch., Charlottesville, Va., 2008—; assoc. surgeon The Children's Hosp., Harvard Med. Sch., Boston, 1988—2003, Dana Farber Cancer Inst., Harvard Med. Sch., Boston, 1988—2003; dir. stereotatic and functional neurosurgery Brigham & Women's Hosp., 1994—2001; active staff mem. dept. surgery divsn. of neurosurgery U. Mass. Med. Ctr., 2001—03, Lynchburg Gen. Hosp.-CentralHealth, Va., 2006—07. Vis. lectr. and panelist dept. neurosurgery U. Va. Sch. of Medicine Internat. Symposium on Stereotactic Radiosurgery, 1989; corp. cons. Gerson Lehman, NY, 2004—06; clin. dir. brain program Focused Ultrasound Surgery Found., Charlottesville, Va., 2008—10; invited lecturer in the field. Editor: (books) Advanced Neurosurgical, 1998, Stereotactic Radiosurgery, 1993; author Proof of Heaven: A Neurosurgeon's Journey into the Afterlife, 2012; mem. of several editl. bds. Mem.: AMA, American Soc. for Stereotactic and Functional Neurosurgery, American Assn. of Neurological Surgeons, World Soc. for Stereotactic and Functional Neurosurgery. Office: University of Virginia School of Medicine Dept of Neuroscience PO Box 801392 Charlottesville VA 22908*

ALEXANDER, F. KING, academic administrator; b. Ky. m. Shenette Alexander; children: Kylie, Savannah, Madison. BA in Polit. Sci., St. Lawrence U.; MS in Comparative Edn. Policy, Oxford U.; PhD in Higher Edn. Adminstrn., U. Wis., Madison. Mgr. Liberty Nat. Bank, Louisville; postdoctoral rschr., office of the provost U. Wis., Madison, vice chancellor for acad. affairs, lectr. ednl. adminstrn.; adminstr., mem. faculty U. Ill., Urbana-Champaign; pres. Murray State U., 2001—05, Calif. State U., Long Beach, 2006—13; pres. & chancellor La. State U., Baton Rogue, 2013—. Found. fellow U. Oxford; faculty affiliate Cornell Higher Edn. Rsch. Inst., Inst. Govt. and Pub. Affairs. Contbr. articles to profl. jours. and publs. Office: Office of the Chancellor Louisiana State University 3810 W Lakeshore Dr Baton Rouge LA 70808 Office Phone: 225-578-2111. Office Fax: 225-578-5524. Business E-Mail: alexander@lsu.edu.*

ALEXANDER, FORBES I.J., electronics executive; BA in Acctg., Dundee Coll. Tech., Scotland. Chartered mgmt. acct. Various fin. positions Hewlett Packard Corp., Apollo Computer, Inc.; fin. controller European mfg. ops. Tandy Electronics Pty Ltd., Scotland; controller Scottish ops. Jabil Circuit, Inc., 1993—96, asst. treas., 1996, treas., 1996—2004, CFO, 2004—. Office: Jabil Circuit Corp Hdqs 10560 Dr Martin Luther King Jr St N Saint Petersburg FL 33716 Office Phone: 727-577-9749.

ALEXANDER, J., energy executive; b. Memphis; m. Cindi Alexander BS, U. Memphis. Sr. mgr. Ernst and Young; sr. v.p., adminstrn. Louis Dreyfus; exec. v.p. TransMontaigne; pres. Refined Solutions Inc. (subs. TransMontaigne); pres., COO Mansfield Oil Co., 2005—; owner Rampensau & Ferke Publ. House. Office: Mansfield Oil Company 1025 Airport Pky SW Gainesville GA 30501 Office Fax: 770-718-3053. Business E-Mail: jalexander@mansfieldoil.com.

ALEXANDER, JAMES PATRICK, lawyer, educator; b. Glendale, Calif., Oct. 14, 1944; s. Victor Elwin and Thelma Elizabeth (O'Donnell) A.; m. Jeanne Elizabeth Bannerman, June 10, 1967; children: Rene Leigh, Amy Lynne. AB, Duke U., 1966, JD, 1969. Bar: Ala. 1969. Assoc. Bradley, Arant, Rose & White, Birmingham, Ala., 1969-75, ptnr., 1975—2008, Littler Mendelson, P.C., share holder, 2008—. Adj. lectr. employment discrimination law U. Ala. Sch. Law, 1981-2003; exec. adv. com. spl. studies program U. Ala., Birmingham, 1991-93; mem. local rules adv. com. U.S. Dist. Ct. (no. dist.) Ala., 1997—. Trustee Ala. chpt. Nat. Multiple Sclerosis Soc. (vice-chmn. 1987-89, chmn. 1990-91); bd. dirs. Birmingham Civil Right Inst. 1998-2004. Fellow Coll. Labor and Employment Lawyers; mem. Birmingham Bar Assn., Ala. State Bar., ABA, Am. Arbitration Assn. (comml. arbitrator, employment disputes arbitrator), Labor Employment Rels. Assn. (Ala. chpt.), Sigma Nu, Duke Law Alumni Assn. (pres. Ala. chpt. 1989-90). Home: 4309 Altamont Rd Birmingham AL 35213-2407 Office: Littler Mendelson PC Wells Fargo Tower Ste 2300 420 20th St N Birmingham AL 35203 Office Phone: 205-421-4778. Business E-Mail: jalexander@littler.com.

ALEXANDER, JEFF, dermatologist; MD, U. Nebr. Med. Ctr., 1977. Diplomate Am. Bd. Dermatology, 1982. Resident dermatology Univ. Okla. Med. Ctr., Oklahoma City, 1978—81; asst. clin. prof. and dermatology instr. med. students and residents Univ. of Okla., Oklahoma City; chmn. dermatology dept. St. Francis Hosp., Tulsa, Okla.; with GlaxoSmithKline, SkinCeuticals, Novartis Pharmaceuticals, SkinMedica; established, med. dir. Skin Care Inst., 1999—. Mem.: Tulsa Dermatol. Soc. (pres.), Okla. Dermatology Soc. (pres.). Office: Skin Care Institute 6565 South Yale Ave Tulsa OK 74136 Office Phone: 918-494-8333. Office Fax: 918-494-8334.

ALEXANDER, JIM R., social sciences educator; b. Gainesville, Tex., Aug. 16, 1946; s. Gordon Lee and Esther Ruby Alexander; m. Mona Sue Beeler, June 7, 1968; 1 child, Jason Fields. AA, North Ctrl. Tex. Coll., Gainesville, 1966; BA in Govt. and Bus. Adminstrn., East Tex. State U., Commerce, 1968, MA in Govt. and Bus. Adminstrn., 1969; PhD in Govt. and Pub. Adminstrn., Am. U., Washington, 1974. Prof., chair, dept. history and govt. Tex. Woman's U., Denton, 1984—2007, dir. Law Enforcement Mgmt. Inst. Tex., 1989—, spl. asst. to pres., 1995—2000, prof. emeritus, 2007. Elected city coun. mem. Denton City Coun., 1986—92; mem. exec. bd. North Ctrl. Tex. Coun. Govts., Arlington, 1989—93, pres. exec. bd., 1991—92; mem., bd. of trustees Denton Ind. Sch. Dist., Denton, Tex., 1993—, pres. bd. trustees, 1999—2000. Contbr. chapters to books, articles to profl. jours. Nat. del. Dem. Nat. Conv., NYC, 1980; conv. del. Tex. Dem. Party, 1974—84; apptd. mem. Governor's Criminal Justice Adv. Bd., Austin, Tex., 1981—83. Recipient Leadership TASB award, Tex. Assn. Sch. Bds., 2004; named Cornaro Prof., Tex. Woman's U., 2008; fellow, Tex. Higher Edn. Coordinating Bd., 1986; Nat. Def. Edn. Act fellow, Am. U., 1969—72, Malone fellow, Coun. on U.S.-Arab Rels., 2006. Mem.: Leadership Summit Adv. Bd. (exec. com. 2007—), World Future Soc., Am. Soc. Pub. Adminstrn., Soc. Police Futurists Internat., Assn. Tex. Law Enforcement Educators (pres. 1978—79), Southwestern Assn. Criminal Justice Educators (pres. 1981—82), Acad. Criminal Justice Sci. (life; bd. dirs. 1982—85), Rotary (Paul Harris Fellow award 1988, 2002).

ALEXANDER, JOHN DAVID, food products executive; b. Camp Lejeune, NC, July 16, 1959; m. Cindy Monroe; children: Britton, Keaton. BS in Agr., U. Fla., 1981. Citrus grower; mem. Dist. 66 Fla. House of Reps., 1998—2002; mem. banking and ins. com., ethics and elections com., rules com., select com. on Fla.'s economy, joint legis. budget commn. Florida State Senate, mem. Dist. 17, 2002—, majority whip, 2004—06; pres., CEO Alico, Inc., 2010—, vice chmn., 2009—. Pres. Polk Farm Bur. Bd. Dirs.; bd. dirs. CNL Macquarie Global

Growth Trust, Inc., 2008—. Republican. Presbyterian. Office: Alico Inc 10070 Daniels Interstate Ct Fort Myers FL 33913-7865 Office Phone: 863-675-2966. Office Fax: 863-675-6928. Personal E-mail: jalexander@alicoinc.com.

ALEXANDER, JOHN MARSHALL, federal prosecutor; b. Greenville, Miss., Feb. 21, 1956; s. William Brooks and Alma Belle (McDonald) A.; m. Melissa Lynne Gordin, Nov. 18, 1989; children: John Marshall Jr., Amanda Margaret, William James. BS, Delta State U., 1977; JD, U. Miss., 1981. Bar: Miss. 1981, U.S. Dist. Ct. (no. dist.) Miss. 1981, U.S. Ct. Appeals (5th cir.) 1983. Atty. Alexander, Johnston and Alexander, Cleveland, Miss., 1981—82; asst. US atty. (northern dist.) Miss. US Dept. Justice, Oxford, Miss., 1982—, interim US atty., 2009—11. Active Inter-Alumni Coun., State of Miss. Recipient Chief Insp.'s Spl. award US Postal Inspection Svc., Washington, 1986, Spl. Achievement award U.S. Dept. Justice, Washington, 1989, 92, Disting. Svc. award Delta State U., Cleveland, 1993. Mem. ABA, Miss. Pros. Assn. (bd. dirs. 1985-89), Delta State U. Alumni Assn. (pres. 1993-94), Rotary Internat. (bd. dirs. 1988-89). Baptist. Avocations: duck hunting, water-skiing, boating, higher education, reading. Office: US Attorneys Office 900 Jefferson Ave Oxford MS 38655-6308 Office Phone: 662-234-3351. Office Fax: 662-234-4818.

ALEXANDER, JOHN W., investment company executive; Ptnr. Meringoff Equities; pres. Mallard Creek Capital Partners, Inc., 1994—. Bd. dirs. Jacor Comm. Inc., 1993—; trustee Equity Residential, 1993—. Mem. Internat. Coun. of Shopping Centers, Urban Land Inst. Office: Mallard Creek Capital Partners Inc 200 S Tryon St Ste 520 Charlotte NC 28202-3214 Office Phone: 704-335-0800.

ALEXANDER, KELLY M., JR., state legislator; BS in Polit. Sci., U. North Carolina, Chapel Hill, MPA in Publ. Admin. Former high sch. tchr.; former tchr. U. North Carolina, Charlotte; mgr. Alexander Funeral Home; mem. Dist. 107 NC House of Reps., 2008—. Democrat. Office: NC House of Representatives 300 N Salisbury St Rm 404 Raleigh NC 27603-5925 Home: 1424 Statesville Ave Charlotte NC 28206 Office Phone: 919-733-5778. Business E-Mail: Kelly.Alexander@ncleg.net.

ALEXANDER, KENNETH C., state legislator; b. Norfolk, Va., Oct. 17, 1966; m. Donna Burnley; 1 child, Kenneth Cooper II. Former mem. Norfolk Econ. Devel. Authority, Norfolk Human Svc. Commn.; mem. Exec. Com. Greater Norfolk Corp., Commn. Study of Popular Election of Office of Mayor; v. chmn. Norfolk Planning Commn.; bd. mem. Tidewater Bus. Financing Corp.; state del. Dist. 89 Va., 2002—. Fellow: Sorenson Inst. Polit. Leadership; mem.: Beacon Light Cmty. Housing Devel. Corp. (former pres.), Beacon Light Civic League (former pres.), Leadership Cir. Pub. Broadcasting Svc. Hampton Rds-WHRO (vol.), Old Dominion U. Alumni Assn. (former bd. mem.), Empowerment 2010, Inc. (bd. mem.), Tidewater Funeral Dirs. Assn., Nat. Funeral Dirs. Assn. (former dist. gov.), Va. Morticians Assn. (former pres., Mortician of Yr. 1998), Norfolk Funeral Dirs. & Embalmers Assn. (former pres., Profl. of Yr. 1998), Antioch Bapt. Ch. Norfolk. Democrat. Baptist. Mailing: Dist Off 7246 Granby St Norfolk VA 23505 Office: Gen Assembly Bldg Rm 412, PO Box 406 Richmond VA 23218 Office Phone: 757-628-1000, 804-698-1089. Office Fax: 804-786-6310. Business E-Mail: Del_Alexander@house.state.va.us.

ALEXANDER, LAMAR (ANDREW LAMAR ALEXANDER), United States Senator from Tennessee, former United States Secretary of Education; b. Maryville, Tenn., July 3, 1940; s. Andrew Lamar and Geneva Floreine (Rankin) Alexander; m. Leslee Kathryn Buhler, Jan. 4, 1969; children: Andrew, Leslee, Kathryn. BA in Latin American Hist., Vanderbilt U., Nashville, 1962; JD, NY Sch. Law, 1965. Bar: Tenn. 1965. Law clk. to Hon. John Minor Wisdom US Ct. Appeals (5th cir.), New Orleans, 1965—66; assoc. Fowler, Rountree, Fowler & Robertson, Knoxville, Tenn., 1965; legis. asst. to Senator Howard Baker US Senate, 1967-68; exec. asst. to Bryce Harlow, Office Congl. Liaison The White House, 1969-70; ptnr. Dearborn & Ewing, Nashville, 1970-76; chmn. Leadership Inst. Belmont Coll., Nashville, 1987-88; gov. State of Tenn., Nashville, 1979—87; pres. U. Tenn., 1988-91; sec. US Dept. Edn., Washington, 1991-93; counsel Baker, Donelson, Bearman & Caldwell, Nashville, 1993-98; pvt. practice atty. Nashville, 1999—2001; US Senator from Tennessee, 2003—; chmn. US Senate Republican Conf., 2007—11. Chmn. Nat. Governors Assn., 1985—86, Pres.'s Commn. America's Outdoors, 1985—87; co-dir. Empower America, 1994—95; Goodman vis. prof. practice of pub. svc. Harvard U., 2001—02. Author: Steps Along the Way, 1986, Six Months Off, 1988, We Know What To Do, 1995; co-editor: Friends, Japanese and Tennesseans: A Model of U.S.-Japan Cooperation, 1986, The New Promise of American Life, 1995, Lamar Alexander's Little Plaid Book, 1998. Chmn. Rep. Exch. Satellite Network, 1993—95; Rep. Presdl. candidate, 1995—96, 2000; campaign mgr. Winfield Dunn for Gov., 1970, chief transition team, 1970—71; Rep. nominee for Tenn. Gov., 1974. Recipient James B. Conant award, Edn. Commn. of States, 1988, Disting. State Leadership award, Am. Assn. State Colleges & Universities, 1989, Teddy Roosevelt award, Nat. Coll. Athletic Assn., 1993, Disting. Congl. award, Nat. League Cities, 2003, Krieble Freedom & Democracy award, Free Congress Found., 2004, Nat. Congl. award, Nat. Recreation and Pk. Assn., 2005, Spirit of Enterprise award, US C. of C., 2005, 2006, 2008, 2010, Congl. Leadership award, Ctr. for Study of Presidency, 2005, Dale E. Kildee Civitas award, We the People, Ctr. for Civic Edn., 2005, Thomas Jefferson award, Internat. Foodservice Distributors Assn., 2006, 2010, Disting. Friend of Sci. award, SW Universities Rsch. Assn., 2006, William Penn Mott Jr. Park Leadership award, Nat. Parks Conservation Assn., 2007, George E. Brown Jr. Sci., Engring. and Tech. Leadership award, Sci., Engring. and Tech. Work Group, 2007, Horst G. Denk Legis. Svc. award, 2007, Pub. Affairs Leadership award, March of Dimes, 2007, Gold Medallion award, Tenn. Ind. Colleges and Universities Assn., 2008, Nat. Geographic Legislator award, 2008, Charles Dick Medal of Merit award, US Nat. Guard, 2008; named one of 100 Most Influential Student-Athletes, NCAA, 2006. Mem.: Phi Beta Kappa. Republican. Presbyn. Office: US Senate 455 Dirksen Senate Office Bldg Washington DC 20510 also: Ste 120 3322 West End Ave Nashville TN 37203-6821 Office Phone: 202-224-4944, 615-736-5129, 202-224-1989. Office Fax: 202-228-3398, 615-269-4803.*

ALEXANDER, LESLIE LEE, professional sports team owner; b. NYC, June 30, 1943; m. Nanci Alexander (div. 2002); 1 child, Jodi. BS, NYU, 1965; JD, Western State Coll., 1977. With Lawrence Kotkin Assocs.; owner, pres. Houston Rockets, 1993—; owner Women's NBA Houston Comets, 1996—2007; former owner Arena Football League Houston ThunderBears. Bd. dirs. First Marblehead Corp., 1995—. Bd. dirs. Humane Soc. US; founder City Clutch Found., Houston, 1995—. Named one of Forbes Richest Ams., 2006. Mem.: Calif. State Bar Assn. Office: Houston Rockets 1510 Polk St Houston TX 77002*

ALEXANDER, MARTHA B., state legislator; m. James F. Alexander. State rep. Dist. 56, NC, 1993—2002; state rep. Dist. 106 NC, 2003—. Mem. Edn. com., Edn. Subcom. on Universities, Health com., Judiciary I com., Mental Health Reform com., vice chmn.; chmn. Appropriations com. Democrat. Office: North Carolina House of Representatives 16 W Jones St Rm 1213 Raleigh NC 27601-1096 Office Phone: 919-733-5807. E-mail: Martha.Alexander@ncleg.net.

ALEXANDER, MILES JORDAN, lawyer; b. Reading, Pa., Nov. 20, 1931; s. Abe Alexander and Sarah (Gold) Fidlow; m. Elaine Eve Barron, May 29, 1955; children: Kent, David, Michael, Paige. BA in Polit. Sci. with honors, Emory U., Atlanta, 1952; LLB cum laude, Harvard U., Cambridge, Mass., 1955. Bar: Ga. 1955, DC 1977. Assoc. Smith, Kilpatrick, Cody, Rogers & McClatchey, Atlanta, 1954—55; tchg. fellow Harvard U., Cambridge, Mass., 1957-58; assoc. ptnr., chmn. Kilpatrick Stockton LLP, Atlanta, 1958—2010, Kilpatrick Townsend & Stockton LLP, Atlanta, 2011—. Lectr. P.L.I., Internat. Trademark Assn., Am. Law Inst., ABA Internat. Franchise Assn., other seminars on trademarks and unfair competition, antitrust, franchising, dispute resolutions and litig. tactics; guest lectr. on trademark law NYU, U.Ga., Ga. State Law Sch., also bd. visitors; bd. visitors Emory U.; chmn. US trademark pub. adv. com. Emory U., 2000-03. Editor-in-chief: The Trademark Reporter, 1978-80; contbr. numerous articles to jours. in trademark field. Mem. City of Atlanta Ethics Bd., chmn., vice-chmn., 1980-92, Emory U. and Harvard Law Sch. Alumni Funds; legal counsel to Mayor Maynard Jackson, 1974-82, 89-93; chmn. City of Atlanta Lic. Rev. Bd., 1976-79; former pres. Am. Jewish Com.; mem. Friends of Morehouse Coll.; adv. bd. Family Outreach Ctr.; mem. adv. coun. J. Thomas McCarthy Inst. Intellectual Property and Tech. Law, 2001-; co-chair ADL S.E. Regional Bd., 2014-. Capt. USAF, 1955-57. Recipient Human Rels. award Anti-Defamation League, 1997, Disting. Alumni award Emory U., 2000, ADL Lifetime Achievement award, 2006, State Bar Ga, Justice Robert Benham Lifetime Achievement Cmty. Svc. award, 2007, IP Legends award, Ga. State U., 2007, Carter Ctr. Bd. Councilors, 2008-, Disting. Svc. award AJC, 2010, Highest Alumni award Emory U., 2012. Fellow Am. Bar Found., Am. Coll. Trial Lawyers; mem. ABA, Internat. Trademark Assn. (counsel 1997-2000, chmn. trademark pub. com.), Ga. Bar Assn. (1st recipient Intellectual Property Sect. Lifetime Achievement award 2006), Ga. State Bar Assn. (former chmn. antitrust sect., advisor to legal counsel 1997—; Hall of Fame 2012), Atlanta Bar Assn. (Leadership award 2009), Lawyers Club Atlanta, Internat. Trademark Assn. (lectr., bd. dirs. 1980-82, rev. commn. 1986, legal counsel 1987-2000, Pres.'s Lifetime Achievement award 2002), Am. Law Inst. (adv. com. restatement of law of unfair competition 1986-95), 191 Club (bd. dirs.), Atlanta City Club (chmn. bd.), Commerce Club, Standard Club, Old War Horse Lawyers Club, Phi Beta Kappa, William Breman Jewish Heritage Mus. Bd., Intellectual Asset Mgmt. (Hall of Fame 2013). Avocations: reading, sports. Office: Kilpatrick Townsend & Stockton LLP 1100 Peachtree St NE Ste 2800 Atlanta GA 30309-4530 Office Phone: 404-815-6410. Business E-Mail: malexander@kilpatricktownsend.com.

ALEXANDER, R. DAVID, retail executive; Sr. v.p. distbn. & transp. Family Dollar Stores, Inc., Charlotte, NC, 1995—2002, exec. v.p., 2000—03, COO, 2000—05, pres., COO, 2003—05; CEO Portrait Corp. of America, Inc. (acquired by CPI Corp.), 2005—07; cons. APAX Ptnrs., 2008; COO Citi Trends, Inc., 2008—09, pres., 2008—, CEO, bd. dirs., 2009—. Office: Citi Trends Inc 104 Coleman Blvd Savannah GA 31408 Office Phone: 912-236-1561. Office Fax: 912-443-3663. Business E-Mail: ralexander@cititrends.com.

ALEXANDER, RODNEY MCKINNIE, state official, former United States Representative from Louisiana; b. Jonesboro, La., Dec. 5, 1946; m. Nancy Sutton; children: Ginger, Rod, Lisa. Attended, La. Tech. U., 1965; BA in Gen. Studies, U. La.-Monroe, 2009. Ins. agent; mem. Jackson Parish Police Jury, 1972—88; mem. Dist. 13 La. House of Reps., Baton Rouge, 1988—2002; mem. US Congress from 5th La. Dist., Washington, 2003—13; sec. La. Dept. Veterans' Affairs, Baton Rouge, 2013—. Mem. Jackson Parish, La. Police Jury, 1970—85, pres., 1978—85. Served in USAFR, 1965—71. Named Legis. of Yr., La. Rural Health Assn., 1997; named to The La. Political Mus. & Hall of Fame, 2010. Republican. Southern Baptist. Office: La Dept Veterans' Affairs PO Box 94095 Baton Rouge LA 70804 Office Phone: 225-219-5000. Office Fax: 225-219-5590.*

ALEXANDER, TERRY, state legislator; b. Florence, Jan. 23, 1955; s. James and Adell Alexander; m. Starlee Davis Alexander; children: Terrill McClain, Matthew. AD, Durham Bus. Coll., 1976; BA, Francis Marion U., 1991; MDiv, Howard U., 1998. Former pres., bd. dirs. Habitat For Humanity; mem. Dist. 59 SC House of Reps., 2007—; mem. Med. Com., Mil. Com., Pub. & Mcpl. Affairs Com., Pee Dee Regional Coun. Govts.; pastor Wayside Chapel Bapt. Ch.; mng. ptnr. Sunrise Of The Pee Dee; adj. prof., religion Limestone Coll. Mem.: NAACP (former Florance Br. pres.), SC Assn. Black County Ofcls., SC Alliance Black Educators, Nat. Assn. Balck County Ofcls., SC Assn. Guidance Counselors, Francis Marion Soc., Am. Red Cross (Pee Dee chpt.), Boys Scouts of Pee Dee (exec. bd. mem.), Mercy Medicine Bd., 100 Black Men of Pee Dee, Nat. Assn. County Ofcls., Boys & Girls Club Florence (former pres.), Florence Breakfast Rotary Club (charter mem.), Kappa Alpha Psi Frat. Inc. Democrat. Home: 1646 Harris Ct Florence SC 29501 Office: 314C Blatt Building Columbia SC 29201 Home Phone: 843-665-7321; Office Phone: 803-734-3004. Business E-Mail: AlexanderT@schouse.org.

ALEXANDER, THOMAS C., state legislator; b. Seneca, SC, Apr. 25, 1956; s. Claude N. and Virginia C. Alexander. AA, Anderson Coll., 1976; BS, Clemson U., 1978. Owner Alexander's Office Supply; mem. Dist. 1 SC State Senate, 1994—, chair Subcommittee on Health and Human Svcs. & Subcommittee on Retirement, chair Gen. Com., mem. Banking and Ins. Com., Fin. Com., Invitations Com. & Labor, Commerce and Industry Com. Recipient Lion of Year, 1984—85. Mem.: Carolina Off Products Assn. (bd.dir. 1986), Walhalla Downtown Assn. (bd.dir. 1985—86, vice pres., pres. 1982—83), Walhalla Sertoma Club (mem.bd. 1982—83, pres. 1982—83), Walhalla C. of C. (bd.dir. 1980—83), Walhalla Sertoma Club, Walhalla Lions Club (pres. 1984—85). Republican. Presbyterian. Mailing: 150 Cleveland Dr Walhalla SC 29691 Office: 402 Gressette Bldg Columbia SC 29201 Home Phone: 864-638-2153, 803-252-0845; Office Phone: 803-212-6220, 864-638-2988. E-mail: tca@legis.lpitr.state.sc.us.

ALEXANDER, WILLIAM OLIN, retired finance company executive; b. Lexington, Ky., Aug. 2, 1939; s. Elby Olin and Louise (Watson) A.; m. Yvonne Davis, Jan. 26, 1961; children: Keith Davis, Hope. BS, U. Ky., 1961. CPA, Fla. Auditor Ring, Mahony & Arner (CPAs), Miami, Fla., 1961-62, sr. auditor, 1964-66; v.p., treas. Seabird Industries, Miami, 1966-70, exec. v.p., 1970-73; controller Belcher Oil Co., Miami, 1973-75, treas., 1976-83; sr. v.p., treas. Mitchell Co., Mobile, Ala., 1983-85; pres. Alexander & Co., PA, CPA, 1985—2006; ret., 2006. Served to 1st lt. AUS, 1962-64. Mem. AICPA, Fla. Inst. CPAs, Porsche Club Am., Beta Alpha Psi, Delta Sigma Pi, Delta Tau Delta. Republican. Home: 10910 Juniperus Pl Tampa FL 33618-3818

ALEXANDER, WILLIAM POWELL, business advisor; b. Buffalo, June 16, 1934; s. James Nelson and Helen (Johnson) A.; m. Eunice Gail Elwood, May 8, 1981; 1 child from previous marriage, Christine Alexander Johnson. BA, Gettysburg Coll., 1956; postgrad., Temple U., 1960-62. With Aetna Casualty & Surety Co., 1956-57, RCA Corp., NYC, 1960-86, asst. sec., 1968-73, sr. asst. sec., 1973-78, sec., 1978-86; also sec. NBC, Coronet Industries, RCA/Ariola, Hertz, Random House; sec. to office of chmn., asst. to chmn. Marine Midland Banks, Inc., 1987-88; adminstrv. dir. The Gt. Atlantic & Pacific Tea Co. Inc., 1988-89. Dir. Westminster-Canterbury Found. 1st lt. USAF, 1957—59. Mem. Am. Soc. Corp. Secs., Phi Kappa Psi. Clubs: Cavalier Golf and Yacht (Virginia Beach, Va.). Home: 3100 Shore Dr PH 42 Virginia Beach VA 23451

ALEXANDER-DAVIS, DEBORAH RADFORD, retired principal, educational consultant; b. Knoxville, Tenn., July 29, 1953; d. Frank Stanley and Elizabeth Anne (Poer) Radford; m. James R. Alexander, 1981 (dec. 1988); m. Bobby Davis, Jan. 3, 1992. BA in Religious Studies, U. Tenn., 1973, MS in Spl. Edn., 1975, EdS in Curriculum and Instrn., 1979, EdD in Curriculum and Instrn., 1982, postdoctoral. Cert. spl. edn. tchr., K-12 adminstr. and supr., career level III tchr. Tenn. Head Start Mideast Community Action Agy., Kingston, Tenn., 1975-77; resource tchr. Roane County Schs., Kingston, 1978-94, designated prin., 1992-94, asst. prin., 1994-96, prin., 1996—2005, leader, 2010; ret., 2005; mem. bd. dirs. Micheal Dunn Ctr., 2012—; chair Leadership Com. Rotary Internat. Dist. 6780, 2013—; mem. bd. dirs. leadership Roane Co., 2009—; mem. Grad. East Tenn. Regional Leadership, 2011. Ednl. cons. in sch. improvement planning and program evaluation, 1998—; adj. faculty mem. Tusculum Coll., 2000—, Roane State CC, 2002—05, Tenn. Technol. U., 2002—; mem. several statewide edn. taskforces; presenter various state, regional and nat. confs.; rsch. assoc. U. Tenn., Inst. Assessment Evaluation, 2006—. Contbr. articles to profl. jours. Pres. Continuing Kingston, 2004—05; mem. Foster Care Rev. Bd., 2004—08; mem. bd. dirs. Leadership Roane County, 2011—; mem. East Tenn. Regional Leadership, Class of 2011; pres. Kingston Rotary Club, 2011—12; mem. Tenn. Jud. Coun., 2005—10. Named Tenn. Prin. of Yr., 2004. Mem. NEA, ASCD, NAESP, Tenn. Assn. for Supervision and Curriculum Devel., Tenn. Prin. Assn., Tenn. Edn. Assn., Tenn. Prins. Study Coun. (pres. East Tenn. divsn. 2002-2005, steering com. 2001-2005, mem. exec. com. 2002-2005), Roane County Edn. Assn. (pres. 1986-87), Am. Contract Bridge League (pres. Tennessee Valley unit 1986-87), Oak Ridge Bridge Assn. (pres. 1983-84), Am. Belgian Malinois Club (sec. 1984-90, pres. 1991-95, bd. dir. 1995-97), Phi Kappa Phi, Kingston Rotary Club (pres. 2011-).

ALEXANIAN, RAYMOND, hematologist; b. NYC, June 8, 1932; s. Hagop and Eleeza (Bynderian) A.; m. Lois Abbott, Jan. 16, 1960; 1 dau., Jane. BA with honors, Dartmouth Coll., 1952; MD, Harvard U., 1955. Diplomate: Am. Bd. Internal Medicine. Intern King County Hosp., Seattle, 1955-56; successively asst. resident in medicine, research fellow in hematology, instr. medicine U. Wash. Med. Sch., 1958-64; mem. faculty U. Tex. M.D. Anderson Hosp., Houston, 1964—, prof. medicine, 1975—. Rsch. fellow in radiobiology Christie Hosp., Manchester, England. Contbr. numerous articles on myeloma and related disorders to med. jours. Served as capt. M.C. AUS, 1956-58. Mem. Am. Contract Bridge League(Bronze Life Master) Home: 4082 Breakwood Dr Houston TX 77025-4033 Office: MD Anderson Hosp Dept Lymphoma-Myeloma 1515 Holcombe Blvd Houston TX 77030-4009 Office Phone: 713-792-2850.

ALEXEFF, IGOR, retired electrical engineering educator; b. Pitts., Jan. 5, 1931; s. Alexander and Tamara (Tchirkow) A.; m. Anne I. Fabina, Feb. 4, 1954; children: Alexander, Helen. BA with honors, Harvard U., 1952; MS, U. Wis., 1955, PhD, 1959. Registered profl. engr., Tenn. Research engr. Westinghouse Corp., Pitts., 1952-53; NSF postdoctoral fellow U. Zurich, Switzerland, 1959-60; group leader controlled thermonuclear fusion Oak Ridge Nat. Lab., 1960-71; prof. elec. engring. U. Tenn., 1971-96, prof. emeritus, 1996—; chief scientist Haleakala R&D Corp., Del., 2004—. Vis. prof. Inst. Plasma Physics, Nagoya, Japan, 1973, Phys. Rsch. Lab., Ahmedabad, India, 1975, physics dept. U. Natal, Durban, South Africa, 1976, U. Fed. Fluminense Niteroi, Brazil, 1978, Birla Inst. Tech., Ranchi, India, 1991; organizer Plasma Physics Workshop, U.S. and India, 1976; chmn. Gordon Rsch. Conf. on Plasma Physics, 1974; pres. So. Appalachian Sci. and Engring. Far, 1985-86. Co-author: High Power Microwave Sources, 1987; contbr. articles to profl. jours. Chancellor's rsch. scholar U. Tenn., 1984; recipient Advanced Tech. award Internat. Hall of Fame, 1989, 91, (with others) R&D 100 award R&D Mag., 1989, 91; named Most Outstanding Tchr. of Yr., U. Tenn. Elec. Engring. Dept., 1992. Fellow IEEE (assoc. editor Trans. on Plasma Sci., organizer 1st Internat. Conf. on Plasma Sci. 1974, former pres. Oak Ridge sect., Centennial medal 1987, Outstanding Engr. in S.E. award 1987), Am. Phys. Soc. (past sec.-treas. div. plasma physics); mem. ASI (co-founder), Tech. Corp., Tenn. Inventors Assn. (founding pres., Inventor of Yr. award 1988), Nuclear and Plasma Scis. Soc. of IEEE (chmn. plasma sect. 1983-84, v.p. 1998, pres. 1999-2000, Shea award for outstanding svc., Plasma Scis. and Applications award 2002). Achievements include 19 issued patents; discovery of propagating ion acoustic waves; ions acoustic waves in plasma. Home: 2790 Turnpike Oak Ridge TN 37830 Personal E-mail: ialexeff@comcast.net. Business E-Mail: ialexeff@utk.edu.

ALFINI, JAMES JOSEPH, dean, lawyer, educator; b. Yonkers, NY, Oct. 12, 1943; s. James Joseph and Olga (Genish) Alfini; m. Carol Miller, Dec. 23, 1966; children: David James, Michael Steven. AB, Columbia U., 1965; JD, Northwestern U., 1972. Bar: N.Y. 1973, Ill. 1976, U.S. Dist. Ct. (no. dist.) Ill. 1976, U.S. Supreme Ct. 1977, U.S. Ct. Appeals (7th cir.) 1982, Tex. 2005. Reginald Heber Smith cmty. lawyer Monroe County Legal Assistance Corp., Rochester, NY, 1972—73; asst. dir. rsch. Am. Judicature Soc., Chgo., 1973—77, dir. rsch., 1977—80, asst. exec. dir. programs, 1980—85; adj. prof. law IIT Chgo.-Kent Sch. Law, 1978—85; assoc. prof. law Fla. State U., Tallahassee, 1985—90, prof. law, 1990—91; dean, prof. No. Ill. U. Coll. Law, 1991—97, prof., 1997—2003; pres., dean South Tex. Coll. Law, Houston, 2003—09, dean emeritus prof. law, 2009—. Co-author: (book) Making Jury Instructions Understandable, 1982, Judicial Conduct and Ethics, 1990, Judicial Conduct and Ethics, 2d edit., 1995, Judicial Conduct and Ethics, 3d edit., 2000, Judicial Conduct and Ethics, 4th edit., 2007, Judicial Conduct and Ethics, 5th edit., 2013, Mediation Theory and Practice, 2000, Mediation Theory and Practice 2nd Edit., 2006, Mediation Theory and Practice, 3rd edit., 2013; bd. editors: jour. Ohio State Jour. Dispute Resolution, 1994—98. Mem. governing bd. Cook County Legal Assistance Found., 1981—83; chmn. coord. coun. Nat. Ct. Orgns., 1982—83; arbitration and mediation rules com. Fla. Supreme Ct., 1988—91; mem. Ill. Jud. Ethics com., 1993—97; bd. govs. Chgo. Coun. Lawyers; exec. com. and bd. dirs. Resolution Sys. Inst., 2001—. 1st lt. US Army, 1965—69. Decorated Commendation medal U.S. Army. Mem.: ACLU, ABA (mem. ho. dels. 2002—, mem. joint commn. evaluate model code jud. conduct 2003—07, sect. dispute resolution 2000, chmn.), Law and Soc. Assn., Am. Law Inst. Democrat. Home: 3928 Southwestern Houston TX 77005 Office Phone: 713-646-1834. Business E-Mail: jalfini@stcl.edu.

ALFORD, BOBBY RAY, otolaryngologist, academic administrator, educator; b. Dallas, May 30, 1932; s. Bryant J. and Edith M. (Garrett) A.; m. Othelia Jerry Dorn, Aug. 28, 1953; children: Bradley Keith, Raye Lynn, Alan Scott. AS, Tyler Jr. Coll., 1951; postgrad., U. Tex., 1951-52; MD, Baylor U., 1956. Diplomate Am. Bd. Otolaryngology (dir. 1972-90, pres. 1985-86, exec. v.p. 1986-90). Intern Jefferson Davis Hosp., Houston, 1956-57; resident Baylor U. Coll. Medicine Affiliated Hosps. Program, 1957-60; mem. faculty Baylor U. Coll.

Medicine, 1962—, prof. otolaryngology, 1966—, chmn. dept., 1967-95, 96—, v.p. and dean acad. and clin. affairs, 1984-88, disting. service prof., 1985—, interim chmn. dept. surgery, 1983—84, exec. v.p., dean medicine, 1988—2004, chancellor, 2004—; pres., CEO BaylorMedCare, Houston, 1994-96; chmn., CEO Nat. Space Biomed. Rsch. Inst., 1997—. Rev. panel surgeon gen. on neurol. and sensory disease USPHS, 1965-67; cons. Nat. Inst. Neurol. Disease and Stroke, 1970-74; cons. to surgeon gen. U.S. Army, 1963-73; nat. adv. coun. Neurol. and Communicative Disorders and Stroke, NIH, 1977-80, Deafness and Other Communicative Disorders, 1991-95, NASA, 1992-95, chmn. aerospace medicine adv. com., 1993-94, chmn. life microgravity scis. and applications adv. com., 1993-95. Author: Neurological Aspects of Auditory and Vestibular Disorders, 1964, Electrophysiologic Evaluation in Otolaryngology, 1997; chief editor: A.M.A. Archives of Otolaryngology, 1970-79. Bd. dirs. Houston Acad. Medicine Tex. Med. Ctr. Libr., 1983-94. Recipient Herman Johnson award Baylor U. Coll. Medicine, 1956, NASA Disting. Pub. Svc. award, 1992, 95, Jeffries Aerospace Medicine and Life Scis. Rsch. award Am. Inst. Aeronautics and Astronautics, 2003, Bobby Alford award for Academic Clin. Professionalism Ben and Margaret Love Found., 2005; spl. NIH fellow Johns Hopkins Hosp., 1961-62. Fellow ACS (bd. govs. 1977-82); mem. AIAA (Jeffries Aerospace Medicine and Life Scis. Rsch. award 2003), NAS Inst. Medicine, Am. Laryngol. Assn., Soc. Univ. Otolaryngologists-Head and Neck Surgeons (sec. 1965-69), Am. Otol. Soc., Assn. Acad. Dept. Otolaryngology-Head and Neck Surgery, Am. Laryngol., Rhinol. and Otol. Soc., Am. Soc. Head and Neck Surgery (councillor 1978-80) Am. Acad. Otolaryngology-Head and Neck Surgery (pres. 1981), Am. Coun. Otolaryngology-Head and Neck Surgery (pres. 1980-81), Am. Bronchoesophagological Assn., Soc. Head and Neck Surgeons, Acoustical Soc. Am., Collegium Oto-Rhino-Laryngologicum Amicitiae Sacrum, Johns Hopkins U. Soc. Scholars, Univ. Space Rsch. Assn. (bd. dirs. 1991-95), Tex. Corinthian Yacht Club (bd. dirs. 1978-80, 94-95), Doctors Club (bd. govs. 1967-70, 91-93), Petroleum Club, Alpha Omega Alpha. Office: 6501 Fannin Ste NA102 Houston TX 77030 Office Phone: 713-798-5906. Business E-Mail: balford@bcm.tmc.edu.

ALFORD, CAROLYN ZANDER, lawyer; B in Math., Duke U., 1989; Jd cum laude, Harvard U. Ptnr. King & Spalding, Atlanta. Named to The 45 Under 45, The American Lawyer, 2011. Fellow: American Coll. Comml. Fin. Lawyers, American Coll. Investment Counsel; mem.: Women's Fin. Exchange, State Bar Ga., Atlanta Bar Assn. Office: King & Spalding 1180 Peachtree St NE Atlanta GA 30309-3521 Office Phone: 404-572-3551. Office Fax: 404-572-5100. Business E-Mail: czalford@kslaw.com.

ALGEO, JOHN THOMAS, association executive, retired educator; b. St. Louis, Nov. 12, 1930; s. Thomas George and Julia Winifred (Wathen) A.; m. Adele Marie Silbereisen, Sept. 6, 1958; children: Thomas John, Catherine Marie. EdB cum laude, U. Miami, Coral Gables, 1955; MA, U. Fla., Gainesville, 1957, PhD, 1960. Instr. Fla. State U., Tallahassee, 1959-61; from asst. to full prof. U. Fla., Gainesville, 1961-71, asst. dean grad. sch., 1969-71, dir. program in linguistics, 1969-71; prof. U. Ga., Athens, 1971-88, dir. program in linguistics, 1974-79, head dept. English, 1975-79, alumni found. disting. prof., 1988-94; nat. pres. Theosophical Soc. in Am., Wheaton, Ill., 1993—2002; internat. v.p. Theosophical Soc., Adyar, India, 2002—08; v.p. sec. Supreme Coun. Eastern Order Internat. Co-Freemasonry & Grand Master North America, 2012—. Mem. gen. coun. Theosophical Soc., Adyar, India, 1993—2008; dir. Manor Found. Ltd., Sydney, 1995-2010, v.p. sec., Supreme Coun. Free Eagtem Order Internat. Co-Freecusaonancy & Grand Master North America, 2012-; accreditation cons. Southern Assn. Colls. and Schs., Atlanta, 1967-90; cons. NEH, Washington, 1974-94; dir. Commn. on the English Lang., Nat. Coun. Tchrs. of English, Urbana, Ill., 1976-82; del. Am. Coun. Learned Socs., NYC, 1984-87; cons. in lang. and lexicography Cambridge Univ. Press, NYC, 1989-93; cons. in English Language Cambridge U. Press, Cambridge Eng., 1987-; cons. in Am. usage Kenkyusha Ltd., Tokyo, 1991-99; cons. Webster's New World Dictionary, 4th edit., Cleve., 1993-95. Author: Problems in the Origins and Development of the English Language, 1966, 7th edit., 2012, On Defining the Proper Name, 1973, Exercises in Contemporary English, 1974, The Origins and Development of the English Language, 1982, 7th edit., 2012, Reincarnation Explored, 1987, Reincarnatie in Kaart gebracht, 1990, Fifty Years "Among the New Words": A Dictionary of Neologisms, 1941-91, 1991, 1993, Eigo no kigen to hattatsu, 1991, Reinkarnation: Evolution der Seele, 1991, 96, Reinkarnation i ny belysning, 1994, Investigando a reencarnacao, 1995, Unlocking the Door: Studies in The Key to Theosophy, 2001, British or American English? A Handbook of Word and Grammar Patterns, 2006, Theosophy: An Introductory Study Course, 4th edit., 2007, Getting Acquainted with "The Secret Doctrine: 3rd. edit, 2007, The Ancient Wisdom of Harry Potter, 2011, Theosophy Fantasy and Mary Poppins, 2012; co-author: English: An Introduction to Language, 1970, Spelling: Sound to Letter, 1971, Elements of Literature, Sixth Course: Literature of Britain, 1989, The Power of Thought, 2001, Pensamento: O que e e como usar, 2003, Tankens Kraft, 2009, Sila Mysli, 2009; editor: American Speech, 1972-81, Thomas Pyles: Selected Essays on English Usage, 1979, Among the New Words, American Speech, 1987-97, Cambridge History of the English Language, vol. 6, English in North America, 2001, 02, The Quest, 1997-03, The Letters of H.P. Blavatsky, vol. 1, 2003, Echoes From the Gnosis, 2006, H.P. Blavatsky: Ein lebun fur die Meister: Die Briefe 1, 1861-1879, 2009; assoc. editor: The Oxford Companion to the English Language, 1992; mem. editl. bd. Jour. of English Linguistics, 1970—, Internat. Jour. Lexicography, 1990-93, World Englishes, 1996—, Names, 1997—. bd. choose best articles, 2011, 12, Language Problems Language Planning, 1997-99, Studies in English Language, 1987—, Theosophy Forward, 2008- Sgt. US Army, 1951-54, Korea. Fellow Guggenheim Found., London, 1986-87; Fulbright scholar U. Coll. London, Eng., 1986-87. Mem. Am. Dialect Soc. (pres. 1979), Am. Name Soc. (pres. 1984), Internat. Assn. Univ. Profs. English, Internat. Linguistic Assn., Ea. Order Internat. Co-Freemasonry, Internat. Phonetic Assn., Linguistic Assn. of the U.S. and Can., Linguistic Soc. Am., Modern Lang. Assn. Am., Philological Soc., Southeastern Conf. on Linguistics (pres. 1970-71), Dictionary Soc. N.Am. (pres. 1995-97), Theosophical Soc. (nat. pres. 1993-2002, internat. v.p. 2002-08), Ea. Order Internat. Co-Freemasonry (adminstr. 2002—). Democrat. Home: 1800 Westen St #1308 Bowling Green KY 42104 Business E-Mail: jalgeo@uga.edu.

ALIBRAHIM, AYMAN, allergist, immunologist; MD, Aleppo Med. Sch., 1986. Diplomate Am. Bd. Pediatrics, 2003, Am. Bd. Allergy and Immunology, 2007, lic. Fla., 2003. Resident pediat. Todd Children's Hosp., 1992—95; fellow allergy and immunology Children's Hospital Med. Ctr., 1995—97; hosp. affiliations include Brooksville Regional Hosp., Citrus Meml. Hosp., Oak Hill Hosp., Spring Hill Regional Hosp. Office: Citrus Memorial Hospital 502 W Highland Blvd Inverness FL 34452-4754 Office Phone: 352-726-1551.

ALLAIN, R.L., II, (BRET ALLAIN), state legislator; b. La. m. Kim McElveen; children: Quin Elise, Emma Marie, Robert Lebreton. B, La. State U. Small bus. owner, La.; mem. Dist. 21 La. State Senate, Baton Rogue, 2012—. Former mem. La. State Mineral Bd.; mem. La. Agrl. Fin. Authority; apptd. mem. I-49 Task Force, La. Republican. Roman Catholic. Office: 600 Main St Ste 1 Franklin LA 70538 also: La State Senate 900 N 3rd St Baton Rouge LA 70804 Office Phone: 337-828-9107. Business E-Mail: allainb@legis.la.gov.

ALLAN, BARRY DAVID, research chemist, government official; b. Steubenville, Ohio, Jan. 20, 1935; s. John Young and Frances Lucy (Halbrunner) A.; m. Inge Elisabeth Bergeler, Aug. 5, 1961; children—Barbara Diane, Stephen Barry. BS, Ariz. State U., Tempe, 1956; MS, U. Ala., 1964, PhD, 1968. Chemist White Sands Missile Range, N.Mex., 1956; aero. fuels research chemist Army Missile Command, Redstone Arsenal, Ala., 1958-62, research chemist-phys., 1962-96, research chemist, 1968-95; prof. J.C. Calhoun Coll., Decatur, Ala., 1969-73, Athens Coll., Ala., 1970-73, U. Ala., Huntsville, 1974-76; rsch. cons. Allan Cons., Huntsville, 1996—. Cons., 1965—; reviewer Nat. Sci. Found., 1973— Publs. in field. Active Huntsville Civic Assn., 1961—. Served to capt. AUS, 1956-58. Recipient Army Research And Devel. Achievement award, 1962, Navy commendation, 1968, Army commendation, 1971, 72 Mem. Am. Chem. Soc. (treas. 1969-73, pres. 1974-76), Combustion Inst., Pasteur Soc., Assn. U.S. Army, N.Y. Acad. Scis., Joint Army, Navy, NASA, Air Force Propellant Characterization Group on Fluids and Materials, Sigma Xi, Gamma Sigma Epsilon, Theta Chi. Office: Barry D Allan Cons 7803 Michael Cir SW Huntsville AL 35802-2900 Office Phone: 256-881-4088. Office Fax: 256-881-4101. Business E-Mail: ballan@hiwaay.net.

ALLARD, DEAN CONRAD, historian, retired historical center director; b. Kansas City, Mo., Oct. 19, 1933; s. Dean Conrad Sr. and Elizabeth Donaldson (Graves) A.; m. Constance Lynne Morgan, June 17, 1955; children: Scott, Hunt, Elizabeth. AB, Dartmouth Coll., 1955; MA, Georgetown U., 1959; PhD, George Washington U., 1967. Head Naval Operational Archives, Washington, 1958-82; sr. historian Naval Hist. Ctr., Washington, 1982-89; dir. naval history USN, Washington, 1989-95. Adj. prof. George Washington U., 1979-89, v.p. Internat. Commn. Mil. History, 2000—05. Author: The United States Navy and the Vietnam Conflict, Vol. I, 1976, Spencer Fullerton Baird: A Study in the History of American Science, 1978; also articles on naval and maritime history; editor: U.S. Naval History Sources in the United States, 1979. Chmn. Hist. Commn., Arlington, Va., 1978-80; pres. Arlington Hist. Soc., 1974-75; mem. coun. Woodlawn Plantation, Fairfax, Va., 1976-84; mem. French-U.S. Sci. Com. on CSS, Ala., 1991-95. Lt. (j.g.) USN, 1955-58. Recipient Superior Civil Svc. award U.S. Govt., 1995, Samuel Eliot Morison award for Disting. Svc., USS Constn. Mus. Found., Boston, 1995. Mem.: Internat. Commn. Mil. History (v.p. 2000—05), Internat. Commn. Maritime History (mem. exec. coun. 1990—2002), U.S. Commn. Mil. History (pres. 1995—99), World War II Studies Assn. (bd. dirs.), Soc. for Mil. History (v.p. 1983—86), N.Am. Soc. for Oceanic History (pres. 1985—89), Cosmos Club (Washington), Phi Beta Kappa. Avocations: gardening, hiking. Home: 3440 S Jefferson ST #377 Falls Church VA 22041

ALLASTER, STACEY, sports association executive; m. John Milkovich; adopted children: Jack, Alexandra. BA in Economics & Physical Edn., U. We. Ontario; MBA, Ivey Sch. Bus., U. We. Ontario. V.p. Tennis Canada, 1990—2006; pres. Sony Ericsson WTA Tour, 2006—09, chmn., CEO, 2009—. Bd. mem., Tournament Coun. Sony Ericsson WTA Tour, 2001—, Tournament Class alt., 2002—. Named Canadian Sports Exec. of Yr., 2002, Exec. of Yr., Sports Media Canada, 2006, Woman of Yr., Women in Sports & Events (WISE), 2011; named one of The Top 25 Leaders in Canadian Sports, Globe & Mail, 2003, 2005, The Most Powerful Women in Sports, Forbes mag., 2010. Office: WTA Corp Hdqs One Progress Plz Ste 1500 Saint Petersburg FL 33701 Office Phone: 727-895-5000. Office Fax: 727-894-1982.

ALLBRIGHT, KARAN ELIZABETH, psychologist, consultant; b. Oklahoma City, Jan. 28, 1948; d. Jack Gahnal and Irma Loise (Keesee) Allbright. BA, Okla. City U., 1970, MAT, 1972; PhD, U. So. Miss., Hattiesburg, 1981. Cert. nat. sch. psychologist, psychometrist, lic. psychologist Okla., Ark. Psychol. technician Donald J. Bertoch, PhD, Okla. City, 1973-76; asst. adminstr. Parents' Assistance Ctr., Okla. City, 1976-77; psychology intern Burwell Psycho-ednl. Ctr., Carrollton, Ga., 1980-81; staff psychologist Griffin Area Psychoednl. Ctr., Ga., 1981-85; clinic dir. Sequoyah County Guidance Clinic, Sallisaw, Okla., 1985-88; psychologist Baker Psychiat. Clinic, Ft. Smith, Ark., 1988-90; cons. Harbor View Mercy Hosp., 1988-90, Integris Bethany Med. Ctr., 1992-99; pvt. practice Okla. City, 1990—, Mercy Health Ctr., 1996—. Cons. Family Alliance (Parents Anonymous) Sequoyah County, 1985-88; lectr. in field.; bd. dir. workshops. Mem. Task Force to Prevent Child Abuse, Fayette County, Ga., 1984-85, Task Force on Family Violence, Spalding County, Ga., 1983-85, Oklahoma County Child Abuse Task Force, 2006; assoc. bd. dir. Lyric Theatre. Named to Outstanding Young Women in Am., 1980. Mem. APA, Okla. Psychol. Assn. Nat. Register Health Svc. Providers in Psychology, Registry Oklahoma City (pres., bd. dirs.), Okla. County Mental Health Assn., Okla. City Orch. League, Psi Chi, Delta Zeta (chpt. dir. 1970-72), Okla. City Mus. Art, Okla Ziol. Soc. Republican. Presbyterian. Home: 3941 NW 44th St Oklahoma City OK 73112-2517 Office: Northwest Mental Health Assocs 3832 N Meridian Ave Oklahoma City OK 73112-2849 Office Phone: 405-949-9322.

ALLDAY, MARTIN LEWIS, JR., retired lawyer; b. El Dorado, Ark., May 30, 1926; s. Martin L. Sr. and Bess (Kavanaugh) A.; m. Patricia Pryor, May 1, 1954; children: Katherine, Elizabeth, Martin III. JD, U. Tex., Austin, 1951. Bar: Tex. 1951. Examiner oil and gas div. R.R. Commn. of Tex., Austin, 1951-53; legal dept. Superior Oil Co., Midland, Tex., 1953-57, Houston, 1957-59; ptnr. Lynch, Chappell, Allday and Alsup, Midland, Austin & Dallas, 1959-89; past solicitor Dept. of Interior, Washington, 1989; chmn. Fed. Energy Regulatory Commn., Washington, 1989-93; of counsel Scott, Douglass and McConnico, Austin, Tex., 1993—2006; pvt. practice, 2006—07; ret., 2007. Past pres. Midland Jaycees, C. of C., Indsl. Found.; past trustee Midland Meml. Hosp.; trustee Petroleum Mus. Hall of Fame; presiding officer Tex. State Cemetery Commn., Austin, 1998-04; pres. Friends of the Cemetery, 2004-. With Inf. U.S. Army, 1944-46. Decorated Purple Heart, Bronze Star, Combat Infantry badge, 96th Presdl. Citation award; recipient Disting. Alumni award Schreiner U., 2004; named Pioneer, Tex. R.R. Commn., 2003; named one of top 50 Oil and Gas Attys. Tex. Monthly Mag. Mem. ABA, Tex. Bar Assn. (chmn. oil, gas and mineral sect. 1970), Tex. Bar Found., Midland County Bar Assn. (pres. 1972-73), Ind. Prodrs. Assn. Am. (Hard Hat award 1992), Midland Country Club (pres.), Petroleum Club (bd. dirs.), Tex. Ind. Prodr. and Royalty Orgn. (Hats Off award 1992). Republican. Episcopalian. Avocations: fishing, hunting, golf. Personal E-mail: martin.allday@yahoo.com.

ALLEGRA, CARMEN J., oncologist, educator; BA in Biology magna cum laude, U. Pa., Phila., 1974; MD, U. Pa. Sch. Med., Phila., 1979. Diplomate Am. Bd. Internal Medicine, 1983, subspecialty cert.in med. oncology 1985. Intern U. Pa., Phila., 1979—80, resident internat med., 1980—82; clin. assoc. dept. medicine & clin. pharmacology Nat. Cancer Inst., NIH, Bethesdam, Md., 1982—85, sr. staff fellow clin. pharmacology br., 1985—88, sr. investigator medicine br., 1988—89, chief sect. biochemical & molecular pharmacology, medicine br., 1989—91, chief NCI- Navy Med. oncology br., 1991—96, acting dir., divsn. clin. sci., 1996, dep. dir., divsn. clin. sci., 1996—2000, chief, medicine br., 1996—2000, vice dep. dir. extramural sci., 2000—01, spl. govt. employee, dir. extramural sci., 2001—05; assoc. dir. clin. & translational rsch. U. Fla., Coll. Medicine. U. Fla. Shands Cancer Ctr., Gainesville, 2000—; med. dir. Network Med. Comm. & Rsch., Atlanta, 2001—07, chief med. officer, 2002—06; staff physician Nat. Naval Med. Ctr., 2002—07; spl. govt. employee US Food & Drug Adminstrn. ODAC, 2003—07; co-dir. Found. Rsch. Program Nat. Surgical Adjuvant Breast & Bowel Project, 2006—; chief, prof. dept. medicine, hematology, oncology U. Fla., Gainesville, Fla., 2007—, prof. dept. pediatrics, 2008—, dir. fellowship program, hematology. oncology, 2008—; assoc. dir. clin. and translational rsch. U. Fla. Coll. Medicine, U. Fla. Shands Cancer Ctr., Fla., 2007—. Contbr. articles to jours.; mem. editl. bd. of several perr-reviewed publications. Recipient Roy G. Williams award for excellence in basic med. rsch., 1977, US Pub. Health Svc. Achievement medal, 1986, US Pub. Health Svc. Commendation medal, 1989, US Pub. Health Svc. Unit Citation, 1989, Nat. Assoc. Govt. Comm., Blue Pencil award, 1990, US Pub. Health Svc. Exceptional Capabilities Promotion, 1992, Gail Garlove Lectureship award, 1995, Fed. Tech. Transfer award, 1996, Director's award, DCS, NCI, 1997, 318 Top Cancer Specialists for Women, Good Housekeeping Mag., 1999, Recognition Excellence, Commander's Award, Dept. Navy, Nat. Naval Med. Ctr., 1999, Exellence Tchg. Fellows award, U. Fl., Dept. Medicine, 2008. Mem.: AMA, AAAS, Am. Soc. Clin. Investigation, Am. Assn. Cancer Rsch., Am. Soc. Clin. Oncology, Alpha Omega Alpha, Phi Beta Kappa, Alpha Epsilon Delta. Office: 1515 SW Archer Rd Gainesville FL 32608

ALLEN, A. WILLIAM, III, (BILL ALLEN), restaurant chain company executive; V.p., ptnr. Restaurant Enterprises Group; gen. mgr. to sr. v.p. The Marriott Corp.; CEO la Madeleine French Bakery and Cafe; pres. West Coast Concepts, 2004—05; CEO OSI Restaurant Partners, LLC, Tampa, Fla., 2005—09, chmn., 2009—. Office: OSI Restaurant Partners LLC 2202 N West Shore Blvd 5th Fl Tampa FL 33607 Office Phone: 813-282-1225.

ALLEN, ALMA A., state legislator; b. Apr. 7, 1939; m. Lawrence Alvin Allen, Sr.; 2 children. BS, MEd, Tex. So. U., Houston; EdD in Curriculum and Instrn., U. Houston. Cert. in curriculum and adminstrn. U. Houston. Tchr. Parker Elementary Sch., Grimes Elementary Sch.; asst. principal Foster Elementary Sch.; principal Peck Elementary Sch.; ret. tchr., adminstr. Houston Ind. Sch. Dist., 1961—2000; mem. Tex. State Bd. Edn., 1992—2004; motivational spkr., ednl. cons. and prof.; mem. Dist. 131 Tex. House of Representatives, 2004—. Adj. prof. Tex. So. U., Prairie View A7M U. Recipient of several awards and honors. Mem.: NAACP, American Assn. of Curriculum and Development, Nat. Assn. of Democratic Women, Tex. Assn. of Sch. Administrators, American Assn. of Supervision and Curriculum, Houston Assn. of Profl. Administrators, Council of Negro Women. Democrat. Office: 10101 Fondren Rd Ste 500 Houston TX 77096 also: Room E2.722 Capitol Extension PO Box 2910 Austin TX 78768 Office Phone: 713-776-0505, 512-463-0744.

ALLEN, BARBARA KIRKMAN, political organization administrator; b. Asheville, NC, July 23, 1931; d. Walter Alfred and Georgia Esmerald (Lewallen) Kirkman; m. Luke C. Allen, Jr., Sept. 9, 1949; 1 child, Michael Kirkman. With Carolina Power and Light Co., Raleigh, 1950—96, mgr. adminstrv. svcs., 1979. Bd. dirs. NC Women's Forum; bd. deacons New Hope Bapt. Ch., Raleigh; mem. J.J. Singers; mem. adv. bd. Wake County coun. Girl Scouts US; mem. adv. council Women in Econ. Devel; chairperson Acad. Women, YWCA; bd. dirs. NC Cmty. Colls., Wake County Coll. Aging; bd. assocs. Meredith Coll.; bd. dirs. NC State U. Humanities Found.; mem. exec. bd. NC Equity Inc.; Dem. chmn., NC, 1998—. Mem. NC Symphony Soc., Greater Raleigh C. of C. (mem. Mayor's com. of '85), Women of Raleigh (trustee). Office: NC Democratic Party 220 Hillsborough St Raleigh NC 27603-1724

ALLEN, BESSIE MALVINA, music educator, organist; b. LaKemp, Okla., Oct. 14, 1918; d. Percy J. and Mary Allen (Hagler) Gheen; m. Edgar Charles Allen, Aug. 29, 1940 (dec. May 1981); children: Stanley Charles, Stephen Wayne. BA in English, Tex. Woman's U., 1939; MA in Music, W. Tex. State U., 1970. Cert. secondary edn. Tchr. English Balko (Okla.) High Sch. and Jr. High Sch., 1939-40; pvt. practice Phillips, Tex., 1950-85; tchr. music Frank Phillips Coll., Borger, Tex., 1960-63, 65-73, 76-85; pvt. practice Borger, 1997. Organist First Bapt. Ch., Borger, 1947-65, Faith Covenant Ch.-Ind., Borger, 1970-81, First Christian Ch., Borger, 1981-82, Faith Covenant Ch., Borger, 1982-2000. Active Nat. Rep. Senatorial Com., Washington, 1988-91; organist First United Meth. Ch., Borger, 2001—03. Recipient Presdl. Order of Merit, Nat. Rep. Senatorial Com., 1991; McCulley Organ scholar, W. Tex. State U., Canyon, 1969. Avocations: gardening, reading. Home and Office: 221 Inverness St Borger TX 79007-8215

ALLEN, DAVID MARK, psychiatrist, educator, director; b. Glendale, Calif., Apr. 26, 1949; s. Emmanuel and Ann Allen; m. Harriet Allen, Dec. 24, 1972; children: Angela, Paula. BA, UCLA, 1970; MD, U. Calif., San Francisco, 1974. Diplomate Am. Bd. Psychiatry and Neurology. Resident in psychiatry U. So. Calif. Med. Ctr., LA, 1977; mem. staff Gateways Hosp., LA, 1977-79; pvt. practice Burbank, Calif., 1979-91; dir. psychiat. residency tng., asst. prof. dept. psychiatry U. Tenn., Memphis, 1992—2008, prof., 2004—. Author: Unifying Individual and Family Therapies, 1988, Deciphering Motivation in Psychotherapy, 1991, Psychotherapy with Borderline Patients - An Integrated Approach, 2003, How Dysfunctional Family Spurs Mental Disorders; A Balanced Approach to Resolve Problems and Reconcile Relationships, 2010. Mem.: Internat. Soc. Study of Personality Disorders, Soc. Psychotherapy Rsch., Tenn. Psychiat. Assn., Soc. Exploration Psychotherapy Integration, Am. Psychiat. Assn. Office: U Tenn Dept Psychiatry 135 N Pauline St 6th Fl Memphis TN 38105-4619 Office Phone: 901-384-8040. Business E-Mail: dmallen@uthsc.edu.

ALLEN, FRANCES L., marketing executive; b. 1962; Sr. v.p. DMB&B, Hong Kong; dir. internat. advt. Frito-Lay PepsiCo Inc., v.p. innovation North America; v.p. mktg. Sony Ericsson Mobile Communications, 2005—07; brand mktg. officer Dunkin Doughnuts Dunkin Brands, Inc., 2007—09; chief mktg. officer Denny's Corp., 2010—. Office: Denny's Corp 203 E Main St Spartanburg SC 29319

ALLEN, FRED, state legislator; Plan commr., Little Rock; mem. Dist .33 Ark. House of Reps., 2007—. Democrat. Baptist. Address: 19 Dover Dr Little Rock AR 72204 Office Phone: 501-225-4979. Fax: 501-225-4762. E-mail: FredAllen99@comcast.net.

ALLEN, GERALD, state legislator; b. Ala., Feb. 8, 1950; m. Shelia Allen; children: Wes, Kellie, Jill. BS in Edn., U. Ala. Owner CASHCO Mktg.; mem. Dist. 62 Ala. House of Reps., Montgomery, 1994—2011; mem. Dist. 21 Ala. State Senate, 2011—. Deacon Gilgal Bapt. Ch. Republican. Baptist. Office: PO Box 71001 Tuscaloosa AL 35407 also: Ala State Senate State House Rm 729 11 S Union St Montgomery AL 36130 Office Phone: 205-556-5310, 334-242-7889. Business E-Mail: gerald.allen@alsenate.gov.

ALLEN, JERRY R., councilman; BBA in Banking & Fin., North Tex. U. Sr. v.p. Colonial Bank; councilman, Dist. 10 Dallas City Coun. Bd. trustees Dallas Police & Fire Pension Bd.; vice chmn. Fin., Audit & Accountability com.; mem. Econ. Devel., Pub. Safety, Transp. & Environ. coms. Chmn. Ethics com. Dallas Area Rapid Transit, vice chmn. Budget & Fin. com. Mem.: Nat. League Cities (Fin., Adminstrn. & Intergovernmental Rels. com.), RISD Tomorrow Found. (former treas.), Lake Highlands Exchange Club (pres. & treas.). Office: City Hall 1500 Marilla St Rm 5FS Dallas TX 75201 Office Phone: 214-670-4068. Office Fax: 214-670-5115.

ALLEN, JESSE OWEN, III, organizational behavior specialist; b. Albany, Ga., Apr. 7, 1938; s. Jesse Owen Jr. and Erma Hazel (Pearson) A.; children by previous marriage: Charlotte Renee, Garrett Owen, Cheryl Hazel; m. Barbara Joanna Smith Ozment, May 23, 1987; 1 stepchild, Pamela Ozment Cartee. LLB, LaSalle Law Sch., 1967; AS, U. State N.Y., Albany, 1978, BS in History, Lit. and Bus., 1986; MA in Philosophy, Calif. State U., 1987; PhD in Organizational Behavior, The Union Grad. Sch., 1991; postgrad., Oxford U., England, 1997. Founder, pres. Specific Action Corp., Greensboro, NC, 1971—; pres. Inst. Christian Studies, Inc., Greensboro, 1987—, Christian Family Online, Inc., 2001—; prof. mgmt. Laurel U., 1993, founder first dean Sch. Mgmt., 2008, exec. v.p., 2010—. Lectr., cons. in field. Author: Weatherization Production Control, 1978, Personal Profile Labs, 1980, Management Power: The Specific Action Way, 1985, Personality Power: The Specific Action Way, 1988, Master of Personal Excellence Program, 1994; contbr. articles to profl. jours., Specific Action Management System, 1996, Specific Action Personality System, 1996, Specific Action Team System, 1997; patentee Allen valve, 1967; Preactive Leadership, 2012. With 40th Congressional Nat. Prayer Breakfast, 1992, Gallup Orgn., Washington, 2002, Carolina Presdl. Bus. Commn., 2004, 54th Congressional Nat. Prayer Breakfast, 2006. With USMC, 1955—64, capt. US Merchant Marines, 1993—99, with US Coast Guard Aux., 1993—95. Named to Hon. Order of Ky. Cols., Commonwealth of Ky., 1978, Hon. Adm. State of Nebr., 1978. Mem. High Point City Club, NC, Piedmont City Club, Winston-Salem, NC. Republican. Avocations: yachting, cruising, deep-sea fishing. Home: 520 Lindley Rd Greensboro NC 27410-4933 Office: Specific Action Corp PO Box 19125 Greensboro NC 27419-9125 Office Phone: 336-854-9494.

ALLEN, JOHN JAY, Spanish language educator; b. May 20, 1932; AB, Duke U., 1954; MA, Middlebury Coll., 1957; PhD, U. Wis., 1960; DLit (hon.), Middlebury Coll., 2004. Prof. Spanish, U. Fla., Gainesville, 1960-83, U. Ky., Lexington, 1983-2000. Home: 1153 Stirling Dr Danville KY 40422-2714 E-mail: jjallen@kih.net.

ALLEN, JON G., psychologist; BS, U. Conn.; D in Clin. Psychology, U. Rochester. Clin. psychology fellowship Karl Menninger Sch. of Psychiatry and Mental Health Scis., faculty, Washburn U., U. Kans., Kans. State U. Author: Coping With Trauma: A Guide to Self-Understanding; editor: (with others) Diagnosis and Treatment of Dissociative Disorders, Contemporary Treatment of Psychosis: Healing Relationships in the Decade of the Brain; co-author: Borderline Personality Disorder: Tailoring the Therapy to the Patient; past editor Bull. of the Menninger Clinic; cons. editor Psychiatry; contbr. chpts. to books and numerous articles to profl. publs. Recipient I. Arthur Marshall Disting. Alumnus award Menninger Alumni Assn. Address: Menningers PO Box 809045 Houston TX 77280

ALLEN, KARL B., state legislator; b. Greenville, SC, Oct. 13, 1960; 1 child, Brittanie Elizabeth. BA, U. SC, 1982, JD, 1986. Mem. Dist. 25 SC House of Reps., 2000—, mem. Judiciary Com. Mem.: Nat. Assn. Blacks in Criminal Justice (past pres.), SC Bar Assn. Democrat. Office: 330B Blatt Bldg Columbia SC 29201 Home: 108 Lavinia Ave Greenville SC 29601 Office Phone: 803-734-3006, 864-235-9049. E-mail: KBA@scstatehouse.net.

ALLEN, LEON HARTWELL, agronomist, educator; b. Opelika, Ala., Oct. 23, 1935; s. Leon and Estelle Vinson Allen; m. Betty Allen, Feb. 21, 1991. BS, Auburn U., Ala., 1958, BS, 1962; MS, Cornell U., Ithaca, NY, 1960, PhD, 1972. Soil scientist physics USDA-Agrl. Rsch. Svc., Ithaca, 1966—73, rsch. soil scientist Gainesville, Fla., 1973; courtesy asst. prof. Dept. Agronomy, Cornell U., 1972—74; courtesy asst. prof. to prof. Agronomy Dept., U. Fla., Gainesville, 1974—. Recipient Sr. Scientist of Yr. award, USDA, Agrl. Rsch. Svc., 1992. Fellow: AAAS, Soil Sci. Soc. America, Crop Sci. Soc. America; mem.: Am. Soc. Agronomy (program chair agroclimatology and agronomic modelling divsn. 1984—85). Achievements include research in determining the impacts of rising CO2 and climate change on plant growth and yield of several globally important crops, led water quality research on land use impacts of surface water flow into Lake Okeechobee; water management for citrus growth and yield on high water table soils. Office: USDA Agricultural Research Service 1700 SW 23rd Dr Gainesville FL 32608 Home: 9120 NW 27th Pl Gainesville FL 32606 Business E-Mail: hartwell.allen@ars.usda.gov.*

ALLEN, MARTI LU, museum director; PhD, U. Mich., Ann Arbor. Dir. Mus. Peoples and Cultures, Brigham Young U., Provo, Utah, 1991—2006, Ark. State U., 2006—. Founder Cert. in Mus. Practices prog. Recipient Merit awards, Utah Humanities Coun., Profl. Faculty award of Excellence, Brigham Young U., Excellence in Peer Review Svc., AAM. Office: ASU Mus PO Box 490 State University AR 72467 Office Phone: 870-972-2074. Office Fax: 870-972-2793. Business E-Mail: mallen@astate.edu.

ALLEN, MIKE, political correspondent; b. 1964; s. Gary Allen. BA in Politics and Journalism, Washington and Lee U., 1986. Reporter The Free Lance-Star, Fredericksburg, Va., Richmond Times-Dispatch, The Washington Post, Richmond, Va., Alexandria, Va., corr. Washington; reporter NY Times; White House corr. Time mag.; chief polit. corr. Politico, 2007—, columnist Playbook. Recipient Merriman Smith Meml. Award, White House Correspondents' Assn., 2004. Office: Politico 1100 Wilson Blvd, Ste 301 Arlington VA 22209

ALLEN, RAY (WALTER RAY ALLEN), professional basketball player; b. Merced, Calif., July 20, 1975; m. Shannon Williams; 3 children. Student, U. Conn., 1996. Shooting guard Milw. Bucks, 1996—2003, Seattle SuperSonics, 2003—07, Boston Celtics, 2007—12, Miami Heat, 2012—. Actor: (films) He Got Game, 1998. Founder Ray of Hope Found. Recipient Gold medal, men's basketball, Summer Olympic Games, 2000, Joe Dumars Sportsmanship award, NBA, 2003; named to Ea. Conf. All-Star Team, 2000, 2001, 2002, 2009, 2011, Western Conf. All-Star Team, 2004, 2005, 2006, 2007. Achievements include winner of the NBA All-Star Weekend Three-Point Shootout, 2001; leading the NBA in: three-point field goals, 2002, 2003, 2006; member of the NBA Championship winning Boston Celtics, 2008; Miami Heat, 2013; breaking the NBA record for career three-point shots made (2,561), February 10, 2011. Office: Miami Heat 601 Biscayne Blvd Miami FL 33132*

ALLEN, ROBERT EUGENE, retired telecommunications industry executive; b. Joplin, Mo., Jan. 25, 1935; s. Walter Clark and Louise (Patton) A.; m. Elizabeth Terese Pfeffer, March 10, 1956; children: Jay Robert, Daniel Scott, Katherine Louise, Ann Elizabeth, Amy Susan. BA, Wabash Coll., 1957, LLD (hon.), 1984; postgrad., Harvard Bus. Sch., 1965; degree (hon.), Wabash Coll., 1984, Rutgers U., 1989, Ill. Inst. Tech., 1990, Babson Coll., 1991, Stevens Inst. Tech., 1992; degree, Norte Dame U., 1993, Pace U., 1990. With Ind. Bell Telephone Co. Inc., Indpls., 1957-74, traffic student, 1957-58, asst. traffic supr. operator services, 1958-61, asst. traffic supr. costs, operator svcs., 1961, dist. traffic supr. Bloomington, 1961-64, dist. comml. mgr., 1964-65, div. comml. mgr. Bloomington, Indpls., 1965-68, asst. to ops. v.p., 1969, gen. comml. mgr., 1969-72, v.p., sec., treas., 1972-74; v.p., gen. mgr. Bell Telephone Co. of Pa., Phila., 1974-76; v.p., COO Ill. Bell Telephone Co., Chgo., 1976-78; v.p. AT&T Corp., Basking Ridge, NJ, 1978-81; pres., chmn. bd. C&P Telephone Cos., Washington, 1981-83; exec. v.p. corp. adminstrn. & fin. ATGT, New York, 1983-84; chmn., CEO AT&T Info. Systems, Morristown, NJ, 1985; pres., COO AT&T Corp., NYC, 1986-88, chmn., CEO, 1988-98. Former mem. bd. dirs. Bristol Myers Squibb Co., Chrysler Corp., PepsiCo, Inc., New Am. Schs. Devel. Corp. Emeritus Trustee Wabash Coll., Mayo Clinic; bd. dirs. Baldridge Found., Coun. Fgn. Rels. Am.-China Soc. Mem. Bus. Roundtable (policy com.), Bus. Coun. (pres.), U.S.-Japan Bus. Coun. Republican. Presbyterian. Home: 11 Country Rd W Village Of Golf FL 33436

ALLEN, ROBERT JOHNSON, plastic surgeon, educator; b. Florence, Mar. 19, 1951; s. James and Lucta Johnson Allen; m. Linda Truluck Perry Allen, June 5, 1976; children: Julia Marshall, Robert Johnson, James Perry, Celeste Blackwell. BS, Wofford Coll., Spartanburg, SC, 1972; MD, Med. U. SC, Charleston, 1976. Diplomate Am. Bd. Surgery, Am. Bd. Plastic Surgery, cert. in surgery of hand, lic. La., NY, SC. Intern/ resident gen. surgery La. State U. Med. Ctr., New Orleans, 1976—82, clin. instr. dept. surgery, 1983—88, clin. asst. prof., 1988—97, program dir. plastic surgery LSU Med. Ctr., 1987—98; microsurgery fellow NYU Med. Ctr., NYC, 1982—83; clin. assoc. prof. La. State U. Health Scis. Ctr., 1997—2004, clin. prof. plastic surgery, 2004—, chief plastic surgery, 1998—2005; staff Ctr. Microsurg. Breast Reconstruction, Charleston, NYC. Clin. prof. plastic surgery Med. U. SC, 2005—, NYU, 2007—. Editor: Seminars in Plastic Surgery, 2002; mem. editl. bd. Jour. Reconstructive Microsurgery, 1996—, Breast Diseases: A Yearbook, 1999—, Annals of Plastic Surgery, 2004; contbr. articles to profl. jours. Vol. celebrity waiter La. Breast Cancer Task Force, New Orleans, 2005. Recipient Spirit award, Am. Cancer Soc., 2003. Mem.: ACS, AMA, Am. Soc. Surgery of Hand, Southern Med. Assn. (sec.-elect 1993—97), New Orleans Surg. Soc., Am. Soc. Plastic & Reconstructive Surgeons, La. State Med. Soc., La. Surg. Soc., La. Soc. Plastic & Reconstructive Surgery (pres. 1990—91), Am. Soc. Reconstructive Microsurgery (edn. com. 1998—99), Southeastern Soc. Plastic Reconstructive Surgeons (bd. dir. 1998—2001), Am. Assn. Plastic Surgeons, World Soc. Reconstructive Microsurgery (coun. mem. 2001—03, sec. gen. 2003—06, founding mem.). Achievements include design of deep inferior episcastric perforator flap; superficial inferior episcastric artery flap; glutal artery perforator flap; first to complete breast reconstruction transplant in identical twins. Avocations: pottery, tennis, running, literature. Office: 1776 Broadway Ste 1200 New York NY 10019 also: Ctr Microsurg Breast Reconstruction 1300 Hospital Dr Ste 110 Mount Pleasant SC 29464-3204 Office Fax: 843-727-3774. Business E-Mail: boballen@diepflap.com.

ALLEN, RONALD W., rental company executive; b. 1941; married. B in Indsl. Engring., Ga. Inst. Tech. Joined Delta Air Lines, Inc., Atlanta, 1963—, asst. v.p. adminstrn., 1967-69, v.p. adminstrn., 1969-70, sr. v.p. pers., 1970-79, sr. v.p. adminstrn. and pers., 1979-83, pres., COO, 1983-87, chmn., CEO, 1987-90, chmn., pres., CEO, 1990-97; chmn. Guided Therapeutics, Inc., Ga., 2011—; interim pres., CEO Aaron's, Inc., Atlanta, 2011—12, pres., CEO, 2012—. Former cons. & adv. dir. Delta Air Lines, Inc.; bd. dirs. Coca-Cola Co., 1991—, Aaron's Inc., 1997—, Aircastle Ltd., 2006—, Guided Therapeutics, Inc., 2008—, Forward Air Corp., 2011—. Office: Aaron's Inc 309 E Paces Ferry Rd NE Atlanta GA 30305

ALLEN, STEVEN GLEN, economics and business professor; b. Louisville, Mar. 17, 1952; s. Charles Freeman and Lois (Crask) A.; m. Linda L. Pattison, May 19, 1978. BA in Math., Mich. State U., 1973, MA in Econs., 1974; PhD in Econs., Harvard U., 1978. Asst. prof. econs. and bus. N.C. State U., Raleigh, 1978—83, assoc. prof., 1983—87, prof., 1987—, dir. MS mgmt. program, 1993—2002, dir. MBA program, 2002—, assoc. dean grad. programs and rsch., 2003—. Rsch. economist Nat. Bur. Econ. Rsch., Cambridge, Mass., 1983-86, rsch. assoc., 1986—; mem. bd. reviewers Indls. Rels., Berkeley, Calif., 1989—. Contbr. articles to profl. jours. Recipient Allyn Young award Harvard Coll., 1975, 76, Disting. Rsch. and Lit. Publ. award Sch. Humanities and Social Scis., N.C. State U., 1986, Outstanding Rsch. award Coll. Mgmt., 1993; NSF grantee, 1984-86, 87-92, five-time U.S. Dept. Labor grantee; Fulbright scholar, 1991, 93. Mem. Am. Econ. Assn., Soc. Labor Economists. Office: NC State U PO Box 7229 Raleigh NC 27695-7229 Office Phone: 919-515-5584. Business E-Mail: steve_allen@ncsu.edu.

ALLEN, THAD WILLIAM, retired military officer; b. Tucson, Jan. 16, 1949; s. Clyde and Wilma Allen; m. Pamela A. Hess, 1975; children: Amanda, Meghan, Lucas. Grad., USCG Acad., 1971; MPA, George Washington U.; MS, Sloan Sch. Mgmt., MIT. Advanced through ranks to admiral USCG, 2006, previous flag assignments include commdg. the Seventh Coast Guard Dist., previous flag assignments include directing all Coast Guard ops, in SC, Ga., Fla., and the Caribbean, dir. resources, comdr. Coast Guard Atlantic Area, Fifth Coast Guard Dist., operational comdr. US Maritime Def. Zone, Atlantic Portsmouth, Va., chief of staff Washington, 2002—06, commdg. officer Coast Guard Hdqs., 2002—06, comdt., 2006—10; chmn. Joints Requirement Coun. US Dept. Homeland Security, 2003—06, prin. fed. ofcl. Hurricanes Katrina & Rita, 2005—06, comdr. Hurricane Katrina Relief Effort, 2005—06, nat. incident comdr. Deepwater Horizon Oil Spill Response, 2010; sr. fellow RAND Corp., Arlington, Va., 2010—. Specialist for Coast Guard cutters Androscoggin, Gallatin, Citrus; coastal ops. assignments include Capt. of the Port Group Long Island Sound, Conn., Group Atlantic City, NJ, and LORAN Sta., Thailand; search and rescue controller Greater Antilles Sect., San Juan; intelligence watch officer DEA/INS El Paso Intelligence Ctr., Tex.; chief budget officer Maintenance and Logistics Command, Atlantic, Governors Island, NY; dep. project mgr. Fleet Modernization and Rehabilitation (FRAM) Project; asst. divsn. chief, programs divsn., Office Chief of Staff Coast Guard Hdqs. Recipient Alumni Achievement award, George Washington U., 2006, Strategic Vision award, Global Strategy Inst., Ctr. for Strtegic & Internat. Studies, 2006, Admiral of the Ocean Sea award (AOTOS), United Seaman's Svc., 2009, Bus. Achievement award, Betta Gamma Sigma, 2009. Fellow: Nat. Acad. Pub. Adminstrn. Office: RAND Corporation 1200 S Hayes St Arlington VA 22202-5050

ALLEN, TONY, professional basketball player; b. Chgo., Jan. 11, 1982; s. Ella Allen. Attended, Butler County CC, Eldorado, Kans., Wabash Valley Coll., Mount Carmel, Ill.; B in Edn., Okla. State U., Stillwater, 2004. Guard Boston Celtics, 2004—10, Memphis Grizzlies, 2010—. Named to NBA All-Defensive 1st Team, 2012, 2013. Achievements include being a member of the NBA Championship winning Boston Celtics, 2008. Office: Memphis Grizzlies 191 Beale St Memphis TN 38103*

ALLEN, WILLIAM HAYES, lawyer, educator; b. Palo Alto, Calif., Oct. 19, 1926; s. Ben Shannon and Victoria Rose (French) Allen; m. Joan Webster Emmett, July 16, 1950 (dec. Oct. 2005); children: Edwin Hayes, Neal French, William Kent. Student, Deep Springs Coll., 1942—44; BA with gt. distinction, Stanford U., 1948, LLB, 1956. Bar: D.C. 1958. Corr. AP, Fresno, Calif., 1948—49, newsman Sacramento, 1950—53; law clk. to Chief Justice Earl Warren U.S. Supreme Ct., Washington, 1956—57; assoc. Covington & Burling, Washington, 1957—64, ptnr., 1964—92; ret., 1993. Acting. prof. Stanford U. Law Sch., 1979; adj. prof. Howard U. Law Sch., 1981—83; lectr. George Mason U. Law Sch., 1983—86; practitioner-in-residence Cornell U. Law Sch., 1992; vis. prof. Deep Springs Coll., 1973, 1996, 2007; chmn. jud. rev. com. Adminstrv. Conf. U.S., 1972—82, sr. conf. fellow, 1982—95, 2011—; mem. steering com. Nat. Prison Project, 1975—93. Pres. Stanford Law Rev., vol. 8, 1955-56; contbr. articles to legal jours. Trustee Deep Springs Coll., 1984-92, chmn. bd. trustees, 1992; mem. Fair Housing Bd., Arlington County, Va., 1974-79. With U.S. Army, 1945-47. Mem. ABA (mem. coun. adminstrv. law sect. 1969-72, 79-81, chmn. 1982-83), D.C. Bar (chmn. legal ethics com. 1976-78), Am. Law Inst., Am. Acad. of Appellate Lawyers, Order of Coif, Cosmos Club. Democrat. Mem. United Ch. Of Christ. Office Phone: 202-662-5420. Personal E-mail: billthedog2012@gmail.com.

ALLEN, WILLIAM LEROY, consumer products company executive; V.p. logistics flow and support Lowe's Companies, Inc., 2003, v.p. logistics planning and forecasting, sr. v.p. logistics, 2011—. Office: Lowe's Companies Inc 1000 Lowe's Blvd Mooresville NC 28117

ALLENDER, JOHN ROLAND, lawyer; b. Boone, Iowa, Oct. 22, 1950; s. John S. and C. Corinne (Hayes) A.; m. Patti Allender; children: Susan A., Andrew J. BS, Iowa State U., 1972; JD, U. San Diego, 1975; LLM in Taxation, NYU, 1976. Bar: Calif. 1976, Tex. 1977, US Ct. Claims 1977, US Tax. Ct. 1977, US Dist. Ct. (so. dist.) Tex. 1977. Assoc. Fulbright & Jaworski LLP, Houston, 1976-83, ptnr., 1983—, and head, tax dept., Norton Rose Fulbright. Mem. adv. commn. Tex. Bd. Legal Specialization, 1986-2000. Bd. dirs. Ronald McDonald House, Houston, 1991—, pres. 2003-05, Cath. Charities, Houston/Galveston; trustee S.W. Rsch. Inst. Mem. State Bar of Tex. (chmn. sect. taxation 1990), Houston Bar Assn. (chmn. sect. taxation 1979). Office: Norton Rose Fulbright Ste 5100 1301 McKinney St Houston TX 77010-3031 Office Phone: 713-651-5151. Office Fax: 713-651-5246. Business E-Mail: jallender@fulbright.com.

ALLINGTON, RICHARD LLOYD, literacy studies educator; b. Grand Rapids, Mich., May 13, 1947; s. George C. and Eldona L. (Weller) A.; m. Susan Gordon, Apr. 6, 1969 (div. May 1979); children: Heidi, Tinker, Bo; m. Anne McGill-Franzen, Jan. 11, 1980; children: Maggie, Michael. BA, Western Mich. U., 1968, MS, 1969; PhD, Mich. State U., 1973. Tchr. Kent City (Mich.) Pub. Schs., 1968-69; adminstr. fed. program Belding (Mich.) Area Pub. Schs., 1969-71; grad. rsch. asst. Mich. State U., East Lansing, 1971-73; from asst. to assoc. prof. SUNY, Albany, 1973-84, prof., 1984-99, chair dept. reading, 1982-89, 94-99; Irving and Rose Fien prof. elem. and spl. edn. U. Fla., Gainesville, 1999—2004; prof. edn. U. Tenn., 2005—. Cons. Dept. Edn., Office Edn. Rsch. and Improvement, Nat. Assessment of Ednl. Progress, Office Spl. Edn. and Rehab., Nat. Faculty, numerous others; sr. rsch. scientist Nat. Ctr. Lit. Tchg., 1990-96; sr. rsch. scientist NRC on English Learning and Achievement, 1996—2000. Author: (children's books), Beginning to Learn About series, 1982; sr. author: (classroom reading series) Celebrate Reading, 1993; author: (with Patricia Cunningham) Classrooms that Work, 1993, Schools That Work, 2006; (with Sean Walmsley) No Quick Fix: Rethinking Literacy Programs in America's Elementary Schools, 1995, Big Brother and the National Reading Curriculum, 2002, What ReEally Matters for Struggling Readers, 2006; contbr. more than 100 articles to profl. jours. Rsch. grantee U.S. Dept. Edn., 1986, 88, 90, 93, 2000. Fellow Nat. Conf. Rsch. in English (bd. dirs. 1992-95), Internat. Reading Assn. (bd. dirs. 1995-98, pres. 2005-06, co-recipient with Anne McGill-Franzen the Albert Harris award 1990, named to Reading Hall of Fame 1995, pres.); mem. Nat. Reading Conf. (v.p. 1995, pres. 1996, bd. dirs. 1988-91), Am. Ednl. Rsch. Assn., N.Y. State Reading Assn. (Outstanding Reading Educator award 1992). Office: University Tenn A209 Bailey Education Complex Knoxville TN 37996 Home Phone: 865-671-6249. E-mail: rallingt@utk.edu.

ALLISON, ANNE MARIE, retired librarian; b. Oak Park, Ill., Oct. 3, 1931; d. Gerald Patrick and Anna Evelyn (Beam) Myers; m. James Dixon Alison, Aug. 28, 1954; children: Mark, Mary, Clare, Ruth, Edward. BA in French, St. Mary of the Woods Coll., 1951; postgrad., U. Fribourg, 1952-53; MLS, Rosary Coll., 1968. Asst. libr. Triton Coll., River Grove, Ill., 1967-68; asst. libr. tech. svcs. Moraine Valley Community Coll., Palos Hills, Ill., 1968-69; dir. learning resources, head libr. Coll. Lake County, Grayslake, Ill., 1969-71; asst. head catalog dept. Kent (Ohio) State U. Librs., 1971-73, head processing dept., 1973-79, asst. dir. libr. svcs., 1979-81; acting dir. Fla. Atlantic U. Libr., Boca Raton, 1980-81; asst. dir., head tech. svcs. Wayne State U. Librs., Detroit, 1981-83; dir. librs. U. Cen. Fla., Orlando, 1983-97, ret., 1997. Past chair, bd. dirs. Fla. Extension Libr., Tampa; bd. dirs. Ctr. for Libr. Automation, Gainesville, Fla., Cen. Fla. Holocaust Meml. Resource Ctr., Orlando; adj. prof. Libr. and Info. Sci., U. S. Fla., Tampa. Editor: OCLC: A National Library Network, 1979; contbr. articles to profl. jours. Arbitrator alternative dispute resolution program Better Bus. Bur. Cen. Fla., Maitland, 1985—; active Friends Winter Park Pub. Libr., Friends of Orlando Pub. Libr. Recognized for Outstanding Leadership in Edn. Cen. Fla. Ednl. Consortium for Women, 1990. Mem. ALA (chair profl. ethics com.), Fla. Libr. Assn., Fla. Assn. Coll. and Rsch. Librs. (pres. bd. dirs.). Avocations: fruit farming, collecting china. Office: U Cen Fla PO Box 25000 Orlando FL 32816-0001

ALLISON, FRED, JR., internist, retired medical educator; b. Abingdon, Va., Sept. 8, 1922; s. Fred and Elizabeth Harriet (Kelly) A.; m. Clara Knox, Oct. 14, 1949; children: Rebecca Allison Parsley, Martha Allison Brown, Fred III, Robert Gardiner. BS, Ala. Poly. Inst., 1944; MD, Vanderbilt U., 1946. Diplomate: Am. Bd. Internal Medicine. Intern Vanderbilt Hosp., Nashville, 1946-47; resident Peter Bent Brigham Hosp., Boston, 1949-50; practice medicine specializing in internal medicine, 1946—; asst. prof. medicine Washington U., St. Louis, 1955; prof. medicine, head infectious disease divsn. U. Miss., Jackson, 1955—68; vis. scientist Rockefeller U., NYC, 1966-67; Edgar Hull prof. medicine, head dept. medicine La. State U., New Orleans, 1968-87; chief medicine La. State U. div. Charity Hosp., 1968—87; prof. medicine emeritus La. State U., 1987—; prof. medicine Vanderbilt U., Nashville, 1987-96, prof. medicine emeritus, 1996—, med. cons. Zerfoss Student Health Svc., 1996-99; physician-in-chief Met. Nashville Gen. Hosp., 1987-93; chief, divsn. gen. internal medicine Vanderbilt U., 1993-96. Bd. dirs. La. State U. Health Network, 1995-01; vice chmn. bd. trustees Hosp. Authority of Metro. Nashville and Davidson County, 1999—2012. With US Army, 1943-46, 47-49. Home: 418 Fairfax Ave Nashville TN 37212-4009 Personal E-mail: allisof@comcast.net.

ALLISON, JONATHAN MACKINNON, university professor; b. Belfast, Northern Ireland, May 8, 1958; arrived in US, 1982, 1989; s. Victor James Frederick and Anne Mackinnon Allison; m. Anna Ruth Bosch, July 17, 1999; children: Victor Paul Mackinnon, Andrew Philip Mackinnon. BA with honors, The Queen's U. of Belfast, Northern Ireland, 1980, Postgrad. cert. of Edn., 1981; MA, U. Mich., Ann Arbor, 1983, PhD, 1988. Tchr. Dunmurry H.S., Northern Ireland, 1982; tchg. asst. U. Mich., Ann Arbor, 1983—85; tutor English lit. U. Coll. London, 1985—87; editl. asst. London Rev. of Books, 1987—87; asst. prof. U. Ky., Lexington, 1988—94, assoc. prof., 1994—2013, prof., 2013—. Gen. editor series U. Press Ky., 1994—2000, mem. editl. bd., 2008—; guest Ky. Ednl. TV, Lexington, 1998—2003; dir. W.B. Yeats Internat. Summer Sch., Sligo, Ireland, 2003—05; mem. nat. adv. bd. U. Ky. Librs., 2008—; chair editl. bd and press com. U. Press Kty., 2011—; mem. U. Press Kty. Senate, 2011—14. Editor: Poetry for Young People: William Butler Yeats, 2002, Yeats's Political Identities, 1996, Bound for the 1890s, 2006, Letters Louis MacNeice, 2010; contbr. articles to profl. jours. Vol. Cub Scouts America, Room in the Inn homeless shelters; vol. youth coach Lexington Youth Soccer Assn. Fellow, U. Edinburgh, 1996, 2003. Mem.: MLA (corr.), Yeats Soc. (corr.), Am. Conf. for Irish Studies (corr.). Presbyterian. Avocations: tennis, travel, golf, fishing. Office: Univ Ky Dept English 1215 Patterson Tower S Limestone Lexington KY 40506-0027 Office Fax: 859-323-1072. Business E-Mail: jalliso@uky.edu.

ALLISON, MERITA ANN, state legislator; b. Spartansburg, SC, Feb. 19, 1940; d. Raymond A. Nichols and Jessie Estell (Caldwell); m. William Ronald Allison, Feb. 14, 1959; 1 child, Katina Maria Degler. Spl. program coord. Springs Indust-Lyman Complex; bd. mem. Miss SC Scholarship Program, 1968—2008; adv. bd. Lyman First Citizens Bank; pres. SC Jaycee Auxiliary, 1968—69; mem. Dist. 5 Spartan Co. Sch. Bd., 1986—92; chmn. Gen. Assembly Women's Caucus, 1994—96, Greer J. Verne Smith Human Resource Ctr. Bd., 1996—99; founder & chmn. GOP Women's Caucus, 1999; mem. SC House of Reps., 1993—2002, mem. Dist. 36, 2008—, mem. Edn. and Pub. Works Com. & Ops. and Mgmt. Com. Republican. Baptist. Home: 209 Spartanburg Hwy Lyman SC 29365-1844 also: PO Box 93 Lyman SC 29365 Office: SC House of Reps 402C Blatt Bldg Columbia SC 29201 Office Phone: 803-212-6788, 803-737-1929. Business E-Mail: RitaAllison@schouse.org.

ALLISON, PAUL D., finance company executive; Head, equity capital markets BMO Nesbitt Burns Inc., Canada; mng. dir., co-head, Can. investment banking Merrill Lynch Can. Inc., 2001—07, exec. v.p., 2001—08; co-pres., co-CEO Raymond James Ltd., 2008—09, pres., CEO, 2009—, chmn. Vice chmn. Merrill Lynch Can., 2007—08. Bd. dirs. Investment Industry Assn. of Can.; dir., deans bus. adv. coun. and trading fl. coms. McMaster U.; vice chmn. Humber River Regional Hosp. Office: Raymond James Financial Inc 880 Carillon Pky Saint Petersburg FL 33716 Office Phone: 727-567-1000. Office Fax: 727-567-8915. Business E-Mail: paul.allison@raymondjames.ca.

ALLISON, STEPHEN, state legislator; b. Mar. 29, 1971; m. Regina Allison; children: Thomas Jackson, Nathanael Greene. BA in Hist., Va. Mil. Inst., 1993; JD, John Marshall Law Sch., 1996. Atty. Allison Firm, 2000—08; mem. Dist. 8 Ga. House of Reps., 2009—. Republican. Christian. Office: 501 Coverdell Legislative Office Bldg Atlanta GA 30334 also: 90 Blue Ridge St Blairsville GA 30512 Office Phone: 404-656-0177, 706-781-3929. Personal E-mail: stephen.allison@house.ga.gov.

ALLISON, STUART ANTHONY, chemistry professor, associate chair, researcher; b. Kalispell, Mont., Mar. 26, 1951; s. Bruce and Arretta Allison; m. Lenong Wang. BA Chemistry, U. Mont., 1973; MS Phys. Chemistry, U. Calif., Berkeley, 1975; PhD Phys. Chemistry, U. Wash., 1980. Postdoctoral fellow U. Oreg., Eugene, 1980—82, U. Houston, Houston, 1982—84; asst. prof. chemistry Ga. State U., Atlanta, 1984—90, assoc. prof. chemistry, 1990—2000, prof. chemistry, 2000—, assoc. chair chemistry, 2011—. Contbr. articles to profl. jours. Recipient Presdl. Young Investigator award, NSF, 1985. Roman Catholic. Achievements include development of numerical methods for computing transport properties of complex model systems. Avocations: hiking, coin collecting/numismatics, stamp collecting/philately. Home: 1605 Rainier Falls Dr Atlanta GA 30329 Office Phone: 404-413-5519. Business E-Mail: sallison@gsu.edu.

ALLRAN, AUSTIN M., state legislator; b. Hickory, NC, Dec. 13, 1951; s. Albert M. and Mary Houser Allran; m. Judy Mosbach, 1980; children: Elizabeth, Catherine. Atty.; state rep., Dist. 45 NC, 1981—86; state senator, Dist 26 NC, 1986—2002; state senator, Dist 44 NC, 2003—04; state senator, Dist 42 NC, 2005—. Author: (short stories) Romilar. Recipient NC Writers' Network Competition Fiction award, 1996. Mem.: NC State U. Alumni Assn., Hickory Mus Art, Duke U. Alumni Assn., Catawba County Hist Assn., Hickory Landmarks Soc, NC State Bar; SAR. Republican. Christian (Ucc) & Catholic. Office: NC Senate 300 N Salisbury St Room 625 Raleigh NC 27603-5925 Office Phone: 828-322-1410, 919-733-5876. Business E-Mail: Austin.Allran@ncleg.net.

ALLRED, JEFFREY A., communications executive; MA, PhD, JD, U. NC. Ptnr. Alston & Bird; exec. v.p. strategic devel. & corp. fin. Premiere Techs., Inc., Atlanta, pres., chief oper. officer, 1999—. Office: Premiere Techs Inc 3399 Peachtree Rd NE Atlanta GA 30326-1120

ALLYN, DAVID L., dermatologist; MD, Case Western Res. U., 1991. Diplomate Am. Bd. Dermatology, 2004. Resident dermatology Univ. Cin., Cin., 1992—95, fellow cosmetic surgery, 1995—96; hosp. affiliations include Fla. Hosp. Waterman, South Lake Hosp. Office: Aesthetic Dermatology Laser and Cosmetic Surgery Center 210 N Hwy 27 Ste 1 Clermont FL 34711 Office Phone: 352-243-2544. Office Fax: 352-243-2745.

ALMAGUER, FRANK, ambassador; m. Antoinette Gallegos, 1970; children: Francisco Daniel, Nina. BA in Polit. Sci., U. Fla., 1967; MS in Govt. and Bus. Adminstrn., George Washington U., 1974. Vol. Peace Corps, Orange Walk Town, Belize, 1967-69; mgmt. analyst Office of Auditor Gen., USAID; mgmt. analyst for health affairs Office of Econ. Opportunity; assoc. country dir. U.S. Peace Corps, Belize City, 1974-76, country dir. Tegucigalpa, Honduras, 1976-79; dep. mission dir. USAID, Panama City, 1979-83, dir. Office of S.Am. and Mex. Affairs Washington, 1983-86, mission dir. Quito, Ecuador, 1986-90; mem. Sr. Seminar Fgn. Svc. Inst., 1990-91; regional mission dir. Eastern Europe USAID, Washington, 1991-93, acting asst. adminstrn. Bur. for Europe, 1993, dep. asst. adminstr. human resources Bur. of Mgmt., 1993-96, mission dir. La Paz, Bolivia, 1996-99; amb. Republic of Honduras Dept. State, Tegucigalpa, 1999—2002; internat. cons. and lectr. on L.Am. and social and econ. devel. issues, 2003—05; sec. adminstrn., fin. Org. Am. States, Washington. U.S. del. UN Commn. on Human Rights, 2004; sr. advisor Pan Am. Devel. Found., 2004—05. Recipient Meritorious award U.S. Peace Corps, 1979, Disting. svc. award USAID, 1989, Spl. Act award, 1992, Presdl. Meritorious awards, 1988, 99, Roger W. Jones Exec. Leadership award, 1996, State Dept. Superior Honor award, 1999, Sec. of State's Career Achievement award, 2002, AID Adminstr.'s Disting. Career award, 2002. Home: 1503 Dulcimer Ct Vienna VA 22182-1607

ALMOND, CARL HERMAN, surgeon, physician, educator; b. Latour, Mo., Apr. 1, 1926; s. Hugh Herman and Sylvia (Morrison) A.; m. Nancy Ginn, June 18, 1964 (div. 1990); children: Carrie, Callie, Carl, Christopher. BS, Washington U., St. Louis, 1949, MD, 1953. Diplomate Am. Bd. Surgery, Am. Bd. Thoracic Surgery. Rotating intern Los Angeles County Gen. Hosp., 1953-54; resident surgery U. Mich., Ann Arbor, 1954-56, jr. clin. instr. surgery, 1956-57, sr. clin. instr., 1957-58; fellow surg. pathology Barnes Hosp.-Washington U., St. Louis, 1956; sr. surg. resident in urology Baylor U. Affiliated Hosps., 1958-59; resident thoracic surgery U. So. Calif., Los Angeles, 1959, fellow thoracic surgery, 1962-63; staff surgeon Univ. Hosp., Columbia, Mo., 1959-78, dir. thoracic and cardiovascular surgery, 1968-77, VA Hosp., Columbia; fellow Brompton Hosp., London, Eng., 1961; asst. prof. surgery U. Mo. Sch. Medicine, Columbia, 1959-64, asso. prof., 1964-69, prof., chief thoracic and cardiovascular surgery, from 1969; prof. and chmn. dept. surgery Sch. Medicine, U. S.C., Columbia, 1978-85, dir. gen. surgery residency program, 1979-85, assoc. dean clin. research and devel., 1986-90. Vis. prof. U. Geneva, Switzerland, 1972—73; mem. med. adv. panel FAA, 1970—75; mem. U.S. Commn. on UNESCO, 1983. Contbr. articles to profl. jours. With USNR, 1944—52. Fellow ACS; mem. AMA, Boone County Med. Soc., Columbia Med. Soc., S.C. Med. Assn., S.C. Thoracic Soc., Am. Assn. Med. Colls., Frederick H. Coller Surg. Soc., St. Louis Surg. Soc., Am. Coll. Cardiology, Am., S.C. heart assns., Am. Soc. Artificial Internal Organs, Soc. Med. Cons. to Armed Forces, Am. Coll. Chest Physicians, So. Thoracic Surg. Assn., Central Surg. Soc., Am. Assn. Thoracic Surgery, So. Surg. Assn., S.C. Surg. Soc., Chest Club, Soc. Surg. Chairmen, Marion S. DeWeese Surg. Soc., Southeastern Surg. Soc., So. Surg. Soc., Internat. Cardiovascular Soc., Soc. Thoracic Surgeons, Sigma Xi, Nu Sigma Nu, Sigma Chi. Home: 1829 Senate St 4E Columbia SC 29201

ALMOND, GILES KEVIN, financial planner; b. Albemarle, NC, June 16, 1956; s. Horace David and Helen Ruth (Hauser) A.; m. Anita Elizabeth Lanier, Oct. 21, 1978; children: Cassandra, Kevin, Alice. BS in Acctg., U. N.C., Wilmington, 1978. CPA, N.C., S.C.; CFP; PFS, CIMA. Revenue agt. IRS, Dothan, Ala., 1978—82; acct. Brittain, Almond & Simpson, P.A., Charlotte, NC, 1982—87; sr. tax mgr. Nasekos, Ryan and Co. CPAs, Charlotte, 1987—90; pres. Matrix Wealth Advisors, Charlotte, 1990—. Mem. N.C. Bd. CPA Examiners, Raleigh, 1986-89; mem. steering com. Queens Coll. Estate Planners Day, 1994-2009; chmn. ednl. needs analysis task force Internat. Bd. Standards and Practices for Cert. Fin. Planners, 1992-94. Mem. council Cen. Ch. God, Charlotte, 1986—. Named one of top fin. planners Worth Mag., 1994, 99, 2001-02, Med. Econs. Mag., 2000-13. Fellow N.C. Assn. CPA; mem. AICPA, Nat. Assn. Personal Fin. Advisors (nat. bd. mem., treas. 2011-), Fin. Planning Assn., Charlotte Estate Planning Coun., Investment Mgmt. Cons. Assn., Kingdom Advisers. Republican. Office: Ste 760 831 E Morehead St Charlotte NC 28202 Home: 1219 Presson Farm Ln Monroe NC 28110 Office Phone: 704-358-3322.

ALMOND, IAN, literature educator; b. Skipton, Eng., Sept. 21, 1969; s. Harry Almond and Margaret Crabtree. BA in English Lit. with honors, Warwick U., Eng., 1991; PhD, Edinburgh U., Scotland, 2000. English tutor Bari (Italy) U., 1990—95; asst. prof. English lit. Erciyes U., Kayseri, Turkey, 1998—2000, Bosphorus U., Istanbul, Turkey, 2000—05; assoc. prof. Ga. State U., 2008—. Author: Sufism and Deconstruction, 2004, The New Orientalists, 2007, Two Faiths, One Banner, 2008; contbr. articles to profl. jours.; author: History of Islam in German Thought, 2010. Avocation: travel. Business E-Mail: ialmond@gsu.edu.

ALMONTE, ROBERT R., US marshal; b. 1957; BS summa cum laude in Criminal Justice Adminstrn., Park U., 2002. With El Paso Tex. Police Dept., 1978—2003, capt., 2000, dep. chief Major Crimes Bur., 2000—03; owner Narcotics Training Specialists. Cons. Gen. Dynamics. Author: Covert Operations Management, 2005, Evolution of Narcotics Investigations, 2005. Recipient Award for Nat. Outstanding HIDTA Task Force Comdr., White House Office of Nat. Drug Control Policy, 1999. Mem.: Nat. Narcotic Officers Assn. Coalition (S.W. regional dir., v.p.), Tex. Narcotic Officers Assn. (pres. 1999—2000, 2001—02, 2005, exec. dir.). Office: Western District of Texas US Courthouse 655 E Durango Blvd, Rm 235 San Antonio TX 78206 Office Phone: 210-472-6540.

ALOFSIN, ANTHONY, architect, art historian, writer, educator, artist; b. Memphis, June 22, 1949; s. Frederick Benjamin and Eleanor (Brodsky) A.; m. Patricia Tierney, June 5, 1993. AB magna cum laude, Harvard U., 1971, MArch with distinction, 1981; MPhil, Columbia U., 1983, PhD, 1987. Registered arch., Tex. Assoc. chmn. divsn. hist. preservation Columbia U., NYC, 1983-84, adminstrv. dir., founder Ctr. Preservation Rsch., 1984-85, asst. prof. architecture, 1984-86; scholar-in-residence The Frank Lloyd Wright Found., 1984-85; from assoc. prof. to prof. architecture U. Tex., Austin, 1987—99, prof. art and art history, Roland Roessner Centennial prof., 1999—. Rsch. dir. A Tense Alliance: Arch. Cen. Europe, Internat. Travelling Exhbn., 1993-96; consulting curator: Frank Lloyd Wright, Arch., Mus. Modern Art, 1994; guest curator Prairie Skycraper, 2005; founder, dir. MS in archtl. studies, history and theory program and PhD program, U. Tex., Austin, 1987-97 2005-06; cons., lectr., spkr. in field. Author: A Modernist Museum in Perspective: The East Building, National Gallery of Art, 2009, Halflife, Fictive Memoir, 2009, Frank Lloyd Wright: Lost Years 1910-1922, 1993, Paperbook edit., 1998, The Struggle for Modernism: Architecture Landscape Architecture and City Planning At Harvard, 2002, Prairie Skyscraper: Frank Lloyd Wright's Price Tower, 2005, When Buildings Speak: Architecture as Language in the Habsburg Empire and Its Aftermath, 1867-1933, 2006, Paperback, 2008, German ed. Architektur beim Wortnehmen, 2011, Frank Lloyd Wright, Art Collector, 2012, Dream Home: What You Need to Know Before You Buy, 2013; editor: Frank Lloyd Wright: An Index to the Taliesin Correspondence, 1988, Frank Lloyd Wright: Europe and Beyond, 1999, Prairie Skyscraper, 2005; contbr. articles to lit. and profl. jours. Recipient Vasari award Dallas Mus. Art, 1989, 2007; Graham Found. Advanced Studies grantee, 1993 96, 97, 05; Santa Fe Workshop Contemporary Art scholar, 1971; fellow Fulbright prof. Acad. Fine Arts, Vienna, Austria, 1989-90, Internationales Forschungzentrum Kulterwissenschaften, Vienna, 1995, Ailsa Mellon Bruce Sr. fellow CASVA Nat. Gallery Art, Washington, 2003-04, MacDowell Colony, 2006, 2010; Bogliasco fellow Liguria Study Ctr. for the Arts and Humanities, 2007, Whiteley Rsch. Ctr., 2011; named Sam and Gene Johnson Disting. Visitor, Carthage Coll., 2011. Mem. AIA, Soc. Archtl. Historians, (nat. bd. dirs. 2005-08), Coll. Art Assn., Spee Club, Fulbright Assn., US Internat. Com. Monuments and Sites, Century Assn., Nat. Adv. Bd. Bogliasco Found. Office: U Tex Sch Arch 1 University Sta B7500 Austin TX 78712-0222 Home: 2207 Camino Alto Austin TX 78746-2436 Office Phone: 512-471-8156. Business E-Mail: alofsin@austin.utexas.edu. E-mail: info@alofsin.com.

ALONSO, CRISTINA, lawyer; BA with distinction, U. N.C., 1997; JD with honors, U. Fla. Coll. Law, 2000. Bar: Fla., U.S. Ct. Appeals (11th cir.), U.S. Dist. Ct., middle and so. dists., Fla. Jud. law clk. 11th Jud. Cir., Miami, 1999; cert. legal intern Office of State Atty., Ocala, Fla., 2000; staff atty. Judge Hazouri, 4th Dist. Ct., West Palm Beach, Fla., 2000—02; shareholder Carlton Fields PA, Miami, 2002—. Mentor Fla. Internat. U. Coll. Law. Author: articles in legal publs. Mentor Fla. Internat. U. Coll. Law, 2003—06; team leader Hands on Miami, 2003, 2005; team capt. American Cancer Soc. Relay for Life Key Biscayne, Fla., 2004; mem. alumni matching program U. Fla., 2009—. Recipient Leader of Yr., Omicron Delta Kappa Nat. Honor Soc. Circle, 1997, Pro Bono Svc. award, Legal Services Greater Miami, 2008; named a Rising Star, Fla. Super Lawyers, 2010, 2011, Top Up-and-Comer, South Fla. Legal Guide, 2010; named an Up-and-Comer, South Fla. Bus. Jour., 2008, 2009; named one of The Most Effective Lawyers, Miami-Dade, Broward & Palm Beach Counties, Daily Bus. Rev., Fla., 2009, Minority 40 Under 40, The Nat. Law Jour., 2011; fellow Criminal Law Tchg., U. Fla. Coun. of Ten, 1998. Fellow American Bar Found.; mem. ABA, Fla. Bar (parliamentarian 2004-05, Young Lawyers divsn. bd. govs. 11th cir. rep. 2005-11, chair diversity com. 2005-06, co-chair govtl. affairs com. 2006-07, chair continuing legal edn. com. 2007-08, chair pro bono and cmty. involvement com. 2009-10), Fla. Legal Svcs. Inc. (bd. dirs. 2004-10, pres. 2009-10), Hispanic Nat. Bar Assn. (law student divsn., regional pres. 1998-99, del. to ABA Young Lawyers divsn., 2004), Dade County Bar Assn. (appellate ct. com. 2002-06, young lawyers sect. pro bono com. 2002-11), Cuban Am. Bar Assn., Fla. Assn. Women Lawyers., Fla. Bar Found. (bd. dirs. 2009-10), Fla. Supreme Ct. Hist. Soc., Third Dist. Ct. Appeal Hist. Soc. Office: Carlton Fields PA 100 SE 2nd St Ste 4200 Miami FL 33131-2113 Office Phone: 305-539-7339. Office Fax: 305-530-0055. Business E-Mail: calonso@carltonfields.com.

ALONZO, MONICA R., councilwoman; Councilwoman Dist. 6 Dallas City Coun., 2011—, mem. Budget, Finance & Audit Com., Econ. Devel. Com., Quality of Life Com. & Trinity River Corridor Project. Chairperson Planning and Design Com.; former mem. Dallas Parks and Recreation Bd. Office: Dallas City Hall Room 5FS 1500 Marilla St Dallas TX 75201 Office Phone: 214-670-4199. Office Fax: 214-670-5117.

ALONZO, ROBERTO R., state legislator; b. Jan. 25, 1956; m. Sylvana Alonzo; children: Roberto Jr., Maria Xiomara, Jose Maria Emeterio. BA, U. Tex., Austin, 1980; JD, Tex. So. U., Houston, 1984. Paralegal Tex. Rural Aid Clinic, Oficina de la Gente Legal Aid Clinic; employee Tex. Dept. Human Resources; legis. aide Tex. State Senate; former asst. atty. gen. Office of Atty. Gen., Tex.; small bus. owner Tex.; pvt. practice atty. Tex.; mem. Dist. 104 Tex. House of Representatives, 1993—97, 2003—. Mem. State Dem. Exec. Com., Tex., 1998—; former mem. bd. dir. Dallas Area Rapid Transit. Recipient of several awards and honors. Mem.: Mex. Am. Dems. (state chmn. 1991—97). Democrat. Roman Catholic. Office: Room CAP 4N.6 Capitol PO Box 2910 Austin TX 78768 Mailing: 312 W 12th St Ste A Dallas TX 75208 Office Phone: 214-942-7104, 512-463-0408. Office Fax: 214-942-8104.

ALPERIN, STANLEY I., writer, editor, consultant; b. Boston, Jan. 3, 1931; s. Herman and Esther (Gorovitz) A.; m. Sondra Price, Sept. 8, 1957; children: Lisa Alperin Rose, Marlene Alperin Hochman, Hillary Baker. Pub., pres. U.S. Directory Service, Miami, Fla., 1966-91; pres. Unicol, Inc., Miami, 1991—. Cons. U.S. Directory Svc., Macmillan Pub., Reed Reference Pub. Author: Careers in the Health Care Field, Careers in Nursing, U.S. Medical Directory, Directory Medical Schools Worldwide, The Hospital Phone Book, The Federal Hospital Phone Book, Insurance Phone Book & Directory, Hospital Telephone Directory, University & College Phonebook, Discover America Directory; editor, researcher numerous medical directories. Home: 8821 SW 103rd St Miami FL 33176-3053 Office: UNICOL Inc PO Box 1690 655 NW 128th St Miami FL 33168-2735

ALPERT, MARTIN JEFFREY, chiropractic physician; b. NYC, Apr. 22, 1951; s. Sheldon Lee and Beatrice (Ostrager) Alpert; m. Gilberta Joachim, May 4, 2000; children: Chad, Mitchell, Eva. BA in Pre-Med. and History, Syracuse U., NY, 1972; DC in Chiropractic Medicine, NY Chiropractic Coll., 1976; MS in Biology and Nutrition, U. Bridgeport, Conn., 1979. Diplomate Am. Bd. Disability Analysts, Am. Acad. Pain Mgmt., Am. Bd. Profl. Disability Cons., Am. Acad. Experts Traumatic Stress, Am. Assn. Integrative Medicine, Coll. Pain Mgmt. Pvt. practice Chiropractic Medicine Career, Yonkers, NY, 1977—84, Hollywood, Fla., 1985, Coconut Creek, Fla., 1987—92, Miami, Fla., 1992—95, Ft. Lauderdale, Fla., 1985—2007, Orlando, Fla., 1994—2003, Palm Bay, Fla., 2008, Boca Raton, Fla., 2009—12, Boynton Beach, 2012—13, Oakland Pk., 2013—. Lt. col. Signal Corps., USA retired, 1970—2005; mil. acad. academic rep. & mil. liaison officer US Mil. Acad. West Pt., 1997—; adj. faculty DDE US Army Command and Gen. Staff Col., Ft. Leavenworth, Kans., 1998—. Mem. Palm Beach County, Florida Med. Rev. Corps. Decorated Meritorious Svc. medal with Two Oak Leaf Cluster, Army Commendation medal with Four Oak Leaf Cluster, Army Achievement medal, Nat. Def. Svc. medal, Army Res. Component Achievement medal, Armed Forces Res. medal, Army Svc. Ribbon, Humanitarian Svc. medal. Fellow: Am. Assn. Integrative Medicine (diplomate mem.), Am. Acad. Experts Traumatic Stress, Am. Back Soc., Internat. Biog. Assn.; mem.: Jewish War Vets. USA, US Army War Coll. Found., Palm Beach County, Fla. Med. Reserve Corps, US Sports Chiropractic Fedn., Fla. Chiropractic Assn., Fla. Chiropractic Soc., Am. Acad. Spine Physicians, Am. Acad. Chiropractic Physicians, Internat. Fedn. Sports Chiropractic, World Fedn. Chiropractic, Am. Pub. Health Assn., NY Acad. Scis., Am. Coll. Sports Medicine, Internat. Chiropractors Assn., Am. Chiropractic Assn., US Army Command and Gen. Staff Coll. Found., Assn. US Army, Naval War Coll. Found., Signal Corps Regimental Assn., Army Hist. Found., Res. Officers Assn. US, Mil. Officers Assn. America, Alpha Phi Omega (life), Nat. Svc. Frat. Republican. Avocations: jogging, chess, basketball, piano. Office: Hollywood Pain and Injury Medical Ctr 2121 Oakland Park Blvd Ste 4 Oakland Park FL 33311 Office Phone: 754-200-8977. Business E-Mail: doctorofchiropractic@hotmail.com.

ALPHIN, JOHN STEELE (STEELE ALPHIN), retired bank executive; b. Windsor, Va., 1951; BS in Mil. History, U. NC, Chapel Hill. With consumer bank Bank of America Corp., Chapel Hill, NC, 1977—80, compensation analyst pers. Charlotte, NC, 1980—84, regional personnel mgr. Tampa, Fla., 1984—85, pers. dir. Fla. bank, 1985—88, corp. pers. divsn. exec. Charlotte, NC, 1988—92, Atlanta, 1992—94, pers. exec. consumer & comml. bank and wealth mgmt. Charlotte, NC, 1994—99, corp. personnel exec., 1999—2006, chief adminstrv. officer, 2006—10. Bd. mem. Bank Adminstrn. Inst.; mem. bd. visitors Class of 2006 U. NC. Bd. trustees Thompson Child & Family Focus.

ALSOBROOK, DAVID ERNEST, museum director, archivist, historian; b. Eufaula, Ala., Sept. 17, 1946; s. Thomas Neville and Frances Joy (Starnes) Alsobrook; m. Ellen Meredith Lester, May 22, 1976; children: Adam, Meredith A. Hobin. BS in Edn., Auburn U., Ala., 1968; PhD in History, Auburn U., 1983; MA in History, W. Va. U., Morgantown, 1972. Tchr. Eufaula HS, 1968—69, Theodore HS,

Mobile County, 1969—72; civil archivist Ala. Dept. Archives & History, Montgomery, 1975—76; supr. archivist Jimmy Carter Libr. and Mus., Atlanta, 1981—91; dir. George Bush Presdl. Libr. and Mus., Coll. Sta., Tex., 1993—2000, William J. Clinton Presdl. Libr. & Mus., Little Rock, 2000—07, Mus. of Mobile, Ala., 2007—. Adj. prof. Dekalb CC, Clarkston, Ga., 1984—91; adv. bd. mem. Ala. Ctr. for the Book, Auburn, 2001—. Contbr. articles to profl. jour. (Milo B. Howard award, 2004). Recipient Milo B. Howard award, Ala. Hist. Assn., 2004. Mem.: Ala. Hist. Assn., Phi Alpha Theta. Avocations: gardening, renovating old houses, history. Office: Museum of Mobile 111 S Royal St PO Box 2068 Mobile AL 36602 Office Phone: 251-208-7569. Office Fax: 251-208-7686. Business E-Mail: alsobrook@cityofmobile.org.

ALSOBROOK, HENRY BERNIS, JR., lawyer; b. New Orleans, Nov. 9, 1930; s. Henry Bernis and Ethel (Smith) A.; children: Eugenie Alsobrook Burglass, John Gleason, Emily Alsobrook Kayton BA, Tulane U., 1952, JD, 1957. Bar: La. 1957. Since practiced in, New Orleans; sr. partner firm Adams & Reese. Past mem. faculty Tulane U. Law Sch.; bd. dirs. Def. Research Inst., 1978-81, 85-88, chmn. med.-legal com., 1967-72; lectr. in field. Author articles in field;: editorial bds. legal jours. Chmn. dean's coun. Tulane U., 1983-88; elder St. Charles Ave. Presbyn. Ch., New Orleans; 1st pres. Les Compagnons du Barreau de La Louisiane, 1985—; treas., bd. dirs. La. State Mus.; bd. dirs. New Orleans Symphony Soc., New Orleans Opera.; mem. La. Gov.'s Commn. on Med. Malpractice, 1989—; mem. Audubon Inst. Aquarium Capital Campaign Commn. With USNR, 1953. Fellow Am. Bar Found., Am. Coll. Trial Lawyers (state chmn.); mem. ABA (past chmn. standing com. commerce, ho. of dels. 1984-89), La. Bar Assn. (pres. 1982-83), New Orleans Bar Assn., Internat. Assn. Def. Counsel (exec. com. 1982-88, pres. 1986-87), Fedn. Ins. Counsel, New Orleans Assn. Def. Counsel (pres.), La. Assn. Def. Counsel (gov. 1965), La. Law Inst. (council 1984-89), Soc. Med. Assn. Counsel (charter), Soc. Hosp. Attys. (charter), AMA (hon.), Confrerie des Chevaliers du Tastevin (grand cellerier 1990-2001), Lakeshore Club, La. Club. Office: Adams & Reese 4500 One Shell Sq New Orleans LA 70139-4501 Office Phone: 504-585-0211. Business E-Mail: alsobrookhb@arlaw.com.

ALSTOTT, MICHAEL JOSEPH (MIKE ALSTOTT), high school football coach, retired professional football player; b. Joliet, Ill., Dec. 21, 1973; m. Nicole Alstott; children: Hannah, Lexie, Griffin. Student, Purdue U. Fullback Tampa Bay Buccaneers, 1996—2008, ret., 2008; head football coach Northside Christian HS Mustangs, St. Petersburg, Fla., 2012—. Founder Mike Alstott Family Found., 2007—. Named NFL All-Pro, 1996—99; named to Nat. Football Conf. Pro Bowl Team, NFL, 1997—2002. Achievements include member of NFL Super Bowl XXXVII championship winning Tampa Bay Buccaneers. Office: Northside Christian HS Football Program 7777 62nd Ave N Saint Petersburg FL 33709 also: Mike Alstott Family Foundation PO Box 40055 Saint Petersburg FL 33743

ALTENBURGER, KARL MARION, allergist; b. Coral Gables, Fla., Nov. 13, 1949; s. Karl and Carol Altenburger; m. Carol Bauer, May 25, 1974; children: Laura Alyson, Ashley Carolyn, Elizabeth Ann, Allison Nicole. BA in Zoology, U. South Fla., 1971, MD, 1974. Diplomate Am. Bd. Pediatrics, Am. Bd. Allergy and Immunology, Nat. Bd. Med. Examiners. Intern in pediatrics U. Colo. Med. Ctr., Denver, 1975-76, resident, 1976-78, fellow in allergy and immunology, 1978-81, Nat. Jewish Hosp. and Rsch. Ctr.-Nat. Asthma Ctr., Denver, 1978-81; pvt. practice, Ocala, Fla., 1981—2006. Instr. dept. pediatrics U. Colo. Sch. Medicine, 1980-81; pres. Fla. Med. Polit. Action Com., 1998-2001 Contbr. articles to profl. jours. Trustee Am. Lung Assn. Ctrl. Fla., 1985—93. Mem. AMA, Fla. Med. Assn. (bd. dirs. 2002-09, v.p. 2004-06, pres.-elect 2006-07, pres. 2007-08), Fla. Med. Assn. (Marion County del. 1990—), Fla. Allergy Asthma and Immunology Soc. (exec. com. 1990-96, pres. 1993-94), Marion County Med. Soc. (bd. dirs. 1983-88, pres. 1985-86, editor Bull. 1986-89), U. South Fla. Coll. Medicine Alumni Assn. (pres. 1983-87), Alpha Omega Alpha. Roman Catholic. Avocations: history, books. Personal E-mail: altenburge@aol.com.

ALTENKIRCH, ROBERT A., academic administrator; b. St. Louis; m. Beth Harsch Altenkirch; 2 children. BS in Mech. Engring., Purdue U., 1970; MS, U. Calif., Berkeley, 1971; PhD, Purdue U., 1975. Grad. instr. rsch. Sch. Mech. Engring. Purdue U., West Lafayette, Ind., 1971—75; asst. prof. mech. engring. U. Ky., Lexington, 1975—80, assoc. prof. mech. engring., 1980—85, prof. mech. engring., 1985—88, chmn. mech. engring., 1985—88; prof. mech. engring., dean Coll. Engring. Miss. State U., Mississippi State, 1988—95, v.p. for rsch., prof. mech. engring., 1998—2002; prof. mech. and materials engring., dean Coll. Engring. and Arch. Wash. State U., Pullman, 1995—98; pres. NJ Inst. Tech., Newark, 2002—11, disting. prof. mech. engring., 2002—11; pres. U. Ala., Huntsville, 2011—. Mem. NASA Microgravity Combustion Discipline Working Group, 1992; mem. com. on microgravity rsch. Space Studies Bd. NRC Commn. on Phys. Scis., Math. and Applications, 1995—99, mem. bd. assessment Nat. Inst. Stds. and Tech., 2000—04; vice-chair governing coun. Partnership for Natural Disaster Relief, 1998—2002; mem. rev., planning and implementation steering com. Govs. Commn. on Health Sci., Edn. and Tng., NJ, 2002—03; trustee Prosperity N.J., 2002; mem. Govs. Commn. on Job Growth and Econ. Devel., NJ, 2003—04, Govs. Blue Ribbon Commn. on Transp., NJ, 2003, NJ Amistad Commn., 2004—, Mayor's Blue (Newark) Ribbon Commn. on downtown core redevelopment, 2004; bd. dirs. Golden Triangle Enterprise Ctr., EPSCoR Found., R&D Coun. N.J.; chmn. Newark Downtown Core Redevel. Corp., 2006—. Recipient Ralph R. Teetor award, Soc. Automotive Engrs., 1979, Outstanding Mech. Engr. Alumnus award, Purdue U. Sch. Mech. Engring., 2001; named one of NJ Monthly 101 Most Influential People, 2009. Fellow: ASME (bd. govs. task force on electronic networking 1993—96, member-at-large coun. on edn. 1993—97, Gustus L. Larson Meml. award 1984); mem.: NSPE, Miss. Engring. Soc., Am. Soc. for Engring. Edn., Combustion Inst., Phi Kappa Phi, Sigma Xi, Tau Beta Pi, Pi Tau Sigma, Phi Eta Sigma. Office: University of Alabama Office of President 301 Sparkman Dr Huntsville AL 35899*

ALTER, NELSON TOBIAS, retail and wholesale distribution executive; b. San Antonio, July 14, 1926; s. William and Celia (Tobias) A.; m. Shirley Ann Jacobs, June 12, 1949; children: Dennis Ira, Keith Alan, Brian Reid, Wendy Ilene. BBA in Acctg., U. Tex., 1948, JD, 1950. Mgr. 9 coin-operated washeterias, 1960-67; mgr. Sta. KOGT radio, Orange, Tex., 1950-65; ptnr. Calder Properties, 1977—; mng. ptnr. Crow Road Devel. Co., Beaumont, Tex., 1976-77, Normandy Townhomes, Beaumont, 1978—, Griffing Devel. Co., Beaumont, 1978—, Griffing Realty Joint Venture, Beaumont, 1983—; comptroller Gem Jewelry Cos., Beaumont, 1950-58; pres. Gem Jewelry Co. of Beaumont, Inc., 1958—, chmn. of bd., 1991—; mng. ptnr. Gem Distbg. Co. Wholesale Jewelry, Beaumont, 1958—; gen. ptnr. Alter's Gem Jewelry, Ltd. (formerly Gem Jewelry Corp.), Beaumont. Also pres., chmn. of bd. Gem Jewelry Co. of Port Artur, Inc., 1991—, Gem Jewelry C. of Orange, Inc., 1991—, Gem. Jewelry C. of Alexandria (La.), Inc., 1991—, Gem. Jewelry C. of Rapides (La.) Inc., 1991, Gem Jewelry Distbg. Co. Inc., 1991—; U.S. rep. Tex. region Habsburg-Feldman Fine Art Auctioneers, Geneva, 1986, 87, 88, 89; real estate developer Normandy Townhomes, Griffing Devel. Co., Joint Venture, Griffing Realty Joint Venture, Partner Calder Properties. Past pres. Downtown Beaumont Unltd.; co-chmn. Beaumont Urban Renewal; drive chmn. United Jewish Appeal, Beaumont, 1954, 67; pres. Temple Emanuel, 1974-75, pres., 1981; mem. Beaumont Heritage Soc., Beaumont Music Commn., Beaumont Symphony Soc., Am. Cancer Soc.; co-founder, mem. BBB S.E. Tex.; bd. dirs. A.W. Schlesinger Geriatric Ctr., 1996-2003. Recipient Paul Harris Fellow, Rotary Internat. Found., 2002. Mem. Tex. Retail Jewelers Assn. (v.p. 1974-75), Jefferson County Bar Assn., Tex. Bar Assn. (50 Yr. Mem. award), Edna Gladney Aux., Beaumont Jewish Fedn., Buckner Benevolences, Tower Club, Masons, Masonic Lodge (50 Yr. membership award), B'nai Brith, Phi Eta Sigma, Beta Gamma Sigma, Phi Alpha Delta, Sigma Alpha Mu. Jewish. Avocations: art collecting, swimming, golf. Office: Alter's Gem Jewelry Ltd 3155 Dowlen Rd Beaumont TX 77706 Office Phone: 409-861-3005.

ALTES, ROBERT DENNIS, state legislator; b. Houston, Tex., May 12, 1948; m to Susasn; children: Bobby & Ana. BS, Ark. Tech. Univ., 1973. Founder, pres. Altes Co. & Environ. Systems, 1974; pres., CEO Resourcet Recycling Inc., 1982—2007; mem. Dist. 14 Ark. House of Reps., 1999—2002, mem. Dist. 63, 2011—; mem. Dist. 13 Ark. State Senate, 2003—11. Former justice of the peace Sebastian County Quorum Ct. Deacon First Bapt. Ch., Ft. Smith, Ark. Served US Army, 1969—71, Korea. Recipient Defender of the Constn. award, NRA, 2003, Support & Leadership award, Profl. Towing Assn., 2005, Senator of Yr. award, Ark. Realtors Assn., 2005, Disting. Legislator award, Ark. Mcpl. League, 2009, Reagan award, Rep. Party Ark. Mem.: Disabled American Vets., American Legion. Republican. Baptist. Mailing: Dist Address 8600 Moody Rd Fort Smith AR 72903 Office Phone: 479-646-8981. E-mail: aaltes@aol.com.

ALTMAN, DONALD, pediatric radiologist, educator; MD, U. Tenn., 1950. Diplomate Am. Bd. of Radiology-diagnostic radiology, 1959, Am. Bd. of Radiology-pediatric radiology, 1995. Resident diagnostic radiology Jackson Meml. Hosp., Miami, Fla., 1951—54; clin. prof. diagnostic radiology Sch. of Medicine Univ. of Miami; hospital affiliations include Miami Children's Hosp. Office: Altman Litt & Greenberg 8356 SW 40th St Apt K Miami FL 33155-3356 Office Phone: 305-223-2825.

ALTMAN, ROBERT, lawyer; b. St. Paul, Feb. 21, 1949; s. Milton and Helen (Horwitz) A.; children by previous marriage: Jesse, David, Aaron. BA, U. Calif., Berkeley, 1970; JD, U. Minn., 1973. Bar: Minn. 2012, Ga. 1978, U.S. Ct. Appeals (5th cir.) 1978, U.S. Ct. Appeals (11th cir.) 1981, U.S. Supreme Ct. 1981. Atty. Team Def. Project, Atlanta, 1976-77; assoc. dir. So. Prisoners Def. Com., New Orleans, 1978-79; exec. dir. Fed. Defender Program, Inc., 1980-84; pvt. practice Atlanta, 1984—; judge Mcpl. Ct. City of Atlanta, 1988-96. Pres. Fed. Defender Program, Inc., 1990-91; instr. Nat. Inst. Trial Advocacy, Emory U., Atlanta, 1983-2000; com. to rev. the criminal justice act U.S. Jud. Conf., 1991-93. Contbr. articles to profl. jours. Co-founder Grounded for good, Centering Youth Yoga and Mindfulness at-risk Youth, 2012—; CEO Centering Youth, Inc., 2013—; bd. dirs. votehealthcare.org, 2007—, Yoga Svc. Coun., 2014—. Mem. ATLA, Ga. Bar Assn., Ga. Trial Lawyers Assn. (chair bad faith ins. litigation group, mem. exec. com. 1999-2004), Ga. Gov.'s Office Children and Families (com. sexual exploitation children prosecution workgroup mem., 2011-), Phi Beta Kappa. Office: PO Box 8238 Atlanta GA 31106 Office Phone: 404-892-8766. Personal E-mail: altlaw@gmail.com.

ALTMAN, THAD, state legislator; b. Macon, Ga., Sept. 8, 1955; m. Mary Pat Altman; children: Hunter, McKenzie, Sullivan. AA, Brevard CC, Cocoa, Fla., 1975; attended, U. Houston, 1975—77; BS, Rollins Coll., 1987. Contractor, cons.; mem. Dist. 30 Fla. House of Reps., Tallahassee, 2003—08; mem. Dist. 24 Fla. State Senate, Tallahassee, 2008—, chair fin. and tax com., mem. policy & steering com. on energy, environment & land use, policy & steering com. on ways & means, cmty. affairs com., health regulation com., mem. transp. com., joint com. on pub. counsel oversight, joint legis. sunset com. Chmn. Brevard County Commn., 1985, 1986, 1992, Brevard Tourist Devel. Coun., 1986, Brevard Met. Planning Coun., 1986, East Ctrl. Fla. Regional Planning Coun., 1992. Republican. Christian. Office: District Office 7025 N Wickham Rd Ste 108 Melbourne FL 32940-7503 also: 324 Senate Office Bldg 404 S Monroe St Tallahassee FL 32399-1100 Office Phone: 321-752-3138, 850-487-5053. Business E-Mail: altman.thad.web@flsenate.gov.

ALTOMARE, JEFFREY, pediatrician; Grad., SUNY, Binghamton, 1978—82; MD, NY Med. Coll., Valhalla, 1986—89. Lic. Fla., diplomate American Bd. Pediatrics, 2004. Resident in pediat. Shands at Univ. Fla., Gainesville, 1986—89; physician Wolfson Children's Hosp. (Bapt. Med. Ctr.), Bapt. Primary Care. Office: Baptist Primary Care 9090 Regency Sq Blvd N Jacksonville FL 32211 Office Phone: 904-724-5576. Office Fax: 904-724-0721.*

ALTONAGA, CECILIA M., federal judge; b. Balt., 1962; BA, Fla. Internat. U., 1983; JD, Yale U., 1986. Atty. Miami-Dade County Atty.'s Office, Fla., 1986—87, asst. county atty., 1988—96; law clk. to Hon. Edward B. Davis US Dist. Ct. (so. dist.) Fla., 1987—88, judge Miami, 2003—; county ct. judge 11th Jud. Cir. Ct. Fla., 1996—99, cir. ct. judge, 1999—2003. Office: US Dist Ct US Courthouse 400 N Miami Ave Rm 12-2 Miami FL 33128 Office Phone: 305-523-5510.

ALTSHULER, KENNETH Z., psychiatrist, educator; b. Paterson, NJ, Apr. 11, 1929; s. Jacob and Altie (Freedman) A.; m. Gloria Seigel, June 14, 1952 (div. 1981); children: Steven, Lori, Dara; m. Ruth Collins Sharp, Dec. 5, 1987. BA, Cornell U., 1948; MD, U. Buffalo, 1952; DSc (hon.), Gallaudet Coll., 1972. Intern Kings County Hosp., Bklyn., 1952-53; resident NY State Psychiat. Inst., NYC, 1955-58; asst. in psychiatry Columbia U., 1958-59, instr., 1959-63, rsch. assoc., 1963-67, asst. clin. prof., 1967-71, assoc. clin. prof., 1971-75, prof., 1975-77; tng. analyst Columbia U. Psychoanalytic Clinic for Tng. and Rsch., 1969-77; project dir. Essential Aspects of Deafness, 1972-76, Trauma and Sleep Physiology, 1975-77; Stanton Sharp prof., chmn. psychiatry U. Tex.-Southwestern Med. Sch., Dallas, 1977-2000, Stanton Sharp prof. psychiatry, 2000—; tng. analyst New Orleans Psychoanalytic Inst., 1979-86, Dallas Psychoanalytic Inst., 1986—. Chief of deafness unit Rockland State Hosp., Orangeburg, NY, 1966-77; cons. to NIH; dir. Am. Bd. Psychiatry and Neurology, 1990-97, pres., 1996; mem. Nat. Bd. Med. Examiners, 1986-89, chmn. Part II psychiatry com., 1988-89; mem. Am. Assn. Chmn. Depts. Psychiatry, 1977-2000, pres. 1990-91. Co-author: Managing Sleep Complaints, 1982; co-editor: Family and Mental Health Problems in a Deaf Population, 1963, Comprehensive Mental Health Svc. for the Deaf, 1966, Psychiatry and the Deaf, 1968, Expanded Mental Health Care for the Deaf, 1970, Depression: Mechanisms, Diagnosis and Treatment, 1986; others.; Contbr. articles to profl. jour. Mem. governing bd. Tex. Sch. for the Deaf, 1986-90; bd. dir. Tex. Dept. Mental Health and Mental Retardation, 1999-2004, Shelter Ministries of Dallas, 2001-; bd. trustees, Callier Ctr. for Comm. Disorders 2005-; Phoenix Houses of Tex., board of advisors, 2001-; Gilda's Club of North Tex., adv. bd., 2001-. Recipient Wilson award in genetics and preventive medicine, 1961, Disting. Cmty. Svc. award Dallas County Mental Health Assn., 1986, Prism award, 1992, Disting. Alumnus award SUNY, Buffalo, 1993, 1st Trailblazer award named in his honor, Dallas County Mental Health and Retardation Ctr., 1996, Tex. Star award for Outstanding Cmty. Svc. Tex. Mental Health Assn., 1997; named Outstanding Psychiatrist, Tex. Soc. Psychiat. Physicians, 1996, Outstanding Alumnus of the 1960s Decade Columbia U., 1996; Kenneth Z. Altshuler Clinic named in honor by Dallas County Mental Health & Mental Retardation Ctr., 1997, Medical Leadership award Turtle Creek Manor, 2003; Cert. of Achievement Bd. of Hosp. Psychiatry, Cert. of Significant Achievement for Deafness Program, NY State, 1976, Cert. of Significant Achievement for Mental Health Connections Program, 1995. Fellow Am. Psychiat. Assn., Am. Coll. Psychiatrists, Am. Coll. Psychoanalysts; mem. AMA, Am. Psychoanalytic Assn., Assn. for Psychoanalytic Medicine (Merit award 1965), Tex. Med. Soc., Dallas County Med. Soc., Am. Psychopathol. Assn., Assn. Dir. Med. Student Edn. in Psychiatry (founder, v.p. 1976-77), So. Assn. Rsch. Psychiatry (pres. 1993-94). Office Phone: 214-648-5588. Business E-Mail: kenneth.altshuler@utsouthwestern.edu.

ALUGUBELLI, VENKAT R., family medicine physician; Diplomate Am. Bd. Family Practice, 1989, Am. Bd. Family Practice-geriatric medicine, 1996. Resident family medicine Detroit Med. Ctr., Detroit, 1986—89; hosp. affiliations include Seven Rivers Regional Med. Ctr., Citrus Memorial Hosp. Office: Beverly Hills Medical Center 3745 N Lecanto Hwy Beverly Hills FL 34465

ALVARADO, CAROL, state legislator; b. Houston, Oct. 26, 1967; d. Frank Sr. and Ida Alvarado BA, U. Houston, 1992, MBA, 2008. Project coord. S.W. Voter Registration Edn. Project, Houston, 1998; clerk Harris County Constables, Houston, 1989-92; legis. asst. to Congressman Gene Green US House of Representatives, Washington, 1993-94; exec. dir. Magnolia Comml. Revitalization Project, 1994-97; sr. exec. asst. to Mayor Lee P. Brown City of Houston, councilwomen, Dist. I, 2002—07; mem., Dist. 145 Tex. House of Representatives, 2008—. Mem. steering com. Al Gore Presdl. Campaign, Houston; mem.-at-large Dem. Nat. Com. Washington, 1998—; mem. exec. com. Texas Dem. Party, 1998—; mentor Latinas on the Rise, 1998—; mem. adv. bd. Hispanic Women in Leadership, 1999—; bd. dirs. Planned Parenthood Action Fund, Houston, 1997—, Habitat for Humanity, Houston, 1998—. Recipient Humanitarian award Harris County Dem. Party, 1997, Adv. Yr. award Houston Hispanic C. of C. Mem. Am. Leadership Forum (Class XVIII). Roman Catholic. Office: 2900 Woodridge Dr Ste 305 Houston TX 77087 also: Room EXT E2.810 Capitol Extension PO Box 2910 Austin TX 78768 Office Phone: 713-649-6563, 512-463-0732. Office Fax: 713-649-6454, 512-463-4781.

ALVARADO, JOSEPH, metal products executive; BA in Economics, U. Notre Dame, 1974; MBA, Cornell U., 1976. Various leadership positions, exec. v.p. Birmingham Steel Corp.; pres. Inland Steel Bar Co.; dir., mktg., long products ArcelorMittal; various leadership positions, dir., mktg. Ispat Internat. N.V (acquired by Arcelor Mittal); various positions, fin., sales and operating positions Inland Steel; pres., Tubular Products Divsn. US Steel Corp.; pres., COO Lone Star Technologies (acquired by US Steel), 2004; v.p., Tubular Ops. US Steel Corp., 2007—09; operating ptnr. Wingate Partners; joined Inland Steel, 1976, pres., Long Product Divsn., 1997; exec. v.p., COO Commercial Metals Co., 2010—11, pres., COO, 2011, pres., CEO, 2011—. Office: Commercial Metals Co 6565 N MacArthur Blvd Ste 800 Irving TX 75039 Office Phone: 214-689-4300. Office Fax: 214-689-5886. Business E-Mail: joseph.alvarado@cmc.com.

ALVAREZ, CESAR L., lawyer; b. Havana, Cuba, June 17, 1947; arrived in US, 1960; m. Kathleen Alvarez; children: Elizabeth, Christopher, Kathryn, Colleen. AA, Miami-Dade CC; BS, U. Fla., 1969, MBA, 1970, JD with high honors, 1972. Bar: Fla. 1973. Joined Greenberg Traurig LLP (formerly Greenberg Traurig Hoffman Lipoff Rosen & Quentel), Miami, 1973, pres., CEO, 1997—2007, CEO, 2007—10, exec. chmn., 2010—; exec. v.p. Air Fla., 1981—82. Mem. U. Fla. Legal Aid and Defender Clinic, 1971-72. Editor U. Fla. Law Rev., 1972. Participant Guardian Ad Litem Program, Miami; trustee Vizcaya Found., Our Kids Inc., Nat. Found. for Advancement in the Arts, Miami Art Mus., Manhattanville Coll., NY, Fla. Internat. U. Found., John S. and James L. Knight Found., 2000—, Miami-Dade Coll., U. Fla. Levin Coll. Law; mem. exec. com. New World Symphony; bd. dirs. Holocaust Documentation and Edn. Ctr. Inc.; chair adv. bd. Fla. Internat U. Law Sch.; chmn. bd. dirs. United Way of Miami-Dade, 2003—04. Recipient Humanitarian of Yr. award, Women's Internat. Zionist Orgn., 1997, Atty. of Yr. award, Hispanic Nat. Bar Assn., 2001, Golden Castanets award, Ballet Hispanico, 2002, Silver Medallion for Svc. to Humanity award, Nat. Conf. for Cmty. and Justice, 2003, New Am. award, Archdiocese of Miami, Inc., 2003, Diversity Works! Advocate-Individual award, So. Fla. Bus. Jour., 2004, FIU Medallion, Fla. Internat. U., 2005, CEO of Yr. award, MultiCultural Law Mag., 2006; named a Top Mng. Ptnr., Fla. Trend. Mag., 2005, 2006; named one of 100 Most Influential Hispanics, Hispanic Bus., 1996, 1998, 100 Most Influential Lawyers in Am., Nat. Law Jour., 1997, 2000, 2006, 50 Most Influential Minority Lawyers in America, 2008, 100 Most Powerful People in Miami, Miami Bus. Mag., 2001, 100 Most Powerful People in So. Fla., So. Fla. CEO Mag., 2002, 50 Most Powerful People in So. Fla., Poder Mag., 2003, 2004, 100 Most Powerful Latinos, 2003, 2004, 2004 Legal Elite, Fla. Trend Mag., 2005 Legal Elite, Top Lawyers in So. Fla., So. Fla. Legal Guide, 2004; named to Miami-Dade CC Hall of Fame, 2003. Mem.: Miami Bus. Forum, Fla. Coun. of 100, Dade County Bar Assn., Fla. Bar, Cuban-Am. Bar Assn. (Pro-Bono Award), ABA, Cuba Study Group, Order of Coif. Office: Greenberg Traurig LLP 333 SE 2nd Ave Ste 4400 Miami FL 33131-2184

ALVAREZ, MICAELA, federal judge; b. Donna, Tex., 1958; BS, U. Tex., 1980, JD, 1989. Pvt. practice atty., McAllen, Tex., 1989—95, 1997—2004; presiding judge 139th Jud. Dist. Ct., Tex., 1995—96; judge US Dist. Ct. (so. dist.) Tex., Laredo, 2004. Office: US Dist Ct US Courthouse 1300 Victoria St Laredo TX 78040 Office Phone: 956-726-2242.

ALVAREZ-ELCORO, SALVADOR, internist, infectious disease; MD, Nat. Autonomous Univ. of Mexico, 1972. Lic. Fla., 1991, diplomate Am. Bd. Internal Medicine, 1977, Am. Bd. Internal Medicine-infectious disease. Intern Tulane Univ. Charity Meml. Hosp.; resident internal medicine Charity Hosp., New Orleans, 1974—77; fellow infectious disease Boston City Hosp., 1977—79; prof. of medicine Univ. of Fla. Coll. of Medicine; physician Mayo Clinic. Co-author: (publs.) Disseminated Bartonella infection following liver transplantation, 2006, Effect of antiviral chemoprophylaxis on adverse clinical outcomes associated with cytomegalovirus after liver transplantation, 2006, Case of Staphylococcus schleiferi subspecies coagulans endocarditis and metastatic infection in an immune compromised host, 2007, Proximal tubular dysfunction associated with tenofovir and didanosine causing Fanconi syndrome and diabetes insipidus, 2009, Left-Sided Pseudomonas aeruginosa Endocarditis in Patients Without Injection Drug Use, 2011, variouse publs. including Visual recovery following Mycobacterium chelonae endophthalmitis, Peritonitis after liver transplantation and Risk stratification and targeted antifungal prophylaxis for prevention of aspergillosis and other invasive mold infections after liver transplantation. Office: Mayo Clinic Division Infectious Disease 4500 San Pablo Rd Jacksonville FL 32224 Office Phone: 904-953-2272. Office Fax: 904-953-2419.

AMACHER, RICHARD EARL, retired literature educator; b. Ridgway, Pa., Dec. 13, 1917; s. Albert and Emma (Luchs) Amacher; m. Cordelia Anne Ward, Aug. 26, 1953; 1 child, Alice Marie. AB, Ohio U., 1939; postgrad., U. Chgo., 1939-42; PhD, U. Pitts., 1947. Instr. English Yale U., New Haven, 1944-45; instr. Rutgers U., New Brunswick, NJ, 1945-47, asst. prof., 1947-53, lectr., 1953-54; chmn. English dept. Henderson State Tchrs. Coll., Arkadelphia, Ark., 1954-57; assoc. prof. Auburn (Ala.) U., 1957-65, prof., 1965-78, Hargis prof. Am. Lit., 1978-84, prof. emeritus, 1984—. Fulbright prof., Würzburg, Germany, 1961—62, Konstanz, Germany, 1969—70. Author: Franklin's Wit and Folly, 1953, Practical Criticism, 1956, Benjamin Franklin, 1962, Edward Albee, 1969, in Spanish, 1972, rev. edit., 1982, American Political Writers, 1588-1800, 1979; author: (with Margaret Rule) Edward Albee at Home and Abroad, 1973; co-editor (with Victor Lange): New Perspectives in German Literary Criticism, 1979; co-editor: (with G. Polhermus) J. G. Baldwin's The Flush Times of California, 1966. Chmn. Auburn Chamber Music Soc., 1980—82, 1985—86, 1988—89; elder Presbyn. Ch. Am. Coun. Learned Socs. grantee, 1972. Mem.: Nat. Soc. Lit. and Arts, Société Historique d'Auteuil et de Passy, Am. Studies Assn. (pres. southeastern sec. 1977—79). Democrat. Home: 515 Auburn Dr Auburn AL 36830-5547 Home Phone: 334-821-8390.

AMADIO, JULIA M., packaging and container manufacturing executive; BS in Acctg., St. Joseph's U., Philadelphia, Pa.; MBA, Drexel U. Mktg. and mgmt. positions Aventis Pharmaceuticals; v.p., mktg., sales and mktg. svcs. Daiichi Pharmaceuticals Inc.; pres. Julia Amadio Consulting LLC; mktg. and mgmt. positions McNeil Pharm., Parexel MMS, Wyeth Pharmaceuticals; v.p., Global Mktg., Healthcare MeadWestvaco Corp., 2009—. Global dir. Healthcare Businesswomen's Assn. (HBA). Office: MeadWestvaco Corp 501 S 5th St Richmond VA 23219 Office Phone: 804-444-1000. Business E-Mail: jamadio@meadwestvaco.com.

AMADOR, JOSE MANUEL, plant pathologist; b. Calimete, Matanzas, Cuba, Mar. 3, 1938; came to U.S., 1957; s. Luis Felipe and Blanca Rosa (Muñiz) A.; m. Silvia G. Garcia, Nov. 25, 1965; children: Silvia G. Amador Bibb, Marian L., Daniel J. BS in Agronomy and Soil Chemistry, La. State U., 1960, MS in Botany, Plant Pathology and Breeding, 1962, PhD in Plant Pathology and Biochemistry, 1965. Rsch. asst. in plant pathology La. State U., Baton Rouge, 1960-65; extension plant pathologist Tex. A&M U. Extension, Weslaco, 1965-91, dir. agrl. rsch. and extension ctr., 1991—. Mem. extension futures task force Tex. A&M U. Extension, 1988, internat. task force agrl. complex, 1989; cons. Rio Grande Sugar Growers, Inc., Santa Rosa, Tex., Big-B Ranch, Belle Glade, Fla., US/AID/U. Fla.-El Salvador, Internat. Planning Svcs., Inc., US/AID Mission, Panama, Citrus Devel. Corp., Chiquita Brands Internat., XAFRA, Inc., Veracruz, Mex. Contbr. articles to profl. and sci. publs. Recipient Svc. to Agriculture award Hidalgo Farm Bur., 1993. Fellow Am. Phytopathological Soc. (long standing, adv. bd. office internat. programs 1989, rep. to Internat. Soc. Plant Pathology 1989, immediate past chmn. tropical plant pathology com. 1989, past chmn. internat. cooperation com. 1980-90, mem. coun., past mem. extension com., counselor Carribean divsn. 1980-89, Excellence in Extension award 1990, F.L. Wellman award 2000); mem. Tex. Vegetable Assn. (bd. dirs.), Tex. Assn. Plant Pathologists and Nematologists, Lower Rio Grande Valley Hort. Soc. (past treas.), Gamma Sigma Delta, Epsilon Sigma Phi. Roman Catholic. Home: 100 Cardinal Ave Mcallen TX 78504-2217 Office: Agricultural Rsch & Extension Ctr 2415 E Us Highway 83 Weslaco TX 78596-8344 E-mail: j-amador@tamu.edu.

AMATO CHIARAMONTE BORDONARO, BARON CARLO CAMILLO, ambassador, consultant; s. Giuseppe Michele Amato and Fernanda Giannini Paolini; m. Lorraine Manville-Dresselhouse, Feb. 22, 1959 (dec. June 1998); m. Irela Fabiola Lopez Fonseca, Nov. 16, 2003. Diploma Archaeology, Mex. U., U. Barcelona, Spain. Appraiser Assn. of Am., N.Y., 1978. Pres., founder Old World Internat., Canada, 1968—; asst. prof. biology Ga. State U., Athens, 1971—81; amb. Sovereign Mil. Order of Malta, Saint Vincent and the Grenadines, 1983—; pres., founder Old World Galleries, NYC, 1977—84; editor-at-large Conde.Nast Publs., Milan and Paris, 1984—91; dir. fgn. rels. Gesfid, Lugano, Switzerland, 1984—98, fin. mgr., 1984—94; mng. dir. Canouan Resort Devel. Co. Ltd, Saint Vincent and the Grenadines, 1994—98; min. plenipotentiary at large Republic of San Marino, 1983—2000. Author: (book) The Wild Boar: History Husbandry The Hunt; editor: (mag.) Artequia Internat., Harper-Bazaar. Recipient Cert. of Appreciation, City of N.Y., 1977, Order of the Trinity, Imperial Ho. of Ethiopia, 1997, Knight of Real Cuerpo de la Nobleza de Madrid, Nobility of Castilla, 1998, Knight Comdr. of St. Maurice and Lazarus, The Savoy Order, 1999, Knight of Grace and Devotion of the Sacred Mil. Order of Malta, 2000; named Man of Yr., World Inst. for Sci. Humanism, Fordham U., 1982. Fellow: Explorer Club; mem.: Knickerbocker Club. Roman Catholic. Avocations: cooking, gardening.

AMBROSE, CHARLES STUART, sales executive; b. Jacksonville, NC, Nov. 28, 1951; s. Samuel Sheridan and Elizabeth (Stansbury) Ambrose. BBA, Emory U., 1974. Asst. mgr. Fifth Quarter Restaurant Shoney's, Birmingham, Ala., 1975; asst. chemist Mackay Paint Co., Birmingham, 1975-76; salesman, sales mgr. Francis & Lusky Co., Nashville, 1976-85; pres. SST Sales Co., Inc., Nashville, 1982—2011. Republican. Presbyterian. Office Phone: 615-447-5658. Business E-Mail: sstsalesco@aol.com.

AMBROZE, WAYNE L., JR., colon and rectal surgeon; Grad. magna cum laude, Baylor U., Waco; MD, Northwestern U., 1983. Diplomate Am. Bd. Surgery, 1999, Am. Bd. Colon and Rectal Surgery, 2003. Resident in gen. surgery NY Presbyn. Hosp./Columbia Univ. Med. Ctr., 1983—88; fellow in colon and rectal surgery Mayo Clinic, Rochester, Minn., 1988—90; hosp. affiliations include Northside Hosp., St. Joseph Hosp.; pvt. practice Ga. Colon and Rectal Surgical Assocs. Author: (articles) The Effect of Stool Consistency on Rectal and Neorectal Emptying, 1991, Let Sleeping Dogs Lie: Role of the Omentum in the Ileal Pouch-Anal Anastomosis Procedure, 1991, Fecal Short-Chain Fatty Acid Concentrations and Effect on Ileal Pouch Function, 1993, Early Results of Laparoscopic Surgery for Colorectal Cancer, 1996, Harmonic Scalpel ® vs. Electrocautery Hemorrhoidectomy: A Prospective Evaluation, 2001, Harmonic Scalpel Hemorrhoidectomy, 2002, Laparoscopic-Assisted Bowel Resection in Pediatric/Adolescent Inflammatory Bowel Disease, 2003, Laparoscopic repair of small bowel and colon A report of 26 cases, 1993. Fellow: Am. Soc. of Colon and Rectal Surgeons, ACS; mem.: AMA, DeKalb Med. Soc., Med. Assn. of Atlanta, Southern Surgical Soc., Southern Surgical Assn., Southeastern Surgical Congress, Soc. of Am. Gastrointestinal Endoscopic Surgeons, Med. Assn. of Ga., Am. Bd. Surgery, Am. Bd. Colon and Rectal Surgeons, Alpha Omega Alpha. Office: Georgia Colon and Rectal Surgical Associates 5445 Meridian Marks Rd Ste 180 Atlanta GA 30342-4755 Office Phone: 770-277-4277.

AMDUR, ARTHUR R., lawyer; b. Houston, Jan. 19, 1946; s. Paul S. and Florence Amdur; m. Dora B. Amdur; children: Josh, Jonny. BA, 1967, JD, 1970, LLM, 1974. Bar: Tex. 1970, D.C. 1974, cert.: Tex. Bd. Legal Specialization (in immigation law) 1988. Pvt. practice, Houston, 1970—76, Washington, 1970—76; asst. U.S. atty. Houston, 1976—82; pvt. practice, 1982—. Adj. prof. law S. Tex. Coll. Law, Houston; lectr. on immigration law. Spl. asst. to gen. counsel Republican Nat. Com., Washington, 1974; bd. dirs. YMCA Internat. Refugee Ctr., 1985—. Named Adj. Prof. Yr., S. Tex. Coll. Law, 1983. Mem.: Immigration Law Examiner (bd. legal specialization 1997—2001), Am. Immigration Lawyers Assn., Tex. State Bar Assn., Fed. Bar Assn., Georgetown U. Alumni (pres., Houston chpt. 1984). Jewish. Office: Amdur Law Office 5909 West Loop S Ste 300 Bellaire TX 77401-2407 Office Phone: 713-268-1000. Business E-Mail: visas@amdurlaw.com.

AMEDEE, JODY, state legislator; b. 1967; m. Jancy Berthelot; 2 children. Former asst. dist. atty.; former atty. Ascension Parish Tourist Comn; mem. Dist. 18 La. State Senate, 2004—, chair environ. quality com., mem. natural resources com., senate and govtl. affairs com. Mem.: ABA, East Ascension Sportsman League, 4-H, Ducks Unlimited, Nat. Assn. Counsel Children, Nat. District Attys. Assn., 23rd Judicial Dist. Bar Assn., La. State Bar Assn., Nat. Wildlife Turkey Fedn., Gonzales Dixie Boys Baseball (pres.). Democrat. Address: 2109 S Burnside Gonzales LA 70737 Office: PO Box 94183 Baton Rouge LA 70804 Office Phone: 225-342-2040, 225-644-1526. Business E-Mail: amedeej@legis.state.la.us.

AMEDEE, RONALD G., otolaryngologist, educator; MD, Louisiana State U. Sch. of Medicine, New Orleans, 1981. Diplomate Am. Bd. Otolaryngology, 1987. Resident Louisiana State Univ. Sch. of Medicine, New Orleans, 1986; fellow otology neurotology and skull base surgery Albert Ludwigs Univ., Freiburg, Germany, 1987; with dept. of otolaryngology - head and neck surgery Tulane Univ. Sch. of Medicine, 1988—, clin. prof. dept. of neurosurgery; Harold G. Tabb prof. and chair Tulane Otolaryngology Head Neck Surgery; assoc. dean grad. med. edn.; chief-of-staff Tulane Univ. Hosp. and Clinic, 2000—02. Recipient Disting. Svc. award, Am. Acad. of Otolaryngology-Head and Neck Surgery, Honor award, Physicians Recognition award, AMA, Disting. Clin. Tchg. award, Alpha Omega Alpha, Attending of the Yr. in Outpatient Surgery, Tulane Owl Club; named one of the Best Doctors in America, 1998, 1999, 2001—04. Office: Tulane University School of Medicine 1430 Tulane Ave New Orleans LA 70112 Office Phone: 504-988-5187.

AMERSON, AMOS, state legislator; b. Washing County, Ga., Jan. 30, 1935; m to Anne; children: Steven, Erin. BS, No. Ga. Coll., 1956, US Naval Postgraduate Sch., 1964; MBA, Univ. Hawaii, 1972; PhD in Econ. & statistics, Am. Univ., London, 1993. Served to Lt. Col., with svc. in Vietnam US Army, 1956—78, mem. Joint Chiefs' Strategic Targeting Staff; mgmt. positions US Dept. Energy, 1978—79; assoc. prof. No. Ga. Coll. & State Univ., 1982—98; city councilman Dahlonega City Coun., 1999—2000; mem. Dist. 9 Ga. House Reps., 2001—. Republican. Methodist. Office: 689 N Chestatee St Dahlonega GA 30355 Business E-Mail: amos.amerson@house.ga.gov.

AMES, RICHARD D., cruise line company executive; B in Acctg., U. Mass., 1975; MBA, George Mason U., 1983. CPA. Mgmt. cons. Internat. Intelligence, Inc. Resorts Internat., Inc., dir. internal audit Miami; sr. v.p. shared svcs., bd. dirs. Awte Uk Ltd.; dir. internal audit Carnival Corp., 1989, v.p. audit svcs., 2002, sr. v.p. audit svcs., 2002—06; sr. v.p. shared svcs. Carnival Corp. & plc, 2006—. Bd. dirs. Bloggingstocks. Office: Carnival Corp 3655 NW 87th Ave Miami FL 33178-2428 Office Phone: 305-599-2600. Office Fax: 305-406-4700. Business E-Mail: rames@carnival.com.

AMES, STEPHEN MICHAEL, professional golfer; b. San Fernando, Trinidad and Tobego, Apr. 28, 1964; m. Jodi Ames. Profl. golfer PGA Tour, 1987—. Mem. Trinidad and Tobago team WGC World Cup, 2000, 2002, 2003, 2006. Achievements include winning the Trinidad and Tobago Open, 1989, Ben Hogan Pensacola Open, 1991, Open V33, 1994, Benson and Hedges Internat. Open, 1996, Cialis Western Open, 2004, Can. Skins Game, 2005, The Players Championship at Sawgrass, 2006 (tied largest margin of victory at event), Skins Game, 2006; Children's Miracle-Disney, 2007.

AMICK, WILLIAM WALKER, golf course architect; b. Scipio, Ind., June 16, 1932; s. George Ellsworth Sr. and Myrtle (Walker) A.; m. Sara Dell Rogers, Apr. 6, 1957; 1 child, David Walker. BA, Ohio Wesleyan U., 1954. Golf course archtl. asst. William H. Diddel, GCA, Carmel, Ind., 1954-55, Charles Adams, GCA, Atlanta, 1957-58; golf course architect Daytona Beach, Fla., 1959—. Capt. USAF, 1955-57. Recipient Disting. Svc. award, ASGCA, 2011. Fellow Am. Soc. Golf Course Architects; mem. Am. Soc. of Golf Course Architects (treas., v.p., pres. 1975-77). Avocation: low handicap golf. Office: PO Box 1984 Daytona Beach FL 32115-1984 Office Phone: 386-767-1449. E-mail: amick@iag.net.

AMIDON, ROGER LYMAN, public health service officer, educator; b. Burlington, Vt., Apr. 8, 1938; s. Ellsworth L. and Mae (Liddle) A.; m. JoAnn Reiland, Aug. 1, 1968. BA, U. Vt., 1960; MA in Hosp. and Health Adminstrn., U. Iowa, 1965, PhD (USPHS trainee), 1968. Asst. prof. hosp. and health adminstrn. U. Iowa, 1968-73, asso. prof., 1973-77; prof., chmn. dept. health adminstrn. U. Okla., 1977-81; prof., chmn. dept. health svcs. policy and mgmt. U. S.C., 1981-88, on sabbatical, 1988-89, prof., grad. dir., 1989—2002, disting. prof. emeritus, 2002—. Exec. sec. Nat. Ctr. Health Svcs. Rsch., 1975-76; dir. Am. Indian Grad. Program in Health Adminstrn., U. Okla., 1977-81; cons. China Med. U. Hosp., 1999-2010, vis. scholar, Nat. Def. Med. Ctr., Taiwan, 2003. Contbr. articles to profl. jours. Chair S.C. Ctr. for Gerontology, 1999-01. Lt., M.S.C. US Army, 1961—62, exec. officer and platoon leader, 418 Med. Co. (Ambulance), XVIII Airborne Hdqs. Mem. APHA (emeritus), AARP (SC) (exec. coun. 2004-10), Am. Coll. Healthcare Execs., Am. Hosp. Assn. (life), Vermont Soc. Colonial Wars (gov. 2006-2011). Home: 234 Saluda Ave Columbia SC 29205-3031 Office: Arnold SPH U SC Health Svcs Policy and Mgmt Columbia SC 29208-0001 Home Phone: 803-252-8993. Personal E-mail: uvmer@sc.rr.com.

AMIN, MOHAMMAD, urology educator; b. Sargodha, Pakistan, Jan. 1, 1942; came to U.S., 1964; s. Mohammad and Gulzar (Begum) Nawaz; m. Elizabeth Anne Howarth, May 25, 1973; children: Daniel, Omar. MB, BS, King Edward Coll., Lahore, Pakistan, 1963. Diplomate Am. Bd. of Urology. Intern Muhlenberg Hosp., Plainfield, NJ, 1964-65; resident in surgery Norton Hosp., Louisville, 1965-66; asst. prof. urology U. Louisville, 1971-74, assoc. prof., 1974-80, prof. urology, 1980—, resident in urology, 1966-69; med. officer Social Security, Pakistan, 1969-70; house officer urology Southmede Hosp., Bristol, England, 1970-71. Contbr. articles and book chpts. to profl. jours. Recipient Health Advancement award Nat. Kidney Found., 1981. Mem.: ACS, Soc. Internat. d'Urologie, Am. Urol. Assn. Democrat. Islamic. Address: VA Med Ctr 800 Zorn Ave Louisville KY 40206 Office Phone: 502-287-4000. Personal E-mail: maminlouky@yahoo.com.

AMOLSCH, ARTHUR LEWIS, publishing executive; b. LA, Nov. 28, 1939; s. Arthur Bruce Amolsch and Mildred Vivian (Guyott) Fry; m. Judith Ann Marolda, Aug. 27, 1963 (div. 1982); children: Christopher Bryan, Kira Leigh; m. Imelda Marie Moore Madden, Mar. 27, 1983. BS, Ea. Mich. U., 1963. Tchr. Edmondson Jr. High Sch., Ypsilanti, Mich., 1963-66; fgn. svc. officer Dept. State, Washington, 1971-72; head speech writer Com. for Re-election of the Pres., Washington, 1972; dep. dir., press rels. Presdl. Inaugural Com., Washington, 1973; dir. pub. info. FTC, Washington, 1973-76; pres., pub. Washington Regulatory Reporting Assocs., 1976—. Capt. USAF, 1967-71. Home: PO Box 356 Basye VA 22810-0356 Office Phone: 202-639-0581. E-mail: ftcwatch@usa.net.

AMOS, BETTY GILES, food service executive, accountant; b. Lebanon, Mo., July 18, 1941; d. Clarence Edgar and Clara Mae (Gann) Giles; m. E.L. Amos, Sept. 18, 1959 (div. Oct. 1965); 1 child, Jeffrey Lee; m. Thomas R. Righetti, Jan. 2, 1983 (dec. Sept. 18, 2002). BBA magna cum laude, U. Miami, Coral Gables, Fla., 1973, MBA, 1976; D of Bus. Adminstrn. honoris causa, Johnson & Wales U., 1990. CPA, Fla. Sec. City of Lebanon, 1959-63; dept. head Empire Gas Co., Lebanon, 1963-68; fin. analyst asst. Biscayne Assocs., Ltd., Miami, Fla., 1968-73; investment mgr. Universal Restaurants Inc., Miami, 1973-77; pvt. practice acct., investment mgr. Miami, 1977-83; pres. The Abkey Cos., Miami, 1983—2013. Founder Mega Bank, Miami, 1983-94; mem. adv. com. Fuddruckers, Inc., Boston, 1986-2002. Trustee Miami Project, 1986-89, United Fund of Dade County, 1992—; pres. Humane Soc. Greater Miami, 1994-2000, bd. dirs., 1993-2000; mem. pres. coun. U. Miami, 1994—, mem. founder's soc., 1994—, bd. trustees, 1997—, vice chair UM Hosp. Bd. Govs., 2011-; mem. presdl. search com. U. Miami, 2000; mem. Orange Bowl Com., 2002—; dir. Wings Over Miami Aviation Mus., treas., 2002-03, pres., 2004-08; bd. dirs. IVAX Corp., 2003—07; mem. audit com. Miami-Dade County Sch. Bd., 2004-06, vice chair, 2007-08, chair, 2008-10. Recipient Philip J. Romano Founders award, 1988. Mem. AICPA, Fla. Inst. CPAs, Am. Women's Soc. CPAs, Coconut Grove C. of C. (trustee 1988-2001), Nat. Assn. Women Bus. Owners (Outstanding Woman Bus. award 1993), U. Miami Alumni Assn. (nat. pres. 1999-2001), Iron Arrow, Internat. Women's Forum (bd. dirs. 2006—08), Women of Tomorrow (bd. dirs. 2006—12, treas. 2008-12), Women's Exec. Leadership (adv. bd. 2005—), Miami Dade Women's History Coalition (Woman Impact award, 2011). Republican. Avocations: skiing, water-skiing, scuba diving, tennis. Home: 8206 SW 171 Ter Palmetto Bay FL 33157 Home Phone: 305-232-1313. Business E-Mail: bgamos@bellsouth.net.

AMOS, DANIEL PAUL, insurance company executive; b. Pensacola, Fla., Aug. 13, 1951; s. Paul Shelby and Mary Jean (Roberts) A.; m. Mary Shannon Landing, Sept. 12, 1972; children: Paul Shelby, Lauren Alyse. BS in Risk and Ins. Mgmt., U. Ga., Athens, 1973. Co-state mgr. Aflac (Am. Family Life Assurance Co.), Columbus, Ga., 1973-78, state mgr., 1978-83, pres., 1983-96, COO, 1987—90; CEO AFLAC, Inc., Columbus, Ga., 1990—, chmn., 2001—; dep. CEO Am. Family Corp., Columbus, Ga., 1996. Dir. Columbus Bank & Trust Co., Synovus Fin. Corp., So. Co. Bd. trustees Children's Healthcare of Atlanta, House of Mercy of Columbus. Recipient Dr. Martin Luther King Jr. Unity award, Torch of Liberty award, Anti-Defamation League. Methodist. Avocation: bridge. Office: Aflac Inc 1932 Wynnton Rd Columbus GA 31999 Office Phone: 706-323-3431.

AMOS, PAUL SHELBY, insurance company executive; b. Enterprise, Ala., Apr. 23, 1926; s. John Shelby and Mary Helen (Mullins) A.; m. Mary Jean Roberts, Oct. 24, 1948; 1 child, Daniel P. Co-founder, v.p. Am. Family Life Assurance Co., Columbus, Ga., 1956-64; state mgr. Ala. Am. Family Life Assurance Co. (W.Fla.), Columbus, Ga., 1964-74; 1st v.p., dir. mktg. Am. Family Life Assurance Co., Columbus, Ga., 1974-78, pres., 1978-83; vice chmn. American Family Life Assurance Co., Columbus, Ga., 1983-90, chmn., 1990—; pres. Am. Family Corp., Columbus, 1981-83, vice chmn., 1983-90; chmn. AFLAC, Columbus, 1990—2001; chmn. emeritus AFLAC, Inc., 2001—. Owner Ben Franklin Stores, Milton, Fla., 1946-66; ptnr., v.p. Service Oil Co., Milton, 1958-66; pres., chmn. First Fed. Savs. & Loan, Milton, 1957-74 Trustee Asbury Theol. Sem. With USCGR, 1944-46, PTO. Named to Worksite Mktg. Hall of Fame, Workplace Benefits Assn., 2010. Mem. Columbus C. of C. Clubs: Country of Columbus; Big Eddy. Republican. Methodist. Home: 939 Overlook Dr Columbus GA 31906-3028 Office: AFLAC 1932 Wynnton Rd Columbus GA 31999-0002

AMOS, PAUL SHELBY, II, insurance company executive, lawyer; b. 1978; B in Economics, Duke U., Durham, NC; MBA, Emory U., Atlanta; JD, Tulane U., New Orleans. With, corp. legal divsn. Skadden, Arps, Slate, Meagher and Flom, Washington; state sales coord., Ga. North AFLAC, Inc., 2002, exec. v.p., US Ops., 2005, pres., COO, 2006—. Office: AFLAC Inc 1932 Wynnton Rd Columbus GA 31999 Office Phone: 706-323-3431. Office Fax: 706-324-6330. Business E-Mail: pamos@aflac.com.

AMOS, TORI, musician, singer, composer; b. NC; d. Edison and Mary Ellen A.; m. Mark Hawley, Feb. 22, 1998, 1 child: Natashya "Tash" Lorien Hawley. Student, Peabody Conservatory. Formed Transmission Galactic, 2013. Albums: Y Kant Tori Read, 1988, Little Earthquakes, 1992, Under the Pink, 1994 (Grammy nomination, Best Alternative Music Performance, 1995), Boys for Pele, 1996, From the Choirgirl Hotel, 1998, To Venus and Back, 1999, Strange Little Girls, 2001, Scarlet's Walk, 2002, Tales of a Librarian: Tori Amos Collection, 2003, The Beekeeper, 2005, A Piano: The Collection, 2006, American Doll Posse, 2007, Midwinter Graces, 2009, Night of Hunters, 2011, Gold Dust, 2012; author: (with Ann Powers) Tori Amos: Piece By Piece, 2005; music and lyrics (musicals) The Light Princess, Nat. Lyttelton Theater, 2013 Supporter Rape, Abuse & Incest Nat. Network (RAINN), 1994—. Office: Tori Amos Galactic LLC 2336 SE Ocean Blvd Ste 177 Stuart FL 34996*

ANAND, KANWALJEET SINGH, pediatrician, researcher; b. Ludhiana, Punjab, India, Nov. 29, 1957; s. Jaswant Singh and Tejinder Kaur Anand; m. Itinder Kaur Anand; children: Amrit K, Tejpartab S. MD, Mahatma Gandhi Meml. Med. Coll., Indore, India, 1980; PhD, Jesus Coll., U. Oxford, Eng., 1985. Diplomate Am. Bd. Pediat., cert. in pediatric critical care, pediatric advanced life support, lic. Ark. Rsch. fellow dept. pediat. U. Oxford, 1983—85; clin. fellow pediat. Harvard Med. Sch., Boston, 1988—91, 1991—93; asst. prof. pediat./anesthesiology Emory U. Sch. Medicine, Atlanta, 1993—97, asst. prof. psychiatry/behavioral scis., 1994—97, dir. critical care rsch., 1994—97, interim dir. office rsch. promotion, dept. pediat., 1995—96; assoc. prof. pediat./anesthesiology U. Ark. for Med. Scis., Little Rock, 1997—2000, sect. chief pediat. critical care medicine, 1997—, assoc. prof. anatomy/neurobiology, 1998—2000, prof. pediat., anesthesiology, pharmacology & neurobiology, 2001—. Dir. pain neurobiology lab. Ark. Children's Hosp., Little Rock, 1999—; bd. dirs. Ark. Children's Hosp. Rsch. Inst., 1997—; Pfizer vis. prof. Wayne State U., Detroit, 2002; vis. prof. Baylor U., Waco, Tex., 2003. Contbr. articles to profl. jours. Mem. Rhodes scholarship selection com. (Ark. sec.), Little Rock, 1997—2003. Recipient Dr. Michael Blacow award, BPA, 1986, Pediat. Resident Rsch. award, AAP, 1992, Young Investigator award, IASP, 1994, Jeffrey Lawson award, Am. Pain Soc., 2000; grantee Rhodes Scholarship, India, 1982-1985, Ark.

Ctr. Pain Rsch., 2001—03, Nat. Inst. Child Health & Human Devel., 1999—2003. Fellow: Am. Coll. Critical Care Medicine (Rsch. Com. 2003—06), Am. Acad. Pediat., Royal Coll. Pediat. & Child Health (Windermere Lectr. award 2004); mem.: Soc. Neurosci., Soc. Critical Care Medicine, Internat. Assn. Study of Pain, Soc. Pediatric Rsch., Am. Assn. Rhodes Scholars. Office: UAMS Pediat AR Childrens Hosp 1 Childrens Way Slot 512 12 Little Rock AR 72202-3500 Office Phone: 501-364-1845. Office Fax: 501-364-3188. E-mail: anandsunny@uams.edu.

ANASTASIO, CURTIS V., energy executive; b. 1956; Pres., COO, Shamrock Logistics Ultramar Diamond Shamrock Corp., v.p., gen. counsel and sec., 1997—99; exec. dir. NuStar GP Holdings LLC (formerly Valero GP Holdings LLC); pres., CEO NuStar GP Holdings, LLC, 2006—; pres. NuStar Energy LP, 1999—2000, pres., CEO, 2002—. Office: NuStar Energy LP 19003 W Interstate 10 San Antonio TX 78257-9518 Office Phone: 210-918-2000. Office Fax: 210-918-5057. Business E-Mail: curtis.anastasio@nustarenergy.com.

ANCHIA, RAFAEL, state legislator; b. Sept. 26, 1968; m. Marissa Anchia; children: Sofia, Maia. B in Latin Am. studies, Spanish, anthropology, So. Meth. U., Dallas; JD, Tulane U., New Orleans. Atty. Patton Boggs, LLP, Haynes & Boone, LLP; mem. Dist. 103 Tex. House of Representatives, 2004—. Former mem. bd. trustees Dallas Ind. Sch Dist. Recipient of several awards and honors. Mem.: Nat. Assn. Latino Elected and Apptd. Officials (nat. chmn. 2006—09, bd. dirs.). Democrat. Office: 1111 W Mockingbird Ln Suite 1330 Dallas TX 75247 also: Room E2.818 Capitol Extension PO Box 2910 Austin TX 78768 Office Phone: 214-943-6081, 512-463-0746.

ANCKER-JOHNSON, BETSY, physicist, engineer, retired automotive executive; b. St. Louis, Apr. 29, 1927; d. Clinton James and Fern (Lalan) Ancker; m. Harold Hunt Johnson, Mar. 15, 1958; children: Ruth P. Johnson, David H. Johnson (dec.), Paul A. Johnson (dec.), Marti H. Gab. BA in Physics with high honors (Pendleton scholar), Wellesley Coll., Mass., 1949; PhD in Exptl. Physics magna cum laude, U. Tuebingen, Germany, 1953; DSc (hon.), Poly. Inst. NY, 1979, Trinity Coll., Northbrook, Ill., 1981, U. So. Calif., LA, 1984, Alverno Coll., Milw., 1984; LL.D. (hon.), Bates Coll., Lewiston, Maine, 1980. Instr., jr. research physicist U. Calif., Berkeley, 1953-54; physicist Sylvania Microwave Physics Lab., 1956-58; mem. tech. staff RCA Labs., 1958-61; rsch. specialist Boeing Co., 1961-70, exec., 1970-73; asst. sec. U.S. Dept. Commerce for Sci. and Tech., 1973-77; dir. phys. rsch. Argonne Nat. Lab., Ill., 1977-79; v.p. for environ. activities Gen. Motors, Warren, Mich., 1979-92. Affiliate prof. elec. engring. U. Wash., 1961-73; mem. US Dept. Energy Rsch. Adv. Bd., 1983-87, adv. com. on inertial confinement fusion Dept. Energy, 1992-94, US Antarctic Safety Rev. Panel NSF, 1987-88; cons. Inland Steel Inc., 1991-96; adv. com. Rowan Sch. Engring., 1993-96; Regents vis. prof. U. Calif., Berkeley, 1988-89; founding dir. Acad. Medicine, Engring. and Sci. Tex., 2004-07. Contbr. articles to profl. jours. Mem. staff Inter-Varsity Christian Fellowship, 1954-56; mem. vis. com. elec. and computer divsn. MIT, US Dept. Def. Sci. Bd.; mem. adv. bd. Stanford U. Sch. Engring., Fla. State U., Fla. A&M U., Congl. Caucus for Sci. and Tech.; bd. dirs. Gen. Mills, 1978-90, Varison Assocs., 1977-79, Motor Vehicle Mfrs. Assn., 1982-92, Enterprise Devel. Internat., U. Tex. Cocknell Sch. Engring. 1997—; trustee Wellesley Coll., 1971-77; chair bd. dirs. World Environ. Ctr., 1988-93, dir. 1988-99; founding trustee Johnson Scholarship Found., 1991-2001; founding dir. Work Place Influence, 1997-2007; bd. dirs. Cocoon-Resources, 2010-; mem. U. Tex. Coll. Engring. Adv. Bd., 1997-2012; bd. dirs. Tex. Environ. Forum, 2000-01. Recipient Nat. Champion Master Swimmer 1500m, 2007, Chmn's. award Am. Assn. Engring. Socs., 1986, Award of Honor, Licensing Execs. Soc.; AAUW fellow, 1950-51, Horton Hollowell fellow, 1951-52; NSF grantee, 1967-72. Fellow AAAS, IEEE, Am. Phys. Soc. (councillor-at-large 1973-76); mem. NRC (bd. engring. edn. 1991-95, com. on women in sci. and engring. 1990-96, office sci. and engring. pers. adv. com. 1993-96), Nat. Acad. Engring. (councillor 1995-2001), Air Pollution Control Assn., Soc. Automotive Engrs. (bd. dirs. 1979-81); Phi Beta Kappa, Sigma Xi Achievements include patents in field. Business E-Mail: betsyaj@gmail.com.

ANCONA, VINCENT M., healthcare company executive; Regional head, Network Ops. Aetna US; v.p., Provider Network Ops. Mid-Atlantic Med. Svcs., Inc.; variety of positions, exec. v.p., Network Ops., dir., ops., Colo. Prudential Ins. Co. America; COO, Amerigroup, Md. Amerigroup Corp., 2006—. Office: Amerigroup Corp Ste 100 4425 Corporation Ln Virginia Beach VA 23462 Office Phone: 757-490-6900. Office Fax: 757-518-3600. Business E-Mail: vancona@amerigroupcorp.com.

ANDERS, JOHN F., state legislator; Mem. Dist. 21 La. House of Reps., 2006—, chair agr., forestry, aquaculture, and rural devel. com., mem. ins. com., house com. on homeland security, joint com. on homeland security. Democrat. Mailing: 200 Advocate Row suite D Vidalia LA 71373 Office Phone: 318-336-5865. Fax: 318-336-9268. E-mail: larep021@legis.state.la.us.

ANDERSEN, SHAZA L., bank executive; m. Marc Andersen; children: Katie, Danny. B in European Studies, George Mason U., Fairfax, Va. Exec. v.p., COO Century Nat. Bank; founder, CEO WashingtonFirst Bank, Reston, Va., 2004—. Former bd. dirs. Fed. Home Loan Bank Va., vice chmn. corp. governance com., mem. housing com.; mem. Va. Treasury Bd.; contbr. CNBC, Fox News. Founder WashingtonFirst Youth Found.; bd. dirs. Wolf Trap Found.; bd. trustees Youth For Tomorrow. Named one of The Top Bankers, Smart CEO Mag., 2010, The Women Who Mean Bus., Wash. Bus. Jour., 2010, The 25 Women to Watch, American Banker, 2011. Mem.: Nat. Assn. Women Bus. Owners Leadership Cir. Office: Washington-First Bank 11636 Plaza America Dr Reston VA 20190

ANDERSON, BARBARA MCCOMAS, lawyer; d. Ben C. Jr. and Elsa A. McComas; m. Roy Ryden Anderson Jr., Dec. 11, 1982; 1 child, Ryden McComas Anderson. BA, Trinity U., San Antonio, 1972; JD, U. Tex., 1978. Bar: Tex. 1978; cert. in estate planning and probate Tex. Bd. Legal Specialization. From assoc. to ptnr. Locke Purnell Rain Harrell, Dallas, 1978-97; of counsel Locke Liddell & Sapp, LLP, Dallas, 1997—2003; pvt. practice Dallas, 1997—. Fellow: Coll. of State Bar of Tex., Tex. Bar. Found., Am. Coll. Trusts and Estates Counsel; mem.: Tex. Acad. Probate and Trust Lawyers (charter, v.p., bd. dirs.), Dallas Bar Assn. (chair probate, trusts and estates sects. 1987—88), Tex. Bar Assn. (chair real estate, probate and trust law sect. 2003—04). Avocations: reading, gardening. Office: PO Box 181147 Dallas TX 75218-8147

ANDERSON, BRADLEY R., computer company executive; BS in Petroleum Engring., Tex. A&M U; MBA, Harvard U. Various mgmt. positions Cray Rsch., Inc.; joined Hewlett-Packard Co., 1996, v.p., Server, Storage, and Infrastructure, sr. v.p., gen. mgr., Industry Std. Servers bus.; sr. v.p., Bus. Product Group Dell, Inc., 2005—09, sr. v.p., Enterprise Solutions Group, 2009—. Mem. Tex. A&M Look Coll. Engring. Adv. Coun. Office: Dell Inc 1 Dell Way Round Rock TX 78682 Office Phone: 512-338-4400. Office Fax: 512-283-6161.

ANDERSON, CARL L., state legislator; b. Georgetown, SC, Feb. 10, 1961; Grad., Horry-Georgetown Tech. Coll., Conway, SC, 1981. Mem. Dist. 103 SC House of Reps., 2004—. Democrat. Mailing: 304C Blatt Bldg Columbia SC 29201 Home: PO Box 694 Georgetown SC 29442 Office Phone: 803-734-2933. Business E-Mail: AndersonC@scstatehouse.net.

ANDERSON, CHARLES (DOC), state legislator; b. June 29, 1945; m. Sandra Anderson; 1 child. Grad., Tex. A&M U. Sch. Vet. Medicine. Small animal veterinarian, Waco, Tex., 1981—; cattle rancher owner McLennan county, Tex.; mem. Dist. 56 Tex. House of Representatives, 2004—. Republican. Office: 900 Austin Ave Ste 804 Waco TX 76701 also: Room E2.502 Capitol Extension PO Box 2910 Austin TX 78768 Office Phone: 254-754-3892, 512-463-0135. Office Fax: 254-754-1604, 512-463-0642.

ANDERSON, CHUCK, retail executive; BA in Merchandising and Fashion Promotion, U. Ariz., Tucson, 1980. Buyer Saks Fifth Ave, 1999—2003; v.p. retail sales support, ops. Theory, 2003—07; sr. v.p. merchandising HSN Interactive, LLC, 2007—. Mem.: Alpha Epsilon Pi. Office: HSN Interactive LLC 1 HSN Dr Saint Petersburg FL 33729 Office Phone: 727-872-1000. Business E-Mail: chuck.anderson@hsn.net.

ANDERSON, CLAYTON C., astronaut; b. Omaha, Nebr., Feb. 23, 1959; s. John T. and Alice J. Anderson; m. Susan Jane Harreld; children: Clayton "Cole", Sutton Marie. BS in Physics, Hastings Coll., 1981; MS in Aerospace Engring., Iowa State U., 1983; PhD (hon.), Hastings Coll., 2004. Mem. mission planning and analysis divsn. NASA, Johnson Space Ctr., Houston, 1983—88, flight design mgr. mission ops. directorate (MOD), 1988—89, supr. MOD ascent flight design sect., 1989—93, chief flight design br., 1993—96, mgr. emergency ops. ctr., 1996—98, astronaut, mission specialist candidate, 1998—. Lead, Enhanced Caution and Warning Sys. Develop. effort within Space Shuttle Cockpit Avionics Upgrade Project; crew support astronaut Internat. Space Station Expedition 4; served as Internat. Space Station Capsule Communicator; astronaut office crew rep. Internat. Space Station Electrical Power Sys.; back-up flight engr. Expeditions 12, 13 and 14 missions to the Internat. Space Station; crew mem. Expedition 15-launch to the Internat. Space Station aboard Shuttle Atlantis with crew of STS-117 and will return to Earth aboard Shuttle Discovery on mission STS-120, 2007; mission specialist STS-131 Discovery Mission, 2010. Recipient Johnson Space Ctr. Cert. Commendation, 1993, NASA Quality and Safety Achievement Recognition award, 1998, Disting. Alumnus award, Nat. Coun. of Alpha Chi, 2001; named Outstanding Young Man Am., 1981, 1985, 1987; named a NCAA Nat. Christian Coll. Basketball Championships Ofcl., 1997, 1998. Mem.: Johnson Space Ctr. Employee Activities Assn., Aircraft Owners and Pilots Assn., Tex./N.Mex. Jr. Coll. Athletic Conf., Lone Star Conf., So. Collegiate Athletic Conf., Men's Coll. Basketball Ofcls., S.W. Basketball Ofcls. Assn., Red River Athletic Conf., Heart of Tex. Conf., Clear Lake Optimist Club (past. pres., past v.p.), Alpha Chi (Disting. Alumnus award, Nat. Coun. Alpha Chi 2001). Avocations: officiating basketball games, flying, reading, writing music, piano/organ playing and vocal performance. Office: Astronaut Office/CB NASA Johnson Space Ctr Houston TX 77058

ANDERSON, CLYDE B., retail executive; married; 4 children. Grad., U. Ala. COO Books-A-Million, Inc., 1987—94, pres., 1987—99, CEO, 1992—2004, chmn., 2000—04, exec. chmn., 2004—09, chmn., CEO, pres., 2009—; founder, mng. ptnr. Anderson Growth Ptnrs., LLC, 1996. Bd. dirs. Hibbett Sports, Inc., 1987—2008, Hat World, Inc., 2001—04. Office: Books A Million Inc 402 Industrial Ln Birmingham AL 35211 Office Phone: 205-942-3737. Office Fax: 205-942-6601. Business E-Mail: clyde.anderson@booksamillion.com.

ANDERSON, DEBORAH GAIL COOK, elementary school educator, special education educator; b. San Antonio, Dec. 26, 1956; d. Clarence Edward Cook, Sr. and Dorothy Mae (Colvin) Phillips; m. Dwight Edward Anderson, June 22, 1980 (div. Sept. 1981). BS, Tex. Woman's U., 1979; MEd in Ednl. Psychology, Spl. Edn., U. Houston, 1989. Tchr. self contained spl. edn., 1979—80; substitute tchr. Marshall Elem. Sch., Detroit, 1980—81; tchr. spl. edn. resource, cons. Ashford Elem. Sch. Houston Ind. Sch. Dist., 1981—95, tchr. spl. edn., pre-sch. program for children with disabilities Ashford Primary Sch., 1996—. Tutor spl. edn., Houston, 1982—; tutor Denton Assn. Student Helpers, Tex., 1977; vol. behavior technician Behavior Studies Ctr. North Tex. State U., Denton, 1976—77; vol. Spl. Olympics, Denton, 1978, Lowry Hall, Denton, 1978. Ashford United Negro Coll. Fund Campus Coord., 1987—95; bd. mem., coord. Divine Dynasphere Christian Ctr. Youth, Inc., adminstrv. contact, Kids Across America; coord. Kids Across Am. Christian Growth Tng. and Leadership Devel. Mentoring Program Divine Dynasphere Program; Ashford Trio Presenter Mem. on Inclusion for Educator Workshops/Conferences, 2001—; Christian debutante com. mem. Soc. America Com.; mem. Young Women's Aux. Mt. Calvary Bapt. Ch., Denton, 1977—79, pres. Young Women's Aux., 1978—79, mem. usher bd. Young Women's Aux., 1977—79, youth worker, 1978—79; youth worker, outreach com., Christian Debutante Soc. Am. Sara Cir. Liberty Bapt. Ch. Gen. Mission; pres. Gen. Mission Liberty Bapt. Ch., 1991—92; UNCF young scholars historian and personal appearance coord. (formerly Little Miss Coll. Fund/United Negro Coll. Fund Pageant); mem. Soc. America Christian Debutante Com.; coord. Ashford Combined Charities Campus, 1996—. Recipient Devoted and Invaluable Svc. award, Liberty Gen. Mission, 1985, Parents' Guild Dedicated Svc. award, Christian Debutante Soc. America, 1989—90, Dedicated Christian Svc. and Christian Leadership award, Liberty Bapt. Ch., 1990—92, Outstanding Leadership award, 1990—92, Loyal and Dedicated Svc. award, 1995, Devoted Christian Svc. award, 1995, Dedicated Missionary Svc. and Labor award, 2001, Faithful Cornerstone award, 2003, award for Excellence in Math. Tchg. Honoree, Ashford Houston Coun. Math., 1993, Annual Fiesta Store Black History Month Local Cmty. Educator Honoree, 2000, Dedicated Svc. award, Divine Dynasphere CCFYI, 2001, Angel of Faith award, 2001, Patience and Perfection award, 2004, Toombs-Brown Prestige awards honoree/The Triumphant 7 Inspiring Great Minds, Profl. Black Women's Enterprise, Inc., 2003, Friend of Precious Jewels Edn. award, Precious Jewels Alpha Learning Ctr., 2005, 1st Rev. George H. Johnson Meml. Scholarship Youth award, The Vision, Divine Dynasphere CCFYI, 2008; named Ashford Exceptl. Edn. Tchr. Yr. and West Dist. Runner-up, 1994, Outstanding Young Educator, Ashford Elem. Sch., 1985, Tchr. of Yr., 1987, Ashford Houston Area Alliance Black Sch. Outstanding Tchr., 1998, Ashford ESL Tchr. of Yr., 2008; Young Scholars, UNCF. Mem.: NAACP (named most prominent black woman Tex. Woman's U. chpt. 1979), NEA, Houston Coun. Edn., Houston Tchrs. Assn., Tex. State Tchrs. Assn., Nat. Assn. Black Social Workers, Assn. Childhood Edn. Internat., Coun. Exceptional Children, Mortar Bd., Delta Sigma Theta, Alpha Chi. Democrat. Baptist. Avocation: baking. Office: Ashford Primary Sch 1815 Shannon Valley Dr Houston TX 77077-4998 Home: 1015 Country Place Dr Apt 112 Houston TX 77079-4744 Office Phone: 281-368-2120.

ANDERSON, DONALD NORTON, JR., retired electrical engineer; b. Chgo., Aug. 15, 1928; s. Donald Norton and Helen Dorothy (Lehmann) A. BS, Purdue U., 1950, MS, 1952. With Hughes Aircraft Co., Culver City and El Segundo City, Calif., 1952-84, sect. head, sr. project engr. Calif., 1960-65, tech. mgr. Apollo program Calif., 1965-66, mgr. visible systems dept. Calif., 1966-69, 70-73, project mgr. Calif., 1969-70, mgr. space sensors lab. Calif., 1973-79, mgr. space electro-optical systems labs. Calif., 1979-80, 80-84, ret. Calif., 1984. Recipient Apollo Achievement award, 1970; Robert J. Collier Landsat award, 1974. Mem. Rsch. Soc. Am., Sierra Club, Sigma Xi (sec. Hughes Labs. br. 1974-75), Eta Kappa Nu. Home: 1885 Craig's Store Rd Afton VA 22920-2013 E-mail: dnafactor@ntelos.net.

ANDERSON, E. KARL, lawyer; b. Huntington, W. Va., Mar. 30, 1931; s. Earle Karl and Helen Emrie (Johnson) A.; m. Mary Elizabeth Williams, Nov. 13, 1953; children: Sharon Elizabeth, Charles Wesley. BBA, So. Methodist U., 1953, LLB, 1960. Bar: Tex. 1960, U.S. Dist. Ct. (no. dist.) Tex. 1963, U.S. Supreme Ct. 1971. Field supr. Travelers Ins. Co., Dallas, 1956-57; claim mgr. Allstate Ins. Co., Dallas, 1958-62; practiced in Dallas, 1963—; pntr. Lastelick, Anderson and Arneson, Dallas, 1968—. 1st lt. USAF, 1954—56. Fellow Tex. Bar Found.; mem. Am. Bar Assn., Dallas Assn. Trial Lawyers (dir. 1964-65, 74-75), Tex. Trial Lawyers Assn., Assn. Trial Lawyers Am., Dallas Country Club, Delta Theta Phi, Sigma Iota Epsilon, Sigma Alpha Epsilon. Presbyterian. Home: 3111 Drexel Dr Dallas TX 75205-2910 E-mail: ekander@flash.net.

ANDERSON, EDWARD R., information technology executive; Degree in Econ., U. Mich.; MBA, Harvard U. Chmn., CEO E-Certify Corp., TorchQuest; COO Vanstar (formerly ComputerLand), Pleasanton, Calif.; CEO CompuCom Sys., 1993—99, Ambrosia Solutions, 2003—05; pres. iPointSystems, 2005—, founder. Bd. dirs. Diamond Mgmt. & Tech. Consultants Inc., 1994—. Office: iPointSystems 3611 Bonnie Rd Austin TX 78703-2644 Office Phone: 512-499-6240. Business E-Mail: edward.anderson@diamondconsultants.com.

ANDERSON, EDWARD RILEY, retired state supreme court justice; b. Chattanooga, Aug. 10, 1932; BS, U. Tenn., 1955, JD, 1957; grad., NYU Appellate Judge & Grad. Programs, 1988, grad., 1994. Bar: Tenn. 1958, U.S. Dist. Ct. (ea. dist.) Tenn. 1965, U.S. Ct. Appeals (4th cir.) 1985, U.S. Ct. Appeals (6th cir.), U.S. Supreme Ct. 1988. Assoc. Joyce & Wilson, Oak Ridge, Tenn., 1957—61; ptnr. Joyce, Anderson & Meredith, Oak Ridge, 1961—87; judge Tenn. Ct. Appeals, Knoxville, 1987—90; justice Tenn. Supreme Ct., Knoxville, 1990—2005, chief justice, 1994—2001. Mem. Tenn. Jud. Conf., 1987—; bd. dirs. Conf. of Chief Justices, 1999-2000, vice chair children and the family com., 1998-99; chmn. Tenn. Jud. Coun., 1990-95, Select Senate/House Com. on Ct. Automation,1990-94, mem. Inst. Jud. Adminstrv. NYU. Past commr. Oak Ridge City Charter. Recipient Vocat. Svc. award Oak Ridge Rotary Club, 2000; named Judge of Yr. Am. Bd. Trial Advocates, 1998. Fellow Am. Bar Found., Tenn. Bar Found.; mem. ABA, Am. Bd. Trial Advocates (pres. Tenn. chpt. 1987-88), Tenn. Bar Assn. (William M. Leech Jr. Pub. Svc. award 2001), Anderson County Bar Assn. (pres. 1961), Tenn. Def. Lawyers Assn. (pres. 1980-81), Am. Inns of Ct. (pres. Tenn. chpt. 1988-90). Avocations: reading, golf, tennis.

ANDERSON, ERIC C., aerospace transportation executive; b. Denver, 1974; BA in Aerospace Engring. magna cum laude, U. Va., 1996. Rsch. positions NASA; bus. develop. lead Analytical Graphics; exec. v.p., co-founder Starport.com (sold to space.com in 2000); co-founder Space Adventures, Ltd., Va., 1998, pres., CEO & bd. dir. Va., 1998—. Bd. dirs. X Prize Found., Zero Gravity Found. Contbr. to tech. papers and articles in the field; author: Space Tourist's Handbook, 2005. Recipient Outstanding Young Engring. Grad. award, U. Va. Engring. Found., 2005. Fellow: World Tech. Network (World Tech. award for Space 2006). Achievements include being an advocate in commercial space transportation and private space exploration/space tourism. Office: Space Adventures Ltd 8245 Boone Blvd Ste 570 Vienna VA 22182-3847 Office Phone: 703-524-7172. Office Fax: 703-524-7176. Business E-Mail: eanderson@spaceadventures.com.

ANDERSON, GARLAND D., obstetrician, gynecologist; b. Dec. 11, 1944; MD, U. Tenn. Intern Hermann Hosp., Houston, 1970—71; resident U. Tex. Health Sci. Ctr., Houston, 1971—74; fellow maternal fetal medicine U. Louisville, Ky., 1974—76, instr. ob-gyn. Ky., 1974—75, asst. prof. Ky., 1975—77, med. dir. Teen Alternative Parent Program Ky., 1975—77, assoc. prof. Ky.; dir. resident edn., div. chief Maternal and Fetal Medicine, prof. Dept. Obstetrics and Gynecology U. Tenn. Coll. Medicine, 1978—89; prof. ob-gyn. U. Tenn., 1983—89; prof., Jennie Sealy Smith disting. chair ob-gyn. U. Tex. Med. Branch Sch. Medicine, Galveston, 1989—2006, exec. v.p., provost, dean, 2006—11, spl. advisor to the pres. for clin. & ednl. programs, 2011—. Steering com. chair Maternal-Fetal Units Network, Nat. Inst. Child Heath and Human Devel., 2003—06. Contbr. articles to profl. jours. Recipient Nicholas and Katherine Leone Award for Adminstrn. Excellence; named a Tex. Super Doc, Tex. Monthly; named one of Best Doctor for Women, Good Housekeeping mag.; named to Best Doctors in Am. Fellow: Am. Coll. of Obstetricians and Gynecologists (FACOG); mem.: Coun. of Univ. Chairs in Ob-gyn. (pres.), Soc. Maternal and Fetal Medicine (former bd. mem., pres., Award for Rsch. Excellence). Office: University of Texas Medical Branch 301 University Blvd Galveston TX 77555-0133 E-mail: ganderso@utmb.edu.

ANDERSON, GEORGE ROSS, JR., federal judge; b. Anderson, SC, Jan. 29, 1929; s. George Ross and Eva Mae (Pooler) A.; m. Dorothy M. Downie, Dec. 2, 1951; 1 son, G. Ross. B.Comml. Sci., Southeastern U., 1949; postgrad., George Washington U., 1949-51; LL.B., U. S.C., 1954, LLD (hon.), 1984, Anderson Coll., 1998. Bar: S.C. 1954. Mem. identification div. FBI, Washington, 1945-47; legislative asst. to Senator Olin D. Johnston US Senate, Washington, 1947-51, Columbia, SC, 1953-54; individual practice law Anderson, SC, 1954-79; judge US Dist. Ct. SC, Anderson, SC, 1980—2009, sr. judge, 2009—. Asst. editor: U. S.C. Law Rev, 1953-54. Bd. dirs. Salvation Army, 1968, YMCA, 1968-79, Anderson Youth Assn., 1978-80. Served with USAF, 1951-52. Recipient War Horse award So. Trial Lawyers Assn., 1990, Dist. Judicial Svc. award The Civil Justice Found., Am. Trial Lawyers Assn., 1997, Ernest F. Hollings Pub. Svc. award, 2002, Order of the Palmetto award, 2002; named for Federal Bldg. Courthouse in Anderson, SC, 2002. Fellow Internat. Acad. Trial Lawyers (dir. 1979-81), Internat. Soc. Barristers; mem. S.C. Bar Assn. (dir. 1977-80, past cir. v.p.), Assn. Trial Lawyers Am. (bd. govs. 1969-71), S.C. Trial Lawyers Assn. (v.p. 1970-71, pres. 1971-72, Outstanding Trial Judge of Yr. 1984), hon. doctor of Laws, U. SC, 1984, bd. dirs., Federal Judges Assn., 1993-97. Democrat. Baptist. Office: US Dist Ct PO Box 2147 Anderson SC 29622-2147

ANDERSON, GERALD LESLIE, finance company executive; b. Washington, May 24, 1940; s. Paul Hash and Edith (Hathaway) A.; m. Margaret Marie Curley, June 8, 1974; children: Paul Charles, Laura Marie. BS in Indsl. Mgmt., Carnegie Mellon U., 1961, MS in Indsl. Adminstrn., 1962. Econ. analyst Sun Oil Co., Phila., 1962-66; asst. treas. Selas Corp. Am., Dresher, Pa., 1966-74; treas. Midrex Corp., Charlotte, NC, 1974-76; v.p., treas. Georgetown Industries, Inc., Charlotte, 1976-85, v.p. fin., chief fin. officer, 1985-95; prin. Anderson Investments, Charlotte, NC, 1995—2000. Active Ch. at Charlotte Evangelical Free Ch. Republican. Home and Office: 4519 N Parview Dr Charlotte NC 28226-3450

ANDERSON, GREG, councilman; m. Beville Anderson; 2 children. BA in Bus. Adminstrn., U. Ga.; MA in Liberal Studies, Duquesne U. Trainee FirstAtlanta; with Global Cash Mgmt. Divsn. Mellon Bank, Pitts.; sr. pvt. banking officer EverBank, Jacksonville, Fla.; councilman-at-large Group 4 Jacksonville City Coun., 2011—. Pres. Riverside Fine Arts Assn.; dir. Daniel Found. Office: Jacksonville City Council 117 W Duval St Jacksonville FL 32202 Office Phone: 904-630-1398. E-mail: GAnderson@coj.net.

ANDERSON, JAMES WINGO, physician; b. Hinton, W.Va., Aug. 6, 1936; s. Fred Wingo and Georgia Lee (Whittaker) A.; m. Gay Veree Gilbert, June 7, 1957; children: Katherine, Steven. BS, W.Va. U., 1957; MD, Northwestern U., 1961; MS, Mayo Clinic, 1965. Intern Presbyn. Med. Ctr., Denver; resident, fellow Mayo Clinic, Rochester, Minn.; asst. prof. medicine U. Calif., San Francisco, 1968-73; prof. medicine, clin. nutrition U. Ky. Coll. Medicine, Lexington, 1973—; pres., founder HCF Nutrition Found., Lexington, 1979—. Author: Diabetes-A Practical Guide to Healthy Living, 1981, Dr. Anderson's High Fiber Fitness Plan, 1994, Dr. Anderson;s Antioxidant Antiaging, 1996. Trustee Georgetown (Ky.) Coll., 1988—, chmn. bd. trustees, 1994-96. Capt. U.S. Army, 1965-68. Fellow Am. Coll. Physicians. Republican. Baptist. Home: 506 Knapp Farm Dr Hermitage TN 37076-1376 Home Phone: 895-269-6642; Office Phone: 859-422-4671.

ANDERSON, JOHN THOMAS, lawyer; b. Gary, Ind., July 13, 1930; s. Jack and Dorothy Genevieve (Gustafson) A.; m. Marvel Nancy Filkey, Aug. 15, 1953; children: Kirsten E. Teevens, Katherine L., Eric M. AB, DePauw U., 1952; LLB, Harvard U., 1955. Bar: Ind. 1955, Ill. 1956. Assoc. Lord, Bissell & Brook, Chgo., 1958-66, ptnr., 1966-95, of counsel, 1996-98. Trustee DePauw U., Greencastle, Ind., 1982—; chmn. bd. dirs. Joyce Found., Chgo., 1979—; Lt. USNR, 1955-58. Methodist. Home and Office: 2313 Cassia Ct Naples FL 34109-3370 Home Phone: 239-596-8218. Personal E-mail: jtand13@embarqmail.com.

ANDERSON, JOSEPH FLETCHER, JR., federal judge; b. Augusta, Ga., Nov. 16, 1949; m. Susan Martha Herlong; 3 children. BA, Clemson U., 1972; JD, U. S.C., 1975. Law clk. to presiding justice US Ct. Appeals (4th cir.), 1975-76; pvt. practice law Anderson, Anderson and Anderson, Edgefield, SC, 1977-86; mem. Ho. of Reps. 3rd Congl. Dist. SC, 1980-86; judge US Dist. Ct. SC, Columbia, 1986—2000, 2007—, chief judge, 2000—07. Chmn. honor coun. U. S.C. Sch. Law, 1976-85, Edgefield Indsl. Devel. Corp., S.C., bd. dirs., 1978-86; mem. local adv. bd. First Citizens Bank and Trust Co., Trenton, SC, 1983-86; chmn., vol. Edgefield County Re-election Campaign for Sen. Strom Thurmond, 1972, 84; chmn. Edgefield County Campaign for Congressman William Jennings Bryan Dorn for Dem. Nomination for Gov. of SC; bd. dirs. Edgefield County United Way, 1983-86; mem. exec. com. Coun. Boy Scouts Am., 1978-86. Named one of Three Outstanding Young Men of SC, 1980. Mem.: SC Trial Lawyers Assn., SC Law Inst. Coun., ABA. Office: Us District Court Judge 901 Richland St Columbia SC 29201-2328

ANDERSON, KENNETH WARD, investor, consultant; b. Evanston, Ill., Dec. 14, 1931; s. Sydney Cleminson and Grey (Simpson) A.; m. Jean Jensen, Mar. 21, 1953; children: Kenneth Ward, Richard Scott, Wendy Lynn. BSBA, Northwestern U., 1953; postgrad. in fin., UCLA, 1955-56, U. So. Calif., 1956-58. Asst. v.p. United Calif. Bank, LA, 1956-63; v.p. fin., asst. sect. T.I.M.E.-DC, Lubbock, Tex., 1963-70; sr. v.p. fin. Campbell-Taggart, Dallas, 1970-80; sr. v.p., CFO Galveston-Houston Co., Houston, 1980-82; pres., CFO, dir. Cook Data Svcs., Dallas, 1983-85; pres., dir. Blockbuster Entertainment Corp., Dallas, 1985-87; pres., dir., chmn. bd. Amtech Credit Corp., Dallas, 1987-90; chmn. exec. com., dir. Amtech Corp., 1987-92; bd. dirs. Lake Area Health Ctr. Found., 1993—, Fossil, Inc., 1993—2009, MarketQuiz, Inc., 2000—08. Bd. dirs. Ch. at Horseshoe Bay Endowment Fund, 1996—2003; trustee Ch. at Horseshoe Bay, 1999—2002. With US Army, 1953—55, Japan. Mem.: Horseshoe Bay Country Club. Republican. Methodist. Address: PO Box 8189 Horseshoe Bay TX 78657-8189

ANDERSON, KERRII B., board member, former food service executive; b. 1957; BS, Elon Coll., 1978; MBA, Duke U., 1987. CPA. With Peat, Marwick, Mitchell & Co., Greensboro, NC, 1978-84, RJ Reynolds Corp., Winston-Salem, NC, 1984-85, Key Co., Greensboro, NC, 1985-87; sec. M/I Schottenstein Homes Inc., Columbus, 1987—94, sr. v.p., CFO, chmn. bd., 1987—2000, asst. sec., 1994—2000; exec. v.p., CFO Wendy's International, Inc., Dublin, Ohio, 2000—06, interim CEO, 2006; pres., CEO Wendy's International, Inc. (merged with Triarc), Dublin, Ohio, 2006—08. Bd. dirs. Worthington Industries, Inc., Tim Hortons Inc., M/I Homes, Inc., Lancaster Colony Corp., 1998—2005, Wendy's Internat. Inc., 2000—08, Laboratory Corp. of America Holdings, 2006—, P.F. Chang's China Bistro, Inc., 2009—, Chiquita Brands Internat., Inc., 2009—. Mem. fin. com. The Columbus Found.; bd. mem. Grant-Riverside Hosp.; mem. dean's adv. com. Fisher Coll. Bus., Ohio State U.; bd. trustees Elon U. Office: Chiquita Brands International Inc 550 S Caldwell St Ste 1010 Charlotte NC 28202-2681 Office Phone: 513-784-8000. Office Fax: 513-784-8030. Business E-Mail: kerrii.anderson@chiquitabrands.com.

ANDERSON, KEVEN L., former legislator; b. Jefferson City, Mo., Nov. 8, 1966; m. Lisa Anderson; children: Chelsea, Joshua. Mem. Loan office, Boatmans Bank, 1989—92; gen. mgr. Sibley Industries Inc., 1993—2001; state rep. Dist.96 Ark., 2003—08; chmn. Utilities subcommittee; mem. Ins. & Commerce Com., Legislature Joint Auditing Comg, Revenue & Taxation Com., Complaints & Remediation Subcommittee; house rep. Ark. Mem.: PTA Westside Elementary Sch. (mem. watch dog bd. 1998—), Rogers Youth Ctr. (coach 1999—), Peace Lutheran Ch., Rogers, Lowell C. of C. (pres. coun. 1997). Republican. Lutheran. Mailing: 1712 S 28th St Rogers AR 72758 Office: Ark House Repr State Capitol Rm 350 Little Rock AR 72201 Office Phone: 479-621-9611. Fax: 479-631-8068.

ANDERSON, LEE, state legislator; b. Jan. 06; m. Donna Robertson; children: Ben, Katie. Attended, Abraham Baldwin Ag. Coll., Brewton Parker Coll. Owner & farmer Anderson Farms; mem. & chmn. Columbia Bd. Edn., 2001—; co. commr. & vice-chmn Columbia Co. Dist. 4, 2005—; mem. Dist. 117 Ga. House of Reps., 2009—. Former pres. Columbia Co. Farm Bur., 1982—2008, mem. bd. dir.; mem. Ga. Cattlemen's Assn.; Deacon Powell Baptist Ch. Republican. Baptist. Office: 608 Coverdell Legislative Office Bldg Atlanta GA 30334 Mailing: 160 Louisville Rd Grovetown GA 30813 Office Phone: 404-656-0298, 706-394-1812. Personal E-mail: lee.anderson@house.ga.gov.

ANDERSON, MARY ANN GRASSO, business executive; b. Rome, NY, Nov. 3, 1952; d. Vincent and Rose Mary (Pupa) Grasso; m. J. Wayne Anderson, Feb. 14, 2004. BA in Art History, U. Calif., Riverside, 1973; MLS, U. Oreg., 1974. Dir. Warner Rsch. Collection, Burbank, Calif., 1975-84; mgr. CBS TV/Docudrama, Hollywood, Calif., 1984-88; v.p., exec. dir. Nat. Assn. Theatre Owners, North Hollywood, Calif., 1988—2007; tourism dir. Bath County, Va., 2010—. Instr. theatre arts UCLA, 1980-85, Am. Film Inst., L.A., 1985-88; founder, CEO Belief Work, motivational speaker; pres., CEO An Affair of the Heart, perform weddings, plan weddings. Screen credits: The Scarlet O'Hara Wars, This Year's Blonde, The Silent Lovers, A Bunnies Tale, Embassy. Mem. Burbank Heritage Commn. Recipient Friend award, Tripod Sch., 1999, Stace award, Dolby, 2002, Intersoc. Ken Mason award, 2004, award of commendation, Sci.-Tech. Acad. Motion Pictures Art Scis., 2007; named ShoWester of Yr., NATO/ShoWest, 2007, Showeast Hall of Fame. Mem.: Found. of the Motion Picture Pioneers, Acad. Motion Picture Arts and Scis., Retinitis Pigmentosa Internat. (The Vision award 1996), Bus. and Profl. Women's Assn. (Woman of Achievement award 1983), Phi Beta Kappa. Avocations: music, dance. Office Phone: 540-997-0203. Personal E-mail: maa21158@aol.com.

ANDERSON, MAXWELL L., museum director; b. NYC, May 1, 1956; AB, Dartmouth Coll., 1977; AM, Harvard U., 1978, PhD, 1981. Asst. curator Met. Mus., 1982-87; dir. Michael C. Carlos Mus., Atlanta, 1987-95, Art Gallery Ont., Toronto, Canada, 1995-98; Alice Pratt Brown dir. Whitney Mus. Am. Art, NYC, 1998—2003; leadership fellow Chief Exec. Leadership Inst., Yale Univ., 2003—04; prin. AEA Consulting, 2004—06; dir. and CEO Indpls. Mus. Art, 2006—11; dir Dallas Mus. Art, Dallas, 2011—. Lectr. Roman art Princeton (N.J.) U., 1985; vis. prof. U. di Roma, 1987; adj. assoc. prof. Emory U., 1989-95. Arranged exhbns. Treasures of the Holy Land, 1986, Roman Portraits in Context, 1988, Souls Grown Deep, 1996, Wired Mus., 1997, 2000 Biennial Exhbn.; contbr. articles to profl. jours.; author "Metrics of Success in Art Muesums:, 2004, Getty Leadership Inst.; co-author "Generating and Sustaining Nonprofit Income", 2004, Yale Sch. Mgmt. Decorated Commendatore dell'Ordine al Merito della Repubblica Italiana; recipient Lotos Club medal, 2003, OTTY award, 2003; named cultural laureate, Hist. Landmarks Preservation Ctr., 1999. Mem.: Assn. Art Mus. Dirs. (pres.), Coll. Art Assn., Am. Assn. Mus. Office: Dallas Mus Art 1717 N Harwood Dallas TX 75201*

ANDERSON, MAYNARD CARLYLE, security firm executive; b. Hesper, Iowa, Aug. 6, 1932; s. Carl Adolph and Mathilda Theodora (Wold) A. BA, Luther Coll., 1954. Mem. spl. ops. group Hqrs. Dept. of Navy, Washington, 1966-68, supervising agt. Naval Investigative Svc. Office Guantanamo Bay, Cuba, 1968-69, asst. head internal security divsn. hqrs. Washington, 1969-73, dir. spl. security and spl. activiites, 1973-78, dir. spl. security, 1978-79; dep. security policy Dept. of Def., Washington, 1979-82, dir. security plans and programs, 1982-88, asst. dep. under sec., 1988-93, acting dep. under sec. def., 1993-94; pres., mng. dir. Arcadia Group Worldwide, Inc., Chantilly, Va., 1994—2006; founder Arcadia Inst., Alexandria, Va., 1997; prin. Strategic Trade Adv. Group, Inc., Washington, 1997—2004. Dir. Nat. Intellectual Property Law Inst., Washington, 1994; chmn. policy com. Security Affairs Support Assn., Washington, 1988—94; former chmn. adv. com. Dept. of Def. Security Inst., Dept. of Def. Polygraph Inst., Def. Pers. Security Rsch. and Edn. Ctr.; chmn. Nat. Adv. Group/Security Countermeasures; hon. faculty mem. Def. Security Inst.; lectr. Sch. Criminal Justice, Coll. Social Sci. Mich. State U., mem. rsch. task force; lectr. Luther Coll., Decorah, Iowa; del. UN Econ. Commn. for Europe, Com. on Sustained Devel., 1999—; dir. VT Group, Inc., Atlanta, 2002—12, mng. dir. multi-sector crisis mgmt. consortium, Arlington, Va., 2003—07; dir. Leader Tech., Inc., Columbus, Ohio, 2007—, Nat. Security Inst., Boston, 1995—, Klastelecom Svc. Inc., 2010—; bd. advisors NC4, LA, 2007—; bd. dirs. Leave No Veteran Behind, Chgo., 2008—. Author/contbr.: Citizen Espionage: Studies in Trust and Betrayal, 1994; contbr. articles to profl. jours. Mem. pres. coun. Luther Coll., Decorah, Iowa, 1990—. Recipient Meritorious Exec. Presdl. Rank award, Washington, 1985, 92, Disting. Svc. award Luther Coll., Decorah, 1989, Donald B. Woodbridge award of excellence Nat. Classification Mgmt. Soc., Washington, 1990, Def. Disting. Svc. medal, 1992. Lutheran. Avocations: tennis, writing, lecturing, travel. Home: 205 S Yoakum Pky Apt 721 Alexandria VA 22304-3818 Office: The Arcadia Inst Inc PO Box 22030 Alexandria VA 22304 E-mail: arcadiagwi@iopener.net.

ANDERSON, MIKE, men's college basketball coach; b. Birmingham, Ala., Dec. 12, 1959; m. Marcheita Anderson; children: Darcheita, Michael Jr., Yvonne, Suney. Attended, Jefferson State Jr. Coll., Birmingham, U. Tulsa, Okla. Vol. asst. coach U. Tulsa Golden Hurricane, 1982—85; part-time asst., asst. head coach, recruiting coord. U. Ark. Razorbacks, 1985—2002, head basketball coach, 2011—, U. Ala. Birmingham Blazers, 2002—06, U. Mo. Tigers, 2006—11. Named Ray Meyer Coach of Yr., Conf. USA, 2004. Office: University Ark Mens Basketball Bud Walton Arena PO Box 7777 Fayetteville AR 72702 Office Phone: 479-575-6389.

ANDERSON, NORMAN DEAN, science education educator, writer; b. Dickens, Iowa, Jan. 29, 1928; s. Eddie and Effie Mae (Condra) A.; separated; children: Brent, Beth, Jeffrey, Todd, Jonathan, Julie. BA, U. Iowa, 1951, MA, 1956; PhD, Ohio State U., 1965. Cert. tchr. and adminstr., Iowa, N.C. Tchr. sci., supr. Burlington (Iowa) Pub. Schs., 1952-59; tchr. sci. Sch. Twp. of Pleasant Valley, Bettendorf, Iowa, 1959-61; instr. Ohio State U., Columbus, 1961-63; prof. sci. edn. N.C. State U., Raleigh, 1963-94. Author: Ozone: A Source Book for Teaching About Ozone in the Troposphere and Stratosphere, 1995; Ferris Wheels: An Illustrated History, 1992; co-author: Science, Students and Schools, 1980, Halley's Comet, 1981, Ferris Wheels, 1984, others (textbook series) Life Science, Physical Science, Earth Science, 1977. Trustee Peace Coll., Raleigh, 1970-75; bd. dirs. N.C. Marine Edn. Found., Raleigh, 1983-89. With U.S. Army, 1946, Japan. With US Army, 1946—47. Recipient Disting. Svc. award N.C. Sci. Tchrs. Assn., 1989; named to Hall Fame, Ohio State U. Coll. Edn., 2006. Fellow AAAS; Mem. NEA (life), Nat. Sci. Tchrs. Assn. (life), Nat. Assn. for Rsch. in Sci. Teaching, Sigma Xi, Phi Kappa Phi, Phi Delta Kappa. Presbyterian. Avocation: woodworking. Home: PO Box 33211 Raleigh NC 27636-3211 Business E-Mail: norman@ncsu.edu.

ANDERSON, PATRICK, state legislator; m. Kelly Anderson; children: Katlyn, Lauren. BS, Okla. State Univ.; JD, Univ. Okla. V.p., financial svc. divsn. Ctr. Nat. Bank & Trust County; mem. Dist. 19 Okla. State Senate, 2004—. Republican. Office: 2300 N Lincoln Blvd Rm 417A Oklahoma City OK 73105 Mailing: 2016 Comanche Trail Enid OK 73703 Address: PO Box 5589 Enid OK 73702 Office Phone: 405-521-5630. Business E-Mail: anderson@oksenate.gov.

ANDERSON, PHILIP SIDNEY, lawyer; b. Little Rock, May 9, 1935; s. Philip Sidney and Frances (Walt) Anderson; m. Rosemary Gill Wright, Sept. 26, 1959 (dec.); children: Sidney Walt Kenyon, Philip Wright, Catherine Gill Askew; m. Annette L. Connaway Anderson, Nov. 24, 2012. BA, LLB, U. Ark., 1959. Bar: Ark. 1960, U.S. Supreme Ct. 1966. Assoc. Wright, Lindsey & Jennings, Little Rock, 1960—65, ptnr., 1965—88, Williams & Anderson PLC, Little Rock, 1988—2007, ptnr. & sr. counsel, 2008—. Lectr. Ark. Law Sch., 1963—66; mem. com. on jury instrns. Ark. Supreme Ct., 1962—97; mem. panel for 8th cir. U.S. Cir. Judge Nominating Commn., 1978—79; mem. fed. adv. com. U.S. Ct. Appeals 8th cir., 1983—88, co-chmn., 1987—88; bd. dirs. WEHCO Media, Inc., Ark. Dem.-Gazette, Inc. Co-author: Arkansas Model Jury Instructions, 1965, 1974, 1989. Pres. Friends of Little Rock Pub. Libr., 1968—69, Little Rock Unltd. Progress, Inc., 1973—74; trustee Ctrl. Ark. Libr. Sys., 1981—87, pres., 1984; trustee George W. Donaghey Found., 1976—, pres., 1979—80. 2d lt. US Army, 1959—60. Fellow: American Acad. Arts & Sciences, Ark. Bar Found. (pres. 1973—74), Am. Bar Found. (Outstanding Svc. award 2013); mem.: ABA (chair ho. of dels. 1992—94, pres. 1998—99), American Law Inst. (mem. coun. 1982—2010, mem. emeritus 2011—), Ark. Bar Assn. (spl. award meritorious svc.), The Grolier Club of the City of N.Y. Episcopalian. Home: 4716 Crestwood Dr Little Rock AR 72207-5436 Office: Williams & Anderson PLC 111 Center St Ste 2200 Little Rock AR 72201-4429

ANDERSON, RALPH, state legislator; b. Greenville, SC, Nov. 2, 1927; s. Johnnie Anderson and Annie M. Anderson.; m. Geraldine Lewis; children: Valerie, Ralph L., Joel T. BA, Allen U., 1949. Postmaster US Postal Svc., 1970—83; city councilman City of Greenville, SC, 1983, SC, 1991; mem. Dist. 23 SC House of Reps., 1991—96; mem. Dist. 7 SC State Senate, 1996—, mem. Edn. Com., Fin. Com., Med. Affairs Com. & Transp. Com. Mem.: Masons, VFW, America Legion, NAACP, Greater Greenville C of C. Democrat. Baptist. Mailing: 315 Elder St Greenville SC 29607 Office: 504 Gressette Bldg Columbia SC 29201 Home Phone: 803-238-0611; Office Phone: 803-212-6032. E-mail: RA@scsenate.org.

ANDERSON, REUBEN V., lawyer, board member; b. Jackson, Miss., Sept. 16, 1942; m. Phyllis Wright; children: Vincent, Raina. BA, Tougaloo Coll., 1964; JD, U. Miss., 1967. Miss. assoc. counsel NAACP Legal Def. and Ednl. Fund, Inc., 1967—75; ptnr. Anderson, Banks, Nichols & Stewart, Jackson, 1968—77; judge Miss. State Municipal Ct., Jackson, Miss., 1975—77, Miss. State County Ct., Hinds County, Miss., 1977—82, 7th Judicial Dist., Miss Cir. Ct., 1982—85; justice Miss. Supreme Ct., Jackson, 1985—90; ptnr. to sr. ptnr. Phelp Dunbar LLP, 1991—. Jamie L. Whitten Chair of Law and Govt. U. Miss., 1995; bd. dirs. Trustmark, 1978—2009, MINACT, Inc., Jackson, Miss., Kroger Co., 1991—, Burlington Resources, 2001—06, BellSouth Corp., 1994—2006, AT&T Inc., 2006—. Bd. dirs. Jackson Med. Mall Found., The Nature Conservancy, United Way Capital; trustee Ole Miss Alumni Assn., Piney Woods Country Life Sch.; past chmn. bd. Tougaloo Coll., Lauren Rogers Mus. of Art; past chair Rhodes Scholarship Selection Com. for Miss. Named U. Miss. Sch. Law Alumnus of the Yr., 2005; named to U. Miss. Alumni Hall of Fame, 1995, Nat. Bar Assn. Hall of Fame, 2009, U. Miss. Sch. Law Alumni Hall of Fame, 2011. Mem. Miss. Bar Assn.(pres. 1997-98, Lifetime Achievement award, 2007), NAACP, ABA, Nat. Bar Assn., Hinds County Bar Assn., American Arbitration Assn. (bd. dirs.), Magnolia Bar Assn., Nat. Bar Assn., 100 Black Men of Jackson, US Fifth Ct. of Appeals Bar Assn., US Supreme Ct. Bar Assn. Democrat. Achievements include being the first African-American graduate of the University of Mississippi Law School; first African-American judge on the Mississippi Supreme Court; first African-American President of the Mississippi Bar Association. Office: Phelps Dunbar LLP 4270 I-55 North Jackson MS 39211-6391 Office Fax: 601-360-9339, 601-360-9777. Business E-Mail: anderson@phelps.com.

ANDERSON, RICHARD A., telecommunications industry executive; b. Ky. BS in Mktg. magna cum laude, Murray State U., 1980, MBA, 1981. Group pres., global bus. svcs. AT&T Corp.; acct. exec. South Ctrl. Bell, 1981—88; v.p., product mgmt., exec. v.p. & COO Universal Comm. Sys., 1988—93; pres., interconnection svcs. Bellsouth Corp., 1993—99, pres., customer markets, 1999—2005, vice chmn., planning & adminstrn., 2005—06, vice chmn., pres., bus. markets, 2006—07; exec. dir. Georgia Regional Transportation Authority, 2008—. Bd. dirs. Cingular Wireless, 2002—07, Adtran, Inc., 2004—06, SciTrek, MetroPCS Comm., Inc., 2009—, Computer Svcs., Inc., 2010—. Chmn. Metro Atlanta C. of C.; mem. dean's adv. coun. Murray State U. Coll. Bus. and Pub. Affairs; bd. dirs. Camp Twin Lakes. Mem.: Atlanta C. of C. (bd. dirs.), Lambda Chi Alpha (bd. dirs.). Office: MetroPCS Communications Inc Bd Directors 2250 Lakeside Blvd Richardson TX 75082 Office Phone: 214-570-5800. Office Fax: 214-570-5859. Business E-Mail: randerson@metropcs.com.

ANDERSON, RICHARD EDMUND, city manager, consultant; b. Ferndale, Mich., Dec. 23, 1938; s. Richard H. and Carolyn Jeanne (Figg) A.; m. Kay Clarke, Nov. 6, 1961 (div.); children: Pam, Mark, Linda; m. Linda (Hawk)Jenkins, Sept. 11, 1997; stepchildren: Travis, Todd. BA, Mich. State U., 1962; postgrad. in advanced mgmt., Harvard U., 1979. Aide to mgr. City of St. Petersburg, Fla., 1962-64; adminstrv. asst. City of Ft. Lauderdale, Fla., 1964-67, dep. mgr., 1967-75, city mgr., 1975-80; v.p. Fla. Innovation Group, Tampa, 1980-81; pres. Intragrated Systems Assocs., Inc., Ft. Lauderdale, 1981-90; city mgr. City of Florida City, Fla., 1990-94, City of Brooksville, Fla., 1995—2007, Holiday Pk. Recreation Dist., Fla., 2008—. Contbr. articles to profl. jours. Mem. Internat. City Mgmt. Assn., Fla. City, County Mgmt. Assn. Office: 215 Holiday Park Blvd Palm Bay FL 32907 Home Phone: 352-796-3734; Office Phone: 321-724-2240. Business E-Mail: reago@bigroot.com.

ANDERSON, RICHARD H., air transportation executive; b. Galveston, Tex., 1956; m. Susan Anderson. BS, U. Houston, 1977; JD, South Tex. Coll. Law, 1981. Various positions Harris County Dist. Atty.'s office, Houston, 1978—87; staff v.p., dep. gen. counsel Continental Airlines, 1987—90; v.p., dep. gen. counsel Northwest Airlines Corp., Eagan, Minn., 1990—94, sr. v.p. labor rels., state affairs and law, 1994—96, sr. v.p. tech. ops. and airport affairs, 1997—98, exec. v.p., COO, 1998—2001, CEO, 2001—04; exec. v.p., CEO Ingenix subs. UnitedHealth Group, Inc., Mpls., 2005—06, exec. v.p., pres. comml. svc. group, 2006—07; CEO Delta Air Lines, Inc., Atlanta, 2007—. Bd. dirs. Mesaba Holdings, Inc., 1999—2003, Northwest Airlines Corp., 2001—05, Medtronic, Inc., 2002—, Xcel Energy, Inc., 2004—06, Cargill, Inc., 2006—, Delta Airlines, Inc., 2007—, Fed. Res. Bank Atlanta. Office: Delta Air Lines Inc PO Box 20706 Atlanta GA 30320-6001 also: 1030 Delta Blvd Atlanta GA 30320-6001*

ANDERSON, RICHARD L., state legislator, retired military officer; b. Roanoke, Va., May 30, 1955; m. Ruth Anderson; children: Scott M., Brooke J. Nines, John R., Bria R. BA in Polit. Sci., Va. Polytechnic Inst. and State U., Blacksburg, 1979; BA in Pub. Adminstrn., Webster U., St. Louis, 1982; grad., Air War Coll., Air U., Maxwell AFB, Ala., 1998. Enlisted USAF, 1979, sr. mil. advisor to the dep. under sec., comdr. Titan II Intercontinental Ballistic Missile combat crew, leader & operator Minuteman II Intercontinental Ballistic Missile squadron, missiles, launch crew, sr. leader Strategic Air Command Hdqs., US Atlantic Command Hdqs., US Pacific Command Hdqs., Pentagon, ret. col., 2009; sr. mil. asst. Office of Sec. Def.; mem. Dist. 51 Va. House of Delegates, Richmond, 2010—. Former nat. comdr. USAF Auxiliary Civil Air Patrol. Mem. Prince William Com. 100, Lake Ridge-Occoquan-Coles Civic Assn.; usher Lake Ridge Bapt. Ch. Decorated Combat Readiness medal, Humanitarian Svc. medal, Meritorious Svc. medal, Def. Meritorious Svc. medal, Global War on Terrorism medal, Legion of Merit. Mem.: Mil. Officers Assn. America, Mt. Vernon Chpt., Air Force Assn. (life), VFW Post 1503, Am. Legion Post 364 (life). Republican. Office: Va House of Dels Gen Assembly Bldg Rm 406 PO Box 406 Richmond VA 23218 also: PO Box 7926 Woodbridge VA 22195 Office Phone: 804-698-1051, 571-264-9983. Office Fax: 804-698-6751. Business E-Mail: delranderson@house.virginia.gov.

ANDERSON, ROBERT E., diagnostic radiologist; MD, U. Minn., 1965. Diplomate Am. Bd. Radiology-diagnostic radiology, 1970. Intern Hennepin County Med. Ctr.; resident diagnostic radiology Univ. of Minn. Med. Ctr., Minneapolis, 1966—69; hosp. affiliation includes Orlando South Seminole Hosp. Office: Orlando South Seminole Hospital 1300 S Orange Ave Orlando FL 32806-2113 Office Phone: 407-423-2581.

ANDERSON, ROBERT J., oil and gas industry executive; BS in Petroleum Engring., U. Wyo., 1986; MBA in Corp. Fin., U. Denver, 1988. Petroleum engr. Anadarko Petroleum Corp., 2000—04; v.p. acquisitions and divestitures ARCO Inc., 2004, Southern Bay Energy LLC., 2005; v.p. bus. devel., acquisitions & divestitures GeoResources, Inc., 2007—. Office: GeoResources Inc Southern Bay Energy 110 Cypress Station Dr, Ste 220 Houston TX 77090 Office Phone: 281-537-9920. Office Fax: 281-537-8324. Business E-Mail: randerson@georesourcesinc.com.

ANDERSON, ROBERT LANIER, III, federal judge; b. Macon, Ga., Nov. 12, 1936; s. Robert Lanier II and Helen Anderson; m. Nancy Briska, Aug. 18, 1962; 3 children. AB magna cum laude, Yale U., 1958; LLB, Harvard U., 1961. Assoc. Anderson, Walkert, Reichert, Macon, Ga., 1963—79; judge US Ct. Appeals (5th cir.), 1979—81, US Ct. Appeals (11th cir.), 1981—2009, chief judge Macon, Ga., 1999—2002, sr. judge, 2009—. With USAR, 1958—61, capt. US Army, 1961—63. Mem.: ABA, Am. Judicature Soc., State Bar of Ga., Macon Bar Assn., Ga. Bar Assn. Office: US Ct Appeals PO Box 977 Macon GA 31202-0977

ANDERSON, STANLEY THOMAS, federal judge; b. Lexington, Tenn., 1953; BS, U. Tenn., 1976; JD, U. Memphis Sch. Law, 1980. Bar: Tenn. 1980. Atty. Davis, Smith & Anderson, 1980—83; asst. commr. Tenn. Dept. Transp., 1983—85; claims commr. Tenn. Dept. Treasury, 1985—87; owner, mgr. Anderson Law Firm PLLC, 1987—2003; magistrate judge US Dist. Ct. (we. dist.) Tenn., 2003—08, judge, 2008—. Office: US Dist Ct Fed Bldg 167 N Main St Memphis TN 38103 Office Phone: 731-421-9273.

ANDERSON, STEPHEN C., diagnostic radiology, educator; MD, U. Md., 1984. Diplomate Am. Bd. Radiology-diagnostic radiology, 1988. Fellow ultrasound, CT and MRI Duke Univ., Durham, 1988—89; resident diagnostic radiology Univ. South Fla., Tampa, 1984—88, asst. clin. prof. Coll. of Medicine. Office: University of South Florida School of Medicine 12901 Bruce B Downs Blvd Tampa FL 33612

ANDERSON, STEVEN C., pharmacy association executive; BA, Cornell Coll., 1975. Clk. House of Commons UK of Gr. Britain and No. Ireland; Rep. candidate U.S. rep. for 16th dist. Ill., 1980; sr. staff mem. for U.S. rep. John B. Anderson US House of Representatives, chmn. Rep. Conf.; pres., CEO Am. Frozen Food Inst.; chmn. Inst. Orgn. Mgmt. U.S. C. of C.; pres., CEO Nat. Restaurant Assn., 1999—2007, Nat. Assn. Chain Drug Stores, 2007—. Vis. lectr. Kellogg Sch. Mgmt. Northwestern U., Wash. Coll. Law Am. U.; Paul E. Wise Exec. in Residence U. Del. Office: Nat Assn Chain Drug Stores 413 N Lee St Alexandria VA 22314-2301 Office Phone: 703-549-3001. Office Fax: 703-836-4869.

ANDERSON, STEVEN GOODWIN, medical products executive; b. St. Paul, Jan. 10, 1939; s. Goodwin S. and Edith (Moon) A.; m. Ann Bernice Bezoier, Nov. 21, 1961; children: Bruce G., Elizabeth M. BA, U. Minn., 1961. Salesman Merck, Sharp & Dohme, West Point, Pa., 1962-67; salesman, regional mgr. Medtronic, Inc., Mpls., 1967-72; divisional mgr. Concept, Inc., Clearwater, Fla., 1972-73; v.p., COO Biotronik GmBH, St. Petersburg, Fla., 1973—76; v.p. mktg., sr. exec. v.p. Intermedics, Inc., Freeport, Tex., 1976-83; chmn., pres. & CEO CryoLife, Inc., Marietta, Ga., 1984—. Inventor pacemaker electrodes. Sgt. U.S. Army. 1961-62. Named Entrepreneur of the Yr., Arthur Young & Co., Inc. mag., 1987. Fellow Kenan Inst. Pvt. Enterprise, Assn. Venture Founders, Inc.; mem. Inst. Am.Entrepreneurs (life). Avocations: golf, raising boxers. Office: CryoLife Inc 1655 Roberts Blvd Kennesaw GA 30144-3632 Office Fax: 770-952-9743. Business E-Mail: steven.anderson@cryolife.com.

ANDERSON, TERENCE JAMES, law educator; b. Chgo., Feb. 26, 1940; s. James E. and Charlotte (Flatley) A.; m. Carolyn Bugh; children: Michael, Kathleen, Jamie, Andrew, Rachel Bugh, Cristina Gonzalez. BA, Wabash Coll., 1961; JD, U. Chgo., 1964. Bar: Ill. 1967, D.C. 1973, Fla. 1977. Local cts. commr. Zomba, Malawa, Africa, 1964-66; assoc. Goldberg, Weigle, Mallin & Gitles, Chgo., 1966-69, ptnr., 1970-73; att. prof. Antioch Sch. of Law, Washington, 1973-78, acad. dean, 1975-76; vis. prof. U. Miami Sch. of Law, Coral Gables, Fla., 1976-78, prof., 1978—. Spl. counsel to gen. counsel SEC, Washington, summers 1980-81; dir. Legal Svcs. of Greater Miami, Inc., 1977-83. Author (with William Twining and David Schum): Analysis of Evidence, 1991, 2d edit., 2005; author: The Battles of Hastings: Four Stories in Search of a Meaning, 1996. Bd. dirs. ACLU of South Fla., 1981-85; counsel to former U.S. Judge Alcee L. Hastings and now mem. Ho. of Reps., 1982-93. Netherlands Inst. Advanced Studies fellow, 1994-95. Mem. ABA, Am. Assn. Law Schs. Office: University Miami Sch Law PO Box 248087 Miami FL 33124-8087 Office Phone: 305-284-2253.

ANDERSON, TIMOTHY J., chemical engineering distinguished professor; PhD, U. Calif., Berkeley, 1980. Prof. chem. engring., assoc. dean rsch. and grad. programs U. Fla., Gainsville. Contbr. articles to profl. jours. Recipient Charles M.A. Stine award in Materials Engring. and Sci., Am. Inst. Chem. Engrs., 1994. Mem.: IEEE, AIChE, Electrochemical Soc., Materials Rsch. Soc. Office: U Fla Coll Engring 300 Weil Hall Gainesville FL 32611-6005 Office Phone: 352-392-0946. Office Fax: 352-392-9673. E-mail: tim@ufl.edu.

ANDERSON, WILLIAM BANKS, JR., ophthalmology educator; b. Durham, NC, June 14, 1931; s. William Banks and Mildred Ursula (Everett) A.; m. Nancy Eldridge Walker, Sept. 17, 1960; children: Mary Banks, Mark Eldridge, Elizabeth Perry. AB, Princeton U., 1952; MD, Harvard U., 1956. Diplomate: Am. Bd. Ophthalmology (dir. 1986-92). Intern Duke U. Med. Ctr., Durham, NC, 1956-57, resident, 1959-62, asst. prof. ophthalmology, 1962-67, assoc. prof. ophthalmology, 1967-76, prof. ophthalmology, 1976—2007, acting chmn., 1991-92, prof. emeritus, 2007—. Mem. profl. adv. com. N.C. Div. Services to the Blind, Raleigh, 1972-84 Chmn. bd. trustees Durham Acad., 1975-77. Served to capt. M.C. U.S. Army, 1957-59. Fellow ACS; mem. Am. Ophthalmol. Soc. (sec.-treas. 1989-98, v.p. 1998-99, pres. 1999-2000), Am. Acad. Ophthalmology (bd. dirs. 1986-89), Am. Bd. Ophthalmology (bd. dirs. 1986-93). Episcopalian. Home: 2401 Cranford Rd Durham NC 27705-1011

ANDERSON-LEHMAN, RON, air transportation executive; married; 3 children. BS in Computer Sci., Iowa State U., Ames. Computer programmer United Airlines, 1986; with Covia, Galileo Internat.; mng. dir. tech. Continental Airlines, Inc., Houston, 2000—03, staff v.p. tech., 2003, sr. v.p., chief info. officer, 2004—. Bd. dirs. OpenTravel Alliance. Office: Continental Airlines Inc PO Box 4607 Houston TX 77210

ANDERSON-MEJIAS, PAMELA L., applied linguistics professor; b. Indpls., May 31; d. George E. and Clara L. Anderson; m. Hugo A. Mejias, Jan. 1982; children: Nicholas A. Mejias, Nathaniel H. Mejias, Joscelyn C. Mejias. PhD, Ind. U., 1980. Prof. U. Tex. Pan Am., Edinburg, 1981—; chair English dept. UTPA. Vis. asst. prof. U. Hawaii, Honolulu, 1980—81. Lang. edn. mem. Valley Grande Inst. Academic Success, Weslaco, Tex., 2000—. Achievements include research in language and sociolinguistics on the US Mexican border. Office: U Tex Pan Am 1201 University Dr Edinburg TX 78539

ANDES, JOAN KEENEN, tax specialist; b. Clarksburg, W.Va., Apr. 23, 1930; d. Ree Martin and Mary Ruth (Pyle) Groghan; m. William Anderson Keenen, Oct. 15, 1949 (dec.); children: Paula Annette Keenen Skelton, William Ree Keenen; 1 foster child, Donald Monroe Dreyer; m. Ralph Paul Andes, Sept. 29, 1976(dec Jan. 6, 2011) Pvt. sec. State Capitol, Charleston, W.Va., 1948-49; statis. typist various acctg. offices, Beaumont, Tex., 1949—60; owner Machine Acctg. and Computing, Beaumont, 1960-70, Automated Enterprises Keypunch Sch., Beaumont, 1962-72; pres. Applied Data Processing, Beaumont, 1970-83; owner Applied Info. Processing, Beaumont, 1983-90, APEX-Bookkeeping and Tax Svc., Beaumont, 1981—2011. Active Westgate Youth Group, 1984-90; vol. Mexican Mission Ch. of Christ, 1984—. Mem. Data Processing Mgmt. Assn. (pres. 1972-73, 80, awards chmn. 1985-86) Republican. Mem. Ch. of Christ. Avocations: counted cross stitch, coin collecting/numismatics. Home: 1410 Marshall Place Dr Beaumont TX 77706-3221

ANDES, LARRY DALE, minister; b. Warrenton, Va., June 7, 1947; s. William Christian and Hilda Elizabeth (Beach) A.; m. Bobbi E. Stephens, July 16, 1966; 1 child, Joshua Dale. BS in Pastoral Studies, North Ctrl. U., 1991; student, U. Richmond, 1991, Bethel Theol. Sem., 1992. Ordained to ministry Assembly of God Ch., 1975, non-denominational, 1987. Assoc. pastor Calvary Assembly of God, Staunton, Va., 1971-72; youth min. Arlington (Va.) Assembly of God, 1972-75; assoc. pastor West End Assembly of God, Richmond, Va., 1975-76; founder, pres., festival dir. Fishnet Ministries Inc., Richmond, Front Royal, Va., 1976—; sr. pastor Fishnet Christian Ctr., Front Royal, 1992—. Named one of Outstanding Young Men of Am., 1984. Office: Fishnet Ministries Inc PO Box 1919 Front Royal VA 22630-1919 Office Phone: 540-636-2961. Personal E-mail: larryandes@hotmail.com. Business E-Mail: fishnet@fishnetministries.org.

ANDRADE, HOPE (ESPERANZA ANDRADE), state commissioner; b. San Antonio, July 1, 1949; d. Elpidio Leon and Eloisa (Gutierrez) Puente; m. Ramiro B. Andrade, Nov. 8, 1968; 1 child, Michael David. Attended, Our Lady of the Lake U., San Antonio. Adminstrv. asst. San Antonio Children's Ctr., 1970-74; adminstr. IBM Corp., San Antonio, 1974-79; CEO The Domestic Agy., Inc., San Antonio; sec. of state State of Tex., Austin, 2008—12; commr. representing employers Tex. Workforce Commn., Austin, 2013—. Group leader U. Tex. San Antonio Entrepreneurship Program, 1987—89; mem. Tex. Transp. Commn., 2003—08, chmn., 2008. Co-author: A Guide for the Household Employer, 1989. Named Woman of Yr., Houston chpt. Women's Transp. Seminar, Mother of Yr., Avance, Small Bus. Advocate of Yr., Small Bus. Adminstrn.; named to San Antonio Leadership Hall of Fame. Mem.: San Antonio Women's Chamber, Hispanic Chamber of Commerce (Lifetime Achievement award). Republican. Roman Catholic. Avocation: reading. Office: Texas Workforce Commission 101 E 15th St Austin TX 78778 Office Phone: 512-463-2222.*

ANDRAS, OSCAR SIDNEY (O.S. ANDRAS), energy executive; b. Bogalusa, La., July 23, 1935; s. Oscar Severin and Rosalyn (Rogers) A.; m. Mary Louise Sisk, June 3, 1957; children: Louis James, David Sisk. BS, La. State U., 1957. With Gulf Oil Corp., Port Arthur, Tex., 1957-59, Dow Chemical Co., Baton Rouge, 1959-67, Dow Chem Co., Houston, 1967-74, Dow Chemical Co., Midland, Mich., 1974-77, Houston, 1977-80, Enterprise Companies, Inc., Houston, 1980—2005; pres. & CEO Enterprise Products Co., 1996—2001, bd. dirs., 2005—; vice chmn., CEO Enterprise Products OLPGP Inc.; pres. Enterprise Products GP, LLC, 1998—2004, CEO, 1998—2005, vice chmn., 2004—05; bd. dirs. Enterprise GP Holdings, LP, 1998—, Enterprise Products Partners, LP, 1998—; vice chmn. EPCO, Inc., 2004—; bd. dirs. EPE Holdings, LLC, 2007—. Bd. dirs. Oasis Pipeline Co., 1974—80. Mem. Tex. Gov.'s Energy Council, Austin, 1975-77; pres. F.U.N. Football, Houston, 1972; bd. dirs. Meyerland Little League, 1970. Served to 2d lt. US Army, 1958. Republican. Roman Catholic. Office Phone: 713-381-6500. Office Fax: 713-381-8200. Business E-Mail: oandras@epplp.com.

ANDREWS, BILLY FRANKLIN, pediatrician, educator; b. Graham, NC, Sept. 22, 1932; s. Dean Franklin and Arlee (Byers) A.; m. Faye Rich, Dec. 25, 1953; children: Ann Elizabeth Feigenbaum, Billy Franklin Jr., David Ashley. Student, Brevard Coll., NC, 1950, Elon Coll., 1951; BS cum laude, Wake Forest Coll., 1953; MD, Duke U., 1957. Diplomate Am. Bd. Pediat., 1963. Commd. 2d lt. U.S. Army, 1956, advanced through grades to maj., 1962; intern Ft. Benning U.S. Army Hosp., Ga., 1957—58; resident in pediat. Walter Reed Gen. Hosp., Washington, 1958—60; with mil. med. and allied scis. course Walter Reed Army Inst. Rsch., Washington, 1960—61; chief pediat. svc. Rodriguez U.S. Army Hosp., Ft. Brooke, PR, 1961—63; chief pediat. Tropical Med. Rsch. Lab., Ft. Brooke, 1963—64; ret. U.S. Army, 1964; dir. newborn svcs. U. Louisville, 1964—76, from asst. prof. pediat. to chmn., 1964—93, chmn. emeritus, 1993—, dir. neonatology tng. program, 1965—86, dir. doctors' and nurses tng. program and regional tng. programs, 1965—93, co-dir. genetic counseling unit, 1965—68, dir. Comprehensive Health Care Ctr. for High Risk Infants and Children, 1968—98, co-dir. health profls. spl. project grant for preceptorship tng., 1974—77; chief staff Kosair Children's Hosp., Louisville, 1969—93, chief-of-staff emeritus, 1993—. Cons. divsn. adult and child health Ky. Dept. Pub. Health, 1966—2003; AOA advisor U. LSM, 1970—79; lectr. Jour. Pediat. Found., 1972; Staley Disting. Christian scholar Mary Baldwin Coll., Washington and Lee U., Sch. Medicine of U.Va., 1990; vis. scholar in med. history and ethics Green Coll., Oxford (Eng.) U., 1993, vis. fellow med. history, ethics and humanities, 1998—2005. Author: Children's Bill of Rights, 1968; editor: Small-for-Date Infants, 1970, The Newborn, Pediatric Clinics of North America, 1977, Aphorisms, Tributes and Tenets of Billy F. Andrews: In Walls, M.E., 1986, Ideals and Inspiration (F.R. Andrews), 1993, Words to Live By (F.R. Andrews), 1993, A Statement on Transplantation and Organ Donors, 1994; contbr. numerous articles to profl. publs.; inventor, poet. Pres. Kornhauser Libr., Health Scis. Ctr., 1981-82, 90-91; mem., tchr., deacon, elder United Ch. of Christ; bd. dirs. Oak Ridge Mil. Acad., 2004-07. Recipient Helen B. Fraser award, 1978, Norton-Children's Hosp. award for leadership in neonatology, 1978, Award of Recognition, XVII Internat. Congress Pediat., Manila, 1983, Wisdom award of honor, eminent fellow The Wisdom Soc., 1991, The Billy F. Andrews, M.D. Endowed Chair in Pediat., U. Louisville, 1993, Winston Churchill medal of Wisdom Soc., Eminent Churchill Fellow of Wisdom Soc., 1993, Disting. Alumnus award Wake Forest U., 1983; Festschrift to Billy F. Andrews, M.D., Jour. of Perinatology, 1995; Billy F. Andrews, MD, scholarship at U. Louisville Sch. Medicine named in his honor, 1986, Billy F. Andrews, MD lectureship in neonatology, U. Louisville, 2002; Named Best Drs. In US, 1979, Col. Ogden C. Bruton Pediat. Svc. Walter Reed Army Hosp., Wash., 2011 Fellow ACP, Am. Acad. Pediat., Royal Soc. Medicine (London); mem. AMA, Am. Pediat. Soc., Am. Osler Soc. (pres. 1996-97), Am. Soc. for Bioethics and Humanities, Soc. for Pediat. Rsch., So. Soc. Pediat. Rsch. (founding), Southeastern Perinatal Soc. (founding), Nat. Assn. Children's Hosps. and Related Instns. (founding), Ky. Med. Assn. (faculty Sci. Achievement award 1971, del. 1981-82, Ednl. Achievement award 1997), Greater Louisville Med. Soc., Ky. Pediat. Soc., Louisville Pediat. Soc., U. Louisville Sch. Medicine Alumni Assn. (bd. govs. 1972-75), Univ. Pediatric Found. Inc. (pres. 1982-93), Internat. Assn. Bioethics, Am. Soc. Law, Medicine and Ethics, Alpha Omega Alpha. Achievements include invention of infant oxygen hood, iontophoresis sweat induction apparatus, radiant open infant warmer, infant blood warmer, diagnostic and treatment table with warmer and position changes, head and extremities transeilluminator, infant transport incubator, others. Office: Kosair Charities Pediat Ctr 571 S Floyd St Ste 449 Louisville KY 40202-3830 Home Phone: 812-944-8087. Business E-Mail: bfandr01@louisville.edu.

ANDREWS, CATHERINE A., family practice physician; MD, U. Va., 1979. Diplomate Am. Bd. Family Practice. Resident family medicine Roanoke Memorial Hosp., Roanoke, Va., 1979—82; hosp. affiliation includes Kennestone Hosp. Office: Main Street Family Physicians 4791 S Main St Acworth GA 30101 Office Phone: 770-422-1400.

ANDREWS, CHARLES EDWARD, federal marshal; b. Monroeville, Ala., 1955; BA in Criminal Justice, U. Ala., 1977. Advanced through ranks to maj. Ala. Dept. Pub. Safety, 1980—2010, numerous positions including ABI area comdr. Mobile, Ala., 1990—94, chief svc. divsn., 1994—99, asst. dir. pub. safety, 1999—2003, chief Highway Patrol Divsn.; US marshal (southern dist.) Ala. US Marshals Svc., US Dept. Justice, Mobile, 2010—. Nat. chair state and provincial steering com. Nat. Orgn. Black Law Enforcement. Mem.: Internat. Assn. Chiefs of Police. Office: US Courthouse 113 St Joseph St Rm 413 Mobile AL 36602 Office Phone: 251-690-2841.

ANDREWS, CHARLES ELLIOTT (CHARLES ELLIOT ANDREWS JR.), management consultant; b. 1952; m. Jean Andrews; 3 children. BA in Acctg., Va. Tech., 1974. Chmn. Sallie Mae Bank, Utah; mng. ptnr., Mid-Atlantic reg. Arthur Andersen LLP, with, 1974—2002, ptnr., 1984—2002, global mng. ptnr., audit & adv. svcs., 2002; exec. v.p. acctg. & risk mgmt. SLM Corp. (Sallie Mae), Reston, Va., 2003—06, exec. v.p., CFO, 2006—07, pres., CEO, 2007—08; pres. RSM McGladrey, 2009—. Bd. adv., acctg. dept. Va. Tech.; bd. adv. R.B. Pamplin Coll. Bus.; bd. dirs. Inova Health Systems, The Greater Wash. Bd. Trade, Six Flags, Inc., U-Store-It Trust, NVR, Inc., 2008—. Chmn. Nat. Capital Chapter, ARC, Leadership Washington; bd. overseers Corcoran Gallery of Art; bd. dirs. Jr. Achievement, Boys' Home, Inc, Washington Performing Arts Soc.; mem. Washington/Balt. Regional 2012 Olympics Coalition, Fed. City Coun., Washington. Mem.: VSCPA, AICPA. Office: RSM McGladrey Inc 3rd Fl 3600 American Blvd W Bloomington MN 55431 Office Phone: 952-921-7700. Office Fax: 952-921-7702. Business E-Mail: candrews@mcgladrey.com.

ANDREWS, E. WYLLYS, archaeologist, educator; b. Phila., Oct. 10, 1943; s. Edward Wyllys IV and Ann (Wheeler) Andrews; m. Patricia Antell Andrews, June 15, 1965; children: Dwen Hardy Andrews-Cita, Edward Wyllys VI, Ruth Wheeler. AB, Harvard U., 1964; PhD, Tulane U., 1971. Asst. prof. anthropology No. Ill. U., DeKalb, 1970-75; dir. Mid. Am. Rsch. Inst., Program Rsch. in Yucatan Tulane U., New Orleans, 1972-74, dir. Mid. Am. Rsch. Inst., gen. editor publs., 1975—2009, assoc. prof. anthropology, 1975-80, prof. anthropology, 1980—2009, prof. emeritus, 2009—. Dir. excavations at Quelepa, El Salvador, Tulane U., 1967—69, dir. excavations at Komchen, Yucatan, Mex., 1980—84, dir. excavations Copan Royal Residence, Honduras, 1990—94. Author: The Archaeology of Quelepa, El Salvador, 1976, Excavations at Dzibilchaltun, Yucatan, Mexico, 1980; co-editor: Late Lowland Maya Civilization: Classic to Postclassic, 1986, Five Hundred Years After Columbus, 1994, Copan: The History of an Ancient Maya Kingdom, 2005; mem. editl. bd. Rsch. and Exploration, 1984-95, Latin Am. Antiquity, 1989-95, U. Pa. Mus., 2013-. Grantee NEA, 1978, NSF, 1980, Nat. Geog. Soc., 1992. Mem. Soc. for Am. Archaeology, Sociedad Mexicana de Antropologia. Avocations: photography, backpacking, cross country skiing, canoeing, skiing.

ANDREWS, JAMES RHEUBEN, orthopedic surgeon; b. New Orleans, La., May 2, 1942; m. Jenelle Andrews; children: Andy, Amy, Archie, Ashley, Amber, Abby. BS, La. State U., 1963, MD, 1967; LLD, Livingston U.; DSc, Troy State U., La. State U. Orthop. resident Tulane Med. Sch., 1969—70; surgical fellow in sports medicine U. Va. Med. Sch., 1972, U. Lyon, Lyn, France, 1972; co-founder Ala. Sports Medicine & Orthopedic Ctr. (ASMOC), 1986—2005; founder, med. dir. American Sports Medicine Inst. (ASMI), Birmingham, Ala.; founding mem. Andrews Sports Medicine & Orthopedic Ctr., Birmingham, Ala., 2005—; med. dir. Andrews Inst. for Orthopaedics & Sports Medicine, Gulf Breeze, Fla., 2007—. Clin. prof. orthopedic surgery U. Ala. Birmingham Med. Sch., Ala. Med. Sch., U. Va. Sch. Medicine, U. SC Med. Sch.; med. dir., intercollegiate sports Auburn U.; sr. orthopedic cons., intercollegiate athletics U. Ala.; orthopedic cons. for athletic teams Troy State U., U. West Ala., Tuskegee U., Samtord U.; spl. med. cons., dept. athletics, Ala.; med. dir. Tampa Bay Devil Rays; sr. orthopedic cons. Washington Redskins; team physician Birmingham Barons Double A, affiliate Chgo. White Sox; med. dir. Ladies Profl. Golf Assn.; mem., sports medicine com. US Olympic Com.; served on NCAA Competitive Safeguards in Medical Aspects of Sports Com.; current mem. med. and safety adv. com. USA Baseball; bd. dirs. Fast Health Corp., Robins Morton Constrn. Co. Author numerous sci. articles and books. Bd. trustees Troy State U. Recipient Disting. Sportsman award, Ala. Sports Hall of Fame, 1992, LSU Cox Communication Acad. Ctr. for Student-Athletes Disting. Alumnus of the Yr. award, 2008, Dave Dixon La. Sports Leadership award, 2008, Excellence in Sports Medicine award, Orthopaedic Found. for Active Lifestyles, 2010, Live the Dream! award, Birmingham Regional Chamber of Commerce, 2009, Disting. American award, Nat. Football Found. & Coll. Hall of Fame (Auburn chapter), 2009, SEC Physician of the Yr. award, 2010; named to The Ala. Sports Hall of Fame, 1992, The La. State U. Alumni Hall of Distinction, 1996, The State of La. Sports Hall of Fame, 2008. Mem.: Ladies Profl. Golf Assn., Internat. Knee Soc. (bd. dir.), Arthroscopy Assn. North America (bd. dir.), American Orthop. Soc. Sports Medicine (bd. dir., sec. bd. dir. 2004—05), American Acad. Orthop. Surgeons, American Bd. Orthop. Surgery. Widely recognized for his role in advancing the field of shoulder, knee and elbow surgery; mentored over 250 fellows throughout the course of his academic career; considered one of the foremost orthopedic surgeons and sports doctors in the world; performed successful operations on dozens of prominent athletes, including Troy Aikman, Roger Clemens and Jack Nicklaus. Address: Andrews Sports Medicine & Orthopaedic Center 805 St Vincent Dr Str 100 Birmingham AL 35205-1616 Office Phone: 205-581-7139. Office Fax: 205-939-3699. Business E-Mail: james.andrews@andrewscenters.com.

ANDREWS, MITCHELL DEWAYNE, internist, dean, educator; b. Enid, Okla., May 24, 1944; s. Mitchell S. and Truel Eva (Melton) A.; m. Rebecca Ellen Meltzer, Aug. 26, 1984. BS, Baylor U., 1966; MD, U. Okla., 1970. Diplomate Am. Bd. Internal Medicine. Resident internal medicine Johns Hopkins Hosp., Balt., 1970-71, U. Okla. Health Sci. Ctr., Oklahoma City, 1971-72, 74-76; asst. prof., assoc. prof., dir. residency program dept. medicine U. Okla., Oklahoma City, 1976-84, vice chmn., chief gen. internal medicine, prof. dept. medicine, 1986—, assoc. dean grad. med. edn. Coll. Medicine, 1994—2000, sr. assoc. dean, 1996—2002, v.p. health affairs, exec. dean, 2002—; chief of medicine regional med. ctr., vice chmn. dept. medicine U. Tenn. Coll. Medicine, Memphis, 1984-86; chief of staff U. Hosp., Oklahoma City, 1992-94, med. dir., 1994-96. Bd. dirs. Nat. Commn. Certification Physician Assts., 1995—2003. Editor: Jour. Okla. State Med. Assn., 1991—; contbr. numerous articles to profl. jours. Bd. dirs. Chamber Orch. Oklahoma City, 1982-84, Lyric Theatre, Oklahoma City, 1996-2000, Oklahoma City Philharm. Found., 2003—; del. Okla. State Leadership Initiative to Soviet Union, 1988. Surgeon CDC, USPHS, 1972-74. Recipient Stollerman award U. Tenn., 1986, Aesculapian award U. Okla. Coll. Medicine, 1989; ACP tchg. and rsch. scholar, 1976-79. Master ACP (bd. govs. Okla. 1995-99); mem. AMA, Alpha Omega Alpha. Episcopalian. Avocation: photography. Office: U Okla Coll Medicine RM 357 BMSB PO Box 26901 Oklahoma City OK 73126-0901

ANDREWS, NANCY CATHERINE, dean, pediatrician, hematologist, educator; b. Syracuse, NY, Nov. 29, 1958; d. William Shankland and Virginia Helen (Rogers) A.; m. Bernard Mathey-Prevot, Aug. 10, 1985; children: Camille, Nicolas. BS in Molecular Biophysics and Biochemistry, MS in Molecular Biophysics and Biochemistry, Yale U., 1980; PhD in Biology, MIT, 1985; MD, Harvard Med. Sch., 1987. Intern Children's Hosp., Boston, 1987-88, resident, 1988-89; fellow in pediat. hematology/oncology Children's Hosp. and Dana-Farber Cancer Inst., Boston, 1989-92; instr., pediatrics Harvard Med. Sch., Boston, 1991—93, asst. prof., 1993—98, assoc. prof., 1998—2003, prof., 2003—07, dean, basic scis. and grad. studies, 2003—07; vice chancellor academic affairs, dean Duke U. Sch. Medicine, Durham, NC, 2007—. Investigator Howard Hughes Med. Inst., Boston, 1993-2006; dir. Harvard MD-PhD Program, Boston, 1999-2003. Author: (chpt.) Hematology of Infancy and Childhood, 1997; contbr. articles to Nature, others. Merck-AFCR Found. fellow, 1991-94; recipient Rosenthal award 1998. Fellow Molecular Medicine Soc., Am. Acad. Arts & Scis.; mem. Soc. Pediat. Rsch. (Young Investigator award 1994), Am. Soc. Hematology (membership com. 1994—), Am. Soc. Clin. Investigation, Inst. Medicine. Democrat. Achievements include being the first women to be appointed dean of Duke University School of Medicine and becomes the only women to lead one of the nation's top 10 medical schools. Avocations: travel, gardening, cooking. Office: Duke U Sch Medicine Box 2927 Med Ctr Durham NC 27710 Office Phone: 919-684-2455. Office Fax: 919-684-0208. E-mail: nancy.andrews@duke.edu.

ANDREWS, RICHARD NIGEL LYON, academic administrator, educator; b. Newport, RI, Dec. 6, 1944; s. Nigel Lyon and Constance Doane (Young) A.; m. Hannah Page Wheeler, June 7, 1969; children: Sarah Huntington, Christopher Page Monteith AB, Yale U., 1966; M in Regional Planning, U. N.C., 1970, PhD, 1972. Vol. U.S. Peace Corps, Bharatpur, Nepal, 1966-68; budget examiner U.S. Office of Mgmt. and Budget, Washington, 1970-72; prof. U. Mich., Ann Arbor, 1972-81; prof. pub. policy U. N.C., Chapel Hill, 1981—, dir. U. N.C. Inst. Environ. Studies, 1981-91, dir. environ. mgmt. and policy program, 1990-94, mem. exec. com. faculty coun., 1994-97, chair of faculty, 1997-00, Thomas Willis Lambeth disting. prof. pub. policy, 2004—09, chmn. dept. pub. policy, 2006—. Cons. NSF, Washington, 1982-85, AID, Yaounde, Cameroon, 1983, U.S.-Asia Environ. Partnership, 2000-06, Kenan Inst. Asia, 2000-06; mem. NC Natural Heritage Adv. Com., Raleigh, 1982-87; sr. staff mem. Commn. on Future of N.C., Raleigh, 1982-84; mem. Bd. Environ. Studies and Toxology, NAS, 1986-88; chmn. study com. on opportunities in applied environ. R&D, NAS, 1988-90; mem. risk reduction subcom. Sci. Adv. Bd., EPA, 1989-90, AID, Czech and Slovak Republics, 1991-94; mem. adv. com. Pew Conservation Scholars Program, 1991-94; mem. adv. com. EPA Decisionmaking, Nat. Acad. of Pub. Adminstrn., 1994-95; chmn. adv. panel new approach to environ. regulation Office Tech. Assessment U.S. Congress, Washington, 1993-95; mem. Multi-State Working Group Environ. Mgmt. Systems, 1997—2004; chmn. adv. panel U.S. registration practices for ISO 14001 environ. mgmt. sys. Nat. Acad. Pub. Adminstrn., 2000-01; mem. adv. com. Environ. Stewardship N.C. dept. environ. and natural resources, 2002-06, mem. study com. on environ. decision making, NAS, 2003-2005, mem.com.human dimensions of global change, 2005-, NC Legislative Commn. Global Climate Change, 2008-10. Author: Environmental Policy and Administrative Change, 1976, Managing the Environment, Managing Ourselves: A History of American Environmental Policy, 1999, 2d edit., 2006; editor: Land in America, 1979, Environmental Change and Public Health-The Next Fifty Years, 1990; contbr. articles to profl. jours. Vestry Episcopalian Ch., Chapel Hill, 1986-89. Resources for the Future Inc. fellow, 1971-72, Rockefeller Found. fellow, 1977-78, Fulbright fellow Vienna U. Econs., 1990, Salzburg Seminar faculty fellow, 1990, fellow Nat. Acad. of Pub. Adminstrn., 1996. Fellow AAAS (nominating com. sect. on societal impacts of sci. and engring. 1987-90, chmn. 1989-90, 96-97, ann. meeting program com. 1988-90, com. on sci. engring. and pub. policy 1997-2003, com. sect. social, econ. and polit. scis. 1998-2002); mem. Assn. Pub. Policy and Mgmt. (ann. meeting program com. 2003, 09), Soc. For Policy Scis., Golden Key, Sigma Xi, Delta Omega. Democrat. Avocations: tennis, sailing, camping, photography, squash. Office: U NC Dept Public Policy CB3435 Abernethy Chapel Hill NC 27599-3435 Office Phone: 919-843-5011.

ANDREWS, WILLIAM FREDERICK, private equity firm executive; b. Easton, Pa., Oct. 7, 1931; s. William Frederick and Lydia Nielson (Cross) Andrews; m. Lin Howard; children: William Frederick III, Whitney, Carter, Clayton, Sloane. BS in Bus. Adminstrn., U. Md., 1953; MBA in Mktg., Seton Hall U., South Orange, NJ, 1961. Product mgr. Scovill Mfg. Co., Waterbury, Conn., 1965-68, v.p., gen. mgr. Raleigh, NC, 1968-73, group v.p. Nashville, 1973-79, pres. Waterbury, 1979-81, chmn., pres., CEO, 1981-86, Singer Sewing Machine Co., 1986-89; pres., CEO, chmn. Massey Investment Co., 1989—90; pres., CEO UNR Industries Inc., 1990—92; CEO, chmn. bd. Amdura Corp., Conn., 1992-94; prin. Kohlberg & Co., LLC, 1992—2013, ptnr., 1997—. Bd. dirs. Corrections Corp. America, 1986—98, chmn. bd. dirs., 2000—08, chmn. exec. com., 2008—; bd. dirs. Black Box, Inc., 1992—2013, Trex Company, Inc., 1999—2013, O'Charleys' Inc., 2004—12; chmn. bd. dirs. Utica Corp., 1992—94, Schrader Bridgeport, 1995—98, Northwestern Steel & Wire Co., 1998—2001, Allied Aerospace Industries, Inc., 2000—06, Katy Industries, Inc., 2001—, Singer Sewing Co., 2004—12, Ctrl. Parking, 2007—12, Thomas Nelson Pub., 2010—12. Capt. USAF, 1953—56. Recipient Significant Sig award, 2000, Silver Beaver award, Boy Scouts of Am.; named ODX Dir. of Yr., 2011. Mem.: Snake River Sporting Club (Jackson, Wyo.), Shooting Star Country Club, Internat. Polo Club Wellington Fla., Old Natchez Country Club (Nashville), Belle Meade Country Club (Nashville, Tenn.), Wanderers Club Wellington, Golf Club Tenn., Tenn. Univ. Club (NYC), Chgo. Club. Republican. Episcopalian. Avocations: horseback riding, swimming, skiing, tennis, golf. Home and Office: Riverstone Farm 1409 Moran Rd Franklin TN 37069 Office Phone: 615-370-0098. Office Fax: 615-370-0013.

ANDREWS, WILLIAM LESTER SELF, chemistry educator; b. Linconton, NC, Jan. 31, 1942; s. William Baker and Clara Adele (Self) A.; m. Marjorie Hare, Jan. 30, 1965; children: Scott Hare, Ross Lester; m. Barbara Beasley, June 26, 2010. BS in Chem. Engring., Miss. State U., 1963; PhD in Phys. Chem., U. Calif., Berkeley, 1966; D (hon.), U. Paul Sabatier, Toulouse, France, 2004. Asst. prof. chemistry U. Va., Charlotteville, 1966-70, assoc. prof., 1970-76, prof., 1976—2008. Fellow chemical engring. Miss. State U., 2002. Editor: Chemistry and Physics of Matrix Isolated Species, 1989; mem. editorial bd. Jour. Molecular Structure, 1978. Scoutmaster Boy Scouts Am., Ivy, Va., 1986-89. Recipient Coblentz award, 1978, Lippincott Vibrational Spectroscopy award 2001; Pimentel award, Matrix Isolation Spectroscopy, 2007, Disting. Scientist award, U. Va., 2008, Plyler prize Am. Phys. Soc., 2010; A.P. Sloan fellow, 1973-75, Fulbright fellow, 1982-83, 94; grantee NSF, 1968—2008; grantee DOE, 2008-2012. Fellow Am. Phys. Soc., Royal Soc. Chemistry; mem. Am. Chem. Soc. Avocations: clarinet, canoeing. Office: U Va Chem Dept McCormick Rd Charlottesville VA 22904-4319 Office Phone: 434-924-6844. Business E-Mail: lsa@virginia.edu.

ANDRIOLE, JOSEPH G., diagnostic radiologist; MD, Howard U., 1980. Diplomate Am. Bd. Radiology-diagnostic radiology, 1985. Resident diagnostic radiology Case Western Univ. Hosps., Cleveland, 1981—84; hosp. affiliations include South Lake Meml. Hosp., Clermont, Fla., Health Ctrl. Hosp., Ocoee, Orlando Regional Healthcare, St. Cloud Regional Med. Ctr. Office: Medical Center Radiology Group 20 W Kaley St Orlando FL 32806 Office Phone: 407-423-5511. Office Fax: 407-423-1930.

ANDRISANI, JOHN ANTHONY, editor, writer; b. Bayshore, NY, Sept. 24, 1949; s. Pat and Gwendoline Mary (Rose) A. Student, SUNY, Stony Brook, 1968—71. Instr. golf in country club, NY, 1971-78; freelance writer golf mags., 1977—; asst. editor Golf Illus. mag., London, 1980-82; sr. editor instrn. Golf mag., NYC, 1982-98; pres. John Andrisani Assoc. Inc. Co-author: (with Sandy Lyle) Learning Golf: The Lyle Way, 1986, (with Seve Ballesteros) Natural Golf, 1987 (Book of Month Club 1987), (with Chi Chi Rodriguez) 101 Supershots, 1990, (with Robin McMillan) The Golf Doctor, 1990 (Brentanos bestseller 1990), (with Mike Dunaway) Hit It Hard!, 1991, (with Phil Ritson) Golf Your Way, 1992, (with John Daly) Grip It and Rip It!, 1992, (with Fred Couples) Total Shotmaking, 1994, (with Craig Stadler) I Am The Walrus, 1995, (with Claude "Butch" Harmon Jr.), The Four Cornerstones of Winning Golf, 1996, (with Jim McLean) The X-Factor Swing, 1996, The Tiger Woods Way, 1997, The Short Game Magic of Tiger Woods, 1998, (with Mark Russell) Golf Rules Plain and Simple, 1999, The Hogan Way, 2000, (with John Anselmo) "A-Game" Golf, 2001, The Bobby Jones Way, 2002, Think Like Tiger, 2002, Everything I Learned about People, I Learned From a Round of Golf, 2002, The Nicklaus Way, 2003, Play Like Sergio Garcia, 2004, (with Jim Hardy) The Plane Truth for Golfers, 2005, Tiger's New Swing, 2005, The Michelle Wie Way, 2007, Golf Heaven, 2007, (with Jim Hardy) The Plane Truth Master Class, 2007; contbr. articles to jours. and mags. Mem. Golf Writers Assn. (assn. champion 1985), Ballybunion Golf Club (life, Ireland), JA/DA Fine Art Antiguls(pres.) Personal E-mail: andrisanij@bellsouth.net.

ANDRUSZKIEWICZ, PETER, healthcare company executive; b. 1957; m. Danielle Andruszkiewicz; 4 children. BS, Springfield Coll., 1980. Chief mktg. officer Blue Cross Blue Shield Nat. Capital Area, DC, 1983—87; sr. v.p., mid. market segment CIGNA HealthCare; v.p., nat. accts. Kaiser Permanente, 2005—06, sr. v.p., health plan ops., regions outside Calif., 2006—08, interim pres. Ga. region Atlanta, 2008, pres., 2008—. Trustee Springfield Coll.; mem. exec. com. Ga. Children's Health Alliance; mem. Buckhead Coalition. Office: Kaiser Permanente Nine Piedmont Ctr 3495 Piedmont Rd NE Atlanta GA 30305 Office Phone: 404-364-7000. Office Fax: 404-364-4998.

ANDRZEJEWSKI, STEPHEN JOSEPH, pharmaceutical executive; b. Buffalo, June 2, 1965; s. Casey Joseph and Maria Martha Andrzejewski; m. Susan Kim Andrzejewski, Sept. 28, 1991; children: Nicole, Ethan, Brian. BA in Liberal Arts and Psychology, Hamilton Coll., 1987; MBA in Fin. and Internat. Bus., NYU, 1992. Mgmt. assoc. Shering-Plough, Kenilworth, NJ, 1987—89, mktg. rsch. mgr., 1989—91, mgr., Managed Care Mktg., 1991—92, product mgr., sr. product mgr., 1992—96, sr. dir., Mktg., 1996—98, v.p., Mktg., 1998—; chief comml. officer King Pharmaceuticals, Inc., 2004—. Trustee No. N.J. Leukemia Soc., 1997—; bd. dirs. Am. Fedn. Aging. Rsch., 1999—. Office: King Pharmaceuticals Inc 501 Fifth St Bristol TN 37620 Office Phone: 423-989-8000. E-mail: sandrzejewski@kingpharm.com.

ANGEL, DENISE HARPER See HARPER ANGEL, DENISE

ANGEL, STEVEN MICHAEL, retired lawyer; b. Frederick, Md., Sept. 19, 1950; s. Charles Robert and Laura Emily (Holland) A.; children: Michael Sean, James Curtis; m. Peggy Whitten, May 4, 1996. BS, U. Md., 1972; MS in Mgmt., U. Md., Lanham, 2007; JD, Okla. City U., 1976; LLM, George Washington U., 1979. Bar: Okla. 1976, Tex. 1979, Tex. 1981. Field atty. NLRB, Balt., 1976-79; supervising trial atty. Fed. Labor Rels. Authority, Dallas, 1979-80; mem. Hughes & Nelson, Oklahoma City and San Antonio, 1980-89; pvt. practice Angel & Assoc., 1984—2003; pres. Human Resources Civil Rights Risk Assessment, LLC, 2003—. Articles editor Oklahoma City U. Law Rev., 1976, 77; contbr. articles to profl. jours. Recipient awards Oklahoma City U., 1975, 76; Spl. Achievement cert. Fed. Labor Rels. Authority, 1980. Mem. ABA, Phi Delta Phi. Democrat. Baptist. Home and Office: 2313 Silverfield Ln Edmond OK 73003-1501 Home Phone: 405-409-0360. Personal E-mail: sangel0484@att.net.

ANGELAKI, DORA E., medical educator; b. Crete, Greece, Oct. 30, 1961; d. Emmanuel Angelakis and Stavroula Angelaki; m. Jerry David Dickman; children: Kristina Deanna, Natalie Nicole. Diploma, Nat. Tech. U. Athens, 1985; MS, U. Minn., 1989, PhD, 1991. Predoctoral fellow U. Tex. Med. Br., Galveston, 1989-91, postdoctoral fellow, 1991-92; predoctoral fellow Physiology U. Minn., Mpls., 1991; postdoctoral fellow Dept. Neurology U. Zurich, Switzerland, 1992-93; assoc. prof. U. Miss. Med. Ctr., Jackson, 1993—99; assoc. prof. biomedical engring., Sch. Engring. and Applied Sci. to Alumni Endowed Prof. of Neurobiology and Prof. Biomedical Engring. Washington U., St. Louis, 1999—2011; Wilhelmina Robertson prof., chair dept. neuroscience Baylor Coll. of Medicine, 2011—; joint appt., prof. dept. psychology and electrical and computer engring. Rice U.; interim dir. Baylor Neuroimaging Center. Contbr. articles to profl. jours.; mem. of several editl. bds. Recipient USAF Scientific Rsch. grants, 1995-98, 97-99, 98-2001, NASA grants, 1995-99, NIH grants, 1995-98, Halpike-Nylen medal, Barany Soc., 2006, Presidential Early Career award for Scientists and Engineers, Pradel Rsch. award in Neurosciene, NAS, 2012. Office: Department of Neuroscience Baylor of Medicine Vivian Smith Building Room S740 One Baylor Plaza Houston TX 77030 Office Phone: 713-798-1468. Office Fax: 713-798-1476. Business E-Mail: angelaki@bcm.edu.

ANGELINI, MARCELLO, performing company executive; b. Naples, Italy, Feb. 11, 1962; m. Daniela Buson. Grad., Kiev Inst. Dance, 1980-81. Dancer Maggio Musicale Fiorentino, 1979, soloist, 1981; prin. dancer Deutsche Oper Berlin, 1983-84, Cin. Ballet, 1983-95, Northern Ballet Theater, England, 1984-87, Ballet West, Salt Lake City, 1988-89, Les Grands Ballets Danadiens, Montreal, 1991-94; artistic dir. Tulsa Ballet, 1995—. Guest prin. dancer San Carlo Opera House, Rome Opera House, the Arena of Verona, Italy, Basler Ballet, Switzerland, English Nat. Ballet, Scottish Ballet, Ballet Ariz., Santiago Teatro Mcpl., Chile. Performer (leading roles in classical repertoire including): Giselle, Sleeping Beauty, Romeo and Juliet, Cinderella; choreographer leading role in Death and the Maiden. Recipient Golden Rose award, Internat. Ballet Competition, Rome, 1982, Leonide Massine Positano prize, 1989, Gov.'s Arts Award, 2002. Office: Tulsa Ballet 1212 45th Place South Tulsa OK 74105 Office Phone: 918-749-6030.

ANGERS, WINSTON THOMAS, lawyer, publishing executive; b. Franklin, La., June 21, 1952; s. Robert John, Jr. and Geraldine Beaulieu Angers; 1 child, Austen John. BA in Polit. Sci. cum laude, U. La., 1974; JD, La. State U., 1976. Bar: La. 1977. Rsch. asst. Inst. for Civil Law Studies La. State U. Law Ctr., Baton Rouge, 1975—76; law clk. 15th Jud. Dist. Ct., New Iberia, La., 1976—77; pvt. practice Lafayette, La., 1977—; pres. Beau Bayou Pub. Co., Lafayette, 1985—. Author: Cajun Cuisine, 1986; editor: History of the Louisiana Society of the Sons of the American Revolution, 1997; co-author: My Wars: Nazis, Mobsters, Gambling and Corruption: Colonel Francis C. Grevemberg Remembers, 2004; contbr. articles to mags. Bd. dirs. Coun. Devel. of French in La.; past chmn. bd. zoning adjustments City of Lafayette; pres. Acadiana Arts Coun., Lafayette, 1990—91; co-founder Citizens of S. Lafayette; pres. Attakapas chpt. SAR, 1994; mem. bd. of election supr. Lafayette Parish, Louisiana; pres. Acadian Civitan Club, Lafayette, 1997—98; bd mem. La. Ctr. Law Civic Edn.; del.-attendee Young Rep. Nat. Fedn. Conv., 1971; alt. del. Rep. Nat. Conv., Dallas, 1984, 7th district elector for pres. La., 2004, del. Houston, 1992, Minneapolis, 2008; past chmn. by laws com. La. Rep. State Ctrl. Com.; chmn. Lafayette Parish Rep. Exec. Com., 1995—96; past chmn. Lafayette Parish Rep. Polit. Action Coun.; del. numerous state convs. La. Rep. Party; chair U. La. at Lafayette Coll. Reps., 1971—72. Recipient Bronze Good Citizenship medal, Attakapas Chpt. SAR, 1992, Oak Leaf Cluster, 1993, Meritorious Svc. medal, 1994, Oak Leaf Cluster, 1995, Oak Leaf Cluster for Meritorious Svc. medal, La. Soc. SAR, 1996. Mem.: La. State Bar Assn. (governing coun. arts, entertainment and sports sect., bd. mem. La. ctr. law and civic edn.), Rotary Internat., Phi Eta Sigma, Phi Delta Phi. Republican. Avocation: collecting rare documents and political memorabilia. Home: 116 Teche Dr Lafayette LA 70503 Office: 131 Audubon Blvd Lafayette LA 70503 Office Phone: 337-233-3268. Personal E-mail: tomangers@aol.com.

ANGLIN, SCOTT, corporate financial executive; Sr. v.p., treas. Amerigroup Corp., 2006—. Office: Amerigroup Corp 4425 Corporation Ln Virginia Beach VA 23462 Office Phone: 757-490-6900. Office Fax: 757-222-2330. Business E-Mail: sanglin@amerigroupcorp.com.

ANGULO, CHARLES BONIN, foreign service officer, lawyer; b. NYC, Aug. 6, 1943; s. Manuel R. and Carolyn C. (Bonin) A.; m. Kathleen Fisher, Oct. 1, 2005. BA, U. Va., 1966; cert., U. Madrid, 1966; JD, Tulane U., 1969. Bar: Va. 1969. Assoc. Michael & Dent, Charlottesville, Va., 1969-73; assoc. editor The Michie Pub. Co., Charlottesville, 1973; fgn. svc. officer U.S. Dept. State, Washington, 1973-75, Am. Embassy U.S. Dept. State, Brussels, 1976-78, Santo Domingo, 1981-85, Office of the Legal Advisor, U.S. Dept. State, Washington, 1978-81; exec. dir. office of insp. gen. U.S. Dept. State, Washington, 1985-86; asst. chief protocol U.S. State Dept., Washington, 1986-88, Am. Consulate Gen. U.S. Dept. State, Jeddah, Saudi Arabia, 1988-93; fgn. svc. officer Am. Embassy U.S. Dept. State, Quito, Ecuador, 1993—. Home and Office: 117 Chestnut Dr River Green Canton GA 30114

ANGULO, GERARD ANTONIO, publishing executive; b. Havana, Sept. 24, 1956; arrived in U.S., 1960; s. Ricardo A. and Rosario (Mestas) Angulo. BA, Princeton U., 1978; MBA, Harvard U., 1980. With office of pres. Consol. Mining & Industries, 1980—84; prof. Grad. Bus. Sch. Columbia University, 1988—90, NYU, 1989—90; host Capital Gains, 1990—91; pres., pub. The San Juan Star Inc., 1994—. Bd. dirs. YMCA of San Juan, PR, Salvation Army, Ballet Concierto; pres., bd. dirs. Better Bus. Bur.; pres. Harvard Bus. Sch. Assn., PR. Mem.: New Eng. Soc. (bd. dirs. 1986—91, v.p., Achievement award 1979—80). Roman Cath. Office: The San Juan Star Inc 5 Calle Acacia San Juan PR 00920-1509 Office Phone: 787-782-4200 2101. E-mail: gangulo@sanjuanstarmedia.net.

ANIK, RUBY K., marketing executive; b. 1957; BA in English Lit., U. Mumbai, M in Mktg. Mgmt. With NW Ayer, 1981—84, Young & Rubicam Advertising, 1984—91; assoc. media dir. Euro RSCG Tatham, sr. partner, grp. media dir., 1991—97; dir. advt., media Pillsbury Co., 1997—2000; v.p. media Best Buy Co., Inc., Mpls., 2000—02, v.p. advt., 2002—05, sr. v.p. advt. & promotional mktg., 2005—07; sr. v.p., dir. brand mktg. J.C. Penney Co., Plano, Tex., 2007—. Bd. trustees Best Buy Children's Found.; dir. in-house agy. Best Buy Advt. Office: JC Penney CO 6501 Legacy Dr Plano TX 75024

ANLYAN, WILLIAM GEORGE, surgeon, educator, academic administrator; b. Alexandria, Egypt, Oct. 14, 1925; s. Armand and Emmy (Nazar) A.; children: William George, John Peter, Louise. BS magna cum laude, Yale U., 1945, MD, 1949; DSc (hon.), Rush Med. Coll., 1973. Diplomate Am. Bd. Surgery, Am. Bd. Thoracic Surgery. Intern, resident, instr., assoc. in surgery Duke Hosp., Durham, NC, 1949-53, asst. prof. surgery, 1953-58, assoc. prof. surgery, 1958—61, prof. surgery, 1961-89; assoc. dean Duke U. Sch. Medicine, 1963, dean, 1964-69, v.p. health affairs, 1969-83, chancellor health affairs, 1983—89, exec. v.p., 1987—89; chancellor Duke U., 1989—90, chancellor emeritus, 1990—. Chmn, Durham VA Chancellor's Com., 1963—89; chmn. Pearle Health Svcs., Inc., 1983—85; surg. cons. Durham VA Hosp.; Markle scholar med. sci., 1953—58; bd. regents Nat. Libr. Medicine, 1971—72; trustee N.C. Sch. Sci. and Math., 1978—85, chmn. phys. facilities com., 1979, vice-chmn. bd. trustees, 1981—84; mem. bd. visitors The U. Tex. Health Sci. Ctr. at Houston, 1980—88, Stanford U., 1985—87; chmn. Yale U. Coun. Com. on Med. Affairs, 1985—93. Mem. editl. bd. Pharos, 1968-93. Trustee The Duke Endowment, 1990—, vice chmn., 2004-, Commn. Future Structure Vet. Health Care, 1990-92; chmn. Gov.'s Task Force Better Health NC in 2000, 1991-97; mem. White House Sci. Coun., 1988-89. Recipient Disting. Achievement award Modern Medicine, 1974; Gov.'s Disting. Meritorious Svc. award, 1978; Abraham Flexner award, 1980, Disting. Surgeon Alumnus award Yale U. Sch. Medicine, 1979, Award of Merit Duke U. Hosp. and Health Adminstrn. Alumni Assn., 1987, Lifetime Achievement award Duke U. Med. Alumni, 1995, Lifetime Achievement award Rsch. Am., 1997, Disting. Meritorius Svc. medal, Duke Univ., 2002, N.C. award in sci., presented by the gov., 2002, Lifetime Achievement award City of Medicine, 2003. Fellow ACS; mem. AMA (adv. com. med. sci. 1972—), Soc. Univ. Surgeons, Soc. Vascular Surgery, Internat. Cardiovasc. Soc., Soc. Clin. Surgery, Am. Heart Assn., Soc. Med. Adminstrs. (pres. 1983-85), Inst. Medicine of NAS, Coun. Deans (chmn. 1968-69), AAMC (exec. com. 1965-71, chmn. 1970-71), AAMC Coun. Deans (chmn. 1968-69), So. Med. Assn., Coord. Coun. Med. Edn. (chmn. 1973-74), Surg. Biology Club II, Am. Surg. Assn., So. Surg. Assn., Halsted Soc., Allen O. Whipple Surg. Soc., Assn. Am. Med. Colls. (chmn. 1970-71), Ind. Rsch. Roundtable NAS, Assn. Acad. Health Ctrs. (pres. 1975), Rsch. Am. (bd. dirs. 1989-2005, chmn. 1992-96), Rotary, Phi Beta Kappa, Sigma Xi, Alpha Omega Alpha. Home: 1516 Pinecrest Rd Durham NC 27705-5817 Office: Duke Med Ctr PO Box 3626 Durham NC 27710-0001 Home Phone: 919-489-3196; Office Phone: 919-684-3438. Business E-Mail: anlya001@mc.duke.edu.

ANNIS, JOSEPH P., anesthesiologist, educator; b. Tallahassee; m. Peggy Annis; 2 children. Grad., Marquette U., Milw.; MD, Med. Coll. Wis., Milw., 1969. Diplomate American Bd. Anesthesiology. Intern surgery Swedish Med. Ctr., Seattle, 1969—70; gen. med. officer US Air Force Med. Corps, Vietnam; resident anesthesiology Long Beach Meml. Hosp., Calif., 1972—73, Stanford U. Hosp., 1973—75; pres. med. staff, vice chair bd. dirs. St. David's Med. Ctr., Austin, Tex.; ptnr. Austin Anesthesiology Group. Bd. dirs. Preferred Physicians Med. Risk Retention Group (PPM), 1990—; adj. assoc. prof. Dartmouth-Hitchcock Med. Ctr./Dartmouth Med. Sch., Hanover, NH; assoc. examiner Am. Bd. Anesthesiology; bd. governers St. David's Health-Care Partnership; former asst. clin. prof. U. Tex. Med. Branch, Galveston, U. Fla. Coll. Medicine. Bd. dirs. Found. Anesthesia Edn. & Rsch. Mem.: AMA (bd. trustees 2006—, former chair Coun. on Med. Svc., sec. 2009—10), American Soc. Anesthesiologists (former mem. bd. dirs.), Tex. Soc. Anesthesiologists (past pres.). Office: Austin Anesthesiology Group Bldg 3, Ste 210 8140 N MoPac Expressway Austin TX 78759 E-mail: joseph.annis@ppmrrg.com.

ANNS, ARLENE EISERMAN, publishing company executive; b. Pearl River, NY; d. Frederick Joel and Anna (Behnke) Eiserman. Student, Fairleigh Dickinson U., 1946—48; BS, Utah State U., 1950; postgrad., Traphagen Sch. Design, 1957, NYU, 1958, Hunter Coll., 1959—60. Rsch. and promotion asst. Archtl. Record, NYC, 1952-56; asst. rsch. dir. Esquire Mag., NYC, 1956-62; rsch. mgr. Am. Machinist publ. McGraw-Hill, Inc., NYC, 1962-67, mktg. svc. mgr., 1967-69, 69-71, sales mgr., 1976-77, dir. mktg., 1977-78; v.p. mktg. svcs. Morgan Grampian, Inc., NYC, 1971-72; mktg. dir. Family Health and Diversion mag., 1972-74; dist. sales mgr. Postgrad. Medicine, 1974-76; advt. sales mgr. Contempory Ob/Gyn, 1976-78, dir. profl. devel., 1978-80; pub. graduating engr., dir. mktg. Aviation Week Group, 1980-90; pub. World Aviation Directory; dir. comms. Aviation Week Group, 1990-92; v.p. Phase, Ltd., 1993—; owner, mgr. Barnahill Loblolly Tree Farm, 1993—. Mem.: Va. Forestry Assn., Am. Soc. Pers. Adminstrs., Employment Mgmt. Assn., Sales Exec. Club, Advt. Club NY, Advt. Women NY, Pharm. Advt. Club, Am. Mktg. Assn., Dir. Assn., Svc. Corps Ret. Execs. (chair), U. Va. Libr. Assn. Bd., Coll. Placement Coun., Nat. Orgn. Disability (bd. dirs.), Internat. Platform Assn., Wings Club, Pi Sigma Alpha. Home: Barnahill Farm 6653 Celt Rd Stanardsville VA 22973-3638 Personal E-mail: theanns@gmail.com.

ANNS, PHILIP HAROLD, brokerage house and pharmaceutical executive; b. London, June 24, 1925; came to U.S., 1950; s. Harold Falkner and Dorothy Louise (Torckler) A.; m. Jacqueline Estelle Wyrtzen, Dec. 27, 1952 (div. 1975); 1 child, Jean Anns; m. Arlene Claire Eiserman, Apr. 1, 1978. BA in Econs., Christ Coll., Cambridge, Eng., 1948, MA in Econs., 1950. Asst. to pres. BASF Inc., NYC, 1954-58; gen. mgr. Squibb Australia E.R. Squibb and Sons, Princeton, NJ, 1958-68, dir. animal health New Brunswick, NJ; gen. mgr. animal health Am. Hoechst, Kansas City, Mo., 1968-72; exec. v.p. Lakeside Labs., Milw., 1972-75; sr. v.p., gen. mgr. internat. div. A.H. Robins Co., Inc., Richmond, Va., 1975-85, sr. v.p. corp. govt. relations Washington, 1986-90; pres. Phase Ltd., Arlington, Va., 1990—; prin., owner Barnahill Tree Farm. Chmn. Va. Dist. Export Coun.; mem. Congl. staff U.S. Ho. of Reps., 1990—. Chmn. Indsl. Devel. Authority, Greene County, Va. Served to lt. pilot Brit. Royal Navy, Indian Ocean, 1943-46, ETO. Mem.: Va. Forestry Assn., Rotary. Home and Office: 6653 Celt Rd Stanardsville VA 22973-3638 Personal E-mail: theanns@earthlink.net.

ANOATUBBY, BILL, Governor of the Chickasaw Nation; b. Nov. 8, 1945; m. Janice Marie Loman, Dec. 23, 1967; children: Chris, Brian. AS, Murray State Coll., 1970; BS, East Ctrl. State Coll., 1972. Acct., office mgr. Am. Plating Co., 1972-74; acct., systems & budgetary contr. Little Giant Corp., 1974-75; dir. health svcs. The Chickasaw Nation, Ada, Okla., 1975-76, dir. acctg., 1976-78, spl. asst. to gov., 1978-79, lt. gov., 1979-87, gov., 1987—. Trustee Morris K. Udall Scholarship and Excellence in Nat. Environ. Policy Found., 1994-2000. Mem. adv. com. Okla. Dept. Commerce, 1990; mem. Trail of Tears Nat. Historic Adv. Com., 1990-92; trustee Oklahoma City U., 1991-98; trustee Native Am. Cultural Edn. Authority, 1998—. Recipient Gov.'s ARTS award, 1997; named Okla. Minority Bus. Advocate of Yr., U.S. SBA, 1995; named to Okla. Hall of Fame, 2004, Honored One and Friend of the Ct., Supreme Ct. Okla., 2005. Mem. Inter-Tribal Coun. of Five Civilized Tribes (past v.p., pres.), Ada Area C. of C. (bd. dirs.), Okla. Indian Affairs Commn. Democrat. Office: Chickasaw Nation PO Box 1548 Ada OK 74821-1548 Office Phone: 405-436-2603. Business E-Mail: bill.anoatubby@chickasaw.net.

ANSARI, ANOUSHEH, digital home and multimedia management technology company executive, entrepreneur; b. Tehran, Iran, 1966; emigrated to the US in 1984; m. Hamid Ansari, 1991. BS in Elec. Engring. & Computer Sci., George Mason U., 1988; MSEE, George Washington U. Engring. positions MCI Telecom. Corp., Comm. Satellite Corp. (COMSAT); co-founder, pres. & CEO Telecom Technologies, Inc. (TTI) (acquired by Sonus Networks, Inc.), 1993—2000; co-founder, chmn. Prodea Systems, Inc., Plano, Tex., 2006—. US Delegate at ITU SG VII, SG XI and SG XVII; rep. Am. Nat. Standard Inst. T1S1 and T1X1. Contbr. to numerous technical papers. Patron Ashoka Found.; mem., trustee X-Prize Found. Vision Circle; past bd. dir. Make-a-Wish Found. (North Tex.), Collin County Children's Advocacy Ctr. Recipient Ernst and Young Entrepreneur of Yr., Southwest Region, Tech. and Comm. category, 1999, Nat. Entrepreneurial Excellence award, Working Women, 2000, George Mason U. Entrepreneurial Excellence award, George Mason Univ. Alumni Assn., 2001, George Wash. U. Disting. Alumni Achievement award; named one of 40 Under 40, Fortune, 2001, 150 Women Who Shake the World, Newsweek, 2011. Mem.: Nat. Soc. Profl. Engineers, IEEE, Eta Kappa Nu. Achievements include with brother-in-law Amir Ansari provided title sponsorship for the Ansari X-Prize, a multi-milion dollar award for the first non-governmental organization to launch a reusable manned spacecraft into space twice within two weeks, 2004; as part of the primary crew on the Soyuz TMA-9 mission launching from Baikonur Cosmodrome, Kazakhstan, became the first Iranian in space and the first female private space explorer, 2006; patents for Automated Operator Services and Wireless Service Node. Office: Prodea Systems Inc 2435 N Central Expy Ste 500 Richardson TX 75080-2750 Office Phone: 214-278-1850. Office Fax: 214-278-1851. Business E-Mail: anousheh.ansari@prodeasystems.com.

ANSARY, HUSHANG, oil industry entrepreneur, philanthropist, private global investment company executive, former diplomat; b. Ahvaz, Iran, 1926; permanent resident in the United States, 1979, United States citizen, 1986. married Shahla Nazemian; 2 children. Newspaper and magazine photographer in Ahvaz, Tehran, and England; served several government positions including Undersecretary of Commerce, Ambassador to many African nations and to Pakistan, and the Minister of Information; Iranian Ambassador to the United States and then the Minister of Economic Affairs and Finance; former CEO National Iranian Oil Company, director, 1977—78; former director Fakhre Iran; chmn. Parman Capital Investment Ltd., 1982, SunResorts Ltd. N.V., 1986; chmn., CEO IRI International Corporation, 1995—2000; director National Oilwell Varco, Inc., 2000—05; founder, chmn., principal stockholder Parman Capital Group, LLC, Houston, 2005—; chmn. Stewart & Stevenson LLC, Houston, 2006—, chmn. executive committee, 2006—. Served on the National Finance Committee of the Bush-Cheney 2004 Presidential Campaign; trustee George Bush Presidential Library Foundation, Asia Society; board overseers Weill Cornell Medical College; member senior advisory board Shorenstein Barone Center for the Press, Politics and Public Policy, Kennedy School of Government; member President's Council of the Center for Middle East Public Policy at RAND; advisory board member America Abroad Media, James Baker Institute. Decorated by the Governments of Japan, South Korea, Italy, Norway, Spain, Egypt, Romania and Pakistan; recipient Ellis Island Medal of Honor, 2003, Woodrow Wilson International Center award. Republican. Achievements include Weill Cornell Medical College of Cornell University establishing the Ansary Center for Stem Cell Therapeutics in 2004 in honor of a grant from Hushang Ansary and wife; involved with the creation of several medical and educational institutions including University of Saint Maarten and the James Baker Institute for Public Policy; involved with projects at the Texas Heart Institute and educational programs in Singapore and at medical facilities in Tanzania; the Ansary name is identified with the following: Ansary fellowship program at Harvard University John F. Kennedy School of Government, Ansary Fellowships at Texas A&M University, Ansary Atrium at The Texas Heart Institute, Ansary Gallery of American History at The George Bush Presidential Library, and the Ansary Series at The American Academy of Diplomacy. Office: Stewart & Stevenson LLC 1000 Louisiana Street Suite 5900 Houston TX 77002 Office Phone: 713-751-2700. Business E-Mail: h.ansary@ssss.com.*

ANSBACHER, BARRY BARNETT, lawyer; b. Jacksonville, Fla., Jan. 7, 1963; s. Lewis and Sybil Ansbacher; m. Lisa Shaken Ansbacher, 2009. BA, U. Fla., 1985, JD, 1988. Bar: Fla. 1989, D.C. 1989; bd. cert. real estate atty. Fla., consultation atty. Atty. Ansbacher & Schneider PA, Jacksonville, 1989—97, Ansbacher Law, Jacksonville, 1997—. Pres. Attys. Real Property Coun. NE Fla., Inc., 2001, Jacksonville; pub. rep. on Pvt. Provider Task Force Fla. Bldg. Commn., 2004. Author: Complex Real Estate Transactions-Subdivisions, 1997, 98, Issues of Transboundary Pollution in North America, 1988. Named Outstanding Young Men of Am., 1986. Mem. Fla. Bar Assn. (exec. coun. cir. rep. real property, probate and trust law sect. 1998-2011, constl. law com. mem. 1998-, chmn. problem studies 2005—09), Jacksonville Bar Assn. (real estate sect. chair 2011-12). Jewish. Office: 8818 Goodbys Executive Dr Ste 100 Jacksonville FL 32217 Office Phone: 904-737-4600. Business E-Mail: info@ansbacher.net.

ANSIN, EDMUND, broadcast executive; divorced; 3 children. BA, Univ. Pa. Wharton Sch. Owner & pres. Sunbeam Broadcasting. Named one of Forbes 400: Richest Americans, 2009. Office: 1401 79th St Cswy North Bay Village FL 33141-4104

ANTHONY, DONALD BARRETT, engineering executive; b. Kansas City, Kans., Jan. 28, 1948; s. Donald W. and Marjorie (Lifsey) A.; m. Darla S. Donovan, Dec. 16, 1972; children: Jennifer L., Danielle S. BSChemE, U. Toledo, 1970; MS, MIT, 1971, DSc, 1974. Asst. prof., practice sch. dir. dept. chem. engring. MIT, Cambridge, Mass., 1974-75; group supr. coal R&D Std. Oil Co. Ohio, Cleve., 1976-77, mgr. marine planning, 1978-79, mgr. synthetic fuels devel., 1980-83, v.p., gen. mgr. Pfaudler Divsn. Rochester, NY, 1983-85; v.p. R&D Std. Oil Co., Cleve., 1985-87, BP Am., Inc., Cleve., 1987-88, BP Exploration, Inc., Houston, 1989-90; v.p. tech. Bechtel, Inc., Houston, 1990-94, v.p. ops., 1994-95, v.p. reference, 1995-96; pres. Bailey Controls Co., 1996-98, Process Ind. Group, ABB Automation, 1999—2000; pres., CEO NineSigma, Inc., Cleve., 2001—03; pres. Coun. for Chem. Rsch., Wash., DC, 2004—07; chief tech. officer Great Point Energy, Chgo., 2007—. Contbr. articles to profl. jours.; patentee in field. Capt. AUS, 1970-78. MIT Esso fellow, 1970-71, Little rsch.-devel. fellow, 1971-72, Procter & Gamble fellow, 1972-73, Bechtel fellow, 1992. Mem. AIChE, Am. Chem. Soc., Sigma Xi, Phi Kappa Phi, Tau Beta Pi, Pi Mu Epsilon, Phi Eta Sigma. Lutheran. Home and Office: Great Point Energy 122 Portofino Dr North Venice FL 34275 Office Phone: 216-396-8664. Business E-Mail: danthony@greatpointenergy.com.

ANTHONY, EVELYN Y., diagnostic radiologist, educator; BS, U. NC, 1985, MA, 1992; MD, Duke U., 1996. Diplomate Am. Bd. Radiology-diagnostic radiology, 2001. Resident diagnostic radiology Wake Forest Univ. Bapt. Med. Ctr., 1996—2001, fellow pediatric radiology, 2001—02; asst. prof. radiology Wake Forest Univ. Mem.: Am. Coll. of Radiology, Radiol. Soc. of N.Am., Soc. of Pediatric Radiology. Office: Wake Forest University 445 ICTAS Bldg Stanger St Blacksburg VA 24061 Office Phone: 336-716-6753. Office Fax: 336-716-2029. E-mail: eanthony@wakehealth.edu.

ANTHONY, HARRY L., mining executive; BS in Engring. Mechanics, Pa. State U., 1969, MS in Engring. Mechanics, 1973. Profl. engr. Project supt., project engr. Union Carbide Corp.; v.p., engring., engring. mgr. Uranium Resources, Inc., sr. v.p., 1990—97; cons. Anthony Engineering Services, 1997—; COO Uranium Energy Corp., 2006—. Bd. dirs. Uranium Resources, Inc., 1984—94, Uranium Energy Corp., 2006—. Recipient Outstanding Citizen of the Yr., Kingsville C. of C., 1999, Disting. Mem. of the South Tex. Mineral Sect. of AIME, 1987. Office: Uranium Energy Corp Ste 230 PO Box 2955 Corpus Christi TX 78403-2955 Office Phone: 512-828-6980. Office Fax: 512-535-0832. Business E-Mail: hanthony@uraniumenergy.com.

ANTHONY, JOAN CATON, retired administrative judge; b. South Bend, Ind., July 28, 1939; d. Joseph Robert and Margaret Catherine (McMeel) Caton; m. Robert Armstrong Anthony, Jan. 3, 1980; 1 child, Peter. BA, Marquette U., Milw., 1961; MA, Northwestern U., Evanston, Ill., 1963; JD, Catholic U. Am., Washington, 1979. Bar: D.C. 1980, Va. 1982. Instr. English Marquette U., Milw., 1963-65, George Washington U., Washington, 1965-69, asst. prof., 1969-70; spl. asst. student affairs HEW, Washington, 1970-72; dir. Office Student and Youth Affairs U.S. Office Edn., Washington, 1972-74, legis. specialist, 1974-78; chief mgmt. ops. br. Fed. Wildlife Permit Office U.S. Fish and Wildlife Svc., Washington, 1978-81; assoc. Cate and Goodbread, Washington, 1981—85; atty., advisor office legis. counsel U.S. Dept. Interior, 1991-95; staff atty. Interior Bd. Land Appeals, 1995—2003; adminstrv. judge Def. Office of Hearings and Appeals, U.S. Dept. Def., 2003—14; ret. Mem. U.S. del. to 2d meeting Conf. Parties to Conv. on Internat. Trade in Endangered Species of Wild Fauna and Flora, San Jose, Costa Rica, 1979. Contbr. lit. revs., essays and articles on univ.-cmty. rels., western settlement and internat. negotiations to various publs. Pres. Franklin Forest Frolickers, 1985—86; den leader Cub Scouts, mem. com. Boy Scouts Am., 1990—2000; parent vol. Fairfax County Pub. Schs., 1987—2001; treas. Greater McLean Rep. Women's Club, 1987—88; bd. dirs. McLean Citizens Assn., 1982—83, Fairfax County Humane Soc., 1983. Recipient Spl. Achievement award U.S. Fish and Wildlife Svc., 1981. Mem.: Warrenton Va. Bd. Zoning Appeals, DAR (Fauquier Ct. House chpt.), Va. Bar Assn., D.C. Bar Assn. Roman Catholic.

ANTHONY, KENNETH C., JR., lawyer; b. Spartanburg, SC, Jan. 23, 1954; s. Kenneth C. Sr. and Carol Ferguson (Burnside) A.; m. Monta Lorraine Moody, Mar. 15, 1980; children: Jay, Mary Sullivan, Dunk, Grady. Student, Rice U., 1972-74; BA, Wofford Coll., 1975; JD, U. S.C., 1977. Bar: S.C. 1978, U.S. Dist. Ct. S.C. 1978, U.S. Ct. Appeals (4th cir.) 1988, U.S. Supreme Ct. 1996; cert. civil and family mediator; cert. civil arbitrator. Ptnr. The Anthony Law Firm, P.A., Spartanburg, 1978—. Adj. prof. Wofford Coll., Spartanburg, 1978-98; bd. advisors U. S.C. Law Sch., Columbia, 1988-92. Recipient Compleat Lawyer award, USC Law School, 2001. Fellow S.C. Bar Found. (life); mem. ABA (mem. editl. bd.ABA/BNA Lawyers; Manual on Professonal Conduct, 1995-98), S.C. Bar Assn. (ho. dels. 1985-96, chmn. Law Related Edn. Commn. 1999-2000, bd. govs. 1996-99, sec. 2000-01, treas. 2001-02, past chmn. ethic adv. com., pres. 2003-04), S.C. Trial Lawyers Assn. (bd. govs. 1996-98), Am. Trial Lawyers Assn, Nat. Bd. Trial Advocacy, Am. Bd. Trial Advs. Office: The Anthony Law Firm PA 250 Magnolia St PO Box 3565 Spartanburg SC 29304-3565 Office Phone: 864-582-2355. Office Fax: 864-583-9772. Business E-Mail: kanthony@anthonylaw.com.

ANTHONY, LOWELL B., medical oncologist, educator; MD, Vanderbilt U., Nashville, 1979. Diplomate Am. Bd. Internal Medicine, 1983, Am. Bd. Internal Medicine-med. oncology, 1989. Intern internal medicine Vanderbilt Univ. Med. Ctr., Nashville, resident internal medicine, 1980—82, fellow med. oncology, 1982—85; assoc. prof. medicine La. State Univ., prof. medicine divsn. hematology and oncology; acting dir. gastrointestinal and neuroendocrine oncology La. State Univ. Health Sciences Ctr., dir. gastrointestinal and neuroendocrine oncology, chmn. cancer com., adv. bd. mem. gen. clinic rsch. ctr.; hosp. affiliation includes Oschner Kenner Med. Ctr. Editl. bd. Jour. Peptide Therapy: Index and Reviews; reviewer Jour. Nuclear Medicine, New Eng. Jour. Medicine, Annals Internal Medicine, Jour. Clin. Oncology and Cancer. Contbr. articles to profl. publs. Fellow: Am. Coll. Physicians; mem.: Southern Soc. Clin. Investigation, Am. Fedn. Med. Rsch., Am. Sov. Hematology, Am. Assn. Cancer Rsch., Am. Soc. Clin. Pharmacology and Therapeutics, Am. Soc. Clin. Oncology. Office: Oschner Kenner Medical Center 200 W Esplanade Ste 200 Kenner LA 70065-2036 Office Fax: 504-464-8525. Business E-Mail: lantho@lsuhsc.edu.*

ANTHONY, MICHAEL A., state legislator; b. Union, SC, Apr. 4, 1950; s. Ernest and Ruth Anne Anthony; m. Kathy Dale Owens Anthony, June 12, 1976; children: Trey, Bret, Will. BS, Gardner-Webb U. Mem. Dist. 42 SC House of Reps., 2003—, mem. Edn. and Pub. Works Com. & Rules Com. Mem.: Coaches Assn. Democrat. Mailing: 322 Mt Vernon Rd Union SC 29379 Office: 432D Blatt Bldg Columbia SC 29201 Office Phone: 864-429-1740, 803-734-3060. E-mail: anthonym@scstatehouse.net.

ANTOKOLETZ, ELLIOTT MAXIM, music educator; b. Jersey City, Aug. 3, 1942; s. Jack and Esther (Leiter) A.; m. Juana Canabal, May 28, 1972; 1 child, Eric. Student, Juilliard Sch. Music, BS in Violin, 1964; BA in Musicology, Hunter Coll., 1968, MA in Musicology, 1970; PhD in Musicology, CUNY, 1975. Instr. violin Brearley Sch., NYC, 1970-76; theory lectr., instr. chamber music Queens Coll., NYC, 1973-76; prof. musicology U. Tex., Austin, 1976—. Author: The Music of Béla Bartók, 1984, Béla Bartók: A Guide to Research, 1988, 97, Twentieth-Century Music, 1992, Musical Symbolism in the Operas of Debussy and Bartok, 2004; editor: Bartók Perspectives, 2000, Georg Von Albrecht Memoirs, 2004, Internat. Jour. of Musicology; contbr. articles to prof. jours. and mags. Recipient Béla Bartók Memorial award Hungarian Govt., 1981, Tacquard Endowed Centennial Chair, U. Tex., 1983-84, Tchg. Excellence award U. Tex., 1981, Achievement PhD Alumni award CUNY, 1987; E.W. Doty professorship, 1994-95, 2007—. Mem. Am. Musicol. Soc. (Subvention award 1982), Coll. Music Soc., Internat. Musicol. Soc. Avocation: oil and water-color painting. Office: U Tex Music School Austin TX 78712 Business E-Mail: antokoletz@mail.utexas.edu.

ANTON, JOHN PETER, philosopher, educator; b. Canton, Ohio, Nov. 2, 1920; s. Peter C. and Christine (Giannopoulos) A.; m. Helen Vezos, Nov. 26, 1955; children: James, Christopher, Peter. BS, Columbia U., 1949, MA, 1950, PhD, 1954, U. Athens, 1954, LHD (hon.), 1992; DHL (hon.), U. Patras, 2004, U. Ioannina, 2005; PhD in Philosophy and Pedagogy, U. Thessaloniki, 2008. Instr. Pace Coll., 1953-54; vis. lectr. U. N.Mex., 1954-55; asst. prof. U. Nebr., 1955-58; assoc. prof. Ohio Wesleyan U., 1958-62; prof. SUNY, Buffalo, 1962-67, assoc. dean grad. sch., prof., 1967-69; Fuller E. Callaway prof. Emory U., 1969-81, chmn. dept. philosophy, 1969-76; prof., provost New Coll., U. South Fla., Tampa, 1982-83, disting. prof. Greek philosophy and culture, 1983—, dir. Ctr. Greek Studies. Woods vis. prof. Mills. Coll., 1981; vis. prof. Columbia U., 1966. Author: Aristotle's Theory of Contrariety, 1957, Science, Philosophy and Educational Tasks, 1966, Naturalism and Historical Understanding, 1967, Philosophical Essays, 1969, Essays in Ancient Greek Philosophy (5 vols.), 1971-92, Science and the Sciences in Plato, 1980, Critical Humanism as a Philosophy of Culture, 1981, Upward Panic: The Autobiography of Eva Palmer-Sikelianos, 1993, The Poetry and Poetics of C.P. Cavafy, 1995, Categories and Experience, 1996, Archetypal Principles and Hierarchies, 2000, American Naturalism and Greek Philosophy, 2005, (book) Eros Politicos, 2010; co-editor (jour.) Diotima: editl. cons. Jour. History of Philosophy, 1968—, The Humanist, 1967—; mem. editl. bd. So. Jour. Philos., 1974—, Eidos, 1974—, Ancient Philosophy, 1979, Idealistic Studies, 1981, Philos. Inquiry, 1981; founding editor (jours.) Jour. of Neoplatonic Studies, 1991, Revue de Philosophie Ancienne, 1984—, Skepsis, 1997, Phronimos, 2004. Bd. govs. St. Lawrence Coll., 1989. With US Army, 1946—47. Mem. Am. Philos. Assn., Soc. Advancement of Am. Philosophy (founding mem.), Am. Philol. Assn., Am. Soc. Aesthetics (trustee 1973-76, 81-84), Ga. Philos. Soc. (v.p. 1972, pres. 1973), Internat. Soc. Neoplatonic Studies (chmn. exec. com., pres. 1997—2004), Soc. Ancient Greek Philosophy (sec., treas. 1973-81, pres. 1981-83), Internat. Assn. Sports Law (hon.), Modern Greek Studies Assn. (v.p. 1969—72), Soc. Macedonian Studies (hon.), Acad. Athens (corr.), Internat. Assn. Greek Philos. (hon. pres. 1993), Soc. Internat. pour l'Etude de la Philosophie Mediévale, Parnassos Lit. Soc. (hon.), Internat. Soc. Arcadia (hon. pres. 2007-), Phi Beta Kappa, Eta Sigma Phi, Phi Sigma Tau. Home: 10012 Oxford Chapel Dr Tampa FL 33647-2870 Office: U South Fla Dept Philosophy Tampa FL 33620 Home Phone: 813-991-7033.

ANTON, RAYMOND F., JR., psychiatrist, educator; b. USA, Jan. 9, 1951; BA in Biol. Sciences, Rutgers U., New Brunswick, NJ, 1972; MMS, Rutgers U., Piscataway, NJ, 1974, MD, 1976. Diplomate Am.

Bd. Psychiatry and Neurology-psychiatry, 1982, Am. Bd. of Addiction Medicine, 2009, cert. Am. Bd. Psychiatry and Neurology-addiction psychiatry, 1997. Intern Greenwich Hosp. Assn., 1976—77; resident psychiatrist sch. medicine Yale Univ., 1977—80; resident psychiatrist Conn. Mental Health Ctr., 1977—80, resident psychiatrist and cons. the drug dependence unit methadone maintenace program, 1979, dir. Naltrexone high intervention program drug dependence unit, 1979—80; consulting psychiatrist Waterbury Gen. Hosp., Conn., 1978—79; asst. prof. dept. psychiatry and behavioral sciences Med. Univ. SC, 1980—85, assoc. prof. dept. psychiatry and behavioral sciences, 1985—91, dir. substance abuse fellowship dept. psychiatry and behavioral sciences, 1989—93, co-sci. dir. alcohol rsch. ctr., 1995—99, acting sci. dir. alcohol rsch. ctr., 1997, dir. alcohol medication studies ctr. for drug and alcohol programs, 1994—2000, sci. dir. rsch. ctr., 1998—2005, dir. rsch. ctr. for drug and alcohol programs, 1999—2000, co-dir. ctr. for drug and alcohol programs, 2000—01, prof. dept. psychiatry and behavioral sciences, 1991—2002, sci. dir. for clin. rsch. alcohol rsch. ctr., 2006—, dir. ctr. for drug and alcohol programs, 2001—, prof. dept. psychiatry and behavioral sciences, disting. univ. prof., 2002—; staff psychiatrist Veterans Adminstrn. Med. Ctr., Charleston, SC, 1980—88, dir. psychopharmacology rsch., 1984—88; dir. inpatient psychotic disorders program Inst. of Psychiatry, Charleston, SC, 1989—92, dir. clin. substance abuse rsch. dept. psychiatry and behavioral sciences, 1990—92, dir. clin.-neurobiology labs., 1988—. Editl. adv. bd. Alcohol Health and Rsch. World, 1996—99; assoc. editor alcoholism Clin. and Exptl. Rsch., 1997—98, editl. bd. alcoholism, 1999—2006, bd. of reviewing editors alcoholism, 2000—; editl. bd. Jour. of Studies on Alcohol, 1997—; guest editor CNS Spectrums, 1999. Co-author: (publs.) Multiple Family Therapy and Naltrexone in the Treatment of Opiate Dependence, Tricyclic Antidepressant Poisoning, 1981, Non-invasive Measurement of Cardiac Ejection Fraction During Desipramine Treatment, 1982, Inhibition of Prostaglandin Synthesis by Indomethacin does not Affect Alcohol Consumption in Inbred Mice, 1983, Efficacy of Amoxapine in Psychotic Depression, 1983, Amoxapine Elevates Serum Prolactin in Depressed Men, 1983, and numerous others. Recipient Disting. Alumni Award, UMDNJ-Robert Wood Johnson Med. Sch., 2000; named one of Best Doctors in America, 1997—98; nominee Golden Appple Award, Med. Univ. SC, 1984. Fellow: Am. Psychiat. Assn., Am. Coll. of Neuropsychopharmacology; mem.: Rsch. Soc. on Alcoholism, Internat. Soc. for Biomedical Rsch. on Alcoholism, Am. Soc. of Addiction Medicine (cert. 1996), Alpha Omega Alpha, Phi Beta Kappa. Office: Medical University of South Carolina Department of Psychiatry 67 President St Box 250861 Charleston SC 29425 Office Phone: 843-792-1226. Office Fax: 843-792-7353. E-mail: antonr@musc.edu.

ANTONELLI, DOMINIC A., astronaut; b. Detroit; married; 2 children. BS in Aeronautics and Astronautics, MIT; MS in Aeronautics and Astronautics, U. Wash.; Disting. grad., US Air Force Test Pilot Sch. (Navy Exchange Pilot). Fleet Naval Aviator and Landing Signal Officer USS Nimitz with Blue Diamonds, Strike Fighter Squadron 146, Flying F/A-18C Hornets in Support of Operation Southern Watch; pilot, astronaut NASA, 2000—. Comdr., pilot STS-119 Mission (Discovery), 2009; pilot STS-132 Mission (Atlantis)-Last Flight for Atlantis, 2010. Decorated Navy Commendation medal, Navy Achievement medals (2), Unit Battle Efficiency awards (2); recipient NASA Return-to-Flight award, NASA Superior Accomplishment award, NASA Exceptional Achievement medal; named CVW-9 Landing Signal Officer Yr. Avocations: snowboarding, NASCAR. Office: NASA Johnson Space Ctr Astronauts Office 2101 NASA Parkway Houston TX 77058

ANTONIA, SCOTT J., medical oncologist, educator; PhD in Immunology, U. Conn., 1987; MD, U. Conn., Storrs, 1989. Diplomate Am. Bd. Internal Medicine, 2002, Am. Bd. Internal Medicine-med. oncology, 2006. Resident internal medicine Yale Univ.-New Haven Hosp., 1990—91, fellow med. oncology, 1991—94, fellow immunology, 1994; assoc. prof. medicine Coll. Medicine Univ. South Fla.; chair dept. thoracic oncology Moffitt Cancer Ctr., co-program leader immunology, med. dir. cellular therapies core. Contbr. articles to profl. publs. Office: H Lee Moffitt Cancer Center & Research Inst 12902 Magnolia Dr Tampa FL 33612 Office Phone: 813-745-8470.

ANTOON, JOHN, II, federal judge; b. Bakersfield, Calif., 1946; BA, Fla. Southern Coll., 1968; JD, Fla. State U., 1971; MS, Fla. Inst. Tech., 1993; LLM, U. Va., 2001. Prosecutor City of Cocoa, Fla., 1971—72; pvt. practice atty., 1971—84; asst. pub. defender 18th Jud. Cir., Fla., 1972—76, cir. judge, 1985—95; judge 5th Dist. Ct. Appeal Fla., 1995—2000, US Dist. Ct. (mid. dist.) Fla., Orlando, 2000—. Office: US Dist Ct US Courthouse 401 W Central Blvd Orlando FL 32801 Office Phone: 407-835-4334.

APODACA, TOM, state legislator; b. Nov. 8, 1957; m. Lisa Apodaca; children: Brandon, Tate. BS in Bus. Adminstrn., Western Carolina U., 1980. Owner A and A Bonding Agy.; pres., owner Fifth Ave. Travel, Inc., Southeastern Sureties Group, Inc.; state senator Dist. 48 NC, 2002—. Republican. Office: NC Senate 16 W Jones St Rm 2010 Raleigh NC 27601-2808 Office Phone: 919-733-5745. E-mail: Tom.Apodaca@ncleg.net.

APPEL, BERNARD SIDNEY, marketing professional, consultant, retired electronics executive; b. Boston, Jan. 10, 1932; s. Max and Sophie (Altshuler) A.; m. Ellen Carey, July 1988; children: Ann, Sharon; children by previous marriage: Arlene R., Gerald I. AA Commercial Sci., Boston U., 1959; D Comml. Sci. (hon.), McKenzie Coll., 1991. Store mgr., buyer S & W Distbg. Co., Boston, 1949-59; buyer Radio Shack Co., Boston, 1959-66, mdse. mgr., 1966-70, v.p. merchandising Ft. Worth, 1970-78, sr. v.p. merchandising and advt., 1978-80, exec. v.p. mktg., 1980-84, pres., 1984-92, chmn., 1992-93; sr. v.p. Tandy Corp., 1992-93; bd. dirs. Uniview Corp., 1995—2002; pres. Appel Assocs., Mktg. Cons., 1993—; vice chmn., bd. dirs. Integrated Tech. Inc., 1994-99. V.p. Holbrook (Mass.) Jewish Cmty. Ctr., 1958-59; bd. dirs. Casa Manana Mus., 1978-79, Dan Danciger Jewish Cmty. Ctr., Ft. Worth, 1989-98, Family Svcs., Inc., 1990—, Non-Profit Svc. Ctr., 1999-04, Crime Prevention Resource Ctr., 1997-2005; v.p., founder Temple Aliyah, Needham, Mass., 1969-70; pres. Congregation Ahavath Sholom, Ft. Worth, 1979-81, bd. dirs., 1972—; bd. dirs. Jewish Fedn. Ft. Worth, 1975-97, v.p., 1981-85, pres., 1985-87; mem. adv. bd. Arts Coun. Ft. Worth, 1985—; project renewal cluster chmn. Acco-East, Israel, 1981-94; mem. exec. com. so. regional campaign cabinet United Jewish Appeal, 1980-89; so. regional chmn. United Jewish Appeal's Passage to Freedom Campaign for Soviet Jewry, 1989; co-chmn. fin. rels. United Jewish Appeal Western Region, Jewish Agy. Com., 1992-93, United Jewish Appeal Ctrl. Region, Jewish Agy Com., 1993; mem. exec. com. Network of Ind. UJA Coms., 1994—; mem. internat. bd. visitors M.J. Neeley Sch. Bus., Tex. Christian U., 1990—; hon. life mem. nat. commn. Anti-Defamation League, 1992. With USCG, 1951-54; mem. adv. bd. Crime Stoppers of N. Tex., 2005-; chmn. crime stoppers com. Safe City Commn., 2006-. Recipient Torch of Liberty award Anti-Defamation League of B'nai B'rith, 1988, Defender of Jerusalem award, 1990, Alumni award Boston U. Sch. Mgmt., 1994; named Man of Yr., B'nai B'rith Ft. Worth Jewish, 1984, Anti-Defamation League Ft. Worth, 1990; named to Consumer Electronics Hall of Fame, 2002. Mem. Electronic VIP Club, Ft. Worth C. of C. (bd. dirs. 1981-84), Masons, Shriners, Frog Club (Tex. Christian U.), Colonial Country Club, City Country Club, Ft. Worth, Rotary (bd. dirs. 2005-). Home: 4917 Ranch View Rd Fort Worth TX 76109-3117 Office: Appel Assocs 301 Commerce St Ste 1415 Fort Worth TX 76102-4114 Office Phone: 817-338-9579. E-mail: bappel@flash.net.

APPEL, CONRAD, state legislator; b. New Orleans, 1951; m. Carol Ann Appel; 2 children. BS in Elec. Engring., La. State U., 1973. Pres. Construction South, Inc., Construction Mgmt. Svcs. Inc., Trinity Co. - Real Estate; mem. Dist. 9 La. State Senate, 2008—, vice chair judiciary C com., mem. edn. com., retirement com. Republican. Address: Capitol Office PO Box 94183 Baton Rouge LA 70804 Mailing: District Office 3525 N Causeway Blvd Ste 602 Metairie LA 70002 Office Phone: 504-838-5550. E-mail: appelc@legis.state.la.us.

APPEL, JOHN C., communications company executive; m. Terry; 2 children. BSBA, U. Fla., 1971. From mgr. to divsn. mgr., dir. ops. GTE Comms. Corp., 1971-88; from south area dir. bus. svc. to regional v.p., mgr. Calif. GTE Tel. Ops., Irving, Tex., 1988-96, exec. v.p. network ops., 1996-97; pres. GTE Network Svcs., Irving, Tex., 1997—. Office: GTE Telephone Ops PO Box 152092 Irving TX 75015-2092

APPEL, MATTHEW W., corporate financial executive; BA in Bus. Adminstrn., Rutgers U., MBA in Acctg. CPA. Audit practice Arthur & Andersen LLP; sr. v.p., fin., acctg. BPO Affiliated Computer Services, Inc. (ACS) (acquired by Xerox Corp.), 2001—03; v.p., fin., adminstrn. BPO Electronic Data Sys. Corp., 2003—05, v.p., BPO product mgmt., 2006—07; v.p., CFO ExlService Holdings, Inc., 2007—09; exec. v.p., CFO Zale Corp., 2009—. Office: Zale Corp 901 W Walnut Hill Ln MS 5B-12 Irving TX 75038-1003 Office Phone: 972-580-5266. Office Fax: 972-580-5523.

APPEL, STANLEY HERSH, neurologist, educator; b. Boston, May 8, 1933; married; 4 children. AB, Harvard U., 1954; MD, Columbia U., 1960. Diplomate Am. Bd. Psychiatry and Neurology. Intern medicine Mass. Gen. Hosp., 1960-61; resident neurology Mt. Sinai Hosp., 1961-62; rsch. assoc. Lab. Moleculat Biology NIH, 1962-64; chief rsch. assoc. Sch. Medicine U. Pa., 1965-66, asst. prof., 1966-67; assoc. of neurology Med. Ctr. Duke U., 1964-65, from assoc. prof. to prof. neurology, 1967-77, assoc. prof. biochemistry, 1968-77, chief divsn. neurology, 1969-77; prof. neurology Baylor Coll. Medicine, 1977—2004, prof., chmn. dept. neurology, 1977—2004, chmn. program neurosci., 1977-89, dir. Jerry Lewis Neuromuscular Disorder Rsch. Ctr., 1977—2004; dir. Vicki Appel MDA/ALS Ctr., 1977—2004; chair dept. neurology Meth. Hosp. Neurol. Inst., Houston, 2005—, dir. MDA/ALS Rsch. and Clin. Ctr., 2005—, Peggy and Gary Edwards disting. endowed chair for the treatment and rsch. of ALS dept. neurology, 2006—; prof. neurology Weill Med. Coll. Cornell U., NYC, 2005—; dir. Methodist Neurol. Inst., 2010—. Recipient Gold medal Columbia Coll. Physicians and Surgeons, 1997, Disting. Faculty award Baylor Coll. Medicine Alumni Assn., 2004, Lifetime Achievement award Tex. Neurol. Soc., 2005, Forbes Norris award Internat. Alliance ALS/MND Assn., 2005, John P. McGavern Compleat Physician award, 2008 Mem. Am. Acad. Neurology (Sheila Essey award, 2003), Am. Neurol. Assn., Soc. Neuroscience, Am. Soc. Neurochemistry. Achievements include research in etiology of amyotrophic lateral sclerosis, Parkinson's disease, and Alzheimer's disease. Office: Methodist Neurological Inst Dept Neurology 6560 Fannin St #802 Houston TX 77030 Office Phone: 713-441-3760.

APPLEBY, C. G., lawyer; BA, Hillsdale Coll., 1968; JD, Wash. Coll. Law, Am. U., 1973. Bar: DC Ct. Appeals 1973, cert.: DC Bar 1974, bar: Fed. Bar Assn. DC 1975, cert.: ABA 1974, bar: US Supreme Ct. 1978, Supreme Ct. Va. 2004, Va. State Bar 2004. Atty. asst. NASA, Washington, 1971—73; atty. US Govt., Washington, 1973—74; sr. v.p. Booz Allen Hamilton Inc., 1975, gen. counsel McLean, Va., 1975—, chief legal officer, sec., 1999—, exec. v.p., 2010—. Pres. Wash. Met. Area Corp. Counsel Assn., Washington, 1989—90, No. Va. Cmty. Found., McLean, 2001—05, bd. mem., 2001—; chmn. Profl. Services Coun., McLean, 2000—02; mem. Wash. Met. Area Corp. Counsel Assn., Washington. Army/specialist 5 sgt. 5 US Army, 1968—70, Vietnam. Recipient Outstanding Alumni Achievement award, Hillsdale Coll., 2001, Diversity award, Minority Corp. Counsel Assn., 2004. Mem.: No. Va. Corp. Counsel Assn. (pres.), Profl. Services Coun. (chmn. 1980—2005, bd. dirs. 1980—2005). Office: Booz Allen Hamilton Inc 8283 Greensboro Dr Mc Lean VA 22102 Office Phone: 703-902-5000. Office Fax: 703-902-3333. Business E-Mail: c_appleby@boozallen.com.

APPLEGATE, WILLIAM BROWN, medical educator, researcher; b. Louisville, July 28, 1946; s. Henry Lovelace and Margaret (Whitesides) A.; m. Gail Reekers, July 31, 1982; children: Elizabeth Marie, Jennifer Michelle. BA, U. Louisville, 1968, MD, 1972; MPH, Harvard U., 1973. Intern Boston City Hosp., 1973—74, resident in internal medicine, 1974—75; R.W. Johnson clin. scholar U. NC, Chapel Hill, 1975-77; asst. prof. medicine U. N.Mex., Albuquerque, 1977-79; chief divsn. geriatric medicine U. Tenn., Memphis, 1979-93, dir. gen. clin. rsch. ctr., 1993-99, chmn. dept. preventive medicine, 1994-99; chmn., prof. dept. internal medicine Wake Forest U., Winston-Salem, NC, 1999—2002, dean sch. medicine, sr. v.p. health scis., 2002—07; pres. Wake Forest U. Health Sciences, Winston-Salem, 2007—11; prof. geriatrics and gerontology Wake Forest Baptist Med. Ctr., Winston-Salem. Mem. coun. Nat. Inst. Aging, 1989-93, nat. adv. bd. Johnson Found. Clin. Scholars Program; bd. regents, ACP, 2002-. Contbr. articles to med. jours., including Jour. AMA, Archives Internal Medicine, others. Named Alumni fellow U. Louisville, 2003; grantee. Mem. ACP (bd. regents, chair bd. regents, 2008), Am. Geriat. Soc. (editor-in-chief jour. 1993-2000), Rotary. Democrat. Avocation: bicycling. Office: Wake Forest Bapt Med Ctr Medical Center Blvd Winston Salem NC 27157-0001 Office Phone: 336-713-8570.

APPLER, THOMAS L., lawyer; b. Washington, Oct. 12, 1943; m. Nancy J. Babb, Dec. 3, 1967; children: Alexandra Whitney. AB in Politics, Princeton U., 1965; JD, George Washington U., 1968. Bar: Va. 1968. Atty. Office of Judge Adv., Surgeon Gen. of Army, 1969-70; ptnr. McGuire, Woods, Battle & Boothe (and predecessor firms), McLean, Va., 1970-99, Crews & Hancock, PLC, Fairfax, Va., 1999—2002, Hancock, Daniel, Johnson & Nagle, P.C., 2002—04, Wilson, Elser, Moskowitz, Edelman & Dicker LLP, McLean, 2005—. Co-author: Damages for Plaintiff and Defense Attorneys, 1987. USAR, 1970-76. Fellow Am. Coll. Trial Lawyers; mem. No. Va. Def. Attys. Assn. (pres. 1975), Va. Assn. Def. Attys. (v.p., bd. dirs. 1977-83), Va. Bar Assn. (bd. dirs. young lawyers sect. 1974-76, appellate judges com. 1989-91, Boyd-Graves Conf. com. chair 2006-08), Va. State Bar (coun. 1985-92, malpractice ins. com. 1989-99), Fairfax Bar Assn. (pres. 1984-85, bd. dirs. 1983-86), No. Va. Young Lawyers Assn. (pres. 1974), Va. Law Found. Home: 9717 Meadowlark Rd Vienna VA 22182-1951 Office: Wilson Elser Moskowitz Edelman & Dicker LLP 8444 Westpark Dr Ste 510 Mc Lean VA 22102 Office Phone: 703-852-7789. Office Fax: 703-245-9301. Business E-Mail: thomas.appler@wilsonelser.com.

AQUINO, PETER D., telecommunications industry executive; BS in Fin. & Economics, Montclair State U, NJ; MBA, George Wash. U., Washington, 1990. Various positions in fin., mktg. and regulatory & corp. devel. Bell Atlantic Corp. (now Verizon), 1983—95; COO, bd. advisors Veninfotel LLC, Caracas, Venezuela, 1995—2000; ptnr. Wave Internat., Inc., 1995—98; sr. mng. dir. Comm. Tech. Advisors, LLC, 2001—04; ops. advisor RCN Corp., 2004, pres., CEO, 2004—. Bd. dirs. Neon Comm., TerreStar Corp. (formerly Motient Corp.), 2003—05, iBasis Inc., 2004—, RCN Corp., 2004—, Comptel Oyj, 2005—, Primus Telecom. Group Inc., 2009—. Bd. trustees United Way America, 2009—. Recipient Best Bus. Turnaround Stevie award, Am. Bus. Awards, 2007. Office: RCN Corp 196 Van Buren St Herndon VA 20170 Office Phone: 703-434-8200. Office Fax: 703-434-8290. Business E-Mail: paquino@rcn.com.

ARASU, THIRU, pediatric gastroenterologist; MBBS, Stanley Med. Coll., 1974. Lic. Fla., 1984, diplomate Am. Bd. Pediatrics, 1980, Am. Bd. Pediatrics-pediatric gastroenterology, 2005. Resident pediat. Wyler Children's-Univ. Health Sciences, 1975—77; fellow pediatric gastroenterology Riley Children's Hosp., 1977—79; hosp. affiliations include St. Joseph's Hosp., Univ. Cmty. Hosp., Brandon Regional Hosp. Office: St Joseph's Hospital 3001 W Martin Luther King Blvd Tampa FL 33607-6387 Office Phone: 813-870-4000.

ARCENEAUX, WILLIAM, historian, educator, foundation administrator; b. Scott, La., Aug. 19, 1941; s. Teddy and Regina (Begnaud) A.; m. Patricia Boozman; children: Ted, Angelle, Leah, Scott. BA, U. La., Lafayette, 1962; MA, La. State U., 1965, PhD, 1969; LHD, Loyola U., 1982. Instr. La. State U., 1966-67; asst. prof. Northwestern State U., Natchitoches, La., 1967-69; assoc. prof., chmn. dept. history So. U., New Orleans, 1969-72; exec. dir. La. Coordinating Council for Higher Edn., 1972-75; commr. higher edn. La. Baton Rouge, 1975-87; pres. La. Assn. Ind. Colls. and Univs., 1987—2007; disting. vis. prof. Tulane U., 2007—. Chmn. CSLA, Inc. Author: Acadian General-Alfred Mouton and the Civil War, 1972, 2d edit., 1981, No Spark of Malice: The Murder of Martin Begnaud, 1999; editor: Postsecondary Education in Transition: Planning for Change in Louisiana, 1975. Bd. dirs., chmn. Student Loan Mktg. Assn., 1979-97; chmn. La. Found. La., 1989—; host, cinema francaise La. Pub. Broadcasting, chair La. Bicentennial Com. of Baton Rouge. Decorated chevalier L'Ordre de la Pleiade, Association Internationale des Parlementaires de Langue Francaise, Officer L'Ordre des Palmes Academique (France); named one of 100 Young Leaders of Academy Change mag., 1978, Am. Com. Bicentennial French Revolutions; recipient Jefferson Davis medal UDC, E.T. Dunlap medal Southeastern Okla. State U. Mem.: French-Am. C. of C. (bd. dirs.), La. Hist. Assn., World Trade Ctr. New Orleans, Am. Hist. Assn., Plimsol Club, City Club of Baton Rouge, Country Club of La., Phi Alpha Theta, Omicron Delta Kappa. Roman Catholic. Office: Found Excellence La Pub Broadcasting 7733 Perkins Rd Baton Rouge LA 70810 Personal E-mail: foundatiomlpb@aol.com.

ARCHAMBAULT, LEE JOSEPH, astronaut; b. Oak Park, Ill., Aug. 25, 1960; s. Lee and Mary Ann Archambault; m. Kelly Renee Raup; 3 children. BSc with hon. in Aero. & Astronautical Engring., U. Ill., Urbana, 1982, MSc with hon. in Aero. & Astronautical Engring., 1984. Commd. 2d lt. USAF, 1985, advanced through grades to lt. col., various assignments, 1985—90; assigned to Operation Desert Shield/Desert Storm, Saudi Arabia, 1990—91, Saudi Arabia, 1991—92, Holloman AFB, N.Mex., 1992—94; various assignments USAF, 1995—98; astronaut NASA, Houston, 1998—. Mem. acad. adv. com. U. Ill. Aero. & Astronautical Engring. Dept.; pilot STS-117 Atlantis Mission, 2007; mission comdr. STS-119 Discovery Mission, 2009. Decorated Disting. Flying Cross USAF, Meritorious Svc. medal with 1 oak leaf cluster, Air medal with 2 oak leaf clusters, Aerial Achievement medal with 4th oak leaf cluster, Commendation medal with 1st oak leaf cluster, Kuwaiti Liberation medal, Achievement medal; recipient Southwest Asia Svc. medal. Mem.: Soc. Exptl. Test Pilots, U. Ill. Alumni Assn., Order of Daedalians. Avocations: weight-lifting, golf, running, ice hockey. Office: Astronaut Office CB NASA Johnson Space Center Houston TX 77058

ARCHBOLD, THOMAS G., corporate financial executive; BS in Profl. Accountancy, 1982. Contr. United Capital Corp.; cons. Taylor White Specialized Staffing Svcs., Inc.; dir., fin. AIL Sys., Inc.; sr. mgr. Ernst & Young LLP, 1982—91; CFO Langer, Inc., Deer Park, NY, 1999—2001; contr. HMS Holdings Corp., 2002—04, CFO, 2004—07; interim CFO, interim prin. acctg. officer Technologies Research Corp., 2008, v.p., fin., CFO, 2008—. Office: Technology Research Corp 5250 140th Ave N Clearwater FL 33760 Office Phone: 727-812-0659. Office Fax: 727-535-4828. Business E-Mail: tarchbold@trci.net.

ARCHER, CHALMERS, JR., retired education educator, military service force; b. Tchula, Miss., Apr. 21, 1928; s. Chalmers Sr. and Eva Alcola (Rutherford) A. AS summa cum laude, Saints Jr. Coll., 1969; BS with honors, Tuskegee Inst., 1972, MEd with honors, 1974; post doctorate, U. Ala., 1980; cert., MIT, 1980; PhD, Auburn U., 1979. Postdoc U. Ala.; asst. to the pres. Saints Coll., Lexington, Miss., 1968-72; asst. v.p. Tuskegee Inst., Ala., 1972—82; prof. No. Va. C.C., Manassas, 1983-2001, prof. emeritus, 2001; with Army Special Forces. Author: Growing Up Black in Rural Mississippi (recipient Miss. Inst. of Arts and Letters award for Nonfiction, Best Seller award, NY Times), Green Berets in the Vanguard: Inside Special Forces, 1953-1963 (Best Seller Local award); contbg. author: The Jackson Advocate; contbr. articles to profl. jours. and newspapers; performing artist (numerous talk shows). Mem. Dem. Spkr.'s Bur. Clinton-Gore Re-election Campaign; vol. Clinton Campaign. Recipient AFRO Achivment Lifetime award; named Hon. Dr. Humanities, St. Coll., 1976, Nat. Edn. Articulation Model, Conf. on Blacks in Higher Edn., Washington, 1986. Mem.: The History Makers Chgo., Leave Rotary Club. Democrat. Baptist. Avocations: writing, motivational speaking, community service, history. Home: 7885 Flager Cir Manassas VA 20109-7435 Home Phone: 703-330-1895; Office Phone: 703-335-5289. Personal E-mail: drarcher97@aol.com.

ARCHEY, WILLIAM T., retired trade association administrator; b. 1943; BS in Econ., Providence Coll.; MBA, Northeastern U.; PhD in Organizational Theory and Behavior, Boston U. With New England Bell Telephone Co., Ford Motor Co.; sr. dep. asst. sec. for enforcement & ops. US Dept. Treasury; vice-chmn. exec. com. Customs Cooperation Coun.; dep. commr. and acting commr. US Customs Svc.; acting asst. sec. for trade adminstrn. US Dept. Commerce, 1983—86; first internat. v.p. then sr. v.p.-policy and congl. affairs US C. of C., 1986—94; pres., CEO AeA, Advancing the Bus. of Tech. (formerly Am. Electronics Assn.), 1995—2008. Adj. faculty George Mason U. Grad. Sch.; disting. vis. lectr. State Dept's Fgn. Svc. Inst. Co-author several publs. on organizational theory; contbr. articles on internat. trade to the Wall Street Journal, Washington Post and other publs. Recipient Medal of Achievement award, AeA, 2007.

ARCHIBALD, LAWRENCE E. (LARRY ARCHIBALD), oil industry executive; b. 1957; BA in Geology, Colgate U., 1979; MS in Geoscience, U. Ariz., 1982; MBA in Fin. & Acctg., Regis U., 1986. With Amoco, 1980—98, BP plc, 1999—2007; v.p. worldwide exploration & appraisal ConocoPhillips, Houston, 2008—09, sr. v.p.

exploration & bus. develop., 2009—. Mem. advisory bd. U. Ariz. Dept. Geosciences; bd. mem. Nat. Ocean Industries Assn. (NOIA). Mem.: Ariz. Geol. Soc. Office: ConocoPhillips PO Box 2197 Houston TX 77252-2197

ARCHIE, JEFFREY B., electric power industry executive; b. Jenkinsville, SC; BS in Mech. Engring., U. SC, 1981. With Virgil C. Summer Nuc. Sta.; joined SC Electric & Gas Co. (subs. of SCANA Corp.), 1978, various managerial positions, gen. mgr., engring., gen. mgr., nuc. plant ops., v.p., nuc. plant ops., sr. v.p., chief nuc. officer, 2010—. Former campaign chmn. Fairfield County United Way, 2006; former area wide campaign chmn. United Way of Midlands, 2007; mem., Future of Learning Strategy Bd., mem., Acad. Coun. Inst. of Nuc. Power Ops.; mem., nuc. strategic issues adv. com. Nuc. Energy Inst.; indsl. bd. adv. U. SC. Office: South Carolina Electric & Gas Co 1426 Main St Columbia SC 29201 Office Phone: 803-217-9000. Office Fax: 803-217-8825. Business E-Mail: jarchie@scana.com.

ARCOS, CRESENCIO S., ambassador; b. San Antonio, Nov. 10, 1943; BA, U. Tex., 1966; MA, Johns Hopkins U., 1973. Various pub. and cultural affairs positions, Leningrad, USSR, Sao Paulo, Brazil; consulate gen. Leningrad, Russia; various pub. and cultural affairs positions Am. Embassy, Lisbon, Portugal, from 1973, counselor pub. affairs Tegucigalpa, Honduras, 1980-85; dep. dir. Nicaraguan Humanitarian Assistance Office, Dept. State, Washington, 1985-86, dep. coord. Latin Am. and Caribbean pub. diplomacy, 1986-87, dep. asst. sec. state for Cen. Am., 1988-89; coord. pub. diplomacy White House Office Communications and Planning, Washington, 1987-88; amb. to Honduras, Am. Embassy, Tegulcigalpa, 1990-93; sr. dep. asst. sec. state for internat. narcotics and crime Dept. State, 1993-95; v.p. for L.Am. and Can. AT&T Corp, IPA, Coral Gables, Fla., 1995—2002; dir. internat. affairs Dept. Homeland Security, Washington, 2003—05, asst. sec. internat. affairs, 2005—06; counselor, govt. affairs Kirkpatrick Lockhart & Gates, 2006—09; sr. advisor Ctr. Hemispheric Def. Studies, 2009—12; adj. prof. Policy St. Mary's U., Tex., 2012—. Mem. White House Pres.'s Fgn. Intelligence Adv. Bd., 1999-2003; mem. res. forces policy bd. Dept. Def. Mem. Hispanic Coun. on Internat. Rels., Washington; bd. dirs. Caribbean-Latin Am. Action, Coun. of the Americas, N.Y.C., Pan Am. Devel. Found.; adv. com. Fla. Internat. Univ. Latin Am. Carribean Ctr.; bd. visitors Zamorano Agr. Sch., Honduras; dir. United Negro Coll. Fund Inst. Internat. Pub. Policy; bd. dirs. Fla. Foster Care Rev., 1999-02; mem. corp. adv. bd. Pacific Coun. on Internat. Policy; mem. Atlantic Coun. Decorated Orden de Morazan (Honduras); recipient awards USIA, Superior Honor awards State Dept.; Regents' fellow U. Calif., 1998-99. Fellow Ctr. Study Presidency (sr.); mem. Coun. Fgn. Rels., Am. Fgn. Svc. Assn., Coun. of Ams. (bd. dirs.), Interam. Dialogue, Pacific Coun. Internat. Policy. (mem. corp. adv. bd.), Cosmos Club Wash., Pan Am. Devel. Found.

ARD, HAROLD JACOB, library administrator; b. Herrick, Ill., Aug. 26, 1940; s. Jacob S. and Hazel E. (Taylor) A.; m. Erma Chapman, Jan. 30, 1960 (div. June 1974); children— Teri Ann, Mark Alan. BS in Edn, Ill. State U., 1962, MS in Psychology, 1964; MLS, Dominicaa U., River Forest, Ill., 1968. Tchr., materials cons. Decatur (Ill.) Pub. Schs., 1962-64; head librarian Barrington (Ill.) Pub. Library, 1964-68; exec. librarian Arlington Heights (Ill.) Meml. Library, 1968-72; library system dir. Jackson (Miss.) Met. Library System, 1972-77; assoc. dir. Rowland Med. Library, U. Miss. Med. Ctr., Jackson, 1978-84; mgr. bus., sci. and tech. units Fort Worth Pub. Libr., 1985-91; mgr. Wedgwood Libr., Ft. Worth, 1991-94; dir. S.W. Regional Libr., Ft. Worth, 1994-97; ret., 1997; part-time instr. U. Tex., Arlington, 2001—05. Reference libr. Burleson Pub. Libr., 2004—09; owner Antiques, Etc., Fort Worth; cons., lectr. in field. Mem. ALA, Tex. Library Assn., Med. Library Assn., Beta Phi Mu. Clubs: Rotary. Methodist. Home: 4952 Stadium Dr Fort Worth TX 76133-1742 Personal E-mail: hard730939@aol.com.

ARDELT, MAXIMILIAN, electronics executive; diploma in Engring., M in Engring., Tech. Univ., Berlin. With Salzgitter AG (merged with Preussag AG); with Telecom. and Logistics Divsn. Viag AG, 1994—2000; CEO Viag Telecom AG (subs. Viag AG), 2000—02; owner, mng. dir. ConDigit Consult GmbH, 2002—. Bd. dirs. Viag AG, 1994—2000; bd. supr. Cinterion Wireless Modules GmbH, Funkwerk AG, Stulz GmbH, Getmobile Europe plc, Tiburon Ptnrs. AG, OHG, CeWeColor AG & Co., Manstaedt GmbH; bd. dirs. Tech Data Corp., 1998—. Chmn., bd. adv. Bavarian Elite Academie; bd. dirs. Tech. U., Graz, Austria. Office: Tech Data Corp 5350 Tech Data Dr Clearwater FL 33760 Office Phone: 727-539-7429. Office Fax: 727-538-5860. Business E-Mail: maximilian.ardelt@techdata.com.

AREA, LEANDRO C., family practice physician; MD, Duke U. Diplomate Am. Bd. Family Practice. Resident family medicine Duke Univ., Durham, NC, 1976—78, fellow; assoc. chmn. family medicine dept. South Shore; hosp. affiliation includes Ochsner Med. Ctr. Office: Ochsner Health Center-Lakeview 101 W Robert E Lee Blvd Ste 201 New Orleans LA 70124 Office Phone: 504-846-9646.

ARENA, JOSEPH, dermatologist; Grad., LeMoyne-Owen Coll.; MD, U. Miami, 1966. Diplomate Am. Bd. Dermatology, 1973. Intern internal medicine LA County Gen. Hosp.; chief flight surgeon USAF; resident dermatology Univ. of Miami Sch. of Medicine, 1969—72, assoc. clin. prof. dermatology; hosp. appointments include Westside Regional Hosp., Aventura Med. Ctr., Meml. Regional Med. Ctr., Hollywood Med. Ctr.; with Skin & Cancer Associates. Fellow: Am. Acad. of Dermatology; mem.: AMA, Broward County Dermatology, Fla. Soc. of Dermatology, Broward County Med. Soc. Office: Skin & Cancer Associates Ste 100 2100 E Hallandale Beach Blvd Hallandale FL 33009 Office Phone: 954-454-1066. Office Fax: 954-456-4025.

ARENS, KATHERINE MARIE, language educator; b. Chgo., Nov. 25, 1953; d. Edward James and Eleanor (Baumgartner) A. BA, Northwestern U., 1975; AM, Stanford U., 1976, PhD, 1981. Tchg. fellow in German studies and humanities Stanford (Calif.) U., 1976-79; asst. prof. German studies U. Tex., Austin, 1980—86, assoc. prof. Germanic langs., 1986-93, prof. Germanic studies, 1993—. Author: Functionalism and Fin de Siècle, 1984, Structures of Knowing, 1989; co-author: (with Swaffar and Byrnes) Reading for Meaning, 1991, Austria and Other Margins, 1996, Empire in Decline, 2001, (with J. Swaffer) Remapping the Foreign Language Curriculum, 2005. Fulbright Hays grantee, 1978-79, NEH grant, 1982; C.G. Whiting Found. fellow, 1979-80. Home: 4806 Red River St Austin TX 78751-3331 Office: Univ Tex Dept Germanic Studies Austin TX 78712-0304 Office Phone: 512-232-6363. Business E-Mail: arens@austin.utexas.edu.

ARGENIO, SANDRA L., family practice physician, educator; MD, Hahnemann Med. Coll. Diplomate American Bd. Family Practice, lic. Fla., 1992. Resident family medicine Geisinger Med. Ctr., Danville, Pa., 1979—82; hosp. affiliations include Mayo Clinic, St. Luke's Hosp.; asst. prof. Mayo Med. Sch. Recipient Patients' Choice award, 2008—09, Women's Leadership award, Young Women's Christian Assn. (YWCA), 1998. Office: Mayo Clinic of Jacksonville 4500 San Pablo Rd Jacksonville FL 32224 Office Phone: 904-953-2000.

ARGENZIANO, NANCY, state legislator; b. Bklyn., Jan. 1, 1955; 1 child, Joseph Hall. Former chairwoman Northern Segment Withlacoochee River DEP Ecosys. Mgmt. Plan; house rep. Fla.; dir. Withlacoochee Basin Initiative, 1995—2002; state rep. Dist. 43 Fla., 1996—2002; chairwoman Elder Affairs & Long-Term Care Com., 1999—2002; mem. Health & Family Svc. Coun., Tourism Com., Real Property & Probate Com., 1999—2002; state senator Dist. 3 Fla., 2003—; real estate investor. Mem.: Nature Conservation, Christian Childrens Fund, DeRosa Civic Assn. (dir. 1994—95). Republican. Roman Catholic. Office: 404 S Monroe Rm 311 Tallahassee FL 32399

ARGIRION, MICHAEL, editor; b. Chgo., May 2, 1940; s. Gus and Angela A.; m. Sherrie Berlant, Feb. 10; children: Carrie, Glen. Student, DePaul U., 1958-59, Northwestern U., 1959-60, U. Chgo., 1961-62. Copy editor Chgo.'s Am., 1959-68, wire editor, 1969; news editor Chgo. Today, 1970-71, Sunday and features editor, 1971-74; asst. Sunday editor Chgo. Tribune, 1974-75, features editor, 1975-79, asst. mng. editor features, 1979-81, asst. mng. editor news editing, 1981-82, exec. news editor, 1982-83, assoc. editor, 1983; editor Tribune Media Services, 1984, v.p., editor, 1985-93. Co-creator internationally syndicated newspaper word puzzle Jumble, That Scrambled Word Game, 1994-2010. Editor: History of Your World, 1969. Served with U.S. Army, 1962. Mem. Legacy Club Alaqua Lakes. Office: Argirion 1212 St Albans Loop Heathrow FL 32746

ARIAS, ILEANA, federal agency administrator, psychiatrist, educator; AB, Barnard Coll., NYC; MA, PhD in Psychology, SUNY Stony Brook. From asst. prof. to clin. psychology prof. & dir. clin. tng. U. Ga., Athens, 1985—2000; chief etiology & surveillance br., divsn. violence prevention Nat. Ctr. Injury Prevention & Control, Atlanta, 2000—04, acting dir., 2004—05, dir., 2005—10; prin. dep. dir. Centers Disease Control & Prevention (CDC), 2010—. Mem. editl. bd. Jour. of Aggression, Maltreatment and Trauma, Rev. of Aggression and Violent Behavior, Violence and Victims; contbr. articles to profl. jours. Office: Centers for Disease Control 1600 Clifton Rd Atlanta GA 30333 Office Phone: 770-488-4696. Office Fax: 770-638-5501. Business E-Mail: iaa4@cdc.gov.*

ARIELY, DAN, behavioral economics educator; b. Apr. 29, 1968; m. Sumi Ariely; children: Amit, Neta. BA in Psychology, Tel Aviv U., 1991; MA in Cognitive Psychology, U. NC, Chapel Hill, 1994, PhD in Cognitive Psychology, 1996; PhD in Bus. Adminstrn., Duke U., 1998. Dir., founder Ctr. for Advanced Hindsight; dir. eRationally Rsch. Group; with MIT, The Media Laboratory, 2000—10; Alfred P. Sloan prof. of Behavioral Economics MIT, Sloan Sch. Mgmt., 1998—2008; with U. Calif., Berkeley, 2001—02, Ctr. for Advanced Studies in the Behavioral Sciences, Stanford U., 2004, Inst. for Advanced Study, Princeton U., 2005—07; James B. Duke Professor of Behavioral Economics Duke U., Fuqua Sch. of Bus., The Ctr. for Cognitive Neuroscience, Sch. of Medicine, Dept. of Economics, 2008—; sr. fellow Duke U. Kenan Inst. for Ethics, 2008—. Adv. bd. mem. Social Sci. Rsch. Network, 2002—; rschr. Fed. Reserve Bank, Boston, 2005—; fellow Diamond (Mgmt. and Tech. Consulting), 2005—; vis. prof. Duke U., Fuqua Sch. Bus. & Ctr. for Cognitive Neuroscience, 2007—08; co-founder BEworks, 2010—; invited lectr. in field. Author: Predictably Irrational: The Hidden Forces That Shape Our Decisions, 2008, The Upside of Irrationality: The Unexpected Benefits of Defying Logic at Work and at Home, 2010, The Honest Truth About Dishonesty: How We Lie to Everyone---Especially Ourselves, 2012; assoc. editor Journal of Economic Behavior and Organization, 2006—, editorial review bd. mem. Journal of Consumer Research, 1999—, Journal of Marketing Research, 2002—, Journal of Interactive Marketing, 2002—; contbr. to published papers; mem. of several editorial review boards; contbr. chapters to books; reviewer for several publications and journals. Recipient Early Career Contribution award, Soc. for Consumer Psychology, 2003, Ig Nobel prize, 2008, U NC at Chapel Hill Psychology Dept. Disting. Alumni award, 2009, William F. O'Dell award for Placebo Effects of Marketing Actions: Consumers May Get What They Pay For, 2010; named one of The 50 Most Influential People in Global Fin., Bloomberg Markets, 2013. Mem.: Judgement and Decision Making Soc. (Hillel Einhorn New Investigator award 2000), Am. Psychological Soc., Am. Psychological Assn., Assn. for Consumer Psychology, Assn. for Consumer Rsch. Avocations: scuba diving, flying, rock climbing, photography. Office: Duke University Fuqua School of Business 100 Fuqua Dr Durham NC 27708 Office Phone: 919-660-7703. Office Fax: 919-681-6246. Business E-Mail: dandan@duke.edu.*

ARILDSEN, RONALD, diagnostic radiologist, educator; MD, Columbia U., 1981. Diplomate Am. Bd. Radiology-diagnostic radiology, 1991. Resident diagnostic radiology St. Lukes Roosevelt Hosp. Ctr., 1987—91; fellow body imaging Vanderbilt Univ. Med. Ctr., Nashville, 1991—92; assoc. prof. radiology Vanderbilt Univ. Office: Vanderbilt University Medical Center N CCC-1121 1161 21st Ave S Nashville TN 37232 Office Phone: 615-322-3801.

ARISON, MARILYN BARBARA (LIN ARISON), art foundation executive; b. NYC, May 10, 1937; d. Louis and Leona (Berger) Hersh; m. Bill Harvey, 1955 (div. 1964); 1 child, Michael; m. Ted Arison, Aug. 6, 1968 (dec. 1999); children: Micky, Sharon. AA, Miami Dade CC, 1974; BA, Skidmore Coll., 1976. Exec. sec. L.I. Water Co., NY, 1955—57; legal sec. Myers, Heiman & Kaplan, Miami, Fla., 1958—64; sec. Judge Lawrence King, Miami, 1965; vice chmn., trustee Nat. YoungArts Found. (previously Nat. Found. Advancement in Arts), Miami, 1981—; co-founder New World Symphony, 1987—. Freelance pub. relations, Miami, 1965—66; columnist Miami Rev., 1965—69; mem. vis. com. U. Miami, 1984—; com. mem. Cultural Arts Found., Miami Beach, Fla., 1985—. Contbr. travel articles to Miami Herald, Miami News. Mem. ARC Com., Miami, 1983—, Gov.'s Mansion Found., Tallahassee, 1984—; trustee Am. Ballet Theatre, NYC, 1984—. Recipient Nat. Medal of Arts, Nat. Endowment for the Arts, 2012. Mem.: Lowe Art Mus. Friends of Art. Republican. Jewish. Office: National YoungArts Found 2100 Biscayne Blvd Miami FL 33137*

ARISON, MICKY, cruise line company executive, professional sports team owner; b. Tel Aviv, June 29, 1949; s. Ted and Mina Wasserman Arison; m. Madeleine Arison; 2 children. Attended, U. Miami; D in Naval Architecture (hon.), U. Genoa. Reservations mgr. Carnival Corp., 1974-76, v.p. passenger traffic, 1976-79, pres., CEO, 1979—90, chmn., CEO, 1990—2013, chmn., 2013—. Bd. dirs. Carnival Corp., 1987—, Carnival PLC, 2003—; mng. gen. ptnr. Miami Heat, Fla., 1995—; chmn. bd. govs. NBA, 2005—. Recipient Onorificenza al Merito della Repubblica Italiana, Pres. of Italy, Decoration of Comdr., 1st Class, of the Order of the Lion of Finland, Pres. of Finland; named Officer of the French Legion of Honor, French Pres. Jacques Chirac; named one of The World's Richest People, Forbes mag., 1999—, The Forbes 400: Richest Americans, 1999—, The Most Influential People in the World of Sports, Bus. Week, 2007. Mem.: Fla. Caribbean Cruise Assn. (chmn.). Jewish. Office: Carnival Corp 3655 NW 87th Ave Miami FL 33178-2428*

ARISON, SHARI, investment company executive; b. NYC, 1957; d. Ted and Mina (Sapir) Arison; m. Ofer Glazer; 4 children. Grad., U. Fl. Chmn. Arison Holdings, 1999—, Arison Investments, 1999—; chmn., pres. Ted Arison Family Foundation, 1999—; controller Bank Ha'poalim, Israel; owner Miya. Founder, chairperson Essence of Life, Tel Aviv, 2001—. Named one of The World's Richest People, Forbes mag., The 100 Most Powerful Women, 2011, The 50 Most Powerful Women in Bus., Fortune Mag., 2008; named to The Internat. Power 50, Forbes mag., 2008. Office: c/o Carnival Corp 3655 NW 87th Ave Miami FL 33178*

ARKIN, J. GORDON, lawyer; b. NYC, Jan. 3, 1946; AB summa cum laude, Lehigh U., 1967; JD cum laude, Harvard U., 1970. Bar: N.Y. 1971, Fla. 1976. Former gen. counsel Greater Orlando Aviation Authority; ptnr. Foley & Lardner, Orlando, Fla. Co-vice-chmn. legal com. Airport Operators Coun. Internat., 1986-88, chmn. legal com., 1989. Founding chmn. Orlando chapter Nat. Conf. Christians and Jews; trustee Cmty. Found. Ctrl. Fla.; bd. mem. Srs. 1st, Inc., New Hope For Kids. Recipient Cmty. Leadership award, Nat. Points Light Found., Humanitarian award, Orlando chapter Nat. Conf. Christians and Jews, Tree of Life award, Jewish Nat. Fund, Svc. to Mankind award, Leukemia & Lymphoma Soc., George Wolly Cmty. Leadership award, Jewish Family Svc. Greater Orlando, Lynford Lardner Cmty. Svc. award, Foley & Lardner LLP., Best Lawyers in Am., Super Lawyer, Law & Politics Media, Inc, 2006. Mem. Fla. Bar (chmn. corps. com. 1979-80), Orange County Bar Assn., Phi Beta Kappa. Office: Foley & Lardner 111 N Orange Ave Ste 1800 PO Box 2193 Orlando FL 32801-2386 Office Phone: 407-244-3225. Office Fax: 407-648-1743. Business E-Mail: jarkin@foley.com.

ARMACOST, MARY-LINDA SORBER MERRIAM, educational consultant; b. Jeannette, Pa., May 31, 1943; d. Everett Sylvester Calvin and Madeleine (Case) Sorber; m. E. William Merriam, Dec. 13, 1969 (div. 1975); m. Peter H. Armacost, July 10, 1993. Student, Grove City Coll., 1961-63; BA, Pa. State U., 1963-65, MA, 1965-67, PhD, 1967-70; HHD (hon.), Carroll Coll., 1991; LLD (hon.), Wilson Coll., 1994. Rsch. assoc. Pa. State U., University Park, 1970-72; asst. prof. speech Emerson Coll., Boston, 1972-79, dir. continuing edn., 1974-77, spl. asst. to pres., 1977-78, v.p. adminstrn., 1978-79; asst. to pres. Boston U., 1979-81; pres. Wilson Coll., Chambersburg, Pa., 1981-91, Moore Coll. Art and Design, Phila., 1991-93; sr. fellow Office of Women in Higher Edn. Am. Coun. on Edn., 1994—; interim pres. Moore Coll. Art and Design, Phila., 1998-99; pres. emerita, 2000; adj. prof. faculty U. Pa. Grad Sch. Edn., 2003—. Cons. Govt. Edn. and Secondary Edn. Act Title III, Alameda County, Calif., 1968. Bd. govs. New Eng. chpt. NATAS, 1980-81; bd. dir. Sta. WITF, Inc., Harrisburg, Pa., 1982-91, chmn. bd., 1988-91; bd. dir. Chambersburg Hosp., 1984-89, vice chmn. bd., 1987-89; bd. dir. Elderhostel, 1997-2002; vice-chmn., 2000-2002; trustee Monmouth U., N.J., 1994-99, Sta. WHYY-FM-TV, Phila., 1992-93, Boston Zool. Soc., 1980-81, Arts Boston, 1979-81, Scotland Sch. Vets. Children, Pa., 1984-90, Randolph-Macon Woman's Coll., Lynchburg, Va., 2001-02; bd. dir. Fla. Orch., 1993-97, co-chair edn. com., 1995-97, exec. com., 1995-97; exec. com. Found. Ind. Colls., 1989-91, WEDU-TV, 1998-2002, chair planning com., exec. com., bd. dir., 1998-2002; pres. Chambersburg Area Coun. Arts, 1988-90; chmn. higher edn. com. Gen. Assembly Presbyn. Ch., 1987-90; elder Falling Spring Presbyn. Ch., 1988-90; fellow Am. Coun. Edn., 1977-78, commn. on govtl. rels., 1985-89, commn. on women, 1992-93; exec. com. Pa. Assn. Colls. and Univs., 1984-90, Assn. Presbyn. Colls. and Univs., 1983-88, pres., 1986-87; edn. adv. com. John S. and James L. Knight Found., 1998-2000; bd. dir., exec. com. Presbyn. Edn. Bd., Lahore, Pakistan 2003-09. Recipient Disting. Alumna award Pa. State U., 1984, Disting. Dau. of Pa., 1986, Athena award Chambersburg C. of C., 1988, Outstanding Alumnae award Sch. Dist. Jeannette, 1991. Mem.: Phi Kappa Phi. Personal E-mail: mlsma@cs.com.

ARMBRISTER, KENNETH L., state legislator; Attended, Sam Houston State U. Former police capt.; dir. Victoria (Tex.) Regional Police Acad.; mem. Tex. House of Reps., 1983-86, Tex. Senate, 1987—, chair state affairs com., mem. fin. com., mem. adminstrn. com., mem. gen. investigating com., others. V.p. Victoria Sch. Bd. Recipeint Legis. Leadership award Tex. State C. of C., award for wildlife resources legislation Tex. Wildlife Assn.; named Outstanding Young Men of Am., others. Democrat. Office: PO Box 12068 Austin TX 78711-2068

ARMES, DON, state legislator; b. Midwest City, Okla., July 31, 1961; s. Donald C. Armes and Elaine O. Oliver Bennett; m. Dede Redlk; children: Katy, Kelsey. Attended, Cameron Univ. Auctioneer; broadcaster; agriculture educator Lawton, Okla.; farmer, rancher; mem. Dist 63 Okla. House of Representatives, 2003—. Recipient Media Appreciation award, OCA, 2001. Mem.: NRA, Okla. Cattlemen's Assn. Republican. Office: 2300 N Lincoln Blvd Rm 440 Oklahoma City OK 73105 Address: Rt 1 Box 87 Faxon OK 73540 Mailing: 10506 SW Tinney Rd Faxon OK 73540 Office Phone: 405-557-7307, 580-351-7909, 580-536-0518. E-mail: donarmes@okhouse.gov.

ARMES, JAMES K., III, state legislator; BS in Botany & Horticulture, McNeese State U., 1974. Landscape contractor; mem. Dist. 30 La. House of Reps., 2008—, mem. edn. com., transp., hwys. and pub. works com., spl. com. on mil. and vets. affairs. Democrat. Office: State Capitol PO Box 44486 Baton Rouge LA 70804 Mailing: 2255 University Pkwy Leesville LA 71446 Office Phone: 225-342-6945, 337-238-7004. Office Fax: 337-238-7007. Business E-Mail: armesj@legis.state.la.us.

ARMISTEAD, WILLIAM COLE, JR., political organization administrator; b. Campbell, Ala., May 29, 1944; s. William C. and Emma Belle (Overstreet) A.; m. Emily Golson, Apr. 6, 1968; children: Allyson Michelle, William C. III. BS, Samford U., 1966. Dist. mgr. Saunders Leasing System Inc., Birmingham, Ala., 1967-73, v.p., regional mgr., 1973-80, sr. v.p., 1980-83; v.p., gen. mgr. McDonnell Douglas, Phila., 1983-86; v.p., sales & mktg. Fontaine Internat., Birmingham, 1986-88; spl. asst. to the gov. State of Ala., Montgomery, 1988-92; v.p. mktg. Hanna Steel Corp., Montgomery, Ala., 1993-95; mem. Dist. 14 Ala. State Senate, 1994—2002; v.p. bus. devel. SBS Corp/Netzee, Inc., 1996-2001; v.p. Fidelity Nat. Info. Services, Inc., 2000—08, product cons., 2008—; exec. v.p. Marketing Solutions, Inc., 2001; chmn. Ala. Rep. Party, Birmingham, 2011—. Bd. dirs. Kings Ranch, Birmingham, Children's Trust Fund, 1996-2000, Dept. Youth Svcs., 1998; former vice chmn. Ala. Rep. Party Districts 3, 6 and 7. Republican. Avocation: family. Office: Alabama Republican Party PO Box 55628 Birmingham AL 35255*

ARMITAGE, RICHARD LEE, consulting firm executive, former federal agency administrator; b. Boston, Apr. 26, 1945; s. Leo Holmes and Ruth H. Armitage; m. Laura Alice Samford, Apr. 15, 1968; children: Beth, Lee, Jenny, Paul. BS, U.S. Naval Acad. Naval ops. coordinator Def. Attache Office, Saigon, Vietnam, 1973-75; cons. US Dept. Def., Washington, 1975-76, Iran, 1975-76; ptnr. Agt.-Export, Bangkok, 1976-78, Washington, 1976-78; adminstrv. asst. to Senator Robert Dole US Senate, Washington, 1978-79; self-employed cons. Fairfax, Va., 1979-80; fgn. policy advisor Reagan for Pres. campaign, Washington, 1980; trans. advisor The White House, Washington, 1980-81; asst. sec. for East Asia US Dept. Def., Washington, 1981-83, asst. sec. for internat. security affairs, 1983—89; presdl. spl. negotiator for Phillippines mil. bases The White House, Washington, 1989—92; US amb. to the Newly Independent States of the former

Soviet Union US Dept. State, 1992—93; pres. Armitage Associates, 1993—2001; dep. sec. US Dept. State, Washington, 2001—05; pres. Armitage International L.C., Arlington, Va., 2005—. Mem. strategy group Aspen Inst.; bd. dirs. ManTech Internat., 2005—, ConocoPhillips, 2006—. Served to lt. USN, 1967-73, Vietnam. Recipient Disting. Pub. Svc. award (4), US Dept. Def., Disting. Honor award, US Dept State. Mem. Assn. Asian Studies Republican. Roman Catholic. Office: Armitage Internat LC 2300 Clarendon Blvd Ste 601 Arlington VA 22201

ARMSTRONG, ALAN S., energy executive; BCE, Univ. Okla., 1985. Engring. positions Williams Companies, Tulsa, Okla., 1986—95, dir. comml. ops., Gulf Coast, 1995—97, v.p. retail energy services, 1997—98, v.p. comml. develop., 1998—99, v.p. gathering & processing, 1999—2002, sr. v.p., pres. midstream, 2002—10, pres., CEO, 2011—. Bd. dir. Williams Companies, 2011—; past pres. Gas Processors Assn.; bd. dir. Nat. Gas Supply Assn., Am. Petroleum Inst., Am. Exploration & Production Coun.; mem. exec. com. Nat. Gas Alliance; mem. US & Okla. Bus. Roundtable. Chmn. bd. vis. Univ. Okla. Coll. Engring.; chmn. Jr. Achievement of Okla.; bd. mem. Tulsa Metro Chamber, Tulsa' s Future II Oversight Com., Williams Found. Office: Williams Companies 1 Williams Ctr Tulsa OK 74172 Office Phone: 918-573-2000.

ARMSTRONG, CATHAL, chef; b. Dublin, 1970; m. Cathal Armstrong; children: Eve, Eamonn. Owner, ptnr. Baytree, Dublin; chef New Heights, Washington, Cities, Washington; sous chef Garbiel Restaurant, Washington, 1994, Vidalia Restaurant, Washington, 1995; head chef Bistro Bis, Washington, 1998; co-owner, chef Restaurant Eve, Alexandria, Va., Eamonn's A Dublin Chipper, Alexandria, Va., 2006—, PX, Alexandria, Va., 2006—. Mem. Share Our Strength Leadership Coun., Am. Farmland Trust. Named one of America's Best New Chefs, Food and Wine mag., 2006, Washington DC's Rising Stars, StarChefs.com, 2006. Office: Restaurant Eve 100 S Pitt St Alexandria VA 22309 Office Phone: 703-706-0450.

ARMSTRONG, DANIEL WAYNE, chemist, educator; b. Ft. Wayne, Ind., Nov. 2, 1949; s. Robert Eugene and Nila Louise (Koeneman) A.; m. Linda Marilyn Todd, June 11, 1972; children: Lincoln Thomas, Ross Alexander, Colleen Victoria. BS, Washington and Lee U., 1972; MS in Chem. Oceanography, Tex. A&M U., 1974, PhD in Chemistry, 1977. Prof. Bowdoin Coll., Brunswick, Maine, 1978-79, Georgetown U., Washington, 1980-83, Tex. Tech. U., Lubbock, 1983-87; Curators' disting. prof., head ctr. environ. sci. and tech.; head dept. analytical chemistry U. Mo., Rolla, 1987-2000; Caldwell prof. chemistry Iowa State U., 2000—06; Robert A. Welch prof. chemistry and biochemistry U. Tex., Arlington, Tex., 2006—; pres., CEO AZYP, LLC, Arlington, 2010—; P.W. West lectr. Louisiana State U., 2014. Bd dirs. Advanced Separations Techs., Whippany, NJ; Moreton lectr. Millsaps Coll., 2001, R.A. Welch lectr., 2002, Dow lectr., 2003; lectr. Columbia U., 2003, pres. & CEO, AZYP LLC, 2010 Host Univ. Forum Radio Show, Washington, 1981-83; writer, host weekly radio show We're Sci. Nat. Pub. Radio, 1993—; author film, radio shows; contbr. articles to profl. jours. Fellow Royal Soc. Chemistry, 2009; Recipient Tchg. Excellence award U. Mo., 1985, 88-89, 92, 94, Faculty Excellence award U. Mo., 1988-89, Martin medal, 1991, EAS Chromatography award, 1990, Isco award, 1992, Presdl. award, 1993, Perkin Elmer award, 1994, R&D 100 award R&D Mag., 1995, Benedetti-Pichler award Am. Microchem. Soc. 1996, ACS Helen M. Free award, 1998, CLDG Merit award, 2001, Weber medal, 2001, Kenneth A. Spencer award for agr. and food chemistry, 2002, Chirality medal, 2003, Dal Nogre award for separation sci., 2005. Slovak Med. Soc. medal. 2007, Chromatography award, Am. Chem. Soc., 1999, Seperation Sci. & Tech. award, 2014, M.J.E. Golay award, 2014; named Disting. Scholar Hope Coll., 1999, Disting. Record Rsch. Creative Activity award, U. Tex., 2012; grantee Rsch. Corp., 1979, Petroleum Rsch. Fund, 1979, 91, NSF, 1981; Rsch. grantee Whatman Corp., 1981, Dept. Energy, 1984, 87, 91, 94, Dow Chem., 1985-90, NIH, 1986, 91, 95, 2000, 03, 05, 10, 12, EPA, 1995, Dept. Agric, 2012, Shell Co., 1989-92, Disting. Record Rsch. Creative Activity award, U. Tex. Arlington, 2012. Fellow Am. Assn. Pharm. Scientists, Am. Chem. Soc., Royal Soc. Chemistry; mem. Am. Chem. Soc. (49th Midwest award for chemistry 1993, award in chromatography 1999), Slovak Pharm. Soc. (hon., Vladimir J. Zuffu medal 2004, ACS award, 2014, MJE Golay award, 2014), Sigma Xi, Phi Lambda Upsilon. Achievements include patents in field. Office: Univ Tex Dept Chemistry & Biochemistry Arlington TX 76019 Business E-Mail: sec4dwa@uta.edu.

ARMSTRONG, DAVID G., journalist; m. Noëlle McAfee; children: Guthrie, Eliza. BA in English, UCLA, 1986; MA in Journalism, U. Tex., 1989, PhD in Am. Studies, 2000. Editorial asst., reporter KPFK Radio, LA, 1981-82; editorial intern LA Weekly, 1983-84; reporter, ops. mgr. Beverly Hills Courier, Calif., 1986; reporter KPFK Radio, LA, 1988; editor Random Lengths News, San Pedro, Calif., 1990-91, Texas Observer, Austin, 1991; freelance journalist, 1992; asst. instr. dept. journalism U. Tex., Austin, 1992-93, tchg. asst. Am. Studies program, 1993-95, asst. instr. Am. Studies program, 1996-97; bureau chief Natl. Security News Service, 2001—08; asst. prof. Am. U., Washington, 2008—10; journalist in residence, sr. lectr. Emory U., Atlanta, 2010—. Lectr. in field; mem. bd. operating trustees Tex. Student Publs., 1994. Mem. editl. bd. Pub. Media Monitor, 1994; co-author (with Joseph Trento) America and the Islamic Bomb: The Deadly Compromise, 2007; contbr. over 50 articles to profl. jours. Judge White House Corrospondents Assoc., 2010, bd. dirs. Liberated Learning, Austin, 1992, Texas Student Pubs., 1994. Recipient Project Censored award, 1990, 91, 2003, Martin Emmet Walter fellowship U. Tex., 1987, 88, 89, Marjorie Kovler fellowship John F. Kennedy Libr. Found., 1993, Livingston fellowship U. Tex., 1997-98; Kennedy Rsch. grantee, 1994, LBJ Found. Moody grantee, 1994, 96; Pat and Jack Maguire scholar U. Tex. Ex-Students' Assn., 1995-96, Edgar A. Poe award, 2010. Mem.: Assn. Edn. Journalism and Mass Communication, Soc. Profl. Journalists, Investigative Reporters and Editors, Atlanta Press Club. Office: Emory University Journalism Program S106 Callaway Ctr 537 Kilgo Cir Atlanta GA 30322

ARMSTRONG, DONALD, biochemistry, pathophysiology educator; b. Hamilton, Ont., Can., July 20, 1933; came to U.S., 1933; s. Alfred George and Dorothy Emma (Burden) A.; m. Christine Marie Medeiros, June 13, 1954; children: Donald, David, Dennis, Sandra, Kenneth, Elizabeth. BS, San Diego State U., 1957; MS, U. Colo., 1969; EdD, Tulsa U., 1974; PhD, Oslo U., Norway, 1980; DSc, Charles U. Med. Sch., Prague, Czech Republic, 1990. Instr. San Diego State U., 1960-62; chief rsch. assoc. U. Oreg., Portland, 1963-70; instr. U. Colo. Med. Ctr., Denver, 1967-70, Tulsa C.C., 1970-74; chief clin. chemist Hillcrest Med. Ctr., Tulsa, 1970-74; asst. prof. U. Colo., Denver, 1974-81; assoc. prof. U. Fla. Med. Ctr., Gainesville, 1981-86; prof., chmn. Kuwait U., 1986-90, SUNY, Buffalo, 1990-95, prof., 1995—; rsch. prof. U. Fla. Vet. Med. Coll., 2000-2001, prof. emeritus, 2001—. Mem. sci. adv. bd. Nat. Inst. on Aging, Bethesda, Md., 1985—86, Internat. Assn. for Exptl. and Clin. Ocular Pharmacology and Pharm., 1997—, ZeptoMetrix Corp., 1999—, Oxford Biomed. Internat., 2008—, Wellness Inst., 2008—; spl. fgn. vis. prof. Japanese Ministry Higher Edn., 1996, 2000; vis. prof. Showa U. Sch. Medicine, Japan, 1996—; adj. prof. U. Fla. Coll. Vet. Medicine, 1986—2001; pres. and CEO Oxidative Stress Assoc., Inc., 2003—; mng. dir. Acad. Sci. Educators, 2005; cons. in field; eminent scholar Union U., Albany, NY, Albany Coll. Pharmacy, 2006; cons. Pharm. Rsch. Inst., 2005—; courtesy rsch. prof. U. Fla. Coll. Medicine, 2007—. Editor: (books) Ceroid-Lipofuscinosis, 1982, Free Radicals in Molecular Biology Aging, and Disease, 1984, Effects of Age and Environment on Vision, 1991, Free Radicals in Diagnostic Medicine, 1994, Free Radical and Antioxidant Protocols, 1998, Oxidative Stress Biomarkers and Antioxidant Protocols, 2002, Ultrastructure and Molecular Biology Protocols for Oxidants and Antioxidants, 2002, Free Radicals in Biosystems, 2007, Advanced Protocols In Oxidative Stress, 2008, 2nd vol., 2010, 3rd edit., 2014, Lipidomics 1 & 2, Methods and Protocls, 2010; author: Oxidative Stress and Nanotechnology, Protocols; reviewer: Jour. Investigative Ophthal. Visual Sci., 1990—, Jour. Biochemica Biophysica Acta, 1994—, Am. Jour. Vet. Med. Assn., 2001, Exp. Eye Rsch., 2001, Jour. Ocular Pharmacological Therapeutics, 2004, editor-in-chief: Jour. Clin. Lab. Sci., 1992—96; editor-in-chief Oxidative Stress in Basic Research and Clinical Practice, 2013—. Chmn. North Fla. Lions Eye Bank, Gainesville, 1983—85; pres. Lions Sight and Hearing Found., 1984—85; trustee Lions Club Internat., Gainesville, 1984—86; chmn. United Way, Gainesville, 1985; pres. Am. Aging Assn., 1984—85; chmn. grad. rsch. edn. com. SUNY Sys. Adminstrn., 1995—98; rsch. prof. Nat. Pigmentosa Found., 1975—78. Rsch. grantee State of Kuwait, 1987-90, Am. Heart Assn., 1992-94,; recipient Rsch. Career Devel. award NIH, 1978-83, Exch. Scientist award NSF/Czechoslovak Acad. of Sci., Prague, 1983, 86, Sr. Scientist award Japan Soc. for Promotion of Sci., 1985, Omicron Sigma award Am. Assn. of Clin. Lab. Scientists, 1994; Norwegian Marshall Fund scholar, 1981, other awards. Fellow Assn. Clin. Scientists; mem. Am. Assn. Clin. Chemists, Assn. for Rsch. in Vision and Ophthalmology, Am. Aging Assn. Avocations: art, hunting, tennis. Personal E-mail: donnchris6@gmail.com.

ARMSTRONG, FRANK, finance company executive; m. Lisa Armstrong; 3 children. B in Math. & Bus., Wake Forest U., 1980; MBA in Fin., Ga. State U., 1986. V.p. NationsBank Corp., 1981—92, Alamo Rent-A-Car, Inc., 1992—98; CFO Terion, Inc., 1998—2001; sr. v.p. JM Family Enterprises, Inc., 2001, exec. v.p., 2001—; v.p., bus. and product devel. World Omni Financial Corp. (subs. of JM Family Enterprises, Inc.), 2001—02, group v.p., 2002—04, sr. v.p., 2004—09, pres., 2009—. Chmn., vehicle fin. divsn., bd. dirs. Am. Fin. Svcs. Assn. Office: JM Family Enterprises Inc 100 Jim Moran Blvd Deerfield Beach FL 33442 Office Phone: 954-429-2000. Office Fax: 954-429-2300. Business E-Mail: frank.armstrong@jmfamily.com.

ARMSTRONG, GREG L., oil industry executive; BS, Southeastern Okla. State U., 1980. CPA. Formerly with Price Waterhouse; corp. sec. Plains Resources, Inc., 1981—88, treas., 1984—87, v.p., CFO, 1984—91, sr. v.p., CFO, 1991—92, exec. v.p., CFO, 1992, pres., COO, 1992, pres., CEO, dir., 1992—2001; chmn., CEO Plains All American Pipeline, LP, Houston, 2001—. Bd. dirs. Petroleum Club of Houston, IPAA Tex. Southeast Regional Bd. of Trustees, Varco Internat., 2004—. Office: Plains All Am Pipeline LP 333 Clay St Ste 1600 Houston TX 77002*

ARMSTRONG, (ARTHUR) JAMES, minister, educator, consultant, writer; b. Marion, Ind., Sept. 17, 1924; s. Arthur J. and Frances (Green) A.; m. Sharon Owen, Apr. 8, 2000; children from previous marriages: Eve Stoughton, Allison Jacob, James, Teresa, John, Rebecca Putens, Leslye Armstrong Hope. AB, Fla. So. Coll., 1948; MDiv, Candler Sch. Theology, Emory U., 1952; DD, Fla. So. U., 1960, DePauw U., 1965; LHD, Ill. Wesleyan U., 1970, Dakota Wesleyan U., 1970, Westmar Coll., 1971, Ind. Ctrl. U., 1982, Emory U., 1982. Ordained to ministry Meth. Ch., 1948. Minister in Fla., 1945-58; sr. minister Broadway Meth. Ch., Indpls., 1958-68; bishop United Meth. Ch., Dakotas area, 1968-80, Ind. area, Indpls., 1980-83; exec. v.p. conflict resolution firm, Washington, 1984-87; vis. prof. preaching and social ministries Iliff Sch. Theology, Denver, 1985-91; sr. min. 1st Congl. Ch., Winter Park, Fla., 1991-99; exec. dir. Ctr. on Dialogue and Devel., Denver, 1984-96. Adj. prof. Rollins Col., 1992—, Fla. Ctr. Theol. Studies, 1999-2007; instr. Christian Theol. Sem., Indpls., 1961-68; del. 4th Gen. Assembly, World Coun. Chs., 1968, 6th Gen. Assembly, 1983; pres. Nat. Coun. Chs., 1982-83; pres. bd. ch. and soc. United Meth. Ch., 1972-76, chmn. com. for peace and self devel. of peoples, 1972-76, pres. Commn. on Religion and Race, 1976-83; exec. v.p. Pagan Internat., 1982-87. Author: Gentlemen, Start Your Engines, 1967, The Journey That Men Make, 1969, The Urgent Now, 1970, Mission: Middle America, 1971, The Pastor and the Public Servant, 1972, United Methodist Primer, 1973, 77, Wilderness Voices, 1974, The Nation Yet To Be, 1975, Telling Truth: The Foolishness of Preaching in a Real World, 1977, From the Underside, 1981, Feet of Clay, on Solid Ground, 2002, Living & Dying With Purpose & Grace, 2010; contbg. author: The Pulpit Speaks on Race, 1966, War Crimes and the American Conscience, 1970, Rethinking Evangelism, 1971, What's a Nice Church Like You Doing in a Place Like This?, 1972, The Miracle of Easter, 1980, Preaching on Peace, 1982, Ethics and the Multi-National Enterprise, 1986, The Best of the Circuit Rider, 1987, Prayerfully Pro-Choice, 1999, Connected Spirits, 2007. Vice-chmn. Hoosiers for Peace, 1968; mem. Ind. State Platform Com. Democratic Party, 1968, Nat. Coalition for a Responsible Congress, 1970. With USNR, 1942. Recipient Disting. Svc. award, Indpls. Jr. C. of C., 1959, Barden Disting. Svc. award, Rollence Coll., 2010. Mem. Fla. Coun. Chs. (pres. 1996-97), Ctrl. Fla. Interfaith Alliance (co-chair 1994-96). Personal E-mail: jarmstrongjsa@aol.com.

ARMSTRONG, JOSEPH E., state legislator; b. Nov. 11, 1956; m. Letonia Armstrong. House rep., Tenn.; state rep. Dist. 15 Tenn., 1989—; majority caucus vice chmn.; dir. Tengasco Oil & Gas Co. Mem.: NAACP, Nat. Ins. Assn., Eastside YMCA, Eastside Optimist Club, U. Tenn. Black Alumni Assn. Democrat. Methodist. Office: 4708 Hilldale Dr Knoxville TN 37914-5069 also: 25 Legislative Plz Nashville TN 37243-0115 Office Phone: 615-741-0768, 865-357-1524. Office Fax: 615-253-0316. Business E-Mail: rep.joe.armstrong@capitol.tn.gov.

ARMSTRONG, RANDY LEE, communications educator; b. Sweetwater, Tex., June 19, 1948; s. Alvin Lee and Essie Lee Armstrong; m. Jody Anne Armstrong, June 12, 1987; 1 child, Eric Lee. BA, Tex. Tech. U., Lubbock, Tex., 1971, MA, 1975, EdD, 1997. Prof. Hardin-Simmons U., Abilene, Tex., 1976—, prof. comm., assoc. dean Cynthia Ann Parker Coll. Liberal Arts, 2004—. Co-dir. Four-O Pub., 1988—. Mem.: Grace Mus. Abilene (trustee), Am. Journalism Historians Assn., Pub. Rels. Soc. Am. (bd. mem.), Book Club Tex. Presbyterian. Avocations: history, coin collecting/numismatics, stamp collecting/philately, films, antiques. Office: Hardin-Simmons Univ 2200 Hickory St Box 16022 HSU Sta Abilene TX 79698 Office Phone: 325-670-1436. Business E-Mail: rarmstrg@hsutx.edu.

ARMSTRONG, TONEY, police director; BA in Psychology, magna cum laude, Christian Brothers U., Memphis. Police officer west precinct Memphis Police Dept., 1989—91, undercover operative, investigator organized crime unit, 1991—97, sgt. robbery divsn., leader organized crime unit, 1997—2000, lt., supr. homicide bur., 2000—08, maj., investigative bur. comdr. homicide, felony assault unit, missing persons and crime stoppers, 2008—10, dep. dir., 2010—11, dir., 2011—. Specialist fourth class US Army, 1983—86. Office: Memphis Police Dept Command Staff 201 Poplar Ave 12th Fl Memphis TN 38103

ARN, PAMELA HAWKS, clinical geneticist, educator; MD, U. Va., 1983. Lic. Fla., 1989, diplomate Am. Bd. Pediatrics, 1987, cert. Am. Bd. Clin. Genetics-Med. Genetics, 1990, Am. Bd. Clin. Biochemical Genetics-Med. Genetics, 1990, Am. Bd. Clin. Molecular Genetics-Med. Genetics, 1990. Intern Children's Hosp., Pitts., 1984, resident pediatric surgery, 1983—86; fellow clin. genetics Johns Hopkins Hosp., 1986—89; asst. prof. pediat. Univ. Fla.; hosp. affiliation includes Nemours Children's Clinic, Wolfson Children's Hosp.; physician Baptist Med. Ctr. Office: Baptist Medical Center Division of Genetics 807 Children's Way Jacksonville FL 32207 Office Phone: 904-697-3586. Office Fax: 904-697-3565.

ARNETT, EDWARD MCCOLLIN, chemistry educator, researcher; b. Phila., Sept. 25, 1922; s. John Hancock and Katherine Williams (McCollin) A.; m. Sylvia Gettmann, Dec. 10, 1970; children: Eric, Brian; stepchildren: Elden, Byron, Colin Gatwood. BS, U. Pa., 1943, MS, 1946, PhD, 1949. Rsch. dir. Max Levy & Co., Phila., 1949-53; asst. prof. Western Md. Coll., Westminster, 1953-54, 1954-55; assoc. prof. chemistry U. Pitts., 1957-61, assoc. prof., 1961-64, prof., 1964-80; R.J. Reynolds prof. Duke U., Durham, NC, 1980-92, prof. emeritus, 1992—. Vis. lectr. U. Ill., 1963; vis. prof. U. Kent, Canterbury, Eng., 1970; dir. Pitts. Chem. Info. Ctr., 1967-70; mem. adv. bd. Petroleum Rsch. Fund, 1968-71; mem. com. on chem. info. NRC, 1969-71. Contbr. 200 articles to sci. jours. DuPont fellow, 1948-49, rsch. fellow Harvard U., Cambridge, Mass., 1955-57, Guggenheim fellow, 1968-69, Mellon Inst. adj. sr. fellow, 1964-80, Inst. Hydrocarbon Chemistry sr. fellow, 1980. Fellow AAAS; mem. Am. Chem. Soc. (James Flack Norris award 1977, Pitts. award Pitts. chpt. 1976, Petroleum Chemistry award 1985), NAS, The Chem. Soc., Sigma Xi, Phi Lambda Upsilon. Personal E-mail: edward.arnett@duke.edu.

ARNING, BILL, museum director; Freelance writer, independent curator; mem. The Student Teachers; dir., chief curator White Columns Alternative Art Space, NY, 1985—96; curator List Visual Art Center, MIT, 2000—09; dir. Contemporary Arts Museum Houston, 2009—. Juror Southern Open, 2010; organized several exhibitions; author of significant interpretive essays for catalogs; published essays in Time Out New York, Aperture, Modern Painters, Honcho, The Village Voice, Art In America, Trans, Out, Frieze and Parkett. Office: Contemporary Arts Museum Houston 5216 Montrose Boulevard Houston TX 77006 Office Phone: 713-284-8253. Office Fax: 713-284-8275.*

ARNOLD, ALBERT JAMES, retired foreign language educator, consultant; b. Ballston Spa, NY, Nov. 8, 1939; s. Albert J. and Florence Emily (Cleveland) A.; m. Josephine Diane Valenza, June 8, 1963; 1 child, Elizabeth. AB, Hamilton Coll., 1961; MA, U Wis. Madison, 1964, PhD, 1968; cert French lang., lit., U. Paris, 1960. Instr. romance langs. Hamilton Coll., Clinton, NY, 1961-62; from asst. to prof. French U. Va., 1966—2008, chair com. comparative lit., 1974-79, 1986-89, prof. emeritus, 2008—, co-chair comparative programs in literature and culture, 1989-95; dir. New World Studies, 1991-92, Caribbean Lit. Archive, 2003—07, Collective Lits. au Sud, Agence U. Francophonie, 2008—; mem. editl. team manuscrits Francophones ITEM, Paris, 2009—13. Vis. exch. prof. U. de Paris III, 1981; external examiner Queensland U., Australia, 1986, U. West Indies, 1991-2013, NYU, 1991, Yale U., 1994, U. West Australia, 2003; external assessor French dept. U. West Indies, 1995, 2002-03; coord. com. on comp. lit. hist. Internat. Comp. Lit. Assoc., 1992-2001; internat. adv. bd. New West Indian Guide, 1992—2012; adv. bd. Review Lit. and Arts Americas, 2003—09; vis. fellow Trinity Coll., Cambridge U., 2007; spkr., cons. in field. Author: Paul Valéry, 1970, Sartre, 1973, Césaire, 1981, 90, 2011-14, Camus, 1984; gen. editor Caraf Books, 1987-93; editor New World Studies, 1992-2005, Plantation Soc. in the Americas, 1999-2007, Critique, 2006; contbr. articles to profl. jours. Fellow ACLS, 1975-76, NEH, 1989-90, Fulbright Found., 1995-96, Queensland U., Australia, 1995, Rock Found. Bellagio Conf. Ctr., 2004, DAAD, 2006; grantee NEH, 1977, 88, 89-90, 2004, U. Va., 1969, 70, 72, 75-76, 78, 80, 81-82, 86, 95-96, 2001-02, Camargo Found., 1981-82, 86, 2001, Va. Found. Humanities, 1992, 94, 2004. Mem. Phi Beta Kappa. Democrat. Avocations: gardening, photography, birding. Home: 310 E Beverley St Staunton VA 24401-4327 Personal E-mail: arnoldajames@yahoo.com.

ARNOLD, BARRY RAYNOR, philosophy educator, medical ethicist, counselor; b. Mooresville, NC, Sept. 29, 1951; s. Adrian Leicester and Cleo Agnes (Fisher) A.; m. Margaret Elizabeth Morelock, Aug. 15, 1984. AB cum laude, Davidson Coll., 1973; MDiv magna cum laude, Emory U., 1976, PhD, 1986. Ordained to ministry Presbyn. Ch., ret. 2012; trappist Lay Cistercians of Gethsemani Abbey, cert. Christian clin. counselor Am. Counseling Assn.; lic. mental health counselor, Ind. Min. various parishes, Ga., Fla., 1976—; instr. religion, assoc. chaplain The Lovett Sch., 1980-82; prof. Andrew Coll., Cuthbert, Ga., 1983-84; from asst. prof. to prof. emeritus U. West Fla., Pensacola, 1986—2007, prof. emeritus, 2007—; pvt. practice clin. counseling, Pace, Fla., 1996—2012; acting chmn. dept. philosophy/religion U. West Fla., Pensacola, 1997—, chmn. dept. interdisciplinary humanities, philosophy, relig., 2000—, exec. dir., creator, founder Univ. Office for Applied Ethics, 2000—, joint prof. biology and philosophy divsn. life and health scis., 2003—; prof. Bioethics and Philosophy, dir. Ctr. for Health Care Ethics U. West Fla./Sacred Heart Hosp., Pensacola, 2003—; supr. interns in palliative care and bio-ethics Sacred Heart Hosp., 2004—; found. dir. Ctr. for Health Care Ethics U. West Fla./Sacred Heart Hosp., 2003—; prof. emeritus biology, allied health U. West Fla., Pensacola, 2007—; creator, founder UWF Ctr. Health Care Ethics. Counselor Pace Counseling Ctr., 1996-97; bd. dirs. Unif Ctr. Aging; reviewer med. edn. Coun. Pensacola Fla., 2006—; spkr. in field. Author: The Pursuit of Virtue, 1989; editor, co-author: Essays in American Ethics, 1992; gen. editor (11 vols.) The Reshaping of Psychoanalysis, 1992-2002; assoc. editor Explorations: Jour. Adventurous Thought, 1999—; featured as med. ethicist on CBS Radio, 2006; contbr. articles to profl. jours. Bd. dirs. Sacred Heart Hosp., Pensacola, Bapt. Hosp., West Fla. Hosp.; mem. instl. rev. bd. U. West Fla., 2006—; conf. spkr. Covenant Hospice, 2003—06; bioethicist, bd. dirs. Sacred Heart Hosp., 2003—, com. on palliative care, com. on blood products, com. on intravenous immunoglobulon, 2006—, keynote spkr. geriatric ethics, ann. symposium on best clin. practice, 2009; pres., bd. dirs. Assn. for Retarded Citizens, Albany, Ga., 1978—79; bioethicist, bd. dirs. West Fla. Regional Med. Ctr., Pensacola, 1990—, Bapt. Hosp., 2003—; adv. bd. mem. McGraw Hill Publs. Bioethics, 2010. Recipient Disting. Tchg. award UWF and Fla. State Legislature, 1988, 90, 95, 6 awards UWF, 1986-2007; fellow Rice U., 1973-75, Emory U., 1975-76, 79-82, U. Glasgow, 1976, Nautilus award, 2007, Nominee Book of Yr., Nat. Assn. Advancement Psychoanalysis. Fellow: Am. Coll. Counselors (cert. Christian clin. counselor, chair examiners for cert.), Am. Assn. Integrative Medicine (chair nat. bd. 2002—03, diplomate, nat. bd. dirs.), Am. Bd. Child Mental Health Providers; mem.: APA, ACA, APA, Fla. Phil. Assn., Am. Assn. Hospice & Palliative Medicine (acad. adv. bd. bioethics), Assn. for Cognitive Behavioral Therapists (cert. cognitive forensic therapist, cert. anxiety disorders specialist), So. Soc. Philosophy and Psychology, Am. Acad. Religion, Internat. Thomas Merton Soc., Rotary (sgt.-at-arms 1982—83), Phi Beta Kappa, AfD (hon.), Alpha Epsilon Delta, Phi Kappa Phi (sec. 1988). Democrat. Avocations: birdwatching, photography. Home: 5820 Kirkland Dr Milton FL 32570-8251 Office: Univ West Fla 11000 University Pkwy Pensacola FL 32514-5750 Home Phone: 850-626-7556. Business E-Mail: barnold@uwf.edu.

ARNOLD, CECIL BENJAMIN, former small business owner; b. Bryantsville, Ky., Jan. 23, 1927; s. Walter Tribble and Ella Mae (Hagan) A.; m. Billie Jean Watkins, July 25, 1947; children: Mary Adrianne Davis, Cecil Benjamin Jr. Student, Heidelburg U., Germany, 1945. Farmer, Lancaster, Ky., 1947-50; grocery store owner, 1950-54; ins. agt. Commonwealth Life Ins., Lancaster, Ky., 1954-57; pres. Cecil Arnold Real Estate, Lancaster, Ky., 1957—; agt. Arnold & Boone Ins., Lancaster, Ky., 1957-81; owner Arnold's Furniture, Inc., Lancaster, Ky., 1971-90; ret., 1992. Chmn. Lancaster-Garrard Indsl. Authority, 1993—, ret. 2000. Author (with Arthur): Lancaster, Kentucky Cemetery, 1995; author: (with Timothy Logan) Garrard County, Kentucky, Revelation War Soldier, Indian Fighter and Spy; author: Descendants that remained and Went elsewhere, 2010. Pres. Lancaster-Garrard Indsl. Devel., 1984-90; mem. Exec. Com. Dem. Orgn., Lancaster, 1965-75; bd. dirs. Ky. Ins. Guaranty Bd., 1972-75; mem. Ky. legis. rsch. com. for revision of Commonwealth of Ky. Ins. Law, 1969-70; dir. Garrard County Habitat for Humanity, Lancaster, Ky., 1995-99. Served with US Army, 1945-46, ETO. Mem. Nat. Assn. Realtors, Ky. Assn. Realtors, Ky. Assn. Profl. Ins. Agts. (pres. 1968-69, bd. dirs. 1963-72, Mr. Chmn. award 1970, Mr. Profl. Agt. 1972, Profl. Agt. of Yr. 1975-76), Nat. Assn. Profl. Ins. Agts. (bd. dirs. 1972-80, v.p. 1979-80, Profl. Agt. of Yr. 1976-77), Dix River Bd. Realtors (pres. 1972), Nat. and Ky. Assn. Auctioneers, Lancaster-Garrard C. of C. (pres. 1966-68), Ky. Ins. Dept. (Ins. Svc. award 1969, 73; Special Recognition award 1975), Rotary (pres. 1966-68). Democrat. Methodist. Avocations: basketball, golf, genealogy. Home: 1015 Danville Rd Lancaster KY 40444-9335 Home Phone: 859-792-3557. Personal E-mail: cbarnold@windstream.net.

ARNOLD, DANIEL CALMES, retired finance company executive, lawyer; b. Houston, Mar. 14, 1930; m. Beverly Bintliff; children: Mrs. Randy Helms, Mrs. Tom Martin, Steven Arnold. BBA, U. Tex., Austin, 1951, LLB, 1953. Ptnr. Vinson & Elkins, Houston, 1953—83; pres., dir. First City Bancorp. Tex., Inc., 1983—85, chmn., pres., dir., 1985—88; chmn., CEO Farm & Home Fin. Corp., 1989—91, dir., 1991—94; pvt. practice. Bd. dirs. Belco Oil & Gas Corp., Pky. Properties, Inc., US Physical Therapy, Baylor Coll. Medicine, 1969—, chmn. bd. trustees, 1996. Bd. dirs. Harris County Hosp. Dist., 1963—69, chmn., 1963—69; bd. dirs. Tex. Med. Ctr., Inc., 1963—89, Houston-Harris County chpt. ARC, chmn., 1970—72; chmn. bd. dirs. Met. Transit Authority Harris County, Tex., 1980—84; bd. dirs. Tex. Med. Ctr., 1996—. Mem.: ABA, Houston Bar Assn., Tex. Bar Assn. Methodist. Office: Ste 720 1001 Fannin St Houston TX 77002-6707

ARNOLD, GARY HOWARD, film critic; b. Princeton, Ind., Aug. 22, 1942; s. Charles Howard and Ferris (Smith) A.; m. Sue Datz, Dec. 29, 1967; children— Pauline, Jane, Esther. Student, NYU, 1959-60, U. Calif., Berkeley, 1960-63. Film critic Diplomat mag., 1966; film critic, reporter Ind. Film Jour., 1968-69; film critic Washington Post, 1969-84; co-host weekly TV commentary show The Moviegoing Family, 1985-90; arts critic The Connection, Reston, Va., 1987-89; movie critic The Washington Times, Washington, 1989—2005, freelance movie columnist, 2006—09. Home: 5133 1st St N Arlington VA 22203-1207 Personal E-mail: garyarnold@verizon.net.

ARNOLD, J(AMES) BARTO, III, marine archaeologist; b. San Antonio, Jan. 9, 1950; s. J. Barto Jr. and Wilnora (Barton) Arnold; children: Kathryn, Julia, Jessica. BA cum laude, U. Tex., 1971, MA, 1973. Rsch. asst. Tex. Archeol. Rsch. Lab. U. Tex., Austin, 1970-72; asst. state marine archaeologist Tex. Antiquities Com., Austin, 1972-75; state marine archaeologist Tex. Hist. Com., Austin, 1975-97; dir. Tex. ops. Inst. of Nautical Archaeology, Tex. A&M U., College Station, 1997—. Cons. NOAA, 1977-91, Nat. Trust Hist. Preservation, Washington, 1979-90, Congl. Office Tech. Assessment, Washington, 1986; mem. Md. Gov.'s Adv. Com. on Marine Archaeology, Annapolis, 1987-90; mem. history area com. nat. park sys. adv. bd. U.S. Dept. Interior, 1994-95; dir. La Salle Shipwreck Project, 1995-96, Confederate Blockade-Runner Denbigh Shipwreck Project, 1997—. Co-author: Nautical Archaeology of Padre Island, 1978, Documentary Sources for the Wreck of the New Spain Fleet of 1554, 1979 (Presidio La Bahaia 1979), others; Plenum series editor Underwater Archaeology, 1995—; contbr. articles to profl. jours. Recipient Achievement award for Hist. Preservation Dept. Interior, 1980. Mem. Soc. Profl. Archaeologists (cert.; sec.-treas. 1987-89, Spl. Achievement award 1990), Soc. Hist. Archaeology (pres. 1993), Tex. Archeol. Soc., Archaeol. Inst. Am., Explorers Club, Phi Beta Kappa. Methodist. Avocations: stamp collecting/philately, science fiction. Office: Tex A&M U Inst Nautical Archaeology PO Drawer HG College Station TX 77841-5137 E-mail: barnold@tamu.edu.

ARNOLD, JEFFERY J., state legislator; Legis. lobbyist, City of New Orleans, 1999—2002; exec. asst. New Orleans Mayor Mar Morial, 1995—2002; mem. Dist. 102 La. House of Reps., 2003—, chair commerce com., mem. house exec. com., spl. com. on mil. and vets. affairs. Democrat. Office: PO Box 94062 Baton Rouge LA 70804 Home: 3520 General Degaulle Dr Ste 3071 New Orleans LA 70114-6761 Office Phone: 504-393-5801. Office Fax: 504-393-5809.

ARNOLD, JESSE CHARLES, retired statistician; b. Bowie, Tex., Sept. 28, 1937; s. Jesse Connally and Lillie Christine Arnold; m. Peggy Lou Peveto; children: Christa Louise, Jesse Charles Arnold, Jr. BS, Southeastern State U., 1960; MS, Fla. State U., 1963, PhD, 1967. Statistician Communicable Disease Ctr., Atlanta, 1961—63; prof. stats. Va. Tech U., Blacksburg, Va., 1968—2002, head Dept. Stats., 1973—82, ret., 2002. Contbr. articles to profl. jours. Sr. asst. health svc. officer USPHS, 1961—63. Fellow, NSF, 1963—67. Fellow: Internat. Statis. Inst., Am. Statis. Assn. (chmn. stat. edn. sect. 1975—76); mem.: Biometric Soc. (pres. 1976—77). Methodist. Achievements include research in sampling, quality control, nutrition. Avocations: tennis, writing. Home: 2011 Northside Drive Blacksburg VA 24060 Office: Virginia Tech University-Retired Hutcheson Hall Blacksburg VA 24061 Business E-Mail: jca@vt.edu.

ARNOLD, JOHN A., state legislator; b. Aug. 23, 1944; Former city councilman; former mayor; physician Chiropractic Med.; mem. Dist. 7 Ky. House of Reps., 1995—; mem. Agr. & Natural Resources Com., Health & Welfare Com., Transp. Com., Labor & Industry Com., Union County Econ. Devel. Bd.; farmer & businessman. Recipient Outstanding Citizen award, Jaycees; named Chiropractor of Yr., 1988. Fellow: Internat. Coll. Chiropractic; mem.: Am. Chiropractic Assn., Ky. Assn. Chiropractors, Kiwanis (past pres.), Sturgis Air Bd. Democrat. Baptist. Mailing: 1301 N Lee PO Box 124 Sturgis KY 42459 Office: Capitol Annex Rm 329E Frankfort KY 40601 Office Phone: 270-333-4641, 502-564-8100 709.

ARNOLD, JOHN DOUGLAS, hedge fund manager; b. 1974; m. Laura Arnold. BS in Economics, Vanderbilt U., Nashville, 1996. Stock trader Enron Corp., 1996—2001; founder, prin., mng. dir. Centaurus Energy, LP (formerly Centaurus Advisors, LLC), Houston, 2002—. Named one of The 40 Under 40, Fortune mag., 2009, 2010, 2011, The 400 Richest Americans, Forbes mag., 2008—, Top 200 Collectors, ARTnews Mag., 2010—. Office: Centaurus Energy LP 3050 Post Oak Blvd Ste 850 Houston TX 77056

ARNOLD, MORRIS SHEPPARD, federal judge; b. Texarkana, Tex., Oct. 8, 1941; BSEE, U. Ark., 1965, LLB, 1968; LLM, Harvard U., 1969, SJD, 1971; MA (hon.), U. Pa., 1977, JD (hon.), 1986; LLD (hon.), U. Ark., Little Rock, 1998, U. Ark., 2009, U. Conn., 2004. Tchg. fellow law Harvard U., 1969-70; from asst. prof. to prof. Ind. U. Law Sch., 1971-76, prof., 1976-77, dean, 1985; prof. law, hist. U. Pa., 1977-81; Ben J. Altheimer disting. prof. law U. Ark., Little Rock, 1981-84; judge US Dist. Ct. (we. dist.) Ark., Ft. Smith, 1985-92, US Ct. Appeals (8th cir.), Little Rock, 1992—2006, sr. judge, 2006—. Vis. fellow commoner Trinity Coll., Cambridge U., 1978; v.p., dir. office of the pres. U. Pa., 1980—81; vis. prof. Stanford U. Law Sch., Calif., 1985. Author: Old Tenures and Natura Brevium, 1974, Yearbook 2 Richard II, 1378-79, 1975, On the Laws and Customs of England, 1980, Unequal Laws Unto a Savage Race, 1985, Select Cases of Trespass from the King's Courts, 1307-1399, 2 vols., 1985, 1988, Arkansas Colonials, 1986, Colonial Arkansas 1686-1804: A Social and Cultural History, 1991, The Rumble of a Distant Drum: Quapaws and Old World Newcomers, 1673-1804, 2000, Arkansas: A Narrative History, 2002. Chmn., Rep. party State of Ark., 1983; gen. counsel, Rep. party Ark., 1982; bd. dirs. Nature Conservancy of Ark., 1982—87, Ark. Arts Ctr., 1981—84. Decorated chevalier Ordre Palmes Acad., France; recipient Porter Lit. prize, 2001, Worthen Lit. prize, 2001, Ragsdale prize, 2002; Frank Knox fellow, Harvard U./U. London, 1970—71, Mus. Sci. Natural Hist. fellow, 1986. Fellow: Am. Soc. Legal Hist. (hon.; pres. 1981—85); mem.: Am. Antiquarian Soc., Grolier Club, Country Club of Little Rock, Union League Club of Phila., Athenaeum Club London. Office: US Ct Appeals PO Box 2060 Little Rock AR 72203

ARNOLD, WILLIAM MCCAULEY, lawyer; b. Waco, Tex., May 3, 1947; s. Watson Caulfield and Mary Rebecca Arnold; m. Karen Axtell, May 17, 1980. BA, Duke U., 1969; JD, U. Tex., 1972. Bar: Tex. 1973, Va. 1975, D.C. 1977, Md. 1983, U.S. Dist. Ct. (ea. dist.) Va. 1975, U.S. Ct. Appeals (4th cir.) 1977, U.S. Ct. Claims 1977, U.S. Supreme Ct. 1978. Spl. atty. U.S. Dept. Justice, Newark, 1973-75; asst. county atty. County of Fairfax, Va., 1975-78; ptnr. Cowles, Rinaldi & Arnold, Ltd., Fairfax, 1978-95, McCandlish & Lillard, Fairfax, 1995—. Instr. No. Va. C.C., Alexandria. Pres. Clifton Betterment Assn., Va., 1979-81; chmn. Clifton Planning Commn., 1980-85, mem. Clifton Town Coun., 1985-2006; bd. dirs. Clifton Gentlemen's Social Club, 1981-84. Mem. Va. State Bar Assn., Fairfax County Bar Assn., Va. Trial Lawyers Assn. Office: McCandlish & Lillard PC 11350 Random Hills Rd Ste 500 Fairfax VA 22030-6044 Office Phone: 703-934-1128. Business E-Mail: marnold@mccandlaw.com.

ARNOLD, WILLIAM TRACY, state legislator; m. Neecy Shook. Attended, Logos Bible Coll. Sr. pastor The Vineyard Ch.; mem. Dist. 3 Miss. House of Reps., Jackson, 2012—. Mem.: NRA, Farm Bur. Republican. Office: Miss House of Reps PO Box 1018 Jackson MS 39215 Business E-Mail: warnold@house.ms.gov.

ARNOTT, HOWARD JOSEPH, biology professor, dean; b. LA, Mar. 9, 1928; s. Andrew Hugh and Evelyn Leonore (Donnelly) A.; m. Wanda Jean Cross, Jan. 28, 1950; children: John Joseph, Catherine Jean Arnott-Thornton, Susan Leonore Arnott Garrett, Virginia Anne Arnott Scott. AB, U. So. Calif., 1952, MS, 1953; PhD, U. Calif., Berkeley, 1958. Asst. prof. biology Northwestern U., Evanston, Ill., 1958-64; assoc. prof. dept. botany U. Tex., Austin, 1965-68, prof., 1968-72, acting chmn. dept., 1970-71; prof., chmn. dept. biology U. So. Fla., Tampa, 1972-74; dean Coll. Sci. U. Tex., Arlington, 1974-90, prof. biology, 1974-91, Ashbel Smith prof. biology, 1991-96, dir. Ctr. for Electron Microscopy Coll. Sci., 1984—, Jenkins Garrett prof. biology emeritus, dean sci. emeritus, 1996—. Vis. mem. dept. biology Tex. A&M U., 1971-75; cons. Ency. Brit. Films, NASA, Alcon Labs., Frito-Lay; bd. dirs. Ft. Worth Nature Ctr., 1985-91; chmn. 2nd Gordon Conf. Calcium Oxalate, 1989, main spkr. 4th Conf., 1993; vis. prof. Purdue U., 1990-91; Bessey lectr. Iowa State U., 1993; visitor Lab. Tree-Ring Rsch., U. Ariz., Tucson, 2006, 07. Advisory editor: Protoplasma; Contbr. articles, abstracts to sci. jours., chpts. to books. With USN, 1946-48. Recipient award for disting. and continued research U. Tex. at Arlington, 1984; postdoctoral fellow U. Tex., NIH, 1964-65; NSF grantee, 1963-65, NIH grantee, 1989. Mem. Am. Soc. Plant Physiology, Bot. Soc. Am., Mycol. Soc. Am., Microscopy Soc. Am., Tex. Soc. Microscopy (hon., pres. 1988-89), Sigma Xi (bd. dirs. S.W. region 1984-91), Phi Sigma (Spl. award 2005). Office Phone: 817-272-2413. Business E-Mail: arnott@uta.edu.

ARNOWITT, RICHARD LEWIS, retired physics professor; b. NYC, May 3, 1928; s. Leon and Belle (Feinberg) A.; m. Young In Rhee, Apr. 21, 1961; children: Michael Paul, Myron Philip. BS, MS, Rensselaer Poly. Inst., 1948; PhD, Harvard U., 1953. Rsch. assoc. Radiation Lab. U. Calif., Berkeley, 1952-54; mem. Inst. Advanced Study, Princeton, NJ, 1954-56; asst. prof. Syracuse (N.Y.) U., 1956-59, assoc. prof., 1959-62; prof. Northeastern U., Boston, 1962-86, Tex. A&M U., College Station, 1986-88, disting. prof. physics, 1988—2004, disting. prof. emeritus, 2004—, dir. Ctr. Theoretical Physics, 1986-95, head dept. physics, 1987-93; disting. prof. emeritus, 2004—. Contbr. over 200 articles to profl. jours. Fellow Guggenheim Found., 1975-76. Fellow Am. Phys. Soc. (Dannie N. Heineman prize 1994, Burgess chair high energy physics 1997-04). Office: Texas A & M U Dept Physics College Station TX 77843-4242 Home Phone: 979-696-1101; Office Phone: 979-845-7746. Business E-Mail: arnowitt@physics.tamu.edu.

ARON, DOUG S., oil industry executive; B in journalism, Univ. Tex., Austin; MBA, Rice Univ. Lending officer Southwest Bank of Tex. (now Amegy Bank); dir. investor rels. Frontier Oil Corp., Houston, 2001—05, v.p. corp. fin., 2005—08, exec. v.p., CFO, 2009—11, HollyFrontier Corp., Dallas, 2011—. Office: HollyFrontier Corp Ste 1300 2828 N Harwood Dallas TX 75201 Office Phone: 214-871-3555.

ARON, JERRY E., lawyer; b. Lancaster, Pa., Oct. 1, 1951; BS, Drexel U., 1974; JD, Stetson U., 1977. Bar: Fla. 1977. Lawyer Gunster, Yoakley, Valdes-Fauli & Stewart, West Palm Beach, Fla.; pvt. practice West Palm Beach, Fla. Teaching asst. legal rsch. and writing Stetson Coll. Law, 1975-76; chmn. Palm Beach County Realtor/Atty. Joint Com., 1983-84. Editor-in-chief Stetson Law Rev., 1976-77. Mem. ABA (real property, probate and trust law sect., econs. of law practice sect., chmn. standing com. lawyers' title guaranty funds), Am. Coll. Real Estate Attys., Fla. Bar (exec. coun. real property probate and trust law sect. 1980—, exec. com. 1985—, sec. 1985-88, dir. real property divsn. 1988-90, chmn.-elect. 1990-91, chmn. 1991-92, chmn. publs. 1980-85, co-chair action line com. 1984-85, liason with title insurers 1984-85, energy law com., environ. land use sect., pub. utilities law com., Annual Svc. award), Palm Beach County Bar Assn., Blue Key, Phi Delta Phi. Office: Ste 301 2505 Metrocentre Blvd West Palm Beach FL 33407 Office Fax: 561-804-6708. Business E-Mail: jaron@aronlaw.com.

ARONOFF, CRAIG ELLIS, business educator, consultant; b. Atlanta, May 18, 1951; s. Marvin Charles and Patricia (Sabin) Aronoff; m. Jane G. Miller; children: Lara Dorfman, Emily Teck, Alexander Samuel Miller. BS in Journalism, Northwestern U., Evanston, Ill., 1971; MA, U. Pa., Phila., 1974; PhD, U. Tex., Austin, 1975. Asst. prof. mgmt. Ga. State U., Atlanta, 1975-79, assoc. prof., 1979-83; prof. mgmt. Kennesaw State U., Marietta, Ga., 1983—2005, Dinos disting. chair pvt. enterprise, 1983—2005, chmn. dept. mgmt., 1984-86, eminent scholar, 1999—2005, prof. emeritus, 2005—. Founder Cox Family Enterprise Ctr., dir., 1987—2005; chmn. Cobb Transit Adv. Bd., Marietta, 1988—90; exec. dir. Bus. Owner Resources, Marietta, 1989—2005; CEO Family Bus. Comm., Inc., 1989—2002; co-founder, prin., dir., chmn. Family Bus. Cons. Group, Inc., 1994—; bd. dirs. Whitacre Oil Co., Nioxin Rsch. Labs., Ga. Oak Ptnrs. Author, co-author, editor: other books, 1979—; co-editor: The Future of Private Enterprise, 3 vols., 1982—84; co-author: Family Business Leadership Series, 22 vols., 1992—, Public Relations: The Profession and the Practice, 4th edit., 1996; contbg. editor, columnist: Family Bus. Planning, Nation's Bus. mag., 1990—99; mem. editl. bd. Jour. Pvt. Enterprise Edn., 1986—, Family Bus. Rev., 1992—2003; exec. editor: Family Bus. Advisor, 1991—2004. With Leadership Cobb, 1986—87; co-pres. West Side Elem. Sch. PTA, 1992—93; bd. dirs. Southeastern Legal Found., 1990—97; commr. Marietta Bd. Zoning and Planning, 1987—90; bd. advisors, v.p. Marcus Jewish Cmty. Ctr., Atlanta, 2007—12; bd. dirs. Temple Kol Emeth, Marietta, 1989—92, co-chmn. capital campaign, 2007—; bd. dirs. Davis Acad., 2009—11. Recipient Leavey award, Freedom Found., 1987, Outstanding Educator award, Nat. Fedn. Ind. Bus. Found., 1989, Disting. Leadership award, Leadership Cobb, 1988; named Craig E. Aronoff Professorship in family bus. in his honor, Kennesaw State U., 2004. Mem.: Ga. Coun. Econ. Edn. (trustee 1983—2004), Family Firm Inst. (bd. dirs. 1989—94, sec., treas. 1990—92, pres. 1992—94, Richard Beckhard award 1997), Family Bus. Forum (founder, bd. dirs. 1987—2005), Assn. Pvt. Enterprise Educators (bd. dirs. 1977—91, pres. 1978—79, Kent-Aronoff award 1988), Cobb C. of C. (vice chmn. 1986, 1991—93), Progressive Club (pres. 1976—77), Kiwanis (Outstanding Kiwanian award 1989). Office: 2061 E Side Dr NE Marietta GA 30062-6426 Office Phone: 678-277-9865. Business E-Mail: aronoff@efamilybusiness.com.

ARONOFF, GEORGE RODGER, medicine and pharmacology educator; b. Peoria, Ill., Mar. 6, 1950; BA in Chemistry with distinction, Ind. U., 1972; MD with honors, Ind. U., Indpls., 1975, MS in Pharmacology, 1984. Diplomate Am. Bd. Internal Medicine; diplomate Am. Bd. Internal Medicine Nephrology. Intern in internal medicine Ind. U., Indpls., 1975-76, resident, 1976-77, clin. fellow div. nephrology, 1977-78, chief resident in internal medicine Wishard Meml. Hosp., 1978-79, rsch. fellow div. nephrology, 1979-80, instr. phys. diagnosis, 1977-78, instr. medicine, 1978-79, from asst. prof. to assoc. prof. medicine, 1980-87, assoc. prof. pharmacology, 1985-87; prof. medicine, prof. pharmacology U. Louisville, 1987—; mem. staff Univ. Louisville (Ky.) Hosp., 1987—. Fellow in clin. pharmacology Eli Lilly & Co., Indpls., 1979-80. Contbr. numerous articles and abstracts to profl. jours. Fellow ACP; mem. Am. Soc. Nephrology, Cen. Soc. Clin. Rsch., Ky. State Med. Assn., Jefferson County Med. Soc. (editorial bd. Louisville Medicine 1989-92, editor 1990), Renal Physicians Assn., Nat. Kidney Found., Phi Eta Sigma, Phi Lambda Upsilon, Phi Beta Kappa, Alpha Omega Alpha, Sigma Xi. Office: U Louisville Kidney Disease Program 615 S Preston St Louisville KY 40202-1715

ARPEY, GERARD J., private equity firm executive, retired air transportation executive; b. NYC, July 26, 1958; m. Lisa Arpey; 2 children. BBA, U. Tex., Austin, 1980, MBA, 1982. Cert. multi-engine instrument pilot FAA. Financial analyst American Airlines, Inc., Ft. Worth, 1982—83, sr. financial analyst, 1983—85, mng. dir. financial analysis & fleet planning, 1985—87, mng. dir. airline profitability analysis, 1987—88, mng. dir. financial planning, 1988—89; v.p. financial planning & analysis AMR Corp., 1989-92, sr. v.p. planning, 1992-95, sr. v.p. financial & planning, 1995—99, exec. v.p. ops., 2000—02, pres., COO, 2002—03, pres., CEO, 2003—04, chmn., pres., CEO, 2004—10, chmn., CEO, 2010—11; ptnr. Emerald Creek Group, LLC, Houston, 2011—. Bd. dirs. S.C. Johnson & Son, Inc., AMR Corp., 2003—11, American Airlines, Inc., 2003—11. Mem.: The Bus. Coun. Avocation: private pilot. Office: Emerald Creek Group LLC 8901 Gaylord Dr Ste 200 Houston TX 77024 Office Phone: 713-468-4050, 713-468-4919.

ARRARÁS, MARIA CELESTE, newscaster, journalist; b. Mayagüez, PR, Sept. 22, 1961; d. Jose Enrique Arrarás; m. Manny Arvesu Arrarás, 1990 (div. Mar. 27, 2004); children: Julian, Lara Giuliana; 1 adopted child, Vadim. Grad., Loyola U. News anchor Primer Impacto Univision TV, 1994—2002, Al Rojo Vivo Telemundo USA, 2002—; co-host Today Show NBC TV, 2006. Actor: (films) Contact, 1997. Office: Telemundo Comm Group Inc 2470 W 8th Ave Hialeah FL 33010

ARRINGTON, JOHN A., diagnostic radiologist, educator; MD, U. South Fla., 1983. Diplomate Am. Bd. of Radiology-diagnostic radiology, 1987, Am. Bd. of Radiology-nuclear radiology, 2006. Resident diagnostic radiology Coll. of Medicine Univ. South Fla., Tampa, 1983—87, assoc. prof. radiology Coll. of Medicine; fellow neurol. radiology John Hopkins Hosp., Baltimore, 1987—88; hops. affiliations include Moffitt Cancer Ctr., Shriners Hosps. for Children. Office: Shriners Hospitals for Children 2900 Rocky Point Dr Tampa FL 33607 Office Phone: 813-281-0300.

ARRINGTON, JOHN LESLIE, JR., lawyer; b. Pawhuska, Okla., Oct. 15, 1931; s. John Leslie and Grace Louise (Moore) A.; m. Elizabeth Anne Waddington, 1956 (div.); children: Elizabeth Anne, John Leslie III, Winifred L., Katherine M.; m. Linda Vance, 1972. Grad., Lawrenceville Sch., 1949; AB, Princeton U., 1953; JD, Harvard U., 1956, LLM, 1957. Bar: Okla. 1956, U.S. Supreme Ct. 1960. Assoc. Arrington, Kihle, Gaberino & Dunn and predecessor firms, Tulsa, 1957-61, ptnr., 1961-93, chmn., CEO, 1994-96; gen. counsel ONEOK, Inc., 1997-98; of counsel GableGotwals, Tulsa, 1998—. Chmn. bd. dirs. Woodland Bank of Tulsa, 1979-94. Prin. draftsman Okla. Supreme Ct. rules governing disciplinary proceedings, 1980-81; bd. dirs. Tulsa County Legal Aid Soc., 1965-70, pres. 1967-70; bd. dirs. Tulsa Family Mental Health Ctr., 1982-89. Named Outstanding Young Man, Tulsa Jaycees, 1963. Mem. ABA, Tulsa County Bar Assn. (Young Lawyer award 1962, pres. 1970, Pres.'s award 1984, Professionalism award 1993), Okla. Bar Assn. (mem. profl. responsiblity commn. 1977-84, vice chmn. 1983-84, Disting. svc. award 1984, Golden Gavel award 1985, Pres.'s award 1991, Masonic award for ethics 1995), So. Hills Country Club (Tulsa), Princeton Club (N.Y.C.). Republican. Episcopalian. Home: 2300 Riverside Dr Unit 3E Tulsa OK 74114-2402 Office: 100 W 5th St Ste 1000 Tulsa OK 74103-4293

ARROWSMITH, MARIAN CAMPBELL, elementary school educator; b. St. Louis, Nov. 12, 1943; d. William Rankin and Elizabeth (Mitchell) Arrowsmith; m. William Earl Schroyer Arrowsmith, July 23, 1983; 1 child, Amy Lynn 1 stepchild, Carey Jo. BS, La. State U., 1961; MEd, Southeastern La. U., 1978. Lic. tchr. La.; cert. practicum supr. Inst. Reality Therapy. 1st grade tchr. McDonough #26, Jefferson Parish Sch. Bd., Gretna, La., 1966, Westminster Elem. Sch., Baton Rouge, 1967—72, Elm Grove Elem. Sch., Harvey, La., 1972—73, St. Andrews Episcopal Sch., New Orleans, 1973—74; 2nd grade tchr. Woodlawn High Sch., Baton Rouge, 1966—67; kindergarten tchr. Univ. Terrace Elem. Sch., Baton Rouge, 1967, Westminster Elem. Sch., Baton Rouge, 1968—71, Elm Grove Elem. Sch., 1973, St. Tammany Parish Sch. Bd., Folsom, La., 1974—77, ednl. cons., 2006—, early childhood specialist Covington, La., 1977—87; prin. Woodlake Elementary Sch., 1987—99; supr. instrn. St. Tammany Parish, 1999—2006; off-campus coordinating asst. St. Tammany Parish Dept. Continuing Edn., Southeastern La. U., 1985—87; condr. workshops in field; ofcl. pres. Sunbelt Region Reality Therapists, 1983; regional dir. La. & Miss. Reality Therapists, Sunbelt Bd. Reality Therapists, 1983. Author: Helping Your Child at Home, 1982—83. Mem.: ASCD, La. Assn. Tchrs. Math., Nat. Assn. Tchrs. Math., La. Assn. Sch. Execs., Jr. League, Regina Coedn. Child Devel. Ctr. (headStart), Ctr. Learning Devel. & Learning, Pontchartrain Yacht Club, Phi Delta Kappa, Kappa Alpha Theta, Alpha Delta Kappa, Delta Kappa Gamma (v.p. 1986). Democrat. Methodist. Avocations: reading, fishing, dance, horticulture. Home: 1000 Montgomery St Mandeville LA 70448-5517 Home Phone: 985-626-5880; Office Phone: 985-892-2276. E-mail: marianarrowsmith@charter.net.

ARROYO, F. THADDEUS, telecommunications industry executive; b. San Francisco; m. Alyssa Arroyo; 1 child. BS in Math., U. Tex., Arlington, 1986; MBA, So. Methodist U. Info. tech. Southwestern Bell; mgr., dir., v.p. Sabre Corp., v.p., strategic infrastructure, 1992—97, v.p., global outsourcing, 1997—99, sr. v.p., info. tech. svcs., 1999, sr. v.p., product mktg. and devel., 2000; chief info. officer Cingular Wireless, LLC, Atlanta, 2001—07; CIO AT&T Inc. (merger of SBC Communications & AT&T Corp.), 2007—. Bd. dirs. National Center for Women & Information Technology. Recipient Disting. Alumna award, U. Tex., Arlington, 2001, Ga. Global Chief Info. Officer of Yr., 2002; named Business 2.0 Dream Team, Business 2.0, 2004; named one of 50 Most Important Hispanics in Tech. & Bus., Hispanic Engr. & Info. Tech. mag., 2004, 2005, 100 Influentials, Hispanic Business, 2005. Mem.: Nat. Soc. of Hispanic MBAs, N. Fulton County C. of C. Office: Cingular Wireless Glenridge Highlands Two 5655 Glenridge Connector Atlanta GA 30342 Office Phone: 866-246-4852.

ARTEAGA, AGUSTÍN, museum director, architect; b. Tierra Blanca, Mex., Feb. 14, 1958; s. Ramón and Balbina (Domínguez) Arteaga. Student, U. Metropolitana, Mexico City; M in Art History, U. Autónoma, Mex., postgrad. Prof. U. Autónoma, Mexico, 1983—89; dep. dir., curator Mus. Modern Art, Mexico City, 1990—94; prof. U. Nuevo Mundo, Mexico, 1993—96; nat. dir. Vis. Arts Inst. Nat. Bellas Artes, Mexico, 1994—98; dir., chief curator Mus. Palacio Belles Artes, Mexico City, 1994—99; founding dir., ch. curator Malba-Constantini Collection, Argentina, 2000—02; curator Gallery Nat. Jeu du Pauma, Paris, 2002—04, Bienal de Mercosur, Porto Alegre, Brazil, 2002—04, Mus Nat. Art, Mexico City, 2002—04; CEO, exec. dir. Mus. Art Ponce, PR, 2004—. Author: Cuerpos Terrenales, 2003. Juror Bienal Monterrey, Mexico, 2003, Found. Nat. Art Min. Culture, Mexico, 2003, Contacto Cultural Rockefeller Found., Mexico, 2003—04. Decorated Chevalier ordre des Arts Letres Republic of France. Roman Catholic. Office: Museum Art Ponce 2325 Ave Las Americas Ponce PR 00717*

ARTHUR, GARY L., JR., energy executive; m. Sheila Arthur; 2 children. BBA, U. Ky.; MBA, Morehead State U. Various positions to v.p. bus. ops. Ashland Petroleum; v.p. supply and distbn. Colonial Grp.; v.p. mktg., supply and transp. Valero Energy Corp., San Antonio, 2000, sr. v.p. retail and speciality products mktg., 2000—. Bd. dirs. St. Peter's/St. Joseph's Children's Home; bd. mem., mem. exec. com. San Antonio Sports Found.; mem. mktg. adv. com. United Way. Office: Valero PO Box 696000 San Antonio TX 78269-6000

ARTHUR, THOMAS D., investor; Grad., U. NC, Chapel Hill, 1966; MBA, East Carolina U., 1971. CFO Havatampa Corp., Tampa, Fla., 1974, COO; pres., CEO, majority shareholder Havatampa Inc., 1978—97. Bd. dirs. Pioneer Natural Resources Co., 2009—. Infantry lt. US Army, 1966—69. Office: Pioneer Natural Resources Co Ste 200 5205 N O Connor Blvd Irving TX 75039 Office Phone: 972-444-9001. Office Fax: 972-969-3576.

ARTHUR, THOMAS HAHN, theater educator, director; b. Chgo., 1937; s. Maxwell Arthur and Josephine Edith (Hahn) A.; m. Carolyn Ruth Dry (div. 1967); 1 child, Michael Dry; m. Ellen Mary Sharkey, Mar. 28, 1968 (div. 1976); children: Adam Stephen, Benjamin Douglas; m. Kathleen Alden Giles, Dec. 28, 1976; 1 child, Robert Kenneth. BS, Northwestern U., 1959; MA, Ind. U., 1969, PhD, 1973. Promotion dir. Graphic Arts Buyer Mag., Chgo., 1960-63; publicity supr., actor Court Theatre, U. Chgo., 1963, 64; teaching asst. Ind. U., Bloomington, 1965-68; co-founder, dir., publicity mgr. Ind. Summer Repertoire Theatre, Ind. U., Bloomington, 1966; asst. prof. theater Ill. State U., Normal, 1969-73; adj. lectr. theater history Ill. Wesleyan U., Bloomington, 1972-73; prof. theater, head dept. theatre and dance James Madison U., Harrisonburg, Va., 1973—93; dir. Sch. Theatre and Dance, 1993—95. Artistic dir. Dinner Theatre, James Madison U., 1977, 82, 85, 88, 91, 92, 93; radio interviewer BBC, 1981, 84; acad. specialist USIA, South Africa and Finland, 1989, Hong Kong, 1993, Hungary, 1994; cons. USIA, Naples, Italy, 1996; individual lectr. Am. Theatre, U. East Anglia, Richmond, Eng., Brit. Inst. Florence, Italy, 1990, Internat. Fedn. Theatre Rsch., Tel Aviv, 1996, Dhaka, Bangladesh, 1997, Ahmedabad, India, 1997, Ankara, Turkey, 1997, Nicosia, Cyprus, 2000, Honolulu, 2002-03, Olympia, Greece, 2003, Ottawa, Ont., 2004, Beijing, 2005, Urbina, Italy, 2006, Pueblo, Mex., 2008; Leicester, Eng., 2010, Vancouver, British Columbia, 2012; theatre workshop, Poly. U. Philipines, Saint Paul U., 2007, Puebla, Mex., 2008, theater workshop, Am. U. Sharjah, UAE, 2009; program evaluator Nat. Assn. Schs. Theatre, 1990—, title II evaluator, 2003; guest dir., actor Sweet Briar Coll., Amherst, Va., 1972-73; reaffirmation com. evaluator So. Assn. Colls., 2002—. Author: See You at the Movies: The Autobiography of Melvyn Douglas, 1986; contbg. editor Dramatics mag., 1979-84; contbr. interviews, articles, revs. and poetry to various mags. and jours.; dir. TV vignettes for NEH grant, 1979-80; prodr. Am. Coll. Theatre Festival prodn. Sizwi Bansi is Dead, Kennedy Ctr., Washington, 1992; dir. Am. Coll. Theatre Festival prodn. Carriage, Kennedy Ctr., 1998; dir. Shakespeare Festival, Williamsburg, Va., 1998; dir. Tex. Shakespeare Festival, 1999, Harrow Prodns., Va., 2000, Bigfork (Mont.) Summer Theatre, 2001, Other: Playworks, Chgo., 2001. Mem. Gov.'s Commn. for 200th Anniversary of Constn., Richmond, 1983-84. NDEA fellow in Am. studies, 1965-68; grantee So. Ednl. Comm. Assn., 1980, Russell B. Nye award, 1981-82, Carl Harter Disting. Tchg. award Mem. World Congress Internat. Theatre, Assn. Theatre in Higher Edn., Comm. Assn. Am., Soc. Theatre Rsch., Nat. Assn. Schs. of Theatre (chmn. com. on nominations 1995, chmn. com. on ethics 1996—), Internat. Fedn. Theatre Rsch., Southeastern Theater Conf., Va. Theatre Assn. (v.p. 1983-84, chair theatre divsn. 1991-95). Avocations: reading, travel. Home: 298 Campbell St Harrisonburg VA 22801-4014 Office: James Madison University Harrisonburg VA 22807-0001 Home Phone: 540-433-8588. Business E-Mail: arthurth@jmu.edu.

ARTILES, FRANK, state legislator; b. LA, Apr. 22, 1973; m. Aimee Sontag; children: Isabella, Giavanna. AA, Miami-Dade CC; BS in Criminal Justice & Criminology, Fla. State U., 1995; JD, St. Thomas U., 2000; LLM in Real Property Devel., U. Miami, 2001. Owner Artiles Solutions, Pinnacle Appraisal and Umpire Svcs.; mem. Dist. 119 Fla. House of Representatives, 2011—. Staff sgt. USMC, 1998—2006. Republican. Avocations: fishing, hunting, scuba diving. Office: 13501 SW 128th St Ste 115A Miami FL 33186-5862 also: Fla House of Reps 1102 The Capitol 402 S Monroe St Tallahassee FL 32399-1300 Office Phone: 305-252-4300, 850-488-9550.

ARUNDEL, JOHN HOWARD, journalist, publisher; b. Washington, June 4, 1965; s. Arthur W. and Margaret C. (McElroy) A.; married; 2 children. BA in Polit. Sci., Duke U., 1988; MA in Internat. Econs., Johns Hopkins U., 1995. Reporter, trainee The New York Times, NYC, 1988-90; bur. chief States News Svc., Washington, 1991-92; corr. The Washington Post, Kuwait City, Kuwait, 1991; v.p. Citigroup, Washington, 1996—; journalist, editor, publisher The Alexandria Times, Alexandria, Va., 2004—08; assoc. pub. Washington Home and Garden Mag., 2009—, Wash. Life Mag., 2009—13. Bd. mem. Va. Film Found.; bd. dirs. The Kennedy Ctr. Camelot Circle, Washington, 1995—. Author: The Student Guide to Duke, 1988, While America Slept, 2003; contbr. articles to profl. jours. Mem. Nat. Press Club. Democrat. Episcopalian. Home: 1900 Belle Haven Rd Alexandria VA 22307-1111 Office Phone: 703-963-4191. Personal E-mail: jonarundel@aol.com. E-mail: john@washingtonlife.com.

ASCENSÃO, JOÃO LUIS AFONSO, physician, researcher, educator; b. Maputo, Mozambique, July 6, 1948; arrived in U.S., 1974; s. Joáo F. A. and Maria (Almeida) A.; m. Vivian Pereyra, June 27, 1993; children: Joáo André, Vítor Luís. MD, U. Lisbon Sch. Medicine, 1972, PhD, 1989. Resident U. Hosp. St. Mary, Lisbon, Portugal, 1972-74; immunology fellow Meml. Sloan-Kettering Cancer Ctr., NYC, 1974-76; internal medicine resident U. Minn. Hosps., Mpls., 1977-78, hematology oncology fellow, 1979-81, instr., 1981-82, asst. prof., 1982-84; assoc. prof., assoc. dir. BMT program N.Y. Med. Coll., Valhalla, 1984-89; assoc. prof., dir. BMT program U. Conn. Health Sci. Ctr., Farmington, 1989-92; prof. medicine, pathology, microbiology and immunology U. Nev. Sch. Medicine, Reno, 1992—2002; prof. medicine George Washington U. Sch. Medicine, Washington, 2002—05; prof. medicine and immunology VA Med. Ctr., Washington, 2005—, chief hematology, 2005—. Adv. bd. mem. Calif. Cancer Ctr., Modesto, 1992—2002; adv. bd. mem., bd. dirs. Nev. Am. Cancer Soc., Reno, 1992—2002. Editor: Regulation of Erythropoiesis, 1987, Molecular Biology of Hemopoiesis, 1988, Molecular Biology of Erythropoiesis, 1989. Portugal Sci. Found. fellow Ministry of Edn., 1974-75, Charles H. Revson Found. fellow, 1984-86; recipient Young Investigator award NIH, 1991-94. Fellow: ACP; mem.: Am. Assn. Immunology, European Soc. Med. Oncology, Internat. Soc. Exptl. Hematology (councillor), Am. Assn. Cancer Rsch., Am. Soc. Clin. Oncology, Am. Soc. Hematology. Avocations: photography, cooking, reading. Office: VA Med Ctr Divsn Hematology 151G 50 Irving St NW Washington DC 20422 Home Phone: 703-850-8441. Business E-Mail: joao.ascensao@med.va.gov.

ASCHOFF, LAWRENCE MICHAEL (MICK), retired computer information scientist; b. NYC, Feb. 14, 1950; s. Edward William and Marie Louise (Marshall) A. BA in Art History, U. Fla., 1971; MBA in Fin., NYU, 1984, advanced profl. cert. in computer applications and info. systems, 1988. Sales rep. VIP Fabrics, NYC, 1979—81; asst. to v.p. mktg. RAM Data, NYC, 1981—82; sales agt. Equitable Life Assurance Soc., NYC, 1982; programmer/analyst Drexel Burnham Lambert, NYC, 1984—86, sr. programmer/analyst, 1986—88, project leader, 1988—89, project mgr., asst. v.p., 1989—90; officer, project mgr. retail banking sys. Mfr.'s Hanover Trust, NYC, 1990—92; asst. v.p. retail banking Chem. Bank (merger with Mfr. Hanover Trust), NYC, 1992—95; v.p. project mgmt. competency ctr. retail banking sys. Nat. Consumer Svcs. Chase Manhattan Bank (merger with Chem.), NYC, 1996—2000; dir. GITSSO Program Mgmt. Office AXA Global I.T. Org., NYC, 2000—01; dir. program mgmt. office AXA Tech. Svcs., NYC, 2002—06, dir. global Sarbanes-Oxley coord., 2006—08, dir., global compliance officer, 2008—10. Treas. Saunders Owners of Queens, Ltd., 1989-91, 2002—2010, pres., 1991-2000 Clin. assoc. Suicide and Crisis Prevention Ctr., Gainesville, Fla., 1972; mem. pres.'s coun. U. Fla., 1992— Mem. IEEE, Mensa, Project Mgmt. Inst. (quality program mgr. N.Y.C. chpt. 2005—08), Phi Beta Kappa (sec. L.I. Alumni Assn. 1985-87, pres. 1987-93), Alpha Lambda Delta. Democrat. Avocations: travel, history, walking, literature, art, music.

ASCOLESE, RICHARD A., insurance company executive; BA in Sociology, Miami U., Ohio; MBA in Mktg. & Mgmt., U. Cin. With General Electric Co.; leadership positions, bus. unit American Home Shield Corp., exec. v.p., sales, mktg., ops., 1997—2004; COO TruGreen LandCare, 2004—05, pres., COO, 2005—. Vol. Boy Scouts of America. Avocations: golf, hiking, camping, reading. Office: TruGreen LandCare 860 Ridge Lake Blvd Memphis TN 38120 Office Fax: 901-681-1805. Business E-Mail: richardascolese@trugreenmail.com.

ASH, DARRON, insurance company executive; BS, Tex. A&M U.; MBA, U. Tex. With Arthur Andersen LLP, Dallas; sr. v.p., fin. Dean Foods Co.; exec. v.p., CFO Hicks Sports Group, LLC.; CFO HM Capital Ptnrs. LLC (formerly Hicks, Muse, Tate & Furst); pub. acctg. Morningstar Group Inc., Dallas, v.p., CFO, 2002; with, public acctg., pvt. equity investments, consumer products manufacturing and professional services Sammons Enterprises Inc., 2006; sr. v.p., CFO and pres. Sammons Enterprises, Inc., 2009—. Bd. dirs. LabNow, Inc. Office: Sammons Enterprises Inc 5949 Sherry Ln Ste 1900 Dallas TX 75225 Office Phone: 214-210-5000. Office Fax: 214-210-5099. Business E-Mail: dash@sammonscorp.com.

ASH, STEPHEN VAUGHAN, history professor, writer; m. Jean Cumming, 1970. BA, Gettysburg Coll., Pa., 1970; MA, U. Tenn., Knoxville, 1974, PhD, 1983. History prof. U. Tenn., 1995—. Author: (history book) A Year in the South: Four Lives in 1865, When the Yankees Came: Conflict and Chaos in the Occupied South, Firebrand of Liberty: The Story of Two Black Regiments That Changed the Course of the Civil War, The Black Experience in the Civil War South, A Massacre in Memphis: The Race Riot That Shook the Nation One Year After the Civil War; co-author (with Paul H. Bergeron and Jeanette Keith): Tennesseans and Their History. Office: Univ Tennessee History Dept 915 Volunteer Blvd Knoxville TN 37996 Office Phone: 865-974-5421. Business E-Mail: sash@utk.edu.

ASHBY, DANNY S., lawyer; b. Jacksonville, Fla., Oct. 1, 1964; BA magna cum laude, U. SC, 1986; JD with highest honors, Baylor Law Sch., Waco, Tex., 1990. Bar: Tex. 1990, US Supreme Ct., US Ct. Appeals (5th, 11th and Fed. Circuits), US Dist. Courts, all Tex. Districts. Clk. to Hon. Edith H. Jones US Ct. Appeals (5th cir.); trial atty. criminal divsn. US Dept. Justice; ptnr., securities & govt. litigation Hughes & Luce, LLP (now K&L Gates LLP), Dallas. Contbr. articles to law jours.; editor (in chief): Baylor Law Rev. Named one of Best Lawyers in Dallas, D Mag., 2005. Mem.: 5th Cir. Bar Assn., Dallas Bar Assn., ABA, Dallas Bar Found., State Bar Tex. Office: K&L Gates LLP Ste 2800 1717 Main St Dallas TX 75201 Office Phone: 214-939-5745. Office Fax: 214-939-5849. E-mail: danny.ashby@klgates.com.

ASHCROFT, JOHN DAVID, lobbyist, law educator, former United States Attorney General; b. Chgo., May 9, 1942; s. James Robert and Grace Pauline (Larson) Ashcroft; m. Janet Elise Roede, 1967; children: Martha, Jay, Andrew. B cum laude, Yale U., 1964; JD, U. Chgo., 1967; PhD (hon.), Truman State U., 2009. Bar: Mo., U.S. Supreme Ct. Asst. prof. S.W. Mo. State U., Springfield, 1967—71, assoc. prof., 1971—73; pvt. practice Springfield, 1967-73; state auditor State of Mo., 1973-75, asst. atty. gen., 1975-77, atty. gen., 1977-84, gov., 1985-92; atty. Suelthaus and Kaplan P.C., 1993-94; US Senator from Mo., 1995-2001; atty. gen. US Dept. Justice, 2001—05; Disting. prof., law & govt. Regent U., Virginia Beach, Va., 2005—; founder, chmn. The Ashcroft Group LLC, Washington, 2005—; founding ptnr. Ashcroft Hanaway, St. Louis, 2009—. Nat. chmn. Edn. Commn. States, 1987-88, Jud. Com., Subcom., chmn. constn.; chmn. Nat. Governors Assn. Task Force on Coll. Quality, 1985, Nat. Governors Assn. Task Force on Adult Literacy; co-chair Renewal Alliance. Author: Lessons From a Father to His Son, 1998, Never Again: Securing America and Restoring Justice, 2006; co-author: (with Janet E. Ashcroft) College Law for Business, 7th, 8th, 9th, 10, 11th edits., It's the Law, 1979-91, (with Gary Lee Thomas) On My Honor: The Beliefs That Shape My Life, 2001; contbr. articles to profl. jours.; gospel singer (records) In the Spirit of Life and Liberty, The Gospel According to John Chmn. Task Force on Adult Literacy, Task Force on College Quality Nat. Governors Assn., 1991; co-chmn. Republican Platform Com., 1992. Recipient Nat. Sheriffs Assn. award, 1996; named Christian Statesman of Yr., 1996. Mem. ABA (house of dels.), Mo. Bar Assn., Cole County Bar Assn., Nat. Assn. Attys. Gen. (pres. 1980-81, chmn. budget com., exec. com., Wyman award 1983), Nat. Governors Assn. (vice chmn. 1990, chmn. 1991-92, chmn. Pres.'s Commn. on Urban Families 1992). Republican. Mem. Assembly Of God Ch. Office: The Ashcroft Group LLC 950 N Glebe Rd Ste 530 Arlington VA 22203-4181 Office Phone: 703-247-5454. Office Fax: 703-247-5446.*

ASHE, HERBERT J., otolaryngologist, educator; MD, La. State U., 1980. Diplomate Am. Bd. Otolaryngology, 1985. Resident surgery Baylor Coll. of Medicine, 1981—82, resident otolaryngology, 1985, asst. clin. prof. otolaryngology head and neck surgery; hosp. affiliations include St. Luke's Episcopal Hosp., Tex. Children's Hosp., Kans. Ambulatory Surgery Ctr.; physician Kelsey-Seybold Clinic, 1985—. Named Super Dr., Tex. Monthly. Fellow: ACS, Am. Acad. of Otolaryngology Head and Neck Surgery; mem.: AMA, Harris County Med. Soc., Tex. Med. Assn. Avocation: jogging. Office: Ear Nose and Throat 4th Fl 2727 W Holcombe Blvd Houston TX 77025 Office Phone: 713-442-0642.*

ASHE, KATHLEEN B., state legislator; b. Nov. 14, 1946; m. Lawrence Ashe; children: Robbie, Sally. Former state rep. Kil Townsend, Dist. 42, Ga.; former mem. Atlanta Charter Rev. Commn., Atlanta Child Care Task Force, Fulton County Rep. Exec. Com.; former bd. mem. Rhodes Hall; treas. House Dem. Caucus. Tchr., 1969—77; state rep. Dist. 46, Ga., 1991—2002, Dist 56, 2004—; ranking mem. edn. com.; mem. Edn. Appropriations, MARTOC, Ways & Means Coms., house rep. Ga.; mem. Women's & Rep. Caucuses, Komen Found., Atlanta Civilian Rev. Bd., Gov.'s Privatization Commn.; cmty. vol. Elder & tchr. Presbyterian Ch. Mem.: Jr. League Atlanta, League Women Voters, Ga. Citzens Arts, Planned Parenthood Atlanta, Ga. Trust Hist. Preservation, Ga. Conservancy, Buckhead Bus. Assn., Midtown Alliance, Atlanta Women's Network, Regional Leadership Inst., Leadership Atlanta. Democrat. Presbyterian. Address: 82 Westminster Dr NE Atlanta GA 30309-3329 Mailing: 417 Legis Off Bldg Atlanta GA 30334 Fax: 404-875-0548. E-mail: kashe46@mindspring.com, kathyashe56@mindspring.com.

ASHE, REID (O. REID ASHE), publishing executive; b. 1948; Student, MIT. With Tech. Rev., Boston, 1971-72; asst. editor Washington (N.C.) Daily News, 1972-73; reporter, editl. writer, editl. page editor Jackson (Tenn.) Sun, 1973-84, exec. editor, 1974-78, editor, pub., pres., 1978-84; gen. exec. Knight-Ridder Inc., 1984; CEO Viewdata Corp. (a subsidiary of Knight-Ridder Inc.), 1984-87; pres., pub. The Wichita (Kans.) Eagle, 1987-96; pres., assoc. pub. The Tampa Tribune, 1996—97, pres., pub., 1997—2001; COO Media General, 2001—05, exec. v.p., COO, 2005—. Bd. dirs. Media General, 2002—. Mem.: Southern Newspaper Publishers Assn. (pres. 2010—). Office: Media General 333 Franklin St Richmond VA 23219

ASHE, VICTOR HENDERSON, former ambassador; b. Knoxville, Tenn., Jan. 1, 1945; s. Robert Lawrence and Martha (Henderson) A.; m. Joan Plumlee, June 11, 1983; children: James Victor, Martha. BA in History, Yale U., 1967; JD, U. Tenn., 1975. Mem. Tenn. House of Reps., 1968-74, Tenn. State Senate, 1975-84; pvt. practice; mayor City of Knoxville, 1988—2003; US amb. to Poland US Dept. State, Warsaw, 2004—09. Mem. Nat. League of Cities; pres. U.S. Conf. of Mayors, 1994-95; resident fellow, Inst. Politics, JOhn F. Kennedy Sch. Govt., Harvard U., 2004; mem. Broadcasting Bd. Govs., 2010-Named Young Man of the Yr., Knox Jaycees, 1972; recipient Disting. Svc. award for Leadership, US Conf. Mayors, 2003 Mem. Civitan Club. Republican. Personal E-mail: vhashe@aol.com.

ASHFORTH, ALDEN, composer, educator; b. NYC, May 13, 1933; m. Nancy Ann Regnier, June 12, 1956 (div. 1980); children— Robyn Richardson, Melissa Adams, Lauren Elizabeth AB, B.Mus., Oberlin Coll, 1958; M.F.A., Princeton U., 1960, PhD, 1971. Instr. Princeton U., N.J., 1961; instr. Oberlin Coll., Ohio, 1961-65, N.Y.U., NYC, 1965-66, Manhattan Sch. Music, NYC, 1965; lectr. CUNY, NYC, 1966-67; asst. prof. music UCLA, 1967-72, assoc. prof. music, 1972-80, prof., 1980—98, prof. emeritus, 1998—. Coordinator electronic music studio, 1969-86. Composer numerous instrumental, vocal and electronic works including: Episodes (chamber concerto for 8 instruments), 1962, The Unquiet Heart (cycle for soprano and chamber orch.), 1968, Big Bang (piano-four hands) 1970, Byzantium (organ and electronic tape), 1971, Sailing to Byzantium (organ and electronic tape), 1973, Aspects of Love (song cycle), 1978, Christmas Motets (a cappella chorus), 1980, The Miraculous Bugle (flugelhorn and percussion), 1989, Palimpsests (organ), 1997; producer, recorder New Orleans Jazz including, New Orleans Parade: The Eureka Brass Band Plays Dirges and Stomps, 1952, Doc Paulins Marching Band, 1982, Last of the Line: The Eagle Brass Band, 1984; contbr. articles to profl. jours. and to New Grove Dictionary of Jazz. Office: UCLA Music Dept Los Angeles CA 90095-0001

ASHWORTH, KENNETH HAYDEN, public administrator; b. Abilene, Tex., Feb. 24, 1932; s. Harold Laverne and Mae Beatrice (Grote) A.; m. Emily Yaung; children: Rodney Brian, Karen Grace. BA, U. Tex., 1958, PhD, 1969; M. Pub. Adminstrn., Syracuse U., 1959. Asst. commr. Tex. Higher Edn. Coordinating Bd., Austin, 1965-69, commr. higher edn., 1976-97; vice chancellor for acad. affairs U. Tex. System, Austin, 1969-73; exec. v.p. U. Tex. at San

Antonio, 1973-76. Adj. prof. govt. and pub. affairs U. Tex., Austin, 1997—, Tex. A &M U., College Sta., 1997—. Author: Scholars and Statesmen, 1972, American Higher Education in Decline, 1979, (with Norman Hackerman) Conversations on the Uses of Science and Technology, 1996, Caught Between the Dog and the Fireplug or How to Survive Public Service, 2001. Served with USN, 1951-55. Mem. Philos. Soc. Tex., Phi Beta Kappa, Phi Delta Kappa, Phi Kappa Phi, Pi Sigma Alpha. Clubs: Town and Gown. Democrat. Unitarian Universalist. Home: 7616 Rustling Rd Austin TX 78731-1365 Office: U Tex LBJ Sch Pub Affairs PO Box Y Austin TX 78713-8925 also: Tex A&M U Bush Sch Govt And Pub Svc College Station TX 77843-0001 Home Phone: 512-345-9521.

ASIABANPOUR, BAHRAM, engineering educator; PhD in Indsl. Engring., U. So. Calif., LA, 2003. Cert. MFGE. Computer-aided design and mfg. engr. Automotive Industry Rsch. and Innovation Ctr., Tehran, 1997—99; rsch. asst. U. of So. Calif., LA, 1999—2003; asst. prof. mfg. engring. Tex. State U., San Marcos, 2003—09, assoc. prof., 2010—. Author: (book chpt.) Rapid Prototyping: Theory and Practice; contbr. scientific papers to profl. jours. Recipient Highly Commended award, Emrald Publ. Literati Club, 2004, Best Paper award, Iran's 6th Indsl. Engring. Conf., 1999, Rsch. and Tchg. assistantship, U. of So. Calif., 1999—2003. Mem.: Inst. of Indsl. Engrs., Soc. of Mfg. Engrs. Office: Ingram Sch Engring 601 University Dr San Marcos TX 78666 Office Fax: 512-245-3052; Home Fax: 512-245-3052. Personal E-mail: asiabanpour@yahoo.com.

ASKEW, KIM JUANITA, lawyer; b. Savannah, Ga., Nov. 14, 1957; BS summa cum laude, Knoxville Coll., 1979; JD, Georgetown U., 1983. Bar: US Supreme Ct., DC 1983, Tex. 1984, US Ct. Appeals (4th, 5th, and 8th cirs.), US Dist. Ct. (no. and ea. dists. Tex.). Law clk. US Dist Ct. (no. dist. Tex.); ptnr., labor & employment practice Hughes & Luce, LLP (now K&L Gates LLP), Dallas. Bd. dirs. Nat. Women's Law Ctr., Baptist Found. Tex., Dallas Com. for a Qualified Judiciary. Contbr. articles to profl. publs. Mem. bd. regents Georgetown U.; bd. dirs. Victims Outreach; dir., treas. Dallas Mus. Art; former dir. Greater Dallas C. of C.; former trustee Paul Quinn Coll.; former dir. Jr. League Dallas. Recipient Louise Raggio award, Dallas Women Lawyers Assn., 2003, Trailblazer award, J.L. Turner Legal Assn., 2003; named Tex. Super Lawyer, Law & Politics Mag., 2003; named one of Best Lawyers in Am., Corp. Counsel, 2003, Best Lawyers in Dallas, D Mag., 2005. Mem.: ABA (mem. com. commn. on women in profession 1993—97, mem. com. on meetings and travel 1997—2000, mem. continuing legal edn. com. 2000—03, sec. litig. sect. 2002—04, chair litig. sect. 2006—, mem. ho. of dels., mem. coun. fund for justice and edn., mem. membership com.), Tex. Women Lawyers, Dallas Bar Assn. (former co-chair judiciary com.), State Bar Tex. (chair continuing legal edn. com. 1997—2000, chair litig. sect. 2001—02, chair bd. dirs. 2003—04, former chair evidentiary panel dist. 6A grievance com., bd. dirs., Presdl. Citation 2000, Gene Cavin award 1999), Am. Law Inst. (chair com. on size, fed. judiciary com.). Office: K&L Gates LLP Ste 2800 1717 Main St Dallas TX 75201 Office Phone: 214-939-5579. Office Fax: 214-939-5849. Business E-Mail: kim.askew@klgates.com.

ASMAN, BUB (HENRY B. ASMAN), sound editor; b. Louisville, Aug. 17, 1949; Editor: (films) Abby, 1974, Sheba, Baby, 1975, Grizzly, 1976, Day of the Animals, 1977, The Manitou, 1978; sound effects editor (films) The Bad News Bears Go to Japan, 1978, Escape from Alcatraz, 1979, North Dallas Forty, 1979, Bronco Billy, 1980, Any Which Way You Can, 1980, The Postman Always Rings Twice, 1981, Nighthawks, 1981, Zorro, the Gay Blade, 1981, Conan the Barbarian, 1982, Firefox, 1982, Honkytonk Man, 1982, Sudden Impact, 1983, Uncommon Valor, 1983, The Last Starfighter, 1984, Red Dawn, 1984, Windy City, 1984, City Heat, 1984, Hard to Kill, 1990, The Last Boy Scout, 1991, Radio Flyer, 1992, True Romance, 1993, Demolition Man, 1993, The Stars Fell on Henrietta, 1995, Quest for Camelot, 1998, The Replacements, 2000, Heartbreakers, 2001, sound editor (films) First Blood, 1982, Vacation, 1983, The Last Starfighter, 1984, Lethal Weapon 2, 1989, White Hunter Black Heart, 1990, Die Hard 2, 1990, New Jack City, 1991, Lethal Weapon 3, 1992, Maverick, 1994, Speed 2: Cruise Control, 1997, supervising sound editor (films) The Bridges of Madison County, 1995, Eraser, 1996, Absolute Power, 1997, Midnight in the Garden of Good and Evil, 1997, True Crime, 1999, co-supervising sound editor (films) Lara Croft: Tomb Raider, 2001, Blood Work, 2003, Star Trek: Nemesis, 2002, Mystic River, 2003, Million Dollar Baby, 2004, The Legend of Zorro, 2005, Flags of Our Fathers, 2006, Letters from Iwo Jima, 2006 (Acad. award for achievement in sound editing, 2007), dialogue editor Up Close & Personal, 1996.

ASP, WILLIAM GEORGE, librarian; b. Hutchinson, Minn., July 4, 1943; s. George William and Blanche Irene (Mattson) A. BA, U. Minn., 1966, MA, 1970; postgrad., U. Iowa, 1972-75. Dir. East Cen. Regional Libr., Cambridge, Minn., 1967-70; asst. prof. Sch. Libr. Sci. U. Iowa, 1970-75; dir. Minn. Office Libr. Devel. and Svcs., St. Paul, 1975-96, Dakota County Libr., Eagan, Minn., 1996—2003. Mem. Nat. Coun. Quality Continuing Edn. for Info., Libr. and Media Pers., 1979-85; bd. dirs. Bakken Libr. Electricity and Life, 1976-2007, Mpls.; vice chmn. White House Conf. on Libr. and Info. Svcs. Task Force, 1980-81, chmn., 1982, mem. adv. com., 1989-91; pres. Continuing Libr. Edn. Network and Exch., 1986-87. Mem. Minn. Regional Network Bd., 1992-96. Mem. ALA (mem. coun. 1985-88, 00-02), Minn. Libr. Assn., Chief Officers State Libr. Agys. (chmn. 1979-80), Minn. Ednl. Media Orgn., Minn. Assn. Continuing and Adult Edn., Assn. Specialized and Coop. Libr. Agys. (pres. 1989-90), Am. Field Svc. Home: 2095 Batello Dr Venice FL 34292

ASPBURY, HERBERT FRANCIS, retired bank executive, board member; b. Millbrook, NY, Dec. 28, 1944; s. James Thomas and Helen Marie (Mulholland) Aspbury; m. Mary Victoria Doran, Sept. 5, 1968; children: Matthew Thomas, Peter Gordon, Pamela Elizabeth. BA in English, Villanova U., Pa., 1967. Mgmt. trainee, asst. sec. Mfrs. Hanover Trust Co., NYC, 1967-72, asst. v.p., 1972-74, v.p., 1974-81, sr. v.p., 1981-85, exec. v.p., 1985-90, group exec., mem. mgmt. com. London, 1990-92; sr. mng. dir. European ops. Chemical Bank, 1992—95; head US industries, then sr. mng. dir. Europe, Africa & Middle East Chase Manhattan Bank, 1995—2000, ret., 2000. Adj. prof. Fisher Grad. Sch. Internat. Bus., Monterey Inst. Internat. Studies, Calif., 2002—; bd. dirs. Exide Technologies, 2006—. Bd. trustees Villanova U., 1999—, chmn. bd. trustees, 2008—; former bd. dirs. Royal Oak Found., chmn., 2004—07. Mem.: Villanova U. Alumni Assn. (past bd. dirs., pres. 2001—03, Alumni Medal 1992). Roman Catholic. Avocations: running, skiing, music. Mailing: Villanova University Bd Trustees 800 Lancaster Ave Villanova PA 19085-1603 Office: Exide Technologies Bd Directors 13000 Deerfield Pky Bldg 200 Milton GA 30004 Office Phone: 610-519-6000, 678-566-9000. Office Fax: 678-566-9188. Business E-Mail: herbert.herbert@villanova.edu.

ASPNES, DAVID ERIK, physicist, researcher; b. Madison, Wis., May 1, 1939; s. Erik A. and Anita L. (Knabe) A.; m. Edna Joyce Hall, Jan. 27, 1964 (dec. 1996); children: James D., Gary E., Ann K.; m. Cynthia Jean Ball, July 26, 1997. BSEE, U. Wis., 1960, MSEE, 1961; PhD, U. Ill., 1965. Postdoctoral rsch. assoc. U. Ill., Urbana, 1965-66, Brown U., Providence, 1966-67; mem. tech. staff Bell Labs., Murray Hill, NJ, 1967-83; sr. scientist Max-Planck-Inst., Stuttgart, Fed. Republic Germany, 1976-77; dist. mgr. Bellcore, Red Bank, NJ, 1983-92; prof. physics dept. NC State U., Raleigh, 1992—99, disting. univ. prof. physics, 1999—. Contbr. more than 500 articles to Phys. Rev., Applied Optics, Thin Solid Films and other jours.; U.S. editor Applied Surface Sci., 1996-2001. Recipient Sr. Scientist award Alexander von Humboldt Found., 1976-77, Wood prize, Optical Soc. America, 1987, John Yarwood medal Brit. Vacuum Coun., 1993, Frank Isakson prize, Am. Phys. Soc., 1996, Max Planck Rsch. award Internat. Coop., 1997, Outstanding Rsch. award NC State U. Alumni Assn., 1997, Medard W. Welch award, Am. Vacuum Soc., 1998, Mentor award Soc. Vacuum Coaters, 2011; elected Nat. Acad. Scis., 1998; named Alumni Disting. Grad. Prof. NC State U. Alumni Assn., 2005; Global Eminent scholar Korean World Class U. Project, 2009, National Academy of Inventors, 2014 Fellow: AAAS, Am. Phys. Soc. (councillor divsn. condensed matter physics 1996-99, exec. coun. 1998-99), Optical Soc. Am., Am. Vacuum Soc. (chmn. electronic materials and processing divsn. 1982-83, chmn. electronics materials and processing divsn. Internat. Union Vacuum Sci., Techniques and Applications 1986-89, bd. dirs. 1991-92, trustee 2001-03, pres. 2005), Soc. Photo-Optical Instrumentation Engrs., World Innovation Found.; mem. Nat. Acad. Scis.(chair sec., 2005-08, chair class III, 2011-14), Materials Rsch. Soc., Alexander von Humboldt Assn. Am., Sigma Xi, Soc. Vacuum Coaters Mem. Lds Ch. Achievements include discovery and development of reflectance-difference spectroscopy and low-field electroreflectance; development of spectroscopic ellipsometry with applications to process control; contributions to solid-state physics including 3rd derivative interpretation of low-field electroreflectance, ordering of the lower conduction bands of GaAs, elucidation of the kinetics of crystal growth by organometallic chemical vapor deposition, virtual-interface theory, anisotropic bond charge model of nonlinear optics. Office: NC State University Physics Dept Campus Box 8202 Raleigh NC 27695-8202 Business E-Mail: aspnes@unity.ncsu.edu.

ASRYAN, LEVON V., physicist, electronics engineer, materials scientist; m. Anna V. Sharonova. MSc in Radiophysics and Electronics, Yerevan State U., 1985; PhD in Physics and Math., Ioffe Inst., St. Petersburg, 1988; DSc in Physics and Math., Ioffe Physico-Technical Inst., St. Petersburg, 2002. Sr. rschr. Ioffe Physico-Tech. Inst., St. Petersburg, Russia, 1992—2005; rsch. assoc. prof. dept. elec. and computer engring. SUNY, Stony Brook, 2000—04; assoc. prof. dept. materials sci. and engring. Va. Tech., Blacksburg, 2004—. Mem. program com. summer topical workshop on nanostructures and quantum dots IEEE LEOS, San Diego, 1999; presenter in field. Contbr. articles, series of papers to profl. publs. Recipient Best Paper award, IEEE Jour. Quantum Electronics, 2001, State Prize in Sci. and Tech., Russia, 2001. Achievements include patent for semiconductor laser with reduced temperature sensitivity; first to theory of threshold characteristics of quantum dot lasers. Office: Va Tech Dept MSE 207 Holden Hall MC 0237 Blacksburg VA 24061

ASSELIN, HEATHER E., lawyer; BA, Calif. State U., Fresno, 1993; JD, Creighton U. Sch. Law, 1996. Bar: Tex., US Dist. Ct. (so. dist.) Tex., US Dist. Ct. (no. dist.) Tex., US Dist. Ct. (ea. dist.) Tex., US Dist. Ct. (we. dist) Tex. Dir. litigation and constrn./surety sects. Coats Rose. Named a Rising Star, Tex. Super Lawyers mag., 2006—09. Fellow: Tex. Bar Found.; mem.: ABA (mem. litig. constrn. surety sect.), Assn. Gen. Contractors (Houston chpt.), Assn. Women Attys. Found. (former mem. jud. reception com., bd. dirs., pres., chair), Houston Bar Assn. Office: Coats Rose Yale Ryman Lee 3 E Greenway Plz Ste 2000 Houston TX 77046 Office Phone: 713-653-7386. E-mail: hasselin@coatsrose.com.

ASTIGARRAGA, JOSE IGNACIO, lawyer; b. Havana, Cuba, July 20, 1953; arrived in US, 1960, naturalized, 1974; AA with honors, Miami Dade CC, 1973; BBA summa cum laude, U. Miami, 1975, JD magna cum laude, 1978. Bar: Fla. 1978, US Dist. Ct. (so. dist.) Fla. 1979, US Dist. Ct. (mid. dist.) 1988, US Ct. Appeals (5th and 11th cir.) 1981, US Supreme Ct. 1990. Chief bailiff Dade County Juvenile and Family Ct., Miami, 1972—74; law clk., bailiff 11th Jud. Cir., Miami, 1974—77; with firm Steel, Hector & Davis, Miami, 1978—84, ptnr., 1984—; adj. faculty U. Miami Sch. Law, Coral Gables, Fla., 1980—81; cons. World Bank; mem. US del. Org. Am. States 6th Conf. Pvt. Internat. Law; with Little Havana Activities and Nutrition Ctrs. Dade County, Inc., 1987—94, NAFTA Adv. Comm. Resolution Pvt. Comml. Disputes, 1994—96; mem. panel arbitrators Comml. Arbitration and Mediation Ctr. Ams., 1996; founder Latin Am. Users Coun. London Ct. Internat. Arbitration. Co-author: Secured Lenders Beware: Particular Issues Affecting Secured Lenders, 1993. Adminstrv. hearing officer Dade County Sch. Bd., Miami, 1982—90; chmn. quality assurance com., mem. fin. com. Miami Children's Hosp., bd. dirs., 1985—88, Miami Children's Hosp. Rsch. Inst., Inc., 1986—87, chmn. nominating com.; bd. dirs. Dade County Beacon Coun. Inc., 1985—95, Miami Coalition, Inc., 1988—94; mem. exec. com., chmn. schs. task force, 1988—90; trustee Fla. Internat. U. Found., 1988—. Recipient Up and Comers Law award Price Waterhouse and South Fla. Bus. Jour., 1988; Harvey T. Reid scholarship, U. Miami Sch. Law, 1975—78, Leonard T. Abess scholarship, U. Miami, 1974—75. Mem.: ABA (com. bus. bankruptcy 1990—, com. comml. fin. svcs., Uniform Comml. Code Com.), Am. Arbitration Assn. (panel commercial fin. disputes 1994—), Greater Miami C. of C. (bd. govs. 1985—86, group chmn. econ. devel. sect. 1986—87), U. Miami Sch. Law Alumni Assn. (bd. dirs. 1981—88), Bankruptcy Bar Assn. (v.p. 1992—94), Cuban-Am. Bar Assn., Dade County Bar Assn. (commr. jud. campaign practices commn. 1986—87), Fla. Bar Assn. (bus. law sect., sec. civil procedure rules com. 1979—84, bankruptcy UCC com. 1992—, lectr. bankruptcy seminar 1993—94), Am. Law Inst. (adv. transnat. insolvency project 1997), Internat. Bar Assn. (com. arbitration, insolvency). Office: Astigarraga Davis 16th Fl 701 Brickell Ave Miami FL 33131 Home: 7667 SW 52nd Ave Miami FL 33143-5937

ASTOR, FRANK, otolaryngologist, educator; Attended, Northwestern U., Pratt Inst., 1970—72; BA in Biology summa cum laude, Inter-Am. U. PR, 1972—74; MD, U. PR, 1974—78; MBA in Mgmt., Bowling Green State U., 1993—97. Diplomate Am. Bd. Otolaryngology, 1984. Resident otolaryngology head and neck surgery Cleve. Clinic. Found., 1978—83; fellow head and neck surgery Univ. of Cin. Coll. of Medicine, 1983—84; fellow facial plastic and reconstructive surgery Oreg. Health and Sci. Univ. Sch. of Medicine, 1984—85; chmn., founder, dir. otolaryngology head and neck surgery, bd. govs. Cleve. Clinic Fla., 1991—2000; assoc. prof. otolaryngology Univ. of Miami Sch. of Medicine, 2000—05; med. dir. Blue Cross and Blue Shield of Fla., 2006—; head and neck surgeon Jackson Meml. Hosp., 2000—05, Univ. of Miami Sylvester Comprehensive Cancer Ctr., 2000—05, Bascom Palmer Eye Inst., 2000—05. Treas. Panamerican Assn. Otolaryngology Head and Neck Surgery, 2000—05. Bd. of editors (jour.) Ear, Nose and Throat, 2000—05. Mem.: Nat. Honor Soc., Am. Acad. of Otolaryngology Head and Neck Surgery (Honor award), Alpha Omega Alpha Honor Med. Soc. Office: Cleveland Clinic Florida 2950 Cleveland Clinic Blvd Weston FL 33331*

ASTRUP, JENS LEO, retired civil engineer; b. Plentywood, Mont., Sept. 21, 1934; s. Jens Legend and Dagmar (Jensen) Astrup; m. Susanne Elizabeth Laime, Nov. 25, 1967 (div. Nov. 1985); children: Moriah Ann, Jens Aaron. BS, ND State U., 1956; MBA, Keller Grad. Sch. Mgmt., 1983. Registered profl. engr., Ill.; patent agt. Civil engr. City of Chgo. Dept. Urban Renewal, 1964—65, Harza Engring. Co., 1965—69; city engr. City of Williston, ND, 1969—70; civil and resident engr. Bauer Engring., Inc., Chgo., 1970—71; civil and structural sr. engr. Brown and Root, Inc., 1971—82; project engr. Lester B. Knight & Assocs., 1983—85, Comstock Engring., Inc., Oak Brook, 1985—86; sr. civil engr. Allen Engring. Co., Villa Park, 1986—88; project engr. Globetrotters Engring. Corp., Chgo., 1988—92; sr. civil engr. Clark Dietz, Inc., 1993—94. Mem.: ASCE, Am. Pub. Works Assn. N.D. (past state sec. 1969—70), Ill. Soc. Profl. Engrs. (state v.p. 1979—80, chmn. state activities com. 1976—77, chpt. pres. 1977—78). Home: 14201 Hobby Ln Apt 16110 Fort Worth TX 76155 Personal E-mail: leoa2@juno.com.

ATALA, ANTHONY JOHN, surgeon; b. July 14, 1958; m. Katherine Atala, May 13, 1985. BA, U. Miami, 1984; MD, U. Louisville, 1985. Cert. Am. Bd. Urology. Intern in surgery U. Louisville Sch. Medicine, 1985-86, resident in surgery, 1985—87, resident in urology, 1987-89, chief resident in urology, 1989-90; rsch. fellow dept. surgery Children's Hosp., Harvard Med. Sch., Boston, 1990-91, clin. fellow dept. surgery, 1991-92, instr., 1992-93, asst. prof., 1993—2003, mem. investigations rev. bd., 1994—; dir. lab. tissue engring. and cellular therapeutics Children's Hosp. and Harvard Med. Sch., 1993—2004; W.H. Boyce prof., chair dept. urology, dir. Wake Forest Inst. for Regenerative Medicine Wake Forest Univ. Baptist Med. Ctr., 2004—. Mem. study sect. NIH, 1996; editor-in-chief Current Stem Cell Rsch. and Therapy, Therapautic Avances in Urology. Cons. Jour. Urology, 1993-, editor investigative urology sect., editor, Lancet, 1994, editor: Jour. Rejuvenation Rsch., Tissue Engring. and Regenerative Medicine, Nanotech. in Engring. and Regenerative Medicine; editor investigative urology sect., Urology, Current Reviews in Urology, The Scientific World: Cell Biology; mem. editl. bd. Expert Opinion on Biol. Therapy; contbr. articles to profl. jours. Rsch. award ACS, 1990, Am. Acad. Pediat., 1993, 94, 96, Am. Soc. Plastic Surgery, 1994, Christopher Columbus Found. award, Gold Cystoscope award, Number 1 Top Sci. Story of Yr., Discover Mag., 2007; named Med. Treatments Leader of the Yr., Scientific American, 56th Most Influential Person of Yr., Time Mag., 2007; named one of 50 People, Fast Co. Mag., 2006, 100 Most Creating People, 2009. Mem. AMA, AAAS, Am. Urol. Assn. (program com. 1995), Soc. for Basic Urol. Rsch. (program com. 1995), Soc. of Regenerative Medicine (bd, dir., v.p.), Tissue Engring. Soc. (bd. gov.), Tissue Engring. and Regerative Medicine Internat. Soc. (chair N.Am. chpt.). Achievements include patents in field, inventions in area of tissue engineering and medicine. First to build a functioning organ from scratch-a bladder made cell by cell. Office: Wake Forest Univ Baptist Med Ctr Dept Urology Medical Ctr Blvd Winston Salem NC 27157 Office Phone: 336-716-4131. Office Fax: 336-716-9042. Business E-Mail: cmontgom@wfubmc.edu, aatala@wfubmc.edu.

ATCHISON, JIM D. (JAMES D. ATCHISON), theme park company executive; b. 1966; m. Elli Atchison; children: Caleb, Nathanael, Bethany. BA in Mktg., U. South Fla., 1989; MBA, U. Ctrl. Fla., 1992. Ops. host Busch Gardens Busch Entertainment Corp., Tampa, Fla., 1985, park ops. supervisor than bus. analyst, mgr. bus. analysis SeaWorld San Antonio, 1992, fin. dir., 1994, fin. dir. Busch Gardens Tampa Bay, 1996, fin. v.p., 1998, mktg. v.p. SeaWorld Orlando, 2002—03, exec. v.p., gen. mgr. SeaWorld Orlando, Discovery Cove and Aquatica Orlando, 2003—07, pres., COO, 2007—09; pres., CEO SeaWorld Parks & Entertainment (formerly Busch Entertainment Corp.), 2009—. Mem. Fla. Commn. on Tourism. Bd. dirs. Spl. Olympics, Boys & Girls Clubs, United Arts, Orlando/Orange County Convention and Visitors Bur., Fla. C. of C., Rosen Coll. of Hospitality Mgmt., U. Ctrl. Fla., Dean's Exec. Coun., U. Ctrl. Fla. Coll. Bus. Recipient Charles Andrews Meml. Hospitality Award for Cmty. Leadership, Ctrl. Fla. Hotel & Lodging Assn., 2009. Avocations: soccer, sailing, basketball. Office: SeaWorld Parks & Entertainment 9205 S Park Center Loop, Ste 400 Orlando FL 32819

ATCHLEY, WILLIAM REID, geneticist, computational biologist, educator; b. Stilwell, Okla., Sept. 6, 1942; s. Reid Kenneth and Velma Alice (Mays) A.; m. Wilinda Landon, Sept. 4, 1964; children: Erika Leigh, Kevin Landon. BS, Ea. N.Mex. U., 1964; MA, U. Kans., 1966, PhD, 1969. Postdoctoral fellow U. Melbourne, 1969-70; postdoctoral fellow U. Wis., 1976-77; NSF trainee U. Kans., 1966-69, asst. prof. entomology, 1970-71; asst. prof. biology and stats. Tex. Tech U., Lubbock, 1971-74, assoc. prof., 1974-77; assoc. prof. entomology and genetics U. Wis., Madison, 1977-80, prof. entomology and genetics, 1980-84, prof. genetics, 1984-86; James prof. pure and applied sci. St. Francis Xavier U., Can., 1991; prof. genetics, prof. stats. N.C. State U., Raleigh, 1986-93, William Neal Reynolds disting. prof. genetics and stats., 1993—. Head dept. genetics N.C. State U., 1986—90, dir. Ctr. for Quantitative Genetics, 1993—98, dir. Ctr. for Computational Biology, 2001—10; vis. rsch. fellow U. Melbourne, Australia, 1974; vis. fellow Australian Nat. U., 1980—81. Author: Multivariate Statistical Methods, 1975, Evolution and Speciation, 1981. Recipient Disting. Internat. Prof. award, Chinese Acad. Sci. Shanghai, 2009, Order Long Leaf Pine, Govs. Office, NC, 2011, Alexander Quarles Holladay medal, NC State U., Raleigh, 2011; NIH postdoctoral fellow, 1977, NSF mid-career fellow, 1989—90, Alfred Sloan Found. fellow, 1993—94, Fulbright scholar, 1969—70, Alexander von Humboldt grantee, 1999—, Internat. fellow, Internat. Grad. Sch. Bioinformatics and Genome Rsch., U. Bielefeld, Germany, 2002—. Fellow AAAS, Am. Acad. Arts and Scis.; mem. Soc. Study Evolution (councillor 1980-82, assoc. editor 1984-86), Soc. Systematic Zoology (councillor 1981-83), Am. Soc. Naturalists (v.p. 1986-87) Office: NC State U Dept Genetics 2560 Gardner Hall Raleigh NC 27695-7614

ATHAS, DOUGLAS, Mayor, Garland, Texas; b. Bergstrom AFB, Tex. m. Robyn Athas; 1 child, Shae. Student, U. Tex., Austin. Land man TNT Land Svcs., 1980—90; site acquisition specialist GTE Mobile Net, 1990—91, AT&T Wireless, 1991—95; sr. mgr. telecom. sales Fluor Daniel, 1995; dir. site devel. Prime Co./Verizon Wireless, 1995—2000; rep. Dist. 1 Garland Plan Commn., 1996—2000, at-large rep., 2002—06; cons., 2000—; mem. Garland City Coun., 2006—12, mayor pro tem, 2007—08; mayor City of Garland, 2013—. Office: Office of the Mayor 200 N 5th St Garland TX 75040 Office Phone: 972-205-2400. E-mail: mayor@garlandtx.gov.

ATHERHOLT, WAYNE DAVID, museum director; BA, Pa. State U.; MA in Internat. Comms., Am. U. With Dali Mus., St. Petersburg, Fla.; dir. mktg. and pub. rels. Salvador Dali Mus., 1989—97; v.p. mktg. and exhibits Fla. Internat. Mus., St. Petersburg, Fla., 1997—2001; v.p. retail enterprises Mus. Sci. and Industry, Tampa, Fla., 2001; exec. dir. Mus. Arts & Scis., Daytona Beach, Fla., 2005—. Tchr. mktg. and tourism Schiller Internat. U., Dunedin. Mem.: Fla. Attractions Assn. (former pres.). Office: Mus of Arts & Scis 352 S Nova Rd Daytona Beach FL 32114 Office Phone: 386-255-0285.

ATKINS, BETSY S., environmental services company executive; b. Boston, June 5, 1953; d. Robert and Barbara Fishkind; m. James Daman, Feb. 1, 1983; children: Ashley Elizabeth, Megan Marie, Needham Stone. BA magna cum laude, U. Mass., 1975; postgrad., U. Copenhagen, Denmark, 1975, Oxford U., Eng., 1976. V.p. sales Data Translation, 1977, Interlan, 1978-80; v.p. internat. ops. Bolt Beranek

Newman, 1981-86; v.p. mktg. Unisys Corp., 1987-88; v.p. sales & mktg. Amdalh Corp., 1989, Ascend Communications, 1989—90, Nellson Candies Inc., Hermosa Beach, Calif., 1990—93; chmn., CEO NCI, Inc., 1991—93; pres., CEO Baja Ventures, Miami, 1994—; chmn., CEO Clear Standards, Inc., 2009—. Bd. dirs. Polycom, Inc., 1999—, Reynolds American Inc., 2004—10, Chico's FAS, 2004—, SunPower Corp., 2005—, NASDAQ Exch., LLC, 2008—, Clear Standards, Inc., 2009—; bd. mem. Pension Benefit Guaranty Corp., 2001—03. Bd. trustees Fla. Internat. U., 2001—. Mem. Phi Beta Kappa. Office: Baja Ventures 10 Edgewater Dr Coral Gables FL 33133 also: Clear Standards Inc 21335 Signal Hill Plz Ste 200 Sterling VA 20164

ATKINS, RODNEY, musician; b. Knoxville, Tenn., Mar. 28, 1969; adopted s. Allan and Margaret Atkins; m. Tammy Jo Atkins (div. Sept. 2012); 1 child, Elijah; m. Rose Falcon, Nov. 10, 2013. Attended, Tenn. Tech., Cookeville. Musician: (albums) Honesty, 2003, If You're Going Through Hell, 2006, It's America, 2009, Rodney Atkins, 2010, Take a Back Road, 2011. Recipient Top New Male Vocalist award, Acad. Country Music, 2007. Office: c/o Creative Artists Agency Inc Ste 500 3310 W End Ave Nashville TN 37203-1087*

ATKINS, TENNELL, councilman; m. Marshella Atkins; children: Todd, Tyler. BA in Bus. Adminstrn., SMU. Former mktg. & devel. dept. lead Ford Motor Co. Tractor Div.; councilman, Dist. 8 Dallas City Coun., 2007—. Vice chmn. Econ. Devel. com.; mem. Housing & Pub. Safety coms.; chmn. Task Force on Southern Sector Econ. Opportunities. Bd. mem. SMU Doak Walker Bd. Mem.: Nat. League Cities, Charlie Taylor Found., Oak Cliff Jaguars Youth Found., SMU Lettermen Assn. Office: City Hall 1500 Marilla St Rm 5FS Dallas TX 75201 Office Phone: 214-670-4066. Office Fax: 214-670-5115.

ATKINSON, RICHARD LEE, JR., internal medicine educator; b. Petersburg, Va., May 15, 1942; s. Richard Lee and Ruth (Scarborough) A.; m. Susan Stayner Hume, Aug. 13, 1966; children: Catherine Crane, Barbara Hill, Deborah Gildea. BA, VA Mil. Inst., 1964; MD, Med. Coll. Va., 1968. Divsn. surgeon 101st Airborne Divsn., 1973; chief, dept. medicine Ft. Campbell Army Hosp., Ft. Campbell, 1973—74; liaison endocrinologist Vanderbilt U., Nashville, 1973-74; chief resident, endocrinology Harbor UCLA Hosp., 1977; asst. prof. internal medicine U. Va. Sch. Medicine, Charlottesville, 1977-83; assoc. prof. internal medicine U. Calif., Davis, 1983-87; prof. internal medicine Ea. Va. Med. Sch., Norfolk, 1987-93; assoc. chief staff for rsch. and devel. VA Med. Ctr., Hampton, Va., 1987-93; prof. medicine and nutritional scis., dir. Beers-Murphy Clin. Nutrition Ctr. U. Wis., Madison, 1993—2002; emeritus prof. medicine and nutritional scis. U. Wis., Madison, 2002—; dir. Obesity Inst. Medstar Rsch. Inst., Washington, 2002—04; pres. Obetech, LLC, Richmond, Va., 2004—, dir. Obesity Rsch. Ctr., 2004—. Clin. prof. pathology Va. Commonwealth U., Richmond, 2005—; vis. prof. molecular medicine Karolinska Inst., Stockholm, 2009-; nutrition study sect. NIH, 1991-95, chair, 1993-95; chair subcom. on obesity in the mil. NAS, 1999-2003; chair USDA Intramural Peer Rev. Com., 2003-04, USDA Retrospective Rev. Panel on Human Nutrition Rsch., 2006-07. Contbr. articles to profl. jours. Maj. US Army, 1970—74. Decorated Army Commendation medal. Mem. N.Am. Assn. Study Obesity (pres. 1990-91), Am. Soc. Clin. Nutrition (pres. 1994-95), Am. Obesity Assn. (pres. 1995-2006), Internat. Assn. Study Obesity (trustee), The Obesity Soc. (regional v.p., editor, Internat. Jour. Obesity, Nutrition and Diabetes, Richard L. Atkinson-Judith S. Stern award, 2006). Office: Obetech LLC Va Biotech Rsch Pk 800 E Leigh St Ste 50 Richmond VA 23219 Home: 486 Calm Creek Rd Manakin Sabot VA 23103-3164 Office Phone: 804-708-0432. Business E-Mail: ratkinson2@vcu.edu.

ATLAS, JAY DAVID, philosopher, linguist, consultant, cognitive scientist, educator; b. Houston, Feb. 1, 1945; s. Jacob Henry and Babette Fancile (Friedman) A. AB summa cum laude, Amherst Coll., Mass., 1966; PhD, Princeton U., NJ, 1976. Mem. common rm. Wolfson Coll., Oxford, England, 1978—; vis. fellow Princeton U., 1979; rsch. assoc. Inst. Advanced Study, Princeton, 1982—84, 1986; vis. lectr. U. Hong Kong, 1986; prof. Pomona Coll., Claremont, Calif., 1989—2013, chair dept. linguistics and cognitive sci., 2001—03, 2006—09, Peter W. Stanley prof. linguistics philosophy, 2003—13. Sr. assoc. Jurecon, Inc., LA; lectr. 2d European Summer Sch. in Logic, Lang. and Info., 1990; examiner U. Edinburgh, Scotland, 1993, U. Groningen, Netherlands, 1991, 93-97, vis. rsch. prof., 1995, 2005; vis. prof. UCLA, 1988-95, Max Planck Inst. for Psycholinguistics, Nijmegen, Netherlands, 1997, 2005; vis. fellow Amherst Coll., 2004; honoree, conf. asserting, meaning & implying Pomona Coll., 2005; disting. scholar faculty linguistics U. Cambridge, 2006, invited lectr., Cognitive Sci. Inst. Rutgers U. NJ, & Cognitive Sci. Inst., CUNY Grad. Ctr., NY, 2010. Author: Philosophy Without Ambiguity, 1989, Logic, Meaning, and Conversation, 2005; contbr. articles to profl. jours., popular mags. Mem. Am. Philos. Assn., Linguistic Soc. Am., Phi Beta Kappa, Sigma Xi. Office: 715 Imlay St San Antonio TX 78209 Office Phone: 210-832-9433. Business E-Mail: jaydatlas@alum.exeter.edu.*

ATLAS, NANCY FRIEDMAN, federal judge; b. NYC, May 20, 1949; BS, Tufts U., 1971; JD, NYU, 1974. Bar: N.Y. 1975, U.S. Dist. Ct. (so. and ea. dists.) N.Y. 1975, U.S. Ct. Appeals (2nd cir.) 1975, U.S. Dist. Ct. (so. dist.) Tex. 1982, U.S. Ct. Appeals (5th cir.) 1982, U.S. Dist. Ct. (no. dist.) Tex. 1989. Law clk. to Hon. Dudley B. Bonsal U.S. Dist Ct. (so. dist.) N.Y., 1974-76; assoc. Webster & Sheffield, 1977-78; asst. U.S. atty. So. Dist. N.Y., 1979-82; shareholder Sheinfeld, Maley & Kay, P.C., Houston, 1982-95, also bd. dirs.; judge US Dist. Ct. (so. dist.) Tex., Houston, 1995—. Lectr. numerous programs CLE. Mng. editor NYU Ann. Survey Am. Law, 1973-74; contbr. numerous articles to profl. jours. Chair Tex. Higher Edn. coord. Bd., 1992-95; mem. Tex. Coun. Workforce and Econ. Competitiveness, 1993-95. Fellow: ABA Found. (chair SCFJI 2009—, mem. SOL task force on jud. independence 2006—, mem. SOL fed. practice task force, chair sect. ann. conf.), Houston Bar Assn., State Bar Tex.; mem.: FBA (South Tex. chpt.), ABA (co-chair ADR com. 1994—95, bus. and litigation joint task force on bankruptcy practice 1994—98, co-divsn. dir. litigation sect. 1996—98, mem. coun. 1998—2001), Am. Law Inst., Houston Bar Found. (trustee), Phi Beta Kappa. Office: US Courthouse 515 Rusk St Ste 9015 Houston TX 77002-2605

ATLAS, SCOTT J., lawyer; b. Austin, Tex., Jan. 15, 1950; s. Morris and Rita Jean (Willner) A.; m. Nancy Ellen Friedman, Mar. 26, 1983; 2 children. BA magna cum laude, Yale U., 1971; JD with honors, U. Tex., 1975. Bar: Tex. 1975, U.S. Dist. Ct. (so. dist.) Tex. 1976, U.S. Ct. Appeals (5th cir.) 1976, U.S. Supreme Ct. 1979, U.S. Ct. Appeals (11th cir.) 1981, U.S. Dist. Ct. (we, no. and ea. dists). Law clk. to judge Thomas Gibbs Gee U.S. Ct. Appeals (5th cir.), Austin, 1975—76; assoc. Vinson & Elkins, Houston, 1976—82, ptnr., 1982—2006, Weil, Gotshal & Manges, Houston, 2006—09; pres. Atlas Counsel Search, 2012—. Mem. bd. visitors U. Tex. Law Sch., 1982-90; mem. Chancellors Coun. U. Tex., exec. com., 2001-; mem. Com. of 125, U. Tex., Austin, 2003--; lectr. numerous law schs. and legal orgns, v.p. U. Tex. Law Sch. Alumni Assn., 2012-, ex-oficio mem. U. Tex Law Sch. Fdn., 2012- Chancellor, Coif, editor-in-chief Tex. Law Rev.; contbr. numerous articles to profl. jours. Founding pres. Houston Shakespeare Festival, 1980-82; vice chair, co-founder Tex. Lyceum Assn. Inc., 1983-85; exec. com. Alley Theatre, Houston, 1983—, ex-officio, 1989—; bd. dirs. ADL S.W. Region, 1998—, exec. com., 1999-, chair, 2010; past bd. dirs. Tex. Opera Theatre, Cultural Arts Coun. of Houston, Young Audiences Houston, others; county coord. U.S. Sen. Lloyd M. Bentsen, 1987-92; fin. chair Bill White Gov. Tex. Campaign, 2009-10, US Senate Campaign, 2009; mem. adv. com. Law Firm Project of the Pro Bono Inst., 1991-2010, chmn., 1997-2001. Named one of Outstanding Young Houstonians, Jaycees, 1984-85, Outstanding Young Lawyer in Houston, Houston Young Lawyers Assn., 1984, Outstanding Young Tex. Exes, Tex. Ex-Students Assn., 1989, Tex. Monthly's Tex. Super Lawyers in Bus. Litigation, 2003-, EEOC's 40th Ann. Civil Rights All Stars, 2005, 100 Best Lawyers in Houston, 2005, 07; named Lawyer of the Yr., Mex.- Am. Bar Assn. Tex., 1996, Disting. Alumnus for Cmty. Svc., U. Tex. Law Alumni Assn., 2000; recipient Azteca Civil Rights award, LULAC Dist. XVIII, 1993, spl. recognition for contbns. to cross-border relationships Tex.-Mex. Bar Assn., 1997, Pub. Interest award Tex. Law Fellowship, 1998, ADL Karen Susman Jurisprudence award, 2002, Orden de Mayo al Merito, Govt. Argentina, 2008, Tex. Bar Found., Lola Wright Pub. Svc. award, 2008, Hon. Bar Assn. Aux., 2008, Leon Jaworski award, Cmty. Svc. Fellow Houston Bar Found. (founder, life), Tex. Bar Found. (life), Am. Bar Found. (life); mem. ABA (chmn. litig. sect. 2002-03, chmn. appellate practice com. litigation sect. 1985-89, coun. mem. litigation sect. 1989-92, 2000-06, exec. com. 1992-96, 2000-06, standing com. on pro bono and pub. svc. 1995-98, dir. divns. litigation sect. 1997-98, co-chair fed. practice task force litigation sect. 1998-2000, liaison to civil adv. com. jud. conf. on rules of practice and procedure 1998-2000, planning com. mem. London 2000 meeting 1996-2000, working group on UCITA 2001-2002, Pro Bono Publico award 1986), Am. Law Inst. 2005-, State Bar Tex. (jud. selection funding com. 1985-87, liaison with law schs. 1988-90, legal aid to indigent com. 1986, numerous coms. 1986-87), Alliance for Jud. Funding (bd. dirs. 1992-95, 2003—), Tex. Law Rev. Assn. (past pres., bd. dirs. 1977-95, ex officio, bd. dirs. 1995— Leon Green award 1997), U. Tex. Ex-Students Assn. (exec. coun. 1992-98), Houston Bar Assn. (ADR sect. coun., 2012-13, ADR annual CLE conf chair, 2013, vol. lawyers program bd. 1998-2000), Houston U. Tex. Ex-Students Assn. (bd. dirs. 1991-92), Yale U. Alumni Club (class sec. 1991-96, coun. 1986-87, 2006-11, local dir. 1982-89, 90-91), Govs. Criminal Justice Adv. Coun. (ex officio). Avocations: golf, reading. Office: PO Box 61606 Houston TX 77208-1606 Office Phone: 713-613-5353.

ATTANASIO, JOHN BAPTIST, law educator, former dean; b. Jersey City, Oct. 19, 1954; s. Gaetano and Madeline (Germinario) A.; m. Kathleen Mary Spartana, Aug. 20, 1977; children: Thomas, Michael. BA, U. Va., 1976; JD, NYU, 1979; diploma in law, Oxford U., 1982; LLM, Yale U., 1985. Bar: Md. 1979, U.S. Dist. Ct. Md. 1980, U.S. Ct. Appeals (4th cir.) 1980, U.S. Supreme Ct. 1983. Pvt. practice, Balt., 1979-81; vis. asst. prof. law U. Pitts., 1982-84; assoc. prof. law U. Notre Dame, Ind., 1985-88, prof. law Ind., 1988-92; John M. Regan, Jr. dir. Joan B. Kroc Inst. for Internat. Peace Studies, U. Notre Dame, 1991-92; dean St. Louis U. Sch. Law, 1992-98, Southern Methodist U. Dedman Sch. Law, Dallas, 1998—2008, prof. law, 1998—2013, Judge William Hawley Atwell Chair of Constitutional Law, 1998—, Judge James Noel Dean, 2008—13; disting. vis. fellow NYU Law Sch., 2013—. Mem. Dallas Com. on Foreign Relations, 2001—, Tex. Supreme Ct. Code of Judicial Conduct Adv. Com., 2002—05, Fifth Circuit Judicial Conf. Host Com., 2002; mem. adv. com. Dallas Com. for Foreign Visitors, 2001—; prin. investigator, dir. Rule of Law Forum, 2002—12; mem. planning com. Corp. Directors' Inst., 2001—03. Co-author: Constitutional Law, 1989, 2008-13, Understanding Constitutional Law, 1993, 2012-2013 and others; contbr. to book chapters Chair adv. bd. Ctr. for Civil and Human Rights, 1990-92; mem. Fulbright awards area com., 1994-96; bd. dirs. Legal Svcs. Ea. Mo., 1996-98; bd. dirs. Ctr. for Internat.; mem. Law Sch. Adv. Com., Access to Justice Comm. Recipient Fulbright Award, 1990, Legal Teaching award Sch. of Law, NYU, 1994. Mem. ABA (chair out-of-the-box com., legal edn. sect., mem. fellows adv. rsch. com., coun. mem. internat. law & practice, 1999-), Dallas Bar assn. (coun. mem.), Ctrl. States Law Sch. Assn. (v.p. 1992-94), Soc. Internat. Bus. Fellows, American Law Inst., Appellate Judges Edn. Inst. (bd. dirs. 2002-13, mem. edn. com., 2002-), Phi Beta Kappa, Alpha Sigma Nu. Roman Catholic. Office: Southern Methodist University Dedman School Law PO Box 750116 3315 Daniel Ave Dallas TX 75205-0116 Business E-Mail: jba@smu.edu, attana7@gmail.com.*

ATTAWAY, JOHN A., JR., lawyer; b. Charleston, W.Va., July 17, 1958; BA in Mgmt. Scis., Duke U., 1980; JD, Stetson U., 1982; LLM in Taxation, U. Fla., 1984. Bar: Fla. 1983. Assoc. atty. Raymond, Rupp & Wienberg, Boca Raton, Fla., 1984—86; ptnr. Lane, Trohn, Bertrand & Vreeland, Lakeland, Fla.; corp. counsel Publix Super Markets, Inc., Lakeland, Fla., 1997—2000, gen. counsel, sec., 2000—04, sr. v.p., gen. counsel, sec., 2005—. Chmn. United Way of Ctrl. Fla., 1997—98. Office: Publix Super Markets PO Box 407 Lakeland FL 33802-0407*

ATWAL, ARJUN, professional golfer; b. Asonsal, India, Mar. 20, 1973; m. Ritika Atwal. Attended, Nassau CC, Garden City, NY. Profl. golfer PGA Tour, 1995—. Mem. Asian team Royal Trophy, 2006. Recipient Order of Merit, Asian Tour, 2003. Achievements include winner Asian Tour events: Wills Indian Open, 1999, Hero Honda Masters, 2000, 2003, Star Alliance Open, 2000, Caltex Singapore Masters, 2002, Carlsberg Malaysian Open, 2003, Maybank Malaysian Open, 2008; winner Nationwide Tour events: Chattanooga Classic, 2008; winner PGA Tour events: Wyndham Championship, 2010; becoming the first golfer to win both the qualifier and the following tournament on the PGA Tour since 1986, 2010; the first Indian born golfer to win on the PGA Tour, 2010. Office: c/o PGA Tour 100 PGA TOUR Blvd Ponte Vedra Beach FL 32082

ATWATER, ROBERT, state legislator; Commr. Chatham County, 2000—04; adminstr. U. NC; state senator Dist. 18 NC, 2005—. Mem. Appropriations/Base Budget com., Fin. com., Health Care com., Judiciary II com., Pensions and Retirement and Aging com., Select Com. on Employee Hosp. and Med. Benefits, Select Com. on Energy, Sci. and Tech., Ways and Means com.; co-chmn. Appropriations on Gen. Govt. and Info. Tech. com.; chmn. Agrl., Environ. and Natural Resources com. Recipient medal Meritorious Svc., Air Force Commendation, 1967. Democrat. Office: NC Senate 300 N Salisbury St Rm 519 Raleigh NC 27603-5925 Office Phone: 919-715-3036. Business E-Mail: Bob.Atwater@ncleg.net.

ATWATER, TODD K., state legislator; b. Greenville, Mar. 9, 1966; s. Harold Jeemes and Mary L. (Joyner) Atwater; m. Elizabeth Jeemes, Aug. 22, 1992; children: Caroline, Jim. BS, Wofford Coll., 1988; JD, U. SC, 1991. Chief counsel to Sen. Strom Thurmond, US Senate Labor and Human Relations Com., 1992—94; vol., Pro-Life Counseling Birthright of Columbia, 1995—96; v.p. governmental relations SC Chamber of Commerce, 1995—97; legislative dir. to Governor David M. Beasley, 1997—99; pres., CEO SC Manufacturer's Alliance, 1999—2003; CEO SC Med. Assn., 2003—; bd. mem. SC Office of Rural Health, 2003—; mem. SC Bus. and Industry Polit. Edn. Com., 2005—, Palmetto Family Council, 2007—; mem. Dist. 87 SC House of Representatives, 2010—. Republican. Address: PO Box 1056 Lexington SC 29071-1056 Office: 320D Blatt Bldg Columbia SC 29201 Home: 109 Sommerford Ct Lexington SC 29072 Office Phone: 803-212-6924, 803-798-6207.

ATWOOD, ALEX, state legislator; b. Oct. 09; m. Cynthia Atwood; children: Melonie, James, Cameron. Attended, Ga. State U., MA in Internat. Rels., JD. Former fed. agent; chief legal tng. Fed. Law Enforcement Tng. Ctr., Brunswick, Ga.; COO, gen. counsel Alpha Protective Services, Inc.; magistrate judge and pvt. practice atty. Glynn County, Ga.; mem. Dist. 179 Ga. House of Representatives, 2011—. Mem. vestry Christ Ch. Frederica. Ret. col. USMC Res. Republican. Office: 1515 Newcastle St Brunswick GA 31520 also: Ga House of Reps 401 Coverdell Legis Office Bldg Atlanta GA 30334 Office Phone: 912-265-5515, 404-656-0152. Business E-Mail: alex.atwood@house.ga.gov.

AUBUCHON, GARY, state legislator; b. Ferndale, Mich., July 10, 1962; m. Andrea Aubuchon; children: Julia, Jennifer, Madison. BA in History, U. Mich., Ann Arbor, 1984. Homebuilder, real estate broker; mem. Dist. 74 Fla. House of Reps., Tallahassee, 2006—, chair roads, bridges and ports policy com., vice chair fin. and tax coun., mem. econ. devel. and cmty. affairs policy coun., health care svcs. policy com., select policy coun. on strategic and econ. planning, mem. transp. and econ. devel. appropriations com. Bd. dirs. Cape Coral Cmty. Redevelopment Agency, Cape Coral Constrn. Industry Assn., Cmty. Bank of Cape Coral, Southwest Fla. Cmty. Found. Named Builder of Yr., Citizen of Yr. Cape Coral C. of C., 2001, Hometown Hero Riverside Bank, 2003, Humanitarian of Yr. Am. Red Cross Lee County Chpt., 2003. Republican. Methodist. Office: 218 House Office Bldg 402 S Monroe St Tallahassee FL 32399-1300 also: 4707 SE 9th Pl Cape Coral FL 33904-9017 Office Phone: 239-344-4900, 850-488-7433.

AUCHINLECK, RICHARD H., energy executive; b. Vancouver, Can., 1952; BS in Chem. Engring., U. BC, 1976. Joined Gulf Can. Resources Ltd., Calgary, Canada, 1976, gas utilization engr., supt., heavy oil ops., joint interest coord., gen. mgr. north bus. unit, mgr. engring., mgr. fin. (major projects group), v.p., 1993—95, sr. v.p., internat. and exploration, 1995—97, COO, 1997-98, CEO Gulf Indonesia Resources, 1997—98, pres., CEO, 1998—2001. Bd. dirs. ConocoPhillips, 2001—, Red Mile Entertainment Inc., 2005—08, Telus Corp., 2003—, Enbridge Comml. Trust. Mem.: Geologists & Geophysicists Alta, Assn. Profl. Engineers, Can. Heavy Oil Assn. (life). Avocations: restoring and driving vintage sports cars, skiing, music. Office: ConocoPhillips Bd Directors 600 N Dairy Ashford Houston TX 77079 Office Phone: 281-293-1000. Personal E-mail: richard.auchinleck@conocophillips.com.

AUCUTT, RONALD DAVID, lawyer; b. St. Paul, Dec. 28, 1945; s. Howard Lewis and Eleanor May (Malcolm) Aucutt; m. Grace Diane Kok, Apr. 3, 1976; children: David Gerard, James Andrew. BA, U. Minn., 1967, JD, 1975. Bar: Minn. 1975, DC 1976, Va. 1978, US Supreme Ct. 1978, US Tax Ct. 1980, US Dist. Ct. DC 1980, US Ct. Appeals (DC cir.) 1980, US Ct. Claims 1980, US Claims Ct. 1982, US Ct. Appeals (fed. cir.) 1982, US Dist. Ct. (ea. dist.) Va. 1986, US Ct. Appeals (4th cir.) 1986, Tex. 1999. Assoc. Miller & Chevalier, Chartered, Washington, 1975-81, ptnr., 1982-98, McGuireWoods LLP, McLean, Va., 1998—. Mem. bd. advisors IRS Practice Alert, NYC, 1987—93; adj. prof. Sch. Law U. Va., 1998—2003; mem. adv. com. Philip E. Heckerling Inst. on Estate Planning U. Miami, 1999—. Bd. advisors Jour. Taxation Exempt Orgns., 1989—, Bus. Entities, 1999—, Tax Mgmt. Estate, Gifts, and Trusts Jour., 1999—, Bus. Valuation Update, Portland, Oreg., 1999—2009, mem. editl. bd. Estate Planning, 1993—; contbr. articles to profl. jours. Orgn. Security and Coop. in Europe internat. observer Bulgarian Parliamentary Election, 1997; sec.-treas. Miller and Chevalier Charitable Found., Washington, 1980—92, pres., 1993—97; bd. dirs. Coun. Ct. Excellence, Washington, 1993—99, Advocates Internat., Fairfax, Va., 1997—2000, vice chmn., 1999—2000; mem. adv. bd. Trinity Law Sch., Santa Ana, Calif., 1998—2001; bd. visitors U. Minn. Law Sch., 1998—2004; bd. regents Trinity Internat. U., Deerfield, Ill., 1993—97, bd. regent, 2000—06, 2007—09; bd. dirs. Evang. Free Ch. Am., Mpls., 1986—92, 1993—95, 2007—11, vice moderator, chmn. bd. dirs., 1993—95, moderator, 1995—97, 2007—09; mem. adv. coun. Internal Revenue Svc., 2014—. Lt. USN, 1970—73. Fellow: Am. Coll. Trust and Estate Counsel (bd. regents 1996—2005, chmn. bus. planning com. 1997—2000, sec. 1999—2000, treas. 2000—01, v.p. 2001—02, pres.-elect 2002—03, pres. 2003—04, chair govt. rels. com. 2009—13), Am. Coll. Tax Counsel, Am. Bar Found.; mem.: ABA (chair taxation sect., com. on estate and gift taxes 1986—88, vice chmn. com. on govt. submissions 1989—91, chmn. com. on govt. submissions 1991—93, coun. 1993—97, vice chair com. ops. 1998—2000), Christian Legal Soc., Internat. Acad. Estate and Trust Law (academician 1993—, exec. coun. 2001—04), U. Minn. Law Alumni Assn. (bd. dirs. 1998—2004), Met. Club Washington. Home: 3417 Silver Maple Pl Falls Church VA 22042-3545 Office: McGuire-Woods LLP 1750 Tysons Blvd Ste 1800 Tysons Corner VA 22102-4215 Office Phone: 703-712-5497. Business E-Mail: raucutt@mcguirewoods.com.

AUERBACH, ANITA L., clinical psychologist; d. Ben and Gussie Weiss; m. Steven Miles Auerbach, May 25, 1969. BA cum laude, SUNY, Buffalo, 1968, MA, 1970; PhD, George Washington U., 1977. Diplomate Am. Bd. Med. Psychotherapists, Internat. Acad. Behavioral Medicine. Chief rsch. Youth Crime Control Project D.C. Dept. Corrections, 1970-74; intern clin. psychology No. Va. Tng. Ctr., Fairfax, 1974-75, staff psychologist, then chief psychol. svcs., 1975-79; pvt. practice clin. psychology Commonwealth Psychol. Assocs. PLC, McLean, Va., 1979—; founder,dir. Commonwealth Psychol. Assocs., 1979—, pres., 1979—; bd. dirs. David H. Lawson Found., 2012—. Lectr. Washington Tech. Inst., 1972-74, George Mason U., 1978—82; clin. prof. psychology George Washington U., 2004—; chair RXP Task Force Va. Acad. Clin. Psychologists, 2006-; cons. in field. Contbr. articles to profl. jours. Mem. family edn. project Joseph P. Kennedy Jr. Found., 1977—79; mem. regional appeals bd. No. Va. Pub. Sch. Sys., 1977—79; mem. adv. bd. Value Options Behavioral Health, 2001—03. Fellow N.Y. State Regents 1968-70; recipient N.Y. State Scholar Incentive award, 1969. Mem. APA, Am. Soc. Clin. Hypnosis (approved cons.), Va. Acad. Clin. Psychologists (exec. com. mem.), Va. Psychol. Assn., No. Va. Soc. Clin. Psychologists, Washington Soc. Study Clin. Hypnosis, Assn. Advancement Applied Sports Psychology, Psi Chi, Alpha Lambda Delta. Office: 6801 Whittier Ave Ste 300 Mc Lean VA 22101 Office Phone: 703-734-0787.

AUKOFER, FRANK ALEXANDER, journalist; b. Milw., Apr. 6, 1935; s. Herbert Anselm and Wanda Mary (Kaminski) A.; m. D. Sharlene Talatzko, Aug. 6, 1960; children: Juliann Navarrete, Matthew P., Becky Hawryluk, Joseph J. BA in Journalism, Marquette U., 1960; Fellowship Cert., Northwestern U., 1967. With The Milw. Jour. Sentinel (merger The Milw. Jour., Sentinel), 1960-2000; with Washington Bur. The Milw. Jour. Sentinel, 1970-2000, bur. chief; ret., 2000. Writer automobile review column, 1975—; syndicated DriveWays, 1985—. Author: City with a Chance, 1968, Never a Slow Day, 2009; co-author: America's Team: The Odd Couple, 1995. Bd. dirs. Haven of No. Va., 2005, pres. 2010-11. With USAF Res., 1952-60. Recipient Byline award for lifetime achievement in journalism Marquette U.,

1992, Profl. Merit award Marquette U., awards from Wis. Press. Assn., Milw. Press Club, Soc. Profl. Journalists; Vis. Profl. Freedom Forum First Amendment scholar Vanderbilt U., 1994-95. Mem. Nat. Press Club (pres. 1978, bd. dirs. bldg. corp., Corr. award), Nat. Press Found. (pres., chmn. bd. 1980-85, bd. dirs., 1978-2005), Soc. Profl. Journalists, Standing Com. Corr. U.S. Congress (sec. 1976), Washington Automotive Press Assn. (pres. 1987-88), Gridiron Club Washington. Roman Catholic. Home: 6325 Beachway Dr Falls Church VA 22044

AULBACH, GEORGE LOUIS, retired real estate company executive; b. York, Pa., July 9, 1925; s. George A. and Mary N. (Goulden) Aulbach; m. Gertrude Frisby, June 24, 1949 (dec. Apr. 2004); children: Jeanne, Cynthia, Patricia, Kathleen, Barbara; m. Florence Hipschman, July 9, 2005. BSCE, Villanova U., 1945. Registered profl. engr., Pa., Ga. Field engr., estimator, chief engr., project mgr., exec. v.p R.S. Noonan, Inc., York, Pa., 1946-63; pres., CEO R.S. Noonan, Inc. & Noonan Engring. Corp., York, Pa., 1963-72; pres. systems bldg. divsn. McCrory-Sumwalt, Columbia, SC, 1972-76; pres., CEO, bd. mem. Laing Properties, Inc., Atlanta, 1976-90; ret., 1990; mem. bd. dirs. Parent Co Laing Properties, London, 1976—90; pres. CEO Contract Complience Svcs, Smyrna, Ga., 2008—. Adv. bd. dirs. Bank South, Atlanta; vice-chmn., dir. Cath. Continuing Care Retirement Cmtys., Inc.; adv. bd. Ga. Tech. Rsch. Inst.; dir., treas. York, Pa. Meml. Osteo. Hosp., 1966—72; pres. York ABC Corp., 1966—72. Bd. dirs. Northside Hosp. Found., Cath. Housing Initiative; trustee So. Tech. Found.; cons. non-profit corp. developing affordable housing; chmn. sch. implementation com. Cath. Archdiocese of Atlanta, chmn. fin. com.; vice chmn. Cath. Continuum Care Com. Lt. (j.g.) USN, 1943—46. Decorated Knight Comdr. St. Gregory Vatican. Roman Catholic. Business E-Mail: imdutchman@comporium.net.

AULD, SKIP (HAMPTON AULD), library director; Grad. in Psychology, Davidson Coll., NC; MLS, U. NC, Chapel Hill, 1980; grad. cert. in Pub. Mgmt., Va. Commonwealth U., 2005. With Pub. Libr. Charlotte and Mecklenburg County, Duke U. Librs.; cons. Montgomery County Md. Pub. Libr. sys.; br. mgr. Carroll County Pub. Libr. sys., Westminster, Md.; asst. libr. dir. Chesterfield County Pub. Libr., Va.; dir. Durham County Libr., NC, 2006—. Contbg. editor pub. librs. Mem.: ALA, Pub. Libr. Assn. Office: Durham County Pub Libr 300 N Roxboro St Durham NC 27701 Office Phone: 919-560-0163. Office Fax: 919-560-0137.

AULL, JAMES STROUD, retired bishop; b. Winnsboro, SC, Mar. 3, 1931; s. Luther Bachman and Ruth (Bull) A.; m. Virginia Kloeppel, Aug. 9, 1958; children: Diane, James Jr. (dec.), Virginia Ruth. AB magna cum laude, Newberry Coll., 1953; MDiv cum laude, Luth. Theol. So. Sem., Columbia, SC, 1960; M in Systematic Theology, Luth. Sch. Theology, Chgo., 1970; PhD, Duke U., 1971; DD (hon.), Newberry Coll., 1988. Ordained to ministry United Luth. Ch. in Am., 1961. Pastor St. Timothy Luth. Ch., Camden, SC, 1961-62; instr., staff mem. Luth. Theol. So. Sem., Columbia, SC, 1962-79; sec. S.C. Synod, Luth. Ch. in Am., Columbia, 1979-87, bishop, 1988-96; ret., 1996. Author: Obey My Voice: a Form Critical Study of Selected Prose in the Book of Jeremiah", 1971. Trustee Newberry Coll., 1972-96, sec., 1977-82; trustee Luth. Homes SC Found., White Rock, 1988-96, 2004-, chair, 2005-; trustee Lutheridge/Lutherock Ministries, Inc., 1988-96; bd. dirs. divsn. edn. Evang. Luth. Ch. Am., Chgo., 1988-91, mem. ch. coun., 1991-96, trustee, mem. bd. pensions, 1997-2003; mem. adv. bd. Lowman Home, 2003-2004. Mem. Soc. Bibl. Lit., Rotary (bd. dirs. 1987-90, pres. 1996-97). Lutheran. Home: PO Box 608 White Rock SC 29177-0608 E-mail: jimaull3@aol.com.

AULL, SUSAN, physician; b. NYC; d. Eugene and Ines Aull. BA, Vassar Coll., 1981; MD, N.Y. Med. Coll., 1986. Diplomate Am. Acad. Phys. Medicine and Rehab., Am. Acad. Pain Mgmt. Intern L.I. Coll. Hosp., Bklyn., 1986-87; phys. medicine and rehab. PGY II, III Westchester County Med. Ctr., Valhalla, NY, 1987-89; phys. medicine and rehab. PGY IV Lincoln Hosp., Bronx, NY, 1989-90, Ctrl. Fla. Physicians Rehab., Orlando, 1990-91; med. dir. dept. phys. medicine and rehab. Halifax Med. Ctr., Daytona Beach, Fla., 1992-99; med. dir. 21st Century Rehab. and Wound Mgmt. Ctr., Maitland, Fla., 1992; staff dept. internal medicine Winter Park (Fla.) Meml. Hosp., 1991-96; pvt. practice WWPM&R, Winter Park and Sarasota, 1991—2002; multi-specialty group practice, dir. phys. medicine and rehab. Ctrl. Fla. Physicians Rehab., Orlando, 1990-91; physician Advanced Sports Medicine Ctr., 2002—04, S. Aull MD PA Phys. Medicine Rehab. Electrodiagnostic Consultation, 2002—, IOM Svcs. Inc., 2004—07. Electrodiagnostic cons. SEA Med. Svcs., PA, Goldenrod, Fla., 1990-96; adj. clin. prof. U. Ctrl. Fla., Orlando, 1991-96. Author: (with others) Strength Conditioning for Preventive Medicine, 1992, ISC Control Points - New Generation of Pressure Points, 1993. Recipient Leadership award Defensive Tactics Newsletter, 1993; grantee PPCT Mgmt. Systems, Inc., 1992. Fellow Am. Acad. Phys. Medicine and Rehab.; mem. AMA, Am. Acad. Pain Mgmt., Am. Coll. Sports Medicine. Office: 5535 Marquesas Cir Sarasota FL 34233 Office Phone: 941-487-7244.

AURELL, JOHN KARL, lawyer; b. Tulsa, Sept. 26, 1935; s. George E. and Maxine (Reagor) A.; m. Jane Brevard Collins, Oct. 1, 1960; 1 child, Jane B. BA, Washington and Lee U., 1956; LLB, Yale U., New Haven, Conn., 1964. Bar: Fla. 1964, D.C 1971, U.S. Dist. Ct. (no., mid. and so. dists.) Fla., U.S. Ct. Appeals (5th and 11th cirs.), U.S. Supreme Ct. Gen. counsel to Gov. State of Fla., Tallahassee, 1979-80; pvt. practice, 1964—79, 1980—. Mem. Fed. Jud. Nominating Commn. Fla.; chmn. No. Dist. Fla., 1993—97, mem., 2009—. Mem. exec. com., v.p. Yale Law Sch. Assn., 1975-80; mem. Orange Bowl Com. 1st lt. U.S. Army, 1956-57. Fellow Am. Bar Found., Internat. Soc. Barristers, Am. Coll. Trial Lawyers; mem. ABA, Fla. Bar Assn. (bd. govs. young lawyers sect. 1966-71), Am. Law Inst., Exch. Club, Econ. Club Fla. (chmn. 1997-98), Havana Country Club, Capital City Country Club, Yale Club (NYC). Democrat. Home: 1225 Live Oak Plantation Rd Tallahassee FL 32312-2509 Office: PO Box 13505 Tallahassee FL 32317 Home Phone: 850-385-8844. Personal E-mail: johnaurell@me.com.

AUSMAN, DAN F., healthcare executive; Pres., CEO Irvine Regional Hosp. and Med. Ctr., Irvine, Calif., 1998—2005; v.p., ops. Vanguard Health Sys., Inc., 2005—06; sr. v.p., ops. Vanguard Health Systems, Inc., 2006—. Office: Vanguard Health Systems Inc Ste 100 20 Burton Hills Blvd Nashville TN 37215 Office Phone: 615-665-6000. Business E-Mail: dausman@vanguardhealth.com.

AUSTIN, JOHN RILEY, surgeon, educator, medical expert consultant; b. St. Louis, Feb. 19, 1960; s. Thomas L. and Barbara (Riley) A.; children: Claire Frances, Emily Grace, John Michael. BS with highest honors, U. Wyo., 1982; MD, U. Utah, 1986. Diplomate Am. Bd. Facial Plastic and Reconstructive Surgery, Am. Bd. Otolaryngolgy, Nat. Bd. Med. Examiners. Surg. intern U. So. Calif., L.A. County Med. Ctr., LA, 1986-87, resident otolarynogology, head and neck surgery dept., 1987-91; fellow in head and neck surg. oncology M.D. Anderson Cancer Ctr. M.D. Anderson Cancer Ctr. U. Tex., Houston, 1991-92; asst. surgeon, clin. instr. U. Tex., Houston, 1992-93; asst. prof., asst. surgeon M.D. Anderson Cancer Ctr. U. Tex., Houston, 1993-95, clin. asst. prof., 1995—; adj. asst. prof. dept. otorhinolaryngology/comm. disorders Baylor Coll. Medicine, 1993-95. Otolaryngologic cons. dept. infectious diseases U. So. Calif., 1988-91; mem. utilization com. M.D. Anderson Cancer Ctr., U.Tex., 1993-95, mem. laser com., 1993-95; presenter in field. Cons. editor Head and Neck, Laryngoscope, Otolaryngology-Head and Neck Surgery, Cancer, 1993—, Archives of Otolaryngology; contbr. articles to profl. jours. Mem. Graduate Edn. com. U. Tex., 1994. Fellow ACS, Am. Acad. Otolaryngology (human resource com.), AMA, Am. Acad. Facial Plastic and Reconstructive Surgery (mem. publs. com.), Tex. Med. Assn. (mem. physician oncology edn. program 1993—, mem. com. cancer 1993—), M.D. Anderson Assocs., Soc. Univ. Otolaryngologists, N.Am. Skull Base Soc., Tex. Assn. Otolaryngology, Sir Charles Bell Soc. (founding), Travis County Med. Soc. (jour. com.), Salerni Colegium, Phi Kappa Phi, Phi Beta Kappa, Sigma Nu. Meth. Avocations: photography, fishing, skiing, reading, hunting. Office: 3705 Medical Pkwy Ste 310 Austin TX 78705-1028 Office Phone: 512-458-6391. Personal E-mail: jraustin98@aol.com.

AUSTIN, LLOYD JAMES, III, career military officer; b. Thomasville, Ga., Aug. 8, 1953; m. Charlene Austin. BS, US Milt. Acad., West Point, NY, 1975; M in Edn., Auburn U.; M in Bus. Mgmt., Webster U. Grad. inf. officer basic and advanced courses US Army Command Gen. Staff Coll., US Army War Coll. 2nd lt. US Army, 1975, advanced through grades to gen., 2010; rifle platoon leader, scout platoon leader in Combat Support Co. 3rd Inf. Divsn.; comdr. Combat Support Co., 2nd. Battalion, 508th Inf., asst. ops. 1st Brigade 82nd Airborne Divsn., Ft. Bragg, NC; ops. officer US Army Indpls. Dist. Recruiting Command; comdr. US Army Recruiting Battalion; co. tactical officer US Milt. Acad., NY; S-3 operations, exec. officer 2nd battalion, exec. officer 1st brigade, dir. plans, tng. mobilization security 10th Mt. Divsn., Ft. Drum, NY; comdr. 2nd Battalion, parachute inf. regiment 82nd Airborne Divsn., Ft. Bragg, 1993, G-3, comdr. 3rd brigade; chief, joint ops. divsn. Pentagon, Washington, DC; asst. divsn. comdr. for maneuver 3rd Inf. Divsn., Ft. Stewart, Ga.; commdg. gen. US 10th Mt. Divsn., Ft. Drum, 2003—05; comdr. Combined Joint Task Force Operation Enduring Freedom, Afghanistan; chief of staff US Ctrl. Command (USCENTCOM), MacDill AFB, Fla., 2005—06; comdr. XVIII Airborne Corps., Ft. Bragg, 2006—09, Multi-Nat. Corps-Operation Iraqi Freedom, Baghdad, 2008—09; dir. The Joint Staff, US Dept. Def., Washington, 2009—10; comdr. US Forces-Iraq, Baghdad, 2010—11; vice chief of staff US Army, Washington, 2012—13; comdr. US Ctrl. Command (USCENTCOM), MacDill AFB, Fla., 2013—. Decorated Def. Disting. Svc. medal, Silver Star, Def. Superior Svc. medal, Legion of Merit with oak leaf cluster, Def. Meritorious Svc. medal, Meritorious Svc. medal with four oak leaf clusters, Joint Svc. Commendation medal, Army Commendation medal with five oak leaf clusters, Army Achievement medal with oak leaf cluster, Expert Infantryman Badge, Master Parachutist Badge, Ranger Tab, Joint Chief Staff Identification Badge; recipient Disting. Svc. medal, 2013, Army Public Svc. medal, 2013. Office: US Central Command (USCENTCOM) 7115 S Boundary Blvd MacDill AFB Tampa FL 33621*

AUSTIN, MILES J., professional football player; b. Summit, NJ, June 30, 1984; s. Miles and Ann Austin. BA in History, Monmouth U., West Long Branch, NJ, 2006. Kick returner, wide receiver Dallas Cowboys, 2006—. Active Make-A-Wish Found. North Tex. Named to Nat. Football Conf. Pro Bowl Team, NFL, 2009. Office: Dallas Cowboys One Cowboys Pky Irving TX 75063

AUSTIN, WANDA MURRY, systems engineer; b. NYC, Sept. 08; d. Murry Pompey and Helen Lewis; m. Wade Austin Jr.; children: Wade, Wendell. BA in Math., Franklin and Marshall Coll.; MS in Sys. Engring. and Math., U. Pitts., 1977; PhD in Sys. Engring., U. So. Calif., 1988. Engr. Rockwell Internat., Anaheim, Calif., 1977-79; with Aerospace Corp., 1979—, gen. mgr., Electronic Sys. Divsn., gen. mgr., Mil. Satellite Comm (MILSATCOM) Divsn., sr. v.p., engring. & tech. group, 2001—03, v.p., spl. studies, 2004, sr. v.p., Nat. Sys. Group Chantilly, Va., 2004—08, pres., CEO, 2008—. Mem. adv. coun. NASA; scientific adv. bd. Air Force; lectr. U. So. Calif.; instr. U. Pitts., Carlow Coll.; treas. bd. dirs. Challenger Ctr. for Space Sci. Edn.; coord. tech. sessions World Space Congress, 2002. Contbr. chpt. to book: Quantitative Simulation, 1991. Recipient Outstanding Achievement award Women in Aerospace, 1996, Martin Luther King Spirit of the Dream award, Air Force Space and Missile Sys. Ctr., 1999, Air Force Scroll Achievement, Nat. Reconnaissance Office Gold medal, US Air Force Meritorious Civilian Svc. medal, Nat. Soc. Black Engrs. Alumni Extension award; named one of America's Best and Brightest, Dollars & Sense Mag.; named to Women In Tech. Internat. Hall of Fame, 2007. Assoc. fellow AIAA; mem. NAE, Soc. Women Engrs. (sr. mem., sr., award 1996, Upward Mobility award, 2002), Internat. Acad. Astronautics (fedn. and corr. mem., bd. trustee); sr. mem. Armed Forces Comm. and Electronics Assn. Office: Aerospace Corp 15049 Conference Ctr Dr Ste 600 Chantilly VA 20151-3824

AUSTIN, WOODY, professional golfer; b. Tampa, Fla., Jan. 27, 1964; Grad. in Bus. Adminstrn., U. Miami, Fla., 1986. Profl. golfer, 1986—. Mem. US Team Presidents Cup, 2007. Recipient PGA TOUR Rookie of Yr., 1995. Achievements include winning PGA Tour events including the Buick Open, 1995, Buick Championship, 2004, Stanford St. Jude Championship, 2007. Office: c/o PGA Tour 112 PGA TOUR Blvd Ponte Vedra Beach FL 32082

AUSTRIAN, NEIL RICHMOND, consumer products company executive; b. NYC, Feb. 21, 1940; s. Joseph H. and Jessie Davis A.; m. Nancy Hewitt, Sept. 8, 1962; children: Neil, John, Jennifer, Jessie Davis, Patrick. B.C.E., Swarthmore Coll., 1961; MBA (Baker scholar), Harvard U., 1968. V.p. Laird Inc., NYC, 1968-70; founder, pres. Dryden & Co., NYC, investment banker, 1970-74; exec. v.p. fin., adminstrn. Doyle Dane Bernbach Internat. Inc., NYC, 1974-76, pres., COO, 1976-82, pres., CEO, 1982-84; chmn., CEO Showtime/The Movie Channel Inc., NYC, 1984-86; mng. dir. Dillon Read & Co., Inc., 1987—91; pres., COO NFL, NYC, 1991—99; interim chmn., CEO Office Depot, Inc., Delray Beach, Fla., 2004—05, Boca Raton, 2010—11, chmn., CEO, 2011—. Bd. dirs. Viking Office Products, 1988-98, Office Depot Inc., 1998-, The DIRECTV Group, 2003-. Chmn. bd. Swarthmore Coll., 1989-97; Lt. USNR, 1963-66. Office: Office Depot Inc 6600 N Military Trail Boca Raton FL 33496

AUSURA, MAUREEN K., human resources specialist; Attended, Albright Coll., 1975; BS in Home Economics, Rutgers U., 1977, MBA, 1982. Sr. human resources positions Campbell Soup Co., 1982—96; sr. v.p., human resources Giant Eagle Supermarkets, 1996—2000; v.p., human resources ADM Alliance Nutrition, Inc., 2000—05; corp. v.p., human resources Archer Daniels Midland Co., 2000—05; sr. v.p., human resources Lowe's Companies, Inc., 2005—11, exec. v.p., human resources, 2011—. Office: Lowes Companies Inc 1000 Lowes Blvd Mooresville NC 28117 Office Phone: 704-758-1000. Business E-Mail: maureen.k.asura@lowes.com.

AUTHEMENT, RAY PAUL, college president; b. Chauvin, La., Nov. 19, 1928; s. Elias Lawrence and Elphia (Duplantis) A.; m. Barbara B. Braud, June 1, 1950; children: Kathleen Elizabeth, Julie Ann. BS, U. Southwestern La., 1950; MS, La. State U., 1952; PhD, 1956. Instr. La. State U., Baton Rouge, 1952-56; asso. prof. McNeese State Coll., Lake Charles, La., 1956-57, U. Southwestern La., 1957-59, prof. math., from, 1959, acad. v.p., 1966-73, pres., 1973—. Vis. prof. U. N.C., Chapel Hill, 1962-63 Mem. Downtown Devel. Com. Lafayette, 1972—; commr., mem. exec. com. Lafayette Econ. Devel. Authority, 1988—94; mem. La. Bicentennial Commn., 1973, Lafayette Bicentennial Commn., 1973, Econ. Devel. Com., Lafayette, 1973, Sch. Bd. Fatima Parish, Lafayette, 1963-65; bd. dirs. United Way, 1973, U. Southwestern La. Found., 1967, Gulf South Rsch. Inst., 1985-91; trustee Lafayette Gen. Hosp., 1981—; mem. bd. advisers John Gray Inst., 1982-91, St. Joseph Sem., 1967; mem. Commn. Colleges So. Assn. Colls., 1981-83; active Cajundome Commn., 1988—; bd. dirs. Lafayette Health Ventures, Inc., 1989—2000, 2007, Enterprise Ctr. of La., Inc., 1990—, Affiliated Blind of La., Inc., 1991—98, La. Partnership for Tech. and Innovation, 1989—, chmn., 1993; chmn. Acadiana Navigation Channel Task Force, 1990—; bd. dirs. Coun. for a Better La., 1992—, La. chpt. Leukemia and Lymphoma Soc., 2005. Named Outstanding Citizen of Acadiana Internat. Rels. Assn. Acadiana, 1991; recipient Lafayette Civic Cup award, 1991. Mem. AAAS, Lafayette C. of C. (dir. 1983—), Blue Key, Phi Kappa Phi, Kappa Mu Epsilon, Sigma Pi Sigma, Phi Kappa Theta. Roman Catholic. Home: PO Drawer 41008 Lafayette LA 70504 Office: U La at Lafayette PO Drawer 41008 Lafayette LA 70504 Office Phone: 337-482-6203. Business E-Mail: president@louisiana.edu.

AVANT, GAYLE, political scientist, educator; b. Mercedes, Tex., Aug. 23, 1940; s. George Clarence and Winnie Lela Avant; m. Patricia Kay Coalson, Sept. 1, 1970; children: Samantha, Celia. BA, U. Tex., 1962; MA, U. N.C., 1965, PhD, 1969. Devel. officer AID/State Dept., Washington, 1966—68; asst. prof. Miami U., Oxford, Ohio, 1968—70; assoc. prof., polit. sci. Baylor U., Waco, Tex., 1970—2010; tchr. Am. & Tex. Govt. McLennan CC. Vis. prof. polit. sci., sr. lectr. U. Ballarat, Australia, 1996—97. Editor: Foundations of Citizenship, 1990. Mem. Founders Lions Club Waco, Social Affairs Commn. of Bapt. World Alliance; dem. candidate Tex. Senate, 2010; state dir. Fellowship of Baptist Educators, 2005; dir. Baylor Washington Program, 1985—92; treas. Am.-Thai Found. Bd., 1993—; sec. treas. Coins for Tchrs., 2001—. Mem.: Internat. Assn. Christian Higher Edn., Am. Polit. Sci. Assn. Baptist, Tex. Coun. Social Studies, Nat. Coun. Social Studies, S.W. Social Sci. Assn. Democrat. Baptist. Office: Centex Ednl Svcs 7601 Tallahassee St Waco TX 76712 Office Phone: 254-772-5572. Business E-Mail: Gayle_Avant@Baylor.edu.

AVARD, STEPHEN LEWIS, retired finance educator; b. Chgo., Feb. 16, 1940; s. William Richard and Helen M. (Gundy) A.; m. Bonnie J. Fulford, Sept. 1, 1962; children: Margaret, Stephen Jr., Jean. BA, Northwestern U., 1961; MBA, Tex. A&M U. Commerce, 1976; PhD, U. North Tex., 1983. CFA, 1987. Asst. city mgr. City of Highland Park, Ill., 1961—64; treas., asst. hosp. adminstr. Sherman Cmty. Hosp., Tex., 1964—69; hosp. cons. and zone supr. Tex. State Dept. Health, Austin, 1969—71; real estate broker John King Realtors, Sherman, 1971—73; pres. Miracle Gardens Tex., Sherman, 1973—79; sec., gen. mgr. Med. Mart, Inc., Sherman, 1979—83; prof. fin. Tex. A&M U., Commerce, 1983—2005, head dept. econs. and fin. dept., 1995—2005. Co-author (monographs): Feasibility Study for a Graduate Program in Health Care Administration, 1984, Accounting for the Non-Accounting Manager, 1984, Overview of the Petroleum Industry, 1983, 89, 98; contbr. dozens of articles to refereed profl. jours. and conf. procs., including Jour. Banking and Fin. (Top Six Best Articles, bd. editors Rsch. Mgmt. jour., 1983). Grad. fellow Gulf Oil, Inc., 1982. Mem.: CFA Inst. (cons. 1999, 2002, 2003), Dallas CFA Soc., Rotary Internat. Avocations: boating, travel. Home: 1111 Western Hills Dr Sherman TX 75092-5523 Business E-Mail: steve_avard@tamuc.edu.

AVEDON, MARCIA J., diversified industrial products company and former pharmaceutical executive; b. 1961; BA in Psychology summa cum laude, U. NC, 1983; MS in Exec. Program, Rutgers U.; MS in Indsl. & Orgnl. Psychology, George Washington U., 1987, PhD in Indsl. and& Orgnl. Psychology with honors, 1989. Intern U.S. Army Civilian Ctr., 1984; various positions including assoc. cons., sr. cons., cons. Booz-Allen & Hamilton, Inc., 1985—90; program mgr. Anheuser-Busch Companies, Inc., 1990—92, sr. cons., 1992—93; mgr., corp. succession planning Anheuser-Busch Cos., Inc., 1993—94; dir., mgmt. & orgn. devel. Campbell Taggart Inc. (divsn. of Anheuser-Busch Cos., Inc.), 1994—95; dir. orgn. & leadership devel. Honeywell Internat., 1995—97, v.p., human resources & comm. Performance Polymers, 1997—2000, v.p., human resources and comm. Performance Polymers and Chemicals, 2000—01, v.p., corp. human resources, 2001—02; v.p., talent mgmt. & orgn. effectiveness Merck & Co., Inc. (formerly Schering-Plough Corp.), Whitehouse Station, NJ, 2002, sr. v.p., human resources, 2003—07; sr. v.p., human resources & comm. Ingersoll-Rand Co. Ltd., Montvale, NJ, 2007—. Adv. bd. Human ResourcesOfficer's Acad., mem. corp. leadership coun. Bd. dirs. Jersey Battered Women's Svcs., 2000—; mem. adv. bd. Masters in Human Resources U. S.C., 1998—; corp. sponsor Cornell Ctr. for Advanced Human Resource Studies, 2001—. Mem.: Pharm. Human Resources Assn., Healthcare Businesswomen's Assn., Am. Psychol. Assn., Human Resources Policy Assn. (mem. personnel roundtable), Soc. for Human Resources Mgmt., Soc. for Indsl. and Orgnl. Psychology. Office: Ingersoll-Rand Co Ltd 155 Chestnut Ridge Rd Montvale NJ 07645 Office Phone: 441-295-2838. Office Fax: 201-573-3448. Business E-Mail: marcia_avedon@irco.com.

AVELLA, JOSEPH RALPH, university professor; b. NYC, Nov. 13, 1942; s. Salvatore Ralph and Bianca (Artoni) A.; m. Felicia Robinson Kauffmann, Oct. 13, 2007, Elizabeth Theresa Eberhardt, Aug. 12, 1967 (dec. Aug. 2000); children: Edward Jay, James Joseph. BS in Chemistry, Rensselaer Poly. Inst., Troy, NY, 1964; MA, Cath. U. Am., Washington, 1992, PhD, 1995; MBA, Capella U., Mpls., 2001. Mgr. Md. ops. Great Atlantic and Pacific Tea Co., Inc., 1978-83; program mgr. Honeywell Fed. Sys., Inc., McLean, Va., 1984-86, mgr. integration svcs., 1987-89; dep. dir. mobilization Office Sec. Def., Washington, 1990-92, dir. internat. programs, 1992-93; sr. fellow global strategy program Potomac Found., McLean, 1995-98; prof. and acad. dean Am. Mil. U., Manassas, Va., 1995-98; exec. v.p. Capella U., 1998—2001, prof. bus., 2001—; adj. faculty U. Phoenix, 2010—, Northcentral. U., 2011—. Seminar moderator US Naval War Coll., Newport, RI, 1989-91; sec. NATO Forces Com., Brussels, Belgium, 1992-94; cons. Masi Rsch. Cons., Inc., Boston, 1995-; pres. Delphic Consulting Inc., 1998. Contbr. articles to profl. jours. With USNR, 1964—95. Recipient Achievement award No. Va. Navy League, 1989, Cert. of Apprecation Sec. of Navy, 1986, 88, Award of Appreciation U.S. Naval Sea Cadet Corps, 1986. Mem. Assn. Naval Aviation (past chpt. sec.), Navy League US (former mem. bd. dirs.), Pi Sigma Alpha. Roman Catholic. Office: Capella Univ 225 S 6th St Fl 9 Minneapolis MN 55402 Home: 313 Pine Glen Way Englewood FL 34223 Office Phone: 612-372-9744. Personal E-mail: javella@aol.com.

AVERA, STEPHEN R., lawyer; b. Tallahassee, Fla., Oct. 19, 1956; m. Anne Avera; children: Harrison, Leigh, Hunter. BA magna cum laude, U. Ala., 1978, JD, 1981. Bar: Ala. 1981, Army Ct. Mil. Rev. 1981, U.S. Ct. Mil. Appeals 1982, Fla. 1987, Ga. 1988. Assoc., asst. gen. counsel Flowers Foods, Inc. (formerly Flowers Industries, Inc.), Thomasville, Ga., 1986—98; v.p., gen. counsel Flowers Bakeries (subs. Flowers Foods, Inc.), 1998—2002; sec., gen. counsel Flowers Foods, Inc. (formerly Flowers Industries, Inc.), Thomasville, Ga., 2002—04, 2002—, sr. v.p., 2004—08, exec. v.p., 2008—. Capt. U.S.

Army JAGC, 1981-86. Mem. ABA, Fla. Bar Assn., Ala. State Bar, State Bar Ga. Office: Flowers Foods Inc 1919 Flowers Cir Thomasville GA 31757-1137 Business E-Mail: savera@flowersfoods.com.

AVERILL, ELLEN CORBETT, retired secondary education science educator, administrator; b. Milledgeville, Ga. d. Felton Conrad and Vivian Iris (Brookins) Corbett; m. George Edmund Averill, July 31, 1971; 1 child, John Conrad BS, U. Ga., 1966, MS, 1971; tchg. cert., Columbus Coll., 1979, EdS, 1994. Cert. master gardener Ga., 2006, Ala., 2005, lic. in amateur radio KE4MSQ, 1994. Grad. tchg. asst. U. Ga., Athens, 1966—68; tchr. sci. Decatur City Schs., Ga., 1971—72; tchr. sci., chair dept. Kendrick H.S., Columbus, Ga., 1980—2004; ret., 2004. Rsch. asst. Caretta Rsch. Project, Savannah (Ga.) Sci. Mus., 1985, NEWMAST, Kennedy Space Ctr., 1986; rsch. assoc. Inhalation Toxicology Rsch. Inst., Albuquerque, summer, 1990; instr. sci. Gov.'s Honor Program Valdosta State Coll., summer, 1991, Woodrow Wilson Biotech. Inst., Princeton, N.J., 1993 Contbr. articles to newspapers, jours.; inventor The Wrap-All, 1992 Vol. Hope Harbour, 2004—; v.p. Russell County Master Gardeners, 2007—12; mem. Valley Master Garderners, 2006—; vol. Columbus Botanical Garden, Callaway Garden, 2006—. Mem. NSTA (program com., regional conf. 1993), Nat. Assn. Biology Tchrs. (Outstanding Biology Tchr. 1990-91), Ga. Sci. Tchrs. Assn. (dist. VI rep. 1988-90, secondary rep. 1990-91, pres.-elect 1991-92, pres. 1992-93, conf. coord. ann. conf. 1992, Dist. VI Sci. Tchr. of Yr. 1995), Coalition for Excellence in Sci. Edn. (orgnl. com. 1992-93), Ga. Sci. Tchrs. Edn. Found. (chair 1994-98), Valley Area Sch. Tchrs. (charter, pres.-elect 1996-97, pres. 1997-98), Muscogee Area Literacy Assn. (treas. 1992-93), Nantahala Hiking Club, Franklin Garden Club, Phi Delta Kappa (Tchr. of Yr. 1992, v.p. 2002-03), Delta Kappa Gamma (treas. 2006—12). Unitarian-Universalist. Avocations: art, gardening, radio, mahjong. Home: 126 Waterway Dr Cataula GA 31804-4407

AVERITT, RICHARD GARLAND, III, diversified financial services company executive; b. Kearney, Nebr., Jan. 27, 1945; m. Sandra Louise Smith, June 7, 1967; children: Dawn, Rick, Scott. BA, Duke U., 1967. Cert. fin. planner. Account exec. Merrill Lynch, Pierce, Fenner & Smith, Atlanta, 1976-78; v.p. Consol. Planning Co., 1978-84; reg. rep. Investment Mgmt. & Rsch. Inc. (now Raymond James Fin. Svcs.), Atlanta, 1978—84, v.p. mktg., 1984—91, sr. v.p., exec. v.p., nat. sales mgr., 1991—2002; chmn., CEO Raymond James Financial Services, Inc. (formerly Investment Management & Research, Inc.), 2002—. Founding chmn. Atlanta Area Marine Corps Coord. Coun. Col. USMCR ret. Mem. Mensa. Republican. Office: Raymond James Fin Svcs 880 Carillon Pky Saint Petersburg FL 33716

AVILA, MARILYN, state legislator; m. Alex Avila; children: David, Katherine. Former asst. plant chemist Hanes Dye & Finishing; with King Finishing Co., Hanes Hosiery; dir. orgn. Wake County Republican Party, 1997, 2nd vice chmn., 2001, chmn., 2003; state rep. Dist. 40 NC, 2007—; founder Dye House Chemist; owner Command Performance-Focus One Hairstyling Salons, 1979—90; adminstrn. dir. John Locke Found., 1991—2005. Mem.: Wake County Rep. Women's Club (treas. 1991, pres. 1992—94). Republican. Office: North Carolina House of Representatives 16 W Jones St Room 2217 Raleigh NC 27601-1096 Office Phone: 919-733-5530. Business E-Mail: Marilyn.Avila@ncleg.net.

AWASTHI, SANJAY, medical oncologist; MD, U. Tex., 1986. Diplomate American Bd. Internal Medicine, 1989, American Bd. Internal Medicine-med. oncology, 2001. Intern Univ. Ark., resident internal medicine, 1987—89; fellow med. oncology Southwestern Med. Sch. Univ. Tex.; physician Tex. Health Arlington Meml., Tex Oncology PA. Office: Texas Oncology PA 515 W Mayfield Rd Ste 101 Arlington TX 76014 Office Fax: 817-465-0680.*

AXEL, BERNARD, finance executive; b. Bklyn., May 23, 1946; s. Joseph and Irene (Rosen) A.; m. Tobie Reznik, Sept. 3, 1995. BS, U. Ala., 1967; grad., Am. Inst. Banking, 1970. Asst. cashier, comptroller Nat. Bank of Commerce (formerly Am. Nat. Bank), Birmingham, Ala., 1967-72; supr. internat. travel Travel Anywhere, Birmingham, 1972; acctg. and purchasing agt. U.S. Dept. Justice, Texarkana, Tex., 1972-74; mgr. Styslinger Realty, Birmingham, 1974-75; pres. Christian's Inc., Birmingham, 1975-92, Christian's Tutwiler, Inc., Birmingham, 1992-98; mgr. Tucker Cos., Tuscaloosa, Ala., 1998—; v.p. Tucker Fin. Co., Tucker Title Co., Tuscaloosa, 1998—; v.p., COO Tucker Fin. Co., 2001—03, pres., 2003—, Tucker Title Co., 2004—, gen. mgr., 2007—, comptroller Tucker Cos., 2011—. Gourmet chef Top of Morning show Sta. WVTM-T-V, Birmingham, 1991—, Good Day Ala. WBRC-TV, Birmingham, 1996—. Contbr. recipes to mags. Judge March of Dimes Gourmet Gala, Birmingham, 1986, Miss Ala.-U.S.A. Pageant, 1990, 91, Miss Teen Ala., 1992; mem. gov.'s staff State of Ala., Montgomery, 1968-70, mem. lt. gov.'s staff, 1980-84; bd. dirs. Temple Beth El, 1969-72; mem. adv. bd. U. Ala. Sch. Restaurant Hospitality Mgmt., 1989—, chmn. adv. bd., 1992—. Awarded Key to City of Birmingham, Ala., 1991. Mem. Nat. Restaurant Assn. (cert. foodsvc. mgmt. profl., mem. adv. bd. polit. action com. 1987-98, state chmn. 1993-98, bd. dirs. 1996-98), Am. Culinary Fedn. (bd. dirs. Birmingham chpt., medal 1986, Appreciation award 1991), Ala. Restaurant and Food Svc. Assn. (bd. dirs. 1983-98, pres. 1990-92, trustee self-ins. fund 1994-96, Restaurateur of Yr. 1992, Polit. Eagle award 1994), Birmingham-Jefferson County Restaurant Assn. (bd. dirs. 1981-83, 89-98, Restaurant Operator of Yr. 1995), Birmingham-Jefferson Restaurant Assn. (pres. 1995), Chaine des Rotisseurs (L'Order Mondial des Gourmets Degustateurs 1989, coord. culinaire south ctrl. 1996-97), Les Disciples d'Auguste Escoffier Assn. Gastronomique, Commanderie des Cordon Bleus France. Republican. Avocations: travel, cooking. Home: 1716 Dauphine Dr Tuscaloosa AL 35406-3070 Office: Tucker Cos 3010 Skyland Blvd E Tuscaloosa AL 35405 Home Phone: 205-366-3660; Office Phone: 205-556-3636. Personal E-mail: bernardaxel.axel@gmail.com.

AXTELL, JAMES LEWIS, retired history professor; b. Endicott, NY, Dec. 20, 1941; s. Arthur James Axtell and Laura (England) Levinsky; m. Susan Carol Hallas, Aug. 31, 1963; children: Nathaniel Harsen, Jeremy England. BA in History, Yale U., New Haven, 1963; PhD in History, U. Cambridge, Eng., 1967. Asst. prof. Yale U., New Haven, 1966-72; assoc. prof. Sarah Lawrence Coll., Bronxville, NY, 1972-75; vis. prof. Northwestern U., Evanston, Ill., 1977-78; prof. Coll. William and Mary, Williamsburg, Va., 1978—2008, William R. Kenan Jr. prof. of humanities, 1986—2008; emeritus, 2008—. Vis. prof. Princeton U., 2009—10. Author: The Educational Writings of John Locke, 1968, The School Upon a Hill, 1974, The European and the Indian, 1981, The Invasion Within, 1985 (prize, 1985, 2 prizes, 1986), After Columbus, 1988, Beyond 1492, 1992, The Indians' New South, 1997, The Pleasures of Academe, 1998, Natives and Newcomers, 2001, The Making of Princeton University, 2006; co-author: Indian Missions, 1978, The Princeton Graduate School: A History, 2000; editor: The Indian Peoples of Eastern America, 1981, The Educational Legacy of Woodrow Wilson, 2012; contbr. articles to profl. jours. in field. Bd. trustee Williamsburg Regional Libr., 2011—. Recipient Outstanding Faculty award Va. State Coun. Higher Edn., 1988; fellow Social Sci. Rsch. Coun., 1965-66, Morse Jr. Faculty Rsch. fellow, Yale U., 1969-70, NEH fellow, 1975-77, 86, 92, J.S. Guggenheim Meml. Found. fellow, 1981-82, Am. Coun. Learned Socs. fellow, 1987; rsch grant Princeton U. Libr., 1999. Fellow Am. Acad. Arts and Scis.; mem. Soc. Am. Historians, Am. Soc. for Ethnohistory (pres. 1988-89), The Champlain Soc., Am. Hist. Assn., Orgn. Am. Historians, Colonial Soc. Mass., Pilgrim Soc, Mass. Hist. Soc., Am. Antiquarian Soc., Phi Beta Kappa. Democrat. Avocation: book collecting. Home: 109 Walnut Hills Dr Williamsburg VA 23185-3426 Personal E-mail: jaxtell3@cox.net. E-mail: jlaxte@wm.edu.

AYAZI, FARROKH, engineering educator; PhD, U. Mich., Ann Arbor, 2000. Prof. Ga. Inst. Tech., Atlanta, 2000—. Dir.: Ctr. MEMS and Microsys. Tech. Fellow: IEEE. Office: Ga Inst Tech 777 Atlantic Ave Atlanta GA 30332-0250*

AYCOCK, JAMES J., lawyer; b. McCamey, Tex., May 1, 1944; BA, U. Tex., Austin, 1966, JD, 1969. Cert.: Tex. Bd. Legal Specialization (estate planning and probate law). Ptnr. Bayern & Aycock, P.C., San Antonio. Named one of Top 100 Attys., Worth mag., 2005. Mem.: Am. Coll. Trust & Estate Counsel, San Antonio Bar Assn., San Antonio Estate Planning and Probate Law Assn., Probate Law Assn., San Antonio Estate Planners Coun. (past pres.), State Bar Tex. (estate and gift tax editor and editor-in-chief of the Reporter, past chair real estate, probate and trust law sect.). Office: Bayern & Aycock PC 745 E Mulberry Ste 300 San Antonio TX 78212 Office Phone: 210-731-8300. E-mail: jjaycock@estplanning.com.

AYCOCK, JIMMIE DON, state legislator; b. Bell County, Tex. m. Marie McKamie, 1967; children: Jimmie, Michelle. Owner & pres. Harker Heights & Copperas Cove, 1972—98, Vet. Clinics Killeen; mem. Dist. 54 Tex. House of Reps., Tex., 2007—. Former treas., trustee Ctrl. Tex. Coll. Bd. Mem.: Harker Heights Econ. Devel. Corp. (former chmn.), Mothers Against Drunk Driving, Tex. Vet. Med. Assn., Greater Killeen C. of C., Harker Heights C. of C. (pres.). Republican. Baptist. Office: Room EXT E2.710 PO Box 2910 Austin TX 78768 Mailing: 2916 Illinois Ave Killeen TX 76543 Office Phone: 512-463-0684. Office Fax: 512-463-8987.

AYCOCK, SHARION, federal judge; b. Tupelo, Miss., 1955; BA, Miss. State U., 1977; JD, Miss. Coll. Sch. Law, 1980. Bar: Miss. 1980. Assoc. A.T. Cleve. Law Office, 1980—83; sole practitioner, 1983—87, 1989—2003; ptnr. Soper, Russell, Richardson & Dent, PA, 1987—89; judge First Cir. Ct., Dist. Miss., 2003—07, US Dist. Ct. (no. dist.) Miss., 2007—. Mem.: Miss. Bar Found. Office: 301 W Commerce St, Rm 218 PO Box 847 Aberdeen MS 39730-0847 Office Phone: 662-369-2628. Office Fax: 662-369-8307. E-mail: Judge_Aycock@msnd.uscourts.gov.

AYERS, EDWARD L., academic administrator, history professor; m. Abby Ayers; children: Hannah, Nate. BA, U. Tenn., 1974; PhD, Yale U., 1980. Asst. prof. U. Va., 1980—86, assoc. prof., 1986—92, prof., 1992—93, Hugh P. Kelly prof. history, 1993—2007, Buckner W. Clay dean Coll. and Grad. Sch. Arts and Scis., 2001—07; pres. U. Richmond, Va., 2007—. John Adams prof. Am. studies U. Groningen, Netherlands, 1995; fellow Ctr. for Advanced Study in the Behavorial Scis., Palo Alto, Calif., 1999—2000. Author: Vengeance and Justice: Crime and Punishment in the Nineteenth-Century American South, 1984, The Edge of the South: Life in Nineteenth Century Virginia, 1991, The Promise of the New South: Life after Reconstruction, 1992 (James Rawley prize Orgn. Am. Historians, 1992), The Strange Career of Thomas Jefferson: Race, Slavery, and American Memory, 1943-1993, 1993 (Frank L. and Harriet C. Owsley award So. Hist. Assn., 1993), All Over the Map: Rethinking American Regions, 1996, The Oxford Book fo the American South: Testimony, Memory, and Fiction, 1997, American Passages: A History of the United States, 2000, The Valley of the Shadow: Two Communities in the American Civil War--The Eve of War, 2000, In the Presence of Mine Enemies: War in the Heart of America, 1859-1863, 2003 (Bancroft prize, 2004), What Caused the Civil War: Reflections on the South and Southern History, 2005. Recipient James Willard Hurst prize, Law and Soc. Assn., 1986, Nat. Humanities Medal, Nat. Endowment for the Humanities, 2012; named Univ. Prof. of Yr., Carnegie Found., 2003. Mem.: Am. Assn. Arts and Scis. Office: University of Richmond / Office of President Maryland Hall, Suite 200 28 Westhampton Way Richmond VA 23173 Office Phone: 804-289-8100. Office Fax: 804-287-6540. E-mail: eayers@richmond.edu.*

AYERS, HOWARD T., lawyer; b. St. Louis, 1944; BA in Econ. & Bus. Adminstrn., Rice U., 1966; JD with honors, U. Houston, 1969. Bar: Tex. 1969. Ptnr., real estate Andrews Kurth LLP, Houston, mng. ptnr. of firm, 1997—2007, sr. ptnr., 2007—, mem. exec. com., chmn. fin. com. Bd. dirs. U. Houston Law Found., Greater Houston Partnership; mem. adv. bd. Tex. State Bank. Recipient Glass Ceiling award, Tex. Diversity Coun., 2008. Mem.: Tex. Coll. Real Estate Attys., ABA, State Bar Tex., Houston Real Estate Lawyers Coun., Houston Bar Assn., Order of Barons, Phi Kappa Phi, Phi Alpha Delta. Office: Andrews Kurth LLP 600 Travis St Ste 4200 Houston TX 77002-3090 Office Phone: 713-220-4044. Office Fax: 713-238-7151. Business E-Mail: hayers@andrewskurth.com.

AYERS, NICK (JAMES NICHOLAS AYERS), political organization executive; b. Ga., 1982; m. Jamie Floyd, 2005. BA, Kennesaw State U., 2009. Mgr. Gov. Sonny Perdue's Re-election Campaign, 2004—06; exec. dir. Republican Governors Assn., Washington, 2007—11; campaign mgr. Tim Pawlenty's Presdl. Exploratory Com., 2011—. Named one of The 50 Politicos to Watch, Politico, 2010, The Politics 40 Under 40, TIME Mag., 2010. Republican.

AYERS, RANDY, professional basketball coach; b. Apr. 16, 1956; m. Carol Ayers; children: Ryan, Cameron. BA in Edn., Miami Univ., Oxford, Ohio, 1978, MA, 1981. Profl. basketball player Reno Bighorns, We. Basketball Assn., 1978—79; grad. asst. Miami U. Red Hawks, 1979—81; asst. coach US Mil. Acad. Black Knights, West Point, NY, 1981—83, Ohio State U. Buckeyes, Columbus, 1983—89, head coach, 1989-97; phys. conditioning coach Phila. 76ers, 1997—98, asst. coach, 1998—2003, 2009—10, head coach, 2003—04; asst. coach Orlando Magic, 2004—07, Washington Wizards, 2007—09, New Orleans Pelicans (formerly New Orleans Hornets), 2010—. Asst. coach, US nat. team Pan Am. Games, 1991; head coach Big Ten Conf. All-Star Team, 1995. Participant NBA's Basketball Without Borders, Johannesburg, 2006. Named Nat. Coach of Yr., AP, 1991, Black Coaches Assn., 1991, Big Ten Coach of Yr., 1991, 1992; named to Springfield North Hall of Fame, Miami U. Hall of Fame. Office: New Orleans Pelicans 5800 Airline Dr Metairie LA 70003*

AYLOR, JAMES HIRAM, engineering professor, dean; b. Charlottesville, Va., May 30, 1946; s. Melvin Winfrey and Mary Yager (Payne) Aylor; m. Sherry Lynn Kendall, Oct. 20, 1973; children: Jennifer K., David A. BSEE, U. Va., 1968, MSEE, 1971, PhD in elec. engring., 1977. Mem. faculty elec. engring. U. Va., Charlottesville, 1978—, chair dept. elec. engring., 1996—2003, assoc. dean. academic programs Sch. Engring. and Applied Sciences, 2003—, interim dean. Sch. Engring. and Applied Sci., 2004—05, dean. Sch. Engring. and Applied Sci., 2005—, Louis T. Rader Prof. Author: Performance and Fault Modeling with VHDL, 1991, Codesign of Embedded Systems: A Unified Hardware/Software Representation, 1996; contbr. articles to profl. jours. Recipient Outstanding Svc. award, Va. Engring. Found., Charlottesville, 1991. Fellow: IEEE (pres. computer soc. 1993, editor-in-chief IEEE Computer). Methodist. Office: U Va Sch Engring and Applied Sciences Box 400246 Charlottesville VA 22904-4246 Office Phone: 434-924-3310. Office Fax: 434-924-3555. Business E-Mail: jha@virginia.edu.

AYMOND, GREGORY MICHAEL, archbishop; b. New Orleans, Nov. 12, 1949; B, St. Joseph's Sem. Coll., St. Benedict, La.; MDiv, Notre Dame Sem., New Orleans, 1975; postgraduate studies, Loyola Univ. Inst. Ministry. Ordained priest Archdiocese of New Orleans, 1975, parish priest, 1975—81; tchr. St. John Vianney Prep. Sem., 1973—79; dir. pastoral edn., prof. pastoral counseling & homiletics Notre Dame Sem., New Orleans, 1981—86, pres., rector, 1986—2000; ordained bishop, 1997; aux. bishop Archdiocese of New Orleans, 1997—2000; coadjutor bishop Diocese of Austin, Tex., 2000—01, bishop, 2001—09; archbishop Archdiocese of New Orleans, La., 2009—. Dir., mem. nat. bd. Pontifical Mission Societies, 1977—2000; chmn. Nat. Catholic Edn. Assn., 2000—04, U.S. Bishops' Com. on Protection of Children & Young People, U.S. Bishops' World Missions Com.; founder & dir. Christ the Healer Med. Mission prog., Granada, Nicaragua. Co-author: Facing Forgiveness, 2007. Mem.: U.S. Conf. Catholic Bishops. Roman Catholic. Office: Archdiocese of New Orleans 7887 Walmsley Ave New Orleans LA 70125-3496 Office Phone: 504-861-9521. Office Fax: 504-866-2906.

AYSCUE, EDWIN OSBORNE, JR., lawyer; b. May 21, 1933; s. Edwin Osborne and Grace Elizabeth A.; m. Emily Mizell Urquhart, Aug. 17, 1957; children: Grace, E. Osborne, Emily Hassel, Margaret Certain. Grad. cum laude, Phillips Acad., Andover, Mass., 1951; AB in Polit. Sci., U. NC, Chapel Hill, 1954, JD with honors, 1960. Bar: NC 1960, US Supreme Ct. 1979. Of counsel Helms Mulliss & Wicker, PLLC (and predecessor firms), 1960—2008; counsel McGuire Woods LLP, 2008—. Mem. Civil Justice Reform Act Com., Western Dist. N.C., 1991—95. Editor-in-chief: NC Law Rev., 1959-60; contbr. articles to profl. jours. Bd. dirs. Legal Svcs. of So. Piedmont, 1983-85, Am. Judicature Soc., 1985-89, Legal Svcs. of NC, 1984-85, 88-94, US Supreme Ct. Hist. Soc., 1999-2003, adv. bd. mem., Inst. Advancement Am. Legal Sys., 2006-; bd. visitors U. NC Chapel Hill, 2000-04; trustee St. Mary's Sch., Raleigh, NC, 2000-04; sr. warden Christ Episcopal Ch., 1990-91. Lt. USNR, 1955-57. Fellow: Am. Coll. Trial Lawyers (pres. 1998—99), Am. Bar Found. (life); mem.: ABA (ho. of dels. 1991—95, standing com. fed. judiciary 2001—04), People's Republic of Cuba Legal Exch. (chair 2001), People's Republic of China Legal Exch. (chair 1987), Anglo-Am. Legal Exch. (co-chair 1999—2000), Mecklenburg County Bar (pres. 1980—81), NC State Bar, NC Bar Assn. (pres. 1984—85, Gen. Practice Hall of Fame), 4th Cir. Jud. Conf., Nat. Conf. Bar Pres., U. NC Chapel Hill Law Alumni Assn. (pres. 1999—2000), Order of Coif, Order Golden Fleece, Charlotte Country Club, Phi Beta Kappa. Democrat. Episcopalian. Office: McGuire Woods LLP PO Box 31247 Charlotte NC 28231-1247 Office Phone: 704-343-2058. Business E-Mail: oayscue@mcguirewoods.com.

AYUS, JUAN CARLOS, nephrologist; b. Buenos Aires, Feb. 25, 1941; arrived in U.S., 1973; s. Jose and Matilde A.; m. Linda Maria Giudici; children: Sebastian, Mariana. BS, Nat. Coll., 1959; MD, U. Buenos Aires, 1967. Diplomate Am. Bd. Internal Medicine, Am. Bd. Nephrology. Resident in internal medicine U. Buenos Aires, 1968-71, fellow in nephrology, 1971-72; resident in internal medicine U. Mass., Worcester, 1973-74, U. Minn., Mpls., 1974-75; fellow in nephrology U. Calif., San Francisco, 1975-77; chief renal svc. Ben-Taub Regional hosp., Houston, 1977-84; from assoc. prof. to prof. medicine Baylor Coll. Medicine, Houston, 1984—2001; prof. medicine U. Tex. Health Sci. Ctr., San Antonio, 2001—. Recipient Gold Insignia, Spanish Soc. Nephrology, 1999. Fellow ACP; mem. L.Am. Soc. Nephrology (sec.-treas. 1993-96, v.p. 1996-99), Argentine Soc. Critical Care (founder). Home: 2412 Westgate Houston TX 77019 Office Phone: 713-502-0543. Personal E-mail: carlosayus@yahoo.com.

AZAR, J. J., engineering educator; b. Tripoli, Lebanon, Sept. 19, 1937; arrived in U.S., 1957; s. Joseph and Sarah Azar; m. Zaetta Jean Bradshaw, Dec. 23, 1961; children: Scott J., Steven Zay. BS, U. Okla., Norman, 1960; MS, U. Okla., 1961, PhD, 1965. Lic. profl. engr., Okla. Asst. prof. U. Tulsa, 1965—69, assoc. prof., 1969—75, prof., 1975—96, McMen Chair prof., 1996—2002, prof. emeritus, 2002—. Dir. U. Tulsa Drilling Rsch. Projects, 1975—96; chmn. award com. AIME, NYC, 1997. Author: Matrix Structural Analysis, 1972, Aircraft Structures, 1982, Drilling Fluids, 1986, Drilling Engineering, 2006; contbr. articles to profl. jours. Mem.: Nat. Acad. Engring., Soc. Petroleum Engrs. (chmn. award com. 1994—, Disting. Achievement Prof. in Petroleum Engring. 1997, Drilling Engring. award 1998, Disting. Mem. award 2004). Republican. Presbyterian. Avocations: tennis, golf, skiing. Office: U Tulsa 600 S College Tulsa OK 74104 Home: 20603 Fairway Meadow Ln Spring TX 77379 Home Phone: 832-717-7938; Office Phone: 918-631-5170. Personal E-mail: adc.training@sbcglobal.net.

AZARENKA, VICTORIA, professional tennis player; b. Minsk, Belarus, July 31, 1989; d. Fedor and Alla Azarenka. Profl. tennis player WTA, 2003—. Mem. Belarusian nat. team Fed Cup, 2005, Summer Olympic Games, 2008, 2012. Recipient Jr. World Girls' Champion 2005 award, ITF, 2006, Gold medal, mixed doubles; Bronze medal, women's singles, Summer Olympic Games, 2012. Achievements include winner 12 career singles titles, 6 career doubles titles, WTA; winner 1 career singles title, 3 career doubles title, ITF; winner Grand Slam mixed-doubles titles: US Open, 2007; French Open, 2008; winner Grand Slam singles title: Australian Open, 2012. Avocations: music, reading. Office: WTA Corp Hdqs 1 Progress Plz Ste 1500 Saint Petersburg FL 33701

AZINGER, PAUL, professional golfer; b. Holyoke, Mass., Jan. 6, 1960; m. Toni Azinger; 2 children. Student, Broward Jr. Coll., Fla., Fla. State U. Profl. golfer, 1981—. Mem. US Team World Cup, 1989, Ryder Cup, 1989, 1991, 1993, 2002, capt. US Team, 2008; co-capt. US Team Pres.'s Cup, 1994, mem. US Team, 2000. Author: Zinger, 1995. Named PGA Tour Player of Yr., 1987, Golf World Player of Yr., 1987; receipient Ben Hogan award Golf Writers Assn. of Am., 1995. Achievements include winning PGA Tour events including the Phoenix Open, 1987, Panasonic Las Vegas Invitational, 1987, Canon Sammy Davis Jr.-Greater Hartford Open, 1987, 89, Hertz Bay Hill Classic, 1988, MONY Tournament of Champions, 1990; winning international events including: BMW International Open, 1990, 92; winner, AT&T Pebble Beach Nat. Pro-Am, 1991, THE TOUR Championship, 1992, Meml. Tournament, 1993, New England Classic, 1993, PGA Championship, 1993, Sony Open in Hawaii, 2000; being a member of the Ryder Cup winning US team, 1991, 1993, 2008. Office: PGA Tour 112 Tpc Blvd Ponte Vedra Beach FL 32082-3077

AZMI, ZALMAI, information technology executive; arrived in USA, 1982, naturalized; married; 3 children. MS in Info. Mgmt. System, George Washington U., 1997. Cert. info. security mgr., tchr. US Marine Corps. With United States Marine Corps, 1984—91; computer scientist US Patent and Trademark Office, 1992—99; chief info. officer Exec. Office US Attys., 1999—2004, Fed. Bur. Investigation,

2004—08; sr. v.p. Strategic Law Enforcement and Nat. Security Progam CACI Internat. Inc., 2008—. Bd. dirs. InfraGard Nat. Members Alliance. Worked US Marine Corps., US Army. With USMC, 1984—91. Recipient Spl. Act award, Mil. Commendations and medal, Bronze medal, Dept. Commerce, Outstanding Performance Ratings award, 1992, Sr. Exec. Svc. Bonus award, 2002—, Arthur S. Flemming Excellence award, 2003, Pres. G.W. Bush award, 2004, Presdl. Disting. Exec. award, 2005. Mem.: IEEE, Info. Security Audit and Control Alliance, Intelligence and Nat. Security Assn., Nat. Def. Indsl. Assn., Info. Tech. Adv. Coun., Nat. Bd. Dirs. Infragard, PADI Diving Soc. Muslim. Avocations: diving, soccer, camping, reading, movies. Office: CACI International Inc 1100 N Glebe Rd Arlington VA 22201 Office Phone: 703-679-3122. Office Fax: 703-679-3130. Business E-Mail: zazmi@caci.com.

BABALIAROS, VASILIS C., cardiologist, educator; BSE in Biomedical Engring. summa cum laude, Duke U., Durham, NC, 2002; MD magna cum laude, Emory U., Atlanta, 1996. Diplomate Am. Bd. Internal Medicine, 1999, Am. Bd. Internal Medicine-cardiovasc. disease, 2003, Am. Bd. Internal Medicine-interventional cardiology, 2004, lic. 44160 Ga., 2007. Asst. prof. medicine Emory Univ. Sch. of Medicine, Atlanta, 1996—, resident, 1996—99, chief resident, 1999—2000, fellow divsn. of cardiology, 2000—03, fellow divsn. of interventional cardiology, 2003—04, assoc. dir. Emory Ctr. for Valvular Intervention and Structural Heart Disease Treatment, 2006—; fellow interventional tng. in valvular heart disease Univ. of Rouen, France, 2004—05; hospital affiliations include Emory Univ. Hosp., Emory Univ. Hosp. Midtown, Grady Meml. Hosp. Participant Am. Coll. of Cardiology Annual Sci. Session, 2004, Osterreichischen Kardiologischen Gesellschaft (Nat. Congress of the Austrian Soc. of Cardiology), Salzburg, Austria, 2004, Internat. Workshop on Interventional Pediatric Cardiology, Milan, 2005, Congresso da Sociedade Brasileira de Hemodinamica e Cardiologia Intervencionista (XXVII Nat. Congress of the Brazilian Soc. of Interventional Cardiology), Goiania, Brazil, 2005, Fundamentals of Critical Care Support (FCCS) Course, 2005, The Tandem of Heart Experience at Emory Univ. Hosp., 2007. Author/co-author: various sci. rsch. articles and manuscripts. Grantee Am. Heart Assn., 2002. Mem.: Alpha Omega Alpha Honor Soc. Office: Emory University Hospital 1364 Clifton Rd Ste F606 Atlanta GA 30322 Office Phone: 404-712-7667. E-mail: vbabali@emory.edu.*

BABB, FLORENCE EVELYN, anthropologist, educator; b. Goshen, NY, Feb. 21, 1951; d. Roland Walker Babb, Marjorie (Knapp) Babb; 1 child, Daniel. BA in Anthropology and French, Tufts U., 1973; MA in Anthropology, SUNY Buffalo, 1976, PhD in Anthropology, 1981. Vis. asst. prof. anthropology Colgate U., Hamilton, NY, 1979—82; asst. prof., prof. anthropology and women's studies U. Iowa, Iowa City, 1982—2004, chair anthropology dept., 2001—03; prof. women's studies U. Fla., Gainesville, 2005—. Resident Bellagio Ctr., 2003. Author: Between Field and Cooking Pot: The Political Economy of Market Women in Peru, 1998, After Revolution: Mapping Gender and Cultural Politics in Neoliberal Nicaragua, 2001, The Tourism Encounter: Fashioning Latin American Nations & Histories, 2011. Recipient Fulbright award, 1990-91, Wenner-Gren award 1991, Rockefeller Found., 1992. Mem. Am. Anthropol. Assn., Latin Am. Studies Assn., Assn. for Feminist Anthropology. Office: Ctr Women's Studies and Gender Rsch Univ Fla PO Box 117352 Gainesville FL 32611 Home Phone: 352-372-5855. Business E-Mail: fbabb@ufl.edu.

BABB, JOSEPH DOLBY, physician; b. Columbus, Ohio, Apr. 16, 1939; s. Joe A. and Dorothe (Dolby) B.; m. Anne Tanner Hammerlund, Sept. 2, 1969 (div. Apr. 1985); children: Elizabeth Anne, Peter Dolby; m. Margo Tregenza, Oct. 6, 1990. BA magna cum laude, Kenyon Coll., Gambier, Ohio, 1961; MD, Johns Hopkins U., Balt., 1966. Diplomate in internal medicine and cardiovasc. diseases, internat. cardiology, Am. Bd. Internal Medicine; cert. physician, Pa., Conn., NC. Intern Mass. Gen. Hosp., Boston, 1966-67, resident in internal medicine, 1967-68, clin. and rsch. fellow, 1970-72; teaching fellow Harvard Med. Sch., Boston, 1970-72; asst. prof. medicine cardiology Pa. State U. Sch. Medicine, Hershey, 1972-76, assoc. prof., 1976-80; chief of cardiology Bridgeport Hosp., Conn., 1980-95; clin. assoc. prof. medicine (cardiology) Yale U., New Haven, 1980-95; prof. medicine (cardiology) East Carolina U. Sch. Medicine, Greenville, 1995—. Bd. dir., pres. Alcohol and Drug Dependency Coun., Westport, Conn., 1987-95. Maj. US Army, 1968—70, Vietnam. Fulbright fellow, Utrecht, Netherlands, 1961-62. Fellow Am. Coll. Cardiology (gov. 1987-90, 2002-05), Am. Heart Assn. (coun. clin. cardiology), Soc. Cardiac Angiography and Intervention (trustee 1993-99, pres. 2001-02), Coalition Cardiovasc. Orgns. (pres. 2004-05). Avocations: fishing, hiking. Office: East Carolina Univ Sch Med 115 Heart Dr Rm 3231 Greenville NC 27834 Business E-Mail: babbj@ecu.edu.

BABB, RALPH W., JR., bank executive; b. Sherman, Tex., Feb. 4, 1949; s. Ralph Wheeler and Billie Margaret (Odneal) B.; m. Barbara Louise Alexander, Aug. 30, 1970; children: Dana P., Derek R. BSBA, U. Mo., Columbia, 1971. CPA, Mo. Audit mgr. Peat, Marwick, Mitchell & Co., 1971-78; contr., sr. v.p. Mercantile Bancorp. Inc., 1978-83, treas., 1979-83, CFO, exec. v.p., 1983-94, vice chmn., 1987-95; exec. v.p. Comerica Inc., 1995—99, CFO, 1995—2002, vice chmn., 1999—2001; chmn., pres., CEO Comerica Inc., 2002—, Comerica Bank (subs. Comerica Inc.), 2002—. Bd. dirs. Tex. Instruments, The Clearing House, Dallas Citizens Coun., Dallas Regional Chamber. Mem. Fin. Execs. Inst. (pres. St. Louis chpt. 1986-87). Methodist. Office: Comerica Inc Comerica Bank Tower 1717 Main St Dallas TX 75201 Office Phone: 214-969-6476. Business E-Mail: rwbabbjr@comerica.com.

BABIN, CLAUDE HUNTER, history professor; b. Baton Rouge, Feb. 6, 1924; s. Ventress Victor and Essie (Bond) B.; m. Barbara Ann Murphy, Dec. 29, 1947; 1 son, Claude Hunter. BA, La. State U., 1945; MA, U. Wis., 1946; PhD, Tulane U., 1954; LLD, Hendrix Coll., 1965. Instr. history U. Miami, Fla., 1946-49; grad. fellow Tulane U., 1949-54; asst. prof., asso. prof., then prof. history Ark. A. and M. Coll., Monticello, 1954-60, acad. dean, 1960-62, pres., 1962-71; chancellor U. Ark. at Monticello, 1971-77, prof. history, 1977-92, chancellor, prof. emeritus, 1992—. Ford fellow, 1951-52 Mem. Am. Hist. Assn., Ark. Hist. Assn., Ark. Farm Bur. Fedn., Drew County Hist. Soc., Kappa Sigma, Phi Alpha Theta, Pi Sigma Alpha. Democrat. Methodist. Home: 135 Ross Ave Monticello AR 71655-4249

BABUSKA, IVO MILAN, mathematics professor; b. Prague, Czechoslovakia, Mar. 22, 1926; PhD in Civil Engring., Tech. U. Prague, 1951; PhD in Math., Czech Acad. Sci., 1955, DSc in Math., 1960. Rsch. fellow Math. Inst., Czech Acad. Sci., 1951—55, dept. head, 1956—68; disting. prof. math. U. Md., College Park, 1968—95; Robert Trull chair engring., ICES sr. rsch. scientist, prof. aerospace engring. engring. mechanics, math. U. Tex., Austin, 1995—; f. Contbr. articles to profl. jours. Recipient Czechoslovak State award for Math., 1968, Alexander von Humboldt Sr. Scientist award, 1977, 1994, Bolzano Medal, Czech Acad. Scis., 1996 (Birkhoff prize AMS/SIAM, 1994) Congress medal IACM. Fellow Soc. Indsl. Applied Math., US Assn. Computational Mechanics; mem. NAE, The Acad. Medicine, Engring., and Sci. Tex., European Acad. Sci., Eng. Acad. Czech Rep. Achievements include rsch. on numerical analysis of partial differential equations, applied mathematics. Office: Inst Computational Engring Sci ACE 4 102 University Tex Austin TX 78712 Office Phone: 512-471-2156. Office Fax: 512-471-8694. E-mail: babuska@ices.utexas.edu.

BACALLAO, MANUEL D., family practice physician; MD, Autonomous U. Guadalajara, 1977. Diplomate American Bd. Family Practice, lic. Fla., 1981. Intern Univ. of Miami, 1980, resident family medicine, 1980—83; hosp. affiliations include Baptist Hosp. of Miami, South Miami Hosp. Recipient Patients' Choice award, 2008, 2010. Office: South Miami Hospital 8525 SW 92 St Ste B-4 Miami FL 33156 Office Phone: 305-279-7446. Office Fax: 305-598-8753. E-mail: Danielle@Alyanimed.com.

BACCHELLI, SANDRO, family practice physician; MD, Facolta Di Medicina E Chirurgia, 1980. Diplomate Am. Bd. Family Practice. Resident family medicine Univ. of Miami-Jackson Memorial Med. Ctr., Miami, Fla., 1990—92; hosp. affiliations include Aventura Hosp. and Med. Ctr., Mt. Sinai Med. Ctr. Office: Aventura Hospital and Medical Center 750 S Federal Hwy Hollywood FL 33020 Office Phone: 954-342-8700. Office Fax: 954-342-8700.

BACHARACH, ROBERT EDWIN, federal judge; b. Clarksdale, Miss., May 20, 1959; s. Marvin Jerome & Norma Sarah (Pries) B.; m. Rhonda Diane Kinsey, Oct. 15, 1994. BA, U. Okla., 1981; JD, Washington U., St. Louis, 1985. Bar: Okla. 1985, US Dist. Ct. (western dist.) Okla. 1985, US Ct. Appeals (10th cir.) 1986, US Supreme Ct. 1989, US Dist. Ct. (eastern dist.) Okla. 1990, US Dist. Ct. (northern dist.) Okla. 1993. Law clk. to Hon. William J. Holloway Jr. US Ct. Appeals (10th Cir.), Oklahoma City, 1985-87; shareholder, dir. Crowe & Dunlevy, Oklahoma City, 1987-94; magistrate judge US Dist. Ct. (western dist.) Okla., 1994—2013; judge US Ct. Appeals (10th Cir.), 2013—. Office: US Courthouse 200 NW 4th St Oklahoma City OK 73102 Office Phone: 405-609-5320.

BACHMANN, BILL, photographer; b. Pa., Mar. 4, 1946; s. Ernest Edward and Helen May B. BS, Roberts Wesleyan Coll., Rochester, NY, 1967; MBA, NYU, 1971; MFA, U. London, 1973; postgrad., Oxford U., U. Calif., Berkeley, Rochester Inst. Tech., U. Pitts., Ft. Lauderdale Art Inst. Freelance comml. and advt. photographer, Miami, NYC, Orlando, 1972—. Worked in over 170 countries worldwide; instr. photography Triangle Inst., 1992, S.E. Ctr. for Creative Arts, Daytona, 1990—; vis. instr. photography at many colls. and univs.; guest numerous TV programs, 1978—; lectr. in field, 1976-. Prin. works include Miami Herald, 1978-80, Fla. Tourism, 1982—, Sheraton Hotels, 1982—, Gen. Mills Restaurants, 1983—, Olive Garden, 1986—, Marriott Hotels, 1992—, Bahamas Tourism, 1984-, Radisson Hotels, 1986—, Grosvenor Hotels, 1988—, Revlon, 1991—, Harris Corp., 1993—, Sea Escape Cruises, 1988—, Century Club, 2000—, Regent China Tours, 1999—, Burger King, 1988—, Oceania Cruises, 2008—, Caribbean Travel & Life, 1990—, Fuji Films, 1990—, Far & Wide, 2000—, Nickelodeon, 1989—, Merv Griffin's Paradise Island, Bahamas, 1990—, Kodak Films, 1976—, McDonalds, 1987—, Stern Mag., 1987—, AAA, 1985—, Regal Boats, 1990—, Renaissance Cruises, 1996-2001, Wingate Realty 2000-1, Universal Studios, 1990—, Citibank VISA, 1990—, Resort Condo, Inc., 1990-, Delta Airlines, 1991—, Am. Showcase, 1991—2012, Creative Black Book, 1994—, PepsiCo, 1994—, Hilton Hotels Internat., 1992—, NuSkin, 1995—, Pizza Hut, 1996—, Grey Poupon, 1995—, Atlantis Resort, 1996—, Arnold Palmer, 1996—, Home Depot, 1996—, Whale Cay, 1997—, Sandals Resorts, 1997—, People Mag., 1998—, Internal Internat., 1980-, La Quinta Hotels, 1998—, Grand Circle Tours, 1999—, Pitcom, 1999, Pep Boys, 2008—, Saga Holidays, 1999-2001, Regent China Tours, 1999—2012, Bachmann Tour Overdrive, 1999—, Backstreet Boys, 2000, MKG Technology, 2013, Cooper Tires, 2000—, Brendan Tours, 2001—, General Tours, 2002—, SIKA, 2002—, Advanced Dermatology, 2003-, Condor Adventures, 2004—, Sony, 2003—, Verigon, 2008-13, Venus Williams, 2003—, Reebok, 2003—, Sony, 2003—, Smithsonian, 2003—, Vantage Tours, 2004, Kodak World Calendar, 2004, United Way, 2004, Sillimam Homes, 2013, Qantas Airlines, 2012, Nat. Geographic Traveler, 2013, Continental Airlines, 2004, Bank of Am., 2004—, Fine & Ice, 2012, Ed McMahon, 2004—Evolution, 2011, Condor Adventures, 2005, Popeyes, 2006-, Tunisia Today, 2009, Tauck World Tours, 2006— (named one of Most Intriguing Woman of the Last 50 Yrs., 2010), Lear Jets, 2006—, SONY, 2006—, Caribbean Travel and Life, 2006, Bank of America, 2006—, Shutterbug Mag., 2007, Pvt. Clubs, 2009-12; dir. TV commls. and videos, 1987—; author: Clicking the Shutter is the Easy Part, 1988, Introspective World, 1996, Welcome Back Berlin, 1990, Bali-Paradise in Indonesia, 1994, Shooting Figure Studies, 1990, Kathmandu, A Jewel Discovered, 1996, One Dream Too Many, 1989, Cuba Revisited, 2004-, Treasures of the Caribbean, 1992, China's Greatest Resource, It's Diverse People, 1997, Orlando-The City Beautiful, 1998, Traveling After Terrorism, 2002, Travel Hints for Photographers, 2003, Images of Woman, 2004, Send Me Anywhere, 2005, Weekend With Bachmann, 2007-13, Remember the Joy, 2006, Stock Strategies for Studio Photographs, 2011, Editorial B&W: A New Year in Photography, 2012, Bachmann Tour Overdrive: Exploring Our Planet, 2007, Cuba: A Step Back in Time, 2007, Caribbean Beauty, 2008, Stock Is Not Dead, 2009; photographer 295-Day Kodak World Photo Tour, 1992-95, Photo Pro Mag., 1991—, Majestic India and Nepal, 2008, Planet China, 2008, Faces, 2008, Vanishing Cultures, 2008, Wandering The Pacific Rim, 2009, Caribbean Blue, 2008, MTV, 2012, Remember the Joy II, 2009, The Beauty of Greece, 2008, Nude Weekend, 2010, Stock Photostrategies, 2011, Talk Stock, 2009, I Never Want A Real Job, 2011, Why Not Be Successful, 2012, Kodak: A Love Story, 2012; photgraphed over 1300 mag. covers; contbr. articles to profl. jours., directs TV commls. Bd. dirs. Big Bros.; active Vols. in Action, 1989—; Fla. pres. ASMP. Named Photographer of Yr. Fla. Peoples Choice Awards, 1987, Photographer of Yr. Asia, 1993, Best Travel Cover Photo in N.Am., 2012; recipient Addy awards, 1976—. Mem. One Club (bd. dirs. 1988—), Sales and Mktg. Execs. (bd. dirs., officer, Photographer of Yr., Asia, 2007), Am. Soc. Media Photographers N.Y., Orlando C. of C. (pres.' club 1983—), Cen. Fla. Photographers Assn. (v.p., bd. dirs. 1983—), Fla. Motion Pictures and TV Guild, PPA, Fla. Profl. Photographers, Heathrow Club (social dir. 1986—), Orlando Camera Club, Rotary, Hilton Vacation Club, Marriott World Vacation Club. Republican. Methodist. Avocations: skiing, tennis, golf, writing, sailing, photography, travel, rock climbing. Home and Office: PO Box 950833 Lake Mary FL 32795-0833 Office Phone: 407-333-9988. Personal E-mail: bill@billbachmann.com.

BACHMANN, RICHARD H., lawyer, energy executive; b. Ft. McClellan, Ala., 1953; BA, Southwestern U., 1974; JD, U. Houston, 1977. Bar: Tex. 1977. Ptnr. Butler & Binion, Houston, 1988—93, Snell & Smith, P.C., 1993—98; chief legal officer Enterprise Products Co., 1999, sec., bd. dirs., 1999—2010, group vice chmn., 2007—10, pres., CEO, 2010; exec. v.p., chief legal officer & sec. Enterprise Products Partners, LP, 1999—, bd. dirs., 2000—04, 2006—10; exec. v.p., chief legal officer, sec. Enterprise GP Holdings, LP, 2005—10; bd. dirs. Enterprise Products Holdings LLC, 2010—; chief legal officer, sec. EPE Holdings, LLC, 2005—10, exec. v.p., 2005—; pres., CEO & bd. dirs. DEP Holdings, LLC, 2006—10, bd. dirs., 2006—10. Bd. mgr. Constellation Energy Ptnrs. LLC, 2006—. Fellow Tex. Bar Found., Houston Bar Found.; mem. ABA, State Bar Tex., Houston Bar Assn., Order Barons, Phi Delta Phi. Office: Enterprise Products Partners LP 10th Fl 1100 Louisiana St Houston TX 77002 Office Phone: 713-381-6500. Office Fax: 713-381-8200. Business E-Mail: rbachmann@eprod.com.

BACHNER, JOHN PHILIP, business consultant; s. Barnard and Bertha (Bellar) B.; m. Patricia Bain, June 14, 1997. AB, Harvard U., 1966. Screenplay writer Screen Presentations Inc., Washington, 1967-68; account exec. Hoffman Assocs. Inc., Silver Spring, Md., 1968-71; pres. Bachner Communications Inc., Silver Spring, 1971—; exec. dir. Nat. Coun. Acoustion Cons., 1972—76. Pres. Bachner Mgmt. Systems, 1973—, eBrownbag.com, LLC, 2009-; exec. v.p. Cons. Engrs. Coun. of Met. Washington, Silver Spring, 1971-96, Property Mgmt. Assn., Silver Spring, 1973-96, Washington Area Coun. Engring. Labs., Silver Spring, 1975-93; exec. v.p. ASFE/The Geoprofl. Bus. Assn., 1973—; pres., chmn. bd. Constrn. Industry Tech. Inc., Silver Spring, 1973—; exec. dir. Nat. Lighting Bureau, 1977-; pres. Most for the Lease, 1982—; v.p. Bachner R.E., 1985-97; exec. v.p. Mid-Atlantic Coun. of Shopping Ctr. Mgrs., 1986-93; exec. v.p. Inst. Profl. Practice, Silver Spring, 1988-94, Coll. Property Mgmt. Found., Silver Spring, 1988-96; pres. Cons. Engrs., Ednl. Found. Inc., 1990-99; exec. dir. Profl. Liability Agts. Network Inc., 1991-98, Mid-Atlantic Cancer Rsch. Found., Silver Spring, 1992-95, Internat. Found. Advancement of Thrombosis and Hematosis Rsch. Inc., Silver Spring, 1992-98, Design and Constrn. Quality Inst., 1992-95, Calif. R.E. Inspection Assn., 1993-98, Metro Washington Heat Pump Assn., 1994-99, Intelligent Bldgs. Inst., 1994; pres. Bus. Art and Graphics, 1993-97; exec. dir. Inst. Brownfield Profls., 2005-09, Engrs. Leadership Found., 2004-. Author: Marketing and Promotion for Design Professionals, 1977, Guide to Practical Property Management, 1991, Practice Management for Design Professionals, 1991, ASFE Contract Reference Guide, 3d edit., 1996, 3.1 edit., 1998, ECS Contract Reference Guide, 1997, 2nd edit., 1999, RA&MCO Contract Reference Guide, 1997, 2d edit., 2002, Derailed by Dispute, 2003; writer 25 motion picture screenplays; contbr. over 2500 articles to profl. publs., popular mags.; columnist, author contract reference guides, 1996-2000. Pres. Engrs.' Leadership Found., 1999—2003; bd. govs. Found. for Profl. Practice, 2001—04. Business E-Mail: john@bachner.com.

BACHUS, SPENCER THOMAS, III, United States Representative from Alabama, lawyer; b. Birmingham, Ala., Dec. 28, 1947; m. Linda Bachus; children: Warren, Stuart, Elliott, Candace, Lisa. BA, Auburn U., 1969; JD, U. Ala., 1972. Pvt. law practice, 1972—92; mem. Dist. 17 Ala. State Senate, 1983—84; mem. Dist. 46 Ala. House of Reps., 1984—87; rep. Dist. 6 Ala. State Bd. Edn., 1987—91; sr. ptnr. Bachus, Dempsey, Carson, & Steed; mem. US Congress from 6th Ala. Dist., Washington, 1993—; ranking minority mem. US House Financial Services Com., Washington, 2007—11, chmn., 2011—13. Mgr. Guy Hunt's Gubernatorial campaign, 1986; del. Republican Nat. Conv., 1988; mem. Ala. Bd. Edn.; chmn. Ala. State Rep. Exec. Com., 1991. Served in USAR, 1969—71. Recipient Commissioner's. Merit award as Outstanding Rep. Ala. Dept. Human Resources, 1986, Henry M. Somerville award U. Ala. Republican. Baptist. Office: US House of Representatives 2246 Rayburn House Office Building Washington DC 20515 also: 1900 Internat Park Dr Birmingham AL 35243 Office Phone: 202-225-4921. Office Fax: 202-225-2082.*

BACIGALUPI, DONALD, museum executive; b. NYC, Apr. 24, 1960; BA in Art History, U. Houston, 1983; MA in Art History, U. Tex., Austin, 1985, PhD in Art History, 1993. Lectr. art hist. U. Tex., Austin, 1988—93; curator contemporary art San Antonio Mus. Art, 1993—95; dir., chief curator Blaffer Gallery, U. Houston, 1996—99; exec. dir. San Diego Mus. Art, 1999—2003; pres., dir., CEO Toledo Mus. Art, 2003—09; dir. Crystal Bridges Mus. American Art, Bentonville, Ark., 2009—13, pres., 2013—. Adj. prof. art history U. Houston, 1996—. Named one of The 50 People to Watch, San Diego Mag., 2000. Office: Crystal Bridges Museum American Art 600 Museum Way Bentonville AR 72712 Office Phone: 479-418-5700.*

BACK, JENIFER C., dentist; Grad, U. Ky., Lexington, 1995. Dentist Sarasota Smile Design. Instr. Nash Inst. Author: (publ.) Woman Dentist Journal. Mem.: Seattle Study Club Saragator Chpt., Sarasota Dental Assn., West Coast Dental Assn., Acad. of Gen. Dentistry, ADA, Fla. Assn. of Cosmetic Dentistry, Am. Acad. of Cosmetic Dentists. Office: Sarasota Smile Design 3800 Clark Rd Sarasota FL 34233 Office Phone: 941-927-5411.

BACKSTROM, NICKLAS (LARS NICKLAS BACKSTROM), professional hockey player; b. Gavle, Sweden, Nov. 23, 1987; s. Anders and Catrin Backstrom. Center Washington Capitals, 2007—. Mem. Team Sweden, Olympic Games, Vancouver, 2010, Sochi, Russia, 2014. Named to NHL YoungStars Game, 2008, 2009, All-Rookie Team, NHL, 2008. Achievements include being a member of silver medal winning Swedish Hockey Team, Sochi Olympics, 2014. Office: c/o Washington Capitals Verizon Center 601 F Street NW Washington DC 20004*

BACON, CHARLES WILSON, mycologist, educator, research scientist; s. Willie Andrew Jackson and Dorether Thomas Bacon; m. Lynda Natalia Solomon, Aug. 15, 1969; children: Jennifer Margaret George, Charles Wilson Bacon Jr. BS, Clarke Coll., 1965; PhD, U. Mich., 1971. Rsch. microbiologist USDA, Athens, Ga., 1973—; prof. U. Ga., Athens, 1981—. Rsch. leader, location coord. USDA, Agrl. Rsch. Svc., Russell Rsch. Ctr., Athens, Ga., 1996—. Author: Microbial Endophytes, Neotyphodium/Grass Interactions, Clavicipitalean Fungi, Biotechnology of Endophytic Fungi. Recipient Superior Svc. award, US Dept. Agr., 1984; named one of Distinguish Scientists of Yr., Agr. Rsch. Svc., 2000. Fellow: Am. Phytopathological Soc. (life); mem.: Internat. Symbiosis Soc. (sec., treas. 1995—97), Am. Soc. Microbiology (assoc. editor), Mycol. Soc. Am. Achievements include research in the cause of tall fescue grass toxicity to livestock and the chemical nature of the toxin; extended production of specific classes of toxins to an entire family of fungi; patents for an endophytic bacterium designed to protect plants from fungal diseases. Home: 125 Plantation Dr Athens GA 30605 Office: USDA 950 College Station Rd Athens GA 30604 Office Fax: 706-546-3116. Business E-Mail: charles.bacon@ars.usda.gov.

BACON, CRAIG, consumer products company executive; b. Mo. m. Debbie Bacon; children: Cassie, Justin, Amanda. Attended, U. Mo., Columbia, 1984; Ph.D, U. Tenn., Knoxville, 1990. Rsch. sci. Oscar Mayer, 1990—91; dir., rsch. and devel. Tyson Foods, Inc., sr. dir., rsch. and devel., v.p., rsch. and devel., 2008, sr. v.p., corp. rsch. and devel., 2008—; adj. asst. prof. Food Sci. and Tech., U. Tenn., Poultry Sci., U. Ark. Spkr. in field. Trustee Benefits Plans for Tyson Foods, 2007—. Mem.: AMSA (Achievement award 1999), IFT. Mem. Christian Ch. Office: Tyson Foods Inc 2200 Don Tyson Pky Springdale AR 72762-6999 Office Phone: 479-290-4000. Office Fax: 479-290-4061. Business E-Mail: craig.bacon@tyson.com.

BACOTE, MAMYE E., state legislator; b. Feb. 18, 1939; m. Theodore Edward BaCote; children: Theodore III, Derek, Marlon. State del. Dist. 95, Va., 2004—; vice chairwoman Hampton Rds. Regional Jail Authority; adj. prof., polit. sci. Democrat. Roman Catholic. Address: Dist Off 2700 Washington Ave PO Box 5154

Newport News VA 23605 Office: Gen Assembly Bldg Rm 507 PO Box 406 Richmond VA 23218 Office Phone: 757-244-4415, 804-698-1095. Fax: 804-786-6310. Business E-Mail: Del_BaCote@house.state.va.us.

BACZKO, JOSEPH RICHARD, JR., retired dean; b. 1945; BS, Georgetown U., 1967; MBA, Harvard U., 1974. CEO Maxfactor Europe, Fort Lauderdale, Fla., 1979-83; pres. internat. divsn. Toys R Us, Inc., Fort Lauderdale, to 1991; pres., COO Blockbuster Entertainment Corp., Fort Lauderdale, Va., 1991-93; chmn., CEO FNC Holdings, Troy, Mich., 1997—2001; dean Pace U. Lubin Sch. Bus, NYC, 2005—10.

BADALAMENTI, ANTHONY, financial planner; b. St. Louis, Apr. 1, 1940; s. Sebastino and Grace (Orlando) B.; 1 child, Annette Marie. BS in Acctg., Washington U., 1970. CPA, Mo.; registered investment advisor. Staff acct. Fischer & Fischer, CPAs, St. Louis, 1959-63; acct. McDonnell Aircraft Corp., St. Louis, 1963-65; asst. chief acct. Dempsey Tegler, Inc., St. Louis, 1965-66; contr. Cummins Mo. Diesel, Inc., St. Louis, 1966-67; sr. acct. Elmer Fox & Co., CPAs, St. Louis, 1967-71; pvt. practice St. Louis, 1972-94; fin. planner Asset Builders Fin. Planners, St. Louis, 1990. Tchr. Meramec C.C., St. Louis, 1973—. Mem. Mo. Soc. CPAs, Crestwood-Sunset Hills C. of C. (pres. 1980-81, Bus. Profl. Month award 1986, 91), Rotary (pres. Crestwood-Sunset Hills chpt. 1982-83). Republican. Roman Catholic. Avocations: basketball, softball, dance. Home: 15612 Crystal Waters Dr Wimauma FL 33598-4015 Personal E-mail: plantornvest@yahoo.com.

BADCOCK, WOGAN STANHOPE, JR., manufacturing executive; b. Mulberry, Fla., Feb. 5, 1932; s. Wogan Stanhope and Evelyn Marie (Clark) B.; m. Mary Robison, Aug. 7, 1953; children: Mary Badcock Stiles, Elizabeth Badcock Daughtrey, Wogan S. III, Henry C., Ben M. BS in Bus. Adminstrn., U. Fla. First v.p. W.S. Badcock Corp., Mulberry, Fla., 1959, bd. dirs., 1959-62, exec. v.p., 1963, pres., 1963-84, chmn. bd., former pres., 1984—, CEO, 1991—. Founding mem. Pres. Coun. U. Fla., Gainesville; bd. dirs. So. Scholarship Found. Inc., Fla. State U., Tallahassee; trustee YMCA, Lakeland. Capt. USAF, 1954-58. Mem. Kiwanis. Episcopalian. Office: W S Badcock Corp PO Box 497 200 N Phosphate Blvd Mulberry FL 33860-2350

BADDELEY, AARON JOHN, professional golfer; b. Lebanon, NH, Mar. 17, 1981; s. Ron Baddeley. Profl. golfer, 2000—; mem. PGA Tour, 2003—. Mem. Australian Team World Golf Championships-World Cup, 2001; mem. internat. team Presidents Cup, 2011. Named Order of Merit Champion, PGA Tour Australasia, 2000—01. Achievements include winning PGA Tour events: Verizon Heritage, 2006; FBR Open, 2007; Northern Trust Open, 2011; winning international events: Holden Australian Open, 1999, 2000, Greg Norman Holden International, 2001. Office: c/o PGA Tour 112 PGA TOUR Blvd Ponte Vedra Beach FL 32082

BADDOUR, ANNE BRIDGE, pilot; b. Royal Oak, Mich. d. William George and Esther Rose (Pfiester) Bridge; m. Raymond F. Baddour, Sept. 25, 1954; children: Cynthia Anne, Frederick Raymond, Jean Bridge. Student, Detroit Bus. Sch., 1948—50; BA, Pine Manor Coll., Chestnut Hill, Mass. Stewardess Ea. Airlines, Boston, 1952—54; instr. aero. Powers Sch., Boston, 1958; co-pilot, flight attendant Raytheon Co., Bedford, Mass., 1958—63; flight dispatcher, ferry Pilot Comerford Flight Sch., Bedford, 1974—76; adminstrv. asst., ferry pilot Jenney Beechcraft, Bedford, 1976; mgr., pilot Balt. Airways, Inc., Bedford, 1976—77; rsch. test pilot Lincoln Lab. Flight Test Facility MIT, Lexington, 1977—97. Aviation cons., corp. pilot Energy Resources, Inc., Cambridge, Mass., 1974-84; holder World Class speed records for single-engine aircraft; Boston to Goose Bay, Labrador, 1985, Boston to Reykjavik, Iceland, 1985, Portland, Maine to Goose Bay, 1985, Portland to Reykjavik, 1985, Goose Bay to Reykjavik, 1985; records for twin-engine aircraft: Sept Isles to Goose Bay, 1988, Mont Joll to Goose Bay, 1988, Presque Isle to Goose Bay, 1988, Millinocket to Goose Bay, 1988, Bedford to Goose Bay, 1988, Goose Bay to Narssassrag, Greenland, 1988, Narssassrag to Klevelevic, Iceland, 1988, Narssassrag to Reykjavik, 1988, Bedford to Narssassrag, 1988, Millinochet to Narssassrag, 1988, Presque Isle to Narssassrag, 1988, Bedford to St. John, 1991, Bedford to Charlottetown, 1991, Charlottetown to Kennebunk, 1991, Charlottetown to Portsmouth, 1991, Muncton to Bedford, 1991, St. John, to Kennebunk, 1991, St. John to Bedford, 1991, World Class Speed Records Single-Engine Aircraft, 1991, Bedford, Mass. to Sydney, Nova Scotia, Bedford, Mass. to Sydney, Nova Scotia to Bedford, Mass., Portsmouth, New Hampshire to Sydney Nova Scotia to Portsmouth, Brunswick to Sydney Nova Scotia to Brunswick; mem. bd. visitors Pine Manor Coll., 2009-13, bd. adv. mem., Mass. Air & Space Mus., 2010-. Mem. campaign coun. Mus. Transp., Boston; mem. coun. assocs. French Libr. in Boston; commr. Commonwealth of Mass., Mass. Aero. Commn., 1979—83; trustee bd. adminstrn. Amelia Earhart Birthplace Mus., 1992—93; trustee Daniel Webster Coll., Nashua, NH, 1995—2009; v.p., trustee Friends of the Libr. Spl. Collections Boston U., 1999—2002; trustee Viscaya Mus., 2002—; bd. dirs. Cambridge Opera, 1977—79, Key West, Fla. Maritime Mus., 2004—13, Smithsonian Nat. Air and Space Mus., 1998—2005. Recipient 1st pl. trophy, Phila. Transcontinental Air Race, 1954, trophy, New Eng. Air Race, 1957, Clifford B. Harmon trophy, Internat. Aviatrix, 1988, recipient Spl. Recognition award, FAA, 1990, Fairchild Tropical Botanic Garden award, 2013; named Pilot of Yr., New Eng. sect. Internat. Women Pilots Orgn./The Ninety-Nines Inc., 1992; named to Internat. Aviation Forest of Friendship, Atchison, Kans., 1991, Women in Aviation Internat. Pioneer Hall of Fame, 2005. Mem.: DAR, Barnacle Soc. Coconut Grove Fla., Women in Aviation Internat. (Pioneer Hall of Fame award 2005), Friends of Switzerland, US Sea Plane Pilots Assn., Assn. Women Transcontinental Air Race, Bostonian Soc., Soc. Exptl. Test Pilots, Aircraft Owners Pilots Assn., Fedn. Aeronautique Internat., Nat. Aero. Assn., Ninety-Nines (New Eng. Safety trophy 1986), Boston Womens Travel Club, Beach Colony Club, Fairchild Tropical Bot. Garden, Harvard Travellers Club, Chilton Club, Belmont Hill Club, Aero Club New Eng. (v.p. 1978—80, dir. 1978—2002).

BADEN, THOMAS JAMES, dermatologist; b. Coral Gables, Fla., Dec. 29, 1951; s. Thomas Benjamin and Helen (Threadgill) B.; m. Sandra Louise Bradley, June 22, 1974; children: Craig, Scott, Michael. AB in Chemistry, Duke U., 1973; MD cum laude, Emory U., 1977. Diplomate Am. Bd. Internal Medicine, Am. Bd. Dermatology. Internal medicine resident N.C. Meml. Hosp., Chapel Hill, 1977-80, dermatology resident, 1983-86; internist Toe Valley Med. Assn., Spruce Pine, NC, 1980-83; dermatologist West Piedmont Dermatology Assn., Morganton, NC, 1986—. Consulting dermatologist Western Carolina Ctr., Broughton Hosp., Morganton, 1986—; staff dermatologist Grace Hosp., Morganton, 1986—. Contbr. articles to profl. jours. Deacon First Bapt. Ch., Morganton. Fellow ACP, Am. Acad. Dermatology; mem. AMA, Christian Med. Soc. Avocations: music, hiking, photography. Home and Office: West Piedmont Dermatology 111 Foothills Dr Morganton NC 28655-5152

BADER, WILLIAM BANKS, historian, former corporate executive, foundation executive; b. Atlantic City, Sept. 8, 1931; s. Edward L. and Celeste Bader (Burkhardt) B.; m. Gretta Lange, Dec. 19, 1953; children: Christopher, Katharine, John, Diedrich. BA, Pomona Coll., 1953; MA, Princeton U., 1960, PhD, 1964. With Libr. of Congress, 1954—55, Office Nat. Estimates, CIA, 1960—64; lectr. history Princeton U., 1964—65; with Dept. State, 1965—66, U.S. Senate Fgn. Rels. Com., 1966—69; program officer, then European rep. Ford Found., Paris, 1969—73; fellow Woodrow Wilson Internat. Ctr. Scholars, 1974—75; dir. fgn. intelligence task force U.S. Senate, 1975—76; asst. dep. under sec. for policy Dept. Def., 1976—78; dir. staff U.S. Senate Fgn. Rels. Com., 1978—81; v.p. SRI Internat.-Washington, Arlington, 1981—87; sr. v.p. SRI Internat., Menlo Park, Calif., 1988—92; pres. Eurasia Found., Washington, 1992—96; with World Bank Group, Washington, 1996—97, Ctr. Strategic and Internat. Studies, 1997—98; asst. sec. of state ednl. and cultural affairs Dept. State, 1998—2001; with World Bank Group, Washington, 2001—02; v.p. Nat. Def. U., 2000—04, Internat. Fin. Corp., 2005—06; prof. internat. history and politics Grad. Inst. Internat. Studies, Geneva, 2006—08. Adj. prof. Georgetown U., Am. U., naval intelligence officer Bombardian Navigator, 1955-58, staff dir. Office Nat. Estimates CIA, 61-65, Com. Fgn. Rels., US Senate, 1978-81, asst. dep. Under Sec. Def., 1974-79. Author: Austria Between East and West: 1945-1955, 1966, The U.S. and the Spread of Nuclear Weapons, 1968, The Taiwan Relations Act: A Decade of Implementation, 1989, Österreich im Spannungsfeld Zwischen Ost und West 1945 bis 1955, 2002; contbr. articles to profl. jours. Bd. dirs. Samuel H. Kress Found, Leave No Vet. Behind, Internat. Student House Inc. Served as naval air capt. USNR, 1954-, ret. 1975. Recipient Meritorious Svc. medal Dept. State, 1966, Sec. Def. medal for outstanding pub. svc., 1979, Österreichische Ehrenkreuz für Wissenschaft und Kunst 1. Klasse Republic of Austria (officer's cross), 1991. Mem. Coun. Fgn. Rels., Cosmos Club Washington Roman Catholic. Office Phone: 703-615-6834.

BADGER, PHILLIP CHARLES, engineer, manager; s. Clifford Russell and Helen Pauline (Fair) B.; m. Cheryl Lynn Baker, Aug. 14, 1971 (div. Feb. 1999); children: Brian, Scott, Mark; m. Bonnie Watkins, Aug. 14, 1999. BS in Agrl. Engring., Ohio State U., 1971, MS in Agrl. Engring., 1973; MBA, Vanderbilt U., 1993. Registered profl. engr., Ohio, Ala. Design engr. Ideanamics, Columbus, Ohio, 1972—74; rsch. assoc., project engr. Ohio State U. and Ohio Agrl. R & D Ctr., Wooster, 1975—78, ext. specialist, rsch. assoc., 1978—79; mgr. waste heat utilization project TVA, Muscle Shoals, Ala., 1979—80, mgr. small scale fuel ethanol project, 1980—82, mgr. fuel ethanol from non-woody cellulose program, 1982—84; mgr. Regional Biomass Energy program US Dept. Energy, Muscle Shoals, 1984—99; leader TVA biomass applications group Dept. Energy, Muscle Shoals, 1994—; pres. Gen. Bioenergy, Inc., Florence, Ala., 1999—; pres., chief mgr. Renewable Oil Internat., Florence, 2000—, ROI Ala. Ops. LLC, Florence, 2002—; com. mem. NSF, DOE, ACS, 2007; CTO and ptnr. Renewable Oil Internat. MD LLC, Woodbine, Ill., 2013—. Mem. biomass and waste energy com. Electric Power Rsch. Inst., Palo Alto, Calif., 1990—99; mem. Renewable Energy and Efficiency Inst. Quality Control Bd., 1996—99; bioenergy tech. advisor Southern States Energy Bd., 1999-. Author: Conserving Energy in Ohio Greenhouses, 1979 (Am. Soc. Agr. Biol. Engrs. blue ribbon award 1979); mem. editl. bd. CIGR Electronic Jour.; contbr. articles to profl. jours. Bd. dirs. New Uses Coun., 1997—. Recipient Tech. Achievement award Dept. Energy, 1985, 96, 98, Outstanding Tech. Presentation award WATTec '89, 1989, Cert. of Environ. Achievement, Nat. Awards Coun. for Environ. Sustainability, 1994-99, Industry Leader award Fiber Fuels Inst., 1993, ASABE Pvt. Enterprise Bioenergy Pioneer award, 2009 Mem. Am. Soc. Agrl. and Biol. Engrs. (v.p. energy com. 1990-91, pres. energy com. 1991-92, trustee 2006-08), Am. Solar Energy Soc., Am. Assn. Indsl. Crops, Internat. Solar Energy Soc., Nat. Mgmt. Assn., Am. Assn. Indsl. Crops, Biomass Energy Rsch. Assn. (bd. dirs. 1987—), New Uses Coun. (bd. dirs. 1997—), Coun. of Forest Engring., Coun. Agrl. Sci. and Tech., Florence Exch. Club (bd. dirs. 1985-86). Office: Gen Bioenergy Inc Renewable Oil Internat LLC and ROI Ala Ops PO Box 26 Florence AL 35631-0026

BADON, AUSTIN J., state legislator; b. New Orleans, Dec. 14, 1964; s. Austin and Brenda Morgan Badon; m. Therese Mitchell-Badon. Program dir. Boy Scouts Of America, 1996—2000; coord., workforce devel. Nunez CC, 2000—; mem. Dist. 100 La. House of Reps., 2004—, chair edn. com. Mem.: New Orleans C. of C. (chmn. 2001—03), Each One Save One (mentor 1999—2003). Democrat. Roman Catholic. Office: Capitol Office 900 N Third St PO Box 94062 Baton Rouge LA 70804 Home: 5555 Bullard Ave Ste 101 New Orleans LA 70128-3455 Office Phone: 504-243-7783. Fax: 504-243-7785. Business E-Mail: larep100@legis.state.la.us.

BAEHR, JOHN J., III, diagnostic radiologist; MD, Tulane U., 1975. Diplomate Am. Bd. Radiology-diagnostic radiology, 1979, cert. added qualification (CAQ) Am. Bd. Radiology-vascular and interventional radiology. Intern Univ. of Calif.; resident diagnostic radiology Univ. of Calif. San Francisco (UCSF) Med. Ctr., 1976—79; hosp. affiliations include Bapt. Hosp., Pensacola, The Andrews Inst. Office: The Andrews Institute 1040 Gulf Breeze Pky Gulf Breeze FL 32563 Office Phone: 850-916-8700.

BAEZ, JOSE ANGEL, lawyer; b. PR, Sept. 17, 1968; BS in Criminology, Fla. State U., 1994; JD, St. Thomas U. Sch. Law, Miami, Fla., 1997. Bar: Fla. 2005. Former intern Miami-Dade Pub. Defender's Office; atty. Baez Law Firm, Kissimmee, Fla. Author: Presumed Guilty, 2012. Served with USN. Mem.: Fla. Bar Assn. Office: Baez Law Firm 625 E Colonial Dr Orlando FL 32803 also: Baez Law Firm 23 S Osceola Ave Orlando FL 32801-2845 Office Phone: 407-705-2626.

BAGBY, MARTHA L. GREEN, real estate holding company and publishing executive, writer; b. West Palm Beach, Fla., June 17, 1937; d. Hampton and Louise (Lambert) Green; m. Joseph R. Bagby, 1966; 1 child, Meredith E. AA, Palm Beach Jr. Coll., 1957; AB, U. Miami, 1959; MA, Pa. State U., 1964. Journalist The Miami Herald; tchr. journalism, english Palm Beach County, 1959—62; instr. journalism Pa. State U., 1962—63; city editor, writer Palm Beach News and Life, 1963—64; editor Alfred Hitchcock Mag., Riviera Beach, Fla., 1964; editor, supr. editl. svc., pub. rels. employee newspaper Nat. Airlines, Inc., Miami, Fla., 1965—73; founder Property Resources Corp., 1970; corp. sec., chmn. bd. Property Resources Co., Palm Beach, Fla., 1971—. Life dir. CareNet Global, 2002—; Ill. franchisee Burger King Corp.; founder Internat. Health Awareness Assn.; lectr. journalism Dade, Palm Beach counties; instr. Barry Coll., Miami; pub. The Bagbys Health Digest, 1985—. Author: Stranglehold, 1977, The Complete Real Estate Dictionary, 1992, The Real Estate Financing Deskbook, 1979-90; author: (with others) The Complete Real Estate Book. Mem. exec. bd. Childbirth and Parent Edn. Assn., Miami. Mem.: Internat. Assn. Corp. Real Estate Execs. (founder, trustee, exec. editor, dir. life), Women in Comm. (pres.), Air Transport Assn. Am., Airline Editors Conf. (chmn.), S. Fla. Indsl. Chmn. Internat. Council Indsl. Editors, Fla. Pub. Relations Assn. Office: Property Resources Co 125 Brazilian Ave Palm Beach FL 33480 Office Phone: 561-655-9510.

BAGGETT, DONNIS GENE, newspaper editor; b. Livingston, Tex., July 16, 1952; s. Sam Jr. and Mavis Baggett; m. Beverly Brown; children: Valerie Shaddix, David Shaddix. BA, Stephen F. Austin State U., 1973. Reporter, photographer East Tex. Eye, Livingston, Tex., 1973-74, co-editor, 1974; reporter Longview (Tex.) Morning Jour., 1974-75, East Tex. editor, 1975-76; reporter The Dallas Morning News, 1976, asst. night city editor, 1977, asst. state editor, 1977-82, state editor, 1982-94, asst. mng. editor, 1994-95; editor The Eagle, Bryan-College Station, Tex., 1996—2007, editor-in-chief, 2007—. Chmn. Tex. Agrl. Summit Exec. Com., 1997—98; bd. dirs., campaign chair Brazos Valley United Way, 2000; v.p. Washington-on-theBrazos State Park Assn. Recipient Mayborn award for Cmty. Leadership, Tex. Daily Newspaper Assn., 2005. Mem.: Soc. Profl. Journalists, Tex. Press Assn. (bd. dirs.), Tex. Daily Newspaper Assn. (pres. 2004), Press Club of Dallas (pres. 1992—94). Methodist. Avocation: ranching.

BAGGETT, W. MIKE, lawyer; b. Waco, Tex., Nov. 8, 1946; s. Bill R. and Jenna (Robertson) B.; m. Jo Kilpatrick, May 28, 1968; children: Carl, Cary. BBA, Tex. A&M U., 1968; JD cum laude, Baylor U., 1973. Bar: Tex. 1973. Law clk. Tex. Supreme Ct., Austin, 1973—74; assoc. Winstead PC, Dallas, 1974-79, equity shareholder, 1979—, chmn. and chief exec. officer, 1992—2006; chmn. emeritus Winstead, Sechrest & Minick, Dallas, 2006—. Chair reverse mortgage rules com., chair home equity loan rules com. Tex. Supreme Ct. Author: Texas Foreclosure: Law & Practice, 1983, Texas Practice Series West, 2nd edit., 2001, Real Estate Litigation, Texas Practice Guide West, 2002; co-author: Lender Liability Law and Litigation, 1989. Trustee Tex. A&M Found., 1989-98, chmn., 1992-93; mem. Joint Select Com. on Judiciary, 1988; bd. dirs. Tex. Higher Edn. Coordinating Bd., 1989-95, Dallas Citizens Coun., bd. mem. exec. com., State Bar of Tex., Baylor Oral Health Found.; vice chmn., trustee Southwestern Bell-SMU Athletic Forum; chmn. Dallas Ft. Worth Regional Sports Commn.; chmn. Cotton Bowl Athletic Assn. 1st lt. US Army, 1968—71, Vietnam. Decorated Bronze Star; named Tex. Aggie Lawyer of Yr., 2004; named one of Top 10 Bus. Litigators in Dallas/Ft. Worth, Dallas Bus. Jour., Best Lawyer in Am., Lawyer of Yr. award, D Mag., Super Lawyer, Top 100 in Dallas/Ft. Worth, Tex. Monthly; recipient Neiman Marcus award, 2002, Judge Sam Williams Leadership award State Bar Tex., 2005, Torch of Conscience award Am. Jewish Congress, 2006, Dallas Bar Found. Fellows award, 2013 Master: Patrick E. Higginbotham Am. Inn Ct.; fellow: Am. Bd. Trial Advocates, Ctr. for Am. and Internat. Law (chair of fellows, chair exec. com., trustee), Tex. Bar Found. (sec./treas. of fellows), Am. Bar Found., Dallas Bar Found. (chmn. and trustee, chmn.); mem.: Dallas Regional C. of C., Tex. Ctr. Legal Ethics & Dallas Bar Assn., Dallas Bar Assn. (pres. chmn., bd. dirs.), Tex. State Bar Assn. (bd. cert. civil trial com. 1983, bd. dirs., exec. com., adminstrn. justice com.), Baylor Law Sch. Alumni Assn. (pres., bd. dirs.), Assn. Former Students Tex. A&M U. (pres. 1988, Outstanding Alumni Coll. Bus. 1996, Disting. Alumni 1998), Ctrl. Dallas Assn. (Downtown Dallas) (chmn.), Crescent Club, Royal Oaks Club. Methodist. Office: Winstead PC 500 Winstead Bldg 2728 No Harwood St Dallas TX 75201 Home Phone: 214-348-4132; Office Phone: 214-745-5303. Business E-Mail: mbaggett@winstead.com.

BAGNELL, PHILIP C., dean, pediatrician, educator; b. Nova Scotia, Can. MD, Dalhousie U., 1968. Residency Izaak Walton Killam Hosp. Children, Halifax, NS, Canada, Children's Hosp. Med. Ctr., Cin., fellowship in pediatric gastroenterology and nutrition; faculty mem. dept. pediat. Ea. Tenn. State U. Quillen Coll. Medicine, Johnson City, 1991—, dir. pediatric residency tng. program, 1996—98, exec. assoc. dean academic and faculty affairs, chief academic officer, 2000—06, dean medicine, 2006—; v.p. med. affairs Johnson City Med. Ctr., 1998—2000. Fellow: Royal Coll. Physicians and Surgeons Can., American Acad. Pediat.; mem.: AMA, N.Am. Soc. Gastroenterology and Nutrition, American Gastroenterol. Assn., American Acad. Pediat., Tenn. Chpt., Tenn. Med. Assn., Alpha Omega Alpha. Office: ETSU Quillen Coll Medicine Stanton Gerber Hall Ste C-200 Box 70694 Johnson City TN 37614-1710 Office Phone: 423-439-6315. Office Fax: 423-439-8090. Business E-Mail: deanofmedicine@etsu.edu.*

BAHL, ROY WINFORD, economist, educator, consultant; b. Miami, Fla., June 28, 1939; s. Roy Winford and Vista Lee (Becks) B.; m. Marilyn Seifried, Dec. 22, 1963; children: Renee, Alexandra, Martin, Ashley. BA, Greenville Coll., Ill., 1961; MA, U. Ky., 1963, PhD in Econs., 1965. Asst. prof. econs. W.Va. U., Morgantown, 1965-67; economist IMF, Washington, 1967-71; prof. econs. Syracuse (N.Y.) U., 1971-88, Maxwell prof. polit. economy, 1985-88; prof. econs. Ga. State U., Atlanta, 1988—2006, dir. Policy Rsch. Ctr., 1988-96, dean Andrew Young sch. policy studies, 1996—2007, regents prof., 2006—. Bd. dirs. N.Y. State Energy Authority, Albany, 1979-87, Lincoln Found., Phoenix, 1986-93; mem. So. Growth Policies Bd., 1997—; cons. World Bank, Washington, 1971—. Author: Urban Public Finance in LDCs, 1992, Economic Growth and Fiscal Plan, 1992, Fiscal Policy in China, 1999; editor: The Jamaican Tax Reform, 1991, Restructuring Local Government Finance, 2003. Recipient Fiscal medal Govt. of Philippines, 1986, Disting. Economist award State of Ky., 1989. Mem. Nat. Tax Assn. (pres. 1986), Am. Econs. Assn., So. Econs. Assn. (v.p. 1993). Democrat. Office: Ga State U Andrew Young Sch Policy Studies 14 Marietta St 14W Ste 138 Atlanta GA 30303 Office Phone: 404-413-0010.

BAHNER, THOMAS MAXFIELD, lawyer; b. Little Rock, 1933; m. Sara M. Bahner; 3 children. BS, Carson-Newman Coll., 1954; JD, U. Va., 1960. Bar: Tenn. 1960, Va. 1960, U.S. Dist. Ct. (ea. dist.) Tenn. 1961, U.S. Supreme Ct. 1970, U.S. Ct. Appeals (6th cir.) 1971, U.S. Ct. Appeals (8th cir.) 1971, U.S. Ct. Appeals (4th cir.) 1975, U.S. Ct. Appeals (3d cir.) 1988, U.S. Ct. Appeals (fed. cir.) 1991, U.S. Ct. Appeals (9th cir.) 1999, U.S. Ct. Appeals (11th cir.) 1999, U.S. Dist. Ct. (we. dist.) Tenn. 2002. Assoc. Kefauver, Duggan and McDonald, Chattanooga, 1960—62; ptnr. Duggan, McDonald & Bahner, Chattanooga, 1962—64, Chambliss, Bahner, Crutchfield, Gaston and Irvine (name changed to Chambliss, Bahner & Stophel), Chattanooga, 1964—. Chmn. adv. commn. civil rules Tenn. Supreme Ct., 1982—89, chair adv. com. drafting Tenn. rules of evidence, 1983—89, mem. bd. profl. responsibility, 1982—85, chmn. fin. com., 1984—85, mem. continuing legal edn. blue ribbon com.; bd. commrs. Hamilton County Law Libr.; chair standing com. on atty. admissions to Chattanooga divsn. US Dist. Ct. Ea. Dist. Tenn., 2007—. Sr. contbg. editor Evidence in America, the Federal Rules in the United States, 1987; contbr. chapters to books. Bd. dirs. Orange Grove Ctr., Chattanooga, 1962—99, pres., 1974—75, chmn., 1976—77; mem. bd. trustees, sec. BOTA Found., 1985—2011; mem. bd. trustees Carson-Newman Coll., Jefferson City, Tenn., 1975—, chmn. bd. trustees, 1983—87, 1990—92, mem. pres. search com., 1977, 1999—2000; mem., dir., organizer Ea. Dist. Tenn. U.S. Dist. Ct. Hist. Soc., v.p. Ea. Dist. Tenn., 1993—; mem., organizer, bd. dirs. Tenn. Supreme Ct. Hist. Soc., pres., 1997; active Hamilton County Sch. Bd., 1970—75; bd. dirs. Chattanooga Symphony, 1980—83, Chattanooga United Way, 1990—96, chmn. fund drive profl. divsn., 1992; mem. merit selection panel for Bankruptcy Judges U.S. Dist. Ct., 1993—94; mem. award com. Liberty Bell; bd. dirs. Chattanooga Cmty. Found., 2005—. Recipient Disting. Alumni award, Carson-Newman Coll., 1984, Bus. Litigation award, John H. Pickering Achievement award, 2011, Disting. Svc.

award, Kiwanis Club of Chattanooga, 2013, Outstanding Svc. award, UTC Alumni, 2014; named Mid-South Super Lawyers, 100 Super Lawyers, Tenn.; named one of Bus. TN's Top 150 Lawyers, 2011. Fellow: Va. State Bar, Chattanooga Bar Found. (life; founder), Tenn. Bar Found. (life; founder); mem.: ABA (Tenn. Bar del. 1984—90, nominating com. 1990—99, bd. govs. 1999—2002, exec. com. 2001—02, exec. dir. search com. 2005—06, standing com. ethics and profl. responsibility 2005—08, super lawyers divsn. chair 2009—10, state del., state adv.), Task Force Revise Jud. Conduct Rules (chair 2009—,), U. Chattanooga Found. Inc. (mem. bd. 2003, exec. com. 2011—), Tenn. Continuing Legal Edn. (Blue Ribbon Com. 2007), Tenn. Supreme Ct., Chattanooga Bar Assn. (pres. 1969—70, med.-legal com. 2004—07, pres.'s award 1995, Ralph H. Kelley Humanitarian award), Tenn. Def. Lawyers Assn., Tenn. Bar Assn. (bd. govs. 1975—82, pres. 1980—81), 6th Cir. Jud. Conf. (life), Conf. So. Bar Pres. (chmn. 1980—81), Am. Bd. Trial Advs., Estate Planning Coun. (bd. dirs. 1971—72), Am. Coll. Trial Lawyers (state com. 1995—99, profl. com. 1998—2000), Am. Judicature Soc., Internat. Assn. Def. Counsel, Chattanooga Rotary Club (sec. 1989—91, 1st v.p. 1997—98, pres. 2001—02), Mountain City Club, Am. Inns Ct. (master), Delta Theta Phi. Baptist. Home: 718 Parsons Ln Signal Mountain TN 37377-2704 Office: Liberty Tower 605 Chestnut St Ste 1700 Chattanooga TN 37450 Office Phone: 423-756-3000. Business E-Mail: mbahner@cbslawfirm.com.

BAHORICH, MICHAEL S., energy executive; Grad., U. Mo., Columbia; M in Geophysics, Va. Poly. Inst. Various positions Amoco Corp., 1981—96; chief geophysicist Apache Corp., 1996—97, v.p., exploration tech., 1997—99, v.p., exploration & prodn. tech., 1999—2000, exec. v.p., exploration & prodn., 2000—09, exec. v.p., tech. officer, 2009—. Bd. advisor Stanford U., Yale U. Mem. Houston Mus. Natural Sci. Patents eight patents. Office: Apache Corp 2000 Post Oak Blvd Ste 100 Houston TX 77056-4400 Office Phone: 713-296-6000. Office Fax: 713-296-6496. Business E-Mail: mike.bahorich@usa.apachecorp.com.

BAIER, LUCINDA M. (CINDY BAIER), parking services company executive; b. 1965; BS in Acctg., Ill. State U., 1984, MS in Acctg., 1987; attended Women's Dir. Devel. Program, Northwestern U., 2002. Self employed, 1984—87; experienced tax staff Arthur Andersen & Co., 1987—89, experienced tax sr., 1989—90, tax mgr., 1990—93; corp. dir., taxes General Dynamics, 1993—97; tax dir. ICI Americas Inc., 1997—98, v.p., taxation, 1998, v.p., fin., 1998—99; sr. v.p., fin. & tax, treas. US Office Products, 1999, sr. v.p., merchandising, 1999—2000; v.p., taxes Sears, Roebuck and Co., 2000—01, v.p., fin. credit svcs. & fin. products, 2001—03, sr. v.p., gen. mgr., credit & fin. products, 2003—04; pres., COO Whitehall Jewelers, Inc., 2004—05; sr. v.p., CFO World Kitchen, LLC, Reston, Va., 2005—08; exec. v.p., CFO Movie Gallery, Inc., Dothan, Ala., 2008—10; sr. v.p., CFO Central Parking System, Inc., Nashville, 2010—. Bd. dirs. The Bon-Ton Stores, Inc., 2007—. Mem.: Executives Club of Chgo. Office: Central Parking System Inc 2401 21st Ave South Nashville TN 37212 Office Phone: 615-297-4255.

BAILE, CLIFTON A., biologist, researcher; b. Warrensburg, Mo., Feb. 8, 1940; s. Harold F. and Salome (Mohler) B.; m. Beth Lucile Hoover, Aug. 21, 1960; children: Christopher A., Marisa B. BS in Agr., Bus., Cen. Mo. State U., 1962; PhD in Nutrition, U. Mo., 1965; MA (hon.), U. Pa., 1979. NIH rsch. fellow Sch. Pub. Health Harvard U., Boston, 1964-66, from. instr. to asst. prof. Sch. Pub. Health, 1966-71; mgr. neurobiol. rsch. SmithKline Animal Health, Phila., 1971-75; from assoc. prof. to prof. Sch. Vet. Medicine U. Pa., Phila., 1975-82; disting. fellow, dir. R & D Monsanto Agrl. Co., St. Louis, 1982-95; adj. prof. nutrition Sch. Medicine Washington U., St. Louis, 1982-95; adj. prof. dept. animal sci. U. Mo., 1982-95; dist. prof. animal sci. and food and nutrition U. Ga., Athens, 1995—; Ga. Rsch. Alliance Eminent scholar Agrl. Biotech., Athens, 1996—; CEO ProLinia, Inc., 1999—2002, InsectiGen, Inc., 2003—, AptoTec, Inc., 2004—. Presenter in field. Contbr. over 350 articles to sci. publs. Rsch. fellow Ralston Purina, 1962-64, spl. postdoctoral fellow NIH, 1969; recipient Georgia Lamar Dodd award, 2002; named D.W. Brooks Dist. Prof. 2008-. Mem. Am. Soc. Animal Sci. (bd. dirs. 1990-93, animal growth and devel. award 1989), Am. Physiol. Soc., Am. Inst. Nutrition, Am. Dairy Sci. Assn. (Am. Feed Mgmt. award 1979), Soc. Neurosci., Endocrine Soc. Achievements include 17 patents in field; research in control and feed intake and regulation of energy balance. Office: U Ga 444 ADS Complex Athens GA 30602-2771 Office Phone: 706-542-4094. Business E-Mail: cbaile@uga.edu.

BAILESS, ROBERT R., lawyer; b. Birmingham, Ala., Nov. 2, 1951; BBA, U. Miss., 1973, JD, 1976. Bar: Miss. 1976, US Dist. Ct. (No. Dist. Miss.) 1976, US Dist. Ct. (So. Dist. Miss.) 1976, US Supreme Ct. 1980, US Ct. Appeals (5th Cir.) 1990. Ptnr. Wheeless Shappley Bailess & Rector LLP, Miss. Mem.: ABA, Warren County Bar Assn., Miss. Bar (pres.-elect 2006—07, pres. 2007—08). Office: Wheeless Shappley Bailess & Rector LLP PO Box 991 Vicksburg MS 39181-0991 Office Phone: 601-636-8451. Office Fax: 601-636-8481.

BAILEY, BILLY WAYNE, state legislator; b. Bluefield, W.Va., June 7, 1957; s. William Wayne and Ellen Jack Lester Bailey; m. Bobbi Jo Thomas. Former sheriff Wyoming County; state senator Dist. 9 W.Va., 1993—; state senate Govt. Orgn. & Mil Com., W.Va.; vice chmn. Govt. Orgn. Com.; mem. Enrolled Bills Com., Confirmations Com., Edn. Com., Fin. Com., Govt. Orgn. & Mil Com., majority whip; pres. W. Va. Young Dem. Clubs; v.p. Voter Regist Com., State Dem. Exec. Com.; salesman; cattle farmer. Mem.: America Legion Varney Cline Post, W. Va. Fedn. Dem. Women, Raleigh County Farm Bur., Sons Italy, Oceana Jaycees, KofC. Democrat. Catholic. Mailing: State Capitol, Rm 214W, Bldg 1 Charleston WV 25305 Home Phone: 304-294-6250; Office Phone: 304-357-7807. E-mail: bwbailey@mail.wvnet.edu.

BAILEY, BYRON JAMES, otolaryngologist, medical association administrator, educator; b. Okla. City, Apr. 5, 1934; s. Jay Gordon and Christine F. (Koehn) B.; m. Margaret Ann Whale, June 6, 1957; children: Michael Jon, Debra Lynn, James Grant, Jennifer Leigh, John Albert. BA, U. Okla., 1955, MD, 1959. Intern UCLA Med. Ctr., Los Angeles, 1959-60, resident in gen. surgery, 1960-61, resident, head and neck specialist, 1961-64, asst. prof., 1964-68; Wiess prof., chair dept. otolaryngology U. Tex., Galveston, 1968—. Treas. Am. Bd. Med. Specialties. Editor The Laryngoscope, 1994—. Chmn. Emergency Med. Svcs. Commn., Galveston, 1975-80. Recipient Mosher award Triological Soc., 1971, Harvey W. Wiley medal U.S. FDA, 1988. Mem. Am. Acad. Otolaryngology (pres. 1988-89), Am. Bd. Otolaryngology (pres. 1992-94), Am. Soc. Head and Neck Surgery (pres. 1992-93), Soc. Univ. Otolaryngologists (pres. 1976), Assn. Acad. Dept. Otolaryngology (pres. 1984), Am. Laryngol. Assn. (pres. 1993-94, DeRoaldes medal 1996, James Newcomb award 2001), Am. Bd. Med. Specialities (treas. 1993-97), Galveston C. of C. (v.p. 1978), Cosmos Club, Triological Soc. (v.p. 1997-98, Gold medal 2001), Nat. Assn. Physicians for the Environ. (pres. 1998-2000), Galveston County Med. Soc. (pres. 2001). Office: U Tex Med Br Dept Otolaryn 7104 JSA 301 University Blvd Galveston TX 77555-0521

BAILEY, DONALD B., JR., medical and special education educator; b. Atlanta, Mar. 23, 1949; married; children: Lara, Rebecca, Nathaniel. BA in Psychology, Davidson Coll., 1971; MEd, U.N.C., 1973; PhD, U. Wash., 1979. Psychol. technician, mental retardation unit Cen. State Hosp., Milledgeville, Ga., 1971-72; tchr., preschool, K-1 Chapel Hill (N.C.) Carrboro City Schs., 1973-76; rsch. asst., teaching asst. spl. edn. Univ. Wash., 1976-79; clin. asst. prof., div. spl. edn. U. N.C., Chapel Hill, 1979-86; dir. early childhood rsch. Frank Porter Graham Child Devel. Ctr., Chapel Hill, 1984—; clin. assoc. prof. of edn. U. N.C., Chapel Hill, 1986—, assoc. prof. med. allied health, 1990-99, prof. med. allied health, dir. child development ctr., 1999—. Advisor/presenter in field. Author: Teaching Infants and Preschoolers With Handicaps, 1984, Effective Teaching: Principles and Procedures of Applied Behavior Analysis With Exceptional Students, 1988, Family Assessment in Early Intervention, 1988, others; contbg. author: Education Handicapped Infants, 1983, Evaluating Early Intervention Programs for Severely Handicapped Children and Their Families, 1986, others; contbr. articles to profl. jours.; editorial bd. various jours. including Jour. of Multihandicapped Person, 1987—. Recipient numerous grants in field. Office: Univ North Carolina Dept Spl Edn 105 Smith-Level Rd Chapel Hill NC 27599-0001 Home: 992 Cleland Dr Chapel Hill NC 27517-5622

BAILEY, DONALD KEITH, music educator, composer, musician; b. Paterson, NJ, Nov. 22, 1954; s. John Alexander and Gertrude Bailey; m. Terri Lee Christensen, June 3, 1983; children: Brooke Renee Cowart, Shane Matthew, Alexis Jordan. MusB in Edn., Iowa Wesleyan Coll., Mt. Pleasant, 1976; MA in Music, U. No. Iowa, Cedar Falls, 1985. Dir. bands Norwalk Mid. Sch., Iowa, 1976—83; grad. asst. jazz studies U. No. Iowa, Cedar Falls, 1983—85; prof., dir. jazz studies U. Ark., Ft. Smith, 1985—. Music min. Faith Assembly God Ch., Ft. Smith, 1985—88; choir dir. Harvest Time Tabernacle Ch., Ft. Smith, 1988—91; worship leader Life Christian Ctr. Ch., Ft. Smith, 1991—2004; tchr, workshop leader Internat. Worship Inst., Dallas, 1997—; studio musician Omega Sound Rec. Studio, Ft. Smith, 1985—; pres., co-founder New Song Pub. Co., Ft. Smith. Composer (producer): (iowa telethon theme song) Reach Out With Love; composer: (arranger) (adventureland theme park musical) Dance to the Music, (sacred work for mass choir & orchestra) Adoration and Exultation, (orchestral ste.) Jazz Suite for Orchestra; composer: (oklahoma city bombing dedication song) Carry On. Clinician performer Ft. Smith Area Pub. Schs., 1985—; musician, event coord. City-wide Cross Denom. Religious Events, 1985—; bd. mem. Ft. Smith Symphony Assn., 2005—. Recipient Addy awards, Greater Ft. Smith Ad Club, 1991—94, Nat. Tchg. Excellece award, U. Tex., Austin, 1987, Lucille Speakman Excellence in Tchg. award, Westark C.C., 1986, Mayor's Civic Honor award Contbns. Arts, Ft. Smith Mayor, Ray Baker, 2007, Master Tchr. award, U. Arks., Ft. Smith, 2009. Mem.: Coll. Music Soc. (corr.), Ark. Sch. Band and Orch. Assn. (corr.), Internat. Assn. Jazz Edn. (corr.; pres. Ark. chpt. 1995—97), Internat. Assn. Jazz Edn. (corr.; v.p. Ark. chpt. 1994—95), Ft. Smith Symphony Assn. (assoc.; bd. mem. 2005—07), Kappa Kappa Psi (hon.), Phi Mu Alpha (corr.). Achievements include development of the first comprehensive summer high school jazz band camp in Arkansas; the only jazz improvisation for orchestral strings camp in Arkansas; a series of jazz improvisation clinics for junior high and high school students; a How to Teach Jazz Improvisation workshop for band directors; a series of music workshops for elementary school students; a concert series bringing world-renowned jazz artists to Eastern Arkansas. Avocations: composing/arranging, travel. Home: 8200 Williamsburg Rd Fort Smith AR 72903 Office: U Ark 5210 Grand Ave Fort Smith AR 72913 Office Fax: 479-788-7559. E-mail: dbailey@uafortsmith.edu.

BAILEY, ELIZABETH ELLERY, economics professor, emerita; b. NYC, Nov. 26, 1938; d. Irving Woodworth and Henrietta Dana (Skinner) Raymond; children: James L., William E. BA magna cum laude, Radcliffe Coll., 1960; MS, Stevens Inst. Tech., 1966; PhD, Princeton U., 1972; LLD (hon.), De Paul U., 1988; Dr.Engring. (hon.), Stevens Inst. Tech., 2003. Successively sr. tech. aid, assoc. mem. tech. staff, mem. tech. staff, supr. econ. analysis group, rsch. head econs. rsch. dept. Bell Labs., 1960-77; commr. CAB, 1977-83, v.p., 1981-83; dean Grad. Sch. Indsl. Adminstrn. Carnegie-Mellon U., 1983-90;, 1990-91; John C. Hower prof. pub. policy and mgmt. Wharton Sch. University of Pennsylvania, Phila., 1991—. Vis. prof. Yale Sch. Ogn. and Mgmt., 1990-91; bd. dirs. Altria Group, CSX Corp., Tchrs. Ins. and Annuity Assn., Bancroft NeuroHealth; adj. assc., then assoc. prof. econs. NYU, 1973-77. Author: Economic Theory of Regulatory Constraint, 1973; editor: Selected Economics Papers of William J. Baumol, 1976; Deregulating the Airlines, 1985; bd. editors Am. Econ. Rev., 1977-79, Jour. Indsl. Econs., 1977-84. Founding mem., v.p. bd. trustees Harbor Sch. for Children with Learning Disabilities; trustee Princeton U., 1978-82, Presbyn. U. Hosp., 1984-91, Nat. Bureau Econ. Rsch., 1993—, Brookings Inst., 1988—, Bancroft Neuro Health, 1996-2004, Catalyst, 1988-90, Am. Assembly Collegiate Schs. of Bus., 1987-90, Nat. Bur. Econs. Rsch., 1993—; mem. exec. coun. Fedn. Orgns. for Profl. Women, 1980-82; chmn. Com. on Status of Women in Econs. Profession, 1979-82; mem. corp. vis. com. Sloan Sch. Mgmt., MIT, 1982-85; mem. adv. bd. Brookings Inst., 1987—, Ctr. Econ. Policy Rsch., Stanford U., 1983—, MIT econs. dept., 1989—, Princeton econs. dept., 1989—. Recipient Alumni Recognition award Radcliffe Coll., 1988, Dirs.' Choice award Nat. Women's Econ. Alliance Found., 1990; Program Design Trainee award Bell Labs; Bell Labs grantee Princeton U., 1972. Mem. Am. Econ. Assn. (exec. com. 1981-83, v.p. 1985, Carolyn Shaw Bell award, 2009), Am. Assn. Collegiate Schs. Bus. (bd. dirs. 1987—), Beta Gamma Sigma. Office: U Pa Wharton Sch Steinberg Hall—Dietrich Hall Philadelphia PA 19104-6372 Home: 11776 Stratford House Pl Apt 1104 Reston VA 20190

BAILEY, F. LEE (FRANCIS LEE BAILEY), lawyer; b. Waltham, Mass., June 10, 1933; m. Florence Gott (div. 1961); m. Froma Portney (div. 1972); m. Lynda Hart, Aug. 26, 1972 (div. 1980); m. Patricia Shiers, June 10, 1985. Student, Harvard U., 1950—52, student, 1957; LLB, Boston U., 1960. Bar: U.S. Dist. Ct. Mass. 1961, U.S. Ct. Appeals (1st cir.) 1963, U.S. Tax Ct. 1964, U.S. Ct. Appeals (6th cir.) 1964, U.S. Supreme Ct. 1964, U.S. Ct. Appeals (2d cir.) 1967, U.S. Ct. Appeals (10th cir.) 1968, U.S. Ct. Appeals (3d cir.) 1969, U.S. Ct. Appeals (9th cir.) 1970, U.S. Ct. Appeals (4th and 7th cirs.) 1971, U.S. Dist. Ct. (we. and no. dists.) Tex. 1980, U.S. Ct. Mil. Appeals 1981, U.S. Ct. Appeals (8th and 11th cirs.) 1984, U.S. Ct. Appeals (5th cir.) 1985, U.S. Dist. Ct. (ea. dist.) Wis. 1991. Formerly with Enstrom Helicopter Mfg. Co., Menominee, Mich., TelShare Publishing Co., Chelsea, Mass., Fairchild Aircraft, San Antonio, Murray Chris Craft Industries, Inc., Sarasota, Fla., Palm Beach Roamer, Inc., West Palm Beach, Fla., Interstate Chem., Inc., West Palm Beach, Fla., Mobile, Ala.; prin. Law Offices of F. Lee Bailey, West Palm Beach, Fla.; chmn. and CEO IMPAC Control Systems, Inc. Author (with Harvey Aronson): The Defense Never Rests, 1971; author: Cleared for the Approach, 1977; author: (with John Greenya) For the Defense, 1976; author: Novel Secrets, 1979, How to Protect Yourself Against Cops In California and Other Strange Places, 1982, To Be a Trial Lawyer, 1983; author: (with Henry Rothblatt) numerous works in field of criminal law. Lt. USMC, 1952—56. Mem.: ATLA, ABA. Office: Impac Control Systems Inc 955 W Retta Esplanada Punta Gorda FL 33950 Office Phone: 941-639-6677.

BAILEY, GEORGE SCREVEN, lawyer; b. Columbia, SC, Feb. 7, 1951; s. Edward E. and Mary S. (Simpson) Bailey. BA in Economics, Wofford Coll., 1972; JD, U. SC, 1975; LLM in Taxation, NYU, 1976. Bar: SC 1976, US Tax Ct. 1979, US Ct. Appeals (4th cir.) 1982; cert. tax specialist. Assoc. Johnson, Smith et al, Sparantanburg, SC, 1976—77, Law Offices R. Young, Columbia, SC, 1976, O'Connor & Young, Columbia, 1976—79; sec.-treas. O'Connor & Bailey, P.A., Columbia, 1979—84; ptnr. Nelson, Mullins, Riley & Scarborough LLP, Columbia, 1984—; state rep. to spl. liaison Tax Com. Southeastern Region, Atlanta, 1980—83. Mem.: Columbia Taxation Study Group, Richland County Bar Assn., Southern Fed. Tax Inst. (trustee 1994—), SC Bar Assn. (chmn. tax sect. 1986—87, sect. estate planning, probate & trust law, chmn. taxation law specialization adv. bd. 1990—91), Am. Coll. Tax Counsel, Palmetto Club, Pine Tree Hunt Club, Columbia Cotillion Club, Forest Lake County Club. Office: Nelson Mullins Riley Law 1320 Main St Columbia SC 29201-3204

BAILEY, GUY H., academic administrator; m. Jan Tillery. BA, U. Ala., MA in English; PhD in English Linguistics, U. Tenn. Provost, exec. v.p. U. Tex., San Antonio, 1999—2005; chancellor U. Mo., Kansas City, 2006—08; pres. Tex. Tech U., Lubbock, 2008—. Contbr. articles to profl. jours. Office: Tex Tech U Office of Pres Box 42005 Lubbock TX 79409-2005 Office Phone: 806-742-2121. E-mail: guy.bailey@ttu.edu.

BAILEY, HAROLD RANDOLPH, surgeon, educator; b. Palestine, Tex., Jan. 20, 1943; m. Kelly Curry Bailey. BA in Biology summa cum laude, Rice U., 1964; MD, U. Tex., Dallas, 1968. Diplomate Am. Bd. Surgery, Am. Bd. Colon and Rectal Surgery. Intern straight surg. Parkland Hosp., Dallas, 1968-69; resident gen. surgery U. Tex. Med. Sch./Hermann Hosp., Houston, 1969-73; fellow colon and rectal surgery Ferguson-Droste-Ferguson Hosp., Grand Rapids, Mich., 1973-74; clin. faculty U. Tex. Med. Sch., Houston, 1974—, dir. residency tng. program colon and rectal surgery, 1984—2005, clin. prof. surgery, 1986—; clin. faculty Baylor Coll. Medicine, 1986—, clin. prof., 1999—2005; chief div. colon rectal surgery Methodist Hosp., Houston, 2006—; clin. prof. surgery Weill Med. Coll., Cornell U., 2007—. Assoc. examiner Am. Bd. Colon and Rectal Surgery, 1985—89, bd. mem., 1988—97, chmn. exam. com., 1995—97, pres., 1996—97, sr. examiner, 1997—; chief staff Park Plaza Hosp., Houston, 1988—90. Bd. dir. Am. Cancer Soc., Greater Houston unit, 1989-93, v.p., 1991-93, pres., 1993-95; mem. vestry Palmer Meml. Episcopal Ch., Houston, 1979-83, 84-86, chmn. fin. com., 1984-86; mem. fund coun. Rice U., Houston, 1993-95, class fund drive chmn. 1993-95). Recipient George Waldron award Hermann Hosp., 1970, Violet Keller award, 1973; named to Good Housekeeping mag. 400 Best Doctors in U.S., 1991, Good Housekeeping mag. Best Cancer Doctors in U.S., 1993; named Disting. Alumnus, Rice U., 2000. Fellow ACS (chmn. adv. coun. colon and rectal surgery 1996-2001, chmn. membership svcs. com. 2005-08, bd. govs. 2002-04, bd. regents 2003—), Am. Surg. Assn., Internat. Soc. Univ. Colon and Rectal Surgeons (program com. 1986), Am. Soc. Colon and Rectal Surgeons (treas., exec. coun. 1993-99, pres. 1999-2000), Tex. Surg. Soc.; mem. AMA, Tex. Soc. Colon and Rectal Surgeons (pres. 1981, exec. sec. 1982-88, exec. sec. 2007-), Tex. Med. Assn., Tex. Soc. Gastrointestinal Endoscopy, Harris County Med. Soc., Houston Surg. Soc., Phi Beta Kappa, Alpha Omega Alpha. Office: Colon & Rectal Clinic 6550 Fannin St Ste 2307 Houston TX 77030-2723 Office Phone: 713-790-9250. Personal E-mail: hrbailey@swbell.net. Business E-Mail: h.randolph.bailey@uth.tmc.edu.

BAILEY, HELEN MCSHANE, historian, consultant; b. Gardner, Kans., Oct. 17, 1916; d. Harry Cramer and Maude Ethel (Kramer) McShane; m. James Edwin Bailey, Feb. 23, 1946; children: James Edwin, Barbara Ann Bailey Crawford. BA, Bethany Nazarene Coll., 1938. Adminstrv. asst. Office Chief of Staff, U.S. Army, Washington, 1941—48; historian U.S. Army ofcl. history of World War II, U.S. Army, Washington, 1948—58; rsch. asst. George C. Marshall Rsch. Found., Washington, 1958—59; historian Orgn. Joint Chiefs of Staff, Dept. Def., Pentagon, Washington, 1968—87; cons., 1987—. Mem.: Am. Hist. Assn., Soc. Historians Am. Fgn. Rels., World War Two Studies Assn., Soc. History in Fed. Govt. Republican. Lutheran. Home and Office: 180 N Henderson Rd Travelers Rest SC 29690 Home Phone: 864-834-8111.

BAILEY, JOHN PRESTON, federal judge; b. Wheeling, W.Va., May 2, 1951; BA, Dartmouth Coll., Hanover, NH, 1973; JD, W.Va. U. Coll. Law, 1976. Bar: W.Va. 1976, US Dist. Ct. (no. and so. dists.) W.Va. 1976, US Ct. Appeals (4th cir.) 1977, Ohio 1981, US Supreme Ct. 1981, US Dist. Ct. (so. dist.) Ohio 2000. Law clk. to Hon. Charles H. Haden, II, US Dist. Ct. (no. and so. dists.) W.Va., 1976—78; atty. Bailey, Riley, Buch & Harman, LC, Wheeling, 1978—2007; asst. prosecuting atty. Ohio County, W.Va., 1985—86; spl. asst. prosecuting atty. Marshall County, W.Va., 1985—90; judge US Dist. Ct. (no. dist.) W.Va., 2007—, chief judge, 2008—. Chmn. Workers' Compensation Appeal Bd., 1985—91. Mem.: ABA, Nat. Assn. Criminal Def. Lawyers, W.Va. Trial Lawyers, W.Va. State Bar (bd. govs. 1992—95, 1998—2001, pres. 2003—04), Ohio County Bar Assn., W.Va. Bar Assn. (exec. coun. 1988—94, pres. 1992—93), Order of Coif, Phi Delta Phi. Office: US Dist Ct PO Box 551 1125 Chapline St Wheeling WV 26003 Office Phone: 304-233-1492.

BAILEY, PAUL, lobbyist; BS, Birmingham So. Coll.; MS in Engring., Vanderbilt U., Nashville; attended exec. mgmt. program, Stanford U., Calif. Analyst Oak Ridge Nat. Lab.; dir. fed. environ. issues Southern Co.; spl. asst. to the dep. sec. US Dept. Energy; dir. health and environ. affairs Am. Petroleum Inst.; mng. dir. Natsource, LLC; v.p. environ. affairs Edison Elec. Inst.; sr. v.p. nat. affairs Am. Coalition Clean Coal Electricity, 2009—. Named one of Washington's Top Lobbyists, The Hill, 2007, 2010. Office: American Coalition Clean Coal Electricity 333 John Carlyle St Ste 530 Alexandria VA 22314

BAILEY, ROBERT ELLIOTT, financial executive; b. Logansport, Ind., Mar. 29, 1932; s. Edwin William and Elizabeth Carolyn (Elliott) B.; m. Geraldine E. Hershberger, Jan. 31, 1954; children: Susan Elaine, Kathryn Jane. BS in Acctg., Ind. U., 1954; LLB, South Tex. Coll. Law, 1962. CPA, N.Y. Ptnr. Arthur Andersen & Co., Chgo., 1958-72; exec. v.p., dir., CFO Damson Oil Corp., NYC, 1972-82, Gearhart Industries, Inc., Ft. Worth, 1985-88; exec. v.p., CFO ENI Cos., Seattle and Houston, 1982-85; corp. fin. cons., 1988-91; chmn. fin. The Turner Corp., NYC, 1991-93; sr. v.p., CFO Rotondo Cos., Avon, Conn., 1993-94; dir. fin. UCAR, Danbury, Conn., 1995-96; acting CFO Tauck Tours, Inc., Westport, Conn., 1996-98, 2005. Bd. dirs. Berlin Steel Constrn. Co., Kensington, Conn., 1995—. Capt. USAFR, 1958. Mem. AICPA, Tex. Bar Assn., N.Y. CPA Soc., Fla. CPA Soc. Home: #209 988 Boulevard of the Arts Sarasota FL 34236-4833

BAILEY, ROBERT SHORT, retired lawyer; b. Bklyn., Oct. 17, 1931; s. Cecil Graham and Mildred (Short) B.; m. Doris Furlow, Aug. 29, 1953 (dec. 2001); children: Elizabeth Jane Goldentyer, Robert F., Barbara A. Jongbloed. AB, Wesleyan U., Middletown, Conn., 1953; JD, U. Chgo., 1956. Bar: Ill. 1965, U.S. Dist. Ct. D.C. 1956, U.S. Supreme Ct. 1960. Atty. criminal divsn. U.S. Dept. Justice, 1956-61, asst. U.S. atty. No. dist. Ill., 1961-65; ptnr. LeFevour & Bailey, Oak

Park, Ill., 1965-68; pvt. practice Chgo., 1968—2008. Panel atty. Fed. Defender Program, 1965-2008. Mem. NACDL (faculty 1976-78, legis. chmn. 1976-78). Home: 113 Canterfield Rd Cary NC 27513-4225 Personal E-mail: bobsbailey@comcast.net.

BAILEY, SALLIE BALLANTINE, construction materials company executive; b. 1959; BA in Economics & German, Wellesley Coll., 1982; MBA in Finance & Acctg., U. Chgo., 1984. Worked Deloitte & Touche, Chgo., Tenneco, Inc. (formerly Tenneco Automotive, Inc.); treas., corporate contr. The Timken Co., Canton, Ohio, dir. finance, 1995, sr. v.p. finance, contr., 2003—07; v.p., CFO Ferro Corp., Cleve., 2007—10; exec. v.p., CFO Louisiana-Pacific Corp., Nashville, 2011—. Bd. dirs. Milacron Inc., 2004—08. Mem. Wellesley Coll. Bus. Leadership Coun. Mem.: In Counsel with Women (bd. dirs.). Office: Louisiana-Pacific Corp 414 Union St Ste 2000 Nashville TN 37219 Office Phone: 615-986-5600. Office Fax: 615-986-5666.

BAILEY, SUSAN RUDD, allergist, immunologist, pediatrician; b. Louisville, Dec. 25, 1955; BS, Tex. A&M U., 1979, MD, 1981. Diplomate American Bd. Pediat., American Bd. Allergy & Immunology. Intern, resident pediat. Mayo Clinic, Rochester, Minn., 1981—84, fellow pediatric allergy & immunology, 1984—86; pvt. practice Ft. Worth Allergy & Asthma Associates, 1988—. Mem. editl. bd. Annals Allergy, Asthma, & Immunology, 1997—2003, asst. editor Allergy Watch; contbr. articles to profl. jours. Treas. Mayo Assn. Fellows, 1984—85; trustee Minn. Med. Assn., 1984—85; bd. visitors Scott & White Clinic, Temple, Tex., 1991—2001; mem. adv. bd. MD Anderson Physicians Network, 1992—94; bd. regents Tex. A&M U. Sys., 1999—2005. Fellow: American Acad. Pediat.; mem.: AMA (chair com. women in medicine 1987—89, mem. House Dels. 1988—, mem. Coun. Med. Edn. 2001—10, chair Tex. del. 2006—11, chair adv. com., Coun. Med. Edn. 2009—10, bd. trustees 2011—, vice spkr. House Dels. 2011—), American Coll. Allergists (Leon Unger award 1985), Tarrant County Med. Soc. (bd. dirs. 1990—, v.p. 1994—95, pres.-elect 1995—96, pres. 1996—97, trustee 1998—2001), American Coll. Allergy & Immunology (bd. regents 1994—97), American Assn. Cert. Allergists, Tex. Med. Assn. (vice spkr. 1997—2001, spkr. 2001—05, pres. 2010—11), Alpha Zeta, Alpha Omega Alpha. Office: Fort Worth Allergy & Asthma Associates 5929 Lovell Ave Fort Worth TX 76107-5029 Office Phone: 817-315-2550. E-mail: susanruddbailey@yahoo.com.

BAILEY, WILLIE L., state legislator; b. Isola, Miss., Apr. 25, 1946; m. Carolyn Trowles; 1 child, Justin. Former judge; mem. Dist. 49 Miss. House of Reps., 1995—, chair judiciary B com.; atty. Mem.: Magnolia Bar Assn., Miss. Bar Assn., Tougaloo Coll. Nat. Alumni Assn. Democrat. Methodist. Mailing: PO Box 189 Greenville MS 38702-0189 E-mail: wbailey@house.ms.gov.

BAILO, CARLA, automotive executive; B in Mech. Engring., Kettering U., Flint, Mich.; M in Mech. Engring., U. Mich. In charge of truck durability testing and test devel. truck and bus divsn. Gen. Motors; vehicle testing engr. Nissan tech. ctr. North America Nissan Motor Co. Ltd., Farmington Hills, Mich., 1989, OEM bus. unit divisional gen. mgr. Japan, dir. vehicle program mgmt., 2003, asst. chief vehicle engr. Nissan Sentra and Nissan Quest, vehicle program dir. Japan, recovery program dir., mem. mgmt. com. Americas, sr. v.p. rsch. and devel. Nissan Americas, 2011—. Office: Nissan Motor Company Limited Nissan North America Incorporated One Nissan Way Franklin TN 37067 Office Phone: 615-725-1000.

BAIN, LORNE DONALD, electronics executive; b. Montreal, QC, Canada, Aug. 26, 1941; s. Lewis S. and Christina (McKay) B.; m. Mary Michelle Fallon, Mar. 8, 1968; children— Christine Elizabeth, David Fallon Completed, Harvard U.; BBA, St. Edward's U., 1967; JD, U. Tex., 1969. Bar: Tex. 1969. Chmn., pres. & CEO WorldOil-.com; Assoc. Baker & Botts, LLP, 1969—72; sr. atty. United Gas Pipe Line, 1972—74; sr. v.p. United Energy Resources, Inc., 1974—78, exec. v.p., bd. dirs., 1979—81, Roy M. Huffington, Inc., 1981—83, pres., COO, 1984—; chmn., CEO Sanifill, Inc., 1991—96; mng. dir. Bellmeade Capital Ptnrs., LLC, 1997—2000. Bd. dirs. Belden Inc., 1993—, Cable Design Technologies Corp., 2004—. Mem. governing bd. Houston Grand Opera, Houston Republican Nat. Com. Served with U.S. Army, 1962-65 Mem. ABA, Houston Bar Assn. Clubs: Forest, Coronado, Thalia Dance. Episcopalian. Home: 3195 Del Monte Dr Houston TX 77019-3215 Office: Belden Inc Bd Directors 1 N Brentwood Blvd Ste 1500 Saint Louis MO 63105-3925 Office Phone: 314-854-8000. Office Fax: 314-854-8001. Business E-Mail: lbain@belden.com.

BAIN, NICK, state legislator; m. Lesley Lewis. B, U. Miss.; JD, Miss. Coll. Atty.; mem. Dist. 2 Miss. House of Reps., Jackson, 2012—. Mem. Oakland Bapt. Ch., Miss. Mem.: Miss. Bar Assn., Miss. Mcpl. Assn., Rotary. Democrat. Baptist. Office: Miss House of Reps PO Box 1018 Jackson MS 39215 Business E-Mail: nbain@house.ms.gov.

BAIN, TRAVIS WHITSETT, II, retired general business executive; b. San Antonio, Mar. 4, 1934; s. Travis Whitsett and Zelma Gladys (Middleton) B.; m. Karlen Jo Bruner, May 30, 1957 (dec. Dec. 09, 2009); children: Travis W. III, James Henry III. BS in Chem. Engring., U. Tex., 1956; MBA, Harvard Bus. Sch., 1958. Mfg. supt. Tex. Instruments, Dallas, 1958-61; sr. assoc. McKinsey and Co., L.A. and Chgo., 1961-65; exec. v.p., COO Trend Line Corp., Jackson, Miss., 1965-81; pres., CEO W.E. Walker Stores, Inc., Jackson, 1981-86; CEO Sunbelt Nursery Group, Inc., Ft. Worth, 1986-87; investor, cons. Bain Assocs., Ft. Worth, 1987-88; pres. Jarman Shoe Co. div. Genesco Inc., Nashville, 1988-92, Bain Enterprises, Inc. dba Sandler Pools, Plano, Tex., 1993-99; chmn. Tex. Custom Pools, Inc., Plano, 1999—2013. Bd. dirs. Atmos Energy Corp., Dallas, 1988—2010, Tex. Commerce Bank, Ft. Worth, 1986-88, Delta Industries, Inc., Jackson, 1984—; chmn. bd. dirs. Master Pools Guild, 1997-99. Bd. dirs. New Stage Theatre, Jackson, 1980-86, Boy Scouts Am., Ft. Worth, 1986-88, Miss. Ballet Internat., Jackson, 1984-86; bd. dirs., exec. com. Nashville Ballet, 1989-92; mem. placement coun. Owen Sch. Mgmt. Vanderbilt U., Nashville, 1984-92; mem. adv. bd. CBA Found. U. Tex., Austin, 1987—. Mem. Dallas Exec. Assn. (pres. 1998-99). Republican. Presbyterian. Avocations: gardening, tennis, jogging, travel, scuba diving.

BAINBRIDGE, FREDERICK FREEMAN, III, architect; b. Charlottesville, Va., Sept. 15, 1927; s. Frederick Freeman and Cornelia Winston (Burnley) B.; m. Binki Baker, Jan. 6, 1948 (div. Nov. 1972); children— Burnley, Susan Winifred, Meriwether, Robin; m. Anna Bacon, Jan. 1976; 1 son, Nicholas Gordon. B.Arch., U. Va., 1950; M. Indsl. Design, Kansas City Art Inst., 1952. Asst. prof. Sch. Architecture Clemson U., SC, 1952-55; asso. firm Toombs, Amisano & Wells (Architects), Atlanta, 1955-62; prin. firm Martin & Bainbridge, Atlanta, 1962-70, Bainbridge & Assos., 1970—. Southeastern project architect U. Ky. civil defense research project, 1964; vis. critic Ga. Inst. Tech., 1964-67 Chmn. archtl. rev. com. Atlanta Civic Design Commn., 1967—. Served with USNR, 1944-46. Recipient honor awards S. Atlantic Region AIA, 1964, 66, 68, 70; honor award prestressed Concrete Inst., 1967 Mem. AIA. Clubs: Fairington Golf and Tennis, Amelia Island Plantation; Farmington Country (Charlottesville, Va.). Home: Oldham Farm PO Box 317 Ivy VA 22945-0317 Office: 6795 Brandon Mill Rd NW Atlanta GA 30328-2028

BAIR, ROYDEN STANLEY, retired architect; b. New Rochelle, NY, Jan. 21, 1924; s. Roy S. and Ruth Irene (Farmer) B.; m. Margaret Davis Powell, Sept. 7, 1946 (dec. July 1972); children: Katherine, David, Laurence (dec. 1990), Andrew, Matthew; m. Martha Ann Cooper, July 7, 1973. BS in Civil Engring., Purdue U., 1947; BArch, MIT, 1950. Registered architect, Tex, Fla.; registered profl. engr., Tex. Construction adminstrn. Skidmore, Owings & Merrill, Chgo., 1950—51; draftsman J.N. MacCammon, Dallas, 1953-56; sr. assoc. Harrell & Hamilton, Dallas, 1956-67; sr. architect Lloyd Morgan Jones, Houston, 1967-68; owner R.S. Bair, Architects, Houston, 1969-95; ptnr. Turner & Bair Architects, Houston, 1996—2002. Capt. U.S. Army, 1942-46, 51-53. Mem. AIA (fellowship 1988, pres. Houston chpt. 1982), Construction Specifications Inst. (nat. pres. 1979, fellowship 1972), Construction Scis. Rsch. Found. (v.p. 1980-87), Tex. Soc. Architects. Home: 9573 Doliver Dr Houston TX 77063-1010 E-mail: stanandmartha@comcast.net.

BAIRD, DUNCAN, state legislator; Mem. Dist. 95 Ark. House of Reps., 2009—. Republican. Office: State Capitol Rm 350 Little Rock AR 72201 also: PO Box 185 Lowell AR 72745 Office Phone: 501-682-6211, 501-682-7771, 479-439-1717. Business E-Mail: bairdd@arkleg.state.ar.us.

BAIRD, EDWARD ROUZIE, JR., retired lawyer; b. Norfolk, Va., Aug. 29, 1936; s. Edward Rouzie and Eleanor Gray (Perry) B.; m. Nell McGlaughon, Oct. 8, 1967 (dec. Oct. 1973); 1 child, Eleanor Gray Demoors; m. Abby St. John Starke, Feb. 5, 1977; children: Abby St. John Kosturko, Edward Rouzie V. BA, U. Va., 1960, LLB, 1967. Assoc. Baird, Creshaw & Ware, Norfolk, 1967—68; asst. dist. counsel U.S. Army C.E., Norfolk, 1968—73; asst. U.S. Atty. U.S. Atty.'s Office, Norfolk, 1973—77; sole practice Norfolk, 1977—82, 1999—2004; ptnr. Willcox & Baird, Norfolk, 1982—99. Served to lt. (j.g.) USN, 1960-63. Mem. Soc. Cin., Va. Club (Norfolk). Home: 1711 Cloncurry Rd Norfolk VA 23505-1717 Home Phone: 747-423-1923.

BAIRD, JAMES KERN, educator, consultant, academic administrator; b. Pitts., Aug. 24, 1941; s. Paul Erwin and Helen Elizabeth (Kern) B.; m. Peggy Lorane Flanagan, 1967; 1 child, David Kern. BS, Yale U., 1963; AM, Harvard U., 1965, PhD, 1969. Physicist Oak Ridge (Tenn.) Nat. Lab., 1970-81; unit mgr. Knolls Atomic Power Lab., Schenectady, N.Y., 1981-82; prof., chmn. chemistry dept. U. Ala., Huntsville, 1982—90, 2001—05. Cons. Chrysler Acutron Div., Huntsville, 1988-89, Morton Thiokol, 1988-89, SCI, Huntsville, 1989, Urisphere, Arlington, Va., 1999-2000, Wilmer and Lee, Huntsville, 2002—; vis. prof. chemistry Yale U., 1998-99, 2007. Contbr. numerous articles to profl. jours. Recipient Def. Atomic Support award, 1970, Student Govt. Assoc. Outstanding Tchr. award, 1996, Coll. Sci. Dean's Service award, 2001, UAH Found. Rsch. award, 2008; disting. summer faculty rsch. fellow Naval Rsch. Lab., Washington, 1993, NASA/MSFC, 2001, Woodrow Wilson Nat. fellowship, 1963, Oak Ridge Grad. fellowship, 1965-68. MEM. Am. Chem. Soc. (Charles H. Stone award Carolina Piedmont sect. 1991), Am. Phys. Soc. Home: 4023 Lucerne Dr SE Huntsville AL 35802-1244 Office: U Ala Dept Chemistry Huntsville AL 35899-0001 Office Phone: 256-824-6441. E-mail: jkbaird@matsci.uah.edu.

BAIRD, ROBERT A., investment company executive; Pub. fin. investment banker Morgan Keegan & Co., Inc., Memphis, 1979, head fixed income investment banking effort, 1996—2010, exec. mng. dir., pres. Investment Banking Divsn., mem. exec. com., 2010—. Mem.: Securities Industry and Fin. Markets Assn. (mem. Mcpl. Securities Exec. Com.). Office: Morgan Keegan Morgan Keegan Tower 50 N Front St Memphis TN 38103 Office Phone: 901-524-4100. Office Fax: 901-524-4797.

BAIRD, ROBERT DAHLEN, retired theology studies educator; s. Jesse Dahlen and Clara (Sonntag) Baird; m. Patty Jo Lutz, Dec. 18, 1954; children: Linda Sue, Stephen Robert, David Bryan, Janna Ann. BA, Houghton Coll., 1954; BD, Fuller Theol. Sem., 1957; STM, So. Meth. U., 1959; PhD, U. Iowa, 1964. Instr. philosophy and religion U. Omaha, 1962-65; fellow Asian religions Soc. Religion in Higher Edn., 1965-66; asst. prof. religion U. Iowa, Iowa City, 1966-69, assoc. prof., 1969-74, prof., 1974-2001, prof. emeritus, 2001—, acting dir. Sch. Religion, 1985, dir., Sch. Religion, 1995—2000; Leonard S. Florsheim Sr. Eminent Scholar's chair New Coll., U. South Fla., Sarasota, 1988-89. Vis. prof. Grinnell Coll., 1983; Goodwin-Philpot Eminent chair in religion Auburn U., 2001—03; adj. prof. Ripon (Wis.) Coll., 2005—10. Author: Category Formation and the History of Religions, 1971, 2d paperback edit., 1991; author: (with W. R. Comstock et al) Religion and Man: An Introduction, 1971, Indian and Far Eastern Religious Traditions, 1972; editor: Methodological Issues in Religious Studies, 1975, Religion in Modern India, 1981, 4th edit., 2001, Essays in History of Religions, 1991, Religion and Law in Independent India, 1993, 2d edit., 2005; book rev. editor: Jour. Am. Acad. Religion, 1979—84; contbr. articles to profl. jours. Ford Found. fellow, 1965—66, Sr. fellow, Am. Inst. Indian Studies, 1972, 1992, Faculty Devel. grantee, U. Iowa, 1979, 1986, 1992. Mem.: Assn. Asian Studies, Am. Acad. Religion. Independent. Office: 12430 Crockett Bend Ln Humble TX 77346 Home Phone: 832-777-6935. E-mail: robert-baird@uiowa.edu.*

BAIRD, THOMAS BRYAN, JR., retired lawyer; b. Newport News, Va., June 21, 1931; s. Thomas Bryan and Mary Florence (Rieker) B.; m. Mildred Katherine Clark, June 23, 1956; children: Sarah, Thomas Bryan III, William, Laura. BA, U. Va., 1952; LLB, U. Tenn., 1960. Bar: Tenn. 1964, Va. 1969, U.S. Dist. Ct. (we. dist.) 1970. With Stat Farm Ins., Knoxville, Tenn., 1960-68; asst. commonwealth atty. Wytheville, Va., 1969-71; commonwealth atty. Wythe County, 1972-98; pvt. practice; ret., 1998. Trustee Simmerman Home for the Aged, 1972-83. Served with U.S. Army, 1953-55. Democrat. Presbyterian.

BAIRSTOW, FRANCES KANEVSKY, arbitrator, mediator, educator; b. Racine, Wis., Feb. 19, 1920; d. William and Minnie (DuBow) Kanevsky; m. Irving P. Kaufman, Nov. 14, 1942 (div. 1949); m. David Steele Bairstow, Dec. 17, 1954; children: Dale Owen, David Anthony. Student, U. Wis., 1937-42; BS, U. Louisville, 1949; student, Oxford U., England, 1953-54; postgrad., McGill U., Montreal, Que., Can., 1958-59. Rsch. economist U.S. Senate Labor-Mgmt. Subcom., Washington, 1950-51; labor edn. specialist U. P.R., San Juan, 1951-52; chief wage data unit WSB, Washington, 1952-53; labor rsch. economist Can. Pacific Ry. Co., Montreal, Que., Canada, 1956-58; asst. dir. indsl. rels. ctr. McGill U., 1960-66, assoc. dir., 1966-71, dir., 1971-85, lectr., indsl. rels. dept. econs., 1960-72, from asst. prof. to assoc. prof. faculty mgmt., 1972—83, prof., 1983-85; lectr. Stetson Law Sch., Fla.; spl. master Fla. Pub. Employees Rels. Commn., 1985-97. Cons. Nat. Film Bd. Can., 1965—69; arbitrator Que. Consultative Coun. Panel Arbitrators, 1968—83, Ministry Labour and Manpower, 1971—83, United Air Lines and Assn. Flight Attendants, 1990—95, Am. Airlines and Transport Workers Union, 1997—98, State U. Sys. Fla., 1990—2003, FDA, 1996—98, Social Security Adminstrn., 1996—2003, Am. Airlines, 1997—, Tampa Gen. Hosp., 1996—, Cargo Internat. Airlines, 2001, Govt. of Fla. and Fla. State Police, 2002—, Bell South and Comm. Workers Am., 2003—, USAF at Warner Robins and AFGE, 2003—; mediator Can. Pub. Svc. Staff Rels. Bd., 1973—85, So. Bell Tel., 1985—, AT&T and Comm. Workers Am., 1986—; cons. on collective bargaining arbitration OECD, Paris, 1979. Contbg. columnist: Montreal Star, 1971—85. Chmn. Nat. Inquiry Commn. Wider-Based Collective Bargaining, 1978; dep. commr. essential svcs. Province of Que., 1976—81. Recipient Sefton award, U. Toronto, 2005, Firside Chat. award, Nat. Acad. Arbirtrators, 2007; Fulbright fellow, 1953—54. Mem.: Ctrl. Fla. Indsl. Rels. Rsch. Assn. (pres. 1999), Nat. Acad. Arbitrators (bd. govs. 1977—80, program chmn. 1982—83, v.p. 1986—88, nat. coord. 1987—90), Indsl. Rels. Rsch. Assn. Am. (mem. exec. bd. 1965—68, chmn. nominating com. 1977), Can. Indsl. Rels. Rsch. Inst. (mem. exec. bd. 1965—68). Home: 4650 54th Ave S Apt 511 Saint Petersburg FL 33711-4638

BAJURA, RITA A., retired research scientist; b. 1941; BS in Chem., Mercyhurst Coll., Erie, Pa., 1963; MS in Mechanical Engring., West Va. U., 1979. With US Dept. Energy, 1980—2005, dir., Nat. Energy Tech. Lab., 1996—2005. Appointed to West Va. State's Energy Task Force, 2001. Recipient Achievement award for contributions to coal industry, Washington Coal Club, 2001, Pitt award, annual award for innovation in coal conversion, Univ. Pitts. Sch. Engring., 2002; named to Acad. of Disting. Alumni of Mech. Engring and Mech., West Va. Univ., 2000.

BAKER, ALAN, state legislator; b. Brewton, Ala., July 15, 1956; m. Kaki Stokes Baker. BS in History, Auburn U., Ala., 1978. Tchr. & coach Phenix City; history tchr. & football coach T.R. Miller HS, Brewton; ret., 2005; mem. Dist. 66 Ala. House of Reps., Montgomery, 2006—. Mem. First Bapt. Ch., Brewton; bd. dirs. Am. Red Cross, Escambia Co., Brewton Area YMCA, Habitat for Humanity. Mem.: Escambia County Ret. Educators Assn. Republican. Baptist. Office: PO Box 975 Brewton AL 36427 also: Ala House of Reps Ala State House 11 S Union St Montgomery AL 36130 Office Phone: 251-867-6514, 334-242-7720. Office Fax: 251-867-8600. Business E-Mail: staterep@co.escambia.al.us.

BAKER, ANITA DIANE, lawyer; d. Byron Garnett and Anita (Swanson) B.; m. Thomas Johnstone Robison. BA summa cum laude, Oglethorpe U., 1977; JD with distinction, Emory U., 1980. Bar: Ga. 1980. Assoc. Hansell & Post, Atlanta, 1980—88, Kitchens, Kelley, Gaynes, Huprich & Shmerling, 1989—90; asst. gen. counsel Nations-Bank Corp., 1991—97; v.p., gen. counsel Adaris Corp., 1997—99; pvt. practice Atlanta, 1999—2004; ptnr. Baker Law Group, LLC, Roswell, Ga., 2005—, Baker & Stalzer, LLC, Roswell, 2006—10. Trustee Oglethorpe U., 2002—05; pres. Oglethorpe U. Nat. Alumni Assn., 2002—04, Estate Planning Coun. North Ga., 2010—11, mem., bd. dirs., 2008—12. Mem.: ABA, Atlanta Bar Assn., North Fulton Bar Assn., Stormy Petrel Bar Assn. (past pres.), Elder Care Matters Alliance, Oglethorpe U. Nat. Alumni Assn. (past pres.), Pace Acad. Alumni Assn., Omicron Delta Kappa, Alpha Chi, Phi Alpha Theta, Phi Alpha Delta, Order of Coif. Office: Baker Law Group LLC 555 Sun Valley Dr Ste N4 Roswell GA 30076 Business E-Mail: info@bakerlg.com.*

BAKER, BILL JOHN, Principal Chief of the Cherokee Nation; b. Cherokee County, Okla. m. Sherry Baker; 6 children. B in Polit. Sci. and History in Edn., Northeastern State U., Tahlequah, Okla., 1972. Owner, operator Baker's Furniture, Tahlequah; mem. Cherokee Nation Tribal Coun., Tahlequah, 1999—2011, prin. chief, 2011—. Active First United Meth. Ch. Mem.: Tahlequah C. of C. (past pres.), Rotary Club. Office: Cherokee Nation 22361 Bald Hill Rd PO Box 948 Tahlequah OK 74465

BAKER, BRENT HAROLD, foundation executive, blogger; b. Pitts., Mar. 15, 1963; s. Burnham H. and Florence E. (French) B. BA with Spl. Honors in Polit. Sci., George Washington U., 1985. With Conservative Digest; editor, Newswatch Nat. Conservative Found., Alexandria, Va., 1985-87; co-creator, exec. dir. Media Rsch. Ctr., Alexandria, 1987—, Steven P.J. Wood Sr. fellow and v.p., rsch. publications, editor, CyberAlert email report, 1996—, editor, newsbusters.org, 2005—, v.p. for rsch. and publications. Author: How to Identify, Expose and Correct Liberal Media Bias, 1994; co-editor: And That's The Way It Isn't: A Reference Guide to Media Bias, 1990; editor Notable Quotables newsletters, 1988-, Media Watch, 1988-99, CyberAlert 1996-; editor-at-large (blog) NewsBusters.org 2005-; oversaw (newsletter) MediaWatch ConventionWatch, 1992, 1996; edited Campaign 2000 Media Reality Check, 2000; contbr. works to NY Post, Wall Street Journal, Investor's Business Daily, Washington Times, Colorado Springs Gazette-Telegraph, Union Leader (Manchester, NH), Orange County Register and Human Events; contbr. articles to National Review and Journalism Quarterly. Republican. Home: 4090 Championship Ct Annandale VA 22003-2425 Office: Media Rsch Ctr 325 S Patrick St Alexandria VA 22314

BAKER, C. MARK, lawyer; BA summa cum laude, Yale Univ., 1981; JD with highest honors, Duke Univ., 1984. Bar: Tex. 1984. Law clk. Hon. John R. Brown US Ct. of Appeals (5th cir.), 1984—85; ptnr., co-head firmwide internat. dept. and arbitration dept. Fulbright & Jaworski, Houston. Arbitrator and mediator World Intellectual Property Assn.; bd. dirs., arbitrator London Ct. Internat. Arbitration. Contbr. articles to profl. journals; lectr. in field. Named one of 100 Most Influential Lawyers, The Nat. Law Jour., 2006, The Decade's Most Influential Lawyers, 2010, 20 Worldwide Experts in Internat. Arbitration, PLC, 2006. Fellow: Tex. Bar Found., Houston Bar Found., Chartered Inst. of Arbitrators, London, England; mem.: ICC Commn., Am. Arbitration Assn. (bd. dir, internat. panel, nat. sports resolution panel), Ct. of Arbitration for Sport, Lausanne, Switzerland, Internat. Bar Assn., Coll. of the Bar of Tex., State Bar Tex. Avocations: fishing, hunting, tennis, opera. Office: Fulbright & Jaworski Ste 5100 1301 McKinney Houston TX 77010-3095 Office Phone: 713-651-5151. Office Fax: 713-651-5246. Business E-Mail: mbaker@fulbright.com.

BAKER, CARLETON HAROLD, physiology educator, scientist; b. Utica, NY, Aug. 2, 1930; s. Harold George and Loretta (Darling) B.; m. Sara Frances Johnson, July 20, 1963; children: Elizabeth Ann Bradshow, Janet Lee Howele. BA, Utica Coll. Syracuse U., 1952; MA, Princeton U., 1954, PhD, 1955. Asst. instr. Princeton U., NJ, 1952—54, asst. rsch., 1954—55; asst. prof. Med. Coll. Ga., Augusta, 1955—61, assoc prof., 1961—67, prof., 1967; prof. physiology and biophysics U. Louisville Health Scis. Ctr., 1967—71; prof., founding chmn. dept. physiology and biophysics U. South Fla. Coll. Medicine, Tampa, 1971—92, dep. dean rsch. and grad. studies, 1980—82, prof surgery, physiology and biophysics, dir. surg. rsch., 1992—95; prof. emeritus U. South Fla., 1995—. Rsch. com. mem. Am. Heart Assn., Louisville, 1969-71; rsch. com., bd. dirs. Am. Heart Assn. Fla., Tampa, 1971-85; NIH program project site visit team, 1982-84, mem. LCME Accreditation Survey Team, 1980-81; cons. U. Louisville Grad. Sch., East Carolina U. Grad. Program; rsch. prof. physiology U. S.C. Coll. Medicine, Columbia, 1994-2001 Editor: Microcirculatory Technology, 1986; mem. numerous editl. bds.; contbr. numerous articles in field Pres. Augusta Choral Soc., 1963; v.p. Blount Rd. Homeowners Assn., Lutz, Fla., 1986-93; bd. dirs. Friends of Augusta;

tech., math & physics to young people. Grantee NIH, 1960-92, Am. Heart Assn., 1968-97; recipient Svc. awards Am. Heart Assn. Fla., 1974, 77, Disting. Scientist award U. South Fla. Coll. Medicine, 1981, Dean's Citation, 1991, Founder award, 1992, Outstanding Artist/Scholar award Phi Kappa Phi, 1991 Fellow: Am. Heart Assn., Am. Physiol. Soc. (fellow cardiovasc. sect.); mem.: Shock Soc. (program coms.), European Microcirculatory Soc., Microcirculatory Soc., Torch Club Internat. Republican. Avocations: golf, fishing, music. Home: 4039 Old Waynesboro Rd Augusta GA 30906-9254 Personal E-mail: microves@bellsouth.net.

BAKER, CHARLES LYNN, management consultant; b. Dallas, Mar. 17, 1934; s. Leonard Allan and Nellie (Boals) B.; m. Joan Heverly, June 1, 1968; 1 child, Annette Lynn. BS in Internat. Rels. summa cum laude, Syracuse U., 1967; MA in Polit. Sci. cum laude, Auburn U., 1975. Commd. USAF, advanced through grades to col., dep. inspector gen. Washington, 1975—80, retired, 1980; mng. ptnr. T.Z. Assocs., Balt., 1980—83; pres. McDermott Internat. Trading A.G., Zurich, 1983—90; mng. dir. McDermott Internat. Gen. Svcs., Hong Kong, 1983—90; pres. Baker Assocs., Rancho Santa Fe, Calif., 1990—. Bd. dirs. T.Z. Assocs., Balt., Environ. Scis., San Diego, Broadleaf Industries, San Diego; adj. prof. U. Redlands Grad. Bus. Sch. Author: Strategic Planning, 1987, Executive Development, 2008. Pres. Redlands Ballet Co., 1987-89; chmn. Redlands Cultural Art Commn., 1988-2000 Mem. Am. C. of C. (v.p. Hong Kong br. 1984-86), Rotary (pres. Redlands chpt. 1989-90, bd. dirs. internat. chpt. in Hong Kong 1983-85, pres. Hong Kong chpt. 1984), Pres.'s Assn. (chmn. 1988-2004), Calif. Cultural Arts Commn. Republican. Episcopalian. Avocations: golf, tennis, reading. Office: Baker Assocs 208 Yellow Rose Trl Georgetown TX 78633-5010 Office Phone: 512-240-4966.

BAKER, DANIEL RICHARD, computer company executive; b. Copenhagen, Mar. 19, 1932; came to U.S., 1936; s. Arthur and Molly (Needman) B.; m. June Ellin Nebenzahl, Oct. 2, 1960; children: David Charles, Jill Alison. Student, Tufts Coll., 1949—51; BA, Bklyn. Coll., 1957; postgrad., Fairleigh Dickinson U., 1961—64, Am. U., 1968—69; grad. Realtors Inst., U. Va., 1972. Math tchr. N.Y.C. Pub. Schs., 1958—59; computer programmer Sys. Devel. Corp., Paramus, NJ, 1959—61; programmer analyst ITT, Paramus, 1961—64; sr. mathematician Melpar Corp., Falls Church, Va., 1964—65; sys. analyst Wolf R & D Corp., Bladensburg, Md., 1965—66, Aries Corp., McLean, Va., 1966—68; sr. sys. analyst N. Am. Rockwell Corp., Roslyn, Va., 1968—70; pres. Data Assocs., Fairfax Station, Va., 1970—, Phoenix. Real estate broker. Group leader Dale Carnegie Sales Courses; vol. Ann. Fund Campaign Tufts Coll., 1976—. With AUS, 1954-55, vet. Korean War. Recipient Eagle Scout, Boy Scouts Am., 1945, 5-yr. Million Dollar Sales Club award, Nat. Assn. Realtors. Mem.: No. Va. Assn. Realtors Pioneer Club, Va. Assn. Realtors (dir. 1977—80, 1983—97, Lifetime award 1992, 1994—2005), Charles Tufts Soc., Silvanus Packard Soc., Washington Tufts Club (v.p. 1975). Avocations: art, music, antique automobiles. Personal E-mail: would_i_kid_you@yahoo.com, data_assocs@yahoo.com.

BAKER, DAVID REMEMBER, lawyer; b. Durham, NC, Jan. 17, 1932; s. Roger Denio and Eleanor Elizabeth (Ussher) B.; m. Myra Augusta Mullins (dec. Sept, 2010), Nov. 2, 1955; m. Lois Avery Gaeta, April 9, 2011. PhB, U. Chgo., 1949; BA, Birmingham-Southern Coll., 1951; JD, Harvard U., 1954; LLD honoris causa, Birmingham-Southern Coll., 2009. Bar: Ala. 1954, NY 1963, US Supreme Ct. 1972. Assoc. Cabaniss & Johnston, Birmingham, Ala., 1957-62, Chadbourne, Parke, Whiteside & Wolff, NYC, 1962-66, ptnr., 1967-86, Jones, Day, Reavis & Pogue, NYC, 1986-93; ret. ptnr. Afridi, Angell & Baker, 1993—96; ptnr. Gersen, Baker & Wood LLP, NYC, 1997-98, Baker, Johnston & Wilson LLP, Birmingham and NYC, 1998—2003; of counsel Haskell Slaughter Young & Rediker, LLC, Birmingham and NYC, 2003—14, Kayser & Redfern, LLP, NYC, 2011—. Gen. counsel Econ. Club NY, 1977—2011; dir. Jr. Achievement NY, 1973—99, Jr. Achievement Greater Birmingham, 1999—2007; pres. NY Legislative Svc., 1975—98, Musica Viva NY, 1994—96; chmn. NY Legislative Svc., 1998—. Co-editor Due Diligence, Disclosures and Warranties in the Corporate Acquisition Practice, 1988, 2nd edit., 1992; author articles and book chpts. Mem. adv. com. Ctr. for NYC Law, 2000—; trustee Birmingham-So. Coll., 1985—2013. With US Army, 1954—57. Mem.: ABA (liaison com. fin. acctg. stds. bd. 1981—2007), Ala. Law Inst., NY State Bar Assn. (exec. com. bus. law sect. 1987—89, exec. com. internat. law and practice sect. 1991—92, chmn. internat. investment and devel. com. 1991—92), Assn. Lloyd's Mems. (N.Am. adv. bd. mem. 2000—), Internat. Bar Assn. (vice chmn. bus. orgn. com. 1986—90, rep. to US mems. NY area 1988—2000, chmn. com. on trusts for bus. 1990—94, prin. rep. to UN in NY 1993—2010), Birmingham Bar Assn. (chmn. history and archives com. 2002, 2008—09, 2014), Ala. Bar Assn., NYC Bar Assn. (chmn. com. on state legis. 1968—70), American Law Inst., American Arbitration Assn. (nat. panel), Met. Club NYC, Harvard Club NYC. Democrat. Unitarian Universalist. Avocation: bridge. Home: 1200 Beacon Pkwy E Apt 500 Birmingham AL 35209-1041 Office: Kayser & Redfern LLP 515 Madison Ave Fl 31 New York NY 10022 Office Phone: 212-752-5507. Business E-Mail: drbaker@515law.com.

BAKER, EDWARD L., JR., public health physician; b. Chattanooga, Nov. 18, 1946; s. Edward Lamar and Sue B. Baker; m. Pamela Taylor, June 21, 1969; children: Justin, Ryan, Lindsay. BA, Vanderbilt U., 1968; MD, Baylor U., 1972; MPH, Harvard U., 1979, MS, 1980. Diplomate Am. Bd. Internal Medicine, Am. Bd. Occupational Medicine. Commd. USPHS, 1974—2003, asst. surgeon gen.; dep. dir. Nat. Inst. for Occupational Safety; asst. prof. Harvard U. Sch. Pub. Health, Boston, 1980-82, assoc. prof., 1982-85; asst. dir. Nat. Inst Occupl. Safety and Health Ctr. Disease Control, Atlanta, 1985-88, dep. dir. Nat. Inst. Occupl. Safety and Health, 1988-90, dir. Pub. Health Practice Program Office, 1990—2003; dir. NC Inst. Pub. Health, Gillings Sch. Global Pub. Health U. NC, Chapel Hill, 2003—, prof. Dept. Health Policy and Mgmt. Bd. dirs. Internat. Commn. on Occupl. Health, 1986-92. Author, editor 100 sci. articles and book chpts. Fellow Am. Coll. Epidemiology; mem. APHA, Am. Coll. Occupl. and Environ. Medicine (authorship award 1988), Soc. Occupl. and Environ. Health, Royal Soc. Medicine (London, vis. fellow). Office: NC Inst Public Health Univ North Carolina Campus Box 8165 Chapel Hill NC 27599-8165 Office Phone: 919-966-1069. Office Fax: 919-966-0478. Business E-Mail: ed_baker@unc.edu.

BAKER, FLOYD WILMER, surgeon, retired military officer; b. Leavenworth, Kans., May 25, 1927; s. Floyd Winfield and Lolita Clare (Somers) B.; m. Darlene Marie Fulk, Apr. 10, 1949; children: Linda Marie, Diane Louise, Barbara Jayne. BA, U. Kans., 1950, MD, 1953; grad., Army Command and Gen. Staff Coll., 1964, Indsl. Coll. Armed Forces, 1967. Diplomate: Am. Bd. Surgery. Commd. 1st lt. U.S. Army, 1953, advanced through grades to maj. gen., 1980; intern Madigan Gen. Hosp., Tacoma, 1953-54; resident in gen. surgery Fitzsimons Army Hosp., Denver, 1955-59; dir. personnel and tng. Office of Surgeon Gen., 1970-71; comdg. gen. Brooke Army Med. Center, Ft. Sam Houston, Tex., 1974-78; Letterman Army Med Center, Presidio of San Francisco, 1978-81; chief surgeon U.S. Army, Europe; comdg. gen. U.S. Army 7th Med. Command, 1981-83, U.S. Army Health Services Command, Ft. Sam Houston, 1983-86; retired U.S. Army, 1986. Served with USNR, 1945-46. Decorated Legion of Merit (2), Meritorious Service medal, Army Commendation medal (3), Air medal (2), Disting. Service medal. Fellow Am. Coll. Physician Execs.; mem. AMA, Soc. U.S. Army Flight Surgeons. Republican. Baptist. Home and Office: 1413 Wiltshire Ave San Antonio TX 78209-6050 E-mail: fbaker1@satx.rr.com.

BAKER, GEORGE HAROLD, III, physicist, educator; b. Cheverly, Md., Mar. 23, 1949; s. George Harold, Jr. and Betty (Fost) Baker; m. Donna Prillaman, June 21, 1975; children: Matthew C., Jeffrey P., Virginia E. BA, Western Md. Coll., 1971; MS, U. Va., 1974; PhD, USAF Inst. Tech., Dayton, Ohio, 1987. Tchg. asst. U. Va., Charlottesville, 1971-73; physicist Harry Diamond Labs., Adelphi, Md., 1973-77, Def. Nuc. Agy., Alexandria, Va., 1977-87, group leader, 1987-89, asst. for program devel., 1989-94; chief innovative concepts divsn., 1994-96; Def. Threat Reduction Agy. dir. Springfield (Va.) Rsch. Facility, 1996-99; sr. scientist Northrop-Grumman, Alexandria, 1999—2000; prof. Coll. Integrated Sci. and Tech. James Madison U., Harrisonburg, Va., 1999—2012, tech. dir. Inst. Infrastructure and Info. Assurance, 2002—11, prof. emeritus, 2012—; mem. Congl. Electromagnetic Pulse Commn., 2002—08; CEO Baycor LLC, 2011—; bd. dirs. Found. Resilient Socs., 2012—. Exec. adv. bd. Inst. Infrastructure and Info. Assurance, 2003—; exec. bd. Nat. Def. Indsl. Assn. Homeland Security, 2005—; infrastructure roundtable NRC, 2005—07, com. on burec security, 2006—08; cons. in field; bd. dirs. Found. Resilient Socs., 2012—; exec. adv. bd. mem. James Madison U. Rsch.; pub. svc. adv. bd. Congl. Task Force on Nat. Homeland Security. Contbr. articles to profl. jours. Canvasser Citizens Sensible County Planning, Fairfax County, Va., 1989—2000; tchr. Agape Christian Fellowship, Chantilly, Va., 1974—94, elder, 1994—2000; music and youth leader New Life Fellowship, Annandale, Va., 1979—83; elder Covenant Presby. Ch., 2008—. Fellow: Nuc. Electromagnetic Soc. (chmn. program com. 1984, co-chair nonproliferation and arms control underground focus group 1996—99, session chair 1998, chmn. nat. HPM conf. steering group 1999, mem. Amerem nat. com. 2001—, session chair 2002); mem.: NAS (mem. infrastructure roundtable 2006—07), IEEE (sr.; session chmn. 1987, 1992), Va. Alliance Secure Computing and Networking (charter mem.), Forum Mil. Application Directed Energy, Directed Energy Profl. Soc. (charter), Assn. Old Crows, Kappa Mu Epsilon, Phi Delta Theta. Achievements include patents for optically coupled differential voltage sensor; co-developer sea-going nuclear EMP simulator concept; development of Defense Nuclear Agency EMP underground test program; High Power Microwave program; space nuclear power program. Office: Baycor LLC 3305 Hemlock St Harrisonburg VA 22801 Business E-Mail: bakergh@jmu.edu.

BAKER, GILBERT R., state legislator; b. Monahene, Tex., Sept. 5, 1956; m. Susan Baker; children: Stephen, Anna, Luke, Nathanael, Philip, Mark, Joshua, Michael. BFA, La. Tech. U., 1977; MM, U. Ariz., 1978. Tchr. U. Ctrl. Ark., 1978-98, acad. advisor, assoc. dean, 1998—; mem. Dist. 30 Ark. State Senate, Little Rock, 2001—; chmn. Ark. State Republican Party, 2005—07. Pres. Life Choices Bd., Crisis Pregnancy Ctr., 1994-99; mem. Conway Home Edn. Fellowship Bd., 1996-99, Ednl. Alliance Steering Com., 1998—; chair Faulkner County Rep., 1997-99. Mem. Greenbrier C. of C., Conway C. of C. Republican. Bible Ch. Office: 17 Cooper Ln Conway AR 72034-7935 also: State Capitol Rm 320 Little Rock AR 72201 Business E-Mail: bakerg@arkleg.state.ar.us.

BAKER, GLEN D. (BUCK BAKER), wholesale distribution executive; Various merchandising mgmt. positions Gates/Arrow Distbg., Inc.; various positions including bus. devel. mgr. & merchandising dir. ScanSource, Inc., 1995—2002, sr. v.p. merchandiising, AIDC/POS sales unit, 2002—05, sr. v.p. merchandising Catalyst Telecom (subs.), 2005—08, pres. ScanSource Comm., 2008—. Office: ScanSource Inc 6 Logue Court Greenville SC 29615 Office Phone: 864-288-2432. Office Fax: 864-288-1165.

BAKER, GLENN, state legislator; b. Sept. 02; m. Janice S. Baker, 1967; 2 children. Exec. Ga. Power, 1966—2001; mgr. client devel. Janice S. Baker & Assoc.; mem. Dist. 78 Ga. House of Reps., 2009—. Pres. Lake Spivey Cmty.; vol. Ga. Transplant Found.; mem. bd. dir. Clayton Co. Cancer Soc. Democrat. Methodist. Office: 611 Coverdell Legislative Office Bldg Atlanta GA 30334 also: PO Box 1529 Jonesboro GA 30237 Office Phone: 404-656-0314. Personal E-mail: glennbakerhr78@bellsouth.net.

BAKER, HOLLIS MACLURE, furniture manufacturing company executive; b. Allegan, Mich., Apr. 27, 1916; s. Hollis Siebe and Ruth (MacClure) B.; m. Betty Jane Brown, Aug. 2, 1947; children: Tomelyn Ann, Susan MacClure; m. Elsie Margarite Leigh, Aug. 27, 2003. Student, U. Va., 1935-37. With Baker Furniture, Inc., Holland, Mich., 1938-40, 45-73, v.p., treas., 1959-61, pres., 1961-70, chmn. bd., 1970-73; v.p., gen. mgr. Grand Rapids Chair Co., Mich., 1959-61, pres., 1961-70. V.p., dir. Manor House, Inc., N.Y.C., 1958-70; pres. Boyne City R.R. Co., Mich., 400 Bldg. Corp., Palm Beach, Fla.; dir. Mich. Nat. Bank, Lansing, 1968-83, Am. Seating Co., Grand Rapids, 1973-83, Mich. Nat. Bank, Grand Rapids, 1959-84, Norton Gallery, Palm Beach, 1984-91. Author: A Brief History of Schloss Branzoll, 1975, A History of the Chateau de Caussade, 1980, A History of the Chateau de la Roque, 1985, Five Castles Are Enough, 1989. Bd. dirs. USCG Found., 1981-91. Lt. (s.g.) USNR, 1941-45. Mem. Nat. Assn. Furniture Mfrs. (dir.), Furniture Mfrs. Assn. Grand Rapids (dir., past pres 1970-84), Zeta Psi. Clubs: Brook (N.Y.C.), River (N.Y.C.), New York Yacht (N.Y.C.), Leash (N.Y.C.); University (Grand Rapids); Everglades (Palm Beach), Bath and Tennis (Palm Beach); Buck's (London). Episcopalian. Home: 301 Chapel Hill Rd Palm Beach FL 33480-4124 Office: 2220 Wealthy St Grand Rapids MI 49506

BAKER, JAMES ADDISON, III, (JIM BAKER), lawyer, former United States Secretary of State; b. Houston, Apr. 28, 1930; s. James A. and Ethel Bonner (Means) Baker; m. Mary Stuart McHenry, 1953 (dec. Feb. 18, 1970); m. Susan Garrett, Aug. 6, 1973; 8 children. BA, Princeton U., 1952; LLB, U. Tex., 1957; LLD (hon.), U. Pa., 2007. Atty. Andrews Kurth Campbell & Jones, Houston, 1957—75; under sec. US Dept. Commerce, Washington, 1975—76; chief of staff to Pres. The White House, 1981—85, chief of staff, sr. counselor to Pres., 1992—93; sec. US Dept. Treasury, 1985—88; chmn. George H.W. Bush Presdl. Campaign, 1988; sec. US Dept. State, 1989—92; sr. ptnr. Baker & Botts, LLP, Washington and Houston, 1993—. Sr. counselor The Carlyle Group, 1993—2005; bd. dirs. Electronic Data Corp., 1996—2003; personal envoy of Sec.-Gen. for Western Sahara UN, 1997—2004; spl. Presdl. envoy to Iraqi for Debt Reduction The White House, 2003; chmn. The B.P. Refineries Ind. Safety Review Panel, 2005—07; co-chair Iraq Study Group, US Inst. Peace, 2006. Author: The Politics of Diplomacy: Revolution, War and Peace, 1989-1992, 1995, "Work Hard, Study...and Keep Out of Politics!": Adventures and Lessons from an Unexpected Political Life, 2006; appeared in (documentaries) Reagan, 2011. Hon. chmn. James A. Baker III Inst. Pub. Policy, Rice U., Houston, 1993—; bd. trustees Woodrow Wilson Internat. Ctr. Scholars, Smithsonian Instn. Recipient Presdl. Medal of Freedom, The White House, 1991, Woodrow Wilson award, Princeton U., 2000, Lifetime Achievement award, American Lawyer mag., 2007, Jefferson award, American Inst. Pub. Svc., Disting. Svc. award, US Dept. State, Alexander Hamilton award, US Dept. Treasury, Hans J. Morgenthau award, George F. Kennan award; named one of America's Best Leaders, US News & World Report, 2007. Fellow: American Acad. Arts & Sciences; mem.: ABA, American Judicature Soc., Houston Bar Assn., Tex. Bar Assn., Phi Delta Phi. Republican. Avocations: hunting, fishing, tennis, golf. Office: Baker & Botts LLP 1 Shell Plz 910 Louisiana Houston TX 77002 Office Phone: 713-229-1234. Office Fax: 713-229-1522. E-mail: jamesbaker@bakerbotts.com.

BAKER, JAMES L., JR., plastic surgeon, educator; b. Somerville, NJ, 1936; MD, U. Amsterdam, 1964. Diplomate Am. Bd. Plastic Surgery. Intern Monmouth Med. Ctr., Long Branch, NJ, 1964—65, resident gen. surgery, 1965—69; resident plastic surgery Orlando Regional Med. Ctr., Fla., 1969—71; fellow hand surgery U. Louisville, 1971; clin. prof. plastic surgery U. South Fla., Tampa, 1991—; pvt. practice Winter Park, Fla. Prof. surgery, dept. med. edn. U. Ctrl. Fla. Coll. Medicine, Orlando; past chmn. dept. plastic surgery Fla. Hosp. Sys. Contbr. articles to profl. jours., chapters to books. Mem.: Fla. Soc. Plastic & Reconstructive Surgeons (pres. 1984), Am. Soc. Aesthetic Plastic Surgery (pres. 1995—96). Office: Pvt Practice 400 W Morse Blvd Ste 203 Winter Park FL 32789-4280 Office Phone: 407-644-5242. Office Fax: 407-644-0236. E-mail: jlbakerjr@msn.com.

BAKER, JANET P., insurance company executive; BS magna cum laude in Mgmt., Troy U., Ala., M in Human Resources Mgmt. Joined AFLAC, Inc., 1982, various positions including second v.p. human resources and second v.p. client svcs., v.p. mktg. svcs., 1999—2002, v.p. account implementation, 2002—04, sr. v.p. client services, then sr. v.p. corp. learning, 2004—10, sr. v.p. human resources, 2010—. Mem.: Kiwanis Club. Office: AFLAC Inc 1932 Wynnton Rd Columbus GA 31999 Office Phone: 706-323-3431.

BAKER, JAY A., diagnostic radiologist; MD, Duke U., 1992. Diplomate Am. Bd. Radiology-diagnostic radiology, 1997. Resident diagnostic radiology Duke Univ. Med. Ctr., Durham, NC, 1990—97, felllow mammography, 1997—98, chief breast imaging divsn. Office: Duke University Medical Center Box 3808 Durham NC 27710 Office Phone: 919-684-7645.

BAKER, JOHN DANIEL, II, trucking executive, crushed stone company executive; b. Jacksonville, Fla., Aug. 7, 1948; s. Thompson Simkins and Cynthia (L'Engle) Baker; m. Anne Davis, Mar. 18, 1972; children: Edward L. II, John D. III, Susan Anne. BA, Princeton U., 1970; JD, U. Fla., 1973. Bar: Fla. 1973. Corp. counsel Fla. Rock Industries Inc., Jacksonville, 1974—75; pres., CEO Fla. Rock Industries, Inc., 1996—2007; div. pres. Aggregates Group, 1975—76, v.p. transp. group, 1976—83, exec. v.p. corp., 1983—89, pres., dir., 1989—, CEO, 1997—; pres., CEO Patriot Transportation Holding, Inc., 2008, chmn., 2010—. Bd. dirs. Fla. Rock Industries, Inc., 1979—2007, Patriot Transp. Holding, Inc., 1986—, Hughes Supply, Inc., 1994—2006; bd.dirs. Wachovia Bank, N.A., 2001—08; bd. dirs. Vulcan Materials Co., 2007—09, Wells Fargo & Co., 2009—, Progress Energy Inc., 2009—12, Tex. Industries, Inc., 2010—, Duke Energy Corp. (formerly Progress Energy Inc.), 2012. Chmn. KIPP Schs., Jacksonville, Tiger Acad.; trustee, YMCA Fla. First Coast; trustee Woodberry Forest Sch. Office: Fla Rock Industries Inc Box 4667 155 E 21st St Jacksonville FL 32206-2136 also: Patriot Transportation Holding Inc 200 W Forsyth St Ste 700 Jacksonville FL 32202-4321 Office Phone: 904-396-5733. Office Fax: 904-396-2715. E-mail: jdbaker@flarock.com.

BAKER, KAREN R., state supreme court justice; BS, Ark. Tech U., 1983; JD, U. Ark., Little Rock, 1987. Pvt. practice, Ark., 1987—95; pub. defender Van Buren County and Searcy County, Ark., 1989—95; juvenile judge 20th Judicial Dist., Ark., 1995—96, chancery judge Ark., 1997—2000; assoc. judge Ark. Ct. Appeals, 2001—10; assoc. justice Ark. Supreme Ct., 2011—. Mem.: ABA, Ark. Assn. Women Lawyers, Faulkner County Bar Assn., Van Buren/Searcy County Bar Assn., Ark. Bar Assn., Ark. Judicial Coun. Office: Arkansas Supreme Court Justice Building 625 Marshall St Little Rock AR 72201*

BAKER, KEITH LEON, lawyer; b. Columbus, Ind., Jan. 22, 1950; s. Richard Leon and Sarah Elizabeth (Wisehart) Baker. BA, Princeton U., 1972; JD, Syracuse U., 1975; LLM with highest honors, George Washington U., 1978. Bar: NY 76, DC 76, Va. 2000, US Ct. Appeals 83, US Ct. Internat. Trade 83. Asst. bank examiner US Treasury Dept., NYC, 1974; law clk. US Dept. of Justice, Syracuse, NY, 1974—75; atty.-adviser GAO, Washington, 1975—78, US EPA, Washington, 1978—80; pvt. practice Washington, 1980—99; ptnr. Barton, Baker, McMahon & Tolle, 1999—. Actor: Small Business Financing, 1983; contbr. articles to profl. jours. Mem.: ABA, Nat. Contract Mgmt. Assn., Fed. Bar Assn. Methodist. Home: 6645 Hawthorne St Mc Lean VA 22101-4423 Office: Barton Baker McMahon & Tolle The Madison Bldg Ste 440 1320 Old Chain Bridge Rd Mc Lean VA 22101 Business E-Mail: kbaker@bbmtlaw.com.

BAKER, KERRY ALLEN, management consultant; b. Selmer, Tenn., Sept. 21, 1949; s. Austin Clark and Betty Ann (Brooks) B.; m. Ellen Fleming. BS in Indsl. & Sys. Engring., Ga. Inst. Tech., 1971; MBA, Ga. State U., 1973; JD, Memphis State U., 1987. With dept. law State of Ga., 1971—73; engr. N.W. Ga. divsn. Gold Kist, Inc., Ellijay, 1977—80; sr. mfg. engr. Schering-Plough Corp., 1980—82, mgr. indsl. engring., 1983—86, supr., mfg. engr., 1986—90; mgr., plant bus. Clorox Co., Dyersburg, Tenn., 1990—95; mgr., ops. Huish Detergents, Inc., Dyersburg, 1995; exec. dir. Mgmt. Recruiters of Dyersburg, 1996—97; pres. Rock Ridge Ventures, Inc., Dyersburg, 1996—2000, Arden, NC, 2000—; mgr., adminstrn. Gabriel Ride Products, Pulaski, Tenn., 1998—99; contr. MAHLE Motorsports, Inc., Fletcher, NC, 2000—07; program mgr. Kearfott Guidance & Navigation Corp., Black Mountain, NC, 2007—08; mgr. spl. programs, motion sys. divsn. Kearfott Corp., Black Mountain, 2008—11. Bd. dirs. Dyersburg Dyer County C. of C., 1995—97, vice chmn., bus. devel., 1997. With US Army, 1973—77. Decorated Order of St. Barbara. Mem. Inst. Indsl. Engrs., Am. Prodn. and Inventory Control Soc., Nat. Def. Indsl. Assn., Scabbard and Blade, Masons, Phi Delta Phi. Methodist. Home: PO Box 87 Arden NC 28704-0087 Office: PO Box 87 Arden NC 28704 Office Phone: 828-654-0349. Personal E-mail: Kb82151@gmail.com.

BAKER, KRISTINE GERHARD, federal judge; b. Colorado Springs, Colo., Mar. 30, 1971; BA, St. Louis U., 1993; JD, U. Ark. Sch. Law, 1996. Law clk. to Hon. Susan Webber Wright US Dist. Ct. (eastern dist.) Ark., 1996—98; assoc. William & Anderson, Little Rock, 1998—2000, Quattlebaum, Groom, Tull & Barrow, Little Rock, 2000—02, ptnr., 2002—12; judge US Dist. Ct. (eastern dist.) Ark., 2012—. Office: US Courthouse 500 West Capitol Ave Little Rock AR 72201*

BAKER, LEE EDWARD, biomedical engineering educator; b. Springfield, Mo., Aug. 31, 1924; s. Edward Fielding and Oneita Geneva (Patton) B.; m. Jeanne Carolyn Ferbrache, June 20, 1948; children: Carson Phillips, Carolyn Patton. BEE, U. Kans., 1945; MEE, Rice U., 1960; PhD in Physiology, Baylor U., 1965. Registered profl. engr., Tex. Asst. prof. electrical engring. Rice U., Houston, 1960-64;

asst. prof. physiology Baylor U. Coll. Medicine, Houston, 1965-69, assoc. prof., 1969-75; prof. biomed. engring. U. Tex., 1975-82, Robert L. Parker Sr. Centennial Prof. Engring. Austin, 1982-2000, prof. emeritus, 2000—. Co-author: Principles of Applied Biomedical Engineering, 1968, 3d edit., 1989; author, co-author scientific papers. Served to lt. USN, 1943-46, PTO, 1951-53. Spl. research fellow NIH, 1964-65. Fellow Am. Inst. Med. and Biol. Engring., Royal Soc. Medicine; mem. IEEE (sr.), Biomed. Engring. Soc. (sr.), Am. Physiol. Soc. Office: Univ Tex Biomed Engring Dept Austin TX 78712 Business E-Mail: leb@mail.utexas.edu.

BAKER, MARK, state legislator; b. Chgo., May 13, 1962; m. Lady Collins Baker. Mem. Dist. 74 Miss. House of Reps., 2004—, mem. apportionment and elections com., conservation and water resources com., fees and salaries of pub. officers com., judiciary A com., mem. judiciary en banc com., pub. utilities com. Republican. Presbyterian. Address: PO Box 947 Brandon MS 39043-0947 Home Phone: 601-824-3297; Office Phone: 601-824-7455. Business E-Mail: mbaker@house.ms.gov.

BAKER, MARK BRUCE, lawyer, educator; b. Bridgeport, Conn., Dec. 27, 1946; s. Phillip and Lillian (Islovitz) Bader; m. Sandra Fay Wolf, June 9, 1968 (div. 1982); 1 dau. Rachel Barrett Bader; m. Nora Kay Mandell, Dec. 30, 1984; 1 dau. Lisa Anne Baker. BBA, U. Miami, Coral Gables, Fla., 1968; JD, So. Meth. U., Dallas, 1974. Bar: Tex. 1974. Assoc. firm Herndon, Girand and Dooley, Dallas, 1974-76; ptnr. firm Pailet and Bader, Dallas, 1976-80; prof. internat. law U. Tex., Austin, 1980—; of counsel Bard and Groves, Houston, 1981—83, Goodall and Davison, Austin, 1991—; gen. counsel Embree Constrn. Group, Inc., Austin, Tex., 1987—2000, LivingDirect.com, 2010—; corp. counsel Kinnect, Inc., Lloyds of London Co., 2005—07. Chmn. bd. Embree Health Care Group, Inc. Contbr. articles to legal publs. Bd. dirs. Jewish Cmty. Coun. Austin, 1983-86, Big Bros./Big Sisters Program, 1999—, Vol. Svcs. of Children's Hosp. of Austin, 2003—. Recipient Outstanding Asst. Prof. award U. Tex., 1982, Outstanding Class Lectr. award, 1984, Tex. Excellence Tchg. award U. Tex. Alumni Assn., 1983. Mem. ABA, Union Internat. des Avocats, Am. Friends Wilton Park (sec.-treas. 1982-84), Tex. Bar Assn. (internat. law sect.), Austin Fgn. Trade Coun., Am. Bus. Law Assn. (internat. law sect., pres. 1990-91). Office: Bldg 3 Ste 601 1250 Capital of Tx Hwy S Austin TX 78746 Home: 2702 Magellan Dr Austin TX 78733-1222 Office Phone: 512-422-3003. Business E-Mail: m.baker@mail.utexas.edu.

BAKER, MERL, engineering educator; b. Cadiz, Ky., July 11, 1924; s. Jesse F. and Argie (Coyle) B.; m. Emily Wilson, Sept. 14, 1946; children: Merl Wilson, Marilyn Ruth. BS in Mech. Engring., U. Ky., Lexington, 1945; MS, Purdue U., 1948, PhD, 1952. Grad. asst. Purdue U., 1946-48; mem. faculty U. Ky., 1948-63, prof. mech. engring., 1955-63; exec. dir. Ky. Rsch. Found., 1953-63; coordinator, dir. U. Ky. coop. programs with AID, 1956-63, exec. dir. research and relations with industry, 1957-63; dean U. Mo. Sch. Mines and Metallurgy, 1963; chancellor U. Mo. Sci. and Tech., Rolla, 1964—73; spl. asst. to pres. statewide system U. Mo., 1973-77; coordinator energy conservation program Oak Ridge Nat. Lab., 1977-79, energy mgmt. specialist, 1979-82; provost U. Tenn.-Chattanooga, 1982-85, prof. engring., 1985-97, dir. Ctr. for Career Enhancement, 1985-97; engring. cons. Lexington, Ky., 1997—. With USN, 1945—46. Recipient Disting. Alumnus award U. Ky., 1965, Disting. Engring. Alumnus award Purdue U., 1968; named Outstanding Mech. Engr., 1991; named to U. Ky. Engring. Hall of Distinction, 2003. Fellow: ASHRAE (award of merit tchg. 1959, chmn. edn. com. 1960-61, Disting. Svc. award 1971, Outstanding Svc. & Achievement award, 1959), Am. Soc. Engring. Mgmt. (bd. dirs.), Am. Soc. Engring. Edn. (bd. dirs.), Acad. Fellows; mem.: U. Mo. Sch. Sci. & Tech., Acad. Engring. Mgmt. (hon.), NSPE (pres. Tenn. Soc. 1995-96), Ky. Acad. Sci., Newcomen Soc. N.Am., Cosmos Club (Washington), Blue Key, Scabbard and Blade, Sigma Xi, Phi Kappa Phi, Phi Eta Sigma, Tau Beta Pi (named Disting. Nat. Alumnus award 2010), Pi Tau Sigma (Gold medal, 1953), Sigma Pi Sigma, Omicron Delta Kappa, Chi Epsilon, Rotary. Home: 2120 Glenway Ave Covington KY 41014-1541 Business E-Mail: m.baker4@insightbb.com.

BAKER, MIKE, food products executive; b. Prairie Grove, Ark., 1955; Grad., Harding U., 1978. V.p., poultry ops. Tyson Foods, Inc., Springdale, Ark., pres., prodn. svcs., 1999—2001, sr. v.p., tech. svcs., 2001, sr. v.p., internat. ops. Office: Tyson Foods Inc 2200 Don Tyson Pkwy Springdale AR 72762 Office Phone: 479-290-4000. Office Fax: 479-290-4061. Business E-Mail: mike.baker@tyson.com.

BAKER, PETER MITCHELL, science association director, laser scientist; b. London, July 18, 1939; arrived in U.S., 1966; s. George Edward and Clarice Baker; m. Sunny Baker, Oct. 15, 1988; 1 child, Scott George. BSc in Physics with honors, London U., 1963. Sr. physicist Itek Corp., Lexington, Mass., 1966-69; sr. v.p. Micronetic Sys., Burlington, Mass., 1969-74; tchr. physics Hillcrest Sch., Nairobi, Kenya, 1975-77; pres. Quantrad Corp., Torrance, Calif., 1977-84, Ebtec Calif., Huntington Beach, 1985-88; exec. dir. Laser Inst. Am., Orlando, Fla., 1988—. Lectr. lasers UCLA Ext., 1986—88; chmn. Bd. Laser Safety Inc., 2003—08. Contbr. articles to profl. jours. Recipient CEO award for Outstanding Small Bus., 1982. Fellow: Laser Inst. Am. (pres. 1987); mem.: Coun. of Engring. and Sci. Soc. Execs. (pres. 2004—05). Avocations: bicycling, walking, tennis. Office: Laser Inst Am 13501 Ingenuity Dr Ste 128 Orlando FL 32826-3009

BAKER, PHILIP STEVEN, dentist, educator; m. Jacqulyn Bennett, June 25, 1995. BS in Biology, Regis Coll., 1974; DDS, Loyola U., 1978. Diplomate Am. Bd. Prosthodontics, 2005. From clin. instr. to asst. prof. Sch. Dentistry Loyola U., Chgo., 1978—85; from asst. prof. to assoc. prof. Coll. Dentistry U. Fla., Gainesville, Fla., 1987—98; assoc. prof. Coll. Dental Medicine, Ga. Regents U., 1998—. Dir. grad. prosthodontics. Recipient Tchg. Excellence award, Coll. Dental Medicine, Ga. Regents U., 2008; named Outstanding Tchr. of Yr., U. Fla. Coll. Dentistry, 1989. Fellow: Am. Coll. Prosthodontists (pres. Ga. sect. 2003—04). Office: Ga Regents University Coll Dental Medicine GC1141 1120 15th St Augusta GA 30912 Office Phone: 706-721-2261.

BAKER, RICHARD, diagnostic radiologist; MD, U. South Fla., 1984. Diplomate Am. Bd. Radiology-diagnostic radiology, 1988. Resident diagnostic radiology Jackson Meml. Hosp., Miami, 1984—88; hosp. affiliations include Holy Cross Hosp. Univ. of Miami, Jackson Meml. Hosp. Office: Jackson Memorial Hospital 1611 NW 12th Ave Miami FL 33136-1096 Office Phone: 305-585-1111.

BAKER, RICK (RICHARD M. BAKER), former mayor, St. Petersburg, Florida; b. Chgo. m. Joyce Baker; 2 children. BS in Mgmt., Fla. State U., Tallahassee, MBA, JD with honors; studied Comparative Law, U. Oxford. Law intern with Fla. Supreme Court Justice Ben Overton; former pres. Fisher and Sauls, P.A., St. Petersburg; mayor City of St. Petersburg, Fla., 2001—10. Group leader Transition Team depts. Transp., Environ. Protection and Cmty. Affairs, Fish and Wildlife Commn.; vice chair. Gov. Crist Action Team on Energy & Climate Change. Author (book): (novels) Mangroves to Major Leagues: A Timeline of St. Petersburg, Florida, 2000. Chmn. Nat. League of Cities Sch. Improvement Task Force; pres. Children's Dream Fund; chmn. St. Petersburg Area C. of C., Fla. Internat. Mus., Leadership St. Pete, Mcpl. Mentoring Initiative, Century Commn. for sustainable Fla.; founder YMCA Neighbor to Neighbor Christmas Program, CONA Neighborhood Leadership Program. Named Pub. Ofcl. of Yr., Governing Mag., 2008. Republican. Avocation: guitar. Home: 1012 N Shore Dr NE #44 Saint Petersburg FL 33701

BAKER, ROBERT JOSEPH, bishop; b. Willard, Ohio, June 4, 1944; BA in Philosophy, Pontifical Coll. Josephinum, Columbus, Ohio; STL, Pontifical Gregorian Univ., Rome, 1974, STD, 1977. Ordained priest Diocese of St. Augustine, Fla., 1970; faculty mem. St. Vincent de Paul Sem., Boynton Beach, Fla.; pastor Cathedral of St. Augustine, 1984—99; ordained bishop, 1999; bishop Diocese of Charleston, SC, 1999—2007, Diocese of Birmingham, Ala., 2007—. Co-editor: (books) Welcome the Stranger: Contemporary Ministry in the Church of Florida, 1983, Historic Catholic Sites of St. Augustine, 1988. Roman Catholic. Office: Diocese of Birmingham 2121 3rd Ave N Birmingham AL 35203 Office Phone: 205-838-8322. Office Fax: 205-836-1910.

BAKER, ROBERT W., lawyer; b. Wilmington, Del., Sept. 7, 1956; B in bus., economics, and acctg., U. Del.; JD, U. Tex., Austin. Bar: Tex. 1981, La. 1986. Joined Tenneco Energy, 1983, named v.p., assoc gen. counsel, 1995, sr. v.p., assoc. gen. counsel; named sr. v.p., assoc. gen. counsel El Paso Corp., Houston, 1996, sr. v.p., dep. gen. counsel, 2002—03, exec. v.p., pres. Merchant Energy, 2003, exec. v.p., gen. counsel, 2004—. Office: El Paso Corp 1001 Louisiana St PO Box 2511 Houston TX 77002-2511

BAKER, ROGER W., consulting firm executive, former federal agency administrator; b. 1956; BS in Computer Sci., U. Mich., MBA. V.p. engring. & ops. VISA Internat.; COO BlueGill Technologies; chief info. officer US Dept. Commerce, 1998—2001; exec. v.p., gen. mgr. telecommunications and info. assurance bus. group CACI Internat.; v.p. info. tech., chief info. officer General Dynamics; pres., CEO Dataline, LLC, Norfolk, Va., 2007—08; asst. sec. for info. & tech. US Dept. Veterans Affairs, Washington, 2009—13; chief strategy officer Agilex, Chantilly, Va., 2013—. Vice chair Industry Adv. Coun.'s Transition Study Group; mem. tech., media, and telecommunication policy group Obama for Am., 2008; mem. Vet. Agency Review Teams Presdl. Transition Team, 2008. Contbr. articles to profl. jours. Democrat. Office: Agilex 5155 Parkstone Dr Chantilly VA 20151 Office Phone: 703-889-3800.*

BAKER, STEPHEN DENIO, physics professor; b. Durham, NC, Nov. 30, 1936; s. Roger Denio and Eleanor Elizabeth (Ussher) B.; m. Paula Eisenstein, June 24, 1962; children: Hannah Hitzhusen, Sarah Topper. BS, Duke U., 1957; MS, Yale U., 1959, PhD, 1963. Lectr. physics Rice U., Houston, 1963-66, asst. prof., 1966-69, assoc. prof., 1969-73, prof., 1973—2004, prof. emeritus, 2004—. Office: Rice Univ Dept Phys & Astron MS 61 6100 Main St Houston TX 77005-1892

BAKER, THOMAS EUGENE, law educator; b. Youngstown, Ohio, Feb. 25, 1953; s. John M. and Helen Marie (Kish) B.; m. Jane Marie Schussler, June 15, 1974; 1 child, Thomas Athanasius. BS cum laude, Fla. State U., Tallahassee, 1974; JD with high honors, U. Fla., Gainesville, 1977. Bars: Fla. 1979, U.S. Dist. Ct. (no. dist.) Tex. 1979, U.S. Supreme Ct. 1982, U.S. Ct. Appeals (5th cir.) 1979, U.S. Ct. Appeals (11th cir.) 1981. Law clk. to presiding judge U.S. Ct. Appeals (5th cir.) Ga., Atlanta, 1977—79; prof. law Tex. Tech. U., Lubbock, 1979—98, Alvin R. Allison prof., 1992—98; jud. fellow U.S. Supreme Ct., Washington, 1985—86, acting adminstrv. asst. to chief justice, 1986—87; James Madison chair constnl. law, dir. constnl. law ctr. Drake U. Law Sch., Des Moines, 1998—2002; mem. founding faculty Coll. of Law, Fla. Internat. U., Miami, 2002—. Mem. adv. bd. Am. Criminal Law Rev., Washington, 1981-85; standing com. rules and procedures US Jud. Conf., 1990-95; vis. prof. U. Fla., 1994, Coll. William and Mary, 2007; Fulbright prof. U. Athens, Greece, 1993; bd. editors Preview US Supreme Ct. Cases, 1991—; bd. acad. advisors Claremont Inst. Ctr. Constitutional Jurisprudence; legal advisory bd. Washington Legal Found.; adv. com. mem. Jour. Legal Edn., 2012-; editl. bd. mem. Jour. Legal Edn., 2012-. Author: Rationing Justice on Appeal: The Problems of the U.S. Court of Appeals, 1994, The Most Wonderful Work: Our Constitution Interpreted, 1996, Federal Court Practice and Procedure: A Third Branch Bibliography, 2001, A Primer on the Jurisdiction of the US Courts of Appeals, 2nd edit., 2009; co-author (with T. Floyd): Can a Good Christian Be a Good Lawyer?, 1998; co-author: (with J. Williams) Constitutional Analysis in a Nutshell, 2d edit., 2003; co-author: (with R. Jarvis and A. McClurg) Amicus Humoriae: An Anthology of Legal Humor, 2004; co-author: (with J. Stack) At War with Civil Rights and Civil Liberties, 2005; co-author: (with A. Hellman & W. Araiza) First Amendment Law: Freedom of Expression and Freedom of Religion, 3d edit., 2014; co-author: (with D. Meador & J. Steinman) Appellate Courts: Structures,Functions, Processes and Personnel, 2d edit., 2006; co-author: (with Araiza, Duhart & Friedland) Skills and Values: Constitutional Law, 2013; mem. editl. bd. Jour. Supreme Ct. History, 1991—93; contbr. articles to profl. jours. Recipient Faculty Rsch. award Tex. Tech U., 1996, 94, 83, Outstanding Law Prof. award, 1988, 89, 2011, 12, Spencer A. Wells U. Tchg. award, SBA Pres.'s award Drake Law Sch., 2002, Pioneer award Fla. Internat. U. Coll. Law, 2004; Justice Tom C. Clark fellow Jud. Fellows, 1986. Fellow Am. Acad. Appellate Lawyers, Am. Bar Fedn.; mem. ABA (various sects. and coms.), Am. Law Inst. (life elected mem. 2009), Am. Judicature Soc. (bd. dirs. 2000-02), Order of Coif. Byzantine Catholic. Avocations: pottery, racquetball. Office: Fla Internat University Coll Law Modesto Maidique Pk RDB Hall Miami FL 33199 Business E-Mail: thomas.baker@fiu.edu.

BAKER, THOMAS J., JR., plastic surgeon; b. Clay, Ky., Nov. 8, 1925; MD, U. Ind., 1949. Diplomate Am Bd. Surgery, Am. Bd. Plastic Surgery, cert. of advanced edn. in cosmetic surgery Am. Soc. Aesthetic Plastic Surgery. Intern plastic surgery Jackson Meml. Hosp., Miami, 1949—50, resident, 1951—55, U. Tex., 1955—57; pvt. practice Miami; clin. prof. plastic surgery U. Miami Sch. Medicine, 1997—. Staff Mercy Hosp., Miami; clin. prof. plastic surgery U. Tex. Med. Ctr., Galveston. Mem.: Am. Assn. Plastic Surgeons (Disting. Fellow award 2000), Am. Soc. Plastic & Reconstructive Surgeons (Spl. Achievement award 1999), Am. Soc. Aesthetic Plastic Surgeons (Disting. Svc. award 1990), Plastic Surgery Ednl. Found. (Disting. Svc. award 1989), Internat. Soc. Aesthetic Plastic Surgery (ednl. found. prof.). Achievements include development of the Baker-Gordon phenol peel which has been used successfully for over 40 years for deep chemical peeling producing reliable results. Office: Pvt Practice 9155 S Dadeland Blvd Miami FL 33156 Office Phone: 305-670-9995.

BAKER, TOM, utilities executive; married; 2 children. BSME, Univ. Tex., Austin. Engring. & mgmt. positions TXU Corp., Dallas, 1968—; sr. v.p. TU Elec. & TU Services, Dallas; prin. fin. officer Tex. Utilities Co., Dallas; chmn., CEO TXU Elec. Delivery, Dallas; vice-chmn. TXU Corp., Dallas, 2007; chmn. emeritus Energy Future Holdings Corp. (formerly TXU Corp.), Dallas. Bd. mem., past. chmn. Greater Dallas C. of C.; exec. bd. mem. Boy Scouts Am. Circle Ten Council; bd. dir. Children's Med. Ctr. Dallas; past chmn. Ctrl. Dallas Assn., Downtown Improvement Dist., Dallas, Dallas Together Forum; past trustee Paul Quinn Coll. Nuclear missile launch officer USAF. Office: Energy Future Holdings Energy Plz 1601 Bryan St Dallas TX 75201

BAKER, TOMMY LEE, state legislator; Alderman Osceola City Coun.; mem. Dist. 55 Ark. House of Reps., 2007—. Democrat. Baptist. Address: PO Box 361 Osceola AR 72370 Office Phone: 870-563-8277. Office Fax: 870-563-7477. Business E-Mail: bakert@arkleg.state.ar.us.

BAKLANOFF, ERIC NICHOLAS, economist, educator; b. Graz, Austria, Dec. 9, 1925; came to U.S., 1937, naturalized, 1943; s. Nicolas W. and Lucille (King) B.; m. H. Christina Janes, June 17, 1956 (div. June 1973); children: Nicholas, Tanya, Ana-Maria; m. Joy Driskell, June 6, 1982. Student, Antioch Coll., 1943-44; AB, Ohio State U., 1949, MA, 1950, PhD, 1958; postgrad. (Fulbright scholar), U. Chile, 1957, Harvard Grad. Sch. Bus. Adminstrn., 1959; postgrad. (NDEA postdoctoral fellow), U. Tex., summer 1963. Instr. econs. Ohio State U., 1957-58; asst. prof. La. State U., 1958-61, assoc. prof., 1961-62; prof. econs., dir. Latin Am. Studies Inst., 1965-68; assoc. prof. econs., dir. Grad. Center for Latin Am. Studies, Vanderbilt U., 1962-65; prof. econs., dean for internat. studies and programs U. Ala., 1969-73, bd. visitors rsch. prof. econs., 1974-92, rsch. prof. econs. emeritus, 1992—. Disting. vis. prof. Luther Coll. summer 1965; cons. Am. Council on Edn., USAF Inst., Pres.'s Southeastern Council on Latin Am. Studies, 1963-64, U.S. Dept. Edn., Centro de Estudios y Communicacion Economica, Am. Enterprise Inst. Pub. Policy Rsch., Fed. Rsch. divsn., Hispanic divsn. Libr. of Congress. Author: Expropriation of U.S. Investments in Cuba, Mexico and Chile, 1975, The Economic Transformation of Spain and Portugal, 1978, La Transformación Economica de Espana y Portugal: La economia del Fanquismo y del Salazarismo, 1980; author: (with Jeffrey Brannon) Agrarian Reform and Public Enterprise in Mexico: The Political Economy of Yucatan's Henequen Industry, 1987; author: (with Edward H. Moseley) Competing for Latin American Markets: A Business Perspective on the Spanish-American War Centennial, 1999; author: (with others) Revolutionary Change in Cuba, 1971, Modern Brazil: New Patterns and Development, 1971, Background to Revolution: The Development of Modern Cuba, 1979, Yucatan: A World Apart, 1980, The Iberian-Latin America Connection: Implications for U.S. Foreign Policy, 1986, State Shrinking: A Comparative Analysis of Privatization, 1987, The Alabama Economy: Issues for the 1990s, 1990, Portugal: Ancient Country, Young Democracy, 1990, Portugal: A Country Study, 1994, Cuba in Transition, 1998, 2001, 2005, 2009, Peripheral Visions: Politics, Society, and the Challenges of Modernity in Yucatan, 2010; co-author (with Edward Moseley): Yucatan in an Era of Globilization, 2008; contbg. author: others, editor, contbg. author: The Shaping of Modern Brazil, 1969, New Perspectives of Brazil, 1966, Mediterranean Europe and the Common Market, 1976, Competing for Latin American Markets: A Business Perspective on the Spanish American War Centennial, 1999, The Handbook of Portuguese Studies, 1999, El Triángulo Económico: España-USA-America Latina, 2002; contbr. articles to profl. jours. Active Boy Scouts Am. Served with USNR, 1944-46, PTO. Decorated Knight of Grace, Hospitaler and Mil. Order St. Lazarus of Jerusalem, Malta obedience; named Outstanding Scholar U. Ala., 1980-81; fellow Ctr. Advanced Study Behavioral Scis., 1964-65; grantee U.S. Dept. State, Spain, 1974; rsch. fellow Andrew W. Mellon Found., 1987. Mem. Delta Chi, Beta Gamma Sigma, Sigma Delta Pi, Omicron Delta Epsilon, Phi Beta Delta. Eastern Orthodox. Office: U Ala PO Box 870224 Tuscaloosa AL 35487-0154 Business E-Mail: ebaklano@cba.ua.edu.

BAKST, DAREN, legal association administrator, think-tank associate; BA, MBA, George Wash. U., Washington; JD, U. Miami; LLM in Law and Govt., American U. Wash. Coll. Law. Founder, pres. Coun. on Law in Higher Edn., 1998—; policy counsel Nat. Legal Ctr. for Pub. Interest (merged into American Enterprise Inst.), Washington, US Chamber of Commerce; dir. legal and regulatory studies John Locke Found., Raleigh, NC, 2006—12; rsch. fellow in agricultural policy, Thomas A. Roe Inst. for Economic Policy Studies The Heritage Found., 2013—. Adj. prof. bus. law Barton Coll.; mem. adminstrv. law and regulation exec. com. Federalist Soc.; mem. energy, environ., and agr. task force American Legis. Exch. Coun. Contbr. columns in newspapers; op-eds and quotes have appeared in Wall Street Journal, Washington Times, USA Today, National Review Online, AOL News, American Enterprise Online, Chronicle of Higher Education and many North Carolina Newspapers. Office: Council on Law in Higher Education 9386 Via Classico West Wellington FL 33411 Address: The Heritage Foundation 214 Massachusetts Ave NE Washington DC 20002-4999 Office Phone: 561-792-4440.*

BALABAN, ANNE R., publishing executive; b. 1957; Grad., SUNY Buffalo, 1979. Formerly with USA Today; account exec. Sunday Mag. Network, 1985; jewelry watch mgr. Vogue, 1986—88; fashion dir. Rolling Stone mag., 1988—93; fashion & luxury goods mgr. In Style, 1993—94; fashion dir. Allure, 1994—97; mass beauty product Self, 1997—98; advt. dir. Fashionmall.com, 1998—2000; online advt. & mag. sales dir. Martha Stewart Living Omnimedia, Inc., 2000—03, sr. v.p., pub. Everyday Food, 2004—07; v.p., pub. Every Day With Rachael Ray Reader's Digest Assn., Inc., 2007—11; consulting pub., chief revenue officer Just A Pinch Recipe Club American Hometown Media, Franklin, Tenn., 2011—. Named Salesperson of Yr., MinOnline Media, 2009. Office: Just A Pinch Recipe Club 110 Third Ave North Franklin TN 37064 Office Phone: 914-238-1000.

BALAGIA, S. JACK, JR., lawyer; b. Austin, Tex., Oct. 26, 1951; BA, Univ. Tex., Austin, 1973, JD, 1976. Bar: Tex. 1976. Law clk. to Hon. W.M. Taylor, Jr. U.S. Dist. Ct., 1976-77; ptnr. McGinnis, Lochridge & Kilgore L.L.P., Austin; atty. ExxonMobil Corp., 1998—99, coord. upstream comml. litigation, 1999—2004, asst. gen. counsel, 2004—10, v.p., gen. counsel, 2010—. Apptd. legal com. Interstate Oil Compact Com., 1981—; pub. affairs com. State Bar Tex., 1989-90. Editor Media Law Handbook, 1980, co-editor, 1985. Fellow: Tex. Bar Found. (life); mem.: ABA, Houston Bar Found. (vice-chmn.), Houston Bar Assn., State Bar Tex., Univ. Tex. Law Sch. Alumni Assn. (pres.). Office: Exxon Mobil Corp 5959 Las Colinas Blvd Irving TX 75039-2298 Office Phone: 972-444-1000. Office Fax: 972-444-1350. Business E-Mail: jack.balagia@exxonmobil.com.*

BALART, LUIS ANTONIO, JR., gastroenterologist; MD, La. State U. Sch. of Medicine, 1973. Diplomate Am. Bd. Internal Medicine-gastroenterology, 1981. Intern Charity Hosp., 1973—74; intern internal medicine La. State Univ., 1974—76; resident internal medicine Naval Regional Med. Ctr., Phila., 1974—76; fellow gastroenterology Ochsner Med. Instns., 1979—81; fellow hepatology Univ. of Southern Calif., 1981—82; physician Tulane Univ. Hosp. and Clinic, Chief Tulane gastroenterology and hepatology. Prof. medicine Tulane Univ. Sch. of Medicine. Office: Tulane University School of Medicine 1415 Tulane Ave Fl 6 New Orleans LA 70112 Office Phone: 504-988-5800.

BALCH, SAMUEL EASON, lawyer; b. Madison, Ala., Sept. 5, 1919; s. Joseph Austin and Clara Irene (Vaughn) B.; m. Elizabeth Gordon Brock, Apr. 17, 1943 (dec.); children: Samuel Eason Jr., Elizabeth Gordon Balch Lanier, Gene Austin Balch Limbaugh, Ann Warwick Balch Miano. BS in Commerce and Bus. Adminstrn, U. Ala.,

1940; LLB, U. Va., 1948, JD, 1970. Bar: Va. 1947, Ala. 1948, U.S. Supreme Ct. 1960, U.S. Ct. Appeals (11th cir.) 1981, U.S. Ct. Appeals (5th cir.) 1965. Assoc. Martin, Turner & McWhorter, 1948; sr. ptnr. Balch & Bingham (and predecessor firms), 1962-89, of counsel, 1990—. Bd. dirs. Ala. Power Co., 1970-90; chmn. legal com. Edison Electric Inst., 1979-81, chmn. econs., pub. policy and strategic planning, exec. adv. com., 1986-88. Served to major AUS, 1941-46, ETO, PTO. Life fellow Am. Bar Found.; mem. ABA (mem. coun. pub. utility law, telecomms. and transp. sect.), Fed. Energy Bar Assn., Ala. Bar Assn., Birmingham Bar Assn., Newcomen Soc., Am. Judicature Soc., Farrah Law Soc., Mountain Brook Club, The Summit Club, The Club (Birmingham, Ala.), Kappa Sigma. Episcopalian. Home: 4227 Old Leeds Rd Birmingham AL 35213-3211 Office: PO Box 306 1710 6th Ave N Birmingham AL 35203-2015 Office Phone: 205-226-3400.

BALCOMB, MELANIE S., women's college basketball coach; b. Princeton, NJ, Sept. 24, 1962; d. Alan and Barbara Balcomb. BS, Trenton State Coll., NJ, 1984; MEd, 1985. Asst. coach Niagara U. Purple Eagles, 1985—89, Ohio U. Bobcats, 1989—90, Providence Coll. Lady Friars, 1990—93; head coach Ashland U. Eagles, Ohio, 1993—95, Xavier U. Musketeers, Cin., 1995—2002, Vanderbilt U. Commodores, Nashville, 2002—. Named Coach of Yr., Atlantic 10 Conf., 2001, NJ Sports Writers Assn., 2001, Greater Cin. Women's Sports Fedn., 2001, Ohio Coll. Coach of Yr., Columbus Dispatch, 2001; named to Greater Cin. Basketball Hall of Fame, 2001. Avocations: golf, travel, reading. Office: Vanderbilt U Womens Basketball McGugin Ctr 2601 Jess Neely Dr Nashville TN 37212 Office Phone: 615-343-8482. E-mail: melanie.balcomb@Vanderbilt.Edu.

BALD, GARY M., cruise line executive; b. 1954; BS in Psychology, U. SC, 1976; M in Forensic Sci., George Washington U., 1981. With Lab Divsn. FBI, 1977—81, with Albany, 1981—84, Phila., 1984—89, with Inspection Divsn., 1989—91, supr., organized crime & drug matters, 1991—95, with, 1995—96, chief, policy planning & analysis unit, criminal investigative divsn., 1996, asst. spl. agent, 1996—99, criminal through inspection divsn., 1999—2002, spl. agent, 2002—03, dep. asst. dir. for counterterrorism ops., 2003—04, asst. dir., Counterterrorism Divsn., 2004, exec. asst. dir., counterterrorism & counterintelligence, 2004—05, dir., Nat. Security Svc., 2005—06; sr. v.p., safety, security & environment, med. pub. health Royal Caribbean Cruises, Ltd., 2006—. Office: Royal Caribbean Cruises Ltd 1050 Caribbean Way Miami FL 33132 Office Phone: 305-539-6000. Office Fax: 305-539-0562. Business E-Mail: gbald@royalcaribbean.com.

BALDANZA, BEN (BASIL BEN BALDANZA), air transportation executive; b. NY, 1961; m. Marcia A. Baldanza. BA in Economics, Syracuse U.; MA in Pub. Affairs, Princeton U. Fin. analyst, mgr. yield mgmt. and fin. depts. Am. Airlines, 1985—91; dir. fin. analysis N.W. Airlines, 1991—93, mng. dir. yield mgmt.; mgr. UPS, 1993—94; joined Continental Airlines, 1994—97, exec. v.p.; mng. dir., COO Grupo Taca, 1997—99; sr. v.p. mktg. & planning US Airways, Inc., Arlington, Va., 1999—2005; pres., COO Spirit Airlines, 2005—06, pres., CEO, 2006—. Office: Spirit Airlines 650 SW 34th St Fort Lauderdale FL 33315 Office Phone: 954-359-0780.

BALDUCCI, LODOVICO, medical oncologist, educator; MD, Cath. U., Rome, 1968. Diplomate Am. Bd. Internal Medicine-geriatric medicine, Am. Bd. Internal Medicine, 1987, Am. Bd. Internal Medicine-hematology, 1978, Am. Bd. Internal Medicine-med. oncology, 1979. Fellow internal medicine A Gemelli Gen. Hosp., Rome, 1968—70; resident internal medicine Univ. Miss. Med. Ctr., 1973—76, fellow hematology and oncology, 1976—79; prof. medicine Coll. Medicine Univ. South Fla.; hosp. affiliation includes Tampa Gen. Hosp.; program leader sr. adult oncology program Moffitt Cancer Ctr., med. dir. affiliates and referring physician relations. Nimmo visiting professorship, Adelaide, Australia, 2009; Mehdi Tavassoli Meml. lecture, Jackson, Miss., 2009; 1st Paul Calabresi Meml. lecture Internat. Soc. Geriatric Oncology, Rome, 2005; visiting expert Univ. Hosp., Singapore. Featured in CBS Evening News with Katie Couric, 2011; contbr. articles to profl. publs. Recipient Claude Jacquillat award, Paris, Am. Cmty. Cancer Ctr. Outstanding Clin. Rsch., 2006. Fellow: Am. Coll. Physicians; mem.: Fla. Soc. Clin. Oncology (bd. dirs.), Am. Soc. Breast Disease, Am. Soc. Hematology, Am. Assn. Cancer Rsch., Am. Geriatrics Soc., Am. Soc. Clin. Oncology (B.J. Kennedy award 2007). Office: H Lee Moffitt Cancer Center & Research Institute 12902 Magnolia Dr Tampa FL 33612 Office Phone: 813-745-3822.*

BALDWIN, BONNIE, physician; b. Dallas, Dec. 18, 1954; d. Eugene and Mary Ellen Jericho; m. Robert Talbot Baldwin, May 28, 1985; children: Robert, Ryan. AB, Duke U., Durham, NC, 1977; MD, Baylor Coll. Medicine, 1985. Gen. surgery resident U. Tex.-Houston, 1985-88; plastic surgery resident Baylor Coll. Medicine, Houston, 1988-91; asst. prof. M.D. Anderson Cancer Ctr., Houston, 1991-97; physician pvt. practice, Houston, 1997—. Med. advisor Reach for Recovery, Houston, 1999, cons. M.D. Anderson, 1998—. Contbr. articles to profl. jours. Named Best Scientific Exhibit Am. Soc. Aesthetic Plastic Surgery, 1997. Fellow ACS; mem. Am. Soc. Plastic Surgery, Soc. Surg. Oncology, Am. Soc. Aesthetic Plastic Surgery. Office: Cons in Plastic Surgery 7737 Southwest Fwy Ste 201 Houston TX 77074-1865 Office Phone: 713-791-1975. Business E-Mail: bjb@bonniebaldwinmd.com.*

BALDWIN, CHUCK (CHARLES O. BALDWIN), minister, radio personality; b. La Porte, Ind., May 3, 1952; s. Ed Baldwin; m. Connie Kay Cole, June 2, 1973; children: Sarah, Christopher, Timothy. Attended, Midwestern Baptist Coll., Pontiac, Mich., 1971—73; Bachelor's in theology, Master's in theology, Liberty U., Lynchburg, Va.; DD (hon.), Christian Bible Coll., Trinity Baptist Coll., Jacksonville, Fla. Founding pastor Crossroad Baptist Ch., Pensacola, Fla., 1975—. Host (radio program) Chuck Baldwin Live, 1994—. Vice-presdl. candidate Constitution Party, 2004, presdl. candidate, 2008; Pensacola chair, state exec. dir. Fla. Moral Majority, 1980—84; vol. chaplain State Prison, Century, Fla.; bd. dirs. Gospel Radio Latin America; bd. regional v.p. Trinity Bapt. Coll., Jacksonville, Fla. Recipient Nat. Medal of Patriotism, Am. Police Hall of Fame; named Hon. Dep. Sheriff, Escambia County Fla. Sheriffs Dept. Constitution Party. Baptist. Office: Crossroad Baptist Ch 6800 Mobile Hwy Pensacola FL 32526 also: Chuck Baldwin Live PO Box 10 Kila MT 59920-0010 Office Phone: 850-944-5709, 850-944-3544. Office Fax: 850-944-0577. E-mail: chuck@chuckbaldwinlive.com.

BALDWIN, HAROLD SCOTT, pediatrician, educator; b. Honolulu, Dec. 22, 1954; MD, U. Va. Sch. Medicine, 1981. Diplomate Am. Bd. Pediat. Intern U. Rochester/Strong Meml. Hosp., NY, 1982—86, resident in pediat. NY; assoc. prof. Children's Hosp., Phila.; fellow in pediatric cardiology U. Iowa Coll. Med., Iowa City, 1986—90; prof. pediatrics, cell and devel. biology, prof. pediat. Vanderbilt U. Med. Ctr., Nashville; chief divsn. pediatric cardiology Vanderbilt Children's Hosp., Nashville. Recipient Established Investigator award, Am. Heart Assn., 1995. Fellow: Am. Heart Assn. (mem. coun. on cardiovasc. disease in young, program com. 1998—2001, mem. nominating com. 2001—03); mem.: Academic Pediat. Soc., Stanley Sarnoff Found. Cardiovasc. Rsch. (sci. bd. mem. 2004), Am. Coll. Cardiology. Office: Vanderbilt U Med Ctr 2204 Childrens Way Ste 5230 Nashville TN 37232 Office Phone: 615-322-7447. Business E-Mail: scott.baldwin@vanderbilt.edu.

BALDWIN, JAMES L., JR., lawyer, beverage company executive; m. Susan Baldwin; children: Sarah, Marie. BA cum laude, Washington & Lee Univ.; JD, So. Methodist Univ. Assoc. Berman, Mitchell, Yeager & Gerber; ptnr. Hutcheson & Grundy, Dallas; asst. gen. counsel Cadbury Schweppes plc, 1995—97; gen. counsel Mott's LLP, Stamford, Conn., 1998—2002; sr. v.p., gen. counsel Dr. Pepper / Seven Up Inc., 2002—03; exec. v.p., gen. counsel Dr. Pepper Snapple Group Inc. (formerly Cadbury Schweppes Americas Beverages), Plano, Tex., 2003—. Office: Dr Pepper Snapple Group 5301 Legacy Dr Plano TX 75024 Office Phone: 972-673-7000.

BALDWIN, JOHN T., wholesale distribution executive; BS, U. Houston, 1978; JD, U. Tex., 1981. Various fin. positions Tenneco, Inc. (formerly Tenneco Automotive, Inc.), Greenwich, Conn., England; treas. Worthington Industries, Inc., 1997—98, v.p., CFO, 1998—2003; sr. v.p., CFO Graphic Packaging Corp., 2003—05. Bd. dirs. The Genlyte Group Inc. (acquired by Koninklijke Philips Electronics N.V.), 2003—08, Metals USA Holdings Corp., 2006—. Office: Metals USA Holdings Corp 2400 E Commercial Blvd Ste 905 Fort Lauderdale FL 33308-4059 Office Phone: 713-965-0990. Office Fax: 713-965-0067.

BALDWIN, MARK E., corporate financial executive; BS in Mech. Engring., Duke U.; MBA, Tulane U. Chmn., CEO Anixter Aerospace Hardware; treas. Keystone Internat. Inc., CFO, pres. indsl. valves and controls group; chmn., CEO Pentacon Inc.; exec. v.p., CFO Nexitra-One, LLC, 2001—02; oper. ptnr. First Resource Corp., 2003—04; exec. v.p., CFO, treas. DGC Inc., 2004—07; exec. v.p., CFO Dresser-Rand Group, Inc., 2007—. Mem. bd. dirs. T-3 Energy Svcs., Inc., 2003, Seahawk Drilling, Inc. Office: Dresser-Rand Group Inc West8 Tower 10205 Westheimer Rd Ste 1000 Houston TX 77042 Office Phone: 713-354-6100. Office Fax: 713-354-6110.

BALDWIN, STANLEY FORREST, lawyer, insurance company executive; b. 1948; BA, JD, U. Tex. Bar: Tex. 1973, Tenn. 1988, Va. 2004. Various sr. officer and gen. counsel positions CIGNA Healthplans, Inc.; sr. v.p., gen. counsel and sec. EQUICOR-Equitable HCA Corp., Nashville, EPIC Healthcare Group, Dallas, 1990—97; exec. v.p., gen. counsel and sec. Amerigroup Corp., Va. Beach, Va., 1997—. Recipient Burton award, 2009. Mem.: Va. State Bar, Va. Bar Assn., State Bar Tex., Tenn. Bar Assn. Office: Amerigroup Corp 4425 Corporation Ln Virginia Beach VA 23462 Office Phone: 757-490-6900. Office Fax: 757-557-6743.

BALÉE, WILLIAM L., anthropology educator; b. Ft. Lauderdale, Fla., Oct. 12, 1954; s. William Lockert Balée and Lorraine Kathryn Monahan; m. Maria da Conceição Bezerra, Mar. 9, 1987; children: Nicholas, Isabel. BA with high honors, U. Fla., 1975; MA, Columbia U., 1979, MPhil, 1980, PhD, 1984. Assoc. rschr. ecology Museu Paraense Emílio Goeldi, Belém, Brazil, 1988-91, chair ecology, 1990-91; assoc. prof. anthropology Tulane U., New Orleans, 1991-98, prof., chair dept. anthropology, 1998-2001, prof. anthropology, 1998—, dir. environ. studies program, Sch. Liberal Arts, 2007—10. Adj. prof. anthropology CUNY, 1983-84, SUNY, Purchase, 1982; adj. prof. social scis. CUNY, 1983; adj. prof. sociology and anthropology Rutgers U., 1984; vis. assoc. prof. Ctr. for L.Am. Studies, U. Fla., 1990; fieldwork with forest peoples in Amazon of Brazil and Bolivia, 1980-2009, Peninsular Malaysia, 2012-; acad. cons. Smithsonian Instn., 2000—04. Author: Footprints of the Forest: Ka'apor Ethnobotany, 1994 (award Soc. Econ. Botany, 1996), Inside Cultures: A New Introduction to Cultural Anthropology, 2012, Indigenous Forests of Malaysia and Amazonia, 2012, Cultural Forests of the Amazon: A Historical Ecology of People and Their Landscapes, 2013; editor: Anthropic Influences on Amazonian Landscapes and Biota, 2009—10, Diversity, Advances in Historical Ecology, 1998, Jour. Ethnobiology, 1999—2002; co-editor: Resource Management in Amazonia: Indigenous and Folk Strategies, Advances in Economic Botany, vol. 7, 1989, Hist. Ecology Series, 1998—2006, Time and Complexity in Historical Ecology, 2006, New Frontiers in Historical Ecology; mem. editl. bd.: Jour. Ethnobiology, 2002—04; mem. editl. bd. Jour. Ethnobiology, 2007—13, Tipití, 2002—08, Diversity, 2009—, Antropologica, Boletim Museu Goeldi Ciencias Humanas, 2012—; contbr. articles to profl. jours., chapters to books. Decorated officer Order of the Golden Ark (Netherlands), 1993; NY Bot. Garden fellow, 1984-88, Fulbright-Hays fellowship, 1980-81, Newcomb Coll. fellowship, 1992-94, Conselho Nacional de Desenvolvimento Tecnológico e Científico fellowship, 1988-91, Fulbright scholarship, 2011-12; grantee OAS, 1981-82, Ford Found., 1989-90, Jessie Smith Noyes Found., 1990-91, World Wildlife Fund, 1991-92, 2003, Tulane U., 1992, 2007-08, Wenner-Gren Found., 1993-94; apptd. to 60th and 61st Coll. Disting. Lectrs., Sigma Xi, 1997-99; recipient Outstanding Book of Yr. award Soc. Econ. Botany. Fellow Am. Anthrop. Assn.; mem. Soc. Ethnobotanists (India), Soc. Ethnobiology (pres.-elect 2011-), Soc. Anthropology of Lowland S.Am. (pres. 2002-05), Phi Beta Kappa (pres. Alpha of La. 1997-98), Phi Kappa Phi, Sigma Xi, Soc. des Americanistes. Office: Tulane U Dept Anthropology New Orleans LA 70118-5238 Office Phone: 504-865-5336. Business E-Mail: wbalee@tulane.edu.

BALES, JIMMY C., state legislator; b. Rose Hill, Va., Sept. 25, 1935; BA, Columbia Coll., 1960; MA, East Tenn. State U., 1966; EEd, U. SC, 1975. Probation officer Richland County Family Ct., 1960—63; dir. career edn., tchr., prin. Richland Sch. Dist. 1, 1959—60, 1963—91; mem. Dist. 80 SC House of Reps., 1999—, chair Subcommittee on Real Estate, sec. Ops. and Mgmt. Com., mem. Labor, Commerce and Industry Com. Democrat. Baptist. Office: 432C Blatt Bldg Columbia SC 29201 Mailing: 1515 Crossing Creek Rd Eastover SC 29044 Home Phone: 803-776-6416; Office Phone: 803-734-3058, 803-776-7355. E-mail: JCB@schouse.org.

BALES, JOHN MALCOLM, federal prosecutor; b. Del Rio, Tex., 1955; m. Betsy Bales; 6 children. BA, U. Tex., Austin, 1977, JD, 1980. Bar: Tex. 1982. Assoc. Hancock, Piedfor, Galton, McGill, Austin, Tex., 1981—82; spl. agent FBI, San Antonio, Mobile & Chgo., 1982—89; asst. US atty. (eastern dist.) Tex. US Dept. Justice, 1989—2009, dep. criminal chief Narcotics Divsn., 1994—95, 2008—09, atty.-in-charge Lufkin, Tex., 1995—2003, criminal chief, 2003—06, 2009, asst. US atty. spl. prosecutions, 2006—08, interim US atty., 2009—11, US atty. (eastern dist.) Tex., 2011—, asst. US atty. Dist. Colo., 1995. Atty. JAG USNR, 1981. Recipient Sustained Superior Achievement Award, US Dept. Justice, 1989, 1992, Atty. Gen.'s Disting. Svc. Award, 2007, Award of Excellence, East Tex. Peace Officers Assn., 1995, J. Michael Bradford Award, Nat. Assn. Former US Attorneys, 2004. Office: Office of US Attorney 350 Magnolia Ave, Suite 150 Beaumont TX 77701 Office Phone: 409-839-2538.*

BALFE, ROBERT CRAMER, III, lawyer, former prosecutor; b. West Palm Beach, Fla., 1968; m. Jennifer Balfe; children: Ryan, Luke. BS, Ark. State Univ.; JD, Univ. Ark., 1994. Bar: Ark. 1995. Dep. pros. atty. Benton County, Ark., 1995—2001, pros. atty. Ark., 2001—04; US atty. (we. dist.) Ark. US Dept. Justice, 2004—09; counsel, head Govt., Investigations, Enforcement and White Collar Crime practice Mitchell Williams Selig Gates and Woodyard PLLC, Little Rock, 2009—. Office: Mitchell Williams 5414 Pinnacle Point Dr, Ste 500 Rogers AR 72758-8131 Office Phone: 479-464-5661. Office Fax: 479-464-5680. E-mail: bbalfe@mwlaw.com.

BALFOUR, DON, state legislator; b. New Brunswick, NJ, May 3, 1957; m. Ginny Balfour; 1 child, Trey. BS, Bob Jones Univ. CPA. V.p. Waffle House Inc.; mem. Dist. 9 Ga. State Senate, 1993—. Mem. America Inst. CPAs, Ga. Inst. CPAs, Gwinett County C. of C. Republican. Baptist. Mailing: 2312 Waterscape Trail Snellville GA 30078 Office Phone: 770-729-5764. Business E-Mail: don.balfour@senate.ga.gov.

BALIGA, PRABHAKAR K., surgeon; m. Kamashki Baliga. MD, Madras Med. Coll., India, 1982. Co dir. Med. Univ. SC, Charleston, 1999—2000, chief, divsn. transplant surgery, 2000—. Grant, NIH, 2002—, HHS, 2004—07. Mem.: ACS, Internat. Liver Transplantation Soc., Soc. U. Surgeons, Am. Soc. Transplant Surgeons. Office: Med Univ SC 96 Jonathan Lucas St Charleston SC 29425 Home: 259 Coinbow Cir Mount Pleasant SC 29464-2535 Office Fax: 843-792-8596. Business E-Mail: baligap@musc.edu.

BALIGA, RADHAKRISHNA, pediatrician, educator, nephrologist; b. Bombay; naturalized, US; m. Mithra Baliga; children: Priya, Divya. Degree, Loyola Coll, Madras, India, 1962, Kasturba Med. Coll., Manipal, 1968; MBBS, Mysore U., India, 1968; diploma in Child Health, Madras U., 1973. Lic. DC, 1976, Calif., 1979, Miss., 1993, diplomate Am. Bd. Pediat., 1979, cert. Sub-Splty. Bd. Pediatric Nephrology, 1982. Internship Govt. Gen. Hosp. Madras U., 1969—70, sr. house surgeon, 1970—71; rsch. fellow, pediat. Inst. Child and Health and Hosp. for Sick Children, Madras U., 1971—73; rsch. fellow, pediat. level I Jewish Hosp and Med. Ctr. Bklyn., 1974—75; rsch. fellow, pediat. level 2 St. Vincent's Med. Ctr., SI, 1975—76; rsch. fellow, pediat. nephrology Children's Hosp Mich. Wayne State U., Detroit, 1976—78; pediatrician New Ctr. Med. Plz. Groups, 1978—80; staff pediatrician South La. Med. Ctr., Houma, 1980—82; clin. asst. prof., pediat. Tulane U. Sch. Medicine, New Orleans, 1980—92, instr., pediat., 1982—83, asst. prof., pediat., 1985—86, rsch. assoc., 1989—90, clin. assoc. prof., pediat., 1992—96, clin. prof., pediat., 1996—; clin. asst. prof., pediat. La. State U. Sch. Medicine, Shreveport, 1985—87, asst. prof., pediat., 1986—92, assoc. prof., pediat., 1992—93; prof., pediat. U. Miss. Med. Ctr., Jackson, 1993—. Rsch. assoc. Tulane U. Sch. Medicine Sect. Nephrology, New Orleans, 1989—90; cons. in pediat. nephrology Handicapped Children Svcs. Program, New Orleans, 1985—93; vis. asst. prof. dept. pediat. U. Calif., San Francisco, 1986—87; med. staff Children Hosp., Detroit, 1978—80; active med. staff South La. Med. Ctr., Houma, 1980—82; med. staff Oschner Hosp. New Orleans, 1980—82, Oschner Hosp., 1980—82, Tulane U. Hosp., 1980—93; vis. physician Charity Hosp., New Oleans, 1980—93; med. staff Child. Hosp., New Oleans, 1981—93, Jackson, 1993—; mem. Credentials Com., 1998—2000, Ethics Com., 2002—10; reviewer Am. Soc. Nephrology Meeting, Toronto, Canada, 2000, San Diego, 2006. Contbr. numerous presentations, articles to profl. jour. Recipient Rsch. Pediat. award, 1998—99; named Best Dr. in America, Woodward White Inc.; grantee Biomedical Rsch. Support Grant, 1991—92, Dept. grant, 1997—98, Dept. Rsch. grant, 2001—03, Kidney Care Found., 1998—2003, Intramural Rsch. Support Program, 2006—07; Dept. grant, South West Pediat. Nephrology Group Merck & Co. Inc, 1996—97, Dept. Rsch. grant, 2001—03, 2008—10. Fellow: Am. Soc. Nephrology; mem.: AHA (kidney coun. sci. coun. mem.), Internat. Soc. Pediat. Nephrology, North Am. Pediat. Renal Transplant Cooperative Study Kidney Coun., Southest Pediat. Nephrology Study Group, Internat. Soc. Nephology, Internat. Soc. Pediat. Nephrology, Am. Soc. Pediat. Nephrology. Achievements include invention of maximum urine concentrating Ability in children with Hb SC Disease effects of Hydroxyurea; research in role of reactive oxygen metabolites in renal disease.

BALL, ARMAND BAER, former association executive, consultant; b. Dubach, La., Sept. 30, 1930; s. Armand Baer and Lovera (Sanderson) B.; m. Beverly Jane Hodges, Sept. 15, 1957; children: Kathryn Lynn, Robin Armand. BA, La. Coll., 1951; MRE, Southwestern Bapt. Theol. Sem., 1953; MS, George Williams Coll., 1960. Royal Ambassador dir. Fla. Bapt. Conv., Jacksonville, 1953-57; program dir. Woodlawn Boys' Club, Chgo., 1957-58; camp/youth dir. YMCA, Nashville, 1958-62; exec. dir. YMCA Camps Widjiwagan/duNord, St. Paul YMCA, 1962-74; exec. Am. Camping Assn., Martinsville, Ind., 1974-88; cons., 1988—2007; assoc. Campaign Assocs., Phila., 1999—2008. Author: (with Beverly H. Ball) Basic Camp Management, 2012; editor: A Cost Study of Resident Camps, 1985; Internat. Camping Fellowship newsletter, 1987-97, Internat. Camp Dir. Curriculum, 2008; co-editor: Business and Finance, Site and Facilities; Trendlines newsletter. Cons. Ctr. Disease Control, St. Petersburg (Russia) & Tyumen (Siberia)Children's Camps, Malaysian Tourist Bd., Pan-Am. Inst. Phys. Edn. (Venezuela), Heritage Conservation and Recreation Svc., Project Reach, Boy Scouts Am., United Ch. of Christ, YMCA, Episcopal Ch.; mem. Internat. Camping Fellowship; past chair Sanibel Parks and Recreation Com., 2001-08, bd. mem. Cmty. Housing Resources Inc.; mem. adv. bd. Ctr. Environ. and Sustainability Edn., Fla. Gulf Coast U., emeritus mem. Internat. Camping Fellowship Bd. Recipient Disting. Svc. award Am. Camping Assn., 1989, Druszba award, 2002; named Citizen Yr., Sanibel, Fla., 1999, Disting. Alumni award, George Williams Coll./Aurora U., 2003. Mem.: Am. Soc. Assn. Execs. (cert. assoc. exec. life), Audubon Soc., Canadian Camping Assn., Kiwanis (Hixon award), Am. Camp Assn. (life). Home and Office: 16502 Cypress Villa Ln Fort Myers FL 33908 Personal E-mail: alphaball@comcast.net.

BALL, CARROLL RAYBOURNE, anatomist, researcher, medical educator; b. Hillman, Miss., Oct. 11, 1925; s. Marvin Hugh and Elizabeth (Hillman) B.; m. Jannie Vee Brooks, Sept. 5, 1947 (dec. 1954); children: Hugh Brooks, Peter Stephen; m. Sally Ann Montgomery, Mar. 22, 1963 (div. 1976); 1 child, Lou Ellen. BA, U. Miss., 1947, MS, 1948, PhD, 1963. Grad. asst. in zoology U. Miss., Oxford, 1946-48; instr. Duke U., 1948-51; instr. anatomy Med. Sch. W.Va. U., 1951-57; asst. prof. biology U. So. Miss., 1957-60; asst. prof. U. Miss. Med. Ctr., Jackson, 1963-66, assoc. prof., 1966-71, prof., 1971-99. Contbr. numerous articles to profl. jours. Pres. Jackson Civil War Round Table, 1983-84; chmn. Hist. Coker House Restoration Project, 1984-99; v.p. Magnolia chpt. Nat. Assn. Watch and Clock Collectors, 1980-82; bd. dirs. Miss. Hist. Soc., 1976-79, 85-88, 93-96. Lt. comdr. USNR, 1944-71, PTO. NIH predoctoral trainee, 1960-63; Miss. Heart Assn. grantee, 1963-66 Mem. Am. Assn. Anatomists, Soc. Exptl. Biology and Medicine, Am. Assn. Pathology, So. Assn. Anatomy, Miss. Acad. Sci., Hattiesburg Jr. C. of C. (sec. 1959-60), Order of First Families of Miss. (Gov. Gen. 2001-2003), Sigma Xi, Alpha Epsilon Delta, Theta Nu Sigma, Beta Beta Beta (pres. 1947-48), Omicron Delta Kappa, Pi Kappa Alpha (sec. 1943-44) Methodist.

BALL, GEORGE L., investment banker; b. Evanston, Ill., 1938; BA, Brown U., 1960. Gov. Am. Stock Exch., Chgo. Bd. Options Exch.; pres. E. F. Hutton Group Inc. and E. F. Inc., 1969-82; mem., exec. office Prudential Ins. Co. America, 1982—91; pres., CEO Prudential

Bache Securities Group, Inc., 1982—91, chmn., 1986-91; cons., prod. devel. J&W Seligman & Co., 1991-92; sr. exec. v.p. Smith Barney Shearson Inc., 1992—94; non-exec. chmn. Sanders Morris Mundy Inc., 1992—97; chmn. Sanders Morris Harris Group, Inc., 2002—, CEO, 2009—; chmn., CEO Sanders Morris Harris Inc. Mem. exec. com. Prudential Ins. Co. Am., 1982—91; bd. dirs. The Edelman Fin. Ctr., LLC, Leonetti & Assocs., LLC, SMH Capital Advisors Inc., RediClinic, LLC, Nestor Inc., 2003—. Trustee Brown U.; mem. Presdl. adv. coun. Pvt. Sector Initiative; mem. bus. com. Met. Mus. Arts.; dir. Paper Mill Playhouse (the State Theatre of N.J.); bd. overseers Duke Comprehensive Cancer Ctr.; trustee Joint Coun. Econ. Edn.; nat. trustee Nat. Symphony Orch.; vice chmn. bd. trustees S. St. Seaport Mus. Mem. Securities Industry Assn., Bond Club N.Y. (v.p.). Office: Sanders Morris Harris Group Inc 5800 JPMorgan Chase Tower 600 Travis Ste 5800 Houston TX 77002 Office Phone: 713-993-4610, 713-224-1101. E-mail: George.Ball@smhgroup.com.

BALL, JOHN ROBERT, healthcare executive; b. Opelika, Ala., July 16, 1944; s. John Cooper Jr. and Ellen Beverly (Williams) B.; m. Cornelia Anne Phillips, Aug. 13, 1966 (div. 1983); children: Kristen Anne, John Robert; m. Pamela Preston Reynolds, Jan. 9, 1988 (div. 2006). AB, Emory U., 1966; JD, Duke U., 1971, MD, 1972. Rsch. assoc. Duke U. Sch. Medicine, Durham, NC, 1971—72, resident in medicine, 1972-74; asst. to dir. office asst. sec. for health USPHS, Rockville, Md., 1974-76; chief med. audit br. bur. quality assurance HEW, Rockville, 1976-77; sr. policy analyst Office Sci. and Tech. Policy Exec. Office of Pres., Washington, 1978-81; assoc. exec. v.p. ACP, Phila., 1981-86, exec. v.p., 1986-94, also master; sr. scholar Assn. Acad. Health Ctrs., Washington, 1994-95; exec. v.p., acting pres., CEO Pa. Hosp., Phila., 1995-96, pres., CEO, 1996-99; sr. v.p. The Lewin Group, Falls Church, Va., 2000; exec. v.p., master Am. Soc. Clin. Pathology, Chgo., 2002—10. Robert Wood Johnson clin. scholar George Washington U., Washington, 1977-79; bd. mgrs. Pa. Hosp., 1988-97; bd. dirs. Milbank Meml. Fund, Holy Cross Hosp., Mission Health Systems. Assoc. editor Jour. Am. Geriatrics Soc., 1984-86; mem. editorial bd. Internat. Jour. Tech. Assessment in Health Care, 1986-89, European Jour. Internal Medicine, 1988-94, Duke U. Law Jour., 1969-71; contbr. articles to profl. jours. Sr. surgeon USPHS, 1974-77. John Gordon Stipe scholar, Nat. Merit scholar, Emory U., 1962. Mem. Inst. Medicine of NAS, N.C. Bar Assn., Am. Clin. and Climatol. Assn., Soc. Med. Adminstrs. Democrat. Personal E-mail: johnrball@hotmail.com.

BALL, MIKE A., state legislator; b. Stockton, Calif., Sept. 17, 1954; m. Debbie Ball; children: Chris, Cara, Mandy. AS in Criminal Justice, Jefferson State Jr. Coll.; BS in Polit. Sci., Athens State U., Ala. Ala. state trooper, hwy. patrol divsn. Ala. Dept. Pub. Safety, 1978—86, maj. crimes unit investigator, Ala. Bur. Investigation, 1986—2003, hostage negotiator; ret., 2003; mem. Dist. 10 Ala. House of Reps., Montgomery, 2003—; owner, operator Ball Roofing. Musician: The Madison Mountaintop Band. Mem. Asbury Meth. United Meth. Ch., Madison, Ala. Sgt. USMC, 1973—77. Republican. Methodist. Office: PO Box 6302 Huntsville AL 35824 also: Ala House of Reps Ala State House 11 S Union St Rm 526-D Montgomery AL 36130 Office Phone: 256-539-5441, 334-242-7683. Business E-Mail: mikeball@knology.net.

BALL, REX MARTIN, urban planner, architect; b. Oklahoma City, June 14, 1934; s. Ralph Martin and Sarah Mae (Kellner) B. BArch, Okla. State U., 1956; MArch, MIT, 1958. Lic. arch. Nat. Coun. Arch. Registration Bd.; cert. planner Am. Inst. Cert. Planners. With HTB Inc. (archtl., engring., planning firm), Oklahoma City, 1958-94; chmn. emeritus HTB Inc., 1958-94; founder, pres. Planning Assocs. Inc., 1960—; founder, pres., chmn., CEO Mid Continent Design Group, 1968—. Presdl. appt. to U.S. Commn. of Fine Arts, 1994-97; former mem. Okla. City Golf & Country Club, Southern Hills Golf & Country Club, Petrolium Clubs, Okla., Tulsa, WBC Ec Club, NH Press Club. Architect U.S./USSR exhibit "The Socially Responsible Environment, 1980-90; contbr. articles to profl. jours. Chair Tulsa Preservation Com., 1997—2007; facilitator Internat. Coalition Art Deco Socs., 2003—05; oversite com. Vision 2025, Tulsa, 2003—; bd. dirs. Price Tower Mus., 1998—2002; past treas. Philbrook Mus.'s Pacers. Recipient Bus. in the Arts award, 1988, 5 Who Care Corp. Humanitarian award, Gannett Found., 1988, Curt Schwartz Bus. in the Arts award, 1989, Phoenix award/Downtown Now, 1992, Cityscape award City of Oklahoma City, 1992, Disting. Alumni award Okla. State U., 1995. Fellow: AIA (mem. nat. com. on design, past pres. ea. Okla. chpt.); mem.: AICp, Tul Fedn. Arch. (bd. dir. 2008—09), Tulsa Found. Arch. (bd. dirs. 2009), Okla. History Ctr. (life; bd. dirs. 2008—), Tulsa Equality Ctr., Soc. Am. Mil. Engrs. (former sustaining mem.), MIT Alumni Assn. (past Okla. pres.), Am. Planning Assn., Oklahoma City C. of C. (bd. dirs. 1980—90, former v.p.), Tulsa C. of C. (past bd. dirs.), Okla. State U. Alumni Assn. (life; past bd. dirs., pres. Tulsa and Okla. counties), Nat. Trust Hist. Preservation, Tulsa Art Deco Soc. (founder & chair), Tulsa Hist. Soc. (bd. dirs. 2000—, chair 6th World Congress on Art Deco 2001), Air Force Assn. (past pres. Gerrity chpt.), Okla. Heritage Assn., Nat. Bldg. Mus., Tulsa Southern Hills, Urban League Greater Oklahoma City (former bd. dirs.), Blue Key Club, OKC Golf & Country Club, NTL Press Club, WOC EC Club, Scabbard and Blade, Sigma Nu, Alpha Rho Chi. Home: 2926 E 39th St Tulsa OK 74105-3704 Fax: 918-748-9688. E-mail: ballrexm@aol.com.

BALL, TRAVIS, JR., editor, retired school administrator; b. Newport, Tenn., July 13, 1942; s. Travis and Ruth Annette (Duyck) Ball. BA, Carson Newman Coll., 1964; MA, Purdue U., 1966. Instr., then asst. prof. English Ill. Wesleyan U., Bloomington, 1966—69; vis. prof. English Millikin U., 1969; asst. headmaster, chmn. English Brewster Acad., Wolfeboro, NH, 1969—72; dir. admissions, asst. to headmaster Park Tudor Sch., Indpls., 1972—88; cons. Selwyn Sch., Denton, Tex., 1988—89; pres. Travis Ball & Assocs., 1988—88; dir. comm. Verde Valley Sch., Sedona, Ariz., 1988—91; editor Projects in Enrollment Mgmt., 1992—2000. Commn. on curriculum and grad. requirements Ind. Dept. Pub. Instrn., 1974—76; adv. coun. Ednl. Records Bur.; reviewer Nat. Stds. Project in Sci., Civics and Govt., 1994—95; cons. in field. Editor: Tchrs. Svc. Com. Newsletter for English Tchrs., 1977—82; dept. editor: English Jour., 1976—82, editor/pub.: Contact: Newsletter for Admissions Mgmt., 1980—88, contbg. editor: The Developing Leader, 2003—05. Editl. cons. The Brewster Story: A Definitive History of Brewster Acad., Wolfeboro, NH, 2011; chair bd. deacons First Bapt. Ch., Newport, Tenn., 2005—08, sec., Bd. Deacons, 2009—12. Mem.: ASCD, Phi Delta Kappa, Pi Kappa Delta, Nat. Assn. Ind. Schs. (workshop faculty 1986, 1997), Coun. Advancement and Support Edn. (adv. com. on ind. schs.), Nat. Coun. Tchrs. English, Ind. Schs. Assn. Ctrl. States, Ind. Non-Pub. Edn. Assn. (treas., dir., vice chmn.), Sigma Tau Delta. Baptist. Office: 1739 Log Church Rd Newport TN 37821-5535

BALLARD, DAVID EUGENE, anesthesiologist; b. Carlsbad, N.Mex., July 30, 1949; s. Samuel Lafayette and Kathleen B.; m. Patricia Ann Lafferty, June 11, 1972; 1 child, Leslie Christine. BA, U. Kans., 1971; MD, U. N.Mex., 1975. Diplomate Am. Bd. Anesthesiology. Intern and resident N.C. Meml. Hosp., U. N.C., Chapel Hill, 1975-78; pvt. practice Anesthesia Cons. Associated, El Paso, Tex., 1978-86; chief anesthesia sect. VA Med. Ctr., Albuquerque, 1986-88; chmn. dept. anesthesiology Lovelace Med. Ctr., Albuquerque, 1988-98; dir. anesthesiology West Mesa Med. Ctr., Albuquerque, 2003—04; clin. assoc. prof. anesthesiology U. NC, Chapel Hill, 2007—. Clin. asst. prof. anesthesiology, U. N.Mex., 1986-88, mem. resident selection com., 1986-88; clin. asst. prof. anesthesiology U. NC, Chapel Hill, 1991-96. Mem. Am. Soc. Anesthesiologists (alt. del. 1988-91, mem. com. on physician resources 1993-94), Tex. Soc. Anesthesiologists (alt. del. dist. 5, 1986), Greater Albuquerque Anesthesia Soc. (pres., v.p. 1987-89), N.Mex. Med. Sch. Alumni Assn. (bd. dirs. 1984-92, exec. com. 1988-90). Avocation: golf. Office: N2201 UNC Hosps CB #7010 Chapel Hill NC 27599-7010 Office Phone: 919-966-5136. Business E-Mail: dballard@aims.unc.edu.

BALLAS, MARK, JR., dancer; b. Houston, May 24, 1986; s. Mark (Corky) and Shirley Ballas. Grad., Italia Conti Acad. Dramatic Arts. Winner Brit. Juvenile Ballroom & Latin Am. dance championships, 1996, US Open to the World, Brit. Open to the World, & Internat. Open to the World Jr. Latin Am. dance championships, Brit. Open to the World, US Open to the World, Internat. Open to the World, UK, Youth Latin Am. dance championships. Co-founding band mem. Almost Amy. Dancer (musicals) Copa Cabana, Maria de Buenos Aires, (TV series) Dancing With the Stars, ABC, 2007— (season 6 winner, with ptnr. Kristi Yamaguchi, 2008, season 8 winner, with ptnr. Shawn Johnson, 2009); musician (with Ballas Hough Band): (albums) BHB, 2009. Recipient Gold medal, Jr. Olympics, 2003, Performer of Yr. award, Italia Conti Acad. Dramatic Arts, 2005. Office: c/o Learning2Dance Ste 550/424 11807 Westheimer Rd Houston TX 77077 E-mail: mark@almost-amy.com.

BALLEN, ANN E., ophthalmologist; b. Geneva, NY, Dec. 2, 1952; 2 children. MD, Tufts U., Medford, Mass., 1979. Diplomate Am. Bd. Ophthalmology. Intern dept. pediat. Montefiore Hosp. Med. Ctr., NYC; fellow in pediatric ophthalmology Nat. Med. Ctr., Washington; ophthalmologist MedEye Lasik, Miami, 1995—; pediatrician Miami Children's Hosp. Office: MedEye Lasik 5950 Sunset Dr South Miami FL 33143 also: Miami Childrens Hosp 3100 SW 62nd Ave Miami FL 33155 Office Phone: 500-883-7866, 305-661-8588.

BALLENGER, ROGER, state legislator; m. Cimone Ballenger; children: Kimberly, Clay 1 stepchild, Lindsay Morrow. Attended, Okla. State Univ. Inst. Tech., Okmulgee. Okmulgee County Commr.; mem. Okmulgee City Coun.; electrical contractor Tulsa; operator, owner Small Beefmaster Cattle Operation, Okmulgee; mem. Dist. 8 Okla. State Senate, Okla., 2006—. Served USN, 1969—73. Democrat. Avocations: hunting, fishing, golf. Address: 19605 Wilson Rd Okmulgee OK 74447 Office: 2300 N Lincoln Blvd Rm 527B Oklahoma City OK 73105 Home Phone: 918-756-7934; Office Phone: 405-521-5588. Business E-Mail: ballenger@oksenate.gov.

BALLENTINE, NATHAN, state legislator; b. Columbia, SC, Dec. 10, 1970; BS, U. SC, 1992. V.p. Wells Fargo Home Mortgage, 1992—; mem. Dist. 71 SC House of Reps., 2004—, mem. Med., Mil., Pub. and Mcpl. Affairs Com. Pres. Riversprings Precinct Rep. Party. Mem.: Irmo C. of C. Republican. Mailing: 320B Blatt Bldg Columbia SC 29211 Home: 1108 Belfair Way Irmo SC 29063 Office: 324 Sienna Dr Chapin SC 29036 Office Phone: 803-734-2969. Business E-Mail: ballentine@scstatehouse.net.

BALLEWEG, DAVID, information technology executive; Sr. dir., bus. devel. Intelligent Decisions, Ashburn, Va.; v.p., strategic programs Access Systems, Inc., 2009—. Office: Access Systems Inc 12011 Sunset Hills Rd Ste 1200 Reston VA 20190-5922 Office Phone: 703-464-6900. Office Fax: 703-464-6990. Business E-Mail: dballeweg@accsys-inc.com.

BALLHAUS, WILLIAM LOUIS, information technology executive; s. William Francis Ballhaus and Susan Elizabeth Berghoff; m. Darrin Jennifer Mollett, Sept. 12, 1998; 2 children. BSME, UC Davis, 1989; MS in Aeronautics and Astronautics, Stanford U., 1990, PhD in Aeronautics and Astronautics, 1994; MBA, UCLA, 1998. Rsch. asst. Stanford Aerospace Robotics Lab., Palo Alto, Calif., 1989—94; program dir. and sys. engring. mgr. Hughes Space and Comm., El Segundo, Calif., 1994—98; dir. Boeing Satellite Systems, Integrated Satellite Factory Ops., 1999—2000; gen. mgr. Boeing Electron Dynamic Devices, Inc., Torrance, Calif., 2000—01, Boeing Satellite Systems, Sys. Products Group, 2001—02; sr. v.p. Boeing Satellite Systems, Sys. Engring., 2002—03; pres. mission solutions BAE Systems, San Diego, 2003, pres. Nat. Security Solutions, 2004, pres. Nat. Security Solutions for Electronics and Integrated Solutions Operating Group Nashua, NH, 2005—08; pres., CEO DynCorp International, Inc., Falls Ch., Va., 2008—10; CEO SRA Internat., Fairfax, Va., 2011—. Mem. of the dean's coun. Loyola Marymount U., Coll. of Sci. and Engring., Westchester, Calif., 2002—; bd. dirs. US Geospatial Intelligence Found.; bd. advisors Geospatial 21. Fellow: Brit. Am. Project, AIAA (assoc.). Achievements include patents for interconnective transponder systems and methods. Office: SRA Internat 4300 Fair Lakes Ct Fairfax VA 22033 Office Phone: 703-803-1500.

BALLY, ALBERT W., retired geologist, educator; PhD, U. Zurich, Switzerland, 1953. Harry Carothers Weiss prof. geology Rice U., Houston, now prof. emeritus. Contbr. articles to profl. jours. Recipient R.J.W. Douglas Meml. medal Can. Soc. Petroleum Geologists, 1996, Signey Powers Meml. award Am. Assn. Petroleum Geologists. Achievements include research in the structure of foreland folded belts, the formation of allochthonous salt sheets in a continental slope environment, mechanical separation of crust and sediments from the underlying lithosphere, inversion of half-grabens in a major orogenic mechanism. Office: Rice U Dept Geology MS126 6100 S Main St Houston TX 77005-1892

BALOGUN, RASHEED ABIODUN, physician and medical educator; s. Ishaq Ayinde and Morinat Bisi Balogun; m. Seki A. Balogun; children: Aisha Ayodele, Zainab Ayoade, Ishaq Opeyemi. MBBS, U. Ibadan, Nigeria, 1991. Diplomate Am. Bd. Internal Medicine, Am. Bd. Nephrology. Assoc. prof. medicine U. Va., Charlottesville, 2001—, asst. dean student affairs, 2010—. Chmn. med. adv. bd. Nat. Kidney Found. of the Virginias, Richmond; asst. dean student affairs U. Va., Sch. Medicine; bd. mem. Am. Soc. Apheresis, 2013; exec. coun. mem., chair Faculty Recruitment, Retirement and Welfare Com., U. Va. Faculty Senate, 2013. Recipient Willem J. Kolff Young Investigator award, ASAIO, 2002, Cmty. Svc. award, U. Va. Health Systems, 2007; named to Acad. Disting. Educators, U. Va. Sch. Medicine, 2005. Fellow: ACP, Am. Soc. Nephrology; mem.: Am. Soc. for Artificial Internat. Organs. Avocations: bicycling, tennis. Office: U VA Nephrology Divsn 1215 Lee St Box 800133 Charlottesville VA 22908-0133 Office Fax: 434-948-2458.

BALSER, JEFFREY R., dean, medical educator; MD, PhD in Pharmacology, Vanderbilt U., 1990. Resident anesthesiology, fellow critical care medicine Johns Hopkins U., faculty mem., 1995—98; assoc. dean physician scientists Vanderbilt U., 1998, James Tayloe Gwathmey prof., chair anesthesiology, 2001; assoc. vice chancellor for rsch. Vanderbilt Med. Ctr., 2004; assoc. vice chancellor health affairs, dean Vanderbilt U. Sch. Medicine, 2008—. Contbr. articles to med. jours. Mem.: NAS (mem. Inst. of Medicine), Assn. of Am. Physicians, Am. Soc. Clin. Investigation. Office: Vanderbilt U Sch Medicine D-3300 MCN 2104 215 Light Hall Nashville TN 37232 Office Phone: 615-936-3030. E-mail: jeff.balser@vanderbilt.edu.*

BALSLEY, PHILIP ELWOOD, entertainer; b. Augusta County, Va., Aug. 8, 1939; s. Henry Elwood and Marjorie Walden (Fielding) B.; m. Wilma Lee Kincaid, July 21, 1962; children— Gregory, Mark, Leah. Grad. high sch. With group Statler Bros., 1961—. Treas. Statler Bros. Prodns., 1973—. Bd. dirs. Happy Birthday U.S.A. Recipient numerous Grammy awards, Country Music Assn. awards. Presbyterian. Office: PO Box 2703 Staunton VA 24402-2703

BALSTER, ROBERT LOUIS, alcohol/drug abuse educator researcher; BS, U. Minn., Mpls., 1966; PhD, U. Houston, 1970. Postdoctoral fellow in psychiatry and pharmacology U. Chgo., 1970-72; rsch. assoc. in psychiatry Duke U., Durham, NC, 1972-73; asst. prof. pharmacology Med. Coll. Va., Richmond, 1973-78, assoc. prof., 1978-84, prof. pharmacology, 1984—2003, Luther A Butler prof. pharmacology, 2003—; dir. Inst. Drug and Alcohol Studies, 1993—2013; coord. Humphrey Fellowship Program in Substance Abuse, 2006—; founder co dir. Internat. Program Addiction Studies, 2008—; Jefferson sci. fellow and sr. sci. advisor US Agy. Internat. Devel. Global Health Bureau, 2011—14. Chmn. Drug Abuse Adv. Com., FDA, Rockville, Md., 1983-84; mem. Robert Wood Johnson Rsch. Network on Etiology of Tobacco Dependence, 1997-2006; mem. adv. bd. Partnership for Drug Free Am. Editor-in-chief Drug Alcohol Dependence, 1998—2010; contbr. 281 articles to profl. jours. Recipient NIH Merit award, 1993-2004, Va. Commonwealth U. Faculty award of Excellence, 1999, Mentoring award Coll. Problems Drug Dependence, 2000, Nathan B. Eddy award, 2009, Faculty Tchg. Excellence award Va. Commonwealth U. Sch. Medicine, 2003, Mentoring award NIDA Internat. Program, 2006. Fellow Coll. on Problems of Drug Dependence (charter fellow, pres. 1995-96), Am. Coll. Neuropsychopharmacology, APA (pres. psychopharmacology divsn. 1989-90, chair bd. sci. affairs 1995-96, Disting. Svc. to Psychol. Sci. award, 2006, Brady-Schuster award 2007, bd. mem. 1994-96, 2008-); mem. European Behavioral Pharmacology Soc. (coun. mem. 1986-94). Achievements include development of laboratory methods for studying the behavioral effects of drugs of abuse and procedures for drug abuse potential evaluation and the management of international training programs in addiction. Office: Va Commonwealth U PO Box 980310 Richmond VA 23298-0310 Business E-Mail: balster@vcu.edu.

BAMBERGER, GERALD FRANCIS, plastics marketing consultant; b. Hannover, Germany, Sept. 20, 1920; came to U.S., 1938, naturalized, 1943; m. Ursula Friede, Mar. 27, 1946; children— Gale, Richard, Annette, Peter. Comml. diploma, Ecole Supérieure de Commerce, Neuchatel, Switzerland, 1938. Pres. A. Bamberger Corp., Bklyn., 1938-54, Interplastics Corp., NYC, 1955-62; prodn. mgr. plastics div. Cities Service Corp., Hicksville, N.Y., 1963-67; pres. Bamberger Polymers, Inc., New Hyde Park, N.Y., 1967-85; plastics mktg. cons., 1985—. Served with M.I. AUS, 1943-46. Decorated Bronze Star. Mem. Soc. Plastics Industry, Soc. Plastics Engrs., Plastics Pioneers Assn. Home Phone: 941-954-5049. Personal E-mail: gfb20906@yahoo.com.

BANCALARI, EDUARDO, pediatrician, educator; b. Santiago, Chile, Sept. 26, 1941; MD, U. Chile, Santiago, 1966. Bd. cert. pediat., bd. cert. neonatal-perinatal medicine. Intern Hosp. Luis Luis Calvo Mackeanna, Santiago, 1966, resident pediat., 1967—69; fellow pediat. cardiology U. Miami, Fla., 1971; staff mem. Jackson Meml. Hosp., Miami; prof. pediat., ob-gyn. U. Miami Sch. Medicine, dir. divsn. neonatology, chief newborn svc. dept. pediat. Recipient Virginia Apgar award, Am. Assn. Pediat., 2003. Office: Jackson Memorial Hosp 1611 NW 12th Ave Room 740 Central Bldg Miami FL 33136

BANDOW, DOUGLAS LEIGHTON, editor, consultant, writer; s. Donald E. and Donna J. B. AA, Okaloosa-Walton Jr. Coll., Niceville, Fla., 1974; BS in Econ., Fla. State U., 1976; JD, Stanford U., 1979. Bar: Calif. 1979 DC 1984. Sr. policy analyst Reagan for Pres. Com., LA, 1979-80, Arlington, Va., 1980, Office of Pres. Elect, Washington, 1980-81; spl. asst. to the Pres. for policy devel. White House, Washington, 1981-82; editor Inquiry Mag., Washington, 1982-84; sr. fellow Cato Inst., Washington, 1984—2005; nat. syndicated columnist Copley News Svc., San Diego, 1983—2005; v.p. Citizen Outreach, 2006—09; Cobden fellow Inst. for Policy Innovation, 2006—12; Bastiat scholar Competitive Enterprise Inst., 2007—09; Taft fellow Am. Conservative Def. Alliance, 2007—10; sr. fellow in internat. religious persecution Inst. Religion Pub. Policy, 2008—; sr. fellow Cato Inst., Washington, 2009—. Author: Unquestioned Allegiance, 1986, Beyond Good Intentions: A Biblical View of Politics, 1988, Human Resources and Defense Manpower, 1989, The Politics of Plunder: Misgovernment in Washington, 1990, The Politics of Envy: Statism as Theology, 1994, Tripwire: Korea and US Foreign Policy in a Changed World, 1996, Foreign Follies: America's New Global Empire, 2006; co-author: The Korean Conundrum: America's Troubled Relations with North and South Korea, 2004; editor: US Aid to the Developing World, 1985, Protecting the Environment, 1986; co-editor: The US-South Korean Alliance, 1992, Perpetuating Poverty, 1994; contbr. articles to periodicals. Recipient Nat. Young Am. award Boy Scouts Am., 1977, Freedom Leadership award Freedoms Found., Valley Forge, Pa., 1977, cert. for polit. and journalistic activities Freedoms Found., Valley Forge, Pa., 1979; named Man of Yr. NY State Coll. Reps., 1982. Mem. Calif. Bar Assn., DC Bar Assn, Chess Collectors Internat. Libertarian. Christian. Avocations: reading, antiques, travel. Office: Cato Inst 1000 Mass Ave NW Washington DC 22153 Business E-Mail: chessset@aol.com.

BANDOWS KOSTER, JANET, science association director; BS in Diplomacy and World Affairs, Occidental Coll., LA, 1983, BA in German Lang. and Linguistics, 1983; MA in Internat. Rels., Troy State U., European Region, 1987; MBA in Internat. Bus., DeVry U. Keller Grad. Sch., McLean, Va., 2000. Program mgr. USO Kaiserslautern, 1983—84; dir. USO Baumholder, 1984—87; regional dir. USO Germany, 1987—89; dir. worldwide ops. USO, 1989—93; asst. dir. internat. activities AARP, Washington, 1993—2000; dir. internat. svcs. Vols. of Am., Alexandria, Va., 2000—04; exec. dir. United German-Am. Com. of USA, Inc., 2004, Assn. for Women in Sci., Washington, 2006—. Mem.: Am. Soc. Assn. Execs. Office: Assn of Women in Sci 1200 New York Ave NW Ste 650 Washington DC 20005 Office Phone: 202-326-8940. Office Fax: 202-326-8960. E-mail: koster@awis.org.

BANDSTRA, EMMALEE S., physician, pediatrician, researcher, educator; b. New Orleans, Oct. 3, 1949; d. James Melvin and Lee (Speir) Shanks; m. Ted E. Bandstra, Feb. 11, 1984; 1 child, Bethany A. BA, U. Ala., Tuscaloosa, 1970; MD, U.Ala., Birmingham, 1974. Diplomate Nat. Bd. of Med. Examiners, 1975, Am. Bd. of Pediat., 1979, Am. Bd. of Pediat. Sub-board of Neonatal-Perinatal Medicine, 1979. Pediat. resident U. Ala., Birmingham, 1974—76, neonatology fellow, 1976—78; asst. prof. pediat. Sch. Medicine, U. Fla., Gainesville, 1978—81, Sch. Medicine, U. Miami, 1982—84, assoc. prof. pediat., 1984—95, prof. pediat. ob-gyn., 1995—, dir. perinatal chem. addiction rsch. and edn. program, 1988—; attending neonatologist

Shands Tchg. Hosp., Gainesville, Fla., 1978—81, Jackson Meml. Hosp., Miami, 1982—. Guest editor: Seminars in Perinatology Journal; contbr. articles to profl. jours., chapters to books. Cons., interagency working group on child maltreatment and juvenile delinquency US Dept. Justice, Washington, 1998; mem. State of Fla. Health and Rehab. Svcs. Task Force on Maternal Child Health, Tallahassee, 1982, Miami-Dade County Cocaine Babies Task Force, Miami, Fla., 1989—91, Miami Coalition for a Safe and Drug-free Cmty., Miami, 1989—, State of Fla. Gov.'s Drug Task Force Subcom. on Substance-exposed Infants and Families, Tallahassee, 1989, Healthy Start Coalition for Miami-Dade County, Miami, Fla., 1996—, bd. dirs., 1994—2000, pres., 1996; mem., consensus panel of drug exposed infants Alcohol and Drug Abuse and Mental Health Adminstrn., Bethesda, Md., 1992; mem., tech. expert group on drug exposed infants and young children Substance Abuse and Mental Health Services Adminstrn., Bethesda, 1992—94. Recipient Disting. Alumnus award, pediat. residency program Children's Hosp., U. Ala. Birmingham, 1990, Genevieve Abraham award med. excellence, Project: New Born, U. Miami, 1994; named to Best Drs. America, 2005—10; Rsch. grant, Nat. Inst. Drug Abuse, 1990—, Substance Abuse and Mental Health Svcs. Adminstrn., 1991—96, Nat. Inst. Health-Office Rsch. Women's Health, 2007—, Svc. grantee, healthy start high risk children's program State of Fla., 1996—99, Health Found. South Fla., State of Fla. Ounce of Prevention Fund, 1998—2001. Mem.: Fla. Soc. Neonatal Perinatologists (pres. 1981—82), So. Soc. Pediat. Rsch. (pres. 1993—94, Founders' award 2007), Soc. Pediat. Rsch., Am. Pediat. Soc. Presbyterian. Avocations: singing, travel, reading, writing, swimming. Office: U Miami Miller Sch Medicine PO Box 016960 R-131 Miami FL 33101*

BANDY, GEORGE C., state legislator; b. Feb. 7, 1945; children: George Jr., Jennifer Mitchell. BA, Morehouse Coll., Atlanta. Mem. Dist. 83 Ala. House of Reps., Montgomery, 1994—. Chmn. Ala. Dem. Conf.; pres. Lee County Alliance. Former mem. Lee County Commn.; former pres. Lee County Concerned Citizens; former pres. pro tem Opelika City Coun; pastor St. James Missionary Bapt. Ch. Mem.: NAACP, Lee County Voters League. Democrat. Baptist. Office: 1307-A Glenn Cir Opelika AL also: Ala House of Reps Ala State House 11 S Union St Rm 529 Montgomery AL 36130 Office Phone: 334-242-7721.

BANE, SANDRA N., retired corporate financial executive, accountant; Grad. in Acctg., Calif. State U., 1975. Ptnr., human resources dept. KPMG LLP, head, merchandising, western region, acct., 1975—96, audit ptnr., 1985—98; cons. Bane Consulting, 1999—. Bd. dirs. AGL Resources Inc., 2008—, Big 5 Sporting Goods Corp., 2002—, Transamerica Premier Investment Funds, 2004—, Petco Animal Supplies, Inc., 2004—. Mem.: Calif. Soc. CPA, AICPA. Office: AGL Resources Inc Ten Peachtree Place Atlanta GA 30309 Office Phone: 404-584-4000. Office Fax: 404-584-3945. Business E-Mail: sandra.bane@Petco.com.

BANG, KI MOON, epidemiologist, professor; b. Korea, Oct. 2, 1940; came to U.S., 1972; m. Hanok Kim Bang, May 30, 1969; children: Sam, David. MPH in Epidemiology, Seoul Nat. U., 1966; MS in Biostats., U. Minn., 1974; PhD in Epidemiology, U. Tex. Med. Br., Galveston, 1981. Chief rsch. and stats. divsn. Nat. Inst. Tuberculosis, Seoul, 1966-72; prof. Howard U., Washington, 1985-88; chief surveillance Nat. Inst. for Occup. Safety and Health, Ctrs. Disease Ctl. and Prevention, Morgantown, W.Va., 1993—. Adj. prof. W.Va. U. Sch. Medicine, Morgantown, 1993—. Author, editor: Occupational Epidemiology, 1997; contbr. chpts. to textbooks, papers and articles to profl. jours. Mem. Coun. Korea Peaceful Unification in N.Y., 1999, Washington, 2005, 13. Fellow Am. Coll. Epidemiology; mem. APHA, Soc. for Epidemiologic Rsch. Presbyterian. Home: 1029 Brettwald Dr Morgantown WV 26508-9413 Office: Nat Inst Occupl Safety and Health CDC 1095 Willowdale Rd Morgantown WV 26505-2845 Office Phone: 304-285-6114. Business E-Mail: kmb2@cdc.gov.

BANGERT, LINDA S., aeronautical engineer; BS in Aero. Engring, MS in Aero. Engring. Aero. rsch. engr. Langley Rsch. Ctr. NASA, Hampton, Va. Avocation: Avocations: flying, reading mysteries and science fiction. Office: NASA Langley Rsch Ctr Mail Stop 254 Bldg 1244 Rm 103 Hampton VA 23681-2199 Business E-Mail: L.S.Bangert@larc.nasa.gov.

BANGS, NELSON A. (TONY BANGS), lawyer; BS, Trinity U., 1975; JD, So. Meth. U., 1978. Bar: Tex. 1979. Assoc. atty. Winstead, McGuire, Sechrest & Trimble, 1979-81; staff atty. Dr. Pepper Co., 1981-83, sr. staff atty., asst. sec., 1983-84; gen. counsel and sec. Dr. Pepper Co. & The Seven-Up Co., Dallas, 1986-88, from v.p. to sr. v.p., sec., gen. counsel, 1988—2001; sr. v.p., gen. counsel Neiman Marcus Group, Inc., 2001—. Mem.: ABA, U.S. Trademark Assn., Am. Soc. of Corporate Secretaries, Dallas Bar Assn. Office: Neiman Marcus One Marcus Square 1618 Main St Dallas TX 75201

BANIKARIM, MARYAM M., marketing executive; b. 1968; married; 2 children. BA in Polit. Sci., Barnard Coll., 1989; MBA, Columbia U., 1993, MA in Internat. Affairs, 1993. Account mgmt. Young & Rubicam; mktg. cons. Time Warner, Deutsche Bank, Bacardi Ltd.; gen. mgr., mktg. dir. CitySearch; mem. mktg. solutions group Turner Broadcasting; pub. Macmillan Pub.; pres. Maryam B Enterprises; joined Univision Comm. Inc., 2002, chief mktg. officer, 2005—11; exec. v.p., chief mktg. officer Gannett Co., Inc., 2011—. Bd. mem. Advertising Week, Sweat Equity Enterprises. Bd. mem. Mt. Sinai Adolescent Healthcare Ctr.; chair Affiliates Coun. for Prep for Prep. Named a Woman to Watch, Multi-Channel News, 2009, Advertising Age, 2011; named one of The 40 under 40, 2006, The 50 Most Powerful Women in NYC, NY Post, 2008, The 40 under 40, Crain's NY Bus., 2008, The Influential Minorities in Cable, Cable-FAX, 2010. Office: Gannett Co Inc 7950 Jones Branch Dr Mc Lean VA 22107

BANKOFF, JOSEPH R., art center president; b. Newark, Dec. 22, 1945; BS, Purdue U., 1967; JD, U. Ill., 1971. Bar: Ill. 1971, Ga. 1972. Law clk. to Hon. Walter P. Gewin U.S. Ct. Appeals (5th cir.), 1971-72; ptnr. King & Spalding LLP, Atlanta, 1972—2006; pres. Woodruff Arts Ctr., Inc., Atlanta, 2006—, CEO, 2006—. Asst. editor U. Ill. Law Forum, 1969-70. Mem. ABA, Ill. State Bar Assn., State Bar Ga., Atlanta Bar Assn., Nat. Inst. Trial Advocacy (trustee 1995-2007, chmn. 2005-07), Am. Law Inst., Order of Coif, Omicron Delta Kappa. Office: Woodruff Arts Ctr Inc 1280 Peachtree St NE Atlanta GA 30309

BANKS, CHARLES AUGUSTUS, III, distribution executive; b. 1940; BA in Internat. Rels., Brown U., 1962. With Cameron Brown Co., 1965-67, Ferguson Enterprises Inc., Newport News, Va., 1967—2001, pres., COO, 1989-93, pres., CEO, 1993—2001; group chief exec. Wolseley PLC, 2001—06; bd. regents Oxford Harris Manchester, 2004—; non-exec. dir., 2004—; ptnr. Clayton, Dubilier & Rice Inc., NYC, 2006—; Mary bd. visitor Coll. William, 2006—; bd. trustees Jamestown Yorktown Found., 2008—. With USN, 1962—64.

BANKS, EARLE S., state legislator; b. Jackson, Miss., June 25, 1954; s. Earl Stewart and Kimberly Celeste. Mem. Dist. 67 Miss. House of Reps., 1993—; funeral dir., atty, ins. exec. Mem.: NAACP, YMCA, 100 Black Men Jackson, Nat. Funeral Dirs. & Morticians Assn. (Miss.), Leadership Jackson, Farish St. Heritage Found Bd., Red Cross, Magnolia & Miss. Bar Assns. Democrat. Catholic. Home: PO Box 2539 Jackson MS 39207 Office Phone: 601-969-2221, 601-359-3755. Fax: 601-961-9450. Personal E-mail: ebanksjax@aol.com. Business E-Mail: ebanks@house.ms.gov.

BANKS, FRED LEE, JR., former state supreme court justice, lawyer; b. Jackson, Miss., Sept. 1, 1942; s. Fred L. and Violet (Mabry) B.; m. Taunya Lovell, June 5, 1967 (div. 1975); children: Rachel R., Jonathan L.; m. Pamela Gipson, Jan. 28, 1978; 1 child, Gabrielle G. BA, Howard U., 1965, JD cum laude, 1968. Bar: Miss. 1968, U.S. Dist. Ct. (no. and so. dists.) Miss. 1968, U.S. Ct. Appeals (5th cir.) 1968, D.C. 1969, U.S. Supreme Ct. 1971. Ptnr. Banks, Owens & Byrd and predecessor firms Anderson, Banks, Nichols & Stewart; Anderson, Banks, Nichols & Leventhal; Anderson & Banks, Jackson, 1968—85; rep. Miss. Ho. of Reps., 1975—85; judge Miss. 7th Cir. Ct., Hinds County and Yazoo County, 1985—91; assoc. justice Miss. Supreme Ct, Jackson, 1991—2000; presiding justice Miss. Supreme Ct., Miss., 2000—01; ptnr., Gen. Litig. Group Phelps Dunbar, LLP, 2001—. Bd. dirs. Sanderson Farms, Inc., 2007—. Bd. dirs. NAACP, 1981—; mem. Nat. Adv. Com. for the Edn. of Disadvantaged Children, 1978-80; del. Dem. Nat. Conv., 1976, 1980; co-mgr. Miss. Carter-Mondale presidl. campaign, 1976; legislator Miss. Ho. of Reps., Jackson, 1976-85; bd. visitors Miss. Coll. Sch. of Law; chmn., Spl. Com. on Jud. Campaign Intervention, 2002, 04; mem. Miss. Bd. Bar Admissions, 1978-81; pres. State Mut. Fed. Savs. and Loan, Jackson, 1976-89; mem. minority adv. com. U. Miss. Sch. of Law. Mem. ABA, Magnolia Bar Assn., Nat. Bar Assn., Hinds County Bar Assn., Am. Inns of Ct., Charles Clark Inn, Miss. Bar Assn., D.C. Bar Assn., Sigma Pi Phi. Roman Catholic. Home: 976 Metairie Rd Jackson MS 39209-6948 Office: Phelps Dunbar LLP Canal Pl 365 Canal St Ste 2000 New Orleans LA 70130-6534 Office Phone: 504-566-1311. Office Fax: 504-568-9130. Business E-Mail: fred.banks@phelps.com.

BANKS, KEITH, bank executive; BA in Economics, magna cum laude, Rutgers U.; MBA in Fin., Columbia U. Equity analyst Home Insurance, 1981; equity rsch. analyst JP Morgan, 1984, head US equity rsch., head global rsch., mng. dir., head US equity; CEO, CIO asset mgmt. org. FleetBoston Fin., 2000—04; joined Bank of America Corp., 2004, pres. CIO Columbia mgmt., 2004—07, pres. global wealth & investment mgmt., 2007—, mem. mgmt. operating com. With Nat. Found. Tchg. Entrepreneurship; mem. bd. overseers Children's Hosp. Boston, mem. fin. com. Mem.: Am. Bankers Assn. (mem. investment adv. com.). Office: Bank of America 100 North Tryon St 18th Fl Charlotte NC 28255

BANKS, LISA JEAN, government official; b. Dec. 19, 1956; d. Bruce H. and Jean P. (Como) Banks. BSBA, Northeastern U., Boston, 1979. Coop. trainee IRS, Boston, 1975-79, revenue officer Reno, 1979-81; spl. agt. Houston, 1981-84, Anchorage, 1984-90; spl. agt. Office Inspector Gen. procurement fraud task force DVA, Boston, 1990-92; spl. agt. Office Inspector Gen. NASA, Kennedy Space Center, Fla., 1992-2000, 2000—03; spl. agt. Computer Crimes Div. NASA-OIG, Kennedy Space Center, Fla., 2000—03; ret., 2003. Fed. womens program mgr., 1980—81. Pres. Make-A-Wish Found. of Cen. Fla., 1994-96, 99-2000, v.p. wish granting, 1996-99. Mem.: Fed. Law Enforcement Officers Assn., Nat. Assn. Fed. Agts. Roman Catholic. Personal E-mail: lisajbanks@comcast.net.

BANKS, RICHARD CHARLES, ornithologist; b. Steubenville, Ohio, Apr. 19, 1931; s. Clinton Seeger and Elizabeth Mae (Harter) B.; m. Gladys Sparks, July 14, 1967; children: Randall C., David R. BS, Ohio State U., 1953; MA, U. Calif., Berkeley, 1957, PhD, 1961. Curator birds and mammals San Diego Natural History Mus., San Diego, 1961-66; zoologist U.S. Fish and Wildlife Svc., Washington, 1966-93, Nat. Biol. Svc., Washington, 1993-97, U.S. Geol. Survey, Washington, 1997—2002. Rsch. assoc. Smithsonian Instn., Washington, 1966—90, 2003—; adj. prof. George Mason U., Fairfax, Va., 1985. Editor: Ornithological Newsletter, 1976-92. 1st lt. U.S. Army, 1953-55, Korea. Fellow: Marion Jenkinson Svc. (AOU award 1998), Am. Ornithologists' Union (sec. 1968—72, v.p. 1987—88, pres.-elect 1992—94, pres. 1994—96); mem.: Washington Biologists Field Club (pres. 1990—93), Biol. Soc. Washington (pres. 1979—80, editor 2004—06), Cooper Ornithol. Soc. (hon.), Wilson Ornithol. Soc. (2d and 1st v.p. 1987—91, pres. 1991—93, Klamm Svc. award 2008), Am. Assn. Zool. Nomenclature (pres. 2001—03). Home: 3201 Circle Hill Rd Alexandria VA 22305-1609 Office: US Geological Survey-MRC 111 Nat Mus Natural History PO Box 37012 Washington DC 20013-7012 Office Phone: 202-633-0783. Business E-Mail: banksr@si.edu.

BANNARD, WALTER DARBY, artist, critic; b. New Haven, Sept. 23, 1934; s. Homes and Janet (Darby) B. BA, Princeton U., 1956. Chmn. dept. art and art history U. Miami, Fla., 1989-97. Lectr. in field, 1969—; vis. prof. Princeton (N.J.) U., 1974, also other univs.; mem. grad. faculty Sch. Visual Arts, N.Y.C., 1984-89; curator Hans Hoffman Hirshorn Mus., 1976; mem. internat. exhbn. com., 1976-78; co-chmn. internat. panel for visual arts Nat. Endowment for Arts, 1979-81; founder, editor newcrit.org, 2001—. Contbr. articles and revs. on modern painting to profl. jours.; contbg. editor: Artforum, 1973-74; 75; one-man shows internat. galleries and mus. include retrospective Balt. Mus. Art, 1973, retrospective U. Tampa, 1997, retrospective Lowe Mus., 1999, Retrospective Rauschenberg Gallery, Edison Coll., 2006, retrospective centre for Visual Comm. Miami, Fla., 2010; numerous internat. group shows; represented in permanent collections at Mus. Modern Art, N.Y.C., Whitney Mus. Am. Art, Met. Mus. Art, N.Y.C., Guggenheim Mus., N.Y.C., others; juror numerous competitions, 1969—; sole juror Australian Bi-Centenary Art Competition, 1988. Recipient Nat. Found. Arts award, 1968-69; Francis J. Greenburger Found. award, 1986; John Simon Guggenheim Meml. Found. fellow, 1968; Richard A. Florsheim Art Fund grantee, 1991. Office: 1540 Levante Ave Miami FL 33124 Home Phone: 305-661-5976; Office Phone: 305-284-2493. Personal E-mail: wbannard@aol.com.

BANNISTER, BRUCE WYCHE, state legislator; b. Greenville, SC, July 21, 1972; s. Oscar W. and Kate Wofford Bannister; m. Mary Margaret A., June 14, 1997; children: Bruce W. Jr., Benjamin A., Margaret Kate. BA, Davidson Coll., 1995; JD, U. SC, 1998. Mng. ptnr. Bannister And Wyatt, LLC; mem. Dist. 24 SC House of Reps., 2006—, mem. Judiciary Com. Mem.: Order Wig and Robe, Leadership Greenville Class 26, Greenville County Bar Assn. Republican. Address: PO Box 10007 Greenville SC 29603 Office: 518B Blatt Bldg Columbia SC 29201 Home: 4 Montrose Dr Greenville SC 29607-3034 Home Phone: 864-676-9250; Office Phone: 864-298-0084, 803-734-3009. E-mail: BannisterB@schouse.org.

BANNISTER, DAVID G., global business advisory firm executive; b. 1956; BA in History, with honors, Stetson U., DeLand, Fla.; MBA, U. NC, Chapel Hill. CPA. Mng. dir. investment banking divsn. Alex. Brown & Sons Inc., 1983—98; gen. ptnr. Grotech Capital Group, 1998—2004; sr. v.p. bus. devel. FTI Consulting, Inc., 2005—06, exec. v.p. corp. devel., 2006—, chief adminstrv. officer, 2008—10, exec. v.p., CFO, 2010—. Bd. dirs. Landstar System, Inc.; past bd. dirs. Allied Holdings, Inc., Simon Delivers, Inc., Trivirix Internat., Inc. Office: FTI Consulting Inc Phillips Point Ste 1500 W Tower 777 S Flagler Dr West Palm Beach FL 33401 Office Phone: 561-515-1900. Business E-Mail: dave.bannister@fticonsulting.com.

BANNISTER, GEOFFREY, academic administrator, geographer; b. Manchester, Eng., Sept. 19, 1945; arrived in US, 1973, naturalized, 1989; s. Leslie and Doris (Shankland) Bannister; m. Margaret Janet Sheridan, Jan. 28, 1968; children: Katherine, Janet; m. Jerri Ross, Apr. 25, 2009. BA, U. Otago, New Zealand, 1967, MA with honors, 1969; PhD, U. Toronto, Can., 1974. Asst. prof. Boston U., 1973-77, acting chmn. geography, 1977-78, dean liberal arts, grad. sch., 1978-87; exec. v.p. Butler U., Indpls., 1987-89, pres., 1989—2000, Forum on Edn. Abroad; pres., chief academic officer CEA Global Edn.; pres. Schiller Internat. U., 2008—09, Hawaii Pacific U., Honolulu, 2011—. Cons. Urban Affairs Ministry of State, Can., 1973; legal cons. U.S. Dept. of State 1982-84; bd. dirs. Somerset Group, Ind. Nat. Bank. Co-author atlas Spatial Dynamics of Postwar County Economic Change, 1977; contbr. articles to profl. jours. Chmn. bd. trustees Cambridge (Mass.) Montessori Sch., 1979-80; mem. corp. Sea Edn. Assn., Woods Hole, Mass., 1979-87; bd. dirs. United Way of Cen. Ind., 1990—, chmn. 1992 Premeire Campaign, edn. chmn.; bd. dirs. Greater Indpls. Progress Com., 1988—; pres. Midwest Collegiate Cons; chmn. World Rowing Championship, 1994. Fellow U. Toronto, 1970-71, Can. Council, 1972. Mem. Nat. Labor/Higher Edn. Coun., Nat. Assn. Scholars, Indpls. Bus. Jour. Blue Ribbon Panel, Indpls. Commn. on African-Am. Males, C. of C., Econ. Club, English Speaking Union U.S. (Indpls. br.), Coun. Urban Coll. of Arts, Letter and Scis., Kiwanis, Phi Beta Kappa. Avocations: bicycling, golf, skiing. Office: Hawaii Pacific University Office of President 1164 Bishop St Honolulu HI 96813 Office Phone: 808-544-0200. E-mail: president@hpu.edu.

BANNISTER, ROBERT CORWIN, JR., historian, educator; b. Bklyn., June 4, 1935; s. Robert C. and Ruth (Allen) B.; m. Joan Turner, June 8, 1958; children: Robert Stanley, Emily E., Paul Andrew, James Peter. BA, Yale U., 1955, Oxford U., Eng., 1957, MA, 1961; PhD, Yale U., 1961. Instr. history Yale U., New Haven, 1960-62; asst. to full prof. Swarthmore Coll., Pa., 1962-98, ret., 1998. Bicentennial prof. U. Helsinki, 1977-78; Fulbright prof. U. Rome, 1985, U. Leiden, Netherlands, 1992; mem. advanced placement program Ednl. Testing Service, Princeton, N.J., 1963-79; vis. prof. U. Queensland, Australia, 1988. Author: Ray Stannard Baker, 1966, Social Darwinism: Science and Myth, 1978, Sociology and Scientism, 1987, Jessie Bernard: The Making of a Feminist, 1991; editor: American Values in Transition, 1972, On Liberty, Society and Politics: The Essential Essays of William Graham Sumner, 1992. Democrat. Home: 1340 Mid Gulf Dr Apt 9C Sanibel FL 33957 E-mail: rbannis1@swarthmore.edu.

BANTA, JAMES ELMER, epidemiologist, educator, dean; b. Tucumcari, N.Mex., July 1, 1927; s. James Elmer and Edna Mae (Murnahan) B. MD, Marquette U., 1950; M.P.H., Johns Hopkins U., 1954; diploma, U.S. Naval Med. Sch., 1952. Med. officer USN, 1950-60; capt. med. officer USPHS, 1960-69; dir. med. program Peace Corps, 1963-65; dir. Office Internat. Health, HEW, 1967-68; med. officer WHO, 1968-70; prof. public health U. Hawaii, 1970-73; dep. dir. Office Health, AID, State Dept., Washington, 1973-75; dean, prof. Sch. Public Health and Tropical Medicine, Tulane U., New Orleans, 1975-87; prof. Sch. Pub. Health U. Hawaii, Honolulu, 1987-88; clin. prof. dept. community and family medicine Georgetown U., Washington, 1990-99. Adj. prof. sch. pub. health and health scis. George Washington U., Washington, 1992-2006. Co-author: How to Travel the World and Stay Healthy, 1969, Year-round Travelers' Health Guide, 1978; Contbr. articles on epidemiology, microbiology and health to profl. jours. Served with USN, 1944-46. Recipient Outstanding Service award Georgetown U., 1965 Fellow AAAS, Am. Coll. Preventive Medicine, Am. Public Health Assn., Am. Heart Assn., Am. Coll. Epidemiology, Coll. Phys. Phila.; mem. ACLU, Common Cause, Environ. Action, Assn. Schs. Public Health (pres. 1979-81), Sigma Xi, Phi Sigma, Delta Omega. Personal E-mail: jebanta@erols.com.

BANZ, GARY W., state legislator; m. Linda Banz; children: Michelle, Mark, Mindy. BS, So. Nazarene Univ., 1968; MEd, Univ. Ctrl. Okla., 1973. Former educator Putnam City Pub. Sch., Ada, Midwest City HS; mem. Dist. 101 Okla. House of Representatives, 2005—. Bd. dir. USS Okla. Meml., Sci. Mus. Okla., 2007—09; pres. Defenders of Dreams Heritage Found.; mem. bd. regents Rose State Coll., 2001—04. Served US Army, 1968—70, served USAR, 1982—90. Decorated Army Commendation medal, Army Achievement medal. Republican. Mailing: 11061 Canterbury Ln Oklahoma City OK 73130 Office: 2300 N Lincoln Blvd Rm 406 Oklahoma City OK 73105 Office Phone: 405-557-7395. E-mail: garybanz@okhouse.gov.

BARAN, GREGG, diagnostic radiology; MD, Vanderbilt U., 1987. Diplomate Am. Bd. Radiology-diagnostic radiology, 1991, Am. Bd. Radiology-neuroradiology, 1995. Resident diagnostic radiology St. Louis Univ., 1987—91; fellow neuroradiology Wash. Univ., St. Louis, 1991; hosp. affiliation includes Bayfront Med. Ctr. Office: Bayfront Medical Center 747 6th Ave S Saint Petersburg FL 33701-4595 Office Phone: 727-898-3647.

BARBALAS, MICHAEL, manufacturing executive; b. Indpls., Aug. 4, 1955; s. Peter Barbalas and Eleanor Barbalas; m. Lorina Cheng Barbalas, Oct. 10, 1981; children: Jonathan, David. BS in Chemistry, Rose-Hulman Inst. Tech., Terre Haute, Ind., 1977; MS in Chemistry, Cornell U., Ithaca, NY, 1979; PhD in Chemistry, Cornell U., NY, 1982. Gen. mgr. Andrew Corp., 1997—2000; mng. dir. Andrew Telecomm. Co. Ltd., Suzhou, China, 2001—06; pres. Goodrich Corp., China, 2010—; group chief Hoffmann-La Roche, 1982—85; mgr. Mgmt. Technologies Internat., 1986—90; exec. dir. Friends of China Foundations, 1991—95; pres. AmCham-China, 2006—10. Exec. dir. Friends of China Found., 1991-95; pres. Am. C. of C., Beijing, China, 2006-10, Board member/Vice Chairman, American Chamber of Commerce in Shanghai, 2003-2005, bd. member, Suzhou University, 2004-, vice chmn., Wuhan Mayor Internat. Adv. Com., 2009- Mem.: Am. Mgmt. Assn., Am. Chem. Soc. Office: Goodrich Corp Four Coliseum Ctr 2730 W Tyvola Rd Charlotte NC 28217-4578 Office Phone: 704-423-7000. Office Fax: 704-423-7002. Business E-Mail: michael.barbalas@goodrich.com.

BARBAN, ARNOLD MELVIN, advertising executive, educator, writer; b. San Antonio, Sept. 17, 1932; s. Sam and Ida Dollie B.; m. Barbara Marie Fox, June 2, 1955; children: Polly Gwen, Pamela Florence. BBA, U. Tex., 1955, MBA, 1959, PhD, 1964. Asst. to v.p. Joske's of Tex., San Antonio, 1955-56; asst. prof. U. Houston, 1959-64; from asst. prof. to prof. in communications U. Ill., Urbana, 1964-83; prof. U. Tex., Austin, 1983-87; prof. advt. U. Ala., Tuscaloosa, 1987-2000, chmn. advt. and pub. rels. dept., 1992-97, prof. emeritus, 2000—. Rsch. prof. communications dept. U. Ill., 1972-83, head advt. dept., 1978-83; cons. Gulf Oil Corp., Houston, 1962, 64, Farm Rsch. Inst., Urbana, 1965-83, Dept. Def., Ft. Sheridan, Ill., 1984; cons. editor Grid Pub. Co., Columbus, Ohio, 1974-84. Author: Readings in Advertising and Promotion Strategy, 1968, Essentials of Media Planning, 1987, 3d edit., 1993, Advertising Media Sourcebook, 4th edit., 1997, Advertising: Its Role in Modern Marketing, 8th edit.,

1994, Advertising Media: Strategy and Tactics, 1992, Advertising Campaign Strategy, 1996, Words From A Rolling Stowe, 2012; editor U. Houston Bus. Rev., 1962-64; cons. editor Jour. Advt., 1979-81; mem. editl. rev. bd. Jour. Current Issues and Rsch. in Advt., 1980-2001, Jour. Advt., 1983-88, 91-94; contbr. articles to profl. jours. Cons. Democratic congl. campaign, Champaign, Ill., 1972. Sgt. U.S. Army, 1956-58. Recipient Outstanding Svc. award Houston Advt. Club, 1964, disting. svc. award Dicionary Internat. Biography, Cambridge, England; fellow U. Tex., Austin, 1960, 1962, Am. Acad. Advt., 1986. Fellow Am. Acad. Advt. (pres. 1981-82, Sandy award 1997), Blanco County Libr. (bd. trustees 2006-13). Home: 4514 Millstone Canyon Ln Sugar Land TX 77479 Personal E-mail: barban@entouch.net.

BARBARA, PAUL FRANK, chemistry professor; b. Jamaica, NY, Apr. 24, 1953; s. Dominic and Virginia (Bambara) B. BA, Hofstra U., 1974; PhD, Brown U., 1978. Postdoctoral fellow Bell Labs., Murray Hill, NJ, 1978-80; asst. prof. chemistry U. Minn., Mpls., 1980-86, assoc. prof., 1986-90, prof., 1990-95, 3M-Alumni Distg. prof. chemistry, 1995—98; Richard J.V. Johnson Welch chair chemistry U. Tex., Austin, 1998—, dir. Ctr. Nano & Molecular Sci. and Tech., 2000—. Cons. Honeywell, 1983—86, 3M, 1985—98; vis. assoc. prof. Nat. Ctr. Sci. Rsch., France, 1988; exec. com. Inter-Am. Photochemical Soc., 1992—96; vis. prof. Cath. U., Belgium, 1996—97; co-chair Ultrafast Phenomena X Optical Soc. Am., 1996—97; co-chair US-Japan coop. prog. on near-field scanning optical microscopy, 1998; mem. devel. resource for biophysical imaging study grp. NIH, 1998; chair radiation chemistry workshop US Dept. Energy, Chesterton, Ind., 1998; vice chair Gordon conf. on radiation chemistry, 2002; internat. lectr. Editl. bd. Jour. Phys. Chemistry, 1990-, Jour. Am. Chem. Soc., 1995-, Accounts Chem. Rsch., 1994-1995, Molecular Physics, 1994-, Chem. Physics, 1994-, Rev. of Sci. Instruments, 1994-1997, Jour. Chem. Physics, 1994-1997, Spectroscopy Letters, 1996-, Chem. Physics Letters, 1997-; assoc. editor Advanced Series in Phys. Chemistry, 1994-, accounts of Chem. Rsch., 1995-. Alfred P. Sloan fellow, Sloan Found., 1983-85; recipient Presdl. Young Investigator award, NSF, 1984-89; George Taylor Disting. Rsch. award, 1990; George Taylor Disting. Svc. award, 1997; Creativity award, NSF, 1998. Fellow Am. Phys. Soc., Am. Acad. Arts Scis.; mem. NAS, Am. Chem. Soc. (exec. com. divsn. phys. chemistry, 1992, vice chair, chmn. elect, chmn., 1993-1995, chair centennial issue com., Jour. Phys. Chemistry, 1997, E. Bright Wilson award in Spectroscopy, 2009), Optical Soc. Am. Office: U Tex Dept Chemistry and Biochem 1 Univ Station A5500 Austin TX 78712

BARBARITO, GERALD MICHAEL, bishop; b. Bklyn., Jan. 4, 1950; s. Anna Marie and Samuel A. Barbarito. BA, Cathedral Coll., Douglaston, NY, 1971; MDiv, Immaculate Conception Sem., Huntington, NY, 1975; licentiate, Cath. U. Am., Washington; LLD (hon.), St. John's U., 1997. Ordained priest Diocese of Bklyn., 1976, asst. chancellor, 1981—82, vice chancellor, 1984—92, master ceremonies, 1984—90, aux. bishop, 1994—99, ordained bishop, 1994, regional bishop, Bklyn. Vicariate East, vicar; with St. Helen's Ch., Howard Beach, NY, 1976—81; bishop Diocese of Ogdensburg, NY, 2000—03, Diocese of Palm Beach, Fla., 2003—. Mem.: Cath. Legal Immigration Network (bd. dirs.), NY State Cath. Chaplains (mem. apostolic com.), Priests' Personnel Bd., Coll. Consultors, Canon Law Soc. America, Cath. Biblical Assn. Roman Catholic. Office: Diocese of Palm Beach 9995 N Military Trail Palm Beach Gardens FL 33410 Office Phone: 561-775-9500. Office Fax: 561-775-9556.

BARBEE, TONY, men's college basketball coach; m. Holly Barbee; children: Hayden Alexandra, Andrew Marsh. BA in Sports Mgmt., U. Mass., 1993. Profl. basketball player, Spain, France, 1993—95; grad. asst., radio color analyst U. Mass. Minutemen, 1995—96, asst. coach, 1996—98, 1999—2000, U. Wyo. Cowboys, 1998—99, U. Memphis Tigers, 2000—06; head basketball coach U. Tex.-El Paso Miners, 2006—10, Auburn U. Tigers, 2010—. Named Coach of Yr., Conf. USA, 2010, Dist. 11 Coach of Yr., Nat. Assn. Basketball Coaches, 2010. Office: Auburn University Basketball c/o Athletics Dept PO Box 351 Auburn AL 36831-0351 Office Phone: 334-844-9760. Business E-Mail: aumensbasketball@auburn.edu.

BARBER, BYRON, II, plastic surgeon; m. Henrietta Barber; 3 children. Grad. magna cum laude, Wofford Coll., Spartanburg, SC; MD, Med. U. SC, Charleston. Diplomate Am. Bd. Plastic Surgery. Gen. surgery residency Bethesda Naval Hosp.; plastic surgery residency Duke Med. Ctr.; chief plastic surgery Moses Cone Hosp. Sys. Christine Kleinert fellow Univ. of Louisville. Contbr. Greensboro News & Record column on Ask the Doctor. Named Top Surgeon, Rrsch. Coun. of America; named one of One of the country's leading plastic surgeons, New Beauty Mag. Fellow: Am. Coll. of Surgeons; mem.: Am. Soc. for Aesthetic Plastic Surgery, Southeastern Soc. of Plastic and Reconstructive Surgeons (v.p.), NC Soc. of Plastic Surgeons (former pres.), Triad Plastic Surgery (former pres.), NC Med. Soc., Guilford County Med. Soc., Am. Soc. of Plastic Surgeons. Office: Barber Center for Plastic Surgery Ste 100 1591 Yanceyville St Greensboro NC 27405 Office Phone: 336-275-3430. Office Fax: 336-275-3420.

BARBER, CHARLES EDWARD, publishing executive, journalist; b. Miami, Fla., Oct. 30, 1939; s. James Plemon (dec.) and Margaret Katherine (Grimes) B. (dec.); m. Judith Margaret Tuck, May 28, 1960 (dec.); children: Janet Lynn Wood, Christopher Edward; m. Magdalena E. Davila, Nov. 7, 2009. AA, Santa Fe Coll., 1971. Prodn. mgr. dept. student publs. U. Fla., Gainesville, 1966-68, ops. mgr., 1968-70, asst. dir., 1970-72, dir. div. publs., 1974; prodn. dir. State Univ. System Press, Gainesville, 1975—76; pres., gen. mgr. Campus Communications, Inc., Gainesville, 1976—2007, pres. emeritus, 2007—. Pres. The Herald Pub. Co., Inc., 1990—2009, Tuck Barber & Assocs., 1995—; pub. The High Springs Herald, 1990—2009, chmn and exec. dir Alliagtor Alumini Assn. Inc.; dir. Campus Press; cons. in field, Columnist, North Fla. Herald, 2010-. Co-author: (with Judy Barber) screenplay This Small Island, 1989; adv. editor Fla. Quar., 1973-74; contbr. articles to profl. jours. Mem. citizens adv. coun. Stephen Foster Elem. Sch., Gainesville, 1976-77, Santa Fe H.S., 1991, Spring Hill Mid. Sch., 1992; mem. Friends of Five, 1975-77, Friends of Libr., 1975-77; mem. Fla. Newspaper Oral History Project, 1996—; chmn. book com. Fla. State Prison, 1973-85, 89-94; bd. dirs. Gainesville H.S. Band Boosters, 1978-79, 83-84, treas., 1984; key communicator Alachua County Sch. Bd., 1980-91, judge countywide spelling bee, 1997-2004; spl. registered dep. sheriff Alachua County Sheriff's Dept., 1979-92, Monroe County Sheriff's Dept., 1997—; mem. gifted students boosters Howard Bishop Mid. Sch., 1980-82; dir. Howard Bishop Band Boosters, 1980-82; mem. pres.'s coun. U. Fla., 1978—95; mem. Leadership Gainesville, 1979, Leadership Fla., 1997—; mentor Coll. Leadership Fla., U. Fla. English Lang. Inst., 1998-2001; mem. steering com. Fla. Alliance for Better Campaigns, chair regional coalition, 1998; mem. Fla. Correct Ct. Com. for 2000 Census, 1998-2000; pack com. chmn. Cub Scouts Am., 1977-78; dir. The Prevention Partnership, 1992-94, Hippodrome State Theatre, 1992-95, bd. advisors. With USCGR, 1957-64, 1966. Recipient Nat. 1st pl. for Editl. Writing Hearst Found., 1965, Svc. award Santa Fe C.C., 1982, Cert. of Appreciation Big Bros. and Big Sisters of Gainesville, 1984, Vols. for Internat. Student Affairs, 1986, 88, 89, 90, Fla. Track Club, 1988, U. Fla. Divsn. Housing, 1990, 91, Addy award Gainesville Advt. Fedn., 1986, 87, 2003, Gold Addy, Fla. and Caribbean Dist., 2003; Recognition for Cold War Svc. U.S. Sec. Def., Disting. Alumnus award, Santa Fe Cmty. Coll., 2007, LeRoy Collins award, Fla. Coll., 2007; named to Ind. Fla. Alligator Hall of Fame, 1996. Mem.: League of Red Herring, Disting. Order of Gator, Soc. Profl. Journalists (treas. No. Fla. chpt. 1972—75, 1986—91, pres.'s club 1994—95, bd. dirs. 2007—, Helen Thomas award for lifetime achievement in journalism 2003), First Amendment Found (trustee 1999—2001), So. Univ. Newspapers (bd. dir. 1980—89), Soc. of News Design, New Media Fedn., Newspaper Assn. Am., Nat. Newspaper Assn. (H.M. for weekly newspaper promotion 1996), Col. Media Advisers, Internat. Newspapers Mktg. Assn., Internat. Newspapers Fin. Execs., Gainesville Advt. Fedn. (bd. dir. 1979—80, Addy award 1986), U. Fla. Coll. Journalism and Comm. (journalism adv. coun. 2000—), Foresight Inst., Fla. Bus. Leadership Network, Fla. Press Found (bd. trustees 2001—, 1st pl. award for newspaper promotion 1992, award for weekly newspaper advt. 1993, 1st pl. award for editl. writing 1994, 1st pl. award for weekly newspaper advt. 1994, Best of Show award weekly newspaper advt. 1994, 1st pl. award weekly newspaper promotion 1995, 1st pl. award for weekly newspaper cmty. svc. 1995, 3rd. pl. award weekly newspaper advt. 1996, 3rd pl. weekly newspaper promotion 1997, award of appreciation,US Census 2000), Fla. Press Assn. (bd. dir. 1992—2001, chmn. continuing edn. com. 1992—2001, v.p. 1997, pres. 1998, chmn. bd. dirs. 1999—2000, Award of Appreciation 1999, Award of Appreciation for 10 years Svc. on Bd. Dirs. 2001, 1st pl. award for Creative Use of Newspaper 2001, Life Mem. award 2006), Fla. Newspaper Advt. and Mktg. Execs. (chmn. edn. com. 1984—87), Fla. Scholastic Press Assn. (newspaper judge 1981—85, Gold Medallion for svc. 2003), Coll. Newspaper Bus. and Advt. Mgrs. (bd. dir. 1980—81), Am. Advt. Fedn., Am. Collegiate Network (adv. com. 1989—91), Leadership Gainesville Alumni Assn., High Springs C. of C., U. Fla. Nat. Alumni Assn. (life Disting. Alumnus award 2007), Alachua C. of C., Gainesville Area C. of C., Alligator Alumni Assn. (bd. dir. 1980—, pres., exec. dir. 2007—, named Mr. Alligator 1986), Am. Red Cross (bd. dir., N.Ctrl. Fla. chpt.), Substance Abuse Prevention Partnership (coun. 1992—95), Tallahassee Social Club, Nat. Press Club, Rotary Internat. (sustaining, sec. 1993—94, Paul Harris fellow), Alpha Phi Gamma. Personal E-mail: cebarber@alligator.org.

BARBER, DOUGLAS E., restaurant chain company executive; b. 1957; BSBA, Ctrl. Mich. U., 1979. Mgr. Metromedia Family Steakhouse, 1979—95, pres., COO, 1995—2003; joined Cracker Barrel Old Country Store, Inc., Lebanon, Tenn., 2003, sr. v.p., restaurant ops., 2006—08, exec. v.p., COO, 2008—10, exec. v.p., chief people officer, 2010—. Office: Cracker Barrel Old Country Store Inc 305 Hartmann Dr Lebanon TN 37088-0787 Office Phone: 615-444-5533. Office Fax: 615-443-9476. Business E-Mail: dbarber@crackerbarrel.com.

BARBER, MARTHA GAYLE, lawyer; b. High Point, NC, Oct. 7, 1953; BA, Duke U., 1975; JD, Wake Forest U., 1981. Bar: NC 1982. Ptnr., chair intellectual property-trademark, copyright group Alston & Bird LLP, Charlotte, NC. Frequent author, spkr. on trademark issues. Mem.: Internat. Trademark Assn. (bd. dirs. 2000—03, mem. leadership devel. subcommittee of Membership Com.). Office: Alston & Bird LLP Ste 4000 Bank of America Plz 101 S Tryon St Charlotte NC 28280-4000 Office Phone: 704-444-1018. Office Fax: 704-444-1688. Business E-Mail: martha.barber@alston.com.

BARBERO, MICHAEL D., career military officer; b. 1953; m. Linda Barbero; 1 child, Emily. BS, US Mil. Acad., West Point, NY, 1976; MS in Nat. Security & Strategic Studies, Nat. Def. U.; M in Mil. Art & Sci., US Army Command & Gen. Staff Course, 1989; Grad., Nat. War Coll., Ft. Lesley J. McNair, Washington DC, 1997. Advanced through grades to lt. gen. US Army, 2009, platoon leader later exec. officer, A Co., 2nd Battalion, 7th Cavalry, 1st Cavalry Divsn. Ft. Hood, Tex., 1977—79, S-3 (Ops) later asst. S-3 (Air) 2nd Battalion, 7th Cavalry, 1st Cavalry Divsn., 1979, aide-de-Camp to Commdg. Gen. 1st Cavalry Divsn., 1979—80; S-1 (Pers.) 3rd Brigade, 2nd Infantry Divsn. Eighth US Army Korea, Republic of Korea, 1982—83, sec. gen. staff, 2nd Infantry Divsn., 1983—84; S-3 (Ops) 3rd Battalion, 327th Infantry, 101st Airborne Divsn. (Air Assault) US Army, Ft. Campbell, Ky., 1984—87, chief current ops., G-3 (ops.) 7th Infabtry Divsn. (Light) & OPERATION JUST CAUSE Ft. Ord, Calif., 1989—90, S-3 (Ops), 1st Brigade, 7th Infantry Divsn. (Light), 1990—91; observer, contr. Battle Command Tng. Program US Army Combined Arms Ctr., Ft. Leavenworth, Kans., 1991—93; comdr. 3rd Battalion, 187th Infantry, 101st Airborne Divsn. US Army, Ft. Campbell, Ky., 1993—95, exec. ops. officer La. Maneuvers Task Force Washington, 1995—96, comdr. 2nd Brigade, 10th Mountain Divsn. Ft. Drum, NY, 1997—99; exec. asst. to comdr. in chief US Joint Forces Command (USJFCOM), Norfolk, Va., 1999—2002; asst. divsn. comdr. 4th Inf. Divsn. US Army, Iraq, 2003—04, chief of staff III Corps & Ft. Hood Ft. Hood, Tex., 2002—03, asst. divsn. comdr. (maneuver) 4th Infantry Divsn. (Mechanized) OPERATION IRAQI FREEDOM, 2003—04; commdg. gen. Joint Readiness Tng. Ctr. & Ft. Polk, Ft. Polk, La., 2004—06; dep. dir. regional ops. (J-3) The Joint Staff, US Dept. Def., Washington, 2006—07; dep. chief of staff strategic ops. (C-3) Multi-Nat. Forces-Iraq OPERATION IRAQI FREEDOM, Iraq, 2007—08; comdr. US Army Inf. Ctr. & Fort Benning, comdt. US Army Infantry Sch. US Army, Ft. Benning, Ga., 2008—09, spl. asst. to chief of staff Washington, 2009, comdr. Multi Nat. Security Transition Command-Iraq, 2009; comdr. NATO Tng. Mission-Iraq OPERATION IRAQI FREEDOM, 2009—11; dep. comdr. for advising & tng. US Forces-Iraq OPERATION IRAQI FREEDOM/NEW DAWN, 2010—11; dir. Joint Improvised Explosive Device Defeat Organization, Arlington, Va., 2011—. Decorated Def. Superior Svc. medal with oak leaf cluster, Legion of Merit with 2 oak leaf clusters, Bronze Star medal with oak leaf cluster, Meritorious Svc. medal with 6 oak leaf clusters, Army Commendation medal with oak leaf cluster, Army Achievement medal. Office: Joint Improvised Explosive Device Defeat Organization 2521 South Clark St Ste 1850 Arlington VA 22202

BARBIER, CARL JOSEPH, federal judge; b. New Orleans, Aug. 21, 1944; m. Peggy Elizabeth McDonald, Jan. 32, 1967. Student, Loyola U., New Orleans; BA cum laude, Southeastern La. U., 1966; JD cum laude, Loyola U., New Orleans, 1970. Cost acct. Michoud Facility, Boeing Co., New Orleans, 1966; tchr. Jefferson Parish (La.) Sch. Bd., 1966-67; law clk. Judge William V. Redmann La. Ct. Appeals, 1969-70; law clk. to Judge Fred J. Cassibry US Dist. Ct., La., 1970-71; assoc. Badeaux & Discon, New Orleans, 1971-73; ptnr. Badeaux, Discon, Cumberland & Barbier, New Orleans, 1974-82; atty. pvt. practice, New Orleans, 1983-84, 93-98; ptnr. Barbier & Cumberland, New Orleans, 1985-92; judge US Dist. Ct. (ea. dist.) La., New Orleans, 1998—. Athletic scholar Southeastern La. U., Hammond, 1963-66. Mem. ABA, Fed. Bar Assn., Assn. Trial Lawyers Am., La. State Bar Assn. (ho. dels. 1994—, com. bar admissins counsel 1974-89), La. Trial Lawyers Assn. (bd. govs. 1985—, exec. com. 1987-91, pres. 1989-90), La. Bar Found. (fellow, strategic planning com. 1997-98), New Orleans Bar Assn., Jefferson Bar Assn., Acad. New Orleans Trial Lawyers, Southeastern La. U. Alumni Assn., English Turn Country Club, Manhattan Athletic Club, Phi Alpha Delta. Office: US Dist Ct 500 Poydras St Rm C256 New Orleans LA 70130

BARBOUR, WILLIAM HENRY, JR., federal judge; b. 1941; BA, Princeton U., 1963; JD, U. Miss., 1966; postgrad, NYU, 1966. Bar: Miss. Ptnr. Henry, Barbour & DeCell, Yazoo City, Miss., 1966-83; judge US Dist. Ct. (so. dist.) Miss., 1983—2006, chief judge, 1989-96, sr. judge, 2006—. Youth counselor Yazoo City, 1971-82. Office: US Dist Ct 245 E Capitol St Ste 430 Jackson MS 39201-2414

BARD, ALLEN JOSEPH, chemist, educator; b. Dec. 18, 1933; m. Fran; children: Eddie, Sara. BSc in Chemistry summa cum laude, CCNY, 1955; MA in Chemistry, Harvard U., 1956, PhD in Chemistry, 1958; PhD (hon.), U. Paris-VII, 1986, U. Tex. A&M U., 2000, Weizmann Inst. Sci., 2003. Instr. chemistry U. Tex., Austin, 1958-60, asst. prof., 1960-62, assoc. prof., 1962-67, prof. chemistry, 1967—, Jack S. Josey Professorship Energy Studies, 1980-82, Norman Hackerman Prof. Chemistry, 1982-85, Hackerman-Welch Regents Chair Chemistry, 1985—, dir., Ctr. for Electrochemistry, 2006—. US nat. com. Internat. Union Pure and Applied Chemistry-Nat. Rsch. Coun., 1983-93, chair, 1988-89, bd. energy and environ. sys., 1983-86, 93-96, bd. chem. scis. tech., 1982-87, co-chair, 1985-87, nat. materials adv. bd. com. on electrochem. aspects of energy conservation and prodn., 1985, com. on chem. scis. and ad hoc panel on DOE rsch., 1980-84, NAS, NRC liaison com. on high temp. sci. and tech. 1984; v.p., Internat. Union Pure and Applied Chemistry, 1990-91, pres., 1991-93; adv. bd. Dept. Energy and Energy Rsch., panel on Cold Fusion, 1989; chem. adv. com. NSF, 1981-84; external adv. com. Beckman Inst., 1989-97; bd. govs. Weizmann Inst., 1995-2000, 2000-05, 2005-10, sci. & acad. adv. com., 1995-98, 2001-; mem. scientific rsch. evaluation panel, Air Force office, 1977-81; adv. bd. mem., Bowling Green State U., Ctr. for Photochemical Sciences, 2002-05; mem. energy rsch. adv. bd., panel on cold fusion, Dept. Energy, mem. low energy nuclear reactions review, 2004; Scientific adv. bd., Biodesign Inst., Ariz. State U., 2006-08; cons. SACHEM, BioVeris (was IGEN), Nucryst Pharma., Konarka Technologies Inc., Nanosys Inc.; past cons. Orchid, Monsanto, CombiChem, Perkin-Elmer, Exxon Rsch. and Engring., ClearFlow, Nat. Sci. Found., Phillips Petroleum, Rockwell Internat., Texas Instruments, Bell Northern, Radian Corp, E.I. DuPont, Electric Power Rsch. Inst.; Woodward vis. prof., Harvard U., 1988; vis. prof., U. of Tokyo, 1975; lectr. in field. Author: Chemical Equilibrium, 1966, Integrated Chemical Systems, 1994; co-author: Electrochemical Methods, 1980; editor Electroanalytical Chemistry, 22 vols., 1966—, Encyclopedia of Electrochemistry, Encyclopedia of the Electrochemistry of the Elements, 16 vols., 1973—, Electrogeneral Chemiluminescence, 2004, (with others) Standard Potentials in Aqueous Solution, Scanning Electrochemical Microscopy; sect. editor Encyclopedia Physical Sci. & Tech., divsn. editor, Jour. Electrochemical Soc., 1970-78, Electrochimica Acta, 1978-80; mem. editl. adv. bd. Analytical Letters, 1967-2004, Chem. Instrumentation, 1967-77, New Journals Chemistry, 1978-93, Jour. Photoacoustics, 1982-84, Ency. Phys. Sci. and Tech., 1984-2004, Analytical Scis., 1985-99, Critical Revs. in Analytical Chemistry, 1985-91, Jour. Supercritical Fluids, 1988-95, Catalysis Letters, 1988-94, Jour. Supercritical Fluids, 1988-95, Academic Press Dictionary Sci. and Tech., 1989-92, Dictionary Modern Sci. and Tech., 1989-92, Ency. Sci. Instrumentation, 1990—, Chem. Physics Letters, 1992-98, Organic Thin Films and Surfaces, 1991—, McGraw-Hill Ency. Sci. and Tech., 1992-97, Heterogeneous Chemistry Revs., 1993-2007, Accounts of Chem. Rsch., 1993-97, Russian Chem. Bull., 1995-2008, Bull. Chemical Soc. Japan, 1995-2004, Ency. Analytical Chemistry: Instrumentation and Applications, 1996-2001, Structure and Bonding, 1996-2005, Nano Letters, 2005-06, NANO, 2007-08; contbr. over 750 articles to profl. jours. Recipient Ward Medal in Chemistry, 1955, Analyst Yr., Dallas Soc. Analystical Chemistry, 1976, Sherman Mills Fairchild scholar Calif. Inst. Tech., 1977, Scientific Achievement award City Coll. N.Y., 1983, Bruno Breyer Meml. award Royal Australian Chem. Inst., 1984, Math. and Phys. Scis. award N.Y. Acad. Scis., 1986, Townsend Harris medal City Coll. N.Y., 1989, Charles N. Reilley award, Soc. Electroanalytical Chemistry, 1984, Edward Mack award Ohio State U., 1989, Outstanding Achievement in Fields of Analytical Chemistry award Eastern Analytical Symposium, 1990, G.M. Kosolapoff award, Auburn U., 1992, Luigi Galvani medal Societa Chimica Italiana, 1992, Sigillum Magnum di Bologna, 1996, Pitts. Analytical Chemistry award, 2001, Welch award in Chemistry, Welch Found., 2004, Disting. Scientist award, Southeastern Universities Rsch. award, 2009, National Medal of Science, 2012; co-recipient Wolf Found. prize in Chemistry, Israel, 2008; NSF Predoctoral Fellowship, 1956-58, Fulbright Fellow, U. Paris, 1973 Fellow Electrochem. Soc. (Carl Wagner Meml. award 1981, Henry Linford award 1986, Olin-Palladium medal 1987, mem. com. edn., 1968-70, vice-chmn., electro-organic divsn., 1968-70, divsn. editor, Jour. Electrochemical Soc., 1970-78, mem. exec. com., S. Tex. sect., 1995-, Heinz Gerischer award-European Section, 2007), World Innovation Found.(fellow, 2004-2006, hon. mem. 2007); mem. AAAS (coun. del. 1992-95, chair-elect chemistry sect. 1996, chair, chem. sect. 1997-98, election panel, 2004), Am. Chem. Soc. (Harrison Howe award Rochester sect. 1980, Fisher award in Analytical Chemistry, 1984, Willard Gibbs award Chgo. sect. 1987, Analytical Chemistry award in Electrochemistry, 1988, Oesper award Cin. sect. 1989, Linus Pauling award, Puget Sound and Portland Sects. 1998, Priestley medal, 2002, William H. Nichols medal, NY, 2004, AdHoc task force to evaluate the Jour. Am. Chem. Soc., 1979, assoc. editor of jour., 1980-81, editor-in-chief, 1982-2001, com. to select editor for Analytical Chemistry, 1990, award com., 1995-97, task force on ethics of the coun. policy com., 2001, mem. governing bd. for publishing's task force on access and pricing for online jour. backfiles, 2001, exec. dir. 2010 com., 2004), NAS (chmn. chemistry sect. 1996-99, chair, selection com., award in chemical sciences, 2002, mem. bd. on energy and environ. sys., 1983-86, 1993-96, 2003-09, governing bd. mem., 2004-05 Acad. Medicine, Engring. and Sciences Tex., com. mem. award in chem. scis. 2006), Am. Acad. Arts and Scis. (award 1990, Chemistry Section Election Panel, 2004, 2007), Internat. Soc. Electrochemists (vice-chmn., chemical physics program, 1978-80), Am. Philos. Soc. (award 2000), Assn. Harvard Chemists (Priestley medal 2002), Soc. Electroanalytical Chemistry, Internat. Union of Pure and Applied Chemistry (mem. commn. on electrochemistry, 1975-83, commn. on chemical kinetics, 1983-87, co-chair CHEMRAWN IV: Conf. on ocean resources, 1987, v.p./pres. elect, 1990-91, pres., 1991-93), Nat. Inst. Standards and Tech. (mem. evaluation panel for Ctr. for Analytical Chemistry, 1983-86), NRC (mem. Nat. Materials Adv. Bd. (NAS/NRC Liaison: com. on high temperature sci. and tech., 1984, mem., com. on chemical sciences and ad hoc panel on Dept. Energy rsch., 1980-84, mem. com. on electrochemical aspects of energy conservation and production, 1985), US Nat. Com. for Biochemistry, 1985, ex-officio mem. US Nat. Com. for Crystallography, 1985, Ad Hoc com. on the future of analytical chemistry, 1984, com. to survey opportunities in chemical sciences, 1984-86, mem. bd. on chemical sciences and tech., 1982-87, co-chair, 1985-87, mem. com. on potential applications of concentrated solar photons, 1990-91, mem. bd. energy and environ. sys., 1983-86, 1993-96, 2003-2006, mem. chemical sciences roundtable, 1997-99, mem. US Nat. Com. for IUPAC, 1983-93, chair, 1988-89, co-chair organizing com., survey workshop on energy and transportation, 2002, co-chair, survey workshop on energy and transportation, 2001, chair review com. Steacie Inst. for Molecular Sciences, NRC-Can., 2004), Nat. Sci. Found. (mem. Nat. Sci. Found.-Dept. Energy Com. for Evaluation of NRCC, chem. adv. com., 1981-84), Solar Energy Rsch. Inst. (panel mem. 1978-80), UNESCO (mem. expert com. on electrochemistry, 1984),

Royal Soc. of Chemistry (hon. fellow), Chinese Chemical Soc. (hon. fellow), Sigma Xi. Achievements include research involving application of electrochemical methods to study of chemical problems and include investigations in electroanalytical chemistry, electron spin resonance, electro-organic chemistry, high resolution electrochemistry, electrogenerated chemiluminescence and photoelectrochemistry; patents in the field. Office: University of Texas Austin Dept Chemistry & Biochemistry 1 University Station A5300 WEL 2-426 Austin TX 78712-0165 Office Phone: 512-471-3761. Office Fax: 512-471-0088. E-mail: ajbard@mail.utexas.edu.

BARDAY, JOHN, office staffing firm executive; Mng. dir. SFN Group Inc. Office: SFN Group Inc 2050 Spectrum Blvd Fort Lauderdale FL 33309 Office Phone: 954-308-7600. Office Fax: 954-308-7666. Business E-Mail: johnbarday@spherion.com.

BARDELAS, JOSE ANTONIO, allergist; b. Havana, Cuba, Feb. 3, 1948; came to U.S., 1961; s. Jose A. and Georgina (Leyva) B.; m. Sallie Young, July 3, 1971; children: Joseph, Mary. BA in Human Biology, Johns Hopkins U., 1970, MD, 1973. Intern, then resident in pediats. Johns Hopkins Hosp., Balt., 1973-75; fellow in allergy and immunology Nat. Jewish Ctr., Denver, 1975-77; pvt. practice Greensboro, NC, 1977—. Asst. clin. prof. pediats. U. N.C., Chapel Hill, 1979—. Named one of Best Doctor, Am., 1996—. Fellow Am. Acad. Allergy and Immunology; mem. AMA, N.C. Soc. Allergy and Immunology (pres. 1982), N.C. Med. Soc. (mem. exec. coun. 1990, 91), High Point Med. Soc. (pres. 1989). Roman Catholic. Avocations: golf, reading. Home: 400 Edgedale Dr High Point NC 27262-2908 Office: 100 Westwood Ave High Point NC 27262-4320 Office Phone: 336-883-1393. Personal E-mail: sybardelas@aol.com, j.bardelas@northstate.net.

BARDEN, GLEN A., orthopedic surgeon; Attended, Abraham Baldwin Agrl. Coll., U. Fla.; MD, Emory Clinic. Cert. American Bd. Orthop. Surgery, American Bd. Orthop. Surgery-hand surgery, 1989. Intern and 1st yr. residency gen. surgery Vanderbilt Univ. Med. Ctr., Nashville; resident orthop. and hand surgery Duke Univ. med. Ctr., Durham; joined Watson Clinic LLP, 1972, found. bd. mem., chmn., orthop. surgeon, bd. dirs.; joined Univ. South Fla., 2009, asst. prof. orthop. surgery, physician; hosp. affiliation includes Lakeland Regional Med. Ctr. Contbr. numerous publs. Capt. orthop. surgeon USAR. Office: Lakeland Regional Medical Center 1324 Lakeland Hills Blvd Lakeland FL 33805 Office Phone: 863-687-1100.*

BAREFOOT, HYRAN EUVENE, academic administrator, educator, minister; b. Mantee, Miss., Jan. 14, 1928; s. James Lee and Martha Caroline (Martin) Barefoot; m. Joyce Lynn Camp, Nov. 24, 1949; children: Judy Barefoot Thomas, June Barefoot Dark, Jane Barefoot Hunter. BA, Miss. Coll., 1949; BD, New Orleans Bapt. Theol. Sem., 1952, ThD, 1955; postdoc., U. N.Mex., 1965—66, Bapt. Theol. Sem., 1971. Asst. prof. religion Union U., Jackson, Tenn., 1957—60, prof. religion, 1962—96, chmn. dept. religion, 1966—75, chmn. div. humanities, 1972—75, v.p. acad. affairs, 1975—87, acad. dean pres., 1987—96, chancellor, 1996; chancellor emeritus; asst. prof. N.T., Southern Bapt. Theol. Sem., Louisville, 1960—62. Pastor Liberty Bapt. Ch., Calhoun, La., 1946—49, Goss Bapt. Ch., Miss., 1949—52, Hebron Bapt. Ch., New Hebron, Miss., 1952—55, First Bapt. Ch., Crowley, La., 1955—57, Woodland Bapt. Ch., Brownsville, Tenn., 1957—60, 1966—75. Recipient Tchr. of Yr. award, Union U., 1967, Disting. Faculty award, 1973; named Jackson Tenn. Man of Yr., 1993. Mem.: Assn. Southern Bapt. Colls. (sec. 1984—85), Jackson Rotary Club. Avocations: antiques, hunting, fishing. Home: 120 Redfield Dr Jackson TN 38305-8526 Office: Union U Office of Chancellor Jackson TN 38305

BARFIELD, KENNY DALE, religious organization administrator; b. Florence, Ala., Nov. 17, 1947; s. Henry Perry and Bernice Elizabeth (Olive) B.; m. Nancy Ann Cordray, Aug.7, 1970; children: Amber Elizabeth, Lora Allyn. BA in Speech Communication, David Lipscomb Coll., 1969; MA in Speech Communication, U. Ala., Tuscaloosa, 1972; EdS in Ednl. Adminstrn., U. North Ala., 1986; EdD in Ednl. Adminstrn., U. Ala., Tuscaloosa, 1989. Dir. debate, instr. Mars Hill Bible Sch., Florence, 1969—, acad. dean, 1986-2000, prin., 1990-95, v.p., 1999-2000, pres., 2001—; minister Highland Park Ch. of Christ, Muscle Shoals, Ala., 1970-74, Jackson Heights Ch. of Christ, Florence, 1974-78, Sherrod Ave Ch. of Christ, Florence, 1978—. Instr. speech communication Internat. Bible Coll., 1972-75, U. North Ala., Florence, 1981-83. Author: 50 Golden Years: The N.F.L. Nationals, 1980, Why The Bible Is Number One, 1988, The Prophet Motive, 1995; editor Pacesetter Panther Notes; contbr. articles to profl. jours. Recipient Outstanding Young Religious Leader award Ala. Jaycees, 1976, Ala. Speech Tchr. of Yr. award 1977, Outstanding Speech and Debate Coach award Comml. Appeal, 1977, Key Coach award Barkley Forum for High Schs., Emory U., 1981, HS Debate Coach of Yr. award Bishop's Guild, Samford U., 1983, Disting. Svc. award Nat. Forensic League, 1981, 86, Gregg Phifer svc. award Fla. State U., 1997; named Five Diamond Coach Nat. Forensic League, 2010, HS Debate Coach of Yr. Carson Newman U., 1992, 2000; named to Nat. Forensic League Hall of fame, 2005; Faulkner fellow U. Miss., 1987. Mem. Am. Forensic Assn. (ednl. practices com. 1984-86, high sch. affairs com. 1988-90, pub. rels. com. 1990-93, v.p. high sch. affairs 1998-00), Ala. Forensic Educators Assn. (pres. 1976-77, 82-83, 85-86, Hall of Fame 2005), Nat. Assn. Secondary Sch. Prins., So. Assn. Colls. and Schs. (cen. rev. com. 1991-95), Deep South Nat. Forensic League (chmn. 1977-79, 81-85), Nat. Debate Coaches Assn. Office: Mars Hill Bible Sch 698 Cox Creek Pky Florence AL 35630-6624

BARFIELD, LISTON DOUGLAS, state legislator; b. Conway, SC, Aug. 9, 1945; s. J. T. and Agnes Jones Barfield; m. Norma Jean Allen, 1967; children: James Douglas, Brett Allen. BA, Coastal Carolina Coll., 1975; MBO, Webster U., 1983; PhD, Francis Marion U., 2005. V.p. Ameritel Comms.; mem. Dist. 105 SC House of Reps., 1985—89, mem. Dist. 58, 1996—, vice chair Invitations and Meml. Resolution Com., mem. Ways and Means Com. Recipient Staff of Yr., Horry-Georgetown Tech. Coll., 1979. Mem.: Ducks Unlimited, Aynor-Lions, Big Brothers Big Sisters. Republican. Baptist. Address: PO Box 1734 Conway SC 29526 Mailing: 503A Blatt Bldg Columbia SC 29201 Home Phone: 803-365-2049, 803-771-8711; Office Phone: 803-734-2968. Business E-Mail: ldb@legis.lpitr.state.sc.us.

BARFIELD, LOWRY, lawyer; BS, Tex. Tech. Univ.; JD, So. Methodist Univ. Atty. Larson King, LLP, 1999—2003, Robins, Kaplan, Miller & Ciresi, 2003—04; pvt. practice Houston, 2004—05; v.p. legal, gen. counsel, sec. Western Refining, Inc., El Paso, Tex., 2005—07, sr. v.p. legal, gen. counsel, sec., 2007—. Office: Western Refining, Inc 6500 Trowbridge Dr El Paso TX 79905 Office Phone: 915-775-3300.

BARGAGLIOTTI, LILLIAN ANTOINETTE, nursing educator; b. Millington, Tenn., Dec. 29, 1949; d. Benard Wood and Georgeanne (Lowe) McIllwain; m. Ronald M. Prentice, Apr. 24, 1970 (div. 1975); m. bill L. Bargagliotti, July 8, 1978; 1 child, William Benard. RN, Tacoma Gen. Hosp., 1971; BSN, U. Tenn., 1976; MS, U. Calif., San Francisco, 1978; D in Nursing Sci., U. Calif., 1984. Staff nurse Tacoma (Wash.) Gen. Hosp., 1971, St. Joseph's Hosp., Tacoma, 1971-75, City of Memphis Hosp., 1975-76; instr. N.W. Miss. Jr. Coll., Senatobia, 1976-78; inservice coord. Eden Hosp., Castro Valley, Calif., 1978-79; instr. Ohlone Coll., Fremont, Calif., 1979-84; assoc. prof. nursing San Francisco State U., 1984-85; assoc. dean, prof. nursing U. San Francisco, 1985-89, interim dean, prof. nursing, 1989-91; assoc. DON Davies Med. Ctr., 1992; dean, prof. nursing Loewenberg Sch. Nursing, U. Memphis, 1992—2005, prof., 2005—. Clin. evaluator SUNY Western Performance Assessment Ctr., Long Beach and Palo Alto, Calif., 1982-85; program evaluator Collegiate Commn. for Nursing Edn. Contbr. articles to profl. jours. Capt. USAR, 1976-78. Fellow Acad. Nursing Edn.; mem. ANA, Tenn. Nurses Assn., Assn. Oper. Rm. Nurses (mem. jour. editl. bd. 1987-90), Nat. League for Nursing (program evaluator, pres. 2005-07, bd. govs. 2003-07, trustee found. bd.), Tenn. Assn. Deans/Dirs. Nursing (pres. 1997-99, 99-2001), Coun. on Grad. Fgn. Nursing Schs. (mem. exam. com. 2008-), Sigma Theta Tau. Republican. Mem. Ch. of Christ. Home: 7423 Wood Rail Cv Memphis TN 38119-9007 Office: U Memphis 308 Admin Bldg Memphis TN 38152 Office Phone: 901-678-5926. Business E-Mail: tbargagl@memphis.edu.

BARHAM, CHARLES DEWEY, JR., electric power industry executive, lawyer; b. Goldsboro, NC, July 7, 1930; s. Charles Dewey and Helen Wilkinson (Douglass) Barham Hughes; m. Margaret Wright Crow, June 17, 1960; children: Margaret Douglass, Charles Dewey III. BS, Wake Forest U., 1952, JD, 1954. Bar: N.C. 1954. Asst. atty. gen. N.C. Dept. Justice, Raleigh, 1958-66; assoc. gen. counsel Carolina Power & Light Co., Raleigh, NC, 1966-73; ptnr. Douglass & Barham, Raleigh, 1974-80; v.p., sr. counsel Carolina Power & Light Co., Raleigh, 1981-82, sr. v.p., gen. counsel, 1982-87, sr. v.p., 1982-90, exec. v.p, 1990-95; bd. of dir., 1990—95; ptnr. Douglass & Barham, 1995—. Chmn. bd., pres. Nuclear Mut., Ltd., Hamilton, Bermuda, 1981-86, bd. dirs. 1973-95; bd. dirs. Nuclear Elec. Ins. Ltd., 1987-95 Hamilton; gen. counsel World Nuclear Fuel Mkt., Atlanta, 1974-80; gen. counsel Meredith Coll., Raleigh, 1977-80, trustee, 1984-87, 90-93, 95—2001; mem. regional bd. dirs. Wachovia Bank of N.C., 1990-95. Pres. Raleigh YMCA, 1982-92; bd. vis. Sch. Law Wake Forest U., 1998—. Capt. USNR, 1955-77. Mem.: ABA, N.C. Bar Assn., Glen Forest Club (pres. 1977), Raleigh Civitan Club (dir. 1974—77, 1999—).

BARHAM, ROBERT JOCELYN, state legislator; b. Jan. 25, 1949; m. Melba Pipes. Mayor, La., 1982—88; alderman, 1988—94; state senator Dist. 33 La., 1994—. Mem.: Ducks Unlimited, Nat. Rifle Assn., Agr. Leaders La., La. Cotton Prodrs., La. Farm Bur. Democrat. Baptist. Address: PO Drawer 10 Oak Ridge LA 71264 Office: PO Box 94183 Baton Rouge LA 70804 Office Phone: 318-244-6965, 318-728-6830. Office Fax: 318-728-3070.

BARIA, DAVID, state legislator; b. Pascagoula, Miss., Dec. 4, 1962; m. Marcie Fyke; children: Merritt, Bess. BS, U. Southern Miss., 1987; JD, U. Miss., 1990. Pvt. practice atty., 1990—2002; ptnr. Baria, Hankins and Stracenes, 2002—05; CEO Rhino Constrn., LLC, 2005—; mem. Dist. 46 Miss. State Senate, 2008—12; mem. Dist. 122 Miss. House of Reps., 2012—. Democrat. Episcopalian. Office: Miss House of Reps PO Box 1018 Jackson MS 39215 Business E-Mail: dbaria@house.ms.gov.

BARILLEAUX, RENE PAUL, curator; b. Lafayette, La., June 29, 1958; s. Ira Charles and Joanna Beyt Barilleaux; life ptnr. Timothy Paul Hedgepeth. BFA, U. Southwestern La., Lafayette, 1975—79; MFA, Pratt Inst., Bklyn., 1979—81. Curator for collections & exhibitions Mus. Holography, NYC, 1983—86; exhibitions curator Madison Art Ctr., Wis., 1986—92; gallery dir., asst. prof. Coll. Charleston, SC, 1992—93; chief curator Miss. Mus. Art, Jackson, 1993—2001, dep. dir. programs, 2002—05; curator art after 1945 McNay Art Mus., San Antonio, 2005—, chief curator, 2006—. Mem.: Coll. Art Assn., Assn. Art Mus. Curators, Am. Assn. Museums. Office: McNay Art Mus PO Box 6069 San Antonio TX 78209 Home: 184 Oakwell Farms Pkwy San Antonio TX 78218 Office Phone: 210-805-1723. Office Fax: 210-824-0218. Business E-Mail: rene.barilleaux@mcnayart.org.

BARISH, CHARLES FRANKLIN, internist, gastroenterologist, researcher; b. Franklin, NJ, Jan. 5, 1955; s. Philip and Laura (Freedman) Barish; m. Debrah Lee Kaufman, Aug. 13, 1977; children: Philip, Stefanie, Jacob. BS in Chemistry with honors, U. Fla., 1976, MD, 1980. Diplomate in internal medicine and gastroenterology Am. Bd. Internal Medicine. Resident, fellow Wake Forest U. Sch. Medicine, Winston-Salem, NC, 1980-85; physician Wake Gastroenterology Divsn. Wake Internal Medicine Cons., Raleigh, NC, 1985—; founder, pres. Wake Rsch. Assocs., Raleigh, 1985—2011, med. dir. GI studies, 2011; clin. asst. prof. medicine U. NC Sch. Medicine, Chapel Hill, 1985—. Chmn. nutritional care com. Rex Hosp., Raleigh, 1987—97; thought leader & cons. Study Design & Protocol Development for Pharmaceutical & Biotech. Industry. Contbr. numerous articles to med. jours., chapters to books. Pres. Jewish Cmty. Ctr., Raleigh, 1995—97; v.p. Jewish Fedn. Greater Raleigh, 1993—97; bd. dirs. Raleigh-Cary Jewish Fedn., 1990—2006. Named one of Top Drs., 2012. Fellow: ACP, Am. Gastroenterology Assn., Am. Coll. Gastroenterology; mem.: AMA, NC Soc. Gastroenterology, Crohn's and Colitis Found. (bd. dirs.), Wake County Med. Soc., N.C. Med. Soc., Am. Soc. Gastrointestinal Endoscopy, Alpha Epsilon Delta, Phi Kappa Phi, Alpha Omega Alpha. Avocations: gardening, golf, travel. Office: Wake Gastroenterology 3100 Blue Ridge Rd Ste 300 Raleigh NC 27612-8035 also: Wake Rsch Assocs 3100 Duraleigh Rd Ste 304 Raleigh NC 27612 Office Phone: 919-781-7515. Business E-Mail: CFBGastro@aol.com.

BARKER, BEN, chef, restaurant owner; m. Karen Barker; 1 child, Gabriel. Grad., Culinary Inst. Am., 1981. Chef Restaurant Le Residence, Chapel Hill, NC; head chef Fearrington House, Pittsboro, NC; chef, co-owner Magnolia Grill, Durham, NC, 1986—. Featured in (TV series) Americas 1996 - Rising Star Chefs, PBS, 1996, Great Chefs of the South, 1997, NY Times, Washington Post, Food & Wine mag., Bon Appetit, Esquire, Restaurant News, Southern Living. Named Rising Star Chef, Esquire, 1992, Best Chef in Southeast, James Beard Found., 2000; named one of Ten Best New Chefs in Am., Food & Wine mag., 1993; named to Who's Who of Southern Cooking, 1988, Fine Dining Hall of Fame, Nation's Restaurant News, 1996; nominee Best Chef in Southeast, James Beard Found., 1992, 1995, 1996, 1997, 1998, 1999. Achievements include creating southern regional menu for Delta Airlines, 1995. Office: Magnolia Grill 1002 9th St Durham NC 27705 Office Phone: 919-286-3609.

BARKER, BILL, publishing executive; b. Nashville; m. Rita Barker; children: Cameron, Caylie. BS in Mgmt., Mktg. & Psychology, Union U., Jackson, Tenn. Various positions Gannett, 1984—90; joined Media General, Inc., Richmond, Va., 1990, chmn. Va. coalition, 2002—04, dir. ops. Richmond Times-Dispatch, 1990—2004, v.p. ops. Fla. comm. group Fla., 2004—12, pres., pub. The Tampa Tribune, 2012—. Office: The Tampa Tribune 200-202 S Parker St Tampa FL 33606 Office Phone: 813-259-7711.

BARKER, GEORGE L., state legislator; b. Eldorado, Ill., Aug. 24, 1951; m. Jane Barker; children: Erik, Emily. AB, Havard Coll.; MS in Health Policy, Mgmt., Harvard U. Planner Health System Agy. of Northern Va.; mem. Dist. 39 Va. State Senate, 2008—. Vice chmn. Springfield Dist. Coun., 2004—; advisor Greater Prince William Cmty. Health Ctr., 2004—; founding mem., chmn. Northern Va. Access to Health Care Consortium. Democrat. Presbyterian. Office: PO Box 10527 Alexandria VA 22310 also: Senate of Virginia PO Box 396 Richmond VA 23218 Office Phone: 703-303-1426, 804-698-7539. Office Fax: 804-698-7651. E-mail: district39@senate.virginia.gov.

BARKER, HOWARD W., JR., accountant; b. 1947; CPA. Joined KPMG LLP, 1972, ptnr., 1982—2002. Bd. dirs. Medco Health Solutions, Inc., 2003—, priceline.com Inc., 2003—, Chiquita Brands Internat. Inc., 2007—. Former treas., bd. dirs. Sr. Svcs. of Stamford; bd. gov. Inst. for Internal Auditors, NYC, 1985-86; bd. dirs., pres. Volunteer Ctr. of Lower Fairfield County, 1990-96; bd. dirs. Darien United Way, 1997-99, Person to Person, 1998-00; mem. AICPA, Conn. Soc. of CPAs, Fla. Inst. of CPAs. Office: Chiquita Brands International Inc Bd Directors 550 S Caldwell St Ste 1010 Charlotte NC 28202-2681 Office Phone: 513-784-8000. Office Fax: 513-784-8030. Business E-Mail: howard_barker@medcohealth.com.

BARKER, JIM (JAMES FRAZIER BARKER), architecture educator, retired academic administrator; b. Kingsport, Tenn., May 1, 1947; BArch, Clemson U., 1970; M in Arch. and Urban Design, Washington U., 1973; PhD (hon.), S.C. State U., Mars Hill Coll. Dean Sch. Arch. Miss. State U., Starkville, 1984—86; pres. Clemson U., 1999—2013, pres. emeritus, prof. architecture, 2013—, dean Coll. Arch., 1986—95, dean Coll. Arch., Arts & Humanities, 1995—99. Bd. dirs. NCAA Divsn. I, 2007—10. Fellow: AIA; mem.: Southern Assn. Colleges & Schools (commr. 2002—04, chmn. 2004—06), Assn. Collegiate Schools Arch. (Nat. Disting. Prof. award). Office: Clemson University Lee-3 135 Clemson SC 29634 Office Phone: 864-656-3884. Business E-Mail: jbarker@clemson.edu.*

BARKER, JOHN ROY, lawyer; b. St. Joseph, Mo., Mar. 9, 1947; s. Frank Otis and Ella Mae (Wiley) B.; m. Mary Lucille Smith, Apr. 17, 1971; children: Sarah J., Kathryn W. Morris, Mary E. BA, U. Mo., 1969; JD, U. Mich., 1974. Bar: US Dist. Ct. (no. dist. Okla.) 1974, Okla. 1974, US Ct. Appeals (10th cir.) 1974. Lawyer Gable Gotwals, Tulsa, Okla., 1974—2004, shareholder, 2012—; sr. v.p., gen. counsel, asst. sec. ONEOK, Inc., Tulsa, Okla., 2004—11; sr. v.p., gen. counsel, sec. ONEOK Partners, LP, Tulsa, Okla., 2006—11. Pres. Jenks (Okla.) Pub. Schs. Found., 1989-91; sec. St. Simeon's Episcopal Home, Tulsa, 1991-96, v.p., 1996-98, pres., 1998-2001; pres St. Simeon's Home Found., 2002-04; vice chmn. Sutton Avian Rsch. Ctr., Bartlesville, Okla., 1994-96; pres. Arts and Humanities Coun., Tulsa, 1994-96, pres., 1993-95. With US Army, 1969—71. Mem. ABA, Okla. Bar Assn. (Outstanding Young Lawyer 1978, chair Young Lawyers 1978), Tulsa County Bar Assn., Okla. Bar Found., Tulsa Title and Probate (pres. 1987-88). Episcopalian. Avocations: running, bicycling. Office: Gable Gotwals 1100 ONEOK Plaza 100 W Fifth St Tulsa OK 74103-4217 Office Phone: 918-595-4815. Business E-Mail: jbarker@gablelaw.com.*

BARKER, ROBERT OSBORNE (BOB BARKER), mediator, retired educator; b. Cleve., June 13, 1932; life ptnr. Pauline Barker; children: Debra, Dawn, Collern, Stephen, Michael. Student, Henry Ford C.C., 1950; BA in Comm. Arts and Sci., Mich. State U., 1954; LLB, LaSalle U., 1969; postgrad. in quality mgmt., U. Wis., 1989; postgrad. in pub. rels., U. Fla., 1996. Cert. mediator Fla. Supreme Ct., cert. dispute resolution, Fla. 1th Circuit Dist., 1995-. With pub. rels. dept. Ford Motor Co., Dearborn, Mich., 1953; mgr. Kaiser Aluminum Co., Chgo., 1956-58; advt. mgr. Bastian Blessing Co., Chgo., 1958-59; dealer tng. regional mgr. Sun Oil Co., Mich., 1959—71; mgr. Goodyear Tire & Rubber Co., Detroit, 1971-72; mgr., v.p. Nat. Assn. Mfrs., Washington, Boston and Detroit, 1972-87, industry exec. & lobbyist; pres., CEO Barker Cons. Inc., 1987-96; mgr., v.p. seminars and materials dept. Am. Supplier Inst. (div. of FoMoCo), 1987-90; nat. mdse./mktg. mgr. Costa del Mar Sunglasses, Ormond Beach, Fla., 1990-91; resort mgr. Oceanside 99 Condo, Ormond Beach, Fla., 1992-93, Outrigger Beach Club, Ormond Beach, Fla., 1994-95; mediator County Ct. Mediation Svcs., 1995—; legislative chair Assoc. Fla. Healthcare Auxiliaries, Volunteers, 2007—08; mem. USO, 2013. Fed. lobbyist Nat. Assn. Mfrs., 1972—87; owner Dolphin Beach Club Condo, 1981—2001, bd. dirs., 1991—99; adj. prof. pub. rels., advt., retailing, sales fundamentals, global and internat. mktg., quality svc. mgmt. Daytona State Coll., 1994—2006, Falcon student athlete mentor, 2003—; FACC mem. Fla. Assn. CC's; bd. dirs. Fla. Hosp. Meml. Med. Ctr., Daytona Beach, 2009—10, bd. mem., 2009—12, pub. PR rels. chair, media chair, 1998—2013, elected aux. pres. adventist hosp. sys., 2008—10; pub. rels. chair Oceanside Hosp. Reflections and Imaging Ctr.; advisor Jr. Achievement, Daytona Beach, 2007—08; with HS Football Players Recruiter Mich. State U., 1956—91; elec bd. mem. Fla. Hosp. Found., 2010—12, planned giving, annual giving com. Twp. trustee, Findlay, Ohio, 1962; lay min. Episcopal ch., 1959-89, vestry, 1981-1989; mem. exec. bd. dirs. Volusia County Rep., 1991-00, Sang Guys & Dolls Defiance, Ohio; bd. dirs. Am. Cancer Soc., 1991-05; bd. dirs. Dearborn Civic Theatre, 1980-84, Volusia Presdl. forum, 1991-99, Dearborn City Beautiful commr. emeritus, 1970-90; commr. Ormond Beach Quality of Life, Beautification and Planning bds., 1990-99, Jazzmatazz exec. com. mem., Ho-Ho parade exec. com. mem., Habitat Humanity, 1995-99; res. police officer, Dearborn, 1968-88; pres. Dearborn High and Lindbergh Elem. PTA; bd. dirs. Bldg. Assn. Mgrs., 1991-95, Cmty. assoc. Inst., 1993-97, Volusia County Pers. Bd., 1991-93; mem. adv. coun. bd. Coun. of Aging, 1991-00; bd. dirs. Daytona and Ormond Beach Rep. Club, 1991-99, 2006-07, heritage mem. Ormond Meml. Art Mus., 1991-01, 04-12; amb. Daytona Internat. Airport, 1996-02; team selection scout Fla. Citrus Sports for New Yr.'s Bowl Capital One Football Game and Russel Athletic Bowls, Orlando, Fla., 1995—; mem. elder voice focus group Genesis Elder Care, 2001; asst. publicity dir. bd. dirs. Ormond Sr. Games, 1994-96; mem. City of Daytona Beach Cmty. Rels. Coun., 2006-09; mem. pers. bd. City of Daytona Beach, 2006—; mem. worship com. & visioning com. St. James Episc. Ch., Ormond Beach, Fla., 2005-08; adv. team US Census Bur. Enumerator & Finger Printing, 2010; survivor Quintuple Bypass Open Heart Surgery, 2010, bd. dirs Navy League PR chair, 2011-, mem. choir and the living christmas tree White Chapel Ch., 2013-. Served with USNR, 1949-58, AFROTC, 1951-54; mem focus group Fla. Healthcare Plans Inc., 2013. Recipient Vol. of Yr. award Am. Cancer Soc., 1998, Outstanding award for faculty bus. Daytona State Coll., award Athletic dept. assistance to student athletes Spl. Needs Awareness Program and Svc. Club, 2000-01, Outstanding Adj. Faculty award Daytona State Coll., 2005-06, Olympian, 1952, Gold, Silver & Bronze medals, Ormond Sr. Olympic Games, 1992-96, Outstanding Leadership award, FHMMC Auxiliary, 2009-10. Mem.: AARP (asst. state coord., driver safety instr., vol.), YMCA, AMD Cancer Inst., GFHE-UF (PR dir. 2011—), Gator Club (advocate 2008, dir.), Premier Health Srs., Fla. Hosp. Meml. Sys., Mich. State U. Spartan Fund, Nat. Football Found., Sr. Friends of Volusia/Flagler Counties (pres. 2000—04), Ormond Beach C. of C. (former amb., chmn. pub. rels. Beautification, JazzMatazz, social com. 1990—2002), Fla. Pub. Rels. Soc. Am. (Chgo. chpt. 1979, mem. Volusia PR chpt. 1994—, v.p. 1996—98, bd. dirs., historian 2011—, sr. advisor 2013—), Assn. Execs., Advt. Fedn., Mil. Officers Assn. America (life), Mich. State U. Football Players Assn. (life), Fla. Sheriffs Assn, Mich. State U. Alumni (life; past pres. 5 alumni clubs,

Dayton area chair Spartan fair club activities, Alumni of Chgo. Bears), Am. Heart Assn. (bd. dirs. Volusia/Flagler 2002—12, advocate award 2008), Navy League US (life; Daytona Beach Area Coun., NL-US bd. dirs. pub. affairs, PR dir. 2011—), Mich. State Varsity Alumni Club (life; volusia flagler mem. 2002—12, 2013—, chair), U. Fla. Alumni Assn. Advocate (life; Gator Club Volusia/ Flagler County, v.p. edn. 1999—2002, outreach v.p. 2007—, Gators For Higher Edn. bd. dirs. mem. 2008—), Fla. Police Benevolent Assn., Exch. Club, Ormond Shrine Club (pres. 1994—95), Shriners (Detroit) (dir. pub. rels. 1984, provost unit, Fez on Wheels and Vets. unit), Moose, South Field Area Rotary (pres. 1987—88), Elks, Am. Legion (life), Masons, Delta Tau Delta. Episcopalian. Home: Unit 613 229 S Ridgewood Ave Daytona Beach FL 32114-4334 Personal E-mail: bobbarker13_99@yahoo.com.

BARKER, SAM L., pharmaceutical executive; BS, Henderson State Coll., 1964; MS, U. Ark., 1966; PhD, Purdue U., 1969. Rsch. scientist Squibb Pharmaceuticals, 1969—75, various exec. positions in rsch. and develop., mfr., fin., bus. develop., sls. and mktg.; former pres., gen. mgr. E.R. Squibb Diagnostics; pres. intercontinental commercial ops. Bristol-Myers Squibb Co., 1990—92, pres. US pharmaceuticals, 1992—97, exec. v.p. worldwide franchise mgmt. and strategy, 1998; co-founder, pres., CEO Clearview Projects, Inc., 2003—04. Bd. dirs. Lexicon Pharms. (formerly Lexicon Genetics), The Woodlands, Tex., 2000—, bd. chmn., 2005—. Office: Lexicon Pharms 8800 Technology Forest Pl The Woodlands TX 77381-1160

BARKER, TOBY, state legislator; b. Meridian, Miss., Dec. 31, 1981; BA, U. Southern Miss., 2004, MS, 2006. Dir. Southern Miss. Bus. Assistance ctr., 2006—, asst. dir., 2006; project mgr. & intern US dept. of agr. rural devel., 2005—06; mem. Dist. 102 Miss. House of Reps., 2008—. Republican. Christian. Home: 409 S 21st Ave Hattiesburg MS 39401 Office: PO Box 1018 Jackson MS 39215 Home Phone: 601-307-3802. E-mail: tbarker@house.ms.gov.

BARKER, WILLIAM DANIEL, hospital administrator; b. New Orleans, July 21, 1926; s. William Daniel and Ada (Will) B.; m. Nancy Pool, Sept. 23, 1949; children: Nancy Louise, Julia Ann, William Daniel III, Marion DeVilbiss. B in Bus. Adminstrn., Emory U., 1949; M in Hosp. Adminstrn., Ga. State U., 1966. Bus. office mgr. Emory U. Hosp., Atlanta, 1949-50; asst. adminstr. Griffin (Ga.) Spalding County Hosp., 1950-51; adminstr. Winder-Barrow (Ga.) Hosp., 1951-52; hosp. field rep. Ga. Dept. Pub. Health, Atlanta, 1952-54, hosp. cons., 1954-55; asst. adminstr. Tri-County Hosp., Ft. Oglethorpe, Ga., 1955-60; asst. dir. Crawford Long Hosp. Emory U., Atlanta, 1960-73, adminstr., 1973-84, dir. hosps., 1984-90, exec. dir. hosp., 1987-90; ret., 1991; prof. Emory U., Atlanta, 1988-93. Bd. dirs. Ga. Fed. Bank, Atlanta, Blue Cross Blue Shield Ga., Inc.; provider affairs com. Blue Cross Blue Shield Assn., United Network for Organ Sharing, bd. dirs., 1991—; bd. govs. SunHealth, Charlotte, N.C., chmn., 1988-89; bd. commrs. Joint Commn. on Accreditation of Healthcare Orgns., 1981-86; v.p. Greater Atlanta Coalition on Health Care, 1983-84; mem. Gov.'s Coun. Malpractice Ins., 1975-83, Medicaid Adv. Com. Ga. Dept. Human Resources, 1973-77, Health Facilities Planning Com. Met. Atlanta Coun. for Health, 1971-74, Atlanta Regional Commn. Emergency Med. Task Force 1969-73, Gov.'s Commn. on Nursing, 1970-71, adv. commn. Internat. Implant Registry, 1989—, vice-chmn., 1991, chmn., 1992; pres. Health Careers of Ga., Inc., 1969-70, Ga. Coun. Paramed. Edn., 1968. Contbr. articles to profl. jours. With U.S. Army, 1944-46. Recipient R.C. Williams award Ga. State U., 1966, Disting. Alumni award, Ga. State U., 1979, Disting. Svc. award. Ga. Med. Assn. Atlanta, 1980; Disting. Guest Lectr. Ga. State U., 1978. Fellow Am. Coll. Healthcare Execs. (regent 1972-75); mem. Am. Hosp. Assn. (chmn. 1979, Speaker of Ho. 1980, Disting. Svc. award 1987), Ga. Hosp. Assn. (pres. 1966-79, Gold Honor award of Excellence 1980), Ansley Golf Club. Baptist. Home: 50 S Prado NE Atlanta GA 30309-3309 Personal E-mail: dbarker@emory.edu.

BARKER, WILLIAM M., retired state supreme court chief justice; b. Chattanooga, Sept. 13, 1941; married; 3 children. BS, U. Chatanooga, 1964; JD, U. Cin., 1967. Bar: Tenn. 1967. Pvt. practice, 1967-83; cir. ct. judge, 1983-95; justice Ct. of Appeals, 1995-98, Tenn. Supreme Ct., 1998—2008, chief justice, 2005—08. Adj. prof. U. Tenn., Chatanooga, 1984—. Chmn. bd. deacons 1st Presbyn. Ch. Chattanooga, 1995-97. Served in USMC, 1967—69. Fellow Tenn. Bar Found., Chattanooga Bar Found.; mem. Am. Legion, Alpha Soc., U. Tenn. Chattanooga Alumni Coun., Chattanooga Rotary Club.

BARKIN, MARVIN E., lawyer; b. Winter Haven, Fla., Nov. 9, 1933; s. Isadore and Jean (Epstein) B.; m. Gertrude Parnes, Sept. 20, 1959; children: Thomas I., Michael A., Pamela L. AB, Emory U., 1955; LLB cum laude, Harvard U., 1958. Bar: Fla. 1958, U.S. Dist. Ct. (mid., no. and so. dists.) Fla., U.S. Ct. Appeals (2d, 5th and 11th cirs.), U.S. Supreme Ct. Research aide Dist. Ct. Appeal Fla., Third Dist., Miami, 1958-60; assoc., then ptnr. Fowler, White, Collins, Gillen, Humkey & Trenam, Tampa, 1960-69; mem. Trenam, Kemker, Scharf, Barkin, Frye, O'Neill & Mullis, Tampa, 1970—, Fla. Bd. Bar Examiners, 1979-84, chmn., 1982-83. Chmn. corp., banking and bus. law sect. Fla. Bar, 1974-75, chmn. appellate ct. rules subcom., 1972-73 Mem. Am. Law Inst., Am. Bar Found., Nat. Conf. Bar Examiners (bd. mgrs. 1985-95, chmn. 1993-94, 11th cir. ct. appeal com. on lawyer qualifications and conduct, chair 2001—, spl. counsel Fla. jud. qualification com. 1985-11, in-term gen. counsel 2006—08), Fla. Bar, Omicron Delta Kappa. Democrat. Jewish. Home: 1605 Culbreath Isles Dr Tampa FL 33629-4824 Office: Trenam Kemker Scharf Barkin Frye O'Neill & Mullis 101 E Kennedy Blvd Ste 2700 Tampa FL 33602-5179 Office Phone: 813-227-7459. Personal E-mail: mebarkin@trenam.com.

BARKLEY, CHARLES WADE, sportscaster, retired professional basketball player; b. Leeds, Ala., Feb. 20, 1963; Student, Auburn U., Ala., 1981—84. Forward Phila. 76ers, 1984—92, Phoenix Suns, 1992—96, Houston Rockets, 1996—2000; co-host Inside the NBA, TNT, 2001—; host Listen Up, TNT, 2002—. Mem. US Olympic team, 1992, 1996. Co-author (with Roy S. Johnson): Outrageous! The Fine Life and Flagrant Good Times of Basketball's Irresistible Force, 1992; co-author: (with Rick Reilly) Sir Charles: The Wit and Wisdom of Charles Barkley, 1994; author: I May Be Wrong But I Doubt It, 2002, Who's Afraid of a Large Black Man, 2005; actor: (films) Forget Paris, 1995. Participant Ante Up for Africa, Las Vegas, Nev., 2008. Recipient Schick Pivotal Player award, 1986—88, IBM award, 1986—88; named NBA All-Star Game MVP, 1991, NBA MVP, 1993; named to All-Rookie team, 1985, NBA All-Star team, 1988—93, Naismith Meml. Basketball Hall of Fame, 2006, Nat. Collegiate Basketball Hall of Fame, 2008. Achievements include leading the NBA in: offensive rebounds, 1987-89; free throw attempts, 1988. Office: Turner Sports One CNN Ctr 13 South Tower Atlanta GA 30303

BARKLEY, PAUL HALEY, JR., architect; b. Washington, Sept. 24, 1937; Paul Haley Sr. and Mary Barrett (Brewer) B.; m. Jeanette Frances Nickerson, Dec. 20, 1975. Student, Ecole D'Art Americaines, Fontainebleau, France, 1959; BArch, U. Va., 1960. Registered architect, Va., Md., D.C. Archtl. designer Strang & Childers Architects, Annandale, Va., 1960-61; project designer Alan J. Lockman Architect, Washington, 1962-63; design assoc. D.G. Chase & Assocs., Alexandria, Va., 1964; pres. Barkley Pierce Assocs., Falls Church, Va., 1965-94; sole practice Paul H. Barkley, FAIA, Architect, Falls Church, Va., 1994—. Bd. dirs. Hist. Falls Church; lectr. archtl. divsn. continuing edn., 1966-91; mng. ptnr. Village Ctr. Assocs., Falls Church, 1983-99. Prin. works includes Falls Ch. Community Ctr., 1967, Vega Precision Labs., 1972, 1st Va. Bank, Arlington, 1979, Sullyfield Commerce Ctr., 1986, Rigg's Nat. Bank, McLean, Va., 1988, Fairfax Meml. Funeral Home 2003; contbr. articles to profl. jours. Chmn. Falls Church Bus. Devel. Commn., 1987—93; mem. exec. com. Citizens for a Better City, Falls Church, 1987—92; mem. Falls Church Econ. Devel. Authority, 2002, Falls Church Pvt. Pub. Partnership, 1991—98, bd. dirs., 1991—98, pres., 1993—94. With USAF, 1960—63. Recipient excellence in design award Falls Church Village Preservation and Improvement Soc., 1979, Indsl. Devel. Vol. of Yr. award So. Indsl. Devel. Coun., 1982, Bus. Person of Yr. award City of Falls Church, 1988; Margaret Thompson Biddle fellow U. Va., 1959. Fellow AIA (bd. dirs. 1986-89, pres. Va. Soc. 1984, regional rep. Coll. of Fellows 1993-95, chair regional reps. 2002-08, numerous other offices, Disting. Svc. award 1983, Outstanding Svc. award No. Va. chpt. 1982, award of recognition of outstanding achievement 1988, Noland award 1991, Leslie N. Boney Spirit of Fellowship award 2005); mem. Falls Church C. of C. (bd. dirs. 1973-75, 99—2006, pres. 1976, 3d v.p. 1977-79, vice chmn. 2003-04 Pillar of the Cmty. award 1977), Va. Found. for Arch. (pres. 1988-89, trustee 1993-99), Fountainbleau Assns. (trustee 1995-), Raven Soc. Lutheran. Avocations: photography, travel, collecting art, art. Home and Office: 311 Chestnut St Falls Church VA 22046-2404 Home Phone: 703-534-1474; Office Phone: 703-532-8500. Personal E-mail: pbarkley@cox.net.

BARKOVSKII, ANDREI L., microbiologist; b. Saratov, Russia, July 16, 1955; s. Lev and Maria B.; m. Marina V. Orlova, Sept. 30, 1989; children: Denis A, Valeria A. BS, Saratov State U., Russia, 1974; MS, Saratov State U., 1977; PhD, Inst. Microbiology, Minsk, Belorussia, 1986. Sr. rsch. scientist Inst. Medicine, Saratov, 1979-87; head of lab. Inst. Indsl. Microbial Genetics, Saratov, 1987-89; head unit of biotech. Inst. Biochem. Physiology of Plants and Microorganisms, Saratov, 1989-92; assoc. rsch. scientist U. Mich., Ann Arbor, 1996—2002; asst. prof. Ga. Coll. and State U., 2002—06, assoc. prof., 2006—10, prof., 2010—. Vis. assoc. rsch. scientist U. Lyon-1, Villeurbanne, France, 1992-93, vis. assoc. prof., 1993-94, vis. assoc. rsch. scientist U. Mich., Ann Arbor, 1994-96. Patentee in field. Active Am. Democracy Project, Ga. River Network. Recipient award for excellence in invention and creativity Soc. of Inventors, Russia, 1985, award CNRS, France, 1992, award Office of Naval Rsch., U.S., 1996, Best Rsch. and Publ. award Ga. Coll. and State U., 2005. Mem. Am. Soc. Microbiology. Achievements include finding evidence of bacterial respiration with polyphenolic compounds, microbial/chemical dechlorination of environmental relevant dioxins and bioavailability and natural attenuation of historical dioxin contaminations; demonstration of positive and negative selection towards tetracycline resistance genes in animal feeding operations, their dischare to the environment and their further association to estuarine sediments; discovery of class 3 integrons associated to oyster reefs; and demonstration of a relationship between microbial diagenesis of soil organic matter and divirgence of soil microbial communities into particle-associated and planctonic consortia. Office Phone: 478-445-4246. Business E-Mail: andrei.barkovskii@gcsu.edu.

BARKSDALE, RHESA HAWKINS, federal judge; b. Jackson, Miss., Aug. 8, 1944; s. John Woodson Jr. and Mary Bryan (Saunders) Barksdale. BS, U.S. Mil. Acad., 1966; JD, U. Miss., 1972. Law clk. to Justice Byron R. White US Supreme Ct., 1972—73; assoc., then ptnr. Butler, Snow, O'Mara, Stevens & Cannada, Jackson, 1973—90; judge US Ct. Appeals (5th Cir.), Jackson, 1990—2009, sr. judge, 2009—. Instr. U. Miss. Sch. Law, Jackson, 1975—76, Miss. Coll. Sch. Law, Jackson, 1976. Chmn. Miss. Vietnam Vets. Leadership Program, Jackson, 1982—85; del. Rep. Nat. Conv., New Orleans, 1988; elector election of Pres. of U.S., Jackson, 1988. Capt. US Army, 1966—70, Vietnam. Decorated Silver Star, Bronze Star for Valor, Purple Heart, Cross of Gallantry with silver star (Republic of Vietnam). Mem.: Phi Delta Phi (Nat. Grad. of Yr. 1972). Episcopalian. Home: 501 E Court St Jackson MS 39201-5022

BARLOW, ANNE LOUISE, pediatrician, medical researcher; b. Skipton-in-Craven, Eng., Jan. 28, 1925; came to U.S., 1951, naturalized, 1954; m. Howard Cadwell, May 19, 1951; children: Barbara Anne, John James Stewart; m. Alastair Ramsay, Dec. 19, 1969. MB BS, London Sch. Medicine for Women, U. London, 1948; diploma in child health, Royal Colls. Eng., 1950; MPH with honors, Yale U., 1952. House physician North Lonsdale Hosp., Barrow-in-Furness, Lancashire, Eng., 1948-49; house surgeon Royal Infirmary (Glasgow), Scotland, 1949; resident to profl. unit of child health Royal Hosp. for Sick Children, Glasgow, 1949-50; jr. hosp. med. officer Knightswood Infectious Diseases Hosp., Glasgow, 1950; Rotary Found. Internat. fellow U. Toronto Med. Sch., Ont., Canada, 1950-51; research asst. Yale U. Sch. Pub. Health, New Haven, 1952-53; clinic physician in cancer prevention Arlington, Va., part-time 1953-54; resident, staff physician William H. Maybury Tb Sanatorium, Northville, Mich., 1954-56; research dir. Detroit Feeding Study with the Detroit City Health Dept., 1954-56; research asst., instr. sch. health U. Pitts. Grad. Sch. Pub. Health, 1957-62; pvt. practice medicine specializing in pediatrics Pitts., 1959-62; mem. courtesy staff St. Margaret Hosp., Pitts., 1959-62; research assoc. Tice Lab for Tb research, Cook County Hosp., Chgo., 1962; med. writer product info. Abbott Labs., North Chicago, Ill., 1963-66, med. specialist antibiotic medicine, 1966-68; mgr. clin. devel. pharm. products div. Abbott Lab., North Chicago, Ill., 1968-71, asst. med. dir., 1971-72, mgr. parenteral nutrition hosp. products div., 1972-73, med. dir., 1973-80, v.p. med. affairs hosp. products div., 1980-84; pres. Albamed, Inc., 1985—2005; asst. clin. prof. Med.Coll. Pa., 1988. Cons. maternal, child and sch. health, dir. well baby clinic Lake County (Ill.) Health Dept., 1963-76; pres. Tb Sanatorium Bd. Lake County Health Dept., Ill., 1976-79; dir., pres. Lake County Bd. Health, 1979-82; health officer Village of North Barrington, Ill., 1964-67; physician-adviser Head Start Lake County Community Action Project, 1970-84; chmn. profl. adv. com. Lake County Health Dept., 1972-84; preceptor Pediatric Nurse Assoc. Program; chmn. bd. Sutton Place Behavioral Health Inc., 2000-05. Contbr. articles on maternal and infant care, pediatrics and nutrition; patentee high calorie solution of low molecular weight glucose polymer mixtures useful for intravenouse adminstrn. Bd. dirs. Heart Assn. of Lake County, 1979-84, chmn. nutrition com. 1980-82, v.p. 1982-83, pres., 1983-84; mem. sch. bd. Grant Twp. Cmty. H.S. (Ill. Dist. 124), 1973-79; sec. to governing bd. Spl. Edn. Dist. of Lake County, 1977-79; assoc. Nat. Coll. Edn., Evanston, Ill., 1976-84; chmn. Am. Women's Hosp. Svc., 1986-95, 2004-; vol. Guardian ad Litem, 1989-2004. Recipient award of merit for outstanding contbns. to pub. health, Ill. Pub. Health Assn., 1975, award of merit for outstanding cmty. svc., Lake County Cmty. Action Project, 1976, award for outstanding and dedicated svc. as pres., Lake County TB Sanatorium Bd., 1979, TWIN award, YWCA, 1983, Charlotte Danstrom award for excellence, Women in Mgmt., 1984, award for volunteering in medicine, AMA Found., 2006. Mem. AAAS, NOW, LWV, AMA (chair sr. physician gov. com. 1996-2005), Am. Med. Women's Assn. (councilor for orgn. and mgmt. 1977-79, treas. 1980, 1st v.p. 1981, pres. 1983, chair found. 1992-95, chair Am. Women's Hosps. Svcs. com. 2004-, Elizabeth Blackwell medal 1992), Fla. Med. Assn. (vice chair Internat. Med. Grad. sect. 1998-2004, coun. on pub. health 2000-05), Med. Women's Internat. Assn. (v.p. N. Am. 1993-95), Pan-Am. Med. Women's Alliance (pres. 2000), Nassau County Med. Soc. (pres. 2002-03). Home: 1900 Amelia Trace Ct Ofc Fernandina Beach FL 32034-6309 Personal E-mail: czardaska@bellsouth.net.

BARNARD, DONALD ROY, medical and veterinary entomologist; BS in Zoology, Calif. State U., 1969, MA in Biology, 1972; PhD in Entomology, U. Calif., Riverside, 1977. Postdoctoral fellow Colo. State U., Ft. Collins, 1977-79; rsch. entomologist agrl. rsch. svc. USDA, Poteau, Okla., 1979-85, supervisory rsch. entomologist, 1985-88, rsch. leader agrl. rsch. svc. Gainesville, Fla., 1988—2003. Prof. entomology Okla. State U., 1988—, U. Fla., 1991—; tech. reviewer NIH, 1989-, NSF, 1995-, Ctrs. for Disease Control and Prevention, 1990; mem. soybean program operating bd., Ill., 1995-96; mem. USDA, NRI Competitive Grants Program, 1994—, Dept. Def., Def. Logistics Agy., 1995-; cons., tech. reviewer WHO/FAO, 1980—, USAID, Somali Dem. Republic, 1981-90, Dept. of Def., AFPMB, 1985-2002, Republic South Africa, 1988-, State of Fla., DOACS, DAI, DOH, 1992-2004, Unilever Rsch., 1999-2004, Consumers Union, 2000—, USDA, APHIS, 1996—, EPA, 2000—, del Cielo Found., 2006-; external reviewer U. Orange Free State, Republic South Africa, 1995-96, Tripura U., India, 1999-2004, Kongunadu Coll., India, 2001-05, Ministry of Health, Brazil, 1988—, Bharathiar U., Coimbatore, India; mem. Coordinating Coun. Mosquito Control, Fla., 1992-2005; rsch. adv. com. Fla. Mosquito Control Assn. Contbr. chpts. to books, articles to profl. jours.; editor Jour. of Med. Entomology, 1999-02; mem. editl. bd. Bull. of the Soc. Vector Ecologists, Jour. Med. Entomology, ISEN Vet. Sci. Mem. Am. Mosquito Control Assn., Internat. Orgn. Biol. Control, Entomol. Soc. Am., Entomol. Soc. Can., Ecol. Soc. Am., Internat. Soc. Travel Medicine, Am. Soc. Tropical Medicine and Hygiene. Office Phone: 352-374-5930. Business E-Mail: don.barnard@ars.usda.gov.

BARNARD, GEOFFREY W., judge; b. Batavia, NY, Apr. 4, 1945; Diploma, U. Madrid, Spain, 1965; BA, Alleghany Coll., 1966; JD, Cornell Univ. Sch. of Law, Ithaca, 1969. Magistrate judge US Dist Ct., St. Thomas, VI, 1986—. Chair Com. of Bar Examiners. Office: US Magistrate Ct 345 US Courthouse 5500 Veterans Dr Charlotte Amalie VI 00802-6424 also: Territorial Ct Virgin Islands PO Box 70 St Thomas VI 00804

BARNARD, RAY F., engineering and construction management company executive; Exec. v.p. ENSCO Corp., 1988—99; v.p. IBM Corp., 1999—2000; sr. v.p. TradeMC, 2000—02; v.p. ops. Fluor Corp., v.p. global systems, various sr. mgmt. positions in info. tech., engring., mfg. and sales, exec. v.p., chief info. officer, 2002—. Mgmt. cons. DuPont, United Techs. Corp., Englehard, Procter & Gamble, Am. Bd. Achievements include patents in field. Office: Fluor Corp 6700 Las Colinas Blvd Irving TX 75039 Office Phone: 469-398-7000. Office Fax: 469-398-7255.

BARNEBEY, KENNETH ALAN, food products executive; b. Fremont, Nebr., Apr. 16, 1931; s. Hoyt F. and Mae S. (Mott) B.; m. Faith Price, May 10, 1969; children: Robert, Mark, Holiday, Cindy, Kendra, Valerie, Bonnie, Laurel, Susan. Student, U. Md., 1950, U. Tampa, 1951; BA in Transp., U. Wash., Seattle, 1953; grad. advanced mgmt. program, Harvard U., 1977. With Tropicana Products, Inc., Bradenton, Fla., 1955-80, gen. sales mgr., then v.p. mktg. and sales, 1957-77, exec. v.p., 1977, pres., chief adminstrv. officer, 1977-79, chmn. bd., chief exec. officer, 1979-81, also dir.; corp. v.p. Beatrice Foods, Inc., 1979-81; pres., dir., dep. chmn. Am. Agronomics Corp., Tampa, Fla., 1981-86; bus. acquisition cons. Bradenton, Fla., 1981—. Bd. dirs. Dependable Ins. Group Inc. Am., Exmart, Cmty. Bank Holding Co.; mem. sch. mktg. program Fla. Citrus Dept., 1973—; dir. First Union Bank. Bd. dirs., pres. Am. Acad. Achievement; bd. dirs. Manatee Jr. Coll., Asolo State Theatre, Blowing Rock (N.C.) Hosp., Blowing Rock Stage Co. Theater; mem. Fla. Coun. of 100; adv. coun. Fla. State U.; exec. svc. corp. pres. Manasota Basin Bd. Served with U.S. Army, 1953-55. Mem. Am. Mgmt. Assn. (lectr.), NAM (mktg. adv. com., dir.), Fla. Canners Assn. (mktg. adv. com.), Manatee County C. of C. (dir., chmn. econ. devel. com.) Clubs: Manatee County Exchange (past pres.), Bradenton Country, Blowing Rock Country (past pres.), State of Fla. Govs. Coun. of 100. Home: 2309 64th St W Bradenton FL 34209-5590

BARNES, ANDREW EARL, former newspaper executive; b. Torrington, Conn., May 15, 1939; s. Joseph and Elizabeth (Brown) B.; m. Marion Otis, Aug. 26, 1960; children: Christopher Joseph, Benjamin Brooks, Elizabeth Cheney. BA, Harvard U., 1961. Reporter, bur. chief Providence Jour., 1961-63; from reporter to edn. editor Washington Post, 1965-73; met. editor, asst. mng. editor St. Petersburg Times, Fla., 1973-75, mng. editor, 1975-84; editor, pres. St. Petersburg (Fla.) Times, 1984-99, CEO, 1988—2004. Chmn. bd. dirs. Congl. Quar., Times Pub. Co., Poynter Inst.; chair Pulitzer prize bd., 2004-05. With USAR, 1963-65. Alicia Patterson fellow, 1969-70 Mem. Newspaper Assn. Am. (chair 2000-01), Am. Soc. Newspaper Editors, Fla. Soc. Newspaper Editors (pres. 1980-81), Internat. Press Inst. (chair, Fla. chpt.), Nature Conservancy. Home: 15724 Puckett Rd Dade City FL 33525-7066 Home Phone: 352-567-6660. E-mail: abarnes@poynter.org.

BARNES, DAVID A., delivery service executive; BBA, U. Mo. Package loader United Parcel Service of America, Inc. (UPS), St. Louis, 1977, various positions UPS Airlines subs., 1986, customer info. mgmt. process mgr., 1998—2001, corp. info. services portfolio coord., 2001—04, sr. v.p., chief info. officer. mem. mgmt. com., 2005—. Bd. mem. St. Joseph's Mercy Found. Named one of The Premier 100 IT Leaders, Computerworld, 2005. Office: United Parcel Svc Inc 55 Glenlake Pkwy NE Atlanta GA 30328

BARNES, GERALD A., retail executive; m. Debbie Barnes. Exec. v.p., merchandising, Neiman Marcus Direct Neiman Marcus Group, Inc., pres., CEO, Neiman Marcus Direct, 2009—. Office: The Neiman Marcus Group Inc 1618 Main St One Marcus Sq Dallas TX 75201 Office Phone: 214-757-2954. Office Fax: 214-573-5320. Business E-Mail: gerald.barnes@neimanmarcus.com.

BARNES, HARRY FRANCIS, federal judge; b. Memphis, May 14, 1932; m. Mary Milburn Mann, four children. Student, Vanderbilt U., 1950-52; BS, US Naval Acad., 1956; LLB, U. Ark., 1964. With Pryor & Barnes, Camden, Ark., 1964-66, Barnes & Roberts, Camden, 1966-68, Gaughan, Laney, Barnes & Roberts, Camden, 1968-78, Gaughan, Laney & Barnes, Camden, 1978-82; mcpl. judge Camden and Ouachita Counties, 1975-82; circuit judge 13th jud. dist. State of Ark., 1982-93; judge US Dist. Ct. (we. dist.) Ark., 1993—2008, sr. judge, 2008—. Mem. Ark. Jud. Discipline and Disability Commn. With USMC, 1956-86, col. res. ret. Named Outstanding Trial Judge in Ark., Ark. Trial Lawyers Assn., 1986, 2000. Mem. ABA, Ark. Bar Assn., Ark. Jud. Coun. (bd. dirs.). Office: 219 US Post Office & Courthouse 101 S Jackson Ave El Dorado AR 71730-6133 Office Phone: 870-862-1303. Business E-Mail: harry_barnes@arwd.uscourts.com.

BARNES, HOYT MICHAEL, professor, wood scientist, consultant; b. Long Beach, Calif., June 9, 1943; s. Hoyt Franklin Barnes and Nellie Ruth Puckett; m. Martha Lou Lasyone, Sept. 5, 1964; children: Bryan David, Brooks Duane, Brandon Lee. BSF, La. State U., Baton Rouge, 1965, MS, 1968; PhD, Suny Coll. Environ. Sci. & Forestry, Syracuse, 1973. Assoc. prof. Miss. State U., 1977—85, prof., 1985—2007, thompson prof. wood sci. & tech., 2007—; vis. prof. Imperial Coll. Sci. Tech. & Medicine, London, 1988—89. Co-owner & v.p. AMBAR INC., Starkville, Miss., 1989—. Contbr. to sci. profl. jours. Com. mem., nat. wood badge task force Boy Scouts Am., Washington, 1978—79; coun. & dist. tng. chmn. Pushmataha Area Coun., Boy Scouts Am., Columbus, Miss., 1972—83; scoutmaster Boy Scouts Am., Starkville, 1972—92. Recipient Ralph E Powe Rsch. Excellence award, Miss. State U., 2005, Silver Beaver, Boy Scouts Am., 1977, Outstanding Svc. to Youth, Mayors office, Starkville, Miss., 1992; named Alumnus of Yr., Sch. Renewable Natural Resources, La. State U., 2004. Fellow: Inst. Wood Sci. (Fellow 1989), Soc. Wood Sci. & Tech. (pres. 2001—02, Fellow 2007), Internat. Acad. Wood Sci. (Fellow 2006); mem.: Soc. Am. Foresters, Rlwy. Tie Assn. (vice chmn. edn. com. 1992—2004, award of Merit 2006), Am. Wood Protection Assn. (chmn. com. t8, vice-chmn. com. p2, vice-chmn. com. s2 1990—, award of Merit 2006), Forest Products Soc. (pres. 2007—, Gottschalk award 2002), Internat. Rsch. Group on Wood Protection (chmn. sect. 4 processes & properties 1998—2001), So. Pressure Treaters Assn., Am. Nat. Stds. Inst., Com. O5, Am. Soc. Testing & Materials, Miss. Forestry Assn., Sigma Xi, Xi Sigma Pi, Gamma Sigma Delta. Conservative. Methodist. Achievements include patents for a novel wood remedial treatment application method. Avocations: gardening, fishing, reading. Business E-Mail: mbarnes@cfr.msstate.edu.

BARNES, JUSTIN T., healthcare information technology executive; b. Amherst, Mass., May 16, 1972; m. Jennifer Barnes. BA, U. Mass., Amherst, BS in Legal Studies, Prelaw & Bus. Cert. clin. diagnostics 1998. With HBO and Co. (merged with McKesson Provider Technologies); nat. ops. exec. McKesson Provider Technologies, 1995—98; v.p., sales ops. and customer devel., mem., founding team Healinx Corp. (now RelayHealth), 1998—2001; v.p., mktg., corp. devel. and govt. affairs Greenway Medical Technologies, Inc., 2003—. Co-founder, chmn. Nat. HIMSS EHR Assn. Pub. (250 journals, magazines and broadcast media outlets relating to national leadership of health IT and EHR adoption). Mem., privacy expert panel Certification Commn. for Healthcare Info. Tech.; mem., health info. protection task force Nat. Govs. Assn.; bd. dirs. Ga. Tech's Ctr. for Health, Healthcare and Eldercare Innovation; chmn. Healthcare Info. and Mgmt. Sys. Soc., 2008—. Served, inf. and communication units US Army. Recipient Leadership in EHR Acceleration award, EHR Assn., 2006, National Health IT Leadership award, 2008—10; named Tech. Mktg. Exec. of Yr., Tech. Assn. Ga., 2007. Mem.: Metro Atlanta Chamber Health IT Subcom./Biosci. Leadership Coun. (chmn.), Integrating the Healthcare Enterprise N.Am. (bd. dirs.), Electronic Health Record Assn. (chmn. emeritus). Avocations: fly fishing, travel. Office: Greenway Medical Technologies Inc 100 Greenway Blvd Carrollton GA 30117-4338 Office Phone: 678-839-4316. Office Fax: 770-836-3200. Business E-Mail: justinbarnes@greenwaymedical.com.

BARNES, RAMON MURRAY, chemistry professor; b. Pitts., Apr. 24, 1940; s. Jack N. and Sally L. (Silver) B.; m. Dorothy M. Soja, May 17, 1969. BS, Oreg. State U., 1962; MA, Columbia U., 1963; PhD, U. Ill., Champaign-Urbana, 1966. Lectr. Baldwin Wallace Coll., Bera, Ohio, 1967-68; materials engr. NASA Lewis Research Ctr., Cleve., 1968-69; postdoctoral fellow Iowa State U., Ames, 1969; asst. to prof. chemistry U. Mass., Amherst, 1969-2000, dir. Univ. Rsch. Inst. for Analytical Chemistry, 2000—, prof. emeritus chemistry, 2000—. Chmn. Winter Conf. on Plasma Spectrochemistry, 1980—. Mem. editl. bd. Jour. Analytical Atomic Spectrometry, Canadian Jour. Analytical Scis. and Spectroscopy, Spectroscopy, Spectroscopy Europe, Analytical Abstracts, Guangpuxue Yu (Spectroscopy and Spectral Analysis), Spectrochimica Acta, Part B, Spectrochimica Acta Electronica; editor, pub., treas. (newsletter) ICP Info. Newsletter, 1975—; editor six books; contbr. articles to profl. jours. Capt. USAR, 1966-68. Fellow AAAS, Soc. Applied Spectroscopy, Optical Soc. Am.; mem. Am. Chem. Soc., Royal Soc. of Chemistry, Spectroscopy Soc. Can., Soc. Toxicology, Sigma Xi. Achievements include inventor in field. Avocation: gardening.: PO Box 666 Hadley MA 01035-0666 Office: 18421 Beauty Berry Ct Lehigh Acres FL 33972 Office Phone: 239-674-9430. Business E-Mail: barnes@chemistry.umass.edu.

BARNES, RICK (RICHARD DALE BARNES), men's college basketball coach; b. Hickory, NC, July 17, 1954; m. Candace, July 31, 1976; children: Nicholas, Caroline. Grad. in Health and Phys. Edn., Lenoir-Rhyne Coll., Hickory, NC, 1977, LHD (hon.), 2005. Head coach North State Acad., 1977-78; asst. coach Davidson Coll., 1978-80, George Mason U., 1980-85, U. Ala., 1985-86, Ohio State U., 1986-87; head coach George Mason U., 1987-88, Providence Coll., 1988-94, Clemson U., 1994-98, U. Tex., Austin, 1998—. Recipient Disting. Alumnus award, Lenoir-Rhyne Coll., 1997; named Dist. I Coach of Yr., Nat. Assn. Basketball Coaches, 1989, Dist. IX Coach of Yr., Nat. Assn. Basketball Writers, 1999, 2001, 2003, Dist. VII Coach of Yr., US Basketball Writers Assn., 1999, 2001, 2011, All-S.W. Coach, Basketball Times, 1999, Big 12 Conf. Coach of Yr., 1999, 2003; named to Hall of Fame, Lenoir-Rhyne Coll., 2002. Achievements include being head coach of the 2006 Big 12 champions. Office: Mens Basketball U Tex Intercollegiate Athletics PO Box 7399 Austin TX 78713-7399 Office Phone: 512-471-5816. E-mail: rick.barnes@athletics.utexas.edu.

BARNES, STEWART EDWARD, physics professor; b. Edenfield, Eng., Dec. 10, 1946; s. George and Hilda Barnes; m. Christiane Kolla; children: Nicole Marie, Laura Anne Kim. PhD, UCLA, 1972. Prof. physics U. Miami, Coral Gables, Fla., 1980—. Office: U Miami Physics Dept Coral Gables FL 33124

BARNES, TIM, state legislator; b. Dec. 28, 1958; married; 3 children. BA, Harding U.; JD, U. Ark. Law Sch. Atty.; mem. Tenn. Bar Assn., Clarksville-Montgomery Co. Bar Assn.; former bd. mem. Montgomery Co. Chpt. Am. Red Cross; mem. C of C Clarksville-Montgomery Co., Cheatham Co.; mem. Dist. 22 Tenn. State Senate, 2008—, sec. Transp. Com. Democrat. Presbyterian. Mailing: 974 Dixie Bee Rd Adams TN 37010 Office: 305 War Memorial Bldg Nashville TN 37243 Office Phone: 931-648-9400, 615-741-2374. Office Fax: 615-253-0193. Business E-Mail: sen.tim.barnes@capitol.tn.gov.

BARNESS, LEWIS ABRAHAM, retired physician; b. Atlantic City, July 31, 1921; s. Joseph and Mary (Silverstein) B.; m. Elaine Berger, June 14, 1953 (dec. Jan. 1985); children: Carol, Laura, Joseph; m. Enid May Fischer Gilbert, July 5, 1987; stepchildren: Mary, Elizabeth, Jennifer, Rebecca. AB, Harvard U., 1941, MD, 1944; MA (hon.), U. Pa., 1971; DS U. Wis. (hon.), 2002. Intern Phila. Gen. Hosp., 1944-45; resident Boston Children's Hosp., 1947-50; asst. chief, then chief dept. pediatrics Phila. Gen. Hosp., 1951-72; vis. physician U. Pa. Hosp., 1952-57, acting chief, then chief, 1957-72. Mem. faculty U. Pa. Sch. Medicine, 1951-72, prof. pediat., 1964-72; chmn. dept. U. So. Fla. Med. Sch., Tampa, 1972-88, prof. pediat., 1988—, Disting. Univ. prof., 2000—; vis. prof. Univ. Wis., 1987-92, prof. emeritus, 1993—. Author: Pediatric Physical Diagnosis Yearbook, edits. 1-6, 1957—; editor: Advances in Pediatrics, 1976-2004, Pediatric Nutrition Handbook, 3d edit., 1991; asst. editor Pediatric Gastroenterology and Nutrition, 1981-91; editl. bd. Cons., 1960-84, Pediatrics, 1978-83, Core Jour. Pediatrics, 1980-96, Contemporary Pediatrics, 1984—, Jour. Clin. Medicine and Nutrition, 1985-95, Nutrition Rev., 1985-87. Served to capt. AUS, 1945-46. Recipient Lindback Teaching award U. Pa., 1963; Borden award nutrition, 1972; Noer Disting. Prof. award, 1980, Joseph B. Goldberger award in clin. nutrition, 1984, Joseph St. Geme Leadership award 7 pediatric socs., 1991, U. So. Fla. Svc. award, 1997, President's Award, U. So. Fla., 2000, Distinguished Prof. award, 2000; inductee Phila. Pediat. Soc. Hall of Fame, 1996. Fellow Am. Inst. Nutrition; mem. AAAS, Am. Pediatric Soc. (recorder-editor 1964-75, pres. 1985-86, John Howland award 1993), Soc. Pediatric Rsch., Am. Acad. Pediatrics (chmn. com. on nutrition 1974-81), Abraham Jacobi award 1991, Hon. Internat. disting. fellow pediatric soc. Thailand, 2004, Med. Edn. Lifetime Achievement award, 1995, Sigma Xi, Alpha Omega Alpha. Office: U South Fla Dept Pediat 17 Davis Blvd Tampa FL 33606 Home: 4415 E Lake Harriet Blvd Minneapolis MN 55419-4746 Office Phone: 813-259-8711. E-mail: eglbert@tgh.org.

BARNET, ROBERT JOSEPH, cardiologist, philosopher; b. Port Huron, Mich., Apr. 27, 1929; s. John A. and Ruth Elizabeth (Wittliff) B.; m Carol R. Taylor; children: Benedict, Maria, Antonia, Peter, Elizabeth, Rebecca, Christina, Jacqueline, Ann. Student, Port Huron Jr. Coll., summers 1947, 49; MD, Loyola U., Chgo., 1951; BS in Chemistry magna cum laude, U. Notre Dame, Ind., 1954, MA in Philosophy, 1988; MA in History, U. Nev., Reno, 1986. Diplomate Am. Bd. Internal Medicine, Nat. Bd. Med. Examiners. Intern Boston City Hosp., 1954—55; rotating intern Mercy Hosp., Chgo., 1955; asst. resident in medicine Boston City Hosp., 1958-59; clin. and research fellow in cardiology Children's Med. Center and House of the Good Samaritan, Boston, 1959-60; cons. fellow in rheumatic fever pediatric service Boston City Hosp., 1959-60; research fellow in pediatrics Harvard U., Boston, 1959-60; clin. fellow in cardiology Mass. Meml. Hosps., Boston, 1960-61; physician-in-charge St. Francis Mission Hosp., Solwezi, No. Rhodesia, 1961-62; dir. clinics, assoc. in medicine Stritch Sch. Medicine, Loyola U., Chgo., 1962-65; physician-in-charge Cardiac Clinic, Loyola U., Chgo., Fantus Outpatient dept. Cook County Hosp., Chgo., 1962-65, Hypertension Clinic, Fantus Outpatient dept. Cook County Hosp., 1962-65; assoc. attending physician dept. medicine Cook County Hosp., 1962-63, attending physician, 1963-65; practice medicine specializing in cardiology Reno, 1965-87; med. staff Washoe Med. Center, 1965—2006, St. Mary's Hosp., 1965—2006; assoc. clin. prof. cardiology U. Nev.; also assoc. dir. Lab. Environ. Patho-Physiology, Desert Research Inst., U. Nev., Reno, 1965-68; dir. Cardiac Care unit Washoe Med. Center, 1965-83, exec. com., 1967-71, 73-77, vice chief dept. medicine, 1969, chief, 1970-71, 78, chief dept. emergency services, 1973-77. Vis physician Solwezi Boma Rural Hosp., 1961-62; cons. in cardiology disability determination unit State of Nev., 1966-87, Crippled Children's Svc., 1966-76, Reno VA Hosp., 1967-80; asst. clin. prof. med. edn. U. Utah, 1968-71; cons. Churchill Pub. Hosp., Fallon, Nev., 1969-87, Pershing Gen. Hosp., Lovelock, Nev., 1969-87; clin. assoc. U. Nev., Reno, 1971-72, assoc. clin. prof. medicine, 1973-77, prof., 1978-2006; vis. scholar U. Notre Dame, 1989-90, 96-97; prof. med. ethics St. Louis U., 1993-95; med. reviewer, cons. Nev. State Bd. Med. Examiners, 1994-2007; sr. scholar-in-residence Ctr. Clin. Bioethics, Georgetown U., Sch. Medicine, 2000—, adj. prof. dept. medicine, 2010-; lectr. in electrocardiography and cardiology Loyola U., Chgo., 1962-65. Contbr. articles to profl. jours. Served with US Army, 1955-58. Recipient Clin. Faculty Honor award Loyola U., 1963-64. Fellow A.C.P. (bd. govs. 1980-85), Am. Coll. Cardiology (bd. govs. 1974-77), Am. Coll. Chest Physicians; mem. Nev. Heart Assn. (bd. dirs., exec. com., pres. 1974-75) Office: Georgetown U Ctr Clin Bioethics Box 571409 Washington DC 20057-1409 Office Phone: 202-687-9385. Personal E-mail: phbobmd@aol.com.

BARNETT, CRAWFORD FANNIN, JR., internist, educator, cardiologist, travel medicine specialist; b. Atlanta, May 11, 1938; s. Crawford Fannin and Penelope Hollinshead (Brown) B.; m. Elizabeth McCarthy Hale, June 6, 1964; children: Crawford Fannin III, Robert Hale. Student, U. Minn., Mpls. Campus, 1957; AB magna cum laude, Yale U., New Haven, Conn., 1960; postgrad., Oxford U., Eng., 1963; MD, Duke U., Durham, NC, 1964. Intern in internal medicine Duke U. Med. Ctr., Durham, NC, 1964-65, resident, 1965; resident in internal medicine Wilmington Med. Ctr., Del., 1965-66; dir. Tenn. Heart Disease Control Program, Nashville, 1966-68; pvt. practice medicine in internal/travel medicine Atlanta, 1968—. Dir. Travel Immunization Ctr., Atlanta; mem. staff Crawford Long Hosp., Atlanta, Northside Hosp., Atlanta, Grady Meml. Hosp., Atlanta, West Paces Hosp., Atlanta, Piedmont Hosp., Atlanta, North Fulton Hosp., Atlanta; mem. tchg. staff Vanderbilt Med. Ctr., Nashville, 1966-68, Crawford Long Meml. Hosp., 1969—; clin. instr. internal medicine, dept. medicine Emory U. Med. Sch., Atlanta, 1969—. Contbr. articles to profl. publs. Bd. councillors Carter Ctr., 2009-, Bd. govs. Doctors Meml. Hosp., 1971-80; bd. dir. Atlanta Speech Sch., 1976-80, 92—, Hist. Oakland Cemetery, 1976-86, So. Turf Nurseries, 1977-92, Tech Industries, 1978-92; bd. dirs. Am. Chestnut Found., 1990; trustee Mary Brown Found. Atlanta, 1998—, Woodward Found., 2001—, George M. Brown Fund Atlanta, 2006-. Surgeon USPHS, 1966-68. Fellow Am. Geog. Soc., Royal Soc. of Tropical Medicine and Hygiene, Royal Geog. Soc., Royal Soc. Medicine, Explorers Club (life, NYC); mem. Am. Soc. Tropical Medicine and Hygiene, Am. Fedn. Clin. Rsch., Coun. Clin. Cardiology, AMA, Ga. Med. Assn., Atlanta Med. Assn., Am. Heart Assn., Ga. Heart Assn., Am. Soc. Internal Medicine, Am. Assn. History Medicine, Ga. Hist. Soc., Atlanta Hist. Soc. (bd. govs. 1976-84), Ga. Trust for Hist. Preservation, Nat. Trust Hist. Preservation, Internat. Hippocratic Found. Soc. (Greece), Faculty of History of Medicine and Pharmacy Worshipful Soc. Apothecaries of London, Atlanta Com. on Fgn. Rels. (chmn. exec. com. 1972-88), So. Coun. Internat. and Pub. Affairs, Newcomen Soc., Atlanta Clin. Soc., Wilderness Med. Soc., Internat. Soc. Travel Medicine (founding), Travelers Century Club, Circumnavigators Club, South Am. Explorers Club, Victorian Soc. Am. (bd. advisers Atlanta chpt. 1971-86), Mensa, Gridiron, Piedmont Driving Club, Yale Club (dir. 1970-74), Nine O'Clocks Club, Pan Am. Drs. Club, Phi Beta Kappa. Episcopalian. Home: 2739 Ramsgate Ct NW Atlanta GA 30305-2817 Office: Ste 302 3193 Howell Mill Rd NW Atlanta GA 30327-2100 Office Phone: 404-262-1414. Personal E-mail: cfbarne@comcast.net.

BARNETT, EDWARD WILLIAM, lawyer; b. New Orleans, Jan. 2, 1933; s. Phillip Nelson and Katherine (Wilkinson) B.; m. Margaret Mauk, Apr. 3, 1933; children: Ann Barnett Stern, Edward William. BA, Rice U., 1955; LL.B., U. Tex.-Austin, 1958. Bar: Tex. 1958. Mem. Baker Botts LLP, Houston, 1958—2004, mng. ptnr., 1984-98, sr. counsel, 1998—2004. Chmn. Cen. Houston, Inc., 1989-91; bd. dirs. Enterprise GP, LLC, 2005-, Westlake Chem. Corp., 2006-13, bd. dirs., GenOn, 2002-12. Trustee Rice U., Houston, 1991-2005, chmn. bd. trustees, 1996-2005; dir. St. Luke's Episcopal Health Sys., 1997-2009, St. Lukes Episcopal Hosp., 2009-2013; life mem. U. Tex. Law Sch. Found., 1992—; dirs. Greater Houston Partnership 1989-, chmn., 1992; bd. dirs. Ctr. Houston's Future, 2000-06; bd. dirs. Houston Zoo, 2002-09, chmn., 2002-04, dir. emeritus 2009-; trustee Baylor Coll. Medicine, 1993-2004, trustee emeritus, 2011-; chair bd. advisors Baker Inst. at Rice U., 2009-. Fellow Am. Coll. Trial Lawyers; mem. ABA (chmn. sect. antitrust law 1981-82), State Bar Tex., Houston Bar Assn., Houston Bar Found., Coronado Club (pres. 1989), Houston Country Club, Old Baldy Club. Office: Baker Botts LLP One Shell Plz 910 Louisiana Houston TX 77002

BARNETT, JOEY VICTOR, pharmacologist, research scientist, educator; b. Evansville, Ind., June 18, 1958; s. Victor Alan and Judy Kay (Kohlmeyer) Barnett. BS in Biology, U. So. Ind., 1980; PhD in Pharmacology, Vanderbilt U., 1986. Rsch. intern Argonne (Ill.) Nat. Lab., U.S. Dept. Energy, 1981; rsch. fellow Brigham & Women's Hosp., Harvard Med. Sch., Boston, 1986-89, instr. medicine, 1989-92; asst. prof. medicine and pharmacology Vanderbilt U., Nashville, 1992-99, assoc. prof., 1999—, dir. grad. studies pharmacology, 2001—05, vice chair pharmacology, 2005—. Rsch. investigator Tenn. affiliate Am. Heart Assn., 1993—95, established investigator, 1996—; mem. devel. mechanisms panel NSF, 1995—98; mem. dev-1 panel NIH, 2003—; chmn. organizing com. Nat. Meeting for Dirs. of Grad. Studies in Pharmacology, 2005—. Co-author: Heart Failure: Basic Science and Clinical Aspects, 1993; contbr. articles to profl. jours. Co-chair cardiovasc. devel. panel Nat. Am. Heart Assn., 1997—98, chair, 1999—2000; founding bd. dirs. Dismas House Ctrl. Mass., Worcester, 1987—90. Recipient Nat. Rsch. Svc. award, Nat. Heart Lung and Blood Inst./NIH, Boston, 1988—90, Disting. Alumni award, U. So. Ind., 1991; Mass. affiliate fellow, Am. Heart Assn., 1986—88. Mem.: AAAS, Am. Soc. for Pharmacology and Exptl. Therapeutics (chmn. grad. edn. com. 2007—), Am. Heart Assn. (basic rsch. coun., vice-chmn. rsch. com. greater southeast affiliate 2007), Ind. Acad. Sci., N.Y. Acad. Scis., Sigma Xi, Sigmz Zeta. Roman Catholic. Achievements include research in molecular mechanisms that regulate development of the cardiovascular system. Office: 460 Prb 2220 Pierce Ave Nashville TN 37232-6600 Business E-Mail: joey.barnett@vanderbilt.edu.

BARNETT, JONATHAN, state legislator; m. Cristy Barnett; 3 children. Mem. Dist. 97 Ark. House of Reps., 2009—, asst. spkr. pro tempore. Republican. Baptist. Office: State Capitol Rm 350 Little Rock AR 72201 also: 1980 Hwy 412 W Siloam Springs AR 72761 Office Phone: 501-682-6211, 501-682-7771, 479-524-6254. Business E-Mail: jonb@msbarnett.com.

BARNETT, LESTER H., state legislator, furniture store executive; b. Biloxi, Miss., Aug. 13, 1958; m. Rosalie Pattison, 2 children. Student, Miss. Gulf Coast C.C., La. State U. State legislator Miss. Ho. of Reps., Jackson, 1995-97. Mem. conservation, pub. health, pub. utilities, and transp. coms. Miss. Ho. of Reps. Mem. Sons. of Confederate Vets., ALEC, Miss. Conservative Coalition; mem. d'Iberville City Coun. Republican. Methodist. Home: 3516 S River Rdg Biloxi MS 39532-8932 Office: State Capitol Bldg PO Box 1018 Jackson MS 39215-1018

BARNETT, MARTHA WALTERS, lawyer; b. Dade City, Fla., June 1, 1947; d. William Haywood and Helen (Hancock) Walters; m. Richard Rawls Barnett, Jan. 4, 1969; children: Richard Rawls, Sarah Walters. BA cum laude, Tulane U., 1969; JD cum laude, U. Fla. Coll. Law, 1973; LLD (hon.), Flagler Coll., 1995, Stetson U., 2000, Nova Southwestern U., 2000; LHD (hon.), DePaul U., 2001; LLD (hon.), Wake Forest U., 2003. Bar: Fla. 1973, U.S. Dist. Ct. (mid. and so. dists.) Fla. 1973, U.S. Ct. Appeals (3d, 4th and 11th cirs.) 1975, DC 1989. Assoc. Holland & Knight LLP, Tallahassee, 1973—78, ptnr., 1979—, chair, dirs. com., past chair. pub. law dept. Bd. dirs., v.p. Fla. Lawyers Prepaid Legal Svc. Corp., 1978—80, pres., 1980—82, legis. com., 1983—84, mem. commn. on access to justice, 1984—86, exec. coun. tax sect., 1987—88, exec. coun. pub. interest. sect., 1989—91; active Fla. Commn. Ethics, 1984—87, chairperson, 1986—87, Fla. Taxation and Budget Reform Commn., 1989—; legal adv. bd. Martindale-Hubbell/Lexis-Nexis, 1990—; chair Ho. of Dels., 1994—96; spkr., lectr. in field. Governor's appointee to the Fla. Commn. on Ethics State Fla., 1984—88, chair, Fla. Commn. on Ethics, 1986—87, mem. Governor's Select Com. on Workforce 2000, 1988—89, Governor's appointee to Constitutional Taxation & Budget Reform Commn., 1990—94, Governor's appointee to Constitution Revision Commn., 1997—98; mem. exec. com. Fla. Tax Watch, 2002; bd. dirs. Lawyers Com. Civil Rights Under Law; bd. adminstrs. Tulane Ednl. Fund; mem. Fla. Commn. on Human Rels., 1977—79; bd. trustee Fla. Tax Watch, 1983—; trustee U. Fla. Coll. Law, 1996—; mem. adv. coun. U. Fla. Law Ctr.; mem. Fla. Blue Key; founding mem., bd. dir. Fla. Women's Alliance; founding mem., past pres. Capital Women's Network, 1977—79; vice-chair Fla. Sales Tax on Svcs. Study Commn., 1986—87; mem. Fla. Coun. Econ. Edn., 1989—96, Fla. Edn. Found., 1991—96, Fla. Supreme Ct. Historical Soc.; bd. govs. Fla. Chamber, 2001. Recipient Arabella Babb Mansfield award, Nat. Assn. Women Lawyers, 1996, Hillary Clinton Glass Cutter award, 1996, Alumnae of Distinction, U. Fla., 1997, Nat. Assn. Pub. Interest Law award, 1998, Newcomb Coll. Outstanding Alumna, 1999, Kate Stoneman award, Albany Law Sch., 1999, Nat. Legal Aid and Defender Assn. award, 2000, Disting. Alumna award, Tulane U., 2001, Medal of Honor award, Fla. Bar. Found., 2002, Rosemary Barkett award, Fla. Assn. Women Lawyers; named Nat. Women of Distinction, Girl Scouts U.S.A., 2002; named one of The 50 Most Influential Women Lawyers in America, Nat. Law Jour., 1998, 2007, 100 Most Influential Lawyers in America, 2006. Fellow: Am. Bar Found. (life); mem.: ABA (exec. coun. sect. on individual rights and responsibility 1974—86, chair, sect. individual rights and responsibilities 1984—85, task force on minorities in profession 1984—86, House of Delegates 1984—, mem. FJE Resources Com. 1985—89, commn. on legal problems of the elderly 1986—88, bd. govs. 1986—89, 1986—89, consortium on legal svcs and the pub. 1987—89, commn. on women in profession 1987—90, chair bd. govs. fin. com. 1988—89, chair, bd. govs. fin. com. 1988—89, long range planning com. 1988—91, chair commn. on pub. understanding about the law 1990—93, chair, commn. on pub. understanding about the law 1990—93, bd. editors ABA Jour. 1990—94, exec. coun. sect. legal edn. and admission to bar 1990—94, bd. editors, ABA Jour. 1990—96, chair, assembly resolutions com. 1991—94, ex-officio, Am. Bar Endowment 1994—96, ex-officio, Am. Bar Found. 1994—96, bd. govs. 1994—96, chair, Consortium on Legal Services and the Public 1996, exec. coun. sect. legal edn. and admission to bar 1996—99, mem. FJE Coun. 1996—99, Ctrl. European and Eurasian Law Initiative (CEELI) Exec. Bd. 1997—, pres.-elect 1999—2000, bd. govs. 1999—2001, bd. editors ABA Jour. 1999—2001, pres. 2000—01, mem. standing com. on legal aid to indigent defendents, mem. standing com. on prepaid legal svcs.), Tallahassee Women Lawyers Assn., Nat. Assn. Women Lawyers, Am. Judicature Soc. (bd. dir. 1986—89), Bar DC, Tallahassee Bar Assn., Fla. Bar Assn. (exec. coun. pub. interest law sect. 1989—91, mem. legis. com., mem. commn. on access to justice, exec. coun. of the tax sect.), Am. Law Inst., Nat. Inst. Dispute Resolution (sec.-treas. 1988—94, bd. dirs. 1988—94, Gov. appt. Fla. Constitution revision Commn. 1997—98), Phi Delta Phi, Phi Kappa Phi. Office: Holland & Knight LLP 315 S Calhoun St Ste 600 Tallahassee FL 32301 Office Phone: 850-425-5620. Business E-Mail: martha.barnett@hklaw.com.

BARNETT, PATRICIA ANN, development professional; b. Culver City, Calif., Jan. 25; d. Howard Taft and Sarah (Ross) B. BJ, U. Tex., 1978; MLA, So. Meth. U., 2002. Program specialist Dallas C. of C., 1978-79, comm. specialist, 1979-81; mgr. pub. rels. Trailways Corp., Dallas, 1981-82, dir. pub. rels., 1982-85; sr. account exec. Keller-Crescent Co., Dallas, 1985-87; dir. comm. Office Pvt. Sector Initiatives The White House, Washington, 1987-89; dir. pub. affairs United Way Am., Alexandria, Va., 1989-91; dir. pub. rels. Dally Advt., Ft. Worth, 1992-94; dir. corp. and found. rels. So. Meth. U., Dallas, 1994-96, dir. major gifts, 1996—2001; exec. dir. devel. Dedman Coll., 2001—07; v.p. donor rels. Baylor Health Care Sys. Found., Dallas, 2007—08; chief devel. officer sch. econ., political & policy scis. U. Tex., Dallas, 2008—. Republican. Avocations: history, travel, literature, folk art, bookbinding. Business E-Mail: tricia.barnett@utdallas.edu.

BARNETT, RICHARD CHAMBERS, historian, educator; b. Davenport, Fla., Apr. 27, 1932; s. Jones Richard and Helen June (Chambers) B.; m. Betty May Tribble, Oct. 18, 1957; children—Amelia Carlton, Colin Warwick BA, Wake Forest Coll., 1953; M.Ed., U. N.C., 1954, PhD, 1963. Instr., acting chmn. dept. social sci. Gardner-Webb Coll., 1956-58; instr. history Wake Forest U., Winston-Salem, NC, 1961-62, asst. prof., 1962-67, assoc. prof., 1967-76, prof., 1976—94, chmn. dept. history, 1968-75, 83-87, acting dean Grad. Sch., 1979; retired. Contbr. articles to profl. jours., chapters to books. Pres Winston-Salem-Forsyth PTA, 1969-71; bd. mgrs. N.C. PTA, 1971-73, exec. com., 1972-73, life mem.; adv. com. N.C. Bd. Edn., 1973-76. Served with CIC, AUS, 1954-56 Southeastern Inst. Medieval and Renaissance Studies fellow, 1974 Mem. Am. Hist. Assn. (pres. elect N.C. conf. 1991-92, pres. 1992-93), AAUP, Carolinas Symposium Brit. Studies (pres. 1979-80), So. Conf. Brit. Studies (pres. 1990-92), N.Am. Conf. Brit. Studies (coun. 1990-92), Danforth Assocs. Home: 6413 Salemtowne Dr Winston Salem NC 27106-3767 Home Phone: 336-767-3106.

BARNEY, MICHAEL E., lawyer; b. Petersburg, Va., Apr. 20, 1947; s. Jack Hansford and Maxine (Scott) Barney; m. Roslyn Ann Weiner, June 7, 1970; children: Jason Ross, Scott Ryan. BA, U. Va., 1969; JD, U. Richmond, 1972. Bar: Va. 1972. Ptnr. Kaufman & Canoles P.C., Norfolk, Va., 1972—. Lectr. in field. Contbr. articles to profl. jours. Officer, bd. dirs. Jewish Cmty. Ctr. Tidewater, Norfolk, 1980—86, Beth El Congregation, Norfolk, 1988—90. Capt. USAR, 1971—79. Mem.: Am. Coll. Real Estate Lawyers, Norfolk and Portsmouth Bar Assn., Virginia Beach Bar Assn., Va. Bar Assn. (coun. real property sect.), Va. State Bar (bd. govs. real property sect., chairperson real property sect. 1988), Va. Assn. Realtors (assoc.), Tidewater Builders Assn. (assoc.). Avocations: hunting, golf, fishing, boating. Office: Kaufman and Canoles PO Box 626 Virginia Beach VA 23451-0626 Office Phone: 757-491-4040. Business E-Mail: mebarney@kaufcan.com.

BARNHARDT, ZEB ELONZO, JR., lawyer; b. Winston-Salem, NC, Dec. 28, 1941; s. Zeb Elonzo and Katie Sue (Taylor) B.; m. Pam Hall; children: Daniel Black, Kathleen Martin. AB, Duke U., 1964; JD, Vanderbilt U., 1969. Bar: N.C. 1969; cert. mediator, N.C. Assoc. Womble Carlyle Sandridge & Rice, PLLC, Winston-Salem, 1969-75, mem., 1975-97, of counsel, 1997-98; owner, mgr. Barnhardt & Assocs., Inc., Greensboro, NC, 1998—; pvt. practice law Greensboro, 1998—; mediator N.C. Superior Ct., 2003—. Arbitrator Fin. Industry Regulatory Authority, 1992—2011, mediator, 2004—11. Alumni admissions adv. com. Duke U., 1970-72; bd. dirs. Industries for Blind, Winston-Salem, 1973-85, vice chmn., 1983-84, chmn., 1985; bd. dirs. Goodwill Industries, Winston-Salem, 1973-80, BarCARES of NC, Inc., 1999-2005, Little Theatre, Winston-Salem, 1979-85, asst. treas., 1980, treas., 1981-82, v.p., 1983-84, pres., 1984-85; adv. bd. Salvation Army, Winston-Salem, 1973-85, chmn., 1979-80, Leadership Winston-Salem, 1984-92, v.p. adminstrn., 1988-89, pres. 1989-90; com. mem. Winston-Salem Found., 1975-84, vice chmn., 1978-80, chmn., 1983-84; trustee High Point U., 1984-96; chmn. Second Journey Inc., 2002-2003, bd. trustees Coastal Horizons Ctr., Inc., Wilmington, NC, 2005-06; bd. dirs. Cmty. Found. Southeastern NC, 2006-07. With USN, 1964—66. Recipient Disting. Service award as Young Man of Yr. Winston-Salem Jaycees, 1974; Disting. Alumni award Duke U., 1979 Mem. ABA (bus. law sect., 1969-2012, dispute resolution sect., 2003—, Commn. on Lawyer Assistance Programs 2002-05), N.C. Bar Assn. (mem. bus. law sect., 1969—, chmn. securities regulation com. 1985-87, vice chmn. bus. law sect. 1987-89, chmn. bus. law sect. 1989-91, mem. dispute resolution sect., 2003—, vice chair dispute resolution sect., 2009-10, chair dispute resolution sect. 2010-2011, bd. govs. 1991-94, chair membership recruitment and retention com. 1997-2000, chair lawyer effectiveness and quality of life com. 2001—04), Winston-Salem Jaycees (life, pres. 1973-74), N.C. Jaycees (regional dir. 1974-75, legal counsel 1975-77), Greater Winston-Salem C. of C. (bd. dirs. 1973-74), Rotary. Democrat. Methodist. Home: 4791 Forest Oaks Dr Greensboro NC 27406 Personal E-mail: zebarnhardt@gmail.com.

BARNHART, JEFF, former state legislator; Former exec. dir.; former state rep. Dist 81 NC; state rep. Dist 82 NC, 2003—11; CEO Cabarrus Cmty. Health Ctrs. Inc. Mem. Appropriations. com., Health com., Homeland Security, Military and Veterans Affairs com., Ins. com.; vice chmn. Mental Health Reform com., Appropriations Subcom. on Health and Human Svcs. Republican.

BARNHILL, HENRY GRADY, JR., lawyer; b. Buena Vista, Ga., Aug. 24, 1930; s. Henry Grady and Imogene (Hogg) B.; m. Sarah Carolyn Haire, Oct. 29, 1953; children: Grady Michael, Stephen Drew, Kevin Scott, Carol Kelly. JD, Wake Forest U., Winston-Salem, NC, 1958. Bar: N.C. 1958, U.S. Dist. Ct. (ea., mid. and we. dists.) N.C. 1958, U.S. Ct. Appeals (4th cir.) 1961, U.S. Supreme Ct. 1983, U.S. Ct. Appeals (fed. cir.) 1985. Assoc. Womble Carlyle Sandridge & Rice, Winston-Salem, 1958-61, ptnr., 1961—. Bd. visitors Sch. of Law Wake Forest U. Lt. USAF, 1951-55. Fellow Am. Coll. Trial Lawyers (state chmn. 1986-88, Named to Best Lawyers in Am. 1984-); mem. Am. Bd. Trial Advs., N.C. Assn. Def. Attys., N.C. Bar Assn. (litigation sect.), 4th Cir. Jud. Conf., Forsyth County Bar (pres. 1979-80), Inns of Ct. (Chief Justice Joseph Branch). Democrat. Presbyterian. Avocation: tennis. Home: 3121 Robinhood Rd Winston Salem NC 27106-5610 Office: Womble Carlyle Sandridge & Rice PLLC One W 4th St Winston Salem NC 27101 E-mail: gbarnhill@wcsr.com.

BARNHILL, JOHN HERSCHEL, retired government administrator, historian; b. Walnut Ridge, Ark., Mar. 2, 1947; s. Herschel and Ada (Rasdon) Barnhill; m. Barbara Leah Clayton, July 19, 1980 (div. 1995); 1 child, William Bryant; m. Valerie Olson, Aug. 2, 2005. AA, Del Mar Coll., Corpus Christi, Tex., 1974; BA, Corpus Christi State U., 1976; MA, Okla. State U., 1978, PhD, 1981. Teaching asst. Okla. State U., Dept. History, Stillwater, 1977-81; dep. dir. 45th Inf. div. Mus., Oklahoma City, 1981-82; videotape archivist Okla. Dept. Libr., Oklahoma City, 1982-84; historian Engring. Installation div. Tinker AFB, Oklahoma City, 1984-85; program analyst 1985th Comm. Computer Systems Group, 1985-93, DISA WE4, 1993—, ret., 2005. Referee Ark. Hist. Quar., 1991, East Tex. Hist. Jour., 2008-. Author: From Surplus to Substitution, 1983; contbr. articles to profl. jours., encyclopedias, book revs. Mem. City Charter Commn., 1991, city planning commr. 1993-98. With USAF, 1966-70. Recipient Disting. Alumnus award Corpus Christi State U., 1984, excellence awards Air Force Orgn., 1985, 87, 89, 91, 93, Beacon of Freedom, 1991, Federal Employee Point of Light, 1991. Mem.: Southwest Hist. Assn., East Tex. Hist. Assn., Phi Kappa Phi. Avocations: reading, writing. Home: 13402 Ensley Wood Dr Houston TX 77082 Personal E-mail: jbarnhil@sbcglobal.net.

BARNUM, WILLIAM DOUGLAS, retired communications executive; b. Denton, Tex., July 28, 1946; s. Billie Douglas and Leticia Christina Barnum; m. Mary Ann Mook, Aug. 10, 1968. BSBA in Econs. with distinction, Georgetown U., 1967; MBA, Fairleigh Dickinson U., 1985. Acct. RCA Corp., Cherry Hill, NJ, 1967-68, Andros Island, Bahamas, 1968-70, budget and cost analyst Cherry Hill, 1970, adminstr. tel. sys., 1970-73; mgr. project adminstrn. white sands radar project RCA Svc. Co., Holloman AFB, N.Mex., 1973-74; coord. profit ctr. acctg. RCA Global Comms., NYC, 1974-76, adminstr. globcom. sys., 1976-77, mgr. spl. project and accts. payable, 1978-79; mgr. fin. RCA Globcom Sys., Inc., NYC, 1979-81; mgr. gateway ops. RCA Global Comms., Edison, NJ, 1981-82, dir. field support svcs., 1982-88; sr. mgr. network svcs. MCI Internat., Piscataway, NJ, 1988-90, sr. mgr. sys. support and adminstrn., 1990-92, sr. mgr. messaging and marine ops., 1992-93, sr. staff internat. alliances, 1994; owner, sr. cons. Lake Road Assocs. Consulting, Far Hills, NJ, 1994-99; ret., 1999. Author: Kroodley Made Knife Catalog, 1977. Mem. Am. Security Coun., 1981—92, Far Hills (N.J.) Bd. Health, 1993—99, vice-chmn., 1994—95, chmn., 1996—99; adviser Jr. Achievement, Cherry Hill, NJ, 1968—69, Cherry Hill Jaycees, 1973—74; mem. spl. commn. Far Hills Police Dept., 1993, 1998; bd. dirs. United Cerebral Palsy Somerset/Morris County, 1989; dam repair project mgr., vol. Beaver Dam Lake Home Owner's Assn. Mem.: NRA (life benefactor mem.), Georgetown U. Legacy Soc., Knifemakers Guild (hon.), RCA Commn. Retirees Assn., S.C. Waterfowl Assn., Mensa, J. Edgar Hoover Found. (life), Am. Knife Throwers Alliance (hon.), Mid-Carolina Rifle Club, Woodcreek Country Club, Wildewood Country Club, Delta Mu Delta, Delta Phi Epsilon. Republican. Presbyterian. Home: PO Box 23329 Columbia SC 29224

BAROFF, GEORGE STANLEY, psychologist, educator; b. Bronx, NY, Nov. 27, 1924; s. Irving and Ida (Herman) B.; m. Rose Kislin, June 15, 1952 (dec. May 1992); children: Marina Binet, Roy James. BS in Zoology, George Washington U., 1948, MA in Psychology, 1950; PhD in Clin. Psychology, NYU, 1955. Research psychologist dept. med. genetics N.Y. State Psychiat. Inst., 1952-60; chief clin. psychologist Vineland (N.J.) Tng. Sch., 1960-63; asso. prof. psychology U. N.C., Chapel Hill, 1963-67, prof., 1967-2000, prof. emeritus, 2000—, dir. devel. disabilties tng. inst., 1964-2000. Forensic psychologist with criminal defendants who may be mentally retarded, 1987—. Author: Mental Retardation: Nature, Cause and Management, 1974, 3d edit. (with J.G. Olley), 1999, Developmental Disabilities: Psychosocial Aspects, 1991, Does Got Exist: A Primer For the Perplexed, 2009; contbr. articles to profl. jours. With US Army, 1943—45. Mem.: APA, Assn., Am. Assn. Intelectual & Devel. Disabilities. Jewish. Home: 417 Granville Rd Chapel Hill NC 27514-2723 E-mail: gbaroff@bellsouth.net.

BARONE, TONY, SR., professional sports team executive; s. Corinne Barone. B in English, Duke U., 1968. Asst. coach Duke University, 1972—74, Bradley U., Peoria, Ill., 1978—85; head coach Creighton U., Omaha, 1985—91, Texas A&M University, Lubbock, Tex., 1991—98; Big 12 color commentator ESPN regional, 1998—2000; dir., player pers. Memphis Grizzlies, 2000—, asst. coach, 2002—04, interim head coach, 2006—07. Host (basketball videos) Drills to Build a Competitive and Fundamentally Sound Team. Named Mo. Valley Conf. Coach of Yr. (twice), Southwestern Conf. Coach of Yr., 1994. Office: Memphis Grizzlies 191 Beale St Memphis TN 38103 Office Phone: 901-888-4667. Office Fax: 901-201-1235.

BARR, ANDY (GARLAND HALE BARR IV), United States Representative from Kentucky; b. Lexington, Ky., July 24, 1973; s. Garland Hale and Donna R. (Faulconer) Barr; m. Eleanor Carol Leavell, 2008; 1 child, Eleanor Dumont. BA in Govt. & Philosophy, U. Va., 1996; JD, U. Ky. Coll. Law, 2001. Legislative asst. to Rep. Jim Talent US House of Representatives, 1996—98; assoc. Stites & Harbison, Lexington, Ky., 2002—04; gen. counsel Governor's Office Local Devel. State of Ky., Frankfort, 2004—07, dep. gen. counsel to Gov. Ernie Fletcher, 2007—08; assoc. Kinkhead & Stilz, Lexington, Ky., 2008—12; mem. US Congress from 6th Ky. Dist., Washington, 2013—, US House Financial Services Com., 2013—. Contributor The Va. Advocate; intern to Senator Mitch McConnell US Senate; mem. Gov.-Elect Ernie Fletcher's Transition Team, 2003—04; part time instr. constitutional law U. Ky. Coll. Law, Morehead State U.; v.p. Fayette County Republican Party. Bd. dirs. Friends of the Isaac Murphy Meml. Art Garden. Mem.: Prevent Child Abuse in Ky. (v.p. 2007, pres. 2008—09), Fayette County Bar Assn., Ky. Bar Assn. Republican. Episcopalian. Office: US House of Representatives 1432 Longworth House Office Bldg Washington DC 20515 also: 2709 Old Rosebud Rd Lexington KY 40509 Office Phone: 202-225-4706, 859-219-1366.*

BARR, JAMES HOUSTON, III, lawyer; b. Louisville, 1941; s. James Houston Jr. and Elizabeth Hamilton (Pope) Barr; m. Sarah Jane Todd, Apr. 16, 1970 (div.); 1 child, Lynn Jamison; m. Cindy Ann Jeffries, May 31, 1997; children: Worden Pope Washington, Augustine Washington Jeffries. Student, U. Va., 1960-63, U. Tenn., 1963-64; BSL, JD, U. Louisville, 1966. Bar: Ky. 1966, U.S. Ct. Appeals (6th cir.) 1969, U.S. Supreme Ct. 1971, U.S. Ct. Mil. Appeals 1978. Law clk. Ky. Ct. Appeals, Frankfort, 1966-67; asst. atty. gen. Ky. Frankfort, 1967-71, 79-82; asst. U.S. atty. U.S. Dept. Justice, Louisville, 1971-79, 83—; 1st asst. U.S. Atty., 1978-79; asst. dist. counsel U.S. Army C.E., Louisville, 1982-83. Lt. comdr. USNR, 1967-81, lt. col. USAR, 1981-91. Mem. FBA (pres. Louisville chpt. 1975-76, Younger Fed. Lawyer award 1975), Ky. Bar Assn., Louisville Bar Assn., Soc. Colonial Wars, SAR (chancellor Louisville Thruston chpt. 2008-10), Washington Family Soc., Pendennis Club, Louisville Boat Club (pres. 2004-05), Filson Hist. Soc., Delta Upsilon. Republican. Episcopalian. Home: 100 Westwind Rd Louisville KY 40207-1520 Office: US Atty 717 W Broadway Louisville KY 40202-2281

BARR, RONALD E., educational association administrator; Tchr. Tex. A&M U.; faculty, Coll. Engring. U. Tex., Austin, 1978—. Contbr.; author: Classroom Testing of Virtual Biomechanics Lab. Learning Modules, 2003 (Best Paper award, Am. Soc. for Engring. Edn., 2002). Mem.: Am. Soc. for Engring. Edn. (pres.-elect 2004—05, pres. 2005—, Disting. Svc. award, Engring. Design Graphics Div. 1999, Spread the Word award 2002, Campus Rep. award). Office: 1 University Station C2200 Mechanical Engring Dept Univ Texas at Austin Austin TX 78712-0292 Office Phone: 512-471-3008. Office Fax: 512-471-7683. E-mail: rbarr@mail.utexas.edu.

BARRAS, TAYLOR F., state legislator; BS in Acctg., La. State U., Baton Rouge, 1979. Market pres. Iberia Bank, New Iberia; mem. Dist. 48 La. House of Reps., 2008—, mem. house and govtl. affairs com., mcpl., parochial and cultural affairs com., ways and means com., joint legis. com. on capital outlay. Democrat. Office: State Capitol PO Box 44486 Baton Rouge LA 70804 Mailing: 800 S Lewis St Ste 206 2nd Fl New Iberia LA 70560 Office Phone: 225-342-6945, 337-373-4051. Office Fax: 337-373-4053. Business E-Mail: barrast@legis.state.la.us.

BARRASSO, TOM, professional hockey coach, retired professional hockey player; b. Boston, Mar. 31, 1965; m. Megan Barrasso; children: Ashley, Kelsey, Mallory. Goaltender Buffalo Sabers, 1983—88, Pitts. Penquins, 1988—2000, Ottawa Senators, 2000, Carolina Hurricanes, 2001, Toronto Maple Leafs, 2002, St. Louis Blues, 2002—03; goaltending coach, dir. goalie devel. Carolina Hurricanes, 2007—09, asst. coach, 2009—. Mem. USA Olympic Hockey Team, Salt Lake City, 2002. Founder Ashley Barrasso Cancer Rsch. Fund. Recipient Calder Meml. Trophy, 1984, Vezina Trophy, 1984, William M. Jennings Trophy, 1985. Achievements include being a member of Stanley Cup Champion Pittsburgh Penquins, 1991, 1992; being a member of silver medal winning USA Hockey Team, Salt Lake City Olympics, 2002; being inducted into the US Hockey Hall of Fame, 2009. Office: Carolina Hurricanes RBC Center 1400 Edwards Mill Rd Raleigh NC 27607

BARRATT, MICHAEL REED, astronaut, internal and aerospace medical doctor; b. Vancouver, Wash., Apr. 16, 1959; s. Joseph and Donna Barratt; m. Michelle Lynne Sasynuik; 5 children. BS in Zoology, U. Wash., 1981; MD, Northwestern U., 1985; M in Aerospace Medicine, Wright State U., 1991. Resident internal medicine Northwestern U., 1988; chief resident VA Lakeside Hosp., Chgo., 1989; aerospace project physician with KRUG Life Sciences NASA Johnson Space Ctr., 1991, mgr., hyperbaric and respiratory subsystems for Space Station Freedom on the Health Maintenance Facility Project, 1991—92; flight surgeon NASA Med. Ops., 1992; assigned to the joint US/Russian Shuttle-Mir Program (in support of the Mir-18/STS-71 Mission Cosmonaut Tng. Ctr., Star City, Russia, 1994; med. ops. lead for Internat. Space Station, 1995—98; lead crew surgeon for first expedition crew to Internat. Space Station, 1998—2000; mission specialist, astronaut NASA, 2000—. Crew mem., flight engr. scheduled to arrive at the Internat. Space Station aboard a Soyuz spacecraft (TMA-14) Expedition-19, 2009; flight engr. Expedition-20, 2009; mission specialist STS-133-Final Flight of Discovery, 2011. Assoc. editor for space medicine Aviation, Space and Environmental Medicine, sr. editor (textbook) Principles of Clinical Medicine for Space Flight. Recipient Flight Surgeons Julian Ward award, 1992, Melbourne W. Boynton award, 1995, W. Randolph Lovelace award, 1998; nominee Rotary Nat. award for Space Achievement Found., 1998. Mem.: Am. Astronautical Soc., Soc. NASA Flight Surgeons, Am. Inst. for Advancement Sci., ACP, Aerospace Med. Assn., Phi Beta Kappa, Alpha Omega Alpha. Avocations: family and church activities, writing, sailing, boat restoration and maintenance. Office: Lyndon B Johnson Space Ctr Astronauts Office 2101 NASA Pkwy Houston TX 77058

BARRERA, ELVIRA PUIG, retired counselor, academic administrator, educational program evaluator; b. Alice, Tex., Dec. 11, 1943; d. Carlos Rogers and Delia Rebeca (Puig) B.; 1 child, Dennis Lee Cheatham, Jr. BA, Incarnate Word Coll., 1971; M Counseling and Guidance, St. Mary's U., San Antonio, 1978; specialist degree marriage and family therapy, St. Mary's U., 1989. Lic. profl. counselor, marriage & family therapist, lic. chem. dependency counselor. Tchr. Edgewood Ind. Sch. Dist., San Antonio, 1965—74, Dallas Ind. Sch. Dist., 1971—72, Northside Ind. Sch. Dist., San Antonio, 1974; ednl. cons. Region 20-Edn. Svc. Ctr., San Antonio, 1974—79; coord. career edn. San Antonio Ind. Sch. Dist., 1979—84, counselor, 1984—91; vice prin., 1998—2005; family coord. CATCH project U. Tex. Health Sci. Ctr., Houston, 1991—94; counselor Austin Ind. Sch. Dist., 1994—97, dist. transition counselor, 1997—98; ret., 2005; program evaluator AOC Solutions, Inc., Chantilly, Va., 2006—11. Cons. SBA, 1981, U.S. Office Edn., Washington, 1981-82, Tex. Edn. Agy., Austin, 1979-80; cons., writer San Antonio Ind. Sch. Dist. and Tex. Edn. Agy., 1985; cons. various edn. publs. Chairperson career awareness exploring divsn. Boy Scouts Am., 1982-87. Named Disting. Alumna, Incarnate Word Coll., 1983, Hall of Fame Internat. Profl. and Bus. Women, 1995; recipient Spurgeon award Boy Scouts Am., 1985, Merit award, 1986, Growth award, 1986 Mem. Am. Assn. Marriage and Family Therapy, San Antonio Hash House Harriers (treas. 1990-91), Incarnate Word Coll. Alumni Assn. (adv. bd. 1990—95), St. Mary's U. Alumni Assn. (v.p. Austin alumni chpt. 2003-10), The Harp and Shamrock Soc. Tex., Delta Kappa Gamma (Kappa Beta chpt. 2d v.p. 1982-84, 1st v.p. 1986-88, sec. 2005-06, pres. 2006-10, parliamentarian 10-12), Tex. State Orgn. (area 6 coord. 2011-13), Pan Am. League (chairperson devel. com., 2011-). Roman Catholic. Avocation: running. Home: 13711 Oak Cabin San Antonio TX 78232-5427

BARRETT, BERNARD MORRIS, JR., plastic and reconstructive surgeon; b. Pensacola, Fla., May 3, 1944; s. Bernard Morris and Blanche (Lischkoff) B.; m. Sandra Neal Barrett; children: Beverly Frances, Julie Blaine, Audrey Blake, Bernard Joseph. BS, Tulane U., 1965; MD, U. Miami, 1969. Diplomate Am. Bd. Plastic Surgery. Surg. intern Meth. Hosp. and Ben Taub Hosp., Houston, 1969-70; resident in gen. surgery Baylor Coll. Medicine, Houston, 1970-71, UCLA, 1971-73; resident in plastic surgery U. Miami (Fla.) Affilated Hosps., 1973-75, chief resident in plastic surgery, 1975; fellow in plastic surgery Clinica Ivo Pitanguy, Rio de Janeiro, 1973; instr. surgery Baylor Coll. Medicine, 1970-71, clin. instr. plastic surgery, 1977-80, clin. asst. prof., 1980-90, clin. assoc. prof., 1991-97, clin. prof. surgery, 1997—; instr. surg. emergencies L.A. County Paramedics, 1972-73; plastic surgery coord. for jr. med. students Sch. Medicine U. Miami, 1975; practice medicine specializing in plastic and reconstructive surgery Houston, 1976—. Pres., chmn. bd. dirs. Plastic and Reconstructive Surgeons, P.A., 1978—; chmn. Tex. Inst. Plastic Surgery, Houston; assoc. chief plastic surgery St. Luke's Episcopal Hosp., Houston, 1991—; attending physician Jr. League Clinic, Tex. Children's Hosp., Houston, 1977—; active staff St. Luke's Hosp., Houston, Meth. Hosp., Houston; clin. assoc. in plastic surgery U. Tex. Med. Sch., Houston, 1976—; instr. surg. emergencies Harris County C.C.; dir. Am. Physicians Ins. Exch., Austin, 1976-2003, vice chmn., bd. dirs., 1995—; bd. dirs. Advocate M.D. Ins., Austin, 2004—; past chief of staff, chief plastic surgery Travis Centre Hosp., Houston, 1985—; dir. Physicians for Peace, Norfolk, Va., 1991—; cons. physician Houston Oilers, 1978-97; attending physician Ontario Motor Speedway, Calif., 1972-73. Author: Patient Care in Plastic Surgery, 1982, 2nd edit., 1996, Manuel de Ciudados en Cirugia Plastica, 1985, Atencion al Paciente de Cirugia Plastica, 1998; contbg. editor: Plastic Surgery Obsession: Brazil's Dr. Ivo Pitanguy Triggered It All, 2011; Professional Adviser: Surgeon: The Man Behind the Mask, Richard H. German, MD, 2011; contbr. articles to med. publs., presentations to profl. confs.; inventor Barrett sterling surgigrip. Bd. dirs. Plastic Surgery Ednl. Found., Chgo.; mem. Fed. Coun. on Aging, Washington, 1991-93, Pres.'s Coun. U. Miami, 1997—; adv. bd. Johnson & Johnson, New Brunswick, N.J. Lt. comdr. M.C., USNR, 1969-74. Recipient Outstanding Tchg. Plastic Surgeon award Baylor Coll. Medicine, 2003; Surg. exch. scholar to Royal Coll. Surgeons, London, 1968; hon. dep. sheriff Harris County, Tex. Fellow ACS; mem. Am. Assn. Plastic Surgery, Am. Soc. Plastic Surgeons, Royal Soc. Medicine, Michael E. DeBakey Internat. Cardiovascular Surg. Soc., Am. Soc. for Aesthetic Plastic Surgery, Denton A. Cooley

Cardiovascular Surg. Soc., Tex. Med. Assn., Tex. Soc. Plastic Surgery, Harris County Med. Soc., Houston Soc. Plastic Surgery, D. Ralph Millard Plastic Surg. Soc. (pres. 1993-94, v.p. 1977-79, sec., treas. 1975-77, historian 1980—), U. Miami Sch. Medicine Nat. Alumni Assn. (bd. dirs. 1975-77, pres. coun. 1997—), Houston City Club, Houstonian Club, Royal Biscayne Racquet Club, Commodore Club, Coral Beach and Tennis Club, Sweetwater Country Club, Alpha Kappa Kappa (pres. 1968-69). Office: 25 West Ln Houston TX 77019-1007 Office Phone: 713-626-4747. Personal E-mail: bbarrettmd@gmail.com.

BARRETT, EUGENE JOSEPH, physician, educator, researcher; b. Jersey City, May 22, 1946; s. Joseph Francis and Margaret (Harney) B.; m. Pauc Marie Quiricani, Jan. 31, 1976; children: Nora, Matthew. BS in Physics, St. Peters Coll., Jersey City, NJ, 1968; MD, U. Rochester, 1975, PhD in Biophysics, 1975. Intern in medicine Strong Meml. Hosp., Rochester, NY, 1975-76, asst. resident in medicine, 1976-77; fellow in endocrinology and metabolism Yale U. Sch. Medicine, New Haven, 1977-80, asst. prof. medicine, 1980-85, assoc. prof. medicine, 1985-91, chief diabetes unit, 1988-91; prof. internal medicine and pediats. U. Va. Sch. Medicine, Charlottesville, 1991—; dir. U. Va. Diabetes Ctr., 1991—. Dir. diabetes unit Yale U. Sch. Medicine, 1987-91; dir. diabetes ctr. U. Va., 1991—. Contbr. over 150 articles to profl. jours. Recipient Rsch. Career award NIH, 1981-85. Mem. NIH (mem. metabolism study sect. 1993-96), Am. Diabetes Assn. (bd. dirs. Va. affiliate 1993-96, v.p. 2002, pres.-elect 2002, pres. 2003-04, mem. nat. profl. practice com., rsch. award 1996), Am. Heart Assn. (Established Investigator 1987-92, mem. Conn. affiliate grant rev. panel 1985-90, mem. grant rev. panel New Eng. region 1986-91, chair 1991), Am. Fedn. Clin. Rsch., Am. Soc. Clin. Investigation. Roman Catholic. Avocations: sailing, tennis. Office: U Va Sch Medicine Diabetes Rsch Ctr PO Box 801410 Charlottesville VA 22908 Business E-Mail: ejb8x@virginia.edu.

BARRETT, LIDA KITTRELL, mathematics professor; b. Houston, May 21, 1927; d. Pleasant Williams and Maidel (Baker) Kittrell; m. John Herbert Barrett, June 2, 1950 (dec. Jan. 1969); children: John Kittrell, Maidel Horn, Mary Louise. BA, Rice U., Houston, 1946; MA, U. Tex., Austin, 1949; PhD, U. Pa., Phila., 1954. Instr. math. U. Conn., Waterbury, 1955-56; vis. appointment U. Wis., Madison, 1959-60; lectr. U. Utah, Salt Lake City, 1956-61; assoc. prof. U. Tenn., Knoxville, 1961-70, prof., 1970-80, head math. dept., 1973-80; assoc. provost No. Ill. U., DeKalb, 1980-87; dean, arts and scis. Miss. State U., Mississippi State, 1987-91; sr. assoc. Edn. and Human Resources Directorate NSF, Washington, 1991-95; prof. math. US Mil. Acad., West Point, NY, 1995-98; adj. prof. U. Tenn., 1998—2001. Math. and math. edn. cons., Knoxville, Tenn., 1964-80, 98—. Contbr. articles on topology, applied math. and math. edn. to profl. jours. Mem. Math. Assn. Am. (pres. 1989, 90), Am. Math. Soc., Soc. Indsl. and Applied Math., Nat. Coun. Tchrs. Math., Am. Assn. Higher Edn., Phi Kappa Phi, Sigma Xi. Episcopalian.

BARRETT, MICHAEL BAKER, historian, educator; b. Honolulu, Oct. 12, 1946; s. John P. and Bernice (Baker) B.; m. Sara Harriet McKerley, Sept. 20, 1969; 1 child, Michael M. AB, The Citadel, 1968; MA, U. Mass., 1969, PhD, 1977; graduate, US Army Command and Gen. Staff Coll., 1980—81, US Army War Coll., Carlisle, PA, 1991. Lectr. history U. Mass., Amherst, 1973-74, 75-76; instr. history The Citadel, Charleston, SC, 1976-78, asst. prof., 1978-82, assoc. prof., 1982—, prof., 2005—, dean of grad. studies, 1985—91. Author: Operation Albion: The German Conquest of the Baltic Islands, 2007; co-author: (with H.P. Willsnott) Clausewitz Reconsidered, 2010; Editor: (Rowman and Littlefield series) Total War: New Perspectives on World War II, 2005-; contbr. articles to profl. jours. Brig. gen. US Army, 1969—2001, comdr. 941st TC Co. US Army, comdr. 812th TC bn. US Army, comdr. 1182d TC Brigade US Army, comdr. 1186th TC Brigade US Army. Recipient Legion of Merit, U.S. Army, others; Fulbright fellow, 1974-75, Citadel Devel. Found. fellow, 1977, 82, NDEA fellow, 1977. Mem. Am. Hist. Assn., Am. Res. Officers Assn., So. History Assn., SC History Assn., Soc. Mil. History, Hibernian Soc., SC Agrl. Assn., US Army Armor Assn., Transp. Corps. Officers Assn., Fulbright Alumni Assn., Phi Alpha Theta, Phi Kappa Phi, Delta Phi Alpha. Office: The Citadel History Dept Charleston SC 29409-0001 Mailing: 1170 Chersonese Rd Mount Pleasant SC 29464-9506 Office Phone: 843-953-4855. Business E-Mail: barrettm@citadel.edu.

BARRETT, MICHAEL JOSEPH, priest; b. NYC, Oct. 6, 1952; s. Patrick Joseph and Margaret Mary (Rogan) B. BA, Columbia Coll., 1974; STD, Pontifical U. Holy Cross, Rome, 1987. Ordained priest by Pope John Paul II, Rome, 1985. Sales rep. Gulf Oil Chems. Co., NYC, 1974-76; acct. exec. Merrill Lynch & Co., NYC, 1976-78; dir. devel. The Heights Found., Inc., NYC, 1978-83; asst. prof. Roman Coll. of Holy Cross, Rome, 1985-88; del. vicar for Tex. Opus Dei Prelature, Houston, 1988-99; dir. Holy Cross Chapel and Cath. Info. Ctr., 1999—; chaplain St. Thomas More Soc. Legal Ethics, 2001—, Bus. Ethics Forum, 2005—. Retreat master Featherock Conf. Ctr., Schulenburg, Tex., 1988—; chaplain Southgate Cultural Ctr., Houston, 1988—99. Co-host (radio talk-show) Faith Matters, 1997—98, Show of Faith, 2004—. Alumnus advisor Columbia U. Secondary Schs. Com., NYC, 1981-83. theologian to archbishop Jose Gomez, 2013-Mem.: Equestrian Order of the Holy Sepulchre of Jerusalem. Roman Catholic. Avocations: classical music, reading. Home: 5505 Chaucer Dr Houston TX 77005-2631 Office: Holy Cross Chapel 905 Main St Houston TX 77002-6408 Home: Cathedral Our Lady of the Angel 555 W Temple St Los Angeles CA 90012 Office Phone: 713-650-1323. Business E-Mail: info@holycrosschapel.org.

BARRETT, O'NEILL, JR., medical educator; b. Baton Rouge, Mar. 21, 1929; s. O'Neill and Hazel (Lohman) B.; m. Elois Stone; children: Deborah Ann, Michael, William. BS in Biology, La. State U., 1949; MSc in Medicine, Baylor U., 1958; MD, La. State U., New Orleans, 1953. Diplomate Am. Bd. Internal Medicine, Am. Bd. Med. Oncology, Am. Bd. Hematology. Commd. 2d lt. U.S. Army, 1953, advanced through grades to col., 1968; intern Brooke Army Med. Ctr., San Antonio, 1953-54, med. resident, 1955-58; chief gen. medicine Madigan Army Hosp., Tacoma, 1960-62; asst. chief medicine Letterman Army Hosp., San Francisco, 1963-68; chief dept. medicine Tripler Army Med. Ctr., Honolulu, 1968-71, Walter Reed Army Med. Ctr., Washington, 1971-73, ret., 1973; chmn. dept. comprehensive medicine U. So. Fla. Sch. Medicine, Tampa, 1973-76; dir. div. gen. medicine U. S.C. Sch. Medicine, Columbia, 1976-86, chmn. dept. medicine, 1987-92, dir. clin. curriculum, 1992-94, disting. prof. emeritus, 1994—. Assoc. counselor So. Med. Assn. Editor: Internal Medicine in Vietnam, 1982; mem. editorial bd. Med. History Vietnam-U.S. Army, 1972—, Archives of Internal Medicine, 1980-91; asst. editor Southern Med. Assn. Jour.; contbr. articles to profl. jours. Recipient 5 Outstanding Tchr. of Yr. awards U. S.C. Sch. Medicine. Fellow ACP, Am. Coll. Clin. Pharmacology; mem. Am. Soc. Hematology, Am. Soc. Clin. Oncology. Avocations: sailing, birding. Office: U SC Sch Medicine Med Libr Bldg Garver's Ferry Rd Ste 316 Columbia SC 29201

BARRETT, STEPHEN, psychiatrist, educator, consultant, swimmer; b. NYC, Sept. 6, 1933; s. Joseph and Rebecca Barrett; m. Judith Barrett; children: Daniel, Deborah, Benjamin. AB, Columbia U., 1954, MD, 1957. Intern Highland Park (Mich.) Gen. Hosp., 1957-58; resident in psychiatry Temple U. Hosp., Phila., 1958-61; chief psychiat. svc. Scott AFB Hosp., Ill., 1961-63; pvt. practice psychiatry, 1963-93; instr. health edn. Pa. State U., 1987-89. Psychiatrist San Francisco Child Psychiatry Clinic, 1963—66, Ctr. Spl. Problems, 1966—67, Allentown Hosp. Psychiat. Clinic, 1968—90, Muhlenberg Med. Ctr. Psychiat. Clinic, 1971—86; cons. San Francisco Dept. Welfare, 1964—65, 1964—65, San Francisco Adult Probation Dept., 1966—67, Pa. Bd. Probation and Parole, 1967—69, Lehigh Valley Mental Health Assn., 1967—69; v.p. Inst. Sci. Medicine, 2009—. Co-author: The Health Robbers-How to Protect Your Money and Your Life, 1976, The Health Robbers-How to Protect Your Money and Your Life, 2d edit., 1980, Consumer Health-A Guide to Intelligent Decisions, 1980;: 8th edit., 2006, 9th edit., 2012, The Tooth Robbers-A Pro-Flouridation Handbook, 1980, Vitamins and "Health" Foods: The Great American Hustle, 1981, Shopping for Helath Care, 1982, Health Schemes, Scams and Frauds, 1990, Your Guide to Good Nutrition, 1991, Reader's Guide to "Alternative" Health Methods, 1993, The Health Robbers-A Close Look at Quackery in America, 1993, The Vitamin Pushers: How the Health Food Industry is Selling America a Bill of Goods, 1994, Chemical Sensitivity: The Truth About Environmental Illness, 1998; editor: Consumer Health Digest, 2001—. Trustee Lehigh Valley Opportunity Ctr., 1970—72; mem. com. on health fraud Pa. Health Coun., 1972—74; mem. com. on quackery Pa. Med. Soc., 1972—79; mem. bd. advisors Calif. Coun. Against Health Fraud, Inc., 1977—84; mem. bd. sci. advisors Am. Coun. on Sci. & Health, 1978—; cons. on unproven health practices Pa. Med. Soc. Coun. on Edn. & Sci., 1979—84; sci. cons. Com. for Sci. Investigation of Claims of Paranormal, 1980—; chmn. bd. dir. Quackwatch, Inc., 1970—2008; v.p. Nat. Coun. Against Health Fraud, 2000—11. Recipient Dr. Francis J. Trembley Outstanding Citizen award, Lehigh Valley Dental soc., 1975, FDA Commr.'s Spl. Citation award, 1984, Hon. Lifetime Meml. award, Lehigh Valley Dietetic Assn., 1986, Disting. Svc. to Health Edn. award, Am. Assn. Health Edn., 2001, 15 medals in Nat. internat, swim compitition, 2012—13, Relay All-Am. award, US Masters Swimming, 2012; fellow, Com. Sci. Investigation of Claims of the Paranormal, 1992. Mem.: Am. Dietetic Assn. (life). Achievements include world champion in swimming. Office: Chatham Crossing 118 Knox Way Chapel Hill NC 27517-6080 Home: 287 Rearrington Post Pittsboro NC 27312 Office Phone: 919-533-6009. Business E-Mail: sbinfo@quackwatch.org.*

BARRIENTOS, GONZALO, advertising and public relations executive, state legislator; b. Galveston, Tex., July 20, 1941; m. Emma Serrato; children: Joseph, Angelina, Alicia, Adelita, Veronica. Student, U. Tex. Mem. Tex. Ho. of Reps., 1975-85, Tex. Senate, 1985—, chair com. of the whole on legis. and congl. redistricting, mem. edn. com., mem. fin. com., mem. nominations com.; vice chair natural resources com., others. Mem. nat. bd. Cmtys. in Schs.; chmn. bd. Mexican Am. State Legislators Policy Inst.; cmty. organizer Nat. Urban League; program officer VISTA/Peace Corps; trainer Leadership Inst. for Cmty. Devel., Washington. Recipient Tex. Outstanding Pub. Servants award, Tex. Rehab. Assns. Legislative Excellence award, Austin Groups for the Elderly 1995 Achievement award, Matt Garcia Pub. Svc. award Mexican Am. Legal Def. and Ednl. Fund, 1996; named Outstanding Legislator of Yr., Tex. Pub. Employees Assn. Democrat. Office: PO Box 12068 Austin TX 78711-2068

BARRINGER, PAUL BRANDON, II, lumber company executive; b. Sumter, SC, Aug. 22, 1930; s. Victor Clay and Gertrude (Hampton) B.; m. Merrill Underwood, May 27, 1957; children: Merrill U., Victor Clay, Ann Hampton. BS, U. Va., 1952; postgrad., George Washington U., 1954. With Human Relations Lab., Washington, 1954; with Coastal Forest ResouLces Co., Weldon, NC, 1954—, chmn. bd., CEO, 1967—. Bd. dirs. BB&T Corp., Sea Pines Co., Inc.; mem. Pres.'s Task Force on Internat. Pvt. Enterprise, Industry Policy Adv. Com. for trade policy matters. Mem. coll. bd. trustees U. Va., 1995-96; trustee U. Va. Found. With USAF, 1952-54. Mem.: NAM (bd. dirs.), Chief Execs. Orgn. (dir.), Farmington Country Coub, Sea Pines Country Club, Chockoyotte Country Club, Lamda Chi, Sigma Delta Psi, Zeta Psi. Episcopalian. Home: 15 S Calibogue Cay Rd Hilton Head Island SC 29928-2912 Office: Coastal Lumber Co PO Box 829 Weldon NC 27890-0829

BARRINGTON, DON, state legislator; b. Pryor, Okla., Sept. 7, 1947; s. Burt and Lura; m. Jennifer Barrington, Feb. 7, 1970; children: Alicia, Gary. A in Engring. Tech., Okla. State U., 1993. Various positions as firefighter, Lawton, 1969—96; fire chief, 1996—2002; mem. Dist. 31 Okla. State Senate, 2004—. Sgt. US Army, 1966—69. Mem.: Lawton Salvation Army Adv. Bd., Gideon's Internat. (sec. 1996—99, v.p. 1999—2001), Lawton Rotary West (bd. mem. 1996—2000, pres. 1999—2000), Okla. Fire Chief's Assn., Okla. Retired Firefighters Assn., Okla. State Firefighters Assn. Republican. Southern Baptist. Mailing: 4506 NE Highlander Cir Lawton OK 73507 Office: 2300 N Lincoln Bldg Rm 515 Oklahoma City OK 73105 Office Phone: 405-521-5563. Fax: 405-521-5573. Business E-Mail: barrington@oksenate.gov.

BARRINGTON, MARTIN J., tobacco company executive; b. Albany, NY, July 16, 1953; BA, Coll. St. Rose, 1977; JD, Albany U., 1980. Bar: N.Y. 1981, Va. 1982. Law clk. U.S. Ct. Appeals (4th cir.), 1980-82; assoc. Hunton & Williams, 1982-89, ptnr., 1990-93; sr. v.p., gen. counsel Philip Morris USA & Philip Morris Internat., NYC; exec. v.p. corp. responsibility Philip Morris USA; exec. v.p., chief adminstrv. officer, chief compliance officer Altria Group Inc., vice-chmn. innovation, pub. affairs, human resources & compliance, 2011—12, chmn., CEO, 2012—. Adj. asst. prof. employment discrimination law U. Richmond, 1988-89. Notes and comments editor Albany Law Rev., 1979-80. Past commr. Va. Port Authority; trustee Coll. St. Rose, Va. Mus. Fine Arts. Mem. ABA (mem. labor and employment sect., com. for devel. of law under NLRA), Justinian Soc. Office: Altria Group Inc 6601 W Broad St Richmond VA 23230

BARRITT, EVELYN RUTH BERRYMAN, nurse, educator, dean; b. Detroit, Sept. 4, 1929; d. George C. and Ruby (Mathews) Berryman; m. Ward LeRoy Barritt, Oct. 28, 1951; 1 dau., Kelli Jo. AA, Graceland Coll., 1949; diploma, Independence Sanitarium and Hosp. Sch. Nursing, Mo., 1952; BSN., Ohio State U., 1956, MA, 1962, PhD, 1971. Asst. instr. nursing Atlantic City Hosp., 1952-53; staff nurse Shore Meml. Hosp., Somers Point, NJ, 1953-54, Ohio State U. Hosp., Columbus, 1954-55; instr. White Cross Hosp., Columbus, 1955-57; asso. dir. nursing service Riverside Meth. Hosp., Columbus, 1957-64; asst. exec. dir. Ohio Nurses Assn., Columbus, 1964-65; dean Capital U. Sch. Nursing, Columbus, 1965-72, Coll. Nursing, U. Iowa, Iowa City, 1972-79, prof. nursing, 1972-80; prof. Sch. Nursing U. Miami, Fla., 1980—, dean Fla., 1980-85. Bd. dirs. Health Coun. South Fla., 1988—, pres., 1990-92; bd. dirs. So. Fla. Perinatal Network, Inc., 1980-89, pres., 1984-86; mem. Fla. Bd. Ind. and Pvt. Colls. and Univs., 1980; co-chmn. Dade County Indigent Care Task Force, 1991-93. Author: Florence Nightingale: Her Wit and Wisdom, 1975; author, editor: Thoughts on CareGiving, 1998; contbr. articles to profl. jours. Mem. ANA, Ohio Nurses Assn. (pres. dist. 1966-68), Iowa Nurses Assn., Fla. Nurses Assn., Graceland Univ. Alumni Assn., Am. Assn. Higher Edn., Am. Assn. Colls. Nursing (pres. 1976-78). Home: 416 Park Blvd N Venice FL 34285-1332

BARRON, ARNOLD S., retired retail executive; BA in Math., Boston U., 1969. With TJX Companies, Inc., 1979, various store operation positions, 1979—84, sr. v.p., dir., stores, 1984—93, sr. v.p., gen. merchandising mgr., TJ Maxx divsn., 1993—96, sr. v.p., group exec., 1996—2000, exec. v.p., COO, Marmaxx Group, 2000—04, sr. exec. v.p., group pres., 2004—09. Bd. dirs. Dollar Tree, Inc., 2008—, rue 21, inc., 2009—. Office: Dollar Tree Inc Bd Directors 500 Volvo Pkwy Chesapeake VA 23320 Office Phone: 757-321-5000. Office Fax: 757-321-5111. Business E-Mail: arnold.barron@dollartree.com.

BARRON, BRADLEY C., energy executive; Counsel, sr. counsel Valero Energy, 2001—03; sr. counsel, refining and procurement NuStar GP, LLC (formerly Valero GP LLC), 2003—06, mng. counsel, corp. sec., 2003—06, v.p., 2006—07; gen. counsel NuStar GP, LLC, 2006—, sr. v.p., 2007—; sec. NuStar Energy LP, 2006—; sec., gen. counsel NuStar GP Holdings, LLC, 2006—, sr. v.p., 2007—. Office: NuStar Energy LP 19003 W Interstate 10 San Antonio TX 78257-9518 Office Phone: 210-918-2000. Office Fax: 210-918-5057. Business E-Mail: bradley.barron@nustarenergy.com.

BARRON, ERIC JAMES, academic administrator, geophysicist, educator; b. Lafayette, Ind., Oct. 26, 1951; married; 2 children. BS, Fla. State U., 1973; MS, U. Miami, 1976, PhD in Geophysics, 1980. Fellow Nat. Ctr. Atmospheric Rsch. (NCAR), Boulder, Colo., 1980—81, rsch. scientist global climate modeling, dir.; assoc. prof. marine geology and geophysics U. Miami, 1985—86; dir. Earth Sys. Sci. Ctr. Coll. Earth and Mineral Scis., Pa. State U., State College, 1986, prof. geosciences, 1989, dir. Environ. Inst., 1998, disting. prof., 1999, dean, 2002—06, Jackson Sch. Geosciences, U. Tex., Austin, 2006—; pres. Fla. State U., Tallahassee, 2009—. Fellow: AAAS, Nat. Inst. Environ. Sci., Cambridge U., Am. Meteorological Soc., Am. Geophysical Union; mem.: Assn. Am. Geographers, Soc. Econ. Paleontologists and Mineralogists, Geol. Soc. Am. Office: Florida State University Office of President 600 W College Ave Tallahassee FL 32306 Office Phone: 850-644-1085. E-mail: ebarron@fsu.edu.*

BARRON, RANDALL FRANKLIN, mechanical engineer, educator, consultant; b. Many, La., May 16, 1936; s. Benjamin Franklin and Inez (Norseworthy) B.; m. Shirley Estelle McDuffie, Mar. 14, 1958; children: Randall Franklin Jr., Donna Carol, Steven Dale, Brian Richard. BS, La. Tech U., 1958; MS, Ohio State U., 1961, PhD, 1964. Registered profl. engr., La. Instr. mech. engring. Ohio State U., Columbus, 1958-64, asst. prof., 1965; assoc. prof. La. Tech U., Ruston, 1965-70, prof., 1970-97, prof. emeritus, 1997—. Engring. cons. Riley-Beaird, Inc., Shreveport, La., 1966-86; mem. La. State Bd. Registration for Profl. Engrs. and Land Surveyors, 1989-94, chmn. bd., 1992-93. Author: Cryogenic Systems, 1985, Cryogenic Heat Transfer, 1999, Industrial Noise Control and Acoustics, 2003, Design for Thermal Stresses, 2011; contbr. articles to profl. jours. Recipient Engring. and Sci. Coun. Profl. Achievement award, 1981; Phi Kappa Phi scholar, 1982. Fellow ASME (Nat. Profl. Devel. lectr. in cryogenics 1988-99); mem. Cryogenic Soc. Am., Am. Soc. for Engring. Edn., Kiwanis, Sigma Xi, Tau Beta Pi, Pi Tau Sigma (Gold medal 1968). Republican. Methodist. Office: La Tech U Mech Engring Dept PO Box 10348 Ruston LA 71272-0001 Office Phone: 318-255-6500. E-mail: rbarron@bayou.com.

BARROS, PAULINO R., JR., communications executive; b. Sao Paulo, Brazil; Degree in Mech. & Elec. Engring.; attended, Escola De Engenharia Indsl. de S.J.Campos, 1978; MBA, Wash. U., 1991. Various positions Nutrasweet Co., Monsanto Co., Brazil; corp. v.p., Latin Am. group personal comm. Motorola, Inc., 1996—2000; pres., Latin Am. Group BellSouth, 2000—04, chief product officer, 2005—06; pres., global ops. AT&T Corp., 2007—. Named one of 50 Most Important Hispanics in Tech. & Bus., Hispanic Engr. & Info. Tech. mag., 2005. Office: AT&T Corp 175 E Houston St Dallas TX 78205-2255 Office Phone: 210-821-4105.

BARROW, JOHN JENKINS, United States Representative from Georgia, lawyer; b. Athens, Ga., Oct. 31, 1955; s. James and Phyllis (Jenkins) B.; m. Victoria Pentlarge, Dec. 19, 1953; children: James, Ruth. AB, U. Ga., 1976; JD, Harvard U., 1979. Bar: Ga., US Dist. Ct. (no. and mid. dists.) Ga., US Ct. Appeals (11th cir.), US Ct. Appeals (5th cir.). Clk. to Hon. Tom Clark US Ct. Appeals, Tampa, Fla., 1979-81; assoc. Winburn & Assocs., Athens, Ga., 1981-83; ptnr. Winburn, Lewis Barrow & Stolz, PC, Athens, Ga., 1983—2004; mem. US Congress from 12th Ga. dist., 2005—, mem. edu. and workforce com., agriculture com. & small bus. com., ranking mem. subcom. on rural enterprise, agriculture, and tech. Mem. rev. panel State Bar Disciplinary Bd., 1997-99; mem. Ga. Com. on Continuing Lawyer Competency, 1984-87. Commr. Athens-Clarke County Commn., Athens, 1990-2004. Mem. Ga. Trial Lawyers Assn., Assn. Trial Lawyers Am. Democrat. Baptist. Avocations: politics, tennis, backpacking, sports. Office: US House of Representatives 2202 Rayburn House Office Bldg Washington DC 20515 also: Ste G 400 Mall Blvd Savannah GA 31406 Office Phone: 202-225-2823. Office Fax: 202-225-3377.*

BARROW, REGINA ASHFORD, state legislator; b. June 14, 1966; Legislature asst. to Rep. Sharon Broome; mem. state dir. Women In Govt.; mem. Dist 29 La. House of Reps., 2005—, chair mcpl., parochial and cultural affairs com., mem. health and welfare com. Recipient Baton Rouge Bus. Report Top 40 under 40, YWCA Young Women of Achievment award. Mem.: America Legislature Exch. Cou (ALEC), Nat. Caucus of Environ. Legislators (NCEL), Nat. Conf. of State Legislators(NSCL). Democrat. Non Demonational. Mailing: State Capitol 900 N Third St, PO Box 94062 Baton Rouge LA 70804 Office: 3552 Monterrey Dr Baton Rouge LA 70814 Office Phone: 225-342-7259. Fax: 225-359-9336. E-mail: larep029@legis.state.la.us.

BARROW, THOMAS DAVIES, retired oil and mining company executive, consultant; b. San Antonio, Dec. 27, 1924; s. Leonidas Theodore and Laura Editha (Thomson) B.; m. Janice Meredith Hood, Sept. 16, 1950; children: Theodore Hood, Kenneth Thomson, Barbara Loyd, Elizabeth Ann BS, U. Tex., 1945, MA, 1948; PhD, Stanford U., 1953; grad. advanced mgmt. program, Harvard U., 1963. With Humble Oil & Refining Co., 1951-72, regional exploration mgr. New Orleans, 1962-64, sr. v.p., 1966—70, pres., 1970-72, also bd. dirs.; exec. v.p. Esso Exploration, Inc., 1964-65; sr. v.p. Exxon Corp., NYC, 1972-78; chmn., CEO Kennecott Corp., Stamford, Conn., 1978-81; vice chmn. Std. Oil Co., Ohio, 1981-85; investment cons. Houston, 1985-89; chmn. GX Tech., Houston, 1990—2004; pres. Thomson-Barrow, 1989—2005; sr. chmn., bd. dir. GeoQuest Internat. Holdings, Inc., Houston, 1990-97; pres. Tecolotita, Inc., 1991—2005, T-BAR-X, Houston, 1995—2005; ret. Chmn. bd. dirs. GPS Tech. Corp., Houston, 1986—98, Petroleum Info./Dwights, 1994—97, Tobin Internat., 1998—2003; mem. commn. on natural resources NRC, 1973—78, commn. on phys. sci., math. and natural resources, 1984—87, bd. on earth scis., 1982—84; trustee Woods Hole Oceanog. Instn., 20th Century Fund-Task Force on U.S. Energy Policy. Pres. Houston Grand Opera, 1985-87, chmn., 1987-91; trustee Am. Mus. Natural History, 1972-82, Stanford U., 1980-90, Tex. Med. Ctr., 1983—, Geol. Soc. Am. Found., 1982-87; trustee Baylor Coll. Medicine, 1984—, vice chmn bd. trustees, 1991-99. Served to ensign USNR, 1943—46. Recipient Disting. Achievement award Offshore Tech. Conf., 1973,

Disting. Engring. Grad. award U. Tex., 1970, Disting. Alumnus, 1982, Disting. Geology Grad., 1985, Disting. Natural Sci. Grad., 1990; named Chief Exec. of Yr. in Mining Industry, Fin. World, 1979. Fellow NY Acad. Scis.; mem. NAE, Am. Mining Congress (bd. dirs. 1979-85, vice chmn. 1983-85), Am. Assn. Petroleum Geologists, Geol. Soc. Am., Internat. Copper Rsch. Assn. (bd. dirs. 1979-85), Nat. Ocean Industry Assn. (bd. dirs. 1982-85), AAAS, Am. Soc. Oceanography (pres. 1970-71), Am. Geophys. Union, Am. Petroleum Inst., Am. Geog. Soc., Houston Country Club, The Hills Club, Petroleum Club, River Oaks Country Club, Houston Club, Sigma Xi, Tau Beta Pi, Sigma Gamma Epsilon, Phi Eta Sigma, Alpha Tau Omega Episcopalian.

BARROWS, FRANK CLEMENCE, journalist; b. Lewes, Del., Nov. 2, 1946; m. Mary S. Newsom, Nov. 16, 1985; 1 child, Margaret S. BA, St. Andrews Coll., Laurinburg, NC, 1968; postgraduate study in Polit. Sci., U. Va., 1969. Reporter, columnist Charlotte Observer, NC, 1969-72, 76-81, asst. sports editor, 1981-82, asst. met. editor, 1982-83, exec. sports editor, 1983-84, 86, dep. features editor, 1985, dep. met. editor, 1986-87, asst. mng. editor, 1987-88, dep. mng. editor, 1988-92, mng. editor, 1992—2005; exec. editor Bus. NC, 2006—07; affiliate Neiman Found. Harvard U., 2007—08. Instr. Queens U., 2011. Contbr. articles to mags. Pres. NC Open Govt. Coalition, 2004—05; bd. dirs. Charlotte Trolley, 2006—. Recipient Reporting awards, NC Press Assn., 1972—80, Pulitzer Prize medal for Pub. Svc. (co-editor), 1988, Ethel Fortner Writer and Cmty. award, 2000. Mem.: Soc. Prof. Journalists (pres. Charlotte chpt. 2011—), Online News Assn., Investigative Reporters and Editors, Am. Soc. News Editors. Office Phone: 704-576-3485. Personal E-mail: fcbarrows@aol.com.

BARRY, BRENT ROBERT, sportscaster, former professional basketball player; b. Hempstead, NY, Dec. 31, 1971; s. Rick Barry and Pamela Hale; m. Erin Barry; children: Quinn, Cade. BA in Sociology, Oreg. State U., Corvallis, 1995. Guard LA Clippers, 1995—98, Miami Heat, 1998, Chgo. Bulls, 1998—99, Seattle Supersonics, 1999—2004, San Antonio Spurs, 2004—08, Houston Rockets, 2008—09; studio analyst NBA TV, 2009—. Active NBA Read to Achieve Program, Blue Ribbon Child Abuse Task Force, San Antonio. Achievements include winning the Nestle Slam-Dunk Competition, 1996; being a member of the NBA Championship winning San Antonio Spurs, 2005, 2007. Avocations: video collecting, golf. Office: NBA TV 1065 Williams St NW Atlanta GA 30309

BARRY, DAVE, columnist, writer; b. Armonk, NY, July 3, 1947; m. Beth Barry, 1976 (div. 1993); 1 child, Robert; m. Michelle Kaufman, 1996; 1 child, Sophie. BA in English, Haverford Coll., Pa., 1969. Reporter, editor West Chester Daily Local News, Pa., 1971-75; with cons. firm Burger Assocs., 1975; columnist The Miami Herald, Fla., 1983—2005, contbg. columnist, 2005—. Author: (non-fiction) Taming of the Screw: Several Million Homeowners' Problems Sidestepped, 1983, Babies and Other Hazards of Sex: How to Make a Tiny Person in Only 9 Months With Tools You Probably Have Around the Home, 1984, Bad Habits: A One Hundred Percent Fact Free Book, 1985, Stay Fit and Healthy Until You're Dead, 1985, Claw Your Way to the Top: How to Become the Head of a Major Corporation in Roughly a Week, 1986, Dave Barry's Guide to Marriage and/or Sex, 1987, Homes and Other Black Holes, 1988, Dave Barry Slept Here: A Sort of History of the United States, 1989, Dave Barry Turns 40, 1990, Dave Barry's Only Travel Guide You'll Ever Need, 1991, Dave Barry's Guide to Life, 1991, Dave Barry Does Japan, 1992, Dave Barry's Gift Guide to End All Gift Guides, 1994, Dave Barry's Complete Guide to Guys, 1995, Dave Barry in Cyberspace, 1996, Dave Barry's Book of Bad Songs, 1997, Dave Barry Turns 50, 1998, My Teenage Son's Goal in Life is to Make Me Feel 3,500 Years Old' and Other Thoughts on Parenting from Dave Barry, 2001, Dave Barry Hits Below the Beltway: A Vicious and Unprovoked Attack on Our Most Cherished Political Institutions, 2001, The Greatest Invention in the History of Mankind is Beer And Other Manly Insights From Dave Barry, 2001, Dave Barry's Money Secrets: Like: Why Is There a Giant Eyeball on the Dollar?, 2006, Dave Barry's History of the Millennium (So Far), 2007, (collected columns) Dave Barry's Bad Habits: A 100% Fact-Free Book, 1987, Dave Barry's Greatest Hits, 1988, Dave Barry Talks Back, 1991, The World According to Dave Barry, 1994, Dave Barry Is Not Making This Up, 1995, Dave Barry Is from Mars and Venus, 1997, Dave Barry is Not Taking This Sitting Down, 2000, Dave Barry: Boogers Are My Beat, 2003, (fiction) Big Trouble, 1999, Tricky Business, 2002, The Shepherd, the Angel, and Walter the Christmas Miracle Dog, 2006; co-author: Mid-Life Confidential: The Rock Bottom Remainders Tour America With Three Chords and an Attitude, 1994, Naked Came the Manatee, 1998; co-author: (with Ridley Pearson) (children's books) Peter and the Starcatchers, 2004, Peter and the Shadow Thieves, 2006, Escape from the Carnivale, 2006, Peter and the Secret of Rundoon, 2007. Recipient Disting. Writing award, Soc. Newspaper Editors, 1987, Pulitzer prize for Commentary, 1988; co-recipient Nat. Journalism award for Investigative Reporting, Scripps Howard Found., 2008. Office: Miami Herald 1 Herald Plz Miami FL 33132-1693

BARRY, DENNIS ROBERT, hospital administrator; b. Chgo., Nov. 1, 1939; married BA, U. Ill., 1961; MA, U. Chgo., 1965. Asst. administr. Evanston (Ill.) Hosp., 1965, administrv. res., 1964-65, dir. patient svcs., 1965-68, dir. mktg., planning, 1968-70; v.p. planning, devel. Samaritan HealthSvcs., Phoenix, 1970-72; administrv. dir. N.C. Meml. Hosp., Chapel Hill, 1972-75, dir. gen. svcs., 1975-80; pres. and ceo Moses H. Cone Meml. Hosp., Greensboro, N.C., 1980—. Office: Moses H Cone Meml Hosp 1200 N Elm St Greensboro NC 27401-1020

BARRY, FRANCIS JULIAN, JR., lawyer; b. New Orleans, Oct. 7, 1949; s. Francis Julian and Bertha Anna (Lion) B.; m. Janice Leigh Gonzales, May 8, 1976; children: Francis III, Marianna. BA, Tulane U., 1970, JD, 1973. Bar: La. 1973, U.S. Dist. Ct. (ea. dist.) La. 1973, U.S. Ct. Appeals (5th cir.) 1973, U.S. Dist. Ct. (we. dist.) La. 1978, U.S. Ct. Appeals (11th cir.) 1982, U.S. Supreme Ct. 1991. Assoc. Deutsch, Kerrigan & Stiles, New Orleans, 1973-78, ptnr., 1978—. Editor Admiralty Law Inst. Symposium Tulane U., New Orleans, 1973. Adv. editor Tulane Maritime Law Jour. (formerly The Maritime Lawyer), 1975—. Served to capt. USAR. Mem. Fed. Bar Assn., La. Bar Assn. (house of del. 2009-), New Orleans Bar Assn., Maritime Law Assn. U.S. (proctor, carriage of goods com. 1982-, com. offshore industries 2004—, com. marine ins. and gen. average 2004—), Admiralty Law Inst. New Orleans (mem. planning com. 1998—, mem. program com. 2000—, chmn. program com. 2004—), U.S. Naval Inst., Southeastern Admiralty Law Inst., La. Assn. Def. Counsel, Def. Rsch. Inst., Assn. Average Adjusters London, Assn. Average Adjusters U.S., Am. Legion, Mil. Order of Fgn. War US, Navy League U.S., Army-Navy Club (Washington), Bienville Club, Univ. Club (N.Y.C.), Mariners Club, The Round Table Club., La. Hist. Soc., La. Landmarks Soc. Republican. Roman Catholic. Home: 4301 Dumaine St New Orleans LA 70119-3617 Home Phone: 504-488-2842.

BARRY, JOYCE ALICE, dietician, consultant; b. Chgo., Apr. 27, 1932; d. Walter Stephen and Ethel Myrtle (Paetow) B. Student, Iowa State Coll., 1950—52, Loyola U., 1952—58; BS, Mundelein Coll., 1955; postgrad., Simmons Coll., 1963—64, U. Ga., 1979, Calif. We. U., 1980. Registered dietitian. Prodn. supr. Marshall Field & Co., Chgo., 1955-59; dir. food svcs. Women's Ednl. and Indsl. Union, Boston, 1959-62, Wellesley Pub. Schs., Mass., 1962-70; regional dietitian Canteen Corp., Chgo., 1970-83; gen. mgr. bus. devel. Plantation-Sysco, Orlando, Fla., 1983-87; dir. product devel., corp. quality assurance, procurement Marriott Internat. Hdqrs., Washington, 1987-95; owner food svc. cons. svc., 1995—. Cons. Stokes Food Svcs., Newton, Mass., 1960-70; vis. lectr. Affiliate Produce for Better Health Found. Mem.: AAUW, Nutrition in Complementary Care, Nat. Assn. Female Execs., Nat. Hist. Trust, Sch. Nutrition Svcs., Am. Dietetics Assn. (career adv. cons.), Food and Culinary Profls., Dietitians in Bus. and Comm., Smithsonian Instn. (assoc.), Washington Opera Guild, Met. Opera Guild. Republican. Roman Catholic. Home and Office: 1009 Pearce Dr Apt 101 Clearwater FL 33764-1107 Office Phone: 727-669-6454. Personal E-mail: joyce4374@yahoo.com.

BARRY, LANCE LEONARD, primary examiner; b. Boston, Dec. 18, 1965; s. Leonard and Theodora Ann Pawlak. BEE, Cath. U. Am., 1988; MS, Johns Hopkins U., 1991; JD, George Mason U., 1995. Bar: Va. 1995, U.S. Ct. Appeals (fed. cir.) 1995, bar: D.C. 1998. Engring. analyst RCI Internat., Vienna, Va., 1987; engring. aide MPR Assocs., Washington, 1987; engring. technician BBN Labs., Arlington, Va., 1988; cons. Booz, Allen & Hamilton, Bethesda, Md., 1988-90, sr. cons., 1990—91; patent examiner U.S. Patent and Trademark Office, Arlington, Va., 1991-95, primary examiner, 1996-99; adminstrv. patent judge US Patent and Trademark Office, Arlington, Va., 1999—2012, primary examiner, 2012—. Pub. adv. com. mem. Lawyers Coop. Pub., Raleigh, NC, 1995; spkr. Va. State Bar, Richmond, 1998—; instr. US Patent and Trademark Office, Arlington, 1996—97, curriculum com., 1999—2005, law lectr., 1997—99, 2005—06, EEO counselor, 1999; substitute law prof. George Mason U., 2005—06. Contbr. articles to profl. jours. Head tutor St. Francis Xavier Sch., Washington, 1997-2001; cmty. svc. v.p. St. Mary's Ch., Alexandria, Va., 2001, Am. Inn Ct., 2011-; vol. Greater DC Cares, Washington, 1999-2002; social officer Holy Trinity Ch., Washington, 1997-98; tutor kids and chemistry program Am. Chem. Soc., 2002-; lector Our Lady of Lourdes Ch., 2002-03, St. Rita Ch., 2010-; vol. Alexandria Christmas in April, 2000-03, house capt., 2003, Camp Invention, 2004. Mem. KC, Am. Intellectual Property Law Assn., Am. Inn of Ct., Patent and Trademark Office Soc. (rep. 1996-98), Usher, St. Rita Ch., Mensa, Phi Theta Kappa, Tau Beta Pi. Avocations: reading, weight-lifting, travel, sports, crossword puzzles. Office: US Patent and Trademark Office PO Box 1450 Alexandria VA 22313-1450

BARRY, RICHARD FRANCIS, III, retired media executive; b. Norfolk, Va., Jan. 18, 1943; s. Richard F. and Mary Margaret (Perry) B.; m. Carolyn Ann Kennett, Aug. 7, 1965; children: Carolyn Michelle, Christopher David. BA, LaSalle Coll., 1964; JD, U. Va., 1967. Bar: Va. 1967. Assoc. Kaufman, Oberndorfer & Spainhour (now Kaufman and Canoles), Norfolk, 1967-71, ptnr., 1972-73; corp. sec. Landmark Media Enterprises LLC (Formerly Landmark Comm., Inc.), Norfolk, 1973—74; pres., COO, dir. Landmark Comm., Inc., Norfolk, 1978—84, CEO, 1984-91, vice chmn., 1991—; pres. Roanoke Times & World-News, Va., 1974-76, The Virginian-Pilot and The Ledger-Star, Norfolk, 1976-78, pub., 1983-90. Bd. dirs. Dominion Enterprises, Greensboro News and Record, Inc., Times World Corp., Capital Gazette Newspapers Inc. Trustee or past trustee Norfolk Acad., Chrysler Mus., U. Va. Colgate Darden Bus. Sch. Found., Cath. H.S. Found., Old Dominion Univ. Ednl. Found., Suffolk Ctr. for Cultural Arts, Mariners' Museum, Obici Healthcare Found.; bd. dirs., past pres., campaign chmn. United Way of South Hampton Rds.; bd. visitors, past rector Old Dominion U., co-chmn. capital campaign Office: 7900 World Trade Ctr Norfolk VA 23510

BARSAM, JEANNIE, retail executive; BSBA in Mktg., Calif. State U., Fresno. With Gottchalk's Dept. Store; with merchandising and planning Mervyn's Dept. Store, Lane Bryant Dept. Stores; v.p. mdse. planning and allocation Gap Inc.; sr. v.p. planning, allocation and co. planning Charlotte Rouse; sr. v.p. inventory mgmt. and merchandise sys. Talbots Inc., 2007; sr. v.p. mdse. planning and allocation Zale Corp., 2011—. Office: Zale Corporation 901 W Walnut Hill Lane Irving TX 75038-1003 Office Phone: 972-580-4000.

BARTEL, HERBERT HERMAN, JR., retired engineering educator; b. Dallas, Mar. 31, 1924; s. Herbert Herman and Freda (Metzger) B.; m. Dorothy Jean Angus, July 19, 1950; children: Peggy Jean and Kathy Jean (twins). BS in Civil Engring., So. Meth. U., 1944; MS, U. Tex., 1950; PhD, Tex. A&M U., 1962. From instr. to prof., chmn. dept. civil and environmental engring. So. Meth. U., Dallas, 1946-72; chmn. dept. civil engring. U. El Paso, Tex., 1972-78, prof., 1972-90, prof. emeritus, 1990—2008. Design engr. Tex. Hwy. Dept., summer 1953, Forrest & Cotton, Inc., summers 1967-68 Commr. Boy Scouts Am., 1952-55; vol. minister Coronado Christian Ch., El Paso, 1990—. Served as ensign C.E.C., USNR, 1943-46, PTO. NSF faculty fellow, 1960-61; Automotive Safety Found. fellow, 1958-59; recipient Excellence in Engring. Teaching award Gen. Dynamics Corp., 1969 Mem. ASCE, Nat. Soc. Profl. Engrs., Tex. Soc. Profl. Engrs. (Outstanding C.E. Faculty Mem. 1982, Engr. of Year award El Paso br. 1973, dir. El Paso br.) Home: 5801 Kingsfield St El Paso TX 79912-4815

BARTELS, JEAN ELLEN, nursing educator; b. Two Rivers, Wis., July 15, 1949; m. Terry D. Bartels, Aug. 14, 1971; children: Justin Dean, Ashlee Jill. Diploma, Columbia Hosp. Sch. Nursing, 1970; BSN with honors, Alverno Coll., Milw., 1981; MSN, Marquette U., Milw., 1983; PhD in Nursing, U. Wis., Milw., 1990. Staff nurse ICU Columbia Hosp., Milw., 1970-76; prof. nursing Alverno Coll., Milw., 1983-99, dean nursing, 1990-99; chair Sch. Nursing Ga. So. U., Statesboro, 1999—, prof. nursing, 1999, clin. nurse leader, 2007—; chair Sch. Nursing, 1999—2010, Coll. Health & Human Scis., 2010; v.p. Academic Affairs & Provost, 2010—. Contbr. articles to profl. jours. Mem.: AACN (past pres.), ANA, Am. Ednl. Rsch. Assn., Am. Assn. Colls. Nursing, Internat. Soc. for Sci. Study Subjectivity, Mu Kappa, Sigma Theta Tau. Home: 912 Brittany Ln Statesboro GA 30461-4499 Office: Ga So U PO Box 8158 Statesboro GA 30460-1000 Office Phone: 912-478-5455. E-mail: jbartels@georgiasouthern.edu.

BARTELS, TERESA HALL, non-profit organization administrator; m. Chuck Bartels; 5 children. BS, Northern Ariz. U.; MSOL, Dominican U. Assoc. regional dir., Mid-Am. region United Way Am., 1982; assoc. campaign and comm. dir. United Way, Lake County, Ill.; owner Manpower Inc.; owner, pres. Hallbart Holdings, LLC., Mundelein, Ill.; pres., CEO United Way Internat., 2007—. Vol. United Way, 1985—; vice chair of bd., chair personnel com. United Way Internat. Vice chair of bd., chair devel. com., mem. capital campaign com. Carmel High Sch.; founding chair Univ. Ctr. Lake County. Office: United Way Internat HQ 701 N Fairfax St Alexandria VA 22314-2045

BARTH, CARIN MARCY, private equity firm executive, former federal agency administrator; b. 1963; BS in Economics summa cum laude, U. Ala.; MBA, Vanderbilt U., 1986. Founder, pres. LB Capital, Inc., Houston, 1987—; CFO US Dept. Housing & Urban Devel., Washington, 2004—06; interim sr. v.p. fin. & adminstrn. Tex. Southern U., 2006—07. Bd. dirs. Western Refining, Inc., 2006—, Encore Bancshares, Inc., 2009—. Bd. regents Texas Tech U., 1999—2005, endowment chair, 2006—; bd. dirs. Methodist Hosp. Rsch. Inst., Ronald McDonald House of Houston; commr. Tex. Dept. Pub. Safety, 2008—. Office: LB Capital Inc PO Box 56048 Houston TX 77256

BARTH, DANNY, professional sports team executive; married; 2 children. Grad., Seattle U. With audit divsn. Price Waterhouse, LLC, Seattle and NYC; dir. fin. and acctg. Cinnabon, Inc.; v.p. fin., contr. Seattle SuperSonics, 1996—2000, exec. v.p., CFO, 2000—06; interim pres., CEO Profl. Basketball Club, LLC (parent co. of NBA Oklahoma City Thunder and WNBA Seattle Storm), Oklahoma City, 2006—08, exec. v.p., chief adminstrv. officer, 2008—. Office: Profl Basketball Club LLC Two Leadership Sq 211 N Robinson Ave Ste 300 Oklahoma City OK 73102

BARTH, ELIZABETH ANNE, former aide; b. Bluefield, W.Va. m. Nick Barth; children: Sally, Claire. BJ, W.Va. U., M in Comm. Sr. aide Senator Robert C. Byrd, 1987—2008, state dir., 1992—2008. Democrat. Office: PO Box 2151 Charleston WV 25328

BARTHEL, WILLIAM FREDERICK, JR., electrical engineer; b. Washington, July 14, 1940; s. William Frederick and Eva (Buday) Barthel; m. Barbara Joan Adams, Nov. 18, 1961; 1 child, William Frederick III. BS, McNeese State U., 1972. Shop mgr. Electronic Unltd., Lake Charles, La., 1968; engr. quality control Rockwell Internat., Cedar Rapids, Iowa, 1974—79, mgr. quality assurance, 1979, sr. engring. scientist, process control devel., 1980—81; engring. mgr. process reliability Digital Equipment Corp., Andover, Mass., 1981—87, engring. mgr. performance assurance, 1987—91; dir. quality Gables Engring., Inc., Coral Gables, Fla., 1991—93, v.p. ops., 1993—2008. With USAF, 1958—62. Mem.: Am. Inst. Chemists, Am. Chem. Soc. Republican. Home: 745 SE 25th Ln Homestead FL 33033-5234 Office: Gables Engring Inc 247 Greco Ave Miami FL 33146-1808

BARTHOLOMAY, WILLIAM C., insurance brokerage company and professional sports team executive; b. Evanston, Ill., Aug. 11, 1928; s. Henry C. and Virginia (Graves) B.; m. Sara Taylor, 1950, (div. 1964); children: Virginia, William T., Jamie, Elizabeth, Sara; m. Gail Dillingham, May 1968 (div. Apr. 1980). Student, Oberlin Coll., 1946-49, Northwestern U., 1949-50; BA, Lake Forest Coll., 1955. Ptnr. Bartholomay & Clarkson, Chgo., 1951-63; v.p. Alexander & Alexander, Chgo., 1963-65; pres. Olson & Bartholomay, Chgo. and Atlanta, 1965-69; sr. v.p. Frank B. Hall & Co. Inc., NYC and Chgo., 1969-72, exec. v.p., 1972-73, pres., 1973-74, vice chmn., 1974—91; chmn. bd., dir. Atlanta Braves, 1966—2004, chmn. emeritus, 2004—; pres. Near North Nat. Group, 1991—2003; vice chmn., chmn. exec. com. Turner Broadcasting Sys., Inc., Atlanta, 2001—; vice chmn. Willis Group Holdings (NYSE), Chgo., 2003—. Bd. dirs. Exec. Coun. Maj. League Baseball, Maj. League Baseball Players Pension Plan; dir. emeritus WMS Industries, Inc., Chgo., 2005—. Commr. Chgo. Park Dist., 1980-2002, Chgo. Pub. Bldg. Commn., 1989-2003; bd. dirs. past trustee Chgo. Maternity Ctr., Lincoln Park Zool. Soc., Mus. Sci. and Industry, Chgo., Ill. Inst. of Tech.; past trustee Lake Forest (Ill.) Coll., Ogelthorpe Coll., Atlanta, Marymount Manhattan Coll., NY With USNR, 1951-54. Mem. Chief Execs. Orgn., World Pres.'s Orgn., Chgo. Pres.'s Orgn., Nat. Assn. CLU, Chgo. Assn. CLU, Chgo. Club, Racquet Club, Saddle and Cycle Club, Econ. Club, Onwentsia Club, Shoreacres Club (Lake Forest), Brook Club, Racquet & Tennis Club (NYC), Piedmont Driving Club, Atlanta Country Club, Peachtree Golf Club, Commerce Club, Old Elm, Pine Valley, Everglades Club. Episcopalian. Home: 180 E Pearson St Chicago IL 60611-2130 also: Atlanta Braves PO Box 4064 Atlanta GA 30302-4064 Office: Willis Tower 233 S Wacker Dr Ste 2000 Chicago IL 60606 Home (Summer): 433 Brazilian Ave Palm Beach FL 33480

BARTHOLOMEW, KEVIN, food service executive; BA in English, Northwestern Louisiana State U., 1984, BS in Zoology, 1984. Joined Ben E. Keith Co., 1984, gen. mgr., Palestine, 1986, gen. mgr. Albania, 1991—93, 1997, v.p., sales & ops., 1999—2000, pres., Beverage Divsn. Office: Ben E Keith Co 601 E 7th St Fort Worth TX 76102-5501 Office Phone: 817-877-5700. Office Fax: 817-338-1701. Business E-Mail: kevenbartholomew@benekeith.com.

BARTLETT, BRUCE REEVES, writer; b. Ann Arbor, Oct. 11, 1951; s. Frank and Majorie (Stern) Bartlett. BA, Rutgers U., 1973; MA, Georgetown U., 1976. Legis. asst. Rep. Ron Paul US House of Representatives, Washington, 1976, spl. asst. to Rep. Jack Kemp, 1977-78; chief legis. asst. to Senator Roger Jepsen US Senate, Washington, 1979-80; dep. dir. Joint Econ. Com., US Congress, Washington, 1981-83, exec. dir., 1983-84; v.p. Polyconomics, Inc., Morristown, NJ, 1984-85; sr. fellow Heritage Found., Washington, 1985-87; sr. policy analyst The White House, Washington, 1987-88; dep. asst. sec. for econ. policy US Dept. Treasury, Washington, 1988-93; sr. fellow CATO Inst., Washington, 1993, Alexis de Tocqueville Instn., 1993-94, Nat. Ctr. for Policy Analysis, 1995—2005; syndicated columnist Creators Syndicate, LA, 1997—2007; columnist Forbes.Com, 2009—10, The Fiscal Times & Tax Notes, 2010—. Author: Cover-up: The Politics of Pearl Harbor, 1941-1946, 1978, Reaganomics: Supply-Side Economics in Action, 1981, Impostor: How George W. Bush Bankrupted America and Betrayed the Reagan Legacy, 2006, Wrong on Race: The Democratic Party's Buried Past, 2008, The New American Economy: The Failure Reaganomics and the New Way Forward, 2009, The Benefit and The Burden, 2012; contbr. columns in newspapers including the Washington Post, NY Times, Wall Street Jour., LA Times, others, articles to profl. jours. including Nat. Tax Jour., Cato Jour., Fin. Analysts Jour., others. Capt. USAFR, 1973. Independent. Office Phone: 703-421-7784.

BARTLETT, DAN (DANIEL JOSEPH BARTLETT), lobbyist, former federal official; b. Jan. 6, 1971; m. Allyson Elizabeth Sikes, 2000; 3 children. BA in Polit. Sci., U. Tex., 1993. With Karl Rove & Associates, Austin, Tex.; dep. to policy dir. Office of Gov., State of Tex., Austin, Tex., 1994—98, issues dir. Governor's Re-Election Campaign, 1998; sr. spokesman, dir. Rapid Response Bush for Pres. campaign; dep. asst. to Pres., dep. to counselor to Pres. The White House, 2001—02, comm. dir., 2001—05, counselor to Pres., 2005—07; sr. strategist Public Strategies, Inc., Austin, 2007—11, chmn., CEO, 2011—13; pres., CEO Hill & Knowlton USA, 2011—13; sr. v.p. corporate affairs Wal-Mart Stores, Inc., Bentonville, 2013—. Republican. Office: Wal-Mart Stores Inc 702 SW 8th St Bentonville AR 72716*

BARTLETT, DEWEY F., JR., mayor, Tulsa, Oklahoma; m. Victoria Bartlett; children: Dewey F. III, Ann, Andrea Petersen. MBA in Fin., Southern Meth. U. Pres. Keener Oil & Gas Co., 1994—; city councilman Tulsa City Coun.; mayor City of Tulsa, Okla., 2009—. Chair Okla. Energy Resources Bd.; mem. Tulsa Airport Authority. Office: Tulsa City Hall 175 E 2nd St Tulsa OK 74103 Office Phone: 918-596-2100. Business E-Mail: MAC@cityoftulsa.org.*

BARTLETT, JERRY, finance company executive; BS in Tech. & Mgmt., U. Md., College Park. Various mgmt. positions St. Paul Co.; various mgmt. positions, mgr., Application Devel. Am. Red Cross; joined Ameritrade Holding Corp., Omaha, 1999, v.p., application devel. & quality assurance, sr. v.p., chief info. officer, 2005—; mgr., Application Devel. USF&G Ins.; sr. v.p., chief tech. officer & sr. v.p.,

Global Product Devel. First Data Corp. Named one of the Premier 100 IT Leaders, Computerworld, 2005. Office: First Data Corp 6200 S Quebec St Atlanta GA 30342 Office Phone: 303-967-8000. Office Fax: 303-967-8388. Business E-Mail: jerry.bartlett@firstdata.com.

BARTLETT, KATHARINE TIFFANY, law educator, former dean; b. New Haven, Feb. 16, 1947; d. Edgar Parmelee and Elizabeth (Clark) B.; m. Christopher Henry Schroeder, Aug. 13, 1975; children: Emily, Ted, Elizabeth. BA magna cum laude, Wheaton Coll., 1968; MA, Harvard U., 1969; JD, U. Calif., Berkeley, 1975. Bar: Calif. 1975, N.C. 1980, U.S. Dist. Ct. (no. dist.) Calif. 1975, U.S. Dist. Ct. (mid. dist.) N.C. Law clk. Childhood and Govt. Project Earl Warren Legal Inst. UC Berkeley, Calif., 1973—74; law clk. to presiding justice Alaska Supreme Ct., Alaska, 1974; law clk. Legal Aid Soc. of Alameda County, Oakland, Calif.; law clk. to presiding justice Calif. Supreme Ct., San Francisco, 1975-76; atty. Legal Aid Soc. of Alameda County, Oakland, Calif., 1976-79; A. Kenneth Pye prof. law Duke University School Law, Durham, NC, 1979—, dean, 2000—07. Vis. prof. UCLA, 1985-86, Boston U., 1990; bd. dirs. Boston Scientific Corp., 2009- Grad. prize fellow Harvard U., 1968-69, fellow Nat. Humanities Ctr., 1992-93, Woodrow Wilson; recipient U. Scholar Teacher of Yr. award Duke U., 1994, Dean of the Yr. award, Equal Justice Works, 2006 Mem. Am. Law Inst., Soc. Am. Law Tchrs., N.C. Women Attys., N.C. Bar Assn., Am. Law Inst. (reporter for principles of family dissolution), Phi Beta Kappa. Democrat. Office: Duke Univ Law Sch Sci Dr and Towerview Rd Box 90362 Durham NC 27708-0362 Office Phone: 919-613-7001. E-mail: bartlett@law.duke.edu.

BARTLETT, RICHARD ADAMS, historian, writer, retired history professor; b. Boulder, Colo., Nov. 23, 1920; s. John Thomas and Margaret Emily (Abbott) Bartlett; m. Marie Regina Cosgrove, Dec. 26, 1945; children: Richard, Margaret, Thomas, Mary. BA, U. Colo., 1942, PhD, 1953; MA, U. Chgo., 1947. Instr. Tex. A&M U., 1945—51; asst. prof. Fla. State U., 1955—63, assoc. prof., 1963—67, prof., 1968—89, prof. emeritus, 1989—. Author: Great Surveys of the American West, 1962, 1966, paperback, 1993, The Wilderness and the Indians: Challenges in the New World, 1970, Nature's Yellowstone, 1974, The New Country: A Social History of the American Frontier, 1776-1890, 1974, paperback, 1976, Freedom's Trail, 1979, 2d edit., 1981, Yellowstone: A Wilderness Besieged, 1985;: paperback, 1989, From Cody to the World: The First Seventy-Five Years of the Buffalo Bill Memorial Association, 1992, Troubled Waters: Champion International and the Pigeon River Controversy, 1995, The World of Ham Radio, 1901-1950; A Social History, 2007, (novels) Yellowstone Holiday, 1998, First Christmas at Muddy Creek, 2007; editor: Rolling Rivers: An Encyclopedia of America's Rivers, 1984; contbr. articles and book revs. to profl. jours. Fellow, Am. Philos. Soc., 1967; Hungtington Libr. fellow, 1967, Woodrow Wilson fellow, Smithsonian Inst., 1979—80. Mem.: Fla. Coll. Tchrs. History (pres. 1974—75), Western History Assn. (governing coun. 1976—79, mem. editl. bd. The Am. West 1980—82), Phi Alpha Theta. Episcopalian. Home: 2205 Mendoza Ave Tallahassee FL 32304-1319

BARTLEY, DONALD CRAIG, internist, infectious disease specialist; MD, U. Fla., Gainesville, 1977. Diplomate Am. Bd. Internal Medicine, Am. Bd. Internal Medicine-infectious disease, 1982. Intern NC Meml. Hosp., Chapel Hill, resident internal medicine, 1978—80; fellow infectious disease Emory U. Med. Ctr., Atlanta, 1980; physician St. Vincent's Med. Ctr. Office: St Vincent's Medical Center 1 Shircliff Way Jacksonville FL 32204-2982 Office Phone: 904-308-7300.*

BARTLING, PHYLLIS MCGINNESS, oil company executive; b. Chillicothe, Ohio, Jan. 3, 1927; d. Francis McGinness and Gladys A. (Henkelman) Bane; m. Theodore Charles Bartling; children: Pamela, Theodore, Eric C. Student, Ohio State U., 1944—47. Bookkeeper Bartling & Assocs., Bartling Oil Co., Houston, 1974—80, sec.-treas., dir. both cos., 1980—. Co-chmn. ticket sales Tulsa Opera, 1956—61; bd. dirs. Tex. Speech and Hearing Ctr., Houston, 1967—70. Republican. Episcopalian. Avocations: gardening, bicycling, cooking, golf. Home and Office: 11 Inwood Oaks Dr Houston TX 77024-6803

BARTLOW, GENE STEVEN, professional society executive, retired military officer; b. Alva, Okla., Dec. 19, 1939; s. C. Merle and Mildred Violet (Stevens) B.; m. Carolyn F. Strickland, Dec. 31, 1960 (div. Apr. 4, 1962); 1 child, Karie Jean Bartlow Parsons; m. Karin C. Jacobsen, Jan. 13, 1967; children: Christina K., Erik K. BA in Ednl. Comm., N.W. Okla. State U., 1962; disting. grad., Indsl. Coll. Armed Forces, Washington, 1972; MPA, Ball State U., 1978; grad., Air War Coll., Maxwell AFB, Ala., 1984; MS in Computers and Info. Mgmt., Webster U., St. Louis, 1995. Cert. assn. exec. Am. Soc. Assn. Execs. Tchr. speech, debate coach Liberal (Kans.) Pub. H.S., 1962-63; commd. 2d lt. USAF, 1964, advanced through grades to full col.; chief logistics plans divsn. 68th tactical air support group Tactical Air Command, Shaw AFB, SC, 1971-73; chief logistics plans inspection br. Hdqs. Tactical Air Command, Langley AFB, Va., 1973-76; chief NATO logistics plans br. Hdqs. USAF in Europe, Ramstein Air Base, Germany, 1976-80; dep. comdr. for resource mgmt. 474th tactical fighter wing Tactical Air Command, Nellis AFB, Nev., 1980-83; chief congl. activities divsn. Office Asst. Sec. Air Force (Acquisition), Washington, 1984-87; dean adminstrn., prof. sys. acquisition mgmt. Indsl. Coll. Armed Forces, Nat. Def. U., 1987-90; ret., 1990; asst. exec. dir., CFO, Assoc. Cath. Charities, Archdiocese of Washington, 1990-91; dep. exec. dir. Internat. Assn. for Dental Rsch.-Am. Assn. for Dental Rsch., Washington, 1991-94; pres., CEO, Am. Wood Preservers Inst., Fairfax, Va., 1995-97; exec. v.p., COO, Painting and Decorating Contractors Am., 1998-2000; exec. dir., COO Assn. Old Crows, Alexandria, Va., 2002—05. Adj. prof. mgmt. Nat.-Louis U., McLean, Va., 1989-97, U. Md. U. Coll., 1998-99; lectr. congl. liaison activities exec. mgmt. course Def. Sys. Mgmt. Coll., Ft. Belvoir, 1986-92. Contbr. articles to profl. jours. Decorated Legion of Merit, others, Def. Superior Svc. medal. Mem.: Greater Washington Soc. Assn. Execs., Air Force Assn., Mil. Officers Assn. Republican. Congregationalist. Avocations: photography, music, history, politics. Home: 6115 Windrose Hollow Ln Spring TX 77379-8906 Personal E-mail: eagle85@gmail.com.

BARTON, BERNARD ALAN, JR., lawyer; b. Glens Falls, NY, Aug. 13, 1948; s. Bernard A. Sr. and Geraldine (Bushey) B.; children: Lindsey, Kylie. BA, U. Fla., 1969, JD, 1975, LLM, 1976. Bd. cert. tax lawyer. Ptnr. Holland & Knight, Tampa, Fla., 1976—. Editor, contbg. author Florida Taxation, State Taxation Series, 1994. Mem. ABA, Nat. Assn. Bond Attys., Fla. Bar Assn. (exec. coun. tax sect., chmn. various coms. 1980-99). Republican. Episcopalian. Office: Holland & Knight PO Box 1288 Tampa FL 33601-1288 Home Phone: 727-577-6916; Office Phone: 813-227-6539. Business E-Mail: bernie.barton@hklaw.com.

BARTON, DAVID, religious studies educator, writer, historian, researcher; b. Austin, Tex., Jan. 28, 1954; s. Charles Grady and Hilda Rose (Seely) B.; m. Cheryl Edith Little, Mar. 18, 1978; children: Damaris Ann, Timothy David, Stephen Daniel. Degree in religious edn., Oral Roberts U., 1976; D.Litt (hon.), Pensacola Christian Coll., 1997. Dir. youth Aledo (Tex.) Christian Ctr., 1974-75, dir. Christian edn., dir. youth, 1977-87, dir. Christian edn., elder, 1987—; dir. youth Jenks (Okla.) 1st Assembly, 1975-76; dir. Christian edn., dir. youth Sheridan Christian Ctr., Tulsa, Okla., 1976-77. Pres. Splty. Rsch. Assocs., Inc./WallBuilders, Aledo, 1987—. Author: America: To Pray or Not to Pray, 1987, The Bulletproof George Washington, 1990, Original Intent, 1995, Benjamin Rush, 1999, The Second Amendment, 2000, Restraining Judicial Activism, 2003, Freemasonry and the Founding Fathers, 2005; prodr.: (video) America's Godly Heritage, Keys to Good Government, Spirit of the American Revolution, Foundations of American Government; prodr.: The Role of Pastors and Christians in Civil Government, The Spiritual Heritage Tour of the U.S. Capitol, Four Centuries of American Education, Setting the Record Straight: American History in Black & White, (video) Influence of the Bible on America, The American Heritage Series, Science, the Bible, and Global Warming, America's War on Terror. Bd. dirs. Youth Leadership Coun., Cin., 1990, Nat. Legal Found., 2008; mem. bd. Nat. Prayer Embassy, Washington, 1988, Providence Found., Madison Project, Oral Roberts U. Alumni Bd., Coun. Faith in Action; mem. adv. bd. Interfaith Stewardship Alliance, Madison Youth Project; Nat. Day of Prayer, Nat. Coun. Bible Curriculum in Pub. Schs.; mem. coun. Nat. Policy Forum, 1994. Recipient Writing award Amy Found., 1989, Angel award for Excellence in Media, 1995, 2000, 07, Telly award, 2000, 01, 08, George Washington medal of honor Freedoms Found. Valley Forge; named one of America's 25 Most Influential Evangelicals Time Mag. Office: WallBuilders PO Box 397 Aledo TX 76008-0397

BARTON, DONALD SCOTT, history professor; b. Columbus, Ohio, Dec. 8, 1958; s. Ruth L. Barton; m. Deanna Mitchelle James, June 6, 1987; 1 child, Allie. BA, Marshall U., 1983; MA, Tex. A&M U., 1987, PhD, 1991. Chair dept. history East Ctrl. U., Ada, Okla., 1999—2006, dean coll. liberal arts and social scis., 2006—. Office: East Central U 1100 E 14th St PMB G-6 Ada OK 74820 Office Fax: 580-436-3329. Business E-Mail: sbarton@ecok.edu.

BARTON, FRITZ ENGEL, JR., plastic surgeon, educator; b. Ft. Worth, Tex., Mar. 5, 1942; BS, So. Meth. U., Dallas, 1963; MD, U. Tex. Southwestern Med. Sch., Dallas, 1967. Diplomate Am. Bd. Surgery, Am. Bd. Plastic Surgery, lic. Tex. Intern gen. surgery NC Meml. Hosp., Chapel Hill, 1967-68; resident plastic reconstructive surgery Parkland Meml. Hosp./U. Tex., 1970-74; resident plastic surgery Inst. Reconstructive Plastic Surgery, NYU, NYC, 1974-76; prof., chmn. divsn. plastic surgery U. Tex. Southwestern Med. Sch., 1977—91, clin. prof. plastic surgery, 1991—; pvt. practice Dallas Plastic Surgery Inst., Dallas, 1976—. Bd. dirs. Am. Bd. Surgery, 1988—95; attending staff Baylor U. Med. Ctr., Dallas, Presbyn. Hosp. Dallas, VA Med. Ctr. Dallas, Zale Lipshy U. Hosp. Contbr. articles to profl. jours., chapters to books. Served with US Army, 1968—70, Vietnam. Recipient Tattinger award, Susan G. Komen Found. Breast Cancer Rsch., 1996. Fellow: ACS; mem.: AMA, Assn. Academic Chmn. of Plastic Surgery (pres. 1991—92), Tex. Med. Assn., Dallas Soc. Plastic Surgeons (pres. 1983—84), Tex. Soc. Plastic Surgery (pres. 1988), Plastic Surgery Ednl. Found. (pres.-elect 1991—92, pres. 1992—93), Am. Soc. Plastic & Reconstructive Surgery (bd. dirs. 1988—91), Am. Soc. Aesthetic Plastic Surgeons, Am. Soc. Aesthetic Plastic Surgery (parliamentarian 1993, v.p. 1997—98, pres. 1999—2000, Simon Fredricks award 1989, 1998), Am. Assn. Plastic Surgeons (trustee 1991), Alpha Omega Alpha. Achievements include development of the high "SMAS" facelift technique which uniquely produces natural, long lasting facial rejuvenation. Office: Dallas Plastic Surgery Inst Pyramids Med Ctr 9101 N Central Expy Ste 600 Dallas TX 75231-5956 Office Phone: 214-821-9355.

BARTON, JAMES E., JR., state legislator; b. Mobile, Ala., June 29, 1968; m. Kim Barton; children: Ward, Georgianne. Degree in polit. sci., U. Southern Ala. Salesperson Accelerated Tech., Inc., 1993—2001; pres. Bay Area Resources, Inc., 1995—; owner Old South Constrn.; mem. Dist. 104; house rep. Ala., 2001—; mem. State Govt. Com. Mem.: Mobile County Young Reps. (pres. 1999—2001), Mobile County Reps. Exec. Com. Republican. Roman Catholic. Office: Ala State House 11 S Union St Rm 540-D Montgomery AL 36130 Address: 3824 Saint Andrews Dr Mobile AL 36693 Office Phone: 334-242-7754. Fax: 334-432-0482, 251-432-0482. E-mail: jbarton@msg-inc.com.

BARTON, JOSEPH LINUS, United States Representative from Texas; b. Waco, Tex., Sept. 15, 1949; s. Larry Linus and Bess Wynell (Buice) Barton; m. Terri Barton; 4 children; 2 stepchildren. BS in Indsl. Engring., Tex. A&M U., College Station, 1972; MS in Indsl. Adminstrn., Purdue U., West Lafayette, Ind., 1973. Various positions to v.p. Ennis Bus. Forms, Tex., 1973-81; White House fellow, aide sec. James B. Edwards US Dept. Energy, Washington, 1981-82; natural gas decontrol cons. Atlantic Richfield Oil & Gas Co., Dallas, 1982-84; mem. US Congress from 6th Tex. dist., 1985—, chmn. energy and commerce com., 2004—. Mem.: Assn. Former Students Tex. A&M U. Republican. Methodist. Office: US House of Representatives 2107 Rayburn House Office Bldg Washington DC 20515 also: 2106 A W Ennis Ave Ennis TX 75119 Office Phone: 202-225-2002.*

BARTON, MANLY, state legislator; m. Sarah Thornton. Attended, Ala. Bus. Coll. Ret. systems analyst Chevron Corp.; former supr. Jackson County, Miss.; mem. Dist. 109 Miss. House of Reps., Jackson, 2012—. Mem.: NRA, VFW, Mil. Order Purple Heart, East Ctrl. Civil Assn., American Legion. Republican. Methodist. Office: Miss House of Reps PO Box 1018 Jackson MS 39215 Business E-Mail: mbarton@house.ms.gov.

BARTON-COLLINGS, NELDA ANN, retired political organization worker, bank executive, entrepreneur; b. Providence, Ky., May 12, 1929; m. Harold Bryan Barton, May 11, 1951 (dec. Nov. 1977); children: William Grant (dec.), Barbara Lynn, Harold Bryan, Stephen Lambert, Suzanne; m. Jack C. Collings, Mar. 28, 1992 (dec. Feb. 2000). Student, Western Ky. U., 1947-49; grad., Norton Meml. Infirmary Sch. Med. Tech., 1950; student, Cumberland Coll., 1978, LLD (hon.), 1991. Lic. nursing home adminstr.; registered med. technician. Pres. Barton & Assocs. Inc., Corbin, Ky., 1977—2002, ret., 2002; past pres. and chmn. Hazard Nursing Home Inc., Ky., 1977—2002, Health Sys. Inc., Corbin, Ky., 1978—2002, Corbin Nursing Home Inc., 1978—2002, Williamsburg Nursing Home, Inc., 1978—2002; pres. Key Distbg. Inc., 1980—2002, pres., chmn. bd., 1981-97; past pres. and chmn. The Whitley Whiz Inc., Williamsburg, 1983—2002; chmn. bd. dirs. and dir. Tri-County Nat. Bank., 1985-97, 2000; bd. dirs. and chmn. Harlan Nursing Home, Inc., 1986—2002; chmn. bd. dirs. Knott Co. Nursing Home, Inc., 1986; pres. Tri-County Bancorp, Inc., 1987—2002; past pres. and chmn. bd. Wolfe County Health Care Ctr., 1990—2002; pres. Bretara, LLC, 2004—; chmn. Tri-County Cineplex, LLC, 2004—. Mem. exec. com. Corbin Deposit Bank, 1982-84; bd. dirs. Greensburg (Ky.) Deposit Bank, Williamsburg (Ky.) Nat. Bank, Campbellsville Nat. Bank, McCreary Nat. Bank, Tri County Nat. Bank, Somerset Nat. Bank, Laurel Nat. Bank; chmn., organizer, dir. Green County Bancorp Inc., 1987—2002; organizer, dir. Laurel Nat. Bank, 1996—2002; mem. nat. adv. com. SBA, 1990-92; active Nat. Policy Forum, 1994—96. Mem. Fedn. Coun. on Aging, 1982-87; bd. dirs. Leadership Ky., 1984-88, adv. com., 1987—92; bd. dirs. Cumberland Coll. Found., 1995, mem. devel. bd., 1981—85; v.p. Southeastern Ky. Rehab. Com., 1981-93; mem. Fair Housing Task Force, Corbin, 1981-84, Ky. Mansions Preservation Found. Inc., 1970-2004, Corbin Comty. Devel. Com., 1970-83; cub scout den mother, 1965-67; pres. Corbin Cen. Elem PTA, 1963-65; vice chmn. 9th dist. PTA, 1958-59; Rep. nat. committeewoman for Ky., 1968-96, sec., 1993-96; del. Rep. Nat. Conv., 1976, 88, 96, 2000, 04, 08; vice-chmn. Rep. Nat. Com., 1984-93; sec.-treas. Nat. Rep. Inst. Internat. Affairs, 1984-86; bd. mem. Ky. Econ. Devel. Fin. Auth., 2000-03, Ky. Econ. Devel. Partnership Bd., 2003-; active numerous other polit. orgns. Recipient Ky. Woman of Achievement award Ky. Bus. and Profl. Women, 1983, Recognition award Joint Rep. Leadership, U.S. Congress, Dwight David Eisenhower award, 1970, John Sherman Cooper Disting. Svc. award Ky. Young Reps. Fedn., 1987, Outstanding Layperson award Ky. Med. Assn., 1992, Nelda Barton Comty. Svc. award Ky. Assn. Health Care Facilities, 1992, 5th Dist. Rep. Party Recognition award, 1996, Tribute to Nelda Barton-Collings Rep. Party of Ky. and 5th Dist. Lincoln Club, 1997, Disting. Recognition award Ky. State Senate, 2002, Hon. Lifetime award Ky. Mansion Preservation Found., 2004; Nelda Barton Collings Rep. internship award established by Rep. Party of Ky., 1997, Jefferson County Ky. Office for Women Hall of Fame, 1999, Ky. State Senate Cert. for Outstanding Women in Bus. and Leadership, 1999, Moral Leadership award U. Cumberlands, 2006, Ky. Woman Remembered award Ky. Com. Women, 2007; named Outstanding Businesswomen U of C, 2008; named Ky. Col., 1968, Ky. Rep. Woman of Yr., Ky. Fedn. Rep. Women, 1969, 2008; named to 5th Dist. Lincoln Club Hall of Fame, 1996; Nelda Barton Day proclaimed by Mayor of Corbin, 1973; Western Ky. U. Acad. scholar, 1947-49. Mem. Am. Coll. Nursing Home Adminstrs., Ky. Assn. Health Care Facilities (legis. com. 1980-97, Ira O. Wallace award 2002), Ky. Assn. Nursing Home Adminstrs. (bd. dirs., polit. action com. 1979—), Ky. Med. Aux. (chmn. health edn. com. 1975-77), Ky. Commn. on Women, Women's Aux. So. Med. Assn. (Ky. counselor), Whitley County Med. Aux. (pres. 1959-60), Aux. Ky. Med. Assn., Ky. Mothers Assn. (parliamentarian 1970—, hon. Mother of Ky. award 1983), Ky. C. of C. (bd. dirs. 1983—, v.p. Region 5 1985—, 1st vice chmn. 1989, chmn. 1990-91). Avocations: fishing, ballroom dancing. Home: 1311 7th Street Rd Corbin KY 40701-2207

BARTOSHUK, LINDA M., psychologist, educator; b. Aberdeen, SD; BA in Psychology, Carleton Coll., Northfield, Minn., 1960; MS in Psychology, Brown U., Providence, 1963, PhD in Psychology, 1965; DSc (hon.), Carleton Coll., 2001. Rsch. psychologist Natick Army Labs, Mass., 1966—70; asst. prof., dept. epidemiology and pub. health Yale U., New Haven, 1971—76, assoc. prof. dept. epidemiology and pub. health, dept. psychology, 1976—85, prof., 1985—88, prof. sect. otolaryngology, dept. surgery, prof. dept. psychology, 1989—2005; Bushnell prof., dept. cmty. dentistry and behavioral sci. U. Fla. Coll. Dentistry, Gainesville, 2005—, also Presdl. endowed prof. cmty dentistry and behavioral sci. Lectr. Brown U., 1966—68; affiliate asst. prof. Clark U., Worcester, Mass., 1966—69; asst. John B. Pierce Found. Lab., Yale U., 1970—73, assoc., 1974—85, fellow, 1985—89; chair Gordon Conf. on Chem. Senses, 1978; mem. various coms. NIH, NRC. Editor: Chem. Senses, 1982—84; cons. editor: Perception and Psychophysics, 1972—86, Sensory Processes, 1976—79; contbr. articles to profl. jours. Recipient Manheimer award, Monell Chem. Senses Ctr., Phila., 1990, Kreshover award, Nat. Inst. Dental Rsch., 1990, Am. Acad. Arts and Scis., 1995, Nat. Acad. Scis., 2003, Disting. Contbn. award, New Eng. Psychol. Assn., 2000, Innovative Rsch. award, 2004. Fellow: AAAS; mem.: APA (mem. NSF working group com. on rsch. support 1985—87, pres. divsn. 6 1988—89, pres. elect divsn. 1 2001), NAS (coun. mem. 2008—), Am. Assn. Dental Schools (mem. women's affairs adv. com.), Soc. Exptl. Psychologists (award 1995), Soc. Study of Ingestive Behavior (bd. govs. 1987—89, 2000—03), Psychonomic Soc. (mem. publ. com. 1987—92), Ea. Psychol. Assn. (mem. program com. 1983—86, bd. govs. 1987—90, pres. 1990—91), Assn. Chemoreception Scis. (exec. chair 1980—81, Max Mozell Outstanding Achievement award 1998), Am. Psychol. Soc. (bd. dirs. 2001—03, pres. 2010), Phi Beta Kappa, Sigma Xi. Achievements include research in the genetic variations in taste perception and how taste perception affects overall health; first to discover that burning mouth syndrome, a condition predominantly experienced by postmenopausal women, is caused by damage to the taste buds at the front of the tongue and is not a psychosomatic condition. Office: University Fla Coll Dentistry 4073 SW 21st Ter Gainesville FL 32608 E-mail: lbartoshuk@dental.ufl.edu.

BARTOW, MURRAY, men's college basketball coach; s. Gene and Ruth (Huffine) Bartow; m. Tammy Earley; children: Alec, Stephen, Connor. BA in Bus. Adminstrn., U. Ala., Birmingham, 1985; M, Ind. U., 1987. Grad. asst. Ind. U. Hoosiers, 1985—87; asst. coach, recruiting coord. Coll. William & Mary Tribe, 1987—89; asst. coach U. Ala.-Birmingham Blazers, 1989—96, head basketball coach, 1996—2002, East Tenn. State U. Buccaneers, 2003—. Named Coach of Yr., Southern Conf., 2004, Atlantic Sun Conf., 2007. Office: East Tenn State University Basketball Memorial Ctr 146-W Corner State of Franklin and JR Bell Dr Johnson City TN 37614 Office Phone: 423-439-4207.

BARTSCH, RICHARD ALLEN, chemist, educator; b. Portland, Oreg., June 7, 1940; s. Harold Emil and Myrtle Blanche (Sitz) B.; m. Nadine Laverne Putnam, Aug. 20, 1966; children: Robert Allen, Lisa Jo. BA in Chemistry, Oreg. State U., 1962, MS in Chemistry, 1963; PhD in Chemistry, Brown U., 1967. NATO postdoctoral fellow U. Wurzburg, Germany, 1967-68; asst. prof. Washington State U., Pullman, 1968-73; asst. program adminstr. Petroleum Rsch. Fund, Washington, 1973-74; assoc. prof., prof. Tex. Tech. U., Lubbock, 1974-88, Horn prof., 1988—. Contbr. more than 400 articles to profl. jours. Office: Dept of Chemistry & Biochemistry Tex Tech U Lubbock TX 79409-1061 Office Phone: 806-742-3069. E-mail: richard.bartsch@ttu.edu.

BARTZ, MARY E., family practice physician; B in Biology cum laude, U. Tex., MD, 1990. Diplomate Am. Bd. Family Practice. Resident family practice Ctrl. Tex. Med. Found., Austin, Tex., 1990—93; hosp. affiliation includes St. David's Med. Ctr. Office: Red River Family Practice 900 E 30th St Ste 300 Austin TX 78705 Office Phone: 512-476-6555. Office Fax: 512-476-5611.

BARZILAY, JOSHUA ISRAEL, endocrinologist, educator; b. NYC, May 11, 1951; s. Isaac and Helly Barzilay; m. Sarah Gilda Goldszer, June 22, 1982; children: Simon David, Aliza. MD, SUNY Downstate, Bklyn., 1976. Cert. in medicine Nat. Bd. Med. Examiners, 1976. Endocrinologist Kaiser Permanente, Tucker, Ga., 1990—; clin. prof. Emory U. Sch. Medicine, Atlanta, 1991—. Author: (book) The Water We Drink. Physician Jewish Health Care Internat., Atlanta, 2000—08. Capt., 1984—86, Israel Air Force. Fellow: Am. Coll. Physicians.

BASH, FRANK NESS, astronomer, educator; b. Medford, Oreg., May 3, 1937; s. Frank Cozad and Kathleen Jane (Ness) B.; m. Susan Martin Fay, Sept. 10, 1960; children: Kathryn Fay, Francis Lee BA, Willamette U., 1959; MA in Astronomy, Harvard U., 1962; PhD, U. Va., 1967; DSc (hon.), Willamette U., 2000. Staff scientist Lincoln Lab. MIT, 1962; assoc. astronomer Nat. Radio Astronomy Obs., Green Bank, W.Va., 1962-64; rsch. asst. U. Va., 1965-67; postdoctoral faculty assoc. U. Tex., Austin, 1967-69, asst. prof. astronomy, 1969-73, assoc. prof., 1973-81, prof., 1981—, Frank N. Edmonds Regents prof., 1985—2006, Edmonds Regents prof. emeritus, 2006—, chmn. dept. astronomy, 1983-86, dir. W.J. McDonald Obs., 1989—2003. Mem. astronomy adv. panel NSF, 1988-91; chmn. vis. com. Nat. Radio Astronomy Obs., 1990, mem., 1990-93; mem. vis. com. Arecibo Obs., 1990-95, chmn., 1994; mem. planning com. NASA Astrophys. Data Systems, 1991-95; bd. dirs., mem. rep. Assoc. Univs. for Rsch. in Astronomy, 1995-2000; chmn. bd. dirs. Hobby-Eberly Telescope, So. African Large Telescope. Author: (with Daniel Schiller and Dilip Balamore) Astronomy, 1977; contbr. articles to profl. jours. Grantee NSF, 1967—, The Netherlands NSF, 1979, W.M. Keck Found., 1988. Mem. Am. Astron. Soc. (councillor 1996-98), Astron. Soc. Pacific (bd. dirs. 1995-97, v.p. 1997-99, pres. 1999-2000), Internat. Astron. Union, Internat. Sci. Radio Union, Tex. Assn. Coll. Tchrs. (pres. U. Tex. chpt. 1980-82), Tex. Philos. Soc., Town and Gown Club (Austin). Office: U Tex McDonald Obs Mail Code C1402 Austin TX 78712 Home Phone: 512-327-3720; Office Phone: 512-471-3373. Business E-Mail: FNB@astro.as.utexas.edu.

BASHORE, THOMAS MICHAEL, cardiologist, educator; b. Paulding, Ohio, Apr. 9, 1946; s. Raymond Earl and Bertha Gladys (Smith) B.; m. Jill Eickhoff; children: Todd Thomas, Tiffany Lynn, Blake William. AB in Zoology, Miami U., 1968; MD, Ohio State U., 1972. Intern, resident U. N.C., Chapel Hill, 1972-75; fellow in cardiology Duke Med. Ctr., Durham, N.C., 1975-77, from asst. prof. to prof., dir. cardiac cath. lab., dir. fellowship tng., prof., 1980-85; asst. prof., dir. nuc. cardiology Ohio State U., Columbus, 1980-85; prof. Duke Med. Ctr., Durham, NC, 1985—, vice chief divsn. cardiology, 2007—. Assoc. editor Am. Heart Jour., 1996—; mem. editl. bd. Am. Jour. Cardiology, 1987—, Catheterization and Cardiovasc. Diagnosis, 1990—, Emergency Medicine, 1992-2002, Circulation, 1995-2001, Duke Med. Update, 1996, Cardiology Today, 1998—, Jour. Am. Coll. Cardiology, 2002—; contbr. articles to profl. jours., chpts. to books; author 3 books on cardiology Recipient endowed professorship, 2008, Housestaff Tchg. award, UNC, Tchg. award, Duke Master Clinician; named one of Top Doctors award. Fellow Am. Coll. Cardiology. (mem. coms. cardiac catheterization 1996-2001, cardiac imaging 1997-2000, adult congenital heart disease com. 2003—, mem. bd. rev. CD ROM 1996-2002, author ACCSAP & CATHSAP questions, mem. com. workforce & tng., chmn. com. on cardiac cath. lab. guidelines 1998-2000, 2009-2012, Com. Competency mem. 2011-12), ACC ValveSAP (editor 2013-, chair ACC Question-writing comm. 2011-, editor, ACC lifelong learning comm., assoc editor ACCSAP 2013), Am. Heart Assn., Alpha Omega Alpha. Avocations: fly fishing, basketball, painting, computers, antiques. Home: 3825 Westchester Rd Durham NC 27707-5072 Office: Duke Med Ctr PO Box 3012 Durham NC 27715-3012 Office Phone: 919-684-2407.

BASKIES, JEFFREY ALAN, lawyer; b. Malden, Mass., Feb. 6, 1966; s. Jack Steven and Bethann (Kravetz) B.; m. Nancy Lynn Alpern, Feb. 29, 1992; children: Jessica Marie, Jon Douglas. BA with highest honors, Trinity Coll., 1988; JD cum laude, Harvard U., 1991. Bar: Fla. 1991, Mass. 1991. Ptnr. Ruden McClosky, Ft. Lauderdale, Fla., Katz Baskies LLC, Boca Raton, Fla. Pres., CEO Lawyers Weekly, Inc., 2000—04. Contbr. articles to profl. jours. Residential campaign chairperson United Way South Palm Beach County, Boca Raton, Fla., 1993-97, Kids in Distress (adv. coun.), Palm Beach County (chair, planned gifts com.) Named a Fla. Super Lawyer, 2006; named one of Top 100 Attys., Worth mag., 2005—06, Legal Elite Fla., Trend mag., 2006. Mem. ABA (chair probate and trust law com. young lawyers divsn. 1994-96), Am. Cancer Soc. (chair planned gifts com. 1993-97, bd. dirs. 1994-97, v.p. 1996-97, pres. 1998—), Fla. Bar Assn., Broward County Bar Assn., Boca Raton C. of C. (chair west area com. 1995-96), Jewish Fedn. Greater Ft. Lauderdale (chair profl. adv. com. found. 1998—, bd. trustees 1998—), Anti-Defamation League (chair planned gifts com. 1994-97), Coun. Villages, Inc., Broken Sound Country Club (bd. dirs. 1994-96, sec. 1994-97, treas. 1995-96), Phi Beta Kappa, Pi Gamma Mu, Broward County Estate Planning Coun. (treas., bd. dirs.), Alzheimers Assn., Planned Giving Coun. Broward County (bd. dirs.). Office: Katz Baskies LLC Suite 240W 2255 Glades Rd Boca Raton FL 33431 Office Phone: 561-910-5700. E-mail: jeff.baskies@katzbaskies.com.

BASNIGHT, MARC, former state legislator; b. May 13, 1947; m. Sandy Tillett; children: Vicki, Caroline. State senator Dist. 1, NC, 1984—2011; pres. Pro Tempore, NC State Senate; owner Lone Cedar Cafe. Recipient President's Pub. Svcs. award, Nature Conservancy, 1989; named Most Effective senator, Ctr. Pub. Policy, 1993, 1995, 1997, 1999; Paul Harris fellowship, North Banks Rotary, 1990. Democrat. Methodist.

BASS, CLAYTON, museum director; Coord. exhbns. Michael C. Carlos Mus., Emory U., Atlanta; dir. Walter Anderson Mus. Art, 1996—2002; pres., CEO Huntsville (Ala.) Mus. Art, 2002—. Office: Huntsville Mus Art 300 Church St South Huntsville AL 35801

BASS, EDDIE, state legislator; b. Giles Co, Tenn., Nov. 3, 1957; 2 children. Mem. Agr. Com., Judiciary Com.; state rep. Dist. 65 Tenn., 2007—. Democrat. Church Of Christ. Office: 1015 Bass Rd Prospect TN 38477-6722 also: 109 War Memorial Bldg Nashville TN 37243-0165 Office Phone: 931-565-3303, 615-741-1864. Office Fax: 615-741-1005. Business E-Mail: rep.eddie.bass@capitol.tn.gov.

BASS, EDWARD P., venture capitalist; b. Fort Worth, Tex., Sept. 10, 1945; married; 3 children. BS in Admin. Sci., Yale Univ., 1967; attended, Yale Sch. Archit., 1968—70. With Bass Enterprises Production; chmn. Fine Line Investment. Pres. bd. dirs Sid W. Richardson Found.; adminstr. & trustee Yale Univ.; vice chmn. Botanical Research Inst. Tex.; founder Philecology Trust, 1986. Named one of Forbes 400: Richest Americans, 2009. Mem.: World Wildlife Fund (exec. com.), New York Botanical Garden (exec. com.). Office: Sid W Richardson Foundation 309 Main St Fort Worth TX 76012 Office Phone: 817-336-0494. Office Fax: 817-332-2176.

BASS, GEORGE FLETCHER, retired archaeology educator; b. Columbia, SC, Dec. 9, 1932; s. Robert Duncan and Virginia (Wauchope) B.; m. Ann Singletary, Mar. 19, 1960; children: Gordon Wauchope, Alan Joseph. MA, Johns Hopkins U., 1955; PhD, U. Pa., 1964; PhD (hon.), Bogazici U., Istanbul, Turkey, 1987, U. Liverpool, 1998. Asst. prof. U. Pa., Phila., 1964-68, assoc. prof., 1968-73; prof. archaeology Tex. A&M U., College Station, 1976-80, disting. prof., 1980-2000, George T. and Gladys H. Abell prof. nautical archaeology, 1986-2000, Yamini Family prof., 1994-2000, prof. emeritus, 2001—. Dir. excavations of ancient shipwrecks off Turkish coast, 1960-2003; pres. Inst. Nautical Archaeology, 1972-82, 96-98; chmn. Inst. Nautical Archaeology Found., 2005-07. Author: Archaeology Under Water, 1966, Cape Gelidonya, 1967, History of Seafaring, 1972, Archaeology Beneath the Sea, 1975, Yassi Ada I, 1982, Ships and Shipwrecks of the Americas, 1988, Serce Limani I, 2004, Serce Limani II, 2009, Beneath the Seven Seas, 2005; adv. editor Am. Jour. Archaeology, 1987-99, Archaeology, 1987-2007, Internat. Jour. Nautical Archaeology, 1987-2007, Nat. Geog. Rsch., 1987-94. Lt. U.S. Army, 1957-59, Korea. Recipient Centennial award Nat. Geog. Soc., 1988, La Gorce Gold medal, 1979, Lowell Thomas award Explorers Club, 1986, Nat. Medal of Sci., 2002 (presented by Pres. George W. Bush); named one of Outstanding Young Men of Yr., Jaycees, 1967. Mem. Inst. Nautical Archaeology (pres. 1973-82), Archaeol. Inst. Am. (Gold medal for disting. archaeol. achievement 1986), Soc. for Hist. Archaeology (J.C. Harrington medal 1999), Nat. Maritime Hist. Soc., Mothers Against Drunk Driving. Presbyterian. Avocation: classical music. Home: 1600 Dominik Dr College Station TX 77840-3623 Office: Tex A&M U Nautical Archaeology College Station TX 77843-4352 Business E-Mail: gfbass@tamu.edu.

BASS, J. KYLE (KYLE BASS), investment company executive; b. Miami, Fla., Sept. 7, 1969; BA in Bus. Admin. & Real Estate Finance, Tex. Christian U., 1992. Broker Prudential Securities, New York, NY, 1992—94; sr. mng. dir. Bear Stearns & Co Inc., Dallas, 1994—2001; mng. dir. Legg Mason, Inc., Dallas, 2001—05; founder, pres. Hayman Capital Mgmt. L.P., Dallas, 2006—. Expert witness US House Financial Services Capital Markets Subcommittee, 2007; speaker American Enterprise Inst. Public Policy Rsch., 2007, Profl. Risk Managers' Internat. Assn., 2007; numerous TV appearances to discuss subprime mortgage crisis, European sovereign-debt crisis, and Japan's economic future. Achievements include research in identifying which residential mortgage back securities composed of low-quality mortgages were most likely to default. Office: Hayman Capital Management LP 2101 Cedar Springs Rd Ste 1400 Dallas TX 75201*

BASS, JAMES ORIN, SR., lawyer; b. Sumner County, Tenn., July 12, 1910; s. Francis Marion and Sadie (Dunn) B.; m. Susanne Warner, June 9, 1937; children: James Orin Jr., Edwin Warner, Francis Marion II, Susan Richardson Bowen BA, U. of the South, 1931, DCL (hon.), 2007; LLB, Harvard U., 1934. Bar: Tenn. 1934. Ptnr. Bass, Berry & Sims, Nashville, 1937—. Mem. Tenn. Ho. of Reps. from Davidson County, 1936-38, Tenn. Senate, 1940-42. Served to lt. col. AUS, 1942-45, ETO. Mem. ABA, Tenn. Bar Assn., Nashville Bar Assn. (pres. 1952), Am. Coll. Trial Lawyers. Presbyterian. Home: 4412 Georgian Pl Nashville TN 37215-4528 E-mail: jbasssr@bassberry.com.

BASS, LEE MARSHALL, food products company executive; b. 1950; s. Perry R. Bass and Nancy Lee; m. Ramona Bass. BA/BS, Yale U., 1979; MBA, U. Pa. Wharton Sch. Bus. With Bass Enterprises Prodn. Co., Ft. Worth, 1970—; chmn. bd. Nat. Farms, Inc., Kansas City, Mo., 1992—, also bd. dirs.; pres. Lee M. Bass Inc., Ft. Worth. Named one of Forbes 400: Richest Americans, 1999—, World's Richest People, Forbes mag., 1999—. Office: Nat Farms Inc 4800 Main St Kansas City MO 64112-2510 also: Bass Bros Enterprises 201 Main St Fort Worth TX 76102-3105 also: Lee M Bass Inc 201 Main St Fort Worth TX 76102-3105 Office: Modern Art Museum 3200 Darnell St Fort Worth TX 76107-2872

BASS, RANDY, state legislator; m. Kelley Bass; children: Zach, Staci, Remi. Attended, Cameron Univ., Lawton, Okla. Operates cattle and wheat farm; power hitter Hanshin Tigers, 1983—88; embassador to Japan, 1986; commentator for baseball games Minichi Broadcasting Systems, Japan; scout Tokyo Giants, 1998—2003; councilman Ward 1 Lawton, Okla., 2001—04; mem. Dist. 32 Okla. State Senate, 2004. Democrat. Avocation: golf. Office: 2300 N Lincoln Blvd Rm 528B Oklahoma City OK 73105 Mailing: 2606 NW Lake Front Dr Lawton OK 73505-1252 Office Phone: 405-521-5567. Business E-Mail: bass@oksenate.gov.

BASS, ROBERT MUSE, financier; b. Ft. Worth, 1948; s. Perry Richardson and Nancy Lee (Muse) B.; m. Anne Thaxton Bass, 1970; 3 children. BA, Yale U., 1970; MBA, Stanford U., 1974. V.p., bd. dirs. Bass Bros. Enterprises Inc., Ft. Worth, until 1985; pres. Robert M. Bass Group Inc. (now The Keystone Group), Ft. Worth, 1985—; founder Oak Hill Capital Partners. Chmn. Aerion Corp. Mem. collector's com. Nat. Gallery, Washington; chmn. emeritus Nat. Trust Historic Preservation; bd. trustees Stanford U. (chmn., 1996-), 1989—, Rockefeller U., Groton Sch., Middlesex Sch., Amon Carter Mus.; commr. Tex. State Hwy. and Pub. Transp. Commn., 1986—87. Named one of Forbes 400: Richest Americans, 1999—, World's Richest People, Forbes Mag., 2000—. Office: Keystone Inc 201 Main St Ste 3100 Fort Worth TX 76102

BASS, SID RICHARDSON, investment company executive; b. 1943; s. Perry R. Bass and Nancy Lee; m. Anne Bass (div. 1986); 2 children; m. Mercedes Bass. BA, Yale Univ., 1965; MBA, Stanford Univ., 1969. Co-founder Idanta Partners, 1971; founder Buena Venture Associates, 1998—. V.p. & dir. Sid. W. Richardson Found. Former sr. fellow of the corp. Yale Univ.; vice chmn. bd. trustees Mus. Modern Art, NYC. Named one of Forbes 400: Richest Americans, 2000—, World's Richest People, Forbes mag., 2000—. Mailing: Buena Venture Associates 1201 Washington Terrace Fort Worth TX 76107

BASS, STEVEN CRAIG, electrical engineering educator, researcher; b. Indpls., July 29, 1943; s. Leland Ellsworth and Isabelle Frances (Ross) B.; m. Sara Ann Hiday, Sept. 4, 1965 (div. Apr. 1988); children: Leland Kai, Marshall Lynn; m. Kevyn Anne Salsburg, Jan. 2, 1989. BSEE, Purdue U., 1966, MSEE, 1968, PhD in Elec. Engring., 1971. Prof. elec. engring. Purdue U., Lafayette, Ind., 1971-88; prof. elec. and computer engring. George Mason U., Fairfax, Va., 1988-91; prin. engr. Mitre Corp., McLean, Va., 1988-91; prof. computer sci. and engring., chmn. dept. U. Notre Dame, Notre Dame, Ind., 1991-2000; founder & co-owner St. John Condos, LLC, USVI, 2007—. Cons. Magnovox Co., Ft. Wayne, Ind., 1971-73, Admiral Corp., Chgo., 1973-76, Kimball Internat., Jasper, Ind., 1978-84, Tektronix Corp., Wilsonville, Oreg., 1987-88. Contbr. over 25 articles to profl. jours., delievered over 35 papers at sci. confs. Rescue officer Stockwell (Ind.) Vol. Fire Dept., 1985-88. Recipient numerous grants from NSF, USAF, IBM, Mitre Corp., others. Fellow: IEEE (life; v.p. circuits and sys. soc. 1981, 91-93); mem.: Tau Beta Pi, Eta Kappa Nu. Roman Catholic. Achievements include 3 U.S. and 6 fgn. patents in the field of digital signal processing. Office Phone: 832-545-3400. Business E-Mail: stevenbass@earthlink.net.

BASS, WILLIAM MARVIN, III, anthropology educator; b. Staunton, Va., Aug. 30, 1928; s. William Marvin II and Jennie Britton (Hicks) B.; m. Mary Anna Owen, Aug. 8, 1953; children— Charles E., William Marvin IV, James O. BA, U. Va., 1951; MS, U. Ky., 1956; PhD, U. Pa., 1961. Diplomate: Am. Bd. Forensic Anthropology. Instr. phys. anthropology Grad. Sch. Medicine, U. Pa., 1956-59; instr. U. Nebr., 1959-60; mem. faculty anthropology dept. U. Kans., 1960-71, prof., 1967-71; prof., head dept. anthropology U. Tenn., Knoxville, 1971-92, founder, Anthropology Forensic Ctr.--The Body Farm, 1988, former dir. Anthropology Forensic Ctr., Alumni Disting. prof., 1978, prof. emeritus. Serves Tenn. State Forensic Anthropologist; active in consultations and lectures across the country. Author: Human Osteology: A Laboratory and Field Manual of the Human Skeleton, 1971, 5th edit., 2005, The Leavenworth Site Cemetery: Archaeology and Physical Anthropology, 1971, (with Jon Jefferson as Jefferson Bass) Carved in Bone, 2006, Flesh and Bone, 2007, The Devil's Bone, 2008, Bones of Betrayal, 2009, The Bone Thief, 2010, The Bone Yard, 2011, The Inqvisitors Key, 2012; co-author: Death's Acre, 2003, Beyond The Body Farm, 2007; contbr. numerous articles. Served with AUS, 1951-53. Named Hill Tchr. U. Kans., 1964; recipient H. Bernerd Fink award for excellence in classroom teaching U. Kans., 1965; Alumni Public Service award U. Tenn., 1975, Hon. award, Bd. Trustees New U. Bldg., 2011; Nat. Prof. of Year award Council Advancement and Support of Edn., 1985. Fellow Am. Assn. Phys. Anthropologists, Am. Acad. Forensic Scis. (Phys. Anthropology award 1985); mem. Am. Anthrop. Assn. Office: Univ Tenn Anthropology Forensic Ctr Dept 250 S Stadium Hall Knoxville TN 37996-0760 Office Phone: 865-974-4408. Office Fax: 865-974-2686. Business E-Mail: wbass@utk.edu.

BAST, ROBERT CLINTON, JR., medical researcher, educator, physician; b. Washington, Dec. 8, 1943; s. Robert Clinton and Ann Christine (Borland) Bast; m. Blanche Amy Simpson, Oct. 21, 1972; 1 child, Elizabeth. BA cum laude, Wesleyan U., Middletown, Conn., 1965; MD magna cum laude, Harvard Med. Sch., Boston, 1971. Diplomate Am. Bd. Internal Medicine, cert. Med. Oncology, Hematology, lic. Tex., NC. Predoctoral fellow dept. pathology Mass. Gen. Hosp., Boston, 1967-69; intern Johns Hopkins Hosp., Balt., 1971-72; rsch. assoc. biology br. Nat. Cancer Inst., NIH, Bethesda, Md., 1972-75; asst. resident Peter Bent Brigham Hosp., Boston, 1975-76; fellow med. oncology Sidney Farber Cancer Inst., Boston, 1976-77; asst. prof. medicine Harvard Med. Sch., 1977-83, assoc. prof., 1983-84; prof. Duke U. Med. Ctr., Durham, NC, 1984-92, Wellcome clin. prof. medicine, 1992-94, co-dir. divsn. hematology-oncology, 1984-94; dir. divsn. med. oncology U. Tex. Health Sci. Ctr., Houston, 1994-2000; head divsn. med. U. Tex. M.D. Anderson Cancer Ctr., 1994-2000, dir., Harry Carothers Wiess chair cancer rsch., 1994—2004, v.p. translational rsch., 2000—, Harry Carothers Wiess disting. Univ. chair, 2004—. Surgeon USPHS, 1972—75; jr. assoc. medicine Brigham & Women's Hosp., Boston, 1977—82; cons. oncologist Boston Women's Hosp., 1978—80; dir. clin. rsch. progs. Duke U. Comprehensive Cancer Ctr., 1984—87; mem. biol. response modifiers decision network com. Nat. Cancer Inst., 1984—87; mem. grant rev. com. Leukemia Soc. Am., 1985—87, Am. Cancer Soc., 1987; lectr. Am. Cancer Soc., Soc. Gyneacologic Oncologists. Contbr. articles to profl. jours., chapters to books. Recipient Dominus award, 1984, Robert C. Knapp award, 1990, Outstanding Leadership and Advocacy award, Nat. Coalition Cancer Rsch., 1995, Smith Kline Beecham Clin. Labs. award, Clin. Ligand Soc., 1996, Abbott award, Internat. Soc. Oncodevel. Biology & Markers, 2001; named Disting. Spkr., Chao Family Comprehensive Cancer Ctr. Symposium, U. Calif., Irvine, 2002, Best Drs. in America, 1992, Americas Top Physicians, 2003, Americas Top Drs., 2009; named an Edward G. Waters Meml. lectr., 1987, John Ohtani Meml. lectr., 1991, D. Nelson Henderson lectr., 1991, Stolte Meml. lectr., 1992, Robert C. Knapp lectr., 1996, Alan Dembo Meml. Keynote lectr., 1997, George Willbanks lectr., 2000; scholar, Leukemia Soc. Am., 1978—83. Fellow: AAAS, ACP; mem.: Am. Clin. & Climatological Assn., Am. Soc. Hematology, Soc. Biol. Therapy (bd. dirs. 1984—86), Internat. Soc. Immunopharmacology, Am. Soc. Clin. Investigation, Am. Fedn. Clin. Rsch., Am. Soc. Clin. Oncology, Assn. Am. Physicians, Am. Assn. Immunologists, Am. Assn. Cancer Rsch., Am. Soc. Microbiology, Reticuloendothelial Soc., Internat. Gynecol. Cancer Soc. (coun. 1997—2002), Soc. Gynecol. Oncology (assoc.; trustee Helene Harris Meml. trust). Achievements include development of techniques for selective elimination of tumor cells from human bone marrow; monoclonal antibodies to react with human ovarian cancer; discovery of molecular changes associated with malignant transformation of ovarian epithelium. Office: 1400 Pressler St Unit 1439 Houston TX 77030 Office Phone: 713-792-7743. Office Fax: 713-792-7864. Business E-Mail: rbast@mdanderson.org.

BASTIAN, EDWARD H., air transportation executive; b. 1957; m. Anna Bastian; 4 children. BBA, St. Bonaventure U., NY, 1979. CPA. Strategic planning ptnr. Price Waterhouse, NY, ptnr. audit practice; v.p. fin., contr. Frito Lay Internat. PepsiCo, Inc., Dallas, v.p. bus. process reengineering Frito-Lay; v.p. fin., contr. Delta Air Lines, Inc., Atlanta, 1998—2000, sr. v.p. fin., contr., 2000—05, exec. v.p., CFO, 2005—07, pres., CFO, 2007—08, pres., 2008—; sr. v.p., CFO Acuity Brands, Inc., Atlanta, 2005; pres., CEO Northwest Airlines Corp., Eagan, Minn., 2008—09. Internat. bd. dirs. Habitat for Humanity; bd. dirs. Woodruff Arts Ctr., Atlanta. Avocations: golf, travel, reading. Office: Delta Air Lines Inc PO Box 20706 Atlanta GA 30320-6001 Office Phone: 404-715-2600.

BATA, RUDOLPH ANDREW, JR., lawyer; b. Akron, Ohio, Jan. 9, 1947; s. Rudolph Andrew and Margaret Eleanor (Ellis) Bata; m. Genevieve Ruth Brannan, Aug. 25, 1968 (div. May 1985); 1 child, Seth Andrew; m. Linda Lee Waldo, Apr. 7, 1985; 1 child, Sarah Ariel. BS, So. Coll., Collegedale, Tenn., 1969; JD, Emory U., 1972. Bar: D.C. 1973, N.C. 1978, U.S. Dist. Ct. N.C. 1991, U.S. Ct. Appeals (4th cir.) 1991, U.S. Supreme Ct. 2004, cert.: Adminstrv. Office of Cts. (arbitrator, mediator), Fin. Industry Regulatory Authority Bd. Arbitrator. Assoc. ICC, Washington, 1972-73; in house counsel B.F. Saul Real Estate Investment Trust, Chevy Chase, Md., 1973-74; staff atty. Martha, Cafferky, Powers & Jordan, Washington, 1974-75; asst. corp. counsel Hardee's Food Systems, Inc., Rocky Mount, NC, 1975-78; ptnr. Bata & Blomeley, Murphy, NC, 1978-87, 88-90, Bata & Sumpter, Murphy, 1987-88; sole practice, 1990—. Arbitrator NASD; bd. dirs. Cherokee County United Fund, Murphy, 1981—83. Mem. ABA, NASD (bd. arbitrators), NC Bar Assn., DC Bar Assn., 30th Jud. Dist. Bar Assn., So. Soc. Adventist Attys. (pres. 1984-85), Cherokee County C. of C. (bd. dirs. 1980-82), FINRA(bd. arbitrators) Avocations: golf, tennis, hiking. Office: 225 Valley River Ave Ste A Murphy NC 28906-3000 Office Phone: 828-837-8684. Personal E-mail: batalaw@yahoo.com. Business E-Mail: batalaw@hotmail.com.*

BATAILLE, GRETCHEN M., former academic administrator, educator; b. 1944; BA in English, Calif. Polytech. State U., 1966, MA in English Edn., 1967; DA, Drake U. Chair dept. English Ariz. State U., assoc. dean acad. personnel, until 1994; provost U. Calif., Santa Barbara, 1994-97; provost, acad. v.p. Wash. State U., Pullman, 1997-2000; sr. v.p., v.p. acad. affairs U. NC Sys., Chapel Hill, 2000—06; interim chancellor NC Sch. Arts, Winston-Salem, 2005—06; pres. U. No. Tex., Denton, 2006—10; cons. GMB Consulting Group LLC, 2010—; bd. trustees Drake U., 2012—. Bd. dirs. SAGE, 2009—. Author: Living the Dream in Arizona: The Legacy of Martin Luther King, Jr., 1992, Native American Women: A Biographical Dictionary, 1994, Ethnic Studies in the United States, 1998, Faculty Career Path., 2006, Managing the Unthinkable, 2014, others. Named one of The 25 Most Influential Women, Dallas Bus. Jour., 2008. Office Phone: 480-510-8373, 480-510-8373. Personal E-mail: gbataille9@gmail.com. Business E-Mail: gbataille@unt.edu.

BATCHELDER, GENE (EUGENE LEWIS BATCHELDER), oil industry executive; b. Enid, Okla., 1947; BS in Acctg., Okla. State U., 1969. CPA. With Ford Motor Co.; gen. sales mgr. wholesale mktg. Phillips 66 Co., 1972—85, mgr. ops. analysis and control, mgmt. info. sys., 1985—89, mgr. comms. networks and computer svcs., 1990, pres. Phillips Driscopipe, Inc. subs., 1990—94; fin. mgr. GMP Gas Co., 1994—99; v.p., chief info. officer Philips Petroleum Co., 1999—2002; sr. v.p. services, chief info. officer ConocoPhillips, Houston, 2002—09, sr. v.p., chief adminstrv. officer, 2009—. With USAR. Office: ConocoPhillips PO Box 2197 Houston TX 77252

BATCHMAN, THEODORE EARL, retired electrical engineering educator, researcher; b. Gt. Bend, Kans., Mar. 29, 1940; s. Jake T. and Dorothy E. (Bardwell) B.; m. Nancy L. Leatherman, Dec. 23, 1961; children: Teddie Suzanne, Timothy Brent, Tracey Nanette. BSEE, U.

Kans., 1962, MSEE, 1963, PhD, 1966. Engr., sci. specialist LTV, Dallas, 1966-70; sr. lectr. U. Queensland, Brisbane, Australia, 1970-75; from asst. prof. to prof. elec. engring. U. Va., Charlottesville, 1975-88; prof., dir. Sch. Elec. Engring. and Computer Sci. U. Okla., Norman, 1988-95; dean Coll. Engring. U. Nev., Reno, 1995—2008, dir. renewable energy ctr., 2008—10, dean & emeritus prof. elec. & biomed. engring. Cons. Commonwealth of Va., Richmond, 1982-83, U.S. Army FSTC, Charlottesville, 1986-90; mem. adv. bd. Chromachron Technology Corp., Columbia, Md., 1988-90. Rsch. grantee NASA, 1978-84, NSF, 1979-84, HHS, 1984-85, Naval Rsch. Labs., 1987-88, U.S. Army, 1989-90, NSF EPSCOR, 1991-94. Fellow IEEE (life, mem. edn. activities bd. 2002-04, Achievement award 1998), Am. Soc. Engring. Edn., Optical Soc. America. Methodist. Avocations: woodworking, model railroading, photography. Home: 42 Preston Path Santa Rosa Beach FL 32459 Business E-Mail: batch_t@unr.edu.

BATEMAN, CATHLEEN P., dermatologist; MD, U. Tex., 1978. Diplomate Am. Bd. Dermatology, 1983. Resident dermatology Univ. New Mex. Med. Ctr.; hosp. affiliation includes Meth. Dallas Med. Ctr. Office: Methodist Dallas Medical Center 1441 N Beckley Ave Dallas TX 75203 Office Phone: 214-947-8181.

BATES, BARRY D., career officer; b. Norman, Okla., Jan. 26, 1947; Commd. U.S. Army, advanced through grades to maj. gen., 1998; comdg. gen. Army and Air Force Exchange Svc., Dallas, 1998—. Office: PO Box 660202 Dallas TX 75265-0202

BATES, GEORGE WILLIAM, obstetrician, gynecologist, educator; b. Durham, NC, Feb. 15, 1940; s. George W. and Lillian M. (Streete) B.; m. Susanne Rayburn, Oct. 18, 1969; children: Jonathan Rayburn, Jeffrey William, Robert Wiser. BS, U. N.C., 1962, MD, 1965; SM, MIT, 1984. Diplomate Am. Bd. Ob-Gyn. (examiner 1984-93). Intern U. Ala., Birmingham, 1965-66; resident ob-gyn U. N.C., Chapel Hill, 1966-70; prof., chmn. ob-gyn U. Tenn., Knoxville, 1972-76; fellow reproductive endocrinology U. Tex., Dallas, 1976-78; prof., dir. reproductive endocrinology U. Miss. Med. Ctr., Jackson, 1978-86; prof. ob.-gyn. Coll. Medicine, Med. U. S.C., Charleston, 1986-90, dean, 1986-89; v.p. med. edn. Greenville (S.C.) Hosp. System, 1990-96; exec. v.p., chief med. officer Prin.Care, Inc., Brentwood, Tenn., 1996-98; v.p. devel. Vanderbilt U. Med. Ctr., Nashville, 1998—. CEO digiChart, Inc. Co-author: Obstetrics and Gynecology for Medical Students, 1992, 95; editor: Manual of Clinical Problems in Obstetrics and Gynecology, 1982, 86, 90; contbr. numerous articles to profl. publs. Commr. coun. Boy Scouts Am., 1989-90, v.p. adminstrn., 1992, pres., 1993-94, bd. dirs. Mid. Tenn. Coun., 2002--; elder Mt. Pleasant Presbyn. Ch., Westminster Presbyn. Ch.; mem. pres.'s adv. coun. Mars Hill Coll., Presbyn. Coll., Nat. Devel. Coun., U. N.C. Maj. USAF, 1970-72. Morehead scholar, 1958; NIH rsch. trainee, 1976-78; Sloan fellow, 1983; recipient Eagle Scout award, 1955, Henry Fordham award, 1966, Golden Apple award, 1987, Silver Beaver award, 1989, Hon. Alumnus award Med. U. S.C., 1990, Disting. Eagle Scout award, 1991; named Prof. of Yr., U. Miss., 1980, Top 100 Healthcare Exec., 2002. Mem. ACOG (chmn. fin. com. 1990-94, health care commn. 1994-97, Jr. Fellow Profl. of Y. award dist. IV 1991), AMA, AAAS, Assn. Profs. Ob-Gyn. Found. (bd. dirs. 1993), Am. Gyn.-Ob. Soc., Nat. Bd. Med. Examiners, Gynecol. Investigation, Am. Fertility Soc. (bd. dirs. 1991-94, treas. 1994-96), Soc. Gynecol. Surgeons, Accreditation Coun. Grad. Med. Edn., So. Atlantic Assn. Obstetricians and Gynecologists, Ctrl. Assn. Obstetricians and Gynecologists, Endocrine Soc., Rotary, Alpha Omega Alpha. Office: digiChart Inc 100 Winners Cir N Ste 450 Brentwood TN 37027-1004 Office Phone: 615-777-2727.

BATES, HAMPTON ROBERT, JR., pathologist; b. Roanoke, Va., Feb. 1, 1933; s. Hampton Robert and Mary Mildred (Crowder) B.; m. Carole Harrison Young, Apr. 12, 1958; children: Hampton Robert III, Catherine Louise Franck. BS in Chemistry, Roanoke Coll., 1953; MD, Med. Coll. Va., 1957. Diplomate Am. Bd. Pathology, Am. Bd. Nuc. Medicine, Nat. Bd. Med. Examiners; cert. radiation safety officer. Intern Med. Coll. Va. Hosp., Richmond, 1957-58, resident in pathology, 1958-62, faculty, 1962-63; practice medicine specializing in pathology and nuc. medicine Richmond, 1963-95; ind. rschr., 1995—. Pathologist Johnston-Willis Med. Ctr., Chippenham Med. Ctr.; v.p. Clin. Lab. Consultants, Inc., Richmond, 1972-95; forensic pathologist Richmond Met. Area, 1959-95. Author (monograph) Card Magic For The Twenty-First Century; contbr. articles on descriptive, exptl. and forensic pathology to med. jours. Fellow Coll. Am. Pathologists (life); mem. AMA, AAAS, Richmond Acad. Medicine, Rokitansky Soc., Diogenes Club, River Road Ch., Baptist. Avocations: dance, card magic. Home: 122 W Square Dr Richmond VA 23238-6156 Home Phone: 804-784-3510; Office Phone: 804-784-3510.

BATES, JOHN WYTHE, III, lawyer; b. Richmond, Va., Aug. 22, 1941; s. John Wythe, Jr. and Virginia (Wellington) B.; m. Beverly Jane Estes, June 20, 1964; children: Elizabeth Puller, Kathryn Wellington. BS, Va. Tech., 1963; LLB, U. Va., 1966. Assoc. McGuire Woods Battle & Boothe, L.L.P., Richmond, 1966-71, pntr., 1971—2005, mng. ptnr., 1989-96. Mem. Va. Racing Commn., 1997-2000; chmn. Richmond Renaissance, Inc., 1998—2001. Chmn. United Way Gtr. Richmond, 1975-76; pres. Family and Children's Svc. Richmond, 1978-80; trustee St. Paul's Coll., 1989-96, Va. Found. Ind. Colls., 1994—; sr. warden St. Stephen's Ch., 1985-86, 2002*05; mem. exec. com. Va. Tech. Found. Bd., 1994-2000. Va. Law Found. fellow, 1997. Mem. Am. Coll. Real Estate Lawyers, Richmond Real Estate Group, Forum Club, River Rd. Citizens Assn. (pres. 1983-84), Country Club Va. (pres. 1987-88), Bull and Bear Club (pres. 1980-81), Commonwealth Club. Episcopalian. Avocations: golf, waterfowl hunting. Office: McGuire Woods LLP One James Ctr 901 E Cary St Richmond VA 23219-4057 Office Phone: 804-775-4302. Business E-Mail: jbates@mcguirewoodsemeritus.com.

BATES, JOSEPH HENRY, internist, educator; b. Little Rock, Sept. 19, 1933; s. Henry Ermer and Susan Elizabeth (Wallis) B.; m. Patsy McGinnis, Aug. 6, 1955 (dec. 2007); children— Patricia, Susan Elizabeth, Joseph Henry, III, Elisabeth Lee; m. Donna Dudney McNair, 2008. BS, MD, U. Ark., 1957, MS, 1963. Diplomate in internal medicine and pulmonary diseases Am. Bd. Internal Medicine, also mem. exam. bd. Med. intern U. Ark. Med. Center, 1957-58, resident in internal medicine, 1958-61, fellow in infections diseases, 1961-63; clin. investigator Little Rock VA Med. Ctr., 1963-66; mem. faculty U. Ark. Med. Ctr., Little Rock, 1967—, prof. medicine, 1973—, vice chmn. dept., 1978-98; assoc. dean U. Ark. Coll. Pub. Health, 2001—, Coll. Pub. Health, U. Ark. for Med. Sci., 2001—. Chief med. service Little Rock VA Hosp., 1970-98, dep. state health officer, chief sci. officer, Ark. Dept. Health, 1998—. Author research papers in field, chpts. in books. Chmn. Ark. chpt. NCCJ, 1980; chmn. biracial commn. Little Rock public schs., 1977-79; bd. dirs. Am. Lung Assn., 1972-90. Served as officer M.C. AUS, 1956-65. Grantee USPHS, 1961-63; Grantee NIH, VA, also pvt. founds. and corps., 1963— Mem. ACP (gov.), Am. Coll. Chest Physicians (gov.), Am. Fedn. Clin. Rsch., Am. Thoracic Soc. (pres. 1988-89), Infectious Disease Soc., So. Soc. Clin. Rsch., Am. Lung Assn. (pres. 1994-95), Assn. Am. Physicians, Assn. Profs. Medicine. Presbyterian. Office: 4815 W Markham St Little Rock AR 72205-3866 Home: 5 Timberlake Dr Little Rock AR 72207-1609 Home Phone: 501-224-3033; Office Phone: 501-661-2412. Personal E-mail: joseph.bates@arkansas.gov.

BATRA, ROMESH CHANDER, engineering educator, researcher; b. Dherowal, Panjab, India, Aug. 16, 1947; arrived in US, 1975, naturalized, 1982; s. Amir Chand and Dewki Bai (Dhamija) B.; m. Manju Dhamija, June 26, 1972; children: Monica, Meenakshi. BSME, Thapar U., Patiala, India, 1968; MASc, U. Waterloo, Ont., Can., 1969; PhD, Johns Hopkins U., 1972; DSc (hon.), Thapar U., Patiala, India, 2006. Postdoctoral rsch. assoc. Johns Hopkins U., Balt., 1972-73; rsch. assoc. McMaster U., Hamilton, Ont., 1973-74; asst. prof. U. Ala., Tuscaloosa, 1976-77; asst. prof. engring. mechanics U. Mo., Rolla, 1974-76, assoc. prof., 1977-81, prof., 1981-94; Clifton C. Garvin prof. Va. Poly. Inst. and State U., Blacksburg, 1994—. Bd. dirs. Midwestern Mechanics Conf., 1989—93, editor procs., 1991; mem. NRC Panel on Armaments, 1996—99, NRC Panel on Survivability and Lethality, 2001—05; organizer, co-chair Mechs. and Mats. Conf., 1999; lectr. S.W. Mechanics Series, 2000; Michael L. Sadowski mechanics lectr. Rensselaer Poly. Inst., 2000; hon. prof. Nanjing U. Sci. and Tech., China, 2004—, Lanzhou U. Tech., 2005—; co-chair 1st internat. conf. Mechanical Engring. and Mechanics; co-chair, organizer 14th US Nat. Conf. Theoretical and Applied Mechanics, 2002; vis. prof. Yangzhou U., China, 2011—; plenary lectr. Internat. Congress Composite Structures, Porto, Portugal, 2009, Ann. Tech. Meeting Soc. Engring. Sci., Blacksburg, Va., 2009, Internat. Congress Computational Mechanics & Simulations, Hyderabad, India, 2012; B. Kannesh meml. lectr. 57th Congress Indian Soc. Theoretical & Applied Mechanics, Pune, India, 2012. Co-editor-in-chief: Internat. Jour. Computational Methods, 2004-; editor: Contemporary Research in Engineering Science, Springer Verlag, 1995; co-editor: Contemporary Research in the Mechanics and Mathematics of Materials, Internat. Ctr. for Numerical Methods in Engring., 1996, Constitutive Laws, Experiments and Numerical Implementation, Internat. Ctr. for Numerical Methods in Engring., 1995, Material Instabilities, Theory and Applications, 1994, Impact, Waves and Fracture, 1994, Contemporary Research in Mechanics, 2002; mem. editl. bd. Internat. Jour. Plasticity, 1989-2003, Internat. Jour. Engring. Design and Analysis, 1992-1995, Continuum Mechanics and Thermodynamics, 1993-2004, Computational Mechanics, 1994-2006, Jour. Engring. Materials and Tech., 1996-2001, Polish Jour. Theoretical and Applied Mechanics, 2000—, Computer Modeling in Engring. and Sci., 2003-04, Iranian Jour. Solid Mechanics, 2010-; editor: Mathematics and Mechanics of Solids, 1995-; author: Elements of Continuum Mechanics, AIAA Publ., 2006; reviewer for various jours. in field; contbr. articles to profl. jours. Grantee NSF, 1980-83, 87—, Army Rsch. Office, 1985—, Office of Naval Rsch., 1994—; recipient Alexander von Humboldt award for sr. scientists, 1992, Jai Krishna award Indian Geotech. Soc., 1994, Eric Reissner medal Internat. Congress in Computational Engrg. Sci., 2000, Engring. Sci. medal Soc. Engring. Sci, 2009, Rsch. award Inst. Metal Rsch. Chinese Acad. Scis., 2009, Outstanding Faculty award, State Coun. Higher Edn. Va., 2010; Va. Outstanding Scientist award, 2011; inducted into Hopkins Soc. Scholars, 1993; lited in ISI Highly Cited Authors, 2010. Fellow ASME (chair elasticity com. 1995-2000, co-editor symposium procs. 1991, 94-95, co-editor meeting procs. 1999, awards nominating com. 1997-2006, organizer, co-chair mechanics and materials conf. 1999), Am. Acad. Mechanics (awards nominating com. 2002-, sec. 2003-05), Am. Soc. Engring. Edn. (Centennial award 1993), Soc. Engring. Sci. (bd. dirs. 1991-96, editor meeting procs. 1982, v.p. 1995, pres. 1996); Soc. Natural Philosophy (treas. 1987-89, editor meeting procs. 1981), U.S. Nat. Congress Theoret. and Applied Mechs. (organizer, co-chmn. 2002), Internat. Soc. Interaction Between Mechanics and Math. Office: Va Polytech Inst & State U Dept Engring Sci & Mechanics 220 Norris Hall Blacksburg VA 24061-0219 Office Phone: 540-231-6051. Business E-Mail: rbatra@vt.edu.

BATSON, RICHARD NEAL, lawyer; b. Nashville, May 1, 1941; s. John H. and Mildred (Neal) B.; m. Jean Elizabeth Flanagan; children: John Hayes, Richard Davis. BA cum laude, Vanderbilt U., 1963, JD, 1966. Bar: Ga. 1967. Law clk. to Judge Griffin B. Bell U.S. Ct. Appeals (5th cir.), Atlanta, 1966—67; assoc. Alston & Bird (formerly Alston, Miller & Gaines), 1967—71, ptnr., 1971—2005, spl. counsel, 2006—. Spkr. Nat. Conf. Bankruptcy Judges, 1982, 86, 87, 88, 94, 96, Bank Lending Inst., 1986-87, also other instns. and assns.; adj. prof. Emory U. Sch. Law, 1994-95; co-lectr. Ga. State U., fall 1984; mem. bankruptcy rules com. Jud. Conf. U.S., 1993-99. Co-author: Problem Loan Strategies, 1985, rev. 1998; contbg. author Bankruptcy Litigation Manual, 1990—; contbg. editor Norton Bankruptcy Law and Practice, 1990—. Sgt. USAF, 1967-73. Fellow Am. Coll. Trial Lawyers, Am. Coll. Bankruptcy (bd. dirs., pres. 1997-2001, chmn. bd. dirs. 2001-03); mem. Atlanta Bar Assn. (pres. 1979-80), Am. Law Inst., Southeastern Bankruptcy Law Inst. (bd. dirs., pres. 1986-87), Nat. Bankruptcy Conf. Avocations: hiking, outdoor activities. Office: Alston & Bird One Atlantic Ctr 1201 W Peachtree St Atlanta GA 30309-3400 Home Phone: 970-923-0122; Office Phone: 404-881-7267. Business E-Mail: neal.batson@alston.com.

BATTAFARANO, FRANK J., healthcare company executive; Pres., Hosp. Divsn. Kindred Healthcare, Inc., 1998—2008, exec. v.p., 2005—08, COO, 2008—. Office: Kindred Healthcare Inc 680 S Fourth St Louisville KY 40202 Office Phone: 502-596-7300. Business E-Mail: frank.battafarano@kindredhealthcare.com.

BATTAGLIA, ANTHONY SYLVESTER, lawyer; b. Binghamton, NY, Aug. 21, 1927; s. Sylvester Anthony and Helen B.; m. Catherine Jean, Oct. 1, 1972; children: Christina, Marc Anthony; children by previous marriage— Anthony, Sandra, Brian, Brenda Lee. AA, U. Fla., 1948, BA, 1949, LLB, 1953, JD, 1967. Bar: Fla. 1953, US Dist. Ct. (mid. and so. dists.) Fla., US Ct. Appeals (5th, 11th cirs.), US Tax Ct., US Ct. Appeals (D.C. cir.), US Ct. Mil. Appeals; cert. ct. approved abritrator US Dist. Ct., US Supreme Ct. 1966. Asst. to U.S. dist. atty., So. Dist. Fla., 1953-56; ptnr. Parker, Parker & Battaglia, St. Petersburg, Fla., 1953-56, Parker, Battaglia & Ross, St. Petersburg, 1965-73, Parker, Battaglia, Parker, Ross & Ross, St. Petersburg, 1973-75, Battaglia, Parker, Ross, Parker & Stolba, St. Petersburg, 1975-76, Battaglia, Ross & Stolba, 1976-77, Battaglia, Ross, Stolba & Forlizzo, 1977-78, Battaglia, Ross & Forlizzo, 1978-80, Battaglia, Ross, Hastings, Dicus & Andrews, 1980-93, Battaglia, Ross, Dicus & Wein PA, 1993—. Mem. Fla. Pub. Svc. Commn., 1971; chmn. bd. Metrocare, Inc., 1975-78; mem. grievance com. U.S. Dist. Ct., 1985-88; pres. Asst. U.S. Attys. Assn. for Mid. Dist. Fla., 1994; guest lectr. Stetson U., 1994; bd. dirs. Intervest Bank, 1st Bankers Tampa Bay, N.A., St. Petersburg, Nat. Bank Fla., St. Petersburg, Operation PAR, Inc.; chmn. adv. bd. 1st Union Nat. Bank, South Pinellas, Fla. Republican nat. committeeman, Fla., 1956-64, bd. dirs., Tampa div.; bd. dirs. San Carlo Opera Fla., 1972-74, pres., chmn. bd. dirs., Pinellas County div., 1974-76; bd. dirs. St. Petersburg Opera Co., 1976-77; chmn. bd. Pinellas County Arthritis Found., 1985; founding sponsor Civil Justice Found.; trustee Ctr. Against Spouse Abuse, 1999. Recipient Jack Edmund award for Herbert G. Goldburg Criminal Law Am. Inn of Ct., 2004; named to U. Fla. Hall of Fame and Fla. Blue Key, 1951. Master Ferguson-White Am. Inn of Ct.; fellow Am. Coll. Mortgage Attys.; mem. ABA, ATLA (sustaining), Fla. Bar Assn. (bd. govs. 1993-99), St. Petersburg Bar Assn. (pres. 1990), Fed. Bar Assn. (v.p. Mid. Fla. dist.), US Attys. Assn. for Mid. Dist. Fla. (pres. 2001), Internat. Bar Assn., Hillsborough County Bar Assn., Acad. Fla. Trial Lawyers (judge student competition 1985), Am. Judicature Soc. (Supreme Ct. Hist. Soc. 1985-89), Nat. Assn. Criminal Def. Lawyers, Acad. Criminal Justice Scis., Fla. Criminal Def. Trial Lawyers, Criminal Def. Lawyers Hillsborough County, Pinellas County Trial Lawyers Assn. Roscoe Pound Am., Trial Lawyers Found. (judicial nominating com.), U. Fla. Nat. Alumni Assn., St. Petersburg C. of C. (gov.), Pinellas Inns Ct. (master bench), Herbert G. Goldberg Criminal Law Am. Inn Ct., Fla. Bar Bd. of Govs. Clubs: Treasure Island Tennis and Yacht (bd. dirs.), Suncoast Tiger Bay, St. Petersburg Yacht, Nat. Italian Am. Found., Italian-Am. Unico Internat., K.C. Roman Catholic. Office: 980 Tyrone Blvd N Saint Petersburg FL 33710-6333 Office Phone: 727-381-2300. Business E-Mail: abatt@brdwlaw.com.

BATTEN, TIMOTHY C., SR., federal judge; b. Atlanta, 1960; m. Beth Batten; 6 children. BS, Ga. Inst. Tech., Atlanta, 1981; JD, U. Ga., Athens, 1984. Assoc. Schreeder, Wheeler & Flint, Atlanta, 1984—93, ptnr., 1993—2006; judge US Dist. Ct. (no. dist.) Ga., Atlanta, 2006—. Office: US Dist Ct Russell Fed Bldg and US Courthouse 75 Spring St SW Rm 1788 Atlanta GA 30303-3309 Office Phone: 404-215-1420.

BATTESTIN, MARTIN CAREY, retired literature and language professor; b. NYC, Mar. 25, 1930; s. Martin Augustus and Marion (Kirkland) B.; m. Ruthe Rootes, June 14, 1963; children: David (dec. 1999), Catherine. BA summa cum laude, Princeton U., 1952, PhD, 1958. English master Westminster Sch., Simsbury, Conn., 1952-53; instr. Wesleyan U., Middletown, Conn., 1956-58, asst. prof., 1958-61, U. Va., Charlottesville, 1961-63, assoc. prof., 1963-67, prof., 1967-75, William R. Kenan, Jr. prof. English, 1975-98, emeritus prof., 1998—, chmn. dept. English, 1983-86. Vis. prof. Rice U., Houston, 1967—68; assoc. Clare Hall, Cambridge (Eng.) U., 1972, Princeton U., 1971. Author: The Moral Basis of Fielding's Art, 1959, 1964, 1975, 2d edit., 1975, The Providence of Wit, 1974, 2d edit., 1989, Henry Fielding: A Life, 1989, 2d edit., 1993, New Essays by Henry Fielding, 1989, 1993, A Henry Fielding Companion, 2000; editor: Joseph Andrews (Henry Fielding), 1961, 2d edit., 1967, Shamela (Henry Fielding), 1961, Tom Jones (Henry Fielding), 1974, 2nd edit., 1975, Amelia (Henry Fielding), 1983, Tom Jones: A Collection of Critical Essays, 1968, British Novelists, 1660-1800, 1 edit., 1985, Tobias Smollett, translator Cervantes' Don Quixote, 2003, The Journal of a Voyage to Lisbon, Shamela and Occasional Writings (Henry Fielding), 2008; co-editor: The Correspondence of Henry and Sarah Fielding, 1993; contbr. Am. Coun. Learned Socs. fellow, 1960-61, 72; Guggenheim fellow, 1964-65; Sr. fellow Coun. Humanities, Princeton U., 1971; Ctr. for Advanced Studies fellow U. Va., 1974-75; NEH Bicentennial Rsch. fellow, 1975-76. Mem. MLA (chmn. sec. VII 1967, adv. editor publs. 1982-86), South Atlantic Modern Lang. Assn., Internat. Assn. Univ. Profs. English (chmn. sect. V 1990-92), Assn. Lit. Scholars and Critics, East Ctrl. Am. Soc. Eighteenth Century Studies, Nat. Assn. Scholars, The Johnsonians. Mem. Ch. of English Home: 2600 Barracks Rd Apt 238 Charlottesville VA 22901-2192

BATTIER, SHANE, professional basketball player; b. Birmingham, Mich., Sept. 9, 1978; s. Ed and Sandee; m. Heidi Ufer, 2004. Graduate, Duke Univ., 2001. Forward Memphis Grizzlies, 2001—06, 2011, Houston Rockets, 2006—11, Miami Heat, 2011—. Mem. USA Basketball Men's Sr. Nat. Team, 2001, 2006—08. Mem. bd. St. Jude, Memphis Zoo. Recipient Wooden award Best Coll. Player, 2001, Naismith award Best Coll. Player, 2001, Gold medal, Goodwill Games, 2001, Cmty. Assist award, NBA, 2002, Southwest Divsn. Sportsmanship award, 2005, 2007, 2008, Magic Johnson award, Profl. Basketball Writer's Assn., 2006—07, Bronze medal, FIBA World Championships, 2006; named Def. Player of Yr., Nat. Assn. Basketball Coaches, 1999—2001, First Team All-Conf., ACC, 2000—01, Co-Player of Yr., 2001, First Team All-Am., AP, USBWA, The Sporting News, 2001, Coll. Basketball Player of Yr., The Sporting News, 2001, Outstanding Young Tennessean, Greater Mid-South C. of C., 2004; named to All-Rookie Team, NBA, 2002. Achievements include member of NCAA Final Four division I national championship winning Duke University Blue Devils, 2001; member of NBA Finals championship winning Miami Heat, 2012, 2013. Office: Miami Heat 601 Biscayne Blvd Miami FL 33132*

BATTIN, R. RAY (ROSABELL HARRIET RAY), audiologist, neuropsychologist; b. Rock Creek, Ohio, May 29, 1925; d. Harry Walter and Sophia (Boldt) Ray; m. Tom C. Battin, Aug. 27, 1949. AB, U. Denver, 1948; MS, U. Mich., 1950; PhD, U. Fla., 1959; postgrad., U. Miami Sch. Medicine, Fla., 1957, U. Iowa, 1958. Diplomate Am. Bd. Forensic Medicine, Am. Bd. Profl. Disability Cons., Am. Bd. Psychol. Specialties, Am. Bd. Forensic Examiners (cert. forensic examiner, cert. med. examiner), forensic neuropsychology, devel. psychology, psychol. assessment, lic. psychologist Tex., audiologist Tex., speech pathologist Tex. Instr. in speech pathology U. Denver, 1949-50; audiologist Ann Arbor (Mich.) Sch., 1950-51, Houston Speech and Hearing Ctr., 1954-56; clin. fellow divsn. Clin. Svcs. U. Fla., Gainesville, 1952-54; dir. speech pathology/psychology Hedgecroft Hosp. and Rehab. Ctr., Houston, 1956-59; audiologist Drs. Guilford, Wright and Draper, Houston, 1959-63; dir. Audiology Lab. Houston Ear Nose and Throat Hosp. Clinic, 1963—73; clin. instr. U. Tex. Sch. Medicine, Galveston, 1964—80; pvt. practice psychology, audiology, and neuropsychology Houston, 1959—. Clin. instr. dept. otolaryngology U. Tex. Sch. Medicine, Galveston, 1964-80; dir. of audiology vestibulography and speech pathology lab. Houston Ear, Nose and Throat Hosp. Clinic, 1963-73; adj. clin. instr. U. Houston, 1981-86; lectr. The First Word program Sta. KUHT-TV, 1959; v.p. Behavioral Perceptual Ctr., 1986-90; neuropsychol. cons. edn. divsn. Environ. Health Screening Lab., 1989-99, adv. bd., 1989-99; lectr. in field in U.S., So. Am., and Europe. Author: (with C. Olaf Haug) Speech and Language Delay, 1964, Vestibulography, 1974, Private Practice: Guidelines for Speech Pathology and Audiology, 1971; editor (with Donna R. Fox) Private Practice in Audiology and Speech and Language Pathology, 1978; contbg. author: Seminars in Speech, Language, Hearing (Northern), Auditory Disorders in School Children (4th edit. Roeser and Downs), Current Therapy of Communications Disorder (Perkins); editor Jour. Acad. Pvt. Practice in Speech Pathology and Audiology, 1981-84; contbr. articles in field to profl. jours.; author: (with Irvin A. Kraft) The Dysynchronous Child (film), 1971, Symposium Brain Plasticity As it Relates to the Remediation of Attention, Auditory Processing, Language and Reading Disorders, 1999; The Battin Clinic Language Learning Screening Test for Preschool Children, 1985, The Battin Scale of Parent's Attitude Toward Family Experience and Need for Child Cochlear Implant Candidates. Bd. dirs. Juvenile Ct. Vols., 1980—83, Children's Resource and Info. Ctr., 1981—85, Dyslexic Adult Support Svcs., 1986—90, Musicfest, 1990—2002, Houston Repretory Theater, 1993—98; mem. adv. bd. Caring Adoptions, 1993—, HS Performing and Visual Arts Friends, 1998—2012, Bayou City Concert Musicals, 2006—. Counselor Women's Army Corps, 1945—46. Recipient Gold award for Ednl. Exhibit, Am. Acad. Pediats., 1969, Lifetime Achievement award Houston Psychol. Assn., 1996, Leadership award Sci. Learning Corp., 2000. Fellow: Am. Acad. Audiology, World Acad. Inc., Am. Speech and Hearing Assn. (profl. svcs. bd. 1967—70, com. on pvt. practice 1971—74); mem.: APA, Soc. Ear Nose and Throat Advances in Children, Tex. Biofeedback Soc., Internat. Assn. Logopedics and Phoniatrics, Acad. of Aphasia, Harris County Biofeedback

Soc. (pres. 1984), Houston Psychol. Assn., Tex. Acad. Audiology, Tex. Psychol. Assn., Tex. Speech and Hearing Assn. (v.p. 1968), Am. Acad. Pvt. Practice in Speech Pathology and Audiology (pres. 1968—70), Am. Coll. Forensic Examiners, Internat. Assn. Applied Psychology. Independent. Unitarian Universalist. Home: 3837 Meadow Lake Ln Houston TX 77027-4029 Office: Battin Clinic Inc 4545 Post Oak Place Dr Ste 375 Houston TX 77027-3121 Office Phone: 713-621-3072. Personal E-mail: rhrb@aol.com.

BATTLE, JAMES A., state legislator; b. Mullins, SC, Oct. 14, 1942; BS, The Citadel, 1964; MBA, U. SC, 1967. Chmn. Marion County Hosp. Dist., 1995—96; mem. Natural Resources Com., Agr. Com., Environ. Affairs Com.; mem. Dist. 57 House of Rep., SC, 1996—. Mem.: SC Aquaculture Assn. (pres.). Democrat. Address: PO Box 536 Nichols SC 29581 Mailing: 333B Blatt Bldg Columbia SC 29201 Home Phone: 803-526-2381; Office Phone: 803-734-3001. Business E-Mail: jab@legis.lpitr.state.sc.us.

BATTLE, THOMAS M., JR., Mayor, Huntsville, Alabama; m. Eula Sammons; 1 child, Drew. Comml. real estate developer; councilman City of Huntsville, Ala., 1984—88, mayor Ala., 2008—. Mem. Met. Planning Org. Bd. mem. Huntsville Emergency Med. Svcs., Early-Works Children's Mus.; adminstrv. coun. Trinity United Meth. Ch. Office: 308 Fountain Cir Huntsville AL 35801 Office Phone: 256-427-5000. Office Fax: 256-427-5257. Business E-Mail: contact@hsvcity.com.*

BATTLES, PAUL, state legislator; b. Sept. 04; m. Marijon B. Battles, 1968; children: Kory McDaniel, Kerron Bonds. Attended, Southern Tech.; BS in Psychology/Min. Rels., Shorter Coll. Banker Cartersville Fed. Savs. & Loan, 1969—2007; co. pres. Crescent Bank, 2005—07, mem. bd. dir.; mem. Bartow Co. Devel. Authority, 2005—, Joint Devel. Authority, 2008—; mem. Dist. 15 Ga. House of Reps., 2009—. Former chmn. Cartersville/Bartow Co. C. of C.; former vice-chmn. Etowah Edn1. Found.; mem. bd. dir. Bartow Co. Cmty. Found.; mem. bd. trustees Ga. Highlands Coll. Found., North Metro Tech Coll. Found.; former min. Macedonia Baptist Ch., Euharlee, 1980, Peoples Valley Baptist Ch., Friendship Baptist Ch., 2000. Staff sgt. 108th Armored Bn. USAR, 1968—74, Ga. Nat. Guard. Republican. Baptist. Office: 404 Coverdell Legislative Office Bldg Atlanta GA 30334 also: 2082 Rd #2 South SW Cartersville GA 30120 Home Phone: 770-382-9965; Office Phone: 404-656-0109. Personal E-mail: p.battles@yahoo.com.

BATTS, MARTIN, literature and language professor; b. Grand Rapids, Mich., May 24, 1941; s. Melania Rose Scherer; m. Reva M. Camp; children: Vanessa Elizabeth, Jeremy Martin. BA, Calvin Coll., Grand Rapids, Mich., 1965; MDiv, Trinity Evang. Div. Sch., Deerfield, Ill., 1973; MST, Dallas Theol. Sem., 1977; MA, U. Dallas, Irving, 1980, PhD, 1983. Bible rep. Am. Bible Soc., Chgo., 1973—74; mem. Village Missions, Canon Beach, Oreg., 1974—76; prof., English & philosophy LeTourneau U., Longview, Tex., 1983—. Mem.: C. S. Lewis and the Inklings Soc. (pres. 2006—07), Conf. Christianity and Lit. (mem., exec. bd. 2003). Conservative. Avocation: horseshoes. Office: LeTourneau Univ 2100 S Mobberly Ave Longview TX 75603 Office Fax: 903-233-3476. Business E-Mail: martinbatts@letu.edu.

BATZLI, TERRENCE RAYMOND, lawyer; b. Dec. 28, 1946; s. Marion Raymond and Kathryn Velma (Hudran) Batzli; m. Sharon Lee Heinatz, Aug. 2, 1969; children: Catherine Barrett, Jonathan Raymond. BS, U. Richmond, 1974, JD, 1975. Bar: Va. 1975, U.S. Dist. Ct. (ea. dist.) Va. 1975, U.S. Dist. Ct. (we. dist.) Va. 1983, U.S. Ct. Appeals (4th cir.) 1984. Ptnr. Mays & Valentine and predecessor firms, Richmond, 1982-93, Durrette & Bradshaw, Richmond, Va., 1993-96; prin. Barnes & Batzli, PC, 1996—2004, Batzli Wood & Stiles, 2004—. Mediator McCammon Group, 1997—2006; adj. prof. law Reynolds C.C., Richmond, 1980—82; lectr. in field. Mem. adv. bd. Nat. Head Injury Found., 1988—, VA Head Injury Found., 1990—91. Capt. US Army, 1966—70. Fellow: Internat. Acad. Matrimonial Lawyers, Am. Acad. Matrimonial Lawyers; mem.: Hanover Assn. Bus. (pres. 1989, bd. dirs.), Va. State Bar (bd. govs. family law sect. 1996—, sec. 1997, vice-chair 1999, chair 2000—), Metro Richmond Family Law Bar Assn. (founding pres. 1994), Hanover County Bar Assn. (treas. 1997, sec. 1998, pres.-elect 1999, pres. 2000), Richmond Bar Assn. (chmn. family law sect. 1982—83, exec. com. 1982—83), Ruritan Club (pres., zone gov., dist. sec.), Rotary (bd.dirs. 1980—84). Republican. Methodist. Office: Batzli Wood & Stiles Ste 200 3957 Westerre Pkwy Ste 400 Henrico VA 23233-1319 Office Phone: 804-545-9800.

BAUER, HENRY HERMANN, chemistry and science educator; b. Vienna, Nov. 16, 1931; came to U.S., 1965, naturalized, 1969; s. Martin Josef and Anne (Rafael) B.; m. Barbara Bush, Aug. 25, 1986; children from previous marriage: Helen Suzanne, Judith Ann. B.Sc., U. Sydney, 1952, M.Sc., 1953, PhD, 1956. Rsch. assoc. U. Mich., 1956-58, vis. scientist, 1965-66; lectr., sr. lectr. U. Sydney, 1958-66; assoc. prof., prof. U. Ky., 1966-78; vis. prof. Southampton (Eng.) U., 1972-73; dean Coll. Arts and Scis. Va. Poly. Inst. and State U., Blacksburg, 1978-86, prof. chemistry and science studies Coll. Arts and Scis., 1986-99. Author: Alternating Current Polarography and Tensammetry, 1963, Electrodics, 1973, Instrumental Analysis, 1978, Beyond Velikovsky, 1984, Enigma of Loch Ness, 1986, (under pseudonym Josef Martin) To Rise Above Principle, 1988, Scientific Literacy and the Myth of the Scientific Method, 1992, Science or Pseudoscience, 2001, Fatal Attractions: The Troubles with Science, 2001, The Origins, Persistence, and Failings of HIV/AIDS Theory, 2007; editor-in-chief Jour. Sci. Exploration, 2000-07. Fulbright fellow, 1956-58; Japan Soc. fellow for promotion of sci., 1974 Mem. Soc. Sci. Exploration (founding mem.) Unitarian Universalist.

BAUER, MISLEN STOL, clinical geneticist; MD, Pontifical U., 1976. Lic. Fla., 1983, diplomate Am. Bd. Pediatrics, 2006, cert. Am. Bd. Clin. Genetics-Med. Genetics, 2010. Intern San Ignacio Hosp., 1976, resident pediat., 1977—80; fellow clin. genetics Univ. Miami Hosps., 1986—88; clin. genetics cons. Genzyme Genetics, Miami, Fla.; med. dir. and pediat. cons. Children's Med. Svcs.; hosp. affiliation includes South Miami Hosp., Plantation Gen. Hosp., Joe Dimaggio Children's hosp., Broward Gen. Hosp. Med. Ctr., Baptist Hosp.; resident pediat. Miami Children's Hosp., 1981—84, dir. neurofibromatois ctr., clin. geneticist. Mem.: Am. Acad. Pediat. Office: Miami Children's Hospital 3100 SW 62 Ave Number 301 Miami FL 33155-3009 Office Phone: 305-663-8595. Office Fax: 305-669-6443.

BAUER, URSULA E., public health service officer; married; 2 children. M in Polit. Sci., Rutgers U., NJ; PhD in Epidemiology, Yale U., New Haven; MPH in Family Health, Columbia U., NYC. Epidemic intelligence officer La. Office Pub. Health; chronic disease epidemiologist Fla. Dept. Health; asst. prof. U. South Fla. Coll. Pub. Health; dir. tobacco control program NY State Dept. Health, 2001—08, dir. divsn. chronic disease and injury prevention, 2008—09; dir. Nat. Ct. Chronic Disease Prevention and Health Promotion Centers Disease Control and Prevention, Atlanta, 2010—. Contbr. articles to profl. jours. Office: Centers Disease Control and Prevention NCCDPHP 1600 Clifton Rd Atlanta GA 30333

BAUGHAN, MICHAEL B., aerospace product and parts manufacturing executive; BA in Economics, U. Va., 1977; MBA, Harvard U., 1984. Lic. pilot. Sales rep. Dow Chemical Co., 1981—84; mgr., Strategic Initiatives The Boston Co., 1986—90; pres. AET Sys., 1990—93; v.p., sales & mktg., Seating Products BE Aerospace, Inc., 1994—99, group v.p., gen. mgr., Seating Products, 1999—2002, sr. v.p., gen. mgr., comml. aircraft, 2002—05, pres., COO, 2005—. Bd. dirs. Novant Health, United Way. Office: BE Aerospace Inc 1400 Corp Ctr Way Wellington FL 33414 Office Phone: 561-791-5000. Office Fax: 561-791-7900.

BAUGHMAN, RAY HENRY, materials scientist; b. York, Pa., Jan. 14, 1943; s. Ray Henry and Ruth Marion (Beers) B.; m. Karen McCarthy, Apr. 30, 1989; children: Lara Crusan, Heather Leigh, Dana Marie, Rebecca Lynn, Alexander Murad. BS in Physics, Carnegie-Mellon U., 1964; MS in Materials Sci., Harvard U., 1966, PhD in Materials Sci., 1971. Staff physicist Allied Signal, Inc. (now Honeywell Internat.), Morristown, NJ, 1970—73, group leader, 1974-78, 1978-90, rsch. fellow, 1990-97, aerospace fellow, 1997—2001; Robert A. Welch prof. chemistry U. Tex., Dallas, 2001—, dir. Alan G. MacDiarmid NanoTech Inst., 2001—. Mem. adv. group for internat. confs. on synthetic materials, 1981—; advisor NATO, NSF, DOE, DARPA, Japan Found. Mem. editl. bd. Synthetic Metals, 1978—; mem. bd. reviewing editors Sci. Mag., 2000—; contbr. articles to profl. jours. Recipient Chem. Pioneer award Am. Inst. Chemists, 1996, New Materials Innovation prize, Avantex Internat. Forum for Innovative Textiles, 2005, Nano 50 award, Nanotech Briefs Mag. Carbon Nanotube Sheets and Yarns, 2006, Fuel Powered Artificial Muscles, 2007, NanoVic prize, Australia, 2006, Outstanding Technol. Leadership, Sci. Am. Mag., 2006, Chancellor's Entrepreneurship and Invention award, 2007, 21 for the 21st Century award 2007, Alumni Disting. Achievement award, Carnegie Mellon U., 2007, Kapitza metal, Russian Academy of Natural Scis., 2007; Named Hon. Prof., 3 Chinese Univs. Fellow Am. Phys. Soc. (mem. exec. com. forum on indsl. and applied physics 1995-99), World Innovation Found.; mem. NAE, AAAS, Am. Chem. Soc. (Coop. Rsch. award in Polymer Sci. and Engring, 1996), Materials Rsch. Soc., Russian Acad. Natural Scis. (elected academedian 1997). Achievements include discovery of new polymeric metals and non-linear optical materials, development of advances in understanding solid-state reactions, conducting polymer structure-property relationships and new carbon phases; invented electrochemical mechanical actuators, improved polymer batteries, improved switchable windows, new processes for the synthesis/fabrication of high temperature superconductors and improved sonar sensors; developed time-temperature indicators and new conducting polymers; pioneering novel applications of conjugated polymers and related nanomaterials; patents in field. Office: Univ Tex Dallas 800 West Campbell Rd BE3 316 Richardson TX 75080 Office Phone: 972-883-6538. Office Fax: 972-883-6529. Business E-Mail: ray.baughman@utdallas.edu.

BAUGHN, RICHARD, state legislator; b. June 9, 1958; Student in gen. studies, Walker Coll. Driver United Parcel Svc. (UPS), 1977—; mem. Dist. 14 Ala. House of Representatives, 2011—. Mem., asst. union steward Teamsters. Mem. Old Zion Meth. Ch. Mem.: NRA. Republican. Office: Ala House of Reps Rm 538-A 11 S Union St Montgomery AL 36130 Office Phone: 334-242-7593.

BAUM, HERBERT MERRILL, consumer products company executive; b. Chgo., Dec. 6, 1936; s. Jack William and Ruth Frances (Ginsburg) Baum; m. Diane Jean Kale, Nov. 1, 1975 (div. Sept. 1977); m. Karen Rochelle Oberman, Dec. 22, 1983. BSBA, Drake U., 1958. Account exec. Stern, Walters & Simmons, Chgo., 1962-66, Doyle, Dane & Bernbach, Chgo., 1966-69; v.p., account dir. Needham, Harper & Steers, Chgo., 1969-78; assoc. dir., dir. new products Campbell Soup Co., Camden, NJ, 1978, v.p. mktg., gen. mgr. soup div., 1978-84, exec. v.p. U.S. divsn., 1984-85; pres. Campbell USA, Camden, NJ, 1985-90, sr. v.p., 1986-89, exec. v.p., 1989-93; pres. Campbell N.Am., Camden, NJ, 1990-92, Campbell North & South Am., Camden, NJ, 1992-93; chmn., CEO Quaker State Corp., Irving, Tex., 1993-98; pres., COO Hasbro Inc., Providence, 1999-2000; chmn., CEO Dial Corp., Scottsdale, Ariz., 2000—05; bd. dirs. Ocean Spicy Cranberris, Inc. Bd. trustees Drake U., Jupiter Med. Ctr. Found., Fla., 2014—. With US Army, 1958—59. Home: 5223 Center St Jupiter FL 33458 Office Phone: 561-747-2321. Personal E-mail: herbertmbaum@gmail.com.

BAUM, VICTOR CURTIS, anesthesiologist; b. NYC, Oct. 18, 1948; MD, Vanderbilt U., 1974. Diplomate Am. Bd. Anesthesiology. Intern U. Calif., San Francisco, 1974-75, resident in pediat., 1975-76, 77-78; fellow in pediat. cardiology, 1985-87; resident in pediat. Mass. Gen. Hosp., Boston, 1976-77; resident in anesthesiology Michael Reese Hosp., Chgo., 1985-87; prof. anesthesiology, pediat. U. Va., Charlottesville. Frederic A. Berry MD prof., pediatric anesthesiology. Mem. Am. Soc. Anesthesiology, Internat. Anesthesia Rsch. Soc., Soc. Cardiovascular Anesthesiology, Substitute Assoc. U. Anesthesiologists. Office: Dept Anesthesiology Box 800710 U Va Med Ctr Charlottesville VA 22901-0710*

BAUMANN, SHELLY, diagnostic radiologist, educator; MD, Tulane U., 1982. Diplomate Am. Bd. Radiology-diagnostic radiology, 1986. Resident diagnostic radiology Univ. South Fla. Affiliated Hosps., Tampa, 1983—86; asst. clin. prof. radiology Coll. of Medicine Univ. South Fla.; hosp. affiliation includes Tampa Gen. Hosp. Office: University of South Florida 2700 University Sq Dr Tampa FL 33612 Office Phone: 813-253-2721.

BAUMGARDNER, JAMES LEWIS, history professor; b. Bristol, Va., Jan. 26, 1938; s. John Richard and Katherine (Lewis) B.; children: Ellen Lorena, James Michael; stepchildren: Joseph Branscome, Sarah Elizabeth Brock. AA, Bluefield Jr. Coll., 1957; BA, Carson-Newman Coll., 1959; MA, U. Tenn., Knoxville, 1964, PhD, 1968. Ordained to ministry Baptist Ch., 1955. Asst. prof. history Carson-Newman Coll., Jefferson City, Tenn., 1964-67, assoc. prof., 1967-73, prof., 1973—, chmn. history-polit. sci. dept., 1974-95. Contbr. articles to learned jours. Interim mem. Jefferson County (Tenn.) Bd. Sch. Commrs., 1978; mem. Anderson County (Tenn.) Bd. Edn., 1990-94; active interim, bivocation pastor. Served with U.S. Army, 1959-62. Named Bivocational Pastor of the Yr., Tenn. Bapt. Conv., 1997. Mem. Am. Hist. Assn., Acad. Polit. Sci., Orgn. Am. Historians, Am. Polit. Sci. Assn., Southern Hist. Assn., Bapt. History & Heritage Soc., Phi Alpha Theta. Office: Carson-Newman University PO Box 71929 Jefferson City TN 37760-7001

BAUR, MICHAEL L., information technology executive; Product mgr. Gates Corp., 1989—90, merchandising dir., 1990—91; pres., gen. mgr. Argent Technologies Inc., 1991—92; pres. ScanSource Inc., Greenville, SC, 1992—2000; bd. dir. ScanSource, Inc., Greenville, SC, 1995—; pres., CEO ScanSource Inc., Greenville, SC, 2000—07; CEO ScanSource, Inc., Greenville, SC, 2007—. Bd. mem. Assn. Automatic identification & Data Capture Technologies. Office: ScanSource Inc 6 Logue Ct Greenville SC 29615

BAWA, RAJ, biotechnologist, inventor, professor, researcher, entrepreneur, patent agent; s. Sukhdev Raj and Sudesh (Bhalla) B. BSc in Microbiology with honors, Panjab U., 1985; MS in Biology, Rensselaer Poly. Inst., Troy, NY, 1987, PhD in Biology, Biophysics, Biochemistry, 1990. Registered patent agent 2002. Rsch. and tchg. asst., biology dept., Rensselaer Poly. Inst., 1985-90; patent examiner, Patent and Trademark Office, US Dept. Commerce, Washington, 1990-96, primary examiner, Patent and Trademark Office, 1996—2002; vis. asst. prof. Rensselaer Poly. Inst., 1999—2002, adj. asst. prof., 2002—04, adj. assoc. prof., 2007—10, adj. prof., 2011—; pres. and patent agt. Bawa Biotech LLC, Ashburn, Va., 2002—; adj. prof. natural and applied scis. Northern Va. CC, Annandale, Va., 2004—. Review panel NIH, Bethesda, Md., 2005, 2013, NSF, Arlington, 2007; prin. investigator NCI/SBIR Contracts, 2009—12; spkr. in field; patent legal advisor Sequoia Pharms. Inc., Gaithersburg, Md., 2008—09; sr. scientist Syner Gene, Therapeutics Inc., Potomac, Md., 2009—12; sci. advisor Teva Pharma. Ltd., Israel, 2012—. Mem. editl. bd.: Internat. Jour. Nanomedicine, Nanotech. Law and Bus., Cancer Nanotechnology, Recent Patents on Biomedical Engineering, WIRES Nanomedicine & Nanobiotechnology, Pharm. Patent Analyst, Jour. Epidemiology and Preventive Medicine Applied Sci. Report, JSM Biotech. & Biomed. Engring., assoc. editor: Nanomedicine, NBM; contbr. articles to profl. jours., chapters to books. Recipient Cert. Appreciation, US Dept. Commerce, 2001, Rensselaer Alumni Assn. Dir.'s award, 2001, Rensselaer Key award, 2005, Innovations prize Inst. Mech. Engrs. London, 2008. Mem.: ABA (co-chair nanotech. com.), NY Acad. Scis., Am. Chem. Soc., Am. Soc. Microbiology, Am. Soc. Nanomedicine (life; founding dir., Lifetime Achievement award 2014), World Future Soc. (life; global adv. coun.), Sigma Xi (life). Achievements include research in isolation and biochemical characterization of a novel potassium transport protein from mammalian mitochondria; research on membrane transport of cationic anticancer drugs and polyamines in mammalian mitochondria, electron microscopy of animal sperm cells; nanotech patent law, targeted nanodrug delivery and lung cancer imaging. Office: Bawa Biotech LLC 21005 Starflower Way Ashburn VA 20147 Office Phone: 703-582-1745. Business E-Mail: bawa@bawabiotech.com.

BAXLEY, DENNIS K., state legislator; b. Ocala, Fla., Aug. 22, 1952; married; 5 children. AA, Ctrl. Fla. CC, Ocala, 1972; BS, Fla. State U., Tallahassee, 1974; AA, Miami-Dade CC, Miami, Fla., 1975. Prin. owner, v.p. Hiers-Baxley Funeral Services; mem. Dist. 24 Fla. House of Reps., Fla., 2000—07, 2011—. Recipient Outstanding Young Religious Leader award, Florida Jaycees, 1989, George Albright Jr award, Coll. Pk. Kiwanis, 1999; named Humanitarian of Yr., Belleview-South Marion C. of C., 1996, Family of Yr., Jr Women's Club Ocala, 1991. Mem.: Rotary Club Belleview (former pres.). Republican. Baptist. Office: 315 SE 25th Ave Ocala FL 34471-2689 also: Fla House of Reps 214 House Office Bldg 402 S Monroe St Tallahassee FL 32399-1300 Office Phone: 352-732-1313, 850-488-0335.

BAXLEY, RICHARD D., family practice physician; MD, U. Miami, 1985. Diplomate Am. Bd. Family Practice. Resident family medicine Florida Hosp., 1986—88; hosp. affiliation includes Arnold Palmer Hosp. for Children. Office: Arnold Palmer Hospital for Children College Park Family Practice 2629 Edgewater DR Orlando FL 32804 Office Phone: 407-246-7001.

BAXTER, LAWRENCE GERALD, financial analyst, law educator, consultant; b. Pietermaritzburg, Republic of South Africa, Dec. 11, 1952; came to U.S. 1985; s. Gerald Robert and Renate Veronica (Volker) B.; children: Chantal, Imogen, Rochelle. B of Commerce, U. Natal, Pietermaritzburg, 1974, LLB, 1976; LLM, Cambridge U., 1977; PhD, U. Natal, 1985. Bar: Republic of South Africa 1978, N.C. 1988. Assoc. Livingston, Doull & Daly, Pietermaritzburg, 1978; sr. lectr. U. Natal, Pietermartizburg, 1978-82, prof. law, 1982-86, Duke U., Durham, N.C., 1986-95; sr. v.p., spl. counsel for strategic devel. Wachovia Corp., Winston-Salem, N.C., 1995-96; exec. v.p., head digital fin. svcs. Wachovia Bank, Winston-Salem, 1996-99, exec. v.p., head eBus. divsn., 2000—. Adj. prof. law Bond U., Australia, 1990—; vis. prof. Duke U., 1996; vis. fellow Wolfson Coll., Cambridge, Eng., 1988; cons. Adminstrv. Conf. of U.S., Washington, 1987-88, 89-93. Author: Administrative Law, 1984; co-editor Natal and Kwazulu, 1980; contbr. articles to profl. jours. Mem. ABA (coun. sect. on adminstrv. law and regulatory practice, chmn. fin. svcs. com., reporter Working Group on Lawyers Representation of Regulated Clients 1992-93), N.C. Bar Assn. (task force on adminstrv. law and procedure 1987-88), Bank Adminstrn. Inst. (chmn. emerging issues 1998—).

BAXTER, RICHARD HENRY GEOFFREY, research scientist; b. Hobart, Tasmania, Australia, Sept. 24, 1975; arrived in US, 1998, permanent resident, 2006; s. Geoffrey Robert and Valerie Joan Baxter; m. Agata Monika Bogusz, Oct. 22, 2005. BSc in Chemistry, with honors, Australian Nat. U., Canberra, 1998; MS, U. Chgo., Ill., 1999, PhD, 2004. Tech. asst. Australian Nat. U., 1998; postdoctoral fellow U. Chgo., 2004; rsch. assoc. Howard Hughes Med. Inst. Southwe. Med. Ctr., Dallas, 2004—. Author: 9 peer-reviewed jour. articles. Recipient Boomery award, Australian Soc. Biochemistry & Molecular Biology. Mem.: Am. Crystallographic Assn., Royal Australian Chem. Soc., Biophysical Soc., Am. Chem. Soc. Office: Univ Tex Southwestern Med Ctr 6001 Forest Park Rd Dallas TX 75390-9050 Office Phone: 214-645-5943. Business E-Mail: richard.baxter@utsouthwestern.edu.

BAXTER, STEPHEN BARTOW, retired historian; b. Boston, Mar. 8, 1929; s. James Phinney 3d and Anne (Strang) B.; m. Ann Sweeney, Aug. 22, 1953; children: Clare, Persis Baxter Andrews, James, Nicholas, Stephen, Michael. AB in Econs. with honors, Harvard U., 1950; PhD, Cambridge U., 1955. Instr. history Dartmouth Coll., Hanover, NH, 1954-57; asst. prof. U. N.C., Chapel Hill, 1958-62, assoc. prof., 1962-66, prof. history, 1966-91, Kenan prof. history, 1975-91. Vis. asst. prof. U. Mo., Columbia, 1957-58; dir. post-doctoral summer seminars Clark Meml. Libr. UCLA, 1973, 88, Clark libr. prof., 1977-78; dir. summer seminars NEH, Chapel Hill, 1974, post-doctoral seminar, 1978-79. Author: The Development of the Treasury, 1660-1702, 1957, William III and the Defense of European Liberty, 1650-1702, 1966; (with Paul R. Sellin) Anglo-Dutch Cross Currents in the Seventeenth and Eighteenth Centuries, 1976; (with others) Major Crises in Western Civilization, vol. 1, 1965, Eighteenth Century Studies Presented to Arthur M. Wilson, 1973, The Revolution of 1688 and the Birth of the English Political Nation, 1973, Biography in the Eighteenth Century, 1980, Changing Views on British History, 1984; editor: Basic Documents of English History, 1968, England's Rise to Greatness, 1660-1763, 1983; mem. editorial bd. Jour. Modern. History, 1971-77, Albion, 1982-92. Guggenheim fellow, 1959-60, 73-74; Charles Henry Fiske III scholar Trinity Coll., 1950-51. Home: 100 Eastwood Lake Rd # B Chapel Hill NC 27514-7501

BAY, ANNELL R., oil industry executive, geologist; b. 1955; m. Robert Suchecki; 2 children. BS in Geology, Trinity U., 1977; MS in Geology, U. Tex., Austin, 1980. With Oryx Energy Co., 1988—99, Kerr McGee Oil and Gas Corp., 1999—2004, exploration mgr. US Onshore, 2000, v.p. N.Am. exploration Denver, 2001—02, v.p. worldwide exploration, 2002; v.p. exploration Americas Shell Exploration and Prodn. Co., Houston, 2004—08; sr. v.p. exploration Marathon Oil Corp., Houston, 2008—. Bd. mem. Nat. Ocean Industries Assn.; trustee Am. Geological Inst. Found.; adv. coun. mem. Jackson Sch. Geology, U. Tex. at Austin Geology Found.; adv. com.

mem. Bur. Econ. Geology, U. Tex. at Austin. Adv. com. bd. Women's Global Leadership Conf. Mem.: Houston Geological Soc., Am. Assn. Petroleum Geologists. Office: Marathon Oil Co 5555 San Felipe Rd Houston TX 77056-2723

BAYAT, EHSAN, broadcast executive; b. 1963; In engring. Founder, CEO Tel. Sys. Internat., 2005—. Office: Telephone Systems International Ste 3 220 Ponte Vedra Park Dr Ste 220 Ponte Vedra Beach FL 32082-6616 Office Phone: 904-686-1470.

BAYER, KARL, lawyer; b. Houston, Feb. 22, 1949; BA in Elec. Engring., cum laude, Rice U., Houston, 1971; MS in Biomedical Engring., MIT, 1973; JD, U. Tex. Sch. Law, 1976. Bar: Tex. 1977, US Ct. Appeals (5th cir.) 1978, US Supreme Ct. 1978, US Dist. Ct. (no., so., ea. and we. dists.) Tex. Staff engr. Concord Rsch. Corp., Boston, 1973; adminstrv./legis. asst. Tex. State Senate, 1974—77; assoc. Grambling, Mounce, Sims, Galatzan & Harris, El Paso, Tex., 1977—79; legis. dir. US House of Representatives, Washington, 1979—80; staff atty., office gen. counsel EPA, Washington, 1980—81; assoc. Brown, Maroney, Rose, Barber & Dye, Austin, Tex., 1981—82; ptnr. Pluymen & Bayer, Austin, 1982—88; spl. counsel Bickerstaff, Heath & Smiley, Austin, 1988—89; ptnr. Gibbins, Winckler & Bayer, Austin, 1989—91; pvt. mediator, arbitrator, dispute resolution expert Austin, 1991—. Instr. U. Tex. Sch. Law, 1987—93, ann. guest lectr. alternative dispute resolution, 2000—; guest lectr. U. Monterrey Law Sch., Mexico, 1993—95, Annahuac Law Sch., Mexico City, 1996; mem. Supreme Ct. Adv. Com. Ct.-Annexed Mediation, 1996—99; ptnr. Resolution Architects, Austin, 1997—99; mem. magistrate selection and rev. com. US Dist. Ct. (we. dist.) Tex., 1999—, mem. disciplinary com., electronic filing com., 2000—. Contbr. articles to profl. jours. Pres. Capital Area Trial Lawyers Assn., 1990—91, Tex. Consumer Assn., 1991—92; bd. dirs. Legal Aid Soc. Ctrl. Tex., 1987—96, pres. bd. dirs., 1991—92. Recipient Cmty. Peacemaker award, Travis County Dispute Resolution Ctr., 1998. Mem.: ABA, Austin Intellectual Property American Inn of Ct., Fed. Bar Assn., Tex. Bar Found., State Bar Tex., Austin Assn. Atty. Mediators (pres. 2004), Austin Bar Assn., American Law Inst., Nat. Acad. Disting. Neutrals. Office: Karl Bayer Dispute Resolution Expert 8911 N Capital of Texas Hwy Ste 2120 Austin TX 78759 Office Phone: 512-345-8537. Office Fax: 512-345-9469. E-mail: karl@karlbayer.com.

BAYERN, SHAWN J., law educator; b. NYC, May 25, 1977; BS in Computer Sci., Yale U., New Haven, 1999; JD, U. Calif., Berkeley Sch. Law, 2006. Cert. former NASD Gen. Securities Registered Rep. Sys. and rsch. programmer Yale U. Info. Tech. Services, Tech. and Planning, New Haven, 1999—2003; mgr. JSP Std. Tag Libr., Java Cmty. Process, 2001—03; jud. extern to Hon. Saundra B. Armstrong US Dist. Ct. (No. Dist.) Calif., Oakland, 2004; summer assoc. Covington & Burling, Washington, 2005; intern appellate staff US Dept. Justice, Civil Divsn., Washington, 2005; editor-in-chief Calif. Law Rev., Berkeley, Calif., 2005—06; mem. office of solicitor gen. US Dept. Justice, 2006; law clk to Hon. Harris J. Hartz US Ct. Appeals (10th cir.); vis. asst. prof. Duke U. Sch. Law, Durham. Vol. Apache Software Found., 1999—2003. Co-author: (Book) Web Development with JavaServer Pages, 2002; author: JSTL in Action, 2003. Achievements include development of timecave.com, online svc. Office: Duke University Sch Law Rm 3015 Box 90360 Durham NC 27708-0360 Office Phone: 919-613-7201. Business E-Mail: bayern@law.duke.edu.

BAYLESS, WILLIAM C., JR., real estate company executive; BS in Bus. Adminstrn., W.Va. U. Resident asst., resident mgr. and area mktg. coord. student housing divsn. Allen & O'Hara Inc., 1984—88; dir. mktg. student housing divsn. Cardinal Industries, 1988—91; dir. ops. student housing divsn. Century Devel., 1991—93; co-founder American Campus Communities, Inc., v.p. devel., 1993—95, COO, 1995—2003, pres., CEO, 2003—, bd. dirs., 2004—. Office: American Campus Communities Inc 12700 Hill Country Blvd Ste T-200 Austin TX 78738-6307 Office Phone: 512-732-1000. Office Fax: 512-732-2450. Business E-Mail: wbayless@studenthousing.com.

BAYLOR, ARTHUR DARROW, federal marshal; b. 1955; BS in Criminal Justice, MS in Criminal Justice, Troy State U., Montgomery, Ala.; diploma, FBI Nat. Acad., Quantico, Va. Rose through ranks from patrol officer to maj. Montgomery Police Dept., 1977—98, chief of police, 2004—10; security coord., dep. marshal Unified Jud. Sys. Ala., 1998—2004; US marshal (mid. dist.) Ala. US Marshals Svc., US Dept. Justice, Montgomery, 2010—. Recipient Alumni of Yr. award, Troy State U., 2005, Montgomery/Tuskegee Achievement award. Mem.: Nat. Orgn. Black Law Enforcement Execs., Kiwanis (past pres.), Kappa Alpha Psi. Office: Frank M Johnson Fed Bldg 15 Lee St Rm 224 Montgomery AL 36104 Office Phone: 334-223-7401.

BAYNE, KATIE J. (KATHERINE J. BAYNE), marketing executive; b. Perth, Australia, 1967; BA, Duke U., MBA, 1989. Joined Coca-Cola Co., 1989; sr. v.p. Coca-Cola brands Coca-Cola N. Am., Coca-Cola Co., chief mktg. officer, 2007—. Bd. dirs. Beazer Homes USA, Inc., 2003—, Imagine It! The Children's Mus. of Atlanta. Named a Woman to Watch, Advt. Age, 2007; named one of The Most Influential People in the World of Sports, Bus. Week, 2007, 2008, 50 Most Influential People in Sports Bus., Street & Smith's SportsBus. Jour., 2009. Office: The Coca-Cola Co PO Box 1734 Atlanta GA 30310

BAYS, YVONNE MARY ERBE, music educator, marketing specialist, guidance counselor; b. Wausau, Wis., Nov. 18, 1947; d. Rudolph Anton and Lucille Virginia Karlen; children: Daniel, Heather. BMus Edn., U. Wis., Madison, 1969, postgrad.; MA in Guidance & Counseling, Eastern Ky. U., Richmond. Lic. music educator, Wis., Ky., guidance counselor, 1999-. Music-vocal tchr. Bayport H.S., Greenbay, Wis., 1969-70; tchr. bassoon, oboe U. Wis., Greenbay, 1969-70; jr. high choral dir. Kenosha Unified Schs., Wis., 1970-76; adjudicator, clinician Wis., 1969—, Ky. Univ. supr.-edn. U. Wis.-Parkside, Kenosha, 1976-78; mem. parent adv. com. Northern Hills Sch. and Onalaska Mid. Sch., 1987-88; mktg. specialist Metro Prodns., La Crosse, Wis., 1984-85; tchr. music elem., jr. high sch., sr. high, LaCrosse, Wis.; secondary high sch. choral dir., Lexington, Ky., 1988-99. Sec. exec. bd. Gt. River Festival of Arts, La Crosse, 1982—83, 1st v.p. exec. bd., chmn. adult choral workshop and performance, chmn. swing choir workshop, 1983—84, pres. bd. dirs., 1984—85; pres. La Crosse Area Newcomers Club, 1982—83; tchr. Confraternity of Christian Doctrine, 1985—88; bd. dirs. La Crosse Boy Choir, 1985—88; condr. Lexington Children's Choir, 1995—96, Ctrl. Ky. Youth Choruses, 1995—98; upward bound instr. Ea. Ky. U., 1994—95; parent vol. coord. Fauver Hill Sch., 1983—84. Mem. NEA, ACA, Ky. Edn. Assn., Ky. Counseling Assn., Ky. Adminstrs. Assn., Sigma Alpha Iota. Roman Catholic. Avocations: tennis, cross country skiing, needlecrafts, gourmet cooking, exercise.

BAYSAL, OKTAY, dean, educator; s. Selim and Servet Baysal; m. Figen Dinckaya, July 11, 1992; children: Celine M., Sarah I. Diploma engring., Istanbul Tech. U., Turkey, 1977; MS, U. Birmingham, England, 1978; PhD, La. State U., Baton Rouge, 1982. Registered profl. engr., Va., 1984. Asst. prof. dept. mech. engring. and mechanics Old Dominion U., Norfolk, Va., 1982—87, assoc. prof. dept. mech. engring. and mechanics, 1988—92, prof. dept. mech. engring. and mechanics, 1992—93, prof. dept. aerospace engring., 1993—, assoc. dean Frank Batten Coll. Engring. and Tech., 1999—2002, interim dean Frank Batten Coll. Engring. and Tech., 2002—04, dean Frank Batten Coll. Engring. and Tech., 2004—. Design, quality control engr. SEBA Dis Ticaret ve Insaat Ltd., Istanbul, 1976—77; tech. dir. SEBA Internat., Inc., Houston, 1982—95, SEBA Dis Ticaret ve Insaat Ltd., Istanbul, 1982—90; tech. cons. Lockheed Missiles and Space Co., Inc., Sunnyvale, Calif., 1989—90, Sci. and Tech. Corp., Hampton, Va., 1998; cons. ICASE, NASA Langley Rsch. Ctr., Hampton, Va., 1997—2002, Bayshore Concrete Products, Cape Charles, Va., 1998—99, Controls Corp. Am., Virginia Beach, Va., 1999—2000. Guest editor Am. Soc. Civil Engrs. Jour. Aerospace Engring., associate technical editor Am. Soc. Mech. Engrs. Jour. Fluids Engring. Bd. dirs. Va. Air and Space Ctr., Hampton, 2005—06, Va. Bd. Edn. Recipient Pub. Svc. medal, NASA, 1993; fellow, NASA Langley Rsch. Ctr., Am. Soc. Engring. Edn. Program, 1999; Eminent scholar, Old Dominion U., 1996—. Mem.: NSPE, ASME, AIAA, Va. Bd. Edn., Va. Microelectronics Consortium (chair exec. coun.), Va. Air and Space Ctr. (bd. mem.), Hampton Rds. Tech. Coun. (bd. mem.), Hampton Rds. C. of C. (bd. mem.), Va. Acad. Sci., US Assn. Computational Mechanics, Va. Soc. Profl. Engrs., Soc. Indsl. and Applied Math., Soc. Automotive Engineers, Am. Soc. Engring. Edn., Chamber Mech. Engrs. Turkey, Phi Eta Sigma, Phi Kappa Phi, Tau Beta Pi, Epsilon Mu Eta. Office: Old Dominion University 102 Kaufman Hall Norfolk VA 23529 Office Fax: 757-683-4898. Personal E-mail: obaysal@aol.com.

BAZELIDES, PHILIP J., utilities executive; b. Iowa; BA in Fin., BS in Fin., Creighton U. Joined Enron, 1971, v.p., human resources, 1992; mng. dir., human resources and adminstrn. Azurix Corp., 1992; sr. v.p., human resources Reliant Resources, Inc., Houston, 2001—. Office: Reliant Resources Inc 5221 N Ocnnor Blvd 290 Connor Irving TX 75039 Office Phone: 972-831-7350. Office Fax: 972-831-7399.

BAZER, FULLER WARREN, science educator, researcher; b. Shreveport, La., Sept. 2, 1938; s. Raymond Richard and Opal Stella (Goolsby) B.; m. Elmire Ann Schaaf, Dec. 29, 1962; children: Amy Elise, Beth Ann. BS in Biology, Centenary Coll. La., Shreveport, 1960; MS in Animal Sci., La. State U., 1963; PhD in Animal Sci., N.C. State U., 1969. From asst. prof. to prof. to grad. rsch. prof. U. Fla., Gainesville, 1968-92; Butler chair in animal sci. Tex. A&M U., College Station, disting. prof., assoc. dir. Tex. Agrl. Expt. Sta., 2001—, assoc. vice chancellor and exec. assoc. dean, agr. and life sci. Dir., mem. org. com. Inst. of Biosciences and Tech., 1994—2001; v.p. rsch., interim dean Grad Sch. of Biomedical Sci., A&M U. Sys. Health Sci. Ctr., 1999—2000. Editor-in-chief: Biology of Reproduction, Soc. for Study of Reproduction, Madison, Wis., 1989-95; contbr. 30 chpts. scientific books, 242 articles to profl. jours. Scientific advisor STOP! Children's Cancer, Gainesville, 1990—; advisor U. Kans. Mental Health program, Kansas City, 1991—. 1st lt. U.S. Army, 1963-65. Recipient physiology and endocrinology award Am. Soc. Animal Sci., 1980, rsch. award Soc. for Study of Reproduction, 1990. Mem. AAAS, Gamma Sigma Delta (sec.-treas., pres.-elect, pres. 1968—), Sigma Xi (sec., pres.-elect, pres.). Office: Tex A&M U Dept Animal Sci 113 Jack K Williams Bldg College Station TX 77843-2471 Office Phone: 979-847-9325. E-mail: fbazer@cvm.tamu.edu.

BEACH, CECIL PRENTICE, librarian; b. Knoxville, Tenn., July 12, 1927; s. Frank Alfred and Lillie Maude (Sims) B.; m. Doris Jean Pardue, Apr. 17, 1949; children: Steven Prentice, Rex Arthur, Keven Sanders, Kyle Alfred, Quentin Anthony; m. Marcia Gibson Buckley, June 20, 1969; children: Stephanie Lynn, Shannon Sue. AB, U. Chattanooga, 1950; MA, Fla. State U., 1952. Bookmobile libr. Chattanooga Pub. Libr., 1948-51; extension libr. Decatur (Ga.)-DeKalb Regional Libr., 1952-54; dir. Piedmont Regional Libr., Winder, Ga., 1954-60, Gadsden (Ala.) Pub. Libr., 1960-64, Tampa (Fla.)-Hillsborough Libr. System, 1965-72; state libr. State of Fla., Tallahassee, 1972-77; dir. div. librs. Broward County, Ft. Lauderdale, Fla., 1977-89, dir. pub. svcs. dept., 1989-93, ret., 1993; appt. bond project coord., 1999—; ptnr. Beach/Willey Cons., Tallahassee, 1993—; prof. Fla. State U. Sch. of Libr. and Infr. Studies, 1993—2009. Instr. dept. libr. sci. U. South Fla.; chmn. Fla. Libr. Study Commn., 1970-72; chmn. bd. dirs. Southeastern Libr. Network; chmn. S.E. Fla. Libr. Info. network; chmn. Fla. del. to The White House Conf. on Libr. and Info. Svcs., 1991; cons. libr. bldgs. and svc. Pres., Gadsden Community Coun., 1963; bd. govs. Nova U.; chmn. adv. coun. Seagull Sch. for Exceptional Children; mem. Fla. Endowment Humanities, 1972—, Ft. Lauderdale Downtown Coun.; bd. dirs. Easter Seal Soc., 1975—, Ft. Lauderdale Art Mus., Multiple Sclerosis Soc., Broward Pub. Libr. Found., Ft. Lauderdale Children's Theater. With USNR, 1944-46. Mem. ALA, Southeastern Libr. Assn. (pres. 1972—), Ala. Libr. Assn., Ga. Libr. Assn., Fla. Libr. Assn. (pres. 1969), Pub. Libr. Assn. (Allie Beth Martin award 1984), Adult Edn. Assn., Tampa C. of C., Greater Ft. Lauderdale C. of C., Fla. State U. Alumni Assn. (pres. 1967, Disting. Alumni award 1985). Lodges: Masons, Rotary. Democrat. Presbyterian. Home and Office: Apt 715 3100 NE 48th St Fort Lauderdale FL 33308-4948 Personal E-mail: cbeach0712@yahoo.com.

BEACH, CHARLES ADDISON, lawyer; b. Albany, NY, Apr. 21, 1945; s. Charles A.W. and Eleanor (Johnston) B.; m. Jane L. Shlionsky, June 8, 1968; children: James E. H. and Jonathan M. BA, Hamilton Coll., 1967; JD, Cornell U., 1973. Bar: N.Y. 1974, U.S. Dist. Ct. (no., ea., we. and so. dists.) N.Y. 1974, U.S. Ct. Appeals (2d and 10th cirs.) 1975, U.S. Supreme Ct. 1982, Tex. 1991, U.S. Dist. Ct. (no. dist.) Tex. 1993, U.S. Ct. Appeals (5th cir.) 1995, U.S. Ct. Appeals (6th cir.) 1998. Assoc. Shearman & Sterling, NYC, 1973-77, 79-81, Paris, 1977-79; sr. counsel, coord. corp. litigation Exxon Mobil Corp., NYC, 1981—90, Irving, Tex., 1990—2010; ind. arbitrator, 2010—. Mng. editor: Cornell Internat. Law Jour. Vol. Peace Corps., Libya and Tunisia, 1968-71; adv. coun. Cornell Law Sch.; v.p., bd. dirs. Irving Symphony Orch., 2006-. Fellow Tex. Bar Found. (sustaining life); mem. Dallas Bar Assn., Inst. Transnat. Arbitration Ctr. Am. and Internat. Law (adv. bd. mem.) Home: 1431 N Travis Cir Irving TX 75038-6238 Office: 1431 Travis Cir N Irving TX 75038-6238 Business E-Mail: charles.beach@verizon.net.

BEACH, ROBERT D., state legislator; b. Morgantown, W.Va., July 31, 1959; m. Rahel Amanda Beach; children: Jennifer, Melanie, Courtney, Samuel, Robert. Attended, Fairmont State Coll. Retail mgr., 1980—2000; realtor J.S. Walker Associates; exec. dir., CEO Garrett Coll. Found., Inc.; mem. Dist. 44 W.Va. House of Delegates, 2003—10; mem. Dist. 13 W.Va. State Senate, 2011—. Mem.: NRA, Nat. Assn. Realtors, Morgantown Bd. Realtors, Garrett County C. of C., W.Va. Farm Bur., American Philatelic Soc. Democrat. Methodist. Office: PO Box 1620 Morgantown WV 26501 also: WVa State Senate Rm 204W Bldg 1 State Capitol Complex Charleston WV 25305 Office Phone: 304-357-7919. Business E-Mail: bob.beach@wvsenate.gov.

BEACHAM, C. WAYNE, wholesale distribution executive; Grad., U. Ala. Joined S.P. Richards Co. (subs. Genuine Parts Co.), 1974, sales rep. distbn. ctr. Tampa, Fla., 1974—83, gen. mgr. distbn. ctr. Orlando, 1983—87, gen. mgr. Western divsn., 1987—88, v.p. Western divsn., 1988—90, sr. v.p. sales, 1990—93, sr. v.p. ops.; various positions including v.p. sales & mktg. and ctrl. group pres. Corp. Express; COO S.P. Richards Co., 2001—04, pres., 2001—, chmn., CEO, 2004—. Recipient The Spirit of Life award, Nat. Office Products Industry, 2005. Office: S P Richards Co 6300 Highlands Pky Smyrna GA 30082 Office Phone: 770-436-6881. Office Fax: 770-433-3586.

BEADLE, BETH MICHELLE, oncologist; b. 1975; BS in Chemistry, Northwestern U., 1996, Ph.D in Structural Biology & Biochemistry, 2002, MD, 2004. Surgical resident, McGaw Med. Ctr. Northwestern U., 2004—05; radiation oncology resident U. Tex. MD Anderson Cancer Ctr., 2005—09, asst. prof. radiology. Recipient Centennial prize, Phi Betta Kappa, 1996, Marple-Schweitzer award for Disting. Chemistry Undergraduate, 1996, Northwestern U. Med. Student Rsch. award, 1997, Drug Discovery Program Symposium Outstanding Poster award, 1998, Finn World Travel Grant award, 2001, Eli Lilly award for Outstanding Poster, 2001, Eleanor Montague Disting. Resident award in Radiation Oncology, Am. Assn. Women Radiologists, 2008, Outstanding ASTRO Presentation award, 2008, Young Oncologist Essay award, Am. Radium Soc., 2008. Office: U Tex MD Anderson Cancer Ctr Unit 097 1515 Holcombe Blvd Houston TX 77030 Office Phone: 713-563-2308. Office Fax: 713-563-2331.

BEADLING, BRENT, family practice physician; BS Biology and Chemistry, Mass. Inst. Tech.; MD, U. Fla. Diplomate Am. Bd. Family Practice, Am. Bd. Family Practice-sports medicine. Resident family practice Halifax Med. Ctr., fellow sports medicine; hosp. affiliation includes Baptist Med. Ctr. Office: Baptist Medical Center 10898 Baymeadows Rd Ste 100 Jacksonville FL 32256 Office Phone: 904-519-5338. Office Fax: 904-519-5664.

BEAIRD, JAMES RALPH, lawyer, educator, dean; b. 1925; BS, U. Ala., 1949; LLB, George Washington U., 1953. Bar: Ga. 1974, Ala. 1951, DC 1973. Atty. US Dept. Labor, 1951—56, asst. solicitor, 1956—59; assoc. gen. counsel NLRB, 1959—60; assoc. solicitor US Dept. Labor, 1960—65; vis. prof. U. Ga., 1965—66, prof. law, 1967—69, prof. emeritus, dean, 1976—87, dean emeritus; John Sparkman vis. disting. prof. U. Ala., 1988—; mem. Sec. Labor's Adv. Coun. Welfare and Pension Plans, 1968—. Mem. adv. com. Ga. SBA, 1969—. Mem.: Farrah Order Jurisprudence. Office: U Ga Sch Law Athens GA 30602 Personal E-mail: jrb@aol.com. Business E-Mail: jrb@bbgbalaw.com.

BEAL, ANDREW, entrepreneur, bank executive; b. Lansing, Mich., 1952; married; 6 children. Student, Baylor U., Waco, Tex. Founder, pres. Beal Bank (formerly Allegiance Savings & Loan Assn.), Dallas, 1988—, Beal Aerospace Technologies, 1997—2000. Named one of Forbes 400: Richest Americans, 2009. Achievements include formulating a conjecture in number theory, Beal's conjecture, 1993; recognition as the poker player who won more money in a poker game in a single day than any other known poker player, earning $11.7 million at the Las Vegas Bellagio on May 13, 2004. Office: Beal Bank 5909 Berkshire Ln Dallas TX 75225 Office Phone: 214-234-0400. Office Fax: 469-467-5258.

BEAL, JOHN M., surgeon, medical educator; b. Starkville, Miss., 1915; m. Mary Lucinda Phemister, Feb. 20, 1943 (dec. July 2005); children: John M., Bruce Phemister, Margaret Anne MD, U. Chgo., 1941. Diplomate Am. Bd. Surgery. Intern N.Y. Hosp., NYC, 1941-42, asst. resident surgery, 1942-44, 46-47, surgeon, 1947-48, attending surgeon, 1953-63; chmn. tumor bd. and staff surgeon Wadsworth Gen. Hosp., West Los Angeles, 1949-50, chief surg. service, 1950-53; cons. staff St. John's Hosp., Santa Monica, Calif., 1950-53; instr. surgery Cornell U., Ithaca, N.Y., 1948-49, assoc. prof. clin. surgery, 1953-63; instr. surgery UCLA, 1949-50, asst. prof., 1950-53; J. Roscoe Miller disting. prof. Northwestern U., 1981-84, prof. emeritus, 1984—, chmn. dep. surgery, 1963-82; clin. prof. surgery U. N.C., Chapel Hill, 1984-88; chmn. dept. surgery Chgo. Wesley Meml. Hosp., 1963-69, Northwestern Meml. Hosp., 1973-82; chief surgery Passavant Meml. Hosp., Chgo., 1963-73. Chmn. Am. Bd. Surgery, 1970-71. Served to capt. M.C. AUS, 1944-46. Fellow ACS (bd. regents 1973-83, pres. 1982-83); mem. Council of Med. Splty. Socs. (sec. 1978-80), Soc. Univ. Surgeons, Soc. Clin. Surgery, AMA, Am. Surg. Assn. Home: 1215 Lake Dr Valdosta GA 31602-1247

BEALL, KENNETH SUTTER, JR., lawyer; b. Evanston, Ill., Aug. 9, 1938; s. Kenneth Sutter and Helen Cantlon (Koenig) B.; m. Blair Hamilton Bissett, May 25, 1975; children: Kevina Anne, Hunter Bissett, Baret Bissett. BA, Washington and Lee U., 1961, LLB, 1963. Bar: Fla. 1964. With Gunster, Yoakley & Stewart, P.A., West Palm Beach, Fla., 1964—, ptnr., 1970—, pres., 1994—2004. Bd. dirs. The Whitehall Found., The Wells Family Found., The Island Sch.; chmn. Palm Beach County Environ. Control Hearing Bd., 1970-92; mem. law coun. Washington and Lee U., 1997-2001; trustee, sec. Caribbean/Latin Am. Action, 2000-03. Served with USMCR, 1963-68. Mem. ABA, Fla. Bar (Pres.'s Pro Bono Svc. award 1983), Palm Beach County Bar Assn., Fed. Bar Assn. (pres. Palm Beach County chpt. 1981). Democrat. Roman Catholic. Office: 777 S Flagler Dr Ste 500E West Palm Beach FL 33401-6121 E-mail: kbeall@gunster.com.

BEALL, LYNN, broadcast executive; Degree in Journalism, U. Kans. With TeleRep Taft Broadcasting (sales and mgmt. training program); account exec., nat. sales mgr. WDCA-TV, Washington; nat. sales mgr. WUSA, Washington; dir., mktg. through dir., mktg. and programming KPNX-TV, 1991—94; v.p., broadcast KSDK-TV, 1997—98, pres., gen. mgr., 1998—; gen. exec., Gannett TV Gannett Co., Inc., 1994—97, sr. v.p., Gannett TV, 2001—06; exec. v.p. Gannett Broadcasting, Inc. (subs. of Gannett Co., Inc.), 2006—; mem., exec. dir. Open Mobile Video Coalition. Nat. v.p. Muscular Dystrophy Assn.; bd. adv. Susan G. Komen Breast Cancer Found.; bd. dirs. Urban League of Met. St. Louis, Cardinal Glennon Children's Hosp., Regional Chamber and Growth Assn., St. Louis; first vice chmn., TV Bd. Nat. Assn. of Broadcasters, 2007-. Recipient Mgr. of the Yr, 2000. Office: Gannett Broadcasting Inc 7950 Jones Branch Dr Mc Lean VA 22102-3302 Office Phone: 703-854-6000. Office Fax: 703-854-2053. Business E-Mail: lbeall@ksdk.gannett.com.

BEALL, ROBERT MATTHEWS, II, retail executive; b. Fresno, Calif., Aug. 7, 1943; s. Egbert Ruffin and Lynda Topp (Matthews) B.; m. Aldona Louise Kupchella, June 15, 1943; children: Jennifer, Lydia, Alexis, Robert. BSBA, U. Fla., 1965; MBA with distinction, NYU, 1969. Asst. buyer Bloomingdale's, NYC, 1969-70; mgr. to chmn. Beall's, Inc., Bradenton, Fla., 1970—. Bd. Fla. Power & Light Corp., Blue Cross Blue Shield Fla., SunTrust Bank, Inc. Divsn. chmn. United Way, Bradenton, 1991; bd. dirs. St. Stephens Sch., Bradenton, 1977-80, Tilton Sch., NH, 1988-92. Capt. U.S. Army, 1965-67. Mem. Nat. Retail Fedn. (bd. dirs. 1982—), Fla. C. of C. (chmn. 1994), Fla. Coun. 100 (bd. dirs., exec. com.), Pi Kappa Phi. Episcopalian. Office: Beall's Inc PO Box 9285 Bradenton FL 34206-9285

BEALL, SAMUEL E., III, (SANDY BEALL), restaurant chain company executive; b. Knoxville, Tenn., June 18, 1950; s. Samuel E. and Mary Ann (Adcock) B.; m. Kreis Bailey, Aug. 28, 1975; children: Sam, David. Student, U. Tenn., 1969-72. Founder, chmn. Ruby Tuesday, Inc., Knoxville, Tenn., 1972-82; pres. specialty restaurant div. Morrison Restaurants, Inc., Mobile, Ala., 1982-84, exec. v.p.,

1985—87, pres., COO, 1987—92, pres., CEO, 1992—95, chmn., CEO, 1995—96; pres., CEO Ruby Tuesday, Inc., Mobile, Ala., 1992—95, chmn., CEO Maryville, Tenn., 1996—2004, chmn., pres., CEO, 2004—. Bd. dirs. Ruby Tuesday Inc., 1982-, Pilot Corp., Pilot Travel Centers, LLC, Windstream Corp., 2006-, SSC Svc. Solutions Co., Blackberry Hotel Co. Inc. Bd. dirs. Mobile council Boy Scouts America, 1986. Served as sgt. USAFR, 1969-74. Office: Ruby Tuesday Inc 150 W Church Ave Maryville TN 37801

BEALS, LOREN ALAN, association executive; b. Glens Falls, NY, Jan. 10, 1933; s. Edgar Vernon and Ruth (Ackley) B.; m. Sandra Gale Campbell, Feb. 26, 1982; children by previous marriage: Vernon Alan, Catherine Ann, Kimberly Ruth; stepchildren: Vicki Lynn Adair, Steven Montgomery Campbell, Gary Britt Campbell, Toby Lane Poston, Jacob David Adair. BA, Colgate U., 1954; M.P.A., Syracuse U., 1955. Intern, City of Richmond, Va., 1955-56; adminstrv. asst. City of Norfolk, Va., 1956; dir. publs., dir. town affiliations Nat. League of Cities, Washington, 1957-59, dir. congl. relations, 1970, dir. fed. affairs, 1971, dep. dir., 1972-75, exec. dir., 1975-90. Exec. sec. Md. Municipal League, College Park, 1959-65; dir. econ. ops. programs Met. Fund, Detroit, 1965-66; sec. Pub. Ofcls. Adv. Coun., Office Econ. Opportunity, Washington, 1966-67, Great Lakes regional dir., Chgo., 1967-70; lectr. govt. and politics U. Md., 1959-65; chmn. Fed. Regional Coun., Chgo., 1968-69; lectr. U. So. Calif., L.A., 1977-81; founding trustee Cmty. Found., Silver Spring, Md., 1971-75; bd. dirs. Nat. Tng. and Devel. Svc., Washington, 1975-82, chmn., 1976-77; bd. dirs. Nat. Assn. Regional Couns., Washington, 1975-79, Coun. for Internat. Urban Liaison, Washington, 1975-85, chmn., 1980-82; bd. dirs. Pub. Tech., Inc., Washington, 1975-90, chmn., 1978-80, 83-85, 86-90; bd. dirs. Acad. for State and Local Govt., Washington 1975-90, United Way of Coastal Empire, Inc., 1995-98; chmn. Acad. for Contemporary Problems, 1977-78; bd. dirs. Ctr. for Renewal Resources, 1980-83; exec. com. Internat. Union Local Authorities, The Hague, 1985-90; pres., CEO Savannah Area C. of C., 1990-99; mem. Ga. Partnership for Excellence in Edn., 1990-99; exec. com. Savannah Olympic Support Coun., 1991-96. Contbg. editor: Nation's Cities Weekly, 1970-75, Editor-in-chief, 1975-90; editor: Md. Municipal News, 1959-65. Pres. Savannah Area Conv. and Visitors Bur., 1990-99, mgmt. cons., 1999-; sr. policy advisor local govt. reform Project Macedonia, 2002-07; assn. devel. advisor Devel. Alternatives, Inc., Romania, 2003-06, PADCO; local govt. cons. Dem. Internat. Inc., Kosovo, 2009-10; pres. Bamboo Farm and Coastal Gardens, Savannah, Ga., 2006—; Mendez Eng., Kosovo, 2012-13, Brown Pelican Consulting, LLC, 2011-. Fellow Nat. Acad. Pub. Adminstrn (trustee 1978-81); mem. Am. Soc. Pub. Adminstrn., City Club of Washington, Savannah Chatham Club. Personal E-mail: labeals@aol.com.

BEAM, RICHARD SQUIRES, theater educator; b. Evanston, Ill., Oct. 12, 1944; s. Robert Edwin and Hope Squires Beam; m. Marilyn Bonnie Jordan, Dec. 27, 1966; children: Katherine, Margaret. AB, Ind. U., 1966, AM, 1969; PhD, U. Ga., 1984. Designer, tech. dir. Theater 65 children's theater, Evanston, 1969—71; instr. Western Carolina U., Cullowhee, NC, 1971—74, asst. prof., 1974—85, assoc. prof., 1985—. Faculty fellow for instrnl. tech., Coulter Faculty Ctr. Western Carolina U., 1993—95, chair faculty, 2006—10. Dir., scenery lighting and designer: (more than 250 theatrical prodns.). Mem.: NC Theater Conf., Southeastern Theater Conf., US Inst. Theater Tech. Home: 52 Smoke Rise Tr Sylva NC 28779 Office: Western Carolina U Sch Stage and Screen Cullowhee NC 28723 Office Phone: 828-227-3800. Business E-Mail: beamr@email.wcu.edu.

BEAMER, FRANK, college football coach; b. Mt. Airy, NC; m. Cheryl Oakley; children: Shane, Casey. BS in Distributive Edn., Va. Poly. Inst. and State U., 1969; MS in Guidance, Radford U., Va., 1972. Grad. asst. U. Md. Terrapins, 1972; defensive coord. The Citadel Bulldogs, 1976, Murray State U. Racers, 1979—80, head football coach, 1981—86, Va. Poly. Inst. and State U. Hokies, 1987—. Recipient Paul "Bear" Bryant award, 1999, Munger award, Maxwell Football Club, 1999; named Eddie Robinson award, Football Writers Assn. America, 1999, Coach of Yr., Big East Conf., 1995, 1996, 1999, Coach of Decade, 1999, Bobby Dodd Coach of Yr., 1999, GTE Coach of Yr., 1999, Woody Hayes Coach of Yr., 1999, Coach of Yr., Walter Camp Football Found., 1999, Nat. Coach of Yr., AP, 1999, Coach of Yr., Atlantic Coast Conf., 2004, 2005; named to Va. Tech Sports Hall of Fame, 1997. Office: Va Tech Univ Athletics Dept 359 Jamerson Athletic Ctr Blacksburg VA 24061 Office Phone: 540-231-4132.

BEANE, JERRY LYNN, lawyer; b. Winnsboro, Tex., Mar. 3, 1944; s. Von Rhea and Charlene (Hawkins) Beane; m. Linda Beane; children: Lucynda, Todd. BA, Baylor U., 1965; JD, Baylor U. Law Sch., 1967. Bar: Tex. 1967, US Dist. Ct. (no. dist.)/Tex. 1968, US Ct. Appeals (5th cir.) 1970, US Dist. Ct. (so. dist.)/Ga. 1971, US Supreme Ct. 1972, US Dist. Ct. (ea. dist.)/Tex. 1972, US Ct. Appeals (10th cir.) 1979, US Ct. Appeals (11th cir.) 1982. Assoc. Strasburger & Price, Dallas, 1967—73, ptnr., 1974—2003, Andrews Kurth LLP, Dallas, 2003—. Adj. prof. law So. Meth. U. Law Sch., 1989-1994. Contbr. articles to profl. jour. Best Lawyers in Dallas D Magazine (May 2001, May 2003, May 2005)., Top 100 Tex. Super Lawyers, Tex. Monthly (Nov. 2003)., Tex. Super Lawyer in Antitrust litig. Tex. Monthly (Sept. 2006)., leading Antitrust lawyers in Tex., Chambers USA Ams. Leading bus. Lawyers (2006)., Whos Who In Am. Colls and U. Fellow: Am. Coll. Trial Lawyers; mem.: chmn. Clients Security Fund Com. State Bar Tex., chmn., Antitrust Sect. Dallas Bar Assn., Am. bd. Trial advs., Tex. Bar Assn., Baylor Law Sch. Alumni Assn., Baylor Ex-Editors Assn., Dallas Assn. Young Lawyers (pres. 1973, chmn. continuing legal edn. com. 1979, chmn. bar activities com. 1980), ABA, Dallas County Health Com. (mem. 1978), Dallas Commn. on Children and Youth (mem. 1977—78), DAC Country Club, City Club. Bapt. Editor in chief Baylor Law Ref., 1967. Office: Andrews Kurth LLP Ste 3700 1717 Main St Dallas TX 75201 Office Phone: 214-659-4520. Office Fax: 214-659-4778. Business E-Mail: jerrybeane@andrewskurth.com.

BEARD, ELIZABETH LETITIA, physiologist, educator; b. New Orleans, Apr. 2, 1932; d. Howard Horace and Irene (Handley) Beard. BA in Biology, Tex. Christian U., Ft. Worth, 1952, BS in Med. Tech., 1953, MS in Med. Tech., 1955; postgrad., Smith Coll., Northampton, Mass., 1953-54, Vanderbilt U., Nashville, 1954-55; PhD in Animal Physiology, Tulane U., New Orleans, 1961. Instr. dept. biol. scis. Loyola U., New Orleans, 1955-58, asst. prof., 1958-62, assoc. prof., 1962-68, prof., 1969—, chmn. premed. com., 1978—; rsch. assoc. dept. physiology Sch. Medicine Tulane U., New Orleans, 1960-63, prof. biology med. reinforcement and enrichment program, 1968-94. Vis. prof. dept. physiology and biophysics Med. Sch. Harvard U., 1983-84, dept. neuropharmacology Scripps Rsch. Inst., La Jolla, Calif., spring 2001; vis. scientist Am. Indian Rsch. Opportunities Programs at Mont. State U., 1994. Contbr. articles on rsch. in physiology to profl. publs. Project rev. com. New Orleans Health Planning Coun., 1974-77, bd. dirs., 1975-78; soprano soloist Holy Name of Jesus Ch., 1978—, pres. sch. bd., 1976-79; grad. rsch. com. La. chpt. Am. Heart Assn., 1970-72, 81-83, undergrad. rsch. com., 1978-81, 89-93; active Met. Mus. Art, New Orleans Mus. Art. Recipient E. L. Bead Disting. prof. biology, Loyola U., New Orleans, 2011; NIH grantee, 1962-64, 67-69, La. Heart Assn. grantee, 1966-67, Edward Schleider Found. grantee, 1974-77, New Orleans Cancer Assn. grantee, 1962-63; Libby Rsch. fellow Sch. Medicine Tulane U., 1961, Named Outstanding Faculty mem., Loyola U., Faculty excellence award, Coll. Humanities and Natural Scis., Loyola U. Mem. AAUP, AAAS, Am. Physiol. Soc., Soc. Exptl. Biology and Medicine, Christian Med. and Dental Soc. Med. Missions Internat. (participant internat. med. missions 1993—), Sigma Xi Office: 6363 St Charles Ave New Orleans LA 70118-6143 Home: # 22 6363 Saint Charles Ave New Orleans LA 70118-6143 Office Phone: 504-865-2768. Business E-Mail: Beard@Loyno.edu.

BEARD, THOMAS REX, economics professor; b. Baton Rouge, Aug. 12, 1934; s. Rex and Gertrude Louise (Hampton) B.; m. Sharon Virginia Petty, Dec. 21, 1957 (dec.); children: Thomas Randolph, Sharon Beard Barber BS, La. State U., 1956, MA, 1958; PhD, Duke, 1963. Asst. prof. La. State U., Baton Rouge, 1961-64, assoc. prof., head econs. dept., 1965-68, prof., head dept. econs., 1969-71, prof., 1972-91, Alumni prof., 1991—97, Alumni prof. emeritus, 1997—. Economist Fed. Res. Bd. of Govs., Washington, 1964-65; 4th Nat. Bank Distinguished prof. Wichita State U., 1968-69; exec. dir. La. Council Econ. Edn., 1972-77; cons. La. Coordinating Council for Higher Edn., 1970, also various fed. govt. agys. Author: U.S. Treasury Advance Refunding, 1966, Financing Government in Louisiana, 1974; Editor: The Louisiana Economy, 1969; assoc. editor: Social Sci. Quar., 1966-70; mem. editorial bd. Pub. Fin. Quar., 1972-74, Rev. Regional Econs. and Bus., 1980-86, Jour. Macroecons., 1987-97; contbr. articles to profl. jours. Chmn. La. Gov.'s Council Econ. Advisors, 1975-77, mem., 1973-80. Earhart Found. fellow, 1957-58; Ford Found. fellow, 1960; James B. Duke fellow, 1958-60; La. State U. Parents Assn. grantee, 1983 Mem. So. Econ. Assn. (exec. com. mem., 1967-1969), Southwestern Econ. Assn. (pres., 1969-1970), Phi Beta Kappa (pres. La. State U. chpt. 1984-86), Kappa Alpha, Omicron Delta Kappa, Phi Kappa Phi. Methodist. Home: 5952 Hibiscus Dr Baton Rouge LA 70808-8891

BEARDEN, JAMES HUDSON, university official; b. Marion, Ala., Sept. 1933; s. Joseph N. and Lula B.; m. Pauline Larkins, Mar. 31, 1961; children: James Hudson, Jr., Pauline B. Simonowich. BS, Centenary Coll. La., 1956; MA, East Carolina U., 1959; PhD, U. Ala., 1966. Bus. mgr. Marion Inst., 1959; mem. faculty East Carolina U., Greenville, NC, 1959—, prof. bus. adminstrn., 1964—, dir. bur. bus. research, 1964, dean, 1968-83, dir. BB&T Ctr. for Leadership Devel., 1983—. Author articles in field. Former trustee Campbell U.; pres., trustee N.C. Council Econ. Edn. Served with AUS, 1956-58. Mem. Assn. Leadership Educators, Fedn. Bus. Honor Socs. (pres. 1991—), Rotary, Beta Gamma Sigma (pres. 1986-1990), Sigma Beta Delta (pres. 1994-2000). Home: 106 Crown Point Rd Greenville NC 27858-5718 Office: BB&T Ctr for Leadership Devel East Carolina U 1100 Bate Bldg Greenville NC 27858-4353

BEASLEY, ANTHONY, astrophysicist, observatory administrator; BSc in Physics, U. Sydney, 1986, PhD in Astrophysics, 1991. Postdoc., sci. staff mem. Nat. Radio Astronomy Obs., Socorro, N.Mex., Charlottesville, Va., 1991—2000, dep. asst. dir., 1997—98, asst. dir., 1998—2000, asst. dir, ALMA project mgr. Santiago, Chile, 2004—08, dir. Charlottesville, 2012—; project mgr., combined array rsch. in millimeter-wave astronomy NSF, Calif., 2000—04; COO, project mgr. Nat. Ecol. Obs. Network, Inc., Boulder, Colo., 2008—12. Recipient Maj. Rsch. Equipment and Facilities Constrn. award, NSF, 2011. Office: National Radio Astronomy Observatory Director's Office 520 Edgemont Rd Charlottesville VA 22903-2475 Office Phone: 434-296-0241. Office Fax: 434-296-0385.*

BEASLEY, BILLY, state legislator; b. Mar. 19, 1940; m. Rebecca Beasley; children: Martin, Brad, Margaret, Tom, Rebecca. BS in Pharmacy, Auburn U., Ala., 1962. Owner Toomer's, Auburn; operator Louisville Drug Store, Clayton Drug Co., Clio Drug Co.; pres. Pratts Station, LLC; mem. Dist. 84 Ala. House of Reps., Montgomery, 1998—2011; mem. Dist. 28 Ala. State Senate, 2011—. Mem. Clayton United Meth. Ch.; bd. dirs. Eufaula/Barbour County C. of C.; mem. Barbour County Hosp. Bd. Capt. med. services corps US Army. Mem.: Ala. Pharm. Assn. (past pres.), Auburn Alumni Assn., Clayton Rotary Club (past pres.). Democrat. Methodist. Office: PO Box 220 Clayton AL 36016 also: Ala Statae Senate State House Rm 737 11 S Union St Montgomery AL 36130 Office Phone: 334-775-3291, 334-242-7868.

BEASLEY, CHERI, state supreme court justice; b. Feb. 14, 1966; d. William James and Lou Beasley; m. Curtis Owens; children: Matthew, Thomas. BA in polit. sci. and economics, Rutgers U., New Brunswick, NJ, 1988; JD, U. Tenn., Knoxville, 1991. Asst. pub. defender 12th Jud. Dist. (Cumberland County), 1994—99, dist. ct. judge, 1999—2008; bus. law instr. Fayetteville Tech. Cmty. Coll., 1995; assoc. judge. NC Ct. Appeals, 2009—12; assoc. justice NC Supreme Ct., Raleigh, 2012—. Mem. First Baptist Ch., Raleigh. Recipient Women of Justice Pub. Ofcl. Award, NC Lawyers Weekly, 2013, Outstanding Achievement Award for Justice, Alliance of NC Black Elected Ofcls. and Advocates, 2013; named to Rutgers U. African-American Alumni Alliance Hall of Fame, 2013. Mem.: Wake County Bar Assn., NC Assn. Women Attys., NC Assn. Black Lawyers, Cumberland County Bar Assn., NC Bar Assn. Found., NC Bar Assn., Nat. Bar Assn., ABA (mem. appellate judges' conf. 2009—, mem. standing com. on diversity in the judiciary 2011—12). Office: NC Supreme Ct PO Box 2170 Raleigh NC 27602-2170

BEASLEY, DIANA F., biology educator; BS in Sci. Edn., Univ. Va. Biology tchr. Hickory HS, NC, 1989—. Named NC Tchr. of Yr., 2007, NW Region Tchr. of Yr., 2006—07, Hickory Pub. Sch. Tchr. of Yr., 2005—06. Mem.: NC Sci. Tchr. Assn., Nat. Sci. Tchrs. Assn., So. Assn. Coll. and Schs. State Accreditation Team, Alpha Delta Kappa. Office: Hickory High Sch 1234 Third St NE Hickory NC 28601 Business E-Mail: beasleydi@hickory.k12.nc.us.

BEASLEY, JAMES W., JR., lawyer; b. Atlanta, 1943; AB cum laude, Davidson Coll., 1965; LLB cum laude, Harvard U., 1968. Bar: N.Y. 1969, DC 1971, Fla. 1972, U.S. Supreme Ct. 1973. With Sullivan & Cromwell, NYC, 1968, Wilmer, Cutler & Pickering, Washington, 1970-72, Miami Law Firms, 1976—89, Cadwalader, Wickersham & Taft, Palm Beach, Fla., 1989-94, Tew & Beasley LLP, West Palm Beach, 1995—97, Beasley Hauser Kramer & Galardi P.A., West Palm Beach, Fla., 1997—. Capt. US Army, 1968—70. Office: Beasley Hauser Kramer & Galardi PA 505 S Flagler Dr Ste 1500 West Palm Beach FL 33401-5923 Office Phone: 561-835-0900.

BEASLEY, MARK V., lawyer; b. Jackson, Mich., Feb. 13, 1954; m. Linda Beasley. AB with distinction, U. Mich., 1976, JD cum laude, 1979. Bar: Texas 1979. Assoc. Johnson & Swanson, 1979—84; counsel Zale Corp., 1984—87; sr. v.p., gen. counsel & sec. Michaels Stores, Inc., Irving, Tex., 1987—. Mem.: ABA, State Bar of Tex. (mem. section on Bus. Law, Corp. Counsel, Labor & Employment Law), Dallas Bar Assn. (mem. sections on Corp. Counsel, Employment Law, Securities). Avocations: stargazing, piano. Office: Michaels Stores Inc 8000 Bent Branch Dr Irving TX 75063 Office Fax: 972-972-1556. Business E-Mail: beasleym@michaels.com.

BEASLEY, MICHAEL PAUL, professional basketball player; b. Frederick, Md., Jan. 9, 1989; s. Michael Beasley and Fatima Smith. Attended, Kans. State U., Manhattan, 2007—08. Forward Miami Heat, 2008—10, 2013—, Minn. Timberwolves, 2010—12, Phoenix Suns, 2012—13. Mem. US Jr. Nat. Basketball Team, 2007. Named Big 12 Payer of Yr., 2008, Nat. Freshman of Yr., CBS Sports.com, Rivals.com, The Sporting News and US Basketball Writers Assn., 2008, First Team All-Am., AP, 2008, First Team All-Rookie, NBA, 2009; named to John R. Wooden Award All-America Team, 2008; finalist John R. Wooden Player of Yr. award, 2008, Naismith Player of Yr. award, 2008. Office: Miami Heat 601 Biscayne Blvd Miami FL 33132*

BEASLEY, WILLIAM REX, retired judge; b. Tulsa, Aug. 29, 1934; s. O. Rex and W. S. B.; m. Donna Knight, Sept. 3, 1954; children: Bradley, Brenda, Barry. BS with honors, U. Tulsa, 1959, JD, 1967; grad., Nat. Jud. Coll., 1977. Bar: Okla. 1967; cert. mediator Okla., 2004-09. Asst. dist. atty., Tulsa County, 1968-71; chief prosecutor McAlester, Okla., 1971-73; assoc. dist. judge Tulsa, 1973—; chief juvenile judge Tulsa County Dist. Ct. Okla., Tulsa, 1981-88; chief criminal judge Tulsa County Dist. Ct., Tulsa, 1998—2000; ret., 2000. Lectr. Okla. Hwy. Patrol Acad., Oklahoma City, 1971—; mem. exec. coun. Okla. Jud. Conf., 1989-92; bd. dirs. Ct. Apptd. Spl. Advs., 1985-88; leader Nat. Jud. Coll., 1978; co-chmn. Tulsa County Ct. Fund; mem. rules com. Criminal Ct. Appeals; mem. judicial legis. com., 1997. Mem. Tulsa Safety Coun.; chmn. State Foster Care Rev. Adv. Bd., 1983-88; mem. Okla. Commn. on Children and Youth; founder, bd. dirs. Ct. Appointed Spl. Advocate, Tulsa, 1985-86; mem. adminstrv. bd. local Meth. ch. Mem. ABA, Okla. Bar Assn., Okla. Jud. Conf. (v.p. 1978, 79, exec. coun. 1989, 90, 91, 92), Nat. Coun. Juvenile Judges, Lions (del. Okla. jud. conf. 1989-92, mem. legis. com. 1997-99), Kappa Sigma. Home: 4640 S Quincy Ave Tulsa OK 74105-4729 Home Phone: 918-742-0205.

BEASLEY-TEAGUE, SHARON, state legislator; b. Feb. 15, 1952; married. AA, Ind. Coll. Bus. and Tech. Former state rep. Dist. 48; state senate candidate, 1988; state rep. Dist. 58, Ga., 1992—2002, Dist. 65, 2004—; mem. Motor Vehicles Com., Indusl. Rels. Com.; house rep. Regulated Beverages & State Inst & Property Coms., Ga., mem.; state rep. Real Estate; cmty. activist; mechanist. Cmty. activist. Baptist. Democrat. Baptist. Address: PO Box 488 Red Oak GA 30272 Mailing: 504 Legis Off Bldg Atlanta GA 30334 Office Phone: 404-656-7859, 770-994-2977.

BEASON, JEFFREY L., corporate financial executive; BBA in Acctg., Tex. Tech U. CPA Tex. Sr. v.p., adminstrn. Mojave Pipeline Oper. Co. (subs. El Paso Corp.), 1993—96; various acctg. and reporting positions including dir., fin. reporting El Paso Corp., 1978—93, sr. v.p., chief acctg. officer, contr., 1996—2005; sr. v.p., prin. acctg. officer, contr. El Paso CGP Co. (formerly The Coastal Corp.), 1996—2005; bd. dirs., treas & contr. El Paso Tenn. Pipeline Co., 1996, v.p., 1996—99, sr. v.p., 1999; interim v.p., v.p., corp. contr., prin. acctg. officer Svc. Corp. Internat., 2006—09; v.p., corp. contr. Heritage Svc. Corp., 2006; v.p., contr., prin. acctg. officer Buckeye Pipeline Services Co., 2009—, Buckeye Partners, LP, 2010—. Office: Buckeye Partners LP 1 Greenway Plz Ste 600 Houston TX 77046 Office Phone: 832-615-8600. Business E-Mail: jbeason@buckeye.com.

BEASON, SCOTT, state legislator; b. Hartselle, Ala., Oct. 13, 1969; m. Lori Beason; children: Keller, Merritt, McCalan. BS in Geology, U. Ala. Owner VFindEm.com, Custom Renovators, Old South Constrn.; mem. Dist. 50 Ala. House of Reps., Montgomery, 1999—2002, mem. Dist. 51, 2003—06; mem. Dist. 17 Ala. State Senate, Montgomery, 2007—. Mem. Jefferson County Rep. Exec. Com., Ala. Rep. Exec. Com., First Bapt. Ch., Gardendale, Ala. Republican. Baptist. Office: Ala State Senate Ala State House 11 S Union St Montgomery AL 36130 Office Phone: 334-242-7794.

BEATLEY, TIMOTHY, architecture educator; b. Alexandria, Va., July 29, 1957; s. Charles Earl and Marjorie Ellen Beatley; m. Anneke Bastiaan, June 6, 1997; children: Emily Carolena Bastiaan Beatley, Jaden Helena Bastiaan Beatley. B in City Planning, U. Va., Charlottesville, 1979; M in Urban Planning, U. Oreg., Eugene, 1981; M in Polit. Sci., U. NC, Chapel Hill, 1984, PhD, 1986. Prof. U. Va., Charlottesville, 1986—, Teresa Heinz prof. sustainable communities, 2002—. Author: (book) Habitat Conservation Planning, 1994, Ethical Land Use, 1994, The Ecology of Place, 1997, Green Urbanism, 2000, An Introduction to Coastal Zone Management, 2002, Native to Nowhere: Sustaining Home and Community in a Global Age, 2005. Home: 1707 Essex Charlottesville VA 22901 Office: U Va Campbell Hall Sch Architecture Charlottesville VA 22904-4122 Business E-Mail: beatley@virginia.edu.

BEATTIE, ART P., utilities executive; b. 1954; B in Fin., U. Tenn.; MBA, U. Ala., Birmingham; completed Standord Exec. program, Stanford U. Dir. Emageon Inc., 2004—09, Southern Co., prin. acctg. officer Ala. Power Co., jr. acct. Ala. Power Co., 1976, comptr. Ala. Power Co., 1997—2005, v.p. Ala. Power Co., 1997—2005, treas. Ala. Power Co., 2005—10, CFO Ala. Power Co., 2005—10, exec. v.p. Ala. Power Co., 2005—10, CFO, 2010—, exec. v.p., 2010—. Office: Southern Company 30 Ivan Allen Jr Blvd NW Atlanta GA 30308 Office Phone: 404-506-5000.

BEATTIE, DONALD A., aerospace scientist, consultant; b. NYC, Oct. 30, 1929; s. James Francis and Evelyn Margaret (Hickey) B.; m. Ann Mary Kean, Mar. 27, 1973; children: Thomas James, Bruce Andrew. AB, Columbia U., 1951; MS, Colo. Sch. Mines, 1958. Regional geologist Mobil Oil Co., 1958-63; Apollo lunar expts. program mgr. NASA, 1963-72, dir. NASA energy systems div. Washington, 1978-82; v.p. Houston ops. BDM Corp., 1983-84; cons. on energy and space tech., 1984—; pres. Endosat Inc., 1991-96. Dir. advanced energy research and tech. NSF, 1973-75; dep. asst. adminstr. ERDA, 1975-77; acting asst. sec. Dept. Energy, Washington, 1977-78; solar energy coordinator U.S./USSR Coop. in Sci. and Tech.; U.S. rep. Vienna Inst. for Comparative Econ. Studies Workshop on Energy. Author, editor: History and Overview of Solar Heat Technologies, 1997; author: Taking Science to the Moon, 2001, Isscapades: The Crippling of America's Space Program, 2006; contbr. numerous articles on lunar sci., energy to profl. jours. Active Boy Scouts Am., 1958-71. Served with AC USN, 1951-56. Recipient Exceptional Service medal NASA, 1971, Sr. Exec. Service and Outstanding Performance award, 1980; Superior Achievement award Dept. Energy, 1978. Fellow AAAS; mem. Geol. Soc. Am., Am. Astronautical Soc., The Planetary Society. Home and Office: 808 Mill Pond Ct Jacksonville FL 32259-3027

BEATTY, DONALD W., state supreme court justice; b. Spartanburg, SC; s. Arthur and Ruth Beatty; m. Angela Chestnut; 3 children. B, SC State U., Orangeburg, 1974; JD, U. SC Sch. Law, Columbia, 1979. Bar: SC 1979. Pvt. practice atty., 1979—95; mem. Spartanburg City Coun., 1988—90, SC House of Reps., 1990—95; judge Cir. Ct. the Seventh Jud. Cir., SC, 1995—2003, SC Ct. Appeals, 2003—07; assoc. justice SC Supreme Ct., 2007—. Mem. fee dispute resolution com. Cir. Ct. the Seventh Jud. Cir., mem. sentencing guidelines commn., com. to review SC drug and common laws. Former vice chmn., chair-elect SC Legis. Black Caucus; judiciary com. SC House of Reps.; trustee Mount Moriah Bapt. Ch., Spartanburg; bd. dirs. Piedmont Legal Services, Spartanburg Residential Devel. Corp.; adv. bd. BB&T; minority adv. bd. BMW Constrn. Project. Commd. officer US Army. Baptist. Office: Supreme Ct SC PO Box 11330 Columbia SC 29211 Office Phone: 803-734-1080.*

BEATTY, KENNETH ORION, JR., chemical engineer, educator; b. East Lansdowne, Pa., Dec. 18, 1913; s. Kenneth Orion and Ada Pearl (Marshall) B.; m. Mary Catharine Carter, Aug. 8, 1936; children: Susan Jennifer, Prudence Carter, Lucy Margaret. BS, Lehigh U., 1935, MS, 1937; PhD, U. Mich., 1946. Registered profl. engr., N.C. Raybestos-Manhattan fellow Lehigh U., 1935-37; chem. engr. Dow Chem. Co., Midland, Mich., 1937-39; asst. prof. chem. engring. U. R.I., Kingston, 1939-44; rsch. assoc. U. Mich., 1944-46; assoc. prof. N.C. State U., Raleigh, 1946-48, prof., 1948—, acting head dept. chem. engring., 1959-60, R.J. Reynolds Industries prof. chem. engring., 1961—, spl. cons. in forensic engring., 1982—. Dir. Carolina Cons. Scientists and Engrs., 1979-87; vis. prof. chem. engring. Ohio State U., summer 1949; vis. engr. Pratt & Whitney Co., Middletown, Conn., summer 1957; resident cons. engr. Nat. Lead Co. of Ohio, Fernald, summer 1959; mem. Max Jakob Award Com., 1963-67, chmn., 1966; mem. Nat. Heat Transfer Conf. Coordinating Com., 1965-71, chmn., 1967; coordinating chmn. 9th Nat. Heat Transfer Conf., Seattle, 1967; U.S. founding del. Assembly for Internat. Heat Transfer Conf., 1967-72; mem. sci. council Internat. Center for Heat and Mass Transfer, Yugoslavia, 1971-90. Contbr. articles to profl. jours. Mem. N.C. Gov.'s Sci. Adv. Com. Rsch. grantee NASA, NSF, Wright Air Devel. Center, AEC, Am. Soc. Refrigerating Engrs.; Princeton U. fellow, 1967-68. Fellow AIChE; mem. Am. Chem. Soc., University Park Homeowners Assn. Home: 323 Shepherd St Raleigh NC 27607-4031

BEATY, JAMES ARTHUR, JR., federal judge; b. Whitmire, SC, 1949; m. Toyoko Christine Beaty; 1 child. BA cum laude, Western Carolina U., 1971; JD, U. N.C., 1974; postgrad., U. Nev., 1985—91; LHD (hon.), Western Carolina U., 2002. With Richard C. Erwin, Winston-Salem, NC, 1974—77; atty. at law Ewrin and Beaty, Winston-Salem, 1977—78, Beaty and Friende, Winston-Salem, 1980—81; pvt. practice Winston-Salem, 1978—79; judge N.C. Superior Ct., 1981—94, US Dist. Ct. (mid. dist.) NC, Winston-Salem, 1994—2006, chief judge, 2006—. Recipient Disting. Alumni award, Western Carolina U., 1994. Mem.: ABA, NAACP (life), N.C. Assn. Black Lawyers (sec. 1976, v.p. 1978), N.C. Acad. Trial Lawyers (named outstanding trial ct. judge of yr. 1990), Winston-Salem Bar Assn., Forsyth County and 21st Jud. Dist. Bar, N.C. State Bar, Rotary Club, Sigma Pi Phi, Alpha Phi Alpha. Office: 251 N Main St Rm 248 Winston Salem NC 27101-3914

BEATY, JAMES HAROLD, pediatric orthopaedic surgeon; b. Atlanta, Feb. 3, 1952; s. James Harold and Stella Cater B.; m. Teresa Stewart, Apr. 8, 1978; children: Eric Christopher, Meredith Ann. BA magna cum laude, Washington and Lee U., 1973; MD, U. Tenn. Coll. Medicine, 1976. Diplomate Am. Bd. Orthop. Surgery. Intern Baptist Meml. Hosp., Memphis, 1977, resident, 1978, U. Tenn.-Campbell Clinic, Memphis, 1979-81, staff mem., prof. orthop. and pediatric trauma, chief-of-staff Germantown, Tenn., 1982—; fellow, pediatric orthop. Alfred I. DuPont Inst., Wilmington, Del., 1982; from instr. to prof. orthop. U. Tenn., Memphis, 1982-96, prof., 1995. Chief Tenn. Crippled Children's Svc., 1984; dir. pediat. orthop. fellowship U. Tenn. Campbell Clinic, Memphis, 1990, program dir. orthop. residency, 1992-99; chief of surgery, 1992-94, med. dir. 1993-; active staff Baptist Meml. Hosp., Regional Med. Ctr., Memphis, VA Hosp.; former pres. Orthop. Learning Ctr.; cons. Meth. Hosp.; lectr. in field. Co-editor: Operative Pediatric Orthopaedics, 1991, 2d edit., 1995, Fractures in Children, 4th edit., 1996; cons. editor Jour. Bone and Joint Surgery, 1994—, editl. cons., 1996—; editl. cons. Jour. Pediat. Orthop., 1991—, Clin. Orthop. and Related Rsch., 1993—, Orthop. Rsch., 1996; editl. bd. Jour. Ped. Ortho., 1997-; editor, Orthop. Knowledge Update VI; contbr. several articles and abstracts to profl. jours., several textbooks. Bd. dirs. Mid-South Down Soc., 1983-89, United Cerebral Palsy, 1983-89, Spina Bifida Found., 1984-89, Safe Kids Coalition, Memphis, 1991—, Children's Mus., Memphis, 1993-98; profl. adv. bd. Nat. Down Syndrome Congress, 1986-89, assoc. bd., 1990-94; sponsor Boy Scouts Am., Memphis, 1994—. J.W. Warner Acad. scholar, 1971-73, Gooch Acad. scholar, 1975-76; named one of Golf Digest Top 250 Golfer Doctors in Am. Fellow Am. Acad. Orthop. Surgeons (evaluation com. 1990-95, com. pediat. orthop. 1992-95, chmn. com. pediat. orthop. 1995—, past chmn. com. on continuing med. edn., bd. dirs. 1993-94, editl. bd. 1996-, pres. 2007-08), Am. Bd. Orthop. Surgery (bd. dirs. 1997-, pres. 2003-04); mem. AMA, Am. Acad. Pediat., Am. Acad. Cerebral Palsy and Devel. Medicine (edn. com. 1988-89), Orthop. Rsch. and Edn. Found. (state solicitor Tenn. 1989-92, state chmn., med. dir. 1993—), Pediat. Orthop. Soc. N.Am. (long range planning com. 1991-92, com. healthcare policy 1994-95, sec. 1995, pres. 2000-01), Am. Orthop. Assn. (traveling fellow 1984, ABC-Traveling Fellow 1991), Orthop. Trauma Assn., Mid-Am. Orthop. Assn. (program com. 1993-96, chmn. program com. 1996, pres. 2002-03), So. Med. Assn., So. Orthop. Assn., Tenn. Med. Assn., Tenn. Orthop. Soc. (chmn. membership com. 1988-89, pres. 1990-91, bd. dirs. 1992-94), Memphis Orthop. Soc., Memphis-Shelby County Med. Soc., Memphis Jour. Club, So. Internat. Chirurgie Orthop. Trauma, Soc. Argentenia Orthop. Trauma Infantil (hon.), Soc. Brazil Orthop. Trauma Infantil (hon.), Soc. Peru Orthop. Trauma Infantil (hon.), Interurban Club, Willis C. Campbell Club, Phi Beta Kappa, Omicron Delta Kappa. Avocation: golf. Office: Campbell Clinic 1400 S Germantown Rd Germantown TN 38138

BEAUCHAMP, ROBERT E., information technology executive; B in Fin., U. Tex., Austin; MS in Mgmt., Houston Baptist U., 2001. Joined BMC Software, Inc., 1988, sr. v.p., rsch.and devel., v.p., strategy mktg. & devel., bus. strategy, 1994, pres., CEO, 2001—, chmn., 2008—. Bd. dirs. Nat. Oilwell Varco, Inc., Meml. Herman Hosp. Sys., Tex. Med. Ctr., NYSE Listed Co. Adv. Bd., Baylor U. With Greater Houston Partnership, Ctr. Houston's Future; adv. Houston Tech. Ctr., Indo-Am.C. of C. Greater Houston. Recipient Distinguished Alumnus, Houston Baptist U. Office: BMC Software Inc 2101 City West Blvd Houston TX 77042-2827 Office Phone: 713-918-8800. Office Fax: 713-918-8000. Business E-Mail: robert.beauchamp@bmc.com.

BEAUDET, ARTHUR L., medical genetics researcher; b. Woonsocket, RI, July 4, 1942; s. Louis George and Sylvia Mary (Lareau) B.; m. Marjorie Adelynn Miller, June 10, 1967; m. Nicole, Alissa. BS in Biology magna cum laude, Holy Cross Coll., Worcester, 1963; MD cum laude, Yale U., 1967. Diplomate Nat. Bd. Med. Examiners, 1968, Am. Bd. Pediatrics, 1973, Am. Bd. Med. Genetics, 1982, 93. Pediatric resident John Hopkins Hosp., Balt., 1967-69; rsch. assoc. NIH, Bethesda, Md., 1969-71; instr. Baylor Coll. Medicine, Houston, 1971-73; active staff Harris County Hosp. Dist., 1973—; active staff, chief of genetic svc. Tex. Children's Hosp., 1973—; cons. staff Methodist Hosp., 1976—; asst. prof. Baylor Coll. Medicine, Houston, 1973-77, assoc. prof., 1977-81, prof., 1981—; investigator Howard Hughes Med. Inst., Houston, 1973-80, 85—; acting chmn. dept. moledular and human genetics Baylor Coll. Medicine, Houston, 1994-95, chmn. dep. molecular and human genetics, 1995—. Mem. bd. dirs. Am. Soc. Human Genetics, Rockville, Md., 1987-90; mem. founding bd. dirs. Am. Coll. Med. Genetics, 1990-94; mem. editl. bds. Human Molecular Genetics, 1991—, Human Mutation, 1991—, Human Gene Therapy, 1994—, Gene Therapy, 1994—, Human Genetics, 1994—. Co-author: (book) The Metabolic and Molecular Bases of Inherited Disease, 7th edit., 1995; editor: (books) The Metabolic Basis of Inherited Disease, 6th edit., 1989, The Metabolic and Molecular Bases of Inherited Disease, 1995; contbr. chpts. to books, articles to profl. jours. Recipient Med. award Alpha Omega Alpha, 1966; grantee numerous orgns. including NIH, March of Dimes, Cystic Fibrosis Found., others. Mem. Am. Acad. Pediatrics, Am. Pediatrics, Am. Pediatric Soc., Am. Soc. Human Genetics (program com. 1984-86, bd. dirs. 1987-90), Am. Soc. Microbiology, Assn. Am. Physicians, Genetics Soc. Am., Tex. Pediatric Soc., Houston Pediatric Soc., Harris County med. Soc., Soc. Inherited Metabolic Disease, Soc. Pediatric Rsch., NAS Inst. Medicine, NAS Achievements include research in the fields of molecular and human genetics, cystic fibrosis, gene therapy, inborn errors of metabolism and gene targeting; discovery of the uniparental disomy in humans. Office: Baylor Coll Med Dept Molecular/Human Genetics 1 Baylor Plz # T619 Houston TX 77030-3411

BEAVER, BONNIE VERYLE, veterinarian, educator; b. Mpls., Oct. 26, 1944; d. Crawford F. and Gladys I. Gustafson; m. Larry J. Beaver, Nov. 25, 1972 (dec. Nov. 1995). BS, U. Minn., 1966, DVM, 1968; MS, Tex. A&M U., 1972. Instr. vet. surgery and radiology U. Minn., 1968-69; instr. vet. anatomy Tex. A&M U., College Station, 1969-72, asst. prof., 1972-76, assoc. prof., 1976-82; prof. Tex A&M U., College Station, 1982-86, prof. vet. small animal clin. scis., 1986—, chief medicine, 1990-99; dir. Cmty. Practice Svc., 2006—. Mem. vet. medicine adv. com. HEW, 1972-74, nat. adv. food and drug com., HEW, 1975, com. on animal models and genetic stocks NAS, 1984-86, 87-89, panel on microlivestock NRC, 1986-87, task force on animal use study Inst. Lab. Animal Resources, 1986, adv. com. for Pew Nat. Vet. Edn. Program, Pew Charitable Trusts, 1987-92, 10th symposium on Vet. Med. Edn. Com., 1988-89; Frank K. Ramsey lects. Iowa State U., 2004; T.S. Williams lectr. Tuskegee U., 2006; spkr. com. Southwest Vet. Symposium, 2006-, vice chair spkr. com., 2008-09, chair spkr. com., 2009-. Mem. editl. bd. Applied Animal Ethology, 1981-82, 83-84, VM/SAC, 1982-85, Applied Animal Behavior Sci., 1982-84, 84-86, 86-88, 88-2000, Bull. on Vet. Clin. Ethology, 1994-1999, Jour. Am. Animal Hosp. Assn., 1995—2008, Jour. Vet. Behavior: Clin. Applications and Rsch., 2005—; contbr. articles to profl. jours. V.p. Brazos Valley Regional Sci. and Engring. Fair, 1974—83, dir., 1983—85; bd. dirs. Brazos Valley unit Am. Cancer Soc., 1976—83, v.p., 1976—83. Named Citizen of Week, The Press, 1981, Outstanding Woman Vet. of 1982, Disting. Practitioner, Nat. Acads. Practice; recipient Friskies PetCare award Am. Animal Hosp. Assn., 2001, Bustad Human-Animal Bond award, 2001, Elanco Disting. Lectr. award, 2002, Frank K. Ramsey Lectr. award, 2004, Lifetime Achievement award TVMA, 2007, Dean's Impact award TAMU, 2007. Mem.: AVMA (exec. bd. 1997—2006, chair exec. bd. 2001—02, pres.-elect 2003—04, pres. 2004—05, Animal Welfare award 1996), AAAS, Am. Coll. Animal Welfare (pres. organizing com. 2007—), Am. Soc. Lab. Animal Practitioners, Am. Assn. Human-Animal Bond Veterinarians, Am. Assn. Food Hygiene Veterinarians, Am. Horse Coun., Ark. Med. Vet. Assn., Am. Quarter Horse Assn., Tex. Palomino Exhibitors Assn., Palomino Horse Breeders Am. (v.p. 1983—88, treas. 1984—85, pres.-elect 1988—89, pres. 1989—90), Nat. Acad. Practice, Am. Coll. Vet. Behaviorists (chair organizing com. 1976—91, pres. 1991—96, charter diplomate 1993—, exec. dir. 1996—), Animal Behavior Soc., Am. Assn. Bovine Practitioners, Am. Assn. Equine Practitioners, La. Vet. Med. Assn., Am. Vet. Soc. Animal Behavior (pres. 1975—80), Am. Animal Hosp. Assn., Brazos Valley Vet. Med. Assn., Tex. Vet. Med. Assn. (3d v.p. 1990, 2d v.p. 1991, 1st v.p. 1992, pres.-elect 1993, pres. 1994, Legacy of Svc. award 2005), Phi Delta Gamma (pres. 1974—75), Phi Zeta (nat. pres. 1979—81), Sigma Epsilon Sigma, Phi Sigma, Delta Soc. Office: Tex A&M Univ Coll Vet Medicine Vet Small Animal Clin Scis College Station TX 77843-4474

BEAVER, HILARY A., medical educator, ophthalmologist; BS in Biology, Coll. William and Mary, Williamsburg, Va., 1987; MD, U. Va., Charlottesville, 1991. Cert. Am. Bd. Ophthalmology, 1997. Intern Baylor Coll. Medicine, Houston, 1991—92, resident in ophthalmology, 1992—95, clin. instr. dept. ophthamology, 1995—98, clin. asst. prof., 1998—2000; asst. prof. U. Iowa Hosps. and Clinics, Iowa City, 2000—06, assoc. prof., 2006—09. Dir. med. student edn. U. Iowa Dept. Ophthlmology, 2001—09, mem. resident edn. com. & task force competences, 2003—09. Contbr. articles to profl. jours. Recipient Janet M. Glasgow Meml. Achievement citation, U. Va. Sch. Medicine, 1991, Physicians Recognition award, AMA, 1997—2000; named Best Dr. in America, 2007—10. Mem.: Tex. Ophthal. Assn., Tex. Med. Assn., Am. Acad. Ophthalmology (mem. task force on aging com. 2001—03, subcom. basic and clin. sci. course sect. 2 2003—09, cataract specialty info. team 2005—07, Achievement award 2006, secretariat award 2009), Am. Soc. Cataract and Refractive Surgery, Alpha Omega Alpha, Phi Sigma Soc. Office: 6560 Fannin Ste 450 Houston TX 77030 Office Phone: 713-441-8843. Business E-Mail: habeaver@tmhs.org.

BEAVER, KEVIN, law educator; BA in Sociology, Ohio U., 2000; MS in Criminal Justice, U. Cincinnati, 2001, PhD in Criminal Justice, 2006. Instr., dept. sociology U. Cin., 2002, instr., divsn. criminal justice, 2003—06; inst. dept. polit. sci. and criminal justice Northern Kentucky U., 2006; asst. prof. Coll. Criminology and Criminal Justice, Fla. State U., 2006—. Invited presenter in field. Contbr. of several articles to profl. jours., chapters to books; author: The Nature and Nurture of Antisocial Outcomes, 2008, Biosocial Criminology: A Primer, 2009; co-editor: Biosocial Criminology: New Directions in Theory ns Rsch., 2009, Criminological Thoery; co-author: Handbook of Crime Correlates, 2009, Why Crime? An Interdisciplinaray Approach to Explaining Crininal, 2010; mem. editl. bd. American Journal of Criminal Justice, 2009—10, manuscript reviewer. Mem.: Southern Sociological Soc., Soc. for the Study of Social Problems, Am. Soc. Criminology (mem. membership com. 2008—09, August Vollmer award com. 2010, mem. program com. 2008, 2007, Ruth Shonle Cavan Young Scholar award 2009), Acad. Criminal Justice Sciences (mem. program com. 2009, 2011), Omicron Delta Kappa. Office: Fla State U Coll Criminology and Criminal Justice 322A Hecht House 634 W Call St Tallahassee FL 32306-1127 Office Phone: 850-644-9180. Office Fax: 850-644-9614. Business E-Mail: kbeaver@fsu.edu.

BEAVERS, ALMA MAE (MAE BEAVERS), state legislator; b. Millport, Ala., Dec. 11, 1947; d. Walter Leon Spruill & Louise Bottens S; m. 1968 to Jerry Wayne Beavers; children: Eric & Jason. BS, Trevecca Nazarene U., Memphis, Tenn. Court reporter, paralegal, Mt. Juliet, Tenn., 1978—; Wilson Co. commr., Dist. 1, 1990—94; finance chmn. Tenn. Ho. of Representatives, 1991—92, Tenn. State Repr., Dist. 57, 1994—2002, former asst. republican floor leader, republican caucus sec., vice chairwoman, freshman caucus, mem. state and local govt. com. and employee affairs com., 1994—2002; Tenn. State Senator, Dist. 17 Tenn. State Senate, 2003—, Republican Caucus Treasurer. Mt Juliet C of C (board member, 95-); Mt. Juliet Lions Club (finance chair, 92-93); Big Brothers Mt. Juliet (secretary, 94-); Lions Club; NRA; Kiwanis Club. Republican. Church Of The Nazarene. Address: 2020 Hunters Pl Mount Juliet TN 37122 Mailing: 317 War Memorial Bldg Nashville TN 37243 Office Phone: 615-754-4632. Fax: 615-758-4383. E-mail: sen.mae.beavers@legislature.state.tn.us.

BEBER, ROBERT H., lawyer, diversified financial services company executive; b. NYC, Aug. 17, 1933; s. Morris and Martha (Pollock) B.; m. Joan Parsons, June 14, 1957; children: Andrea, Judith, Deborah. AB in Econs, Duke U., 1955, JD, 1957. Bar: N.Y., N.C. With Everett, Everett & Everett, NC, 1957—58; atty. SBA, Washington, 1961—63; with RCA, 1963—81; sr. v.p., gen. counsel, sec. GAF Corp., NYC, 1981—83, exec. v.p., dir., 1983—84, dir. subs.; sr. v.p., gen. counsel, sec. Phlcorp, Inc. (formerly Baldwin United Corp.), Phila., 1984—88; asst. gen. counsel litig. W.R. Grace & Co., NYC, 1988—89, v.p., dir. litig., 1988—91, sr. v.p., gen. counsel, 1991—93, exec. v.p., 1993—98, ret., 1999, cons., 1999—2009. Bd. vis. Sch. Law, Duke U., 1996—; chmn. bd. Health Care Plan N.J., 1975-78; v.p. South Jersey C. of C., 1974-77; dir. Advantage Bank, Palm Beach, Fla., 1999-2003. Served with U.S. Army, 1958-61. Mem. ABA. Republican. Jewish. Home: 7228 Queenferry Cir Boca Raton FL 33496-5953 Office: WR Grace & Co 5400 Broken Sound Blvd NW Boca Raton FL 33487-3511 Personal E-mail: rhb11682@yahoo.com.

BEBIN, E. MARTINA, neurologist, educator; MD, U. Miss., 1986. Diplomate American Bd. Psychiatry and Neurology-child neurology, 2003. Resident in neurology Mayo Clinic, Rochester, 1986—91; assoc. prof. in neurology Univ. Ala.; dir. tuberous sclerosis clinic Univ. Ala. Hosp. Office: University of Alabama Hospital at Birmingham 619 19th St S Birmingham AL 35249 Office Phone: 205-934-4011.*

BECHAMPS, GERALD JOSEPH, surgeon; b. Flushing, NY, 1937; MD, Georgetown U., 1963. Diplomate Am. Bd. Surgery. Intern Meadowbrook Hosp., East Meadow, NY, 1963-64, resident in surgery, 1964-65; fellow surgery Mayo Clinic-Found., Rochester, 1965-69; clin. instr. U. Va. Sch. Medicine, 1971—; pvt. practice Winchester Surg. Clinic, Ltd., 1971—; asst. clin. prof., dept family medicine Va. Commonwealth U., 2003—09, clin. prof. surgery, dept. surgery, 2009—. Past pres. Fedn. State Med. Bds. of U.S.; surgeon Winchester Med. Ctr., Surgi-Ctr. of Winchester; mem. Va. State Bd. Medicine, pres., 1985-86, 87-88. Mem. ACS (past pres. Va. chpt.), So. Soc. Clin. Surgeons. Office: Winchester Surg Clinic Ltd 20 S Stewart St Winchester VA 22601 Office Phone: 540-536-0130. Office Fax: 540-536-0135.

BECHTOLD, ROBERT, diagnostic radiologist, educator; MD, Wash. U., 1979. Diplomate Am. Bd. Radiology-diagnostic radiology, 1983. Intern Vanderbilt Univ. Med. Ctr., Nashville, 1980, resident, 1983; fellow NC Baptist Hosp., 1984; prof. radiology Wake Forest Univ. Office: Wake Forest University Medical Center Radiology Department Medical Center Blvd Winston Salem NC 27157 Office Phone: 336-716-2471.

BECK, ALBERT, manufacturing executive; b. NYC, Jan. 14, 1928; s. Albert Christian and Mabel Agnes (Dunn) B.; m. Jean Norma Russ, June 16, 1951; children— Nancy, Richard, Douglas BS, Fairleigh Dickinson U., 1950; MS, Rutgers U., 1956. Product line mgr. Tung Sol Electric Inc. div. Wagner Electric, Bloomfield, NJ, 1951-66; dir. quality control IT&T, Brussels, 1966-69, asst. dir. product ops. NYC, 1969-72, dir. N.Am. staff, 1972-73; v.p. ops. Grinnell Fire Protection Co., Providence, 1973-79, exec. v.p., 1979, Grinnell Corp., 1986—2002. Mem. bd. edn. curriculum com. Wayne, N.J., 1964. Served with A.C., USN, 1945-47 Mem. Nat. Fire Sprinkler Assn. (bd. dirs. 1990), Sigma Xi. Republican. Avocations: golf, travel.

BECK, ANDREW H., farm equipment manufacturing executive; BBA in fin., Emory U.; MBA in acctg., U. NC. Auditor Arthur Andersen; joined AGCO Corp., Duluth, Ga., 1994, asst. treas., contr., internat. oper., chief acctg. officer, contr., sr. v.p., CFO, 2002—. Office: AGCO Corp 4205 River Green Pkwy Duluth GA 30096

BECK, DANE, advertising executive; Attended, Ind. U., Ball State U. Contr. Verizon; v.p., chief acctg. officer SuperMedia, Inc. Office: SuperMedia Inc 2200 W Airfield Dr Dallas TX 75261 Office Phone: 972-453-7000. Business E-Mail: dane.beck@supermedia.com.

BECK, DAVID EDWARD, surgeon; b. Geneva, Ill., May 1, 1953; s. George R. and Gloria M. (Zesch) B.; m. Sharon Meier, Aug. 30, 1983; children: Allison, Lauren, John. BS, USAF Acad., 1975; MD, U. Miami, Fla., 1979; postgrad., USAF Aerospace Medicine Primary Course, Brooks AFB, Tex., 1978, Combat Casualty Care Course, Ft. Sam Houston, Tex., 1980, Hyperbaric Oxygen CourseB, Brooks AFB, 1982, ATLS Instr. Course, Ft. Sam Houston, 1986, Squadon Officers Sch., 1987-88, Mgmt. for Chief of Hosp. Svcs., Sheppard AFB, Tex., 1988, Sch. Pub. Health, Harvard U., 1990. Diplomate Am. Bd. Colon and Rectal Surgery. Lt. Col. USAF, 1975-93; resident in gen. surgery Wilford Hall USAF Med. Ctr., Lackland AFB, Tex., 1979-84, chief colorectal surgery, 1986-92, staff surgeon, chief colorectal surgery svc., 1986-92, asst. chmn. dept. gen. surgery, 1988, chmn. dept. gen. surgery, residency program dir., 1988-92; staff gen. surgeon Patrick AFB Hosp., Fla., 1984-85; fellow in colorectal surgery Cleve. Clinic Found., 1985-86; residency program dir. gen. surgery Joint Mil. Med. Command, San Antonio, 1989-91; clin. assoc. prof. surgery U. Tex. Health Sci. Ctr., San Antonio, 1990-92, F. Edward Herbert Sch. Medicine, U. Health Scis., Bethesda, Md., 1992—; chief surgery 870 USAF Contingency Hosp., RAF Little Rissington, England, 1993; staff colorectal surgeon Ochsner Clinic, New Orleans, 1993—, chmn. dept. colon and rectal surgery, 1994—; med. dir. Ochsner Endoscopy Ambulatory Surgery Ctr., 2003—06. Cons. USAF Surgeon Gen., Washington, 1986-92. Author chpts. to books; co-editor (textbooks); (with David R. Welling) Patient Care in Colorectal Surgery, 1991, (with Steven D. Wexner) Fundamentals of Anorectal Surgery, 1992, 2nd edit., 1998, (with T.C. Hicks, F.E. Opelka, A.E., Timmcke) Complications of Colon and Rectal Surgery, 1996; editor: Handbook of Colorectol Surgery, 1997, 2d edit., 2002, ASCRS Textbook of Colon and Rectal Surgery, 2007; mem. editl. bd. Current Surgery, 1990-2006; reviewer Diseases of the Colon and Rectum, 1990—, mem. editl. bd., 1992-98, So. Me. Jour., 1988-92; mem. editl. bd. Perspectives in Colon and Rectal Surgery, 1997-2000; editor-in-chief Clinics in Colon and Rectal Surgery, 2001—, Ochsner Jour.; contbr. articles to profl. jours. Decorated Air Force Achievement medal with oak leaf cluster, Air Force Meritorious Svc. medal with oak leaf cluster; recipient Pres. award United Ostomy Assn., 2000. Fellow ACS; mem. AMA, Am. Soc. Colon and Rectal Surgeons (mem. socioecon./legis. com. 1991-94, pub. rels. com. 1993-99, chmn. 1996-99, mem.-at-large exec. coun. 2004-07, pres.-elect 2009-, Outstanding Young Investigator award, 1992), Assn. Mil. Surgeons U.S., La. State Med. Soc., Soc. Air Force Clin. Surgeons (treas. 1989-90, v.p. 1990-92, pres. 1992-93, Excalibur award 1992), Soc. Surgery of Alimentary Tract, So. Med. Assn. (mem. colon and rectal sect., sec. 1988-91, v.p. 1990-91, pres. 1991-92), Soc. Med. Cons. to Armed forces, St. Tamminy Parish Med. Soc., Tex. Soc. Colon and Rectal Surgeons (sec. 1991-93), Air force Assn., USAF Acad. Assn. Grads. Avocations: fishing, wood working, gardening. Home: 127 Deloaks

Rd Madisonville LA 70447-9597 Office: Oschner Clin Found 1514 Jefferson Hwy New Orleans LA 70121-2429 Home Phone: 985-845-1063; Office Phone: 504-842-4060. Personal E-mail: dbeckmd@aol.com. Business E-Mail: dbeck@oschner.org.

BECK, DAVID JOSEPH, lawyer; b. Pitts., Apr. 8, 1940; BS, Lamar U.; LLB, U. Tex., Austin. Bar: Tex. 1964. Sr. ptnr. Fulbright & Jaworski, LLP, Houston; founding ptnr. Beck, Redden & Secrest, LLP, Houston, 1992—. Mem. Judicial Conf. Standing Com. on Rules of Practice and Procedure, 2004—. Author: Legal Malpractice in Texas, 1991; co-author: O'Connor's Annotated Civil Practice and Remedies Code, 1999—2010; contbr. articles to law jours. Recipient U. Tex. Law Sch. Outstanding Alumnus Award, 2000, Jurisprudence Award, Anti-Defamation League, 2005, Professionalism Award for Fifth Cir., American Inns of Court, 2011; named a Disting. Alumnus of Lamar U., 1999; named one of The 25 Greatest Lawyers of the Past Quarter Century, Tex. Lawyer Mag., Top 10 Super Lawyers, Tex. Monthly Mag., The Nation's Top Litigators, The Nat. Law Journal, 2010. Fellow: Internat. Acad. Trial Lawyers; mem.: Comml. Bar Assn. (hon. overseas mem.), American Bd. Trial Advocates (advovate), American Coll. Trial Lawyers (pres. 2006—07), Internat. Assn. Def. Counsel (past pres.), State Bar Tex. (pres. 1995—96). Office: Beck, Redden & Secrest, LLP One Houston Center 1221 McKinney St, Suite 4500 Houston TX 77010-2010 Office Phone: 713-951-6209. E-mail: dbeck@brsfirm.com.

BECK, GEORGE LAMAR, JR., federal prosecutor; b. Geneva, Ala., 1941; m. Carlotta Beck; 3 children. BA, Auburn U., 1963; LLB, U. Ala., 1966. Bar: Ala. 1966. Assoc. St. John & St. John, 1966—71; dep. atty. State of Ala., 1971—79; sole practitioner Ala., 1979—82, Ala., 1986—2003; ptnr. Baxley, Beck, Dillard & Dauphin, 1982—86; shareholder Capell & Howard, P.C., 2004—11; US atty. (middle dist.) Ala. US Dept. Justice, Montgomery, 2011—. Col. Ala. Army Nat. Guard, mem. JAGC, 1966—98. Master: American Inns of Ct.; mem.: Nat. Criminal Def. Attorneys, Ala. Assn. Criminal Def. Attorneys, Montgomery County Trial Lawyer's Assn., Ala. Law Found., American Trial Lawyers Assn., Ala. Trial Lawyers Assn. Office: US Attorney's Office Middle District of Alabama 131 Clayton St Montgomery AL 36104 Office Phone: 334-223-7280. Office Fax: 334-223-7560.*

BECK, JEFFREY S., oil industry executive; BS in Chemistry, SUNY, 1980—84; PhD in Chemistry, U. Pa., 1984—89. Group leader Mobil Oil, 1996—98, mgr. reforming & isomerization, 1998—2000; dir. catalyst tech. ExxonMobil, 2000—04, tech. mgr. Baytown refinery, 2004—06, mgr. corp. rsch., 2006—10; mktg. mgr. ExxonMobil Chem. Co., 2010—. Mem.: Mobil Oil Corp. Alumni, NAE. Office: ExxonMobil Chemical Co 13501 Katy Fwy Houston TX 77079--139 Office Phone: 281-870-6050.

BECK, MORRIS, allergist; b. Miami, Fla., Oct. 12, 1927; s. Max and Anna (Luks) B.; m. Hollis Schwartz, Aug. 6, 1960; children: Gayle Beck Finan, Anne Lin. BA, UCLA, 1949; MD, U. Zurich, Switzerland, 1957. Diplomate Am. Bd. Allergy and Immunology, Am. Bd. Pediatrics. Intern Queens Hosp. Ctr., 1958, resident in pediatrics, 1959-60; preceptor in allergy U. Miami (Fla.) Med. Sch., 1961-77; pvt. practice pediatrician Miami, 1961—78; pvt. practice allergist, 1979—; chief dept. allergy Miami Children's Hosp., 1986—2003; clin. prof. pediatrics Nova U. Southeastern Med. Sch., 1998—; clin. asst. prof. U. Miami Med. Sch. With U.S. Army, 1950-52. Fellow: Am. Assn. Cert. Allergists, Am. Acad. Pediatrics, Am. Acad. Asthma, Allergy and Immunology, Am. Coll. Allergy and Immunology; mem.: Am. Coll. Chest Physicians. Republican. Jewish. Avocations: photography, fishing, travel. Office: 7800 SW 87th Ave # C-340 Miami FL 33173-3570 Home Phone: 305-667-3090. E-mail: beckmd123@aol.com.

BECK, SANDRA J., colon and rectal surgeon, educator; MD, Wright State U., Dayton, 1995. Diplomate Am. Bd. Surgery, 2002, Am. Bd. Colon and Rectal Surgery, 2003. Resident in surgery Allegheny Gen. Hosp., Pitts., 1995—2001; fellow in colon and rectal surgery Cleve. Clinic, Ohio, 2001—02; hosp. affiliation includes Univ. Ky. Albert B. Chandler Hosp.; asst. prof. surgery coll. medicine Univ. Ky.; assoc. prof. Office: University of Kentucky Albert B Chandler Hospital Department of Surgery 800 Rose St Lexington KY 40536 Office Phone: 859-323-6346.

BECK, THOMAS MARTIN, health facility company executive, former federal agency administrator; b. 1966; BA, U. Va., Charlottesville, 1988, JD, 1992. Ptnr. Jones Day, Washington, 1992—2007; chmn. Fed. Labor Rels. Authority (FLRA), Washington, 2008—09, mem., 2009—12; v.p. labor rels. HCA, Inc., Nashville, 2012—. Adj. prof. separation of powers, legislative & public policy George Mason U. Sch. Law, Va., 2007—10. Author: Constitutional Separation of Powers: Cases & Commentary, 2010. Vol., dir. then pres. Ct. Appointed Spl. Advocates of Fairfax County, 2005—12; bd. dirs. Tenn. Voices for Children, 2013—. Republican. Office: HCA 1 Park Plz Nashville TN 37203*

BECK, TONY, energy executive; B in Social Sci., U. Cape Town; diploma in Journalism, Western Media Inst., Victoria. With Duke Energy Gas Transmission, Westcoast Energy; group v.p. internal and externa; affairs Spectra Energy Corp., 2006—11; group v.p. corp. comm. Entergy Corp., 2011—. Office: Entergy Corporation 3700 Tulane Ave New Orleans LA 70119 Office Phone: 504-593-3449. Office Fax: 504-593-3475.

BECK, WENDY ANN, cruise line company executive; b. Norwalk, Conn., Oct. 21, 1964; d. Walter Rudolph Jr. and Lois Ann (Brahm) Gartner; m. Basil K. Beck, Jr., Dec. 23, 1989. BS in Acctg., U. South Fla., 1987. CPA, Fla. Sr. tax acct. Lincare Holdings, Inc., Clearwater, Fla., 1987-93; treas., v.p. fin. Checkers Drive-In Restaurants, Inc., Clearwater, 1993—2002; sr. v.p., CFO, treas. Whataburger Restaurants, Corpus Christi, Tex., 2001—08; exec. v.p., CFO Domino's Pizza, Inc., Ann Arbor, Mich., 2008—10, Norwegian Cruise Line, Miami, Fla., 2010—. Bd. dirs. Women's FoodService Forum, Spartan Stores, Inc., 2010—. Mem. AICPA, Fla. Inst. of CPA, Inst. of Mgmt. Accts. (spl. activities dir. 1992-93), American Mgmt. Assn. Republican. Avocations: boating, water-skiing, gardening, antiques. Office: Norwegian Cruise Line 7665 Corporate Ctr Dr Miami FL 33126 Office Phone: 305-436-4000. Office Fax: 305-436-4120.

BECKER, BRUCE, family practice physician; MD, Rosalind Franklin U., 1978. Diplomate Am. Bd. Family Practice. Resident surgery Univ. NC Hosp., 1978—79; resident family medicine St. Mary's Hosp., 1979—81; hosp. affiliation includes Odessa Regional Med. Ctr. Office: Odessa Regional Medical Center 520 E 6th St Odessa TX 79761 Office Phone: 432-582-8000.

BECKER, CHARLES MAXWELL, economics professor; b. SI, NY, Oct. 31, 1954; s. Edward J. and Joanna Maxwell Becker; m. Mary Chrestenson, June 4, 1977; children: Stephen R., Andrew L. BA, Grinnell Coll., Iowa, 1976; PhD, Princeton U., NJ, 1981. Asst. prof. Vanderbilt U., Nashville, 1982—86; acad. v.p. Econs. Inst., U. Colo., Boulder, 1987—89, pres., 1990—96, assoc. prof., 1987—96, full prof., 1996—98; sr. economist Internat. Mgmt. & Consulting Corp., Arlington, Va., 1998—2001, dir., 1999—2003; rsch. prof. U. Colo., Denver; rsch. scientist Duke U., Durham, NC, 2003, rsch. prof., 2004—. Team leader, tech. assistance project IMCC, Asian Devel. Bank, Bishkek, Kyrgyzstan, 1998—99; sr. advisor Nat. Bank, Ministry Labor & Social Protection, Ministry Fin., Almaty, Kazakhstan, 1999—2001, Kazakhstan Actuarial Ctr., 2001—06; dir. Am. Econ. Assn. Summer Program & Minority Scholarship Program, Denver, 2001—03, Durham, NC, 2001—07. Bd. dirs. Nat. Econ. Assn., 2004—07. Mem.: Am. Econ. Assn. (life). Avocation: bicycling. Office: Duke Univ Dept Economics Box 90097 Durham NC 27708 Office Fax: 919-660-1879. Business E-Mail: cbecker@econ.duke.edu.

BECKER, FERDINAND F., facial plastic surgeon, otolaryngologist, educator; MD, Tulane U. Sch. of Medicine, La. Diplomate Am. Bd. Otolaryngology, 1972, cert. Am. Bd. Facial Plastic and Reconstructive Surgery. Intern, resident Charity Hosp., La.; asst. clin. prof. otolaryngology Univ. Of Fla. Coll. of Medicine; hosp. appointment includes Indian River Med. Ctr. Nat. tng. ctr. physician Botox Cosmetic Network Perceptorship Tng. Program. Supporter Samaritan Ctr., Women's Refuge, The Ctr. for the Arts, Riverside Theatre. Recipient Guide to America's Top Physicians, Consumer Rsch. Coun. of America, William Wright award, Am. Acad. Facial Plastic and Reconstructive Surgery; named Guest of Honor at the ann. conv., Fla. Soc. of Dermatol. Surgeons, Amateur Outdoor Photographer; named one of The Best Doctors in America, 1992, America's Top Doctors, Castle Connolly, America's Cosmetic Doctors and Dentists, Orlando's Top Doctors, Orlando Mag., the foremost facial plastic surgeon in Fla., Fla. Soc. of Dermatol. Surgeons. Avocation: walking. Office: Indian River Medical Center 1000 36th St Vero Beach FL 32960 Office Phone: 772-567-4311.

BECKER, GAIL ROSELYN, museum director; b. Long Branch, NJ, Oct. 22, 1942; d. Joseph and Adele (Michelsohn) B. BA, Vassar Coll., 1964. Exhibit project officer U.S. Info. Agy., Washington, 1967-87, chief devel. and prodn. exhibits, 1987-91; exec. dir. Louisville Sci. Ctr. (formerly Mus. History and Sci.), 1991—2008. Bd. dirs. Louisville Advanced Tech. Coun., 1993-2000, Louisville Com. Fgn. Rels., Main St. Assn., 1998-2009, Arts and Cultural Attractions Coun., 1999—2008; active Leadership Louisville. Recipient Presdl. Design awards Nat. Endowment for the Arts, Washington, 1984, 88, 92, Special Achievement award U.S. Info. Agy., Washington, 1988. Mem. Am. Assn. Mus. (bd. dirs. 1994-97), Assn. Sci.-Tech. Ctrs. (bd. dirs. 1992—2003, pres. 1999-2001), Vassar Coll. Alumnae Assn., Rotary.

BECKER, LAWRENCE CARLYLE, philosopher, educator, writer; b. Lincoln, Nebr., Apr. 26, 1939; s. Albert Carlyle and Harriette (Toren) B.; m. Charlotte Ann Burner, June 10, 1967. BA in History, Midland Coll., 1961; MA in Philosophy, U Chgo., 1963, PhD in Philosophy, 1965; LHD (hon.), Midland Luth. Coll., 1994. Instr. philosophy Hollins Coll., Roanoke, Va., 1965-67, asst. prof. philosophy, 1967-71, assoc. prof., 1971-78, prof., 1978-89, fellow of coll., 1989—, dir. summer inst. for ethics and pub. policy, 1990-92; prof. philosophy, William R, Kenan, Jr. prof. humanities Coll. William and Mary, Williamsburg, Va., 1989-2001. Author: On Justifying Moral Judgments, 1973, Property Rights: Philosophic Foundations, 1977, Reciprocity, 1986, A New Stoicism, 1998; editor: (with Kenneth Kipnis) Property: Cases, Concepts and Critiques, 1984 (with Charlotte B. Becker) A History of Western Ethics, 1992, Encyclopedia of Ethics, 2 vols., 1992, 2d edit., 3 vols., 2001; mem. edit. bd. Ethics, 1979-85, 2000, assoc. editor, 1985-2000. Woodrow Wilson grad. fellow, 1961-62, Danforth grad. fellow, 1961-65, Woodrow Wilson dissertation fellow (hon.), 1964-65, fellow NEH, 1971-72, 93-94, Oxford (Eng.) U., 1971-72, Harvard U., 1975-76, Am. Coun. Learned Socs., 1975-76, humanities fellow Rockefeller Found., 1982-83, Ctr. for Advanced Study in Behavioral Scis., 1983-84. Mem. Am. Philos. Assn. (com. on philosophy and law 1984-87, adv. com. to program com. ethics divsn. 1989-92, com. on status and future of profession 1993-96), Am. Soc. for Legal and Polit. Philosophy, Va. Philos. Assn. (sec. 1978-79, v.p. 1979-80, pres. 1980-81).

BECKER, MARK PAUL, academic administrator, statistician, educator; s. Alvin John and Mildred Theresa (Hines) B.; m. Laura Lynn Voisinet, July 16, 1983; children: Matthew Brian, Julia Marie. BS in Math. magna cum laude, Towson State U., 1980; PhD in Stats., Pa. State U., 1985. Asst. prof. U. Fla., Gainesville, 1985-89; sr. fellow U. Wash., Seattle, 1987-89; asst. prof. U. Mich., Ann Arbor, 1989-92, assoc. prof., 1992-98, assoc. dean, 1997—2000, prof., 1998—2000; prof. biostatistics, dean Sch. Pub. Health, asst. v.p. pub. health preparedness and emergency response U. Minn., 2000—04; exec. v.p. academic affairs, provost U. SC, 2004—08; pres. Ga. State U., 2009—. Cons. Am. Coll. Emergency Physicians, 1991, Kellogg Co., Battle Creek, Mich., 1993-96, Pa. State U., 1999; mem. spl. study sect. NIH, Bethesda, Md., 1994-97. Editor Sociol. Methodology jour., 1998—; assoc. editor Biometrics Jour., 1998-2000; contbr. articles to profl. jours. Recipient Fellow, Am. Statis. Assn., 1999, Hon. Mem., Honor Soc. of Phi Kappa Phi, Mary Hudson Scarborough Award for Excellence in Math., Towson State U., 1980; fellow Postdoctoral Rsch. Fellowship, NIH, 1987-1989. Fellow Royal Statis. Soc., Am. Statistical Assn.; mem. Population Assn. Am., Am. Sociol. Assn., Internat. Biometric Soc., Inst. Math. Stats., Phi Kappa Phi (hon.). Office: Ga State U Office of Pres PO Box 3999 Atlanta GA 30302-3999 Office Phone: 404-413-1300. E-mail: mbecker@gsu.edu.

BECKER, MICHAEL J., air transportation executive; married. BSBA, St. John's U.; M in Human Resources and Indsl. Rels., U. Minn. Various human resources, compensation and planning positions Dow Chemical Co.; Joined NW Airlines Corp., Minn., 1993, mng. dir. corp. human resources, v.p. internat., 2000—01, sr. v.p. human resources, 2001—05, sr. v.p. human resources and labor rels., 2005—08, exec. v.p., COO, 2008—09; exec. v.p. Delta Air Lines, Inc., 2008—. Office: Delta Air Lines Inc PO Box 20706 1030 Delta Blvd Atlanta GA 30320 Office Phone: 612-726-2111.

BECKER, QUINN HENDERSON, orthopedic surgeon, military officer; b. Kirksville, Mo., June 11, 1930; s. Quinn Henry B. and Sarah Lucille (Henderson) Finley; m. Gladys Marie Roussell, Aug. 11, 1951; children: Quinn E., Terri K., Paul Eric. Grad., N.E. La. State Coll., 1952; MD, La. State U., 1956; student, Armed Forces Staff Coll., 1969-70, Command and Gen. Staff Coll., 1971, U.S. Army War Coll., 1974-75. Diplomate Am. Bd. Orthop. Surgery. Commd. 2d lt. U.S. Army, advanced through grades to lt. gen., 1985; intern Tripler Gen. Hosp., 1956-57; resident in orthopedic surgery Confederate Meml. Med. Ctr., Shreveport, La., 1958-61; orthopedic surgeon Ft. Gordon, Ga., 1962-63; chief orthopedic service Ft. Rucker, Ala., 1963-64; comdg. officer 5th Surg. Hosp. (Mobile Army), Heidelberg, W. Ger., 1964-65; surgeon 3d Inf. Div., Wurzburg, W. Ger., 1965-66; chief orthpedic surgery 33d Field Hosp., Wurzburg, 1965; asst. chief orthopedic service Walter Reed Gen. Hosp., 1966-69; chief profl. services 85th Evacuation Hosp., Vietnam, 1970; div. surgeon and bn. comdr. 15th Med. Bn. 1st Cavalry Div., Vietnam, 1970-71; chief orthopedic service and orthopedic residency tng. Tripler Army Med. Ctr., 1971-74; surgeon 18th Airborne Corps., Ft. Bragg, 1975-77; comdr. Med. Activity Womack Army Hosp., Ft. Bragg, 1976-77; dir. health care ops. Office Surgeon Gen., 1977-80; comdt. Acad. Health Scis., U.S. Army, Ft. Sam Houston, Tex., 1980-81; dep. surgeon gen. Washington, 1981-83; comdr. 7th Med. Command, Heidelberg, 1983-85; Surgeon Gen. Dept. Army, 1985-88, ret., 1988. Asst. prof. orthopedic surgery Howard U., Washington, 1967-69; clin. assoc. prof. Sch. Medicine U. Hawaii, Honolulu, 1973-74; chief of staff VA Hosp., Asheville, N.C., 1989-92, ret. 1992; mem. Congl. Commn. on Svc. Mems. and Vets. Transition Assistance, 1998; mem. adv. bd. Ind.-Ohio Ctr. Traumetic Amputation Rsch. Vietnam, 2006-. Contbr. papers to publs. and confs. in field. Pres. ARC Golden K- Kiwanis Club, 2007—08; team tchr. Ramp Project San Antonio Br., 2007—; chmn. bd. Army Med. Mus. Found. Ft. Sam, Houston, 2005—08. Decorated Legion of Merit, Meritorious Service medal, Bronze Star, Air medal, Disting. Service medal. Fellow Am. Acad. Orthopedic Surgeons (chmn. mil. affairs com. 1981-85), ACS, Am. Coll. Physician Execs. (disting.); mem. AMA (ho. of dels.), Am. Orthopaedic Assn., Masons (33d degree, Grand Cross 1993), Civitan (pres. Asheville club 1992, chmn. internat. rsch. com. 1996-98). Home: 2111 Peninsula Dr San Antonio TX 78239-3085

BECKER, RALPH EDWARD, broadcast executive, consultant; b. Carbondale, Ill., Sept. 18, 1931; s. Ralph Walter and Ola (Goetz) B.; m. Jane Mulholland, May 9, 1959; children: Susan B. McDermott, Nancy B. Gunzenhauser. BS, So. Ill. U., 1955. Gen. sales mgr. Sta. KPLR-TV, St. Louis, 1966-68, Sta. KNEW-TV Metromedia, Inc., San Francisco, 1968-70, Sta. KBHK-TV Kaiser Broadcasting, 1970-72; v.p., gen. mgr. Sta. WJKS-TV Rust Craft Broadcasting, Jacksonville, Fla., 1972-73; exec. v.p. Rust Craft Broadcasting Co., Pitts., 1973-79; pres. Ziff-Davis Broadcasting Co., NYC, 1979-83; pres., COO Toledo TV Investors, 1986-97, TV Sta. Ptnrs. L.P., Greenwich, Conn., 1983—93; pres., CEO, WHP TV L.P., Darien, Conn., 1993—95; pres., owner Becker Global Investments Inc., 2012—. Mem. tech. adv. coun. Grad. Sch. Edn., Harvard U., 1996—; pres., CEO, bd. dirs. Catamount Holdings Inc., Norwalk, Conn., 2002-12. Mem. Carbondale, 1985—; bd. dirs. So. Ill. U. Found., 1986-2003. Capt. USAF, 1956—59. Recipient Profl. Achievement award So. Ill. U. Alumni Assn., 1985, 95, Radio-TV Dept. Alumnus of Yr. award, 1985. Mem. Broadcast Foundation, Libr. Am. Broadcasting. Republican. Presbyn. Avocation: travel. Home and Office: 121 Copperfield Ridge Ct Winston Salem NC 27106-3592 Office Phone: 336-923-5216. Personal E-mail: rebecker_2000@yahoo.com.

BECKER, RICHARD CHARLES, retired academic administrator; b. Chgo., Mar. 1, 1931; s. Charles Beno and Rose Mildred (Zak) B.; m. Magdalene Marie Kypry, June 19, 1954; children: Richard J., Daniel P., Douglas F., Steven G., Pamela J. BS in Elec. Engring, Fournier Inst. Tech., 1953; MS in Elec. Engring, U. Ill., 1954, MS in Math., 1956, PhD in Elec. Engring, 1959; postgrad., Harvard Inst. Ednl. Mgmt., 1976. Engr. Ill. Bell Tel. Co., Chgo., 1952, Andrew Corp., Chgo., 1953; rsch. asst. U. Ill., Urbana, 1954-58, asst. prof., 1959; sr. staff engr. Amphenol Corp., Chgo., 1959-60, sr. rsch. scientist, 1961-64, dir. program mgmt., 1965-67; dir. Amphenol Corp. (Far Eastern ops.), 1968; group v.p., corporate dir. adminstrn. Bunker Ramo Corp., Oak Brook, Ill., 1968-73; chief exec. officer and chmn. bd. Fortune Internat. Enterprises, Inc., Oak Brook, 1973-76; pres. Benedictine Univ. (formerly Ill. Benedictine Coll.), Lisle, 1976-95, pres. emeritus, 1995—. Trustee, prof. Midwest Coll. Engring., Lombard, Ill., 1968—86; trustee Ill. Benedictine Coll., Lisle, 1973—76; bd. dirs. Amphenol Tyree Proprietary, Ltd., Australia, Amphetronix, Ltd., India, Oxbow Resources, Ltd., Canada; v.p. Bonita Springs Incorporation Com., Inc., 1998—99, pres., 1999—2000; bd. dirs. Arthur J. Schmitt Found., 1970—, pres., 1995—2007, pres. emeritus, dir., 2007—; mem. exec. adv. bd. Internat. Engring. Consortium, 2000—. Contbr. articles and chpts. to profl. jours. and books. Gov. Brook Forest Community Assn., 1971-74; del. Oak Brook Caucus, 1970; trustee, pres. Arthur J. Schmitt Found., Ill. Benedictine Coll.; chmn. Coun. West Suburban Colls., Chgo. Met. Higher Edn. Coun., officer Fedn. Ind. Ill. Colls. and Univs.; chmn. Associated Colls. of Ill., West Suburban Regional Acad. Consortium. Named Disting. Eagle Scout, 1989, Regent, Nat. Eagles Scout Assn., Disting. Alumnus, U. Ill.; Arthur J. Schmitt fellow, 1953—56. Mem. Am. Phys. Soc., Nat. Assn. Ind. Colls. and Univs. (bd. dirs.), Albertus Magnus Guild, Rotary (Paul Harris fellow), Equestrian Order of the Holy Sepulchre of Jerusalem (knight commdr. with star), KC (4th deg. color corps. office), Laity Support Retired Priests Inc. (exec. com. mem.), Sigma Xi, Eta Kappa Nu, Tau Beta Pi. Home: 4790 Aston Gardens Way Apt 104 Naples FL 34109-3568 Personal E-mail: papinani2@aol.com.

BECKER, RICHARD K.A., lawyer; b. Phila., May 10, 1958; s. Richard H. and Jane M. (Duckworth) Becker; m. Dorothea W. Dickerman, May 24, 1986; 1 child, Alexander. AB cum laude, Princeton U., NJ, 1980; JD, Harvard Law Sch., 1983. Bar: DC 1983, Va. 1984, Pa. 1984, US Ct. Appeals (4th and DC cirs.), US Supreme Ct. Assoc. Shaw, Pittman, Potts & Trowbridge, Washington, 1983-85; founding ptnr. Northern Va. office Hogan Lovells US LLP (formerly Hogan & Hartson LLP), McLean, 1985—, co-head pvt. equity practice. Adj. prof. corp. acquisitions George Mason U. Sch. Law, Arlington, Va. Named a Top Washington Lawyer in Corp. Mergers & Acquisitions, Washington Bus. Jour., 2006, Va. Super Lawyer, Law & Politics mag., 2006—09, Washington, DC Super Lawyer, 2007—09. Mem.: Va. Bar Assn., Va. State Bar, DC Bar. Office: Hogan Lovells US LLP Park Place II Ninth Fl 7930 Jones Branch Dr Mc Lean VA 22102-3390 Office Phone: 703-610-6123. Office Fax: 703-610-6200. Business E-Mail: richard.becker@hoganlovells.com.

BECKER, STEVEN RICHARD, beverage corporation executive; b. NYC, Mar. 28, 1952; s. Isidore A. and Adele (Sandler) B.; m. Abbe Dale Kligman, Feb. 27, 1982; chldren: Robert Sandler, Meredith Brooke. BS, Syracuse U., 1973; JD, Boston U., 1976; MBA, U. Pa., 1978. Bar: N.Y. 1977, U.S. Supreme Ct. 1980. Gen. counsel, asst. to pres. Knickerbocker Liquors Corp., Syosset, NY, 1978-85; exec. v.p., dir. Beauvignot Internat., Syosset, 1979-86; v.p. So. Wine and Spirits Am., Inc., Miami, Fla., 1985-91, 1st v.p., treas., 1991—2006, also bd. dirs., exec. v.p., treas., 2007—. Cons. Ion Technols., Inc., N.Y., 1984-85. Jewish. Office: So Wine and Spirits 1600 NW 163rd St Miami FL 33169

BECKETT, CHARLES JIM, state legislator; b. Bruce, Miss., Jan. 25, 1958; m. Susan Bryant Beckett. Mem. Dist. 23 Miss. House of Reps., 2004—, mem. forestry com., judiciary A com., judiciary en banc com., transp. com., univs. and colls. com. Republican. Address: PO Box 722 Bruce MS 38915 Office Phone: 662-983-7358. E-mail: jbeckett@house.ms.gov.

BECKHAM, WALTER HULL, III, lawyer; b. Boston, Feb. 12, 1948; s. Walter Hull Beckham Jr. and Ethel Brooks (Koger) Beckham. BA, Emory U., 1970, JD, 1977; MBA, U. Mich., 1972. Bar: Ga. 1977, U.S. Dist. Ct. (no. dist.) Ga. 1978, U.S. Dist. Ct. (mid. dist.) Ga. 1988, U.S. Ct. Appeals (11th cir.) 1982. Investment analyst, portfolio mgr. Life of Ga., Atlanta, 1972-74; assoc. Jessee, Ritchie & Duncan, P.C., Atlanta, 1977-81, ptnr., 1981-82; pvt. practice Atlanta, 1982—. Bd. dirs. YMCA Blue Ridge Assembly, 2010—, Cmty. Outreach YMCA, Atlanta, 1973—75; Brookhaven Boys Club Atlanta, 1976; pres. Sr. Hon. Soc. Emory U., Atlanta, 1984—85, mem. Law Sch. Coun., 1993—2001, bd. govs., 2001—05. Mem.: ABA (tort and ins. practice sect., long range planning com. 1986—90, coun. 1990—93, sect. chmn. 1995—96), Ga. Trial Lawyers Assn. (long range planning com. 1982—86), Internat. Acad. Trial Lawyers (state chmn. 2002—12, internat. rels. com. 2004—07), Atlanta Bar Assn. (state ct. com. 1985), Ga. Bar Assn. (co-chmn. com. on professionalism 1997—2000, jud. procedure and adminstrn. com. 2000—08), Kappa Alpha (Hardeman Province Ct. of Honor). Avocations: hunting, fishing, skiing. Home: 1208 Village Run NE Atlanta GA 30319-5303 Office: Ste 2600 75 14th St Atlanta GA 30309 Office Phone: 404-873-8000.

BECKINGHAM, KATHLEEN MARY, education educator, researcher; b. Sheffield, Yorkshire, Eng., May 8, 1946; arrived in U.S., 1976; d. Philip and Mary Ellen (Flint) B.; m. Alan Edward Smith, Oct. 7, 1967 (div. Oct. 1978); m. Robert Bruce Weisman, July 25, 1986; 1 child, Caroline Mary Weisman. BA, U. Cambridge, Eng., 1967, MA, 1968, PhD, 1972. Grad. student Strangeways Rsch. Lab., Cambridge, 1967-70; postdoctoral Inst. Molecular Biology, Aarhus, Denmark, 1970-72; rsch. assoc. Nat. Inst. Med. Rsch., London, 1972-76; rsch. assoc., instr. U. Mass. Med. Sch., Worcester, 1976-80; asst. prof. Rice U., Houston, 1980-85, assoc. prof. biochemistry, cell biology, molecular biology, 1985-92, prof., 1992—. Recipient award, Camille and Henry Dreyfus Found., 1979. Office: Rice U Dept Biochemistry and Cell Biology PO Box 1892 Ms-140 Houston TX 77251-1892

BECKLES, INGRID, investment company executive; b. Washington, May 27, 1961; d. Frank Neville Beckles and Maria Beckles Jenkins; m. David Alan Fountain, July 3, 1981 (div. Jan. 1987); children: Kaiesha Nicole. BS, U. Md., 1988. Asst. br. mgr. Chevy Chase (Md.) Savs. Bank/B.F. Saul Mortgage Co., 1983-84, staff auditor, 1984-87, v.p., mgr., policies & procedures dept., 1989-91, v.p., mgr., ctrl. processing divsn., 1991, v.p., mgr., quality control dept., 1986-91; asst. v.p., regional ops. & mgr., SouthEast Region PNC Mortgage Corp. Am., Vernon Hills, Ill., 1991-93, 2nd v.p., underwriting mgr., Nat. Mortgage Ctr., 1993-96, mem., corp. fair lending initiatives staff, 1993—96, v.p., chief underwriter, 1996-98, v.p., customer focused intiatives, 1998-99, v.p., credit policy & quality assurance, 1999—2001; sr. v.p, default asset mgmt. Freddie Mac, 2001—10; founder, CEO IBK, LLC, 2007—; pres. Velocity Capital Defense, 2010—. Spkr. HUD and Joint Ctr. for Housing Studies, 1994, HUD Working Group for Underwriring and Bus. Practices, 1994—, Nat. Assn. Real Estate Brokers, 1995, Fannie Mae Nat. and Regional Risk Adv. Coun., 1995-96, VA Working Group on Underwriting and Bus. Practices, 1996—, Mortgage Bankers Assn., Nat. Underwriting Conf., 1997, Freddie Mac-Nat. Mgr.'s Meeting, 1998. Bd. dirs. Robert Taylor Boys and Girls Club, Chgo., 1998—. Mem. NAFE, Mortgage Bankers Assn. Am., Women in the Arts. Episcopalian. Avocations: horseback riding, piano, tennis, bicycling. Office: Velocity Capital Defense 7880 Bent Branch Dr Ste 150 Irving TX 75063 Office Phone: 972-715-1000. Office Fax: 917-644-3356. Business E-Mail: ibeckles@velocitycapitaldefense.com.

BECKMAN, PAUL, state legislator; m. Linda Beckman; 1 child, Jamie. BS in Edn., Fla. State U., Tallahassee; JD, Faulkner U., Montgomery, Ala. Fin. profl. with emphasis in banking and shopping centers; atty. Capouano, Beckman and Russell, LLC; mem. Dist. 88 Ala. House of Representatives, 2011—. Mem. St. Joseph's Cath. Ch., Prattville, Ala. Mem.: ABA, KC, Nat. Assn. Retail Collection Attys., Ala. State Bar Assn., Montgomery County Bar Assn., Bankruptcy and Comml. Law League, Prattville Civitan Club. Republican. Office: Ala House of Reps Rm 538-B 11 S Union St Montgomery AL 36130 also: PO Box 36068 Prattville AL 36068 Office Phone: 334-242-7499, 334-323-5918. Personal E-mail: paulbeckmanjr@yahoo.com.

BECKMANN, BILL, mortgage company executive; BA in Mathematical Economics, Brown U.; MS in Mgmt., Stanford Sloan Program. Various positions consumer and info. bus. Citibank; v.p. strategy & new bus. develop. IBM Corp., global internet divsn.; chmn., CEO Student Loan Corp. Citigroup Inc., 1997—2003, pres., COO CitiMortgage, 2005—08; pres. Beckmann Insights, LLC, 2008—11; pres., CEO MERSCORP Inc., Reston, Va., 2011—. Bd. trustees Enterprise Cmty. Partners. Office: Merscorp Inc 1818 Library St Ste 300 Reston VA 20190

BECKNER, WILLIAM, mathematician; b. Kirksville, Mo., Sept. 15, 1941; s. William Horace and Bessie Mae Beckner; m. Chandra Muller; children: Amalia Marise, Chiara Lisa. BS in Physics, U. Mo., Columbia, 1963; PhD in Math., Princeton U., NJ, 1975. L.E. Dickson instr. U. Chgo., 1975-76, asst. prof., 1976-83; assoc. prof. U. Tex., Austin, 1983-90, prof., 1992—, Montgomery prof. math., chair dept. math., 2007—11. Lectr. Princeton U., 1975; vis. prof. Columbia U., NYC, 1984-85, U. Chgo., 1990-91, UCLA, 1992; asst. dir. Inst. Computational Engring. and Sci., U. Tex., 2006-, mem. adv. bd.; chair-elect, Faculty Coun., U. Tex., 2013-14. Mng. editor: Transactions of Am. Math. Soc., 2000—05; contbr. articles to profl. jours. Recipient Salem prize French Math., 1975; Sloan fellow, 1976-78, fellow Am. Math. Soc. Mem.: Inst. Computational and Engr. Sci., Am. Math. Soc. Office: U Tex Dept Math One University Sta C1200 Austin TX 78712 Business E-Mail: beckner@math.utexas.edu.

BECKWITT, RICHARD, construction executive; Mem. Mergers & Acquisitions Dept. and Corp. Fin. Depts. Lehman Brothers Inc., 1986—93; exec. v.p. D.R. Horton, Inc., 1993—98, bd. dirs., 1993—2003, pres. investments divsn., 1996—98, pres., 1998—2000; owner EVP Capital, L.P., 2000—02; exec. v.p. Lennar Corp., Miami, Fla., 2006—. Office: Lennar Corp 700 NW 107th Ave Miami FL 33172 Office Phone: 305-559-4000.

BEDAPUDI, PRAKASH, manufacturing executive; b. Chittoor, Andhra, India, Aug. 25, 1966; came to U.S. 1989; s. Bhaskar Naidu and Ambujakshi (Bhaskar) B. BS in Mech. Automotive Engring., Karnataka U., India, 1987; MS in Mech. Aero. Engring., U. Cin., 1991. Sr. engring. leadership positions General Electric Co.; mktg. engr. Avanti KoppElec. Ltd., Hyderabad, India, 1986-87; project engr. Escorts India Ltd., New Delhi, 1987-89; cons. Escorts Rsch. Ctr., New Delhi, 1989; rsch. asst. University of Cincinnati, 1989—91; project engr. Cummins Engine Co., Inc., Columbus, Ind., 1990, sr. performance devel. engr., 1991—; v.p., Engring. & Tech., Residential Sys. Divsn. Trance Inc., 2003—06; v.p., Global Engring. & Program Mgmt., Comml. Sys. Trane Inc., 2006—08; exec. v.p., chief tech. officer Lennox International, Inc., 2008—. Author tech. reports on high pressure injection systems. U. Cin. grad. scholar, 1989-91. Mem. ASME, AIAA, India Student Assn., Assn. Auto. Engrs. India (pres. 1987). Achievements include design and development of lean burn combustion system for 2-stroke gasoline engines; designed fuel manifold which solved the start of injection variation problem of a 6-cylinder DI diesel engine. Home: 4559 Voyageur Dr Erie PA 16505-5421 Office: Lennox International Inc 2140 Lake Park Blvd Richardson TX 75080 Office Phone: 972-497-5000. Office Fax: 972-497-5292. E-mail: prakash.bedapudi@lennoxintl.com.

BEDARD, ERIK JOSEPH, professional baseball player; b. Navan, Ontario, Can., Mar. 5, 1979; Attended, Norwalk CC, Conn. Pitcher Balt. Orioles, 2002, 2004—07, Seattle Mariners, 2008—11, Boston Red Sox, 2011, Pitts. Pirates, 2012, Houston Astros, 2013—. Achievements include leading the American League in: strikeouts per nine innings pitched (10.93), 2007. Office: Houston Astros 501 Crawford St Houston TX 77002*

BEDEIAN, ARTHUR GEORGE, business educator; BBA, U. Iowa, 1967; MBA, U. Memphis, 1968; DBA, Miss. State U., 1973. Instr. mgr. Miss. State U., Mississippi State, 1969-71; asst. prof. Ga. So. Coll., Statesboro, 1971-73; adj. asst. prof. Boston U., 1973-74; Edward L. Lowder prof. mgmt. Auburn (Ala.) U., 1974-85; Ralph and Kacoo G. Olinde Disting. prof. mgmt. La. State U., Baton Rouge, 1985-96, Boyd prof., 1997—. Dir. Found. for Adminstrv. Rsch., 1982-93, pres., 1989-90; cons. in field. Author: Organizations: Theory and Design, 1991, Management Laureates, 1992, 6th edit., 2002, Evolution of Management Thought, 2009, 6th edit.; Standardization of Selected Management Concepts, 1986, Management, 3d edit., 1993, Management in Extension, 3d edit., 1995; editor Jour. of Mgmt., 1977-79, Evolution Mgmt. Thought, 2012. With USAR, 1968—73. Recipient Ronald G. Greenwood Lifetime Achievement award, 2003, Richard M. Hodgetts Disting. Career award, 2007, Disting. Faculty award, LSU, 2006, Disting. Faculty Tchg. award, Disting. Svc. award, Acad. Mgmt. Fellow Acad. Mgmt. (pres. 1987-89, dean 1997-99), Internat. Acad. Mgmt., So. Mgmt. Assn.; mem. APA, Inst. Decision Scis. (nat. coun. 1976-79), Southeastern Inst. Decision Scis. (pres. 1978-79), So. Mgmt. Assn. (pres. 1982-83), Am. Sociol. Assn., Soc. Organizational Behavior, Beta Gamma Sigma, Delta Mu Delta, Phi Kappa Phi, Sigma Iota Epsilon, Soc. Indsl. & Organisational Psychology Armenian Orthodox. Home: 838 High Plains Ave Baton Rouge LA 70810-4349 Office: La State University 2709 Business Education Complex Dept Mgmt Baton Rouge LA 70803-6312 Office Phone: 225-578-6141. Business E-Mail: abede@lsu.edu.

BEDFORD, ROGER H., JR., state legislator; b. Ft. Belvadere, Va., July 2, 1956; m. Maudie Darby; children: Roger H., III. BS, U. Ala., 1978; JD, Samford U. Cumberland Sch. Law, 1981. Mem. Dist. 6 Ala. State Senate, Montgomery, 1982—90, 1996—; spl. atty. gen. State of Ala., 1988—; mcpl. judge Town of Phil Campbel; atty. Roger Bedford & Associates. Del. Dem. Nat. Convention, 1982, 84, 92, 2000; treas. Young Dem. America, 1981-83, legal counsel, 1983-85; mem. Dem. Nat. Fin. Coun.; pres. Ala. Dem. Leadership Coun., 1992-93; exec. mem. Boy Scouts America, Tenn. Valley Coun.; mem. First Bapt. Ch. Recipient Outstanding Legislator award Ala. Probate Judges Assn., 1984, Cert. of Merit, AFL-CIO, 1996; named Legislature Conservationist of Yr. Ala. Wildlife Fedn., 1984, Citizen of Yr. Franklin County, 1990, Outstanding Legislator of Yr., 1996. Mem. ABA, NRA (life), Ala. Bar Assn., Franklin County Bar Assn., Ala. Cattlemen's Assn., Ducks Unlimited, Am. Cancer Soc., Russellville C. of C., Rotary, Jaycees. Democrat. Baptist. Office: Ala State Senate Ala State House 11 S Union St Rm 730-B Montgomery AL 36130 Office Phone: 256-332-2880, 334-242-7862. Business E-Mail: senbedford@aol.com.

BEDINGFIELD, ERIC M., state legislator; b. Greenville, Jan. 30, 1967; s. Burgess Michael and Fielding Petty Carmouche Bedingfield; m. Sabrina Tumblin Bedingfield; children: Joshua Michael, Jared Seth, Clinton Tucker, Gracie-Tate. AA, Greenville Tech. Coll., 1988. Vice chmn. County Pub. Svc. Planning & Devel., Greenville, SC, 2002—04; mem. Greenville County Pub. Svc. Planning & Devel. Commn., 2004—; mem. Dist. 28 SC House of Reps., 2007—; mem. Edn. & Pub. Works Com. Republican. Office: 312B Blatt Building Columbia SC 29201 Home: 945 Cooley Bridge Rd Belton SC 29627-9276 Home Phone: 864-335-8937; Office Phone: 864-230-7044, 803-734-2962. Business E-Mail: BedingfieldE@schouse.org.

BEDKE, MICHAEL A., lawyer; b. Oct. 19, 1960; BA with high honors, Univ. Fla., 1981, JD with honors, 1984. Bar: Fla. 1984. Ptnr. DLA Piper LLP US, Tampa, Fla., 2004—09. Adj. prof. Stetson Coll. Law, Fla.; bd. dirs., past pres. Bay Area Legal Svcs., Fla. Recipient William Reece Smith Jr. Public Svc. award, 1994. Mem.: Hillsborough County Bar Assn., ABA (bd. govs. 2004—07), Fla. Bar Assn. (Outstanding Young Lawyer, Pres. Pro Bono award). Office: DLA Piper LLP US Suite 2200 100 N Tampa St Tampa FL 33602-5809 Office Phone: 813-222-5924.

BEDNAR, MICHAEL JOHN, architecture educator; b. Cleve., Mar. 19, 1942; s. Peter and Mary (Rohal) B.; m. Mary Kathryn Gillman; children: Richard Earl, Matthew Scott, Rachel Catherine; m. Elizabeth Waddel Lawson. BArch, U. Mich., 1964; MArch, U. Pa., Phila., 1967. Registered architect, Pa., NY, Va. Jr. designer I.M. Pei & Ptnrs., NYC, 1965-66; project architect Geddes, Brecher, Qualls, Cunningham, Phila., 1967-68; asst. prof. Renselaer Polytech. Inst., Troy, 1968-72; assoc. prof. U. Va., Charlottesville, 1972—2007, prof. architecture, 2007—09, emeritus prof. architecture, 2009—, co-chmn. div. architecture, 1976-81, assoc. dean for academics, 1992-95, assoc. dean for students, 2006, dir. advising, 2007—09. Prin. Michael Bednar, FAIA Architect, Charlottesville, 1973-90, Bednar Lawson Architects, 1990—. Author: Architecture for Handicapped, 1973, The New Atrium, 1986; Interior Pedestrian Places, 1989, L'Enfant's Legacy, 2006; editor: Barrier-Free Environment, 1977. Mem., chair City Planning Commn., Charlottesville, 1982—; chmn. Urban Design Task Force, Charlottesville, 1985-88; mem. Bd. of Architectural Review, Charlottesville, 1983-86; bd. dirs. Charlottesville Habitat for Humanity, 2006. Booth fellow U. Mich., 1972, NEA fellow, 1984, Graham Found. fellow, 1988-2003; recipient Nat. Book award Am. Assn. of Publ., 1986, Nichols award Preservation Alliance Va., 1997, Cmty. Svc. award AIA Ctrl. Va., 1997. Fellow Am. Inst. Architects (Disting. Achievemnt award 1997), Assn. for the Preservation of Va. Antiquities (bd. dirs. Jefferson chpt. 1999-2000). Avocations: jazz, travel, sculpting, singing. Home: 1201 E Jefferson St Charlottesville VA 22902-5414 Business E-Mail: mjb6g@virginia.edu.

BEDNAR, RAY, bank executive; Grad., US Mil. Acad., West Point, NY; MBA, Harvard U. Bus. Sch. Leadership positions General Electric Co., Brown-Forman Corp.; CEO, North and South America PRISM, 2002—06; sr. v.p., global sponsorship mktg. exec. Bank of America Corp., 2006—. Author: Sponsorship's Holy Grail, 2005. Named one of Most Influential People in the World of Sports, Bus. Week, 2008. Office: Bank of America Corp 100 N Tryon St Charlotte NC 28255-0001

BEEBE, MIKE DALE, Governor of Arkansas, former state attorney general, lawyer; b. Amagon, Ark., Dec. 28, 1946; s. Lester Kendall and Meadean Louise (Quattlebaum) Beebe; m. Ginger Croom, Mar. 2, 1979; children: Kyle, David, Tammy. BA in Polit. Sci., Ark. State U., 1968; JD, U. Ark. Sch. Law, Fayetteville, 1972. Bar: Ark. 1972. Ptnr. Lightle, Beebe, Raney, Bell & Simpson, Searcy, Ark., 1972—2003; mem. Dist. 21 Ark. State Senate, Little Rock, 1983—2003, pres., 2001—03; atty. gen. State of Ark., Little Rock, 2003—07, gov., 2007—. Mem. exec. com. Dem. Governors Assn., 2008—09. Trustee Ark. State U., Jonesboro, 1974—79, chmn. bd. trustees, 1977—79; chmn. Ctrl. Ark. Gen. Hosp., Searcy, 1985—93. Served in USAR, 1968—74. Mem.: Searcy C. of C., Ark. Mcpl. League (Dist. Svc. award 1985). Democrat. Episcopalian. Avocation: golf. Office: Office of Governor State Capitol Room 250 Little Rock AR 72201 Office Phone: 501-682-2345. Office Fax: 501-682-1382.*

BEECH, ELAINE, state legislator; m. Wayne Beech (dec.); children: Leslie, Daniel. Pharmacist, former owner B&F Drugs, Chatom, Ala.; supervising pharmacist Wash. County Hosp., Chatom; mem. Dist. 4 Wash. County Sch. Bd. Edn., Chatom, 2006—10; mem. Dist. 65 Ala. House of Reps., Montgomery, Ala., 2009—. Democrat. Office: PO Box 1256 Chatom AL 36518 also: Ala House of Reps 11 S Union St Montgomery AL 36130 Office Phone: 334-242-7702.

BEEHLER, BRUCE MCPHERSON, research zoologist, ornithologist, conservationist; b. Balt., Oct. 11, 1951; s. William Henry Jr. and Cary (Baxter) B.; m. Carol Hare, June 7, 1982; children: Grace Bryant, Andrew McPherson, Cary Elizabeth Selden. BA, Williams Coll., 1974; MA, Princeton U., 1978, PhD, 1983. Sci. asst. to sec. Smithsonian Instn., Washington, 1981-84, sci. asst. to sec. emeritus, 1984-88, zoologist, 1988-91; assoc. rsch. zoologist N.Y. Zool. Soc., Washington, 1991-93; sr. ecologist Conservation Internat., 1993-95; natural resource mgmt. officer U.S. Dept. State, Washington, 1995-97; dir. environ. conservation Counterpart Internat., 1997-99, v.p. environ. and nat. resources, 1999-2001; sr. rep. Conservation Internat., 2001—02, sen. dir. Melanesia, 2002—03, v.p. Melanesia, 2003—06, v.p. Pacific, 2006—08, sr. rsch. scientist, 2008—10, sr. dir. biodiv. assessment, 2010—. Leader expdns. to Papua New Guinea, 1975-76, 78-84, 86-87, 89, 91-93, 2005-09, to India, 1983, 85-86, 88; rsch. assoc. dept. vertebrate zoology Nat. Mus. Natural History, 1985—. Author: Birdlife of the Adirondack Park, 1978, Upland Birds of Northeastern New Guinea, 1978, A Naturalist in New Guinea, 1991, 12 Lost Worlds, 2008; sr. co-author: Birds of New Guinea; jr. co-author: The Birds of Paradise, 1998, Ecology of Papua, 2007; contbr. articles to sci. jours. Thomas J. Watson Found. fellow, 1974; rsch. grantee Nat. Geog. Soc., 1980, 86, 89, 94, N.Y. Zool. Soc., 1986. Fellow Am. Ornithologists Union (elective). Democrat. Co-discoverer with John P. Dumbacher of toxicity in the Pitohui, a genus of bird that uses as a chemical defense the alkaloid homobatrachotoxin. Office: Conservation Internat 2011 Crystal Dr Arlington VA 22202 Office Phone: 703-341-2434, 301-221-5654. Business E-Mail: bbeehler@conservation.org.

BEER, KENNETH ROBERT, dermatologist; b. May 7, 1963; BS in Zoology magna cum laude, dean's list and honors, U. Oxford; AB, Duke U., 1981—85; MD, U. Pa., 1985—89. Diplomate Am. Bd. of Dermatology, 1993, Am. Bd. of Dermatology-Dermatopathology, 1995, cert. recertified in dermatology with specialization in dermatologic surgery and dermatopathology 2001, lic. Fla. Bd. of Health, Calif. Bd. of Medicine, Ill. Dept. of Profl. Regulation, NY State Dept. of Medicine. Internship in internal medicine Grad. Hosp., Pa., 1989—90; resident in dermatology Univ. Chgo., 1990—93, fellow in dermatopathology, 1993—94; fellow Am. Soc. for Laser Medicine and Surgery, Am. Soc. for Dermatologic Surgery, Am. Soc. for Mohs Surgery; founder & dir. Cosmetic Bootcamp LLC; founder Dermsoftware; voluntary assoc. prof. dermatology Univ. Miami, 1995—; consulting assoc. dept. of medicine Duke Univ., 1998—; section chief dermatology Good Samaritan Med. Ctr., mem. exec. bd. Instr. Am. Acad. of Dermatology, 2001—; preceptor Am. Soc. for Dermatologic Surgery, 2002—; instr. allergan Medicis, Sanofi Aventis, Stiefel, 2004—. Mem.: Assn. for the Study of Lung Cancer, Am. Soc. of Cosmetic Dermatology & Aesthetic Surgery, Am. Soc. for Dermatopathology, Am. Acad. of Dermatology, Phi Beta kappa, Duke Univ., Assn. of Clin. Rsch. Professionals. Office: 1500 North Dixie Hwy Ste 305 West Palm Beach FL 33401 Office Phone: 561-655-9055. Office Fax: 561-655-9233.

BEER, PETER HILL, federal judge; b. New Orleans, Apr. 12, 1928; s. Mose Haas and Henret (Lowenburg) B.; children: Kimberly Beer Bailes, Kenneth, Dana Beer Long-Innes; m. Marjorie Barry, July 14, 1985. BBA, Tulane U., 1949, LLB, 1952; LLM, U. Va., 1986. Bar: La. 1952. Successively assoc., ptnr., sr. ptnr. Montgomery, Barnett, Brown & Read, New Orleans, 1955-74; judge La. Ct. Appeal, 1974-79, US Dist. Ct. (ea. dist.) La., New Orleans, 1979—94, sr. judge, 1994—. Vice chmn. La. Appellate Judges Conf.; apptd. by chief justice of U.S. to state-fed. com. Jud. Conf. U.S., 1985-89; apptd. by chief justice of U.S. to Nat. Jud. Coun. State and Fed. Cts., 1993—. Mem. bd. mgrs. Touro Infirmary, New Orleans, 1969-74; mem. exec. com. Bur. Govtl. Rsch., 1965-69; chmn. profl. divsn. United Fund New Orleans, 1966-69; mem. New Orleans City Coun., 1969-74, v.p., 1972-74. Capt. USAF, 1952-55. Decorated Bronze Star, Air Force Commendation medal; recipient Justice William Brennan award U. Va. Sch. Law, 2005. Mem. ABA (mem. ho. dels.), Am. Judicature Soc., Fed. Bar Assn., La. Bar Assn., Nat. Lawyers Club, So. Yacht Club, St. John Golf Club. Jewish. Home: 133 Bellaire Dr New Orleans LA 70124-1008 Office: US Dist Ct US Courthouse 500 Poydras St New Orleans LA 70130-3313 Home Phone: 504-482-8745; Office Phone: 504-589-7510.

BEERS, CHARLOTTE LENORE, retired advertising executive, former federal agency administrator; b. Beaumont, Tex., July 26, 1935; d. Glen and Frances (Bolt) Rice; m. Donald C. Beers, 1971; 1 child, Lisa. BS in Math. and Physics, Baylor U., Waco, Tex., 1958. Group product mgr. Uncle Ben's Inc., 1959-69; sr. v.p., dir. client services J. Walter Thompson, 1969-79; COO, mng. ptnr., chmn., CEO Tatham-Laird & Kudner, Chgo., 1979—92; vice chmn. RSCG Group Roux Seguela, Cayzac & Goudard, France; chmn., CEO Ogilvy & Mather Worldwide, Inc., NYC, 1992—97, chmn. emeritus, 1997-99; chmn. J. Walter Thompson Worldwide, NYC, 1999—2001; under sec. for pub. diplomacy & pub. affairs US Dept. State, Washington, 2001—03. Bd. dirs. Martha Stewart Living Omnimedia, Inc., 1999—2001, 2008—. Author: I'd Rather Be in Charge, 2012. Recipient Matrix award, NY Women in Comm., 1996, Legend in Leadership award, Yale Sch. Mgmt. Chief Exec. Leadership Inst., 1999, Distinguished Svc. medal, US Dept. State; named Nat. Advt. Woman of Yr., Am. Advt. Fedn., 1975; named one of Most Powerful Women in America, Fortune mag., 1997; named to Advt. Hall of Fame, Am. Advt. Fedn., 2009. Mem.: Am. Assn. Advt. Agy.'s, Women's Advt. Club Chgo. Republican. Episcopalian.

BEGEMAN, GARY D., lawyer; BFA in Music Edn., U. SD, 1980; JD, Ohio State U., 1983. Ptnr. Jones, Day, Reavis & Pogue; sr. v.p., gen. counsel XO Comm., Inc., 1999—2003; pres., gen. counsel Nextel Comm., Inc., 1997—99, v.p., 2003—06; sr. v.p., dep. gen. counsel Sprint Nextel Corp., 2003—06; joined NII Holdings, Inc., 2006, v.p., gen. counsel, 2007—11, exec. v.p., gen. counsel, 2011—. Office: NII Holdings Inc Ste 1000 1875 Explorer St Reston VA 20190 Office Phone: 703-390-5100.

BEHNKE, MARYLOU, pediatrician, educator; b. Orlando, Fla., Sept. 1, 1950; d. Ernest Edmund and Elizabeth (Kolb) Behnke. BS in Chemistry, U. Fla., 1972, MD, 1976. Diplomate Am. Bd. Pediatrics, Am. Bd. Neonatology-Perinatology. Intern dept. pediat. Coll. Medicine U. Fla., Gainesville, 1976-77, resident, 1977-79, chief resident, 1979-80, fellow in neonatology, 1981-83, asst. prof., 1979-81, 83-89, assoc. prof., 1989-99, prof., 1999—, adj. asst. prof. Coll. Nursing, 1988-89, adj. assoc. prof., 1989-99, mem. senate-at-large, 1984-89, 2004—10, mem. grad. studies faculty, 1988-2000. Presenter nat. and internat. meetings, 1981—; med. dir. ICU Shands Hosp., Gainesville, 1983—89, neonatal devel. follow-up program, 1989—; ad hoc mem. spl. rev. com. human devel. rsch. NIH, 1991—96, chair, 1993, 1994, mem. human devel. and aging-3 study sect., 1998—99; mem. BBBP-6 study sect., 1999—2002. Mem. editl. bd.: Death Studies, 1983—94; mem. editl. bd. Jour. Addiction Medicine, 2007—; contbr. chpts. to books, articles to profl. jours. Grantee, NIH, 1984—87, 1991—, Nat. Inst. Drug Abuse, 1991—, Ctr. Substance Abuse Treatment,

1993—95. Fellow: Am. Acad. Pediat. (sect. perinatal pediat. com. substance abuse 2003—09); mem.: Soc. Rsch. in Child Devel., Fla. Pediat. Soc., Am. Pediatric Soc., Soc. Pediatric Rsch., Southern Soc. Pediat. Rsch., Fla. Med. Assn. Mem. Ch. Of Christ. Avocation: reading. Home: 426 SW 40th St Gainesville FL 32607-2749 Office: J Hillis Miller Health Ctr Dept Pediatrics PO Box 100296 Gainesville FL 32610-0296 Business E-Mail: behnkem@peds.ufl.edu.

BEHNKEN, ROBERT L., astronaut; b. Creve Coeur, Mo. BSME, Wash. U., 1992, BS in Physics, 1992; MSME, Calif. Inst. Tech., 1993, PhD in Mech. Engring., 1997. Active duty, Air Force, Eglin AFB, Fla.; tech. mgr., develop. engr. for new munitions systems; assigned to F-22 Combined Test Force Edwards AFB; lead test engr. for Raptor 4004 and spl. projects test dir.; mission specialist, astronaut NASA, Johnson Space Ctr., 2000—. Technical duties, Astronaut Office Shuttle Br. Kennedy Space Ctr., Fla.; mission specialist 1 for ascent and entry, perform 3 spacewalks, serve as the IV (internal spacewalk coord.) and operate the space station robotic arm STS-123 Mission (Endeavor), mission to deliver the Japanese Logistics Module and the Canadian Spl. Purpose Dexterous Manipulator to the Internat. Space Station (ISS), 2008; mission specialist STS-130 Mission (Endeavour), 2010. Recipient Air Force Rsch. Lab. Munitions Directorate, USAF Achievement medal, 1997, USAF Commendation medal, 1998, USAF Test Pilot Sch. Col. Ray Jones award as the top flight test engr./flight test navigator in class 98B, USAF Commendation medal, 2000, USAF Meritorious Svc. medal, 2004, NASA Space Flight medal, 2008; named Eglin AFB Fla. Co. Grade Officer Yr., 1997; NSF Grad. Rsch. Fellow, 1993—96. Avocations: mountain biking, skiing, backpacking. Office: Astronaut Office NASA Lyndon B Johnson Space Ctr 2101 NASA Pky Houston TX 77058

BEHRENS, LEANN, public health service officer; CEO, Amerigroup DFW and Corpus Christi Health Plans Amerigroup Corp. Office: Amerigroup Corp Ste 100 4425 Corporation Ln Virginia Beach VA 23462 Office Phone: 757-490-6900. Office Fax: 757-518-3600. Business E-Mail: lbehrens@amerigroupcorp.com.

BEHRENS, WILLIAM BLADE, television program syndication and professional sports team executive; b. Burlington, Vt., Oct. 17, 1956; s. Robert Allen and Elizabeth (Husk) B. BA in Psychology, Emory U., 1978. Video/audio tech. WXII-TV, Winston-Salem, 1979-80; v.p. sales Behrens Co.-Behrens Prodns., Miami, Fla., 1980-87; S.E. sales mgr. Access Syndication, Studio City, Calif., 1987-88, The Great Entertainment Co., NYC, 1988-90; dir. syndication World Sports Syndication, Atlanta, 1988-91; S.E. sales mgr. Colbert TV Sales, LA, 1988—; v.p. Litton TV Syndications, Balt., 1989-94; pres. Show Bus., Inc., Atlanta, 1989—; dir. southeast sales Polygram Television/ITC, Beverly Hills, Calif., 1994-98; v.p. Nat. Wrestling Alliance, 1998—2002, pres., 2003—04; dir. Total Non-Stop Action Entertainment, 2003—05, 2006—08; pvt. practice cons. Atlanta, 2005—. Cons. World Wrestling Entertainment, 2006. Music editor Emory Wheel, 1977-78; contbr. articles to profl. jours. Mem.: Nat. Assn. TV Program Execs., Nat. Assn. TV Arts and Scis., Am. Film Inst. Avocations: collecting films, animation cells, records and comic books, fishing. Home: PO Box 941787 Atlanta GA 31141-0787 Office Phone: 770-621-9533. E-mail: showbis@aol.com.

BEHRING, ALEXANDRE, food service executive; b. 1967; BSEE, Pontificia Universidad Catolica; MBA, Harvard Bus. Sch, 1995. CEO America Latina Logistica S.A., 1998—2004; mng. dir. 3G Capital Partners Ltd., 2005—; co-chmn. Burger King Holdings, Inc., Miami, 2010—. Bd. dirs. CSX Corp., 2008—. Office: Burger King Holdings Inc 5505 Blue Lagoon Dr Miami FL 33126 Business E-Mail: alexandre.behring@3gcapital.com.

BEHYMER, CHRISTOPHER GLENN, insurance company executive; b. LA, Feb. 2, 1954; s. Howard Glenn and Mary Bernice (Pickerel) B.; m. Tracy Lynn Wilkinson, Mar. 30, 1985; 1 child, Jeffrey. BBA, U. Wis., 1976. Chartered Property and Casualty Underwriter, Cert. Ins. Counselor. Underwriter Sentry Ins., Scottsdale, Ariz., 1977—79, underwriting mgr., 1979—82, mktg. specialist, 1982—85, sales tng. mgr., 1985—87; dir., tng. and devel. Scottsdale Ins., 1987; dir., mktg., Market West Markel Corp. Chmn. Semi Ann. Blood Dr., Scottsdale, 1988—, Co. United Way Fund Raiser, Scottsdale, 1988—; advisor Jr. Achievement, Scottsdale, 1988—; chmn. corp. team sales Ariz. State U. Pres.'s Club Golf Tournament, 1990—. Mem. CPCU (ctrl. Ariz. chpt.), Cert. Ins. Conselors (chmn. edn. com. 1988—), Soc. Ins. Trainers and Educators (v.p. Western region 1993—). Office: Markel Corp 4521 Highwoods Pkwy Glen Allen VA 23060-6148 Office Phone: 804-747-0136. Office Fax: 804-965-1600. Business E-Mail: cbehymer@markelcorp.com.*

BEICHNER, ROBERT J., physics professor; BS with high distinction in Physics and Math., Pa. State U., 1977; MS in Physics, U. Ill., Urbana-Champaign, 1979; PhD in Sci. Edn., SUNY, Buffalo, 1989. Instr. then asst. prof. physics Erie CC, Buffalo, 1980—89, chair Physics Dept., 1986; co-dir. then dir. Ctr. for Learning and Tech. SUNY, Buffalo, 1989—92, vis. asst. prof. sci. edn., 1989—92; asst. prof. physics NC State U., Raleigh, NC, 1992—98, assoc. prof., 1998—2003, prof., 2003—, dir. physics grad. program, 2005—06, founding dir. STEM Edn. Initiative, 2007—. Vis. prof. physics Old Dominion U., 2005—; adj. prof. physics U. Sydney, Australia, 2007. Contbr. articles to profl. jours. Recipient Harold W. McGraw, Jr. Prize in Edn., McGraw-Hill Rsch. Found., 2011; named NC State Prof. of Yr., Carnegie Found. for Advancement of Tchg. and Coun. for Advancement and Support of Edn., 2009. Office: North Carolina State University Physics Dept Riddicks Labs, Rm 246 Raleigh NC 27695-8202 Office Phone: 919-515-7226. E-mail: beichner@ncsu.edu.

BEIRNE, MARTIN DOUGLAS, lawyer; s. Martin Douglas and Catherine Anne Beirne; m. Kathleen Harrington; children: Martin, Shannon, Kelley. BS, Spring Hill Coll., 1966; JD with honors, St. Mary's U., 1969. Bar: Tex. 1969, US Dist. Ct. (ea. dist.) Tex. 1972, US Dist. Ct. (so. dist.) Tex. 1971, US Dist. Ct. (no. dist.) Tex., US Dist. Ct. (we. dist.) Tex., US Dist. Ct. DC, US Ct. Appeals (5th and 11th cirs.) 1974, US Dist. Ct. (ea. dist.) Calif., US Supreme Ct. 1975. Ptnr. Fulbright & Jaworski, Houston, 1971-85; chmn. Beirne, Maynard & Parsons, Houston, 1985—. Editor-in-chief St. Mary's Law Rev. Bd. dirs. St. Thomas U., Houston Law Rev. Found.; bd. trustees St. Mary's U., chmn. law sch. found.; trustee Tex. Bar Found.; commr. Tex. Access to Justice Commn. Capt. US Army, 1969—71. Fellow Am. Bar Found., Tex. Bar Found. (bd. dirs.); mem. ABA, Tex. Bar Assn., Houston Bar Assn., Coronado Club, Houstonian Club, Legatus-U. Houston Law Sch. Found. Am. Law Inst., Inst. for Transnat. Arbitration, Houston Bar Found. (bd. dirs.). Roman Catholic. Office: Beirne Maynard & Parsons LLP 1300 Post Oak Blvd Fl 25 Houston TX 77056-3028 Office Phone: 713-623-0887. Business E-Mail: mbeirne@bmpllp.com.

BELANGER, TERRY, historian, educator; b. Hartford, Conn., Mar. 21, 1941; BA, Haverford Coll., 1963; MA, Columbia U., 1964, PhD, 1970. Faculty Columbia U. Sch. Libr. Svc., 1971—92; assistant dean Columbia U., 1980—86, founder Book Arts Press bibliog. lab., 1971—92, founder Rare Book Sch., 1983—; moved Book Arts Press and Rare Book Sch. to U. Va., 1992; prof., hon. curator spl. collections U. Va., 1992—2009. Named MacArthur fellow, John D. and Catherine T. MacArthur Found., 2005. Mem.: Bibliographical Soc. U. Va. (coun. 1992—), Bibliographical Soc. Am. (chair nominating com. 1995, 2007), Bibliographical Soc. London, Assn. Coll. Rsch. Libr. (bd. dir. 1976—78, chair rare books and manuscripts sect. 1978—79), Am. Antiquarian Soc., Am. Printing History Assn. (trustee 1974—81, pres. NY chpt. 1979—82, Laureate 1994). Office: Univ Va PO Box 400103 114 Alderman Libr Charlottesville VA 22904-4103 Office Phone: 434-924-8851. Business E-Mail: belanger@virginia.edu.

BELANGER, WILLIAM JOSEPH, chemist, consultant; b. Chgo., Mar. 20, 1925; m. Keltah Long, Feb. 1, 1947; children: William Joseph, Thomas, Kathryn, Michael, Jeanne, Judith, Elizabeth, John, Anne. BS in Chemistry, St. Louis U., 1948; PhD in Organic Chemistry, Notre Dame U., 1951. Research chemist duPont Co., 1951-53; research chemist, then tech. service mgr. Devoe & Reynolds Co., 1953-60; tech. mgr. resin devel. Celanese Coatings & Specialties Co., Louisville, 1960-69; v.p. tech. and engring. Celanese Polymer Specialities Co., Jeffersontown, Ky., 1970-79; v.p. Specialties Group, Celanese Plastics & Specialties Co., 1979-82; Splty. polymer applications cons., 1982—. Tchr. polymer chemistry U. Louisville, 1957; tchr. organic chemistry Ind. Univ. Southeast, 1986. Patentee in field. Vice chmn. Jefferson County Housing Authority, 1975-78; trustee Audubon Hosp., 1979-82. Served with USNR, 1943-45. Mem. Am. Chem. Soc., Nat. Paint and Coatings Assn. Home and Office: 1208 Creighton Hill Rd Louisville KY 40207-2244 Personal E-mail: billb1208@insightbb.com.

BELCHER, CAROLYN R., state legislator; b. Dec. 11, 1953; CPA. State rep. Dist. 72, Ky., 1999—; mem. Econ. Develop Com., Tourism Com., Energy Com., State Com., Local Govt. Com.; house rep. Ky. Mem.: America Inst. CPA's, DAV Auxiliary, Ky. Farm Bureau, Bath County Salvation Army, C of C, Owingsville Woman's Club, Kiwanis Club. Democrat. Christian. Office: Capitol Annex Room 457E Frankfort KY 40601 Mailing: 51 Blevins Valley Rd Owingsville KY 40360 Home Phone: 606-674-3280; Office Phone: 606-674-2417, 502-564-8100 ext 752.

BELCHER, DENNIS I., lawyer; b. Wheeling, W.Va., Aug. 24, 1951; s. Finley Duncan Belcher and Ellen Jane (Huffman) Good; m. Vickie Marie Early, Aug. 2, 1975; children: Sarah Anne, Matthew Irl, Benjamin Scott. BA, Coll. William and Mary, 1973; JD, U. Richmond, 1976. Bar: Va. 1976, U.S. Tax Ct. 1978. Assoc. McGuireWoods LLP (formerly McGuire, Woods, Battle & Boothe), Richmond, Va., 1976—83, ptnr., 1983—, mem. exec. com., 1996—2001, mem. bd. ptnrs., 2005—. Adj. prof. taxation Va. Commonwealth U., Richmond, 1985-88. Co-author: Business Tax Planning Forms for Businesses and Individuals, 1985. Chmn. Richmond chpt. Am. Heart Assn., 1984-85; trustee St. Christopher's Sch., 1993-2003. Named one of The Most Influential Lawyers, The Nat. Law Jour., 2011; named to Hall of Fame, Nat. Assn. Estate Planners and Couns., 2010. Fellow Am. Coll. Trust and Estate Counsel (bd. regents 1999-05, sec. 2005-06, treas. 2006-); mem. ABA (real property and probate sect., sec. 1997-98, chmn. marital deduction com., vice chmn. lifetime transfers com., ho. of dels. 1998-99, vice chair probate divsn. 1999-01, chair 2002-03), Va. Bar Assn. (wills and trusts and taxations sects.), Country Club of Va., Kinloch Golf Club. Presbyterian. Avocations: golf, farming. Office: McGuireWoods LLP One James Center 901 East Cary St Richmond VA 23219-4030 Office Phone: 804-775-4304. Office Fax: 703-712-5050. Business E-Mail: dbelcher@mcguirewoods.com.

BELCHER, LINDA, state legislator; b. Sept. 20, 1948; BS in Elem. Edn., Eastern Ky. U.; MS in Elem. Edn., Western Ky. U. Ret. tchr., prin. & dir. U. Louisville; mem. Dist. 49 Ky. House of Reps., 2009—. Democrat. Baptist. Office: 702 Capitol Ave Rm 429D Frankfort KY 40601 also: 4804 Hickory Hollow Ln Shepherdsville KY 40165 Office Phone: 502-564-8100 Ext. 663, 502-957-2793. Office Fax: 502-957-4182.

BELEW, JOHN SEYMOUR, academic administrator, chemist; b. Waco, Tex., Nov. 3, 1920; s. George H. and Mary (Seymour) B.; m. Ruth Edna McAtee, June 3, 1944; children— James Seymour, Janet Elizabeth. BS, Baylor U., 1941; MS, Wichita State U., 1947; PhD, U. Wis., 1951; LLD, Hong Kong Bapt. U., 1995. Instr. U.S. Army Air Corps Tech. Tng. Command, 1941-43; rsch. assoc. Brown U., Providence, 1951-53; acting. asst. prof. U. Va., 1953-56; asst. prof., then assoc. prof. and prof. chemistry Baylor U., Waco, Tex., 1956-91, prof. emeritus, 1991—, assoc. dean Coll. Arts and Scis., 1973-74, dean Coll. Arts and Scis., 1974-79, chief acad. officer, 1979-91, Jo Murphy chair in internat. edn., 1990-96, provost emeritus, 1991—. Vis. fellow Manchester Coll., Oxford U., summer 1995; mem. team advs. to Tech. U. Liberec, Czech Rep., 1999. Mem. various cmty. bds.; trustee Midway Ind. Sch. Dist., Waco, 1962-72; bd. dirs. Tex. High Speed Rail Authority, 1992-1996; del. Nat. Dem. Conv., 2000. With USAAF, 1943-46. Wilton Park fellow, 1976; recipient Disting. Alumnus award Baylor U., 1993. Mem.: Royal Soc. Chemistry, Am. Chem. Soc., Turner Soc. London, Grolier Club, Sigma Xi. Office: Provost Emeritus Baylor Univ Waco TX 76798-7121 E-mail: seymourbelew@earthlink.net.

BELFIGLIO, VALENTINE JOHN, political science professor; b. May 28, 1934; s. Edmond Liberato and Mildred Elizabeth (Sherwood) B.; 1 child by previous marriage, Valentine Edmond; m. Ellie K. Belfiglio; stepchildren: Andy, Kevian Navid. BS, Union U., 1956; MA, U. Okla., Norman, 1967; PhD, U. Okla., 1970. Registered pharmacist, Fla., Okla., Tex.; cert. cons. pharmacist., pharmacy based immunization delivery, sterile pharmaceutical compounding. Grad. asst., instr. U. Okla., 1967-70; prof. polit. sci., instr. drug law and policy Tex. Woman's U., Denton, 1970—; cons. pharmacist Whitaker Med., Ltd. Assoc. editor Common Ground Pub.; lectr. in field to Great Britain, Spain, Italy and Greece. Contbr. textbooks in the practice of pharmacy Holbrook Press, Boston, 1973-75, contbr. articles to profl. jours. With USAF, 1959—67, ret. col. tex. State Guard, mem. Dept. DEf. ESGR. Decorated knight Order of Merit, Republic of Italy; recipient Guido Dorso prize U. Naples, 1985, C.K. Chamberlain award East Tex. Hist. Assn., 1990, Cornaro award Tex. Woman's U., 2003, Faculty Devel. leave, Rome, 2001, Cornaro award Tex. Woman's U., 2003, Counseling Excellence award in pharmacy Pharmacy Today, 2006, One-to-One award in pharm. counseling Am. Pharm. Assn., 2006; Instnl. Rsch. grantee Tex. Woman's U., 1973-74, 76-77, Faculty Devel. fellow, Rome, 2001. Fellow Am. Soc. Cons. Pharmacists; mem. AAUP, Internat. Studies Assn. (sec.-treas. region 1974-76), Am. Polit. Sci. Assn., Am. Italian Hist. Assn. (col., ret.), Tex. State Def. Forces, US Dept. Def. (ESGR Com. mem. 2009-), Fourth degree Knight of Columbus, Mensa, Kappa Psi Republican. Roman Catholic. Avocations: chess, dance, gourmet cooking. Office: Tex Woman's Univ PO Box 425889 Denton TX 76204-5889 Home: 11505 Sonnet Dr Dallas TX 75229-2629 Office Phone: 940-898-2144. Business E-Mail: vbelfiglio@twu.edu.

BELICH, JOHN PATRICK, SR., journalist, private investigator; b. Peekskill, NY, Dec. 6, 1938; s. John Andrew and Iris Patricia (Brown) B.; m. Louise Daniel, June 4, 1971; children: Mary Louise, John P. Jr., Andrew J. Student, N.Y. Inst. Photography, St. Petersburg Jr. Coll. Cert. Fla. Bd. Cert. Investigators Inc. Staff news photographer UPI, 1963-69; So. div. photo mgr. Atlanta, 1969-72; photo editor, dir. photography St. Petersburg Times and Evening Independent, 1972-87, mgr. newsroom projects, 1987-94, asst. to pres., 1994—2006; pvt. investigator J. Belich & Assocs., 2006—. V.p., bd. dirs. N.W. Fla. Little Maj. League Assn.; mem. photography adv. com. St. Petersburg Vocat. Tech. Inst.; guardian ad litem 6th Jud. Ctr., Fla.; Skywarn vol. Amateur Radio Emergency Svc. Corp., Nat. Weather Svc.; bd. advisors Coll. Comm., Fla. State U. Recipient Pres.'s medal Nat. Press Photographers Assn., 1978, citation of excellence, 1979, James E. Reddick Sr. Meml. award, Fla. Bd. Cert. Investigators, 2011. Mem.: Nat. Press Photographers Assn. (bd. dirs., chmn. info. com. 1978), Atlanta Press Photographers Assn. (past treas., v.p.), Fla. News Photographers Assn., Nat. Press Photographers Found., Am. Meteorol. Soc., Nat. Weather Assn., Am. Radio Relay League, Amateur Radio Satellite Corp., NRA, Clearwater Amateur Radio Soc., Fla. Assn. Lic. Investigators (bd. dirs. 2004-06, 2007-13, sec., 2013-), Am. Soc. Indsl. Security, Nat. Coun. Investigation and Security Svcs., Nat. Assn. Legal Investigators, Fla. Assn. Security Cos., Computer Security Inst., Info. Sys. Security Assn., Sigma Delta Chi. Office: J Belich & Assoc Inc 6822 22nd Ave N 304 Saint Petersburg FL 33701 Home Phone: 727-345-1021; Office Phone: 877-724-9253. Business E-Mail: jbelich@jbelich.com.

BELK, H.W. MCKAY, retail executive; BS in Indsl. Rels., U. NC, Chapel Hill, MBA. Joined Belk Inc., 1979; pres., mdse., sales promotion Belk Stores Svcs., Inc., 1995—97, pres., chief mdse. officer, 1997—98; pres., merchandising, mktg., mdse. planning Belk Inc., 1998—2004; pres., chief merchandising officer Belk, Inc., 2004—. Bd. dirs. Coca-Cola Bottling Co., 1994—, Belk Inc., 1998—. Chmn. Charlotte C. of C.; former bd. trustee Charlotte Latin Sch.; former bd. dirs. North Carolina C. of C.; bd. inst., arts, humanities U. of NC, Chapel Hill; bd. trustee Crossnore Sch. Office: Belk Inc 2801 W Tyvola Rd Charlotte NC 28217-4500 Office Phone: 704-357-1000. Office Fax: 704-357-1876. Business E-Mail: hw_belk@belk.com.

BELK, IRWIN, retail executive; b. Charlotte, NC, Apr. 4, 1922; s. William Henry and Mary Leonora (Irwin) B.; m. Carol Grotnes, Sept. 11, 1948; children: William Irwin, Irene Belk Miltimore, Marilyn Belk Wallis, Carl Grotnes. BS in Commerce, U. NC, 1946; LLD (hon.), Mo. Valley Coll., 1977, Elon Coll., 1990, East Carolina U., 1997, St. Andrews Presbyn. Coll., 2001, Fayetteville State U., 2001; LLD, Lynchburg Coll., Va., 2006; HHD (hon.), Erskine Coll., 1979, U. NC, 1991, Wingate U., 1995, Johnson C. Smith U., 1999, Western Carolina U., 1999, Furman U., 2000, Livingston Coll., Salisbury, NC, 2004, Presbyn. Coll., Clinton, SC, 2005, Christopher Newport U., Va., 2006, U. NC, Pembroke, 2007, U. NC, Greensboro, 2007, U. NC, Wilmington, 2008, Va. Wesleyan Coll., Norfolk, 2008; LHD, Appalachian State U., 2010; PhD, Va. Wesleyan Coll., 2008; LHD, UNC Wilmington, 2008, UNC Pembroke, 2007, Lenoir-Rhyne U., 2009. Officer and dir. Belk Group, Inc., Charlotte; past dir. PMC, Inc., Raleigh, NC; chmn. bd. Monroe Hardware Co. Past dir. First Union Nat. Bank of NC, Charlotte, Lumbermen's Mut. Casualty, Co., Chgo., Stonecutter Mills, Spindale, NC; Past pres. men's council NC Synod, Presbyn. Ch.; mem. exec. com. Hist. Found. Presbyn and Reformed Chs. (Montreat), NC. Past pres. NC div. Am. Cancer Soc.; trustee NC Symphony Soc.; chmn. US Olympic Com. for NC; past mem. City of Charlotte Urban Redevel. Com.; mem. NC Ho. of Reps., 1959-60, 61-62, NC Senate, 1963-66, NC Legis. Coun., 1963-64, Legis. Rsch. Commn., 1965-66, Democratic nat. committeeman for, NC, 1969-72; del. Dem. Nat. Convs., 1956, 60, 64, 68, 72; bd. dirs. Med. Found. NC, NC State Bus. Found. NC, Chapel Hill, Ednl. Found., Found. of U. NC, Charlotte, Sch. of Design, NC State U.; bd. dirs., mem. exec. com. NC Assn. for Blind; bd. dirs., past pres. N.C. chpt. Nat. Soc. Prevention Blindness; ho. dels. Am. Cancer Soc.; bd. dirs. Charlotte Opera Assn.; bd. govs. U. NC, Presbyn. Coll., Clinton, SC; bd. advisors Belk Found.; former bd. assocs. Meredith Coll., Raleigh; bd. counselors Erskine Coll., Due West, SC; bd. advisers Western Carolina U., Cullowhee, NC; former bd. advisers Campbell Coll., Buies Creek, NC; dir. NC Citizens for Bus. and Industry, Raleigh, NC, 1990-94. Served with USAAF, World War II. Recipient Outstanding Young Man award Charlotte, 1954-57, Algenon Sydney Sullivan award Queens Coll., Charlotte, 1971, William Davie award U. NC, 1992, univ. award U. NC, 1993. Mem. Charlotte Mchts. Assn., Charlotte C. of C. (exec. com., dir.), NC Presbyn. Hist. Soc. (past pres.), Charlotte Country Club, Myers Park Country Club, Charlotte City Club, Sky Club, Masons, Shriners, Lions (past pres., past dist. gov.), Kappa Alpha, Delta Sigma Pi. Democrat. Presbyterian (elder, past deacon). Clubs: Masons (Charlotte, dist. gov.), Shriners (Charlotte, dist. gov.), Lions (Charlotte, dist. gov.) (past pres.); Charlotte City (Charlotte), Charlotte Country (Charlotte), Charlotte Execs. (Charlotte) (past pres.), Charlotte Carrousel (Charlotte) (past pres.), Myers Park Country (Charlotte); Sky (N.Y.C.). Home: 9200 Winged Bourne Rd Charlotte NC 28210-5948 Office: Belk Group 6100 Fairview Rd Ste 640 Charlotte NC 28210-4258

BELK, JOHN R., retail executive; s. Thomas M. Belk and Katherine Belk Cook. BA in Economics, Political sci., U. NC, Chapel Hill; MBA, U. Va. Various positions Irving Trust Co., 1981—83; mgmt. trainee Belk Inc., NC, 1986, buyer, mdse. mgr., Matthews Belk store NC, 1986—89, store mgr., Monroe Belk store NC, 1989—90, v.p., dir. Charlotte, NC, 1990—92, sr. v.p., 1992—97, pres., fin., sys. and ops., 1998—2004; pres., COO Belk, Inc., Charlotte, NC, 2004—. Bd. dirs. Alltel Corp., Bank of Am. Corp., Ruddick Corp. Bd. dirs. Ctrl YMCA, United Way Ctrl. Carolinas. Office: Belk Inc 2801 W Tyvola Rd Charlotte NC 28217 Office Fax: 704-357-1876. Business E-Mail: john_belk@belk.com.

BELK, THOMAS MILBURN, JR., (TIM), retail executive; s. Thomas Milburn and Katherine (McKay) Belk. BS in Economics, Williams Coll., Williamstown, Mass.; MBA, U. NC, Chapel Hill, 1981. Joined Belk, Inc., Charlotte, NC, 1981; pres., store divsn. Belk Inc., Charlotte, NC, 1998—2004; chmn., CEO Belk, Inc., Charlotte, NC, 2004—. Trustee NC Blumenthal Performing Arts Ctr.; mem. adv. bd. Kenan-Flagler Bus. Sch., Univ. NC, Chapel Hill, Univ. NC, Charlotte; bd. mem. Carolinas Healthcare Sys., Rsch. Triangle Found. NC. Office: Belk Inc 2801 W Tyvola Rd Charlotte NC 28217 Office Fax: 704-357-1876. Business E-Mail: thomas_belk@belk.com.

BELL, BETH P., public health service officer; BA, Brown U., Providence; MD, Yale U., New Haven; MPH, U. Rochester Sch. Medicine, NY. Epidemic intelligence officer Wash. State Dept. Health; mem. hepatitis br., divsn. viral and rickettsial diseases Centers Disease Control an Prevention, Atlanta, chief epidemiology br., divsn. viral hepatitis, leadership positions during fed. responses to major pub. health events including 2001 anthrax attacks, Hurricane Katrina and 2009 H1N1 flu response, acting dep. dir. then acting dir. Nat. Ctr. Immunization and Respiratory Diseases, 2008—09, assoc. dir. epidemiol. sci. Nat. Ctr. Immunization and Respiratory Diseases, 2009—10, dir. Nat. Ctr. Emerging and Zoonotic Infectious Diseases, 2010—. Contbr. articles to profl. jours. (Alexander Langmuir prize, Iain Hardy award). Fellow: Infectious Disease Soc. America, American Acad. Family Medicine, American Acad. Preventive Medicine; mem.: American Epidemiol. Soc. Office: Centers Disease Control and Prevention NCEZID 1600 Clifton Rd Atlanta GA 30333

BELL, CHARLES EUGENE, JR., retired industrial engineer; b. NYC, Dec. 13, 1932; s. Charles Edward and Constance Elizabeth (Verbelia) Bell; m. Doris R. Clifton, Jan. 14, 1967 (dec. May 8, 2013);

1 child, Scott Charles. B in Engring., Johns Hopkins U., 1954, MS in Engring., 1959. Registered Calif. Indsl. engr. Signode Corp., Balt., 1957—61, asst. to plant mgr., 1961—63, plant engr., 1963—64, divsn. indsl. engr. Glenview, Ill., 1964—69, asst. to divsn. mgr., 1969—76, engring. mgr., 1976—93; cons., 1993—2004; ret., 2004. Host committeeman Internat. Indsl. Engring. Conf., Chgo., 1984, Chgo., 1992. With US Army, 1955—57. Mem.: NSPE, Soc. Plastics Engrs., Tenn. Soc. Profl. Engrs., Indsl. Mgmt. Club Ctrl. Md. (pres. 1964), Am. Inst. Indsl. Engrs. (pres. 1981), Druid Hills Country Club. Republican. Roman Catholic. Home: 207 Markham Ln Crossville TN 38558

BELL, DONNIE, state legislator; b. Tupelo, Mar. 3, 1963; m. Nelda Higginbotham. BS, Miss.State U.; attended, Itawamba CC. Teacher; mem. Dist. 21 Miss. House of Reps., 2008—, vice chair transp. com., mem. conservation and water resources com., county affairs com., forestry com., ports, harbors and airports com., univs. and colls. com. Democrat. Home: 836 Tucker Rd Fulton MS 38843 Office: PO Box 1018 Jackson MS 39215 Home Phone: 601-862-3385. E-mail: dbell@house.ms.gov.

BELL, GRIFFIN BOYETTE, JR., lawyer; b. Richmond, Va., Feb. 16, 1944; AB, U. Ga., 1965; JD, Emory U., 1970. Bar: Ga. 1970. Law clk. to Hon. Alexander A. Laurence U.S. Dist. Ct. (so. dist.) Ga., 1970-72; ptnr. Fisher & Phillips, Atlanta. Capt. field arty. U.S. Army, 1965-71. Mem. ABA, Fed. Bar Assn., State Bar Ga., Lawyers Club Am., Phi Delta Phi. Office: Fisher & Phillips 1500 Resurgens Plz 1075 Peachtree St NE Ste 3500 Atlanta GA 30309-3900

BELL, HANEY HARDY, III, lawyer; b. Staunton, Va., Aug. 20, 1944; s. Haney Hardy Jr. and Maud (Deekens) B.; m. Alice Tester, Feb. 17, 1968; 1 child, Landon D. BA, U. Va., 1966; JD cum laude, U. Wis., 1973. Bar: Va. 1974. Group ins. rep. Prudential Ins. Co. Am., Milw., 1969-70; assoc. Woods, Rogers & Hazelgrove, Roanoke, Va., 1973-78; assoc. counsel R.J. Reynolds Industries, Inc., Winston-Salem, NC, 1978-79; sec., gen. counsel RJR Foods, Inc., 1979-80; sr. internat. counsel R.J. Reynolds Tobacco Internat., Inc., 1980-87; assoc. gen. counsel Fieldcrest Cannon Inc., Eden, NC, 1987-95, Lorillard Tobacco Co., Greensboro, 1996—2002; v.p., asst. gen. counsel Santa Fe Natural Tobacco Co., 2002—07, v.p., gen. counsel, 2007—09. Lt. AUS, 1967-69. Mem. Va. State Bar, Order of Coif. Home: 2 Champions Ct Frisco TX 75034 Home Phone: 336-414-3577. Personal E-mail: wtrn534@gmail.com.

BELL, HEATH JUSTIN, professional baseball player; b. Oceanside, Calif., Sept. 29, 1977; m. Nicole Bell; children: Jasmine, Jordan, Reece. Attended, Rancho Santiago CC, Calif. Relief pitcher NY Mets, 2004—06, San Diego Padres, 2007—11, Miami Marlins, 2011—12, Ariz. Diamonbacks, 2013, Tampa Bay Rays, 2013—. Recipient Nat. League Rolaids Relief award, 2010; named Delivery Man of Yr., Maj. League Baseball, 2010; named to Nat. League All-Star Team, 2009, 2011. Achievements include leading the National League in: saves (42), 2009. Office: Tampa Bay Rays One Tropicana Dr Saint Petersburg FL 33705*

BELL, JAMES A.H., lawyer; b. Knoxville, Tenn., Nov. 10, 1948; BS, East Tenn. State U., 1970; JD, U. Tenn., Knoxville, 1973. Bar: Tenn. 1974, US Dist. Ct. (ea. dist.) Tenn. 1975, US Supreme Ct. 1981, US Ct. Appeals (6th cir.) 1983. Pvt. practice, Knoxville, Tenn. Lectr. in field. Fellow: Am. Bd. Criminal Lawyers; mem.: ABA, Tenn. Trial Lawyers Assn., Assn. Trial Lawyers of Am., Nat. Assn. Criminal Defense Lawyers (chmn. By Laws Com. 1990—), Tenn. Assn. Criminal Defense Lawyers (bd. dirs. 1977, pres. 1983—84). Office: James AH Bell Attorney 10 Emory Pl Knoxville TN 37917-7317 Office Phone: 865-637-2900. Office Fax: 865-971-4298. E-mail: jbell@jamesahbell.com.

BELL, JERRY NATHAN, state legislator; b. Mena, Ark., July 17, 1969; m. Phyllis Bell; 2 children. Founder, mng. ptnr. Quad B Specialties, LLC; mem. Dist. 22 Ark. House of Representatives, 2010—. Republican. Office: PO Box 2103 Mena AR 71953 Office Phone: 479-394-5665. Business E-Mail: nate@natebell4arkansas.com.

BELL, JOHNNY W., state legislator; b. June 15, 1965; Mem. Dist. 23 Ky. House of Reps., 2007—; mem. Banking & Ins. Com., State Govt. and Transp. Com. Mem.: Barren County Bar Assoc., KY Bar Assoc., Nat. Golden Key Honor Soc. Democrat. Baptist. Mailing: 108 N Green St Glasgow KY 42141 Office Phone: 502-564-8100 ext. 688. E-mail: Johnny.Bell@lrc.ky.gov.

BELL, KENNETH B., lawyer, former state supreme court justice; married; 4 children. BA in History, Davidson Coll., NC, 1978; JD cum laude, Fla. State U., 1982. Bar: Fla. 1982. Pvt. practice, real estate atty., Pensacola, 1982—91; trial judge 1st Jud. Cir. Fla., 1991—2002; justice Fla. Supreme Ct., Tallahassee, 2003—08; ptnr. Clark, Partington, Hart, Larry, Bond & Stackhouse, Pensacola, Fla., 2008—. Mem. cir. com. on professionalism Supreme Ct., 2000—08. Founding pres. of bd. dirs. Friends of Children's Hosp. at Sacred Heart, Inc.; bd. dirs. Escambia County 4-H Found., Waterfront Rescue Mission; c-founder Yan-Bian Chinese-Korean Tech. U., China. Mem.: Am. Judicature Soc., AMA (mem. real property, probate and trust law sections), Fla. Bar Assn. (mem. real property, probate and trust law sections), Escambia-Santa Rosa Bar Assn. Office: Clark Partington Hart Ste 800 1 Pensacola Plz Pensacola FL 32502 Mailing: Clark Partington Hart PO Box 13010 Pensacola FL 32591-3010 Office Phone: 850-432-9200. Office Fax: 850-432-7340.

BELL, LARRY M., SR., state legislator; b. Sampson Co., NC, Aug. 18, 1939; widowed; 1 child, Larry Jr. BS, North Carolina Agrl. & Tech. State U., 1961, MA, 1976; EdS, East Carolina U., 1983. Tchr. Sampson Co. Schs., 1961—76, prin., 1976—85, asst. supt., 1985—90, supt., 1990—96; commr. Sampson Co. Bd. Commrs., 1990—2000; mem. Dist. 97 NC House of Reps., 2001—02, mem. Dist. 21, 2003—, majority whip. Democrat. Baptist. Office: North Carolina House of Representatives 300 N Salisbury St Rm 606 Raleigh NC 27603-5925 Office Phone: 919-733-5863. E-mail: Larry.Bell@ncleg.net.

BELL, NORMAN HOWARD, retired endocrinologist, educator; b. Gainesville, Ga., Feb. 11, 1931; s. Kenneth Rush and Henrietta Maria (Howard Rankin) Bell; m. Claude Handy Bell, June 27, 1959 (dec. 1967); children: Douglas Howard, Julianne Rankin; m. Mary Virginia Baughman, Aug. 24, 1968 (div. July 1972); m. Ledlie Laird Dinsmore, Dec. 16, 1972; 1 child, Bayard Gardiner. AB, Emory U., 1951; MD, Duke U., 1955. Intern Duke U. Med. Ctr., Durham, NC, 1955-56, resident, 1956-57; clin. assoc. Nat. Inst. Allergy and Infectious Diseases, NIH, Bethesda, Md., 1957-59; mem. staff clin. endocrinology br. Nat. Heart, Lung and Blood Inst., NIH, Bethesda, 1959-63, assoc. in medicine, 1963-65; asst. prof. medicine Northwestern U. Sch. Medicine, Chgo., 1965-68; assoc. prof. Ind. U. Med Sch., Indpls., 1968-71, prof., 1971-79; prof. medicine and pharmacology Med. U. SC, Charleston, SC, 1979—2006, disting. univ. prof., 1998. Mem. gen. medicine B study sect. NIH, Bethesda, 1982—86, chmn., 1985—86, mem. spl. grants rev. com. Nat. Inst. Arthritis, Musculo-Skeletal and Skin Diseases, 1990—95, chmn., 1993—94. Mem. editl. bd. Calcified Tissue Internat., 1978—83, 1994—2002, Jour. Clin. Endocrinology and Metabolism, 1982—87, Jour. Bone and Mineral Rsch., 1989—93, Italian Jour. Mineral and Electrolyte Metabolism, 1990—, Current Drug Targets-Immune, Endocrine and Metabolic Disorders, 2000—06, Reviews in Endocrine & Metabolic Disorders, 2000—05. Trustee Nat. Osteoporosis Found., Washington, 1984—88, chmn. sci. adv. bd., 1985—88. With USPHS, 1957—63. Recipient Career Devel. award, USPHS, 1965—68, VA Med. Investigator award, 1979, 1981—87, Thomas A. Roe Found. award, S.C. Med. Assn., 1982, William S. Middleton VA award, 1983, Frederic C. Bartter award, Am. Soc. Bone and Mineral Rsch., 1992, Career Recognition award, Vitamin D Workshop, 1997. Mem.: Endocrine Soc., Assn. Osteobiology (councillor 1997—98, sec.-treas. 1999, pres. 2000—02), Assn. Am. Physicians, Am. Soc. Pharmacology and Exptl. Therapeutics, Am. Soc. Bone and Mineral Rsch. (sec.-treas. 1978—85, pres. 1986—87, Shirley Hohl Svc. award 1998), Am. Soc. Clin. Investigation, Alpha Omega Alpha. Democrat. Episcopalian. Home: 1 Johnson Rd Charleston SC 29407-7514 E-mail: belln@musc.edu.

BELL, RICHARD M., critical care surgeon, educator; BS, Ctr. Coll. Ky., Danville; MD, U. Ky., 1979. Diplomate Am. Bd. of Surgery, 1980. Resident gen. surgery Univ. Ky. Coll. Medicine/Chandler Med. Ctr., Lexington, 1979; faculty mem. Univ. Ky.; flight surgeon 123rd Tac Hosp., Ky.; prof. surgery dept. Sch. Medicine Univ. SC, 1985—, chmn. surgery dept. Sch. Medicine, 1998; critical care surgeon Palmetto Health Richland. Chmn. subcommittee Advanced Trauma Life Support. Lt. col. USAF, chief aeromedical svcs. Blytheville Air Force, Ark., chief aeromedical svcs. Ky. Air Nat. Guard, Louisville. Recipient Meritorious Svc. award, Advanced Trauma Life Support, Dean's medal, Univ. SC Sch. Medicine. Mem.: ACS (trauma com. mem.), Assn. Surg. Edn. (pres.). Office: Palmetto Health Richland 5 Richland Medical Park Dr Columbia SC 29203 Office Phone: 803-256-2657.

BELL, RICHARD P. (DICKIE BELL), state legislator; b. Staunton, Va., Oct. 26, 1946; m. Anne Starr Littlejohn; children: Erin, Brian. BS, James Madison U., Harrisonburg, Va., 1988; grad. student in spl. edn., Old Dominion U., Norfolk, Va. HS tchr., Va.; mem. Staunton City Coun., 1996—2009; mem. Dist. 20 Va. House of Dels., Richmond, 2010—. Deacon, Sunday sch. tchr. Meml. Bapt. Ch. Hosp. corps USN, 1967—73. Mem.: Va. HS Coaches Assn., Fellowship Christian Athletes. Republican. Office: Va House of Dels Gen Assembly Bldg Rm 517 PO Box 406 Richmond VA 23218 also: Staunton City Hall PO Box 239 Staunton VA 24402 Office Phone: 804-698-1020, 540-448-4763. Office Fax: 804-698-6720. Business E-Mail: deldbell@house.virginia.gov.

BELL, ROBERT B., state legislator; b. Palo Alto, Calif., Apr. 23, 1967; m. Jessica Sweeney; 1 child, Robert IV. BS, U. Va., 1988; JD, U. Va. Law Sch., 1995. Tchr.; mem. Dist. 58 Va. House of Delegates, 2002—. Deacon, Sunday sch. tchr. Meml. Bapt. Ch. Served with hosp. corps USN, 1967—73. Mem.: Fellowship Christian Athletes, Va. HS Coaches Assn. Republican. Methodist. Office: Capitol Office Gen Assembly Bldg Rm 517 PO Box 406 Richmond VA 23218 also: PO Box 239 Staunton VA 24402 Office Phone: 804-698-1020, 540-332-3998. Office Fax: 804-698-6720. Business E-Mail: DelDBell@house.virginia.gov.

BELL, RONALD MACK, university foundation administrator, consultant; b. Atlanta, Mar. 4, 1937; m. Deborah Jean Slaton, Dec. 28, 1989. BS in Indsl. Mgmt., Ga. Inst. Tech., 1959; MBA, U. Mich., 1965; attended, Cornell U., 1980. Commd. USN, 1959, advanced through grades to capt., 1979, ret., 1985; assoc. dir. rsch. contracts Ga. Inst. Tech., Atlanta, 1985-88; v.p., gen. mgr. Ga. Tech. Rsch. Corp., Atlanta, 1988-97; exec. dir. S.C. Rsch. Inst., Columbia, 1997-2001; v.p., bd. dirs. Pisgah Astrol. Rsch. Inst., 1999—2003; pres., CEO UCRF Support Assoc., St. Simons Island, Ga., 1998—. Bd. dirs., past pres., now dir. emeritus Nat. Supply Corps. Assn.; cons. Wesvaco/Post, Buckley, Coastal Cons., Inc., also others, 1985—; expert witness ELSCO, U. Tenn., others, 1987-90; nat. chmn. Univ. Connected Rsch. Found., 1990-91. Past chmn., dir. emeritus Naval Supply Corps. Sch. Mus. Com., Athens, mem., 1983—; mem. Exec. Roundtable, Atlanta, 1985-97; resource staff Gov.'s Com. Tech. & Devel., Atlanta, 1992-97; bd. dirs. Ga. Tech. Sch. Mgmt., 1995-98; bd. grad. studies advisors Ga. So. U., 2004—08. Decorated Legion of Merit (2), Meritorious Svc. medal (2), Navy Commendation medal (2); named to Honor Roll of Mentors, U. Connected Rsch. Found., 2004. Mem. Soc. Rsch. Adminstrs. (nat. coms., chair regional com. 1985-2002), Licensing Execs. Soc., Nat. Coun. Univ. Rsch. Adminstrs. (chair regional com., nat. panelist 1985-2001), Coun. Rsch. and Tech. (dir. workshop, tax com. 1986-92), Ga. Tech. Nat. Alumni Assn. (various coms.), Nat. Conf. on the Advancement of Rsch. (conf. com. 2000), Assn. Univ. Tech. Mgrs., Theta Chi (past chpt. pres.), Phi Kappa Phi, Beta Gamma Sigma. Avocations: golf, woodworking. Home: 113 Thompson Cv Saint Simons Island GA 31522-3768 Office: UCRF Support Assoc PO Box 20272 Saint Simons Island GA 31522 E-mail: bellssi@earthlink.net.

BELL, SIMONE, state legislator; b. Detroit; Grad., Agnes Scott Coll., Ga. Cmty. organizer and activist, Atlanta; rep. Dist. 58 Ga. House of Reps., Atlanta, 2009—. Democrat. Office: Ga Gen Assembly 18 Capitol Sq Coverdell Legis Office Bldg Ste 612 Atlanta GA 30334 Office Phone: 404-656-0330. Business E-Mail: simone.bell@house.ga.gov.

BELL, THOMAS DEVEREAUX, JR., real estate company executive; b. Niagara Falls, Nov. 2, 1949; s. Thomas Devereaux and Lenore (Chisholm) B.; m. Margaret McDaniel, Jan. 17, 1975 (div.); 1 child, Thomas Devereaux III; m. Jennifer Holtzman, Dec. 27, 1987; children: Kevin Holtzman Bell, Hannah Holtzman Bell. Student, U. Tenn., 1967-70, George Washington U., 1973, NYU, 1983—84. Exec. dir. Presdl. Inaugural Ball Com., Washington, 1972; dep. div. dir. Com. to Reelect the Pres., Washington, 1971-72; adminstrv. asst. U.S. Senator William Brock, Washington, 1973-75; pres., CEO Bell and McDaniel, Washington, 1975-76, Holder, Kennedy, Dye & Bell, Nashville, 1976-79, Creative Com. Corp., Washington, 1979-82, Hudson Inst., Indpls., 1982-87; exec. v.p. Ball Corp., Muncie, Ind., 1987-89; vice chmn., COO Burson-Marsteller, 1989-94; vice chmn. Gulfstream Aerospace Corp., Savannah, Ga., 1994-95; pres., CEO Burson-Marsteller, NYC, 1995-98; also bd. dirs. Gulfstream Aerospace Corp., Savannah, Ga.; chmn., CEO Young & Rubicam Advt., NYC, 1998-99; pres., COO Young & Rubicam Inc., NYC, 1999—2000, pres., CEO, 2000; vice chmn., pres. Cousins Properties Inc., 2001—, CEO, 2002—, chmn., CEO, 2006—, Regal Entertainment, 2003—, AGL Resources, 2004—. Mem. Transition Team for Pres. Ronald Reagan, Washington, 1981. Mem. Burning Tree Club (Bethesda, Md.), Georgetown Club (Washington), Blind Brook Club (Harrison, N.Y.), Capital Club, Peachtree Golf Club (Atlanta). Republican. Office: Cousins Properties Inc 191 Peachtree St Ste 3600 Atlanta GA 30303 Office Phone: 404-407-1000. Office Fax: 404-407-1003.

BELL, WILLIAM A., SR., mayor, Birmingham, Alabama; b. Birmingham, Ala. m. Sharon Carson Bell; children: William A., Jr., Jillian. BA in Psychology, U. Ala., Birmingham, 1971, Masters in Psychology and Guidance Counseling, 1974; JD, Miles Coll., 1980. Probation officer Jefferson County Family Court; sales cons. Xerox Corp.; spl. asst. to v.p. U. Ala., Birmingham; mem. Dist. 5 Birmingham City Coun., pres., 1985—87, 1997; interim mayor City of Birmingham, 1999, mayor, 2010—; commr. Jefferson Country Commn., 2008, pres. pro-tem, 2008. Mem. Am. Com. on Africa; worked with merchants of 4th Ave. Bus. Dist. to transform area back into a productive bus. corridor, worked with local, state and federal authorities to ensure present means funding and implementing future legislation to protect urban governing, improved public-private partnership in Birmingham. Panel mem. invited to U.S. State Dept. to discuss diplomatic and military strategies of U.S. govt. around the world with emphasis on Middle East; mem. North Pratt Civic League. Recipient Peggy Spain McDonald Award, 1986, West End Adv. Coun. Humanities award, 1990, Operation New Birmingham's Achievement award 1997, Gamma Phi Delta Political Achievement award 1986, Alpha Kappa Alpha Pub. Svc. award, 1986, Outstanding Leadership award bd. dirs. office of Black Cath. ch., 1986; named Govt. Pers. of the Year Nat. Bus. League, 1989. Bd. dirs. Ops. New Birmingham, Met. Devel., 101 Black Men (founder, pres.), Nat. League Cities Human Devel. Steering Com.; life mem. Kappa Alpha Psi Frat (Pole March's award, 1990). Roman Catholic. Office: Office of City Coun 710 North 20th St Birmingham AL 35203-2216*

BELL, WILLIAM (BILL) V., mayor, Durham, North Carolina; b. Washington; m. Judith C. Bell; children: William V. II, Tiffany Anne, Kristen Vaughn Bell-Hughes, Anjanee Nicole. BS in Elec. Engring., Howard U., Wash. DC, 1961; MS in Elec. Engring., NYU, 1968. Ret. sr engr. IBM Corp.; commr. Durham County, 1972—94, 1996—2000; chmn. Durham County Bd. Commrs., 1982—94; exec. v.p. & chief oper. officer UDI/CDC, 1996—; mayor City of Durham, 2001—. Bd. mem. Durham Com. on Affairs of Black People, 1968—, Durham C. of C., 1982—94, 2001—, TTA bd. trustees, 1989—96, 2000—, NCCU bd. trustees, 2001, Greater Triangle United Way, 2003—. 1st lt. Signal Corps US Army, 1961—63. Democrat. Office: Office of Mayor 101 City Hall Plaza Durham NC 27701 Office Phone: 919-560-4333. Fax: 919-560-4801. E-mail: Bill.Bell@durhamnc.gov.*

BELL, WILLIAM WOODWARD, lawyer; b. May 15, 1938; s. Charles Smith and Janie Mae (Woodward) B.; m. Mary Elizabeth Beniteau, May 31, 1969; children: Susan Elizabeth, Carol Ann. BBA, Baylor U., 1960, JD, 1965. Bar: U.S. Dist. Ct. (we. dist.) Tex. 1967, U.S. Dist. Ct. (no. dist.) Tex. 1993, U.S. Supreme Ct. 1971. Ptnr. Sleeper, Boynton, Burleson, Williams & Johnson, Waco, Tex., 1965-68, Holloway, Slagle & Bell, Brownwood, 1968-71, Johnson, Slagle & Bell, Brownwood, 1971-74; pvt. practice Brownwood, 1974—. Capt. USMC, 1960-63. Named Vol., 1991, Developer of Yr., Tex. Indsl. Devel. Coun. Fellow Tex. Bar Found.; mem. ABA, Tex. Bar Assn., Brown County Bar Assn., Am. Judicature Soc., Phi Alpha Delta. Baptist. Home: PO Box 1564 Brownwood TX 76804-1564 Office: PO Box 1726 115 S Broadway Brownwood TX 76804-1726 Office Phone: 325-646-5547.

BELL, ZACHARIAH XAVIER, chef; b. Clermont, Fla. m. Jennifer Reed, Apr. 25, 2005. Grad., Johnson & Wales U. With William's Island Yacht Club, Biz Bistro, Miami; banquet kitchen cook Le Cirque 2000, NYC, chef de partie, saucier, Café Boulud, NYC, 1998, sous chef, chef de cuisine Palm Beach, Fla. Guest chef (TV series) South Florida Today. Involved with Daily Bread Food Bank, March of Dimes, Share Our Strength. Named one of South Fla.'s Rising Stars, StarChefs.com, 2008. Office: Boulud Cafe 301 Australian Ave Palm Beach FL 33480

BELLATTI, LAWRENCE LEE, lawyer; b. Oklahoma City, Apr. 19, 1944; s. Lawrence Fitzhugh and Esther Lee (Swank) Bellatti; m. Barbara Gail Wolfinger, June 25, 1977; children: Julie M., Jenny E., Jill N. BS, Okla. State U., 1966; JD, Okla. U., 1969. Bar: Okla. 1969, Tex. 1974, U.S. Dist. Ct. (so., we, ea. and no. dists.) Tex., U.S. Dist. Ct. (no., we. and ea. dists.) Okla., U.S. Ct. Mil. Appeals, U.S. Ct. Appeals (5th cir., 10th and 11th cirs.). Assoc. Andrews, Kurth, Campbell & Jones, Houston, 1974-80; ptnr. Andrews Kurth LLP, Houston, 1980—. Bd. dirs. Samaritan Counseling Ctrs., Inc., Houston, 1984—2001. Mem. Harris County Flood Control Dist. Task Force, Houston, 1984. Lt. comdr. JAGC USNR, 1969—74. Mem.: Houston Bar Assn., Okla. Bar Assn., State Bar Tex., Order of Coif, Phi Delta Phi, Sigma Chi, Phi Kappa Phi. Republican. Baptist. Office: Andrews Kurth LLP 600 Travis St Ste 4200 Houston TX 77002-2910 Office Phone: 713-220-4196.

BELLE, GERALD, pharmaceutical executive; BSBA Mktg., cum laude, Xavier U., Cin., 1968; MBA, Northwestern U., 1969. Mem. staff Merrell-Nat. Labs., Cin., 1969-77, mem. sales and mktg. staff U.S. and Philippines Manila, 1978-82; East Asia regional mgr. pharms. Dow Chem. Pacific Ltd., Hong Kong, 1982-83; product group dir. Merrell-Nat. Labs., Cin., 1983-85; dir. product planning and promotion Lakeside Pharms., Cin., 1985-87; dir. mktg. Merrell Dow Pharms. KK, Tokyo, 1987-90; v.p. mktg. and sales Marion Merrell Dow Europe AG, Zurich, Switzerland, 1990-95; pres. Hoechst Marion Roussel Can., Montreal, Que., 1995-97; pres., N.Am., CEO Hoechst Marion Roussel, Inc. Hoechst Marion Roussel, Kansas City, Mo., 1997—99; pres. Aventis, N. Am. Pharm. (from merger of Hoechst Marion Roussel and Rhône-Poulenc Rorer), 1999—2004; exec. chmn. Merial Ltd., Duluth, Ga., 2004—07. Bd. dirs. Nat. Pharm. Coun., Mid-Am. Coalition on Health Care. Mem. Civic Coun. Greater Kansas City. Office: Merial Ltd Bldg 500 3239 Satellite Blvd Duluth GA 30096 Office Phone: 678-638-3000.

BELLEAU, ASHLEY L., lawyer; BA cum laude, Newcomb Coll., New Orleans, 1980; JD, Tulane U. Law Sch., New Orleans, 1984. Bar: Tex., La., Wis., US Dist. Cts. (ea., we., mid. dists.) La., US Ct. Appeals (5th cir.), US Supreme Ct. Law clk. to Judge Henry A. Mentz, Jr. US Dist. Ct. (Ea. Dist.) La.; pub. co. owner; mng. mem. Patrick, Miller, Burnside & Belleau, LLC; ptnr. Montgomery Barnett, New Orleans, 2008—. Mem. FINRA, 1996—, ADR, 2011—; mem. panel of mediators La. Dept. Ins. Hurricane Mediation Program, 2006—07; dir. Federal Bar Building Corp., 2012—14. Contbr. articles to profl. jours.; editor: The La. US Ct. Newsletter, 1988—98; co-author: Louisiana Chapter, Fifty State Construction Lien and Bond Law, 2nd Edition, 2013, Louisiana Chapter, State-by-State Guide to Architect, Engineer, and Contractor Licensing, 2013. Hearing examiner for property assessment tax appeals City of New Orleans, 2007, hearing officer, 2008—09. Named Louisiana Super Lawyers, 2007—13; named to New Orleans Magazine, Top Lawyers in New Orleans, Louisiana, 2013. Fellow: ABA (chair Young Lawyers Divsn. securities law com. 1989—91, young lawyers divsn. fellow 1995—, vice-chair tort trial & ins. practice sect. fidelity & surety law gen. 2012—13, mem. bus. law sect.; mem. alternative dispute resolution sect.), ABA Found., La. Bar Found. (chair IOLTA banking com. 2000—03), Found. of Fed. Bar Assn. (life), Litigation Counsel of America; mem.: Internat. Soc. of Primerus Law Firms (mem. exec. com. of construction practice group 2012—), Defense Research Inst. (mem. 2010—), Fed. Bar Assn. (gen. counsel 2006—08, nat. treas. 2008—10, nat. pres.-elect 2009—10, nat. pres. 2010—11), Assn. Women Attorneys, La. State Bar Assn. (mem. house of delegates 1997—, vice-chair bankruptcy law sect. 2007—13), La. Bankers Assn., The Federalist Soc., La. Chpt. (mem. exec. com. 2004—06),

American Inns of Ct., Tulane Chpt. (barrister 1987—), Phi Alpha Delta, Kappa Alpha Theta. Office: Montgomery Barnett 3300 Energy Ctr 1100 Poydras St New Orleans LA 70163-3300 Office Phone: 504-585-3200. Office Fax: 504-585-7688. Business E-Mail: abelleau@monbar.com.*

BELLER, GEORGE A., cardiologist, educator; b. NYC, Dec. 23, 1940; children: Michael, Amy, Leslie, Ray Wadlow, Jeff Wadlow. B in Philosophy, Dartmouth Coll., Hanover, NH; MD, U. Va., 1966. Diplomate Am. Bd. Cardiovascular Disease, Am. Bd. Internal Medicine. Internship in internal medicine U. Wis. Hosp., Madison; sr. resident in internal medicine Boston City Hosp.; clin. fellow in cardiology Harvard U. Med. Sch.; rsch. fellow in cardiovascular diseases, asst. prof. Mass. Gen. Hosp.; prof. cardiology and internal medicine, chief cardiovasc. divsn. U. Va. Health Sys., Charlottesville, 1977—2004, pres. clin. staff, U. Va. Med. Ctr., 1999—2005, Ruth C. Heede prof. cardiology and prof. internal medicine, 1977—2012, clin. prof., 2012—. Editor-in-chief: Jour. Nuc. Cardiology, 2003—; contbr. articles to profl. jours. Maj. US Army, 1970—73. Recipient Disting. Achievement award, Am. Heart Assn., Herrick award, 2000, Walter Reed Disting. Achievement award, U. Va., 2006, Lifetime Achievement award, Paul Dudley White Soc., Mass. Gen. Hosp., 2006, Disting. Scientist award, Am. Coll. Cardiology, 2010. Mem. Am. Soc. Clin. Investigation, Am. Fedn. Clin. Rsch., Assn. Am. Physicians, Am. Coll. Cardiology (chmn. bd. govs. 1994-95, pres. 2000-01, trustee), Assn. Profs. Cardiology (pres. 1995). Office: U Va Health Sys Box 800158 Charlottesville VA 22908 Business E-Mail: gbeller@virginia.edu.

BELLER, STEPHEN MARK, retired academic administrator; b. Chgo., Aug. 14, 1948; s. I.E. and De Vera (Jameson) B.; m. Luanne Evelyn Heyl, June 28, 1970; children: Clancy Dee, Corby Lu. BS, U. Ill., 1970; MS, Western Ill. U., 1972; PhD, Oregon State U., 1977. Asst. head ed. Awards of Rotary Found., Evanston, Ill., 1972-73; asst. dean of students SUNY, Geneseo, N.Y., 1977-81; dean of student svcs. Tenn. Wesleyan Coll., Athens, 1981-83, MacMurray Coll., Jacksonville, Ill., 1984-88, Capital U., Columbus, Ohio, 1988-99, v.p., dean of student svcs., 1999—2003, v.p. emeritus, 2003—. Mem.: Phi Delta Kappa, Phi Kappa Phi. Methodist. Avocations: railroading, photography. Home: 174 W Bristol Oak Cir The Woodlands TX 77382-1272

BELLOWS, THOMAS JOHN, political scientist, educator; s. Charles Everett and Dorothy (Morrison) B.; m. Marilyn Denise Corbell; children: Scott Anthony, Justin Thomas, Trevor Cullen, Ethan Forrest; children by previous marriage: Roderick Alan, Adrienne Marie, Jeannine Louise, Derek John, Marshall Everett. Student, Am. U., 1956, UCLA, 1956-57; BA, Augustana Coll., 1957; MA, U. Fla., 1958, Yale U., 1960, PhD, 1968. From asst. prof. to prof. polit. sci. U. Ark., Fayetteville, 1967-81, chmn. dept., 1971-78; dir. divsn. social policy scis. U. Tex., San Antonio, 1981-88, prof. polit. sci., 1981—. Vis. lectr. depts. history, polit. sci. Nanyang U., Singapore, 1965; vis. prof. Nat. Chengchi U., Taiwan, 1979. Author: The People's Action Party of Singapore: Emergence of a Dominant Party System, 1970; (with S. Erikson and H. Winter) Political Science: Introductory Essays and Readings, 1971, Taiwan's Foreign Policy in the 1970's, 1976, (with H. Winter) People and Politics: An Introduction to Political Science, 1985, Bridging Tradition and Modernization: The Singapore Bureaucracy, 1989, (with H. Winter)Conflict and Compromise: An Introduction to Political Science, 1992; Taiwan and Mainland China, 2000, The Republic of China's Legislative Yuan: A Study of Institutional Evolution, 2003; (with Felix Almaraz) State Craft of Modern Texas: Perspectives on Politics and History, 2007, No Change in Sight: Party Politics and Taiwan's Legislative Yuan During the Global Economic Crisis, 2010; editor: Am. Jour. Chinese Studies, 1999—. Mem.: Am. Assn. for Chinese Studies (pres. 1998—2000), Assn. Asian Studies, S.W. Conf. Asian Studies (pres. 1995), Phi Beta Kappa, Phi Kappa Phi. Methodist. Office: U Tex Dept Polit Sci San Antonio TX 78249 Office Phone: 210-458-4628. Business E-Mail: thomas.bellows@utsa.edu.

BELTRAN, EUSEBIUS JOSEPH, archbishop emeritus; b. Ashley, Pa., Aug. 31, 1934; s. Joseph C. and Helen Rita (Kozlowski) Beltran. Grad., St. Charles Sem., Overbrook, Pa. Ordained priest Diocese of Atlanta, 1960, pastor, 1960; notary, then vice officialis Atlanta Diocesan Tribunal, 1960—62; vice chancellor Archdiocese of Atlanta, 1962, officialis Archdiocesan Tribunal, 1963—74, pastor, 1963—66, vicar gen., 1971—78; pastor St. Anthony's Ch., Atlanta, 1972—78; ordained bishop, 1978; bishop Diocese of Tulsa, Okla., 1978—92; archbishop Archdiocese of Okla. City, 1992—2010, archbishop emeritus, 2010—. Liturgy com. Nat. Conf. Cath. Bishops; com. mem. Am. Coll., Louvain, Belgium; bd. regents Conception Sem.; bd. dirs. St. Gregory's Coll., Shawnee, Okla. Mem.: NCCJ, Equestrian Order Holy Sepulchre, K.C. Roman Catholic. Office: Archdiocese of Oklahoma City 7501 NW Expy Oklahoma City OK 73132-2180

BELTRE, ADRIAN, professional baseball player; b. Santo Domingo, Dominican Republic, Apr. 7, 1979; m. Sandra Beltre; 1 child, Cassandra. Third baseman LA Dodgers, 1998—2004, Seattle Mariners, 2005—09, Boston Red Sox, 2010, Tex. Rangers, 2011—. Mem. Dominican Republic nat. team World Baseball Classic, 2009. Recipient Nat. League Silver Slugger award, Maj. League Baseball, 2004, American League Silver Slugger award, 2010, 2011, American League Gold Glove award, 2007, 2008, 2011, 2012; named to American League All-Star Team, 2010, 2011. Achievements include leading the National League in: home runs (48), 2004; leading the American League in: doubles (49), 2010; hits (199), 2013. Office: Tex Rangers 1000 Ballpark Way Arlington TX 76011 Office Phone: 206-346-4000.*

BEMBRY, LEONARD L., state legislator; b. Jasper, Fla., Aug. 24, 1947; m. Susan Bembry; children: Lori, Jacquelyn, Leonard Jr. AA, North Fla. Cmty. Coll.; grad., Fla. State U. Gen. mgr. U. Homes; mem. Dist. 10 Fla. House of Reps., 2008—, ranking mem. agr. and natural resources policy com., econ. devel. policy com., natural resources appropriations com. Mem. Madison County Devel. Coun., Madison County Farm Bur. Recipient Outstanding Alumni, North Fla. Cmty. Coll., Pres. Club, Clayton Homes, Outstanding Mgmt. award. Mem.: NRA, Fla. Manufactured Housing Assn., Wild Turkey Fedn., Habitat for Humanity, Chi Delta Tau. Democrat. Baptist. Office: The Capitol 402 S Monroe St Rm 1003 Tallahassee FL 32399-1300 also: 304 NW Crane Ave Bldg 36 Madison FL 32340-1423 also: 23 SE 2nd Ave Chiefland FL 32626 Office Phone: 850-488-7870, 850-973-5630. Business E-Mail: leonard.bembry@myfloridahouse.gov.

BENACQUISTO, LIZBETH, state legislator; b. Rockville Centre, NY, Dec. 23, 1967; 3 children. BA in Orgnl. Mgmt., Palm Beach Atlantic U. Realtor; mktg. and spl. events cons.; councilwoman Village of Wellington, Fla., 2002—10; mem. Dist. 27 Fla. State Senate, 2011—. Republican. Office: 175 S Tamiami Trail Ste 200-9 Fort Myers FL 33908 also: Florida State Senate 326 Senate Office Bldg 404 S Monroe St Tallahassee FL 32399-1100 Office Phone: 239-433-6599, 850-487-5356. Business E-Mail: benacquisto.lizbeth.web@flsenate.gov.

BENARIO, HERBERT WILLIAM, classicist, educator; b. NYC, July 21, 1929; s. Frederick and Ilse (Kessler) Benario; m. Janice M. Martin, Dec. 23, 1957; children: Frederick M., John H. BA, CCNY, 1948; MA, Columbia U., 1949; PhD, Johns Hopkins U., 1951. Instr. Greek and Latin Columbia U., 1953-58; asst. prof. Greek and Latin Sweet Briar Coll., 1958-60; mem. faculty Emory U., Atlanta, 1960—, prof. classics, 1967-87, chmn. dept., 1968-73, 76-78, prof. emeritus, 1987, Heilbrun disting. fellow emeritus, 2001—02, 2010—11. Dir. Vergilian Soc. Summer Sch., Italy, 1963, Italy, 1967, Italy, 1973, Italy, 1981, asst. dir., Italy, 1957, Italy, 1959; dir. Roman Britain Tour, 1977, 1986, Roman Germany Tour, 1981, 1988, Rome and North Italy, 1982, Roman Germany Tour Mediterranean Soc., 1998, North Italy Tour Mediterranean Soc., 1999; vis. prof. Intercollegiate Ctr. Classical Studies, Rome, 1967, co-prof. in charge, 1984—85; vis. prof. U. Colo., 1969, Brigham Young U., 1999; Fulbright Sr. prof. U. Passau, Germany, 1990; co-exec. sec. Vergilian Soc., 1992—93; mem. Latin achievement test com. Coll. Entrance Exam. Bd., 1963—66. Author: (book) Tacitus, Agricola, Germany, Dialogue on Orators, 1967, Tacitus, Agricola, Germany, Dialogue on Orators, rev. edit., 1991, 2006, An Introduction to Tacitus, 1975, A Commentary on the Vita Hadriani in the Historia Augusta, 1980, Tacitus Annals 11 and 12, 1983, The Classical Association of the Middle West and South, 1989, Caesaris Augusti Res Gestae et Fragmenta, 1990, Thusnelda: A German Princess in Ancient Rome, 1993, Tacitus Germany, 1999, Julius Caesar's Gallic War, 2012, The Romans and Germany, 2012; co-editor: Basil Lanneau Gildersleeve: An American Classicist, 1986. With AUS, 1951—53. Recipient Distinguished Emeritus award, 2008; grantee Fulbright, 1956, Rsch., Am. Philos. Soc.; fellow Am. Coun. Learned Soc., 1978. Mem.: Classical Soc. Am. Acad. Rome (pres. 1965), Am. Classical League, Vergilian Soc. Am. (trustee 1960—65, 1969—73, pres. 1980—82), Classical Assn. Mid. West and South (pres.so. sect. 1968—70, pres. 1971—72), Am. Philological Assn., Phi Beta Kappa (pres. Emory U. chpt. 1968—69). Home: 1717 N Decatur Rd NE #119 Atlanta GA 30307 Office: Emory U Classics Dept Atlanta GA 30322-0001 Personal E-mail: hwbenario@yahoo.com.

BENAVIDES, FORTUNATO PEDRO (PETE BENAVIDES), federal judge; b. Mission, Tex., Feb. 3, 1947; BBA, U. Houston, 1968, JD, 1972. Atty. Rankin, Kern & Martinez, McAllen, Tex., 1972—74, Cisneros, Beery & Benavides, McAllen, 1974, Cisneros, Brown & Benavides, McAllen, 1975, Cisneros & Benavides, McAllen, 1976; pvt. practice McAllen, 1977; judge Hidalgo County Ct.-at-Law # 2, Edinburg, Tex., 1977—79; prin. Law Offices of Fortunato P. Benavides, McAllen, 1980—81; judge 92nd Dist. Ct. of Hidalgo County, Tex., 1981—84, 13th Ct. Appeals, Corpus Christi, Tex., 1984—91, Tex. Ct. Criminal Appeals, Austin, 1991—92; atty. Atlas & Hall, McAllen, 1993—94; judge US Ct. Appeals (5th cir.), Austin, 1994—2012, sr. judge, 2012—. Commr. Tex. Juvenile Probation Commn., 1983—89; vis. judge to cts. in Tex., 1993. Active Mustangs of Corpus Christi, 1990—91, hon. mem., 1992; active Mex.-American Democrats of Tex., 1990—92; mem. St. Michael Episc. Ch., Austin, 1992—. Mem. ABA, Hidalgo County Bar Assn., State Bar Tex. Office: US Ct Appeals 5th Cir Homer Thornberry Judicial Bldg 903 San Jacinto Blvd Rm 450 Austin TX 78701 Office Phone: 512-916-5796.*

BENBENEK, R. SCOTT, wholesale distribution executive; Grad., U. S.C. Product mgr. Gates/Arrow, 1990—92, dir., merchandising, 1992—95, v.p., merchandising, 1995—98; joined ScanSource, Inc., 1998, v.p., merchandising, dir., merchandising, exec. v.p., corp. ops., 2002—07, pres., worldwide ops., 2007—. Office: ScanSource Inc 6 Logue Ct Greenville SC 29615 Office Phone: 864-288-2432. Office Fax: 864-288-1165.

BENBOW, CAMILLA PERSSON, dean, psychology professor; b. Lund, Sweden, Dec. 3, 1956; came to U.S., 1965, naturalized, 1985; m. David Lubinski; children: Wystan R., Bronwen G., Trefor A., Evan M., Lovisa D., G. Byron, Lena C. BA in Psychology with honors, Johns Hopkins U., 1977, MA in Psychology, 1978, MS in Edn. of the Gifted, 1980, EdD with distinction in Edn. of Gifted, 1981. Dir. Office of Precollegiate Programs for Talented & Gifted Iowa State U., 1987-98, Johns Hopkins U., Balt., 1977—79, asst. dir. Study of Mathematically Precocious Youth, 1979—81, assoc. dir., 1981—85, co-dir., 1985—86, dir., 1986, assoc. rsch. scientist dept. psychology, 1981—86, asst. prof. sociology, part-time, 1983—86; assoc. prof. psychology Iowa State U., Ames, 1985—90, prof. psychology, 1990—95, chair dept. psychology, 1992—98, disting. prof., 1995—98, interim dean coll. edn., 1996—98; Patricia and Rodes Hart dean edn. and human devel. Peabody Coll., Vanderbilt U., Nashville, 1998—. Mem. Nat. Sci. Bd., NSF, 2006—, chair Com. on Edn. and Human Resources; vice chmn. Nat. Math Panel, 2006—. Sr. editor: Academic Precocity: Aspects of Its Development, 1983, Intellectual Talent: Psychometric and Social Issues, 1996; contbr. articles to profl. jours. Recipient John Curtis Gowan prize Nat. Assn. Gifted Children, 1980, 81; Rsch. award Am. Ednl. Rsch. Assn., 1982; Spencer fellow, alt., 1984, 85, 86, Rsch. paper award Mensa, 1985, 86, 89, 94, 95 Mensa Lifetime Achievement award, 2004; Early Scholar award Nat. Assn. Gifted Children, 1985, Disting. Scholar award 1992, George A. Miller award APA, 1999. Mem. Johns Hopkins Soc. Scholars, Phi Beta Kappa, Sigma Xi. Office: Vanderbilt University Peabody College MSC 329, Peabody Station Nashville TN 37203 Office Phone: 615-322-8407. Office Fax: 615-322-8501. Business E-Mail: camilla.benbow@vanderbilt.edu.

BENCINI, SARA HALTIWANGER, concert pianist; b. Winston Salem, NC, Sept. 2, 1926; d. Robert Sydney and Janie Love (Couch) Haltiwanger; m. Robert Emery Bencini, June 26, 1954; children: Robert Emery III, Constance Bencini Waller, John McGregor. MusB, Salem Coll., 1947; postgrad., Juilliard Sch. Music, 1950; MA, Smith Coll., 1951; D in Mus. Arts, U. NC, Greensboro, 1989. Solo piano performance Winston-Salem Symphony, 1948; pianist Conservatoire Americain, Fontainebleau, 1951; head piano dept. Mary Burnham Sch. Girls, Northampton, Mass., 1949—51; pianist Smith Coll., composer dance and drama dept., 1951—52; head music dept. Walnut Hill Sch. Girls, Natick, Mass., 1952—54; pvt. piano tchr. High Point, NC, 1954—66; concert pianist appearing, Europe, 1968—; duo-piano performances PBS-TV, Columbia, SC, 1967, Winston Salem Symphony, NC, 1965, Eastern Mus. Festival, Greensboro, NC, 1969. Mem. Jr. League. Mem.: DAR, High Point Country Club. Presbyterian.

BENDELIUS, ARTHUR GEORGE, engineering firm executive; b. Passaic, NJ, May 21, 1936; s. Arthur Leopold and Lydia Ella (Flach) B.; m. Virginia Brown, June 21, 1958; children: Linda Ellen, Bonnie Sue, Heidi Ann Mitchell. BE, Stevens Inst. Tech., 1958, MMS, 1966. Registered profl. engr. Engr. Syska & Hennessey, NYC, 1958-60, Parsons Brinckerhoff Quade & Douglas, Inc., NYC, 1960-62, Nat. Biscuit Co., NYC, 1962—63; asst. dept. head Parsons Brinckerhoff Quade & Douglas, Inc., NYC, 1963-68, dept. head, 1968-70, project mgr., 1970-73, regional mgr. Atlanta, 1973-76, asst. v.p., 1976-78, v.p., 1978-82, sr. v.p., 1982-89; regional mgr. Energy Sys. Group, NYC, 1989-93, prin. profl. assoc., 1991—2004, sr. v.p., 1989—2004, tech. dir., 1992—2004. Divsn. mgr. PBES, NYC, 1994-96, Parsons Brinckerhoff Quade & Douglas, Inc., NYC, 1996-2002, Atlanta, 2002-04; pres. A & G Cons., Inc., 2004—; presenter in field. Co-author: Tunnel Engineering Handbook, 1982, 2d edit., 1996, ASHRAE Handbook Applications, 1978, 5th edit., 2007, 2011, Fire Protection Handbook, 19th edit. 2003, 20th edit., 2008, Handbook of Tunnel Fire Safety, 2005, 2nd edit., 2012, Fire & Smoke Control in Road Tunnels, 1999; co-editor Equipment and Systems for Fire Smoke Control in Road Tunnels, 2007; contbr. articles to profl. jours. Pres. Brookside Home Sch. Orgn., Westwood, NJ, 1972-73; co-v.p. Dunwoody Band Booster Club, Ga., 1975-76, co-pres., 1976-77. Named Atlanta Engr. of Yr. in Pvt. Practice, 1978; recipient Harold R. Fee Alumni award, 1978. Fellow Soc. Am. Mil. Engrs. (pres. Atlanta chpt. 1978-79, nat. bd. dirs. 1983-86), ASHRAE (life, chmn. tech. com. 1975-79, rsch. promotion com. 1980-82, life mem. com., tech. com. 5.9 1982—); mem. NSPE (life), ASME (life), Ga. Soc. Profl. Engrs. (bd. dirs. 1976-78, life), Nat. Coun. Examiners Engring. and Surveying (cert.), Ga. Engring. Found. (life 1983—, bd. dirs. 1977-89, 2007-, sec. 1979, v.p. 1980, pres. 1982-83, bd. dir.2007-, chair life mem. com. 2007-), Steven's Alumni Assn., Brit. Tunneling Soc., SC Transp. Assn. (bd. dirs. 1987, treas. 1987-89), Nat. Fire Protection Assn. (tech. com. 130, 1992-2004, task group ventilation, tech. com. 502 1993—1995, chair NPPA 502 subcom. 1994-97, chair tech. com. 502, 1996-2004, World Road Assn. (PIARC) (tech. com. C5 and C3.3 on Rd. Tunnel Operation, 1999-2007, working group Ventilation & Fire Control 1992—, chmn., 1999-2007), Aircraft Owners and Pilots Assn., Tau Beta Pi, Sigma Nu (pres. alumni assn. 1966-70, comdr. 1971-73), Atlanta Stevens Club (pres. 1974-90, 2002-), ASHRAE Life Club (bd. dir. 2005-10). Lutheran. Office: A&G Consultants Inc 11391 Big Canoe Big Canoe GA 30143-5108 Office Phone: 706-268-1965. Personal E-mail: bendelius@tds.net. Business E-Mail: abendeliis@agconsultantsinc.com.

BENDER, JANE, furniture manufacturing company executive; Dir. mktg. Henredon Furniture Industries, Inc. Office: Furniture Brands Internat Inc 1 N Brentwood Blvd 15th Fl Saint Louis MO 63105 Office Phone: 828-438-1257. Office Fax: 314-863-5306. Business E-Mail: jbender@henredon.com.

BENDER, JOHN HENRY, JR., (JACK BENDER), editor, cartoonist; b. Waterloo, Iowa, Mar. 28; s. John Henry and Wilma (Lowe) B.; divorced; children: Thereza, John Henry IV, Anthony; m. Carole R. Suggs, 1995. BA, U. Iowa, 1953; postgrad., Art. Inst. Chgo., 1956, Washington U., St. Louis, 1957; MA, U. Mo., 1962. Art dir., asst. editor Commerce Pub. Co., St. Louis, 1953-54, 56-58; editor Florissant Reporter, Mo., 1958-61; editl. cartoonist Waterloo Courier, 1962-84, assoc. editor, 1975-83; art. dir., editor Alpha VII Corp., Tulsa, 1984-87; head dept. prodn. art Platt Coll., Tulsa, 1987-92; cartoonist Don Martin Studio, Miami, Fla., 1989-92; artist Alley Oop comic strip United Feature Syndicate, NYC, 1991—2011, Universal Uclick Syndicate, Kans. City, 2011—. Sports cartoonist Basketball Weekly, Baseball Digest Mag., U. Iowa, others. Author: Pocket Guide to Judging Springboard Diving, (with Dick Smith) Inside Diving, (with Ed Gagnier) Inside Gymnastics; exhibited at Grout Mus., Waterloo, Iowa, 2002, Iowans of Impact Exhibit, Grout Mus., Waterloo, Iowa, 1998, Okie Cartoonists Exhbn., Okla. History Ctr., 2010-11. With USAF, 1953-56, col., ret. 1983. Recipient Best Editl. award Mo. Press Assn., 1960, Grenville Clark Editl. Page award, 1968, Freedoms Found. award, 1969, 75, Freedoms Found. Honor medal, 1971, Ignatz award Orlandocon, 1992, Air Force Commendation medal, 1981, Golden Lion award Edgar Rice Burroughs Bibliophiles, 2008; named to Hall of Fame East H.S., Waterloo, Iowa, 1972, Names on Main, Cedar Falls, Iowa, 1997, Okla. Cartoonists Hall of Fame, 2005. Mem. Assn. Am. Editl. Cartoonists, Nat. Cartoonists Soc., Comic Art Profl. Soc., Sigma Chi, Kappa Tau Alpha. Office: RR 1 Box 540 Terlton OK 74081-9740

BENDITT, THEODORE MATTHEW, humanities educator; b. Phila., Oct. 23, 1940; m. Anne Rosamond Shaw, Feb. 3, 1968; 1 child, David Shaw. AB, U. Pa., 1962, JD, 1965, MA, 1967; PhD, U. Pitts., 1971. Instr. Duke U., Durham, N.C., 1970-71, asst. prof., 1971-75, U. So. Calif., Los Angeles, 1975-78; assoc. prof. U. Ala., Birmingham, 1978-83, prof., 1983—, dean, Sch. Arts and Humanities, 1984-98. Author: Law as Rule and Principle, 1978, Rights, 1982, Normality, Disease, and Enhancement, 2007, Why Respect Matters, 2008. Recipient Younger Humanist Fellowship, NEH, 1974-75. Mem. Am. Philos. Assn. Office: Univ of Ala at Birmingham Dept Philosophy Birmingham AL 35294-1260

BENEDETTO, ANTHONY R., religious mediator; BS in Nuc. Engring., Tex. A&M U., Coll. Station, 1968, M in Nuc. Engring., 1970; MBA, Sul Ross State U., Alpine, Tex., 1976; PhD in Nuc. Engring., Tex. A&M U., Coll. Station, 1984; JD, South Tex. Coll. Law, Houston, 2005. Lic.: Tex. 2005; cert. in nuc. medicine physics and instrumentation Am. Bd. Sci. in Nuc. Medicine, 1979, in med. nuc. physics Am. Bd. Radiology, 1980, in healthcare mgmt. Am. Coll. Healthcare Execs., 1998. Asst. prof. dept. radiology U. Tex. Health Sci. Ctr., San Antonio, 1979—84; assoc. prof. to full prof. dept. radiology U. Tex. Med. Branch, Galveston, 1984—94; sr. sys. engr. ADAC Labs., Inc., Milpitas, Calif., 1994—95; prof., dir. ops. dept. diagnostic radiology U. Ky. Chandler Med. Ctr., Lexington, Ky., 1995—99; film lib. performance improvement project adminstr. M.D. Anderson Cancer Ctr., Houston, 2000—02; med. physicist Guidant Corp., Houston, 2002—03; scripture based conflict resolution conciliator Woodlands Conciliation Ctr., The Woodlands, 2005—09, Christian Dispute Resolution Ministry, 2010—. Mem. nuc. sci. com. Am. Coll. Nuc. Physicians, 1983—96, mem. quality assurance and practice cert. com., 1984—96, mem. publs. com., 1984—96, mem. com. single photon emission computed tomography quality control, 1992—96; dir. U. Tex. Med. Branch Diagnostic Radiology and Nuc. Medicine Sci. Lecture Series, 1984—94, instr., 1984—94; mem. sci. com. Nat. Coun. Radiation Protection and Measurements, 1989—2002, chmn. sci. com., 1992—95; cons. to standards com. Health Physics Soc., 1991—99; mem. comml. affairs com. Soc. Nuc. Medicine, 1992—95, chmn. advertising subcom., 1992—95, publs. com., 1992—95, mem. bylaws com., 1993—95, vice chmn. comml. affairs com., 1994—95; com. physics and instrumentation Am. Bd. Sci. in Nuc. Medicine, 1993—97; dir. UK Diagnostic Radiology Sci. Lecture Series, 1995—99, instr., 1995—99; profl. devel. com. Healthcare Info. and Mgmt. Sys. Soc., 1998—2000, ann. meeting proposal reviewer, session coach, 2000—03, chmn. clin. sys. spl. interest group, 2000—01, mem. evaluation task force edn. com., 2001; presenter in field. Contbr. articles to profl. jours., chapters to books; referee: Jour. Nuc. Medicine, 1983—96, reviewer:, 1984—96, mem. editl. bd.:, 1986—96; contbg. editor: Health Physics Soc. Newsletter, 1983—95; referee: Health Physics, 1983—96, book reviewer:, 1984—96, Med. Physics, 1984—96, referee:, 1987—95, RadioGraphics, 1992—98; contbg. editor: Jour. Nuc. Medicine Tech., 1995—97, credits reviewer: Am. Healthcare Radiology Adminstrs., 2000, mem. editl. review bd.:, 2001—03. Named one of Top 100 Vols., Harris County Dispute Resolution Ctr., 2006—11. Fellow: Am. Coll. Radiology (mem. com. standards and accreditation 1992—97), Am. Coll. Healthcare Execs., Am. Assn. Physicists in Medicine (chmn. publs. com. 1993—96, mem. com. electronic archival and comm. 1993—96); mem.: ABA, Assn. for Conflict Resolution. Office Phone: 832-585-4215. Business E-Mail: tony@cdrmtw.org.

BENEDICT, LORI A., state legislator; b. Chgo., Ill. m. Don Benedict; children: Sherry Jackson, Rick Gicla. With, checking dept. Fed. Res. Bank, 1963—66; payroll, ins., positions Hines Lumber Co.,

1965—70; owner, mgr. Corral Western Wear, 1973—79; mem., women's commn. Fulton County Farm Bur., 1979—90; owner Sunrise Cattle Co., 1980—91; chmn. Fulton County Rep. Party, 1987—92; mem. Fulton County Election Commn., 1987—92; candidate Ark. House of Representatives, 1992; pres., gen. mgr., mountain home flight svc. Ozark Regional Flight Svc. Inc., 1992—; mem. Bus. & Profl. Women's Assn., 1993—96, State of Ark. Election Commn., 1994—98; bd. dirs., scholarship com. Cowboy Mounted Shooting Assn., 2006—; mem. Dist. 82 Ark. House of Representatives, 2011—. Republican. Office: PO Box 22 Sturkie AR 72578 Office Phone: 870-481-5966. Office Fax: 870-481-5967. Business E-Mail: sunrisecattleco@centurytel.net.

BENEDIK, MICHAEL J., microbiologist, educator; b. Indianapolis, Jan. 29, 1955; s. Peter Rajko and Luigina Benedik; children: Chris K., Jeremy K. BA with honors, U. Chgo., 1976; PhD, Stanford, 1982. Prof. U. Houston, 1989—2003, Tex. A&M U., Coll. Station, 2003—. Grantee, NIH, NSF. Achievements include research in studies on the extracellular nuclease of Serratia marcescens; using bacterial enzymes for the bioremedation of cyanide. Office: Tex A&M Univ Biology - TAMU 3258 College Station TX 77843-3258 Office Fax: 979-845-2891. Business E-Mail: benedik@tamu.edu.

BENENATI, SUSAN VENTO, allergist, immunologist; MD, U. South Fla., 1984. Diplomate Am. Bd. Internal Medicine, 1988, Am. Bd. Allergy and Immunology, 1999, lic. Fla., 1990. Intern internal medicine Ind. Univ. Hosp., 1985, resident internal medicine, 1987, fellow hematology, 1988; fellow allergy and immunology Johns Hopkins Hosp., 1990; hosp. affiliations include Doctors Hosp., Meml. Regional Hosp., Miami Children's Hosp., South Miami Hosp., Baptist Hosp. of Miami. Office: Baptist Hospital of Miami 8900 North Kendall Dr Miami FL 33176-2197 Office Phone: 786-596-1960.

BENFER, DAVID WILLIAM, hospital administrator; b. Toledo, May 28, 1946; s. Wilson L. and Marjorie (Baringer) B.; m. Mary Sturner, Sept. 5, 1970; children: Emily, Matthew, Andrew. BA, Wittenberg U., 1968; MBA in Hosp. Adminstrn., Xavier U., 1970. Asst. adminstrn. Med. Coll., Ohio Hosp., Toledo, 1971-76, exec. dir., CEO, 1976-81, Bon Secours Hosp., Grosse Pointe, Mich., 1982-84, Henry Ford Hosp., Detroit, 1985-92; pres., CEO, St. Joseph Med. Ctr., Joliet, Ill., 1992-99; CEO St. Raphael Healthcare System, New Haven, 1999—2010; chair The Benfer Group LLC, 2010—; advs. healthcare supplier, ptnr., 2010—. Dir. Merchants and Mfrs. Bank, Stereotaxis, Inc.; fellow Berkeley Coll. Yale U., 2002—. Co-author: Issues in Health Care Management, 1982; contbg. author: Sisters of Bon Secours Centennial, 1982. Trustee, chmn. Family Svcs., Detroit and Wayne County, 1982-92; chmn. AIDS Consortium Southeastern Mich., Toledo, 1988-921 v.p. Med. Value Plan, Inc., 1986-91; chmn. S.E. Mich. Hosp. Coun.; bd. dirs. U. St. Francis, Joliet, 1993-2002; vice chmn. New Ctr. Area Coun., 1991-92; mem. Mich. Tastefest, 1996; bd. dirs., chmn. Ctr. Econ. Devel., Will County C. of C., Ill., New Haven Symphony, v.p. bd. Recipient Commendation 114th Ohio Gen Assembly, 1981, Torch of Liberty award Anti Defamation League, 2005. Fellow Am. Coll. Health Care Execs. (coun. regents 1989-92, bd. govs. 1992—2000, Robert S. Hudgens award 1982, chair 1998-99); mem. Am. Hosp. Assn. (regional policy bd.), Conn. Hosp. Assn. (bd. dirs. 2003-09), Cath. Health Assn. (bd. dirs. 2003-09), Quinnipiack Club (New Haven), Country Club Detroit (Grosse Pointe), New Haven Country Club. Roman Catholic. Avocations: jogging, golf. Home: 7618 Silver Wood Ct Bradenton FL 34202

BENFEY, PHILIP N., botanist, educator; m. Elisabeth Benfey; 2 children. Diplome d'Etudes Universitaire Generale, Univerisite de Paris, 1981; PhD in Cell Biology, Harvard Univ., 1986; post-doctoral study in Plant Molecular Biology, Rockefeller Univ. Asst. prof. Rockefeller Univ., NYC, 1990—91; prof. NYU, 1991—2002; prof. dept. biology Duke U., Durham, NC, 2002—03, chmn. dept. biology, 2002—, Paul Kramer prof. biology, 2003—. Author: Genomics, 2005. Mem.: NAS. Office: Dept Biology Duke Univ B353 LSRC Durham NC 27708 Office Phone: 919-660-7338 919 660 7338.

BENFIELD, STEPHANIE STUCKEY, state legislator; b. Eastman, Ga., Dec. 25, 1965; m. Robert H. Benfield; children: Robert III, Beverly. Attended, Vanderbilt U., 1984—87; BA, U. Ga., 1989; JD, U. Ga. Sch. Law, 1992. Staff atty. Prisoner Legal Counseling Project, 1992—94, Fulton Co. Public Defender's Office, 1994—96; sole practicioner Law Offices of Stephanie Stuckey, 1996—99; partner Law Offices of Stuckey & Manheimer, LLC., 1998—2002; mem. Dist. 67 Ga. House of Reps., 1999—2002, mem. Dist. 56, mem. Dist. 85, 2004—. Del. Dem. Nat. Conv., 1988, 1996, 2000. Co-author: Women and the Law: A Guide to Women's Legal Rights in Georgia. V.p. Jeannette Rankin Found.; bd. mem. Nature Conservancy Ga., 1997—2001. Recipient Golden Shoe award, Pedestrians Educating Drivers About Safety, 2001, Outstanding Pub. Svc. in Child Advocacy award, Ga. Younger Lawyers Assn., 2001; named one of 40 under 40 promising Georgians, Georgia Trend Mag., 2002, 16 Attorneys to Watch, Fulton County Daily Report, 2003. Mem.: LWV (former DeKalb County and state bd. mem.), Ga. Commn. Women (former treas.), State Bar Ga. (vice chair emerging issues com.). Democrat. Methodist. Office: 512 Coverdell Legis Office Bldg Atlanta GA 30334 also: 940 Artwood Rd NE Atlanta GA 30307 Home Phone: 404-377-7014; Office Phone: 404-656-7859. Personal E-mail: stuckey@mindspring.com.

BENGE, CHRIS, state official, former state legislator; b. Tulsa, Okla., Sept. 9, 1962; s. Glenn and Barbara (Langley) Benge; m. Allison Fox; children: Garrett, Hayden. BSBA, Okla. State U. Sr. v.p. govt. affairs Tulsa Regional Chamber; dir. intergovernmental & enterprise devel. City of Tulsa; mem. Dist. 68 Okla. House of Reps., Oklahoma City, 1999—2011, spkr., 2008—11; sec. of state State of Okla., Oklahoma City, 2013—. Recipient Disting. Svc. award, Okla. State Regents for Higher Edn., 2009, Defender of Free Enterprise award, Okla. State Chamber of Commerce, 2009, Tulsa Icon award, Okla. State U., 2009, Jim Close Humanitarian award, Southwest Tulsa Chamber, 2010; named Legislative Advocate of the Yr., Okla. Econ. Development Coun., 2008, Legislator Yr., Natural Gas Vehicles of America, 2010. Republican. Baptist. Office: Secretary of State 2300 North Lincoln Blvd Ste 101 Oklahoma City OK 73105 Office Phone: 405-521-6434. Office Fax: 405-521-2031.*

BENGTSON, ROGER DEAN, physicist, department chairman; b. Wausa, Nebr., Apr. 29, 1941; s. Fridolph M. and Edith E. (Pearson) B.; m. Billie A. Spies, June 15, 1963; children— Nissa C., Hans E. BS, U. Nebr., 1962; MS, Va. Poly. Inst. and State U., 1964; PhD, U. Md., 1968. Aerospace engr. NASA-Langley Research Ctr., Hampton, Va., 1962-67; research assoc. U. Tex., Austin, 1968-70, asst. prof. physics, 1970-75, assoc. prof., 1975-81, prof., 1981—, chmn. dept., 1984-88. Mem. Am. Phys. Soc., AAAS, Sigma Xi Home: 411 Honeycomb Rdg Austin TX 78746-5324 Office: U Tex Dept Physics C-1600 Austin TX 78712 Business E-Mail: bengtson@physics.utexas.edu.

BENHAM, ROBERT, state supreme court justice; m. Nell (Dodson) B.; children: Corey Brevard, Austin Tyler. BS in Polit. sci. (hon.), Tuskegee U., 1967; JD, U. Ga. Lumpkin Sch. of Law, 1970; LLM, U. Va., 1989. Former trial atty. Atlanta Legal Aid Society, Inc.; judge Ga. Ct. Appeals, Ga., 1984-89; justice Ga. Supreme Ct., Atlanta, 1989—, presiding justice, former chief justice, 1995. Mem. adv. bd. 1st So. Bank. Chmn. Gov.'s Commn. on Drug Awareness and Prevention, State of Ga.; mem. Ga. Hist. Soc.; trustee Ga. Legal Hist. Found.; bd. dirs. Cartersville (Ga.) Devel. Authority, Cartersville-Bartow C. of C.; deacon, former Sunday Sch. supt. The Greater Mt. Olive Bapt. Ch. Captain USAR. Recipient Ben F. Johnson, Jr. Pub. Svc. award, Ga. State Univ. Sch. Law, 2004. Mem Atlanta Bar Assn. (bd. dirs. jud. sect.), Ga. Bar Found., Lawyers Club Atlanta, Masons, Shriners, Elks. Office: Ga Supreme Ct 244 Washington St SW Rm 572 Atlanta GA 30334-9007 Fax: (404) 657-4329.*

BENJAMIN, BRENT D., state supreme court justice, lawyer; b. Marietta, Ohio, July 3, 1957; m. Janice Benjamin; 5 children. BA in Political sci., Ohio State U., 1981, JD, 1984. Bar: W.Va. 1984, U.S. Fourth Circuit Ct. of Appeals, U.S. Dist. Ct. Southern W.Va., W.Va. Supreme Ct., Ky. Supreme Ct. 2001. Atty. Robinson and McElwee, Charleston, W.Va., 1983—90, ptnr., 1990—2004; justice W.Va. Supreme Ct. of Appeals, 2004—, chief justice, 2009. Mem. Hocking Coll. Archeol. Mission; former treas. W.Va. Republican Party. Mem.: ABA, Kanawha County Bar Assn., W.Va. State Bar Assn. Office: WVa Supreme Ct Appeals Capitol Complex Bldg 1 Rm E302 Charleston WV 25305 Office Phone: 304-558-2602.*

BENJAMIN, CECIL, political organization administrator; m. Ferryneisa Hodge; children: Lawrence, Ofari. BS in Biology, Inter-Am. U. of PR; MS in Sci. Edn., Temple U. Nat. v.p. Am. Fedn. of Tchrs., 1984; commr. VI Dept. Labor, 2005; chmn. VI Dem. Party. Chief negotiator St. Thomas/St.John Fedn. of Tchrs. Mem.: St. Croix Fedn. of Tchrs. Democrat. Office: Virgin Islands Democratic Party PO Box 222848 St Croix VI 00822*

BENJAMIN, REGINA MARCIA, physician, former federal official; b. Mobile, Ala., Oct. 26, 1956; d. Clarence and Millie Benjamin. BS in Chemistry, Xavier U., New Orleans, 1979; MD, U. Ala., Birmingham, 1984; MBA, Tulane U., New Orleans, 1991; DSc (hon.), Dartmouth Coll., Hanover, NH, 2010; PharmD (hon.), Albany Coll. Pharmacy & Health Scis., NY, 2010; LHD (hon.), Rensselaer Poly. Inst., Troy, NY, 2011. Diplomate American Bd. Family Medicine. Intern, resident Med. Ctr. Ctrl. Ga., Macon; pvt. med. practice Bayou La Batre, Ala.; assoc. dean rural health U. South Ala. Coll. Medicine, Mobile; founder, CEO Bayou La Batre Rural Health Clinic, Inc., 1990—; surgeon gen. US Dept. Health & Human Services (HHS), Washington, 2009—13. Mem. Kaiser Commn. Medicaid & Uninsured; past v.p. Ala. Governor's Commn. Aging. Bd. dirs. Physicians for Human Rights. Recipient Nelson Mandela award for health & human rights, Kaiser Family Found., 1997, Nat. Caring award, Caring Inst., 2000, President's award, U. Ala. Birmingham, 2001, Pro Ecclesia et Pontifice Disting. Svc. medal, Pope Benedict XVI, 2006, NAACP Chairman's award, 2011; named Woman of Yr., CBS This Morning, 1996; named a MacArthur Fellow, The John D. & Catherine T. MacArthur Found., 2008; named one of The Nation's 50 Future Leaders Age 40 and Under, TIME mag., 1995, America's Best Leaders, US News & World Report, 2008; Kellogg Nat. Fellow, 1993—96, Next Generation Leadership fellowship, Rockefeller Found. Fellow: American Acad. Family Physicians; mem.: NAS, AMA (Women in Medicine Panel 1986—87, pres. Edn. & Rsch. Found. 1997—98, bd. trustees 1995—, Found. Leadership award 2009), Med. Assn. State of Ala. (pres. 2002—03). Achievements include featured in Nat. Libr. Medicine exhibit Changing the Face of Medicine honoring women physicians, 2003. Office: Bayou Clinic 13833 Tapia Lane Bayou La Batre AL 36509 Office Phone: 301-443-4000. Office Fax: 301-443-3574.*

BENKISER, TINA JOHNS, lawyer, former political organization administrator; b. 1963; m. Eric Benkiser. BA, Miss. U. for Women; JD, U. Ala. Bar: Tex. 1988, US Ct. Appeals (fed. cir.). Atty., counselor at law, Houston; chmn. Tex. Rep. Precinct; mem. Tex. State Rep. Exec. Com., 1998—; chmn. Tex. Rep. Party, 2003—09. Mem. Harris County Execution Com., 1994—2003; chair Daughters of Liberty Rep. women, 1995—2000. Del. Nat. Rep. Conv., Tex. Precinct Conv., Tex. Senate Dist. Conv., Tex. State Conv. Mem.: State Bar Tex., Nat. Sports Lawyers Assn., Houston Bar Assn., Nat. Fedn. Rep. Women, Tex. Fedn. Rep. Women (Tribute Honoree 2000), Gospel Movie Assn. Republican. Office: 7500 San Felipe Ste 600 Houston TX 77284

BENKOVICH, CARL, consumer products company executive; BS in Acctg., Wright State U., 1979. CFO, N.Am. Tupperware Brands Corp., 2000—05, v.p., internal audit, 2005—07, CFO, beauty group, 2007—09, v.p., strategy and bus. devel., 2009—. Office: Tupperware Brands Corp 14901 S Orange Blossom Trail Orlando FL 32837 Office Phone: 407-826-5050.

BENN, JAMIE, professional hockey player; b. Victoria, BC, Canada, July 18, 1989; Center, left wing Dallas Stars, 2009—; captain, 2013—. Mem. Team Canada, Olympic Games, Sochi, Russia, 2014. Named to NHL All-Star Game, 2012. Achievements include being a member of gold medal winning Canadian Hockey Team, Sochi Olympics, 2014. Office: c/o Dallas Stars 2601 Avenue of the Stars Frisco TX 75034*

BENNETT, ALAN M., retired finance company executive; b. July 11, 1950; BS in Acctg., Susquehanna U., 1972. Cert. Pub. Acct. Audit mgr. Ernst & Young LLP; various positions Pirelli Armstrong Tire Corp.; CFO, Aetna Bus. Resources Aetna, Inc., 1995—97, v.p., dir., internal audit, 1997—98, v.p., corp. contr., 1998—2001, sr. v.p., CFO, 2001—07; interim CEO H&R Block, Inc., Mo., 2007—08, pres., CEO & bd. dirs., 2010—11. Bd. dirs. Bausch & Lomb Inc., 2004—07, Haliburton Co., 2006—, The TJX Companies, Inc., 2007—. Mem. bd. dirs. Gaylord Hosp.; mem. acctg. adv. bd. U. Conn.; former trustee Conn. Policy and Econ. Coun. Mem.: Conn. Soc. Cert. Pub. Accts., Am. Inst. Cert. Pub. Accts., New Haven Lions Club (past pres.).

BENNETT, ARCHIE WAYNE, academic administrator; b. Rocky Mount, Va., May 5, 1937; s. Archie Conrad and Catherine (Purdue) B.; m. Shirley Turner Bennett; children: Elizabeth Anne, David Wayne. BSEE with hons., Va. Tech., 1960, MSEE, 1963; PhD Elec. Engring., U. Fla., 1966. Registered profl. engr., S.C., Va., Miss. Systems engr. GE, Salem, Va., 1960-62; instr. Va. Tech., Blacksburg, 1962-64, asst. to assoc. profl. elec. engring., 1966-81; NASA doctoral fellow U. Fla., Gainesville, 1964-66; head elec. and computer engring. Clemson (S.C.) U., 1981-88, assoc. dean engring., 1988-92, sr. vice provost/dean grad. sch., 1992—96; dean engring. Miss. State U., 1996—2004; sr. devel. counselor Clemson (SC) U., 2004—. Cons. numerous nat. and internat. cos. Editor: Applied Micro Electronics, 1978, Linear Systems, 1976; author: Introduction to Computer Simulations, 1974, Effective Technical Communications Manual, 1988. Fellow IEEE, Internat. Engring. Consortium; mem. ACM, Am. Soc. Engring. Edn., Rotary (pres. Clemson club 1984). Baptist. Avocations: woodworking, tennis, photography. Home: 205 Stonebridge Dr Clemson SC 29631 Office: Clemson U 110 Daniel Dr Clemson SC 29631 Office Phone: 864-650-6007.

BENNETT, BOB, energy executive; BSc in Civil Engring., U. Strathclyde, UK, MSc in Petroleum Engring. V.p., tech., Hughes Christensen Baker Hughes, Inc.; v.p., tech. Baker Oil Tools, v.p., N.Am ops., 2008—09, pres., 2009—. Mem. Soc. for Petroleum Engrs. Office: Baker Hughes Inc Ste 2100 2929 Allen Pky Houston TX 77019-2118 Mailing: Baker Hughes Inc P O Box 4740 Houston TX 77210-4740 Office Phone: 713-439-8600. Office Fax: 713-439-8699. Business E-Mail: bob.bennett@bakerhughes.com.

BENNETT, CHRISTOPHER A., electric power industry executive; BSChemE, Princeton U., 1980; MBA in Gen. Mgmt., Harvard U., 1987. Sr. engr. Intel, 1980—84; mgr., advanced mfg. engring. Digital Equipment Corp., 1984—85; exec. mgr., corp. bus. devel. General Electric Co., 1993—95; v.p. Dean & Co., 1995—2007; v.p., bus. strategy & policy FPL Group, Inc., 2007—08, exec. v.p., chief strategy, policy & bus. process improvement officer, 2008—. Office: FPL Group Inc 700 Universe Blvd North Palm Beach FL 33408 Office Phone: 561-694-6311. Office Fax: 561-694-4999. Business E-Mail: christopher_bennett@fpl.com.

BENNETT, CLAYTON IKE, professional sports team owner; m. Louise Gaylord; 3 children. Grad., U. Okla. Chmn. Profl. Basketball Club, LLC (owns NBA Oklahoma City Thunder and WNBA Seattle Storm), 2006—, Dorchester Capital, Oklahoma City. Chmn. emeritus bd. dirs. Okla. Heritage Assn. Office: Dorchester Capital Okla Tower 210 Park Ave Ste 3121 Oklahoma City OK 73102 also: Profl Basketball Club LLC Two Leadership Sq 211 N Robinson Ave Ste 300 Oklahoma City OK 73102

BENNETT, G. KEMBLE (GEORGE KEMBLE BENNETT), engineering professor, dean; b. Jacksonville, Fla., Apr. 2, 1940; s. George K. and Murla E. (Weeks) Bennett; m. Jill Alison McMaster, June 5, 1982; children: Russell William, Paige E., Alison Kemly. BA in Math., Fla. State U., 1962; MS in Engring. Math., San Jose State U., 1968; PhD in Indsl. Engring., Tex. Tech. U., 1970. Cert. profl. engr., Fla., Tex. Assoc. engr. Martin Co., Orlando, Fla., 1962—63; engr. Lockheed Rsch. Labs., Palo Alto, Calif., 1963—64, sr. engr., 1964—66; asst. dir. Computer Ctr. Tex. Tech. U., Lubbock, 1966—69; vis. scientist NASA Manned Spacecraft Lab., Houston, 1969—70; asst. profl. indsl. engring. Va. Poly. Inst., Blacksburg, 1970—73; prof., chmn. indsl. and mgmt. sys. engring. U. South Fla., Tampa, 1973—86; pres., CEO G. Kemble Bennett & Assocs., 1975—79; staff engr. avionics divsn. Honeywell, 1984—86; prof., head indsl. engring. Tex. A&M U., Coll. Sta., 1986—91, assoc. dean engring., 1991—2002, dir. Tex. Engring. Extension Svc., 1992—2002, assoc. vice chancellor engring., 1992—2002, dir. Tex. Engring. Expt. Sta., vice chancellor engring., dean Dwight Look Coll. Engring., 2002—. Assoc. editor: IIE Transactions, mng. editor: Logistics Spectrum; contbr. articles to nat. and internat. jours. Fellow: Soc. Logistics Engrs. (bd. referees The Annals, Eccles medal 1997), Inst. Indsl. Engrs. (Fla. West Coast Engr. of Yr. 1979, 1982, Albert G. Hozlman Disting. Educator award 1996); mem.: Inst. Mgmt Scis., Am. Soc. Engring. Edn., Phi Kappa Phi, Tau Beta Pi. Republican. Methodist. Office: Dwight Look Coll Engring Texas A&M U 3126 TAMU College Station TX 77845-3126

BENNETT, JAMES THOMAS, economics professor; b. Memphis, Oct. 19, 1942; m. Sara Ellen Dorman, Sept. 2, 1967. BS in Ops. Research magna cum laude, Case Inst. Tech., 1964, MS in Mgmt. Sci., 1966; PhD in Econs., Case Western Res. U., 1970; student Grad. Sch. Bus., Columbia U., 1964-65. Teaching fellow Case Inst. Tech., 1968-69; instr. bus. Cleve. State U., 1967-68; asst. prof. econs. George Washington U., Washington, 1970-75; assoc. prof. econs. George Mason U., Fairfax, Va., 1975-77, Eminent Scholar and William P. Snavely prof. polit. economy and pub. policy, 1975—. Dir. John M. Olin Inst. for Employment Practice and Policy; chmn. faculty senate George Mason U., 2002-05; trustee Horowitz Found., 2008-; bd. dirs. transaction Pubs., 2007-. Co-author: The Political Economy of Federal Government Growth: 1958-1978, 1980, Better Government at Half the Price, 1981, Deregulating Labor Relations, 1981, Underground Government: The Off-Budget Public Sector, 1983, Destroying Democracy: How Government Funds Partisan Politics, 1985, Unfair Competition: The Profits of Nonprofits, 1989, Patterns of Corporate Philanthropy: Ideas, Advocacy and the Corporation, 1989, Health Research Charities: Image and Reality, 1990, Health Research Charities II: The Politics of Fear, 1991, Official Lies: How Washington Misleads Us, 1992, Unhealthy Charities: Hazardous to Your Health and Wealth, 1994, Cancer Scam: The Diversion of Federal Cancer Funds to Politics, 1998, The Food and Drink Police: America's Nannies, Busybodies and Petty Tyrants, 1999, From Pathology to Politics: Public Health in America, 2000, Public Health Profiteering, 2001, The Future of Private Sector Unionism in the United States, 2002, Tax-Funded Politics, 2004, Information Technology and the World of Work, 2004, Homeland Security Scams, 2006, The Politics of American Feminism: Gender Conflict in Contemporary Society, 2007, What Do Unions Do? A Twenty-Year Perspective, 2007, Stifling Political Competition: How Government Has Rigged the System to Benefit Demopublicans and Exclude Third Parties, 2008, Not Invited to the Party: How The Demopublicans Have Rigged The System and Left Independents Out in the Cold, 2009, The Doomsday Lobby: Hype and Panic from Sputniks, Marians and Maurading Meteors, 2010, They Play, You Pay: Why Taxpayers Build Ballparks, Stadiums, and Arenas for Billionaire Owners and Millionaire Players, 2012; editor Jour. Labor Rsch., 1980—2007, sr. assoc. editor, 2008—; contbr. chapters to books, articles to profl. jours.; co-author: Unfunded Mandates: How Congress Forces States and Localities to Do Its Bidding and Pay for the Privilege, 2013. Trustee Horowitz Found. Social Policy, 2006—, Trans. Pubs., 2007—. Ford Found. scholar, 1960-64; Continental Grain Corp. fellow; McKinsey scholar; Case Inst. fellow, 1965-67; Fed. Res. Bank Cleve. fellow, 1969-70 Mem. Am. Econ. Assn., So. Econ. Assn., Pub. Choice Soc., Western Econ. Assn., Am. Statis. Assn., Phila. Soc., Mont Pelerin Soc., Phi Beta Kappa, Sigma Xi, Tau Beta Pi, Alpha Lambda Delta, Phi Theta Kappa. Office: George Mason U Dept Econs Fairfax VA 22030 Business E-Mail: jbennett@gmu.edu.

BENNETT, JAMES TOLIVER, pediatric orthopedist; b. New Orleans, Nov. 29, 1953; s. Joseph Walter and Alberta (Toliver) B.; m. Susan Pardue, Oct. 20, 1972; children: James Jr., Robert Clifton. BS in Engring., Tulane U., 1974, MD, 1978. Cert. Am. Bd. Orthopedic Surgery., Am. Bd. Spine Surgeons. Resident U. NC, Alfred Dupont Inst.; fellow Scottish Rite Hosp./ Emory, Atlanta; prof. orthopaedics, chief pediatric orthopaedics Tulane U., New Orleans. Contbr. articles to profl. jours. Bd. dirs. United Cerebral Palsy, New Orleans. Mem. Am. Acad. Orthop. Surgery, Am. Acad. Pediat., Scoliosis Rsch. Soc., Pediatric Orthop. Soc. N.Am. Republican. Presbyterian. Avocation: sailing. Office: Tulane U 1430 Tulane Ave New Orleans LA 70112-2699 also: Tulane University Hospital Clinic 129 New Camellia Blvd Covington LA 70433-7813

BENNETT, JAY D., lawyer; children: Summer, Lillian, Sky. AB with honors, U. NC, Chapel Hill, 1974; JD cum laude, Harvard U., 1977. Bar: Ga., US Dist. Ct. (no. and mid. dists.) Ga., US Ct. Appeals (4th, 5th, 9th and 11th cirs.), US Supreme Ct. Assoc. Alston & Bird, Atlanta, 1977-83, ptnr., 1983—. Morehead scholar Morehead Found. 1970-74. Mem. State Bar Ga., Atlanta Bar Assn., Lawyers Club Atlanta, Trial Attys. Am., Phi Beta Kappa. Avocations: flying, skydiving, motorcycling, fishing. Office: Alston & Bird LLP One Atlantic Ctr 1201 W Peachtree St Atlanta GA 30309-3449 Office Phone: 404-881-7643. Office Fax: 404-253-8485. E-mail: jay.bennett@alston.com.

BENNETT, JIM (JAMES RONALD BENNETT), state official; b. Red Oak, Iowa, Jan. 3, 1940; s. George T. and Florence B. (Olson) B.; m. Andrea Roberts; children: Donald B., Tara L. BS, Jacksonville State U., 1961; MA, U. Ala., 1980. Political editor Birmingham Post-Herald, 1961—71; dir. public affairs Ala. Labor Coun., 1971—76, Birmingham-Southern Coll., 1976—81; mem. Ala. House of Reps., 1978-83, Ala. State Senate, 1983-93; gen. ptnr. Marshall-Bennett Advt., 1981—83; sec. of state State of Ala., 1993—2003, 2013—; commr. Ala. Dept. Labor, Montgomery, 2003—13. Author: Fire in the Furnace, 1976; Old Tannehill, A History of the Pioneer Ironworks in Roupes Valley, 1829-1865, 1986; Tannehill and the Growth of the Alabama Iron Industry, 1999, Historic Birmingham and Jefferson County, 2008. Chmn. bd. trustees Jacksonville State U.; bd. dirs. Tannehill Ironworks Hist. State Park, 1970. Recipient Assoc. Press Newswriting award, 1963; Award for Public Affairs Reporting, American Polit. Sci. Assn., 1969; Merit award, Pub. Relations Coun., 1974 & 1976-78; Lantern award, Southern Public Rels. Fedn., 1975; Citation for Excellence, Nat. Collegiate Baseball Writers Assn., 1978; Legislator of the Year, Nat. Assn. Soc. Workers, 1984, Ala. Child Support Assn., 1986; Montgomery Advertiser's Meritorious Public Svc. award, 1989 & 1990; Named one of The Top Five Senators, Ala. Senate, 1989-90. Mem. Nat. Assn. Secs. of State (pres. 1999-2000, chair elections com., 1995-98). Republican. Methodist. Office: Alabama Secretary of State PO Box 5616 Montgomery AL 36103 Office Phone: 334-242-7200. E-mail: jim.bennett@sos.alabama.gov.*

BENNETT, MICHAEL S., state legislator; b. Brainerd, Minn., Jan. 1, 1945; m. Diane Bennett. BA, Drake U., Des Moines, Iowa, 1975, MBA, 1976. Elec. contractor; mem. Fla. House of Reps., Tallahassee, 2000—02; mem. Dist. 21 Fla. State Senate, Tallahassee, 2002—, chair policy and steering com. on commerce and industry, cmty. affairs com., mem. policy and steering com. on govtl. ops., policy and steering com. on ways and means, banking and ins. com., fin. and tax com., mem. health regulation com., mil. affairs and domestic security com., reapportionment com., select com. on Fla.'s economy. Mem. Suncoast Found. Bd., 2002, Suncoast Work Force Devel. Bd. Served with USN, 1963—67, Vietnam. Recipient Gov. Lawton W. Chiles Religious Freedom award Am. Jewish Com., 2003. Mem. Greater Sarasota Sertoma Club (pres., bd. chmn. 1985-2000), Manasota Specialties Contractors (pres. 1997-2000), Am. Subcontractors Assn. (pres. 1993-99), Elec. Coun. Fla. (pres. 1986-89). Republican. Baptist. Office: 322 Senate Office Bldg 404 S Monroe St Tallahassee FL 32399-1100 also: Wildewood Profl Pk Ste 90 400 S Monroe St Tallahassee FL 32399-6536 Office Phone: 941-727-6349, 850-487-5078. Business E-Mail: bennett.mike.web@flsenate.gov.

BENNETT, PETER BRIAN, medical researcher, educator; b. Portsmouth, Hampshire, Eng., June 12, 1931; s. Charles Risby and Doris Isobel (Peckham) B.; m. Margaret Camellia Rose, July 7, 1956; children: Caroline Susan, Christopher Charles BSc, U. London, 1951; PhD, U. Southampton, 1964, DSc, 1984; Dr. honoris causa, U. de la Mediterranean, France, 2001. Asst. head surg. sect. Royal Navy Physiol. Lab., Alverstoke, England, 1953-56, head inert gas narcosis sect., 1953-66; dep. dir., prin. sci. officer, head pressure physiology sect. Royal Naval Physiol. Lab., Alverstoke, 1968-72; head pressure physiology group Can. Def. and Civil Inst. for Environ. Rsch., Toronto, Ont., 1966-68; prof. biomed. engring. Duke U., Durham, NC, 1972-75, assoc. prof. physiology, 1975—80, prof. anesthesiology, 1972—2007, founder, pres. Nat. Divers Alert Network, 1980—2003, dir. rsch. dept. anesthesiology, Duke Med. Ctr., 1980, 2007; dep. dir. F.G. Hall Lab. Environ. Rsch., 1973-74; co-dir. F.G. Hall Lab. Environ. Research, 1974-77, dir., 1977-88; sr. dir. Hyperbaric Ctr., 1988—2007; exec. dir. Underseas and Hyperbaric Med. Soc., 2007—. Cons. in field Author: The Aetiology of Compressed Air Intoxication and Inert Gas Narcosis, 1966; author, editor: The Physiology and Medicine of Diving and Compressed Air Work, 1969, Russian edit., 1987, 4th edit., 1993, (autobiography) To The Very Depths, 2008; contbr. over 200 articles to profl. jours. With RAF, 1951-53. Recipient Letter of Commendation, Pres. Ronald Reagan, 1981, Sci. award Underwater Soc. Am., 1980, Leonard Greenstone Safety award Nat. Assn. Underwater Instrs., 1985, 1st Prince Tomohito of Mikasa Japan prize, 1990, Craig Hoffman Meml. award, 1992, Dan Seap Mentor award, 1998, Ernst & Young Entrepreneur of Yr. in Life Scis. award, NC and SC, 2002, Reaching Out award Diving Equipment Mfrs., 2002, Colin McLeod award Brit. Sub Aqua Jubilee Trust, 2011. Fellow Nat. Underwater Explorers Club; mem. Undersea Med. Soc. (pres. 1975-76, mem. exec. com. 1972-75, editor jour. 1976-79, 1st Oceaneering Internat. award 1975, Albert R. Behnke award 1983), Am. Physiol. Soc., European Undersea Biomed. Soc., Russian Acad. Sci. (fgn. mem., Pavlov medal 2001), Aerospace Med. Soc., Marine Tech. Soc., Croatian Undersea and Hyperbaric Med. Soc. (hon.), Nat. Acad. Scuba Educators (Meritorious Svc. award 1997). Avocations: gardening, swimming, boating. Home: 213 Lancaster Dr Chapel Hill NC 27517-3430 Home Phone: 919-932-5879; Office Phone: 919-490-6161. Business E-Mail: peterbennett@uhms.org. E-mail: pbennett25@nc.rr.com.

BENNETT, RICHARD, state legislator; b. June 25, 1957; m. Tricia Clark. Attended, Gulf Coast Jr. Coll., U. Southern Miss. Ret. employee Dupont; mem. Dist. 120 Miss. House of Reps., 2008—. Republican. Catholic. Home: 20108 Daugherty Rd Long Beach MS 39560 Office: PO Box 1018 Jackson MS 39215 Home Phone: 228-863-6483. E-mail: rbennett@house.ms.gov.

BENNETT, STEVEN ALAN, lawyer, insurance company executive; b. Rock Island, Ill., Jan. 15, 1953; s. Ralph O. and Anne E. B.; m. Jeanne Aring; children: Preston, Spencer, Hunter, Whitney. BA in Art History, U. Notre Dame, Ind., 1975; JD, U. Kans., Lawrence, 1982. Bar: Tex. 1983, Ohio 1995, US Dist. Ct. (no. dist. Tex.) 1983, US Ct. Appeals (5th cir.) 1983, US Supreme Ct. 1995. Atty. Freytag, Marshall et al, Dallas, 1982-84, Baker, Mills & Glast, Dallas, 1984-87; ptnr. Shank, Irwin, Conant et al, Dallas, 1987-89; gen. counsel Bank One, Tex., N.A., Dallas, 1989-94; sr. v.p., gen. counsel, sec. Banc One Corp., Columbus, Ohio, 1994-99; exec. v.p., chief legal officer, sec. Cardinal Health, Inc., Dublin, Ohio, 1999-2001; pvt. practice atty. Columbus, 2001—03; sr. v.p., gen. counsel Fed. Savs. Bank USAA (United Svcs. Automobile Assn.), San Antonio, 2003—04, exec. v.p., gen. counsel, sec., 2004—. City councilman, Mesquite, Tex., 1984-86, mayor pro tem, 1985; trustee Meadowview Sch., Mesquite, 1985-92; chair fin. com. St. Brendan Ch., Hilliard, Ohio, 1998-2003; pres., bd. dirs. Dallas Dem. Forum, 1993-94; bd. dirs. Ohio Hunger Task Force, Columbus; trustee Woodrow Wilson Internat. Ctr. for Scholars, Washington, 1996-2002, vice-chmn., 1999-2002; bd. dirs. Capital U. Law Sch., Columbus, 1998-2003, Ctr. Thomas More Studies, Dallas; mem., Citizens Commn. for City-County Svc. Integration, San Antonio, 2003-04. Fellow Am. Bar Found., Ohio State Bar Found.; mem. ABA, Dallas Bar Assn., Ohio State Bar Assn., Columbus Bar Assn., St. Thomas More Soc. (Dallas bd. dirs. 1990-94), Am. Corp. Counsel Assn. (sec. 1999-2000, bd. dirs. 1996-2002, chair policy com. 1997-99), Phi Beta Kappa. Avocation: landscape photography. Office: Gen Counsel C3E USAA 9800 Fredericksburg Rd San Antonio TX 78288 Office Phone: 210-498-1888. E-mail: steven.bennett@usaa.com.*

BENNETT, TONY (ANTHONY G. BENNETT), men's college basketball coach; b. 1969; s. Dick Bennett; m. Laurel Bennett; 3 children. Student, U. Wis., Green Bay, 1989—92. Profl. basketball player Charlotte Hornets, NC, 1992—95; basketball player North Harbor Kings, Auckland, New Zealand, 1996, player/coach, 1997, head coach, 1998—99; various basketball positions including recruiting and player devel. U. Wis. Badgers, Madison, 1999—2003; asst. coach Wash. State U. Cougars, 2003—04, assoc. head coach, 2004—06, head coach, 2006—09, U. Va. Cavaliers, 2009—. Recipient Naismith Men's Coll. Coach of Yr. award, Atlanta Tipoff Club, 2007; named Nat. Coach of Yr., AP, 2007, Coach of Yr., Pacific-10 Conf., 2007, Dist. IX Coach of Yr., US Basketball Writers Assn., 2007, Dist. III Coach of Yr., 2012. Achievements include ranking as the NCAA all-time leader in 3-point percentage (.497). Office: Univ Va Men's Basketball John Paul Jones Arena PO Box 400823 Charlottesville VA 22904-5425 Office Phone: 434-982-5400.

BENNETT, VANN, cell biologist, educator; AB in Chemistry and Biology, Stanford U., Calif.; MD, PhD, The Johns Hopkins U. Sch. Medicine, Balt. Investigator U. Md. Howard Hughes Med. Inst., 1987—; James B. Duke prof. dept cell biology, biochemistry and neurology Duke U., Durham, NC. Contbr. articles to profl. jours. Recipient Merit award, NIH; named Outstanding Young Md. Scientist of Yr. Mem.: NAS, Am. Soc. Clin. Investigation, Johns Hopkins Soc. Scholars, Am. Acad. Arts and Sciences. Office: Duke University Med Ctr 361 CARL Bldg Box 3892 Durham NC 27710 Office Phone: 919-684-3538, 919-684-3105. Office Fax: 919-684-3590. Business E-Mail: benne012@mc.duke.edu.

BENNETZEN, JEFFREY L., molecular biologist; BA in Biology, U. Calif., San Diego, 1974; PhD in Biochemistry, U. Wash., 1980; postdoctoral study, Wash. U., 1980—81, Stanford U., 1980—81, U. Calif., Berkeley, 1980—81. Rsch. scientist Internat. Plant Rsch. Inst., 1981—83; asst. to full prof. Purdue U., 1983—99, Umbarger prof. genetics, 1999—2003; Norman Giles Eminent Scholar chair in molecular biology and functional genetics U. Ga., 2003—. Vis. prof. U. Calif., Davis, 1998. Mem. editl. bd. Current Opinion in Plant Biology, Ency. Life Scis. Recipient McKnight Found. award, Plant Biology, 1986, Fulbright award, 1990, Faculty Rsch. award, Sigma Xi, 1995, Nehru Centenary Professorship, U. Hyderabad, 2002. Fellow: AAAS; mem.: NAS. Office: U Ga C426A Life Sci Bldg Athens GA 30602 Business E-Mail: maize@uga.edu.

BENOIT, GARY, insurance company executive; Ptnr. Stewart Info. Svcs. Corp. Office: Stewart Information Services Corp 1980 Post Oak Blvd Houston TX 77056 Office Phone: 713-625-8100. Office Fax: 713-552-9523. Business E-Mail: gbenoit@stewart.com.

BENSON, EDWIN WELBURN, JR., retired trade association executive; b. Nashville, Feb. 18, 1945; s. Edwin Welburn and Mildred B.; m. Jamie Suzanne Parks, Aug. 14, 1982; 1 child, Edwin III. BA, Vanderbilt U., 1967. V.p. The Benson Co., Nashville, 1970-78; assoc. exec. dir. Country Music Assn., Nashville, 1979-91, exec. dir., 1992—2005, chief strategic officer, 2006—08; pvt. practise, 2009—. Bd. govs. Nashville C. of C., 1994-97; bd. dir. Crescendo Music Cmty. Fund., 2001-, Leadership Music, 2004-, Tenn. Repertory Theatre, 2007-; bd. trustees, Country Music Found., 2000-05, Nash. Centennial Hosp., 2007-. With U.S. Army, 1967-70. Decorated Bronze Star for Svc. in Vietnam US Army; named a Tennessean of Yr., Nashville Tennessean newspaper, 2005. Mem. Leadership Music Alumni, Leadership Nashville Alumni, The Rec. Acad., Acad. TV Arts and Scis., Am. Soc. Assn. Execs. Avocations: golf, travel, music. Office: Country Music Assn 1 Music Cir S Nashville TN 37203-4312

BENSON, JOHNNY, professional race car driver; b. Grand Rapids, Mich., June 27, 1963; s. John and Judy Benson; m. Debbie Benson; children: Katelyn and Mikayla 1989 Berlin Raceway Champion, competed Amer. Speed Assoc. Series, 1990-93 with 9 wins, 48 top-10 finishes; winner 1995 NASCAR Busch Series Grand Nat. Divsn. championship, 1995, NASCAR Winston Cup Series, 1996—, ranked 11th in 1997 with 8 top-10 finishes. Named Rookie of Yr. 1990, Rookie of Yr. 1994, Busch Grand National, NASCAR Craftsman Truck Series Champion, 2008. Office: care NASCAR Bahari Racing 208 Rolling Hill Rd Mooresville NC 28117-6845 also: care NASCAR PO Box 2875 Daytona Beach FL 32120-2875

BENSON, RICHARD CARTER, mechanical engineering professor, dean; b. Newport News, Va., July 29, 1951; s. Willard Raymond and Helene Antonia (Kraus) B.; m. Leslie Ellen Brault; children: Stephanie A., James P., Kenneth C. BSE with hons., Princeton U., 1973; MS, U. Va., 1974; PhD, U. Calif., Berkeley, 1977. Registered profl. engr., NY. Tech. specialist Xerox Corp., Rochester, NY, 1977-80; asst. prof. mech. engring. U. Rochester, 1980-83, assoc. prof., 1983-89, prof. mech. engring., 1989-95, assoc. dean grad. studies, 1989-92, chmn. dept. mech. engring., 1992-95; sabbatical vis. U. Calif., San Diego, 1986-87; prof. mech. engring. Pa. State U., University Park, 1995—2005, head dept. mech. engring., 1995-98, head dept. mech. and nuc. engring., 1998—2005; dean Coll. Engring. Va. Poly. Inst. and State U., Blacksburg, 2005—. Founder, dir. Mechanics of Flexible Structures, 1982-97. Contbr. more than 60 articles to profl. jours. concerning mechanics of flexible structures. Fellow ASME (press oversight com. 1990—, Henry Hess award 1984); Am. Soc. Engring. Edn. Avocations: squash, game of go. Office: College of Engineering Virginia Tech 3046 Torgersen Hall Blacksburg VA 24601 Office Phone: 540-231-9752. Office Fax: 540-231-3031. E-mail: deaneng@vt.edu.

BENSON, ROBERT L., mining executive; Contract adminstr., Falkirk Mining Co. North Am. Coal Corp. (NACoal, subs. NACCO Industries, Inc.), 1976, v.p., eastern and southern ops., 2001—05, COO, exec. v.p., 2005—06, pres., CEO, 2006—; ops. mgr. NuCoal, 1998—2001; gen. mgr. Miss. Lignite Mining Co. (MLMC)(subs. NuCoal), 1998—2005, v.p. eastern and southern ops. Office: North American Coal Corp 5340 Legacy Dr Ste 300 Plano TX 75024-3141 Office Phone: 972-239-2625. Office Fax: 972-387-1328.

BENSON, ROBERT SCOTT, child and adolescent psychiatrist; MD, Emory U., Ga., 1968. Diplomate Am. Bd. Psychiatry and Neurology-pediatric psychiatry, Am. Bd. Psychiatry and Neurology-child and adolescent psychiatry, 1985, Am. Bd. Psychiatry and Neurology-forensic psychiatry, 1999. Resident pediat. Univ. Minn., Minneapolis, 1969—70; resident psychiatry Duke Univ. Med. Ctr., 1972—79, fellow; hosp. affiliation includes Sacred Heart Hosp. Pensacola. Office: Sacred Heart Health System Creekside Psychiatry 5190 Bayou Blvd Bldg 6 Pensacola FL 32503 Office Phone: 850-476-0977. Office Fax: 850-476-2558.

BENSON, TOM (THOMAS BENSON), professional sports team owner; b. New Orleans, 1927; s. Tom Sr. and Carmen B. Benson; m. Grace Trudeau; children: Rene, Tootsie, Donn, Susan, Rick, Mirian. Student, Loyola U., New Orleans, HHD (hon.); DSc and Bus. (hon.), Cleary Coll. Bookkeeper Cathey Chevrolet Co., New Orleans, 1948; mgr. Chevrolet Dealership, San Antonio, 1956-62; founder Tom Benson Chevrolet Co. name changed to Benson Automobile World, San Antonio, 1962; owner, chmn. New Orleans Saints, 1985—, New Orleans Pelicans (formerly New Orleans Hornets), 2012—. Mem. pres. coun. Loyola U., New Orleans; trustee Pensacola Naval Mus. Served with USN, 1945, USS South Dakota. Recipient Brotherhood award NCCJ, Order St. Louis medallion Archdiocese of New Orleans. Avocations: ranching, horse racing. Office: New Orleans Saints 5800 Airline Dr Metairie LA 70003-3876*

BENSON LEBLANC, RITA, professional sports team executive; BS in Agribus., Tex. A&M U.; cert. in internat. bus., Lowry May Sch. Bus.; grad. NFL mgmt. program, Stanford U. Exec. Edn. Grad. Sch. Bus., Calif. Various positions NFL, NYC, NFL Properties Pub. Group, LA, NFL Films, Mount Laurel, NJ; various positions in fiscal responsibility, bus. devel. and stadium rsch. New Orleans Saints, co-owner, exec. v.p., 2005—12, vice chmn., 2012—. Chair employee benefits com. NFL, mem. internat. com.; bd. dirs. La. Entertainment Co. Exec. prodr.: Horizon Entertainment. Mem. New Orleans Bus. Coun.; bd. trustees United Way, Loyola U., Shirley Landry Benson PACE Ctr. at St. Cecilia, Oblate Missionary Partnership. Recipient Pop Warner Female Achievement award, Pop Warner Little Scholars, 2008, Changing La. award, Lt. Gov. Mitch Landrieu, 2008; named one of 40 Most Influential Sports executives Under 40, Street and Smith's Sports Jour., 2007, 10 Most Powerful Women in Sports, Forbes mag., 2009; named to Women of Yr., Women in Sports and Events, 2008. Office: New Orleans Saints 5800 Airline Dr Metairie LA 70003

BENTLEY, CLARENCE EDWARD, savings and loan association executive; b. Ranger, Tex., Oct. 9, 1921; s. Clarence Edward and Rosa Estelle (Bryant) B.; m. Gloria Gill(dec. dec. 01, 2006), Dec. 9, 1943; children: Jon (dec.), Kitty, Perry (dec.). Student, McMurry U., Abilene, Tex., 1939-42. Pres. Abilene Savs. Assn., 1944-77, Southwestern Group Fin. Co., Houston, 1976-77; pres. United Savs. Assn. Tex., Houston, 1977-80, chmn. bd., 1980-85; dir., chmn. bd. Sandia Fed. Savs. & Loan, Albuquerque, 1986-89; dir. Kaneb Pipeline Partners, 1990—; gen. ptnr. Cels Oil & Minerals LP., 1998. Chmn. bd. dirs. United Fin. Mortgage Co., Dallas, United Fin. Group, Inc., Houston, 1980-86; bd. dirs. Kaneb Services Inc., Investors Mortgage Ins. Co., Boston; adb.bd. FNMA, 1980-81; trustee Thrift Instns. Short Term Liquidity Fund, N.Y.C., N.Y., 1982-83. Contbr. articles to profl. publns. Pres. Abilene Indsl. Found., 1970, United Fund Abilene, 1962, United Way, 1960; mem. bd. Tex. State Hosps., 1962-64; mem. Tex. Fin. Commn., 1964-76, chmn., 1971. Served with USAAF, 1942-43. Recipient Outstanding Citizen award City of Abilene, 1964, Disting. Alumnus award McMurry U., 1971, John T. Mahone award 1981. Mem. Nat. Savs. and Loan League (pres. 1970-71), Tex. Savs. and Loan League (pres. 1970-71), Assn. Thrift Holding Cos. (chmn. bd. 1985-87), Abilene C. of C. (pres. 1964). Clubs: Abilene Country (pres. 1951). Episcopalian. Home: 52 Rue Maison St Abilene TX 79605-4710 E-mail: cbent63@yahoo.com.

BENTLEY, DIERKS, singer; b. Phoenix, Nov. 20, 1975; m. Cassidy Black, Dec. 17, 2005; children: Evelyn Day, Jordan Catherine, Knox. Attended, U. Vermont; degree, Vanderbilt U., Nashville. Rschr. TNN TV; signed with Dangling Rope Records, 2001, Capitol Records, Nashville, 2002—. Musician: (albums) Don't Leave Me In Love, 2001, Dierks Bentley, 2003, Modern Day Drifter, 2005, Long Trip Alone, 2006, Greatest Hits: Every Mile a Memory, 2008, Feel That Fire, 2009, Up on the Ridge, 2010, Home, 2012, Riser, 2013; singer: (singles) What Was I Thinkin', 2003; narrarator The Rise of Kahne, 2009. Recipient Horizon award, Country Music Assn., 2005; named Top New Artist, Acad. Country Music, 2003. Office: Vector Management PO Box 120479 Nashville TN 37212 also: Capitol Records 11th Fl 3322 W End Ave Nashville TN 37203*

BENTLEY, FRED DOUGLAS, SR., lawyer; b. Marietta, Ga, Oct. 15, 1926; s. Oscar Andrew and Ima Irene (Prather) B.; children from previous marriage: Fred Douglas, Robert Randall; m. Jane Morrill McNeel, Nov. 7, 1997. BA, Presbyn. Coll., 1949; JD, Emory U., 1948; HHD (hon.), PhD (hon.), LHD (hon.), Kennesaw State U., 2000. Bar: Ga. 1948. Sr. mem. Bentley & Dew, Marietta, 1948-51; ptnr. Bentley, Awtrey & Bartlett, Marietta, 1951-56, Edwards, Bentley, Awtrey & Parker, Marietta, 1956-75, Bentley & Schindelar, Marietta, 1975-80, Bentley, Bentley & Bentley, Marietta, 1975—. Pres. Beneficial Investment Co., Newmarket, Inc., Happy Valley, Inc., Bentley & Sons, Inc.; founder, chmn. emeritus bd. Charter Bank and Trust Co.; founder, trustee emeritus Kennesaw State U. Mem. Ga. Ho. Reps., 1951-57, Ga. Senate, 1958; past pres. Cobb County (Ga.) C. of C.; founder, hon. curator Bentley Rare Book Galleries-Brenau U., Kennesaw State U.; mem., past chmn. Ga. Coun. Arts, 1976-89; mem. Gov.'s Fine Arts Com., 1990-92, Cummer Mus. of Art (hon. life); attache Ghana Olympic Com.; founder Cobb Emergency Svc.; fell. US Supreme Ct. Museum Acquisition Com., US Constitution Museum, mem. Corpus Cordis Aureum Emory U.; Served with USN. Recipient Blue Key Cmty. Svc. award, Founder's award, 1992, Clarisse Baqwell award for outstanding svc., Spl. Svc. award Kennesaw State U., Robert Cleveland award for lifetime achievement in law; named Citizen of Yr., C. of C., 1951, Leader of Tomorrow, Time mag., 1953, 1st Golden Cir. award Vol. Citizen of Yr., Atlanta Jour. Constn., 1981, Kennesaw Hist. Soc. Man of Yr., 1996, Brenau U. Man of Yr. award, 1996, President's award Kennesaw State U., 1999, Disting. Alumna Marietta HS, Bus. Assoc. of Yr. award ABWA, 2002, The Extra Mile trophy, 2003, Most Disting. Alumna, Emory U. Law Sch., 2004; Bridge named in his honor, 2000; Oct. 15th Day named in his honor City and Coun., City of Kennesaw, Kennesaw State U., 2006; fellow J. Pierpont Morgan Libr., Visionary Philanthropy Trophy, award United Supreme Ct. Fellow Am. Trust Brit. Libr., Marietta Cobb Mus. Art (founder), U.S. Supreme Ct. Hist. Soc., U.S. Const. Ctr.; mem. Ga. Bar Assn., Ga. Mus. Art (bd. advisors, hon. life), Nat. PTA (hon. life), Cobb Landmarks Soc. (founder), Kennesaw Mountain Jaycees (founder), Rotary (hon. life), Georgian Club (bd. dir.), Corpus Cordis Anceum Emory U. Republican. Presbyterian. Home: 1441 Beaumont Dr Kennesaw GA 30152-3201 Office: 241 Washington Ave NE Marietta GA 30060-1958 Office Phone: 770-422-2300.

BENTLEY, ROBERT JULIAN, Governor of Alabama, dermatologist, former state legislator; b. Columbiana, Ala., Feb. 3, 1943; s. David Harford and Mattie Boyd (Vick) Bentley; m. Martha Dianne Jones, July 24, 1965; children: John, Paul, Luke, Matthew. BS in Chemistry & Biology, U. Ala., 1964; MD, Med. Coll. of Ala., 1968. Cert. American Bd. Dermatology. Dermatology resident U. Ala., Birmingham, 1974, dermatologist, 1974—98; founding ptnr., pres. Ala. Dermatology Associates, 1974—2009; mem. Dist. 63 Ala. House of Reps., Montgomery, 2003—11; gov. State of Ala., 2011—. Deacon Sunday sch. tchr. First Bapt. Ch., mem. youth for Christ adv. bd., mem. family counseling adv. bd. Capt. USAF, 1969—75. Mem.: Med. Assn. Ala., American Acad. Dermatology, American Legion, VFW (life). Republican. Southern Baptist. Office: Office of Governor State Capitol 600 Dexter Ave Montgomery AL 36130 Office Phone: 334-242-7100. Office Fax: 334-242-0937.*

BENTON, JANINE SCHOLLNICK, lawyer; d. Arnold Schollnick and Eileen Hecht Levy, Chauncey Frederick Levy (Stepfather) and Ethel Schollnick (Stepmother). BA, Binghamton U., NY, 1991; JD, George Mason Univ., Arlington, Va., 1991—95. Bar: Va. 1995, DC 1998, US Dist. Ct. (ea. dist.), Va. 1998, US Dist. Ct. (DC dist.) 2004, Fed. Claims Ct. 2005. Paralegal supr. Epstein Becker & Green, PC, 1988—93, law clk. DC, 1993—95, assoc., 1995—2003; sr. counsel, chair govt. contracts group Albo & Oblon, LLP, Arlington, Va., 2003—04, ptnr., chair govt. contracts group, 2004—06; ptnr. Benton & Potter, PC, Falls Church, Va., 2006—. Deans scholar faculty George Mason Univ. Sch. Law, Arlington, 1993—94; dir. Holocaust Art Restitution Project, DC, 1997—2002, Women's Soccer Initiative, Inc., DC, 2004—, Creative Cauldron, Inc., Falls Church, Va., 2005—, Found. Youth At Risk, Falls Church, 2006—. Assoc. editor (jour.) George Mason Univ. Sch. Law Review, 1993—95; co-author (with D.B. Abrahams and R. Fioravanti): (book) Public Official's Guide to E-Government, 2001; contbg. writer (book) Government Contracts Compliance Guide, 1994; contbr. articles to profl. jours. Bd. dirs. Holocaust Art Restitution Project, DC, 1997—2002, Women's Soccer Initiative, Inc., DC, 2004—06, Creative Cauldron, Inc., Falls Church, 2005—06; bd.dirs. Nicholas F. Benton Found., Falls Church, 2005—06; bd. dirs. Found. for Youth at Risk, Falls Church, 2006. Mem.: ABA (assoc.), D.C. Bar Assn., Va. State Bar Assn., Arlington Bar Assn. (assoc.), Bd. Contract Appeals Bar Assn. (assoc.), Ct. Fed. Claims Bar Assn. (assoc.). Office: Benton Potter & Murdock PC 400 S Maple Ave Ste 210 Falls Church VA 22046 Office Phone: 703-992-9255. Personal E-mail: janinebenton@yahoo.com. Business E-Mail: jb@bentonpotter.com.

BENTON, NICHOLAS FREDERICK, publisher; b. Ross, Calif., Feb. 9, 1944; s. Frederick C. H. and Jeanne Emma (Brun) B.; m. Donna Carley, Apr. 15, 1979 (div. Oct. 1984); m. Janine Schollnick, Oct. 20, 1985 (div. Apr. 2000). AA, Santa Barbara City Coll., Calif., 1963; BA, Westmont Coll., 1965; MDiv cum laude, Pacific Sch. Religion, Berkeley, Calif., 1969. Reporter Santa Barbara News Press, 1961-66; dir. Christian edn. Plymouth Ch., Oakland, Calif., 1966-69; chief corr. Berkeley Barb, 1970-72; dir. advt. display Syufy Enterprises, San Francisco, 1973-76; regional dir. Exec. Intelligence Rev., San Francisco, LA, Houston, Washington, 1976—87; pres., CEO Benton Comms., Inc., 1987—; founder, owner, editor Falls Church News Press, 1991—. Author: The Gay Science Pagers, 2010—12, Metro Weekly. Clk. Emmaus Ch., 1989-92; bd. dirs. Arlington Symphony, Va., 1992-93, bd. dirs., mem. Falls Church Edn. Found., 2003-; founder N.F. Benton Diversity Affirmation Education Fund, 2005; mem. 1st Congl. United Ch. Christ. Recipient Bus. of Yr. award Falls Church City Coun., 1991, Bus. Contbn. to Cmty. award, 1997, Bus. of Yr. award Fall Church City Coun., 2001, Grand Marshall Falls Church Meml. Day Parade, 2001, Outstanding Varginian award, Equality Va., 2012; named Bus. Person of Yr., 2007; named to Media Honor Roll, Va. Sch. Bd., 1998, 2005, 09, 12. Mem. Greater Falls Church C. of C. (bd. dir. 1991—, pres. 1993-94, Pillar of Cmty. award 1993, 2003), LWV of Falls Church, mem. Falls Church City Dem. Com., Optimists Club, White House Corr. Assn., Nat. Press Club (Washington), Kennedy Ctr. Cirs. (Washington). Office: Falls Church News Press 450 W Broad St Ste 321 Falls Church VA 22046-3318 Office Phone: 703-532-3267. Personal E-mail: nfbenton@aol.com. Business E-Mail: nfbenton@fcnp.com.

BENTON, OBIE FOLSOM, publishing executive, writer; b. Elba, Ala., Dec. 28, 1932; s. Charlie D. and Johnnie Victoria Benton; m. Mary Rebel Bennett, July 3, 1952; 1 child, Sharon Jean. Cert. bldg. inspector So. Std. Bldg. Code Congress, 1992. Comml. bldg. insp. City of Nashville, 1987—98; CEO AAA-Writer's Inkhorn Pub., Winter Haven, Fla., 1998—. Pres. Ambassador Bible Inst. Pub.: The Great Deception, Full Moon Dance, Seniorscene Mag., World To Come Mag.; author: The Book of Prophecies, The Apocalypse. Min., dir. Ch. of God, Congregation Beth-el, Auburndale, Fla., 1981—2003. Independent. Avocations: writing, landscaping, travel. Mailing: AAA-Writer's Inkhorn Pub PO Box 7483 Winter Haven FL 33883

BENTON, THOMAS H. (TOMMY BENTON), state legislator; b. Athens, Ga., May 20, 1950; s. Thomas Frazer and Matilda Housch Benton; m. Karen Compton Benton; children: Leigh Ann, Thomas H., Jeff Jr., Zach. Clk. Commerce Drug, 1966—68; clk. & asst. mgr. Wt Grant County, 1969—74; clk. Mcdonald Ace Hardware, 1974—; tchr. Jackson County Bd. Edn., 1974—2004; mem. Jefferson Historic Preservation Com., 1994—; state rep. Dist. 31 Ga., 2005—; ret. Mem.: Jackson County Hist. Soc., Sons America Revolution, Mil. Order Stars & Bars, Sons Confederate Vets. (life), Nat. Rifle Assn. (life). Republican. Methodist. Mailing: 177 Martin St Jefferson GA 30549 Office: 501 C Legis Off Bldg Atlanta GA 30334 Office Phone: 404-656-0177. Business E-Mail: tbenton@legis.state.ga.us.

BENVENISTE, LAWRENCE M., dean; 1 child, Jeffrey. BS in math., U. Calif., Irvine, 1972; PhD in math., U. Calif., Berkeley, 1975. Staff economist for bd. governors FRS, Washington; mem. faculty U. Rochester, University of Pennsylvania, Northwestern U.; assoc. prof. fin. Wallace E. Carroll Sch. Mgmt., Boston Coll.; US Bancorp prof. fin. Carlson Sch. Mgmt., U. Minn., Twin Cities, 1996—99, chair fin. dept., 1999—2000, assoc. dean faculty and rsch., 2000—01, interim dean, 2001, dean, prof. fin., 2001—05; dean Goizueta Business School, Emory University, Atlanta, 2005—, Asa Griggs Candler prof. fin. Bd. dirs. Rimage Corp., 2003—, Alliance Data Systems. Office: Emory U Goizueta Bus Sch 1300 Clifton Rd Atlanta GA 30322 Office Phone: 404-727-6377. Office Fax: 404-727-6313. Business E-Mail: Larry_Benveniste@bus.emory.edu.

BENYUNES, ABRAHAM JOSEPH, pediatrician; b. NYC, June 30, 1938; MD, Georgetown U., Washington, DC, 1963. Cert. Am. Acad. Pediatrics; conservative Mohel Jewish Theological Seminary America (cert. by Rabbinical Assembly). Intern pediatrics Downstate NY Sch. Medicine, Kings County Hosp., Bklyn., 1963—64, resident pediatrics, 1964—65; resident Mt. Sinai Hosp., NYC, 1965—66; sr. attending pediatrician Miami Children's Hosp., Baptist Hosp.; clin. assoc. prof. pediatrics U. Miami Sch. Medicine, Fla.; with South Dade Pediatrics, Miami. Chief pediatrics US Pub. Health Svc. Hosp., Baltimore, Md. Fellow: Am. Acad. Pediatrics. Office: 7800 SW 87th Ave Miami FL 33173 Office Phone: 305-271-4711. Office Fax: 305-271-8732.

BENZLE, CURTIS MUNHALL, artist, educator; b. Lakewood, Ohio, Apr. 20, 1949; s. Arthur George and Martha (Munhall) B; m. Wendy Sue Wilson, 2007; children: Elliott, Kyle, Marisa. Student, Hillsdale Coll., 1967-69; BFA, Ohio State U., 1972; postgrad., Rochester Inst. Tech., 1973; MA, No. Ill. U., 1978. Owner, mgr. Oz Crafts, Hilton Head, SC, 1973-76, Benzle Porcelain Co., Columbus, Ohio, 1980—, Benzle Applied Arts, Huntsville, Ala., 1988—. Owner Creative Spirit Workshop; exec. dir. Ohio Designer Craftsmen, 1996—99; instr. U. SC, Beaufort, 1978—79; prof., chair dept. dimensional studies Columbus Coll. Art and Design, 1982—2007, dir. com. art project, prof. emeritus, 2007; pres. Japan-USA Exch. Exhbn., 1988—92; bd. overseers Am. Crafts Assn., 1991—96; trustee Am. Crafts Coun., 1992—96; chair Ala. Clay Conf., 2007—09. One-man show U. SC, 1979, Indpls. Mus. Art, 1984, Lawrence Gallery, Portland, Oreg., 1986, Running Ridge Gallery, Santa Fe, 1986, Akasaka/Green Gallery, Tokyo, 1987, 90, Zanesville Art Ctr., 1988, Swidler Gallery, 1990, Tsukushi Gallery, Kitakyushu, Japan, 1991, del Mano Gallery, 1998, Canton Mus. Art, Ohio, 2004-05, Sherrie Gallery, Columbus, 2004-05, 09, also others; exhibited in numerous group shows, 1971—, including Smithsonian Instn., 1980, 83, Leeuwarden, Suntory Art Mus., Tokyo, 1984, Cermaic Nat. Everson Mus., Syracuse, 1988, Internat. Competition of Ceramics, Mino, Japan, 1989, Seto Ceramic and Glass Ctr., Japan, 2003 21st Century Ceramics, Canzani Gallery, Columbus, Ohio, St. Joseph Gallery, Netherlands, 2004-05; represented in numerous permanent collections, including Smithsonian Instn., Everson Mus. Art, LA County Mus. Art, Cleve. Mus. Art., White House Collection Contemporary Craft., Taiwan Biennale, 2008., Met. Mus. of Art, Tucson Mus. Art, Crockaw Mus. Mem. Ohio Citizens Com. for Arts, 1986—. Nat. Endowment for Arts fellow, 1980, Ohio Arts Coun. fellow, 1981, 83, 84, 86, 88, 2005, Greater Columbus Arts Coun. fellow, 1987. Mem. Am. Crafts Coun. (bd. overseers 1991-96, trustee 1992-96), Nat. Coun. on Edn. in Ceramic Art, Ohio Designer Craftsmen (bd. dirs. 1984-88, pres. 1985-87). Avocation: gardening. Home: 706 Randolph Ave Huntsville AL 35801 Personal E-mail: curtisbenzle@gmail.com, info@www.benzleporcelain.com.

BEOHM, RICHARD THOMAS, safety engineering consultant; b. Youngstown, Ohio, Nov. 15, 1943; s. John and Eleanor (Leverence) B.; m. Rose Elizabeth Ralston, Oct. 25, 1968; children: Michael F., Eric R. B.E.E.T., Devry Inst. Tech., Chgo., 1969. Registered profl. engr., Ga., Fla., Mass., cert. NC. Asst. engr. North Electric Co. (ITT), Galion, Ohio, 1966-69; engr. Gen. Dynamics, Ft. Worth, 1969-71; fire protection engr. State of Ga. Self Ins. Program, Atlanta, 1971-80, acting dep. dir., 1980; fire protection cons. State of Ga. Risk Mgmt. Svc., Atlanta, 1981-87, acting field support supr., 1987-88, sr. loss control engring. cons., 1988-97; consulting engr. Atlanta, 1997—; consulting engr., fire marshal Ga. Tech., 2001—. Cartoonist Upson Home Jour., 1986-88; creator several safety coloring books; editor ASSE Refresher Guide for the Bd. Cert. Safety Profls. Safety Fundamentals Exam., 2002; author SFPE Reference Manual for F.P.E.Exam, 3d edit., 2005, 4th edit. safety engineering, 2012; contbr. articles to profl. jours Past mem. Fire Safe Ga. Commn.; vol. safety engr. and fire marshall Olympics and Paralympics, 1996; Ga. state games risk mgr. Mem.: NSPE, Soc. Fire Protection Engrs. (chpt. pres. 1998—99, nat. FPE-PE lic. com. problem review chair, S.E. chpt. Person of Yr. 1992, Nat. Hats Off award), Fed. Criminal Investigation Assn. (sec. Atlanta chpt. 1989), Am. Soc. Safety Engrs. (adminstrv. engring. divsn. 1997—99, editor 3rd edit. Safety Engring. 2000, past pres. Ga. chpt., past chair com. safety engring. tech. gorup engring divsn., editor refresher guide for BCSP Safety Fundamentals Exam. 2002, Engring. Divsn. Safety Profl. of Yr. 1996, cert. safety profl., bd. cert. bldg. inspection engr.). Democrat. Avocations: bird watching, butterfly collecting, illustrating, german language, church trustee. Home and Office: 981 Waymanville Rd Thomaston GA 30286-4759 Office Phone: 706-647-1380. E-mail: rtboehm@windstream.net.

BEPKO, GERALD LEWIS, retired academic administrator, law educator; b. Chgo., Apr. 21, 1940; s. Lewis V. and Geraldine S. (Bernath) B.; m. Jean B. Cougnenc, Feb. 24, 1968; children: Gerald Lewis Jr., Arminda B. BS, No. Ill. U., DeKalb, 1962; JD, Chgo. Kent Coll. Law Ill. Inst. Tech., 1965; LLM, Yale U., New Haven, 1972; D of Juridicial Sci. (hon.), Chgo. Kent Coll. Law Ill. Inst. Tech., 2003; LLD (hon.), Ind. U., Bloomington, 2007; LHD (hon.), Purdue U., 2009. Bar: Ill. 1965, U.S. Supreme Ct. 1968, Ind. 1973. Assoc. Ehrlich, Bundesen, Friedman & Ross, Chgo., 1965; spl. agt. FBI, 1965-69; asst. prof. law Ill. Inst. Tech.-Chgo. Kent Coll. Law, 1969-71; prof. Ind. U., Indpls., 1972-86, assoc. dean acad. affairs, 1979-81, dean, 1981-86, v.p., long-range planning, 1986—2003, chancellor, 1986—2002, interim pres., 2002—03, chancellor emeritus, 2003—, trustees prof., 2003—. Vis. prof. Ind. U.-Bloomington, summers, 1976, 1977, 1978, 1980, U. Ill., 1976—77, Ohio State U., 1978—79; cons. and reporter Fed. Jud. Ctr.; bd. dirs. First Ind. Bank/Corp., 1988—2007, Ind. Energy Inc. & Ind. Gas Co., Inc., 1989—97, Indpls. Life Ins. Co., One Am. Ins. Co., M&I Ind. Regional Bd., 2008—; mem. Conf. Commrs. on Uniform State Laws, 1982, mem. permanent editl. bd. for the Uniform Comml. Code, 1993—2004; mem. Ind. Lobby Registration Commn., 1992—2004, vice chair, 1992—96, chair, 1996—2000; mem. Ind. Commn. Higher Edn., 2006—. Author: (with Boshkoff) Sum and Substance of Secured Transactions, 1981; contbr. articles on comml. law to profl. jours. Bd. dirs. Lumina Found. for Edn., Riley Children's Found., 1998—, chair. exec. com., 2004—; bd. trustees Citizen's Energy, 2002—. Indpls. Chgo. Title and Trust Co. Found. scholar 1962-65; Ford Urban law fellow, 1971-72. Fellow Am. Bar Found., Ind. State Bar, Indpls. Bar Found.; mem. ABA, Ind. State Bar Assn., Indpls. Bar Assn., Country Club Indpls., Colliers Reserve Country Club Naples, Fla. Methodist. Office: Ind U Sch Law Indpls Inlow Hall 219 530 W New York St Indianapolis IN 46202-3225 Home: The Dorchester 406 6075 Pelican Bay Blvd Naples FL 34108 Office Phone: 317-278-9240.

BERAN, DAVID R., food products executive; BS in Acctg., U. Va., 1976; MBA, U. Richmond, Va. Various positions with fin. group Philip Morris USA, Inc., 1976—90, v.p. mktg. rsch. & planning, 1990—94, v.p. discount brands, 1994—96, v.p. Marlboro promotions, 1996—98, sr. v.p. planning & info., 1998—2000, sr. v.p. ops., 2000—02, exec. v.p. strategy, comm. & consumer contact, 2002—05, exec. v.p. fin., planning & info., 2005—07; exec. v.p., CFO Philip Morris U.S.A., Inc. Altria Group, Inc., 2007—10, vice chmn. bus. ops., 2011—. Head Philip Morris Capital Corp. Mem. exec. com., bd. dirs. Venture Richmond; bd. dirs. Richmond Ballet; mem. exec. adv. coun. U. Richmond Robins Sch. Bus. Office: Altria Group Inc 6601 W Broad St Richmond VA 23230 Office Phone: 804-274-2200.

BERCE, DANIEL EUGENE, financial services company executive, accountant; b. Milw., Nov. 10, 1953; s. Eugene Daniel and Mary (Mullen) B.; m. Mary Anne Tiger, Oct. 9, 1977; children: Sarah, Emily, Eric. BS in Acctg., Regis U., 1975. Staff auditor Coopers & Lybrand, 1975—86, ptnr., 1986—90; CFO AmeriCredit Corp., 1990—2003, pres., 2003, pres., CEO, 2005—10, GM Financial Co., Inc., 2010—. Bd. dir. Cash Am. Internat. Inc., 2006—; bd. dirs. AZZ, Inc.; ind. dir. Arlington Asset Investment Corp. Com. chmn. United Way, Ft. Worth, 1987—; bd. dirs. Lena Pope Home, Ft. Worth, 1989—, Cath. Charities, Ft. Worth, 1990—. Mem. AICPA, Tex. Soc. CPAs, Ft. Worth Club (fin. com. 1987—), Ridglea Country Club. Avocations: golf, basketball, bicycling, reading, travel. Office: General Motors Financial Co Inc 801 Cherry St Ste 3500 Fort Worth TX 76102 Office Fax: 817-882-5614. Personal E-mail: daniel.berce@americredit.com.

BERCHUCK, ANDREW, gynecologic oncologist, educator; married; 3 children. MD, Case Western Reserve U., Ohio, 1980. Resident, ob-gyn. Case Western Reserve U., Cleve., 1980—84; rsch. and clin. tng. gynecologic oncology U. Tex. Southwestern, Dallas, Meml. Sloan-Kettering Cancer Ctr., NYC, 1985—87; with Duke U. Med. Ctr., 1987—, F. Bayard Carter Disting. Professorship; dir., gynecologic cancer rsch. prof. gynecologic oncology, dept. ob-gyn. Duke Comprehensive Cancer Ctr. Chair scientific adv. com. Ovarian Cancer Rsch. Fund. Contbr. several articles to profl. jours.; editor of several books. Recipient award for best scientific presentation, Internat. Gynecologic Cancer Soc., Barbara Thomason Ovarian Cancer Rsch. Professorship, Am. Cancer Soc., 2006. Mem.: Soc. Gynecoligic Oncologists (pres. 2007—08). Office: Duke U Med Ctr DUMC 3079 Durham NC 27710 Office Phone: 919-684-3765. Office Fax: 919-684-8719.

BERENDZEN, RICHARD, astronomer, educator, author; b. Walters, Okla., Sept. 6, 1938; s. Earl Emmanuel and Florine Adora (Harrison) B.; m. Gail Anita Edgar, Nov. 26, 1964; children: Deborah Carol, Natasha Karina. BS, MIT, 1961; MA, Harvard U., 1967, PhD, 1969; LLD (hon.), W.Va. Wesleyan U., 1979; LHD (hon.), Bridgewater Coll., 1983; LLD (hon.), Kean Coll. of NJ, 1984, Seton Hall U., 1985; DS (hon.), U. Columbo, Sri Lanka, 1985; LLD (hon.), U. Charleston, 1986, U. Balt., 1990. Staff scientist Geophysics Corp. Am., 1959-64, Ling-Temco-Vought, 1961-62; lectr. Harvard U., 1964, 66; mem. staff Project Physics, 1965; mem. faculty Boston U., 1965-73, assoc. prof. astronomy, 1971-73, acting dept. chmn., 1971-72; prof. physics, dean Coll. Arts and Sci., Am. U., Washington, 1974-76; univ. provost Am. U., Washington, 1976-79, pres., 1980-90, prof., 1990—2006, prof. emeritus, 2006—; commentator on edn. and astronomy Stat. WUSA-TV/WTOP, Washington, 1984-90; cons. NASA, 1991, 98; sr. scholar Woodrow Wilson Internat. Ctr. Scholars, 2005—. Commentator on NASA for NBC-TV, 2003; cons. space sci. bd. NAS, 1973-74, mem. panel astron. survey com., 1971-73; cons. acad. affairs Am. Coun. on Edn., 1973-74; cons. to pub. cos.; Am. specialist in Asia Am. Council Edn. and Dept. State; adv. Am. Inst. Physics, Library of Congress, Internat. Comm. Agy., UNESCO, Smithsonian Instn., NSF; univ. evaluator Commn. Higher Edn. Middle States Assn. Colls. and Secondary Schs.; chmn. priorities and planning com. Assn. Am. Colls., 1978-80, chmn. pres.'s adv. com., 1977-79; program evaluator US Armed Forces Inst.; mem. rev. panel human resources NRC; lectr. USIA; host spls. on astronomy and higher edn. NBC-TV, 1976-77; organizer Space 2000 Symposium, 1999; frequent guest radio and TV shows; researcher on cosmology, history of astronomy, sci. and soc., Am. and internat. edn. Author: Education in and History of Modern Astronomy, 1972, Life Beyond Earth and the Mind of Man, 1973, Man Discovers the Galaxies, 1976, Is My Armor Straight? A Year in the Life of a University President, 1986, Come Here: A Man Overcomes the Tragic Aftermath of Childhood Sexual Abuse, 1993, Pulp Physics: Humankind in Space & Time Audio Series, 2000; founding editor Jour. Coll. Sci. Teaching; contbr. numerous articles and revs. to profl. jours. Bd. dirs. Bus. Coun. for Internat. Understanding, 1980-84, Assn. Am. Colls., 1981-83, European Inst., Group Hospitalization Med. Svc. Inc., Nat. Network for Youth, Inc., 1994-97; chmn. Com. on Fng. Students and Instl. Policy, 1981-82; chmn. Employment/Edn. Bur. Greater Washington Bd. Trade, 1989; co-chmn. AIDS project Meyer Found., 1988-90; mem. DC Com. on Pub. Schs., 1988-90; chmn. DC Commn. on Budget and Fin. Priorities, 1989-90, 94; mem. NASA Exploration Adv. Task Force, 1988-91; chmn. bd. dir. Orphan Found. Am., 1996-97; dir. NASA's DC Space Grant Consortium, 2000—. Named one of Top Young Educators Change: Mag. of Learning, 1978; recipient Mortar Bd. Faculty award, 1977, Freedoms Found. Valley Forge award, 1982, Glenn T. Seaborg award Internat. Platform Assn., 1997, Tchr. of Yr. award American U., 2006; fellow Com. Scientists Investigating Claims of the Paranormal, 1977-78. Fellow AAAS; mem. Internat. Astron. Union, Internat. Assn. Univ. Pres., Am. Astron. Soc., Am. Assn. U. Adminstrs., Am. Assn. for Higher Edn., Internat. Assn. Univs., NY Acad. Scis., Am. Assn. Physics Tchr., Astron. Soc. Pacific, History of Sci. Soc., Nat. Sci. Tchrs. Assn., Am. Assn. Higher Edn., Am. Conf. Acad. Deans, Washington Inst. Fgn. Affairs, Cosmos Club, Sigma Xi, Kappa Mu Epsilon, Phi Eta Sigma, Phi Kappa Phi. Home: 1300 Crystal Dr 1402 Arlington VA 22202-3234 Office: Am U Dept Physics Washington DC 20016-8058 Personal E-mail: rberendzen@aol.com.

BERENSON, GERALD SANDERS, physician; b. Bogalusa, La., Sept. 19, 1922; s. Meyer A. and Eva (Singerman) B.; m. Joan Seidenbach, Mar. 7, 1951; children— Leslie, Ann, Robert, Laurie. BS, Tulane U., 1943, MD, 1945. Intern U.S. Navy Hosp., Great Lakes, Ill., 1945-46; practice medicine specializing in cardiology New Orleans; mem. staff Charity Hosp., U. Hosp.; instr. dept. medicine Tulane U., 1948—52, prof. epidemiology Sch. Pub. Health, 1992—; asst. prof. medicine La. State U. Med. Sch., 1954-58, assoc. prof., 1958-63, prof., 1963-92, disting. Boyd prof., 1988-92, prof. emeritus, 1992—; prof. medicine, biochemistry and pediatrics Tulane U. Sch. Medicine, New Orleans, 1992—. Dir. Specialized Ctr. Rsch. Arteriosclerosis, New Orleans, 1972-87, Nat. Rsch. and Demonstration Ctr. in Arteriosclerosis, 1984-87, Nat. Ctr. Cardiovascular Health, Sch. Pub. Health and Tropical Medicine Tulane U., 1992—; sr. vis. physician Charity Hosp. La., New Orleans, 1948—; cons. Touro Infirmary, 1967—. Contbr. articles to profl. jours. Served with USNR, 1945-48. USPHS fellow U. Chgo., 1952-54 Mem. Am. Coll. Cardiology (gov. La. 1985-88, trustee 1988, chmn. prevention com. 1990-93), Am. Heart Assn. (Population Rsch. award, 2006, Disting. Scientist award, 2008), So. Soc. Clin. Investigation (pres. 1969), La. Heart Assn. (pres. 1971), New Orleans Acad. Internal Medicine (pres. 1966), Musser-Burch Soc. (pres. 1981), Soc. Geriatric Cardiology (pres. 1999-00), Sigma Xi, Alpha Omega Alpha. Office: Tulane Sch Pub Health Nat Ctr Cardiovascular Health 1440 Canal St Ste 1838 New Orleans LA 70112-2750 Office Phone: 504-988-7197. Business E-Mail: berenson@tulane.edu.

BERENZWEIG, JACK CHARLES, lawyer; b. Bklyn., Sept. 29, 1942; s. Sidney A. and Anne R. (Dubowe) B.; m. Susan J. Berenzweig, Aug. 8, 1968; children: Mindy, Andrew. BEE, Cornell U., 1964; JD, Am. U., 1968. Bar: Va. 1968, Ill. 1969. Examiner U.S. Pat. Off., Washington, 1964-66; pat. adviser U.S. Naval Air Systems Command, Washington, 1966-68; ptnr. Brinks, Hofer, Gilson & Lione and predecessor firm, Chgo., 1968—. Editorial staff Am. U. Law Rev., 1966-68; contbr. articles to profl. jours. Mem. ABA, Chgo. Bar Assn., Ill. State Bar Assn., Bar Assn. 7th Fed. Cir., Va. State Bar, Internat. Trademark Assn. (bd. dirs. 1983-85), Brand Names Edn. Found. (bd. dirs. 1993-2000), Meadow Club (Rolling Meadows, Ill.), Island Country Club (Marco Island, Fla.), Delta Theta Phi. Office: 1876 Calusa Ct Marco Island FL 34145 Business E-Mail: jcb@brinkshofer.com. E-mail: jberenzweig@gmail.com.*

BERG, CHARLES G., health products executive, lawyer; m. Casey Wiggins; 3 children. Degree in Law, Georgetown U.; BA in Polit. Sci., Macalester Coll., St. Paul, Minn., 1978. Founder, CEO Health Ptnrs., Inc.; exec. v.p., med. delivery Oxford Health Plans, Inc., 1998—2000, exec. v.p., med. delivery and tech., 2000—01, pres., COO, 2001—02, pres., CEO, 2002—04; CEO, Northeast region UnitedHealth Group, Inc., 2004—05, exec., 2005—06; sr. adv. Welsh, Carson, Anderson & Stowe, 2007—09; exec. chmn. WellCare Health Plans, Inc., Tampa, Fla., 2008—10, non-exec. chmn., 2011—. Bd. dirs. America's Health Ins. Plans, DaVita, Inc. Office: WellCare Health Plans Inc 8725 Henderson Rd Renaissance 1 Tampa FL 33634 Office Phone: 813-290-6200. Office Fax: 813-262-2802. Business E-Mail: charles.berg@wellcare.com.

BERG, DONALD CROWLEY, beverage company executive; b. Lincoln, Ill., Apr. 21, 1955; s. LaVerne C. and Bernice M. (Crowley) B.; m. Fran Lisa Swerling, Nov. 30, 1985; children: Courtney Ilyssa, Logan Patrick, Addison Amelia. BA in Acctg., Augustana Coll., 1977; MBA in Fin., U. Pa., 1983. CPA, Ill. Sr. auditor Ernst & Whinney,

Chgo., 1977-79; sr. internat. auditor Abbott Laboratory, Inc., North Chgo., 1979-81; asst. product mgr. Carnation Co., Los Angeles, 1983-84; dir. fin. planning Erbamont, Inc., Stamford, Conn., 1984-86, dir. fin. Far East area, 1986-88; asst. to pres. Brown-Forman Corp., Louisville, 1988-90, AVP dir. fin. and adminstrn. Nashville Mktg., 1990-91, v.p. beverage cons. group, 1992, dir. bus. devel. Advancing Marketing Group, sr. v.p. sales, mktg. dir., pres. Advancing Marketing Group, 1999—2001, sr. v.p., dir. corp. devel. and strategy, 2001—03, pres. Spirits Americas, 2003—06, sr. v.p., dir. corp. finance, 2006—08, exec. v.p., CFO, 2008—. Office: Brown-Forman Corp 850 Dixie Hwy Louisville KY 40210 Office Phone: 502-585-1100. Office Fax: 502-774-6633. Business E-Mail: dberg@bf.com.

BERG, STACEY LYNN, pediatric oncologist; AB, Harvard U., 1981; MD, U. Pitts., 1985. Diplomate Am. Bd. Pediatrics, Am. Bd. Pediatric Hematology-Oncology, Am. bd. Pediat. Hospice and Palliative Medicine. Resident Children's Hosp. Pitts., 1985-88; fellow pediatric hematology-oncology pediatric br. Nat. Cancer Inst., Bethesda, Md., 1988-91, biotech. fellow, 1991-94; asst. prof. pediatrics Uniformed Svcs. U. Health Scis., Bethesda, 1993-94, Tex. Childrens Hosp., Baylor Coll. Medicine, Houston, 1994—. Recipient travel award Am. Soc. Clin. Oncology, Washington, 1990. Mem. Am. Assn. Cancer Rsch., Am. Soc. Clin. Oncology, Children's Oncology Group, Pediatric Brain Tumor Consortium, Phi Beta Kappa. Office: Tex Childrens Cancer Ctr 1102 Bates Ave Ste 1220 Houston TX 77030-2303 Business E-Mail: sberg@txccc.org, sberg@txch.org.

BERGANT, PAUL R., marketing executive; b. 1946; married. With Sullivant Assocs., 1972-78; asst. gen. counsel Kansas Corp. Commn; gen. counsel J.B. Hunt Transport Services, Inc., Lowell, Ark., 1978; v.p., mktg. J. B. Hunt Transport Svcs. Inc., Lowell, Ark., 1980-86, exec. v.p., mktg., 1986, exec. v.p., chief mktg. officer & pres., Intermodal. Office: JB Hunt Transport Services Inc 615 JB Hunt Corp Dr Lowell AR 72745-0130 Office Phone: 479-820-0000. Office Fax: 479-820-3418. Business E-Mail: paul_bergant@jbhunt.com.

BERGAU, FRANK CONRAD, real estate, commercial and investment properties executive; b. NYC, Sept. 17, 1926; s. Frank Conrad and Mary Elizabeth (Davie) B.; m. Rita I. Korotkin; children: Mary, Rita, Francis, Theresa, Veronica. BA in English, St. Francis Coll., Loretto, Pa., 1950; MS in Edn. and English, Potsdam State U., NY, 1969. Cert. tchr., supr., adminstr., NY; cert. comml. investment mem. Tchr. English, Gouverneur Schs., NY, 1962-81, dir. continuing edn., 1968-81, summer prin., 1974-80; project dir. St. Lawrence County Bd. Co-op Ednl. Svcs., Canton, NY, 1974; pres. Irenicon Assocs., Clermont, Fla. Bd. dirs. St. Lawrence County Assn. Retarded Children, 1965—; pres. bd. dirs. Gouverneur Libr.; mem. Family Care Coun., Fla. Dist. 13. Mem.: KC (fin. sec. coun. 13240), NEA, NY Assn. Continuing Edn. (dir.), South Lake County Devel. Coun. (pres.), Lake County Bd. Realtors, Nat. Assn. Realtors, Gouverneur C. of C. (bd. dirs. 1963—66), Kiwanis (creator Terrific Kids award 1985), Gouverneur Luncheon Club. Personal E-mail: fconradb@gmail.com.

BERGER, DAN (BRIAN DANIEL BERGER), lobbyist; b. Allentown, Pa., Feb. 4, 1966; s. Richard D. and Joyce Berger; m. Aimee Elizabeth Hines, Nov. 17, 1990; 1 child, Shelby Elizabeth. AA in Econs., Appalachian State, Boone, NC, 1986; BS in Econs., Fla. State, Tallahassee, 1989; MA, Harvard U., Cambridge, 1999. Asst. dir. legis. and pub. affairs Farm Bur., Homestead, Fla., 1989—90; mng. ptnr. Power Rels., Inc., St. Petersburg, 1990—93; dir. govt. and pub. affairs Assn. of Realtors, 1992—93; dir. corp. and govt. rels. Fla. Employers Exch., Sarasota, 1993—95; dir. govtl. and legis. affairs Riscorp, Inc., 1995—97; dir. govt. & regulatory affairs Ins. Data Resources, Inc., Boca Raton/Sarasota, 1997—98; co-founder, mng. dir. eCapital Group, Sarasota, 1999—2001; sr. v.p. bus. devel. & strategic planning Indigo Investment Software, Inc., 2000—01; mng. ptnr. & co-owner ScoreCast Golf Tournament Software, Inc., 2001—; campaign mgr. and gen. cons. Katherine Harris for Congress, 2001—02; chief of staff to Rep. Katherine Harris US Congress, Washington, 2002—03; v.p. govt. rels. America's Cmty. Bankers, Washington, 2003—05; sr. v.p. govt. affairs Nat. Assn. Fed. Credit Unions (NAFCU), Arlington, Va., 2006—. Aide re-election campaign Senator George Kirkpatrick, Gainesville, Fla., 1986; campaign coord. Stop State Mandates, Tallahassee, 1987; campaign mgr. David Flagg for State Rep., Gainesville, 1988, Don Sullivan for State Senate, St. Petersburg, 1990; adviser Charlie Crist for State Senate, 1992; cons. Katherine Harris for State Senate, Sarasota, 1993—94; county coord. Bob Dole for Pres., 1996; advisor Katherine Harris for Fla. Sec. of State, 1998; county coord. George W. Bush for Pres., 2000. Found. dir. Boys & Girls Clubs, 1999—; bd. dir. Sarasota County Sports Commn., Fla., 2000—02, Juvenile Diabetes Found., 1999—2000; founding mem. Coun. for Emerging Nat. Security Affairs, Washington, 1999. Recipient Outstanding Young Man in Am. Mem.: Nat. Rifle Assoc, Congl. Sportsmen 's Found., B.A.S.S., Harvard Club of Sarasota, Seminole Boosters, Harvard Alumni Assn., Seminole Club of Greater Wash., DC, FSU Alumni Assoc, Pi Kappa Phi. Lutheran. Avocations: exercise, reading, golf, fishing, hunting. Office: Nat Assn Fed Credit Unions (NAFCU) 3138 10th St N Arlington VA 22201

BERGER, DOUG, state legislator; b. Miami, Fla., 1960; married. Former atty. 9th Jud. Dist.; dep. commr. NC Indsl. Commn.; state senator Dist. 7 NC, 2005—. Democrat. Baptist. Mailing: PO Box 1101 Youngsville NC 27596 Office: NC Senate 300 N Salisbury St Rm 518 Raleigh NC 27603-5925 Office Phone: 919-715-8363. Business E-Mail: Doug.Berger@ncleg.net.

BERGER, IRENE CORNELIA, federal judge; b. Richlands, Va., 1954; BA in Math., W.Va. U., 1976; JD, W.Va. U. Coll. Law, 1979. Bar: W.Va. 1979. Staff atty. Legal Aid Soc., Charleston, W.Va., 1979—82; asst. pros. atty. Kanawha County, W.Va., 1982—94; asst. US atty. (so. dist.) W.Va. US Dept. Justice, Charleston, 1994; Kanawha County cir. judge, thirteenth jud. cir. W.Va. Supreme Ct. Appeals, 1994—2009; judge US Dist. Ct. (so. dist.) W.Va., 2009—. Recipient Outstanding Alumna award, W.Va. U., 2006, Cmty. Champion award, Kanawha Inst. Social Rsch. & Action, Disting. W.Va. award. Fellow: ABA; mem.: Mountain State Bar Assn. (Merit award). Achievements include recognition as the first African-American female federal judge in West Virginia's history. Office: US Courthouse PO Box 5009 110 N Heber St Rm 336 Beckley WV 25801 Office Phone: 304-253-2438.

BERGER, JERRY J., anesthesiologist, educator; MD, Duke U., 1977. Diplomate Am. Bd. Anesthesiology, 1981, Am. Bd. Anesthesiology-pain medicine, 2004, lic. Fla., 1979, Colo., 2005. Intern Shands Hosp. at Univ. Fla., 1978, resident anesthesiology, 1981; intern St. Vincent's Hosp, 2005; hosp. affiliation includes Malcom Randall VA Med. Ctr.; assoc. prof. anesthesiology Univ. Fla. Coll. of Medicine, Gainesville, Fla. Office: Shands at the University of Florida 1600 SW Archer Rd Gainesville FL 32608 Office Phone: 352-265-0943.

BERGER, JOYCE MURIEL, foundation administrator, writer, editor; b. NYC, Oct. 20, 1924; d. Samuel and Daisy (Lichtenstein) Zeitlin; m. Arthur Seymour Berger, Feb. 11, 1946. BA magna cum laude, NYU, 1944, MA, 1946. Editor Theta Psychical Rsch. Found., Durham, NC, 1978-80; sec.-treas., libr. Survival Rsch. Found., adminstr. Internat. Inst. for Study of Death, Miami, Fla., 1980—. Convener confs. Internat. Inst. Study of Death, Miami, 1985, 87, Survival Rsch. Found., Miami, 1986. Co-author: Reincarnation Fact or Fable, 1991, Encyclopedia of Parapsychology, 1991, Fear of the Unknown, 1995; co-editor: To Die or Not to Die, 1990, Perspectives on Death and Dying, 1989; lectr. and seminar coord. in field. Right to Die conf. grantee Fla. Endowment of the Humanities, Tampa, 1987. Mem. Am. Soc. for Psychical Rsch., Soc. for Psychical Rsch., The Book Group of South Fla., Phi Beta Kappa. Avocations: bridge, tennis, travel, recording for the blind.

BERGER, PHIL, state legislator; Former state senator Dist 12, NC; state senator Dist 26 NC, 2003—; atty. Mem. Appropriations on Dept. of Transp. com., Appropriations/Base Budget com., Commerce com., Edn./Higher Edn. com., Fin. com., Judiciary I com., State and Local Govt. com., Transp. com. Republican. Address: PO Box 1309 Eden NC 27289 Office: NC Senate 16 W Jones St Rm 2008 Raleigh NC 27601-1026 Office Phone: 919-733-5708. E-mail: Phil.Berger@ncleg.net.

BERGER, WILLIAM BENEDICT, SR., federal marshal; b. 1953; BA in Criminal Justice, St. Thomas U., Miami, Fla., MPA; JD, Shephard Broad Law Ctr., Nova Southeastern U., Ft. Lauderdale, Fla. Cert. mediator Fla. Supreme Ct. Advanced through ranks to police capt. City of Miami Police Dept., 1974—89; chief of police City of North Miami Beach, Fla., 1989—2004, City of Palm Bay, Fla., 2004—10; US marshal (middle dist.) Fla. US Marshals Svc., US Dept. Justice, Tampa, 2010—. Past chmn. Commn. Fla. Law Enforcement Accreditation. Past pres. Greater North Miami Beach C. of C., North Dade American Cancer Soc.; past chair adv. coun. Miami-Dade Cmty. Coll. Sch. Justice & Safety Adminstrn. Recipient President's award, Fla. Crime Prevention Assn., 1991, Partnership award for innovation & tech., Beyond Computing Mag., 1999; named Police Chief of Yr., Fla. Police Chiefs Assn., 1992, 2003, 2006; named a Top Local Govt. Ofcl., Price Waterhouse/South Fla. Mag., 1993. Mem.: Fla. Police Chiefs Assn. (past pres.), Internat. Assn. Chiefs of Police (past pres.), Golden Glades Rotary Club (past pres.). Office: US Courthouse 801 N Florida Ave 4th Fl Tampa FL 33602 Office Phone: 813-274-6401.

BERGERON, WILTON LEE, physician; b. Scott, La., Feb. 13, 1933; s. Lee and Ida (Duhon) B.; m. Juanita Marie Landry, Aug. 3, 1957; children: David, Marcel, René, Jeanne. BS, U. South La., 1956; MD, La. State U., 1958. Diplomate Am. Bd. Allergy and Immunology. Intern Confederate Meml. Med. Ctr. (now La. State U. Med. Sch.), Shreveport, 1958-59; resident Lafayette (La.) Charity Hosp., 1959-60; fellow in allergy Tulane U. Med. Sch., New Orleans, 1968-70; pvt. practice Lafayette and Scott, La., 1960—; allergist, 1970—. Pres. Secular Franciscan Order, 1990-93. Mem. La. Allergy Soc. (former pres.). Republican. Roman Catholic. Avocations: fishing, computers. Home and Office: PO Box 98 # 90 Scott LA 70583-0098

BERGES, JAMES G., retail executive; BSEE, U. Notre Dame. Various engring. and mgmt. positions GE Co.; various positions, mfg. Emerson Electric Co., 1976, pres., Emerson Splty. Motors, group v.p., 1988—89, exec. v.p., 1989—97, vice chmn., 1997—99, pres., 1999—2005; chmn. HD Supply, Inc.; mgr. Clayton, Dubilier & Rice Funds, 2006—; ptnr., oper. prin. Clayton, Dubilier & Rice, Inc., 2006—; chmn. Sally Beauty Holdings, Inc., 2006—. Bd. dirs. Diversey, Inc., PPG Industries, Inc., 2000—, MKS Instruments, Inc., 2002—, NCI Bldg. Sys., Inc., 2009—. Chmn. bd. commr. St. Louis Sci. Ctr.; bd. dir. St. Louis Children's Hosp.; mem. adv. council Coll. Bus., Univ. Notre Dame. Office: Sally Beauty Holdings Inc 3001 Colorado Blvd Denton TX 76210 Office Phone: 940-898-7500. Office Fax: 940-898-7927. Business E-Mail: jberges@sallybeautyholdings.com.

BERGMANN, CARL, ecologist; PhD in Organic Chem., Ohio State U. With UGA Complex Carbohydrate Rsch. Ctr., Athens, 1985—, rsch. sci.; co-dir. Savannah River Ecology Lab., 2007—. Office: Complex Carbohydrate Rsch Ctr 315 Riverbend Rd Athens GA 30602 Office Phone: 706-542-4478. Office Fax: 706-542-4412. Business E-Mail: cberg@ccrc.uga.edu.

BERGNER, KEVIN J., insurance company executive; Exec. v.p., chief adminstrv. officer United Svcs. Automobile Assn. (USAA). Office: United Services Automobile Association 9800 Fredericksburg Rd San Antonio TX 78288 Office Phone: 210-498-2211.

BERGSTRESSER, PAUL RICHARD, dermatologist, educator; b. Ottawa, Kans., Aug. 24, 1941; s. Karl Samuel and May (Holmes) B.; m. Rebecca Louise Baird, Jan. 4, 1969; children: Daniel Baird, Laura Suzanne. AB, Coll. of Wooster, 1963; MD, Stanford U., 1968. Diplomate Am. Bd. Dermatology (bd. dirs. 1996-2005, v.p. 2003-05). Asst. prof. dept. dermatology U. Miami, 1975-76; asst. prof. to prof. Southwestern Med. Ctr. U. Tex., Dallas, 1976—, chmn. dept., 1984—2007. Mem. dermatologic drugs adv. com., FDA, 1986-88; mem. gen. medicine study sect. GMIA, NIH, 1989-93; mem. adv. coun. Nat. Inst. Arthritis and Musculoskeletal and Skin Disease, 1999-2003. Editor Photodermatology, Photoimmunology and Photomedicine, 1990-99; editor Jour. Investigative Dermatology, 2007-12; contbr. numerous articles to profl. jours. Odland lectr., Dept. Medicine Dermatology, U. Wash., 2011. Maj. U.S. Army, 1970-72. Recipient John Lathrop award, Coll. Wooster, 1963, Hopkins award, Stanford U. Sch. Medicine, 1968, Dermatitis Rsch. award, Am. Skin Assn., 1994, Marion B. Sulzberger Meml. award, 2000, Dohi Lecture award, Japanese Dermatological Soc., 2008; Fogarty Sr. Internat. fellowship, Dept. Dermatology, U. Vienna, 1993—94. Fellow AAP, AAAS, ACP, Am. Acad. Dermatology; mem. Am. Assn. Immunologists, Assn. Am. Physicians, Soc. Investigative Dermatology (bd. dirs. 1987-92, sec.-treas. 1999-2004; Stephen Rothman Meml. award, 2013), Am. Assn. Tissue Banks, Am. Dermatol. Assn., Assn. Profs. Dermatology (bd. dirs. 1990-95, pres.-elect 1998-2000, pres. 2000-02), Polish Dermatological Assn. (hon.), Finnish Dermatol. Assn. (hon.), Austrian Dermatol. Assn. (hon.), Norwegian Dermatol. Assn. (hon.), Japanese Dermatol. Soc. (hon.), Chinese Dermatology Soc. (internat. fellow mem. 2008), Philippine Dermatol. Soc. (hon.). Democrat. Methodist. Avocations: choral music, running. Home: 3758 Pallos Verdas Dr Dallas TX 75229-2740 Office: U Tex Southwestern Med Ctr Dept Dermatology 5323 Harry Hines Blvd Dallas TX 75390-9069 Business E-Mail: paul.bergstresser@utsouthwestern.edu.

BERK, STEVEN LEE, dean, internist, educator; b. NYC, Mar. 12, 1949; s. Sidney and Freida (Blank) B.; m. Shirley Anne Holtsclaw, Oct. 10, 1981; children: Jeremy Charles, Justin Lee. BS, Brandeis U., 1971; MD, Boston U., 1975. Diplomate Am. Bd. Internal Medicine, Am. Bd. Infectious Disease, Am. Bd. Geriatrics. Intern Boston City Hosp., 1975-76, resident, 1976-78; chief of infectious disease VA Med. Ctr., Johnson City, Tenn., 1979-83, chief of medicine, 1982-88; chief of infectious disease East Tenn. State U., Johnson City, 1982-88, dir. clin. clerkships in medicine, 1981—99, prof. medicine, 1986—99, chmn. dept. internal medicine, 1988—99, dir. internal medicine residency program, 1988—99; regional dean, prof. medicine Tex. Tech U. Health Sci. Ctr. Sch. Medicine, Lubbock, 1999—2006, Mirick-Myers endowed chmn. in geriatric medicine, 2001—06, dean, 2006—, v.p. med. affairs, 2006—10, exec. v.p., provost, 2010—. Author: Infections in the Nursing Home, 1990, Manual of Clinical Infectious Diseases, 1994; contbr. articles to profl. jours. Recipient Tchr. of Yr. award students East Tenn. State U. Coll. Medicine, 1982-93. Fellow ACP, Am. Coll. Chest Physicians, Am. Geriatric Soc., Infectious Disease Soc. Am.; mem. Alpha Omega Alpha, Am. Osler Soc., Phi Beta Kappa. Avocations: medical history, tennis. Office: Tex Tech University Sch Medicine Office of Dean 3601 4th St Stop 6207 Lubbock TX 79430-6207 Office Phone: 806-743-3000. Business E-Mail: steven.berk@ttuhsc.edu.

BERKE, ANDY, mayor, Chattanooga, Tennessee; b. Chattanooga, Tenn., Mar. 31, 1968; married; 2 children. BS, Stanford U.; JD, U. Chicago Law Sch. Former law clk. for Honorable Judge Deanell US Ct. Appeals, 10th Circuit; former legis. asst. to Bart Gordon US House of Representatives, Washington; former adj. prof. Kansas U. Law Sch.; atty. & ptnr. Berke, Berke, & Berke Law Firm; mem. Dist. 10 Tenn. State Senate, 2007—13; mayor City of Chattanooga, Tenn., 2013—. Democrat. Office: City of Chattanooga Mayor's Office 101 E 11th St Chattanooga TN 37402 Office Phone: 423-643-7800. Business E-Mail: mayor@chattanooga.gov.*

BERKE, RICK (RICHARD LELAND BERKE), newspaper editor; b. 1958; BA, U. Mich., 1980; MS, Columbia U. Graduate Sch. Journalism, 1981. Reporter, city desk Mpls. Tribune, 1980; reporter, then chief Washington correspondent Balt. Evening Sun, 1981—86; reporter, editor, then nat. political correspondent The NY Times, Washington, 1986—2002, Washington editor, 2002—05, asst. mng. editor for news NYC, 2006—10, nat. editor, 2010—11, asst. mng. editor, 2011—13; exec. editor POLITICO, 2013—. Fellow Inst. of Politics, John F. Kennedy Sch. Govt., Harvard U., 1997, mem. sr. adv. bd., 1999; vis. fellow Hoover Inst., Stanford Univ., 1997, 1999, 2001. Named one of The 25 Most Influential People in American Media, Brill's Content mag., 1999. Office: POLITICO 1000 Wilson Blvd Ste 601 Arlington VA 22209*

BERKEBILE, CHARLES ALAN, geology educator, hydrogeology researcher; b. Queens, NY, Mar. 4, 1938; s. Charles Dean and Bernice (Manlove) B.; 1 child, Patricia Berlowe; m. Martha S. Berkebile, May 17, 2003. BS, Allegheny Coll., 1960; MA, Boston U., 1961, PhD, 1964. Mem. rsch. staff MIT, Cambridge, 1963—64; asst. prof. Southampton Coll. L.I. U., NY, 1964—67, assoc. prof., dept. chair Southampton Coll., 1969—75, prof., assoc. dir. Southampton Coll., 1975—81; rsch. mineralogist Corning Glass Works, NY, 1967—69; prof., dept. chair Corpus Christi State U., Tex., 1981—91; prof., dir. Tex. A&M U., Corpus Christi, 1991—2004, prof., asst. dean, 1994—98, Regents prof., 2001—04, prof. emeritus, 2004—. Vis. assoc. chemist Brookhaven Nat. Lab., Upton, N.Y., 1966-67; vis. sr. rsch. geologist Princeton (N.J.) U., 1979-80. Contbr. articles to profl. jours. Mem. Regional Stormwater Master Plan Adv. Com., Corpus Christi, 1989-90, Mayor's Adv. Com. on Water Issues, Corpus Christi, 1991-92; treas., bd. dirs. Rockport (Tex.) Country Club Estates Homeowners Assn., 1991-94. Named Outstanding Educator, Koch Industries, 2001. Fellow Geol. Soc. Am.; mem. Tex. Ground Water Assn. (hon., life, bd. dirs., v.p. ground water sci. 1994, pres. 1995-96), Corpus Christi Geol. Soc. Avocations: golf, music. Home: 314 Champions Dr Rockport TX 78382-6906 E-mail: alanberk@wildblue.net.

BERKELHAMER, JAY ELLIS, pediatrician; b. Tuscaloosa, Ala., Apr. 8, 1942; s. Louis H. and Belle F. B.; m. Jacqueline Beth Colman, June 12, 1966; children: Beth Carolyn, Sara Kay, Adam Colman. BS, U. Mich., 1963, MD, 1967. Resident U. Chgo., 1967-70, asst. prof., 1972-78, assoc. prof., 1978-84, prof., 1984-93, assoc. chair, dir. residency program, 1986-93, assoc. dean ambulatory care, 1983-88; chair pediatrics Henry Ford Health Sys., Detroit, 1993-99. Prof. pediatrics Case Western Res. U., Cleve., 1994-99; clin. prof. pediatrics and communicable diseases U. Mich., Ann Arbor, 1994-2006; sr. v.p. for med. affairs Children's Healthcare of Atlanta, 1999—2007; clin. prof. pediats. Emory U., Atlanta, 1999—; sr. v.p. academic affairs Children's Healthcare Atlanta, 2007-10, sr. physician advisor, 2010-; adj. clin. prof. Morehouse Sch. Medicine. Lt. comdr. USPHS, 1970-72. Robert Wood Johnson Health Policy fellow NAS, Washington, 1978-79. Mem. Am. Acad. Pediatrics (pres. Ill. chpt. 1992, pres. 2006-07), Chgo. Pediatric Soc. (pres. 1987, Archibald L. Hoyne award 1993), Ambulatory Pediatric Assn. (pres. 1986). Office Phone: 404-785-7005. Personal E-mail: javeb@att.net.

BERKLEY, PETER LEE, lawyer; b. Newark, Mar. 10, 1939; s. Irving S. and Goldie A. (Karp) Berkley; m. Nancy R. Margolis, Aug. 2, 1964; children: James, Alison Wagonfield, John. BA, Williams Coll., 1960; JD, Harvard U., 1963. Bar: N.J. 1963, U.S. Dist. Ct. N.J. 1963. Assoc. Riker, Danzig, Scherer & Brown, Newark, 1963—68; ptnr. Riker, Danzig, Scherer & Hyland, Newark and Morristown, NJ, 1969-83; mng. ptnr. Riker, Danzig, Scherer, Hyland & Perretti, L.L.P., Morristown, 1984—95; ptnr. Riker, Danzig, Scherer, Hyland & Perretti, LLP, 1996—99, of counsel, 1999—2009, ret. ptnr., 2009—. Trustee Livingston (N.J.) Symphony Orch., 1975-89. Mem. ABA, N.J. State Bar Assn., Am. Coll. Real Estate Lawyers, Eagleton Estates Homeowners Assn. (pres. 2007-12), Harvard Law Sch. Alumni Assn. N.J. (pres. 1980-81), Williams Coll. Alumni Assn. Ctrl. N.J. (pres. 1986-89), Phi Beta Kappa. Home Phone: 561-627-8983. Personal E-mail: plberkley@gmail.com.

BERKMAN, LANCE, professional baseball player; b. Waco, Tex., Feb. 10, 1976; s. Larry and Cynthia Berkman; m. Cara Berkman, 1998; children: Hannah Leigh, Carly Anne, Katie Mae. Attended, Rice U., Houston. First baseman, outfielder Houston Astros, 1999—2010; first baseman, outfielder, designated hitter NY Yankees, 2010; first baseman, outfielder St. Louis Cardinals, 2011—12; first baseman, outfielder, designated hitter Tex. Rangers, 2013—. Named Nat. League Comeback Player of Yr., Maj. League Baseball Players Assn., 2011; named to Nat. League All-Star Team, Maj. League Baseball, 2001—02, 2004, 2006, 2008, 2011. Achievements include becoming the first switch-hitter in history with 50 doubles and 30 homers in the same season, 2001; leading the National League in: doubles, 2001, 2008; RBI, 2002; member of World Series championship winning St. Louis Cardinals, 2011. Avocations: golf, ballroom dancing. Office: Texas Rangers 1000 Ballpark Way #400 Arlington TX 07601*

BERKOFF, CHARLES EDWARD, pharmaceutical and biotech consultant; b. London, Sept. 29, 1932; arrived in US, 1963, naturalized, 1975; s. Maurice and Dora (Landy) B.; children: Timothy, David, Kevin; m. Heide-Gisela Triesch, 1997. BS in Chemistry (1st class honors), U. London, 1956; DIC, PhD, Imperial Coll., U. London, 1959. Chartered chemist. Dir. GlaxoSmithKline, Phila., 1964-83; exec. v.p. ImuTech, Inc., Huntingdon Valley, Pa., 1983-84; pres., CEO Antigenics, Inc., Horsham, Pa., 1984-89, Creative Licensing Internat., Inc., Sarasota, Fla., 1987—, CEBRAL, Inc., 1987—. Research fellow Johns Hopkins U., Balt., 1959-60; sr. research fellow Southampton U., Eng., 1960-61; mem. Adv. Council Smithsonian Sci. Info. Exchange, Washington, 1976-82. Contbr. articles to profl. jours.; patentee numerous U.S. and fgn. patents. Monsanto Research fellow Imperial Coll. Sci. and Tech., 1956-59; Fulbright scholar, 1959-60; recipient Statue of Victory World Culture prize Centro Studi e Ricerche Delle Nazioni, 1985. Fellow Am. Chem. Soc., Royal Soc. Chemistry; mem. Am. Arbitration Assn., Entomol. Soc., Am. Inst. Chem. Engrs.,

Licensing Execs. Soc. Clubs: Engrs. Club of Phila. Republican. Unitarian Universalist. Avocations: writing, tennis, guitar, bridge, swimming. E-mail: cebral@verizon.net.

BERKOWITZ, BRUCE R., equity fund manager; b. 1958; s. Barney and Hennie Berkowitz; m. Tracey Berkowitz, 1980; 3 children. BA in Economics, U. Mass., 1980. With Strategic Planning Inst., Cambridge, Mass., 1980—81, Merrill Lynch & Co., London, 1983—87; with fixed income divsn. Lehman Brothers Holdings, Inc., London, 1987—89, sr. portfolio mgr. NYC, 1989—93; mng. dir. Salomon Smith Barney, Inc., NYC, 1993—97; founder, mng. mem., chief investment officer Fairholme Capital Management, LLC, Miami, 1997—; pres. Fairholme Funds, Inc., Miami; chmn. The St. Joe Co., WaterSound, Fla., 2011—. Bd. dirs. Fairholme Funds, Inc., 1999—, White Mountains Ins. Group, Ltd., 2004—, AmeriCredit Corp., 2008—, The St. Joe Co., 2011—. Named Fund Mgr. of the Decade, Morningstar, 2010. Jewish. Office: Fairholme Capital Management LLC 4400 Biscayne Blvd 9th Fl Miami FL 33137 Office Phone: 305-358-3000. Office Fax: 305-358-8002. Business E-Mail: bruce@fairholme.net.

BERKOWITZ, PETER, public policy and government educator; b. Chgo., Aug. 5, 1959; s. Howard and June (Golten) B. BA English lit., Swarthmore Coll., 1981; MA philos., Hebrew U., Jerusalem, 1985; PhD Polit. sci., Yale U., 1987, JD, 1990. Asst. prof. govt. Harvard U., Cambridge, Mass., 1990-94, assoc. prof. govt., 1994—; assoc. prof. George Mason U., Arlington, Va. Co-founder, dir Israel Prog. on Constl. Govt.; sr. cons. Pres.'s Coun. on Bioethics; mem. Policy Adv. Bd. Author (Book): Virtue and the Making of Modern Liberalism, 1999, Nietzsche: The Ethics of an Immoralist, 1995; contbr. Mem.: Hoover Instn. (Tad and Dianne Taube sr. fellow). editor Varieties of Conservatism in American and Varieties of Progressivism in America, The Future of American Intelligence, Terrorism, the Laws of War, and the Constitution: Debating the Enemy Combatant Cases, and Never a Matter of Indifference: Sustaining Virtue in a Free Republic, co-editor Preventing Surprise Attacks: Intelligence Reform in the Wake of 9/11. Home: 18 Banks St Cambridge MA 02138-6039 Office: George Mason U 3301 Fairfax Dr Ste 370 Arlington VA 22201 Office Phone: 703-993-8020, 703-993-8247. Office Fax: 703-993-8012. Business E-Mail: berkowit@gmu.edu.

BERLIN, KENNETH DARRELL, chemistry professor, consultant, researcher; b. Quincy, Ill., June 12, 1933; s. Kenneth Marion Fischer and Mary Esther (Beckley) B.; m. Grace Frances Smith, Apr. 3, 1937; children: Grace Esther, James Darrell. BA cum laude, North Ctrl. Coll., Naperville, Ill., 1955; PhD, U. Ill., 1958. Postdoctoral fellow U. Fla., Gainesville, 1958-60; asst. prof. chemistry Okla. State U., Stillwater, 1960-63, assoc. prof., 1963-66, prof., 1966-71, Regents prof., 1971—. Spl. cons. Nat. Cancer Inst., Bethesda, Md., 1969—; cons. E.I. DuPont Co., Wilmington, Del., 1969-70, Am. Heart Assn., Oklahoma City, 1983-86, Ariz. Disease Control Commn., 1989—. Co-author: Organic Chemistry, 1972, Phosphorous Stereochem, 1977; contbr. rsch. Jour. Organic Chemistry, 1960, articles to profl. jours. Recipient Regents Disting. Tchg. award, 1998, Sigma Xi rsch. award Okla. State U., Stillwater, 1969, Okla. Chemist of Yr. award, 1977, named one of Top 20 Scientist Okla., 2013. Fellow ACS, Okla. Acad. Sci. (scientist of yr. 1976), Burlington No. Faculty Achievement award 1988, Eminent Faculty award 1998, Okla. medallion Excellence in Tchg. at Coll.-Univ. Regents Disting. Rsch. award 2003), Am. Chem. Soc. (elected fellow, 2011; Internat. Golden Torch award 2008, 10, Rall medal, 2011); mem. Internat. Soc. Heterocylic Chemists, Nat. Acad. Inventors (elect. mem. 2012, named Top 20 Scientists and Engrs., 2013, Outstanding Prof. award, Coll. Arts and Sci., 2014), Alpha Chi Sigma. Mem. Assembly Of God Ch. Office Phone: 405-744-5950. Business E-Mail: kdb@okstate.edu.

BERLINER, DANA, lawyer; b. 1967; d. Michael and Judith Berliner. BA in Psychology, Yale U., 1987; JD, Yale Law Sch., 1991. Bar: Pa. 1993, D.C. 1999. Law clk. to Hon. Jerry Smith U.S. Ct. Appeals (5th cir.), Houston, 1991—92; sr. atty. Inst. Justice, Washington, 1994, Arlington, Va. Achievements include winning case saving elderly widow's home from condemnation for Donald Trump's casino across the street; co-representing a Mississippi family whose home was being condemned for Nissan; state withdrew the condemnation; winning suit declaring New Orleans' prohibition on street vending of books a free speech violation; winning case declaring that would-be limousine drivers had been subjected to an unconstitutional application process by state agency. Office: Inst For Justice Ste 900 901 N Glebe Rd Arlington VA 22203 Office Fax: 703-682-9321. Business E-Mail: dberliner@ij.org.

BERMAN, BRUCE JUDSON, lawyer; b. Roslyn, NY, Oct. 9, 1946; s. Howard M. Berman and Soosha T. (Draizen) Hurwitz; m. Susan Leigh Readinger, Dec. 29, 1991; children: Andrew J., Josie A.;children from previous marriage: Daniel H., Ann N. BA, Williams Coll., 1968; MBA, Columbia U., 1972; JD, Boston U., 1972. Bar: Fla. 1973, U.S. Supreme Ct. 1976, U.S. Dist. Ct. (so. dist.) Fla. 1980, U.S. Ct. Appeals (5th cir.) 1980, U.S. Ct. Appeals (11th cir.) 1981, U.S. Dist. Ct. (mid. dist.) Fla. 1990, U.S. Ct. Appeals (3rd cir.) 2008. Assoc. Guggenheimer & Untermyer, NYC, 1973-79; from assoc. to ptnr. Myers, Kenin, Levinson, Frank & Richards, Miami, Fla., 1979-85; ptnr. Weil, Gotshal & Manges LLP, Miami, 1985-2000, McDermott, Will & Emery LLP, Miami, 2000—10, Carlton Fields Pa., 2010—. Spl. ad hoc trial com. Dade County Cir. Ct., Fla., 1988—2000; apptd. ct. reporter cert. planning com. Fla. Supreme Ct., 1995; apptd. Workgroup on access to pub. records, Fla. Supreme Ct., 2000, Fla. Supreme Ct. Com. Std. Jury Instrns. Civil Cases, 2000—06. Author: Berman's Florida Civil Procedure, West Group, 1998—2014; contbr. chapters to books. Mem. New World Symphony Cmty. Bd., Miami Beach, Fla., 1991—2000; bd. dirs. Feeding South Florida (formely Daily Bread Food Bank), 2002—10, v.p., 2002—08, pres., 2008—10. Mem.: Dade County Bar Assn., Fla. Bar (mem. civil procedure rules com. 1984—2004, chmn. 1988—90, mem. jud. adminstrn. rules com. 1988—2002, chmn. 1993—94), Internat. Bar Assn. Office: Carlton Fields PA 100 SE 2nd St Ste 4200 Miami FL 33131-9101 Home Phone: 305-665-4211; Office Phone: 305-539-7415. Business E-Mail: bberman@carltonfields.com.

BERMAN, LEO, state legislator; b. NYC, Oct. 21, 1935; s. Abraham Berman and Rose Sensor b.; m. Cara Sue Hughey, 1967 (dec.); m. Lou Ann Kuck, 2001; children: A.Y., Jennings, David S., Dean B., Susan Bourbonnais. BA in Polit. Sci. with honors, So. Meth. U., Dallas, 1969. Liaison officer to the sec. of army US House of Representatives, 1971—75; mem. Arlington City Coun., Tex., 1979—85; ret. pub. affairs exec. Sun Exploration and Prodn. Co., 1980—91; mayor pro tem City of Arlington, 1983—84; mem. Dist. 6 Tex. House of Representatives, 1998—. Alt. del. Rep. Nat. Conv., 1976; mem. adv. bd. Tex. Nat Guard Armory; chmn. Tex. Adv. Commn. Intergovtl. Rels.; bd. mem. Tyler Assn. Retarded Citizens; mem. adv. com. occupational med. residency & environ. sci. masters prog. U. Tex. Health Ctr. Ret. lt. col. US Army. Mem.: Tex. Assn. Bus. and C. of C. (life; former bd. dir.), American Legion, VFW, Tex. State Rifle Assn. (life), NRA (life), Mason, Lions. Republican. Meth. Office: PO Box 6028 Tyler TX 75711 also: Room EXT E2.908 Capital Extension PO Box 2910 Austin TX 78768 Office Phone: 903-939-2400, 512-463-0584.

BERMAN, LORI BETH, state legislator; b. NYC, June 27, 1958; d. George Gilbert and Sara Ann (Abrams) B.; m. Jeffrey Ganeles, Nov. 26, 1983; children: Caryn Elissa, Steven Aaron. BA magna cum laude, Tufts U., 1980; JD, George Washington U., 1983; LLM, U. Miami, 2002. Assoc. Margolies, Edelstein & Scherlis, Phila., 1983-84, White and Williams, Phila., 1984-87, Brownstein Zeidman & Schomer, Washington, 1987-89; v.p. legal & compliance Pointe Savs. Bank, Boca Raton, Fla., 1990-95; dist. rep. Congressman Robert Wexler, Boca Raton, 1997-99; assoc. Belson & Lewis, Boca Raton, Fla., 2002; mem. Dist. 86 Fla. House of Reps., 2011—. Mem., Jour. Internat. Law and Econs. Mem. exec. coun. United Jewish Appeal Fedn., Washington, 1987-89, Boca Raton, 1990—, Leadership Boca, 1992. Mem. ABA, D.C. Bar Assn., Fla. Bar Assn., Boca Raton C. of C. Democrat. Jewish. Office: 203 Northeast 1st Ave Delray Beach FL 33444-3714 also: Capitol Office 1401 The Capitol 402 South Monroe St Tallahassee FL 32399-1300 Office Phone: 561-266-6645, 850-488-1662.

BERMAN, ROBERT S., marketing consultant; b. NYC, Apr. 13, 1932; s. Sydney and Beatrice (Lipman) B.; m. Eleanor Rae Greenwald, June 16, 1956 (div. 1973); children: Thomas, Eric, Terry; m. Sherry Rona Frawley, May 29, 1975 (div. 1992); m. Sharon Louise Erbe, Oct. 5, 1996. BA, Cornell U., 1953, MA, 1954; advanced mgmt. certificate, Harvard U., 1964. Vice pres. Marschalk, Inc., NYC, 1962-64; exec. v.p. DeGarmo, Inc., NYC, 1964-70, 1970-80; exec. v.p., gen. mgr. D'Arcy MacManus & Masius, NYC, 1980-83; chmn. exec. com. Margeotes Fertitta & Weiss, 1984-88; ptnr. Ber/Cam Ptnrs., 1987-89; pres. Berman Mktg. Network, Naples, 1983—. Instr. dept. communications Parsons Sch., 1968-70, Pratt Inst., 1974-76; columnist Madison Ave. Mag., N.Y.C., 1968-72. Dir. Collier County Spl. Olympics Internat. Served to 1st lt. U.S. Army, 1954-56. Named Advt. Accountman of the Yr. N.Y. Advt. Council, 1969 Mem. Unity of Naples (bd. dirs.), The Conservancy, Civil War Roundtable N.Y., Komos Aiden Theatrical Assn., Quill and Dagger Club, Cornell Club, The Vineyards Golf Club, Naples Bath and Tennis Club. Home: 232 Silverado Dr Naples FL 34119-4651

BERMAN, STEPHEN ALAN, neurologist; b. Oak Park, Ill., Mar. 15, 1948; s. Edward and Esther Ruby Berman; m. Sherry Bursztajn. BS, U. Ill., Champaign-Urbana, 1970; MD, U. Ill., 1974, PhD in Biochemistry; MBA, U. Tenn., 2008. Diplomate Am. Bd. Psychiatry and Neurology, Am. Bd. Clinical Neurophysiology. Intern Greater Balt. Med. Ctr., 1976—77; resident in neurology Baylor Coll. Medicine, Houston, 1977—80, fellow in genetics and muscle disease, 1980—83; asst. prof. neurology U. Chgo., 1983—89, U. Tex. and MD Anderson Cancer Ctr., Houston, 1989—90; instr. neurology Harvard Med. Sch., Boston, 1990—92, asst. prof., 1992—96; prof. neurology La. State U., Shreveport, 1996—2000; prof. medicine neurology Dartmouth Med. Coll., Hanover, NH, 2000—; chief neurology White River Junction Vets. Med. Ctr., White River Junction, Vt., 2000—. Med. dir. lab. clinical neurophysiology La. State U., Shreveport, 1997—2000. Contbr. articles to profl. jours.; mem. editl. bd. E-Medicine, 1999. Med. adv. com. Multiple Sclerosis Soc., Shreveport, La., 1997—2000. Recipient Rsch. award, Clarence A. Hawkinson Meml. Fund, 1983—84, Brain Rsch. Found., 1984—87, Tchr. Investigator Devel. award, NIH, 1985—89, Physician Scientist award, Nat. Inst. Aging, 1992—96; grantee, Alzheimer Found., 1984—85, Louis Bloch Fund grant, 1984—87; fellow, Muscular Dystrophy Assn., 1981—83. Mem.: Soc. for Neurorehabilitation (cert.), Am. Acad. Neurology (quality stds. subcom., therapeutics and tech. assessment subcom. 1998), Alpha Omega Alpha (v.p. Ill. chpt. 1973—74), Phi Beta Kappa. Jewish. Office: University Central Fla Coll Medicine 6850 Lake Nona Blvd Orlando FL 32827 Office Phone: 407-266-1190. Business E-Mail: stephen.berman@ucf.edu.

BERMUDEZ, EUGENIA M. See DIGNAC, GENY

BERN, RONALD LAWRENCE, management consultant, writer; b. Anderson, SC, Aug. 23, 1936; s. Samuel Harris and Minnie (Siegel) B.; m. Elaine Kay Lefkowitz, Dec. 25, 1960; children: Brett Alan, Melissa Lynn. BA in Journalism, U. S.C., 1958, MA in Journalism, 1961. Writer William Barton Marsh Co., NYC, 1958-59; editor, writer Univac div. Sperry Rand, NYC, 1959-60; editor, mgr. Bell Tel. Labs., NYC, 1961-63; pres. Ronald Bern Co., NYC, 1965—85, 1990—2000; corp. sr. v.p. The LVI Group, Inc., NYC, 1985-90. Cons. AT&T Co., NY, NJ, 1966-85, The LVI Group, Nico Constrn.; bd. dir. Talon Corp., The Bern Cos., Inc., Healing Images Inc., Riverstone Svc., Inc. Author: An American in the Making, 1960, The Successful Salesman, 1972, The Legacy, 1975; Gone Fishin': The 100 Best Spots in New Jersey, 1998, Gone Fishin': The 100 Best Spots in New York, 1999, Mule Maddox, 2005, Sport Fish of Now Jerrey: An Anglees Guide, 2012; contbr. articles to profl. publ. Bd. dir. North Brunswick Little League, NJ, 1975-79; mem. North Brunswick Planning Commn., 1984. With US Army, 1958-59, 61-62. Fellow SC Press Assn., 1960. Mem. South Caroliniana Soc. Democrat. Jewish. Avocations: fishing, reading, travel. Home: 3306 Twilight Ln #6403 Naples FL 34109

BERNAL, DIEGO M., councilman; BA, MSW, JD, U. Mich. Social worker Communities in Schools (CIS), Harlingen, Tex.; atty. NAACP Legal Def. Fund, NYC, Mexican American Legal Def. and Ednl. Fund (MALDEF), San Antonio; pvt. practice San Antonio; councilman Dist. 1 San Antonio City Coun., 2011—. Office: City Hall PO Box 839966 San Antonio TX 78283 also: 1310 Vance Jackson San Antonio TX 78201 Office Phone: 201-207-7279, 210-207-0900.

BERNARD, H. RUSSELL, anthropologist, educator, editor; b. NYC, June 12, 1940; s. Herman Fink and Lillian (Rosenfeld) B.; m. Carole May Phillips, Jan. 28, 1962; children: Elyssa Lynn, Sharyn Kymm. BA, CUNY, 1961; MA, PhD, U. Ill., 1968. From asst. prof. to assoc. prof. Wash. State U., Pullman, 1966-72; rsch. assoc. Scripps Inst. Oceanography, La Jolla, Calif., 1972; from assoc. prof. to prof. W.Va. U., Morgantown, 1972-79; prof., chmn. dept. anthropology U. Fla., Gainesville, 1979—90, prof. anthropology, 1990—2007, prof. anthropology emeritus, 2007—. Guest prof. Nat. Mus. Ethnology, Osaka, Japan, 1991; vis. prof. U. Cologne, 1994-95, U. Mich. 2005, U. Kent, Canterbury. Editor (with B.P. Pelto): (books) Technology and Social Change, 1972; editor:, 1987; editor: (with J. Salinas) The Otomi, 1978; editor: Native Ethnography, 1989, Handbook of Methods in Cultural Anthropology, 1998, (jours.) Cultural Anthropology Methods Jour., 1989—98, Field Methods, 1999—; author: (books) Research Methods in Cultural Anthropology, 1988, 1994, 2002, 2006, Social Research Methods: Qualitative and Quantitative Approaches, 2000; co-author (with W. Penn Handwerker): Data Analysis with MYSTAT, 1994; collaborator: (films) Aegean Sponger Divers (Chris Plaque award 1975), 1969—; contbr. articles to profl. jours. Recipient Alexander von Humboldt Rsch. award, 1994-95; Fulbright Rsch. scholar, 1969-70; grantee NSF, 1967—, NEH, 1976-85, Am. Philol. Soc., 1972. Mem. NAS, Soc. for Applied Anthropology (editor Human Orgn. 1976-81), Am. Anthrop. Assn. (editor-in-chief Am. Anthropologist 1981-89, Franz Boas award 2003). Business E-Mail: ufruss@ufl.edu.

BERNARD, LOUIS JOSEPH, surgeon, educator; b. Laplace, La., Aug. 19, 1925; s. Edward and Jeanne (Vinet) B.; m. Lois Jeannette McDonald, Feb. 1, 1976; children: Marie Antonia, Phyllis Elaine. BA magna cum laude, Dillard U., New Orleans, 1946; MD, Meharry Med. Coll., 1950. Diplomate: Am. Bd. Surgery. Instr. surgery Sch. Medicine, Meharry Med. Coll., Nashville, 1958-59, prof., 1973-90, chmn. dept. surgery, 1973-87, dean, 1987-90, v.p. for health svcs., 1988-90; practice medicine specializing in surgery, 1959-69; mem. clin. faculty U. Okla., 1959-69, assoc. prof., vice chmn. dept. surgery, 1969-73, chmn. dept. surgery, 1973-87, disting. prof. emeritus, 1990—. Dir. Drew-Meharry Morehouse Consortium Cancer Ctr., 1990-96. Contbr. articles in field to profl. jours. Mem. Okla. State Bd. Corrections, 1968-69. With M.C. U.S. Army, 1951-53. USPHS research fellow NCI, U. Rochester, 1953-54 Fellow ACS, Southeastern Surg. Congress; mem. Soc. Surg. Oncology, Internat. Surg. Soc., Am. Assn. Cancer Edn., Alpha Omega Alpha. Democrat. Roman Catholic. Home: 156 Queens Ln Nashville TN 37218-1826

BERNARD, MACKENSON, state legislator; b. Mar. 4, 1976; m. Shawn Bernard; children: Macall, Mackenna. BS, Fla. State U., 1997; JD, U. Fla., 2002, LLM in Taxation, 2003. Traffic hearing officer 15th Jud. Cir., 2008; mem. code enforcement bd. City of Delray Beach, 2008, dep. vice mayor, 2008—09; atty.; mem. Dist. 84 Fla. House of Reps., 2009—, mem. fin. and tax coun., govt. ops. appropriations com., mil. and local affairs policy com., pub. safety and domestic security policy com. Adventist. Office: 303 House Office Bldg 402 S Monroe St Tallahassee FL 32399-1300 also: 526 24th St West Palm Beach FL 33407-5404 Office Phone: 850-488-8632, 561-650-6880.

BERNARD, PAMELA JENKS, lawyer; b. Montgomery, Ala., Nov. 27, 1955; d. Harford Perry and Mable (Sawyer) Jenks; m. Geoffrey Pedrick Bernard, Sept. 19, 1981. BA, U. Fla., 1976, JD, 1981. Bar: Fla. 1982, U.S. Dist. Ct. (mid. dist.) Fla. 1983, U.S. Ct. Appeals (11th cir.) 1983. Asst. atty. U. Fla., Gainesville, 1982-83, assoc. gen. counsel, 1983-87, gen. counsel, 1987—2006; v.p., gen. counsel Duke U., Durham, NC, 2006—. Pvt. investment trustee, Gainesville, 1976-83. Mem. Nat. Assn. Coll. and Univ. Attys. (former pres.). Office: Duke University Office of Univ Counsel Box 104124 Durham NC 27710 Office Phone: 919-684-3955. Business E-Mail: pam.bernard@duke.edu. E-mail: pamela.bernard@duke.edu.

BERNARD, STEPHEN ALAN, oncologist; b. High Point, NC, 1947; MD, U. N.C., 1973. Diplomate Am. Bd. Internal Medicine, Am. Acad. Internal Medicine, Am. Bd. Oncology, Am. Bd. Hospice & Palliative Medicine, 2008. Intern Colum-Presbyn. Med. Ctr., 1973-74, resident in medicine, 1974-76; fellow in hematol. oncology Washington U. Hosps., St. Louis, 1976-78; mem. staff U. N.C. Hosp., Chapel Hill, 1981—; prof. U. NC Sch. Medicine, Chapel Hill, 1990—. Mem. ACP, Am. Soc. Clin. Oncology. Office: U NC Sch Medicine Cb # 7305 Chapel Hill NC 27599-0001

BERNER, LEO DE WITTE, JR., retired oceanographer; b. Pasadena, Calif., Feb. 11, 1922; s. Leo De Witte and Maude Alena (Wright) B.; m. Arvetta Jo Hankins, June 28, 1947; children: Jo Anne Berner Thomas, Ernestine Elizabeth Berner Ice. BA, Pomona Coll., 1943; MS, UCLA-Scripps Instn. Oceanography, 1952, PhD, 1957. Fishery biologist U.S. Fish and Wildlife Svc., La Jolla, Calif., 1957-58; asst. rsch. biologist Scripps Instn. Oceanography, La Jolla, Calif., 1958-60, acting curator marine invertebrates, 1960-61; vis. asst. prof. U. Oreg., Oreg. Inst. Marine Sci., 1961; asso. program dir. NSF, Washington, 1961-65; adminstrv. scientist Tex. A&M U., College Station, 1965-66, asso. prof., 1966-72; asst. dean Tex. A&M U. (Grad. Coll.), 1967-71, assoc. dean, 1971-84, dean, 1984-87, prof. oceanography, 1972-87, prof. emeritus, dean emeritus, 1987—. Vol. George Bush Presdl. Libr. Archives, 1990-2002. Served with USNR, 1943-47. Fellow AAAS; mem. Am. Soc. Limnology and Oceanography, Oceanographic Soc., Assn. Tex. Grad. Schs. (1st v.p. 1981-82, pres. 1982-83), Sigma Xi. Home: 514 Helen Greathouse Cir Midland TX 79707-6116 E-mail: bunsen@suddenlink.net.

BERNEY, RAND C., oil industry executive; b. Phillipsburg, Kans., June 2, 1955; BS in Acctg., Kans. State U., 1977; MBA, Okla. State U., 1985. CPA, cert. Mgmt. Acct., Internal Auditor. Sr. staff acct. controllers for exploration and prodn. Phillips Petroleum Co., 1981, supr. controllers divsn. exploration and prodn., 1982—85, sr. supr. gas and gas liquids, 1985, staff dir. corp. tax, 1986—88, dir. corp. tax, 1989—92, assoc. tax officer, 1992—93, asst. treas., 1993—95, asst. contr., 1995—97, gen. auditor, 1997—99, v.p., contr., 1999—2002; v.p., contr. fin. ConocoPhillips, Houston, 2002—09, sr. v.p. corporate shared services Bartlesville, Okla., 2009—. Mem. Conf. Bd. Controllers Coun., Inst. Internal Auditors, Inst. Mgmt. Accts.; mem. acctg. com. American Petroleum Inst.; mem. bus. adv. coun. Kans. State Coll.; mem. growth com. Bartlesville Wesleyan Coll. Named to Acctg. Hall of Fame, Kans. State Coll., 2003. Mem.: Tax Execs. Inst. (treas., fed. tax chmn.), Fin. Execs. Inst., Okla. Soc. CPA's. Office: ConocoPhillips 511 S Keeler Ave Bartlesville OK 74003 Office Phone: 918-661-5500. Business E-Mail: rand.c.berney@conocophillips.com.

BERNHARD, JAMES M., JR., engineering executive; m. Dana Bernhard. Grad., La. State U., 1976. Founder Shaw Group, Inc., Baton Rouge, 1987—, CEO, 1987—, pres., 1987—2003, 2006—, chmn., 1990—, La. State Dem. Party, 2005. Mem. Pipe Fabricators Inst. Mem. Com. of 100 for State of La.; chmn. Select Coun. for Revenues and Expenditures for La.'s Future; active La. State U. Alumni Assn., Tiger Athletic Found., La. Tech. U. Found., St. George Cath. Ch. and Sch., Ducks Unltd., Krewe of Endymion; supporter United Way, Baton Rouge Area Found., St. George Cath. Ch., St. George Cath. Sch., East La. Tech. U. Recipient Prevent Child Abuse La.'s Corp. Champions for Children award, 1997, Ernst and Young Entrepreneru of Yr. award, 2001, Ace award, La. State U. Golf Program, Tiger Athletic Found. Augie Cross Meml. Mem. of Yr. award; named Marketer of Yr., 1994, Entrepreneur of Yr. in La., 1995, Perpetual Founder of Cath. H.S.; named one of Top Ten CEOs, Greater Baton Rouge Bus. Report, 1993. Mem.: Associated Building Contractors, American Welding Society, Associated Gen. Contractors. Avocations: golf, duck hunting, horseback riding, bill fishing, coaching Little League sports. Office: Shaw Group Inc 4171 Essen Ln Baton Rouge LA 70809 Office Phone: 800-747-3322, 225-932-2500. Office Fax: 225-932-2661.

BERNHARD, RICHARD HAROLD, industrial engineer, educator; b. NYC, Dec. 11, 1933; s. Harold Christian and Clara Cladel Bernhard; m. Cynthia Aline Petersen, May 22, 1969; children: Barbara Bernhard Windom, Harold Christia II, Hans Petter. B in Mech. Engring., Cornell U., Ithaca, NY, 1956; MS in Mgmt., MIT, Cambridge, 1958; PhD in Ops. Rsch., Cornell U., 1961. Asst. prof. indsl. engring. Cornell U., 1961—69; assoc. prof. indsl. engring. NC State U., Raleigh, 1969—80, prof. indsl. & sys. engring., 1980—2011, prof. emeritus. indsl. & systems engring., 2011—. Editor Inst. Indsl. Engrs., Atlanta, 1970—2004, fellow, 2008; vis. prof. Am. U. Armenia, 1993—94, vis. prof. Norwegian Sch. Economics, 1977—78; vis. prof. sch. econ. U. Canterbury, New Zealand, 1982, Norwegian Inst. Tech., 1988—89. Mem. & v.p. Raleigh Chamber Music Guild, 1995—. Recipient Nat. Engring. Economy Tchg. Excellence award, Am. Soc. for Engring. Edn., 2012; Scholarship, Fulbright Brazil, 1986. Mem.: Am. Soc. for Engring. Edn., Inst. Indsl. Engrs. Lutheran. Avocation: genealogy. Office: NC State University 488 Daniels Hall Raleigh NC 27695-7906 Home: 8811 Cypress Lakes Dr Unit 107-B Raleigh NC 27615-2128 Office Fax: 919-515-5281. Business E-Mail: bernhar@ncsu.edu.*

BERNHARDT, MARCIA BRENDA, mental health counselor; b. Jersey City, Aug. 22, 1938; d. Jerome and Mitzie (Cohen) B. BA, Fairleigh Dickinson U., 1960; MA, Columbia U., 1960-63, postgrad., 1968-70, Hunter Coll., 1973-74. Nat. cert. counselor. Rsch. asst. Tchrs. Coll., Columbia U., NYC, 1963-64; counselor JOIN, NYC, 1965-66; project assoc. Bd. Higher Edn. N.Y., NYC, 1966-68, Tchrs. Coll, Columbia U., NYC, 1968-70; counselor Nassau Community Coll., Garden City, N.Y., 1970-72; rsch. scientist Div. for Youth, NYC, 1972-73; rsch. assoc. Family Svc. Assn., NYC, 1974-76; counselor Div. Blind Svcs., West Palm Beach, Fla., 1984-96. Sec., chairperson adv. bd. com. Lighthouse for the Blind, West Palm Beach, 1984-90. Mem. AAUW, Am. Mental Health Counselors Assn. Democrat. Jewish. Avocations: theater, ballet, opera, art, swimming. Home: 40 Chatham B West Palm Beach FL 33417-1807 Personal E-mail: marciabrend@aol.com.

BERNHARDT, MONA LEIGH, oil and gas company executive; BA in Comm., Va. Poly. Inst. & State U., 1984; MS in Orgnl. Comm., Purdue U., 1988. With Exxon, 1990—96; joined Newfield Exploration Co., 2000, mgr. human resources, v.p. human resources, 2005—. Mem.: Soc. Human Resources Mgmt., Inst. Mgmt. Consultants, Houston Chpt. Office: Newfield Exploration Co 363 N Sam Houston Pky E Ste 100 Houston TX 77060 Office Phone: 281-847-6000. Office Fax: 281-847-6006.

BERNIER, DAVID, state official, odontologist; b. Patillas, PR, Jan. 21, 1977; m. Alexandra Fuentes; children: Adrián David, Miranda. B in Medical Science, U. of PR, Doctorate in Odontology. Exec. dir. PR Office of Youth Affairs, 2003—05, 2006; sec. PR Dept. of Sports and Recreation, 2005—08; pres. PR Olympic Com., 2008—12; sec. of state Commonwealth of PR, San Juan, 2013—. Former athlete, mem. PR Nat. Fencing Team. Popular Democratic Party. Office: Office of the Secretary of State Department of State Box 9023271 San Juan PR 00902 Office Phone: 787-722-2121. Office Fax: 787-722-2684.*

BERNS, KENNETH IRA, physician; b. Cleve., June 14, 1938; s. Charles and Delnet (Cohn) Berns; m. Laura Louise Lawless, June 26, 1964; children: Jonathan Charles, Deborah Louise. Student, Harvard U., 1956—59; AB, Johns Hopkins U., 1960, PhD, 1964, MD, 1966. Intern Johns Hopkins Hosp., 1966—67; asst. prof. microbiology Johns Hopkins U. Sch. Medicine, 1970—74, asst. prof. pediat., 1970—76, asso. prof. microbiology, 1974—76; dir. Johns Hopkins U. Sch. Medicine (Yr. I program), 1973—76; prof., chmn. dept. immunology and med. microbiology, prof. pediat. U. Fla. Coll. Medicine, Gainesville, 1976—84, disting. prof., 2006—, dean, 1997—2002, v.p. health affairs, 2000—02; R.A. Rees Pritchett prof., chmn. dept. microbiology Cornell U. Med. Coll., 1984—97; pres., CEO Mt. Sinai Med. Ctr., NYC, 2002—03; dir. U. Fla. Genetics Inst., 2003—. Howard Hughes med. investigator, 1970—75; mem. microbiology test com. Nat. Bd. Med. Examiners, 1979—82, chmn., 1983—86, mem. exec. bd., 1986—95; mem. Recombinant DNA adv. com. NIH, 1980—83, chmn., 1982—83, mem. virology study sect., 1985—89; mem. genetic biology panel NSF, 1981—84; Fogarty sr. internat. fellow virology dept. Weizmann Inst. Sci., Rehovot, Israel, 1982—83; ad hoc mem. Bd. Sci. Counselors Nat. Inst. Allergy and Infectious Diseases, 1982, permanent mem., 1992—96; del. U.S.-Japan Coop. Program on Recombinant DNA, 1981; mem. Internat. Com. Taxonomy of Viruses, 1981—98; mem. virology and microbiology adv. com. Am. Cancer Soc., 1985—89, mem. liaison com. on med. edn., 1989—92; mem. composite com. U.S. Med. Licensing Exam., 1995—98; nat. adv. coun. Nat. Ctr. Rsch. Resources, 1999—2003. Bd. trustees Johns Hopkins U., 2000—06; bd. dir. Rosalind Franklin Soc., 2007—. With USPHS, 1967—70. Recipient Faculty Rsch. award, Am. Cancer Soc., 1975—76, Disting. Svc. award, Nat. Bd. Med. Examiners, 1995; named Disting. Svc. Mem., Assn. Am. Med. Coll., 2003; grantee Am. Cancer Soc., 1970—72, NIH, 1970—76, 1980—2005, NSF, 1973—75, 1979—80; fellow Shell Oil, 1963—64; Fogarty Sr. Internat. Fellowship, 1982—83. Fellow: AAAS; mem.: NAS, Inst. Medicine of NAS, Internat. Union Microbiol. Socs. (v.p. 1990—94), Soc. Pediatric Rsch., Soc. Gen. Microbiology, Am. Soc. Virology (pres. 1988—89), Assn. Med. Sch. Microbiology Chairmen (chmn. com. pub. policy 1979, counselor 1980—83, pres. 1985), Am. Soc. Microbiology (chair Public and Scientific Affairs Bd. 1990—96, pres. 1996—97), Am. Soc. Biol. Chemists, Am. Acad. Microbiology (bd. govs. 2003—), Alpha Omega Alpha, Sigma Xi, Phi Beta Kappa. Office: Univ Fla Coll of Medicine PO Box 103610 Gainesville FL 32610-3610 Office Phone: 352-273-8100. Business E-Mail: kberns@ufl.edu.

BERNSEN, HAROLD JOHN, political scientist, educator, businessmen, retired military officer; b. Boston, Nov. 25, 1936; s. Harold Arthur and Solveig Bachrud (Birkrem) B.; m. Doris Ann Champion, Mar. 5, 1960. BA, Dartmouth Coll., 1958. Commd. ensign USN, 1958, advanced through grades to rear adm., 1988, comdg. officer USS LaSalle, 1980-82, comdg. officer USS Lexington Pensacola, Fla., 1983-84, dir. plans and policy, staff comdr. in chief U.S. Cen. Command Tampa, Fla., 1985-86, comdr. Mideast Force, 1986-88, dir. plans and policy staff comdr. in chief Atlantic Fleet Norfolk, 1988-91; dep., chief of staff, comdr. in chief Atlantic Fleet, 1991; ret., 1991. Spkr. on Mid. East issues. Dir. Middle East Ops. Advanced Bio Catalytics Corp.; bd. dirs. Am. Bahraini Friendship Soc., Hampton Rds. World Affairs Coun. Decorated Disting. Svc. Medal, Def. Superior Svc. Medal, Legion of Merit; Royal Norwegian Order of Merit (Norway); Order 1st Class (Bahrain). Mem.: Assn. Naval Aviation, Sons of Norway, Army Navy Club, N.Y. Yacht Club. Avocations: sailing, cooking, gardening, skiing. Office Phone: 757-651-4811. E-mail: hbernsen@cox.net.

BERNSTEIN, IRA HARVEY, clinical science professor; b. NYC, Aug. 10, 1938; s. Louis and Sally (Cantor) B.; m. Linda Jean Greif, June 4, 1961; children: Cari Gaye, Dina Louise. BA, U. Mich., 1959; MA, Vanderbilt U., 1961, PhD, 1963. Instr. U. Ill., Urbana, 1963-64; clin. prof. U. Tex. S.W. Med. Sch., Dallas, 1976-78, 80-89; asst. prof. to prof. U. Tex., Arlington, 1965—2007. Vis. prof. North Tex. State U., Denton, 1972, prof. Dept Clin. Scis. Sch. Allied Health, U. Tex. Southwe. Med. Ctr., adj. prof. U. Tex.-Arlington, 2007. Author: (with C.G. Garbin and G.K. Teng) Applied Multivariate Analysis, 1988, (with J.C. Nunnally) Psychometric Theory, 3d edit., 1994, Computer Literacy: Getting the Most From Your PC, 1998,(with P.Havig), (with N. Rowe) Statistical Data Analysis for the Personal Computer, 2001; editor: Behavior Rsch. Methods; contbr. over 120 articles to profl. jours. Recipient award Am. Med. Assn., 1969, Am. Acad. Ophthalnology-Otolaryngology, 1969. Fellow: APA; mem.: Psychonomic Soc. Democrat. Jewish. Avocations: jazz, travel. Home: 5809 Brookstown Dr Dallas TX 75230-2617 Office: Florence Bioinfo Ctr 5th Floor Suite 506 5323 Harry Hines Blvd Dallas TX 75390-9066 Office Phone: 214-648-9543. Personal E-mail: irahbernstein@gmail.com. Business E-Mail: ira.bernstein@utsouthwestern.edu.

BERNSTEIN, JOSEPH, lawyer; b. New Orleans, Feb. 12, 1930; s. Eugene Julian and Lola (Schlemoff) Bernstein; m. Phyllis Maxine Askanase, Sept. 4, 1955; children: Jill, Barbara, Elizabeth R., Jonathan Joseph. BS, U. Ala., 1952; LLB, Tulane U., 1957. Bar: La. 1957. Clerk to Justice E. Howard McCaleb of La. Supreme Ct., 1957; assoc. Jones, Walker, Waechter, Poitevent, Carrere & Denegre, 1957—60, ptnr., 1960—65; pvt. practice New Orleans, 1965—. Former gen. counsel Alliance for Affordable Energy. Past pres. New Orleans chpt. March of Dimes, New Orleans Jewish Cmty. Ctr.; past nat. exec. com. Am. Jewish Com.; trustee New Orleans Symphony Soc.; past mem. adv. council New Orleans Mus. Art. 2d lt. AUS, 1952—54. Mem.: ABA, La. Bar Assn., Zeta Beta Tau, Phi Delta Phi. Republican. Jewish. Home: 708 Explanade Ave Bay Saint Louis MS 39520 Office Phone: 228-466-4423. E-mail: Joelou1@bellsouth.net.

BERNSTEIN, MICHELLE, chef; Grad., Johnson & Wales U., 1994. With Ailey Dance Theater, NYC; chef Red Fish Grill, Coral Gables, Fla., Christy's, Coral Gables, Tantra, Miami Beach; tng. Alison on Dominick, Le Bernardin, NYC; exec. chef, co-owner The Strand; exec. chef Azul, Miami; owner, exec. chef Michy's, Miami, 2006—. Co-host (TV series) Melting Pot, The Food Network, participant Iron Chef, 2005, appeared on Today Show, featured in NY Times, Bon Appetit, Gourmet, Food & Wine mag. Named Most Creative Chef in Miami, O Mag., 2006, Best Chef: South, James Beard Found., 2008. Office: Michys 6927 Biscayne Blvd Miami FL 33138

BERRARD, STEVEN R., investment company and former automotive retail company executive; b. 1954; BS in Acctg., Fla. Atlantic U. Auditor Coopers & Lybrand; pres. Huizenga Holdings, Inc.; sr. v.p., treas., CFO Blockbuster Entertainment Corp., 1987—93, pres., COO, 1993—94, pres., CEO, 1994—96, vice chmn.; co-founder, co-CEO AutoNation, Inc. (formerly Republic Industries Inc.), 1996—99; co-founder, mng. ptnr. New River Capital Ptnrs., Ft. Lauderdale, 1997—; pres., CEO Spelling Entertainment Group, 1993—96. Bd. dirs. Blockbuster Entertainment Corp., 1989—94, Viacom, Inc., 1994—96, Boca Resorts, Inc., 1996—2004, HealthSouth Corp., 2004—. Office: New River Capital Ptnrs Ste 1220 PO Box 19190 Fort Lauderdale FL 33318-0190

BERREY, ROBERT FORREST, lawyer; b. Oak Park, Ill., Dec. 7, 1939; s. Rhodes Clay and Regina (Kasprovich) B.; m. Rebecca L. Newell, Apr. 10, 1993; children from previous marriage: Adam Forrist, Ellen Catherine, Kevin Joseph. AB, Harvard U., 1962; JD, U. Chgo., 1968. Bar: Ill. 1969, Ohio 1986. Atty. Torshen, Fortes & Eiger, Chgo., 1970-75; atty. Jewel Cos., Inc., Chgo., 1975-76, sec., 1976-80, v.p., sec., gen. counsel, 1980-85; v.p., gen. counsel Tomkins (formerly Philips) Industries, Inc., 1986-91; ptnr. Chernesky, Heyman & Kress, Dayton, Ohio, 1991-98; formerly of counsel Bieser, Greer & Landis LLP, Dayton, Ohio; venture capital investments Chapel Hill, NC. With AUS, 1962-65. Mem. Governors Club, Old Chatham Golf Club. Office Phone: 919-358-5005.

BERRIGAN, HELEN GINGER, federal judge; b. New Rochelle, NY, Apr. 15, 1948; m. Joseph E. Berrigan Jr. BA, U. Wis., 1969; MA, Am. U., 1971; JD, La. State U., 1977. Staff rschr. Senator Harold E. Hughes, 1971-72; legis. aide Senator Joseph E. Biden, 1972-73; asst. to mayor City of Fayette, Miss., 1973-74; law clk. La. Dept. Corrections, 1975-77; staff atty. Gov. Pardon, Parole and Rehab. Commn., 1977-78; prin. Gravel Brady & Berrigan, New Orleans, 1978-94, Berrigan, Litchfield, Schonekas, Mann & Clement, New Orleans, 1984-94; judge US Dist. Ct. (ea. dist.) La., New Orleans, 1994—2001, 2008—, chief judge, 2001—08. Active La. Sentencing Commn., 1987. Active Com. of 21, 1989, pres., 1990-92, ACLU of La., 1989-94, Forum for Equality, 1990-94, Amistad Rsch. Ctr. Tulane U., 1990-95. Mem.: New Orleans Assn. Women Attys., La. Assn. Criminal Def. Lawyers, La. State Bar Assn. Office: US Dist Courthouse 500 Poydras St Rm C556 New Orleans LA 70130-3313

BERRY, BRIAN JOE LOBLEY, geographer, urban planner, political economist, educator; b. Sedgley, Stafford, Eng., Feb. 16, 1934; arrived in U.S., 1955, naturalized, 1965; s. Joe and Gwendoline Alice (Lobley) B.; m. Janet Elizabeth Shapley, Sept. 6, 1958; children: Duncan Jeffrey, Carol Anne (dec.), Diane Leigh, Karen. BSc with honors, Univ. Coll., London, 1955; MA, U. Wash., 1956, PhD, 1958; AM (hon.), Harvard U., 1976. Instr. geography, civil engring. U. Wash., Seattle, 1957-58; asst. prof. geography U. Chgo., 1958-62, assoc. prof., 1962-65, prof., 1965-72, Irving B. Harris prof. urban geography, 1972-76, dir. Ctr. Urban Studies, chmn. dept. geography, 1974-76; Frank Backus Williams prof. urban and regional planning Harvard U., 1976-81, chmn. Ph.D. Program in Urban Planning, dir. Lab. for Computer Graphics and Spatial Analysis, fellow Inst. Internat. Devel., 1976-81, prof. sociology, 1978-81; dean H. John Heinz III Sch. of Pub. Mgmt. Carnegie-Mellon U., 1981-86, Univ. prof. urban studies and pub. policy, 1981-86; founders prof. U. Tex., Dallas, 1986-91, prof. polit. econ., 1986—, Lloyd Viel Berkner Regental prof., 1991—, chmn. Bruton Ctr. for Devel. Studies, 1988-95, dean Sch. Econ., Polit. and Policy Scis., 2005—10. Author numerous books; contbr. articles to profl. jours. Recipient Victoria medal, Royal Geog. Soc., 1988, Rockefeller prize, Dartmouth U., 1992; named Lord of Hastingleigh, County Kent, 2000, Dist. Alumnus award in Social Scis., U. Wash., 2005, Vautrin Lud Laureate in Geography, 2005; fellow, Univ. Coll., U. London, 1983. Fellow AAAS, Am. Acad. Arts and Scis., Am. Inst. Cert. Planners, Urban Land Inst., Brit. Acad. (corr.), Weimer Inst. Real Estate and Land Econs., Royal Geog. Soc., So. Regional Sci. Assn.; mem. NAS (coun. 1999-2002), Assn. Am. Geographers (Hon. award 1968, pres. 1978-79, Anderson medal 1987), Acad. Medicine, Engring. and Sci. Tex., Regional Sci. Assn., Inst. Brit. Geographers, Sigma Xi, Royal Geog. Soc. Office: University Tex Dallas Sch Econ Polit and Policy Scis Richardson TX 75083 Home Phone: 972-562-1058. Business E-Mail: brian.berry@utdallas.edu.

BERRY, DENNIS (G. DENNIS BERRY), publishing executive; B in Advt. and Pub. Rels., U. Ga.; JD, Boston Coll., 1973; MBA, Northwestern Univ., 1980. Pub. Atlanta Jour.-Constn.; pres., CEO Manheim Auctions, 1995—2000; pres., COO Cox Enterprises, Inc., 2000—05, vice chmn., 2005—. Bd. dirs. Cox Comm., Inc., Cox Radio, Inc.; chmn. bd. AutoTrader.com. Mem. adv. bd. Grady Coll. Journalism and Mass Comm.; bd. dirs. Atlanta Area Coun., Boy Scouts Am., Ctrl. Atlanta Progress, Advt. Coun., United Way, Emory Bd. Visitors, Mission New Hope; mem. bd. advisors Ga. State U.; past chair bd. dirs. Better Bus. Bur. Met. Atlanta. Mailing: Cox Enterprises PO Box 105357 Atlanta GA 30348 Office: Cox Enterprises 6205 Peachtree Dunwoody Rd Atlanta GA 30328

BERRY, LEONARD L., humanities educator, board member; b. 1942; PhD, Texas A&M U. Prof., mktg. and M.B. Zale Chair in Retailing and Marketing Leadership, Mays Bus. Sch. Texas A&M U., 1982—; bd. dirs. Genesco Inc., 1999—, Darden Restaurants, Inc., 2001—, Lowe's Companies, Inc.; prof., Humanities in Medicine Texas A&M U., 2004—, disting. prof., Mktg. Mailing: Darden Restaurants Inc PO Box 593330 Orlando FL 32859-3330 Office: Darden Restaurants Inc 1000 Darden Center Dr Orlando FL 32837-4032 Office Phone: 407-245-4000. Business E-Mail: berryle@tamu.edu.

BERRY, LORRAINE LEDEE, state senator; b. St. Thomas, VI, Nov. 15, 1949; d. Joseph and Emelda Ledee; m. Richard Berry; children: Roxanne, Kurt. Student, U. V.I. Mem. V.I. Legis., 1982—, pres., 1997-99, 2005—. Mem. econ. devel., agr., consumer protection, health, govt. and operation coms.; chair fin. com. Office: Capitol Bldg PO Box 1690 St Thomas VI 00804-1690 Home Phone: 340-774-4414; Office Phone: 340-693-3507. E-mail: LBerry19@hotmail.com, lberry@senate.gov.vi.

BERRY, NANDITA VENKATE, state official, lawyer; b. Hyderabad, Andhra Pradesh, India, Apr. 14, 1968; arrived in U.S., 1989; d. Anant Kumar and Srutha Keerthi Venkateswaran; m. Michael C. Berry; 2 children. BA, U. Bangalore, India, 1988, U. Houston, 1991; JD, U. Houston Law Ctr., 1995. Intern Hindustan Times, New Delhi, 1989; intern to Hon. Judge Leal US Bankruptcy Ct., Houston, 1992; intern to Hon. Judge Hal DeMoss US Ct. Appeals (5th Cir.), Houston, 1992; assoc. Haynes & Boone LLP, Houston, 1995—97; sr. counsel El Paso Corp., Houston, 1997—2005, Locke, Liddell & Sapp, LLP, Houston, 2005—13; sec. of state State of Tex., Austin, 2014. Bd. dirs. Houston Zoo, 2005—, Houston Area Women's Ctr., 2002. Republican. Avocations: running, reading, gemology. Office: Secretary of State PO Box 12887 Austin TX 78711 Office Phone: 512-463-5770. Office Fax: 512-475-2761. E-mail: secretary@sos.state.tx.us.*

BERRY, WILLIAM E., automotive executive; BBA, Va. Polytechnic Inst. and State U. CPA NC. Various fin. mgmt. position Dr. Pepper Co.; contr. ITCO Tire Co., 1984, sr. v.p., fin., 1984—96, exec. v.p., 1996—98; various positions including, sr. v.p., fin., SE divsn. The Speed Merchant, Inc. (merger with ITCO Tire Co. and Am. Tire Distributors, Inc.), 1998—2003; exec. v.p., CFO Am. Tire Distbrs. Holdings, Inc., 2002—03, pres., COO, 2003—09; pres., CEO, bd. dirs. American Tire Distributors Holdings, Inc., 2009—. Mem.: AICPA, NCCPA. Office: American Tire Distributors Holdings Inc 12200 Herbert Wayne Court Ste 150 Huntersville NC 28078-3145 Office Phone: 704-992-2000. Office Fax: 704-992-1384. Business E-Mail: wberry@americantiredistributors.com.

BERRY, WILLIAM LEE, business administration educator; b. Indpls., Dec. 24, 1935; s. George Lee and Anna Marie (Hansert) B.; m. Carol M. Berry; children: Ann Kathleen, Lee Michael, Lynn Colleen, Kimberly Ann. BS, Purdue U., West Lafayette, Ind., 1957; MS, Va. Poly. Inst., Blacksburg, 1964; DBA, Harvard U., Cambridge, Mass., 1969. Mfg. trainee GE, various locations, 1957-60, supr. mfg. Salem, Va., 1960-64; from asst. prof. to assoc. prof. indsl. mgmt. Purdue U., West Lafayette, Ind., 1968-76; prof. prodn. mgmt. Ind. U., Bloomington, 1976-82; C. Maxwell Stanley prof. prodn. mgmt. U. Iowa, Iowa City, 1982-87, sr. assoc. dean Coll. Bus. Adminstrn., 1983-87, dir. Mfg. and Productivity Ctr., 1986-87; Belk prof. bus. adminstrn., chmn. ops. mgmt. area U. N.C., Chapel Hill, 1988-92; prof. bus. adminstrn. Ohio State U., Columbus, 1992—2007, Richard Ross chair in mgmt., dir. Ctr. Excellence in Mgmt., 1995—2006, prof. emeritus, 2007. Vis. prof. IMD, Lausanne, Switzerland, 1987-88; cons. in field. Co-author: Operations and Logistics Management, 1972, Production Planning, Scheduling and Inventory Control: Concepts, Techniques and Systems, 1974, Master Production Scheduling: Principles and Practice, 1979, Manufacturing Planning and Control for Supply Chain Management, 1984, 6th edit., 2011, ITEC: Manufacturing Planning and Control/Manufacturing Strategy Simulation, 1992, Production and Inventory Control Integrated, 1992; contbr. articles to profl. jours. 1st Enterprise fellow Kenan Inst., 1988-90. Fellow Decision Scis. Inst. (v.p. 1983-84, sec. 1985-86, pres.-elect 1987, pres. 1988); mem. Inst. Indsl. Engrs. (v.p. 1979-81, dir., Disting. Service award 1979), Ops. Mgmt. Assn. (v.p. 1981-85, pres.-elect 1985-86, pres. 1986-87, dir., Disting. Leadership award 1987), Am. Prodn. and Inventory Control Soc., Inst. Mgmt. Sci., Ops. Research Soc.

BERRY, WILLIAM WILLIS, retired utilities executive; b. Norfolk, Va., May 18, 1932; s. Joel Halbert and Julia Lee (Godwin) B.; m. Elizabeth Mangum, Aug. 23, 1958; children: Preston Blackburn, John Willis, William Godwin. BSEE, Va. Mil. Inst., 1954; MC in Commerce, U. Richmond, 1964. Registered profl. engr., Va. Engr. Gen. Electric Co., 1954-55; with Va. Power, Richmond, 1957-92, v.p. divsn. ops., then sr. v.p. comml. ops., 1976-78, exec. v.p., 1978-80, pres., COO, 1980-83, pres. CEO, 1983-85, chmn., CEO, 1985-86, Dominion Resources Inc., Richmond, 1986-90, chmn., 1990-92. Bd. dirs. New Market Corp., Richmond, 1983—2005. Chair ISO New Eng., Holyoke, Mass., 1997-2006. Mem. Commonwealth Club, Country Club Va. Republican. Home Phone: 804-285-2656. Personal E-mail: wwberry@earthlink.net.

BERRYHILL, HENRY LEE, JR., retired geologist; b. Charlotte, NC, Nov. 6, 1921; s. Henry Lee and Viola Estelle (Johnston) B.; m. Louise Randall Russell, Sept. 13, 1947; children: Stuart Randall, Keith Courtney. BS, U. N.C., 1947, MS in Geology, 1949. With U.S. Geol. Survey, 1948-86, chief publs. officer Denver, 1963-65, research marine geologist, 1965-66, chief marine geology Gulf of Mexico-Caribbean region office Corpus Christi, Tex., 1967-70; chief Office Marine Geology, Washington, 1970-73, sr. research marine geologist Corpus Christi, 1973-86; gen. cons., 1986-99; ret., 1999; Tech. adviser offshore prospecting com. ECAFE, 1972-73; Dept. Interior rep. Fed. Intragy. Com. on Marine Sci. and Engring., 1970-73; program mgr. integrated environ. assessment Outer Continental Shelf N.W. Gulf of Mexico, 1973-86; U.S. rep. marine geology panel U.S.-Japan Coop. Programs in Natural Resources, 1973-95; ret. Cons. Nat. Center for Geoscis., India, 1981-87. Author: Geology and Coal Resources of Belmont County, Ohio, 1963, Geology of the Ciales Area, Puerto Rico, 1965, Coal-Bearing Upper Pennsylvanian and Lower Permian Rocks, Washington Area, Pennsylvania, 1971, The Worldwide Search for Petroleum Offshore-A Status Report for the Quarter Century, 1947-72, 1974, Seismic Models of Late Qua ternary Facies and Structure, Northern Gulf of Mexico, 1986. Contbr. articles to sci. pubIs. Served with USAAF, 1942-45. Decorated DFC, Air medal with 3 oak leaf clusters; recipient Outstanding Performance award U.S. Geol. Survey, 1969, a seafloor feature of the Gulf of Mexico named Berryhill Basin in his honor, 1995. Fellow Geol. Soc. Am.; mem. Am. Assn. Petroleum Geologists (co-recipient Jules Braunstein meml. award 1987), Sierra Club (chmn. Coastal Bend group 1980-81, 86-89), Sigma Xi. Episcopalian. Home: 982 Bolingbrook Dr SW Marietta GA 30064-2900

BERT, CHARLES WESLEY, mechanical and aerospace engineer, educator; b. Chambersburg, Pa., Nov. 11, 1929; s. Charles Wesley and Gladys Adelle (Raff) B.; m. Charlotte Elizabeth Davis (June 29, 1957); children: Charles Wesley IV, David Raff. BSME, Pa. State U., 1951, MS, 1956; PhD in Engring. Mechanics, Ohio State U., 1961. Jr. design engr. Am. Flexible Coupling Co., State Coll., Pa., 1951-52; aero. design engr. Fairchild Aircraft div. Fairchild Engine and Airplane Corp., Hagerstown, Md., 1954—56; prin. M.E. Battelle Inst., Columbus, Ohio, 1956-61; sr. research engr., 1961-62; program dir., solid and structural mechanics research, 1962-63; cons., 1964-65; assoc. prof. U. Okla., 1963-66, prof., 1966—2004; Benjamin H. Perkinson Chair prof. engring. Sch. Aerospace and Mech. Engring., 1978—2004; George L. Cross rsch. prof. U. Okla., 1981—2004, prof. emeritus, 2004—. Instr. engring. mechanics Ohio State U., Columbus, 1959-61; dir.Sch. Aerospace and Mech. Engring. U. Okla., 1972-77, 90-95; vis. scholar U. Calif., San Diego, 1996; cons. in field; chmn. Midwestern Mechanics Conf., 1973-75; Honor lectr. Mid-Am. State Univs. Assn., 1983-84; seminar lectr. Midwest Mechanics, 1983-84; Plenary lectr. Internat. Conf. on Composite Structures, Paisley,

Scotland, 1987. Mem. editl. bd. Composite Structures Jour., 1982—, Jour. Sound and Vibration, 1988—, Composites Engring., 1991-95, Mechanics of Composite Materials and Structures, 1993-2001, Applied Mechanics Revs., 1993—, Composites, 1996-98, Internat. Jour. Structural Stability and Dynamics, 2000—06, Jour. Sandwich Structures and Materials, 1997—, Mechanics of Advanced Materials and Structures, 2002-06; assoc. editor: Exptl. Mechanics, 1982-87, Applied Mechanics Revs., 1984-87; contbr. chpts. to books, articles to profl. jours. 1st lt. USAF, 1952-54. Sr. Rsch. scholar U. Calif., San Diego, 1996; recipient Disting. Alumnus award Ohio State U. Coll. engring., 1985; named to Higher Edn. Hall of Fame, 2011. Fellow AAAS, AIAA (nat. tech. com. structures 1969-72, chmn. Ctrl. Okla. sect. 1966-67), ASME (Cen. Okla. sect. exec. com. 1973-78, 90-95, 99-01, sec. 1990-91, region X mech. engring. dept. heads com. 1972-77, 90-95, chmn. 1975-77, 10-session symposium named in his honor 1999), Am. Soc. Composites (bd. dirs. 1996-98, Disting. Rsch. award 1999), Am. Acad. Mechs. (bd. dirs. 1978-82, pres.-elect 2001-02, pres. 2002-03), Soc. Exptl. Mechanics (monograph com. 1978-82, chmn. 1980-82, sec. Mid-Ohio sect. 1958-59, chmn. 1959-60, adv. bd. 1960-63), Soc. Engring. Sci. (bd. dirs. 1982-88); mem. NSPE, Okla. Acad. Sci., Okla. Soc. Profl. Engrs., Scabbard and Blade, Pa. State Alumni Assn. (Outstanding Engring. Alumnus award 1992), Sigma Xi, Sigma Tau, Pi Tau Sigma, Sigma Gamma Tau (Disting. Engr. award), Tau Beta Pi (Disting. Engr. award), Okla. Higher Edn. Heritage Soc. (elect. mem., Okla. Higher Edn. Hall of Fame). Achievements include co-development of world's smallest pressure transducer capable of measuring both steady and fluctuating pressures; first general solution of cylindrically orthotropic plates of radially varying thickness under arbitrary body forces; origination of several minimum-weight optimal designs for multicell cylindrical pressure vessels, experimental techniques and associated data reduction equations for determining residual stresses in both flat-sheet and thick-walled cylindrical specimens of composite materials; first successful application of Kennedy-Pancu system identification method to shell structures, noninteger polynomial version of Rayleigh's method to heat conduction; first application of differential quadrature method to static structural problems, structural vibration problems and nonlinear structural problems; first application of noninteger polynomial method to finite element analysis; first dynamic stability analysis of unicycles and monocycles; origination of concept of stress gages for composite materials; research on sandwich structures with bimodular facings, prediction of ply steer behavior of automobile tires, nonlinear flutter of laminated composite panels; many others. Home and Office: 2516 Butler Dr Norman OK 73069-5059 Office: U Okla Sch Aerospace and Mech Engring 865 Asp Ave Norman OK 73019-1052 Office Phone: 405-329-4459. Personal E-mail: cbert@cox.net.

BERTE, NEAL RICHARD, academic administrator; b. May 7, 1940; s. Edward H. and Wenonah Maureen (Stevens) B.; m. Anne; children: Becky, Julie, Mark, Scott. BS in Polit. Sci, U. Cin., 1962, MS (Ford Found. scholar), 1963, EdD, 1966; Rockefeller Found. fellow, Union Theol. Sem., NYC, 1962-63; postgrad., Garrett Theol. Sem., Evanston, Ill., 1966-67, Harvard U., Cambridge, Mass., 1966; LHD (hon.), U. Cin., 1993. Asst. dir. Coll. Entrance Exam. Bd., Evanston, 1966-68; exec. asst. to pres., asst. prof. Ottawa U., Kans., 1968-70; dean New Coll.; assoc. prof. U. Ala., 1970-74; v.p. ednl. devel., dean New Coll., 1974-76; pres. Birmingham-So. Coll., Ala., 1976—, chancellor, 2004—, pres. emeritus, 2004—. Project dir. NSF grants, 1972; chmn. session Internat. Coun. on Edn. for Tchg. World Assembly, Nairobi, Kenya, 1973; faculty Danforth Found. sponsored CC Inst., Stephens Coll., 1973; steering com. Carnegie Found. funded project Coop. Assessment of Experiential Learning, 1974-77; mem. Commn. on Ednl. Credit, Am. Council Edn., 1975-81, Danforth Found. exec. com. for Danforth Fellows Program, 1974-75; nat. adv. council for career edn. HEW, Office Edn., 1976-79; sec.-treas. So. U. Conf., 1977-80, v.p., 1984-85, pres., 1985-86; vis. scholar Inst. for Ednl. Mgmt., Harvard Grad. Sch Edn., 1990-91; co-chmn. Region 2020, Ala., 1997—; bd. dirs. Ala. Ctr. for Law and Civic Edn, Robins and Morton Group, 2008-. Contbr. articles to edn. jours. Mem. adminstrv. bd. Canterbury United Meth. Ch., Birmingham, 1977—, univ. senate United Meth. Ch., 1986-88; chmn. Univ. United Fund campaign, 1973; bd. dirs., mem. exec. com. United Fund, Tuscaloosa, Ala., 1974-75, chmn. edn. div., 1975; chmn. sect. for pvt. ednl. insts. Jefferson-Shelby-Walker Counties United Appeal, 1977; chmn. pub. employees div. United Way campaign, 1978; v.p. Coun. for Advancement Pvt. Colls. in Ala., 1977-82, pres., 1982-83; chmn. com. to select Man of Year in Birmingham, 1977; chmn. selection com. Rhodes Scholarships for Ala., 1976-81; bd. dirs. Jefferson-Shelby Counties Lung Assn., 1978-79, Ala. Partners for Progress with Guatemala Program, 1977—, Carraway Meth. Hosp., 1977-80, Brookwood Hosp., 1982-90, Neighborhood Housing Svc., Birmingham, 1977-78, Birmingham Symphony Assn., 1976-80, 82-87, Cmty. Affairs Com., 1976-87, Operation New Birmingham, 1976-89, 2006-09, Nature Conservancy of Ala., 2007; bd. govs. Relay House Club, Birmingham, 1983-87, Circle S Industries, Selma, Ala., 1983—, Parisian, Inc., Birmingham, 1983-88; bd. dirs. NCCJ, 1978—, Birmingham Summerfest, 1979—, March of Dimes, 1979-86, Am. Heart Assn., 1980-84, So. Rsch. Inst., 1982—, Leadership Birmingham, 1981—; bd. dirs., chmn. long range planning com., chmn. program for Scout Expn. Jefferson County coun. Boy Scouts Am., 1977—; exec. com. Men's Com., Birmingham Symphony Assn., 1977-84; bd. dirs. Jefferson Fed. Savs. and Loan Assn., Birmingham, 1978-91, Birmingham Festival Arts, 1982-89, bd. advisors, 1989, trustee, 1990, pres., 1981—; chmn. Birmingham Area United Way, 1983; trustee Advent Episc. Day Sch., 1977-87, Gorgas Scholarship Found., 1976-88, New Coll.-Sarasota, U. South Fla., 1977-79; founding mem., bd. dirs. Progressive Alliance, 1986—; bd. dirs. Met. Devel. Bd., 1987-88, Greater Birmingham Conv. and Visitors Bur., 1988; commn. pub. rels. Nat. Assn. Ind. Colls and Univs., 1992-94, bd. dirs., 1994; adv. bd. pub. Edn. Found. Jefferson County Bd. Edn., 1999—; bd. dirs. Civil Rights Inst., 2000; co-chair Campaign for Restoration of Birmingham's Hist 16th St. Bapt. Ch., mem. found. bd., 2004—; chmn. steering com. McWane Cmty. Adv. Panel, 2004—; bd. dirs. U. Ala. Health Svcs. Found., 2004—; v.p. Birmingham Civil Rights Inst., 2005, chmn. 2005-06; mem. adv. bd. Cmty. Grief Support Svc., 2005-; bd. dirs. Operation New Birmingham, 2006—, vice chmn. 2007, chmn. 2008; nat. adv. com. Robert Wood Johnson Found., 2007; bd. dirs. Cmty. Found. Greater Birmingham, 2008, co-chair 50th Anniversary Campaign, 2008. Recipient Outstanding Citizens award Lawson State CC, 1977, Outstanding Citizen award in Birmingham Erskine Ramsay Award Com., 1978, Brotherhood award NCCJ, 1984, Outstanding Svc. award Black Student Union, 1986, Outstanding Cmty. Svc. award Mortar Bd., 1986, James M. Tingle award, 1986, Disting. Svc. award, Sigma Alpha Epsilon, 1991, Medal of Honor, DAR, 1995, Leadership award Birmingham Regional Planning Commn. promoting regional cooperation, 2000, award of distinction Nat. Interfrat. Coun., 2004, Outstanding Svc. award Martin Luther King, Jr. Unity Breakfast, 2005, James A. Head Lifetime Achievement award Nat. Conf. for Cmty. and Justice, 2007, Bi-Racial Friendship award Birmingham Urban League, 2008; elected to Ala. Acad. Honor, 1979; named one of 10 Outstanding Cmty. Leaders Birmingham Post-Herald, 1984, one of Top 10 Current Leaders in Birmingham, The Birmingham News, 1990, 99, one of 10 leaders Bus. First jour., 1990, Birmingham Citizen of Yr. award for outstanding civic and cmty. svc., 1986, Outstanding Ala. Civic Leader Nat. Soc. Fund-Raising Execs., 1991, Disting. Citizen City Coun. of Birmingham, 1992, one of top ten mems. of 1997 Class of Movers and Shakers, Birmingham Bus. Jour.; named to Sigma Alpha Epsilon Leadership Sch. Hall of Fame, 1994; named one of 2 recipients Ala. Humanities Found. award, 2005; honoree Ann. Benefit Am. Cancer Soc., 2005; King Beaux Arts Krewe Ball, Birmingham Mus. Art benefit, 2005. Mem. Am. Assn. Univ. Adminstrs. (pres. Alpha chpt. 1978-79), Greater Birmingham Area C. of C. (bd. dirs., exec. com. 1978-80, v.p. for govtl. rels., policy com. 1986, pres. 1988, chmn. exec. com. 1989), Am. Assn. Colls. (pres.'s adv. coun. 1977-78), Am. Assn. for Higher Edn. (chmn. Southeastern Regional Coun. 1973, chmn. panel on three-year degree programs 1973, program chmn. 1974, adv. bd. NEXUS Project 1974-75), Assn. for Innovation in Higher Edn. (adv. bd. 1973), Kiwanis Internat. (Disting. Pres. award 1992-93, George F. Hixon fellow 1995), Phi Beta Kappa (pres. 1975), Phi Delta Kappa. Clubs: The Redstone Club, The Jefferson Club, Downtown Birmingham Kiwanis (chmn. Ministers Day 1977, chmn. Youth-of-the-Year selection com. 1978, pres. 1992-93, Disting. Pres. award, Kiwanian of Yr. 2007). Office: Pres Emeritus Birmingham So Coll 2100 First Ave N Ste 410 Birmingham AL 35203 E-mail: nberte@bsc.edu.

BERTELSMAN, WILLIAM ODIS, federal judge; b. Cin., Jan. 31, 1936; s. Odis William and Dorothy B.; m. Margaret Ann Martin, June 13, 1959; children: Kathy, Terri, Nancy. AB, Xavier U., 1958; JD, U. Cin., 1961. Bar: Ky. 1961, Ohio 1962. Law clk. firm Taft, Stettinius & Hollister, Cin., 1960-61; mem. firm Bertelsman & Bertelsman, Newport, Ky., 1962-79; judge US Dist. Ct. (ea. dist.) Ky., Covington, 1979—91, 1998—2001, chief judge, 1991—98, sr. judge, 2001—; instr. Coll. Law U. Cin., 1965-72; city atty., prosecutor Highland Heights, Ky., 1962-69. Adj. prof. Chase Coll. of Law, 1989—. Contbr. articles to profl. jours. Served to capt. AUS, 1963-64. Mem.: U.S. Jud. Conf. (standing com. on practice and procedure 1989—95, liaison mem. adv. com. on civil rules 1989—95, 6th cir. rep. 2004—06), Ky. Bar Assn. (bd. govs. 1978—79), ABA. Republican. Roman Catholic.

BERTHELOT, JOHN A., state legislator; m. Paula Chauvin Berthelot; children: Shelley, Kelley, Brad. Mem. Gonzales Town Coun., La., 1976, Gonzales City Coun., 1980; mayor pro-tempore City of Gonzales, mayor, 1984; mem. Dist. 88 La. House of Reps., 2012—, mem. Appropriations Com., House and Govtl. Affairs Com., Mcpl., Parochial and Cultural Affairs Com. & Joint Legislative Com. on Budget. Republican. Office: District Office 1024 S Purpera Gonzales LA 70737 Office Phone: 225-647-5646. Office Fax: 225-644-7207. E-mail: berthelotj@legis.la.gov.

BERTOLONE, SALVATORE J., pediatric medicine educator; b. Bronx, NY, July 31, 1944; BS in Biology, Fordham U., 1966; MD, U. Louisville, 1970. Med. lic., Ky.; cert. Am. Bd. Pediatrics, Supspecialty Bd. Pediatric Hematology/Oncology. Pediatric intern U. Louisville (Ky.) Sch. Medicine, 1970-71, pediatric resident, 1971-72; fellow dept. pediatrics U. Colo., Denver, 1972-74; asst. clin. prof., dept. pediatrics, dept. neurosurgery U. Colo., Sch. Medicine, Denver, 1974-76; asst. prof. pediatrics, dept. pediatrics U. Louisville (Ky.) Sch. Medicine, 1976-82; assoc. in oncology U. Louisville (Ky.), James Graham Brown Cancer Ctr., 1977; assoc. prof. pediatrics, dept. pediatrics U. Louisville (Ky.) Sch. Medicine, 1982-92, prof. pediatrics, dept. pediatrics, 1992—, dir. pediatric Hematology, Oncology, 1998—. Cons. Crippled Children's Svcs., State of Ky., 1976—, State of Ind., 1976, Hemophilia Clinic, Kosair Children's Hosp., Louisville, 1979—, Dept. Pediat. Ireland Army Hosp., Fort Knox, Ky., 1979—, Jefferson County Dept. Health, Lead Poisoning Program, Louisville, 1983—; founder, bd. dirs. Pediat. Hospice Louisville, 1979—, med. dir., 1979-84; com. mem. U. Louisville Sch. Medicine and Kosair Children's Hosp., others; asst. chief pediat. clinic Fitzsimons Army Med. Ctr., Denver, 1974-76, chief pediatric hematology/oncology, 1974-76; active med. staff Kosair Children's Hosp., Louisville, 1976—, Humana Hosp., Audubon, Louisville, 1979—, U. Gen. Hosp., Louisville, 1979—, Humana Hosp., U., Louisville, 1986—, Meth. Evang. Hosp., Louisville, 1987-93; med. staff Home of Innocents, Louisville, 1980-83; courtesy staff Humana Hosp. Suburban, Louisville, 1981—, Jewish Hosp., Louisville, 1982—. Mem. editl. bd. Jour. Cancer Edn., 1986—; contbr. chpts. in books and numerous articles to profl. jours. Adv. com. on childhood cancer Am. Cancer Soc., Louisville, 1979-80; mem. med. adv. com. ARC, Louisville, 1979—; bd. dirs. Help Our Parents Endure, Parent Support Group, Louisville, 1980-85; med., bd. dirs. Ronald McDonald House, Louisville, 1980—, chmn. planning com., 1980-82; co-chmn. Affiliate Instn. Com., Children's Cancer Group, 1984—; others. Maj. U.S. Army, 1972-76. Recipient WLKY Bell award, 1991, Nat. Jefferson award, Washington, 1992; grantee Nat. Cancer Inst., 1977-82, Crusade for Children, 1978, 80, 82, 86, 90, 91, 92, Ky. Adv. Bd. on Hemophilia, State of Ky., 1981, 82, 83-85, 86-90, 91, Am. Cancer Soc., 1982, Louisville and Jefferson County Bd. of Health, 1983-90, 91, Children's Cancer Group, 1984-87, 87, 88, 89, 90, 91, 92, 93, Cabinet for Human Resources, 1988, 89, 90, Alpha Therapeutic Corp., 1991, others. Fellow Am. Acad. Pediatrics; mem. Am. Soc. Clin. Oncology, Am. Soc. Pediatric Hematology/Oncology, Am. Assn. Cancer Educators, So. Soc. for Pediatric Rsch., Ky. Chpt. Am. Acad. Pediatrics, Ky. Med. Assn., Jefferson County Med. Soc., Louisville Pediatric Soc., Alpha Omega Alpha. Office: Dept Pediats Hemtology/Oncology 601 S Floyd St Ste 403 Louisville KY 40202-1837

BERTSCH, PAUL M., ecologist, educator; b. Oct. 28, 1956; BS in Plant Sci., U. Conn., 1978; MS in Soil Chemistry, Va. Poly. Inst., 1980; PhD in Soil Phys. Chemistry-Mineralogy, U. Ky., 1983. Rsch. specialist dept. agronomy U. Ky., Lexington, 1983, asst. prof. dept. agronomy, 1984; asst. rsch. prof. divsn. biogeochemistry Savannah River Ecology Lab., U. Ga., Aiken, SC, 1984—89, assoc. rsch. prof. divsn. bigeochemistry, 1989—95, prof., dir. Advanced Analytical Ctr. for Environ. Scis., 1995, dir., 1999—2007; vis. scientist applied and atomic physics Nat. Synchrotron Light Source, Brookhaven Nat. Lab., Upton, NY, 1992—93; faculty mem. Marine Biomedicine and Environ. Scis. Program Med. U. SC, Charleston, 2001—; affiliate faculty mem. engring. U. Ga., 2002—. Vis. scientist European Ctr. for Environ. Geosciences, France, 2004; presenter in field. Contbr. articles to profl. jours. Fellow: Soil Sci. Soc. Am. (assoc. editor 1994—2001, selection com. 1999—, evaluation com., chmn. divisn. soil chemistry 2003—04, Career Achievement award 2004, Jackson award 1996), Am. Soc. Agronomy; mem.: AAAs, Internat. Soil Sci. Soc., Internat. Clay Minerals Soc., Clay Minerals Soc. (coun. 1997, awards com. 2001, v.p. 2001, program devel. com. 2004—), Am. Geophysical Union, Am. Chem. Soc., Sigma Xi, Phi Sigma, Phi Kappa Phi, Gamma Sigma Delta. Achievements include patents for in-situ groundwater remediation by selective colloid mobilization, 1998. Office: Med U SC 171 Ashley Ave Charleston SC 29403

BESCH, EMERSON LOUIS, physiologist, educator, retired dean; b. Hammond, Ind., June 9, 1928; s. Ernest Henry and Carolyn (Dieckmann) B.; m. H. Jean Whitstine, May 28, 1955; children: Karen J., Kevin D., Kathleen L., Kristine A. BS in Biology/Chemistry, S.W. Tex. State U., 1952, MA in Biology/Chemistry, 1955; PhD in Physiology, U. Calif., Davis, 1964. Grad. instr. biology dept. S.W. Tex. State U., San Marcos, 1954-55; research asst., NIH trainee U. Calif., Davis, 1960-64, research physiologist, lectr., 1964-67; research assoc. Pacific Missile Range, USN, Point Mugu, Calif., 1960-64; from assoc. to full prof., head dept. physiology Kans. State U., Manhattan, 1967-74, from assoc. to full prof. mech. engring., 1967-74; prof. mech. engring. U. Fla., Gainesville, 1974-93; prof. physiology U. Fla. Coll. Vet. Medicine, Gainesville, 1974-93, assoc. dean, 1974-87, acting dean, 1980-81, exec. assoc. dean, 1987-88, prof. emeritus, 1993—. Capt. USNR. Fellow Aerospace Med. Assn. (exec. council 1985-88, profl. excellence award 1987); mem. Am. Physiology Soc., Soc. for Exptl. Biology & Medicine, Aerospace Physiologist Soc. (pres. 1984-86), Am. Soc. Heating, Refrigerating & Air Conditioning Engring. Achievements include research in environmental physiology and acceleration biology. Home: 15207 Rompel Trail Dr San Antonio TX 78232-4255 Office: U Fla Coll Vet Medicine PO Box 100144 Gainesville FL 32610-0144 Office Phone: 352-392-2246. Personal E-mail: ebesch@satx.rr.com.

BESH, JOHN, chef, television personality, restaurateur; b. New Orleans; m. Jenifer Besh; children: Luke, Andrew, Jack, Brendan. Grad., Culinary Inst. Am. Chef Maxim's, NYC, Windsor Ct. Grill Room, New Orleans, Cinnamon Tree, Balt.; apprentice Romantik Hotel Spielwet, Germany; chef Graham's; owner, chef La Provence; exec. chef Artesia, Abita Springs, La.; owner, exec. chef Restaurant August, 2001—; owner Besh Steak, Domenica, Lüke, New Orleans, Lüke San Antonio, Soda Shop, The America Sector, Borgne, La. Author: My New Orleans: The Cookbook, 2009, My Family Table: A Passionate Plea for Home Cooking, 2011; co-author (with David A. Newsome): New Orleans Program: Eat, Exercise, and Enjoy Life, 2006; contbr. Wild Abundance: Ritual, Revelry & Recipes of the South's Finest Hunting Clubs; guest chef The Today Show, guest appearances on top programs on The Food Network and the Sundance Channel, host (cooking show) John Besh's Family Table, 2013—. Served in USMC. Recipient Four Star rating, Mobil Restaurant Guide, Four Diamonds, AAA, Five Beans, Gregory Roberts, Times Picayune, Silver Spoon award, Food Arts, Best French Restaurant in New Orleans award, Zagat's, 2000, Best Chef: Southeast award, James Beard Found., 2006; named Best New Chef, New Orleans Mag., 1998, Hot Table, Condé Nast Traveler, 2002; named one of America's Best New Chefs, Food & Wine mag., 1999, New Orleans' Best Restaurants, Gourmet, 2002, Top New Orleans Restaurants, Travel & Leisure, 2002. Office: 301 Tchoupitoulas St New Orleans LA 70130

BESHEAR, STEVEN LYNN, Governor of Kentucky, lawyer; b. Dawson Springs, Ky., Sept. 21, 1944; m. Jane Klingner, 1969; children: Jeff, Andy. AB, U. Ky., Lexington, 1966, JD, 1968. Bar: NY 1969, Ky. 1971. Assoc. White & Case, NYC, 1968-70; ptnr. Beshear, Meng and Green, Lexington; mem. Dist. 76 Ky. House of Reps., 1974-79; atty. gen. State of Ky., Frankfort, 1980—83, lt. gov., 1983-87, gov., 2007—; ptnr. Stites & Harbison, Lexington, 1987—2007. Bd. editors Ky. Law Jour., 1967—68. Mem. CommerceLexington, Inc., God's Pantry Food Bank, Ky. Horse Park Found., Ky. World Trade Ctr., Bluegrass Tomorrow, U. Ky. Vis. Com. Mem.: ABA, Ky. Bar Assn., Fayette County Bar Assn., Omicron Delta Kappa, Phi Delta Phi, Phi Beta Kappa. Democrat. Baptist. Office: Office of the Governor 700 Capitol Ave Ste 100 Frankfort KY 40601 Office Phone: 502-564-2611. Office Fax: 502-564-2517.*

BESOSA, FRANCISCO AUGUSTO, federal judge; b. San Juan, 1949; AB, Brown U., 1971; JD, Georgetown U. Law Ctr., 1979. Ptnr., chmn. litig. dept. Adsuar Muniz Goyco & Besosa, PSC, San Juan, 1979—83, 1986—2006; asst. US atty. US Dept. Justice, 1983—86; judge US Dist. Ct. PR, 2006—. US Army, 1971—77. Office: Clemente Ruiz-Nazario US Courthouse CH-119 150 Carlos Chardon St San Juan PR 00918 Office Phone: 787-772-3241.

BESSANT, CATHY (CATHERINE POMBIER BESSANT), bank executive; b. Jackson, Mich., 1961; m. John E. Clay; 2 children. BBA in Fin., Mktg. & Eng. Lit., U. Mich., 1982. Joined NationsBank, 1982; pres., cmty. devel. bank Bank of America Corp. (formerly NationsBank), 1998—2000, pres., mortgage lending ops., pres., consumer real estate banking, 1999—2000, pres., Fla. ops., 2000—01, chief mktg. officer, 2001—06, pres. global treasury services, 2006—09, pres. global corporate banking, 2009—10; global tech. & ops. exec. Bank of America Corp., Charlotte, NC, 2010—. Trustee Enterprise Found. Bd. dirs. Children's Theatre Charlotte, Blue Cross Blue Shield Fla., Inc. Named one of The Most Powerful Women in Banking, US Banker, 2003, 25 Women to Watch, 2009, 2010, 25 Most Powerful Women in Banking, American Banker, 2011. Office: Bank of America Corp 100 N Tryon St Charlotte NC 28255

BESSETTE, DIANE J., construction executive; Joined Lennar Corp., Miami, 1995, contr., 1997—2008, v.p., 2000—, treas., 2008—. Office: Lennar Corp 700 NW 107th Ave Ste 400 Miami FL 33172-3154 Office Fax: 305-228-8383. E-mail: dbessette@lennar.com.

BEST, LAURENCE EDWARD, lawyer; b. New Orleans, June 14, 1949; s. Kermit Roosevelt and Frances Elizabeth (Hicks) Best; m. Julie B. Guten (div.); children: Erin Lynn, Mark Edward, Kevin John; life ptnr. Kory Chatelain, Oct. 13, 2001. BS in Acctg., U. New Orleans, 1971; JD, Tulane U. Sch. Law, 1974. Bar: La. 1974, U.S. Dist. Ct., ea. dist., La. 1974, U.S. Dist. Ct., western dist., La., U.S. Dist. Ct., middle dist., La. 1974, U.S. Supreme Ct. 1979, U.S. Dist. Ct., so. dist., Tex. 1991, U.S. Dist. Ct., so. dist., Miss. 1991. Atty. Waitz & Downer, Houma, La., 1974—78, Waitz, Downer & Best, Houma, 1978—83, Hebert & Abbott, New Orleans, 1983—84; ptnr. Abbott, Webb, Best & Meeks, New Orleans, 1984—88, Abbott, Best & Meeks, New Orleans, 1988—91, Best Koeppel, New Orleans, 1991—2012, Loutace E Bart LLC, 2012—. Presenter, panelist numerous radio shows, meetings, TV shows. Treas. Forum for Equality, 1992-93, chair-elect and chair, 1993-95; mem. Forum for Equality/Equality Club; cmty. dir. Forum for Equality, 2001; founder, bd. mem. New Orleans Lesbian and Gay Cmty. Ctr., 1994-95; mem. adv. com. City of New Orleans Human Rels. Commn., 1994-96; mem. La. Log Cabin Reps. 2003, Human Rights Campaign Fed. Club, Svc. Members Legal Def. Network, Parents and Friends of Lesbians and Gays, 1996-; mem. Lambda Legal Def. Fund. Recipient Legal Eagle award, La. Electorate of Gays and Lesbians, 1996, award for outstanding leadership and svc. to the Lesbian and Gay Counsel, New Orleans Human Rights Campaign, 2001, Annual Acclaim award for lesbian and gay polit. activism, New Orleans Forum for Equality, 2003, Founders award, New Orleans Lesbian & Gay Cmty. Ctr., 2009, Top 100 Verdicts, 2010; named one of La. Top Lawyers, 2012. Mem.: La. Assn. Justice (La. Super Lawyers 2012, Top 100 Verdicts 2010), Nat. Lesbian and Gay Bar Assn., Fed. Bar Assn. New Orleans, Tex. Bar Assn., La. Bar Assn., U. New Orleans Alumni Assn., Tulane U. Alumni Assn. Democrat. Avocations: reading, cooking, wine. Office Phone: 504-598-1000. Office Fax: 504-524-1024.

BEST, RHYS JOHN, board member; b. Hartford, Conn., Sept. 14, 1946; s. Robert John and Eunice Marie (Spencer) B.; m. Sue F. Ewing, Apr. 18, 1969; children: Paul S., Anne E. BBA in Acctg., U. North Tex., 1969; MBA in Banking, So. Meth. U., 1971. Chmn. Crosstex Energy, L.P.; asst. v.p. FNB-Dallas, 1969—73; v.p. Mfr.'s Hanover, 1973—80, Paul R. Ray & Co., 1980—81; exec. v.p. First City Bank Dallas, 1982—84, vice chmn., 1984—86, pres., COO, 1986—88; chmn., pres. & CEO Lone Star Technologies, Inc., v.p., treas., 1988—89; pres., CEO Lone Star Steel Co., 1989—. Bd. dirs. Child Care Partnership, Dallas, 1985-89, Tex. Superconductor/Collider, Dallas, 1987-88, Family Place, Dallas, 1991—. Mem. Dallas Bankers Assn. (pres. 1987). Office: LONE STAR TECHNOLOGIES PO BOX

803546 Dallas TX 75380-3546 also: Trinity Industries Inc Bd Directors 2525 Stemmons Fwy Dallas TX 75207-2401 Office Phone: 214-631-4420. Office Fax: 214-589-8810. Business E-Mail: rhys.best@trin.net.

BEST, ROBERT WAYNE, gas transmission company executive, lawyer; b. Nappanee, Ind., Oct. 8, 1946; s. Wayne and Helen F. (Kendall) B.; m. Mary Beth Hoffman, Apr. 7, 1967; children—Stephanie, Sean, Ashley BS, Ind. State U., 1968; JD, Ind. U., 1974. Bar: Ky., Ind. Atty. Tex. Gas Transmission Corp., Owensboro, Ky., 1974-79, sr. atty., 1979-81, gen. counsel, 1981-82, v.p., gen. counsel, 1982-85, pres., chief exec. officer, 1985-89, pres., chief operating officer, 1989-1995; chmn., pres. & CEO Atmos Energy Corp., Dallas, 1997—2008, chmn., CEO, 2008—10, chmn., 2010—. Dir. Cardinal Fed. Savs. Bank. Bd. dirs. Leadership Owensboro, Brescia Coll., Mercy Hosp., Ky. Ind. Coll. Fund., United Way Owensboro-Daviess County; mem. exec. com. Strategies for Tomorrow; mem. Ky. Econ. Devel. Corp. Mem. ABA, Ky. Bar Assn., Ind. Bar Assn., Fed. Energy Bar Assn. Democrat. Roman Catholic. Avocations: golf, reading. Office: Atmos Energy Corp PO Box 650205 Dallas TX 75265-0205

BETHEA, LOUISE HUFFMAN, allergist; b. Jackson, Miss., Mar. 27, 1947; d. Theodore G. and Frances (Allen) Huffman; m. Henry L. Bethea, Sept. 15, 1946; children: Mary, Samuel, Sarah. BS, Miss. Coll., Clinton, 1968; MD, U. Miss., 1974. Diplomate Am. Bd. Allergy and Immunology, Am. Bd. Pediatrics. Resident pediatrics U. Miss., Jackson, 1973-75; fellow allergy and immunology U. Fla., 1977-79; pvt. practice Houston, 1983—. Instr. pediatrics U. Miss., 1975-77, U. Fla., 1979-80; active staff Houston Northwest Med. Ctr., 1983—, Meml. Hermann Hosp. The Woodlands, St. Luke's Hosp. The Woodlands; cons. in field. Fellow Am. Acad. Allergy, Asthma and Immunology, Am. Coll. Allergy, Am. Acad. Pediatrics. Republican. Episcopalian. Avocations: photography, travel, arts and crafts. Home: 92 Hollymead Dr The Woodlands TX 77381-5121 Office Phone: 281-298-8132. Office Fax: 281-298-8213. Business E-Mail: bethea@dbmed.net.

BETHEL, CHARLES JONES, state legislator; b. Mar. 03; s. Jim and Trisha Bethel; m. Lynsey Nix; children: Jeb, Henry. BBA in Mgmt. cum laude, U. Ga., 1998, JD, 2001. Clk. to Judge Charles A. Pannell, Jr. US Dist. Ct. No. Dist. of Ga.; atty. Minor, Bell & Neal, 2003—05; asst. city solicitor City of Dalton, Ga., 2003—04; councilman Dalton City Coun., 2005—10; dir. corp. affairs J&J Industries, Inc., Dalton; mem. Dist. 54, coun. mem. Ga. State Senate, 2011—. Mem. ABA, State Bar Ga., Conasauga Bar Assn. Republican. Office: 1701 Briarcliff Cir Dalton GA 30720-5178 also: Georgia State Senate 324 A Coverdell Legis Office Bldg Atlanta GA 30334 Office Phone: 706-270-1685, 404-656-6436. Business E-Mail: charlie.bethel@senate.ga.gov.

BETTI, JOHN ANSO, federal official, retired automotive executive; b. Ottawa, Ill., Jan. 6, 1931; s. Louis and Ida (Dallari) B.; m. Joan Doyle, Aug. 22, 1953; children: Diane, Denise, Donna (dec.), Joan. BSMechE, Ill. Inst. Tech., 1952; MS in Engring., Chrysler Inst. Engring., 1954. Registered profl. engr., Mich. Student engr. to asst. chief engr. Chrysler Corp., 1952-62; with Ford Motor Co., 1962-89, from exec. engr. body engring. to v.p., gen. mgr. truck ops., 1962-76; v.p. product devel. Ford of Europe, Inc., Warley, England, 1976-79, also dir.; with N.Am. Automotive Ops., Dearborn, Mich., 1979-84, v.p. powertrain and chassis ops., 1979-83, v.p. mfg. and bus. devel., 1983-84; exec. v.p. tech. affairs and operating staffs Ford Motor Co., Mich., 1984—88, bd. dirs. fin. and exec. coms., 1985—89, exec. v.p. diversified products ops. Dearborn, Mich., 1988-89; undersecretary of def., acquisition and nat. armaments dir. Dept. Def., Washington, 1989-91. Instr. Lawrence Inst. Engring., Wayne State U., Detroit, 1953-59; chmn. bd. Ford Motor Co., Caribbean Inc., 1979-84, Ensite Ltd. Can., 1979-84, Ford Aerospace corp., 1988-89, Ford Electronics and Refrigeration Corp., 1988-89; dir. collins & Aikman Corp., 1991-94; mem. dir. compensation com. Breed Tech., 1992-94, Kaysor-Roth Corp., 1993-94. Bd. dirs. Mich. Opera Theatre, 1984-87; trustee Detroit Inst. for Children, 1985-89; mem. nat. adv. com. U. Mich. Engring. Sch., 1985-89; chmn. bd. trustees GMI Engring. and Mgmt. Inst., 1985-89, Nat. Acad. Engring., 1989. Recipient Alumni Profl. Achievement award Ill. Inst. Tech., 1980, OTHS Hall of Fame, 2008, Hon. Citizen award, Montese Italy, 2010; John Morse Meml. scholar. Mem. Lost Tree Club (North Palm Beach, Fla.), Tau Beta Pi, Pi Tau Sigma, Alpha Sigma Phi, Beta Omega Nu.

BETTMAN, JAMES ROSS, management educator; b. Laurinburg, NC, Sept. 15, 1943; s. Roland David and Virginia Gertrude (Hare) B.; m. Joan Carol Scribner, Dec. 16, 1967; 1 child, David James. BA, Yale U., 1965, MPhil, PhD, Yale U., 1969. Prof. mgmt. Grad. Sch. Mgmt., UCLA, 1969-82; IBM rsch. prof. Fuqua Sch. Bus., Duke U., Durham, NC, 1982-83, Burlington Industries prof., 1983—. Author: An Information Processing Theory of Consumer Choice, 1979, The Adaptive Decision Maker, 1993, Emotional Decisions: Tradeoff Difficulty and Coping in Consumer Choice, 2001; co-editor Jour. of Consumer Rsch., 1981-87 (Disting. Svc. award, 2008), editor monographs, 2002-07; contbr. chpts. to books, articles to profl. jours. Named ISI Highly Cited Rschr., Econs./Bus., 2003; recipient Melamed prize bus. rsch., 2000, Disting. Sci. Achievement award Soc. for Consumer Psychology, 2006. Fellow APA, Am. Psychol. Soc.; mem. Assn. Consumer Rsch. (bd. dir. 1976-79, pres. 1987, fellow in consumer behavior 1992), Inst. Ops. Rsch. and Mgmt. Sci., Am. Mktg. Assn. (Harold M. Maynard award 1979, Paul D. Converse award 1992, Irwin/McGraw-Hill Disting. Mktg. Educator award 2000, Paul Green award 2009, Consumer Behavior Special Interest Group Lifetime Achievement award, 2013). Democrat. Episcopalian. Home: 213 Huntington Dr Chapel Hill NC 27514-2419 Office: Duke U Fuqua Sch of Bus Durham NC 27708-0120 Office Phone: 919-660-7851. Business E-Mail: jrb12@duke.edu.

BETTS, EUGENE KOHLER, pediatric anesthesiologist; b. Boston, June 2, 1942; MD, Wake Forest U., 1968. Diplomate Am. Bd. Anesthesiology. Intern N.C. Bapt. Hosp., Winston-Salem, N.C., 1968-69, resident in anesthesiology, 1969-72; fellow in pediat. anesthesiology Childrens Hosp., Phila., 1971, assoc. in chief anesthesiology, 1974—98; staff anesthesiology Hosp. U. Pa., 1979—98; assoc. prof. anesthesiology U. Pa.; prof. anesthesiology and pediat. Ga. Regents U. Augusta. Maj. US Army, 1972—74. Decorated Bronze Star US Army; recipient 500th Anniversary medal, Nicolaus Copernicus Med. Acad. Krakow, Poland, 1982. Mem. Am. Soc. Anesthesiologists, Soc. Pediat. Anesthesia, Assn. Univ. Anesthesiologists, Ga. ANES Soc. Republican. Presbyterian. Office: Ga Regents University MCG Children's Med Ctr 1120 15th St BT-2651 Augusta GA 30912-2700 Home Phone: 706-738-7124; Office Phone: 706-721-5271. Office Fax: 706-721-5287. Business E-Mail: ebetts@gru.edu.*

BETTS, JAMES EDWARD, lawyer; b. Holyoke, Mass., Oct. 9, 1940; s. James Archibel and Ruth Owen Betts; m. Carol Sue Hanser, June 19, 1962; children: James Hanser, Laurie Jane Betts Hemler. AB, Colgate U., Hamilton, NY, 1962; JD, U. Richmond, Va., 1965; LLM, Harvard Law Sch., Cambridge, Mass., 1966. Bar: Va. 1965. Assoc. Christian & Barton, LLP, Richmond, Va., 1966—72, ptnr., 1972—, mng. ptnr., 1990—2013. Adj. assoc. prof. antitrust law U. Richmond Law Sch., Richmond, Va., 1973—83, 2005—10; chmn. antitrust sect. Va. State Bar, 1977, mem. lawyer disciplinary bd., 1990—93, chmn. com. on lawyer discipline, 1999—2000. Sec. Richmond First Club, 1972; pres. Friends of Richmond Libr., Va., 1974; chmn. Profls. Divsn. United Way Svcs. Greater Richmond, 1996; mem., moderator diaconate First Presbyn. Ch., Richmond, 1989—95, elder, clk. of session, 1996—2002; sec. and mem. Mary Baldwin Coll. Bd. Trustees, Staunton, Va., 1976—89, 1991—96; v.p. and mem. bd. dir. The Steward Sch., Richmond, 1977—79; chmn. U. Richmond Nat. Alumni Coun., 1979—80; mem. com. on spl. issues Nat. and State Importance, 2003—. Fellow: Am. Bar Found. (Va. state chair); mem.: Nat. and State Importance (mem. com. on spl. issues 2003—), Com. on Special Issues of Nat. & State Importance, Va. Found. Ind. Coll. (trustee 2009—), John Marshall Found. (pres. 2006—07), U. Richmond Law Sch. Assn. (pres. 1979—80), Va. Bar Assn. (pres. 2002), Farmington Country Club (Charlottesville, Va.), US Supreme Ct. Hist. Soc. (Va. state chmn. 2004), Phi Delta Phi, Omicron Delta Kappa. Presbyterian. Avocations: reading, exercise, sports. Office: Christian and Barton LLP 909 E Main St Richmond VA 23219 Office Phone: 804-697-4156. Business E-Mail: jbetts@cblaw.com.

BETTS, REBECCA A., lawyer; b. Memphis, Nov. 25, 1951; BA, Dickinson Coll., 1972; JD, W.Va. U., 1976. Bar: W.Va., US Dist. Ct. (so. dist.) W.Va. 1976, US Ct. Appeals (4th cir.) 1978, US Supreme Ct. 1984. Assoc. Spilman, Thomas, Battle & Klostermeyer, Charleston, W.Va., 1976—77; asst. US atty. US Atty.'s Office, 1977—81, chief civil divsn., 1979—81; founding ptnr. King, Betts & Allen, Charleston, W.Va.; US atty. US Dist. Ct. (So. Dist.), W.Va., 1994—2001; ptnr. Allen Guthrie McHugh & Thomas PLLC, 2001—. Adv. com. on rules & procedures 4th Cir., 1995—2001; civil justice reform act adv. com. So. Dist. W.Va., 1991, com. for local rules and subcom. on criminal rules, 1992. Mem. editl. bd.: W.Va. Law Rev. Mem.: The Legal Aid Soc. of Charleston (bd. dirs.), W.Va. State Bar (past mem. com. on legal ethics), Order of Coif. Office: Allen Guthrie McHugh & Thomas PO Box 3394 Charleston WV 25333 Office Phone: 304-345-7250. Business E-Mail: rabetts@agmtlaw.com.

BETZ, DONALD, academic administrator; b. Anacortes, Wash., Feb. 16, 1945; s. Donald L. and Mary Ann (Sarno) Betz; m. Mona Seymour, Aug. 19, 1967; 1 child, Nick. BA with honors, U. San Francisco, 1967; MA, U. Denver, 1970, PhD, 1973. Exec. dir. Northeastern State U. Ednl. Found., Tahlequah, Okla., 1978-80; asst. to pres. Northeastern State U., Tahlequah, 1980-86, dir. univ. relations, 1984-85, prof. polit. sci., 1979—, dean continuing studies, 1986-88, v.p. univ. rels., 1988, pres., 2008—11; provost, v.p. academic affairs Palmer Coll., Davenport, Iowa, 1994—99; provost, v.p. academic affairs, prof. polit. sci. U. Ctrl. Okla., Edmond, 1999—2005, pres., 2011—; chancellor U. Wis.-River Falls, 2005—08. Vis. prof. World Campus Afloat Chapman Coll., Orange, Calif., 1974, Orange, 1975, Semester-at-Sea U. Pitts., 1981. Author: Cultivating Leadership, 1981. Named Tchr. of Yr., 1975; named one of Outstanding Educators of America, 1973, Outstanding Young Men of America, 1979. Roman Catholic. Avocations: exercise, travel. Office: University of Central Oklahoma Office of President, Box 105 100 N University Dr Edmond OK 73034 Office Phone: 405-974-2311. E-mail: betz@uco.edu.

BETZ, RANDAL R., orthopedist; MD, Temple U. Fellow pediatric orthopaedics Alfred I duPont Inst.; Am.-Brit.-Can. traveling fellow Can. Orthopaedic Assn., North Am. traveling fellow; Berg-Sloat traveling fellow Orthopaedic Rsch. and Edn. Found.; intern gen. surgery Temple Univ. Hosp., resident orthopaedic surgery; prof. orthopaedic surgery Temple Univ. Sch. Medicine; staff Temple Univ. Children's Med. Ctr.; chief staff Shriners Hosps. for Children, med. dir. spinal cord injury unit. Editl. bd. Jour. Pediatric Orthopaedics, SpineUniverse, assoc. editor Spinal Frontiers, reviewer Jour. of Bone And Joint Surgery, Jour. Pediatric Orthopaedics, Spine. Mem.: Spinal Deformity Edn. Group, Internat. Functional Elec. Stimulation Soc., Brit. Scoliosis Soc., Am. Spinal Injury Assn., Am. Paraplegia Soc., Am. Orthopaedic Assn., Am. Acad. Orthopaedic Surgeons, Am. Acad. Cerebral Palsy and Devel. Medicine, Am. Orthopaedic Soc., Alpha Mega Alpha. Office: Shriners Hospitals for Children 2900 Rocky Point Dr Tampa FL 33607 Office Phone: 813-281-0300.

BETZER, SUSAN ELIZABETH BEERS, physician, geriatrician; b. Evanston, Ill., Aug. 24, 1943; d. Thomas Moulding and Mary Ella (Waidner) Beers; m. Peter Robin Betzer, June 18, 1965; children: Sarah Elizabeth, Katherine Hannah. AB in Biol. Scis. magna cum, Mount Holyoke Coll., 1965; PhD in Oceanography, U. R.I., 1972; MD, U. Miami, 1978. Diplomate Am. Bd. Family Practice, Am. Bd. Geriat. Rsch. assoc. dept. marine sci. U. South Fla., St. Petersburg, 1973-74, rsch. scholar, scientist, 1975-76; resident in family practice Bayfront Med. Ctr., St. Petersburg, 1978-81; clin. asst. prof. dept. family medicine U. South Fla., Tampa, 1982—2007; pvt. practice St. Petersburg, 1982—. Cons. physician Fed. Employee Health Clinic, Honolulu, 1981-82. Contbr. articles to profl. jours. Adv. com. St. Petersburg H.S., 1996-2002; bd. dir. Fla. Orch., St. Petersburg, 1983-86, 88-, pres., 1985-86, mem. exec. com., 1988-, vice-chair bd. trustees 1996-2002, sec., 2002-, founder, chair audience devel. com., St. Petersburg, 1990-94; bd. dirs. Suncoast Ctr. Cmty. Mental Health, St. Petersburg, 1992-93; trustee Bayfront Health Found., 1996-2004, chmn., 2001-03; trustee Bayfront Health Svcs., 1992-96, vice-chair, 1993-96; vol. physician St. Petersburg Free Clinic, 1979-2003. Recipient Golden Baton award, St. Petersburg Fla. Orch. Guild, 1994, Chmns. award, Fla. Orch., 1997, Svc. award, Pinellas County Med. Soc., 1999, Philanthropy Vol. of Yr., Tampa Bay chpt. Assn. Fundraising Profls., 2003, Humanitarian Physician of Yr., Tampa Bay Area, Fla. Med. Bus., 2004; named Woman of Distinction, Suncoast coun. Girl Scouts U.S., 1994; named one of Best Doctors in Am., 1996—. Mem.: Mt. Holyoke Coll. Campaign Steering Com., Fla. Acad. Family Physicians (Dr. of the Day, Fla. Legislature 1995, 1996), Am. Med. Women's Assn., Am. Acad. Family Physicians (Mead Johnson award 1980), Mount Holyoke Alumnae Assn. (alumnae honor rsch. com. 1988—91, alumnae devel. com. 1996—2003, pres. 2003—06, Alumnae medal of honor 2000), Phi Beta Kappa. Avocations: symphony, birding, cooking, reading. Home: 1830 7th St N Saint Petersburg FL 33704-3322 Office: 461 7th Ave S Saint Petersburg FL 33701-4818 Office Phone: 727-823-0402.

BEUTLER, BRUCE A., geneticist, immunologist; b. Chgo., Dec. 29, 1957; s. Ernest and Brondelle May Beutler; children: Daniel Edward, Elliot Karl, Jonathan David. BA, U. Calif., San Diego, 1976; MD, U. Chgo. Pritzker Sch. Medicine, 1981; MD (hon.), Tech. U. Munich, 2007. Med. tng. U. Tex. Southwester Med. Ctr., Dallas, 1981—83, asst. prof., 1986—90, assoc. prof., 1990—96, founding dir., Ctr. Genetics of Host Defense, 2011—, prof., 1996—2000; fellow Rockefeller U, NY, 1983—85, asst. prof., 1985; assoc. physician Rockefeller U. Hosp., 1984—86; prof. dept. immunology Scripps Rsch. Inst., La Jolla, Calif., 2000—11, chmn. dept. genetics, 2007—11. Investigator Howard Hughes Med. Inst., 1986—2000. Recipient Young Investigator award, American Fedn. Clin. Rsch., 1994, Charles-Léopold Mayer prize, French Acad. Scis., 2006, William B. Coley award, Cancer Rsch. Inst., 2006, Will Rogers Inst. Ann. prize for rsch., 2009; co-recipient Robert Koch prize, Germany, 2004, Internat. Balzan Found. prize, 2007, Albany Med. Ctr. prize, 2009, Nobel Prize in Physiology or Medicine, 2011, Shaw Found. prize for Life Sci./Medicine, Hong Kong, 2011. Mem.: NAS, Inst. Medicine, Assn. American Physicians, American Soc. Clin. Investigation, European Molecular Biology Orgn. (assoc.; fgn. assoc.). Achievements include first to isolate mouse tumor necrosis factor-alpha (TNF) and to demonstrate the inflammatory potential of this cytokine, proving its important role in endotoxin-induced shock; invention of recombinant molecules expressly designed to neutralize TNF used extensively in the treatment of rheumatoid arthritis, Crohn's disease, psoriasis, and other forms of inflammation. Office: UT Southwestern Med Ctr 5323 Harry Hines Blvd Dallas TX 75390 Office Phone: 214-648-5838. Business E-Mail: bruce.beutler@utsouthwestern.edu.

BEUTTENMULLER, RUDOLF WILLIAM, lawyer; b. St. Louis, Dec. 20, 1953; s. Paul A. and Doris R. (Henle) B.; m. Ragina Lee Winters, July 14, 1984. AB cum laude, Princeton U., 1976; JD with distinction, Duke U., 1980. Bar: Tex. 1980, U.S. Dist. Ct. Tex. 1980. Assoc. Jenkens & Gilchrist, Dallas, 1980-83; ptnr. Gregory, Self & Beuttenmuller, Dallas, 1983-88, Bradley, Bradley & Beuttenmuller, Irving, Tex., 1988-93; dir. Thomas Cinclair & Beuttenmuller, Dallas, 1994—. Articles editor Duke Law Jour., Durham, 1979-80. Mem. Rep. Nat. Com., Washington, 1984. Mem. ABA, Dallas Bar Assn., Duke Law Alumni Assn., Princeton Alumni Assn. Office: 5335 Spring Valley Rd Dallas TX 75254-3009 Home: 4617 Livingston Ave Dallas TX 75209 Office Phone: 972-991-2121. Business E-Mail: rudybeutt@tcblawfirm.com.

BEVARD, HERBERT ARMSTRONG, bishop; b. Balt., Md., Feb. 24, 1946; s. Charles Wright and Catherine (Schafer) Bevard. Attended, Dickinson Coll.; grad., St. Charles Borromeo Sem., 1972. Ordained priest Archdiocese of Phila., Pa., 1972, parochial vicar in various parishes, 1972—83; asst. pastor St. Charles Borromeo parish, Bensalem, Pa., 1983—89; parochial vicar St. Anastasia parish, Newtown Sq., Pa., 1989—94; pastor St. Athanasius parish, Phila., 1994—2008; vicar Phila. North Archdiocese of Phila., Pa., 2007—08; ordained bishop, 2008; bishop Diocese of St. Thomas, U.S.V.I., 2008—. Newman chaplain Pa. State Univ., 1972—73, Widener Univ., 1973—78. Roman Catholic. Mailing: Diocese of St Thomas PO Box 301825 St Thomas VI 00803-1825 Office: Diocese of St Thomas 29A Princesse Gade St Thomas VI 00803 Office Phone: 340-774-3166. Office Fax: 340-774-5816.

BEVERIDGE, NORWOOD PIERSON, retired law educator; b. Boston, Nov. 5, 1936; s. Norwood Pierson and Dorothy Winifred (Woodrow) Beveridge; children: Norwood Pierson Jr., Richard W., Susan C. Mapp. AB, Harvard U., 1958, LLB, 1962; LLM, NYU, 1985. Bar: N.Y. 1963. Assoc. Kramer, Marx, Greenlee & Backus, NYC, 1962—68, ptnr., 1968—71; asst. sec., asst. gen. counsel Amerace Corp., NYC, 1971—73, sec., corp. counsel, 1973—84; asst. prof. Lubin Sch. Bus. Pace U., Pleasantville, NY, 1985—86; assoc. prof. We. State U. Coll. Law, Fullerton, Calif., 1986—89, Oklahoma City U. Law Sch., 1989—92, prof., 1992—2010, assoc. dean, 1999—2003, prof. emeritus, 2010—. Fellow: Am. Bar Found. (life); mem.: ABA (mem. com. corp. law depts. 1974—86, mem. com. partnerships and unicorp. bus. orgns. 1990—, mem. com. corp. gov. 1998—, fed. regulation of securities com. 2003—), Harvard Club. Home: 7400 NW 115th Street Oklahoma City OK 73162

BEVERLY, JAMES, state legislator; BS in Biology, Guilford Coll., Greensboro, NC, 1990; DO, Pa. Coll. Optometry, Phila., 1994; MBA, Wesleyan Coll., Macon, Ga., 2006; MPA, Harvard U., Cambridge, Mass., 2010. Pvt. practice optometrist, Ga., 1986—; CEO Goggles Eyecare 4 Kids, Inc., Macon, Ga.; mng. mem. Midtowne Vision Ctr., LLC, Macon; mem. Dist. 139 Ga. House of Reps., Atlanta, 2011—. Vol. optometrist Chijan Internat. Found., Nigeria, Uganda, Jamaica. Democrat. Office: Ga House of Reps 509-D Coverdell Legis Office Bldg Atlanta GA 30334 Office Phone: 404-656-0220. Business E-Mail: james.beverly@house.ga.gov.

BEVILLE, LEWIS E., insurance company executive; BS in Fin., U. Ala., 1974. Chartered property and casualty underwriter Am. Inst. Property and Liability Underwriters, 1981. Ins. broker Beville Ins. Agency, 1974—90; ptnr., v.p., treas. Thames, Batre, Mattei, Beville and Ison, Mobile, Ala., 1990—; bd. dirs. Colonial BancGroup, Inc., 1997—2009, pres., CEO, 2009. Mem. Dauphin Way Meth. Ch.; dir. Mobile Area C. of C., Mobile Area Edn. Found. Mem.: Gulf Coast Chpt. CPCU's (dir., past pres.). Office: Thames Batre Mattei Beville & Ison 2065 Old Shell Rd Mobile AL 36660 Office Phone: 251-473-9000. Office Fax: 251-473-9010. Business E-Mail: lewis@tbmbi.com.

BEYER, DON (DONALD STERNOFF BEYER JR.), former ambassador; b. Trieste, Free Territory of Trieste, June 20, 1950; arrived in U.S., 1952. s. Donald Sternoff Sr. and Nancy Prew (McDonald) B.; m. Carolyn Anne (McInerney), July 15, 1972 (div.); children: Donald III, Stephanie; m. Megan Carroll, Sept. 19, 1987; children: Clara, Grace. BA in Economics, magna cum laude, Williams Coll., 1972. Owner Don Beyer Volvo, Falls Ch., Va., 1974—; lt. gov. Commonwealth of Va., Richmond, 1990-98; US amb. to Switzerland & Liechtenstein US Dept. State, Bern, 2009—13. Urban at large mem. Commonwealth Transp. Bd., Va., 1987-90; chmn. Va. Poverty & Welfare Reform Commn., 1994-95, Transp. & Land Use Group, Va. Commn. on Climate Change, 2008 Chmn. Baliles for Gov., Northern Va., 1985; Paul Simon for Pres., Va., 1988; Bill Clinton for Pres., Va., 1992; mem. 11th Dist. Democratic Com., Vienna, Va., 1992; Dem. nominee Gov. of Va., 1998. Named TIME Mag. Quality Dealer of Yr., Va., 1991; Dealer of Excellence Award; Grand Award for Highway Safety, Nat. Safety Fedn.; James Wheat Award for Svc. to Virginians with Disabilities; Earl Williams Leadership in Tech. Award. Mem. Land Rover Alexandria (pres. 1997); Northern Va. Bus. Roundtable; Northern Va. HighTech. Coun. (co-founder), American Internat. Automobile Dealers Assn., 2006-07; Bd. mem. Youth for Tommorrow; Washington Cmty. Found. & the Red Cross. Democrat. Episcopalian. Avocations: golf, skiing, climbing.*

BEYER, GERRY WAYNE, lawyer, educator; b. Sept. 12, 1956; s. O. Frank and Lorraine Hazel (Kopper) B.; m. Margaret Mary Brewer, June 17, 1983. BA summa cum laude, Ea. Mich. U., Ypsilanti, 1976; JD summa cum laude, Ohio State U., 1979; LLM, U. Ill., 1983, JSD, 1990. Bar: Ohio 1980, Ill. 1980, Tex. 1984, US Ct. Mil. Appeals 1990, US Supreme Ct. 1991. Assoc. Knisley, Carpenter, Wilhelm & Nein, Columbus, Ohio, 1980; instr. law U. Ill., Champaign, 1980-81; asst. prof., assoc. prof. law St. Mary's U., San Antonio, 1981-87, prof., 1987—2005; Gov. Preston E. Smith regents prof. Tex. Tech. U., Sch. Law, Lubbock, 2005—. Vis. prof. Boston Coll. Law Sch., 1992-93, U. N.Mex., 1995, So. Meth. U. Sch. Law, 1997, Santa Clara U. Sch. Law, 1999-2000; La Trobe U. Sch. Law, Melbourne, Australia, 2008, 10, Ohio State U., 2012; lectr. Inst. Tex. Bar Rev., Austin, 1984-88, BAR/BRI Bar Rev., Houston, 1984-90, 99—, SMH Bar Rev., Boston, 1990-95, West Bar Rev., 1996-97; adv. bd. paralegal divsn. S.W. Sch. Ct. Reporting, 1990-92. Author quar. jour. articles in Estate Planning Devels. for Tex. Profls., 1981—, Texas Wills and Estates: Cases and Materials, 1987, 6th rev. edit., 2008, Tex. Estate Planning Statutes Student Edit., 2006, 2008, 10, 12, Teaching Materials on Estate Planning, 1995, 2005, 2013, Wills, Trusts, and Estates: Examples and Explanations, 1999, 5th rev. edit., 2012, West's Legal Forms- Real Estate Transactions - Residential (vols. 19 & 19A), 4th edit. 2008, Texas Law of Wills, 3d ed., 2002; co-author: West's Legal Forms - Real Estate Transactions (vols. 19-23), 1986, West's Texas Forms - Probate and Administration of Estates (vols. 12, 12A, 12B), 1996,

2007, Texas Law of Wills, 2d edit., 1992, 3d edit., 2007, ann. supplement to Tex. Will Manual, 1986-2004, Modern Dictionary for the Legal Profession, 1993, 4th edit., 2008, Wills, Trusts and Estates for Legal Assistants, 2002, 06, 09, 13, Fat Cats and Lucky Dogs - How to Leave (some of) Your Estate to Your Pet, 2010. Mem. ALI, ABA (vice chair significant current lit. com., probate and trust divsn. of real property, probate and trust law sect. 1990-95, vice-chair non-tax issues in drafting wills and revocable trusts 1996-99), ACTEC, ALI, Tex. Bar Assn., Ill. State Bar Assn., South Plains Trust & Estate Coun. (pres. 2010-11), Lubbock County Bar Assn. (treas. 2009-10), Order Coif, Order Barristers, Southwest Found. for Biomed. Rsch. (animal rsch. com. 1986-91). Home: Ste 212 4414 82nd St Lubbock TX 79424 Office: Tex Tech Univ Sch Law 1802 Hartford St Lubbock TX 79409-0004 Office Phone: 806-742-3990 ext. 302. Business E-Mail: gwb@ProfessorBeyer.com.

BEYER, RICHARD MICHAEL, manufacturing executive; b. NYC, Oct. 12, 1948; s. Thomas Robert Sr. and Madeline Frances B.; m. Nikki Cole Greene, Nov. 5, 1983; children: Laura, Christopher. BS in Russian, Georgetown U., 1970, MS in Russia, 1974; MBA, Columbia U., 1977. V.p. mktg. ITT, Raleigh, N.C., 1984-86, v.p., gen. mgr. PABX sys. divsn., 1986-87, Alcatel, Alexandria, Va., 1987-89; v.p., gen. mgr. Rockwell Internat., Downers Grove, Ill., 1989-93; pres. comm. & computing group National Semiconductor Corp., Sunnyvale, Calif., 1993-95, exec. v.p., COO, 1995-96; pres., COO VSLI Tech. Inc., San Jose, Calif., 1996-98; pres., CEO FVC.COM, Inc., Santa Clara, Calif., 1999—2000; CEO Elantec Semiconductor, Inc., Irvine, Calif., 2000—02, Intersil Corp., Milpitas, Calif., 2002—08; chmn., CEO Freescale Semiconductor, Inc., Austin, Tex., 2008—. Bd. dirs. VLSI Tech., Inc., 1996-98, FVC.COM, Inc., 1999-2000, Elantec Semiconduxtor, Inc., 2000-02, Credence Systems Corp., 2003-08, Xceive Inc., 2006-08, Semiconductor Ind. Assn. Bd. dirs. San Jose Symphony, 1995—96, 2003—. 1st lt. USMC Res., 1970—73. Mem. Am. Electronics Assn. (bd. dirs. 1997-98). Republican. Methodist. Avocations: skiing, bicycling, reading, tennis, wine. Office: Freescale Semiconductor Inc 6501 William Cannon Dr W Austin TX 78735 Business E-Mail: rich.beyer@freescale.com.

BEYTAGH, FRANCIS X., law educator; b. Savannah, Ga., July 11, 1935; BA magna cum laude, U. Notre Dame, Ind., 1956; JD, U. Mich., 1963. Bar: Ohio 1964, US Supreme Ct 1967, Ind. 1972. Clk. Fuller, Seney, Henry, and Hodge, Toledo, 1961; sr. law clk. to Chief Justice Earl Warren US Supreme Ct., Washington, 1963-64; assoc. Jones, Day, Cockley, and Reavis, Cleve., 1964-66; asst. to solicitor gen. US Dept. Justice, Washington, 1966-70; prof. law U. Notre Dame, 1970-74, 75-76; prof., dean U. Toledo, 1976-83; Cullen prof. law U. Houston, 1984-85; prof., dean Ohio State U. Coll. Law, 1985-93, prof., 1993-97; spl. counsel Jones, Day, Reavis, and Pogue, Columbus, Ohio, 1993-96; pres., prof. Fla. Coastal Sch. Law, Jacksonville, 1997-98, prof., 1998—, founders' chair, 2000—. Vis. prof. law U. Va., Charlottesville, 1974—75, U. Mich., 1983—84, So. Meth. U., Dallas, 1997. Editor in chief: Mich. Law Rev., 1962—63; author: Supplement to Kauper's Constitutional Law: Cases and Materials, 1977, Constitutional Law: Cases and Materials, 5th edit., 1980, supplements, 1981, 1984, Constitutionalism in Contemporary Ireland, 1997; contbr. articles to profl. jours. Ret. capt. USNR. Fulbright fellow, 1994. Fellow: Am. Bar Found. (life); mem.: ABA, Jacksonville Bar Assn., Fla. Bar, Am. Jud. Soc. (assoc.), Order of Coif. Home: 49 Marsh Creek Rd Amelia Island FL 32034-6414 Office: Fla Coastal Sch Law 8787 Baypine Rd Jacksonville FL 32256-8528 Business E-Mail: fbeytagh@fcsl.edu.

BHADA, ROHINTON KHURSHED, chemical engineering educator; b. Bombay, Mar. 23, 1935; s. Khurshed A. and Goola K. (Press) B.; m. Patricia Ann Bergman, Jan. 18, 1959; children: John, James, Sarah, Naomi, Jenny, Nikki, Cyndie. BS, U. Mich., 1955, MS, 1957, PhD, 1968; MBA, U. Akron, 1964. Registered profl. engr., Tex. Rsch. asst. U. Mich., Ann Arbor, 1955-59; rsch. engr. Babcock & Wilcox, Alliance, Ohio, 1959-64, group leader, 1964-72, sect. mgr., 1972-77, dept. mgr., 1977-88; assoc. dean, prof. N.Mex. State U., Las Cruces, 1988-92, prof., assoc. dean of engring., 1992—99, assoc. dean emeritus, dir., 1978—85; pvt. practise, cons., 1999—. Dir. Wast Edn. & Rsch. Consortium, Las Cruces, 1989-99. Contbr. articles to profl. jours.; patentee in field. Local pres. Alliance Jaycees, 1964-65; state v.p. Ohio Jaycees, Marion, 1965-66; nat. dir. US Jaycees, Tulsa, 1966-67; vice-chair City Environment Com., Las Cruces, 1989—. Named Outstanding Pres. U.S. Jaycees, 1965, Outstanding Nat. Dir., 1967. Mem. AIChE (chmn. 1967-68), NSPE (Outstanding Engring. Achievement award 1991), Am. Acad. Environ. Engrs. (diplomate, Grand Prize award 1998), Am. Soc. Engring. Edn., N.Mex. Soc. Profl. Engrs., Phi Lambda Upsilon, Beta Gamma Sigma, Tau Beta Pi. Jehovah'S Witness. Avocations: racquetball, religious study, gardening. Office Phone: 678-313-0938. Personal E-mail: ronbhada@aol.com.

BHARUCHA, KERSI J., neurologist, educator; MD, Jawaharlal Inst., India, 1984. Diplomate American Bd. Psychiatry and Neurology-neurology, 2006. Resident in internal medicine Nat. Health Svc. Hosps., 1985—89; resident in neurology Mayo Clinic, Rochester, Minn., 1990—94; fellow in movement disorders Med. Coll. Ga., 1994—95; assoc. prof. in neurology Univ. Okla.; physician OU Med. Ctr. Office: OU MedicalCenter 1200 Everett Dr Oklahoma City OK 73104-5047 Office Phone: 405-271-5911.*

BHASIN, MADAN MOHAN, research scientist; b. Lahore, India, June 23, 1938; came to U.S., 1959; s. Late L. Mela Ram and Bahain Devi (Sahni) B.; m. Anand Kumari Chugha, Aug. 5, 1961; children: Madhu Lata, Anoop Kumar. BS with hon., Delhi U., New Delhi, India, 1958; postgrad., Indiana U., 1959-60; PhD, U. Notre Dame, 1964. Chemist Union Carbide Corp., South Charleston, W.Va., 1963-69, project scientist, 1969-77, research scientist, 1977-81, group supr., 1981-82, sr. research scientist, group supr., 1982-88, corp. fellow., group supr., sr. scientist, 1988—. Spkr., lectr. in field. Patentee in field; contbr. articles to profl. jours. Chmn. India Ctr., Charleston, W.V., 1986-96, co-chair, India Heritage Fair, 1996—; bd. dirs. United Way, 2000. Recipient Eugene J. Houdry Award in Applied Catalysis, Catalysis Soc. N. Amer., 1995, Scientific Achievement Awd., Kanawka Valley Section of ACS (Am. Chem. Soc.), 1995, Amer. Chem. Soc. Awd. in Indsl. Chem., 1999, AZKO Nobel. Mem. AIChE, NAE, Am. Chem. Soc. (chmn. summer symposium Indsl. and Engring. Chem. div. 1986-88, exec. com. mem. 1983-87, chmn. I & EC div. 1990), Catalysis Secretariat (chair 1997), India Assn. (pres. 1979-80). Avocations: photography, tennis, badmington, gardening. Office: Union Carbide Corp 437 Maccorkle Ave SW South Charleston WV 25303 E-mail: bhasin2m@excelonline.com.

BHIDE, MANOHAR GOPAL, retired nuclear scientist; b. Pune, Maharashtra, India, Nov. 9, 1935; arrived in U.S., 1994, naturalized, 2001; s. Gopal Ramchandra and Manorama Gopal Bhide; m. Meena Mohiniraj Joshi, Jan. 7, 1981; children: Unmesh, Amit, Sonia. BSc in Math., U. Mumbai, India, 1954; MSc in Physics, U. Mumbai, 1956; PhD, U. Mumbai, India, 1971. Registered profl. engr., Argonne Nat. Lab., IL., USA, 1958, cert. Atomic Energy Rsch. Establishment, Harwell, U.K., 1960; yoga tchr. Kaivalyadham, Lonavala, Maharashtra, India, 1984. Fellow Ramnarain Ruia Coll., Mumbai, Maharashtra, 1954—56; sci. officer Bhabha Atomic Rsch. Ctr., Trombay, Mumbai, 1956—94; adj. faculty physics No. Va. CC, Annandale, 1997; substitute tchr. Fairfax County Pub. Schs., Va., 1998—2007. Exch. scientist Atomic Energy Rsch. Establishment, Harwell, Didcot, Berkshire, United Kingdom, 1958—60; affiliate Internat. Inst. Nuc. Sci. & Engring., Argonne, Ill., 1960—62; sec. disarmament study group Govt. of India, Dept. Atomic Energy, Mumbai, 1962—67; sci. sec. XII Pugwash Conf. on Sci. & World Affairs, Udaipur, Rajasthan, India, 1964; Indian del. IAEA Seminar on Physics of Fast & Intermediate Reactors, Vienna, 1961, Second UN Conf. on Peaceful Uses of Atomic Energy, Geneva, 1958; adj. prof. Southeastern U., Washington, 1999—2009. Editor: Vidnyan Kutuhal, Marathi Mahasangh-Vidnyan; contbr. articles to profl. jours. Co-founder, treas. Marathi Vidnyan Mahasangh, Mumbai, 1980—82; founder, treas., sec. Madhyamumbai Marathi Vidnyan Sangh, Mumbai, 1971—93; co-founder, treas. Mumbai Shubham Karoti Parivar, 1979—88; camp leader Student Voluntary Work Camps, Turbhe, Gorkamat & Kadav, Maharashtra, 1953—54; active Bhabha Atomic Rsch. Ctr. Maharashtra Mandal, Mumbai, 1970—94, Kokannagar Yuvak Mandal (Youth Club), Mumbai, 1965—75; vis. lectr. Shramik Vidyapeeth Ministry Non-formal Edn. Govt. India, 1973—82. Recipient V. K. Bhagwat prize, Ramnarain Ruia Coll., Mumbai, India, 1954, Homi J. Bhabha Commemorative Medallion, Bhabha Atomic Rsch. Ctr., Trombay, Mumbai, 1982. Fellow: Soc. for Advancement Electrochem. Sci. and Tech. (life; internal auditor Mumbai chpt. 1988—93); mem.: ACLU, AAUP, Am. Nuc. Soc., Indian Nuc. Soc. (life), Nat. Assn. for Applications Radiation and Radioactive Isotopes (life), Assn. Med. Physicists India (life), Indian Assn. for Radiation Protection (life; organizing com. ann. conf. 1990), Indian Physics Assn. (life), Vienna Photographic Soc., Sierra Club. Avocations: photography, nature walks, music, museums, yoga. Personal E-mail: mhbhide@hotmail.com.

BIARD, JAMES ROBERT, retired electrical engineer, consultant; b. Paris, Tex., May 20, 1931; s. James Christopher and Mary Ruth (Bills) B.; m. Amelia Ruth Clark, May 23, 1952; children: James Clark, Jan Elaine; 1 adopted child, Becky Dell. AS, Paris Jr. Coll., 1951; BSEE, Tex. A&M U., 1954, MSEE, 1956, PhD in Elec. Engring., 1957. Sr. engr. Tex. Instruments, Inc., Dallas, 1957-69; v.p. R & D Spectronics, Inc., Richardson, Tex., 1969-78; chief scientist Honeywell Optoelectronics, Richardson, 1978-88, Honeywell Micro Switch, Richardson, 1988-98; ret., 1998. Prof. elec. engring. dept. Tex. A&M U., College Station, 1980—; presenter at nat. and internat. symposia, 1957—; cons. in field. Contbr. over 23 articles to profl. jours. Entertainer for various svc. clubs, radio, TV, bus. and chs., 1957—, bd. dirs. City Sq. Recipient Disting. Alumnus award Tex. A&M U., 1986, Paris Jr. Coll., 1993, Patrick E. Haggerty Innovation award from Tex. Instruments, Honeywell Lund award. Fellow IEEE; mem. Am. PHys. Soc., Nat. Acad. Engring., Sigma Xi, Tau Beta Pi, Eta Kappa Nu, Phi Kappa Phi, Nat. Acad. Engring. Republican. Mem. Ch. of Christ. Achievements include 69 U.S. and foreign patents for gallium arsenide light emitting diode, schottky clamped silicon integrated logic circuits, metal-oxide-semiconductor read only memory, others. Office: Advanced Optical Products 6000 Millennium Dr Allen TX 75013 Office Phone: 214-509-2731. Business E-Mail: bob.biard@finisar.com.

BIBBY, HENRY (CHARLES HENRY BIBBY), professional basketball coach; b. Franklinton, NC, Nov. 24, 1949; children: Hank, Mike, Charisle. BS, UCLA, 1972. Guard NY Knicks, NYC, 1973-75, New Orleans Jazz, 1975-76, Phila. 76ers, 1977-80, asst. coach, 2006—08; guard San Diego Clippers., 1981; asst. coach Ariz. State U. Sun Devils, 1983-85; head coach Balt. Lightning, Continental Basketball Assn., 1986, Savannah Spirits, Ga., 1988, Tulsa Fast Breakers, Okla., 1989-91, Oklahoma City Cavalry, 1992-94, Club Team, Venezuela, 1995; asst. coach U. So. Calif. Trojans, LA, 1995, head coach, 1996—2004, LA Sparks, 2005; asst. coach Memphis Grizzlies, 2009—. Program dir. Henry Bibby Basketball Schools, Torrance, Calif. Recipient UCLA Alumni Assn. award, 1972. Achievements include member of the NCAA National Championship winning UCLA Bruins, 1970, 71, 72; member of the NBA championship winning New York Knicks, 1973. Office: Memphis Grizzlies 191 Beale St Memphis TN 38103 also: Henry Bibby Basketball 2785 Pacific Coast Hwy C#113 Torrance CA 90505 Office Phone: 213-725-3197. Business E-Mail: henrybibbycamps@msn.com.

BIBLE, DARYL N., bank executive; b. Cinn., Ohio, Mar. 18, 1961; BBA, MBA, U. Cinn., Ohio. Chartered Fin. Analyst. Position with mgmt. develop. program Star Banc; with US Bancorp (formerly Firstar Corp.), 1984—2008, treas., 1998—2008; asst. CFO BB&T Corp. (Branch Banking and Trust Co.), Winston-Salem, NC, 2008—09, sr. exec. v.p., CFO, 2009—. Named Bank Borrower of the Yr., Euromoney Mag., 2007. Mem.: Chartered Fin. Analyst NC Soc. Office: BB&T Corp 200 W Second St Winston Salem NC 27101

BICE, BO (HAROLD ELWIN "BO" BICE JR.), singer, musician; b. Huntsville, Ala., Nov. 1, 1975; s. Harold Elwin and Nancy Bice; m. Caroline Merrin Fisher, June 15, 2005; children: Aiden Michael, Caleb James, Ean Jacob, Merrin Elizabeth Joy. Musician: (albums) (with Purge) Ex Gratia, 1999, (with SugarMoney) Recipe for Flavor, 2000, (solo) The Real Thing, 2005, See the Light, 2007, 3, 2010, (movie soundtrack CD) Blades of Glory, 2007; guest star, grand prize winner: Don't Forget the Lyrics!, 2010. Performed for troops in Kuwait & Afghanistan, 2008; performer Jerry Lewis MDA Telethon, Las Vegas, 2008, Share the Beat Benefit, Ga. Transplant Found. & the James Redford Inst. for Transplant Awareness, 2008; vol. more than 4,000 hrs of his time for worthy causes. Recipient Lifetime Presidential Volunteer Service award, 2009. Presbyterian. Achievements include in Alabama, May 24 was declared "Bo Bice Day" by governor Bob Riley; runner up to Carrie Underwood on American Idol, May 25, 2005. Office: c/o Buddy Lee Attractions 38 Music Sq East Ste 300 Nashville TN 37203

BICHER, ANNETTE, gynecologic oncologist, director; MD, U. Mich. Diplomate Am. Bd. Ob-Gyn, Am. Bd. Ob-Gyn-gynecologic oncology. Intern George Wash. Univ. Hosp., 1988, resident DC, 1991; fellow NIH Warren Grant Magnuson Clin. Ctr., Bethesda, 1992; fellow gynecologic oncology Univ. Tex.-MD Anderson Cancer Ctr., Houston, 1994; dir. gynecologic oncology dept. Suburban Hosp., Inova Fairfax Hosp.; physician Mid-Atlantic Pelvic Surgery Assocs.; hospital affiliation includes inova Alexandria Hosp. Mem.: Soc. of Gynecologic Investigation, Soc. of Gynecologic Oncologists, Felix Rutledge Soc. of Gynecology/Oncology, Am. Coll. of Obstetricians and Gynecologists. Office: Inova Fairfax Hospital 3300 Gallows Rd Falls Church VA 22042 Office Phone: 703-776-4001.

BICK, KATHERINE LIVINGSTONE, neuroscientist, educator, researcher; b. Charlottetown, Can., May 3, 1932; came to U.S., 1954; d. Spurgeon Arthur and Flora Hazel (Murray) Livingstone; m. James Harry Bick, Aug. 20, 1955 (div.); children: James A., Charles L. (dec.); m. Ernst Freese, 1986 (dec. 1990). BS with honors, Acadia U., Can., 1951, MS, 1952; PhD, Brown U., 1957; DSc (hon.), Acadia U., 1990. Rsch. pathologist UCLA Med. Sch., 1959-61; asst. prof. Calif. State U., Northridge, 1961-66; lab. instr. Georgetown U., Washington, 1970-72, asst. prof., 1972-76; dep. dir. neurol. disorder program Nat. Inst. Neurol. and Communicative Disorders and Stroke, NIH, Bethesda, Md., 1976-81, acting dep. dir., 1981-83, dep. dir., 1983-87; dep. dir. extramural rsch. Office of Dir. NIH, 1987-90; sci. liaison Centro Studio Multicentrico Internazionale Sulla Demenza, Washington, 1990-95. Cons. Nat. Rsch. Coun., Italy, 1991-97, The Charles A. Dana Found., N.Y.C., 1993-98, Edn. Commn. of the States, 1996-99. Editor: Alzheimer's Disease: Senile Dementia and Related Disorders, 1978, Neurosecretion and Brain Peptides, Implications for Brain Functions and Neurol. Disease, 1981, The Early Story of Alzheimer's Disease, 1987, Alzheimer Disease, 1994, 2d edit., 1999, Alzheimer Disease: The Changing View, 2000; contbr. articles to profl. jours. Pres. Woman's Club, McLean, Va., 1968-69; bd. dirs. Fairfax County (Va.) YWCA, 1969-70; pres. Avenel Homeowner's Assn., 1998; pres. Emerson Unitarian Ch., 1964-66; mem. Bethesda Pl. Cmty. Coun., 1992-95, pres., 1993-94; mem. Dana Alliance for Brain Initiatives, 1993—; bd. dirs. Wilmington NC Child Advocacy Commn., 1998-2002; mem. vol. guild St. John's Mus. Art, Wilmington; chair Vol. Guild Cameron Art Mus., Wilmington, 2002-03, Cameron Art Mus. Bd., 2003-06; vestry St. Andrew's on the Sound, Wilmington, 2004-06, St. Stephens Epis. Ch. Durham NC, 2013-. Recipient Can. NRC award Acadia U., 1951-52, NIH Dir.'s award, 1978, Spl. Achievement award NIH, 1981, 83, Superior Svc. award USPHS, 1986, Presdl. Rank award meritorious sr. exec., 1989, Genesis award Alzheimer's Assn., 2005; Universal Match Found. fellow Brown U., 1956-57, Fed. Exec. Inst. Leadership fellow, 1980 Fellow AAAS, Internat. Brain Rsch. Orgn., World Fedn. Neurology Rsch. Group on Dementias (exec. sec. Am. region 1984-86, chmn. 1986-93), Alzheimer's Disease Internat., Soc. for Neurosci. (emeritus), Acad. of Medicine Washington (emeritus), Dana Alliance for Brain Initiatives, Am. Neurol. Assn. Home: 528 Cedar Club Cir Chapel Hill NC 27517 Business E-Mail: Kitbick@aol.com.

BICKEL, JOHN W., II, lawyer; b. Champaign, Ill., Sept. 9, 1948; s. John William and Virginia Bickel; children: Hannah, Molly, Sarah. BS, U.S. Mil. Acad., 1970; JD, So. Meth. U., 1976. Bar: N.Y. 1988, Tex. 1976, U.S. Ct. Appeals (5th and 11th cirs.) 1980, U.S. Supreme Ct. 1983. Assoc. Thompson & Knight, Dallas, 1980-83; ptnr. Brown, Thomas, Karger & Bickel, Dallas, 1983-84; co-mng., co-founder, ptnr. Bickel & Brewer, Dallas, 1984—; co-founding ptnr. Bickel & Brewer Storefront, PLLC, Dallas; founder Bickel & Brewer Foundation. Adv. mem. Tex. Supreme Ct. Jury Charge Task Force, 1992; mem. com. for qualified judiciary. Co-author: "Exhibits and other Evidence," Chpt. 13, Lawyers Cooperative Fed. Practice Guide. Mem. exec. bd. So. Meth. U. Sch. Law.; mem. Hiram A. Boaz Soc. So. Meth. U.; mem. Tex. Com.: A Time to Lead--The Campaign for So. Meth. U.; mem. adv. com. Southwestern Ball, 1997-2000, co-founder Future Leaders Program, Bickel & Brewer Nat. Pub. Policy Forum. Named a Tex. Super Lawyer, Tex. Monthly Mag., 2003—07, Best Lawyer in Dallas, D Mag. Fellow Tex. Bar Found., Dallas Bar Found. (sustaining life); mem. ABA, State Bar Tex. (past chmn. litigation com. of environ. and natural resource law sect.), N.Y. Bar Assn., Dallas Bar Assn., Markey/Wigmore Inns of Ct. (Chgo. chpt.), West Point Assn. Grads. (trustee 1997-2000, strategic planning com. 1997-2005, adv. com. to bd. trustee, 2006-), West Point Soc. North Tex. (bd. dirs. 1992-2002). Office: Bickel & Brewer 4800 Bank One Ctr 1717 Main St Ste 4800 Dallas TX 75201-4651 E-mail: jwb@bickelbrewer.com.

BICKETT, BRENT B., insurance company executive; BSBA, U. So. Calif., LA, 1986; MBA, UCLA, 1990. Mem. investment banking divsn. Bear, Stearns & Co. Inc., 1990—99, mng. dir. real estate, gaming, lodging and leisure group, 1997—99; exec. v.p. fin. Fidelity National Financial, Inc., Jacksonville, Fla., 1999—2006; corp. exec. v.p. bus. develop. Fidelity National Information Services, Inc., Jacksonville, Fla., 2006—. Office: Fidelity Nat Fin Inc 601 Riverside Ave Jacksonville FL 32204 Office Phone: 888-934-3354.

BIDIC, SEAN MICHAEL, plastic surgeon, orthopedist; b. Vineland, NJ, May 29, 1970; s. Reiner Paul and Christine Angela Bidic; m. Gretchen Ann Hays; children: Emma Gretchen, Leyna Raine. BA, U. Pa., Phila., 1992, BS in econ., 1992; MD, Columbia U., NYC, 1996; MFA, Carnegie Mellon U., Pitts., 2002. Cert. Am. Bd. Plastic Surgery, 2006, added qualification in hand surgery 2007. Resident in gen. surgery U. Pitts. Med. Ctr., 1996—99, resident in plastic surgery, 2002—04; fellow in bone substitutes, robotic hands and human computer interfaces Carnegie Mellon U., 1999—2001; fellow in hand and microsurgery UCLA Dept. Orthopaedic Surgery, 2004—05; asst. prof. U. Tex. Southwestern, Dallas, 2005, dir. hand surgery fellowship, 2007—. Video, In The Absence Of Voyeurism. Mem.: Dallas Soc. Plastic Surgeons, Am. Soc. Plastic Surgeons. Office: Univ Tex Southwestern Med 1801 Inwood Rd Dallas TX 07530 Office Fax: 214-645-3105. Business E-Mail: sean.bidic@utsouthwestern.edu.

BIECK, ROBERT BARTON, JR., lawyer; b. Wiesbaden, Germany, Apr. 13, 1952; arrived in US, 1954; s. Robert Barton and Mary-Jean (Boeck) B.; m. Julia A. Dietz, Apr. 20, 1991. BA in Polit. Sci., U. Nebr., 1974; JD with high honors, Tex. Tech. U., 1977. Bar: Tex. 1977, La. 1977, US Dist. Ct. (ea. dist.) La. 1977, US Dist. Ct. (mid. dist.) La. 1978, US Dist. Ct. (we. dist.) La. 1979, US Supreme Ct. 1980, US Ct. Appeals (5th and 11th cirs.) 1981, US Dist. Ct. (no. and so. dists.) Tex. 1991, DC 1992, US Ct. Appeals (DC cir.) 1992, US Dist. Ct. DC 1994, US Dist. Ct. (ea. dist.) Tex. 2006. Assoc. firm Jones, Walker, Waechter, Poitevent, Carrere & Denegre, New Orleans, 1977-82, ptnr., 1982—. Chmn. profl. liability practice group Jones, Walker, et al. Recipient West Horn Book award West Pub. Co., 1976; Fulbright and Jaworski scholar, 1976. Mem. ABA (litigation sect., bus. law sect.), Securities Industry and Fin. Markets Assn., Nat. Soc. Compliance Profls., New Orleans Bar Assn., La. Bankers Assn., 5th Cir. Bar Assn., Order of Coif, Phi Kappa Phi, Phi Delta Phi. Home: 5708 Annunciation St New Orleans LA 70115 Office: Jones Walker Waechter Poitevent Carrere & Denegre 201 Saint Charles Ave Ste 5200 New Orleans LA 70170-5100 Home Phone: 504-891-3901; Office Phone: 504-582-8202.

BIEGLER, DAVID W., energy executive; b. 1946; m. Diane Knape; 1 child, Mallory. BS, St. Mary's U., 1968; postgrad., Harvard U., 1979. Joined Enserch Exploration Inc., 1966, petroleum engr., 1968—70, dist. petroleum engr., 1970—72, staff petroleum engr., mgr. revenue control, 1972—74, chief engr., 1974—75, dir., engring. mktg. planning, v.p. processing engring. mktg., 1975—77, v.p., land and mktg., 1977—78; exec. v.p. Pool Arabia, 1978—79; exec. v.p.,Eastern Hemisphere Pool Intairdril, 1979—80; pres. Pool Well Servicing Co., 1980—84; pres., US ops. Pool Co., 1984—85; chmn., pres., COO & CEO Enserch Corp., 1985—97; pres., COO, vice-chmn. TXU Corp. (formerly Tex. Utilities), Dallas, 1997—2001; CEO Estrella Energy, LP, 2003—; chmn., CEO Southcross Energy, LLC, Dallas, 2009—; interim pres., CEO Dynegy Inc., Houston, 2011. Bd. dirs. Trinity Industries, Inc., 1992—, Dynegy Inc., 2003—11, Southwest Airlines Co., 2006—, Animal Health Internat., Inc., 2007, Guaranty Financial Group, Inc., 2008—09. Bd. dirs. Children's Med. Ctr. Office: Southcross Energy 1700 Pacific Ave Ste 2900 Dallas TX 75201

BIELAK, KENNETH M., medical educator; s. Stanley and Eleanor Bielak; married. MD, Mich. State U. Coll. Human Medicine, East Lansing, 1986; MBA, U. Tenn., Knoxville, 2002. Prof. Dept. Family Medicine, Grad. Sch. Medicine, U. Tenn. Health Sci. Ctr., Knoxville,

1994—. Bd. dirs., vol. Interfaith Health Clinic, Knoxville, 2000. Office: University Family Physicians 1924 Alcoa Hwy Knoxville TN 37920 Office Fax: 865-305-9314. Business E-Mail: kbielak@utmck.edu.*

BIELEMA, BRET ARNOLD, college football coach; b. Prophetstown, Ill., Jan. 13, 1970; BA in Mktg., U. Iowa, Iowa City, 1992. Grad. asst. U. Iowa Hawkeyes, 1994—95, linebackers coach, 1996—2001; co-defensive coord. Kans. St. U. Wildcats, 2002—03; defensive coord. U. Wis. Badgers, 2004—05, head football coach, 2006—12, U. Ark. Razorbacks, 2013—. Named Big 10 Conf. Coach of Yr., 2006. Office: University of Arkansas Football Program Reynolds Razorback Stadium 350 N Razorback Rd Fayetteville AR 72701

BIELSS, OTTO WILLIAM, JR., secondary school educator; b. Weatherford, Tex., Nov. 12, 1933; s. Otto William and Ada Susan (Thomas) B.; m. Patsy Lee Woolsey, Dec. 23, 1958; children: Otto William III, Paul Lee. BA, Hardin-Simmons U., 1954; MS, N. Tex. State U., 1971; postgrad., So. Meth. U., 1957-58, U. Tex., Arlington, 1965-67, U. Tex., Dallas, 1984-87. Engr. Tex. Hwy. Dept., Weatherford, 1954, Gen. Dynamics Corp., Fort Worth, 1956-59; tchr. Tarleton State Coll., Stephenville, Tex., 1959-65; math. tchr. Highland Park High Sch., Dallas, 1965-72, Skyline High Sch., Dallas, 1972-90; travel cons. Travelco, Irving, Tex., 1990-96; asst. prof. math. Paul Quinn Coll., Dallas, 1994—. Cluster coord. and dept. chairperson Skyline Math., 1983-90; instr. Dallas County C.C. Dist., various campuses, 1972—; grader coll. bd. advanced placement exams ETS. Author: Computer Mathematics, 1975; contbr. articles to profl. jours. Vol. various polit. campaigns, Stephenville, Tex., 1959-65, Irving, Tex., 1965—; bd. dirs. coun. airport noise, Irving, 1982—, Irving Cmty. Concerts, 1991—; mem. antiracism team N. Tex. Conf. United Meth. Ch., 2000--. Served with U.S. Army, 1954-56, Korea. Recipient scholarship, Hardin Simmon U., Abilene, Tex., 1951—54; grantee, NSF, 1961, 1967. Mem. AAUP, Math. Assn. Am., Greater Dallas Coun. Tchrs. (pres. 1974-76, bus. mgr. 1980-86, nat. rep. 1980-86), Tex. Coun. Tchrs. Math. (bus. mgr. 1980-86, pres. 1988-90), Nat. Coun. Tchrs. Math. (referee jour., rep.), Greater Dallas Tchrs. Math. (pres. 1988-90), Lions (bd. dirs. Irving 1985-87, treas. 1987-89, v.p. 1988-89, pres. 1989-91), Masons, Shriners (bd. dirs. 1988-89, 91, v.p. 1989-90, pres. 1990-91). Methodist. Avocations: photography, camping, gardening. Home: 2900 Normandy CT Euless TX 76039-4082

BIEN-AIME, TONY, family practice physician; Diplomate American Bd. Family Practice, lic. Fla., 1989. Intern Jackson Memorial Hosp., 1988, resident family medicine, 1988—90; hosp. affiliations include Jackson North Med. Ctr., Memorial Hosp. West Comprehensive Cancer Ctr., Parkway Regional Med. Ctr.; clin. preceptor Nova Southeastern Univ., Univ. of Miami Sch. of Medicine. Recipient Charles E. Aucermann MD Art of Medicine award, 1995. Office: Memorial Hospital System 19503 NW 57th Ave Ste A Opa Locka FL 33055 Office Phone: 305-621-8080. Office Fax: 305-624-2671.

BIERLEY, MARK RUSSELL, retail executive; b. 1966; BS in Bus. & Acctg., Mich. State U., 1988; MBA, U. Mich. Ross Sch. Bus., 2008. CPA. Various fin. mgmt. positions Price Waterhouse, 1988—92, Federal-Mogul Corp., Southfield, Mich.; mgr. fin. planning/reporting Dunham's Sporting Goods, 1993—96; mgr. store inventory control Borders Group, Inc., 1996—97, dir. inventory control, 1997, v.p. fin. planning/reporting, 2003—07, sr. v.p. fin., 2008, exec. v.p. fin., CFO, 2009—10, exec. v.p., CFO, COO, 2010; sr. v.p., CFO The Pantry, Inc., 2010—. Mailing: The Pantry Inc PO Box 1410 Sanford NC 27331-1410 Office Phone: 919-774-6700.

BIERMAN, JAMES L., health products executive; BA, Dickinson Coll., 1974; MBA, Cornell U., 1976. Ptnr. Arthur Andersen LLP, 1976—98; sr. v.p. corp. devel. Quintiles Transnational, Research Triangle Park, NC, 1998—2000, exec. v.p., CFO, 2000—07; sr. v.p., CFO Owens & Minor, Inc., Mechanicsville, Va., 2007—. Spkr. in field. Contbr. articles to profl. jours. Mem.: N.C. Assn. CPAs. Office: Owens & Minor Inc 9120 Lockwood Blvd Mechanicsville VA 23116

BIERRIA, MYRA COLEMAN, gas industry executive; Grad., U. Calif., Berkeley; degree in Law, Georgetown U. Bus. and tech. atty. Brobeck, Phleger & Harrison LLP, NY; joined AGL Resources, Inc., 2002, exec. v.p., corp. governance, corp. sec., securities counsel, 2005—, v.p., 2008—. Bd. dirs. Aid Atlanta, Inc. Amb. ABA; mem., bd. dirs. AGL Resources Inc. Pvt. Found., Girl Scouts of Greater Atlanta, Inc. Recipient Ga. Bus. Ethics award, 40 under 40 Up and Comer award, Atlanta Bus. Chronicle, 2006. Office: AGL Resources Inc 10 Peachtree Pl NE Atlanta GA 30309 Office Phone: 404-584-4000. Office Fax: 404-584-3714. Business E-Mail: MBierria@aglresources.com.

BIERY, EVELYN HUDSON, lawyer; b. Lawton, Okla., Oct. 12, 1946; d. William Ray and Nellie Iris (Nunley) Hudson. BA in English and Latin summa cum laude, Abilene Christian U., Tex., 1968; JD, So. Meth. U., 1973. Bar: Tex. 1973, US Dist. Ct. (we. dist.) Tex. 1975, US Dist. Ct. (so. dist.) Tex. 1977, US Dist. Ct. (no. dist.) Tex. 1979, US Ct. Appeals (5th cir.) 1979, US Ct. Appeals (11th cir.) 1981, US Supreme Ct. 1981. Atty. Law Offices of Bruce Waitz, San Antonio, 1973-76; mem. LeLaurin & Adams, PC, San Antonio, 1976-81; ptnr. Fulbright & Jaworski, San Antonio, 1982—2003, head bankruptcy, reorgn. and creditors' rights sect. Houston, 1990—2009. Policy com. Fulbright & Jaworski, 1996-98; spkr. on creditors' rights, bankruptcy and reorganization law; lectr. Southwestern Grad. Sch. Banking, Dallas, 1980, La. State U. Sch. Banking, 1994; presiding officer, U. Tex. Sch. of Law Bankruptcy Conf., 1976, 94, State Bar Tex. Creditors' Rights Inst., 1985, 88, State Bar Tex. Advanced Bus. Bankruptcy Law Inst., 1985, State Bar Tex. Inst. on Advising Officers, Dirs. and Ptnrs. in Troubled Bus., 1987, U. Tex. Sch. Law Bankruptcy Conf. 2006; mem. bankruptcy adv. com. 5th cir. jud. coun., 1979-80; vice-chmn. bankruptcy com. Comml. Law League Am., 1981-83; mem. exec. bd. So. Meth. U. Sch. Law, 1983-91; founding dir., com. chair, Internat. Insolvency Inst., 1998-. Editor: Texas Collections Manual, 1978, Creditor's Rights in Texas, 2d edit., 1981; author: (with others) Collier Bankruptcy Practice Guide, 1993. Del. to US/Republic of China joint session on trade, investment and econ. law, Beijing, 1987; designated mem. Bankruptcy Judge Merit Screening Com. State of Tex. by Tex. State Bar Pres., 1979-82; patron McNay Mus., San Antonio; rsch. ptnr. Mind Sci. Found., San Antonio; diplomat World Affairs Coun., San Antonio. Fellow: Soc. Internat. Bus. Fellows (chair bd. dirs.), San Antonio Bar Found. (life), Tex. Bar Found. (life); mem.: San Antonio Young Lawyers Assn. (pres. 1979—80, Outstanding Young Lawyer award 1979), Tex. Assn. Bank Counsel (bd. dirs. 1988—90, 2001—04), Tex. Bar Assn. (chair bankruptcy com. 1982—83, chair corp., banking and bus. law sect. 1989—90), Am. Coll. Bankruptcy Attys. (chair bd. dirs. 2006—07, pres. 2003—05), Zonta (Chair Z club com. 1989—90), Plaza Club San Antonio (bd. dirs. 1982—), Order of Coif. Office: Fulbright & Jaworski LLP 1301 McKinney St Ste 5100 Houston TX 77010-3031 Office Phone: 713-651-5544. Office Fax: 713-651-5246. Business E-Mail: ebiery@fulbright.com.

BIERY, SAMUEL FRED, JR., (FRED BIERY), federal judge; b. McAllen, Tex., Nov. 11, 1947; s. Samuel F. and Clara Belle (Martin) B.; m. Marcia Mattingly, May 25, 1989; children: Anna Lisa, Molly. BA, Tex. Luth. Coll., 1970; JD, So. Meth. U., 1973. Bar: Tex., U.S. Dist. Ct. (fed. dist.) Tex. 1974. From assoc. to shareholder Biery, Biery, Davis & Myers, P.C., San Antonio, 1973-78; judge County Ct. Two, San Antonio, 1979-82, 150th Dist. Ct., San Antonio, 1983-88, 4th Ct. of Appeals, San Antonio, 1989-94, US Dist. Ct. (we. dist.) Tex., San Antonio, 1993—2010, chief judge, 2010—. Regent Tex. Luth. Coll., Seguin, 1970—. Served USAR, 1970-76. Recipient Disting. Alumni award Tex. Luth. Coll., 1980; named Outstanding Young Dem., Bezar County Dems., 1978. Mem. ABA, State Bar Tex., San Antonio Bar Assn. (pres. 1987-88, Outstanding Young Lawyer 1980), Am. Inns of Ct. (pres. 1990-92). Avocations: basketball, gardening. Office: US Dist Ct 655 E Durango Blvd Fl 1 San Antonio TX 78206-1100

BIEVER, ANGELA MARY, diversified financial services company executive; b. Lloydminster, Sask., Can., Aug. 19, 1953; came to U.S., 1977; d. Vernon Adam and Lila Mae (Enzenauer) B. B in Commerce with honors, Queen's U., Kingston, Ont., Can., 1975; MBA, Harvard U., 1979. Chartered acct., 1977. Auditor Peat, Marwick, Mitchell & Co., Toronto, Canada, 1975-77, Ottawa, Canada, 1975—77; cons. McKinsey & Co., 1979-82; gen. mgr., Ofcl. Olympic Souvenir Program Sports Illustrated (subs. Time Inc.), 1983-84; dir., fin. and planning, Books Group divsn. Time, Inc., 1984-87, v.p., mktg., Time-Life Home Video divsn., 1986-87; v.p., corp. strategic planning American Express Co., 1987-91; pres. Anasazi Inc. (subs. First Data Corp.), 1993-94; sr. v.p., fin. and planning First Data Corp. (formerly Am. Express Info. Svcs. Corp.), 1991-92, sr. v.p., chief adminstrv. officer, 1992-93, exec. v.p., Integrated Svcs. divsn. Englewood, Colo., 1995-97; ind. cons., 1997-98; v.p., mng. dir., consumer internet sector Intel Capital, dir., sector leader, 1999-2000; gen. mgr., new bus. initiatives Intel Corp., 2000—; chief adminstrv. officer Raymond James Financial, Inc., 2008—. Bd. advisors Search Alternatives Inc., Princeton, N.J., 1987-89. Bd. dirs. Girl Scouts Am. Mile Hi Coun., Denver, 1995-96, Raymond James Fin., Inc., St. Petersburg, Fla., 1997—; mem. Century Club Harvard Bus. Sch., 1978. Mem. Colo. Women's C. of C. (Wise Women Colo. 1995—). Office: Raymond James Financial Inc 880 Carillon Pky Saint Petersburg FL 33716 Office Phone: 727-567-1000. Office Fax: 727-567-8915. Business E-Mail: angela.biever@raymondjames.com.

BIFFLE, GREG, race car driver; b. Vancouver, Wash., Dec. 23, 1969; s. Jack and Sally Biffle. Race car driver Rousch Fenway Racing, 2001—. 1st pl. Pepsi 400 Daytona Internat. Speedway, 2003; 1st pl. Mich. 400 Mich. Internat. Speedway, 2004, 2005, 1st pl. Pure Mich. 400, 2012; 1st pl. Ford 400 Homestead-Miami Speedway, 2004, 2005, 2006; 1st pl. Auto Club 500 Calif. Speedway, 2005; 1st pl. Samsung/Radio Shack 500 Tex. Motor Speedway, 2005, 1st pl. Samsung Mobile 500, 2012; 1st pl. MBNA Am. 400 Dover Internat. Speedway, 2005, 1st pl. Camping World RV 400, 2008; 1st pl. Carolina Dodge Dealers 400 Darlington Raceway, 2005, 1st pl. Dodge Charger 400, 2006; 1st pl. LifeLock 400 Kans. Speedway, 2007, 1st pl. Price Chopper 400, 2010; 1st pl. Sylvania 300 NH Motor Speedway, 2008; 1st pl. Pa. 500 Pocono Raceway, 2010. Founder Greg Biffle Found. Named Rookie of Yr., Busch Series, 2001, Champion, 2002. Office: c/o Roush Racing 7020 Aviation Blvd Concord NC 28027-8196

BIFFLE, TONY, editor; Copy editor Sun Herald, Biloxi, Miss., 1993—94, mem. editorial bd., assoc. editor, 1994—. Recipient Walker Stone award for editorial writing, Scripps Howard Found., 2006. Office: The Sun Herald 205 DeBuys Rd Gulfport MS 39507 Mailing: The Sun Herald PO Box 4567 Biloxi MS 39535-4567 Office Phone: 228-896-2387. Office Fax: 228-896-2104. E-mail: tdbiffle@sunherald.com.

BIGELOW, CAROLYN L., hematologist, educator; MD, U. Miss., 1979. Diplomate Am. Bd. Internal Medicine, 1982, Am. Bd. Internal Medicine-hematology, 1988. Intern Univ. Miss. Med. Ctr., 1980, resident internal medicine, 1980—82; fellow hematology and oncology Univ. Wash. Med. Ctr., 1983—87; prof. medicine Univ. Miss.; hosp. affiliation includes Univ. Miss. Health Care. Office: University of Mississippi Health Care 2500 N State St Jackson MS 39216 Office Phone: 601-815-2005.

BIGELOW, MARTHA MITCHELL, retired historian; b. Talladega Springs, Ala., Sept. 19, 1921; children: Martha Frances, Carolyn Letitia. BA, Montevallo U., 1943; MA, U. Chgo., 1944, PhD, 1946. Assoc. prof. history Miss. Coll., Clinton, 1946-48, Memphis State U., 1948-49; Assoc. prof. history U. Miss., 1949-50; assoc. curator manuscripts Mich. Hist. Collections, U. Mich., Ann Arbor, 1954-57; prof. history Miss. Coll., 1957-71, chmn. dept. history and polit. sci., 1964-71. Dir. Bur. of History, Mich. Dept. State, 1971-90; sec. Mich. Hist. Commn., Mich. Dept. State, state historic preservation officer, 1971-90; coord. for Mich., Nat. Hist. Publs. and Recs. Commn., 1974-90. Contbr. articles to profl. publs. Fellow, Ency. Britannica, 1944—45; scholar Julius Rosenwald scholarship, 1943—44, Cleo Hearson scholarship, 1944. Mem. Am. Assn. State and Local History (v.p. 1979-80, pres. 1980-81, fellow summers 1958, 59), Orgn. Am. Historians, Nat. Assn. State Archives and Recs. Assn., So. Hist. Assn., Mich. Hist. Soc., Miss. Hist. Soc. Home: 201 Jefferson St Clinton MS 39056-4237 Office Phone: 601-924-2822. Personal E-mail: bigelowmartha@gmail.com.

BIGGERS, NEAL BROOKS, JR., federal judge; b. Corinth, Miss., July 1, 1935; s. Neal Brooks and Sara (Cunningham) B.; 1 child, Sherron. BA, Millsaps Coll., 1956; JD, U. Miss., 1963. Sole practice, Corinth, 1963-68; pros. atty. Alcorn County, 1964; dist. atty. 1st Jud. Dist. Miss., 1968-75, cir. judge, 1975-84; judge US Dist. Ct. (no. dist.) Miss., Oxford, 1984—98, chief judge, 1998—2000, sr. judge, 2000—. Contbr. articles to profl. jours. Office: US Courthouse 911 Jackson Ave Oxford MS 38655-1238

BIGGINS, J. VERONICA (JACQUELINE VERONICA BIGGINS), executive search company executive; b. Belmont, NC, Oct. 19, 1946; d. Andrew Williams & Jacqueline McDonald; m. Franklin Biggins; children: Dawn, Kenzie. BA, Spelman Coll., 1968; MA in Edn., Ga. State U.; postgrad., U. Md. Asst. br. mgr. Citizens & Southern Nat. Bank, Atlanta, affirmative action officer, compliance mgr., employee relations mgr., mgr. Atlanta personnel, exec. v.p., dir. human resources; asst. to Pres., dir. presdl. personnel The White House, Washington, 1994—95; mng. ptnr. Diversity Svc. Practice Heidrick & Struggles Internat., Atlanta, 1995—2007; ptnr. Diversified Search, LLC (formerly Hodge Partners), Atlanta, 2007—. Bd. dirs. Avnet Corp., 1997—, AirTran Airways, 2001—11, Zep, Inc., 2007—, Southwest Airlines Co., 2011—. Mem. exec. com. Leadership Atlanta, 1983; bd. mem. East Lake Found., mem. Atlanta advisory bd. Savannah Coll. Art & Design; bd. trustees Woodruff Arts Ctr. Recipient Outstanding Performance award Inroads, Atlanta, 1986, Urban Bankers, 1987, trail blazer award Nat. Assn. Negro Bus. & Profl. Women's Clubs, Inc. Mem.: Internat. Bus. Fellows, Chautaugua Cir., Dogwood City Links, American Bankers Assn. (chmn. human resource divsn.), Atlanta Rotary Club. Episcopalian. Office: Diversified Search LLC 3500 Lenox Rd Ste 1500 Atlanta GA 30326 Office Phone: 404-419-2350.

BIGGIO, CRAIG (ALAN), baseball coach, retired professional baseball player; b. Smithtown, NY, Dec. 14, 1965; m. Patty Biggio; children: Conor Joseph, Cavan Thomas, Quinn Patricia. Attended, Seton Hall U. Catcher Houston Astros, 1988—89, catcher, outfielder, 1990—91, second baseman, 1992—2002, 2005—07, outfielder, 2003—04; ret., 2007; head baseball coach St. Thomas HS, 2008—. Lead spokesperson Sunshine Kids Found. Recipient Nat. League Silver Slugger award, 1989, 94, 95, 97, 98, Nat. League Gold Glove award, 1994, 95, 96, 97, Branch Rickey award for exceptional cmty. svc., 1997, Hutch award, 2005, Heart & Hustle award, 2006, Roberto Clemente award, 2007; named Houston Astros Player of Yr., 1998; named one of Sporting News' Good Guys, 2004; named to Nat. League All-Star Team, 1991, 92, 94, 95, 96, 97, 98, Tex. Baseball Hall of Fame, 2004, Tex Sports Hall of Fame, 2004. Achievements include becoming the 27th player in major league history to reach 3,000 hits, June 28, 2007; becoming the first Astro in franchise history to accumulate 3,000 hits; being the only player in Major League baseball's history with 3,000 hits, 600 doubles, 400 stolen bases and 250 home runs; being the first player in the history of baseball to make the All-Star team as a catcher and then second baseman; having his number (7) retired by the Houston Astros, 2008. Mailing: c/o Sunshine Kids Found 2814 Virginia Houston TX 77098 Office: St Thomas HS 4500 Memorial Dr Houston TX 77007

BIGGS, ALAN RICHARD, plant pathologist, educator; b. Lewisburg, Pa., June 22, 1953; s. Edgar Harold and Yvonne S. Biggs; m. Lise N. Sade, Oct. 3, 1981 (div) 2005; children: Benjamin Jesse Biggs Sade, Skylar Rose Biggs Sade. BS, Pa. State U., 1976, MS, 1978, PhD, 1982. Rsch. scientist Can. Dept. Agr., Vineland, Ont., 1983-89; assoc. prof. W.Va. U., Kearneysville, 1989-95, prof., 1995—. Editor: Defense Mechanisms of Woody Plants Against Fungi, 1992, Cytology, Histology and Histochemistry of Fruit Tree Diseases, 1992; assoc. editor Phytopathology, 1986-88, Plant Disease, 1994-96; sr. editor Plant Disease, 1998-2000, editor-in-chief, 2001-2003. Recipient Lee M. Hutchins award, 1993, USDA Sec. Honor award, 2001, 2002. Mem. Am. Phytopath. Soc. (Lee M. Hutchins award 1993). Avocations: photography, bicycling, jazz guitar. Office: WVa U Tree Fruit Rsch and Edn Ctr PO Box 609 Kearneysville WV 25430-0609 Office Phone: 304-876-6353.

BIGGS, ARTHUR EDWARD, retired chemicals executive, social services administrator; b. NYC, Jan. 3, 1930; s. Arthur Edward and Pauline B.; m. Charlotte Marion Elliott, Sept. 10, 1955; children—Arthur Edward III, William Elliott, Nancy Catherine, Andrew David. BS in Acctg. and Fin. Magna cum laude, U. Md., 1951; MBA in Fin. and Prodn. with distinction, Harvard U., 1957. Mgmt. cons. McKinsey & Co., Inc., NYC, 1957-62; asst. controller Mobil Oil Co., NYC, 1963-66, controller, 1966-68; v.p., gen. mgr. plastics div. Mobil Chem. Co., Rochester, NY, 1969-73, exec. v.p. NYC, 1974-82, pres., 1982-86. Chmn. bd. dir. The Century Group, 1987-91. Vice pres. bd. dir. Vis. Nurse Svc. N.Y., 1975-88; bd. advisers Pace U., N.Y.C., 1976-88; trustee Quinnipiac Coll., Hamden, Conn., 1982-92, chmn., 1986-90; bd. dirs. Ptnrs. in Care, N.Y.C., 1983-88, chmn., 1983-88; trustee Conn. Conf. Ind. Colls., chmn., 1987-89; trustee Harvard Sch. Bus. 1st lt., pilot USAF, 1951-55. Baker scholar, Harvard U., 1957. Mem. Monarch Country Club, Woodfield Country Club (Boca Raton). Avocation: tennis. Personal E-mail: arthurebiggs@aol.com.

BIGGS, JEFFERY LADON, social welfare administrator; b. Andalusia, Ala., Mar. 21, 1975; s. Carroll Ladon and Judy Gail Edgar Biggs. BS in Journalism & Pub. Rels., Troy State U., Ala., 1997. Reporter, graphic designer Boone Newspapers, 1997—2002; copy editor Birmingham (Ala.) Post-Herald, 2000—01; ad designer Andalusia Star-News, 1997—2000, editor, composing & pre-press mgr., 2002, mng. editor, 2002—06; exec. dir., Covington County Chapter Am. Red Cross, 2006—09; various positions, Advanced Pub. Affairs Team Am. Red Cross, 2007—09; cmty. outreach coord. Dothan-Houston County Substance Abuse Partnership, 2009—. Newspaper advisor Andalusia H.S., 2004—. Mem. publicity com. Lions Club Internat., Andalusia, 2003—; chmn. Christmas com. Andalusia Area C. of C., 1999, newsletter designer, 2002—; team recruitment chair Covington County Relay for Life, Andalusia, 2000. Recipient 2d pl. in graphic design, Ala. Press Assn., 2003. Mem.: Lions Club Internat. (publicity com. 2003—). Baptist. Avocations: photography, travel, cooking. Office: Dothan-Houston County 812 S Appletree St Dothan AL 36301 Office Phone: 334-699-2813. Office Fax: 334-699-2815. Business E-Mail: jbiggs@wiregrasspartnership.com.

BIGHAM, WANDA DURRETT, religious organization administrator; b. Barlow, Ky., June 19, 1935; d. Herbert Martin and Ada Florene (Baker) Durrett; m. William M. Bigham, Jr., June 7, 1958; children: William M. III, Janet Kaye, Julia Lynn. BME, Murray State U., 1956; MM, Morehead State U., 1971, MHE, 1973; EdD, U. Ky., 1978; cert., Inst. For Ednl. Mgmt. -Harvard U., 1982; LittD (hon.), Loras Coll., 1989. Dir. TRIO programs Morehead (Ky.) State U., 1972-85, assoc. dean acad. affairs, dir. instructional sys., 1982-85, acting dean grad. and spl. acad. programs, 1984-85; exec. asst. to pres. Emerson Coll., Boston, 1985, v.p. for devel., 1986; pres. Marycrest Coll., Davenport, Iowa, 1986-92, Huntingdon Coll., Montgomery, Ala., 1993—2003; asst. gen. sec. for schs., colls. and univs. The United Meth. Ch., Nashville, 2003—. Bd. dirs. Nat. Assn. Ind. Coll. U., 2002-03, Secretariat, 2007-; bd. dirs., pres. Asia-Pacific Fedn. Christian Schs.; bd. dirs. Internat. Assn. Meth.-Related Schs., Colls. and Univs., Montgomery Symphony Orch., 1993-2003, Ala. Shakespeare Festival, 1996-2003, NASCUMC, 1996-2003; exec. com., pres. Univ. Senate United Meth. Ch., Ctrl. Ala. chpt. ARC, Montgomery, 1995-2003, pres, 2001-2002; mem. Leadership Ala., 1994—; co-chair Quad Cities Vision for the Future, Davenport, 1987-92. Recipient Pres.'s award Davenport C. of C., 1988, Women of Spirit and Note award Cmty. Com. of Davenport, 1991, Hope for Humanity award Jewish Fedn. of QC, Rock Island, Ill., 1993, Women's Acad. of Honor award Ala. Bus. and Profl. Women's Found., 2004; named to Alumni Hall of Fame, Morehead State U., 1988, Disting. Alumna, Murray State Coll., 1988, Woman of Distinction award Girl Scouts South Ctrl. Ala., 2001. Mem. Am. Coun. on Edn. (mem. coun. of fellows, bd. dirs. 1994-97, fellow in higher edn. adminstrn. 1983-84), Internat. Assn. Univ. Pres., Montgomery C. of C., Com. of 100, Sigma Alpha Iota (Sword of Honor 1956), Phi Kappa Phi, Kappa Delta Pi. Office: United Meth Ch Gen Bd Higher Edn and Ministry 1001 19th Ave S PO Box 340007 Nashville TN 37203-0007 Mailing: PO Box 340007 Nashville TN 37203-0007 Office Phone: 615-340-7406. Business E-Mail: wbigham@gbhem.org.

BIGLAISER, GARY, economics professor; s. Leo and Marcia Biglaiser; m. Alison Hagy, May 2, 1999; children: Anna, Catherine. BS, U. Ariz., Tucson, 1982; PhD, U. Calif., San Diego, 1987. Prof. U. NC, Chapel Hill, 1988—. Editor to profl. econ. jours. Office: Univ NC Dept Economics Chapel Hill NC 27599-3305 Business E-Mail: gbiglais@emai.unc.edu.

BIGLARI, SARDAR, diversified financial services company executive; b. Iran, Aug. 30, 1977; BS in Fin. & Internat. Bus., Trinity U. Co-founder INTX Networking LLC, 1996; founder, gen. ptnr. The Lion Fund, L.P., 2000—; chmn., CEO Biglari Holdings Inc., 2008—. Bd. dirs. Western Sizzlin Corp., 2005—, chmn., 2006—, pres., CEO, 2007—; bd. dirs. CCA Industries, Inc. Named one of America's 20 Most Powerful CEOs 40 and Under, Forbes mag., 2012. Office: Biglari Holdings, Inc Suite 400 17802 IH 10 West San Antonio TX 78257 Office Phone: 210-344-3400. Office Fax: 210-344-3411. Business E-Mail: Sardar.Biglari@steaknshake.com.

BIGWOOD, DAVID P., librarian, writer; b. Feb. 23, 1953; BA in Arts, Assumption Coll., 1976; MLS, U. North Tex., 1993. Sr. libr. Ctr. Info. and Rsch. Svcs. Lunar and Planetary Inst., Houston. Mem.: Tex Libr. Assn., SLA, OLAC, Beta Phi Mu. Office: Lunar and Planetary Inst 3600 Bay Area Blvd Houston TX 77058 Office Phone: 281-486-2134. E-mail: dbijwood@hou.usra.edu.

BIKAS, ERIC J., state legislator; b. Aug. 13, 1986; s. Jimmy and Kathy. AS, Orlando Culinary Academy, 2006. Businessman; mem. Dist. 26 SC House of Representatives, 2010—. Republican. Home: 103 Monaghan Ave Greenville SC 29617 Address: 434C Blatt Bldg Columbia SC 29201 Home Phone: 864-982-0046; Office Phone: 803-212-6892, 864-246-6009.

BILAS, RICHARD A., economist; b. Passaic, NJ, Feb. 3, 1935; s. Nestor Joseph and Helen Evelyn (Smith) B.; m. Janet Lianne Harris, June 23, 1956; children: Cathy, David, Ami. AB in Math., Duke U., 1956; PhD in Econs., U. Va., 1963. Asst., then assoc. prof. U. So. Calif., LA, 1962-67; from assoc. prof. to prof. Ga. State U., Atlanta, 1967—70; E.C. Reid prof. econs. Calif. State U., Bakersfield, 1970-87, prof. emeritus Calif., 2002—; commr. Calif. Energy Commn., Sacramento, 1987-95; Brock chair in energy econs. and policy Sarkeys Energy Ctr., Norman, Okla., 1995—96; commr. Calif. Pub. Utilities Commn., San Francisco, 1997—2002. Program on workable energy regulation bd. U. Calif., 1990—95; pres. Calif. Pub. Utilities Commn., 1998—99; adj. prof. bus. adminstrn. The Citadel, Charleston, 2006—12; adj. prof. economics Coll. Charleston, 2007—. Author: Microeconomics, 1967, 71, Problems in Microeconomics, 1972, Macroeconomics, 1974; mem. editl. bd. Western Econ. Assn.'s Contemporary Econ. Policy, 1990-. Active Rep. Ctrl. Com., Kern County, Calif., 1978-82; pres. bd. dirs. Mendocino Art Ctr., 2000-05; treas. Cmty. Found. Mendocino County, 2003-05; vestryman Cathedral Ch. St. Luke and St. Paul, Charleston, SC, 2008-10; bd. mem. Drawing Near to God Ministry, 2012-. Nat. Def. fellow U. Va., 1959-62, Fulbright fellow to the Philippines, 1966-67; recipient Honor cert. Freedoms Found., 1977, 79. Mem. Mont Pelerin Soc., Masons, Phi Beta Kappa. Republican. Anglican. Avocations: reading, golf. Home: 1513 Oakhurst Dr Mount Pleasant SC 29466 Personal E-mail: richardbilas@comcast.net.

BILECA, MICHAEL, state legislator; b. Miami, Fla., Mar. 8, 1970; m. Vivian Salazar; children: Nathan Bileca, Benjamin Bileca, Gabriel Bileca. BS in Mgmt., Tulane U., 1992; MBA, Northwestern U., 2002. Entrepreneur; mem. Dist. 117 Fla. House of Representatives, 2011—. Republican. Office: 1000 SW 57th Ave Ste 202 West Miami FL 33144-5120 also: Fla House of Reps 1003 The Capitol 402 S Monroe St Tallahassee FL 32399-1300 Office Phone: 305-442-6868, 850-488-6506.

BILES, CHARLES LEE, plant pathologist, physiologist, educator; b. Ft. Worth, Nov. 24, 1957; s. Betty LaRue Biles; m. Merrianne Densie Daughtery, May 24, 1986; children: Robert Josiah, Caleb Lincoln, Peter Battle. BS, Stephen F. Austin State U., Nacogdoches, Tex., 1980; MS, Colo. State U., Ft. Collins, 1984; PhD, Tex. A&M U., College Station, 1988. Asst. prof. N.Mex. State U., Las Cruces, 1990—93; prof. biology East Ctrl. U., Ada, Okla., 1993—. Cons. Ada Biolab Cons., LLC, 2002—. Author: Human Physiology Laboratory Workbook. Recipient Tchg. Excellence award, East Ctrl. U., 1997, 2004; Summer Acad. Forensic Biology grantee, Okla. State Regents for Higher Edn., 1998—2005, Grantee for preformed and induced disease def. mechanisms of cantaloupe, USDA Agr. Rsch. Svc., 1996—2000, Rsch. and Engring. Apprenticeship Program grantee, Acad. Applied Sci., 2006, 2007. Mem.: Okla. Acad. Scis. (vice-chair microbiology 2006—07), Brit. Mycol. Soc., Beta Beta Beta (sponsor East Ctrl. U. Campus Soc., Psi Delta 1994—2007). Conservative. Avocations: bicycling, hiking. Office: East Central Univ 1100 East 14th St Ada OK 74820 Business E-Mail: cbiles@ecok.edu.

BILGER, BRUCE R., lawyer; b. Balt., Feb. 27, 1952; BA, Dartmouth Coll., 1973; MBA, JD, U. Va., 1977. Bar: Tex. 1977. Mem. Vinson & Elkins LLP, Houston, chair Energy Practice Group, co-head Bus. & Internat. Law Sect.; chmn. global energy practice Lazard Ltd., 2008—10, sr. advisor, 2010—. Mem. Phi Beta Kappa. Home: Lazard Ltd JP Morgan Chase Tower 600 Travis St Ste 2300 Houston TX 77002

BILIR, ALI F., poet; b. Mersin, Turkey, 1945; Grad., U. Istanbul, 1969. Reception clk. Tourist Youth Hostel, Istanbul, Turkey, mgr. Author: (books) Üsüyen Sicak Düslerim, 1994, Göç Türküsü, 1995, Elestiriden Günceye, 1996, Güz Anımsamalari, 2003, Ortaasyadan Toroslara Gülnar, 2007, Migration Ballads, 2008, (poems) A Dervish of the Bektashi, Cyclamen, Intimate Questions, and various others. Recipient Fiction Story award, Günes Mag. (Sweden), 1990, Ibrahim Yildiz Poetry award, 1996, S. Avni Olez Poetry award, 2004; co-recipient Fiction Story award, Orhan Kemal, 1993, Samim Kocagöz Fiction Story award, 1998. Mem.: Florida State Poets Assn., Turkish Writers Syndicate, Turkish Authors Assn., Nat. Fedn. of State Poetry Socs. (NFSPS), Language Assn. Mailing: c/o Florida State Poets Association 310 South Adams St Beverly Hills FL 34465

BILIRAKIS, GUS MICHAEL, United States Representative from Florida, lawyer; b. Gainesville, Fla., Feb. 8, 1963; s. Michael Bilirakis; m. Eva Lialios; children: Michael, Theodore, Emmanuel, Nicholas. BA, U. Fla., 1986; JD, Stetson U. Coll. Law, DeLand, Fla., 1989. Atty. Bilirakis Law Group, Holiday, Fla.; mem. Dist. 48 Fla. House of Reps, 1999—2006; mem. US Congress from 9th Fla. Dist., Washington, 2007—13, sr. whip, 2006—08; mem. US Congress from 12th Fla. Dist., 2013—. Intern to Pres. Ronald Reagan The White House; staff mem., Rep. Don Sundquist US House of Representatives; adj. prof. St. Petersburg Jr. Coll., 1997; mem. Pinellas County Republican Exec. Com., 1996—. Mem.: West Pasco Chamber of Commerce, Tarpon Springs Chamber of Commerce, Palm Harbor Chamber of Commerce, Clearwater Bar Assn., American Hellenic Edn. Progressive Assn., Tarpon Springs Rotary, Masons, Elks, Moose Lodge. Republican. Greek Orthodox. Office: US House of Representatives 2313 Rayburn House Office Bldg Washington DC 20515 also: Palm Harbor Profl Ctr Ste 3 35111 US Hwy 19 N Palm Harbor FL 34684 Office Phone: 727-773-2871, 202-225-5755. Office Fax: 202-225-4085.*

BILLINGS, HAROLD WAYNE, retired library director, editor, writer; b. Cain City, Tex., Nov. 12, 1931; s. Harold Ross and Katie Mae (Price) B.; m. Bernice Schneider, Sept. 11, 1954; children: Brenda, Geoffrey, Carol. BA, Pan Am. Coll., 1953; MLS, U. Tex., 1957. Tchr. Pharr-San Juan-Alamo (Tex.) H.S., 1953-54; catalog libr. U. Tex., Austin, 1954-57, asst. chief catalog libr., 1957-65, chief acquisitions libr., 1965-67, asst. univ. libr., 1967-72, assoc. dir. gen. librs., 1972-77, acting dir. gen. librs., 1977-78, dir. gen. librs., 1978—2003. Sec. Tex. Bd. Libr. Examiners; mem. adv. com. Tex. Higher Edn. Coordinating Bd. Libr. Formula, 1987-92, Acad. Support Formula Adv. Com., 1993-94; mem. steering com. Tex-Share Project, 1993-94; trustee Amigos Bibliographic Coun., 1980-83; chmn. Coun. Acad. Rsch. Librs., 1979-81; chmn. Rsch. Librs. Adv. Com. Online Computer Libr. Ctr. (OCLC), 1980-82, 87-88, mem. OCLC Users Coun.; bd. dirs. Ctr. Rsch. Librs., Chgo., 1989-96, Assn. Rsch. Librs., 1989-92; mem. Tex. Coun. State Univ. Librs., Assn. Rsch. Librs. Preservation Com., Collection Devel. Com., Coun. on Libr. Resources Preservation and Access Com., Coun. on Libr. Resources/Assn. Am. Pubs. Joint Working Group on Electronic Info., 1993-94; mem. adv. bd. Project Muse-Johns Hopkins U. Press, Balt., 1995-98; mem. N.Am. adv. bd. Lit. Online, 1997—2003; assoc. Tex. Telecomm. Policy Inst., 1996-2003; mem. Coun. Libr. & Info. Studies Area Studies Materials Task Force ACLS, 1998-99; mem. adv. coun. for Stanford U. Librs., 1998-2003; mem. steering com. Digital Libr. Fedn., 1999-2003; vis. coms. U. Tenn., U. Wyo.; project dir. numerous fed. grants. Author: Education of Librarians in Texas, 1956, Edward Dahlberg: American Ishmael of Letters, 1968, A Bibliography of Edward Dahlberg, 1972, The Leafless American, 2d edit., 1986, Magic and Hypersystems: Constructing the Information-Sharing Library, 2002, Texas Beast Fables, 2007, M.P. Shiel: A Biography of His Early Years, 2005; M.P. Shiel: The Middle Years 1897-1923, 2010, A Dead Church, 2014, editor books in field; contbr. The Texas Book, 2007, A Remarkable Mixture(Sherlock Holmes), 2007, Faunus 19, 2009, Faunus 22, 2010, Translation of The Flesh, 2013, to profl. jours.; mem. editl. bd. Libr. Chronicle, 1970-97. Sec., trustee Littlefield Fund for So. History, 1977-2003. Recipient Morley-Montgomery Meml. award, Baker St. Irregulars, 2007. Mem. ALA (Hugh C. Atkinson Meml. award 2002), Tex. Libr. Assn., Assn. Coll. Rsch. Librs. (chmn. tech. svcs. group, 1979-80), Friends Arthur Machen. Democrat. Protestant. Avocations: book collecting, pottery, literature.

BILLIOT, ROBERT E., state legislator; BA, Nicholls State U., 1976. Former educator; mem. Dist. 83 La. House of Reps., 2008—, vice chair mcpl., parochial and cultural affairs com., mem. natural resources and environment com., transp., hwys. and pub. works com., house exec. com., joint legis. com. on capital outlay. Democrat. Office: Capitol Office PO Box 44486 Baton Rouge LA 70804 also: 10 Westbank Expressway Westwego LA 70094 Office Phone: 504-431-1535, 225-342-6945, 504-436-8929. Office Fax: 504-431-1550, 504-436-8994. E-mail: billiotr@legis.state.la.us.

BILLY, LISA J., state legislator; b. Purcell, Okla., Feb. 21, 1967; d. Frank and Beverly (Jones) Johnson; m. Phillip Billy; children: Masheli, Nahinli, Anoli. BA, Northeastern State Univ.; MEd, Univ. Okla. Former educator; small bus. owner; mem. Chickasaw Legislature, 1996—2001; nat. bd. mem. Girl Scouts of U.S.A., 1996—2004; bd. mem. Girl Scouts Sooner Coun., 2006—08; mem. Dist. 42 Okla. House of Representatives, 2005—. Mem.: NRA. Republican. Mailing: PO Box 1412 Purcell OK 73080 Office: 2300 N Lincoln Blvd Rm 302-A Oklahoma City OK 73105 Office Phone: 405-557-7365. E-mail: lisajbilly@okhouse.gov.

BILNEY, JODY LYNN, health care company executive; b. 1961; BS in Economics, Clemson U., 1983. V.p. mktg. Verizon Communications, Inc., 1996—97, v.p., gen. mgr. consumer sales, 1997—99, v.p. consumer markets group, 2000—01, sr. v.p. brand mgmt. & mktg. comm, 2001—02; exec. v.p., chief mktg. officer Charles Schwab, Inc., 2002—04, Openwave Systems, Inc., 2005—06; chief mktg. officer Outback Steakhouse (subs. OSI Restaurant Ptnrs., LLC), 2006—08; exec. v.p., chief brand officer Bloomin' Brands, Inc., Tampa, 2008—13; sr. v.p., chief consumer officer Humana Inc., Louisville, 2013—. Office: Humana Inc 500 W Main St Louisville KY 40202 Office Phone: 502-580-1000.

BILTONEN, RODNEY LINCOLN, biochemistry and pharmacology educator; b. Ont., Can., Aug. 24, 1937; came to U.S., 1941; s. Frank Emil and Frances Cecilia (Castren) B.; m. Margaret Jane Kobel, Aug. 6, 1960; children— Michael Andrew, Eric Franklin AB, Harvard Coll., 1959; PhD, U. Minn., 1965. Asst. prof. Johns Hopkins U., Balt., 1966-72; assoc. prof. biochemistry and pharmacology U. Va., Charlottesville, 1972-77, prof., 1977—2003, prof. emeritus, 2003—, assoc. dean, 1979-81, assoc. provost, 1981-84. Vis. prof. Gulbenkian Inst., Portugal, 1970-71, U. Lund, Sweden, 1971, Cayetano, Lima, Peru, 1976, U. N.C., Chapel Hill, 1980, CNR, Genoa, Italy, 1993, The Technical U. Denmark, 1995; James Disting. prof. physics St. Francis Xavier U., Antigonish, N.S., 1984; cons. in field. Assoc. editor Biophys. Jour., 1991-95; mem. editl. bd. Chemistry and Physics of Lipids, 1995—2000; contbr. over 150 articles to profl. jours. Recipient G.T. Walker award, Sigma Xi, 1965, Huffman Meml. award, Calorimetry Conf., 1989; grantee, NSF, 1968—99, NIH, 1970—2005; fellow, 1965—66, Biophysics Soc., 2000—. Fellow: Biophys. Soc. (councilor 1984—86); mem.: Am. Calorimetry Conf. (chmn. 1976—77). Office: University Va Dept Pharmacology 1300 Jefferson Park Ave Charlottesville VA 22908-0735 Personal E-mail: rlb1t@virginia.edu.

BINA, WILLIAM F., III, dean, medical educator; BS in Nuc. Sci., US Naval Acad., Annapolis; MD, U. Nebr.; MPH in Internat. Health, Johns Hopkins U., Balt. Family practice residency Naval Regional Med. Ctr., Camp Pendelton, Calif., 1975—78; gen. preventive medicine residency Johns Hopkins U., 1982—84; joined Mercer U. Sch. Medicine, Macon, Ga., 1991, various positions in the family medicine dept. including prof., practicing physician and program dir. family residence program, assoc. dean, 2007—08, dean, 2008—. Dir. family practice residency program Med. Ctr. of Ctrl. Ga., 1992—97; bd. dirs. Ctrl. Ga. Health Network, 1996—99, Secure Health Plans Ga., 1996—; pres., chmn. bd. dirs. Ga. Acad. Family Physicians, 1998—2000. Project and med. dir. Ctrl. Ga. Cancer Coalition, 2002—08; mem. steering com. to establish a primary health care facility in Macon and Bibb counties Ga., 2004—07. Served with USN. Office: Mercer University Sch Medicine Office of Dean 1550 College St Macon GA 31207*

BINFORD, JESSE STONE, JR., chemistry professor; b. Freeport, Tex., Nov. 1, 1928; s. Jesse Stone and Eglan Lee (Bracewell) B.; m. Lolita Ramona Fritz, June 8, 1955; children: Lincoln Bracewell, Jason Jolly. BA in Chemistry, Rice U., 1950, MA in Chemistry, 1952; PhD in Phys. Chemistry, U. Utah, 1955. Instr. chemistry U. Tex., Austin, 1955-58; asst. prof. U. of the Pacific, Stockton, Calif., 1958-60, assoc. prof., 1960-61; Fulbright prof., chmn. dept. chemistry Univ. Nacional Autonoma de Honduras, Tegucigalpa, 1968-69; vis. rsch. prof. Thermochemistry Lab., U. Lund, Sweden, 1971, researcher, 1982-83; rsch. fellow Chelsea Coll., U. London, 1983; assoc. prof. U. South Fla., Tampa, 1961-72, prof., 1972—2003, emeritus prof., 2004—. Cons. Fla. consortium AID, Honduras, 1969, Exxon Prodn. Rsch. Co., Houston, 1974; chmn. State Univ. Faculty Senate Coun., Fla., 1975-76; dir. gen. chemistry program U. South Fla., 1978-82, 98-2003; vis. prof. dept. chem. engring. Rice U., 1993-94, rschr. Cox Lab. for Biomed. Engring., Inst. Bioscis. and Bioengring., 1993-94; mem. Inst. for Biomolecular Sci., U. South Fla., pres. faculty senate, 1999-2000. Author: (textbook) Foundations of Chemistry, 1977, 2nd edit., 1985; contbr. articles to profl. jours., 1956—2003. Active bicycle adv. com. Hillsborough County, Tampa, 1975-93, chairperson bicycle adv. com., 1990-93; faculty advisor U. South Fla. Bicycle Club, 1972-2004; coord. spl. tutoring program Danforth Found., Tampa, 1968. Grantee Petroleum Rsch. Fun, 1960-62, USPHS (NIH), 1966-68, Rsch. Corp., 1986. Mem. AAUP, AAAS, Am. Chem. Soc. (nat. and Tex. sect.), Calorimetry Conf., League of Am. Bicyclists, Golden Key, Sigma Xi, Phi Beta Kappa, Phi Lambda Upsilon, Sigma Pi Sigma, Omicron Delta Kappa, Advocate Nuc. Power. Avocations: bicycling, travel, reading. Office: U South Fla Dept Chemistry 4202 E Fowler Ave Tampa FL 33620-8000 Home: 5600 Bull Creek Rd Austin TX 78756-1010 Office Phone: 813-974-9676. Personal E-mail: infordb@sbcglobal.net.

BINFORD, MICHAEL WILLIAM, professor physical geography; b. Hutchinson, Kans., May 21, 1951; s. Raymond Wilbur and Elizabeth (Wyse) B.; m. Patricia Woodall, May 20, 1973 (div.); 1 child, Elizabeth; m. Mary Virginia Lowry, May 11, 1985; 1 child, Katherine; 1 stepchild, Erin. BS, Kans. State U., Manhattan, 1973; MS, La. State U. and A&M Coll., Baton Rouge, 1976; PhD, Ind. U., Bloomington, 1979. Rsch. assoc. Fla. State Mus., Gainesville, 1980—86, U. Fla., Gainesville, 1980—86; asst. prof. Grad. Sch. Design, Harvard U., Cambridge, Mass., 1986—91, assoc. prof., 1991—96, U. Fla., Dept. Geography, Gainesville, 1997—2001, prof., 2001—. Assoc. editor: Jour. of Paleolimnology, 1987—. Mem. bd. dirs. Alachua Conservation Trust, Gainesville, 2001—06. U. Fla. Rsch. Found. Professorship, 2002-2005, Rsch. grantee NSF, Haiti, 1985-1986, US Man & The Biosphere Program, Bolivia, 1989, Bolivia, 1992-1996, Mass., 1994-1997, Thailand/Cambodia, 2002-2006, Uganda/Tanzania/Botswana/Namibia, 2004-2009; NASA, Fla. 2001-2004, Botswana/Namibia 2009-. Mem. AAAS (fellow 1991), Ecol. Soc. Am. (paleoecology sect. chair 1985, chair to com. to obtain internat. travel grants 1985-86), Assn. Am. Geographers. Achievements include development of 210Pb-assay method for measuring whole-lake sedimentation rates, of first empirical tests of agricultural sustainability from ecological perspectivein Andean agroecosystems; paleoecological studies in unstudied areas of tropical Americas; demonstration of links between economic well-being and environmental variation in Thailand and Cambodian rural agricultural systems; demonstration of underlying factors determining the conservation and social successes of protected areas in East and southern Africa. Office: Univ Florida 3141 Turlington Hall PO Box 117315 Gainesville FL 32611 Office Fax: 352-392-8855. Business E-Mail: mbinford@geog.ufl.edu.

BINGHAM, KENNETH A., state legislator; b. Columbia, SC, Aug. 3, 1962; s. William Harold Bingham Sr. and Marylynn Bingham; m. Jennie Lynn Bingham, Aug. 3, 1962; children: Kayla McKenzie, Kellie Nicole. BCE, U. SC, 1984. V.p. Hercules Contractors & Engrs. Inc., 1984—; mem. City of Cayce Planning Com., 1994—96; owner Am. Engring. Consultants, 1994—; bd. of trustees mem. Lexington Sch. Dist. Two, 1996—2000; mem. Dist. 89 SC House of Reps., 2000—, majority leader. Deacon Trinity Bapt. Ch. Republican. Baptist. Office: PO Box 2025 West Columbia SC 29171 also: Capitol Office 518C Blatt Bldg Columbia SC 29201 Office Phone: 803-796-9300, 803-734-3138. E-mail: KAB@schouse.org.

BINGHAM, STAN, state legislator; Former state senator Dist. 38, NC; former owner Lumber Co.; state senator Dist 33 NC, 2003—. Mem. Agrl., Environ. and Natural Resources com., Appropriations on Justice and Pub. Safety com., Appropriations/Base Budget com., Judiciary II com., Pensions and Retirement and Aging com., Ways and Means com.; co-chmn. Health Care com. Republican. Office: NC Senate 16 W Jones St Rm 2117 Raleigh NC 27601-2808 Address: 292 N Main St Denton NC 27239 Office Phone: 919-733-5665, 336-859-0999. E-mail: Stan.Bingham@ncleg.net.

BINGMAN, BRIAN, state legislator; b. Tulsa, Dec. 9, 1953; m. Paula Bingman; children: Annie, Blake, Rebecca. BBA in Petroleum Land Mgmt., Univ. Okla., 1976. V.p., land and ops. Uplands Resources, Inc.; mayor Sapulpa, 1992—2004; mem. Dist. 30 Okla. House of Representatives, 2004—06; mem. Dist. 12 Okla. State Senate, 2006—. Mem. Creek Nation, Sapulpa C. of C. Mem.: Okla. Independent Producers Assn., Tulsa Ass. of Petroleum Landman, American Assn. of Petroleum. Republican. Avocation: golf. Address: 1502 E McKinley Ave Sapulpa OK 74066 Office: 2300 N Lincoln Blvd Rm 422 Oklahoma City OK 73105 Office Phone: 405-557-7414, 405-521-5528. Business E-Mail: bingman@oksenate.gov.

BINKLEY, DAVID MARTIN, electrical engineer, educator, musician; b. Knoxville, Tenn., July 19, 1955; s. Jerry White and Carol Dexter Binkley; m. Jacqueline Lee Wimsatt, Apr. 23, 1988; children: Anna Marie, Christopher Michael Dexter. PhD in Elec. Engring., U. Tenn., 1992, MS in Elec. Engring., 1984, BS in Elec. Engring., 1978. Registered profl. engr., Tenn., 1983. Devel. engr. Tech. for Energy Corp., Knoxville, Tenn., 1978—85; sr. scientist CTI PET Systems, Knoxville, 1985—98; v.p. integrated circuit devel. Concorde Microsystems, Knoxville, 1998—2000; assoc. prof., elec. and computer engring. U. NC, Charlotte, 2000—09, prof., 2010—. Bd. dirs. Concorde Microsystems, Knoxville, 1992—2008, cons., 2000—04, Siemens Molecular Imaging, 2011—. Contbr. articles to profl. jours.; author: (book) Tradeoffs and Optimization in Analog CMOS Design, —; performer: WUOT, 1995—97, Tenn. Jazz Festival, 1999, NCAA, 2001. Pres. West Forest Neighborhood Assn., Knoxville, 1988—2000. Recipient Most Influential Engring. Prof., Tau Beta Ph, U. NC at Charlotte, 2000. Mem.: IEEE (sr.), Research! America. Achievements include patents in field. Avocations: photography, amateur radio, jazz.

BINKLEY, WILLIAM, healthcare industry executive; Field engr. Computer Innovations; network engr. Dialogic Comm. Corp.; consulting network engr. HCA, Inc.; ptnr. HCA Holdings, Inc. Office: HCA Holdings Inc 1 Park Plz Nashville TN 37203 Office Phone: 615-344-9551. Office Fax: 615-344-2266.

BINTLIFF, BARBARA ANN, library director, law educator; d. Donald Richard and Frances Arlene (Appling) Hay; m. Byron A. Boville, Aug. 20, 1977 (dec. 2006); children: Bradley, Bruce. BA in Political Sci. with hon., Cen. Wash. U., Ellensburg, 1975; JD, U. Wash., Seattle, 1978, MLL, 1979. Bar: Wash. 1979, U.S. Dist. Ct. (ea. dist.) Wash. 1980, Colo. 1983, U.S. Dist. Ct. Colo. 1983. Atty., libr. Gaddis and Fox, Seattle, 1978-79; reference libr. U. Denver Law Sch., 1979-84; assoc. libr., sr. instr. Sch. Law U. Colo., Boulder, 1984-88, assoc. prof., libr. dir., 1989—2001, prof., dir. Law Libr., 2001—10, Nicholas Rosenbaum prof. law, 2002—10; Joseph C. Hutcheson prof. law, dir. Tarlton Law Libr. U. Tex. Sch. Law, Austin, 2010—. Legal cons. Nat. Ctr. Atmospheric Rsch., Environ. and Societal Impacts Group, Boulder, 1980; vis. prof. U. Wash., Seattle, 1996, chair U. Colo. Boulder, Faculty Assembly, 2003-05, cons., Legal Resources Ctr., Johannesburg, South Africa. Co-author: Colorado Legal Resources: An Annotated Bibliography, 2004; co-editor, Public Services in Law Libraries: Evolution and Innovation in the 21st Century, 2007, Teaching Legal Research, 2010; editor: A Representative Sample of Tenure Documents for Law Librarians, 1988, 2nd edit., 1994, Chapter Presidents' Handbook, 1989, Representatives Handbook, 1990, Marketing Toolkit for Academic Law Libraries, 2004, Colorado Legal Research, 2009; assoc. editor: Legal Reference Svcs. Quarterly,

Perspectives: Teaching Legal Research and Writing Recipient Boulder Faculty Assembly Excellence Svc. award, 2001, Calhoun Svc. award, U. Colo., 2002, Robert L. Stearns award, 2008; named Disting. Alumnus, Ctrl. Wash. U., 2000, Disting. Alumna, U. Washington Info. Sch., 2012; named to Hall of Fame, Am. Assn. Law Libraries, 2012. Mem. Am. Assn. Law Librs. (v.p./pres.-elect 2000-01, pres. 2001-02; Frederick Charles Hicks award 2005, Presdl. Citation award 2006, 2010, Spectrum article of Yr. 2007), Am. Law Inst. (elected), Colo. Assn. Law Librs. (pres. 1982), Southwestern Assn. Law Librs. (pres. 1987-88, 91-92); fellow Am. Bar Found. (elect 2011). Episcopalian. Office: Tarlton Law Library University of Texas School Law 727 E Dean Keeton St Austin TX 78705-3224 Office Phone: 512-471-7735. Business E-Mail: bbintliff@law.utexas.edu.

BIONDI, MANFRED ANTHONY, physicist; b. Carlstadt, NJ, Mar. 5, 1924; s. Manfred Anthony and Helen Biondi; m. Elaine Theresa Leitkam, May 12, 1952; children: David Mark, George Philip BS in Physics, MIT, 1944, PhD, 1949. Research assoc. MIT, Cambridge, 1948-49; with Westinghouse Research Labs, Pitts., 1949-60, adv. physicist, 1952-57, mgr. physics dept., 1957-60; prof. physics U. Pitts., 1960-86, prof. emeritus, 1987—; also dir. Atomic Scis. Inst., 1968-79; exchange prof. U. Paris, 1976-86. Trustee Upper Atmosphere Rsch. Corp.; mem. adv. com. Army Rsch. Office, Durham, N.C., NAS, 1962-64; mem. exec. coun. Fedn. Am. Scientists, 1966-68; mem. adv. panel physics NSF, 1970-72; mem. Army basic rsch. steering com. NRC, 1985-88, chmn., 1987-88. Mem. editl. bd. Jour. Applied Physics, 1966-68. Served with USNR, 1943-46. Fellow AAAS, Am. Phys. Soc. (chmn. div. electron and atomic physics 1957, chmn. gaseous electronics conf. 1962-64, Davisson-Germer prize 1984); mem. Am. Geophys. Union, Earth and Sky (adv. bd. 1992-94). Home: 109 Tierra Verde Trl Panama City Beach FL 32407-3811

BIRBAHADUR, DINDIAL, secondary school educator; b. Albion Estate, Guyana, Oct. 28, 1944; came to the U.S., 1980; s. Pandit and Mangree Birbahadur; m. Rabby Devi Jaikaran, Feb. 23, 1969; 1 child, Devendra. BA, U. Guyana, 1971, diploma in edn., 1972; advanced diploma in ednl. studies, U. Leeds., 1976; MEd, U. V.I., 1984. Elem. tchr. Dept. Edn., Guyana, 1963-71, secondary tchr., 1971-74; math. lectr. Lilian Dewar Coll. Edn., Guyana, 1974-80; secondary math. tchr. V.I. Dept. Edn., 1980-89, master tchr., 1989—, chmn. math. dept., 1986—99, registrar/sys. analyst, 1999—. Math. lectr. U. Guyana, 1975-80; instr. U. V.I., 1981-89; math. examiner Caribbean Examination Coun., Barbados, 1978-80; statis. advisor U. V.I., 1982—; mem. Territorial Tech. Com., V.I., 1994—; state coord. for Presdl. award in elem. and secondary math. Author: Use of Objective Testing in Mathematics, 1976. Fellow Govt. of U.K., 1975; recipient Presdl. award for excellence in math. teaching Pres. of U.S., 1995. Mem. Nat. Coun. Tchrs. Math., Math. Assn. Am., V.I. Math. Tchrs. Assn., St. Croix Fedn. Tchrs., Coun. Presdl. Awardees in Math., Lions. Avocations: reading, playing chess, swimming, fishing, touring. Office: Arthur A Richards Jr High 20 & 21 Stoney Ground Frederiksted VI 00840 Personal E-mail: dbirbah@yahoo.com.

BIRCH, ADOLPHO A., JR., retired state supreme court justice; b. Washington, Sept. 22, 1932; 3 children. Attended, Lincoln U., Pa., 1950—52; BA, JD, Howard U., 1956. Bar: Tenn. 1957. Pvt. practice, Nashville, 1958—66; asst. pub. defender Davidson County, 1963—66, asst. dist. atty., 1966—69; judge Davidson County Gen. Sessions Ct., 1969—78, Tenn. Criminal Ct. (20th Jud. Dist.), 1978—87; presiding judge Trial Cts. of Davidson County, 1981—82; mem. Ct. of the Judiciary, 1983—86; judge Tenn. Ct. Criminal Appeals; chief justice Tenn. Supreme Ct., Nashville, 1996—97, assoc. justice, 1994—2006. Former assoc. prof. legal medicine Meharry Medical Coll.; former law lecturer Fisk U., Tenn. State U.; assoc. prof. Nashville Sch. of Law, 1991—; disting. jurist-in-residence U. Memphis. Mem. Howard Law Review, 1954—56. With USNR, 1956—58. Mem.: ABA, Nat. Bar Assn. Jud. Coun., Napier Looby Bar Assn. (past pres.), Nashville Bar Assn., Tenn. Bar Assn., Nat. Bar Assn.

BIRCH, GLYNN R., non-profit organization administrator; children: Courtney(dec.), Adrian, Rahmlee. Vol. speaker MADD Ctrl. Fla. Chpt., Orlando, bd. dirs., 1998, pres., 1999; nat. bd. dirs. Mothers Against Drunk Driving (MADD), Irving, Tex., 2000—; nat. v.p. victims issues MADD, Irving, Tex., 2003—05, nat. pres., 2005—08. Spkr. in field. First male and minority to become president of MADD. Office: MADD Nat Office 511 E John Carpenter Frwy Ste 700 Irving TX 75062

BIRD, CHRISTOPHER M., heath services company executive; BS, Colo. State U.; MBA, Harvard U.; M in Health Policy & Mgmt., Columbia U. V.p., western divisn. DaVita, Inc., 2001—06; v.p., ops., bus. devel., outpatient svcs. divsn. Tenet Healthcare Corp., 2006—08; pres., Peoplefirst Rehabilitation divsn. Kindred Healthcare, Inc., 2008—. Office: Kindred Healthcare Inc 680 S Fourth St Louisville KY 40202 Office Phone: 502-596-7300. Business E-Mail: Christopher_Bird@kindredhealthcare.com.

BIRD, HECTOR RAMÓN, child psychiatrist, psychoanalyst, educator; b. San Juan, P.R., Feb. 5, 1939; s. Hector F. and Yvette (Baker) B.; m. Sandra Lopez, May 23, 1970; 1 child, Alejandra Y. BA, U. Mich., 1960; MD, Yale U., 1965; cert. in psychiatry and child psychiatry, Columbia U., 1972; cert. in psychoanalysis, W.A. White Inst., NYC. Diplomate Am. Bd. Psychiatry and Neurology. Asst. dir. child psychiatry St. Luke's Hosp., NYC, 1972-78; dir. tng. in child psychiatry Columbia U., NYC, 1978-80, prof. emeritus clin. psychiatry, 2006—; dir. child psychiatry U. P.R. Med. Sch., San Juan, 1980-86; dep. dir. child psychiatry N.Y. State Psychiat. Inst., NYC, 1986—2006. Contbr. articles to profl. jours. Founding dir., pres. bd. dirs. Teatro de la Opera, San Juan, 1982-86; dir. Pro-Arte Musical, San Juan, 1982-86, 2007-. Lt. USN, 1966-68. Recipient Profl. Achievement award Boricua Coll., N.Y.C., 1987, Wilfred C. Hulse Meml. award N.Y. Coun. on Child and Adolescent Psychiatry, 2001. Fellow Am. Acad. Child and Adolescent Psychiatry (Riger award 2007), Am. Acad. Psychoanalysis (trustee); mem. Am. Psychopathological Assn., Soc. Rsch. in Child and Adolescent Psychopathology, William A. White Psychoanalytic Soc. Roman Catholic. Office: 1452 Ashford Ave 403 B San Juan PR 00907 Home: 60 W 66th St Apt 15J New York NY 10023-6288 Office Phone: 212-874-5311. Personal E-mail: hecbird@aol.com.

BIRD, WENDELL RALEIGH, lawyer; s. Raleigh Milton and R. Jean Bird. BA summa cum laude, Vanderbilt U., 1975; JD, Yale Law Sch., 1978; DPhil, U. Oxford, 2012. Bar: Ga. 1978, Ala. 1980, Calif. 1981, Fla. 1982, U.S. Ct. Appeals (2d, 3d, 4th, 5th, 6th, 7th, 8th, 9th, 10th and 11th cirs.) 1979-83, U.S. Supreme Ct. 1983. Law clk. to judge U.S. Ct. Appeals (4th cir.), Durham, NC, 1978-79, U.S. Ct. Appeals (5th cir.), Birmingham, Ala., 1979-80; atty. Parker, Johnson, Cook & Dunlevie, Atlanta, 1982-86; sr. ptnr. Bird Loechl Brittain & McCants LLC, Atlanta, 1986—. Adj. prof. Emory U. Law Sch., Atlanta, 1985—90; lectr. Washington Non-Profit Tax Conf., 1982—. Contbg. author: Federal and State Taxation of Exempt Organizations, 1994, CCH Federal Tax Service, 1988—; mem. bd. editors Yale U. Law Jour., 1977-78, others; contbr. articles to profl. jours. Recipient Egger prize Yale U., 1978. Mem.: ABA (litigation sect., taxation sect., com. on exempt orgns., past chmn. subcom. on religious orgns., past chmn. subcom. on state and local taxes, co-chmn. subcom. on charitable contbns. 2002—), Am. Bar. Found., Am. Law Inst., Ga. Bar Assn., Fla. Bar Assn., Calif. Bar Assn., Ala. Bar Assn., Phi Beta Kappa. Republican. Avocations: piano, skiing, photography, genealogy, architecture. Home: 92 Blackland Rd NW Atlanta GA 30342-4420 Office: Bird Loechl Brittain & McCants LLC 1150 Monarch Plz 3414 Peachtree Rd NE Atlanta GA 30326-1153 Office Phone: 404-264-9400.

BIRDWELL, BRIAN, state legislator; m. Mel Birdwell; 1 child, Matt. BS in Criminal Justice, Lamar U., Beaumont, 1984; MPA, U. Mo., Kansas City, 1996; grad., Command and Gen. Staff Coll., Ft. Leavenworth, Kansas, 2000. Deployed to Operation Desert Shield/Desert Storm during first Gulf War, 1990; deployed to Ctrl. America as Joint Ops. Officer for Joint Task Force Aguila to conduct humanitarian ops. after Hurricane Mitch, 1998; serving on the Dept. of the Army staff as mil. aide to the Dep. Asst. Chief of Staff for Installation Mgmt.; co-founder, nat. spkr. Face The Fire Ministries; mem. Dist. 22 Tex. State Senate, 2010—. Nat. spkr. WallBuilders. Co-author (with wife): Refined by Fire: A Family's Triumph of Love and Faith; guest appearances Fox News, Today Show, CBS Early Show, and CNN, panelist Sean Hannity's, Great American Panel, featured in Washington Post, US News & World Report and Los Angeles Times. Ret. lt. col. US Army. Decorated Bronze Star for Exceptional Meritorious Achievement, Purple Heart for wounds received on September 11, 2001 in the Pentagon, Legion of Merit. Republican. Office: PO Box 12068 Capitol Station Austin TX 78711 also: 900 Austin Ave Ste 500 Waco TX 76701 also: 1315 Waters Edge Dr Ste 116-2 Granbury TX 76048 Office Phone: 512-463-0122, 254-772-6225, 817-573-9622.

BIRDWHISTELL, TERRY L., library director; BA in Am. Studies, Georgetown Coll.; MA in History and Libr. and Info. Sci.; D in Ednl. Policy Studies, U. Ky. Dir. oral history program and Louis B. Nunn Ctr. Oral History U. Ky., Lexington, 1974—2005, univ. archivist, 1985—2001, assoc. dean spl. collections and digital programs, 2005—10, dean, 2010—. Adj. assoc. prof. dept. ednl. policy studies and evaluation U. Ky., grad. sch. faculty mem. Co-gen. editor Kentucky Remembered: An Oral History Series, U. Press Ky.; prodr.: (documentaries) Kentucky's New Dealer: Ed Prichard Remembers, 1983, Long Road Back: Vietnam Remembered, 1985; author: (books) An Educated Difference: Women at the University of Kentucky through the Second World War, 1994; contbr. articles to profl. jours. Advisor Ky. Oral History Commn. Named to U. Ky. Coll. Edn. Alumni Hall of Fame, 2006. Mem.: Ky. Coun. on Archives, Am. Studies Assn. (former pres.), Nat. Oral History Assn. (former pres.), Assn. Centers for Study of Congress. Office: University of Kentucky Libraries Young Library West Wing 1st Fl Lexington KY 40506 Office Phone: 859-257-0500 2087. Business E-Mail: tlbird@uky.edu.

BIRK, JOHN RICHARD, management consultant; b. Boston, Aug. 11, 1951; s. Harold F. and Jane Birk; m. Susan Arnold, Feb. 9, 1980; children: John R. Jr., Andrew A. BA in Econs. and English, Colgate U., 1974; Advanced Mgmt. Program, Harvard Bus. Sch., 1991. Sales rep. Procter & Gamble, NYC, 1975-76, dist. field rep. White Plains, NY, 1976, unit mgr. Dallas, 1976-78; sales devel. mgr. Pepsi Cola Co., Purchase, NY, 1978-80, regional sales mgr. San Francisco, 1980-83; dir. sales and mktg. MCI Comm. Inc., Atlanta, 1983-84, v.p. sales and mktg., 1984-85; pres., bd. dirs. U.S. Telecomm Svcs. Co., Kansas City, 1985; pres. N.E. divsn. US Sprint, Purchase, 1986-87, pres. we. group San Francisco, 1987-88; exec. v.p., COO, dir. ADVO, Inc., 1988—89; pres., COO, dir. ADVO Inc., Windsor, 1989-92; pres., CEO, dir. Wright Express Corp., South Portland, Maine, 1992-94, chmn., 1994-95; pres. Ideon Group Inc. (formerly Safe Card Svcs., Inc.), Jacksonville, Fla., 1995; mgmt. cons. John R. Birk & Assocs., Ponte Vedra Beach, Fla., 1995—; oper. ptnr. Evercore Ptnrs., 1996—. Bd. dirs. Nat. Sys., Inc. Bd. dirs. Prevent Blindness, Atlanta, 1984-85, United Way, White Plains, 1986-87, Westchester County Assn., 1986-87, Bay Area Coun., 1987-88, United Way Greater Portland, 1993-95, Found. for Blood Rsch., Inc., 1993-95, Colgate U. Alumni Corp., 1995-99; chmn. Colgate U. Pres. Club, 1996-99. Mem.: Shelter Harbor Golf Club (bd. overseers, treas. 2008—). Republican. Roman Catholic. Avocations: tennis, golf, skiing. Office Phone: 904-273-7819. Personal E-mail: jrbirk@aol.com.

BIRLE, JAMES ROBB, investor; b. Phila., Jan. 25, 1936; s. John George and Mildred C. (Donnelly) B.; m. Mary Margaret McDaniels, Jan. 28, 1961; children— James Robb, Jr., Anne Margaret, Alexandra Lea, John George II BSM.E., Villanova U., 1958. With Gen. Electric Co., San Jose, Calif., 1958, gen. mgr. nuclear energy bus., 1969-77, v.p., gen mgr. far east business div. NYC, 1977-81, v.p., gen mgr. air condition div. Louisville, 1981-82, sr. v.p., group exec. constrn. and engring. svcs. group Westport, Conn, 1982-85, sr. v.p. corp. trading ops. NYC, 1985-88; ptnr. The Blackstone Group, NYC, 1988-94; co-chmn., CEO Collins & Aikman Group, NYC, 1988-94; chmn. Resolute Ptnrs., LLC, Village of Golf, Fla., 1994—; non-exec. chmn. Mass. Mut. Fin. Svcs. Co., 2005—. Bd. dirs. Mass. Mut. Fin. Svcs. Co. 1992-, chmn. bd. Mass Mutual Fin. Group; former mem. Transparency Internat. Former trustee Villanova U., 2005-. Republican. Avocations: tennis, golf, reading, sailing. Office: Resolute Ptnrs LLC 2 Pine Ln East Village Of Golf FL 33436 Home: 2 Pine Ln E Village Of Golf FL 33436

BIRMINGHAM, RICHARD GREGORY, lawyer; b. Buffalo, Aug. 14, 1929; s. William Anthony and Laura Louise (Reimann) B.; m. Suzanne M. Cannon, May 20, 1961; children: Barbara A. McCarty, Maureen E., Gregory S. BA, U. Notre Dame, 1951; JD, SUNY, Buffalo, 1957. Bar: N.Y. 1957, Del. 1984, Pa. 1993. Law clk. to justices appellate div. N.Y. Supreme Ct. (4th dept.), Rochester, 1957-60; ptnr. Phillips, Lytle, Hitchcock, Blaine & Huber, Buffalo, 1960-84, 90-94, ret., 1994, ptnr. Wilmington, Del., 1984-90; of-counsel Beck & Thomas, 2010—. Lt. comdr. USN, 1951-54, Korea. Mem. ABA, N.Y. State Bar Assn., Del. Bar Assn., Erie County Bar Assn., Rivermont Country Club. Republican. Roman Catholic. Office: 510 Shelli Ln Roswell GA 30075-2988

BIRNBAUM, LINDA S., federal agency administrator, toxicologist; b. Passaic, NJ, Dec. 21, 1946; BA in Biology, U. Rochester, NY, 1967; MS in Microbiology, U. Ill., Urbana, 1969, PhD in Microbiology, 1972. Diplomate Am. Bd. Toxicology. Vis. asst. prof. microbiology U. Ill., 1972; postdoc. fellow biochemistry U. Mass., Amherst, 1973—74; asst. prof. sci. Kirkland Coll., Clinton, NY, 1974—75; rsch. assoc., rsvh. fellow Masonic Med. Rsch. Lab., Utica, NY, 1975—79; sr. staff fellow nat. toxicology program Nat. Cancer Inst., Research Triangle Park, NC, 1979—80; rsch. microbiologist Nat. Inst. Environ. Health Svcs. (NIEHS) NIH, Research Triangle Park, NC, 1980—89, dir. NIEHS, 2009—, dir. Nat. Toxicology Program, 2009—, sr. investigator, Nat. Cancer Insi., 2009—; dir. exptl. toxicology divsn., Nat. Health & Environ. Effects Rsch. Lab., EPA, Research Triangle Park, NC, 1989—2008, acting dir. human studies divsn. Chapel Hill, NC, 2001—02, sr. toxicologist, 2008—09. Adj. prof. genetics SUNY Inst. Tech., Utica, 1976; adj. asst. prof., dept. environ. sci. U. NC Sch. Pub. Health, Chapel Hill, 1980—82, adj. assoc. prof., 1982—88, adj. prof., 1988—; adj. faculty Duke U., Durham, NC, 1995—. Mem. editl. bd. AGE, 1985—, Environ. Health Perspectives, 1988—, Human & Exptl. Toxicology, 1993—, Toxicology & Applied Pharmacology, 1989—, Chemosphere, 1999—; contbr. numerous articles to profl. jours., chapters to books. Mem. exec. bd. Am. Aging Assn., 1979—83, v.p., 1980—81; ofcl. avvisor Endometriosis Assn., 2007—. Recipient Conservation Achievement award, Nat. Wildlife Fedn., 1996, Ahlborg Memorial award, Karolinska Inst., Sweden, 1996; grantee, NIH, 1967—72, Mellon Found., 1974—75; fellow, Damon Runyon Found., 1973—74. Fellow: Acad. Toxicological Scis.; mem.: AAAS, Soc. Risk Analysis, Inst. Medicine, Women in Toxicology (Elsevier Mentoring award 2008), Internat. Union Toxicology (pres. 2010—), Gerontol. Soc., Internat. Soc. Study Xenobiotics, Am. Aging Assn. (former v.p.), Soc. Toxicology (pres. 2004—05, Pub. Comm. award 2006, Amb. award 2006), Am. Soc. Pharmacology & Exptl. Therapeutics (former chairperson, divsn. toxicology), Sigma Xi, Phi Kappa Phi, Phi Beta Kappa. Office: NIEHS Bldg 101 Rall Bldg B242 111 T Alexander Dr Research Triangle Park NC 27709 Office Phone: 919-541-3201. Office Fax: 919-541-2260. Business E-Mail: linda.birnbaum@nih.gov.

BIRNS, IRA MICHAEL, corporate financial executive; b. Long Beach, NY, Sept. 12, 1962; s. Alfred and Edith (Moskovich) B.; m. Francine Silver, Mar. 19, 1988. BBA in Pub. Acctg., Hofstra U., 1983. CPA, Cert. Treas. Profl. Internal auditor Culbro Corp., NYC, 1983-85, fin. analyst, 1985-86, asst. treas., 1986-89, Arrow Electronics, Inc., Melville, NY, 1989—96, treas., 1996—2003, v.p., treas., 2003—04, v.p. investor rels. & treas., 2004—07; exec. v.p., CFO World Fuel Services, Inc. (subs. World Fuel Services Corp.), Miami, Fla., 2007—. Mem., past vice-chmn., Assn. Fin. Professionals; mem. AICPAs, N.Y. State Soc. CPAs, Nat. Corp. Cash Mgmt. Assn., Treasury Mgmt. Assn. L.I. (co-founder 1991). Republican. Jewish. Avocation: rare coin collecting. Office: World Fuel Services Ste 400 9800 NW 41st St Miami FL 33178

BISCHOFF, SUSAN ANN, foundation executive; b. Indpls., July 31, 1951; d. Thomas Anthony and Betty Jean (Coons) Bischoff; m. Jim B. Barlow, June 20, 1975; 1 child, Samantha Lynn Barlow Martinez. BA, Ind. U., 1973. Rschr., reporter Congl. Quar., Washington, 1973-74; city desk reporter Houston Chronicle, 1974-75, bus. reporter, 1975-79, asst. bus. editor, 1979-84, bus. editor, 1984-86, asst. mng. editor, 1986-2000, dep. mng. editor, 2000—03, assoc. editor, 2003—06; pres. Houston Pub. Libr. Found., 2007—. Houston corr. Kiplinger, Tex. Letter, Washington, 1980-85; juror Pulitzer Prizes in Journalism, 2004, 05. Mem. class policy Leadership Houston, 1992—94; mem. exec. com. Gulf Coast affiliate United Way, 1994—2002; pres. Friends of Houston Girl Scouts, 2002—06; bd. dirs. Houston Chronicle Employees Fed. Credit Union, 1980—87, San Jacinto Coun. Girl Scouts US, 1997—2003, Child Adv., 1999—2005, US Olympic Festival VII, Houston, 1985—86, Gulf Coast Mar. of Dimes Birth Defects Found., 1989—2001, YES Coll. Prep. Sch., 1999—2002, AIDS Found., Houston, 2002—10, Psychology Works, 2006—09, Houston A+ Challenge, 2007—; founding bd. dir. Greater Houston Women's Found.; mem. bd. visitors Anderson Cancer Ctr. U. Tex. Recipient Outstanding Vol. Achievement award, Gulf Coast United Way, 1995, Outstanding Media award, Nat. Soc. Fund Raising Execs., 1997, Nat. Thanks award, San Jacinto Girl Scouts, 2001, Mayborn award, Cmty. Leadership Tex. Daily Newspaper Assn., 2001, honoree, Jewish Cmty. Ctr. of Houston Children's Scholarship Ball, 2002, Strong, Smart and Bold award, Houston Girls, Inc., 2003, Urban Campout Honoree, Girls Scouts, 2010; named Outstanding Woman in Houston Journalism, YWCA, 1989, Fabulous Femme, Greater Houston Women's Found., 1994, Woman of Distinction, Crohn's & Colitis Found., 1996. Mem.: Am. Assn. Sunday and Feature Editors (named to Features Hall of Fame 2003), Am. Soc. Newspaper Editors (bd. dirs.). Home: 2929 Buffalo Speedway # 112 Houston TX 77098 Office: Houston Pub Libr Found 500 McKinney St Houston TX 77002

BISHER, JAMES FURMAN, journalist, writer; b. Denton, NC, Nov. 4, 1918; s. Chisholm and Mamie (Morris) B.; m. Lynda Landon; children: Roger, James Furman Jr., Monte. Student, Furman U., Greenville, SC, 1934—36; AB in Journalism, U. NC, Chapel Hill, 1938; D in Arts and Letters (hon.), Furman U., Greenville, SC, 1999; PhD in Arts and Letters (hon.), Furman U. Editor Lumberton (N.C.) Voice, 1938-39; reporter High Point (N.C.) Enterprise, 1939-40; reporter, state editor Charlotte (N.C.) News, 1940-42, sports editor, 1946-50, Atlanta Constn., 1950-57, Atlanta Jour., 1957—; columnist The Sporting News, St. Louis; moderator weekly TV show, Football Rev., 1950-68. V.p. Bisher Hosiery Mill, Denton, N.C. Author: With A Southern Exposure, 1962, Miracle in Atlanta, 1966, Strange But True Baseball Stories, 1966, Arnold Palmer— The Golden Year, 1971, Aaron, 1974, The College Game, 1974, The Masters, 1976, The Furman Bisher Collection, 1989, Thankful, 1997, Atlanta Half-Century, 1997, Peachtree Golf Club, 2004, Face to Face, 2005, also numerous articles; contbr. to: anthologies including Best Sports Stories of Year, 23 times. Chmn. Ga. Christmas Seal campaign, 1961; charter mem. Atlanta-Fulton County Stadium Authority.; mem. selection com. Pro Football Hall of Fame, Coll. Football Hall of Fame, Ga.; bd. dirs. Salvation Army Boys Club, mem. adv. bd. Sarazen World Open Golf Tournament; mem. Atlanta Sports Coun. Served to lt. USNR Air Corps, 1943-46. Named Ky. col., 1958, Sportswriter of Yr. Ga. (19 times); hon. Tar Heel, 1961; Disting. Alumnus of Yr. Furman U., 1978, Disting. Alumnus 20th Century, 2006; named to U. NC Journalism Hall of Fame, 1985; Nat. Sportscasters and Sportswriters Hall of Fame, 1989, Internat. Golf Writers Hall of Fame, 1989, Ga. Sports Hall of Fame, 1990, N.C. Sports Hall of Fame, 1995, Ga. Soccer Hall of Fame, 1997, Ga. Golf Hall of Fame, 2004; recipient Ga. A.P. Sports Writing award, 18 times; UPI Sports Writing award, 4 times; Turf Writing award Fla. Throughbred Breeders Assn., 1972, 75; Jake Wade award Coll. Sports Info. Dirs. Am., 1979; Sigma Delta Chi awards best sports commentary, 1982, 93, 90; Bert McGrane award disting. svc. to coll. football, 1982; N.C. Gov.'s award, 1986; Red Smith award disting. and meritorious contbn. to art of sportswriting, 1988, Bobby Jones Sportsman of Yr. award, 1994, Lifetime Achievement in Journalism award PGA in Am., 1996, Meml. Golf Journalism award, 1997, Marvin Francis Svc. award, 2001, Nat. Conf. Cmty. and Justice award, 2001, Lincoln Werden Meml. award, N.Y. Golf Assn., 2001, Furman Bisner medal UNC Sch. Journalism, 2008, Lifetime Achievement award, Ga. Writers Assn., 2009; sponsor Furman Bisher Acad.-Athletic scholarship Furman U., Roger C. Bisher Scholarship Ga. Tech. Mem. Nat. Sportscasters and Sportswriters Assn. (pres. 1974-76), Football Writers Assn. Am. (pres. 1959-60), Golf Writers Assn. Am. (pres. 1992-94), Assn. Golf Writers (Europe) (life), Canongate Golf Club, Legends at Chateau Elan, Capital City Club, The European Club, Sea Island Golf Club, Gridiron Club, Chi Psi. Presbyterian. Home: 431 Lester Rd Fayetteville GA 30215-4930 Office: 72 Marietta St NW PO Box 4689 Atlanta GA 30302-4689: 21 Dunbar Creek Pte Saint Simons Island GA 31522 Office Phone: 404-526-5335. Personal E-mail: furman@ajc.com.

BISHOP, ANNE HUGHES, retired nursing educator; b. Charlottesville, Va., June 27, 1935; d. Aubrey Scott and Virginia May (Flint) Hughes; m. Bobby Nelson Bishop, June 15, 1957; children: Kathryn B. Bartholf, Barry S. Bishop (Dec.). BSN, U. Va., 1958; MEd, Lynchburg Coll., Va., 1968; MSN, U. Va., 1986, EdD, 1980. Staff nurse Va. Bapt. Hosp., Lynchburg, 1958-59, instr., 1959-63, asst. dir., 1963-72, dir. Sch. Nursing, 1972-79; prof. and dept. chmn. nursing Lynchburg Coll., 1979-85, prof. nursing, 1979—97; DON Ctr. for Health Promotion, 1992—97; ret., 1997. Presenter in field. Co-author:

The Practical, Moral and Personal Sense of Nursing, 1990, Nursing: The Practice of Caring, 1991, Nursing Ethics: Therapeutic Caring Presence, 1995, Nursing Ethics: Holistic Nursing Practice, 2001, Japanese translation, 2005, Beyond Friendship & Eros: Unrecognized Relationships Between Men & Women, 2001, Voice of Hope & Despair, 2004, Yes and Thanks: Seeking the Spiritual in the World, 2012; co-editor: Caring, Curing, Coping, 1985; contbr. articles to profl. jours. Sec., dir. Free Clinic of Ctrl. Va., Lynchburg, 1987-96. Named Outstanding Scholar Lynchburg Coll., 1992, named to YWCA Acad. Women in Health/Sci., 1996; recipient Humanitarian award Nat. Conf. for Cmty. & Justice, 2003. Democrat. Mem. Christian Ch. (Disciples Of Christ). Avocations: genealogy, reading, travel. Personal E-mail: abbishop107@comcast.net.

BISHOP, BRUCE TAYLOR, lawyer; b. Hartford, Conn., Sept. 13, 1951; s. Robert Wright Sr. and Barbara (Taylor) B.; m. Sarah M. Bishop, Aug. 31, 1974; children: Elizabeth, Margaret. BA in Polit. Sci., Old Dominion U., 1973; JD, U. Va., Charlottesville, 1976. Bar: Va. 1977, U.S. Supreme Ct., Va. 1976, U.S. Dist. Ct. (ea. dist.) Va., U.S. Dist. Ct. (we. dist.) Va., U.S. Ct. Appeals (4th cir.); diplomate Am. Bd. Trial Advocates. Law clk. to chief judge U.S. Dist. Ct. (ea. dist.) Va., 1976-77; assoc. Willcox & Savage, P.C., Norfolk, Va., 1977-82, ptnr., 1983—. Bd. dirs. Nautical Adventures, Inc., Norfolk FestEvents, Ltd., 1981—, pres., 1982-85; pres. Va. OpSail 2000 Found.; bd. visitors Old Dominion U., 1972-83, sec., 1979-81, chmn., com. mem.; speaker in field. Treas. Norfolk Reps., 1978-82, com. mem.; bd. dirs., chmn. regional Key Club campaign United Way South Hampton Roads; chmn., co-chmn. United Negro Coll. Fund, 1981, Four Cities United Way Campaign; trustee Va. Stage Co., 1982; pres. Cmty. Promotion Corp.; commr. Norfolk Redevel. and Housing Authority, chmn., 2000-02; pres. Old Dominion U. Ednl. Found., 2003-2005. Named Outstanding Young Man in Norfolk, Norfolk Jaycees, 1982; recipient Disting. Alumni award Old Dominion U., Dominion Vol. of Yr. award, 1993. Mem. ABA, Fed. Bar Assn. (pres. Tidewater chpt. 1980-81), Am. Bd. Trial Advocates, Va. Assn. Def. Lawyers, Va. Bar Assn., Norfolk-Portsmouth Bar Assn., Def. Rsch. Inst., Internat. Assn. Def. Counsel (nat. trial acad. faculty 1997), Assn. Def. Attys., Def. Rsch. Inst., Old Dominion U. Alumni Assn. (bd. dirs. 1978-83), Old Dominion U. Ednl. Found. (bd. dirs. 1987—, sec. 2000-02, pres. 2003-05), Norfolk C. of C. (chmn. downtown devel. com. 1980-81), James Kent Am. Inn of Ct. (master). Avocations: basketball, tennis, gardening. Office: Willcox & Savage PC 440 Monticello Ave Ste 2200 Norfolk VA 23510 Office Phone: 757-628-5573. Business E-Mail: bbishop@wilsav.com.

BISHOP, BUDD HARRIS, retired museum director; b. Canton, Ga., Nov. 1, 1936; s. James M. and Mary E. (Ponder) B.; m. Julia Crowder, Nov. 30, 1968. AB, Shorter Coll., Rome, Ga., 1958; M.F.A., U. Ga., 1960; student, Arts Adminstrn. Inst. Harvard, 1970. Instr. art Ensworth Sch., Nashville, 1961-63; dir. creative services Transit Advt. Assn., NYC, 1964-66; dir. Hunter Mus. of Art, Chattanooga, 1966-76, Columbus (Ohio) Mus. Art, 1976-87, Samuel P. Harn Mus. Art, U. Fla., Gainesville, 1987-98, dir. emeritus. Vis. lectr. Vanderbilt U., 1962; past pres. bd. Intermuseum Conservation Lab., Oberlin, Ohio Past trustee Fla. Arts Celebration, Gainesville; mem. Gainesville Art in Pub. Places Trust; mem. faculty Ctr. for Arts and Pub. Policy, Tenn. Arts Commn., 2007—11; bd. dirs. Fla. Assn. Mus. Found., Inc.; mem. nat. adv. bd. Philharm. Ctr. for Arts, Naples, Fla.; trustee Hist. Rugby, Inc., Tenn.; bd. dirs. Cordell Hull Mus. and Bhplace, Upper Cumberland Arts Alliance; pres. Livingston-Overton County C. of C. Recipient gov.'s award Tenn. Art Commn., 1971, 73, Alumni Arts achievement award Shorter Coll., 1979, arts leadership award Columbus Day, 1986, Person of Yr. award in arts Gainesville Sun, 1995, Lifetime Achievement Mus. Svc. award Fla. Assn. Mus., 1997. Mem. Am. Assn. Museums, Assn. Art Mus. Dirs. (past trustee), Southeastern Museums Conf. (James R. Short award 1998), Fla. Art Mus. Dirs. Assn. (Lifetime Achievement award 1998). Office Phone: 931-823-1106.

BISHOP, CHARLES EDWIN, academic administrator, economist, educator; b. Campobello, SC, June 8, 1921; s. Fred and Hattie Bess (Wall) B.; m. Lee N., June 1, 2002; children from a previous marriage: Susan Ann, Mary Catherine, Charles Edwin. BS, Berea Coll., 1946; MS, U. Ky., 1948; PhD (Farm Found. fellow 1948-49), U. Chgo., 1952. Research asst. agrl. econs. U. Ky., 1947-48; research assoc. econs. U. Chgo., 1949-50; mem. faculty N.C. State U., 1950-70, prof. agrl. econs., 1956-70, head dept. agrl. econs., 1957-65, head dept. econs., 1965-66, William N. Reynolds Disting. prof., 1957-70; v.p. U. N.C., Chapel Hill, 1966-70; exec. dir. Agrl. Policy Inst., 1960-66; chancellor U. Md., College Park, 1970-74; pres. U. Ark., Fayetteville, 1974-80, U. Houston System, 1980-86. Vis. prof. Grad. Sch. Bus., U. Va., 1961-63; cons. Universidad Agraria, Lima, Peru, 1961-65; mem. Nat. Com. Agrl. Policy, Nat. Planning Assn., 1958-70; agrl. bd. Nat. Acad. Scis., 1963-68; sci. adv. com. to sec. agr., 1962-68; mem. Nat. Manpower Adv. Com., 1962-68; exec. dir. Pres. Johnson's Nat. Adv. Com. on Rural Poverty, 1966-67; mem. food adv. com. Pres. Nixon's Cost of Living Council, 1972; mem. Pres. Carter's adv. com. White House Conf. on Balanced Nat. Growth and Econ. Devel., 1978 Co-author: Introduction to Agricultural Economic Analysis, 1958. Mem. com. on vet. med. edn. So. Regional Edn. Bd., 1974; trustee Farm Found., 1968-78; bd. dirs. Winthrop Rockefeller Found., 1975-78, Resources for the Future, 1976-90, chmn., 1987-90; co-chmn. bd. Nat. Rural Ctr., 1975-79; mem. N.C. Rural Econ. Devel. Ctr., 1986-96, chmn., 1991-96; mem. Pres. Carter's Commn. on Agenda for Eighties, 1980; bd. dirs. Houston Industries, 1984-92. Sr. fellow M.D.C., 1991-2000. Fellow Am. Agrl. Econ. Assn. (pres. 1967-68); mem. Internat. Assn. Agrl. Econs., Commn. on Cen. European Econ. Devel., Alpha Zeta, Phi Kappa Phi, Gamma Sigma Delta.

BISHOP, CLAIRE DEARMENT, small business owner, retired librarian; b. Youngstown, Ohio, Oct. 12, 1937; d. Eugene Howard and Ruth (Bright) DeArment; m. Carl R. Meinstereifel, 1956 (div. 1964; children: Paul, Dawn; m. Olin Jerry Dewberry, Jr., 1974 (div. 1979); m. J. Bruce Bishop, May 6, 1992 (dec. Oct. 2005). BS, Clarion State U., 1967; MLS, Ga. State U., 1977. Cert. libr. media specialist, Ga. Libr. Henry County, Stockbridge, Ga., 1967-69; head libr. Russell H.S., East Point, Ga., 1969-84; engring. libr. Rockwell Internat., Duluth, Ga., 1984-88; rep. Govt. Industry Data Exch. Program, Corona, Calif., 1984-88; libr. Raytheon Co., 1990, Missile Sys. Divsn., Bristol, Tenn., 1988-90; owner, mgr. Claire's Collectibles, rubber stamp store, St. Augustine, Fla. Author newsletter Grin and Stamp It. Sec. San Marco Avenue Mchts. Assn. Mem. St. Augustine IBM Users Group (sec.), Six-Ninety-Six Investment Club (fin. officer), Mensa. Democrat. Avocations: writing, computers. Office Phone: 904-825-1122. Personal E-mail: clairebishop@bellsouth.net.

BISHOP, INA SUE MARQUIS, retired dean; b. Charleston, W.Va., Sept. 30, 1939; d. Harold Edwin and Ina Mabel (Walkup) Marquis; m. Randal Young Bishop, Feb. 27, 1960: children: Jon Marquis, Heather Suzanne. RN, Norton Infirmary Sch. Nursing, 1960; BSN, Murray State U., 1963; MSN, Ind. U., 1967, PhD, 1983. RN, Ky., Ind., Fla., N.C. Ind. staff nurse psychiatry Norton Infirmary, Louisville, 1960-61; head nurse obstetrics, nursing supr. Murray (Ky.) Gen. Hosp., 1961-62; primary care nurse, crisis counselor infirmary Murray State U., 1962-63; staff nurse, clin. instr. Madison (Ind.) State Hosp., 1963-65; instr. through assoc. prof. Ind. U. Sch. Nursing, Indpls., 1967-89, developer child/adolescent psychiat., mental health nursing program, 1982-83, chairperson grad. dept., 1983-89; prof., asst. dean Coll. of Nursing U. South Fla., Tampa, 1989-91; dean Coll. Nursing U. N.C., Charlotte, 1992-95, dean Coll. of Nursing and Health Professions, 1995—2004, dean Coll. Health and Human Svcs., 2002—04, dean emerita, 2004—; ret., 2004. Pvt. practice marital and family therapy, 1975-89; cons. in field. Founding editor-in-chief Jour. of Child and Adolescent Psychiatric and Mental Health Nursing, 1987-91; contbr. articles to profl. jours. Bd. dirs. Carolinas blood svcs. region ARC, 1997-2002, chmn. bd. dirs., 2000—. NIMH trainee Ind. U., 1965-67, USPHS profl. nurse trainee Ind. U., 1977-78; recipient Youth Advocacy award Ind. Advs. for Child Psychiat. Nursing, 1987, Disting. Svc. award Ind. U. Sch. Nursing Alumni Assn., 1989, Nat. Youth Advocacy award Advs. for Child Psychiat. Nursing, 1990, Disting. Alumni award Ind. U. sch. Edn., 2000. Fellow Am. Acad. Nursing; mem. ANA, Psychiat. Mental Health Nursing Coun., Soc. for Edn. and Rsch. in Psychiat. Mental Health Nursing (pres. 1988-90), Am. Assn. Marital and Family Therapy, So. Nursing Rsch. Soc., So. Piedmont Alzheimer's Assn. (bd. dirs. 1999-2000), New South Hospice of Charlotte and Lincoln County (bd. dirs. 1995—2004, chair 2002-04), Sigma Theta Tau.

BISHOP, LISTON, II, (BO BISHOP), lawyer, insurance company executive; b. 1947; AB, U. NC, Chapel Hill, 1969, JD, 1972. Atty. corp. and securities law Miller & Martin PLLC, 1979—2005, atty. corporate & securities law, 2007—08; dep. gen. counsel, corporate sec. Coco-Cola Enterprises Inc., 2005—07; interim gen. counsel Unum Group, Chattanooga, 2008, exec. v.p., gen. counsel, 2008—. Office: Unum Group 1 Fountain Square Chattanooga TN 37402*

BISHOP, RAND, retired humanities educator; b. Lansing, Mich., Feb. 3, 1933; s. David Rand and Myra Lu (Deacon) B.; 1 child, Andrew Nelson. BA, U. Mich., 1954, MA, 1961; cert., Fgn. Svc. Inst., 1964; PhD, Mich. State U., 1970. Cultural affairs officer USIA, Lomé, Togo, 1964-66, acting pub. affairs officer, 1965-66; asst. prof. Calif. State U., Sacramento, 1966-69, Mich. State U., East Lansing, 1970-71; prof. SUNY, Oswego, 1971-95; ret., 1995. Scholar-in-residence Fulbright program USIA, Washington, 1983-84; Fulbright prof. U. Nat. du Gabon, Libreville, 1974-75; vis. prof. McGill U., Montreal, Que., Can., 1974; U. Fla., Gainesville, 1979. Author: African Literature, African Critics: The Forming of Critical Standards, 1947-66, 88, Be Weatherwise: A Brief Account of the Life of Horace "Stormy" Meredith, 2007; contbr. articles to profl. jours.; poems, short stories, to lit. mags. Fellow NEH, UCLA, 1978. Avocation: poetry.

BISHOP, SANFORD DIXON, JR., United States Representative from Georgia, lawyer; b. Mobile, Ala., Feb. 4, 1947; s. Sanford and Minnie Bishop; m. Vivian Creighton; 1 child, Aayesha J. Reese. BA in Polit. Sci., Morehouse Coll., 1968; JD, Emory U., 1971. Ptnr. Bishop & Buckner, P.C., Columbus, Ga., 1972—92; mem. Ga. House of Reps. from 94th dist., 1977—90, Ga. State Senate, 1991—92, US Congress from 2nd Ga. dist., 1993—, mem. appropriations com. Del. Dem. Nat. Conv. 1980, 84, 88. Named Man of the Yr. Men's Progressive Club Columbus, Ga., 1977, Black Georgian of the Yr., 1983, Most Influential Black Men in Ga.; recipient Outstanding Legis. award Ga. NOW, 1983-84, Legis. Svc. award, Ga. Mcpl. Assn., 1984, 86, Friend of the Children award Child Adv. Coalition, Disting. Eagle Scout award; Earl Warren fellow, 1971-72; named one of Most Influential Black Americans, Ebony mag., 2006; named to Power 150 Ebony mag., 2008. Mem. ABA, Nat. Bar Assn., Ga. Bar Assn., Ala. Bar Assn., Am. Judicature Soc., Shriners, Masons (32 degree), Phi Delta Phi, Pi Sigma Alpha, Kappa Alpha Psi, Sigma Pi Phi. Democrat. Baptist. Office: US House of Representatives 2429 Rayburn House Office Bldg Washington DC 20515-1002 also: Albany Towers Ste 114 235 Roosevelt Ave Albany GA 31701 Office Phone: 202-225-3631. Fax: 202-225-2203. Business E-Mail: bishop.email@mail.house.gov.*

BISHOP, SID GLENWOOD, union official; b. Gladehill, Va., Nov. 11, 1923; s. Clarence Glenwood and Lillian Helen (Onks) B.; m. Patrice Frances Collier, Nov. 14, 2004. Grad., US Naval Trade Sch., 1942; cert. in labor rels., Concord Coll., Athens, W.Va., 1961. Telegraph operator Virginian R.R., 1946-47, C & O R.R., 1947-62; local chmn. Order R.R. Telegraphers, 1960-62; gen. chmn. C & O-Virginian R.R.'s, 1962-68; 2d v.p. Transp-Communication Employees Union, St. Louis, 1968-69; v.p. transp. com. divsn. Brotherhood Ry. and Airline Clks., Rockville, Md., 1969-73, asst. internat. v.p., 1973—. Mem. subcom. Labor Rsch. Adv. Coun., Dept. Labor, 1975, mem. com. on productivity, tech., growth Bur. Labor Statistics, 1975-77. With USN, 1941-46. Mem. AFL-CIO, Can. Labor Congress, Hunting Hills Homeowners Assn., VFW, Chantilly Nat. Golf and Country Club, Elks, Masons, K.T., Shriners. Home and Office: 676 NE 28th Ave Okeechobee FL 34972-3323 Personal E-mail: bishlite@comcast.net.

BISHOP, STUART J., state legislator; m. Kim Dugas; children: Donald, Cooper. BA, La. State U. Aide La. State Senate, 1995—97; co-owner, sales mgr. Baldwin Redi-Mix, 1998—; mem. Dist. 43 La. House of Reps., Baton Rogue, 2012—. Mem. Holy Cross Cath. Ch., La.; bd. dirs. Downtown Lafayette Unlimited, 2008—, Lafayette Edn. Found., 2010—. Mem.: Concrete and Aggregate Assn. La. (bd. dirs.), Nat. Ready Mix Concrete Assn. (bd. dirs.), Coastal Conservation Assn., Ducks Unlimited. Republican. Office: 101 W Farrell Rd Bldg 5 Ste 100 Lafayette LA 70508 also: La House of Reps 900 N 3rd St Baton Rouge LA 70804 Office Phone: 337-981-7409. Business E-Mail: bishops@legis.la.gov.

BISHOP, WESLEY T., state legislator; m. Shannon Bishop; 1 child. BS in Criminal Justice, Southern U., New Orleans, 1990; MPA, U. Miss., 1991; JD, Ohio State U., 1995. Counsel Spears and Spears Law Firm; asst. vice chancellor academic affairs, asst. prof. criminal justice Southern U., New Orleans; mem. Dist. 99 La. House of Reps., 2012—, mem. Edn., Mcpl., Parochial and Cultural Affairs Com. & Ways and Means Com. Fellow Harvard U., 2009. Democrat. Office: District Office 7240 Crowder Blvd Ste 402 New Orleans LA 70127-1923 Office Phone: 504-242-4198. Office Fax: 504-242-6116. E-mail: bishopw@legis.la.gov.

BISHOP, WILLIAM, councilman; m. Melody Bishop; children: Melody Starr, William H. IV. BArch, Lawrence Tech. U.; MArch, MBA, U. Detroit Mercy. V.p. & prin. Akel, Logan & Shafer Architects & Planners; councilman, Dist. 2 Jacksonville City Coun., Fla. Former v.p. JaxPride, 1997; former bd. dirs. & exec. com. Jacksonville Cmty. Coun. Inc., chmn. Affordable Housing Study, 2000; mem. Econ. Devel. Adv. Com. Downtown Jacksonville Master Plan, Mayor's Downtown Green Com., Pub. Health & Safety Com.; chmn. Transp., Energy & Utilities Com.; leader Coun. Floor; mem. Downtown Devel. Rev. Bd.; chmn. Jacksonville Waterways Commn.; mem. Northeast Fla. Regional Coun.; alt. Transp. Planning Org. Bd. mem. Jacksonville Arboretum & Gardens, First Coast Tiger Bay; mem. Jacksonville Transp. Authority North-Southeast Corridor Mass Transit Citizen's Adv. Com.; former bd. mem. Riverside Avondale Preservation Inc.; founding bd. mem. & former corp. sec. Mellon C. Greeley Found. Mem.: Fla. Planning & Zoning Assn., Am. Inst. Arch. (Jacksonville pres. 1995, Fla. pres. 2003—04, John Dyal Cmty. Svc. award 1997), Urban Land Inst., Meninak Club, Southside Businessmen's Club. Republican. Office: 117 W Duval St Ste 425 Jacksonville FL 32202 Office Phone: 904-630-1386, 904-630-1392. Business E-Mail: wbishop@coj.net.

BISIGNANO, FRANK J., payment processing company executive, former diversified financial services company executive; b. Bklyn., Aug. 9, 1959; m. Tracy Bisignano; 3 children. BA in Finance, Newport U. Sr. v.p. Shearson Lehman Brothers, 1986—90; exec. v.p., chief consumer lending officer First Fidelity Bancorporation, 1990—94; with Smith Barney, 1994—2000; sr. exec. v.p., chief adminstrv. officer, Global Corp. and Investment Banking Group Citgroup, Inc., NYC, 2000—02, CEO global transactions services (GTS), 2002—05; chief adminstrv. officer JPMorgan Chase & Co., NYC, 2005—12, chief adminstr. officer, CEO Mortgage Banking, 2012, co-COO, 2012—13; CEO First Data Corp., 2013—. Bd. dirs. First Data Corp., 2013—. Bd. mem. PENCIL, Nat. Sept. 11th Meml. & Mus.; trustee Battery Conservancy, St. Patrick's Cathedral. Recipient Award for Outstanding Corporate Leadership, Bklyn. Children's Mus., 2008, Chancellor's Medal for Outstanding Achievement, Syracuse U., 2010. Office: First Data Corp 5565 Glenridge Connector NE Ste 2000 Atlanta GA 30342 Office Phone: 303-967-8000.

BISSETTE, WINSTON LOUIS, JR., lawyer, mayor; b. Statesville, NC, Sept. 18, 1943; s. Winston Louis and Rubye (Goode) B.; m. Sara Oliver, Aug. 21, 1965; children: W. Louis III, Thomas Anderson. BA, Wake Forest U., 1965; JD, U. N.C., Chapel Hill, 1968; MBA, U. Va., 1970. Bar: N.C. 1968. Asst. v.p. Wachovia Bank & Trust Co., Winston-Salem, 1970-74; v.p., treas. Western Carolina Bank, Asheville, N.C., 1974-76; pres. McGuire, Wood & Bissette, P.A., Asheville, 1976—; chmn. Forest Comml. Bd. Co-chmn. I-26 corridor Assn., 1987—; chmn. West NC Devel. Assn., 1995—98; regional adv. coun. HUD, 1986—90; mem. Gov.'s Task Force on Urban Transp., 1986, Yr. of the Mtns. Commn., 1995—97; chmn. Asheville Sports Com., 1991—97, Buncombe County Econ. Devel. Commn., 1997—2013, Asheville Buncombe Econ. Devel. Coalition, 2013—, NC Arboretum Soc., 2003—09, Asheville Cmty. Betterment Found., 1992—; bd. dirs. AB Tech. Coll. Found., 2005—11; vice-chmn. Wake Forest Bd., 2009—11; mayor City of Asheville, 1985—89, city coun., 1983—89; bd. trustees Wake Forest U., 1996—, Western Carolina U., 1995—2003; chmn. Advantage Asheville, 1996—2000, Grove Arcade Pub. Mkt. Found., 1992—2010; bd. dirs. Mission-St. Joseph's Health Sys., Inc., 1996—99; vice chmn. Sisters of Mercy Svcs. Corp., 1999—2013; bd. dirs. Blue Ridge Pkwy. Found., 2000—08, Inst. at Biltmore, 2001—07; chmn. Asheville Merchants Corp., 2002—12, Met. Sewerage Dist. Buncombe County, 2005—11, Western Carolina Industries, 2002—; bd. govs. UNC Sys., 2011—, Biltmore Forest Country Club, 2007—13. Mem. ABA, N.C. Bar Assn., Asheville Area C. of C. (pres. 1991-92, 1992-93), Bald Head Island Club, Biltmore Forest Country Club, Cliffs at Walnut Cove. Republican. Methodist. Avocations: golf, running. Home: 321 Old Toll Rd Asheville NC 28804 Office: McGuire Wood & Bissette PA 48 Patton Ave PO Box 3180 Asheville NC 28802-3180 Office Phone: 828-254-8800. Business E-Mail: lbissette@mwbavl.com.

BITTNER, VERA, cardiologist; b. Mainz, Germany, July 31, 1957; d. Friedrich and Lieselotte Bittner. MD, U. South Ala., Mobile, 1981; MSPH, U. Ala., 1995. Asst. prof. medicine U. Ala., Birmingham, 1987—93, assoc. prof. medicine, 1993—2000, dir. cardiovasc. disease residency program, 1998—, prof. medicine, 2000—, sect. head preventive cardiology, 2005—. Contbr. articles to profl. jours. Fellow, CDC and Am. Heart Assn., 1995. Fellow: ACP, Am. Heart Assn. (clin. exercise com. 2005—, chair clin. exec. prevention com. effective 2009, fellow 1991), Am. Coll. Cardiology (cardiovasc. disease prevention com. 2004—, chair prevention com. effective 2009—, edit. bd. mem. circulations); mem.: ULA (past pres.), Birmingham Cardiovasc. Soc. (pres. 2004—05), SE Lipid Assn. (pres. 2003—04), Nat. Lipid Assn. (bd. dirs. 2005—, pres. 2009—), Am. Assn. Cardiovasc. and Pulmonary Rehab. (bd. dirs. 2001—03), Delta Omega, Alpha Omega Alpha. Office: U Ala 701 19th St S - LHRB 310 Birmingham AL 35294

BITZER, DONALD LESTER, electrical engineer, educator, retired lab administrator; b. East St. Louis, Ill., Jan. 1, 1934; s. Jess L. and Marjorie (Look) B.; m. Maryann Drost, July 2, 1955; 1 son, David. BS, U. Ill., 1955, MS, 1956, PhD, 1960; PhD (hon.), MacMurray Coll., Jacksonville, Ill. Mem. faculty U. Ill.-Urbana, 1955—, asst. prof., 1960-63, assoc. prof., 1963-67, prof. elec. engring., 1967—, dir. Computer-Based Edn. Research Lab., 1967-89; disting. prof. rsch. N.C. State U., 1989—. Cons. in field. Contbr. articles to profl. jours.; pioneer PLATO-large computer-based edn. system; co-inventor plasma display panel. Recipient Indsl. Rsch. 100 award, 1966, Bobby Connelly Meml. award Miami Valley Computer Assn., 1973, Recognition award Soc. for Info. Display, 1979, Edn. award Am. Fedn. Info. Processing Socs., 1989, Elec. Engring. Disting. Alumni award U. Ill., 1992, Emmy award NATAS, 2002; named to Consumer Electronics Hall of Fame, 2006, named to Nat. Inventors Hall of Fame, 2013; named laureate Lincoln Acad of Ill., 1982; Internat. Engring. Consortium fellow, 1994. Fellow AAAS, IEEE, Assn. Devel. Computer-Based Instrnl. Sys., Internat. Engring. Consortium; mem. NAE (Vladimir K. Zworykin award), Data Processing Mgmt. Assn. (Computer Sci. Man of Yr. award), Am. Soc. Engring. Edn. (Chester Carlson award), Nat. Acad. Engring. Home: 104 Christofle Ln Cary NC 27511-6473 Office: NC State U Dept Computer Sci PO Box 8206 Raleigh NC 27695-0001

BIVIANO, MARK, state legislator; b. Blytheville, Ark. m. Barbara Biviano; 3 children. Grad. in Fin., U. Ark. Mem. St. Paul United Meth. Ch.; owner Re/Max Real Estate, Heber Springs, Searcy; mem. Dist. 50 Ark. House of Representatives, 2011—. Republican. Home: PO Box 436 Searcy AR 72145-0436 Office Phone: 501-230-5751. Business E-Mail: mkbiv@cablelynx.com.

BIZIOS, HARRY J., electronics executive; BS in Engring. Ops., Iowa State U. Indsl. engr., mfg. facility Lennox International, Inc., Marshalltown, Iowa, 1976, v.p., gen. mgr., Lennox Industries Comml., 1998—2003, v.p., gen. mgr., Lennox N. Am. Comml. Products, 2003—05, v.p., gen. mgr., LII Worldwide Comml. Sys., 2005—06, exec. v.p., pres., COO, Comml. Heating, Cooling Segment, 2006—. Office: Lennox International Inc 2140 Lake Park Blvd Richardson TX 75080 Office Phone: 972-497-5000. Office Fax: 972-497-5292. Business E-Mail: Harry.Bizios@lennoxintl.com.

BJORKMAN, DAVID JESS, dean, gastroenterologist, educator; b. Salt Lake City, Oct. 28, 1952; s. Jesse Harold and Violet Maureen (Neese) B.; m. Kaye Hansen, Aug. 20, 1975; children: D. James, Michael. BA, U. Utah, 1976, MD, 1980. Diplomate Am. Bd. Internal Medicine, Am. Bd. Gastroenterology. Intern Brigham and Womens Hosp., Harvard U. Med. Sch., 1980-81, resident in internal medicine, 1981-83; clin. fellow, rsch. fellow Harvard U. Med. Sch., Boston, 1983-85; instr. medicine U. Utah Sch. Medicine, Salt Lake City, 1985-88, asst. prof. medicine, 1988-92, assoc. prof. medicine, 1992—99, dir. endoscopy, 1993—95, assoc. chief divsn. gastroenterology, 1995—2000, asst. dean continuing med. edn. & ednl. assessment, 1998—2000, prof. medicine, 1999—2011, sr. assoc. dean, 2000—03, interim dean, 2004, dean, 2004—11; exec. med. dir. U.

Utah Med. Group, Salt Lake City, 2000—11; prof., dean Fla. Atlantic U. Charles E. Schmidt Coll. Medicine, Boca Raton, Fla., 2011—. Staff physician VA Med. Ctr., Salt Lake City, 1985—96, asst. chief, 1990—93, acting chief, 1990—91, med. dir. alcohol & drug detoxification unit, 1990—93, consulting physician, 1996—2011; mem. sci. rev. com. Nat. Cancer Inst., Bethesda, Md., 1991. Contbr. articles to profl. jours.; author over 100 reviews, books, book chpts., and abstracts. Fellow ACP, Am. Coll. Gastroenterology (chair publs. com. 1994-97), Royal Coll. Physicians, London, Am. Soc. Gastrointestinal Endoscopy (mem. governing bd. 1999-2007); mem. Utah State Med. Assn. (mem. legis. com.), Am. Soc. Laser Medicine and Surgery, Phi Beta Kappa, Alpha Omega Alpha (bd. dirs. 1979-82). Achievements include laser identification of colonic cancer using photoactive agent; research on therapeutic endoscopy, changes in intestinal membrane composition and fluidity. Office: Florida Atlantic University Charles E Schmidt College of Medicine 777 Glades Rd Bldg 71 Boca Raton FL 33431

BJORKMAN, JONAS, professional tennis player; b. Vaxjo, Sweden, Mar. 23, 1972; s. Lars Bjorkman and Margaretha; m. Petra Bjorkman, Dec. 2, 2000; 1 child, Max. Profl. tennis player, 1991—. Mem. ATP Player Coun., 1998—2001, pres., 2000—01. Achievements include winner 6 career singles titles, 52 career doubles titles, ATP. Avocations: golf, hockey, soccer, golf, hockey, soccer. Office: c/o ATP Tour 201 Atp Tour Blvd Ponte Vedra Beach FL 32082-3211

BLACHLY, JACK LEE, lawyer; b. Dallas, Mar. 8, 1942; s. Emery Lee and Thelma Jo (Budd) B.; m. Lucy Largent Rain, Jan. 15, 1972; 1 son, Michael Talbot. BBA, So. Meth. U., 1965, JD, 1968. Bar: Tex. 1968, U.S. Ct. Appeals (5th cir.) 1969, U.S. Supreme Ct. 1975, U.S. Tax Ct. 1977. Trust officer First Nat. Bank in Dallas, 1968-70; ptnr. firm Reese & Blachly, Dallas, 1970-71; assoc. firm Rain Harrell Emery Young & Doke, Dallas, 1971-76; staff atty. Sabine Corp., Dallas, 1976-77, mgr. legal dept., 1977-80, v.p., gen. counsel, 1980-89; asst. gen. counsel Pacific Enterprises Oil Co. USA (merger Sabine Corp. and Pacific Enterprise Oil Co. USA), Dallas, 1989-90; pvt. practice Dallas, 1990—2005; v.p., gen. counsel Cornerstone Credit Union League, Farmers Br., Tex., 2005—. Mem.: Dallas Bar Assn., Tex. Bar Assn., Dallas Gun Club. Baptist. Office: Cornerstone Credit Union League 4455 LBJ Freeway Farmers Branch TX 75244 Office Phone: 469-385-6411.

BLACK, CLIFFORD MERWYN, academic administrator, sociologist, educator; b. Lafayette, Ohio, Mar. 6, 1942; s. Richard Allen and Ivaloo Mae (Mosher) B.; m. Angelica Hernandez; children: Jonathan Andrew, Marisela, Jose Angel, Carlos Alberto. BA, Adrian Coll., 1963; MDiv, Meth. Theol. Sch., 1966; PhD, Northwestern U., 1972. Cert. clin. sociologist; lic. profl. counselor. Asst. prof. Wilberforce (Ohio) U., 1973-74, The Ohio State U., Mansfield, 1974-78; instr. U. North Tex., Denton, 1978-79, asst. prof., 1979-83, sociology program dir., 1982-83, assoc. prof., 1983-89, chair Ctr. for Pub. Svc., 1984-86, chair dept. sociology, 1986-87, assoc. dean Sch. Cmty. Svc., 1986-88, 91-92, acting dean Sch. Cmty. Svc., 1988-90, prof., 1989-92, Tex. A&M Internat. U., Laredo, 1992—2001, dean Sch. Edn. and Arts and Scis., 1992-94, dean Coll. of Arts and Humanities, 1994-96, 96-2001, Webb Co. Tex. Planning Coun., 1996-2001, Webb Co. Tex. Drug Planning Com., 1996-2001, Webb Co. Tex. Jail Case Mgmt. Supervision, 1998-2001, Webb Co. Drug Ct. Supervising Com., 1998-2001; prin. investigator US Dept. Justice/Webb Co. Tex., Laredo, Tex., 1996—2001, 3d Party Payment Com.; adminstrv. cons. Webb County Sheriff's Dept., 2005—; dir. Internat. Justice Ctr., 1996—2002; pres. CJUS Rsch. and Program Cons. Internat. Inc., 2002—; adminstrv. coord. Webb County Sheriff's Dept., 2005—08. Cons. Denton County Sheriff's Dept., Denton, 1984-89; mem. state coordinating bd. com. on Two Yr. Coll. Curriculum, 1986-89. Author: (book) Alternative Sentencing: Electronically Monitored Correction Supervision, 1992; contbg. editor for Clin. Sociology Newsletter, 1983-84; mem. editorial bd. Sociol. Practice, 1984-89; contbr. numerous articles to profl. jours. Pres. Sam Houston Elem. PTA, Denton, 1985-86; trustee Denton Ind. Sch. Dist., 1986-89; mem. United Way Bd., Laredo, 1994-95; active St. Martin de Porres Cath. Ch. Recipient U.S. Dept. Justice award for Rsch. Prgms. for Elimination of Illegal Drugs. Mem. Nat. Clin. Sociology Assn. (v.p. 1984-86, certification bd. mem. 1984-90, nat. certifier 1985-92, nat. program chair for ann. meeting 1984-85), Clin. Sociology Assn. Tex. (pres. 1982-84), Nat. Sociol. Practice Assn. (exec. bd. 1990-91), Nat. Sociol. Practice Assn. (certification bd. 1990-91), Am. Sociol. Assn. (sect bd. 1981-84, sociol. practice sect. sec./treas. 1981-84), Southwestern Sociol. Assn. (chair com. on professions 1983-86), Am. Criminology Soc., Acad. Criminal Justice Scis. Avocations: walking, reading, writing, drawing. Home and Office: 8506 Callow Ct Laredo TX 78045-1983

BLACK, COFER (JOSEPH COFER BLACK), consulting firm executive, former federal official; b. Stamford, Conn., 1950; BA in Internat. Relations, U. Southern Calif., 1973, MA in Internat. Relations, 1974. With CIA, 1974—2002, station chief Khartoum, Sudan, 1993—95, task force chief near East, South Asia divsn., 1995, deputy chief Latin American divsn., 1998—99, dir. Counterterrorist Ctr., 1999—2001; coord. US Office of Counterterrorism US Dept. State, Washington, 2002—04; vice chmn. Blackwater USA, Moyock, NC, 2005—07; founder Total Intelligence Solutions, 2007—08; v.p. global ops. Blackbird Technologies, Inc., Herndon, Va., 2009—. Recipient Distinguished Intelligence medal, George H.W. Bush Medal for Excellence, Exceptional Collector award, 1994. Office: Blackbird Technologies Inc 13900 Lincoln Park Dr Ste 400 Herndon VA 20171 Office Phone: 703-796-1420. Office Fax: 703-464-9381.

BLACK, DIANE LYNN, United States Representative from Tennessee, former state legislator; b. Balt., Jan. 16, 1951; m. David Black; 3 children. ADN, Anne Arundel Coll., Annapolis, Md., 1971; BSN, Belmont U., Nashville, 1991. RN. Asst. prof. allied health Vol. State Cmty. Coll., Gallatin, Tenn., 1988—93; exec. dir. Summer Regional Health Sys. Found., Gallatin, Tenn., 1993—98; mem. Dist. 45 Tenn. House of Reps., Nashville, 1999—2005; mem. Dist. 18 Tenn. State Senate, Nashville, 2005—10, Republican Caucus chmn., 2008—11; mem. US Congress from 6th Tenn. Dist., Washington, 2011—, US House Budget Com., Washington, 2011—, US House Ways & Means Com., Washington, 2011—. Pres. Hendersonville Rotary Found.; past v.p. Sumner County Habitat for Humanity; past chair Sumner County United Way; bd. dirs. Tenn. Ctr. Nursing, Vol. State Cmty. Coll. Found., Children Are People, Inc.; past bd. dirs. Sumner County YMCA, Sumner County chpt. ARC, Sumner County chpt. Am. Heart Assn. Recipient State Pub. Policy Leadership award, American Diabetes Assn., 2007, Statesman award, Tenn. Home Edn. Assn., 2008, Champions for Seniors in Assisted Living award, Assisted Living Fedn. America, 2008, Hon. Chair award, Tenn. Assn. Homes & Services for Aging, 2008, Guardian of Small Bus. award, Nat. Fedn. Ind. Bus., 2008; named Vol. of Yr., Sumner County YMCA, 2001, Legislator of Yr., American Cancer Soc., 2003, Tenn. Right to Life, 2004, Tenn. Nurse Assn., 2005, Tenn. Devel. Dist. Assn., 2008, Jr. Leagues Tenn., 2008, American Heart Assn., 2008, Tenn. Assn. Assessing Officers, 2008; named an Outstanding State Senator, County Officials Assn. Tenn., 2005. Mem.: Hendersonville League Women Voters, Leadership Sumner Alumni Assn. (past pres., Disting. Alumni award 1998), Gallatin Toastmasters (past pres.), Hendersonville Rotary Club (past pres., Rotarian of Yr. 1993). Republican. Lutheran. Office: US House of Representatives 1531 Longworth HOB Washington DC 20515 also: 355 N Belvedere Dr RM 308 Gallatin TN 37066-5410 Office Phone: 202-225-4231, 615-896-1986. Office Fax: 202-225-6887.*

BLACK, ELLIS, state legislator; b. July 28; m. Aletha Black. Former state rep. Dist. 144, Ga.; state rep. Dist. 178 Ga.; house rep. Ga.; state rep. Dist. 144, 2004—; mem. Agr. & Consumer Affairs Com., Retirement Com., State Planning & Cmty. Affairs Com. Mem.: Southeast Ag Coalition, Lowndes County Hist. Soc., Lake Pk. Hist. Soc., Echols County Hist. Soc., Brook's County Hist. Soc., Valdosta-Lowndes County C. of C. Democrat. Methodist. Office: 609 Legislative Off Bldg Atlanta GA 31601 Mailing: 5900 Jumping Gully Rd Valdosta GA 31601 Office Phone: 404-656-0305, 912-559-7546. Fax: 912-599-1592. E-mail: ellblack@surfsouth.com, webmaster@legis.state.ga.us.

BLACK, JOHN K., wholesale distribution executive; Grad., Clemson U., SC. Various sales & mgmt. positions including bus. unit exec. for fin. industry IBM Corp., 1977—94; gen. mgr. RightSource, 1994—98; pres. Catalyst Commerce divsn. ScanSource, Inc., 1998—99, pres. Catalyst Telecom divsn., 1999—. Office: ScanSource Inc 6 Logue Ct Greenville SC 29615 Office Phone: 864-288-2432. Office Fax: 864-288-1165.

BLACK, MARCEL, state legislator; b. Mar. 25, 1951; m. Martha Black; children: Edgar, Virginia Fern. BA, JD, U. Ala. Ptnr. Black and Hughston, PC; mem. Dist. 3 Ala. House of Reps., Montgomery, 1990—. Past chmn. Colbert County Dem. Exec. Com.; mem. First Presbyn. Ch., Tuscumbia; former dir. Tenn. Valley Art Assn.; former bd. mem. Boy Scouts America; former profl. chmn. United Way of the Shoals. Democrat. Presbyterian. Office: 210 N Main St Tuscumbia AL 35674 also: Ala House of Reps Ala State House 11 S Union St Rm 516-C Montgomery AL 36130 Office Phone: 256-383-2435, 334-242-7667.

BLACK, RICHARD HAYDEN, state legislator; b. Balt., May 15, 1944; m. Barbara Jean Hale; children: Michelle Cope, Richard H., Ronald. BSBA in Acctg., U. Fla., 1973, JD, 1976. Mem. Va. State Assembly, 1998—2006; mem. Dist. 13 Va. State Senate, 2012—, mem. Agr., Conservation and Natural Resources Com., Gen. Laws and Tech. Com., Edn. and Health Com. & Rehab. and Social Services Com. Col. US Army. Republican. Roman Catholic. Office: Senate of Virginia PO Box 396 Richmond VA 23218 also: PO Box 650370 Sterling VA 20165 Office Phone: 804-698-7513. Office Fax: 804-698-7651. E-mail: district13@senate.virginia.gov.

BLACK, ROY, lawyer; b. NYC, Feb. 17, 1945; s. Richard and Minna (Benett) B. BA, U. Miami, Fla., 1967, JD, 1970. Bar: Fla. 1970; US Dist. Ct. Fla. (so. dist.) 1975, US Dist. Ct. Colo. 2001, US Dist. Ct. Fla. (mid. dist.) 2007, US Dist. Ct. Fla. (no. dist.) 2008, US Dist. Ct. Ind. (so. dist.) 2010, US Ct. Appeals (5th cir.) 1975, US Ct. Appeals (11th cir.) 1981, US Ct. Appeals (2d, 4th, 6th and 9th cirs.) 1984, US Ct. Appeals (DC cir.) 1984, US Ct. Appeals (8th cir.) 1985, US Ct. Appeals (10th cir.) 2003, US Supreme Ct. 1976. Sr. asst. pub. defender Miami-Dade County, 1971-76; ptnr. Roy E. Black, PA, Miami, 1976-79, Black and Furci, PA, 1979-93, Black & Seiden, Miami, 1993-96, Black, Srebnick & Kornspan, Miami, 1996—2002, Black Srebnick Kornspan & Stumpf, P.A., Miami, 2002—. Tchr. advanced criminal def. U. Miami, 1973—; legal analyst NBC, 2003—05; legal commentator several nat. TV networks. Author: Black's Law: A Criminal Lawyer Reveals his Strategies in Four Cliffhanger Cases, 1999. Fundraising events sponsor Bay Point Sch., Miami, 1998—2009, Consequences Charity, 2010—. Recipient Nelson Poynter award ACLU, 1982, Criminal Justice award Dade County Bar Assn., 1991, U. Miami William R. Butler Cmty. Svc. award, 2005; named Best of the Bar South Fla. Bus. Jour., 2003-, Fla. Super Lawyer, 2006; named one of Fla.'s Legal Elite Fla. Trend, 2004-2009, Top Lawyers South Fla. Legal Guide, 2008-. Fellow: Am. Coll. Trial Lawyers (mem. exec. com.); mem.: ABA, NACDL (life), Eugene Spellman Inns of Ct., Dade County Bar Assn., Internat. Acad. Trial Lawyers, Fla. Assn. Criminal Def. Lawyers, Fla. Bar Assn. Office: Black Srebnick Kornspan and Stumpf PA 201 S Biscayne Blvd Ste 1300 Miami FL 33131-4311 Office Phone: 305-371-6421. Business E-Mail: rblack@royblack.com.

BLACK, STANLEY WARREN, III, retired economics professor; b. Charlotte, NC, July 8, 1939; s. Stanley Warren Jr. and Julia Settle (Wilkes) B.; m. Roberta Burr Callison, June 26, 1965; children: Stanley Wilkes, Sarah Constance. AB in Econs. with honors, U. N.C., 1961; MA in Econs., Yale U., 1963, PhD, 1965. Acting instr. econs. Yale U., New Haven, 1964-65, vis. prof., 1980-81; mem. staff Pres.'s Coun. Econ. Advisers, Washington, 1965-66; asst. prof. Princeton (N.J.) U., 1966-71; vis. prof. Bd. Govs., Fed. Res. System, Washington, 1971-72; assoc. prof. Vanderbilt U., Nashville, 1972-76, prof., 1977-83; spl. asst. to undersec. econ. affairs U.S. Dept. State, Washington, 1977-78; Georges Lurcy prof. U. NC, Chapel Hill, 1983—2008, chmn. dept. econs., 1985—90; dir. econ. studies Am. Inst. Contemporary German Studies, Washington, 1994-97. Cons. U.S. Agy. for Internat. Devel., Washington, 1974-75, Ulan Bator, 1998, U.S. Fgn. Svc. Inst., Arlington, Va., 1981-90; vis. scholar IMF, Washington, 1989, IMF Inst., 2000-01; guest scholar Brookings Inst., Washington, 1992; Bundesbank vis. prof. Free U., Berlin, 1997. Author: Floating Exchange Rates and National Economic Policy, 1977, A Levite Among the Priests: E.M. Bernstein and the Origins of the IMF, 1991; editor and contbr.: Europe's Economy Looks East, 1997; contbr. articles to profl. publs.; contbr. chpts. to econ. books. Fgn. Affairs fellow Coun. Fgn. Rels., N.Y.C., 1975-76; Fulbright Disting. lectr. Coun. Internat. Exch. of Scholars, U. Siena, Italy, 1988. Mem. Am. Econ. Assn., Econometric Soc., So. Econ. Assn. (v.p. 1983), Coun. on Fgn. Rels., Cosmos Club, Rotary Club, Phi Beta Kappa. Democrat. Episcopalian. Avocations: hiking, singing. Home: 100 Rhododendr Dr Chapel Hill NC 27517 Home Phone: 919-967-6059. Business E-Mail: swblack@unc.edu.

BLACK, SUSAN HARRELL, federal judge; b. Valdosta, Ga., Oct. 20, 1943; d. William H. and Ruth Elizabeth (Phillips) Harrell; m. Louis Eckert Black, Dec. 28, 1966. BA, Fla. State U., 1965; JD, U. Fla., 1967; LLM, U. Va., 1984. Bar: Fla. 1967. Atty. US Army Corps of Engrs., Jacksonville, Fla., 1968—69; asst. state atty. Gen. Counsel's Office, Jacksonville, 1969—72; judge County Ct. of Duval County, Fla., 1973—75; judge 4th Jud. Cir. Ct. of Fla., 1975—79; judge US Dist. Ct. (middle dist.) Fla., Jacksonville, 1979—90, chief judge, 1990—92; judge US Ct. Appeals (11th cir.) Fla., Jacksonville, 1992—2011, sr. judge, 2011—. Faculty Fed. Jud. Ctr.; mem. U.S. Jud. Conf. Com. on Inns of Ct., 1984—87; trustee American Inns Ct. Found., 1985—91; pres. US Dist. Judge's Assn (11th Cir.), 1987—88; mem. Jud. Improvements Com., 1987—90, Com. on Court Admin. and Case Mgmt., 1990—92, Jud. Conference Com. on Fed.-State Jurisdiction, 1998—2004, Fed. Judicial Ctr. Bd., 2008—. Trustee emeritus Law Sch. U. Fla.; past pres. Chester Bedell Inn of Ct.; emeritus mem. Jacksonville Bar Assn., Fla. Bar Assn. Presbyterian.

BLACKBURN, MARSHA, United States Representative from Tennessee; b. Laurel, Miss., June 6, 1952; m. Chuck Blackburn; 2 children. BS, Miss. State U., 1973. Dir. retail fashion Caster Knott Co., Nashville, 1975—78; owner Mktg. Strategies, Williamson County, Tenn., 1978—; mem. Dist. 23 Tenn. State Senate, Nashville, 1998—2002; mem. US Congress from 7th Tenn. dist., 2003—. Exec. dir. Tenn. Film, Entertainment & Music Commn., 1995—97. Bd. dirs. Nashville Symphony Guild, Arthritis Found. Recipient Spirit of Enterprise award, US C. of C., 2004. Mem.: Am. Coun. Young Political Leaders, National Assn. Retail Merchants, Found. Women Legislators, Country Music Assn. Republican. Office: US House of Representatives 217 Cannon House Office Bldg Washington DC 20515-4305 also: 7975 Stage Hill Blvd Ste 1 Memphis TN 38133 Office Phone: 202-225-2811.*

BLACKBURN, RICHARD WALLACE, retired board member, lawyer; b. Detroit, Mich., Apr. 21, 1942; s. Wallace Manders and E. Jean (Beetham) B.; m. Dede Frances Reid, Aug. 29, 1964; children: David Thomas, Jeffrey Manders, Megan Louise. Attended, Baldwin-Wallace Coll., 1962; AB, Mich. State U., 1964; JD, George Washington U., 1967; grad. in Advanced Mgmt. Program, Harvard Bus. Sch., 1988. Labor atty. Chesapeake & Potomac Tele. Co., Washington, 1967-70; gen. corp. atty. Chesapeake & Potomac Telephone Co., Richmond, Va., 1970-74; regulatory atty. AT&T Inc. (merger of SBC Communications & AT&T Corp.), NYC, 1974-76; gen. atty. New Eng. Tele. Co., Boston, 1976-81, v.p., gen. counsel, 1981—91; sr. positions NYNEX World Wide Svc. Group, 1991; pres., group exec. NYNEX Worldwide Comm., 1995—96; exec. v.p., gen. counsel & sec. Duke Energy Corp., Charlotte, NC, 1997—2004, chief adminstrv. officer, 2003—04. Bd. dirs. Enesco Group, Inc., OM Group, Inc., 2005—. Bd. dirs. New Eng. Legal Found., 1988; mem. Concord (Mass.) Zoning Bd. Appeals, chmn., 1984, 87; trustee Mass. Eye & Ear Infirmary., George Washington U. Mem. Fed. Communications Bar Assn., Am. Bar Assn., Newcomen Soc. N.Am., Boston Bar Assn. Republican. Episcopalian. Office: OM Group Inc Bd Directors 127 Public Sq 1500 Key Tower Cleveland OH 44114 Office Phone: 216-781-0083. Office Fax: 216-781-1502. Business E-Mail: richard.blackburn@omgi.com.

BLACKBURN, SHARON LOVELACE, federal judge; b. Pensacola, Fla., May 7, 1950; BA, U. Ala., Tuscaloosa, 1973; JD, Samford U., 1977. Law clk. to Hon. J. O. Sentell Ala. Supreme Ct., 1977; law clk. to Hon. Robert Varner US Dist. Ct. (mid. dist.) Ala., 1977—78; staff atty. Birmingham Area Legal Svcs., 1979; asst. US atty. civil divsn. US Atty's. Office (no. dist. Ala.), 1979—85, asst. US atty. criminal divsn., 1985—91; judge US Dist. Ct. (no. dist. Ala.), Birmingham, 1991—, chief judge, 2006—. Mem. Birmingham Bar Assn. Office: US Dist Ct 730 Hugo L Black US Courthouse 1729 5th Ave N Birmingham AL 35203-2000

BLACKBURN, WYATT DOUGLAS, insurance company executive; b. July 6, 1954; s. Wyatt W. and Marjorie C. (Wyre) B.; m. Deborah L. Garland, Feb. 28, 1987; children: Wyatt Woodrow, Taylor Lynne. BBA in Acctg., West Tex. A&M U., 1976. CPA. Staff acct. Harvey, Messenger & Co., Amarillo, 1974-77; audit mgr. Martin W. Cohen & Co., 1977-78, sr. v.p., adminstrv. ops., 1978-88, CFO, 1988-94, sr. v.p., 1988—97, COO, 1995-97; exec. v.p., COO State Nat. Companies, Inc., 1997—. Bd. dirs. Nat. Splty. Ins. Co., State & County Mut. Fire Ins. Co., State Nat. Ins. Co., United Splty. Ins. Co. Tex. Mem. AICPA, Tex. Soc. CPAs, Omicron Delta Epsilon. Home: 1028 Diamond Blvd Southlake TX 76092-6208 Office: State National Companies Inc 1900 L Don Dodson Dr Bedford TX 76201 Office Phone: 817-265-2000. Office Fax: 817-861-1051. Business E-Mail: wblackburn@statenational.com.

BLACKFORD, ROBERT NEWTON, lawyer, director; b. Cin., Feb. 5, 1937; s. Robert Criley and Virginia Pendleton (Yowell) B.; m. Margaret Ann Williams, July 22, 1961; children: William Pendleton, John Whitner. BSBA, U. Fla., Gainesville, 1960; JD, Emory U., Atlanta, 1968. Bar: Fla. 1968, Ga. 1968. Mem., dir. Maguire, Voorhis & Wells, P.A., Orlando, Fla., 1972-98, sec., treas., 1972-95; ptnr. Holland & Knight LLP, Orlando, 1998—2001. Dir. Hughes Supply, Inc., Orlando, 1970-2006, sec., 1972-96, asst. sec., 1996-98; dir., sec. Princeton Fin. Corp., 1987-94. Mem. Orlando Mcpl. Planning Bd., 1969-75, Orlando Downtown Devel. Bd., 1972-77, chmn., 1975-77, bd. dirs. Crime Commn., Inc., 1985-88; mem. Orange County's Refuse Disposal Citizens Coordination Com., 1988-90, Orange County Solid Waste Adv. Bd., 1992-96; mem. neighborhood concerns com. Orlando Naval Tng. Ctr. Base Closing Commn., 1994-96; trustee Chelsey G. Magruder Found., Inc., 1981—, pres., 1982-85, 92-94, 2000-02, 2008-10, sec./treas., 1998-2000; trustee Orlando Mus. Art, 1980-82, 85-91, pres. 1985-86, chmn. bd., 1986-87, v.p. 1989-91; ruling elder First Presbyn. Ch., Orlando, 1989-2003, tchr., 1970-2000; bd. dirs. Univ. Club Orlando, 1994-97, sec., 1994-96; active The Cathedral Ch. of St. Luke, 2004—, chpt. mem., 2010-14. With US Army, 1954—56. Mem. Fla. Bar Assn., State Bar Ga. (emeritas), Orlando Area C. of C. (pres. 1980, chmn. bd. dirs. 1981), Orange County Hist. Soc. (bd. dirs. 1980-83), Country Club Orlando, Rotary Club Orlando (pres. 1991-92). Democrat. Episcopalian. Personal E-mail: rblackf398@aol.com.

BLACKLEDGE, BRETT J., reporter; b. Baton Rouge; married; 1 child. Grad., La. State U., 1986. Reporter AP, New Orleans, Jackson, Miss., Tulsa, Okla., Jour. Newspapers, Washington, Edn. Daily, Washington; local govt. reporter, edn. & state govt. reporter Mobile (Ala.) Register, 1993—98; gen. assignment & spl. projects reporter Birmingham (Ala.) News, 1998—. Recipient Pulitzer Prize for Investigative Reporting, 2007. Office: Birmingham News PO Box 2553 Birmingham AL 35202 E-mail: bblackledge@bhamnews.com.

BLACKMAN, JOHN CALHOUN, IV, lawyer; b. Monroe, La., Dec. 13, 1944; s. John Calhoun Blackman III and Marie (Collens) Bernstein; m. Judy Swayze, Apr. 19, 1986; children: Carrie Marie, Caroline Frances, Mary Winston. BA, La. State U., 1966, JD, 1969. Bar: La. 1969, U.S. Ct. Appeals (5th cir.) 1969, U.S. Tax Ct. 1972, U.S. Supreme Ct. 1976. Ptnr. Hudson, Potts & Bernstein, Monroe, 1969-79, Blackman, Arnold & Pettway, Monroe, 1979-88, Jones, Walker, Waechter, Poitevent, Carrere & Denegre, Baton Rouge, 1988—. Adj. prof. law La. State U., Baton Rouge, 1990-93; mem. com. of 100 econ. devel., 1993—; mem. trust code com. La. State Law Inst., 1982—. Mem. La. State U. Found.; mem. adv. commn. Estate Planning and Adminstrn. Cert., 1994—99, chmn., 1998—99. Fellow Am. Coll. Trusts and Estates Counsel (bus. planning com.), Am. Coll. Tax Counsel; mem. ABA (litigation task force, employee benefits com., taxation sect.), La. Bar Assn. (bd. cert. tax specialist, cert. estate planning and adminstrn. specialist, cert. LA Bd. Legal Specialization, chmn. taxation sect. 1976-77, chmn. liaison com. with dist. dir. IRS 1981-82, liaison com. with regional commrs. office), Estate Planning Coun. N.E. La. (pres. 1975-76), Estate and Bus. Planning Coun. Baton Rouge, La. State Found. (planned giving com.), Baton Rouge Area Found. (profl. adv. com.). Republican. Episcopalian. Office: Jones Walker et al 8555 United Plaza Blvd Ste 500 Baton Rouge LA 70809 Home Phone: 225-921-3724; Office Phone: 225-248-2070. Personal E-mail: jcbandjsb@bellsouth.net. Business E-Mail: jblackman@joneswalker.com.

BLACKMAN, ROLANDO ANTONIO, professional sports team executive, retired professional basketball player; b. Panama City, Panama, Feb. 26, 1959; m. Tamara Blackman; 4 children. B, Kans.

State U., Manhattan, 1996. Guard Dallas Mavericks, 1981—92, player devel. coach, 2000, asst. coach, 2005—06, dir. basketball devel., 2006—; guard NY Knicks, NY, NY, 1992—94, AEK Athens BC, Greece, 1994—95, Stefanel Milano, Italy, 1995—96; broadcaster ESPN, CBS Sports; asst. coach German Nat. Basketball Team, 2001—02. Bd. dirs. Assist Youth Found. Named Italian Cup MVP, 1996; named to We. Conf. All-Star Team, NBA, 1985—87, 1990, Kans. State U. Athletic Hall of Fame, Kans. Sports Hall of Fame, 1998. Office: Dallas Mavericks The Pavilion 2909 Taylor St Dallas TX 75226

BLACKMON, DOUGLAS A., newspaper reporter, writer; married; 2 children. Grad., Hendrix Coll., Conway, Ark. Reporter Ark. Dem., 1986—87; mng. editor Daily Record, Little Rock, 1987—89; reporter Wall St. Jour., Atlanta, 1995—, Atlanta bur. chief, 2004—. Author: (books) Slavery by Another Name: The Re-Enlsavement of Black Americans from the Civil War to World War II, 2008 (Pulitzer prize for gen. nonfiction, 2009). Office: Wall St Jour 303 Peachtree St NE 4200 Atlanta GA 30308 Business E-Mail: doug.blackmon@wsj.com.

BLACKMON, EDWARD, JR., state legislator; b. Canton, Miss., Feb. 21; m. Barbara A. Martin; children: Madison Edward, Bradford Jerome, Janessa. Mem. Dist. 57 Miss. House of Reps., 1979—80, 1984—; atty.; real estate developer. Mem.: NAACP, Magnolia Bar Assn., Am. Bar Assn., Miss. Trial Lawyers Assn., Am. Trial Lawyers Assn. Democrat. Baptist. Mailing: PO Drawer 105 Canton MS 39046 Office Phone: 601-859-1567, 601-359-3388. E-mail: eblackmon@house.ms.gov.

BLACKMON, RONALD H., biologist, science educator; s. Henry L. and Lillian Blackmon. BS, Del. State U., 1980; MS, Howard U., 1985, PhD, 1988. Postdoctoral rsch. assoc. USDA-Insect Attractants, Behavior/Basic Biology Rsch. Lab., Gainesville, Fla., 1988-89; asst. prof. Elizabeth City State U., 1989-94, assoc. prof., 1994-96, prof., 1996—2008, chmn., 1995—2002, dean sch. math sci. tech., 2002—05, sr. res. prof., 2008—. Mem. acad. ops. com. Program for Minority Advancement in Biomolecular Scis., Chapel Hill, NC, 1991-2002; mem. Historically Minority Univs. program adv. bd. NC Biotech. Ctr., Research Triangle Park, NC, 1997-2003. Mem. adv. bd. State Employees' Credit Union, Elizabeth City, 1999. Recipient Biotech. Leadership award N.C. Inst. for Minority Econ. Devel., Durham, N.C., 1993. Mem. AAAS, Soc. for In Vitro Biology, N.C. Acad. Sci., Port Discover Hands on Sci. Ctr. (chmn., bd. dirs.)Sigma Xi. Avocations: reading science fiction, piano. Office: Elizabeth City State U ECSU Campus Box 930 Elizabeth City NC 27909 Office Phone: 252-335-3240. Office Fax: 252-335-3697. Business E-Mail: rhblackmon2@mail.ecsu.edu.

BLACKSHEAR, A. T., JR., lawyer; b. Dallas, July 5, 1942; s. A. T. and Janie Louise (Florey) Blackshear; m. Stuart Davis Blackshear. BBA cum laude, Baylor U., 1964, JD cum laude, 1968. CPA Tex.; bar: Tex. 1968, U.S. Ct. Appeals (5th cir.) 1970, U.S. Tax Ct. 1970. Acct. Arthur Andersen & Co., Dallas, 1964-66; assoc. Fulbright & Jaworski, Houston, 1969-75, ptnr., 1975—2004, chmn. exec. com., 1992—2002, of counsel, 2005—. Bd. dirs. Tex. Med. Ctr., Inc. Bd. dirs. Sam Houston Area coun. Boy Scouts Am.; bd. dirs. Meml. Hermann Healthcare System, Faith in Practice Tex. Med. Ctr., Inc. Mem.: Houston Bar Assn., State Bar Tex., Houston Country Club, Coronado Club. Baptist. Office: Fulbright & Jaworski 1301 Mckinney St Fl 51 Houston TX 77010-3031

BLACKSTOCK, JAMES FIELDING, lawyer; b. LA, Sept. 19, 1947; s. James Carne and Justine Fielding (Gibson) B.; m. Kathleen Ann Weigand, Dec. 12, 1969; children: Kristin Marie, James Fielding. AB, U. So. Calif., 1969, JD, 1976. Bar: Calif. 1976, Tenn. 1994, U.S. Dist. Ct. (ctrl. dist.) Calif. 1977, U.S. Supreme Ct. 1980. Assoc. Hill Farrer Burrill, LA, 1976-80, Zobrist, Garner, Garrett, LA, 1980-83; ptnr. Zobrist & Vienna, LA, 1983; v.p., gen. counsel Tatum Petroleum, La Habra, Calif., 1983; atty. Thorpe, Sullivan, Workman & Thorpe, LA, 1984; ptnr. Sullivan, Workman & Dee, LA, 1985-91; prin. James F. Blackstock, 1992-93; prof. Law Corp., LA; v.p., gen. counsel Nat. Auto/Truckstops, Inc., Nashville, 1993-97, Cracker Barrel Old Country Store, Inc., Lebanon, Tenn., 1997-98; sr. v.p., gen. counsel CBRL Group, Inc., Lebanon, 1998—2005; exec. v.p., gen. counsel Shoney's USA, Inc., Nashville, 2007—09; prin. James F. Blackstock Counsellor at Law, Brentwood, Tenn., 2009—10; prin James F. Blackstock PLLC, 2010—. Pres. Commerce Assocs., U. So. Calif., 1990-93. Mem. Town Hall, L.A., 1980-90; bd. dirs. Tenn. Valley Region ARC, 2002-04, Nashville chpt. ARC, 2004—; interim CEO, Nashville area chpt. ARC, 2006. Served to lt. USN, 1969-73; capt. USNR ret. Mem. ABA, Tenn. Bar Assn., Nashville Bar Assn., U. So. Calif. Alumni Assn. (bd. govs. 1990-92), Pasadena Tournament of Roses Assn., Saddle and Sirloin Club, Rancheros Visitadores. Republican. Roman Catholic. Home: 533 Turtle Creek Dr Brentwood TN 37027-5632 Office: PO Box 2687 Brentwood TN 37024 Home Phone: 615-371-5183; Office Phone: 615-500-5173. Personal E-mail: jim.blackstock@comcast.net.

BLACKSTONE, W. C., architectural firm executive; Owner Blackstone Partnership, Houston. Office: The Blackstone Partnership 1502 Augusta Dr Ste 270 Houston TX 77057-7401

BLACKWELL, GUS, state legislator; b. Wichita, Kans., Nov. 4, 1955; s. Carl Raymond and Myrl Kathryn (O'Dell) B.; m. Joanna Jett, May 12, 1990. BA, Okla. Baptist Univ., 1976; MDiv, Southwestern Baptist Theol. Sem.; BBA, Okla. Panhandle State Univ., 1991; MBA, Southwestern Okla. State Univ., 1998. Lic. to ministry Bapt. Ch., 1974. Youth dir. Soldier Creek Bapt. Ch., 1982—83; BSU dir. Okla. Bapt. Gen. Conv., 1983—; campus minister Baptist Collegiate Ministries; mem. Dist. 61 Okla. House of Representatives, 2003—. Speaker seminars in field. Coach Spl. Olympics, Oklahoma City, 1985; commnr. Kiwanis Little League, 1987; tchr. First Bapt. Ch., Sayre, 1984-87; bd. dirs. Ventilator Dependent Quadraphlegics Assn., 1983, 86. Named one of Outstanding Young Men of Am., 1985, one of Outstanding Community Leaders of Am., 1989. Mem. Okla. Sec. Sch. Activities Assn., U.S. Wrestling Assn., Am. Softball Assn., Community Leaders of Am., Internat. Register of Profiles, Phi Eta Sigma. Clubs: Sayre Wrestling (pres. 1985-86); Hobie Fleet 131 (Oklahoma City) (rep. 1986, 87). Republican. Baptist. Office: 2300 N Lincoln Blvd Rm 305-A Oklahoma City OK 73105 Home: PO Box 790 Laverne OK 73848-0790 Office Phone: 405-206-2770, 580-349-2263, 508-921-3349, 405-557-7384. Business E-Mail: gusblackwell@okhouse.gov.

BLACKWELL, HUGH, state legislator; Atty.; mem. Dist. 86 NC House of Reps., 2009—. Mem. Appropriations com., Appropriations Subcom. on Edn., Edn. com., Commerce, Small Bus. and Entrepreneurship com., Judiciary II com., Local Govt. II com., Pub. Utilities com., Water Resoureces and Infrastructure com. With USAR. Republican. Office: 300 N Salisbury St Rm 541 Raleigh NC 27603-5925 Home: 321 Mountain View Ave SE Valdese NC 28690 Office Phone: 919-733-5805. Business E-Mail: Hugh.Blackwell@ncleg.net.

BLACKWELL, KEITH R., state supreme court justice; m. Angela Blackwell; 3 children. BA summa cum laude in polit. sci., U. Ga., 1996, JD summa cum laude, 1999. Law clk. to Judge J.L. Edmondson US Ct. Appeals (11th cir.), 1999—2000; assoc. Alston & Bird; asst. dist. atty. Cobb County, 2003—05; assoc. Parker, Hudson, Rainer & Dobbs, Atlanta, 2005—08, ptnr, 2008—10; dep. spl. atty. gen. State of Ga., 2010; judge Ga. Ct. Appeals, 2010—12; assoc. justice Ga. Supreme Ct., Atlanta, 2012—. Mem. bd. advisors Atlanta chpt. Federalist Soc. for Law and Pub. Policy Studies. Master: Columbus American Inn of Ct., Joseph Henry Lumpkin American Inn of Ct.; mem.: Cobb Bar Assn. Office: Georgia Supreme Ct 244 Washington St Atlanta GA 30334

BLACKWELL, KIMBERLY LYNN, oncologist, educator; b. Aug. 12, 1968; MD, Mayo Med. Sch., Minn., 1994. Diplomate American Bd. Internal Medicine-med. oncology, 2000. Resident internal medicine Duke Univ. Med. Ctr., Durham, NC, 1994—97, fellow med. oncology, 1997—2000, assoc. medicine divsn. hematology-oncology; assoc. prof. medicine Duke Univ. Contbr. articles to profl. publs. Profl. adv. bd. Breastcancer.org. Named one of The 100 Most Influential People in the World, TIME mag., 2013. Office: Duke University Medical Center 2301 Erwin Rd 3893 Durham NC 27710 Office Phone: 919-668-1748. Office Fax: 919-681-0874.*

BLACKWELL, LARRY G., computer company executive; BS in Engring., U. Miss.; MS, Ga. Inst. Tech.; PhD in Environtl. Systems Engring., Clemson U. Registered profl. engr., Ill., Pa., SC. Co-founder, chmn. bd. EDI Tech. Cos.; pres. Datastream Systems divsn. subsidiary Wis. Power and Light; founder, CEO, pres., chmn. bd. Datastream Systems, Greenville, S.C., 1986—. Named Entrepreneur of Yr. INC. mag., 1994. Office: Datastream Systems Inc 50 Datastream Plz Greenville SC 29605

BLACKWELL, PATTON, artist; b. Columbia, SC, May 6, 1949; d. Charles Shannon and Dorothy Mitchell (Kelly) B. BA in Cultural Geography, Macalester Coll., St. Paul, 1974; Cert. Moyen, French Lang./Lit., Sorbonne, Paris, 1977; postgrad., Escola de Artes Visuais, Rio de Janeiro, 1984-86; M in Internat. Adminstrn., Sch. for Internat. Tng., 1997. Owner Blackwell Studios, Camden, S.C., 1993—, Rio de Janeiro, 1982—96. Dorland Mountain Arts Colony residency, Temecula, Calif., 1994; art columnist Rio Life, 1987-89. One woman shows include: Sao Jose dos Campos, Brazil, 1987, Sao Paulo, Brazil, 1987, N.Y.C., 1988, Museu de Arte Contemporaneo, Goiania, Goias, Brazil, 1993, Brasilia, Brazil, 1993, Recife, Pernambuco, Brazil, 1993, Louisville, 1995, Camden, 1996; group shows in cities including Rio de Janeiro, Brasilia, Sao Paulo, Asheville, N.C., Salvador, Bahia, Brazil, Cairo, Camden, Burlingame, Calif., Boca Raton, Fla., Greenville, S.C., Charleston, S.C., Tegucigalpa, Honduras, Guatamala, Doha, Qatar, Bucharest, Romania and private and corp. collections in U.S., France, Brazil and Japan, Honduras, Doha, Qatar. Mem. S.C. Arts Alliance, Camden Tree Found. Episcopalian. Avocations: golf, travel, visiting museums, nature. Office: Blackwell Studios PO Box 399 Camden SC 29020-0399 Business E-Mail: studio@pattonblackwell.com.

BLACKWELL, PAUL EUGENE, SR., military officer; b. York, SC, Aug. 19, 1941; s. Paul Webb and Ruby Mae (Hartness) B.; m. Janet Gail Glenn, June 23, 1963; 1 child, Paul Eugene Jr. BS, Clemson U., SC, 1963, MS, 1965, postgrad., 1970-72, LLD, 1992. Commd. 1st lt. U.S. Army, 1963, advanced through grades to lt. gen., 1994, comdr. 1st Bn., 4th inf., 3d inf. divsn. Aschaffenburg, W. Ger., 1980-82, ops. officer 9th Inf. Div. Ft. Lewis, Wash., 1983-85, chief staff 9th Inf. Div., 1985-86, comdr. 1st Brigade, 9th Inf. Div., 1986-88, dep. dir. ops. Nat. Mil. Command Ctr., Joint Staff Washington, 1988-89; asst. div. comdr. 3d Armored Div., Germany, 1989-91; comdg. gen. 2d Armored Div., Garlstedt, Germany, 1991-92; comdr. 24th Inf. Div., Ft. Stewart, Ga., 1992-94; dep. chief staff ops. Dept. Army, Washington, 1994-96; v.p. integrated command ctrl. and comm. Raytheon Co., 2000—03; v.p. RayTheon, NCS, 2003—09; v.p., bus. devel. Network Centric Sys., RayTheon, 2009—12; ind. cons., 2012—. Ruling elder Presbyn. Ch., Puyallup, Wash., 1985—88, Beth Shiloh Presbyn. Ch., 1998—2001, 2003—06, 2009—, clerk of session, 1999—2001, 2003—06, 2009—, supt., 1997—99; bd. mem. Clemson U. Found., 1997—2001, bd. pres., 2001. Decorated DSM with oak leaf cluster, Silver Star with oak leaf cluster, Legion of Merit with oak leaf cluster, Bronze Star with V device with eight oak leaf clusters, Purple Heart, Air medal, Army Commendation medal with V device and three oak leaf clusters, Combat Infantryman's Badge, Sr. Parachutist Badge, others.; recipient Clemsm Disting. Svc. award, 2002. Mem. 82d Airborne Div. Assn., 9th Inf. Div. Assn. (pres. 1986-88), Marine Corps Assn., Assn. of U.S. Army, Tiger Brotherhood (hon.), Am. Ordnance Assn., Octofoil Assn., 3d Armored Div. Assn., 2d Armored Div. Assn., 24th Inf. Div. Assn., Assn. U.S. Army, DAV, Masons, Shriners, Ft. Stewart Skeet Club, Phi Kappa Phi, Gamma Sigma Delta, Alpha Zeta, Alpha Tau Alpha. Avocations: hunting, skeet shooting, running. Home: 650 N Shiloh Rd York SC 29745-8378 Home Phone: 803-628-6963. Personal E-mail: geneblackwell@hughes.net.

BLACKWELL, SLADE, state legislator; b. Miss., June 14, 1968; m. Sally Salter; children: Colby, Grant, Hagen. BS in Art, U. Montevallo, Ala. Cert. comml. investment mem. Owner real estate devel. co., Birmingham, Ala.; mem. Dist. 15 Ala. State Senate, Montgomery, 2011—. Vol. youth basketball coach; mem. Covenant Presbyn. Ch.; bd. dirs. Shelby Arts Coun. Republican. Office: Ala State Senate State House Rm 733 11 S Union St Montgomery AL 36130 Office Phone: 334-242-7851, 205-396-1144. Business E-Mail: sb@sladeblackwell.com.

BLACKWELL, WILLIAM ERNEST, broadcast executive; b. Rocky Mount, NC, Apr. 1, 1932; s. Rosser I. and Ellen W. (Wilkinson) Blackwell; m. Elizabeth Levitan Blackwell, Mar. 22, 1973. BS, Davidson Coll., 1954; MBA, U. N.C., 1958. Security analyst Jefferson Standard Life Ins. Co., Greensboro, NC, 1958—66, asst. treas., 1966—69, 2d v.p., 1969—81; v.p. corp. devel. Jefferson-Pilot Corp., Greensboro, 1981—83, sr. v.p. corp. devel., 1983—85, exec. v.p., 1986; pres. Jefferson-Pilot Comm. Co., 1991—97, OmniVest Svcs., 1998—. Served in US Army, 1954—56. Mem.: Nat. Assn. Life Underwriters, N.C. Soc. Fin. Analysts, Inst. Chartered Fin. Analysts. Office: OmniVest Svcs 601 Woodland Dr Greensboro NC 27408-7416

BLACKWELL-TAFFEL, CAMELLIA ANN, art educator, consultant; b. Balt., Feb. 21, 1949; BS, Morgan State U., Balt.; MFA, MEd, Md. Inst. Coll. Art, Balt.; PhD in Art Edn., U. Md. Art tchr. Balt. City Pub. Schs., 1971—76; art dir., asst. art dir. McKeldin Ctr., lectr. art dept. Morgan State U., 1971-76, art dir., asst. art dir. McKeldin Ctr. Balt., 1976-81; assoc. prof. Bowie (Md.) State Coll., 1981-83; mus. specialist Smithsonian Instn., Washington, 1984, dir. mus. publs., 1984-88; asst. prof. Howard U., Washington, 1988-89; assoc. prof. Prince George's C.C., Largo, Md., 1989-91; artist-in-residence Montpelier Cultural Arts Ctr., Laurel, Md., 1991-97; prof. U. D.C., Washington, 1991-95; exec. dir. Internat. Ctr. for Artistic Devel. Inc., 1991—; art specialist Montgomery County Pub. Schs., 1993—2004; owner art studio, gallery and gift shop Historic Savage Mill, Savage, Md., 1997—2010; owner, propr., educator, Camp Camellia Tree Firm, art, nature, tech. and wildlife ctr. divsn. Internat. Ctr. Artistic Devel., Goldvein, Va.; owner proprietor Lamp Camilliatree Farm Art Nature Tech. & Wildlife Ctr., Va.; featured artist 911-Art Exhbn. Columbia Art Ctr., 2011. Panelist individual artists' grants Indpls. Arts Commn., 1991; del. U.S./USSR Emerging Leaders Summit-Russia, Kazakhstan, 1990; art cons. to Cultural Ctr. of Nagyatad, Hungary, 1994, 95; owner art studio, gallery and gift shop, Historic Savage Mill, Savage, Md., 1997—. One-women shows include Blackwell Home Gallery, Balt., 1974-77, U. Ife, Ile-Ife, Nigeria, 1979, McCrillis Gardens Gallery, Bethesda, Md., 1991, Johns Hopkins Space Sci. Telescope Inst., 1992, State Fine Arts Mus. of Almaty, Kazakhstan, 1993, Howard C.C., 1996, Montpelier Cultural Art Ctr., 1996, Bowie State U., 2001, No Worries for Tomorrow, Bowie State U., 2006 (P.C. Arts Coun. grant), The Business for art lecture Series; curator, Herbert Bearman Art Gallery at Frederick Douglass-Isaac Myers Maritime Pk. Mus., Mica Alumni & Friends Art Exhbn. at Maryland Inst. Coll. Arts Wellness Ctr., 2013; exhibited in group shows The Finnish Sch. Design, Finland, 1977, Chgo. Southside Community Art Ctr., 1991, Museu Da Gravura Cidade De Curitiba, Brazil, 1991, McCrillis Gardens Gallery, Bethesda, 1991, Katzenstein Gallery, Balt., 1991, The Print Club, Phila., 1991, James E. Lewis Mus. Art, Balt, 1992, Montpelier Cultural Arts Ctr., Morgan State U., Balt., 1992, Cergy-Pontoise, France, Sister City Artist Exch., 1999, Ctr. de Cuidad de Tres Canto, Spain, 2000, Sister City Artist Exch., Internat. Art Edn. Inst., U. Alaska, Fairbanks, 2001, Nat. Art Edn. Assn., New Orleans, 1997, San Francisco, 1988, Chgo., 1999, Washington, 2000, Prince George's Juried Exhbn., The Sky's The Limit, 2011, Howard County Arts Coun., 2011, Oakland Mills Multicultural Art Show, 2011; executed mural Howard County Rehab. Ctr., Columbia, Md., 1996, New Art Studies Gallery, 2007, camellist Art Studio Gallery, 2007; dir., TV Series, ICAD Historic Overview U. Meryland, Balt. Country Collaboration Project, 2008, Nat. Eubie Blake Cultural Ctr. Art Exhibition, 2012, Oakland Mills Village Ctr. Art Exhibition: Art in The Mills, 2011, Brentwood Arts Exchange Art Exhibition, 2011; painter Smithsonian's Anacostia Cmty. Mus., 2013. Founder, exec. dir. Internat. Ctr. Artistic Devel., Inc.; mem. cultural arts exch. France, Spain. Recipient Jurors' Choice award Md. Fedn. Art, Annapolis, 1977, NEA Grant to African Am. Mus. Assn. Conf., 1984, Merit award-design Printing Industries of Commonwealth of Va., 1985, First Pl. in Design, Printing Industries of Met. Washington, 1986, Best in Category Printing Industries of Md. Ann. Competition, 1987, Robert Rauschenberg's Learning Disabilities Workshop award, 1995, Network Jour. Mag. award, 2002, Women in Bus. award, 2002, Artist award, Prince Georges County Md. Arts Coun., 2005, Cmty. Arts award, Md. State Arts Coun. Howard County Arts Coun., 2001-04, Bus. award Network Jour. Mag., 2002, Cmty. Arts award Md. State Arts Coun., 2000-05, Individual Artist award Md. State Arts Coun., 2006; print selected to travel to the Belgium Congo Embassy, 1996; named Outstanding Advisor to Art League, Prince George's C.C., 1990; grantee to direct students to design and produce a mural for the Md. Sci. Ctr., Balt., Montgomery County Pub. Schs., 1996; Grant award for May Arts Expo Festival, Coun. Cmty. Arts, 2004, Sister City Artist Exch., Columbia, Md. and Cergy Pontrios, France, 1999, Va. State Dept. Forestry Stewardship award Goldvein, Va. at Camp Camellia Tree Farm, Art Natural & Utilities Ctr., 2012, Forestry Stewardship award, 2013; 3 yr. grants Dep. Agr., 2013. Mem.: Nat. Art Edn. Assn., The Smithsonian, Md. Printmakers, So. Graphics Coun., Nat. Mus. Native Americans, Assn. Am. Museums, African Am. Museums Assn., Balt. Mus. Art, Walters Art Gallery, U. Md. Alumni Assn., Md. Inst. Coll. Art Alumni Assn., Morgan State U. Alumni Assn., Lake Clifton/Ea. High Sch. Alumni Assn. Home and Office: 6001 Jamina Downs Columbia MD 21045-3819 Studio: Camp Camellia Tree Farm Art Nature and Wildlife Ctr 13766 Sillamon Rd Goldvein VA 22720 Office Phone: 410-730-6008. Personal E-mail: ctaffel@comcast.net. Business E-Mail: cab@icadev.org.

BLACKWOOD, ROBERT E., family practice physician; BS, MD, U. Fla. Diplomate Am. Bd. Family Practice. Resident family medicine Shands Hosp., Gainesville, Fla., 1970—71; hosp. affiliation includes Blake Med. Ctr. Recipient People's Choice award, Bradenton Herald, 2008; named Chief of Staff, Blake Hosp., 1979—80, Doctor of the Year, Blake Med. Ctr., 1992; named one of Top Doctors, Sarasota Mag., 2004, 2005. Mem.: Am. Acad. of Family Physicians, Fla. Med. Assn. Office: Blake Medical Center 7005 Cortez Rd W Bradenton FL 34210 Office Phone: 941-792-2122.

BLADES, JOHN MICHAEL, museum director; b. Decatur, Ill., Jan. 19, 1952; s. Robert Ray and Beverly Ann B.; m. Sandra Jean Barghini, Feb. 11, 1995; 1 child, Erin R. BS, Calif. Poly. State U., 1981; postgrad., Tex. Christian U., 1981-84; cert., U. Calif., Berkeley, 1994. From guide supr. to head pub. affairs office Hearst Castle, San Simeon, Calif., 1986-95; instr. Cuesta Coll., San Luis Obispo, Calif., 1987-90; exec. dir. Henry M. Flagler Mus., Palm Beach, Fla., 1995—. Grant reviewer Inst. Mus. & Libr. Svcs., D.C., 1996—; presenter, lectr. in field. Contbr. articles and photographs to profl. jours. Pres. Mozart Festival, San Luis Obispo, 1993; chmn. Cultural Execs. Coun., Palm Beach County, 1996-98; bd. dirs. Cambria (Calif.) C. of C., 1994-95, Ctrl. Coast Tourism Coun., San Luis Obispo, 1993-95. Sgt. USAF, 1970-74. Mem. Am. Assn. Mus. (surveyor, adv. com. Mus. assessment program, programming com. 2000, historic house profl. interest com. 1996—, accreditation reviewer 1999—), Fla. Art Mus. Dirs. Assn. Republican. Episcopalian. Avocations: sailing, salt water aquariums, collecting antiquities. Home: PO Box 705 Palm Beach FL 33480-0705 Office: Flagler Mus One Whitehall Way PO Box 969 Palm Beach FL 33480-0969 Fax: 561-655-2826. E-mail: executivedirector@flaglermuseum.us.

BLAIR, BRYCE, real estate company executive; BS in Civil Engring. magna cum laude, U. NH; MBA, Harvard U. Ptnr. Trammell Crow Residential, 1985—93; sr. v.p., devel., acquisitions and constrn. AvalonBay Cmtys., Inc., Alexandria, Va., COO, 1999, pres., 2000; CEO AvalonBay Communities, Inc., Alexandria, Va., 2001—, chmn. bd., 2002—. Mem.: Nat. Assn. Real Estate Investment Trusts (bd. govs.), Real Estate Roundtable, Nat. Multi Housing Coun., Urban Land Inst. Office: AvalonBay Communities Inc 671 N Glebe Rd Ste 800 Arlington VA 22203-2138 Business E-Mail: bryce_blair@avb.com.

BLAIR, CRAIG P., utilities executive, former state legislator; b. Martinsbusrg, W.Va., Oct. 17, 1959; m. Andrea Blair; children: Phillip, Saira. Cert. water specialist Water Quality Assn., 1993. Engr. Cassco Ice/Reddy Ice, 1986—2003; pres. Sunset Water Svcs., 1989—; mem. Dist.52 W.Va. House of Delegates, W.Va., 2002—10. Republican. Protestant. Office: Sunset Water 191 Wasser Dr Martinsburg WV 25403-0884 Office Phone: 304-754-9031. Office Fax: 304-754-5121. Business E-Mail: craig@sunsetwater.com.

BLAIR, GARY, women's college basketball coach; b. Aug. 10, 1945; m. Nan Smith-Blair; children: Paige, Matt. BS in Health & Phys. Edn., Tex. Tech. U., 1972, MA in Phys. Edn., 1974. Head coach Dallas South Oak Cliff HS, 1973—80; asst. coach La. Tech. U., 1980—85; head coach Stephen F. Austin Coll., Tex., 1985—93, U. Ark., Fayetteville, 1993—2003, Tex. A&M U., College Station, 2003—. Asst. coach US nat. team Jones Cup, Taiwan, 1996. Served with USMC. Named Nat. Coach of Yr., Women's Basketball News, 1995, Basketball Times, 1995, Coach of Yr., Tex. Assn. Basketball Coaches, 2006, 2007, Nat. Coach of Yr., Women's Basketball News Svc., 2006, Coach of Yr., Big 12 Conf., 2007; named to Tex. HS Basketball Hall of Fame, 2002, Stephen F. Austin Athletics Hall of Fame, 2008; finalist Naismith Coach of Yr., 2003, 2007. Achievements include head coach of the NCAA Women's Final Four national championship winning Texas A&M University Aggies, 2011. Office: Tex A&M Univ Athletic Dept PO Box 30017 College Station TX 77842-3017 Office Phone: 979-862-3218.

BLAIR, MARGARET MENDENHALL, economist, consultant, law educator; b. Bartlesville, Okla., Nov. 8, 1950; d. Harold Leroy and Mary Winifred (Simmons) Mendenhall; m. Forrest Randall Blair, May 29, 1971 (div. Sept. 1979); m. Roger Lisle Conner, June 22, 1991; 2 children, Elizabeth LeeAnn Conner, Joshua David Conner. BA, U. Okla., 1973; postgrad., Harvard U., 1982-83; MA, MPhil, PhD, Yale U., 1989. Reporter Houston Chronicle, 1973-75; reporter, bur. mgr. Fairchild Publ., Houston, 1975-77; corr. Bus. Week, Houston, 1977-79, bur. chief, 1979-82; economist Fed. Res. Bank N.Y., NYC, 1985; rsch. asst. Yale U., New Haven, 1985-86, lectr., 1986-87; rsch. assoc. Brookings Instn., Washington, 1987-94, sr. fellow, 1995-99; dir. Brookings Project on Corps. and Human Capital, 1996-99; co-dir. Brookings Project on Intangible Sources of Value, 1998-2001; rsch. dir., vis. prof. Sloan-GULC Project on Bus. Inst. Georgetown U. Law Ctr., 2000—04; prof. law Vanderbilt U., Nashville, 2004—; prin. investigator Vanderbilt-Sloan project on corps., pvt. law and governance global econ. activity. Adj. faculty U. Md. Coll. Bus. and Mgmt., 1993—94; vis. prof. Georgetown U. Law Ctr., 1996—2004; steering com., rapporteur Woodstock Seminar Series on Bus. Ethics, Washington, 1989—90; subcoun. on capital allocation Competitiveness Policy Coun., 1993—96; rapporteur Salzburg (Austria) Seminar on Internat. Fin. Markets, 1989; steering com. time horizons project Coun. on Competitiveness, Washington, 1990; mem. Task Force on Restructuring America's Labor Market Instns., MIT/Sloan Sch. Mgmt., 1997—2001, World Econ. Forum Corp. Performance Coun., 1999—2003; non-resident sr. fellow Brookings Instn., 2000—04; bd. advisors George Washington U. Sloan Program on Bus. and Soc., 1998—2002; trustee Woodstock Theol. Ctr., 2001—04; bd. dir. Worldwide Responsible Apparel Prodn. Author: The Deal Decade Handbook, 1993, Ownership and Control: Rethinking Corporate Governance for the Twenty-first Century, 1995; co-author: Unseen Wealth: Report of the Brookings Task Force on Intangibles, 2001; editor: The Deal Decade: What Takeovers and Leveraged Buyouts Mean for Corporate Governance, 1993, Wealth Creation and Wealth Sharing: A Colloquium on Corporate Governance and Investments in Human Capital, 1996, Employees and Corporate Governance, 1999, The New Relationship Human Capital in the American Corporation, 2000; contbr. articles to profl. jours. Vol. Big Sisters Washington Met. Area, 1989-92; organizer neighborhood watch group, Washington, 1990; mem. bd. advisors Ctr. for Cmty. Interest, 1993-98; mem. bd. dir. Christ Edn. Rock Spring United Ch. Christ, 2000-03; mem. Arlington County Adv. Coun. Instrn., 1999-2003, foster parent, Davidson County, 2007-08. Univ. fellow Yale U., 1983-86, Leo Model fellow Brookings Instn., 1987-88; rsch. grantee Boston U. Mfrs. Roundtable, 1990, Columbia U. Instnl. Investor Project, 1994, Alfred P. Sloan Found., 1995, 96, 98, 99, 06. Mem.: ABA (assoc.), Am. Law Econs. Assn., Am. Econ. Assn. Avocations: ballet, religious studies, cooking. Office: Vanderbilt University Law School 131 21st St S Nashville TN 37203-1181

BLAIR, MARIE LENORE, elementary school educator; b. Maramec, Okla., Jan. 9, 1931; d. Virgil Clement and Ella Catherine (Leen) Strode; m. Freeman Joe Blair, Aug. 26, 1950; children: Elizabeth Ann Crump, Roger Joe. BS, Okla. A&M Coll., Stillwater, 1956; MS, Okla. State U., Stillwater, 1961, postgrad., 1965—68. Reading specialist Pub. Schs., Stillwater, Okla., 1966-88. Past bd. dirs. Okla. Reading Coun.; active 1st Christian Ch. Mem. Internat., Okla., Cimarron (past pres.) reading assns., NEA, Okla. Edn. Assn., Stillwater Edn. Assn., Pawnee County Ret. Tchrs. Assn., Demoley Mothers Club, Rainbow Mothers Club, Lahoma Club, White Shrine Jerusalem (past worthy high priestess), Order White Shrine Jerusalem (past supreme queen's attendent), Internat. Order of Rainbow for Girls (Okla. exec. com. emeritus), Order Ea. Star (past grand Martha, past grad rep. of Nebr. in Okla., past grand rep. of Manitoba in Okla.), Order of Amaranth, Kappa Kappa Iota. Democrat. Home: 351200 E 5500 Rd Maramec OK 74045-6124

BLAIR, PATRICK, healthcare company executive; CEO, sr. svcs. unit Amerigroup Corp. Office: Amerigroup Corp 4425 Corporation Ln Virginia Beach VA 23462 Office Phone: 757-490-6900. Office Fax: 757-518-3600. Business E-Mail: pblair@amerigroupcorp.com.

BLAIS, ROGER NATHANIEL, physics professor, academic administrator; b. Duluth, Minn., Oct. 3, 1944; s. Eusebe Joseph and Edith Seldina (Anderson) Blais; m. Mary Louise Leclerc, Aug. 2, 1971; children: Christopher Edward, Laura Louise. BA in Physics and French Lit., U. Minn., 1966; PhD in Physics, U. Okla., Norman, 1971; cert. in computer programming, Tulsa Jr. Coll., 1981; cert. in bus., UCLA, 1986. Registered profl. engr., Okla. Instr. physics Westark C.C., Ft. Smith, Ark., 1971-72; asst. prof. physics and geophys. scis Old Dominion U., Norfolk, Va., 1972-77; asst. prof. engring. physics U. Tulsa, 1977-81, assoc. prof., 1981-98, prof., 1998—; assoc. dir. Tulsa U. Artificial Lift Projects, 1983—98, chmn. physics, 1986-88, vice-provost, 1989-92, provost, v.p. acad. affairs, 1998—. Contbr. articles to profl. jours. Active Leadership Okla. XVI, 2003; bd. dirs. Look Musical Theatre, 2003—13, Okla. Acad. Exec. Com., 2008—; bd. trustees Brock Internat. Prize in Edn. Stearing Com., 2001—, All Socs. Unitarian Ch., 2008—. Fellow Internat. Soc. Automation (dir. test measurement divsn. 1995-97, v.p. automation and tech. dept. 2003-04), Governors Comn. on Sci. & Tech., 2012-; mem. AAAS, AAUP, NSPE, Am. Phys. Soc., Am. Geophys. Union, Soc. Petroleum Engrs., Am. Assn. Physics Tchrs., Am. Soc. Engring. Edn., NY Acad. Scis., Iron Wedge Soc., Phi Beta Kappa, Sigma Xi, Sigma Pi Sigma, Tau Beta Pi, Phi Kappa Phi. Home: 5348 E 30th Pl Tulsa OK 74114-6314 Office: U Tulsa Office of Provost 800 S Tucker Dr Tulsa OK 74104-3189 Office Phone: 918-631-2554. Personal E-mail: rblais71@att.net. Business E-Mail: roger.blais@utulsa.edu.

BLAISS, MICHAEL S., allergist, immunologist; MD, U. Tenn. Health Sci. Ctr., 1967. Diplomate Am. Bd. Pediat., Am. Bd. Allergy & Immunology. Intern, resident U. Tenn./Le Bonheur Children's Med. Ctr., Memphis, 1976—80; fellowship in allergy/immunology Ochsner Hosp. & Med. Found., New Orleans, 1980—82; clin. prof. pediat. and medicine U. Tenn. Health Sci. Ctr.; pvt. practice Allergy & Asthma Care, Memphis. Bd. dirs. World Allergy Orgn., Am. Bd. Allergy & Clin. Immunology. Co-editor: Atlas of Allergic Diseases, 2005; mem. editl. bd. Jour. Asthma, Annals of Allergy, Asthma & Immunology; contbr. articles to profl. jours. Named one of The Most Influential Physicians in Asthma Care, USA Today, 2009. Fellow: Am. Acad. Allergy, Asthma, & Immunology, Am. Coll. Allergy, Asthma, & Immunology (past pres.); mem.: AMA. Office: Allergy & Asthma Care 7205 Wolf River Blvd Ste 200 Germantown TN 38138 Office Phone: 910-757-6100. Office Fax: 910-757-6109.

BLAKE, ELIZABETH K., lawyer; b. June 1951; m. Frank Blake, 2005; 2 stepchildren; 3 children from previous marriage. BA with honors, Smith Coll., 1973; JD, Columbia U., 1977; degree (hon.), Cin. State Tech. CC, Coll. Mt. St. Joseph. Bar: NY, Ohio. Assoc. Davis Polk & Wardell, NYC, 1977—82; assoc., ptnr. Frost & Jacobs (now Frost Brown Todd LLC), Cin.; gen. counsel S.W. Ohio Regional Transit Authority; dir. Star Gas Corp.; v.p., chief of staff Cinergy Corp., 1996—98; v.p., gen. counsel GE Power Sys., 1998—2002; sr. v.p., gen. counsel Trizec Properties, 2002; exec. v.p., corp. affairs, gen. counsel US Airways Group, Inc., US Airways, Inc., Arlington, Va., 2003—04, exec. v.p., corp. affairs, gen. counsel, corp. sec., 2004—05; sr. v.p. advocacy & corp. affairs, gen. counsel Habitat for Humanity Internat., Inc., Atlanta, 2006—. Bd. dirs. Patina Oil & Gas Corp. Chmn. Aronoff Ctr.; vice chmn. Cin. Arts Assn.; mem. adv. bd. Civic Forum; bd. dirs. Ohio Bd. Regents, 1990, sec. of the bd., 1994, 1995, chmn., 1996; bd. dirs. Cin. Parks Found., Greater Cin. Conv. and Visitors Bur., Lighthouse Youth Svcs., World Affairs Coun., Children's Svcs. Levy Com. Harlan Fiske Stone scholar, Columbia U. Sch. Law. Office: Habitat for Humanity Internat Inc 270 Peachtree St Atlanta GA 30303 Office Phone: 404-962-3403. Business E-Mail: eblake@habitat.org.

BLAKE, FRANK (FRANCIS STANTON BLAKE), consumer products company executive, lawyer; b. Boston, July 30, 1949; s. George Baty and Rosemary (Shaw) Blake; m. Anne McChristian, Jan. 1, 1977; children: Francis S., Margaret D. BA, Harvard U., 1971; JD, Columbia U. Sch. Law, 1976. Bar: DC 1978. Legis. aide to Joint Com. on Social Welfare Mass. Legis., Boston, 1971—73; law clk. to Hon. Wilfred Feinberg US Ct. Appeals (2nd Cir.), NYC, 1976—77; law clk. to Justice John Paul Stevens US Supreme Ct., Washington, 1976—78; assoc. Leva, Hawes, Symington, Martin & Oppenheimer, Washington, 1978-81; dep. counsel to v.p. The White House, Washington, 1981-83; ptnr. Swidler Berlin & Strelw, Washington, 1983-85; gen. counsel EPA, Washington, 1985—88; v.p., gen. counsel GE Power Systems, Schenectady, NY, 1991—95, v.p. bus. devel. & alliances, 1995—98, v.p. bus. devel., 1998—2000; sr. v.p. corp. bus. devel. General Electric Co., 2000—01; dep. sec. US Dept. Energy, Washington, 2001—02; exec. v.p. bus. devel. & corporate ops. The Home Depot, Inc., Atlanta, 2002—07, vice-chmn., 2006—07, chmn., CEO, 2007—. Bd. dirs. Southern Co., Atlanta, 2004—, The Home Depot, Inc., 2006—. Republican. Episcopalian. Office: The Home Depot Inc 2455 Paces Ferry Rd Atlanta GA 30339-4024*

BLAKE, GERALD RUTHERFORD, retired banker; b. Knoxville, Tenn., Apr. 2, 1939; s. Roy Carl and Katherine Marie (Rutherford) B.; m. Jeanne Avonne Jones, May 11, 1962; children: Robert Alan, Douglas Mark. Student, U. Tenn., 1957-58, Sch. Bank Adminstrn., U. Wis., 1971-73. With Miller's. Inc., Knoxville, 1959—62, First Tenn. Bank, Knoxville, 1963—, eastern regional bldg. mgr., 1973—. Vice-chmn. planning com. Knoxville United Way, 1973—; pres. Ramsey Cmty. Club, 1966-67, Ramsey Elem. Sch. PTO, 1976-80; bd. dirs. Planned Parenthood Assn., 1976-77. Mem. Am. Inst. Banking, Bank Adminstrn. Inst. (pres., dir. Smoky Mountain chpt. 1976-77, state dir. 1977-79, 2d vice-chmn. Tenn. Title XX com.) Baptist.

BLAKE, HARRIS DURHAM, state legislator; State senator Dist. 22, NC, 2002—. Mem. Appropriations on Health and Human Svcs. com., Appropriations/Base Budget com., Commerce com., Fin. com., Health Care com., State and Local Govt. com. Republican. Mailing: Dist Off PO Box 4266 Pinehurst NC 28374 Office: NC Senate 300 N Salisbury St Rm 408 Raleigh NC 27603-5925 Office Phone: 919-733-4809. Business E-Mail: Harris.Blake@ncleg.net.

BLAKE, THOMAS BENJAMIN, III, colon and rectal surgeon; MD, U. South Ala., 1984. Lic. Fla., 1993, diplomate Am. Bd. Colon and Rectal Surgery, 2007, Am. Bd. Surgery, 2009. Resident in surgery St. Agnes Hosp., Balt., 1984—90; fellow in colon and rectal surgery Orlando Regional Med. Ctr., Fla., 1993—94, hosp. affiliations include, South Seminole Hosp., Winter Pk. Meml. Hosp., Fla. Hosp. Altamonte, Fla. Hosp. Fellow: ACS. Office: Florida Hospital 331 N Maitland Ave Ste A2 Maitland FL 32751 Office Phone: 407-629-5141.

BLAKELY, ROBERT T., chemicals executive; b. Dec. 16, 1941; B in Mech. Engring., Cornell U., 1964, MBA, 1965; PhD, MIT, 1970; postgrad., Dartmouth U., 1976. Mng. dir. Morgan Stanley & Co., 1970—81, CFO, 1996—99; v.p., CFO U.S. Synthetic Fuels Corp., 1981; CFO Tenneco Inc, 1981—99, exec. v.p., 1981—99; exec. v.p., CFO Lyondell Chemical Co, 1999—2002; pres. Performance Enhancement Group, Inc., 2002—03; exec. v.p., CFO MCI, Inc., 2003—05; CFO, exec. v.p Federal National Mortgage Association, 2006—. Bd. dirs. Solutia, Inc., Vlasic Foods Internat., Inc. Trustee, mem. audit and fin. coms. Cornell U.; bd. dirs. N.Y.C. Ballet, Manhattan and Bronx Coun. Boy Scouts Am., United Way Greenwich. Office: Westlake Chemical Corp 2801 Post Oak Blvd Ste 600 Houston TX 77056 Office Phone: 713-960-9111. Office Fax: 713-963-1590. Business E-Mail: rblakely@westlake.com.

BLAKELY, SARA, apparel executive; b. Clearwater, Fla., Feb. 21, 1971; m. Jesse Itzler, 2008; 1 child, Lazer Blake. BA in Legal Comm., Fla. State U., 1993. Employee Disney World, Orlando, 1993; saleswoman Danka, Fla., 1993—2000; founder Spanx, Atlanta, 2000—. Founder Sara Blakely Found., 2006—. Named Entrepreneur of the Yr., Ernst & Young; named one of The 100 Most Influential People in the World, TIME mag., 2012, The 100 Most Powerful Women, Forbes mag., 2013. Mem.: Delta Delta Delta. Office: Spanx 3344 Peachtree Rd Ste 1700 Atlanta GA 30326*

BLAKEY, MARION CLIFTON, aerospace association executive, former federal agency administrator; b. Gadsden, Ala., Mar. 26, 1948; m. William Ryan Dooley; 1 child, Mona. BA Internatl Studies, Mary Washington Coll., U. Va., 1970; postgrad., Johns Hopkins U. Dir. pub. affairs NEH, 1982—84; dir. pub. affairs & spl. asst. to the sec. US Dept. Edn., Washington, 1985—87; adminstr. Nat. Hwy. Traffic Safety Adminstrn. US Dept. Transp., 1992—93; prin. Blakey & Associates, Washington, 1993—2001; chmn. Nat. Transp. Safety Bd. (NTSB), 2001—02; adminstr. FAA US Dept. Transp., 2002—07; pres., CEO Aerospace Industries Assn. America (AIA), Arlington, Va., 2007—. Bd. dirs. Alaskan Air Group, Inc., 2010—; bd. trustees Noblis; mem. advisory coun. NASA. Office: Aerospace Industries Assn America (AIA) 1000 Wilson Blvd Ste 1700 Arlington VA 22209 Office Phone: 703-358-1000.

BLALOCK, REBECCA A., information technology specialist; BS in Mktg., State U. West Ga.; M in Fin., Mercer U., Ga. Sr. v.p., chief info. officer Southern Co.; pmd Harvard Bus. Sch., 1994. Chair Bd. Leadership Atlanta. Named Ga. CIO of Yr., Ga. CIO Leadership Assn., 2003, Power Woman of the Yr., Atlanta Woman Mag., 2006; named one of Premier 100 IT Leaders, Computerworld, 2006; named to Acad. of Woman Achievers, YWCA Atlanta, 2005. Office: Southern Co 241 Ralph McGill Blvd Atlanta GA 30308

BLANCHARD, JAMES HUBERT, retired bank executive; b. Augusta, Ga., July 22, 1941; BBA, U. Ga., 1963, LLB, 1965. Atty. Page, Scranon, Harris, McGalley and Chapman, 1964-70; CEO Synovus Fin. Corp., Columbus, Ga., 1971—2005, chmn., 2005—06. Chmn. exec. com., bd. dirs. TSYS; bd. dirs. AT&T, Total Systems Services Inc., Synovus Fin. Corp. & Columbus Bank and Trust Co. subs.; past chmn. Fin. Service Roundtable. Trustee Columbus State U. Found.; Emory Com. Robert T. Jones, Jr. Scholarship; Carter Center Board of Councilors mem.; bd. visitors Morehouse Sch. Med.; mem. Trust for Public Land Chattahoochee River Land Protection Campaign Com.; bd. councilors Carter Ctr.; bd. visitors, mem. Advisory Com. Ga. Partnership Excellence in Education; bd. curators Ga. Historical Society. 1st Lt. and Finance Officer US Army, 1965—67. Mem.: Ga. C. of C. (dir.), Ga. Rsch. Alliance (dir., past chmn.), Ga. Dept. Econ. Develop. (past chmn.), Banker Information Technol. Secretariat (dir., former chmn.), Financial Services Roundtable (dir.), Am. Bankers Assn. (dir.). Office: Synovus Fin Corp 901 Front Ave Columbus GA 31901-2722

BLANCHARD, LEONARD ALBERT, writer, consultant, educator; b. New Britain, Conn., July 30, 1947; s. Albert Edward and Sophie Marian (Lemanski) B.; children: Sarah Hunter Blanchard, Henry Wyche Hunter. BA in English cum laude, Washington & Lee U., 1969; MA, Emory U., 1974, PhD, 1975. Instr. English, coach Oak Ridge (N.C.) Mil. Inst., 1969-71, St. Mark's Sch., Dallas, 1974-75; instr. English El Centro Coll., Dallas, 1975-79; writer, developer, liaison Southland Corp., Dallas, 1979-87; dir. devel. Franchise Group Internat., Little Rock, 1987-88; cons. Len Blanchard, Bradenton, Fla., 1988—. V.p. human resources Harken Internat., Bedford, Tex., 1989—90; mgmt. cons. Tropical Breeze Inn, Sarasota, 1996—99; instr. English State Coll. Fla. Manatee-Sarasota, Bradenton, Fla., 1999—. Author: An American Passion, 2001, Provocations of the Birds and the Beach, 2005, The First Day, 2012, Not Most People, 2013;: Beach Synchronization, 2013, Not Most People: The Pornographists Tale, 2013;: Beach Synchronization, 2013. Mem.: Southern Poverty Law Ctr., Pub. Citizen, Acad. Am. Poets, Amnesty Internat. Democrat. Avocations: swimming, hiking, classical music. Office: State Coll Fla Manatee-Sarasota Dept Lang and Lit 5840 26th St W Bradenton FL 34207-3522 Business E-Mail: blanchl@scf.edu.

BLANCHARD, RICHARD EMILE, SR., retired management services executive, consultant; b. Thompson, Conn., July 13, 1928; s. Lionel A. and Bernadette L. (Jolicoeur) B.; m. Lorraine Patricia Lachapelle, July 3, 1954; children: Michele Welling, Richard E., Danielle Wornstaff, Marie Blanchard Oser, Robert Allen, Janine Lippert. BS in Biology, Providence Coll., 1952; postgrad., U. Conn. Sch. Law, West Hartford, 1952-53. Cert. mgmt. cons. Chemist Charles Pfizer Co., Inc., NYC, 1953-56, med. salesman, 1956-60, coll. rels. mgr., 1960-63, pers. mgr., 1963-67; dir. manpower and orgn. devel. Sky Chef divsn. Am. Airlines, NYC, 1967-70; dir. manpower ARA Svcs., Inc., Phila., 1970-72, v.p., 1972-76; v.p. pers. Jerrico, Inc., Lexington, Ky., 1976-78; chmn., CEO Career Mgmt., Inc., C.M. Temporary Svcs., C.M. Mgmt. Svcs., Lexington, 1978-99; ret., 1999. Cons. pers. svcs. Bd. dirs. Ky. Higher Edn. Coun., Bluegrass United Way, 1979-99, Jr. Achievement, 1979—, Better Bus. Bur., 1985—, United Way of the Bluegrass, 1998-2000, U. Ky. Small Bus. Devel. Ctr., Ky. Econ. Devel. Coun.; v.p. Bluegrass Ednl. Work Coun., 1980—, Bluegrass Better Bus. Bur., 1990-98, bd. dirs., past pres.; chmn. adv. bd. U. Ky. C.C., 1987—; divsn. chmn. United Way, 1990, 92—; Bd. dirs., vice-chmn. Human Rights Commn., 1991-94; co-chmn. bd. dirs. Bluegrass MS Soc., 1996; mem. adv. bd. C.C. divsn. U. Ky., Muscular Dystrophy Bluegrass Coun. With USN, 1946-48. Mem. Inst. Mgmt. Cons., Am. Mgmt. Assn., Am. Soc. Pers. Assocs. (past pres. N.Y. chpt.), Nat. Assn. Temporary Svcs., Ind. Temporary Svcs. Assn., Ky. Assocs. Temporary Svcs. (past pres.), Ky. State C. of C. (bd. dirs.), Lexington C. of C. (bd. dirs. 1996-99), Lexington Country Club, Exec. Fitness and Sports Ctr., Lexington Tennis Club, Rotary (bd. dirs. 1996-99, Bluegrass Bus. Hall of Fame, 2003). Republican. Roman Catholic. Home: 16279 Edgemont Dr Fort Myers FL 33908-3658 Personal E-mail: chezmemere@aol.com.

BLANCHARD, TERENCE, musician, composer; b. New Orleans, Mar. 13, 1962; s. Joseph Oliver Blanchard; m. Robin Burgess, 1996; 2 children. Studied with Ellis Marsalis, New Orleans Ctr. Creative Arts; studied wwith Paul Jeffrey-Bill Fielder, Rutgers U., 1980-82. Former trumpet player New Orleans Civic Orch., Dixieland and big bands, New Orleans; with Lionel Hampton's band, 1980-82, Art Blakey's Jazz Messengers, 1982-86, mus. dir., 1983-86; with Donald Harrison in a quintet, 1986-90; founder, leader Terence Blanchard Quintet, 1990—; artistic dir. Thelonius Monk Inst. Jazz, U. So. Calif., 2000—. Performed concerts Equitable Ctr., JVC Jazz Festival, NYC, 1991, Orpheum Theater, New Orleans, Jazz Tent, New Orleans Jazz and Heritage Festival, 1992, (with Sonny Rollins), Carnegie Hall, NYC, 1993; performer as leader Jazz at Lincoln Ctr., 1993, Terence Blanchard Quinted, Village Vanguard, NYC, 1993, Jazz Showcase, Chgo., 1994; performed internationally; albums include (with Donald Harrison) New York Second Line, 1983, Discernment, 1986, Nascence, 1986, (with Blakey) New York Scene, 1984, Live at Kimball's, 1987, Blue Night, 1991, Dr. Jekyle, 1992, Hard Champion, 1992, New Year's Eve at Sweet Basil, 1992, (with Harrison and others) Fire Waltz, 1993, Eric Dolphy and Booker Little Remembered Live at Sweet Basil, 1993; The Malcolm X Jazz Suite, 1993, In My Solitude: The Billie Holiday Songbook, 1993, Simply Stated, 1993, Romantic Defiance, 1994, The Heart Speaks, 1995, Clockers Original Orchestral Score, 1995, Jazz in Film, 1999, Wandering Moon, 2000, Let's Get Lost, 2001, 25th Hour, 2003, Bounce, 2003, McCoy Tyner's Illuminations, 2004 (Grammy award for Best Jazz Instrumental Album, 2005), Flow, 2005, A Tale of God's Will (A Requiem for Katrina), 2007 (Grammy award, Best Large Jazz Ensemble Album, 2008), Live at the 2007 Monterey Jazz Festival (Grammy award for Best Jazz Instrumental Solo, 2009); composer (films) Jungle Fever, 1991, Malcolm X, 1992, Sugar Hill, 1994, The Inkwell, 1994, Crooklyn, 1994, Trial by Jury, 1994, Clockers, 1995, Get on the Bus, 1996, 'Til There was You, 1997, 4 Little Girls, 1997, Eve's Bayou, 1997, Summer of Sam, 1999, Next Friday, 2000, Love & Basketball, 2000, Bamboozled, 2000, The Caveman's Valentine, 2001, Original Sin, 2001, Glitter, 2001, Barbershop, 2002, People I Know, 2002, Dark Blue, 2002, 25th Hour, 2002, Negroes with Guns, 2004, She Hate Me, 2004, Drum, 2004, All the Invisible Children, 2005, Inside Man, 2006, Waist Deep, 2006, Who the #$&% is Jackson Pollock?, 2006, Talk to Me, 2007, Steep, 2007, Miracle at St. Anna, 2008, Cadillac Records, 2008, (TV films) Assault at West Point, 1994, Gia, 1998, The Tempest, 1998, A Saintly Switch, 1999, The Color of Courage, 1999, Free of Eden, 1999, Having Our Say, 1999, Navigating the Heart, 2000, The Truth About Jane, 2000, A Girl Thing, 2001, Bojangles, 2001, Jim Brown, 2002, Sucker Free City, 2004, Their Eyes Were Watching God, 2004, Heartless, 2005, (TV miniseries) The Promised Land, 1995, When the Levees Broke: A Requiem in Four Acts, 2006. Named one of America's Best Leaders, US News & World Report, 2008. Office: care Burgess Mgmt 6110 St Charles Ave New Orleans LA 70118 Office Phone: 504-897-2958. Office Fax: 504-897-1267.

BLANCHARD, TOWNSEND EUGENE, retired service companies executive; b. Du Quoin, Ill., Jan. 30, 1931; s. Townsend and Anna Belle Blanchard; m. Norma Louise Barr, Dec. 18, 1960, (died) Apr. 8, 2008; children: John Barr, Susan Melody, Jayne Ann Blanchard Reishus, Stephen Eugene, m. Phyllis Morris, May 9, 2009. BS, U. Ill., 1952; MBA, Harvard U., 1957. Cons. Ill. Sch. Bond Svc., Monticello, 1958-62; co-founder, treas., chief fin. officer Americana Nursing Ctrs., Monticello, 1962-75; v.p. fin., treas., CFO, chief of staff Cenco, Inc., Chgo., 1975-79; sr. v.p., CFO DynCorp., Reston, Va., 1979-97. Chmn. Employee Stock Ownership Plan DynCorp, 1997—2003. Elder, deacon Presbyn. Ch.; bd. dirs. Combined Health Appeal, 1986-96; bd. advisors Cameron Glen Care Facility, 1989-92, dir., Augusta HOA, 2003-11; v.p. Bantley Village Resident Coun., 2014-. Lt. USNR, 1952-55. Decorated Spl. Commendation letter. Mem. Fin. Execs. Inst. (chpt. pres. 1988-89, nat. v.p. and bd. dirs. 1991-94), U. Ill. Alumni

Club, Harvard U. Bus. Sch. Club, Harvard Club, Am. Legion, Delta Sigma Phi (trustee nat. found. 1982-89, pres. nat. found. 1988-89, Harvey W. Herbert award 1975, Mr. Delta Sig award 1988). Personal E-mail: g_blanchard@comcast.net.

BLANCHETT, MICHAEL G., family practice physician; MD, U. Tex., 1978. Diplomate Am. Bd. Family Practice. Resident family medicine UTSA Affil Hosp., San Antonio, 1978—81; hosp. affiliation includes Santa Rosa Hosp. Office: Santa Rosa Hospital 4241 Woodcock Ste A100 San Antonio TX 78228 Office Phone: 210-785-5255.

BLANCK, SUSAN R., insurance company executive; BS in Edn., U. Mo., Columbia. With actuarial dept. in US pricing area AFLAC, Inc., 1993, second v.p., asst. actuary, 1998—2000, v.p., assoc. actuary, 2000—04, sr. v.p., dep. corp. actuary, 2004—06, sr. v.p., corp. actuary, 2006—, 1st sr. v.p., Japan, 2008—. Bd. mem. Fla. Health Reinsurance Program. Bd. mem. Chattahoochee Riverkeeper. Fellow: Soc. Actuaries (chair cancer experience studies com.); mem.: Am. Acad. Actuaries. Office: AFLAC Inc 1932 Wynnton Rd Columbus GA 31999 Office Phone: 706-323-3431. Office Fax: 706-324-6330. Business E-Mail: sblanck@aflac.com.

BLANCO, RAFAEL, territorial banking agency administrator; b. San Juan, Dec. 2, 1948; s. José Rafael and Luisa María (Latorre) B.; m. Aida Méndez, Aug. 5, 1972; children: Rosaida Luisa, Mariela Marta. BA in Econs., U. Notre Dame; JD, U. PR. Bar: PR. Pers. officer Banco Popular de PR, 1971-73; account exec. Citibank N.A., 1973-76, v.p. credit, 1977-82; assoc. McConnel, Valdes et al, 1976-77; former sr. v.p. Banco de Ponce; former v.p. BBVA; dep. sec. adminstrn. PR Dept. Edn.; commr. PR Bur. Financial Institutions, San Juan, 2011—. Bd. dirs. Better Bus. Bur., San Juan; mem. budget com. United Fund, San Juan, 1982-83, housing and urban com. Commonwealth PR Senate, San Juan, 1982; head PR Bankers Assn., 2007-09. Mem. PR Bar Assn., ABA, PR Fin. Analysis, Robert Morris Assocs. (sr.). Roman Catholic. Office: Office of Commissioner Financial Institutions Edif Centro Europa Ste 600 1492 Ave Pnce de Leon San Juan PR 00907 Office Phone: 787-723-8004. Business E-Mail: comisionado@ocif.gobierno.pr.

BLAND, JAMES THEODORE, JR., lawyer; b. Memphis, June 16, 1950; s. James Theodore and Martha Frances (Downen) B.; m. Pattie L. Martin, Apr. 12, 1974. BBA magna cum laude, Memphis State U., 1972, JD, 1974. Bar: Tenn. 1975, U.S. Dist. Ct. (we. dist.) Tenn. 1976, U.S. Tax Ct. 1976, U.S. Supreme Ct. 1983, U.S. Ct. Claims 1987; cert. Estate Planning specialist; CPA Tenn., 1975, VI, 2008. Estate tax atty. IRS, Memphis, 1974—76; atty. Armstrong, Allen, Braden, Goodman, McBride & Prewitt, Memphis, 1976—91; prin. James T. Bland, Jr. and Assocs., Memphis, 1991—. Instr. in taxation, bus. law State Tchr.'s Inst., Memphis, 1975-83; bd. dirs. Thomas W. Briggs Found., Memphis, bd. dirs. pres. St Croix Branch Rep. Party, 2008-13. Bd. dir. St George Village Bot. Gardens, Inc., 2007—11, treas., 2007—10. Fellow Am. Coll. Trust and Estate Counsel, Tenn. Bar Found., Memphis Bar Found., Shelby County Bar Found. (pres. 1991-93); mem. ABA (legis. initiatives com., taxation sect., specialization in estate planning real property, probate and trust sect., Achievement award 1983, 85), Fed. Bar Assn. (pres. 1987-88, nat. coun. 1979—, bd. dirs. young lawyers divsn. 1979-84, pres. Memphis mid south chpt. 1979-80), Tenn. Bar Assn. (chmn. tax sect. 1984-85, bd. govs. 1984-85, 89-90, 90-91), Tenn. Young Lawyers Conf. (pres. 1985), Memphis Bar Assn. (bd. dirs. 1990-91), Tenn. Soc. CPA Republican. Methodist. Office: PO Box 25345 Christiansted VI 00824 Business E-Mail: blandjr@viaccess.net.

BLAND, JOHN LLOYD, lawyer; b. Wichita Falls, Tex., Sept. 20, 1944; Student, Vanderbilt U.; BA, U. Tex., 1967, JD with honors, 1969. Bar: Tex. 1969. Mem. Bracewell & Giuliani, LLP, Houston, 1969—. Mem. State Bar Tex., Houston Bar Assn., Phi Delta Phi. Office: Bracewell & Giuliani LLP 2300 S Tower Pennzoil Pl 711 Louisiana St Houston TX 77002-2781 Home Phone: 713-522-0787; Office Phone: 713-221-1310. E-mail: john.bland@bracewellgiuliani.com.

BLANDA, MICHAEL THOMAS, chemist, researcher; b. Orange, Tex., Nov. 21, 1960; s. Michael Thomas and Mary Ann Blanda; m. Connie Lynn Bell; children: Nicholas Paul, Nathaniel Thomas. PhD, Tex. A&M U., College Station, 1989. Post doctoral fellow UCLA, 1989—92; prof. Tex. State U., San Marcos, Tex., 1992—. Mem.: Am. Chem. Soc. Office: Texas State Univ 601 University Dr San Marcos TX 78666

BLANK, ARTHUR M., professional sports team executive, retired retail executive; b. Queens, NY, 1942; BS, Babson Coll., LLD (hon.), 1998. Acct. Arthur Young & Co., NYC, 1963-67; with Daylin Inc., Los Angeles, 1967-74; v.p., treas. Handy Dan Home Improvement Ctrs. Inc., Los Angeles, 1974-78; co-founder Home Depot Inc., Atlanta, 1978, pres., COO, 1978—97, pres., CEO, 1997—2000, co-chmn., 2000—01; chmn. Arthur M. Blank Family Found., 1995—; chmn., pres., CEO AMB Group LLC, 2001—; owner, CEO Atlanta Falcons Football Club, 2002—. Bd. dir. Cox Enterprises, Staples Inc.; disting. exec. in residence Goizueta Bus. Sch., Emory Univ., 2001. Trustee Carter Ctr., Emory Univ., Cooper Inst.; bd. mem. NC Outward Bound Sch. Recipient Brotherhood / Sisterhood award, Nat. Conf. of Christians & Jews, 1994; co-recipient Ga. Philanthropist of the Year, Nat. Soc. Fundraising Exec., 2000, Abe Goldstein Human Rels. award, Anti-Defamation League, 2001; named Ga. Most Respected CEO, Ga. Trend mag., 2001, 2003; named one of 50 Most Generous Philanthropists, BusinessWeek, 2005, Forbes 400: Richest Americans, 2006—; named to Acad. Disting. Entrepreneurs, Babson Coll., 1995, Bus. Hall of Fame, Junior Achievement Atlanta, 2001, Ga. State Univ., 2002. Mem.: Commerce Club. Office: Atlanta Falcons 4400 Falcon Pkwy Flowery Branch GA 30542

BLANK, IRVING MICHAEL, lawyer; b. Richmond, Va., Dec. 29, 1943; s. Lewis and Evelyn (Rosenstein) Blank; m. Rhona Mandel Blank, June 26, 1966; children: Lisa Rae, Jonathan Todd. BS in Pub. Adminstrn., Va. Tech., 1965; JD, U. Richmond, 1967. Bar: Va. 1967, US Supreme Ct. 1972, DC 1978, US Ct. Appeals (4th cir.) 1983. Assoc. Paul & Smith and Predecessors, Richmond, 1967—71; ptnr. Paul, Smith & Blank, Richmond, 1972—83, Smith, Blank, Isaacs & Hinton, 1983—85, Smith, Moncure, Blank, Isaccs & Hinton, 1985—88, ParisBlank, LLP, 1989—. Active Nat. Coun. Am.-Israel Pub. Affairs; chmn. cmty. rels. com. Richmond Jewish Fedn., 1980—87, 1989—90, 1993—95; treas. Jewish Cmty. Fedn., Richmond, 1988—91; mem. cmty. rels. com. Richmond Jewish Cmty. Ctr.; mem. exec. com. Nat. Jewish Cmty. Rels. Adv. Com., 1980—84, 1989—92, 1994; bd. dirs. Jewish Family Svcs., Richmond Jewish Cmty. Fedn.; mem. exec. com., bd. dirs. Richmond Multiple Sclerosis Soc.; mem. internat. affairs commn. and equal opportunity commn. Anti-Defamation League, 1981—; active Tom Bliley Adv. Com. Richmond Tennis Patrons, 1982, Nat. Jewish Cmty. Rels. Adv. Coun.; commr. Vir. Brael Commn., 1987—88, 1992—95. Capt. JAGC US Army. Recipient Tree of Life award, Jewish Nat. Fund, 1992. Mem.: AAJ, Va. State Bar (coun. mem. 2003, exec. com. 2006, pres.-elect 2009—10, pres. 2010—11), Va. Assn. Def. Attys., Richmond Criminal Law Assn. (sec. 1973), Am. Judicature Soc., Am. Arbitration Assn. (panel arbiters), Richmond Bar Assn. (com. adminstrn. of justice 1981—83, exec. com. 1982—85), Va. Bar Assn., Va. Trial Lawyers Assn., ABA (criminal justice sect. 1974—76, 1974—76, com. privacy, environ. matters in criminal law com., com. specialization). Home: 17 E Square Ln Richmond VA 23233-6147 Office: ParisBlank, LLP 1804 Staples Mill Rd Ste 100 Richmond VA 23230-3530 Office Phone: 804-355-0691. Office Fax: 804-353-1839.

BLANK, STEVEN A., energy executive; B in History, SUNY; M in Internat. Bus., Columbia U. V.p. fin., treas. Ultramar Diamond Shamrock Corp., 1996—2002; chief acctg. officer, CFO Valero GP, LLC, San Antonio, 1999—2002, sr. v.p., CFO, 2002—07; sr. v.p., CFO, treas. NuStar Energy LP, San Antonio, 2007—. Office: NuStar Energy LP 19003 W Interstate 10 San Antonio TX 78257-9518 Office Phone: 210-918-2000.

BLANKENBEKER, LYNNE FERRARI, state legislator; married; 1 child. BS in Nursing, U. Ala.; JD, Fanklin Pierce Law Ctr. Nurse Concord Hosp., NH; atty. pvt. practice NH; mem. Merrimack, Dist. 11 NH House of Reps., 2010—, mem. Local and regulated revenues. Mem. Concord Rep. City Com. Lt. comdr. USNR. Republican. Home: 2586F S Arlington Mill Dr Arlington VA 22206-3354 Home Phone: 603-225-7758; Office Phone: 603-369-1464. E-mail: 64ferrari@comcast.net.

BLANKENSHIP, CHARLES P., JR., (CHIP BLANKENSHIP), diversified technology and services company executive; b. 1966; m. Belinda Blankenship; 4 children. BS in Materials Sci. & Engring., Va. Poly Inst. & State U., 1988; PhD in Materials Sci. & Engring., U. Va., 1992. Gen. mgr., Aero Energy bus. GE Co., gen. mgr., Small Comml. Engine Operation, GE Aviation, mgr., CF34 EMBRAER programs, Comml. Engines, GE Aviation; leader, CF6 Airline Support Engring. team, Comml. Engines GE Aviation, program mgr., staff scientist, corporate rsch. & devel Schenectady, NY; gen. mgr. Aero Energy GE Energy, Houston, 2006—08; v.p., gen. mgr. comml. engines GE Aviation, 2008—11; pres., CEO GE Appliances, Louisville, 2012—13, GE Home & Bus. Solutions, 2013—. Office: GE Appliances 4000 Beuchel Bank Rd Louisville KY 40225 Business E-Mail: Charles.Blankenship@ge.com.

BLANTON, HOOVER CLARENCE, retired lawyer; b. Green Sea, SC, Oct. 13, 1925; s. Clarence Leo and Margaret (Hoover) B.; m. Cecilia Lopez, July 31, 1949; children: Lawson Hoover, Michael Lopez. JD, U. S.C., 1953. Bar: SC 1953; ordained deacon Bapt. Ch. Assoc. Whaley & McCutchen, Columbia, SC, 1953—66; ptnr. McCutchen, Blanton, Johnson and Barnette LLP, Columbia, 1967—2007; of counsel Hopkins & Campbell LLP, 2008—09, McCutchen Blanton Hopkins & Campbell LLP, 2009—10, McCutchen Blanton LLP, 2010—12; ret. Dir. Legal Aid Service Agy., Columbia, chmn. bd., 1972-73. Gen. counsel S.C. Rep. Party, 1962-65; del. Rep. State Conv., 1962, 64, 66, 68, 70, 74; bd. dirs. Midlands Cmty. Action Agy., Columbia, vice chmn., 1972-73; bd. dirs. Wildewood Sch., 1976-78; mem. Gov.'s Legal Svcs. Adv. Coun., 1976-77, Commn. on Continuing Legal Edn. for Judiciary, 1977-84, Commn. on Continuing Lawyer Competence, 1988-92, Commn. on Continuing Legal Edn. and Specialization, 1992-2000, sec. 1995, chmn., 1996-99. Mem. ABA. SC Bar (ho. of dels. 1975-76, chmn. fee disputes bd. 1977-81), Richland County Bar Assn. (pres. 1980), Assn. Def. Trial Attys. (state chmn. 1971-77, 80-95, exec. coun. 1977-80), Am. Bd. Trial Advs. (pres. SC chpts. 1989, Trial Lawyer of Yr. 2001), Toastmasters Club (pres. 1959), Palmetto Club, Phi Delta Phi. Home: 3655 Deerfield Dr Columbia SC 29204-3730

BLANTON, VALLYE J. JEAN, educator; b. Valdosta, Ga., Sept. 4, 1953; d. Louie Sloan and Tomie Jean (Roberts) B. BS in edn., U. Ga., 1975; MEd, Valdosta State Coll., 1977, cert., 1977-79. Tchr. Lowndes County Sch. System, Valdosta, Ga., 1975-89; assessment specialist Coastal Plains Regional Assessment Ctr., Valdosta, Ga., 1989-90; tchr. Lowndes County Sch. System, Lake Park, Ga., 1990—2007, Valwood Sch, 2007—. Bd. dirs. Ga. Partnership for Excellence in Edn., Atlanta, 1994-97; tchr. adv. com. Southeastern Regional Vision for Edn., Greensboro, N.C., 1994-2003; editorial bd. Tchr. Learning Resource Ctr., Dayton, Ohio, 1994-99; scholarship selection com. U.S. Space & Rocket Ctr., Huntsville, Ala., 1994-97. Bd. dirs. Valdosta Jr. Svc. League, 1985—, Valdosta State U. Alumni Bd., 1993-2002, U. Ga. Booster Club, 1982-2000. Named Ga. Tchr. of Yr. Ga. Dept. Edn., 1994; recipient Milken Nat. Educator award Milken Family Found., 1994, Presdl. award, excellence in math. tchg., 2000, Valdosta State U. Disting. Alumna, 2000, Ga. Christa McAuliffe fellowship, 2001. Mem. Ga Assn. Educators (profl. devel. chmn. 1975-94), Profl. Assn. Ga. Educators, Ga. Coun. Tchrs. Math., Nat. State Tchrs. of Yr. Orgn., Kappa Delta Pi, Phi Delta Kappa. Baptist. Avocations: reading, walking, volunteer work. Home: 3288 Jordon Way Valdosta GA 31605

BLATT, GREGORY R., broadcast executive, lawyer; b. 1968; BA, Colgate U., Hamilton, NY, 1990; JD, Columbia Law Sch., NYC, 1995. Assoc. Wachtell, Lipton, Rosen & Katz, 1995—97, Grubman, Indursky & Schindler PC, 1997—99; sr. v.p. Martha Stewart Living Omnimedia, Inc., 1999, sec., 1999, gen. counsel, 1999—2003, exec. v.p., 1999—2001; exec. v.p., Bus. Affairs Martha Stewart Living Omnimedia Inc., 2001—03; sr. v.p., gen. counsel & sec. IAC/InterActiveCorp., 2003—09, exec. v.p., 2005—09, CEO Match.com, 2009—10, CEO, 2010—. Bd. dirs. HSN Interactive LLC, 2008—, Interval Leisure Group, Inc., 2008—, Meetic S.A., 2009—, IAC/InterActiveCorp., 2010—, Ticketmaster Entertainment, Inc. Office: IAC InterActiveCorp 555 W 18th St New York NY 10011 also: HSN Interactive LLC Bd Directors 1 HSN Dr Saint Petersburg FL 33729-0001 Office Phone: 212-314-7300, 727-872-1000. E-mail: gregory.blatt@hsn.net.

BLATT, SOLOMON, JR., federal judge; b. Sumter, SC, Aug. 20, 1921; s. Solomon and Ethel (Green) B.; m. Carolyn Gayden, Sept. 12, 1942; children: Gregory, Sheryl Blatt Hooper, Brian. AB, U. S.C., 1941, LLB, 1946, LLD (hon.), 1987, The Citadel, 1990, Coll. of Charleston, 1992. Bar: S.C., 1946. Ptnr. Blatt & Fales, Barnwell, S.C., 1946-71; judge US Dist. Ct. SC, Charleston, 1971-86, chief judge, 1986-90, sr. judge, 1990—. Office: US Dist Ct SC PO Box 835 Charleston SC 29402-0835 Personal E-mail: Badputton7@hotmail.com.

BLATTBERG, ROBERT CHARLES, marketing consultant, business educator; b. Chgo., Oct. 19, 1942; s. Abbey and Helen (Weil) B.; m. Rebecca Donelson BA, Northwestern U., 1964; MS, Carnegie-Mellon U., 1966, PhD, 1971. Prof. U. Chgo. Sch. Bus., 1969—80; Charles H. Kellstadt prof. mktg. Grad. Sch. Bus. U. Chgo., 1980—91; Polk Bros. disting. prof. retailing Kellogg Grad. Sch. Mgmt. Northwestern U., 1991—2008; pres. Robert C. Blattberg Cons., Chgo., 1986—. Bd. dirs. First Tenn. Bank Corp., SuperMedia Inc. (formerly Idearc Inc.), 2010—. Author: The Economy in Transition, 1975, Sales Promotions, 1990; contbr. numerous articles to profl. jours. Bd. dirs. Chgo. Food Depository, 1985— Mem. Am. Mktg. Assn. Office: SuperMedia Inc Bd Directors 2200 W Airfield Dr Dallas TX 75261 Office Phone: 972-453-7000. Office Fax: 972-453-3969. Business E-Mail: robert.blattberg@supermedia.com.

BLAUL, FRANK, finance company executive; Attended in Bus. & Computer Sci., Frostburg State U. V.p., global govt. sales & mktg. Clear Cube, Austin, Tex.; worked GTSI, Ruben H. Donnelley Corp.; various positions in sales, mktg. & bus. devel. Electronic Data Sys., 1997—2006, Internat. Bus. Machines Corp., 1997—2006, ViON Corp., 1997—2006; exec. v.p., sales & mktg. Emtec, Inc., 2007; sr. v.p., pub. sector svcs. Equifax, Inc., 2009—. Mem. Armed Forces Electronics Assn., Industry Adv. Coun., Potomac Officers Club, The Northern Va. Tech. Coun. Office: Equifax Inc 1550 Peachtree St NW Atlanta GA 30309 Office Phone: 404-885-8000. Office Fax: 404-885-8682. Business E-Mail: frank.blaul@equifax.com.

BLAYDES, SOPHIA BOYATZIES, English language educator; b. Rochester, NY, Oct. 16, 1933; d. James George and Helene (Bougdanos) Boyatzies; m. David Fairchild Blaydes, June 4, 1961; children: Stephanie Anne, Jeffrey Glenn. BA, U. Rochester, 1955; MA, Ind. U., 1958, PhD, 1962. Teaching asst. English Ind. U., 1955-62; instr. to asst. prof. Am. Thought and Lang. dept. Mich. State U., 1962-65; instr. to prof. English W.Va. U., Morgantown, 1966-99, prof. emerita, 1990—, chair faculty senate, 1990-91, coord. program for sr. and retired faculty, 1994—2007, chair faculty senate standing com. of retired faculty, 2007—, mem. faculty senate representing ret. faculty, 2007—, mem. athletic dept. liaison ret. faculty, 2010—; pres. Carolinas Symposium for British Studies, 1990-91. Co-dir. Lit. Discussion Group for Sr. Citizens, 1978—; mem. faculty Elderhostel, 1985, 87, 88, 90, 94; mem. ctrl. exec. com. Folger Inst., 1992-99; rep. to adv. coun. to bd. trustees, 1993-99; state del. to the 1995 White House Conf. on Aging; bd. trustees Univ. Sys., 1998-99, Women in Sci. and Health, Robert C. Byrd Health Scis. Ctr., 2004-10, ret. faculty rep. athletic dept., 2009-, ret. faculty liaison with WVU found. 2012-. Author: Christopher Smart as a Poet of His Time: A Re-Appraisal, 1966, Sir William Davenant, 1981, (with others) Sir William Davenant: An Annotated Bibliography, 1986; editor: (with others) Selected Papers from the W.Va. Shakespeare and Renaissance Association, 1976, The Literary Discussion Group, 1982, 85; contbr. chpts. to books, articles to profl. jours., encys., dictionaries, bibliographies. Mem. cen. exec. com. Folger Inst., 1992-99. Recipient Disting. Manuscript award Mich. State U., 1965, Gerontology Ctr. award, 1983; named Disting. West Virginian, W.Va. Gov., 1995; grantee W.Va. Found., 1973, W.Va. Humanities, 1980; W.Va. U. Senate rsch. grantee, 1984, 89; Folger fellow, 1981, Folger grantee, 1988, 91; recipient Sigma Tau Delta Outstanding Tchg. award, 1996, induction W.Va. U. Order of Vandalia, 2007. Mem. Am. Soc. 18th Century Studies, MLA, W.Va. Assn. Coll. English Tchrs. (pres. 1977), Shakespeare and Renaissance Soc. W.Va. (chmn. 1978, 84), Carolinas Symposium on Brit. Studies (chair program 1989, pres. 1990, conf. chair 1993). Home: 652 Bellaire Dr Morgantown WV 26505-2421

BLAYLOCK, JAMES CARL, clergyman, librarian; b. Guntown, Miss., Jan. 27, 1938; s. Carl Houston and Katie Lee (Pugh) Blaylock; m. Jo Ann Enlow, May 3, 1962; children: Jacquelyn Ann, John Thomas. AA, Southeastern Bapt. Coll., 1962; BTh, N.Am. Theol. Sem., 1964; BA, U. Tex., Tyler, 1976; MRE, Bapt. Missionary Sem., 1977; MSLS, Tex A&M U., 1980; DD, Bapt. Mission Sem., 2011. Ordained to ministry Bapt. Ch., 1962. Pastor Mt. Pleasant Ch., Bedias, Tex., 1962—64, Buena Vista Ch., Timpson, Tex., 1964—70, 1st Bapt. Ch., Maydelle, Tex., 1970—86, Corinth Ch., Jacksonville, Tex., 1986—; asst. dir. Bapt. News Svc., Jacksonville, 1969—88, dir., 1988—99; asst. editor Directory and Handbook of Bapt. Missionary Assn., Jacksonville, 1969—88, editor, 1988—99; libr. Bapt. Missionary Assn. Theol. Sem., Jacksonville, 1972—. Editor: Mt. Olive Evangel, 1965—70; author: History of 1st Baptist Church Maydelle, Texas, 1966, Buena Vista Baptist Church, 1986, Glimpses from the Past, 2003. Mem.: ALA, Tex. Libr. Assn., Am. Theol. Libr. Assn. Office: Bapt Missionary Assn Theol Sem 1530 E Pine St Jacksonville TX 75766-5407 Home: 1105 Robs Rd Jacksonville TX 75766-3527 Home Phone: 903-586-4594; Office Phone: 903-586-2501.

BLAZE, DOUG A., dean, law educator; BS magna cum laude, Dickinson Coll., Carlisle, Pa., 1976; JD summa cum laude, Georgetown U. Law Ctr., Washington, 1984. Geologist U. SD State Geol. Survey, Vermillion, 1976—78; dir. resource mgmt. Appalachian Trail Conf., Harpers Ferry, W.Va., 1978—81; law fellow Georgetown U. Law Ctr., 1982—83; assoc. Fennemore Craig, Phoenix, 1984—86; prof. law, dir. cmty. legal services clin. program Ariz. State U. Coll. Law, Tempe, 1986—93; prof. law U. Tenn. Coll. Law, Knoxville, 1993—, dir. clin. programs, 1993—2006, Art Stolnitz disting. prof., 2002—, dir. Ctr. Advocacy and Dispute Resolution, 2004—06, Art Stolnitz and Elvin E. Overton disting. prof., 2004—, interim assoc. dean academic affairs, 2006—08, dean, 2008—. Contbr. articles to profl. jours. Mem.: ABA, Knoxville Bar Assn., Tenn. Bar Assn. Office: University of Tennessee College of Law 1505 W Cumberland Ave Room 278 Knoxville TN 37996-1810 Office Phone: 865-974-2521. Business E-Mail: blaze@utk.edu.*

BLAZER, DAN GERMAN, II, psychiatrist, epidemiologist; b. Nashville, Feb. 23, 1944; s. Dan German and Mary Elizabeth (Owsley) Blazer; m. Sherrill Walls, Aug. 19, 1966; children: Dan German III, Natasha Leigh. BA, Vanderbilt U., 1965; MD, U. Tenn., 1969; MPH, U. N.C., 1979, PhD, 1980. Diplomate Am. Bd. Psychiatry and Neurology, cert. geriatric psychiatry. Fellow Montefiore Hosp. and Med. Ctr., NYC, 1975—76; asst. prof., assoc. prof., then prof. psychiatry Duke U. Med. Ctr., Durham, NC, 1976—, J.P. Gibbons prof. psychiatry, 1990—, interim chair of psychiatry, 1990—93, prof. cmty. and family medicine, 1986—; dean of med. edn. Duke U., 1992—99. Chair, bd. dirs. Am. Geriat. Soc., NY, 1983; bd. dirs. ret. persons svcs. Am. Assn. Ret. Persons, Alexandria, Va., 1987—92; pres. Psychiat. Rsch. Soc., Salt Lake City, 1988; chmn. epidemiology and disease control study sect. NIH, Bethesda, Md., 1988—. Author: Life is Worth Living, 1987, Depression in Late Life, 1993, Freud vs. God, 1998, Introduction to Clinical Research in Psychiatry, 1998, The Age of Melancholy, 2005. Recipient Rsch. Career Devel. award, NIMH, 1977, Alex Haley award, East Tenn. Bapt. Hosp., Knoxville, 1986, Disting. Svc. award, U. N.C. Sch. Pub. Health, Chapel Hill, 1989, Milo Leavitt award, Am. Geriat. Soc., 1997, Rema LaPouse award, APHA, 2001, Disting. Faculty award, Duke U. Med. Ctr., 2005; named Outstanding Alumnus, U. Tenn. Coll. Medicine, 2003. Fellow: Am. Assn. Geriatric Psychiatry (disting. life) (pres. 2005—06), Am. Psychopathol. Assn., Gerontol. Soc. Am. (Kleemeier award 2005), Am. Psychiat. Assn. (Oscar Pfister award 2008), Am. Coll. Psychiatrists (Geriatric Psychiatry Rsch. award 2003); mem.: Inst. Medicine NAS, 1995. Democrat. Avocations: hiking, reading. Office: Duke U Med Ctr PO Box 3003 Durham NC 27715-3003 Office Phone: 919-684-4128. Business E-Mail: blaze001@mc.duke.edu.

BLAZINA, JANICE FAY, pathologist; d. Joseph and Cordelia Evelyn B. BS, Youngstown State U., 1975; MD, Ohio State U., 1978. Diplomate Am. Bd. Pathology. Resident in anat. and clin. pathology U. Ala. Med. Ctr., Birmingham, 1978-82; assoc. pathologist various hosps., Bryan, Tex., 1982-83, High Plains Bapt. Hosp., Amarillo, Tex., 1983-84; fellow in blood banking Baylor U. Med. Ctr., Dallas, 1984-85; asst. prof. dept. pathology Ohio State U., Columbus, 1985-93, asst. prof. Sch. Allied Med. Professions, 1987-93. Asst. dir. transfusion svc. Ohio State U. Hosp., 1985-89, assoc. dir., 1989-90, dir., 1990-93, med. dir. histocompatibility, paternity, apheresis and phlebotomy svcs., 1987-93, divsn. med. tech., 1987-93; asst. med. dir.

Carter Blood Ctr., Ft. Worth, 1993-95, med. dir., 1995-96. Contbr. articles to profl. publs. Bremer Found. grantee, 1987. Mem. AMA, Am. Soc. Apheresis, Am. Soc. Histocompatibility and Immunogenetics, Am. Assn. Blood Banks (insp. 1987—), Ohio Assn. Blood Banks (trustee 1990-93, sec. 1992-93), Assn. Women Sci. Cen. Ohio (v.p. 1989-90, pres. 1990-91), Nat. Alliance Mentally Ill Tarrant County (sec. 2003-05, treas, 2006-07). Mem. Church of Christ. Avocation: gardening. Personal E-mail: bbpathd1@yahoo.com.

BLAZZARD, NORSE NOVAR, lawyer; b. St. Johns, Ariz., July 8, 1937; s. Howard N. and Viola (Greer) B.; m. Mary Elizabeth Jecker, June 15, 1958; children: Howard Norse, Mary Catherine; m. Judith A. Hasenauer, July 2, 1977. AB, Stanford U., 1959; JD, U. Calif., Hastings, 1962. Bar: Calif. 1963, US Dist. Ct. (no. dist.) Calif. 1966, Conn. 1974, US Dist. Ct. Conn. 1975, US Supreme Ct. 1975, US Ct. Appeals (DC cir.) 1977, US Ct. Appeals (2d cir.) 1978, Fla. 1993; CLU. Counsel Calif. Western Life Ins. Co., Sacramento, 1966-70; sr. v.p., gen. counsel NARE Life Svc. Co., Palo Alto, Calif., 1970-74; pres. Blazzard & Hasenauer, P.C., Westport, Conn., 1974—. Chmn. ins. products task force Fin. Products Stds. Bd., 1988-89; chmn. Nat. Assn. Variable Annuities, 1994. Bd. govs. Norwalk Symphony, 1979. Capt. JAGC, U.S. Army, 1962-66. Inductee Variable Annuity Hall of Fame, 1998. Mem. FBA, Calif. Bar Assn., Fla. Bar Assn., D.C. Bar Assn. Republican. Mem. Lds Ch. Business E-Mail: norse.blazzard@blazzardlaw.com.

BLEAKNEY, DANA A., family practice physician; married; 1 child. MD, U. Tex., 1999. Diplomate Am. Bd. Family Practice. Intern family practice Baylor Univ. Med. Ctr., Garland, Tex., resident family practice, hosp. affiliation includes. Mem.: AMA, Tex. Med. Assn., Am. Acad. of Family Physicians. Avocations: walking, yoga, cooking. Office: Family Medical Center at Baylor 3600 Gaston Ave Barnett Tower Ste 1109 Dallas TX 75246 Office Phone: 214-820-8300. Office Fax: 214-820-8313.

BLECHSCHMIDT, EDWARD ALLAN, healthcare industry executive; b. Harvey, Ill., Aug. 4, 1952; s. Edward and Virginia Blechschmidt; m. Kathleen Nash, Sept. 22, 1984; children: Jenica, Michael, Jeffrey. BSBA, Ariz. State U., 1973; MBA, San Diego State U., 1977. Various positions, including contr., bus. info. systems group, v.p. fin. and adminstrn. Burroughs Corp., 1983—86, pres., bus. forms divsn. Rochester, NY, 1986; pres., Memorex media products group Unisys Corp., Santa Clara, Calif., 1986—87, v.p., spl. projects office of pres. Blue Bell, Pa., 1987; v.p., pres. Unisys Japan Ltd., 1987—90; pres., Pacific Asia Ams. divsn. Unisys Corp., Blue Bell, 1990—95, corp. sr. v.p., Pacific Asia Ams. divsn., 1994—96, pres., US and Can. divsn., 1995—96, CFO, 1996; pres., CEO Siemens Nixdorf Americas, 1996—98, Siemens Pyramid Tech., 1996—98; pres., COO Olsten Corp., Melville, 1998—99, bd. dirs., CEO, 1999—2000; chmn., CEO, pres. Gentiva Health Services, Inc., 2000—02; CEO Novelis, Inc., 2006—07. Bd. dirs. Nihon Unisys Ltd., Oki Unisys Kaisha, Tata Unisys Ltd., India, Aiesec U.S., Lionbridge Technologies, Inc., 2003—, Neoforma, Inc., 2003—06, HealthSouth Corp., 2004—, Columbia Labs., Inc, 2004—; former bd. dirs. Option Care, Inc., 2005; bd. dirs. VWR Funding, Inc., 2007—, Diamond Foods, Inc., 2008—. Office: HealthSouth Corp 3660 Grandview Pkwy Ste 200 Birmingham AL 35243 Office Phone: 205-967-7116. Office Fax: 205-969-3543. Business E-Mail: edward.blechschmidt@healthsouth.com.

BLEDSOE, CECILE H., state legislator; b. June 26, 1944; m. James Bledsoe; children: Greg, Sam, Tricia. BA, Univ. Ga. Asst. mgr., v.p. surgical clin.; mem. Dist. 95 Ark. House of Reps., 1999—2004; mem. Dist. 8 Ark. State Senate, 2009—. Bd. dir. Agy. on Aging; mem. Rogers Civil Svc. Commn. Republican. Baptist. Office: 709 Sky Mountain Dr Rogers AR 72757 Business E-Mail: bledsoec@arkleg.state.ar.us.

BLEICHER, MICHAEL NATHANIEL, mathematics professor; b. Cleve., Oct. 2, 1935; s. David B. and Rachel (Faigin) B.; m. Betty Isack, June 4, 1957; children: Helene, Laurence, Benjamin; m. E. Jeanne Smith, Dec. 31, 1980; stepchildren: Kathryn, Robert, Zaka. BS, Calif. Inst. Tech., 1957; MS, Tulane U., 1959, PhD, 1961; doctorate degree, U. Warsaw, 1961. Teaching and research asst. Tulane U., 1957-60; fellow U. Warsaw, Poland, 1960-61; NSF fellow U. Calif., Berkeley, 1961-62; mem. faculty U. Wis., Madison, 1962—93, dept. chmn., 1972-74, prof. dept. math., 1968—93, prof. emeritus, 1993—; chief adv. and liaison U.S. Dept. Energy, 1979-81. Assigned to coll. preparatory studies Inst. of Tech. Mara, Shah Alam, Selangor, Malaysia, 1987-90; founder Wis. Emerging Scholars program; chair Dept. Math. Sci. Clark Atlanta U., 1998-05.; prof. Kennesaw State U., 2005—06, prof. chair, Eternal U., 2011; disting. vis. prof. Indian Inst. Tech., Hyderabad, 2011, Indore, 2013. Author: (with A. Beck, D. Crowe) Excursions into Mathematics, 1968; co-translator: A. Mathematical Guidebook for Technologists and Engineers, 1962. Mem. Dem. Nat. Com., 1972-79; chmn. Dem. Party Wis., 1977-79. Recipient Regents award of distinction, U. Wis., 1973. Mem. Am. Math. Soc., Math. Assn. Am., Polish Math. Soc. Democrat. Jewish. Achievements include research on length and size of denominators of Egyptian fractions, least length subdivision of a region into cells of a given area. Home: 540 Calaveras Dr Atlanta GA 30350-4002 Office Phone: 404-403-2888. Business E-Mail: bleicher@math.wisc.edu.

BLESZINSKI, CLIFF (CLIFFORD MICHAEL BLESZINSKI), game designer; b. North Andover, Mass., Feb. 12, 1975; With Epic Games, Inc., Cary, NC, 1994—, now lead designer. Creator video games The Palace of Deceit: Dragon's Plight, 1992, Dare to Dream Volume One: In a Darkened Room, 1993, Jazz Jackrabbit, 1994, Unreal, 1998, Unreal Tournament series, Unreal Championship series, Unreal II: The Awakening, 2003, Brothers in Arms: Road to Hill 30, 2005, Gears of War, 2006, Gears of War 2, 2008. Co-recipient Rave award-Games, WIRED Mag., 2007; named one of The 100 Agents of Change, Rolling Stone mag., 2009.

BLEUER, T. CORY, software company executive; BS in Bus. Adminstrn. Acctg., Ind. U. CPA. Mgr. PricewaterhouseCoopers, LLP; corp. contr. HNC Software Inc. (acquired by Fair Isaac Corp.), 2000—02; dir. corp. fin. and acctg. Fair Isaac Corp., 2002—04, corp. contr., 2004—05; v.p., corp. contr. Captiva Software Corp. (acquired by EMC Corp.), 2005; v.p., contr. Captiva Software Group EMC Corp., 2005—06; v.p., contr., chief acctg. officer BMC Software, Inc., 2006—. Office: BMC Software Inc 2101 CityWest Blvd Houston TX 77042 Office Phone: 713-918-8800. Office Fax: 713-918-8000. Personal E-mail: cory_bleuer@bmc.com.

BLEVINS, CHARLES RUSSELL, publishing executive; b. Kittaning, Pa., Apr. 6, 1942; s. Clarence Ray and Elizabeth Sarah (Warren) B.; m. Gale Watkins Crittenden, Dec. 16, 1967; children: Charles Jr., Rush. BS, Ind. U., 1964. Asst. prodn. exec. Wall St. Jour., Cleve., D.C. and Princeton, 1964-71, Gannett Co. Inc., El Paso Agy., El Paso, Tex., 1971-76; prodn. exec. Rockford Newspapers, Rockland, Ill., 1976-77; corp. prodn. dir. Gannett Corp. Hdqrs., Rochester, N.Y., 1977-79, v.p., prodn. Arlington, Va., 1979-89; CEO Blevins Harding Group, Vienna, Va., 1989-98; pres., CEO Chuck Blevins & Assocs., Vienna, 1998—. Speaker European Printing Conf., Newspaper Quality Meeting Conf.; chmn. Conf. Quality-Newspaper Assn., Conf. Research & Engring. Council, Chgo., Rsch. and Engring. Coun. Com. Graphic Arts Techs. Standards Unit Loading. Creator quality standards, operating procedures USA Today, 1981-86. Judge RIT/USA Today Quality Cup for Individuals and Teams, 1992-2000; chmn. long range planning com. Vanderbilt Country Club. Mem. Am. Newspaper Pub. Assn. (tech. com. 1985-89, officer internat. newspaper group 1989—), Rsch. and Engring. Coun. of Graphic Arts (v.p. 1985-94), Rochester Inst. Tech. Coun., W.Va. Inst. Tech. Adv. Coun., Inca Fiej Rsch. Assn. (press com. 1984-89), Vanderbilt Country Club (chmn. long range planning com.), Hillside Cox Mountain Condominium Assn.(pres., bd. dir.) Office: Chuck Blevins & Assocs 8396 Northhampton Naples FL 34120 Office Phone: 239-595-3840. Business E-Mail: crblevins@aol.com.

BLEVINS, HARRY BURNS, state legislator; b. Elk Park, NC, Aug. 22, 1935; m. Margie White; children: Harry Jr., Marsha B., Danny, Linda. Former mem. Chesapeake Crime Line; state del. Dist. 78 Va., 1999—2002; mem. Transp. Com., Fin. Com., Counties Cities & Towns Com., Chesapeake & Tributaries Com., 1999—; state senator Dist. 14 Va., 2003—. Named Outstanding Sec. Sch. Prin., Va., Chesapeake First Citizen; named to Hall of Fame, Va. HS League. Mem.: Chesapeake C. of C. (former bd. dir.), Chesapeake Rotary Club (former pres.), Chesapeake Civitan Club (former pres.). Republican. Baptist. Mailing: Senate of Virginia PO Box 396 Richmond VA 23218 also: PO Box 16207 Chesapeake VA 23328 Office Phone: 804-698-7514, 757-546-2435. Business E-Mail: district14@sov.state.va.us. E-mail: hbblevins@erols.com.

BLEVINS, WALTER, state legislator; b. Paintsville, Ky., Mar. 29, 1950; s. Walter Clayton Blevins and Dorothy C. Beculhimer B.; m. Carla Elaine Justice, 1982; children: Kristen Lauren, Lacy Morgan, Leah Kathryn. Former chmn. Water Mgmt. Task Force; Ky. state rep. Dist. 71, 1982—92; house rep. Ky.; mem. econ. devel. & tourism, local govt., labor & industry state govt. & transp. coms. State Senate, Ky.; dentist, 1978—; Ky. state senator Dist. 27, 1992—. Recipient Outstanding Consumer Advisor award, 1986; named Commonwealth Commr., Ky. Jaycees, 1982, Health Edn. Legislator of Yr., 1988. Mem.: Mason, Shriner, America Legion, Morehead Optimist (pres. 1982—83), Morehead Jaycees (pres. 1982—83). Democrat. Bapt. Mailing: 777 Broadway West Liberty KY 41472-1023 Office: Capitol Annex Rm 251 Frankfort KY 40601 Home Phone: 606-743-1200; Office Phone: 606-743-1212, 502-564-8011 793. Office Fax: 606-743-1214. Business E-Mail: walter.blevins@lrc.state.ky.us.

BLEVINS, WILLIAM EDWARD, management consultant; b. Boissevan, Va., Oct. 18, 1927; s. Howard Muncey and Elsie Jane (Wire) B.; m. Mary Hester Jenkins, Aug. 25, 1951 (dec.); children— Jeffrey Alexander (dec.), Jennifer Lynn, Bradley Edward. AB, Marshall Coll., 1951; MPA, CCNY, 1960. Personnel mgr. Equitable Life, NYC, 1951-66; asst. v.p., dir. mgmt. devel. Nat. Bank Detroit, 1966-69, v.p., dir. personnel, 1969-74, sr. v.p., dir. personnel, 1974-91; exec. v.p., dir. human resources NBD Bancorp, Inc., Detroit, 1980-92; pres. WEB Communications Co., Detroit, 1993—2004, adv. com. mem. Trustee Bon Secour Hosp., Grosse Pointe, Mich., 1975-84; chmn. St. John Sr. Cmty., 1995-2004, St. John Health Sr. Svcs., 2000-04; bd. dirs. Oxford Inst., 1987-89, Holy Cross Hosp., 1996-98, Mich. Diabetes Assn., 1982-86, Mich. Soc. for Mental Health, 1984-87, Lancaster Heart and Stroke Found. 2006--2008, chmn. 2008-2012, Susquehanna Assn. Blind and Visually Impared, 2005-11; corp. adv. bd. Am. Heart Assn., 1995-98; trustee Frances Rhodes, M.D. Meml. Found., 1999-2004; personnel com. Lancaster County Coun. Chs., 2005-08. Recipient Outstanding Alumnus award Marshall U., 1976, Hall of Fame award Lambda Chi Alpha, 1996. Mem. Am. Bankers Assn. (bd. dirs. 1974-75), Am. Inst. Banking (bd. dirs., bd. regents, chmn. 1983-90), Am. Soc. Employers (bd. dirs. 1970-94, treas. 1970-90, vice chmn. 1991-92, chmn. 1992-94), Alpha Bank Pers Group (founder, chmn. 1972-74, 86), Mich. Pers. Indsl. Rels. Group (chmn. 1980-92), Bank Adminstr. Inst. (human resources commn. 1983-88), Detroit Athletic Club, Country Club Detroit. Republican. Office: 3241 Tradition Cir Mount Pleasant SC 29466 Office Phone: 843-881-3614. Personal E-mail: webmjb@comcast.net.

BLINN, MARK A., manufacturing executive; b. 1962; m. Heather Blinn. BA, Southern Meth. U., 1984, JD, 1987, MBA, 1998. CFA. Atty. Smith, Barshop, Stoffer & Millsap; v.p. Comml. Capital Funding, Inc.; divsn. mgr. corporate strategy & strategic devel. EDS, Dallas; sr. v.p., treas. FIRSTPLUS Financial Group, PL; v.p., chief acctg. officer, mng. dir. corporate finance Centex Corp., 2000—02; v.p. treasury & tax Kinko's, Dallas, 2002—03, sr. v.p., CFO, 2003—04; CFO Flowserve Corp., Irving, Utah, 2004—09, pres., CEO, 2009—. Bd. dirs. Flowserve Corp., 2009—. Mem. investment com. Dallas Symphony Found.; bd. mem. Dallas Ctr. for Nonprofit Mgmt., The Leukemia and Lymphona Soc. Mem.: State Bar Assn. Tex. Office: Flowserve Corp Ste 2300 5215 N O'Connor Blvd Irving TX 75039

BLISK, BRENDA PACK, financial consultant; b. McMinnville, Tenn., May 29, 1948; d. James A. and Wanda Sunelle (Campbell) Pack; m. Alan Flowers, Sept. 7, (div. 1982); 1 child, Jason Alan; m. David L. Blisk, May 7, 1983; 1 child, Laura Marie. Student, Tenn. Tech. U., 1986-88, Vanderbilt U., 1988-89. CFP. Dept. mgr. Hudson-Belk, Raleigh, N.C., 1976-83, The Denver, 1983-84; realtor cons. Billings & Co., Denver, 1984-85; fin. advisor Prudential Bache Securities, Dayton, Ohio, 1985-88, Washington, 1988-90; co-founder, CEP Blisk Fin. Group, McLean, Va., 1987—; fin. cons. Shearson Lehman Bros., McLean, Va., 1990—97; investor advisor rep. Legacy Advisors, LLC (now Spire Wealth Mgmt., LLC), 1997—. Recipient Charlie Eisemann Clients First award, 2007; named one of The Top 100 Women Fin. Advisors, Barron's, 2007, 2008. Republican. Lutheran. Avocations: reading, gardening, travel. Office: Spire Wealth Mgmt 7918 Jones Branch Dr Ste 750 Mc Lean VA 22102

BLISS, ROBERT HARMS, lawyer; b. Paris, Tex., Nov. 20, 1940; s. Jack Edward and Ruth Eugenia (Harms) B.; m. Juliee Dixie Fuselier, Dec. 29, 1964; 1 child, Katherine Elaine. BA, U. Colo., 1964; JD, U. Tex., 1967. Bar: Tex. 1967; cert. civil trial specialist, mediator-arbitrator, spl. master. Since practiced in, Dallas; assoc. Johnson, Bromberg, Leeds & Riggs, 1967-72; ptnr. Bliss, Danner & Bishop, 1972-74; individual practice, 1974; pres. Bliss & Hughes, P.C., Dallas, 1978-88; pvt. practice Robert Harms Bliss P.C., 1988-98; ptnr. Glast, Phillips & Murray, PC, 1998—2002; pvt. practice, 2002—. Mem. faculty CLE series So. Meth. U. Sch. Law, Dallas, 1989, 92, 94, 97, 98, 99, 2000, mem. faculty The Leasing Inst., 2004-05, course dir., 2007, 2009, 2011, 2012; mem. faculty Mortgage Lending Inst., U. Tex. Sch. Law, 1994, 97, 98, 99, 2000, mem. faculty advanced real estate drafting course, 1995, 2000-04, course dir., 2002. Contbr. articles to profl. jours. Bd. dirs. Dallas Symphony Orch., Dallas Symphony Orch. Guild, Dallas Classic Guitar Soc.; mem. Gov.'s Task Force on Immigration, 1983-84, Tex. Real Estate Commn., 1983-87; adv. bd. Tex. Real Estate Rsch. Ctr., Tex. A&M U., 1985-87; ch. atty. Episcopal Diocese Dallas, 1997-2009. Recipient Disting. Tex. Real Estate Atty. Lifetime Achievement award, Real Estate Probate and Trust Law Sect. State Bar Tex., 2009. Fellow Tex. Bar Found. (sustaining life); mem. Am. Coll. Real Estate Lawyers, State Bar Tex. (mem. faculty advanced real estate law 1985, 92-93, 95, 97, 99, 2000, 2002, 2009-10, 2013, course dir., 2014, mem. faculty advanced real estate strategies course 1997, 2007, 09-10, past chair real estate, probate and trust sect., named Disting. Tex. Real Estate Atty. Lifetime Achievement award, Real Estate Probate & Trust Law Sect. 2009), Dallas Bar Assn. (past chmn. real property sect.), Assn. Atty.-Mediators (pres. North Tex. chpt.), Acad. Ct. Appointed Masters, U. Tex. Tchg. Quiz-Masters Assn., Mc. Donald Obs. U. Tex. (bd. visitors), Phi Delta Phi. Home: 29 Ashton Ct Dallas TX 75230-1977 Office: PO Box 12825 Dallas TX 75225 Home Phone: 972-726-0605; Office Phone: 214-521-0190.

BLISSIT, DOUG W., air transportation executive; b. Atlanta; BA in Economics, Wake Forest U., Winston-Salem, NC, 1981. With computer svcs. divsn. Delta Air Lines, Inc., 1981—84, various network planning positions, 1984—98, v.p. network planning, 1998—2004, v.p. network planning & scheduling, 2004—05, v.p. pub. affairs, 2005—, v.p. corp. real estate, 2006—, v.p. Delta AirElite, 2007—08. Bd. advisors. Metro Atlanta C. of C., Atlanta History Ctr.; bd. dirs. Ga. C. of C. Office: Delta Air Lines Inc PO Box 20706 Atlanta GA 30320 Office Phone: 404-715-2600. Office Fax: 404-715-5042. Business E-Mail: doug.blissit@delta.com.

BLOCH, RALPH JAY, professional association executive, marketing consultant; b. NYC, Sept. 21, 1942; s. Alexander and Catherine (La Bue) B.; m. Patricia Ann Cassone, Aug. 18, 1963 (div.); 1 child, Marci Suzanne; m. Helen Lightstone, June 19, 1988. BS, UCLA, 1965. Sales rep. Lowell Wood Co., LA, 1967-68; mgr. Home Furniture, LA, 1968-72, co-owner, gen. mgr., 1972-78; pres. Concepts III, Inc., Greenville, S.C., 1978-79; from western exec. v.p. to mktg. v.p. Nat. Home Furnishings Assn., 1979-83; pres., owner The Access Group, Inc., Chgo., 1984-99, Ralph J. Bloch & Assocs., Inc., Chgo., 1999—. Mem. Chgo. Soc. Assn. Execs., Am. Soc. Assn. Execs. Avocations: backpacking, hiking, sailing, cooking. Office: Ralph J 7132 Dornough Ln Bradenton FL 34202-4004

BLOCK, NELSON RICHARD, lawyer; b. San Antonio, Mar. 24, 1951; s. Norman and Ethel (Poliakoff) B. BA, Johns Hopkins U., 1973; JD, U. Tex., 1976. Bar: Tex. 1976. Law clk. 14th Ct. Appeals, Houston, 1976-77; assoc. Sheinfeld, Maley & Kay, P.C., Houston, 1977-83, shareholder, 1983-2001, Winstead PC, Houston, 2001—. Spkr. in field, 1991. Author: Commercial Law Manual: Ch. 40 Contractural Subordination, A Thing of the Spirit: The Life of E. Urner Goodman (BSA 2000); co-editor and author: Scouting Frontiers: Youth and the Scout Movement's First Century. Bd. dirs. legal counsel Sam Houston Area coun. Boy Scouts America, 1984—, mng. trustee The Green Bar Bill Hillcourt Trust; mem. Baden-Powell World Fellowship; co-chair "Scouting: A Centennial History Symposium," Johns Hopkins U., 2008; mem. Nat. Order Arrow Com., BSA, 2010, Nat. Jewish Com. Scouting, 2010. Recipient Boy Scouts Am.: Eagle Scout, Disting. Eagle Scout, Silver Beaver, Silver Antelope, Order Arrow Disting. Svc. award, UK Scout Assn.; Founder Gilwell Fellow. Mem. ABA, Tex. Bar Assn. (chmn. uniform comml. code com. 1982-84), Houston Bar Assn., Tex. Bar Found., Selden Soc. (state corr. 1978—), Houston Comml. Fin. Lawyers Forum (founder, chmn.), Am. Coll. Comml. Fin. Lawyers. (former regent) Avocations: camping, hiking, reading, history, sketching. Office: Winstead PC 1100 JPMorgan Chase Tower 600 Travis St Houston TX 77002 Business E-Mail: nblock@winstead.com.

BLOCK, NORMAN LOUIS, oncologist, educator; b. NYC, Aug. 31, 1938; s. Abraham Harold and Rose (Bodatsky) B.; m. Carolyn Lee Peck, May 12, 1967; children: Joseph, David, Adam, Nathaniel, Jessica. BA, NYU, 1959, MD, 1963. Diplomate Am. Bd. Urology. Intern Baylor U. Med. Ctr., Dallas, 1963-64, resident in surgery, 1966—67; resident in urology NYU Med. Ctr., NYC, 1967—71; fellow in urologic oncology Meml. Sloan Kettering Cancer Ctr., NYC, 1971-72; attending physician Miami VA Med. Ctr., 1972-96, Jackson Meml. Hosp., Fla., 1972—; chief urology VA Med. Ctr., 1975—85; assoc. prof. urology U. Miami, 1976-82, prof. urology, 1982—, prof. biomed. engring., 1982—, L. Austin Weeks prof., 1982—, prof. oncology, 1985—, prof. pathology, 2009—. Editl. reviewer 6 jours. Contbr. numerous articles to profl. jours., including Cancer Jour. Urology, Jour. Urology, Jour. Surg. Oncology. Capt. U.S. Army, 1964-66. Recipient numerous awards, fellowships, lectureships; named Best Doctor in Am. Super Doctors, South Fla., Best Oncologist. Mem. AMA, ACS, AAAS, Internat. Urology Soc., Internat. Soc. for Artificial Organs, Am. Fertility Soc., Am. Urol. Assn. (Southeastern sect.), Am. Soc. for Artificial Internal Organs, Am. Assn. Lab. Animal Sci. (Fla. divsn.), Southeastern Cancer Rsch. Assn., Soc. Surg. Oncology, Soc. Univ. Urologists, Southeastern Coop. Oncology Group, Soc. Govt. Svc. Urologists, So. Med. Assn., Confedn. Am. Urologists, Soc. Urologic Oncology, Colombian Urol. Soc., Fla. Med. Assn., Fla. Urologic Assn., Greater Miami Urologic Soc., Dade County Med. Soc., Bellevue Urologic Alumni Assn. Republican. Jewish. Achievements include holder six patents; research in new treatment for prostate cancer; development of new diagnostic test for bladder cancer; applied a new model for prostate cancer in animals; development of an artificial bladder, ureter, urethra sphincter. Avocation: wildlife photography. Office: U Miami Sch Medicine Dept Pathology R-5 PO Box 16960 Miami FL 33101-6960 Business E-Mail: nblock@med.miami.edu.

BLOCK, RYAN, consumer electronics media startup company executive, technology journalist and critic; Attended, New Sch. U., NYC. Programming dir. AOL; mem. mgmt. team Weblogs, Inc.; part-time reporter Engadget, 2004—05, reporter, 2005, editor-in-chief, 2007—08, editor-in-chief emeritus, 2008; co-host weekly podcast; co-founder gdgt, 2009—. Founding editor, contbr. Joystiq, quoted by BBC, Business Week, Chicago Tribune, New York Times, The Guardian, The Times and The Wall Street Journal, guest appearances BBC, CNN, NPR, PRI, G4, and Leo Laporte's This Week in Tech., regular panelist The Engadget Show. Named one of Paper Mag.'s Beautiful People, 2006, Top 25 Web Celebs, Forbes mag., 2007. Personal E-mail: contact@ryanblock.com.

BLODGETT, J. KEVIN, lawyer, consulting firm executive; BA in Polit. Sci., Tex. A&M U., 1993; JD, U. Houston, 1997. Bar: Tex. 1997. Assoc. Baker Botts LLP, Houston, 1997—2000; asst. gen. counsel, corporate counsel Dynegy Inc., 2000—03, group gen. counsel, corp. fin. & securities, corp. sec., 2003—04, sr. v.p., human resources, 2004—05; gen. counsel, exec. v.p. adminstrn. Dynegy, Inc., 2005—11; mng. dir Huron Consulting Group, Inc., Houston, 2011—. Bd. mem. Junior Achievement. Recipient Corporate Sector Achievement award, U. Houston Law Alumni Assn., 2007, Award for Outstanding Corporate Counsel, Houston Bus. Journal, 2008, Magna Stella Award for Best Large Legal Dept. General Counsel, General Counsel Forum, 2009; named a Tex. Super Lawyer Rising Star, 2007, 2008, 2009. Mem.: Houston Young Lawyers Assn., Houston Bar Assn., Tex. Bar Assn. Office: Huron Consulting Group Inc 2929 Allen Pkwy 27th Fl Houston TX 77019 Office Phone: 713-222-5980. Office Fax: 713-222-5901. E-mail: kblodgett@huronconsultinggroup.com.

BLODGETT, LYNN R., information technology executive; Grad., Brigham Young U., Utah Tech. Coll. Co-founder Unibase Technologies, Inc. (acquired by Affiliated Computer Svcs., Inc.), 1985; pres. ACS Bus. Process Solutions, Inc., 1990—99; exec. v.p., group pres., comml. solutions Affiliated Computer Svcs., Inc. (ACS) (acquired by

Xerox Corp.), Dallas, 1999—2005, v.p., COO, 2005—06, bd. dirs., 2005—, pres., CEO, 2006—; corp. exec. v.p. Xerox Corp., 2010—. Office: Affiliated Computer Services Inc 2828 N Haskell Dallas TX 75204 Office Phone: 214-841-6111. Business E-Mail: lynn.blodgett@acs-inc.com.

BLODGETT, TOM, information technology executive; Attended, Brigham Young U. Worked, sales and mktg. team Siemens Nixdorf Info. Sys.; led Adminstrn. and Customer Care Svc. Delivery Unit Affiliated Computer Services, Inc. (ACS) (acquired by Xerox Corp.), sr. mng. dir., profl. svcs. bus., Comml. Solutions Group, v.p., ops. Sandy, Utah, 1992—98, pres., mng. dir., Bus. Process Solutions Group, 1998—2007, exec v.p., group pres., Bus. Process Solutions, 2007—09, COO, comml. ops., 2009—; pres. ACS Data Entry Inc. Office: Affiliated Computer Svcs Inc 2828 N Haskell Ave Dallas TX 75204 Office Phone: 214-841-6111. Office Fax: 214-823-9369. Business E-Mail: Tom.Blodgett@acs-inc.com.

BLOEM, JAMES H., managed health care executive; BA, Calvin Coll., Grand Rapids, Mich.; MBA, Harvard U., Mass.; JD, Vanderbilt U. Sch. Law, Nashville. CPA. Ptnr. Law, Weathers and Richardson; various sr. mgmt. positions including CFO and gen. counsel Herman Miller, Inc.; pres. personal care divsn. Perrigo Co., 1998—99; pvt. fin. and bus. cons., 1999—2001; sr. v.p., CFO, treas. Humana, Inc., Louisville, 2001—; chmn. ResCare, Inc., 2011—. Bd. dir. Rotech Healthcare Inc., NeighborCare Inc., Warner Chilcott, ResCare, Inc., 2007—. Office: Humana Inc 500 W Main St Louisville KY 40202

BLOISE, MICHAEL, chef; b. Va. 1 child. Grad., Johnson & Wales U., 1998. Chef 1220, Tides Hotel, Miami; exec. sous chef Gaucho Room, Miami, Wish, Miami, 2001—02, exec. chef, 2003—, Tantra, Miami, 2002. Named one of Southern Fla.'s Rising Stars, StarChefs.com, 2008. Office: Wish Hotel of South Beach 801 Collins Ave Miami Beach FL 33139

BLONDY, STEVEN M., corporate financial executive; BA magna cum laude, U. Mich., MBA. Sr. v.p., CFO Grundy Worldwide; exec. v.p., CFO Poppe Tyson; sr. v.p., corp. devel. Young & Rubicam, Inc.; investment banker Chase Manhattan, 1988—94; dir., investment banking Merrill Lynch, 1988—94; sr. v.p. Dex One Corp. (formerly R.H. Donnelley Corp.), 2002—06, CFO, 2002—, exec. v.p., 2006—. Recipient Triangle Top CFO, Bus. Leader Media, 2010. Office: Dex One Corp 1001 Winstead Dr Cary NC 27513 Office Phone: 919-297-1600. Office Fax: 919-297-1285. Business E-Mail: steven.blondy@dexone.com.

BLOOM, MICHAEL K., retail executive; b. 1960; Mgr. Fla. Divsn. Shopper's Drug Mart; mgr. People's Drug Stores, Va.; joined CVS Caremark Corp., Woonsocket, RI, 1991, category mgr., v.p. consumer healthcare, sr. v.p. merchandising, 2003—09, sr. v.p. merchandising and supply chain, 2009—10, exec. v.p. merchandising, supply chain, mktg. and advertising, 2010—11; pres., COO Family Dollar Stores, Inc., Charlotte, NC, 2011—. Office: Family Dollar Stores, Inc 10401 Monroe Rd PO Box 1017 Charlotte NC 28201-1017 Office Phone: 704-847-6961. Office Fax: 704-847-5534.

BLOOMER, JOSEPH ROBERT, physician, educator; b. Indpls., Sept. 29, 1940; s. Betty Glore Bloomer; m. Anne Vaughn Macintyre, June 26, 1965; children: Jennifer Anne Jeans, Jeffrey Neil. BS, MIT, Cambridge, 1962; MD, Western Res. Med. Sch., Cleve., 1966. Diplomate Am. Bd. Internal Medicine. Assoc. prof. medicine Yale U Sch. Medicine, New Haven, 1976—79; prof. medicine U. Minn., Mpls., 1979—95, dir. gastroenterology, 1983—95; prof. medicine and genetics, dir. liver ctr. U. Ala., Birmingham, 1995—. Investigator Howard Hughes Med. Inst., 1974—79; bd. govs. Am Bd. Internal Medicine; lectr. in field. Pres. Am. Assn. for Study of Liver Diseases, 1998—99. Lt. comdr. USPHS, 1968—71. Recipient Merit award, NIH, 1994—2002. Mem.: Am. Assn. Study Liver Diseases (Disting. Svc. award 2009), Am. Clin. Climatol. Assn. (Theodore Woodward award 1999), Assn. Am. Physicians. Office: University Ala 1720 2nd Ave 1720 2nd Ave S BDB 398 Birmingham AL 35294*

BLOOMFIELD, LOUIS AUB, physicist, researcher; b. Boston, Oct. 11, 1956; s. Daniel Kermit and Frances (Aub) B.; m. Karen Shatkin, Aug. 28, 1983; children: Elana, Aaron. BA in Physics, Amherst Coll., 1979; PhD in Physics, Stanford U., 1983. Postdoctoral physicist AT&T Bell Labs., Murray Hill, NJ, 1983-85; asst. prof. U. Va., Charlottesville, Va., 1985-91, assoc. prof., 1991-96, prof, 1996—. Author: (Book) How Things Work: The Physics of Everyday Life, 2010, How Everything Works: Making Physics Out of the Ordinary, 2008. Recipient Alumni Tchr. award U. Va., 1992, Pres.'s Rsch. prize, 1994; named Presdl. Young Investigator NSF, 1986, Young Investigator Office of Naval Rsch., 1988, Va. Outstanding Faculty award, 1998; Alfred P. Sloan fellow, 1989. Fellow Am. Phys. Soc. (Apker award 1980, Pegram medal 2001). Jewish. Office: University Va 382 McCormick Rd Charlottesville VA 22904 Office Fax: 434-924-4576. Business E-Mail: lab3e@virginia.edu. E-mail: bloomfield@virginia.edu.

BLOOMFIELD, MICHAEL J., astronaut; b. Flint, Mich., Mar. 16, 1959; s. Rodger and Maxine Bloomfield; m. Lori Miller; 2 children. BSc in Engring. Mechanics, USAF Acad., 1981; MSc in Engring. Mgmt., Old Dominion U., 1993. Commd. 2d lt. USAF, 1981, advanced through grades to lt. col., various assignments, 1981—83; assigned to Holloman AFB, N.Mex., 1983—85, Bitgurg Air Base, Germany, 1987—89, Langley AFB, Va., 1989—92, Edwards AFB, Calif., 1992—95; astronaut NASA, Houston, 1995—. Astronaut Space Shuttle Atlantis, 1997, Space Shuttle Endeavour, 2000. Capt. USAF Acad. Football Team, 1980. Decorated Meritorious Svc. medal USAF, Commendation medal, Aerial Achievement medal. Mem.: Air Force Assn., USAF Acad. Assn. Graduates. Avocations: reading, gardening, all sports, family. Office: Astronaut Office CB NASA Johnson Space Center Houston TX 77058 Business E-Mail: Michael.Bloomfield@nasa.gov.

BLOSSMAN, ALFRED RHODY, JR., banker; b. Madisonville, La., Oct. 21, 1931; s. Alfred Rhody and Mabel (Perrin) Blossman; m. Royanne Elaire Hurd, Dec. 28, 1957; children: Alfred Rhody III, Roy Edward, Gary Bennett, Christopher Hurd, David Quintin, John Eric. AB in Gen. Bus., La. State U., 1955. Pres. Blossman Hydratane Gas, Inc., Covington, La., 1963—67; chmn. First Nat. Corp. First Nat. Bank, Covington, 1968—84, pres., CEO, 1980—84, Parish Nat. Bank, Covington, 1986—2008, also chmn. bd. dirs.; mem. bd. dir. First Bank and Trust, NOLA. Capt. USAF, 1956—58. Mem.: Phi Delta Theta. Republican. Roman Catholic. Home: 10 Blossman Ln Covington LA 70433-4707 also: 503 Norriego Dr Destin FL 32541 E-mail: fredb@abita.com.

BLOUNT, BEN B., JR., administration and finance executive; Attended, Auburn U., Ga. So. Coll., Ga. State U. From indsl. engr. to corp. v.p. Oxford Industries, Atlanta, 1961-82; pres. Kayser Roth Apparel, Atlanta, 1982-86; exec. v.p. Oxford Industries, Inc., Atlanta, 1986—. Office: Oxford Industries Inc 222 Piedmont Ave NE Atlanta GA 30308-3391

BLOUNT, BENROE WAYNE, physician, department chairman; b. Augusta, Ga., Feb. 8, 1950; s. Benroe and Loreen Moellering B.; m. Merry Teresa Van Dam, Feb. 14, 1974 Dec. May 8, 1974); m. Young Hui Cho, Nov. 23, 1976; children: Teresa Jana, Daniel Paul. BS, US Mil. Acad., 1972; MA, U. Calif., Berkeley, 1975; MD, U. Miami, 1983; MPH, U. Wash., Seattle, 1990. Commd. 2d lt. U.S. Army, 1972, advanced through grades to lt. col., 1990, ret., 1994; intern, resident DeWitt Army Hosp., Alexandria, Va., 1983-86; divsn. chief, dept. vice-chair Emory Sch. Medicine, Atlanta, 1994-99, 2004—13; chair dept. family medicine U. Tenn., Memphis, 1999—2002; prof. Emory U., 2002—; chief family practice Kaiser, S.E., 2002—04; market med. dir. JenCare, 2013—. Contbr. articles to profl. jours., chpts. to books. Recipient Chmn. of Joint Chief of Staff award for Excellence in Mil. Medicine, 1993; named one of Outstanding Young Men of Am., Nat. Jaycees, Top Family Physicians in US, 2007—, 2013, Best Dr. in Am., 2000, 2001, 2002. Independent. Business E-Mail: benreb@jencaremed.com.

BLOUNT, DANIEL J., lumber company executive; BS, U. Ill., Urbana; MBA, St. Ambrose U. Sr. v.p. fin. Montgomery Elevator Co., 1989-97; v.p. Riverwood Holding, Inc., Atlanta, 1998; sr. v.p., CFO and treas. Riverwood Holding Inc., Atlanta, 1999—2003; sr. v.p., CFO, integration Graphic Packaging Holding Corp., Atlanta, 2003—. Office: Graphic Packaging Holding Corp 814 Livingston Ct Marietta GA 30067 Office Phone: 770-644-3000. Office Fax: 770-644-2962. Business E-Mail: daniel.blount@graphicpkg.com.

BLOUNT, DAVID, state legislator; b. Apr. 19, 1967; m. Katherine Drayne; children: Susanna, Charles. Attended, Davidson coll., U. Va. Comm. dir. Miss. sec. of State's Office; mem. Dist. 29 Miss. State Senate, 2008—. Democrat. Episcopal. Home: 1305 St Mary St Jackson MS 39202 Office: PO Box 1018 Jackson MS 39215 Office Phone: 601-359-3232. E-mail: dblount@senate.ms.gov.

BLOWERS, HELENE, library and information scientist; m. David Blowers; children: Kathryn, Jessica. BS, U. Wis., Stevens Pt., 1986. Cert. project mgmt. trainer. Staff trainer Pub. Libr. Charlotte & Mecklenburg County, NC, 1996—98, web dir. NC, 1998—, pub. svcs. tech. dir. NC. Co-author: Weaving a Library Web: A Guide to Developing Children's Websites, 2004; developer Learning 2.0 online discovery program, co-developer (websites) Readersclub.org, 1998 (Nat. Assn. Counties Achievement award, 2001), BookHive.org, 1999 (Assn. Libr. Svc. to Children Notable award, 2000, Nat. Assn. Counties Achievement award, 2000, Learning Mag. Teacher's Choice award, 2001, StudyWeb Academic Excellence award for Literature), StoryPlace.org, 2000 (USA Today Edn. Best Bet Web Site, Lightspan StudyWeb Academic Excellence award, Bonus.com Editor's Choice award), Brarydog.net. Named one of the Movers & Shakers, Libr. Jour., 2007. Office: Pub Libr Charlotte & Mecklenburg County 310 N Tryon St Charlotte NC 28202 E-mail: hblowers@plcmc.org, helene.blowers@gmail.com.

BLUE, DANIEL T., state legislator; b. Lumberton, NC, Apr. 18, 1949; s. Daniel T. Blue and Allene Morris B.; m. Edna Earle Smith; children: Daniel III, Kanika, Dhamian. Former chmn. small bus. com.; former mem. Appropriations, Judiciary I & Ways & Means Coms., Appropriation Subcom. on Transp. & Select Com. on Tobacco Settlement; former assoc. Sanford, Adams, Mccullough & Beard, Raleigh; state rep. Dist. 21 NC, 1980—2002; chmn. Black Caucus, 1984—89; mgn. ptnr. Thigpen, Blue, Stephens & Fellers, Raleigh, 1976; NC state rep. Dist. 33, 2006—09; state senator Dist. 14, 2009—. Recipient Outstanding Legislator award, NC Assn.Trial Lawyers, 1985, NC Black Lawyers Assn., 1985, Friend of Working People award, NC AFL-CIO, 1991, Adam Clayton Powell Leadership award, Congl. Black Caucus, 1991, Nat. Alumni of Yr. award, 4-H, 1992. Mem.: America, NC & Wake County Bar Assns., Kiwanis, Raleigh-Wake Citizen's Assn. Democrat. Presbyn. Mailing: PO Box 1730 Raleigh NC 27602 Office: NC Senate 300 N Salisbury St Rm 1117 Raleigh NC 27603-5925 Office Phone: 919-733-5752. E-mail: Dan.Blue@ncleg.net.

BLUE, JOHN RONALD (J. RONALD BLUE), evangelical mission executive; b. Milw., Sept. 4, 1935; s. Earl R. and Wretha J. (Teater) B.; m. Elizabeth F. Wood, Sept. 7, 1962; children: Elisa, Laurie, David. BA, U. Nebr., 1957; cert. contact lens fitter, Ohio State U., 1960; ThM, Dallas Theol. Sem., 1965; PhD, U. Tex., Arlington, 1983. Contact lens fitter Ohio State U., Columbus, 1960-61; field dir. Ctrl. Am. Mission, 1965—75; dept. chmn. Dallas Theol. Sem., 1975-92; pres. CAM Internat., Dallas, 1992-2000; coord. Spanish-lang. Doctor Minsitries program Dallas Theol. Seminary, 2001—. Mem. adv. bd. Proclamation, Inc., Dallas, 1998—, Christar, Reading, Pa., 1999—; mem. edit. bd. Evang. Missions Quar. Contbg. author: Walvoord: A Tribute, 1982, Bible Knowledge Commentary, 1983, 85, Essays in Honor of J.D. Pentecost, 1986, Devotions for Kindred Spirits, 1995, Basic Theology Applied, 1996; author: Evangelism and Missions, 2001; editor Una Vida Transformada, 2007. Lt. USN, 1957-59. Mem. Pi Epsilon Pi, Theta Xi. Republican. Avocation: travel. Home: 3504 Halifax Dr Arlington TX 76013-1909 Office: Dallas Theol Seminary 3909 Swiss Ave Dallas TX 75204 Business E-Mail: rblue@dts.edu.

BLUE, MONTE LYNN, college president; b. Ft. Worth, Feb. 25, 1945; s. Bert Leonard and Mary Lee (Cooper) B.; m. Sheryl Doris O'Connor, July 1, 1966; children: Michelle Denea, Laura Lynn. BA, North Tex. State U., 1967, MA, 1972; EdD, U. Houston, 1979. Illustrator Gen. Dynamics, Ft. Worth, 1967-71; instr. advt. art, Cen. Campus San Jacinto Jr. Coll., Pasadena, Tex., 1971-74, dist. dir., instr. media, 1975-79, dean student services, South Campus, 1979-81, dean student services, Cen. Campus, 1981-83, pres., 1983—. Bd. dirs. Deer Park Ednl. Found., 1996-07; bd. dirs. Southeast Econ. Devel. Coun., 1995—, chmn. bd., 1997-98; moderator Bd. of Southmore Med. Ctr.; consumer credit counselor svc. bd. dirs., 1999-2000; spkr. numerous presentations to various comty., civic and profl. groups. Contbr. articles to profl. jours.; speaker numerous presentations to various community, civic and profl. groups. Vice chmn. bd. dirs. San Jacinto YMCA, Pasadena, 1986-87, chmn., 1987-88. Named Outstanding Alumni, Ft. Worth Ind. Sch. Dist., 1984. Mem.: Tex. Pub. Cmty. Jr. Coll. Assn., Assn. Tex. Colls. and Univs., Nat. Orgn. on Legal Problems in Edn., Am. Assn. Higher Edn., Am. Assn. Cmty. Jr. Colls., LaPorte/Bayshore C. of C. (bd. dirs. 1987—89, pres. 1989), Rotary (local pres. 1986—87), Phi Theta Kappa (hon. mem. Mu Omicron Chpt., Hall of Honor 1985). Republican. Baptist. Avocation: painting. Office: San Jacinto Coll Cen 8060 Spencer Hwy Pasadena TX 77505

BLUE, ROBERT M., lawyer, energy executive; BA, Univ. Va., 1989, MBA; JD, Yale Univ., 1994. Bar: Va. 1994. Ptnr. Hogan & Hartson; counselor & policy dir. for Va. Gov. Mark Warner, 2002—05; mng. dir. state affairs & pub. policy to v.p. state & federal affairs Dominion Resources, Inc., Richmond, Va., 2005—08, sr. v.p. pub. policy & corp. communications, 2008—10, sr. v.p. law, pub. policy & environment, 2010—11, 2011—14; pres. Dominion Virginia Power, 2014—. Bd. dir. Va. C. of C., Maymont Found., American Civil War Ctr., Va. Commonwealth Univ. Health System Authority, Virginiaforever, Virginia21, Va. Found. for the Humanities, Va. Healthcare Found., Sports Backers. Office: Dominion Resources 100 Tredegar St Richmond VA 23219 Office Phone: 804-771-4517.

BLUEDORN, TODD M., manufacturing executive; BS with distinction, U.S. Mil. Acad., West Point, 1985; MBA with distinction, Harvard Univ., 1992. Engagement mgr. McKinsey & Co.; dir. strategic planning United Technologies, 1995—96, v.p. N.Am. truck & trailer, Carrier Transicold, 1996—98, v.p. SE Asia, Carrier Corp., pres. Hamilton Sundstrand Indsl., pres. N.Am. HVAC, Carrier Corp., 2002—04, pres. Otis Elevator, 2004—07; CEO Lennox International, Inc., Richardson, Tex., 2007—12, chmn., CEO, 2012—. Ranger, combat engr. US Army, 1985—90. Office: Lennox Internat 2140 Lake Park Blvd Richardson TX 75080

BLUESTEIN, DANIEL A., family practice physician; MD, U. Mass., Worcester, 1975. Diplomate Am. Bd. Family Practice, Am. Bd. Family Practice-geriatric medicine. Intern Univ. of Iowa Hosps. & Clinics, 1979—81; resident family medicine Univ. Md. Affil Hosp., Baltimore, Md., 1975—78; fellow family medicine Univ. of Iowa, 1979—81; hosp. affiliation includes Sentara Norfolk Gen. Hosp.; assoc. prof. family medicine Eastern Va. Med. Sch. Office: EVMS Ghent Family Practice 825 Fairfax Ave Norfolk VA 23507 Office Phone: 757-446-7360. Office Fax: 757-622-2651.

BLUESTEIN, EDWIN A., JR., lawyer; b. Hearne, Tex., Oct. 16, 1930; s. Edwin A. and Frances Grace (Ely) B.; m. Marsha Kay Meredith, Dec. 21, 1957; children: Boyd, Leslie. BBA, U. Tex., 1952, JD, 1958. Bar: Tex. 1957, U.S. Ct. Appeals (5th cir.) 1960, U.S. Dist. Ct. (so. dist.)Tex. 1959, U.S. Dist. Ct. (ea. dist.)Tex. 1965, U.S. Supreme Ct. 1967, U.S. Ct. Appeals (11th cir.) 1982. Law clk. U.S. Dist. Ct., Houston, 1958-59; assoc. Fulbright & Jaworski, Houston, 1959-65, participating atty., 1965-71, ptnr., 1971-97, head admirality dept., 1984-93, sr. ptnr., 1990-97, of counsel, 1998—. Mem. permanent adv. bd. Tulane Admiralty Law Inst., New Orleans, 1983-2001; mem. planning com. Houston Marine Ins. Seminar, 1970-76; lectr. profl. seminars Assoc. editor: American Maritime Cases; contbr. articles to profl. jours. Mem. Tex. Coastal Mgmt. Adv. Com., Austin, 1975—78, Planning & Zoning Commn., Morgan's Point, Tex., 2008—; chair Morgan's Point Beach Preservation Restoration Assn., 2001—03; bd. dirs. Barbour's Cut Seafarers Ctr., 1992—2004, Houston Internat. Seafarers Ctr., 1993—2003. With US Army, 1952—54. Recipient Yachtsman of Yr. award Houston Yacht Club, 1978, Outstanding Alumnus award Atlanta, 2006; Eagle Scout, Boy Scouts Am., 1944. Mem. Tex. Bar Found., Maritime Law Assn. U.S. (mem. exec. com. 1980-83), Houston Maritime Arbitrators Assn. (dir., sec.-treas. 1999-2005), Houston Mariners Club (pres. 1970), Southeastern Admiralty Law Inst. (dir. 1983-85, Houston C. of C. (chmn. ports and waterways com. 1978-79), Propeller Club U.S., Theta Xi (chpt. pres. 1952). Clubs: Houston Yacht (commodore 1979-80). Methodist. Home: 603 Bayridge Rd Morgan's Point TX 77571-3512 Office: Fulbright & Jaworski 1301 Mckinney St Houston TX 77010-3031

BLUM, ALAN M., family practice physician, educator; MD, Emory U.; BA in English Lit., Amherst Coll. Resident family medicine Univ. of Miami, 1976—78, fellow family medicine, 1978—79; prof. faculty of medicine Baylor Coll. of Medicine, 1987—99; prof. family medicine Univ. of Ala., dir. ctr. for the study of tobacco and soc. Dir. DOC (Doctors Ought to Care), 1977—2002. Author of 100 articles in peer-reviewed jours.; editor: (jour.) New York State Journal of Medicine, Medical Journal of Australia. Recipient Surgeon General's Medallion, National Public Health award, Am. Acad. of Family Physicians, Gleitsman Foundation award, McGovern Achievement award, Am. Sch. Health Assn., Washington Monthly Journalism award. Office: University Medical Center 850 5th Ave E Tuscaloosa AL 35401 Office Phone: 205-348-2886.

BLUM, EDWARD HOWARD, investment banker; s. Irwin Ellis and Esther (Wolff) Blum; m. Marlene H. Witman, June 8, 1965; children: Daniel Joseph, Matthew Alan. BS, Carnegie-Mellon U., 1961; MS, Princeton U., 1963, PhD, 1965. Asst. prof. Princeton (N.J.) U., 1965-67; sr. scientist, project leader, dir. rsch., v.p. Rand Corp., NYC and Santa Monica, Calif., 1967-76; dir. advanced tech. U.S. Dept. Energy, Washington, 1976-80; v.p., exec. dir. Merrill Lynch Capital Markets, Washington and NYC, 1980-86; pres., CEO, vice-chmn. bd. Md. Nat. Investment Banking Co., Greenbelt, 1986-89; pres., CEO Blum & Co., Inc., Reston, Va., 1989—; CEO OG Co., Inc., Houston, 1991—2005. Mem. adv. bd. Solar Energy Rsch. Inst., Denver, 1983—90; bd. dirs. Fed. Pvt. Sector Partnership; bd. dirs., audit com. chair Periphonics Corp., 1995—99; chmn. bd. Sterlington Resources & Sterlington Resources Gold Ltd., 2011—. Editor: Jour. Urban Analysis, 1970—77; contbr. articles to profl. jours. Chmn. Fairfax (Va.) County Info. Tech. Adv. Com., 2000—; trustee U. Detroit, 1970—79. Recipient award, Inst. Mgmt. Sci., 1974, Ops. Rsch. award, NATO, 1976. Home: 2417 Luckett Ave Vienna VA 22180-6818 Office: Blum & Co Inc 2417 Luckett Ave Vienna VA 22180 Office Phone: 703-860-3736. Business E-Mail: eblum@blumandco.com.

BLUM, JACOB JOSEPH, physiologist, educator; b. Bklyn., Oct. 3, 1926; s. Paul and Anna (Brown) B.; m. Ruth Marsey, June 3, 1960; children: Mark, Douglas, Lisa, Laura. BA, NYU, 1947; MS, U. Chgo., 1950, PhD, 1952. Mem. staff Naval Med. Rsch. Inst., Bethesda, Md., 1953-56; chief biophysics sect. gerontology br. NIH, Balt., 1958-62; prof. physiology Duke U., Durham, NC, 1962—, James B. Duke prof., 1980-97, James B. Duke prof. emeritus, 1997—. With AUS, 1945-46. Merck postdoctoral fellow, 1952, Guggenheim fellow, 1969, Fogarty sr. internat. fellow, 1992. Mem. Am. Physiol. Soc., Soc. Protozoologists (pres. 1991). Home: 16 Stoneridge Cir Durham NC 27705 Office Phone: 919-684-6937. Business E-Mail: j.blum@cellbio.duke.edu.

BLUM, JONATHAN D., restaurant company executive, lawyer; Undergraduate, George Washington U.; JD, Western New England Coll. V.p., pub. affairs Taco Bell, 1993—97; sr. v.p., chief pub. affairs officer Yum! Brands, Inc. (formerly TRICON Global Restaurants, Inc.), 1997—. Bd. dirs. Kindred Healthcare, Inc., 2008—. Office: YUM! Brands Inc 1441 Gardiner Ln Louisville KY 40213 Office Phone: 502-847-8300. Office Fax: 502-874-8790. Business E-Mail: jonathan.blum@yum.com.

BLUM, KRISTEN E., apparel executive; b. 1965; BA, Ohio State U. Sr. mgr. KPMG/Bearing Point; dir. supply chain solutions & internat. retail Apple Computer Inc., Cupertino, 2002—06; sr. v.p., chief info. officer Abercrombie & Fitch Co., 2008—10; sr. v.p., chief info. officer Enterprise Transformation PepsiCo, 2010—12; exec. v.p., chief tech. officer J.C. Penney Co., Inc., Plano, Tex., 2012—. Mem. Big Brothers Big Sisters North dallas. Mem.: Nat. Retail Fedn. CIO Coun. Office: JC Penney Co Inc 6501 Legacy Dr Plano TX 75024 Office Phone: 972-431-1000. Office Fax: 972-431-1362.

BLUM, TERRY CHRISTINE, management educator, former dean; b. Bklyn., Dec. 25, 1953; m. Paul M. Roman; children: Luke, Faith Elisabeth. BA in Sociology with honors, Bklyn. Coll., 1976; MA, Columbia U., 1978, MPhil, 1980, PhD, 1982. Asst. prof. Dept. Sociology, adj. prof. biostatistics and epidemiology Sch. Pub. Health and Tropical Medicine, Tulane U., 1982—86; asst. prof. orgnl. behavior and human resource mgmt. Ga. Inst. Tech. Coll. Mgmt., 1986—88, assoc. prof., 1988—92, prof., 1992—99, dir. Ctr. Entrepreneurship and New Venture Devel., 1996—2000, Tedd Munchak chair in entrepreneurship, 1999—, dean, 1999—2006, dir. Inst. Leadership and Entrepreneurship, 2006—. Mem. Prevention and Epidemiology Initial Review Group Nat. Inst. Alcohol Abuse and Alcoholism, 1988—92; mem. cmty. prevention and control study section NIH, 1997—2000. Grantee, Nat. Inst. Alcohol Abuse and Alcoholism, 1982, 1983, 1987, 1988, Nat. Inst. Drug Abuse, 1991, 1999, NIH, 1993, 1994, Coleman Found., 1999; special opportunities grant, Whitaker Found., 1998. Office: Inst Leadership and Entrepreneurship Ga Inst Tech 800 W Peachtree St NW Atlanta GA 30332-0520 Office Phone: 404-894-4924. Office Fax: 404-894-1517. Business E-Mail: terry.blum@ile.gatech.edu.

BLUMBERG, EDWARD ROBERT, lawyer; b. Phila., Feb. 15, 1951; BA in Psychology, U. Ga., 1972; JD, Coll. William and Mary, 1975. Bar: Fla., 1975, U.S. Dist. Ct. Fla. 1975, U.S. Ct. Appeals, 1975, U.S. Supreme Ct. 1979. Assoc. Knight, Peters, Hoeveler & Pickle, Miami, Fla., 1976-77; ptnr. Deutsch & Blumberg, P.A., Miami, 1978—. Adj. prof. U. Miami Sch. Paralegal Studies; mem. adv. coun. legal studies Fla. Internat. U., 2004—. Author: Proof of Negligence, Mathew Bender Florida Torts, 1988. Mem. ABA (ho. of dels. 1996-2002), ATLA, Dade County Bar Assn., Fla. State Bar (bd. govs., pres.-elect 1996-97, pres. 1997-98), Acad. Fla. Trial Lawyers, Nat. Bd. Trial Advocacy (cert. civil trial adv.), Fla. Bar Found. (bd. dirs. 1996-99, bd. govs. 1996-99), Bankers Club (chmn. bd. govs. 2003-05). Office: Deutsch & Blumberg PA 100 Biscayne Blvd Fl 28 Miami FL 33132-2304 Home Phone: 305-667-4884; Office Phone: 305-358-6329.

BLUMBERG, HENRY MICHAEL, internist, infectious disease, educator; MD, Vanderbilt Univ., 1983. Diplomate Am. Bd. Internal Medicine, 1986, Am. Bd. Internal Medicine-infectious disease, 2000. Resident internal medicine Crawford-Long Hosp., Atlanta, 1978—88, Emory Univ. Hosp., Atlanta, 1984—86, fellow infectious disease, 1988—92, physician; prof. medicine Emory Univ.; physician Grady Meml. Hosp. Office: Emory University 49 Jesse Hill Jr Dr Atlanta GA 30303 Office Phone: 404-616-6145.

BLUMBERG, MICHAEL ZANGWILL, allergist; b. Phila., July 29, 1945; s. Jerome Blumberg and Vivian Rose (Liebman) Steiger; m. Barbara Sue Gurman, June 9, 1973; children: Jessica Lynn, Jason Mark. AB, Brandeis U., 1967; MD, Jefferson Med. Coll., 1971; MSHA., Va. Commonwealty U., 1998. Diplomate Am Bd Pediatrics, Am Bd Allergy and Immunology. Intern, resident N.Y. Hosp., Cornell U. Med. Ctr., 1971-73; fellow in allergy and immunology Nat. Jewish Hosp.-U. Colo. Med. Ctr., 1973-75; chief allergy sect. major Scott Air Force Base, Ill., 1975-77; physician-ptnr. Va. Adult and Pediat. Allergy and Asthma, Richmond, 1977—, mng. ptnr., 1998—; assoc. clin. prof. pediatrics Med. Coll. Va., Richmond, 1977—2002, 2000—; chief of allergy Children's Hosp. of Richmond, 1987-2000; ptnr. Clin. Rsch., Richmond, 1998—. Med advisor Sanofi-Aventis, Astra Zeneca, Glaxo SmithKline, Merck; mem. editl. bd. Annals Allergy, Asthma and Immunology, 2010—. Contbr. articles and abstracts to profl jours; contbg. editor: Review in Allergy, 1978; mem ed bd: Jour Asthma, 1996—. Mem exec comt, pres, bd dirs, chmn Beth Shalom Home Va, Richmond, 1987—95; bd. dirs. Allergy Ptnrs., 1977—2010; vice chmn. bd. medicine Adv. Com. on Respiratory Care, 2010—; bd. dirs Jewish Community Ctr, Richmond, 1984—87, Va. Endowment Jewish Aged, 2009; bd dirs endowment fund, mem budget comt Jewish Fedn; pres. Richmond Jewish Found., 2002. Recipient Maimonides award, Jewish Fedn. Richmond, 2006, Chased award, Rudlin Torah Acad. Co. Svc., 2009; named one of Best Drs. in America, 2007—10, 2011—13. Fellow: Am Acad Pediatrics, Col Chest Physicians, Am Col Allergy, Asthma and Immunology (pub. rels.com.); mem.: Allergy Ptnrs., Allergy and Asthma Soc. Va. (pres. 2002—04), Am Thoracic Soc, Am Acad Allergy, Asthma and Immunology (managed care com.), Am Col Allergy Sports Med (practice standards com. 1994—95), Friends of Brandeis Athletics, Masons, Phi Kappa Phi. Jewish. Avocations: exercise, history. Office: Allergy Partners-Richmond Hub 7605 Forest Ave Ste 103 Richmond VA 23229-4936 Home: 149 W Square Court Richmond VA 23238 Office Phone: 804-288-0055, 804-285-8465. Personal E-mail: mshadoc@comcast.net. Business E-Mail: mblumberg@allergypartners.com.

BLUMENCRANZ, PETER WILLIAM, surgeon; b. NYC, Mar. 8, 1946; s. Bernard and Evelyn (Guttman) B.; m. Ann Frances Garfes, June 6, 1970; children: Brett, Lisa, Jennifer, Deborah, Todd. BA, U. Pa., 1966; MD, Cornell U., 1970. Diplomate Am. Bd. Surgery. Resident in surgery N.Y. Hosp.-Cornell U. Med. Ctr., NYC, 1970-76; fellow in surg. oncology Meml. Hosp.-Sloan Kettering Cancer Ctr., NYC, 1976-77; surgeon Diagnostic Clinic, Largo, Fla., 1977-79, Fla. Surg. Assocs., Clearwater, Fla., 1980-95; pres. Surg. Assocs. West Fla., Clearwater, 1995—2009; med. dir. Comprehensive Breast Care Ctr. Tampa Bay, 2009—. Bd. dirs. Morton Plant Mease Health Care; trustee Morton Plant Hosp., Clearwater, Fla., 1992—98, 2005—11; med. dir. Moffitt Morton Plant Cancer Care, Tampa, Fla., 2001—. Trustee Shorecrest Prep. Sch., St. Petersburg, Fla., 1982-88; bd. dirs. Pinellas unit Am. Cancer Soc., 2006-09. Lt. comdr. USN, 1972-74. Fellow Soc. Surg. Oncology, Am. Coll. Surgeons, Southeastern Surg. Congress; mem. Am. Soc. Breast Diseases, Fla. Soc. Clinical Oncology, Am. Soc. Clin. Oncology, Am. Soc. Breast Surgeons, State Fla. Cancer Coun., Fla. Soc. Gen. Surgeons. (bd. dirs. 1998—2011). Avocations: tennis, running. Office Phone: 727-462-2131.

BLUMENSHINE, W. MARK, oil and gas company executive; B in Petroleum Land Mgmt. & Adminstrn., U. Tex. Gen. mgr. land Dominion Exploration & Prodn. Co.; mgr. land Newfield Exploration Co., 2001—05, v.p. land, 2005—. Mem.: Profl. Landman's Assn. of New Orleans, North Houston Assn. of Prof. Landmen, Houston Land Mgrs. Assn., Houston Assn. Profl. Landmen, Am. Assn. of Profl. Landmen. Office: Newfield Exploration Co 363 N Sam Houston Pky E Ste 100 Houston TX 77060 Office Phone: 281-847-6000. Office Fax: 281-847-6006.

BLUMROSEN, ALFRED WILLIAM, law educator, consultant, arbitrator; b. Detroit, Dec. 14, 1928; s. Sol and Frances (Netzorg) B.; m. Ruth L. Gerber, July 3, 1952; children: Steven Marshall, Alexander Bernet, Ruth(dec.) BA, U. Mich., Ann Arbor, 1950, JD, 1953. Bar: Mich. 1953, N.J. 1961, N.Y. 1981. Solo practice, Detroit, 1953-55; mem. faculty Rutgers Law Sch., Newark, 1955—, prof., 1961—, acting dean, 1974-75, Herbert J. Hannoch scholar, 1984, Thomas A. Cowan prof., 1986—2002, emeritus prof., 2002—. Dir. fed.-state rels., chief conciliations U.S. EEOC, 1965-67, cons. to chmn., 1977-79; advisor U.S. Dept. Justice, HUD, 1968-72, U.S. Dept. Labor, 1995-96; of counsel Kaye, Scholer, Fierman, Hays & Handler, N.Y.C., 1979-82; dir. Ford Found. intentional discrimination project Rutgers U., Law Sch., 1998—. Author: Black Employment and the Law, 1971, Modern Law: The Law Transmission System and Equal Employment Opportunity, 1993; author: (with Ruth Blumrosen) The Realities of Intentional Job Discrimination in Metropolitan America, 1999, Slave Nation: How Slavery United the Colonies and Sparked the American Revolution, 2005; contbr. articles to profl. jours. Fulbright scholar, South Africa, 1993, Rockefeller Inst. Resident scholar Bellagio Conf. Ctr., 1995, Ross Essay award, Am. Bar Assn., 1983 Mem. ABA (Ross essay prize 1983), Internat. Soc. for Labor Law and Social Security, Indsl. Relations Rsch. Assn., Order of Coif. Democrat. Jewish. Office: Rutgers U Sch Law 123 Washington St Newark NJ 07102-3026 Home (Summer): 54 Riverside Dr Bonita Springs FL 34134 Office Phone: 917-670-8878. Office Fax: 239-992-9916. Business E-Mail: theblumrosen@aol.com.

BLUMSTEIN, JAMES FRANKLIN, lawyer, educator, consultant; b. Bklyn., Apr. 24, 1945; s. David and Rita (Sondheim) B.; m. Andree Kahn, June 25, 1971 BA in Econs., Yale U., 1966, MA in Econs., LLB, 1970. Bar: Tenn. 1970, U.S. Ct. Appeals (6th cir.) 1970, U.S. Dist. Ct. (mid. dist.) Tenn. 1971, U.S. Supreme Ct. 1974, N.Y. 1985. Instr. econs. New Haven Coll., 1967-68; pre-law adviser office of dean Yale U., New Haven, 1968-69, sr. pre-law adviser office of dean, 1969-70, asst. in instrn. law shc., 1969-70; asst. prof. law Vanderbilt U., Nashville, 1970-73, assoc. prof., 1973-76, prof., 1976-99, spl. advisor to chancellor for acad. affairs, 1984-85, Centennial prof., 1999—2003, Univ. prof. constl. law and health law and policy, 2003—, chair faculty senate, 2001—02, univ. prof., 2003—. Assoc. dir. Vanderbilt Urban and Regional Devel. Ctr., 1970-72, dir. ctr., 1972-74; sr. rsch. assoc. Vanderbilt Inst. for Pub. Policy Studies, 1976-85, sr. fellow, 1985—, dir. health policy ctr., 1995—; Commonwealth Fund fellow, vis. assoc. prof. law and policy scis. law sch. Duke U. and Inst. of Policy Scis. and Pub. Affairs, 1974-75; adj. prof. health law med. sch. Dartmouth U., scholar-in-residence intermittently, 1976-; John M. Olin vis. prof. Sch. Law, U. Pa., 1989; elected mem. Inst. Medicine NAS, 1990—; bd. dirs. St. Thomas Health Scis. Found., Alive Hospice, Nashville; cons. law, health policy, civil and voting rights, land use, state taxation, torts; scholar-in-residence Robert Wood Johnson Found. Ctr. Health Policy, Meharry Med. Coll., 2010-11, mem., Nat. Adv. Bd., 2011-; lectr. in field. Editor: (with Eddie J. Martin) The Urban Scene in the Seventies, 1974, (with Benjamin Walter) Growing Metropolis: Aspects of Development in Nashville, 1975, (with Lester Salamon) Growth Policy in the Eighties (Law and Contemporary Problems Symposium), 1979; (with Frank A. Sloan and James M. Perrin) Uncompensated Hospital Care: Rights and Responsibilities, 1986, (with Frank A. Sloan and James M. Perrin) Cost, Quality, and Access in Health Care: New Roles for Health Planning in a Competitive Environment, 1988; (with Frank A. Sloan) Organ Transplantation Policy: Issues and Prospects, 1989, (with Frank A. Sloan) Antitrust and Health Care Policy (Law and Contemporary Problems Symposium), 1989, (with Clark C. Havighurst and Troyen A. Brennan) Health Care Law and Policy, 1998, supplement, 2007, editl. bd. Jour. Health Politics, Policy and Law, 1981-01, Jour. Health Care poor and Unmarried; mem. adv. bd. Nat. Fedn. Ind. Bus. Legal Found., 2003-11; mem. pub.'s adv. bd. Nashville Banner, 1982-98; contbr. articles to profl. jours., op-ed articles to newspapers. Mem. Health Econs. Task Force, Middle Tenn. Health Sys. Agy., 1979; mem. Nashville Mayor's Commn. on Crime, 1981; chmn. Yale Alumni Schs. Com. Middle Tenn., 1983—; sec. Martin Luther King Jr. Holiday Com., State of Tenn., 1985—87; mem. Tenn. Gov.'s Task Force Medicaid, 1992—94; active Inst. Medicine Com. on Adequacy of Nursing Staffing, 1994—96; chmn. Tenn. adv. com. U.S. Commn. on Civil Rights, 1985—91, mem., 1991—97; bd. dirs. Alive Hosp., 2005—11, St. Thomas Health Svcs. Found.; mem. adv. bd. LWV, 1979—80; bd. dirs. Jewish Fedn. Nashville and Middle Tenn., 1981—90, mem. exec. com., 1988—90, chmn. cmty. rels. com., 1980—82, chmn. campus com., 1987—89; chmn. task force cost containment and med. malpractice Rand Corp., 1991—92; mem. adv. panel Office Tech. Assessment study of defensive medicine and use of med. tech., 1991—94; mem. adv. com. on The Records of Congress, 1997—99; cons. Leadership Nashville, 1977—, Tenn. Motor Vehicle Commn., 1986—87, Leadership Music, 1989—2002, Tenncare Reform Project, Office Gov. Phil Bredesen, 2004—07, Acad. Country Music, 2005; panelist Am. Arbitration Assn., 1977—2002. Bates Jr. fellow, 1968-69; grantee Ford Found./Rockefeller Found. Population Program, 1970-73, Health Policy grantee HCA Found., 1986-90; grantee State Justice Inst., 1991—2000, Robert Wood Johnson Found., 1994—2000; named One of Outstanding Young Men in Am., 1971; recipient award Univ. Rsch. Coun., 1971-72, 73-74, 79-80, 94-95, Earl Sutherland prize achievement in rsch. Vanderbilt U., 1992, Paul J. Hartman award Outstanding Prof., 1982. Mem. ABA (sec. sect. legal edn. and admissions to bar 1982-83, chmn. subcom. on state and local taxation com. on corp. law and taxation sect. on corp., banking and bus. law 1983—, mem. accreditation com. sect. legal edn. and admissions to bar 1983-89, mem. com. on state and local taxation sect. on taxation 1983—), NAS (inst. of medicine), Assn. Am. Law Schs. (chmn. law, medicine and health care sect. 1987-88, mem. exec. com. 1988-92, 2d vice chmn. sect. local govt. law 1976-78, mem. sect. coun. 1980-86), Tenn. Bar Assn. (Pres.'s award 2004), N.Y. State Bar Assn., Nashville Bar Assn. (Liberty Bell award 1987), Poly Prop (Disting. Achievement award 2012), Assn. Yale Alumni (del.), Yale U. Law Sch. Alumni Assn. (exec. com. 1985-88), Univ. Club (Nashville). Home: 2113 Hampton Ave Nashville TN 37215-1401 Office: Vanderbilt U Sch Law 21st Ave S Nashville TN 37240-0001 Office Phone: 615-322-2615.

BLUNTZER, ELENA C., real estate company executive; Cert. GRI Fla. State Assn. Realtors. Formerly with RE/MAX Advance Reality, Miami, Fla.; realtor, owner Bluntzer Grp., Miami, 2004—. Recipient Chmn.'s Club award, RE/MAX Internat. Conv., 2003. Office: Town & Country Real Estate Svcs 5724 SW 76th Terrace Miami FL 33143 Office Phone: 305-667-8644. Business E-Mail: elena@bluntzergroup.com.

BLUST, JOHN M., state legislator; Former state senator Dist. 32, NC; state rep. Dist. 27 NC, 2001—02; state rep. Dist. 62 NC, 2003—. Republican. Address: PO Box 8146 Greensboro NC 27419 Office: North Carolina House of Representatives 16 W Jones St Rm 2208 Raleigh NC 27601-1096 Office Phone: 919-733-5781, 336-274-4658 ext. 121. E-mail: John.Blust@ncleg.net.

BLUTH, B. J. (ELIZABETH JEAN CATHERINE BLUTH), sociologist, aerospace technologist; b. Phila., Dec. 5, 1934; d. Robert Thomas and Catherine Cecelia (Boxman) Gowland; m. Thomas Del Bluth, Aug. 20, 1960 (dec. Aug. 6, 1980); children: Robert Thomas, Richard Del. BA in Sociology (Washington semster fellow), Bucknell U., 1953; MA, Fordham U., 1960; PhD, UCLA, 1970. Teaching fellow in methods of social research Fordham U., 1957-58; reading instr. St. Margaret's High Sch., Tappahannock, Va., 1958-59; instr. history, civics and English, Rosary High Sch., San Diego, 1959-60; successively instr., asst. prof. sociology Immaculate Heart Coll., Los Angeles, 1960-65; prof. sociology Calif. State U., Northridge, 1965-87; grantee NASA Ames Research Ctr., Moffett Field, Calif., 1982-83; grantee space sta. program NASA, Washington, 1983-87, aerospace technologist system engring. div. space sta. program office Reston, Va., 1987-90, spl. asst. to dep. program dir. space sta. freedom program and ops., 1990-94, spl. tech. asst. to dir. edn. divsn., mgr. edn. evaluation Washington, 1994—2006, program mgr. on-line edn. evaluation program, 1994—2006, cons. services, 2006—. Cons. Immaculate Heart Cmty., L.A., 1967-69; engring. rsch. NASA Space Sta. design Boeing Aerospace Co., 1982-83; mem. Presdl. Citizens Adv. com. on Space, Coun. Nat. Space Policy, Nat. Tech. Com. on Soc. and Tech., UN team on relevance of space activities to econ. and social devel.; professor emeritus Calif. State U., 1987—; computational scis. and informatics inst. dir.'s search com. George Mason U., 1992-93. Editor: (with others) Search for Identity Reader, vol. I and II, 1973, (with S.R. McNeal) Update on Space, vol. I, 1961, Parson's General Theory of Action, 1982, Space Station Habitability Report, 1983, Soviet Space Station Analog, 1983, Space Station Human Productivity Study NASA, 1986, Russian Mir Space Station Analog, 1993, Marching with Sharpe, 2001; contbr. articles to profl. jours. Recipient Alpha Omega faculty awards, 1966, 1974. Fellow Am. Astronautical Soc.; mem. AIAA (chpt. award for outstanding program 1980, tech. com. mem. on space colonization, 2010), Am. Sociol. Assn., L5 Soc., Brit. Interplanetary Soc., Inst. Social Sci. Study of Space (acad. adv. bd.), Space Studies Inst., Internat. Acad. Astronautics (com. on space econs. and benefits, chmn. bylaw com.), Nat. Space Soc. Loudoun County Rep. Womens Club(1st v.p. programs), Va. Fedn. Rep. Women, Loudoun County Rep., Smart Girls Politics (state com. co-chair), Phi Beta Kappa. Republican. Office Phone: 703-967-0522. Personal E-mail: bjb@patriot.net.

BLYNN, GUY MARC, retired lawyer; b. Bklyn., May 26, 1945; s. S. Jerry and Viola T. Vogel Blynn; children: Daniel Scott, Harlan Sterling, Aaron Seth. BS in Econs. cum laude, U. Pa., Wharton Sch. of Fin. Commerce, 1967; JD cum laude, Harvard U., 1970. Bar: N.C., N.Y., U.S. Ct. of Appeals for Fed. Cir., U.S. Ct. of Appeals for the 2d Cir., U.S. Dist. Cts. for the Middle Dist. of N.C., Southern and Eastern Dist. N.Y. Assoc. Kaye, Scholer, Fierman, Hays & Handler, NYC, 1970-78; assoc. counsel R.J. Reynolds Industries Inc., Winston Salem, N.C., 1978-79; sr. counsel RJR Nabisco Inc., Winston Salem, N.C., 1979-86; dep. gen. counsel R.J. Reynolds Tobacco Co., Winston Salem, NC, 1986—2006, v.p., 1989—; dep. gen. counsel R.J. Reynolds Global Products, Inc., 1989—2006, v.p., gen. counsel, 2006—08. Lectr. Wake Forest U. Sch. of Law, 1980-93; cons. Dept. Commerce, 1987-90. Contbr. articles to profl. jours. Chmn. Brand Names Edn. Found., 1988-94; bd. dirs. N.C. Vol. Lawyers for the Arts, 1985-91, pres., 1987-91; bd. dirs. Urban League Winston-Salem. Mem. ABA, Am. Arbitration Assn. (panel of arbitrators 1975-95), Carolina Patent Trademark & Copyright Law Assn. (v.p. 1979-80, pres. 1980-81), Am. Intellectul Property Law Assn. (chmn. taxation and fin. matters com. 1991-92), Am. Bar Assn. Forum Com. on Entertainment And Sports Industries, Assn. of Bar of City Of N.Y. (chmn. com. on trademarks and unfair competition 1975-78, subcommittee on patent and trademark office practice 1976-77), Anti-Defamation League (N.C. regional adv. bd. 1987—, chmn. elect 1991-93, chmn. 1993—, vice chmn. 1990-91), U.S. Trademark Assn. (bd. dirs. 1982-90, v.p. 1984-85, exec. v.p. 1985-86, pres., chmn. 1986-87). Home: PO Box 20383 Winston Salem NC 27120-0383

BOADLE-BIBER, MARGARET CLARE, physiologist, educator; b. Melbourne, Australia, Jan. 18, 1943; arrived in U.S., 1967; d. Campbell Dean and Constance Ellen (Browne) Boadle; m. Thomas Ulrich Leonard Biber, Oct. 8, 1969; 1 child, Eric Gustav Nicholas Biber. BS, U. Coll. London, 1964; DPhil, Oxford U., Eng., 1967. Rsch. assoc. pharm. dept. Yale U. Sch. Medicine, New Haven, 1968-69, instr. pharm. dept., 1969-71, asst. prof. pharm. dept., 1971-75; assoc. prof. physiology dept. Va. Commonwealth U., Richmond, 1975-87, prof., 1987—, interim chair, 1991-93, chair, 1993—2007. Contbr. articles to profl. jours. Mem.: Soc. Neuroscience, Am. Soc. Pharm. and Exptl. Therapeutics, Am. Soc. Neurochemistry. Office: Va Commonwealth U 1101 E Marshall St Richmond VA 23298-0551 Office Phone: 804-628-3325. Business E-Mail: mbiber@vcu.edu.

BOARDMAN, WILLIAM PENNIMAN, retired bank executive; b. Columbus, Ohio, June 22, 1941; s. John King and Eleanor Susan (Penniman) Boardman; m. Nancy Louise Staby, Sept. 10, 1971; children: Abigail Blair, Anna Neel, Elizabeth Penniman. BA, Washington & Lee U., Lexington, Va., 1963, JD summa cum laude, 1969. Mgmt. trainee First Nat. City Bank, NYC, 1963-64; ptnr. Porter, Wright, Morris & Arthur, Columbus, Ohio, 1969-81; gen. counsel, exec. v.p. BancOhio Nat. Bank, Columbus, 1981-84; v.p. Banc One Corp., Columbus, 1984-88, sr. v.p., 1988-90, exec. v.p., 1990-93, sr. exec. v.p., 1993-98, Chgo., 1998-99, vice chmn., 1999—2001; chmn. Visa Internat. Inc., 1996—2005; chmn., CEO First USA, Inc., 1999—2001; sr. adv. Goldman Sachs & Co., 2001—03. Bd. dirs. Bank One Corp., 1984—2001, CheckFree Corp., 1996—, Ohio Casualty Corp., 2003—05, Bank of America Corp., 2009—11. Bd. trustees Washington & Lee U., Columbus Sch. for Girls. 1st lt. artillery US Army, 1964—66, Korea. Republican. Episcopalian.

BOAZ, DAVID DOUGLAS, foundation executive; b. Mayfield, Ky., Aug. 29, 1953; s. Seth Thomas Jr. and Martha Elizabeth (Pruitt) B. BA, Vanderbilt U., 1975. Exec. dir. Young Am.'s Found., Sterling, Va., 1975-76; editor New Guard Mag., Sterling, Va., 1976-78; exec. dir. Coun. for a Competitive Economy, Washington, 1978-80; rsch. dir. Clark for Pres. Com., Washington, 1980; v.p. Cato Inst., Washington, 1981-89, exec. v.p., 1989—. Bd. dirs. Ctr. for Ind. Thought, NYC, Women's Freedom Network; bd. regents Congl. Schs. Va., 1991-2003. Author: Libertarianism: A Primer, 1997, The Politics of Freedom, 2008; co-author: The Libertarian Vote, 2012; co-editor: Beyond the Status Quo, 1985, An American Vision, 1989, Market Liberalism: A Paradigm for the 21st Century, 1993, Cato Handbook for Congress, 2001; editor: Left, Right and Babyboom, 1986, Assessing the Reagan Years, 1988, The Crisis in Drug Prohibition, 1990, Liberating Schools: Education in the Inner City, 1991, The Libertarian Reader, 1997, Toward Liberty, 2002, Cato Handbook for Policymakers, 2009; contbr. Encyclopedia Brittanica, also books and newspapers. Office: Cato Inst 1000 Massachusetts Ave NW Washington DC 20001-5400

BOBRUFF, JEROME, physician; b. Hartford, Conn., June 18, 1930; s. Nathan and Mildred (Dobin) B.; m. Bernice S. Gendron, July 22, 1990; m. Carole Marks, June 20, 1954 (div. 1986); children: Ellen, Neal, Paul, Mark; stepchildren: Jeffrey Reynolds, Michael Reynolds. BA, Wesleyan U., 1952; MD, Yale U., 1955. Diplomate Am. Bd. Internal Medicine. Instr. Seton Hall Coll. Medicine, Jersey City, N.J., 1961-62; physician Lawrence Meml. Hosp., New London, Conn., 1962-95, chief gastroenterology, 1975-80; dir. Yale Club Southwest Fla., 2008—; v.p. Naples Lions Club, 2010—; dir. Ret. Physicians Collier County, 2010—; ret. physician bd. dirs. Collier County; dir. Tiger Island Estates HOA, Naples, Fla. Pres. Digestive Disease Assocs., New London, 1969—95; cons. med. dir. MD Health Plan, New Haven, 1995—97; med. dir. Americares Free Clinic, 1999—2002; bd. dirs. Colonial IPA, New London. Contbr. articles to profl. jours. Mem. Gov.'s Commn. on Reading, Conn., 1968, Charter Rev. Com., New London, 1970, Zoning Bd. Appeals, New London, 1986-91, 2002-. Capt. USAF, 1957-59. Fellow: Am. Soc. Gastrointestinal Endoscopy; mem.: AMA (ho. of dels. 1989—2000), New London County Med. Assn. (pres. 1979—80, Disting. Physician award 1993), Conn. Med. Soc. (councillor 1979—88), Yale Club SW Fla. (v.p.), Lions (v.p. naples, Fla.), Phi Beta Kappa. Democrat. Jewish. Avocations: skiing, sailing, golf, bowling. Home: 7928 Tiger Lily Dr Naples FL 34113-2633

BOCHATON, PHILIPPE, hospital administrator; Chief adminstrv. officer HCA Holdings, Inc. (subs. HCA). Office: HCA Holdings Inc 1 Park Plz Nashville TN 37203 Office Phone: 615-344-9551. Office Fax: 615-344-2266.

BOCK, WILLIAM C., cardiac electrophysiologist; MD, Med. U. SC. Diplomate Am. Bd. Internal Medicine, 1988, Am. Bd. Internal Medicine-cardiovasc. disease, 2001, Am. Bd. Internal Medicine-clin. cardiac electrophysiology, 2004, cert. Nat. Com. for Quality Assurance Heart/Stroke Recognition. Resident internal medicine Carolinas Med. Ctr., 1986—88, hosp. affiliations include, Presbyn. Hosp.; fellow cardiovasc. disease Emory Univ., 1988—91. Office: Sanger Heart and Vascular Institute-Mercy 2001 Vail Ave Ste 340 Charlotte NC 28207 Office Phone: 704-304-1110. Office Fax: 704-304-1159.

BOCKSTRUCK, LLOYD DEWITT, librarian; b. Vandalia, Ill., May 26, 1945; s. Harry Earl and Olive Elsie (Blankenship) B. AB cum laude, Greenville Coll., Ill., 1967; MA, So. Ill. U., 1969; MS, U. Ill., 1973; student, Samford U., 1973. Teaching asst. So. Ill. U., Carbondale, 1967—69; tchr. Mombasa (Kenya) Bapt. High Sch., 1969—71; teaching asst. U. Ill., Urbana, 1972—73; libr. Dallas Pub. Libr., 1973—2009. Instr. Inst. Genealogy and Hist. Rsch., Samford U., Birmingham, Ala., 1973—2013; instr. Sch. Continuing Edn., So. Meth. U., Dallas, 1974-91; instr. Geneal. Inst. of Mid-Am., U. Ill., Springfield, 1994-2005; columnist Dallas Morning News, 1991-2008, Eastman Online Genealogy Newsletter, 2008-09. Author: Virginia's Colonial Soldiers, 1988, Genealogical Research in Texas, 1992, Revolutionary War Bounty Land Grants Awarded by State Governments, 1996, Family Tree Weekly Newspaper Columns from the Dallas Morning News, 1991-1996, 1999, Naval Pensioners of the United States, 1800-1851, 2002, Denizations and Naturalizations in the British Colonies in America, 1607-1775, 2005, Bounty and Donation Land Grants in British Colonial America, 2007, Revolutionary War Pensions: Awarded by State Governments 1775-1874, the General and Federal Governments Prior to 1814, and by Private Acts of Congress to 1905, 2011, The Name Is the Game: Onomatology and the Genealogist, 2013; contbr. articles to profl. jours. Recipient Scholarship Key award Phi Alpha Theta, 1967, History award DAR, 1989, Profl. award for hist. preservation Dallas County Hist. Commn., 1992, Filby prize for Genealogical Librarianship, 1999, Lifetime Achievement award N.E. Tex. Libr. Sys., 2003; Nat. Geneal. Soc. fellow, 1992; Gold Good Citizenship award, SAR, 2005, Lillian Moore Bradshaw award, Friends Dallas Pub. Libr., 2008. Mem. ALA (life), SAR (libr. gen. 1981-83), SCW (dep. gov. gen. 2000), Soc. of the Cincinnati, Jamestowne Soc., Order of Ams. of Armorial Ancestry (genealogist gen. 1993-99), Order of Founders and Patriots of Am. (genealogist gen. 1986-2000), Dallas Geneal. Soc. (dir. 1979—2009). Republican. Avocation: genealogy. Home: 3955-C Buena Vista St Dallas TX 75204-1667

BODDE, DAVID LEO, technology educator; b. Kansas City, Mo., Jan. 27, 1943; s. Leo Antony and Frances (Henkes) B.; m. Priscilla Anne Dick, Aug. 5, 1967; children: Mark David, Douglas Somers, Daniel Philip, Katherine Elizabeth. BS, U.S. Mil. Acad., 1965; MS, MIT, 1972, MS, 1973; DBA, Harvard U., 1976. Mgr. engring. analysis office, energy sys. planning divsn. TRW, Inc., 1976-78; dep. asst. sec. for coal, nuc. and synthetic fuels US Department of Energy, 1978-81; asst. dir. Congl. Budget Office, Washington, 1981-86; exec. dir. Commn. Engring. and Tech. Sys., NAS, Washington, 1986-91; v.p. Midwest Rsch. Inst., 1991-96; Charles N. Kimball chair tech. and innovation U. Mo., 1996—2004; sr. fellow & prof. Arthur M. Spiro Inst. for Entrepreneurial Leadership Clemson University, 2004—. Bd. dirs. Great Plains Energy, 1994—, The Commerce Funds, 1995—, chmn. Environ. Mgmt. Adv. Bd. U.S. Dept. Energy; mem adv. coun. Electric Power Rsch. Inst. Contbr. articles to profl. jours. Capt. U.S. Army, 1965-70. Decorated Bronze star, Army Commemdation medal; AEC fellow, 1970-73, Harding Found. fellow, 1974-75. Mem. AAAS. Episcopalian. Office: Spiro Inst Clemson Univ 346 Sirrine Hall Clemson SC 29634-1345

BODE, JOYCE SCRUGGS, lawyer; b. Waco, Tex., Nov. 18, 1953; d. James Harry and Jane Reese (Rich) Scruggs BA Criminology with highest honors, U. Calif., Berkeley, 1975; JD cum laude, Harvard U., 1979. Bar: Tex. 1979, U.S. Dist. ct. (no. dist.) Tex. 1986, U.S. Tax Ct. 1979, U.S. Ct. Appeals (5th cir.) 1985. Jud. clk. to Judge Richard C. Wilber US Tax Ct., Wash., 1979-81; assoc. Vinson & Elkins, Houston, Fulbright & Jaworski, Dallas, 1987-89, ptnr. Austin, 1989—. Spkr. in feilds. Contbr. Recipient Best Lawyers in Am. Tax, Tex. Super Lawyer, Tex. Monthly mag., Best of Bus. Attys. & Corp. Counsel, Austin Bus. Jour. Mem. ABA (taxation sect.), Nat Assn. Bd. Lawyers, State Bar Tex. (taxation sect., tax exempt fin. com., vice chmn. fed. ct. procedure). Republican. Methodist. Avocations: travel, hiking. Office: Fulbright & Jaworski 2200 Ross Ave Ste 2800 Dallas TX 75201 Office Phone: 214-855-8007. Office Fax: 214-855-8200. Business E-Mail: jbode@fulbright.com.

BODE, WILLIAM ERNEST, colon and rectal surgeon; MD, Tex. Tech U., 1977. Lic. Tex., 1977, diplomate Am. Bd. Colon and Rectal Surgery, 1984, Am. Bd. Surgery, 2001. Intern Univ. Tex. Health Sci. Ctr., San Antonio, 1978, resident in surgery, 1982; fellow in colon and rectal surgery Mayo Clinic, Rochester, Minn., 1982—83; hosp. affiliations include St. Lukes Hosp., Christus Santa Rosa Hosp., Meth. Specialty and Transplant Hosp., Bapt. Med. Ctr., SW Tex. Meth. Hosp.; pvt. practice Colon and Rectal Surgical Assocs., Tex. Named one of Best Doctors in America. Fellow: ACS; mem.: Am. Soc. of Colon and Rectal Surgeons. Office: Colon and Rectal Surgical Associates 7950 Floyd Curl Dr Ste 101 San Antonio TX 78229 Office Phone: 210-614-0880.

BODENCHUK, MICHAEL J., wildlife biologist; b. Jacksonville, Fla., May 7, 1957; s. John M. and Martha H. Bodenchuk; m. Deborah G. Godley, Mar. 3, 1984; children: Hunter A., Leigh A. BS, N.Mex State U., Las Cruces, 1979. State dir. Utah Wildlife Svcs. Program, Salt Lake City, 1996—2007, Tex. Wildlife Svcs. Program, San Antonio, 2007—. Contbr. chapters to books. Dir. Coleman County C. of C., Tex., 1983—86. Recipient Strategic Vision award, USDA-APHIS-Wildlife Svcs., 1997, Conservation award, Utah Trappers Assn., 2000, Administrators Civil Rights award, USDA-APHIS, 2000, award, Utah Dept. Agr. and Food, 2003. Mem.: NRA, SCI, Wildlife Soc. Avocations: travel, hunting. Office: USDA-APHIS-Wildlife Svcs Box 690170 San Antonio TX 78269 Office Phone: 210-472-5451.*

BODEY, GERALD PAUL, retired medical educator; b. Hazelton, Pa., May 22, 1934; s. Allen Zartman and Marie Frances (Smith) B.; m. Nancy Louise Wiegner, Aug. 25, 1956; children: Robin Gayle Sparwasser, Gerald Paul Jr., Sharon Dawn Brantley. AB magna cum laude, Lafayette Coll., 1956; MD, Johns Hopkins U., 1960. Diplomate Nat. Bd. Med. Examiners, Am. Bd. Internal Medicine, Am. Bd. Infectious Diseases, Am. Bd. Oncology. Intern Johns Hopkins U., Balt., 1960-61, resident, 1961-62; clin. assoc. Nat. Cancer Inst., Bethesda, Md., 1962-65; resident U. Wash., Seattle, 1965-66; internist to prof. medicine U. Tex./M.D. Anderson Cancer Ctr., Houston, 1975—95, emeritus prof. medicine, 1995—, ret., 2004. Mem. Am.-Soviet Meetings on Cancer Chemotherapy, 1974—78; adj. prof. microbiology, immunology and medicine Baylor Coll. of Medicine, Houston, 1975—99; active collaborative cancer treatment rsch. program Pan Am. Health Orgn., 1976—84; prof. internal medicine and pharmacology Med. Sch. U. Tex. Health Sci. Ctr., Houston, 1976—2004, clin. prof. Dental Sch., 1977—95; mem. orphan products devel. initial rev. group FDA, 1984—95; mem. lunar quarantine ops. team Apollo 11-14, Manned Spacecraft Ctr., NASA, Houston, 1987—89; mem. joint commn. accreditation healthcare orgns. Hospitalwide Indicators Task Force; hon. prof. U. Peruana Cayetano Heradia, Lima, 2007—. Former mem. editl. bd., European Jour. Clin. Microbiol. Infectious Diseases; Cancer Rsch., Antimicrobial Agts. and Chemotherapy, Brazilian Jour. Infectious Disease; contbr. 1100 articles to profl. jours. Past trustee Nat. AIDS Prevention Inst. Recipient Am. Chem. Soc. prize, 1956, Merck award, 1956, Robert B. Youngman Greek prize Lafayette Coll., 1956, Eugene Yourassowsky award U. Libre de Bruxelles, Belgium, 1995, Gran Ofcl. de Orden, Hipolito Unanue, Peru, 2007; scholar Leukemia Soc. Am., 1969-74; Henry Strong Denison fellow Johns Hopkins Sch. Medicine, Balt., 1958-60, Great Ofcl. of Order Hipolito Unanue award, Peru, named one of 300 Most Cited Authors award, Disting. Med. Alumnus award Johns Hopkins U., 2012. Fellow ACP, Am. Coll. Chest Physicians, Infectious Diseases Soc. Am., Am. Coll. Clin. Pharmacology, Royal Coll. Medicine, Royal Soc. Promotion Health; mem. AMA, Nat. Acad. Medicine Peru (hon.), Am. Soc. Clin. Oncology, Infectious Diseases Soc. Am., Am. Soc. Clin. Pharmacology and Therapeutics, Am. Soc. Hematology, Am. Soc. Microbiol., Am. Sci. Affiliation, Internat. Soc. Complexity, Info. and Design, Christian Med. Soc., Tex. Med. Assn., Academia Peruana de Cirugia (hon.), Academia Nacional Medicina (hon.), Mediterranean Med. Soc. (hon.), Le Soc. Peruana Cancerologia (hon.), La Costarricensa Oncologie (hon.), Soc. Brasileira Cancerologia (hon.), Phi Beta Kappa, Sigma Xi. Methodist. Achievements include named awards to others from University of Texas MD Anderson Cancer Center: Gerald Paul Bodey Senior Immunocompromised Host Fellowship Training Award; Gerald Paul Bodey Senior Distinguished Professorship in Infectious Diseases, Gerald Paul Bodey Award for excellence in education, division of medical oncology. Avocations: reading, travel. Office: University Tex MDACC 1515 Holcombe Blvd Houston TX 77030-4009 Business E-Mail: drbodey@live.com.

BODRUZZAMAN, MOHAMMAD, engineering educator; m. Selina Banu; children: Samia, Milia, Jabir. PhD in Elec. Engring., Vanderbilt U., Nashville, 1990. Prof. Tenn. State U., Nashville, 1985—. Mem.: IEEE (sr.), Phi-Kappa-Phi, Eta-Kappa-Nu. Avocation: music. Office: Tennessee State Univ 3500 John A Merritt Blvd Nashville TN 37209

BOE, ERIC A., pilot, astronaut; b. Miami, Fla., Oct. 1, 1964; m. Kristen Newman; 2 children. BS in Astronautical Engring., USAF Acad., 1987; MSEE, Ga. Inst. Tech., 1997; attended, USAF Test Pilot Sch., Edwards AFB. Calif., 1997. Completed Euro-NATO Joint Jet Pilot Tng., Sheppard AFB, Tex., 1988; combat ready pilot in the F-4E 3rd Tactical Fighter Squadron, Clark Air Base, Philippines; T-38 instr. pilot 50th Flying Tng. Squadron, 1991; AT-38B instr. pilot 49th Fighter Squadron, Columbus AFB, Miss., 1991; F-15C flight comdr. 60th Fighter Squadron, Eglin AFB, Fla., 1994; dir. Test, Air-to-Air Missile Test Divsn., test pilot flying of F-15 and UH-1N 46th Test Wing, Eglin AFB, Fla., 1997; pilot, astronaut NASA, 2000—. Assigned technical duties, astronaut office advanced vehicles br., station ops. br. and space shuttle br.; dir. ops., Gagarin Cosmonaut Tng. Ctr. NASA, Star City, Russia, 2005—06; worked on new Crew Launch Vehicle and Crew Exploration Vehicle NASA, Exploration Br.; pilot (will be first shuttle pilot in his astronaut class to reach orbit) STS-126 Endeavour Mission, 2008; pilot STS-133-Final Flight of Discovery, 2010. Decorated Meritorious Svc. medal (2), Air medal (2), Aerial Achievement medal (5), Commendation medal (3), Achievement medal, Outstanding Unit award (3), Combat Readiness medal; Fannie and John Hertz Found. Fellowship for grad. studies, 1987. Mem.: Soc. Exptl. Test Pilots, Civil Air Patrol. Avocations: outdoor sports, reading, scuba diving, skiing. Office: NASA Johnson Space Center 2101 NASA Pkwy Houston TX 77058

BOE, MYRON TIMOTHY, lawyer; b. New Orleans, Oct. 30, 1948; s. Myron Roger and Elaine (Tracy) B. BA, U. Ark., 1970, JD, 1973; LLM in Labor, So. Methodist U., 1976. Bar: Ark. 1974, Tenn. 1977, US Ct. Appeals (4th, 5th, 6th, 7th, 8th, 9th, 10th, 11th cirs.) 1978, US Supreme Ct. 1978. City atty. City of Pine Bluff, Ark., 1974-75; sec.-treas. Ark. City Atty. Assn., 1975; sr. ptnr. Rose Law Firm, Little Rock, 1980—. Author: Handling the Title VII Case Practical Tips for the Employer, 1980. Served to 2d lt. USAR, 1972-73. Recipient Florentino-Ramirez Internat. Law award, 1975; Named one of The Best Lawyers in Am., Ark. Leading Employment Lawyer. Fellow Coll. Labor and Employment Lawyers, Inc., Ark. Bar Found. (bd. dirs.), Ark. Bd. Legal Specialization (sec. 1982-85, chmn. 1985-89, labor, employment discrimination, civil rights).; mem. ABA (labor sect. 1974—, employment law com. 1974—), ARC of Ark. (bd. dirs., v.p.), Ark. Bar Assn. (sec., chmn. labor sect. 1978-81, ho. of dels. 1979-82, Golden Gavel award 1983, bd. dirs., v.p., pres.), Def. Rsch. Inst. (employment law com. 1982—), Am. Employment Law Coun. (charter), Ark. Assn. Def. Counsel. Office: Rose Law Firm 120 E 4th St Little Rock AR 72201-2893

BOECKMANN, ALAN L., engineering and construction management company executive; BSEE, U. Ariz., Tucson. Engr. Fluor Corp., 1974; pres., CEO Fluor Daniel; pres. Fluor Daniel's Energy & Chem. group; pres., COO Fluor Corp., 2001—02, chmn., CEO, 2002—11, chmn., 2011—. Dir. Burlington No. Santa Fe, Am. Petroleum Inst., Bus. Coun. Internat. Understanding, Nat. Petroleum Coun., Archer Daniels Midland Co. Dir. Orange County Performing Arts Ctr., Hearing & Speech Found.; mem. Bus. Roundtable; chmn. engring. & constrn. gov. World Econ. Forum; mem. adv. coun. U. Ariz. Coll. Engring. & Mines; dir. So. Meth. U. Cox Sch. Bus. Office: Fluor Corp 6700 Las Colinas Blvd Irving TX 75039 Office Phone: 469-398-7000. Office Fax: 469-398-7255.

BOEHLE, WILLIAM RANDALL, music educator emeritus; b. Waxahachie, Tex., July 1, 1919; s. Wilhelm Reinhold and Ruby (Connally) B.; m. Emma Jean Belk, Dec. 10, 1943; children: Dulcy Jean, Alison Lee. Mus.B., Hardin-Simmons U., 1941; Mus.M., La. State U., 1948; PhD, U. Iowa, 1954. Asst. prof. music Chadron (Nebr.) State Coll., 1949-52, chmn. div. fine arts, 1952-60; chmn. dept. music U. N.D., Grand Forks, 1960-77, acting dean Coll. Fine Arts, 1971-73, prof. music, 1977-84; prof. emeritus, 1984—; profl. musician, 1985—. Mem. N.D. Council Arts and Humanities, 1966-77; pres. Internat. Music Camp, 1978-84. Served with AUS, 1942-46. Boehle Lodge at Internat. Music Camp, Internat. Peace Garden, named in his honor, 1990, William & Jean Boehle Music Scholarship established by Chadron State Coll. Alumni, 1993. Mem. Music Tchrs. Nat. Assn. (past nat. chmn. student activities), Nat. Assn. Composers U.S.A., Nebr. Music Tchrs. Assn. (past pres.).

BOEHM, KENNETH, legal association administrator; 1 child, Christine. BA, Pa. State U., 1971; JD, Widener Sch. of Law, 1976. Talk show host Sta. WWDB-FM, Phila.; prosecutor; adminstrv. asst. to Congressman Christopher Smith; legis. dir. Howard Jarvis' Am. Tax Reduction Movement; co-founder, chmn. Nat. Legal Policy and Ctr., Falls Church, Va., 1991—. Counsel to bd. dirs. Legal Svcs. Corp. Office: Nat Legal and Policy Ctr 107 Park Washington Ct Falls Church VA 22046 Office Phone: 703-237-1970.

BOER, F. PETER, chemical company executive; b. 1940; AB, Princeton U., 1961; PhD, Harvard U., 1965. With Tex Div. Lab. Dow Chem. Co., 1965-78, dir; v.p., mgr. R & D Am. Can Co., 1978-83; v.p., pres. rsch. div., corp. tech. group W.R. Grace & Co., from 1983, sr. v.p., until 1989, exec. v.p., until 1995; pres., CEO, Tiger Scientific Inc., 1995—. Bd dirs. Nova Corp., ENSCO, Inc., Rhodes Techs. Inc.; former adj. prof. Sch. Mgmt. and chem. engring. Yale U.; mem. evaluation com. for nat. medals of tech. Dept. Commerce, 1990-97. Author: Valuation of Technology, 1999, The Real Options Solution, 2002, Technology Valuation Solutions, 2004. Mem. Nat. Acad. Engring. Office: Tiger Scientific Inc 47 Country Rd S Village Of Golf FL 33436-5615 Business E-Mail: fpboer@boer.org.

BOFF, KENNETH RICHARD, engineering research psychologist; b. NYC, Aug. 17, 1947; s. Victor and Ann (Yunko) B.; m. Judith Marion Schoer, Aug. 2, 1969 (dec. Apr. 1997); children: Cory Asher, Kyra Melissa; m. Jacque Aelanda Coppler, Aug. 20, 1999. BA, CUNY, 1969, MA, 1972; MPhil, Columbia U., 1975, PhD, 1978. Research scientist Human Resources Lab., Wright Patterson AFB, Ohio, 1977-80; sr. scientist Armstrong Aerospace Med. Rsch. Lab. (now Airforce Rsch. Lab.), Wright Patterson AFB, Ohio, 1980—, dir. design tech., 1980-91, dir. human engring. div., 1991—97; chief scientist, human effectiveness directorate Air Force Rsch. Lab., 1997—2007; Edenfield Exec.-in-Residence Sch. Ind. & Sys. Engring. Georgia Inst. Tech., 2002—04; prin. scientist Tennebaum Inst. Ga. Inst. Tech., Atlanta, 2007—; chief scientist Socio Tech. Scis., Sarasota, Fla. Project custodian Internat. Air. Standard Coordination Com., Washington, 1984; chmn. com. Tri-Service Human Factors Tech. Adv. Group, Washington, 1984—; chair human factors com. NATO Adv. Group Aerospace R&D, Paris, 1992—; chair human sys. tech. panel Dept. Def., 1994-97; U.S. coord. NATO Rsch. and Tech. Orgn. Human Factors, 1997—. Editor: Handbook of Perception and Human Performance, 1986, Human Engineering Data Compendium, 1988, System Design: Behavioral Perspectives on designers, Tools and Organizations, 1987, Organizational Simulation, 2005; contbr. articles to profl. jours. Travel grantee Rank Prize Found., Cambridge, Eng., 1984; named Air Force Scientist of the Quarter, 1989; recipient Patent award for rap-com display tech., 1989, Human Factors Soc. award for best publ., 1989. Fellow Internat. Ergonomics Assn., Human Factors and Ergonomics Soc.; mem. IEEE (sr.), Human Factors Soc., Am. Psychol. Assn. (div. 21 engring. psychology). Avocations: computers, photography. Business E-Mail: ken.boff@ti.qatch.edu.

BOGAN, RICHARD KEITH, medical educator, director; s. Jesse Cleveland Bogan and Edna Louise Putman Bogan; m. Shannon Marie Thornton; children: Martin Keith, Richard Larkin, Stephanie Ann, Laura Alyson Bogan Herpel, Ross Thornton. BS, Wofford Coll., 1996; MD, MUSC, Charleston, 1970. Diplomate Med. U. SC, 1970. Asst. prof. medicine U. Ala. Hosps., Birmingham, 1976—78; pulmonologist Pulmonary Assocs. SC, Columbia, 1978—94; med. dir. respiratory therapy Palmetto Bapt. Med. Ctr., Columbia, 1978—98; asst. clin. prof. U. SC Sch. Medicine, Columbia, 1978—; pres., med. dir. Sleep Disorder Ctrs.Am., Columbia, 1994—99; pres. Bogan Consulting, Columbia, 1994—; chmn., CMO SleepMed, Inc., Columbia, 1999—; dir., co-founder First Cmty. Bank, Lexington, SC, 1996—; intern. Internal U. Ala. Medicine Hosps., Birmingham, Ala., 1970—91; resident internal medicine Internal U. Ala. Hosps., 1971—72, 1974—75, chief med. resident, 1975—76; CMO R Bogan@sleepmed.md; assoc. clin. prof. USC, 2009—. Lt. comdr. USN, 1972—74, US Naval Base, Albany, Ga. Fellow: Am. Acad. Sleep Medicine, Am. Coll. Chest Physicians. Avocations: golf, skiing, scuba diving. Office: SleepMed Inc 1333 Taylor St Columbia SC 29201 Office Fax: 803-376-1876. Business E-Mail: rbogan@sleepmed.md.

BOGARDUS, CARL ROBERT, JR., radiologist, educator; b. Hyden, Ky., June 26, 1933; s. Carl Robert and Jeannette Wanda (Eversole) B.; m. Norma Gail Shields, June 24, 1956; children: Carl Robert III, Cynthia Gail. BA, Hanover Coll., 1955; MD, U. Louisville, 1959. Diplomate: Am. Bd. Radiology, Am. Bd. Nuc. Medicine. Intern Penrose Cancer Hosp., Colorado Springs, Colo., 1959-60, resident, 1960-63; prof. U. Okla. Med. Ctr., 1963—, mem. staff, 1963—. Cons. Okla. hosps.; pres. Bogardus Med. Sys. Inc. Author: Practical Applied Physics of Radiology and Nuclear Medicine, 1969; contbg. author: Benign and Malignant Tumors of the Bladder, 1971, Radiation Biology for the Physician, 1973; contbr. articles to profl. jours. Fellow Am. Coll. Radiology (bd. chancellors, sec.-treas. 1987-91, pres. 1991-92); mem. Okla. Soc. Nuc. Medicine (charter pres. 1966), Am. Soc. Therapeutic Radiology (nat. sec. 1968-70, treas. 1987-88, pres. 1989-90), S.W. Regions Soc. Nuc. Medicine, Okla. Radiol. Soc. (treas. 1970, pres. 1974-75, counselor to Am. Coll. Radiology 1976-85), Okla. County Radiol. Soc. (pres. 1974). Office: U Okla Med Ctr 825 NE 101st Oklahoma City OK 73104 Home: 15021 Dourdan Ct Oklahoma City OK 73142-1807 Office Phone: 405-271-3577. Business E-Mail: carl-bogardus@ouohsc.edu.

BOGDAN, MICHAEL ANDREW, plastic surgeon; b. Washington, Apr. 12, 1971; s. Victor Michael and Ulla Eva-Maria Bogdan; m. Isidra Veve, Mar. 13, 1999; children: Alexander Michael, Andrew Edwin. BS in Zoology, BS in Chemistry, U. of Md., College Park, 1993; MD, Stanford U., Calif., 1998. Lic. Med. Bd. Calif., Bd. Med. Examiners, Colo., Edn. Dept., NY, Tex. Med. Bd., 2007, diplomate Am. Bd. Plastic Surgery, 2006. Intern in gen. surgery U. Calif.-San Francisco, Stanford Health Care, 1998—99; resident in plastic surgery Stanford U. Med. Ctr., 1999—2003, chief resident in plastic surgery, 2003—04; fellow in aesthetic surgey Manhattan Eye, Ear and Throat Hosp., NYC, 2004—05; cosmetic surgeon Napa Valley Plastic Surgery, Inc., Napa, Calif., 2005—07, Southlake Plastic Surgery, Tex., 2007—08; pvt. practice, 2008—14. Presenter in field. Author: (book chpt.) Advances in Plastic and Reconstructive Surgery; contbr. articles to profl. jours. and presentations (Tiffany award Am. Soc. of Aesthetic Plastic Surgery, 2004). Mem.: AMA, Rhinoplasty Soc., Dallas Soc. Plastic Surgery, Tex. Soc. Plastic Surgeons, Am. Soc. Aesthetic Plastic Surgery, Internat. Soc. Aesthetic Plastic Surgery, Am. Soc. Plastic Surgeons, ZedPlast, Alpha Lambda Delta, Phi Kappa Phi. Office: 410 N Carroll AVe Ste 170 Southlake TX 76092 Business E-Mail: info@drmichaelbogdan.com.

BOGDANOFF, ELLYN SETNOR, state legislator; b. North Miami, Fla., Oct. 17, 1959; m. Steven Bogdanoff; children: Matthew, Alec, Danna. BS in Ins., Risk Mgmt., U. Fla., 1980; JD, Nova Southeastern U., Shepard Broad Law Sch., 2003. Atty.; mem. Dist. 91 Fla. House of Reps., Tallahassee, 2004—10, majority whip, 2006—08, chair fin. and tax coun., vice chair rules and calendar coun., mem. joint legis. budget commn., select com. on Seminole Indian compact rev., full appropriations coun. on edn. and econ. devel.; mem. Dist. 25 Fla. State Senate, 2011—. Mem. The Human Rights Bd., Broward County, 1997—2000; mem. edn. adv. com. City of Ft. Lauderdale, 1997—2000; mem. transition team Gov. Jeb Bush, Fla., 1998—99; mem. The State Bd. Dirs., WAGES Program, 1998—2000; mem. adv. bd. The Homeless Initiative Partnership, Broward County, 2000; mem. State Elections Commn., 2000—01, Ft. Lauderdale Planning & Zoning Bd., 2002; chair Broward County Children's Services Bd., 2003—05; mem. Fed. Jud. Nominating Commn., 2005—08. Mem.: The Fla. Bar. Republican. Jewish. Office: Ste 202 1845 Cordova Rd Fort Lauderdale FL 33316 also: Fla State Senate 212 Senate Office Bldg 404 South Monroe St Tallahassee FL 32399-1100 Office Phone: 954-467-4205, 850-487-5100. Business E-Mail: bogdanoff.ellyn.web@flsenate.gov.

BOGER, JOHN CHARLES (JACK BOGER), law educator, dean; b. Concord, NC, Sept. 8, 1946; s. Charles Edgar Jr. and Mary (Snead) B.; m. Jennifer Lynn Brackenbury, May 13, 1947; children: Gretchen Elisabeth, Peter Grayson. BA, Duke U., 1968; MDiv, Yale U., 1971; JD, U. N.C., 1974. Bar: N.Y. 1975, U.S. Ct. Appeal, U.S. Supreme Ct. Assoc. atty. Paul, Weiss, Rifkind, Wharton & Garrison, NYC, 1974-75, 76-78; law clk. to Justice Samuel Silverman N.Y. Appellate Divsn., NYC, 1975-76; asst. counsel NAACP Legal Def. and Edn. Fund, Inc., NYC, 1978-90; assoc. prof. law U. NC Sch. Law, Chapel Hill, 1990-94, prof. law, 1994—, assoc. dean for acad. affairs, 1995—98, dean, 2006—, Wade Edwards Disting. Prof. of Law. Chair Poverty and Race Rsch. Action Coun., Washington, 1989—; dep. dir. Ctr. for Civil Rights at U. N.C., 2002—2004. Co-editor: Race, Poverty and American Cities, 1996; contbr. articles to profl. jours. Mem.: Order of the Coif, Phi Beta Kappa. Home: 104 Emerywood Pl Chapel Hill NC 27516-8718 Office: UNC School of Law Van Hecke-Wettach Hall 160 Ridge Road CB #3380 Chapel Hill NC 27599-3380 Office Phone: 919-962-4417. Office Fax: 919-962-1170. Business E-Mail: jcboger@email.unc.edu.*

BOGGS, CHARLES HARMON, JR., retired surgeon; b. Washington, July 4, 1923; MD, Northwestern U., Evanston, Ill., 1950. Diplomate Am. Bd. Surgery. Intern Emergency Hosp., Washington, 1951, resident, 1952—53; intern Passavant Meml., Chgo., 1952; resident Northwestern U., Chgo., 1953—56; with VA Hosp., Roanoke, Va., 1956—57; pvt. practice Morgantown, W.Va., 1957—58, VAMC, Salem, Va., 1958—91; clin. instr. U. Va. Sch. Medicine, 1971—79, asst. prof. surgery, 1979—91; ret., 1991.

BOGGS, DANNY JULIAN, federal judge; b. Havana, Cuba, Oct. 23, 1944; s. Robert Lilburn and Yolanda (Pereda) Boggs; m. Judith Susan Solow, Dec. 23, 1967; children: Rebecca, David, Jonathan. AB cum laude, Harvard Coll., Cambridge, Mass., 1965; JD, U. Chgo., 1968; LLD (hon.), U. Detroit Mercy, 1994. Dep. commr. Ky. Dept. Econ. Security, 1969—70; legal counsel, adminstrv. asst. to Gov. State of Ky., 1970—71; legis. counsel to Rep. legislators Ky. Gen. Assembly, 1972; asst. to solicitor gen. US Dept. Justice, Washington, 1973—75; asst. to chmn. FPC, Washington, 1975—77; dep. minority counsel US Senate Energy Com., Washington, 1977—79; of counsel Bushnell, Gage, et al., Washington, 1979—80; spl. asst. to Pres. The White House, Washington, 1981—83; dep. sec. US Dept. Energy, Washington, 1983—86; judge US Ct. Appeals (6th cir.), Cin., 1986—, chief judge, 2003—09. Mem. adv. com. on appellate rules Jud. Conf. US, 1991—94, com. on automation and tech., 1994—2000. Mem. vis. com. U. Chgo. Law Sch., 1984—87, 1999—2002; trustee Lexington Sch., 1999—2005; del. Rep. Nat. Conv., 1972; staff dir. energy subcom. Rep. Platform Com., 1980. Mem.: ABA (chair appellate judges conf. 2001—02), Jud. Conf. US (exec. com. 2008—09), Mont Pelerin Soc., Ky. Bar Assn., Phila. Soc., Phi Delta Phi, Order of Coif. Office: US Ct Appeals US Courthouse 601 W Broadway Ste 220 Louisville KY 40202-2227 Office Phone: 502-625-3900.

BOGGS, JACK AARON, retired banker, municipal government official, publisher; b. Easley, SC, July 4, 1935; s. Walter Benston and Bessie Mae (Jones) B.; m. Isabel Thomas Brown, July 7, 1965; children— James Benston, Renee Chaplin, Edward Cunningham, Donn Lester. BS in Bus. Econs, U. S.C., 1964; grad., Sch. Banking, U. Wis., 1974. Cert. internal auditor, chartered bank auditor. With USN, 1952—56, USNR, 1956—60, SC Air Nat. Guard, 1960—62; Sec.-treas. Cedarpoint Farms Corp., Columbia, SC, 1963-67; auditor S.C. Nat. Bank, Columbia, 1967-76; pres. S.C. Automated Clearing House Assn., 1976—2008, ret., 2009; sec., treas. Arcadia Publs., 2002—; sec.-treas. E.C. Boggs Law Firm, 2002—; treas. SC Arch. Soc., 2008—11. Mem. 5th dist. ops. adv. com. Fed. Res. Bank of Richmond, 1997-99; instr. S.C. Bankers Sch., 1972-80; sec., treas. Five Star Pubs., 1986-88; bd. dirs. NACHA, Inc., 1989-2000; vice chmn. ACH Exec. Dirs. Group, 1989-90, chmn., 1991-93. Mem. town coun., Town of Arcadia Lakes, SC, 1977-85, mayor, 1985-89, chief of police, 1990-91; treas. SC Fedn. Older Ams., 1982-84; pres. Fairfield 600 Hunt Club, 1983-2009. Recipient 1st award, Bank Adminstrn. Inst. Mem. Inst. Internal Auditors (bd. govs. 1971-74, pres. 1973-74, internat. rsch. com. 1972-75, internat. membership com. 1976), Bank Adminstrn. Inst. (1st award 1972), S.C. Ducks Unltd. (treas. 1984-92, 98-2002, state chmn. 1992-94), Explorers Club (treas. 2013-), Woodward Hunt Club (treas. 2013-), Sigma Delta Pi, Chi Psi. Democrat. Unitarian Universalist. Achievements include one of first in development of electronic payment systems. Avocations: stamp collecting/philately, hunting, fishing. Home: 804 Arcadia Lakes Dr Columbia SC 29206-1321 Personal E-mail: duckboggs@aol.com.

BOGGS, JAMES ERNEST, chemistry professor; b. Cleve., June 9, 1921; s. Ernest Beckett and Emily (Reid) B.; m. Ruth Ann Rogers, June 22, 1948 (dec. 2002); children: Carol, Ann, Lynne. AB, Oberlin Coll., 1943; MS in Chemistry, U. Mich., 1944, PhD, 1953. Rsch. chemist Manhattan Dist. Project, Linde Air Products, Tonawanda, NY, 1944-46; asst. prof. dept. chemistry Eastern Mich. U., Ypsilanti, 1949-52; instr. U. Mich. at Ann Arbor, 1952-53; asst. prof. dept. chemistry U. Tex., Austin, 1953—58, assoc. prof., 1958-66, prof., 1966-98; emeritus prof., 1998—; asst. dean Grad. Sch. U. Tex., Austin, 1958-67, dir. Center for Structural Studies, 1969-79, acting dir. Inst. Theoretical Chemistry, 1979-81. Program officer for theoretical and computational chemistry NSF, 1991-94; founder, organizer series Austin Symposia on Molecular Structure, 1966—2010; chmn. subcom. on theoretical chemistry Internat. Union Pure and Applied Chemistry, 1995-01; internat. lectr. in field. Mem. editl. bd. Jour. Molecular Structure, Structural Chemistry, Asian Jour. of Spectroscopy; contbr. over 340 articles to profl. jours. Recipient Starck prize, 2010. Fellow Am. Chem. Soc.; mem. Am. Phys. Soc. Nat. Acad. Scis. (India), Phi Beta Kappa, Sigma Xi, Phi Lambda Upsilon, Gamma Alpha. Achievements include research in structural chemistry, microwave spectroscopy, quantum chemistry. Office: U Tex Dept Chemistry 1 University Sta A5300 Austin TX 78712 Home Phone: 512-466-9145; Office Phone: 512-466-9145. Business E-Mail: james.boggs@mail.utexas.edu.

BOHAC, DWAYNE A., state legislator; b. Houston, Sept. 4, 1956; m. Dawn Bohac; children: Foster, Faith, Sterling, Reagan. B in Polit. Sci. and Mktg., Tex. A&M U. Small retail bus. owner, Tex.; mem. Dist. 138 Tex. House of Representatives, 2002—. Mem.: Heights C. of C., Justice for All, White Oak Bayou Assn., Oaks Dad Club, Candlelight Woods & Estates Civic Club. Republican. Office: 2600 Gessner Rd Ste 212 Houston TX 77080 also: Room E2.904 Capitol Extension PO Box 2910 Austin TX 78768 Office Phone: 713-460-2800, 512-463-0727.

BOHANON, RICHARD LEE, federal bankruptcy judge; b. Oklahoma City, Feb. 9, 1935; s. Luther L. and Marie F. (Swatek) Bohanon; m. Ann L. Eddleman; children: Christopher, David, Philip. BA, Dartmouth Coll., 1957; LLB, Okla. U., 1960; LLM, NY U., 1962. Bar: Okla. 60, US Ct. Appeals 61, US Supreme Ct. 76. Ptnr. Bohanon & Barth, Okla. City, 1964—79, Andrews, Davis, Legg, Bixler, Milsten & Price, Okla. City, 1979—82; judge US Bankruptcy Ct., Western Dist. Okla., Okla. City, 1982—. Mem.: Nat. Conf. Bankruptcy Judges (bd. of govs.). Office: US Ct House 215 Dean A Mcgee Ave Oklahoma City OK 73102-3440

BOHN, ROBERT G., board member, retired manufacturing executive; Dir., Ops., European Automotive Group Johnson Controls; v.p., ops. Oshkosh Truck Corp., Wis., 1992—94, pres., COO, 1994—97, pres., CEO, 1997—2000, chmn., pres., CEO, 2000—07, chmn., CEO, 2007—10. Bd. dirs. Menasha Corp., Graco Inc., 1999—2008, Carlisle Companies Inc., 2008—, Parker Hannifin Corp., 2010—. Office: Carlisle Companies Inc Bd Directors 13925 Ballantyne Corporate Pl Ste 400 Charlotte NC 28277 Office Phone: 704-501-1100. Office Fax: 704-501-1190. E-mail: rbohn@carlisle.com.

BOHNERT, BRAD C., retail executive; Attended, Murray State U., 1985. Dir., pub. rels., events HSN, Inc. Office: HSN Inc 1 HSN Dr Saint Petersburg FL 33729 Office Phone: 727-872-1000. Business E-Mail: brad.bohnert@hsn.net.

BOINEAU, FRANKLIN GIRARD, pediatric nephrologist; b. Orangeburg, SC, July 13, 1943; s. Franklin Girard Jr. and Rachel (Pratt) B.; m. Margaret Kizer, Aug. 14, 1965; children: Stephen Kizer, Girard Cullen. BS, Coll. Charleston, 1965; MD, Med. U. S.C., Charleston, 1969. Diplomate Am. Bd. Pediat., Am. Bd. Pediat. Nephrology. Intern Children's Hosp. Phila., 1969-70; asst. resident pediat. Strong Meml. Hosp., Rochester, NY, 1970-71, assoc. resident pediat., 1971, chief resident pediat., 1972; fellow pediat. nephrology Med. Ctr. Cornell U., NYC, 1972-74, rsch. fellow physiology Med. Coll., 1974-75; asst. prof. pediat. U. Rochester, 1975-78; from asst. prof. pediat. to assoc. prof. Tulane U. Sch. Medicine, New Orleans, 1978-89, prof. pediat., 1989—2005; dir. pediat. nephrology Tulane U. Hosp., 1978—2005; med. dir. pediat. nephrology Children's Hosp. Sys., Greenville, SC, 2005—. Invited cons.nephrology U. South Ala. Sch. Medicine, Mobile, 1980-81; med. adv. com. La. High Blood Pressure Control Program, 1979-85; Coralie Virginia Schafer chair pediat. nephrology Tulane U. Sch. Medicine, 1998. Contbr. numerous articles, papers to profl. and med. jours. Mem. adv. bd. Handicapped Children's Services Program State of La., 1984—88. Fellow Am. Acad. Pediat. (exec. com. nephrology sect. 1984-87); mem. Am. Soc. Pediatric Nephrology, Am. Soc. Nephrology, Am. Soc. Transplant Physicians, Greater New Orleans Pediat. Soc., Internat. Soc. Nephrology, Nat. Kidney Found., Nat. Kidney Found. La., La. State Med. Soc. (subcom. on hypertension 1980-85), Orleans Parish Med. Soc., Southern Soc. for Pediat. Rsch., Southwest Pediat. Nephrology Study Group. Avocation: sailing. Office: Children's Hosp Outpatient Ctr 200 Patewood Dr Ste A200 Greenville SC 29615 Office Phone: 865-454-5105. Business E-Mail: fboineau@ghs.org.

BOLAND, CLEMENT RICHARD, gastroenterologist, educator; s. Clement Richard and Catherine Jane Boland; m. Patricia Ellen Sweeney, Sept. 4, 1970; children: Tara Sweeney Boland-Maggiotto, Maureen Sweeney, Brigid Sweeney. MD, Yale U., New Haven, 1973. Lic. Am. Bd. Internal Medicine, 1981. Asst. prof. medicine U. Calif., San Francisco, 1981—84; prof. medicine U. Mich. Sch. Medicine, Ann Arbor, 1984—95; prof. medicine, chief of gi U. Calif. Sch. Medicine, San Diego, 1995—2003; chief divsn. gastroenterology Baylor U. Med. Ctr., Dallas, 2003—. Contbr. scientific papers and manuscripts in field. Fellow: Am. Gastroent. Assn.; mem.: Assn. Am. Physicians. Avocations: jogging, opera.

BOLAND, JAMES PIUS, surgeon, educator; b. Phila., Mar. 6, 1931; s. John Patrick and Beatrice Christine (Murphy) B.; m. Kathryn Ann Watts, May 18, 1963; children: Beatrice, James, Kathryn, Sara, Angela, Genevieve. BS, St. Joseph's Coll., Phila., 1948-52; MD, Jefferson Med. Coll., Phila., 1952-56; MPH, U. South Fla., 1998. Diplomate Am. Bd. Surgery, Am. Bd. Thoracic Surgery, Am. Bd. Surg. Critical Care. Asst. prof. to prof. Med. Coll. Pa., Phila., 1964-76; prof. surgery W.Va. U., Charleston, 1976—, chmn. dept. surgery, 1976—. Capt. USNR, ret. Decorated Navy Commendation medal. Fellow ACS. Roman Catholic. Office: W Va U/CAMC 3110 Maccorkle Ave SE Charleston WV 25304-1210 Home: 1108 Kanawha Blvd Charleston WV 25301

BOLAND, JOHN KEVIN, bishop; b. Monkstown, Ireland, Apr. 25, 1935; s. John Joseph and Gertrude (O'Brien) Boland. B, Catholic Univ., Washington, 1964; M, Fordham Univ., NYC, 1989. Ordained priest Diocese of Savannah, Ga., 1959; assoc. pastor St. Mary on the Hill, Augusta, Ga., 1959—61, Cathedral of St. John the Baptist, Savannah, 1961—62; vice chancellor Diocese of Savannah, 1965—68; pastor St. Michael's, Tybee Island, Ga., 1967—68; rector Cathedral of St. John the Baptist, 1970—72; pastor Blessed Sacrament, Savannah, 1972—83; vicar gen. Diocese of Savannah, 1973—95, personnel advisor, 1976—95, chancellor, 1978—83; pastor St. Anne parish, Columbus, Ga., 1983—95; ordained bishop, 1995; bishop Diocese of Savannah, 1995—2011, bishop emeritus, 2011—. Roman Catholic. Office: Diocese of Savannah 601 E Liberty St Savannah GA 31401-5196 Office Phone: 912-201-4100. Office Fax: 912-201-4101.

BOLAS, GERALD DOUGLAS, museum director, art historian, educator; b. LA, Nov. 1, 1949; s. Norman Theodore and Elizabeth Louise (Douglas) B.; children: Ellen Claire, John David. BA, U. Calif., Santa Barbara, 1972, MA, 1975; PhD, CUNY, 1998. Tchg. asst. U. Calif., Santa Barbara, 1973-74; NEH mus. intern Yale U. Art Gallery, New Haven, 1975-76, asst. to dir., 1976-77; dir. Washington U. Gallery of Art, St. Louis, 1977-88, Portland Art Mus., Oreg., 1988-92, Ackland Art Mus., U. NC, Chapel Hill, 1994—. Adj. prof. art history Washington U., 1982-88, U. NC, Chapel Hill, 1994—; advisor Mo. Arts Coun., St. Louis, 1981-82; field reviewer Inst. Mus. Svcs., Washington, 1980-83; panelist NEA, 1989, NEH, 1990, 95, NC Arts Coun., 1995; bd. dirs. Asian Art Soc. of Washington U., 1983-88; mem. No. Calif. adv. com. Archives of Am. Art; active Lake Oswego Arts Commn., 1993-94. Author: Illustrated Checklist of Washington University Collection, 1981; contbr. to books: Ketav: Flesh and Word in Israeli Art, 1996, Paris in Japan: The Japanese Encounter with European Painting, 1987; also contbr. articles to other publs.; numerous catalog forewords. Organizer numerous exhbns. Fellow Winterthur Mus., 1993, Smithsonian Instn., 1993. Mem. Coll. Art Assn., Assn. Art Mus. Dirs.

BOLCH, CARL EDWARD, JR., oil industry executive, lawyer; b. St. Louis, Feb. 28, 1943; s. Carl Edward and Juanita (Newton) Bolch; m. Susan Bass; children: Carl, Allison, Natalie, Melanie, Jordan. BS in Econs, U. Pa., 1964; JD, Duke U., 1967. Cert. Fla., 1967. CEO, chmn. bd. dirs. RaceTrac Petroleum,Inc., Atlanta, 1967—. Chmn. bd. dir. Nat. Assn. Convenience Stores (NACS), 2000—. Edition editor Close Corporations, 1967. Mem.: Nat. Assn. Convenience Stores (bd. dirs. 1994—), Soc. Ind. Gasoline Marketers (pres. 1987—89), Fla. Bar Assn., ABA. Office: RaceTrac Petroleum Inc PO Box 105035 Atlanta GA 30348-5035 also: Racetrac Petroleum 3225 Cumberland Blvd SE Ste 100 Atlanta GA 30339-6408

BOLCH, JAMES R., industrial electrical equipment company executive; b. Shreveport, La. BS in Mechanical Engring., Tulane U.; MS in Mechanical Engring., U. Fla.; attended Advanced Mgmt. Program, Harvard Bus. Sch. Several positions including engring. and program mgmt. roles, bus. area mgr. United Technologies Optical Systems and Otis Elevator Co., United Technologies Corp. (UTC); service and product adminstrn. positions Otis Elevator Co., United Technologies Corp. (UTC), 1991, 1999; v.p. Otis Services, United Technologies Corp. (UTC); v.p., ops UTC Power Divsn.; exec. v.p., service bus., N.Am. services functions Schindler Elevator Corp., 2005; sr. v.p., pres., indsl. technologies sector Ingersoll Rand Co., 2005—10; pres., CEO Exide Technologies, 2010—. Bd. dirs. Exide Technologies, 2010—. Office: Exide Technologies 13000 Deefield Parkway Bldg 200 Milton GA 30004

BOLES, JAMES L., JR., state legislator; m. Melissa Boles; 4 children. AA, Sandhills Cmty. Coll.; BA in Funeral Svc., Cincinnati Coll. Mortuary Sci. Owner & pres. Boles Funeral Home & Crematory Inc., 1984—; mem. Dist. 52 NC House of Reps., 2009—. Republican. Office: North Carolina House of Representatives 300 N Salisbury St Rm 528 Raleigh NC 27603-5925 Home: 425 W Pennsylvania Ave Southern Pines NC 28387 Home Phone: 910-692-6262; Office Phone: 919-733-5903. Business E-Mail: Jamie.Boles@ncleg.net.

BOLEY, DONNA JEAN, state legislator; b. Bens Run, W.Va., Dec. 9, 1935; d. Glen A. and Grace Jones Northcraft; m. Jack Edward Boley, 1956; children: Kari Lynn, Brian Lee. Mem. Dist. 3 W.Va. State Senate, 1985—, minority leader, 1991—97, mem. Edn. Com., Fin. Com., Govt. Orgn. Com., Health and Human Resources Com., Mil. Com. & Rules Com. Mem.: Pleasant County Rep. Women, St. Mary's Women's Club (pres. 1972—74, 1980—81, dir.). Republican. Methodist. Office: State Capitol, Rm 213 W Bldg 1 Charleston WV 25305 Mailing: 2332 Greens Run Rd Saint Marys WV 26170 Office Phone: 304-684-3266. E-mail: donnaboley@suddenlink.net.

BOLIAN, GEORGE CLEMENT, healthcare executive, psychiatrist; b. New Orleans, May 24, 1930; s. George William and Effie (McQuaid) B.; m. Patricia Ruth Green, July 27, 1957 (div. 1984); children— Mark Geoffrey, Gregory Wayne; m. Patricia Ann Morrison, Mar. 26, 1984; children— Joshua Sean, Zachary Ryan. BA, U. Chgo., 1950, Harvard U., 1952; MD, Tulane U., 1957. Diplomate Am. Bd. Psychiatry and Neurology. Intern Nassau County Med. Ctr., East Meadow, N.Y., 1957-58; resident psychiatry and child psychiatry U. Cin., 1958-62; instr., asst. prof. U. Wash., Seattle, 1965-70; dir. dept. psychiatry Children's Orthopaedic Hosp. and Med. Ctr., Seattle, 1968-70; assoc. prof. U. Hawaii, Honolulu, 1970-86; dir. community mental health ctr. Queen's Med. Ctr., Honolulu, 1971-83, sr. v.p., 1976-83, pres., 1983-86; practice medicine, Nashville, 1986-87; assoc. prof., acting dir. child and adolescent psychiatry Vanderbilt U., Nashville, 1987—89, prof., 2003—, dir. resident edn., 1988-93, dir. child and adolescent psychiatry, 1999—2007, vice chmn. dept. psychiatry, 1988—; interim chmn. dept. psychiatry, 2002—05; chmn. Med. Sch. Acad. Programs Vanderbilt U., Nashville, 1993—; med. dir. The Psychiat. Hosp. Vanderbilt, Nashville, 1999—2008. Contbr. numerous articles to profl. jours. Served to capt. U.S. Army, 1962-65 Fellow Am. Psychiat. Assn. (life), Am. Acad. Child Psychiatry, Am. Orthopsychiat. Assn. (life); mem. AMA. Home: 6002 Hickory Valley Rd Nashville TN 37205-1306

BOLIN, MICHAEL F., state supreme court justice; b. Jefferson County, Ala. m. Rosemary Bolin; 1 child. BS in Bus. Admin. (hon.), Samford U., 1970; JD, Cumberland Sch. of Law, 1973. Atty. pvt. practice, Birmingham, Ala., 1973—88; probate judge Jefferson County, Ala., 1988—2003; assoc. justice Ala. Supreme Ct., 2005—. Former chmn. Education and Adoption Com.; former mem. Children's Code Com., Probate Procedures Com., Adoption Com., Paternity Com. Ala Law Inst.; chief election official Jefferson County; chmn. Ala. Electronic Voting Com.; mem. Governor's Commn. on Consolidation, Efficiency, and Funding, Jefferson County Republican Exec. Com. and Steering Com.; campaign coordinator Senator Jeff Sessions, 2002; county party chmn. Jefferson County Republican Party, 2003; mem. Jefferson County Republican Assembly. Mem.: Mid-Ala. Republican Club, Ala. Probate Judges Assn. (pres., sec., treasurer, v.p., pres.). Office: Ala Supreme Ct 300 Dexter Ave Montgomery AL 36104*

BOLING, DAVID ALAN, health policy center executive, former legislative staff member; m. Mine Sasaguri; children: Christopher, Ellen. BA in History, U. Ark., Fayetteville, 1987, JD with honors, 1991; LLM, Columbia U. Sch. Law, NYC, 1994. Bar: Ark. 1993, DC 1996. Asst. English tchr. Fujishiro Town Bd. Edn., Japan, 1988—89; Mansfield fellow Maureen & Mike Mansfield Found., 1999—2001; trial atty., antitrust divsn. US Dept. Justice, Washington, 1995—2005; counsel Mitchell, Williams, Selig, Gates & Woodyard, Little Rock, 2005—07; chief of staff Office US Rep. Vic Snyder, Washington, 2007—10; legal cons. Williams & Anderson PLC, Little Rock, 2010; sr. policy & legal analyst Ark. Ctr. Health Improvement, Little Rock, 2011—. Adj. prof. U. Ark. Little Rock Sch. Law, 2011—. Candidate from 2nd Congl. dist. Ark. US House of Reps., 2010. Mem.: Sigma Nu. Democrat. Office: Arkansas Center for Health Improvement 1401 West Capitol Ste 300 Victory Bldg Little Rock AR 72201 Office Phone: 202-225-2506. E-mail: david.boling@mail.house.gov.

BOLING, EDWARD JOSEPH, retired academic administrator; b. Sevier County, Tenn., Feb. 19, 1922; s. Sam R. and Nerissa (Clark) B.; m. Carolyn Pierce, Aug. 8, 1950; children: Mark Edward, Brian Marshall, Steven Clark. BS in Accounting, U. Tenn., 1948, MS in Stats., 1950; EdD in Ednl. Adminstrn, Vanderbilt U., 1961; LLD (hon.), U. Richmond, 1984. With Wilby-Kinsy Theatre Corp., Knoxville, Tenn., 1940-41, Aluminum Co. Am., 1941-42; instr. statistics U. Tenn., 1948-50; research statistician Carbide & Carbon Chem. Corp., Oak Ridge, 1950; supr. source and fissionable materials accounting Carbide & Carbon Chem. Corp. (K-25 plant), 1951-54; budget dir. Tenn., 1955-59; commr. finance and adminstrn., 1959-61; v.p. U. Tenn., 1961-70, pres., 1970-88, pres. emeritus, 1988—, univ. prof., 1988-92. Mem. So. Regional Edn. Bd., 1957-61, 70-81, 83-90, 92-96, mem. exec. com., 1974-75, 79-81, vice chmn., 1986-88; mem. Edn. Commn. of States, 1970-82; trustee, chmn. Am. Coll. Testing Program, 1983-85; dir. emeritus Allied Signal Corp., CSX, N.A. Philips, United Foods, Home Fed. Bank. Author: (with D. A. Gardiner) Forecasting University Enrollment, 1952, Methods of Objectifying The Allocation of Tax Funds to Tennessee State Colleges, 1961. Mem. Nat. Govs. Conf. Good Will Tour to Brazil and Argentina, 1960; Mem. com. on taxation Am. Council on Edn. Served with AUS, 1943-46, ETO. Mem. Am. Statis. Assn., Assn. Higher Edn., Nat. Assn. Land-Grant Colls. (com. on financing higher edn.), Am. Coll. Pub. Rels. Assn. (trustee chmn. com. taxation and philanthropy), Am. Coun. on Edn., Knoxville C. of C. (bd. dirs., chmn. bd. 1989-91), Tenn. Resource Valley (dir., chmn. bd. 1991-92, chmn. supr. com. 1992-02, chmn. 21st century jobs initiative), Am. Legion, Phi Kappa Phi (Scholarship award 1947), Beta Gamma Sigma (charter pres. Alpha chpt. 1948), Phi Delta Kappa, Omicron Delta Kappa, Beta Alpha Psi. Democrat. Office: U Tenn System Andy Holt Towers Ste 731 Knoxville TN 37996-0001 Office Phone: 865-974-3500.

BOLING, PETER A., geriatrician, educator; MD, U. Rochester, 1981. Diplomate Am. Bd. Internal Medicine, 1984, Am. Bd. Internal Medicine-geriatric medicine, 2000. Intern Med. Coll. Va. Hosp., 1982, resident internal medicine, 1984; hosp. affiliation includes: Va. Commonwealth Univ. Med. Ctr.; prof. medicine Med. Coll. Va. Hosp. Office: Virginia Commonwealth University Medical Center 1250 East Marshall St Richmond VA 23219 Office Phone: 804-828-9000.

BOLLER, PAUL FRANKLIN, JR., retired American history educator, writer; b. Spring Lake, NY, Dec. 31, 1916; s. Paul Franklin and Grace (Hall) B. BA, Yale U., 1939, PhD, 1947; DLitt, Tex. Wesleyan U., 1993; Degree, US Navy, 1946. From asst. to full prof. So. Meth. U., Dallas, 1948-66; prof. U. Mass., Boston, 1966-76; Lyndon Johnson prof. history Tex. Christian U., Ft. Worth, 1976-83, prof. emeritus, 1983—. Vis. prof. U. Tex., Austin, 1963-64. Author: (with J. Tilford) This Is Our Nation, 1961, George Washington and Religion, 1963, Quotemanship, 1967, American Thought in Transition, 1865-1900, 1967, American Transcendentalism, 1830-1860, 1974, Freedom and Fate in American Thought, 1978, Presidential Anecdotes, 1981, Presidential Campaigns, 1984, (with R. Story) A More Perfect Union, 1984, (with R.L. Davis) Hollywood Anecdotes, 1987, Presidential Wives, 1988, (with J. George) They Never Said It, 1989, Congressional Anecdotes, 1991, Memoirs of an Obscure Professor, 1992, Not So!, 1995, Presidential Inaugurations, 2001, Presidential Diversions: the Presidents at Play from George Washington to George W. Bush, 2007, Essays on the Presidents: Principles and Politics, 2012. Lt. (j.g.) USNR, 1942-46. Mem. Tex. Inst. Letters, Authors Guild, Phi Alpha Theta, Phi Beta Kappa. Democrat. Avocations: music, films, swimming. Office: 1600 Tex St # 908 Fort Worth TX 76102 Office Phone: 817-257-7288.

BOLLINGER, RALPH RANDAL, surgeon, researcher; b. Dearborn, Mich., Oct. 3, 1944; s. Ralph Perry and Edith Delores (Algren) B.; m. Monika Irmgard Koch, May 1, 1965; children: Christine Laura, Mark Randal. BS in Biology, Tulane U., 1966, MD, 1970, MS in Biochemistry, 1970; PhD in Immunology, Duke U., 1977, MBA with cert. in Health Svc. Mgmt., 1997. Diplomate Am. Bd. Surgery. Stress physiology rsch. physician USAF Sch. of Aerospace Medicine, Brooks AFB, Tex., 1972-74; postdoctoral fellow, instr. in surgery, dept. immunology Duke U., Durham, NC, 1974-76; resident in surgery Duke U. Med. Ctr., 1970—72, 1977—79, chief resident in surgery, 1979—80, asst. prof. surgery, 1980—86, asst. prof. immunology, 1981—86, chief of surg. transplantation, 1983—99, assoc. prof. immunology, 1986—95, assoc. prof. surgery, 1986—91, prof. surgery, 1991—2008, prof. emeritus, 2008—, prof. immunology, 1995—2008, chief gen. surgery, 1994—2003, vice chair surgery, 2004—06, sr. ednl. advisor, 2006—07. Vice councillor United Network for Organ Sharing, Richmond, Va., 1986-88, councillor, 1989-91, v.p., 1991-92, pres., 1992-93; sec. Southeastern Organ Procurement Found., Richmond, 1988-89, v.p., 1989-90, pres., 1990-91; v.p. Carolina Organ Procurement Agy., Greenville, N.C., 1985-87, pres., 1987-89; trustee N.C. Kidney Found., Chapel Hill, 1983-90; pres. elect Durham-Orange County Med. Soc. 2004, pres. 2005. Contbr. numerous articles to profl. jours.; editor: Transplant Management, 1988; mem. editl. bd. Am. Surgeon, 1988, Jour. Surg. Rsch., 1993—96, Jour. ACS, 1996, Graft, 1998, Jour. Investigative Surgery, 2001. Com. chmn. Troop 408, Boy Scouts Am., Durham, N.C., 1982-89; mem. staff/parish rels. com. Duke Meml. Meth. Ch., Durham, 1985-87, 2009-12, chmn., 2003-2004, admin. bd., 2004-06, coun. on ministries, 1983-85, 2009-12. Maj. USAF, 1972—74. Recipient La. Pathology Soc. award Tulane U., 1979, Golden Apple award Duke U., 1984, 89. Fellow ACS; mem. Aerospace Med. Assn. (environ. sci. award 1978), Am. Soc. Transplant Surgeons (membership com. 1988, councillor 1989-93), Transplantation Soc., Soc. Univ. Surgeons, Am. Surg. Assn., So. Surg. Assn., N.C. Assn. Biomed. Rsch. (sec. 2001-03, vice chmn. 2003-05, chmn. 2005-07). Republican. Avocations: scuba diving, gardening, white water canoeing. Home: 1120 Infinity Rd Durham NC 27712-9765 Office: Duke U Med Ctr PO Box 2910 Durham NC 27710-2910

BOLOTIN, IRVING, retired construction executive, board member; b. US, 1933; m. Joan M. Bolotin; 1 child, Nancy Ruth. Sr. v.p. Lennar Corp., 1972—98. Bd. dirs. Lennar Corp., 1974—, Rechtien Internat. Trucks Inc., WPBT TV. Office: Lennar Corp Bd Directors 700 Northwest 107th Ave Suite 400 Miami FL 33172 Office Phone: 305-559-4000. Office Fax: 305-226-4158. Business E-Mail: Irving.Bolotin@lennar.com.

BOLSTERLI, MARGARET JONES, English professor, writer; b. Watson, Ark., May 10, 1931; d. Grover Clevel and Zena (Cason) Jones; m. Mark Bolsterli, Dec. 30, 1953 (div. Dec. 1964); children: Eric, David. BA with honors, U. Ark., 1952; MA, Washington U., St. Louis, 1953; PhD, U. Minn., 1967. Asst. prof. Augsburg Coll., Mpls., 1967-68; prof. English, U. Ark., Fayetteville, 1968-93, prof. emeritus, 1993—, dir. Ctr. for Ark. and Regional Studies, 1984-87. Fulbright lectr., Portugal, 1986; vis. rsch. fellow Yale U., 1997-98; bd. dirs. Ark. Humanities Coun., 1992-94. Author: The Early Community at Bedford Park, 1977, Vinegar Pie and Chicken Bread, 1982, Born in the Delta, 1991, A Remembrance of Eden, 1993, During Wind and Rain, 2008, Things You Need To Hear, 2012; contbr. articles and stories to Jour. Modern Lit., So. Quar., others. Recipient Porter prize, 2012; NEH Younger Humanist grantee, 1970-71; Ark. Endowment for Humanities grantee, 1980, 81 Mem. MLA (pres. women's caucus), South Cen. MLA. Democrat. Personal E-mail: mbolster3206@att.net.

BOLTE, TONY, retail executive; Grad., Midland Luth. Coll., Fremont, Nebr. V.p. Dillard's, Inc., 2009—. Office: Dillards Inc 1600 Cantrell Rd Little Rock AR 72201 Office Phone: 501-376-5200. Office Fax: 501-399-7831. E-mail: tony.bolte@dillards.com.

BOLTON, JOSEPH D., lawyer; b. La Crosse, Wis., Feb. 20, 1948; s. James R. Bolton; m. Alison Miller, June 15, 1975; children: Reid, Scott, Elizabeth. BA, Univ. Wis., 1970; JD, Univ. Chgo., Ill., 1974. Bar: Minn. 1974, Fla. 1976, US Dist. Ct. (so. dist.) Fla. 1991. Atty., ptnr. Shutts & Bowen, Miami, Fla., 1976—, mem. exec. com., mng. ptnr. of firm. Former troop leader Boy Scouts America; hon. bd. mem. Baptist Hosp. Found., Miami; mem. Miami-Dade cmty. bd. American Heart Assn. Named one of The Best Lawyers in America, 2010, 2011; named to Fla. Super Lawyers, 2006, 2007, 2009. Mem. Fla. Bar (cert. real estate law specialist), Deering Bay Yacht and Golf Club. Avocations: golf, swimming. Office: Shutts & Bowen LLP 201 S Biscayne Blvd Ste 1500 Miami FL 33131-4308 Office Phone: 305-379-9106. Office Fax: 305-347-7806. Business E-Mail: jbolton@shutts.com.

BOLTON, MARTHA O., writer; b. Searcy, Ark., Sept. 1, 1951; d. Lonnie Leon and Eunice Dolores Ferren; m. Russell Norman Bolton, Apr. 17, 1970; children: Russell Norman II, Matthew David, Anthony Shane. Freelance writer for various comedians, 1975-86; newspaper columnist Simi Valley Enterprise, Simi, Calif., 1979-87; staff writer Bob Hope, 1986—, The Mark and Kathy Show, 1995-96. Author: A Funny Thing Happened to Me on My Way Through the Bible, 1985, A View from the Pew, 1986, What's Growing Under Your Bed?, 1986, Tangled in the Tinsel, 1987, So. How'd I Get To Be in Charge of the Program?, 1988, Humorous Monologues, 1989, Let My People Laugh, 1989, If Mr. Clean Calls Tell Him I'm Not In, 1989, Journey to the Center of the Stage, 1990, If You Can't Stand the Smoke, Get Out of My Kitchen, 1990, Home, Home on the Stage, 1991, TV Jokes and Riddles, 1991, These Truths Were Made for Walking, 1991, When the Meatloaf Explodes It's Done, 1993, Childhood Is a Stage, 1993, Honey, It's Time To Weed the Carpets Again, 1994, Walk A Mile in His Truths, 1994, The Cafeteria Lady on the Loose, 1994, On the Loose, 1994, If the Pasta Wiggles, Don't Eat It, 1995, Bethlehem's Big Night, 1995, Club Family, 1995, When the Going Gets Tough, The Tough Start Laughing, 1995, Who Put The Pizza in the VCR?, 1996, And Now a World from Our Maker, 1997, A Lamb's Tale, 1998, Race You to The Fountain Of Youth, 2007, Rick and Bubba's Expert Guide to God, Country, Family and Anything Else We Can Think Of, 2006, The Rick and Bubba Code, 2007, Josiah for President, 2012; (lyrics) Mouth in Motion, Sermon on the Stage, 1998, Never Ask Delilah For A Trim, 1998, (with Mark Lowry) Piper's Night Before Christmas, (with Gene Perret) Talk About Hope, The Twelve Plays of Christmas, 1999, Don't Jump to Conclusions Without a Bungee Cord, 1999, I Love You...Still, 2000, Didn't My Skin Used to Fit, 2000, Piper Steals the Show, 2000, The "Official" Book series, 2002—, I Think Therefore I Have a Headache, 2003, Cooking with Hot Flashes, 2004, Growing Your Own Turtleneck, 2005, My Life As A Bystander (co-written with Jeff Allen), 2005, (with Brad Dickson) Maybe Life's Just Not That Into You, 2006, (with Phil Callaway) It's Always Darkest Before the Fridge Door Opens, 2006, 2010, If A Womans Hair is her Glory Why am I Tweezing my Chin?, 2010, Josiah for President, 2012, Bro: The Confession Musical, Librettist, 2010, Bear in the Burbs, 2010, Bethlehem or Bust Musical, 2011, Half Stitched Musical, 2012. Pres. Vista Elem. Sch. PTA, Simi, 1980-81. Recipient Emmy nomination for outstanding achievement in music and lyrics, 1988, Internat. Angel award, 1990, 91, 2001, 02, Amb. award Media Fellowship Internat., 1995. Mem. ASCAP, NATAS, Nat. League Am. Pen Women (pres. Simi Valley br. 1984-86, 96-98, Woman of Achievement award 1984, Pen Woman of Yr. award 1995, pres. 1996-98), Writers Guild Am. West. Avocation: travel. Home: PO Box 3046 Brentwood TN 37024 Personal E-mail: martha@marthabolton.com.

BOLTZ, BILL, retail executive; Attended, Northwestern U., Mont. State U., Billings. V.p., gen. mdse. mgr. Sears, Roebuck & Co.; v.p. merchandising lawn & garden outdoor living Home Depot, Inc. Office: Home Depot Inc 2455 Paces Ferry Rd NW Atlanta GA 30339-4024 Office Phone: 770-433-8211. Office Fax: 770-384-2356. E-mail: bill_boltz@homedepot.com.

BOMAN, DANIEL H., state legislator, lawyer; b. Tupelo, Miss., Dec. 7, 1974; children: Brooklyn, John Daniel. AA, Bevill State CC, Sumiton, Ala.; BA in Psychology, Auburn U., Ala.; JD, Birmingham Sch. Law, Ala. Pvt. practice atty.; mem. Dist. 16 Ala. House of Representatives, 2011—. Republican. Baptist. Office: Ala House of Reps Rm 536-C 11 S Union St Montgomery AL 36130 also: 55314 Hwy 17 Ste B Sulligent AL 35586 Office Phone: 334-242-7494, 205-999-2904. Business E-Mail: daniel_boman@thebomanfirm.com.

BOMMANNA, VASUDEVA M., allergist, immunologist; b. India, Oct. 3, 1959; MBBS, 1983. Diplomate Am. Bd. Pediats., Am. Bd. Allergy and Immunology. Rotating intern Jawaharlal Nehru Med. Coll., Belgaum, India, 1982-83; resident in pediatrics St. Luke's Roosevelt Med. Ctr., NYC, 1993-95; fellow in allergy and immunology State U. - Children's Hosp., Buffalo, N.Y., 1995-97; asst. clin. instr. pediatrics SUNY, Buffalo, 1995-97; pvt. practice, 1997—. Mem.: AMA, Am. Coll. Allercy and Immunology, Am. Acad. Allergy and Immunology, Am. Acad. Pediatrics. Office: 607 Russell Blvd Nacogdoches TX 75965-1247

BOMMIER, BERNARD, beverage company executive; V.p. process optimization. & SAP implementation Coca-Cola Enterprises, Inc., 2010—, v.p., SAP ops., European Group, 2010—. Office: Coca Cola Enterprises Inc 2500 Windy Ridge Pky Atlanta GA 30339 Office Phone: 770-989-3000. Office Fax: 770-989-3788. Business E-Mail: BBommier@na.cokecce.com.

BONANNO, PHYLLIS O., transportation executive; b. Andover, Mass., 1943; m. Evan R. Berlack. Attended, U. Conn. Personal asst. to pres. Lyndon Johnson; v.p., internat. trade Warnaco, Inc., 1986—97; pres., CEO Columbia Coll., 1997—2000; pres. Trade-Builders, Inc, 2000—01; pres., CEO International Trade Solutions, Inc., 2002—. Bd. dirs. U.S. Trade Representative's (USTR), 1977—86, Adams Express Co., 2003, BorgWarner Inc., 1999—, Petroleum & Resources Corp., 2003—, Mohawk Industries, Inc., 2004—. Former bd. dirs. Can. Am. Bus. Coun. Office: Mohawk Industries Inc 160 S Industrial Blvd Calhoun GA 30701 Office Phone: 706-629-7721. Office Fax: 706-624-3825.

BONAPARTE, RUDOLPH, engineering company executive; BS in Civil Engring., U. Tex., Austin, 1977; MS in Geotechnical Engring., U. Calif., Berkeley, 1978, PhD in Geotechnical Engring., 1981. Pres., CEO GeoSyntec Consultants, Inc., Atlanta, 1988—. Mem., civil and environ. engring. adv. coun. U. Calif., Berkeley. Contbr. articles to profl. jours., chapters to books. Recipient Award of Excellence, North Am. Geosynthetics Soc., 1991, IGS award, Internat. Geosynthetics Soc., 1994; named Overall Engr. of Yr., Ga. Soc. Profl. Engrs., 2004. Mem.: ASCE (J. James Croes medal 2000), NAE. Office: GeoSyntec Consultants Inc 2002 Summit Blvd NE Ste 885 Atlanta GA 30319 Office Phone: 404-267-1101. Office Fax: 404-267-1102. Business E-Mail: rudyb@geosyntec.com.

BOND, JULIAN, history professor, former civil rights association executive; b. Nashville, Jan. 14, 1940; s. Horace Mann and Julia Agnes (Washington) Bond; m. Pamela S. Horowitz, Mar. 17, 1990; children from previous marriage: Phyllis Jane, Horace Mann, Michael, Jeffrey, Julia. BA, Morehouse Coll., 1971; LLD (hon.), Dalhousie U., 1969, U. Bridgeport, 1969, Wesleyan U., Conn., 1969, U. Oreg., 1969, Syracuse U., 1970, Eastern Mich. U., 1971, Tuskegee Inst., 1971, Howard U., 1971, Morgan State U., 1971, Wilberforce U., 1971, Patterson State Coll., 1972, NH Coll., 1973, Detroit Inst. Tech., 1973; DCL (hon.), Lincoln U., Pa., 1970, Bates Coll., 1998, Northeastern U., 1999, Edward Waters Coll., 1995, Gonzaga Sch. Law, 1997, Calif. State U., Monterey Bay, 1998, Washington U., 2000; LLD (hon.), Audrey Cohen Coll., New York, 2001, Williams Coll., 2005, U. Ill., 2006, Loyola U., New Orleans, 2007, George Washington U., 2008, Va. State U., 2009. A founder Com. Appeal for Human Rights, 1960, Student Nonviolent Coordinating Com., 1960, comm. dir., 1961-66; reporter, feature writer Atlanta Inquirer, 1960-61, mng. editor, 1963; mem. Ga. House of Reps., from Fulton County, 1965-75, Ga. State Senate, 1975-87; Disting. prof. in-Residence American U., Washington, 1991—; prof. history U. Va., Charlottesville, Va., 1998—; chmn. NAACP, Baltimore, Md., 1998—2010. Vis. prof. history Drexel U., 1988—89; Arnold Bernhard vis. prof. polit. sci. Williams Coll., 1992. So. corr.: Reporting Racial Equality Wars; narrator Eyes on the Prize, Part 1, Part 2. Mem. adv. bd. Harvard Bus. Sch., Initiative Social Enterprise; bd. dirs. So. Conf. Edn. Fund, Coun. for a Liveable World, So. Poverty Law Ctr., pres. emeritus. Recipient Nat. Freedom award, 2002, Spingarn medal, NAACP, 2009, Living Legend award, Library of Congress, 2008; named to Power 150, Ebony mag., 2008. Office: University of Virginia Dept History PO Box 400180 Randall Hall Charlottesville VA 22904 Office Phone: 434-924-7972. Office Fax: 434-924-7891. E-mail: hjb7@virginia.edu.

BONDERMAN, DAVID, investment company executive, lawyer; b. Nov. 27, 1942; BA, U. Wash., Seattle, 1963; JD magna cum laude, Harvard U., 1966. Asst. prof. Tulane U. Sch. Law, New Orleans, 1967—68; spl. asst. to atty. gen. US Dept. Justice, Washington, 1968—69; fellow fgn. & comparative law Harvard University, 1969—70; ptnr. Arnold & Porter LLP, Washington, 1971—83; COO Keystone Inc. (Robert M. Bass Group), Fort Worth, Tex., 1983—92; co-founding ptnr., mng. gen. ptnr. TPG Capital (formerly Texas Pacific Group), Ft. Worth, 1993—; chmn. Ryanair Holdings PLC, 1996—. Bd. dirs. Burger King Holdings, Inc., Ducati Motor Holding SPA, Gemplus Internat., Korea First Bank; bd. dirs Mobilcom AG; bd. dirs. Washington Mutual, Inc., CoStar Group, Inc., 1995—, Ryanair Holdings PLC, 1996—, Gemalto N.V., 2006—, Harrah's Entertainment, Inc., 2007—, Gen. Motors Co., 2009. Mem. gov. council Wilderness Soc.; trustee Grand Canyon Trust; bd. dirs. Am. Himalayan Found.; dir. & past chmn. U. Wash. Found. Named one of Forbes 400: Richest Americans, 2009; Sheldon Fellow. Mem.: Phi Beta Kappa. Office: TPG Capital 301 Commerce St Ste 3300 Fort Worth TX 76102-3128 Business E-Mail: david.bonderman@armstrong.co.in.

BONDI, JOSEPH CHARLES, JR., education educator, consultant; b. Tampa, Fla., Aug. 15, 1936; s. Joseph C. and Virginia B.; m. Patsy L. Hammer, Aug. 6, 1960; children: Pamela, Beth, Bradley. BS, U. Fla., 1958, M.Ed., 1964; Ed.D., U. Fla, 1968. Tchr., adminstr. Hillsborough County (Fla.) Pub. Schs., 1958-65; instr. U. South Fla., Tampa, 1965-66, asst. prof., 1966-68, assoc. prof., 1968-74, prof. edn., 1974—2003; ptnr. Wiles, Bondi & Assocs. Edn. cons. in field, South Africa, Hong Kong, China, Taiwan, Can., Am. Internat. Schs. Author 28 textbooks including Developing Middle Schools, 1972, Curriculum Development, 1979, 8th edit., 2010, Practical Politics for School Administrators, 1981, The Essential Middle School, 1981, 1993, 2000, 2005, Supervision: A Guide to Practice, 6th edit., 2004, The New American Middle School, 2001. Councilman City of Temple Terrace, Fla., 1970—74, mayor, 1974—78. With USNR, 1958—63. Mem.: Fla. ASCD (pres.). Republican. Lutheran. Personal E-mail: josephbondi@aol.com.

BONDI, PAMELA JO, state attorney general; b. Tampa, Fla., Nov. 17, 1965; d. Joseph Bondi. BA in Criminal Justice, U. Fla., Gainesville, 1987; JD, Stetson U. Law Sch., Fla., 1990. Bar: Fla. 1991. Asst. states atty., felony bur. chief Fla. 13th Jud. Cir., Tampa, 1992—2009; atty. gen. State of Fla., Tallahassee, 2011—. Bd. dirs. Tampa Bay United Way, The Children's Bd., Jr. League, U. Fla. Gator Club. Recipient Leadership award, Nat. Assn. Drug Diversion Investigators, 2011, Chairman's Recognition award, Fla. Bd. Medicine, Disting. Alumna award, Stetson U. Law Sch., 2011, Lawyer of Distinction award, Tampa Review. Mem.: Fla. Bar Assn. (mem. grievance com.). Republican. Office: Office of the Attorney General State of Florida The Capitol PL 01 Tallahassee FL 32399-1050 Office Phone: 850-414-3300.*

BONDINELL, STEPHANIE, counselor, academic administrator; d. Peter Jr. and Gloria Lucille (Burden) Honcharuk; m. Paul Swanstrom Bondinell, July 31, 1971; 1 child, Paul Emil. BA, William Paterson U., 1970; MEd, Stetson U., 1983. Cert. elem. educator Fla., guidance counselor grades K-12 Fla. Tchr. Bloomingdale Bd. Edn., NJ, 1971-80; edn. dir. Fla. United Meth. Children's Home, Enterprise, 1982-89; guidance counselor Volusia County Sch. Bd., Deltona, Fla., 1988—. Coord. sch. improvement svcs., Deltona Lakes, 1996—98, Deltona Lakes, 2002—05. Sec. adv. com. Deltona Jr. HS, 1996—98, sec. PTA, 1982; vice-chmn. adv. com. Deltona Mid. Sch., 1988, chmn., 1991—92, 1991—92; mem. adv. com. Deltona HS, 1995—96; secondary sch. task force Volusia County Sch. Bd., 1986—; team leader Volusia County Sch. Accreditation Quality Assurance Team, 2003—13; mem. exec. com. Volusia County Reps.; mem. Rep. Presdl. Task Force; bd. dir. Deltona Arts Hist. Ctr., 2008—; mem. state adv. bd. Fla. Future Educators Am., 1990—92, 2003—09. Recipient Outstanding Ednl. Partnership award, S.W. Volusia C. of C., 1998, Sunshine State Medallion award, Fla. Pub. Rels. Assn., 1998, award, Volusia/Flagler Alcohol & Drug Abuse Prevention Coun., 1998—2010, Fla. Lottery Creative Tchg. award, 2002; named Deltona Lakes Tchr. of Yr., Volusia County Sch., 1991, 1996, Volusia County Sch. Dist. Accreditation Steering Com. Team Leaders, 2003—10, Volusia County Guidance Counselor of Yr., Volusia/Flagler Counseling Assn., 2006; Acad. scholar, Becton, Dickinson & Co., 1966, NJ State scholar, 1966—70. Mem.: AAUW, Am. Counseling Assn., Fla. Edn. Assn., Internat. Platform Assn., Volusia Tchrs. Orgn., NJ Edn. Assn., Fla. Assn. Counseling and Devel., Disvn. Learning Disabilities, Coun. Exceptional Children, Stetson U. Alumni Assn., Deltona Civic Assn., 4 Townes Federated Rep. Women's Club (sec., v.p.), Deltona Rep. Club (v.p. 1991—93). Avocations: painting, dance, writing. Office: Volusia County Sch Bd 2022 Adelia Blvd Deltona FL 32725-3976 E-mail: sbondine@mail.volusia.k12.fl.us.

BONELLO, WILLIAM B., medical products executive; Grad. in Fin. & Health Svc.Mgmt., J.L. Kellogg Grad. Sch. Mgmt. Cons. BDC Advisors, LLC; mng. dir., sr. equity rsch. analyst Wachovia Capital Markets; sr. v.p., investor rels. Laboratory Corp. of America Holdings, 2008—. Office: Laboratory Corporation of America 358 S Main St Burlington NC 27215 Office Phone: 336-584-5171. Business E-Mail: william_bonello@labcorp.com.

BONESIO, WOODROW MICHAEL, lawyer; b. Hereford, Tex., Dec. 27, 1943; s. Harold Andre and Elizabeth (Ireland) B.; m. Michaele Ann Dougherty; children: Elizabeth Eaton, Jo Kristin Simpson, William Michael. BA, Austin Coll., 1966; JD, U. Houston, 1971. Bar: Tex. 1971, US Dist. Ct. (We., No., So., and Ea. Dists.) Tex., US Ct. Appeals (5th Cir.) 1973, US Ct. Appeals (11th Cir.) 1981, US Supreme Ct. 2004. Law clk. to US Dist. Judge We. Dist. Tex., San Antonio, 1971—73; ptnr. Akin, Gump, Strauss, Hauer & Feld, Dallas, 1973—92, Kuntz & Bonesio LLP, Dallas, 1992—2002, Shackelford, Melton & McKinley LLP, Dallas, 2003—12, Law Office of W. Michael Bonesio, Dallas, 2013—. Spkr. in field. Bd. dirs. Grace Presbytery Devel. Bd., 1986—89; ruling elder First Presbyn. Ch., Dallas, 1999—2001, bd. dirs., 2004—06. Named Tex. Super Lawyer, Tex. Monthly Mag., 2006; named a Top Lawyer in Tex., The Legal Network, 2013. Fellow: Dallas Bar Found., Tex. Bar Found.; mem.: FBA, ABA, Tex. Comptroller Pub. Accts. Panel of Arbitrators, FINRA Panel Arbitrators, Assn. Attorney Mediators, Tex. Mediator Credentialing Assn. (advanced), Tex. Assn. Mediators, Nat. Assn. Rec. Artists, U. Houston Law Alumni Assn. (Dallas chpt. pres. 1982), Austin Coll. Alumni Bd. (mem. bd. 2006—12, Disting. Alumni award 2001), Common Cause Tex. (bd. dirs. 1999—2006), Tex. Bar Coll., Dallas Bar Assn., Vocal Majority Chorus (bd. dirs. 1990—2005, pres. 2002—03), Barbershop Harmony Soc. (Internat. Chorus champion 1975, 1979, 1982, 1985, 1988, 1991, 1994, 1997, 2000, 2003, 2006), Order of Barons, Phi Alpha Delta. Business E-Mail: mbonesio@bonesiolaw.com.

BONILLA, ERNESTO, family practice physician; Grad., Colegio Andino; MD, Escuela Colombiana de Medicina, 1987. Diplomate Am. Bd. Family Practice. Intern family practice Bronx-Lebanon Hosp. Ctr., 1997, resident family practice, 1999; assoc. staff family medicine Cleve. Clinic; primary care physician Ind. Health Ctrs., site med. dir.; supr. med. students Ind. Univ.; primary care provider Emerald Hills Med. Ctr. Mem.: AMA, Am. Acad. of Family Practice. Office: Weston Family Health Center 1825 N Corporate Lakes Blvd Weston FL 33326 Office Phone: 954-349-1111.

BONILLA-FELIX, MELVIN A., pediatrician, educator; b. San Juan, June 20, 1962; MD, U. Puerto Rico, 1986. Cert. pediat., pediat. nephrology, 1993. Intern U. San Juan Pediat. Hosp., 1986-87, resident in pediat., 1987-89; fellow in pediat. nephrology St. Louis Childrens, 1992; asst. prof. pediat. U. Tex., Houston, 1992-99; with U. P.R., Guaynabo, 1999—. Recipient Minority Scientist Devel. award Am. Heart Assn., 1995-96. Mem. Am. Assn. Pediat. Office: Univ PR Med Scis Campus Dept Pediat PO Box 365067 San Juan PR 00936-5067 Office Phone: 787-777-3535 ext. 7300. Business E-Mail: mabonill@coqui.net.

BONNEFOUX, JEAN-PIERRE, choreographer, dancer; b. Bourg-en-Bresse, France, Apr. 9, 1943; s. Laurent and Marie-Therese (Noel) Bonnefoux; m. Patricia McBride, Sept. 8, 1973. Student, Paris Opera Sch.; DFA (hon.), Goucher Coll., 1987. Prin. dancer NYC Ballet, 1970—77; ballet master and choreographer Pitts. Ballet; founder Patricia McBride & Jean-Pierre Bonnefoux Ctr for Dance, Charlotte, NC; artistic dir. and pres. NC Dance Theatre, Charlotte, 1996—. Faculty Sch. Am. Ballet, 1977—80; ballet artist-in-residence Goucher Coll., Towson, Md., 1984—94; chmn. and artistic dir. Ind. U. Sch. Music, Bloomington, 1985—96; artistic dir., choreographer, and tchr. Chautauqua Inst., New York. Danseur entoile Paris Opera Ballet, 1958—70; dancer NYC Ballet, 1970—81, choreographer Peter Pan, Cinderalla, Nutcracker, Romeo & Juliet, Carmina Burana. Decorated Officier L'Ordre du Merite France; recipient Illona Copen Award, New York Internat. Ballet Competition, 2011, Chautauqua Artist Teacher Award, 2011. Office: NC Dance Theatre 622 E 28th St Ste 113 Charlotte NC 28205 Office Phone: 704-372-0101. Business E-Mail: jpbonn@ncdance.org.

BONNELL-MIHALIS, PAMELA GAY SCOGGINS, library director; b. Monterey, Calif., Feb. 2, 1948; d. Dewey L. and Marlyce I. (Hansen) Scoggins; m. Verneil S. Henerson, June 18, 1966 (div. 1971); 1 child, V. Samuel Henerson III; m. Chrisman E Bonnell, Mar. 2, 1974 (div. 1983); m. Hugh R. McElroy, Nov. 10, 1990 (div. 1996); m. Stephan S. Mihalis, Oct. 5, 2002 (dec. Sept. 11, 2009). BA, Cameron U., Lawton, Okla., 1972; MLS, U. Okla., 1972—73; CPM, S.W. Tex. State U., 1998. Libr. Met. Libr. Sys., Oklahoma City, 1974—75, Office of City Mgr., Dallas, 1977—80; dir. audience devel. Dallas Symphony Orch., 1980—81; libr. Dallas Morning News, 1981—83; libr. mgr. Plano (Tex.) Pub. Libr. Sys., 1983—91; dir. libr. svcs. Waco-McLennan County Libr. System, Waco, Tex., 1992—2001; exec. dir. Elyria (Ohio) Pub. Libr., 2002—05; realtor Scoggins Realty, Lawton, Okla., 2006—. Bd. trustees Lawton Pub. Libr., 2006—. Author: Fund Raising for Small Libraries, 1983; contbr. chapters to books, articles to profl. jours. Gala chair Easter Seal Soc., Dallas, 1988; exec. bd. Am. Heart Assn., 1997—99; chmn. Lorain County Librs. Coun., 2003—04; trustee Freedom to Read Found., 1999—2003, liaison, 2004—; chmn. Oboler award com. Intellectual Freedom Round Table, 2004—05; program com. Fund, 2004—05; ops. com. Main St. Elyria, 2004—05; bd. dirs. Women's Shelter, Plano, 1991; trustee Dallas Symphony Orch., 1981; bd. dirs. Salvation Army, 2003—05; pres. Townbluff Homeowners Assn., Plano, 1984—90, Hippodrome Theatre Guild, 1996; treas. YWCA, 1995—96. Recipient Telecom. Excellence award, Ctrl. Tex. Edn., 1997. Mem.: ALA (councilor-at-large 1990—99, pres. Intellectual Freedom Round Table 1993—94, constn. and bylaws chair 1994—97, Shirley Olofson Meml. award 1974, cert. of Spl. Thanks 1986, John Phillip Immroth award 1990), Ctrl. Tex. Women's Alliance (bd. dirs. 1992—96), Tex. Libr. Assn. (chmn. Adminstrs. Roundtable 1994—95, trustee Leroy C. Merritt Trust Fund 1997—2000, chair intellectual freedom com. 2000—02, SIRS Intellectual Freedom award 1990), Tex. Mcpl. Librs. Dirs. (pres. 1994—95), Jr. League, Leadership Waco Alumni Assn., Rotary (bd. dirs. 2007—). Avocations: reading, travel. Office: Scoggins Realty Co 1401 W Gore Blvd Lawton OK 73501 Home: 825 NW 44th St Lawton OK 73505 Home Phone: 580-591-0055; Office Phone: 580-357-5700, 580-583-8046. Personal E-mail: pbonnell39@hotmail.com.

BONNEN, DENNIS H., state legislator; b. Mar. 3, 1972; Small businessman, Tex.; mem. Dist. 25 Tex. House of Representative, 1996—. Republican. Office: 122 E Myrtle St Angleton TX 77515 also: Room CAP 4N.5 Capitol Austin TX 78768 Office Phone: 979-848-1770, 512-463-0564. Office Fax: 979-849-3169.

BONNER, BILLY EDWARD, physics professor; b. Oak Grove, La., Dec. 12, 1939; s. James Wilbur and Julia (Deer) B. BS, La. Tech. U., 1961; MA, Rice U., 1963, PhD, 1965. Prin. scientific officer Rutherford High Energy Lab., Didcot, Berkshire, England, 1966-70; post-doctoral fellow U. Calif., Davis, 1971-72; physicist Los Alamos (N.Mex.) Nat. Lab., 1972-85; scientific assoc. CERN, Geneva, 1983-84; prof. physics Rice U., Houston, 1985—2009, chmn. dept. physics, 1986-91, dir. Bonner Nuclear Lab., 1987—2009. Editor 3 books; contbr. articles to profl. jours. Avocations: squash, fishing, cooking. Office: Rice Univ Bonner Nuclear Labs Houston TX 77005-1892 Home and Office: PO Box 1846 Montgomery TX 77356-1846 Home Phone: 713-664-5276; Office Phone: 713-348-4897. Business E-Mail: bonner@rice.edu.

BONNER, JACK WILBUR, III, psychiatrist, educator, administrator; b. Corpus Christi, Tex., July 30, 1940; s. Jack Wilbur and Irldene (Turner) B.; m. Myra Lynn Taylor; children: Jack Wilbur, IV, Katherine Lynn, Shelley Bliss AA, Del Mar Coll., Corpus Christi, 1960; BA with honors, U. Tex., Austin, 1961; MD, S.W. Med. Sch., U. Tex., Dallas, 1965. Diplomate Am. Bd. Psychiatry and Neurology. Intern U. Ark. Med. Center, 1965-66; resident Duke U. Med. Center, 1966-69; assoc. in psychiatry Highland Hosp. divsn. Duke U. Med. Center, Asheville, NC, 1971, asst. prof. psychiatry, 1972-80, dir. outpatient services, 1972-75, med. dir., 1975-81; chmn. bd. dirs., CEO, med. dir. Highland Hosp., Asheville, NC, 1981-92; med. dir. The Oaks Psychiat. Health Sys., Austin, Tex., 1992-93, exec. med. dir., 1993-94; med. dir. Behavioral Health Svcs. Greenville (S.C.) Hosp. Sys. Univ. Med. Ctr., 1994—2009, adminstr. Behavioral Health Svcs., 1996—2000, acad. chair, 1994—2009. Asst. clin. prof. Duke U. Med. Ctr., Durham, NC, 1982—87, asst. cons. prof. psychiatry, 1987—; clin. assoc. prof. U. NC Sch. Medicine, Chapel Hill, 1986—92, Quillen-Dishner Coll. Medicine, Johnson City, Tenn., 1989—92, U. Tex. Health Sci. Ctr., San Antonio, 1993—94, U. SC Sch. Medicine, Columbia, 1995—2004, GHS prof. clin. neuropsychiatry and behavioral sci., 2004—. Author: (with others) The Psychology of Discipline, 1983, Unmasking the Psychopath: Antisocial Personality and Related Syndromes, 1986; contbr. articles to profl. jours. Chmn. bd. dirs. The Highland Found., 1980-93; bd. dirs. Western N.C. Med. Peer Rev. Found., 1975-78; trustee La Amistad Found., Maitland, Fla., 1985-95, N.C. Symphony, 1987-92, Cooper Riis Found., Mill Spring, N.C., 2000- (exec. com. 2007-). Recipient Disting. Mentor award, 2009. Fellow: APA (trustee 1999—2005, chair fin. and budget com. 2002—09, Disting. Life Fellow, Warren Williams award 2002, Nancy C.A. Roeske cert. of recognition for excellence in med. student edn. 2005, Spl. Presdl. Commendation 2011), Am. Coll. Psychiatrists (treas. 1992—95, 2d v.p. 1999—2000, 1st v.p. 2000—01, pres.-elect 2001—02, pres. 2002—03, sec.-gen. 2006—, E.B. Bowis award 2000), So. Psychiat. Assn. (v.p. 1984—85, chmn. bd. regents 1988—89, pres. 1992—93); mem.: AMA, Found. Excellence Mental Health Care (sci. adv. bd. 2011—), Group Advancement Psychiatry (treas. 1991—99, pres.-elect 1999—2001, pres. 2001—03), Ctrl. Neuropsychiat. Hosp. Assn. (councillor 1981—85, pres. 1983—84), So. Med. Assn. (sec. sect. on neurology, neurosurgery and psychiatry 1977—80, chmn.-elect 1980—81, chmn. 1981—82), Nat. Anorexic Aid Soc. (nat. anorexia adv. coun. 1979—86), NC Psychiat. Assn. (pres. 1982—83), Buncombe County (NC) Med. Soc. (pres. 1983), Nat. Acads. Practice, Am. Group Psychotherapy Assn., Nat. Alliance on Mental Illness Greenville (bd. dirs. 2005—12, v.p. 2006—08, pres. 2008—10), Nat. Assn. Psychiat. Health Sys. (trustee 1989—94, 1st v.p. 1990—91, pres.-elect 1991—92, pres. 1992—93), Benjamin Rush Soc. (exec. coun. 2006—, sec.-treas. 2008—10, v.p. 2010—12, pres. 2012—), U. Tex. Southwestern Med. Sch. Alumni Assn. (bd. dirs. 1988—95, pres. 1989—91), Phi Theta Kappa. Office: Greenville Hosp Sys U Med Ctr Academic Svcs 701 Grove Rd Greenville SC 29605-5601 Home: One Pg Ave Ste 501 Asheville NC 28801-2388 Office Phone: 864-455-7834. Business E-Mail: jwb2@att.net.

BONNER, JAMES RYAN, allergist, immunologist, educator; MD, U. Mich., 1971. Diplomate Am. Bd. Internal Medicine, 1974, Am. Bd. Internal Medicine-infectious disease, 1976, Am. Bd. Allergy and Immunology, 1979. Resident internal medicine Univ. Ala. Med. Ctr., 1972—74, fellow allergy & immunology, 1974—77; prof. pulmonary, allergy and critical care medicine divsn. Univ. Ala. Sch. of Medicine; staff Veterans Adminstrn. Hosp.; hosp. affiliations include Univ. of Ala. Hosp., Ala. Allergy and Asthma Ctr. Fellow: ACP (mem. ala. chpt.), Am. Coll. of Allergy, Asthma and Immunology; mem.: Med. Assn. of the State of Ala. Office: Veterans Affairs Medical Center 700 S 19th St Birmingham AL 35233-1927 Office Phone: 205-933-8101.

BONNER, JO (JOSIAH ROBINS BONNER JR.), academic administrator, former United States Representative from Alabama; b. Selma, Ala., Nov. 19, 1959; s. Josiah Robins and Imogene Virginia (Lyons) Bonner; m. Janée Lambert; children: Jennifer Lee, Josiah Robins III. BA in Journalism, U. Ala., 1982. Press sec. to Rep. Sonny Callahan, US House of Reps., 1984—89, chief of staff, 1989—2002; mem. US Congress from 1st Ala. Dist., Washington, 2003—13; chmn. US House Ethics Com., Washington, 2011—13; vice chancellor govt. rels. & econ. development U. Ala. System, Montgomery, Ala., 2013—. Mem. pres. adv. coun. U. Mobile; mem. bd. cmty. advisors Jr. League Mobile. Named Outstanding Alumnus in Pub. Rels., U. Ala. Coll. Comm., 2000. Mem.: Mobile Area C. of C. (bd. dirs.), U. Ala. Alumni Assn. (Mobile chpt., bd. dirs.), Leadership Mobile (bd. dirs.), Rotary Club (bd. dirs.). Republican. Episcopalian. Office: University Alabama System 401 Queen City Ave Tuscaloosa AL 35401 Office Phone: 205-348-5861.*

BONNER, JUDY L., academic administrator; b. 1947; d. Josiah Robins and Imogene (Lyons) Bonner. BS, MS, U. Ala.; PhD, Ohio State U., 1976. Faculty mem. U. Ala., Tuscaloosa, 1981—, asst. acad. v.p., 1985—90, dean Coll. Human Environ. Scis., 1990—2003, provost, v.p. acad. affairs, 2003—06, exec. v.p., provost, 2006—12, pres., 2012—. Office: Univ Ala Office of Provost and Vp Tuscaloosa AL 35487 Office Phone: 205-348-4892. Business E-Mail: judy.bonner@ua.edu.*

BONNEY, HAL JAMES, JR., federal judge; b. Norfolk, Va., Aug. 27, 1929; s. Hal J. and Mary (Shackelford) B.; m. Marie McBee, July 4, 1963 (div. 1979); children: David James, John Wesley. BA, U. Richmond, 1951, MA, 1953; JD, Coll. William and Mary, 1969. Bar: Va. 1969. Instr. Norfolk public schs., 1951-61; supt. Douglas MacArthur Acad., 1961-67; practiced law, 1969-71; law clk. US Dist. Ct., 1969; prof. U. Va., 1964-71, Coll. William and Mary, 1969-71; US bankruptcy judge Norfolk, 1971—96; ret., 1996. Adj. prof. law Regent U. Law Sch., 1987—97; prodr. Hal Bonney Prodns. Author: Overturning Applecarts, 2002. Tchr. Wesleymen Bible Class Sta. WTAR-AM, 1962-98, tchr. emeritus, 1998—; tchr. Good News TV Network, 1989—; treas. Wesleymen Found., Inc., Billy Graham Crusades, 1974-76; pres. adv. coun. CBN U., 1986-95; vice-chmn. Va. Meth. Bd. Edn., Inc., 1991-99; bd. visitors Duke Div. Sch., 1991—; 1st v.p., bd. dirs. Norfolk Union Mission, 1994—; task force on pub. housing City of Norfolk, 1995-96; advisor Film Sch., Regent U., 1996-2000, assoc. prodr. 2000-04; commr. City of Norfolk Parks and Recreation, 2003—, chmn. 2003-07; vice chair rules com. Va. United Meth. conf., 1996-2004; bd. ordained ministry United Meth. Ch., Va; active World Affairs Coun.; pres. coun. Old Dominion U., mem. planning com. Recipient S.A.R. Good Citizenship medal, Woodmen of the World History medal, U. Richmond Gold medal, George Washington honor medal Freedoms Found., Alli award Cultural Alliance Greater Hampton Rds., 1998; Judge Hal Bonney Day named in honor by City of Norfolk, Jan. 27, 1998. Mem. Nat. Conf. Bankruptcy Judges (pres. 1983-84, chmn. editl. bd. Am. Bankruptcy Law Jour.), Va. State Bar, Norfolk and Portsmouth Bar Assn., Nat. Film Soc., Am. Film Inst. (Premiere Circle), Brit. Film Inst., US Naval Inst., Am. Cinematheque (moving picture ball benefit com.), Drama League (NYC), Women in Film (exec. com.), James Kent Inn of Ct. (hon., pres. 1994-96), Phi Alpha Theta, Pi Sigma Alpha, Phi Alpha Delta, Masons, Shriners, Elks, Kiwanis Internat. Club (Norfolk) (dir., George F. Hixson award 2011). Home: 1357 Windsor Point Rd Norfolk VA 23509-1311 Home Phone: 757-853-4770. Personal E-mail: bonney@cox.net.

BONNIE, RICHARD JEFFREY, lawyer, educator, consultant; b. Richmond, Va., Aug. 22, 1945; s. Herbert Herman and Helene Selma (Berz) B.; m. Kathleen Ford, June 15, 1967; children: Joshua Ford, Zachary Andrew, Jessica Katherine. BA, Johns Hopkins U., 1966; LLB, U. Va., 1969. Var: Va. 1969, U.S. Dist. Ct. (ea. dist.) Va. 1969; U.S. Ct. Appeals (4th cir.) 1969, U.S. Supreme Ct. 1986. Asst. prof. law U. Va., Charlottesville, 1969—70, assoc. prof., 1973—77, prof., 1977—87, John S. Battle prof., 1987—2007, Harrison found. prof. medicine and law, 2007; dir. Inst. Law, Psychiatry, and Pub. Policy, 1979—, prof. psychiatry, 2001—, prof. pub. policy, 2009—. Vis. fellow Inst. Criminology, Cambridge U., 1977; vis. prof. Cornell Law Sch., 1993-94, Parsons visitor Sydney Law Sch., 2005; vis. prof Columbia Law Sch., 2012; assoc. dir. nat. Commn. Marijuana and Drug Abuse, 1971-73; reporter Nat. Conf. Commrs. on Uniform State Laws, 1972-74; cons. Spl. Action Office for Drug Abuse Prevention Exec. Office of the Pres., 1973-75; spl. asst. to US Atty. Gen., 1975; sec. Nat. Adv. Coun. on Drug Abuse, 1975-80; mem. Com. on Problem of Drug Dependence, Inc., 1979-84; charter fellow Coll. Problems of Drug Dependence, 1992—; cons. Am. Psychiat. Assn., Coun. Psychiatry and Law, 1979—, Am. Acad. Neurology, Com. Law, Ethics and Humanities, 2007-; mem. U.S. State Dept. Del. to investigate psychiat. practices in the Soviet Union, 1989; mem. World Psychiat. Assn. rev. team to investigate Soviet psychiatry, 1991; adv. bd. permanent coordination office Reforms in psychiatry in Ctrl. and Ea. Europe, former Soviet Union, 1993—; bd. dirs. Geneva Initiative on Psychiatry, 1996-2005, Global Initiative on Psychiatry, 2005-2007; pres. Am. Friends of Geneva Initiative on Psychiatry, 1997 - 2011; treas. Global Initiative Psychiatry, 2011—; mem. MacArthur Found. Network on Mental Health and the Law, 1988-96; bd. dirs. Va. Capital Representation Resource Ctr., 1994-97, 2002—; mem. MacArthur Found. Network on Mandated Treatment, 2000-10, MacArthur Found. Network on Neurosci. and Law, 2007—; mem. Max Plank Network on Aging, 2005—; co-chair, bd. dirs. Physicians and Lawyers for Nat. Drug Policy, 2004—; steering com. underage drinking Nat. Inst. Alcohol Abuse and Alcoholism, 2004—; nat. commn. diversion and abuse of prescription Ctr. Addiction and Substance Abuse, 2003-04; chair commn. on mental health law reform Va. Supreme Ct., 2006-11; cons. in field Author: The Marijuana Conviction: The History of Marijuana Prohibition in the United States, 1974, 2d edit. 1999, Legal Aspects of Drug Dependence, 1975, Psychiatrists and the Legal Process: Diagnosis and Debate, 1977, Marijuana Use and Criminal Sanctions: Essays in the Theory and Practice of Decriminalization, 1980, Criminal Law: Cases and Materials, 1982, 2d edit., 1986, The Trial of John W. Hinckley, Jr.: A Case Study in the Insanity Defense, 1986, rev. edit., 2000, 2008, Criminal Law, 1997, 2d edit., 2004, 3rd edit., 2010, Growing Up Tobacco Free, 1994, Mental Disorder, Work Disability and the Law, 1997, Reducing the Burden of Injury, 1999, The Evolution of Mental Health Law, 2001, Elder Mistreatment, 2002, Adjudicative Competence, 2002, Reducing Underage Drinking, 2003, Ending the Tobacco Problem, 2007, Law Touched Our Hearts, 2009, Reforming Juvenile Justice: A Developmental Approach, 2013. Chmn. Va. Human Rights Com., Dept. Mental Health and Mental Retardation, 1979-85; chair Commn. on Mental Health Law Reform, Va. Supreme Ct., 2006-11; bd. dirs. Coll. on Problem of Drug Dependence, 1996-2000; mem. Steering Com. Underage Drinking, Nat. Inst. Alcohol Abuse and Alcoholism, 2005-10, IOM, Comm. Increasing Rates of Organ Donation, 2005-07; ABA (criminal justice-mental health stds. project adv. bd. 1981—87, task force on mental illness and the death penalty 2003—05, criminal justice standards task force mental health, 2013-), Nat. Inst. on Alcohol Abuse and Alcoholism (mem. steering com. on underage drinking 2005-10); World Psychiat. Assn. (rev. team to investigate Soviet psychiatry 1991), Va. Bar Assn. (chmn. com. mentally disabled 1981—90, criminal law sect. coun. 1992—96), Am. Psychiat. Assn. (Isaac Ray award 1998, Spl. Presdl. Commendation 2003), Nat. Rsch. Coun. (com. on data and rsch. for policy on illicit drugs 1998—2000, chair com. elder abuse and neglect 2001—02, com. on law and justice 2002—, chair com. underage drinking 2002—, exec. com. divsn. com. behavioral & social scis. & edn. 2003—08, bd. behavioral, cogmitive & sensory sci. 2009—, mem., com. informing juvenile justice 2010-13, Inst. Medicine of NAS (bd. neurosci. and behavioral health 1992—2001, vice chair com. preventing nicotine dependence in children and youth 1993—94, chair com. on opportunities in drug abuse rsch. 1995—96, membership com. 1995—98, chair com. injury prevention control 1997—98, com. to assess sci. base for tobacco harm reduction 1999—2001, com. to assess sys. for protection of human rsch. subjects 2000—02, chair com. to propose strategy to prevent/reduce underage drinking 2002—03, chair com. on reducing tobacco use 2004—07, com. on increasing rates of organ donation 2005—07, chair, comm health, safety and wellbeing young adults, 2013-) Jefferson award, 2007; Inst. Criminology fellow Cambridge U., 1977. Fellow: Va. Law Found.; mem.: APA (hon. disting. mem. 2007), NAS (nat. assoc.), ABA (criminal justice-mental health stds. project adv. bd. 1981—87, task force on mental illness and the death penalty 2003—05, stashforce to revise criminal justice mental health standards 2012—), Nat. Inst. on Alcohol Abuse and Alcoholism (mem. steering com. on underage drinking 2005—), Inst. Medicine (Yarmolinsky medal 2002), Am. Acad. Psychiat. Law (Amicus award 1994), World Psychiat. Assn. (rev. team to investigate Soviet psychiatry 1991), Va. Bar Assn. (chmn. com. mentally disabled 1981—90, criminal law sect. coun. 1992—96), Am. Psychiat. Assn. (Isaac Ray award 1998, Spl. Presdl. Commendation 2003), Nat. Rsch. Coun. (com. on data and rsch. for policy on illicit drugs 1998—2000, chair com. elder abuse and neglect 2001—02, com. on law and justice 2002—, chair com. underage drinking 2002—, exec. com. divsn. com. behavioral & social scis. & edn. 2003—08, bd. behavioral, cogmitive & sensory sci. 2009—, vice-chmn., com. informing juvenile justice 2010—13), Inst. Medicine of NAS (bd. neurosci. and behavioral health 1992—2001, vice chair com. preventing nicotine dependence in children and youth 1993—94, chair com. on opportunities in drug abuse rsch. 1995—96, membership com. 1995—98, chair com. injury prevention control 1997—98, com. to assess sci. base for tobacco harm reduction 1999—2001, com. to assess sys. for protection of human rsch. subjects 2000—02, chair com. to propose strategy to prevent/reduce underage drinking 2002—03, chair com. on reducing tobacco use 2004—07, com. on increasing rates of organ donation 2005—07, comm. on improving health, safety and well being of young adults 2013—). Office: U Va Sch Law 580 Massie Rd Charlottesville VA 22903 Business E-Mail: rjb6f@virginia.edu.

BONOMETTI, ROBERT JOHN, technology management and strategy executive; b. NYC, Sept. 29, 1953; s. Joseph Patrick and Fortunata Mary (Barba) B.; m. Virginia Anne Scyphers, Oct. 26, 1997. BS summa cum laude, US Mil. Acad., 1975; MS in Physics, MIT, Boston, 1981, PhD in Physics, 1985; MBA, LI U., 1987. Registered profl. engr., Va., 2012. Assoc. prof. physics U.S. Mil. Acad., West Point, NY, 1985-88; program mgr. Def. Advanced Rsch. Projects Agy., Arlington, Va., 1988-93; sr. policy analyst White House Sci. and Tech. Office, Washington, 1993-95; exec. dir. tech. strategy Bell Atlantic Corp., Arlington, Va., 1995-98; pres. MGB Enterprises, LLC, Winchester, Va., 1998—2012; Byrd prof. info. sys. and computer tech. Shenandoah U., Byrd Sch. Bus., 1999—. Industry adv. bd. Ctr. for Satellite and Hybrid Comm. Networks, U. Md., 1994-2000; chmn. rev. com. commercialization of space NASA, Washington, 1996; exec. dir. info. and comm. R & D com. Nat. Sci. and Tech. Coun., Washington, 1993-95; adj. prof. various univs., 1981—; chmn. Tek-Xam content exec. com. Va. Found. for Ind. Colls., 2000-01 Contbr. articles to profl. jours. Pres. SPCA of Winchester, Frederick and Clarke Counties, 2007-09, bd. dirs. Blue Ridge Wildlife Ctr., 2013-; active animal rights and environ. orgns. Lt. col. US Army, 1975—95. Recipient Laurel award Aviation Week and Space Tech., 1990, Wilkins award, Shenandoah U., 2006, Outstanding Svc. award, Byrd Sch. Bus., 2006, Excellence Tchg. award, 2010, Rsch. scholarship, 2007; Sci. and Tech. fellow Dept. Commerce, 1993-94; Hertz Found. fellow, 1981-85. Mem. IEEE (sr.), AIAA (sr., Van Allen Conf. award, 1993), Am. Phys. Soc., Am. Astron. Soc., Beta Gamma Sigma, Phi Kappa Phi. Avocations: music, guitar, weightlifting, tennis, running. Home and Office: 260 Golds Hill Rd Winchester VA 22603-3129 Office Phone: 540-545-7272. Business E-Mail: rbonomet@su.edu.

BONTE, FREDERICK JAMES, radiologist, educator, physician; b. Bethlehem, Pa., Jan. 18, 1922; s. Frederick R. and Harriett (Stoudt) B.; m. Cecile Poetzel; children: Frederick W., Stephen J., John A., Therese A., Suzanne M., Ann E. BS, Western Res. U., 1942, MD, 1945. Diplomate: Am. Bd. Radiology, Am. Bd. Nuclear Medicine. Intern Huntington Meml. Hosp., Pasadena, Calif., 1945-46; resident Univ. Hosp., Cleve., 1948-52; practice medicine, specializing in radiology and nuclear medicine Dallas, 1956—; mem. faculty Western Res. U. Sch. Medicine, 1952-56, asst. prof., 1952-56, chief radiotherapy and nuclear medicine, 1954-56; prof. U. Tex. Southwestern Med. Sch., Dallas, 1956—; prof. emeritus, 2013—; chmn. dept. radiology U. Tex. Southwestern Med. Sch., 1956-73, dean, 1973-80; dir. Nuclear Medicine Research Center, 1980—2013, Effie and Wofford Cain disting. chair in diagnostic imaging; Dr. Jack Krohmer prof. in radiation physics. Mem. bd. Nat. Coun. Radiation Protection and Measurements, 1966-71; radiology tng. com. Nat. Insts. Gen. Med. Scis., USPHS, 1966-70, Ad Hoc Study Sects., 1970-96, cons. adv. com. US DOE Oak Ridge Los Alamong Nat. Labs, residency rev. com. radiology AMA, 1966-69, adv. and rev. coms. VA, 1972—; trustee Am. Bd. Radiology, 1969-75; founding trustee Am. Bd.

Nuclear Medicine, 1971-73, chmn., 1977-80 Contbr. more than 250 papers and 2 books. Capt. M.C., USAAC, 1946-48. Recipient Lifetime award, 2009, Am. Bd. Radiology, 2010. Fellow Am. Coll. Radiology, Am. Coll. Nuclear Physicians (Pres.'s award 1997), Am. Coll. Nuc. Medicine; mem. AMA (del., chmn. grad. med. edn. com., Roentgen Centennial Hartman medal 1995), Soc. Nuclear Medicine (De Hevesy Nuclear Pioneer award 1995), Am. Roentgen Ray Soc. (exec. com.), Radiol. Soc. N.Am., Sigma Xi, Alpha Omega Alpha, Dallas Co-Med. Soc.(pres., Cole award, 1993), Tex. Radiological Soc.(pres., Gold medal award, 1991), Soc. Nuc. Med. Achievements include research on experimental nuclear medicine and radiology, international consultant medical education. Home: 11138 Wonderland Trl Dallas TX 75229-3943 Office: 5323 Harry Hines Blvd Dallas TX 75390-9061 Home Phone: 214-352-4781; Office Phone: 214-648-2025. Business E-Mail: frederick.bonte@utsouthwestern.edu.

BONURA, LARRY SAMUEL, writer; b. Galveston, Tex., Jan. 4, 1950; s. Leo Bonura and Beatrice Sadie (Maiorka) Immel; m. Marilyn Esther Ward, Feb. 17, 1990; 1 child, Sean Joseph Sullins. BS in Journalism, U. Kans., 1977; MA in Am. History, Emporia State U., Kans., 1982. Cert. trainer Microsoft, 2013; in geographical info. sci. La. Tech. U., Shreveport, 2006. Asst. libr. U. Kans. Librs., Lawrence, 1975-77; instr. Butler County Community Coll., El Dorado, Kans., 1982-83; dir. bikelibrary, Emporia, 1977—84; mng. editor Agora Assocs., Balt., 1983-84; dir. Word Workers, Richardson, Tex., 1984—2005; mgr. editorial svcs. Convex Computer Corp., Richardson, 1987-94; sr. instr. No. Telecom Meridian Info. Products, Richardson, 1994-95; sr. tech. writer DSET Corp., 1999—2001, Presagis USA, 2001—11; sr. tech. trainer FTS Internat., 2011—14; epic credentialed trainer Presbyn. Healthcare Svcs., 2014—. Instr. Richland C.C., Dallas, 1988-91; leader seminar Solutions Inc., Boston, 1991-93; participant 2nd World Congress on Sports Documentation, Vienna, Austria, 1982; mem. Sch. Advanced Rsch., 2009-; pres. STC Kachina Chpt., 2009-10. Author: Fruit of a Fleeting Joy, 1975, Desktop Publisher's Dictionary, 1989, Desktop Publisher's Thesaurus, 1990, Indexing Technical Documents, 1991, The Art of Indexing, 1994, Engulfed from Within, 2002, Genesis of the Bicycle in the United States: 1865-1893, 2010. Coach Richardson Sports Inc., 1990-95. Petty officer 2nd class, journalist USN, 1971—75. Mem. Am. Hist. Assn., N.Am. Soc. Sports History, Soc. for Am. Baseball Rsch., USS Forestal Assn., Am. Soc. Training & Devel., U. Kans. Alumni Assn., Pi Gamma Mu. Avocations: history, music, reading. Personal E-mail: lbonura@hotmail.com.

BOOK, JOHN KENNETH (KENNY), retail store owner; b. Hillsboro, Ill., June 26, 1950; s. Vern Ray Book and Pearl Iva (Foster) Book Alford Carroll; m. Betty L. Christy, Dec. 23, 1981; children: Elizabeth Marie Dunn Rose, Leslie Michelle Dunn Edge. Assoc. in Acctg., Ky. Bus. Coll., 1974. Laborer Lexington (Ky.) Army Depot, 1968-70; machine operator A.O. Smith, Mt. Sterling, Ky., 1971-72; laborer Irvin Industries, Lexington, Ky., 1973-75; owner Kenny's Signs & Bus. Svcs., Winchester, Ky., 1977-90, Book's Bookkeeping & Tax Svc., Winchester, Ky., 1990—; rsch. bd. advisors ABI, 1990—. Active Winchester Sch. Bd., 1976, 78; candidate for commr. City of Winchester, 1977, 79, 81, 83, 87, elected commr., 1989, re-elected commr., 1993, 96, 98, 2000, 02, 04, 06, 08, 10, 12, candidate for mayor, 1985; city commr., 2008, KLC, DOT; bd. dirs. Blue Grass Rails to Trails; bd. dirs. People Helping People, 2008. Named to Hon. Order Ky. Cols., 1973; Road scholar Ky. Dept. Transp., 2002, Road Master, 2003; Leadership Fellow Cert., Ky. League Cities, 1999, Leadership Exec. Cert., 2000, Leadership Amb. Cert., 2001, Leadership Bronze Cert., 2003, Leadership Silver Cert., 2003, Leadership Gold Cert., 2004, 05. Mem. Nat. Assn. Tax Profls., Ky. Sheriffs Assn. (hon.), NATP/Am. Inst. Profl. Bookkeepers. Democrat. Office: Book's Bookkeeping & Tax Svc PO Box 840 Winchester KY 40392-0840

BOOKBINDER, ROBERT MAX, retired school system administrator, educational consultant, writer, arbitrator, negotiator; b. Newark, Apr. 28, 1923; s. Harry and Pearl (Barenberg) B.; m. Natalie Sonya Gelfand, Sept. 10, 1946 (dec. Feb. 1996); children: Howard, Susan Blauel, Pamela Spears. BA, U. Ky., 1947; MA, Columbia U., 1948, profl. diploma, 1952; EdD, East Coast U., 1971. Owner, dir. summer day camp Camp Gelfand, Mountaindale, NY, 1947—66; tchr. BOCES 3d Dist., Huntington, NY, 1948-50, Harborfields Ctrl. Sch. Dist., Greenlawn, NY, 1950-54, elem. prin., 1954-61, jr. HS prin., 1961-64, dist. curriculum and adminstrv. coord., 1964-67, asst. supt., 1967-73; supt. East Stroudsburg Sch. Dist., Pa., 1973-87; prof. East Stroudsburg U., 1987-90; supr. student tchrs. Lynn U., Boca Raton, Fla., 1996-99. Ednl. cons. Careers/Cons. in Edn., Pompano Beach, Fla., 1977—; arbitrator Am. Arbitration Assn., N.Y.C., 1987—. Author: Critical Issues in Education, 1972, The Principal, 1992, Amusing Definitions, 1999, Witty Remarks, 1999, Noteworthy Proverbs, 1999, Concise Quotations, 1999, Funny School Excuses, 1999, An Educator's Scrapbook, 2000, Toasts for All Occasions, 2000, Best of Satire and Wit, 2002, Golf's Best Jokes and Quips, 2002, The Colonel's Combat Team 343 in WWII, 2003, Sparkling Gems, 2003, Thoughts to Live By, 2004, On the Firing Line With The 86th Blackhawk on WWII, 2004, Bookbinder's Book of Yiddish Proverbs, 2005, Bookbinder's Book of Poetry, Verse and Rhyme, 2005, Bookbinders Book of Sayings, Idioms and Maxims, 2008, Bookbinders Book of School Humor and Laughter, 2008; (weekly article) Pocono Today, 1975-84. Pres. Torch Internat., 1976-78, Monroe Arts Coun., 1980-81, Kiwanis, 1980-81, C. of C., 1983-84, United Way of Monroe County, 1983-84, 86th Black Hawk Infrentry Divsn. Orgn., Inc., 2010-, City Hope Charter, 2011-12. 1st lt. US Army, 1943-46, 51-52, World War 11 and Korean War, PTO. Decorated Bronze Star; recipient Combat Infantryman's badge. Mem. ASCD, Am. Assn. Sch. Adminstrs., 86th Blackhawk Divsn. Assn. (pres. 2000-04), 86th Blackhawk Divsn. Orgn. (pres., 2010-), B'nai B'rith (pres. 1996-00), Sabals Exec. Golf Assn. (pres. 2000-05), City of Hope Palm Aire Chpt. (pres. 2011-12), Phi Delta Kappa, Zeta Beta Tau, Phi Epsilon Kappa. Democrat. Jewish. Avocations: golf, theater, public speaking, writing, swimming. Home and Office: Careers/Cons in Edn Press 3050 N Palm Aire Dr Apt 310 Pompano Beach FL 33069-3424 Office Phone: 954-974-3511. Personal E-mail: carconed@aol.com.

BOOKER, LEWIS THOMAS, lawyer; b. Richmond, Va., Sept. 22, 1929; s. Russell Eubank and Leslie Quarles (Sessoms) B.; m. Nancy Electa Brogden, Sept. 29, 1956; children: Lewis Thomas Jr., Virginia Frances, Claiborne Brogden, John Quarles. BA, U. Richmond, 1950, LLD, 1977; JD, Harvard U., 1953. Bar: Va. 1953, U.S. Ct. Mil. Appeals 1954, U.S. Supreme Ct. 1958. Assoc. Hunton & Williams, Richmond, Va., 1956-63, ptnr., 1963-95, sr. coun., 1995—; substitute Judge 13th Dist., Va., 1996—. Lectr. in law Seinan Gakuin U., Fukuoka, Japan, 1985; vis. lectr. in law St. Thomas U., Miami, Fla., 1993; maj. gen., sr. mil. aide to Gov. of Va., 1997-2001. Active Va. Coun. on Human Rights, 1987; commr. chmn. Richmond Redevel. and Housing Authority, 1961-70; mem., vice chmn. Richmond Sch. Bd., 1971-80; trustee U. Richmond, 1972-2002, trustee emeritus, 2002—, rector, 1973-77, 81-85, 91-94, vice rector, 1985-87, chmn. exec. commn., 1977-81; trustee Va. Inst. Sci. Rsch., 1981-94, Richmond Symphony, 1987-92, Rouse-Bottom Found., 1989—; pres., 2004-07; active Westminster-Canterbury Found. Richmond, 1995-2001, chmn., 1998-2001; active Robins Found., 1996—, Richmond Symphony Orch. Found., 1999—2011, Christian Children's Fund, 2000—08, ChildFund Internat., 2002-08, Richmond Eye and Ear Hosp., 2000—08, Homeward, 2001-07; chmn. Richmond Eye and Ear Found., 2001-07. With U.S. Army Res., 1959-83, col. ret. Fellow Am. Coll. Trial Lawyers, Am. Bar Found.; mem. ABA, Va. Bar Assn., Va. Law Found. (chmn. fellows coun. 1996-2001), Richmond Bar Assn., Westwood Racquet Club. Democrat. Baptist. Office: Hunton & Williams East Tower Riverfront Pla PO Box 1535 Richmond VA 23218-1535 Home Phone: 804-282-1391; Office Phone: 804-788-8496. Business E-Mail: lbooker@hunton.com.

BOOKER, NANA LAUREL, art gallery owner, honorary consul; b. Waco, Tex., Aug. 5, 1946; d. Karl and Helen Dorothy (Keene) B. BA, Baylor U., 1968; MA, U. Fla., 1970; MBA, Pepperdine U., 1980. Asst. prof. comm. U. New Orleans, 1970-74, 1977-78; pub. rels. cons. New Orleans, 1974-78; dir. pub. rels. Touro Infirmary, New Orleans, 1976-78; dir. comm. Lifemark Corp., Houston, 1978-81; pres. Comm. Alliance, Houston, 1981-82; dir. internat. rels., comm. Mayor's Office, City of Houston, 1982-84; pres. Nana Booker & Assocs. (now Booker/Hancock & Assocs.), Houston, 1984—2004; owner Booker-Lowe Gallery of Australian Aboriginal Art, 2002—. Hon. consul of Australia, State Tex., 1999—. Co-author: Introduction to Theatrical Arts, 1972. Active South Tex. Dist. Export Coun., Houston, 1988-92; press aide campaign K. Whitmire for Mayor, Houston, 1982; exec. adv. bd. coll. bus. adminstrn. U. Houston, 1990-95; bd. dirs. Escape Ctr., 1990-93, YWCA, Houston, 1991-92, Greater Houston Partnership, 2003—06; co-chair Asia-Pacific Arts Cir. Asia Soc., Tex., 2006-. Recipient Internat. Assn. Bus. Communicators awards, Women in Comms. awards, Crystal award Am. Mktg. Assn., Outstanding Pub. Rels. Practitioner award Tex. Pub. Rels. Assn., 1996, Vol. of the Yr. award Houston Area Women's Ctr., 1998, Order of Australia, 2005. Mem. Pub. Rels. Soc. Am. (accredited, chairperson internat. sect. 1993-95, Excalibur award 1988, Cert. of Appreciation 1993, 94, 95; mem. U.S. coun. 1994-96), Internat. Pub. Rels. Assn., Houston World Trade Assn. (bd. dirs. 1986—2005), Houston-Shenzhen Sister City Assn. (bd. dirs. 1987-94), Swiss-Am. C. of C. (bd. dirs. 1987-90), River Oaks Breakfast Club (bd. dirs. 1997), Asia Soc. Tex. (bd. dirs. 1995—). Avocations: photography, design, art. Business E-Mail: nana@bookerlowegallery.com, art@bookeriowegallery.com.

BOOKHARDT, FRED BARRINGER, JR., architect; b. New Orleans, May 14, 1934; s. Fred B. and Leticia (Chevez) B. BArch, Tulane U., 1959; postgrad., U. Pa., 1960-61. Designer Freret and Wolf, Architects, 1959-60, Kenneth Ripnen, Architect, 1961-63, Francis X. Gina, Architects, 1963-64, Smith, Smith, Haines, Lundberg and Waehler, NYC, 1965; ptnr., v.p. William F. Pedersen & Assocs., NYC and New Haven, 1965-77; prin. Fred B. Bookhardt, Architect, NYC, 1977—. Dir. 28 E. 4th St. Housing Corp.; cons. Engring. Cons. Group, Cairo, Heliopolis and Alexandria, Egypt, 1983—; dir. The Network of Bus. & Profl. Orgns. Contbg. editor Uptown mag., New Orleans; archtl. works include: Superior Cts. Bldg., New Haven, 1974, Hall Minerals and Gems of Am. Mus. Natural History, 1976, Fed. Office Bldg., New Haven, 1978, Restaurant Claire, Key West, Fla., 1978, Woodmere Kingdom of Minerals, 1980, exec. offices So. Container Corp., Hauppauge, N.Y., 1981, Mus. Shop Am. Mus. Natural History, N.Y.C., 1982, renovation of pub. spaces lower level, 1984, employees cafeteria, 1984, Children's Reception Ctr., 1986, Sadowsky residence, Northport, N.Y., 1987, Kaufman residence, N.Y.C., 1987, Grossman residence, Montauk, N.Y., 1983, St. Barts, W.I., 1990, Zweibel residences, N.Y.C., 1983, Ft. Lauderdale, Fla., 1984, exec. offices Bon Temps Employment Agy., N.Y.C., 1984, Dieckmann residence, Manhasset, N.Y., 1985, master plan Am. Mus. Natural History, N.Y.C., 1989, space analysis The Trotting Horse Mus., Goshen, N.Y., 1989, addition and renovation, 1990, De Roy residence, N.Y.C., 1991, Zweibel residence, Boca Raton, Fla., 1993, Kelley residence, St. James, N.Y., 1983, HIV Law Project, 1994, Hinlein residence, 1995, Price/Uribe Residence, East Northport, N.Y., 1996, Branford (Conn.) H.S. with David M. Chin, 1996-97, Mancini Residence, N.Y.C., with Charles Burke, 1998, Fitz Simons Residence, 1999, Cary Grossman Residence, 1999, Bookhardt-Gaskell Residence, New Orleans, 2000. With U.S. Army, 1954-56. Recipient Lumen award Illuminating Engrs. Soc., 1977, 1st pl. award Home Mag. ceramic tile competition. Mem. AIA, N.Y. State Assn. Architects, Architects Coun. N.Y.C., N.Y. Soc. Architects, Am. Assn. Mus., N.E. Mus. Conf., Nat. Cert. Archtl. Rev. Bd. (cert.) Home and Office: 819 Marigny St New Orleans LA 70117-8525 Personal E-mail: catfred@cox.net.

BOOKOUT, PAUL, state legislator; b. El Dorado, Ark., June 30, 1962; m. Sheryl Bookout. Funeral dir., Jonesboro, Ark.; mem. Ark. House of Reps., 1998—2004; mem. Dist. 14 Ark. State Senate, 2006—, asst. pres. pro tempore, 2007, asst. pres. pro tempore 1st Dist., 2009—. Democrat. Baptist. Office: 2104 Catharine Dr Jonesboro AR 72404-6963 Office Phone: 870-932-6662. Office Fax: 870-932-6701. Business E-Mail: bookoutp@arkleg.state.ar.us.

BOOKSPAN, MARTIN, broadcaster, writer; b. Boston, July 30, 1926; s. Simon and Martha (Schwartz) Bookspan; m. Janet Sylvia Sobel, Oct. 24, 1954; children: Rachel Raissa, David Israel, Deborah Joy. BS, Harvard U., 1947; MusD (hon.), Mannes Coll. of Music, 1991; LHD (hon.), Suffolk U., 1995. Music dir. Sta. WBMS, Boston, 1946—50; concert music dir. Sta. WCOP, 1950—54; exec. dir. New Eng. Opera Theater, 1952—54; media dir. Boston Symphony, 1954—56; program dir. Sta. WQXR, NYC, 1956—67; dir. concerts ASCAP, 1968—83; commentator N.Y. Philharm., 1975—88, Live from Lincoln Ctr., 1976—2006; v.p. Moss Music Group, 1983—88. Cons. Rockefeller Found., NYC, 1963—67, Madison Sq. Garden, 1984—86, Nat. Westminster Bank, 1987—91; panelist Nat. Endowment Arts, Washington, 1978—86; expert classical music Prodigy On-Line Computer Svc., 1990—95; web moderator Livefromlincolncenter.org, 1997—. Author: 101 Masterpieces Music, 1968, Consumer Reports Recs., 1973; author: (with others) Zubin, 1978, Andre Previn, 1982. Recipient Peabody award, 1948, Letter of Merit, Am. Music Ctr., 1977, medal of Honor, Nat. Arts Club, 1984, Spl. award, Concert Artists Guild, 1986, Lifetime Achievement award, Fine Arts Radio Internat., 2002; named one of Am. Classical Music Hall of Fame, 2006. Mem.: SAG, The Bohemians, ASCAP, AFTRA. Home and Office: Apt 806 21205 NE 37th Ave Aventura FL 33180 Office Phone: 212-496-0740, 305-936-0191.

BOOM, MARC L., hospital administrator; m. Julie Boom; 3 children. BS in Biology with high honors, U. Tex., Austin; MD with high honors, Baylor U. Coll. Medicine, Waco, Tex.; MBA, The Wharton Sch. of U. Pa., Phila. Cert. in internal medicine and geriatric medicine. Resident in internal medicine Mass. Gen. Hosp., Harvard Med. Sch.; fellow in geriatric medicine and gen. medicine Hosp. of U. Pa.; asst. prof. clin. medicine Weill Cornell Med. Coll., NY; part-time practice in preventive medicine, lipid disorders and hypertension; pres., CEO, med. dir. Baylor-Meth. Primary Care Associates, Tex.; pres., CEO The Meth. Diagnostic Hosp., Tex.; sr. v.p., COO The Meth Hosp., Houston, exec. v.p., CEO, 2012—. Bd. dirs. Univ. Health Sys. Consortium; adj. prof. mgmt. Rice U., Tex. Bd. mem. Houston Ballet. Named a Modern Healthcare Up & Comer, 1999. Fellow: American Coll. Physicians, American Coll. Healthcare Executives; mem.: American Coll. Physician Executives, American Heart Assn. (past pres. Houston office, Disting. Svc. award 2007), Leadership Inst. Office: The Methodist Hosp 6565 Fannin Dunn Tower 200 Houston TX 77030 Office Phone: 713-441-2671. Office Fax: 713-441-1995. Business E-Mail: mboom@tmhs.org.

BOOMERSHINE, DONALD EUGENE, bureau executive, development official; b. Brookville, Ohio, Oct. 5, 1931; s. Harold Everett and Elsie (Rhoads) B.; m. Marilyn Sullivan, Aug. 29, 1953 (dec.); children: Jeffrey, Alan; stepson: Andrew Raine; m. Patti Watson, May 29, 1985. BS, Bowling Green State U., Ohio, 1953; grad., Northwestern U. Bank Mktg. Grad. Sch., 1965; M in Bank Mgmt., Rutgers U., 1969-72; postgrad., U. Okla. Nat. Sr. Comml. Lending Sch., 1974. With jr. exec. program Frigidaire div. Gen. Motors Corp., Dayton, 1955-57; sr. sales rep. IBM, Dayton, 1957-61; bus. devel. rep., asst. cashier Exchange Security Bank, Birmingham, 1961-65; v.p. charge nat. divsn. Birmingham Trust Nat. Bank, 1965-78, v.p., 1978—80; v.p., sales mgr. Cir. S divsn., v.p. cmty. devel. Met. Devel. Bd., 1980—82; pres., CEO Better Bus. Bur. Ctrl. Ala., Birmingham, 1982—2006. Chmn. Bus. Tomorrow Conf. Auburn U., 1975, U. South Alabama, 1976; ednl. chmn. Assoc. Industries Ala., 1975—77; mem. Atlanta-Birmingham br. Fed. Res. Bd., 1990—97, chmn., 1993, 1996; bus. adv. coun. Sorrell Coll. Bus., Troy U., 1991—; interim exec. dir. Ala. Pub. TV. Gen. chmn. US World Youth Games, 1973; v.p. Nat. Vet.'s Day, 1972—2010; mem. Blue and Gold Bd. US Naval Acad., designated info. officer, 1982—2004; pres. North Ctrl. Ala. chpt. Muscular Dystrophy Found., 1964; trustee Birmingham YWCA, 1972—75; charter mem. Downtown Action Com., 1966; mem. ARC, 1967—, bd. dirs., 1968—80, Birmingham Children's Theatre, 1974—75, Downtown YMCA, Met. YMCA, 1992—97; mem. steering com. Mobile Coll., 1987—90; mem. adv. bd. U. South Ala., 1975—78; chmn. Am. Cancer Crusade, 1976; alumnus Leadership Birmingham, 1991; mem. adv. bd. Ala. State Bd. Edn., 1976—78; bd. govs. Ala. Assn. Ind. Colls. and Univs.; mem. exec. com. Birmingham Cmty. Svc. award; mem. Ala. com. Employers Support of the NG and Res.; bd. dirs., 2d v.p. Birmingham BBB, 1980—82; founding bd. dirs. Ala. Jump Start Coalition, 2002; bd. dirs. Birmingham Zoological Soc., 1972—76. 2nd lt. USMC, 1953, Occ i Commd., retired colonel USMCR, 1984. Recipient Comdt. award U.S. Naval Acad., 1994, Comdts. Dir. award, 1999, Outstanding Broadcasters Cooperation award Ala. Broadcasters Assn., 1998, Alumni Cmty. Svc. award Bowling Green State U., 2001; Res. Day proclaimed in his honor, Birmingham, 1983, Donald E. Boomershine Day proclaimed in his honor, 1985; named to Brookville HS Alumni Hall of Fame, 1991, Ala. Sr. Citizen Hall of Fame, 2005, Better Bus. Bureau, Inc. Hall of Fame, 2006; recipient lifetime achievement award Fed. Res. Bank of Atlanta, 2009, award, Yacht Leadership Devel. Program, 2011, CAC Youth Leadership award, 2011. Mem. Bank Mktg. Assn. (nat. dir. 1971-75, nat. v.p. devel. 1971), Ala. Indsl. Devel. Coun., So. Indsl. Coun., World Trade Assn. Ala., Diplomats of Birmingham (founder, chmn. 1973), Marine Corps Res. Officers Assn. (nat. dir. 1974-76), Ala. Native Sons and Daus. (chmn. 1971-72), Newcomen Soc. of U.S., Birmingham C. of C. (life), Vestavia Country Club, The Club, Touchdown Club (Birmingham, founder, dir., treas), Kiwanis (officer, dir., Birmingham 1971, Diamond Leuch Hixson fellow 2003, Legion Honor award, 2006, Tablet of Honor, 2010, Diamond Level, 2011), Vestavia Country Club, The Club, Summit Club (founding mem., bd. dirs. 2004), Nat. Sigma Chi (Significant Sig award 2011), Ala. Pub. television (appointed interim exec. dir. 2012), US Marine Corps League (life, founding mem., 2013-). Home: 183 Highland Park Dr Birmingham AL 35242

BOONE, MERRILL, healthcare management executive; B in Acctg., U. So. Miss. Asst. contr. Nat. Am. Companies, Biloxi, Miss.; numerous positions of increasing responsibility including dir. fin. planning and local market fin. Kaiser Permanente, v.p., regional contr. Ga., 2003—. Office: Kaiser Permanente Nine Piedmont Ctr 3495 Piedmont Rd NE Atlanta GA 30305 Office Phone: 404-364-7000. Office Fax: 404-364-4998. Business E-Mail: M.Boone@kp.org.

BOORAS, CHARLES H., family practice physician; b. Jacksonville; married. Grad., U. South Fla., 1974—78, MD, 1978—81. Diplomate Am. Bd. Family Practice. Resident family medicine St. Vincent's Med. Ctr., Jacksonville, Fla., 1981—84; hosp. affiliation includes Baptist Med. Ctr. Named one of Best Doctors. Avocations: surfing, fishing, hiking, golf. Office: Baptist Primary Care 1922 University Blvd S Jacksonville FL 32216 Office Phone: 904-721-7844. Office Fax: 904-727-3597.

BOORSTEIN, LAURENCE, economist, project manager; b. Neuilly, France, Jan. 22, 1951; arrived in U.S., 1951; s. Edward and Regula Boorstein. BA, Columbia U., 1972, MS, 1974, CE, 1978, MBA, 1988. Sys. analyst Frederic R. Harris, Inc. divsn. Planning Rsch. Corp., NYC, 1974—77, prin. sys. engr. Frederic R. Harris, Inc., 1977—79, sr. sys. planner Frederic R. Harris Inc., 1979—83, sr. economist Frederic R. Harris, Inc., 1983—86; sr. economist Soros Assocs., 1988—94; project mgr., prin. economist AECOM, NYC, 1994—2005, Arlington, Va., 2005—. Mem.: Soc. Civil Engrs. Office: AECOM 2101 Wilson Blvd 8th Fl Arlington VA 22201-3044 Office Phone: 703-340-3027. Office Fax: 703-340-3101. Business E-Mail: larry.boorstein@aecom.com.

BOOTH, JANE SCHUELE, real estate company officer, broker; b. Cleve. d. Norman Andrew and Frances Ruth (Hankey) Schuele; m. George Warren Booth, Dec. 6, 1968. AA, Stephens Coll., 1946; student, U. Mo., 1946—47. Lic. real estate broker, Fla. Assoc. J.M. Mathes Inc., NYC, 1947-48; dept. supr. Lord and Taylor, Scarsdale, N.Y., 1948-50; art coord. J. Walter Thompson, Inc., NYC, 1953-58; art buyer SSC&B Inc. Advt., NYC, 1959-80; pres. Jane Schuele Booth Realty, Ocala, Fla., 1982—. Mem. Fla. Thoroughbred Fillies, Ocala, 1980—; charter mem., trustee Royal Dames for Cancer Rsch., Inc., Ocala, 1986—; treas. Ladies Aux. Fla. H.C.H. Inc., Ocala, 1986-90; bd. visitors Fla. Horsemen's Children's Home, Inc., 1983-90. Mem. Ocala/Marion County Assn. Realtors, Ocala/Marion County C. of C. (agribus./equine com.), Nat. Assn. Realtors, Fla. Assn. Realtors. Office: PO Box 5538 Ocala FL 34478-5538 Home: PO Box 1270 Pisgah Forest NC 28768-1270 Personal E-mail: janeschuelebooth@aol.com.

BOOTHBY, LEE K., energy executive; Degree in Petroleum Engring., La. State U.; MBA, Rice U. Worked Tenneco Oil Co., Cockrell Oil Corp., British Gas; mng. dir. Newfield Exploration Australia Ltd., 1999—2001; joined as v.p., gen. mgr., Australian bus. unit Newfield Exploration Co., 1999, pres., v.p., Mid-Continent, 2002—07, sr. v.p., acquisitions and bus. devel., 2007—09, pres., CEO, 2009—. Bd.dirs. Newfield Exploration Co., 2009—; currently serving as bd. dirs. Okla. Energy Resources Bd. Mem. Soc. Petroleum Engrs., Ind. Petroleum Assn. America; bd. dirs. Okla. Ind. Petroleum Assn. (OIPA). Office: Newfield Exploration Co Ste 100 363 N Sam Houston Pkwy E Houston TX 77060 Office Phone: 281-847-6000. Office Fax: 281-405-4242. Business E-Mail: lboothby@newfld.com.

BOOTHE, ALAN C., state legislator; b. Opp, Ala., Nov. 14, 1945; m. Anne Boothe; children: Melissa, Jason. BS, MS, Troy State U., Ala. Former city councilman & county coroner; dir. govtl. rels. Troy State U.; mem. Dist. 89 Ala. House of Reps., Montgomery, 1998—. Mem. First Bapt. Ch., Troy. Mem.: Rotary Club. Democrat. Baptist. Office:

PO Box 36081 Troy AL 36081 also: Ala House of Reps Ala State House 11 S Union St Rm 627-A Montgomery AL 36130 Office Phone: 334-242-7710. Business E-Mail: alan.boothe@alhouse.gov.

BOOTHROYD, HERBERT, insurance company executive; b. Mason City, Iowa, Dec. 23, 1928; s. Herbert L. and Clara (Schmitt) B.; m. Barbara Elizabeth Dunne, Feb. 9, 1962; children: Diane Lea, John Herbert. AB in Math. with honors, U. Mich., 1952, AM, 1953. Enrolled actuary, 1976; cert. in exec. mgmt. programs, Columbia, 1964, MIT, 1971. With Mass. Mut. Life Ins. Co., 1953-57; with New Eng. Mut. Life Ins. Co., Boston, 1957-87, v.p., 1967-77, sr. v.p. pension ops., 1977-82, exec. v.p. group ops., 1983-87; dir. New Eng. Pension and Annuity Co., 1980-87, pres., 1981-87; pres., dir. New Eng. Gen. Life, 1983-85. Dir. New Eng. Mut. Life Ins. Co., 1984-87, New Eng. Variable Life Ins. Co., 1984-87. Contbg. author: (book) Hammett Families, 1983, Cockrill Families of No. Virginia, 2002; contbg. author: Life and Health Insurance Handbook, 1973. Bd. dirs. New Eng. chpt. Am. Diabetes Assn., 1979-84; bd. govs. Handel and Haydn Soc., 1984-94, sec., 1986-94, overseer, 1994—2003; mem. nat. campaign com. U. Mich., 1983-90; bd. dirs. Better Bus. Bur. Ea. Mass., 1980-88, vice chmn., mem. exec. com., 1985-88. With US Army, 1946—47. Fellow Soc. Actuaries; mem. SAR, Am. Acad. Actuaries, Internat. Congress Actuaries, New Eng. Hist. Geneal. Soc.(mem. coun., 2010-), Ky. Hist. Soc., U. Mich. Alumni Assn. (v.p. 1st dist. 1989-91, pres. 1991-93, nat. bd. dirs. 1997-2000, chair nat. clubs coun. 1999-2000), Soc. Colonial Wars Comm. Mass., Haile Plantation Golf and Country Club, Phi Beta Kappa, Theta Delta Chi. Avocations: genealogy, music, skiing, travel. Home and Office: 4205 SW 96th Dr Gainesville FL 32608 E-mail: herbbooth@aol.com.

BOOZMAN, JOHN NICHOLS, United States Senator from Arkansas, former United States Representative from Arkansas; b. Shreveport, La, Dec. 10, 1950; m. Cathy Marley; 3 children. Student, U. Ark., Fayetteville, 1969—72; OD, Southern Coll. Optometry, 1977. Pvt. practice eye clinic, 1977; mem. US Congress from 3rd Ark. Dist., Washington, 2001—11; US Senator from Ark. Washington, 2011—; mem. US Senate Commerce, Sci. & Transp. Com., Washington, 2011—, US Senate Environment & Public Works Com., Washington, 2011—, US Senate Agrl., Nutrition & Forestry Com., Washington, 2011—, US Senate Veterans Affairs Com., Washington, 2011—. Co-founder Boozman-Hof Regional Eye Clinic, P.A., Rogers, Ark., 1977. Mem. Rogers (Ark.) Bd. Edn., 1994—2001; establisher low vision program Ark. Sch. for Blind for Little Rock. Recipient Spirit of Enterprise award, US Chamber of Commerce, 2001, 2002, 2003, Hero of the Taxpayer award, American for Tax Reform, 2001, 2002, 2003, Small Bus. Advocate award, Small Bus. Survival Com., 2004, Brighter Vision award, Age-Related Macular Degeneration Alliance Internat., 2006, Award for Manufacturing Legislative Excellence, Nat. Assn. Manufacturers, 2010, A in English award, US English, Inc., 2010, Disting. Advocate award, Assn. Edn. & Rehabilitation of the Blind & Visually Impaired (Ark. chapter). Mem.: Internat. Acad. Sports Vision, Ark. Optometric Assn., American Optometric Assn., Fellowship Christian Athletes. Republican. Baptist. Office: US Senate 320 Senate Hart Office Building Washington DC 20510 also: 1401 W Capitol Ave Plz F Little Rock AR 72201 Office Phone: 202-224-4843, 501-372-7153. Office Fax: 202-228-1371, 501-372-7163.*

BORCHELT, MARK D., endocrinologist; Grad., Kent State U.; MD, Northeastern Ohio U. Coll. Medicine, 1983. Diplomate Am. Bd. Internal Medicine, 1986, Am. Bd. Internal Medicine-endocrinology, diabetes and metabolism, 1989. Resident internal medicine Akron City Hosp., Ohio, 1984—86; fellow endocrinology Cleve. Clinic Found., Ohio, 1986—88; physician Heart and Family Health Inst., Port St. Lucie, Fla., St. Lucie Med. Ctr., Port St. Lucie. Office: St Lucie Medical Center Ste 200 1700 SE Hillmoor Dr Port Saint Lucie FL 34952 Office Phone: 772-335-9600. Office Fax: 772-335-9699.*

BORCHERT, ROBERT, information technology executive; BBA in Mktg. & Fin., Pace U.; attended, SUNY, Albany. Account exec. to v.p. Cameron Assocs.; v.p., Investor & Corp. Comm. Coastal Physician Group; sr. v.p. Edelman Pub. Rels.; sr. investor rels. cons. Healthways Inc.; asst. v.p. Morgen-Walke Assocs.; v.p., investor rels. & corp. comm. NDCHealth (acquired by Per-Se Technologies), Per-Se Technologies; sr. v.p. Robinson Lerer & Montgomery; dir., corp. comm. The Multicare Companies; sr. investor rels. and corp. comm. positions CNET Networks, 1999—2003, Ziff-Davis, 1999—2003; joined MedAssets, Inc., 2007, v.p., investor rels. Bd. dirs. NIRI Atlanta, 2009—. Named Best IR Officer and Best Overall Investor Rels. award, Investor Rels. Mag., 2002. Office: MedAssets Inc 100 N Point Ctr E Ste 200 Alpharetta GA 30022 Office Phone: 678-323-2500. Office Fax: 678-323-2501. Business E-Mail: rborchert@medassets.com.

BORDELON, JOHN, bank executive; m. Suzzane Bordelon; children: Kate Bordelon, Molly Bordelon, Olivia Bordelon. Pres., CEO, bd. dirs. Home Bank (subs. of Home Bancorp, Inc.), 1993—, Home Bancorp, Inc., 1993—. Office: Home Bancorp Inc 503 Kaliste Saloom Rd Lafayette LA 70508 Office Phone: 337-237-1960. Office Fax: 337-264-9280.

BORDLEY, WILLIAM CLAYTON (CLAY), pediatrician, educator; b. Washington, Dec. 14, 1959; Grad., U. NC, Chapel Hill, 1982; MD, John Hopkins Sch. Medicine, 1986; MPH, U. NC, Chapel Hill, 1993. Cert. in pediat. Intern, pediat. Children's Hosp. Phila., Pa., 1986—87, resident, pediat. Pa., 1990; fellow Robert Wood Johnson Clin. Scholars Program, Duke U. Med. Ctr., NC, 1993; chief, divsn. hosp. and emergency medicine, dept. pediat. Duke U. Med. Ctr., NC, med. dir., pediat. emergency dept.; chief, hospitalist svc. Duke Children's Hosp., 2002—; assoc. prof. pediat. Duke U., Durham, NC, assoc. prof., surgery. Recipient Samuel L. Katz Tchg. award, 2004; named a Health Care Hero-Category-Hospitalist, Triangle Bus. Jour., 2008. Avocation: soccer. Office: Duke Med Ctr Divsn Pediatrics and Emergency Medicine DUMC 3096 Durham NC 27710 Office Phone: 919-681-1850. Office Fax: 919-681-8521.

BORDONE, ADRIAN, information technology executive; Attended, US Navel Acad., 1989; BA, U. Balt., 1994; MLA, St. John's Coll., 1996. Asst. dir. The Learning Bank of Balt., 1996—97; program dir. The Learning Bank, 1996—98; COO Md Ctr. for Arts & Tech., 1997—2000; v.p. Social Solutions Global, Inc.; co-founder, treas. & bd. dirs. Social Solutions Inc.; co-founder, v.p. Citrix Sys., Inc. Office: Citrix Systems Inc 851 W Cypress Creek Rd Fort Lauderdale FL 33309 Office Phone: 954-267-3000. Office Fax: 954-267-9319. Business E-Mail: adrian.bordone@citrix.com.

BORDSEN, ALICE L., state legislator; State rep. Dist. 63, NC, 2002—. Mem. Aging com., Edn. com., Judiciary II com.; vice chmn. Appropriations com., Edn. Subcom. on Cmty. Colleges; chmn. Appropriations Subcom. on Justice and Pub. Safety. Democrat. Mailing: Dist Off 411 S Fifth St Mebane NC 27302 Office: North Carolina House of Representatives 300 N Salisbury St Rm 602 Raleigh NC 27603-5925 Office Phone: 919-733-5820, 919-563-5264. E-mail: Alice.Bordsen@ncleg.net.

BOREL, CALVIN H., jockey; b. St. Martin Parish, La., Nov. 7, 1966; m. Lisa Funk. Profl. horse racing jockey, 1982—. Recipient George Woolf Meml. Jockey award, Santa Anita Pk., Calif., 2010. Achievements include winning horse racing titles including: Delta Downs, 1985-87; Louisiana Downs, 1991, 1992, 1994; Oaklawn Park, 1995, 2001; Ellis Park, 1995; Churchill Downs, 1998, 2007, 2009, 2010; Turfway Park, 2000; Kentucky Downs, 2005; winning US Triple Crown/Breeders' Cup races including: Breeders' Cup Juvenile, (aboard Street Sense) 2006; Kentucky Derby (Street Sense) 2007, (Mine That Bird) 2009, (Super Saver) 2010; Preakness Stakes (Rachel Alexander), 2009. Office: c/o Churchill Downs 700 Central Ave Louisville KY 40208

BOREN, DAVID LYLE, academic administrator, former United States Senator from Oklahoma; b. Washington, Apr. 21, 1941; s. Lyle H. and Christine (McKown) B.; m. Molly Shi, Dec. 1977; children: David Daniel, Carrie Christine. BA summa cum laude, Yale, 1963; MA (Rhodes scholar), Oxford U., Eng., 1965; JD (Bledsoe Meml. prize as outstanding law grad.), U. Okla., 1968. Bar: Okla. 1968. Practiced law in, Seminole, 1968-74; prof. polit. sci., chair divsn. social scis. Okla. Bapt. U., Shawnee, 1969-74; mem. Okla. House of Reps., 1967-75; gov. State of Okla., Oklahoma City, 1975-79; US Senator from Okla., 1979-94; chmn. US Senate Select Com. on Intelligence, 1987—95; pres. U. Okla., Norman, 1994—; co-chmn. President's Intelligence Advisory Bd. (PIAB), 2009—. Bd. mem. Bloomberg Family Found., 2010—. Author: A Letter to America, 2008. Trustee Yale U., 1988-97. Named One of 10 Outstanding Young Men in U.S., U.S. Jaycees, 1967. Mem. Assn. U.S. Rhodes Scholars, Phi Beta Kappa. Democrat. Methodist. Office: University of Oklahoma Office of President 660 Parrington Oval Rm 110 Norman OK 73019-3003 Office Phone: 405-325-3916. E-mail: dboren@on.edu.*

BOREN, LYNDA SUE, gifted education educator; b. Leesville, La., Apr. 1, 1941; d. Leonard and Doris (Ford) Schoenberger; m. James Lewis Boren, Sept. 1, 1961; 1 child, Lynda Carolyn. BA, U. New Orleans, 1971, MA, 1973; PhD, Tulane U., 1979. Prof. Northwestern State U., Natchitoches, La., 1987-89; propr. Colony Country House, New Llano, La., 1992-94; tchr. of gifted Leesville HS, La., 1992—2010. Vis. prof. Newcomb Coll., Tulane U., New Orleans, 1979-83, U. Erlangen-Nuremburg, Germany, 1981-82, Middlebury (Vt.) Coll., 1983-84, Ga. Inst. Tech., Atlanta, 1985-87, Srinakharinwirot U., Bangkok, 1989-90; mem. planning com. 1st Kate Chopin Internat. Conf., Natchitoches, La., 1987-89; Fulbright lectr. USIA and Bd. Fgn. Scholars, 1981-82, 89-90. Author: Eurydice Reclaimed: Language, Gender and Voice in Henry James, 1989; co-editor, author: Kate Chopin Reconsidered, 1992; contbg. author: Encyclopedia of American Poetry, 1998, Awakenings: The Story of the Kate Chopin Revival, 2009; contbr. numerous articles to profl. jours. Founding mem. John F. Kennedy libr. Recipient awards for watercolors; Mellon fellow Tulane U., 1977-78; NEH seminar fellow Princeton U., 1986. Mem. MLA, DAR, Fulbright Alumni Assn. Avocations: painting, video film documentaries, photography. Home: 1492 Fords Dairy Rd Newllano LA 71461-4530 Personal E-mail: lyboren@suddenlink.net.

BORKOWSKI, FRANCIS THOMAS, music educator; b. Weirton, W.Va., Mar. 16, 1936; s. Francis Thomas and Felicia Josephine (Pawlowski) B.; m. Kay Kaiser, Aug. 22, 1959; children: Stanley, Anne-Marie, Christian. BS, Oberlin Coll., Ohio, 1957; M.Mus., Ind. U., 1959; PhD, W.Va. U., 1967; LLD (hon.), St. Leo Coll., Fla., 1989. Clarinetist Indpls. Symphony Orch., 1957-59; music dir. Bishop Kenny High Sch., Jacksonville, Fla., 1959-61; dir. bands W.Va. U., 1961-67; assoc. prof. music edn. Ohio U., Athens, 1967-69, asst. dir. Sch. Music, 1969-70, assoc. dean faculties, 1970-75; prof. music, vice chancellor, dean faculty Ind. U.-Purdue U., Ft. Wayne, 1975-78; v.p. Ft. Wayne Philharmonic Orch., 1976-78; provost U. S.C. System, 1978-83, exec. v.p., provost, 1983-88; pres. U. South Fla., Tampa, 1988-93; chancellor Appalachian State U., Boone, NC, 1993—2003, prof. music, 2003—. Bd. dirs. Fla. Nations Bank. Author articles. Mem. nat. adv. coun. John F. Kennedy Ctr., 1978-80; pres. S.C. Orch. Assn., 1982; bd. dirs. United Way of Columbia, 1981; chmn. Moffitt Cancer Ctr. Bd., United Way Bd., Tampa; mem. urban affairs com. Nat. Assn. Land Grant Colls. Recipient Amicus Poloniae award Poland mag., 1971, award for research Sigma Xi; named Polonian of Yr., 1989, Gold medal with Diamond, INTERPROM, 1997, Commdr. of the Cross of the Rep. of Poland, 2001. Mem. Am. Coun. Edn. (bd. dirs.), Am. Assn. Higher Edn., Music Educators Nat. Conf., Phi Beta Kappa, Mortar Bd., Omicron Delta Kappa, Eta Sigma Gamma, Golden Key, Phi Beta Delta. Roman Catholic. Office Phone: 828-262-7537. Business E-Mail: borkowskif@appstate.edu.

BORMAN, J. RICHARD, automotive executive; BA in Economics, Creighton U., 1984. Various positions Genuine Parts Co., exec. v.p. Rayloc, 2005—06, pres. Rayloc, 2006—09, v.p. American parts group, Southern divsn., 2009—. Office: Genuine Parts Co 2999 Cir 75 Pky Atlanta GA 30339 Office Phone: 770-953-1700. Office Fax: 770-956-2211. Business E-Mail: j.borman@genpt.com.

BORMAN, MICHAEL J., information technology executive; BS in Computer Science & Engg., U. Ill., 1977; MBA, Northwestern U., 1983. Programmer IBM Software Group, 1977, various positions including v.p. worldwide sales & ops., web servers and v.p. small and medium bus. North America, dir. strategy, Asia Pacific, gen. mgr. distbn. and SMB, Asia Pacific, gen. mgr. global bus. ptnrs., 2003—04, gen. mgr. i-Series and p-Series, 2004, v.p. worldwide sales, 2005—08; head software sales International Bus. Machines Corp., 2005—08; pres., COO Blue Martini Software, Inc.; CEO Avocent Corp., 2008—, chmn. bd. dirs., 2008—09. Mem. adv. bd. Northwestern U. Kellogg Sch. Mem.: Econ. Club Chgo., Comml. Club. Office: Avocent Corp 4991 Corporate Dr Huntsville AL 35805 Office Phone: 256-430-4000. Office Fax: 256-430-4030. Business E-Mail: michael.borman@avocent.com.

BORNHORST, DONALD T., air transportation executive; Grad., Eastern Ky. U. Mgr., then dir. internal audits & special projects Comair, Inc. (subs. of Delta Air Lines, Inc.), Cin., 1991—98, v.p. info. svcs., 1998—2000, v.p. performance mgmt., 2000—02, sr. v.p. customers, 2002—05, CFO, 2005—06, pres., 2006—07, sr. v.p. Delta Connection, 2007—. Office: Delta Air Lines Inc PO Box 20706 Atlanta GA 30320-6001 Office Phone: 404-715-2600. Office Fax: 404-715-5042. E-mail: Don.Bornhorst@delta.com.

BORTON, SARA JOHNSON, publishing executive; Pub. Lowcountry Newspapers, 2009, pres., Lowcountry Ops., 2009—; pres., pub. The Island Packet, 2009—, Beaufort Gazette, 2009—. Office: The Beaufort Gazette 1809 Boundary St Beaufort SC 29902-3951 Office Phone: 843-524-3183. Business E-Mail: sborton@islandpacket.com.

BORTZ, WALTER M., III, academic administrator; m. Lorraine Bortz; children: Catherine, Walter. BS, Bethany Coll.; PhD in Policy Studies, George Washington U.; EdD in Ednl. Policy Studies. Dir. admissions Bethany Coll., East Carolina U.; dean admissions Tex. Christian U.; exec. dir. admissions and student fin. assistance U. Hartford, v.p. institutional advancement, acting v.p. adminstrn., acting v.p. student svcs.; v.p. adminstrn. and info. svcs. George Washington U.; pres. Hampden-Sydney Coll., Va., 2000—. Mem. exec. com. Coun. Independent Colls. in Va.; trustee Va. Found. Independent Colls.; head President's coun. Old Dominion Athletic Conf.; mem. and NCAA pres. coun. commn. on colls. So. Assn. Colls. and Univs. Office: Hampden-Sydney Coll Hampden Sydney VA 23943 Office Phone: 434-223-6110. E-mail: prez@hsc.edu.

BORZINO, BRUCE EDWARD, federal agency administrator; b. 1950; Grad., U. Conn., 1972. Various mgmt. & consulting positions Anteon Corp.; ret. lt. col. US Army; dir. electronic bus. systems GSA; dep. dir., chief ops. officer Nat. Tech. Info. Svc. (NTIS), US Dept. Commerce, Alexandria, Va., dir., 2009—. Office: National Technical Information Service 5301 Shawnee Rd Alexandria VA 22312 Office Phone: 703-605-6405. E-mail: bborzino@ntis.gov.*

BOSAH, FRANCIS N., molecular biochemist, educator; b. Onitsha, Anambra, Nigeria, Sept. 13, 1959; s. Michael and Comfort (Odiari) Bosah. BS, Shaw U., 1985; MS, N.C. Ctrl. U., 1988; PhD, Clark Atlanta U., 1995. Rsch. asst. N.C. Ctrl. U., Durham, 1985-88, instr., 1988-90; rsch. assoc. Rsch. Triangle Inst., Research Triangle Park, NC, 1989-90; rsch. assoc. dept. biochemistry Morehouse Sch. Medicine, Atlanta, 1990-95, NASA postdoctoral rsch. fellow dept. medicine, 1995-98, rsch. instr. dept. biochemistry, 1998—2004; asst. prof. Clark Atlanta U., 2004—09. Coord. health career Atlanta Met. Coll., 1993—94, instr. dept. biol. sci., 1993—; instr. DeKalb Coll., Clarkston, Ga., 1998—99; presenter in field. Contbr. articles to profl. jours. Recipient Minority Biochemical Rsch. Support award, 1990—93. Mem.: AAAS, Soc. Exptl. Biology and Medicine, Minority Biomedical Rsch. Soc., N.Y. Acad. Scis., Am. Chem. Soc., Am. Physiol. Soc. (predoctoral fellow 1993—95), Am. Soc. Cell Biology, Beta Kappa Chi. Roman Catholic. Avocations: photography, ping pong/table tennis, handball, racquetball, basketball, travel. Home: 5056 Rails Way Norcross GA 30071-4514 Office Phone: 404-880-8134. Personal E-mail: bosahf@hotmail.com.

BOSCHINI, VICTOR JOHN, JR., academic administrator; b. Cleve. m. Megan Boschini; children: Elizabeth, Mary Catherine, Edward Mark, Margaret. B in Sociology and Psychology, Union Coll.; M in Coll. Student Pers., Bowling Green State U.; D in Higher Edn. Adminstrn., Ind. U. Asst. to the dir. of residence life Bowling Green State U., 1978—79; student adviser Western Ill. U., Macomb, 1979—82; asst. dean of students DePauw U., Greencastle, Ind., 1982—84; asst. dean studies Ind. U., Bloomington, 1984—90; assoc. provost Butler U., Indpls., 1990—97; v.p., dean student affairs, edn. prof. Ill. State U., Normal, 1997—99, pres., 1999—2003; chancellor, prof. edn. Tex. Christian U., Ft. Worth, 2003—. Bd. dir. State Farm Mutual Funds Co. Bd. dir. Fort Worth Symphony, Tex.; bd. dir. Van Cliburn Found., Fort Worth, Tex.; bd. trustee Brite Divinity Sch. Office: Texas Christian University Box 297080 3861 Bellaire Circle Fort Worth TX 76109 Office Phone: 817-257-7783. Office Fax: 817-927-7518. E-mail: v.boschini@tcu.edu, chancellor@tcu.edu.*

BOSE, BIMAL KUMAR, electrical engineering educator; b. Calcutta, India, Sept. 1, 1932; came to US, 1971; s. Rajendra and Nirmala (Ghosh) B.; m. Arati Ghosh, June 26, 1961; children: Papia, Amit. BE, Calcutta U., 1956, PhD, 1966; MS, U. Wis., 1960; DSc (hon.), Bengal Engring. & Sci. U., 2013. Asst. engr. Tata Hydro Power Co., Bombay, 1956-59; asst. prof. Bengal Engring. Coll., Calcutta, 1960-71; assoc. prof. Rensselaer Poly. Inst., Troy, NY, 1971-76; rsch. engr. GE R & D Ctr., Schenectady, NY, 1976-87; prof. Condra Chair of Exellence U. Tenn., Knoxville, 1987—2002; emeritus prof., 2013. Disting. scientist Power Electronics Appliance Ctr., Knoxville, 1987—; cons. PCI Ozone Corp., NJ, 1971-73, GE, 1971-76, Rsch. Triangle Inst., NC, 1991-95, Bendix Corp., Electric Power Rsch. Inst., Lutron Electronics, UN for tech. devel. in People's Republic China and India;; sr. advisor to Beijing Power Electronics R&D Ctr.; lectr. in field; hon. prof. Shanghai U. Tech., 1991, China U. of Mining and Technology, 1996, Xi'an Mining Inst., 1998. Author: Power Electronics and AC Drives, 1986, Modern Power Electronics and AC Drives, 2002; editor: Adjustable Speed AC Drive Systems, 1981, Micro Computer Control of Power Electronics and Drives, 1987, Modern Power Electronics, 1992, Power Electronics and Variable Frequency Drives, 1996, Power Electronics and Motor Drives, 2006; patentee in field; contbr. articles to profl. jours. Recipient Mouat Gold medal Calcutta U., 1967, Publ. award GE, 1982, Silver Patent medal GE, 1983. Fellow IEEE (life, chmn. power electronics, chmn. indsl. power converter com., Trans. Rev. chmn., static power converter com., assoc. editor Trans., neural network coun., Industry Applications Soc. outstanding achievement award 1993, Region 3 outstanding engr. award, 1994, Lamme Gold medal 1996); mem. IEEE Indsl. Electronics Soc. (Eugene Mittlemann Achievement award 1994, chmn. power electronics coun., Cont. Edn. award 1997, Millennium medal 2000, Newell award 2005). Hindu. Avocations: travel, gardening. Home: 404 Dixieview Rd Knoxville TN 37934-2609 Office: University Tenn Dept Elec Engring 610 Min Kao 1520 Middle Dr Knoxville TN 37996-0001 Office Phone: 865-974-8398. Business E-Mail: bbose@utk.edu, b.bose@ieee.org.

BOSH, CHRIS, professional basketball player; b. Dallas, Mar. 24, 1984; s. Noel and Freida Bosh; m. Adrienne Williams; 1 child, Jackson. Student, Ga. Inst. Tech., 2002—03. Forward Toronto Raptors, Ont., Canada, 2003—10, Miami Heat, 2010—. Mem. US nat. team FIBA World Championship, Japan, 2006, Summer Olympic Games, Beijing, 2008. Founder Chris Bosh Found. Recipient Sportsmanship award, NBA, 2008, Gold medal, men's basketball, Beijing Olympic Games, 2008; named a McDonald's All-American; named to All-Rookie 1st Team, NBA, 2004, Ea. Conf. All-Star Team, 2006—11, 2013. Achievements include member of NBA Finals championship winning Miami Heat, 2012, 2013. Office: Miami Heat 601 Biscayne Blvd Miami FL 33132*

BOSSEN, WENDELL JOHN, retired financial planner; b. Vienna, SD, Nov. 11, 1933; s. Hans Simonsen and Clara Patrina (Vorseth) B.; m. Jean Davidson, Jan. 6, 1956; children: Mark, Monica. Student, S.D. Sch. Mines, 1952. CLU. Agt. Northwestern Nat. Life Ins. Co., Mpls., 1957-61, dist. mgr., staff mgr., 1961-68, br. mgr., 1968-72, div. v.p., 1972-77; exec. v.p., chief operating officer Inter-Ocean Ins. Co., Cin., 1977-84; exec. v.p. corp. mktg. Mut. Benefit Life Ins. Co., Newark, 1984-92; pres. Internat. Corp. Mktg. Group, Hartford, Conn., 1992-99, retired, 1999. Cons. Newark Performing Arts Corp., 1986. Author: Businessmens Guide to Insurance, 1981; contbr. articles to profl. jours. Chmn. ARC, Watertown, S.D., 1962, Northeast S.D. chpt. United Way, Watertown, 1963, Watertown County Reps., 1963-64; mem. exec. com. S.D. Reps., Pierre, 1964; bd. dirs. Am. Luth. Ch., Cin., 1979, Apostles' House, 1989, chmn. Beijing Wenda Mgmt. Cons. Ltd., 2007-, Global Benefit Mgmt. Group, Bermuda, 2007-, Global Benefit Funding Group, 2007-. Recipient Danforth Found. award, 1952. Mem. Nat. Assn. Life Underwriters (pres. Watertown chpt. 1960-61, v.p. state chpt. 1961-62), Chartered Life Underwriters, Life Ins. Mktg. Research Assn. (com. chmn. 1975). Clubs: Golden Valley Country (Mpls). Lodges: Elks (pres. 1962-63), Lions (pres. 1961, 73), Kiwanis. Avocations: golf, tennis, photography. Home: 111 Sugarberry Ln Hendersonville NC 28739-6933 Office: Internat Corp Mktg Group 100 Campus Dr Florham Park NJ 07932-1006 Personal E-mail: wbossen@aol.com.

BOSSHART, ANDI, healthcare services company executive; Grad., St. Louis U., Mo. Registered health Info. adminstr.; cert. healthcare compliance. V.p., corp. compliance, privacy officer Cmty. Health Sys., Inc. Mem. AHIMA, Tenn. HIMA, Health Care Compliance Assns.

Office: Community Health Systems Inc 4000 Meridian Blvd Franklin TN 37067 Office Phone: 615-465-7000. Office Fax: 615-371-1068. Business E-Mail: andi_bosshart@chs.net.

BOSTETTER, MARTIN V. B., JR., federal judge; b. Balt., Mar. 11, 1926; s. Martin V.B. Bostetter and Louella Jane (Smith) Rice; m. Joanne Rushworth, March 28, 1955; children: Martin III, David W., Jonathan A., Lisa A. BA, U. Va., 1950, LLD, 1952. Bar: Va. 1952, Md. 1953, D.C. 1962. City prosecutor City of Alexandria, Va., 1953-57; chief judge U.S. Bankruptcy Ct. for Ea. Dist. Va., Alexandria, 1985-99. Bd. dirs. Fed. Jud. Ctr., Washington, 1984-87, chmn. edn. com. for all bankruptcy judges, Washington, 1986-89; mem. Fed. State Jud. Rels. Com. of Commonwealth of Va.; chmn. Juvenile Detention Com., Alexandria, 1957-74. Recipient Distinguished Svc. awd. Jr. C.of C., Alexandria, 1959; U.S. Courthouse named Martin V.B. Bostetter U.S. Courthouse by act of Congress, Alexandria, Va., 1998. Office: 200 N Fairfax St Alexandria VA 22314

BOSTICK, CHARLES DENT, retired lawyer; b. Gainesville, Ga., Dec. 28, 1931; s. Jared Sullivan and Charlotte Catherine (Dent) B.; m. Susan Oliver, Sept. 8, 1956; children: Susan, Alan. Student, Emory-at-Oxford U., 1948-49; BA, Mercer U., 1952, JD, 1958. Bar: Ga. 1957, Tenn. 1974, U.S. Dist. Ct. (no. dist.) Ga. 1958, U.S. Ct. Appeals (5th cir.) 1959. Pvt. practice, Gainesville, Ga., 1958-66; asst. prof. law U. Fla., Gainesville, 1966-68, assoc. prof., 1968, Vanderbilt U., Nashville, 1968-71, prof., 1971-92, assoc. dean, dir. admissions, 1975-79, acting dean, 1979-80, dean, 1980-85; ret., 1992. Vis. prof. law U. Leeds, Eng., 1985-86, prof. law emeritus, dean emeritus Sch. Law, 1992. Served to lt. USNR, 1952-55. Mem. Tenn. Bar. Assn. Episcopalian. Office: Vanderbilt U Sch Law 21st Ave S Nashville TN 37240-0001

BOSTON, WALLACE ELLSWORTH, JR., academic administrator; b. Salisbury, Md., May 28, 1954; s. Wallace Ellsworth Sr. and Barbara Ellen (Widdowson) B.; m. Sharon K. Ochs, May 25, 1991; children: Sarah, Grace. AB, Duke U., 1975; MBA, Tulane U., 1978; PhD in Higher Edn. Mgmt., U. Pa., 2010. CPA Md. Mktg. trainee John Deere Indsl. Equipment Co., Moline, Ill., 1978; acct. PriceWaterhouseCoopers, Balt., 1978—80, sr. cons., 1980—83, mgr., cons., 1983; v.p. fin., CFO Nat. Realty Svcs., Inc., Vienna, Va., 1984—85; sr. v.p. syndications Nat. Realty Services, Inc., Vienna, Va., 1985—86; v.p. fin. Meridian Healthcare, Towson, Md., 1986—90, v.p. bus. devel., 1991—92; v.p. fin. Manor HealthCare Corp., Silver Spring, Md., 1993—96; sr. v.p. acquisitions devel. ManorCare Health Svcs., Gaithersburg, Md., 1996—98; exec. v.p., COO NeighborCare, Inc., Balt., 1998—99, pres., CEO, 1999—2001; CFO Sun Healthcare Group, Inc., 2001—02; exec. v.p., CFO American Public Education, Inc., 2002—04, pres., CEO, bd. mem., 2004—, pres., CEO American Public University System, 2004—. Bd. visitors Montebello Rehab. Hosp., Balt., 1988-96; bd. trustees McDonogh Sch., Balt., 1990-99. Contbr. articles to profl. jours. Recipient Honoris Causa, APUS. Fellow Healthcare Fin. Mgmt. Assn.; mem. AICPA, Md. Assn. CPAs (mem. mgmt. adv. services com. 1980-84, mem. industry com. 1988-89), Inst. Mgmt. Acctg., Fin. Execs. Inst., McDonogh Sch. Alumni Assn. (pres. 1986), Duke Univ. Alumni Assn. (pres. Balt. chpt. 1983-84). Clubs: Balt. Country, Ctr. (Balt.). Republican. Methodist. Avocations: squash, golf, photography, bowling. Office: American Public Education Inc 111 W Congress St Charles Town WV 25414 Office Phone: 304-724-3700. Office Fax: 304-724-3780. Personal E-mail: wboston@apus.edu.

BOTBOL, ELIAS, wholesale distribution executive; Grad. in Computer Engring., Simon Bolivar U. Developer Compusoftware; founder, pres. Groupo Netpoint Internat., Inc., Venezuela, Netpoint Internat., Inc.(acquired by ScanSource, Inc.), 1995—2001; pres., L.Am. ScanSource, Inc., 2001—. Office: ScanSource Inc 6 Logue Ct Greenville SC 29615 Office Phone: 864-288-2432. Office Fax: 864-288-1165.

BOTSFORD, DAVID L., lawyer; b. Phila., Aug. 18, 1952; s. Thomas C. and Lois A. (Yarrison) B. BA, U. Conn., 1974; JD, So. Meth. U., 1977. Bar: Tex., 1977, U.S. Supreme Ct., 1981, U.S. Ct. Appeals (5th & 9th cir.), U.S. Dist. Ct. (all dists.), Tex.; cert. Tex. Bd. Legal Specialization, criminal law. Law clerk Emmett Colvin, Dallas, 1974-77; assoc., ptnr. Emmet Colvin, Dallas, 1978-81; briefing atty. Hon. Truman Roberts Ct. Criminal Appeals Tex., 1977-78; treas. bond trader Chgo. Bd. Trade, 1981-82; assoc. Frank Maloney, Austin, Tex., 1982-88; ptnr. Alvis, Carssow, Cummins, Hoeffner & Botsford, P.C., 1988-93, Botsford & Sauer, L.L.P., 1993-96; pvt. practice Austin, 1996—. Contbr. articles to profl. jours. Tex. Criminal Def. Lawyers Ednl. Inst. fellow, 1990. Mem.: Travis Bar Assn., Tex. Criminal Def. Lawyers Assn. (assoc. dir. 1985, 1986, dir. 1987—91, asst. sec.-treas. 1991—92, sec.-treas. 1992—93, 2d v.p. 1993—94, 1st v.p. 1994—95, pres.-elect 1995—96, pres. 1996—97, Presdl. Excellence award 1989, 1990, 1993, 1994, 1995), Tex. Assn. Bd. Cert. Specialists Criminal Law (pres. 1991—92), State Bar Tex. (criminal law exam. commn. 1985—2005, Coll. State Bar 1991, criminal justice sect.Outstanding Criminal Def. Lawyer of Yr. 1993), Nat. Assn. Criminal Def. Lawyers, Barristers, Order of Coif. Office: 1307 W Ave Austin TX 78701-2948 Office Phone: 512-479-8030. Personal E-mail: dbotsford@aol.com.*

BOTTLE, LISA, aerospace and defense parts manufacturing company executive; Attended, Helenswood Sch., Hastings, 1985, Kingston U., 2000. Dir., comm. Thales, 1994—2001, TRW Aero. Sys., 2001—02; v.p., corp. comm. Goodrich Corp., 2002—. Office: Goodrich Corp 4 Coliseum Centre 2730 W Tyvola Rd Charlotte NC 28217-4578 Office Phone: 704-423-7000. Office Fax: 704-423-7002. Business E-Mail: lisa.bottle@goodrich.com.

BOTTORFF, DENNIS C., banker; b. Clarksville, Ind., Sept. 19, 1944; s. Irvin H. and Lucille H. B.; m. Jean Brewington, Aug. 21, 1964; children: Todd, Chad. BE, Vanderbilt U., 1966; MBA, Northwestern U., Evanston, Ill., 1968. Exec. v.p. Commerce Union Corp., Nashville; chmn., CEO Commerce Union Bank and Commerce Union Corp., Nashville, 1984-87; vice chmn., COO Sovran Fin. Corp., Norfolk, Va., 1987—89, pres., COO, 1989—91, C&S/Sovran Corp., Norfolk, Va., 1990—, C&S/Sovran Corp. (merger Citizens & So. Corp. and Sovran Fin. Corp.), 1991—; chmn., CEO First Am. Corp., Nashville, 1991-99; chmn. AmSouth Bancorp., 1999—2001. Chmn. Tenn. State Lottery Edn. Corp., 2003-, Capstar Bank, 2007; bd. advisors The Jack C. Massey Grad. Sch. Bus., Belmont, Coll., Nashville; bd. dirs. Ingram Industries, Dollar Gen. Corp., TVA, 2006-. Vice-chair Vanderbilt Bd. of Trustees, Nashville; trustee Leadership Nashville; former chmn. United Way Mid. Tenn., Nashville Area C. of C., Tenn. Performing Arts Ctr., Nashville Symphony, Titans Adv. Bd.; former bd. mem. Am. Bankers Assn., Fin. Services Roundtable Mem. Belle Meade Country Club. Presbyterian. Office: Council Ventures 150 2nd Ave N Ste 415 Nashville TN 37201

BOUCHER, BRIAN, professional hockey player; b. Woonsocket, RI, Jan. 2, 1977; m. Melissa Boucher; 1 child, Tyler. Goaltender Phila. Flyers, 1999—2002, 2009—11, Phoenix Coyotes, 2002—06, Calgary Flames., 2006, Chgo. Blackhawks, 2006—07, Columbus Blue Jackets, 2007, Phila. Phantoms, 2007—08, San Jose Sharks, 2008—09, Carolina Hurricanes, 2011—. Goaltender Team USA World Jr. Championships, 1997, 1998. Charity work Children's Miracle Network. Named to All-Rookie Team, NHL, 2000. Achievements include setting NHL record for most consecutive regular season shutouts (5 games). Avocation: golf. Office: Carolina Hurricanes Hockey Club RBC Center 1400 Edwards Mill Rd Raleigh NC 27607

BOUCHER, WAYNE IRVING, policy analyst; b. Bay City, Mich., Dec. 12, 1934; s. Harold Oscar and Mildred Christine (Born) B.; m. Donna Lou Collins, June 12, 1961 (div. 1973); children: Michèle Annette, Robert Alain. BA in English Lang. and Lit., U. Mich., 1956, MA in English Lang. and Lit., 1960; postgrad. in philosophy, U. Mo., 1959-61. Instr. English U. Mo., Columbia, 1958-63; dep. asst. to pres. Rand Corp., Santa Monica, Calif., 1963-69; rsch. assoc. Inst. for the Future, Middletown, Conn., 1969-71; co-founder, v.p. The Futures Group, Glastonbury, Conn., 1971-76; dept. dir., dir. rsch. Nat. Commn. on Electronic Fund Transfers, Washington, 1976-78; sr. rsch. assoc. Ctr. for Futures Rsch., U. So. Calif., LA, 1978—84; exec. v.p. Benton Internat., Torrance, Calif., 1984-93; pres. The Ark. Inst., Little Rock, 1993-94; pres., COO Electronic Funds Transfer Assn., Herndon, Va., 1994—95; co-founder, mng. dir. Strategic Futures Internat., Harpers Ferry, W.Va., 1995—2007; pvt. practice Harpers Ferry, 2007—. Author: (with J.L. Morrison and W.L. Renfro) Futures Research and Strategic Planning, 1984; Spinoza in English, 1991, 2d edit., 1999, Spinoza: 18th and 19th Century Discussions, 6 vols., 1999; editor: (with J.L. Morrison and W.L. Renfro) Applying Methods and Techniques of Futures Research, 1983; author, editor: The Study of the Future, 1977; editor (with E.S. Quade) Systems Analysis and Policy Planning, 1968; mem. editorial bd. Technol. Forecasting and Social Change, 1978-82, Futures Rsch. Quar., 1984—2008; contbr. articles to profl. jours. Independent. Home and Office: 87 Lakeside Dr Harpers Ferry WV 25425-4731 Personal E-mail: wib@frontier.com.

BOUCOUVALAS, MARCIE, adult development and learning educator, professor, researcher, author; d. Stellios Efstathios and Georgia (Foundas) B.; m. Nicholas Gregory Gianourakos; 1 child, Anastasia Starr Boucouvalas-Gianourakos. BS in Psychology & Sociology, Boston State U. Mass., 1968; MEd, Boston U., 1971; PhD, Fla. State U., 1980. Social worker social work careers program Roxbury Neighborhood House, Boston, 1966; rsch. assoc. Postgrad. Med. Inst., Boston, 1968-71; program info. coord. Bd. Health Columbia, S.C., 1971-72; human resources devel. staff Dept. Corrections, Columbia, 1972-76; editor Career Edn. Ctr. Fla. State U., Tallahassee, 1978; tutor, cons. Adult Pub. Sch., Charlottesville, Va., 1978-79; freelance editor Tallahassee, 1979-80; asst. prof. adult learning Va. Poly. Inst. and State U., No. Va. Grad. Ctr., Falls Church, 1980-86, assoc. prof., 1986-95, prof., 1996—, program leader, 1993—96, 2004—. Rsch. adv. bd. Va. State Dept. Adult Edn.; internat. task force/steering com. internat. linkages in adult edn. Va. State Dept. Edn.; U.S. del. World Congress Adult Edn. Bangkok, 1990, Cairo, 1994, Jamaica, 2001, steering com.; Non-Govtl. Orgn. del., observer to 5th Internat. UNESCO Assembly Adult Edn., 1997; U.S. del., UNESCO Assembly Adult Edn., Sofia, Bulgaria, 2002, 09, Belem, Brazil, 2009, UNESCO WNED Assembly Hishin Edn. del. Farco, 2009, Adult Learning, Australia, 2005, Belem, Brazil, 2009, del., World Assembly Internat. Coun. Adult Edn., 2011; chair internat. task force Coalition of Lifelong Learning Orgn., 2005—; pres. elect coalition, Lifelong Learning Orgns, 2009-10,pres. Collo, 2010-12, dir. comm. Internat. Adult Edn., 2005—, editor Jour. Transpersonal Psychology, 2002-; field editor, 1981-2002, bd. editor, Adult Learning Manuscript Review Several Jours., bd. dirs., Internat. Adult & Continuing Edn.; mem. editl. bd. Adult Learning. Field editor Jour. Transpersonal Psychology, 1981-2001, editor, 2002—; author: Interface: Lifelong Learning and Community Education, 1979, Adult Education in Greece, 1988; cons. editor: Adult Education Quarterly; contbr. articles to profl. jours., chpts. to books. Counselor, trainer Contact-help, Columbia, S.C., 1972-76; rape educator YWCA, 1975-76; mem. Soc. for Rsch. in Adult Devel. Inst. for Noetic Scis. Named one of 35 Internat. Scholars Consciousness Studies, Princeton U., 1994; named to Internat. Adult and Continuing Edn. Hall of Fame, 2003; Kellogg faculty devel. grantee, 1987; Fla. State U. fellow, 1977; Kellogg exch. prof., Eng., 1984, sr. fulbright rsch. scholar, Greece, 2012, Hall of Fame. Mem.: ASTD (nat. rsch. com. 1990—93), United Nations Assn. US, Am. Assn. U. Profs., Interdisciplinary Acad. Consciousness Studies (selected as one of 35 internat. scholars 1994—95, mem. steering com.), N.Y. Acad. Scis., Assn. Transpersonal Psychology (field editor jour., selected editor Jour. of Transpersonal Psychology), Met. Washington Area Assn. Adult and Continuing Edn., Va. Assn. Adult and Continuing Edn. (mem. rsch. adv. bd., rsch. colloquy), Commn. on Profs. Adult Edn. (co-chmn. task force on internat. adult edn. 1984—, exec. com. 1986—88, futures com. 2001—), Am. Assn. Adult and Continuing Edn. (head commn. on status of women 1977—78, head adult psychology 1980—83, program chair Nat. Conf. Empowering the Adult Learner 1987, head adult psychology 1989—2000, bd. dirs. 2005—, Svc. award 1978, 1982, 1998, Pres. award for exemplifying outstanding svc. to the assn. and profl. field internationally 2006, Outstanding Svc. medal 2013), Soc. Rsch. Adult Devel., Internat. Assoc. in Adult Edn. (program com. 1986—88, apptd. dir. 1990—95, pres. 1996—), Internat. Soc. Comparative Adult Edn. (bd. dirs.), World Future Soc., Phi Beta Delta, Hellenic Soc. of Paideia (Va. br.), Phi Delta Kappa (rsch. rep. 1981—86, pres. 1989—90, faculty-student liaison person to exec. bd. 1995—96, Disting. Acad. Svc. award 1985, Golden Key award 1986), Psi Chi. Greek Orthodox. Avocations: music, dance, ice skating. Office: Va Poly Inst & State University Grad Ctr Nat Capital Reg Dept Human Devel 7054 Haycock Rd Falls Church VA 22043-2311 Office Phone: 703-538-8469.

BOUDINOT, FRANK DOUGLAS, dean; b. NB, NJ, Mar. 31, 1956; s. Frank Lins and Dorothy Jean (Libourel) B.; m. Sarah Garrett, Sept. 1992; 1 child, Frank Garrett. BS in Biology, Springfield Coll., 1978; PhD in Pharmaceutics, SUNY, Buffalo, 1986. Vet. technician Afton Animal Hosp., Williamsville, N.Y., 1978-79; rsch. technician SUNY-Millard Fillmore Hosp., Buffalo, 1979-80; grad. asst. SUNY, 1980-85; asst. prof. pharmaceutics U. Ga., Athens, 1986-90, assoc. prof., 1990-98, head dept. pharm., 1992-98, prof., head dept. pharm. & biomed. scis., 1998-99, prof. dept. pharm. and biomed. scis., 1998—, assoc. dean grad. sch., 1999—2001, sr. assoc. dean Grad. Sch., 2001—02; dean Grad. Sch. Va. Commonwealth U., Richmond, 2002—, prof. dept. pharmaceutics, 2002—. Mem. sci. adv. bd. Pharmassett Ltd., 1999-2002; adj. prof. dept. pharm. and biomed. scis. U. Ga., 2002-07; mem. Grad. Record Exam Bd., 2011-. Mem. editl. bd.: Jour. Pharmacy Tchg., 1989—2001, Biopharm. and Drug Disposition, 1994—2007, Antimicrobiol. Agts. and Chemotherapy, 1998—2001, Archives of Pharmacal Rsch., 1999—2001, Jour. Pharm. Rsch., 2007—, N.Am. editor: Jour. Biopharmaceutics and Drug Disposition, 1998—2007; contbr. over 100 articles to profl. jours.; editl. bd. mem. Jour. Pharm. Rsch., 2007—, adv. bd. mem. Sci. Jours. Internat., 2008—. Vice chair govt. svcs. subcom. Oconee 2000, Watkinsville, Ga., 1986—87; vol., event svcs. agt. Summer Olympics, Athens, Ga., 1996; rollerhockey coach Athens YMCA, 2001—02; Little League baseball coach Midlothian, Va., 2003—06; del. Ga. State Rep. Conv., Atlanta, 1989, 1991, 1992; bd. dirs. Oconee Animal Shelter, Watkinsville, Ga., 1986—88. Named one of Outstanding Young Men of Am., 1987. Fellow Am. Assn. Pharm. Scientists (mem. abstract screening com. 2001-02, rsch. achievement com., 2002, fellow selection com., 2008-); mem. Am. Assn. Coll. Pharmacy (del. 1989-90, profl. affairs com. 1990-91, chair mentoring com., 2002—, task force on faculty workforce 2006—08), Am. Soc. Microbiology, Am. Assn. Advancement Sci. (nominating com., 2007-11), Conf. Southern Grad. Schs. (chair masters thesis award com., 2005-12, mem. exec. com., 2013-); Rho Chi, Phi Kappa Phi (v.p. for scholarships and awards 2003-04, pres.-elect 2004-05, pres. 2005—06). Presbyterian. Achievements include research in pharmacokinetics of antiviral drugs, effects of age in drug disposition, veterinary pharmacokinetics, and drug pharmacodynamics. Office: Va Commonwealth U Grad Sch PO Box 843051 Richmond VA 23284-3051 Home Phone: 804-379-6790; Office Phone: 804-828-2233. Business E-Mail: fdboudinot@vcu.edu.

BOUDREAUX, KENNETH JUSTIN, economist, educator; b. New Orleans, Dec. 22, 1943; s. Aldwin John and Beverly Estelle (Swanton) B.; m. Carole Jean Barnette, May 28, 1966; 1 child, Beau Justin AB, Princeton U., 1965; MBA, Tulane U., 1967; PhD, U. Wash., 1970. Asst. prof. Sch. Bus., Tulane U., New Orleans, 1970-73, assoc. prof., 1973-78, prof., 1978—2010, assoc. dean faculty, 1981-83, prof. emeritus, 2010—. Cons. City of New Orleans Author: Basic Theory of Corporate Finance, 1977, Finance, 1990; editorial bd. Jour. Econs. and Bus., Jour. Fin. Rsch.; contbr. articles to scholarly jours. AACSB fellow, 1969-70; recipient Wissner award Tulane U., 1972, 75, Outstanding Prof., 1972, 75, Disting. Prof., 1973 Fellow Fin. Analysts Fedn.; mem. Am. Econ. Assn., Am. Fin. Assn., Western Fin. Assn., Western Econ. Assn. Clubs: Cannon (Princeton U.), Pickwick, So. Yacht Club. Office: Tulane U Sch Bus New Orleans LA 70118 Office Phone: 504-895-8741.

BOULDING, WILLIAM, dean, business professor; b. 1955; BA with honors, Swarthmore Coll., 1977; PhD, U. Pa., 1986. Faculty mem. Fuqua Sch. Bus., Duke U., 1984—, academic program dir. Mktg. Leadership Forum, 1991—99, mktg. area coord., 1996—99, co-dir. Teradata Ctr. for Customer Relationship Mgmt., 2002—05, assoc. dean, 2003—07, sr. assoc. dean programs, 2007—09, dep. dean, 2009—11, J.B. Fuqua prof. bus. adminstrn., 2009—, dean, 2011—. Contbr. articles to profl. jours. Office: Fuqua School of Business Duke University 100 Fuqua Dr Durham NC 27708-0120 Office Phone: 919-660-7822. Office Fax: 919-684-8742. E-mail: bb1@duke.edu.

BOUNDS, C. SCOTT, state legislator; b. Phila., Miss., Feb. 12, 1962; m. Jennifer Cheatham Bounds. Mem. Dist. 44 Miss. House of Reps., 2004—, mem. conservation and water resources com., juvenile justice com., labor com., pub. property com., wildlife, fisheries and pks. com. Democrat. Baptist. Address: 45 Carla Dr Philadelphia MS 39350 Office Phone: 601-656-5541. Business E-Mail: sbounds@house.ms.gov.

BOUNDS, SARAH ETHELINE, historian; b. Nov. 5, 1942; d. Leo Deltis and Alice Etheline (Boone) Bounds. AB, Birmingham-So. Coll., 1963; MA, U. Ala., 1965, EdS in History, 1971, PhD, 1977. Tchr. social studies Huntsville City Sch., 1963, 65-66, 1971-74; residence hall adv., dir. univ. housing U. Ala., Tuscaloosa, 1963-65, 68-71; instr. history N.E. State Jr. Coll., Rainsville, Ala., 1966-68, U. Ala., Huntsville, 1975, 1978—80, 1985—2012. Dir. Weeden House Mus., 1981-83, com. mem., 1981-2000; asst. prof. edn., supr. student tchr. U. North Ala., Florence, 1978. Fin. com. First United Meth. Ch., 2004—07, mem. older adult ministries com., 2007—, history com., 2007—09. Mem.: AAUW, NEA, Assn. Tchr. Educators, Huntsville Music Study Club, Huntsville Hist. Soc. (bd. mem. 2010—), Historic Huntsville Found., Gladlin Club, Aladdin Club (pres. 2004—05), Twickenham Study Club, Huntsville Pilot Club (pres. 1990—91, club builder 1991—93, Ala. dist. lt. gov. 1995—96, Ala. dist gov. elect 1996—97, Ala. dist gov. 1997—98), Phi Alpha Theta, Kappa Delta Pi, Alpha Delta Kappa (state pres. Ala. 1990—92, regional sec. 1991—93, mem. internat. com. 1993—97, chmn. internat. com. 1995—97, state parliamentarian 1998—). Methodist. Personal E-mail: sebounds@knology.net.

BOURGEOIS, DOSS R., oil and gas industry executive; Various positions including prodn. engr., offshore prodn. mgr., drilling engring. supr. & workovers and completion supt. CNG Producing Co., 1982—93; v.p. prodn. Ocean Energy, Inc., 1993—2003; v.p. Eastern devel. Plains Exploration & Prodn. Co., 2003—06, v.p. devel., 2006; exec. v.p. exploration & prodn. Plains Exploration and Production Co., 2006—. Office: Plains Exploration and Production Co Ste 3100 700 Milam St Houston TX 77002 Office Phone: 713-579-6000. Office Fax: 713-579-6611.

BOURNE, PETER GEOFFREY, physician, educator, writer; b. Oxford, Eng., Aug. 6, 1939; arrived in US, 1957, naturalized, 1963; s. Geoffrey Howard and Gwen (Jones) B.; m. Mary Elizabeth King, Nov. 9, 1974. MD, Emory U., 1962; MA in Anthropology, Stanford U., 1969. Fellow dept. psychiatry Med. Sch.; co-dir. Alcoholism Project, Emory U., 1962-63; intern King County Hosp., Seattle, 1963-64; rsch. psychiatrist Walter Reed Army Inst.; rschr. Washington, 1964-67; chief neuropsychiat. br. U.S. Army Med. Research Team, Vietnam, 1965-66; cons. S.E. Asia Health Br. (AID), Dept. State, 1966-67; resident dept. psychiatry, Stanford U. Med. Center, Palo Alto, Calif., 1967-69; dir. mental health unit Southside Comprehensive Health Center, Atlanta, 1969-71; founder, dir. Atlanta S Ctrl. Cmty. Mental Health Ctr., 1970-71; dir. Ga. Office Drug Abuse, 1971-72; spl. adviser for health affairs to Gov. Jimmy Carter of Ga., 1971-73; asst. dir. White House Spl. Action Office for Drug Abuse Prevention, 1972-74; cons. Drug Abuse Coun., Washington, 1974-76; pres. Found. for Internat. Resources, 1975-76; Mid-Atlantic coord., dep. campaign dir. Jimmy Carter Presdl. Campaign, 1975-76; spl. asst. for health issues to U.S. Pres., Washington, 1976-78; mem. U.S. del. to Exec. Coun. UNICEF, 1977; asst. sec. gen. UN, NYC, 1979-81; pres. Global Water, 1981-98; exec. v.p., pub. Devel. Internat., 1986-90; mem. U.S. Pres. Commn. on White House Fellows; head U.S. del. UN Devel. Program Governing Coun., 1978; emergency rm. physician Casualty Hosp., Washington, 1966-67; emergency room physician Kaiser Permanente Hosp., Santa Clara, Calif., 1967-69; psychiat. cons. Santa Clara County Hosp., 1968-69, San Mateo County Hosp., 1969; cons. WHO, Geneva, 1972, UN Divsn. on Narcotic Drugs, 1976; asst. prof. dept. psychiatry Emory U. Med. Sch., 1969-72, asst. prof. dept. preventive medicine and cmty. health, 1969-72; lectr. dept. psychiatry Harvard U. Med. Sch., 1974; v.p. Nat. Coordinating Coun. on Drug Abuse Edn., 1971-72; dir. White House Office Drug Abuse Policy, 1977—78; asst. sec. gen. UN, 1978—82; prof. psychiatry, chmn. dept. St. Georges Med. Sch., Grenada, 1979-98; pres. Peter Bourne Assocs., Washington, 1985-98; vice chancellor St. Georges U., Grenada, 1998—2002; vis. sr. rsch. fellow Green Templeton Coll., U. Oxford, England, 2002—. Mem. of jury The Lasker Awards, 1978—79; vice chancellor St. Georges U., Grenada, 1998—2001, vice chancellor emeritus, Grenada, 2001—; chmn. Med. Edn. Coop. with Cuba, 2000—; vis. fellow Green Templeton Coll., Oxford U., England, 2001—; bd. dir. Inst. Human Virology, Balt., Nat. Grad. U., Wash., Student Partnerships Worldwide, London. Author: Men, Stress and Viet Nam, 1970; editor: Psychology and Physiology of Stress, 1969, (with R. Fox) Alcoholism: Progress in Research and Treatment, 1973, Addiction, 1974, Acute Drug Abuse Emergencies, 1976, Water Resources: Social and Economic Aspects, 1983, Fidel, A Biography of Fidel Castro, 1986, Jimmy Carter: A Comprehensive Biography from

Plains to the Post-Presidency, 1997; mem. editorial bd. Psychiatry, 1968—, Am. Jour. Drug Alcohol Abuse, 1973—; contbr. articles to profl. jours. and chpts. to books. Bd. dirs. Save the Children Fedn., Inst. for So. Studies; chmn. global bd. dirs. Hunger Project; chmn., bd. trustees Council on Hemispheric Affairs, 1986—; chmn. bd. dirs. Am. Assn. World Health, 1982-98, Health and Devel. Internat., 1997—, Youth Advocate Program, 1998—, Med. Edn. Collaboration with Cuba, 1998—, Inst. Caribbean and Internat. Studies, Windward Islands Rsch. and Edn. Found. Served to capt. U.S. Army, 1964-67. Decorated Bronze Star medal, Air medal, Combat Medics badge; recipient William C. Menninger award Central Neuropsychiat. Assn., 1967, Pub. Svc. award Nat. Assn. State Drug Abuse Program Coordinators, 1974, Pub. Svc. award Assn. Chinese Ams., 1978; named one of Five Outstanding Young Men, Atlanta Jaycees, 1971, one of Five Outstanding Young Men in Ga., Ga. Jaycees, 1972. Fellow Am. Psychiat. Assn. (disting. life, chmn. task force on drugs and drug abuse edn. 1969-73); mem. AAAS, Ga. Psychiat. Assn., Washington Psychiat. Soc., Royal Soc. Medicine, Med. Assn. Ga., Soc. for Internat. Health (pres. 1988-92), Am. Med. Soc. on Alcoholism, Am. Anthrop. Assn., World Fedn. for Mental Health. Democrat. Methodist. Avocation: running. Home and Office: 10500 Kings Ln Spotsylvania VA 22553 Business E-Mail: pbourne@igc.org.

BOUSAMRA, MICHAEL, II, cardiothoracic surgeon; b. Highland Park, Mich., Aug. 12, 1959; married; 3 children. BS in Biochemistry, summa cum laude, U. Mich., Dearborn, 1981; MD, U. Mich., Ann Arbor, 1985. Diplomate Am. Bd. Thoracic Surgery. Intern gen. surgery Med. Coll. Va. Hosp., Richmond, 1985-86, resident gen. surgery, 1986-87, 88-91, cardiovasc. surgery rsch. fellow, 1987-88; resident cardiothoracic vascular surgery Washington U. Med. Ctr./Barnes Jewish Hosp., St. Louis, 1991-93; asst. prof. dept. cardiothoracic surgery Med. Coll. Wis., Milw., 1993—99; assoc. prof. dept. surgery U. Louisville, 1999—, dir. thoracic surgery, James Graham Brown Cancer Ctr., 2005—; pres. (non-profit) Drive Cancer Out, Louisville, 2006—. Attending staff Milw. County Med. Complex, 1993—95, Zablocki Vets. Adminstrn. Med. Ctr., Milw., 1993—99; assoc. attending staff Froedtert Meml. Luth. Hosp., Milw., 1993—99; dir. lung transplant prog. Jewish Hosp., Louisville, 1999—. Mem. editl. bd. Annals of Thoracic Surgery, Jour. Thoracic & Cardiovasc. Surgery; contbr. articles to profl. jours. Office: Univ Cardiothoracic Surgical Assoc 201 Abraham Flexner Way Ste 1200 Louisville KY 40202-3841 Business E-Mail: mbousamra@louisvilleheartsurgery.com.

BOUSTANY, CHARLES WILLIAM, JR., United States Representative from Louisiana, surgeon; b. Lafayette, La., Feb. 21, 1956; s. Charles William and Madlyn M. (Ackal) Boustany; m. Bridget Edwards, 1979; children: Erik, Ashley. BS, U. Southwestern La., 1978; MD, La. State Univ., New Orleans, 1982. Surgeon, pvt. practice, Lafayette, La., 1990—2004; mem. US Congress from 7th La. Dist., Washington, 2005—13, US Congress from 3rd La. Dist., 2013—, US House Ways & Means Com., 2013—. Mem. Lafayette Parish Rep. exec. com., 1996—2001. Bd. dir. Greater Lafayette C. of C, 2001, v.p. govt. affairs, 2002; mem. tissue adv. bd. La. Organ Procurement Agy.; bd. dir. Lafayette Gen. Med. Ctr. Mem.: Lafayette Parish Med. Soc. (pres. 2000). Republican. Episcopalian. Office: US House of Representatives 1431 Longworth House Office Bldg Washington DC 20515 also: 800 Lafayette St Ste 1400 Lafayette LA 70501 Office Phone: 202-225-2031, 337-235-6322. Office Fax: 202-225-5724, 337-235-6072.*

BOUTTE, TRACIE L., electric power industry executive; b. New Orleans; Grad., New Orleans Leadership Inst., 2004; B in Mech. Engring., U. New Orleans; MBA, Tulane U. Nat. accounts exec., comml. segment coord. & maj. accounts mgr. Entergy Corp., dir., sales & svc., dir., retail ops. & v.p., retail strategic market planning, mktg. rep., power & light La., 1986; v.p., gas distbn. Entergy Svcs., Inc., 2002—04; v.p., gas & C&I svcs. Entergy New Orleans, Inc. (subs. Entergy Corp.), 2000—02; v.p., regulatory affairs Entergy New Orleans, Inc., 2004—, bd. dirs., 2005—. Mem. Nat. Assn. of Female Execs., Soc. of Women Engrs., Am. Soc. of Mech. Engrs.; nat. bd. dirs. La. State Mus. Bd., Women's Leadership Initiative, Local Initiatives Support Corp., Com. for a Better New Orleans & Met. Area, New Orleans Coun. for Cmty. & Justice, LSUHC Found. Bd., YWCA, Am. Assn. of Blacks in Energy, WYES, Pres. of Coun. on Alcohol and Drug Abuse, New Orleans Jr. Achievement Bd., Sisters of the Holy Family, Downtown Devel. Dist., U. New Orleans Found. Bd. Recipient Top 40 Under 40, City Bus., 2002, Disting. Engring. Alumni award, U. New Orleans, 2003. Office: Entergy New Orleans Inc Bldg 529 1600 Perdido St New Orleans LA 70112 Office Phone: 504-576-4000. Office Fax: 504-576-4269. Business E-Mail: tracie.boutte@entergy.com.

BOUVETTE, MARIA L., bank executive; B in Acctg., U. Louisville. Mgr. Deloitte, Haskins & Sells (now Deloitte & Touche); pres., CEO Porter Bancorp, Inc., 1983—. Bd. dirs. PBI Bank, Porter Bancorp Inc., 1988—. Mem. Ky. State Bd. Accountancy; trustee Norton Healthcare, Inc. Mem.: Ky. Soc. Cert. Pub. Accountants, Am. Inst. Cert. Pub. Accountants. Office: Porter Bancorp Inc 2500 Eastpoint Pkwy Louisville KY 40223 Office Phone: 502-499-4800. Office Fax: 502-499-4811. Business E-Mail: mbouvette@pbibank.com.

BOVA, BENJAMIN WILLIAM, writer, editor; b. Phila., Nov. 8, 1932; s. Benjamin P. and Giove (Caporiccio) B.; m. Rosa Cucinotta, Nov. 28, 1953 (div. 1973); children: Michael Francis, Regina Marie; m. Barbara Ellen Berson, June 28, 1974 (dec. 2009); m. Rashida Gani Loya, March 20, 2013 BS in Journalism, Temple U., 1954; MA in Communications, SUNY Albany, 1987; EdD, Calif. Coast U., 1996. Formerly newspaper reporter; mktg. mgr. Avco Everett Rsch. Lab.; formerly tchr. sci. fiction Harvard U.; formerly tchr. sci. fiction, dir. film courses Hayden Planetarium, N.Y.C.; editor Upper Darby News, Pa., 1954-56; tech. editor Project Vanguard, 1956-58; motion picture scriptwriter Phys. Sci. Study Com., Ednl. Svcs., Inc., Watertown, Mass., 1958-60; mgr. mktg. Avco Everett Rsch. Lab., Avco Corp., Everett, Mass., 1960-71; editor Analog Sci. Fiction-Sci. Fact mag. Conde Nast Pub. Co., NYC, 1971-78; fiction editor Omni mag., NYC, 1978-79, exec. editor, 1979-81, v.p., editorial dir., 1981-82. Past mem. panel Office Tech. Assessment, U.S. Congress; lectr. Nat. Geog. Soc., major govt. and corp. exec. groups, univs.; adv. bd. Post Coll.; bd. contbrs. USA Today; publ. Galaxy Online.com, 1999-2000. Author: (fiction) The Star Conquers, 1959, Star Watchman, 1964, The Weathermakers, 1967, Out of the Sun, 1968, The Dueling Machine, 1969, Escape!, 1969, Exiled From Earth, 1971; author: (with George Lucas) THX 1138, 1971; author: Flight of Exiles, 1972, As On a Darkling Plain, 1972, When the Sky Burned, 1972, Forward in Time, 1973; author: (with Gordon R. Dickson) Gremlins, Go Home!, 1974; author: End of Exile, 1975, The Starcrossed, 1975, City of Darkness, 1976, Millennium, 1976, The Multiple Man, 1976, Colony, 1978, Maxwell's Demons, 1978, Kinsman, 1979, The Exiles Trilogy, 1981, Voyagers, 1981, Test of Fire, 1982, The Winds of Altair, 1983, Escape Plus, 1984, Orion, 1984, The Astral Mirror, 1985, Privateers, 1985, Prometheans, 1986, Voyagers II: The Alien Within, 1986, Battle Station, 1987, The Kinsman Saga, 1987, Vengeance of Orion, 1988, Peacekeepers, 1988, Cyberbooks, 1989, Voyagers III, Star Brothers, 1990, Orion in the Dying Time, 1990, Future Crime, 1990; author: (with Bill Pogue) The Trikon Deception, 1992; author: Mars, 1992; author: (with A.J. Austin) To Save the Sun, 1992; author: Triumph, 1993, Empire Builders, 1993, Challenges, 1993, Sam Gunn, Unlimited, 1993, Orion and The Conqueror, 1994, Death Dream, 1994; author: (with A.J. Austin) To Fear the Light, 1995; author: Orion Among the Stars, 1995, Brothers, 1996, Moonrise, 1997, Moonwar, 1998, Sam Gunn Forever, 1998, Twice Seven, 1998, Return to Mars, 1999, Venus, 2000, Jupiter, 2001, The Precipice, 2001, The Rock Rats, 2002, Saturn, 2003, Tales of the Grand Tour, 2004, The Silent War, 2004, Powersat, 2005, Mercury, 2005, Titan, 2006, The Green Trap, 2006, The Sam Gunn Omnibus, 2007; fiction, The Aftermath, 2007; author: (fiction) Mars Life, 2008, The Immortality Factor, 2009, Laugh Lines, 2008, The Hittite, 2010, Able One, 2010, Leviathans of Jupiter, 2011, Power Play, 2012, Mars Inc., 2013, (fiction) Orion and King Arthur, 2012, Farside, 2013, New Earth, 2013, Transhuman, 2014, New Frontires, 2014, Rescue Mode, 2014, (nonfiction) The Milky Way Galaxy, 1961, Giants of the Animal World, 1962, Reptiles Since the World Began, 1964, The Uses of Space, 1965, In Quest of Quasars, 1970, Planets, Life and LGM, 1970, The Fourth State of Matter, 1971 (Best Sci. Book award ALA, 1988), The Amazing Laser, 1972, The New Astronomies, 1972, Starflight and Other Improbabilities, 1973, Man Changes the Weather, 1973; author: (with Barbara Berson) Survival Guide for the Suddenly Single, 1974; author: The Weather Changes Man, 1974, Workshops in Space, 1974, Through Eyes of Wonder, 1975, Science: Who Needs It?, 1975, Notes to a Science Fiction Writer, 1975, Closeup: New Worlds, 1977, Viewpoint, 1977, The Seeds of Tomorrow, 1977, The High Road, 1981, Vision of the Future: The Art of Robert McCall, 1982, Assured Survival, 1984, Star Peace, 1986, Welcome to Moonbase!, 1987; author: (with Sheldon Glashow) Interactions, 1988; author: The Beauty of Light, 1988, First Contact, 1990, The Craft of Writing Science Fiction That Sells, 1994, Space Travel, 1997, Immortality, 1998, The Story of Light, 2001, Faint Echoes, Distant Stars, 2004; author: (with Jon Paul) Visions of Lake Tahoe, 2004; editor: The Many Worlds of SF, 1971 (SFWA Hall of Fame, 1974, Nebala Showcase, 2008). Recipient 6 Sci. Fiction Achievement awards for best profl. editor (Hugo), E.E. Smith Meml. award for imaginative fiction, New Eng. Sci. Fiction Soc., 1974, Balrog award, 1983, Inkpot award, 1985, Disting. Alumnus award, Temple U., 1982, Isaac Asimov Meml. award, 1996, Lifetime Achievement award, Arthur C. Clarke Found., 2005, John W. Campbell Meml. award for best sci. fiction novel, Titan, 2006, First Ann. Ben Bova award, Omegacon, 2008, Robert A. Heinlein award, 2008. Fellow AAAS, Brit. Interplanetary Soc.; mem. AIAA, Nat. Space Soc. (pres. 1982-88, pres. emeritus, chmn. bd. 1988-92), N.Y. Acad. Scis., Sci. Fiction Writers Am. (charter, pres. 1990-92), Planetary Soc., Nature Conservancy, Nat. Space Club, Explorers Club, Amateur Fencer's League Am.

BOVO, ESTEBAN L., JR., county official, former state legislator; b. Queens, NY, July 12, 1962; m. Viviana Bovo; 4 children. BA, Miami-Dade Cmty. Coll., 1983; BS, Fla. Internat. U., 1987. Mem. Hialeah City Coun., 1998—2008, pres., 2005—08; mem. Dist. 110 Fla. House of Reps., 2008—11, vice chair elder and family svcs. policy com., mem. energy and utilities policy com., mil. and local affairs policy com., transp. and econ. devel. appropriations com.; mem. Dist. 13 Miami-Dade County Bd. County Commissioners, 2011—. Mem. Bay of Pigs Mus. & Libr. Mem.: Lions Club. Republican. Roman Catholic. Office: 3794 W 12th Ave Hialeah FL 33012-4126 also: Miami Dade County Bd County Commissioners Stephen P Clark Ctr 111 NW 1st St Ste 320 Miami FL 33128 Office Phone: 305-820-8424, 305-375-4831. Business E-Mail: district13@miamidade.gov.

BOWDEN, BOBBY (ROBERT CLECKLER BOWDEN), retired college football coach; b. Birmingham, Ala., Nov. 8, 1929; s. Robert Pierce and Sunset (Cleckler) Bowden; m. Julia Ann Estock, Apr. 1, 1949; children: Robyn Hines, Steve, Tommy, Terry, Ginger Madden, Jeff. BS, Howard U., 1953; grad. degree, Peabody Coll. Asst. football coach, head track coach Howard Coll., Homewood, Ala., 1954—55, head football coach, 1959—62; head football coach, athletic dir. South Ga. Coll., Douglas, Ga., 1955—58; wide receivers coach Fla. State U., Tallahassee, 1963—65; offensive coord. W.Va. U. Mountaineers, Morgantown, 1966—69, head football coach, 1970—75, Fla. State U. Seminoles, Tallahassee, 1975—2010. Co-author (with Terry Bowden): Winning's Only Part of the Game: Lessons of Life and Football, 1996; co-author: (with Setve Bowden) The Bowden Way: 50 Years of Leadership Wisdom, 2001; co-author: (with Jim Bettinger) The Book of Bowden, 2001; co-author: (with Steve Ellis) Bobby Bowden's Tales from the Seminole Sidelines, 2004; co-author: (with Mark Schlabach) Called to Coach: Reflections on Life, Faith and Football, 2010. Named So. Ind. Coach of Yr., 1977, 79, ABC-Chevrolet Nat. Coach of Yr., 1979, Bobby Dodd Coach of Yr., 1980, Region II Coach of Yr., 1987, Coach of Yr. Walter Camp Football Found., 1991, Atlantic Coast Conf. Coach of Yr., 1993, 1997, Gold medal Nat. Football Fedn. awards, 2006; named to Fla. Sports Hall of Fame, 1983, Ala. Sports Hall of Fame, 1986, Coll. Football Hall of Fame, 2006; recipient Neyland Trophy, Contributions to Coll. Football award Nat. Coll. Football Awards Assn., 2008, Bryant Lifetime Achievement award Nat. Sportscasters and Sportswriters Assn., 2011. Baptist. Achievements include the only coach in college football history to win 11 consecutive bowl games, 1985-95; head coach of NCAA Bowl Championship Series national championship winning Florida State University Seminoles, 1993, 1999.

BOWDEN, HENRY LUMPKIN, JR., lawyer; b. Atlanta, Aug. 2, 1949; s. Henry Lumpkin and Ellen Marian (Fleming) B.; m. Roberta Jeanne Johnson, June 30, 1973; children: Caroline Bruton, Henry Lumpkin III. BA, U. Va., 1971; JD, Emory U., 1974. Bar: Ga. 1974. Law clk. for Hon. Griffin B. Bell U.S. Ct. Appeals (5th cir.), Atlanta, 1974-75; ptnr. King & Spalding, Atlanta, 1975-95; prin. Bowden Sprott Law Firm, P.C., Atlanta, 1995—. Trustee Atlanta Ballet, Inc., 1976-85, chmn., 1983-84; trustee Emory U., Atlanta, 1986—; trustee Hist. Oakland Found., Inc., Atlanta, 1987-95, chmn. 1992-95; trustee Westminster Schs., Atlanta, 1995-2000. Fellow Am. Coll. Trust and Estate Counsel (state chair 1991-96), Am. Bar Found.; mem. ABA, State Bar Ga. (chair fiduciary sect. 1990-91), Lawyers Club Atlanta, Piedmont Driving Club (dir. 1996-99), Capital City Club, Nine O'Clocks (pres. 1977-78), Farmington Country Club, Gridiron Secret Soc., The Ten, Phi Beta Kappa, Omicron Delta Kappa, Phi Delta Theta. Methodist. Home: 2542 Habersham Rd NW Atlanta GA 30305-3566 Office: 191 Peachtree St NE Ste 4400 Atlanta GA 30303-1741

BOWDEN, JESSE EARLE, editor, writer, cartoonist; b. Altha, Fla., Sept. 12, 1928; s. Jesse Walden and Earlene (Rackley) B.; m. Mary Louise Clark, Feb. 4, 1951; children: Steven Earle, Randall Clark. BS in Journalism and Polit. Sci, Fla. State U., 1951; DHL, U. West Fla., 1985. Reporter, columnist Panama City (Fla.) News-Herald, 1950; sports editor Pensacola (Fla.) News-Jour., 1953-57, news editor, 1957-65, editl. page editor, 1965-66, editl. cartoonist, 1965—, editor-in-chief, 1966-97, v.p., editor, 1969-97, editor emeritus, 1998—; prof. journalism U. West Fla., 1983—2007; charter mem., chmn. Pensacola Hist. Commn., 1967-2001; chmn. Gulf Islands Nat. Seashore Adv. Com., 1990-93; pres. U. West Fla. Found., 1977-79, Pensacola Hist. Soc., 1978-86. Pres. West Fla. Hist. Preservation, Inc., U. West Fla., 2001—. Author: Always the Rivers Flow, 1979, Fla. Classic edit., 2002, Iron Horse in the Pinelands, 1982, Pensacola: Florida's First Place City, 1989, The Write Way, 1990, When You Reach September, 1990, Fla. Classic edit., 2005, Gulf Islands: The Sands of All Time, 1994, Earle Bowden: Drawing from an Editor's Life, 1996, Look and Tremble: A Novel of West Florida, 2000, Texas Desperado in Florida: The Capture of John Wesley Hardin in 2, 2002, Embrace an Autumnal Heart, 2003, Chipola Moon Rising, 2009; editor Emerald Coast Rev., Vol. V 1993, Vol. VI, 1995, Vol. VII, 1997, Vol. IX, 1999, Vol. X, 2001. Trustee Pensacola Jr. Coll.; bd. dirs. Fla. Hist. Soc. Served to capt. USAF, 1951-53. U. West Fla. Found. fellow, 1982; recipient Disting. Citizen award Pensacola Jr. Coll., 1966, Nat. Editl. Writing award Freedoms Found. at Valley Forge, 1967, 68, 69, 70, 72, 74, awards for editls. and cartoons, 1967, 68, 69, 72, 86, George Washington Medallion Lifetime award, 2004, DeLuna award Pensacola Founders' Day, 1979, Pensacola Kiwanis Civic award, 1982, award Am. Assn. State and Local History, 1984, Founder's award Inspiring Pensacola Bus. awards, 1992, Bob Graham Hon. AIA Archtl. Awareness award Fla. Assn. Archs., 1992, Malcolm B. Johnson Fellowship award James Madison Inst., 1994, Spirit of Pensacola award, 1998; named Pensacola Profl. Bus. Leader of Yr., 1980, J. Earle Bowden Jr. Historian award named in honor Pensacola Jr. League, 1983, Preservationist of Yr., Fla. Trust Hist. Preservation, 1985, West Fla. Lit. Hall of Honor, 1989, Dorothy Dodd Lifetime Achievement award Fla. Hist. Soc., 2000; Gulf Island Nat. Seashore Hwy. named J. Earle Bowden Way, 1997, Mary Call Darby Collins award, Fla. Sec. of State, 2002, Lifetime Achievement award Pensacola Heritage Found., 2002. Mem. Am. Soc. Newspaper Editors, Nat. Conf. Editl. Writers, Fla. Soc. Newspaper Editors (pres. 1970), Rotary. Achievements include establishment of J. Earle Bowden history endowment U. West Fla. Home: 2220 McCutchen Pl Pensacola FL 32503-3422 Office: One NewsJour Pla Pensacola FL 32501 Personal E-mail: jeb2220@aol.com.

BOWDRE, KARON O., federal judge; b. Montgomery, Ala., 1955; BA, Samford U., 1977, JD, 1981. Law clk. to Hon. J. Foy Guin Jr. US Dist. Ct. (no. dist. Ala.), 1981—82; pvt. practice atty. Ala., 1982—90; prof. law Samford U. Cumberland Sch. Law, 1990—2001; judge US Dist. Ct. (no. dist. Ala.), 2001—. Office: US Dist Ct No Dist Ala Hugo Black Courthouse 1729 5th Ave N Birmingham AL 35203

BOWEN, DON C., state legislator; b. Charleston, May 7, 1945; s. Carson and Rebecca Bowen; m. Tomilyn Forrester; children: Amy, Don Jr., Ward. BS, U. SC, 1971. Mem. Dist. 8 SC House of Reps., 2007—; mem. Med. Com., Mil. Com., Pub. & Mcpl. Affairs Com., Anderson Ad Hoc Property Tax Study Com.; chmn. United Way For Bilo Supermarkets. Mem.: Anderson Area Accountability Assn. (chmn.). Republican. Home: 1176 Embassy Dr Anderson SC 29625 Office: 306C Blatt Building Columbia SC 29201 Home Phone: 864-287-2009; Office Phone: 864-934-3272, 803-734-3038. Business E-Mail: BowenD@schouse.org.

BOWEN, DUDLEY HOLLINGSWORTH, JR., federal judge; b. Augusta, Ga., June 25, 1941; AB in Fgn. Lang., U. Ga., 1964, LLB, 1965; profesor invitado (hon.), Universidad Externada de Bogotá, 1987. Bar: Ga. 1965, U.S. Dist. Ct. (so. dist.) Ga. 1997-. Pvt. practice law, Augusta, 1968-72; bankruptcy judge So. Dist. Ga., Augusta, 1973—75; ptnr. firm Dye, Miller, Bowen & Tucker, Augusta, 1975-79; judge US Dist. Ct. (so. dist.) Ga., Augusta, 1979—97, 2004—06, chief judge, 1997—2004, sr. judge, 2006—. Bd. dirs. Southeastern Bankruptcy Law Inst., 1976-87; mem. Ct. Security Com. Jud. Conf. U.S., 1987-92. Mem. bd. visitors U. Ga. Sch. Law, 1987-90. Served to 1st lt. inf., U.S. Army, 1966-68. Decorated Commendation medal. Mem. State Bar Ga. (chmn. bankruptcy law sect. 1977), Fed. Judges Assn. (bd. dirs. 1985-90), 11th Cir. Dist. Judges Assn. (sec.-treas. 1988-89, pres. 1991-92, chief judge So. Dist. Ga., 1997-2004). Presbyterian. Office: US Dist Ct PO Box 1130 Augusta GA 30903

BOWEN, JIMMIE CARL, manufacturing executive; b. Palmdale, Calif., Dec. 27, 1955; s. Charles Richard and Majorie Elizabeth (Cole) B.; m. Marsha Corrine Nuckolls, Apr. 30, 1978; 1 child, Allison Tiffany. Diploma in Word Processing, Ameritech Colls., Inc., Van Nuys, Calif., 1988, Diploma in Computerized Acctg., 1988; AA, Antelope Valley Coll., Lancaster, Calif., 1988; AS, Antelope Valley Coll., 1989. 1st asst. mgr. Thrifty Corp., Lancaster, Calif., 1974-88; bus. edn., computer instr. Ameritech Colls., Inc., Van Nuys, 1988-93; software cons. Calif. Freeware, Palmdale, 1989-90, Barbara's Choice Software, Lancaster, 1991; hardware, software cons. Bowen's Computer Consultant, Palmdale, 1991; computer, software instr. A-1 Computer School, Lancaster, 1992; hardware, software instr. and cons. ABC Computer Learning Centers, Lancaster, Calif., 1992-94, Computer Sci. Corp., Edwards AFB, 1994-96; tng. supr. GTE, 1996; joined Sonoco Products Co., 1972, sr. v.p., global paper ops., 2000—02, sr. v.p., 2002—08, sr. v.p., recycling & internal supply, 2008—09, sr. v.p., Primary Materials Group, 2009—. Contbr. articles to profl. jours. Mem. Nat. Assn. Desktop Pubrs., Antelope Valley Microcomputer Users Group, L.A. Amiga Users Group, Antelope Valley Commodore Users Group (pres., newsletter editor 1990—). Avocations: hiking, camping, travel. Home: 3156 E Avenue H4 Lancaster CA 93535-1626 Office: Sonoco Products Co 1 N 2nd St Hartsville SC 29550-3305 Office Phone: 843-383-7000. Office Fax: 843-383-7008. Business E-Mail: jim.bowen@sonoco.com.

BOWEN, JOE R., state legislator; b. Evansville, Ind., Apr. 22, 1950; m. Vicki Bowen. BSBA, U. Ky., 1972. Owner, ptnr. Bowen Tire Co. Inc., 1972—; mem. Ky. House of Reps., Frankfort, 2005—06; mem. Dist. 8 Ky. State Senate, Frankfort, 2011—. Republican. Office: Kentucky State Senate Annex Rm 228 702 Capitol Ave Frankfort KY 40601 Office Phone: 502-564-8100 ext. 662.

BOWEN, JOHN METCALF, pharmacologist, toxicologist, educator; b. Quincy, Mass., Mar. 23, 1933; s. Loy J. and Marjorie (Metcalf) B.; m. Jean Alma Schmidt, Dec. 26, 1956; children: Mark John, Richard Kelley. DVM, U. Ga., 1957; PhD, Cornell U., 1960. Asst., then assoc. prof. Kans. State U., Manhattan, 1960-63; assoc., then prof. U. Ga., Athens, 1963-98, assoc. dean, dir. veterinary med. expt. sta., 1976-98. Cons. vet. medicine, 1998—. Mem. Am. Vet. Med. Assn., Soc. Neuroscis., Soc. for In Vitro Biology. Office: U Ga Coll Vet Medicine Athens GA 30602-7371

BOWEN, RAY MORRIS, academic administrator, engineering educator; b. Ft. Worth, Mar. 30, 1936; s. Winfred Herbert and Elizabeth (Williams) Bowen; m. Sara Elizabeth Gibbens, July 5, 1958; children: Raymond Morris, Marguerite Elizabeth. BS in Mech. Engring., Texas A&M U., 1958, PhD in Engring., 1961; MS in Mech. Engring, Calif. Inst. Tech., 1959. Registered Ky. Assoc. prof. Mech. Engring. La. State U., Baton Rouge, 1965-67; prof. Mech. Engring. Rice U., Houston, 1967-83, chmn. dept., 1972-77; dir. divsn. NSF, Washington, 1982-83, from acting asst. dir. to dep. asst. dir., engr., 1990-91; prof. Engring., dean U. Ky., Lexington, 1983-89; v.p. acad. affairs Okla. State U., Stillwater, Okla., 1991-93, interim pres., 1993—94; pres. Tex. A&M U., College Station, 1994—2002, pres. emeritus, 2002—, prof. mech. engring., 1994—. Staff Sandia Corp., Albuquerque, 1966—67, Albuquerque, 1972, cons., 1970—78, US Army Ballistic Rsch. Lab, Aberdeen Proving Ground, Md., 1970; chmn. budget NSF Com.; mem. Nat. Sci. Bd., NSF, 2002—, chmn., 2010—. Author: Introduction to Continuum Mechanics for Engineers, 1989; co-author: Introduction to Vectors and Tensors, 1976; contbg. author

Rational Thermodynamics, 1984; contbr. articles to profl. jours. Capt. USAF, 1961—64. Mem.: Soc. Scholars Johns Hopkins U., Sigma Xi, Phi Kappa Phi, Tau Beta Pi. Office: Tex A&M Univ Evans Library Annex 252C College Station TX 77843-5000 Office Phone: 979-862-2955. Business E-Mail: rbowen@tamu.edu.

BOWEN, STEPHEN G., astronaut; b. Cohasset, Mass., Feb. 13, 1964; m. Deborah Alden; 3 children. BSEE, US Naval Acad., 1986; Degree in Ocean Engring., MIT, 1993. Submarine tng. pipeline; serve with USS PARCHE (SSN 683); completed qualification in submarines USS POGY (SSN 647); engring. officer USS AUGUSTA (SSN 710); reported to US Spl. Ops. Command (USSOCOM), Office Plans and Policy, 1997; reactor and propulsion inspector Navy Submarine Bd. Inspection and Survey, 1999; first exec. officer, pre-commissioning unit VIRGINIA (SSN 774), 2000; mission specialist NASA, 2000—. Assigned technical duties in the Astronaut Office Station Ops. Br.; crew mem., mission specialist (performed three spacewalks in first spaceflight) STS-126 Mission (Endeavour), 2008; mission specialist STS-132 Mission (Atlantis)-Last Flight for Atlantis, 2010, STS-133 Mission-Final Flight of Discovery, 2011. Decorated Def. Meritorious Svc. medal, Navy Commendation medal (3), Navy Achievement medal (2). Mem.: Sigma Pi Sigma, Phi Kappa Phi, Tau Beta Pi. Office: NASA Johnson Space Center 2101 NASA Pkwy Houston TX 77058

BOWEN, STUART W., JR., federal official; b. 1958; BA, U. South, 1982; attended, Vanderbilt Law Sch.; JD, St. Mary's Law Sch., 1991. Lic.: Tex. State Bar, bd. cert. in Adminstrv. Law: Tex. Bd. Legal Specialization. Briefing atty. to Justice Raul Gonzalez Supreme Ct. Tex., 1991—92; asst. atty. gen. adminstrv. law litig. State of Tex., 1992—94, asst. gen. counsel to Gov., dep. gen. counsel; counsel Bush-Cheney Transition Team, 1999—2000; assoc. counsel, spl. asst. to Pres. The White House, dep. asst. to Pres., dep. staff sec.; ptnr. Patton Boggs LLP, Washington, 2003—04; insp. gen. Coalition Provisional Authority, 2004; spl. insp. gen. for Iraq Reconstruction (SIGIR), 2004—. Intelligence officer USAF, capt. USAF. Republican. Office: Office of Insp Gen 400 Army Navy Dr Arlington VA 22202*

BOWEN, WILLIAM JACKSON, retired gas industry executive; b. Sweetwater, Tex., Mar. 31, 1922; s. Berry and Annah (Robey) Bowen; m. Annis K Hilty, June 6, 1945; children: Shelley Ann, Barbara Kay, Berry Dunbar, William Jackson. BS, U.S. Mil. Acad., 1945. Registered profl engr, Tex. Petroleum engr. Delhi Oil Corp., Dallas, 1949-57; v.p. Fla. Gas Co., Houston, 1957-60, pres. Winter Park, Fla., 1960-74; pres., CEO Transco Cos., Inc., Houston, 1974-81; chmn. Transco Cos., Inc. (name changed to Transco Energy Co.), Houston, 1976-92; CEO Transco Energy Co., Houston, 1981-87; ret., 1992; also bd. dirs. Transco Energy Co., Houston; ret., 1992. Bd. dir. J.P. Poindexter and Co., Inc.; hon. vice chmn. World Energy Coun. Bd. dirs. YMCA, Houston; trustee emeritus bd Baylor Coll. Medicine; trustee emeritus bd. Jesse H Jones Grad. Sch. Bus., Rice U. With AUS, 1945—49. Mem.: U.S. Energy Assn. (past chmn.). Episcopalian. Office: Williams 2800 Post Oak Blvd Level 16 Houston TX 77056-6100 Home Phone: 713-850-0454; Office Phone: 713-215-2301.

BOWER, DOUGLAS WILLIAM, counseling administrator, psychotherapist, clergyman; b. Niagara Falls, NY, Jan. 6, 1948; s. Charles Henry Bower and Phyllis June (Rank) Ayres; m. Cheryl Stewart, May 25, 1980; children: Katherine Elizabeth, Erin Colleen. AA, Manatee Jr. Coll., Bradenton, Fla., 1969; BS, Oglethorpe U., 1972; PhD, U. Ga., 1989. RN, Ga.; ordained to ministry United Meth. Ch., 1981; cert. counselor, Ga.; life cert. diplomate Am. Psychotherapy Assn.; cert. in sports psychology, US Sports Acad. Nurse Northside Hosp., Atlanta, 1970-80; assoc. pastor 1st United Meth. Ch., Griffin, Ga., 1980-82; pastor, pastoral counselor Oconee Street United Meth. Ch., Athens, Ga., 1982-86; dir. Counseling Ministeries, Athens, 1986—. Adj. faculty Ft. Valley State U., 1999—2005. Contbr. articles to profl. jours. Commr. Oglethorpe County, Dist. 1, 2002-06. Fellow: Am. Psychotherapy Assn.; mem.: Ga. Sheriffs Assn. (hon.), Pilot Club Oconee County. Avocations: music, walking, reading. Office: PO Box 143 Bishop GA 30621-0143

BOWER, JAMES MASON, neuroscientist, educator, science administrator; b. Northampton, Mass., Feb. 17, 1954; s. Mason James and Dorothe Gule Bower; m. Carolina Becker Livi, Dec. 11, 1997; children: Katherine Gule, John Hywel, Ian Ferrera, Lucas Pohlman. BS in zoology, Mont. State U., Bozeman; PhD, U. Wis., Madison, 1981. Prof. biology Calif. Inst. Tech., Pasadena, 1985—2001; prof. computational biology U. Tex., San Antonio, 2001—. Chmn. bd. Numedeon Inc., Pasadena, Calif., 1999—, CEO, 1999—. Pro-dr.(founder): (ednl. web site) Whyville (named Children's Best Site, iParenting, 2006). Grantee, NIH, 1982—2007, NSF, 1982—2007. Independent. Achievements include research in computational neuroscience; cerebellum as non-motor device; development of GENESIS neural simulation system; patents pending for web use safety technology. Avocations: horse breeding, polo, musician.

BOWERS, KIM (KIMBERLY SMITH BOWERS), retail executive, lawyer; b. Ohio, 1964; BA in Spanish & Internat. Studies, Miami U., Ohio; MA in Internat. Rels., Baylor U., Waco, Tex.; JD, U. Tex. Sch. Law, Austin, 1991; Grad., Stanford Exec. Program, 2009. Atty. Kelly, Hart & Hallman, Ft. Worth, 1991—97; corporate counsel to sr. comml. counsel Valero Energy Corp., San Antonio, 1997—2002, mng. counsel, 2002—03, v.p. legal services, 2003—06, sr. v.p., gen. counsel, 2006—08, exec. v.p., gen. counsel, 2008—13; chmn., pres., CEO CST Brands, Inc., San Antonio, 2013—. Bd. dirs. WPX Energy, Inc., 2011—, CST Brands, Inc., 2013—. Bd. dirs. Family Svc. Assn., 2002—09, chair, 2007—09. Named one of The 50 Most Powerful Women in Bus., Fortune mag., 2013. Office: CST Brands Inc 1 Valero Way San Antonio TX 78249 Office Phone: 201-692-5000.*

BOWERS, RONALD E., critical care specialist; MD, U. Va., 1972. Diplomate Am. Bd. Internal Medicine, 1976, Am. Bd. Internal Medicine- pulmonary disease, 1978, Am. Bd. Internal Medicine-critical care medicine, 2005. Resident in internal medicine Vand Univ. Med. Ctr., Nashville, Tex., 1973—75, fellow in pulmonary critical care medicine, 1975—78; critical care specialist Morton Plant Hosp., Largo Med. Ctr., Fla. Office: Largo Medical Center 1301 2nd Ave SW Largo FL 33770 Office Phone: 727-581-8767. Office Fax: 727-581-2739.

BOWERS, THOMAS ARNOLD, journalism educator, dean; b. Plymouth, Ind., Sept. 27, 1942; s. Merritt Edward and Beulah Irene (Burkhart) Bowers; m. Patricia Mills Shane, July 29, 1966 (div.); children: Matthew, Lisa; m. Mary Ellen McKay Woolley, Jan. 10, 2002. BA in Journalism with distinction, Ind. U., 1964, MA in Journalism, 1969, PhD in Communication Rsch., 1971. Asst. prof. Sch. Journalism U. N.C., Chapel Hill, 1971-76, assoc. prof., 1976-80, prof., 1980-93, assoc. dean, 1980—2005, interim dean, 2005—06; James L. Knight prof. Sch. Journalism and Mass Comm. U. N.C., 1993—2006, dean emeritus, 2006—. Author: Making News: One Hundred Years of Journalism Mass Communication at Carolina, 2009; co-author: Fundamentals of Advertising Research, 1979, 4d edit., 1991; editor Journalism Educator, 1983-88; also articles, chpts. in books. Capt. U.S. Army, 1965-68. Recipient Silver medal, Triangle Advt. Fedn., N.C., 1994, Sanders award Tchg. Excellence, U. N.C., 1997; grantee, Freedom Forum. Mem. Assn. Edn. Journalism and Mass Communication (pres. 1988-89), Am. Advt. Fedn.(Disting. Advt. Educator award, 2007), Am. Acad. Advt., Newspaper Assn. Am., Phi Beta Kappa, Kappa Tau Alpha. Avocation: reading. Home: 17 Dartford Ct Chapel Hill NC 27517-8667

BOWERS, W. PAUL, utilities executive; b. 1956; Grad., U. West Fla., Pensacola; M in Mgmt. Residential sales rep. Gulf Power Southern Co., 1979, sr. v.p. retail mktg. Ga. Power, 1995—98, pres., CEO Western Power Distbn. Bristol, England, 1998—2000, sr. v.p. Southern Co. Svcs. Inc., chief mktg. officer, 2000—01, exec. v.p. Southern Co. Svcs. Inc., 2001, bd. dirs., pres., CEO Southern Power, 2001—05, pres. Southern Co. Generation, 2001—08, exec. v.p., CFO, 2008—10, pres., CEO Ga. Power subs., 2011—. Office: Southern Co Generation 30 Ivan Allen Jr Blvd NW Atlanta GA 30308 Office Phone: 404-506-5000.

BOWERS, WILLIAM K., state legislator, accountant; b. Brunson, SC, July 25, 1952; s. William Lonnie Bowers and Betty Jean Hubbard Wall. BS, Clemson U., SC, 1974; MBA, U. SC, 1980, PhD, 1994. CPA. Mem. Dist. 120 SC House of Reps., 1997—. Bd. dirs. Friends Colleton County Libr. Paul Harris fellow. Democrat. Office: State Capitol 310C Blatt Bldg Columbia SC 29211 Home: PO Box 686 Hampton SC 29924 E-mail: WKB@scstatehouse.net.

BOWLES, ERSKINE BOYCE, former academic administrator, former White House chief of staff; b. Greensboro, NC, Aug. 8, 1945; s. Hargrove "Skipper" Bowles & Jessamine Woodward (Boyce); m. Crandall Close, 1971; children: Samuel, Annie, William BS in Bus. Adminstrn., U. N.C., 1967; MBA, Columbia U., 1969. With Morgan Stanley & Co., NYC, Bowles Hollowell Conner & Co., Charlotte, NC, 1975-93; adminstr. Small Bus. Adminstrn. (SBA), Washington, 1993-94; asst. to the Pres. & dep. chief of staff The White House, Washington, 1994—95, chief of staff to Pres., 1996—98; ptnr. Forstmann Little & Co., NYC, 1999—2001; mng. dir., co-founder Carousel Capital Co., LLC, 1999—2001, sr. adv., 2002—; chmn. Erskine Bowles & Co., LLC, 2003—; dep. spl. envoy for Tsunami Recovery UN, 2005; pres. U. NC System, Chapel Hill, 2006—10, pres. emeritus Chapel hill, 2011—. Co-chmn. Nat. Commn. on Fiscal Responsibility & Reform, 2010—; bd. dirs. Merck & Co., 1999—2001, VF Corp., 1999—2001, First Union Corp., 1999—2001, Wachovia Corp., 2001, Krispy Kreme Doughnut Corp., 2003, Cousins Properties, Inc., 2003—, Gen. Motors Corp., 2005—09, Morgan Stanley, 2005—, Facebook, Inc., 2011—, Norfolk Southern Corp., 2011—, Belk, Inc., 2011—. Pres. Juvenile Diabetes Found.; Democratic nominee for US Senate, NC, 2002, 04. Democrat. Office: Erskine Bowles & Co LLC Ste 2450 c/o Carousel Capital 201 N Tryon St Charlotte NC 28202

BOWLES, GROVER CLEVELAND, JR., pharmacist, educator; b. Piedmont, Mo., Feb. 15, 1920; s. Grover Clevel and Oca (Newton) B.; m. Mary Lois Van Inwagen, Dec. 23, 1947; children: Rebecca R., Deborah M. Student, S.E. Mo. State Coll., 1938-39; BS in Pharmacy, U. Tenn., 1942; DSc (hon.), Phila. Coll. Pharmacy and Sci., 1968. Intern hosp. pharmacy U. Mich. Hosp., 1946-47; instr. U. Tenn. Coll. Pharmacy, 1947-48; chief pharmacist Strong Meml. Hosp., also U. Rochester Sch. Medicine and Dentistry, 1948-55; assoc. adminstr. Meml. Hosp. Assn., Washington, 1955-56; dir. dept. pharmacy Bapt. Meml. Hosp., Memphis, 1956-85; prof. U. Tenn. Coll. Pharmacy, 1959-93, prof. emeritus, 1993—. Mem. revision com. U.S. Pharmacopeia, 1960-70; mem. Tenn. Hosp. Licensing Bd., 1961-82 Bd. dirs. Am. Coun. on Pharm. Ecn., 1978-86, pres., 1982-86; trustee Bapt. Meml. Coll. Health Scis., 1995—2010. Served with USNR, 1942-46. Recipient Meritorious Svc. citation Tenn. Hosp. Assn., 1976, Disting. Svc. award U. Tenn. Coll. Pharmacy, 1979, Outstanding Alumnus award U. Tenn. Coll. Pharmacy, 1989 Mem. Am. Pharm. Assn. (pres. 1965-66, chmn. bd. trustees 1966-67, treas. 1967-78, Remington Honor medal 1973, Hugo H. Schaffer medal 1979, Practice Excellence award 1993), Am. Soc. Hosp. Pharmacists (pres. 1952, Harvey A.K. Whitney lectr. 1962), Am. Soc. Hosp. Pharmacists (hon.), Tenn. Soc. Hosp. Pharm. Edn. (pres. 1982-85), Trezevant Episcopal Home (bd. dirs. 2008-11), Phi Delta Chi. Home: Apt 808 177 N Highland St Memphis TN 38111-4755 Home Phone: 901-324-5825. Personal E-mail: gbowles177@comcast.net.

BOWLSBY, BOB, sports association executive; b. Waterloo, Iowa, Jan. 10, 1952; m. Candice Bowlsby; children: Lisa, Matt, Rachel, Kyle. BS, Moorhead State U., 1975; MS, U. Iowa, 1978. Asst. athletic dir. No. Iowa U., athletic dir., 1984-91, U. Iowa, Iowa City, 1991—2006; Jaquish & Kenninger dir. athletics Stanford U., Calif., 2006—12; commr. Big 12 Conf., 2012—. Chmn. NCAA Divsn. I Mgmt. Coun., 1997—99; mem. NCAA Divsn. I Basketball Com., 2000—05, chmn., 2004—05, Big Ten Administrator's Coun., 2002—04; mem. Commn. on Opportunities in Athletics, 2002—03, NCAA/US Olympic Com. Task Force; chmn. NCAA Olympic Sports Liaison Com.; bd. dirs. US Olympic Com., 2007—, San Jose Sports Authority. Named Regional Nat. Athletics Dir. of Yr., Sports Bus. Jour. Mem. Nat. Assn. Collegiate Dir. Athletics (mem. exec. com.; Ctrl. Region Athletic Dir. of Yr. 2001-02), NCAA Divsn. I Athletic Directors' Assn. (pres. 2002-03) Office: Big 12 Conference 400 E John Carpenter Freeway Irving TX 75062 Office Phone: 469-524-1000.*

BOWMAN, BRUCE ALAN, civil engineer; b. Garmisch-Partenkirchen, Bavaria, Germany, Mar. 12, 1959; s. Walter Earl and Ingeborg Marie Bowman; m. Leslie Suzanne Thompson, Sept. 19, 1981; children: Gregory, Douglas. BS Chemistry, Ind. U., 1981; MS Ops. Rsch., USAF Inst. Tech., 1988; PhD Civil Engring., Columbia U., 1995. Analyst Office of the Dep. Chief of Staff for Pers., Hdqs., US Army, Washington, 1990—92; asst. prof. US Mil. Acad., West Point, NY, 1996—99; sect. chief and divsn. chief, joint warfighting analysis divsn. (j8) Office of the Chmn. of the Joint Chiefs of Staff, Washington, 1999—2001; prin. cons. PricewaterhouseCoopers Mgmt. Consulting LLP, Fairfax, Va., 2001—01; sr. profl. staff Johns Hopkins U. Applied Physics Lab., Laurel, Md., 2001—03; sr. scientist Anser, Inc., Arlington, Va., 2003—04; sr. cons. IBM Bus. Cons. Svcs., Fairfax, 2004; dir. sys. engring. SAIC, McLean, Va., 2005; prin. Hilltop Cons. Ptnrs., Oak Hill, Va., 2005—07; dean, Sch. Engring. Norwich U., 2007—10, dir., Ctr. Innovation Leadership, 2010—11; dean, sci., tech. & bus. divsn. Northern Va. CC, 2011—13; dean Sch. Bus., Letourneau U., Tex., 2013—. Co-chmn. sys. dynamics in nat. security conf. Nat. Def. U., Washington, 2000; mem. adv. bd. MobilePro Corp.; profl. lectr. George Washington U., Washington, 2004—05, adj. prof., 2005—07; mem. adv. bd. Worcester Poly. Inst., Mass., 2009—12; fellow Kern Entrepreneurship Edn. Network, 2008—11; mem. bd. dirs. Vt. Environ. Consortium, 2009—10, Vt. Tech. Coun., 2008—11. Contbr. book Pipeline Risk Management Manual, 1996; author: (novels) The Flanagan Option, 2009, Money Baby, 2012. Coo and founding exec. dir. The ACE Mentor Program of the Greater Wash. DC Met. Area, Inc., 2000—04; elder Presbyn. Ch. U.S.A., 1991; youth soccer coach Springfield, Va., 1989—91, Rockland County, NY, 1992—95. Lt. col. US Army, 1981—2001. Fellow, Kern Entrepreneurship Ed Network, 2008—. Mem.: ASCE, Vt. Environ. Consortium (mem. bd. dirs. 2009—), Vt. Tech. Coun. (mem. bd. dirs. 2008—), Mil. Ops. Rsch. Soc. (chmn. weapons of mass destruction nat. symposium 2001—01). Avocations: reading, chess, soccer, jogging. Business E-Mail: brucebowman@letu.edu.

BOWMAN, C. MICHAEL, physician; married; two children. BS in Chemistry with honors, U. Ill., 1968; PhD in Genetics, U. Wis., 1972, MD, 1975. Diplomate Am. Bd. Pediatrics, Am. Bd. Pediatric Pulmonology. Pediat. resident Vanderbilt U., 1975-78, chief resident, 1978-79; dir. comprehensive cystic fibrosis ctr. Med. U. S.C.; divsn. head Divsn. Pediat. Pulmonolgy; prof. pediats. Med. U. S.C., Charleston, 2000—. Fellow Am. Acad. of Pediat., mem. Am. Bd. of Pediat., Am. Thoracic Soc. Achievements include research in lung disorders in children. Office: Med U S C Ste 281 MSC 561 135 Rutledge Ave Charleston SC 29425-5610 Office Phone: 843-876-1555. Office Fax: 843-876-1583. Business E-Mail: bowmanm@musc.edu.

BOWMAN, CATHERINE MCKENZIE, lawyer; b. Tampa, Fla., Nov. 10, 1962; d. Herbert Alonza and Joan Bates (Baggs) McKenzie; m. Donald Campbell Bowman, Jr., May 21, 1988; children: Hunter Hall, Sarah McKenzie. BA in Psychology and Sociology, Vanderbilt U., 1984; JD, U. Ga., 1987. Bar: Ga. 1987, U.S. Dist. Ct. (so. dist.) Ga. 1987. Assoc. Ranitz, Mahoney, Forbes & Coolidge, P.C., Savannah, Ga., 1987-91; ptnr. Forbes and Bowman, 1991—2007; mem. The Bowman Law Office, L.L.C., 2007—. Bd. dirs. Greenbriar Children's Ctr., 1994-98, exec. com. 1995, pres. 1996-98; mem. distbn. com. Savannah Found., 1994-2002; ball com. Telfair Arts Acad., 2002, Historic Savannah Found., 2002, 09; chmn. Savannah Country Day Sch. Fair, 2004; founder, co-chair Savannah Country Day Sch. Auction, 2004; sec. Savannah Country Day Sch. Parents Assn., 2005, pres.-elect, 2011-12, pres., 2012-13, Savannah County Day trustee, Creative Minds Com., 2005-08, 12-13, Atheletic Com. SCDS, 2009-11. Named Best Lawyer, Savannah Mag., 2012. Mem. Am. Employment Law Coun., Internat. Assn. Def. Counsel, Ga. Def. Lawyers Assn. (chmn. employment com. 2006-07), Savannah Bar Assn. (pres. younger lawyer divsn., 1996-97, mem. exec. com., 2010-11, treas., 2011-13, pres.-elect, 2013-), Ga. Trends Legal Elite, 2000 Club (membership chair 1990-91, pres. 1992), South Atlantic Found. (bd. dirs. 1992). Office: 7505 Waters Ave Ste D3 Savannah GA 31406 Office Phone: 912-401-0121. Business E-Mail: catherine@thebowmanlawoffice.com.*

BOWMAN, GILES, retail executive; B in Math., U. NC, Chapel Hill, 1985. Various merchandising positions, lumber, millwork and hardware Lowe's Companies, Inc.; joined Home Depot, Inc., 1996, divisional merchandise mgr., SW Divsn., millwork merchant, SW Divsn., merchandising v.p. Canada, merchandising v.p. bldg materials, merchandising v.p., Eastern Divsn., v.p., sales and svc., SW Divsn., sr. v.p., Merchandising, Hardlines, 2007—. Bd. dirs. The Home Depot Hispanic Coun., Habitat for Humanity of NW Metro Atlanta, The Home Depot Found. Office: The Home Depot Inc 2455 Paces Ferry Rd NW Atlanta GA 30339 Office Phone: 770-433-8211. Office Fax: 770-384-2356.

BOWMAN, JEFFREY T., insurance company executive; CPA. Fin. acct. Esperanza PLC, England, 1982—84; fin. dir. Graham Miller Group, England, 1984—91; fin. dir. overseas ops. Crawford & Co., London, 1991—94, v.p. internat. fin., 1995—96, v.p. internat. strategic planning, 1996—97, regional mng. dir. of Americas Canada, 1997—2001, pres. internat. ops., 2001—05, exec. v.p., COO global property & casualty, 2006—08, pres., CEO, bd. dirs., 2008—. Fellow: Chartered Cert. Accountants, UK. Office: Crawford & Co 1001 Summit Blvd Atlanta GA 30319 Office Phone: 404-300-1000. Office Fax: 404-300-1905. Business E-Mail: jeffrey.bowman@crawfordandcompany.com.

BOWMAN, KATHLEEN GILL, academic administrator; BS in English & Spanish, U. of Minn., 1964, MA in English Edn., 1967, PhD in English Edn., 1977. Rsch. assoc. Legis. Adv. Coun. on the Econ. Status of Women, St. Paul, 1976-77; asst. dir. of grad. studies, asst prof. of edn. Reed Coll., Portland, OR, 1977-79, exec. asst. to the pres., dir. of spl. programs, 1979-82; assoc. dir., program officer Fred Meyer Charitable Trust, Portland, OR, 1982-84; assoc. v.p. for rsch. U. of Oreg., Eugene, OR, 1985-89, vice-provost for internat. affairs, 1989-94; pres. Randolph-Macon Woman's Coll., Lynchburg, VA, 1994—. Fullbright Sr. Scholar award, Japan & Korea, 1993. Office: Randolph-Macon Womans Coll Office of the Pres 2500 Rivermont Ave Lynchburg VA 24503-1555

BOWMAN, SCOTTY (WILLIAM SCOTT BOWMAN), professional sports team executive, retired professional hockey coach; b. Montreal, Can., Sept. 18, 1933; s. John and Jane (Scott) Bowman; m. Suella Belle Chitty, Aug. 16, 1969; children: Alicia Jean, David Scott, Stanley Glen, Nancy Elizabeth, Robert Gordon. Student, Sir George Williams Bus. Sch., 1954; LHD (hon.), Canisius Coll., Buffalo, 2003; D in Pedagogy (hon.), Niagara U., Niagra Falls, NY, 2009. Scout exec. Montreal Canadiens, 1956—66, head coach, 1971—79; head coach, gen. mgr. St. Louis Blues, 1966—71; head coach, gen. mgr., dir. hockey ops. Buffalo Sabres, 1979—86; TV analyst Hockey Night in Can., 1987—90; dir. player devel. Pitts. Penguins, 1990—91, interim head coach, 1991—92, head coach, 1992—93, Detroit Red Wings, 1993—2002, dir. player pers., 1993—2002; cons. Detroit Red Wings Stanley Cup Champions, 2002—08; sr. advisor hockey ops. Chgo. Blackhawks Hockry Ops., 2008—. Mem. Hockey Hall of Fame Selection Com.; head coach Team Can., 1976. Recipient Jack Adams Award, 1977, 1996, Victor award for NHL Coach of Yr., 1993, 1996, 2002, Lester Patrick Trophy, 2001, Award, Can. Soc. NY, 2001, Wayne Gretzky Award of Excellence, US Hockey Hall of Fame, 2002; named NHL Exec. of Yr, Sporting News, 1980, NHL Coach of Yr., 1996, Hockey News, 1977, 1993—97, NHL Exec. of Yr., 1997; named to Mich. Sports Hall of Fame, 1999, Buffalo Sports Hall of Fame, 2000, Can. Walk of Fame, 2003, Can.'s Sports Hall of Fame, 2004, Quebec Sports Hall of Fame, 2005, St. Louis Sports Hall of Fame, 2011. Achievements include being the head coach of Stanely Cup Champion, Montreal Canadiens, 1973, 1976, 1977, 1978, 1979, Pittsburgh Penguins, 1992, Detroit Red Wings, 1997, 1998, 2002; being the only head coach in NHL history to win Stanley Cup with 3 different teams; being inducted into the Hockey Hall of Fame, 1991; holding NHL career regular season records for wins (1,244) and winning percentage (.670); holding NHL career playoffs records for wins (223) and games (353). Office: Chgo Blackhawks United Ctr 1901 W Madison St Chicago IL 60612

BOWNE, SHIRLEE PEARSON, real estate consultant; b. High Shoals Twp., NC, Mar. 11, 1936; d. Lloyd E. Pearson and Parnell (James) Garland; divorced; 1 child, Gregory Charles. Grad. h.s., Gaffney, SC. Various secretarial positions, 1955-64; sales repr., pres. Real Estate Marketers, Inc., Tallahassee, 1964-80; chief exec. officer Shirlee Bowne Mktg. & Devel. Inc., Tallahassee, 1980-91; vice chmn. Nat. Credit Union Adminstrn., Washington, 1991-97. Cons. in field. Treas. Rep. Party Fla., 1988-91. Episcopalian. Avocation: bridge. Personal E-mail: shirleebrowne@earthlink.net.

BOW WOW, See MOSS, SHAD

BOWYER, E. CARLTON, board member; PhD. Bd. dirs. Commonwealth Bankshares, Inc., 2001—. Worked Va. Beach Sch., adv. bd. dirs. Mailing: Bank of the Commonwealth PO Box 1177 Norfolk VA 23501 Office Phone: 757-446-6900.

BOYATT, THOMAS DAVID, retired ambassador; b. Cin., Mar. 4, 1933; s. Lynn Craig Haven and Florine (Cloar) B.; m. Maxine Lorraine Shearwood, Dec. 30, 1971; children: Thomas Benton, Christopher Lynn, Jessica Allyn, Alexander Shearwood, Catherine Jordan. BA, Princeton U., 1955, MA, 1956. Vice consul US Dept. State, Antofagasta, Chile, 1960-62; with US Dept. Treasury, 1962-64; 2d sec. Am. Embassy, Luxembourg, 1964-66, 1st sec. Nicosia, Cyprus, 1967-70; dir. Cypriot affairs Near East Bur. US Dept. State, Washington, 1970-74, assigned to Sr. Seminar, 1974-75; dep. chief mission, minister counselor Am. Embassy, Santiago, Chile, 1976-78; US amb. to Upper Volta US Dept. State, Ouagadougou, 1978-80, US amb. to Colombia Bogota, 1980—84; v.p. market devel. Sears World Trade Inc., Washington, 1984-87; ptnr. IRC Group, 1988-96; pres. US Def. Systems, 1990-96; pres., CEO Fgn. Affairs Coun. Trustee Princeton U., 1984-89; bd. dirs. Patterson Sch./U. Ky., Inst. for Study of Diplomacy/Georgetown U.; mem. State Dept. Adv. Com. on Leadership and Mgmt., 2004. 1st lt. SAC, USAF, 1956-59. Decorated Legion d'Honneur (Upper Volta), Gran Cruz Order of San Carlos (Colombia); recipient Meritorious Honor award US Dept. State, 1969, William R. Rivkin award Am. Fgn. Service, 1970, Christian A. Herter award, 1976 Mem.: Am. Fgn. Svc. Assn. (treas.), Washington Inst. Fgn. Affairs (bd. dirs.), Acad. of Diplomacy (bd. dirs.), Am. Fgn. Svc. Assn. (pres. 1971—74, award for post-retirement contbns. to fgn. affairs 1999, Lifetime Achievement award 2001, Lifetime Contbn. to Am. Diplomacy award 2008).

BOYCE, DONALD NELSON, water transportation executive; b. Buffalo, May 4, 1938; s. Nelson W. and Mary A. (Gillis) B.; m. Jeris Jane Smith, Sept. 22, 1956; children: Mark D., Tammy J., Timothy R., Daniel E. BS, Rochester Inst. Tech., 1967, postgrad., 1971. Acct. Sylvania Electric Products Co., Buffalo and Batavia, NY, 1956—59; acct., sys. mgr., contr. Constrn. Equipment (divsn. Eaton Corp.), Batavia, 1959—69; contr. Strippit div. Houdaille Industries, Inc., Akron, NY, 1969—72; treas. Houdaille Industries, Inc., Northbrook, Ill., Buffalo, Ft. Lauderdale, Fla., 1972-79, v.p., fin. and adminstrn., dir., 1979—84, exec. v.p., 1984—86, pres., 1986-87, CEO, 1987—88; chmn., pres. & CEO IDEX Corp., Northbrook, 1988—98; pres., CEO Walter Industries, Inc. (now Walter Energy, Inc.), 2000, chmn., 2000—02, bd. dirs., 2002—06. Mem adv. bd. Marine Bank-Western, Batavia, 1967-69; bd. dirs. United Dominion Industries, Charlotte, Metromail Corp., Lombard, Ill., Band-It Inc., Denver, Lubriquip Inc., Cleve., Vibratech Inc., Buffalo, Strippit Inc., Akron, N.Y., Viking Pump, Cedar Falls, Iowa, Warren Rupp Inc., Mansfield, Ohio, Corken, Inc., Oklahoma City, Pulsafedder Inc., Rochester, N.Y., Hale Products, Inc., Conshohocken, Pa., Micropump, Inc., Vancouver, Wash., Fluid Mgmt., Inc., Wheeling, Ill.; bd. dirs., Mueller Water Products, Inc., 2006-. Bd. adv., Sch. Food, Hospitality and Travel, Rochester Inst. Tech.; Trustee Oakton C.C. Found. Bd.; mem. bd. edn. Oakfield-Ala. Cen. Sch., 1970-77. Mem. Mfrs. Alliance (trustee), Am. Mgmt. Assn., Monroe Club, Chgo. Exec. Club, Econs. Club Chgo. Republican. Methodist. Home: 370 N Western Ave Lake Forest IL 60045-2133 Office: Mueller Water Products Inc Bd Directors 1200 Abernathy Rd NE Ste 1200 Atlanta GA 30328 Office Phone: 770-206-4200. Office Fax: 770-206-4235. Business E-Mail: dboyce@muellerwp.com.

BOYCE, H. WORTH, gastroenterologist, educator; b. Clinton, NC, Sept. 21, 1930; s. Henry Worth and Lena Craft Boyce; m. Jean Murphy Boyce, June 21, 1952; children: Henry, Steve, Cindy, Gregory, Mary. BS, MD, Wake Forest U., 1955; MS, Baylor U., 1961. Intern Tripler Army Med. Ctr., Honolulu, 1955—56; resident in internal medicine Brooke Army Med. Ctr., Ft. Sam Houston, Tex., 1957—59, resident in gastroenterology, 1960; chief gastroenterology svc. Walter Reed Army Med. Ctr., Washington, 1966—75; prof. medicine U. South Fla., Tampa, 1975—. Dir. gastroenterology U. South Fla., Tampa, 1975—90, dir. Swallowing Ctr., 1987—. Author: Techniques of Clinical Gastroenterology, 1975; contbr. chapters to books, articles to profl. jours. Col. US Army, 1955—75. Decorated Legion of Merit. Mem.: Am. Gastroent. Assn., Am. Soc. Gastrointestinal Endoscopy (pres. 1973—74, gov. 1985—88, Disting. Svc. award 1989, Rudolph Schindler award 1982). Republican. Methodist. Avocations: photography, gardening, golf. Office: Univ S Fla Coll Medicine Box 72 12901 Bruce B Downs Blvd Tampa FL 33612 Office Phone: 813-974-3374. Office Fax: 813-974-7031.

BOYCE, RICHARD W., investment company executive; B with honors, Princeton U., 1976; MBA, Stanford Bus. Sch., 1980. Ptnr. TPG Capital (formerly Texas Pacific Group), 1997—. Bd. dirs. LPL Investment Holdings, Burger King Holdings, Inc., 2002—. Office: TPG Capital Ste 3300 301 Commerce St Fort Worth TX 76102 Office Phone: 817-871-4000. Office Fax: 817-871-4010.

BOYD, BARBARA BIGSBY, state legislator; b. Anniston, Ala., Jan. 31, 1937; children: Frank Jr., Reginald M. BA in French and English, Miles Coll., Birmingham; MA in Supervision and Curriculum Devel., U. Ala., EdD in Instructional Leadership and Reading. Retired educator in pub. & pvt. and secondary sch. edn. and two-year & four-year colleges including Jacksonville State U. and Gadsden State CC; mem. Dist. 32 Ala. House of Reps., Montgomery, 1994; assoc. prof., coll. edn. Miles Coll., Fairfield, Ala. Mem. trustee bd., Christian edn. Murray Temple Christian Meth. Episc. Ch.; bd. mem. NAACP, Ala. Dem. Conf., SCLC. Mem.: Ala. Coun. Negro Women (life), Kappa Delta Si, Phi Delta Kappa, Alpha Kappa Alpha. Democrat. Christian. Office: 2222 McDaniel Ave Anniston AL 36202 also: Ala House of Reps Ala State House 11 S Union St Rm 530 Montgomery AL 36130 Office Phone: 256-741-8683, 334-242-7692. Business E-Mail: bboyd@calhouncounty.org.

BOYD, DAN STEWART, lawyer; b. Waco, Tex., Sept. 30, 1949; s. Will Carr and Elizabeth Lockey (Stanton) B.; m. Terry Mae Riddlesperger, Mar. 20, 1976; children: Daniel James, Caroline Elizabeth, Catherine Terry. BA with honors, U. Tex., 1972, JD with honors, 1975. Bar: Tex. 1975, U.S. Dist. Ct. (so. dist.) Tex. 1976, U.S. Dist. Ct. (ea. dist.) Tex. 1978, U.S. Dist. Ct. (no. dist.) Tex. 1982, U.S. Ct. Appeals (5th cir.) 1978, U.S. Ct. Appeals (11th cir.) 1978, U.S. Supreme Ct. 1979, bd Cert. Civil Trial Law and Civil Appellate Law, Tex. bd of Legal Specialization. Assoc. Vinson & Elkins, Houston, 1975-81, Johnson & Swanson, Dallas, 1982; ptnr. Johnson & Gibbs, P.C. (formerly Johnson & Swanson), Dallas, 1982-93, Baker & McKenzie, Dallas, 1993—2002; founder The Boyd Law Firm, PC, Dallas, 2003—. Adj. Prof. Law, Trial and Appellate Procedure, SMU Law sch., 1984-1987. Author: (autobiographical novel) Grand Aspirations, 2006; co-author: Texas Pre-Trial Practice, 2007; contbr. articles to legal jours. Bd. dirs. F.D. Roosevelt Four Freedoms Found., N.Y.C., 1986-87, Franklin and Eleanor Roosevelt Inst., Hyde Park, N.Y., 1987—. Fellow Am. Bar Found.; mem. Tex. Young Lawyers Assn. (bd. dirs. 1980-82), Houston Young Lawyers Assn. (bd. dirs. 1979-80, Outstanding Dir. award 1980), Dallas Bar Assn. (chmn. bus. litigation sect. 1990), Friars Soc., Phi Delta Phi. Methodist. Office: The Boyd Law Firm PC 400 Providence Towers E 5001 Spring Valley Rd Dallas TX 75244 Home: 8316 Coral Dr Dallas TX 75243 Office Phone: 972-383-1260. Office Fax: 214-292-8491, 214-292-8491. Business E-Mail: dan@boydlawfirmpc.com.

BOYD, DANA KRISTIN, elementary school educator; Advanced from tchr. to lead tchr. Dolphin Terrace Elem. Sch., El Paso, Tex., 2000—06, asst. prin., 2006—. Named Tex. Tchr. of Yr., 2007. Avocation: running. Office: Dolphin Terrace Elem Sch 9700 Pickerel El Paso TX 79924 Office Phone: 915-434-6502. Office Fax: 915-757-8073. Business E-Mail: dboyd@yisd.net.

BOYD, GWENDOLYN LOUISE, anesthesiologist, educator; b. Houston, Apr. 22, 1943; d. Louise VanDeventer and David Milton Boyd, Jr.; children: Noelle Suzanne, Lauren Louise. MD, U. Ill. Coll. Medcine, Chgo., 1968. Diplomate Am. Bd. Anesthesiology, 1973. Asst. prof. U. Ill., 1973—77; assoc. prof. Tulane U., New Orleans, 1977—84; prof. U. Ala., Birmingham, 1984—. Chief anesthesiology Callahan Eye Found. Hosp., Birmingham, 2006—. Contbr. scientific papers to profl. pub. on anesthesiology. Found. bd. mem. Vestavia Hills United Meth. Ch., Birmingham, 2005; v.p. Med. Mission Ecuador, Birmingham, 2001—06, Tunguragua, 2001—06; bd. mem. FOCUS on Recovery, Birmingham, 2007—09. Mem.: Assn. U. Anesthsiologists (ednl. bd. mem. 1999—2001), Am. Soc. Anesthesiologists (house of delgates 1975—77), Alpha Omega Alpha (elected mem. 1968). Office: Univ Alabama at Birmingham Dept Anesthesiology 619 South 19th St 845 JT Birmingham AL 35233 Office Fax: 205-325-8316.

BOYD, JAMES ROBERT, retired energy executive; b. Nashville, July 29, 1946; s. James Clinton and Mary Avon (Motlow) B.; m. Elise White, June 27, 1970; children: Elizabeth, Mary Franklin. BSEE, U. Ky., 1969; MBA, NYU, 1972. Sales engr. Westinghouse Electric Co., NYC and St. Louis, 1970-75, mgr., generation sales St. Louis, 1975-77, cons. planning Pitts., 1977-79, mgr., Divsn. Planning, 1979-81; mgr., strategic planning Ashland Oil Co., Ky., 1982-84, dir., corp. planning Ky., 1984-86, sr. v.p., group oper. officer Ky., 1989—2002; sr. v.p. adminstrn. Ashland Exploration, Houston, 1986-87, pres., 1987-89; chmn. Arch Coal, Inc., 1998—2006. Bd. dirs. Arch Coal Inc., 1998—, Halliburton, Inc. Avocations: golf, hunting, swimming. Office: 2333 Alexandria Dr Ste 134 Lexington KY 40504 also: Arch Coal Inc Bd Directors 1 City Pl Dr Saint Louis MO 63141 Office Phone: 314-994-2700. Office Fax: 314-994-2878. Business E-Mail: jboyd@archcoal.com.

BOYD, JANEGALE, former state legislator, lobbyist; b. Reno, Nev., Nov. 30, 1952; m. Hines Boyd; children: Whit, Beth, Erin. ASN, Tallahassee CC, Fla., 1975. Lic. ins. agt., life and health, Fla., Ga.; RN, Fla., Ga. Quality assurance coord., instr. critical care, head nurse Tallahassee Cmty. Hosp., 1979-85; adminstr. HMO Am., Inc., Tallahassee, 1986-87; exec. dir. Ga. Fla. Preferred, Inc. (Health Alliance of the South), Thomasville, Ga., 1987-92; dir. North Fla. ops. Family Health Plan of Fla., Inc., Tallahassee, 1992-93; area dir. Tallahassee market Humana/PCA Health Plans of Fla., 1993—; mem. Fla. Ho. of Reps., Tallahassee, 1996—2000; pres., CEO Fla. Assn. Homes and Services for the Aging. Vice chair water and resource mgmt. com.; mem. edn. com., utilities and comm. com., jt. legis. auditing com., fiscal responsibility coun., gen. appropriations com., procedural coun.; mem. Women's Caucus, Dem. Caucus, Blue Dawg Caucus; presenter in health care field. Chair United Way, Jefferson County; pres. Big Bend br. Am. Lung Assn., 1984-90; mem. exec. com. Monticello Opera House; mem. 1st United Meth. Ch., Monticello; grad. Leadership Tallahassee; mem. adv. bd. Tallahassee C.C. Sch. Nursing, 1988-92; instr., trainer BLS, Am. Heart Assn.; chmn. City of Monticello Planning Agy., 1989-96, Healthyways, Inc., 1989-96. Named 1 of Top 40 Legislators, Fla. C. of C., 1997, 98, 2000, Freshman Legislator of Yr., Fla. Sch. Bds. Assn., 1997, 98, Legislator of Yr., Fla. Assn. Dist. Sch. Supts., 1998; recipient Freshman Courage award Small Sch. Dist. Coun. Consortium, 1997, award Fla. Assn. HMO, 1997, 98, Legis. award Fla. Sheriffs Assn., 1997, Fla. Landscape Designers Assn., 1998, Regional I & II Correctional Officers, 1998, Small Sch. Dist. Coun. Consortium, 1998, Fla. Farm Bur., 1998, Quality Floridian award Fla. League of Cities, 1998, award Fla. Assn. Managed Care Orgns., Inc., 1999, cert. of appreciation Fla. Rural Health Assn., 1999, Outstanding Fla. Legislator award Fla. Nurses Assn., 1999, recognition for leadership and support Small County Coalition, 1999, Outstanding Leadership award Dept. Corrections, 1999, award Fla. Tchg. Profession-NEA Bd. Dirs., 1999, Friend of Edn. award, 1999, Spl. Recognition award Fla. Conf. Judges of Compensation Claims, 1999. Democrat. Methodist. Avocations: swimming, reading, volunteer work. Home: 735 W Washington St Monticello FL 32344-1118

BOYD, JEFFREY S., state supreme court justice; m. Jackie Boyd; children: Hanna, Abbie, Carter. Grad., Abilene Christian U.; law degree summa cum laude, Pepperdine U. Law clk. for Judge Thomas M. Reavley US Ct. Appeals (5th cir.); atty. Thompson & Knight, sr. ptnr., 2003—11; dep. atty. gen. for gen. litig. Office of Tex. Atty. Gen., 2000—03; gen. counsel to Gov. Rick Perry State of Tex., 2011, chief of staff to Gov. Rick Perry, 2011—12; justice Tex. Supreme Ct., Austin, 2012—. Bd. pres., dir. Vol. Legal Svcs. of Ctrl. Tex.; chair, dir. Goodwill Industries of Ctrl. Tex.; dir. Freedom of Info. Found. Tex. Named a Tex. Super Lawyer, 2004, 2006—10. Office: Texas Supreme Ct PO Box 12248 Austin TX 78711

BOYD, JIM, state legislator; b. Bradenton, Fla., Oct. 22, 1956; m. Sandy Boyd; children: Ansley, Austin. AA, Manatee Cmty. Coll., 1976; BS, Fla. State U., 1978. Lic. real estate broker. Co-owner, CEO Boyd Ins. & Investment Svcs.; pres. The Boyd Group; councilman, vice mayor, mayor Palmetto City Coun., 1989—93; mem. Dist. 68 Fla. House of Representatives, 2011—. Bd. dirs. First America Bank; bd. governors Manatee Meml. Hosp. Mem.: Fla. Assn. Ins. Agents (bd. mem. 1994—97), Manatee County Ind. Ins. Agents Assn. Republican. Avocations: golf, hunting, reading, travel, quail hunting, spending time in North Carolina with family. Office: 717 Manatee Ave W Ste 100 Bradenton FL 34205-8654 also: Fla House of Representatives 1102 The Capitol 402 S Monroe St Tallahassee FL 32399-1300 Office Phone: 941-708-4968, 850-488-4086.

BOYD, JOHN WESLEY, JR., trade association administrator, farmer; b. NYC, Sept. 4, 1965; s. John Wesley and Betty J. Boyd; m. Kim Hardy, 1988 (div. 1994); 1 child. Attended, Southside Cmty. Coll., 1983, Clemson U., 1984—85. Farmer, 1983—; founder, pres. Nat. Black Farmers Assn. (NBFA), 1995—. Mem. Va. Tobacco Indemnification & Cmty. Revitalization Commn., 1999—2001, Gov.-Elect Tim Kaine's Policy Com. on Agrl. & Forestry, 2001—02. Named one of 100 Most Influential Black Americans, Ebony mag., 2006; named to The Power 150, 2008. Mem.: NAACP. Democrat. Achievements include founded the association to fight the racism in the USDA loan programs; led class action law suit of 1000 black farmers against the USDA in 1997 that led to a historic agreement in 1999; Staged a protest in 2003 on behalf of black farmers by traveling 200-plus miles from his farm in Virginia to Washington on a wagon pulled by his two mules, Struggle and 40 Acres. Office: Nat Black Farmers Assn 68 Wind Rd Baskerville VA 23915 Office Phone: 434-848-1865. E-mail: Johnboyd@johnwboydjr.com.

BOYD, RALPH F., JR., mortgage company executive, former federal agency administrator; b. Schenectady, NY, Feb. 7, 1957; BA, Haverford Coll., 1979; JD, Harvard U., 1984; LLD (hon.), Suffolk U., 2001. Law clk. to Hon. Joseph H. Young U.S. Dist. Ct. Md., Md.; assoc. Ropes & Gray, 1987—91; asst. U.S. atty. major crimes unit U.S. Attys. Office, 1992—98; ptnr. Goodwin Procter, LLP, 1998—2001; asst. atty., Gen. Civil Rights Divsn. U.S. Dept. Justice, Washington, 2001—03; sr. ptnr. Alston & Bird LLP, Washington, 2003—04; chmn. Freddie Mac Foundation, 2005—; exec. v.p., gen. counsel Fed. Home Loan Mortgage Corp. (Freddie Mac), McLean, Va., 2004—05; exec. v.p., cmty. rels. Freddie Mac - Federal Home Loan Mortgage Corp., McLean, Va., 2005—. Mem. exec. com. Mass. Jud. Nominating Commn., 1996—2001; mem. U.S. Magistrate Judge Selection and Rev. Panel, 1998. Office: Freddie Mac 8200 Jones Branch Dr Mc Lean VA 22102-3110 Office Phone: 703-918-8599. Business E-Mail: ralph_boyd@freddiemac.com.

BOYD, RANDY P., state legislator; m. Sherry Holland. Attended, Itawamba CC, Fulton, Miss., Miss. State U. Forester, land surveyor; mem. Dist. 19 Miss. House of Reps., Jackson, 2012—. Mem.: Miss. Forestry Assn., Soc. American Foresters, Mantachie Lion's Club. Republican. Office: Miss House of Reps PO Box 1018 Jackson MS 39215 Business E-Mail: rboyd@house.ms.gov.

BOYD, WILLIAM PINCKNEY, gastroenterologist; MD, Med. U. of SC, 1972. Lic. Fla., 1975, diplomate Am. Bd. Internal Medicine, 1975, Am. Bd. Internal Medicine-gastroenterology, 1977, Am. Bd. Internal Medicine-transplant hepatology, 2006. Intern Akron Gen. Med. Ctr., 1973, resident internal medicine, 1975; fellow gastroenterology Tampa Gen. Hosp., 1977; hosp. affiliations include Bayfront Med. Ctr. Inc., James A. Haley Veterans' Hosp., St. Anthony's Hosp. Office: James A Haley Veterans Hospital 13000 Bruce B Downs Blvd Tampa FL 33612-4798 Office Phone: 813-972-2000.*

BOYER, LORI N., councilwoman; b. SD; m. Ron Nemeyer (dec.); m. Tyrie W. Boyer; children: R.J. Nemeyer, Quinn Nemeyer, Kimberly Boyer Hellmuth, Kelley Boyer. BA, Georgetown U.; JD, U. Fla., 1978. Pvt. practice; councilwoman Dist. 5 Jacksonville City Coun., Fla., 2011—. Mem. Women's Giving Alliance, Women's Bd. of Wolfson Children's Hosp. Mem.: San Marco Preservation Soc. Office: Jacksonville City Council 117 W Duval St Jacksonville FL 32202 Office Phone: 904-630-1382. E-mail: LBoyer@coj.net.

BOYER, TYRIE ALVIS, lawyer; b. Williston, Fla., Sept. 10, 1924; s. Alton Gordon and Mary Ethel (Strickland) B.; m. Elizabeth Everett Gale, June 9, 1945; children: Carol, Tyrie, Kennedy, Lee. BA, U. Fla., 1953, LLB, JD, 1954. Bar: Fla. Atty. Crawford, May & Boyer, Jacksonville, Fla., 1954-58, Boyer Law Offices, Jacksonville, 1958-60; judge Civil Ct. of Record, Jacksonville, 1960-63; cir. judge 4th Jud. Cir. of Fla., Jacksonville, 1963-67; atty. Dawson, Galant, Maddox, Boyer, Sulik & Nichols, Jacksonville, 1967-73; appellate judge 1st Dist. Ct. Appeal, Tallahassee, 1973-79; chief judge 1st Dist. Ct. Appeals, Tallahassee, 1975-76; atty. Boyer, Tanzler, Blackburn & Boyer, Jacksonville, 1979-84, Boyer, Tanzler & Sussman, Jacksonville, 1984—. Adj. prof. Fla. Coastal Sch. Law, Jacksonville, 1996—, U. North Fla., 1998—; chmn. Supreme Ct. Com. on Standard Conduct Governing Judges, Tallahassee, 1976—79. Contbr. articles to profl. jours. Chmn. Duval County Hosp. Authority, Jacksonville, 1970-73, Jacksonville Bldg. Fin. Authority, 1980-81; pres. Jacksonville Legal Aid Assn., 1954-61; bd. dirs. Jones Coll., Jacksonville, 1978-85; bd. advs. Fla. Coastal Sch. Law, 1996—; adj. prof. U. North Fla., 1998—. With USN, 1942—45, PTO. Mem. Am. Judicature Soc., Fla. Bar, Jacksonville Bar Assn., Am. Bd. Trial Advs., SCV (comdr.), Mil. Order Stars and Bars (comdr.), Masons, dir., Safari Club Internat., Fla. Blue Key, Order of Coif, Phi Beta Kappa, Phi Kappa Phi. Methodist. Home: 3966 Cordova Ave Jacksonville FL 32207-6019 Office: Boyer Tanzler & Sussman 210 E Forsyth St Jacksonville FL 32202-3320 Office Phone: 904-358-3030. Business E-Mail: tab3030@bellsouth.net.

BOYES, PATRICE FLINCHBAUGH, lawyer; b. York, Pa., Aug. 1, 1957; d. Glenn Dale Flinchbaugh and Patricia Ann (Frey) Shultz. BA, Dickinson Coll., 1978; MA, U. Mich., 1980; JD, U. Fla., 1991. Bar: Fla. 1991, Fed. 1994, US Supreme Court, 2006. Law clk. Rakusin & Ivey, Gainesville, Fla., 1989; summer assoc. Hopping, Boyd, Green & Sams, Tallahassee, 1990; gen. counsel GeoSolutions, Inc., Gainesville/Tallahassee, Fla., 1986—2002; pres. Patrice Boyes, Pa., Gainesville, Fla., 1991—. Pres. Hist. Gainesville, Inc.; chair City's Hist. Preservation Adv. Bd.; vol. Kanapha Bot. Gardens; counsel Duckpond Neighborhood Assn., Inc., mem. nominating commn. Boy Scouts America. Recipient Keystone Press award Pa. Soc. Newspaper Editors and Pubs., 1981, City Beautification award, 1994, Hist. Preservation award, 1994, Fla. Trust for Hist. Preservation award, 1996; grad. fellow Modern Media Inst., St. Petersburg, Fla. Mem. Fed. Bar Assn., Fla. Bar Assn. (environ. and land use sect., real property sect.), Am. Inn Ct. (Master), 8th Jud. Cir. Bar Assn., Fla. Assn. Women Lawyers, Gainesville C. of C., Gainesville Coun. Econ. Outreach, Pi Delta Epsilon, Gainesville Country Club, Gainesville Woman's Club (bd. dirs. 2010-11), Sebastian Ferrero Found. (v.p.), Altar Guild and Sec. of Congregation, Abiding Savior Luth. Ch., Rotary (Paul Harris fellow, Disting. Lawyers Directory, 2010), Santa FE CC Spring Arts Festival House (founding patron), Newberry Jonesville C. of C. (bd. dirs. 2014). Avocations: tennis, golf, photography, gardening, reading, travel. Office: 414 SW 140th Ter Newberry FL 32669-3363 Office Phone: 352-372-2684. Personal E-mail: pboyes@boyeslaw.com.

BOYES, STEPHEN RICHARD, hydrogeologic consultant; b. Evanston, Ill., May 17, 1950; s. Will W. and Beth (Henry) B. AA, U. South Fla., 1972, BA, 1974. Lic. profl. geologist, Fla. Geophys. engr. seismic process ctr. Geophys. Svcs., Inc., Midland, Tex., 1974, geophys. engr. field ops. Chickasha, Okla., 1975, geophys. engr. Saudi, Arabia, 1975-77; geologist Fla. Dept. Environ. Regulation, Tallahassee, 1978-82, hydrogeologist Tampa, 1982-84; sr. hydrogeologist Groundwater Technology, Tampa, 1984-86, Handex Corp., Odenton, Md., 1986; pres. GeoSolutions, Inc., Gainesville, Fla., 1986—. Contbr. to profl. publs. Mem.: Nat. Groundwater Assn. Avocations: canoeing, computers, snorkeling, racquetball. Office Phone: 352-378-7026. Personal E-mail: geosolutions86@yahoo.com.

BOYETTE, RICHARD T., lawyer; b. Fayetteville, NC, Aug. 4, 1952; BA, Univ. NC, Chapel Hill, 1974, JD, 1977. Bar: NC 1977, cert.: mediator. Law clerk, Hon. Walter E. Brock NC Ct. of Appeals, 1977—78; asst. dist. atty. 12th Judicial Dist., 1978—80; ptnr., mediation, comml. litig. Cranfill Sumner & Hartzog, Raleigh, NC. Mem.: Internat. Assn. Def. Counsel, NC Assn. Def. Attys. (pres. 1990—91, Award for Profl. Excellence 2004), NC Bar Assn., Wake County Bar Assn., Def. Rsch. Inst. (bd. dir. 1998—2001, pres. 2004—05). Office: Cranfill Sumner & Hartzog Ste 300 224 Wash Pk Blvd PO Box 27808 Raleigh NC 27611 Office Phone: 919-863-8729. Office Fax: 919-863-3915. Business E-Mail: rtb@cshlaw.com.

BOYKIN, FRANK H., textiles executive; Sr. mgr. Deloitte & Touche, KPMG LLP; corp. contr. Mohawk Industries, Inc., Calhoun, Ga., 1993—99, v.p., corp. cont., 1999—2004, v.p. fin., 2004—05, v.p. fin., CFO, 2005—. Office: Mohawk Industries, Inc PO Box 12069 160 S Industrial Blvd Calhoun GA 30701

BOYKIN, GLADYS, retired religious organization administrator; b. NYC, Dec. 10, 1929; d. Jacob Allen and Annie Mae (Alston) McClendon; m. Eugene S. Callender (div. 1963); 1 child, Renee

Denise; m. John R. Strachan (dec. 1982); m. Elton Boykin, 1996 (dec. Nov. 13, 2007). Student, NYU, 1947-49. Dep. asst. Presbyn. Ch. of East Africa, Nairobi, Kenya, 1964-67; assoc. for women's program Presbyn. Ch. of U.S., NYC, 1970-83; exec. dir. United Presbyn. Women, NYC, 1983-97; ret., 1997. Cons. Peace Corps, Nairobi, 1964-67, Operation Crossroads Africa, Nairobi, 1964-67, Afro-Am. Ednl. Inst., Teaneck, N.J., 1977-79, various women's orgns. in Asia, Australia, Europe, Africa. V.p. Addicts Rehab. Ctr. Bd., N.Y.C., 1957—; mem. N.Y. Coalition of 100 Black Women, N.Y.C., 1972—; v.p., bd. dirs. La. Internat. Cultural Ctr.; bd. dirs. aging resource ctr. Sister Cities of Louisville. Recipient Cert. of citation borough pres. N.Y.C., 1977, Harlem Peacemaking award Harlem Peacemaking Com., 1983, Vol. award Louisville Internat. Culture Ctr., 1996. Mem. World Affairs Couns. America, La. C. of C., River City Assn. Bus. and Profl. Women., Downtown Resident Assn. (pres.), Jefferson Club (bd. govs.). Avocations: music, reading, travel, needlepoint, theater. Home: 211 W Oak St Apt 1119 Louisville KY 40203-5404

BOYKO, ALAN, publishing executive; BS in Geography, U. South Fla., Tampa, 1978; attended, Rollins Coll. Crummer Grad. Sch. Bus., winter Pk., Fla., 1995—97. Joined Scholastic Corp., 1988, various positions in mktg., sales and product devel. including pub. Tangerine Press; v.p. product devel. Scholastic Book Fairs, sr. v.p., 2004—05, pres., 2005—. Office: Scholastic Book Fairs Inc 1080 Greenwood Blvd Lake Mary FL 32746 Office Phone: 407-829-7300.

BOYLE, COLEEN A., public health service officer; MS in Biostatistics, U. Pitts., PhD in Epidemiology. Post. doc. tng. in epidemiol. methods Yale U., New Haven; faculty mem. in epidemiology U. Mass. Program in Pub. Health; joined Centers Disease Control and Prevention, Atlanta, 1984, joined divsn. birth defects and devel. disabilities, 1988, assoc. dir. Nat. Ctr. Birth Defects and Devel. Disabilities, 2001—10, dir. Nat. Ctr. Birth Defects and Devel. Disabilities, 2010—. Recipient Charles C. Shepard award, CDC, 1997. Office: Centers Disease Control and Prevention NCBDDD 1600 Clifton Rd Atlanta GA 30333

BOYLE, JAMES T., JR., health services company executive; Dir., litigation, asst. gen. counsel Laboratory Corp. of America Holdings, 1999—2004, v.p., managed care, 2004—06, sr. v.p., managed care, 2006—09, sr. v.p., occupl. testing and employer group svcs., 2008—09, exec. v.p., COO, 2009—. Office: Laboratory Corporation of America Holdings 358 S Main St Burlington NC 27215 Office Phone: 336-229-1127. Office Fax: 336-513-4510. Business E-Mail: boylej@labcorp.com.

BOYLE, JANE J., federal judge; b. Sharon, Pa., Dec. 15, 1954; BS, U. of Tex., Austin, 1977; JD, So Meth. U., Dallas, 1981. Asst. dist. atty. Dist. Atty.'s Office, 1981-87; asst. U.S. atty. US Dist. Ct. (no. dist.) Tex., 1987-90, magistrate judge U.S. Dallas, 1990—2002, U.S. atty., 2002—04; judge US Dist. Ct. (no. dist.) Tex., 2004—. Office: US Courthouse 1100 Commerce St Rm 1452 Dallas TX 75242

BOYLE, JOANNE, women's college basketball coach; B in Economics, Duke U., Durham, NC, 1985; MS in Health Sci. and Adminstrn., U. NC, 1989. Profl. basketball player, Luxembourg, Germany; asst. coach Duke U. Blue Devils, 1993—2002; head coach U. Richmond Spiders, 2002—05, U. Calif. Golden Bears, Berkeley, 2005—11, U. Va. Cavaliers, 2011—. Asst. coach, under 20 nat. team USA Basketball, 2006, jr. nat. team com. mem., 2009—; bd. dirs. Women's Basketball Coaches Assn. Recipient Carol Eckman award, Women's Basketball Coaches Assn., 2011; named Coach of Yr., Pac-10 Conf., 2007, Region VIII Coach of Yr., Women's Basketball Coaches Assn., 2008. Office: University Virginia Womens Basketball John Paul Jones Arena PO Box 400827 Charlottesville VA 22904-4827 Office Phone: 434-982-5800. Office Fax: 434-982-5822. Business E-Mail: jb4xd@virginia.edu.

BOYLE, TERRENCE WILLIAM, federal judge; b. Passaic, NJ, Dec. 22, 1945; married; 3 children. BA, Brown U., 1967; JD, Am. U., 1970. Minority counsel US House Housing, Banking, & Currency Subcommittee, 1970-73; legislative asst. to Senator Jesse Helms US Senate, 1973; judge US Dist. Ct. (eastern dist.) NC, 1984—, chief judge, 1997—2004. Office: US Dist Ct 306 E Main St Ste 1 Elizabeth City NC 27909-4865

BOYLEN, JIM, professional basketball coach; b. East Grand Rapids, Mich., Apr. 18, 1965; m. Christine Boylen; children: Ashlen Clare, Layla Blue. B in Bus., U. Maine, 1987. Grad. asst. Mich. State U. Spartans, 1987—89, asst. coach, 1989—92, 2005—07; video coord. Houston Rockets, 1992—94, asst. coach, 1994—2003, Golden State Warriors, 2003—04, Milw. Bucks, 2004—05; head basketball coach U. Utah Utes, 2007—11; asst. coach Ind. Pacers, 2011—13, San Antonio Spurs, 2013—. Office: San Antonio Spurs One AT&T Center San Antonio TX 78219 Office Phone: 801-581-5451.*

BOYLES, FREDERICK HOLDREN, historian; b. Gainesville, Fla., Nov. 9, 1954; s. Eugene Harry and Frances Louise (Holdren) B.; m. Deborah Anne Beverly, Aug. 21, 1976; children: Cynthia Beverly, Joseph Holdren. A in Edn. and History, Abraham Baldwin Coll., 1974; BS in Edn. and History, U. Ga., 1976; M in Recreation and Parks Adminstrn., Clemson U., 1981. Dir. trail camp Goshen (Va.) Scout Camps, 1975-79; tchr. history and geography Waycross (Ga.) City Schs., 1976-78; instr. grad. students Clemson (S.C.) U., 1978-79; outdoor recreation planner Nat. Park Svc., Atlanta, 1979-81; historian Cumberland Gap Nat. Hist. Park, Middlesboro, Ky., 1981-85; supt. Moores Creek Nat. Battlefield, Currie, NC, 1985-89, Andersonville (Ga.)-Jimmy Carter Nat. Hist. Sites, 1989—. Adj. faculty Lincoln Meml. U., Harrogate, Tenn., 1983-84, U. N.C., Wilmington, 1987. Scoutmaster troop 231 Boy Scouts Am., Americus, Ga., 1994; elder 1st Presbyn. Ch., Americus, 1991—. Comdr. USNR, 1987, comdg. officer Surface Deployment Distribn. Command, Richmond, VA. Recipient Superior Achievement award, U.S. Dept. Interior, 1980, Good Citizenship award, SAR, 1989; named Supt. of Yr., Nat. Pk. Svc., 1998; scholar Grad. alumni scholar, Clemson U., 1979. Mem. Sumter C. of C. (bd. dirs. 1992—), Americus Rotary Club, Burgaw N.C. Rotary Club (bd. dirs. 1988, 90), Burgaw Area C. of C. (pres. 1989). Office: Nat Park Svc 496 Cemetery Rd Andersonville GA 31711-9707 Home: 709 Margaret St Saint Marys GA 31558-8678 Office Phone: 229-924-0343. E-mail: fred_boyles@nps.gov.

BOZALIS, JOHN RUSSELL, physician; b. St. Louis, Sept. 19, 1939; s. George Sauter and Ruth (Russell) B.; m. Sharon Louise Sabo, June 21, 1963; children: John Jr., David L., Diana. BA, U. Okla., 1961, MD, 1965; MS, U. Mich., 1971. Diplomate Am. Bd. Internal Medicine, Am. Bd. Allergy and Immunology. Intern Henry Ford Hosp., Detroit, 1965-66, resident, 1966-68, chief resident, 1968-69; fellow in allergy-immunology U. Mich., Ann Arbor, 1969-71, instr., 1969-71; clin. asst. prof. U. Tex., San Antonio, 1972-73; pvt. practice Okla. Allergy Clinic, Oklahoma City, 1973—. Clin. instr. Coll. Medicine, U. Okla., 1973, clin. asst. prof., 1977-83, clin. assoc. prof., 1983-89, clin. prof., 1989—; mem. courtesy staff Mercy Hosp., Bapt. Hosp., Deaconess Hosp., St. Anthony Hosp., Presbyn. Hosp., Children's Hosp., Okla. Tchg. Hosp., S.W. Med. Ctr. Trustee Casady Sch., 1977-85, United Way Okla. City, chmn. profl. divsn. 1983, Okla. Health Scis. Found.; bd. dirs. Infant Ctr., 1983-86, Allied Arts Okla. City, 1984-86, 92, Hosp. Hospitality House, 1983-86, United Way Greater Okla. City, 2006; vice chmn. health scis. ctr. U. Okla. Centennial Commn.; bd. trustees McGee Eye Inst., search com. for chmn. dept. ophthalmology and dir., 1991, Okla. City Mus. Art., 2003—, U. Okla. Found., 2003—; active Com. of 100, 1991; bd. trustees Okla. City Pub. Schs. Found., 1989—, Okla. Orthopedic and Arthritis Found., Inc., Bone and Joint Hosp., 1993; trustee Oklahoma City Mus. Arts, 2003—, U. Okla. Found., 2003; chmn. legis. task force for promotion of children's health State of Okla., 2002-06; pres. bd. Schs. Healthy Lifestyles, 1997—. Maj. USAF, 1971-73. Recipient Regents' Alumni award U. Okla., 1992; named Physician of Yr.-Pvt. Practice, U. Okla. Coll. of Medicine Alumni Assn., 1993, recipient dean's award, 1998. Fellow ACP, Am. Coll. Chest Physicians, Am. Acad. Allergy; mem. AMA, Am. Thoracic Soc., Okla. State Med. Assn. (del. 1993—, vice spkr. ho. dels. 1997, trustee 1993—), Okla. Lung Assn., Okla. Thoracic Soc. (pres. 1979), John M. Sheldon Soc., Okla. County Med. Soc. (editor Bull. 1978-83, chmn. orientation com. 1989—, pres. 1996, bd. trustees 1996—), Osler Soc. (pres. 1984), Okla. City Acad. Medicine, Robert M. Bird Soc., U. Okla. Coll. Medicine Alumni Assn. (chmn. rsch. com., pres. 1983-85), Okla. City C. of C. (bd. dirs. 1988-90). Republican. Episcopal. Avocations: hunting, golf, fly fishing, travel, gardening. Office: Okla Allergy and Asthma Clinic PO Box 26827 Oklahoma City OK 73126-0827 also: Okla Allergy and Asthma Clinic 750 NE 13th St Oklahoma City OK 73104 Home Phone: 405-843-7115; Office Phone: 405-235-0040. Business E-Mail: jbozalis@oklahomaallergy.com.

BOZEMAN, FRANK CARMACK, retired lawyer; b. Greenwood, Miss., Oct. 16, 1933; s. Frank Carmack and Mamie Hyatt (Pyle) B.; m. Mary Ireland Callcott, Dec. 29, 1961; children: Frank C. III, William Pyle, Thomas Anderson. BA, U. of South, 1955; MA, U. Va., 1956; JD, Washington and Lee U., 1960. Bar: Fla. 1960, Va. 1960. Assoc. Beggs and Lane, Pensacola, Fla., 1960-65; ptnr. Harrell, Wiltshire, Bozeman, Clark & Stone, Pensacola, 1965-75, Carlton, Fields, Ward, Emmanuel, Smith & Cutler, P.A., Pensacola, 1975-93, Bozeman, Jenkins & Matthews, Pensacola, 1993—98; ret., 1998. Editor Washington and Lee Law Rev., 1960. Chmn. Eagle Scout rev. com. Boy Scouts Am., Pensacola, 1961-63; trustee U. of the South, 1990-96. Capt. USAF, 1956-57. Mem. Am. Bd. Trial Advs. (pres. Pensacola chpt. 1989-90), Fla. Def. Lawyers Assn., Fedn. Ins. and Corp. Counsel, Register of Pre-Eminent Lawyers, Def. Rsch. Inst., Order of Coif, Phi Beta Kappa, Phi Delta Phi (Grad. of Yr. award 1960). Republican. Episcopalian. Home: 122 W Lloyd St Pensacola FL 32501-2637

BOZER, AHMET C., beverage company executive; b. 1960; BSBA, Middle East Tech. U., Ankara, Turkey; M in Bus. Info. Sys., Ga. State U., US. Various audit, consultancy and mgmt. positions Coopers & Lybrand, 1985—90; various positions The Coca-Cola Co., Belarus, Ukraine, Russia, financial contr. mgr., 1990—92, region fin. mgr. Turkey, 1992—94, fin. dir., mgr., dir., bottling ops., 1994—2000; CFO Coca-Cola Bottlers (now Coca-Cola Icecek A.S.), Turkey, 1994—98, mng. dir., 1998—2000; pres., Eurasia Divsn. The Coca-Cola Co., 2000—02, pres., Eurasia, Middle East Divsn., 2002—07, pres, Eurasia Group, 2007—08, COO, Eurasia & Africa Group, 2008—10, pres., Eurasia & Africa Group Istanbul, Turkey, 2008—12, exec. v.p., pres. Coca-Cola Internat. Atlanta, 2013—. Bd. dirs. The Coca-Cola Found., Atlanta, Ga.; with US-Pakistan Bus. Coun.; founding mem., bd. trustees The Coca-Cola Turkey Life Plus Found.; chmn. Bus. Coun. for Internat. Understanding (BCIU), 2013 Office: The Coca Cola Co 1 Coca Cola Plz Atlanta GA 30313 Office Phone: 404-676-2121. Business E-Mail: abozer@na.cokecce.com.*

BRABENDER, JOHN, political consultant; b. 1956; m. Rebecca Robinson Brabender, Aug. 16, 1980. BS, Gannon U., 1978; MBA in Mktg., Cleve. State U., 1981. Chief creative officer, mng. ptnr. BrabenderCox, 1982—. Adj. prof. Perley Isaac Reed Sch. Journalism, W.Va. U.; mem. ad-making team Rudy Giuliani for Pres. Campaign, 2007—08; mem. McCain for Pres. Advertising Coun.; sr. advisor, media cons. Rick Santorum's Presdl Campaign, 2011—. Guest Politically Incorrect with Bill Maher, Talk of the Nation, NPR, Inside Politics, CNN, NBC Nightly News, The Today Show, CBS Evening News. Named one of Rising Stars of 1996, Campaigns & Elections, Sy Snyder's Power 50, PoliticsPA, 2002, 2003, Republican Dream Team, Top 10 Republicans in Pa., 2010. Republican. Office: BrabenderCox 932 Edwards Ferry Rd, Suite 107 Leesburg VA 20176 also: 1218 Grandview Ave Pittsburgh PA 15211 Office Phone: 703-896-5306, 412-434-6320. Office Fax: 703-896-5315, 412-434-6391. E-mail: john@brabendercox.com.*

BRACKEN, RICHARD M., hospital administrator; b. Richmond, Va., 1977; m. Judith Bracken; 4 children. B, 1974; M, Med. Coll. Va., 1977. CEO Centennial Med. Ctr., Green Hosp. of Scripps Clinic & Rsch. Found.; various exec. positions HCA, Inc., 1981—95, pres. Pacific divsn., 1995—97, pres. Western Group, 1997—2001, COO, 2001—09, pres., 2002—09, chmn., CEO, 2009—. Bd. dirs. United Way of Met. Nashville; mem. Am. Soc. of Corp. Execs., Bus. Coun., Nashville Healthcare Coun., Cmty. Found. of Middle Tenn. Bd.; fellow Am. Coll. of Healthcare Exec. Mem.: Fedn. Am. Hosps. (bd. dirs.), Calif. Hosp. Assn. (bd. dirs.). Office: HCA Inc 1 Park Plz Nashville TN 37203 Office Phone: 615-344-9551. Business E-Mail: richard.bracken@hcahealthcare.com.*

BRACKETT, MARTIN LUTHER, JR., lawyer; b. Charlotte, NC, Feb. 23, 1947; s. Martin Luther and Helen Virginia (Smith) Brackett; m. Lisa Nichol Brackett; children: Martin Hunter, Alexander Jones, Amelia Kathleen, Lauren Hart. BA, Davidson Coll., 1969; JD, U. NC., 1972. Bar: NC 72, US Dist. Ct. NC 73, US Ct. Appeals 75. Ptnr. Bailey, Brackett & Brackett, PA., Charlotte, NC, 1973—83, Brackett & Sitton, Charlotte, 1983—85, Robinson, Bradshaw & Hinson PA, 1985—. Mem. Auditorium-Coliseum-Conv. Ctr. Authority, Charlotte, 1981—87, chmn., 1985—87. Capt. US Army, 1972—73. Recipient Van Hecke-Wettach award, U. NC, 1972. Fellow: Am. Coll. Trial Lawyers; mem.: NC Acad. Trial Lawyers (bd. govs. 1980—86, 1988—95, v.p. 1984—86). Democrat. Presbyterian. Office: 1900 Independence Ctr 101 N Tryon St Charlotte NC 28246-0100 Office Phone: 704-377-8347.

BRACKETT, THOMAS G., corporate financial executive; BA in Polit. Sci., Fla. Internat. U., 1980; MA in Mgmt., Webster U., 1990. Branch mgr. The Terminix Internat. Co. LP, Miami, Fla., 1992—97, divsn. v.p., 1997—2005; COO Terminix International Co., LP, Miami, Fla., 2005—, pres., 2006—. Office: The Terminix International Co LP 860 Ridge Lake Blvd Memphis TN 38120 Business E-Mail: tbrackett@terminix.com.

BRACY, NAPOLEON, JR., state legislator; b. Prichard, Ala. s. Napoleon and Ernestine Bracy; m. Melody Bracy; children: Kena, Brooklyn. BA in Sociology/Social Welfare, Dillard U., New Orleans, 2000. Site coord. Mobile County Pub. Sch. Sys. & Health Dept., Ala.; mem. Dist. 3 Prichard City Coun., 2008—11, pres., 2008—11; exec. dir. Beyond Expectations Tutoring, Inc., Ala.; mem. Dist. 98 Ala. House of Reps., 2011—. Patron American Red Cross; former advisor Prichard Police Dept. Explorers; chmn. Mobile County Dem. Party; mem. First Bapt. Ch. Prichard, Inc.; pres. Prichard Regional Cmty. Action Group; bd. mem. Habitat for Humanity. Mem.: 100 Black Men Greater Mobile, Prince Hall Masonry, Alpha Phi Alpha. Democrat. Office: Ala House of Reps Rm 540-A 11 S Union St Montgomery AL 36130 also: 150 Edision St Prichard AL 36610 Office Phone: 334-242-7756, 251-622-8118. Business E-Mail: napoleon@napoleonbracy.com.

BRADBEER, CLIVE, biochemistry educator; b. Tynemouth, Northumberland, Eng., Feb. 20, 1933; came to U.S., 1962, naturalized, 1994; s. Joseph Walter and Mary (Hall) B.; m. Wilma Jean Youngert, Sept. 1, 1960; children: Suzanne Mary, Thomas Clive. BSc with first class honors, Durham U., Newcastle Upon Tyne, Eng., 1954, PhD, 1957. Jr. rsch. biochemist U. Calif., Berkeley, 1957-59, Davis, 1959; postdoctoral fellow U. Wis., Madison, 1959-60; lectr. Queen Mary Coll., London U., 1960-62; asst. prof. Sch. Medicine, U. Va., Charlottesville, 1964-69, assoc. prof., 1969-79, prof., 1979—. Vis. scientist NIH, Bethesda, Md., 1962-64, ad hoc mem. study sect., 1980-84; vis. prof. U. Otago, Dunedin, New Zealand, 1982-83, 93. Contbr. articles to profl. jours. Mem. Am. Soc. for Biochemistry and Molecular Biology. Episcopalian. Achievements include contbns. in elucidation of the molecular mechanisms involved in utilization of vitamin B12 in microbial and animal cells. E-mail: cb7f@virginia.edu.

BRADBURN, NORMAN M., behavioral science educator; s. Hubert Benjamin and Mary Celeste (Marshall) B.; m. Wendy McAneny, Dec. 15, 1956; children: Isabel Stuart, Andrew Marshall, Laura Humphreys. BA, U. Chgo., 1952, Oxford U., Eng., 1955; MA, Harvard U., 1958, PhD in Social Psychology, 1960. From asst. prof. to assoc. prof. behavioral sci. U. Chgo., 1960-67, prof., 1967—, chmn. dept. behavioral sci., 1973-79, Tiffany and Margaret Blake Disting. Service prof., 1977-99, provost, 1984-89, prof. emeritus, 1999—. Sr. study dir. Nat. Opinion Rsch. Ctr., Chgo., 1961—, dir., 1967-71, 79-84, 89-92, rsch. dir., 1992-2000, sr. fellow, 2004—; asst. dir. NSF, 2000—04. Author: (with D. Caplovitz) Reports on Happiness, 1967, The Structure of Psychological Well-Being, 1970, (with S. Sudman, G. Gockel) Side by Side: A Study of Integrated Neighborhoods, 1971, (with S. Sudman) Response Effects in Surveys, 1974, Asking Questions: A Practical Guide to Questionnaire Construction, 1982, revised edit. (with Sudman and Wansinik), 2004, Polls and Surveys: Understanding What They Tell Us, 1988, (with others) Improving Questionnaire Design and Interview Method, 1979, (with S. Sudman and N. Schwarz) Thinking About Answers, 1996. Alexander von Humboldt scholar U. Cologne (Germany), 1970-71 Fellow AAAS, Am. Statis. Assn.; mem. Internat. Statis. Inst., World Assn. Pub. Opinion Rsch., Am. Assn. Pub. Opinion Rsch. (pres. 1991-92), Am. Acad. Arts and Scis. Office Phone: 301-634-9331. Business E-Mail: bradburn-norman@norc.uchicago.edu.

BRADDOCK, PAULETTE RAKESTRAW, state legislator; b. May 07; m. Jeff Braddock; 3 children. Grad. in Bus. Adminstrn. & Mktg., Kennesaw State U. Contract adminstr. Ga. Inst. of Tech., 1985—87; special projects co-ord. The Weather Channel, 1987—88; editor, pub. The Pulse Mag., 2006—08; pres., CEO Atlanta Mktg. Solutions, 1988—; mem. Dist. 19 Ga. House of Representatives, 2011—. Republican. Office: PO Box 580 Powder Springs GA 30127 also: Georgia House of Reps 501 Coverdell Legis Office Bldg Atlanta GA 30334 Office Phone: 770-439-9056, 404-656-0177. Business E-Mail: paulettehouserep@gmail.com.

BRADFORD, BARBARA REED, retired lawyer; b. Cleve., June 13, 1948; d. William Cochran and Martha Lucille (Horn) Bradford; m. Warren Neil Davis, Oct. 9, 1976 (div. 1989); m. S. Jack Odell, Dec. 12, 1991. BA, Pitzer Coll., 1970; JD, Georgetown U., 1975, MBA, 1985. Bar: N.Y. 1976, DC 1976. Staff asst. Sen. Edward M. Kennedy, Washington, 1970-71; assoc. Breed, Abbott & Morgan, NYC, 1975-76, Verner, Liipfert Law Firm, Washington, 1976-78; atty. AID, Washington, 1978-83; pres. Georgetown Export Trading, Inc., Washington, 1984-86; regional dir. U.S. Trade and Devel. Agy., Washington, 1986-2000, agy. dep. dir., 2000—05; ret., 2005. Bd. dirs. Jr. League, Washington, 1977—78. Democrat. Avocations: art, golf, reading. Home: 300 Three Islands Blvd Apt 819 Hallandale Beach FL 33009-2826

BRADFORD, C.O. (BRAD BRADFORD), councilman, former protective services official; b. La., Aug. 25, 1955; m. Dee Jackson; children: Cole, Claire. BA in Criminal Justice, Grambling U.; JD, U. Houston; MBA, Tex. So. U.; grad., FBI Acad. Patrolman Houston Police Dept., 1979—91, asst. chief police, 1991—97, chief of police, 1997—2004; councilman-at-large, Position 4 Houston City Coun., 2010—. Lectr. in field. Mem. Criminal Justice Adv. Bd., Grambling State U., Wiley Coll. Criminal Justice Inst.; adv. bd. Harris County Constable Precinct 7. Mem.: Edn. Found. of Harris County. Office: City Hall Annex 900 Bagby, 1st Fl Houston TX 77002 Office Phone: 832-393-3012. Office Fax: 832-393-3327. E-mail: atlarge4@cityofhouston.net.

BRADFORD, DANA GIBSON, II, lawyer; b. Coral Gables, Fla., Sept. 29, 1948; s. Dana Gibson and Jeanette (Ellis) B.; m. Mary E. Bradford, June 20, 1970 (div. Jan. 1982); 1 child, Jeffrey Dana; m. Donna P. Bradford, Apr. 14, 1984; 1 child, Shannon Claire. BA, U. Fla., 1970; JD, Duke U., 1973. Bar: Fla. 1973, U.S. Dist. Ct. (mid. dist.) Fla. 1974, U.S. Dist. Ct. (so. and no. dists.) Fla. 1979, U.S. Ct. Appeals (5th cir.) 1974, U.S. Ct. Appeals (11th cir.) 1982, U.S. Supreme Ct. 1977. Lawyer, ptnr. Mahoney, Hadlow & Adams, Jacksonville, Fla., 1973-82, Baumer, Bradford & Walters, Jacksonville, 1982—2000, Smith, Gambrell & Russell, LLP, Jacksonville, 2000—. Mem. Fla. Bd. Bar Examiners, 1989-94, chmn. bd., 1992-93; mem. Fla. Supreme Ct. Commn. on Professionalism, 1996-98; seminar lectr. Contbr. chpt. to book, articles to profl. jours. Mem. Leadership Jacksonville, 1982; spl. counsel Jacksonville Sports Authority. Capt. U.S. Army Res., 1972-80. Mem. ABA, ABOTA, Jacksonville Bar Assn. (bd. govs. young lawyers sect. 1976-78, chmn. trial sects. 1989-90), Jacksonville Assn. Def. Counsel (pres. 1978-79), Am. Bd. Trial Advocates, Boys & Girls Clubs NE Fla. (bd. mem.) Republican. Methodist. Office: Smith Gambrell & Russell LLP 50 N Laura St Ste 2600 Jacksonville FL 32202-3659 Office Phone: 904-598-6103. Business E-Mail: dgbradford@sgrlaw.com.

BRADFORD, JAMES WARREN, JR., (JIM BRADFORD), dean, finance educator; b. Newport News, Va., May 3, 1947; s. James Warren and Blanche B. Bradford; m. Susan Garrision; children: Geoffrey, Emily, Alexander, Laura. BA in Polit. Sci., U. Fla., 1969; JD, Vanderbilt U., Nashville, 1973. Ptnr. Hunter, Smith & Davis, Kingsport, Tenn., 1973-84; v.p., gen. counsel AGF Industries, Inc., Kingsport, 1984-92, pres., CEO, 1992—99, United Glass Corp., 1999—2001; clin. prof. mgmt. Owen Grad. Sch. Mgmt., Vanderbilt U., 2002—04, assoc. dean corp. rels., clin. prof. mgmt., 2002—04, acting dean, 2004—05, dean, Ralph Owen prof. practice of mgmt., 2005—. Bd. dirs. Genesco Inc., 2005—, Clarcor Inc., 2006—, Granite Constrn. Inc., 2006—, Cracker Barrel Old Country Store, Inc., 2011—. Mem.: ABA, Kingsport Bar Assn., Tenn. Bar Assn. Avocations: golf, running, bicycling, gardening. Office: Vanderbilt University Owen School of Management 2201 West End Ave Nashville TN 37235 Office Phone: 615-343-5705, 615-322-7311. Office Fax: 615-343-7177. E-mail: jim.bradford@owen.vanderbilt.edu.

BRADFORD, REAGAN HOWARD, JR., ophthalmology educator; b. Lawton, Okla., July 31, 1954; s. Reagan Howard Sr. and Conita Ann (Hargraves) B.; m. Cynthia Ann McGough, Apr. 22, 1988. BS, U. Okla., 1976; MD, U. Okla., Oklahoma City, 1980. Diplomate Am. Bd. Ophthalmology. Intern Bapt. Med. Ctr., Oklahoma City, 1980-81; resident Dean A. McGee Eye Inst. U. Okla., 1981-84; fellow in vitreo retina Bascom Palmer Eye Inst. U. Miami, Fla., 1984-85; clinical prof. Dean A. McGee Eye Inst., U. Okla., Oklahoma City, 1985—. Author: (with others) Basics of Neurophthalmology; contbr. articles to profl. jours. Fellow Am. Acad. Ophthalmology; mem. Okla. County Med. Soc., Okla. State Med. Assn., AMA, Okla. State Acad. Ophthalmology. Republican. Baptist. Avocation: golf. Office: Dean A McGee Eye Inst 608 Stanton L Young Blvd Oklahoma City OK 73104-5065 Office Phone: 405-271-1092. Business E-Mail: reagan-bradford@dmei.org.

BRADFORD, TONI C., state legislator; b. Hot Springs, Ark., Oct. 31, 1942; m. Thomas Bradford; children: Renee Bennett, T. Hal. BSE, Univ. Ark., Pine Bluff, 1976. Tchr., ret. Watson Chapel Sch. Sys.; mem. Dist. 18 Ark. House of Reps., 2007—, asst. spkr. pro tempore. Democrat. Baptist. Address: 8410 Wildcat Dr Pine Bluff AR 71603 Office Phone: 870-879-5270. Business E-Mail: bradfordt@arkleg.state.ar.us.

BRADFORD, WILLIAM DALTON, pathologist, educator; b. Rochester, NY, Nov. 2, 1931; s. William Leslie and Lenora Dee (Dalton) B.; m. Anne Bevington Harden, July 8, 1961; children—Scott Harden, Lisa B. Lee BA, Amherst Coll., 1954; MD, Western Res. U., 1958. Diplomate Am. Bd. Pediatrics, Am. Bd. Anatomic Pathology. Intern in pathology Boston Children's Med. Ctr., 1958-59, resident in pediatrics, 1959-61; teaching fellow in pathology Harvard Med. Sch., 1963-64; fellow Mead Johnson, 1963—64; asst. prof. pathology Duke U., Durham, NC, 1966-70, assoc. prof., 1970-81, prof., 1981—, assoc. dean, 1970-71, 74-78, 84-87, asst. to chancellor for health affairs, 1987-89, dir. pediatric pathology, 1966—2002, dir. pathology tng. program, 1974-2001. Pres. Durham YMCA, 1978, bd. dirs., 1976-83, 90-95; mem. bd. visitors YMCA Camps Sea Gull/Seafarer, chair, 2002-07; faculty chmn. athletics Duke U., 1979-85. Lt. comdr. USN, 1961-63. Recipient Golden Apple award Student Med. Assn., 1969, 93, 95, 98, Layman of Yr. award YMCA, 1974, 78, Disting. Tchr. award Duke Med. Alumni Assn., 1989, Life Time Achievement award, YMCA The Triangle, 2008. Mem. Internat. Acad. Pathology, Am. Assn. Pathologists, Soc. Pediatric Research, Group for Rsch. in Pathology Edn., Soc. for Pediatric Pathology (pres. 1987-88), Nat. Collegiate Athletic Assn. Council, Nat. Faculty Athletics Reps. Forum (chmn. 1985), Atlantic Coast Conf. (pres. 1982-83), Duke Med. Alumni Coun. (pres. 2000-01, exec. com. med. sch. admissions, vice-chmn. 2007—11), Sigma Xi, Alpha Omega Alpha, YMCA Triangle (trustee). Office: Duke U Med Ctr PO Box 3712 Durham NC 27710-0001 Office Phone: 919-684-5112. Business E-Mail: william.bradford@dm.duke.edu.

BRADFORD, WILLIAM EDWARD, manufacturing executive; b. Dallas, Jan. 8, 1935; m. JoDeane Browning, Aug. 18, 1955; children: William B., A. Kathleen, Jon E. BS in Geology, Centenary Coll., 1958; grad., Tex. A&M U., 1975. Salesman Hycalog, Inc., 1958-61; v.p., gen. ptnr. Analytical Logging, Inc., 1961-70; product mgr. Oilfield Products Group Dresser Industries, Inc., Dallas, 1970-72, mgr. Mid-cont. Oilfield Products Group, 1972-73, mgr. Europe, Africa, Middle East Oilfield Products Group, 1973-76, v.p. Security Divsn., 1976-78, pres. Security Divsn., 1980-83, group pres. Oilfield Products Group, 1983-84, v.p. ops., 1984-92, sr. v.p., 1988-92; pres. CEO Dresser-Rand Co., Corning, NY, 1992-95; pres., COO and dir. Dresser Industries, Inc., Dallas, 1995-96, pres., CEO, dir., 1996-98, chmn. pres., 1998-2000; chmn. Halliburton Co. (formerly Dresser Industries, Inc.), Dallas, 2000—. Bd. dirs. Valero Energy Corp. Mem.: Petroleum Equipment Suppliers Assn., Am. Assn. Petroleum Geologists, Soc. Petroleum Engrs., Dallas Country Club. Office: Two Turtle Creek Village 3838 Oak Lawn Ave Ste 777 Dallas TX 75219

BRADLEY, BRIAN S., retail executive; BS in Engring., U. Mich.; MBA, Duke U. Various positions including, process mgr., worldwide ops. IBM Corp., 1992—97; sr. mgr. McKinsey & Co., 1997—2002; dir., strategy and implementation Capital One Financial Corp., 2002—05; v.p., gen. mgr., strategy, bus. devel., innovation Circuit City, 2005, sr. v.p., multi-channel, 2005—09; exec. v.p., HSN.com, advanced svcs. HSN, Inc., 2009—. Office: HSN Inc 1 HSN Dr Saint Petersburg FL 33729 Office Phone: 727-872-1000. Business E-Mail: brian.bradley@hsn.net.

BRADLEY, C. ALLEN, JR., insurance company executive; Joined Amerisafe, Inc., 1994—2002, sec., 1997—2002, gen. counsel, 1997—2003, COO, 2002—03, pres., 2002—, CEO, bd. dirs., 2003—, chmn., 2005—. Office: Amerisafe Inc 2301 Hwy 190 W Deridder LA 70634 Office Phone: 337-463-9052. Office Fax: 337-463-7298. Business E-Mail: abradley@amerisafe.com.

BRADLEY, CHARLES MACARTHUR, retired architect; b. Chgo., Sept. 26, 1918; s. Harold Smith and Helen Francis (MacArthur) B.; m. Joan Marie Daane, July 27, 1946 (dec.);children: Mary Barbara, Nancy Ann, Sally Joan, William Charles (dec.); m. Letricia L. Bradley, June 29, 2007. BS in Architecture, U. Ill., 1940. With Holabird & Root, architects, Chgo., 1940-41, Giffels & Vallet, architects and engrs., Detroit, 1941-44; ptnr., corp. pres. Bradley & Bradley, architects and engrs., Rockford, Ill., 1947-2001; ret., 2001. Pres. Bradley Bldg. Corp., 1962—. Prin. works include North Sheboygan HS and addition, Wis., 1960-68, J.F. Kennedy Middle Sch., Rockford, 1968, Singer Health Clinic, Rockford, 1964, Jacobs HS, Algonquin, Ill., 1976, Atwood plant, Rockford, 1977, Admiral Home, Chgo., 1978, Bushnell Jr. HS, Ill., 1980, Bloom HS, 1983, Evenglow Lodge, 1984, East Aurora HS addition, 1992, Erie HS, 1994; author papers on life cycling old schs., roofing procedures. Active Blackhawk coun. Boy Scouts Am. Served with C.E., US Army, 1945-46. Recipient Meritorious Svc. award Ill. Assn. Sch. Bds., 1976. Mem. AIA (pres. No. Ill. chpt. 1962, treas. Ill. coun. 1973-74), Ill. Soc. Architects (pres. 1974), Edn. Facilities Planners Inst., Ill. Assn. Sch. Bd. Officers, Rotary, Union League, Univ. Club, Lauderdale Lakes Sailing Club, Meridian Club. Republican. Congregationalist. Home and Office: Meridian Club 1103 4901 Gulfshore Blvd N Naples FL 34103

BRADLEY, GLEN A., state legislator; b. Portsmouth, Va., Sept. 11, 1973; Owner, operator Ohmega.comm, Inc.; mem. Dist. 49 NC House of Representatives, 2011—. Republican. Southern Baptist. Office: 144 Ridgewood Rd Youngsville NC 27596 Address: North Carolina House of Representatives 300 N Salisbury St Room 536 Raleigh NC 27603-5925 Office Phone: 919-374-2973, 919-733-5860, 919-733-0449. Business E-Mail: Glen.Bradley@ncleg.net.

BRADLEY, GUS (PAUL CASEY BRADLEY), professional football coach; b. Zumbrota, Minn., July 5, 1966; m. Michaela Bradley; children: Carter, Anna, Eli, Ella. BA in Bus. Adminstrn., N.Dak. State U., 1989, BA in Phys. Edn., 1990, MA in Athletic Adminstrn., 1992. Grad. asst. coach N.Dak. State U. Bisons, 1990—91, defensive coord., 1996—2005; defensive coord., linebackers coach Fort. Lewis Coll. Skyhawks, 1992—95, head coach, 1995—96; defensive quality control coach, linebackers coach Tampa Bay Buccaneers, 2006—08; defensive coord. Seattle Seahawks, 2009—12; head coach Jacksonville Jaguars, 2013—. Office: Jacksonville Jaguars One EverBank Field Dr Jacksonville FL 32202

BRADLEY, LAURENCE ALAN, psychologist; b. Cleve., Sept. 13, 1949; s. Irving and Jeanne (Weil) B.; m. Gifford Weary, Dec. 28, 1974 (div. 1979); m. Elizabeth Wrenn, Oct. 3, 1981 (div. 1991), Virginia Wadley, March 26, 2007. BA cum laude in Psychology with honors, Vanderbilt U., Nashville, 1971, PhD in Psychology, 1975. Clin. intern Duke U. Med. Ctr., Durham, NC, 1975-76; asst. prof. U. Tenn., Chattanooga, 1976-77, Fordham U., Bronx, NY, 1977-80, Bowman Gray Sch. Med., Winston-Salem, NC, 1980-82, assoc. prof., 1982-89, adminstrv. head sect. med. psychology, 1981-89; assoc. prof., dir. epidemiology, edn. & health svcs. rsch. Multipurpose Arthritis & Musculoskeletal Disease Ctr U. Ala., Birmingham, 1989-92, prof., dir. epidemiology, edn. & health svcs. rsch., 1992-99; prof., dir. neurobehavioral medicine rsch. Multidisciplinary Clin. Rsch. Ctr., Birmingham, 1999—2012. Adj. assoc. prof. U. NC, Greensboro, 1983-89; vis. behavioral scientist Orebro Med. Ctr. Hosp., Sweden, 1986-92. Co-author: Health Psychology: Clinical Methods and Research, 1991; co-editor: Medical Psychology: Contributions to Behavioral Medicine, 1981, Coping with Chronic Disease: Research and Applications, 1983; assoc. editor: Clin. Psychology, Pain, 1995—2000, editl. bd.: Health Psychology, 1999—2001, Arthritis Care and Rsch., 1995—2004, Jour. Back and Musculoskeletal Rehab., 1999—2010. Rsch. grantee Robert Wood Johnson Found., 1983-86, Am.-Scandinavian Found., 1986, Am. Fibromyalgia Syndrome Assoc., 1996, Fetzer Inst., 2000-05, NIH, 1989— Fellow APA, Soc. Personality Assessment; mem. Internat. Assn. Study of Pain, Am. Pain Soc., Soc. Behavioral Medicine, Am Coll. Rheumatology, Osteoarthritis Rsch. Soc. Internat., Arthritis Health Professions Assoc. (Disting. scholar, 1992), Sigma Xi, Phi Beta Kappa. Democrat. Achievements include research to determine that relaxation training and psychological therapy reduces pain behavior and number of painful joints among patients with rheumatoid arthritis, functional brain activity abnormalities are associated with chronic pain, ethnic differences in pain biomakers and endogenous regulation of pain in patients with knee osteoarthritis, evidence of central sensitization that influences pain among persons with knee osteoarthritis. Office: Univ Ala Divsn Clin Immunol and Rheumatol 177A Shelby Rsch Bldg 1825 Univ Blvd Birmingham AL 35294-0001 Office Phone: 205-934-8550. Business E-Mail: braddog@uab.edu.

BRADLEY, MELVIN LEROY, communications executive; b. Texarkana, Tex., Jan. 6, 1938; s. S.T. and David Ella (Garth) B.; m. Ruth Ann Terry, Mar. 3, 1958; children: Cheryl, Eric, Jacqueline, Tracy. Student, Los Angeles City Coll., 1955, Compton Coll., 1965; BS, Pepperdine U., 1973; LLD (hon.), Shaw U., 1982, Bishop Coll., 1984, Lane Coll., 1986. Real estate broker, Los Angeles, 1960-63; dep. sheriff Los Angeles County, 1963-70; asst. to Gov. Ronald Reagan, 1970-75; dir. public relations Drew Med. Sch., Los Angeles, 1975-77; asst. v.p. United Airlines, 1977-81; sr. policy advisor to Pres. U.S., White House, 1981-82, asst. to Pres. U.S., 1982-89; pres. Garth & Bradley Assocs., Washington, 1989—. Bd. dirs. SMA MicroSys. Republican. Baptist. Office Phone: 301-237-7043. Personal E-mail: garthbrad@yahoo.com.

BRADLEY, STERLING GAYLEN, microbiology and pharmacology researcher; b. Springfield, Mo., Apr. 2, 1932; s. Benn and Lora (Brown) B.; m. Lois Evelyn Lee, May 13, 1951; children: Don, Evelyn, John, Phillip; m. Judith Bond, July 24, 1974; 1 son, Kevin. BA, BS, Mo. State U., 1950; MS, Northwestern U., 1952, PhD (NSF fellow), 1954; PhD certificate med. mycology, Duke U., 1957. Grad. teaching asst. Northwestern U., Evanston, Ill., 1950-51, Abbott research asst., 1951-52, instr. biology, 1954; instr. dept. bacteriology and immunology U. Minn., 1956-57, asst. prof. dept. bacteriology, 1957-59, assoc. prof. dept. microbiology, 1959-63, grad. faculty genetics, 1961-68, prof., 1963-68, chmn. genetics faculty group, 1964; chmn. dept. microbiology Va. Commonwealth U., Richmond, 1968-82, prof. depts. pharmacology and microbiology, 1979-96, dean basic health scis., 1982-93, dean emeritus, 1996—; v.p. acad. affairs U. Md. Biotech Inst., Balt., 1996-99, Pa. State Hershey Med. Ctr., sr. assoc. dir. rsch. affairs, 1999—2005, vis. prof., humanities, 1999—2002, vis. prof., pharmcalogy, 2001—07, vis. prof., biochemical molecular biology, 2005—12, interim dir. technol. devel., 2010—11, BB BioCritique Inc., 2008—11, prin., 2009—11. Vis. worker in pharmacology Cambridge (Eng.) U., 1978; mem. bd. sci. counselors NIH, 1968-72, chmn., 1970-72; mem. Internat. Com. Bacteriol. Systematics, 1966-74, exec. bd., 1970-74; mem. U.S. Pharmacopeial Com. of Revision, 1980-85; coord. Project 3 U.S.-USSR Joint Working Group on Microbiology, 1979-82; v.p. Found. Immunotoxicology, 1985-91, pres., 1991-97. Mem. editl. bd. Proc. Soc. Exptl. Biol. Medicine, 1966-72, Conf. on Anti-microbial Agts., 1960, Jour. Indsl. Microbiology, 1985-95; editor Jour. Bacteriology, 1970-78; contbr. articles to profl. jours. Trustee Southeastern U. Rsch. Assn., Inc., 1990-93; bd. dirs. Sci. Mus. Va. Found., 1993-98. Recipient Charles Porter award, 1983; named Mo. State U. Outstanding Alumnus, 1991, Life Achievement award Sci. Mus. Va., 1996; Eli Lilly postdoctoral fellow U. Wis., 1954-55; NSF postdoctoral fellow dept. genetics, 1955-56; NIH Sr. Fogarty internat. fellow, 1978. Fellow AAAS (life), Va. Acad. Sci. (life, past mem. coun., sec. 1976-77, publs. com., 2012-); mem. Assn. Practical Profl. Ethics, Am. Acad. Microbiology, Am. Chem. Soc., Am. Soc. Microbiology (past mem. council, treas. 1985-91, ethics com. 1997-99, centennial com. chair 1994-99), Soc. Protozoologists, Soc. Indsl. Microbiology (past pres.), Am. Inst. Biol. Sci. (past dir., gen. chmn. 41st Meeting, 1989-90, bd. dirs. 1996-99), Soc. Toxicology, U.S. Fedn. Culture Collections (pres. 1984-86), Internat. Union Microbiol. Socs. (treas. 1994-99), Mycol. Soc. Am. (life), Torrey Bot. Club (life), N.Y. Acad. Scis. (life), Am. Soc. Pharm. and Exptl. Therapeutics, Am. Assn. Immunologists, Sigma Xi (life, pres. chpt. 1975-76, fin. com. 1991-99, audit com., 2010-12), Am. Soc. Biochem. Molecular Biol., Internat. Soc. Proteolysis. Achievements include research in the field of immunotoxicology, interactions between drugs and toxins, role of the protease 'meprin', research integrity. Home: 5300 Longwood Dr Durham NC 27713 Office Phone: 717-903-7533. Personal E-mail: sgbradley1932@alumni.vcu.edu.

BRADLEY, WALTER G., neurologist, educator; MD, Eng., 1963. Cert. American Bd. Psychiatry and Neurology-neurology, 1979. Fellow in neurological apthology Mass. Gen. Hosp., Boston, 1968—69; prof. in neurology Univ. Miami; hosp. affiliation includes Univ. Miami,Jackson Meml. Hosp. Office: University of Miami,Jackson Memorial Hospital 1611 NW 12th Ave Miami FL 33136-1094 Office Phone: 305-585-1111.*

BRADSHAW, JOHN, diagnostic radiologist; MD, Med. U. SC, 1980. Diplomate Am. Bd. Radiology-diagnostic radiology, 1986. Resident surgery Strong Meml. Hosp., Rochester, NY, 1981—82; resident radiation oncology Rochester Gen. Hosp., 1983—86; fellow angiography Presbyn. Univ. Hosp., Pitts., 1986, fellow interventional radiology, 1986; hosp. affiliation includes Lakeland Regional Med. Ctr. Office: Lakeland Regional Medical Center 1324 Lakeland Hills Blvd Lakeland FL 33805 Office Phone: 863-603-6565.

BRADSHAW, KELLIE K., history professor, department chairman; MA in History, Coll. Charleston, SC, 2001. History instr. Germanna Cmty. Coll., Fredericksburg, Va., 2001—, dept. chair humanities, 2004—. Office: Germanna Cmty Coll 10000 Germanna Point Hwy Fredericksburg VA 22408

BRADSHAW, MAJOR WILLIAM, dean, medical educator; b. Marlin, Tex., Feb. 2, 1940; m. Susan Robertson, 1964; children: Heather, Jennifer, Major. BA in Zoology with highest honors, U. Tex., 1962; MS in Anatomy with honors, Baylor Coll. of Medicine, 1966, MD with highest honors, 1967. Diplomate Am. Bd. Internal Medicine, Am. Bd. Infectious Diseases. Intern Osler Med. Svc., Johns Hopkins Hosp., 1968, med. resident, 1969; clin. fellow infectious diseases The Meth. Hosp., Houston, 1971-72; clin. assoc. NIH, 1969-71; asst. prof. medicine and microbiology and immunology Baylor Coll. of Medicine, 1972-76, assoc. prof. medicine, 1976-84, assoc. prof. microbiology-immunology, 1976—, assoc. dean, 1976-93, sr. assoc. dean, 1993-95, prof. medicine, 1984—, prof. molecular virology & microbiology, 2001, John S. Dunn prof. medicine, sr. v.p., dean of med. edn., 2004—06; founding dean U. Botswana Sch. Medicine, 2006—09; dir. Global Health Programs, Baylor Coll. Medicine, 2010—11; physician advisor devel. & alumni, 2011—. Adv. coun. U. Tex. Marine Sci. Inst. Contbr. articles to profl. jours. Fellow ACP (past dir. S.E. dist. Tex.), Infectious Diseases Soc. Am.; mem. AMA, AAUP, Tex. Med. Assn., Harris County Med. Soc., Houston Soc. of Internal Medicine, Am. Soc. Microbiology, Assn. of Am. Med. Colls., Found. for Advanced Edn. in the Scis., Inc., S.W. Assn. of Student Pers. Adminstrs., Tex. Acad. of Physicians, Johns Hopkins U. Alumni Assn., Johns Hopkins Med. and Surg. Soc., Michael E. DeBakey Cardiovascular Soc., Infectious Diseases Soc. of Tex., Alpha Omega Alpha, Sigma Xi, Phi Beta Kappa, Phi Eta Sigma. Avocations: reading, fly fishing, fishing, scuba diving, travel. Office: Baylor Coll Medicine One Baylor Plaza Houston TX 77030 Business E-Mail: majorb@bcm.edu.

BRADY, JAMES JOSEPH, labor arbitrator; b. Jersey City, Mar. 2, 1936; s. James and Anna (Shine) B.; m. Sheila Hartney, July 24, 1965; children: Matthew, Michael, James. BA, U. Notre Dame, 1959, MA in Econs., 1963, PhD in Econs., 1969. Profl. baseball player Detroit Tigers, 1955-60; asst. prof. econs. Ind. U., South Bend, 1965-69; asst. prof., assoc. prof., prof. econs. Old Dominion U., Norfolk, Va., 1969-79; dean Coll. Arts and Scis. Jacksonville (Fla.) U., 1979-83, dean Coll. Bus., 1983-84, v.p. acad. affairs, 1984-88, pres.-elect, 1988-89, pres., 1989-95, prof. econs., 1995—. Spl. magistrate Fla. Pub. Employees Rels. Commn., Tallahassee, 1985—; pvt. labor cons., Jacksonville, 1978-88; mem. Fed. Mediation and Conciliation Svc. Labor Panel, 1985—; perm. arbitrator State Fla. dept. mgmt. svcs., 1999— Author: Arbitration Principles: Layoffs, 1989; co-author: Transportation Noise Pollution, 1970. With U.S. Army, 1959-61. NASA grantee, Norfolk, Va., 1970. Mem. Am. Arbitration Assn. (labor arbitrator 1965—, comml. arbitrator 1987-89), Indsl. Rels. Rsch. Assn., Soc. Profls. in Dispute Resolution, Jacksonville C. of C. (bd. dirs. 1989—). Avocations: fishing, cooking, tennis. Home: 1072 Meadow View Ln Saint Augustine FL 32092-1055 Personal E-mail: jimbrady@sjcgcc.com.

BRADY, JAMES JOSEPH, federal judge; b. St. Louis, Mo., Feb. 29, 1944; s. Robert M. and Arlene (Coleman) B.; m. Karen Nix, June 10, 1967; children: James Sean, Kathleen Melissa. BA in History, Southeastern La. Coll., 1966; JD, La. State U., 1969. Bar: La. 1969, US Ct. Claims 1969, US Ct. Appeals (5th. cir., 11th cir.) 1969, US Supreme Ct. 1969. Ptnr. Gravel, Brady & Berrigan, Alexandria, La., 1969-93; bd. mem. La. Bd. Tax Appeals, 1975—80; pvt. practice atty. La., 1993—2000; pres. Assn. State Dem. Chairs, Washington, 1997; judge US Dist. Ct. (mid. dist.) La., Baton Rouge, 2000—. Chmn. La. Dem. Party, 1990-97, vice chmn., 1996; mem. Dem. Nat. Com., Washington, 1985. Mem. Assn. State Dem. Chairmen (exec. com. 1985-96). Baptist. Office: US Dist Ct 777 Florida St Ste 139 Baton Rouge LA 70801

BRADY, JOAN B., state legislator; b. NYC, May 13, 1952; BA in Journalism, U. SC, 1974. Mayor Town of Arcadia Lakes, SC, 1997—2000; mem. Richland County Coun., SC, 2000—04; mem. Dist. 78 SC House of Reps., 2004—, mem. Ethics Com. & Labor, Commerce and Industry Com. State dir. Nat. Found. Women Legislators, 2008—. Republican. Office: 414B Blatt Bldg Columbia SC 29201 Mailing: PO Box 61047 Columbia SC 29260 Home Phone: 803-786-9786; Office Phone: 803-734-3027. Business E-Mail: BradyJ@schouse.org.

BRADY, KATHLEEN T., psychiatrist, educator; PhD in Pharmacology; MD, Med. U. SC, 1985. Diplomate Am. Bd. Psychiatry and Neurology-psychiatry, 1992, Am. Bd. Psychiatry and Neurology-addiction psychiatry, 2002. Resident psychiatry Med. Univ. SC, 1986—89, fellow addiction psychiatry, 1986—89, asst. dean for clin. rsch., 2005, dir. gen. clin. rsch. ctr., 2005, assoc. dean clin. and translational rsch., dir. clin. and translational rsch. ctr., prof. psychiatry; dir. Addiction Psychiatry Fellowship Program, 1994—2004. Pres. Am. Assn. of Edn. and Rsch. in Substance Abuse, 1994—96. Recipient Betty Ford award, 2001, Women of Achievement award, Gov. Jim Hodges, 2010; grantee First Mid-career Devel. Grant (K-24), Med. Univ. SC, 1999. Mem.: Am. Acad. of Addiction Psychiatry (pres.). Office: Medical University of South Carolina Department of Psychiatry 67 President St Box 250861 Charleston SC 29425 Office Phone: 843-792-5205. Office Fax: 843-792-4817. E-mail: bradyk@musc.edu.

BRADY, KEVIN PATRICK, United States Representative from Texas; b. Vermillion, SD, Apr. 11, 1955; m. Cathy Patronella Brady; 2 children. BS in Mass Comm., U. SD, Vermillion, 1990. Pres. South Montgomery County-Woodlands C. of C., 1985—96; mem. from Dist. 15 Tex. House of Reps., 1991—97; mem. US Congress from 8th Tex. dist., 1997—, dep. whip. Active Saints Simon and Jude Cath. Ch. Recipient Achievement award, Tex. Conservative Coalition, Scholars Achievement award, Excellence in Pub. Svc., North Harris Montgomery Cmty. Coll. Dist., Support for Family Issues award, Tex. Ext. Homemakers Assn., Victims Rights Equalizer award, Texans for Equal Justice Ctr.; named Outstanding Young Texan, Tex. Jaycees, Legis. Standout, Dallas Morning News; named one of 10 Best Legislators for Families and Children, State Bar Tex. Mem.: Rotary. Republican. Roman Catholic. Office: US House of Representatives 301 Cannon House Office Bldg Washington DC 20515 also: 200 River Pointe Ste 304 Conroe TX 77304 Office Phone: 202-225-4901.*

BRADY, PATRICK GEORGE, gastroenterologist; BS in Pre-Medicine, Seton Hall U., 1964; MD, U. of Medicine and Dentistry of NJ, 1968. Diplomate Am. Bd. Internal Medicine, 1972, Am. Bd. Internal Medicine-gastroenterology, 1973, lic. Fla., 1973. Intern internal medicine Shands Jacksonville, 1969, resident internal medicine, 1971, fellow gastroenterology, 1975, The Johns Hopkins Hosp., 1972; hosp. affiliation includes Tampa Gen. Hosp. Office: Tampa General Hospital 1 Tampa General Circle Tampa FL 33606-3508 Office Phone: 813-844-7000.

BRADY, ROBERT, communications educator; Chmn. dept. comm. U. Ark., Fayetteville, 1993—. Contbr. articles to profl. jours. Office: Dept Comm/Univ Ark 417 Kimpel Hall Fayetteville AR 72701 Business E-Mail: rbrady@uark.edu.

BRADY, THERESA L., state banking agency administrator; b. Columbus, Miss. BS in Banking, Miss. State U.; JD, Miss. Coll., Clinton. Joined as a bank examiner Miss. Dept. Banking and Consumer Fin., 1981, dir. consumer fin. divsn., 1998—2000, dep. commr., 2000—11, commr., 2011—; former bond dir. Miss. State Treasury Dept.; former asst. city atty. City of Jackson, Miss. Mem.: Nat. Assn. Consumer Credit Administrators (sec.-treas., v.p., past pres.), American Assn. Residential Mortgage Regulators, Miss. Bar Assn. Office: Mississippi Dept Banking and Counsumer Finance PO Drawer 23729 Jackson MS 39225-3729 Office Phone: 601-359-1031. Business E-Mail: theresa.brady@dbcf.ms.gov.

BRADY, THOMAS M., federal agency administrator, educator; BA in Edn. (Social Scis.), Niagara U., NY; MA in Human Resources Mgmt., Pepperdine U., Calif.; grad., Broad Supts. Acad. COO Fairfax County Pub. Schs., DC Pub. Schs.; CEO Sch. Dist. Phila.; supt. Providence Sch. Dept., RI; COO GEMS Edn.; sr. advisor Pub. Sector Svcs. Team Alvarez & Marsal; dir. Dept. Def. Edn. Activity, Alexandria, Va., 2014—. Former commd. officer US Army. Office: Department of Defense Education Activity 4800 Mark Center Dr Alexandria VA 22350

BRAFFMAN, BRUCE, diagnostic radiologist; MD, Yeshiva U., 1982. Diplomate Am. Bd. Radiology-diagnostic radiology, 1982. Resident diagnostic radiology Montefiore Med. Ctr., Bronx, 1983—86; fellow neuroradiology Univ. Penn. Hosp., Phila., 1986; hosp. affiliations include Meml. Regional Hosp., Radiology Assocs. of Hollywood. Office: Radiology Associates of Hollywood Ste 200 9050 Pines Blvd Hollywood FL 33024 Office Phone: 954-437-4800. Office Fax: 954-437-6628.

BRAITHWAITE, WILFRED JOHN, retired physics professor; b. Ferndale, Wash., Apr. 11, 1940; s. John Alfred and Joyce Elinor (Gunderson) B.; m. Wanda Pearl Chism, June 3, 1961 (div. 1975). BS in Physics with honors, Seattle Pacific U., 1962; MS in Physics, U. Wash., 1965, PhD in Physics, 1971; postgrad, Sci. Edn. U. Tex., 1988—89. Instr. physics Princeton U., NJ, 1970-72; asst. prof. physics U. Tex., Austin, 1972-79, rsch. scientist faculty, 1979-81; tech. and sci. cons. Austin, 1981-89; assoc. prof. physics U. Ark., Little Rock, 1989-95, prof. physics, 1995—2007, prof. emeritus, 2007—. Vis. staff mem. Los Alamos Nat. Lab., N.Mex., 1975-76, 78-79; vis. scientist Ind. U., Bloomington, 1990-96; affiliate prof. physics U. Wash., Seattle, 1991-96; sci. assoc. PPE divsn. CERN, Geneva, Switzerland, 1992-2007; guest scientist Brookhaven Nat. Lab., Upton, NY, 1992-2007; grant referee Ark. Sci. and Tech. Authority, 1990-2007; cons. for GE Corp. R&D, 2002-07; lectr. in field. Numerous unedited contbns.; jour. referee Phys. Rev. C and Phys. Rev. Letters, 1970-2007, Found. Physics, Assoc. Ed. Ark. Acad. Sci., 2000-07. U.S. Dept. Energy rsch. grantee, 1992-95, 99-2007, Ark. Sci. and Tech. Authority rsch. grantee, 1993-94, 96-98; numerous grants from NSF, Dept. of Energy, Robert A Welch Found. Mem. IEEE, Am. Phys. Soc., Nat. Assn. for Rsch. in Sci. Teaching, N.Y. Acad. Sci., Ark. Acad. Sci. Achievements include rsch. on time reversal invariance; high excitation neutron particle-hole states; charge-dependent matrix elements in light nuclei; method for determining rotational symmetries of nuclear states using heavy ions; multiply-excited atomic states in helium-like and lithium-like oxygen; strength of the 3-alpha process in stellar helium burning; method for identifying antimatter stars; large isospin mixing in light nuclei via scattering comparisons of positive and negative pions near the pion-nucleon resonance, microwave refrigeration; measurement limits on source sizes formed in symmetric collisions of ultra-relativistic heavy nuclei; method for separating charged kaons and pions in Time Projection Chambers via in-flight decays using their known isotropic emissions in both COM frames; instrument design for high-energy nuclear physics, examining models to slow aging. Home: 1 Broadmoor Dr Little Rock AR 72204-4818

BRAMAN, NORMAN, automotive and former sports team executive; b. West Chester, Pa., Aug. 22, 1932; s. Harry and Katie (Rappaport) B.; m. Irma Miller, Sept. 30, 1956; children: Debra Braman Shack, Susan Lynn. BA, Temple U., 1955. With mktg. and sales dept. Seagrams Distbrs., NYC, 1955-57; founder Keystone Stores, Phila., 1957-72; pres. Braman Enterprises, Miami, Fla., 1972—; owner Phila. Eagles, 1985—94; chmn. ARCONA, Miami, 1985-87. Mem. U.S. Holocaust Meml. Council; campaign chmn. United Jewish Appeal, Miami; bd. govs. U. Miami Med. Sch.; bd. dirs. Am. Israel Pub. Affairs Com., Miami; mem. Dade County Planning and Adv. Bd.; founder, trustee Mt. Sinai Med. Ctr., Miami; bd. govs. Tel Aviv U.; trustee United Israel Appeal Named one of Top 200 Collectors, ARTnews Mag., 2004—12, Forbes 400: Richest Americans, 2009. Mem. Greater Miami C. of C. Republican. Office: Braman Enterprises 2060 Biscayne Blvd Fl 2 Miami FL 33137-5024

BRAMANTI, FRANK J., retired insurance company executive; CPA. Mgmt. positions through exec. v.p., CFO, interim pres. HCC Ins. Holdings, Houston, 1980—2001; bd. dir. HCC Insurance Holdings, Inc., Houston, 2001—; CEO HCC Ins. Holdings, Houston, 2006—09. Office: HCC Insurance Holdings 13403 Northwest Fwy Houston TX 77040

BRAMBLE, FRANK P., bank executive; b. 1948; Chmn. U. Md.; with Md. Nat. Bank, 1968—78, v.p., 1978—85, sr. v.p., 1985, MNC Financial, Inc., 1987—91, COO, 1991—, CEO, pres., chmn.; pres., CEO Allfirst Bank, 1994—99; CEO, USA Allfirst Fin. Inc. (subs. of Allied Irish Banks, PLC), 1998—2002; chmn. Allfirst Fin. Inc., 1999—2002, Allfirst Bank, 1999—2002; exec. vice chmn., vice chmn. MBNA Bank, 2002, MBNA Corp., 2002. Bd. dirs. Allfirst Bank, 1994—2002, Allfirst Fin. Inc., 1994—2002, Constellation Energy Group Inc., 2002, Bank of America Corp., 2006. Office: Bank of America Corp 100 N Tryon St Charlotte NC 28255 Office Phone: 704-386-5681. Office Fax: 704-386-6699. Business E-Mail: frank.bramble@bankofamerica.com.

BRAMLETTE, DAVID C., III, federal judge; b. New Orleans, Nov. 27, 1939; BA, Princeton U., 1962; JD, U. Miss., 1965. Assoc., then ptnr. Adams, Forman, Truly, Ward & Bramlette, Natchez, Miss., 1975-91; spl. cir. judge Dist. Ct. (6th dist.) Miss., 1977, 79; judge US Dist. Ct. (so. dist.) Miss., Natchez, 1991—2006, sr. judge Jackson, 2006—. Trustee Miss. Nature Conservancy, 1990—; pres. BBCHA, 1989-90; active Arcole Hunting Camp, Ducks Unlimited, Nat. Wild Turkey Fedn.; mem. adv. bd. Natchez Lit. Celebration. Office: US Dist Ct PO Box 928 Natchez MS 39121-0928 Office Phone: 601-442-3006.

BRANAN, CLIFF, state legislator; b. Okla. City, 1961; m. Connell Branan; children: Ford, Langley. BBA, Univ. Okla. Broker CB Richard Ellis Comml., 1984—95; founder pres. Branan Property Co., 1995—; mem. Dist. 40 Okla. State Senate, 2002—. Mem.: Okla. Philharmonic (assoc. bd. mem.), City Arts Ctr., Okla. Bethany C. of C., Comml. Real Estate Coun., Rotary Club. Republican. Episcopalian. Office: 2300 N Lincoln Blvd Rm 417C Oklahoma City OK 73105 Office Phone: 405-521-5543, 405-843-5064. Business E-Mail: branan@oksenate.gov.

BRANCH, DANIEL HUGH, state legislator, lawyer; b. Montreal, Quebec, Can., Mar. 5, 1958; arrived in US, 1968; s. Charles Leon and Sylvia Lee (Boswell) Branch; m. Stacey Jeane Salvino, Sept. 15, 1984; children: Daniel H. Jr., Spencer Hollon, Catherine Lee, Charles Victor, Sarah Jeane. BA in Am. Studies summa cum laude, BS in Acctg. summa cum laude, Okla. Christian Coll., 1980; JD, So. Meth U., 1983. Bar: Tex. 1983, NY 1986, DC 1989. Mem. staff U.S. Senator John Tower of Tex., Washington, 1980; law clk. to Chief Justice Jack Pope Supreme Ct. of Tex., Austin, 1983-84; assoc. Gibson, Dunn & Crutcher, NYC, 1984-86, Baker & Botts, Dallas, 1987-91; founding shareholder Langley & Branch PC, Dallas; atty., shareholder Winstead Sechrest and Minick, 1999—; mem. Dist. 108 Tex. House of Representatives, 2002—. Bd. dirs. Tex. Pub. Fin. Authority, Austin, John G. Tower Ctr., So. Meth. U., 1997—; mem. US exec. com. British-Am. Project, Washington, chmn., 1995—97. Contbr. articles to profl. jours. Tex. state adminstr. Victory Fund Reagan/Bush 1984 Campaign; spl. counsel for debates Luce Gov. Campaign, Tex., 1990, George W. Bush Gov. Campaign, 1994; Tex. state vice chair Bush/Quayle, 1992; bd. dirs. Christian Svcs. SW, Dallas, 1988—, chmn., 1991—96; hon. mem. Tex. Inangural Com., 1995; trustee Fund for Am. Studies, Washington, 1995. Fellow Birtish-Am. Project, Johns Hopkins U., 1992; Dewitt Wallace Reader's Digest Scholar, Okla. Christian Coll., 1976—80, Barry M. Goldwater Scholar, Georgetown U., 1977, Inst. Comparative Politics and Econ. Sys. diplomate, 1977. Mem.: ABA, DC Bar Assn., Assn. of Bar of City of NY, Dallas Bar Assn., Tex. Bar Assn. Republican. Church Of Christ. Avocations: golf, tennis, hockey, sailing, horseback riding. Office: Room E1.308 Capitol Extension PO Box 2910 Austin TX 78768 Address: 3953 Maple Ave Ste 100 Dallas TX 75219 Office Phone: 512-463-0367, 214-745-5768. Fax: 512-463-5896.

BRANCH, JOHN CURTIS, biology professor, lawyer; b. Buffalo, Okla., Oct. 1, 1934; s. Ernest Samuel and Ethel Imogene (Parsons) B.; m. Jacqueline Joyce Davis, July 20, 1960; children: Kim Renee, Karla Jean, Kay Lynn. BS, Northwestern Okla. State U., 1959; MS, U. Okla., 1963, PhD, 1965; JD, Okla. City U., 1980. Bar: Okla. 1980. Asst. prof. biology dept. Okla. City U., 1964-67, assoc. prof. biology dept., 1967-75, prof. biology dept., 1975—. With U.S. Army, 1955-57. Mem. Okla. County Bar Assn., Okla. Acad. Sci., Okla. Bar Assn., Beta Beta Beta. Methodist. Avocations: reading, sports, travel. Home: 2705 Abbey Rd Oklahoma City OK 73120-2702 Office: 1525 SW 89th St Oklahoma City OK 73159 Office Phone: 405-634-7600.

BRAND, BILL, retail executive; b. Buffalo; BS in Comm., Ohio U., 1983. Prodr. WSYX-TV, 1987—88; assoc. prodr. KCAL-TV, 1990—91; asst. news dir. KHQ-TV, 1991—93, WKMG-TV, 1992—94; news dir. WPRI, 1994—96; v.p., programming, prodn. VH1, 1996—2001; sr. v.p., reality programming Lifetime, 2001—06; sr. v.p., programming HSN, Inc., 2006—08, sr. v.p., programming, advanced svcs., 2008—09, exec. v.p., programming, mktg. and bus. development, 2009—. Recipient Edward R. Murrow award. Office: HSN Inc 1 HSN Dr Saint Petersburg FL 33729 Office Phone: 727-872-1000. Business E-Mail: bill.brand@hsn.net.

BRAND, EDWARD CABELL, retail executive; b. Salem, Va., Apr. 11, 1923; s. William F. and Ruth (Cabell) B.; m. Shirley Hurt, June 20, 1964; children: Sylvia, Miriam, Liza, Richie (dec.), John, Edward (dec.), Marshall (dec.), Caroline. Grad., Va. Mil. Inst., 1944; HHD (hon.), Roanoke Coll., 1997, Washington and Lee U., 1999, Ferrum Coll., 2005, Va. Western Coll., 2005. Dept. of State econ. analyst, intelligence office Berlin Mil. Govt., 1947-49; v.p. Ortho-Vent Shoe Co., 1949-62; pres. Brand Edmonds Assocs. Advertising, 1962-66, chmn. bd., 1962-81; founder, pres. Stuart McGuire Co., Salem, Va., 1962-85, chmn. bd., chief exec. officer, 1973-85; chmn. emeritus, cons. Stuart McGuire Co. (merged with Home Shopping (TV) Network), 1985-86; pres. Recovery Systems, Inc., Salem, Va., 1986—2005, Brand-Edmonds Assoc. Advertising, 1956—66, chmn. bd., 1962—81. Rsch. assoc., former instr. bus. adminstrn. and sales mgmt. Roanoke Coll., 1986-2005 Author: If Not Me Then Who, 2008. Chmn. Va. State Bd. Health, 1989-93; pres., founder, chmn. Cabell Brand Ctr. for Internat. Poverty and Resource Studies, 1988-; former dir. Southeast Rural Assistance Project Inn; cons. Rainwater Mgmt. Solutions; former mem. Bus. Leadership Adv. Council.; founder, pres. Total Action Against Poverty, Roanoke Valley, 1965-95; pres. Pvt. Sector Commn. Va. Community Action Agys., 1986-88; mem. Gov.'s Commn. on Fed. Funding of State Domestic Program, 1986-88; trustee Council on Religion and Internat. Affairs, Ethics Resource Ctr., Heinz Ctr. Sci., Econs. and Environ.; bd. dirs. Roanoke Coun. Cmty. Svcs., Woodlands Conf. divsn. Woodlands Ctr. for Future Research and the Houston Area Research Ctr., Global Water, Washington, Va. Health Care Found., Richmond, Va., 1993-2000, Va. Found. for the Humanities and Pub. Policy, Charlottesville, 1993-99, Blue Ridge Pub. TV, Roanoke, Va., 1993—2006, Action Alliance for Va. Children and Youth, Richmond, 1994-2000, Va. Conservation Network, Richmond, 1996—2009; bd. trustees Western Va. Land Trust, Roanoke, Va., 1995-2000; assoc. World Resources Inst., Washington, 1985., dir. Found. Alternative & Intrative medicine, 2005-, advisor to pres. Lynchburg, 2010-, Served from pvt. to capt. AUS, 1942-46, ETO. Decorated Bronze Star. Named Businessman in U.S. who has done most to help disadvantaged people, Vista, 1980; recipient LBJ Humanitarian nat. award, 1989, Outstanding Citizen Rotary Club, 1999, Lifetime Achivement award Salem Rocule County C. od C., 2010, John W Hancoch award, 1996, medal Nat. Soc. Daughters Am. Revolution, 2010, Heros award Am. Red Cross, 2010 Mem. NAS (coun., pres. cir.), Social Venture Network, Direct Selling Assn. (past dir., chmn. named to Hall of Fame), U.S. C. of C., Conf. Bd. (exec. coun.), World Pres. Assn. (past dir., chmn. Argentina Conf. 1988), Roanoke Touchdown Club (past pres.), Valley Torch Club (past pres.), Roanoke Sales Execs. (past dir.), Rotary (past. pres. Salem), US Assn. Club Rome, Roanoke Valley Hist. Soc, Home: 701 W Main St Salem VA 24153-3513 Office: PO Box 429 Salem VA 24153-0429 Office Phone: 540-389-6367. Personal E-mail: scbrand25@comcast.net.

BRAND, ELTON TYRON, professional basketball player; b. Peekskill, NY, Mar. 11, 1979; m. Seneca Shahara Simmons, 2006. Attended, Duke U., Durham, NC, 1997—98. Forward Chgo. Bulls, 1999—2001, LA Clippers, 2001—08, Phila. 76ers, 2008—12, Dallas Mavericks, 2012—13, Atlanta Hawks, 2013—. Mem. USA Basketball Men's Sr. Nat. Team, 2003. Founder Elton Brand Found., 2000—. Recipient Magic Johnson award, Profl. Basketball Writers Assn., 2002, Sportsmanship award, NBA, 2004, 2006; named Player of Yr., Atlantic Coast Conf., 1999, USA Basketball Man of Yr., 1999, Nat. Coll. Basketball Player of Yr., AP, 1999, First Team All-Am., 1999, Rookie Challenge MVP, NBA, 2000, Co-Rookie of Yr., 2000; named to All-Rookie First Team, 2000, Western Conf. All-Star Team, 2002, 2006, All-NBA Second Team, 2006. Achievements include becoming the first Duke University Blue Devil selected #1 overall in the NBA Draft, 1999. Office: Atlanta Hawks Centennial Tower 101 Marietta St NW Ste 1900 Atlanta GA 30303*

BRANDENBURG, DAVID SAUL, gastroenterologist, educator; b. Linz, Austria, Apr. 12, 1948; arrived in US, 1948; s. Mayer and Syda Brandenburg; m. Bette Ellen Hirschberg, Aug. 8, 1971; children: Stacey, Mark, Marci. BA, Rutgers U., 1968; MD, Georgetown U., 1972. Bd. cert. internal medicine; bd. cert. GI. Intern, resident R.I. Hosp.-Brown U. Affiliated, Providence, 1972-75; gastroenterology fellow Emory U., Atlanta, 1975-77; pvt. practice Atlanta Digestive Diseases and Internal Medicine, 1977-82, Brandenburg and Kramer M.D., P.C., Atlanta, 1983-97; clin. asst. prof. medicine Emory U. Sch. Medicine, Atlanta, 1977—2008; with Atlanta Gastroenterology Assocs., 1997—. Med. dir. North Atlanta Endoscopy Ctr., Atlanta, 1986-2002; sec., v.p., pres. Ga. Soc. GI Endoscopy, Atlanta, 1980-86; chmn., med. adv. com. Ga. chpt. Crohn's and Colitis Found., Atlanta, 1995-97. Bd. trustees Temple Emmanuel, Dunwoody, Ga., 1985-91, 95-96, treas., 1988-89, v.p., 1990-91. Fellow Am. Coll. Gastroenterology (gov. 1991-95); mem. Am. Gastroenterol. Assn., Am. Soc. Gastrointestinal Endoscopy. Office: 5671 Peachtree Dunwoody Rd Ste 600 Atlanta GA 30342-2311 Office Phone: 404-257-9000.

BRANDENSTEIN, DANIEL CHARLES, astronaut, retired military officer; b. Watertown, Wis., Jan. 17, 1943; s. Walter C. and Agnes (Holzworth) B.; m. Jane A. Wade, Jan. 2, 1966; 1 dau., Adelle. BS, U. Wis., River Falls, 1965; postgrad., U.S. Naval Text Pilot Sch., Patuxent River, Md., 1971. Commd. officer U.S. Navy, 1965, advanced through grades to capt., 1984, ret., 1993, student aviator Pensacola, Fla., 1965-67, aviator Whidbey Island, Wash., 1967-71, test pilot Patuxent River, Md., 1971-74, aviator Whidbey Island, Wash., 1974-78; astronaut NASA Johnson Space Ctr., Houston, 1978-93, chief astronaut office, 1987-93; dir. program development Loral Space Info. Sys., Houston, 1993-96; exec. v.p. Kistler Aerospace Corp., Kirkland, Wash., 1996-99; v.p. Lockheed Martin Space Ops., 1999—2007; exec. v.p., coo United Space Alliance, 2007—12. Decorated Legion of Honor (France), 34 medals and awards USN, 1968-93; recipient Disting. Alumnus award U. Wis., 1982, Yuri Gagarin Gold medal Fedn. Aeronautique Internationale, 1990, Laurel Award, Space/Missiles, Aviation Week & Space Tech., 1993, Haley Space Flight award Am. Inst. of Aeronautics and Astronautics, 1993; named to Astronaut Hall Fame, 2003. Mem. AIAA (Haley Space Flight award 1993), Soc. Exptl. Text Pilots (Ivan C. Kinchloe award 1992), Astronaut Scholarship Found. (chmn.), U.S. Naval Inst., Assn. Space Explorers. Business E-Mail: danb25m@aol.com.

BRANDES, JEFF PAUL, state legislator; b. St. Petersburg, Fla., Feb. 12, 1976; m. Natalie Brandes; children: Charlotte. BS in Bus. Adminstrn., Carson-Newman Coll., Jefferson City, Tenn., 1999. Real estate profl.; mem. Dist. 52 Fla. House Of Representatives, 2011—. Bd. dirs. Bay Cities Bank, Christian Legacy Found., First Night of St. Petersburg, Haines City Econ. Devel. Coun. Transp. officer USAR, 1996—2007, 1st lt. USAR, 2003—04, Iraq. Republican. Office: 3637 4th St N Ste 101 Saint Petersburg FL 33704-1300 also: Fla House of Reps 1301 The Capitol 402 S Monroe St Tallahassee FL 32399-1300 Office Phone: 727-552-2573, 850-488-5719.

BRANDMAIER, JEFF, information technology executive; MS in Info. Sys., Stockton State Coll.; MBA in Fin., Pace U. Sr. v.p., in terim chief info. officer First Union; CEO Fiserv SourceOne; mgr. IBM Corp.; sr. mgr. KPMG Nolan, Norton & Co.; chief info. officer The Money Store, 1995—2001; sr. v.p., chief info. officer H&R Block, Inc., Kans. City, Mo., 2001; CEO Mgmt. & Tech. Consultants. Avocation: amateur competitive equestrian. Office: Management & Technology Consultants Inc 160 Green Oaks Ln Southlake TX 76092-6130 Office Phone: 972-333-6766.

BRANDON, MARCUS, state legislator; b. Jan. 18, 1975; Attended, NC Agrl. & Tech. State U., Greensboro. Founder KMB Consulting; nat. account exec. NGP Software; nat. fin. dir. to Dennis Kucinich, 2008; mem. Dist. 60 NC House of Representatives, 2011—. Democrat. Mailing: 200 Oak St Apt 3 High Point NC 27260 Office: North Carolina House of Representatives 16 W Jones St Room 1209 Raleigh NC 27601-1096 Office Phone: 336-307-3917, 919-733-5825, 336-987-3357. Business E-Mail: Marcus.Brandon@ncleg.net.

BRANDOW, PETER B., lawyer; b. 1961; Atty. Simpson Thatcher & Bartlett, 1989—99; v.p. Regal Cinemas, Inc., 1999—2000, gen. counsel, sec., 1999—2001, sr. v.p., 2000—01; exec. v.p., gen. counsel & sec. Regal Entertainment Group, Knoxville, Tenn., 2001—. Office: Regal Entertainment Group 7132 Regal Ln Knoxville TN 37918 Office Phone: 865-922-1123. Office Fax: 865-922-3188. Business E-Mail: peter.brandow@regmovies.com.

BRANDS, JAMES EDWIN, retired medical products executive; b. Lebanon, Ind., July 5, 1937; s. Edwin Herman and Pearl Irene (Brown) B.; m. Gail Marian Knight, Sept. 12, 1959; children: Jeffrey, Scot, Alan, Susan. AB, Wesleyan U., Middletown, Conn., 1959; MBA, U. Chgo., 1961; JD, Kennedy-Western U., Boise, Idaho, 1992. CPA, Mo. Staff acct., mgr. Arthur Andersen, Chgo., 1961-71, ptnr. St. Louis, 1971-82; sr. v.p. Scherer-Storz, Inc., St. Louis, 1982-86, bd. dirs.; vice chmn., CFO Scherer Healthcare Inc., Atlanta, 1982-95; exec. v.p. Scherer Sci. Ltd., Atlanta, 1986-95; chmn., CEO Marquest Med. Products, Inc., Denver, 1993-95; CFO Wilson Pest Control, Inc., Atlanta, 1997-99; sr. exec. v.p. Able Telcom Holding Corp., Atlanta, 1999—2001. Pres. Brands & Co, 1981—. Mem. AICPA, Mo. Soc. CPAs, Bellerive Country Club (St. Louis), Country Club of the South (Atlanta). Home: 4330 Bancroft Valley Alpharetta GA 30022-5175 Personal E-mail: brandsj@bellsouth.net.

BRANDT, FREDRIC S., dermatologist; Attended, Drexel U., Phila., 1975. Diplomate Am. Bd. Internal Medicine, Am. Bd. Dermatology. Cancer rschr. Sloan-Kettering; cons. and prin. investigator Medicis Aesthetics, Mentor Biologics, Dermik, ColBar, Contura, Revance, Isolagen, Merz, Lumenis, Cutera, Palomar, Johnson & Johnson, Stiefel-GSK, Allergan. Author: (profl. manuscripts) 10 Minutes 10 Years, Age-Less, (profl. publs.) Brunner's gland adenoma associated with high output congestive heart failure, 1976, Guttate psoriasis following sterptococal throat infection, 1979, Topical nitrogen musard therapy in multicentric reticulohistiocytosis, 1982, and numerous others. Office: Advanced Cosmetic Dermatology Ste 200 4425 Ponce de Leon Blvd Miami FL 33146 Mailing: Advanced Cosmetic Dermatology 2nd Fl 323 East 34th St New York NY 10016 Office Phone: 305-443-6606, 212-889-7096. Office Fax: 305-443-4890, 212-686-7305.

BRANDT, MARY L., medical educator; MD, Baylor Coll. Medicine, Houston, Tex., 1983. Prof. surgery, pediat. and ethics Baylor Coll. Medicine, Houston, 1990—. Office: Baylor College Medicine One Baylor Plz Houston TX 77030 Business E-Mail: mary.brandt@bcm.edu.*

BRANDWEIN, RUTH ANN, social welfare educator, professor, dean emeritus, social services administrator, writer; b. Bklyn., Apr. 24, 1940; d. Charles and Kate (Berkowitz) Solin; divorced; children: Lorena Lisa Epstein, Garth Whitman. BA magna cum laude, Bklyn. Coll., 1960; MSW, U. Wash., 1970; PhD, Brandeis U., 1978. Libr. trainee Bklyn. Pub. Libr., 1960—61; substitute tchr. N.Y.C. Bd. Edn., 1961—63; recreation dir. Seattle Park Dept., 1964—66; exec. dir. Ctrl. Seattle Commn. Coun., 1967—69; rsch. assoc. Harvard U./Lab.

Comm. Psychiatry, Boston, 1971—72; asst. prof., chair, comm. org. Boston U. Sch. Social Work, 1973—78; dir., assoc. prof. U. Iowa Sch. Social Work, Iowa City, 1978—81; dean Sch. Social Welfare SUNY, Stony Brook, 1981—89, prof. Sch. Social Welfare, 1981—2010, dir. Social Justice Ctr., 2001—10; commr. Suffolk County Dept. Social Svcs., Hauppauge, NY, 1989—93; holder Spafford Endowed chair U. Utah Sch. Social Work, 1994—96. Vis. prof. U. Wash. Sch. Social Work, 2000-01, Addis Abada U., Ethiopia, 2009; co-founder Women's Rsch. Ctr. of Boston, 1971-78; co-dir. Women's Com. of 100, 1995—; cons. U.S. Senate Subcom. on Vets.' Affairs, 1971; guardian ad litem Family Ct., Middlesex County, Mass.; expert witness Grevatt vs. U. Minn., Duluth; vis. assoc. Inst. Policy Studies, 1986-87; lead reviewer Nat. Inst. Justice, 1997-98; presenter in field. Author: Battered Women, Children and Welfare Reform: The Ties That Bind, 1999; editor: Affilia; founding editor, mem. corp. bd. Affilia: Jour. Women and Social Work, 1985—, mem. editl. bd., 2004-, book rev. editor, 2004—09; contbr. articles to profl. jours. and chpts. to books and encyclopedia. Mem. Nat. Adv. Coun. Violence Against Women, 1997—2000; mem. steering com. LI Fund for Women and Girls, 1993—2000; mem. alumni bd. Heller Sch. Brandeis U., 2003—09; chair Nominating Com., 2008—09; mem. adv. bd. LI Housing Svcs., 2004—; bd. dirs., v.p. Kehillath Shalom Synagogue, Cold Spring Harbor, NY, 1987—90, bd. dirs., 2001—06, chair social action com., 2001—06; bd. dirs. gov.'s mental health coun. NY, 1990—2002; chmn. mental health coun. NYS Govs., 1992—95; chmn. exec. task force family violence Suffolk County, 1988—94; bd. dirs. United Way LI, Melville, NY, 1982—88, mem. allocations com., 2002—05; bd. dirs. Suffolk Cmty. Coun., Islandia, NY, 1981—97; bd. dirs., mem. exec. com. Am. Jewish Congress, LI, 1989; bd. dirs. NY Civil Liberties Union, 1994—98; adv. bd. LI Progressive Coalition, 1998—2010; bd. dirs. LI Cmty. Found., 1994—96, Hudson- Peconic Planned Parenthood, 1997—2005; mem. Action Fund bd. Hudson-Peconic Planned Parenthood, 2003—10, sec., 2007—; bd. dirs. LI Health and Welfare Coun., 1996—2001, Suffolk Coalition Against Domestic Violence, 2003—10, v.p., 2006—. Recipient Disting. Alumnus award U. Wash. Sch. Social Work, Seattle, 1989, Congrl. award Congressman Mrazek, Suffolk County, N.Y., Hon. Supporter award Women on the Job; Vol. Svc. award, Suffolk County Human Rights Commn., 2003, Stony Brook Hillel Found. award, 2005, Jewish Reconstructionist Fedn. award, 2005, Social Justice award, Stony Brook U., 2010. Mem.: NASW (bd. dirs. 1991—96, 2d v.p. 1994—96, pres.-elect NY state chpt. 1997—98, pres. 1998—2000, nat. com. on women's issues 2000—03, Suffolk County Social Worker of Yr. 1989, Lifetime Achievement award 2003), Huntington NY NOW (bd. dirs. 1982—91, chair 1988—91), Coun. Social Work Edn. (chair women's commn. 1980—83, bd. dirs. 1987—89, chair internat. commn. 1988—89), NY Pub. Welfare Assn. (bd. dirs. 1990—93), Phi Beta Kappa. Office: SUNY Stony Brook Sch Social Welfare Health Sci Ctr Level 2 Rm 093 Stony Brook NY 11794-0001 Home: 1503 Clower Creek Dr HA162 Sarasota FL 34231

BRANHAM, LESTER P., JR., state legislator; b. Camden, Dec. 14, 1933; s. Lester P. and Roberta H. Branham; m. Dorothy Ruth Hayes Branham, Aug. 10, 1956; children: Lester P. III, Maria Ruth Matthews. BA, Wake Forest U., 1955. Mem. Dist. 61 SC House of Reps., SC, 2003—, mem. Edn. and Pub. Works Com. Mem.: Palmetto Health Alliance, Midwestern Bapt. Theol. Seminary (chmn. exec. com. 1971—72), Furman U. (trustee 1973—79), SC Bapt. Conv. (gen. bd. mem. 1967—72). Democrat. Baptist. Mailing: 118 Lockewood Dr Lake City SC 29560 Office: 314B Blatt Bldg Columbia SC 29201 E-mail: branham@scstatehouse.net.

BRANHAM, MACK CARISON, JR., retired religious organization administrator, minister; b. Columbia, SC, Apr. 20, 1931; s. Mack Carison and Laura Pauline (Sexton) Branham; m. Jennie Louise Jones, Dec. 17, 1953; children: Kenneth Gary, Charles Michael, Keith Robert, Laurie Lynn. BS, Clemson U., 1953; MDiv, Luth. Theol. Sem., 1958, STM, 1963; MS, George Washington U., 1968; PhD, Ariz. State U., 1974; DD (hon.), Newberry Coll., 1990; LLD (hon.), Clemson U., 1991. Ordained to ministry Luth. Ch., 1958. Commd. 2d lt. USAF, 1953, advanced through grades to col., 1959; pastor Providence Nazareth Luth. Ch., Lexington, SC, 1958-59; adminstrv. asst., registrar Luth. Theol. So. Sem., 1979-81, v.p. adminstrn., 1981-82, pres., 1982-92, pres. emeritus, 1992—. Instr., counselor in field. Editor: Air Force Chaplain newsletter, 1975—77. Decorated Bronze Star, Legion of Merit; named to Order of Palmetto (S.C.), Sr. Sports Hall of Fame, 2012. Mem.: Greater Chapin C. of C. (bd. dirs. 1998—2000, pres. 2000), Rotary (dist. gov. 2004—05). Lutheran. Home: 109 Laurent Way Irmo SC 29063 Personal E-mail: mbranham@hotmail.com.

BRANN, RICHARD R., lawyer; b. Olney, Ill., June 9, 1943; s. Roland John and Margaret (McVay) B.; m. Penny Sue Farrington, June 5, 1965; children: Wesley R., Patrick T. BA, Miss. State U., 1965; JD, U. Tex., 1968. Bar: Tex. 1968, U.S. Dist. Ct. (so., no., ea. and we. dists.) Tex. 1970, U.S. Ct. Appeals (5th and 11th cirs.) 1973, U.S. Supreme Ct. 1973; bd. cert. in labor and employment law Tex. Bd. Legal Specialization. Assoc. Baker Botts, Houston, 1968—76, ptnr., 1976—2008; labor & employment arbitrator & mediator, 2009—. Chmn. fed. judiciary rels. com. State Bar Tex., 1996-98, pattern jury charge oversight com., 2005-10; chmn. Houston Mgmt. Lawyers Forum, Houston, 1981. Editor: Tex. Assn. of Bus. and C. of C. Labor Law Quar. Rev., Tex. Labor Letter; chmn. bd. editors Tex. Bd. Legal Specialization, 2000-2003. With USMC, 1961-66. Fellow Coll. Labor and Employment Lawyers; mem. ABA, Tex. Bar Assn., Tex. Bar Coll., Houston Bar Assn. (chmn. labor and employment law sect. 1997-98), Def. Rsch. Inst., Am. Employment Law Coun., Houston Club, Order of Coif, Phi Kappa Phi. Republican. Methodist. Avocations: fitness activities, reading. Home: 13 Stonegate Dr Houston TX 77024-2703 Home Phone: 713-464-9301; Office Phone: 713-229-1563. Business E-Mail: richard.brann@bakerbotts.com.

BRANNAN, ANTHONY NETTERVILLE, colon and rectal surgeon; MD, Vanderbilt U., Nashville, 1980. Diplomate Am. Bd. Colon and Rectal Surgery, 1987, Am. Bd. Surgery, 2006. Resident in surgery Mayo Clinic, Rochester, Minn., 1981—86, fellow in colon and rectal surgery, 1985; hosp. affiliations include St. Joseph's Hosp.-North, Fla., St. Joseph's Hosp. Office: St Josephs Hospital 4700 N Habana Ave Ste 101 Tampa FL 33614 Office Phone: 813-879-5010.

BRANNAN, EULIE ROSS, educational consultant; b. Norwood, Ohio, Sept. 6, 1928; s. Olin Hiram and Bernice Cleo (Beall) Brannan; m. Ruby Merle Moore, Dec. 16, 1945 (dec.); children: Stephen Earl, Deborah Brannan Watkins, Rebecca Brannan Hagan, Julie Ross Brannan-Williams; m. Willie Metta Strong, Mar. 7, 1981. AA, Ala. Christian Coll., 1947; BA, Huntingdon Coll., 1949; MS, Auburn U., 1953, EdD, 1960; postgrad., Harding Grad. Sch., 1960—63, Oxford U., Eng., 1981; LHD, Faulkner U., 2005. HS tchr., Montgomery, Ala., 1949-51; guidance counselor Montgomery Bible HS, 1951-53; prin. Ala. Christian HS, Montgomery, 1953-55; prof. Ala. Christian Coll., Montgomery, 1953-55, asst. to pres., 1955-56, acad. dean, 1956-69, acad. v.p., 1969-73, pres., 1973-81; field dir. Nat. Edn. Program, Huntsville, Ala., 1981-82; pres. Jefferson Christian Acad., Birmingham, Ala., 1982-90; assoc. J. Robert Clark & Assocs., 1990-91; spl. counsel to pres. Faulkner U., Montgomery, 1991—2004; involvement min. Madison (Ala.) Ch. of Christ, 2004—. Chaplain Madison Police Dept., 1996—; bd. trustees Faulkner U., 2005—. Mem.: Phi Delta Kappa. Home: 103 Manningham Dr Madison AL 35758-7419 Office: Madison Ch of Christ 556 Hughes Rd Madison AL 35758 Office Phone: 256-772-3911. E-mail: eulieb@bellsouth.net.

BRANNON, NORMAN DOUG, state legislator; b. Detroit, Mich., Apr. 22, 1961; s. Norman and Marion E. Brannon; m. Tracey S. Brannon, Aug. 28, 2004; children: Cody Brannon, Lexi Brannon, Chris Brannon, Spike Brannon. BS, U. SC, 1996, JD, 2000. Mayor, Landrum, 1993—97; mem. Dist. 38 SC House of Representatives, Spartanburg, 2011—. Republican. Office: South Carolina House of Representatives District 38 404D Blatt Bldg Columbia SC 29201 Home: 201 Clearwater Rd Landrum SC 29356 Office Phone: 803-212-6876. Business E-Mail: NormanBrannon@schouse.gov.

BRANSCOMB, HARVIE, JR., lawyer; b. Dallas, Mar. 24, 1922; s. Bennett Harvie and Margaret (Vaughan) B.; m. Mary Josephine Goodearle, Dec. 28, 1951; children: Mary Margaret, Bennett Hill, Richard Lee. AB, Duke U., 1943; LL.B., Yale U., 1948. Bar: Tex. 1948, D.C. 1980, CPA, Tex. Shareholder Branscomb P.C., Attys.-at-Law, Corpus Christi, Tex., 1948—. Contbr. articles to profl. jours. Trustee emeritus Southwestern Legal Found.; trustee, chmn. Una Chapman Cox Found. Served with USNR, 1943-46. Fellow Am. Coll. Tax Counsel; mem. ABA, (chmn. tax sect. 1979-80), State Bar Tex. (chmn. sect. taxation 1961-62), Am. Law Inst., Am. Inst. CPA's, Phi Beta Kappa, Phi Delta Phi. Episcopalian. Home: 4500 Ocean Dr Apt 8B Corpus Christi TX 78412-2500 Office: 802 N Carancahua St Ste 1900 Corpus Christi TX 78470-0102 Home Phone: 361-853-6032; Office Phone: 361-888-9261.

BRANSCUM, DAVID L., state legislator; m. Judith Branscum; 5 children. BA in Agr. Bus., U. Ark., 1982. Mem. First Bapt. Ch., Marshall; owner, operator Branscum Farms; pres. Branscum and Harness Lumber, Inc., Marshall; mem. Dist. 90 Ark. House of Representatives, 2011—. Republican. Mailing: PO Box 370 Marshall AR 72650 Office Phone: 870-448-2408. Business E-Mail: davidlbranscum@hotmail.com.

BRANSFIELD, MICHAEL JOSEPH, bishop; b. Phila., Sept. 8, 1943; BA in Philosophy, St. Charles Borromeo Sem., Overbrook, Pa., MDiv; MPhil, Cath. U. America, Washington, 1973. Ordained priest Archdiocese of Phila., 1971; asst. pastor St. Albert the Great Parish, Huntington Valley, Pa., 1971—73; tchr., chaplain, chmn. religion dept. Lansdale Cath. HS, 1973—80; asst. dir., dir. liturgy Nat. Shrine of the Immaculate Conception, 1980—82, fin. dir., 1982—86, dir., 1986—90; first rector Basilica of the Nat. Shrine of Immaculate Conception, 1990—2004; ordained bishop, 2005; bishop Diocese of Wheeling-Charleston, W.Va., 2005—. Liaison US Conf. Cath. Bishops to the Nat. Coun. Cath. Women. Trustee Papal Found.; bd. trustees Cath. U. America, Cath. Distance U., Washington, Pontifical Coll. Josephinum, Columbus, Ohio; mem. bd. regents St. Vincent Sem., Latrobe, Pa. Named a Prelate of Honor, His Holiness Pope John Paul II, 1987. Mem.: Knights of the Holy Sepulchre, KC. Roman Catholic. Office: Diocese of Wheeling-Charleston 1300 Byron St PO Box 230 Wheeling WV 26003 Office Phone: 304-233-0880. Office Fax: 304-233-0890.

BRANTLEY, CURTIS, state legislator; b. Jan. 20, 1940; s. Marshall and Rose Brantley; m. Doris Fagan; 1 child, Kendrick. BS, NC Agrl. & Tech. State U., 1969; MA, Elmira Coll., NY; EdD, SC State U., 1988. Tchr. Elmira Free Acad., 1969—75, Elmira Correctional Facilities, 1970—75; prin. Ridgeland HS, SC, 1975—86; dir., ops. Jasper County Sch. Dist., Ridgeland, 1986—88, dist. supt., 1998—2000; asst. prin. West Hardeeville Elem. Sch., SC, 1988—89, prin. SC, 1989—97, Ridgeland Mid. Sch., 1997—98; mem. Dist. 122 SC House of Reps., 2007—. Mem.: Prince Hall Masons, Citizens Orgn. Pub. Svc. (former pres.), Rotary Club (former pres.). Democrat. Home: 194 Bees Creek Rd Ridgeland SC 29936 Office: 314D Blatt Building Columbia SC 29201 Home Phone: 843-726-5998; Office Phone: 803-734-2965. Business E-Mail: BrantleyC@schouse.org.

BRANTLEY, JOHN C., III, airport executive; b. 1942; Degree in Civil Engring., NC State U., Northwestern U. With Fed. Aviation Adminstrn., Atlanta, 1966-69, Wilbur Smith & Assocs., Columbia, S.C., 1969-71; airport planning and design cons. Aviation Sys. Inc., Raleigh, N.C., 1971-77; with Raleigh-Durham Airport Authority Raleigh-Durham Internat. Airport, 1977-82, former devel. mgr., dir., 1982—. Office: Raleigh-Durham Airport Authority PO Box 80001 Raleigh NC 27623-0001

BRAS, RAFAEL LUIS, academic administrator, engineering educator; b. San Juan, Oct. 28, 1950; s. Rafael and Amalia Antonia (Muniz) B.; m. Patricia Ann Brown, June 29, 1974; children: Rafael Edmundo, Alejandro Luis. BSCE, MIT, 1972, MSCE, 1974, DSc in Water Resources and Hydrology, 1975; Laurea (hon.), U. Perugia, Italy, 1991. Registered profl. engr., Mass., PR. Asst. prof. U. PR, Mayaguez, 1975—76; from asst. prof. hydrology to assoc. prof. MIT, Cambridge, Mass., 1976—82, prof., 1982—, head water resources and environ. engring. divsn., 1983—91, dir. Ralph M. Parsons Lab., 1983—91, dir. Minority Intro. to Eng. and Sci., 1987, William E. Leonhard prof. engring., 1988—95, head dept. civil and environ. engring., 1992—2001, Bacardi and Stockholm Water Founds. prof., 1995—2004, chair faculty, 2002—05, Edward A. Abdun-Nur prof. civil and environ. engring., 2004—08; assoc. dir. Ctr. Global Change Sci., 1990—2008; dir. Terrascope Program Ctr. for Global Change Sci., 2006—08; dean Henry Samueli Sch. Engring., U. Calif., Irvine, 2008—10; provost, exec. v.p., K. Harrison Brown family chair Ga. Inst. Tech., 2010—. Vis. assoc. prof. U. Simon Bolivar, Caracas, Venezuela, 1982-83; vis. scholar Internat. Inst. Applied Sys. Analysis, Vienna, 1983; vis. prof. Iowa Inst. Hydraulic Rsch., U. Iowa, 1989-90; mem. adv. bd. engring. divsn. NSF, 1988-91; earth scis. and applications divsn. adv. subcom. NASA, 1990, sci. team TRMM mission, 1991-94, chair Earth Sys. Sci. and Applications Adv. Com., 1998-2002; sci. steering group GCIP-Global Energy and Water Cycle Experiment, 1991-95; adv. coun. for com. Nat. Insts. for Environment; mem. adv. com. civil engring. dept. Rensselaer Poly. Inst., 2000-02, Johns Hopkins U., 1998—,dept. civil and environ. engring. Cornell U., 2001-11; mem. adv. coun. Princeton U., 1999-10; mem. nominating com. Stockholm Water Prize, 1996-2004; mem. exec. com. Clarke Prize, 2002-04; mem. sci. com. Inter Poly. Sch., Milan, Italy, 2003-2006; vis. prof. Harvard U., 2001-2002; mem. com. New Orleans regional hurricane protection program, NAS, 2005-09; mem. rels. com. UCAR, 2006—07; cons. in field; lectr. in field. Author: (with I. Rodriguez-Iturbe) Random Functions and Hydrology, 1985, 94, Hydrology: An Introduction to Hydrologic Science, 1990; editor: The World at Risk: Natural Hazards and Climate Change, 1993; editor Nonlinear Processes in Geophysics, 1996-2000; contbr. articles to profl. jours.; assoc. editor Water Resources Rsch., 1980-88, Jour. Geophys. Rsch.-Atmospheres, 1996-98; mem. editl. bd. Jour. Hydrology, Internat. Jour. Environ. Tech.; mem. editl. adv. bd. SERRA, 1998-07. Recipient Walter L. Huber Civil Engring. prize, 1993, Giants in Sci. award, Quality Edn. for Minorities Math., Sci. and Engring. Network, 2001, Albert Baez Jr. award and Outstanding Educator award, Hispanic Engr. Nat. Achievement Conf., 1999, MLK-MIT Leadership award, 2000, Clarke prize, 1998, Hispanic Engr. Nat. Achievement award hall of fame, 2003, AGU Lorenz Lecture, 2003, NASA Pub. Svc. Medal, 2002, Anthony J. Drexel Exceptional Achievement Award, 2010; named to Top 100 Most Influential Hispanics, Hispanic Bus., 1997; grantee Guggenheim fellow, 1982, P.R. Econ. Devel. Adminstrn. fellow; Horton lectr., AMS, 1999, Kisiel Disting. lectr., 2002, William Mong Disting. lectr., U. Hong Kong, 1999—2000, Boussinesq-KNAW lectr., 2005. Fellow: AMS, AAAS (mem. electorate nominating com. engring. sect. 2007—09), ASCE (task com. 1996—97, Huber prize 1993, Simon W. Freese Environ. Engring. award 2008), Am. Meteorol. Soc. (Robert E. Horton lectr. award 1999), Am. Geophys. Union (chmn. bd. jous. editors 1984—88, chair budget and fin. 1990—94, pres. Hydrology sect. 2003—06, statutes and bylaws com. 2006—08, assoc. editor, bd. dirs. 2010—, Horton award 1981, James B. Macelwane award 1982, Lorenz lectr. 2003, Hydrology Days award 2006, Horton medal 2007); mem.: Nat. Acad. Arts and Scis. Puerto Rico, Internat. Water Acad., Nat. Acad. Scis. Mex. (corr.), Nat. Acad. Engring. Mex. (corr.), U.S. Nat. Acad. Engring., Soc. Presdl. Fellows Lectrs., Boston (Mass.) Soc. Civil Engrs., MIT Alumni Assn. (Bronze Beaver award 2005), Tau Beta Pi, Sigma Xi, Chi Epsilon. Roman Catholic. Office: Georgia Institute of Technology Office of Provost Box 0325 Atlanta GA 30332 Office Phone: 404-385-2700. E-mail: provost@gatech.edu.

BRASFIELD, EVANS BOOKER, lawyer; b. Richmond, Va., Sept. 21, 1932; s. George Frederick and Minna (Booker) B.; children: Evans Booker, John McDonald, Elizabeth Lee; m. Anne Dobbins Heilig, June 28, 1980; stepchildren: J. Randall Heilig, Mollie H. Storey. BA, U. Va., 1954, LLB, 1959. Bar: Va. 1959. Pvt. practice, Richmond; ptnr. Hunton & Williams, Richmond, 1965-99; gen. counsel Va. Electric & Power Co., Richmond, 1976-94, Dominion Resources, 1983-91. Pres. Children's Home Soc. Va., 1972-73, bd. dirs., 1965-91; chmn. Cen. Va. Ednl. TV Corp., 1980-84, bd. dirs., 1965-2004; bd. dirs. Richmond Cmty. Action Program, 1974-76, Richmond Area Cmty. Coun., 1973-75, Big Bros. Richmond, 1970-75, Sheltering Arms Hosp., 2001—. With USNR, 1954-56. Fellow Am. Bar Found., Va. Law Found.; mem. ABA (chmn. sect. pub. utility law 1996-97), Va. Bar Assn. (exec. com. 1981-86, pres. 1985), Richmond Bar Assn.,, Va. State Bar, Phi Beta Kappa (pres. Richmond chpt. 1982-83). Clubs: Country of Va., Commonwealth, (Richmond). Presbyterian. Home: 2 Ampthill Rd Richmond VA 23226-2233

BRASHER, GEORGE WALTER, physician, consultant; b. Jackson, Tenn., Dec. 7, 1936; s. George W. and Verla S. Brasher; m. Martha S. Brasher, Dec. 23, 1960; children: Suzanne Cheshier, George Brasher, John Brasher, David Brasher. BA, Lambuth U., 1959; MD, U. Tenn., 1961. Diplomate Am. Bd. Allergy and Immunology, Am. Bd. Pediatrics. Cons. Scott & White Clinic & Hosp., Temple, Tex., 1966—2007; emeritus prof. medicine Tex. A & M Coll. Medicine, 2008—. Dir. Allergy and Immunology Scott and White Clinic and Hosp., Temple, Tex., 1976-2006; prof. Medicine and Pediatrics Tex. A&M U. Coll. of Medicine, Temple, Tex., 1977-08. Contbr. articles to profl. jours. Fellow Am. Acad. Allergy and Immunology, Am. Acad. Pediatrics, Am. Coll. Allergy and Immunology; mem. AMA, Tex. Med. Assn., Bell County Med. Soc., Tex. Allergy Soc. Avocations: civil war history, amateur radio. Personal E-mail: gbrasher@excite.com.

BRASWELL, JACKIE BOYD, state agency administrator; b. Leon County, Fla., Feb. 15, 1938; d. Chalmer Parks and Kathryn Iris (Johnson) Boyd; m. Fletcher Braswell, Nov. 28, 1957; children: Flecia Lori, Carmen Ethelee. BS, Fla. State U., 1964; M in Ednl. Adminstrn., 1976. Cert. educator Valdosta State Coll., 1968, lic. real estate sales assoc. Fla., 2005, cert. Rayner Real Estate, Tallahassee, Fla. Lic. tchr., adminstr. Fla. single mgr., ammunition, base clothing fund, security clearance USAF, Moody AFB, 1958-61; tchr. bus. edn. Berrien H.S., Nashville, Ga., 1966-69, Rickards H.S., Tallahassee, 1970-75; bus.-vocat. tchr., chmn. dept. career edn. Lincoln H.S., 1975—99; dir. ednl. affairs and policy Fla. Lottery, 1999—2005; real estate assoc. Rayner Real Estate, 2005—. Co-owner, fin. mgr. Rundown Farms, Tallahassee, 1969—; pres. Eight Out Investment Group, 1993-2003; mem. Gov.'s Mentoring Initiative Lottery Mentoring Program, 1999-2005. Editor: In Touch, 1979-80; contbr. articles to profl. jours. Apptd. Fla. State Bd. Pub. Schs., Gov. Fla., 1987-90, vice chmn., 1990-91; chmn.; apptd. mem. by Spkr. House of Reps. to Fla. Commn. Edn. Reform and Accountability, Spkr. Fla. House Reps., 1991-93; invited del. Citizens Amb. Program People Internat., Beijing, Hangzhou, Shanghai, China, 1995; fundraising chmn. Dist. Sch. Supts. Campaign, 1996; sponsorship chair Capital Cultural Ctr., Chukker Challenge, 1997-98; mem. fundraising com. Boys and Girls Club Big Bend, mem. fundraising com. ann. dinner, 2005-06; mem. ann. fundraiser com. Pace Ctr. Girls, 2005-08. Recipient Merit award Future Farmers Am., 1974; selectee Harvard Inst., 1991. Mem. Nat. Mus. Women in the Arts (charter), Nat. Bus. Edn. Assn., Fla. Vocat. Assn., Fla. Bus. Edn. Addn., Leon Vocat. Assn. (pres. elect 1987-88, pres. 1988-89), Leon Classroom Tchrs. Assn. (sec.-treas. 1987-88, chair pub. rels., parliamentarian 1988-89, govtl. rels. 1991), Dance Arts Guild, Leon County Farm Bur., Capital Gains Club (treas., 2000), Quill and Scroll, Phi Kappa Phi. Republican.

BRASWELL, LOUIS ERSKINE, lawyer; b. Selma, Ala., Mar. 11, 1937; s. Erskine McKinley and Leota (Grubb) B.; m. Moren, Nov. 4, 2005; children by previous marriage: Margaret, Anne, Helen. AB, Birmingham So. Coll., 1959; JD, Harvard U., Cambridge, Mass., 1962. Bar: Ala. bar 1962. Assoc. firm Hand, Arendall, Bedsole, Greaves & Johnston, Mobile, Ala., 1963-68; ptnr. Hand Arendall LLC, Mobile, 1968—2006. Participant Nat. Conf. on Discovery Reform, U. Tex. Law Sch., 1982; program participant 11th Cir. Jud. Conf., 1984, others Bd. dirs. Children's Dental Clinic, Mobile, 1965-75; past pres. Friends of Mobile Publ. Libr.; bd. dirs. Jr. Achievement of Mobile; past pres. YMCA Rockies Alumni Assn.; bd. dirs. Kidney Found. South Ala., 1978-85, Ecumenical Ministries, Inc., 2001-04. With US Army, 1962-63. Mem. Athelstan Club, Rotary Internat., Point Clear Rotary Club (bd. dirs. 1997-2000, pres. 1998-99). Presbyterian. Home: 250 N Bayview St Fairhope AL 36532 Office: PO Box 123 Mobile AL 36601-0123

BRASWELL, ROBERT M., state banking agency administrator; m. Amy Braswell; children: Nathan, Jessica. BBA in Fin., Ga. So. Coll., 1984. Fin. examiner Ga. Dept. Banking and Fin., supervisory examiner NW region, dir. NW dist. 1, dep. commr. mortgage, 2003—05, commr., 2005—. Office: Georgia Department Banking and Finance 2990 Brandywine Rd Ste 200 Atlanta GA 30341-5565 Office Phone: 770-986-1628. E-mail: robertb@dbf.state.ga.us.

BRATCHER, KEVIN, state legislator; b. Apr. 17, 1961; m. Maria Bratcher. Tech. sch. instr.; mem. Dist. 29 Ky. House of Reps., 1997—. Mem.: Coalition Advan Regional Transp., Masons, Ky. Railway Mus. Republican. Baptist. Address: 5205 Constance Dr Louisville KY 40272 Home: 10215 Landwood Dr Louisville KY 40291 Office: Capitol Annex Rm 405F Frankfort KY 40601 Home Phone: 502-231-3311; Office Phone: 502-564-8100 ext 680. E-mail: kevin.bratcher@lrc.state.ky.us.

BRATHOVDE, JAMES ROBERT, chemistry professor; b. Glasgow, Mont., June 8, 1926; s. Arnold Morgan and Ebbie Rozella (Hevener) B.; m. Bonnie Dee Cornwell, Oct. 28, 1949; children: James Edgar, Robert Dean, Liné, Tonna. BA, Eastern Wash. Coll., 1950, BA in Edn., 1950; MS, U. Wash., 1955, PhD (Army Ordnance

Research fellow), 1956. Tchr. pub. schs., Spokane, 1950-51; assoc. prof. chemistry, chmn. dept. Whitworth Coll., Spokane, 1956-60; research scientist Sandia Corp., Albuquerque, 1960-63; program dir. undergrad. sci. edn. NSF, Washington, 163-64; dir. computer ctr., prof. chemistry SUNY, Binghamton, 1964-67; chmn. chemistry dept. No. Ariz. U., Flagstaff, 1967-70, dean Coll. Sci. and Humanistic Studies, 1970-72, prof. environ. sci. and chemistry, 1972-84, prof. emeritus, 1984—. Pres. Brathovde Lands, Inc., Elk, Wash., 1967—, JRB Enterprises, Inc., Elk, 1967—; dir. Wash. State Sci. Talent Search, 1959-60; pres. Human Growth, Inc., N.Y.C., 1964-70 Bd. dirs. Human Growth Found., 1970—. Served with USMC, 1944-46, 51-52. NSF Research grantee, 1958-60; Research Corp. grantee, 1957 Mem. Am. Crystallographic Assn., AAAS, Sigma Xi. Lutheran. Home: 555 Lewis Ln Morganton GA 30560-1805

BRATTON, IDA FRANK, retired secondary school educator; b. Glasgow, Ky., Aug. 31, 1933; d. Edmund Bates and Robbie Davis (Hume) Button; m. Robert Franklin Bratton, June 20, 1954; 1 child, Timothy Andrew. BA, Western Ky. U., 1959, MA, 1962. Cert. secondary tchr., Ky. Tchr. math. and sci. Gottschalk Jr. H.S., Louisville, 1959-65; tchr. math. Iroquois H.S., Louisville, 1965-79; tchr. Waggener HS, Louisville, 1979—98, chair dept. math., 1993—98, ret., 1998. Mem. NEA, AAUW, Ky. Edn. Assn., Jefferson County Tchrs. Assn. Democrat. Methodist. Avocations: travel, needle crafts. Home: 304 Paddington Ct Louisville KY 40222-5541

BRATTON, JAMES HENRY, JR., lawyer; b. Pulaski, Tenn., Oct. 9, 1931; s. James Henry and Mabel (Shelley) B.; m. Alleen Sharp Davis, Oct. 15, 1960; children: Susan Shelley McGonigle, James Henry III, Margaret Alleen Schilling. BA optime merens, valedictorian, U. South, 1952; BA, Oxford U., Eng., 1954, MA, 1978; LL.B., Yale U., 1956. Bar: Tenn. 1956, Ga. 1957. With antitrust div. Dept. Justice, summer 1955; since practiced in Atlanta; of counsel Smith, Gambrell & Russell. Vis. lectr. U. Ga. Law Sch., 1967; adj. prof. law Emory U., 1984-2001. Editor Yale Law Jour.; contbr. articles to profl. jours. Mem. Gov.'s Citizens Adv. Council on Environ. Affairs, 1970-74, U. South Sch. Theology Visiting Com., 2004-10; trustee Pembroke Coll. Found., Inc., Trust Fund for Sibley Park, Ga. chpt. Multiple Sclerosis Soc., U. of the South, 1984-87, 95-98, Peachtree Rd. United Meth. Ch., 1997-2000, chmn. bd. trustees; bd. dirs. Soccer in the Streets, Buckhead Christian Ministry, pres., 1996; pres. Peachtree Heights West Civic Assn., 1984-99; co-chmn. Sewanee Parents Council, 1987-88; v.p. Pembroke Coll. Soc. of N.Am.; mem. Williams Parents' Fund, 1984-86; mem. parents adv. coun. Hamilton Coll., 1988-91. Named Alumnus of Yr., Sewanee Club Atlanta, 1990; John R. Crawford Disting. Svc. Award, U. of South, 2003. Fellow Lawyers Found. Ga., Am. Law Inst.(life); mem. ABA (standing com. on aero. law 1962-84, chmn. 1977-80), State Bar Ga. (founding chmn. environ. law sect. 1970-73), Fed. Bar Assn., Atlanta Bar Assn., Lawyers Club Atlanta, Old Warhorse Lawyers Club (11th cir. Hist. Soc.), Am. Acad. Polit. and Social Scis., Am. Judicature Soc., Associated Alumni U. of South (v.p. admissions 1993-95, pres. 1995-97), Yale Law Alumni Assn. (exec. com. 1976-79), Pembroke Coll. Found., Inc. (treas. 2003-), Inquiry Club, Buckhead Heritage Soc., Phi Beta Kappa, Phi Delta Phi, Pi Gamma Mu, Gridiron, Am. Bar Found. Democrat. Methodist. Home: 63 N Muscogee Ave NW Atlanta GA 30305-3542 Office: 1230 Peachtree St NE Atlanta GA 30309-3592 Home Phone: 404-237-9781; Office Phone: 404-815-3510. Business E-Mail: jbratton@sgrlaw.com.

BRATTON, TERESA SUE, pediatrician; b. Nashville, Oct. 14, 1948; m. Gustav Blomquist; children: Gus, Kerstin, Michael. BS, Vanderbilt U., Nashville, 1970, MD, 1974. Cert. master gardener Guilford County Agrl. Extension Agy. Asst. prof. U. Miss., 1979—81; pvt. practice pediatric allergist, 1982—2006; adj. clin. asst. prof., dept. pediat. U. NC, Chapel Hill, 1987—; physician, allergy & asthma clinic Guilford Child Health, 1985—. Chmn. Greensboro Med. Symposium, 1993, Blue Cross Blue Shield NC Physician Adv. Group, 1997—2004, Cmty. Health Improvement Fund, Moses Cone-Wesley Long Cmty. Health Found., 2000—04, Guilford County Asthma Coalition, 2004—. Co-chair Sawbones-Jawbones Charity Fund Raiser, 1994; pres. Greater Greensboro Soc. Medicine, 1994, Am. Lung Assn., Piedmont Br., 1994—95, bd. mem., 1992—98. Democrat. Avocations: tennis, hiking, bicycling, gardening. Office: Guilford Child Health 1046 E Wendover Ave Greensboro NC 27408

BRAUN, MICHAEL A., securities firm executive, retired federal agency administrator; m. Kathleen A. Mayfield; 3 children. BS in Criminal Justice, S.E. Mo. State U., 1977. Spl. agent St. Louis divsn. Drug Enforcement Adminstrn. (DEA), US Dept. Justice, 1985—91, supervisory spl. agent Latin America, 1991—94, exec. asst. to adminstr., 1997—99, asst. spl. agent in charge, 1999—2001, spl. agent in charge Detroit divsn., 2001, asst. adminstr., chief ops., 2005—08; chief of staff Ministry Interior, Coalition Provisional Authority, Iraq, 2003, head Office Spl. Intelligence, 2003—05; founder Spectre Group Internat. LLC (SGI), Alexandria, Va., 2008—. Infantryman USMC, 1971—73. Office: Spectre Group International LLC (SGI) 211 N Union St Ste 100 Alexandria VA 22314 Office Phone: 703-519-4201. Office Fax: 703-683-4707. E-mail: mb@spectregi.com.

BRAUN, MICHAEL RENE, lawyer; b. New Orleans, June 26, 1967; s. Paul H. and Carol Anne (robinson) B.; m. Henther B. Braun, Sept. 4, 1998. BA in Econs., U. Ga., 1989; JD, Atlanta Law Sch., 1993. Bar: Ga. 1993, U.S. Ct. Appeals (11th cir.) 1993, U.S. Dist. Ct. (no. dist.) 1993, US Supreme Ct. Assoc. Buchanan & Assoc., Atlanta; atty. Braun & Ree LLP, Marietta, Ga., 2002—. Mem. Atlanta Bar Assn., State Bar Ga., Assn. Trial Lawyers Am. Office: Braun And Ree Llp 3225 Shallowford Rd Ste 500 Marietta GA 30062-7024 Office Phone: 770-421-6888. Office Fax: 770-421-6959. Business E-Mail: mrbraun@braunree.com.

BRAUN, ROBERT DAVID, aerospace engineer, educator, former federal agency administrator; b. 1965; BS in Aerospace Engring., Pa. State U., 1987; MS in Astronautics, George Washington U., 1989; PhD in Aeronautics and Astronautics, Stanford U., Calif., 1996. With NASA Langley Rsch. Ctr.; David and Andrew Lewis assoc. prof. space tech. Ga. Inst. Tech., 2003—10, David and Andrew Lewis prof. space tech., 2011—, co-dir. Space Systems Design Lab.; chief technologist NASA, Washington, 2010—11. Mem. aircraft design group Stanford U., Calif., 1991—96; development mgr. Mars Sample Return Earth Entry Vehicle, 1998—2000; chief engr. NASA Intelligent Synthesis Environment Prog., 2000—01; mission arch. Aerial Regional-scale Environ. Survey Mars Scout mission, 2001—03. Contbr. articles to sci. jours. Recipient NASA Exceptional Achievement medal, NASA Group Achievement award. Fellow: AIAA (Disting. lectr. 2003—06, mem. multidisciplinary optimization tech. com. 2004—06, mem. space systems tech. com. 2006, Lawrence Sperry award 1999). Office: Dept Aerospace Engring Ga Inst Tech 270 Ferst Dr Rm 321-3 Atlanta GA 30332-0150 Office Phone: 404-385-6171. Business E-Mail: robert.braun@aerospace.gatech.edu.

BRAVENDER, TERRILL (TERRY) D., pediatrician; b. Feb. 7, 1966; MD, U. Mich. Med. Sch., 1992; MPH, Harvard Sch. Pub. Health, 1999. Cert. Am. Bd. Pediatrics, Adolescent Medicine. Intern, adolescent medicine Duke U. Med. Ctr., Durham, NC, 1992—96, staff, 1999—; fellow, internal medicine Children's Hosp. Boston, 1996—98, physician, pediat., 1998—99; instr., pediat. Harvard Med. Sch., Boston, 1998—99; assoc. prof. Duke U. Med. Sch., dir., adolescent medicine; private practice Duke Children's Primary Care, NC. Course dir., adolescent medicine rotation in the pediat. residency program Duke U. Sch. Medicine; co-founder, med. dir. Duke Eating Disorders Program (DEDP). Contbr. several articles to profl. jours. Office: Duke Childrens Primary Care 4020 N Roxboro Rd Durham NC 27704 Office Phone: 919-620-5374. Office Fax: 919-471-3820.

BRAVERMAN, YUVAL, stone manufacturing company executive; Grad., U. Md. Pres., Retail Sales divsn. Gematic Internat., Inc.; co-founder J & J Zaidman, Inc., 1981, pres., 1981—. Bd. dirs. Zale Corp., 2008—. Office: Zale Corp 901 W Walnut Hill Ln Irving TX 75038-1003 Office Phone: 972-580-4000.

BRAWLEY, JOEL VINCENT, mathematician, educator; b. Mooresville, NC, Feb. 2, 1938; s. Joel Vincent Brawley, Sr. and Dorothy Cavin Brawley; m. Mary Frances Owen, Aug. 22, 1959; children: Albert Vincent, Daniel Owen, Frances Brawley Barnes. BS, N.C. State U., 1956—60, MS, 1960—62, PhD, 1962—64. Instr. N.C. State U., 1964—65; asst. prof. Clemson U., 1965—68, assoc. prof., 1968—72; vis. assoc. prof. N.C. State U., 1971—72; prof. of math. sciences Clemson U., 1972—82; vis. prof. U. of Tenn., 1979—80; alumni disting. prof. of math. sciences Clemson U., Clemson, 1982—2006, alumni disting. prof. emeritus, 2006—. Author: (book) Infinite Algebraic Extensions of Finite Fields; contbr. numerous jour. articles. Recipient Southeastern Sect. Award for Disting. Coll. or U. Tchg. of Math., Math. Assn. of Am., 1998, Deborah and Franklin Tepper Haimo Award for Disting. Coll. or U. Tchg. of Math., 1999, SC Governor's Prof. of the Yr., 2001—02, award, Thomas G. Clemson Acad. Scientists & Engrs., 2007, Disting Svc. award, Math. Assn. Am. SE Sect., 2007. Avocations: golf, folk, guitar. Office: Clemson U Dept of Math Sci Clemson SC 29634-0975 E-mail: brawley@clemson.edu.

BRAWLEY, OTIS WEBB, oncologist, educator; b. Detroit, July 4, 1959; MD, U. Chgo.-Pritzker Sch. Medicine, 1985. Cert. American Bd. Internal Medicine, American Bd. Med. Oncology. Resident, internal medicine U. Hospitals Cleve., Case Western Reserve U., Cleve., 1985—88; fellow, oncology Nat. Cancer Inst., Bethesda, Md., 1988—90; attending physician NIC Clin. Ctr., 1990, Nat. Naval Med. Ctr., Bethesda, Md., 1990; chief, Intramural Prostate Cancer Clinic Nat. Cancer Inst., Bethesda, Md., 1993—95, asst. dir., Spl. Populations Rsch., 1995—2001, sr., divsn. cancer prevention and control; prof., hematology, oncology & epidemiology Ga. Ctr. for Excellence, Grady Meml. Hosp., 2001—07; prof., hematology, oncology and medicine Emory U. Sch. Medicine; prof., epidemiology Emory Rollins Sch. Pub. Health; assoc. dir. to dep. dir., Winship Cancer Inst. Emory U.; chief, hematology and oncology svcs., med. dir., Ga. Cancer Coalition Ctr. of Excellence Grady Meml. Hosp.; exec. v.p., chief med. officer American Cancer Soc., 2007—; sr. rsch. fellow Internat. Prevention Rsch. Inst., 2011—. Sr. investigator NIH, mem. adv. com. on women's health; mem. adv. com. NIH Office of Disease Prevention; chair NIH Consensus Panel on the Treatment of Sickle Cell Anemia; mem. oncologic drug adv. com. FDA; mem. Uniformed Svcs. U, Health Sci. Bd. Regents, Dept. Def., 2004, CDC; mem. adv. com. Prevention Breast and Cervical Cancer Early Detection and Control; co-chair Surgeon General's Task Force in Cancer Health Disparities; bd. dirs. Theragenics Corp., 1995; invited lectr. in field. Contbr. articles to profl. jours.; editl. roles Contemporary Oncology, Prostate Cancer and Prostatic Diseases, Cancer Epidemiology Biomarkers and Prevention, & British Jour. Urology and Cure; co-author (with Paul Goldberg): How We Do Harm: A Doctor Breaks Ranks About Being Sick in America, 2012. Vol. Am. Cancer Soc. Prostate Cancer Com. Recipient Nat. Cancer Inst. and the Equal Employment Opportunity Officer's Commendation, 1991, 1993, US Pub. Health Svc. Crisis Response Svc. award, 2006, US Pub. Health Svc. Disting. Svc. Commendation, Key to St. Bernard Parish for work in New Orleans with Hurricane Katrina; Ga. Cancer Coalition Eminent Scholar. Mem.: American Assn. for Clin. Rsch., American Soc. Clin. Oncology, Nat. Med. Assn., ACP. Office: American Cancer Society 1599 Clifton Rd Atlanta GA 30329

BRAWLEY, WILLIAM M., state legislator; Mem. Dist. 103 NC House of Representatives, 2011—. Republican. Office: 13612 O'Toole Dr Matthews NC 28105 Address: North Carolina House of Representatives 16 W Jones St Room 1313 Raleigh NC 27601-1096 Office Phone: 704-574-0894, 919-733-5800. Business E-Mail: Bill.Brawley@ncleg.net.

BRAXTON, HERMAN HARRISON, JR., lawyer, judge; b. Durham, NC, May 15, 1936; s. Herman Harrison and Anne Grimm Braxton; m. Patricia Gail Galway, June 26, 1965; children: Herman Harrison III, Grace Anne, William Marshall. AB in Polit. Sci., U. NC, 1958; JD, U. Va., 1961. Bar: Va. 1961. Ptnr. Willis, Braxton, Ashby & Bass, Fredericksburg, 1965—96; commonwealth atty. City of Fredericksburg, 1974—82; gen. dist. judge 15th Dist, 1996—2005; cir. judge 15th Jud. Cir., Stafford, Va., 2005—07, Fredericksburg, Va. Pres. Fredericksburg Chpt. Va. Mus. Fine Arts, 1970—72. Chief Golf Rules Official Special Olympic World Games Shanghai, China, 2007. Served to capt. JAGC USAF, 1961—64. Recipient Disting. Svs. award, Fredericksburg Jr. C. of C. Mem.: Fredericksburg Area Bar Assn. (pres. 1972—73, 1980), 15th Jud. Circuit Bar Assn., Va. Bar Assn., Fredericksburg C. of C., Phi Alpha Delta, Pi Kappa Alpha. Episcopalian. Home: 1204 Charles St Fredericksburg VA 22401-3706 Personal E-mail: hhblaw@aol.com.

BRAY, GEORGE AUGUST, internist, researcher, educator; b. Evanston, Ill., July 25, 1931; s. George A. and Mary H. B.; m. Martha, Aug. 8, 1959 (div. July 1983); children: George, Thomas, Susan, Nancy; m. Marilyn Rice, Jan. 1, 1984. BA summa cum laude, Brown U., 1953; MD magna cum laude, Harvard U., 1957. Diplomate Am. Bd. Internal Medicine; cert. Nat. Bd. Med. Examiners, Mass. Bd. Registration Medicine, Calif. Bd. Med. Examiners, La. Bd. Med. Examiners. Intern Johns Hopkins Hosp., Baltimore, Md., 1957-58; rsch. assoc. NIH, Bethesda, Md., 1958-60; resident U. Rochester, NY, 1960-61; rsch. assoc. Mill Hill Nat. Inst. Med. Rsch., London, 1961-62; asst. prof. medicine Tufts U., Boston, 1964-69, assoc. prof., 1969-70, UCLA, 1970-72, prof., 1972-81, U. So. Calif., Los Angeles, 1981-89, prof. medicine and physiology, 1983-89, chief of Diabetes and Nutrition Los Angeles County USC Med. Ctr., 1981-89; prof. medicine, vice chancellor Med. Ctr. La. State U., Baton Rouge, 1989-99; exec. dir. Pennington Biomed. Rsch. Ctr., Baton Rouge, 1989-99; prof., chief clin. sci., 1999—; Boyd prof. La. State U., Baton Rouge, 1999—. Vis. prof. U. Ill., 1981; cons. FDA, 1971, 95, Can. Dept. Health and Welfare, Ottawa, Ont., 1974, Nat. Inst. on Aging; mem. adv. coun. Nat. Inst. Diabetes, Digestive and Kidney Diseases, 1985-90; lectr. Furth meml. lectr. East Carolina U., 2006; Sommer meml. lectr., Portland, 2004. Author: Obese Patient, 1976; editor: Obesity in America, 1979, Obesity in Perspective, 1976, Treatment of Obesity, 1985, 89, Obesity: Basic Aspects and Clinical Applications, 1989, Battle of the Bulge, 2007, Metabolic Syndrome and Obesity, 2007; contbr. articles to profl. jours. Recipient Travel award Am. Thyroid Assn., 1970, Sam E. Roberts award Kans. Nutrition Soc., 1977, Wellcome Vis. Prof. award Mich. State U., 1978, U. Chgo., 1985, Alumni Day spkr. Harvard Med. Sch., Boston, 1982, Osborne and Mendel award Am. Inst. Nutrition, 1989, E.V. McCollum award Am. Soc. Clin. Nutrition, 1989, Joseph Goldberger award in Clin. Nutrition AMA, 1994, TOPS award NAASO, 1999, W. Henry Sebrell award Weight Watchers Found., 2000, Bristol-Myers Squibb/Mead Johnson Nutrition award, 2000, Stunkard Lifetime Achievement award, NAASO, 2003; grantee NIH, 1965—, Weight Watchers Found., 1979-81, Kroc Found., 1980-81; fellow NSF, 1961-62, NIH, 1962-64. Master: Am. Coll. Endocrinology (pres. 1993—95, editor Endocrine Practice 1993—95), ACP, APC (chmn.-elect con. med. spltys. 1987—88, bd. regents 1987—91, chmn. 1988—91); fellow: AAAS, Am. Inst. Nutrition (Osborne-Mendal award 1988), Am. Dietetic Assn. (hon.), Am. Soc. Nutrition Sci.; mem.: Johns Hopkins U. Soc. Scholars, Internat. Assn. Study Obesity (pres.-elect 1990—94, pres. 1994—98, Willendorf award 1980), Am. Soc. Clin. Investigation (hon.), Assn. Am. Physicians (hon.), N.Am. Assn. Study Obesity (chmn. organizing com. 1980—82, councilor 1984—88, pres.-elect 1988—89, pres. 1989—90, editor Internat. Jour. Obesity 1974—91, Obesity Rsch. 1991—97, TOPS award 1999, Stunkard Lifetime Achievement award 2003), Am. Fedn. Clin. Rsch., Am. Diabetes Assn. (bd. dirs. So. Calif. 1984—88, 1988—89), Endocrine Soc., Am. Soc. Clin. Nutrition (councilor 1982—84, v.p. 1985—86, pres.-elect 1986—87, pres. 1987—88, McCollum award 1989), Am. Assn. Clin. Endocrinology (bd. dirs. 1990—96), Peripatetic Club (hon.), Alpha Omega Alpha, Sigma Xi, Phi Beta Kappa. Avocations: medical history, travel. Office: Pennington Ctr 6400 Perkins Rd Baton Rouge LA 70808-4124

BRAYNON, OSCAR, II, state legislator; b. Corpus Christi, Tex., Feb. 1, 1977; m. Melissa Fung; 1 child, Oscar III. BS in Polit. Sci., Fla. State U. Legis. aide pub. rels. coord. Miami-Dade County Commn. Dist. 1; intern Former State Rep. Kendrick Meek; page Fla. House of Reps. Messenger Program; govt. cons. Pittman Law Group; coun. mem. City of Miami Gardens, 2003—08, vice mayor, 2005—07; mem. Dist. 103 Fla. House of Reps., 2008—11; mem. Dist. 33 Fla. State Senate, 2011—. Exec. bd. mem. Adrienne Arsht Ctr. Performing Arts Miami-Dade County. Recipient Men of Tomorrow Svc. Recognition award, Egelloc Civic & Social Club, Appreciation award, Fla. Meml. U. Manhood Youth Devel. Camp, Svc. Above Self award, Opa-Locka Rotary Club, Cmty. Svc. award, Success South Fla.; named New Guard, D'Luxe Mag.; named one of 30 Leaders Under 30, Ebony Mag., 40 Under 40 Most Influential Black Profl., Success Mag. Mem.: 5000 Role Models, Kappa Alpha Psi. Democrat. Episcopal. Office: 606 NW 183rd St Miami Gardens FL 33169 also: Fla State Senate 213 Senate Office Bldg 402 S Monroe St Tallahassee FL 32399-1100 Office Phone: 305-654-7150, 850-487-5116. Business E-Mail: braynon.oscar.web@flsenate.gov.

BREAKIRON-EVANS, MAUREEN, corporate board member, accountant; b. 1954; m. Jim Evans. BBA in Acctg. & Mathematics, Stetson U., 1976; MBA, Harvard Bus. Sch., 1980; MA in Liberal Arts & Art History, Stanford U., 1996. CPA. Audit ptnr. Arthur Andersen & Co., 1980—94; pres., Transamerica Bus. Technologies Corp. Transamerica Corp., 1994—99, v.p., gen. auditor, 1994—99; exec. v.p., CFO Inovant LLC, 2001—04; v.p., gen. auditor CIGNA Corp., 2005—07; CFO Towers Perrin, 2007—08; co-founder, CEO Strategic Forge, 2008—. Bd. dirs. Cognizant Tech. Solutions Corp., 2009—, Fed. Home Loan Bank Pitts., 2011—, Heartland Payment Systems, 2012—. Trustee Stetson U. Mem.: Forum Exec. Women (FOEW). E-mail: maureen@strategicforge.com.

BREAKSTONE, ROBERT ALBERT, information technology and consumer products company executive, consultant; b. NYC, Feb. 20, 1938; s. Morris and Minnie B.; m. Eileen Fogel, Nov. 5, 1966; children: Warren, Ron, David. BS in Math., CCNY, 1960, MBA in Mgmt., 1964. Sys. engring. mgr. IBM, NYC, 1960-64; dir. mgmt. sys. Continental Copper & Steel Industries, Inc., NYC, 1964-68; v.p., CFO Sys. Audits, Inc., NYC, 1968-70; v.p., group exec. Chase Manhattan Bank, NYC, 1970-74; group v.p., bd. dirs. Chesebrough-Pond's, Inc., Greenwich, Conn., 1974-85; pres., CEO Health-Tex Inc., NYC, 1985-88; exec. v.p., COO GTech Corp., West Greenwich, RI, 1988-95; pres., CEO Landmark Internat. Group, Inc., Boca Raton, Fla., 1995—. Adj. asst. prof. Pace U. and NYU, 1964-71; adj. prof. Mercy Coll. Grad. Sch. Bus., 1999—; bd. dirs. Cion Investment Corp., State of Conn. Conix Program, OSF, Inc., By Design Internat. Ltd.; bd. advisors Hoffinger Industries; spkr. in field. Bd. dirs. Stamford Mus. and Nature Ctr., Bi-Cultural Sch.; pres. United Jewish Fedn. of Stamford, 1996-98; treas., Rockrimmon Country Club, Broken Sound Club, 2009-13. Mem. N.Am. Soc. Corp. Planning, Am. Apparel Mfrs. Assn. (dir.), Mu Gamma Tau (pres.). Mem. N.Am. Soc. Corp. Planning (v.p.), Mu Gamma Tau (pres.). Office: 95 Lynam Rd Stamford CT 06903-4527 Office Phone: 203-322-3679, 561-893-0500. Business E-Mail: rab@landmarkinternational.com.

BREAULT, KEVIN D., social studies educator, researcher; b. NYC, May 24, 1954; s. Roland E. and Vera A. Breault; m. Joy Dworkin, June 27, 1982 (div. Sept. 1985); m. Lynn E. Egan, July 30, 1988; 1 child, Lucy. BA, Reed Coll., 1978; MA, U. Wash., 1983; PhD, U. Chgo., 1986. Asst. prof. U. Cin., 1985-87, Washington U., St. Louis, 1988-91, U. Ill., Chgo., 1991-92; assoc. prof. Austin Peay State U., Clarksville, Tenn., 1993-97; assoc. prof. sociology Mid. Tenn. State U., Murfreesboro, 1997-98, prof., 1998—; editor Sociol. Spectrum, 2013—. Author: (monograph) Four Hundred Years of Social Thought, 1986, (children's book) With Wings To Fly, 2000; contbr. articles and book revs. to profl. jours., including Am. Jour. Sociology, Jour. Interpersonal Violence, jour. Quantitative Criminology, Social Forces, Brit. Jour. Sociology, Contemporary Sociology, Sociol. Focus, Am. Sociol. Rev., Jour. Marriage and Family, Sociol. Quar., Social Sci. Rsch., also chpts. to books. Grantee U. Cin., 1986, Austin Peay State U., 1994, G.H. Weems Ednl. Found., 1997, Mid. Tenn. State U., 1999; fellow Ctr. for Advanced Study in Behavioral Scis., Ogburn-Stouffer fellow U. Chgo., 1987-88. Mem. Am. Sociol. Assn., Am. Birding Assn. Avocations: birding, travel, chess, writing young adult books. Office: Middle Tenn State U Dept Sociollogy Murfreesboro TN 37132 Home: 9413 Atherton Ct Brentwood TN 37027-8700 Office Phone: 615-221-5113. Personal E-mail: kbreault@bellsouth.net.

BREAUX, RANDALL P., manufacturing executive; Various positions including v.p. customer svc. & nat. sales mgr. Baldor Electric Co., v.p. mktg., 2001—. Office: Baldor Electric Co 5711 R S Boreham Jr St Fort Smith AR 72901 Office Phone: 479-646-4711. Office Fax: 479-648-5792. Business E-Mail: rbreaux@baldor.com.

BREAZEALE, JAMES DANIEL, philosopher, educator; b. Houston, Tex., Jan. 23, 1945; s. Melba Pauline (Copeland) Breazeale; m. Viviane Cecile Chabas, Aug. 10, 1965; children: Nicole Danielle, Rebecca Cecile. BA, Austin Coll., Sherman, Tex., 1966; PhD, Yale U., New Haven, Conn., 1971. Prof. U. Ky., Dept. Philosophy, Lexington, 1971—. Translator numerous books. Recipient Disting. Prof., Arts and Scis., U. Ky.; fellow, Woodrow Wilson Found., Nat. Endowment Humanities; Sr. Rsch. fellowship, Alexander von Humboldt Stiftung. Mem.: Phi Beta Kappa. Home: 358 South Upper St Lexington KY 40508 Office: Univ Kentucky Limestone St Lexington KY 40506 Business E-Mail: breazeal@uky.edu.

BREAZEALE, WILL, pilot, military officer; b. Charleston, SC, June 24, 1968; adopted s. William and Madeleine Breazeale; divorced; 1 child, Darienne. BS in Polit. Sci., Francis Marion U., Florence, SC; postgrad. in theology, Liberty U. Theol. Sem. Lic. airline transport pilot with Boeing 737 capt. rating Pan Am Aviation Acad., cert. single engine and multi-engine instrument flight instr. Ft. Bragg Flying Club, NC. Maj., bn. exec. officer US Army Res., Lumberton, NC, 1990—, Stinger and Vulcan Air Def. officer, 24th inf. divsn. Saudi Arabia and Iraq, 1991, air def. leader, 24th inf. divsn. Cairo, 1993, chief of protocol, 3rd. US Army Hdqs. Camp Arifjan, Kuwait, 2004—05, bn. mil. transition team chief, divsn. staff officer, Iraqi Assistance Group Iraq, 2006—07; Dornier 328 pilot PSA Airlines, 1998—2003; Boeing 737 pilot Airtran Airways, 2003—. Mem. Angel Flight Network, Elizabethtown Bapt. Ch. Decorated Bronze Star Medal, Joint Svc. Commendation Medal, Army Commendation Medal with 1 Oak Leaf Cluster, Joint Svc. Achievement Medal, Nat. Def. Svc. Medal, Southwest Asia Svc. Medal with Bronze Svc. Star, Iraq Campaign Medal, Global War on Terrorism Svc. Medal, Global War on Terrorism Expeditionary Medal, Armed Forces Res. Medal, Army Svc. Ribbon, Overseas Svc. Ribbon, Kuwait Liberation Medal Kingdom Saudi Arabia, Govt. Kuwait, SC Nat. Guard Membership Ribbon, Parachutist Badge. Mem.: NRA, Evang. Theol. Soc., Bladen County Ministerial Assn., Ducks Unlimited Fairmont Chpt., Elizabethtown Am. Legion Post, Elizabethtown VFW (life). Republican. Office: c/o Airtran Airways 9955 AirTran Blvd Orlando FL 32827

BRECHER, ARMIN GEORGE, lawyer; b. Prague, Czechoslovakia, July 7, 1942; s. Gerhard and Eleanor Brecher; m. Elizabeth Pardue Rountree, July 2, 1966; children: Lindsay Brecher Cobb, Stefan Ryan Brecher, Alden Kelsey Brecher. BA summa cum laude, Emory U., Atlanta, 1966; LLB, U. Va., 1969. Ptnr., chair exec. com. Powell, Goldstein LLP, Atlanta, 1969—, bd. ptnrs., 1992—2004. Mem. The ESOP Assn. Presbyterian. Office: Powell Goldstein LLP 1201 W Peachtree St NW Fl 14 Atlanta GA 30309-3488 Office Phone: 404-572-6634. Business E-Mail: abrecher@pogolaw.com.

BRECHER, DAVID B., family practice physician; MD, Autonomous U., Guadalajara, Mexico. Diplomate Am. Bd. Family Practice, Am. Bd. Family Practice-hospice and palliative medicine. Chief resident family medicine Kings County Hosp. Med. Ctr.; palliative care physician Mease Countryside Hosp., Mease Dunedin Hosp.; assoc. med. dir. Suncoast Hospice. Recipient Excellence in Medicine award, 2009. Office: Mease Countryside Hospital 3231 McMullen Booth Rd Safety Harbor FL 34695 Office Phone: 727-725-6111.

BREDEHOFT, ELAINE CHARLSON, lawyer; b. Fergus Falls, Minn., Nov. 22, 1958; d. Curtis Lyle and Marilyn Anne (Nesbitt) Charlson; m. Keenan P. Frank; children: Alexandra Charlson, Michelle Charlson. BA, U. Ariz., 1981; JD, Cath. U. Am., 1984. Bar: Va. 1984, DC 1994, admitted to practice: US Ct. Appeals (4th Cir.) 1984, US Bankruptcy Ct. (Ea. Dist.) Va. 1987, US Ct. Appeals (DC Cir.) 1994. Assoc. Walton and Adams, McLean, Va., 1984-88, prin., 1988-91; founding atty., prin. Charlson Bredehoft Cohen Brown & Sakata, Reston, Va., 1991—. Spkr. Fairfax Bar Assn. CLE, 1992—, spkr. VB Assn., 1993—; spkr. Labor and Employment Law Update, 1993—, Va. Women's Trial Lawyers Assn. Ann. Conf., 1998, Va. Bar Assn. Labor and Employment Conf., 1994—97, 1999—, Va. Trial Lawyers Assn., 1995, 1997, Va. Law Found., 1995—, 1995—, Va. Assn. Def. Attys., 1996, 2001; mem. faculty Va. State Bar Law Student Professionalism Com.2, 2001—04; invitee Boyd Graves Conf., 1999—2009; substitute judge 19th Jud. Dist., 1998—, steering com. mem., 2004—09; mem. 4th Cir. Jud. Conf.; assoc. editor Cath. U. Law Rev. Bd. dir. Va. Commn. on Women and Minorities in the Legal Sys., 1987—90, sec., 1988—90; faculty mem. Va. State Bar Professionalism Com., 1997—2000, Va. State Bar Professionalism Com. for Law Students, 2001—05. Named Best Individual Employment Lawyer of Yr., 2012; named one of Best Lawyers in America, 1997—, 50 Best Lawyers in Washington, Washingtonian Mag., 1997, 40 Top Lawyers Under 40, 1998, 75 Best Lawyers, 2002, Best Employment Lawyers, 2004, Top 20 Attys. in Washington Area, 2007, Best Employment Lawyers, 2009, Top 12 Employment Lawyers in the Washington Met. Area, Legal Times, 2004, Almanac of Leading Lawyers, 2008, Top Va. Super Lawyers, Super Lawyers Mag., 2006, Va.'s Most Influential Women, Va. Lawyer's Weekly, 2009, Top 10 Lawyers in Met. Washington Area, DC Mag., 2009—11, Top 500 Plaintiff's Lawyers in America, Law Dragon, 2010, Top Lawyers, Labor & Employment Mag., 2010, Northern Va. Mag., 2011, Washington Best Lawyers, The Washington, 2011, Top Lawyers in Va., Richmond Times Dispatch, 2011. Master: George Mason Inns of Ct. (master 1996—); fellow: Western Counsel America, Internat. Acad. Trial Lawyers, Am. Coll. Trial Lawyers; mem.: Va. Women Attys. Assn., Litig. Counsel America, Fairfax Bar Assn. (chair diversity taskforce 1998—99, co-chair subcom. on minorities, Pres.'s Vol. award 1998, 1999), Minn. State Soc., Va. Trial Lawyers Assn. (mem. com. on long-range planning 1996—97, vice chmn. ann. conv. 1996—98), Va. Bar Assn. (spkr. 1995, 1997, mem. exec. com. young lawyers sect., mem. litig. com., mem. nominating com., chmn. model jud. com., mam., sect. on labor and employment law, mem. governing coun. 1994—2008). Office: Charlson Bredehoft Cohen Brown & Sakata 11260 Roger Bacon Dr Ste 201 Reston VA 20190-5252 Home: 11990 Market St Unit 614 Reston VA 20190 Home Phone: 703-444-0805; Office Phone: 703-318-6800. Personal E-mail: ecb@cbcblon.com. Business E-Mail: ebredehoft@charlsonbredehoft.com.

BREDEMEIER, MARY ELIZABETH, counselor, educator; b. Eden, NC, Sept. 4, 1924; d. William Thomas and Cora May (Lewis) Robertson; m. Harry C. Bredemeier, Nov. 16, 1953; 1 child, Suzanne Leaphart. BS, James Madison U., 1944; MA, Columbia U., 1946; EdD, Rutgers U., 1972. Instr. Finch Coll., NYC, 1945-46; tchr. Ben Franklin Jr. H.S., Yonkers, N.Y., 1949-53; instr. Douglass Coll., New Brunswick, N.J., 1953-54; tchr., counselor Middlesex County Vocat. and Tech. H.S., Woodbridge, N.J., 1955-67; prof. edn. Montclair State Coll., Upper Montclair, N.J., 1967-88, prof. emeritus, 1988—. Cons. Miami (Fla.)-Dade Pub. Schs., 1989—2005. Author: Labor Problems in America, 1970, Social Forces in Education, 1980, Urban Classroom Portraits, 1988; contbr. numerous articles to profl. jours. Democrat. Avocations: tennis, swimming, reading, jewelry-making. Office: 7441 Wayne Ave Apt 15C Miami Beach FL 33141-2566 Home (Summer): Box 741 North Truro MA 02652

BREDFELDT, JOHN CREIGHTON, economics educator, writer, retired military officer; b. Oct. 31, 1947; s. Willis John and Geraldine Elizabeth (Creighton) Bredfeldt; m. Janice Elaine Hamilton; children: Jason Caulter, Bryan Thomas. BBA, Wichita State U., 1969, MA in Econs., 1971; PhD in Pub. Adminstrn., La Salle U., 1995; grad., Air Command and Staff Coll., 1984, Nat. Security Mgmt. Coll., 1987. Dir. Brennan Halls Wichita State U., 1969-71; commd. 2d lt. USAF, 1971, advanced through grades to lt. col., 1987, ret., 1993; budget/cost analyst Aero. Sys. Divsn., Dayton, Ohio, 1971-76; insp. Air Force IG, Andrews AFB, Md., 1976-79; chief economist Dir. Programs AF/PRP, Pentagon, Va., 1979-83; chief cost analyst divsn. USAF Europe, 1985-87, dep. dir. program control, engine program office Dayton, 1987-89; dir. program control spl. ops. forces USAF, 1989-93; project leader econs., fin. analyst Bering Straits Aeorspace Svc., Warner Robins, Ga., 1993—. Instr. econs. Wichita State U., 1969-71; bus. prof. Bowie State Coll., 1980-83; econs. instr. European divsn. U. Md., Germany, 1985-87, Sinclair CC, Dayton, 1988-93, adj. prof. Macon State Coll., Ga., 1994—2012; adj. prof. Mercer U., 1996, Wesleyan Coll., 1998. Author of 2 books; contbr. articles to profl. jours. Rep., Sunday sch. tchr. Ramstein Protestant Parish Coun. Germany, 1984-86; asst. scoutmaster Ramstein coun. Boy Scouts Am., 1984-87, den leader, 1998, charter rep., 1999—2012; v.p. St. Timothy Lutheran Ch., Dayton, 1989-91; prayer team leader Wesley United Meth. Ch., Macon, 2004, chmn. fin. com., 2005-07. Mem. Internat. Cost Estimating and Analysis Assn., Am. Soc. Mil. Comptrollers, Nat. Eagle Scout Assn., Air Force Assn., Mil. Officers Assn. America, Am. Legion.

BREEDEN, DOUGLAS TOWER, finance educator, consultant, former dean; b. Leavenworth, Ind., Sept. 29, 1950; s. Russell E. and Annabelle (Tower) B.; m. Josie Chao-Chih Pian, June 4, 1972; children: Jennifer, Laurel, Mark, David. BS in mgmt. sci., MIT, 1972; postgrad., Harvard U., 1973—74; MA in econs., Stanford U., 1976, PhD in fin., 1978. Asst. prof. fin. U. Chgo., 1978—79, Stanford U., 1979—81, assoc. prof. fin., 1981—85; vis. assoc. prof. fin. Yale U., 1981—82, Sloan Sch. Mgmt., MIT, 1984-85; area coord. for fin. and econs. Fuqua Sch. Bus., Duke U., Durham, NC, 1985—86, 1987—88, assoc. prof. fin., 1985—89, co-dir. Futures and Options Rsch. Ctr., 1987-90, prof. fin. Durham, NC, 1989—91, rsch. prof. fin., 1991—99, dean, 2001—07, William W. Priest prof. fin., 2001—; vis. prof. fin. Kenan Flagler Bus. Sch., U. NC, Chapel Hill, 2000, Dalton McMichael Prof. Fin., 2000-01; co-founder Smith Breeden Assocs., Chapel Hill, NC, 1982—, chmn. bd., 1982—2005, chmn. emeritus, 2005—, pres., 1988-2000; chmn. bd. Smith Breeden Mut. Funds, 1992-2000; chmn. bd., prin. shareholder Harrington Fin. Group, 1988—2001. Chmn., owner Wyandotte Cmty. Corp., 1989—; co-owner, Old Capital Golf Course, Corydon, IN, 1998-; chmn. bd., prin. shareholder, Cmty. First Fin. Group, 1986-; cons. Chgo. Bd. Trade, 1977-82; exec. tchr. Nomura Sch. Adv. Mgmt., Tokyo, 1987, 89-92. Editor Jour. Fixed Income, 1990-2001; assoc. editor Jour. of Fin., 1988-91, Rev. of Fin. Studies, 1987-89, Jour. Fin. Quantitative Analysis, 1985-87, Jour. Fin. Econs., 1982-88, Jour. Money, Credit and Banking, 1980-83; contbr. articles to profl. jours. Bd. dirs. Chapel Hill-Carrboro City Schs., 1989-93, Chapel Hill-Carrboro Pub Sch. Found., 1987-89; chmn. Breeden Family Found., 1989—; bd. dirs. Fund for Human Possibilities, 1995—; bd. visitors Fuqua Sch. Bus., Duke U., 1995-99; mem. deans adv. coun. Sloan Sch. Mgmt., MIT, 1999—, mem. vis. com., 1999—, mem. Pres. adv. com., 2000-01; donor Smith Breeden prize Jour. of Fin., 1989—. Rotary Internat. Grad. Fellow in Bus., 1972-73, Batterymarch Fin. Mgmt. Fellow, 1981-82, Dean Witter Fellow in Fin., 1981-82. Mem. Am. Fin. Assn. (bd. dirs. 1988-91), Western Fin. Assn., Applied Capital Markets Group of Nat. Bur. Econ. Rsch. Methodist. Avocations: golf, skiing, basketball. Office: Duke U Fuqua Sch Bus One Towerview Dr Box 90120 Durham NC 27708-0120

BREEDEN, MIMI, bank executive; B in English and French, Fla. State U.; MBA, Ga. State U. Analyst R & D dept. SunTrust Banks, Inc., mgr. Ga. In-Store Banking unit, with retirement svcs. area of instl. trust, 2001, mgr. instl. trust, 2002—05, mgr. pvt. wealth mgmt. line of bus., 2005—06, corp. exec. v.p., dir. human resources, mem. mgmt. com., 2006—. Office: SunTrust Banks Inc PO Box 4418 Atlanta GA 30302-4418 Office Phone: 404-588-7711. Office Fax: 404-827-6173.

BREEN, JOHN DANIEL, federal judge; b. Jackson, Tenn., July 10, 1950; m. Linda Turnbo; two children. BA summa cum laude, Spring Hill Coll., 1972; JD, U. Tenn., 1975. Bar: Tenn. 1975, U.S. Ct. Appeals (6th cir.) 1977, U.S. Supreme Ct. 1979. Atty. Waldrop and Hall, Jackson, Tenn., 1975—2003; magistrate judge US Dist. Ct. (we. dist.) Tenn., 1991—2003, dist. judge, 2003—. Mem. exec. com. West Tenn. Boy Scouts of Am.; lifetime bd. dirs. West Tenn. Cerebral Palsy Ctr. appointed U.S Dist. Judge, Western Dist. of Tenn., 2003. Mem. ABA, Fed. Bar Assn., Memphis Bar Found., Am. Bar Found., Fed. Magistrate Judges Assn. (cir. dir. 6th cir. 2000-03), Fed. Judges Assn. (cir. dir. 6th cir. 2009-11), Tenn. Bar Found. (chair 2002-03), Tenn. Bar Assn. (pres. 1996-97), Jackson-Madison County Bar Assn. (pres. 1983-84), Howell Jackson Inn of Ct. (master). Office: US Dist Ct 444 US Courthouse 111 S Highland Ave Rm 262 Jackson TN 38301-6101 Office Fax: 731-421-9255.

BREEN, JOHN EDWARD, civil engineer, educator; b. Buffalo, May 1, 1932; s. Timothy J. and Alice C. (Keenan) B.; m. Marian T. Killian, June 20, 1953; children: Mary L., Michael T., Dennis P., Sheila A., Sean E., Kerry T., Christopher D. B.C.E., Marquette U., Milw., 1953; DSc (hon.), Marquette U., 2004; MS in Civil Engring., U. Mo., 1957; PhD, U. Tex., Austin, 1962. Registered profl. engr., Tex., Mo. Structural designer Harnischfeger Corp., Milw., 1952-53; asst. prof. U. Mo., Columbia, 1957-59; mem. faculty U. Tex., Austin, 1959—, prof. civil engring., 1969—, J.J. McKetta prof. engring., 1977-81, Carol Cockrell Curran chair engring., 1981-84, Nasser I. Al-Rashid chair civil engring., 1984—; dir. P.M. Ferguson Structural Engring. Lab., Balcones Research Center, 1967-85. Cons. in field. Contbr. articles to profl. jours. Served to lt. USNR, 1953-56. Recipient Tchg. Excellence award Gen. Dynamics Corp., 1971, Tchg. Excellence award U. Tex. Student Assn., 1963, Teaching Excellence award Std. Oil Found. Ind., 1968, Fedn. Internat. Precontrainte medal, 1990, Internat. award of merit in structural engring. Internat. Assn. Bridge and Structural Engring., 2000, Freyssinet medal Internat. Assn. for Structural Concrete, 2002, Caquot medal French Assn. Civil Engring., 2004, John A. Roebling medal Engrs. Soc. Western Pa., 2005. Mem.: ASCE (T.Y. Lin medal 1985, A.J. Boase Reinforced Concrete Rsch. Coun. award 1987, T.Y. Lin medal 1989, 1991, Croes medal 1999, T.Y. Lin medal 2009), Swiss Acad. Engring., Nat. Acad. Engring., Am. Concrete Inst. (hon.; bd. dirs. 1974—77, Wason medal 1972, Raymond C. Reese Rsch. medal 1972, Raymond Davis lectr. 1978, Raymond C. Reese Rsch. medal 1979, Kelly medal 1981, Wason medal 1983, Anderson medal 1987, Bloem award 1989, Alfred E. Lindau award 1994, Structural Engring. award 2002, C.P. Siess Structural Rsch. award 2008), Austin Yacht Club (commodore 1977), Sigma Xi. Democrat. Roman Catholic. Home: 8603 Azalea Trl Austin TX 78759-7501 Office: Univ Tex Ferguson Lab 10100 Burnet Rd PRC Bldg 177 Austin TX 78758-4445 Office Phone: 512-471-4578. Business E-Mail: jbreen@mail.utexas.edu.

BREEN, MARILYN, mathematics educator; b. Anderson, SC, Nov. 8, 1944; d. Marvin and Martha Louise (Lesser) B.; m. Walter Gill Kelley, May 24, 1975; 1 child, Joyce Elizabeth. BA, Agnes Scott Coll., 1966; MS, Clemson U., 1968, PhD, 1970. Mem. faculty dept. math. U. Okla., Norman, 1971—, instr., 1971-73, asst. prof., 1973-77, assoc. prof., 1977-82, prof., 1982—. Contbr. rsch. articles to math. jours. Mem. Am. Math. Soc., Math. Assn. Am., Phi Beta Kappa, Sigma Xi, Phi Kappa Phi. Office: U Okla Dept Math 601 Elm Ave Norman OK 73019-3100

BREES, DREW (ANDREW CHRISTOPHER BREES), professional football player; b. Austin, Tex., Jan. 15, 1979; s. Chip and Mina Brees; m. Brittany Dudchenko, 2003; children: Baylen Robert, Bowen Christopher, Callen Christian. BA in Indsl. Mgmt. & Mfg., Purdue U., West Lafayette, Ind., 2001. Quarterback San Diego Chargers, 2001—06, New Orleans Saints, 2006—. Co-author (with Chris Fabry): Coming Back Stronger: Unleashing the Hidden Power of Adversity, 2010; appeared in (TV series) Entourage, 2010. Co-founder The Brees Dream Found., 2003—. Recipient Maxwell award, Maxwell Football Club, 2000, Bert Bell award, 2009, Bart Starr Man of the Yr. award, 2011; co-recipient Walter Payton Man of Yr. award, 2006; named Big Ten Player of Yr., 1998, 2000, NFL Comeback Player of Yr., AP, 2004, Sports Illustrated, 2004, Dallas Morning News, 2004, Most Improved Player of Yr., Pro Football Weekly, 2004, Pro Football Writers of America, 2004, CBSSportsline.com, 2004, FoxSports.com, 2004, Nat. Football Conf. Offensive Player of Yr., 2006, 2008, 2009, 1st Team All-Pro, AP, 2006, NFL Offensive Player of Yr., 2008, 2011, The Sporting News, 2008, 2009, FedEx Air NFL Player of Yr., 2008, Super Bowl XLIV MVP, NFL, 2010, Sportsman of Yr., Sports Illus., 2010, Male Athlete of Yr., AP, 2010; named to The American Football Conf. Pro-Bowl Team, NFL, 2004, The Nat. Football Conf. Pro Bowl Team, 2006, 2008—11. Mem.: Sigma Chi. Achievements include leading the NFL in: passing yards 2006, 2008, 2011, 2012; pass attempts, 2007; pass completions, 2007, 2011; passing touchdowns, 2008, 2009, 2011, 2012; member of Super Bowl XLIV championship winning New Orleans Saints, 2010; holding the: NFL single season record for passing yards (5,476 yards), 2011; NFL record for consecutive games with a touchdown passes, including the playoffs (54), 2012. Office: New Orleans Saints 5800 Airline Dr Metairie LA 70003*

BREEZE, WILLIAM HANCOCK, academic administrator; b. Cin., Nov. 25, 1923; s. William T. and Nancy (Hancock) B.; m. JoAnne Robertson Watson, Oct. 8, 1949 (dec. Jan. 1983); 1 child, Nancy Louise Breeze; m. Barbara L. Hall, Dec. 15, 1990. Student, Berea Coll., 1943-44; AB, Centre Coll., Danville, Ky., 1945; MA, U. Ky., 1948. Various actuarial positions Ohio Nat. Life Ins. Co., Cin., 1948-56, actuary, 1956-65, asst. to pres., 1965-67, sr. v.p., 1967-72, exec. v.p., 1972-86; v.p., gen. sec. Centre Coll., Danville, Ky., 1987-88, 89-91, acting pres., 1988-89, spl. asst. to pres. for endowment, 1991—. Bd. dirs. Ohio Nat. Life Ins. Co., 1966-88. Bd. dirs. Jr. Achievement Greater Cin., 1974-84; trustee Centre Coll., 1980-86. Served to lt. (j.g.) USNR, 1943-46, PTO. Fellow: Soc. Actuaries. Republican. Presbyterian. Avocations: reading, classical music. Home: 468 W Broadway St Danville KY 40422-1420 Office: Centre Coll Danville KY 40422 Home Phone: 859-236-1816; Office Phone: 859-238-5207. Business E-Mail: breeze@centre.edu.

BREGMAN, ARTHUR, child and adolescent psychiatrist; MD, NY Med. Coll., Valhalla, NY, 1974. Resident psychiatry Univ. Miami Jackson Meml. Hosp.; asst. chief psychiatry Miami Children's Hosp., chief psychiatry; founder PsychSolutions, Inc., 1993. Office: PsychSolutions Incorporated 701 SW 27th Ave Ste 500 Miami FL 33135 Office Phone: 305-668-9000. Office Fax: 305-662-1788.

BREGMAN, MITCHELL S., manufacturing executive; BS in Indsl. Engring., Cornell U.; MBA, Harvard U. Joined GNB Technologies Inc., 1979, pres., Indsl. Battery divsn., mfg. mgr., Transp. divsn., plant mgr., Transp. divsn., dir., sales, Transp. divsn., product mgr., Transp. divsn.; joined Exide Technologies, 2000, v.p., gen. mgr., GNB Indsl. Power, v.p., gen. mgr., stationary power, GNB Indsl. Power, v.p., ops., GNB Indsl. Power, pres., Global Network Power, pres., Indsl. Energy Americas, 2003—. Office: Exide Technologies Bldg 200 13000 Deerfield Pky Milton GA 30004 Office Phone: 678-566-9000. Office Fax: 678-566-9188. Business E-Mail: mbregman@exide.com.

BREHL, ROBERT J., real estate company executive; b. Feb. 23, 1962; BS in Acctg., U. Louisville. Various positions through gen. mgr. Ernst & Young LLP, Louisville, Ky., 1985—98; sr. v.p., contr. Atria Sr. Living Group, Inc., 1998—2005; chief acctg. officer ElderTrust; chief acctg. officer, contr. Ventas, Inc., 2006—. Mem. AICPA, Ky. Soc. CPAs. Office: Ventas Inc 10350 Ormsby Park Pl Ste 300 Louisville KY 40223 Office Phone: 502-357-9000. Office Fax: 502-357-9001. Business E-Mail: rbrehl@ventasreit.com.

BREIDENBACH, WARREN CONRAD, III, plastic surgeon, hand surgeon; b. June 21, 1946; Grad., U. Calgary, Can.; MD, Harvard Med. Sch., 1975. Cert. Plastic Surgery, Hand Surgery. Postgraduate tng. in plastic surgery McGill U., Montreal; microsurgery fellow Eastern Vir. Med. Sch., Norfolk; Christine M. Kleinert hand fellow; ptnr. Kleinert, Kutz and Associates Hand Care Ctr., PLLC; asst. clin. prof. surgery (plastic and reconstructive) U. Louisville. Author of several articles. Recipient Clin. Rsch. Scholarship award, Am. Soc. Plastic Surgery and Reconstructive Surgery, Senior award. Mem.: Am. Soc. for Peripheral Nerve (sec.), Am. Soc. for Surgery of the Hand. Achievements include being appointed the first hand scholar with the Louisville Institute for Hand and Microsurgery; being the lead surgeon in all three successful hand transplant surgeries that took place in the US in 1999, 2001 and 2006. Office: Kleinert Kutz and Associates Hand Care Ctr PLLC Ste 700 225 Abraham Flxner Way Louisville KY 40202 Office Phone: 502-561-4263.

BREITFELD, PHILIP PAUL, pharmaceutical executive, oncologist; b. Geneva, NY, Mar. 4, 1953; m. Susan Gail Kreissman. AB in Chemistry, Princeton U.; MD, U. Rochester, 1979. Cert. Pediat., 1984, Pediat. Hematology-Oncology, 1998. Intern pediatrics U. Rochester, NY, 1979—80, resident pediatric hematological oncology NY, 1980—82; fellowship Children's Hosp.-Harvard, Boston, 1982—85; staff mem. Dana-Farber/Children's Hosp. Cancer Inst., Boston, 1985—88, U. Mass. Med. Ctr., Worcester, 1988—91, Riley Hosp. for Children, Ind. U., 1991—2000; staff mem. pediat. Duke U. Med. Ctr., Durham, NC, 2000—; assoc. cons. prof. pediat. Duke U., Durham, NC; med. dir. oncology EMD Pharm., Inc.; exec. dir. oncology devel., assoc. chief med. officer BioCryst Pharmaceuticals, Inc., Birmingham, 2007—. Vice chair Soft Tissue Sarcoma Com. Children's Oncology Group. Contbr. articles to med. jours. Office: BioCryst Pharmaceuticals Inc 2190 Parkway Lake Dr Birmingham AL 35244 Office Phone: 205-444-4600. Office Fax: 205-444-4640.

BREKHUS, MELVIN G., construction executive; b. ND; BS in Engring. Sci., Univ. Mont., 1972. Various positions including, chemist, production mgr. and plant mgr. Lehigh Portland Cement Co., 1972—83; tech. mgr., plant mgr. Mo. Portland Cement Co., 1984—89; v.p., cement prodn. Texas Industries, Inc., 1989, exec. v.p., cement, aggregates and concrete, 1998—2004, pres., CEO & bd. dirs., 2004—. Pres. Am. Portland Cement Alliance; chmn. Innovative Paving Rsch. Found., Portland Cement Assn., 2001—02, bd. dirs. Mem.: Portland Cement Assn. (chmn. 2001—02, bd. dirs.). Office: Texas Industries Inc 1341 W Mockingbird Ln Ste 700W Dallas TX 75247-6913 Office Phone: 972-647-6700. Office Fax: 972-647-3964. Business E-Mail: mbrekhus@txi.com.

BREMER, PAUL (LEWIS PAUL BREMER III, JERRY BREMER), security firm executive, former ambassador; b. Hartford, Conn., Sept. 30, 1941; s. L. Paul and Nina (Struthers) B.; m. Frances Winfield, June 11, 1966; children: Paul, Leila. BA, Yale U., 1963; cert., Inst. d'etudes Politiques, U. Paris, 1964; MBA, Harvard U., 1966; LLD (hon.), Ave Maria U., 2005. With Diplomatic Svc., 1966; exec. asst. to sec. US Dept. State, Washington, 1974-76, dep. exec. sec., 1979-81, exec. sec., spl. asst. to sec. of state, 1981—83; dep. amb., chief of mission US Embassy, Oslo, 1976—79; US amb. to The Netherlands US Dept. State, The Hague, 1983—86, amb.-at-large for counter-terrorism Washington, 1986—89; mng. dir. Kissinger Associates, 1989—2000; chmn. Nat. Commn. on Terrorism, 1999—2001; chmn., CEO Marsh Crisis Consulting Co., 2001—03; mem. Homeland Security Adv. Coun., 2002—04; presdl. envoy to Iraq The White House, Baghdad, 2003; dir. Office of Reconstruction & Humanitarian Assistance Coalition Provisional Authority, Baghdad, Iraq, 2003—04; chmn. advisory bd. Global Secure Corp., Washington, 2009—; pres., CEO World T.E.A.M. Sports, Washington, 2010—. Co-author (with Malcom McConnell): My Year in Iraq: My Struggle to Build a Future of Hope, 2006; appeared in (documentaries) No End in Sight, 2007. Recipient Superior Honor award US Dept. State, 1974, Presdl. Merit Pay award, 1983, Presdl. Medal of Freedom, 2004, Joseph H. Sherick award, US Dept Def., 2004, Victory of Freedom award, Nixon Library Mem. Internat. Inst. Strategic Studies, Coun. on Fgn. Rels. (bd. dirs.), Netherlands-American Found., Conner Peripherals Inc., Air Products & Chemicals Inc. Republican. Roman Catholic. Avocations: skiing, jogging, history. Office: Global Secure Corp 1033 N Fairfax St Ste 302 Alexandria VA 22314 also: World TEAM Sports 1300 17th St N Ste 750 Arlington VA 22209-3872 Office Phone: 703-299-0033, 855-987-8326. Office Fax: 703-299-9033, 855-288-3377. E-mail: paulbremer@worldteamsports.org.

BRENDER, JEAN DIANE, epidemiologist, educator, nurse, university administrator; b. Bellingham, Wash., Nov. 23, 1951; d. Otto and Jennie Wilma Tolsma; m. Dennis Ray Brender, Aug. 30, 1975; 1 child, Valerie. BSN summa cum laude, Whitworth Coll., 1974; MN in Nursing, U. Wash., 1979, PhD in Epidemiology, 1983. RN Tex. Staff nurse, infection control Sacred Heart Med. Ctr., Spokane, Wash., 1974-80; instr. nursing Intercollegiate Ctr. for Nursing Edn., Spokane, 1979-80, asst. prof. nursing, 1982-84; teaching asst. epidemiology U. Wash., Seattle, 1981-82; rsch. health scientist Audie L. Murphy Vets. Hosp., San Antonio, 1984-85; staff epidemiologist bur. epidemiology Tex. Dept. Health, Austin, 1986-87, acting program dir. environ. epidemiology program, 1987, dir. environ. epidemiology program, 1987-93, dir. noncommunicable disease epidemiology and toxicology, 1993-97; infectious disease epidemiologist Bur. Disease Control, 1997-99; also state environ. epidemiologist Tex. Dept. Health, Austin, 1993-97; assoc. prof. health svcs. rsch. Tex. State U., 1999—2005; assoc. prof. epidemiology Sch. Pub. Health Tex. A&M Health Sci. Ctr., College Station, Tex., 2005—08; prof. epidemiology Tex. A&M Health Sci. Ctr., Sch. Pub. Health, Tex., 2008—; assoc. dean rsch. Tex. A&M Health Sci. Ctr., Sch. Rural Pub. Health, 2009—; fellow Am. Coll. Epidemiology. Bd. dirs. Agr. Resources Protection Authority; adj. instr. allied health scis. and health adminstrn. Tex. State U., 1988-90; adj. asst. prof. epidemiology U. Tex. Health Sci. Ctr.-Houston Sch. Pub. Health, 1985-93, adj. assoc. prof., 1993-2010. Contbr. articles to profl. jours. Recipient H.E.A.L.T.H. award, 1994; grantee in field. Fellow Am. Coll. Epidemiology; mem. Internat. Soc. Environ. Epidemiology, Soc. Epidemiologic Rsch., Tex. Pub. Health Assn. (editl. bd.), Nat. Rsch. Coun.(com. mem.) Avocations: reading, church activities, skiing. Home: 6902 Alder Cove Austin TX 78750-8161 Office Phone: 979-862-1573. Business E-Mail: jdbrender@srph.tamhsc.edu. E-mail: jdbrender@aol.com.

BRENHOLT, JOHN, corporate financial executive; BBA in Acctg, U. Wis., Milwaukee, WI, 1986. CPA. Sr. v.p., CFO Vistar Corp., Corp. Express, Inc.; auditor Deloitte & Touche, 1986—91; various positions TEREX Corp., 1991—95; v.p., fin. Hickory Farms, 1995—99; exec. v.p., CFO Schneider Nat. Inc., 2008—10, Florida East Coast Railway, 2010—. Office: Florida East Coast Railway 7411 Fullerton St Ste 100 Jacksonville FL 32256-3628 Office Phone: 904-538-6100. Office Fax: 904-538-6480. Business E-Mail: jbrenholt@fecrwy.com.

BRENNAN, ELLA, restaurant manager; b. New Orleans, Nov. 27, 1925; d. Owen Edward Brennan Sr. and Nellie Brennan; m. Paul Martin, May 1957 (div.); children: Alex Brennan-Martin, Ti Adelaide Martin. Mgr. The Vieux Carre; ptnr. Brennan's, Houston, Commander's Palace, New Orleans, 1969—, Mr. B's, New Orleans, Palace Cafe, New Orleans, Ristorante Bacco, New Orleans, Third Coast, Houston. Co-author: The Commander's Palace New Orleans Cookbook, 1984. Recipient Lifetime Achievement award, Southern Foodways Alliance, 2002, James Beard Found., 2009. Office: Commanders Palace 1403 Washington Ave New Orleans LA 70130

BRENNAN, LAWRENCE EDWARD, retired electronics engineer; b. Oak Park, Ill., Jan. 29, 1927; s. Lawrence John and Lillian Irene (Day) B.; m. Mary Ellen Green, Aug. 9, 1947; children: Kathleen, Marianne, Teresa, James. BSEE, U. Ill, 1948; PhD in Elec. Engring., U. Ill., 1951. Mem. tech. staff Rand Corp., Santa Monica, Calif., 1957-67; chief scientist Tech. Svc. Corp., Santa Monica, 1967-80; v.p. Adaptive Sensors, Inc., Santa Monica, 1980-93; cons. pvt. practice, Orange Beach, Ala., 1993—99; ret., 1999—. Served with USN, 1944-46. Fellow: IEEE. Home Phone: 251-987-1526. E-mail: lbrennan@gulftel.com.

BRENNAN, NORMA JEAN, retired professional society administrator; b. Helena, Mont., Apr. 16, 1939; d. Harland Sanford Herrin and Elizabeth (Wardlaw) Brumfield; m. Anthony E. Brennan, Dec. 4, 1964 (div. Mar. 1986); children: Christopher E., Kimberly A. BA, U. Pacific, 1960. Editl. asst. Am. Rocket Soc., NYC, 1961-62, asst. mng. editor, 1962-65; mng. editor AIAA, NYC, 1978-80, publs. divsn. dir. NYC, Washington, Reston, Va., 1980—2008. Mem. Young Republicans, Stockton, Calif., 1958-60; vol. Mt. Sinai Hosp., N.Y.C., 1962-64. Fellow: AIAA (Space Shuttle Flag award); mem.: Washington Women's Info. Network, N.Am. Serials Interest Group, Coun. Engring. and Sci. Soc. Execs., Assn. Am. Pubs., Coun. Sci. Editors, Soc. for Scholarly Pub. (bd. dirs.). Avocations: reading, travel, gardening. Home: 11551 Links Dr Reston VA 20190-4820 Personal E-mail: nbre1@verizon.net.

BRENNAN, THOMAS EMMETT, lawyer; b. Detroit, May 27, 1929; s. Joseph Terence and Jeannette Frances (Sullivan) B.; m. Pauline Mary Weinberger, Apr. 28, 1951; children: Thomas Emmett, Margaret Ann and John Seamus (twins), William Joseph, Marybeth, Ellen Mary. LL.B., U. Detroit, 1952; LL.D., Thomas M. Cooley Law Sch., 1976. Bar: Mich. 1953. Assoc. Kenny, Radom, Rockwell & Mountain, Detroit, 1952-53; ptnr. Waldron, Brennan & Maher, Detroit, 1953-61; judge Detroit Ct. Common Pleas, 1962-63, Wayne County Circuit Ct., 1963-66; justice Mich. Supreme Ct., 1967-73, chief justice, 1969-70; adj. prof. polit. sci. U. Detroit, 1970-72; founder, dean emeritus Thomas M. Cooley Law Sch., Lansing, 1972—. Mem. Mich. Commn. Law Enforcement and Criminal Justice, 1969-70; bd. dirs. Motor Wheel Corp., 1987-89. Author: Judging the Law Schools, 1997, The Bench, 2000. Founder Conv. US, 2008, chmn., 2010; bd. dir. Cath. League for Religious & Civil Rights, 1993—. Fellow Am. Bar Found., Mich Bar Found.; mem. ABA, Ingham County Bar Assn., State Bar Mich. (bd. commrs. 1979-83), Mich. Assn. of Professions (Disting. Citizens award 1982), Assn. of Ind. Colls. and Univs. Mich. (bd. dirs., exec. com., sec. 1990, chmn. 1991), Cath. Lawyers Soc. (Thomas More award 1987), Am. Jurisprudence Soc., Inc. Soc., Irish Am. Lawyers, Cooley Legal Author's Soc. (charter), Mich. State C. of C. (bd. dirs. 1988-94), Walnut Hills Country Club (bd. dirs. 1992-95), KC, Delta Theta Phi. Roman Catholic. Home: 2174 Golfview Ct Harbor Springs MI 49740-9276 Personal E-mail: thosbrennan@aol.com.

BRENNEN, DAVID A., dean, law educator; B in Fin., Fla. Atlantic U., Boca Raton, 1988; JD, U. Fla. Coll. Law, 1991, LLM in Tax Law, 1994. Bar: Fla. Atty. Moody & Salzman, PA, Gainsville, Fla., Bobo, Spicer & Ciotoli, PA, West Palm Beach, Fla., Messer, Vickers, Caparello, Madsen, Lewis, Goldman & Metz, PA, Tallahassee, State Fla. Dept. Revenue; adj. prof. Fla. A&M U., 1994; prof. Syracuse U. Coll. Law, NY, U. Richmond Sch. Law, Va., Mercer U. Sch. Law; prof. law U. Ga. Law Sch., 2006—09; dean U. Ky. Coll. Law, 2009—, W.T. Lafferty prof. law, 2009—10, Laramie L. Leatherman prof. law, 2010—. Co-founder, co-editor Nonprofit Law Prof Blog; founding editor Nonprofit and Philanthropy Law Abstracts; vis. prof. U. Ala., Temple U., Phila. Mem.: ABA Sect. Taxation, Nat. Bar Assn., Assn. Am. Law Schools (dep. dir.), Am. Law Inst., Soc. Am. Law Teachers. Office: University of Kentucky College of Law Rm 209 620 S Limestone Lexington KY 40506-0048 Office Phone: 859-257-1678. Office Fax: 859-323-1061. Business E-Mail: david.brennen@uky.edu.*

BRESALIER, ROBERT SCOTT, gastroenterologist, educator; BS in Biol. Sci. with honors, SUNY, 1973; MD, U. of Chgo., 1978. Diplomate Am. Bd. Internal Medicine, 1981, Am. Bd. Internal Medicine-gastroenterology, 1983. Resident internal medicine Barnes-Jewish Hosp., 1978—81; fellow gastroenterolgy Univ. of Calif., San Francisco, 1981—84. Prof. gastrointerology, hepatology and nutrition internal medicine divsn. The Univ. of Tex. MD Anderson Cancer Ctr., 2003—. Author: (articles) Management of Barrett's Esophagus. Cases and Questions, 2005, Chemoprevention of colorectal neoplasia: advances and controversies (the COX-2 story), 2007, Neutrophil Gelatinase-Associated Lipocalin: A Novel Suppressor of Invasion and Angiogenesis in Pancreatic Cancer, 2008, Chemoprevention of colorectal cancer: why all the confusion?, 2008, Plasma glycoprotein profiling for colorectal cancer biomarker identification by lectin glycoarray and lectin blot, 2008, Barrett's esophagus and esophageal adenocarcinoma, 2008, Colorectal Adenomas in a Randomized Folate Trial: The Role of Baseline Dietary and Circulating Folate Levels, 2008, Cardiovascular events associated with rofecoxib: Final Analysis of the APPROVe Trial, 2008, Polyphenon E inhibits the growth of human Barrett's and aerodigestive adenocarcinoma cells by suppressing cyclin D1 expression, 2009, Nonsteroidal anti-inflammatory drug use after 3 years of aspirin use and colorectal adenoma risk: observational follow-up of a randomized study, 2009, Folic acid and risk of prostate cancer: results from a randomized clinical trial, 2009; editor: (books) Current Opinion in Gastroenterology. In: Large Intestine, 2008. Office: The University of Texas MD Anderson Cancer Center Unit 1466 Rm FCT13 6008 1400 Pressler Houston TX 77030-4009 Office Phone: 713-745-4340. Office Fax: 713-745-9295.

BRESLAWSKY, MARC C., retired security firm executive; b. NYC, Sept. 26, 1942; s. Graham and Mollie (Sofferman) B.; m. Deborah Rose Breslawsky; children: Adam, Cindy. BA, NYU, 1963. V.p. mktg. and devel. bus. sys. Pitney Bowes, Inc., Stamford, Conn., 1980—82, v.p., gen. mgr. Facsimile Divsn., 1982—85, v.p. fin. and adminstrn., 1985—87, CEO Facsimile Divsn., 1985—2001, pres., CEO Dictaphone Corp. Stratford, Conn., 1987—90, pres. office sys. Pitney Bowes Copier Trumbull, Conn., 1990—98, CEO Pitney Bowes Copier, 1990—94, vice chmn. Stamford, Conn., 1994—96, pres., COO, 1996—2001; chmn., CEO Imagistics Internat., Inc. (formerly Pitney Bowes Office Sys.), 2001—05. Bd. dirs. The United Illuminating Co., C.R. Bard, Inc., Imagistic Internat. Inc., Oce Holdings USA Inc. (subs. Oce N.V.), UIL Holdings Corp., Brink's Co., 1999—. Mem. corp. coll. coun. Western Conn. State U., 1987. Mem. Am. Inst. CPA's, Conn. Soc. CPA's, Fin. Execs. Inst. Office: Brink's Co Bd Directors 1801 Bayberry Ct Richmond VA 23226-8100 Office Phone: 804-289-9600. Office Fax: 804-289-9746. Business E-Mail: mbreslawsky@brinkscompany.com.

BRETT, THOMAS RUTHERFORD, federal judge; b. Oklahoma City, Oct. 2, 1931; s. John A. and Norma (Dougherty) B.; m. Mary Jean James, Aug. 26, 1952; children: Laura Elizabeth Brett Tribble, James Ford, Susan Marie Brett Crump, Maricarolyn Swab. BBA, U. Okla., 1953, LL.B., 1957, JD, 1971. Bar: Okla. 1957. Asst. county atty., Tulsa, 1957; mem. firm Hudson, Hudson, Wheaton, Kyle & Brett, Tulsa, 1958-69, Jones, Givens, Brett, Gotcher, Doyle & Bogan, 1969-79; judge U.S. Dist. Ct. (no. dist.) Okla., Tulsa, 1979—2003; of counsel Crowe and Dunlevy, 1996—2003. Bd. regents U. Okla., 1971-78; mem. adv. bd. Salvation Army; trustee Okla. Bar Found. Col. JAG, USAR, 1953-83. Named to Okla. Heritage Assn. Hall of Fame, 2000. Fellow Am. Coll. Trial Lawyers, Am. Bar Found.; mem. Okla. Bar Assn. (pres. 1970), Tulsa County Bar Assn. (pres. 1965), U. Okla. Coll. Law Alumni Assn. (bd. dirs.), Order of Coif (hon.). Democrat.

BREWBAKER, DICK LANSDEN, state legislator; b. Jan. 28, 1961; m. Ruth Wible Brewbaker; children: Alex Brewbaker, Ben Brewbaker, Mac Brewbaker, Tom Brewbaker, David Brewbaker. Grad., Vanderbilt U., Nashville, 1983. Tchr. The Montgomery Acad., Trinity Presbyn. Sch.; wrestling coach Ga. Washington Jr. High; pres., CEO Brewbaker Motors Inc.; rep. Ala. House of Representatives, 2002—11; mem. Dist. 25 Ala. State Senate, 2011—. Del. Rep. Nat. Conv., 1996, 2000; mem. Montgomery County Rep. Com., Ala.; bd. dirs. Salvation Army, Father Walter's Children Ctr. Mem.: NRA, Spina Bifida Assn. America. Republican. Presbyterian. Office: Alabama State Senate State House Rm 734 11 S Union St Montgomery AL 36130 Office Phone: 334-242-7895. Business E-Mail: dick.brewbaker@alsenate.gov.

BREWER, CLINT, editor; b. Knoxville, Tenn. m. Amy Brewer; children: Emma Grace, Davis Clinton. Music critic Knoxville (Tenn.) Jour.; staff reporter Lebanon (Tenn.) Democrat, mng. editor, 2002—06; editor Gannett Corp. Middle Tenn. Newspaper Group, 2000; owner Mt. Juliet (Tenn.) News, 2000—02; exec. editor City Paper, Nashville, 2006—. Recipient Malcolm Law Meml. award for Investigative Reporting (4-time winner), Tenn. AP Mng. Editor's Contest. Mem.: Tenn. Press Assn., Soc. Profl. Journalists (pres. elect). Office: City Paper 624 Grassmere Park Ste 28 Nashville TN 37221 Office Phone: 615-301-9229. E-mail: cbrewer@nashvillecitypaper.com.

BREWER, EILEEN D. (L. EILEEN DOYLE BREWER), nephrologist, educator; b. Houston, Oct. 27, 1944; MD, Washington U., St. Louis, 1971. Cert. Am. Bd. Pediat., Am. Bd. Pediat. Sub-Bd. in Pediatric Nephrology. Intern pediat. Children's Hosp., Washington U., St. Louis, 1971—72; resident pediat. nephrology U. Calif. San Francisco, 1972—74, fellow, 1974—77; chief renal sect. Tex Children's Hosp.-Baylor Coll. Medicine, Houston, 1994—, dir. Pediat. Nephrology Fellowship Program, prof. pediat. Mem.: So. Soc. Pediat. Rsch., Soc. Pediat. Rsch., Nat. Kidney Found., Women in Nephrology, Renal Physicians Assn. (bd. mem.), Internat. Soc. Peritoneal Dialysis, Internat. Soc. Nephrology, Internat. Pediat. Nephrology Assn., Am. Soc. Transplant Physicians, Am. Soc. Pediat. Nephrology, Am. Soc. Nephrology, Am. Pediat. Soc., Am. Fedn. Clin. Rsch. Office: Baylor Coll Medicine 6621 Fannin St, MC 3-2482 Houston TX 77030-2399 Office Phone: 832-824-3800. Office Fax: 832-825-3889. E-mail: ebrewer@bcm.tmc.edu.

BREWER, ROSALIND GATES (ROZ BREWER), retail executive; b. Mich., 1962; m. John Brewer; 2 children. BS in Chemistry, Spelman Coll., Atlanta, 1984; completed advanced mgmt. program, Wharton Sch. Bus., U. Pa.; grad., Directors' Coll., Stanford Law Sch. Chemist, various sr. mgmt. positions Kimberly-Clark Corp., 1984—2004, pres. global nonwovens divsn., 2004—06; regional v.p. ops. Wal-Mart Stores, Inc., Ga., 2006, pres. southeast operating divsn., 2007—10, exec. v.p., pres. Wal-Mart South, 2010—11, exec. v.p., pres. Wal-Mart East Atlanta, 2011—12, pres., CEO Sam's Club Divsn. Bentonville, Ark., 2012—. Bd. dirs. Molson Coors Brewing Co., 2006—11, Lockheed Martin Corp., 2011—. Bd. trustees Spelman Coll., 2006—, chair, 2011—. Recipient Legacy of Leadership award, Spelman Coll., 2005, Millennium Pacesetter award, Atlanta Bus. League, Woman of Achievement award, YWCA of Atlanta, 2013; named one of The 25 Power Women to Watch, Atlanta Women Mag., 2005, The 50 Most Powerful Women in Bus., Fortune mag., 2010—13, The 100 Most Powerful Women, Forbes mag., 2012—13. Office: Wal-Mart Stores Inc 702 SW 8th St Bentonville AR 72716-8611 Office Phone: 479-273-4000. Office Fax: 479-277-1830. Business E-Mail: rosalind.brewer@walmart.com.*

BREWER, W. KEITH, tobacco company executive; V.p., dir. internat. processing Universal Corp., Richmond, Va., 1993—2002, pres. Universal Leaf No. America, 2002—06; exec. v.p. Universal Leaf Tobacco Co., Richmond, Va., 2006—07; v.p. Universal Corp., Richmond, Va., 2007—08, exec. v.p., COO, 2008—. Office: Universal Corp 1501 N Hamilton St Richmond VA 23230 Mailing: Universal Corp PO Box 25099 Richmond VA 23260 Office Phone: 804-359-9311. Office Fax: 803-254-3582.

BREWER, WILLIAM E., JR., lawyer; AB in Economics, U. NC, Chapel Hill, 1973, JD with honors, 1976. Bar: NC, cert.: NC State Bar (specialist in consumer bankruptcy law), bar: US Supreme Ct., US Ct. Appeals (4th Cir.). Law clk. to Hon. R.A. Hedrick NC Ct. Appeals; pvt. practice atty. Raleigh, NC. Fellow: American Coll. of Bankruptcy; mem.: NC State Bar, NC Bar Assn., Nat. Assn. Consumer Bankruptcy Attorneys (mem. bd. dirs. 1997—, v.p. 2007—10, pres. 2010—12). Office: The Brewer Law Firm 311 E Edenton St Raleigh NC 27601 Office Phone: 919-832-2288. Office Fax: 919-834-2011. Business E-Mail: wbrewer@williambrewer.com.*

BREWSTER, OLIVE NESBITT, retired librarian; b. San Antonio, July 19, 1924; d. Charles Henry and Olive Agatha (Nesbitt) Brewster. BA, Our Lady of Lake Coll., 1945, BS in LS, 1946. Asst. librarian aeromed. library U.S. Air Force Sch. Aviation Medicine, Randolph AFB, Tex., 1946-60; chief cataloger aeromed. library Sch. Aerospace Medicine, Brooks AFB, Tex., 1960-83, chief tech. processing, 1983-88; ret., 1988. Mem.: ALA, Mensa. Home: 602 Babcock Rd San Antonio TX 78201-3101 Personal E-mail: olivenbrewster@yahoo.com.

BREWSTER, WILLIAM HOWARD, lawyer; b. Takoma Park, Md., Nov. 10, 1962; s. William and Maridell (Baker) B.; m. Karen McCue, Aug. 16, 1986; children: Kristina Baker, William Howard, Katherine Marie. BA, MA, Emory U., 1984; JD, U. Va., 1987. Bar: Ga. 1987, U.S. Dist. Ct. (no. dist.) Ga. 1988, U.S. Dist. Ct. (mid. dist.) Ga. 1992, U.S. Ct. Appeals (11th cir.) 1989, U.S. Ct. Appeals (4th cir.) 1992, (9th cir.), 2004, (7th cir.), 2010 U.S. Supreme Ct. 1992. Assoc. Kilpatrick & Cody, Atlanta, 1987-94, ptnr., 1994—97, Kilpatrick Stockton, LLP, Atlanta, 1997—2001, 2007—10, mng. ptnr., 2001—06; ptnr. Kilpatrick Townsend & Stockton LLP, 2011—. Barrister Lumpkin Am. Inns of Ct., Atlanta, 1989—97; adj. prof. U. Va. Sch. Law, 2000, Emory U. Sch. Law, 2001—. Bd. dirs., chair Special Olympics, Ga.; bd. dirs. Metro Atlanta C. of C.; bd. visitors Emory U. Mem.: U. Va. Sch. Law (bd. advisors), State Bar Ga. (intellectual property and sports & entertainment secs.), Am. Intellectual Property Law Assn. (trademake litig. com.), Internat. Collegiate Licensing Assn., Internat. Trademark Assn., Commerce Club (operating bd.), Lawyers Club Atlanta. Office: Kilpatrick Townsend & Stockton LLP 1100 Peachtree St NE Ste 2800 Atlanta GA 30309-4530 Business E-Mail: bbrewster@kilpatricktownsend.com.

BRICE, LEE, singer; b. Sumter, SC, Sept. 25, 1980; m. Sara Reeveley; children: Takoda, Ryker Mobley. Attended, Clemson U. Singer: (albums) Love Like Crazy, 2010, Hard 2 Love, 2012, (songs) I Drive Your Truck, 2012 (Song of Yr., Country Music Assn. Awards, 2013, Song of Yr., Acad. Country Music Awards, 2014). Office: Curb Records 48 Music Square East Nashville TN 37203*

BRICKER, HARVEY MILLER, retired anthropology educator; b. Johnstown, Pa., June 29, 1940; s. George Harry and Florence Helen (Miller) B.; m. Victoria Evelyne Reifler, Dec. 27, 1964. BA, Hamilton Coll., 1962; MA, Harvard U., 1963, PhD, 1973. Successively instr., asst. prof., assoc. prof. to prof. anthropology Tulane U., New Orleans, 1969—2005, emeritus prof. anthropology, 2005—; courtesy prof. anthropology and rsch. assoc. Fla. Mus. Natural History, U. Fla., Gainesville, Fla., 2006—. Co-author: The Analysis of Certain Major Classes of Upper Palaeolithic Tools, 1969, Excavation of the Abri Pataud: The Perigordian VI Assemblage, 1984, Astronomy in the Maya Codices, 2011; co-editor: Hunting and Animal Exploitation in the Later Palaeolithic and Mesolithic of Eurasia, 1993; editor: La Paléolithique Supérieur de l'abri Pataud (Dordogne), 1995; contbr. articles on French prehistory and Maya archaeoastronomy to profl. jours. Decorated Order Palmes Académiques, France, 1987; recipient John Frederick Lewis award, Am. Philos. Soc., 2011, Donald E. Osterbrock Book prize, Hist. Astronomy Divsn. of Am. Astron. Soc., 2013. Fellow AAAS; mem. Soc. Am. Archaeology, Soc. French Prehistory. Office Phone: 504-866-1669. Business E-Mail: hbricker@tulane.edu.

BRICKER, VICTORIA REIFLER, anthropologist, educator; b. Hong Kong, June 15, 1940; arrived in US, 1947, naturalized, 1953; d. Erwin and Henrietta (Brown) Reifler; m. Harvey Miller Bricker, Dec. 27, 1964. AB, Stanford U., 1962; A.M., Harvard U., 1963, PhD, 1968. Vis. lectr. anthropology Tulane U., 1969-70, asst. prof., 1970-73, assoc. prof., 1973-78, prof., 1978—2005, chmn. dept. anthropology, 1988—91, 2003—05. Author: Ritual Humor in Highland Chiapas, 1973, The Indian Christ, The Indian King: The Historical Substrate of Maya Myth and Ritual, 1981 (Howard Francis Cline meml. prize Conf. Latin Am. History), A Grammar of Mayan Hieroglyphs, 1986, (with Gabrielle Vail) Papers on the Madrid Codex, 1997, (with Eleuterio Po'ot Yah and Ofelia Dzul de Po'ot) A Dictionary of the Maya Language as Spoken in Hocaba, Yucatan, 1998, (with Helga-Maria Miram) An Encounter of Two Worlds: The Book of Chilam Balam of Kaua, 2002; book rev. editor: Am. Anthropologist, 1971-73; editor: Am. Ethnologist, 1973-76; gen. editor: Supplement to Handbook of Middle American Indians, 1977—2008. Guggenheim fellow, 1982; Wenner-Gren Found. Anthropol. Rsch. grantee, 1971; Social Sci. Rsch. Coun. grantee, 1972; NEH grantee, 1990. Fellow Am. Anthrop. Assn. (exec. bd. 1980-83); mem. NAS, Am. Philos. Soc., Am. Soc. Ethnohistory (exec. bd. 1977-79).

BRICKMAN, BLAKE (JAMES BLAKE BRICKMAN), lawyer, former legislative staff member; BA in History and Spanish cum laude, Vanderbilt U., Nashville, 2000; JD, U. Ky., 2009. Bar: Ky., US Dist. Ct. (eastern dist.) Ky. Legis asst. for Senator Jim Bunning US

Senate, Washington, 2002—04, chief of staff, 2004; polit. dir. for Senator Jim Bunning's Re-election campaign, 2004; law clk. for Judge Amul Thapar US Dist. Ct. (eastern dist.) Ky.; assoc. Litig. Dept. Dinsmore & Shohl LLP, Lexington, Ky., 2010—. Republican. Office: Dinsmore & Shohl LLP Lexington Financial Center 250 W Main St, Suite 1400 Lexington KY 40507 Office Phone: 202-224-4343, 859-425-1029. Office Fax: 859-425-1099. Business E-Mail: blake_brickman@bunning.senate.gov. E-mail: blake.brickman@dinslaw.com.

BRICKMAN, CHRISTIAN ANDERS, consumer products company executive; b. 1964; BS in Economics, Occidental Coll., L.A., 1986. Mktg. dir., Aspartame NutraSweet Co.; mng. cons. CSC Index Consulting; gen. mgr. Guinness & Co; v.p., strategic planning, v.p., gen. mgr., Guinness Brewing Worldwide Latin American region Guinness Co., 1994—98; with McKinsey & Co. (Consumer Packaged Goods & Ops. Practices); assoc. prin. McKinsey & Co., 2001—03, prin. Dallas, 2003—08; pres., CEO Whitlock Packaging, 1998—2001; sr. v.p., chief strategy officer Kimberly-Clark Corp., 2008—10; pres. Kimberly-Clark Profl., 2010—12, Kimberly-Clark Internat., 2012—. Office: Kimberly Clark Corp 351 Phelps Dr Irving TX 75038 Office Phone: 972-281-1200. Office Fax: 972-281-1490. Business E-Mail: cbrickman@kimberly-clark.com.

BRIDENSTINE, JIM (JAMES FREDERICK BRIDENSTEIN), United States Representative from Oklahoma; b. Ann Arbor, Mich., June 15, 1975; m. Michelle Ivory; children: Walker, Sarah, Grant. BS in Economics, Bus. & Psychology, Rice U., 1998; MBA, Cornell U., 2009. Def. cons. Wyle Laboratories, 2007—08; exec. dir. Tulsa Air & Space Mus. & Planetarium, 2008—10; mem. US Congress from 1st Okla. Dist., Washington, 2013—, US House Armed Services Com., 2013—, US House Sci., Space & Technology Com., 2013—. Aviator USN, 1998—2007, lt. comdr. USNR, 2010—. Decorated Air medal, Navy Commendation medal with V medal, Navy & Marine Corps Achievement medal (2), Nat. Def. Svc. medal, Armed Forces Expeditionary medal, Iraq Campaign medal, Global War on Terrorism Expeditionary medal, Naval Sea Svc. Deployment Ribbon, Expert Pistol medal, Battle Efficiency Ribbon. Republican. Southern Baptist. Office: US House of Representatives 216 Cannon House Office Bldg Washington DC 20515 also: 2448 E 81st St Ste 5150 Tulsa OK 74137 Office Phone: 202-225-2211, 918-935-3222. Office Fax: 918-935-2716.*

BRIDGEFORD, GREGORY M., consumer products company executive; BS in Psychology, U. Va.; MBA, Wake Forest U. Various pos., including exec. asst. to chmn., v.p. corp. devel. Lowe's Companies, Inc., Wilkesboro, NC, sr. v.p. merchandising/gen. merchandising mgr., 1996—98, sr. v.p. mktg., 1998—99, sr. v.p. bus. devel., 1999—2004, exec. v.p. bus. devel., 2004—. Office: Lowes Cos Inc 1605 Curtis Bridge Rd Wilkesboro NC 28697

BRIDGES, ALAN LYNN, physicist, researcher, application developer; BS in Physics, Ga. Inst. Tech., 1972, MS in Physics, 1974, postgrad., 1975—78, postgrad., 1994—95. Cert. C-130J R&M HUD, BIU, MC, FMECA. Asst. rsch. scientist Ga. Tech. Rsch. Inst., Atlanta, 1975—78; asst. mgr. product Humphrey Instruments Inc., San Leandro, Calif., 1978; pres., cons. ETC West Ltd., 1979—; with Lockheed Aero Sys. Co., 1983—88; sr. prin. engr. new bus. devel. Lockheed Electronics Co., Atlanta, 1988—90; sr. engr., program mgr. Flat Panel & Graphics Display Sys. SCI Tech., Inc., Hunstville, Ala., 1990—92; software engr. specialist life cycle software support and F22 & C130JRM & S sys. engring. Lockheed Martin Aero. Sys. Co., Marietta, Ga., 1992—2001, sr. S.W. software specialist, 1998—; reliability, supportability and safety staff engr., lead engr. visiona display server Barcoview LLC, 2001—03; staff reliability/safety engr. L-3 Comm. Display Sys., Alpharetta, Ga., 2003—, reliability and safety mgr. joint strike fighter panoramic cockpit display, supportability mgr. and system, software safety engr., 2005—, common criteria NIAP vulnerability testing and certification JSF PCD, PCD system/sub system safety, 2007—, writing internal L-3DS DO-254 Assurance ISO STD, 2008; software safety engr. FAA Software & Complex Electronics Hardware, 2006—. Mem. Lockheed Software Process Std. ISO 9000/SEI CMM software and sys. engring. CMM process action team, ACM stds. com. tech. adv. group ISO 9241 Contbg. editor Computer Tech. Rev., PC Graphics & Video Mag.; bi-monthly columnist Hardcopy, 1983-93; contbr. articles to profl. jours Mem. IEEE (sr., dir. Atlanta sect., 1987-88, sec. 1988-89, treas. 1989-90, chmn. student activities com. 1985-87, sec.-treas. computer soc. chpt. 1985-86, chmn. computer soc. chpt. 1986-89, vice-chmn. 1987-88, gen. chmn. Atlanta software tech. conf. 1987, P1226 ABBET com., P1498/12207 stds. com., SW stds. com.), Assn. for Computing Machinery, Optical Soc. Am., Soc. Photo-Optical Instrumentation Engrs., Nat. Security Indsl. Assn. (integrated diagnostic working group, co-chair integrated avionics task group), Soc. for Tech. Comm., Computer Press Assn., Soc. for Info. Display, Nat. Telesys. Conf., Control and Displays Session Orgn., Am. Nat. Stds. Inst./Internat. Stds. Orgn., Sigma Pi Sigma Avocations: amateur radio, woodworking. Home: 8523 Colony Club Dr Alpharetta GA 30022-5407 Office: L-3 Comm Display Sys 1355 Bluegrass Lakes Pkwy Alpharetta GA 30004-8458 Office Phone: 770-752-5135. Personal E-mail: alan.bridges@l-3com.com.

BRIDGES, CHRISTOPHER BRIAN See LUDACRIS

BRIDGES, DUWAYNE, state legislator; m. Pat Bridges; children: DuWayne Jr., Karen. BBA, Faulkner U., Montgomery, Ala.; MA in Human Resources Mgmt., Troy State U., Ala. Owner, pres. Bridges Travel Plz. and Western Wear; mem. Dist. 38 Ala. House of Reps., Montgomery, 2000—. Past vice chmn. Ala. State Dept. Mental Health and Mental Retardation; former bd. mem. Assn. Retarded Citizens, Greater Valley Area C. of C.; bd. trustees Colonial Bank; bd. dirs. Chattahoochee Valley Hosp. Recipient Outstanding Vol. award, Assn. Retarded Citizens, 1991; named Gentleman of Yr., Chambers County, 1996. Republican. Assembly Of God. Office: Ala House of Reps Rm 120 11 S Union St Montgomery AL 36130 also: PO Box 729 Valley AL 36854 also: 5495 County Rd 388 Cusseta AL 36852 Office Phone: 334-242-7708, 334-756-6373.

BRIDGES, JUDY CANTRELL, gifted and talented education educator; b. Dallas, Feb. 17, 1947; d. William and Jewel Alexandria (Autrey) C.; m. Gary L. Bridges, Aug. 17, 1969; children: John Drewry, Judith Alexandria. BA, Tex. Tech. U., 1969; gifted/talented endorsement, Sul Ross State U., Alpine, Tex., 1992, MEd, 1993; cert. in mid-mgmt., Sul Ross State U., 1994. Lic. secondary edn. math. and English. Tchr. New Deal (Tex.) Ind. Sch. Dist., 1969—70, Indpls. Pub. Schs., 1970, USDESEA, Zweibruecken, Germany, 1971—73, Lubbock (Tex.) Ind. Sch. Dist., 1973—76, Ector County Ind. Sch. Dist., Odessa, Tex., 1976-85, 87-90, tchr. gifted spl. edn., 1990—92, gifted/talented coord., 1992—97, dir. advanced acad. svcs., 1977—2001; ednl. cons., self employed Odessa, 2001—02; prin., dir. gifted and talented svcs. Midland Ind. Sch. Dist., 2002—. Acct. Walter Smith CPA, Odessa, 1977—82; real estate appraiser Appraisal Assocs., Odessa, 1985—87; vis. lectr. Sul Ross State U., Alpine, 1994, Alpine, 1997—98, Alpine, 2001; mem. gifted/talented adv. com. Region 18 Edn. Svc. Ctr., Midland, Tex., 1993—; adv. dir. Ptnrs. for Excellence, 2002—. Author: (poem) Paradigm Shifts in the West Texas Sand, 1991. Advisor, officer Jr. League of Odessa, Inc., 1980—, treas./treas. elect, 1986—88; with State Bd. for Educator Cert. Math. Stds. Com., 2000; chair math. Gifted/Talented Performance Stds. Com. Tex., 2000; treas. Campaign to Elect County Judge, Odessa, 1991; mem. bd. Permian H.S. Football Booster Club, 1993; dir. region I Tex. Acad. Decathlon, 1999, 2000; bd. dirs. ECISD Edn. Found., 2002—03, Odessa Symphony Guild, 1996—2004, 2005—; mem. Tex. Edn. Agy. Commr.'s Adv. Coun. on Gifted and Talented Edn., 2004—. Recipient Dept. of Def. Commendation, U.S. Dependent Edn. System, Zweibruecken, 1973, Cert. of Appreciation-Stop of Felony Odessa Police Dept., 1992. Mem. ASCD, NEA, Nat. Assn. Gifted Children, Tex. State Tchrs. Assn. (treas. Ector County unit 1991-92), Tex. Assn. Gifted and Talented (bd. dirs. 1999-2001, sec.-treas. 2002, pres.-elect 2003, pres. 2004, immediate past pres., 2005—), Am. Creativity Assn., Nat. Coun. Tchrs. Math, Ptnrs. for Excellence (bd. dirs. 2002—), West Tex. Reading Coun. Baptist. Avocations: skiing, floral design, reading, travel. Office: 1300 E Wall St Midland TX 79701 E-mail: jcbridges@sbcglobal.net.*

BRIDGEWATER, HERBERT JEREMIAH, JR., radio personality; b. Atlanta, July 3, 1942; s. Herbert Bridgewater and Mary Sallie (Clark) Bridgewater-Hughes. BA, Clark Coll., Atlanta, 1968; postgrad., Atlanta U.; L.H.D., Faith Coll., 1978; LL.D., Heed U., 1978. Cert. ordained min. in theology Interdenominational Theol. Ctr. CITCO, Atlanta, 2004; ordained minister Gospel, 2005; apptd. First Chaplain, City of East Point Police Dept. Tchr. bus. edn. and English Atlanta Pub. Sch. System, 1964-67; relocation and family svcs. cons. Atlanta Housing Authority, 1967-70; columnist, writer Atlanta Daily World, 1968—, Lovely Atlanta; consumer protection specialist FTC, Atlanta, 1970-83; pres. Bridgewater's Personnel Service, 1971—; assoc. prof. bus. edn. and mass communication Clark Coll., instr., 1983-86, Atlanta Jr. Coll., 1986—, The Univ. System of Ga., 1986—; with reservations sales Delta Airline Inc., Atlanta, 1984—. Host program Enlightenment Radio Sta. WGKA-AM, 1975-79; host pub. affairs program Confrontation Radio Sta. WZGC FM and WIGO AM, 1975-79, WYZE AM, 1979—; TV talk show host Bridging the Gap Mem. Epilepsy Found. Am., Nat. Urban League, Big Bros. Council of Atlanta, Met. Boys Clubs of Atlanta, YMCA, NAACP; active So. Christian Leadership Conf., Ga. and nationwide civil rights movements; bd. dirs. Atlanta Dance Theater, Ralph C. Robinson Atlanta Boys Club, Proposition Theater Co., Am. Cancer Soc., Just-Us Theatre Task Force. Recipient Pres.'s award Clark Coll. United Negro Coll. Fund, 1960, 61, Best Citizens award Delta Sigma Theta, 1962, Humanitarian award Future Soc. Orgn., 1975, award Atlanta Dance Theatre, 1978-79, also; Met. Atlanta Boys Club; FTC Superior service medal, 1978; Bronner Bros. Nat. Beauticians Conv. Excellence in Communication award, 1978; named One of Most Outstanding Young Men in Am., Nat. Jr. C. of C., 1969, One of Most Eligible Bachelors in Am., 1970, One of 1,000 Successful Black Americans, 1973; both Ebony Mag.; One of 10 Outstanding Young People of Atlanta, 1977-78; One of 20 Most Progressive Young People in Atlanta, 1977; Herbert Bridgewater Day proclaimed in his honor Atlanta. Mem. Atlanta Jr. C. of C., Young Men on the Go, Clark Coll. Alumni Assn., Clark Coll. Assn., Heritage Valley Community Civic Orgn., Hungry Club Forum, Internat. Assn. for African Heritage and Black Identity (founding) Baptist (founder, chmn. bd. jr. deacons). Home: 2963 Duke Of Windsor East Point GA 30344-5606 Personal E-mail: HerbertBridgewater@yahoo.com.

BRIGGS, DICK DOWLING, JR., physician, educator; b. Electric Mills, Miss., Jan. 28, 1934; s. Dick Dowling and Anita (Carnathan) B.; m. Susan Hunt Davis, June 20, 1959 (dec. 2006); children: Adrienne Davis, Dick Dowling, III, Daniel Roth. BS, U. of South, 1956; MD, Washington U., 1960. Resident, fellow, chief resident U. Ala. Hosp., Birmingham, 1960-62, 64-68; prof. medicine U. Ala., Birmingham, 1964-95, prof., 1971—92, dir. divsn. pulmonary critical care, 1971-92, vice chmn. dept. medicine, 1981-95, eminent scholar chair in pulmonary diseases, 1989-95, emeritus eminent scholar chair, 1995—; pres., CEO, med. dir. U. Ala. Health Svc. Found., P.C., Birmingham, 1988-92; corp. med. dir. Complete Health, 1985—88, Triton Health Sys., Birmingham, 1995-97; chief med. officer Best Drs. Worldwide Health Svcs., Boston, 1997—2005. Cons. VA Med. Ctr., Birmingham, 1966-2003; trustee AmSouth Funds, Birmingham, 1992-2005. Assoc. editor (CDROM) UpToDate, 1994—; sr. editl. bd. Archives Internal Medicine, 1985-97; contbr. articles to profl. publs. Bd. dir. Am. Bd. Emergency Medicine, 1994—2002. Recipient Pulmonary Acad. award NIH, 1972-77, Breath of Life award Cystic Fibrosis Found., 1994; named to Ala. Tennis Hall Fame, 2003. Master: ACP (Laureate award 1995), Am. Coll. Chest Physicians (pres. 1984—85, master fellow 2002); mem.: Am. Bd. Pulmonary Disease (chmn. 1988—90), So. Med. Assn. (chmn. sect. medicine 1973—74), Am. Thoracic Soc. (pres. Ala. chpt. 1978—79), Assn. Pulmonary and Critical Care Medicine Program Dirs. (founding mem. 1984, pres. 1986—87), Newcomen Soc., US Tennis Assn. (Ala. Tennis Hall of Fame 2003), Rotary Club. Episcopalian. Avocations: tennis, music, travel, wine. Home: 2925 Southwood Rd Birmingham AL 35223-1232 Office: Univ Ala Birmingham Sch Medicine 1808 7th Ave S Birmingham AL 35294-0012 Personal E-mail: dickbriggsjr@gmail.com.

BRIGHAM, BEN M. (BUD BRIGHAM), oil industry executive; BS in Geophysics, U. Tex. Seismic data processing geophysicist Western Geophysical, Houston; exploration geophysicist Rosewood Resources; founder, pres., CEO, chmn. Brigham Exploration Corp., Austin, Tex., 1990—. Mem.: Soc. Ind. Profl. Earth Scientists, Ind. Prodrs. of America, Soc. Exploration Geophysicists, Am. Assn. Petroleum Geologists, Nat. Petroleum Coun. Office: Brigham Exploration Corp 6300 Bridge Point Pkwy Bldg 2 Ste 500 Austin TX 78730-5073 Office Phone: 512-427-3300. Office Fax: 512-427-3400.

BRIGHAM, KENNETH LARRY, medical educator; b. Tenn., Oct. 29, 1939; m. Arlene A. Stecenko; 1 child, Heather. BA, David Lipscomb Coll., 1962; MD, Vanderbilt U., 1966. Intern Osler Med. Service, Johns Hopkins Hosp., Balt., 1966-67, asst. resident in medicine, 1967-68; with cholera research unit Johns Hopkins Ctr. for Med. Research and Tng., Calcutta, India, 1968; med. epidemiologist Ecol. Investigations program USPHS Nat. Communicable Disease Ctr., Phoenix, 1968-70; instr. in medicine, fellow in pulmonary diseases Vanderbilt U. Sch. Medicine, Nashville, 1970-71, dir. pulmonary research, 1973-76, asst. prof. medicine, 1973-74, assoc. prof., 1974-78, dir. Ctr. for Lung Research, 1976—, assoc. prof. biomed. engring., 1977-86, prof. of medicine, 1978-95, dir. div. pulmonary medicine, 1978—, asst. prof. physiology, 1983-85, assoc. prof. molecular physiology and biophysics, 1985—, Joe and Morris Wethan prof. investigative medicine, 1984-94, prof. biomed. engring., 1986—, now dir. divsn. allergy, pulmonary, & crit. care med., 1998—; research fellow Cardiovascular Research Inst., U. Calif. Med. Ctr., San Francisco, 1971-73; dir. of Div. Allergy, Pulmonary & Critical Care Med. Vanderbilt U. Sch. Med., Nashville, 1995. Mem. council on cardiopulmonary disease Am. Heart Assn., investigator, 1975-80; mem. cardiovascular and pulmonary study sect. USPHS, Nat. Heart Lung Inst., 1975-79, mem. pulmonary nat. research service award group, 1975; mem. lung research rev. com. VA, 1976; mem. A program project rev. com. Nat. Heart Lung and Blood Inst., 1982-85, chmn., 1984-85, mem. pulmonary disease adv. com., 1986—; prin. investigator Specialized Ctr. Research in Pulmonary Vascular Disease, 1976—, Parker B. Francis Found. Fellowships in Pulmonary Research, 1977-83, Multidisciplinary Lung Research Tng. Grant, 1975—; mem. Am. Lung Assn./Am. Thoracic Soc. steering com., 1988-89; chmn. pulmonary diseases adv. com. NIH, 1988-90. Mem. editorial bd. Jour. Applied Physiology, 1978-84, Respiratory, Environ. and Exercise Physiology, 1978-84, Circulation Research, 1982—, Exptl. Lung Research, 1982—, Am. Jour. Med. Scis., 1983—, Am. Rev. Respiratory Diseases, 1984—, Jour. Clin. Investigation, 1985—, Intensive Care Medicine, 1985—; contbr. articles to profl. jours. Mem. planning com. Am. Lung Assn., 1983—; rep. Vanderbilt Univ. Senate, Nashville, 1986—. Grantee NIH, 1985—. Mem. Am. Physiol. Soc. (circulation and respiration groups), Am. Fedn. for Clin. Research (pres. So. sect. 1980-81), Am. Thoracic Soc. (pres.-elect pulmonary circulation sect. assembly on structure and function 1979-80, pres. pulmonary circulation sect. 1980-81, chmn.-elect assembly on respiratory structure function and metabolism 1981-82, chmn. assembly 1982-83, fed. lung program com. 1987—, pres.-elect 1988-89, bd. dirs. 1988-89, budget com. 1988-89), AAAS, Johns Hopkins Med. and Surg. Assn., Microcirculatory Soc., So. Soc. for Clin. Investigation (councilor 1988-89), Am. Soc. for Clin. Investigation, N.Y. Acad. Scis., Assn. Am. Physicians, ACP, Am. Soc. for Cell Biology, Nashville Soc. for Internal Medicine (v.p. 1985-86), Am. Lung Assn. (exec. com. 1988-89, planning com. 1988-89, program coordinating/program and budget com. 1988-89)) Office: Emory University 550 Peachtree St Ste 1850 Atlanta GA 30308 Business E-Mail: kbrigha@emory.edu.

BRIGHT, CRAIG BARTLEY, lawyer; b. Mineola, NY, May 23, 1931; s. Herbert Lester and Gertrude Lillian (Smith) Bright; m. Judith Alice Pollard, July 31, 1955 (dec. Aug. 1956); m. Ann Sharpe, July 18, 1959. BA summa cum laude, Colgate U., 1952; JD magna cum laude, Harvard U., 1955. Bar: N.Y. 1956, U.S. Dist. Ct. (so. and ea. dists.) N.Y. 1961, U.S. Dist. Ct. Conn. 1961, U.S. Ct. Appeals (2d cir.) 1961. Staff judge adv. Judge Adv. Gen.'s Group, 1955—57; assoc. Patterson, Belknap, Webb & Tyler, NYC, 1957—64, ptnr., 1965—92. Co-author: The Law and the Lore of Endowment Funds, 1969, The Developing Law of Endowment Funds, 1974; contbr. articles to law jours. Capt. USAF, 1955—57. Mem.: ABA, Assn. of Bar of City of N.Y., N.Y. State Bar Assn. (chmn. com. on profl. ethics 1981—84), Hermitage Club Goochland, Va. Republican. Presbyterian. Home and Office: 21 Hunting Ridge Rd Manakin Sabot VA 23103-2614 Personal E-mail: cbbasb@comcast.net.

BRIGHT, LEE, state legislator; b. Greer, SC, Mar. 20, 1970; s. Marvin L. and Virginia Bright; m. Amy Byers, July 24, 1993; children: Kaylee, Kendyl. Bd. mem. Palmetto Family Coun.; mem. Southeastern Theol. Sem. Bd. of Dirs., Spartanburg Co. Taxpayers Assn., Atty. Gen. Com. on the Family, 2001, Dist. 6 Sch. Bd., 1999—2003; mem. Dist. 12 SC State Senate, 2008—. Republican. Bapt. Mailing: PO Box 589 Roebuck SC 29376 Office: Capitol Office 502 Gressette Bldg Columbia SC 29201 Home Phone: 864-576-6742; Office Phone: 864-587-1800, 803-212-6108. E-mail: leebright@scsenate.org.

BRIGHT, WILLARD MEAD, retired manufacturing executive, director; b. NYC, Mar. 26, 1914; s. William Van Horn and Bernice Hartwell (Reynolds) B.; m. Martha Norris Land, May 15, 1944 (dec.); 1 child, Willard Mead; m. Virginia L. Jones, Mar. 14, 1981 (div. Aug. 1996). BS, U. Toledo, 1936, MS, 1937; postgrad., U. Pitts., 1937-38; A.M., Harvard U., 1941, PhD, 1942. Research chemist Kendall Co., Boston, Chgo., 1942-52; asst. lab. dir. Kendall Co. (Bauer & Black div.), 1944-48; lab. dir. (Theodore Clark Lab. div.), Cambridge, Mass., 1948-52; asst. research dir. Lever Bros. Co., 1952-54, research dir., 1954-60, v.p. research and devel., 1960-64; chmn. bd. W. H. Norris Lumber Co., Houston, 1957-64; treas. Border Lumber Co., Weslaco, Tex., 1957-64; v.p. R.J. Reynolds Tobacco Co., 1964-68; sr. v.p., pres. profl. products group Warner-Lambert Pharm. Co., 1968-70; pres., chief exec. officer Kendall Co., Boston, 1970-73; pres. Curtiss-Wright Corp., 1973-74, Boehringer Mannheim Corp., 1974-81; chmn. Zoll Med. Corp, 1982-96; ret., 1996. Bd. dirs. Zoll Med. Corp.; mem. adv. com. on patents U.S. Dept. Commerce, 1966-69; mem. bd. visitors dept. chemistry Boston U. Recipient Gold T award U. Toledo, 1960 Mem. N.A.M. (chmn. sci. tech. com. dir. 1970-73), Am. Chem. Soc., N.Y. Acad. Scis., Assn. Rsch. Dirs., Indsl. Rsch. Inst. (dir. 1963-69, pres. 1967-68), Dirs. Indsl. Rsch., Sigma Xi, Phi Kappa Phi, Harvard Club (Boston), Comml. Club (Boston), The Country Club (Brookline, Mass.), Bent Pine Golf Club (Vero Beach, Fla.). Home: 211 Seaside Pathway Vero Beach FL 32963-5025

BRIGHTMAN, ROSS I., biology professor; b. Washington, Mar. 21, 1963; s. Milton W. and Harriet E. Brightman. PhD, U. South Fla., St. Petersburg, 1993. Prof. St. Petersburg Coll., 1993—. Achievements include research in energetics, photosynthesis. Office: St Petersburg Coll PO Box 13489 Saint Petersburg FL 33733 E-mail: brightmanr@spcollge.edu.

BRIGHTMAN, STUART M., energy executive; m. Randi Brightman; children: David, Lauren. BS, U. Pa., Phila., 1978, MBA, 1982. With Arthur Young, Boston, 1978—82; asst. contr. oil tools divsn. Cameron Iron Works, Houston, plant mgr., gen. mgr. ball valve products Scotland; product sales mgr. transmission and distbn. products Cooper Oil Tools, Houston, 1991—93; sr. v.p. ops. Wheatley TXT Corp., 1993—94; sr. v.p. oilfield valve divsn. Dresser, Inc., 1994—95, pres. oilfield valve divsn., 1995—98, pres. Americas ops. energy valve divsn., 1998—2002, pres. flow control divsn., 2002—04; self employed, 2004—05; exec. v.p., COO TETRA Technologies, Inc., 2005—09, pres., CEO, bd. dirs., 2009—. Bd. dirs. Compressco Ptnrs. GP Inc. (subs. TETRA Technologies, Inc.). Office: TETRA Technologies Inc 24955 Interstate 45 N The Woodlands TX 77380 Office Phone: 281-367-1983. Office Fax: 281-364-4346. Business E-Mail: sbrightman@tetratec.com.

BRILES, ART (ARTHUR RAY BRILES), college football coach; b. Tex., Dec. 3, 1955; s. Dennis and Wanda Briles; m. Jan Allison; children: Jancy, Kendal, Staley. Attended, U. Houston, 1974—77; BA, Tex. Tech U., Lubbock, 1979; MEd, Abilene Christian U., Tex., 1984. Asst. coach Sundown HS, Tex., 1979, Sweetwater HS, Tex., 1980—83; head coach, athletic dir. Hamlin HS, Tex., 1984—85, Georgetown HS, Tex., 1986—87, Stephenville HS, Tex., 1988—99; running backs coach Tex. Tech. U. Red Raiders, Lubbock, 2000—03; head coach U. Houston Cougars, 2003—07, Baylor U. Bears, Waco, 2007—. Former pres. Tex. HS Coaches Assn. Co-author (with Nick Eatman): Art Briles, Looking Up: My Journey From Tragedy to Triumph, 2013. Named Conf. USA Coach of Yr., 2006, Big 12 Conf. Coach of Yr., 2013; named to The Tex. HS Football Hall of Fame, 2008, The Big Country Athletic Hall of Fame. Christian. Office: Baylor Athletic Dept 150 Bear Run Waco TX 76711

BRILEY, STEPHEN MORRIS, lawyer; b. Denison, Tex., Jan. 4, 1954; s. J. I. and Patsy Ruth (Scoggins) Briley; m. Mary Ann Reinert, Nov. 16, 1973; children: John, Mark, Stephanie, Katheryne. BA, Northwestern State U., Natchitoches, La., 1975; MS in English, Midwestern State U., Wichita Falls, Tex., 1996; JD, U. Tex., Austin, 1978. Bar: Tex., Okla., U.S. Dist. Ct. (northern and western dist.) Tex., cert.: Tex. Bd. Legal Specialization (personal injury trial law and civil trial law). Assoc. Law Offices Dale Muller, Austin, 1976—81; ptnr.

Fillmore, Purtle, Lambert & Lee, Wichita Falls, Tex., 1981—86, Banner Briley, Wichita Falls, 1986—92, Banner, Briley & White, LLP, Wichita Falls, 1992—96, Banner, Briley, & White, Wichita Falls, 1997—. Bd. dirs. Assn. for Retarded Citizens, 1983—92, Girl Scouts USA, 2004—05. Fellow: Tex. Bar Found. (life); mem.: AAJ, BAFFC, TTLA, OBA, ABOTA, OAJ, Wichita Co. Bar Assn., TBA. Avocations: reading, cooking, skeet shooting, skiing, bird hunting. Office: Banner Briley & White PO Box 4867 Wichita Falls TX 76308-0867 Office Phone: 940-692-5000. E-mail: sbriley@wf.net.

BRILL, AARON BERTRAND, nuclear medicine educator; b. NYC, Dec. 19, 1928; s. Louis And Cecile (Sroge) B.; m. Joan Booth Morrison, Sept. 1, 1950; children: Paul, David, Laurie. AB, Grinnell Coll., 1949; MD, U. Utah, 1956; PhD in Biophysics, U. Calif., Berkeley, 1961. Statistician Contra Costa County Health Dept., Martinez, Calif., 1949—50; res. asst. U. Calif., Donner Lab, 1950—52; biophysicist U. Utah Pediatrics Dept., Salt Lake City, 1952-56; intern Salt Lake City Gen. Hosp., 1956-57; USPHS officer Div. of Radiol. Health, Rockville, Md., 1957-64; asst. prof. radiology dept. radiology scis. Johns Hopkins Hosp. and Sch. of Hygiene, 1961-64; assoc. prof. radiol. Vanderbilt U. Sch. Medicine, Nashville, 1964-72; assoc. prof. medicine, biomed. engring. and physics, 1964-79; prof. radiology Vanderbilt U. Sch. Medicine, Nashville, 1972-79, SUNY, Stony Brook, 1979-87; sr. scientist, nuc. medicine coord. Brookhaven (N.Y.) Nat. Lab., 1979-87; prof. nuclear medicine U. Mass. Sch. Medicine, Worcester, 1987—97. Rsch. affiliate HST MIT, Cambridge, 1993-2005; affil. prof. Worcester Poly. Inst., Worcester, 1995-97; rsch. prof. radiol. sci. Vanderbilt U. Sch. Medicine, Nashville, 1997—, rsch. prof. physics, adj. prof. biomed. engring. Editor: Low Level Radiation Fact Book, 1st edit. 1982, 2d edit., 1985; editor: IEEE Trans Med. Imaging, 1986-92. Med. dir. USPHS, 1957-64, U. Calif. at Berkeley fellow, 1959-61. Fellow IEEE, Am. Coll. Nuclear Physicians, Am. Inst. Med. and Biol. Engring.; mem. NAS (com. on atomic casualties 1964-70, com. on biol. effects of ionizing radiation 1978-80; com.to assess sci. info. for radiation exposure and edn. program 2004-06, com. on assessment of CDC and prevention radiation studies from DOE contractor sites 2002-04, nat. assoc, 2004-, coun. radiation protection and measurement 1972-82, 92-97). Avocation: sailing. Office: Vanderbilt U Med Sch Dept Radiol Sci Mcn S1314 Nashville TN 37232-2675 Office Phone: 615-322-3190. Business E-Mail: aaron.brill@vanderbilt.edu.

BRILLANT, PATRICK T., colon and rectal surgeon; MD, U. Miami, 1988. Diplomate Am. Bd. Surgery, 2003, Am. Bd. Colon and Rectal Surgery, 2006. Intern Parkland Meml. Hosp., Dallas, 1989, resident in surgery, 1993; fellow in colon and rectal surgery Mayo Clinic, Rochester, Minn., 1993—94; hosp. affiliation includes Pitt County Meml. Hosp., NC; pvt. practice Physicians East, P.A. Office: Pitt County Memorial Hospital 2100 Stantonsburg Rd Greenville NC 27834 Office Phone: 252-847-4100.

BRIM, ORVILLE GILBERT, JR., former foundation administrator, writer; b. Elmira, NY, Apr. 7, 1923; s. Orville G(ilbert) and Helen (Whittier) B.; m. Kathleen J. Vigneron, May 30, 1944; children: John G., Scott W., Margaret L., Sarah M. BA, Yale U., 1947, MA, 1949, PhD in Sociology, 1951. Instr. sociology U. Wis., 1952-53, asst. prof., 1953-55; sociologist Russell Sage Found., NYC, 1955-64, asst. sec., 1959-64, pres., 1964-72, trustee, 1964-72, cons., 1972-74; pres. Found. for Child Devel., 1974-85; mem. core study group MacArthur Found. Rsch. Program Successful Aging, 1985-89; dir. MacArthur Found. Rsch. Network on Successful Mid Life Devel., 1989—2002; pres. Life Trends, Inc., 1991—2002; vis. scholar Russell Sage Found., 1985-86; interim pres. Social Sci. Rsch. Coun., 1998-99. Vice chmn. Am. Inst. for Rsch., 1971-88, chmn. 1988-91; chmn. bd. dirs. Automation Engring. Lab., 1959-67; dir. Consumer Behavior, Inc., 1957-61; chmn. environ. panel U.S. Office Edn., 1962-64; mem. drug rsch. bd. NAS., 1964-66, adv. com. on child devel., 1971-76; mem. mental health tng. com. NIMH, 1959-62; chmn. commn. social scis. NSF, 1968-69; nat. adv. food and drug coun. HEW, 1967-69; chmn. com. on work and personality in mid. years Social Sci. Rsch. Coun., 1972-79; trustee Found. for Child Devel., 1972-85, Ctr. for Creative Leadership, 1972-78, Mental Health Law Project, 1973-77, William T. Grant Found., 1975-84, Greenwich Hosp., 1972-77 Author: Sociology and the Field of Education, 1958, Education for Child Rearing, 1959, Personality and Decision Processes, 1962, Intelligence: Perspectives 1965, 1966, Socialization after Childhood: Two Essays, 1966, American Beliefs and Attitudes Toward Intelligence, 1969, The Dying Patient, 1970, Learning to Be Parents, 1980, Ambition: How We Manage Success and Failure Throughout Our Lives, 1992; editor: Lifespan Development and Behavior, Vol. 2-6, 1979-83, Constancy and Change in Human Development, 1980, How Healthy Are We? A Nat. Study of Well-Being at Midlife, 2004, Look At Me: The Fame Motive From Childhood to Death, 2009; cons. editor Child Devel., 1958-61, Sociology of Edn., 1963-69, Sociometry, 1959-62; mem. publ. com. The Public Interest, 1967-75. Served as 1st lt. USAAF, 1943-46. Recipient Wilbur Lucius Cross medal Yale Grad. Sch. Assn., 1975; Kurt Lewin Meml. award Soc. Psychol. Study Social Issues, 1979, Disting. Career Contbns. to the Sci. Study of Life Span Devel., Soc. for the Study of Human Devel., 2005. Fellow APA, AAAS, Am. Sociol. Assn., Am. Acad. Arts and Scis., Am. Orthopsychiat. Assn. (pres. 1974-75), Ea. Sociol. Soc. (pres. 1971-72); mem. Inst. Medicine of NAS, Soc. Rsch. Child Devel. (Disting. Sci. Contbns. award, 1985).

BRIMER, KENNETH KIMBERLIN, JR., state legislator; b. Houston, Mar. 5, 1945; s. Kenneth Kimberlin and Frances Louie (Hughes) B.; m. Sharon Elizabeth Graves, Mar. 15, 1969 (div. 1984); children: Kimberly Dawn, William Robert; m. Janna Kay Patton, Nov. 8, 1987. BS, Stephen F. Austin State U., 1967. Former chmn. Bus. & Indsl. Com.; former mem. Calendars & State Affairs Com.; mem. bd. Bracos River Authority, 1986—88; precinct chmn. Tarrant County Rep. Com., 1987—88; state rep. Tex., 1984; state rep. Dist. 96, 1989—2002; state senator Dist. 10, 2003—; ins. agt, 1976—. Bd. dirs. Interfirst Bank, S.W., Arlington, 1982-87, Brazos River Authority, Waco, Tex., 1987-88; adv. bd. NCNB Tex. S.W., Arlington, 1988—. Precinct chmn. Rep. Party Tex., Ft. Worth, 1987; state rep. Tex. Legis., Austin, 1989—; mem. Tarrant Task Force 2000, Ft. Worth, 1988. With USAFR, 1969-75. Named Alumni of the Yr., Tex. Eta, Phi Delta Theta, 1985. Mem. Ind. Ins. Agts. of Am., Ind. Ins. Agts. of Tarrant County (pres. 1985-86), Cert. Ins. Counselors, Arlington West Rotary (dir. 1983—), Petroleum Club. Republican. Methodist. Avocations: geneology, wood crafts. Address: 617 Averett Kennedale TX 76060 Mailing: 1600 W 7th St Ste 650 Fort Worth TX 76102 Office: PO Box 12068 State Capitol E1-810 Austin TX 78711 Fax: 817-572-3370.

BRIN, ROYAL HENRY, JR., lawyer; b. Dallas, Oct. 9, 1919; BA, JD, U. Tex., 1941. Bar: Tex. 1941. Postgrad. fellow Harvard U., 1941—42; atty. OPA, Washington, 1942; assoc. firm Strasburger & Price, Dallas, 1946-56, ptnr., 1956—. Editor-in-chief Tex. Law Rev., 1940-41; contbr. articles to profl. jours. Fellow Am. Bar Found. (life); mem. ABA, Am. Acad. Appellate Lawyers, State Bar Tex., Tex. Assn. Def. Counsel (pres. 1981-82), Dallas Bar Assn., Dallas Assn. Def. Counsel, Def. Rsch. Inst., Internat. Brotherhood Magicians (pres. 1969-70), The Chancellors (grand chancellor 1940-41), Order of Coif, Phi Beta Kappa, Phi Eta Sigma. Home: 6506 Lupton Dr Dallas TX 75225-2323 Office: 4300 Bank of Am Plz 901 Main St Dallas TX 75202-3714 Home Phone: 214-368-8110; Office Phone: 214-651-4604. Business E-Mail: royal.brin@strasburger.com.

BRIND'AMOUR, ROD, professional hockey coach, retired professional hockey player; b. Ottawa, Ont., Canada, Aug. 9, 1970; married; 3 children. Grad., Mich. State U. Center St. Louis Blues, 1988—91, Phila. Flyers, 1991—99, Carolina Hurricanes, 1999—2010, capt., 2005—10, dir. forwards devel., 2010—11, asst. coach, devel. coach, 2011—. Mem. CCHA All-Rookie Team, 1988—89; player NHL All-Star Game. Recipient CCHA Rookie of Yr. award, 1988—89, Frank J. Selke Trophy, 2006, 2007. Achievements include being a member of Stanley Cup Champion Carolina Hurricanes, 2006. Office: Carolina Hurricanes RBC Center 1400 Edwards Mill Rd Raleigh NC 27607-3624

BRINK, ROBERT HENDRICKS, state legislator; b. Chgo., Nov. 27, 1946; m. Deborah Harrison Schanck; children: David Harrison, Eliza Page. BA, Monmouth Coll., Ill.; JD, Coll. William & Mary, Va. Legis. cons.; vol. listener North Va. Hotline, 1972—75, mem. adv. bd., 1985—93; mem. Arlington County Fiscal Affairs Adv. Com., 1983—85, chmn., 1984—85; mgr. Arlington Sch. Bonds Campaign, 1988, gen. coord., 1996; mem. Arlington County Transp. Commn., 1996—97; mem. Dist. 48 Va. House of Delegates, Richmond, Va., 1999—. Served with US Army, 1969—71, served with US Army, 1970—71, Vietnam. Recipient Honored Citizen award, Arlington Sch. Bd., 1991. Democrat. Office: PO Box 7668 Arlington VA 22207 also: Capitol Address Gen Assembly Bldg Rm 711 PO Box 406 Richmond VA 23218 Office Phone: 703-513-1048, 804-698-1048. Business E-Mail: DelRBrink@house.virginia.gov.

BRINKEMA, LEONIE MILHOMME, federal judge; b. NJ, June 26, 1944; d. Alexander Juste and Modeste Leonie Milhomme; m. John Robert Brinkema, Dec. 22, 1966; children: Robert Aaron, Eugenie Alexandra. BA with honors, Douglass Coll., 1966; MLS, Rutgers U., 1970; JD with honors, Cornell U., 1976. Bar: D.C. 1976, Va. 1978. Trial atty. U.S. Dept. Justice, Washington, 1976-77, 1983-84; asst. U.S. atty. U.S. Atty's Office Ea. Va., Alexandria, 1977-83; prin. Leonie M. Brinkema Atty., Alexandria, 1984-85; U.S. magistrate judge U.S. Dist. Ct. (ea. dist.) Va., Alexandria, 1985-93, U.S. dist. judge, 1993—. Legal lectr. Va. State Bar Professionalism Faculty, 1990-92, No. Va. Criminal Justice Acad., 1984-85; guest lectr. Alexandria Bar Assn., Alexandria Women Attys. Assn., Va. Women Attys. Assn., U.S. Dept. Justice Advocacy Inst., Va. Law Found. Active Fairfax Choral Soc., Alban Chorale. Woodrow Wilson grad. fellow, 1966, Danforth Found. grad. fellow, 1966. Mem. ABA, Va. State Bar, D.C. Bar, Nat. Assn. Women Judges, Va. Women Attys. Assn., George Mason Inn of Ct. (master), Phi Beta Kappa. Avocation: singing. Office: US Dist Ct 401 Courthouse Sq Alexandria VA 22314-5704

BRINKER, NANCY GOODMAN, foundation administrator, former ambassador; b. Peoria, Ill., Dec. 6, 1946; d. Marvin L. & Eleanor (Newman) Goodman; m. Robert Leitstein (div. 1978); 1 child, Eric Blake; m. Norman E. Brinker, Feb. 14, 1981 (div. 2001) B in Sociology, U. Ill., 1968; PhD (hon.), Southern Meth. U. Founder, CEO Susan G. Komen Breast Cancer Found., 1982—2012, found, chair global strategy, 2012—; founder edn. & fundraising event Susan G. Komen Race for the Cure, 1983—2012; founder, chair, CEO In Your Corner, Inc., 1994—98; US amb. to Hungary US Dept. State, Budapest, 2001—03, chief of protocol Washington, 2007—09. Spkr. in field; advocate for women's health issues in Congress; collaborating ptnr., Nat. Dialogue on Cancer; bd. dirs. LHC Group, Inc., 2006-. Co-author: (with Catherine McEvily Harris) The Race Is Run One Step at a Time: Every Woman's Guide to Taking Charge of Breast Cancer and My Personal Struggle, 1995, (with Chriss Anne Winstone) Winning the Race: Taking Charge of Breast Cancer, 2001, (with Joni Rodgers) Promise Me: How A Sister's Love Launched the Global Movement to End Breast Cancer, 2010; articles published in nat. and internat. media. Bd. dirs. Physicians Reliance Network, Harvard Sch. Pub. Health, NYU Med. Sch. Found., Nat. Surg. Adjuvant Breast Project, Susan Komen Breast Cancer Found., Palm Beach Fellowship of Christians and Jews, Manpower, Inc., 2004-, US Oncology, Inc., Netmarket, Inc., Meditrust Corp.; mem. Nat. Cancer Adv. Bd.; bd. govs. Nat. Jewish Coalition.; mem. adv. bd. Harvard Ctr. for Cancer Prevention, Women's Health Initiative, Nat. Coalition of Cancer Suvivorship, Nat. Cancer Inst. Recipient Jefferson award for Hero award Coping Mag., 1996, Pub. Svc. award Oncology Nursing Soc., 1996, Greatest Pub. Svc. by a Pvt. Citizen, American Inst. Pub. Svc., 1997, Lifetime Achievement award Nat. Breast Cancer Awareness Month, 1997, Albert Einstein's Sarnoff Vol. award, Humanitarian of Yr. award Mt. Sinai, James Ewing Layman's award, Soc. Surg. Oncology, Humanitarian of Yr. award Rep. Women's Leadership Forum, Healthcare Humanitarian award, Global Conf. Inst., Tex. Gov. award, outstanding nat. svc., the first Salomon Smith Barney Extraordingary Achievement award, Champion of Prevention award, Nat. Found. for Ctrs. for Disease Control, internat. achievements in support of breast cancer rsch., Sword of Ignatius Loyola award, St. Louis Univ., Spl. Recognition award, American Soc. Clin. Oncology, Caring award, 1999, Cino del Duca award, 2000, Toastmasters Internat. Top Five Speakers award, 2001, Lifetime Achievement award, Sisters Network, 2001, Mary Woodward Lasker Pub. Svc. award in Support of Med. Rsch. & the Health Sciences, Lasker Found., 2005, Global Pathfinder award, American Soc. Breast Disease, 2006; named EVIE Profl. of the Yr., Profl. & Bus. Forum, 2005, Centennial Medal for Disting. Pub. Svc., American Assn. Cancer Rsch., 2007, Presdl. Medal of Freedom, The White House, 2009; named one of The 100 Most Important Women of 20th Century, Ladies Home Jour., The 25 Most Powerful Women in America, Biography Mag., Top 10 Champions of Women's Health, Ladies Home Jour., 100 Most Influential People in the World, TIME mag., 2008; named to The Cancer Rsch. & Treatment Fund, Inc. Cancer Survivors Hall of Fame. Office: Susan G Komen Breast Cancer Foundation PO Box 650309 Dallas TX 75265-0309*

BRINKLEY, DOUGLAS G., historian, writer, educator; b. Atlanta, Dec. 14, 1960; married; 3 children. BA, Ohio State U., 1982; MA, Georgetown U., Washington, 1983, PhD in Mil. and Diplomatic Hist., 1989; LHD (hon.), Trinity Coll., Hartford, Conn., 1997; PhD (hon.), Conn. U., NOVA Southeastern U., Ft. Lauderdale, Fla., 2004. Rsch. asst. for Smith Simpson Inst. of Diplomacy, Sch. of Foreign Svc., Georgetown U., 1985, rsch. asst. for Douglas Kinney, 1994; grad. tchg. asst. dept. history Georgetown U.; instr. dept. history US Naval Acad., Annapolis, Md., 1987; lectr. dept. history Princeton U., NJ, 1988; assoc. prof. history, tchg. fellow, New Coll. Hofstra U., Hempsted, NY, 1989—94; vis. assoc. dir. Eisenhower Ctr. for American Studies, assoc. prof. history U. New Orleans, 1993—94, dir. Eisenhower Ctr. for American Studies, 1994—2005, Stephen E. Ambrose prof. history, 1998—2005; dir. Theodore Roosevelt Ctr. for American Civilization, prof. American History Tulane U., New Orleans, 2005—07; prof. history Rice U., Houston, 2007—, fellow in history James A. Baker III Inst. Pub. Policy, 2007—. Vis. rsch. fellow Woodrow Wilson Sch. of Pub. Policy and Internat. Affairs, 1987—88; co-dir. Hofstra U. Dutch Study Summer Abroad, Roosevelt Study Ctr., Middleburg, Netherlands, Ctr. for American-Netherlands Studies, 1990—95; vis. fellow European U. Institute, Florence, Italy, 1991; vis. prof. history U. Innsbruck, Austria, 1996; creator, cons. C-SPAN Yellow School Bus Program; invited spkr. Author: Dean Acheson: The Cold War Years, 1953-1971, 1992 (New York Times Notable Book of the Yr., 1993), The Majic Bus: An American Odyssey, 1993 (Lushman Fellowship at Davenport Coll., Yale U., 1994), The Unfinished Presidency: Jimmy Carter's Journey Beyond the White House Years, 1998 (New York Times Notable Book of the Yr., 1998), American Heritage History of the United States, 1998 (Benjamin Franklin award for best political/history book, 1999), Rosa Parks: A Biography, 2000, Wheels for the World: Henry Ford, His Company, and a Century of Progress, 1903-2003, 2003 (New York Times Notable Book of the Year, 2004, Mich. Notable Book honor, 2004, Henry Ford Heritage Assn. Book award, 2004), Tour of Duty: John Kerry and the Vietnam War, 2004, The Boys of Pointe du Hoc: Ronald Reagan, D-Day, and the US Army 2nd Ranger Battalion, 2005, The Great Deluge: Hurricane Katrina, New Orleans and the Mississippi Gulf Coast, 2006 (Robert F. Kennedy Book prize, 2007, New York Times Notable Book of the Yr., 2006, Humanities Book of the Yr., La. Endowment for the Humanities, 2007), Gerald R. Ford, 2007, Wilderness Warrior: Theodore Roosevelt and the Crusade for America, 2009, The Quiet World: Saving Alaska's Wilderness Kingdom, 1979-1960, 2011, Cronkite, 2012; co-author (with Townsend Hoopes): Driven Patriot: The Life and Times of James Forrestal, 1992 (Theodore and Franklin Roosevelt Naval History prize, 1993, New York Times Notable Book of the Yr., 1993), Franklin Roosevelt and the Creation of the United Nations, 1997; co-author: (with Stephen E. Ambrose) Rise to Globalism: American Foreign Policy Since 1939, 1997;: The Mississippi and the Making of a Nation, 2002, Theodore Roosevelt, the U.S. Navy, and the Spanish-American War, 2003; co-author: (with Ronald J. Drez) Voices of Valor: D-Day, June 6, 1944, 2004, Voices of Courage: The Battle for Khe Sanh, Vietnam, 2005; co-author: (with Julie M. Fenster) Parish Priest: Father Michael McGivney and American Catholicism, 2006; editor: Dean Acheson and the Making of US Foreign Policy, 1993, John F. Kennedy and Europe, 1997, Strategies of Enlargement: The Clinton Doctrine and US Foreign Policy, 1997, Hunter S. Thompson: The Proud Highway: Saga of a Desperate Southern Gentleman 1955-1967, 1997, Hunter S. Thompson: Fear and Loathing in Ameica, 2001, The World War II Memorial: A Grateful Nation Remembers, 2004, Windblown World: The Journals of Jack Kerouac 1947-1954, 2004, The Reagan Diaries, 2007, American History Magazine, 2004—05; co-editor (with Clifford P. Hackett): Jean Monnet: The Path to European Unity, 1991; co-editor: (with D. Facey-Crowther) The Atlantic Charter, 1992; co-editor: (with Gable and Naylor) Theodore Roosevelt: The Many-Sided American, 1993; co-editor: (with Richard Griffiths) John F. Kennedy and Europe, 1999; co-editor: (with Stephen Ambrose, Allen Nevins & Henry Steele Commager) Witness to America: An Illustrated Documentary History of the United States from the Revolution to Today, 1999; co-editor: (with Andrew Carroll) War Letters: Extraordinary Correspondence from Wars, 2001; co-editor: (with Patricia Limerick) The Bernard DeVoto Reader, 2001; co-editor: (with Michael Haskew) The World War II Desk Reference, 2004; general editor The New York Times Living History: World War II: The Axis Assault, 1939-1942, 2003, The New York Times Living History, World War II: The Allied Counteroffensive, 1942-1945, 2004, adv. editor The Penguin Encyclopedia of American History, 2003; contbr. chapters to books, of articles to magazines and newspapers; contributing editor Vanity Fair, American Heritage, mem. editl. bd. Presidential Studies Quarterly, Soc. for Historian of American Foreign Relations. Recipient Stessin award, Hofstra U., 1993, Stuart Bernath Lecture prize for 1995, Soc. of Historians of American Foreign Relations, 1996, Bernath Lecture prize, 1996, Humanities Alumni award of Distinction, Ohio State U., 2002; named La. Endowment for the Humanities, Humanist of the Yr., 2004; Leah Goldman Karp Found. Lecture Fellowship, 1999. Mem.: Coun. on Foreign Relations, Soc. of American Historians, The Century Assn. of NYC, Theodore Roosevelt Assn. Office: Baker Institute Rice University 6100 Main St Baker Hall Room 220 Houston TX 77005 Office Phone: 504-621-3939. Business E-Mail: Douglas.Brinkley@Rice.edu.

BRINKLEY, JACK THOMAS, lawyer, former United States Representative, Georgia; b. Faceville, Ga., Dec. 22, 1930; s. Lonnie Elester and Pauline (Spearman) B.; m. Alma Lois Kite, May 29, 1955 (dec. Apr. 24, 2001); children: Jack Thomas Jr., Fred Alen II; m. Sally Posey, May 25, 2009 Student, Young Harris Coll., 1947-49, Okla. A. and M. Coll., 1952; LL.B. cum laude, U. Ga., 1959. Bar: Ga. 1958, DC 1973. Sch. tchr., Ga., 1949-51; assoc. firm Young, Hollis & Moseley, Columbus, Ga., 1959-61; ptnr. firm Coffin & Brinkley, Columbus, 1961-66; mem. Ga. Ho. Reps., 1965-66; sr. ptnr. Brinkley and Brinkley, 1983-95, of counsel, 1996-2000, of counsel emeritus, 2001—; mem. 90th-97th Congresses from 3d Ga. dist.; chmn. mil. facilities and installations subcom. 97th Congress. Mem. Ga. Ho. Rep., 1965-66. Trustee Young Harris Coll. Mem. Ga. Bar Assn., Columbus Bar Assn., Young Lawyers Club of Columbus (pres. 1963-64), Blue Key, Muscogee Civitan Club (pres., 2005), Masons. Democrat. Baptist. Office: 812 Timber Creek Ct Columbus GA 31904 Home Phone: 706-505-8258; Office Phone: 706-576-5322. E-mail: jackandsallybrinkley@gmail.com.

BRINKLEY, WILLIAM ROBERT, cell biologist, educator; b. Weldon, Tex., May 31, 1936; s. Lee Elmore and Saline (Bass) B.; m. Shirley Wise, June 4, 1955; 1 child, William Kevin BS, Sam Houston State U., MS, 1961; PhD, Iowa State U., 1964. Prof., dir., divsn. cell structure and function, dept. cell biology Baylor Coll. Medicine, 1973—85, disting. svc. prof., dean, grad. Sch. Biomed. Scis., 1991—; prof. and chair, dept. cell biology U. Ala., Birmingham, 1985—91. Dir. Gregory Fleming Cystic Fibrosis Rsch. Ctr., U. Ala., Birmingham, 1985; cons. Eli Lilly Rsch. Labs., Indpls., 1981-85; chmn. biomed. sci. study sect. NIH, HHS, Bethesda, Md., 1985-89. Author 2 books; editor-in-chief jour. Cell Motility and the Cytoskeleton; contbr. numerous articles to profl. jours. Recipient Disting. Alumnus award U. Tex. M.D. Anderson Hosp., 1984, Disting. Alumnus award Sam Houston State U., 1985, Merit award Nat. Cancer Inst., Bethesda, 1988—. Mem. Am. Soc. Cell Biology (pres. 1979-80), Internat. Fedn. Cell Biology (pres. 1980-84), Sigma Xi (nat. lectr. 1982-85). Avocations: travel, birdwatching. Home: 2602 Glen Haven Blvd Houston TX 77025 Home Fax: 713-798-5762. Personal E-mail: brinkley@bcm.edu.

BRINSMADE, LYON LOUIS, retired lawyer; b. Mex. City, Feb. 24, 1924; s. Robert Bruce and Helen (Steenbock) B. (Am. citizens); m. Susannah Tucker, June 9, 1956 (div. 1978); children: Christine Fairchild, Louisa Calvert; m. Carolyn Hartman Lister, Sept. 22, 1979 (dec. 2003); m. Elizabeth Bonnet Markland, May 26, 2009. Student, U. Wis., 1940-43; BS, Mich. Technol. U., 1944; JD, Harvard U., 1950. Bar: Tex. 1951. Assoc. Butler, Binion, Rice, Cook & Knapp, Houston, 1950-58, ptnr. in charge internat. dept., 1958-83, Porter & Clements, Houston, 1983-91; sr. counsel Porter & Hedges (formerly Porter & Clements), Houston, 1991-99. Bd. dirs. Houston br. English-Speaking Union of U.S., 1972-75. Served with AUS, 1946-47. Mem. ABA (chmn. com. internat. investment and devel. of sect. internat. law and practice 1970-76, council 1972-76, 81-82, vice chmn. 1976-79, chmn.-elect 1979-80, chmn. 1980-81, co-founder and co-chmn. com. Mex. 1982-85), Internat. Bar Assn., Inter-Am. Bar Assn. (co-chmn. sect. oil and gas laws, com. natural resources 1973-76, council 1984-87), Houston Bar Assn., State Bar Tex. (chmn. internat. law com. 1970-74, mem. council sect. internat. law 1975-78), Am. Soc. Internat. Law (exec. council 1984-86), Houston World Trade Assn. (sec., dir. 1967-70), Houston World Trade Assn. (chmn. legis. com. 1967-72), Houston C. of C. (chmn. legis. subcom. internat. bus. com. 1970-72), SAR, Harvard Club (Houston), Sigma Alpha Epsilon. Episcopalian. Home: PO Box 550451 Houston TX 77255

BRIONES, DAVID, federal judge; b. El Paso, Tex., Feb. 26, 1943; m. Delia Garcia; 4 children. BA, U. Tex., El Paso, 1969; JD, U. Tex., Austin, 1971. Ptnr. Moreno & Briones, 1971-91; judge El Paso County Ct. No. 1, El Paso, 1991-94, US Dist. Ct. (we. dist.) Tex., El Paso, 1994—2009, sr. judge, 2009—. Mem. Jud. Conf. Com. Adminstrn. Magistrate Judges Sys., 2003—. With US Army, 1964—66. Fellow: Tex. Bar Found.; mem.: Mex.-Am. Bar Assn., El Paso Bar Assn., State Bar Tex. Office: US Courthouse Courtroom 1 511 E San Antonio Ave El Paso TX 79901-2401 also: 525 Magoffin Ave Ste 761 El Paso TX 79901-2577 Office Phone: 915-534-6744. Business E-Mail: David_Briones@txwd.uscourts.gov.

BRISCOE, ANNE M., retired science educator; b. NYC, Dec. 1, 1918; m. William A. Briscoe, Aug. 20, 1955 (dec. Dec. 1985); m. Theodore H. Heinly Sr., Jan. 21, 1989 (dec. Dec. 2002), Irwin H. Slater, Oct. 12, 2009. MA, Vassar Coll., 1945; PhD, Yale U., 1949. From rsch. assoc. to asst. prof. Cornell U. Med. Coll., NYC, 1950-56; faculty Columbia U. Coll. Physicians and Surgeons, NYC, 1956—, prof. emeritus, 1987. Spl. lectr., 1987-89; lectr. Harlem Hosp. Center Sch. Nursing, 1968-77; adj. asst. prof. Hunter Coll., 1951-64, 73-75; mem. N.Y.C. Commn. on Status of Women, 1979-93, vice chair, 1982-93; non-govtl. orgn. del. to UN; adv. coun. Inst. Nuc. Power Ops., 1979-84. Contbr. articles to profl. jours. Sterling Jr. fellow, USPHS fellow, Yale U., 1949; recipient Yale medal, 1986, Susan B. Anthony award, 1989, Wilbur Cross medal Yale Grad. Sch. Sesquicentennial Convocation, 1997, Yale Fund Chmns. award, 2000. Fellow: AAAS (mem. coun. 1982—85, chmn.'s award Yale Alumni Fund 2001), Assn. Women in Sci. (editor newsletter 1971—74, nat. pres. 1974—76), N.Y. Acad. Sci. (chair women in sci. com. 1978—92, bd. govs. 1981), Am. Inst. Chemists (sec. N.Y. chpt. 1981—83); mem.: ACS, Assn. Women in Sci. Ednl. Found. (pres. 1978—82), Fedn. Orgns. for Profl. Women (treas. 1978—80), Harvey Soc., Am. Fedn. Clin. Rsch., Am. Soc. Clin. Nutrition, Yale Grad. Sch. Alumni Assn. (pres. 1981—86), Assn. Yale Alumni (assembly rep. 1978—88, bd. govs. 1982—85). Home: 200 Lake Ave NE Apt 419 Largo FL 33771-1655 E-mail: drannieb@aol.com.

BRISSETTE, MARTHA BLEVINS, lawyer; b. Salisbury, Md., Apr. 30, 1959; d. Reuben Wesley and Miriam Rebecca (Walters) Blevins; m. Henry Joseph Brissette III, May 24, 1980; children: Madeline Rose, William Roy. BA, U. Richmond, 1981, JD, 1983. Bar: Va. 1983, US Supreme Ct. 1987. Law clk. Supreme Ct. Va., Richmond, 1983-84; atty. Dept. Justice, Washington, 1984-88; staff atty. Office of the Exec. Sec., Supreme Ct. Va., Richmond, Va., 1988; asst. atty. gen. Office of the Atty. Gen. of Va., Richmond, 1989-92; v.p. counsel Lawyers Title Ins. Corp., Richmond, 1992-97; asst. counsel State Farm Ins. Cos., 1997-99; asst. atty. gen. Office of Atty. Gen. of Va., Richmond, 1999—2001; pvt. practice Richmond, 2002—05; assoc. Ukrops Supermarkets, Inc., 2004—05; atty. Va. Divsn. Legis. Svcs., Richmond, 2005—07; policy analyst Va. State Bd. Elections, Richmond, 2007—. Mem.: Henrico County Bar Assn. Roman Catholic. Avocation: cake decorating. Home: 8307 Forge Rd Henrico VA 23228-3127 Office Phone: 804-864-8925. Personal E-mail: marthabrissette@aol.com. Business E-Mail: marthabbrissette@justice.com, mbrissemarthaobrissette@sbc.virginia.gov.

BRISSON, WILLIAM D., state legislator; m. Brenda Brisson; 1 child, Alan. Farmer; state rep. Dist. 22 NC, 2007—. Mem. Appropriations com., Appropriations Subcom. on Health and Human Svcs., Transp. com., Wildlife Resources com.; chmn. Mental Health Reform com. Democrat. Mailing: PO Box 531 Dublin NC 28332 Office: North Carolina House of Representatives 16 W Jones St Room 1325 Raleigh NC 27601-1096 Office Phone: 919-733-5772. Business E-Mail: William.Brisson@ncleg.net.

BRISTER, BILL H., lawyer, former bankruptcy judge; b. Sieper, La., Mar. 5, 1930; s. Clayton Houston and Era (Price) Brister; m. Carolyn Lee McDowell Brister, June 11, 1955; children: Jeff, Julie. BS in Chemistry, Northwestern State U., Natchitoches, La., 1948; JD, U. Tex., 1958. Bar: Tex. 1957, US Dist. Ct. (no. dist.) Tex. 1959, US Ct. Appeals (5th cir.) 1971, US Supreme Ct. 1971. Pvt. practice, Lubbock, Tex., 1958—79; bankruptcy judge US Dist. Ct. (no. dist.) Tex., 1979—85; of counsel Winstead, Sechrest & Minick & Predecessor Firm, 1986—. Served to col. USMC, 1951—52. E-mail: billbrist@aol.com.

BRISTER, SCOTT ANDREW, lawyer, former state supreme court justice; b. Waco, Tex., Jan. 8, 1955; s. Miller Robbins and Annette Josephine (Scott) B.; m. Julia Upton Brister, 4 children. BA summa cum laude, Duke U., 1977; JD cum laude, Harvard U., 1980. Bar: Tex. 1980, U.S. Dist. Ct. (so. dist.) Tex. 1981, U.S. Ct. Appeals 1981 (5th cir.), U.S. Supreme Ct. 1986. Briefing atty. to presiding justice Tex. Supreme Ct., Austin, 1980-81; atty. Andrews & Kurth, Houston, 1981-89; judge 234th Dist. Ct., Harris County, Houston, 1989—2000; justice First Dist. Ct. of Appeals, Houston, 2000—01; chief justice 14th Dist. Ct. of Appeals, 2001—03; justice Tex. Supreme Ct., Austin, 2003—09; ptnr. Andrews Kurth LLP, Austin, 2009—. Former mem. Jud. Panel on Multidistrict Litigation, Supreme Ct. Advisory Com., Supreme Ct. Jury Task Force. Co-author Texas Pretrial Practice; author law review articles in Baylor Law Review, St. Mary's Law Jour. Fellow Houston Bar Found., Tex. Bar Found. Office: Andrews Kurth LLP 111 Congress Ave Ste 1700 Austin TX 78701 Office Phone: 512-320-9220. Office Fax: 512-542-5220. E-mail: sbrister@andrewskurth.com.

BRISTOW, ROBERT O'NEIL, writer, educator; b. St. Louis, Nov. 17, 1926; s. Jesse Reuben and Helen Marjorie (Utley) Bristow; m. Gail Hamiter Rosen, Aug. 25, 2003; children from previous marriage: Cynthia Lynn, Margery Jan Wu, Gregory Scott, Kelly Robert. BA in Journalism, U. Okla., 1951, MA in Journalism, 1965. Asst. advt. mgr. Altus (Okla.) Times Democrat, 1951-53; freelance writer Altus, 1951-60; prof. English Winthrop Coll., Rock Hill, SC, 1960-87, prof. emeritus, 1987—. Author: Time for Glory, 1968, Night Season, 1970, A Faraway Drummer, 1973, Laughter in Darkness, 1974. With USNR, 1944—45. Recipient award for Lit. Excellence, U. Okla., 1969, award for novel, Friends of Am. Writers, 1974. Mem.: Alpha Tau Omega. Home: 210 Cantrell Ave Fort Mill SC 29715-1604 Personal E-mail: bobbristow@comporium.net.

BRITO, DAGOBERT LLANOS, economics professor; b. Mex., Apr. 6, 1941; came to U.S., 1945, naturalized, 1958; s. John L. and Guadalupe G. (Llanos) B.; m. Patricia Ann Kendrick, June 29, 1968. BA, Rice U., 1967, MA, PhD, Rice U., 1970. Asst. prof. econs. U. Wis., Madison, 1970-72; asso. prof. econs. and polit. sci. Ohio State U., Columbus, 1972-75, prof., 1976-79; dir. Murphy Inst. Polit. Economy; chmn., prof. econs. Tulane U., New Orleans, 1979-84; Peterkin prof. polit. econs. Rice U., Houston, 1984—. Cons. Dept. State, Dept. Def. Author: A Dynamic Model of the Armaments Race, 1972, Strategic Nuclear Weapons and the Allocation of International Rights, 1977, Conflicts and Outbreak of War, 1985, Stock Externalities, Pigovian Taxation and Dynamic Stability, 1987, Richardsonian Arms Race Models, 1989, On the Limits of Economic Control, 1990, Externalities and Compulsory Vaccinations, 1991, The Economic and Political Incentives to Acquire Nuclear Weapons, 1993; (with M.D. Intriligator) The Economics of Disarmament, Arms Races and Arms Control, 1993, Minimizing the Risks for Accidental Nuclear War: An Agenda for Action, 1993; (with P.R. Hartley) Consumer Rationality and Credit Cards, 1995, Proliferation and the Probability of War: A Cardinality Theorem, 1996, Pricing Natural Gas in Mexico, 2002; editor: Strategies for Managing Nuclear Proliferation, 1983; assoc. editor Jour. Optimization Theory and Applications. Served with U.S. Army, 1963-66. NSF grantee, 1972, 74, 77, 78, 81; Mershon Center grantee, 1973, 78; Rice scholar Baker Inst. Mem. Econometric Soc., Public Choice Soc., Houston Philo. Soc. Office: Rice U PO Box 1892 Houston TX 77251-1892 Office Phone: 713-348-5792. Business E-Mail: brito@rice.edu.

BRITT, KENNY (KENNETH LAWRENCE BRITT), professional football player; b. Bayonne, NJ, Sept. 19, 1988; s. Jack Britt and Michelle Johnson; 1 child, Aiden. Student in criminal justice, Rutgers U., New Brunswick, NJ. Wide receiver Tenn. Titans, 2009—. Active Ch. of Living Water, Newark. Office: Tenn Titans One Titans Way Nashville TN 37213

BRITT, WILLIAM EARL, federal judge; b. McDonald, NC, Dec. 7, 1932; s. Dudley H. and Martha Mae (Hall) B.; m. Judith Moore, Apr. 17, 1976. Student, Campbell Jr. Coll., 1952; BS, Wake Forest U., 1956, JD, 1958. Bar: N.C. 1958. Pvt. practice law, Fairmont, N.C., 1959-72, Lumberton, N.C., 1972-80; judge US Dist. Ct. (ea. dist.) NC, 1980—83, 1990—97, chief judge, 1983-90, sr. judge, 1997—. Mem. Jud. Conf. Com. on Automation and Tech., 1990-95; 4th cir. dist. judge rep. to Jud. Conf. U.S., 1991-97. Trustee Southeastern Community Coll., 1965-70, Southeastern Gen. Hosp., Lumberton, 1965-69, Pembroke State U., 1967-72; bd. govs. U. N.C. Served with U.S. Army, 1953-55. Mem. N.C. Bar Assn., Fed. Judges Assn. (bd. dirs., v.p., 1993-95, pres. 1995-97). Baptist. Office: US Dist Ct PO Box 27504 Raleigh NC 27611-7504 Home: 51 Holly Hill Ct Littleton NC 27850-8928

BRITTAIN, JAMES EDWARD, science and technology educator, researcher; b. Mills River, NC, May 20, 1931; s. Randall Francis and Velma Hassie (Gillespie) B.; m. Louise Mary Lambert, March 29, 1969 (dec. Mar. 27, 1972); m. Jo Ann Layne, Apr. 14, 1973. BS, Clemson U., 1957; MS, U. Tenn., 1959; MA, Case Western Res. U., 1969, PhD, 1970. Jr. rsch. engr. U. Tenn., Knoxville, 1958-59; asst. prof. elec. engring. Clemson (S.C.) U., 1959-66; asst. prof. history of sci. and tech. Ga. Inst. Tech., Atlanta, 1969-71, assoc. prof., 1972-91, prof., 1992-94; prof. emeritus, 1994—. Author: Engineering the New South, 1985, Alexanderson: Pioneer in American Electrical Engineering, 1992, Scanning The Past: A History of Electrical Engineering and Its Pioneers, 1999, Gun Fights, Dam Sites and Water Rights, 2001; editor: Turning Points in American Electrical History, 1977. With USAF, 1950-54. Smithsonian Instn. rsch. fellow, 1972-73; recipient rsch. contract Nat. Park Svc., 1974-75; grantee NSF, 1979. Fellow IEEE (chmn. history com. 1978-79, 88-89, assoc. editor proceedings 1990-, Centennial medal 1984), Royal Soc. Arts, Radio Club Am. (Batcher Meml. prize 1989); mem. Soc. History of Tech. (mem. exec. coun. 1978-80, 89-91, Usher prize 1971). Home: 600 Carolina Village Rd # 2509 Hendersonville NC 28792

BROACH, DAVID E., architectural firm executive; CEO BSW Internat., Tulsa, Okla. Office: Bsw International PO Box 1046 Tulsa OK 74101-1046

BROAD, AARON, healthcare service company executive; Dir., investor rels. Vanguard Health Sys., Inc. Office: Vanguard Health Systems Inc Ste 100 20 Burton Hills Blvd Nashville TN 37215 Office Phone: 615-665-6000. Office Fax: 615-665-6099. Business E-Mail: abroad@vanguardhealth.com.

BROADWATER, CHRISTOPHER, state legislator; BA, La. Coll., 1995; MDiv, New Orleans Baptist Theol. Seminary, 1998; JD, La. State U., 2002. Mem. Dist. 86 La. House of Reps., 2012—, vice chair Labor and Industrial Relations Com., mem. Edn. Com., Ways and Means Com. & Joint Legis. Com. on Capital Outlay. Republican. Office: District Office 112 S Cypress St Hammond LA 70403 Office Phone: 985-543-4900. E-mail: broadwaterc@legis.la.gov.

BROADWATER, JAMES E., retired publisher; s. Robert L. and June J. B.; m. Diane K. Plummer, Apr. 22, 1967; children: James Tegan, Kelly Diane, Robert Charles, Krista Dawn. BS in Journalism, U. Fla., 1967. Acct. mgr. Young & Rubicam, Inc., Detroit, Kansas City, NYC and Houston, 1968-73; assoc. pub. Tex. Monthly Mag., Austin, 1973-78; pres., pub. Saturday Rev. Mag., NYC, 1978-80; regional pub. dir. Baker Publs., Houston, 1980-85; pres. HBC, Inc., Houston, 1985-87; assoc. pub. Tex. Sportsworld Mag., 1985-86; pub. Washington Journalism Rev., 1987-92; pres. The Broadwater Co., Houston, 1993—. Mem. Mag. Pub. Assn., Nat. Press Club, Am. Mgmt. Assn., Direct Mail Mktg. Assn., Lambda Chi Alpha. Baptist. Personal E-mail: jbroadwater@sbcglobal.net.

BROCHIN, ROBERT M., lawyer; b. May 14, 1955; m. Cristina E. Brochin. BA, U. Fla., 1977; JD, U. Fla. Law Sch., 1980. Bar: Fla. 1981. Dep. gen. counsel Fla. Gov. Office, 1991—92, Fla. Chief Inspector Gen., 1992—93; ptnr., litig. practice group Morgan, Lewis & Bockius LLP, 1993—, chmn. recruiting com-Miami Office. Mem.: Fla. Partnership Am. (chmn.), Dade County Bar Assn., Fla. Bar Assn., Fla. Constn. Revision Commn. (1997-1998). Office: Morgan Lewis & Bockius LLP 5300 Wachovia Fin Ctr 200 S Biscayne Blvd Miami FL 33131-2339 Office Phone: 305-415-3456. Office Fax: 305-415-3001. Business E-Mail: rbrochin@morganlewis.com.

BROCK, ANDREW C., state legislator; b. Mocksville, NC, Apr. 9, 1974; Vol. Howard House, 1998; field repr. Faircloth Senate, 1998—99; state senator Dist. 34 NC, 2002—; cons. RCS Comm. Group. Mem.: Davie County C. of C. Republican. Methodist. Office: NC Senate 300 N Salisbury St Room 623 Raleigh NC 27603-5925 Office Phone: 919-715-0690. E-mail: Andrew.Brock@ncleg.net.

BROCK, CAROLYN PRATT, chemist, educator; b. Chgo., July 25, 1946; d. Charles Stebbings and Grace (Goodman) Pratt; m. Louis Milton Brock, July 22, 1972. BA, Wellesley Coll., Mass., 1968; PhD, Northwestern U., 1972. Asst. prof. chemistry U. Ky., Lexington, 1972-78, assoc. prof. chemistry, 1978-87, prof., 1987—. Vis. scientist organic chemistry lab. Swiss Fed. Inst. Tech., Zurich, 1980—81, 1988—89; bd. govs. Cambridge Crystallographic Data Centre, 2001—09, vice chmn., 2003—05, chmn., 2005—07. Co-editor: Acta Crystallographica, 1993—2002; editor: Sect. B of Acta Crystallographica, 2002—11; editor in chief internat. Tables Crystallography, 2010—; contbr. articles to profl. jours. Mem. Am. Chem. Soc., Am. Crystallographic Assn., U.S. Nat. Com. for Crystallography (sec.-treas. 1989-91), Phi Beta Kappa, Sigma Xi. Home: 133 Sycamore Rd Lexington KY 40502-1841 Office: U Ky Dept Chemistry Lexington KY 40506-0055 Home Phone: 859-266-2414; Office Phone: 859-257-1959. Business E-Mail: cpbrock@uky.edu.

BROCK, DEE SALA, television executive, writer, consultant, educator; b. Covington, Okla., June 7, 1930; d. Lester Edward and Vera Mae (Bowers) Sala; m. Robert Wesley Brock, June 8, 1952 (div. 1979); children: Baron Sala, Bishop Chapman, Bevin Bowers. BA, U. North Tex., 1950, MA, 1956, PhD, 1985. Tchr. high sch. Dallas Ind. Sch. Dist., 1952-66; dir. Dallas Cowboy Cheerleaders, 1960-75; mem. faculty, adminstr. Dallas County Cmty. Coll. Dist., 1966-74, telecourse writer, prodr., adminstr., 1974-75, dir. mktg. info., 1975-80; dir., v.p. PBS, Washington, 1980-89, sr. v.p. edn. Alexandria, Va., 1989-90; pres. Dee Brock & Assocs., Plano, Tex., 1991-98; pub. FAQs Press, 1999—. Bd. dirs. Pub. Svc. Satellite Consortium, U.S. Basics; adv. bd. Learning Link, 1987-90, Telcon Industry, 1990-91; chair exec. coun. U. of the World, 1989-91; adv. coun. Triangle Coalition, 1989-91; spkr. in field. Author: Writing for a Reason: Study Guide, 1974; author: (with Jeriel Howard) Writing for a Reason, 1978; author: (with Laura Derr) The World of F. Scott Fitzgerald, 1980; author: (with Deborah Burkett and Carole Wilson) Troup Goes to War: World War II, A Collection of Memories, 1999; author: (with Linda Resnik) Food FAQs: Substitutions, Yields & Equivalents, 2000; author: (with JoAnna Lewis) 100 Great Fundraising Ideas Celebrating 100 Years of Texas Library, 2002; mem. editl. bd.: American Jour. Distance Edn., 1987—90; prodr.: (internat. teleconf.) Out of the Red, 1991; prodr., writer: TV series and workbook Communicating in English in the Healthcare Workplace, 1994; contbr. articles to profl. jours. Trustee Coun. for Adult and Experiential Learning, 1989—99; chair spl. task force Mcpl. Libr. Friends of Libr., 1996, pres., 1997—; chair planning to plan com. NE Tex. Libr. Sys., 1997—98, adv. coun., 1998—2004, vice chair, 1998—2000, chair, 2000—04; chmn. Strategic Planning Com., 1999; fundraising co-chair Komen Tyler Race for the Cure, 1999; active PTA, Dallas; pres. Littera, 2002—04, Friends of the Troup Libr., 1998—; chair Libr. Friends, Trustees and Advs., 2001—04; bd. LWV, 2000—, v.p. comm., 2001, pres., 2002—06, v.p. cmty. rels., 2006—10, v.p. program, 2010—; pres. Friends Arts, UT Tyler, Tex.; bd. dirs. Tyler Civic Theatre Ctr., 2002, Coalition for the Advancement of Citizenship, 1988—90; chair Smith County Lilmaries Together, 2006—; bd. dirs. LWV Tex., 2008—, v.p. orgn., 2009—; chair East Tex. Book Fest, 2009—. Reynolds Econ. fellow U. NC, 1966; Literacy award North Tex. Reading Coun., 1980, Nat. Person of Yr. award Nat. Coun. on Cmty. and Continuing Edn., 1985, Award for Excellence in TV Programming NEA, 1986; recipient Outstanding Career Achievement award ITC American Assn. Cmty. and Jr. Colls., 1990, named Woman in Tyler 2009, recipient. Liberty Bell award, Smith County Bar Assn. Mem. NEH (nat. bd. cons. 1980-85), LWV (bd. dirs., v.p. cmty. rels. Tyler chpt. 2002-03, pres. 2003—bd. dirs.,Tex.,2008, bd. mem. 2008-), US Distance Learning Assn. (bd. dirs. 1989-91, adv. bd. 1989), So. Assn. Colls. and Schs. (project 1990 task force 1984-86), Nat. Assn. Ednl. Broadcasters (steering com. 1979-81), Assn. Ednl. Comms. Tech., Nat. Coun. Tchrs. English (pres. SW regional coun. 1972-74), Tex. Libr. Assn. (legis. com. 1999—, chair roundtable 2001-2003, chair pub. rels. com. 2005—07). Methodist. Achievements include being co-patentee video indexing system; design of and management of PBS Adult Learning Service and PBS Adult Learning Satellite Service. Home and Office: 3529 Woods Blvd Tyler TX 75707

BROCK, HORACE RHEA, finance educator; b. Leggett, Tex., Aug. 26, 1927; s. Hobby B. and Winona (Epperson) Brock; m. Frances Euline Williams, May 24, 1955; children: Alan Howard, Mary Ann, Charles. BS, Sam Houston State U., 1946, BBA, MA, Sam Houston State U., 1951; PhD, U. Tex., 1954. Prof. U. Ark., 1954-55; disting. prof. North Tex. State U., Denton, 1965-93, chmn. dept. accounting, 1966-74, acting dean Coll. Bus. Adminstrn., 1983-85; dir. Chief Execs. Round Table U. North Tex., Denton, 1993—99. Adviser AID, Istanbul, Turkey, 1967—69; cons. taxation and fin. reporting. Author: Accounting for Oil and Gas Producers, 1960, Intermediate and Advanced Accounting, 1966, Introduction to Taxation, 1972, 17th edit., 1988, Cost Accounting, 1970, 8th edit., 2006, College Accounting, 1974, 11th edit., 2005, Accounting for Oil and Gas Producing Companies, 1982, 6th edit., 2007. With USAF, 1946—49. Mem.: AICPA, Tex. Soc. CPAs, Beta Gamma Sigma. Home: 1900 Westridge St Denton TX 76205-6925 Office: U North Tex 302 Marquis Hall Denton TX 76203 Personal E-mail: brocks3@verizon.net. Business E-Mail: horace.brock@unt.edu.

BROCK, JOHN F., beverage company executive; m. Mary Brock. BS chem. engring., MS chem. engring., Ga. Inst. Tech. Positions in product develop. Proctor & Gamble, 1972—83; sr. v.p. ops. & tech. Cadbury Schweppes USA, 1983—90; pres. Cadbury Beverages Internat., 1990—92, Cadbury Beverages Europe, 1992—93, Cadbury Beverages No. Am., 1993—96; mng. dir. global beverages Cadbury Schweppes plc, 1996—2000, COO, 2000—02; CEO Interbrew, 2003—04, InBev, Brussels, 2004—06; pres., CEO Coca-Cola Enterprises, Inc., Atlanta, 2006—08, chmn., CEO, 2008—. Bd. dir. Reed Elsevier plc, 1999—2005, Campbell Soup Co., 2004—06. Office: Coca-Cola Enterprises Inc 2500 Windy Ridge Pkwy Atlanta GA 30339

BROCK, JOHN WILLIAM, III, surgeon, urologist, educator; b. Louisville, Apr. 13, 1952; s. John W. and Sara (Fisher) Brock; m. Lisa Ann Trusler; children: Elizabeth Draper, Grace Ann, Anna Fisher. BS, Vanderbilt U., Nashville, 1974; MD, Med. Coll. Ga., Augusta, 1978. Diplomate Am. Bd. Urology. Resident urology Vanderbilt U., Nashville, 1979—82, chief resident, 1982—83; clin. asst. prof. Vanderbilt U. Sch. Medicine, 1983—91, assoc. prof. urology, pediat., 1992—99, prof. urology, pediat., 1999—; assoc. program dir. urology residents Bapt. Hosp., Nashville, 1989—91; dir. pediat. urology Vanderbilt U. Med. Ctr., 1992—, vice-chair surg. sciences sect., 2002—; surgeon-in-chief Vanderbilt Children's Hosp., 2002—. Sr. investigator Vanderbilt Cancer Group; invited vis. prof. Baylor U., Brown U., Boston Children's, U. Calif. San Francisco, U. Colo., Germany, Egypt, Bolivia, Argentina, Columbia, Guatemala; presenter in field. Mem. editl. bd.: Internat. Pediatric Surgery, Jour. Urology, Pediatric Urology Sect., mem. exec. com.: Jour. Pediatric Urology; contbr. articles to profl. jours., chapters to books. Mem. C. of C., Nashville. Recipient Eliot V. Newman award, Vanderbilt U., 1994, 2006, Best Rsch. Trainee award, Radiology Soc. N.Am., 1994, First prize, Resident Rsch. award, Soc. Pediat. Rsch., 1997, First prize, Fellow Rsch. award, 1997; named Best Doctor in Nashville, Nashville Life, 1996; named one of Best Doctors in Nashville, 1998; grantee, NIH Ctr. Excellence in Pediatric Nephrology and Urology, 1996—, Am. Found. Urol. Disease, 1998—99; scholar, 1993, 1995. Fellow: ACS, Soc. Pediat. Urology (ex-officio bd. mem., pres.-elect 2008), Am. Acad. Pediat.; mem.: AMA, Pediatric Urology Fellowship Dirs. (pres. 2007—08), Vanderbilt Urology Soc., Urodynamics Soc., Tenn. Urol. Assn., Spina Bifida Assn., Soc. Genitourinary Reconstructive Surgery, Soc. Fetal Urology, Nashville Surg. Soc., Nashville Acad. Medicine, Mid. Tenn. Urology Soc., Davidson County Pediat. Assn., Cumberland Pediat. Found., Am. Urol. Assn. (bd. mem. southeastern sect. 2003, Frank Hinman award 2002), Am. Fertility Soc., Rotary Club, Sigma Chi. Avocations: gardening, golf, outdoor activities. Office:

Vanderbilt Children's Hosp 4102 Doctors Office Tower 2200 Childrens Way Nashville TN 37232-9820 Office Phone: 615-936-1060. Office Fax: 615-936-1061. E-mail: john.brock@Vanderbilt.edu.

BROCK, KARENA DIANE, dancer, educator; b. LA, Sept. 21, 1942; d. Orville DeLoss and Sallie Alice (Anderson) B.; m. Ted Kivitt, Apr. 16, 1965 (div. 1978); m. John Robert Carlyle, June 28, 1985; 1 child, Timothy John. Grad. H.S., Kansas City, Mo. Tchr. master classes Radford (Va.) Coll., U. Louisville, U. Tampa; staff tchr. Bklyn. Coll.; mem. faculty SUNY-Purchase; artistic dir., choreographer, tchr. and founder Hilton Head Dance Theater and Sch., Hilton Head Island, SC, 1985—. Guest tchr. S.C. Dance Inst., Columbia, 1993-94, Walnut Hill Sch., Boston, Savannah Ballet, Cleve. Ballet; tchr. master classes Florence, S.C., Columbia; guest choreographer Towson (Md.) U., 2000, 05, Carolina Ballet Theatre, Greeville, S.C., 1998, Island Dance Theatre Ga., 2005, Ron Jones Dance, Ga., 2004. Dancer, David Lichine Concert Group, L.A., 1960-61, Netherlands Nat. Ballet Co., Amsterdam, 1961-62, mem. corps, Am. Ballet Theatre, N.Y.C., 1963-68, soloist, 1968-73, prin. ballerina, 1973-79, artistic dir., prima ballerina, choreographer, Savannah (Ga.) Ballet Co., 1979-85; co-artistic dir. and choreographer Ballet South, Savannah, 1992-96; guest artist, Miami (Fla.) Civic Ballet, Macon (Ga.) Civic Ballet, Tampa (Fla.) Civic Ballet, U. Ill. Ballet Co., Champaign, San Jose (Calif.) Civic Ballet, Ballet de San Juan, P.R., Gala Ballet, Amarillo (Tex.) Civic Ballet, Maywood Ballet Co., Phila., U. Wis., Milw. Civic Ballet, Stars of Am. Ballet, various TV shows, White House, 1966, 69. Mem. adv. bd. S.C. Arts Commn., Columbia, 1988—; hon. mem. bd. dirs. Columbia City Ballet. Mem.: AFTRA, AGVA, Am. Guild Mus. Artists. Office: Hilton Head Dance Theater and Sch 24 Palmetto Business Park Rd Hilton Head Island SC 29928-3234 Office Phone: 843-785-5477. Personal E-mail: balletkbc@yahoo.com.

BROCK, LOUIS MILTON, JR., engineering educator, researcher; b. Davenport, Iowa, Apr. 16, 1943; s. Louis Milton and Mary Elizabeth (Creech) B.; m. Carolyn Starbuck Pratt, July 22, 1972. BS, Northwestern U, 1966, MS, 1967, PhD, 1972. With Black and Veatch, Kansas City, Mo., 1962, Gen Dynamics/Convair, San Diego, 1963-64, Sargeant-Welch Co., Skokie, Ill., 1964, Am. Can Co., Barrington, Ill., 1965; prof. mech. engring. U. Ky., Lexington, 1971—. Contbr. articles to profl. jours. NSF grantee; USN/Am. Soc. Engring. Edn. fellow, 1983, 85, 87, 90; recipient rsch. award Rsch. Found. U. Ky., 1977, rsch. prof. award, 1986. Fellow ASME; mem. ASCE (corr. award 1989), Sigma Xi, Chi Epsilon. Avocations: riding, reading, horse care, jogging. Home: 133 Sycamore Rd Lexington KY 40502-1841 Office: U Ky Dept Mech Engring Lexington KY 40506-0503

BROCK, MACON F., JR., retail company executive; BA, Randolph-Macon Coll., Ashland, Va., 1964. Pres., COO K&K Toys, Inc.; founder Dollar Tree Stores, 1986, pres., 1986—2001, CEO, 1993—2003, chmn., 2001—. Bd. dirs. K&K Toys, Inc., Dollar Tree, Inc., 1986—, Landmark Comm. Inc., 2004—09, Lumber Liquidators, Inc., 2007—, rue21, Inc., 2010—. Past chmn., dir. Va. Beach Found.; past pres., trustee Va. Beach Ctr. for Contemporary Art; chmn. Randolph-Macon Coll.; dir. Greater Norfolk Corp., Hampton Roads Econ. Develop. Alliance, Va. Bus. Coun. Capt. USMC, Vietnam Vet., spl. agt. US Naval Intelligence. Named Entrepreneur-in-Residence, Christopher Newport U., Sch. Bus., 2003. Office: Dollar Tree Stores 500 Volvo Pkwy Chesapeake VA 23320 Office Phone: 757-321-5000. Office Fax: 757-321-5111. Business E-Mail: macon.brock@dollartree.com.

BROCKENBROUGH, HENRY WATKINS, retired lawyer; b. Richmond, Va., Aug. 28, 1923; s. Benjamin Willard and Kathleen Reading (Watkins) B.; m. Mary Lane Williams, Oct. 30, 1948; children: Henry Watkins, Rebecca Lane, John Reading, Willson Williams. BA cum laude, Hampden-Sydney Coll., 1944; LLB, U. Va., 1948; grad. degree, Rutgers U., 1957. Bar: Va. 1949. With Crestar Bank, Richmond, 1948-88, v.p., trust officer, 1963-67, sr. v.p., trust officer, 1967—88, trust cons., 1988-91; ptnr.unsel Taylor, Hazen, Kauffman & Pinchbeck, Richmond, 1991—2003; of counsel Kimberly, Pinchbeck, P.C., Richmond, 2003—07; ret., 2007. Chmn. trust com. Va. Bankers Assn., 1970-71. Past pres. Estate Planning Coun., Richmond; chmn. bd. dirs. Tuckahoe YMCA, 1975; with Westminster Canterbury. Lt. (j.g.) USNR, 1943-46. Mem. The Cohoke Club (West Point, Va., past pres.), Lambda Chi Alpha, Delta Theta Phi. Home: 1600 Westbrook Ave Apt 620 Richmond VA 23227-3320

BROCKERT, JOSEPH PAUL, government executive, writer, designer; b. Tipp City, Ohio, Sept. 17, 1954; s. Paul Edwin and Mary (Aten) B.; m. Deborah Sue Schaefer, Apr. 10, 1976; children: Jonathan Andre, Jason Anthony. BS in Journalism with honors, Ohio U., 1975. Sr. editor Linn's Stamp News, Sidney, Ohio, 1976—84; program mgr. stamp program specialist US Postal Svc., Washington, 1984—87, program mgr. stamp design, 1987—93, coord. Citizen's Stamp Adv. Com., 1985, art dir. US stamps and stationery, 1986—97, designer, 1988—95, prodn. mgr., Stamps OnLine website, 1999, head speechwriter, 2001, sr. writer, editor, 2002, curator spl. collections, 2003—06, stamp mfg. specialist, 2006—07, program mgr. stamp manufacturing, 2008—. Guest curator Smithsonian Nat. Postal Mus., 2005—06; agy. rep. Commn. Bicentennial of U.S. Constn., 1986-91, affiliated staff, Smithsonian Inst., 2012-13. Author: Basic Knowledge for the Stamp Collector, 1978, 4th rev. edit., 1983 (Silver medal Am. Philatelic Soc. 1979, Internat. Bronze medal 1986), (with Elaine Durnin Boughner) Stamp Collecting Made Easy, 1984, 3d rev. edit., 1986; editor: The Postal Service Guide to U.S. Stamps, 20th-22d edits., 1993-95, Stamps etc., 1993-1996, USA Philatelic, 1996-98; composer Mass of the Good Shepherd, 2000, Good Shepherd Celebrates!, 2001; contbr. articles to profl. and hobby jours. Chmn. publicity Gunston (Va.) Elem. PTA, 1985, pres., 1986-87; budget chmn. Fairfax County (Va.) Coun. PTA, 1988-92, sec., 1992; pres. Newington Forest (Va.) Elem. PTA, 1989-91; coach Lorton Little League, 1987-88. Mem.: AARP, Am. Philatelic Soc. Roman Catholic. Avocations: music, photography, bowling, stamp collecting/philately. Home and Office: 8605 Village Way Unit F Alexandria VA 22309-1605 Office Phone: 202-268-3260. Business E-Mail: joseph.p.brockert@usps.gov.

BROCKMAN, LESLIE RICHARD, social worker; b. St. Paul, Aug. 10, 1940; s. Leslie Blair Brockman and Mary Emma (Miller) Hemenway; m. Rosemarie Lemus, Aug. 18, 1962; 1 child, Christopher Scott. BA, Loyola U. of L.A., 1963; MS, Troy State U., Ala., 1977; MS in Social Work, U. Tex., Arlington, 1984. Lic. profl. counselor; lic. chem. dependency counselor, marriage and family therapist; lic. clin. practitioner ACSW; diplomate clin. social work; cert. criminal justice specialist. Exec. dir. Family Assessment Consultation Therapy Svc., Ft. Worth, 1984—; commd. 2d lt. USAF, 1963, advanced through grades to maj., retired, 1983. Fellow NASW (diplomate); mem. ACA, Am. Assn. Marriage and Family Therapists, Am. Mental Health Counselors Assn., Am. Assn. Behavioral Therapists. Home: 6400 Trail Lake Dr Fort Worth TX 76133-4810 Home Phone: 817-294-1729; Office Phone: 817-913-0039. Personal E-mail: facts@sbcglobal.net. Business E-Mail: facts1@swbell.net.

BROCKWAY, BUZZ, state legislator; b. Lawrenceville, Ga., July 22, 1966; m. Christa Brockway; 3 children. BS in Mgmt. Sci., Ga. Inst. Tech., Atlanta, 1990. Ops. mgr. Felicity Internat., Inc.; campaign mgr. to Melvin Everson Ga. House of Representatives, 2005, campaign mgr. to David Casas, 2008, mem. Dist. 101, 2011—; Gwinnett chmn. to Gov. Sonny Perdue Office of Gov., 2006; campaign mgr. to Mike Beaudreau Gwinnett County Commn., 2008. Republican. Office: PO Box 491355 Lawrenceville GA 30049 also: Georgia House of Reps 504 Coverdell Legis Office Bldg Atlanta GA 30334 Office Phone: 678-895-9064, 404-656-0188. Business E-Mail: buzz.brockway@house.ga.gov.

BRODBECK, WILLIAM JAN, marketing professional; b. Platteville, Wis., Feb. 14, 1944; s. Richard W. and Helen (Stoneman) B.; m. Janet Piwonka, Feb. 4, 1967; children: Allison S., Courtney K., Stephanie L. BA, Hillsdale Coll., Mich., 1966; PhD (hon.), Hillsdale Coll., 2004. Asst. to v.p. Hillsdale Coll., 1966-68; mgr. advt. Brodbeck Enterprises, Inc., Platteville, 1968-72, v.p., 1972-79, pres., CEO, 1980-96; pres. Relationship Mktg., Sanibel, Fla., 1996—. Gov. Uniform Product Code Coun., Dayton, Ohio, 1977—86; chmn. First Nat. Bank, Platteville, 1986—92; chmn Hillsdale Coll., 2003—, chmn., presdl. search com., 1999—2000, trustee, 1991—, vice chmn., 2000—03; bd. dirs. Neenah Springs, Inc., Oxford, Wis., 1997—2006, Noodles and Co., Boulder, Colo., 1997—2007. Contbr. articles to profl. jours Nat. adv. coun. Heritage Found., Washington, 2003—; pres. Platteville Area Indsl. Devel., 1976—79; bd. govs. The Sanctuary, 1999—2004, v.p., 2001—03, pres., 2003—04; chmn. 3d Congl. Dist. Reagan Campaign, 1976; bd. dirs. Thursday's Child, Madison, Wis., 1983—96, Wis. Shakespeare Festival, Platteville, 1986—96, CROW (Care and Rehab. of Wildlife), 1999—2002. Mem. Nat. Grocers Assn. (bd. dirs. 1977-85), Food Mktg. Inst. (bd. dirs. 1982-96, mem. efficient consumer response exec. com. 1993-96), U. Wis. Platteville Found. (pres. 1980-81), Platteville C. of C. (pres. 1972-73), Omicron Delta Kappa (chpt. v.p. 1966). Office: Relationship Mktg The Cliffs at Keowee Vineyards 124 Wood Sage Ct Sunset SC 29685 Personal E-mail: wjbrod@aol.com.

BRODEUR, JASON, state legislator; b. Daytona Beach, Fla., June 7, 1975; s. Tim Brodeur, Rene Brodeur; m. Wendy Brodeur; children: Katie, Bailey. BS in Economics, U. Fla., MBA. Healthcare cons.; mem. Dist. 33 Fla. House of Representatives, 2011—. Republican. Office: 114 W First St Sanford FL 32771-1273 also: Fla House of Reps 1003 The Capitol 402 S Monroe St Tallahassee FL 32399-1300 Office Phone: 407-302-4800, 850-488-0468.

BRODHEAD, RICHARD H., academic administrator; b. Dayton, Apr. 17, 1947; m. Cynthia Degnan Brodhead; 1 child, Daniel. BA in English summa cum laude, Yale U., 1968, MPhil, 1970, PhD in English, 1972. Asst. prof. English Yale U., 1972—77, assoc. prof. English, 1977—85, prof. English, 1985—90, Bird White Housum Prof. English, 1990—95, chair dept. English, 1988—93, dean Yale Coll., 1993—2004, A. Bartlett Giamatti prof. English, 1995—2004; prof. English Duke U., 2004—, pres., 2004—. Vis. prof. Ecole Normale Superieure, Paris, 1989, 1991; faculty mem. Yale-New Haven Tchrs.' Inst., 1982; summer faculty Bread Loaf Sch. English, 1975—76, 1978, 1980, 1989—92. Bd. dirs. J. William Fulbright Fgn. Scholarship Bd., 2002—05; trustee Carnegie Corp., 2004—. Recipient Bicentennial medal, Middlebury Coll., 1998, DeVane Outstanding Scholarship and Tchg. medal, Yale U., 1979, Wilbur Lucius Cross medal, 2006. Fellow: Am. Acad. Arts and Scis. Office: Duke University Office of the President 207 Allen Bldg Box 90001 Durham NC 27708*

BRODIE, HARLOW KEITH HAMMOND, psychiatrist, educator; b. Stamford, Conn., Aug. 24, 1939; s. Lawrence Sheldon and Elizabeth White (Hammond) B.; m. Brenda Ann Barrowclough, Jan. 26, 1967; children: Melissa Verduin, Cameron Keith, Tyler Hammond, Bryson Barrowclough. AB, Princeton U., 1961; MD, Columbia U., 1965; LLD hon., U. Richmond, 1987; LHD (hon.), High Point U., 1992. Diplomate Am. Bd. Psychiatry and Neurology. Intern Ochsner Found. Hosp., New Orleans, 1965-66; resident in psychiatry Columbia-Presbyn. Med. Center, NYC, 1966-68; clin. assoc. intramural research program NIMH, 1968-70; asst. prof. psychiatry, dir. gen. clin. research center Stanford U. Med. Sch., 1970-74; prof. psychiatry, chmn. dept. Duke U. Med. Sch., 1974-82, James B. Duke prof. psychiatry and behavioral scis., 1981—, prof. dept. psychology, prof. law, 1980—2004; psychiatrist-in-chief Duke U. Med. Center, 1974-82; chancellor Duke U., 1982-85, pres., 1985-93, pres. emeritus, 1993—. Mem. Pres. Biomed. Rsch. Panel, 1975; mem. Carnegie Coun. on Adolescent Devel., 1986-97; trustee Com. for Econ. Devel., 1986-93, subcom. on edn. and child devel., 1990; trustee Nat. Humanities Ctr., 1988-93; nat. rev. and adv. panel for improving campus race rels. Ford Found., 1990-94; bd. dirs. Mental Health and Behavioral Medicine, 1981-83, chmn., 1981-82; chmn. Com. on Substance Abuse and Mental Health Issues in AIDS Rsch., 1992-95; mem. Com. on Leadership Devel., Am. Coun. on Edn., 1990-93. Co-author: The Importance of Mental Health Services to General Health Care, 1979, Modern Clinical Psychiatry, 1982; co-editor: American Handbook of Psychiatry, vols. 6, 7 and 8, 1975, 81, 86, Controversy in Psychiatry, 1978, Psychiatry at the Crossroads, 1980, Critical Problems in Psychiatry, 1982, Signs and Symptoms in Psychiatry, 1983, Consultation-Liaison Psychiatry and Behavioral Medicine, 1986, AIDS and Behavior: An Integrated Approach, 1994, Keeping an Open Door: Passages in a University Presidency, 1996, The Research University Presidency in the Late Twentieth Century, 2005; assoc. editor Am. Jour. Psychiatry, 1973-81. Recipient A.E. Bennet Rsch. award, 1970, Soc. Biol. Psychiatry, Strecker award Inst., Pa. Hosp., 1980, Disting. Alumnus award Ochsner Found. Hosp., 1984, Disting. Med. Alumni award Columbia U., 1985, N.C. award for sci., 1990, William C. Menninger Meml. award ACP, 1994. Mem.: Royal Soc. Med., Inst. Medicine, Internat. Soc. Sport Psychiatry, Royal Coll. Psychiatrists, Am. Psychiat. Assn. (sec. 1977—81, pres. 1982—83). Home: 63 Beverly Dr Durham NC 27707-2223 Office: Devonwood Co 3211 Shannon Rd Ste 603 Durham NC 27707

BRODY, AARON LEO, food and packaging consultant; b. Boston, Aug. 23, 1930; s. Nathan and Lillian (Gorman) Brody; m. Carolyn Goldstein, Apr. 11, 1953; children: Stephen, Glen, Robyn. BS, MIT, Cambridge, 1951, PhD, 1957; MBA, Northeastern U., Boston, 1970. Cert. food scientist 2013. Head food rsch. labs. Whirlpool Co., St. Joseph, Mich., 1957-61; packaging and product devel. mgr. Mars, Inc., Hackettstown, NJ, 1961-66; packaging coord. Arthur D. Little, Inc., Cambridge, Mass., 1967-73; new ventures mgr. Mead Packaging, Atlanta, 1973-81; mgr. mktg. devel. Container Corp. Am., Oaks, Pa., 1981-85; v.p. strategic studies Schotland Bus. Rsch. Inc., Princeton, NJ, 1985-91; mng. dir. Rubbright/Brody, Inc., Duluth, Ga., 1991-2001; pres., CEO Packaging/Brody, Inc., 2001—. Course dir. Mich. State U., East Lansing, 1959—61; instr. Emory U., 1979; adj. assoc. prof. dept. food sci. U. Del., Newark, 1983—86; vis. prof. St. Joseph's U., Phila., 1990; adj. prof. Spring Garden Coll., Phila., 1990, U. Ga., 1995—, Clemson U., 2010—; sr. instr. Keller Grad Sch. Mgmt., 1996—2011. Mem. Nat. Def. Exec. Res., 1978—88; mem. food svc. adv. com. USN, 1958—62; mem. optimal program edn., sec. DeKalb County, Ga., 1975; active Kerry for Congress campaign, 1972, Levitas for Congress campaign, 1974; mem. pres.'s coun. Spring Garden Coll., Phila., 1984—89. With US Army, 1952—54. Recipient Willis H. Carrier award, ASHRAE, 1960, Braverman Meml. award, Israel Inst. Tech., 1976, Outstanding Alumnus award, Northeastern U., 1982, George P. Morgan award, Alumni Assn. MIT; named Packaging Man of the Yr., Nat. Inst. Packaging, Handling and Logistics Engrs., Carolyn and Aaron Brody Fund for Packaging Rsch. and Edn. in their honor, Mich. State U. Sch. Packaging, 2005, Aaron Brody disting. lectureship in food packaging named in honor, Mich. State U., 2007; named to Packaging Hall of Fame, 1995; William Underwood fellow, 1955—56. Fellow: AAAS, Inst. Food Technologists (Indsl. Achievement award 1964, Riester-Davis Food Packaging Achievement award 1988, Inds. Scientist award 1994, Nicholas Appert award 2000), Packaging Inst. (v.p. 1973—79); mem.: Product Devel. and Mgmt. Assn., NY Acad. Scis., Inst. Packaging Profls. (hon. Mem. of the Yr. 1994—95, lifetime cert. profl), Planning Execs. Inst., League Internat. Food Edn., Soc. Packaging Profls., Mich. State U. Beaumont Tower Soc., Toastmasters, MIT Club (pres. 1977—79, mem. exec. com., v.p. ednl. coun.), Sigma Xi. Achievements include patents in field. Home: 4981 Trevino Cir Duluth GA 30096-6072 Office: PO Box 956187 Duluth GA 30095 Office Phone: 770-613-0991. Personal E-mail: aaronbrody@aol.com.

BRONAUGH, EDWIN LEE, retired electrical engineer; b. Salina, Kans., July 22, 1932; s. Edwin and Violet Mary (Dryden) B.; m. Geraldine Kelley, Dec. 10, 1955: children: Cecilia Ann Bronaugh Snodgrass, Dana Lea Bronaugh Weinberg. BA in Physics, Math. and Language, Tex. A&M U., Commerce, 1955. Commd. USAF, 1955, advanced through grades to capt., 1961, various comm. and ops. assignments, 1955-68; major USAFR, 1968; rsch. scientist Southwest Rsch. Inst., San Antonio, 1968-70, sr. rsch. scientist, 1970-76, rsch. dir., 1976-82; dir. R & D, tech. dir. Electro-Metrics Divsn. Penril, Amsterdam, NY, 1982-89; prin. electromagnetic compatibility scientist Electro-Mechanics Co., Austin, Tex., 1989-92, v.p. engring., 1992-94; prin. EdB EMC Cons., Austin, 1994—2004; lead engr. comm. devices divsn. Siemens Info. and Comm. Products, LLC, Austin, 1997-2000; ret., 2005. Author: Electromagnetic Interference Test Methodology and Procedures, 1988; contbr. over 150 articles to profl. jours.; patentee in field. Decorated Bronze Star, Air Force Commendation medal. Fellow IEEE (life; Third Millennium medal 2000); mem. IEEE Stds. Assn. (life), Electromagnetic Compatibility Soc. of IEEE (stds. com. 1980—, dir. tech. svcs. 1981-87, v.p. 1988-90, pres. 1990-92; Cert. of Appreciation 1979, Cert. of Achievement 1983, Cert. of Acknowledgement 1985, Richard R. Stoddart award 1985, Stds. Medallion 1992, Lawrence G. Cumming award 1992), Am. Nat. Stds. Inst. (vice chmn. accredited stds. com. C63 on electromagnetic compatibility 1986-2002, mem. emeritus C63 2002—), Electromagnetic Compatibility Soc. (hon. life.). Avocations: music, model railroads, engineering history, learning additional languages. Home and Office: 10210 Prism Dr Austin TX 78726-1364 Home Phone: 512-258-6687. E-mail: ed.bronaugh@ieee.org.

BRONCZEK, DAVID J., transportation executive; BBA, Kent State U., 1976. Joined FedEx Corp., 1976, various sales and ops. management positions, 1976—87, v.p., Canadian ops. FedEx Express, 1987—93, sr. v.p., Europe, Africa and Mediterranean FedEx Express, 1993—95, sr. v.p., Europe, Mid. East and Africa FedEx Express, 1995—98, exec. v.p., COO FedEx Express, 1998—2000, pres., CEO FedEx Express, 2000—. Bd. dirs. FedEx Express Corp., Internat. Paper Co., 2006—. Mem. Toronto Bd. Trade, Memphis Tomorrow; bd. dirs. Internat. Sch. Brussels, United Way, Nat. Safe Kids Campaign, Washington, DC, U. NC, Chapel Hill, Internat. Air Transport Assn. Office: International Paper Co 6400 Poplar Ave Memphis TN 38197 Office Phone: 901-419-9000. Office Fax: 901-214-9682. Business E-Mail: david.bronczek@fedex.com.

BRONSON, DAVID M., corporate financial executive; BS in Acctg., Calif. State U.; M in Mgmt., Northwestern U. Held sr. fin. roles Baxter Healthcare Inc., 1975—95; v.p., contr., Dade Divsn. Baxter Diagnostics, 1988—92; v.p., fin. and bus. devel. Baxter Sci. Products, 1992—95; sr. v.p., fin., CFO VWR Sci. Products (acquired by Merck KGaA), 1995—99; sr. v.p., CFO Digineer Inc., 1999—2001; sr. v.p. PSS World Med. Inc., 2002—03; CFO PSS World Medical, Inc., 2002—, exec. v.p., 2003—. Office: PSS World Medical Inc 4345 Southpoint Blvd Jacksonville FL 32216 Office Phone: 904-332-3000. Office Fax: 904-332-3395. Business E-Mail: dbronson@pssd.com.

BROOK, SCOTT JONATHAN BRADLEY, mayor, lawyer; b. Bronx, NY, Apr. 3, 1964; s. Seymour and Marcia Marion (Handelman) B.; m. Brenda Post-Brook, Dec. 14, 1997; 5 children. BS in Psychology, Tulane U., 1985, MBA, 1987; JD, U. Miami, Coral Gables, Fla., 1992. Sr. advisor Tulane U., New Orleans, 1985-87, tchr. asst., 1987; rsch. asst. Howard, Weil, Labouisse, Friedrichs, Inc., New Orleans, 1986-87; career cons. Bus.Week Careers, NYC, 1987; securities legal asst. Milberg Weiss Bershad Specthrie & Lerach, NYC, 1988-89; pres. Brook Cons., Forest Hills, N.Y., 1989; law clk. Faber & Gitlitz, Coral Gables, Fla., 1989-90, Traveller's Insur., 1990-91, Conroy Simberg & Lewis, Hollywood, Fla., 1991—2000; pres. Scott J. Brook, P.A., Coral Springs, Fla., 2000—, Premier Networking Alliance, Inc.; commr. City of Coral Springs, 2002—, mayor, 2006—. Chair affordable housing task force Broward County Planning Coun., 2005—; mayor City Coral Springs, 2006—. Named Freeman fellow, 1985-87; recipient Merit scholarship, Tulane U., 1981-85, Best Brief award State Workers Compensation Competition, 1991. Mem. ABA (founder, chmn. ABA/LSD informational interview network), Soc. Bar and Gavel (pres.), U. Miami Student Bar Assn. (treas.). Office Phone: 954-757-5551. Business E-Mail: scottbrook@scottjbrookpa.com.

BROOKE, FRANCIS JOHN, III, retired academic administrator; b. Charleston, W.Va., Mar. 4, 1929; s. Francis John Jr. and Elizabeth (Baird) B.; m. Helen Holmes Morgan, Dec. 20, 1958; children: Francis John, Haynes Morgan, David Tucker. BA, Hampden-Sydney Coll., 1949; MA, U. Chgo., 1951; PhD, U. N.C., 1954. Instr. German Roanoke Coll., Salem, Va., summers 1950-52; teaching fellow, part-time instr. U. N.C., Chapel Hill, 1951-54; mem. faculty, to assoc. prof. German U. Va., Charlottesville, 1956-65, asst. dean. Coll. Arts & Scis., 1959-62, acting chmn. dept. modern langs., 1962-63; exec. dean, prof. German Centre Coll., Danville, Ky., 1965-68; v.p. acad. affairs Va. Commonwealth U., Richmond, 1968-74, provost, acad. campus, 1973-79, spl. asst. to pres., 1979-80, prof. German, 1968-80; pres. Columbus (Ga.) Coll., 1980-87; spl. asst. to chancellor Univ. System of Ga., Atlanta, 1988; Pacific N.W. regional rep. Presbyn. Ch. Found., Seattle, 1989-99, ret., 1999. Vice chmn. So. Humanities Conf., 1965; pres. South Atlantic region Am. Assn. Tchrs. German, 1965-67; exec. com. South Atlantic chpt. MLA, 1963-66. Mem. gen. assembly com. on theol. edn. Presbyn. Ch., 1989-99. With AUS, 1954-56. Old Dominion Found. grantee, 1960; intern acad. adminstrn. Ellis L. Phillips Found., Cornell U., 1963-64. Mem. Assn. State Colls. and Univs. (com. on humanities 1984-86, com. on urban affairs 1986-87), Omicron Delta Kappa.

BROOKS, BEN, state legislator; b. Mobile, Ala., Aug. 11; m. Kathy Brooks; 3 children. BA, U. South Ala., 1980; JD, U. Ala., 1983. Atty., Mobile, Ala.; spl. judge Mobile County Dist. Ct.; councilman Mobile City Coun., 2001—06, chmn. fin. com., 2001—06; mem. Dist. 35 Ala. State Senate, Montgomery, 2006—. Apptd. Ala. Law Inst. Republican. Office: 1495 University Blvd Mobile AL 36619 also: Ala State Senate Ala State House 11 S Union St Rm 735-A Montgomery AL 36130 Office Phone: 251-344-7744, 334-242-7882. Office Fax: 251-343-9629. Business E-Mail: benbrooksiii@aol.com.

BROOKS, CARLA JO, financial services manager; b. Cedar Rapids, Iowa, July 9, 1956; d. Carleton Paul and Gladys Jane (Benning) Groszkruger; m. Thomas Robert Brooks, Sept. 28, 1979; children: Chera MoRae, Erica Love, Heather Joyzelle, Victoria JoLee. BS in Bus. and Economics, Coe Coll., Iowa, 1978; MS in Fin., U. Tex., Dallas, 1983. Cert. insolvency and reorganization accountant. Fin. analyst Fed. Res. Bank of Dallas, 1978-83, mgr., 1983-85; sr. mgr. KPMG Peat Marwick LLP, Dallas; first v.p. corp. acquisitions, Office of Chmn. Calif. Fed. Bank, FSB; with SAMCO Capital Markets, Inc.; dep. portfolio mgr., mng. dir., ptnr. Commerce Street Capital, LLC, Dallas, 2002—; COO Svc. Equity Partners, LP, Genesis Bank Fund, LP. Instr. FRS Bd. Govs., Washington, 1985-87, 96; instr. Southwestern Grad. Sch. Banking, Dallas. Named one of 25 Most Powerful Women in Fin., US Banker, 2008—10. Mem.: P.E.O. (Richardson, Tex.). Republican. Methodist. Office: Commerce St Capital LLC 1445 Ross Ave Dallas TX 75202-2711 Office Phone: 214-545-6800.

BROOKS, DOUGLAS H., food service executive; From asst. mgr. to sr. v.p. ops. Chili's Grill & Bar, 1978—92, pres., 1994—99; COO Brinker International, Inc., Dallas, 1998—2004, pres., 1999—2004, chmn., pres., CEO, 2004—. Office: Brinker Internat 6820 LBJ Freeway Dallas TX 75240

BROOKS, FREDERICK PHILLIPS, JR., computer scientist, educator; b. Durham, NC, Apr. 19, 1931; s. Frederick Phillips and Octavia Brooks; m. Nancy Lee Greenwood, June 16, 1956; children: Kenneth Phillips, Roger Greenwood, Barbara Brooks LaDine. AB in Physics, Duke U., 1953; SM, Harvard U., 1955, PhD, 1956; D Tech. Sci. (hon.), ETH-Zurich, 1991. Engr. IBM, Poughkeepsie, NY, 1956—59, Yorktown Heights, NY, 1959—60, mgr. devel. computer System/360 Poughkeepsie, 1960—64, mgr. devel. Operating System/360, 1964—65; founder computer sci. dept. U. N.C., Chapel Hill, 1964, prof., 1964—75, chmn. dept. computer sci., 1964—84, Kenan prof., 1975—. Bd. dirs. Triangle U. Computation Ctr., 1966—84, chmn., 1975—77, N.C. Edni. Computing Svc., 1965—; active Def. Sci. Bd., 1982—86, Nat. Sci. Bd., 1987—92. Author: The Mythical Man-Month-Essays on Software Engineering, 1975, 1995; author: (with K.E. Iverson) Automatic Data Processing, 1963, Automatic Data Processing System/360 Edition, 1969; author: (with G.A. Blaauw) Computer Architecture: Concepts and Evolution, 1997; contbr. articles to profl. jours.; inventor (with D.W. Sweeney) program interruption system, alphabetical read-out device. Trustee Durham Acad., pres., 1977—80; trustee, chmn. Trinity Sch. Durham and Chapel Hill, 2003—; chmn. exec. com. Ctrl. Carolina Billy Graham Crusade, 1972—73; mem. corp. Inter-Varsity Christian Fellowship, 1968—77. Recipient McDowell award, IEEE Computer Soc., 1970, Man of Yr. award, Data Processing Mgmt. Assn., 1970, Bower award and prize for achievement in sci., Franklin Inst., 1975, Nat. Medal Tech., 1985, Harry Goode Meml. award, Am. Fedn. Info. Proc. Socs., 1989, Fellow award, Computer History Mus., 2001; grantee, NSF, AEC, NIH, NASA, Def. Advanced Projects Rsch. Agy.; fellow Guggenheim Found., 1975. Fellow: IEEE (John von Neumann medal 1993, Eckert-Manchly award 2004), Brit. Computer Soc. (disting.), Assn. Computing Machinery (coun. mem.-at-large 1966—70, Disting. Svc. award 1987, Allen Newell award 1994, Alan M. Turing award 1999), Am. Acad. Arts and Scis.; mem.: NAE, NAS, Royal Acad. Engring. (U.K.), Royal Netherland Acad. Arts and Scis. Methodist. Home: 413 Granville Rd Chapel Hill NC 27514-2723 Office: Univ NC Dept Computer Sci Brooks Computer Sci Bldg CB# 3175 Chapel Hill NC 27599-3175 Office Phone: 919-962-1931. Business E-Mail: brooks@cs.unc.edu.

BROOKS, GARTH (TROYAL GARTH BROOKS), musician; b. Tulsa, Okla., Feb. 7, 1962; s. Troyal Raymond and Colleen Carroll Brooks; m. Sandy Mahl, 1986 (div. 2001); children: Taylor Mayne Pearl, August Anna, Allie Colleen; m. Trisha Yearwood, Dec. 10, 2005. BS in Advertising and Journalism, Okla. State U., 1984. Recording artist (albums) Garth Brooks, 1989, No Fences, 1990 (Album of Yr. Acad. Country Music, 1991), Ropin' The Wind, 1991, Beyond the Season, 1992, The Chase, 1992, In Pieces, 1993, The Hits, 1994, Fresh Horses, 1995, Sevens, 1997, The Limited Series, Double Live, 1998, In the Life of Chris Gaines, 1999, Scarecrow, 2001, The Lost Sessions, 2005, The Ultimate Hits, 2007, (songs) The Dance (Video of Yr. award Country Music Assn., 1991, Song of Yr. and Video of Yr. awards Acad. Country Music, 1991), Friends in Low Places (Single Record of Yr. Acad. Country Music, 1991), If Tomorrow Never Comes (Am. Music award for Country Song of Yr., 1991), The Thunder Rolls, We Shall Be Free (Video of Yr., Acad. Country Music), Somewhere Other Than The Night, Learning to Live Again, (TV spls.) This is Garth Brooks, 1992, This is Garth Brooks, Too, 1994, Garth Brooks: The Hits, 1995, Garth Brooks Live in Central Park, 1997; performer: Encore Hotel and Casino. Las Vegas, 1999—. Founder Teammates for Kids Found., 1999. Recipient Entertainer of Yr. award, Acad. Country Music, 1991, Male Vocalist of Yr. award, 1991, Crystal Milestone award, Acad. Country Music Awards, 2008, Horizon award, Entertainer of Yr. award, Country Music Assn., 1991, 1992, Grammy award for Best Male Country Vocalist, 1992, Grammy award for Best County Collaboration with Vocals, 1998, Best Male Musical Performer award, People's Choice Awards, 1992, Favorite Country Artist award, Am. Music Awards, 2000, Favorite Country Album award, 2000; named Artist of Decade, Acad. Country Music Awards, 1999, Best Male Country Music Performer, 1992, 1993; named to Grand Ole Opry, Country Music Hall of Fame, 2012. Office: c/o GB Management 1111 17th Ave S Nashville TN 37212-2203

BROOKS, HARRY, state legislator; b. Sept. 4, 1946; m. Mary Brooks; children: Ben, Adam(dec.). Mem. State & Local Com., Edn. Com., Joint Bus. Tax Com., K-12 Subcom., Local Govt. Com.; budget dir. Knox County Sheriff'S Dept., 1978—2000; pres. Security Svc., Knoxville, 2000—; state rep. Dist. 19 Tenn., 2003—. Mem.: NRA, Hall's Bus. & Profl. Assn., Gideon's Internat., United Way, C. of C., East Knox Bus. & Profl. Assn., Knoxville Civitan, NE Preservation Assn., Powell Bus. & Profl. Assn., America Soc. Indsl. Security. Republican. Baptist. Office: 6600 Washington Pike Knoxville TN 37918 also: 212 War Memorial Bldg Nashville TN 37243-0119 Office Phone: 615-741-6879. Office Fax: 615-253-0212. Business E-Mail: rep.harry.brooks@capitol.tn.gov.

BROOKS, JEFFREY MARTIN, marketing and sales executive; b. Charlotte, NC, Oct. 14, 1958; s. Jack M. and Margaret Anne (Reap) B.; m. Kim Marie Whitaker, Sept. 26, 1981; 2 children: Justin Jeffrey Whitaker, Evan Martin Whitaker. BSBA in Acctg., East Carolina U.; MS in Econs., N.C. State U. Staff acct. Ernst & Whinney, Raleigh, N.C., 1980-82; acct. rep. Data Gen. Corp., Charlotte, 1982-85; mgr. systems mktg. AT&T, Charlotte, 1985-86; pres. Fastfly Corp., 1985-89; v.p. sales and distbn. Vanguard Cellular Systems, Inc., Greensboro, N.C., 1989-94; v.p. mktg. and sales So. Comm. (subs. So. Co.), Atlanta, 1994—97; asst. v.p. corp. mktg. BellSouth, Atlanta, 1997—2001; v.p. N.Am. channel Vigilinx, 2001—03; exec. v.p. mktg. and sales W.V. Fiber, 2003—04; CEO Ulanji, Charleston, SC, 2004—07; COO ITO LLC, Rsch. Triangle Pk., NC, 2007—. Cons. Charlotte Hornets, GTE, Sequent My Southern Sons. Vol. Jr. Achievement, Habitat for Humanity, YMCA Youth Sports, Mecklenburg Coun. on Aging; mem. Christ King Luth. Ch., Cary, NC; advisor Low Country Continuum Care Charleston, SC, past chmn. Palmetto House, Summerville, SC. Mem. AICPA, Aircraft Owners and Pilots Assn., Nat. Bus. Aircraft Assn., U.S.A. Soccer, Nat. Youth Coaches Assn., Tech. Coun. Charleston C. of C. (vice chmn.). Office Phone: 919-662-2662. Business E-Mail: jbrooks@itoonline.com.

BROOKS, KATHLEEN, communications professional; d. William Chesley and Sara (Brooks) Howton. BA, Stephens Coll., Columbia, Mo., 1978. Mktg. asst. The Laitram Corp., New Orleans, 1978-79; reporter Daily Home, Talladega, Ala., 1979-80, copy editor, 1980-81; asst. wire editor, reporter Gastonia Gazette, NC, 1981, wire editor, 1981-84; asst. wire editor Comml. Appeal, Memphis, 1984-88, Washington editor, 1988-91, nat. editor, 1991—2005; comm. advisor FedEx Freight, 2006—08; prin. KB Comm., 2008—. Co-author: My Homeland Tennessee, My Georgia Home, 2012, Proud to Call Arkansas Home, 2014. Methodist. Personal E-mail: katbr@bellsouth.net.

BROOKS, KEVIN D., state legislator; b. May 4, 1967; Mem. Children & Family Affairs Com., Consumer & Employee Affairs Com., Dem. Affairs. Subcommittee, Employee Affairs Subcommittee; chmn. Blue Ribbon Advisor Coun., Cleveland City Sch.; state rep. Dist. 24 Tenn., 2007—. Mem.: Religious Conf. Mgmt. Assn., Main St. Cleveland (former bd. mem.), United Way Bradley County (divsn. chmn.), Cleveland Rotary Club (officer, bd. mem.). Republican. Church Of God. Mailing: PO Box 4801 Cleveland TN 37320 Office: 104 War Memorial Bldg Nashville TN 37243-0124 Office Phone: 615-741-1350. Office Fax: 615-253-0346. Business E-Mail: rep.kevin.brooks@capitol.tn.gov.

BROOKS, KIX (LEON ERIC BROOKS), musician; b. Shreveport, La., May 12, 1955; m. Barbara Brooks; children: Molly, Eric. Grad., La. Tech. Staff songwriter Tree Pub.; songwriter Highway 101, The Nitty Gritty Dirt Band; with Brooks & Dunn, 1988—; rec. artist Arista, 1991—. Prodr. clothing line "Panhandle Slim Western Wear" with Ronnie Dunn. Musician: (albums) (with Ronnie Dunn) Brand New Man, 1991 (Acad. Country Music award Album of Yr., 1992), Hard Workin' Man, 1993 (Grammy award Best Country Vocal Performance by Duo or Group for Hard Workin' Man, 1993), Waitin' on Sundown, 1994, Borderline, 1996 (Grammy award Best Country Vocal Performance by Duo or Group for My Maria, 1996), Greatest Hits Collection, 1997, If You See Her, 1998, Tight Rope, 1999, Super Hits, 1999, Steers and Stripes, 2001, It Won't Be Christmas Without You, 2002, Red Dirt Road, 2003, Greatest Hits Collection: Volume II, 2004, Hillbilly Deluxe, 2005 (Single of Yr., Song of Yr., & Music Video of Yr. for Believe, Country Music Assn. Awards, 2006, Song of Yr. for Believe, Acad. Country Music, 2006), Cowboy Town, 2007, Kix Brooks, 1993, Common Thread: The Songs of the Eagles, 1994 (Country Music Assn. Album of Yr., 1994), (singles) Boot Scootin' Boogie, 1992, We'll Burn That Bridge, 1993, Rock My World (Little Country Girl), 1993, (songs) (8 Seconds (soundtrack) Ride 'Em High, Ride 'Em Low, 1994, (with Hank Thompson) Hooked on Honky Tonk, 1997, (with Reba McEntire) If You See Him, If You See Her, 1998, (with Ronnie Dunn) Indian Summer, 2009 (Duo Video of Yr., CMT Music Awards, 2010). Co-recipient Top New Vocal Duo or Group award, Acad. Country Music, 1991, Entertainer of Yr. award, 1995, 1996, 2001, Top Vocal Duo award, 1991—97, 2000—03, 2005—07, 2008, 2010, Vocal Event of Yr. award, 2007, Home Depot Humanitarian award, 2007, Vocal Duo of Yr. award, Country Music Assn., 1992—99, 2001—06, Entertainer of Yr. award, 1996, Favorite Country Group award, Am. Music Awards, 2004, 2005. Office: Brooks and Dunn PO Box 120669 Nashville TN 37212-0669

BROOKS, MARY ELIZABETH, bank executive; m. Tim Brooks; 3 children. BSBA in Fin. Mgmt., U. Ark.; MBA in Banking, U. Wis. With Arvest Bank Group, Nat. Bank of Commerce, Memphis, Bancorp South, Ark. State Bank Dept.; pres., CEO Bank of Fayetteville, Ark., 2005—. Mem. founders' cir. Fayetteville Cmty. Found.; bd. dirs. Kappa Kappa Gamma House, The New Sch.; mem. exec. com. NWA Coun.; bd. dirs. Boys & Girls Club, Fayetteville, Fayetteville C. of C., Fayetteville Pub. Libr. Found., Northwest Ark. Coun., Beaver Water Dist. Named Ark. Bus. Exec. of Yr., 2007; named one of 25 Women to Watch, US Banker, 2007. Office: Bank of Fayetteville One South Block Fayetteville AR 72701 Office Phone: 479-444-4444. Office Fax: 479-443-1529.

BROOKS, MORRIS J. (MO BROOKS), United States Representative from Alabama, lawyer; b. Charleston, SC, Apr. 29, 1954; s. Jack and Betty Brooks; m. Martha Jenkins, 1976; 4 children. BA, Duke Univ.; JD, Univ. Ala., 1978. Atty. Tuscaloosa Dist. Atty. Office, 1980; law clk. Cir. Ct. Judge John David Snodgrass, 1980—82; mem. Dist. 18 Ala. House of Representatives, 1982—84, mem. Dist. 10, 1984—92; dist. atty. Madison County, Ala., 1991—92; commr. Madison County Commn., 1996—2010; spl. asst. atty. gen. State of Ala., 1995—2002; pvt. law practice, 2002—; mem. US Congress from 5th Ala. Dist., Washington, 2011—, US House Homeland Security Com., 2011—, US House Armed Services Com., 2011—, US House Science, Space & Technology Com., 2011—. Republican. Office: US House of Represetatives 1230 Longworth House Office Bldg Washington DC 20515 Office Phone: 202-225-4801, 202-225-4392.*

BROOKS, PHILIP COOLIDGE, JR., archivist, curator, historian, editor, writer; b. Dec. 1, 1940; s. Philip Coolidge and Dorothy Hamilton (Holland) Brooks; m. Susan Mary Fox, Dec. 21, 1965; 1 child, Anthony Franklin Coolidge. BA, U. Kans., 1962, MA, 1966; Exchange fellow, U. Reading, Eng., 1962—63, postgrad., 1964—65, Stanford U. Law Sch., 1963—64. Mus. specialist polit. history Smithsonian Instn., Washington, 1967—71; asst. to exec. dir. Nat. Archives, Washington, 1971—74, asst. to asst. archivist, pub. programs, 1974—83, also curator archives reception room, 1974—83, acting dir., dir. edn. divsn., 1979—83, sr. archives specialist, records centers, 1983—96, devel. officer, 1986—87; ret., 1996. Historian archivist Pres. Inaugural Com., 1968, 1989, 1993; consulting editor RROC Desk Diary and RROC Travel Guide, 1997—2012. Contbr. articles on history to profl. jours. Mem. Gadsby's Tavern Acquisitions Commn., Alexandria, Va., 1974—78, Historic Records Adv. Com., Alexandria, 1975—77, Historic Alexandria Restoration and Preservation Com., 2001—06; vice chmn. Historic Alexandria Resources Com., 1983—97, chmn., 1995—97; mem. Alexandria Libr. Co., 1989—, U. Kans. Internat. Students Program Adv. bd., 2006—; vice chmn. Alexandria Assn., 1976—78; chmn. Alexandria Ad Hoc Lyceum Com., 1981—82, The Lyceum Co., 1983—87, vice chmn., 1987—91; mem., vice chmn. Alexandria Bicentennial Commn., 1972—83; chmn. Alexandria Mus. Task Force, 1979—80, Alexandria 250th Anniversary Com., 1997—2000; dir. RROC Found., 1984—92; pres. Rolls-Royce Found., 2000—03; mem. adv. bd. Coun. Internat. Nontheatrical Events, 1989—97. Recipient Commendable Service award, Nat. Archives, 1976, Archivist's Achievement awards, 1985, 1996, Appreciation cert., City Alexandria, 1976, 1981, 1984, Va. Senate Joint Resolution of Commendation, 2000, Rolls-Royce Found. Commendation, 2003. Mem.: Fords Colony Model Railroad Club (pres. 2012—), Nat. Trust Historic Preservation, Am. Assn. State and Local History, Rolls-Royce Owners Club (dir. 1978—84, editor The Flying Lady 1986—89, v.p. regions 1992—94), Bentley Drivers Club (rep. 1968—), Zeta-Iota House Corp. Bd., Lambda Chi Alpha. Home: 102 Carnoustie Williamsburg VA 23188 Personal E-mail: kexbyphil@gmail.com.

BROOKS, ROBERT FRANKLIN, SR., lawyer; b. Richmond, Va., July 13, 1939; s. Robert Noel Brooks and Annie Mae (Edwards) Miles; m. Patricia Wilson, May 6, 1972; children: Robert Franklin Jr., Thomas Noel, Courtenay M. Brooks Rainey. BA, U. Richmond, 1961, M of Humanities, 1993; JD, 1964. Bar: Va. 1964, N.Y. 1985, U.S. Dist. Ct. (ea. and we. dists.) Va. 1964, U.S. Ct. Appeals (4th cir.) 1965, U.S. Ct. Appeals (5th cir.) 1972, (2d cir.) 1979, (11th cir.) 1981, D.C. 1977, U.S. Supreme Ct. 1979. Assoc. Hunton & Williams, Richmond, 1964-71, ptnr., 1971—. Chmn. sect. II 3d Dist. Com., 1983; mem. rules evidence com. Supreme Ct. Va., 1984-85; mem. Fourth Cir. Judicial Conf. Trustee U. Richmond, chmn. exec. com., 1998-99, 99—. Fellow ABA, Am. Coll. Trial Lawyers (com. atty.-client relationships 1983-91, chmn. Va. state com. 1993-94), Am. Bar Found., Va. Law Found.; mem. N.Y. Bar Assn., D.C. Bar Assn., Va. State Bar (coun. 1986—, bd. govs. litigation sect. 1984-90, sec. 1985-86, chmn. 1986-87, com. lawyer fin. responsibility 1986-89, nominating com. 1990, spl. com. election methods 1989, chmn. bench-bar rels. com. 1987-88, faculty professionalism course 1988-90, governance com. 1990-91), Richmond Bar Assn. (chmn. judiciary com. 1985-87, chmn. com. on unprofl. conduct 1979-80, com. on improvement of adminstrn. of justice 1981-84), Va. Bar Assn. (profl. responsibility com. 1981-84). Home: 1804 Weather Vane Ct Richmond VA 23238-4158

BROOKS, ROGER LEON, retired academic administrator; b. El Dorado, Ark., Apr. 14, 1927; s. Roger Spurgeon and Lumae (Jackson) B.; m. Martha Edwina Withers, Aug. 25, 1950; children:Leslie, Roger, Geoffrey, Stephen, Douglas. BA, Baylor U., 1949; MA, U. Ill., 1950; PhD, U. Colo., 1959. Instr. English U. Colo., 1955-57, 58-60; prof. Tex. Tech U., Lubbock, 1960-64, assoc. dean Grad. Sch., 1964-67; dean Coll. Arts and Scis. Tex. A&M U., Commerce, 1967-72; pres. Howard Payne U., Brownwood, Tex., 1972-79; v.p. adminstrv. affairs Houston Bapt. U., 1979-87; dir. Armstrong Browning Libr., Baylor U., 1987-96. Cons. Victorian Studies, 1967, Choice, 1970, Can. Coun., 1971. Editor: Studies in Browning and His Circle, 1987-96, Robert Browning and Victorian Culture, 1992, Elizabeth Barrett Browning and Victorian Culture, 1994; contbr. articles to profl. jours. Pres., bd. advs. Baylor U., 2000-02, libr. fellow, 2002—. With USNR, 1945-51; lt. col. USMC, 1972-87, ret. Rsch. grantee U. Colo. at Oxford and Brit. Mus., 1957-58, Tex. Tech. U. at Bibliotheque Nationale, Paris, 1964, Am. Philos Soc. at N.Y. Public Libr., 1963, Brit. Mus., 1980, the Suratt-Lewis Libr. award, 1997. Mem. London Browning Soc., Grolier Club (N.Y.C.), Westlake Club (Houston). Office: Baylor U Armstrong Browning Lib Waco TX 76798

BROOKS, SALLY, healthcare service company executive; BS in Pharmacy & Biology, Ohio Northern U., 1984; MD, Wright State U., 1986, Marshall U., 1988. Registered pharmacist., cert. internist and geriatrician. Dir., section of geriatric medicine, The Christ Hosp. Health Alliance of Greater Cincinnati, 1991—99; asst. prof., Coll. of Medicine University of Cincinnati, 1993—2009; nat. med. dir., Govt. Programs Anthem Blue Cross Blue Shield, 1999—2004; nat. med. dir. Evercare, 2004—09; v.p., physician svcs. United Health Group, 2004—09; physician exec. Cons., 2009; with Transitional Care Ctrs., Transitional Care Units Kindred Healthcare, Inc., v.p., med. dir. Fellow, bd. dirs. Am. Geriatrics Soc.; fellow Am. Coll. of Physicians. Office: Kindred Healthcare Inc 680 S Fourth St Louisville KY 40202 Business E-Mail: Sally.Brooks@kindredhealthcare.com.

BROOKS, SCOTT WILLIAM, professional basketball coach; b. French Camp, Calif., July 31, 1965; m. Sherry Brooks; children: Chance, Lexi. Attended, Tex. Christian U., Fort Worth, San Joaquin Delta Coll., Stockton, Calif., 1983—84; grad., U. Calif., Irvine, 1987. Guard Albany Patroons, Continental Basketball Assn., 1988, Phila. 76ers, 1988—90, Minn. Timberwolves, 1990—92, Houston Rockets, 1992—95, Dallas Mavericks, 1995—96, NY Knicks, 1996—97, Cleve. Cavaliers, 1997—98, LA Clippers, 1998—99; guard, asst. coach LA Stars, ABA, 2000; head coach So. Calif. Surf, ABA, 2001; asst. coach Denver Nuggets, 2003—06, Sacramento Kings, 2006—07, Seattle Supersonics, 2007—08, Okla. City Thunder, 2008—, interim head coach, 2008—. Recipient Red Auerback trophy (Coach of Yr.), NBA, 2010; named to All-Rookie Team, Continental Basketball Assn., 1988. Achievements include member of the NBA Championship winning Houston Rockets, 1994. Office: Okla City Thunder Two Leadership Sq 211 N Robinson Ave Ste 300 Oklahoma City OK 73102

BROOKS, TIMOTHY LLOYD, federal judge; b. Detroit, July 17, 1964; BBA, U. Ark., 1986; JD, U. Ark. Sch. Law, 1989. Assoc. Taylor Law Partners, LLP, 1989—93, ptnr., 1993—2014; judge US Dist. Ct. (western dist.) Ark., 2014—. Office: US District Court 35 East Mountain St Fayetteville AR 72701 Office Phone: 479-444-7876.*

BROOKS, TYRONE L., state legislator; b. Warrenton, Ga., Oct. 10, 1945; s. Mose Brooks and Ruby Cody B.; married; children: Tyrone Jr., Naheede Teresa. Former exec. dir. Dr. Martin Luther King Jr.'s Southern Christian Leadership Conf., Atlanta, former dir. nat. field dir. & nat. comm. dir.; former Ga. state rep. Dist. 47; mem. Dr. Martin Luther King Jr.'s Southern Christian Leadership Conf., 1967—69; chmn. Rainbow Coalition of Ga., Universal Humanities; Ga. state rep. Dist. 54, 1981—2002; mem. Coms. on Govt. Affairs, Econ. Devel., Tourism; chmn., Jesse Jackson for pres. campaign Ga., 1984; elected. pres. Ga. Assn. Black Elected Office, 1993; nat. pres. Tyrone Brooks & Assoc., 1973—; founder & chmn. Visions Of Literacy; v. p. African America Bus. Syst.; chmn. & Chief Exec. officer Bus. & Polit. Firm; former Ga. state rep. Dist. 63, 2004—; spkr.; human rights activist. Recipient Ann. Legislature award, A. Phillip Randolph Labor Inst., 1984, Best Pub. Servant award, Ga. Coalition Black Women, 1996, Roy Wilkins award, NAACP, 1984, Ann. Pub. Servant award, Atlanta City Coun., 1986, Civil Rights award, 1990, Thurgood Marshall award, Atlanta NAACP, 1992, Leadership award, 2001; named One of 50 most influential men in Ga., Ga. Coalition Black Women, 1984, Father of Yr., Concerned Black Clergy, 1996; named to Hall of Fame, NAACP, 1986. Mem.: Nat. Youth Connection, Ga. Coalition Black Women, Georgia Coun. Internat. Visitors, Ralph David Abernathy Found. (mem. bd. trustees), America Civil Liberties Union, NAACP, Atlanta Chpt., Atlanta SCLC (former exec. dir.). Democrat. Bapt. Mailing: Sta A Box 11185 Atlanta GA 30310-0185 Office: 511 Legis Office Bldg Atlanta GA 30334 Home Phone: 404-753-3361; Office Phone: 404-524-5531, 404-656-6372. Office Fax: 404-656-0238. Business E-Mail: tbrooks@legis.state.ga.us.

BROOME, OSCAR WHITFIELD, JR., finance educator; b. Monroe, NC, Feb. 3, 1940; s. Oscar Whitfield and Irma (Hinson) B.; m. Julia Carol Renegar, June 14, 1964; children: Christine Irma, Michael Whitfield. AB, Duke U., 1962; MS, U. Ill., 1964, PhD, 1971. Prof. acctg. U. Va., Charlottesville, 1967-91, prof. law, 1998—, Frank S. Kaulback Jr. prof. commerce, 1991—, assoc. dean, 1992-98, interim dean, 1997, dir. grad. studies, 1986-92, dir. Ernst & Young master's program, 1998—2001; exec. dir. Inst. Chartered Fin. Analysts, Charlottesville, 1978-84. Faculty fellow Price Waterhouse & Co., NYC, 1964; vis. prof. U. Tex., Austin, 1975, Duke U., Durham, NC, 1977-78, Tulane U., New Orleans, 2002; vis. rsch. scholar, Lancaster (Eng.) U., 1994; adminstr. exams. Inst. CFAs, 1973-77; bd. regents Coll. Fin. Planning, 1984-89, chmn., 1987-89; mem. CPA Exam. Rev. Bd., 1984-87, chmn., 1986-87; mem. exams. com. Nat. Assn. State

Bds. Accountancy, 1995-2000, 04-06; bd. dirs. Internat. Bd. Stds. and Practices for CFPs, 1989-91; mem. vis. adv. com. DePaul U. Sch. Accountancy, 1991-97; mem. Va. Bd. Accountancy, 2003—, vice chair, 2008-09, chair 2009-10. Named Outstanding Educator Va. Soc. CPAs, 1979; recipient Outstanding Faculty award Z Soc., 1988, Commendation Career Contribution award, Va. Soc. CPAs, 2006 Mem. AICPA (bd. examiners 1977-82, 2006—), CFA Inst. (investment analysis stds. bd. 1984-86), Nat. Assn. Accts. (pres. chpt. 1974), Phi Beta Kappa, Phi Kappa Phi, Beta Gamma Sigma, Beta Alpha Psi, Omicron Delta Kappa.

BROOME, PATRICK J., dentist; BS in Biol. Sci. and Mktg., Clemson U., SC; MBA, Wingate U., NC; grad., Med. U. SC. Served as an adviser and cons. for many dental equipment and product mfrs.; clin. instr. Southeast Regional Tng. Ctr.; dentist Charlotte Ctr. for Cosmetic Dentistry. Named one of TopDentists, 2007—. Master: World Clin. Laser Inst.; fellow: Acad. of Gen. Dentistry; mem.: ADA, SC Dental Assn., NC Dental Assn., Am. Acad. Cosmetic Dentistry. Office: Charlotte Center for Cosmetic Dentistry 6849 Fairview Rd Ste 200 Charlotte NC 28210 Office Phone: 704-364-4711. Office Fax: 704-364-1963.

BROOME, SHARON WESTON, state legislator; b. Chgo., Oct. 1, 1956; d. Willie Weston and Lucille Fuller W. Asst. pol. action dir. Regional Devel. Office, 1980—82, 1985; pub. rels. cons. & spkr. Finesse & Assoc., Baton Rouge, 1985—; mktg. & promotion asst., 1986; communication dir, 1987; pub. affairs & traffic dir. TV. Sta., 1987—90; city councilwoman Baton Rouge, 1989—92; mayor, v.p. Pro Tem, 1991—92; mem. Dist. 29 La. House of Reps., 1992—2004; mem. Dist. 15 La. State Senate, 2005—, mem. fin. com., select com. on women and children. Fellow: Christian Athletes; mem.: Nat. Black Caucus State Legislators, Leadership La., Touch Life Found., Women Need Gain Support, La. Ctr. Women Govt. (hon.), Southern U. Ctr. Women Studies (advisor bd.), North Baton Rouge Women's Health Ctr., East Baton Rouge Parish Coun. Aging (bd. mem.). Democrat. Christian. Address: PO Box 52783 Baton Rouge LA 70892 Office: LA State Legislature PO Box 94183 Baton Rouge LA 70892 E-mail: lasen15@legis.state.la.us.

BROOMFIELD, BILLY FRANK, state legislator; b. Moss Point, Miss., Jan. 15, 1945; m. Vera DuBose; children: Vernonia, Chanda. Mem. Dist. 110 Miss. House of Reps., 1992—; mem. Jackson County Dem. Com., Moss Point Pk. & Recreation Com.; sr. planner Ingalls Shipbldg. Mem.: Shriner, Miss. Vietnam Vet. Assn., Mason Club, Am. Legion. Democrat. Methodist. Mailing: 4512 Hawkins St Moss Point MS 39563 Home Phone: 228-475-1293; Office Phone: 228-935-1640, 601-359-9382. Business E-Mail: bbroomfield@house.ms.gov.

BROPHY, ALFRED LAURENCE, III, law educator; b. Champaign, Ill., Sept. 6, 1966; s. Alfred Laurence Jr. and Athena (Logothetis) B. AB, U. Pa., 1987; JD, Columbia U., 1987—90; AM, Harvard U., 1993, PhD, 2001. Bar: N.Y. 1992. Law clk. hon. John D. Butzner, Jr. U.S. Ct. Appeals (4th Cir.), Richmond, Va., 1990-91; assoc. Skadden, Arps, Slate, Meagher & Flom, NYC, 1991-92; Mellon fellow in the humanities Harvard U., Cambridge, Mass., 1992-94; asst. prof. law Oklahoma City (Okla.) U., 1994-97, assoc. prof. law, 1997-99, prof. law, 1999—2001, U. Ala., 2001—08; Reef C. Ivey II prof. law U. NC, Chapel Hill, 2008—11, Judge John J. Parker Disting. prof. law, 2011—. Bd. dirs. Okla. Indian Legal Svcs.; book reviews editor Law and History Review, 2003-10. Co-author: Integrating Spaces: Property Law and Race, 2011; author: Reconstructing the Dreamland: the Tulsa Rist of 1921, 2002, Reparations Pro and Con, 2006; co-editor: Transformations in American Legal History, 2 vols., 2009 & 2010, A Companion to American Legal History, 2013; contbr. articles to profl. jours. Mem. Am. Soc. Legal History (mem. exec. com., bd. dirs. 2007-10), Phi Beta Kappa. Democrat. Unitarian Universalist. Office: Univ NC CB #3380 Chapel Hill NC 27599-3380 Office Phone: 919-962-4128. Business E-Mail: abrophy@email.unc.edu.*

BROPHY, JEREMIAH JOSEPH, retired finance company executive, military officer; b. NYC, Mar. 19, 1930; s. John Joseph and Mary Margaret (Moran) B.; m. Jane Guthrie, June 4, 1955; children: John, Sandy, Greg, Elizabeth, Diane, Stephen. Student, Manhattan Coll., 1947-48; BS, U.S. Mil. Acad., 1953; postgrad., Army Command and Gen. Staff Coll., 1963, Armed Forces Staff Coll., 1964, Army War Coll., 1969, Monmouth Coll., 1981. Commd. 2d lt. U.S. Army, 1953; advanced through grades to brig. gen., 1976; advisor 12th Vietnamese Inf. Rgt., Vietnam, 1963-64; US Army staff The Pentagon, Washington, 1965—68; comdr. 1st Bn., 327th Inf. 101st Airborne Divsn., Vietnam, 1969-70; G3 advisor I Corps, Vietnam, 1970; comdr. US Army garrison Aschaffenburg, Germany; comdr. 3d Brigade, 3d Inf. divsn., 1973-75; G1 and G3 VII corps. staff Germany, 1975—76; comdr. US Army garrison Baumholder, Germany; asst. comdr. 8th Inf. div., 1976-78; dep. comdr. Combined Arms Tng. Devels. Agy., 1978-80; dep. comdr. U.S. Army Tng. Ctr. Ft. Dix, NJ, 1980-83; stockbroker Merrill, Lynch, Pierce, Fenner & Smith, Nashville; agt. Franklin Life Ins. Co.; exec. v.p. Gen. Trust Co.; divsn. mgr. Waddell & Reed Inc., Nashville, 1983-94; cert. fin. planner BMA Fin. Svcs. Inc., and others, Nashville, 1995—2001; leader US Army Europe Team, Four Day Int'l Marches Nijmegen, Netherlands, 1976. Decorated D.S.M., Bronze Star valor with oak leaf cluster, Purple Heart, Legion of Merit with oak leaf cluster, Vietnamese Cross of Gallantry (3 awards), Meritorious Svc. medal, Army Commendation medal with oak leaf cluster. Mem. Assn. Grad. U.S. Mil. Acad., West Point Soc. Mid. Tenn., Mil. Officers Assn. Am. (Mid Tenn. chpt. bd. dirs. 1998-2011, chmn. middle Tenn. chpt. scholarship com. 2003-10). Roman Catholic. Home: 6071 Bethany Blvd Nashville TN 37221-4314 Personal E-mail: planner30@aol.com.

BROPHY, STEPHEN JEREMIAH, lobbyist, former legislative staff member; b. 1966; s. Jeremiah and Jane Brophy; m. Deborah Brophy; children: Hannah Jane, Peter. BA, Middle Tenn. State U., 1989. With US Dept. Labor, Washington, Ctr. Naval Analyses, KPMG Cons.; legis. asst. to Senator Bill Frist US Senate, 2002—03; chief of staff to Rep. Marsha Blackburn US House of Representatives, 2003—09; v.p. govt. affairs Dollar Gen. Corp., 2009—. Recipient Adjutant General's Disting. Patriot Medal, Tenn. Nat. Guard, 2009; Stennis Fellow. Republican. Office: Dollar General Corp 100 Mission Ridge Goodlettsville TN 37072 E-mail: sbrophy@dollargeneral.com.

BROSMAN, CATHARINE SAVAGE, retired language educator, poet; b. Denver, June 7, 1934; d. Paul Victor and Della (Stanforth) Hill; m. Patric Savage, 1955 (div. 1964), m. July 11, 2008; m. Paul William Brosman Jr., Aug. 21, 1970 (div. 1993); 1 child, Katherine Elliott. BA, Rice U., Houston, Tex., 1955, MA, 1957, PhD, 1960. Instr. in French Rice U., Houston, 1960-62; asst. prof. French Sweet Briar Coll., Va., 1962-63, U. Fla., Gainesville, 1963-66; assoc. prof. French Mary Baldwin Coll., Staunton, Va., 1966-68; vis. assoc. prof. U. Waterloo, Ont., Can., 1970; from assoc. prof. French to prof. emerita Tulane U., New Orleans, 1968—97, Andrew Mellon prof. humanities, 1992, prof. emerita, 1997—. De Velling & Willis vis. prof. U. Sheffield, U.K., 1996. Author: André Gide: L'évolution de sa pensée religieuse, 1962, Malraux, Sartre, and Aragon as Political Novelists, 1964, Roger Martin du Gard, 1968, Watering, 1972, Jean-Paul Sartre, 1983, Abiding Winter, 1983, Jules Roy, 1988, Art as Testimony: The Work of Jules Roy, 1989, An Annotated Bibliography.on André Gide, 1990, Journeying from Canyon de Chelly, 1990, Simone de Beauvoir Revisited, 1991, The Shimmering Maya and Other Essays, 1994, Passages, 1996, Visions of War in France, 1999, The Swimmer and Other Poems, 2000, Places in Mind, 2000, Existential Fiction, 2000, Albert Camus, 2000, Finding Higher Ground: A Life of Travels, 2003, The Muscled Truce, 2003, Range of Light, 2007, Breakwater, 2009, Trees in a Park, 2010, Under the Pergola, 2011, On The North Slope, 2012, Louisiana Credle Literature, 2013; editor: French Novelists 1900-1930, 1988, French Novelists 1930-1960, 1989, French Novelists Since 1960, 1989, Nineteenth-Century French Fiction Writers 1800-1860, 1992, Nineteenth-Century French Fiction Writers 1860-1900, 1992, French Culture 1900-1975, 1994; asst. editor French Rev., 1974—77, 1984—77, mng. editor, 1977—80; co-editor: Retour aux Norritures terrestres, 1997. Fulbright scholar, 1957—58. Home (Winter): 2001 Holcombe Blvd #1705 Houston TX 77030 Home (Summer): 417 E Kiowa #406 Colorado Springs CO 80903 Business E-Mail: cbrosman@tulane.edu.

BROSSETT, JARED C., state legislator; BA in Polit. Sci., Xavier U. Mgmt. cons.; mem. Dist. 97 La. House of Reps., 2009—, mem. commerce com., ins. com., mcpl., parochial and cultural affairs com., mem. Dem. caucus, La. legis. black caucus, Orleans del. Democrat. Office: 6305 Elysian Fields Ave Ste 404 New Orleans LA 70122 Office Phone: 504-286-1033. Office Fax: 504-286-1035. E-mail: brossettj@legis.state.la.us.

BROTT, WALTER HOWARD, retired cardiac surgeon, educator, military officer; b. Alamosa, Colo., Sept. 5, 1933; s. Walter Hugo and Viola Helen (Roscher) B.; m. Marie Helen Kuzniewski; children: Cheryl Marie, Michelle Marie, Kevin Walter. BA, Yale U., 1955; MD, U. Kans., 1959. Diplomate Am. Bd. Surgery, Am. Bd. Thoracic Surgery. Commd. 1st. lt. U.S. Army, 1959, advanced through grades to col., 1974; intern Walter Reed Army Med. Ctr., Washington, 1959; resident in gen. surgery William Beaumont Gen. Hosp., El Paso, Tex., 1960-64; resident in thoracic surgery Fitzsimmons Army Med. Ctr., Denver, 1967-69; comdr. 3d Surg. Hosp., Vietnam, 1969, 18th Surg. Hosp., 1970; asst. chief thoracic and cardiovascular surgery Walter Reed Army Med. Ctr., 1971-76, chief cardiothoracic surgery, 1977-84; ret. U.S. Army, 1982. Chief surg. cons. Surgeon Gen. Army, Washington, 1976-77; prof. surgery and subsequent adjuvant prof. surgery Uniformed Svcs. U. Health Scis., 1976—; assoc. clin. prof. surgery U. Tenn., Knoxville, 1984-94, hon. clinical prof., 1994—; mem. joint rev. com. Coun. for Perfusion Edn. and Accreditation, 1981-87, 1st chief cardiothorasic surgery uniformed svc. U. Health Sci., Herbert Sch. Medicine. Contbr. articles to profl. jours.; chmn.: NATO editorial bd., sr. editor Emergency War Surgery Handbook, 1977-82. Mem. physicians' panel Heritage Found., 1991—. Decorated Legion of Merit with oak leaf cluster; decorated Bronze Star (U.S.), Cross of Gallantry (Vietnam), 1st class Action medal Vietnam; recipient Cert. of Achievement Surgeon Gen. U.S., 1973 Fellow ACS (grad. edn. com. 1977-78); mem. AMA (cons. panel coun. allied health edn. accreditation 1981-87), Walter Reed Assn., Soc. Thoracic Surgeons, Washington Med. Soc., Thoracic and Cardiovascular Surgeons, Thoracic Surgery Program Dirs. Assn., Am. Assn. for Thoracic Surgery, Assn. Med. Cons. to Armed Forces, Assn. Mil. Surgeons, Heritage Found. (Physicians Coun.), Internat. Platform Assn., Alpha Omega Alpha. Clubs: Yale (Washington); Marine Meml., Univ. Faculty Club (U. Tenn.). Lutheran.

BROUILLARD, JACK (JOHN CHARLES BROUILLARD), automotive parts company executive; b. Brockton, Mass., Apr. 7, 1948; s. Francis Arthur Brouillard and Marie Virginia Carroll; m. Elaine Ferguson, Oct. 12, 1974; children: John Jr., Carolyn, Michael, Diane, Jeffrey. BMechE, U. Mass., 1970; MBA, U. Pa., 1974. CPA, Mass. Sr. cons. Arthur Andersen & Co., Boston, 1974-77; with Hill Dept. Stores, Canton, Mass., 1977—91, pres., COO, 1990—91; CFO, chief adminstrv. officer H.E. Butt Grocery Co., San Antonio, 1991—2005; interim chmn., pres., CEO Advance Auto Parts, Inc., Roanoke, Va., 2007—08, chmn., 2008—. Bd. dirs. HE Butt Grocery Co., 2003—, Advance Auto Parts, Inc., 2004—, Eddie Bauer Holdings, 2005—. Served with U.S. Army, 1971-73. Office: Advance Auto Parts Inc 5008 Airport Rd Roanoke VA 24012

BROUILLETTE, FREDERICK, JR., corporate financial executive; BS in Acctg. with honors, U. Va., 1973. CPA. Audit positions Peat, Marwick Mitchell & Co.; with PricewaterhouseCoopers LLP, Richmond, Va.; v.p., risk mgmt. King Pharmaceuticals, Inc., 2001—03, exec. v.p., fin., 2003, corp. compliance officer, 2003—. Mem. Inst. of Internal Auditors, Va. Soc. of CPAs. Mem.: AICPA. Office: King Pharmaceuticals Inc 501 Fifth St Bristol TN 37620 Office Phone: 423-989-8000. Office Fax: 423-274-8677. Business E-Mail: frederick.brouillette@kingpharm.com.

BROUN, PAUL COLLINS, JR., United States Representative from Georgia, physician; b. Athens, Ga., Dec. 7, 1946; s. Paul C. and Gertrude Margaret (Beasley) Broun; m. Niki Bronson; children: Carly, Lucy, Collins. Grad., U. Ga.; MD, Med. Coll. Ga., 1971. Mem. US Congress from 5th Ga. dist., 2007—, homeland security com., sci. & tech. com. Founding pres. Ga. Rep. Assembly. Mem. Rotary Club, Athens-Clarke County C. of C. Mem.: NRA, Gun Owners Am., Ga. Sport Shooting Assn. Republican. Baptist. Office: US House of Representatives 2437 Rayburn House Office Bldg Washington DC 20515*

BROUSSARD, BRUCE D., health care company executive; b. 1962; MBA, U. Houston, 1989. CFO, bd. dirs. Sun Healthcare Group, Inc., 1993—96; exec. v.p., CFO Regency Health Svcs., Inc., 1996—97; CEO Harbor Dental Inc., 1997—2000; CFO US Oncology, Inc., Houston, 2000—06, pres., 2006—08, exec. v.p., pharm. svcs., 2003—06, pres., CEO, 2008—10, chmn., 2009—10; CEO US Oncology (divsn. McKesson Corp.), 2010—11; pres. Humana, Louisville, 2011—12, pres., CEO, 2013—. Bd. dir. U.S. Physical Therapy Inc. Office: Humana 500 W Main St Louisville KY 40202 Office Phone: 281-863-1000. Business E-Mail: Bruce.Broussard@usoncology.com.*

BROWN, ALVIN, mayor, Jacksonville, Florida; m. Santhea Brown; children: Joshua, Jordan. BS, MBA, Jacksonville U., Fla.; postgrad. studies, Harvard U. JFK Sch. Govt., Cambridge, Mass.; doctorate (hon.), Edward Waters Coll., Jacksonville. Intern to Bill Nelson US House of Representatives, Washington; exec. asst. Clinton-Gore Transition Team; dep. assoc. dir. White House Office Presdl. Pers., Washington; sr. advisor for urban policy to Al Gore Office of Vice Pres. of US; sr. advisor to Ron Brown US Dept. Commerce, Washington; sr. advisor to Andrew Coumo US Dept. Housing and Urban Devel., Washington; pres., CEO Willie Gary Classic Found.; exec. dir. Bush/Clinton Katrina Interfaith Fund; exec.-in-residence Jacksonville U. Davis Sch. Bus.; mayor City of Jacksonville, Fla., 2011—. Vice-chmn. White House Cmty. Empowerment Bd.; co-chmn. White House Task Force on Livable Communities. Recipient Frederick Douglass award, So. Christian Leadership Conf., Excellence in Cmty. Svc. award, 100 Black Men America, Govt. Svcs. award, Nat. Bapt. Conv., Chmn.'s award, Congl. Black Caucus. Mem.: Nat. Black MBA Assn. (former chmn., H. Naylor Fitzhugh award). Office: Mayors Office City Hall at St James Bldg 117 W Duval St Ste 400 Jacksonville FL 32202 Office Phone: 904-630-1776. Business E-Mail: mayorbrown@coj.net.*

BROWN, AVERT HAYDEN, animal scientist, educator; s. A. Hayden and Imogene Wanda Brown; m. Helen Virginia Gann, Nov. 9, 1977; 1 child, Ashley. BSc, Tenn. Tech. U., 1968; MSc, U. Tenn., 1974, PhD, 1976. Cert. Am. Coll. Animal Genetics, 1995, registered Am. Registry Profl. Animal Scientist. Prof. U. Ark., Fayetteville, Ark., 1977—. Mem. editl. bd.: Jour. Animal Sci., 2001—03; contbr. articles to profl. jours. Named to American Cattle Breeders Hall Fame, 1982. Mem.: American Registry Profl. Animal Scientists (pres. 1999—2000), Sigma Xi. Office: University Arkansas AFLS B 106 Fayetteville AR 72701 Office Phone: 479-575-4855, 479-575-4845. Business E-Mail: hbrown@uark.edu.

BROWN, BENJAMIN A., investment advisor; b. NYC, Feb. 13, 1943; s. Horace A. and Lillian A. (Hurwitz) B.; m. Elinore Carole Abravanel, Aug. 8, 1968; children— Adam Howard, Dina Lauren BBA in Acctg., Adelphi U., 1964; MBA in Fin. and Investments, Baruch Coll. CUNY, 1971. Registered investment advisor prin. Fin. Mgmt. Svcs. Acct. Samuel Greiff C.P.A., Atty., Forest Hills, NY, 1963-66; v.p. research dept. Walston & Co., NYC, 1967-73; treas. ENSERCH Corp., Dallas, 1974-78, v.p. fin., 1978-82, v.p. fin. relations, 1982-96. V.p. Enserch Exploration, Inc., 1995-96; v.p. fin. and investor rels. EEX Corp., Houston, 1997-98; chief investment officer, mng. dir. Fin. Mgmt. Svcs., Ltd., Dallas, 1999—. Mem. Am. Assn. Individual Investors, NY Soc. Security Analysts, DAC Country Club, Houston City Club. Avocations: walking, golf, coin collecting/numismatics, oenology. Home: 5200 Keller Springs Rd Apt 1225/1227 Dallas TX 75248-2744 Office: Candy & Schonwald Bldg 3116 Live Oak St Ste 201 Dallas TX 75204-6190 Office Phone: 214-826-6660. Business E-Mail: ben@financialmanagementservices.com.

BROWN, BILL, state legislator; b. Henryetta, Okla. m. Linda Brown; 4 children. BA, Northeastern State Univ. Former tchr.; insurance business; owner Lake Eufala Marina; mem. Dist.36 Okla. State Senate, 2006—. Mem.: Gatesway Found (pres.), Broken Arrow Rotary Club (former pres.). Republican. Office: 2300 N Lincoln Blvd Rm 513A Oklahoma City OK 73105 Home: PO Box 140866 Broken Arrow OK 74014-0008 Office Phone: 918-258-5526, 405-521-5602. E-mail: brownb@oksenate.gov.

BROWN, C. DAVID, II, lawyer; b. West Palm Beach, Fla., Nov. 29, 1951; s. Clyde David and Peggy R. B.; children: Teresa Michelle, Kristin.; m. Wanda Leigh, Jan. 1, 1984. BSBA in Acctg., U. Fla., 1973, JD, 1978; student, U. N.D., 1975, U. Utah, 1976. Bar: Fla. Assoc. Broad & Cassel, Orlando, Fla., 1978-83, ptnr., 1983-89, mng. dir., 1989—, chmn. exec. com., 2003—. Resident mem. The Fla. Coun. of 100, mem. bd. dirs., exec. com., CVS/Caremark; mem. bd. dirs. Rayonier. Chmn. aviation com. Naval Tng. Ctr. Reuse Com., Orlando, Fla.; dist. chmn. Heart of Fla. United Way, Orlando; bd. dirs. Orange County Pub. Schs.; bd. govs. Multiple Sclerosis Soc., Orlando; bd. of 100 Rep. Party, Orlando, 1997; past chmn. Fla. Transp. Commn.; fin. chmn. Jeb Bush for Gov., bd. trustees U. Fla. Mem. ABA, The Fla. Bar, Isleworth Golf and Country Club (bd. govs.), Wade Hampton Golf Club (bd. dirs.). Avocations: golf, flying, salt water fly fishing. Office: Broad & Cassel Bank of America 390 N Orange Ave Ste 1400 Orlando FL 32801-4961 Office Phone: 407-839-4200. Office Fax: 407-425-8377. Business E-Mail: dbrown@broadandcassel.com.

BROWN, C. HAROLD, lawyer; b. Mendenhall, Miss., July 28, 1931; children: Tracey Gwen, Terry Lynne, Allison Anne, Harold Allen. BA, Vanderbilt U., 1957; LLB, U. Tex., 1960. Bar: Tex. 1960. Sr. ptnr. Brown Pruitt Peterson & Wambsganss, P.C., Ft. Worth, 1960—. Pres. A.J. and Jessie Duncan Found.; past chmn. Ft. Worth Civil Svc. Commn.; past chmn. bd. dirs., past pres. Tarrant County Conv. Ctr., 1980; active Com. for Greater Tarrant County; past bd. dirs. Ft. Worth Camp Fire Girls, Nat. Com. for Adoption, Gladney Ctr. Hall of Fame, Adopt a Spl. Kid/Tex., Tex. Assn. Licensed Children's Svcs.; mgr. campaign R.M. Stovall for Mayor of Ft. Worth, 1969, 71, 73, Richard T. Andersen for Tarrant County Commr., 1972, 76, 80, 84, Senator Al Gore for Pres., Tarrant County, Tex., 1988; past deacon U. Christian Ch., Ft. Worth. Sgt. U.S. Army, 1953-55. Recipient cert. Carnegie Hero Fund Commn., 1972; named Outstanding Young Texan, 1976; named to Gladney Ctr. Hall of Fame. Fellow Tex. Bar Found. (life), Southwestern Legal Found., Tarrant County Bar Found. (life), Ft. Worth-Tarrant County Bar Assn. (charter, life, bd. dirs. family law sect. 1978-80); mem. ABA, Tex. Bar Assn., Tarrant County Probate Bar, Ft. Worth Jr. Bar Assn. (pres. 1963), Am. Acad. Adoption Attys., Am. Acad. Hosp. Attys., Nat. Health Lawyers Assn., Pro Bono Coll. of State Bar of Tex., Badge and Shield, Vanderbilt U. Alumni Assn. (pres. 1966-67), Am. Brittany Club (Hall of Fame), Ridotto Club (pres. 1974), Petroleum Club, River Crest Country Club, Steeplechase Club, Nat. Commodore Club (adm.), Rotary, Masons, Shriners, Jesters, Alpha Tau Omega, Phi Delta Phi. Office: Brown Pruitt Peterson & Wambsganss PC 201 Main St Ste 801 Fort Worth TX 76102-3817 Office Phone: 817-338-4888. E-mail: hbrown@brownpruittlaw.com.

BROWN, CARLTON E., academic administrator; m. T. LaVerne Ricks-Brown; children: Kwame, Jamila. BA in English, U. Mass., 1971, EdD in Multicultural Edn., 1979. Faculty Sch. of Edn. Old Dominion U., Va., 1979-87; various to Dean Sch. Edn. Hampton U., 1987-90, dean Sch. Liberal Arts and Edn., 1990-96, v.p. for planning, dean Grad. Coll., 1996-97; pres. Savannah State U., Ga., 1997—2006; exec. v.p., provost Clark Atlanta U., 2007—08, pres., 2008—. Mem. bd. Hampton City Sch. Bd., 1992-97, vice-chair 1995-97; bd. dirs. Savannah Econ. Devel. Coun., 1998—, Nat. Assn. for Equal Opportunity, 1999—; vice chair Savecon Devel. Authority, 2002—. Mem. Savannah C. of C. (bd. dirs. 1999—), Savannah Econ. Devel. Authority (chmb. 2004), Youth Futures Assn. (vice chmn. 2004). Office: Clark Atlanta U 205 Harkness Hall 223 James P Brawley Dr SW Atlanta GA 30314 Office Phone: 404-880-8566. E-mail: cbrown@cau.edu.

BROWN, CECIL C., state legislator; b. Meridian, Miss., June 22, 1944; m. Nancy Hass. Former state fiscal officer, Miss.; former exec. dir. dept. fin. & adminstrn.; mem. Dist. 66 Miss. House of Reps., 1999—. Mem.: Greater Jackson Found., Jackson Redevel. Author, ALCAA, Miss. Soc. CPA. Democrat. Episcopalian. Mailing: PO Box 55502 Jackson MS 39296 Office: Capitol Rm 201, PO Box 1018 Jackson MS 39215 Home Phone: 601-362-8383; Office Phone: 601-359-3330, 601-982-4123. E-mail: cbrown@house.ms.gov.

BROWN, CHRIS, state legislator; m. Ryksie Brown; 5 children. RV dealership owner; mem. Dist. 20 Miss. House of Reps., Jackson, 2012—. Mem. Jayco Dealer Adv. Coun. Active Appleseed Project of Revolutionary War Veterans America; mem. Miss. Rep. State Exec. Com.; former pres. Aberdeen Visitors Bur. Mem.: NRA. Republican. Office: Miss House of Reps PO Box 1018 Jackson MS 39215 Business E-Mail: crbrown@house.ms.gov.

BROWN, COLIN, automotive executive; m. Cynthia Brown; 3 children. BA, Williams Coll.; JD, Duke U. Assoc. Simpson, Thacher & Barnett, NYC; sr. v.p., gen. counsel Cannon Mills, Kannapolis, NC; sr. v.p., sec., gen. counsel Fuqua Industries, Atlanta; v.p., gen. counsel JM Family Enterprises, Deerfield Beach, Fla., 1992—97, COO, 1997—2000, pres., 2000—, CEO, 2003—. Mem. Fla. Council of 100, 2005—; bd. dir. Broward Workshop, 2003—, Broward County United Way, 2005—, Automotive Hall of Fame, 2008—; past bd. mem. Nat. Conf. for Cmty. & Justice. Mem.: Tocqueville Soc. Office: JM Family Enterprises 100 Jim Moran Blvd Deerfield Beach FL 33442 Office Phone: 954-429-2000.

BROWN, CORRINE, United States Representative from Florida; b. Jacksonville, Fla., Nov. 11, 1946; 1 child, Shantrel. BS, Fla. A&M U., 1969, MS, 1971; EdS, U. Fla., 1974; LLD (hon.), Edward Waters Coll. Prof. Fla. Cmty. Coll., Jacksonville, 1977—82, guidance counselor, 1982—92; mem. Dist 17 Fla. House of Reps., 1983—93; mem. US Congress from 3rd Fla. Dist., 1993—2013, US Congress from 5th Fla. Dist., 2013—. Recipient Legislative Leadership award, Nat. Coalition for Homeless Veterans, 2002; named one of The Most Influential Black Americans, Ebony mag., 2006; named to The Power 150, 2008. Mem.: Sigma Gamma Rho. Democrat. Baptist. Office: US House of Representatives 2111 Rayburn House Office Bldg Washington DC 20515-0903 also: Ste 202 101 E Union St Jacksonville FL 32202 Office Phone: 202-225-0123, 904-354-1652. Office Fax: 202-225-2256, 904-354-2721.*

BROWN, DANIEL T., councilman; m. Cathy Smith; 1 child. BS in History, Tenn. State U. Ret. US Postal Svc.; councilman, Dist. 6 City of Knoxville, Tenn., 2009—, interim mayor, 2011. Mem. Dandridge Ave. Neighborhood Assn., First African Meth. Episcopal Zion Ch., Beck Cultural Exch. Ctr. Inc. Served with US Army, Vietnam. Mem.: NAACP. Office: City of Knoxville City County Bldg 400 Main St Knoxville TN 37902 E-mail: dbrown@cityofknoxville.org.

BROWN, DAVID A.B., oil industry executive; b. Newcastle Upon Tyne, Eng., Nov. 6, 1943; came to U.S., 1968; s. David Lumsden and Joyce Ethel (Johnstone) B.; m. Karin Monica Wenham, Aug. 3, 1968; children: Sanford, Andrew. B in Commerce, McGill U., Montreal, Que., Can., 1966; MBA with distinction, Harvard U., 1970. Chartered acct., Can. Chmn. Layne Christensen Co.; dir., planning Teradyne Inc., 1978-79; ptnr. Braxton Assocs., 1980-84; pres. Windsor Group, Inc., 1984—2005; chmn. Comstock Group, Inc., 1988—90; bd. dirs. Marine Drilling Companies, Inc. (acquired by Pride Internat., Inc.), 1995—2001; chmn. Pride International, Inc., 2005—. Bd. dirs. EMCOR Group, Inc., BTU Internat., Inc., Billerica, Mass., Marine Drilling Cos., Houston, Emcor Corp., Norwalk, Conn., Tech. Comm. Corp., Concord, Mass.; bd. dirs. Boston Cons. Group, 1970-78., Comstock Group, Danbury, Conn., 1984-90, chmn., 1989-90., bd. dirs. NS Group, Inc., 2001-06., Petrohawk Energy Corp., 2006-07. Mem. Vineyard Haven Yacht Club (commodore 1991-93), Psi Upsilon (bd. govs. 1979—, treas. Found. 1983—, pres. 1994-98). Home: 31 Everett Ave Winchester MA 01890-3544 Office: Pride International Inc 5847 San Felipe St Ste 3300 Houston TX 77057 Office Phone: 713-789-1400. Office Fax: 713-789-1430. Business E-Mail: dbrown@prde.com.

BROWN, DAVID G., academic administrator; AB in Econs. with honors, Denison U., 1958; PhD, MA in Econs., Princeton U., 1961. From asst. to assoc. prof. econs. U. N.C., Chapel Hill, 1961-66; Am. Coun. on Edn. fellow U. Minn., 1966-67; provost, v.p. for acad. affairs Drake U., 1967-70; provost, exec. v.p. for acad. affairs Miami U., 1970-82; pres. Transylvania U., 1982-83; spl. cons. Assn. Governing Bds., 1983-84; chancellor U. N.C., Asheville, 1984-90; provost Wake Forest U., Winston-Salem, NC, 1990—98, v.p., dean Internat. Ctr. for Computer Enhanced Learning, 1998—2003, provost emeritus, 2004—; interim pres. Ga. Coll. and State U., 2003; coord., Inter-Instl. Collaborative Atlantic Coast Conf., 2002—; exec. dir. Asheville Hub Alliance, 2007—. Chair Asheville's Econ. Devel. Summit, 1986, Nat. Small Pub. Ivys Conf., 1988, Asheville Hills Cabinet, 2006-; coord. Interinstl. Academic Collaborative, Atlantic Coast Conf. Univs., 2001—; exec. dir. Asheville Hub Alliance, 2007-; leader numerous workshops. Author: The Market for College Teachers, 1965, The Mobile Professors, 1967, Leadership Vitality, 1979, Leadership Roles of Chief Academic Officers, 1984, (monograph) Economic Development: 1987 and Beyond, 1986, Electronically Enhanced Education, 1999, Always in Touch, 1999, Interactive Learning, 2000, Teaching with Technology, 2000, Ubiquitous Computing, 2003, Developing Faculty to Use Technology, 2003, Univ Presidents As Moral Leaders, 2006; contbr. articles and papers to profl. bulls. and jours., also book chpts. Recipient Big A award Asheville Area C. of C., 1990; named one of 100 Young Leaders of the Acad., Change Mag., 1978; rsch. grantee Carnegie, 1979, U.S. Dept. Edn., 1965, NSF, 1965. Mem. Nat. Assn. State Univs. and Land Grant Colls. (chair coun. on acad. affairs 1975-76), Nat. Coun. Chief Acad. Officers (chair ACE 1978-80), Nat. Am. Assn. for Higher Edn. (chair 1981-82), Nat. Higher Edn. Colloquium (chair 1984-86), Phi Beta Kappa, Omicron Delta Kappa. Office: 439 Vanderbilt Rd Asheville NC 28803 Office Phone: 828-274-0828. Business E-Mail: brown@wfu.edu.

BROWN, DAVID O., police chief; m. Cedonia Brown. BS in Bus. Adminstrn., Dallas Baptist U., 1999; MBA, Amberton U., 2001; grad., FBI Nat. Acad. Joined Dallas Police Dept., Tex., 1983, chief police Tex., 2010—; interim asst. city mgr. City of Dallas, Tex., 2007. Mem.: Black Police Assn., Dallas Chap., Nat. Assn. Black Law Enforcement Execs., Police Exec. Rsch. Forum, Internat. Assn. Chiefs of Police (IACP). Office: Dallas Police Department 1400 S Lamar Dallas TX 75215 Office Phone: 214-671-3901.

BROWN, DEBRA MARIE, federal judge; b. Yazoo City, Miss., 1963; BA in Architecture, Miss. State U., 1987; JD, U. Miss. Sch. Law, 1997. Pvt. architect practice, Washington, 1987—94; assoc. Phelps Dunbar LLP, Jackson, 1997—2011; shareholder Wise Carter Child & Caraway, P.A., Jackson, Miss., 2012—13; judge US Dist. Ct. (northern dist.) Miss., Greenville, 2013—. Mem.: Miss. Women Lawyers Assn. (pres. 2003—04). Office: US District Court 305 Main St Ste 329 Greenville MS 38701 Office Phone: 662-334-1971.*

BROWN, DEIRDRE A., energy executive; BS in Acctg., Fla. State U.; MBA in Mgmt. summa cum laude, U. South Fla. CPA; cert. internal auditor, fraud examiner. Auditor Clerk of the Circuit Ct., Pinellas; pres. TEPAC Fla., 2003—04; dir., regulatory affairs Tampa Electric Co., 1998, v.p., customer svc. & regulatory affairs, 2006—09, v.p., bus. strategy & compliance, chief ethics officer & chief compliance officer, 2009—; dir., audit svc. group TECO Energy, Inc., internal auditor, audit svcs. dept., 1990, v.p., customer svc. & regulatory affairs, 2001—09, v.p., bus. strategy & compliance, 2009—, chief ethics officer, chief compliance officer, 2009—. Regional bd. dirs., devel. Enterprise Village, Hillsborough, 1995-98; bd. dirs. Heritage Propane, Southern Gas Assn., Am. Gas Assn., Fla. Natural Gas Assn., Enterprise Fla., The Fla. Orchestra; trustee U. Tampa; active Jr. Achievement West Coast Fla.; mem. Fla. Inst. CPAs. Mem.: AICPA. Office: TECO Energy Inc 702 N Franklin St Tampa FL 33602 Office Phone: 813-228-1111. Office Fax: 813-228-1670. Business E-Mail: dbrown@tampaelectric.com.

BROWN, DEL M. MAUHRINE, lawyer, educator; BA, U. Md., College Park, 1987, JD, 1991. Bar: Va. 1993, U.S. Dist. Ct. (ea. dist.) Va. 1994, U.S. Ct. Appeals (4th cir.) 1994. Tchg. asst. Sch. Law U. Md., Balt., 1990, instr., 1991, assoc. dir. devel., mem. faculty College Park, 1991-92; Asper fellow, law clk. Md. Ct. Spl. Appeals, Balt., 1991; pvt. practice Virginia Beach, Va., 1993—; asst. prof., dir. recruitment Norfolk (Va.) State U., 1993-98; assoc. Poindexter and Brown, 1995-98; asst. pub. defender Office Pub. Defender Portsmouth, Va., 1998—2000. Vis. prof. U. Minn., Mpls., 1994. Editor: report N.J. Gov.'s Commn., 1991. Bd. dirs. Md. Women's Polit. Caucus, College Park, 1989—91; candidate Va. Ho. Dels., 1995, 1997. Mem.: ABA (mem. planning bd. young lawyers divsn. 1993—94), Va. Bar Assn. (6th cir. rep. young lawyers divsn.), Va. Trial Lawyers Assn., Hopewell Bar Assn., Golden Key, Delta Sigma Theta, Omicron Delta Kappa. Office: PO Box 1506 Prince George VA 23875 Office Phone: 804-919-1777.

BROWN, DENNISON ROBERT, mathematician, educator; b. New Orleans, May 17, 1934; s. Elihu Thomson and Floy Clements (Edwards) B.; m. Janet Madden, June 9, 1956 (dec. June 1986); children: Robert Leslie, Alan Madden; m. Betty Rieger, May 30, 1987; children: Mary; stepchildren: Robert, Sally, Ann. BS, Duke U., 1955; MS, La. State U., 1960, PhD, 1963. Instr. math. La. State U., New Orleans, 1958-61, 1962-63; asst. prof., then assoc. prof. U. Tenn., Knoxville, 1963-67; mem. faculty U. Houston, 1967—, prof. math., 1970—2003, deptl. dir. grad. studies, 1969-72, emeritus prof., 2003—; rsch. prof. MD Anderson Cancer Ctr., 2003—10. Vis. lectr. Math. Assn. Am., 1965-72, cons., 1972-2003; vis. prof. Rice U., 2006-07, La. State Univ., 1987-88; speaker Oberwolfach Conf. on Topological Semigroups, 1989. Editor: Semigroup Forum, 1970—2003; Contbr. profl. jours. Baseball coach Strake Jesuit Coll. Prep. Sch., 1981-86. Lt. USN, 1955-58. NSF grantee, 1965-69; sr. investigator NASA Contract, 1972-79; recipient Coll. Tchg. Excellence award, U. Houston Coll. Natural Sci. Maths., 1995. Mem. Am. Math. Soc., Math. Assn. Am., USS Lake Champlain Assn., Sigma Xi, Kappa Sigma. Episcopalian. Home: 777 North Post Oak Rd Apt 1704 Houston TX 77024 Personal E-mail: dbrown9057@att.net.

BROWN, DONALD VAUGHN, retired engineer; b. Fairfield, Maine, May 16, 1919; s. Walter C. and Hazel (Fogg) Brown; m. Christine R. Bishop, Mar. 14, 1945 (dec. Oct. 2000); 1 child, Donald V. Jr.; m. Wanda Jean Grant, June 1, 2002. BS, U. Maine, Orono, 1943; MS, Brigham Young U., 1963; EdD, Utah State U., 1965. Registered engr., Maine. Apprentice engr. U.S. Steel Corp., Elwood City, Pa., 1943-47; works metallurgist Aluminum Co. of Am., Alcoa, Tenn., 1947-55; asst. v.p. Penobscot Fibre Co., Old Town, Maine, 1955-60; assoc. prof. Inst. Paper Chemistry, Appleton, Wis., 1960-62; instr. Brigham Young U., Provo, Utah, 1962-63, Utah State U., Logan, 1963-65; dean Fla. Keys C.C., Key West, 1965-66; dean, prof. Western Piedmont C.C., Morganton, N.C., 1966-68; prof. U. Tenn., Knoxville, Tenn., 1968—2005; ret., 2005. Cons. Assn. Am. States, Washington, 1976—, San Jose Costa Rica, S.A., Tenn. State Dept. Edn., Nashville, 1970—84, Maine State Libr., Augusta, 1970—; coord. Surname Index Project, 2001, Am. Adventure, Inc., Orlando, Fla., 1986—96, Thousand Trails Resorts, 1989—95, Coast to Coast Camping, Inc., Washington, 1986, Lincoln Acad., New Castle, Maine, 1994; cons. Capetown South Africa Mission, 2003—05; bd. dirs. Goodwill-Hinckley, Maine. Author: A Teaching Partnership, 1972, Metallurgy Basics, 1978; contbr. articles to profl. jours. Scoutmaster Boy Scouts Am., Elwood City, Pa., Alcoa, Tenn., 1946—52, scout commr. Massena, NY, Orono, Maine, 1952—60; trustee Hinkley Sch., Maine, 1978—. Lt. USN, 1944—46, PTO, lt. USN, 1950—52, Korea. Recipient Presdl. USN Unit citation, 1945. Mem.: Engring. Edn. Assn. (editing. bd. 1968—79), Am. Tech. Edn. Assn., Am. Vocat. Assn. Achievements include patents in field. Avocations: photography, sailing, hiking, camping. Home: 6423 Honeywood Knoxville TN 37918 Personal E-mail: wdonbrown@yahoo.com.

BROWN, EDWARD J, III, automotive executive; B in Indsl. Mgmt., Ga. Inst. Tech.; M in Fin., Harvard U., 1972. Credit analyst Nations-Bank, 1972—79, sr. v.p., dir., Southern dept., 1979—80, sr. v.p., specialized industries divsn., 1980—82, Tampa Bay area exec., 1982—84, Tampa Bay region exec., 1984—85, mid. market group exec., 1985—88, pres., corp. banking, 1988, pres., global fin., 1997; pre. global capital raising and global capital markets Bank Am. Corp. (formerly NationsBank), 1998—2000; pres., global corp. and investment banking Bank America Corp., 2000—04; CFO Hendrick Automotive Group, 2010—. Bd. dirs. Inst. Internat. Fin., Carolinas Health Care Sys., PGA TOUR Golf Course Properties. Commr. San Francisco Asian Art Mus. Office: Hendrick Automotive Group 6000 Monroe Rd Ste 100 Charlotte NC 28212 Office Phone: 704-568-5550. Office Fax: 704-566-3295.

BROWN, FRANK, social sciences educator; b. Gallian, Ala., May 1, 1935; s. Tom and Ora L. (Lomax) B.; m. Joan Drake, July 6, 1963; children: Frank G., Monica J. BS, Ala. State U., 1957; MS, Oreg. State U., 1962; MA, U. Calif., Berkeley, 1969, PhD, 1970; grad. studies, Tenn. State U., U. Puget Sounds, San Francisco State U., Calif. State U., East Bay, SUNY, Buffalo. Chem., physics tchr. Oakland Pub. Schs. (Calif.), 1962-68; assoc. dir. N.Y. State Commn. on Higher Edn., NYC, 1970-72; dir. Urban Inst., prof. CCNY, 1971-72; prof., coll. master SUNY, Buffalo, 1972-77; dean U. N.C., Chapel Hill, 1983-90, Cary C. Boshamer prof. edn., dir. ednl. rsch. and policy project studies for rsch. in social sci., 1990—. Vis. scholar U. Calif., Berkeley; dir. sponsored rsch. Ford Found., N.Y.C., SUNY, Nat. Inst. Edn., Spencer Found., Buffalo, NSF, Washington, Rockefeller Found., US Dept. Edn., IBM Corp., Burroughs Corp.; speaker, presenter in field. Author: (with others) Fleischmann Commn. Report, Vols. I & II, 1973, Vol. III, 1974, Minority Enrollment in U.S. Institutions of Higher Education, Readings on the State of Education in Urban America, 1991, Challenges of Urban Education and Efficacy of School Reform, 2003; contbr. articles to Ednl. Forum, Ednl. Researcher, Jour. Negro Edn., Jour. Black Studies, Am. Sch. Bd. Jour., numerous others; book series editor: Educational Excellence, Equity; editor: Emergent Leadership; book review editor: Education and Urban Society; editorial bds. Afro-Am. History in NY State, Brigham Young U. Edn. & Law Jour., Jour. Black Students, Jour. Negro Edn., Jour. Ednl. Policy, Edn. and Urban Soc., Jour. Equity and Leadership, NABSE Jour., NOLPE Law, others. Bd. dirs. Buffalo Urban League, Langston Hughes Black Culture Ctr., Buffalo; trustee White Rock Bapt. Ch., Durham, N.C.; founder, first chair Black Faculty/Staff caucus CUNY, SUNY, U. N.C., Chapel Hill; established Inst. for AFrican Am. Rsch., U. N.C. With U.S. Army. Grad. fellow Tenn. State U., San Francisco State U., Washington U., Oreg. State U., U. Calif.-Berkeley, fellow Rockefeller Found., 1979. Mem. NAACP, Am. Assn. Colls. for Tchr. Edn. (bd. dirs.), Am. Ednl. Fin. Assn., Am. Ednl. Rsch. Assn. (sec. div. A, v.p., com. on minority affairs), Assn. Sch. Bus. Ofcls. Internat., Edn. Law Assn., Assn. Social and Behavioral Scientists, Nat. Alliance Black Sch. Ednl. Fin. Assn. of Sch. Bus. Assn., Educators, Nat. Assn. Multicultural Edn., Nat. Orgn. Legal Problems of Edn. (editorial bd. 1979-80, bd. dirs. 1990—), Politics of Edn. Assn., Phi Delta Kappa, Alpha Phi Alpha (chpt. pres.). Democrat. Baptist. Office: U NC 121B Peabody Hall CB 3500 Chapel Hill NC 27599-3500 Office Phone: 919-962-2522. Office Fax: 919-966-1533. Personal E-mail: fkbrown@frontier.com.

BROWN, FRED, former state legislator; Mem. Dist. 14 Tex. House of Reps., 1999—2011. Republican. Office: 1920 W Villa Maria Rd Ste 303 Bryan TX 77802 Office Phone: 979-822-9797, 512-463-0698.

BROWN, GARY SANDY, electrical engineering educator; b. Jackson, Miss., Apr. 13, 1940; s. John Leo and Welma (Kelley) B.; m. Mary Kathleen Connaughton, Mar. 16, 1970; children: Joshua John, Nathan Matthew. BSEE, U. Ill., 1963, MS, 1964, PhDEE, 1967. Grad. rsch. asst. Antenna Lab. U. Ill., Urbana, 1963-67; mem. tech. staff TRW Systems Group, Redondo Beach, Calif., 1969-70; sr. engr. Rsch. Triangle Inst., Durham, NC, 1970-73; sr. scientist Applied Sci. Assocs., Apex, NC, 1973-85; prof. elect. engring. Va. Poly. Inst. and State U., Blacksburg, 1985—, apptd. Bradley disting. prof. electromagnetics, 2002. With Wallops Flight Facility, NASA, Wallops Island, Va., 1974; cons. Naval Rsch. Lab., Washington, 1988-91, Decision Scis. Applications, Arlington, Va., 1988-91, DTI Inc., Torrance, Calif., 1987-91, Applied Physics Lab., Laurel, Md., 1987-88, Waste Policy Inst., Blacksburg, Va., 1991—, Motorola Corp., Chandler, Ariz., 1991-93; mem. NATO AGARD Electromagnetic Propogation Panel, 1993—; dir. Electromagnetic Interactions Lab. Contbr. chpts. to books, articles to profl. jours. Capt. U.S. Army, 1967-69. Recipient Best Paper awards R.W.P. King, 1978, Schelkunoff, 1999, Bradley Disting. Prof. Electromagnetics, 2002. Fellow IEEE (Third Millenium award 2000); mem. Antennas and Propagation Soc. of IEEE (pres. 1988), Am. Geophys. Union (editor's citation Radio Sci., Am. sects. 1986), Internat. Union of Radio Sci. (mem.-at-large 1987, sec. U.S. nat. com. 1997-99, chair U.S. nat. com. 2000-2002), NATO AGARD Sensors and Propagation Panel. Avocations: backpacking, jogging. Office: Va Poly Inst & State U Bradley Dept Elec & Computer Engr Blacksburg VA 24061

BROWN, GEO. GARVIN, IV, food products executive; Joined Brown-Forman Corp., 1996, chmn., CEO, 2002—04, v.p., Brown-Forman Beverages, Europe, 2004—07, v.p., brand dir., Jack Daniel's, Europe & Africa, 2004—08, chmn., 2007—, sr. v.p., mng. dir., Western Europe & Africa & bd. dirs., 2009—. Office: Brown Forman Corp 850 Dixie Hwy Louisville KY 40210 Office Phone: 502-585-1100. Office Fax: 502-774-7876. Business E-Mail: geo_brown@b-f.com.

BROWN, GLENDA ANN WALTERS, ballet director; b. Buna, Tex., July 22, 1937; d. Jesse Olaf and Kathryn Jeanette (Rogers) Walters; m. David Dann Brown, Dec. 13, 1958 (div. 1995); children: Kathryn, Jean, Vanessa Lea. Grad. h.s., Beaumont, Tex. Mem. Melody Maids, Beaumont, 1950-60; asst. tchr. Widman Sch., Beaumont, 1952-55; owner, tchr. Walters Sch. of Dance, Jasper, Tex., 1955-59; assoc. tchr. Emmamae Horn Sch., 1964-81, artistic dir., 1981—; assoc. dir. Allegro Ballet Houston, 1974-81, artistic dir., 1981—; owner, dir. Allegro Acad. Dance, Houston, 1981—. Dir. Regional Dance American Nat. Craft Choreography Conf., 1987—2001; mem. adv. bd. Dance Tchr. Mag., 1998—2003; founder, dir. Glenda Brown Choreography Project, 2002—. Dance panel Cultural Arts Coun., Houston, 1979, Tex. Commn. on the Arts, 1988-90; sec. Riedel Estates Civic Club, Houston, 1975-78; Rep. poll worker, Houston, 1970-81; bd. dirs. Austrian Alps Performing Arts Festival, 1996-98; coord. First Nat. Regional Dance American Festival, 1997, bd. dirs. Tanzsommer/Austria, 1998—; dir. Young Tanzsommer, 2006-. Mem. Dance Masters American (exam. chair chpt. 3 1980-86), Regional Dance American S.W. (exec. v.p. 1981-2001), Dance American, Nat. Assn. Regional Ballet (bd. dirs. 1985-88), Regional Dance American (nat. bd. dirs., v.p. 1988-95, pres. 1995-2001, dir. emeritus 2002—). Meth. Avocations: camping, singing, golf, travel. Office: Allegro Ballet and Dance Acad 12680 Goar Rd Houston TX 77077-3870 Office Phone: 281-496-4670. Business E-Mail: glendabrown@allegroballetofhouston.com.

BROWN, GRADY A., state legislator; b. May 1, 1944; s. Arthur and Maude Atkinson Brown; m. Laura Annette Webster, 1971; children: Johnathan Everett, Grady Allen. Mem. Lee County Coun., 1973—80; mem. Dist. 50 SC House of Reps., 1985—; mem. Labor Com., Commerce Com.; adv. bd. First Citizens Bank & Trust, Bishopville, SC. Named Outstanding Young Man of Yr., Lee County, 1976. Mem.: Lee County Chap America Cancer Soc., Lee United Way, Jaycee, Lee County C. of C. (pres. 1974—75). Democrat. Address: 106 E Cedar Ln Bishopville SC 29010 Mailing: 304B Blatt Bldg Columbia SC 29201 Office: 420 S Main St Bishopville SC 29010 Home Phone: 803-484-6918; Office Phone: 803-734-2934, 803-484-6832. Business E-Mail: gb@legis.lpitr.state.sc.us.

BROWN, GREGORY NEIL, academic administrator, forester, educator; b. Detroit, Feb. 10, 1938; s. Robert Octavus and Dorothy Etta May (Kingsbury) B.; m. Patricia Lee Talbott, Dec. 16, 1961 (div. 1974); children: Kathryn Duket, Julie Ann, Deborah Louise; m. Janeth Christine Hartman, May 24, 1974 (dec. 1997); children: Kimberly Suzanne, Kevin Scott; m. Laura Jean Dale, June 27, 1998. BS, Iowa State U., 1959; MF, Yale U., 1960; DF, Duke U., 1963. Cert. forester Soc. Am. Foresters, 2003. Plant physiologist Oak Ridge Nat. Lab., 1963—66; asst. prof. forestry to prof. U. Mo.-Columbia, 1966—77, dir. grad. studies Sch. Forestry, 1969—74; prof. Iowa State U., Ames, 1977—78; dept. head, prof. U. Minn.-St. Paul, 1978—83; dean, prof. U. Maine-Orono, 1983—86, acting v.p. acad. affairs, 1986-87, 91-92, v.p. rsch. and pub. svc., 1987—92; dean, prof. Coll. Natural Resources, Va. Poly. Inst. and State U., Blacksburg, 1992—2004, interim dean Coll. Agrl. and Life Scis., 2003; ret., 2004. Assoc. dir. Maine Agrl. Exptl. Sta., Orono, 1983-86, acting pres., 1992; assoc. dir. Va. Agrl. Exptl. Sta., Blacksburg, 1992-2004, interim provost, 1995; chair, bd. dirs. Powell River Project, 1996-2004; mem. sci. adv. bd. Nat. Ctr. Housing and the Environment, 2002-05; bd. dirs. Friends of Blue Ridge Pkwy., 2004—, adminstrv. v.p., 2006—08, pres, 2008-. Author-editor: Seedling Physiology and Reforestation Success, 1984; editor International Directory of Woody Plant Physiologists, 1974-84, Jour. Forest Sci., 1979-82; editl. bd. Renewable Resources Jour., 2002—. Contbr. articles to profl. jours. Scoutmaster Boy Scouts Am., 1965-66; mem. Forestry Rsch. Adv. Coun., U.S. Sec. Agr., 2000-02. With USNR, 1955—63. Fellow Soc. Am. Foresters (chmn. physiology working group 1983-84, chmn. ednl. policies com. 2006—); mem. Nat. Assn. Profl. Forestry Schs. and Colls. (north Ctrl. rsch. chmn. 1981-82, nat. sec. treas. 1984-85, nat. pres. elect 1986-87, 94-95, pres. 1996-97), Internat. Union Forest Orgns. (chmn. working parties 1970-86), Nat. Assn. State Univs. and Land-Grant Colls. (chair bd. on natural resources 1997, chair U.S. geol. survey partnership com. 1997-2000), Soc. for Preservation and Encouragement of Barbershop Quartet Singing in Am. (pres. 1973-74), Sigma Xi, Xi Sigma Pi, Gamma Sigma Delta (jr. faculty award 1971), Rotary (chair, youth exch. com., 2007-08). Independent. Home: PO Box 63 Fairview NC 28730-0063 Personal E-mail: browngn@att.net.

BROWN, H. BOYD, state legislator; b. Columbia, SC, Oct. 27, 1986; s. R. David and Melinda (Meng) Brown. BA, U. SC, 2007. Bus. devel. mgr.; intern rep. John Spratt US Congress, 2006; asst. to candidate Tommy Moore for Govt., 2006; pres. U. SC Coll. Dem., 2006; legis. aide SC Gen. Assembly, 2005—07; 3rd vc Fairfield Co. Dem. Party, 2006—; mem. Dist. 41 SC House of Reps., SC, 2008—. Democrat. Presbyn. Office: Dist/Home Office 424 Bratton St Winnsboro SC

29180 also: Capitol Office 532A Blatt Bldg Columbia SC 29201 Home Phone: 803-815-0716; Office Phone: 803-718-2992, 803-212-6789. E-mail: boydbrown@schouse.org.

BROWN, HARRY, state legislator; State senator Dist. 6, NC, 2005—; dep. Rep. leader; owner Auto Dealereships. Mem. Agrl., Environ. and Natural Resources com., Appropriations on Dept. of Transp. com., Appropriations/Base Budget com., Edn./Higher Edn. com., Fin. com., Health Care com., Judiciary I com., Select Com. on Energy, Sci. and Tech., Transp. com. Republican. Mailing: 2223 N Marine Blvd Jacksonville NC 28546 Office: NC Senate 300 N Salisbury St Rm 300 B Raleigh NC 27603-5925 Office Phone: 919-715-3034. Business E-Mail: Harry.Brown@ncleg.net.

BROWN, HELENA, councilwoman; Grad. with honors, U. St. Thomas. Councilwoman Dist. A Houston City Coun., 2012—. Mem.: Houston Property Rights Assn., Moritz Village Townhomes Assn. (pres.), Pachyderm Club of Northwest Houston (co-founder). Office: City Hall Annex 900 Bagby, First Floor Houston TX 77002 Office Phone: 832-393-3010. Office Fax: 832-393-3302. E-mail: districta@houstontx.gov.

BROWN, J. E. (J.E. BUSTER BROWN), lawyer, consultant; b. Dec. 10, 1940; BS, Tex. A&I U., 1963; JD, U. Tex., 1967. Mem. Tex. Senate, 1980—2002, chmn. natural resources com., chmn. sunset adv. com., chmn. natural resources interim com., chmn. water resources devel. com.; chmn. Gulf States Marine Fisheries Commn., Tex. Water Found. Mem. Criminal Justice Com., So. Legis. Conf. Energy Commn., Am. legis. Exch. Coun. Telecom. Commn., Nat. Conf. State Legis. Comm. and Info. Policy, Legis. and Congl. Redistricting Com., Fin. Com., Nominations Com., Vets. Affairs and Mil. Installations Com., alt. Environ. com., Legal Com. Interstate Oil and Gas Compact Commn.; past chmn. Energy Coun.; adj. prof. U. Tex. Sch. Law. Home Phone: 512-482-0404; Office Phone: 512-457-0600. E-mail: buster-brown@austin.rr.com.

BROWN, JAY A., telecommunications industry executive; CPA. With Arthur Andersen LLP; various positions corp. devel. & corp. fin. Crown Castle Internat., 1999, treas., 2004—08; sr. v.p., CFO Crown Castle International Corp., 2008—. Office: Crown Castle International Corp 1220 Augusta Dr Ste 500 Houston TX 77057-2261 Office Phone: 713-570-3000. Office Fax: 713-570-3100. Business E-Mail: jabrown@crowncastle.com.

BROWN, JEFF, state supreme court justice; m. Susannah Brown; children: Kathleen, Rob, Gus. B in English, U. Tex.; law degree with high honors, U. Houston. Briefing atty. to Justices Jack Hightower and Greg Abbott Tex. Supreme Ct.; atty. Baker Botts, Houston; judge 55th Dist. Ct., 2001—07; justice 14th Ct. Appeals, Houston, 2007—13, Tex. Supreme Ct., Austin, 2013—. Mem. Tex. Multi-Dist. Litig. Panel, 2009; adj. prof. law U. Houston. Mem. Bellaire United Meth. Ch., Houston. Named Outstanding Young Lawyer of Tex., Tex. Young Lawyers Assn., 2006, Appellate Judge of Yr., Tex. Assn. Civil Trial & Appellate Specialists, 2011; named one of Five Outstanding Young Texans, Tex. Jaycees, 2008. Office: Texas Supreme Ct PO Box 12248 Austin TX 78711

BROWN, JEFFREY P., lawyer; BA with honors, U. Waterloo, 1991; MA, Carleton U., 1995; LLB, U. Ottawa, 1995. Ptnr., mem., corp. and securities team Hunton & Williams; sr. mgmt. positions, legal dept., including v.p., gen. counsel, internat. unit. BellSouth Corp., v.p. and group counsel, domestic, wireless, Internet, video and long-distance units; sr. level counsel AGL Resources, Inc., 2001, v.p., assoc. gen. counsel, 2002—09, sr. v.p., dep. gen. counsel, 2009—. Mem. Assn. Corp. Counsel, State Bar Ga.; mem. bd. dirs., Atlanta Chpt. Juvenile Diabetes Rsch. Found. Office: AGL Resources Inc Ten Peachtree Pl NE Atlanta GA 30309 Office Phone: 404-584-4000. Office Fax: 404-584-3714. Business E-Mail: jefbrown@aglresources.com.

BROWN, JEFFREY WARNER, state legislator; m. Shirely Scott; 1 child: Greg. BA in Polit. Sci., Ursinus Coll., 1963; M in Psychology, Temple U., 1969; postgrad., Fla. State U., UCLA, U. Ga. Coun. mem. City of LaGrange, Ga., 1990-94; rep. Ga. House, Atlanta, 1994—. Mem. Hi Tech Task Force, LaGrange Devel. Authority, West Point Lake Task Force. Bd. dirs. LaGrange Symphony Orch.; trustee Troup County Hist. Soc.; mem. LaGrange Telecomm. Com.; elder Presbyn. Ch. Mem. Rotary Club. Republican. Home: 2010 Foxcroft Dr Lagrange GA 30240-6306 Office: Legis Office Bldg Rm 612 Atlanta GA 30334 Fax: 706 884-4106. E-mail: jbrown@legis.state.ga.us.

BROWN, JERRY A., federal judge; b. Detroit, Jan. 31, 1932; m. Florence Freedman; three children. BA, Murray State Univ., 1954; LLB, Tulane U., 1959. Bar: La. 1959, Ky. 1959, U.S. Ct. Appeals (5th cir.) 1960, U.S. Ct. Appeals (11th cir.) 1981, U.S. Dist. Ct. (ea. dist.) La. 1960, U.S. Dist. Ct. (we. dist.) La. 1961, U.S. Dist. Ct. (mid. dist. La.) 1973, U.S. Dist. Ct. (we. dist.) Ky. 1981. Law clk. to Hon. John Minor Wisdom US Ct. Appeals (5th cir.), 1959-60; assoc. Monroe & Lemann, New Orleans, 1960-63, ptnr., 1963-90; spl. counsel Bronfin & Heller, New Orleans, 1991-92; bankruptcy judge US Bankruptcy (ea. dist.) La., New Orleans, 1992—2004, chief bankruptcy judge, 2005—. With US Army, 1954—56. Office: US Bankruptcy Ct Ea Dist LA 500 Poydras St Rm B-741A New Orleans LA 70130-3319 Office Phone: 504-589-7886.

BROWN, JODY A., information technology executive; Joined CACI International, Inc., 1991, v.p. pub. rels. & bus. comm., sr. v.p. pub. rels., exec. v.p. pub. rels. & bus. comm. Office: CACI International Inc 1100 N Glebe Rd Arlington VA 22201 Office Phone: 703-841-7801. Office Fax: 703-841-7882. Business E-Mail: jbrown@caci.com.

BROWN, JOE BLACKBURN, judge; b. Louisville, Dec. 9, 1940; s. Knox and Miriam (Blackburn) B.; m. Marilyn McGowen, Aug. 10, 1963; children: Jennifer Knox, Michael McGowen. BA cum laude, Vanderbilt U., 1962, JD, 1965. Bar: Ky. 1965, Tenn. 1972, U.S. Supreme Ct. 1979. Asst. U.S. atty. Dept. Justice, Nashville, 1971-73, 1st asst. U.S. atty., 1974-81, U.S. atty., 1981-91, spl. asst. U.S. trustee, 1991-98; U.S. magistrate judge, U.S. Dist. Ct. (mid. dist.) Tenn., Nashville, 1998—. Lectr. law Atty. Gen.'s Advocacy Inst., 1982—; vice chmn. Atty. Gen.'s Adv. Com., 1986-87, chmn. subcom. on sentencing guidelines, mem. subcommittee on budget and office mgmt., 1982-91; instr. math. and bus. law Augusta Coll., Ga., 1966-69; instr. law Nashville Sch. Law, 1999—; adj. prof. law, Vanderbilt U., 2006-. Contbr. articles to legal jours. Bd. dirs. Mid-Cumberland Drug Abuse Coun., Nashville, 1977-86; asst. scoutmastr Boy Scouts Am.; vestryman St. David's Episcopal Ch., sr. warden, 1982, 90; ch. atty. Episcopal Diocese of Tenn., 1995-98; lt. col. CAP, 1996—. Maj. U.S. Army, 1965-71; col. JAGC, USAR ret. Decorated Legion of Merit, Meritorious Svc. medal with 3 oak leaf clusters; recipient Disting. Svc. award Atty. Gen.'s Adv. Com., 1988. Fellow Tenn. Bar Assn., Nashville Bar Found.; mem. FBA (treas. 1978), Nashville Bar Assn. (bd. dirs. 1995-97, exec. com. 1996-97, v.p. 1997, bd. dirs. 2004-07, 1st v.p. 2007—), Radio Amateur Transmitting Soc. (pres. 1997-98), Nat. Assn. Flight Instrs., Profl. Assn. Div Instrs., Ky. Bar Assn., NRA (life, Disting. Rifleman award), Harry Phillip Inn of Ct. (master of bench and bar 1994—), Order of Coif, Phi Beta Kappa. Republican. Home: 3427 Woodmont Blvd Nashville TN 37215-1421 Office: US Courthouse Rm 704 801 Broadway Nashville TN 37203-3816

BROWN, JOHN ROBERT, lawyer, librarian; b. Muskogee, Okla., 1948; s. John Robert and Betty Jane (Singleterry) B. BA, MA, Cambridge U., 1972; STB, Gen. Theol. Sem., 1973; STM, Union Theol. Sem., 1978; grad resident, Harvard U., 1982; MA, STL, Cath. U. Louvain, Belgium, 1979; JD, Howard U., 1991; MLIS, Valdosta State U., Ga., 2009. Bar: Ga. 1991, D.C. 1991, U.S. Supreme Ct. 1997; admitted Middle Temple, London, 2000; ordained priest Episcopal Ch., 1972, received into Roman Cath. Ch., 2001. Tchr., headmaster St. John's Sch., Oklahoma City, 1973-77; novice Soc. St. John the Evangelist, Cambridge, Mass., 1979-81; minor canon Pro-Cathedral of Holy Trinity, Brussels, 1982—83; assoc. rector St. James Ch., LA, 1983-87; hon. assisting priest Ch. of the Ascension and St. Agnes, Washington, 1987-91; legis. aide US House of Representatives, Washington, 1987-91; hon. asst. priest Ch. of Our Savior, Atlanta, 1991—2001; staff atty. Ga. Legal Svcs., Atlanta, 1991-1995; asst. gen. counsel State Bar Ga., Atlanta, 1996—2003; novice Quarr Abbey, Isle of Wight, 2003—05; intern chaplain clin. edn. program St. Elizabeths Hosp., Washington, 2005—06; libr. assoc. Atlanta Fulton Pub. Libr., 2007—. Reader Ecumenical Inst. World Coun. Ch., Geneva, 1978, Huntington Libr., San Marino, Calif., 1985-86, Coll. of Preachers, Nat. Cathedral, Washington, 1987, fellow Ctr. for Ethics in Public Policy and the Professions, Emory U., 1996-98. Contbr. articles to profl. jours. Vol. NIH, 1987—88, Fed. Charitable Campaign, Washington, 1988—89, Atlanta Project, 1991—96; spiritual adv. com. AIDS Project, LA, 1984—86; mem. Mayor's Task Force on Family Diversity, LA, 1984—86, Mcpl. Elections Com. L.A., 1984—86; governing bd. Robert Wood Johnson Homeless Health Care Project, LA, 1985—87; trustees com. Opera Am., 1996—99; co-trustee Freeman Found., 1994—97; adv. bd. Caring Hands Programs, 1983—87; adv. bd. mem. United Way of Metro Atlanta, 1993—97; adv. bd. Metro Atlanta Cmty. Found., 1994—97; co-chmn. social justice grants com. Threshold Found., 1994—96; capt. The Old Guard of The Gate City Guard, Atlanta, 1998—; bd. dirs. S.W. Assn. Episcopal Schs., 1974—77, Cmty. Counseling Svc., LA, 1983—86, Acad. Performing Arts, LA, 1984—86, Right to Life League So. Calif., 1984—86, Cape Coast Outreach Found., 1984—86, Coun. Battered Women, Atlanta, 1991—94, AID Atlanta, 1993—2002, Atlanta Opera, 1993—2003, ACLU of Ga., 1994—2002, Fund for So. Cmtys., 1995—98, Funding Exch., 1997—99, Cathedral of St. Philip Bookstore, 1999—2003. Named one of Outstanding Young Men of Am., 1974, Yale U. rsch. fellow, 1983, Chaplain Venerable Order of St. John of Jerusalem, 1996-, Knight of Malta, 2005-; recipient: Mayor's Phoenix award, Atlanta, 1997, Disaster Relief medal, Katrina, Order of Malta, 2011. Fellow: Ga. Bar Found. (life); mem.: ALA, ABA (vice-chmn. fed. legis. com. gen. practice sect. 1989—91), Harvard Faculty Club (Cambridge), Sons of Revolution, Soc. Colonial Wars, Patrons of the Vatican Mus., Commerce Club (Atlanta), City Tavern Assn. (Washington), Oxford and Cambridge Club (London).

BROWN, KEITH LAPHAM, retired ambassador; b. Sterling, Ill., June 18, 1925; s. Lloyd Heman and Marguerite (Briggs) B.; m. Carol Louise Liebmann, Oct. 1, 1949; children: Susan, Briggs (dec.), Linda, Benjamin. Student, U. Ill., 1943-44, Northwestern U., 1946-47; LLB, U. Tex., 1949. Bar: Tex., Okla., Colo. Assoc. Lang, Byrd, Cross & Ladon, San Antonio, 1949-55; v.p., gen. counsel Caulkins Oil Co., Oklahoma City, 1955-70, Denver, 1955-70; founder, developer Vail Assocs., Colo., 1962; pres. Brown Investment Corp., Denver, 1970-87; developer Colo. State Bank Bldg., Denver, 1971; amb. to Lesotho Dept. State, 1982-84, amb. to Denmark Copenhagen, 1988-92; ret., 1992; chmn. Brown Investment Corp., Denver, 1993—. Mem. adv. bd. Ctr. for Strategic and Internat. Studies. Chmn. Rep. Nat. Fin. Com., 1985-88; hon. trustee, past pres. bd. Colo. Acad.; mem. Am. Acad. Diplomacy. Ensign USN, 1943-46. Mem. Coun. Am. Ambs. (pres.), San Antonio Country Club, Bohemian Club. Republican. Presbyterian. also: 11 Auburn Pl San Antonio TX 78209-4739 Office: 1490 Colo State Bank Bldg 1600 Broadway Denver CO 80202-4927 Home Phone: 210-804-0556; Office Phone: 303-830-7379.

BROWN, KENYEN RAY, federal prosecutor; b. Detroit, 1969; BA in Comm., U. Ala., 1991; JD, U. Tenn. Law clk. Lloyd, Schreiber & Gray, Birmingham, Ala., Foshee & Associates, Montgomery, Ala.; dep. dist. atty. Montgomery County, Ala., 1995—96; asst. US atty. (southern dist.) Ala. US Dept. Justice, 1996—99; counsel US Senate Ethics Com., Washington, 1999—2007, sr. counsel to dir. edn. & training, 2007—08; dep. chief counsel to dir. advice & edn. US House Com. on Standards Ofcl. Conduct, 2008, acting chief counsel, staff dir., 2008—09; dir. advice & edn. US House Ethics Com. (formerly Com. on Standards of Ofcl. Conduct), 2009; US atty. (southern dist.) Ala. US Dept. Justice, Mobile, 2009—. Named one of Fabulous Fifty Movers and Shakers Behind the Scenes of Capitol Hill, Roll Call, 2008, 2009. Office: Office of US Attorney 63 S Royal St, Ste 600 Mobile AL 36602 Office Phone: 251-441-5845. Office Fax: 251-441-5277.*

BROWN, KOVEN L. (K.L. BROWN), state legislator, funeral director; b. Lineville, Ala., June 27, 1951; m. Amanda Anne Mitchell; children: Allison, Emily. Grad., Ky. Sch. Mortuary Sci., Louisville, 1971. Cert. funeral svc. practitioner Acad. Profl. Funeral Svc. Practice, lic. funeral dir., embalmer, cremationist. Owner, pres. K. L. Brown Funeral Home, Jacksonville, Ala., 1978—; co-founder, pres. K.L. Brown Memory Chapel, Anniston, Ala., 1999—; mem. Dist. 40 Ala. House of Reps., 2010—. Mem. adv. bd. Wachovia Bank Calhoun County; mem. adminstrv. bd. 1st United Meth. Ch. Jacksonville; bd. dirs. Northeast Ala. Regional Med. Ctr.; co-chair bd. dirs. Internat. House at Jacksonville State U.; bd. dirs., past chmn. Leadership Calhoun County. Served with Ala. Army Nat. Guard, Montgomery, Mobile. Mem.: Ala. Funeral Directors Assn. (past pres.), Internat. Order Golden Rule (bd. dirs., past pres.), Anniston Rotary Club, Jacksonville Exch. Club (past pres.). Republican. Office: Alabama House of Reps 11 S Union St Ste 524 B Montgomery AL 36130 also: K L Brown Funeral Home 322 Nisbet St NW Jacksonville AL 36265 Office Phone: 256-435-7042. Office Fax: 256-435-2702. E-mail: klbrown@cableone.net.

BROWN, LARRY (LAWRENCE HARVEY BROWN), men's college basketball coach; b. Bklyn., Sept. 14, 1940; Student, U. NC, Chapel Hill, 1959—63. Amateur basketball player Akron Goodyears, Ohio, 1963-65; asst. coach U. NC Tar Heels, Chapel Hill, 1965-67; profl. basketball player New Orleans Buccanneers, 1967-68, Oakland Oaks, 1968-69, Washington Caps, 1969-70, Va. Squires, 1970-71, Denver Rockets, 1971—72; head coach Carolina Cougars, 1972-74, Denver Rockets, 1974-76, Denver Nuggets, 1976-79, UCLA Bruins, 1979-81, NJ Nets, 1981-83, U. Kans. Jayhawks, Lawrence, 1983-88, San Antonio Spurs, 1988-92, LA Clippers, 1992-93, Ind. Pacers, 1993-97, Phila. 76ers, 1997—2003, exec. v.p., 2007—08; head coach Detroit Pistons, 2003—05, NY Knicks, 2005—06, Charlotte Bobcats, 2008—10, Southern Meth. U. Mustangs, Dallas, 2012—. Mem. US nat. team Summer Olympic Games, Tokyo, 1964, asst. coach US nat. team, Sydney, 2000, head coach US nat. team, Athens, Greece, 2004. Recipient Gold medal, men's basketball, Summer Olympic Games, 1964, Espy Award for Best Coach/Mgr., ESPN, 2004; named All-Star Game MVP, American Basketball Assn., 1968, Coach of Yr., 1973, 1975, 1976, NBA, 2001; named to American Basketball Assn. All-Star Team, 1968—70, The Naismith Meml. Basketball Hall of Fame, 2002. Achievements include member of the American Basketball Association championship winning Oakland Oaks, 1969; head coach of the NCAA Final Four men's national championship winning University of Kansas Jayhawks, 1988; head coach of the NBA Finals championship winning Detroit Pistons, 2004; being the only coach in history to win both NCAA and NBA titles. Office: Southern Methodist University Basketball Program PO Box 750216 5800 Ownby Dr Dallas TX 75275 Office Phone: 214-768-3501.

BROWN, LARRY, sportscaster, retired professional football player; b. Miami, Fla., Nov. 30, 1969; Attended, Southwestern Coll., Calif.; B in Criminal Justice, Tex. Christian U., Fort Worth. Cornerback Dallas Cowboys, 1991-96, 1998, Oakland Raiders, 1996—97; co-host, Dallas Cowboys Radio Network pregame and postgame shows Sta. KRLD, 105.3 The Fan, Dallas/Fort Worth, Tex. Named Super Bowl XXX MVP, NFL, 1996. Achievements include member of Super Bowl championship winning Dallas Cowboys, 1993, 1994, 1996. Office: KRLD 1005.3 the Fan 4131 N Central Expressway Fl 5 Dallas TX 75204

BROWN, LEE PATRICK, retired mayor, former federal official; b. Wewoka, Okla., Oct. 4, 1937; s. Andrew and Zelma (Edwards) B.; m. Yvonne Carolyn Streets, July 14, 1958 (dec.); children: Patrick, Torri, Robyn, Jenna; m. Frances M. Young, Dec. 29, 1995. BA, Fresno State U., 1960; MA, San Jose State U., 1964; MS, U. Calif., 1968; PhD in Criminology, U. Calif., Berkeley, 1970; D of Pub. Affairs (hon.), Fla. Internat. U., 1982; LLD (hon.), John Jay Coll., 1985; HHD (hon.), Portland State U., 1990; LHD (hon.), Fresno State U., 1994; LLD (hon.), SUNY Brockport, 1995; doctorate (hon.), Howard U.; Doctorate (hon.), Paul Quinn Coll., 2002; doctorate (hon.), Wiley Coll.; PhD (hon.), Lee P Brown inst. Criminal Justice. Police officer San Jose Police Dept., Calif., 1960-68; prof. Portland State U., Oreg., 1968-72; assoc. dir. Urban Affairs Inst. Howard Inst., Washington, 1972-75; sheriff Sheriff's Dept., Mulnomah County, Oreg., 1975-76; dir. Dept. Justice Services, Mulnomah County, 1976-78; commr. Dept. Pub. Safety, Atlanta, 1978-82; chief of police Houston Police Dept., 1982-90; rsch. fellow John F. Kennedy Sch. Govt, Harvard U.; police commr. NYC Police Dept., 1990-92; prof. Tex. So. U., 1992-93; dir. Office Nat. Drug Control Policy (ONDCP), Washington, 1993—95; prof. Rice U., Houston, 1996-98, vis. scholar, 2004—05; mayor City of Houston, 1998—2004; chmn., CEO Brown Group Internat., 2005—. Adj. prof. U. Houston, U. Tex. Health Sci. Ctr., Houston, Tex. So. U., Houston; vis. prof. Dalian Sch. Tech., China; hon. prof. Beijing Normal Sch., Tongji U.; guest prof. Tianjin U., China; cons. U.S. Dept. Justice, Washington, Police Found., Washington, various state and local govts., Houston; chmn. Nat. Minority Adv. Council on Criminal Justice; mem. Nat. Adv. Commn. on Criminal Justice Standards and Goals, Washington, Nat. Commn. on Higher Edn. for Police, Washington, Commn. on Accreditation for Law Enforcement Agencies, Washington, Presdl. Task Force, 1993—; mem. chmn. bd. Unity Nat. Bank, Houston, CAMA Internat., Scicom Infrastructure; mem. adv. bd. Carbon Motors. Co-author: Attitudes of Black Police Officers, 1976, Police and Society, 1981; editor: Neighborhood Team Policing, 1976, Violent Crime, 1981, Policing in The 21st Century: Community Policing, 2013, Growing 4P to be Mayor, 2013; author of numerous articles and book chpts. Bd. dirs. Boy Scouts Am., United Way, Urban League, Blue Bonnet Bowl, "Just Say No", Peoples Workshop for Visual and Performing Arts, Houston, 1987—, Nat. Black Child Devel. Inst., Washington, 1987—, Nat. Alliance Against Violence, N.Y., 1986—, Sheltering Arms, Houston, 1985—; task force mem. Nat. Ctr. for Missing and Exploited Children, Washington, 1986—; mem. adv. bd. Nat. Inst. Against Prejudice and Violence, Balt., 1987—; mem. Police Activities League, Houston, 1987—90; mem. adv. policy bd. Nat. Incident Based Reporting System, 1988—90; mem. adv. com. Fannie Mae, Washington, 1999; bd. dirs. Police Found., 2000, Camac Energy; mem. U.S. Conf. of Mayors, Mayors and CEOs. Recipient Peace and Justice award Martin Luther King Jr., 1981, Nat. Law Enforcement award Nat. Black Police Assn., 1982, Disting. Alumnus of Yr. award Fresno State U., 1983, Police Leadership award, Police Exec. Research Forum, 1987, Liberty Bell award Houston Young Lawyers Assn., 1987, August Vollmer award Am. Soc. Criminology, 1988, Cartier Pasha award Cartier Internat., 1992, Exemplary Leader award Am. Leadership Forum, 1994, Mikey Leland Lifetime Achievement award Mickey Leland Ctr. for World Hunger; named to Gallup Hall of Fame by Gallup, Inc., 1993; named Mgr. of Yr., Nat. Mgmt. Assn., Practitioner of Yr., Nat. Assn. of Blacks Criminal Justice, 1984, Communicator of Yr. Washington News Service, 1986, Father of Yr. Nat. Father's Day com., 1991, Politician of Yr. Libr. Jour., Technologist of Yr., Pub. Tech., Inc., 2002, Alumnus of Yr., U. Calif., Berkeley, 2004; named one of 100 Most Influential Black Ams., Ebony Mag., 2003; rsch. fellow Harvard U., 1988; Berkeley fellow, 2002. Mem. Internat. Assn. Chiefs of Police (past pres.), Nat. Orgn. of Black Law Enforcement Execs. (v.p. 1985, Robert Lamb Jr. Humanitarian award 1987), Police Exec. Research Forum, Internat. Narcotic Enforcement Officers Assn., Nat. Forum for Black Pub. Adminstrs., N.Y. Police Chiefs Assn., Tex. Police Assn., Tex. Criminal Justice Task Force, Nat. Police Athletic League, Mich. State U. (adv. council nat. neighborhood foot patrol ctr.), Nat. Research Council (com. on research on law enforcement and the adminstrn. of justice, com. on status of Black Ams.), Harvard U. (com. exec. session on community policing), Nat. Coun. Crime and Delinquency (bd. dirs.; Roscoe Pound award 2008), Nat. Acad. Pub. Adminstrn. (Nat. Pub. Svc. award 1988), Am. Soc. Pub. Adminstrn. (Nat. Pub. Svc. award 1988), Am. Leadership Forum, Forum Club of Houston (bd. dirs. 1987—), Calif. Alumni Club of Tex., Houston Bus. and Profl. Men's Club, Alpha Phi Alpha (Award of Merit 2000), Sigma Pi Phi. Democrat. Avocations: travel, reading, writing. Office Phone: 832-366-1584. Personal E-mail: leepbrown1@aol.com. Business E-Mail: lbrown@bgi-intl.com.

BROWN, LORENE B(YRON), retired library educator; b. Plant City, Fla., Nov. 9, 1933; d. Benjamin and Sallie (Barton) Byron; m. Paul L. Brown, Aug. 1, 1974. BS, Fort Valley State Coll., 1955; MSL.S., Atlanta U., 1956; PhD, U. Wis., Madison, 1974. Cataloguer N.C. Central U., Durham, 1956-58, Gibbs Jr. Coll., St. Petersburg, Fla., 1958-60, Fort Valley State Coll., Ga., 1960-65, Norfolk State U., Va., 1965-70; assoc. prof., dean Atlanta U., 1970-89, prof., 1989—2003, v.p., Friends Coun. Robert W. Woodruff Libr.; dir. Info. Retrieval Workshops, Atlanta, 1976-78; evaluator Coop. Coll. Library Ctr., Atlanta, 1979-82; cons. United Bd. Coll. Devel., Atlanta, 1976-79. Mem. southeastern/Atlantic regional adv. coun. Nat. Network Librs. Medicine, 2001—03. Author: Subject Access for African American Material, 1995. Mem. Friends of Library, Atlanta, 1982. Recipient Rachel Schenk award Library Sch. U. Wis., Madison, 1971; So. Fellowship Found. fellow Atlanta, 1972-74; Libr. and Info. Studies Centennial Celebration Alumnus of Yr. award in Libr. Edn., U. Wis. Libr. and Info. Studies, Madison, 2006. Mem. ALA, Am. Soc. for Info. Sci., Assn. Library and Info. Sci. Edn., Ga. Library Assn., Met Atlanta Library Assn., Beta Phi Mu. Democrat. Baptist. Home: 855 Flamingo Dr SW Atlanta GA 30311-2402 Personal E-mail: lorenebrown119@comcast.net.

BROWN, MARILYN A., research scientist, educator; BA in Polit. Sci., Rutgers U., 1971; MRP in Resource Plannin; PhD in Geography, Ohio State Univ., 1977. Cert. Energy Mgr., Assn. Energy Engineers. Rsch. analyst Conn. Dept. Environ. Protection, 1973; tchg. asst., univ. fellow Ohio State U., 1973—76; lectr., dept. geogrpahy and geology Ohio Wesleyan U., 1976—77; asst. prof. U. Ill., 1977—83, assoc. prof. geography, 1983—84; group leader, sr. rsch. staff Oak Ridge Nat. Lab., 1984—95, dep. dir., 1996—99, dir. engring. sci. and tech. divsn., 2005—06, dir. energy efficiency and renewable energy program, 2000—05; prof., Sch. Pub. Policy Ga. Inst. Tech., 2006—. Commr. Nat. Comm. on Energy Policy, 2002—08; co-founder, chair bd. dirs. Southeast Energy Efficiency Alliance, 2006—09; bd. dirs. Home Energy, 1995—2003, Alliance to Save Energy, 1998—, American Coun. for an Energy-Efficient Economy, 2001—, Tenn. Valley Authority (TVA), 2010—. Contbr. several artilces to profl. jours.; mem. several editl. bds., reviewed articles and monographs for several publications. Recipient C.C. Huntington Meml. award, Ohio State Univ., Dept. Geography, 1976, Award for Disting. Contribution to Sci. Mgmt. and Policy Implementation, American Women in Sci., 1992, Ivan-Allen Coll. Endowed Professorship, 2008; named Corp. Honoree, YWCA Tribute to Women, 1994; Univ. Fellow, Ohio State Univ., 1973. Mem.: Assn. for Pub. Policy Analysis and Mgmt., Tech. Transfer Soc. (Gold medal award 1987), Assn. Energy Engineers, Assn. Am. Geographers (nat. councilor 1988—91, chair, energy and environ. specialty group 1986—88, 1994—96, Anderson medal of Applied Geography 2003), Nat. Academies (Com. on Alternatives to the Indian Point Nuclear Plant 2004—07, Bd. Energy and Environ. Systems 2006—09, Panel on America's Energy Choices: Energy Efficiency 2007—09, Panel on America's Climate Choices 2008—). Office: Georgia Inst Technology DM Smith 312 685 Cherry St Atlanta GA 30332-0345 Office Phone: 404-385-0303. Office Fax: 404-385-0504. Business E-Mail: Marilyn.Brown@pubpolicy.gatech.edu.*

BROWN, MARTIN S., JR., lawyer; b. Indpls., Mar. 28, 1964; BA, Yale U., New Haven, 1986; JD, Vanderbilt U., Nashville, 1992. Law clk. to Hon. Boyce F. Martin, Jr. US Ct. Appeals (6th cir.), 1992—93; ptnr. Stokes & Bartholomew, P.A., 1999—2005, Adams & Reese LLP, Nashville, 2005—. Bd. dirs. Brown-Forman Corp., 2006—. Mem.: ABA, Tenn. Bar Assn., Nashville Bar. Assn. Office: Adams & Reese LLP Fifth Third Ctr 424 Church St Ste 2800 Nashville TN 37219 Office Phone: 615-259-1479. E-mail: martin.brown@arlaw.com.*

BROWN, MARY ROSE, energy executive; B in Comm., SW Tex. State U. V.p., pub. rels. Atkins Agy., 1983—97, Valero Energy Corp., 1997, sr. v.p., corp. comm., 1997—2007, NuStar GP, LLC, 2007—08, sr. v.p., adminstrn., 2008—. Trustee Our Lady of The Lake U. Recipient Women's Leadership award, San Antonio Bus. Jour., Silver Anvil award, Pub. Rels. Soc. Am. Mem.: Pub. Rels. Soc. Am., Tex. Pub. Rels. Assn. (nearly 20 Silver Spur and Best of Texas awards). Office: NuStar GP LLC 2330 N Loop 1604 W San Antonio TX 78248 Office Phone: 210-918-2000. Office Fax: 210-345-2646. Business E-Mail: mary.brown@nustarenergy.com.

BROWN, MICHAEL K., retail executive; Various pos., including store mgr., mgr. and dir. re-merchandising, retrofits and splty. sales Lowe's Companies, Inc., 1984—96, merchandising v.p., lawn and garden, bag goods/chems. and outdoor power equipment, 1996—98, regional v.p., northeast divsn., 1998—99, v.p., splty. sales, 1999—2001, sr. v.p., store ops., we. & so. ctrl. divisions, 2001—06, exec. v.p., store ops., 2006—11, exec. v.p., CIO, 2011—. Office: Lowes Cos Inc 1605 Curtis Bridge Rd Wilkesboro NC 28697

BROWN, MICHAEL STUART, geneticist, educator; b. Bklyn., Apr. 13, 1941; s. Harvey and Evelyn (Katz) Brown; m. Alice Lapin, June 21, 1964; children: Jane Elizabeth, Ellen Sara. BA in Chemistry, U. Pa., 1962; MD, U. Pa. Sch. Medicine, 1966; DSc (hon.), Rensselaer Poly. Inst., 1982, U. Chgo., 1982, U. Pa., 1986, U. Buenos Aires, 1988, U. Paris, 1988, So. Meth. U., 1993, U. Miami, 1996, Rockefeller U., 2001, Duke U., 2009. Diplomate Am. Bd. Internal Medicine. Intern, resident in medicine Mass. Gen. Hosp., Boston, 1966-68; fellow digestive & hereditary disease, Nat. Inst. Arthritis & Metabolic Diseases NIH, 1968-70, fellow biochemistry, Nat. Heart Inst., 1970—71; asst. prof. U. Tex. Southwestern Med. Ctr., Dallas, 1971-74, prof., 1976—, Paul J. Thomas chair in medicine, dir. Jonsson Ctr. Molecular Genetics, 1977—, W. A. Moncrief disting. chair in cholesterol & arteriosclerosis rsch., 1989—. Bd. dirs. Pfizer Inc., 1996—. Co-editor: The Metabolic Basis of Inherited Disease, 1983. Recipient Pfizer award, Am. Chem. Soc., 1976, Passano Found. award, 1978, Lena Annenberg Hazen award, 1982, Louisa Gross Horwitz prize, Columbia U., 1984, Albert D. Lasker award for basic med. rsch., 1985, Nobel prize in physiology/medicine, 1985, Nat. Med. Sci., 1988, Warren Alpert Found. prize, 2000, Albany Med. Ctr. prize in medicine & biomed. rsch., 2003. Mem.: NAS (Lounsbery award 1979), Inst. Medicine, Royal Soc. London (fgn.), Assn. Am. Physicians, Am. Soc. Clin. Investigation. Office: UT Southwestern Med Ctr Dept Molecular Genetics 5323 Harry Hines Blvd Dallas TX 75390-9046 E-mail: mike.brown@utsouthwestern.edu.

BROWN, MIKE, state legislator; m. Tammy Brown; children: Brandi, Dustin. Owner, operatot Okla. Sign Co., Tahlequah; mem. Dist. 4 Oklahoma House of Representatives, 2005—. Democrat. Mailing: Oklahoma House of Representatives 2300 N Lincoln Blvd Rm 545 Oklahoma City OK 73105 Office Phone: 405-557-7408. E-mail: mikebrown@okhouse.gov.

BROWN, MYRA SUZANNE, retired university librarian; b. Gainesville, Fla., Jan. 6, 1949; d. Samuel Jackson and Myra Frances (Whiddon) B.; m. Roman Jonas Yoder, Jan. 5, 1973 (dec.); m. Jeremy Gallaudet Hole, May 3, 1986. Student European divsn., U. Md., West Berlin, 1967-69; BA, U. South Fla., 1971; MSLS, Fla. State U., 1972; postgrad., U. Cin., 1974. Libr. asst. Strozier Libr., Fla. State U., Tallahassee, 1973, libr. serials dept., 1973; libr. sci. and tech. dept. Pub. Libr. of Cin. and Hamilton County, 1973-74; libr. assoc. II Coll. Design, Architecture and Art Libr. U. Cin., 1975-77; assoc. u. libr. State U. Sys. of Fla. Extension Libr., St. Petersburg, Fla., 1979-81, Edn. Libr. U. Fla. Librs., Gainesville, 1982-84, head and edn. bibliographer, 1984-90; asst. dept. chair humanities and social scis. svcs. dept. Smathers Librs. U. Fla., Gainesville, 1990—92, head and edn. bibliographer Edn. Libr., 1992—2002, asst. edn. libr., 2002—07, U. libr., 2002—, humanities and social scis. reference, 2007—, librs. liaison to U. div. Student svcs. common reading books selection and campus program, 2007—11; emeritus honor by pears. Reference liaisons discussion group Rsch. Librs. Group, Inc., 1990-92; reviewer Gale Rsch. Co., Inc., 1988—Edn1. Librs., 1995—; rsch. panel Univ. Microfilms Internat., 1992, Libr. Supplies, 1999; nat. user group Libr. of Congress Cataloging Distbn. Svc., 1992-96; cons. Mus. Fine Arts Libr., St. Petersburg, Fla., 1981-82, Design, Architecture and Art Libr., U. Cin., 1975-77; focus group ISI, 1998-99; cons. New Bus. Devel. Edn. titles Gale Rsch., 1998-2004; presenter in field. Mem. SLA, 1979-2010, host group to winter mtg., 1992, 2005, edn. div. editl. bd. edn. librs., 1999—2009; publications include Freshman Common Reading Program U. Fla. Librs. Coordr., 3-D Displays, 2-D Bibliographies Online Resource Guides with Multi-Media Resources for Each Year's Common Reader, 1999-2011, Building Managerial Competancies, contbr. chapter to staff development com., hr section, Libr. Admin. and Mgmt. Assn., Am. Libr. Assn. Chgo.: ALA editions, 2001, pp. 63-69, 2001, (with Abby Kratz, Julie Alexander, Patricia Finney, Awilda Reyes, and Julie Todara) How to Learn More and Keep Up: A Guide to Bibliographic and Web Resources, contbr. chapter to staff development: A Practical Guide, Third Ed.; a project of the staff development com., HR section, Libr. Admin. and Mgmt. Assn. Am. Libr. Assn., Chgo.: ALA Ed., pp. 172-182, 2001; Libr. TV Video Com. for Creating and Producing Video, Libraries to the Rescue, assisted in story/theme development and filming video targeting Freshmen and Sophmores on U. Fla. Campus, dorm TV Objective: U. Fla Librs. Orientation, 2006, (with Leilani Freund) Services for Users with Disabilities, Spec. AIT 321, Wash DC Assn. Rsch. Librs. (ARL), 2011, contbr. World Architecture Index: A Guide to Illustrations, 1991; contbr. chpts. to books, articles to profl. jours. Aux. mem., vol. Shands Hops. of U. Fla., Gainesville, 1993-96, nominating com., 1995-96, sustaining mem., 1997-2002; advocate for homeless; outreach com., evangelism com., implementation team VIA media program Holy Trinity Episcopal Ch.; advocate for animal rights; vol. Interfaith Hospitality Network, 2003—2009; co-chair Holiday Bazaar-Jewelry Room, 2004-07; Holiday Bazaar vol., 2013-, Gift Shop, 2014-; exec. bd. Cedar Creek Homeowners Assn., 2004-07, v.p., 2004-07. Mem. ALA (chmn., planner, moderator preconf. and conf. program, mem. divsns., reference svcs. in medium-sized rsch. librs. discussion group 1992—2001, presenter), ALA/Assn. Coll. and Rsch. Librs. (edn., behavioral and social scis. sect., ERIC users forum 2005—2011, ERIC users forum steering com. 2005—2009), Reference and User Svcs. Assn., Fla. Ednl. Rsch. Assn., U. Fla. Librs. Assn. (v.p. 1983-84), U. Faculty Fla. (U. Fla. chpt. sec. 2004-05, v.p. 2005—2006). Democrat. Episcopalian. Avocation: art. Personal E-mail: myrasuzanne.brown@gmail.com.

BROWN, NANCY A., health science association administrator; Grad., Ctrl. Mich. U., Mt. Pleasant, 1985. Spl. events dir. Mt. Carmel Mercy Hosp., Detroit; dir. devel./dep. dir. endowment campaign Mich. Cancer Found.; joined as metro Detroit dir. American Heart Assn., 1986, exec. v.p. Mass. to exec. v.p. New Eng. affiliate, nat. exec. v.p. sci. ops., COO, 2001—08, CEO, 2009—. Achievements include being the first female to be elected CEO of the the American Heart Association, 2008. Office: American Heart Association Nat Ctr 7272 Greenville Ave Dallas TX 75231 Office Phone: 214-706-1158. Business E-Mail: nancy.brown@heart.org.

BROWN, NANNETTE JOLIVETTE, federal judge; b. Lafayette, La., 1963; BA, U. Southwestern La., Lafayette, 1985; JD, Tulane U. Law Sch., New Orleans, 1988, LLM in Energy & Environment, 1998. Atty. Adams & Reese, LLP, 1988—92; clin. law prof. Tulane U. Law Sch., 1992—94; dir. New Orleans Dept. Sanitation, 1994—96; atty. Onebane Law Firm, 1996—98; asst. law prof. Southern U. Law Ctr., Baton Rogue, 1998—2000; atty. Milling, Benson, Woodward, LLP, 2000—03, Chaffe McCall, LLP, 2004—07; clin. law prof. Loyola U. New Orleans Coll. Law, 2007—09; city atty. City of New Orleans, 2009—11; judge US Dist. Ct. (eastern dist.) La., 2011—. Office: US District Court 500 Poydras St Rm C-151 New Orleans LA 70130 Office Phone: 504-589-7600. Office Fax: 504-589-7697.

BROWN, NEIL, publishing executive, newspaper editor; m. Gelareh Asayesh; 2 children. BA in Polit. Sci. and Journalism, U. Iowa, Iowa City. Reporter, editor Miami Herald, Fla., 1981—89; mng. editor Congl. Quarterly, 1989—93; world editor Tampa Bay Times (formerly St. Petersburg Times), Fla., 1993—95, mng. editor, 1995—2004, v.p., 2001—, exec. editor, 2004—10, editor, 2010—. Vis. faculty mem. Poynter Inst.; journalism juror Pulitzer Prize. Mem., past chmn. U. Iowa Sch. Journalism Adv. Bd. Named to U. Iowa Sch. Journalism Hall of Fame. Mem.: Am. Soc. News Editors (bd. dirs.), Fla. Soc. Newspaper Editors (bd. dirs., past pres.), Phi Beta Kappa. Office: Tampa Bay Times 490 First Ave S Saint Petersburg FL 33701 Office Phone: 727-893-8441. Office Fax: 727-893-8675. Business E-Mail: nbrown@tampabay.com.

BROWN, NORMAN DONALD, history professor; b. Pitts., June 28, 1935; s. Donald Madden and Regina Deborah (Koehler) B.; m. Betty Jane Aldrich, Apr. 2, 1966; children: David, Tracy. BA summa cum laude, Ind. U., 1957; MA, U. N.C., 1959, PhD, 1963. Instr. history U. Tex., Austin, 1962-65, asst. prof., 1965-69, assoc. prof., 1969-83, prof., 1983-84, Barbara White Stuart Centennial prof. Tex. history, 1984—. Author: Daniel Webster and the Politics of Availability, 1969, Edward Stanly, 1974, Hood, Bonnet, and Little Brown Jug, 1984; editor: One of Cleburne's Command, 1980, Journey to Pleasant Hill, 1982. Woodrow Wilson fellow, 1957. Fellow: Tex. State Hist. Assn. (coun. 1989—93, 2d v.p. 1997—98, 1st v.p. 1998—99, pres. 1999—2000, coun. 2000—02); mem.: East Tex. Historical Assn., Tex. State Historical Assn., Civil War Preservation Trust, Civil War Round Table Assocs., Soc. Civil War Historians (adv. bd. 1986—2008), Soc. Historians Early Am. Republic, So. Hist. Assn., Orgn. Am. Historians, Sons of Union Vets. of the Civil War, Phi Kappa Phi, Phi Alpha Theta, Phi Beta Kappa. Democrat. United Methodist. Avocation: book collecting. Home: 2607 Barton Skyway Austin TX 78704-4602 Office: Univ Tex Dept History Austin TX 78712 Office Phone: 512-475-7216.

BROWN, PAUL, curator; b. Baton Rouge; children: Amy, Isabelle, Jackson. BA in Art History, Skidmore Coll., Saratoga Springs, NY, 1993, MA in Ancient Art, 1995. Admin. asst. BlumHelman Gallery, 1993—95; studio mgr. Peter Tunney Photography, 1996—98; exhibition asst. The Catholic Mus., 1999—2003; curator Meriks & Brown Gallery, 2003—11, exec. curator, 2012—, curator, art of the middle ages. Cons. Orchid Arts, Meridian, Miss., 2001—05, Emporium Arts, Gulfport, Miss., 2005—10, Creative Corner, Tupelo, Miss., 2009—. Author: (book) Georgia O'Keefe: A Psyche Explained Through Flowers, 2003, Vol. 2, 2012. Mem.: Am. Assn. Museums (life). Roman Catholic. Avocations: bonsai, birdwatching, acting. Office: Meriks & Brown Gallery 164 Quail Ridge Dr Madison MS 39110-8253

BROWN, PAUL A., medical services executive; b. Boston, Apr. 1, 1938; s. Morton G. and Helen C. (Appleton) B.; m. Cynthia R. Shrier, June 4, 1961; children: Richard, Mark. AB, Harvard U., 1960; MD, Tufts U., 1964. Intern Tufts New Eng. Med. Ctr., Boston, 1964-65; resident in pathology Columbia Presbyn. Hosp., NYC, 1965-69; chmn., chief exec. officer Metpath Inc., Teterboro, NJ, 1970-83, chmn., 1983-84, Sci/Med Advances Corp., Teaneck, NJ, 1983-88, HearUSA, West Palm Beach, Fla., 1986—. Chmn., chief exec. officer Permark Corp., Hacksensack, N.J., 1985-89; lectr. pathology Columbia U., 1981—. Trustee Tufts U., 1978—88; mem. vis. com. Boston U. Sch. Medicine, 1987—2000; trustee, chmn. bd. overseers Tufts U. Sch. Medicine, 1978—82. Home: 223 Grand Pointe Dr Palm Beach Gardens FL 33418 Office: HearUSA Inc 1250 Northpoint Pkwy West Palm Beach FL 33407 Office Phone: 561-478-8770 x 123. Personal E-mail: pbrown@hearusa.com.

BROWN, PAUL J., travel company executive; BS in Mgmt., Ga. Inst. Tech., 1989; MSc in Engring. Mgmt., McCormick Sch. Engring. & Applied Sci.,Northwestern U., Evanston, Ill.; MBA, Kellogg Grad. Sch. Mgmt., Northwestern U. Sr. cons. Andersen Consulting; mgr. Boston Consulting Group, Inc.; sr. v.p. strategic svcs. Intercontinental Hotels Grp.; ptnr. McKinsey & Co.; sr. v.p., strategy devel., Expedia N. Am. & Hotels.com Expedia Inc., pres., ptnr. svc. grp., 2005—06, pres., Expedia N. Am., 2006—08; pres., Global Brands and Comml. Svcs. Hilton Hotels Corp., 2008—. Adv. bd. mem. Cornell Ctr. Hospitality Rsch.; bd. dirs. Travel Industry Assn., Borders Group, 2009—. Mem.: World Travel Tourism Coun. Office: Hilton Hotels Corp 7930 Jones Branch Dr Ste 1100 Mc Lean VA 22102 Office Phone: 703-883-1000. Business E-Mail: Paul_Brown@hilton.com.

BROWN, PETER C., information technology executive; b. 1957; m. Kate Brown; 5 children. BBA, U. Kans., 1979. Various exec. positions AMC Entertainment Inc. (AMC), 1990—91, sr. v.p., CFO Kansas City, Mo., 1991—99, exec. v.p., 1994—97, co-chmn., 1998—99, chmn., pres. & CEO, 1999—2009; founder, chmn. Entertainment Properties Trust, 1997—2003; chmn. Midway Games, Inc. (formerly Midway Manufacturing), 2008—. Bd. dirs. LabOne, Inc., 1999—2001, Protection One, Inc., 1999—2001, Midway Games Inc., 2005—, Nat. CineMedia, Inc., 2006—, Embarq Corp., 2006—, CenturyLink, Inc. (formerly CenturyTel, Inc.), 2009—. Bd. trustees Rockhurst High School; bd. dirs. Nat. Assn. Theatre Owners; bd. adv. Will Rogers Motion Pictures Pioneers Found.; mem. Variety Internat. Movie Industry Advisory Coun., Internat. Coun. Shopping Centers (ICSC). Recipient Hope award, Nat. Multiple Sclerosis Soc., 2007, Salah M. Hassanein Humanitarian award, 2003, "Get on Board for Entrepreneurial Success" Outstanding Director award, Kans. City Bus. Jour., 2003; named a Disting. Alumni, Kans. U., 2008. Office: CenturyLink Inc Bd Directors 100 Centurytel Dr Monroe LA 71203 Office Phone: 318-388-9000. Office Fax: 318-388-9562. Business E-Mail: brown@centurylink.com.

BROWN, RAYNE, state legislator; m. Clark Brown; 1 child, Jordan Brown. BA in Social Work, East Carolina U., 1975; MEd, U. NC, Greensboro, 1985. Bd. dirs. Friends of the Libr.; teacher, compensatory edn. Davidson County Cmty. Coll.; social worker, 1975—; bd. dirs. Humane Soc. of Davidson County, 1986—2000, Animal Ctr. of Davidson County, 1994—98; candidate Dist. 81 NC House of Representatives, 2008, mem. Dist. 81, 2011—. Republican. United Methodist. Office: 416 Lee Ave Lexington NC 27295 Address: North Carolina House of Representatives 300 N Salisbury St Room 638 Raleigh NC 27603-5925 Office Phone: 336-249-2608, 919-715-0873. Business E-Mail: Rayne@Rayne4House.com, Rayne.Brown@ncleg.net.

BROWN, REGINALD L., councilman; Exec. dir. Project Reach Found.; councilman, Dist. 10 Jacksonville City Coun., Fla. Mem. Land Use & Zoning, Recreation & Cmty. Devel., Transp., Energy & Utilities Coms., Spl. Com. on City Pension Reform. Warrant officer US Army. Democrat. Office: 117 W Duval St Ste 425 Jacksonville FL 32202 Office Phone: 904-630-1386, 904-630-1684. Business E-Mail: rbrown@coj.net.

BROWN, RICHARD LEE, lawyer; b. Ft. Worth, Dec. 7, 1925; s. Marvin H. and Janie (McIntosh) B.; m. Elizabeth McPherson, Nov. 19, 1949; children: Beverly Elizabeth, Leigh Ann (dec.). Student, Rice U., 1942-43; LLB, U. Tex., 1949; LLM, George Washington U., 1954. Bar: Tex. 1949. Asst. dist. atty., Tarrant County, 1949- 50; spl. atty. Chief Counsel's Office, IRS, Washington, 1953-56; partner Friedman & Brown, 1956-60, Stone, Parker, Snakard & Brown, 1961-66, Law, Snakard, Brown & Gambill, 1967-81, 83-84; of counsel Bishop Payne Harvard & Kaitcer, Ft. Worth, 1984-89, 91—; judge Ct. Appeals Tex. 2d Dist., 1981-83; chief civil div. Tarrant County Dist. Atty's Office, 1989-91. Former mem. bd. commrs. Pub. Housing Authority Ft. Worth, chmn., 1976-77; Chmn. bd., chmn. competition Van Cliburn Internat. Piano Competition, 1966-69. Served with AUS, 1944-46; Served with U.S. Army, 1950-53. Decorated Bronze Star medal, Combat Infantry badge and 3 battle stars. Fellow Tex. Bar Found. (life); mem. Tex. Bar Assn., Tarrant County Bar Assn. (pres. 1977-78) Office: 4609 Washburn Ave Fort Worth TX 76107

BROWN, ROBERT DALE, wildlife science educator, dean; b. Red Bluff, Calif., July 31, 1945; s. Charles Arthur and Carol Joyce (Dale) Brown; m. Regan Mensch, June 30, 1981; children: Alex, Jason, Adam. Student, U. Calif., Davis, 1963—65; BS, Colo. State U., Ft. Collins, 1968; PhD, Pa. State U., State Coll., 1975. From asst. prof. to assoc. prof. Tex. A&I U., Kingsville, 1975-81; from assoc. rsch. scientist to rsch. scientist C. Kleberg Wildlife Rsch. Inst., Kingsville, 1981-87; dept. head Miss. State U., Starkville, 1987-93, Tex. A&M U., College Station, 1993—2006, coord. Gulf Coast Coop. Ecosys. Studies Unit, 2002—06; dean Coll. Natural Resources N.C. State U., Raleigh, 2006—. Editor: Antler Development in Cervidae, 1983, Translocation of Wild Animals, The Biology of Deer, 1991. Lt. col. USMCR, 1968—93. Fellow Am. Inst. Nutrition, Wildlife Soc. (past pres.), mem. NC Forestry Coun., Nat. Assn. Univ. Fish and Wildlife Programs (past pres.). Episcopalian. Avocations: hunting, fishing, kayaking. Office: Dean Coll Natural Resources NC State Univ 2028 Biltmore Hall Campus Box 8001 Raleigh NC 27695-8001 Office Phone: 919-515-2883. Business E-Mail: bob_brown@ncsu.edu.

BROWN, ROBERT L., state legislator; b. Hollywood, SC, July 24, 1950; s. James Brown and Alice Brown-Grant; m. Alfreda E. Brown, Jan. 21, 1978; children: Tremayne, Donell. AS, Trident Tech. Coll., Charleston, SC, 1976; grad., Barber Coll., Charleston, 1979; grad. enterpreneur program, Charleston Southern U., 1995. Pres., CEO Brown & Stewart Inc.; mem. Dist. 116 SC House of Reps., 2001—. Planning/zoning commr. Town of Hollywood, 1990—93, councilman, 1993—99, chmn. econ. develop. com., 1995—99. Svc. with US Army, 1970—71. Democrat. Office: State Capitol 330D Blatt Bldg Columbia SC 29211 Home: 5925 Hwy 162 Hollywood SC 29449 Business E-Mail: RLB@schouse.org.

BROWN, ROBERT LAIDLAW, lawyer, former state supreme court justice; b. Houston, June 30, 1941; s. Robert Raymond and Warwick (Rust) B.; m. Charlotte Banks, June 18, 1966; 1 child, Stuart Laidlaw. BA, U. of the South, 1963; MA in English and Comparative Lit., Columbia U., 1965; JD, U. Va., 1968. Bar: Ark. 1968, U.S. Dist. Ct. (ea. and we. divs.) Ark. 1968. Assoc. Chowning, Mitchell, Hamilton & Burrow, Little Rock, 1968-71; dep. prosecuting atty. 6th Jud. Dist., Prosecuting Atty. Office, Little Rock, 1971-72; legal aide Office Gov. Dale Bumpers, Little Rock, 1972-74; legis. asst. US Senator Dale Bumpers, Washington, 1975-76; adminstrv. asst. Congressman Jim Guy Tucker, Washington, 1977-78; ptnr. Harrison & Brown, P.A., Little Rock, 1978-85; pvt. practice law, 1985-90; assoc. justice Ark. Supreme Ct., Little Rock, 1991—2012; of counsel Friday Eldredge & Clark, Little Rock, 2012—. Contbr. articles to profl. jours. Trustee U. of the South, Sewanee, Tenn., 1983-89, bd. regents, 1989-95. Recipient Disting. Alumnus award, U. of South, 2006. Fellow ABA, Ark. Bar Found (cert. of recognition 1981); mem. Ark. Bar Assn. Episcopalian. Office: Friday Eldredge & Clark 400 W Capitol Ave Ste 2000 Little Rock AR 72201-3522 Office Phone: 501-370-1522. Office Fax: 501-376-2147. E-mail: rbrown@fridayfirm.com.

BROWN, SAMUEL JOSEPH, JR., engineer, scientist; b. New Orleans, May 6, 1941; s. Samuel Joseph and Camille (Trumbatory) B.; m. Josephine Monistere; children: Troy Joseph, Tricia Maria Brown Kenworthy, Kamryn Leigh Brown Johnson. BS in Mech. Engring., Math., U. La., Lafayette, 1966; MS in Applied Mechanics, U. Fla., 1968; PhD in Civil Engring. & Appl. Mechanics, U. Akron, 1982; MA in Human Behavior, Devel., Counseling, ACPE, Sch. Theology, U. St.

Thomas, Houston; grad., Baylor U.; MDiv, Liberty U. Registered profl. engr., Ohio, Tex., La., Okla., Pa., Ala., Miss., AE residential, comml. design. New constrn. inspector New Orleans Port Authority, 1964; project mech. engr. Mid South Utilities, New Orleans, 1966; R&D cons. U. Fla., Gainesville, 1969-70; with design and devel. of prototype equipment Babcock & Wilcox McDermott Co., Akron, Ohio, 1970-78; cons. Sci. Mgt. Corp./O'Donnell & Assocs., Pitts., 1979-80, Quest Engring. Devel. Corp., Humble, Tex., 1980—; bd. dirs. Intertech Svcs. Inc., Houston, 1984—; clin. chaplain intern Meml. Hermann NE Hosp., Humble, Tex. Univ. faculty, vis. lectr., profl. devel. instr. in courses on computer simulation, failure analysis, fluid structure dynamics, component design and analysis, explosions and hazardous release protection, forensic engring. Author: Pressure Systems Energy Release Protection, 1986; co-author: Am. Soc. Metals Handbook of Engineering Mathematics, 1983, Handbook of Case Histories in Failure Analysis, 1993, 1994, Non-Linear Analysis of Light Water Reactor Components: Areas of Investigation/Benefits/Recommendations, 1980, Forensic Engineering: Part I, 1995; editor (and author): 20 tech. volumes; co-editor: Jour. Process Mech. Engring. (U.K.), 1990—92, Accident Investigation Quarterly, 2007—; contbr. articles to profl. jours. Sponsor U. La. Alumni Assn., 1990, U. Akron Alumni Assn., U. Fla. Alumni Assn., 1991; pres. Lakeside Terrace Cmty. Assn., 1995-97. Fellow NASA, 1981, NDEA, 1966, Wisdom Soc., 1989; Personalities in Am. award ABI, 1990. Fellow: Am. Inst. Chem. Engrs. (tech. divsn. 1989—), Am. Soc. Metals, Am. Soc. Mech. Engrs. (edn. honors and awards subcom. OAC vice-chmn. 1974—83, pressure vessel and piping divsn. 1974—, high pressure codes & stads. com. 1979—82, newsletter editor 1982—83, chmn. OAC com. 1982—85, codes and standards divsn. 1982—, chmn. conf. tech. program com. 1985, vice chmn. & chair, high pressure sys. std. com. 2000—08, lectr. 2003, chmn. subcom. on hazardous release protection, tech. divsn., PVP divsn., Outstanding Tech. Paper award 1984, Bd. Govs. Svc. award 1992, Dedicated Svc. award 1995, lectr. in field, risk & safety); mem.: Houston C. of C., Post Tng. Inst., Nat. Assn. Accident Reconstrn. Specialists (jour. review com. mem.), Human Factors and Ergonomics Soc., Soc. Mfg. Engrs., Am. Soc. Exptl. Mechanics (tech. divsn. 1978—), Am. Soc. Civil Engrs. (tech. divsn. 1984—), ASM, Sigma Xi. Achievements include design of PWR, LWR, breeder, naval nuclear and geothermal power systems, and new mechanical-civil-aeronautical-chem. sys., equipment and structural concepts, redesign of systems, equipment and components following forensic anlaysis, and recognized as expert in forensic engineering, accident reconstruction, safety. Office: Quest Engring Devel Corp 7500 Old North Belt Dr Humble TX 77396-2625 Office Phone: 281-441-2525. Personal E-mail: drsambrownii@aol.com. Business E-Mail: questisi@qed-isi.com.

BROWN, SANDRA LEE, art association administrator, consultant, artist; b. Chgo., July 9, 1943; d. Arthur Willard and Erma Emily (Lange) Boettcher; m. Ronald Gregory Brown, June 21, 1983; 1 child, Jon Michael. BA in Art and Edn., N.E. Ill. U., 1966; postgrad., No. Ill. U. Cert. K-9 tchr., Ill. Travel agt. Weiss Travel Bur., Chgo., 1959-66; tchr. Chgo. Sch. Sys., 1966-68, Schaumburg (Ill.) Sch. Dist. 54, 1968-94, creator coord. peer mentoring program for 1st-yr. tchrs., 1992-96; cons. Yardstick Ednl. Svcs., Monroe, Wis., 1994—2003; exec. dir. Monroe Arts Ctr., 1996—2001, Monroe Area Coun. for the Arts, Madisonville, Tenn., 2002—03; arts mgmt. cons. Helping Hands, Non-Profit Consulting, Knoxville, Tenn., 2003—, Tenn. Arts Commn. Arts cons.; mem. adv. bd. Peer Coaching and Mentoring Network, Chgo. suburban region, 1992-94; peer cons. Schaumburg Sch. Dist. 54, 1988-94. Exhibited in solo and group exhibitions, Court House Gallery, Woodstock, Ill., Millburn (Ill.) Gallery, Gallerie Stefanie, Chgo., Monroe Arts Ctr., Athens Art Ctr., Athens, Tenn., Chumley/Orr Gallery, Cleve., Tenn. Campaign chmn. for mayoral candidate, Grayslake, Ill., 1989; campaign chmn. for trustee Citizens for Responsible Govt., Grayslake, 1991. Mem. Lakes Region Watercolor Guild, Delta Kappa Gamma (chmn. women in arts Gamma chpt. Ill. 1992-94, Alpha Mu chpt. 1995-97), Cmty. Arts League (Athens, Tenn.). Avocations: gardening, musician for barn dances, pre-war Appalachian, blues and cajun music, research collecting 78 rpm records. Home and Office: Helping Hands Non-Profit Consulting PO Box 1456 Athens TN 37371

BROWN, SANDRA LYNN, writer; b. Waco, Tex., Mar. 12, 1948; m. Michael Brown; children: Ryan, Rachel. LHD (hon.), Tex. Christian U. Mgr. Merle Norman Cosmetics Studios, Tyler, Tex., 1971-73; weather reporter KLTV-TV, Tyler, 1972-75, WFAA-TV, Dallas, 1976-79; model Dallas Apparel Mart, 1976-87. Author: (novels) Tomorrow's Promise, 1983, Relentless Desire, 1983, Heaven's Price, 1983, Temptations Kiss, 1983, Tempest in Eden, 1983, In a Class by Itself, 1984, Thursday's Child, 1985, Riley in the Morning, 1985, 22 Indigo Place, 1986, Sunny Chandler's Return, 1987, Demon Rumm, 1987, Slow Heat in Heaven, 1988, Tidings of Great Joy, 1988, Hawk O'Toole's Hostage, 1988, Best Kept Secrets, 1989, Long Time Coming, 1989, Temperatures Rising, 1989, A Whole New Light, 1989, Mirror Image, 1990, Breath of Scandal, 1991, French Silk, 1992, Shadows of Yesterday, 1992, Where There's Smoke, 1993, Charade, 1994, The Witness, 1995, Exclusive, 1996, Fat Tuesday, 1997, Unspeakable, 1998, The Alibi, 1999, Standoff, 2000, The Switch, 2000, Envy, 2001, The Crush, 2002, Hello, Darkness, 2003, White Hot, 2004, Chill Factor, 2005, Ricochet, 2006, Play Dirty, 2007, Smoke Screen, 2008 (#1 Publishers Weekly bestseller), Smash Cut, 2009, Rainwater, 2009, Tough Customer, 2010, Lethal, 2011, Low Pressure, 2012, Deadline, 2013, (Bed & Breakfast series) Breakfast in Bed, 1983, Send No Flowers, 1984, (Coleman Family Saga series) Sunset Embrace, 1985, Another Dawn, 1985, (Mason Sisters series) Fanta C, 1987, Adam's Fall, 1988, (Texas! Tyler Family Saga series) Texas! Lucky, 1990, Texas! Chase, 1991, Texas! Sage, 1991, (under pseudonym Rachel Ryan) Love's Encore, 1981, Love Beyond Reason, 1981, Eloquent Silence, 1982, A Treasure Worth Seeking, 1982, Prime Time, 1983, (under pseudonym Laura Jordan) Hidden Fires, 1982, The Silken Web, 1982, (under pseudonym Erin St. Claire) Not Even for Love, 1982, Seduction by Design, 1983, A Kiss Remembered, 1983, A Secret Splendor, 1983, Words of Silk, 1984, Bittersweet Rain, 1984, Tiger Prince, 1984, Sweet Anger, 1985, Led Astray, 1985, Above and Beyond, 1986, Honor Bound, 1986, Two Alone, 1987, The Devil's Own, 1987, The Thrill of Victory, 1989; editor: Love is Murder, 2012. Recipient Tex. Medal of Arts award for Lit., 2007, Disting. Circle of Success award, Am. Bus. Women's Assn., B'nai B'rith's Disting. Lit. Achievement award, AC Greene award, Romance Writers America Lifetime Achievement award. Mem.: Internat. Thriller Writer's Assn. (founding mem., Thriller Master 2008), Literacy Partners, Novelists, Inc, Internat. Assn. Crime Writers, Mystery Writers America, Author's Guild. Office: Sandra Brown Mgt Ltd 1306 W Abram St Arlington TX 76013-1703 Mailing: c/o Tracey Guest Simon & Schuster 1230 Ave of Americas New York NY 10020*

BROWN, SHELAGHMICHAEL, bank executive; 5 children. BA, Wheaton Coll., 1972; MBA, U. Chgo., 1975; grad., Am. Leadership Found. With Morgan Guaranty; predecessor JP Morgan Chase, 1979—2002; pres. Rediclinic Inc., 2002—07; CEO Telecheck Internat., 2002—07; joined Compass Bancshares, Inc., Birmingham, 2007; sr. exec. v.p., head retail banking BBVA Compass, Birmingham, 2007—. Bd. dirs. BBVA Compass, 2011—. Bd. mem. CanCare. Named one of 25 Most Powerful Women in Banking, US Banker, 2009, 2010. Mem.: Consumers Bankers Assn. (bd. dirs. 2008—). Office: BBVA Compass 15 20th St S Birmingham AL 35233-2011

BROWN, STEPHEN F., health facility administrator; BS, U. Ala. Joined Am. Med. Internat., 1976; CIO Am. Med. Internat. (now Tenet Healthcare Corp.), 1990—95; sr. exec. v.p., CIO Tenet Healthcare Corp., Dallas, 1995—99, exec. v.p., CIO, 1999—. Active The Wharton Sch., Info. Week mag., CEO mag., The Healthcare Collaboration Group, Sheldon I. Dorenfest and Assocs. Consulting; mem. adv. bd. Nat. Health Founds. Ctr. for Health Info. Tech. Contbg. author: Financial Information Systems Manual, 1992. Office: Tenet Healthcare Corp 13737 Noel Rd Ste 100 Dallas TX 75240

BROWN, STEPHEN H., lobbyist; BA, Am. U., Washington, 1977. Counsel to Steve Boucher US House of Representatives, Washington, chief of staff to Ken Bentsen, polit. advisor to minority leader Richard Gephardt, 2000—01; lobbyist Vorys, Sater, Seymour and Pease, LLP, 1998—2001; sr. v.p., counsel Dutko Group, 2001—07; v.p. fed. govt. affairs Tesoro Petroleum Corp., 2007—. Named one of Washington's Top Lobbyists, The Hill, 2010. Office: Tesoro Petroleum Corp 19100 Ridgewood Pky San Antonio TX 78259

BROWN, STEPHEN IRA, mathematics and philosophy of education professor emeritus; b. Bklyn., July 14, 1938; s. Milton Frank and Ruth (Mittman) B.; m. Eileen Thaler, June 12, 1960; children: Jordan David, Sharon Jean. AB, Columbia Coll., 1960; MA in Teaching (Sloan fellow 1960-61), Harvard U., 1961, Ed.D., 1967. Instr. math. and edn. Simmons Coll., Boston, 1962-65; asst. prof. edn. Harvard U., 1966-72; vis. prof. Hebrew U., Jerusalem, 1970-71; asso. prof. Syracuse U., NY, 1972—73; mem. faculty SUNY, Buffalo, 1973-98, prof. math. edn., 1979-98, prof. philosophy of edn., 1982-98, prof. emeritus, 1998—. Vis. prof. U. Ga., Athens, 1979-80; vis. scholar Harvard U., Cambridge, Mass., 1993-94; participant ethics workshops Coll. Jewish Studies, Buffalo, 1974-76. Author: Some Prime Comparisions, 1978, Student Generations, 1987, Posing Mathematically, 1996, Reconstructing School Mathematics: Problems with Problems and the Real World, 2001, Educational Transformations: The Influences of Stephen I. Brown, 2006; co-editor (Francis Rosamond & Larry Copes): The Art of Problem Posing, 1983, rev. edit., 2005; co-author: Mathematics, Pedagogy and Secondary Teacher Education, 1996; co-editor: Progresssive Education: A Movement and Its Professional Journal, 1988, Problem Posing: Reflections and Applications, 1993; editor: Creative Problem Solving, 1989; mem. rev. bd. Ednl. Theory, 1983-87; mem. editl. bd. Math. Tchr., 1977-80, For Learning of Math., 1980-97; mem. adv. bd. Humanistic Math. Network Jour., 1995-2003; contbr. articles to profl. jours. Mem. adv. council Inst. Jewish Life, 1973-75. Grantee Dewey Found., 1979-80, NSF, 1983-86, 90-97; John Dewey sr. fellow, 1986-87, Ednl. Advancement Found., 2006-10. Fellow Philosophy Edn. Soc.; mem. John Dewey Soc. (bd. dirs. 1976-78), Math. Assn. Am., Nat. Council Tchrs. Math., Phi Beta Kappa, Phi Delta Kappa.

BROWN, TERRY R., state legislator; BA, Northwestern State U., Natchitoches, La. Ret. La. Dept. Transp. and Devel.; mem. Dist. 22 La. House of Reps., Baton Rogue, 2012—. Independent. Office: La House of Reps 900 N 3rd St PO Box 94062 Baton Rouge LA 70804 Business E-Mail: browntr@legis.la.gov.

BROWN, TERRY WAYNE, state legislator; b. Columbus, Miss., Mar. 14, 1950; m. Andra Leonar Dobbel; children: Andrew Cody, Charles Randolph, Terry Wayne Jr. Former mem. Convenience Store Bus.; former mem. bd. trustees Eastern Miss. Jr. Coll.; mem. Dist. 40 Miss. House of Reps., 1980—81; mem. Dist. 17 Miss. State Senate, 2004—; gen. ins. agt. Mem.: Columbus-Lowndes C. of C., Lions Club, Exch. Club. Republican. Baptist. Mailing: 22 Hillside Dr Columbus MS 39702 Home Phone: 662-329-3399; Office Phone: 662-386-6732. Office Fax: 601-359-3938; Home Fax: 662-329-3399. Business E-Mail: tbrown@senate.ms.gov.

BROWN, THADDEUS B., professional sports team executive; m. Janice Brown; children: Kennedy, Addison, Nicolette, Chloe. Grad., Colgate U. Founder, pres. Streetball Ptnrs. Internat.; v.p. corp. devel. Houston Rockets/Clutch City Sports & Entertainment, 2001, sr. v.p. sales, mktg. and broadcasting, 2004—06, CEO, 2006—. Office: Houston Rockets Toyota Ctr 110 Polk St Houston TX 77002

BROWN, THEODORE LAWRENCE, chemistry professor; b. Green Bay, Wis., Oct. 15, 1928; s. Lawrence A. and Martha E. (Kedinger) B.; m. Audrey Catherine Brockman, Jan. 6, 1951; children: Mary Margaret, Karen Anne, Jennifer Gerarda, Philip Matthew (dec.), Andrew Lawrence. BS in Chemistry, Ill. Inst. Tech., 1950; PhD, Mich. State U., 1956. Mem. faculty U. Ill., Urbana, 1956—, prof. chemistry, 1965-93, prof. chemistry emeritus, 1993—, vice chancellor for rsch., dean Grad. Coll., 1980-86, dir. Beckman Inst. for Advanced Sci. and Tech., 1987-93. Vis. scientist Internat. Meteorol. Inst., Stockholm, 1972; Boomer lectr. U. Alta., Edmonton, Can., 1975; Firth vis. prof. U. Sheffield, Eng., 1977; mem. bd. govs. Argonne Nat. Lab., 1982-88, Mercy Hosp., Urbana, 1985-89, Chem. Abstracts Svc., 1991-96, Arnold and Mabel Beckman Found., 1994-2008, Am. Chem. Soc. Pub., 1996-2001 Author: (with R.S. Drago) Experiments in General Chemistry, 3d edit., 1970, General Chemistry, 2d edit., 1968, Energy and the Environment, 1971, (with H.E. LeMay B.E. Bursten C.J. Murphy, P.A. Woodward and Mathew W. Staltzfus) Chemistry: The Central Science, 1977, 13th edit., 2014, Making Truth: Metaphor in Science, 2003; Imperfect Oracle: The Epistemic and Moral Authority of Science, 2009, Bridging Divides: The Origins of The Beckman Institute at Illinois, 2009; assoc. editor Inorganic Chemistry, 1969-78; contbr. articles to profl. publs. Mem. Govt.-Univ.-Industry Roundtable Coun., 1989-94; bd. dirs. Champaign County Opportunities Industrialization Ctr., 1970-79, chmn. bd. dirs., 1975-78. With USN, 1950-53. Sloan rsch. fellow, 1962-66, NSF sr. postdoctoral fellow, 1964-65, Guggenheim fellow, 1979. Fellow AAAS, Am. Acad. Arts and Scis., Am. Chem. Soc. (award in inorganic chemistry 1972, award for disting. svc. in advancement of inorganic chemistry 1993, Harry and Carol Mosher award, 2008); mem. Philosophy Sci. Assn., Sigma Xi, Alpha Chi Sigma. Avocations: films, literature. Home: 26455 S Tamiami Trl Ste 5208 Bonita Springs FL 34134-7842 Personal E-mail: tlbrown1@earthlink.net.

BROWN, THOMAS CARTMEL, JR., lawyer; b. Marion, Va., June 20, 1945; m. Sally Guy Lynch; children: Preston, Taylor. AB, Davidson Coll., 1967; JD, U. Va., 1970. Bar: Va 1971. Assoc. Boothe, Prichard & Dudley, Alexandria, Va., 1971-76, ptnr., 1976-86, McGuireWoods LLP and predecessors, McLean, Va., 1986—. Lawyers com. Nat. Ctr. State Cts., 1993—2003, Warren E. Burger Soc.; sec., gen counsel Potomac KnowledgeWay, 1995—99; chmn. bd. dir. No. Va. Health Found., 2006—08. Mem. Va. Child-Day Coun., Richmond, 1987—91, No. Va. Roundtable, 1995—2001; pres. Alexandria Libr. Co., 2002—04; bd. visitors Davidson Coll., 2006—; mem. exec. bd. Nat. Capital Area Coun. Boy Scouts Am., 2002—07. Fellow: Va. Law Found. (bd. dirs. 1997—2005, pres. 2003), Am. Bar Found.; mem.: Va. State Bar (chmn. bus. law sect. 1987—88, chmn. health law sect. 2002—03), Va. Bar Assn. (pres. 1992), Omicron Delta Kappa. Office: McGuireWoods LLP 1750 Tysons Blvd Ste 1800 Mc Lean VA 22102-4231 Home Phone: 703-370-1963; Office Phone: 703-712-5393. Business E-Mail: tbrown@mcguirewoods.com.

BROWN, TOMMIE FLORENCE F., state legislator, social work educator; b. Rome, Ga., June 25, 1934; d. Phillip and Mary Louise (Murden) B. BA, Dillard Univ., 1957; MSW, Washington Univ., St. Louis, 1964; DSW, Columbia Univ., 1984. Social svc. supr. Tenn. Dept. Pub. Welfare, Chattanooga, 1964-67, dir. tng., 1967-71; asst. prof. sociology Univ. Tenn., Chattanooga, 1971-73, head social work dept., 1973-82, UC Found. assoc. prof. social work, ret.; mem. Dist. 28 Tenn. House of Reps., Nashville, 1992—. Named Nat. Social Worker of Yr., NASW, 1971. Democrat. Baptist. Office: Tenn Gen Assembly Legislative Plz Ste 36 Nashville TN 37243-0128 Mailing: 603 N Highland Park Chattanooga TN 37404 Office Phone: 615-741-4374. Office Fax: 615-253-0203. Business E-Mail: rep.tommie.brown@capitol.tn.gov.

BROWN, TREG S., automotive executive; Asst. pres. customer fin. svcs. Genuine Parts Co., v.p. customer fin. svcs., v.p. planning and acquisitions. Mem.: ACG Atlanta. Office: Genuine Parts Co 2999 Cir 75 Pky Atlanta GA 30339 Office Phone: 770-953-1700. Office Fax: 770-956-2211. Business E-Mail: treg_brown@genpt.com.

BROWN, TROY ANDERSON, JR., retired electric power industry executive; b. Tampa, Fla., July 7, 1934; s. Troy Anderson and Valerie Aldona (Mohler) B.; m. Jean Thompson, Aug. 22, 1962; children: Troy Anderson, III, George Albert, Douglas Alan. AB, Harvard U., 1956; JD, U. N.C., 1959. Bar: Fla. bar 1959. With Raybro Electric Supplies Inc., Tampa, 1960-99, exec. v.p., 1964-74, pres., 1974-99. Dir. Exchange Nat. Bank, 1978—83, 1st Fla. Bank, 1983—90, 1st Fla. Holding, 1989—91; bd. dirs. founding dir. Bay Cities Bank, 1999—. Mem. exec. com. Tampa Com. 100, 1975, U. South Fla. Found., 1974-75; chmn. bd. fellows U. Tampa, 1978; bd. dirs., vice chmn. Tampa Mus., 1977-79; bd. dirs. Tampa YMCA, 1977-79, Tampa Marine Inst., 1976-77. With USAFR, 1959. Mem.: Tampa Mchts. Assn. (bd. dirs. 1980), Pres. Round Table Tampa (pres. 1971), Exch. Club Tampa (pres. 1970), Greater Tampa C. of C. (gov. 1968—74), Nat. Assn. Elec. Distbrs. (bd. dirs. 1989—91), Harvard Club of Fla. (pres. 1984), Tampa Yacht and Country Club (bd. dirs. 1982—83). Episcopalian. Home: 1013 S Skokie St Tampa FL 33629-5237

BROWN, TROY E., state legislator; BS, So. U., New Orleans. CEO Home-Care PCA, LLC; mem. Dist. 2 La. State Senate, 2012—. Democrat. Office: PO Box 974 Napoleonville LA 70390 also: La State Senate 900 N 3rd St Baton Rouge LA 70804 Office Phone: 985-369-3333. Business E-Mail: brownte@legis.la.gov.

BROWN, WARREN JOSEPH, physician; b. Bklyn., July 17, 1924; s. Benjamin Oscar and Angela Marie (Cahill) B.; m. Greet Roos, July 3, 1970; children: Warren James, Robert E., Suzanne J., Annemarie, Eric Jan. Student, Ursinus Coll., 1942-43; BS, Bethany Coll., 1945; MD, Ohio State U., 1949. Diplomate Am. Bd. Family Practice. Intern U.S. Naval Hosp., Long Beach and Oceanside, Calif.; resident Pottstown Hosp., Pa., 1950-51; assoc. Roos Loos Med. Group, Alhambra, Calif., 1951; practice medicine specializing in family practice Largo, Fla., 1953—2004; mem. Sampson NTS, Sampson, NY, Bainbridge NTS, Bainbridge, MD., USN Tng. Unit, Bethany Coll.; Bethesda Naval Hosp. staff USN Tng Unit, Ohio State U., USNH Long Beach, Calif.; staff USNH Santa Margarita Ranch, Oceanside, Calif., USNS Gen Sturgis, USNS Gen. Leroy Eltinge, USNS Gen. Stuart Heintzelman, USNS Gen. Henry Gibbins, USN Station Key West, Fla., hosp. corpsman, med. officer. Sr. civilian flight surgeon FAA, 1964-2004; pres. Aero-Med. Consultants, Inc., Largo, 1969-. Author: Florida's Aviation History, 1980, 2d edit., 1993, Child Yank Over the Rainbow, 1977, Patients' Guide to Medicine, 10th edit., 1987, The World's First Airline: The St. Petersburg-Tampa Airboat Line, 1914, 1981, 2d edit., 1984. Historian Fla. Aviation Hist. Soc., 1978—, pres., 2004-05; chmn. Fla. Aviation Hall of Fame, 2002—: historian St. Petersburg-Clearwater-Tampa Hangar Order of Quiet Birdmen, 1969—. With USN, 1943-45, 49-50, 51-53. With USN, 1943—54. Fellow Am. Acad. Family Physicians; mem. Pinellas County Med. Assn., Fla. Med. Assn., Aircraft Owners and Pilots Assn., Am. Radio Relay League, Med. Amateur Radio Coun. (Southeastern, USA dir.). Avocations: history, aviation, amateur radio. Home: 14607 Brewster Dr Largo FL 33774-4822 Home Phone: 727-595-2773; Office Phone: 727-542-4158. Personal E-mail: warenbrown@aol.com.

BROWN, WILLIAM M., telecommunications industry executive; BS in Mech. Engring., Villanova U., Pa.; MS in Mech. Engring., Villanova U.; MBA, U. Pa., Phila. Project engr. Air Products and Chems. Inc.; sr. engagement mgr. McKinsey and Co.; dir. strategic planning United Technologies Corp., Hartford, Conn., 1997, gen. mgr. replacement components bus., pres. Carrier Transicold, 2001, head Carrier Asia Pacific ops. Conn., 2004—06, pres. UTC Fire & Security Hartford, Conn., 2006—11, sr. v.p. corp. strategy & develop., 2011; dir., pres., CEO Harris Corp., 2011—. Active Easter Seals Capital Region & Ea. Conn.; supporter United Way; bd. dirs. Fire Dept. NY Found.; mem. dean's adv. bd. Villanova U. Coll. Engring. Office: Harris Corporation 1025 W NASA Blvd Melbourne FL 32919-0001

BROWN, WILLIAM SAMUEL, JR., communication sciences and disorders educator; b. Pottstown, Penn., Apr. 25, 1940; s. William Samuel and Elizabeth (Gallager) B.; m. Elaine Kay Whitehouse, Aug. 18, 1962; children: William Samuel III, Allen Reed. MA, SUNY, Buffalo, 1967, PhD, 1969. Speech therapist Crawford Cty. Schools, Meadville, Pa., 1962-65; rsch. asst. SUNY, Buffalo, 1965-68; prof. U. Fla., Gainesville, Fla., 1970—. Contrib. numerous articles to sci. jours. Postdoctoral fellow U. Fla, Gainsville, 1968-70. Fellow Internat. Soc. Phonetic Sci. (coun. rep. 1980—), Am. Speech-Lang.-Hearing Assn., Acoustical Soc. Am.; mem. Am. Assn. Phonetic Sci. (exec. sec. 1980—). Republican. Presbyterian. Office: U Fla IASCP Dauer 63 Gainesville FL 32611 Business E-Mail: wsbrown@csd.ufl.edu.

BROWN, WILLIAM VIRGIL, internal medicine educator; b. Royston, Ga., Sept. 25, 1938; m. Alice Brown; 2 children. BA in Physics and Chemistry, Emory U., 1960; MD, Yale U., 1964. Diplomate Am. Bd. Internal Medicine, Am. Bd. Endocrinology. Intern, asst. resident Osler Med. Svc. Johns Hopkins Hosp., Balt., 1964—66; clin. assoc. Nat. Heart and Lung Inst., Bethesda, Md., 1966—69; fellow in endocrinology and metabolism Yale-New Haven Hosp., 1969—70; asst. prof. medicine U. Calif. Dept. Medicine, San Diego, 1970—74, assoc. prof. medicine, 1974—78; dir. lipid rsch. clinic U. Calif., San Diego, 1972—78; prof. medicine Mt. Sinai Sch. Medicine, NYC, 1978—87, dir. divsn. arteriosclerosis and metabolism, 1978—87; pres., CEO Medlantic Rsch. Found., Washington, 1987—91; Charles Howard Candler prof. internal medicine, dir. divsn. arteriosclerosis and lipid metabolism Emory U., Atlanta, 1991—2009, pres. faculty coun. and univ. senate, 1998—99, prof. medicine emeritus Sch. Medicine, 2009—; chief of medicine Atlanta VA Hosp., 1998—2009. Chmn. Gordon Conf. on Lipid Metabolism, 1984; metabolism study sect. NIH, 1985; pres. Am. Bd. Clin. Lipidology, 2004—. Editor: Jour. Clinical Lipidology, 2007—. Fellow, Alexander von Humboldt. Master: ACP; mem.: Internat. Atherosclerosis Soc. (pres. 2009—13), Nat.

Lipid Assn. (pres. 2002—03), Am. Bd. Bioanalysis (high-complexity clin. lab. dir.), Am. Soc. Exptl. Biology, Am. Soc. Clin. Investigation, Am. Fedn. Clin. Rsch., Am. Heart Assn. (mem. physiology study sect. 1978—80, mem. credentials com. aterioselerosis coun. 1978—80, chmn. credentials com. arteriosclerosis coun. 1979—82, mem. nutrition com. 1981—86, mem. several rsch. con., chmn. nutrition com. 1982—86, bd. dirs. 1983, vice chmn. edn. and cmty. program com., nat. pres. 1991—92, gold heart award 1996, R. Bruce Logue award 2000, fellow arteriosclerosis coun., fellow epidemiology and preventive cardiology coun., numerous others), Alpha Omega Alpha, Phi Beta Kappa. Achievements include research in structure and metabolism of lipoproteins; lipolytic enzymes, including their molecular and kinetic characteristics, diagnosis and treatment of the hyperlipoproteinemias; the relationship of lipoprotein metabolism to atheromatous vascular disorders. Office: 3208 Habersham Rd Atlanta GA 30305

BROWNE, ANN APRIL, purchasing manager; b. Washington, Apr. 9, 1945; d. Benjamin and Sarah (Barr) Mudrick. BA in Bus. Mgmt., Eckerd Coll., 1987. Cert. purchasing mgr.; accredited purchasing practitioner. Purchasing mgr. Gen. Kinetics, Rockville, Md., 1972-73; assoc. buyer Control Data Corp., Rockville, 1973-74; outside sales rep. Mid Atlantic Industries, Bladensburg, Md., 1974, U.S. C. of C., San Antonio, 1975; inside sales coord. Frabimore Equipment & Controls, Inc., Elk Grove Village, Ill., 1976-77; customer svc. rep. Viracon, Inc., Bensenville, Ill., 1977; purchasing mgr. Vectrol div. Westinghouse Elec. Corp., Oldsmar, Fla., 1978-83; purchasing agt. Helen Ellis Meml. Hosp., Tarpon Springs, Fla., 1987—2001; sr. purchasing specialist St. Petersburg Coll., Pinellas Park, Fla., 2001—. Nat. Assn. Purchasing Mgmt. (cert.), Phi Theta Kappa. Avocations: photography, weightlifting, reading, spectator sports.

BROWNE, DONALD VICTOR, retired broadcast executive; b. Passaic, NJ, May 16, 1943; s. Donald James and Roseanna (Hopp) Browne; m. Maria Junquera, May 9, 1981; children: Christopher Barret, Ryan Alexander. BS in Mktg., Fairleigh Dickinson U., 1971. Traffic expediter CBS News, NYC, 1967-70, prodr., 1970-71, reporter, assignment editor, 1971-75, prodr., dep. bur. chief Atlanta, 1975-79; bur. chief, Fla., Latin America NBC News, Miami, Fla., 1979-88, bur. chief, Latin America, Southeast US, 1988-89, exec. news dir. NYC, 1989-90, exec. v.p., 1990-93; pres., gen. mgr. Sta. WTVJ-TV, NBC, Miami, 1993—2003; COO Telemundo Network, Hialeah, Fla., 2003—05, pres., CEO, 2005—11. With USCG, 1967—73.

BROWNE, FREDERICK DOUGLAS, physiologist, educator; b. Springfield, Ohio, June 3, 1929; s. Charles David and Ruth Noami Browne; m. Joyce Louise Burton, June 11, 1955; children: Fred, Sharon, Michael, Regina, Stephan, Monica. BS, U. Dayton, Ohio, 1956; MS, Miami U., Oxford, Ohio, 1958; postgrad., Case Western Res. U., Cleve., 1963-66; postgrad. in Instrn. Anatomy, Coll. Medicine Case Western U., 1966; EdD, Nova U., Fort Lauderdale, Fla., 1981. Ordained permanent deacon Maronite Cath. Ch., 1992. Rschr. artificial organs and exptl. heart surgery Cleve. Clinic, 1958-63; predoctoral fellow Coll. Medicine Case Western Res. U., Cleve., 1963-66; instr. sci. Cleve. Bd. Edn., 1966-69; asst. prof. St. John's Coll., Cleve., 1969-73; instr. Sch. Anesthesia Cleve. Clinic, 1973-74; prof. anatomy and physiology Cuyahoga C.C., Warrensville, Ohio, 1973-92; chair/CEO Rameso, Inc., Copley, Ohio, 1993—. Contbr. articles to profl. jours. Pres., Bd. Cath. Edn., Diocese of Cleve., 1972-73; chmn. Civil Svc. Commn. Warrensville Heights, Ohio, 1970-72; councilman Warrensville Heights, 1982-85; bd. dirs. Summit County Cath. Social Svc.; parish rep. Boy Scouts Am., Cuyahoga County, 1958-63; mem. precinct com., AMA minority affairs com., Rep. Nat. Conv., 2004; pres. Holy Name Soc., St. Cecilia Cath. Ch., 1958-63. 2d lt. U.S. Army, 1952-54. NIH fellow, 1963-66, nominee Dr. of Yr. Summit County, 2007. Mem. AAUP, AMA, NRC, Nat. Assn. Advancement Sci., N.Y. Acad. Scis., Ohio Coll. Biology Tchrs. Assn., Secular Franciscan, Am. Legion, Knights of Columbus, Alpha Phi Alpha. Republican. Home and Office: 5612 Greenevers Dr Raleigh NC 27613 Personal E-mail: hrtdr02@roadrunner.com.

BROWNE, JAMES DALE, otolaryngologist, educator; BS, Mercer U., 1978; MD, Med. Coll. Of Ga., 1982. Diplomate Am. Bd. Otolaryngology. Intern surgery NC Bapt. Hosp., 1983, resident otolaryngology, 1987; fellow otolaryngology Univ. Zurich Med. Fac-Switzerland, 1991; James A. Harrill prof. and chmn. dept. of otolaryngology-head and neck surgery Wake Forest Sch. of Medicine. Fellow: ACS; mem.: AMA, Ga. Med. Assn., Forsyth-Davie-Stokes Med. Soc., Am. Neurotological Soc., Am. Broncho-Esophagological Assn., Am. Acad. of Otolaryngology-Head and Neck Surgery. Office: Wake Forest Baptist Medical Center Medical Center Blvd Winston Salem NC 27157 Office Phone: 336-716-2011.

BROWNE, RICHARD HAROLD, statistician, consultant; b. St. Louis, Sept. 24, 1946; s. Basil Campbell and Evelyn Beatrice (Biver) B.; m. Dennise Marie Richardson, Aug. 10, 1970. AS, Meramec C.C., 1966; BS, U. Mo.-Rolla, 1968; MS, Okla. State U., 1970, PhD, 1973. Statistician M.D. Anderson Hosp., Houston, 1971-72; asst. prof. U. Tex. Health Sci. Ctr., Dallas, 1973-79; statistician Criterion Inc., Dallas, 1979-81; sr. mgmt. analyst Sun Co., Dallas, 1981-83; sr. biostatistician Teams, Inc., Dallas, 1983-85; sr. cons. RHB Cons. Svcs., Dallas, 1979—; rsch. program adminstr. Tex. Scottish Rite Hosp, Dallas, 1988—2004, dir. divsn. rsch. support, 2004—. Adj. asst. prof. So. Meth. U., Dallas, 1974-77, Health Sci. Ctr., U. Tex.-Dallas, 1979-82; adj. assoc. prof. Tex. Women's U., Dallas, 1984-95; asst. prof. U. Tex. Southwestern Med. Ctr., 1997—. Contbr. articles to profl. jours. Mem. Am. Statis. Assn. (pres. North Tex. chpt.), Nat. Coun. Univ. Rsch. Adminstrs., North Tex. SAS Users Group, Alzheimers Assn. (group leader), Pediatric Orthopedic Soc. N.Am., Phi Kappa Phi. Republican. Avocation: photography. Home: 12045 Inwood Rd Dallas TX 75244-8016 Business E-Mail: rich@tsrh.org.

BROWNELL, BRADLEY ROBERT, men's college basketball coach; b. Evansville, Ind., Nov. 15, 1968; B, DePauw U., Greencastle, Ind., 1991; M, U. Indpls., 1994. Grad. asst. coach U. Evansville Purple Aces, 1991—92; asst. coach U. Indpls. Greyhounds, 1992—94; asst. coach, assoc. head coach U. NC Wilmington Seahawks, 1994—2002, head basketball coach, 2002—06, Wright State U. Raiders, 2006—10, Clemson U. Tigers, 2010—. Named Coach of Yr., Colonial Athletic Assn., 2003, 2006, Mid-Major Coach of Yr., Foxsports.com, 2006, Dist. 10 Coach of Yr., Nat. Assn. Basketball Coaches, 2007; finalist Hugh Durham Coach of Yr. award, 2007. Office: Clemson University Basketball Jervey Athletic Ctr PO Box 31 Clemson SC 29633-0031

BROWNELL, EDWIN ROWLAND, retired banker, civil engineer, land surveyor; b. Tampa, Fla., Sept. 19, 1924; s. Clarence DeWolf and Helen Lucy (Hill) B.; m. Helen Marie Kegel, Jan. 22, 1948 (dec. Apr. 1967); 1 child, Nancy (dec. Apr. 2013); m. Blanche Rosina Parisi, Dec. 26, 1967; children: Elizabeth (dec. Mar. 2012), Elaine, Evelyn. BCE, U. Fla., 1947. Registered profl. surveyor, Fla., Ark., Ga., Miss., Nev., N.D., S.D., S.C., Tenn., W.Va. Cadastral engr. City of Miami, Fla., 1948-53; pres., CEO, chmn. E.R. Brownell & Assocs., Inc., Miami, 1953-93, real estate salesman, 1975—2012; founding dir. Total Bank, 1983—85, Am.'s Bank, 1980—83; pres., chief exec. officer, chmn. Brickellbanc Savs. Assn., Miami, 1985-89, also bd. dirs.; pres. Tri-County Engring. Co., 1983-89, Naples Title and Abstract Co., Fla., 1st Title and Abstract Co. Chmn. surveying com. Geomatics Surv. Com.U. Fla., Gainesville, 1974—2012, mem. pres.'s coun.; mem. nat. engring. degree accreditation team Nat. Coun. Engring. Examiners, Balt., Md., 1985-95, mem. team evaluating engring. readiness U.S. Armed Forces, 1980-81; chmn. engring. adv. com. Fla. Bd. Regents, Tallahassee, 1982-85; chmn., pres., CEO Bricbell Bank, 1990, vice-chmn. legal grievance com. Fla. Bar 11th Dist., 1992-94. Elected county surveyor State of Fla., Dade County, 1956-60; chmn. Zoning Bd. Adjustment, Coral Gables, Fla., 1978-87; chmn. Coral Gables Planning and Zoning Bd., 1987-95; mem. Coral Gables Code Enforcement Bd., 1995-97, City of Coral Gables Historic Preservation Com., 1997, City of Coral Gables Constrn. Regulation Bd., 1997-05, 07—; emergency preparation com. City of Coral Gables, 1995-2007; bd. dirs. Boys Club of Miami, 1980-83, Salvation Army South Fla., dir., 1990-94. Named Man of Yr., Dade County, Fla., 1989. Master (life) Am. Contract Bridge League (nat. mem; Silver award); fellow Am. Congress Surveying and Mapping (hon. life, pres. 1980-81, Surveying Excellence award 1977, Miami Man Yr. 1990, Presdl. award 1994, U. Fla. 1st Profl. Excellence in Geomatics award, 2013), NSPE, Nat. Soc. Profl. Surveyors (pres. 1978-79), Fla. Surveying and Mapping Soc. (hon., life), Profl. Surveyors and Mappers (pres. 1981), Fla. Soc. Profl. Land Surveyors (hon. life mem., Fla. Land Surveyor of Yr. 1973, pres. 1972, pres. Dade County chpt. 1965-69, hon., life mem. Dade County chpt. 1993); mem. AIA, NSF, Profl. Surveyors of Fla. (bd. dirs., chmn. 1993-94), Am. Soc. Photogrammetry and Remote Sensing (Presdl. citation 1982, 91, Merit award 1992), Am. Soc. Photogrammetry Found. (vice chmn. 1985-91), Am. Mil. Engrs., Am. Planning Assn., Internat. Geog. Info. Found. (vice-chmn.), Miami Bd. Realtors, Fla. Engring. Soc. (bd. dirs. 1992-94), Fla. Planning and Zoning Assn. (S. Fla. chpt.), Fla. Assn. Cadastral Mappers, Bus. Inc., Sierra Club (pres. 1977), Com. of 100, Bus. Inc., Granada Golf Assn., 10th Holers Golf Assn. (treas. 1995-96, pres. 1996-97, pres. 2003-04, bd. dirs. 2006-09), Coral Gables Country Club Fleet, Coral Gables 30 Yr. Club, Coral Gables Fin. Club (pres. 1998-01), U. Miami Yacht Club, Century Club Coral Gables (exec. sec., treas. 1993-96), Coral Gables Country Club (dir., pres. 1991-97, chmn., vice chmn. found. 1992-94, pres. fin. club 1998-02), Riviera Country Club (fin. com., house commn., duplicate bridge com.), Holly Hills Country Club (NC), Computer Club Coral Gables (bd. dirs.), U. Miami Sailing Club, Kiwanis (pres. Southwest Miami chpt. 1979-81), Elks, Duplicate Bridge Silver Life Master, Lambda Alpha Internat., Kappa Alpha Fraternity. Republican. Roman Catholic. Avocations: golf, bridge, travel. Home: 1207 Sorolla Ave Coral Gables FL 33134-3515 Personal E-mail: ebrow40862@aol.com.

BROWNELL, KELLY DAVID, dean, psychologist, educator; b. Evansville, Ind., Oct. 31, 1951; s. Arnold Buffum and Margaret Elizabeth (Egly) Brownell; m. Mary Jo Gabriele, Aug. 20, 1977; children: Matthew Joseph, Kevin David, Kristy Elizabeth. BA, Purdue U., 1973; PhD, Rutgers U., 1977. Postdoctoral fellow Brown U., Providence, 1977; from asst. prof. to assoc. prof. U. Pa., Phila., 1977—87, prof., 1987-90; prof. psychology Yale U., New Haven, 1991—, dir. Yale Ctr. Eating and Weight Disorders, 1994-2000, prof. epidemiology and pub. health, 2003—06, chair dept. psychology, 2003—06, dir. Rudd Ctr. for Food Policy and Obesity, 2005—08, master, Silliman Coll.; dean Sanford Sch. Pub. Policy, prof. pub. policy, psychology, and neuroscience Duke U., Durham, NC, 2013—. Dir. Rudd Ctr. Food Policy and Obesity; bd. dirs. Duke Global Health Inst. Author: (books) Handbook of Eating Disorders, 1986, Handbook of Behavioral Medicine, 1988, Eating Disorders in Athletes, 1991, Eating Disorders and Obesity, 1995, vol. 2, 2002, Behavioral Medicine and Women, 1998, Food Fight, 2004; contbr. articles to profl. jours. Recipient Cattell award, N.Y. Acad. Scis., 1978, Choice award, ALA, 1989, Disting. Alumni award, Purdue U., 2001; named one of World's 100 Most Influential People, Time Mag., 2006. Fellow: APA (pres. divsn. health psychology 1989—90), Acad. Behavioral Medicine Rsch., Soc. Behavioral Medicine (pres. 1988—89); mem.: Inst. of Medicine, Assn. Advancement Behavior Therapy (pres. 1988—89). Office: Sanford School of Public Policy Duke Box 90239 Durham NC 27708-0239 Office Phone: 919-613-7309. E-mail: kelly.brownell@duke.edu.*

BROWNING, CHRISTOPHER, lawyer; m. Margaret Browning; 2 children. B, JD, U. NC, Chapel Hill. Law clk. to Hon. James C. Hill US Ct. Appeals (11th Cir.); atty. Hunton & Williams, Raleigh, NC, Office of Atty. Gen., NC, solicitor gen. NC, 2004—. Mem.: Phi Beta Kappa. Office: NC Atty Generals Office 114 W Edenton St 9001 Mail Svc Raleigh NC 27699-9000 Office Phone: 919-716-6900. Business E-Mail: cbrowning@ncdoj.gov.

BROWNING, CHRISTOPHER R., historian, educator; b. Durham, NC, May 22, 1944; s. Robert Willard and Eleanor (Oechsli) B.; m. Jennifer Jane Horn; children: Kathryn, Anne. BA, Oberlin Coll., 1967; MA, U. Wis., 1968, PhD, 1975. Instr. history Allegheny Coll., Meadville, Pa., 1969-71; asst. prof. history Pacific Luth. U., Tacoma, 1974-79, assoc. prof., 1979-84, prof., 1984-97, disting. univ. prof., 1997-99; Frank Porter Graham prof. history U. NC, Chapel Hill, 1999—. J.B. and Maurice C. Shapiro sr. scholar in residence U.S. Holocaust Mus., 1996, Ina Levine scholar, 2002-03; George Macaulay Trevelyan lectr. Cambridge U., 1999, Bertelsmann lectr., Oxford U., 2007; George L. Mosse lectr. U. Wis., Madison, 2002. Author: The Final Solution and the German Foreign Office, 1978, Fateful Months, 1985, Ordinary Men, 1992 (Nat. Jewish Book award 1993), The Path to Genocide, 1992, Nazi Policy, Jewish Workers, German Killers, 2000, Collected Memories: Holocaust History and Post-War Testimony, 2003, The Origins of the Final Solution, 2004 (Nat. Jewish Book award, 2004), Remembering Survival: Inside a Nazi Slave Labor Camp, 2010 (Nat. Jewish Book award, 2011, Yad Vashem Internat. Book prize, 2012); co-editor, Every Day Lasts a Year, 2007. Woodrow Wilson fellow, 1967-68, Alexander von Humboldt fellow, Germany, 1980-81, Forschungspreis, 2003; Fulbright rsch. fellow, Israel, 1989, Inst. for Advanced Studies fellow, Princeton, NJ, 1995. Fellow: Nat. Human Ctr., Am. Acad. Arts and Scis. Office: U NC Dept History Chapel Hill NC 27599-0001

BROWNING, GRAYSON DOUGLAS, philosophy educator; b. Seminole, Okla., Mar. 7, 1929; s. Grayson Douglas and Dorothea (Cook) B.; m. Becky Beck, July 15, 1972; children by previous marriage— Tony Louis, Luke Matthew, Lauren Beth. BA, U. Tex., Austin, 1954, MA, 1955, PhD, 1958. Instr., asst. prof., assoc. prof., prof. U. Miami, Coral Gables, Fla., 1958-69; vis. instr. U. Tex., Austin, summer 1963, vis. prof., 1969-71, prof. philosophy, 1971—98, prof. emeritus, 1998—, chmn. dept. philosophy, 1972-76. Author: Act and Agent, 1964, Poems and Visions, 1965, Ontology and the Practical Arena, 1990; editor: Philosophers of Process, 1965, 2d rev. edit., 1998; contbr. articles to profl. jours., contbr. poems to anthology. Served with USAF, 1948-52. Mem. Am. Philos. Assn., Southwestern Philos. Assn. (pres. 1977), Fla. Philos. Assn. (pres. 1967), So. Soc. for Philosophy and Psychology (pres. 1972), Soc. for Advancement of Am. Philosophy. Home: 211 Faubion Dr Georgetown TX 78628-9604

BROWNING, JAY D., energy executive, lawyer; BBA in Fin., Tex. Tech. U., MBA, JD, Tex. Tech. U. Atty. corp./transactional divsn. Baker & Botts, LLP, Austin, Tex.; assoc. corp. and securities divsn. Akin, Gump, Strauss, Hauer & Feld, LLP, San Antonio; various legal positions Valero Energy Corp., San Antonio, 1993, corp. sec., mng. atty. corp. law, v.p. corp. law, 2002—06, sr. v.p., sec., 2006, corp. sr. v.p., general counsel, 2013—; sr. v.p., general counsel Valero Energy Partners GP LLC, San Antonio, 2013—; general ptnr. Valero Energy Partners LP, 2013—. Office: Valero Energy Corpn PO Box 696000 San Antonio TX 78269-6000*

BROWNING, JONATHAN, automotive executive; b. Tauton, England, June 21, 1959; Degree in Indsl. Econs., Nottingham U., Eng.; MBA, Duke U., Durham, NC. With Vauxhall Motors Ltd., England, 1981; mng. dir. GM Turkey, 1992—93; exec. dir. mktg. GM Europe, Zurich, Switzerland, 1993—97, v.p. sales, mktg. & aftersales, 2001—08; head European mktg. to mng. dir. Jaguar Cars Ltd. Ford Motor Co., England, 1997—2001; v.p. global sales, svc. & mktg. GM Corp., Detroit, 2008—09; global head nat. sales companies Volkswagen Group of America, Herndon, Va., 2010, CEO, 2010—. Chmn. Vauxhall Motors Ltd., 2006—08. Office: Volkswagon Group of America 2200 Ferdinand Porsche Dr Herndon VA 20171 Office Phone: 703-364-7000.

BROWNING, KEITH D., automotive executive; Contr. we. coast div. Circuit City, 1984—87, asst. corp. contr., 1987—90, corp. contr., 1990—96; exec. v.p., CFO CarMax Inc., Richmond, Va., 1996—2010; exec. v.p. fin. CarMax, Inc., Richmond, Va., 2010—. Office: CarMax Inc 12800 Tuckahoe Creek Pkwy Richmond VA 23238-1115

BROWNING, NICKEY REED, state legislator; b. Pontotoc, Miss., Nov. 19, 1951; m. Brenda Smithey; children: Tracey, Jason, Brea Klair. Mem. Dist. 3 Miss. State Senate, 1996—; businessman. Mem.: Lions Club. Democrat. Methodist. Address: PO Box 1051 Pontotoc MS 38863 Home Phone: 662-489-5979. Fax: 601-359-3938. Business E-Mail: nbrowning@senate.ms.gov.

BROWNING, PETER CRANE, manufacturing executive; b. Boston, Sept. 2, 1941; s. Ralph Leslie and Nancy (Crane) Browning; m. Carole Ann Shegog, Dec. 14, 1963 (div. 1974); children: Christina, Jennifer; m. Kathryn Anne Klucharich, July 27, 1974; children: Kimberley, Peter. AB in History, Colgate U., Hamilton, NY, 1963; MBA, U. Chgo., 1976. Salesman, mktg. mgr. White Cap Divsn. Continental Can, Northbrook, Ill., 1964-75; mgr. mktg. Conally Venture divsn. Continental Can, 1975-79; gen. mktg., sales mgr. Bondware Divsn. Continental Can, 1979-81, v.p., gen. mgr., 1981-84; v.p. gen. mgr. White Cap. divsn. Continental Can, 1984-86, exec. v.p., oper. officer, 1987-89; pres. Gold Bond Bldg. Products Divsn. Nat. Gypsum Co., Charlotte, 1989-90; pres., chmn. and CEO National Gypsum Co., Charlotte, 1990-93; exec. v.p. Sonoco Products Co., Hartsville, SC, 1993-96, COO, 1996-98, pres., CEO, 1996—2000; chmn. bd. dirs. Nucor Corp., 2000—06, lead dir., 2006—; mng. dir. Peter C. Browning & Assocs., LLC, 2009—. Bd. dirs. Lowe's Companies, Inc., 1998—, Acuity Brands, Inc., 2001—, ENPRO Industries Inc., 2002—; dean McColl Grad. Sch. Bus. Queens U., Charlotte, 2002—06; bd. dirs. Nucor Corp., 2006—, Wachovia Corp., 2008—09, Phoenix Companies, Inc., 2008—09. Life mem. coun. U. Chgo. Grad. Sch. Mem.: DeBordieu Country Club, Quail Hollow Country Club. Republican. Episcopalian. Avocations: mountain climbing, running, reading. Office: Peter C Browning & Associates LLC ? 2038 Providence Rd Charlotte NC 28211 Office Phone: 704-442-8559. Office Fax: 704-442-5334. Business E-Mail: Peter@peterbrowning.com.

BROWNLEE, JOHN LESLIE, lawyer, former prosecutor; b. 1965; s. Les and Nancy Brownlee; m. Lee Ann Necessary, Aug. 30, 1997; children: Thompson Ann, Catherine Harris. BA, Washington and Lee U., 1987; MBA, Golden Gate U.; JD, Coll. William and Mary, 1994. Law clk. to Hon. Samuel G. Wilson US Dist. Ct. (we. dist.) Va., 1994—96; asst. US atty. DC US Dept. Justice, 1997—2001, US atty. (we. dist.) Va. Roanoke, Va., 2001—08; assoc. Woods, Rogers and Hazelgrove, Richmond, Va., 2001; ptnr. Holland & Knight LLP, 2009—. Adj. prof. law U. Va. Sch. Law. Lt. US Army, 1987—91, capt. JAG USAR, 1991—. Recipient Spl. Achievement for Sustained Superior Performance, US Dept. Justice, 2000, Award for Excellence, President's Coun. on Integrity & Efficiency, 2007, Chief's award, IRS Criminal Investigation Divsn., US Dept. Treasury. Mem.: Va. State Bar Assn. Office: Holland & Knight LLP 1600 Tysons Blvd Ste 700 Mc Lean VA 22102 Office Phone: 702-720-8053. E-mail: john.brownlee@hklaw.com.

BROWNLEE, PAULA PIMLOTT, higher education consultant; b. London, June 23, 1934; came to US, 1959; d. John Richard and Alice A. (Ajamian) Pimlott; m. Thomas H. Brownlee, Feb. 10, 1961; children: Kenneth Gainsford, Elizabeth Ann, Clare Louise. BA with honors, Somerville Coll., Oxford U., 1957; MA with honors, Oxford U., Eng., 1957, PhD in Organic Chemistry, 1959. Postdoctoral fellow U. Rochester, NY, 1959-61; rsch. chemist Am. Cyanamid Co., Stamford, Conn., 1961-62; lectr. U. Bridgeport, Conn., 1968-70; asst. prof., then assoc. prof. Rutgers U., NJ, 1970-76, assoc. dean, then acting dean Douglass Coll. NJ, 1972-76; dean faculty, prof. chemistry Union Coll., Schenectady, NY, 1976-81; pres., prof. chemistry Hollins U., Va., 1981-90; pres. Assn. Am. Colls. and Univs., Washington, 1990-98; prin. Pres.' Group, LLC, 1997—2003; founding prin. Nat. Acad. for Acad. Leadership; bd. dirs. Acad. Search Inc., 2010—11. Vice chmn. bd. dirs. Am. Academic Leadership Inst., 2007—11. Contbr. articles to profl. jours., chapters to books. Life trustee U. Rochester. Hon. fellow Somerville Coll., Oxford, Eng., 1996—. Mem. Am. Chem. Soc., Sigma Xi. Avocations: gardening, writing, hiking, art. Personal E-mail: ppbrownlee1@gmail.com.

BROWNLEE, ROBERT CALVIN, pediatrician, educator; b. Due West, S.C., Mar. 13, 1922; s. Robert Calvin and Eleanor Louise (Pressly) B.; m. Judith Frances Irby; children: Eleanor Koets, Susan, Katherine Chambers, Jonathan, Robert Calvin. AB, Erskine Coll., 1943; MD, Vanderbilt U., 1945. Diplomate Am. Bd. Pediat. (pres. 1975), Am. Bd. Family Practice. Intern Vanderbilt U. Hosp., Nashville, 1945-46, resident, 1948-49, U. Va., Charlottesville, 1949-50; chief resident Vanderbilt U., Nashville, 1950-51; practice medicine, specializing in pediat. Christie Pediatric Group, Greenville, SC, 1951-70; dir. pediat. Greenville Hosp. Sys., 1970-75; assoc. exec. sec. Am. Bd. Pediat., Chapel Hill, NC, 1976, exec. sec., 1977-87, pres., 1987-92. Clin. prof. pediat. U. Pa., 1976-78; prof. pediat. U. S.C., 1971-75; clin. prof. U. N.C., 1978-96. Contbr. articles to med. jours. With AUS, 1943-45; with M.C. USAF, 1946-48, 53. Mem. Am. Acad. Pediat., Ambulatory Pediat. Assn. Presbyterian.

BROWNLEE, THOMAS MARSHALL, manufacturing executive; b. Omaha, Nebr., Oct. 11, 1926; s. John Templeton and Reed (Marshall) B.; children: Linda Sue, Thomas John, Curtis Marshall, Reed Ann; m. Lenora A. Hollingsworth, Mar. 31, 1994. BSBA, U. Nebr., 1950. Asst. mgr. Daytona Beach (Fla.) C. of C., 1950, Tampa (Fla.) C. of C., 1952-53; exec. mgr. Tallahassee C. of C., 1953- 58; exec. v.p. Greater Columbia (S.C.) C. of C., 1959-63, Winston-Salem (N.C.) C. of C., 1963-64, Orlando Area (Fla.) C. of C., 1964-78;

chmn. Brownlee Lighting Co., Orlando, 1978—. Mem. energy policy com. Orange County (Fla.) Schs.; mem. Fla. Energy Action Com.; mem. energy com. Nat. League Cities Contbr. articles to profl. jours. Bd. dirs. Loch Haven Art Mus.; bd. dirs. Chamber Inst., U. Ga.; mem. Orlando City Council.; pres. Christian Service Ctrs. Daily Bread. Served with USNR, 1944-46; as 1st lt. AUS, 1951-52. Mem. Fla. Energy Mgmt. Assn. (pres.), Illuminating Engring. Soc. (pres. Ctrl. Fla. chpt., bd. dirs., pres. internat. soc. 1996), Am. C. of C. Execs. Assn. (hon., pres. 1966), S.C. C. of C. Execs. Assn., Fla. C. of C. Execs. Assn. (pres. 1971), Better Bus. Bur. Ctrl. Fla. (chmn.), Knights Temple, Scottish-Am. Soc. Ctrl. Fla. (bd. dirs.), Orlando Scottish Games (exec. coun.), St. Andrews Soc. Ctrl. Fla. (pres.), Coun. Scottish Clans and Assn., Scottish Coalition (chmn.), Caledonian Found. (dir.), Country Club Orlando, Univ. Club, Tiger Bay Club (pres.), Clan Hamilton Soc. (Fla. commr.), Rotary, Phi Delta Theta. Episcopalian. Office: Brownlee Lighting 4600 Dardanelle Dr Orlando FL 32808-3832 Office Phone: 407-297-3677.

BROWN-OLMSTEAD, AMANDA, public relations executive; b. Oct. 7, 1943; Founder ABOA (formerly a divsn. Shandwick PLC), 1972; pres., CEO A Brown Olmstead Assocs., Atlanta. Mem. Atlanta Pub. Rels. Seminar Group. Bd. dirs. Ctrl. Atlanta Progress, Councilors for The Carter Ctr.; former bd. dirs. Atlanta Bot. Garden; mem. adv. bd. Sheperd Spinal Ctr.; former mem. adv. bd. U. Miss. Bus. Sch.; former mem. adv. guild Clark U.; former pres. Ga. chpt. Internat. Women's Forum; former mem. exec. com. Regional Bus. Coalition, bd. dirs., Atlanta Regional Health Forum; mem. exec. com. Robinson Coll. Bus., chair Hall of Fame program. Recipient Gold medal, N.Y. Film and TV Festival; named a Recognized Woman of Achievement, Internat. Women's Forum; named one of The Ten Outstanding Atlantans; named to Georgia Pub. Rels. Hall of Fame; YWCA honoree, Salute to Women of Achievement. Fellow: Pub. Rels. Soc. Am. (mem. Counselors Acad., mem. eligibility bd., Silver Anvil award); mem.: Order of the Phoenix, Leadership Atlanta. Achievements include being featured in Mademoiselle magazine, Business Week, Savvy, Atlanta Weekly, Atlanta magazine, and Movers and Shakers in Georgia. Office: A Brown Olmstead Assocs 274 W Paces Ferry Rd NW Atlanta GA 30305-1167 Business E-Mail: amanda@newaboa.com.

BROWN-WAITE, VIRGINIA (GINNY BROWN-WAITE), former United States Representative from Florida; b. Albany, NY, Oct. 5, 1943; m. Anthony M. Selvaggio (dec.); children: Jeannine Bradford, Danene Mitchell, Lorie Sue Busiere. BS, SUNY, Albany, 1976; grad. Labor Studies Prog., Cornell U., NYC, 1980; MPA, Russell Sage Coll., Troy, NY, 1984. Legis. dir. NY State Senate, 1970—87; commr. Hernando County, Fla., 1990—92; mem. Fla. State Senate, 1992—2002, pres. pro tempore, 2001—02; mem. US Congress from 5th Fla. Dist., 2003—11. Owner (franchise) Mr. Donut; adj. prof. Springfield Coll., Tampa, Fla.; chair Congl. Concrete Caucus; co-chair Congl. Women's Caucus, Unexploded Ordinances Caucus, Congl. Coalition Adoption; vice-chair Speaker's Prescription Drug Action Team. Active United Way; bd. dirs. Boys & Girls Club, Habitat for Humanity; founder, bd. dirs. Dawn Ctr. Hernando County; hon. bd. dirs. Hernando County Spouse Abuse Shelter; adv. bd. mem. Oak Hill Hosp., Brooksville, Fla. Mem.: Bus. & Profl. Women USA, Suncoast MG Club, Nature Coast British Car Club. Republican. Roman Catholic.

BROXSON, DOUGLAS VAUGHN, state legislator; b. Pensacola, Fla., Mar. 10, 1949; m. Mary Bernhardt; children: Julie, Jason, Juddsen, Marian Jill. BS, Evangel U., Springfield, Mo., 1971. Ins. profl.; mem. Dist. Fla. House Of Representatives, 2011—. Mem. Brownsville Assembly of God Ch. Republican. Office: 2990-C Gulf Breeze Pky Gulf Breeze FL 32563-3100 also: Fla House of Reps 1003 The Capitol 402 S Monroe St Tallahassee FL 32399-1300 Office Phone: 850-626-3113, 850-916-5436. Business E-Mail: doug.broxson@myfloridahouse.gov.

BROYLES, ROBERT HERMAN, biochemistry and molecular biology educator; b. Kingsport, Tenn., Feb. 16, 1943; s. Herman Harrison and Nancy (Larkin) Broyles; m. J. Dianne Fields, Sept. 3, 1966; children: David C., James R. BS in Chemistry, Wake Forest Coll., 1965; postgrad., Marine Biolog. Lab., Mass., 1969; PhD in Biochemistry, Wake Forest U., 1970; postdoctoral studies, Fla. State U., 1970-72. Rsch. asst. dept. biochemistry Bowman Gray Sch. Medicine, Winston-Salem, NC, 1966; rsch. assoc. dept. chemistry Fla. State U., Tallahassee, 1970-72; asst. prof. dept. zoology U. Wis.-Milw., 1972-77; assoc. prof. dental biochemistry U. Okla. Health Scis. Ctr., 1977—, prof. biochemistry and molecular biology, 1985—2009. Mem. Ctr. for Gt. Lakes Studies, U. Wis.-Milw., 1975-77; assoc. prof. dept. biochemistry and molecular biology U. Okla. Health Scis. Ctr., 1977-85; adj. prof. dept. pediatrics U. Okla. Coll. Medicine, 1988—, asst. dir. MD/PhD program, 1991—99; sr. scientist divsn. kidney, urol. and hematol. diseases and lab. of chem. biology NIH, 1989, 90, adj. rsch. mem Free radical Biology and Aging Program, Oklahama Med. Rsch. Found., 2000-08; pres. Sickle Cell Cure Found.,Inc.,2006-; invited participant workshop NSF, 1973, confs., NIH, 1978, 80, 82, 84, 86, 88, 90, 92, 94, 96, 98, 2000, 02, 04; lectr. Marine Biol. Lab., 1983; vis. sr. scientist NIH, 1991-97; adj. prof. dept. biochemistry & molecular biology U. Okla. Health Scis. Ctr., Coll. Medicine, 2009-; mentor numerous rsch. students; mem. numerous univ. and profl. coms.; presenter in field. Contbr. numerous articles to profl. jours. Hon. scholar Wake Forest Coll., 1961-63; Title IV Predoctoral fellow NDEA, 1965-68; Wilder fellow Bowman Gray Sch. Medicine, 1968-70, postdoctoral fellow NIH, 1970-72; recipient numerous research grants; grant Bill & Melinda Gater Found. Mem. AAAS, Am. Soc. Cell Biology, Am. Soc. Biolog. Chemists, Am. Soc. Hematology, Am. Soc. Zoologists, N.Y. Acad. Scis., Soc. Devel. Biologists, Sigma Xi (chpt. pres.-elect 1988-89, 91-92, pres. 1992-93), Am Assn. Cancer Rsch., Am. Soc. Gene Therapy, Internat. BioIron Soc., Internat. Soc. Differention, Internat. Soc. Stem Cell Rsch., Soc. Free Radical Biology Medicine. Unitarian Universalist. Avocations: exercise, music, photography. Office: Sickle Cell Cure Found Inc 755 Research Pky Ste 451/MB24 Oklahoma City OK 73104 Office Phone: 405-706-5802. Business E-Mail: robert-broyles@ouhsc.edu, robert.broyles@sicklecellcurefoundation.org.

BROZOVSKY, JOHN A., accounting educator; b. Spokane, Wash., Apr. 30, 1951; s. Victor Jerald and Orise (Watson) Brozovsky; m. Sue Ellen King, Apr. 14, 1984; 1 child, Joseph Victor. AAS, Spokane CC, 1971; BBA, U. Tex., 1975, M in Profl. Acctg., 1978; PhD in Bus. Adminstrn., U. Colo., 1990. CPA Tex.; cert. data processor, computer programmer. Computer programmer U. Tex., Austin, 1974-77; computer programmer II Tex. State Health Dept., Austin, 1978-80; EDP auditor City of Austin, 1980-81; sr. internal auditor Enserch Corp., Dallas, 1981-83; lectr. Calif. State U., Fresno, 1983-86; rsch. and tchg. asst U. Colo., Boulder, 1986-89; asst. prof. Va. Tech., Blacksburg, 1989-96, assoc. prof., 1996—. Presenter in field. Author: Advanced Accounting, 2000; contbr. articles to profl. jours. Grantee, Calif. CPA Found., 1986—89, AICPA, 1988, Pamplin, 1992; Gerald Hart fellow, 1987, Wayne Lieninger Jr. fellow, 2010—13, grant, Pamplin, 2009, Deloitte, 2008, Price Waterhouse Coopers, 2012. Fellow: Wayne Lieninger (sr.); mem.: Inst. Mgmt. Accts. (coach nat. championship team student case competition 1995, nat. finalists 1996, 1997, nat. semifinalist 1998, 1999, 2005, 2006, Roanoke chpt. v.p. profl. edn. 1997—98), Am. Acctg. Assn. Avocation: wood turning. Home: 9000 Newport Rd Catawba VA 24070-3018 Office: Va Tech Pamplin # 3007 Blacksburg VA 24061 Office Phone: 540-231-5971. Business E-Mail: jbrozovs@vt.edu.

BRU, JULIE O., lawyer; B cum laude, U. South Fla., Tampa; JD, Stetson U. Coll. Law, Gulfport, Fla., 1988. Cert.: (in city, county and local govt. law). Dep. city atty. City of Miami, Fla., city atty., 2008—. Recipient American Jurisprudence Book award, Ethics and Profl. Responsibility. Office: City of Miami Office of City Atty 444 SW 2nd Ave Ste 945 Miami FL 33130 Office Phone: 305-416-1816. Office Fax: 305-416-1801. Business E-Mail: jobru@miamigov.com.

BRUBAKER, HAROLD J., state legislator; b. Mt Joy, Pa., Nov. 11, 1946; s. Paul Nissley Brubaker and Verna Mae B.; m. Geraldine Baldwin Brubaker, 1972; children: Jonathan Nissley, Justin Andrew. Pres. Mktg. Enterprises, 1970—, Asheboro Carpet & Supply Co., 1973—76, Harold Brubaker & Assocs.; asst. sec. NC Rep. Party, 1972—76; chmn. Randolph County Bd Electorate, 1974—76; Joint Caucus Leader, 1979—80; majority leader, 1980—84; state rep. Dist. 38 NC, 1976—2002; state rep. Dist. 78 NC, 2003—. Recipient North Atlantic Regional State Star Farmers award, 1965, Disting. Svc. award, Randolph County Jaycees, 1980, Outstanding 4-H Alumni award, NC 4-H, 1981. Mem.: Soc. Real Estate Appraisers, Bd. Realtors, Am. Inst. Real Estate Appraisers, Home Builders Assn. Republican. Luth. Address: 138 Scarboro St Asheboro NC 27203 Office: North Carolina House of Representatives 300 N Salisbury St Room 302 Raleigh NC 27603-5925 Home Phone: 336-629-5128; Office Phone: 919-715-4946. Business E-Mail: Harold.Brubaker@ncleg.net.

BRUCE, JACKSON MARTIN, JR., lawyer; b. Milw., Apr. 10, 1931; s. Jackson Martin and Harriet (Edgell) B.; m. Lilias M. Morehouse, June 30, 1954; children: Lilias Stephanie, Andrew Edgell. AB magna cum laude, Harvard U., 1953, JD cum laude, 1957; MA with 1st class honors in Law, Cambridge U., 1955. Bar: Wis. 1957, Fla. 1973. Assoc. Quarles & Brady, Milw., 1957-64, ptnr., 1964-96; shareholder Dunwody, White & Landon, Naples, Fla., 1996—; counsel Michael Best & Friedrich, Milw., 1996—. Mem. joint editl. bd. Uniform Trusts and Estates Acts; contbr. articles to profl. jours. Bd. dirs. Living Ch. Found., Inc., 1965-98; trustee Univ. Sch. Milw., 1973-79. Fellow Am. Coll. Trust and Estate Counsel (bd. regents 1976-82, treas. 1990-91, sec. 1991-92, v.p. 1992-93, pres. 1994-95); mem. ABA (bd. govs. 1994-97, chmn. sect. real property, probate and trust law 1984-85, ho. dels. 1988-97, ethics com. 1998-2001), State Bar Wis. (chmn. bd. govs. 1979-80), Am. Bar Found., Am. Law Inst., Internat. Acad. Estate and Trust Law (mem. exec. coun. 1980-86), Town Club, Milw. Club (bd. dirs. 1985-2001), The Club Pelican Bay. Home: 6101 Pelican Bay Blvd Apt 1201 Naples FL 34108-8183 also: 9008 N Bayside Dr Milwaukee WI 53217-1913 Office: Dunwody White & Landon 4001 Tamiami Trl N Ste 200 Naples FL 34103-3591 also: Michael Best & Friedrich 100 E Wisconsin Ave Ste 3300 Milwaukee WI 53202-4107 Home Phone: 239-591-1512; Office Phone: 239-263-5885, 414-225-4963. Business E-Mail: jbruce@dwl-law.com, jmbruce@michaelbest.com.

BRUCE, MARYANN, bank executive; Grad., Duke U. Sr. v.p. OppenheimerFunds, 1985—97; sales exec. Allstate Ins. Co., 1998—99; pres., retail, high net worth sales, mktg. First Union Evergreen Investment Services (now Wachovia), Boston, 1999—. Named one of Most Powerful Women in Banking, USBanker Mag., 2005. Office: Evergreen Investment Services 17th fl 200 Berkeley St PO Box 2121 Boston MA 02106 also: Evergreen Investment Services 401 S Tryon St Charlotte NC 28288

BRUCE, ROGER, state legislator; b. NYC, May 9, 1953; m. Angela Bruce; 3 children. Former state rep. Dist. 45, Ga.; state rep. Dist. 64 Ga., 2004—; mem. Judiciary Coms., Edn. Coms.; vice chmn. Fulton County Del.; sec. Ins. Com. Recipient TV Svc. award, WSB-TV Cmty. Democrat. Methodist. Mailing: 511 LOB Atlanta GA 30334 Office: 410 Stone Arbor Ct Atlanta GA 30331 Office Phone: 404-656-6372, 770-612-7210. E-mail: rbruce5347@aol.com.

BRUCE, STEVE, construction executive; V.p., gen. mgr. Carolina Divsn., Greensboro Dist. Martin Marietta Aggregates, Martin Marietta Materials, Inc., v.p., gen. mgr. Greensboro Dist. Office: Martin Marietta Materials Inc Carolina Division / Greensboro District 413 S Chimney Rock Rd Greensboro NC 27409 Office Phone: 336-668-3253.

BRUCE, THOMAS ALLEN, physician, educator; b. Mountain Home, Ark., 1930; s. Rex Floyd and Dora Madeline (Fee) B.; m. Dolores Fay Montgomery; children: T.K. Montgomery, Dana Fee Thomas. BSM, MD, U. Ark., 1955, DSc (hon.), 1995. Intern Duke Hosp., 1956-57; resident medicine Bellevue Hosp., NYC, 1957, Meml. Ctr. Cancer and Allied Diseases, NYC, 1958, Parkland Meml. Hosp., Dallas, 1958—59; cardiopulmonary trainee Southwestern Med. Sch. of U. Tex., 1959—60; cardiac rsch. fellow Hammersmith Hosp. and U. London Postgrad. Med. Sch., London, 1960—61, Harvard Bus. Sch., 1974. From instr. to prof. medicine Wayne State U., 1961—68, also asst. dean Sch. Medicine; prof. medicine, head cardiovascular sect. U. Okla. Med. Ctr., 1968—74; prof. medicine, dean Coll. Medicine U. Ark. Med. Scis., 1974—85, emeritus prof., 1997—, dean pro tem Coll. Pub. Health, 2001—02, prof. health policy and mgmt., 2001—; prof. U. Ark. Clinton Sch. Pub. Svc., 2002—07, dean pro tem, 2003—04, Heifer Found. Bd., 2013—; assoc. dean U. Ark. Clinton Sch. Pub. Svc., 2004—07, prof. emeritus, 2007—; med. dir. Barton Rsch. Inst., 1974—85; coord. Sino-am. Med. Exch. Program, 1979—85; rsch. support rev. com. NIH, 1983—85; program dir. W.K. Kellogg Found., 1985—97; co-chair session 312 Salzburg Seminar, Austria; mem. History of Medicine Assocs.; chair nat. adv. bd. cmty. health leadership program Robert Wood Johnson Found., 2004—06; policy adv. bd. Ark. Ctr. for Health Improvement, 1995—2009; chmn. bd. trustees Watershed Found.; adj. staff Ark. Cmty. Found.; bd. dirs. Heifer Internat., 1996—2006, chair, 2003—04, emeritus bd. mem., 2013—. Master gardener, chmn. garden docents Wildwood Park Arts; pres. Taiwan-US Sister Rels. Alliance; coord. STAR Health Initiative, Ark. Dept. Health, 2008—11; bd. dirs. Garvan Woodland Gardens, 2000—06, Wise Old Goats Club, 2014. Named Profl. of Yr., U. Ark. at Little Rock, 2003; named to U. Ark. Med. Scis. Coll. Medicine Hall of Fame, 2004; recipient Ark. Gov. Meritorious Achievement award, 1974, Lugene Chilcote award, 1999, Double Helix award U. Ark. Med. Sci., 2001, Lucy Lockett Cabe award Wildwood Park Arts, 2001, Giving Tree Soc. award, 2003, Ctrl. High Mus. Appreciation award, 2001, Ark. Ctr. Health Improvement award, 2002, Sen. David Pryor Carelink award, 2004, Bruce Commons Dedication award U. Ark. Med. Scis. Coll. Publ Health, 2004, Martin Luther King Salute to Greatness award, 2005, Humanitarian of Yr. award Just Communities Ark., 2007, Lifetime Achievement award Ark. Med. Soc., 2009; named Philanthropist of the Yr., Ark. Assn. Fundraising Profls., Merit award, Kaohsiung Med. U., 2009, Resolution Appreciation award, U. Ark. Bd. Trustees, 2009, Disting. Cmty. Svc. award Ark. Med. Dental Pharm. Assn., 2009, Visionary Pub. Health award, Ark. Minority Health Commn., 2011, Friend of Children award Ark. Advs. Children & Families, 2013. Fellow: ACP, Am. Coll. Cardiology; mem.: AMA, APHA, Leila Arboretum Soc. (pres. 1989—92), Am. Rhododendron Soc., Ark. Caduceus Club, Alpha Omega Alpha, Sigma Xi. Rsch. and publs. on cardiovascular disease including left ventricular function in cardiac denervation, coronary heart disease, myocardial metabolism relating to phospholipids in graded cardiac ischmia, med. edn. with particular reference to rural health care, health promotion and disease prevention, primary health care, community-based pub. health. Home: 6 Spy Glass Ln Little Rock AR 72212-4418

BRUCK, BILL, business owner; b. Dayton, Ohio, Aug. 1, 1951; s. Emil J. and Lucy A. (Lombardi) B.; m. Jacqueline Youden, June 6, 1984 (div. Dec. 1987); m. Anita M. Brack, June 15, 1996; 1 child, Abby Elizabeth. AB, Brown U., 1973; MA, Duquesne U., 1974; PhD, U. Fla., 1977. Lic. clin. psychologist, Va. Asst. prof. psychology Seattle U., 1978-79, West Ga. Coll., Carrollton, 1979-81; prin. Leadership Resources, Inc., Fairfax, Va., 1981-83; assoc. prof. psychology Marymount U., Arlington, Va., 1983-91, dir. instnl. rsch., 1986-91, prof. psychology, 1991-99; owner/operator Bill Bruck & Assocs., Falls Church, Va., 1986—2003; prin. Caucus Systems, Inc., Arlington, Va., 1999-2001; ptnr. Q2Learning LLC, 2001—. Author: Special Edition Using WordPerfect Office, 1994, Special Edition Using PerfectOffice 3, 1995, Special Edition Using Novell GroupWise 4, 1995, Using Corel WordPerfect Suite 7, 1996, Using Corel WordPerfect Suite 8, 1997, The Essential Book for Microsoft Office 95, 1996, The Essential Book for Microsoft Office 97, 1997, The Essential Book for Microsoft Office 2000, 1999, Make Your Mouse Roar, 2001, Taming the Information Tsunami, 2002. Avocations: martial arts, racquetball, gardening, folk music. Office: 2686 Hillsman St Falls Church VA 22043 Office Phone: 877-751-2200.*

BRUECKHEIMER, WILLIAM ROGERS, social sciences educator; b. Gary, Ind., Aug. 19, 1921; s. Albert Gustav and Lucille (Schwartz) B.; m. Mary Ellen Roe, Nov. 7, 1942; children: William Rogers, David Rogers, Suzanne Rogers. Student, Wabash Coll., Crawfordville, Ind., 1941-42; MA in Social Sci., U. Chgo., 1949; MA in Geography, U. Mich., Ann Arbor, 1952, PhD, 1953. Instr. geography Fla. State U., 1949-51; teaching fellow, instr. geography U. Mich., 1951-53; asst. prof., then asso. prof. geography So. State Coll., Magnolia, Ark., 1953-55; faculty Western Mich. U., Kalamazoo, 1955-64, prof. geography and geology, head dept., 1958-64; prof., head dept. geography Fla. State U., Tallahassee, 1964-71; dir. London Study Center, 1971-72; prof. dept. geography Fla. State U., 1972-90, dir. interdisciplinary program in social sci., 1979-85; vis. scholar U. Mich., 1974. Mem. Fla. Gov.'s Resource Use Edn. Com., 1964-71; mem. adv. bd. Tall Timbers Research, Inc.; Found. Econ. Edn. fellow, summer 1955; Henry L. Beadel fellow Tall Timbers Rsch. Sta., summers 1973-92. Contbr. articles to profl. jours.; sect. editor Atlas of Fla., 1981, The Hunting Plantations of Northern Leon County, Fla., 1988, The Legacy of a Red Hills Hunting Plantation, 2012. Served with AUS, 1942-46, ETO. Fellow Royal Geog. Soc.; mem. Assn. Am. Geographers (chmn. East Lakes div. 1957-58), Mich. Schoolmasters Club (chmn. geography sect. 1958-59), Fla. Soc. Geographers, Leon County Soc. Geographers and Anthropologists, Exch. Club. Home: St Augustine Plantation Apt 2602 2507 Old St Augustine Rd Tallahassee FL 32301

BRUEL, IRIS BARBARA, psychologist; b. NYC, June 10, 1933; d. Herman and Anna (Cohen) Goldstein; m. Robert Bruel, Apr. 1953 (div. 1957); adopted children: Michael Abraham, Russell Emanuel. BA in Psychology, CCNY, 1956, MS in Sch. Psychology, 1961; PhD in Clin. Psychology, U. Miami, Fla., 1972. Cert. profl. psychologist, Fla., diplomate Am. bd. Assessment Psychology. Child supr. Linden Hill Sch., Hawthorne, N.Y., 1957-59; tchr., therapist The League Sch. for Severely Disturbed Children, Bklyn., 1959-61, Assn. for Mentally Ill Children, Yonkers, N.Y., 1961-63; asst. psychology rsch. U. Miami, Coral Gables, Fla., 1964-67; trainee VA Hosp., Miami, 1967-68; intern diagnostic testing and psychotherapy Henderson Clinic, Ft. Lauderdale, Fla., 1968-69; intern child psychol. svcs. San Fernando Valley Child Guidance Clinic, Van Nuys, Calif., 1970-71; cons. Sorensen Group, NYC, 1972; clin. psychologist Dade County Dept. Youth and Family Devel., Miami, 1972-77; co-dir. Ctr. for the Whole Family, Inc., Coral Gables, 1976-79; pvt. practice clin. psychology, South Miami, Fla., 1979—; clin. psychologist Juvenile Ct. Assessment Ctr., Miami, 1989—2004. Cons. Jewish Vocat. Svc., 1980-85; mem. affiliate staff Grant Ctr. Hosp., 1977—; med. staff Charter Hosp., 1991—; allied health staff Highland Park Hosp., 1988—; adj. prof. Nova U., Ft. Lauderdale, 1977; field supr. practicum students So. Fla. Sch. Profl. Psychology, Miami, 1978-80; cons. Guardian Ad Litem program, 1988—. Vol. ARC, 2001—; Sec. Reform Dem. Club, NYC, 1962—63. Mem. APA, Am. Soc. Clin. Hypnosis, Nat. Acad. Neuropsychology, Fla. Soc. Clin. Hypnosis (sec. editor newsletter), Dade County Mental Health Assn., Cousteau Soc., N.Y. Acad. Scis., Assn. for Play Therapy, Am. Bd. Profl. Disability Cons. (diplomate),Amnesty Internat., Am. Bd. Assessment Psychology, Am. Coll. Forensic Examiners, Am. Acad. Experts in Traumatic Stress, EMDR Internat. Assn. Jewish. Office: 7800 S Red Rd Ste 310ph Miami FL 33143-5528 Office Phone: 305-444-6005. Personal E-mail: dririsbruel@bellsouth.net.

BRUEN, JOHN DERMOT, management consultant; b. Glen Cove, NY, Oct. 19, 1930; s. John D. and Kathleen M. (Halferty) B.; m. Ann Theone Lee, June 22, 1957; children: Michael J., Kathleen A., Thomas L., Lisa M. BS, U. Md., 1959; MBA, U. Pitts., 1963; grad., Naval War Coll. Command and Staff Course, 1966, Army War Coll., 1972. Enlisted in Ill. Nat. Guard, 1948; active duty, 1952; attended Loyola U., Chgo., 1951—52, Infantry Officer Candidate Sch., 1952; commd. 2d lt. US Army, 1953, advanced through grades to lt. gen., 1983; service in Korea, Germany, Azores, Thailand and Vietnam; dir. resources and mgmt. Office Dep. Chief Staff Logistics Hqrs., DA, 1977—79; comdr. Mil. Traffic Mgmt. Command Washington, 1979-83; comdr. 21st Support Command Europe, 1983-86; ret., 1986; pres. Bruen & Assocs., Springfield, Va., 1986—; hon. col. US Army Transp. Corps Regt., 1997—2001, pres., 1997—2001. Contbr. articles on leadership, mgmt. to profl. jours. Internat. vice chmn. US Continuous Acquisition and Life Cycle Support; bd. dirs. Industry Steering Group, 1990—96. Decorated Def. D.S.M., Army D.S.M., Legion of Merit with two oak leaf clusters, Bronze Star with one oak leaf cluster, Meritorious Svc. medal with one oak leaf cluster, Army Commendation medal with one oak leaf cluster, Meritorious Unit Citation with one oak leaf cluster; decorated grand officer Order of the Crown (Belgium) NATO; named to US Inf. Officer Candidate Sch. Hall of Fame, 1979, US Army Transp. Corps Hall of Fame, 2000; recipient Computer-Aided Acquisition and Life-Cycle Support Meritorious Svc. award, 1996. Mem. U.S. Army Transp. Corps Regiment Assn. (pres. 1997-2001), Nat. Def. Transp. Assn., Assn. U.S. Army, Mil. Officers Assn. Am. (bd. dirs. 1986-94). Roman Catholic. Office: 6104 Greenlawn Ct Springfield VA 22152-1314 Home Phone: 703-644-7072; Office Phone: 703-644-7072. Personal E-mail: jdbruen@aol.com.

BRUGGEWORTH, ROBERT A., communications executive; BSEE, Wilkes U. Various mfg. and engring. mgmt. positions, including area dir., v.p., Asia Pacific ops., divisional v.p., global computer and consumer electronics AMP Inc. (now Tyco Electronics), Hong Kong, China, 1983—99; v.p., wireless products RF Micro Devices, Inc., 1999—2002, pres., wireless products, 2002, pres., 2002—, CEO,

2003—. Bd. dirs. LightPath Technologies, Inc., 2001—07, RF Micro Devices, Inc., 2003—, Mine Safety Appliances Co., Pittsburgh, Pa. Bd. trustee Wilkes U., Wilkes-Barre, Pa., Guilford Tech. Cmty. Coll., Greensboro. Office: RF Micro Devices Inc 7628 Thorndike Rd Greensboro NC 27409-9421 Office Phone: 336-664-1233. Office Fax: 336-664-0454. Business E-Mail: b.robert@rfmd.com.

BRUKARDT, GARY A., health facility administrator; Undergrad., Univ. Wisc.; grad., Am. Grad. Sch. Internat. Mgmt. With St. Luke's Med. Ctr., Phoenix, Presbyterian St. Luke's Med. Ctr., Denver; found., sr. officer Partners Nat. Health Plans; with VHA; chmn., pres. Healthnet, 1991—96; exec. vice-pres. Baptist Healthcare Affiliates, Nashville, 1991—96; pres., COO Renal Care Group, Nashville, 1996—2003, pres., CEO, 2003—06; chmn., CEO Specialty Care Services Group, Nashville, 2006—. Office: Specialty Care Services Corp One American Ctr 3100 West End Ave Ste 150 Nashville TN 37203 Office Phone: 615-345-5510. Office Fax: 615-345-5565.

BRUMBY, ANDREW M., lawyer; b. Feb. 4, 1954; BA with high distinction, U. Va., Charlottesville, 1976, JD, 1979. Bar: Ga. 1979, Fla. 1987. Assoc. Kilpatrick & Stockton LLP, Atlanta, 1979—86; shareholder Swann & Haddock, P.A., Orlando, Fla., 1987—90; ptnr. Shutts & Bowen LLP, Orlando, 1990—; chmn. Creditor Rights & Bankruptcy Practice Group. Named one of Best Lawyers in America, 2006—14, Best Lawyers in Orlando, 2006—14, Fla. Super Lawyers, 2006—14, Fla.'s Legal Elite, Fla. Trend, 2007—08. Mem.: Am. Bankruptcy Inst., Ctrl. Fla. Bankruptcy Law Assn. (pres. 1991, bd. mem. 1991—95). Office: Shutts and Bowen Ste 1000 300 S Orange Ave Orlando FL 32801-5403 Office Phone: 407-835-6901.

BRUMELLE, KENNETH COY, retired business owner; b. Odessa, Tex., Mar. 18, 1945; s. Clarence Lee and Leota (Jones) B.; m. Sharon Jean Suther, Dec. 21, 1967; 1 child Jenni Rebecca. AS, Odessa Coll., 1966; BBA, Tex. Tech U., 1968. Buyer trainee Sanger Harris, Dallas, 1969—71, buyer, 1971—73, White House Dept. Stores, Beaumont, Tex., 1973—74, mgr. mdse., 1974—77; owner Outlaw Jean Store, Odessa, 1977—97; pres. SOLD COLAM, Inc., 1997—2008. Bd. dirs. Better Bus. Bur. With US Army, 1968—69, Tex., with NG, 1969—74. Mem. Nat. Fedn. Ind. Bus., Tex. Retail Mchts. Assn. (bd. dirs.), Tex. Retail Assn. (state chmn. membership com. 1991—), Odessa C. of C., Optimist (v.p. Odessa club), Masons Republican. Methodist. Home: 1809 East 52 nd St Odessa TX 79762-8138 Home Phone: 432-367-4588. Personal E-mail: KB@KenBrumelle.com.

BRUMFIELD, WILLIAM CRAFT, Slavic studies educator, photographer, writer; b. Charlotte, NC, June 28, 1944; s. Lewis F. and Pauline Elizabeth (Craft) Brumfield. BA, Tulane U., New Orleans, 1966; PhD in Slavic langs., U. Calif., Berkeley, 1973. Vis. lectr. U. Wis., Madison, 1973-74; asst. prof. Harvard U., Cambridge, Mass., 1974-80; assoc. prof. Tulane U., New Orleans, 1984-91, prof. Slavic langs., 1992—. Resident dir. Am. Coun. Tchrs. Russian Pushkin Inst. Program, Moscow, 1979—80; co-dir. Summer INst. Coll. Faculty, NEH, 1994; adv. dir. Russian Children's Welfare Soc.; lectr. architecture, photography and lit. mus. and univs. throughout US and Europe. Author: Gold in Azure: One Thousand Years of Russian Architecture, 1983, The Origins of Modernism in Russian Architecture, 1991, A History of Russian Architecture, 1993, 2004 (Notable Book of Yr. NY Times Book Rev., 1993), An Architectural Survey of St. Petersburg: 1840-1916, 1994, Lost Russia: Photographing the Ruins of Russian Architecture, 1995, Landmarks of Russian Architecture: A Photographic Survey, 1997, Vologda Album: Photographing Architectural Monuments in the Volodga Region, 2005, Totma: Architectural Heritage in Photographs, 2005, Irkutsk: Architectural Heritage in Photographs, 2006, Tobolsk: Architectural Heritage in Photographs, 2006, Solikamsk: Architectural Heritage in Photographs, 2007, Cherdyn: Architectural Heritage in Photographs, 2007, Velikii Ustiug, 2007, Kargopol: Architectural Heritage in Photographs, 2007, Chita: Archtl. Heritage Photogs., 2008, Buriatiia: Archtl. Heritage Photogs., 2008, Solovki: Archtl. Heritage Photogs., 2008, Kirillov, Ferapontovo, 2009, Sotsialnyi Proekt V Russkoi Literature XIX Veka, 2009, Kolomna: Architectural Heritage in Photographs, 2009, Suzdal: Architectural Heritage in Photographs, 2009, Ustiuzhna, 2010, Torzhok: Architectural Heritage in Photographs, 2010, Belozersk, 2011, Vologda, 2012, Usole: Architectural Heritage in Photographs, 2012; editor, contbr.: Reshaping Russian Architecture: Western Technology, Utopian Dreams, 1990, Christianity and the Arts in Russia, 1991, Russian Housing in the Modern Age: Design and Social History, 1993, Commerce in Russian Urban Culture: 1861-1914, 2001, Zhilischche V Rossil: vek XX, 2001, Predprinimatelstvo i gorodskaia kultura V Rossii, 2002, Vologda Album, 2005; contbr. articles to profl. jours.; exhibitions include Duke U. Mus. Art, 1996, New Orleans Mus. Art, 1996, U. Mich. Mus. Art, 1997, Arkhangelsk Mus. Art, 1999, Shchusev Mus. Architecture, Moscow, 2001, Represented in permanent collections Photog. Archives, Nat. Art Gallery, Washington, Libr. Congress, New Orleans Mus. Art; author: Usole: Zemlia Stroganovykh na Kame, 2013. Grantee, Samuel H. Kress Found., 1996—97, Nat. Coun. Eurasian and E. European Rsch., 1999—2000; fellow, Harvard Russian Rsch. Ctr., 1980—81; Woodrow Wilson fellow, 1966, NEH fellow, Nat. Humanities Ctr., 1992—93, John Simon Guggenheim fellow, 2000—01, NEH Collaborative fellow, Am. Coun. Internat. Edn., 2001—02, Sr. Exch. scholar, Internat. Rsch. Exchs. Bd./Am. coun. Learned Socs. US-USSR Exch., 1983—84, Rsch. scholar, Kennan Inst., 1989. Fellow: Russian Acad. Architecture and Constrn. Sci., Russian Acad. Art; mem.: Soc. Historians E. European and Russian Art and Architecture, Am. Coun. Tchrs. Russian, Inst. Modern Russian Culture (head photography sect.), Soc. Archtl. Historians, Am. Assn. Advancement Slavic Studies, Phi Beta Kappa. Home and Office: Tulane U Slavic Dept 305 Newcomb Hall New Orleans LA 70118 Office Phone: 504-865-5276. Business E-Mail: brumfiel@tulane.edu.

BRUMLEY, ELIZABETH D., construction company executive, accountant; b. 1958; 2 children. Student, Baylor U., 1976—77; BA in English, Rice U., 1981, MS in Acctg., 1981. CPA. Sr. auditor Arthur Andersen LLP, 1981—87; mgr. Jennings, Hawley, Cederberg & Co., 1987; contr. GulfMark Offshore, Inc. (formerly GulfMark Internat., Inc.), 1987—96; v.p., prin. acctg. officer MAXXAM Inc., 1996—97, v.p., prin. acctg. officer, asst. contr., 1997—99, v.p., prin. acctg. officer, contr., 1999—2005; v.p., contr. Noble Drilling Svcs., Inc., 2005; contr. Bristow Group, Inc., 2005—07, v.p., chief acctg. officer, 2005—08, v.p. finance, 2008—11, interim CFO, 2010—11; chief acctg. officer, contr. Sterling Construction Co., Inc., Houston, 2011, exec. v.p., CFO, chief acctg. officer, contr., 2011—. Office: Sterling Construction Co Inc 20810 Fernbrush Rd Houston TX 77073

BRUMLEY, FRANK W., real estate company executive; m. Blanche Brumley; children: Jane, Leigh, Kate. BBA in Fin., U. Ga., Athens, 1962; grad., Ga. Banking Sch., U. NC Kenan Exec. Program. Comml. banker, 1962—69; various exec. positions Sea Pines Co., Kiawah Island Co.; founder, chmn., CEO Daniel Island Co., 1997—. Bd. dirs. Synovus Fin. Corp., 2004—, Nat. Bank SC. Bd. overseers U. Ga. Terry Coll. Bus.; state trustee Nature Conservancy; trustee, past pres. Hist. Charleston Found.; bd. mem. Lowcountry Open Land Trust, Charleston Civic Design Ctr., Coastal Cmty. Found. Recipient Disting. Alumni award, U. Ga. Terry Coll. Bus., 2008. Mem.: Sigma Alpha Epsilon. Office: The Daniel Island Co Ste 201 230 Seven Farms Dr Charleston SC 29492 Office Phone: 843-971-3500. Office Fax: 843-971-3540.

BRUMLEY, JON S., oil industry executive; b. 1971; BBA, U. Tex. Dir., bus. devel. MESA; mgr., commodity risk & comml. projects Pioneer Nat. Resources Co., 1997—98; exec. v.p., bus. devel., corp. sec. Encore Acquisition Co., Fort Worth, Tex., 1998—2002, bd. dirs., 1999—2001, pres. Fort Worth, Tex., 2002—, CEO, 2006—. Named Entrepreneur of the Yr., Forbes mag., 2005; named one of America's 15 Most Powerful CEO's 40 and Under, 2010. Office: Encore Acquisition Co 5320 Legacy Dr Ste 100 Plano TX 75024-3124 Office Phone: 817-877-9955. Office Fax: 817-877-1655.

BRUNDAGE, GERTRUDE BARNES, pediatrician; b. Neptune, NJ, May 13, 1941; d. John Holt and Mary Downey (Chatham) B. BS in Chemistry, Marietta Coll., 1964; MD, Jefferson Med. Coll., 1971. Diplomate Am. Bd. Pediatrics. Chemist Lederle Labs., Pearl River, NY, 1964-67; intern pediatrics Harrisburg Polyclinic Hosp., Pa., 1971-72; resident pediatrics Wilmington Med. Ctr., Del., 1972-74; pediatrician St. Barnabas Med. Ctr., Livingston, NJ, 1974—2006, Coastal Family Health Svc., Biloxi, Miss., 2008—09. Chief dept. pediat. Hosp. Ctr. At Orange, 1990—98. Moderator Presbytery of Newark, 1996; active 1st Presbyn. Ch., elder, trustee, 1982—87, 1989—92, 2004—07. Mem. Am. Med. Women's Assn., Alpha Gamma Delta. Republican. Presbyterian. Avocations: choral singing, needlecrafts, gardening. Home: 3911 Baywood Ln Ocean Springs MS 39564 Home Phone: 228-447-3254. Personal E-mail: trudyb18@yahoo.com.

BRUNETTI, WAYNE HENRY, energy executive; b. Cleve., Oct. 13, 1942; s. Henry Joseph and Lillian (Lupo) B.; m. Mary Kelly, Aug. 17, 1963; children: Kelly Christine, Andrew Wayne. BSBA in Acctg., U. Fla., 1964; program for mgmt. devel., Harvard U., 1974. Chmn., pres. & CEO Southwestern Pub. Svc. Co.; acct. Florida Power & Light Co., Miami, Fla., 1964-68, systems analyst, 1968-69, project coordinator, 1969-72, mgr., property acctg., 1972-73, mgr., corp. acctg., asst. comptroller, 1973-77, asst. to v.p. pub. affairs, 1977-80, dir., energy mgmt., 1980, v.p., energy mgmt., 1980-83, v.p., divs., 1983-84, group v.p., 1984-87, exec. v.p., 1987-91; pres., CEO Mgmnt. Sys. Internat., Fla., 1991-94; pres., COO Public Svc. Co. of Colo., 1994-96, CEO, chmn., 1996; chmn., pres. & CEO New Century Energies, Inc., 2000; pres. Xcel Energy, 2001—03, chmn, CEO, 2001—05. Bd. dirs. OGE Energy Corp. Bd. adv. US Dept. of Energy; mem. Nat. Petroleum Coun., Sec. Energy Nat. Petroleum Coun., 2002—03; chmn. Edison Electric Inst., Nat. Trade Assn., Colo. Assn. of Commerce & Industry. Mem.: Minn. Bus. Partnership, Inc., Juran Ctr. for Leadership and Quality (exec. adv. bd.), Capital City Partnership (bd. dirs.). Democrat. Roman Catholic. Office: OGE Energy Corp Bd Directors 321 N Harvey Oklahoma City OK 73101 Office Phone: 405-553-3000. Office Fax: 405-553-3567. Business E-Mail: wayne.brunetti@oge.com.

BRUNK, WILLIAM EDWARD, astronomer; b. Cleve., Nov. 24, 1928; s. Edgar Rea and Mabel Mowbray (Pearson) B.; 1 dau., Anna Kathryn. BS, Case Inst. Tech., 1952, MS, 1954, PhD, 1963. Aero. research scientist Lewis Flight Propulsion Lab., NACA, Cleve., 1954-58; aerospace engr. Lewis Research Center, NASA, Cleve., 1958-64; staff scientist for planetary astronomy NASA Hdqrs., Washington, 1964-65, program chief planetary astronomy, 1965-77, discipline scientist planetary astronomy, 1977-82, chief planetary sci. br., 1982-85; mgr. solar system sci. Univ. Space Rsch. Assn., Washington, 1985-94; ret., 1994. Recipient Exceptional Service medal NASA, 1985. Fellow AAAS; mem. Am. Astron. Soc. (Harold Mazursky Meritorious Svc. award 1995), Internat. Astron. Union; Mem. Sigma Xi. Home: 4802 51st St W Apt 710 Bradenton FL 34210-5107 Home Phone: 941-794-6142. E-mail: webrunk@earthlink.net.

BRUNNER, GEORGE MATTHEW, management consultant, retired manufacturing executive; b. Newark, Jan. 17, 1925; s. Mathias J. and Mary E. (Fuith) Brunner; m. Ruth E. Owens, Nov. 16, 1953. AB in Chemistry, Columbia U., 1949, MChemE, 1950. Devel. engr. J.T. Baker Chem. Co., Phillipsburg, NJ, 1950—53; plant mgr. Internat. Minerals & Chem. Corp, Niagara Falls, NY, 1953—62, Houston, 1953—62; mfg. engring. mgr. Gen. Foods Corp., Hoboken, NJ, 1962—71, Houston, 1962—71, Lafayette, Ind., 1962—71; v.p. mfg. W.R. Grace & Co., St. Simons Islands, Ga., 1971—73; pres. & CEO S.A. Schonbrunn & Co., Inc., Palisades Pk., NJ, 1973—82; v.p. ops. Am. Maize Products Co., Stamford, Conn., 1982—84, mgmt. cons., 1984—. Contbr. articles to profl. pubuls. With US Army, 1943—45. Decorated Purple Heart. Mem.: 5th Armored Divsn. Assn. (pres. 1980—81), Electrochem. Soc., Am. Inst. Chem. Engrs., Am. Chem. Soc., Pres.'s Assn., Nat. Coffee Assn. (dir.). Achievements include patents in field. Home and Office: 1221 Clays Trl Oldsmar FL 34677-4866 Home Phone: 727-787-0068.

BRUNO, IRENE EVELYN, application developer, educator; b. Pitts., Mar. 6, 1962; d. Joe Stephen and Ann Laurene (Lally) Hitt; m. Mark J. Bruno; children: Joseph Michael, Anna Michelle, Maria Elizabeth. BS in Math., U. Pitts., 1984; MEd in Math., The Pa. State U., U. Pk., Pa., 1991; PhD in Orgnl. Mgmt., Capella U., Mpls., 2003. Secondary cert. in math. and computer sci. Pa., 1985, Va., 2002. Tchr. State Coll. Area Sch. Dist., Pa., 1985—91; prof., assoc. dean, chmn. dept. Strayer U., Manassas, Va., 1995—2002; asst. prof. George Mason U., Fairfax, Va., 2002—09, assoc. prof., 2010—12, assoc. chair, undergrad. studies Applied Info. Tech. Dept., 2013—. Trainer, lead software devel. team Am. Online, Dulles, Va., 1996—98; program evaluator ABET. Recipient Prof. of Yr. award, Strayer U., 1997. Mem.: Assn. Computing Machinery, Spl. Interest Group Info. Tech. Edn. Office: George Mason University 10900 University Boulevard MS4F5 Manassas VA 20169 Office Fax: 703-995-8450. Business E-Mail: ibruno@gmu.edu.

BRUNO, NICK JOSEPH, academic administrator; b. 1951; m. Linda Capra; children: Steven, Victoria, Christina. BA in Acctg., Southeastern La. U.; PhD in Ednl. Leadership, U. Miss. Dir. auxiliary svcs. Southeastern La. U., Hammond, asst. v.p. spl. initiatives, adj. faculty mem. Coll. Bus.; assoc. v.p. bus. affairs then v.p. bus. affairs U. La., Monroe, 2002—05, pres., 2010—; v.p. bus. and fin. U. La. Sys., Baton Rouge, 2005—10. Mem.: Nat. Assn. Coll. and Univ. Bus. Officers, KC, Beta Alpha Psi. Roman Catholic. Office: University of Louisiana at Monrow Office of President - LIB 632 700 University Ave Monroe LA 71209 Office Phone: 318-342-1010. E-mail: bruno@ulm.edu.

BRUNS, DAVID EUGENE, medical educator, researcher; s. Eugene H. and Ellen E. B.; m. M. Elizabeth Hirst; children: Elizabeth, David. BSChemE, Washington U., 1963, AB, 1965; MD, St. Louis U., 1973. Diplomate Nat. Bd. Med. Examiners, lic. Va. State Bd. Medicine. Instr. pathology Sch. Medicine Washington U., St. Louis, 1973—77, vis. prof. pathology, 1985—86; asst. prof. U. Va., Charlottesville, 1977—81, assoc. prof. dept. pathology, 1981—90, prof. pathology Sch. Medicine, 1990—, assoc. dir. clin. chem. and toxicology, 1977—2003, assoc. dir. molecular diagnostics, 1986—, dir. clin. chemistry, 2003—. Lectr. in field. Author, editor (with Mills, Gaffey and Stoler): Yearbook of Pathology and Laboratory Medicine, 1994—97; author, editor, with Lo and Wittwer: Molecular Testing in Laboratory Medicine, 2002, editor: Clin. Chemistry, 1990—2007; co-editor: Yearbook of Pathology and Laboratory Medicine, 1995—97; editor: Fundamentals of Molecular Diagnostics, 2007; contbr. articles to profl. jours.; author, editor (with Burtis and Ashwood): Tietz Textbook of Clinical Chemistry and Molecular Diagnostics, 4th edit., 2005, Tietz Fundamentals of Clinical Chemistry, 6th edit., 2008, Tietz Textbook of Clinical Chemistry and Molecular Diagnostics, 5th edit., 2012, Tietz Fundamentals of Clinical Chemistry and Molecular Diagnostics, 7th edit., 2014. Bd. dirs. Little League Baseball, Charlottesville. Recipient Rsch. Grant awards, NIH, Am. Cancer Soc., Am. Dairy Coun., St. Louis-San Francisco RR Scholarship, Washington U., 1959—63, Disting. Scientist award, Nat. Acad. Clin. Biochem., 2007, Partnership award, Abbott Diagnostics, Edwards Sci., Siemens, Nichols Institute/Quest,OptiScan. Mem.: Am. Assn. Clin. Chemistry (bd. dirs. 2009—11, Outstanding Contbns. to Rsch. award 1987, Outstanding Contbns. to Clin. Chemistry award 1998, Norman Kubasik award 2001, Presdl. Citation 2001, Bernard Gerulat award 2001, Miriam Reiner award 2003, Speaker Award 2003, Presdl. Citation 2005, Outstanding Contrbns. to Edn. award 2013), Acad. Clin. Lab. Physicians and Scientists (mem. exec. coun. 1990—93, pres. 2003—04, Gerald T. Evans award 2007), Assn. Clin. Scientists (pres. 1985—86, Sunderman award 1987). Achievements include patents for immunochemical assays for human amylase isoenzymes and related monoclonal antibodies, 1993. Avocations: travel, reading, theater. Office: Dept Pathology University Virginia Sch Medicine PO Box 800168 Charlottesville VA 22908 Office Phone: 434-924-9432. Business E-Mail: dbruns@virginia.edu.

BRUNSTETTER, PETER SAMUEL, state legislator; b. San Francisco, Feb. 28, 1956; s. Richard Worstall and Roberta Sandra (Bessin) B.; m. Jodie Bray, July 1, 1978; children: Peter Jr., Rebecca, Daniel, Timothy. BA, Tulane U., 1977; JD, U. Va., 1984. Bar: Va. 1984, DC 1985, NC 1986. Assoc. McGuire, Woods & Battle, Richmond, Va., 1984-85; assoc. to ptnr. Kilpatrick Stockton LLP, Winston-Salem, NC, 1985—, mem. Fin. Practice Group; mem. Dist. 31 NC State Senate, 2007—. Chmn. Forsyth County (NC) Bd. Elections, 1990-91; mem. Forsyth County Bd. Commrs., 1991—, chmn., 1994—; bd. visitors N.C. State U., Raleigh, 1997, U. NC, Wilmington, 1998-99; trustee Novant Health, Inc., Winston-Salem, 1997, NC Hosp. Assn., 2001—; mem. State Health Coord. Coun., 1998—; mem. Piedmont Triad Internat. Airport Authority, 1999-2003; bd. mem. Winston-Salem Business, Inc. Lt. USN, 1977—81. Named fellow NC Inst. Polit. Leadership, 1988, one of Emerging Leaders of South, Lamar Soc., 1995. Mem.: Am. Health Lawyers Assn., NC State Bar, YMCAs of Northwest NC (chmn.), Winston-Salem Downtown Rotary, Order of Coif. Republican. So. Bapt. Avocation: flying. Office: Kilpatrick Stockton LLP 1 W 4th St Winston Salem NC 27101 also: NC Senate 16 W Jones St Room 2022 Raleigh NC 27601-2808 Address: PO Box 5401 Lewisville NC 27023 Office Phone: 919-733-7850. Business E-Mail: Peter.Brunstetter@ncleg.net. E-mail: pbrunstetter@kilpatrickstockton.com.

BRUTTO, DANIEL J., delivery service executive; Grad. in bus. and acctg., Loyola U., Chgo.; MBA, DeVry U. Keller Grad. Sch. Mgmt., Oakbrook Ter., Ill. Part-time assoc. to sr. mgmt. positions in ops., fin., mktg., and bus. devel. United Parcel Svc. America, Inc., mem. internat. acquisition and fin. integration team, v.p., gen. mgr. North and South America supply chain solutions, corp. controller, pres. global transportation and shared services, pres. global freight forwarding; pres. United Parcel Service International, 2008—. Mem. mgmt. com. United Parcel Svc. America. Office: United Parcel Svc America Inc 55 Glenlake Pky NE Atlanta GA 30328

BRYAN, CHARLES STONE, internist, educator; b. Columbia, SC, Columbia, South Carolina, Jan. 15, 1942; s. Leon Stone and Mary Morrill (Leadbeater) Bryan; m. Donna Hennesee, Oct. 30, 1982; children: Eleanor Chandlee, Emily Singleton. Student, Harvard U., Cambridge, Mass., 1960-62; BA, Johns Hopkins U., Balt., 1964, MD, 1967. Diplomate Am. Bd. Internal Medicine, Am. Bd. Infectious Diseases. Intern in pathology Johns Hopkins Hosp., Balt., 1967-68; intern in medicine Vanderbilt U. Hosp., Nashville, 1968-69, resident, fellow, 1971-74; pvt. practice Columbia, SC, 1974-77; dir. infectious diseases U. SC Sch. Medicine, Columbia, 1977-93, Heyward Gibbes disting. prof. medicine, chmn. dept., 1992-2000; dir. Ctr. Bioethics and Med. Humanities, 2000—08; cons. Providence Hosp. Columbia SC, 2008—. Pres. Am. Osler Soc., 2010—11, Columbia Med. Soc., 1992—93; editor Jour. of the SC. Med. Assn., 1977—2012; dir. Midlands Care Consortium, 1993—2004. Author: A Most Satisfactory Man, 1996, Osler: Inspirations from a Great Physician, 1997, Infectious Diseases in Primary Care, 2002, For Goodness Sake: The Seven Basic Virtues, 2006, A Hound Dog in Anderson: Essays on Medicine and Life, 2008; editor: Jour. S.C. Med. Assn., 1977—; author: A Oliver Wendell Homes: Physician And Man of Letters, 2009; contbr. articles to profl. jours. Chmn. Midlands Care Consortium, Columbia, 1993—2006. Surgeon USPHS, 1969—71. Recipient William Osler Medal, Am. Assn. for the History of Medicine, Theodore E. Woodward Award, Am. Clin. and Climatol. Assn., Laureate, ACP, Nicholas E. Davies Meml. Scholar Award, Lifetime Achievement Award, Am. Osler Soc. Master: ACP (Laureate award 1993, Nicholas E. Davies award 2007); fellow: Infectious Diseases Soc. Am., Royal Coll. Physicians (Edinburgh); mem.: Columbia Med. Soc. (pres. 1992), S.C. Infectious Diseases Soc. (pres. 1994), Am. Osler Soc. (sec.-treas. 2000—, pres. 2010), Am. Assn. History Medicine (William Osler medal 1967), Am. Clin. and Climatological Assn., Waring Libr. Soc. (pres. 1988). Avocations: medical history, golf. Office: Providence Hosp 2435 Forest Dr Columbia SC 29204 Office Phone: 803-256-5359. Personal E-mail: cboslerian@gmail.com, charles.bryan@providencehospitals.com.

BRYAN, J(AMES) P(ERRY), JR., energy executive; b. Houston, Jan. 17, 1940; s. James Perry Bryan Sr. and Gretchen (Smith) Josey; m. Mary Jon Lewis, Jan. 24, 1964; children: Alicia and John Bracken. BA, U. Tex., 1962, LLB, 1965; BFT, Am. Inst. Foreign Trade, 1966. V.p. Morgan Guaranty Trust Co., NYC, 1966-69; v.p. dir. investment banking Dominick & Dominick, NYC, Houston, 1969-74; pres., CEO The MortgageBanque, Inc., Houston, 1974-78; v.p. regional dir. corp. fin. dept. E.F. Hutton & Co., Inc., Houston, 1978-81; chmn., CEO Torch Energy Advisors, Inc., Houston, 1981—; Neuvo Energy Energy Assets Internat. Corp., Houston, 1987—95; chmn. & CEO Bellwether Exploration Co., Houston. Bd. dirs. Torch Energy Advisors, Inc., Bellwether Exploration Co., Neuvo Energy Co., Park Nat. Bank, Torchmark Corp., Republic Waste Inds. Founder, editor Internat. Law Jour.; contbr. reviews and articles on Tex. history to mags. and jours. Chmn. endowment fund, other offices Tex. State Hist. Assn.; chmn. fund raising com., past. chmn., pres. Tex. Hist. Found.; chmn. devel., adv. bd. Inst. Texan Cultures; trustee Nita Stewart Haley Meml. Libr.; past trustee, chmn. nominating com. Harris County Heritage Soc; mem. adv. bd. Bazoria County Hist. Mus.; founding chmn., past bd. dirs. South Main Ctr. Assn.; founder, bd. dirs. Collector's Inst.; bd. dirs. The Book Club of Tex.; chmn., dir. fund raising River Oaks Bapt. Sch., others. Mem. ABA, Tex. Bar Assn., Houston Bar Assn., Univ. Tex. Ex-Students Assn. (life), Philos. Soc. Tex., Houston Country Club, Tex. Breakfast Club (treas. Houston), Tejas Club, Argyle Club, Nat. golf Links Am., Phi Delta, Delta Phi Epsilon.

BRYAN, JOHN STEWART, III, newspaper publisher; b. Richmond, Va., May 4, 1938; s. David Tennant and Mary Davidson Bryan; m. Alice Pyle Zimmer, 1963 (div. 1985); children: Elizabeth Talbott, Anna Saulsbury; m. Lisa-Margaret Stevenson, 1993. BA, U. Va., 1960; LHD (hon.), Hampden-Sydney Coll., 1997, Emory and Henry Coll., 1999, Coll. of William and Mary, 2001, Randolph Macon Coll., 2004. Former advt. salesman Burlington (Vt.) Free Press; former reporter The Tampa (Fla.) Times; pub. The Tampa Tribune and Times, 1976—77, Richmond Times-Dispatch, Richmond News Leader, 1978—2004. Bd. dirs. Media Gen., Inc., Richmond, vice-chmn., exec. v.p., 1985—90, chmn., pres., CEO, 1990—2005, chmn., 2005—. Past pres. or chmn. Tampa Bay Art Ctr., Tampa Citizens Safety Coun., Tampa United Way, Gulf Coast Symphony, Jr. Achievement Richmond, Goodwill Industries Richmond, United Way Greater Richmond; trustee Va. Found. Ind. Coll., chmn., 1993—95, Va. Hist. Soc., 2008—, trustee, George C. Marshall Found.; former dir., trustee Episc. H.S., U. Tampa, St. Catharine's Sch., Hoover Instn. at Stanford, Tampa Bay Buccaneers, Fla. State Fair, Tampa Rowdies, Richmond C. of C., Maymont Found., Valentine Mus., Mutual Ins. Co., Bermuda, Richmond World Affairs Coun., Tampa Bay Coun. on Fgn. Rels., Va. Coalition for Open Govt., U. Va. Coll. Found., Va. Adv. Coun. Freedom of Info.; Va. Performing Arts Fedn.; with Thomas Jefferson Fedn.; mem. Inst. Bill of Rights Law, Coll. William & Mary; World Bus. Coun. Va. Business Coun. With USMC, 1960—62. Mem.: Soc. Profl. Journalists, Newspaper Assn. Am. (dir. 1990—93, 1997—2005), Newspaper Advt. Bur. (chmn. 1991—92), Va. Press Assn. (bd. dirs. 1980—86), So. Newspapers Pub. Assn. (found. chmn. 1978—79, pres. 1981—82), Fla. Press Assn. (life; pres. 1971—72, Disting. Svc. award 1975), Fla. Soc. Newspapers Editors (life), Soc. Colonial Wars, Fla. Coun. of 100, Soc. Cin., Nantucket Yacht Club, Farmington Country Club, Tampa Yacht and Country Club, Commonwealth Club, Country Club Va., Bohemian Club. Home: 4608 Sulgrave Rd Richmond VA 23221-3119 Office: Media Gen Inc PO Box 85333C Richmond VA 23293-5333

BRYAN, JOSEPH SHEPARD, JR., lawyer; b. Wilson, NC, Nov. 8, 1922; married; five children. BS, U.S. Naval Acad., 1944; JD, Harvard U., 1950. Bar: Fla., N.C. Asst. prof. pub. law and govt. U. N.C., 1950-54; counsel Winn-Dixie Stores, Inc., Jacksonville, Fla., 1954-61; gen. counsel Winn-Dixie Stores Inc., Jacksonville, Fla., 1961-66, sec., 1961-66, v.p., gen. counsel, sec., 1966-91, also bd. dirs.; of counsel Holland & Knight, Jacksonville, 1991—. Mem. adv. bd. 1st Union Nat. Bank of Fla., Inc.; bd. dirs. Shands Tchg. Hosp. Clins., Inc., Gainesville, Fla., Jacksonville Cmty. Found., Bok Tower Gardens Found., Jacksonville Symphony Assn., Cultural Coun. Greater Jacksonville, Inc.; exec. com., bd. dirs. Baptist St. Vincent's Health Sys., Jacksonville; bd. govs. The Nat. Conf. Chmn. Westminster Retirement Cmtys., 1998—. With USN, 1944-47, 51-52. Recipient Individual award Arts Assembly of Jacksonville, Inc., Humanitarian award Nat. Conf. Christians and Jews. Mem. ABA, Am. Arbitration Assn., Am. Corp. Counsel Assn., Riverside Presbyn. Ch. Home: 1651 Beach Ave Jacksonville FL 32233-5840

BRYAN, LUKE (THOMAS LUTHER BRYAN), musician; b. Leesburg, Ga., July 17, 1976; m. Caroline Boyer, Dec. 8, 2006; children: Thomas Boyer, Tatum Christopher. Attended, Ga. Southern U. Musician: (albums) I'll Stay Me, 2007, Doin' My Thing, 2009, Tailgates & Tanlines, 2011, Spring Break...Here to Party, 2013, Crash My Party, 2013, (songs) Do I, 2009 (USA Weekend Breakthrough Video of Yr., CMT Music Awards, 2010), I Don't Want This Night to End, 2011 (Male Video of Yr., CMT Music Awards, 2012), The Only Way I Know (with Jason Aldean and Eric Church), 2012 (Vocal Event of Yr., Acad. Country Music Awards, 2013, Collaborative Video of Yr., CMT Music Awards, 2013). Named Top New Solo Vocalist of Yr., Acad. Country Music Awards, 2010, Top New Artist, 2010, Entertainer of Yr., 2013, Favorite Country Male Artist, American Music Awards, 2012, 2013. Office: c/o Capitol Records Nashville 3322 West End Ave 11th Fl Nashville TN 37203-1100*

BRYAN, ROBERT ARMISTEAD, academic administrator, educator; b. Lebanon, Pa., Apr. 26, 1926; s. Morris Armistead and Katherine (Maulfair) B.; m. Kathryn Elizabeth Williams, Feb. 3, 1953; children: Lyla, Matthew. BA, U. Miami, 1950; MA, U. Ky., Lexington, 1951, PhD, 1956. Tchg. asst. U. Ky., Lexington, 1950-54, instr., 1956-57; lectr. extension div. U. Calif., Tokyo, 1955-56; dean advanced studies, dir. sponsored rsch. Fla. Atlantic U., 1969-70; mem. faculty, adminstrn. U. Fla., Gainsville, 1957-90, prof. English, 1968-90, dean faculties, 1970-71, assoc. v.p. acad. affairs, 1971-75, v.p. acad. affairs, 1975-85, provost, 1985-89, interim pres., 1989-90, ret., 1990; interim pres. U. Cen. Fla., 1991-92, U. South Fla., 1993-94. Reader Coll. Bd. Exams., Ednl. Testing Svc., 1958-61; cons. So. Assn. Schs. and Colls., 1965-73, also chmn. visitation com., 1966-67; cons. HEW, Nat. Assn. of State Univs. and Land Grant Colls., 1990-91; cons. Fla. Bd. Regents, 1994-95; trustee Bethune-Cookman Coll., 1994-2001; mem. Fla. Postsecondary Edn. Planning Commn., 1996-2000. Bibliographer: Twentieth Century Literature, 1958-61. Served with U.S. Mcht. Marine, 1944-47, with AUS, 1954-56. Decorated Royal Order North Star (Sweden) Mem. MLA, Southeastern Renaissance Conf., S. Atlantic Mod. Lang. Assn., Sigma Chi. Episcopalian. Home: 2680 SW 53rd Ln Unit 1527 Gainesville FL 32608-8911 Personal E-mail: rbryan@gator.net.

BRYAN, TOMMY ELIAS, state supreme court justice; b. May 16, 1956; s. Marge Spivey and Elias Daniel Bryan; m. Pamela Mizzell; children: Thomason, Tucker. BS in edn., Troy State U., 1978, MS in edn., 1979; JD, Jones Sch. Law, 1983. Staff atty. Ala. Ct. Criminal Appeals, 1984—86; asst. atty. gen., assoc. gen. counsel environ. dept. State of Ala., 1987—2005; judge Ala. Ct. Civil Appeals, 2005—13; assoc. justice Ala. Supreme Ct., Montgomery, 2013—. Deacon First Bapt. Ch., Montgomery. Named Judge of Yr., Ala. State Bar Family Law Sect., 2012. Mem.: Montgomery County Bar Assn., Ala. Bar Assn. (mem. environ. law and appellate practice sects.). Office: Alabama Supreme Ct 300 Dexter Ave Montgomery AL 36104*

BRYAN, WENDELL HOBDY, II, (HOB BRYAN), state legislator; b. Amory, Miss., Dec. 5, 1952; s. Wendell and Nadine. BA, Miss. State U., 1974; JD, U. Va., 1977. Bar: Miss. 1977. Atty. pvt. practice, Amory, 1977—; mem. Dist. 7 Miss. State Senate, 1984—. Chmn. Fin., Elections, Constn. coms. Democrat. Baptist. Office: PO Box 1018 Rm 212 D Jackson MS 39215 Office Phone: 662-256-9601, 601-359-3234.

BRYANT, ANGELA R., state legislator; State rep. Dist. 7, NC, 2007—; atty.; sr. cons. Angela Bryant Consulting; co-founder Visions Inc. Mem. Appropriations com., Edn. com., Election Law and Fin. Reform com., Juvenile Justice com., Pub. Utilities com.; vice chmn. Univ. Bd. Govs. Nominating com.; chmn. House Select Com. on Use of 911 Funds, Energy and Energy Efficiency com. Democrat. Office: North Carolina House of Representatives 300 N Salisbury St Rm 542 Raleigh NC 27603-5925 Office Phone: 919-733-5878. E-mail: Angela.Bryant@ncleg.net.

BRYANT, HUBERT HALE, retired lawyer; b. Tulsa, Jan. 4, 1931; s. Roscoe Conkling and Curlie Beatrice (Marshall) B.; m. Elnora Geraldine Roberson, Oct. 25, 1952; children: Cheryl Denise, Tara Kay. BA, Fisk U., 1952; LLB, Howard U., 1956. Bar: Okla. 1956, U.S. Dist. Ct. (no. dist.) Okla 1956, U.S. Ct. Appeals (10th cir.) 1967, U.S. Supreme Ct. 1980. Individual practice law, Tulsa, 1956—67, 1981—84, 1986—2013. Asst. city prosecutor, City of Tulsa, 1961-63, chief city prosecutor, 1963-67, asst. U.S. atty., No. Dist. Okla., 1967-77, U.S. atty., 1977-81; mcpl. ct. judge City of Tulsa, 1984-86. Trustee 1st Bapt. Ch., Tulsa, 1970-75, 96-2002; bd. dirs. Tulsa Urban League, 1962-64. Recipient Outstanding Alumni award Howard U. Sch. Law, 1981, 30 Yr. Outstanding African Am. Lawyer award Met. Tulsa Urban League, 1997, Amos T. Hall award, Northeastern Okla Black Lawyers Assn., 2010. Mem. NAACP, Nat. Bar Assn. (Named to Hall of Fame), Okla. Bar Assn. (50 Yr. Membership award 2006), Tulsa County Bar Assn., Okla. Trial Lawyers Assn., Nat. Set, Masons (named Mason of Yr. local chpt. 1963, Outstanding Citizen award 1978), Sigma Pi Phi, Alpha Theta Boule, Alpha Phi Alpha. Democrat. Home: 1818 N Boston Ave Tulsa OK 74106

BRYANT, JOHN BRADBURY, economics professor, consultant; b. July 7, 1947; s. Royal Calvin and Martha Preble (Jones) B.; m. Evelyn Sandra Seltzer, June 24, 1973; 1 child, Aryn Royale. BA, Oberlin Coll., 1969; MS, Carnegie-Mellon U., 1973, PhD, 1975. Economist, bd. govs. FRS, Washington, 1974-77; sr. economist Fed. Res. Bank, Mpls., 1977-81; assoc. prof. U. Fla., Gainesville, 1980-81; cons. Fed. Res. Bank, Dallas, 1983-86, 91-92; Fox assoc. prof. Rice U., Houston, 1981-84, Fox prof. econs., 1984—, prof. mgmt., 1987—. Vis. scholar Hoover Inst., Stanford U., 1988-89; vis. fellow Center, Tilburg U., Netherlands, 1998-99. Contbr. articles to profl. jours., chapters to books. Office: Rice U Dept Econs MS22 6100 Main St Houston TX 77005-1892 Business E-Mail: jbb@rice.edu.

BRYANT, KEITH LYNN, JR., history professor; b. Oklahoma City, Nov. 6, 1937; s. Keith Lynn and Elsie L. (Furman) B.; m. Margaret A. Burum, Aug. 14, 1962; children: Jennifer Lynne, Craig Warne. BS, U. Okla., 1959, MEd, 1961; PhD, U. Mo., 1965. From asst. prof. to prof., assoc. dean U. Wis., Milw., 1965-76; prof. Tex. A&M U., College Station, 1976-88, head dept. history, 1976-80, dean Coll. Liberal Arts, 1980-84; prof. history U. Akron, Ohio, 1988-2000, head dept., 1988-95, prof. emeritus Ohio, 2000—. Cons. So. Ry., NEH. Author: Alfalfa Bill Murray, 1968, Arthur E. Stilwell, Promoter with a Hunch, 1971, History of the Atchison, Topeka and Santa Fe Railway, 1974, William Merritt Chase: A Genteel Bohemian, 1991, Culture in the American Southwest, 2001; co-author: A History of American Business, 1983; bd. editors Western Hist. Quar., 1984-87, Southwestern Hist. Quar., 1980-87; editor Railroads in the Age of Regulation, 1900-1980, 1988. Served to 1st lt. U.S. Army, 1959-60. Recipient William H. Kiekhofer award U. Wis., 1968, George W. and Constance M. Hilton book award Ry. and Locomotive Hist. Soc., 1990, David P. Morgan Article award Ry. and Locomotive Hist. Soc., 1998; grantee Am. Philos. Soc., 1968, NEH, 1984. Mem. So. Hist. Assn. (chmn. Frank Owsley book award com. 1988), Western History Assn., Tex. Hist. Assn., Lexington Group, S.W. Conf. Humanities Consortium (pres. 1982-83). Home: PO Box 5366 Bryan TX 77805-5366

BRYANT, KEVIN L., state legislator; b. Anderson, SC, Feb. 19, 1967; m. Ann Barinowski, 1989; 3 children. BS in Pharmacy, U. Ga., 1989. Pres. Bryant Pharmacy & Supply, 1989—; chmn. Anderson County Rep. Party, 1997—2001; del. Rep. Nat. Conv., 2000; mem. Dist. 3 SC State Senate, 2004—, mem. Agr. and Natural Resources Com., Fin. Com., Gen. Com., Labor, Commerce and Industry Com. & Med. Affairs Com. Mem.: Anderson Area C. of C., 10th Dist. Pharmacy Assn., Concord Cmty. Ch. (treas. & deacon 1993—). Republican. Office: 606 Gressette Bldg Columbia SC 29201 Mailing: 104-A North Ave Anderson SC 29625 Office Phone: 803-212-6024. E-mail: bryantk@scsenate.org.

BRYANT, L. GERALD, management consultant; b. Norman, Okla., July 27, 1942; s. Lewis Cullen and Ludie A. (Skacel) B.; m. Linda Sue Farris, June 12, 1964; children: David Graham, Heather Leigh. BBA, U. Okla., 1964; MHA, Washington U., St. Louis, 1968. Acct. Pan-Am. Petroleum Corp., Tulsa, 1964-66; adminstrv. asst. Baylor U. Med. Ctr., Dallas, 1968-70, adminstr. C.P.C.H., 1970-72, assoc. dir., 1972-75, assoc. dir. planning and budget, 1975-80, sr. v.p., 1980-81, Baylor Health Care System, Dallas, 1981-84, COO, exec. v.p., 1984-92, exec. v.p. strategy devel., 1992—2000; pres. Bryant Consulting Group, 2000—. Bd. dirs. Regional Health Planning Agy., Irving, Tex., 1979—83; adj. faculty Wahington U. Sch. Med., St. Louis, 1983—2000, U. Ala., Birmingham, 1992—2000, Trinity U., San Antonio, 1996—2000; active Blue Ribbin Task Force on Health Care Reform, Tex. Hosp. Assn., 1992—93; devel. bd. dirs. Allied Bank, Dallas. Contbr. chpts. to books. Bd. dirs. Arthritis Found. Dallas, 1980-84; bd. dirs. Preservation Dallas, 1995—; deacon Wilshire Bapt. Ch., Dallas, 1976—; bd. dirs. Dallas Sci. Pl., 1995—. Fellow Am. Coll. Health Care Execs.; mem. Am. Hosp. Assn. (coun. regents 1994—, ho. of dels. 1996—, region 7 policy bd. 1994—), Tex. Hosp. Assn. (coun. on health planning 1981-84, coun. on pre-paid health plans 1984—), Am. Soc. Hosp. Planning, Am. Mgmt. Assn. Lodges: Rotary. Republican. Baptist. Avocations: antique furniture collecting, travel, gardening. Home: 8648 Cherry Hill Dr Dallas TX 75243-7030

BRYANT, MYNORA JOYCE, not-for-profit fundraiser; EdD, U. Md. Coord. counseling svcs. and student activities No. Va. CC; internat. grand basileus Sigma Gamma Rho. Named one of 100 Most Influential Black Americans, Ebony mag., 2006; named to Power 150, 2008. Office: Ste 200 1000 Southhill Dr Cary NC 27513 Office Phone: 919-678-9721. E-mail: Mbryant@nvcc.edu.

BRYANT, PAMELA L., chemistry professor; d. Richard W. and Ruth C. Davis; m. Kenneth M. Bryant, Feb. 22, 1969; children: Suzanne R. George, Michele B. Babuchna. PhD, La. State U., Baton Rouge, 2000. Postdoc. MIT, Cambridge, 2000—01; head dept. phys. sci. Howard Payne U., Brownwood, Tex., 2001—. Mem. Bangs Sch. Bd., Tex., 2007—. Named Outstanding Faculty Mem. of Yr., Howard Payne U. Mem.: Am. Chem. Soc. Baptist. Avocation: raising cattle. Home: 5000 County Rd 147 Brownwood TX 76801 Office: Howard Payne Univ 1000 Fisk Brownwood TX 76801 Office Fax: 325-649-8948. Business E-Mail: pbryant@hputx.edu.

BRYANT, PAUL THOMPSON, language educator; b. Oklahoma City, Aug. 24, 1928; s. Paul Dewey and Lynnis (Thompson) B.; m. Genevieve Dale Bryant, Aug. 27, 1949; children: Elaine Lynette Bryant Smyth, Christopher Dale. BS, U. Okla., 1950, MS, 1952, MA, 1956; PhD, U. Ill., 1965. Editor Inst. of Tech., Wash. State U., Pullman, 1954-56, Am. Soc. Engring. Edn., Urbana, Ill., 1958-64; dir engring. pubs. U. Ill., Urbana, 1958-64; chmn. Dept. English Colo. State U., Ft. Collins, 1969-75, faculty English, 1964-84, assoc. dean grad. sch., 1980-84; prof. English, dean Grad. Coll. Radford U., Va., 1984-93; ind. scholar, writer, cons., 1993—. Author essays, poems, short stories; author: H.L. Davis, 1978, The Homestead Cabin, 1998, Confessions of an Habitual Administrator, 2005, Old Men, 2009; editor, compiler essay collection: Geography to Geotechnics, 1969; co-editor essay collection: Frontier Experience and the American Dream, 1989. Bd. dirs. NRV Cmty. Sentencing, Christiansburg, Va., 1985-91; bd. dirs. Buncombe County Friends of Libr., 1999-2004, v.p., 2000-2002, pres., 2002-2004; trustee Sci. Mus. of Western Va., Roanoke, 1989-92; adv. coun. Assn. for the Study of Lit. and the Environment, 1994-2000. With U.S. Army, 1946-47. Mem. MLA, Coll. English Assn. (pres. 1982-83), Western Lit. Assn. (exec. com. 1989-91), conf. of So. Grad. Schs. (pres. 1991-92). Personal E-mail: pgbryant@bellsouth.net.

BRYANT, PHIL, Governor of Mississippi; b. Moorhead, Miss., Dec. 9, 1954; m. Deborah Hays; children: Katie, Patrick. AA, Hinds Cmty. Coll., Raymond, Miss.; BS in Criminal Justice, U. Southern Miss., Hattiesburg, 1977; MS in Polit. Sci., Miss. Coll., Clinton, 1988. Dep. sheriff Hinds County, Miss., 1976—81; ins. fraud investigator, 1981—91; mem. Miss. House of Reps., Jackson, 1991—96; auditor State of Miss., Jackson, 1996—2008, lt. gov., 2008—12, gov., 2012—; pres. Miss. State Senate, Jackson, 2007—12. Part-time faculty Miss. Coll., 2008—. Contbg. author 21st Century Government: Digital Promise, Digital Reality, Leadership Secrets of Government Financial Officials, Best Case Practices. Active Habitat for Humanity, Miss. Mentoring Network, Mission Miss.; mem. Gov.'s Commn. Recovery & Renewal, Law Enforcement & Fire Fighter Relief Fund; active St. Marks United Meth. Ch. Recipient Disting. Alumnus award, Miss. Coll. Dept. Hist & Polit. Sci., 1997, Mississippian of the Yr. award, Assn. Info. Tech. Professionals (AITP), 2003, Kirk Fordice Freedom award, Ctrl. Miss. Nat. Rifle Assn., 2005, In the Arena award, Ctr. for Digital Govt.; named Crime Victims Advocate of the Yr. award, 2003, Statesman of Yr., American Family Radio, 2004; named to The Southern Miss. Alumni Assn. Hall of Fame, 1999; Henry Toll fellow, 1998. Mem.: NRA, Miss. Rep. Elected Officials Assn. (past pres.), Nat. Assn. State Auditors (chmn. bylaws com., exec. com.), Miss. Fire Investigators Assn., Internat. Assn. Arson Investigators, Leadership 2000, Ducks Unlimited, Greater Jackson Law Enforcement Officers Assn. (pres.), Jaycees, Reservoir Lions Club. Republican. Methodist. Office: Office of the Governor PO Box 139 Jackson MS 39205 Office Phone: 601-359-3150.*

BRYANT, ROBERT, state legislator; b. Savannah, Ga., Aug. 11, 1944; Supt., Savannah, 1999—2000; state rep. Dist. 160 Ga., 2004—. Democrat. Baptist. Office: Rm 608 Legis Off Bldg Atlanta GA 30334 Mailing: 4110 4th St Savannah GA 31408 Office Phone: 404-656-0298.

BRYANT, TIMOTHY CLARK, financial advisor; b. Akron, Ohio, Apr. 11, 1943; s. Alan Willard and Clara Sherman (Clark) Bryant; m. Mary Esther Snell, Jan. 17, 1981. AB, Dartmouth Coll., 1967; MBA, U. Chgo., 1971; MS in Taxation, DePaul U., 1975. CPA, Ill. Dir. fin. and adminstrn. Fibre Box Assn., Chgo., 1975—77, Akers Packaging Co., Middletown, Ohio, 1977—78; dir., sec., treas. CompuShop, Inc., Dallas, 1978—80, dir., 1980—85; v.p. fin., dir. Rubicon Corp., Richardson, Tex., 1980—82, Automated Mgmt. Inc., Dallas, 1982—83, Avian Corp., Clearwater, Fla., 1983—85, pres., bd. dirs., 1985—87; v.p. investments Wells Fargo Advisors, St. Petersburg, Fla., 1990—2012, Ameriprise Fin., St. Petersburg, 2012—. Chmn. bd. dirs. Adventures Away, Inc., Chgo., 1983-87; pres., treas., bd. dirs. Talk2 Corp., Clearwater, 1987-90; cons. Nevada Brake Corp., 1985-91, So. Conf. Bur., Inc., 1987-90, Innovative Products Group, Inc., 1987-90. With U.S. Army, 1965-66, Korea. Mem. AICPA, Vinoy Club. Home: 307 Brightwaters Blvd NE Saint Petersburg FL 33704-3709 Office: Ameriprise Financial 100 2d Ave S # 904-S Saint Petersburg FL 33701 Office Phone: 727-369-3203. Office Fax: 727-369-3223.

BRYCE, WILLIAM DELF, lawyer; b. Georgetown, Tex., Aug. 7, 1932; s. D.A. Bryce and Frances Maxine (Wilson) Bryce Bakke; m. Sarah Alice Riley, Dec. 20, 1954; children: Douglas Delf, David Dickson. BA, U. Tex., 1955; LLB, Yale U., 1960. Bar: Tex. 1960. Briefing atty. Tex. Supreme Ct., Austin, 1960-61; sole practice, 1961—. Lectr. U. Tex., 1965—66. Served to 1st lt. USAF, 1955—57. Fellow Tex. Bar Found.; mem. ABA, State Bar Tex., Austin Bar Assn., Williamson County Bar Assn., Rotary Internat. (dist. 5870 gov. 1999-2000). Office: 511 S Main St Georgetown TX 78626-5609 Home: 308 E University Ave Georgetown TX 78626 Office Phone: 512-930-3725.

BRYNJOLFSSON, ARI, nuclear physicist; b. Akureyri, Iceland, Dec. 7, 1926; arrived in U.S., 1965, naturalized, 1970; s. Brynjolfur and Gudrun (Rosinkarsdottir) Sigtryggsson; m. Marguerite Reman, Dec. 22, 1950; children: Ariane, Olaf, Erik, John, Alan Cand. Phil., U. Copenhagen, 1949, Cand. Mag., 1954, Mag. Scien., 1954; Dr.Phil., Niels Bohr Inst., U. Copenhagen, 1973; post grad., Advanced Mgmt. Program, Harvard U., 1971. Dir. radiation rsch. Danish Atomic Energy Rsch. Establishment, Roskilde, Denmark, 1957-65; chief radiation rsch. U.S. Army Natick (Mass.) Lab., 1965—72, dir. U.S. food irradiation program, 1972—80, spl. asst. for physics, 1980—88; project dir. Facility for Food Irradiation Tech. UN Joint FAO/IAEA Divsn., Wageningen, Netherlands, 1988-90; project dir. internat. tng. ctr. joint FAO/IAEA divsn. Internat. Atomic Energy Agy., Vienna, 1990-92; pres. Applied Radiation Industries, Wayland, Mass., 1992—. Contbr. articles to profl. jours. Subspecialties: Nuclear physics; radiation biology. Current work: Astrophysics, plasma red shift cosmology, theoretical physics, general theory relativity. Biological effects radiation. Spl. scholar NRC and U. Iceland, 1954-55, Alexander von Humboldt scholar U. Göttingen, Fed. Republic Germany, 1955-57; recipient Mollers Found. award for exceptional svc. to Danish industry, 1965, Tech. award Am. Nuc. Soc. Radiation Sci., 1988. Mem.: Am. Phys. Soc. Home: 15486 N Nebraska Ave Ste A Lutz FL 33549-6103 Personal E-mail: aribrynjolfsson@comcast.net.

BRYSON, VALRICA, music educator; Grad., Coll. VI (now U. VI). Music tchr. St. Croix Ednl. Complex, Kingshill, V.I. Named St. Croix Dist. Tchr. of Yr., 2006, V.I. Tchr. of Yr., 2007. Office: St Croix Ednl Complex RR 1 Box 10360 Kingshill VI 00850-9701 E-mail: valricab@yahoo.com.

BRYSON, WILLIAM HAMILTON, law educator; b. Richmond, Va., July 29, 1941; s. William Alexander and Lillian Sutton (Wilkinson) B. BA, Hampden-Sydney Coll., 1963; LLB, Harvard U., 1967; LLM, U. Va., 1968; PhD, Cambridge U., Eng., 1972. Bar: Va. 1967. Asst. prof. U. Richmond Sch. Law, 1973-76, assoc. prof., 1976-80, prof., 1980—; Blackstone prof. law U. Richmond Sch. Law, 2001. Mem. adv. com. on rules of ct. Jud. Coun. Va. Author: Equity Side of the Exchequer, 1975, Legal Education in Virginia 1779-1979: A Biographical Approach, 1982, Virginia Civil Procedure, 1997, 4th edit., 2005, Virginia Circuit Court Opinions, 1985—, Virginia Law Books, 2000, Samuel Dodd's Reports, 2000, Cases Concerning Equity, 2001; mem. editl. bd., asst. editor Am. Jour. Legal History, 1999—2009. William Senior scholar, 1970-72; Max Planck Inst. fellow, Frankfurt, Germany, 1972-73; Fulbright grant, 1963, Am. Coun. Learned Socs. grant, 1980; recipient Yorke prize Cambridge U., 1973 Fellow Royal Hist. Soc.; mem. Selden Soc. (Va. corr.), Va. Hist. Soc., Va. Bar Assn. (Boyd-Graves Conf. 1982-), Am. Soc. Legal History (bd. dirs. 1981-84), Supreme Ct. Va. Hist. Commn., John Marshall Inn of Ct. (exec. com.), Phi Beta Kappa. Episcopalian. Office: University Richmond Sch Law 28 Wesrhampton Way Richmond VA 23173

BUBRICK, MELVIN PHILLIP, surgeon; b. Chgo., June 2, 1944; m. Barbara Lynn Jacobs, Jan. 26, 1969; children: Jerome Bradley, Ellen Jeanne, Dena Beth. BA with honors, U. Ill., 1964, MD, 1968.

Diplomate Am. Bd. Surgery, Am. Bd. Colon and Rectal Surgery; lic. Minn. Intern in surgery Univ. Hosps., Madison, Wis., 1968-69; resident in gen. surgery Hennepin County Gen. Hosp., Mpls., 1969-74; postdoctoral fellow colon and rectal surgery U. Minn. Health Scis. Ctr., Mpls., 1974-75; clin. instr. div. colon and rectal surgery U. Minn., Mpls., 1975-77, clin. asst. prof., 1977-78, clin. asst. prof. dept. surgery, 1978-80, asst. prof., 1980-87, assoc. prof., 1987—; chief surgery, program dir. surg. residency Hennepin County Med. Ctr., 1988-94; pres. Hennepin Facility Assocs., 1995—2000, chmn. bd. dirs., 1991—2001. V.p. Mpls. Med. Rsch. Found., 1991-2000; chmn. bd. dirs. Hennepin Faculty Assocs., 1991-2000, CEO, 1991-2001. Author: (with others) Conn's Therapy, 1985, The Pancreas. Principles of Medical and Surgical Practice, 1985, Applied Therapeutics: The clinical use of drugs, 4th rev. edit., 1988; contbr. over 90 articles to Minn. Med. jour., Am. Surg. jour., Diseases of Colon and Rectum, Surgery, others. Bd. dirs. Mpls. Med. Rsch. Found., Inc., 1981-89. Mem. AMA, ACS, Am. Assn. Surgery of Trauma, Am. Soc. Colon and Rectal Surgeons (co-chair Self Assessment Exam. Com. 1984-85), Am. Soc. Microbiology, Assn. Program Dirs. of Surgery, Cen. Surg. Assn., Collegium Internat. Chirurgiae Digestivae, Soc. Surgery of Alimentary Tract, Minn. Assn. Pub. Teaching Hosps., Minn. Surg. Soc., Minn. Med. Assn., Mpls. Surg. Soc., Hennepin County Med. Soc. (mem. and chair various coms. 1975—, Hennepin faculty assoc. 1983—). Achievements include research in assessment of bursting strength and healing of intestinal anastomoses, predictive value of surface oximetry in assessing healing in irradiated bowel, use of antibiotic microspheres for infected vascular grafts and peritonitis, clinical and anatomic assessment of first rib-clavicular decompression on subclavian catheters and pacemaker leads, influence of nutritional deficits in intestinal anastomotic strength, iron chelation with a Deferoxamine (DFO) conjugate in hemorrhagic shock. Personal E-mail: mbubrick@comcast.net.

BUCAY, VIVIAN W., dermatologist; m. Moises Bucay; 3 children. Grad., John Hopkins U., Baylor Coll. of Medicine. Asst. prof. physician asst. studies Univ. of Texas Health Sci. Ctr., San Antonio; dermatology tng. Univ. of Miami, Baylor Coll. of Medicine, Houston. Author many publications. Named Texas Super Doctor, Texas Monthly Mag., 2004, 2005, 2006. Fellow: Am. Acad. of Dermatology; mem.: Am. Soc. for Laser Medicine and Surgery, Soc. for Pediatric Dermatology, Internat. Soc. of Dermatology, Am. Soc. of Dermatologic Surgery. Office: Vivian W Bucay 326 W Craig Pl San Antonio TX 78212 Office Phone: 210-692-3000. Office Fax: 210-692-3056.

BUCHAN, DOUGLAS CHARLES, gas industry executive, government agency administrator; b. Bklyn., Aug. 4, 1936; s. Charles J. and Amelia P. (Petraca) B.; 1 son, Paul Douglas. Student, U. Fla., 1954—56. Pres. Buchan Gas Co., St.Petersburg, Fla., 1955—88, Buchan Oil Co., St.Petersburg, 1966-89, 1994—97, Grill Parts Distbrs., 1983—89, Site Mgmt., Inc., 1983—; dep. asst. sec. energy US Department of Energy, 1989—93; energy expert US Govt., 1994—99. Mem. U.S. Senate Bus. Adv. Com., 1984—, Petr Equipment Inst., Common Ground Alliance, Pinellas County Gas Bd., Pinellas County Plumbing and Mech. Bd., So. Bldg. Code Congress, Internat. Code Coun., Nat. Fire Protection Assn., Nat. Fire Investigators Assn., Petroleum Equipment Inst., Energy Tng. Network, Energy U. Pres. Pinellas County Rep. Ivory Club; chmn. Pinellas campaign Reagan-Bush, Fla. campaign George Bush for Pres., dep. asst. sec. energy, spl. asst. pres. consumer affairs pub. liaison, energy cons., The White Ho., US Govt. 1st lt. US Army, 1958—65. Recipient Meritorious Svc. award, US Dept. Energy. Mem. Nat. Oil Jobbers Coun., Nat. Liquified Petroleum Gas Assn., Nat. Assn. Fire Investigators (mem. Internat. Code Coun., Energy Tng. Network), Nat. Fire Protection Assn., Fla. Petroleum Marketers Assn. (v.p.), Oil Fuel Inst. Fla (pres., chmn. bd.), St. Petersburg Yacht. Episcopalian. Home: 1067 42nd Ave NE Saint Petersburg FL 33703-5235 Office: Site Mgmt Inc PO Box 60485 Saint Petersburg FL 33784 Personal E-mail: buchandoug@msn.com.

BUCHAN, JONATHAN EDWARD, JR., lawyer; b. Mullins, SC, Sept. 1, 1950; s. Jonathan Edward and Margaret Alice (Liles) B.; m. Suzette Rogers Phillips, Nov. 22, 1986; 1 stepchild, Geoffrey Eliot Eloge; 1 child, Caroline Phillips. AB magna cum laude, Princeton U., 1972; JD, Duke U., 1978. Bar: N.C. 1978. Co-founder, sr. editor, Osceola News Weekly, Columbia, SC, 1973—74; govt. reporter Charlotte Observer, Columbia, SC, 1974—75, govt. editor, 1983—84; ptnr. Helms Mulliss & Wicker and predecessor firms, Charlotte, 1984—2008, McGuire Woods LLP, Charlotte, 2008—. Mem. adj. faculty dept. mass media law Wake Forest Law Sch., 1992-2002; bd. dirs. Legal Svcs. for So. Piedmont, Inc., 1993-98. Co-author: 50-State Survey of Libel Law, NC Sect., 1981—; contbg. author: North Carolina Media Law Handbook, 2007. Pres., bd. dirs. Hospice at Charlotte, Inc., 1982-88; adv. bd. Trust for Pub. Land, Carolinas. 2001-08. Mem.: WFAE (bd. dirs. 2011—), Mecklenburg County Bar Assn. (pres. 2004—05). Avocations: fly fishing, tennis, reading. Office: McGuire Woods LLP PO Box 31247 100 N Tryon St Ste 2900 Charlotte NC 28202 Home: 2019 Meadowood Ln Charlotte NC 28211-4081 Office Phone: 704-343-2063. Personal E-mail: Buchan247@aol.com. Business E-Mail: jbuchan@mcguirewoods.com.

BUCHANAN, BRUCE, II, political science professor; b. Shelby, Mont., July 28, 1945; s. Neil and Dorothy Jean (Gallup) B.; m. Susan Safford Bright, June 10, 1964 (div. June 1976); m. Stephanie Ann Sokolewicz, Jan. 3, 1981; children: Kathryn Elaine, Douglas Neil, Jacqueline May. BA, Stanford U., 1967; MA, Yale U., 1969; MPhil, 1970, PhD, 1972. Prof. U. Ga., Athens, 1973-74, U. Tex., Austin, 1974—. Author: The Presidential Experience, 1978, The Citizens Presidency, 1987, Electing A President, 1991, Renewing Presidential Politics, 1996, Presidential Campaign Quality, 2004, The Policy Partnership, 2004, Presidential Power and Accountability, 2013. Exec. dir. Markle Commn. on Media and Electorate, 1988-90; rsch. dir. Markle Found. Presdl. Election Study, 1992, dir. Markle Presdl. Watch, 1996. Mem. Am. Polit. Sci. Assn. (award for best paper on presidency 1997), Presidency Rsch. Group, Western Polit. Sci. Assn. Avocations: cello, sports, gardening. Home: 1304 Wilshire Blvd Austin TX 78722-1127 Office: University Tex Dept Govt 1 University Sta A1800 Austin TX 78712-1087 Office Phone: 512-232-7212. Business E-Mail: bruceb@mail.la.utexas.edu, bruceb@austin.utexas.edu.

BUCHANAN, GEORGE R., oncologist, hematologist, educator; b. Bloomington, Ill., Apr. 21, 1944; m. Chris Buchanan. BA with honors, Drake U., 1966; MD, U. Chgo., 1970. Cert. Am. Bd. Pediat., Am. Bd. Pediat. Sub-Bd. Hematology-Oncology. Intern pediatrics Children's Meml. Hosp., Chgo., 1970—71, resident hematologic oncology, 1971—73; fellowship hematology Children's Hosp., Boston, 1973—75; fellowship pediatric oncology Dana-Farber Cancer Inst., Boston, 1974—75; instr. Harvard U.; med. dir. Ctr. Cancer and Blood Disorders Children's Med. Ctr., Dallas; asst. prof. to. prof. pediat. U. Tex. Southwestern Med. Ctr., Children's Cancer Fund disting. chair pediat. oncology and hematology Dallas, dir. Barrett Family Ctr. for Pediat. Oncology; dir. pediat. hematology / oncology Southwestern Comprehensive Sickle Ctr. & North Tex. Hemophilia Ctr. Co-chair working group of strategic planning com. Nat. Heart, Lung and Blood Inst. (NHLBI); chair protocol review com. Sickle Cell Disease Clin. Rsch. Network. Contbr. articles to med. jours. Mem.: Soc. Pediat. Rsch., Hemophilia Thrombosis Rsch. Soc., Am. Soc. Pediat. Hematology-Oncology (pres. 1999—2002, Disting. Career award 2007), Am. Soc. Hematology (exec. com. 2001—05), Am. Pediat. Soc., Alpha Omega Alpha, Phi Beta Kappa. Office: Children's Med Ctr - Dallas 1935 Motor St Dallas TX 75235 also: UT Southwestern Med Ctr at Dallas 5323 Harry Hines Blvd Dallas TX 75390-9063 Office Phone: 214-648-8594, 877-445-1234. Office Fax: 877-445-1234. E-mail: george.buchanan@utsouthwestern.edu.

BUCHANAN, JOHN D., lawyer; B in Economics, Washington & Lee U.; JD, Vanderbilt U.; LLM, NYU. Exec. v.p., gen. counsel, corp. sec. AmSouth Bancorporation; gen. counsel Regions Financial Corp., Birmingham, Ala., 2007—, sr. exec. v.p., corp. sec., 2008—; gen. counsel SouthTrust Bank; officer, helicopter pilot US Army. Office: Regions Financial Corp 1900 5th Aveune North Birmingham AL 35203 Office Phone: 205-944-1300. Office Fax: 901-580-3915.

BUCHANAN, PAT (PATRICK JOSEPH BUCHANAN), journalist, author, political commentator; b. Washington, Nov. 2, 1938; s. William Baldwin and Catherine E. (Crum) B.; m. Shelley Ann Scarney, May 8, 1971. AB in English cum laude, Georgetown U., 1961; MS in Journalism, Columbia U., 1962. Editorial writer St. Louis Globe-Dem., 1962-64, asst. editl. editor, 1964—65; exec. asst. to Pres. The White House, 1966-69, spl. asst. to Pres., 1969-73, cons. to Pres., 1973-74; commentator NBC Radio Network, 1978-82; columnist TV Guide, 1975—77; syndicated columnist NY Times Spl. Features, 1975-78, Chgo. Tribune-NY News Syndicate, 1978-85; dir. comm. The White House, Washington DC, 1985-87; syndicated columnist Tribune Media Svcs., 1987-91, 93-95, Creators Syndicate, 1997—99, 2001—. Co-host Buchanan-Braden Show, Sta. WRC, 1978-83, columnist; co-host Crossfire (TV show) Cable News Network, 1982-85, 87-91, 93-95, 97-99; panelist The McLaughlin Grp., NBC/PBS, 1982-85, 88-92, 97-99, 2001—, After Hours WTOP-TV, 1979-1982; moderator Capital Gang (TV Show) Cable News Network, 1988-91; co-host Buchanan and Press, MSNBC, 2002-2003; editor-in-chief newsletter PJB-From the Right, 1990-91; co-founder, editor The American Conservative, 2002-07; candidate for Republican Nomination for Pres., 1992, 96, Reform Party candidate for Pres., 2000; founder, chmn. The American Cause, 1993-95, 97-99, 2001—, Buchanan & Co., Mut. Broadcasting System, 1993-95; polit. analyst MSNBC, 2003-12 Author: The New Majority: President Nixon at Mid-Passage, 1973, Conservative Votes, Liberal Victories: Why the Right Has Failed, 1975, Right from the Beginning, 1988, America Asleep, 1991, The Great Betrayal: How American Sovereignty and Social Justice Are Being Sacrificed to the Gods of the Global Economy, 1998, A Republic, Not an Empire: Reclaiming America's Destiny, 1999, Death of the West: How Dying Populations and Immigrant Invasions Imperil Our Country and Civilization, 2002, Where the Right Went Wrong: How Neoconservatives Subverted the Reagan Revolution and Hijacked the Bush Presidency, 2004, State of Emergency: The Third World Invasion and Conquest of America, 2006, Day of Reckoning: How Hubris, Ideology, and Greed are Destroying America, 2007, Churchill, Hitler and "The Unnecessary War": How The Britain Lost Its Empire and The West Lost The World, 2008, Suicide of a Superpower: Will America Survive to 2025?, 2011 Mem. Pres.'s Commn. White House Fellowships, 1969-73; v.p. American Coun. of Young Polit. Leaders, 1974-75, 76-79. Named Knight of Malta, 1987. Independent. Roman Catholic.

BUCHANAN, RICHARD KENT, retired electronics company executive; b. Schenectady, Sept. 10, 1951; s. Richard Linton and Jeanette (Dunn) B.; m. Diane Carolyn Laffler, Oct. 14, 1984; 1 child, Lindsay Sarah. BSEE, USAF Acad., 1973; MBA, Harvard U., 1980. Commd. 2d lt. USAF, 1973, advanced through grades to capt., 1976; resigned, 1978; mgmt. cons. Bain and Co., Boston, 1979-82; corp. dir. strategy Gen. Instrument Corp., NYC, 1982-84; mgr. strategic planning GE Med. Systems Group, Milw., 1984-86, mgr. mktg. magnetic resonance, 1986-87, product gen. mgr. magnetic resonance bus. unit, 1987-89; dir. strategic mktg. Motorola Communications Sector, Schaumburg, Ill., 1989-91; dir. internat. networks svcs. Motorola Land Mobile Sector, Schaumburg, Ill., 1991-94; v.p., gen. mgr. Am. Parts Divsn., Motorola, Schaumburg, Ill., 1994-97, Radio Products Group, N.Am. Divsn., Motorola, Rolling Meadows, Ill., 1997-2000; v.p., gen. mgr. Global eBusiness, Motorola, Deer Park, Ill., 2000—05; v.p. corp. tech. and devel, chief growth officer Harris Corp., Melbourne, Fla., 2005—07, chief tech. officer, v.p., engring., 2007—13; bd. mem. Terion, 2009—11, Authentec, 2009—11; ret., 2013. Contbr. numerous articles on time div. multiple access comm. systems to profl. jours. Scholar, NSF, 1968. Mem. IEEE, N.Y. Acad. Scis. Republican. Avocations: skiing, travel, art, swimming. Home: 146 Lansing Island Dr Indian Harbor Beach FL 32937 Personal E-mail: rkentb333@aol.com.

BUCHANAN, VERN (VERNON GALE BUCHANAN), United States Representative from Florida; b. Detroit, May 8, 1951; m. Sandy Buchanan; children: James, Matt. BBA, Cleary U., Mich., 1975; MBA, U. Denver, 1986. Founder, chmn. Am. Speedy Printing, 1976—91; chmn. Buchanan Enterprises, 1994—; mem. US Congress from 13th Fla. Dist., Washington, 2007—13, US Congress from 16th Fla. Dist., 2013—. State finance chair Mel Martinez's Election Campaign, 2004. Active Boys and Girls Club, Cmty. Found. Sarasota. Served in Mich. Air Nat. Guard, 1970—76. Mem.: US C. of C. (bd. dirs., mem. exec. com.), Sarasota C. of C. (past chmn.), Fla. C.of C. (chmn. bd. dirs.). Republican. Baptist. Office: US House of Representatives 2104 Rayburn House Office Bldg Washington DC 20515 also: 111 South Orange Ave Fl 2R Ste 202W Sarasota FL 34236 Office Phone: 941-951-6643. Office Fax: 941-951-2972.*

BUCHANAN, WALTER WOOLWINE, electrical engineer, educator, academic administrator; b. Lebanon, Ind., Oct. 6, 1941; s. Eugene Neptune and Amy Malvina (Woolwine) B.; m. Carol Ann Saunders, Dec. 28, 1968 (div. 1978); children: William Saunders, John Douglas; m. Charlotte Jane Drake, 1985. BA in Math, Langs., Ind. U., 1963, JD, 1973; BS in Engring., Purdue U., 1982, MS in Elec. Engring., 1984; PhD, Ind. U., 1993. Bar: Ind.; registered profl. engr., Ind., Fla., Tenn., Oreg., Mass., Tex. Aerospace engr. Martin Co., Denver, 1963-64, Boeing Co., New Orleans, 1964-65; audit coord. Ind. Tax Bd., Indpls., 1970-73; atty. VA, Indpls., 1973-79; electronics engr. Naval Avionics, Indpls., 1979-86; asst. prof. Ind. U.-Purdue U., Indpls., 1986-93, U. Ctrl. Fla., Orlando, 1993-95; assoc. prof., chmn. Mid. Tenn. State U., Murfreesboro, 1995—96; prof., dean Oreg. Inst. Tech., Klamath Falls, 1996-99; prof., dir. Northeastern U., Boston, 1999—2005; prof. and J.R. Thompson chair Tex. A&M U., College Station, 2005—. Evaluator Accreditation Bd. for Engring. and Tech., Balt., 1987—, mem. tech. accreditation commn., 1998—2003, mem. exec. com., 2004—07, ABET disting. vol., 2010; dir. Lowell Inst. Sch.; chmn. Nat. Engring. Tech. Ednl. Clearinghouse; grants reviewer NSF, Washington; cons. in field; mem. editl. bd. Internat. Jour. Engring. Rsch. & Innovation, Jour. Engring. Edn., Tech. Interface Internat. Jour., Am. Jour. Engring. Edn. Mem. editl. bd. Jour. Engring. Tech.; mem. editl. bd.: Nat. Engring. Tech. Ednl. Clearinghouse, Internat. Jour. of Modern Engring.; contbr. over 200 articles to profl. publs. Faculty coun. Ind. U.-Purdue U., Indpls., 1989-92, exec. com., 1991-92; fundraiser Ind. U. Found., Indpls.; tech. com. Ind. Bus. Modernization Corp., Indpls., 1990-93; vestry St. Paul's Ch., Klamath Falls, Oreg., 1998-99; vestry King's Chapel, Boston, 2004-05. Lt. comdr. USN, 1965-69, Vietnam. Recipient Glenn W. Irwin award, Peter Marbaugh award Ind. U.-Purdue U. Indpls., 1988, Crawford Disting. Svc. award Tex. A&M U., 2012, Internat. Engring. Educator Honoris Causa, 2013; Wright scholar Ind. U., 1961; Rsch. grantee Ctr. on Philanthropy, 1992, Fla. Engring. and Indsl. Experimentation Sta., 1993, NSF, 2004, 2nd 2008. Fellow: NSPE (bd. dirs. 2008—10, educator, exec. bd., past chmn., Profl. Engr. in Edn. award 1993, 1997, 2008, 2010), Am. Soc. for Engring. Edn. (exec. bd. ednl. rsch. and methods divsn. 1986—92, exec. com. engring. tech. divsn. 1994—, bd. dirs. 2003—08, pres. 2012—13, past chmn. engring. tech. divsn., internat. engring. tech. Listserv adminstr., Centennial award 1993, Frederick J. Berger award 2000, James H. McGraw award 2003, Disting. Svc. Citation award 2009, rsch. grantee); mem.: IEEE (sr.; com. tech. accreditation activities, press electronics tech. editl. bd., past chmn.), Nat. Acad. Engring. (mem. engring. tech. edn. com.), Planetary Soc. Trip Antarctica, Mass. Soc. Profl. Engrs. (past pres.), Engring. Tech. Coun. (exec. com. 2002—, chmn. 2006—08), Indpls. Sci. and Engring. Found. (bd. dirs. 1988—92), Soc. Mfg. Engrs. (sr.), Profl. Engrs. in Oreg. (chmn. engring. edn. 1997—99, pres. elect 1999), Tenn. Soc. Profl. Engrs. (chmn. engring. edn. 1996), Fla. Engring. Soc. (chmn. engring. edn. 1993—95), Ind. Soc. Profl. Engrs. (chmn. engring. edn. 1988—92), Engring Tech. Leadership Inst. (past chmn.), Ancient and Honorable Arty. Co. Mass., Univ. Faculty Club (bd. dirs. 1988—93), Scientech Club (bd. dirs. 1990—92), Phi Kappa Tau, Sigma Epsilon Rho, Epsilon Pi Tau, Alpha Phi Omega, Phi Beta Delta, Delta Phi Alpha, Tau Alpha Pi (past pres.), Order of Engr., Engring. and Sci. Hall of Fame. Republican. Episcopalian. Achievements include systems test evaluation on the Apollo booster rocket. Home: 2240 Rockingham Loop College Station TX 77845-4854 Office: Tex A&M Univ Dept Engring Tech and Indsl Distbrn 3367 TAMU College Station TX 77843-3367

BUCHHOLZ, DONALD ALDEN, stock brokerage company executive; b. LaPorte, Tex., Mar. 10, 1929; s. Fred T. and Chrystine (McCombs) B.; m. Ruth Vernon, May 17, 1958; children: Robert, Chrystine Louise. BBA, North Tex. U., 1952. C.P.A., Tex. Acct., staff auditor Peat, Marwick & Mitchell, Dallas, 1952-54; asst. sec.-treas., chief acct. ICT Discount Corp., 1954-56; comptr. Eppler-Guerin & Turner, Inc., 1956-59; ptnr. Cheshier-Buchholz, pub. accts., 1959-60; comptroller, sec. Parker Ford, Inc., stock brokers, Dallas, 1960-63, also dir., 1962-63; v.p., chief adminstrv. officer, sec. Weber, Hall, Cobb & Caudle, Inc., Dallas, 1963-72, also bd. dirs.; ptnr., chmn. bd. S.W. Securities Group, 1972—; chmn. bd. Buckley Oil Co., Dallas, 1994-99, 1st Savs. Bank, Arlington, Tex., 1994—. Bd. govs. N.Y. Stock Exch., 1969-71; assoc. mem. Am. Stock Exch.; mem. Chgo. Bd. Trade, Midwest Stock Exch.; bd. dirs. Security Bank N.A., Garland, Tex., 1987-2003; mem. found. bd. U. North Tex., 1998—; dir. Nat. Ctr. for Policy Advisors, 2003—, U.S. Home Systems, 2003--; bd. regents, U. North Tex., 2007. Trustee Garland Ind. Sch. Bd., 1971-74, pres., 1973-74; trustee Dallas County C.C. Dist., 1978-97, pres., 1982-84, 90-92; bd. dirs. Garland Meml. Hosp., 1981-85, Garland Meml. Hosp. Found., 1981, Alliance of Higher Edn., 1994-96, Coun. for Higher Edn. Accreditation, 1996-97, Dallas Citizens Coun., Old Red Found. 1997-2002, Nat. Ctr. Policy Analysis, 2003—.; dir. Dallas County C.C. Dist. Found., 2003--; mem. bus. adv. bd. Baylor U., 1991-94, pres. adv. bd. Hankamer Sch. Bus., 1995-97; bd. North Tex. U. Found, 2004-08, Mannatech Corp., 2004-2005; mem. blue ribbon com. Parkland Hosp., 2005-2006, regent U. North Tex., 2008-. Recipient U. North Tex. Outstanding Alumnus Svc. award, 1999, U. North Tex. Disting. Alumnus award, 2001; named Disting. Alumni, Garland HS, 2006. Mem. Nat. Security Dealers Assn. (chmn. bus. conduct com. dist. 6 1985-87, bd. govs. 1988-91), Securities Industry Assn. (exec. com. south ctrl. dist. 1986—, exec. bd. 1990-93), Dallas Security Dealers Assn. (sec. 1961), Tex. Stock and Bond Dealers Assn. (treas. 1982, v.p. 1986-87, pres. 1987-88), Chief Execs. Round Table, Alto Lakes Golf and Country Club, Dallas Country Club, City Club Dallas, Kiwanis (pres. 1957-58). Baptist. Home: 7712 Glenshannon Cir Dallas TX 75225- Office: SWS Group Inc 1201 Elm St Ste 3500 Dallas TX 75270-2180 Office Phone: 214-859-9140.

BUCHMAN, KENNETH WILLIAM, lawyer; b. Plant City, Fla., Nov. 20, 1956; s. Paul Sidney and Beryle (Solomon) B.; m. MarDee H. Buchman, May 9, 1985; 1 child, Katherine Elizabeth. AA, U. Fla., 1976, BBA, 1978, JD, 1981. Bar: Fla. 1981; U.S. Dist. Ct. (Mid. dist.) Fla. 1981; U.S. Ct. Appeals (11th cir.) 1986; U.S. Supreme Ct. 1988; bd. cert. city, county, local govt. law., 1996. Ptnr. Buchman and Buchman, Plant City, 1981-85, Buchman and Buchman, PA, Plant City, 1985-91; pvt. practice Plant City, 1991-2000; asst. city atty. City of Plant City, 1982-91, city atty., 1991—. City atty. San Antonio, Fla., 1995-2000; mem. exec. coun. city, county and local govt. law sect. Fla. Bar., 1997—2005, chair, 2003-04. Recipient Paul S. Buchman Municipal Attorney of Yr. Award, Fla. Mcpl. Atts. Assn., 2009; Paul S. Buchman award, City, County and Local Government Law Sect. Fla. Bar, 1999, Osee R. Fagan award, 2002 Mem.: Plant City Bar Assn. (v.p. 2013—), Fla. Mcpl. Attys. Assn. (steering com. 1999—2002, exec. bd. 2002—04, treas. 2004—05, pres. 2005—06), Masons. Jewish. Office: 302 W Reynolds St Plant City FL 33563

BUCHMANN, MOLLY O'BANION, choreographer, educator; b. Baton Rouge, Nov. 22, 1949; d. James Dennis and Annie Laurie (Joffrion) O'Banion; m. Fred J. Buchmann, Aug. 23, 1969; children: F. Jason (dec.), Dennis Andrew. BS in Secondary Edn., La. State U., 1971, MS in Dance, 1973. Artistic dir. Baton Rouge Ballet Theatre, 1976—; choreographer Baton Rouge Little Theatre, 1983—; tchr. dance Baton Rouge Magnet H.S., 1979-85; owner, mgr. The Dancers' Workshop, Baton Rouge, 1973—; dir. dance Scotlandville Magnet H.S., 1986-98; dance dir., profl.-in-residence dept. theatre La. State U., Baton Rouge, 1999—. Vis. artist Arts and Humanities Council of Greater Baton Rouge, 1976; choreographer Aubin Lane Dinner Theatre, Baton Rouge, 1980-82; mem. cultural caucus steering com. La. State Div. of Arts, cons., 1986. Editor La. Dance News, 1976-77. Choreographer numerous ballets. Mem. cmty. fund for the arts com. and campaign cabinets, 2004-07; vol. La. Public Broadcasting, Baton Rouge Symphony, La. Arts and Sci. Ctr., Magnolia Mound, others. John W. Barton award for Excellence in Non-Profit Mgmt., 2007, Outstanding Undergraduate Tchg. award, La. State U. Tiger Athletic Found., 2002; recipient Mayor-Pres. award for Excellence in the Arts, 1999; State of La. Div. Arts Choreographic grantee, 1982; Baton Rouge Alumni Fedn. scholar, 1967. Mem. Southwest Regional Ballet Assn. (bd. dirs., sec. 1984-88, parliamentarian 1993). Democrat. Roman Catholic. Office: Baton Rouge Ballet Theatre PO Box 82288 Baton Rouge LA 70884-2288 Home Phone: 225-926-6248. Business E-Mail: mbuchm1@lsu.edu.

BUCK, JENNIFER COONEY, consulting firm executive, former federal agency administrator; b. Bethesda, Md., Jan. 18, 1954; d. Allan Stedman and Mavis Eugenia (England) Cooney; m. Gerome Seymour Buck, June 8, 1974 (dec. Feb. 1993); children: Sandra Lynne, Steven Eric, Christopher Allan, Ryan Michael. BA, U. Va., 1974; postgrad., George Mason U., 1974-77; MBA, Auburn U., 2009. Mgmt. intern Naval Sea Sys. Command, Arlington, Va., 1974-75, civilian manpower analyst, 1975-79; chief program and budget Army N.G., Arlington, Va., 1979-81; chief civilian manpower budgeting Naval Material Command, Arlington, Va., 1981-85; budget officer Def. Contract Audit Agy., Alexandria, Va., 1983-85; dir. guard/reserve programs US Dept. Def., Arlington, 1985-94, dep. asst. sec. for reserve affairs, 1994—2009; pres. J. Buck Enterprises, 2009—. Soccer coach Springfield (Va.) Youth Club, 1993-96; treas. Homeowner's Assn., Fairfax Station, Va., 1989. Recipient Va. State Young Career Woman award Bus. and Profl. Women's Club, 1980, Presdl. Rank award, 2000, Roger W. Jones award for Exec. Excellence, American U., 2004 Avocations: gardening, needlecrafts, bridge.

BUCK, KELVIN O., state legislator; b. Tupelo, Miss., Feb. 23, 1961; Former city alderman Holly Springs; mem. Dist. 5 Miss. House of Reps., 2004—, vice chair univs. and colls. com., mem. edn. com., juvenile justice com., Medicaid com., pub. utilities com., select com. on utility cost recovery, select com. on poverty, transp. com., mem. ways and means com. Mem.: NAACP, Boy Scouts America. Democrat. Methodist. Address: 700 Martin Luther King Dr Holly Springs MS 38635 Office Phone: 901-323-2430. Business E-Mail: kbuck@house.ms.gov.

BUCK, KIMBERLY CAMPBELL, state legislator; b. Jackson, Miss., Jan. 13, 1972; m. Kelvin Buck. BA, Miss. State U., 1994; MA, Auburn U., 1998; JD, U. Miss., 2001. Adj. prof. Belhaven coll., 2006—; sloe practitioner Law Office of Kimberly L. Campbell, 2005—; policy analyst Jackson City Council, 2005—06; law clk. Miss. Supreme Court, 2001—02; mem. Dist. 72 Miss. House of Reps., 2008—. Democrat. Methodist. Home: 1062 Devonshire Dr Jackson MS 39206 Office: PO Box 1018 Jackson MS 39215 Home Phone: 601-982-4277; Office Phone: 601-956-5771. E-mail: kcampbell@house.ms.gov.

BUCK, PETER, musician; b. Berkeley, Calif., Dec. 6, 1956; m. Stephanie Dorgan (div.); children: Zoe, Zelda. Student, Emory U., U. Ga. Guitarist R.E.M., 1980—2011. Albums include Chronic Town, 1982, Murmur, 1983 (Rolling Stone Critics Poll Best Album of Yr. 1983), Reckoning, 1984, Fables of the Revolution, 1985, Life's Rich Pageant, Dead Letter Office, Document, 1987, Eponymous, 1988, Green, 1988, Out of Time, 1991 (7 Grammy nominations, 3 Grammy awards for Best Pop Vocal Performance, Best Alternative Music Performance, and Best Music Video, 1992), Automatic for the People, 1992 (4 Grammy nominations), Monster, 1994, New Adventures in Hi-Fi, 1996, Up, 1998, Reveal, 2001, Around the Sun, 2004, Live, 2007, Accelerate, 2008, Collapse into Now, 2011, Part Lies, Part Heart, Part Truth, Part Garbage 1982-2011, 2011; songs include The One I Love, Losing My Religion, Everybody Hurts (4 MTV Video Music awards, 1994), The Great Beyond, Imitation of Life, It's the End of the World As We Know It. Recipient 2 Billboard Music awards for Top Modern Rock Artist & Top World Album, 1991, MTV Video Music Best Video of Yr. award, 1992, Brit award for Best Internat. Group, 1993, 1995, Patrick Lippert award, Rock the Vote, 1994, Video Vanguard award, MTV Video Music Awards, 1995; named Rolling Stone Critics Poll Best New Group, 1983, Best Band, 1995, 1996, Rolling Stone Group Artist of Yr., 1992; named to Rock & Roll Hall of Fame, with R.E.M., 2007. Office: REM/Athens Ltd 170 College Ave Athens GA 30601 Office Phone: 706-353-6689.

BUCK, RICHARD PIERSON, chemistry educator, researcher; b. L.A., July 29, 1929; s. Richard Maurice and Lucile Frances (Pierson) B.; m. Mary Ann Kenney, May 23, 1959; children: Nancy Elizabeth Buck McKenna, Pierson Kenney, Margaret Ruth. BS, Calif. Inst. Tech., 1950, MS, 1951; PhD, MIT, 1954. Teaching asst. MIT, Cambridge, 1951-52, NSF fellow, 1952-53, Dupont teaching fellow, 1953-54; rsch. chemist Chevron Rsch. Corp., Richmond, Calif., 1954-61, asst. to gen. mgr., 1956-58; prin. rsch. chemist Bell & Howell Rsch. Ctr., Pasadena, Calif., 1961-65; sr. scientist Beckman Instrument Co., Fullerton, Calif., 1965-67; assoc. prof. chemistry U. N.C., Chapel Hill, 1967-75, prof., 1975—, adj. prof. biomed. engring. and math. Sch. Medicine, 1990—99, prof. emeritus chemistry, 1999—. Kenan prof.-on-leave U. Bristol, Eng., 1976-77; vis. prof. Imperial Coll., London, 1987, Bundeswehr U. Munich, 1989-91; cons. Eastman Kodak, Rochester, N.Y., 1969-77, E.I. duPont de Nemours & Co., Wilmington, Del., 1979-84; mem. adv. bd. I-Stat Corp., Princeton, N.J., 1984-90, Broadley-James Corp, Irvine, Calif. 2002—, NIH resource at Case Western Res. U., Cleve., 1977-84, Ctr. for Solid State Sensors, U. Pa. Moore Sch. Engring., Phila., 1980-84; chmn. A Nomenclature Commn., Internat. Union Pure and Applied Chemistry, 1991—. Author: (with V.V. Cosofret) Pharmaceutical Applications of Membrane Sensors, 1992; mem. editorial bd. 4 internat. chemistry jours.; contbr. over 350 articles to sci. jours. Recipient C.N. Reilley award Soc. Electroanalytical Chemistry, 2000; Von Humboldt grantee, Bonn, Germany, 1989-91, grantee Advanced Rsch. Projects Agy., 1967-71, NSF, 1971—, N.C. Biotech. Ctr., 1990-94. Fellow Electrochem. Soc. (div. chmn., outstanding achievement award sensor divsn. 1996); mem. Am. Chem. Soc., Internat. Soc. Electrochemistry (bd. dirs. 1988-91), Bohemian Club (San Francisco). Avocations: performing chamber music, solo piano playing. Mailing: 312 Carolina Meadows Villa Chapel Hill NC 27517 Personal E-mail: richardpbuck@earthlink.net.

BUCKELEW, ALAN B., cruise line company executive; B, MBA, UCLA. COO Cunard Line; mgr. mgmt. info. Sitmar Cruises (acquired by Princess Cruises), 1977—84, sr. v.p. corp. planning, 1984; exec. v.p. corp. svcs., Princess Cruises, Ltd., 2000—04, pres., 2004—, CEO, 2007—. Office: Carnival Corp 3655 NW 87th Ave Miami FL 33178 Office Phone: 305-599-2600. Office Fax: 305-406-4700. Business E-Mail: abuckelew@princess.com.

BUCKELEW, JOHN D., insurance company executive; Grad., US Naval Acad.; PhD in History, U. Calif., San Diego. Bd. dirs. USAA, 1994—. Combat engr. officer, data sys. officer USMC. Recipient Fulbright scholar, U. Vienna, U. Bonn. Office: USAA Bd Directors 9800 Fredericksburg Rd San Antonio TX 78288 Office Phone: 210-498-2211. Business E-Mail: john.buckelew@usaa.com.

BUCKHORN, BOB, mayor, Tampa, Florida; b. Evanston, Ill., July 29, 1958; m. Catherine Lynch; 2 children. Grad., Penn State U., 1980. Dir. govtl. affairs Builders Assn. of Greater Tampa, Fla., 1985—87; spl. asst. to mayor City of Tampa, 1987—95; mem. Tampa City Coun., 1995—2003; prin. Dewey Square Group, 2003—07; founder Buckhorn Ptnrs., Tampa, 2007; mayor City of Tampa, 2011—. Co-chair John Glenn for Pres. Campaign, Hillsborough County, Fla.; chair MacDill Reuse Adv. Com., 1991; mem. Fla. Def. Transition and Conversion Commn.; co-chair Base Closure Commn.; polit. analyst Bay News 9, 2005. Recipient Up and Comers Award, Tampa Bay Bus. Jour. & Price Waterhouse; named one of America's 100 to Watch, Dem. Leadership Coun. Mem.: Builders Assn. of Greater Tampa (dir.). Democrat. Office: Office of the Mayor 306 East Jackson St Tampa FL 33602 Office Phone: 813-274-8251.*

BUCKLEW, NEIL S., former academic administrator, educator; b. Morgantown, W.Va., Oct. 23, 1940; s. Douglas Earl and Lanah L. (Martin) B.; children— Elizabeth, Jennifer, Jeffrey. AB, U. Mo.; MS, U. N.C.; PhD (grad. fellow), U. Wis. Dir. personnel Duke U., 1964-66; dir. employee relations U. Wis., 1966-70; prof., v.p. Central Mich. U., Mt. Pleasant, 1970-76; prof., provost Ohio U., Athens, 1976-80; pres. U. Mont., Missoula, 1981-86, W.Va. U., 1986-95, prof., 1995—. Vis. rsch. fellow Pa. State U.; arbitrator in field. Author: Public Sector Collective Bargaining, Planning in Higher Education. Mem. Nat. Assn. State Univs. and Land Grant Colls. Office: West Va U PO Box 6025 Morgantown WV 26506-6025 Business E-Mail: nbucklew@wvu.edu.

BUCKLEW, SUSAN CAWTHON, federal judge; b. Tampa, Fla., May 12, 1942; BA, Fla. State U., 1964; MA, U. South Fla., 1968; JD, Stetson U., 1977; LLD (hon.), Stetson Coll. Law, 1994. Tchr. Plant HS, 1964-65, 70-72, Seminole HS, 1965-67, Chamberlain HS, 1969; instr. Hillsborough CC, 1974-75; corp. legal counsel Jim Walter Corp., 1978-82; county ct. judge Hillsborough County, 1982-86; cir. ct. judge 13th Jud. Cir., 1986-93; judge US Dist. Ct. (mid. dist.) Fla., Tampa, 1993—2008, sr. judge, 2008—. Mem. Gender Bias Study Commn., 1988-90, Fla. Bar Bench Bar Commn., 1990-92; bd. overseers Stetson Coll. Law, 1994—. Recipient award Disting Svc., Fla. Coun. Crime and Delinquincy, 1990, Disting. Alumnus award Stetson Lawyers Assn., 1994. Mem. ABA, Fla. Gar Assn., Fla. Assn. Women Lawyers, Hillsborough Assn. Women Lawyers (award Outstanding Pub. Svc. ADvancing Status Women 1991), Hillsborough County Bar Assn. (Robert W. Patton Outstanding Jursit award young lawyer's sect. 1990), Fla. State U. Alumni Assn., Am. Inns Ct. (LII, William Glenn Terrell chpt.), Athena Soc., Tampa Club, Delta Delta Delta Alumnae. Office: US Dist Ct Gibbons US Courthouse 801 N Florida Ave Rm 1430 Tampa FL 33602-3849

BUCKLEY, CHARLES ROBINSON, III, lawyer; b. Richmond, Va., Oct. 9, 1942; s. Charles Robinson and Eleanor (Small) B.; m. Virginia Lee, Apr. 17, 1971; children: Richard, Rebecca. BS, U. N.C., 1965, JD, 1969. Bar: N.C. 1969, U.S. Supreme Ct. 1979. Asst. city atty. City of Charlotte, NC, 1969-78; ptnr. Constagny, Goines, Buckley & Boyd, 1978-81, Taylor & Buckley, Charlotte, 1981-85, Buckley McMullen & Buie, P.A., Charlotte, 1994—2010, Cranford, Buckley, Schultze, Tomchin, Allen & Buie, P.A., 2010—. Town atty. Town of Matthews, N.C., 1978—; faculty Ctrl. Piedmont C.C., 1970; interim town atty. Town Huntersville, NC, 2013. Bd. dirs. Charlotte City Employees' Credit Union, 1974-78; pre. PTA, 1980-82; bd. visitors Luth. Theol. So. Sem., 1989-93. Recipient Cert. of Merit, City of Charlotte, 1982. Mem.: Internat. Mcpl. Lawyers Assn., N.C. Assn. Mcpl. Attys. (bd. dirs. 1979—81, v.p. 1995—96, 1st v.p. 1996—97, pres. 1997—98), N.C. State Bar, Optimist Club (pres. 1982—83), Rotary Club (pres. Charlotte South Rotary Found. 2003—10), Phi Alpha Delta. Republican. Lutheran. Home: 135 Oxford Dr Mooresville NC 28115 Office: 7257 Pineville-Matthews Rd Ste 2100 Charlotte NC 28226 Office Phone: 704-442-1010. E-mail: CRB3@southcharlottelawfirm.com.*

BUCKLEY, CLIFFORD JAMES, surgeon, educator; b. Rahway, NJ, Nov. 24, 1936; BS in Chemistry, U. Pa., 1958; MD, Hahnemann U., 1962. Vascular surgeon USAF, 1963—78, Vascular Surg. Assocs., 1978—93; dir., divsn. vascular surgery, exec. com. mem., dept. surgery Scott & White Meml. Healthcare Sys., 1993—, exec. vice-chair, dept. surgery, 2008—; assoc. chief staff for surg. svc. Ctrl. Tex. Vets. Health Care Sys., 2007—. Clin. prof. surgery Uniformed Svcs. U. Health Scis., 1986—; prof. surgery Tex. A&M U. Health Sci. Ctr. Coll. Medicine, 1998—; cons. Endologix, Inc., 2006—; bd. mem. Internat. Soc. Endovascular Specialists, 2009—. Recipient Physicians Recognition award, AMA, Excellence in Health Care Delivery and Svc. award, Tex. A&M U. Health Sci. Ctr., Malcolm C. Grow award, USAF, Sys. Command Mederi award, Cert. of Merit; named Flight Surgeon of Yr., Mil. Airlift Command Flight Surgeon of Yr. Fellow: ACS, Royal Soc. Medicine, Southwestern Surg. Congress, Soc. Vascular Surgery; mem.: Tex. Surg. Soc. Avocations: travel, reading, snorkeling. Office: 2401 S 31st St Temple TX 76504-7115 Office Fax: 254-724-3173. Business E-Mail: cbuckley@swmail.sw.org.*

BUCKLEY, JOHN JOSEPH, JR., healthcare executive; b. Evanston, Ill., Oct. 5, 1944; s. John Joseph and Mary Ruth (Smith) B.; m. Sarah Amelia Puceloski, May 16, 1970; children: Ruth Mary, Patricia Kimberly, John Joseph III. AB, Kenyon Coll., 1966; MBA, George Washington U., 1969. Asst. adminstr. Maricopa County Gen. Hosp., Phoenix, 1969-71, St. Joseph's Hosp. and Med. Ctr., Phoenix, 1971-74, assoc. adminstr., 1974-76, v.p., 1976-79, pres., 1984-88, St. Anthony's Hosp., Amarillo, Tex., 1979-84, St. Anthony's Devel. Corp., Amarillo, 1982-84; chief operating officer Harrington Cancer Ctr., Amarillo, 1982-84; sr. v.p. Mercy Health System, Cin., 1988-91; pres. So. Ill. Healthcare Enterprises, Carbondale, Ill., 1992—2001, Jack Buckley & Assocs., College Station, Tex., 2001—; interim pres., CEO St. Mary's Hosp. of East St. Louis, Ill., 2002; interim COO, St. Joseph Campus of Via Christi Med. Ctr., Wichita, Kans., 2003; interim CEO St. Joseph Regional Health Ctr., Bryan, Tex., 2003—04, CEO, 2004—08; pres., CEO, St. Joseph Health Sys., Bryan, Tex., 2005—09. Pres. So. Ill. Hosp. Svcs., Health Svcs. So. Ill., Regional Health Plan, 1992-2001,external adv. bd. mem, 2004- TAMU Health Sci. Ctr. Sch. Rural Pub. Health, chmn., 2004-11; exec.-in-residence TAMU Health Sci. Ctr. Sch. Rural Pub. Health, HPM Dept. MHA Program, 2009-; mem. external adv. bd. Coll. Bus. and Adminstrn., So. Ill. U., 2000-. Active Amarillo Alliance of Cmty. Svc. Execs., Amarillo Area Acad. Health Ctr. Corp., Amarillo Area Hosp. Home Care, Amarillo Found. Health and Sci., Panhandle chpt. Tex. Soc. to Prevent Blindness, Amarillo Jr. League, Children's Oncology Svcs. Tex. Panhandle; Amarillo diocesan coord. health affairs; adminstrv. com. Amarillo; pres. Mercy Svcs. Corp., 1984-88; bd. dirs. Greater Phoenix Affordable Health Care Found., 1984-88; trustee Kenyon Coll., Gambier, Ohio, 1991-95, alumni coun., 1998-2003, pres., 2001-02; active SI Edge, 1995-2003. Fellow: Am. Coll. Healthcare Execs. (regent Ariz. 1984—88, regent So. Ill. 1998—2002); mem.: St. Mary's Cath. Ch. (chair. leadership coun. 2009—), Tex. Assn. Voluntary Hosp. (sec. treas. 2008—09, bd. mem. and chair membership com.), HOSPAC (polit. action com. Tex. Hosp. Assn. 2006—09), Ariz. Hosp. Assn., Ariz. Kidney Found., Cath. Health Assn. U.S. (trustee 1985—91, chair Govt. rels. com. 1986—91), Ill. Hosp. Assn. (trustee 1995—2001, chmn. 2000), Tex. Hosp. Assn. (trustee 1983—84), The George Washington U. Alumni Assn. for Health Svcs., Mgmt. and Leadership (Tex. Health bd. advisors 2010—, dir. ACHE-Southeast Tex. Chpt 2011—, parliamentarian 1995—97, bd. trustee 1988—2013), Delta Phi (pres. alumni assn. 1988—2000). Republican. Roman Catholic. Office Phone: 979-731-8235. Business E-Mail: jackbuckleyjr@earthlink.net.

BUCKLEY, REBECCA HATCHER, allergist, immunologist, pediatrician, educator; b. Hamlet, NC, Apr. 1, 1933; d. Martin Armstead and Nora (Langston) Hatcher; m. Charles Edward Buckley, III, July 9, 1955; children: Charles Edward IV, Elizabeth Ann, Rebecca Kathryn, Sarah Margaret. BA, Duke U., 1954; MD, U. NC, 1958. Intern Duke U. Med. Ctr., Durham, NC, 1958-59, resident, 1959-61, pediat. allergist and immunologist, 1961—. Dir., chair exam. com. Am. Bd. Allergy and Immunology, Phila., 1971—73, co-chair bd. dirs., 1982—84; chair Diagnostic Lab. Immunology, 1984—88; mem. staff Duke U. Med. Ctr., asst. prof. pediat. and immunology, 1968—72, assoc. prof. pediat., 1972—79, prof. pediat., 1976—79, prof. immunology, J. Buren Sidbury prof. pediat., 1979—; chief Divsn. Allergy and Immunology, 1974—2003. Contbr. more than 300 articles to profl. jours. Recipient Thomas Waldmann award, Found. Primary Immunodeficiency Diseases, 2013, March of Dimes Colonel Sanders award, Am. Coll. Med. Genetics, 2014, John Howland award, Am. Pediat. Soc., 2014. Fellow: AAAS (chair med. scis. sect. 2001—03); mem.: NAS (elected mem. 2011), Assn. Am. Physicians, Inst. Medicine of NAS, Am. Pediat. Soc. (coun. mem. 1991—, pres. 1999—2000, chmn. immune deficiency found. med. adv. com. 2003—), Southeastern Allergy Assn. (pres. 1978—79), Am. Acad. Pediat. (Bret Ratner award 1992), Soc. Pediat. Rsch., Am. Assn. Immunologists, Am. Acad. Allergy and Immunology (exec. com. 1975—82, pres. 1979—80, hon. fellow award 1999). Republican. Episcopalian. Home: 3621 Westover Rd Durham NC 27707-5032 Office: Duke University Medical Ctr 362 Jones Bldg Box 2898 Durham NC 27710 Office Phone: 919-684-2922. Business E-Mail: buckl003@mc.duke.edu.

BUCKLEY, THOMAS HUGH, historian, educator; b. Elkhart, Ind., Sept. 11, 1932; s. Bernard Leroy and Martha B. (Swoveland) B.; m. Julie Griffith; children: Christopher, Kathryn, Elizabeth, Thomas, Barbara. Student, Northwestern U., 1950-53; AB, Ind. U., 1955, MA, 1956, PhD (grad. fellow), 1961. From instr. to prof. U. S.D., 1960-69; vis. prof. Ind. U., 1969-71; prof., chmn. dept. U. Tulsa, 1971-81, chmn. humanistic studies, 1975-81, Jay Walker research chair Am. History, 1981—, assoc. dean Grad. Sch., 1995-2000; cons. on overseas edn. to Nat. Edn. Corp. Author: The United States and the Washington Conference, 1921-1922, 1970 (award as best first book by an historian 1971); co-author: American Foreign and National Security Policies, 1914-1945, 1987; editor: Research and Roster Guide of Soc. Historians of Am. Fgn. Relations, 1980-86; contbr. chpts. in books. Postdoctoral fellow Stanford U., 1968, U. Wis., 1983, Brown U., 1986, U. Tex., 1991; Fulbright fellow, U. Western Australia, 1986. Mem. Orgn. Am. Historians, Soc. Historians of Am. Fgn. Relations, Tulsa Com. Fgn. Relations, Phi Alpha Theta, Lambda Chi Alpha. Republican. Methodist. Home: 1301 Terrace Dr Tulsa OK 74104-4409 Office: Univ Tulsa Dept History Tulsa OK 74104 Office Phone: 918-631-2824. Business E-Mail: thomas-buckley@utulsa.edu.

BUCKLEY, VINCENT H., lawyer; BA, Rice U., 1947; LLB, U. Tex., 1950. Various legal and mgmt. positions including asst. gen. counsel, pres., gen. mgr., Oil & Gas Divsn. Dow Chem., gen. counsel Pacific region; with Lock, Liddell, and Sapp, 1990—2002; bd. dirs. Adams Resources & Energy, Inc., 2003—05, exec. v.p., gen. counsel, 2005—. Office: Adams Resources & Energy Inc 4400 Post Oak Pky Ste 2700 Houston TX 77027 Office Phone: 713-881-3600. Office Fax: 713-881-3491. Business E-Mail: vincentb@adamsresources.com.

BUCKNER, DEBBIE G., state legislator; b. Atlanta, Ga., Mar. 4, 1955; d. Eugene Jr. and Mildred (Marshall) Gignilliat; m. Michael Harvey Buckner, June 19, 1976; children: Joshua Edlow, John Gignilliat, Olivia Georganna. BS in Health Edn., Columbus Coll., 1977; postgrad., Ga. Southwestern, 1985. Cert. health edn. specialist, 1989. Former state rep. Dist. 109, Ga.; state rep. Dist. 130 Ga., 2004—; sec. State Insts. & Property Com.; mem. Health & Ecology Coms., Natural Resources & Environ. Coms. Bd. dirs., 1985—, state bd. pres. 1995-96, Am. Lung Assn. of Ga.; health chmn. Muscogee County PTA Coun., 1987-90; pres.-elect Columbus Coalition Children and Youth. Bd. dirs. March of Dimes, 1987-93; mem. Citizens for Safe Progress, Taylor County, Ga., 1987-90; mem. adv. coun. Drug Free Schs. and Community, 1987—; sec. Zion Ch. Restoration, Inc., Talbotton, Ga., 1987—; chmn. Talbot County Recycling Task Force; co-founder Talbot Country Friends of Environment; mem. Toastmasters Internat., 1997, Coastal Heritage Soc., Savannah, Ga.; pres.-elect Network of Profls. & Execs. Named Woman of Achievement Girl Scouts Concharty Council 1988. Mem. Perennial Garden Club (Talbotton). Democrat. Baptist. Avocations: collecting antiques, needlecrafts, gardening, flower arranging. Mailing: Rt 1 Box 76 Junction City GA 31812 Office: 511 Legislative Office Bldg Atlanta GA 30334 Office Phone: 706-269-3630, 404-656-6372. Business E-Mail: dbuckner@legis.state.ga.us.

BUCKNER, SALLY BEAVER, literature and language professor, writer; b. Statesville, NC, Nov. 3, 1931; d. Henry George and Foda Leigh (Stack) Beaver; m. Robert Lynn Buckner, Aug. 21, 1954; children: George Robert, Sally Lynn, Theodore Warren. AB in English, U.N.C., Greensboro, 1953; MA in English, N.C. State U., 1970; PhD in Curriculum and Instrn., U. N.C., Chapel Hill, 1980. Tchr. Arlington Jr. H.S., Gastonia, N.C., 1953-54, Protestant Sch., Goldsboro, N.C., 1962-65; journalist Raleigh Times, N.C., 1966-68; tchg. asst. N.C. State U., Raleigh, 1968-70; prof. English Peace Coll., Raleigh, 1970-98. Mem. scholar's adv. bd. MotheRead; chair N.C. Writers' Conf., 1988-89. Author: (poetry collections) Strawberry Harvest, 1986, Collateral Damage, 2007, 19 Visions of Christians, 2011; editor: (anthologies) Our Words, Our Ways, 1991, 95, Word and Witness: 100 Years of North Carolina Poetry, 1999. Mem. Legis. Study Commn. for Emotionally Disturbed Children, N.C., 1970-71, Women's Good Will Com., Goldsboro, N.C., 1963-65; co-chair arts edn. panel Dept. Cultural Resources, Raleigh, 1977-81; bd. dirs. N.C. Autism Soc., 1969-73, N.C. Lit. and Hist. Soc., 1981-86. Recipient Ragan-Rubin award N.C. English Tchr.'s Assn., 1993, Sam Ragan award, St. Andrew's Coll, Laurinburg, N.C., 1993, R. Hunt Parker award N.C. Lit. and Hist. Soc., 1999, Alumni Disting. Svc. award UNC Greensboro, 2008, Human Rights award Wake County Ch. Women United, 2007, Disting Alumna award UNCG, 2008; named Alumnae Disting. Prof., Peace Coll., 1991. Mem. N.C. Poetry Soc. (poet laureate festival chair 1988-89), N.C. Lit. Hall of Fame (chair selection com.). Democrat. Baptist. Avocations: music, gardening, reading. Personal E-mail: sbuckner14@yahoo.com.

BUCKNER, THOMAS RANDOLPH, lawyer; b. Goldsboro, NC, Aug. 23, 1947; s. Samuel Lee and Helen Faris Buckner; m. Karen Renée Wagner; children: Kelly Buckner Dallas, Susan Elizabeth, Samuel Randolph. BA, Va. Mil. Inst., 1969; JD, Vanderbilt U., 1972. Bar: Tenn. 1972. Sole practitioner, Memphis, 1972—81; assoc. Wildman Harrold Allen, Dixon, McDonnell, Memphis, 1981—84, ptnr., 1985—87; mem. Apperson, Crump & Maxwell, PLC, Memphis, 1987—. Bd. editors Vanderbilt Jour. Transnat. Law, 1970—71. Chmn. planned giving com. Boys & Girls Club, Memphis, 2003—. Capt. USAF, 1972. Named one of Best Lawyers in Am., Woodward, Best 101 Lawyers in Tenn., Bus. Tenn. Mag., 2004, Best 150 Lawyers in Tenn., 2005—10. Mem.: Planned Giving Coun. of Greater Memphis, Estate Planning Coun. of Memphis, Tenn. Bar Assn. (vice chair tax, probate and trust sect. 1999), Memphis Bar Assn. (chmn. wills and probate sect. 2000—03, chmn. CLE com. 2005), Am. Coll. Trust and Estate Counsel. Methodist. Avocations: tennis, golf, running, reading. Home: 6589 May Hollow Cove Memphis TN 38119 Office: Apperson Crump & PLC 6070 Poplar Ave Ste 600 Memphis TN 38119-3954 Office Phone: 901-756-6300. Office Fax: 901-756-9782. Business E-Mail: tbuckner@appersoncrump.com.

BUCKSTEIN, MARK AARON, lawyer, mediator, educator; b. NYC, July 1, 1939; s. Henry Al and Minnie Sarah (Russ) B.; children: Robin Beth, Michael Alan. BS in Math., CCNY, 1960; JD, NYU, 1963. Bar: N.Y. 1963, U.S. Dist. Ct. (so. and ea. dists.) N.Y. 1965, U.S. Supreme Ct. 1981. Assoc. Russ & Weyl, Massapequa, NY, 1963-64; assoc. counsel Mut. Life Ins. Co. N.Y., NYC, 1964-65; assoc. Moses & Singer, NYC, 1965-67, Leinwand, Maron & Hendler, NYC, 1967-68; sr. ptnr. Baer Marks & Upham, NYC, 1968-86; sr. v.p. external affairs, gen. counsel TWA, Inc., NYC, 1986-92; exec. v.p. Am. Arbitration Assn., NYC, NJ, 1992-93; exec. v.p., gen. counsel GAF Corp. and Internat. Specialty Products, Wayne, NJ, 1993-96;

counsel Greenberg Traurig, Ft. Lauderdale, Fla., 1996-99, Profl. Dispute Resolution, Inc., Boca Raton, Fla., 1999—. Spl. prof. law Hofstra U. Law Sch., Hempstead, N.Y., 1981-93; adj. prof. law Rutgers U. Law Sch., Newark, 1994-96; adj. prof. Fla. Atlantic U., Grad. Sch. Bus., 2004-06; bd. dirs. Bayswater Realty & Capital Corp., N.Y.C., Travel Channel Inc., N.Y.C., TWA, GAF Corp., Internat. Specialty Products, Consultis; mem. exec. com. Herzfeld & Stern, N.Y.C., 1981-84; mem. nat. arbitration and mediation com. NASD, 1998-2001. Trustee Bronx H.S. Found., 1984-96. Mem. ABA, N.Y. Bar Assn., Assn. of Bar of City of N.Y., KP (past dep. grand chancellor 1978). Jewish. Avocations: tennis, music, theater, puzzles. Office: Profl Dispute Resolution 2424 N Federal Hwy Boca Raton FL 33431 Home: 8654 Valhalla Dr Delray Beach FL 33446 Office Phone: 561-417-6602. Personal E-mail: mabresolve@aol.com.

BUDALUR, THYAGARAJAN SUBBANARAYAN, chemistry professor; b. India, July 14, 1929; came to U.S., 1969, naturalized, 1977; s. Subbanarayan Subbuswamy and Parvatham (Gopalakrishnan) B.; children: Chitra, Poorna, Kartik. MA, U. Madras, 1951, M.Sc., 1954, PhD, 1956. Postdoc. assoc. Northwestern U., Evanston, Ill., 1956—58, U. Wis., Madison, 1958—59; Reader organic chemistry U. Madras, 1960-68; prof. chemistry U. Idaho, Moscow, 1968-74; vis. prof. U. Southern Calif., LA, 1965—66; prof. chemistry, dir. div. earth phys. sci. U. Tex., San Antonio, 1974-2000, emeritus prof., 2000—. Lectr. in field. Author: Mechanisms of Molecular Migrations; Selective Organic Transformations; Editorial bd. chem. jours.; contbr. articles to profl. jours.; 3 patents in field. Recipient Intra Sci. Research award, 1966 Fellow Am. Chem. Soc.; mem. Chem. Soc. London, Soc. Cosmetic Chemistry N.Y. Acad. Sci., Am. Inst. Chemists, Sigma Xi, Phi Kappa Phi. Clubs: Lions. Home: 6119 Amble Trl San Antonio TX 78249-2108

BUDD, RICHARD WADE, academic administrator, dean, priest; b. Henderson, Md., Aug. 24, 1934; s. Bryan William and Dorothea Marie (Fouvy) B.; m. Claudia L. Wolff; children: Kimberly, Richard Wade, Janna, Eric, Gary, Stephanie. BA, Bowling Green U., 1956; MA, U. Iowa, 1962, PhD, 1964. Ordained priest Episcopal Ch., 2001. Reporter, staff writer Dayton (Ohio) Daily News, 1956-57; rsch. assoc., instr., asst. prof., dir. Inst. Comm. Studies, U. Iowa, Iowa City, 1960-71; prof., disting. prof., assoc. dean Rutgers Coll. Rutgers U., New Brunswick, NJ, chmn. dept. human comm., 1971-80, dir. Sch. Comm. Studies, 1980-83, founding dean Sch. Comm., Info. and Libr. Studies, 1983-97; v.p. for info. and technology Regent U., Virginia Beach, Va., 1997—2000, disting. scholar, 2000—; chmn. bd. Newstatements Comm. Cons., 1973-80; cons. in field.; rector Ch. of the Good Shepherd, Richmond, Va., 2002—06, Christ the King Episcopal Ch., Tabb, Va., 2006—09, Ch. of Advert Norfolk, Va., 2009—13, St. Pauls Newport News, Va., 2014—. Author: Introduction to Content Analysis, 1964, Content Analysis of Communication, 1967, Approaches to Human Communication, 1972, Human Communication Handbook Simulations and Games, 1975, Mass Communication: Dialogue and Alternatives, 1976, Interdisciplinary Approaches to Communication, 1979, Beyond Media, 1988; assoc. editor Human Communication Research, 1974-83, Communication Quar, 1975-83; mem. editorial bd. Jour. Communication, 1976-82, Communication Yearbook, 1977-86, Mass Communications Yearbook, 1979—95. Mem. Cmty. Arts Coun. East Brunswick, 1973—80; exec. coun. East Brunswick Youth Baseball Program, 1974; active Boy Scouts Am.; priest Episcopal Diocese of So. Va., 2001; chmn. bd. dirs. Anglican Ctr. for Theology and Spirituality, Diocese of So. Va., 2003—05; dean Sch. of Ministry Formation, Diocese of So. Va., 2003—11. Lt. USNR, 1957—60. Mem. Internat. Comm. Assn. (pres. 1976-77), AAAS, Nat. Comm. Assn., Am. Assn. Public Opinion Rsch., Assn. Edn. in Journalism, ALA (com. on accrediting 1995-99), Assn. Libr. Info. Edn. Episcopalian. Avocations: golf, harmonica, painting. Home: 120 Cypress Crk Williamsburg VA 23188-7804 Office: Church Advent 9629 Norfolk Ave Norfolk VA 23503 Office Phone: 757-587-0125. E-mail: rwbudd@msn.com.

BUDD, ROSE ANTOINETTE, language educator; d. Cyprian Alexander and Zerish May Leslie; m. Theophilus N. Budd, Dec. 22, 2001. BA in English, So. Meth. U., Dallas, 1973, MA in English, 1977; MLS, U. North Tex., Denton, 1980. Tchr. Ministry Edn., Jamaica, West Indies, 1956—70; libr. assoc. Dallas Pub. Libr., 1972—80; adminstrv. asst. So. Meth. U., Fondren Libr., 1980—84; libr. Ft. Worth Pub. Libr., 1984—86, Dallas Pub. Libr., 1986, Greiner Mid. Sch., Dallas, 1986—89; prof. English, devel. writing Eastfield C.C., Mesquite, Tex., 1983—. Cons. in field. Author: Yes, You Can Write!, 2003. Co-founder, presenter African-Am. read-in Eastfield Coll., Mesquite, 1990; vol. Heritage Pl. Nursing Home, Mesquite, 2005—06; mem. Polit. Congress African Am. Women, Dallas, 1998—; pianist First United Meth. Ch., Seagoville, Tex., 2004—. Recipient award, Eastfield Coll. Bapt. Student Assn., 1995, Image award, Eastfield Coll. African Am. Support Group, 1995, Excellence in Tchg. award, Eastfield Coll., 1999, Vol. award, Dallas Ind. Sch. Dist., 1995. Mem.: Eastfield Coll. Faculty Assn., Tex. C.C. Tchrs. Assn., Conf. Coll. Composition and Comm., Nat. Coun. Tchrs. English. Methodist. Avocations: travel, reading, piano, movies, music. Office: Eastfield Coll 3737 Motley Dr Mesquite TX 75150 Office Phone: 972-860-8351.

BUDENHOLZER, MIKE, professional basketball coach; b. Holbrook, Ariz. s. Vince Budenholzer; m. Mary Beth Budenholzer; children: William Vincent, Savoia Elizabeth, Hanna Louise, John Bent. B in Politics, Philosophy & Economics, Pomona Coll., Claremont, CA, 1993. Profl. basketball player & coach Vejle Basketball Klub, Denmark, 1993—94; video coord. San Antonio Spurs, 1994—96, asst. coach, 1996—2013; head coach Atlanta Hawks, 2013—. Advance scout, US nat. team Summer Olympic Games, Athens, Greece, 2004. Office: Atlanta Hawks 101 Marietta St NW #1900 Atlanta GA 30303*

BUDNER, CRAIG W., lawyer; b. Dallas, Dec. 2, 1964; AB cum laude, Dartmouth Coll., 1987; JD, U. Tex., 1990. Bar: Tex. 1990, US Dist. Ct. (all Tex. districts), US Ct. Appeals (2nd, 4th, 5th, 7th and 9th cirs.), US Supreme Ct. Ptnr. Hughes & Luce, LLP, Dallas, K&L Gates LLP, Dallas, 2007—, adminstrv. ptnr. Dallas office. Barrister Patrick E. Higginbotham Inn of Ct.; chmn. Dallas Urban Debate Alliance. Mem. Lamplighter New Families Com., Dallas; bd. mem., past pres. Vogel Alcove Childcare Ctr. for Homeless, Dallas; bd. dir. Children's Eye Found., Temple Emanu-El; bd. mem. Dallas Furniture Bank. Named one of Best Lawyers in Dallas, D Mag., 2005. Mem.: Dallas Assembly, Dallas Bar Assn., ABA. Office: K&L Gates LLP Ste 2800 1717 Main St Dallas TX 75201 Office Phone: 214-939-5806. Office Fax: 214-939-5849. Business E-Mail: craig.budner@klgates.com.

BUECHLER, MARK ALAN, insurance company executive; b. Hamilton, Ohio, Sept. 16, 1952; s. R. Lee and Betty Ann (Little) B.; m. Frances Elaine Harms, Aug. 1, 1981; children: David Alan, Elizabeth Marie. BA in Chemistry, Rice U., 1974; MA in Human Resources Mgmt., Pepperdine U., 1980; MBA, U. Houston, 1987. CPA, Tex. Constrn. mgr. Home Builders, Houston, 1980—84; mgr., MIS Rep. Mineral Corp., Houston, 1984—87; audit sr. Coopers & Lybrand, Houston, 1987—89; v.p., contr. Houston Casualty Co. (subs. of HCC Insurance Holdings, Inc.), Houston, 1989—94, sr. v.p., fin., 1995; v.p., fin. reporting HCC Insurance Holdings, Inc., v.p., fin. reporting and budgeting, 2006—. Lt. USMC, 1974-80. Avocations: reading history, chess, bridge, sports. Home: 3507 Mckean Dr Houston TX 77080-1711 Office: HCC Insurance Holdings Inc 13403 Northwest Freeway Houston TX 77040-6094 Office Phone: 713-690-7300. Office Fax: 713-462-2401. Business E-Mail: mbuechler@hcch.com.

BUELL, L. DICK, marketing executive; m. Marcia Buell; 2 children. BS in Engring., Purdue U.; MBA, U. Chgo. Cons. McKinsey & Co, 1979—83; v.p., mktg., Kraft Grocery Products Kraft Foods, Inc., 1983—90; CEO Griffith Labs., Inc., 1992—99; pres., COO Foodbrands America, Inc., 2000—01; CEO WS Brands, 2002—04; chmn. Checkout Holding Corp.; chmn., CEO Catalina Marketing Corp., 2004—. Bd. dirs. Smarter Agent, LLC, Bolthouse Farms, Prestige Brands Holdings, Inc., 2004—. Mem. Chgo. Club. Office: Catalina Marketing Corp 200 Carillon Pky Saint Petersburg FL 33716 Office Phone: 727-579-5000. Office Fax: 727-556-2700. Business E-Mail: ldick.buell@catalinamarketing.com.

BUERGEL, ROGER M., curator, art historian, educator; b. Berlin, 1962; Attended, Acad. Fine Arts, Vienna, Austria, U. Vienna. Cofounder Springerin-Hefte für Gegenwartskunst; artistic dir. Documenta 12, Kassel, Germany, 2007; chief curator, dep. dir. programs Miami Art Mus., 2008—. Lectr. Luneberg U., Germany, 2001—05; vis. prof. art history Acad. Fine Arts, Karlsruhe, Germany, 2007. Curator (exhibitions) Painting Between Vulgarity and the Sublime, 1999, Things We Don't Understand, 2000, Governmentality, 2003. Recipient Walter Hopps award for Curatorial Achievement, Menil Collection, 2002. Office: Miami Art Mus 101 W Flagler St Miami FL 33130 Office Phone: 305-375-1844.

BUFANO, KATHRYN, retail executive; b. Chgo. BS in Retailing, U. Ill., Urbana. Various positions, Macy's East and Lord & Taylor divsns. Federated Dept. Stores.; pres., chief merchandising officer Dress Barn, Inc.; exec. v.p., gen. mgr., soft-lines Sears Roebuck & Co., Hoffman Estates, Ill.; CEO Vanity Shops, Inc., Fargo, ND, 2006—08; pres., merchandising and mktg. Belk, Inc., 2008—. Office: Belk Inc 2801 W Tyvola Rd Charlotte NC 28217-4500 Office Phone: 704-357-1000. Office Fax: 704-357-1876. Business E-Mail: kathy_bufano@belk.com.

BUFFALO, ELIZABETH A., medical educator, researcher; BA magna cum laude, Wellesley Coll., 1988—92; vis. student, U. Oxford, 1990—91; MA in Philosophy, U. Calif., San Diego, 1993—95, PhD in Neuroscience, 1996—98; postdoc. tng., NIH, 1998—2005, NIMH, 1998—2005. Undergraduate rsch. asst., dept. Exptl. Psychology Oxford Univ., England, 1990—91; undergraduate rsch. asst. Wellesley Coll., 1992; rsch. asst., dept. Univ. of Calif., San Diego, 1993—98; intramural rsch. fellow, lab. Neuropsychology NIMH, 1998—2004; asst. prof. Neurology at Yerkes Nat. Primate Rsch. Ctr. Emory Univ. Sch. of Medicine. Recipient Nat. Insts. of Health Intramural Rsch. Tng. award, 1998—2005; co-recipient Troland Rsch. award, NAS, 2011; grantee Predoctoral Humanities Fellowship, Univ. of Calif., San Diego, 1993—97; fellow McDonnell-Pew Ctr. for Cognitive Neuroscience, San Diego, 1994—98. Achievements include innovative, multidisciplinary study of the hippocampus and the neural basis of memory. Office: Yerkes National Primate Research Center 954 Gatewood Rd NE Atlanta GA 30329 Office Phone: 404-727-9294, 404-712-9431. E-mail: Buffalo@emory.edu.

BUFORD, R.C., professional sports team executive; m. Beth Buford; 1 adopted child, Alexis Wangmene children: Chase, C.C. Student, Tex. A&M U., Okla. State U.; grad., Friends U. Coach U. Kans., 1983—88; asst. coach San Antonio Spurs, 1988—92, head scout, 1994—97, dir. scouting, 1997—99, v.p., asst. gen. mgr., 1999, gen. mgr., 2002—, sr. v.p., 2004—08, pres. of sports franchises, 2008—; asst. coach LA Clippers, 1992—93, U. Fla., 1993—94. Bd. mem. Roy Maas' Youth Alternatives; bd. dirs. Playing for Peace; hon. bd. mem. Juvenile Diabetes Found. Office: San Antonio Spurs One AT&T Ctr San Antonio TX 78219

BUFORD, TED, information technology executive; Grad., Sam Houston State U., Huntsville, Tex.; attended, U. Kans. Various positions CACI International, Inc., founder GSA Program, now sr. v.p., program mgr. govt. svcs. adminstrn. & government wide acquisition contracts. Active Coalition Fed. Procurement; chmn. GSA Subcommittee TechAmerica. Office: CACI International Inc 1100 N Glebe Rd Arlington VA 22201 Office Phone: 703-841-7800. Office Fax: 703-841-7882. Business E-Mail: tbuford@caci.com.

BUFORD, TOM, state legislator; b. Nicholasville, Ky., May 26, 1949; s. William B. and Miriam Hill Buford; m. Carol Tweeddale; children: Stephanie, Beau. State senatore Dist. 22, Ky., 1991—; rep. whip, 1991—92; rep chmn. Senate Caucus, 1993—; chmn. Banking & Ins. Com.; state senate Ky.; v.p. bank holding div. Ctrl. Bank & Trust Co., 1972—76; pres. Buford Constrn., 1976—91, Ky. Bank. Elder Nicholasville Christian Ch., 1984. Named Legislator of Yr., RNC, 1992, Most Ethical Legislator of Yr., Common Cause, 1992. Mem.: Home Builders Assn. Bluegrass, United Way, Jessamine Co. Arts County (dir.), C. of C., Kiwanis (v.p.), Rotary. Republican. Disciple Of Christ. Address: 105 Crosswoods Pl Nicholasville KY 40356 Office: Capitol Annex Rm 230 Frankfort KY 40601 Home: 409 W Maple St Nicholasville KY 40356-1215 Home Phone: 859-885-0606; Office Phone: 502-564-8100 ext. 610. Fax: 859-885-0606.

BUHAIN, WILFRIDO JAVIER, medical educator; b. Bacoor, Cavite, Philippines, Oct. 12, 1940; m. Carlota Torres; children: Ronald, Edgar. AA, BS, U. Philippines, 1959, MD, 1964. Diplomate Am. Bd. Internal Medicine, Am. Bd. Pulmonary Diseases. Rsch. fellow in cardiology U. Philippines, Philippine Gen. Hosp., 1964-65; rotating intern Queens Hosp. Ctr., NYC, 1965-66, resident in internal medicine, 1965-68; clin. fellow in pulmonary diseases Hosp. of U. Pa., 1968-69, chief pulmonary function lab. dept. medicine, 1971-72; rsch. fellow in pulmonary diseases Hosp. of U. Pa., VA Hosp., Phila., 1969-71; assoc. in medicine, cardiovascular-pulmonary div. med. dept. U. Pa. Sch. Medicine, 1971-72; assoc. in medicine, dept. medicine Mt. Sinai Sch. Medicine, CUNY, 1972-74; clin. instr. medicine Georgetown U., 1976-95; ret. Chief pulmonary function lab. dept. medicine Mt. Sinai Hosp. Svcs./City Hosp. Ctr. at Elmhurst, 1973-74; med. dir. respiratory therapy dept. Mt. Vernon Hosp., 1978—2003, chmn. dept. medicine, 1987-88, pres. med. staff, 1996-98; mem. exec. com. Alexandria Hosp., 1983; trustee, chmn. med. affairs coun. Inova Health Sys., 1998-99. Contbr. articles to profl. jours. Grantee, Queensborough Soc., Pa. Thoracic Soc. Fellow ACP, Am. Coll. Chest Physicians; mem. Alexandria Med. Soc., Va. Med. Soc., Philippine Med. Assn. (exec. dir., past pres. Metro-Washington), Assn. Philippine Physicians in Am. (v.p.). Avocations: golf, ballroom dancing.

BUILDER, J. LINDSAY, JR., lawyer; b. Miami, Fla., Feb. 6, 1943; s. John Lindsay and Majorie (Merrell) L.; m. Jean Fern, Aug. 3, 1968; children Thompson Merrell Builder, John Lindsay III. BE, Vanderbilt U., 1965, JD, 1970. Bar: Fla. 1970, U.S. Dist Ct. (mid. dist.) Fla. 1971, U.S. Supreme Ct. 1976. Assoc., ptnr. Maguire, Voorhis & Wells P.A, Orlando, Fla., 1970-84; ptnr. Godbold, Allen, Brown & Builder P.A., Winter Park, Fla., 1984-88, Allen, Brown & Builder P.A., Winter Park, 1988-90, Honigman, Detroit, Orlando, 1991-96, Graham, Builder, Jones, Pratt and Marks, Winter Park, Fla., 1996—2008, Burr & Forman LLP, 2009—. Mem. Vanderbilt U.(bd Trust, 1990 - 1992, mem. 1989 - 1999, and chmn. 1994 - 1999), Winter Park Health found., Winter Park Mem. Hosp., chmn. 1994-96. Lt. (j.g) USN, 1965-67. Mem. Fla. Bar (Realtor-atty Joint Com. 1985-1987), Orange County Bar Assn. (exec. coun., 1979-1985, v.p. 1982-1983, pres. 1983-84), Vanderbilt U. Law Sch. Alumni (mem. 1983-1992, bd. dirs. 1985, pres. 1989-1990), Vanderbilt U. Alumni (pres. bd. dirs. 1989-90), Moot Ct. bd. Republican. Episcopalian. Avocations: golf, running. Office Phone: 407-647-4455. Office Fax: 407-740-7063. Business E-Mail: lbuilder@burr.com. E-mail: lbuilder@grahambuilder.com.

BUJA, L. MAXIMILIAN, pathologist, academic administrator, educator; b. New Orleans, Dec. 30, 1942; s. Louis Marcus and Fay Maxine (Kofler) B.; m. Donna Steele Kinney, Apr. 7, 1966; children: Maximilian Kinney, Evan Louis, Gregory James. BS in Biology magna cum laude, Loyola U., New Orleans, 1964; MD with honors, Tulane U., 1967, MS in Anatomy, 1968. Diplomate Am. Bd. Pathology. Resident in pathology Nat. Cancer Inst./NIH, Bethesda, Md., 1970—72; sr. investigator pathology Nat. Heart and Lung Inst./NIH, Bethesda, Md., 1972—74; asst. prof. pathology U. Tex. Health Sci. Ctr. at Dallas, 1974—77, assoc. prof. pathology, 1977—81; prof. pathology U. Tex. Southwestern Med. Ctr. at Dallas, 1981—89, acting chmn. dept. pathology, 1988—89; prof. pathology and lab. medicine U. Tex. Health Sci. Ctr. at Houston, 1989—, chmn. dept. pathology and lab. medicine, 1989—96; chmn. dept. clin. lab. scis. U. Tex.-Houston Health Sci. Ctr., 1993—96, disting. chair pathology and lab. med., 1995—, dean, 1996—2003, exec. v.p. acad. affairs, 2003—, H. Wayne Hightower disting. prof. in med. scis., 2000—03; chief of svc. clin. pathology lab. Hermann Hosp., Houston, 1989—96; pathologist-in-chief clin. pathology lab. Lyndon Baines Johnson Gen. Hosp., Houston, 1990—96; prof. lab. medicine U. Tex. Anderson Cancer Ctr., Houston, 1990—. Lectr. pathology; mem. autopsy svc.; mem. Tex. Heart Inst. St. Luke's Episcopal Hosp., Houston, 1989—, dir. Cardiovascular Pathology Rsch., 1989—95, chief cardiovasc. pathology, 2000—; 1st Chancellor's Health fellow in edn. U. Tex. System; cons. in field. Author (with Hillis and Willerson): Ischemic Heart Disease-Clinical and Pathophysiological Aspects, 1982; author: (with others) Calcium Antagonists and Cardiovascular Disease, 1984; author: Physiology and Pathophysiology of the Heart, 1984, Cardiovascular Imaging, 1991, Cardiovascular Medicine, 1995; co-author: Netter's Illustrated Human Pathology, 2005; contbg. editor: Clin. Nuc. Cardiology, 1979; mem. editl. bd. Am. Jour. Cardiovascular Pathology, 1985—95, Am. Jour. Cardiology, 1982—88, 1999—, Am. Jour. Pathology, 1980—92, Archives of Pathology and Lab. Medicine, 1985—96, assoc. editor, 2006—, mem. editl. bd. Cardiovascular Pathology, 1991—, Circulation, 1983—88, Circulation Rsch., 1990—99, Lab. Investigation, 1984—2005, Tex. Medicine, 1984—87, Exptl. Molecular Pathology, 1999—, Jour. Am. Coll. Cardiology, 2000—04, Jour. Burns, 2001; assoc. editor: Circulation, 1993—2004; contbr. articles to profl. jours. Surgeon with USPHS, 1968-74. Recipient Joseph Diaz award Loyola U., Order of the Gold-Tipped Stethoscope award Tulane U., John Herr Musser Meml. prize; Sabbatical fellow German Sci. Found., U. Cologne, West Germany, 1988; grantee NIH, 1979, 80, 81, 84, 86-87, 89-90, 93-98, U. Tex., 1993—. Fellow: AAAS, Internat. Soc. for Heart Rsch., Am. Heart Assn. (fellow coun. on basic sci. on clin. cardiology, on atherosclerosis, on circulation, inaugural fellow basic cardiovasc. scis.), Am. Coll. Cardiology; mem.: AMA, U.S. and Can. Acad. Pathology, Tex. Soc. Microscopy, So. Soc. for Clin. Investigation, Soc. Exec. Leadership in Acad. Medicine, Histochem. Soc., Assn. Am. Med. Colls. (coun. deans 1996—2003), Am. Soc. Clin. Pathologists, Am. Soc. Clin. Investigation, Tex. Soc. Pathologists (pres. 1998, George T. Caldwell, M.D. Disting. Svc. award 2005), Tex. Med. Assn., Soc. Cardiovasc. Pathology (Merit award 1998), Internat. Acad. Pathology, Houston Soc. Clin. Pathologists (pres. 1995—96, Harlan J. Spjut award 1997), Harris County Med. Soc. (bd. dirs. 1997—), Coll. Am. Pathligsts, Am. Soc. Cell Biology, Am. Fedn. Med. Rsch., Am. Coll. Healthcare Execs. (assoc.), ACP Execs., Am. Soc. Investigative Pathology, Houston Philos. Soc., Sigma Xi Sci., Beta Beta Beta, Alpha Omega Alpha. Achievements include rsch. on cardiovascular pathology; on mechanisms of cell injury, with emphasis on cell membrane integrity and intracellular electrolyte balance; on measurement of intracellular electrolytes, electron probe x-ray microanalysis and fluorescent probes; on the devel. and regenerative potential of cardiac muscle. Office: U Tex Health Sci Ctr 7000 Fannin St Ste 1715 Houston TX 77030-1501 Office Phone: 713-500-3062.

BULICH, MICAELA NIVEN, energy executive; BEE, U. Hartford, 1981—85; MEE, Rensselaer Poly. Inst., NY, 1985—87. Mfg. leader DuPont, 1988—97; gen. mgr. global supply chain leader SABIC Innovative Plastics (formerly GE Plastics), 2006—09; gen. mgr. lean six sigma GE Electric, 2004—07, gen, mgr. quality and regulatory compliance, 2009; v.p. sourcing GE Energy, 2011—. Office: GE Energy 4200 Wildwood Pky Atlanta GA 30339 Office Phone: 678-844-6000. Office Fax: 678-844-6690.

BULL, FRANK JAMES, retired architect; b. Chattanooga, June 25, 1922; s. Louis H. and Augusta (Clausius) B.; m. Betty Frances Graham, May 7, 1949; 1 child, Birney O'Brian. BS in Architecture, Ga. Inst. Tech., Atlanta, 1948, BArch, 1949. Registered architect, Ga., 1951; cert. Nat. Coun. Archtl. Registration Bds. Pilot Pan Am. World Airways, NY, Fla., 1942—46; arch. Aeck Assocs. Architects, Atlanta, 1948-57; ptnr. Bull & Kenney Architects, Atlanta, 1957-88, Bull, Brown & Kilgo, Architects, Atlanta, 1988—2003; ret., 2003. Cons. Fed. Republic of Germany Embassy, Washington, 1986-93; archtl. cons. for golf clubhouse Quinta do Peru, Sesimbra, Portugal and Palheiro Golfe, Funchal, Madeira Island, Portugal, 1991; lectr. in field. Co-author: Asbestos Abatement: Vol. 5 The Sourcebook on Asbestos Diseases, 1991; contbr. articles to profl. jours.; prin. works include Sanctuary for Holy Innocents Episc. Ch., Atlanta, Atlanta Speech Sch. and Clin., Hummel Hall Episc. H.S., Alexandria, Va., Jekyll Island Golf Clubhouse, McLarty Hall, Tull Hall, Turner Gymnasium, Westminster Schs., Atlanta, Dunwoody Country Club, Atlanta, East Lake Golf Clubhouse Restoration, Atlanta, others. Charter trustee Holy Innocents Episcopal Sch., Atlanta, 1962-68, chmn., 1966; founder Galloway Schs., Atlanta, 1969-75. Recipient Rambusch prize, Ecole de Beaux Arts, 1940, Lifetime Achievement award, Nat. Environ. Info. Assn., 2009. Mem. AIA (mem. emeritus, treas. Atlanta chpt. 1976-78, bd. dirs. Ga. assn. 1971-74), Am. Arbitration Assn. (mem. nat. panel constrn. industry arbitrators 1977-2002), Nat. Asbestos Coun. (founder, charter v.p., bd. dirs. 1983-86, 89-90, treas. 1987, exec. com. 1983-87), Cherokee Town and Country Club (charter, bd. govs. 1976-79, chmn. capital appropriations com., chmn. green com.), Omicron Delta Kappa, Tau Beta Pi, Phi Kappa Phi, Phi Eta Sigma, ANAK, Beta Theta Pi. Republican. Episcopalian. Avocations: golf, writing.

BULLARD, DENNY B., oil and gas company executive; BS in Petroleum Engring., Tex. Tech U., 1970. With Conoco, Inc., 1970—84, Damson Oil Corp., 1984—91; ops. mgr. Permian Divsns., South Tex., Appalachia and La. Parker & Parsley Petroleum Co., 1991—93, v.p. Gulf Coast Divsn., 1993—96, v.p. Oklahoma City Divsn., 1996—97; joined Pioneer Natural Resources Co., 1997, v.p.

engring. and devel., v.p. ops., v.p. ops. svcs., 2007—. Mem.: Internat. Assn. Drilling Contractors, Soc. Profl. Well Log Analyst, Am. Soc. Mech. Engrs., Soc. Petroleum Engrs. Office: Pioneer Natural Resources Co Ste 200 5205 N O'Connor Blvd Irving TX 75039 Office Phone: 972-444-9001. Office Fax: 972-402-7023.

BULLARD, DWIGHT, state legislator; b. Philadelphia, Pa., Feb. 4, 1977; s. Edward and Larcenia. BA in Hist., Fla. A&M U., 1999. Tchr. Coral Reef Sr. High Sch., 2000—; mem. Dist. 118 Fla. House of Reps., 2008—, ranking mem. preK-12 policy com., mem. agr. and natural resources policy com., preK-12 appropriations com. Mem.: NAACP (life), South Dade Dem., Ron Brown Dem. Caucus, Redlands Dem., Richmond Heights Homeowners Assn., Kappa Alpha Psi. Democrat. Episcopal. Office: 1401 The Capitol 402 S Monroe St Tallahassee FL 32399-1300 also: 16201 SW 95 Ave Ste 214 Miami FL 33157-3459 Office Phone: 850-488-5430, 305-234-2208. Business E-Mail: dwight.bullard@myfloridahouse.gov.

BULLARD, EDGAR JOHN, III, museum director; b. LA, Sept. 15, 1942; s. Edgar John and Katherine Elizabeth (Dreisbach) B. BA, UCLA, 1965, MA, 1968; LHD (hon.), Loyola U., New Orleans, 1987. Asst. to dir., curator spl. projects Nat. Gallery Art, Washington, 1968-73; Montine McDaniel Freeman dir. New Orleans Mus. Art, 1973—2010, dir. emeritus, 2011—. Alternate mem. Citizens Stamp Adv. Com., 1969-71; mus. adv. panel Nat. Endowment for Arts, 1974-77; bd. vis. Xavier U., La., 2006—, bd. dirs. LSU Mus. Art, 2010- Author: Edgar Degas, 1971, John Sloan 1871-1951, 1971, Mary Cassatt: Oils and Pastels, 1972, A Panorama of American Painting, 1975. Nerdrum: The Drawings, 1994, Henry Casselli: Master of the American Watercolor, 2000, In Celebration of Light: Photographs from the Pierce Collection, 2004, George Rodrigue: Catalogue Raisonné of Prints, 2008. Bd. dirs. New Orleans Jazz and Heritage Found., 1974-78; trustee New Orleans Opera Assn., 2001-06, Ga. Mus. Art, U. Ga., Athens, 1975-80, Kneisel Hall Chamber Music Sch., Blue Hill, Maine, 1986-02, La. Soc. for Prevention Cruelty to Animals, 1986-93, New Orleans Jazz Orch., 2003-06, Haystack Mountain Sch. of Crafts, Deer Isle, Maine, 2003—; mem. adv. bd. Tulane Univ. Coll., 1999-2001; trustee Amistad Rsch. Ctr., Tulane U., 2001—; bd. visitors Xavier U. La., 2007—, bd. govs., Nat. Hospice Found., 2011-. Decorated Order of Republic of Egypt, officer Am. Soc. Venerable Order St. John Jerusalem, Comdr., Order of Arts and Lettres of France; Samuel H. Kress Found. fellow, 1967-68; recipient New Orleans Mayor's Art award, 1993. Mem.: Am. Assn. Mus. (bd. dirs. 1996—98), Assn. Art Mus. Dirs. Democrat. Episcopalian. Home: 1805 Milan St New Orleans LA 70115-5443 also: Greenlea Reach Rd Deer Isle ME 04627 Home Phone: 504-897-2655, 207-348-6137; Office Phone: 504-658-4102. Business E-Mail: jbullard@noma.org.

BULLARD, JOHN MOORE, religious studies educator, church musician; b. Winston-Salem, NC, May 6, 1932; s. Hoke Vogler and May Evangeline (Moore) B. AB, U. N.C., 1953; AM, 1955; MDiv, Yale U., 1957; PhD, 1962. Ordained to ministry United Meth. Ch., 1955. Asst. in instrn. Yale U., New Haven, 1957-61; asst. prof. religion Wofford Coll., Spartanburg, SC, 1961-65, assoc. prof., 1965-70, Albert C. Outler prof. religion, 1970—, chmn. dept., 1962—, faculty sec., 1988—2001. Minister music, organist-choirmaster Central United Meth. Ch., Spartanburg, 1961-72, Bethel United Meth. Ch., 1972-88, Second Presbyn. Ch., Spartanburg, 1994, Palmetto Moravian Fellowship, 1994—; lectr. Eureka Coll., 1967, Furman U., 1982, Barton Coll., 1992; vis. prof. Biblical Lit. U. NC, Chapel Hill, 1966-67, U. NC, Charlotte, 1974; vis. prof. comparative religion Converse Coll., Spartanburg, 1984. Author: History of the Spartanburg Chapter, American Guild of Organists, 1954-2004, 2004; editor: Wofford Lectures in Religion, Ethics, and Society, 2004; co-author (with Hugh Sanborn): The Prophetic Call: Celebrating Community, Earth, Justice and Peace, 2004; contbr. articles and book reviews to profl. jours. With Naval ROTC, 1950-52. Grantee NEH summer seminar Harvard U., 1982, U. Pa., 1986, Yale U., 1987; Fulbright-Hays grantee, Pakistan 1973, Fund for the Study of Gt. Religions in Asia, 1970-71; James fellow Yale U.; NEH/Wofford rsch. grantee U. London, 1975; named to Ky. Cols., 1977; Dana Fellow Emory Univ's. Grad. Inst. Liberal Arts, 1989-90. Mem. Soc. Bibl. Lit. (pres. so. sect. 1968-69), Am. Acad. Religion, Am. Guild Organists (dean chpt. 1965-67), Organ Hist. Soc., S.C. Acad. Religion (pres. 1974-75), Southeastern Hist. Keyboard Soc., New Bach Soc. (Leipzig), Moravian Music Found. (bd. trustees), Phi Mu Alpha Sinfonia. Home: 104 Hickman Ct Hillbrook Forest Spartanburg SC 29307 Office Phone: 864-582-8589. Business E-Mail: bullardjm@wofford.edu.

BULLOCH, JOHN D., JR., state legislator; b. Thomas County, Ga., Mar. 19, 1947; m. Miriam Bulloch; children: Dee, Joni, Ashley. Attended, Abraham Baldwin Coll., U. Ga. Owner Bulloch Farms; mem., house rep. Ga., 1999—2002; mem., state senate Dist. 11 Ga., 2002—. Republican. Baptist. Mailing: 3554 Bulloch Rd Ochlocknee GA 31773 Office Phone: 229-683-3420. Business E-Mail: john.bulloch@senate.ga.gov.

BULLOCK, ELLIS WAY, JR., architect; b. Birmingham, Ala., Sept. 11, 1928; s. Ellis Way Sr. Bullock and Martha (Foute) Alexander; m. Ann Ardelia Pope, Nov. 28, 1950; children: Ellis Way III, Elbert Pope, John Howard Keith, William Frank. BArch, Auburn U., 1954. Registered architect, Fla., Ala., Ga., Miss., S.C., N.C. Apprentice architect Yonge, Look & Morrison, Pensacola, Fla., 1954-58; owner Ellis Bullock Architect, Pensacola, 1958-73; pres., CEO Bullock-Tice and Assocs. Arch., Inc., Pensacola, 1973—96. Pres. Fla. AIA, 1977, treas. AIA Rsch. Corp., Washington, 1980-81; chmn. Energy in Arch., Washington, 1980-82; mem. faculty adv. com. Auburn U. Sch. Architecture, 1980—, chmn., 1988-89; mem. Nat. Architecture Accrediting Bd., Washington, 1982-86; mem. adv. coun. U. Fla. Coll. Architecture, 1986—. Contbr. articles to profl. jours. Chmn. Pensacola Hist. Commn., 1967; chmn. City of Pensacola Archtl. Review Bd., 1968, Pensacola Bldg. Bd. of Appeals, 1970—; bd. dirs. Pensacola Symphony, 1998-2000, Fla. Bd. Architecture and Interior Design, 2002-06, chair, 2005; exec. bd. Auburn U. Coll. Architecture, Design and Constrn., 2000—; mem. Blue Ribbon Task Force on Edn., Escambia County, Fla., 1985-86; mem. adv. coun. U. Fla., 1986—; mem. sesquicentennial commn. State of Fla. 1st lt. U.S. Army, 1950-54. Recipient 1st Honor AIA-Navy, 1977, 78, Award of Merit, 1976; recipient Outstanding Design award for Air Force Systems Command Hdqrs., 1980, Gov.'s Design award, 1982, 84, Merit award for U.S. Air Force Design, 1983, Design Excellence award Air Force Regional Civil Engrs., 1984, award of merit Navy Youth Ctr., 1990, award of merit Navy Bowling Ctr. Complex, 1990; named Profl. of Yr., Pensacola News Jour., 1977. Fellow AIA (bd. dirs. 1979-82, v.p. 1981-82, jury coll. of fellows 1988-91, exec. com. coll. of fellows 1993—, bursar 1993—, vice chancellor 1994-95, chancellor 1995-96, regional rep. Fla. Caribbean 1990—, numerous awards N.W. chpt. 1974—, award of excellence Fla. N.W. chpt. 1980, 82, 86, 89, 90, Gold medal Fla. chpt. 1988, Millennium award of honor Fla. chpt. 2000), Am. Archtl. Found. (regent 1995-96, EXCOM 1995-96, task force account and reason 1988, program chmn. nat. conv. com. 1986); mem. Fla. Assn. AIA (pres. 1977, govtl. liaison com. 1984—, Gold medal 1988, gold medal noiminating com. 1990-91, balanced curriculum task force 1990, chmn. design awards jur. Ctrl. Fla. chpt. 1980, speaker ann. conf. 1997-98), Fla. Archtl. Found. (trustee 1988—, chmn. 1993), Inst. Bus. Designers (award for contractual interiors 1977), NRA, St. Andrews Soc., Rotary (Paul Harris fellow 1994). Office: Bullock Tice Assocs 909 E Cervantes St Ste B Pensacola FL 32501-3281 Home: 608 Bayshore Dr Pensacola FL 32507 Office Phone: 850-434-5444. E-mail: ewbjr@ewbullock.com.

BULLOCK, FRANK WILLIAM, JR., lawyer, retired federal judge; b. Oxford, NC, Nov. 3, 1938; s. Frank William and Wilma Jackson (Long) B.; m. Frances Dockery Haywood, May 5, 1984; 1 child, Frank William III BSBA, U. N.C., 1961, LLB, 1963. Bar: N.C. 1963. Law clk. to Hon. Algernon L. Butler US Dist. ct. (ea. dist.) NC, 1963—64; assoc. Maupin, Taylor & Ellis, Raleigh, NC, 1964-68; asst. dir. Adminstrv. Office of Cts. of N.C., Raleigh, NC, 1968-73; ptnr. Douglas, Ravenel, Hardy, Crihfield & Bullock, Greensboro, NC, 1973-82; judge US Dist. Ct. (mid. dist.) N.C., Greensboro, NC, 1982—2006, chief judge, 1992-99; ptnr. Womble Carlyle Sandridge & Rice LLP, Greensboro, NC, 2006—. Mem. bd. editors N.C. Law Rev., 1962-63; contbr. articles to profl. jours. Mem. N.C. Bar Assn., Greensboro Bar Assn., N.C. Soc. of Cin., Fla. Soc. Colonial Wars, Greensboro Country Club. Republican. Presbyterian. Avocations: golf, tennis, running, history. Office: Womble Carlyle Sandridge & Rice LLP PO Box 21104 Greensboro NC 27402 Office Phone: 336-574-8061.

BULLOCK, MARY BROWN, history, political science professor, former academic administrator; m. George Bullock; children: Ashley, Graham. BA, Agnes Scott Coll., Atlanta, 1966; MA in Chinese history, Stanford U., 1968, PhD in Chinese history, 1973. Profl. assoc. Com. on Scholarly Comm. with People's Republic of China, 1973—77, dir., 1977—88; dir. Asia program Woodrow Wilson Internat. Ctr. Scholars, Washington, 1988—95; pres. Agnes Scott Coll., Decatur, Ga., 1995—2006; disting. prof. China studies Emory U., 2007—. Chair, bd. trustees China Med. Bd. of N.Y.; dir. Nat. Com. on U.S.-China Rels.; mem. adv. coun. on U.S.-China cooperation in sci., policy, rsch. and edn. NSF; chair Nat. Assn. Ind. Colls. and Univs., 2002—04, Women's Coll. Coalition, 2004—06; bd. dirs. Genuine Parts Co.; trustee Asia Found., Luce Found. Recipient Elizabeth Luce Moore Visionary Leadership award, Dist. Svc. award, NAS; grantee, Ford Found., Henry Luce Found., Rockefeller Found., NSF; fellow, Woodrow Wilson Internat. Ctr. Scholars, Rockefeller Conf. Ctr., Bellagio, Italy. Mem.: Coun. on Fgn. Rels., Carter Ctr. Bd. of Councilors.

BULLOCK, ROGER V., motor and generator manufacturing company executive; Gen. mgr., drives Baldor Electric Co., v.p., drives sales, 2002—. Office: Baldor Electric Co 5711 R S Boreham Jr St Fort Smith AR 72901 Office Phone: 479-646-4711. Office Fax: 479-648-5792. Business E-Mail: RBullock@baldor.com.

BULLOCK, WILLIAM L., JR., oil industry executive; Pres., gen. mgr. Indonesia ConocoPhillips, pres. Middle East and North Africa, 2007—. Office: ConocoPhillips PO Box 2197 Houston TX 77252-2197

BULOVA, DAVID L., state legislator; b. Fairfax, Va., May 6, 1969; m. Gretchen Marie Reimer; children: Alex, Josette. BA in Govt., Coll. William & Mary, Va., 1991; MPA, Va. Polytechnic Inst. and State U., Blacksburg, 1996. Environ. planner; bd. dir. Northern Va. Soil & Water Conservation Dist., 2004—06; mem. Dist. 37 Va. House of Delegates, 2006—; mem. Gen. Laws Com., Agr. Chesapeake & Natural Resources Com., 2006—. Mem. St. Mary's of Sorrows Cath. Ch.; bd. trustees Brain Injury Svcs., 1997—; former chmn. Fairfax County Consumer Protection Commn.; former mem. Chesapeake Bay Local Assistance Bd. Recipient Citation of Merit award, Fairfax Federation Citizen Assns., 2002, Watershed Connections award, Va. Assoc. Soil & Water Dist., 2005. Democrat. Office: PO Box 106 Fairfax Station VA 22039 Office Phone: 703-310-6752. Office Fax: 888-816-2660. Business E-Mail: DelDBulova@house.virginia.gov.

BULOVA, SHARON, county official; m. Lou DeFalaise; 4 children. Supr. Braddock Dist., Va., 1988—2009, chmn. Budget Com. Va.; chmn. Fairfax County Bd. Suprs., Va., 2009—. Chair Gov.'s Commn. on Rail Enhancement for the 21st Century in the Commonwealth of Va., 2004; mem., past chmn. No. Va. Transp. Com., No. Va. Regional Commn.; founder Virginia Railway Express (VRE). Gov. bd. Fairfax County's Initiative to Prevent and End Homelessness. Named one of The 100 Most Powerful Women in DC, Washingtonian mag., 2009. Office: Fairfax County Bd Supervisors Ste 530 12000 Government Center Parkway Fairfax VA 22035 Office Phone: 703-324-2321.

BUMPAS, STUART MARYMAN, lawyer; b. Little Rock, Oct. 7, 1944; s. Hubert Wayne Bumpas and Martha Conway (Maryman) Gaylord; m. Diane Ellen DeWare, Oct. 1, 1977. BA, Brown U., 1966; JD, U. Tex., 1969; LLM, George Washington U., 1973. Bar: Tex. 1969, D.C. 1972. Atty.-advisor Office of Chief Counsel, Washington, 1969-72; asst. to commr. IRS, Washington, 1973-74; ptnr. Locke, Purnell, Rain, Harrell, Dallas, 1974-98, Locke, Liddell & Sapp, Dallas, 1999—2007, Locke Lord, 2008—. Adj. prof. employee benefits So. Meth. U., Dallas, 1975; lectr. Washington Non-Profit Tax Conf., Am. Law Inst., Ann. Non-Profit Orgns. Inst. Contbr. articles to profl. jours. Exec. com. Meadows Sch. of Arts, So. Meth. U., Dallas; bd. dirs. Callier Ctr. for Comm. Disorders, Dallas, 1984—, Friends of Alzheimer's Dis. Ctr., Southwestern Med. Sch., Goodwill Industries, Dallas; bd. dirs., v.p. Dallas Grand Opera Assn., 1984; mem. Mayor's Commn. on Internat. Devel. Task Force on Arts and Culture, Dallas, 1988; nat. counsel Am. Heart Assn., Dallas, 1979—; trustee The Lamplighter Sch.; gen. counsel The Hockaday Sch.; gen. counsel, trustee, mem. exec. com. Dallas Mus. Art; trustee Southwestern Med. Found.; mem. chancellor's coun. U. Tex. Sys.; mem. adv. com. Meadows Mus. Mem. ABA (mem. exempt orgns. com.), Tex. Bar Assn. (former chmn. legal aspects of arts com.), Dallas Bar Assn., Bus. Adv. Com., Am. Coun. on Germany, Coun. on Fgn. Rels. Clubs: Dallas Petroleum, Brook Hollow Golf, Idlewild (Dallas); Soc. Cin. (Washington), Coral Beach and Tennis (Bermuda). Episcopalian. Home: 5306 Surrey Cir Dallas TX 75209-2427 Office: Locke Lord LLP 2200 Ross Ave Ste 2200 Dallas TX 75201-6776 Office Phone: 214-740-8000. E-mail: sbumpas@lockelord.com.

BUNDY, CHARLES ALAN, retired foundation executive; b. Cheraw, SC, Jan. 5, 1930; s. Jackson Corbett and Ruby Jones (Hughes) B.; m. Margaret Ellen Jackson, Feb. 27, 1954; children: Charles Alan, Robert Jackson, Dan Hughes. AB, Wofford Coll., 1951; DH (hon.), Charleston So. U. Mgr. prodn. planning J.P. Stevens & Co., Inc., Rockingham, NC, 1951-54; mgr. Jesup (Ga.) C. of C., 1954-56, Lancaster (S.C.) C. of C., 1956-61; dist. mgr. U.S. C. of C., Birmingham, Ala., 1961-65; exec. v.p. Macon (Ga.) C. of C., 1965-71, Greg Enterprises, Lancaster, 1971-72; pres. Springs Found., Inc. and Close Found., Inc., Lancaster, 1972-97, ret., 1997; pvt. practice cons., 1997—; ret., 2004. Chmn. Lancaster County Higher Edn. Commn. Chmn. SC Parks, Recreation and Tourism Commn., 1983—89; mem. SC Coordinating Coun. for Econ. Devel., 1986—89; mem., past chmn. S. E. Coun. on Founds.; trustee Columbia Coll., 1976—88, SC Found. Ind. Colls., 1982—93; chmn. Gov.'s Freshwater Wetlands Forum, 1989, Lancaster County Strategic Plan, 1990; past pres. U. SC Lancaster Ednl. Found.; mem. State Govt. Reorgn. Commn., 1991; chmn. bd. 1st Meth. Ch., 1978—; past chmn. bd. dirs. Springs Meml. Hosp. Mem. Lancaster County C. of C. (past pres.), Rotary (past pres.). Home: 518 Briarwood Rd Lancaster SC 29720-1802

BUNGO, MICHAEL WILLIAM, cardiologist, educator, administrator; b. Passaic, NJ, July 18, 1950; s. John C. and Mary Bungo; children: Elise Nicole, Jonathan Michael. BS in Chemistry, Rensselaer Poly. Inst., 1971; MD, N.J. Med. Sch., 1975. Diplomate Am. Bd. Internal Medicine, Subsplty. Bd. Cardiovasc. Diseases, Am. Coll. Physician Execs., Bd. Cardiovas. Computed Tomography. Intern in internal medicine New England Deaconess Hosp., Boston, 1975-76, resident, 1976—78; asst. in medicine Peter Bent Brigham Hosp., 1976—77; cardiology fellow New England Deaconess Hosp., Harvard Med. Sch., 1978—80; head cardiovascular lab. NASA Johnson Space Ctr., Houston, 1980—85; mem. Aerospace Medicine Bd., 1980—91; dir. Space Biomed. Rsch. Inst. NASA Johnson Space Ctr., 1986—90; chief scientist med. scis. divsn. NASA, 1990—91; prof. medicine U. Tex., Galveston, med. dir. heart sta. divsn. cardiology, 1995—2002, vice chmn. dept. internal medicine, 1999—2002; assoc. dean U. Tex. Med. Sch., Houston, 2002—05, vice dean, 2005—07; chief of staff LBJ Gen. Hosp., 2002—06; pres. and CEO UT Physicians, 2005—07, CMO! Tomography, 2010—. Chmn. dept. medicine St. John Hosp., Houston, 1987—89; fellowship advisor NRC, Washington, 1984—89. Editor: Results of Life Sciences Aboard the Space Shuttle, 1987, CMO: Tomography, 2010-; contbr. abstracts and articles to jours., chpts. to books; tech. reviewer Circulation, Aviation, Space and Environ. Medicine, 1989—; mem. editl. bd. Aviation, Space and Environ. Medicine, 1997-2000. Recipient medal NASA, 1986. Fellow ACP, Am. Coll. Cardiology; mem. Am. Heart Assn., Aerospace Med. Assn. (Louis H. Bauer Founders award 1987), Tex. Med. Assn., Am. Coll. of Physician Exec., Phi Lambda Upsilon. Office: U Tex Houston Med Sch MSB Ste 1242 6431 Fannin St Houston TX 77030 Office Phone: 713-500-5532.

BUNNING, DAVID L., federal judge; b. Ft. Thomas, Ky., 1966; s. James Paul David Bunning and Mary Catherine Theis. BA, U. Ky., 1988, JD, 1991. Law clk. US Atty.'s Office (ea. dist.) Ky., 1991, asst. US atty., 1991—2002; judge US Dist. Ct. (ea. dist.) Ky., Covington, 2002—. Office: US Dist Ct Ste 410 35 W 5th St Covington KY 41011 Office Phone: 859-392-7907.

BUNZL, RUDOLPH HANS, retired manufacturing executive; b. Vienna, July 20, 1922; arrived in U.S., 1940, naturalized, 1944; s. Robert Max and Nellie Margaret (Burian) Bunzl; m. Rema R. Templeton, Apr. 6, 1947 (div.); children: Ann Mary Bunzl Kamoe, Carol Elizabeth Bunzl Showker; m. Esther R. Mendelsohn, Nov. 14, 1970. BSChemE, Ga. Inst. Tech., 1943; MA in History, U. Richmond, 1994. With Shell Chem. Co., Calif., 1943-54; v.p. Am. Filtrona Corp., Richmond, Va., 1954-59, pres., 1959-83, CEO, 1983-87, chmn. bd., 1987-95. Pres. R.E.B. Found.; trustee Richmond Symphony Found. With US Army, 1944—46.

BURATYNSKI, THERESA JOAN, physician; b. Steubenville, Ohio, Apr. 21, 1964; d. Raymond Stanley and Anna Sue Buratynski; m. Peter Randall Daspit, Apr. 1, 2000. BSc, U. Akron, 1986; MPH, Johns Hopkins U., 1999; MD, Case We. Res. U., 1995. Student fellow pathology U. Hosps. Cleve., 1992—93; gen. med. officer Naval Hosp., Yokosuka, Japan, 1996—98; resident Navy Aerospace Medicine Inst., Pensacola, Fla., 1999—2000; head dept. aviation medicine Med. Clinic Kaneohe Bay, 2000—01; flight surgeon Marine Heavy Helicopter 363, Kaneohe, 2001—04; sr. med. officer Marine Aircraft Group 24, Kaneohe, 2004—05, 3rd Navy Constrn. Regiment, 2009—12; med. officer Navy Health Clinic, Kaneohe, 2006—08; sr. med. officer 1NCR, 2013—. Contbr. articles to profl. jours. Activist Kailua Neighborhood, Hawaii, 2004—09; med. support and aid USN, 2000. Comdr. USN, 1996—. Decorated Navy Achievement medal, Navy Commendation medal; recipient Dr. Roger Keller, Jr. award for Genetics and Biotech., U. Akron, 1986, Daniel Lewis Raven, MD award, Case We. Res. U. Sch. Medicine, 1995, Physician Recognition award, AMA, 2003—06; Rsch. grantee, Am. Heart Assn., 1986, Armed Forces Health Scis. Edn. and Tng. scholar, USN, 1990—95, Betty Ford Ctr. Resident in Tng. scholar, 1991, March of Dimes rsch. scholar, 1991, fellow in pathology, U. Hosp. Cleve., 1992—93, Chattanooga Corp. grantee, 1985, Ohio Bd. Regents scholar, 1982—86. Mem.: APHA, Am. Coll. Occupl. and Environ. Medicine, Aerospace Med. Assn., Soroptimists Internat., Phi Sigma Alpha. Avocations: running, gardening, community service, reading. Office Phone: 808-778-4541. Personal E-mail: doctjb@hotmail.com.

BURBRIDGE, MICHAEL FRANCIS, bishop; b. Phila., June 16, 1957; s. Francis and Shirley Burbridge. BA in Philosophy, St. Charles Borromeo Sem., MA in Theology; MA in Edn. Adminstrn., Villanova U.; EdD, Immaculata Coll. Ordained priest Archdiocese of Phila., 1984; parochial vicar St. Bernard Ch., Phila., 1984—86; faculty mem. Cardinal O'Hara HS, Archbishop Wood HS, St. Charles Borromeo Sem., 1986—92; adminstrv. sec. to Anthony Cardinal Bevilacqua Archbishop of Philadelphia, 1992—99; rector St. Charles Borromeo Sem., 1999—2002; ordained bishop, 2002; aux. bishop Archdiocese of Phila., 2002—06; bishop Diocese of Raleigh, NC, 2006—. Dean of students St. Charles Borromeo Sem. Roman Catholic. Office: Diocese of Raleigh 715 Nazareth St Raleigh NC 27606 Office Phone: 919-821-9700. Office Fax: 919-821-9705.

BURCH, JAMES LEO, science research institute executive; b. San Antonio, Nov. 28, 1942; s. Joseph Leo Jr. and Doris Babette (Hagy) B.; m. Kathleen Marie Dowdy, Dec. 30, 1965; children: Angela Marie, Charles Joseph, Kenneth James. BS in Physics, St. Mary's U., San Antonio, 1964; PhD, Rice U., 1968; MS in Adminstrn., George Washington U., 1973. Space physicist Goddard Space Flight Ctr. NASA, Greenbelt, Md., 1971-74, space physicist Marshall Space Flight Ctr. Huntsville, Ala., 1974-77; sr. rsch. physicist S.W. Rsch. Inst., San Antonio, 1977-78, sect. mgr., 1978-80, dept. dir., 1980-85, v.p., 1985—. Prin. investigator NASA Dynamics Explorer Mission, 1978-92, Nasa Atlas Shuttle Mission, 1989-93, ESA Rosetta Comet orbiter, 1996—, NASA Image Midex mission, 1996—2005, NASA Magnetosphere Multiscale Mission, 2005—; mem. space sci. and applications adv. com. NASA, 1990-93; mem. NAS Space Studies Bd., 2000-04; chair NAS com. Solar and Space Physics, 2000-04. Assoc. editor Jour. Geophys. Rsch., 1977-79, 94-96, Geophys. Rsch. Letters, 1978-82, editor, 1989-90, editor-in-chief, 1990-93; contbr. numerous articles to profl. jours. Capt. U.S. Army, 1968-71. Recipient Disting. Alumnus award St. Mary's U., 1987. Fellow Am. Geophys. Union (pres. space physics and aeronomy sect. 1996-98, fellow 95, Van Allen Lecturership award 2001, Fleming medal 2010), Internat. Acad. Astronautics. Roman Catholic. Avocation: golf. Office: SW Rsch Inst 6220 Culebra Rd San Antonio TX 78238-5100 Business E-Mail: jburch@swri.edu.

BURCH, JIM, former mayor; m. Janet Burch; children: Zachary, Kelsey, Joseph. BA in English, Secondary Edn., Va Commonwealth U., Richmond. Profl. surveyor & mapper; councilman, Dist. 1 Cape Coral City Coun., Fla., 2007—08; mayor City of Cape Coral, Fla., 2008—09. Mem. Lee County Met. Planning Org.; coach Cape Coral Nat. League Baseball, Cape Coral Parks and Recreation Basketball. Mailing: PO Box 150027 Cape Coral FL 33915-0027

BURCH, JOHN CHRISTOPHER, JR., investment banker; b. Nashville, Jan. 18, 1940; s. John Christopher and Frances Vivian (Harris) B.; m. Susan Marie Klein, Sept. 13, 1969; children: Frances Marie, Christina Polk, John Christopher III. BA, Vanderbilt U., 1966. Credit analyst Bank N.Y., NYC, 1966-70; v.p. instl. sales Loeb Rhoades & Co., NYC, 1970-75, J.C. Bradford & Co., Nashville, 1976-82; mng. dir. SunTrust Equitable Securities Corp., Nashville, 1982-2001; pres. Capital Markets Advisors LLC, Nashville, 2001—. Co-author: Capital Markets Handbook, 1999, 6th edit., 2013. With U.S. Army, 1962-65. Mem.: CFA Soc. Nashville (bd. dirs. 2006—08), Fin. Industry Regulatory Authority (arbitrator), Securities Industry Assn. (chmn. syndicate com. 1998—2000, bd. dirs. chair so. dist. 2001), CFA Inst., Soc. of the Cincinnati, Belle Meade Country Club (Nashville). Episcopalian. Home: 705 Hillwood Blvd Nashville TN 37205-1315 Office: Capital Markets Advisors LLC Ste 228 2200 Twenty First Ave S Nashville TN 37212 Office Phone: 615-292-6323. Fax: 615-292-6757. E-mail: jburch@capitalmarketsadvisors.com.

BURCH, VORIS REAGAN, retired mediator, arbitrator, lawyer; b. Liberty, Tex., Feb. 10, 1930; s. Voris Reagan and Jessamae (Coffey) B.; m. Claudia Ramsland, Dec. 30, 1978; children: Melissa Burch Lively, Voris Reagan III. BBA, Tex. A&M U., 1952; JD, U. Tex., 1957. Bar: Tex. 1957. Assoc. Baker & Botts, Houston, 1957-69, ptnr., 1969-95, ret., 1995. Served to 1st lt. USAF, 1952-54. Mem. State Bar Tex. (chmn. labor law sect. 1970-71), Houston Bar Assn., Phi Delta Phi. Home and Office: 5761 Indian Cir Houston TX 77057-1302 Office Phone: 713-780-0196. Personal E-mail: reagan.burch@att.net.

BURCHFIELD, TERESA C., corporate financial executive; BS in Acctg., U. Ctrl. Okla., 1982. Dir., acctg., fin. BeautiControl, Inc., v.p., CFO, 2001—07, contr., 2004—07; v.p., investor rels. Tupperware Brands Corp., 2007—. Office: Tupperware Brands Corp 14901 S Orange Blossom Trail Orlando FL 32837 Office Phone: 407-826-5050.

BURD, JOHN STEPHEN, retired academic administrator, music educator; b. Lock Haven, Pa., Apr. 6, 1939; s. John Wilson and Lily (Fye) Burd; m. Patricia Ayers, June 3, 1961; children: Catherine Elizabeth, Emily Susanne. B in Music Edn., Greenville Coll., 1961; MS in Sacred Music, Butler U./Christian Theo. Sem., 1964; PhD, Ind. State U., 1971. Adj. music instr. Rose Hulman Inst. Tech., Terre Haute, Ind., 1969-71; assoc. prof. Greenville (Ill.) Coll., 1971-76; prof. edn. Lindenwood Coll., St. Charles, Mo., 1976-80; v.p. acad. affairs Maryville U., St. Louis, 1980-85; pres. Brenau U., Gainesville, Ga., 1985—2004, ret., 2004; pres. emeritus, 2004—. Team evaluator Nat. Coun. Accreditation Tchr. Edn., 1979—84, 1985—; mem. exec. coun. Women's Coll. Coalition, 1989—92, NAICU Commn. State Rels. Bd., 1991—93; adv. bd. Wachovia Bank, Gainesville, 1991—. Editor: New Voices in Education, 1969—71; contbr. articles to profl. jours. V.p. Christian Arts, Inc., NJ, 1965—, pres.; choir dir. Maryville U., St. Louis, 1983—85; bd. dirs. Gainesville Symphony, 1991—94, W. Crawford Long Mus.; chair Gainesville Redevelopment Authority, Chicopee Pk. Commn.; choir dir. Ctr. Presbyn. Ch., St. Louis, 1984—85; adv. bd. N.E. Ga. Med. Ctr.; bd. dirs. Met. Atlanta Arts Fund, bd. mem., 2004—. Recipient Outstanding Young Alumnus award, Greenville Coll., 1982, Disting. Alumnus award, 1991. Mem.: Ga. Assn. Colls. (pres. 1989—90, 2003—04), Ga. Found. Ind. Colls. (exec. bd. 1986—, vice chmn. 1993, 2002), So. Assn. Women's Colls. (pres. 1988—89), Am. Assn. Higher Edn., Am. Assn. Tchr. Edn., Gainesville C. of C. (bd. dirs.). Methodist. Avocations: tennis, travel, art. Office: Brenau Univ 500 Washington St Gainesville GA 30501-3697 Home Phone: 770-535-7673; Office Phone: 770-297-5952. Business E-Mail: jburd@brenau.edu.

BURDINE, GREG, state legislator; b. Florence, Ala., May 1, 1959; m. Susan Burdine; 2 children. BS in Fin., U. Northern Ala., 1982; JD, Cumberland U., 1988. Mem. Dist. 1 Ala. House of Reps., 2011—. Democrat. Office: Ala House of Reps Rm 536-D 11 S Union St Montgomery AL 36130 also: 207 Indian Springs Dr Florence AL 35634 Office Phone: 334-242-7265, 256-766-9201. Office Fax: 256-766-9220.

BURFORD, RICHARD T., state legislator; Dairy & beef farmer; mem. Dist. 7 La. House of Reps., 2008—, mem. agr., forestry, aquaculture, and rural devel. com., civil law and procedure com., health and welfare com. Republican. Office: State Capitol PO Box 44486 Baton Rouge LA 70804 Mailing: 671 Hwy 171 Ste E Stonewall LA 71078 Office Phone: 225-342-6945, 318-925-9588. Office Fax: 318-925-9590. Business E-Mail: burfordr@legis.state.la.us.

BURG, JOHN PARKER, construction panel executive; b. Great Bend, Kans., Dec. 17, 1931; s. Kenneth Edwin and Viola Mae (Parker) B.; m. Ida Elizabeth Groome; children Ida Elizabeth, Clarence Oscar Edwin; m. Shirley Joan Steele, Apr. 10, 1976; children: Nathan Parker, Emily Diane, Paul Andrew. BS in Physics, BA in Math., U. Tex., 1953; MS in Physics, MIT, 1960; PhD in Geophysics, Stanford U., 1975. Asst. engr. Tex. Instruments, Inc., 1956-57, engr. Dallas, 1960; sr. rsch. geophysicist Geophys. Svc., Inc., Dallas, 1960-73; chmn. bd. dirs. Time and Space Processing, Inc., Santa Clara, Calif., 1973-83; pres. Entropic Processing, Inc., Cupertino, Calif., 1983—, also chmn. bd. dirs. Cons. oil cos., ESL, Inc., Naval Undersea Ctr., 1969-75; cons. Digicon, Inc., Houston, 1982-83; chmn. bd. dirs. Entropic Rsch. Lab., Washington, 1984-98, Entropic Geophysical, Inc., 1984-91, Entropic Speech Inc., 1984-02, Affordable Bldg. Sys., 2000—. Inventor patent predictive seismic deconvolution, multichannel filtering. Recipient Rsch. Publication award Naval Rsch. Lab., 1984; named Life Master Am. Contract Bridge League. Fellow IEEE (contbr. to jour.). Avocation: bridge theory. Office: Durra Bldg Systems LLC 2747 State Hwy 160 PO Box 10 Whitewright TX 75491 Home: 350 Windsor Ave Apt #142 Terrell TX 75160 Business E-Mail: john.burg@durra.com.

BURG, RALPH, art association executive; b. Malden, Mass., Jan. 2, 1914; s. Joseph and Bessie (Meyer) B.; m. Fay E. Pristaw, Jan. 10, 1937; children: Stephen, Harvey. BA, Boston U., 1936. V.p. Beacon Musical Inst. Co., Boston, 1939-70; pres., owner Quisisana Lodge, Center Lovell, Maine, 1946-76; chmn. Edna Hibel Soc., Coral Springs, Fla., 1979-99, pres., 1979—2009. Mem. Friends for Life, B'Nai B'rith. Recipient Cultural award Minister of Culture, Flanders, Belgium, 1983. Mem. Kiwanis (various coms. Boston chpt. 1946-70), Synergistic Assn. (pres. Boston chpt. 1962-70), Edna Hibel Soc. (pres., chmn. 1979-2009, editor Hibeletter newsletter 1979-2008), Woodlands Country Club. Avocations: golf, tennis, writing, bridge, saxophone. Office: Edna Hibel Soc PO Box 9721 Coral Springs FL 33075-9721 Home: 48 Park Rd Marlborough CT 06447-1134 Personal E-mail: maestroralph@cs.com.

BURGE, JOHN WESLEY, JR., management consultant; b. Mobile, Ala., Sept. 11, 1932; s. John Wesley and Mary Jo (Guest) Burge; m. Shirley Paulette Roberts, Mar. 29, 1958; children: John, Delene, Eric, Kurt, Karen. BSEE, Centenary Coll.; MBA, UCLA, PhD in Aerospace Program Mgmt., 1967. Engring. and mgmt. staff ITT Gilfillan, 1954-69; pres., gen. mgr. Rantec, Calabasas, Calif., 1969-71, chmn. bd. dirs.; pres., gen. mgr. electronics and space divsn. Emerson Electric Co., St. Louis, 1971-80, corp. group v.p. govt., def., 1977-89; ret., 1989; pvt. practice Pensacola, Fla., 1975—. With USAF, 1950—54. Decorated Grand Cordon Order Al-Istiqlal (Jordan).

BURGERT, DAVID LEE, lawyer; b. Kansas City, Kans., Jan. 30, 1959; s. Marion Lawrence and Barbara Jean (Marmont) B.; children: Melissa Christine, Grace Josephine. BS summa cum laude, Ohio U., 1980; JD, U. Mich., 1983. Bar: Tex. 1983, U.S. Dist. Ct. (so. dist.) Tex. 1984, U.S. Dist. Ct. (we. dist.) (no. dist., 2002) Tex. 1999, U.S. Ct. Appeals (5th cir.) 1984, U.S. Tax Ct. 1993, U.S. Ct. Appeals (fed. and 8th cirs.) 1996, U.S. Dist. Ct. (ea. dist.) Tex. 2006; bd. cert. civil trial lawyer, 1990, Tex. Bd. Legal Spec. Assoc. Vinson & Elkins, Houston, 1983-86, Porter Hedges LLP, Houston, 1986-90, ptnr., 1991—2013, Am. Bd. Trial Advs., 2008—, Jones Day, Houston, 2013—; leader intellectual property litig. Chambers and Ptnrs., 2009—. Named Tex. Superlawyer in Intellectual Property Litigation, Tex. Monthly mag., 2003—, One of Houston's Top Lawyers, Tex. Mag., 2005, 2007—09, 2011—12. Office: Jones Day 717 Texas Ste 3300 Houston TX 77002 Office Phone: 832-239-3737. Business E-Mail: dlburgert@jonesday.com.

BURGESS, MICHAEL CLIFTON, United States Representative from Texas; b. Rochester, Minn., Dec. 23, 1950; s. Harry Meredith Burgess and Norma Crowhurst; m. Laura Burgess; 3 children. BS, North Tex. State U., 1972, MS, 1976; MD, U. Tex. Med. Ctr., Houston, 1977; MA in Med. Mgmt., U. Tex., Dallas, 2000; D of Pub. Svc. (hon.), U. North Tex. Health Scis. Ctr., 2009. Resident Parkland Meml. Hosp., Dallas; pvt. practice Ob-Gyn. Assocs., Lewisville, Tex.; chief obstetrics, chief of staff Lewisville Med. Ctr.; mem. US Congress from 26th Tex. dist., 2003—, chair Congl. Health Care Caucus, 2009—. Recipient Guardian of Small Bus. award, Nat. Fedn. Ind. Bus., Taxpayer Hero award, Coun. Citizens Against Govt. Waste; named Legislator of Yr., Am. Acad. Nurse Practitioners, 2005, House Legislator of Yr., Multiple Sclerosis Soc., 2008. Mem.: Denton County Med. Soc. (past pres.). Republican. Office: US House of Representatives 2336 Rayburn House Office Bldg Washington DC 20515 also: Ste 230 1660 S Stemmons Fwy Lewisville TX 75067 Office Phone: 202-225-7772.*

BURGESS, R(OY) BRANDON, communications executive; m. Saira Burgess. Grad., European Bus. Sch.; MBA, Wharton Sch. Bus. Investment banker Goldman Sachs, London; CFO NBC TV Network, London, dir., bus. devel.; exec. v.p., devel. NBC Universal, 2002—04, exec. v.p., internat. channels, bus. devel., 2004—05; corp. planner PesiCo, Purchase, NY, 2004—05; CEO Paxson Comm., 2005—. Mem. bd. NBC U., A&E Networks, MSNBC, Miss Universe. Office: Paxson Communications Inc 601 Clearwater Pk Rd West Palm Beach FL 33401-6233 Office Phone: 561-659-4122.

BURGHARDT, WALTER FRANCIS, JR., veterinarian; b. Columbus, Ohio, Sept. 18, 1952; s. Walter Francis and Helen Wanda (Watrobinski) B.; m. Charleen S. Horkott, July 24, 1993; stepchildren: Joel Webster, Christopher Webster; 1 child, Kurt. BA, Fla. Atlantic U., 1974, MA, 1975; DVM, U. Fla., 1980; PhD in Biopsychology, U. Md., 1988. Diplomate Am. Coll. Vet. Behariorists. Prin. investigator, dept. exec. officer Armed Forces Radiobiology Research Inst., Bethesda, Md., 1980-84; animal behavior cons. Behavior Clin. for Animals, Washington, 1985-95; assoc. veterinarian Colonial Animal Hosp., Boynton Beach, Fla., 1985; chief mil. pub. health 482d Med. Squadron, Homestead AFB, Fla., 1984-95; hosp. dir. Abacus Animal Hosp., Coral Springs, Fla., 1985-95; chief pub. health 433 Med. Squadron, Kelly AFB, Tex., 1995-97, hosp. admin., 1998—2001; chief behavioral medicine and mil. working dog studies Mil. Working Dog Vet. Svc., Lackland AFB, Tex., 1995—; IMA to cmdr. USAF Force Protection Battlelab, 2002—08; med. IMA Hdqs. USAF Lackland AFB Tex., Security Force Ctr., 2008; IMA med. dir. USAF Res., AF Pentagon, Washington, 2008—10. Cons. Am. Vet. Med. Assn.; exec. dir. Internat. Working Dog Breeding Assn., 1999—. Contbr. articles and papers in field. Capt. USAF, 1980-84, Res. maj. 1989-97, Lt.C. 1997-2004, Col. 2004, ret. 2010. Research fellow U. Fla. Coll. Vet. Medicine, 1977. Mem. AVMA, Am. Vet. Soc. Animal Behavior (sec.-treas. 1984-88, pres. 1989-92), Bexar County Vet. Med. Assn., Internat. Working Dog Breeding Assn. (dir. 2003—), Blue Key. Republican. Avocations: bicycling, boating, scuba diving. Office: LTC Daniel E Holland Mil Working Dog Hosp 1219 Knight St Lackland AFB TX 78236 Business E-Mail: walter.burghardt.1@us.af.mil.

BURGIN, CHARLES EDWARD, retired lawyer; b. Marion, NC, Dec. 16, 1938; m. Ellen Salsbury Burgin; children: Ellen, Lucy. BA, U. N.C., 1961; LLB, Duke U., 1964. Bar: N.C.; U.S. Supreme Ct. Law clk. to Hon. J. Braxton Craven Jr. U.S. Dist. Ct., U.S. Ct. Appeals, 1964—66; pros. atty. McDowell County Criminal Ct., 1966—68; sr. ptnr. Dameron, Burgin & Parker, P.A., Marion, 1968—2008. Bd. dirs. Shadowline, Inc.; lectr. in field. Contbr. articles to profl. jours. Bd. dirs. McDowell County Recreation Commn. 1977-87, First Union Nat. Bank; McDowell County Mountain Rescue Team, McDowell Arts and Crafts Assn. Named Legal Elite in N.C., Bus. N.C., 2004; named one of N.C.'s Super Lawyers, 2006. Fellow Am. Coll. Trial Lawyers (state chmn. 1996-98, named Best Lawyers in Am. 1993—, N.C. Super Lawyer 2006), Internat. Soc. Barristers, Am. Bar Found.; mem. ABA, N.C. Bar Assn. (pres. 1993-94), Def. Rsch. Inst., Am. Soc. Hosp. Attys., N.C. Assn. Def. Lawyers, U.S. Supreme Ct. Bar Assn. Office: 186 Pleasant Meadow Ests Marion NC 28752

BURGIN, RACHEL V., state legislator; b. Brandon, Fla., July 23, 1982; Grad., Bob Jones U., 2004. Aide Hillsborough County Bd. Commrs., 2005—06; legis. aide Hillsborough County, 2006—08; mem. Dist 56 Fla. House of Reps., 2008—, mem. agr. and natural resources policy com., elder and family svcs. policy com., preK-12 policy com., state univs. and pvt. colls. appropriations com. Bd. mem. Brandon Cmty. Advantage Bd.; mem. Hillsborough County Rep. Exec. Com.; vol. Plant City Pregnancy Care Ctr. Mem.: Plant City Federated Rep. Women's Club. Republican. Office: House Office Bldg 402 S Monroe St Rm 317 Tallahassee FL 32399-1300 also: 410 S Ware Blvd Ste 105 Tampa FL 33619-4439 Office Phone: 850-488-9910, 813-740-7655. Business E-Mail: rachel.burgin@myfloridahouse.gov.

BURGUIERES, PHILIP J., energy executive; b. Franklin, La., 1943; BS in Mech. Engring, U. Southwestern La., 1965; MBA, U. Pa., 1970. Chmn. J.M. Burguieres Co., Ltd., Franklin; adminstrv. asst. Cameron Iron Works, Inc., Houston, 1971, fin. mgr. European ops., 1972-75, v.p. corp. svcs., 1975-77, v.p. and gen. mgr. forged products div., 1977-79, exec. v.p. ops., 1979-81, pres., chief oper. officer, 1981-85, pres., chief exec. officer, 1986—89, chmn., 1987—89; chmn., pres. & CEO Panhandle Eastern Corp., Houston, 1990; pres., CEO Weatherford Internat. Inc., Houston, 1991—96, chmn., 1992-96; chmn., pres., CEO Weatherford Enterra Inc. (formerly Weatherford Internat.), 1996; chmn., CEO EMC Holdings, LLC, 1998—. Bd. dirs. Tex. Commerce Bankshares, McDermott Internat., Cogen Technologies; FMC Technologies, Inc.; Newfield Exploration Co., 2010-. Pres. Duchesne Acad. Sacred Heart, Houston, 1987-90. With USAR, 1966-69. Mem. Petroleum Equipment Suppliers Assn. (pres. 1986-87), Petroleum Club Houston (pres. 1988-89), Tau Beta Pi, Pi Tau Sigma. Roman Catholic. Avocation: golf. Office: Newfield Exploration Co 363 N Sam Houston Pky E Ste 2020 Houston TX 77060 Office Phone: 281-847-6000. Office Fax: 281-405-4242. Business E-Mail: pburguieres@newfield.com.

BURK, RAYMOND FRANKLIN, JR., internist, educator, researcher; b. Kosciusko, Miss., Dec. 9, 1942; s. Raymond Franklin and Florence Annie (Davis) B.; m. Enikoe Vikor, June 17, 1967; children: Teresa Marie, Stephen Morrison. BA, U. Miss., 1963; MD, Vanderbilt U., 1968. Diplomate Am. Bd. Internal Medicine. Intern Vanderbilt Hosp., Nashville, 1968—69; resident in medicine Vanderbilt Hosp., Nashville, 1969—70; asst. prof. medicine and biochemistry U. Tex. S.W. Med. Sch., Dallas, 1975—78; assoc. prof. medicine and biochemistry La. State U. Sch. Medicine, Shreveport, 1978—80; assoc. prof. medicine U. Tex. Health Sci. Ctr., San Antonio, 1980—82, prof., 1982—87; prof. medicine Vanderbilt U., 1987—. Rschr. in field; mem. staff Vanderbilt U. Hosp., Nashville. Contbr. articles to med. jours. Maj. M.C., U.S. Army, 1970-73. Grantee NIH, 1974—. Mem. Am. Soc. Biol. Chemists, Am. Soc. Clin. Investigation, Am. Inst. Nutrition. Business E-Mail: raymond.burk@vanderbilt.edu.

BURKART, BURKE, geology educator, researcher; b. Dallas, Feb. 23, 1933; s. Herman Frederick and Velma Viola (Ball) B.; m. Marilyn Caskey; children: Patrick Caskey, Michael David BS in Geology, U. Tex., 1954, MA in Geology, 1960; PhD in Geology, Rice U., Houston, 1965. Asst. prof. geology Temple U., Phila., 1965-70; asst. prof. U. Tex., Arlington, 1970-73, assoc. prof. geology, 1973-82, prof., 1982—2001, prof. emeritus, 2001—. Cons. in field. Contbr. articles, maps. to profl. publs. Served to 1st. lt. USAF, 1955-58 Fulbright fellow, 1972 Fellow Geol. Soc. Am.; mem. Am. Geophys. Union, Am. Assn. Petroleum Geologists, Am. Inst. Profl. Geologists (registered), Sigma Xi. Achievements include research in tectonics of Central America and Southern Mexico, strike slip faults, environmental geochemistry. Home: 2307 Wild Turkey Trail Arlington TX 76016 Office: U Tex Dept Geology PO Box 19049 Arlington TX 76019-0001 Home Phone: 817-272-2989. Personal E-mail: b_burkart@sbcglobal.net.

BURKE, KELLY HOWARD, retired military officer, entrepreneur; b. Mobile, Ala., June 7, 1929; s. Kelly Howard and Vesta (Trussell) B.; m. Denny Ray Hosey, Dec. 30, 1951; children: Bethany, Patricia, Kelly Howard, III. BS in History, Auburn U., 1952; MS in Internat. Rels., George Washington U., 1968; postgrad., Naval War Coll., 1967-68, RAF Staff Coll., 1969-71, Indsl. Coll. Armed Forces, 1964-65. Commd. 2d lt. U.S. Air Force, 1953, advanced through grades to lt. gen., 1979; comdr. 379th Bomb Wing Wurtsmith AFB, Mich., 1973-74; comdr. 2d Bomb Wing Barksdale AFB, La., 1974-75; dep. chief of staff/plans SAC, 1975-78; dir. operational requirements Hdqrs. U.S. Air Force, Washington, 1978-79, dep. chief of staff/research, devel. and acquisition, 1979-82; ret., 1982; chmn. bd. Stafford, Burke and Hecker, Inc., Alexandria, Va., 1982—2000. Bd. dirs. Singer Co., Tiger Internat. Inc., Flying Tigers Line Inc., Orbital Scis. Corp., OWC Found., Children's Advocacy Ctr.; cons. White House Sci. Office, NRC, Def. Sci. Bd., Sci. Adv. Bd., others; frequent lectr. Chmn. editl. bd. Aerospace Am.; contbg. editor Armed Forces Jour.; contbr. numerous articles on nat. security issues to publd. Decorated D.S.M. with oak leaf cluster, Legion of Merit, D.F.C., Meritorious Svc. medal, Air medal with oak leaf clusters; established Burke Scholarship Endowment for 15 4-yr. coll. scholarships annually to needy students, established Burke Scholarship for outstanding AFROTC cadet, Auburn U.; named Fla. Benefactor of Yr. for this and other charitable activities, 1995. Mem. Nat. Space Club, Nat. Aviation Club Episcopalian. Home: 803 Choctaw Ln Shalimar FL 32579-2248 Personal E-mail: kbxel@aol.com.

BURKE, KEVIN CHARLES ANTONY, geologist; b. London, Nov. 13, 1929; came to U.S., 1973, naturalised, 1979; s. Charles Henry and Kathleen B.; m. Angela Marion Phipps, Jan. 23, 1960; children: Nicholas, Matthew, Jane. BSc, Univ. Coll., London, 1951, PhD, 1953. Lectr. U. Ghana, 1953-56; geologist Brit. Geol. Survey, 1956-61; head geology dept. U. West Indies, Kingston, Jamaica, 1961-65; prof. geology U. Ibadan, Nigeria, 1963-71, SUNY-Albany, 1973-83; prof. U. Houston, 1983—; dir. Lunar and Planetary Inst., 1983-88; scholar in residence NRC, Washington, 1989-92, Crosby Lecturer Dept Earth, Atmospheric & Planetary Scis. MIT, 2004—. Vis. prof. U. Toronto, 1971-73, Calif. Inst. Tech., 1976, U. Minn., 1977, U. Calgary, 1979; cons. in field. NSF grantee, 1976—, NASA grantee; recipient Holmes medal European Geoscientists Union, 2014. Fellow: Geol. Soc. Am. (Penrose medal 2007); mem.: AAAS, Nigerian Mining, Geol. and Metall. Soc. (pres. internat. com. on the lithosphere 1992—95, Du Toit Meml. lectr. 1995), Am. Geophys. Union. Achievements include research in plate tectonics. Office: University Houston Dept Earth & Atmosphere Scis Bldg S & R1 Calhoun Blvd Houston TX 77204-5007 Home: 20 Pleasant St Rockport MA 01966 Home Phone: 978-309-3305, 978-309-8662; Office Phone: 713-743-3399.

BURKE, KIERAN E., water park company executive; b. 1957; JD, Harvard Law Sch., 1982. V.p. Drexel Burnham Lambert Group, Inc., NYC, 1978-87, vice chmn., mng. dir., 1987-89; pres., CEO The Tierco Group, Inc., Oklahoma City, 1989, Premier Parks, Inc. (formerly The Tierco Group, Inc.), Oklahoma City, 1989—94, chmn., CEO, 1994—2000, Six Flags Theme Parks, Inc., 2000—05; co-founder Nashville Shores Holdings, LLC, Nashville, 2009—. Office: Nashville Shores Holdings LLC 4001 Bell Rd Hermitage TN 37076

BURKE, MICHAEL DONALD, oil and gas company executive; b. Salem, Oreg., Feb. 27, 1944; s. James Michael Burke and Mary Jane (Farrington) Gage; m. Louise Mennow, June 3, 1972; children: Kendra Anne, Michael John. BSChemE, Tex. A&M U., 1966; MBA in Fin. and Mktg., U. Tex., Austin, 1970. Chem. and process engr., mktg., product mgr. Houston Chem. Co. subs. PPG Industries, Pitts., 1966-76; cons. PACE Cons., Houston, 1976-78; mktg. mgr. ICI Americas (CCPC), Houston, 1978-80, dir. tri-states synfuel project, 1980-81; v.p. synfuels Tex. Ea. Corp., 1981-82; v.p. mfg. and refining La Gloria Oil & Gas Co. subs. Tex. Ea. Corp., Houston, 1982-84, pres., 1984-86, Tex. Eastern Products Pipeline Co. subs. Tex. Eastern Corp., Houston, 1986-90; group v.p. Tex. Ea. Corp., 1986-90; pres., CEO, Tex. Ea. Products Pipeline Ltd., Houston, 1990-92, Tesoro Petroleum Corp., San Antonio, 1992-95, EOTT Energy Corp., Houston, 1998-2000; pres. MDB Capital Ventures, Houston, 2000—. Chmn. bd. dirs. Fiber Dynamics; bd. dirs. Nutraceutical Internat. Inc., Premier Instruments, Inc., Visual Intelligence Systems, Inc; pres., CEO M.D. Burke and Co., 1995—, Personal Devel. Forum, Houston, 1982-85; nat. fellow Am. Leadership Forum, 1985. Chmn. Tex. Ea. Polit. Action Com., Houston, 1985-86, United Way Campaign Effectiveness Coun., Houston, 1986, Houston chpt. Am. Leadership Forum, 1987-89; bd. dirs. Houston Mental Health Assocs., 1987-91, Gulf Coast chpt. ARC, 1987-92, vice chmn., 1989-92, mem. bd. and exec. com., 1990-92, chmn. elect, 1992; bd. dirs., mem. exec. com. Sam Houston Coun. Boy Scouts Am., 1987-92, vice chmn. exploring, 1989-92; mem. adv. bd. U. Houston, 1990-92; Alamo area coun. Boy Scout Am., exec. com., 1994-96; chmn. Alamadoma Task Forces, 1994; bd. dirs., exec. com. San Antonio Bexar County United Way, 1994—, Our Lady of Lake U., 1995—, World Affairs Coun., 1994-97, San Antonio Via Met. Transit Bd., 1996-98, South Tex. YMCA, 1994—, Free Trade Alliance San Antonio, 1996—, Tex. Pub. Policy

Found., 1996—, Mind Sci. Found., 1996—; mem. San Antonio Mayor's Commn. on Brooks AFB Redevel., Econ. Vitality and Workforce Edn.; bd. dires. U. Tex. Houston Health Sci. Ctr., Ctr. for Houston's Future, Houston Tech. Ctr., Greater Houston YMCA. Mem. Nat. Petroleum Refiners Assn. (bd. dirs. 1984—), Am. Petroleum Inst. (gen. refining com. 1982-84, pipeline transp. com. 1986-92), Nat. Petroleum Coun., Tex. Ea. Toastmasters (pres. 1984), Houston C. of C. (chmn. Houston Bus. Group 1986-88, founder Innovate Houston 1986), Corpus Christi Jaycees (past. dir.), Southbriar Community Assn. (past pres.), Assn. Oil Pipelines (bd. dirs. 1986-92), Mt. Belvieu Industry Assn. (chmn. 1987-89), San Antonio C. of C. (bd. dirs., exec. com., 1994-97), Petroleum Club. Republican. Roman Catholic. Office: MDB Capital Ventures 5252 Westchester Ste 250 Houston TX 77005 E-mail: mdburkesa@aol.com.

BURKE, REDMOND PAUL, cardiologist, surgeon; b. Honolulu, Hawaii, Nov. 4, 1958; married; 1 child. BA, Stanford U., Palo Alto, CA, 1980; MD, Harvard Med. Sch., Boston, MA, 1984. Lic. Mass., 1989, Fla., 1995, cert. Nat. Bd. Med. Examiners Diplomate, 1985, Advanced Trama and Life Support, 1986, Advanced CPR and Emergency Cardiac Care, 1989, Am. Bd. Surgery Diplomate, 1990, Am. Bd. Thoracic Surgery Diplomate, 1993, Am. Bd. Surgery Recertification, 2002. Rsch. asst., dept. immunology Stanford U. Children's Hosp., Palo Alto, Calif., 1977; rsch. asst., statistician, dept. radiology Palo Alto Veteran's Adminstrn. Hosp., Palo Alto, Calif., 1978; rsch. fellow, surgery Harvard Med. Sch., Boston, 1989—90, instructor, surgery, 1992—95; intern, surgery Brigham and Women's Hosp., Boston, 1984—85, resident, surgery, 1985—89, chief resident, cardiothoracic surgery, 1990—91, assoc., cardiac surgery, 1991—95, attending surgeon, 1992—95; clin. fellow, surgery Children's Hosp., Boston, 1984—89, assoc., cardiac surgery, 1991—95, attending surgeon, 1992—95, chief resident, cardiovascular surgery, 1992; chief, divsn. cardiovascular surgery Miami Children's Hosp., Fla., 1995—2002, mem. mortality review com. Fla., 1995—, divsn. chief, daily adminstrn. pediatric cardiovascular surgery program Fla., 1995—; apptd. cardiac surgeon, cardiac surgeon program Arnold Palmer Hosp., Orlando, Fla., 2002—. Vis. scientist MIT, Cambridge, Mass., 1989—92, mem. adv. com., spectroscopy lab., 1994—; vis. instr., dept. biomedical engring. U. Miami, Fla., 1995—; attending surgeon Boston Adult Congenital Heart Svc., Mass., 1992—95; mem. adv. com. Premier Cardiac Surgery Physician, 1999—; founder, co-dir. Congenital Heart Inst., Miami, Fla., 2002—; lectr. in field. Contbr. articles to profl. jours., chapters to books; reviewer Jour. Thoracic and Cardiovascular Surgery, 1995—, Annals of Thoracic Surgery, 1995—, mem. editl. bd. Heart Surgery Forum, 1999—, Jour. Laparoendoscopic & Advanced Surgical Techniques, 1999—, mem. med. team Miracle Workers, ABC, 2006—, guest appearance The View, 2006. Vice-chmn. American Heart Walk, Miami, Fla., 2000; mem. med. adv. bd. Children's Heart Found., 2004—; bd. dir. Island Dolphin Cove, Key Largo, Fla., 2000—. Recipient Best Doctor in Am. award, 2001—02, Fla. Med. Bus. Healthcare award, 2002, Valor award, Am. Diabetes Assn., 2004; named Best Doctors in South Fla., Miami Metro Mag., 1998—2000, Most Wired Physician, State Fla., 2002. Fellow: Am. Coll. Surgeons, Coun. on Cardiothoracic and Vascular Surgery, Am. Heart Assn.; mem.: Internat. Soc. for Heart and Lung Transplantation, Candidate Soc. Thoracic Surgeons, Mass. Med. Soc., Southern Thoracic Surgical Assn., Soc. Thoracic Surgeons (active mem. 1998—), Internat. Soc. for Minimally Invasive Cardiothoracic Surgery, Cardiothoracic Surgery Network, Harvard Med. Sch. Alumni Assn. (class rep. 1985—), Phi Beta Kappa. Achievements include performing the first pediatric heart lung transplant in New England in 1992; developing and refining of minimally invasive surgical techniques in pediatric cardiothoracic surgery; patents in field. Office: Miami Children's Hosp Dept Cardiovascular Surgery 3200 SW 60th Ct Ste 102 Miami FL 33155 Office Phone: 305-663-8401. Office Fax: 305-669-6574. Business E-Mail: redmond111@aol.com.

BURKE, ROBERT D., diagnostic radiologist; MD, U. Louisville, 1981. Diplomate Am. Bd. Radiology-diagnostic radiology, 1985. Resident diagnostic radiology Michael Reese Hosp., Chgo., 1982—85; fellow neurol. radiology Strong Meml. Hosp., Rochester, 1985—86; hosp. affiliation includes Wellington Regional Med. Ctr. Office: Wellington Regional Medical Center 10101 Forest Hill Blvd West Palm Beach FL 33414

BURKE, THOMAS M., consulting company executive; B in Mktg. & Mgmt., U. North Fla. Mgr., human resources leader Headstrong Corp., Hercules Chemicals, Inc., SunTrust Banks, Inc., Thrifty Car Rental; dir. global human resources Deloitte Consulting; sr. v.p. human resources MPS Group Soliant Health, Inc.; sr. v.p. human resources MPS (Modis Professional Services) Group, Inc. (acquired by Adecco). Office: MPS Group Inc 10151 Deerwood Park Blvd Ste 200-400 Jacksonville FL 32256-0557 Office Phone: 904-360-2000. Office Fax: 904-360-2814.

BURKE, WILLIAM TEMPLE, JR., lawyer; b. San Antonio, Oct. 30, 1935; s. William Temple and Adelaide H. (Raba) B.; m. Mary Sue Johnson, June 8, 1957; children: William Patrick, Michael Edmond, Karen Elizabeth. BBA, St. Mary's U., San Antonio, JD, 1961. Bar: Tex. 1961; cert. scuba dive master, PADI. Practice law, Dallas; founder, pres. Burke Wright & Keiffer, PC, 1985-98, 2007; coun. Hance/Scarborough/Wright, Dallas, 1998-2000, Hance, Scarborough, Wright, Ginsberg and Brusilow, Dallas, 2000—07, Wright, Ginsberg and Brusilow, 2008—. Co-founder, v.p., dir. Tex. Cath. Cmty. Credit Union, 1966—69, vice-chmn. bd. dirs., 1990—91; v.p. Dallas County Hist. Survey Com., 1966; pres. Dallas Mil. Govt. Assn., 1962—63; trustee Montserrat Jesuit Retreat House, 1999—2000, treas., 1997; pres. Dallas County Small Bus. Devel. Corp., 1981—82; trustee Dallas Ecol. Found., 2004—, sec. bd., 2008—10; chmn. scout troop com. St. Patrick's Parish Roman Cath. Ch., 1976—78, chmn. fin. com., 1984—87, bldg. com., 1978—87, chmn. bd. consultors, 1978—82; vice-chmn. Cath. Diocese Dallas Cath. cmty. Appeal, 1993—97; pres. men's club St. Patrick's Parish Roman Cath. Ch., 1963, prin. jr. H.S. Christian devel. program, 1970; bd. dirs. Dallas County War on Poverty, 1965—66. 1st lt. US Army, 1958—60, capt. USAR, ret. Fellow Tex. Bar Found. (life), Dallas Bar Found. (sr., life); mem. ABA, Tex. Bar Assn., Dallas Bar Assn. (co-founder, chmn. bankruptcy and comml. law sect. 1976-77, 86-87, courthouse liaison com. 1985—96, lectr. 1985—, chmn. spkrs. com. 2001-02), John C. Ford Am. Inn Ct. (co-founder, pres. 2000-04, emeritus and mem. exec. com. 2000—, hon. sgt. of the Inn 2003), Dallas Safari Club (life), Serra Internat. Met. Club (pres. Met. Dallas 1997-98, dist. gov. 2004-05, Outstanding Mem. award 1995), Internat. Order Alhambra (exemplar 1978-95), KC (co-founder Greater Dallas chpt., coun. 799 grand knight, trustee 1964-69, dist. examplar 4th degree coun. 799 1968-69, Man of Yr. award 1970), Optimists (v.p., bd. dirs. Dallas 1965-66, Man of Yr. award 1966, Pres.'s award 1968), Phi Delta Phi (life, magister Tarlton INN 1960-61, mem. of yr. 1961), Tau Delta Sigma Fraternity (pres. 1957). Home: 9751 Larchcrest Dr Dallas TX 75238-2112 Office: Wright Ginsberg Brusilow PC Republic Ctr Suite 4150 325 N St Paul St Dallas TX 75201 Business E-Mail: wburke@wgblawfirm.com.

BURKE, WILLIAM W., corporate financial executive; BBA in Fin., U. Tex., Austin, 1977; MBA, U. Pa., 1983. Past cons. DJO, Inc., Blackstone Capital Ptnrs.; mng. dir. Everen Securities Inc., 1991—95, Prin. Fin. Securities Inc. (acquired by Everen Securities, Inc.), 1995—98, Bear, Stearns & Co., Inc., 1998—2001; CFO Cholestech Corp., 2001—04; exec. v.p., CFO ReAble Therapeutics Inc. (sold to Blackstone Capital Ptnrs.), 2004—07; cons. Medical Action Industries, Inc., bd. dirs., 2004—; pres. Emergent Technologies, Inc., 2009—; exec. v.p., CFO IDev Technologies, Inc., 2009—. Office: Emergent Technologies Inc Ste 300 11412 Bee Caves Rd Austin TX 78738 Office Phone: 512-263-3232. Office Fax: 512-263-3236. Business E-Mail: wburke@etibio.com.

BURKET, LYSCHEL, healthcare company executive; Pres., prin., adminstr. Team Health Holdings, Inc. Office: Team Health Holdings Inc 265 Brookview Town Centre Way Ste 400 Knoxville TN 37919 Office Phone: 865-693-1000. Office Fax: 865-539-3073. Business E-Mail: lyschel_burket@teamhealth.com.

BURKHART, HAROLD EUGENE, forester, educator; b. Wellington, Kans., Feb. 29, 1944; s. Walter F. and Zelma (Lutz) B.; m. Katherine West, June 12, 1971; 1 child, Anna Katherine. BS, Okla. State U., 1965; MS, U. Ga., 1967, PhD, 1969. From asst. prof. to profl. Va. Poly. Inst. and State U., Blacksburg, 1969—81, Thomas M. Brooks prof., 1981-99, univ. disting. prof., 1999—. Author: Forest Measurements, 1983, 94, 2002; contbr. sci. articles to profl. jours. Sr. Rsch. fellow NRC, 1976-77; recipient Sci. Achievement award Internat. Union Forestry Rsch. Orgns., 1981, J. Shelton Horsley Rsch. award Va. Acad. Sci., 1983, Outstanding Faculty award State Coun. for Higher Edn. in Va., 1988, Disting. Agr. Alumnus award Okla. State U., 1993. Fellow AAAS, Soc. Am. Foresters (Barrington Moore Meml. award 1991); mem. Biometric Soc., Am. Forestry Assn., Sigma Xi, Phi Kappa Phi, Xi Sigma Pi. Presbyterian. Avocations: gardening, running. Office: Va Poly Inst and State U Dept Forestry Blacksburg VA 24061 Home Phone: 540-951-0605; Office Phone: 540-231-6952. Business E-Mail: burkhart@vt.edu.

BURKI, FRED ALBERT, labor union official; b. Chgo., Apr. 8, 1926; s. John and Helen (Kramer) B.; children— Bill, Ken, Scott. Student, Northwestern U., U.Ill. Started as grocery clk., 1947; pres. local 470 United Retail Workers Union, Westchester, Ill., 1951-53, rep., 1953-62, field supr., 1963-65, nat. v.p., 1966-71, nat. exec. dir., 1971-81; internat. v.p. United Food and Comml. Workers Union, AFL-CIO, 1981—; pres. local 881, 1981—. Guest lectr. labor edn., advisor U. Ill. Circle Campus, Chgo.; labor edn. adv. U. Ind., 1967—, Loyola U., 1978—; mem. Midwest Com. Labor Study in Europe; labor adv. com. Senator Charles Percy, 1977—; chmn. Westchester Bldg. Corp., 1971-83; guest instr. WWU, WWII, Experiences IENk & Tulsa, Mid. HS. Bd. dirs. Chgo. Regional Blood Bank/Blood Services, Blood Ctr. of No. Ill., 1983—, Midwest Assn. for Sickle Cell Anemia, 1986—; trustee United Retail Workers Union-Super-Valu Trust Fund.; mem. Ill. Detection of Deception Com., 1982—; pres. Human Services Ltd., 1984—. Served with AUS, 1943-47; battalion exec. officer, maj. Res., 1947-67, ret. Decorated Bronze Star medal; named Man of Year Combined Counties Police Assn., 1977 Mem. V.F.W. (past officer), Mil. Police Assn., Res. Officers Assn. Home Phone: 918-296-3513; Office Phone: 918-296-3513. Personal E-mail: fburki@aol.com.

BURKS, ANDREW CHARLIE, JR., councilman, communications consultant, minister; b. Houston, Nov. 22, 1950; s. Andrew Charlie Sr. and Lillie Savannah (Cooper) B.; m. Thyra Lois Smith, Dec. 21, 1985; children: Lisa Denise Randon, Cardena Marie Fontenette, Adam Joseph Fontenette III. Student, San Jacinto Jr. Coll., Pasadena, Tex., 1968-70, Houston Community Coll., 1973-75, Tex. So. U., 1978-80. Ordained elder in Christian Meth. Episcopal Ch., 1988. Installer Western Electric Co., Houston, 1971-76; installer, repairman Southwestern Bell Corp., Houston, 1976-81; pres., CEO AM-PM Telephone Svc. Inc., Houston, 1982—; councilman-at-large Position 2 Houston City Coun., 2012—. Bd. dirs. Assn. of Afro Am. Bus., Houston; pres. Assn. of Better Communication Dealers, Houston, 1984-88; pastor Washington Chapel Christian Meth. Episcopal Ch., Sweeney, Tex. Pres. Precinct Club 276, Houston, 1988, 89, 90; alternate del. Nat. Dem. Conv., Atlanta, 1988, del. Tex. State Dem. Conv., Houston, 1988, del. Nat. Dem. Party Conv., N.Y.C., 1992; mem. Nat. Rainbow Coalition, Washington, 1989; candidate State Rep. of Tex., 1988, 90, U.S. Ho. of Reps., 1992. With USAF, 1970. Mem. Harris County Coun. of Orgns., Tex. Coalition of Black Dems., Houston Profl. and Businessmen's Club, Southeast Tex. Ann. Conf., Houston Dist. Christian Meth. Episcopal Ministers Alliance. Avocations: arts and crafts, fishing, racquetball, chess, reading the bible. Office: CIty Hall Annex 900 Bagby, First Floor Houston TX 77002 Home: 5643 Beldart St Houston TX 77033-3101 Office Phone: 832-393-3013. Office Fax: 832-393-3336. E-mail: atlarge2@houstontx.gov.

BURKS, CHARLOTTE, state legislator; 3 children. State senator Dist. 15, Tenn., 1999—. Democrat. Office: 18131 Crossville Hwy Monterey TN 38574 also: 304 War Memorial Bldg Nashville TN 37243-0215 Office Phone: 615-741-3978. Office Fax: 615-741-8744. Business E-Mail: sen.charlotte.burks@capitol.tn.gov.

BURLAGE, PETER J., energy executive; BS in Mech. Engring., U. Tex., Arlington, 1991; MBA, Baylor U., 2006. With an indsl. equipment mfg. co.; joined Peerless Manufacturing Co., 1992, various positions including v.p. environ. bus. segment, 1992—97, mgr. SCR divsn., 1997—2000, v.p. engring., 2000—01, v.p. environ. sys. bus., 2001—05, exec. v.p., COO, 2005—06, pres., CEO, bd. dirs., 2006—. Bd. dirs. Peerless Europe, Ltd., 2006—, PMFG, Inc., 2006—. Office: Peerless Mfg Co 14651 N Dallas Pky Ste 500 Dallas TX 75254 Office Phone: 214-357-6181. Office Fax: 214-351-0194. Business E-Mail: pburlage@peerlessmfg.com.

BURLEIGH, WILLIAM ROBERT, retired media executive; b. Evansville, Ind., Sept. 6, 1935; s. Joseph Charles and Emma Bertha (Wittgen) B.; m. Catherine Anne Husted, Nov. 28, 1964; children: David William, Catherine Anne, Margaret Walden. BS, Marquette U., Milw., 1957; LLD (hon.), U. So. Ind., 1979; LLD, Thomas More Coll., 2009. From reporter to editor, pres. Evansville Press, 1951-77; editor Cin. Post, 1977-83; v.p., gen. editl. mgr. Scripps-Howard Newspapers, Cin., 1984-86, sr. v.p. newspapers and publs., 1986-90, exec. v.p., 1990-94, pres., COO, 1994-96, pres., CEO, 1996-99; chmn., CEO E.W. Scripps Co., Cin., 1999-2000, chmn., 2000—09. With AUS, 1957-58. Mem. Queen City Club, Cin. Lit. Club, Cin. Country Club, Cin. Comml. Club, Alpha Sigma Nu. Roman Catholic.

BURMAN, DARRYL MICHAEL, lawyer; b. 1958; m. Valerie Burman; children: Dean, Miles. BS in Finance, U. South Fla., 1980; JD, South Tex. Coll. Law, 1983. Bar: Tex. 1984. Assoc. Dotson, Babcock & Scofield, 1983—88; ptnr. Meyer & Cribbs, 1989—93, Brill & Byrom, 1994—95; ptnr., head corp. & securities sect. Fant & Burman, LLP, Houston, 1995—2005; ptnr., head corp. & securities practice Epstein, Becker & Green, Houston, 2005—06; v.p., gen. counsel, corp. sec. Group 1 Automotive, Inc., Houston, 2006—. Avocation: golf. Office: Group 1 Automotive Ste 500 800 Gessner Houston TX 77024 Office Phone: 713-647-5700.

BURNAM, LON, state legislator; b. July 11, 1953; m. Carol Roark, 1979. B in Govt., U. Tex., Austin; M in Regional and City Planning, U. Tex., Arlington. Former spl. asst. to regional adminstr. Tex. Dept. Human Svc.; former city planner; exec. dir. Dallas Peace Ctr.; mem. Dist. 90 Tex. House of Representative, 1997—. Recipient New Leadership Environ. award, Sierra Club, Tex. Chpt., 1997, Best Pub. Ofcl. award, Ft. Worth Weekly, and several others. Democrat. Office: 1067 W Magnolia Fort Worth TX 76104 also: Rm CAP GW.8 Capitol PO Box 2910 Austin TX 78768 Office Phone: 817-924-1997, 512-463-0740.

BURNER, DAVID L., management consultant; b. Lodi, Ohio; m. Rosemary Burner; 3 children. BS in Acctg. & Fin., Ohio U., 1962. Joined B.F. Goodrich Co. (now Goodrich Corp.), 1983, pres., aerospace divsn., 1987, pres., 1995—2002, CEO, 1996—2003, chmn., 1997—2003. Bd. dirs. Briggs & Stratton Corp., Milacron, Inc., 1998—2007, Progress Energy, Inc., 1999—2009, Lance, Inc., 2002—06, Engelhard Corp., 2003—06. Office: Bearingpoint Inc Bd Directors 100 Crescent Ct Ste 700 Dallas TX 75201-2112 Office Phone: 214-459-2770. Business E-Mail: dburner@briggsandstratton.com.

BURNESS, JOHN F., political science professor, former academic administrator; m. Anne D. Williams; children: Evan, Sam. BA, Franklin & Marshall Coll., 1967. Asst. to pres. then dep. to pres. for univ. affairs, sec. Stony Brook Coun. SUNY, Stony Brook, 1970—80; dir. pub. affairs U. Ill., 1981—83, assoc. chancellor pub. affairs, 1984—86; v.p. univ. rels. Cornell U., 1986—90; sr. v.p. pub. affairs and govt. rels. Duke U., Durham, NC, 1991, vis. prof. practice of pub. policy DeWitt Wallace Ctr. for Media and Democracy, Terry Sanford Sch. Pub. Policy; interim pres. Franklin & Marshall Coll., Lancaster, Pa., 2010—11. Dir. Nat. Assn. Coll. and Univ. Bus. Officers (NACUBO); chmn. Pun. Issues Com. Consortium of Financing Higher Edn.; dir. MDC, Chapel Hill, NC; sr. counsel, mem. Higher Edn. Adv. Panel Widmeyer Comm. Trustee Durham Tech. CC; mem. Eisenhower Found. Fellows Selection Com.; adv. bd. Duke's Ctr. for Child and Family Policy. Recipient Josephine Clement Award for Exemplary Cmty. Leadership for Pub. Edn., 2002; grantee RIAS Commn. Fellowship, Berlin, Germany. Mem.: NAACP, NC Press Assn. (hon.). Office: Duke University PO Box 90241 Durham NC 27708-0241 Office Phone: 919-613-7369. Office Fax: 919-684-4270. E-mail: john.burness@duke.edu.

BURNETT, CLARA HENDERSON, state legislator; b. Tunica, Miss., Aug. 28, 1941; Mem. Dist. 9 Miss. House of Reps., 2004—, vice chair gaming com., mem. edn. com., enrolled bills com., judiciary B com., judiciary en banc com., juvenile justice com., tourism com., univs. and colls. com. Democrat. Methodist. Address: PO Box 469 Tunica MS 38676 Office Phone: 662-363-2531. Business E-Mail: cburnett@house.ms.gov.

BURNETT, E. C., III, former state supreme court justice; b. Spartanburg County, SC, Jan. 26, 1942; s. E. C., Jr. and Lucy (Byers) Burnett; m. Jami Grant, 1963; children: Curry, Sharon, Jeffrey. AB, Wofford Coll., 1964; JD, U. S.C., 1969. Bar: S.C. 1969, US Dist. Ct., SC, Fourth Circuit Ct. of Appeals, US Supreme Ct. Pvt. practice atty., Spartanburg; mem. SC Ho. of Reps., 1973-74; probate judge Spartanburg County, 1976-80; judge family ct., 1980-81, Seventh Jud. Cir., 1981-95; assoc. justice SC Supreme Ct., 1995—2007. Elder Mt. Calvary Presbyn. Ch. Maj. USAR, 1964—66. Mem.: ABA, Spartanburg County Bar Assn., S.C. Bar Assn. Home: 200 Burnett Rd Pauline SC 29374-2610

BURNETT, HENRY, retired lawyer; b. NYC, Feb. 24, 1927; s. Lucien Dallam and Ruth (Hinkle) B.; m. Florence Stewart, July 19, 1952; children: Marian Starr, Betsy Callaway, Henry Stewart. BA, U. Va., 1947, LLB, 1950. Bar: Va. 1950, Fla. 1951. Ptnr. Fowler, White, Burnett, Miami, Fla., 1957—93, pres., 1957—93, ptnr., 1993. Bd. dirs. Dade County Citizens Safety Council, Travelers Aid, United Family and Children's Services(Episcopal chapt.), Served with USN, 1945-46. Recipient Unsung Hero award, USMC, So. Dist. Fellow Am. Coll. Trial Lawyers; mem. Am., Fla., Dade County bar assns., Fla. Def. Lawyers Assn. (pres. 1967-68), Dade County Def. Bar Assn. (pres. 1966-67), Internat. Assn. Def. Counsel (exec. com. 1972-74, pres. 1976-77), Riviera Country Club. Episcopalian. Home: 8871 SW 68th Ave Miami FL 33156 Home Phone: 305-666-6363. E-mail: hburnett@fowler-white.com.

BURNETTE, ADA M. PURYEAR, program coordinator; b. Darlington, SC; d. Theodore and Floia (King) Peoples; m. Paul Lionel Puryear, March 27, 1954 (div. 1975); children: Paul Lionel, Jr., Paula Lynn. BA in Math., Talladega Coll., 1953; postgrad., Chgo. State U., 1954-56; MA in Reading, U. Chgo., 1958; PhD, Fla. State U., 1986; postgrad., Fla. A&M U., 1994, Oxford U., 2005. High sch. math tchr., Winston-Salem, NC, 1953-54; elem. tchr. Chgo. Pub. Schs., 1954-58; reading clinician U. Chgo., 1958; dir. reading clinic, asst. prof. Norfolk State U., 1958-61, Tuskegee Inst., 1961-66; coord. freshman math., asst. prof. math. Fisk U., 1966-70; adminstr. early childhood basic skills and elem. edn. State of Fla. Dept. Edn., Tallahassee, 1973-88; assoc. prof., program dir., grad. studies dir. Bethune-Cookman Coll., Daytona Beach, Fla., 1988-90; dir., supt. Fla. A&M U. Devel. Rsch. Pub. Sch. Dist., Tallahassee, 1990-93; coord., prof., dept. chmn., dir. PhD program devel. Fla. A&M U., 1993-98, coord., prof., 1998—2003, prof., dir. Robert H. Anderson Ednl. Leadership Libr., 1998—2003, prof. emerita, 2003—; assoc. prof., coord. off campus programs Valdosta State U., 2005—. Hostess radio talk show, 1977—79; sec.-treas. Afro-Am. Rsch. Assocs., 1968—74; tutor, diagnostician, lectr., cons., planner, 1958—; cons. Job Corps, N.C. Advancement Sch., pub. co.; lectr. univ. classes; trustee Fla. A&M U., 2003, pres. faculty senate, 1999—2003, adj. prof., 2003—05. Regular columnist profl. jours., 1974—; writer grants proposals; weekly columnist Capital Outlook, 1991-97; contbr. articles to profl. publs. Pres. PTA, 1975—76, v.p., 1983—84; edn. commentator Sta. WFSU, 1993—94; mem. United Fund com., Leon County 4C Bd.; pres. Norfolk Women's Interracial Coun., 1960; mem. Dem. Exec. Com. Leon County, 1981—88, 1991—93; deacon Presbyn. Ch., 1981—2004, AME ch. grief chmn., 2004—; bd. dirs. Tallahassee Coalition for the Homeless, 2002—, sec., 2004—. Mem.: AAUW (regional dir. 2003—, pres. Tallahassee chpt. 2005—, dir. Fla. 2005—), Am. Acad. Cert. Pub. Mgmt., Fla. Assn. Cert. Pub. Mng. NF (bd. dirs. 2004—), Nat. Assn. African Am. Studies (coord. 1999—), Fla. Soc. Cert. Pub. Mgrs. (newsletter bd., pres. North Fla. chpt. 2004, pres. North Fla. chpt. 2004—, state bd. 2004—), Am. Assn. Sch. Adminstrs., Socs. Docta Inc. (co-founder, sec. 1987—93), So. Assn. Colls. and Schs. (elem. and mid. sch. commn.), Assn. Childhood Edn. Internat., Leon Assn. Children Under Six (pres. 1977), So. Assn. Children Under Six, Fla. Assn. Children Under Six, Nat. Assn. Edn. Young Children, Nat. Assn. Elem. Sch. Prins., Internat. Reading Assn. (pres. Concerned Educators Black Students 1983—86, nat. early childhood com., nat. textbook com., libr./media com., nat. med. com., nat. awards com., nat. media com.), Fla. ASCD (regional dir. policy rev. jour. editl. bd. 1995—), Alliance of Black Sch. Educators, Assn. State Cons. on Early Childhood Edn., Fla. State Reading Assn., Fla. Coun. Elem. Edn., Fla. Assn. Suprs. and Adminstrs., The Holidays (nat. sec. fin. 1993—97, nat. v.p. 1997—2001, nat. pres. 2001—, chpt. pres.), Drifters (nat. membership chmn. 1977—79, Nat. Now Black

Woman 1984, historian, reporter 1992—94, pres. 1994—99, cluster coord. 2000—), FAMU Ladies Art and Social Club (pres.), Alpha Kappa Alpha (treas., summer sch. dir., undergrad. adv., parliamentarian, sec.), Pi Lambda Theta, Phi Kappa Phi (pres. 1985—86, v.p. pub. rels. chair), Phi Delta Kappa (advisor 2004—). Home: PO Box 1513 Valdosta GA 31603 Office: Valdosta State U 1800 N Patterson St Valdosta GA 31698 Home Phone: 229-671-9670. Personal E-mail: draburnette@wmconnect.com. Business E-Mail: amburnette@valdosta.edu.

BURNETTE, BRANDON R., librarian; b. Evansville, Ind., Apr. 27, 1965; s. Charles Dent and Carol Burnette. BFA, Tex. Christian U., Fort Worth, Tex., 1989; MSLS, U. Ky., Lexington, 1999. Reference libr. Murray State U., Ky., 1999—2000; govt. docs. reference libr. Southeastern Okla. State U., Durant, 2000—. Mem.: Govt. Docs. Roundtable, Okla. Libr. Assn., ALA. Office Phone: 580-745-2702. Office Fax: 580-745-7463. Personal E-mail: brandrb@yahoo.com. Business E-Mail: bburnette@se.edu.

BURNETTE, RALPH EDWIN, JR., judge; b. Lynchburg, Va., Sept. 25, 1953; s. Ralph Edwin and Carlease (Samuels) B. BA, Coll. William & Mary, 1975, JD, 1978. Bar: Va. 1978. Assoc. Edmunds & Williams, Lynchburg, 1978-83, ptnr., 1983-2001; gen. dist. ct. judge 24th Jud. Dist. Ct. Va., 2001—. Adj. prof. law Coll. William and Mary, 1996-2002, Washington & Lee U., 2003—. Deacon Peakland Bapt. Ch., Lynchburg, 1983-86; pres. Kaleidoscope Festival, Lynchburg, 1985, Lynchburg Symphony Orch., 1989-91; bd. dirs. Centra Health, Inc., 1987-97, United Way Cen. Va., 1989-90, Amazement Sq. Children's Mus. Mem. Va. Bar Assn., Va. State Bar (pres. 1993-94, pres. young lawyers conf. 1985, chmn. com. on alternative dispute resolution 1985-89, mem. bar coun., 1986-95, vice chmn. standing com. on legal ethics 1986-88, chmn. com. on long range planning 1988-91, mem. exec. com. 1990-95), Lynchburg Bar Assn. (pres. 1991-92), Avocations: golf, music, boating. Office: Lynchburg Gen Dist Ct 905 Court St Lynchburg VA 24504 Office Phone: 434-455-2630. Business E-Mail: reburnette@courts.state.va.us.

BURNHAM, J. V., retired sales executive; b. Pascagoula, Miss., May 23, 1923; s. George Luther and Eli Vashti (Hough) B.; m. Patti Lauri Latham, May 18, 1946 (dec. Aug. 6, 2006); children: James Steven, Jon Douglas, Richard Scott, Bruce Edward, Vernon Alan. AA, Jones County Jr. Coll., Miss., 1946; AS, Rochester Inst. Tech., 1948; BS, U. Houston, 1951, MEd, 1963. Mgr. The Progress-Item, Ellisville, Miss., 1948-50; asst. prof., asst. mgr. U. Houston Journalism and Printing Plant, 1950-57; estimator, product supt. purchasing Chas. P. Young Co., Houston, 1957-67, asst. sec.-treas., 1967-69, v.p. sales, 1969-91, sr. v.p., 1991—2001, ret., 2001. Assoc. editor Am. Oceanography, 1968-71; southwest corr. Inland Printer and Nat. Lithographer, 1952-60. Founding mem. Am. Air Mus. in Britain; pres. Printing Industries of Gulf Coast, Houston, 1971—73; chmn. emeritus, bd. dirs. Tex. Printing Edn. Found., Houston; active The Heritage Found., The Concord Coalition, Adm. Nimitz Found., St. Joseph Found., Hist. Mt. Vernon, Young America's Found.; treas. emeritus & founding life mem. Mus. Printing History, Houston; with Nat. WWII Mus. Charter, Am. Air Mus. Britain Founding, Colonial Williamsburc Founding, Mus. Am., Indian Charter; active Rep. Presdl. Task Force, Nat. Rep. Senatorial Com. Order of Merit, Nat. Rep. Congl. Com.; life, chmns. adv. bd. Rep. Nat. Com.; active Rep. Party of Tex., Rep. Nat. Candidate Trust, George Bush Pres. Libr. & Mus., Reagan Pres. Found., Young Am. Found., Judicial Watch, Presdl. Coalition. Lt. USNR, 1943—46. Named Man of Yr., Houston Graphics Soc., 1968, Printing Industry of Gulf Coast, 1970. Mem.: BAMPAC, Rochester Inst. tech. Alumni Assn., Tex. Police Officers Assn., Pres's. Club of Chas. P. Young Co. (charter, Outstanding Sales Achivement award), Mt. Vernon Ladies Assn., Citizens Against Govt. Waste, Claremont Inst., United Srs. Assn., Naval Aviation Mus. Found., Second Amendment Found. (charter), USS Constitution Mus. Found., Houston Lithographic Club, Rep.-Presdl. Legion of Merit, U.S. Golf Assn., Houston Golf Assn., Hummel Collectors Club (Houston), Crime Stoppers of Houston (gold cir. member), U.S. Navy Meml. Found., Tex. State Rifle Assn. (life), Naval Airship Assn. (life), Am. Legion (life), U. Houston Alumni (life), Jones County Jr. Coll. Alumni (life), U.S. Navy Pub. Affairs Alumni Assn. (life), VFW (life), PGA Ptnrs. Club (life; charter), Am. Fedn. Police, Gun Owners Am., NRA (life), U.S. Hist. Soc. (life), Nat. Eagle Scout Assn. (life), Houston Public TV, WWII Meml. Found., High Frontier, Am. Kidney Found., Juvenile Diabetes Found., Am. Diabetes Assn., NRA Whittington Ctr. Founders Club, Braeburn Country Club, Houston Craftsmens Club (hon.; life, past pres., Ben Franklin award 1971), Santa Fe Trail Gun Club (life), Nat. Home Gardening Club (life), 100 Club Houston, Kappa Delta Pi, Phi Delta Kappa, Sigma Delta Chi. Republican. Episcopalian.

BURNHAM, TOM, retired school system administrator; b. Jackson, Miss., May 5, 1946; 1 child, Cassondra Burnham Vanderford. BBA, Miss. Coll., Clinton, 1969, MEd, 1975; EdS, Delta State U., Cleveland, Miss., 1983, EdD, 1985. Tchr., dept. chair Pearl HS, Miss., 1969-72; asst. prin. McLuarin Jr. HS, Pearl, 1973-81; asst. dean Delta State U., 1981-86; prin. Solomon Jr. HS, Greenville, Miss., 1986-87; supt. Biloxi Pub. Schools, Miss., 1987-92; supt. edn. Miss. Dept. Edn., Jackson, 1992-97, 2010—12; exec. dir. Gulf Coast Edn. Consortium, Long Beach, Miss., 1998-99; supt. Henderson County Schools, NC, 1999—2004; dean U. Miss. Sch. Edn., 2004—09. Mem.: Nat. Coun. Accreditation Tchr. Edn., American Assn. Coll. Tchr. Edn., Miss. Assn. Sch. Supts., Miss. Profl. Educators, American Assn. Sch. Administrators, Phi Delta Kappa. Baptist.

BURNHAM, WALTER DEAN, political science professor; b. Columbus, Ohio, June 15, 1930; s. Alfred Huntington Jr. and Gertrude Elinor (Hamburger) B.; m. Patricia Ann Mullan, June 7, 1958; children: John Patrick, Anne More. BA, Johns Hopkins U., 1951; AM, Harvard U., 1958, PhD, 1962; LittD (hon.), Rutgers U., 1982. Instr. polit. sci. Boston Coll., 1958-61; asst. prof. Kenyon Coll., Gambier, Ohio, 1961-64, Haverford Coll., Pa., 1964-66; from assoc. to full prof. Washington U., St. Louis, 1966-71; prof. MIT, Cambridge, Mass., 1971-88, Ruth and Arthur Sloan prof. polit. sci., 1984-88; Frank C. Erwin Jr. Centennial prof. govt. U. Tex., Austin, 1988—94, prof. emeritus, 1994—. Author: Presidential Ballots, 1955, 2d. edit., 1976, Critical Elections, 1970, The Current Crisis in Am. Politics, 1982, Democracy in the Making, 1983, 2d edit., 1986; contbr. articles to profl. jours. With US Army, 1953-56. Fellow Social Sci. Rsch. Coun., 1963, Guggenheim Found., 1974, Ctr. Advanced Study in Behavioral Sci., 1979. Fellow Am. Acad. Arts and Scis.; mem. Am. Polit. Sci. Assn. (mem. coun. 1984-86, pres. organized sect. on politics and history 1993-94), Phi Beta Kappa (vis. scholar 1995-96). Avocation: opera. Home: 4203 Greenridge Pl Austin TX 78759 Office: Univ Tex Dept Govt Burdine Hall # 536 Austin TX 78712 Personal E-mail: tishmb@aol.com.*

BURNS, ARTHUR LEE, architect; b. Indpls., July 5, 1924; s. Charles Raymond and Dorothy Frances (Young) B.; m. Dorothy Maxine Kingsland, Oct. 26, 1946 (dec.); children— Stephen Robert (dec.), Melody Lee; m. Frances C. Mathers, Jan. 12, 1988. BS in Architecture, U. Cin., 1949. Archtl. draftsman Foster Engring. Co., Ltd., Indpls., 1941-42; archtl. draftsman Albert V. Walters (Architect), Cin., 1946-48; chief draftsman Arend & Arend (Architects), Cin., 1948-49; architect The McGuire & Shook Corp., Indpls., 1949-84, v.p., 1964-71, sec.-treas., 1972-73, pres., 1974-75, exec. v.p., 1976-77, v.p., 1978-79, sec.-treas., 1980-84; archtl. cons., 1984—. Bd. dirs. Friends of Winter Haven Pub. Libr., 1995—2001, 2002—, pres., 1997—98. With USAF, 1943—46. Fellow AIA (sec.-treas. Indpls. chpt. 1965-66, v.p. 1967, pres. 1968, mem. documents bd. 1973-85, chmn. 1978-79); mem. Ind. Soc. Architects (bd. dirs. 1968-69, v.p. 1971, pres. 1972, Edward D. Pierre medal 1972), Constrn. Specifications Inst. (v.p. Indpls. chpt. 1966-67, pres. 1967-68), Broad Ripple Sertoma Club Indpls. (v.p. 1973-74, pres. 1974-75, Gold Honor Club), Cypress Gardens Sertoma Club Winter Haven (bd. dirs. 1991-99, 2000-02). Republican. Methodist. Home: 805 N Collins St Plant City FL 33563-3325

BURNS, C(HARLES) PATRICK, hematologist, oncologist; b. Kansas City, Mo., Oct. 8, 1937; s. Charles Edgar and Ruth (Eastham) B.; m. Janet Sue Walsh, June 15, 1968; children: Charles Geoffrey, Scott Patrick. BA, U. Kans., 1959, MD, 1963. Diplomate Am. Bd. Internal Medicine, subsplty. bds. hematology, med. oncology. Intern Cleve. Met. Gen. Hosp., 1963-64; asst. resident in internal medicine Univ. Hosps., Cleve., 1966-68, sr. resident in hematology, 1968-69; instr. medicine Case Western Res. U., Cleve., 1970-71; asst. chief hematology Cleve. VA Hosp., 1970-71; asst. prof. medicine U. Iowa Hosps., Iowa City, 1971-75, assoc. prof. medicine, 1975-80, prof., 1980—2006, prof. emeritus, 2006—, dir. sect. med. oncology, co-dir. divsn. hematology/oncology, 1980-85, dir. div. hematology, oncology, blood marrow transplantation, 1985-99. Vis. scientist Imperial Cancer Rsch. Fund Labs., London, 1982-83; cons. U.S. VA Hosp.; mem. study sect. on exptl. therapeutics NIH, Cancer Ctr. Support Rev. Commn. Nat. Cancer Inst., NIH, NIH Cancer Clin. Investigation Rev. Com., Com. H Nat. Cancer Inst., VA Med. Rsch. Svc. Career Devel. Com.; mem. external adv. com. U. Oreg. Cancer Ctr., 1994-2000; mem. oncology group external adv. com., ACS, 2004-08; cons. Irish Rsch. Bd., Dublin, 2000— Mem. bd. assoc. editors Cancer Rsch., 1988-2000, rsch. and publs. on hematologic malignancies, tumor lipid biochemistry, leukemia and oncology, role of oxidation in cancer treatment. Chair Med. Exec. Com.; mem., bd. dirs., vol. Medicine Clinic, Hilton Head, SC. Served to capt. USMC, 1964—66. Am. Cancer Soc. fellow in hematology-oncology, 1968-69, USPHS fellow in medicine, 1969-70; USPHS career award, 1978; Outstanding Paper Presentation, Am. Oil Chemists Soc., 1992. Master ACP; mem. AAAS, Am. Bd. Internal Medicine (subsplty. bd. hematology test writing com. 1992-98, com. on recent advances in hematology, 2002—11, chair 2006—11), Am. Soc. Hematology (disting. emeritus mem.), Am. Assn. Cancer Rsch., Internat. Soc. Hematology, Ctrl. Soc. Clin. Rsch., Am. Soc. Clin. Oncology, Soc. Exptl. Biology and Medicine, Oxygen Soc., Royal Soc. Medicine, Am. Fedn. Clin. Rsch., Internat. Soc. for the Study of Fatty Acids and Lipids, Phi Beta Pi, Lambda Chi Alpha, Alpha Omega Alpha. Avocations: music, racquet sports, computer software. Home: 341 Greenwood Dr Hilton Head Island SC 29928 Home Phone: 843-671-2555. Business E-Mail: c-burns@uiowa.edu.

BURNS, HENRY L., state legislator; BA in Upper Elem. Ed., Northwestern State U.; MA in Sch. Admin., Pepperdine U. Owner/operator Wooden Spoon Bakery, Bossier City; thoroughbred owner/breeder; mem. Dist. 9 La. House of Reps., 2008—, mem. agr., forestry, aquaculture, and rural devel. com., natural resources and environment com., transp., hwys. and pub. works com. Republican. Office: State Capitol PO Box 44486 Baton Rouge LA 70804 Mailing: 954 Hwy 80 Ste 400 Haughton LA 71037 Office Phone: 225-342-6945, 318-949-2463. Office Fax: 318-949-5019. Business E-Mail: burnsh@legis.state.la.us.

BURNS, JON G., state legislator; b. Effingham County, Ga., Sept. 04; m. Dayle Burns; children: Jon Guerry Jr., Wilson. House rep., Ga.; state rep. Dist. 157 Ga., 2004—; mem. Transp. Com., Agr. Com., Games, Fish & Pks. Com. Mem.: Effingham County Young Farmers Orgn., Effingham C. of C., Ga. Agribusiness Coun. & Sigma Chi Fraternity, Ga. Southern U. Alumni Assn. (bd. dirs.), Rotary Club Effingham Sunrise. Republican. Methodist. Office: 411 Legis Off Bldg Atlanta GA 30334 Mailing: 5829 Clyo-Kildare Road Newington GA 30446 Office Phone: 912-754-3439. Business E-Mail: jon.burns@house.ga.gov.

BURNS, KEITH B., consumer products company executive; BSEE, Lawrence Technological U., 1974; MBA, Va. Commonwealth U., 1995. V.p., engring. and new product devel. Hamilton Beach Brands, Inc. (subs. NACCO Industries, Inc.), 2004—08; v.p., engring. and info. tech. Hamilton Beach Brands, Inc., 2008—. Office: Hamilton Beach Brands Inc 4421 Waterfront Dr Glen Allen VA 23060 Office Phone: 804-273-9777. Office Fax: 804-527-7142. Business E-Mail: keith.burns@hamiltonbeach.com.

BURNS, NED HAMILTON, civil engineering educator; b. Magnolia, Ark., Nov. 25, 1932; s. Andrew Louis and Ila Mae (Martin) B.; m. Martha Ann Fontaine, June 11, 1955; children: Kathryn Jane, Stephanie Ann, Michael Everett. BS, U. Tex., 1954, MS, 1958; PhD, U. Ill., 1962. Registered profl. engr., Tex. Instr. U. Tex., Austin, 1957-59, asst. prof., 1962-65, assoc. prof., 1965-70, prof. civil engring., 1970-83, Zarrow Centennial prof. engring., 1983—; assoc. dean engring. for acad. affairs, 1989-93; dir. Ferguson Structural Engring. Lab., 1994-97. Rsch. asst. U. Ill., Urbana, 1959-62. Author: (with T. Y. Lin) Design of Prestressed Concrete Structures, 1981 (McGraw Hill Book of Month 1982), S.I. Version-Design of Prestressed Concrete Structures, 1982, Legend of Post-Tensioning, 2005; contbr. articles to profl. jours. With US Army, 1955—57. Recipient Gen. Dynamics Tchg. award U. Tex. Coll. Engring., 1965, AMOCO Tchg. award, 1983, Martin P. Korn award, 1993, Blunk Meml. Professorship Tchg. award U. Tex., 1996-97; named Disting. Grad. U. Tex., 2005. Fellow: Post-Tensioning Inst. (bd. dirs. 1975-2010, Legends award, 2005), Am. Soc. Civil Engrs.(com. chmn. 1975—, T. Y. Lin award 1994), Prestressed Concrete Inst. (com. mem. 1968-, Martin Korn award for best paper 1993, Disting. Educator award 2000); mem. NAE, NSPE (chpt. pres. 1970), Am. Concrete Inst. (bd. dirs. 1983-87, Joe Kelley award 1990, Structural Rsch. award 2005, Arthur Anderson award 2006), Tex. Soc. Profl. Engring. (Young Engr. of Yr. award 1970, Travis chpt. Engr. of Yr. award 1987). Democrat. Baptist. Home: 3917 Rockledge Dr Austin TX 78731-2921 Office: U Tex Dept Civil Engring Austin TX 78712

BURNS, PAUL YODER, forester, educator; b. Tulsa, Okla., July 4, 1920; s. Paul Patchin and Mary Emily (Knowles) B.; m. Kathleen Iola Chase, Dec. 4, 1942; children: Virginia B. Belland, Margaret B. Feierabend, Nancy B. McNeill. BS, U. Tulsa, 1941; M in Forestry, Yale U., 1946, PhD, 1949. Asst., assoc. prof. U. Mo., Columbia, 1948-55; prof. forestry La. State U., Baton Rouge, 1955-86, prof. emeritus of forestry, 1986—. Dir. sch. forestry La. State U., Baton Rouge, 1955-76; commr. La. Forestry Commn., Baton Rouge, 1955-76. Editor: Forest Management in Plan & Practice, 1956, Southern Forest Soils, 1959; co-editor: Southern Forestry in Practice, 1977, Christmas Tree Production & Marketing, 1983. Pres. bd. dirs. La. State U. YMCA-YWCA, Baton Rouge, 1957-59; mem. La. Conf. Ch. Bd., Baton Rouge, 1967-73; pres. La. Coun. Human Rels., Baton Rouge, 1987-89; chair bd. dirs. The FISH Good Samaritans, Baton Rouge, 1996. Recipient Disting. Alumnus award U. Tulsa, 1974, Humanitarian award Baton Rouge Coun. Human Rels., 1984, Peacemaking award, Bienville House Ctr. for Peace, Baton Rouge, 1991, Vol. Activist award Baton Rouge, La., 1992, Brotherhood award Baton Rouge chpt. NCCJ, 1995. Fellow Soc. Am. Foresters, La. Soc. Am. Foresters (chmn. 1990, Disting Svc. to Forestry 1989), Phi Kappa Phi, Sigma Xi, Xi Sigma Pi. Presbyterian. Achievements include inductee Hall of Fame, La. State University School of Renewable Natural Resources. Avocations: tennis, piano. Office: La State Univ Sch Renewable Natural Resources Baton Rouge LA 70803-0001 Home: 208 Lovedale Dr Bristol TN 37620-6604 Office Phone: 225-578-4204. Personal E-mail: pburns@lsu.edu.

BURNS, SANDRA, lawyer, educator; b. Bryan, Tex., Aug. 9, 1949; d. Clyde W. and Bert (Rychlik) B.; 1 son, Scott. BS, U. Houston, 1970; MA, U. Tex., 1972, PhD, 1975; JD, St. Mary's U., 1978. Bar: Tex. 1978, US Supreme Ct., US Dist. Ct. (no. dist.), Tex.; cert. tchr., adminstr., supr. instrn., Tex., qualified mediator, arbitrator, Tex., ad litem, Tex. Tchr. Austin Ind. Sch. Dist., Tex., 1970—71; prof. child devel./family life and home econs. edn. Coll. Nutrition, Textiles and Human Devel. Tex. Women's U., Denton, 1974—75; instrnl. devel. asst. Office of Ednl. Resources divsn. instr U. Tex. Health Sci., San Antonio, 1976—77; legis. aide William T. Moore Tex. Senate, Austin, 1978, com. clk.-counsel, 1979; legal cons. Colombotti & Assocs., Aberdeen, Scotland, 1980; corp. counsel 1st Internat. Oil and Gas, Inc., 1983; contracted atty. Humble Exploration Co., Inc., Dallas, 1984; assoc. Smith, Underwood, Dallas, 1986—88; pvt. practice Dallas, 1988—; mem. grad. faculty Tex. A&M U., Commerce, 2003—04. Atty. contracted to Republic Energy Inc., Bryan, Tex., 1981-82, ARCO, Dallas, 1985; vis. lectr. Tex. A&M U., fall 1981, summer, 1981; lectr. home econs. Our Lady of the Lake Coll., San Antonio, fall, 1975; pres. Tex. Old Missions & Fts. Restoration Assn., 2009-11; chair First Internat. Oil & Gas Conf.; grant reviewer Tex. Edn. Agy., Austin, Title I Part F, No Child Left Behind Act, 2004.; peer reviewer Interest Based Mediation, Consortium for Appropriate Dispute Resolution Spl. Edn., Washington, 2006. Contbr. articles to profl. jours. Mem. Daughters of the Am. Revolution and Daughters of Republic Tex. French Legation Mus., 2007—09. Mem.: Dallas Bar Assn. (chair ADR sect. 2006), Coll. of the State Bar of Tex., Learning Disabilities Assn. Tex. (bd. mem. 2005—06). Achievements include development of a special needs church program that provides care for all ages. Office: Preston Commons West 300 8117 Preston Rd Dallas TX 75225

BURNS, THOMAS SAMUEL, history professor; b. Michigan City, Ind., June 7, 1945; m. Carol Ann Morris, June 29, 1968; 1 child, Catherine Elizabeth. AB, Wabash Coll., 1967; postgrad., Am. Sch. Classical Studies, Athens, summer 1967; MA, U. Mich., 1968, PhD, 1974. Asst. prof. history Emory U., Atlanta, 1974-80, assoc. prof., 1980-85, Samuel Candler Dobbs prof. history, 1985—, chmn. dept. history, 1989-92, 2006—07, prof. emeritus, 2010. Dir. summer seminar for sch. tchrs. NEH, 1985, 88; adj. prof. U. Windsor, Ont., 1978, 79; vis. rsch. prof. Kommission für alte Geschichte und Epigraphik des deutschen archäologischen Inst. in München, 1982; vis. rsch. prof. Römisch-Germanische Kommission des deut. arch. Inst., Frankfurt, 1982; Gastprof. U. Augsburg, 1986; co-dir. of Archaeological excavations in Passau, Germany, 1978-79, Manching, Germany, 1985, Pecs, Hungary, 1998. Author: The Ostrogoths: Kingship and Society, 1980, A History of the Ostrogoths, 1984, (with B.H. Overbeck) Rome and the Germans as Seen in Coinage, 1987, Barbarians within the Gates of Rome, 1994; (with J.W. Eadie) Urban Centers and Rural Realities, 2000, Rome and the Barbarians 100 B.C.-A.D. 400, 2003; (with H. Bender, F. Fazekas, Z. Visy) The Roman Settlement near Barbac, Komitat Baranya, Hungary, 2007; contbr. articles to profl. jours. With U.S. Army, 1969-71. Recipient Emory Williams Disting. Teaching award Emory U., 1982, Thomas Jefferson award Emory U., 2004, Student Govt. Disting. Tchg. award Emory U., 2007; Fulbright fellow Fed. Republic Germany, 1986, Hungary, 2010, Boak fellow in ancient history U. Mich., 1971-74; Disting. Vis. scholar-in-residence U. Adelaide, Australia. Mem. Medieval Acad. Am. (nominating com. 1987-88), Ga. Classical Assn., AAUP (pres. Emory U. chpt. 1983-84), Phi Beta Kappa, Omicron Delta Kappa. Avocations: camping, fishing, wilderness canoeing, kayaking. Office: Emory U Dept History Atlanta GA 30322-0001 Office Phone: 404-727-6555. Business E-Mail: histsb@emory.edu.

BURNS, TIMOTHY G., state legislator; Mem. Dist. 89 La. House of Reps., 2004—, chair civil law and procedure com. Republican. Office: Capitol Off 900 N Third St PO Box 94062 Baton Rouge LA 70804 Mailing: Dist Off 1 Sanctuary Blvd Ste 306 Mandeville LA 70471 Office Phone: 985-624-4492. Fax: 985-624-4496. Business E-Mail: larep089@legis.state.la.us.

BURNS, TIMOTHY H., investment company executive; BA in Polit. Sci., East Carolina U., 1982. V.p. OTC trading Drexel Burnham Lambert, 1984—88; sr. v.p., OTC trading Bear, Stearns & Co., Inc., 1988—92, mng. dir., 1994—98; sr. v.p. instl. equities JP Morgan & Co., 1993—94; head sales trading, mng. dir. sales trading Friedman, Billings, Ramsey Group, Inc., 1998—2007; CEO, pres. Friedman, Billings, Ramsey Internat., Ltd., 2007—07. Mem. Mid- Atlantic Security Traders Assn. Office: FBR Capital Markets Corp 1001 Nineteenth St N Arlington VA 22209 Office Phone: 703-312-9500. Office Fax: 703-312-9501. Business E-Mail: TBurns@fbr.com.

BURR, JUSTIN P., state legislator; Lic. real estate broker. Owner Burr Realty Inc.; bail enforcement agent Burr Bail Bonds; intern US Senator Jesse Helms, 2002, US Senator Elizabeth Dole, 2004; vice chmn. NC 8th US Congl. Dist., 2007—; mem. Dist. 67 NC House of Reps., 2009—. Republican. Office: North Carolina House of Representatives 300 N Salisbury St Rm 538 Raleigh NC 27603-5925 Home: 125 South Third St Albemarle NC 28001 Office Phone: 919-733-5908. Business E-Mail: Justin.Burr@ncleg.net.

BURR, RICHARD MAUZE, United States Senator from North Carolina; b. Charlottesville, Va., Nov. 30, 1955; m. Brooke Fauth; children: Tyler, William. BA in Comm., Wake Forest U., Winston-Salem, NC, 1978. Nat. sales mgr. Carswell Distributing, Winston-Salem, NC, 1978-94; state co-chmn. NC Taxpayers United, 1993-98; mem. US Congress from 5th NC Dist., 1995—2005; US Senator from NC, 2005—. Co-chmn. Partnership Drug Free NC; bd. dirs. Brenner Children's Hosp., Winston-Salem, NC; mem. Forsyth County Earning by Learning. Recipient Alfred & Alma Hitchcock Tribute award, Cystic Fibrosis Found., 1999, Mfg. Legis. Excellence award, Nat. Assn. Mfrs., 1999, Ground Water Protector award, Nat. Ground Water Assn., 2000, Jefferson award, Citizens for Sound Econ., 2001; named Legis. of Yr., Biotechnology Industry Orgn., 2002. Mem.: Optimist Soccer League, Rotary Club. Republican. Office: US Senate 217 Russell Senate Office Building Washington DC 20510 also: District Office Ste 508 2000 West First St Winston Salem NC 27104 Office Phone: 202-224-3154, 336-631-5125. Office Fax: 202-228-2981, 336-725-4493.*

BURRAGE, SEAN, state legislator; b. Durant, Okla., 1968; s. Michale and Aletha Burrage; m. Carole Burrage; children: Truman, Carter. BBA in Acctg., Univ. Okla., 1990, JD, 1993. Former legislature dir. to United States senator David Boren, Washington; former spl. asst. and dir. of state and fed. relations to Pres. David Boren U.

Okla.; former bd. mem. U. Hospitals Authority & Trust, Okla. U. Med. Ctr., Tri-County CASA; pres. Share the Spirit; mem. Dist. 2 Okla. State Senator, Okla., 2006—. Named Atty. Yr., Tri-County CASA, 2001. Mem.: Share Spirit (former pres.). Democrat. Home: 1510 NE Oakridge Dr Claremore OK 74017-1463 Office: 2300 N Lincoln Blvd Rm 529B Oklahoma City OK 73105 Home Phone: 918-341-8128; Office Phone: 405-521-5555. E-mail: burrage@oksenate.gov.

BURRELL, ROY A., state legislator; Mem. Dist. 2 La. House of Reps., 2004—, mem. adminstrn. of criminal justice com., mcpl., parochial and cultural affairs com., ways and means com., joint legis. com. on capital outlay. Democrat. Mailing: District Off 820 Jordan St Ste 315A Shreveport LA 71101 Office Phone: 318-676-7137. Fax: 318-676-7139. Business E-Mail: larep002@legis.state.la.us.

BURRIS, CRAVEN ALLEN, retired college administrator, professor; b. Wingate, NC, Sept. 11, 1929; s. Craven Cullom and Virginia Neulin (Currie) B.; m. Jane Russell Burris, June 19, 1955; children: Christa Cullom, David Allen. AA, Wingate Coll., 1949; BS, Wake Forest U., 1951; BDiv, Southeastern Bapt. Sem., Wake Forest, NC, 1958; MA, Duke U., 1959, PhD, 1964. Prof. history and govt. Gardner-Webb U., Boiling Springs, NC, 1958-66; prof. history, govt. and interdisciplinary studies St. Andrews Presbyn. Coll., Laurinburg, NC, 1966-69; v.p., dean of coll., prof. history and politics Meredith Coll., Raleigh, NC, 1969-98, ret., 1998, acting pres., 1971. Vis. lectr. in politics N.C. State U., Raleigh, 2003, tchr. ENCORE Program, 2000—10. Contbr. articles to profl. jours. Precinct officer State Conv. del., N.C. Dem. Party, 1969, 71; pres., dir. Tammy Lynn Found./Retarded Children, Raleigh, 1980—; chmn. Raleigh Hist. Dists. Commn., 2000-01; ch. sch. tchr. Lt. USNR, 1951-55, Italy and Atlantic Fleet. Recipient Disting. Alumni award Wingate U., 1983, Fulbright Study Trip, U.S. Govt., Pakistan, 1973, Study Trip USSR, 1988, Rsch. Brit. Mus. and Libr., 1963, 97. Mem. Civitan Internat. (v.p. bd. dirs. 1970—), Lions Club (editor 1965), Masons. Baptist. Avocations: tennis, racquetball, golf, sailing, gardening, swimming. Home: 1322 Duplin Rd Raleigh NC 27607-3721 Office: Meredith Coll 3800 Hillsborough St Raleigh NC 27607-5237 E-mail: burri@bellsouth.net.

BURRIS, JOHN, state legislator; Mem. Dist. 85 Ark. House of Reps., 2009—. Republican. Baptist. Office: State Capitol Rm 350 Little Rock AR 72201 Home: PO Box 7585 Little Rock AR 72217-7585 Office Phone: 501-682-6211, 501-682-7771, 870-688-6181. Business E-Mail: burrisforstaterep@gmail.com.

BURRIS, JOHN EDWARD, academic administrator, biologist, educator; b. Feb. 1, 1949; s. Robert Harza and Katherine (Brusse) Burris; m. Sally Ann Sandermann, Dec. 21, 1974; children: Jennifer, Margaret, Mary. AB, Harvard U., 1971; postgrad., U. Wis., 1971—72; PhD, U. Calif., San Diego, 1976. Asst. prof. biology Pa. State U., University Park, 1976—83, assoc. prof. biology, 1983—85; dir. bd. biology NRC/NAS, Washington, 1984—89; exec. dir. Commn. Life Scis., 1988—92; dir., CEO Marine Biology Lab, Woods Hole, Mass., 1992—2000; pres. Beloit College, Beloit, Wis., 2000—08, Burroughs Wellcome Fund, Rsch. Triangle Pk., 2008—. Adj. assoc. prof. biology Pa. State U., University Park, 1985—89, adj. prof., 1989—2001; chmn. adv. com. student sci. enrichment program Burroughs Wellcome Fund, 1995—2002; life and microgravity scis. and applications adv. com. NASA, 1997—2001; trustee Krasnow Inst., 1999—2002. Bd. dirs. Radiation Effects Rsch. Found., Grass Found., 2001—07, Naples Stazione Zoological, Consiglio Sci., Morgridge Inst. Rsch., 2009—. Mem.: AAAS (bd. dirs. 2002—06), Am. Inst. Biol. Sci. (pres. elect 1995, pres. 1996), Phi Beta Kappa. Business E-Mail: jburris@bwfund.org.

BURROW, HAROLD, retired gas industry executive; b. Navasota, Tex., Dec. 1, 1914; s. Benjamin Donald and Minnie (Weaver) B.; m. Vassa Woodley; children: Larry W., Harry W., Janice K. With Tenneco, Inc., Houston, 1943-66, pres., mem. exec. com., 1960-66; chmn. bd., mem. exec. com. Colo. Interstate Gas Co., Colorado Springs, 1974—, also bd. dirs.; vice chmn. bd., mem. exec. com. Coastal Corp. (formerly Coastal States Gas Corp.), Houston, 1974—2001; chmn. bd., CEO Coastal Natural Gas Co., 1995-2001; mng. ptnr. H&V B Partnership, Houston. Mem. exec. bd., bd. dirs., mem. exec. com. Am. Nat. Resources, Detroit. Mem. Petroleum Club (Houston), Ramada-Tajas Club (Houston). Methodist.

BURRUS, ROBERT LEWIS, JR., lawyer; b. Richmond, Va., Sept. 16, 1934; s. Robert Lewis and Bessie (Hart) Burrus; children: David Curran, Peter Tandy, Lewis Graves. BA, U. Richmond, 1955, LLD (hon.), 2005; LLB, Duke U., 1958. Bar: Va. 1958. Assoc. McGuire-Woods LLP, Richmond, Va., 1959-63, ptnr., 1963—, chmn., 1990—2006, chair emeritus, 2007—. Former dir. CSX Corp., Smithfield Rds. Apter Riverton, Amvest Corp., Best Products, Inc., O'Sullivan Corp., Riverton Investment Corp. Trustee U. Richmond, chmn. presdl. search coms., 1997-98 and 2005-06, rector, 1998-2002; bd. visitors Duke U. Law Sch., Durham, NC; dir. R.E.B. Found., Richmond, Va.; past trustee Va. Mus. Fine Arts and It's Found.; dir. Mus. Confederacy, former trustee, Va. Hist. Soc.; past chmn. State Coun. Higher Edn. for Va.; past dir., chmn. exec. com. Richmond Renaissance; past mem. Gov.'s Commn. Intercollegiate Athletics, 1991-92; past pres. St. Christopher's Sch. Found., Richmond. Capt. USAR. Recipient Charles S. Rhyne Award Duke U., 1998, Alumni of Yr. Award U. Richmond, 1998, Trustees Disting. Svc. Award, 2002, Silver Hope Award Nat. Multiple Sclerosis Soc., 2000, Humanitarian Award Nat. Conf. for Cmty. and Justice, 2001. Fellow Am. Bar Found., Va. Law Found.; mem. ABA, Va. Bar Assn. (chmn. corp. law com. 1975-77, chmn. bus. sect. 1976-77), Richmond Bar Assn., Commonwealth Club, Chgo. Club, Country Club Va., Kinloch Golf Club, Forum Club, Omicron Delta Kappa. Episcopalian. Office: McGuireWoods LLP One James Ctr 901 E Cary St Richmond VA 23219-4030 Office Phone: 804-775-4306. Office Fax: 804-698-2023. Business E-Mail: rburrus@mcguirewoods.com.

BURRUS, SIDNEY (CHARLES SIDNEY BURRUS), engineering professor, dean; b. Abilene, Tex., Oct. 9, 1934; s. Charles Hooker B. and Aleta (Hunter) Hoffman; m. Mary Lee Powell, June 7, 1958; children: Mary Virginia, Charles Stephen. BA, Rice U., 1957, BSEE, 1958, MS, 1960; PhD, Stanford U., 1965. Registered profl. engr., Tex. Lectr. Stanford U., Calif., 1964-65; asst. prof. elec. engring. Rice U., Houston, 1965-70, assoc. prof., 1970-74, prof., 1974—, chmn. dept. elec. engring., 1984—92, dir. Computer and Info. Tech. Inst., 1992—, dean George R. Brown Sch. Engring., 1998—2005, interim dean, 2010—, Maxfield and Oshman prof. emeritus elec. and computer engring. Vis. prof. Universitaet Erlangen-Nürnberg, Germany, 1975, 79, MIT, 1989-90; vis. fellow Trinity Coll., Cambridge, Eng., 1984.cons. IBM, Tex. Instruments, VA Hos., 1975— Author: Algorithms for DSP, 1984, Digital Filter Design, 1987; contbr. articles to profl. jours. Served to lt. USN, 1958-62. Recipient Humboldt Award, 1975, Signal Processing Soc. Award, 1995; Sr. Fulbright Fellowship, 1985. Fellow IEEE (Sr. Paper award 1974, Tech. Achievement award 1985, Jack S. Kilby Signal Processing medal, 2009); mem. Am. Soc. Elec. Engring., Sigma Xi, Tau Beta Pi Democrat. Baptist. Office: Rice U Dept Elec Engring PO Box 1892 Houston TX 77251-1892 Office Phone: 713-348-5484. Business E-Mail: csb@rice.edu.

BURRUSS, TERRY GENE, architect; b. Dec. 30, 1950; s. Alvin Eugene and Fern (Pelton) B.; m. Merilyn Kloss, Dec. 20, 1981; children: Mamie Christine, Gracie Aline. BArch, BA, U. Ark., 1973. Registered architect, Ark. Intern architect firm Robinson and Wassell, Inc., Little Rock, Ark., 1973-75; practice architecture Evo-Tech Prodn., Little Rock, Ark., 1976-78, I.D.E.A., Eureka Springs, Ark., 1976-78; architect Store Planning Assocs., San Francisco, 1978; assoc. Design 3, Architects, Little Rock, 1979; v.p., divsn. mgr. Mehlburger, Tanner, Renshaw and Assocs., Little Rock, 1980-84; v.p. Mehlburger, Tanner, Robinson & Assocs., Little Rock, 1984-87; pres. Terry Burruss Architects, Little Rock, 1987—. Instr. Hatha Yoga Community Edn. Program, 1976-77, St. Francis House, Little Rock, 1978, Parapsychology Ctr., 1978-79; vis. prof. constrn. mgmt. program U. Ark., Little Rock, 1999-2002; mem. Ark. Environ. Barriers Coun. Author: Flow Gently Sweet Alpha, 1972, Inflatables, an Alternative to the Deflated Classroom, 1973, Accessibility Guidelines for Meeting and Lodging Facilities, 1981, Housing for the Developmentally Disabled, 1986. Chmn. ministerial rels. Unity Ch. of Little Rock, 1986-87, pres. bd. dirs., 1987; pres. Montessori Children's Ctr. Parent Tchrs. Orgn., 1986-87; pres. Unity Ch., 1987, Ctrl. High Neighborhood Assn., 1989-90; chmn. Gov.'s Mansion Area, 1998-2000; mem. bd. adjustment City of Little Rock, 2003—. Mem. AIA (state chmn. 1981), U. Ark. Alumni Assn., Little Rock Jaycees (dir. 1981-83, sec. 1982-83, chmn. TV auction 1982), Alpha Phi Omega, Pi Kappa Alpha. Home: 12 Tallyho Ln Little Rock AR 72227-2416 Office: 1202 Main St Ste 230 Little Rock AR 72202-5076 Home Phone: 501-228-5783; Office Phone: 501-376-3676. E-mail: tbartichoke@aristotle.net.

BURSEY, MAURICE M., retired chemistry professor; b. Balt., July 27, 1939; s. Reginald Price and Edna Frances (Moyer) B.; m. Joan Marie Tesarek, Dec. 28, 1970; children— John Thomas Kieran, Sara Helen Moyer. BA, Johns Hopkins U., 1959, MA, 1960, PhD, 1963. Lectr. Johns Hopkins U., Balt., 1963-64; asst. prof. Purdue U., Lafayette, Ind., 1964-66; asst. prof. chemistry U. N.C., Chapel Hill, 1966-69, assoc. prof., 1969-74, prof., 1974-96, prof. emeritus, 1996—. Editor Mass Spectrometry Revs., 1990-93; contbr. articles to profl. jours. Recipient various research grants. Fellow Am. Inst. Chemists, Royal Soc. Chemistry; mem. Am. Chem. Soc. (council, 1976-2001, bd. dirs. 1993-2001), Am. Soc. Mass Spectrometry, Alpha Chi Sigma (Grand Master Alchemist nat. pres. 1986-88). Democrat. Roman Catholic. Home: 101 Longwood Pl Chapel Hill NC 27514-9584 Personal E-mail: mauricebursey@aol.com.

BURSON, BETSY LEE, librarian; b. Olney, Tex., Dec. 16, 1942; d. James Hollis and Lora Elizabeth (Talbott) B.; m. Winston Rabb Henderson, June 26, 1976. BS in Edn., Kans. State Tchrs. Coll., 1964; MLS, Tex. Woman's U., 1967, PhD in Libr. Info. Studies, 1987. With Phoenix Pub. Libr., 1967-74; libr. dir. Glendale (Ariz.) Pub. Libr., 1974-75; project archivist Phoenix History Project, 1975-77; adj. faculty U. Ariz., Tucson, 1979, Tex. Woman's U., Denton, 1980; libr. cons. La. State Libr., Baton Rouge, 1982-85; libr. dir. El Paso Pub. Libr., Tex., 1987-90, Arlington Pub. Libr., Tex., 1990—2001, cons., 2001—. Named Librarian of the Yr. Tex. Library Assn., 1995. Home Phone: 817-795-2194.

BURT, ALVIN MILLER, III, anatomist, cell biologist, writer, educator; b. Bridgeport, Conn., Aug. 14, 1935; s. Alvin Miller and Esther Louise (Carey) B.; m. Dorothy Hanlin, July 15, 1961 (div.); children: Constance Walker, Carolyn Marie; m. Judith Nath, July 13, 1991; 1 stepchild, Stephen Jacob Nath. BA, Amherst Coll., 1957; PhD (USPHS fellow 1960-61), U. Kans., 1962. Asst. prof. anatomy Med. Coll. Va., Richmond, 1962-63; instr. Yale U. Med. Sch., 1963-66; mem. faculty Vanderbilt U. Med. Sch., 1966—, prof. anatomy, 1974-85, prof. cell biology, 1985-2000, prof. cell biology emeritus, 2000—; prof. cell biology Nursing Sch. Vanderbilt U., Nashville, 1994-2000, prof. cell biology in nursing emeritus, 2000—; adj. prof. biology Vol. State Cmty. Coll. Gallatin, Tenn., 2008—; sole proprietor Old Hickory Design, Hendersonville. Vis. scientist Agrl. Rsch. Coun., Inst. Animal Physiology, Babraham, Cambridge, Eng., 1972-73. Author: Textbook of Neuroanatomy, 1993; contbr. articles to profl. jours. Vestryman Episcopal Ch. of Advent, Brentwood, Tenn., 1977-81, sr. warden, 1979-81, lay reader, chalice bearer, 1975-87, tchr. adult classes, mem. diocesan lay ministry com., 1981-85; lay reader, chalice bearer St. Philips Episcopal Ch., Donelson, Tenn., 1989-92, vestryman, 1991-92, mem. diocesan total ministry com., 1990-93; mem. Stephen Ministry Diocese of Tenn., 1991—95; dir. pastoral care St. Ann's Episcopal Ch., Nashville, 1993-96, lay reader, 1994—2010, chalice bearer, 1996—2010, vestryman, 2002-05, Saint Joseph Aramathea Episcopal Ch., Hendersonville, Tennessee, 2012-; mem. steering com. Interfaith AIDS Ministry, 1994-96; vol. ombudsman rep. Mid Cumberland Human Resources Ctr., 2001—, vestry mem., St. Joseph Arimathea Episcopal Ch., 2012-, pastoral care, 2012-. Recipient Research Career Devel. award USPHS, 1968-73 Mem. Am. Assn. Anatomists, Am. Soc. Neurochemistry, Human Anatomy & Physiology Soc., Internat. Soc. Neurochemistry, Internat. Brain Rsch. Orgn., Soc. Neurosci., Tenn. Outdoor Writers Assn. (v.p. 1985-86, pres.-elect 1986-87, pres. 1987-88, chmn. bd. dirs. 1988-89), Southeastern Outdoor Press Assn. (Webmaster 2002-2005), Bass Anglers Sportsmens Soc., Tenn. Spoonplugging Club (bd. dirs. 1980-88, editor newsletter 1980-85), Sigma Xi. Home and Office: 149 Bay Dr Hendersonville TN 37075-4040

BURTLESS, GARY THOMAS, economist, consultant; b. Cayuga County, NY, Apr. 11, 1950; s. Charles Bernie and Patricia Ann (MacCone) B.; m. Elise Kathe Bruml, Nov. 27, 1976; children: Andrew B., Matthew B. BA, Yale U., 1972; PhD, MIT, 1977. Economist Office Sc., HEW, Washington, 1977-79, U.S. Dept. Labor, Washington, 1979-81; John D. and Nancy C. Whitehead chair in econ. studies Brookings Instn., Washington, 1981—. Vis. prof. pub. affairs U. Md., College Park, 1993; cons. various orgns., 1981—, U.S. Dept. Lab., 1985—, World Bank, Washington, 1990-97. Author: Can America Afford To Grow Old, 1989, Growth With Equity: Economic Policymaking for the Next Century, 1993, Globaphobia: Confronting Fears about Open Trade, 1998; co-editor Jour. Human Resources, 1988-96, Brookings-Wharton Papers on Urban Affairs, 2004-09, A Future of Lousy Jobs?, 1990, Five Years After: Long Term Effects of Welfare-to-Work Programs, 1995, Does Money Matter? Effect of School Resources, 1996, Work, Health and Income Among the Elderly, 1997, Aging Societies: The Global Dimension, 1998; mem. editl. bd. Jour. Policy Analysis and Mgmt., 1999-, Australian Econ. Rev., 2006-; contbr. articles to profl. jours. Commn. mem. panel on fin. adequacy Trustees Social Security, 1989; mem. tech. panel Adv. Coun. on Social Security, 1994—95; mem. com. on health and safety needs of older workers NAS, 2001—04. Recipient Leontief prize Ea. Econ. Assn., 1978. Mem.: Assn. Pub. Policy Analysis & Mgmt., Nat. Acad. Social Ins. (commn. mem. panel on Social Security notch 1988, panel on privatizing Social Security 1997—98), Am. Econ. Assn. Avocations: history, hiking. Office: Brookings Instn 1775 Massachusetts Ave NW Washington DC 20036-2103 Office Phone: 202-797-6000, 202-797-6130. Business E-Mail: communications@brookings.edu.

BURTON, ALLEN W., pain medicine specialist, educator; MD, Baylor Coll. Medicine, 1991. Diplomate American Bd. Anesthesiology, 1996, American Bd. Anesthesiology-pain medicine, 1998. Resident anesthesiology Brigham & Women's Hosp., Boston, 1992—95; fellow pain medicine Univ. Tex. Med. Br. Hosp., 1997—98, assoc. prof. anesthesiology; physician St. Luke's Episcopal Hosp. Office: St Luke's Episcopal Hospital 6720 Bertner Ave Houston TX 77030-2697 Office Phone: 832-355-1000.*

BURTON, CLAUDE S., III, dermatologist, educator; MD, Duke U., 1979. Diplomate Am. Bd. Internal Medicine, 1982. Resident internal medicine Duke Univ. Med. Ctr., Durham, NC, 1979—82, resident dermatology, 1982—84, hosp. affiliation include; prof. dermatology Duke Univ. Sch. of Medicine, Durham, NC. Office: Duke University Medical Center Department of Dermatology PO Box 3511 Durham NC 27710 Office Phone: 919-684-3432. Office Fax: 919-681-7991.

BURTON, DONALD W., venture capitalist; BA in Am. Studies, Yale U.; MBA, Harvard U. Chmn., founder Fidelity Ventures Assocs., Inc., Boston, 1973; gen. ptnr. Burton Partnership, LP, 1979—; mng. gen. ptnr. South Atlantic Venture Fund, 1981—, chmn., pres., South Atlantic Capital, Inc., 1981—, founder, 1983; mem., investment adv. coun. Fla. State Bd. of Adminstrn., 2001—07. Bd. dirs. BlackRock Equity Bond, Ballast Point Ventures, L.P., 1996—, Knology, Inc., 1996—, Capital SW Corp., 2006—. Mem.: Nat. Venture Capital Assn. (bd. dirs.). Office: South Atlantic Capital Inc 614 W Bay St Tampa FL 33606 Office Phone: 813-253-2500. Office Fax: 813-253-2360. Business E-Mail: dwburton@southatlantic.com.

BURTON, E. JAMES, board member, business school dean; married; 2 children. BA in Economics, MacMurray Coll.; MBA in Mgmt., Murray State U.; PhD in Acctg., U. Ill. CPA, cert. fraud examiner. Asst. prof. acctg. Fla. State U.; pres. Profl. Growth Assocs., Profl. Credit Corp., Flagman, Inc.; prof. acctg. Middle Tenn. State U., 1990, assoc. dean, external rels., 1990—99, dean, Jennings A. Jones Coll. Bus. Murfreesboro, Tenn., 1999. Bd. dirs. Piedmont Natural Gas Co., 2006—. Contbr. 50 articles to profl. jours.; author (& co-author) 5 books in acctg. & fin. Past trustee Middle Tenn. State Univ. Found.; bd. dir. Leadership Middle Tenn., Area IX Workforce Investment Bd., Jennings & Rebecca Jones Found.; pres. Southern Bus. Adminstrn. Assn.; v.p. Mid. Tenn. Coun. Boy Scouts America. Named Tenn. Acctg. Educator of Yr., 2002. Avocations: boating, fishing, woodworking. Office: Piedmont Natural Gas Co Bd Directors 4720 Piedmont Row Dr Charlotte NC 28210 Office Phone: 704-364-3120. Office Fax: 704-365-3849. Business E-Mail: eric.burton@piedmontng.com.

BURTON, JEFF BRIAN, race car driver; b. South Boston, Va., June 29, 1967; m. Kim Burton; children: Kimberle Paige, Harrison. Race car driver NASCAR Nationwide Series Burton Autosports, 1988—89, NASCAR Nationwide Series for Sam Ard, 1990—91, NASCAR J&J Racing, 1991—92, NASCAR Filmar Racing, 1992—93, NASCAR Stavola Brothers Racing, 1993—95, NASCAR Roush Fenway Racing, 1996—2004, NASCAR Richard Childress Racing, 2004—; part-time race car driver Nationwide Series. 1st pl. (First NASCAR Nationwide win) Zerex 150, Martinsville Speedway, Va., 1990; 1st pl. (First NASCAR win) Interstate Batteries 500, Texas Motor Speedway, Ft. Worth, 1997; 1st pl. Hanes 500, Martinsville Speedway, Va., 1997, Jiffy Lube 300, NH Internat. Speedway, 1997, Jiffy Lube 300, NH Motor Speedway, 1998, Exide NASCAR Select Batteries, Richmond, Va., 1998, Las Vegas 400, Las Vegas Motor Speedway, 1999, TranSouth Financial 400, Darlington Raceway, 1999, Coca-Cola 600, Lowe's Motor Speedway, 1999, Jiffy Lube 300, NH Internat. Speedway, 1999, Pepsi Southern 500, Darlington Raceway, 1999, Popsecret Microwave Popcorn 400, NC Speedway, 1999, CarsDirect.com 400, Las Vegas Motor Speedway, 2000, Pepsi 400, Daytona Internat. Speedway, 2000, DuraLube 300 sponsored by Kmart, NH Internat. Speedway, 2000, Checker Auto Parts/Dura Lube 500, Phoenix Internat. Raceway, 2000, Coca Cola 600, Lowe's Motor Speedway, 2001, Checker Auto Parts 500 presented by Pennzoil, 2001, Dover 400, Dover Internat. Speedway, 2006, Samsung 500, Tex. Motor Speedway, 2007, Food City 500, Bristol Motor Speedway, Tenn., 2008, Bank of America 500, Lowe's Motor Speedway, 2008. Actively involved with wife Duke Children's Hosp. Named NASCAR Cup Rookie of Yr., 1994, Person of Yr., NASCAR Illustrated, 2007. Achievements include First NASCAR Nationwide Series, Grand National Division Race: March 13, 1988 Miller Classic at Martinsville Speedway, Virginia (started 16th, finished 28th); First NASCAR Nationwide Series top-five: July 4, 1989 at Myrtle Beach Speedway in SC (started 5th, finished 4th); First NASCAR Nationwide Series top-10: March 12, 1989 at Martinsville Speedway in Virginia (started 27th, finished 10th); First NASCAR Nationwide Series pole position: June 8, 1990, at Orange County Speedway in Rougemont, NC (finished 5th); First NASCAR Cup Race: July 11, 1993, Slick 50 300 at the New Hampshire International Speedway (started 6th, finished 37th); First NASCAR Cup top-five and top-10 finish: March 13, 1994, Atlanta Motor Speedway in Hampton, Ga. (started 13, finished 4th); First NASCAR Cup pole position: August 18, 1996, Michigan International Speedway, Brooklyn, Michigan (finished 9th); In September of 2000, for first time in his NASCAR career, led every lap of a Cup Series Race. It came at New Hampshire Motor Speedway; NASCAR Career: 20 wins & 196 Top 10; NASCAR Nationwide Series Career: 27 Wins & 136 Top 10. Avocations: basketball, boating, deep sea fishing, golf. Office: Richard Childress Racing 425 Industrial Dr Welcome NC 27374

BURTON, TERRY C., state legislator; m. Darleen Allday Burton; children: Ben Jones, Dawn Jones. Mem. Dist. 31 Miss. State Senate, 1992—; owner, operator Real Prodns. Henry Toll fellow, Coun. State Govt., 1993. Mem.: Hamasa Shrine, Newton Chap-Coun. & Commandery, York Rite Mason, Newton Jaycees (gov.), Miss. Assn. Broadcasters, Rotary Club, Newton Lodge No. 57. Republican. Methodist. Mailing: 101 Rew St Newton MS 39345 Home Phone: 601-683-7050; Office Phone: 601-359-3234. Fax: 601-683-6695; Office Fax: 601-359-5345. Business E-Mail: tburton@senate.ms.gov.

BURTON, TROY, parks director, museum association administrator; b. Dallas, Tex. BA in Hist., Eng., U. Ala., 1993; MA in Pub. Hist., NC State U., 1998. Cur. Raleigh City Mus., 1996; edn. cur. Hist. Oak View, 1996—98, asst. park mgr., 1998—2000, park. mgr., 2000—05; site mgr. Mordecai Hist. Park, Raleigh, 2005—. Grad. tchg. asst. NC State U. Vol. Habitat for Humanity; elder Cary Presbyn. Mem.: NC Museums Coun. (pres.). Avocations: photography, fly fishing, sailing. Office: Mordecai Hist Park 1 Mimosa St Raleigh NC 27604

BURZIK, CATHERINE M., corporate board member, retired medical products executive; b. Nov. 11, 1950; m. Frank Burzik. BS in Math., Canisius Coll., 1972; MS in Math., U. Buffalo. Gen. mgr. electronic imaging products Eastman Kodak Co., 1991—93, v.p. corporate mktg., 1996—97; gen. mgr. Critikon, Inc., 1997—98; pres. Ortho-Clinical Diagnostics, Inc., 1998—2003; exec. v.p. Applied Biosystems (subs. of Applera Corp.), 2003—04, pres. Foster City, Calif., 2004—06; sr. v.p. Applera Corp., Foster City, Calif., 2004—06; pres., CEO Kinetic Concepts, Inc., San Antonio, 2006—12; founder, CEO CFB Interests LLC, San Antonio, 2012—; chair VitaPath Genetics, Inc., Foster City, Calif., 2012—. Bd. dirs. Kinetic Concepts, Inc., 2006—11, Fed. Res. Bank Dallas, San Antonio, 2010—, Allscripts, LLC, 2011—12, VitaPath Genetics, Inc., 2012—, ViroXis Corp., 2012—, Becton, Dickinson & Co., 2013—; co-founder Catherine M. & Francis N. Burzik Found., 2012—. Chair bd. trustees Canisius Coll., bd. trustees Keck Graduate Inst. Applied Life Sciences Office: CFB Interests LLC 222 Primrose Pl San Antonio TX 78209

BURZYNSKI, NORMAN STEPHEN, editor; b. Pitts., Nov. 21, 1928; s. Ladislaus and Eleanor Marie B.; m. Ann Louise Adams, June 11, 1951; children: Michael Derek, Stephanie Ann, Eric Adams, Karen Ruth, John Kerstan, Joan Lorraine. BA in Journalism, U. Pitts., 1953; MS in Bus. Adminstrn., George Washington U., 1971; A. Applied Sci. summa cum laude in Aviation Tech.— Airport Mgmt., No. Va. Community Coll., Manassas, 1977, A. Applied Sci. summa cum laude in Aviation Tech.— Air Traffic Control, A. Applied Sci. magna cum laude in Comml. Art, 1982. Editor corporate publs. PPG Industries, Pitts., 1958-72, pub. relations rep., 1972-73; air res. forces liaison officer Office of Info., U.S. Air Force, Washington, 1968-72; chief Office of Info., U.S. Air Force Res., 1973-76; editor The Officer, Res. Officers Assn. U.S., Washington, 1976-95. Editor Civil War Camera, Luray, Va., 1998—. Served to lt. U.S. Army, 1951-52; to col. USAF, 1968-76. Mem. Res. Officers Assn., Air Force Assn., Mil. Officers Assn. America, Aircraft Owners and Pilots Assn., Exptl. Aircraft Assn., Aviation and Space Writers Assn. Home: 384 West Lu Dr Luray VA 22835 Business E-Mail: n_s_b@comcast.net.

BURZYNSKI, STANISLAW RAJMUND, internist; b. Lublin, Poland, Jan. 23, 1943; came to U.S., 1970; s. Grzegorz and Zofia Miroslawa (Radzikowski) B. MD with distinction, Med. Acad., Lublin, 1967, PhD, 1968. Tchg. asst. Med. Acad., 1962-67, intern, resident, 1967-70; rsch. assoc. Baylor U., 1970-72, asst. prof., 1972-77; pvt. practice specializing in internal medicine Houston, 1977—; pres. Burzynski Clinic, 1979—. Dir. Burzynski Rsch. Lab., 1977-83; pres. Burzynski Rsch. Inst., Inc., 1983-; prof. neuro-oncology Capital U. Beijing, 2012-. Contbr. articles to profl. jours. Nat. Cancer Inst. grantee, 1974, West Found. grantee, 1975. Mem. AMA, AAAS, Am. Assn. Cancer Rsch., Harris County Med. Soc., Polish Nat. Alliance (pres. Houston chpt. 1974-75), Soc. Neurosci., Soc. Neuro-oncology, Tex. Med. Assn., Sigma Xi. Roman Catholic. Achievements include discovery of antineoplastons components of biochem. def. system against cancer; described structure of Ameletin, 1st substance known to be responsible for remembering sound in animal's brain; invented new treatment for cancer, AIDS, viral infections, autoimmune diseases, neurofibromatosis, and Parkinson's disease; gene silencing theory of aging. Home: 20 W Rivercrest Dr Houston TX 77042-2127 Office: 9432 Katy Freeway Ste 200 Houston TX 77055-6330 Home Phone: 713-781-4782. Business E-Mail: info@burzynskiclinic.com.

BUSBY, CHARLES, state legislator; m. Felicia Hillman. Attended, Miss. Gulf Coast CC, U. South Ala., Mobile. Small bus. owner, engr.; mem. Dist. 111 Miss. House of Reps., Jackson, 2012—. Active Jackson County Econ. Devel. Found., Miss. Mem.: ASME, NRA, Jackson County C. of C., American Coun. Engrng. Companies, Pascagoula Rotary Club. Republican. Episcopalian. Office: Miss House of Reps PO Box 1018 Jackson MS 39215 Business E-Mail: cbusby@house.ms.gov.

BUSCH, KURT THOMAS, professional race car driver; b. Las Vegas, Aug. 4, 1978; s. Tom and Gaye Busch; m. Eva Bryan, July 27, 2006. Race car driver NASCAR Roush Racing, Concord, NC, 2001—05, Penske Racing South, 2006, Penske Racing, 2007—11. 1st pl. Auto Club 500 Calif. Speedway, 2003; 1st pl. Pa. 500 Pocono Raceway, 2002, 2003, 2005, 2007; 1st pl. Subway 500 Martinsville Speedway, 2002; 1st pl. Siemens 300 NH Internat. Speedway, 2004, 1st pl. Sylvania 300, 2004; 1st pl. Lenox Indsl. Tools 301 NH Motor Speedway, 2008; 1st pl. Food City 500 Bristol Motor Speedway, 2002, 2003, 2004, 2006, 1st pl. Sharpie 500, 2003; 1st pl. NAPA 500 Atlanta Motor Speedway, 2002, 1st pl. Kobalt Tools 500, 2009, 2010; 1st pl. Ford 400 Homestead-Miami Speedway, 2002; 1st pl. Sirius 400 Mich. Internat. Speedway, 2003, 1st pl. 3M Performance 400, 2007; 1st pl. Subway Fresh 500 Phoenix Internat. Raceway, 2005; 1st pl. Chevy Rock and Roll 400 Richmond Internat. Raceway, 2005; 1st pl. Dickies 500 Tex. Motor Speedway, 2009; 1st pl. Coca-Cola 600 Charlotte Motor Speedway, 2010; 1st pl. Toyota/Save Mart 350 Infineon Raceway, Sonoma, Calif., 2011; 1st pl. AAA 400 Dover Internat. Speedway, 2011. Founder Kurt Busch Found. Named NASCAR Nextel Cup Series Champion, 2004. Office: Kurt Busch Inc 151 Lugnut Ln Mooresville NC 28117 Office Fax: 704-799-2326.

BUSCH, KYLE, race car driver; b. Las Vegas, Nev., May 2, 1985; Race car driver NASCAR Hendrick Motorsports, 2003—07, Joe Gibbs Racing, 2008—. 2nd pl. UAW-DaimlerChrysler 400 Las Vegas Motor Speedway, 2005, 1st pl. Shelby 427, 2009; 2nd pl. MBNA RacePoints 400 Dover Internat. Speedway, 2005, 1st pl. Best Buy 400, 2008, 1st pl. Autism Speaks 400, 2010; 1st pl. Sony HD 500 Calif. Speedway, 2005; 1st pl. Checker Auto Parts 500 Phoenix Internat. Raceway, 2005; 2nd pl. Pepsi 400 Daytona Internat. Speedway, 2006, 2007, 1st pl. Coke Zero 400, 2008; 1st pl. Lenox Indsl. Tools 300 NH Internat. Speedway, 2006; 2nd pl. Sharpie 500 Bristol Motor Speedway, Tenn., 2006, 1st pl. Food City 500, 2007, 2009, 1st pl. Sharpie 500, 2009, 1st pl. IRWIN Tools Night Race, 2010, 1st pl. Jeff Byrd 500, 2011; 2nd pl. Chevy Rock and Roll 400 Richmond Internat. Raceway, 2006, 2nd pl. Jim Stewart 400, 2007, 1st pl. Crown Royal Health Calhoun 400, 2010, 1st pl. Crown Royal Matthew & Daniel 400, 2011, 1st pl. Richmond 400, 2012; 1st pl. Kobalt Tools 500 Atlanta Motor Speedway, 2008; 1st pl. Aaron's 499 Talladega Superspeedway, 2008; 1st pl. Dodge Challenger 500 Darlington Raceway, 2008; 1st pl. Toyota Save Mart 350 Infineon Raceway, 2008; 1st pl. Quaker State 400 Ky. Speedway, 2011; 1st pl. Mich. 400 Mich. Internat. Speedway, 2011. Named NEXTEL Cup Rookie of Yr., 2005. Achievements include being the youngest driver ever, at 20, to win a race in the Nextel Cup series, 2005; being the first driver in NASCAR history to win three road races in one year: the Nationwide Series, Mexico, the Cup Race at Sonoma, the Centurion Boats at The Glen at Watkins Glen International, 2008. Avocation: surfing. Mailing: c/o Joe Gibbs Racing 13415 Reese Blvd W Huntersville NC 28078

BUSER, BOYD RICHARD, dean, osteopath; b. Iowa City, Jan. 19, 1955; s. Charles L. and Ruth M. (Walker) B.; m. Pamela K. Lowe, Dec. 18, 1976; children: Michelle, Morgan, Charles. BA in Gen. Sci., U. Iowa, 1977; DO, Coll. Osteo. Medicine and Surgery, 1981. Diplomate Am. Bd. Gen. Practice, Am. Bd. Osteo. Manipulative Medicine. Intern Cranston Gen. Hosp., RI, 1981-82; asst. prof. family practice U. Osteo. Medicine and Health Scis., Des Moines, 1982-86; dir. Immediate Care Clinic South, Immediate Care Clinic West, Des Moines, 1982-86, Dietz Family Practice Clinic, Des Moines, 1982-84, West Des Moines Family Practice Clinic, 1984-86; prof. dept. osteo. manipulative medicine U. New Eng. Coll. Osteo. Medicine, Biddeford, Maine, chmn. dept. osteo. manipulative medicine, 1986—99, assoc. dean clin. affairs, 1999—2007, interim dean, 2005—07; v.p., dean U. Pikeville Ky. Coll. Osteopath. Medicine, 2007—. Mem. faculty-student forum U. Osteo. Medicine and Health Scis., clinic edn., scholarship, honors and awards, product standardization com., univ. self-study com., 1982-86; mem. curriculum U. New Eng. Coll. Osteo. Medicine, student promotion and evaluation, univ. self-appraisal, dean's steering com., faculty senate; presenter in field. Recipient Pre-doctoral fellowship Coll. Osteo. Medicine and Surgery, 1980. Mem. Am. Osteo. Assn. (editorial cons. 1989, osteo. manipulative medicine certifying bd. 1992, third v.p., trustee), Am. Acad. Osteopathy (program chmn. ann. convocation 1991, bd. govs. 1991—, bd. trustees, 1993—, coll. assistance com., chmn. membership com. 1989-91, edn. com. chmn. 1991—, component soc.'s com., undergrad. academies com., pres.-elect 1994), Ednl. Coun. Osteo. Prins., New Eng. Acad. Osteopathy (v.p. 1987-88, pres. 1988-89), Maine Osteo. Assn. (bd. dirs. 1989, pres. 1999-2001), Nat. Bd. Osteo. Med. Examiners (bd. dirs. 1993—, chmn. test constrn. com.), Am. Coll. Osteo. Family Physicians. Avocations: golf, racquetball. Office: University Pikeville Ky Coll Osteopath Medicine Office of Dean Armington 220 147 Sycamore St Pikeville KY 41501 Office Phone: 606-218-5411. Business E-Mail: boydbuser@upike.edu.*

BUSH, BARBARA PIERCE, former First Lady of the United States, volunteer; b. NYC, June 8, 1925; d. Marvin and Pauline (Robinson) Pierce; m. George Herbert Walker Bush, Jan. 6, 1945; children: George Walker, Pauline Robinson (Robin) (dec. Oct. 11, 1953), John Ellis, Neil Mallon, Marvin Pierce, Dorothy Walker. Student, Smith Coll., 1943-44; degree (hon.), Stritch Coll., Milw., 1981, Mt. Vernon Coll., Washington, 1981, Hood Coll., Frederick, Md., 1983, Howard U., Washington, 1987, Judson Coll., Marion, Ala., 1988, Bennett Coll., Greensboro, NC, 1989, Smith Coll., 1989, Morehouse Sch. Medicine, 1989. First Lady of the US, Washington, 1989—93; oper. & facilities divsn. Dept. Administration, Washington, 1992. Author: C. Fred Story, 1984, Millie's Book, 1990, Barbara Bush: A Memoir, 1994, Reflections: Life After the White House, 2003. Hon. chair adv. bd. Reading is Fundamental; hon. mem. Bus. Coun. for Effective Literacy; mem. adv. coun. Soc. of Meml. Sloan-Kettering Cancer Ctr.; hon. mem. bd. dirs. Children's Oncology Svcs. of Met. Washington, The Washington Home, The Kingsbury Ctr.; hon. chmn. nat. adv. coun. Literacy Vols. of America, Nat. Sch. Vols. Program; sponsor Laubach Literacy Internat.; nat. hon. chmn. Leukemia Soc. of America; hon. mem. bd. trustees Morehouse Sch. of Medicine; hon. nat. chmn. Nat. Organ Donor Awareness Week, 1982-86; pres. Ladies of the Senate, 1981-88; mem. women's com. Smithsonian Assocs., Tex. Fedn. of Rep. Women, life mem., hon. mem.; hon. chairperson Nat. Com. on Literacy and Edn. United Way, Washington Parent Group Fund, Girls Clubs of America, 10th Anniversary Harvest Nat. Food Bank Network, Nat. Com. for the Prevention of Child Abuse, Childhelp USA, Leukemia Soc. Am., Children's Literacy Initiative, Read Am., Boarder Baby Project, Barbara Bush Found. for Family Literacy, 1989-, hon. mem.; hon. pres. Girl Scouts U.S; hon. chair Nat. Com. for Adoption; mem. bd. trustees Mayo Clinic Found.; mem. bd. visitors M. D. Anderson Cancer Ctr.; hon. mem. Reading is Fundamental; ambassador-at-large Americares. Recipient Nat. Outstanding Mother of Yr. award, 1984, Woman of Yr. award USO, 1986, Disting. Leadership award United Negro Coll. Fund 1986, Disting. Am. Woman award Mt. St. Joseph Coll., 1987, Free Spirit award Freedom Forum, 1995. Mem. Tex. Fedn. Republican Women (life), Internat. II Club (Washington), Magic Circle Rep. Women's Club (Houston), YWCA. Episcopalian. Avocations: reading, gardening, needlepoint.*

BUSH, GEORGE HERBERT WALKER, 41st President of the United States; b. Milton, Mass., June 12, 1924; s. Prescott Sheldon and Dorothy (Walker) B.; m. Barbara Pierce, Jan. 6, 1945; children: George Walker, Pauline Robinson (Robin) (dec. Oct. 11, 1953), John Ellis (Jeb), Neil Mallon, Marvin Pierce, Dorothy Walker BA in Economics, Yale U., 1948; LHD (hon.), U. NH, 2007. Co-founder Bush-Overbey Oil Devel. Co., 1951; co-founder, dir. Zapata Petroleum Corp., Midland, 1953-59; pres. Zapata Off Shore Co., Houston, 1956-64, chmn. bd., 1964-66; mem. US Congress from 7th Dist. Tex., 1967-71; US amb. to UN US Dept. State, NYC, 1971-73; chmn. Republican Nat. Com. (RNC), Washington, 1973-74; chief US Liaison Office, People's Republic of China US Dept. State, Peking, 1974—76; dir. CIA, Washington, 1976-77; chmn. First Internat. Bank, Houston, 1977—80; Vice Pres. of the US, 1981-89; Pres. of the US, 1989-93; sr. adv. Carlyle Group, 1998—2003. Adj. prof. adminstrv. sci. Rice U. Jones Sch. Bus., Houston, 1978; bd. visitors M.D. Anderson Cancer Ctr., Houston; chmn. Nat. Constitution Ctr., Phila., 2007—08. Co-author (with Victor Gold): Looking Forward, 1987; co-author: (with Brent Scowcroft) A World Transformed, 1998; author: All The Best, George Bush: My Life and Other Writings, 1999, All The Best, George Bush: My Life and Other Writings, revised edition, 2013; appeared in (documentaries) 41, 2012. Co-founder (with Bill Clinton), fundraiser Bush-Clinton Tsunami partnership, 2005—, Bush-Clinton Katrina Fund, 2005—; del. Republican Nat. Conv., San Francisco, 1964, Miami Beach, Fla., 1968; Republican candidate US Senate, Tex., 1964, 1970. Served in USN, 1942—45, WWII. Decorated Disting. Flying Cross, 3 Air medals; recipient Internat. Security Leadership award, 1993, Albert Schweitzer Gold Medal for Humanitarianism, 1997, George C. Marshall award, 2002, Dwight D. Eisenhower medal, 2003, Ronald Reagan Freedom award, 2007, Presdl. Medal of Freedom, The White House, 2010, 5,000th Daily Point of Light award, Points of Light Found., 2013, Profile in Courage award, John F. Kennedy Library Found., 2014; co-recipient Liberty medal, Nat. Constitution Ctr., 2006; named Man of Yr., TIME mag., 1990; named a Knight Comdr. of the British Empire (KBE), Her Majesty Queen Elizabeth II, 1993; named one of The 100 Most Influential People in the World, TIME mag., 2006. Fellow: American Acad. Arts & Sciences. Republican. Episcopalian. Office: 10000 Memorial Dr Ste 900 Houston TX 77024-3422*

BUSH, GEORGE WALKER, 43rd President of the United States; b. New Haven, July 6, 1946; s. George Herbert Walker and Barbara (Pierce) Bush; m. Laura Lane Welch, Nov. 5, 1977; children: Barbara, Jenna. BA in Hist., Yale U., 1968; MBA, Harvard Bus. Sch., 1975. Founder, CEO Arbusto Energy Inc., Midland, Tex., 1977—82, Bush Exploration (formerly Arbusto Energy Inc.), Midland, Tex., 1982—84; chmn. Spectrum 7 Energy Corp. (formerly Bush Exploration), Midland, Tex., 1984—86; bd. dirs. Harken Energy Corp. (formerly Spectrum 7 Energy Corp.), Midland, Tex., 1986—99; sr. adv. George Herbert Walker Bush Presidential Campaign, 1988; mng. gen. ptnr. Tex. Rangers, 1989—94; gov. State of Tex., Austin, 1994—2000; pres. US, Washington, 2001—09. Bd. dirs. Caterair Internat., Inc., 1990—94. Co-author (with Karen Hughes): A Charge to Keep, 1999; author: Decision Points, 2010 (#1 NY Times bestseller). Pilot Texas Air Nat. Guard, 1968—70. Recipient Big D award, Dallas All Sports Assn., 1989; named Person of Yr., TIME mag., 2004; named one of The 100 Most Influential People in the World, 2004, 2005, 2006, 2008, The 50 Highest-Earning Polit. Figures, Newsweek, 2010. Mem.: Delta Kappa Epsilon (pres. 1965—68). Republican. Methodist. Achievements include becoming the first governor in the history of Texas to be elected to two consecutive four-year terms.*

BUSH, JACK EUGENE, retail executive; b. Skidmore, Mo., Oct. 10, 1934; s. Harold Travis Bush and Aletha Virginia (Case) Quinn; m. Mary June Birbeck, June 28, 1953; children: Paula Annette, Tracy Lynn. Student, Air Force Inst., 1953-58; BS, U. Mo., 1958. Owner Bush Seed Co., King City, Mo., 1953-56; various mgmt. and exec. positions J.C. Penney Co., NYC, 1958-80; v.p. Zayre Corp., Framingham, Mass., 1980-85, Roses Stores, Henderson, N.C., 1985-86, sr. v.p., 1986, pres., chief operating officer, 1986—, also bd. dirs. Bd. dirs. YMCA, Henderson, 1986-88. Served to capt. USAF, 1953-58. Named Hon. Citizen, City of Memphis, 1982, State of Tenn., 1980, Hon. State Trooper, State of Ga., 1980, Lt. Col., Gov.'s Staff State of Ga., 1981; named to Hon. Order Ky. Cols. Mem. Internat. Mass Retailers Assn., Am. Mgmt. Assn., Nat. Retail Mgmt. Inst., Pres.'s. Assn., Beta Gamma Sigma. Clubs: Henderson Country, Ky. Cols. Republican. Avocations: art, writing, tennis. Home: 6222 Raintree Ct Dallas TX 75254-8602

BUSH, LAURA WELCH, former First Lady of the United States; b. Midland, Tex., Nov. 4, 1946; d. Harold Bruch and Jenna Louise (Hawkins) Welch; m. George Walker Bush, Nov. 5, 1977; children: Jenna, Barbara. BS in Edn., So. Meth. U., 1968; MLS, U. Tex., Austin, 1973. Tchr. Longfellow Elem. Sch., Dallas, 1968—69, John F. Kennedy Elem. Sch., Houston, 1969—72; libr. Houston Pub. Lib., 1973—74, Dawson Elem. Sch., Austin, 1974—77; First Lady State of Tex., 1995—2001; First Lady of the U.S., 2001—09. Established Adopt-A-Caseworker programs, Tex., Rainbow Rooms, Tex.; launched National Book Festival, 2001; speaker Republican Nat. Convention, NYC, 2004. Co-author (with Jenna Bush): (children's books) Read All About It!, 2008; author: (memoirs) Spoken from the Heart, 2010 (#1 NY Times bestseller). Vol. Hurricane Help for Schools. Recipient President's Crystal Apple award, American Assn. Sch. Librarians, 2006; named one of The 100 Most Powerful Women, Forbes mag., 2004—08. Republican.*

BUSH, NORMAN, research and development company executive; b. NYC, Dec. 10, 1929; s. Louis and Ida (Trembola) B.; m. Audrey Faith Blumberg, Dec. 28, 1952; children: Stewart Alan, I. Jeffrey, Ellen Gail Dash. BBA, CUNY, 1951, MBA, 1952; PhD, N.C. State U., 1962. Statistician Army Chem. Ctr., Edgewood, Md., 1952-56, RCA Svc. Co., Patrick AFB, Fla., 1956-58, DBA and ICF, Melbourne, Fla., 1962-64, Pan Am Airlines, Patrick AFB, Fla., 1964-72; div. mgr. ENSCO Inc., Melbourne, Fla., 1972-83, pres., chief oper. officer Springfield, Va., 1983-94, chmn. bd., 1989-95. Contbr. articles to statis. jours. With U.S. Army, 1952-54. Mem. Am. Statis. Assn. Republican. Avocation: travel.

BUSH, WESLEY G., aerospace transportation executive; b. 1961; BS in Elect. Engring., MIT, 1983, MSEE. With engrng. staff Serospace Corp.; corp. v.p., pres. space tech. Comsat Labs; from. sys. engr. to v.p., gen. mgr. telecomm. programs divsn. TRW Aero. Sys., 1987—99, pres., CEO, 2001—03; v.p., gen. mgr. TRW Ventures, 2000—01; pres., CEO, global aeronautical sys. TRW-United Kingdom, 2001—03; corp. v.p., pres. space tech. Northrop Grumman Corp., L.A., 2003—05, corp. v.p., CFO, 2005—06, pres., CFO, 2006—07, pres., COO, 2007—09, pres., CEO, 2010—. Bd. dirs. Northrop Grumman Corp., 2009—; mem. Nat. Infrastructure Advisory Coun., 2008—. Bd. dir. Nat. Action Coun. for Minorities in Engring.; bd. mem. Bus.-Higher Edn. Forum, Smithsonian Air & Space Mus.; bd mem. Conservation International. Office: Northrop Grumman Corp 2980 Fairview Park Dr Falls Church VA 22042-4511*

BUSH HAGER, JENNA (JENNA WELCH BUSH), language educator, writer, volunteer, former first daughter; b. Dallas, Nov. 25, 1981; d. George Walker and Laura (Welch) Bush; m. Henry Chase Hager, May 10, 2008; 1 child, Margaret Laura. BA in English, U. Tex., Austin, 2004. Spanish immersion instr. Elsie Whitlow Stokes Cmty. Freedom Pub. Charter Sch., Washington; edn. policy vol. UNICEF, Panama, 2006; reading coord.; correspondent The Today Show, NBC, 2009—; editor-at-large Southern Living Magazine, 2012—, contributor, Paper Napkin Interview column and blogger The Daily South, 2012—. Author: Ana's Story: A Journey of Hope, 2007; co-author (with Laura Bush): (children's books) Read All About It!, 2008; co-founder, co-blogger (blog site) The Novo Project. Mem.: Kappa Alpha Theta. Republican. Office: NBC News 4001 Nebraska Ave NW Washington DC 20016 also: Southern Living Magazine Attn: Editorial Offices 2100 Lakeshore Drive Birmingham AL 35209 Office Phone: 205-445-6000. Office Fax: 205-445-6700.*

BUSKEY, JAMES E., state legislator; b. Greenville, Ala., Apr. 10, 1937; m. Virgia Buskey. BS in Secondary Edn., Ala. State U., Montgomery; MA in Tchg. Math., U. NC, Chapel Hill; EdS, U. Colo., Boulder. Counselor, job developer CETA; asst. prin. Williamson HS; prin. ES Chastang Mid. Sch.; dir. Franklin Meml. Clinic; organizer Commonwealth Nat. Bank; mem. Dist. 99 Ala. House of Reps., Montgomery, 1976—; asst. prin. Toulmmville HS(LeFlore High). Mem. Ala. Dem. Conf., Aimwell Bapt. Ch. Mem.: Omega Psi Phi. Democrat. Baptist. Office: 104 S Lawrence St Mobile AL 36617 also: Ala House of Reps Ala State House 11 S Union St Rm 540-C Montgomery AL 36130 Office Phone: 251-208-5480, 334-242-7757. Business E-Mail: jamesebuskey@alhouse.org.

BUSMIRE, BRUCE W., corporate financial executive; BBA in Acctg., Lamar U.; MBA, Northwestern U. CPA. Various fin., aactg. & investor rels. positions Amoco Corp., mgr., exploration prodn. acctg.; contr. Altura Energy Ltd.; v.p., investor rels. Ocean Energy, 2000—04; mng. dir. Pickering Energy Ptnrs. Inc., 2004—05; v.p., sr. v.p., CFO, treas. & contr. Noble Corp., 2005—06; v.p., chief acctg. officer Anadarko Petroleum Corp., 2006—08, v.p., fin., treas., 2008—. Mem. Petroleum Investor Rels. Assn., Tex. Soc. of CPAs., Tex. Parent Tchrs. Assns., Fin. Execs. Inst., Nat. Investor Rels. Inst. Mem.: AICPA, FEI. Office: Anadarko Petroleum Corp 1201 Lake Robbins Dr The Woodlands TX 77380 Office Phone: 832-636-1000. Office Fax: 832-636-8220. Business E-Mail: Bruce.Busmire@anadarko.com.

BUSSMAN, PAUL DAVID, state legislator, dentist; b. New Orleans; m. Holly Bussman; children: Melissa Bussman, Phillip Bussman, Kendall Bussman, Noah Bussman. BS, Troy State U., Ala.; DDM, U. Ala. Dentist, Cullman, Ala., 1983—; owner FUNZONE, Cullman; exec. dir. Ala. Acad. Gen. Dentistry; mem. Dist. 4 Ala. State Senate, 2011—. Bd. dirs. Cullman Savs. Bank, Cullman Savs. Bank Found. Mem. Grace Episc. Ch., Cullman. Mem.: ADA, Acad. Gen. Dentistry. Republican. Episcopalian. Office: 1625 Main Ave SW Cullman AL 35055 also: Ala State Senate State House Rm 729 11 S Union St Montgomery AL 36130 Office Phone: 265-734-1700, 334-242-7855. Personal E-mail: p_bussman@bellsouth.net.

BUSTAMANTE, NESTOR, lawyer; b. Havana, Cuba, Apr. 20, 1960; came to the U.S., 1961; s. Nestor and Clara Rosa (Sanchez) B.; m. Marilyn Gonzalez, Sept. 20, 1986; children: Tiffany Alexandra, Nestor C. AA, U. Fla., 1980, BS in Journalism, 1982, JD, 1985. Bar: Fla. 1986, U.S. Dist. Ct. (so. dist.) Fla. 1989, U.S. Supreme Ct. 1991. Asst. state atty. State Atty.'s Office 11th Cir., Miami, 1986-88; juvenile serious offender prosecutor State Atty.'s Office, Miami, 1987-88, spl. prosecutor, gang prosecutor, 1987-88; asst. divsn. chief State Atty.'s Office-11th Jud. Cir., Miami, 1987-88; of counsel Fernandez-Caubi, Fernandez & Aguilar et al., Miami, 1988-89; atty. Ferencik, Libanoff, Brandt, Bustamante and Williams PA, Ft. Lauderdale, Fla., 1989—; ptnr. Ferencik, Libanoff, Brandt, Bustamante and Goldskin PA, Ft. Lauderdale, Fla., 1996—. Mem. code and rules of evidence com. The Fla. Bar, 1989—90, jud. evaluation com., 2000; chmn. Dade County Constrn. Trades Qualifying Bd.; adj. faculty dept. constrn. mgmt. Fla. Internat. U. Contbr. articles to newsletters. Chmn. Miami-Dade Constrn. Trades Qualifying Bd. Named Hon. mem. Quien es Quien Publs., Inc., N.Y.C., 1990, Fla. Super Lawyers, Best Lawyers in Am., Fla. Top Attorneys, Best Attorneys in Fla. Mem. ATLA (scoring judge nat. finals student trial advocacy competition 1994, 95), Fed. Bar Assn., Dade County Bar Assn. (mem. juvenile divsn. com. 1988-92, mem. media and pub. rels. com. 1989-91, mem. constrn. law com. 1990—), Phi Delta Phi, U. Fla. Alumni Assn. Office: Ferencik Libanoff Brandt Bustamante & Williams PA 150 S Pine Island Rd Ste 400 Fort Lauderdale FL 33324-2667 Office Phone: 305-949-8003. Business E-Mail: nbustamante@flbbwlaw.com.

BUSTER, JOHN EDMOND, obstetrician, researcher; b. Oxnard, Calif., July 18, 1941; s. Edmound B. and Beatrice (Keller) B. Student, Stanford U., 1959-62; MD, UCLA, 1966. Diplomate Am. Bd. Obstetrics and Gynecology. Intern Harbor UCLA Med. Ctr., Torrance, Calif., 1966-67, resident, 1967-71, rsch. fellow, 1971-73, faculty, 1975—; prof. ob-gyn. UCLA Sch. Medicine, 1983, U. Tenn., Memphis, 1987-94; prof. ob-gyn., dir. divsn. reproductive endocrinology Baylor Coll. Medicine, Houston, 1994—; div. divsn. reproductive endocrinology UCLA Sch. Medicine. Examiner Am. Bd. Ob-Gyn. Contbr. articles to profl. jours. Served to lt. col. U.S. Army, 1973-75. Fellow: Am. Coll. Obstetricians and Gynecologists; mem.: Soc. Reproductive Endocrinologists, Am. Gynecol. and Obstet. Soc., Am. Soc. Reproductive Medicine, Soc. Gynecologic Investigation, Endocrine Soc. Presbyterian. Home: 1709 Dryden Rd Ste 1100 Houston TX 77030-2414 also: 3030 Post Oak Blvd Houston TX 77030

BUSWELL, ARTHUR WILCOX, physician, surgeon; b. Oklahoma City, Jan. 6, 1926; s. Albert Currier and Enid May (Scott) Buswell; m. Loleta JoAnn Sherrill, June 11, 1950; children: Arthur Lee, Robert Joseph, Barbara JoAnn, Brian A., Gayla, Richard; m. Jane Marie Fuksa, Mar. 1, 1969. BS in Medicine, U. Okla., 1950, MD, 1952; AA in Med. Svcs., U.S. Army, 1963, student, 1963, Army Command and Gen. Staff Coll., 1966; postgrad., U. So. Calif., 1969. Intern Fitzsimons Army Hosp., Aurora, Colo., 1952—53; surg. resident Wesley Hosp., Oklahoma City, 1954—55; practice medicine and surgery Hennessey, Okla., 1955—63; dep. surgeon Ft. Wainwright and Yukon Command, 1963—65; chief staff Kingfisher Cmty. Hosp., 1956—57; supt. health Kingfisher County, 1960—61; chief profl. svc. Bassett Army Hosp., 1963—65; div. surgeon 1st Armored Div., Ft. Hood, Tex., 1965—67; 1st Inf. Div. Vietnam, 1967—68; med. project officer U.S. Army Combat Devels. Command Experimentation Command, Ft. Ord, Calif., 1968—72; also chief human factors div. and chief experimentation div. of experimentation command; chief profl. svcs. Reynolds Army Hosp., Ft. Sill, Okla., 1972—73; comdr. med. dept. activities Ft. Stewart, Ga., 1973—77; chief profl. svcs. Kenner Army Hosp., Ft. Lee, Va., 1977—78; comdr. med. dept. activities Alaska, 1979—83. Adj. asst. prof. med. scis. Baylor U., 1973—. Mem. Kingfisher Meml. Libr. Bd.; pres. Ft. Stewart Sch. Bd., 1977; bd. dirs. Ft. Stewart Fed. Credit Union, 1977, Chisholm Trail Mus., 1986—, Friends of Librs. in Okla., 1987—; pres. Friends of Libr. for Kingfisher County, 1984—88. With AUS, 1944—46, 1st lt. US Army, 1952—54, maj. to col. US Army, 1961—83. Decorated Legion of Merit with 2 oak leaf clusters, Soldier's medal, Bronze Star for Valor with oak leaf cluster, Meritorious Service medal, Air medal with 3 oak leaf clusters, Army Commendation medal, Gallantry cross with palm, Honor medal 1st class (both Vietnam); named Citizen of Yr., Kingfisher C. of C., 1988; named to Kingfisher H.S. Hall of Fame, 1987. Fellow: Royal Soc. Health; mem.: AMA, Garfield-Kingfisher County Med. Soc., Assn. Mil. Surgeons U.S., Army Aviation Med. Assn., Aerospace Med. Assn., Okla. State Med. Assn. Home: PO Box 703 Kingfisher OK 73750-0703

BUTCHER, DANIEL L., lawyer; BS cum laude, U. Denver, 1981; JD with honors, U. Tex., 1984; LLM in Taxation, So. Meth. U., Dallas, 1989. Bar: Tex. Ptnr. Strasburger & Price, LLP, Dallas, former chief operating ptnr., mng. ptnr. of firm, 2005—. Contbr. articles to profl. jours. Former gen. counsel. US-Mex. C. of C. Southwestern Chpt. Named one of The Best Lawyers in America, 2005—10; named to Tex. Super Lawyers, Tex. Monthly Mag., 2003—08. Mem.: State Bar Tex. Tax Sect. (chmn. corp. tax com. 1991—93, chmn. state tax com. 1992—94). Office: Strasburger & Price LLP 901 Main St Ste 4400 Dallas TX 75202-3794 Office Phone: 214-651-4640. Office Fax: 214-659-4054. Business E-Mail: dan.butcher@strasburger.com.

BUTCHER, GREG, state legislator; b. Logan, W.Va., May 11, 1952; s. Namon, Ethel Mae Hanna; married; 1 child, Gregory A. Mem. W.Va. House of Delegates, 1996—2004, mem. Dist. 19, 2008—, mem. Energy, Industry and Labor/Econ. Devel. and Small Bus. Com., Govt. Orgn. Com., Roads and Transp. Com. & Sr. Citizen Issues Com. Democrat. Baptist. Office: Rm 219E, Bldg 1 Charleston WV 25305 Mailing: HC 74, Box 3220 Chapmanville WV 25508 Home Phone: 304-573-9918; Office Phone: 304-340-3113. E-mail: gbutcher@mail.wvnet.edu.

BUTCHER, HARRY WILLIAM, workplace learning development executive, educator, writer, teacher; b. Frederick, Okla., May 15, 1948; s. Harry William Hobbs and Alice Marie (Brownrigg) Butcher Able; m. Susan Mary Howell, Nov. 11, 2000; children: Jonathan Hobbs Butcher, Megan Butcher George. BS in Communication, Okla. State U., Stillwater, 1971; postgrad., Okla. State U., 1971; postgrad. in Bus., Southern Meth. U., Dallas, 1999; postgrad. in History, U. Tex., Arlington, 2002. Cert. tchr. U. Tex., Arlington, 2002. Investigator to C level officer Pinkerton Security Investigations, Baton Rouge, New Orleans, Houston, Memphis, San Antonio NYC, LA, Ft. Worth, Oklahoma City, 1971—2000; founder, exec. dir. Ctr. Edn., 2000—; tchr. Ft. Worth Ind. Sch. Dist., 2000—04; chair Ft. Worth Cmty. Devel. Coun., 2009—. Cons. Ft. Worth Police Dept., Crime Ctr. Prevention Dist.; staff vol. FWISD Pub. Engagement Group; dir. Mere Anglicanism" Spkr. Series; bd. mem. Brotherhood St. Andrew. Recipient Minot Dodson Outstanding Leadership award, 1997. Mem. Am. Mgmt. Assn. (pres.'s assn.), Pinkerton Pres. Club NYC, Tex. Hist. Soc., Okla. Hist. Soc., Golden Key Soc., Ft. Worth Episcopal Diocesan Youth Com., Phi Alpha Theta History Frat., Pi Kappa Phi Social Frat. Conservative. Anglican. Avocations: gardening, historical studies, collectables. Office Phone: 817-994-9169. Personal E-mail: butcherhw@aol.com.

BUTCHER, RICHARD O., II, sports association administrator, former legislative staff member; BA in Sociology, Harvard U., 1988; MBA, Georgetown U. McDonough Sch. Bus., 2005. Dir. DNA synthesis facility Salk Inst. Biol. Studies, La Jolla, Calif., 1989—94; asst. coach women's basketball U. Calif., Irvine, 1994—95; HS tchr. San Diego County Sch. Dist., 1995—97; asst. coach Australian Women's Nat. Basketball League, 1997—2000; attache to amb. Federated States of Micronesia US Dept. State, 2000—01; legis. corr. Office US Rep. Diane Watson, Washington, 2001, legis. asst., 2001—06, chief of staff, 2007—09; v.p. sports internat. govt. rels. (SIG) Atlanta Dekalb Internat. Training Ctr., 2009—. Office: Atlanta Dekalb International Training Center 4770 N Peachtree Rd Atlanta GA 30338

BUTHMAN, MARK A., corporate financial executive; m. Tammy Buthman; 3 children. BA in Fin., U. Iowa, 1982. Fin. assoc., corp. acctg. and procedures and controls Kimberly-Clark Corp., Neenah, Wis., 1982, cost analyst Memphis, 1983, project analyst, sr. strategic analyst, dir. corp. strategic analysis Neenah, Wis., 1984—95, v.p. strategic planning and analysis Dallas, 1997—2002, v.p. fin. Irving, Tex., 2002—03, sr. v.p., CFO, 2003—. Office: Kimberly-Clark Corp PO Box 619100 Dallas TX 75261-9100 Office Phone: 972-281-1200. Business E-Mail: mbuthman@kcc.com.

BUTHOD, MARY CLARE, school superintendent; b. Tulsa, Aug. 20, 1945; d. Arthur Paul and Mary Rudelle (Dougherty) B. MA in Teaching, Tulsa U., 1969; M Christian Spirituality, Creighton U., 1981. Joined Order of St. Benedict. Asst. tchr. HeadStart, Tulsa, 1966; tchr. Madalene Parish Sch., Tulsa, 1968-69, Monte Cassino Pvt. Sch., Tulsa, 1969-79; prin. Monte Cassino Elem. Sch., Tulsa, 1979-86; dir. Monte Cassino Sch., Tulsa, 1986—2010. Mem. convent coun. Benedictine Sisters, Tulsa, 1975-88, dir. formation programs, 1983—; examiner Okla. Quality Found., 2004. Active State Congl. Ednl. Com., Tulsa, 1989-90; co-chair for edn. and human devel. Tulsa Coalition Against Illegal Use of Drugs, 1990-91; adv. com. Okla. State Schs. Attuned, 2002—, Tulsa Pub. Sch. Quality Bd., 2005-06; adv. bd. Ret. Sr. Vol. Program, 2004—; min. Stand in the Gap, 2010-. Recognized for Excellence in Edn. U.S. Dept. Edn., 1993-94; Innovator of Yr., Jour. Recosol, 2007, Pinnacle Edn. award, 2010, Spl. Recognition award, Cath. Diocese St. Clare of Assisi, 2010; named Tulsa Person, Tulsa People, 2007, Woman of Yr., 2008; Jour. Record Woman of Yr., 2010. Mem. Tulsa Reading Coun. (sec. 1975-77), Nat. Cath. Edn. Assn., Advance Ed Quality Assurance (review chair 2008), Delta Kappa Gamma. Home: 2200 S Lewis Tulsa OK 74114-3117 Office Phone: 918-585-6112. Personal E-mail: sistermaryclarebc@gmail.com.

BUTLER, ALBERT, state legislator; m. Malinda Boyd; children: Shelia A. Morgan, Antoinette R. Gant, Albert Jr., Alton D. Student, Alcorn State U., Jackson State U., U. Ark., Conway. Academic mgr. Miss. Job Corp.; mem. Dist. 36 Miss. State Senate, 2010—, mem. appropriations com., constn. com., drug policy com., ethics com., forestry com., judiciary B com., labor com., oil, gas and other minerals com. Mem.: NAACP (life), Jackson State U. Alumni Assn., Alcorn State U. Alumni Assn. Democrat. Mailing: PO Box 614 Port Gibson MS 39150 Office: State Capitol PO Box 1018 Jackson MS 39215 Home Phone: 601-437-4089; Office Phone: 601-892-3348. Office Fax: 601-892-1250. E-mail: abutler@senate.ms.gov.

BUTLER, AMANDA, women's college basketball coach; d. Stephen and Barbara Butler. BS in Exercise and Sports Sci. with honors, U. Fla., Gainesville, 1995; M in Exercise and Sports Sci., U. Fla., 1997. Asst. coach U. Fla. Gators, 1995—97, head coach, 2007—; asst. coach Austin Peay State U. Lady Governors, Tenn., 1997—2001, U. NC Charlotte 49ers, 2001—03, assoc. head coach, 2003—05, head coach, 2005—07. Named Coach of Yr., Atlantic 10 Conf., 2006. Office: c/o Univ Athletic Assn Univ Fla PO Box 14485 Gainesville FL 32604

BUTLER, CHARLES RANDOLPH, JR., federal judge; b. NYC, Mar. 28, 1940; BA, Washington and Lee U., 1962; LLB, U. Ala., 1966. Assoc. Hamilton Butler Riddick and LaTour, Mobile, Ala., 1966-69; asst. pub. defender Mobile County, 1969-70, dist. atty., 1971-75; ptnr. Butler and Sullivan, Mobile, 1975-84, Hamilton Butler Riddick Tarlton and Sullivan P.C., Mobile, 1984-88; judge US Dist. Ct. (so. dist.) Ala., Mobile, 1988—94, 2003—05, chief judge, 1994—2003, sr. judge, 2005—. Adj. prof. criminal justice program U. So. Ala., 1972-76; mem. jud. coun. 11th cir., 1994-2003, jud. conf. com. on criminal law, 1993-99, jud. conf. com., 1999-2002; past liaison mem. to long-range planning com. of the AO; past mem. program and adminstrn. subcom., planning for the future and automation subcom., probaton and pretrial umbrella group; mem. exec. com. Jud. Conf. of U.S., 1999-2002. 1st lt. USAR, 1962-64. Recipient Jud. award of merit Ala. State Bar, 2003; named One of Outstanding Young Men of Am., Mobile County Jaycees, 1971. Office: US Dist Ct So Dist Ala 113 Saint Joseph St Mobile AL 36602-3683 Office Phone: 251-690-2175.

BUTLER, DAVID, museum director; BA in Art History magna cum laude, Fla. State U., 1976, MA in Art History, 1980; PhD, Wash. State U., 1991. Curatorial asst. John and Mable Ringling Mus. Art, Sarasota, Fla., 1978—79; edn. coord., registrar Mus. Art and Archeology, U. Mo., Columbia, 1980—84, asst. dir., 1984—86; asst. project coord. St. Louis Arts in Transit, Metrolink Light Rail, 1987—88; art history instr. U. Mo., St. Louis, 1988—91; dir. Emerson Gallery, Hamilton Coll., Clinton, NY, 1992—95, Swope Art Mus., Terre Haute, Ind., 1995—2000, Ulrich Mus. Art, Wichita State U., Kans., 2000—06; exec. dir. Knoxville Mus. Art, 2006—. Art history instr. Wash. U., St. Louis, 1987—92. Contbr. articles to profl. publs. Sec. Friends of Hist. Allen Chapel, 1997—2000; design com. co-chair Downtown Terre Haute, 1999—2000; mem. design coun. City of Wichita, 2003—06; bd. dirs. Trees, Inc., 1996—2000. Mem.: Arts Illiana (v.p. 1995—2000), Assn. Coll. and Univ. Mus. and Galleries (bd. sec. 2000—05), Am. Assn. Mus. Office: Knoxville Mus Art 1050 Worlds Fair Pk Dr Knoxville TN 37916 Office Phone: 865-525-6101 ext. 244. Office Fax: 865-546-3635. Business E-Mail: dbutler@kmaonline.org.

BUTLER, DONALD PHILIP, educator; s. Clifton Aubrey and Helen Eunice (Roy) B.; m. Zeynep Celik, Aug. 23, 1986; children: Melissa, Susan. BS in Engring. Sci., Physics Option, U. Toronto, 1980; MS in Elec. Engring., U. Rochester, NY, 1981, PhD in Elec. Engring., 1986. Prof. So. Meth. U., Dallas, 1987—2002, U. Tex., Arlington, 2002—. Prof., elec. engring.; disting. lectr. Electron Device Soc.; topical editor Applied Optics, Optical Tech. & Biomed. Optics, 2003—09. Contbr. articles to Applied Physics Letters, Jour. Applied Physics, others. Mem. IEEE (sec.-treas. Dallas chpt. electron device soc. 1984—), Am. Phys. Soc. Achievements include investigation of nonequilibrium properties of superconductors, observing dynamic intermediate state, transient magnetic superheating and phase-slip, microbridge mixers, uncooled infrared detectors MEMS sensors; patents. Office: University Tex Arlington 500 S Cooper St Arlington TX 76019 Business E-Mail: dbutler@uta.edu.

BUTLER, DWIGHT D., state legislator; b. Nov. 21, 1963; Auctioneer farmer; mem. Dist. 18 Ky. House of Reps., 1995—; mem. Agr. & Natural Resources Coms., Appropriations & Revenue, Energy Coms., State Govt. Coms. Mem.: Nat. Rifle Assn., Ky. Cattlemens Assn., Ky. Auctioneers Assn. Republican. Baptist. Mailing: PO Box 9 Harned KY 40144 Office: Capitol Annex Rm 405D Frankfort KY 40601 Home Phone: 270-756-0100; Office Phone: 270-756-5931, 502-564-8100 ext. 640. Business E-Mail: butlerdd@bbtel.com.

BUTLER, GLORIA S., state legislator; b. Daytona Beach, Fla., Dec. 25, 1941; c Felicia & Leslie, two grandchildren. BA, Perimeter Coll., 1984. Acctg. asst. Emory Univ., 1981—93; legis. asst. Congresswoman Cynthia McKinney, 1993—95; asst. to dir. AmeriCorps Team for Nat. Svc., 1996; exec. asst. DeKalb County Sheriff's Office, 1997—99; mem. Dist. 55 Ga. State Senate, 1999—. Nat Coun Negro Women; Nat Organization Women; DeKalb Women's Polit Caucus; gov member Nat Women's Polit Caucus; DeKalb Co Nat Association Advan Colored People (life, exec. bd. mem.), South DeKalb Bus. Assn. (bd. mem.), The World C. of C. (bd. mem.). Democrat. Baptist. Mailing: 420-C State Capitol Atlanta GA 30334 Office Phone: 404-656-0075. Business E-Mail: gloria.butler@senate.ga.gov.

BUTLER, HENRY NOLDE, law and business educator; b. Roanoke, Va., Feb. 16, 1954; s. Manley Caldwell and June Parker (Nolde) B.; m. Mary Graham Cravens, Aug. 22, 1982; children: Sarah Elizabeth, Andrew Graham, Henry Adams. BA, U. Richmond, 1977; MA, Va. Tech., 1979; JD, U. Miami, Coral Gables, Fla., 1982; PhD, Va. Tech., 1982. John M. Olin fellow Sch. Law U. Miami, Coral Gables, 1979-82; asst. prof. dept. mgmt. Tex. A&M Univ., College Station, 1982-86; John M. Olin fellow Law Sch. U. Chgo., 1985-86; asst. prof. Sch. Law George Mason U., Arlington, Va., 1986-88, assoc. prof. Sch. Law, 1988-90, prof. Sch. Law, 1990-93, assoc. dean Sch. Law, 1989-91, dir. law and economics ctr., 1989-91, prof. law, exec. dir. law & economics ctr., 2010—; Koch disting. teaching prof. law and econs. U. Kans., Lawrence, 1993—2001; Farley prof. economics Chapman U., Orange, Calif., 2001, dean George L. Argyros Sch. Bus. and Economics, 2001; exec. dir. Searle Ctr. on Law, Regulation, and Economic Growth Northwestern U. Sch. Law. Republican. Episcopalian. Office: Sch Law George Mason U 3301 Fairfax Dr Arlington VA 22201

BUTLER, JAY C., epidemiologist, former public health service officer; MD, U. NC, Chapel Hill, 1985. Med. epidemiologist Ctr. Disease Control and Prevention, Atlanta; dir. CDC Arctic Investigations Program, Alaska, 1998—2005; state epidemiologist Alaska Dept. Health and Social Services, 2005—07, dep. dir. sci. and medicine Divsn. Pub. Health, 2006—07, dir. Divsn. Pub. Health, 2007, chief med. officer, 2007—09; program dir. Divsn. Emerging Infections and Surveillance Services Nat. Ctr. for Preparedness, Detection and Control of Infectious Diseases, Centers for Disease Control and Prevention (CDC), Altanta, 2009—. Spkr. in field. Office: Centers for Disease Control and Prevention 1600 Clifton Rd Atlanta GA 30333 Office Phone: 907-465-3092. Office Fax: 907-586-1877. Business E-Mail: jay.butler@alaska.gov.

BUTLER, KELVIN E., state legislator; b. Apr. 8, 1956; children: Kelvin Jr., Kendric, Destiny. Employee Delphi Packard Elec. Sys.; mem. Dist. 38 Miss. State Senate, 2004—. Mem.: IUE, Mason. Democrat. Baptist. Office: PO Box 1018 Jackson MS 39215 Mailing: 2018 Hawthorne Dr Mccomb MS 39648 Home Phone: 601-783-2706; Office Phone: 601-783-2706, 601-359-3244. Fax: 601-783-3668; Office Fax: 601-359-9210. E-mail: kbutler@senate.ms.gov.

BUTLER, MICHAEL WARD, economics professor; b. Great Bend, Kans., June 11, 1939; s. George Ward and Mary Jane (Lambert) B.; m. Regina Ann Hammond, Sept. 8, 1995; 1 child, Alexander Ward. BSBA, Fort Hays State U., 1963, MS in Econs., 1964; PhD in Econs., U. Ark., 1974. Diplomate Am. Bd. Forensic Examiners. Data processing sales rep. IBM, Wichita, Kans., 1964-66; instr. econs. Butler County C.C., El Dorado, Kans., 1966—70; asst. prof. econs. U. North Ala., Florence, 1973-75, assoc. prof. econs., 1975-78, prof. econs., 1978-97, dean coll. bus., 1997-2001; dean Coll. Bus. and Profl. Studies, Angelo State U., San Angelo, Tex., 2001—06, prof. economics, 2006—. Referee Jour. Forensic Econs., Kansas City, Mo., 1988-2005; editl. adv. Ark. Bus. Econs. Rev., Fayetteville, Ark., 1976-99; editl. bd. Am. Bd. of Forensic Examiners, Springfield, Mo., 1995-98; mem. mgmt. adv. com. Wise Alloys, L.L.C., 1999-2001; pres. Region 3, Assn. of Collegiate Bus. Schs. and Programs, 1999-2000; bd. dirs. Wells Fargo Cmty. Bank; chmn. Concho Valley Ctr. for Entrepreneurship; mem. adv. bd. South-West Tex. SBDC, 2004-06; bd. trustees San Angelo Cmty. Med. Ctr., 2006. Editor: Jour. Legal Econs., 1991—2005. Bd. govs. Soc. Litig. Economists, 2000-02. Recipient Outstanding Achievement award Am. Higher Ed., 1985; Disting. Svc. award Ala. C. of C., Montgomery, 1976. Mem. Assn. Collegiate Bus. Schs. and Programs (pres. region 3 1999-2000), Nat. Assn. Forensic Economists, Am. Assn. Wine Economists, Am. Rehab. Econs. Assoc. (adv. bd. 1992-94), MidSouth Acad. Econs. and Fin. (pres. 85-86), Am. Acad. Econ. Fin. Experts (pres. 1994-96, svc. award 1995), Am. Econs. Assn., San Angelo C. of C. Avocations: wine collecting, boating. Home: 3101 Clearview Dr San Angelo TX 76904 Business E-Mail: michael.butler@angelo.edu.

BUTLER, PATRICK HAROLD, media executive; b. Hartselle, Ala., Oct. 25, 1949; s. Arthur L. and Christine (Stewart) B.; m. Donna Therese Norton, Sept. 10, 1977; children: Katharine, Anna, Sydney. Student, U. Tenn., 1967-69, 74, Am. U., 1993, MA in Comm., 1996; postgrad. Cert. in Fin. and Acctg., U. Pa., 1997. Reporter Chattanooga Times, 1968-69; asst. dir. pub. info. Appalachian Regional Commn., Washington, 1969-70; press sec. U.S. Rep. Wilmer D. Mizell, Washington, 1970-75; speechwriter to Pres. The White House, Washington, 1975-77; dir. corp. pub. relations Bristol-Myers Co., NYC, 1978; spl. asst. U.S. Sen. Rep. leader, Washington, 1978-80; staff v.p. RCA Corp., NYC and Washington, 1980-82; pres. Patrick Butler and Co., Washington, 1982-85; v.p. Times Mirror, Washington, 1985-91, Washington Post Co., 1991—2008; founder and pres. Newsweek Productions, Inc., 1997—2008; pres., CEO Assoc. Pub. TV Stas., 2011—. Cons. to chief of staff The White House, 1987 Mem. Nat. Coun. on Humanities, 1988-94, chmn. pub. programs com.; vice chmn. bd. trustees Am. U. Found. Nat. Archives, Pew Rsch. Ctr., Children's Charities Found.; mem., Bd. Coll. Success Program; chmn. emeritus Md. Pub. Television Found., chmn., dean's coun. Sch. Comm. Am. U. Mem. Kenwood Club. Avocation: golf. Office: Assoc Pub TV Stations 2100 Crystal Dr Arlington VA 22202 Business E-Mail: pbutler@apts.org.

BUTLER, PAUL BASCOMB, JR., lawyer; b. Charleston, SC, Nov. 27, 1947; s. Paul B. and Mary Anna (Tisdale) B.; m. Virginia Eldridge, June 14, 1969; children: Jeffrey Bryan, Robert Paul. BA, Emory U., 1969, MDiv cum laude, 1972, JD with distinction, 1976. Bar: Ga. 1976, Fla. 1977, cert.: Fla. Supreme Ct. (mediator); ordained to ministry United Meth. Ch., 1970. United Meth. Ch., 1970—; assoc. min. First United Meth. Ch., Phoenix, 1972-73; assoc. Swift, Currie, McGhee and Hiers, Atlanta, 1976-79; ptnr. Butler Pappas, Tampa, Fla., 1979-97, founder/of counsel, 1998—; cert. mediator Fla. Supreme Ct., 2002—; pres., chmn. Faces In Need, Inc., 2012—. Chancellor Fla. Ann. Conf. United Meth. Ch., 1997—. Contbr. articles to profl. jours. Chair com. on new church devel. Fla. annual conf. United Meth. Ch., 1996-2000, chair bd. missions and ch. ext. Tampa dist. United Meth. Ch., Inc., 1992-96; pastor Temple Terrace United Meth., Tampa, 1998-2000, sr. pastor, 2000-02; vision pastor Tampa Dist. United Meth. Ch., 2002-03; exec. pastor Van Dyke United Meth. Ch., 2004; bd. dirs. United Meth. Ch. Found., 1999-2000. Mem. ABA (chmn. Nat. Inst. sect. of trial tort and ins. practice 1987-89, ho. of dels. 1993-95, coun. mem. sect. of trial tort and ins. practice 1990-93, chmn. task force on civil justice reform, chmn. property ins. law com. 1985-86, editor So. Region Annotated Homeowner's Policy), Fedn. of Def. and Corp. Counsel (dean Litigation Mgmt. Coll. 1996-98, chair litigation mgmt. coll. adv. coun. 1998-2000, bd. deans 2000-02, vice chair 2005-06), Def. Rsch. Inst. (chmn. ins. law com. 1989-92, chmn. Amicus com. 1994-97, bd. dirs. 1995-98, vice chair law inst. 1998-99, chair law inst. 1999-2001, immediate past chair 2001-03), Fla. Def. Lawyers Assn., Hillsborough County Bar Assn., Internat. Assn. Def. Counsel (vice chair property ins. com. 1993-96), Assn. Def. Trial Attys. Clubs: Temple Terr. (Fla.) Golf and Country, HIV/AIDS Ministry (chair), St. James United Methodist, Maggie Valley Club. Democrat. Avocations: golf, tennis. Office: Butler Pappas One Harbour Pl Ste 500 777 South Harbour Island Blvd Tampa FL 33602 Home Phone: 813-988-5870; Office Phone: 813-281-1900. Business E-Mail: pbutler@butlerpappas.com.

BUTLER, ROBERT CLIFTON, retired construction executive; b. Newark, Aug. 29, 1930; s. Thomas C. and Helen V. (Woods) B.; m. Eileen Hudson, Apr. 14, 1956; children: Christopher R., John H., Thomas C. BS, U. Notre Dame, 1952; MBA, U. Pa., 1956. Dir., planning Gen. Tele. & Electronics Internat., 1955-66; v.p., treas. Isotopes Inc., 1966-67; sr. v.p., contr. Inmont Corp., 1967-72; v.p., fin. analysis RCA, 1972-76, v.p., contr., 1976-79; exec. v.p., fin. NBC, 1979-84, group exec. v.p., 1984-87; sr. v.p., CFO International Paper Co., 1988-95, Celgene Corp., Warren, NJ, 1996—98. Bd. dirs. Studio One Networks, Inc., Hanley & Assocs., NVR, Inc., 2002—. Served with AUS, 1954-55. Home: 146 Rensselaer Rd Essex Fells NJ 07021-1307 Office: NVR Inc Bd Directors Plz America Tower I 11700 Plz America Dr Reston VA 20190 Office Phone: 703-956-4000. Office Fax: 703-956-4750. Business E-Mail: robert.butler@nvrinc.com.

BUTLER, ROBERT OLEN, writer, educator; b. Granite City, Ill., Jan. 20, 1945; s. Robert Olen Sr. and Lucille Frances (Hall) B.; m. Carol Supplee, Aug. 10, 1968 (div. Jan. 1972); m. Marylin Geller, July 1, 1972 (div. July 1987); 1 child, Joshua Robert; m. Maureen Donlan, July 21, 1987 (div. Mar. 1995); m. Elizabeth Dewberry, Apr. 23, 1995 (div. 2007); m. Kelly Lee Daniels, June 19, 2012 BS summa cum laude in Oral Interpretation, Northwestern U., 1967; MA in Playwriting, U. Iowa, 1969; postgrad., New Sch. Social Rsch., 1979-81; LHD, McNeese State U., 1994; LHD (hon.), SUNY. Editor-in-chief Energy User News, NYC, 1975-85; assoc. prof. fiction writing McNeese State U., Lake Charles, La., 1985—93, prof., 1993—2001; Francis Epps prof. Fla. State U., 2001—, Michael Shaara Chair in Creative Writing. Summer faculty Iowa Summer Writing Festival U. Iowa, Port Townsend (Wash.) Writers Conf., New Orleans Writers' Conf., Southampton Writers' Conf., Long Island U., N.Y., Hofstra U. Summer Writing Conf., Hempstead, N.Y., others, 1988-, McNeese State U., 1985-2000. Author: The Alleys of Eden, 1981 (also wrote screenplay 1991-92), Sun Dogs, 1982, Countrymen of Bones, 1983, Fragments, 1984, On Distant Ground, 1985, Wabash, 1987, The Deuce, 1989, They Whisper, 1994, The Deep Green Sea, 1997, Mr. Spaceman, 2000, Fair Warning, 2002, Hell, 2009, A Small Hotel, 2011, The Hot Country, 2012; (non-fiction) From Where You Dream: The Process of Writing Fiction, 2005; (short story collection) A Good Scent from a Strange Mountain, 1992 (The Southern Review/La. State U. prize for Short Fiction, 1992, Citation for Notable Book for 1993, Notable Books Coun. of the ALA, 1993, Pulitzer Prize for fiction 1993, Richard and Hinda Rosenthal Found. award Am. Acad. Arts & Letters 1993, nominee PEN/Faulkner award 1993, Notable Book 1993 Notable Books Coun. Am. Libr. Assn.), Tabloid Dreams, 1996, Had a Good Time: Stories from American Postcards, 2004, Severance, 2006, Intercourse, 2008, Weegee Stories, 2010; contbr. articles, book reviews to jours., newspapers, screenplays; works translated to 12 langs. Sgt. U.S. Army, 1969-72, Vietnam; mayor of Capps, Fla. Recipient Charter Recipient TuDo Chinh Kien award outstanding contbns. to Am. culture by Vietnam Vet. Vietnam Vets. Am., 1987, Emily Clark Balch award for the best work of fiction to appear in the Virginia Quarterly Review in 1990, 1991, Medal of Merit, Lotos Club, 1996, Nat. Mag. award in Fiction for short story The One in White, 2005; grantee NEA, 1994; fellow John Simon Guggenheim Found., 1993. Mem. PEN, WGAWest. Office: English Dept Fla State U 411 Williams Bldg Tallahassee FL 32306-1580 E-mail: rbutler@english.fsu.edu.

BUTLER, WILLIAM THOMAS, academic administrator, physician, educator; b. Boston, Aug. 10, 1932; s. Albert Quigg and Elizabeth West (Visknisski) B.; m. Marilou Beutel, Apr. 26, 1957; children: Marilyn West, Thomas Charles, Robin Eileen; m. Carol Ann Pike, Nov. 23, 1977. AB, Oberlin Coll., 1954; MD, Western Res. U., 1958; grad. program for health systems mgmt., Harvard U., 1974, A.M.P., 1979. Intern and asst. resident in internal medicine Mass. Gen. Hosp., Boston, 1958—61, clin. fellow in medicine, 1960—61, resident in internal medicine, 1964—65; rsch. fellow in bacteriology and immunology Harvard Med. Sch., 1960—61; clin. assoc. Lab. Clin. Investigations, Nat. Inst. Allergy and Infectious Diseases, NIH, Bethesda, Md., 1961—62, chief clin. assoc., 1962—63, clin. investigator, 1963—64, acting head clin. immunology sect., 1965—66; asst. prof. Baylor Coll. Medicine, Houston, 1966—68, assoc. prof., 1968—71, prof. microbiology and immunology, prof. internal medicine, 1971—2001, prof. immunology, 2001—, assoc. dean, 1973—74, dean admissions, 1974—77, acting exec. v.p., 1976—77, exec. v.p., dean, 1977—79, pres., 1979—96, chancellor, 1996—2004, chancellor emeritus, 2004—08, 2010—; interim pres. CEO Baylor Coll. Medicine, 2008—10. Mem. spl. med. adv. group VA, 1981-91, chmn., 1984-91; bd. dirs. Lyondell Chem. Co., chmn. bd., 1997-2007; mem. Am. Quality and Productivity Ctr., 1991-2004, chmn. S.W. CEO Coun., 1997-98, mem., 1994—2004. Mem. forward planning com. Tex. Med. Ctr., 1981-96; bd. dirs. South Main Ctr. Assn., exec. com., 1980-94, chmn., 1989-91, coun. advisors, 1994—2004; past assoc. chmn. key group United Way Campaign, Flagship Divsn., group chmn., 1990; mem. Houston Econ. Summit Host Com., 1990; bd. dirs. Blvd. Oaks Civic Assn., 1982-85, Sci. Engring. Fair of Houston, 1985—2005, United Way Tex. Gulf Coast, trustee, 1993-99, exec. com. 1998-99; nat. bd. dirs. Points of Light Found., 1995-2004; mem. coordinating bd. Tex. Coll. and Univ. System, Health Professions Edn. Adv. Com., 1984-95, chmn., 1988-95, rsch. adv. com., 1987-90; mem. The Houston Forum, 1981—2004, bd. govs., 1983-92, 1996-2004; mem. Tex. Sesquicentennial Celebration Com., 1984-86; mem. bd. edn. blue ribbon com. Houston Ind. Sch. Dist., 1986; adv. bd. Covenant House Tex., 1987-90; HISD City-Wide Com., 1987; vice-chmn. health svcs., 1990 U.S. Savs. Bond Program. Mem. AMA, Am. Assn. Immunologists, Am. Soc. Clin. Investigation, N.Y. Acad. Scis., Infectious Diseases Soc. Am., Inst. Medicine, Nat. Acad. Scis. (membership com. 1992-96, sect. 12 1992—, vice chmn., 1992-94, chmn. 1994-96, com. on prevention and control of sexually transmitted diseases 1995-96, chmn. 1995-96), Assn. Acad. Health Ctrs., Assn. Am. Med. Colls. (chmn. coun. deans 1987-89, adminstrv. bd. 1983-90, exec. coun. 1984-92, mgmt. edn. programs planning com. 1986-96, chmn.-elect 1989-90, chmn. 1990-91, project 3000x2000 implementation com. chmn. 1991-2002, nominating com. chmn. 1982), Harris County Med. Soc., Houston Acad. Medicine, Tex. Med. Assn. (adv. coun. med. edn.), Houston C. of C. (bd. dirs. 1981-82, 83-89), Greater Houston Partnership, Inc. (bd. dirs. 1989, 92-99, co-chair healthcare task force 1994-97, bus. issues adv. com. 1994-99, govtl. rels. adv. com. 1995-97), Houston Mus. Nat. Sci. (ex officio 1989-94), River Oaks Country Club, Doctors' Club (bd. govs. 1980-84, pres. 1982), Harvard Bus. Sch. of Houston Club, Sigma Xi, Alpha Omega Alpha. Methodist. Achievements include research in numerous publs. on infectious disease and immunology. Office: Baylor Coll Medicine 1 Baylor Plz Ste 177A Houston TX 77030-3498

BUTT, CHARLES CLARENCE, food service executive; b. Houston, 1938; BS in Econs., U. Pa., 1959; grad. advanced mgmt. program, Harvard U. Pres. H.E.B. Grocery Co., San Antonio, 1971-84; chmn., CEO H.E. Butt Grocery Co., San Antonio, 1984—. Dir. Tex. Commerce Bancshares, 1974—89. Mem. bd. overseers The Wharton Sch.; mem. bd. dirs. of the assocs, Harvard Bus. Sch.; chmn. adv. coun. U. Tex. Marine Sci. Inst., 1976-86; chmn. M.D. Anderson Cancer Hosp. ann. campaign, 1981; mem. coord. bd. Tex. Coll. and Univ. Sys., 1978-83, chmn. faculty salaries com.; mem. Harvard Bus. Sch.'s Bd. Dirs. of Assocs. Recipient Conservation award Winedale Hist. Ctr., U. Tex., Amanda Cartwright Taylor award San Antonio Conservation Soc., Mr. South Tex. award Washington's Birthday Celebration Assn., 1996; named one of Forbes 400: Richest Americans, 2006-. Mem.: San Antonio German Club, Order of the Alamo, NY Yacht Club, Nantucket Yacht Club, Corpus Christi Yacht Club, Argyle Club. Avocations: sailing, historical preservation, photography. Office: H E Butt Grocery Co 646 S Main Ave San Antonio TX 78204-1210

BUTTERFIELD, CHARLES EDWARD, JR., educational consultant; b. Urbana, Ill., Mar. 31, 1928; s. Charles E. and Bessie J. (Winters) B.; m. Gayle Coberley, Jan. 27, 1952; children: Jeffrey M., Carey J. BS in Biology, Chemistry, Physics, Psychology, Edn., U. Ill., 1951, MS, 1953; postgrad., Murray State U., 1957, Duke U., 1958, No. Ill. U., 1958—59, Mich. State U., 1959, postgrad., 1972, Knox Coll., 1962, Fla. State U., 1969, U. Colo., 1970. Field exec. Nottawa Trails Coun. Boy Scouts Am., Battle Creek, Mich., 1953—54; instr. sci. Gardner-South Wilmington Twp. H.S., Ill., 1954—59; pub. rels. cons., edn. cons. Dresden Nuc. Power Plant Consol. Edison, Braidwood, Ill., 1958—60; biology coord. Lake Park H.S., Medinah, Ill., 1959—65; sr. sci. project editor Singer/Random House Pub. Co., NYC, 1965—68; sci. supr. K-12 Ramsey Pub. Schs., NJ, 1968—82; sci. edn. cons., 1981—; pres., CFO, Shield Cons., 1977—. Instr. radiation physics N.W. Cmty. Hosp., Arlington Heights, Ill., 1963-65; cons. Rand McNally Pubs., 1972-80; peer reviewer NSF proposals, 1979-84; mem. sci. adv. bd. Raintree Publs., Milw., 1981-86; assoc. Thomas A. Edison Found., 1981-88; condr. various workshops for sci. tchrs., 1965—; assoc. dir. U.S./Japan Sci. Educator Leadership Exch., 1978-81. Contbg. author: NSSA Sourcebook for Science Supervisors, 2d edit., 1976, 3d edit., 1988. Pres. Bd. Edn., Gardner, Ill., 1956-57, Foxwood Village Fedn. Mfrd. Home Owners of Fla., 1988-92; co-project dir., fin. officer suprs. programs NSF/NSSA/PEEC, 1979-83; pres., treas., bd. dirs. Highland Fairways Property Owners Assn., 1993-96, 99-2002, fin. cons., 1996—; judge Nat. Seiko Youth Challenge, 1994, 95. With USN and USMC, 1946-48. Recipient Allendale (N.J.) Cmty. Lifesaving award, 1976; NSF/AAAS fellow Mich. State U., 1964-66, fellow 1st Southeastern NASA Aerospace Conf., 1961. Fellow AAAS; mem. NEA, ACLU, Nat. Sci. Ednl. Leadership Assn. (exec. com. 1974-80, pres. 1977-78, sr. staff leader U. Calif. at San Diego State Leadership Conf., 1979-, U. Iowa 1979-80, chair summer leadership conf., supr. nat. elections 1982-2000, editl. adv. bd. 1986-91, Outstanding Svc. award 1990, 98, 1st hon. lifetime exec. bd. award for outstanding svc. 2000—), NSTA (exec. bd. 1977-78, Disting. Svc. Sci. Edn. citation 1981), Am. Humanist Assn., N.J. Sci. Tchrs. Assn., N.J. Sci. Suprs. Assn. (Disting. Svc. award 1982), Ramsey Suprs. Assn. (founding pres. 1980-81), Bergen County Sci. Suprs. Assn. (pres. 1971-73, Outstanding Svc. award 1974, 78), pres., mem. bd. dirs., Nat. Sci. Supervisors Assn., 1977-80, Sch. Sci. and Math. Assn., Am. Inst. Biol. Scis. (cons. biol. sci. curriculum study 1965—), Nat. Assn. Biol. Tchrs., Coun. Elem. Sci. Internat., Assn. Edn. Tchrs. Sci., N.J. Prins. and Suprs. Assn., Am. Assn. Notaries, Nat. Notary Assn., U. Ill. Alumni Assn. (life), Fla. So. Coll. Sixth Man Club, Cmty. Assns. Inst., 1st Marine Divsn. Assn., Fleet Marine Force Combat Med. Pers. Assn., Am. Legion, USN Meml. Found., Lakeland (Fla.) North C. of C., Mensa, Masons, DeMolay Internat. (chevalier), Order Ea. Star, Humanist Assn. West Ctrl. Fla. (charter), Norwalk H.S. Alumni Assn., Psi Chi. Office: 22 Spring Ave Oakland NJ 07436-1930 Office Phone: 863-859-4306. Personal E-mail: chargayb3121@earthlink.net.

BUTTERFIELD, GEORGE KENNETH, JR., (G.K. BUTTERFIELD), United States Representative from North Carolina, former state supreme court justice; b. Wilson, NC, Apr. 27, 1947; s. G. K. and Addie (Davis) Butterfield; children: Valeisha Monique, Jenetta Lenai. BS in Polit. Sci. and Sociology, NC Ctrl. U., 1971; JD, NC Ctrl. U. Sch. Law, 1974. Bar: NC 1975. Sr. ptnr. Butterfield, Fitch & Wynn, 1974—88; judge NC Resident Superior Ct. Dist. 7B, 1989—2001; justice NC Supreme Ct., 2001—02; judge NC Spl. Superior Ct., 2002—04; mem. US Congress from 1st NC Dist., 2004—; 2nd vice chair Congressional Black Caucus, 2011—. Specialist US Army, 1968—70. Recipient Lawyer of Yr. award, NC Assn. Black Lawyers; named one of Most Influential Black Americans, Ebony mag., 2006; named to Power 150, 2008. Mem.: NC Bar Assn. (v.p. 2003—). Democrat. Baptist. Office: US House of Representatives 2305 Rayburn House Office Bldg Washington DC 20515 Office Phone: 202-225-3101. Office Fax: 202-225-3354.*

BUTTERS, RONALD RICHARD, language educator; b. Cedar Rapids, Iowa, Feb. 12, 1940; s. Richard Orton and Dorothy Mae B.; children: Rebecca, Catherine, Rachel. BA, U. Iowa, 1962, PhD, 1967. Asst. prof. English Duke U., Durham, N.C., 1967-74, assoc. prof. English, 1974-90, prof. English, 1990—2007, prof. anthropology, 2000—07, prof. emeritus, 2007. Editor Am. Speech Jour. Am. Dialect Soc., 1981-95; mem. editl. adv. bd. New Oxford American Dictionary. Author: The Death of Black English, 1989; co-author: Displacing Hompohobia, 1989 (CEW best spl. issue award 1989); chief editor Am. Dialect Soc. publs., 1996—2007; co-editor Internat. Jour. Speech, Language, and Law, 2007—10. Recipient Rsch. grant NEH, 1973-74. Mem. Am. Dialect Soc. (v.p. 1997-99, pres. 2000-02), Internat. Assn. Forensic Linguists (v.p. 2007—08, pres. 2009-), Linguistic Soc. Am., Southeastern Conf. Linguistics (pres. 1983), Law and Soc. Assn., Dictionary Soc. N.Am. Home: 6710 Huntington Lakes Cir Apt 201 Naples FL 34119-7800 Home Phone: 919-423-8866; Office Phone: 919-423-8866. Personal E-mail: ronbutters@aol.com.

BUTTERWORTH, JIM B., military officer, former state legislator; b. Apr. 30; m. Amy Butterworth; children: Blake, Claire, Jack. BS in Polit. Sci., U. Ga. Pilot Delta Airlines; former chmn. Habersham Co. Bd. Commrs.; exec. bd. mem. Ga. Mountains Regional Devel. Ctr., Ga. Dept. Cmty. Affairs All Hazard Coun., Ga. DCA Regional Adv. Com.; mem. Dist. 50 Ga. State Senate, 2008—11; adj. gen. Ga. Dept. of Def., 2011—. Served 12 yrs USAF, finished svc. with Ga. Air Nat. Guard. Republican. Baptist. Office: The Adj Gen of Ga Ga Dept of Defense PO Box 1970 Marietta GA 30061 Office Phone: 678-596-6001. Office Fax: 678-596-6005. Business E-Mail: james.b.butterworth@us.army.mil.

BUTTERWORTH, S. KENDALL, lawyer; d. Charles Kenneth and Sue (Anderson) Butterworth. BA with honors, U. Va., 1991; JD cum laude, U. Ga., 1994. Bar: Ga. 1994, U.S. Dist. Ct. (no. dist.) Ga. 1994, U.S. Ct. Appeals (11th cir.) 1994. Assoc. Kilpatrick Stockton LLP, 1994—97; atty. Bellsouth Telecom., 1997—98, Bellsouth Cellular Corp., 1999—2000; litigation counsel Bellsouth Corp., 2001; sr. litigation counsel AT&T Southeast (formerly Bellsouth Corp.), 2007—07, chief litigation counsel, 2007—; corp. atty. Mueller Water Products, Inc. Mem. adv. bd. Atlanta Legal Aid Soc., 2002—, chief litigation counsel; spl. asst. to chair Supreme Ct. Commn. on Indigent Def., Atlanta, 2001—04. Named Up and Comer Under 40, Atlanta Bus. Chronicle, 2004—05, Ga. Rising Star, Atlanta mag., 2005. Mem.: Ga. State Bar (mem. bd. govs. 1999—, pres. Young Lawyers divsn. Atlanta chpt. 2000—01), ABA (mem. Ho. of Dels., Chgo. 2000—04, mem. jury commn. 2004—05, named Star of the Quarter 1999, 2004, 2005), Atlanta Bar Assn. Avocations: running, travel, music. Office: Mueller Water Products Inc 1200 Abernathy Rd NE Ste 1200 Atlanta GA 30328 Office Phone: 770-206-4200. Office Fax: 770-206-4235. Business E-Mail: Sbutterworth@muellerwp.com.

BUTTRAM, MARVIN, state legislator; m. Pam Buttram; children: Lara Lee, Lindsey, Carter. BS in History, U. North Ala., Florence, 1969; MDiv, Emory U., 1983. Chaplain Cullman County Sherriff's Dept.; pastor Red Ridge United Meth. Ch., 1981—84, Camp Hill United Meth. Ch., 1981—84, Taylorville United Meth. Ch., 1984—86; assoc. pastor Trinity United Meth. Ch., 1986—95; pastor St. Andrew's United Meth. Ch., 1995—2003, Hamilton United Meth. Ch., 2003—09; mem. Dist. 12 Ala. House of Representatives, 2011—. Mentor Volunteers in Pub. Schs. Program; mem. Cullman C. of C., Cullman County Rep. Party. Republican. Office: Ala House of Reps Rm 207-B 11 S Union St Montgomery AL 36130 Office Phone: 334-242-7775. Personal E-mail: mbuttram@att.net.

BUX, WILLIAM JOHN, lawyer; b. Wadsworth, Ohio, Nov. 10, 1946; s. William J. and Helen M. (Sybelnik) B.; m. Linda Alice Zenar, Feb. 13, 1971. BSME, Ohio State U., 1969, MS, 1970; JD cum laude, So. Meth. U., 1977. Bar: Tex. 1977, U.S. Dist. Ct. (so. dist.) Tex. 1978, U.S. Ct. Appeals (5th cir.) 1978, U.S. Dist. Ct. (no. dist.) Tex. 1980, U.S. Dist. Ct. (ea. and we. dists.) Tex. 1981, U.S. Ct. Appeals (11th cir.) 1981, U.S. Supreme Ct. 1982; cert. Labor & Employment Law Tex. Bd. Legal Specialization. Assoc. Vinson & Elkins, Houston, 1977-85; ptnr. Hughes & Luce, Dallas, 1985-93; shareholder Locke Purnell Rain Harrell, Dallas, 1994-97; ptnr. Liddell, Sapp, Zivley, Hill & La Boon, Houston, 1997-98, Locke, Liddell & Sapp, Houston, 1999—2007, Locke Lord LLP, Houston, 2007—. Author: Developing and Enforcing Drug and Alcohol Abuse Work Rules: A Primer for Texas Employers, 1984. Sec. So. Meth. U. Law Sch. Alumni Council, Dallas, 1986-88. Capt. USAF, 1971-74. Mem. ABA, Tex. Bar Assn. (chmn. labor and employment law sect. 1992-93), Houston Bar Assn., Dallas Bar Assn., 5th Cir. Bar Assn. (named a Tex. Super Lawyer 2003-13, named one of Best Lawyers Am. 2006-14), Order of the Coif. Republican. Roman Catholic. Office: Locke Lord LLP 600 Travis St 2800 JP Morgan Chase Twr Houston TX 77002-3095 Home: 5063 Fieldwood Dr Houston TX 77056 Office Phone: 713-226-1275. Business E-Mail: bbux@lockelord.com.

BUXTON, BARRY MILLER, academic administrator, writer, educator; b. Blowing Rock, NC, Aug. 5, 1949; s. Augustin Kinnard and Carrie (Miller) Buxton; m. Deborah Keyes, June 15, 1984; children: Loren Augustin, Peter I. BS, Appalachian State U., 1971, MA, 1973; PhD, U. Nebr., 1976. Dean Southeast CC, Lincoln, Nebr., 1977-81; exec. dir., dir. press Appalachian Consortium, Boone, NC, 1982-90; exec. dir. Health Adventure Mus., Asheville, NC, 1991-95; dir. Mus. Health and Med. Sch., Houston, 1995-98; pres., CEO Eighth Air Force Heritage Mus., Savannah, Ga., 1998-2000; v.p. instl. advancement Savannah Coll. Art and Design, 2000—05, Atlanta, 2005—06, v.p. spl. projects Savannah, Ga., 2006—10; pres. Lees-McRae Coll., Banner Elk, NC, 2010—. Cons. Howard Hughes Med. Inst., Chevy Chase, Md., 1993-95, Girl Scouts US, NYC, 1984; prin. rschr. Nat. Park Svc., Asheville, 1987-90; project dir. Nat. Humanities Coun., Washington, 1986-87. Editor: The Great Forest, 1985, Emerging Patterns in the Southern Highlands Appalachian Consortium Press, 1986, Parkways: Past, Present, Future, American Society of Landscape Architects, 1989; co-editor: The Blue Ridge Parkway: Agent of Transition, 1985, The Many Faces of Teaching, 1986; author: Moses H. Cone Memorial Historic Study, 1987, Brinegar Cabin Historic Study, 1988, Mabry Mill Historic Study, 1989, A Village Tapestry: The History of Blowing Rock, 1989, Davey Farm Historic Study, 1990. Trustee Tex. A&M U., Inst. Bioscis., Houston, 1996-98, Historic Savannah Found. YMCA, Savannah, Ga., 1998-99, Bethesda Home for Boys, 2000—, Lucas Theater, 2003—; mem. policy coun. Tex. Med. Ctr., Houston, 1995-98, chmn., 2003, chmn. bd. dirs.; bd. dirs. Conv. and Visitors Bur., Savannah, 1998-99, C. of C. Sanavannah, 2002—; bd. dirs. NC Health Alliance, 1993-95, Savannah Econ. Devel. Authority, 1998-99; v.p. Project ASSIST, 1994-95. Recipient Cmty. Historian of Yr. award NC Soc. Historians, 1989, Disting. Svc. award N.C. Soc. Historians, 1987; named Outstanding Fund Raiser, Nat. Soc. Fundrising Execs., 1996; Lovill fellow Appalachian State U., 1971. Mem. Houston Museums Assn. (v.p., 1996-98), NC Sci. Museums (v.p. 1993-95). Republican. Episcopalian. Avocations: tennis, bicycling, hiking, landscape architecture, history. Home: 114 W Gaston St Savannah GA 31401-4903 Office: Lees-McRae College Office of President/Historic Rock House PO Box 128 Banner Elk NC 28604 Office Phone: 828-898-8785.

BUZZARD, JAMES A., paper, packaging and chemical company executive; BS in Pulp and Paper Tech., N.C. State U.; MBA in Fin., U. Pa. Joined WestVaco, 1978, purchasing mgr., Kraft Divsn., 1982—84, adminstrv. mgr., Container Divsn., 1984—86, area sales mgr., container plant Eaton, Ohio, 1986—88, corp. mktg. mgr., 1988—90, mgr., mktg. svcs., 1990—91, mgr., bus. planning, analysis, Envelope Divsn., 1991—92, mgr., Envelope Divsn., corp. v.p., 1992—94, interim mktg., sales mgr., Fine Papers Divsn., 1994—95, sales, mktg. mgr., 1995—98, asst. divsn. mgr., Fine Papers Divsn., 1998—99, sr. v.p., 1999—2000, mgr., Fine Papers Divsn., 1999—2000; exec. v.p. Westvaco Corp., 2000—02, MeadWestvaco Corp., Stamford, Conn., 2002—03, pres., 2003—. Mem.: Web Offset Assn. (mem. supplier adv. bd.). Office: MeadWestvaco 501 S 5th St Richmond VA 23219-0501

BYARS, LEISA, marketing professional, music company executive; b. Warren, Ohio, 1967; m. Delfon McSpadden. BA in Econs. and Govt., Oberlin Coll.; MA in Pub. Policy, U. Mich.; MBA in Mktg. and Fin., U. Pa. From mem. staff to group mgr. Innovative Mktg. Solutions Group Ford Motor Co., Dearborn, Mich., 1995—2000, group mgr. Innovative Mktg. Solutions Group, 2000, mgr., global media, agency, events and alliances; v.p. mktg. EMI Christian Music Group EMI, Tenn., 2005—. Recipient Outstanding Women in Mktg. and Comms. award, Ebony Mag., 2001. Office: EMI CMG PO Box 5010 Brentwood TN 37024-5010

BYARS, MICHAEL D., retail executive; Dir., merchandising, meat ops., Ctrl. Divsn. Food Lion Stores, 1995—97; COO Kash 'n Karry Food Stores (subs. Delhaize America Inc.), Fla., 1997—2005; joined Minyard Food Stores, Inc., 2005, exec. v.p., ops., pres., CEO, 2006—09, BI-LO, LLC (subs. of BI-LO Holdings LLC), 2009—. Former mem. Tex. Health Harris Meth. Found., The Children's Med. Ctr., Dallas; mem. Project Return of Tampa Bay, Tampa Children's Hosp., St. Joseph; bd. dirs. Associated Wholesale Grocers, Nat. Grocers Assn.; chmn. Tampa Bay's U.S. Govt. Bond Com. Office: BI-LO LLC 208 BI-LO Blvd Greenville SC 29607 Office Phone: 864-213-2500. Business E-Mail: michael.byars@bi-lo.com.

BYARS, WALTER RYLAND, JR., lawyer; b. Birmingham, Ala., Oct. 5, 1928; s. Walter Ryland and Essie (Hopper) B.; m. Mildred Lucile Rhodes, Dec. 22, 1950; children: Debra Leigh Byars Patterson, Walter Ryland Byars III, Rebecca Lynn Byars Pradat, John Baxter Byars. BS, U. Ala., 1948, LLB, 1952, JD, 1969. Bar: Ala. 1952, U.S. Ct. Appeals (5th and 11th cirs.), U.S. Dist. Ct. (no., mid. and so. dists.) Ala., U.S. Supreme Ct. Pvt. practice, Troy, Ala., 1953-57; atty. legal dept. So. Bell. Tel. & Tel. Co., Atlanta, 1957-59, gen. atty. Birmingham, 1959-68; ptnr. Steiner, Crum & Baker, 1968—; city atty. Montgomery, Ala., 2002—09; mng. ptnr. Steiner, Crum & Byars, PC, Montgomery, 2003—, chief legal advisor to mayor, 2009—. Bd. editors Ala. Law Rev., 1951-52. Lt. (j.g.) USNR, 1952-53. Fellow: Am. Bar Found., Ala. Bar Found., Internat. Soc. Barristers (gov.

1977-83, sec.-treas. 1979-80, 2d v.p. 1980-81, 1st v.p. 1981-82, pres. 1982-83), Am. Coll. Trial Lawyers; mem.: ABA (Young Lawyers past mem. exec. council, com. chmn.), Ala. Bar Assn. (pres.-elect 1983-84, pres. 1984-85, past pres. Young Lawyers, past sect. chmn., past com. chmn.), Pike County Bar Assn. (past pres.), Birmingham Bar Assn. (past com. chmn.), Montgomery County Bar Assn. (past com. chmn., bd. dirs. 1976-79, v.p. 1978, pres. 1979), Ala. Law Inst. (coun.), Montgomery Area Com. of 100, Masons, Sigma Chi (Significant mem. 2012), Phi Alpha Delta. Methodist. Home: 1744 Fairforest Dr Montgomery AL 36106-2602 Office: PO Box 668 Montgomery AL 36101-0668 Office Phone: 334-832-8800. Business E-Mail: wbyars@steinercrum.com.

BYBEE, STEWART M., legislative staff member; b. 1975; m. Ronda L. Bybee. Legis. corr. to Senator Richard Bryan US Senate, Washington, legis. corr. to Senator John Ensign, 2001—03; mgr. govt. affairs Solid Waste Assn. North America, Silver Spring, Md., 2003; press sec. to Rep. Dean Heller US House of Representatives, Washington, 2007—11; dep. chief of staff, comm. dir. for Senator Dean Heller US Senate, Washington, 2011—. Republican. Office: US Senate 4 Russell Courtyard Washington DC 20510 Office Phone: 202-224-6244. E-mail: stewartbybee@heller.senate.gov.

BYE, RAYMOND ERWIN, JR., academic administrator; b. Mobile, Ala., Feb. 22, 1944; s. Raymond Erwin and Frances (Bain) Bye; m. Katherine Jackson, Dec. 28, 1971; children: Philip Jackson, Eleanor Ashley. BA, Rhodes Coll., Memphis, 1966; MA, Kent State U., 1968, PhD, 1974. Resident dir., 1966-68; area residence dir. Kent (Ohio) State U., 1968-69, asst. to pres., 1969-71, asst. to vice pres. student affairs, 1971-72; asst. to dir., deputy head, head congl. affairs NSF, Washington, 1973-83, dir. office of legis. and pub. affairs, 1983-94; assoc. v.p. rsch. Fla. State U., Tallahassee, 1994-98, v.p. rsch., 1999—2003, dir. fed. rels., 2004—; cons. Oldaker Group, 2011—. Adv. bd. Knight Found., 2002—; bd. dirs. Tallahassee Chamber, 1995—2005, Econ. Devel. Commn., 1995—98, TMH Hosp., 1998—2001, Oak Ridge Assn. Univs., 2001—03, Coun. Gov. Affairs, pres., 1998—2000, Fla. State U. Rsch. Found., 1998—2003; bd. dirs. Nat. Assn. State Univ. Land Grant Colls., 1999—2000, chair coun. govt. affairs, 1999—2001; bd. govs. Oak Ridge Nat. Lab., 2000—03; mem., exec. com. Assn. Pub. and Land-Grant U. Coun. Govtl. Affairs, 2004—06; bd. mem. Economic Club Fla., 2002—08, Cmty. Found. North Fla., 2007—11, 2008—12, St. John's Episcopal Ch. Found., 2013—; chair St. John's Found. Bd., 2014—. Recipient Disting. Svc. award, NSF, 1989, Pres. Meritorious Exec. award, 1991, Disting. Alumnus award, Rhodes Coll., 2009, Career Excellence award, Assn. Pub. and Land-Grant U., 2010. Mem.: AAAS, Acad. Mgmt., So. Polit. Sci. Assn., Fla. Econ. Club (bd. dirs. 2002—08). Office: Fla State University Westcott N Bldg Tallahassee FL 32306-1330 Office Phone: 850-645-1410. Personal E-mail: rebye@comcast.net. Business E-Mail: rbye@fsu.edu.

BYERLEIN, ANNE P., human resources specialist, food products executive; b. Birmingham, Mich. BA, Michigan State. Various positions PepsiCo., v.p. corp. human resources, 1988—96; v.p. human resources Yum Brands, Inc. (formerly Tricon Global Restaurants), Louisville, 1997—2002; chief people officer KFC, 2000—02, Yum! Brands, Inc. (formerly TRICON Global Restaurants, Inc.), Louisville, 2002—. Past pres. Leadership Palm Beach County. Office: Yum Brands Inc 1441 Gardiner Ln Louisville KY 40213 Office Phone: 502-874-8300. Office Fax: 502-874-8790.

BYERS, JOHN R., insurance company executive, lawyer; b. Pickens, SC, Jan. 20, 1955; s. A.R. and R.S. (Simmons) B.; m. Cheryl Ann Fowler, June 18, 1978; children: Kristen, Kailey. BA, Clemson U., 1977; JD, Vanderbilt U., 1980. Bar: Fla. 1980, U.S. Ct. Appeals (5th and 11th cirs.) 1981. Atty. Smith & Hulsey, Jacksonville, Fla., 1980-85, U.S. Shelter Corp., Greenville, S.C., 1985-87, Smith & Hulsey, Jacksonville, Fla., 1987-88; ptnr. Dewey & LeBoeuf LLP, Jacksonville, Fla., 1988—98; exec. v.p., gen. counsel FPIC Ins. Group, Inc., 1999—2000, pres., CEO, 2000—. Mem. ABA, The Fla. Bar, Jacksonville Bar Assn. Home: 2795 Via Baya Ln Jacksonville FL 32223-7200 Office: FPIC Insurance Group Inc PO Box 4220 East Lansing MI 48826-4220 Office Phone: 904-354-2482. Office Fax: 904-475-1159. Business E-Mail: byers@fpic.com.

BYNER, EARNEST ALEXANDER, professional football coach, retired professional football player; b. Milledgeville, Ga., Sept. 15, 1962; m. Tina Byner; 5 children. BS in Exercise Sci., East Carolina U., Greenville, NC. Running back Cleve. Browns, 1984—88, 1994—95, Washington Redskins, 1989—93, running backs coach, 2004—07; running back Balt. Ravens (formerly the Cleve. Browns), 1996—97, dir. player pers., 1998—2004; running backs coach Tenn. Titans, 2008—09, Jacksonville Jaguars, 2010—11, Tampa Bay Buccaneers, 2012—. Recipient Ed Block Courage award, 1986, Extra Effort award, NFL, 1996, Unsung Hero award, NFL Players Assn., 1997; named Ravens Man of Yr., 1997; named one of 70 All-Time Greatest Redskins, 2002; named to Am. Football Conf. Pro Bowl Team, NFL, 1990, 1991, East Carolina Univ. Sports Hall of Fame, Ravens Ring of Honor. Achievements include leading the NFL in: touches (328), rushing attempts (297), 1990. Office: Tampa Bay Buccaneers One Buccaneer Pl Tampa FL 33607

BYNUM, RICHARD CARY, author, former publisher; b. Atlanta, Mar. 15, 1937; s. Paul Cary and Ethel Avious (Rutherford) B.; m. Brenda Sue Storey, Apr. 12, 1964; children: Brennon Franklin, Quinlan Ashby. BFA, U. Ga., 1962; MA, CUNY, 1973. Prodn. editor Holt, Rinehart and Winston, NYC, 1965-67; publ. mgr. Assn. Am. U. Presses, NYC, 1967-69; mng. editor R.R. Bowker Co., NYC, 1969-73; founding dir. Ga. State U. Bus. Press, Atlanta, 1973-95; ret. Ga. State U., 1997. Co-dir. So. Poets Theatre, 1974-87. Author: Cabbagetown: 3 Women, 1984, Six Short Plays, 1993, The Chinaberry Tree and Other Poems, 2002, Sea Vigil: Poems, 2008, Reunion in Thera & Other Stories, 2012, Woodhall Stories, 2014; editor: Scholarly Books in America, 1968-69. With USAR. Recipient John Golden award CUNY, 1972, Sparks award Ga. State U., 1985, medal AAUP, 1995. Mem. Dramatists Guild. Avocation: reading.

BYRD, ANDREW WAYNE, investment company executive; b. Nashville, Apr. 16, 1954; s. Benjamin F. and Allison (Caldwell) B.; m. Marianne Menefee; children: Marianne, Valere, Andrew Jr. BA, Vanderbilt U., 1976, JD, 1979; LLM, Georgetown U., 1981. Bar: Tenn., 1979, US Dist. Ct. (mid. dist.) Tenn. 1979, US Supreme Ct. 2001. Atty. Stokes & Bartholomew, Nashville, 1981-84; exec. v.p. Gen. Cap Am. Inc., 1987-94, Gen. Capital Corp., Nashville, 1984-89, pres., 1989-94; CEO Andrew W. Byrd & Co., LLC, 1994—. Chmn., bd. dirs. Multi-Link, Inc., Lexington, Ky., 2000—11, Albertville Quality Foods, Inc., Ala., 2000—10, Precision Boilers, Inc., Morristown, Tenn., 1999—2010, So. Quality Meats, Inc., Pontotoc, Miss., 2002—10, Indco, Inc., Louisville, 2005—, Critical Solutions Internat. Inc., Dallas, 2011—, Big 3 Precision Products Centralia, Ill., 2012—, Bigham Brothers, Lubbock, Tex., 2012—. Mem. Leadership Nashville, 1984-85; deacon 1st Presbyn. Ch., 1982-92, elder, 2005-11, chair, Missions Coun., 2009-11; bd. dirs. Tenn. divsn. Am. Cancer Soc., 1982-88, 92-97, Cheekwood, 1987-93; bd. dirs. Boy Scouts of Am., Mid. Tenn. Coun., 1995—, v.p. manpower, 2002-04, treas., 2005-06, v.p. fin., 2007-08, pres.-elect, 2009, pres., 2010, chmn., 2011; bd. dirs. Exch. Club Charities, 2003-06, bd. dirs. Vanderbilt Children's Hosp., 1987-93, chmn., 1991-93; bd. dirs. Vanderbilt Ingram Cancer Ctr., 2007—. Recipient Silver Beaver award, Boy Scouts Am., 2006, Celtic Cross award, First Presbyn. Ch., 2007. Mem. ABA, Tenn. Bar Assn., Nashville Bar Assn., Nashville Area C. of C. (bd. dirs. 2003-09), Exch. Club (pres. 1993-94). Democrat. Avocations: tennis, gardening, travel. Home: 4419 Harding Pl Nashville TN 37205-4530 Office: Andrew W Byrd & Co LLC 201 4th Ave N Ste 1250 Nashville TN 37219-2092 Office Phone: 615-256-8061.

BYRD, CAROLYN H., financial consultant; b. 1950; Fin. mgmt. positions through chief internal audits & dir. corp. auditing dept. Coca-Cola Co., 1977—97; pres. The Coca-Cola Financial Corp., 1997—2000, GlobalTech Fin., LLC, Atlanta, 2000, chmn., CEO, 2000—. Bd. dirs. RARE Hospitality Internat., AFC Enterprises Inc., 2001—, Freddie Mac (Fed. Home Loan Mortgage Corp.), 2008—, Regions Fin. Corp., 2010—. Bd. trustee Fisk U. Office: GlobalTech Financial LLP Ste 810 PO Box 421308 Atlanta GA 30342-8308 Office Phone: 678-816-2200. Office Fax: 678-816-2222. Business E-Mail: carolynb@globaltechfinancial.com.

BYRD, DARYL GLYNN, bank executive; b. Columbia, SC, June 1, 1954; m. Laura Edwards; children: Martha, Bennett. BSBA, Samford U., 1976; MBA, U. Birmingham, 1978. Sales rep. Vulcan Materials Co., Birmingham, Ala., 1978-81; banking officer Trust Co. of Ga., Atlanta, 1981-83; v.p., comml. lending officer First Nat. Bank, Columbia, S.C., 1983-84; v.p. Br. Banking & Trust Co., Wilson, N.C., 1984; exec. v.p., corp. banking First Nat. Bank, Lafayette, La., 1985—90; pres., CEO Rapides Bank & Trust Co. (subs. of 1st Commerce Corp.), Alexandria, La., 1990—92; exec. v.p. First Commerce Corp., 1992—99; pres. IBERIABANK Corp., 1999—, CEO, 2000—. Bd. dirs. United Way of Cen. La., 1990—, ARC. Mem. Cen. La. C. of C. (bd. dirs.), Alexandria Golf and Country Club, Rotary. Avocation: tennis. Office: IBERIABANK Corp 200 W Congress St Lafayette LA 70501 Office Phone: 337-521-4012. Office Fax: 337-364-1171. Business E-Mail: dbyrd@iberiabank.com.

BYRD, LARRY, state legislator; b. Aug. 1, 1948; m. Karen Devereaux. Vet. US Army 82nd Airborne Divsn.; contractor; mem. Dist. 104 Miss. House of Reps., 2008—, vice chair county affairs com., mem. agr. com., marine resources com., mil. affairs com., oil, gas and other minerals com., transp. com. Republican. Southern Baptist. Home: 17 Byrd Rd Petal MS 39465 Office: PO Box 1018 Jackson MS 39215 Home Phone: 601-544-1877. E-mail: lbyrd@house.ms.gov.

BYRD, LARRY DONALD, behavioral pharmacologist; b. Salisbury, NC, July 14, 1936; s. Donald Thomas and Mildred (Gardner) B.; m. Corrinne Williams, Dec. 23, 1961; children: Kay, Lynn, Renee, Andrew. AB, E. Carolina U., Greenville, NC, 1962; MA, E. Carolina U., 1964; PhD, U. N.C., 1968; postgrad., Harvard U., 1967-70. Faculty E. Carolina U., 1962-64; tchg. and rsch. asst. exptl. psychology U. N.C., Chapel Hill, 1964-67; rsch. fellow pharmacology, instr. psychobiology Harvard Med. Sch., 1967-70; assoc. scientist Lab. Psychobiology New Eng. Reg. Primate Rsch. Ctr., 1969-74; psychobiologist, chmn. divsn. primate behavior Yerkes Primate Rsch. Ctr., Emory U., Atlanta, 1974-79, assoc. rsch. prof., chmn. divsn. primate behavior, 1979-80, lectr. dept. psychology, 1974-81, assoc. rsch. prof., chief divsn. behavioral biology, 1980-82, prof., chief divsn. behavioral biology, 1982-97, prof. dept. pharmacology, 1995-97; prof. emeritus, 1998. Adj. prof. dept. psychology Emory U., 1981-97; cons. Dept. Pharmacological and Physiol. Scis. U. Chgo., 1973, MIT Press, Cambridge, 1975, Nat. Ctr. for Toxicological Rsch. FDA, Jefferson, Ark., 1976-77, S.W. Found. for Rsch. and Edn., San Antonio, 1977, Naval Aerospace Med. Rsch. Lab. U.S. Naval Air Sta., Pensacola, Fla., 1977, G.D. Searle and Co., Skokie, Ill., 1986, Battelle Meml. Inst., Columbus, Ohio, 1989-94; mem. spl. rev. com. Contract Rev. Unit Nat. Inst. on Drug Abuse, Lexington, Ky., 1979-81, mem. spl. rev. com. biomed. rsch. rev. com., 1981-82, spl. rev. cons. clin., behavioral and psychosocial rsch. rev. com., 1981-82, mem., 1982-85, chmn., 1984-85, others; spl. rev. cons. dept. medicine and surgery VA, Washington, 1983, NSF, Washington, 1984, div. of rsch. resources NIH, Washington, 1983, mem. spl. study sect. div. rsch. grants, 1984, panel mem. Workshop on Implementation of Pub. Health Svc. Policy on Humane Care and Use of Lab. Animals, 1989, others; panel mem. USPHS Animal Welfare Forum Alcohol, Drug Abuse and Mental Health Adminstrn., 1985; active numerous other career related orgns. Editorial bd. Jour. Exptl. Analysis of Behavior, 1969-79, 87-91; assoc. editor Jour. Exptl. Analysis of Behavior, 1970-76; cons. editor Am. Jour. Primatology, 1980-83; editor Psychopharmacology Newsletter, 1976-82; editorial advisor Jour. Pharmacology and Exptl. Therapeutics, Jour. Exptl. Analysis of Behavior, others; contbr. numerous articles to profl. jours. Mem. sci. adv. com. Nat. Families in Action, 1991—95. Recipient Outstanding Alumnus award, E. Carolina U., 1977, Disting. Alumnus award, U. N.C., 1987. Fellow AAAS, Am. Psychol. Assn. (exec. com. psychopharmacology divsn. 1976-95, neurobehavioral toxicity test standards com. 1980-97, coord. Young Psychopharmacologist award 1985-95, bd. sci. affairs com. on animals in rsch. and ethics 1990-93); mem. Assn. for Assessment and Accreditation Lab. Animal Care (trustee 1990-98, exec. com. 1991-98, sec. 1993, vice chmn. 1994-96, chmn. 1996-98), Am. Soc. Pharmacology and Exptl. Therapeutics, Nat. Families in Action (sci. adv. com. 1991-95), Am. Soc. Primatologist, Behavioral Pharmacology Soc. (pres. 1984-86), Soc. Exptl. Analysis of Behavior (v.p. 1975-76, bd. dirs. 1970-78), European Behavioral Pharmacology Soc., Southeastern Pharmacology Soc., Am Pub. Health Assn., Behavioral Toxicology Soc., Southeastern Assn. for Behavior Analysis, Internat. Study Group Investigating Drugs as Reinforcers, Emory Neurosci. Group, Phi Sigma Pi. Home: 2730 Camp Branch Rd Buford GA 30519-4455 Business E-Mail: lbyrd@emory.edu.

BYRD, LORI, legislative staff member; BA in Polit. Sci., NC State U., 1988. Online columnist Townhall.com, 2005—; blogger wizbangblog.com, 2006—; comm. dir. Office US Rep. Renee Ellmers, NC, 2010—. Republican. Office: Dist Office US Rep Renee Ellmers 609 N First St Lillington NC 27546 Office Phone: 910-814-0335. Office Fax: 910-814-2264. E-mail: lori.byrd@mail.house.gov.

BYRD, RICK, men's college basketball coach; m. Cheryl Byrd; children: Andrea, Megan 1 stepchild, Robert Duke. B in Phys. Edn., U. Tenn., Knoxville, 1976, M in Phys. Edn., 1977. Student asst. coach U. Tenn. Volunteers; asst. coach Maryville Coll. Scots, Tenn., 1976—78, head basketball coach, 1978—80; asst. coach Tenn. Tech U. Golden Eagles, 1980—83; head basketball coach Lincoln Meml. U. Railsplitters, Tenn., 1983—86, Belmont U. Bruins, Nashville, 1986—, dir. athletics, 1986—91, acting dir. athletics, 1996. Recipient Reese L. Smith award, Nashville Area Athletic Club, 1995, Hugh Durham Nat. Coach of Yr. award, CollegeInsider.com, 2011; named Tenn. Valley Athletic Conf. Coach of Yr., Area V Coach of Yr., 1989, Tenn. Collegiate Athletic Conf. Coach of Yr., 1995, Dist. 24 Coach of Yr., Nat. Assn. Intercollegiate Athletics, 1989, Nat. Coach of Yr., 1995, Tenn. Men's Basketball Coach of Yr., Tenn. Sports Writers Assn., 1999, Atlantic Sun Conf. Coach of Yr., 2008, 2011. Office: Belmont University Mens Basketball c/o Athletics Dept 1900 Belmont Blvd Nashville TN 37212-3757

BYRD, STEVE (HENRY STEPHENSON BYRD), plastic surgeon, educator; BA with honors, North Tex. State U., 1968; MD with honors, U. Tex., Galveston, 1972. Diplomate Am. Bd. Surgery, 1978, Am. Bd. Plastic Surgery, 1980, lic. Tex., Utah. Surg. intern U. Tex. Southwestern Med. Ctr., Dallas, 1972—73, resident plastic surgery, 1977—79, prof., vice chair plastic surgery, 1979—2000, prof. clin. surgery, chief pediat. plastic surgery sect., 1979—; resident gen. surgery U. Utah Med. Ctr., Salt Lake City, 1973—77. Sec.-treas., bd. mem. Selected Readings in Plastic Surgery, 1980—; treas. Rhinoplasty Soc., pres., 1999—2001, Bd. Cert. Plastic and Cosmetic Surgeons Dallas, 1999—2001; chmn. Bd. Pediat. Surg. Alliance; bd. mem. Health Tex. Provider Network; sec. Preferred Surg. Specialist Tex.; attending staff Parkland Meml. Hosp., Dallas, U. Med. Ctr., Dallas; dir. plastic surgery svc., mem. cleft lip-craniofacial team Children's Med. Ctr., Dallas; dir. Dallas Day Surgery Baylor U. Med. Ctr., 1992—, chief plastic and reconstructive surgery svc., 1996—2002. Contbr. articles to med. jours. Mem. long-range planning task force Plastic Surgery Ednl. Found., 1991—, mem. mktg. com., 1991, bd. mem., 1993—95, mem. select com. on forward planning, 1996, bd. dirs., 1996—98, mem. internat. svc. com., 1997—99. Fellow: ACS; mem.: Dallas County Med. Soc., Dallas Soc. Plastic Surgeons (sec.-treas.), Tex. Soc. Plastic Surgeons, Tex. Med. Assn., Am. Cleft Palate Assn., Am. Soc. for Aesthetic Plastic Surgery (mem. edn. commn.), Am. Assn. Plastic Surgeons, Am. Soc. Plastic and Reconstructive Surgeons (mem. sci. program com. 1991, James Barrett Brown award 1984), Alpha Omega Alpha, Blue Key Honor Soc. Office: Dallas Plastic Surgery 9101 N Central Expy Ste 600 Dallas TX 75231-5956 Office Phone: 214-821-9662. Office Fax: 214-828-2609. Business E-Mail: info@drstevebyrd.com.

BYRNE, BRADLEY ROBERTS, United States Representative from Alabama, lawyer, former state legislator; b. Mobile, Ala., Feb. 16, 1955; s. Arthur LaCoste and Elizabeth Patricia (Langsdale) B.; m. Rebecca Dow Dukes, May 16, 1981; children: Patrick MacGuire, Kathleen Roberts, Laura Ann, Colin Arthur. BA, Duke U., 1977; JD, U. Ala. Sch. Law, 1980. Bar: Ala. 1980, US Dist. Ct. (southern dist.) Ala. 1980, US Ct. Appeals (5th and 11th cirs.) 1981, US Dist. Ct. (middle dist.) Ala. 1985, US Ct. Appeals (8th cir.) 1985, US Dist. Ct. (northern dist.) Ala. 1986, U.S. Supreme Ct. 1987. Assoc. Miller, Hamilton, Snider & Odom, Mobile, 1980-85, ptnr., 1985-95, ptnr., mem. mgmt. com., 1989-95; mem. Jackson Myrick Chambers & Byrne, Mobile, 1995—2013; mem. Dist. 32 Ala. State Senate, 2003—07; chancellor Ala. Dept. Postsecondary Edn., 2007—09; mem. US Congress from 1st Ala. Dist., Washington, 2014—, US House Armed Services Com., 2014—, US House Natural Resources Com., 2014—. Active Ala. State Bd. of Edn., 1994-2002; sec. Mobile City Planning Commn., 1990-94; hon. life mem. Ala. PTA. Named one of Outstanding Young Men of America, 1981, 82; recipient Phi Delta Phi Outstanding Lay Person award, 1998, Ala. Assn. Sch. Boards' Champion for Children award, 2004; Coun. for Leaders in Ala. Schools Legis. Leadership award, 2004, Legis. of Yr. award, Ala. Wildlife Fedn., 2005, South Ala. Literacy Champion award, 2006, Leadership award, Ala. Civil Justice Reform Com., 2007. Mem. ABA (litigation sect.), Ala. Bar Assn., Ala. State Bar, Mobile Bar Assn., Mobile Area Chamber of Commerce (vice chmn. 1989-91), Leadership Ala. Republican. Episcopalian. Office: US House of Representatives 2236 Rayburn House Office Bldg Washington DC 20515 Office Phone: 202-225-4931.*

BYRNE, C. WILLIAM, JR., athletics program director; b. Boston; m. Marilyn Kent; children: Bill, Greg. BBA, Idaho State U., 1967, MBA, 1971. Dir. alumni rels. Idaho State, 1971—76; exec. dir. Lobo Club, U. N.Mex., Albuquerque, 1976-79; asst. athletic dir. San Diego State U., 1980-82; assoc. dir., adminstr. Duck Athletic Fund, U. Oreg., Eugene, 1983-84, dir. athletic dept., 1984-92; dir. athletics U. Nebr., Lincoln, 1992—2002, Tex. A&M U., Coll. Sta., 2003—. Bd. dir. Nat. Football Found.; chair Big 12 Bd. Athletic Dirs. Recipient Carl Maddox Sports Mgmt. award, US Sports Acad., 2007; named Ctrl. Region NACDA/Continental Athletic Dir. Yr., Hall of Champions dedicated in his honor, Autzen Stadium, 1993, Nat. Fundraiser Yr., Nat. Athletic Fundraisers Assn. Mem. Nat. Assn. Collegiate Dirs. of Athletics (exec. com., pres., John L. Toner award 2002), U.S. Collegiate Sports Coun. (v.p., bd. dirs.), All-Am. Football Found. (v.p.), Football Assn. (bd. dirs.), NCAA (spl. events com., mktg. com., cert. com.), Nat. Football Found. (bd. dirs.), Big 12 Bd. of Athletic Dirs. (chair). Office: Tex A&M Univ Athletics Dept PO Box 30017 College Station TX 77842-3017

BYRNE, GRANVILLE BLAND, III, lawyer; b. San Antonio, Jan. 26, 1952; s. Granville Bland and Mary (Dowling) B.; divorced; children: Peyton Smith, Fulton Buckner; m. Monique Renée Wise, 1999; 1 child, Monique Renée-Christienne. AB, U. N.C., Chapel Hill, 1974; JD, Harvard U., 1978. Bar: Ga. 1978, U.S. Dist. Ct. (no. dist.) Ga. 1978, U.S. Ct. Appeals (5th cir.) 1978, U.S. Ct. Appeals (11th cir.) 1981. Assoc. Swift, Currie, McGhee & Hiers, Atlanta, 1978-84, ptnr., 1984-94; prin. Byrne, Eldridge, Moore & Davis, P.C., Atlanta, 1994—99, Byrne, Moore & Davis, PC, Atlanta, 1999—2002, Byrne & Davis, PC, Atlanta, 2003, Byrne, Davis & Hicks, PC, Atlanta, 2003—. Elder, mem. session 1st Presbyn. Ch. Atlanta, 1993-96, 99-2002. Mem. ABA, Ga. Bar Assn., Atlanta Bar Assn. Democrat. Presbyterian. Home: 3555 Castlegate Dr NW Atlanta GA 30327-2601 Office: Byrne Davis & Hicks PC 3340 Peachtree Rd NE Atlanta GA 30326-1000 Home Phone: 404-262-7626; Office Phone: 404-266-7260. Personal E-mail: gbb3@bellsouth.net.

BYRNE, JAMES FREDERICK, banker; b. Fairmont, NC, July 30, 1931; m. Daphne Martin, July 22, 1955; children: Paula Jean, Daphne Ann, Laura. BS, Wake Forest U., 1953; MBA, U. NC, 1959. Ptnr. Byrne-Floyd Realty, Fairmont, NC, 1961-80; v.p., city exec. So. Nat. Bank, Fairmont, 1963-69, mgr. master charge Lumberton, NC, 1969-71, v.p., dir. mktg., 1971-77, sr. v.p., dir. customer services, 1977-83, exec. v.p., 1983, exec. v.p., dir. retail banking, 1985-89, sr. exec. v.p., chief adminstrv. officer, 1989-94. Mem. endowment bd. Pembroke State U., NC, 1985—87, chmn. libr. bd., NC, 1995—96. Pres. Am. Lung Assn. NC, Wilmington, 1971, Raleigh, 1972, NC rep. dir., NY, 1977-89, nat. v.p., 1989; pres. Robeson County Cmty. Found., 2005-06, 06-07. Recipient Vol. of Yr. award, Am. Lung Assn. of N.C., 1972—90, Nat. Humanitarian award, 1993. Mem. Bank Mktg. Assn., NC Bankers Assn., Shrine Club (pres. 1996-97), Rotary (pres. 1968), Masons. Home: 1709 Waterway Dr North Myrtle Beach SC 29582

BYRNE, JOHN G., surgeon; BS in Biochemistry, U. Calif., Davis, 1982; MD, Boston U., 1987. Cert. Am. Bd. Surgery, 1996, Am. Bd. Thoracic Surgery, 1998. Intern and jr. resident U. Ill. Affiliated Hospitals, Chgo., 1987—89, sr. and chief resident in gen. surgery, 1992—95, adminstrv. chief resident in gen. surgery, 1994—95; rsch. fellow in cardiac surgery Harvard Med. Sch., Boston, 1989—92, assoc. prof. surgery; resident and chief resident in cardiothoracic surgery Brigham and Women's Hosp., Boston, 1995—97, assoc. chief and residency program dir., divsn. cardiac surgery; chair dept. cardiac surgery, William S. Stony prof. surgery Vanderbilt U. Med. Ctr., Heart and Vascular Inst., Nashville, 2004—. Contbr. articles to profl. jours. Fellow: ACS, Am. Coll. Cardiology. Office: Vanderbilt Heart and Vascular Inst 1215 21st Ave S MCE-N Tower Ste 5025 Nashville TN

37232-8802 also: Vanderbilt Med Ctr 1211 Med Ctr Dr Nashville TN 37232 Office Phone: 615-343-9195. Office Fax: 615-936-2815. Business E-Mail: john.byrne@vanderbilt.edu.

BYRNE, TIM, real estate company executive; b. Dallas, Tex. BBA, U. Tex. Founder, pres. Byrne Co.; joined Lincoln Property Co., 1976, pres. & CEO, residential divsn. Dallas, 1984—. Bd. dirs. Nat. Multi Housing Coun., Real Estate Coun., Urban Land Inst. Office: Lincoln Property Co 2000 McKinney Ave Ste 1000 Dallas TX 75201 Office Phone: 214-740-3300. Office Fax: 214-740-3313. Business E-Mail: wgibson@lpsi.com.

BYRNES, JOHN P., medical products executive; Joined Lincare Holdings, Inc., Clearwater, Fla., 1986, pres., 1996—2003, COO, 1996, CEO, 1997—, chmn., 2000—. Bd. dirs. Kinetic Concepts Inc., US Renal Care Inc. Office: Lincare Holdings inc 19387 US 19 N Clearwater FL 33764 Office Phone: 727-530-7700. Office Fax: 727-532-9692. Business E-Mail: jbyrnes@lincare.com.

BYRON, GLENN, advertising executive; Chief tech. officer Super-Media LLC (Idearc Search Mktg.). Office: SuperMedia LLC 2200 W Airfield Dr DFW Airport TX 75261 Office Phone: 800-555-4833. Business E-Mail: glennbyron@supermedia.com.

BYRON, KATHY J., state legislator; b. Abingdon, Pa., Sept. 5, 1953; m. John T. Bryon; children: Amy Manzi, John Jr., Joe. CEO B & B Presentations, Inc.; mem. Dist. 22 Va. House of Delegates, Va., 1999—; mem. Corps. Com., Ins. & Banking Com., Agr. Com., Sci. & Tech. Com., Mining & Mineral Resources Com., 1999—. Mem.: Greater Lynchburg C. of C., Rep. Women's Club. Republican. Baptist. Office: 523 Leesville Rd Lynchburg VA 24502 also: Capitol Office Gen Assembly Bldg Rm 816 PO Box 406 Richmond VA 23218 Office Phone: 434-582-1592, 804-698-1022. Business E-Mail: DelKByron@house.virginia.gov.

BZOCH, KENNETH RUDOLPH, speech and language educator, department chairman; b. Chgo., Nov. 6, 1927; s. Rudolph and Mildred (Novotny) B.; m. Lorrayne M. Cali, Oct. 29, 1950; children: Kathleen Marie, Kevin Jude. BA, DePaul U., Chgo., 1951; MA, Northwestern U., 1952, PhD, 1956. Cert. clin. competence-speech pathology, CCC-audiology; lic. speech pathologist, Fla. Asst. prof. Loyola U., Chgo., 1953—57, Northwestern U., Chgo., 1957—59; assoc. prof. U. Fla., Gainesville, 1960—64, prof., chair, 1964—96, prof. emeritus. Program dir. Communicative Disorders and Craniofacial Ctr., Shands Hosp., U. Fla.; researcher in field. Author: Communicative Disorders Related to Cleft Lip and Palate, 5th edit., 2004, Receptive-Expressive Language Test: A Method of Assessing Language Skills in Infancy, 3d edit., 2004, How Babies Learn To Talk: A Book for New Parents and Grandparents, 2004. Cpl. USMC, 1946-47. Fellow Am. Cleft Palate Assn. (past pres.), Fla. Cleft Palate Assn. (hon., past pres.), Fla. Speech Lang. and Hearing Assn. (hon., past pres.). Home and Office: 640 NW 57th St Gainesville FL 32607-6103 Home Phone: 352-331-7171; Office Phone: 352-331-7171. Personal E-mail: bzoch@aol.com.

CABANISS, THOMAS EDWARD, lawyer; b. Farmville, Va., Oct. 16, 1949; s. Frank Edward and Myrtle (Stembridge) C.; 1 child, Clara Louisa. BS, N.C. State U., 1972; JD, U. Va., 1975. Bar: Va. 1975, US Dist. Ct. (wc. and ea. dists.) Va. 1975, US Ct. Appeals (4th cir.) 1975, US Supreme Ct. 1975. Ptnr. Kaufman & Oberndorfer, Norfolk, Va., 1975-81; mem. Kaufman & Canoles P.C., Norfolk, 1982-85; ptnr. McGuireWoods LLP (formerly McGuire, Woods, Battle & Boothe), 1985—, mng. ptnr., 2007—. Del. Va. Rep. Conv., 1969-72; alt. del. Rep. Nat. Conv., Miami, Fla., 1972. Mem. ABA, Va. Bar Assn. (bd. governors bankruptcy law sect., 1990-), Harbor Club (Norfolk), Phi Kappa Phi, Tau Beta Phi. Office: McGuireWoods LLP One James Ctr 901 E Cary St Richmond VA 23219-4030 Office Phone: 804-775-4733. Office Fax: 804-225-5444. Business E-Mail: tcabaniss@mcguirewoods.com.

CABANISS, WILLIAM JELKS, JR., former ambassador, machining company executive; b. Birmingham, Ala., July 11, 1938; s. William Jelks and Florence Pierson (Sanson) Cabaniss; m. Catherine Hood Caldwell, July 20, 1962; children: Mary C., Frances C. BA, Vanderbuilt U., 1960. Dir. mktg. Southern Cement Divsn. Martin Marietta Corp., Birmingham, Ala., 1964—71; pres. Precision Grinding Inc., 1971—. Mem. Ala. House of Reps., 1978—82, Ala. State Senate, 1982—90; US amb. to Czech. Repub. US Dept. State, Prague, 2003—06. Past. pres., bd. dirs. Jr. Achievement Jefferson County. Served with US Army, 1960—64.

CABELL, MATTHEW D., oil and gas industry executive; b. Auburn Hills, Mich. m. Deborah Cabell; 1 children. BS in Geology, U. Mich.; MBA, Cornell U., Ithaca, NY. Various positions Texaco Exploration & Prodn., Inc., New Orleans; divsn. geologist Amerada Hess Corp., Houston, 1990—97; v.p. Gulf of Mex. exploration Texaco Corp., Houston, 1997—2001; exec. v.p., gen. mgr. Marubeni Oil & Gas Inc., Houston, 2003—06; pres. Seneca Resources Corp. (subs.) National Fuel Gas Co., Houston, 2006—, sr. v.p. Nat. Fuel, 2010—. Mem.: Am. Exploration & Prodn. Coun., Am. Natural Gas Alliance. Office: Seneca Resources Corp Ste 400 1201 Louisiana St Houston TX 77002 Office Phone: 713-654-2600. Office Fax: 713-654-2654.

CABRERA, ÁNGEL, academic administrator, finance educator; b. Madrid, Aug. 5, 1967; arrived in US, 1991; s. Angel and Virtudes (Izquierdo) Cabrera; m. Elizaebth Jean Frazer, Mar. 19, 1994; 2 children. BS, Madrid Polytechnical U., Spain, MS in Engring.; MS in Psychology, Ga. Inst Tech, 1993, PhD in Psychology, 1995. Rsch. engr., asst. prof. U. Politecnica, Madrid, 1990—91; mgr. Accenture, 1995—96; vis. prof. Carlos III U., 1997—98; prof. Instituto de Empresa, Madrid, 1998—2004, dir. Human Resource Dept., 1999—2000, dean, 2001—04; pres. Thunderbird Sch. Global Mgmt., Glendale, Ariz., 2004—12, George Mason U, Fairfax, Va., 2012—. Contbr. articles to profl. jours. Named a Crown Fellow, Aspen Inst., 2008; Goethe Inst. Scholar, DAAD, 1989, Fulbright Scholar, 1991—95. Mem.: APA, Cognitive Sci. Soc., European Soc. Cognitive Psychology. Office: Office of the President George Mason University 4400 University Dr Fairfax VA 22030*

CABRET, MARIA M., territorial supreme court justice; b. Frederiksted, St. Croix, VI; d. Miguel Angel and Epifania C. Cabret. BA, Marymount Manhattan Coll., NYC, 1971; JD, Howard U. Sch. Law, Washington, 1978; grad., Am. Acad. Jud. Edn., Nat. Jud. Coll. Bar: VI, US Ct. Appeals (3rd cir.). ESL tchr. Claude O. Markoe Elem. Sch., Frederiksted, VI, 1971—75; law clerk Hon. Raymond L. Finch Territorial Ct. the VI, 1978—80, judge, 1987—2006, adminstrv. judge, 1994—99, presiding judge, 2000—06, sr. judge, 2006; atty. Legal Svcs. the VI, Office the Territorial Pub. Defender; pvt. practice atty.; assoc. justice Supreme Ct. the VI, 2006—. Former mem. Conf. of Chief Justices, Am. Law Inst., Nat. Assn. Ct. Mgrs., Howard U., Law Revision Comm. Recipient Am. Jurisprudence award, Howard U., 1978; named Tchr. of Yr., Claude O. Markoe Elem. Sch., 1975; named to VI Women's Hall of Fame, 2005; fellow, ASTAR Sci. and Tech., 2009. Fellow: ABA; mem.: Jud. Coun., Nat. Assn. Women Judges, Am. Judicature Soc., Am. Judges Assn., Nat. Bar Assn. Office: Supreme Court of the US VI PO Box 590 St Thomas VI 00804*

CACCAMISE, ALFRED EDWARD, real estate executive; b. LeRoy, NY, June 9, 1919; s. Joseph Peter and Rose Marie (Petrella) C.; m. Louise Ball, July 7, 1974. Student, Officers' Candidate Sch., Camp Davis, NC, 1943, Cen. Calif. Comml. Coll., 1946-47. Lumber co. and hardware store owner, Chili, N.Y., 1956-65; motel owner DeLand, Fla., 1965-71; real estate salesman, 1974-75; real estate investments co. owner, 1972—2005; real estate broker Alliance Realty, DeLand, 1976—2005; ret. Served with U.S. Army, 1940-46. Recipient John McCready award Community Outreach Services, DeLand, 1979, 81. Mem. Nat. Assn. Realtors, Fla. Assn. Realtors, DeLand and West Volusia Bd. Realtors (bd. dirs. 1978-79, grievance com. chmn. 1983, bldg. com. chmn. 1985-87), Alhambra Villas Home Owners' Assn. (pres. 1979-80), DeLand C. of C., DeLand Com. of 100. Lodges: Kiwanis (Sav-a-Life chmn. 1977, membership chmn. 1979), Lions (charter). Democrat. Roman Catholic. Avocations: golf, travel, reading. Home: PO Box 241 Deland FL 32721-0241

CACCAMISE, GENEVRA LOUISE BALL (MRS. ALFRED E. CACCAMISE), retired librarian; b. July 22, 1934; d. Herbert Oscar and Genevra (Green) Ball; m. Alfred E. Caccamise, July 7, 1974. BA, Stetson U., DeLand, Fla., 1956; MLS, Syracuse U., NY, 1967. Tchr. grammar sch., Sanford, Fla., 1956-57; tchr. elem. sch. Longwood, Fla., 1957-58; tchr., libr. Enterprise Sch., Fla., 1958—63; libr. media specialist Boston Ave. Sch., DeLand, Fla., 1963-83; head media specialist Blue Lake Sch., DeLand, 1983-87; ret., 1987. Author: Volusia County manual Instructing the Library Assistant, 1965, Echoes of Yesterday: A History of the DeLand Area Public Library, 1912-1995, 1995, A Quest for Beauty: A History of the Garden Club of DeLand, Florida, 1927-97, 1997, Index to Reflections: West Volusia County, 100 Years of Progress, 2002, (compilation) The Minutes and Memorials of the Old Settlers of DeLand, Fla., 1882-1926, 2003, Memory Lane: A History of the Street Names of DeLand Fla., 2013. Charter mem. West Volusia Meml. Hosp. Aux., DeLand, 1962—81; leader Girl Scouts US, 1955—56; area dir. Fla. Edn. Assn., Volusia County, 1963—65; bd. dirs. Alhambra Villas Home Owners Assn., 1972—75; trustee DeLand Pub. Libr., 1977—86, sec., 1978—80, v.p., 1980—82, pres., 1982—84; v.p. Friends of DeLand Pub. Libr., 1987—88, 1998—2005, bd. dirs., 1987—, pres., 1989—90, 1995—97, 2006—, newsletter editor, 1992—95, 1999—2005; charter mem. Guild Fla. Mus. Art (formerly Guild of the DeLand Mus. Art), 1988—, pres., 1991—92, co-rec. sec., 1997—98, rec. sec., 2005—08, treas., 2011—13; bd. dirs. DeLand Mus. Art, 1991—95. Recipient Woman's Club Lit. award for contbns. to arts in West Volusia County, 1995. Mem.: DAR (asst. chief page Continental Congress, Washington 1962—65, chpt. registrar 1969—80, Excellence in Cmty. Svc. award 1995), AAUW (rec. sec. 1961—65, 2d v.p. chpt. 1965—67, rec. sec. 1978—80, pres. 1980—82, parliamentarian 1982—84), Volusia County Ret. Educators Assn. (pres. Unit II 1988—90, scholarship chmn. 1992—95, corr. sec. 2003—05), Volusia County Assn. Media in Edn. (treas. 1977), Fla. Libr. Assn., Assn. Childhood Edn. (corr. sec. 1963—65, 1st v.p. 1965—66), Roots and Brs. Gen. Soc. West Volusia County (corr. sec. 2006—08, pres. 2012—13), Nat. League Am. Pen Women, DeLand Br. (corr. sec. 1996—98, pres. 1998—2000, corr. sec. 2000—04), Magna Carta Dames, Stetson U. Alumni Assn. (class chmn. for ann. fund dr. 1968), Soc. Mayflower Descendants (lt. gov. Francis Cook Colony 1988—90), Pilgrim John Howland Soc., Colonial Dames XVII Century, Nat. Soc. New Eng. Women (v.p. Daytona Beach Colony 1990—91), Nat. Soc. US Daus. of 1812 (rec. sec. Peacock chpt. 1989—90), Fla. Hist. Soc., West Volusia Hist. Soc. (libr. 1993—, bd. dirs. 1993—, sec. 1996, v.p. 2000—02, pres. 2002—03, sec. 2013—14, Vol. of Yr. 1999, Historian of Yr. 2002, 2013), Morning Glory Garden Cir. (v.p. 2011—13, pres. 2013—14), Hibiscus Garden Cir. (treas. 1988—89, v.p. 1990—93, 1996—97, pres. 1997—99, treas. 2001—03), DeLand Garden Club (corr. sec. 1993—95, editor newsletter 1993—95, v.p. 1997—99), Bus. and Profl. Women's Club (corr. sec. DeLand 1968—71, 2d v.p. 1969—70), Delta Kappa Gamma (pres. Beta Psi chpt. 1982—84). Address: PO Box 241 Deland FL 32721-0241

CACCIATORE, S. SAMMY, lawyer; b. Tampa, Fla., Aug. 2, 1942; s. Sam and Margarita C.; m. Carolyn Michels, Aug. 10, 1963; children: Elaine Michel, Sammy Michel. BA, JD, Stetson U., DeLand, Fla., 1966. Bar: Fla. 1966, U.S. Ct. Appeals (5th cir.) 1967, U.S. Supreme Ct. 1971, U.S. Ct. Appeals (11th cir.) 1981, U.S. Dist. Ct. (mid. dist. 1966) Fla.; cert. bd. civil trial lawyer, med. malpractice, Am. Bd. Profl. Liability Lawyers. Asst. public defender 9th jud. cir. State of Fla., Fla., 1966; assoc. firm Orlando, Fla., 1966-67; pvt. practice Melbourne, Fla., 1967—; ptnr. Nance, Cacciatore, Hamilton, Barger, Nance & Cacciatore, Melbourne, Fla., 1970—. Mem. 5th Dist. Appellate Nomination Commn., 1979-83; mem. Fla. Med. Malpractice Adv. Com., 1982; mem. jud. nominating commn. Fla. Supreme Ct. 1986-90, mem. Supreme Ct. Jury Instrn. Com., 2001-10; bd. overseers Stetson U. Coll. Law, 1995-, chairperson, 2006-08; trustee Stetson U., 2000—; lectr. in field. Contbr. articles to profl. jour., chpt. to books. Trustee A. Max Brewer Meml. Law Libr., Brevard County, Fla., 1972-76, chmn., 1972-75. Mem. ABA, Am. Assn. for Justice (formerly ATLA), Am. Law Inst., Internat. Acad. Trial Lawyers, Am. Bd. Profl. Liability Lawyers, Am. Bd. Trial Advocates, Nat. Bd. Trial Advocacy, Fla. Justice Assn. (formerly Acad. Fla. Trial Lawyers; fellow, bd. dir. 1970—, pres. 1984-85, Pres.'s award 1983), Fla. Bar (bd. govs. 1994-99, exec. com. 1995-99, vice chmn. advt. task force 1995-97, budget com. 1994-97, chmn. 1996, mem. exec. com. trial lawyer sect. 1975, chmn. constl. revision com. 1997—, mem. legis. com. 1995-99, chmn. 1998-99, mem. jury instrn. com. Fla. Supreme Ct., 2001—10), So. Trial Lawyers Assn., Stetson Lawyers Assn. (1st v.p. 1992-93, pres.-elect 1994-95, pres. 1995-96), Brevard County Bar Assn. (bd. dir., Pres.'s award 1975, Lifetime Achievement award for professionalism), Vassar Carlton Inn of Ct. (emeritus), Eau Gallie Yacht Club (gov., vice commodore 1981-82, commodore 1983-84). Democrat. Roman Catholic. Avocations: fishing, boating, travel. Office: 525 N Harbor City Blvd Melbourne FL 32935-6837 Home Phone: 321-773-1711; Office Phone: 321-777-7777. Business E-Mail: sammy@nancelaw.com.

CACHERIS, JAMES C., federal judge; b. Pitts., Mar. 30, 1933; BS in Econs., U. Pa., 1955; JD cum laude, George Washington U., 1960. Bar: D.C. 1960, Va. 1962. Asst. corp. counsel, Washington, 1960-62; assoc. Miller Brown & Gildenhorn, Washington, 1962-64; pvt. practice Washington and Alexandria, Va., 1964-70; ptnr. Howard. Stevens, Lynch, Cake & Cacheris, Alexandria, Va., 1970-71; judge 19th Jud. Cir. Ct. Va., Fairfax, 1971-81, U.S. Dist. Ct. (ea. dist.) Va., Alexandria, 1981—98, sr. judge, 1998—. Mem. Va. Bar Assn., Fairfax County Bar Assn. Office: US Dist Ct 401 Courthouse Sq Alexandria VA 22314-5704

CADDY, MICHAEL DOUGLAS, lawyer, real estate broker; b. Long Beach, Calif., Mar. 23, 1938; s. Frank Edward and Tabitha (Miles) C. BS in Fgn. Svc., Georgetown U., 1960; JD, NYU, 1966. Bar: DC 1970, Tex. 1979. Practiced in, Washington and, Tex.; exec. dir. com. on pub. affairs McGraw-Edison Co., NYC, 1960-61; asst. to lt. gov. State of N.Y., 1962-65; asst. to exec. v.p. NAM, NYC, 1966-67; Washington liaison Gen. Foods Corp., 1968-70; assoc. Gall, Lane, Powell & Kilcullen, 1970-74; legis. counsel Nat. Assn. Realtors, Washington, 1975-76; atty. Office Tex. Sec. of State, Austin, 1980-81. Author: The Hundred Million Dollar Payoff, 1974, How They Rig Our Elections, 1975, Understanding Insurance, 1984, Legislative Trends in Insurance Regulation, 1985, Exploring America's Future, 1987, Watergate Exposed, 2010 Mem. Rep. County Com., N.Y.C., 1965-66; nat. dir. Young Ams. for Freedom, 1960-62. Scholar Intercollegiate Studies Inst., 1957-59. Mem.: FBA, ACLU, ABA, ATLA, Nat. Lesbian and Gay Law Assn., Nat. Trust Hist. Preservation, People for Am. Way, Supreme Ct. Hist. Soc., Nat. Coun. Crime and Delinquency, Internat. Platform Assn., Am. Acad. Polit. and Social Sci., Am. Econ. Assn., Assn. Former Intelligence Officers, Am. Judicature Soc., Stonewall Lawyers Assn. Houston, Houston Bar Assn., Tikkun Cmty. Office: 7941 Katy Fwy Ste 296 Houston TX 77024-1924 E-mail: douglascaddy@justice.com.

CADENHEAD, ALFRED PAUL, lawyer; b. LaGrange, Ga., Oct. 14, 1926; s. Roy E. and Omie (Bishop) C.; m. Sara Davenport, Oct. 14, 1945; children: Steven Paul, David James. Jr. coll. certificate, W. Ga. Coll., 1944; LLB, Emory U., 1949; LHD (hon.), U. West Ga., Carrollton, 2012. Bar: Ga. 1949. Sr. counsel, ptnr. Hurt, Richardson, Garner, Todd & Cadenhead, Atlanta; with Hurt, Richardson, 1977-92; of counsel Fellows La Briola LLP, Atlanta, 1993—. Pres. Atlanta Legal Aid Soc., 1958. Pres. Met. Atlanta Mental Health Assn., 1964-65, Ga. Assn. Mental Health, 1968; past trustee Queens Coll., Charlotte, NC; lifetime trustee West Ga. Found. Served with paratroops US Army, 1944-46. Recipient West Ga. Coll. Disting. Svc. award, 1993, Emory U. Law Sch. Disting. Alumnus award, 1996, Ben F. Johnson Pub. Svc. award Ga. State U., 1999, Founders award State U. West Ga., 2001; named to Hall of Fame State Bd. Regents, 2013. Fellow Am. Bar Found., Am. Acad. Matrimonial Lawyers, Am. Coll. Trial Lawyers, Internat Soc. Barristers; mem. State Bar Ga. (past bd. govs.), Atlanta Bar Assn. (pres. 1970-71, Charles E. Watkins award for disting. and sustained svc. 1992, Leadership award 2000, Professionalism award, 2004), Atlanta Estate Planning Coun. (pres. 1976, U.W. Ga. Thelma Harman Tarner Loyalty award, 2012). Presbyterian. Office: South Tower Peachtre Ctr Ste 2300 225 Peachtree St NE Atlanta GA 30303-1731 Home: 4094 S Creek Ct Austell GA 30106 Business E-Mail: pcadenhead@fellab.com.

CADIEUX, CHESTER, retail executive; b. Tulsa, 1932; m. Debbie Cadieux; 6 children; 1 child, Chester III. BBA, U. Okla., 1954. Salesman Maneke-Kinzie Printing Co., Tulsa, Okla., 1954—58; co-founder (with Burt B. Holmes) QuikTrip, Tulsa, Okla., 1958, CEO. Bd. trustees U. Tulsa; pres. Nat. Assn. Convenience Stores; mem. bd. C. of C., Tulsa; chmn. Tulsa Area United Way, River Parks Authority; mem. bd. Nat. Benevolent Assn., Tulsa Cmty Found., Okla. Bus. and En. Coalition, Trust for Public Lands. Named Ernst and Young Southwest Retail-Wholesale Entrepreneur of Yr.; named to Okla. Commerce and Industry Hall of Fame. Avocations: reading, running. Office: QuikTrip Corp 4705 S 129th East Ave Tulsa OK 74134

CAETANO, RAUL, psychiatrist, educator; b. São Paulo, Brazil, May 5, 1945; came to U.S., 1978; s. Silvestre Vieira and Vera Vieira (Barbosa) C.; m. Patrice Vaeth, Sept. 30, 1995; children: Izabel, Lauren, Helena. MD, U. Rio de Janeiro, 1969, diploma in Psychiatry, 1971; MPH, U. Calif., Berkeley, 1979, PhD, 1983. Psychiatrist Pinel Hosp., Rio de Janeiro, 1969-73; asst. prof. State U., Rio de Janeiro, 1969-73; rsch. psychiatrist Inst. Psychiatry U. London, 1973-76; asst. prof. Inst. Psychiatry, Rio de Janeiro, 1976-78; vis. scholar Alcohol Rsch. Group, Berkeley, 1978-83, assoc. scientist to sr. scientist, 1983-94, dir., 1992—. Adj. prof. Sch. Pub. Health, U. Calif., Berkeley, 1991-98; assoc. dir. Calif. Pacific Med. Ctr. Rsch. Inst., San Francisco, 1992-93; prof., regional dean Sch. Pub. Health, U. Tex., 1998—, prof., dean Sch. Health Professions, U. Tex. Southwestern Med. Ctr., 2006-. Contbr. articles to profl. jours. WHO fellow, 1973-76; rsch. grantee Nat. Inst. Alcohol Abuse and Alcoholism, 1985—. Mem. APHA, Am. Coll. Epidemiology, Rsch. Soc. Alcoholism. Roman Catholic. Office: V8112 5323 Harry Hines Blvd Dallas TX 75390-9128 Office Phone: 214-648-1080. Business E-Mail: raul.caetano@utsouthwestern.edu.

CAFARO, DEBRA A., real estate company executive; b. Dec. 15, 1957; m. Terrence Livingston; 2 children. BA in Govt. magna cum laude, U. Notre Dame, 1979; JD, U. Chgo., 1982. Bar: Ill., Pa. Jud. clk. Hon. J. Dickson Phillips 4th cir. US Ct. of Appeals, 1982—83; founding mem. Barack Ferrazzano Kirschbaum Perlman & Nagelberg LLP, Chgo., 1986—97; pres. Ambassador Apartments, Inc., 1997—98; pres., CEO Ventas, Inc., Louisville, 1999—2003, chmn. bd., pres., CEO, 2003—. Adj. prof. law Northwestern U. Law Sch., 1988—92; bd. dirs. Ambassador Apartments, Inc., 1997—98, Weyerhaeuser Co., 2007—, chair fin. com., mem. compensation com.; bd. dirs. General Growth Properties, Inc., 2010—. Recipient Aiming High award, Legal Momentum, 2009; named Female Leader of the Yr., Comml. Property News, 2007, Outstanding Woman, Nat. Real Estate Investor Mag., 2008, Woman of Influence, Real Estate Forum, 2008, Best CEOs, Forbes, 2010; named one of Best of the Best, Real Estate Investment Trust (REIT) CEOs, 2003, 50 Women to Watch, Wall St. Journal, 2004, Top 25 Women in Healthcare, Modern Healthcare mag., 2011, Women to Watch, Crain's Chgo. Bus., 2011. Mem.: Nat. Assn. of Corp. Dirs., Nat. Assn. of Real Estate Investment Trusts (bd. dirs., immediate past chair). Office: Ventas Inc Ste 300 10350 Ormsby Park Pl Louisville KY 40223

CAFFARELLI, LUIS ANGEL, mathematician, educator; b. Buenos Aires, Dec. 8, 1948; came to U.S., 1973; s. Luis and Hilda Delia (Cespi) C.; m. Irene Andrea Martinez-Gamba; children: Alejandro, Nicolas, Mauro. MS, Univ. Buenos Aires, 1969, PhD, 1972; D (hon.), Univ. Autonoma de Madrid, 1992, Univ. del la Plata, Argentina, 2003, Ecole Normal Superieur, Paris, 2003, Universidad de San Luis, 2007, U. Norte Dame, 2012; D, U. Buenos Aires, 2012. Postdoctoral asst., asst. prof. U. Buenos Aires, 1972-73; postdoctoral Univ. Minn., 1973—74, asst. prof., 1975—77, assoc. prof., 1977—79, prof., 1979—83; prof. math. Univ. Chgo., 1983-86, Courant Inst., NYU, 1980—82, 1994—97, Inst. for Advanced Study, Princeton, NJ, 1986—96; prof. math. and the Inst. for Computational Engring. and Sciences Univ. Tex., Austin, 1997—. Hon. prof. math. Univ. de Buenos Aires, Univ. de Mar del Plata. Contbr. articles to profl. jours. Co-Recipient Stampacchia prize Scuola Normale de Pisa, 1982, Wolf Found. prize in Mathematics, 2012; recipient Premio Konex Platimo-Brillante, 2003, Rolf Schock prize, Royal Swedish Acad. Sciences, 2005; Guggenheim Fellowship, 1985. Mem. NAS, Am. Acad. Arts & Sciences, Acad. Medicine, Engring., and Sci, Tex., Pontifical Acad. Sci.(Pius XI Gold medal, 1988), Am. Math. Soc.(Bocher prize, 1984, Leroy P. Steele prize for Lifetime Achievement, 2009), Union Matematica Argentina, Soc. for Industrial and Applied Mathematics; fgn. mem. Accademia dei XL, Academia Argentina de Ciencias, Accademia Nazionale delle Scienze, Italy, Accademia Nazionale dei Lincei, Italy, Academia Nacional de Ciencias, Buenos Aires and Cordoba, Istituto Lombardo, Accademia di Scienze e Lettere, Italy. Office: University of Texas Dept Math RLM 10.150 1 University Station C1200 Austin TX 78712-1082 Office Phone: 512-471-3160. Office Fax: 512-471-9038. Business E-Mail: caffarel@math.utexas.edu.

CAFFEY, HORACE ROUSE, academic administrator, agricultural company executive; b. Grenada, Miss., Mar. 24, 1929; s. C. Horace and Anna Belle (James) C.; m. Lois (Granger) Stevens, Mar. 13, 1999; children: Brenda, Jerry, Belle, Rex. BS, Miss. State U., 1951, MS, 1955; PhD, La State U., 1959. Agronomist in charge rice project Miss. Agrl. Exptl. Sta., Stoneville, 1958—62; supt. La. State U. Rice Sta.,

La. Agrl. Exptl. Sta., Crowley, 1962—70; assoc. dir., prof. La. State U., La. Agrl. Exptl. Sta., Baton Rouge, 1970—79; vice-chancellor adminstrn. La. State U. Agrl. Ctr., 1979—80, vice-chancellor internat. programs, 1980—81, chancellor, 1981—84, 1984—97, interim chancellor, 2007—08; chancellor La. State U., Alexandria, 1981—84; pres., CEO Caffey Internat. Inc., 1997—; interim v.p. acad. affairs La. Coll., 2005. Internat. rice cons. AID, World Bank, other orgns., 1965—; mem. pub. health study team Nat. Acad. Sci., Washington, 1973-74; mem. adv. bd. Bd. Regents Masters Plan Higher Edn., Baton Rouge, 1977; Nat. co-chair joint coun. for Food and Agr., 1989-94, Internat. Sci. and Edn. Coun., 1986-90; chmn. Nat. Assn. State Univs. and Land Grant Colls. divsn. Agr. Budget Com., 1989; spring semester interim v.p. acad. affairs La. Coll., Pineville, 2005. Contbr. articles to profl. jours., chapters to books. Pres. Internat. Rice Festival, Crowley, 1968; bd. dirs. Boy Scouts U.S.A., United Way, others. Served to 1st lt. 82nd airborne US Army, 1951—54. Recipient Internat. award of Merit Gamma Sigma Delta, 1970, 81; honoree Internat. Rice Festival, 1974; named Man of Yr. Crowley C. of C., 1969-70, Progressive Farmer Man of Yr. in Svc. to La. Agr., 1986, Outstanding Alumnus Coll. Agr. of La. State U., 1992, Alumnus of Yr., La. State U., 1993, Outstanding Alumnus of Yr., Coll. Agr., Miss. State U., 1993. Mem. Sigma Xi, Gamma Sigma Delta, Phi Delta Kappa, Omicron Delta Kappa, Phi Delta Phi, Phi Zeta. Lodges: Rotary. Democrat. Baptist. Home: 10471 Barry Dr Baton Rouge LA 70809-3265 Office: Chancellor Emeritus La State U 4560 Essen Ln Baton Rouge LA 70809-3424 Personal E-mail: hrcaffey@aol.com.

CAGLE, CASEY (LOWELL S. CAGLE), Lieutenant Governor of Georgia; b. Hall County, Ga., Jan. 12, 1966; m. Nita Cagle; children: Jared, Grant, Carter. Attended, Gainesvill Coll., Ga. Southern U. Mem. dDst. 49 Ga. State Senate, 1995—2007; pres. Casey Cagle Properties; lt. gov. State of Ga., 2007—. Ga. rep. environment com. Nat. Conf. State Legislatures. Republican. Office: Office of Lieutenant Governor 240 State Capitol Atlanta GA 30334 Office Phone: 404-656-5030. Office Fax: 404-656-6739.*

CAGLE, JAMES DOUGLAS, retail executive; s. J. Douglas Cagle; children: George Douglas, James David. Pres. Cagle's, Inc., 1970—93, CEO, 1970—, chmn., 1993—, pres., 2004—. Bd. advisor PotatoFinger Snack Foods, Inc. Past pres. Ga. Poultry Fedn., Ga. Poultry Processors Assn., Ga. Poultry Improvement Assn.; trustee, pension plan RWDSU; bd. dirs. Georgia Net; trustee Mercer U. Mem.: US Poultry & Egg Assn. (bd. dirs.). Office: Cagles Inc 1385 Collier Rd NW Atlanta GA 30318 Office Phone: 404-355-2820. Office Fax: 404-350-9605. Business E-Mail: jcagle@caglesinc.com.

CAHILL, GERALD R., cruise line company executive; BBA, U. Miami, 1973. With Price Waterhouse LLP, Resorts Internat., Inc., 1979—88; CFO then COO Safecard Svcs., Inc.; v.p. fin. Carnival Corp., 1994—98, sr. v.p. fin., 1998—2003, exec. v.p., CFO, 1998—2007; pres., CEO Carnival Cruise Lines Carnival Corp. & plc, 2007—. Office: Carnival Corp 3655 NW 87th Ave Miami FL 33178-2428 Office Phone: 305-599-2600. Office Fax: 305-406-4700. Business E-Mail: gerald.cahill@carnivalcorp.com.

CAHILL, HARRY AMORY, diplomat, educator; b. NYC, Jan. 10, 1930; s. Harry Amory and Elaine Olga (Loumena) C.; m. Angelica Margarita Ravazzoli, Dec. 12, 1956; children— Alan, Daniel, Sylvia, Irene, Madeleine, Steven BA, Manhattan Coll., NYC, 1951; postgrad., Johns Hopkins U., 1964-65; MS, George Washington U., Washington, 1972. Sales exec. Johns Manville Corp., NY, 1954-56; fgn. service officer U.S. Dept. of State, Washington, 1956-59, Oslo, 1959-61, Warsaw, 1961-64, Belgrade, Yugoslavia, 1965-68, Montevideo, Uruguay, 1968-71, Lagos, Nigeria, 1975-78, Colombo, Sri Lanka, 1979-81; dir. comml. service U.S. Dept. Commerce, 1982-83; U.S. consul gen. Dept. of State, Bombay, 1983-87; U.S. Mission to UN, dep. U.S. rep. UN Econ. and Social Coun., NYC, 1987-89; pres. Amory Assoc., Inc., McLean, Va., 1990—, World of Film Found., NYC. Prof. Pepperdine U., 1992—, Georgetown U., 1995; cons. U.S. Dept. State, 1991—, U.S. Dept. Def., 1999—. Author: The China Trade and U.S. Tariffs, 1973. Pres. Hinduja Found., NYC, 1993—2002. Woodrow Wilson Nat. Fellowship found. fellow, 1990-93. Mem. Am. Fgn. Svc. Assn. Roman Catholic. Avocation: photography. Office: 1240 Daleview Dr Mc Lean VA 22102-1539 E-mail: hacahill@aol.com.

CAHILL, JOHN T., former private equity firm executive; b. 1957; m. Betsy Cahill; 4 children. AB in Economics, Harvard U., 1979; MBA in Bus. Adminstrn., Harvard Bus. Sch., 1983. CFO RKO Pictures; sr. v.p. finance, CFO KFC, 1993—96; v.p. corporate finance, asst. treas. PepsiCo, Inc., 1989—93, sr. v.p., treas., 1997—98; sr. v.p., CFO PepsiCo North America, 1996—97; exec. v.p., CFO Pepsi Bottling Group, Inc., 1998—2000, pres., COO, 2000—01, chmn., CEO, 2001—06, chmn., 2006—07; industrial ptnr. Ripplewood Holdings, LLC, 2008—11; chmn. Kraft Foods Group Inc., 2012—. Bd. dirs. Woodward/White Pub. Co., Pepsi Bottling Group, Inc., 1999—2007, Colgate-Palmolive Co., 2005—, Legg Mason, Inc., 2010—.

CAHILL, MARY BETH, political strategist; BA in Polit. Sci., Emmanuel Coll. Receptionist and caseworker to Senator Robert Drinan, Rep. Barney Frank, Senator Patrick Leahy; asst. to pres., dir. pub. liaison The White House, Washington; chief of staff to Senator Ted Kennedy; campaign manager to Senator John Kerry's presdl. campaign, 2003; fellow Harvard Inst. of Politics John F. Kennedy Sch. of Govt., Harvard U., 2005. Former exec. dir. EMILY's List; spkr. in field. Democrat. Office: c/o Washington Speakers Bur 1663 Prince St Alexandria VA 22314

CAILLAT, COLBIE MARIE, singer; b. Malibu, Calif., May 28, 1985; Singer: (albums) Coco, 2007, Breakthrough, 2009, All of You, 2011, Christmas In The Sand, 2012, (songs) Bubbly, 2007 (Song of Yr., BMI Pop Awards, 2009), Realize, 2008, (with Jason Mraz) Lucky, 2008 (Best Pop Collaboration with Vocals, Grammy awards, 2010), (with Taylor Swift) Breathe, 2008, Fallin' for You, 2009, I Never Told You, 2010. Named Songwriter of Yr., Broadcast Music, Inc. (BMI) Awards, 2009. Office: c/o Fitzgerald Hartley Co 1908 Wedgewood Blvd Nashville TN 37212

CAIN, HAROLD D., critical care specialist; MD, U. Tex. Southwestern Med. Ctr., Dallas, 1971. Diplomate Am. Bd. Internal Medicine, 1974, Am. Bd. Internal Medicine- pulmonary disease, 1978, Am. Bd. Internal Medicine- critical care medicine, 1999. Resident in internal medicine NC meml. Hosp., Chael Hill, 1972—74; fellow in pulmonary disease Baylor Univ. Med.Ctr., Houston, 1976—78; critical care specialist St. David North Austin Med. Ctr. Office: Saint David North Austin Medical Center 12201 renfert Wat Ste 260 Austin TX 78758 Office Phone: 512-977-0123. Office Fax: 512-977-0126.

CAIN, HERMAN, entrepreneur; b. Memphis, Dec. 13, 1945; s. Luther and Lenora (Davis) Cain; m. Gloria Etchison, 1968; children: Melanie, Vincent. BA in Mathematics, Morehouse Coll., Atlanta, 1967; MS in Computer Sci., Purdue U., West Lafayette, Ind., 1971. Ballistics positions Dept. Navy; computer sys. bus. analyst Coca-Cola Co., Atlanta, 1971—77; various positions to v.p. Pillsbury Co., 1977—82, regional v.p. Burger King divsn. Phila., 1982—86; pres., CEO Godfather's Pizza, Omaha, 1986—88, chmn., CEO, 1988—96; chmn. Nat. Restaurant Assn., Washington, 1994—95, pres., CEO, 1996—99, RetailDNA, 1999—2000; founder, chmn., CEO THE New Voice, Inc., Morrow, Ga., 2004—. Bd. dirs. Fed. Res. Bank Kansas City, 1992—96, dep. chmn., 1992—94, chmn., 1995—96; bd. dirs. Whirlpool Corp., 1992—2003, Aquila, Inc., 1992—2008, Reader's Digest Assn. Inc., 2001—07, AGCO Corp., 2004—11; candidate for Republican nomination 2012 US Presdl. Election. Author: Leadership is Common Sense, 1997, Speak as a Leader, 1999, CEO of Self: You Are in Charge, 2001, They Think You're Stupid: Why Democrats Lost Your Vote and What Republicans Must Do to Keep It, 2005, This Is Herman Cain!: My Journey to the White House, 2011; commentator Fox Bus. Network, syndicated columnist North Star Writers Group, host The Herman Cain Show, Atlanta Radio News Talk 750 WSB. Mem. Nat. Commn. Econ. Growth & Tax Reform, 1995; sr. econ. adviser Dole/Kemp presdl. campaign, 1996; Rep. candidate for US Senate Ga., 2004; Rep. presdl. candidate, 2012. Recipient Operator of Yr./Gold Plate award, Internat. Foodservice Mfrs. Assn., 1991, Horatio Alger award, 1996; named one of The 100 Most Influential Black Americans, Ebony mag., 1997, 1999, The 10 Most Fascinating People of 2011, Barbara Walters Special. Republican. Baptist. Office: THE New Voice Inc PO Box 278 Stockbridge GA 30281-0278

CAIN, JAMES DAVID, state legislator; b. Pitkin, La., Oct. 13, 1938; s. Alton J Cain and Mary Etta Thornton; m. Goldie Bonds, 1961; children: Melissa Ann, James David Jr. Sch tchr. & head coach East Beauregard High Sch., 1962—72; state rep. Dist. 32, 1972—92; state senator Dist. 30, 1992—; v. chmn. Ins. Com.; mem. Coms. on Judiciary, Natural Resources & Joint Budget; farmer & rancher. Named Outstanding Coach in Dist., La Coach Yr.; named to La Coaches Hall of Fame, 1992. Mem.: Allen Parish Assn., La Farm Bur., Beauregard C. of C., McNeese Alumni Assn., Nat & La Coaches Assns., Am. Brahman Breeder's Assn., Beauregard Parish Cattlemen's Assn. Democrat. Bapt. Address: PO Box 460 Dry Creek LA 70637 Office Phone: 225-342-2040. Fax: 318-491-2027.

CAIN, JAMES PALMER, lawyer, former ambassador; b. NC, 1957; m. Helen Cain; children: Cameron, Laura. BA in Politics, Wake Forest U., 1979, JD cum laude, 1984. Bar: NC 1984. Atty., co-founder Kilpatrick Stockton, LLP, Raleigh, NC, 1985—2000, ptnr., 2002—05; counsel Kilpatrick Stockton LLP, Raleigh, NC, 2009—; pres. Carolina Hurricanes NHL/Gale Force Holdings, 2000—02; US amb. to Denmark US Dept. State, Copenhagen, 2005—09. NC vice chair Bush-Cheney Presdl. Campaign, 2004; mem. Rep. Nat. Com. Recipient Nat. Outstanding Cmty. Svc. award, Am. Diabetes Assn., 2003, Grand Cross of the Order of the Dannebrog, H.M. Queen Margrethe of Denmark, 2008, John Ross Leadership award, Greater Raleigh Convention & Visitors Bur. Republican. Office: Kilpatrick Stockton LLP Ste 400 4208 Six Forks Rd Ste 1400 Raleigh NC 27609-5764 Office Phone: 919-420-1776. Office Fax: 919-510-6179. E-mail: JCain@KilpatrickStockton.com.

CALABRESE, MICHAEL RAPHAEL, manufacturing executive, lawyer, consultant; b. Atlantic City, May 28, 1956; s. Angelo William and Sally (Snyder) C.; m. Kitty R. Calabrese. BS in Fgn. Svc., Georgetown U., 1978; JD, U. Va., 1982. Law clk. to cir. judge U.S. Ct. Appeals (4th cir.), Washington, 1982—83; assoc. Mudge, Rose et al, Washington, 1983—84, Finley, Kumble et al, Washington, 1984—86, Morgan, Lewis & Bockius, Washington, 1986—92; ptnr. McKenna & Cuneo, Washington, 1992—95; asst. gen. counsel Lockheed Martin Corp., Bethesda, Md., 1995—99; ptnr. Coudert Bros., Washington, 1999—2003; cons. investment banking, corp. and internat., 2004—06; sr. v.p. Cajun Industries, LLC, 2006—. Mem.: Columbia Country Club, Univ. Club, Army and Navy Club, Phi Beta Kappa. Republican. Home: 17907 E Augusta Dr Baton Rouge LA 70810

CALADO, MIGUEL MARIA, consumer products company executive; b. Lisbon, Portugal, July 25, 1955; came to U.S., 1994; s. Jose Maria and Maria Rosario (Oliveira) C.; m. Maria Da Gama, Apr. 15, 1980; children: Maria Gama, Filipa Gama, Andre Gama. BS in Acctg., Pontifical Cath. U., Rio de Janeiro, Brazil, 1979, BS in Bus. Adminstrn., 1981. Asst. contr. Samarco SA, Belo Horizonte, Brazil, 1976—81; contr. Renz-Zanini, Sao Paulo, Brazil, 1981—82, fin. dir., CFO, 1982—83; v.p. fin., CFO Pepsi Cola do Brazil, Rio de Janeiro, 1983—87; v.p., Fin., CFO Pepsi Cola Far East, Singapore, 1987—90; v.p. Fin., CFO Pepsi Cola Asia, Hong Kong, 1990—92; v.p., Fin., CFO Gamesa SA, Monterrey, Mexico, 1992—94; v.p., Fin. Pepsico Foods Internat., NYC, 1994—95; sr. v.p., Fin., CFO Frito-Lay Internat., Dallas, 1996—98; exec. v.p., pres. Internat. Suiza Foods Corp., Dallas, 1998—2006; exec. v.p., pres., Internat. Ops. Dean Foods, 1998—2005; bd. dirs., CEO Hovione, LLC, East Wintsoc, NJ, 2006—; pres. GAMCAL, LLC, 2006. Bd. dirs. HNI Corp., 2004—. Mem.: European Corp. Governance Inst. Office: Dean Foods 2575 Mckinney Ave # 1200 Dallas TX 75201-1949 Home: 3924 Stanford Dallas TX 75225-7110 Office: HNI Corp Bd Directors 408 E Second St Muscatine IA 52761-0071 Office Phone: 563-272-7400. Office Fax: 563-272-7655. E-mail: caladom@honi.com.

CALAVIA, JOSE EMILIO, physics professor; s. Benigno and Marta Elena Calavia. BS in Physics, Fla. Internat. U., Miami, 1974; postgrad., Johns Hopkins U., Balt., 1979—81, MS in Physics, 1984. Engr. Bendix, Columbia, Md., 1978—87; sr. scientist McDonnell Douglas Astronautics, Huntington Beach, Calif., 1987—89; prof. physics Miami Dade Coll., 1991—. Author: (60 web-based tutorials) Physics and Mathematics for Physics. Vol. Cat Network, Miami, 1994—2008.

CALDERON, JOSE, professional basketball player; b. Villanueva de la Serena, Spain, Sept. 28, 1981; married; 1 child. Guard LEB Lucentum Alicante, 1999—2000, ACB Lucentum Alicante, 2000—01, ACB Fuenlabrada, 2001—02, Tau Ceramica, Spanish League, 2002—03, Tau Saski Baskonia Vitoria, Spanish League, 2003—04, Tau Vitoria, Spanish League, 2004—05, Toronto Raptors, 2005—13, Detroit Pistons, 2013, Dallas Mavericks, 2013—. Mem. Spanish Nat. Team World Championship Basketball, Indpls., 2002, FIBA European Championship, Sweden, 2003, Spain, 2007, Lithuania, 2011, Summer Olympic Games, Athens, Greece, 2004, Beijing, 2008, Loondon, 2012, FIBA World Championship, 2006. Recipient Silver medal, FIBA European Championship, 2003, 2007, Gold medal, 2011, FIBA World Championship, 2006, Silver medal, men's basketball, Summer Olympic Games, 2008, 2012. Achievements include member of Spanish National Cup winning Tau Saski Baskonia Vitoria, 2004. Office: Dallas Mavericks The Pavilion 2909 Taylor St Dallas TX 75226*

CALDWELL, BARRY H., waste management executive; Atty. Kutak Rock & Campbell, Washington, Cole Corette & Abrutyn, Washington; counsel to chief of staff US Senator Arlen Specter; v.p. fed. affairs Pharm. Rsch. and Mfrs. of Am.; v.p. govt. rels. CIGNA Corp., 2000—02; sr. v.p. govt. affairs and corp. comm. Waste Management, Inc., 2002—. Bd. dirs. Keep Am. Beautiful, 2005. Office: Waste Mgmt Inc 1001 Fannin Ste 4000 Houston TX 77002 Office Phone: 713-512-6200.

CALDWELL, BILLY RAY, geologist; b. Newellton, La., Apr. 20, 1932; s. Leslie Richardson and Helen Merle (Clark) C.; m. Carolyn Marie Heath; children: Caryn, Jeana, Craig. BA, Tex. Christian U., 1954, MA, 1970; PhD, Cambridge Grad. Sch., 2004. Cert. petroleum geologist, profl. geologist; lic. geoscientist, Tex. Geologist Geol. Engring. Svc. Co., Ft. Worth, 1954-60; sci. tchr. Ft. Worth and Lake Worth Sch. Dists., 1960-63; mgr. Outdoor Living, 1963-71; adjunct prof. geology Tarrant County Coll., Ft. Worth, 1971—. Petroleum and environ. geologist cons., Ft. Worth, 1971—. Bd. dirs. Ft. Worth and Tarrant County Homebuilders Assn., 1973; past chmn. Ft. Worth Environ. Coun. Named Dir. of Yr. Ft. Worth Jaycees, 1966-67. Mem. Am. Inst. Profl. Geologists, Am. Assn. Petroleum Geologists, Geol. Soc. Am., Ft. Worth Geol. Soc. Republican. Baptist. Avocations: travel, cruiseship lecturer. Home: 305 Bodart Ln Fort Worth TX 76108-3804 Office: PO Box 150989 Fort Worth TX 76108-0989 Office Phone: 817-246-5477. Personal E-mail: bcgeology@sbcglobal.net.

CALDWELL, BUDDY (JAMES DAVID CALDWELL, JR.), state attorney general; b. Columbia, La., May 20, 1946; s. James David and Genevieve (Minsky) Caldwell; m. Pat Caldwell; 7 children. BA in Psychology, Tulane U., New Orleans; JD, Tulane U. Law Sch., 1973. Pvt. practice atty., Tallulah, La., 1973—79; dist. atty. Sixth Jud. Dist. Ct. La., 1979—2008; atty. gen. State of La., 2008—. Bd. dirs. La. Dist. Attorney's Assn., 1983—96. Mem.: Tallulah Lions Club (past pres.). Democrat. Office: Office of the Attorney General PO Box 94005 Baton Rouge LA 70804-4095 Office Phone: 225-326-6079.*

CALDWELL, DAVID, professional sports team executive; b. Buffalo; m. Joelle Caldwell; 1 child, David Michael II. BS in Finance/Bus. Adminstrn., John Carroll U., University Heights, Ohio. Scouting asst. Carolina Panthers, 1996—97; area scout Indpls. Colts, 1998—2007; dir. coll. scouting Atla. Falcons, 2008—11, dir. player personnel, 2012—13; gen. mgr. Jacksonville Jaguars, 2013—. Office: Jacksonville Jaguars One EverBank Field Dr Jacksonville FL 32202

CALDWELL, GARNETT ERNEST, lawyer; b. Houston, July 2, 1934; s. William Ernest and Ethel Leona (Jones) C. BA, U. Houston, 1957, JD, 1959. Bar: Tex. 1958. Pvt. practice law, Houston, 1959-64; ptnr. Ginther, Erwin, Dillard & Caldwell, Houston, 1964-65, Prappas, Caldwell & Moncure, Houston, 1965-77, Caldwell & Baggott, Houston, 1977-82, Caldwell, Wallis, Pruitt & Baggott, Houston, 1982; pvt. practice Houston, 1982-85, 87-90, Houston and Galveston, 1990—; ptnr. Caldwell & Lareau, 1985-87. Lectr. govt. U. Houston, 1961—62. 2d lt. U.S. Army, 1957, lt. col. Res., 1977—. Decorated knight and knight comdr. Royal Yugoslavian Order St. John of Jerusalem. Mem. Galveston County Bar Assn. (dir. 2006-07), Houston Bar Assn., Houston Sr. Lawyers Forum, Houston Bankruptcy Conf., Res. Officers Assn., Houston Early Music Soc., K.C., Delta Theta Phi. Roman Catholic. Home and Office: 1619 Post Office St Galveston TX 77550-4813 Office Phone: 409-762-3500.

CALDWELL, JAMES D., hotel executive; married; 3 children. BBA in Acctg. with highest honors, U. Tex., 1977, JD with honors. Acct. Peat Marwick, Houston, Corpus Christi; ptnr. law firm Tex.; v.p., gen. counsel TRT Holdings, Inc., 1991-96; pres. TRT Devel. Co., Omni Hotels Mgmt. Corp., 1996—2004, CEO, 2004—. Office: Omni Hotels 420 Decker Dr Irving TX 75062-3952

CALDWELL, KAREN K., federal judge; b. Stanford, Ky., 1956; BA, Transylvania U., 1977; JD, U. Ky., 1980. Fields claims rep. State Farm Fire & Casualty, 1980—87; asst. US atty. US Dist. Ct. (ea. dist.) Ky., Lexington, 1987—90; US atty. Ea. Dist. Ky., 1991—93; pvt. practice atty. Ky., 1993—2001; of counsel Breeding, McIntyre & Cunningham, Lexington, Ky.; judge US Dist. Ct. Ky., Lexington, 2001. Adj. prof. Eastern Ky. U., 1984—85, 1987, Transylvania U., 2000. Office: US Dist Ct 101 Barr St Ste 136 Lexington KY 40507 Office Phone: 859-233-2828. Office Fax: 859-233-2413.

CALDWELL, MATTHEW H., state legislator; b. Gainesville, Fla., Aug. 12, 1981; s. Stephen and Delina Caldwell; m. Yvonne Medina; 1 child, Ava. AA, Edison CC, Fort Myers, Fla., 2001; BA in History, Fla. Gulf Coast U., Fort Myers, 2004. Real estate appraiser, Fla.; mem. Dist. 73 Fla. House Of Representative, 2011—. Republican. Office: 2120 Main St Ste 208 Fort Myers FL 33901-3010 also: Florida House Of Representative 1102 The Capitol 402 S Monroe St Tallahassee FL 32399-1300 Office Phone: 239-533-2411, 850-488-1541.

CALDWELL, NIKKI, women's college basketball coach; b. Oak Ridge, Tenn., 1972; BS in Pub. Rels., U. Tenn., 1994. Analyst FOX Sports Net South, 1994—97; cable TV sports host Shop at Home, 1997—98; grad. asst. U. Tenn. Lady Volunteers, 1998—99, asst. coach, 2002—08, U. Va. Cavaliers, 1999—2002; head coach UCLA Bruins, 2008—11, La. State U. Lady Tigers, 2011—. Recipient Gloria Ray Leadership award. Avocations: golf, movies. Office: La State University Womens Basketball Athletics Dept PO Box 25095 Baton Rouge LA 70894-5095 Office Phone: 310-825-8699.

CALDWELL, RICHARD H., lawyer; b. Pine Bluff, Ark., 1939; BS cum laude, U. Houston, 1960; LLB, Harvard Law Sch., 1963. Bar: Tex. 1963, US Ct. Appeals (5th cir.), US Ct. Appeals (11th cir.), US Dist. Ct. (no. dist.) Tex., US Dist. Ct. (so. dist.) Tex., US Dist. Ct. (ea. dist.) Tex., US Dist. Ct. (we. dist.) Tex., US Supreme Ct. Ptnr., co-chmn. Litig. Sect. Andrews Kurth LLP, Houston, mem. mgmt. com. Named one of Best Lawyers in Am. Fellow: Internat. Acad. Trial Lawyers, Houston Bar Found., Tex. Bar Found.; mem.: State Bar Tex., Phi Kappa Phi, Omicron Delta Kappa. Office: Andrews Kurth LLP Ste 4200 600 Travis St Houston TX 77002-3090 Office Phone: 713-220-4712. Office Fax: 713-238-7361. Business E-Mail: rcaldwell@andrewskurth.com.

CALDWELL, RODNEY KENT, lawyer; b. Washington, Feb. 19, 1937; s. Rodney Huntington and Marion Elizabeth Caldwell; m. Marjorie Lee Zink, Apr. 15, 1965 (div. 1975); children: Dana Kent, Susan Ashley; m. Yolanda Silva, June 22, 1979; 1 child, David Huntington. BChemE, U. Va., 1959; JD, U. Houston, 1969. Bar: Tex. 1969, U.S. Supreme Ct. 1975. With Howrey LLP (formerly Arnold, White & Durkee), Houston, 1970—, Pirkey Barber LLp, Austin, 2011—. Lt. USAF, 1959-62. Fellow Tex. Bar Found., Houston Bar Found.; mem. ABA, Am. Intellectual Property Law Assn., Internat. Assn. for the Protection of Intellectual Property, Army and Navy Club. Methodist. Home: 4021 Ella Lee Ln Houston TX 77027-3910 Office: Pirkey Barber LLP 600 Congress Ave Ste 2120 Austin TX 78701 Office Phone: 713-787-1441, 512-322-5200, 713-355-9135. Business E-Mail: rcaldwell@pirkeybarber.com.

CALDWELL, WILLIAM B., IV, (BILL CALDWELL), career military officer; b. 1954; s. William B. and Tudy (Dismuke) Caldwell; m. Stephanie Caldwell; 5 children. Grad., US Mil. Acad., 1976; MS in Sys. Tech., US Naval Post Grad. Sch.; M in Mil. Arts and Scis., Sch. Advanced Mil. Studies, US Army Command and Gen. Staff Coll. Commd. 2d. lt. US Army, 1976, advanced through grades to lt. gen., 2007; chief of plans 82nd Airborne Divsn., Panama; brigade ops. officer 3rd Brigade, 82nd Airborne Divsn.; politico-mil. officer Operation Restore/Uphold Democracy, Haiti; comdr. 1st Brigade, 10th Mountain Divsn., Fort Drum, NY; with Office of Dir. for Strategic Plans and Policy Joint Chiefs of Staff, Washington, exec. asst. to chmn.; asst. divsn. comdr. 25th Infantry Divsn.; dep. dir. ops. US

Pacific Command, Hawaii; sr. mil. asst. to dep. sec. of def. US Dept. Def., 2002—04; commdg. gen. 82nd Airborne Divsn., 2004—06; dep. chief of staff for strategic effects, spokesperson Multi-Nat. Force-Iraq; commdg. gen. Combined Arms Ctr., Fort Leavenworth, Kans., 2007—09; commandant US Army Command and Gen. Staff Coll.; dep. commdg. gen. Combined Arms, US Army Training and Doctrine Command; dir. Joint Ctr. for Security Force Assistance (JCSIFA); comdr. NATO Training Mission, Afghanistan, 2009—, Combined Security Transition Command, Afghanistan, 2009—11; commdg. gen. US Army North (5th US Army), Ft. Sam Houston, Tex., 2011—; sr. comdr. Ft. Sam Houston & Camp Bullis, 2011—. Decorated Legion of Merit (with 2 Oak Leaf Clusters), Bronze Star (with 1 Oak Leaf Cluster), Def. Meritorious Svc. Medal (with 3 Oak Leaf Clusters), Joint Svc. Commendation Medal, Army Achievement Medal (with 2 Oak Leaf Clusters), Joint Meritorious Unit Award (with 2 Oak Leaf Clusters), Army Meritorious Unit Commendation, Philippine Presdl. Unit Citation, Nat. Def. Svc. Medal (with Bronze Svc. Star), Armed Forces Expeditionary Medal (with 1 Oak Leaf Cluster), S.W. Asia Svc. Medal with Bronze Svc. Star, Iraq Campaign Medal, Global War on Terrorism Medal, Humanitarian Svc. Medal (with 3 Oak Leaf Clusters), Mil. Outstanding Vol. Svc. Medal, Presdl. Svc. Identification Badge, Office of Sec. of Def. Identification Badge, Joint Chiefs of Staff Identification Badge; recipient La. Cross of Merit, La. Humanitarian Svc. Award; named Hon. ROCK of Yr., 2008; Sr. Svc. Coll. Fellow, John F. Kennedy Sch. Govt., Harvard U. Mem.: Sergeant Audie Murphy Club (hon.). Office: US Army North (5th Army) 1400 East Grayson Ste 152 Fort Sam Houston TX 78234

CALDWELL DYSON, TRACY ELLEN, astronaut, researcher; b. Arcadia, Calif., Aug. 14, 1969; d. James and Mary Ellen C. m. George Dyson BS in Chemistry, Calif. State U., Fullerton, 1993; PhD in Phys. Chemistry, U. Calif., Davis, 1997. Journeyman electrician J.C. Electric Co., Cherry Valley, Calif., 1987-92; environ. lab. asst. Rsch. and Instrnl. Safety Office Calif. State U., Fullerton, 1990-93, rsch. asst. chemistry, 1991-93; tchg. asst. chemistry U. Calif., Davis, 1993-94, rsch. asst. chemistry, 1994-96, rsch. asst. physics, 1996-97, Camille and Henry Dreyfus postdoctoral fellow in Environ. Sci. Irvine, 1997; astronaut, 1998—. Private pilot and conversational in Am. Sign Language (ASL) and Russian; Russian crusader Astronaut Office ISS Ops. Branch, 1999; prime crew support astronaut 5th Internat. Space Station (ISS) Expedition Crew; ISS spacecraft communicator (CAPCOM) inside mission control; with Astronaut Shuttle Ops. Branch assigned to flight software verification in the Shuttle Avionics Integration Lab, 2003; mission specialist STS-118 Mission (Endeavour) to Internat. Space Station; flight engineer Expedition 24 Mission, 2010. Contbr. articles to profl. jours. including Polyhedron, Jour. Am. Chem. Soc., Surface Sci., and Jour. Phys. Chemistry. Recipient U. Calif., Davis Graduate Rsch. award, 1996, U. Calif., Davis Grad. Student award for Scientific Travel, 1996, Pro Femina Rsch. Consortium Grad. Rsch. award, 1996, Pro Femina Rsch. Consortium Grad. award for Scientific Travel, 1996, Nellie Yeoh Whetten award, Am. Vacuum Soc., 1996, Grad. Rsch. award, 1996, NASA Superior Accomplishment Award, 2000, NASA Performance Award, 2001, 2002, NASA Group Achievement award-Russian Crusader Team, 2000, NASA Go the Extra Mile award, 2001; Patricia Roberts Harris Grad. Fellowship in Chemistry, 1993—97. Mem. Am. Chem. Soc., Am. Vacuum Soc. (Nellie Yeoh Whelton award 1996, Grad. Rsch. award 1996), Sigma Xi. Presbyterian. Achievements include mem. Russian Crusader Team, Office ISS Operations Branch, 1999; Crew Support Astronaut, 5th ISS Expedition crew, 2000. Avocations: running, weightlifting, hiking, softball, auto repair/maintenance. Office: NASA Johnson Space Ctr Astronaut Office Houston TX 77058

CALE, WILLIAM GRAHAM, JR., university administrator, environmental sciences educator, researcher; b. Phila., Dec. 10, 1947; s. William Graham and Kathryn (Rowland) Cale; m. Betty Jean Byrd, June 8, 1974. BS, Pa. State U., 1969; PhD, in Zoology, U. Ga., 1975. Asst. prof. ecology and environ. scis. U. Tex., Dallas, 1975—80, assoc. prof. environ. scis., 1980—87, prof., 1987—89; assoc. dean Sch. Natural Scis. and Math., 1983—85, 1987—89, chmn. dept. environ. scis., 1984—89; dean Coll. Natural Scis. and Math. Ind. U., Pa., 1989—94; exec. v.p. acad. affairs Lamar U., Beaumont, 1994—2000; CEO, dean Pa. State U., Altoona, 2000—05; pres. U. North Ala., Florence, 2005—; vis. sci. Oak Ridge Nat. Lab., 1981, 1984, 1985. Grantee NSF grantee, 1985; NSF grant adv. panel, 1985—88, Dept. Energy grant rev. panel, 1989—90, NSF grantee, 1981, 1983. Mem.: Internat. Soc. Ecol. Modelling, Internat. Assn. for Ecology, Am. Inst. Biol. Scis., Ecol. Soc. Am., Phi Kappa Phi, Sigma Xi, Delta Mu Delta, Omicron Delta Kappa. Avocations: bridge, golf. Office: Univ North Ala 1 Harrison Plaza Florence AL 35632 Office Phone: 256-765-4211. Business E-Mail: wgcale@una.edu.*

CALHOUN, CREDELL, state legislator; b. Natchitoches, La., May 20, 1945; Former admin. asst. to mayor, Jackson; former auditor gov.'s off job devel. & tng.; mem. Dist. 68 Miss. House of Reps., 1979—92, 2005—. Mem.: Miss Boy Scouts Coun., Elks, Mason. Democrat. Baptist. Address: PO Box 3406 Jackson MS 39207 Home Phone: 601-949-7561; Office Phone: 601-948-1217, 601-359-3327. E-mail: ccalhoun@house.ms.gov.

CALHOUN, PEGGY JOAN, fundraising executive; b. La Salle, Ill., Sept. 14, 1957; d. Floyd Anthony and Sophia (Regula) Sarwinski; m. James R. Calhoun, Apr. 19, 1989; children: (twins) Robert Blair and Christina Sophia. Student, Ill. Valley C.C., Oglesby, 1975, So. Ill. U., 1976-77; MA, St. Mary's Coll., Minn., 1994. Assoc. dir. United Way, Sarasota, Fla., 1979-85; devel. dir. Boy Scouts Am., Sarasota, 1985-86; assoc. campaign dir. United Way, Ft. Lauderdale, Fla., 1986-87; dir. devel. YMCA, Sarasota, 1987-88, Salvation Army, Ft. Lauderdale, 1988-91, Diabetes Rsch. Inst. Found., U. Miami Sch. Medicine, 1992-93; pres. Calhoun & Co., Inc., Ft. Lauderdale, 1997—; owner Miller, Calhoun & Co., Inc. Instr. Nova U., Ft. Lauderdale, Barry U., 1996—. Mem.: Pub. Rels. Soc. Am. (bd. dirs. 1991—93, pres. 1993), Broward Planned Giving Coun. (bd. dirs. 1991), Assn. Fundraising Profls. (pres. bd. dirs. 1985, bd. dirs. 1990—97, pres. 1996, advanced cert. fund raising exec. 1997, cert. fund raising exec. 1985), Jr. League. Republican. Avocations: water sports, reading, travel. Home and Office: 2741 NE 57th Ct Fort Lauderdale FL 33308-2723

CALIEL, MICHAEL J., electric power industry executive; BS in Indsl. Distbn., Clarkson U., Potsdam, New York. Various sr. mgmt. positions in the process automation divsn. Asea Brown Boveri, 1981—91; dir. mktg. for hydrocarbon processing industries Honeywell, 1991—93; various sr. mgmt. positions Invensys Sys., Inc., 1993—2006, pres. North America and Europe, Mid. East and Africa ops., 2001—03, pres. Invensys process systems, 2003—06; pres., CEO, bd. dirs. Integrated Electric Services, Inc., 2006—, acting head IES comml. and indsl., 2010—. Office: Integrated Electrical Services Inc 1800 W Loop S Se 500 Houston TX 77027 Office Phone: 713-860-1500. Office Fax: 713-860-1599.

CALIFF, ROBERT MCKINNON, cardiologist, educator; b. Anderson, SC, Sept. 29, 1951; m. Lydia Carpenter, 1974; children: Sharon, Sam, Tom. Grad. summa cum laude, Duke U., 1973; MD, Duke U. Sch. Medicine, 1978. Cert. in internal medicine 1984, in cardiology 1986. Intern, cardiology U. Calif., San Francisco, 1978—79, resident, medicine, 1979—80; fellow, cardiology Duke U. Med. Ctr., Durham, NC, 1978, 1980—83, attending physician, 1983—, Donald F. Fortin Prof. Cardiology, prof. internal medicine, 1995—, dir., Clin. Rsch. Inst., 1995—2006, assoc. vice chancellor clin. rsch., 1995—2005, vice-chancellor, clin. rsch., 2005—, dir., Translational Medicine Inst., 2006—. Mem. cardiorenal adv. panel US FDA; mem. pharm. roundtable Inst. Medicine; dir., coord. ctr. Ctrs. for Edn. & Rsch. on Therapeutics. Cons. ABCNews.com OnCall+ Heart Disease Ctr.; editor: (textbook) Acute Coronary Care (1st and 2nd edits.); editor or co-editor (textbooks) Comprehensive Cardiovascular Medicine, Interventional Cardiovascular Medicine, and Atlas of Heart Diseases, sect. editor Textbook of Cardiovascular Medicine, editor-in-chief Am. Heart Jour.; contbr. several articles to peer-reviewed jours.; contbg. editor (online resource) theheart.org, serves on numerous editl. bds. Recipient Clin. Rsch. prize, Am. Heart Assn., 2006; named one of 10 Most Cited Authors in the field of medicine, Inst. for Scientific Information. Fellow: Am. Coll. Cardiology; mem.: Alpha Omega Alpha, Phi Beta Kappa. Avocations: golf, basketball, listening to music. Office: Duke U Med Ctr PO Box 17969 DCRI 2400 Pratt St Rm 0311 Terrace Level Durham NC 27705 Office Phone: 919-668-8820. Office Fax: 919-668-7103.

CALIKOGLU, MUGE GUCSAVAS, clinical geneticist, educator; MD, U. Ankara, Turkey, 1983. Diplomate Am. Bd. Pediatrics, 1996, cert. Am. Bd. Med. Genetics-clin. genetics, 1996, Am. Bd. Med. Genetics-clin. biochemical genetics, 2009. Resident Univ. Hacettepe, Ankara, Turkey, 1985—88; fellow HA Chapman Inst., Tulsa, Okla., 1991—93, Cecil G. Sheps Ctr., NC, 1996—99; resident Univ. NC, 1995—96, assoc. prof.; physician pediat. dept. Univ. NC Health Care. Office: University North Carolina Health Care Pediatrics Department Wing E Campus Box 7487 Chapel Hill NC 27599-7487 Office Phone: 919-966-1401.

CALIPARI, JOHN VINCENT, men's college basketball coach; b. Moon Twp., Pa., Feb. 10, 1959; m. Ellen Calipari; children: Erin Sue, Megan Rae, Bradley Vincent. Attended, U. NC, Wilmington; B, Clarion State U., Pa., 1982. Asst. coach U. Kans. Jayhawks, 1982-85; recruiting coord. U. Vt. Catamounts, 1983; asst. coach U. Pitts. Panthers, 1985-88; head coach U. Mass. Minutemen, Amherst, 1988-96; head coach, exec. v.p. basketball ops. NJ Nets, East Rutherford, 1996—99; asst. coach Phila. 76ers, 1999; head coach U. Memphis Tigers, 2000—09, U. Ky. Wildcats, 2009—. Asst. Buckler Challenge All-Star Team, 1993, head coach, 1994; coach East squad US Olympic Festival, Denver. Author: Players First, 2014. Vol. Camp Good Days and Spl. Times; chmn. Children's Miracle Network Telethon, Springfield. Named Eastern Basketball Coach of Yr., 1992, Atlantic 10 Coach of Yr., 1993, 1994, 1996, Dist. I Coach of Yr. US Basketball Writers Assn., 1993, Dist. IV Coach of Yr., 2009, The Sporting News Nat. Coach of Yr., 1996, Naismith Nat. Coach of Yr. Atlanta Tip-off Club, 1996, 2008, East Region Coach of Yr. Basketball Times, 1996, South Region Coach of Yr, 2007, Dist. VII Coach of Yr. Nat. Assn. Basketball Coaches, 2004, Co-Coach of Yr., 2009, Conf. USA Coach of Yr., 2006, 2008, 2009, Sports Illus. Nat. Coach of Yr., 2009, Jim Phelan Nat. Coach of Yr., 2009, Southeastern Conf. Coach of Yr., 2012; recipient Lombardi award UNICO Nat., 2003, Adolph Rupp Cup Commonwealth Athletic Club Ky., 2010; named to Nat. Italian Am. Sports Hall of Fame, 2004, U. Mass. Athletic Hall of Fame, 2004. Achievements include head coach of the NCAA Final Four Division I National Championship winning University of Kentucky Wildcats, 2012. Office: Univ Ky Athletics Joe Craft Ctr 338 Lexington Ave Lexington KY 40506-0604 Office Phone: 859-257-1916.*

CALKINS, SUSANNAH EBY, retired economist; b. Bucyrus, Ohio, Jan. 16, 1924; d. Samuel L. and Mae (McClure) Eby; m. G. Nathan Calkins, Nov. 19, 1949 (dec.); children: Helen E. (dec.), Margaret S. Van Auken, Sarah A. (dec.), Abigail Calkins Aguirre. AB, Goucher Coll., 1945; MS in Econs. (Univ. scholar 1946-47), U. Wis., 1947. Fiscal analyst U.S. Bur. Budget, 1945-50; economist U.S. Council Econ. Advisors, 1950-51, U.S. Office Price Stabilization, 1951-53, U.S. Bur. Budget, 1953-55; cons. U.S. Adv. Commn. on Intergovtl. Rels., Washington, 1972-73, 74-75, cons. on counter-cyclical aid programs, 1977-78, sr. analyst, 1979-87, exec. asst. to dir., 1987-89. Cons. revenue sharing Brookings Instn., Washington, 1973—74. Author (with R. Nathan and A. Manvel): Monitoring Revenue Sharing, 1975. Sponsor S.S. Goucher Victory, Balt., 1945; bd. dirs. Bread for the City, 1994—2002. Mem.: Am. Econs. Assn., George Towne Club (Washington), Cosmos Club (assoc.), Phi Beta Kappa. Presbyterian. Home: 3440 S Jefferson St Apt 1124 Falls Church VA 22041-3130

CALL, ROBERT SOMERVILLE, allergist, immunologist, educator; m. Mary Call; 4 children. BA in Biology, U. Va., MD, 1987. Diplomate Am. Bd. Allergy and Immunology, 2003. Tng. internal medicine Mich. State Univ.; resident internal medicine Blodgett Meml. Med. Ctr., 1988—90; fellow allergy and immunology Univ. of Va. Med. Ctr., 1990—92; instr. medicine Univ. of Va.; owner Commonwealth Clin. Rsch. Specialists, pres.; appointed commonwealth health rsch. bd. Commonwealth of Va., 2005, chair commonwealth health rsch. bd.; physician Richmond Allergy & Asthma Specialists. Mem.: Allergy and Asthma Soc. of Va. (pres.), Richmond Acad. of Medicine (former pres., bd. chmn.). Office: Richmond Allergy & Asthma Specialists Ste 100 9920 Independence Park Dr Henrico VA 23233 Office Phone: 804-285-7420.

CALLAHAN, BILL (WILLIAM E. CALLAHAN), professional football coach; b. Chgo., July 31, 1956; m. Valerie J. Callahan; children: Brian, Daniel, Cathryn, Jaclyn. B in Phys. Edn., Benedictine Coll., Ill., 1978. Assoc. coach U. Ill. Illini, 1980—81, tight ends coach, 1982—83, offensive line coach, 1984—85, quarterbacks coach, 1986; offensive line coach Northern Ariz. U. Lumberjacks, 1987—88, U. Wis. Badgers, 1990—94, Phila. Eagles, 1995—97; offensive coord. Southern Ill. U. Salukis, 1989, Oakland Raiders, 1998—2001, head coach, 2002—03, U. Nebr. Cornhuskers, Lincoln, 2004—07; asst. head coach, offensive line coach NY Jets, East Rutherford, NJ, 2008—11; offensive coord., offensive line coach Dallas Cowboys, Irving, Tex., 2012—. Founder Coach Callahan Charities. Named to Benedictine Coll. Hall of Fame, 2005. Achievements include becoming the fourth NFL rookie head coach to reach the Super Bowl, 2002. Office: Dallas Cowboys 1 Cowboys Pky Irving TX 75063

CALLAHAN, ELIZABETH F., dermatologist; BA, U. Vermont, 1988, MD, 1997. Diplomate Am. Bd. of Dermatology. Resident in dermatology Cleve. Clinic Found., chief resident in dermatology, 1997—2001; fellow in dermatologic surgery Mayo Clinic, fellow in MOHS surgery, 2001—02; founder SkinSmart Dermatology, dir. Mem.: Sarasota County Med. Soc., Am. Soc. for Dermatologic Surgery, Women's Dermatol. Assn., Am. Coll. of MOHS Surgery, Am. Acad. of Dermatology. Office: Skin Smart Dermatology Suite 214 5911 N Honore Ave Sarasota FL 34243 Office Phone: 941-308-7546. Office Fax: 941-308-7550.

CALLAHAN, REBECCA, corporate financial executive; Various sr. sales positions Blue Pumpkin Software, PageNet; sr. v.p. sales Spherion Corp., v.p. assessment group, 2003, sr. v.p. RPO svcs., SourceRight Solutions, 2008—09, pres. SourceRight Solutions, 2009—. Mem. bd. dirs. RPO Alliance. Office: SourceRight Solutions 2050 Spectrum Blvd Fort Lauderdale FL 33309 Office Phone: 954-308-7600. Office Fax: 954-351-8117.

CALLAHAN, RICKEY DON, business owner; b. Dallas, Mar. 17, 1956; s. Dayton Easton and Alice Jane (Holloway) C. AA, Eastfield Coll., 1976; BA in Polit. Sci., U. Tex.-Dallas, 1978; MBA in Gen. Mgmt., Amberton U., 1986; degree, Dallas City Coun. Dist., 2013. Cert. secondary tchr., Tex. Real estate assoc. ERA Sage Realty, Inc., Dallas, 1979-80, First Mark Real Estate, Dallas, 1980-81; adminstrv. asst. Dallas Precious Metal Plating, Inc., Garland, Tex., 1981-84; legis. asst. to state rep. Alvin R. Granoff, Dallas, 1984-87; owner, broker Callahan Properties Comml. Real Estate Svcs., Dallas, 1987—. Sub-com. chair, neighborhood restoration & econ. devel. Pleasant Grove Weed & Seed. Pres. Dallas County East Dem. Orgn., 1986-88, Clean Dallas-S.E., Inc., 1987-88, Tex. Jr. C. of C. Found.; bd. dirs. Dallas Conv. and Visitors Bur., 1995-98; mem. Dallas Bond Campaign Com., 1995; bd. dirs. S.E. Emergency Food Ctr., 1996-99, v.p. 1998-99; treas. Pleasant Grove Hist. Soc., 2000-02; mem. Lake Pointe Ch. Town East in Mesquite, Tex. Mem. Nat. Assn.Realtors, Tex. Assn. Realtors, North Tex. Comml. Assn. of Realtors (arbitration panel), S.E. Dallas C. of C. (bd. dirs. 1987—, vice chmn. econ. devel. 1991-92, chmn. 1994-95, vice chmn. 2002-03, vice chmn. econ. divsn., 2011-13, elected Dallas city coun. dist., 2013, steering com. mem. Cmty. and Economic b Dev. Nat. League Cities), U. Tex. Dallas Alumni Assn., Amber U. Alumni Assn., Tex. Jaycees (dist. dir. 1981-82, Prestigious J.C.I. Senator award #38931, pres. Mesquite chpt. 1980-81, 82-83, bd. dirs. Dallas 1990-91), Mayor's Task Force for Economic Devel. Southern Dallas, Phi Theta Kappa, Tex. Mpcl. League. Democrat. Baptist. Avocations: scuba diving, guitar, genealogy, reading, attending football games. Office: Callahan Properties 8344 E R L Thornton Fwy Ste 308 Dallas TX 75228-7134

CALLAHAN, RYAN, professional hockey player; b. Rochester, NY, Mar. 21, 1985; m. Kyla Allison, June 25, 2011; 1 child, Charlotte. Right wing Hartford Wolf Pack (American Hockey League), 2006—07, NY Rangers, 2006—14, Tampa Bay Lightning, 2014—; capt. NY Rangers, 2011—14. Mem. Team USA, Olympic Games, Vancouver, 2010, Sochi, Russia, 2014. Recipient Steven McDonald Extra Effort award, NY Rangers, 2008—09, 2009—10, 2011—12, 2012—13. Achievements include being a member of silver medal winning United States Hockey Team, Vancouver Olympics, 2010. Office: c/o Tampa Bay Lightning 401 Channelside Dr Tampa FL 33602*

CALLAHAN, VINCENT FRANCIS, JR., state legislator, retired publishing executive; b. Washington, Oct. 30, 1931; s. Vincent Francis and Anita (Hawkins) C.; children from previous marriage: Vincent Francis III, Elizabeth Lauren, Anita Marie, Cynthia Helen, Robert Bruce; m. Yvonne Weight, Feb. 15, 2006. BS in Fgn. Svc., Georgetown U., 1957; LHD (hon.), No. Va. C.C., 1997; PhD (hon.), Marymount U., Arlington, Va, 2008. Pres. Callahan Publs., 1957-2000; mem. Va. Hos. of Dels., 1968—2008, minority leader, 1982-85, chmn. appropriations com. Author eight books including: Missile Contracts Guide, 1958, Space Guide, 1959, Underwater Defense Handbook, 1963, Military Research Handbook, 1963. Candidate for lt. gov. Va., 1965; state fin. chmn. Rep. Party of Va., 1966-68; candidate for U.S. Congress, 1976; chmn. No. Va. Cmty. Found.; chmn. Jamestown-Yorktown Found; chmn. emeritus Jamestown-Yorktown Found.; bd. visitors, George Mason U., bd. mem. 2008-2012, With USMC, 1950-53; as lt. USCGR, 1959-63. Mem. U.S. Naval Inst. (bd. mem. 2008-2012), Nat. Press Club, Kiwanis (past pres. McLean, Va.). Republican. Roman Catholic.

CALLAN, JOSEPH PATRICK, social service administrator; b. Washington, July 29, 1944; s. G. Christopher and Mary Jane (Gorsuch) C.; m. Judith Marie Bell, June 14, 1980; children: Kimberly Jane, Kathleen Marie. AA, St. Petersburg Jr. Coll., Fla., 1964; BA, U. So. Fla., 1972, MSW, 1985; MS, Nova U., 1985. Group work supr. Eckerd Found., Clearwater, Fla., 1968-72, dir. tng., 1977-83; coord. Collier County Mental Health, Naples, Fla., 1972-76; pvt. practice psychotherapy Tampa, Fla., 1985—; dir., owner Univ. Psychotherapy Group, P.A., Tampa, 1987—2011. Psychotherapist Employee Assistance Programs and Sex Therapy, Tampa, 1987—; vis. faculty U. So. Fla., Tampa, 1987-; clin. dir. Traverse Equestrian Therapy Program for traumatized youth, Tampa, 1995—; pres. Tng. and Edn. Ctr., Naples, 1972-77, Immokalee (Fla.) Adult Refuge, 1972-77; cons. social svcs. agys. Tampa area, 1987—. Sgt. U.S. Army, 1966-71. Mem. NASW, Am. Acad. Clin. Sexologists, Clin. Social Wk. Assn., Collier County Assn. Retarded Citizens, U. So. Fla. Social Work Alumni Assn. (pres. 1986-88), Profl. Assn. Therapeutic Horsemanship Internat. (bd. trustee), Equine Facilitated Mental Health Assn. (bd. dirs.), Phi Kappa Phi, Pi Gamma Mu. Avocation: horseback riding. Home: 3450 Lake Padgett Dr Land O Lakes FL 34639-6514 Office: Traverse Inc 1101 Anclote Blvd Tarpon Springs FL 34689 Office Phone: 813-980-3488, 813-924-0488. Personal E-mail: jcallanlcsw@gmail.com.

CALLEGARI, WILLIAM (BILL), state legislator; m. Ann Callegari; 4 children. B in Agrl. Engring., La. State U.; M in Civil Engring., U. Houston. Lic. profl. engr. Founder, chmn., CEO Am-Tex Corp., 1974—93; founder, engring. cons. WC Engineers, Inc.; mem. Dist. 132 Tex. House of Representatives, 2000—. Recipient of several awards and honors; named to Louisiana State U. Alumni Wall of Honor, 2000. Republican. Office: 1550 Foxlake Dr Ste 120 Houston TX 77084 also: Room GN.12 Capitol PO Box 2910 Austin TX 78768 Office Phone: 281-578-8484, 512-463-0528. Office Fax: 281-578-1674.

CALLEN, JEFFREY PHILLIP, dermatologist, educator; b. May 30, 1947; s. Irwin R. and Rose P. (Cohen) C.; m. Susan B. Manis, Dec. 21, 1968; children: Amy, David. BS, U. Wis., 1969; MD, U. Mich., 1972. Diplomate Am. Bd. Internal Medicine, Am. Bd. Dermatology. Intern, resident in internal medicine U. Mich., Ann Arbor, 1972-75, resident in dermatology, 1975-77; from asst. clin. prof. to dir. residency tng. program U. Louisville Sch. Medicine, 1977-84, dir. residency tng. program, 1984—; chief dermatology svc. Louisville VA Hosp., 1984-93, prof., chief dermatology divsn., 1988—. Author: Manual of Dermatology, 1980, Cutaneous Aspects of Internal Disease, 1981, Neurology Clinics North America, 1987, Dermatologic Signs of Systemic Disease, 1988, 3d edit., 2003, 4th edit., 2009; asst. editor Dermatology, 2nd edit., 2007, 3rd Edit., 2012, Color Atlas of Dermatology, 1993, 2d edit., 2000, Current Practice of Dermatology, 1995; editor: Clinics in Rheumatic Disease, 1982, Dermatologic Clinics, 1985, 89, 2002, Medical Clinics of North America, 1982, 84, 86, 89, Dermatologic Therapy, 2007, 12; editor-in-chief Dermavision video program; mem. editl. bd. Internat. Jour. Dermatology, 1990-95, Jour. Watch Dermatology, 1999-, dep. editor 2005-; asst. editor Internat. Jour. Dermatology, 1993-95, Jour. Am. Acad. Dermatology, 1995-2003; assoc. editor Archives Dermatology, 2003-; editor-in-chief Dermatology Up-to-Date, 2010-. Bd. dirs. Actor's Theater of Louisville, 1982-98, 2000-2009, 2012-, sec., 1986-87, Ky. Arts and Crafts Found., 1991-97; bd. govs. JB Speed Art Mus., 1995-2003 Fellow ACP, Am. Acad. Dermatology (chmn. audio/visual edn. com., task force therapeutic agts., internal med. symposium 1978-83, chmn. sci. and tech. exhibits 1986-89, dir. various symposiums, mem. coun. sci. assembly 1993-98, chair 1997-98, chair com. to evaluate ann.

meeting, 1999-2003, vice chair coun. on edn. 2002-2003, chair coun. on edn. 2003-07, v.p. elect 2003-04, v.p. 2004-05, bd. dirs. 1995-99, mem. exec. com. 1997-99, 2003-05, co-chair program for 21st century 1999-2000, chair psoriasis edn. conf. 2002, chair unity summit, chair task force on psoriasis edn. 2005, com. on maintenance cert. 2006—11), Am. Coll. Rheumatology (founder, chair skin disease study group 1996-98, 2000-02); mem. AMA, Am. Fedn. Clin. Rsch., Am. Dermatol. Assn. (bd. dirs. 2008-13), Dermatology Found. (trustee 1984-90), Louisville Theatrical Assn. (bd. dirs. 1999-2002), Am. Bd. Dermatology (bd. mem. 2000-11, v.p. 2011), Maintanance Cert. Com., (chair, 06-10). Achievements include research on condition in which systemic disease has cutaneous manifestations, lupus erythematosus, psoriasis, dermatomyositis. Office: University Louisville Dept Dermatology 3810 Springhurst Blvd Louisville KY 40241 Office Phone: 502-583-1749. Business E-Mail: jpcall01@louisville.edu.

CALLENDER, NORMA ANNE, counselor, public relations executive; b. Huntsville, Tex., May 10, 1933; d. C.W. Carswell and Nell Ruth (Collard) Hughes Bost; m. B.G. Callender, 1951 (div. 1964); remarried 1967 (div. 1973); children: Teresa Elizabeth, Leslie Gemey, Shannah Hughes, Kelly Mari; m. E Purfurst, June 1965 (div. Aug. 1965). BS, U. Houston, 1969; MA, U. Houston-Clear Lake, 1977; postgrad., Tex. So. U., Houston, 1971, Lamar U., Beaumont, Tex., 1972-73, U. Houston-Clear Lake, 1979, 87, 89-93, postgrad., 1998, St. Thomas U., 1985-86, Aerospace Inst., NASA, Johnson Space Ctr., 1986, San Jacinto Coll., Houston, 1988—99, postgrad., 2001—03; PhD, Cornerstone U., 1998. Cert. profl. reading specialist, Tex.; lic. profl. counselor. Tchr. Houston Ind. Schs., 1969-70; co-counselor, instr. Ellington AFB, Houston, 1971; tchr. Clear Creek Schs., League City, Tex., 1970-86; owner, dir. Bay Area Tutoring and Reading Clinic, Clear Lake City, Tex., 1970—, Bay Area Tng. Assocs., 1982-98, Bay Area Family Counseling, 1995—, Bay Area Speech and Lang., 2003—11; cons., LPC intern Guidance Ctr., Pasadena Ind. Sch. Dist., Tex., 1993-95; prin., dir. pub. rels. Gateway Supply, Inc., 2005—10, Gateway Foods USA, 2005—10. Instr. San Jacinto Coll., Pasadena, 1980-81, 91-93; adj. instr. U. Houston, Clear Lake, 1986-91; founder, editor BATA Books Pub., 1997—. Author: numerous poems. State advisor U.S. Congl. Adv. Bd., 1985-87; vol., bd. dirs. Family Outreach Ctr., 1989-92; vol. Bay Area Coun. on Drugs and Alcohol, Nassau Bay, Tex., 1993-94; bd. dirs. Ballet San Jacinto, 1985-87; adv. bd. Cmty. Ednl. TV, 1990-92; charter mem. Nat. Women's History Mus., Washington, 2005. Recipient Franklin award U. Houston, 1965-67; Delta Kappa Gamma/Beta Omicron scholar, 1967-68, PTA scholar, 1973, Berwin scholar, 1976, Mary Gibbs Jones scholar, 1976-77, Found. Econ. Edn. scholar, 1976, Insts. Achievement Human Potential scholar, Phila., 1987. Mem.: ACA, Am. Contract Bridge League (life master 2011), The NET: Bay Area Mental Health Providers Network, Clear Creek Educators Assn. (past, honorarium 1976, 1977, 1985), Sam Houston Chpt., Daughters of Am. Revolution, Leadership Clear Lake Alumni Assn. (edn. com. 1985, program and projects com. mem. 1986—87, charter), U. Houston Alumni Assn. (life), Phi Theta Kappa, Phi Delta Kappa, Kappa Delta Pi, Psi Chi (life), Phi Kappa Phi (life).

CALLI, PAUL ALBERT, lawyer; b. New Haven, 1967; BA in Polit. Sci., U. Conn., 1989; JD, U. Miami Sch. Law, Coral Gables, Fla., 1993. Bar: Fla. 1993, US Dist Ct. (southern & middle districts) Fla., US Ct. Appeals (11th cir.). Asst. pub. defender Miami-Dade County Pub. Defender's Office, 1993—97; asst. fed. pub. defendr So. Dist. Fla., 1997—2000; of counsel Zuckerman Spaeder LLP, Miami, 2000—08; shareholder Carlton Fields, P.A., Miami, 2008—. Bd. dirs. Miami Light Project, 2006—07, YWCA Criminal Ct. Care Program, 2007—08. Named Best of the Bar, South Fla. Bus. Jour., 2003; named one of Florida's Legal Elite, Fla. Trend mag., 2005, 2006, 2008, Top 100 Lawyers in South Fla., South Fla. Legal Guide, 2009, The Nation's Top Litigators, The Nat. Law Journal, 2009. Mem.: ABA, Dade County Bar Assn., Fla. Assn. Criminal Def. Lawyers (bd. dirs. Miami chpt. 2002—09), Nat. Assn. Criminal Def. Lawyers, Fla. Bar. Office: Carlton Fields PA Miami Tower 100 SE Second St Ste 4200 Miami FL 33131 Office Phone: 305-530-4065. Office Fax: 305-530-0055. E-mail: pcalli@carltonfields.com.

CALLOWAY, MARK T., lawyer, former prosecutor; married. Grad. in Polit. Sci., NC State U., 1980; JD, Campbell Univ., 1983. Bar: NC 1983, US Dist. Ct. (we., mid., ea. dists.) NC, US Ct. Appeals (4th cir.), US Supreme Ct. Rsch. asst. to Hon. Jack L. Cozort NC Ct. Appeals; law clk. to Hon. Robert D. Potter US Dist. Ct. (we. dist.) NC; assoc., then ptnr./shareholder James, McElroy & Diehl, PA, Charlotte, NC, 1987-94; US atty. for we. dist. NC U.S. Dept. Justice, Charlotte, 1994—2001; ptnr., govt. investigations, compliance group Alston & Bird, LLP, Charlotte, NC, 2001—. Office: Alston & Bird LLP Bank Amer Plz Ste 4000 101 S Tryon St Charlotte NC 28280 Office Phone: 704-444-1089. Business E-Mail: mcalloway@alston.com.

CALOBRACE, M. BRADLEY, plastic surgeon, educator; b. Marion, Ind., Dec. 15, 1962; BS in Biology-Chemistry summa cum laude, Manchester Coll., North Manchester, Ind., 1981—85; MD, Ind. U., Indpls., 1985—89. License to practice Ky. (lic. number 32666), diplomate Am. Bd. Medical Examiners, 1990, Am. Bd. Surgery-expired, 1995, Am. Bd. Plastic Surgery, 1999, cert. Ky. State Med. Bd., 1997. Clin. instr. surgery divsn. plastic and reconstructive surgery Univ. Louisville; hosp. affiliations include Calobrace Plastic Surgery Ctr., Jewish Hosp., Baptist East Hosp., Dupont Surgery Ctr., Health-South Surgery Ctr.; resident gen. surgery Univ. Southern Calif., LA, 1989—94, resident plastic and reconstructive surgery, 1994—96; fellow aesthetic surgery/reconstructive and aesthetic breast surgery Aesthetic and Reconstructive Inst. Baptist. Hosp., Nashville, 1996—97; owner Calobrace Plastic Surgery Ctr., CaloSpa, Cosmetic Breast Ctr. Speaker; mentor; luminary physician ptnr. Syneron; certified faculty speaker on injectables CME Scholar; nat. edn. faculty Allergan, roundtable cons. Juvederm, acad. faculty; with breast cancer task force Caritas Med. Ctr., 1998; cancer com. mem. Alliant Health System, 1998; emergency room com. mem. Jewish Hosp., 2000, surgical svcs. com. mem., 2001—04. Author: (articles) Cosmetic Surgery-Not Just for Women Anymore, 2001, Post-partum Rejuvenation-The Mommy Makeover, 2006, Men-On the Cutting Edge, 2006, The Medispa Makeover, 2007, numerous others; co-author: (book chpt.) Large Volume Ultrasound Assisted Lipoplasty, 1998. Recipient 1st place Sci. Exhibit for Rsch., Ind. Med. Assn., Summer Rsch. Stipend, 1986, Groves-Hardiman Scholarship for Rsch., 1986. Fellow: Am. Coll. Surgeons; mem.: LA County-Univ. Southern Calif. Soc. Grad. Surgeons, Botox Cosmetic Physicians Network, Ky. Soc. Plastic Surgeons, Greater Louisville Med. Soc., Ky. Med. Assn., AMA, Alpha Omega Alpha Honor Soc., Am. Soc. Plastic Surgeons, Am. Soc. Aesthetic Plastic Surgery, Patient Care Fund Com., Joint Coun. Interns and Residents, Univ. Southern Calif. House Officers' Assn., Am. Coll. Surgeons (southern Calif. chpt.). Office: Calobrace Plastic Surgery Center 2341 Lime Kiln Lane Louisville KY 40222 Office Phone: 502-899-9979. Office Fax: 502-899-9939.

CALVER, RICHARD ALLEN, retired dean; b. Chillicothe, Ohio, Feb. 16, 1939; s. Robert K. Calver and Catherine Mae (Roush) Bryan; m. Susan Jane Yost, Oct. 9, 1988 (dec. Feb. 2012); children: Mark R. Fortney, Sherry Skinner, Alan D. Fortney; m. Glenda Leigh Davidson, Mar. 13, 1965 (div.). Student, U. Hawaii, 1959-61; degree in Bus. Admin, W.Va. U., 1963; MS in Bus., Va. Commonwealth U., 1970; C.A.G.S.E., Va. Tech. U., 1983, EdD in C.C. Edn., 1984. Mgmt. trainee Sears Roebuck & Co., 1963, Reuben H. Donnelley Corp., 1963-64, state publs. and customer rels. mgr., 1964-68; state analyst Va. Divsn. Pers., Richmond, 1968-70; dean adminstrv. svcs. S.W. Va. C.C., Richlands, 1970-88, Thomas Nelson C.C., Hampton, Va., 1988—2002, interim pres., 1994-95, ret., 2002, spl. asst. to pres., 2002—05. Accreditation team So. Assn. Colls. and Schs., 1976-95, Mid. States Assn., 1983-94. Mem. Lebanon (Va.) Town Coun., 1978-82; spl. edn. adv. com. Russell County Sch. Bd., 1984-88, Va. Peninsula Inst. Leadership Inst. Program, 1989; planning com. Greater Williamsburg Area Crossroads, 1999-2005; bd. mem. Thomas Nelson C.C., 2005-07. With USAF, 1957-61. Mem. So. Assn. Coll. and Univ. Bus. officers, Ea. Assn. Coll. and U. Bus. Officers, Coll. and Univ. Pers. Assn., Lions (pres. Lebanon club 1976-77), Shriners (pres. club 1974-75), Scottish Rite (32d degree), Masons, Delta Tau Delta, Phi Kappa Phi, Phi Theta Kappa (hon.). Unitarian Universalist. Home: 4302 Creek View East Williamsburg VA 23188 Home Phone: 757-565-4140.

CALVERT, DAVID VICTOR, soil science educator; b. Chaplin, Ky., Feb. 26, 1934; s. Stanford Byron and Willia Neal Calvert; m. Joyce Faye LeMay, July 27, 1957; children: Victor Neal Calvert, Yvonne Carole Calvert. BS, U. Ky., 1956, MS, 1958; PhD, Iowa State U., 1962. Cert. profl. soil scientist, Am. Registry of Cert Profls. in Agronomy, Crops and Soils, Ltd. Grad. rsch. asst. U. Ky., Lexington, 1956-58, Iowa State U., Ames, 1958-62; asst. prof. soil and water sci. U. Fla., Ft. Pierce, 1962-68, assoc. prof., 1968-76, prof., 1976—2003, prof. emeritus, 2003—, dir. Indian River Rsch. & Edn. Ctr., 1979-94. Ofcl. collaborator S.E. region USDA, Athens, Ga., 1965-79; cons. World Bank, Jamaican Sch. Agr., Kingston, 1970-71; cons. soil sci. Coun. for Agrl. Sci. and Tech., St. Louis; presenter in field. Contbr. over 175 articles to profl. jours. including Soil Sci. Soc. Am. Proceedings, Jour. Agrl., Food Chem., Jour. Environ. Quality, Soil Sci., Proceedings Internat. Soc. Citriculture. Recipient Soil-Water-Air-Plant grant USDA Agrl. Rsch. Svc., Fla., 1968-80; grantee EPA, 1970-73, Water Quality Rsch. City of Okeechobee, Fla., 1990-93, St. Johns and South Fla. Water Mgmt. Dists., Palatka and West Palm Beach, 1993-96; award Fla. Dept. Agr. and Consumer Svcs., Tallahassee, 1996—; recipient Rsch. Achievement award Fla. Fruit and Vegetable Assn., 1979, Agrl. Hall of Fame award Saint Lucie County Farm Bur., 1997; U. Ky. fellow; named Outstanding Conservationist of Yr., Soil Conservation Svc. USDA, Fla., 1983, Disting. Out-of-State Alumnus for the U. Kys. Coll. of Agrl., 1997. Fellow Am. Soc. Agronomy; mem. Soil Sci. Soc Am., Internat. Soc. Soil Sci., Am. Soc. Hort. Sci., Coun. of Agrl. Sci. and Tech., Soil and Crop Sci. Soc. Fla. (pres. 2000, hon. membership award, 2006), Fla. State Hort. Soc. (hon. membership award 1997), Internat. Soc. Citriculture, Rsch. Ctr. Adminstrs. Soc., Am. Soc. Agronomy, Farmhouse Fraternity, Scovell Soc. U. Ky. (charter mem.), Sigma Xi, Gamma Sigma Delta, Alpha Zeta. Achievements include contbns. to development and deployment of working water quality standards to guide growers using low-volume sprinkler and micro irrigation systems; development of a soil and water management strategy for control of nitrates and phosphates leaching from citrus groves into surface water and ground water. Home: 1007 Grandview Blvd Fort Pierce FL 34982-4323 Home Phone: 772-464-3393; Office Phone: 772-332-2821. Personal E-mail: cgator1@bellsouth.net.

CALVERT, JACK GEORGE, atmospheric chemist, educator; b. Inglewood, Calif., May 9, 1923; s. John George and Emma (Eschstruth) C.; m. Doris Arlene Breimon, Nov. 8, 1946; children: Richard John, Mark Steven. BS in Chemistry, UCLA, 1944, PhD, 1949. Mem. faculty Ohio State U., 1950-81, prof. chemistry, 1960-81, Kimberly prof. chemistry, 1974-81, prof. emeritus, 1981—, chmn. dept., 1964-68; sr. scientist Nat. Ctr. Atmospheric Rsch., Boulder, Colo., 1982-94, sr. rsch. assoc., 1994—2002, sr. scientist emeritus, 2002—. Vis. scientist Oak Ridge (Tenn.) Nat. Lab., Environ. Scis. Divsn., 2002-12; cons. air pollution tng. com. USPHS, 1964-66; cons. World Innovation Found., 2001—; mem. Nat. Air Pollution Control Manpower Devel. Com., 1966-69, chmn., 1968-69; bd. dirs. Gordon Rsch. Confs., 1969-71; mem. air pollution control rsch. grants com. EPA, 1970-72, chmn., 1971-72, mem. chemistry and physics adv. com., 1973-75; chmn. air pollution com. Conservation Found., 1968-70; mem. air conservation commn. Am. Lung Assn., 1973-75; chmn. EPA environ. chemistry/physics grants rev. panel, 1979-83; mem. State of Colo. Air Quality Control Commn., 1987-90, Disting. Acad. Adv. Group of Auto/Oil Air Quality Improvement Rsch. Program, 1989-96; mem. panel on atmospheric effects of aviation NRC/NAS, 1995-98, mem. com. on ozone potential of reformulated gasoline, 1997-99; atmospheric chemistry tech. implementation panel Am. Chem. Coun., 1998-2004. Author: (with J. N. Pitts, Jr.) Photochemistry, 1966, Graduate School in the Sciences, 1972; also articles. Ensign USNR, 1944-46. Named Honor Prof. of Year Coll. Arts and Scis., Ohio State U., 1957; recipient Alumni award for disting. tchg., 1961, Disting. Rsch. award, 1981; fellow NRC Can., 1949; Guggenheim fellow, 1977-78 Fellow Ohio Acad. Sci., Am. Inst. Chemists, Am. Geophys. Union; mem. AAUP, Am. Chem. Soc. (award for creative rsch. in environ. sci. and tech. 1981, Columbus sect. award 1981), Air Pollution Control Assn. (Chambers award 1986, Haagen-Smit prize 2011), Phi Beta Kappa, Sigma Xi, Pi Mu Epsilon, Phi Lambda Upsilon, Alpha Chi Sigma. Achievements include research on photochemistry, reaction kinetics, atmospheric chemistry, mechanisms free radical reactions.

CALVERT, JERRY L., bank executive; BA in Economics, Wofford Coll., 1974. Ret. lt. col., Reserves USMC; sr. v.p., regional mgr. Am. Fed. Bank, 1984—99; pres., CEO First Nat. Bank of the South, First Nat. Bancshares Inc. Bd. dirs. First Nat. Bancshares, Inc. Office: First National Bancshares Inc 215 N Pine St Spartanburg SC 29302 Office Phone: 864-281-0830. Business E-Mail: jcalvert@ebankfirstnational.com.

CALVERT, WILLIAM PRESTON, radiologist; b. Warrensburg, Mo., July 2, 1934; s. William Geery and Elizabeth (Spaulding) C.; m. Mary Kay Kersh, Apr. 4, 1976. BS, MIT, 1956; MD, U. Pa., 1960. Diplomate Am. Bd. Nuclear Medicine, Am. Bd. Radiology. Intern Pa. Hosp., Phila., 1960-61, resident in medicine, 1961-62, 64-66, chief med. resident, chief resident physician, 1965-66; resident in gastro-enterology U. Miami, 1966-67, NIH fellow in gastroenterology, 1967-68, resident in radiology, 1968-71; radiologist Meml. Hosp., Hollywood, Fla., 1971-72; chief dept. radiology Larkin Gen. Hosp., South Miami, Fla., 1972-80, radiologist, 1980-89, Jackson Meml. Hosp., U. Miami, 1989-93, Univ. Hosp., Tammarac, Fla., 1993-95; part-time radiologist Northern Navajo Med. Ctr., Shiprock, N.Mex., 1995-2000; ret., 2000. Clin. instr. radiology U. Miami Sch. Medicine, 1971-76, clin. asst. prof. radiology, 1984-88, clin. assoc. prof. radiology, 1988-94. Bd. dirs. Wediko Farms Children's Svcs., Carbondale, Ill. Served with M.C., USAF, 1962-64. Mem. AMA, Fla. Med. Assn., Fla., Greater Miami radiol. socs., Soc. Nuclear Medicine, Radiol. Soc. N.Am., Explorers Club. Personal E-mail: calvertb12@aol.com, billcalvert100@gmail.com.

CAMBEL, ALI B., engineering educator; b. Merano, Italy, Apr. 9, 1923; came to U.S., 1943, naturalized, 1951; s. H. Cemil and Remziye (Hakki) C.; m. Marion dePaar, Dec. 20, 1946; children: Metin, Emel, Leyla, Sarah. BS, Robert Coll., Istanbul, Turkey, 1942; postgrad., U. Istanbul, 1942-43, MIT, 1943-45; MS, Calif. Inst. Tech., 1946; PhD, U. Iowa, 1950. Registered profl. engr. Instr. U. Iowa, 1947-50, asst. prof., 1950-53; from assoc. prof. to prof. mech. engring. Northwestern U., 1953-61, Walter P. Murphy disting. prof., 1961-68, dir. gas dynamics lab., 1955-66, chmn. dept. mech. engring. and astronautical scis., 1957-66; from dir. research and engring. support divsn. to v.p. rsch. IDA, 1966-68; dean Coll. Engring., Wayne State U., Detroit, 1968-70; exec. v.p. for acad. affairs Wayne State U., 1970-72; v.p., dir. system rsch. divsn. Gen. Rsch. Corp., 1972-74; dep. asst. dir. for sci. and tech. NSF, 1974-75; prof. engring. and applied sci. George Washington U., Washington, 1975-88, prof. emeritus, 1988—, chmn. dept. civil, mech. and environ. engring., 1978-80, dir. energy programs, 1976-88. Cons. in field; staff dir. Pres.'s Interdeptl. Energy Study, 1963-64; engring. scis. adv. com. USAF Office Sci. Research, 1961-63; mem. Commn. Engring. Edn., 1966-68, Army Sci. Advisory Panel, 1966-72; nat. lectr. Sigma Xi, 1961-62. Author: Plasma Physics and Magnetofluidmechanics, 1963, Applied Chaos Theory: A Paradigm for Complexity, 1993; co-author: Gas Dynamics, 1958, Real Gases, 1963, Plasma Physics, 1965; co-editor: Transport Properties in Gases, 1958, The Dynamics of Conducting Gases, 1960, Magnetohydrodynamics, 1962, Second Law Analysis of Energy Devices and Processes, 1980, Dissipative Structures in Integrated Systems, 1989; co-editor AIAA Jour., Jet Propulsion, 1955-60, Energy, The Internat. Jour., 1975-95; mem. editl. bd. Energy, Environment, Economics, 1991; contbr. articles to profl. jours. Bd. dirs. YMCA. Recipient citation for solar satellite power system evaluation Dept. Energy/NASA, 1981, Immigrant Achievement award Immigration Law Found., 2005; cert. for patriotic service Sec. of Army; award for excellence NSF/RANN; award for contbns. to sci. and edn. U.S. Immigrants League.; Washburn scholar, 1938. Fellow AIAA (J. Edward Pendray award 1959, nat. dir.), 1996, Am. Soc. Engring. Edn. (Curtis McGraw award 1960, George Westinghouse award 1966, chmn. engring. and pub. policy divsn. 1986-87), ASME (founding chmn. energy systems analysis tech. com. 1980-82), Am. Immigration Law Found. (Achievement award 2005), Cosmos Club (Washington), Sigma Xi, Pi Tau Sigma, Tau Beta Pi. Mem. Soc. Of Friends. Home: 7621 Provincial Dr Apt 208 Mc Lean VA 22102-7623 Personal E-mail: alibcambel@msn.com.

CAMBER, DIANE WOOLFE, association president; b. Miami Beach, Fla. m. Isaac Camber. BA in Art History, Barnard Coll.; postgrad., Columbia U., Mass. Coll. Art; MEd in Arts Edn., Boston State Coll. Mus. lectr., pub. rels. specialist Albright-Knox Art Gallery, Buffalo, 1962—64; mus. educator De Cordova and Dana Mus., Lincoln, Mass., 1967—68; mus. lectr. Mus. Fine Arts, Boston, 1968—69; art specialist LA Pub. Schs., 1970—77; instr. Ft. Lauderdale Art Inst., 1978—79; assoc. dir. Miami Design Preservation League, 1978—80; acting dir. Bass Mus. Art, Miami, 1980—82, exec. dir., chief curator, 1982—2007, dir. emeritus, 2007—; pres. Diane W Chambers Assn. Co-author: Frank Lloyd Wright: Decorative Objects, Prints, Drawings, Florida Projects, 1984. Campaigned to place Miami's Art Deco Dist. on the Nat. Register of Historica Places; bd. dirs. Chaim Gross Found., NY. Recipient Chevalier des Arts et Lettres, French Govt., 1989. Mem.: Fla. Art Mus. Dirs. Assn. (v.p. 1984—86, pres. 1986—88), Mus. Trustees Assn. (mem. adv. coun. dirs.), Am. Assn. Art Mus. Dirs. Office: Diane W Camber Associates 4474 Sheridan Ave Miami Beach FL 33140

CAMBRE, RONALD C., construction executive; m. Gail Cambre. BSCE, La. State U.; postgrad., Harvard U. Chmn. Rio Tinto Minera SA; various positions, including pres., CEO Freeport-McMoRan Resource Ptnrs. (subs. Freeport-McMoRan Inc.), 1964-93; v.p., sr. tech. adviser to chmn. Freeport-McMoRan Inc., 1988-93; vice chmn. Newmont Mining Corp., Denver, 1993, pres., 1994—99, chmn., 1995—2001, CEO, 1993—2000; chmn. McDermott Internat. Inc., 2008—. Bd. dirs. Cliffs Natural Resources, Inc. (formerly Cleveland-Cliffs Inc.), 1996—, W.R. Grace & Co., 1998—, Inco Ltd., 2000—06. Office: McDermott International Inc 777 N Eldridge Pky Houston TX 77079 Office Phone: 281-870-5000. Office Fax: 281-870-5095. Business E-Mail: rcambre@mcdermott.com.

CAMBURN, CLYDE, oil industry executive; Mng. dir. SEACOR Holdings Inc. Office: SEACOR Holdings Inc 2200 Eller Dr Fort Lauderdale FL 33316 Office Phone: 954-523-2200. Office Fax: 954-524-9185. Business E-Mail: clyde.camburn@seacorholdings.com.

CAMERON, ANGELA R., dentist; b. Morristown, Tenn. m. Jason Cunningham; children: Andrew, Alexis. BS in Biochemistry, Furman U., Greenville, SC, MS in Biophysical Chemistry; DDS with honors, U. Tenn. Cert. dentistry, diplomate Am. Bd. Surgery. Dentist Sophisticated Smiles, Johnson City, Tenn. Author: (publ.) Smile Line. Recipient Richard L. Sullivan Award for Excellence in Dental Rsch. (Oral Cancer), 2000, ACE Award, Tenn. Dental Assn., 2003—; named one of America's Top Dentists, Consumer's Rsch. Coun. of America, 2003—10, 40 Under 40, Bus. Journal, 2006. Fellow: Dental Orgn. for Conscious Sedation; mem.: First Dist. Dental Soc., Tenn. Dental Assn., Am. Assn. of Women Dentists, Am. Acad. of Dental Sleep Medicine, ADA, Acad. of Gen. Dentistry, Am. Acad. of Cosmetic Dentistry (sustaining mem.). Avocation: reading. Office: Sophisticated Smiles 189 Corporate Dr Ste 20 Johnson City TN 37601 Office Phone: 423-928-8359. Office Fax: 423-282-6018.

CAMERON, CAM (MALCOLM G. CAMERON III), college football coach; b. Chapel Hill, NC, Feb. 6, 1961; m. Missy Cameron; children: Tommy, Daniel, Christopher, Elizabeth BS in Bus. Mgmt., Ind. U., 1983. Grad. asst. U. Mich. Wolverines, 1983—84, wide receivers coach, 1986—89, quarterbacks & receivers coach, 1990—93; quarterbacks coach Washington Redskins, 1994-96; head football coach Ind. U. Hoosiers, 1997—2001; offensive coord. San Diego Chargers, 2002—06, Balt. Ravens, 2008—12; head coach Miami Dolphins, 2007—08; offensive coord., quarterbacks coach La. State U. Tigers, 2013—. Recipient Trester award for Mental Attitude, 1979; named Vigo County's Athlete of Yr., 1978-79, Nat. Athlete of Yr., Fellowship Christian Athletes, 1979 Office: LSU Athletic Dept PO Box 25095 Baton Rouge LA 70894

CAMERON, NICHOLAS ALLEN, manufacturing executive; b. Phila., Jan. 6, 1939; s. Nicholas Guyot and Katherine (Rogers) C.; m. Leslie Wood, Dec. 14, 1974; children: Christopher Wilson, Pamela Wilson. BS, Yale U., 1960. Treas. Allied Corp., Morristown, NJ, 1979-81, v.p. and treas., 1981-82, v.p. fin., 1982-83, v.p. planning and devel., 1983-85; sr. v.p. planning, devel. and adminstrn. Allied-Signal Inc., Morristown, NJ, 1985-86; sr. v.p. tech. and bus. devel. Bendix Aerospace-Allied-Signal, Inc., Arlington, Va., 1986-87; group pres. Allied-Signal Aerospace, 1988; sr. v.p. ops. svcs. Allied-Signal, Inc., Morristown, NJ, 1988-90, sr. v.p., gen. mgr. chem. intermediates, 1990-95. Bd. dirs. Morristown Meml. Health Found., 1996—2001, United Way of Morris County, Morristown, 1980-86, 90-98, campaign chmn., 1991, chief vol. officer, 1993-95, bd. chmn., 1996-98; bd. dirs. Morris 2000, 1990-97, 99-2003, chmn., 1993-96; adv. bd. Morristown Hosp., 1998-2008; mem. Morris County Park Commn., 1999—2010, pres., 2005-07. Mem. Morris County C. of C. (bd. dirs. 1975-86, 1990-98), Tau Beta Pi. Clubs: St. Elmo Soc. (New Haven); Morris County Golf, Essex Yacht Club, Old Lyme Country Club, The Moorings Club. Republican. Episcopalian. Home: 2165 Sea Mist Ct Vero Beach FL 32963 Personal E-mail: ncame1639@aol.com.

CAMERON, THOMAS WILLIAM LANE, investment company executive; b. Newton, Mass., Feb. 19, 1927; s. Percy G. and Mary W.D. (Mitchell) C. AB cum laude, Harvard, 1949, MBA, 1951. With sales dept. Procter & Gamble, Boston, 1951-53; with Hopper, Soliday, & Co., Inc., Phila., 1953—86, ptnr., 1961—, pres., 1966-72, chmn., 1972-83; dir. Hopper, Soliday & Co., Inc., 1983-86; sr. v.p. Interstate/Johnson Lane, Johns Island, SC, 1986—99; chmn. Sovereign Investors Inc., 1979-91; vice chmn. John Hancock Sovereign Investors, 1991-96; chmn. Cameron & Assocs., Inc., 1999—2008, Rising Dividend Growth Fund, 2004—. Chmn. Phila.-Balt.-Washington Stock Exch., 1970-74, bd. govs., 1963-75; chmn. Dividend Growth Advisers, 2004—. Bd. mgrs. Franklin Inst., 1970-90, chmn., 1978-81; bd. dirs. Holling Cancer Ctr., Med. U. SC, 1992—2002. Served with USNR, 1944-46. Mem.: Waynesborough Country (Paoli, Pa.) (pres. 1965-67); Harvard (Phila.) (pres. 1965-66), Harvard Bus. Sch. (Phila.) (pres. 1962-64). Office: Dividend Growth Advisors 58 Riverwalk Blvd Bldg 2 Ste A Ridgeland SC 29936 Office Phone: 843-645-9700.

CAMILLERI, MICHAEL, lawyer, educator; b. NYC, July 16, 1953; s. Joseph and Lena (Calatozzo) C.; m. Debralyn Fisher, Aug. 5, 1989; children: Bryan, Brandon, Brooke. BA, L.I. U., 1974; JD, Fordham U., 1977. Bar: N.Y. 1978. Sr. v.p., gen. counsel Nat. Coun. Compensation Ins., NYC, 1978-91; ptnr. Adorno & Zeder, Miami, Fla., 1991-99; pres. AmTrust Ins. Group, Boca Raton, Fla.; prin. Preferred Ins. Capital Cons., Boca Raton, 2001—; pres. Newport Star Reins. Co., Columbia, SC, 2003—; CEO USA Title Co., 2006—; pres. Am. Fin. Security Life Ins. Co., Mo., 2010—, USA Title Ins., Columbia, SC, 2008—; prin. Matrix Ins. Cons., 2009—. Pres. Ins. Data Resources, 1997-2000; cons. Family Counseling Ctr., Bklyn., 1980-85; adj. prof. law Coll. Ins., NYC, 1981-91; arbitrator civil ct., NYC, 1983-91; bd. dirs., gen. counsel First Comml. Co., 2001—. Author: Matthew Bender's Accident and Health Law, 1989; editor: Werbel's N.Y. Worker's Compensation Law, 1986-94. Mem. ABA, N.Y. State Bar Assn., D.C. Bar Assn., Profl. Bowlers Assn. Home Phone: 561-703-0457; Office Phone: 561-241-9974.

CAMISA, CHARLES, dermatologist, educator; BS, Cornell U.; MD, Mt. Sinai Sch. of Medicine, 1977. Diplomate Am. Bd. Dermatology, 1981, cert. clin. & lab. dermatologic immunology. Resident dermatology NYU Med. Ctr., NYC, 1978—81, chief resident skin & cancer dept.; affiliate assoc. prof. dermatology Coll. of Medicine Univ. of South Fla.; dir. dermatology divsn. Ohio State Univ.; vice-chmn. dermatology dept. Cleve. Clinic Found., dir. residency program, 1987—2001; dir. phototherapy dept. Riverchase Dermatology. Editor: (jour.) Cutis, author 40 peer-reviewed articles and textbook chpts. on skin and oral disease, editor three textboooks on psoriasis. Named one of Best Doctors in America. Achievements include discovery of Camisa disease, a rare genetic variant of Vohwinkel's Syndrome. Office: Riverchase Dermatology and Cosmetic Surgery Naples Center 1015 Crosspointe Naples FL 34110 Mailing: Riverchase Dermatology and Cosmetic Surgery Fort Myers 7331 Gladiolus Fort Myers FL 33908 Office Phone: 239-596-9075, 239-437-8810. Office Fax: 239-596-9076, 239-437-8875.

CAMP, DAMON D., JR., law educator; BS, Ga. State Univ., 1971, MS, 1975, JD, 1993; PhD, Claremont Grad. Sch., 1981. Bar: Ga. 1993. Assoc. prof. emeritus of criminal justice Ga. State Univ., Atlanta; faculty assoc. Inst. of Public Health, Ga. State Univ.; atty., private practice. Editor: Criminal Justice Rev. Mailing: Ga State Univ 1210 UL PO Box 4018 Atlanta GA 30302-4018 Office Phone: 404-413-1023. Business E-Mail: dcamp@gsu.edu.

CAMP, ELIZABETH W., investment company executive, lawyer; BBA magna cum laude, U. Ga., Athens, JD; M in Tax Law, Georgetown U. Law Ctr., Washington. Tax acct.; pvt. practice atty. Washington, Atlanta; various positions including pres., CEO Camp Oil Co.; pres., CEO DF Management, Inc., 2000—. Bd. dirs. Blue Cross Blue Shield Ga., 1992—2001, Synovus Fin. Corp., 2003—. Former trustee Ga. Dept. Industry, Trade & Tourism; mem. campaign adv. task force U. Ga. Terry Coll. Bus. Adv. Coun., 2008—. Office: c/o Synovous Bd Directors PO Box 120 Columbus GA 31902 Office Phone: 706-649-2311.

CAMP, THOMAS HARLEY, economist; b. Charlotte, NC, Aug. 13, 1929; s. Thomas Franklin and Agnes Mae (Davis) C.; m. Frances Ann Rogers, Mar. 20, 1953 (dec. Feb. 1998); children: Thomas Harley Jr., Landon G.; m. Sheila M. Schell, Apr. 24, 1999. BSc, U. N.C., 1956; postgrad, Am. U., 1965-67. Industry econ. USDA, Washington, 1959-70, location leader Austin, Tex., 1970-74, rsch. leader College Station, Tex., 1974-86, program leader Weslaco, Tex., 1986-88, agrl. mktg. specialist Lane, Okla., 1988-90; cons. Georgetown, Tex., 1990—. Author, co-author 44 sci. publs.; contbr. articles to profl. jours. Cubmaster Boy Scouts Am., Springfield, Va., 1965-69, asst. scoutmaster, 1966-70, scoutmaster, Round Rock, Tex., 1970-72, asst. scoutmaster, Austin, 1972-74. With USN, 1946-51, Korea. Mem. Am. Soc. Agrl. Engrs., Animal Air Transp. Assn., Food Distbn. Rsch. Soc., Transp. Rsch. Forum, Masons. Presbyterian. Avocations: photography, boating. Home and Office: 1005 Fountainwood Dr Georgetown TX 78628-1906 Office Phone: 512-809-0731. Personal E-mail: northstar13@suddenlink.net.

CAMPANA, PHILLIP JOSEPH, German language educator; b. Jersey City, Apr. 10, 1941; s. Ralph Joseph and Alberta Alphonsine (Lepis) C.; m. Paulette Monique Beauregard, 1968 (div. 1978); children: Lisa Marie, Michael Phillip; m. Nancy June Parr Hendricks, 2005(dec. 2012). BA in German magna cum laude, St. Peters Coll., Jersey City, 1962; postgrad. (Fulbright scholar), U. Saarbrücken, Germany, 1962-63; PhD, Brown U., 1970. Instr. German St. Peter's Coll., Jersey City, summer 1964; grad. asst. in German Brown U., Providence, 1965-67; assoc. prof. German Tenn. Tech. U., Cookeville, 1970-74, prof. German, 1974—2007, adj. prof., 2007—11, chmn. dept. fgn. langs., 1970—2003, founder and 1st dir. English Lang. Inst., 1977, dir. Interactive Videodisc Project, 1984-94, prof. emeritus, adj., 2007—11. State chmn. So. Conf. on Lang. Tchg., 1981-85; reviewer grant proposals (EESA, Title II) Tex. Coord. Bd. for Higher Edn., 1986, U.S. Dept. Edn., 1987; evaluator Nat. Tchrs. Exam in German for Ednl. testing Svc., 1990; lectr., presenter in field. Assoc. editor Schatzkammer, 1980-89, cons. editor, 1990-93, editl. bd., 1993—; evaluator: the materials Ctr. of Am. Assn. Tchrs. German, 1980-81, Modern Lang. Jour., Fgn. Lang. Annals, Seminar; mem. editl. bd. Unterrichtspraxis, 2000—10; book rev. editor Unterrichtspraxis, 2002—2010; contbr. numerous articles and revs. to profl. jours. Mem. faculty adv. group on master plan for higher edn. Tenn. Higher Edn. Comm., 1973, steering com. on tchr. edn., 1983-84; chmn. Tenn. Bd. Regents Task Force on Improvement of Quality in Tchr. Edn., 1982; mem. Com. on Bus. and Fiscal Affairs, Tenn. Bd. Regents, 1975-76. Recipient Outstanding Faculty award in Tchg., Tenn. Tech. U., 1976, Goethe-Inst. award, 1977, 84, 99, Nat. Endowment for the Humanities, 1981, Meritorious Svc. award Nat. Coun. State Suprs. of Fgn. Langs., 1981, Svc. award Rural Educators Alliance for Lang., 1993, Outstanding Faculty award for Profl. Svcs., Tenn. Tech. U., 1995; Fulbright scholar, 1962-63, 80, 88; Woodrow Wilson fellow, 1962-64, NDEA fellow, 1963-66; grantee Tenn. Tech., 1984, 86-87, 87-88, 88-89, Govt. of Germany, 1983, Tenn. Higher Edn. Commn., 1986-87, 88, 89, 97, 98, 99, Tenn. Bd. Regents, 1989, Tenn. Humanities Coun., 1990. Mem. MLA, Am. Assn. Tchrs. German (Tenn. chpt. pres. 1975-77, treas. 1980-92, cert. of Merit award 1982), Tenn. Fgn. Lang. Tchg. Assn. (bd. dirs. 1974-77, 80-81, 82-85, 98-2001, pres. 1977-80, mem. com. 1990-96, rep. Ctrl. States Conf. bd. 1990-93, Jacqueline C. Elliott award 1984), Ctrl. States Conf. on Tchg. Fgn. Langs. (chmn. 1984-87, bd. dirs. 1979-80, 81-84, 91-94, adv. coun. 1978—2008, co-editor annual volume 1995, co-chair Leadership CSC, 1995-96, Founders award 2006), Am. Coun. on Tchg. Fgn. Langs. (exec. coun. 1985-86, 91-94, chmn. pub. com. 1993-94, Florence Steiner award 1987), Tenn. Fgn. Lang. Inst. (bd. govs. 1986-2001, v.p., sec.-treas.), Tenn. Coun. Internat. Edn. (bd. dirs. 1976-78), Ill. Fgn. Lang. Tchrs. Assn. (mem. adv. bd. 1986-88, nominating com. 1987-88, Land of Lincoln Svc. award 1986, 87), Consortium for German in S.E. (founding mem., treas. 1991-96), Omicron Delta Kappa. Roman Catholic. Home: 1135 Meadow Rd Cookeville TN 38501-2035 Office: Tenn Tech U Dept Fgn Langs PO Box 5061 Cookeville TN 38505-0001 E-mail: pcampana@tntech.edu.

CAMPBELL, ANDREW WILLIAM, immunotoxicology physician; b. Beirut, Apr. 3, 1948; s. William Alexander and Gisela (Landes) C.; children: Denia Giselle, Michelle Elise, Colin Alexander, Ian William. BA in Pre-med., Psychology, Franklin Piere Coll., Rindge, NH, 1970; MD, U. Autonoma de Guadalajara, Mex., 1974. Diplomate Am. Bd. Family Practice, Am. Bd. Forensic Examiners, Am. Bd. Forensic Medicine. Intern Pediat. Hosp. Infantil, Ob-gyn., Clin. Santa Monica, Guadalajara, Mex., 1974-75, Pub. Health Dept., Guadalajara, Mex., 1975-76; resident gen. surgery Orlando (Fla.) Regional Med. Ctr., 1977-78; resident family practice Med. Coll. Ga., Augusta, 1978-81; pvt. practice family physician Two Physician Practice, Sarasota, Fla., 1981, with former chief surgeon Eisenhower Med. Ctr., Augusta, Ga.; pvt. practice Augusta, Wrens and Louisvlle, Ga., 1983-84, Houston, 1985—; med. dir. Med. Ctr. for Immune and Toxic Disorders, Houston, 1993—. Staff mem. Meml. City Med. Ctr., Spring Branch Med. Ctr.; chmn. dept. family practice Sam Houston Meml. Hosp., Houston, 1987, chmn. credentials com., 1988, exec. com., 1987—89; lectr. and spkr. at Artificial Implants and Toxic Exposure Symposia; faculty U. Tex. Sch. Medicine, 1993—98; cons., presenter in field; editl. bd. mem. Integrative Medicine: A Clinician's Jour.; editor-in-chief Advances in Mind Body Medicine, Alternative Therapies in Health & Medicine; med. editor Alternative Medicine Consumer Mag.; mng. ptnr. Clinica del Barrio. Author (with others): Health Effects of Toxic Chemicals, 1994, Textbook of Nephrology (2 vols.), 1995; co-editor: Internat. Jour. Occupl. Medicine and Toxicology, 1992—95; mem. editl. bd.: Toxicology and Indsl. Health, 1994—96; contbr. articles to profl. jours., chapters to books. Founder Clinic for the Indigent, St. John Vianney Ch., Houston, 1987; bd. trustees Sam Houston Meml. Hosp., 1987-93. Recipient Consumer's Choice award Am. Nurses in Bus. Assn., Houston, 1994. Fellow: Am. Acad. Family Physicians; mem.: Am. Bd. Forensic Examiners, Am. Assn. Physicians & Surgeons. Republican. Avocation: golf. E-mail: answerwellness@gmail.com.

CAMPBELL, ANN-MARIE, retail executive; BA in philosophy, Ga. State U., MBA. Cashier Home Depot, Inc., 1985, store mgr., dist. mgr. and regional v.p., v.p. ops., v.p. merchandising and spl. orders, v.p. retail mktg. and sales Home Depot Direct, v.p. vendor svcs., now pres. So. Divsn. Adv. bd. mem. The Atlanta Union Mission. Mem.: Nat. Scholars Honor Soc., Beta Gamma Sigma. Office: Home Depot, Inc 2455 Paces Ferry Rd NW Atlanta GA 30339 Office Phone: 770-433-8211. Office Fax: 770-384-2805.

CAMPBELL, BARRY G., information technology executive; b. 1941; Pres., CEO & bd. dirs. Allied Aerospace Industries, Inc.; with CIA, Langley, Va., 1968—71; exec. v.p. Vitro Corp., Rockville, Md., pres., CEO, 1993—97; with Tracor Systems Technologies, Inc., Rockville, Md., 1971, chmn., CEO, 1997. Bd. dirs. ManTech Internat. Corp., 2002—. Office: ManTech International Corp 12015 Lee Jackson Hwy Fairfax VA 22033 Office Fax: 703-218-6000, 703-218-8296. Business E-Mail: barry.campbell@mantech.com.

CAMPBELL, BERT LOUIS, lawyer, arbitrator, mediator; b. Tyler, Tex., Aug. 11, 1939; s. Bert M. and Jocelyn M. (Day) C.; m. Mary Ann Suatoni, July 17, 1965; children: Stephen, Brian, Rebecca. BA, U. Tex., 1961, B in Journalism, 1970, JD with honors, 1970. Ptnr. Vinson & Elkins, Houston, 1970—2001. Writer, lectr. in field. Trustee Cullen Found. Lt. (j.g.) USN, 1963-66. Mem. ABA, Tex. Bar Assn., Houston Bar Assn., Am. Health Lawyers Assn. (ADR panel), Am. Arbitration Assn. Office: 3017 Nottingham Blvd Houston TX 77005 Home Phone: 713-667-6003; Office Phone: 713-349-8923. Personal E-mail: bcampbell-houston@comcast.com.

CAMPBELL, BOBBY JACK, academic administrator; b. Ft. Worth, Oct. 12, 1929; s. Jack Bryan and Ruby Opal (Lamberth) C.; m. Frances Carol Alexander, Aug. 24, 1957; children: Carol Stuart Davis, John William Campbell. BA, Tex. Christian U., 1951, MA, 1953; PhD, U. N.C., 1960. Asst. dir. U. N.C. Inst. of Govt., Chapel Hill, 1957-59; chief accident rsch. br. Cornell U. Aero. Lab., Buffalo, 1959-66; dir. U. N.C. Hwy. Safety Rsch. Ctr., Chapel Hill, 1966-91, sr. investigator, dir. emeritus, 1992—; interim dir. Nat. Driving Ctr., 1990—91, UNC Inst. Trans. Res. & Edvc. Chm. com. accident stats. Nat. Safety Coun., 1964-68; chmn. nat. motor vehicle safety adv. coun. U.S. Dept. Transp., 1975-76, mem., 1987-89, chmn. nat. driver register adv. com., 1983-86; chmn. panel on automotive assessment into 21st century U.S. Congress Office Tech. Assessment, 1976-77; chmn. com. to study CB radios on buses NRC, 1983-84, mem. com. to identify measures to improve safety of sch. bus transp., 1987-88; chmn. Global Traffic Safety Trust, Melbourne, Australia, 1988-92; lectr. or cons. in Australia, Azerbaijan, Brazil, Can., China, Denmark, Dominica, France, Germany, India, Hong Kong, Japan, Republic of Korea, Malawi, Malaysia, New Zealand, Russia, Saudi Arabia, Spain, Switzerland, Uruguay. Author: Driver Improvement: The Point System, 1958, Reducing Traffic Injury: A Global Challenge, 1988; (with others) Reflections on the Transfer of Highway Safety to Developing Nations, 1998, Collier's Encyclopedia, 1962, Human Factors in Technology, 1963, Trauma and the Automobile, 1966, Traffic Safety: A National Problem, 1967, Key Issues in Highway Loss Reducation, 1970, Restraint Technologies: Rear Seat Occupant Protection, 1987; contbr. numerous articles to profl. jours. SFC US Army, 1948—49. Recipient Leadership award Nat. Gov. Safety Rep. Orgn., 1997, Gerin Medal for Rsch. Internat. Assn. for Accident and Traffic Medicine, 1992, Gustafson Leadership award Hwy. Users Fedn., 1989, Volvo Internat. Traffic Safety prize, 1988, Volvo Pub. Safety award 1984, Disting. Svc. award Am. Assn. for Automotive Medicine, 1978, N.C. Pub. Health Assn., 1972, Alvah Lauer award Human Factors Soc., 1976, Met. Rsch. prize, 1960, Commendation Nat. Safety Coun., 1971, 60. Avocations: astronomy, classical music, opera, sports, history. Home: 502 Belmont St Chapel Hill NC 27517-3000

CAMPBELL, BRIAN WESLEY, professional hockey player; b. Strathroy, Ont., Canada, May 23, 1979; s. Ed and Lorna Campbell. Defenseman Buffalo Sabres, 2001—08, San Jose Sharks, 2008, Chgo. Blackhawks, 2008—11, Fla. Panthers, 2011—. Recipient Lady Byng Trophy, 2012; named to NHL All-Star Game, 2007, 2008, 2009, 2012, Second All-Star Team, NHL, 2008. Achievements include being a member of Stanley Cup Champion Chicago Blackhawks, 2010. Office: Florida Panthers BankAtlantic Center One Panther Parkway Sunrise FL 33323

CAMPBELL, BYRON CHESSER, newspaper publishing executive; b. Evanston, Ill., Feb. 6, 1934; s. Chesser Milburn and Hallie (Calhoun) C.; m. Barbara Mace, Aug. 16, 1958 (div. Apr. 1982); children: Evan Chesser, Aimee Campbell Wood; m. Meta Pierce, Aug. 13, 1983; stepchildren: Marc Wise, Meier Wise, Matthew Wise, Miles Wise. BA, Yale U., 1955; MBA, Harvard U., 1959. Various positions Burlington (Vt.) Free Press, 1959-61; prodn. engr., asst. labor rels. mgr. Chicago Tribune, 1961-68, prodn. mgr., 1970-73; bus. mgr. Chicago Today, 1968-70; asst. to pres. Tribune Co., 1973-75; pres., gen. mgr. Area Publs. Corp., Merrill Printing Co., Chgo., 1975-77; pres., chief exec. officer News and Sun-Sentinel Co., Ft. Lauderdale, Fla., 1977-83; pres., pub. L.A. Daily News; pres., chief exec. officer Tribune Newspapers West, Inc., LA, 1983-87; pres., pub. The Record, Hackensack, NJ; v.p. Macromedia Inc., Hackensack, 1988-91. Bd. dirs. Home News Pub. Co., New Brunswick, N.J., Newspapers of New Eng., Concord, N.H., George W. Prescott Pub. Co., Quincy, Mass., Journal-Star Printing Co., Lincoln, Nebr., Freedom Comm., Inc., Irvine, Calif. Bd. dirs. Lyric Opera Chgo., Newberry Libr. Chgo., Sta. WPBT, Miami, Fla., Rush-Presbyn.-St. Luke's Med. Ctr., Chgo.; bd. dirs., campaign chmn. United Way of Bergen County, 1989-91; adv. bd. Bergen 2000; bd. dirs., pres., campaign chmn. United Way of Broward County, Fla.; bd. dirs., chmn. San Fernando Valley Cultural Found., L.A.; bd. dirs., pres. Chgo. Youth Ctrs., Broward Community Blood Ctr.; bd. dirs., exec. com. Broward Workshop; bd. dirs. United Way, L.A., campaign chmn. San Fernando Valley; bd. dirs., 1st v.p. Ft. Lauderdale Symphony. Lt. USNR, 1955—57. Mem. AP (nominating com.), Am. Newspaper Pubs. Assn. (govt. affairs com., newsprint com. 1989-92), Am. Press Inst. (bd. dirs. 1984-93), Inland Press Assn. (pres., bd. dirs.), Greater L.A. C. of C. (bd. dirs.), Econ. Club (Chgo.), Yale Club (Chgo., bd. dirs., pres.), Lotos Club (N.Y.C.), Univ. Club (Chgo., bd. dirs., admissions com.), Saddle and Cycle Club (Chgo., bd. dirs., admissions com.), Lauderdale Yacht Club (Ft. Lauderdale, Fla.), Ristigouche Salmon Club (Matapedia, Que.). Congregationalist. Avocations: tennis, wine, fly fishing, travel, golf. Home: 70 Indianhead Dr Ormond Beach FL 32174-3059

CAMPBELL, CHAD, professional golfer; b. Andrews, Tex., May 31, 1974; B, UNLV, 1996. Profl. golfer, 1996—. Mem. US Team Ryder Cup, 2004, 2006, 2008. Named Rookie of Yr., Hooters Tour, 1997. Achievements include winning PGA Tour events: Tour Championship, 2003; Bay Hill Invitational, 2004; Bob Hope Chrysler Classic, 2006; Viking Classic, 2007; being a member of the Ryder Cup winning US team, 2008. Avocation: hunting. Office: c/o PGA Tour 112 PGA Tour Blvd Ponte Vedra Beach FL 32082

CAMPBELL, CHARLES ALTON, private equity instructor, transportation executive; b. Brunswick, Ga., Mar. 10, 1944; s. Rayford Monroe and Cecelia Elizabeth (Camilla) C.; m. Mary Alla Traber, Aug. 15, 1970; children: Christine Beensen, Elizabeth Traber, Charles Traber. B Indsl. Engring., Ga. Inst. Tech., 1966; MBA, Harvard U., 1973. Mgr. ops. projects Camak Lumber Ops. ITT Rayonier, Thomson, Ga., 1974-75, mgr. ops. projects Wood Products Group, 1975-77, dir. chems. devel. parent co., 1977-79, dir. operational planning and control, 1979-80; pres. Fox Mfg. Co., Rome, Ga., 1980-81, Camtec, Inc., Rome, 1981-88; chmn. Universal Ceramics, Inc., Adairsville, Ga., 1984-87; exec. v.p. Saunders, Inc., Birmingham, Ala., 1987-88, pres. CEO, 1988-90; pres. North Am. Tech. Corp., Birmingham, 1990—2007; pres. & CEO Cacet Inc., 2008—; chmn. HLCC Ltd. Mem. Lake Oconee Cmty. Ch. Lt. CE, USNR, 1967-69. Office: Cacet Inc 1060 Early Pl Greensboro GA 30642

CAMPBELL, CHRISTIAN LARSEN, lawyer, food service executive; b. Chgo., Nov. 21, 1950; s. William Joseph and Marie Agnes (Cloherty) C.; children from previous marriage: Chris, Brent; m. Heather Gilchrist, Mar. 7, 1987; children: Amelia, Colleen BA in Economics, Northwestern U.; MA in Economics, Harvard U., completed Advanced Mgmt. Program, JD, 1975. Bar: Ill. 1975, U.S. Dist. Ct. (no. dist.) Ill. 1975, U.S. Ct. Appeals (7th cir.) 1975, U.S. Ct. Appeals (5th cir.) 1980, U.S. Supreme Ct. 1980. Assoc. Sidley & Austin LLP, Chgo., 1975-83, ptnr., 1983—90; v.p., gen. counsel, sec. Nalco Chem. Co., Naperville, Ill., 1990—94; sr. v.p., gen. counsel, sec. Owens Corning, Inc., 1995—97, Yum! Brands, Inc. (formerly TRICON Global Restaurants, Inc.), 1997—, chief franchise policy officer, 2003—. Mem. ABA, Ill. State Bar Assn., Ky. Bar Assn., Chgo. Bar Assn., Louisville Bar Assn., Am. Mgmt. Assn. (lectr.1976—). Clubs: Barclay (Chgo.). Avocations: tennis, jogging, jogging, fishing. Office: Yum! Brands Inc 1441 Gardiner Ln Louisville KY 40213-1914 Office Phone: 502-874-2467. Office Fax: 502-874-8790. Personal E-mail: chris.campbell@yum.com.*

CAMPBELL, COLIN GOETZE, foundation president; b. NYC, Nov. 3, 1935; s. Joseph and Marjorie (Goetze) C.; m. Nancy Nash, June 20, 1959; children: Elizabeth, Jennifer, Colin, Blair. AB, Cornell U., 1957; JD, Columbia U., 1960; LLD (hon.), Amherst Coll., 1972, Williams Coll., 1973, Dickinson Coll., 1982, U. Hartford, 1983, Wesleyan U., 1989, Conn. Coll., 1990, Fairfield U., 1999; DHL (hon.), Trinity Coll., 1981, Georgetown U., 1984; PhD in Pub. Sci. (hon.), Cedar Crest Coll., 1997. Bar: Conn. 1961. Atty. Cummings & Lockwood, Stamford, Conn., 1960-62; asst. to pres. Am. Stock Exch., NYC, 1962-63, sec., 1963-64, v.p., 1964-67; adminstrv. v.p. Wesleyan U., Middletown, Conn., 1967-69, exec. v.p., 1969-70, pres., 1970-88, pres. emeritus, 1988—; pres. Rockefeller Bros. Fund, 1988-2000, Colonial Williamsburg Found., Va., 2000—. Bd. dirs. Pitney Bowes, Sysco Corp. Bd. dirs. Rockefeller Fin. Svcs. Mem.: Phi Delta Phi, Century Assn., Coun. on Fgn. Rels., Am. Acad. Arts and Scis., Knickerbocker Club, Psi Upsilon. Episcopalian. Office: Colonial Williamsburg Found PO Box 1776 Williamsburg VA 23187-1776 Home: Light Foot House 120 E Francis St Williamsburg VA 23185 Office Phone: 757-220-7200. E-mail: ccampbell@cwf.org.

CAMPBELL, DAPHNE, state legislator; b. Cap-Haitian, Haiti, May 19, 1957; m. Hubert Campbell; 5 children. BA, SOD Nursing Sch., 1981. Registered nurse; mem. Dist. 108 Fla. House of Representatives, 2011—. Democrat. Office: 9999 NE 2nd Ave Ste 309 Miami Shores FL 33138-2346 also: Fla House of Reps 1401 The Capitol 402 S Monroe St Tallahassee FL 32399-1300 Office Phone: 305-795-1210, 850-488-4233.

CAMPBELL, DAVID, electric power industry executive, lawyer, utilities executive; BA, Yale U.; JD, Harvard U.; MPhil, Oxford U. Prin. McKinsey & Co., Dallas; exec. v.p. corp. planning, strategy and risk TXU Corp., Dallas, 2004—06, CFO, chief risk officer, 2006—08; CEO Energy Future Holdings Corp. (subs. of Energy Future Holdings Corp.), Dallas, 2008—. Trustee Dallas Theater Ctr.; past. mem. Rhodes Scholarship selection com. Rhodes Scholar. Mem.: Council on Fgn. Rels., Dallas Assembly. Office: Energy Future Holdings Corp Energy Plz 1601 Bryan St Dallas TX 75201 Office Phone: 214-812-4600. Business E-Mail: david.campbell@energyfutureholdings.com.

CAMPBELL, DAVID GWYNNE, retired petroleum executive, geologist; b. May 2, 1930; s. Lois Raymond Henager and La Vada (Ray) Henager Campbell; m. Janet Gay Newland, March 1, 1958; 1 child, Carl David. BS in Geology, Tulsa U., 1953; MS in Geology, U. Okla., Norman, 1957. Geologist Lone Star Producing Co., Oklahoma City, 1957-65; dist. geologist, geol. cons. Tenneco Oil Co., Oklahoma City, 1965-77; exploration mgr. Leede Exploration, Oklahoma City, 1977-80; pres. Earth Hawk Exploration, Inc., Oklahoma City, 1980—; ret. Divsn. exploration mgr. PetroCorp., Inc., Oklahoma City, 1983-92, divsn. gen. mgr. 1992-96; cons. Jr. Achievement, Oklahoma City, 1996-2005; active U. Okla. Sch. Geology and Geophysics Alumni 1985—, bd. dirs. adv. coun. 1988-90, sec. 1990-91, vice chmn., 1991-92, chmn., 1992-93, life mem., 1994, centennial com., 2000-01, U. Okla. Trailblazer award com., 2003—. Contbr. articles to Jour. Cherokee Studies. Active Last Frontier Coun. Boy Scouts Am., 1960-73, edn. chmn. Eagle Dist. 1963-67; gubernatorial appointee Native Am. Cultural and Edn. Authority, 2002—; Okla. Cultural Coalition Gala com., 1999. Recipient Okla. Gov.'s Arts award for cmty. svc., 2003, Disting. Alumni award, Mewbourne Coll. Earth Energy, 2008, OU Inaugural Disting. Alumni award. Mem. AAAS, Internat. Assn. Energy Economists, Soc. Ind. Profl. Earth Scientists (pres. Okla. chpt. 1988, chmn. 1989, 91), Soc. Profl. Well Log Analysts, Am. Assn. Petroleum Geologists (hon. mem. 1995, chmn. house of dels. 1981-82, ho. of dels. 1982—, exec. com. 1981-82, 90-91, found. trustee assoc. 1983—, corp. mem. Am. Assn. Petroleum Geologists Found. 1996—, mem. adv. coun. 1984-87, councillor mid-continent sect. 1984-87, nominating com. 1984-85, 86-87, astrogeology com. 1984-2004, 2006-, honors and awards com. 1984-85, 85-86, adv. bd. Treatise of Petroleum Geology 1986-91, nat. membership adv. coun. 1987-90, membership com. chmn. mid-continent sect. 1987-90, Disting. Svc. award 1989, nat. v.p. 1990-91, mid-continent councillor energy minerals divsn. 1992-94, chmn. com. of coms. 1992-98, charter mem. divsn. Environ. Geoscis. 1992, candidate for nat. pres. 2001), Oklahoma City Geol. Soc. (hon. life mem. 1992, pub. rels. chmn. Spkrs. Bur. 1963-64, chmn. stratigraphic code com. 1967-68, presdl. appointee 1969-70, advt. mgr. Shale Shaker 1969-71, bylaws and incorp. rev. com. 1986), Oklahoma City Geol. Found. (founding pres. 1993-98, bd. dirs. 1993-2001), Ind. Petroleum Assn. Am. (Okla. chpt. regulatory affairs com. 1991-93), Houston Geol. Soc., Tulsa Geol. Soc., Petroleum Exploration Soc. Great Britain, Oklahoma City Petroleum Club (bd. dirs. 1987-90, 1995-98, sec. 1989, 2d v.p. 1990, chmn. membership com. 1988-90), Geol. Soc. Moscow, NY Acad. Scis., Oklahoma City C. of C., Okla. Hist. Soc., Cherokee Nat. Hist. Soc. (devel. com. 1987-95, trustee nat. soc. 1983-96), Ctr. Am. Indian (bd. dir. 1988-92), Red Earth Indian Ctr. (bd. dirs. 1992—, co-founder Red Earth Amb. of Yr. award, v.p. 1994-97, pres. 1997-98, Spirit award, 1999), Nat. Mus. Am. Indian, Am. Indian Cultural Soc., Houston Mus. Fine Arts, Okla. Pilots Assn., Exptl. Aircraft Assn., Aircraft Owners and Pilots Assn., First Families of Twin Ters., Clan Campbell N.Am., Okla. Geol. Found. (Legends award 2010), Okla. Corp. Commn. Regulatory Affairs Adv. Com., Sigma Xi, Pi Kappa Alpha. Home: 6109 Woodbridge Rd Oklahoma City OK 73162-3220

CAMPBELL, DENNIS MARION, academic administrator, theologian, educator; b. Dalhart, Tex., Aug. 23, 1945; s. Francis Marion and Margaret (Osterberg) C.; m. Leesa Heydenreich, June 13, 1970; children: Margaret Heyden, Robert Trevor. AB, Duke U., 1967, PhD, 1973; BD, Yale U., 1970; DD (hon.), Fla. So. U., 1986. Ordained to ministry United Meth. Ch., 1974. Min. Trinity United Meth. Ch., Durham, NC, 1973-74; chmn. dept. religion Converse Coll., Spartanburg, SC, 1974-79; dir. continuing edn. Div. Sch. Duke U., Durham, 1979-82, prof. theology, 1982—, dean. Div. Sch., 1982-97; headmaster Woodberry Forest (Va.) Sch., 1997—. Mem. Oxford (Eng.) Inst. Theol. Studies, 1982, 87, 92, Denver, 1996; gen. conf. United Meth. Ch., Balt., 1984, St. Louis, 1988, Louisville, 1992; del. World Meth. Coun., Nairobi, Kenya, 1987, World Coun. Chs. 7th Assembly, Canberra, Australia, 1991. Author: Authority and the Renewal of American Theology, 1976, Doctors, Lawyers, Ministers: Christian Ethics in Professional Practice, 1982, The Yoke of Obedience: The Meaning of Ordination in Methodism, 1988, Who Will Go For Us?, 1994. Chmn. Protection of Human Subjects Com.; bd. dirs. Family Health Internat., Research Triangle Park, 1986—, Internat. Coalition Boys Schs; bd. visitors Perkins Sch. Theology So. Meth. U., Dallas, 1987—; overseers com. Harvard U., 1992—; trustee Duke Endowment, 2004-. Mem. Am. Theol. Soc., Am. Acad. Religion, Soc. Christian Ethics, Assn. Theol. Schs. (accrediting com. 1986—), Phi Beta Kappa, Omicron Delta Kappa. Methodist. Home: PO Box 48 Woodberry Forest VA 22989-0048 Office: The Residence Woodberry Forest VA 22989-0048 Office Phone: 540-672-6000.

CAMPBELL, EILEEN M., oil industry executive; married; 2 children. Bachelor's, U. Md. Lobbyist Gov. NJ; with Nat. Assn. Mfrs.; lobbyist United Gas Pipe Line Co.; mgr. govt. affairs Marathon Oil Corp., Houston, 1991—98; dir. state govt. affairs USX, 1998—2000; v.p. human resources Marathon Oil Corp., Houston, 2000—10, v.p. pub. policy, 2010—. Office: Marathon Oil Corp Corp Hdqrs 5555 San Felipe Rd Houston TX 77056-2723

CAMPBELL, GILBERT SADLER, surgeon, educator; b. Toronto, Ont., Can., Jan. 4, 1924; s. Gilbert S. and Ellen (Thorson) Campbell; m. Dorothy Jean Nugent, Sept. 18, 1947 (div. 1960); children: Kathryn Elln, Rebecca Sadler, Thomas Kim, William Riley; m. Joan Louise Hancock, Sept. 28, 1961; children: Susan Muffin, John Gilbert. Student, Hampden-Sydney Coll., Va., 1939-40; BA, U. Va., Charlottesville, 1943, MD, 1946; MS, U. Minn., Mpls., 1949, PhD, 1954. Intern U. Minn. Hosps., Mpls., 1946-47, tchg. asst., 1947-49, researcher Am. Cancer Soc., 1951-53, sr. surgery resident, 1953-54; instr. physiology U. Minn., Mpls., 1948-49, instr. surgery, 1954-55, asst. prof., 1955-58; prof. surgery U. Okla., Oklahoma City, 1958-65; prof. surgery and thoracic surgery U. Okla. Med. Ctr., Oklahoma City, 1958-65; prof. surgery, chief thoracic surgery U. Ark. for Med. Scis., Little Rock, 1965-90; cons. surgery Little Rock VA Hosp, 1965-90, Ark. Children's Hosp., Little Rock, 1973-90; mem. courtesy staff Ark. Bapt. Med. Ctr., Little Rock, 1972-90; prof. emeritus, 1990—. Contbr. articles in field to med. jours. Served to capt. US Army, 1949-51. Decorated Purple Heart, Bronze Star with oak leaf cluster, Silver Star with oak leaf cluster US Army; Mary R. Markle scholar, 1954-59; recipient Horsley prize U. Va., 1954; named Surgery Alumnus of Yr. U. Minn., 1983; named to U. Ark. Medicine Hall of Fame. Mem. Am. Assn. Thoracic Surgery, AMA (ho. of dels. 1976-82), Am. Physiol. Soc., Am. Surg. Assn., Halsted Soc. (pres. 1978), Internat. Cardiovascular Soc. (v.p. N. Am. Chpt. 1973), Societe Internationale de Chirurgie, Soc. Thoracic Surgeons, Soc. Univ. Surgeons, Soc. Vascular Surgery, So. Surg. Assn. (1st v.p. 1981), Western Surg. Assn., S.W. Surg. Congress (pres. 1980), Raven Soc., Alpha Omega Alpha Home: 66 River Ridge Rd Little Rock AR 72227-1526

CAMPBELL, GLEN, musician; b. Delight, Ark., Apr. 22, 1936; s. Wesley and Carrie (Stone) C.; m. Diane Campbell, 1954 (div. 1958); a child, Debby; m. Billie Jean Nunley, Sept. 20, 1959 (div. 1976); children: Kelli, Travis, Kane; m. Sarah Barg Davis, 1977 (div. 1980); 1 child, Dillon; m. Kimberly Woollen, 1982; children: Cal, Shannon, Ashley. Student, pub. schs., Ark. and N.Mex. Prin. Glen Campbell Goodtime Theatre, Branson, Mo., 1994-96. Appearances include: N.Mex.-Bick Bills, 1953, Hollywood Champs, 1960, 63-64, Shindig, 1964, Baby the Rain Must Fall, 1965, The Cool Ones, 1967, True Grit, 1969, Norwood, 1970, Any Which Way You Can, 1980, Uphill All the Way, 1986, Rock-A-Doodle (voice), 1991; studio musician, 1962-66; host summer: Smothers Bros. Show, 1968; film appearance in True Grit, 1969, Norwood, 1970; host TV shows: Glen Campbell Good Time Time Hour, 1969-71, Glen Campbell Music Show, 1981; co-sponsor, Glen Campbell-Los Angeles Open Golf Tournament; composer (song) Less of Me; performer, over 75 albums (albums include): Too Late to Worry, Too Blue to Cry, 1963, The Big Band Rock Guitar of Glen Campbell, 1964, Mr. 12 String Guitar, 1964, Burning Bridges, 1967, Gentle on My Mind, 1967, By the Time I Get to Phoenix, 1968, Hey, Little One, 1968, A New Place in teh Sun, 1968, Wichita Lineman, 1968, Galveston, 1969, True Grit, 1969, Where's the Playground Susie, 1969, Norwood, 1970, Oh Happy Day, 1970, Try a Little Kindness, 1970, Christmas with Glen Campbell, 1971, The Last Time I Saw Her, 1971, Satisfied Mind, 1971, I Knew Jesus (Before He Was a Star), 1973, I Remember Hank Williams, 1973, Houston (I'm Comin' to See You), 1974, I'll Paint You a Song, 1975, Rhinestone Cowboy, 1975, Bloodline, 1976, Southern Nights, 1977, Basic, 1978, Highwayman, 1979, Something 'Bout You Baby I Like, 1980, It's the World Gone Crazy, 1981, Old Home Town, 1983, Letter to Home, 1984, It's Just a Matter of Time, 1986, Still Within the Sound of My Voice, 1987, Country Boy, 1988, Light Years, 1988, Unconditional Love, 1988, Walkin' in the Son, 1990, Show Me Your Way, 1991, Merry Christmas, 1991, Wings of Victory, 1992, Favorite Hymns, 1992, Somebody Like That, 1993, The Boy in Me, 1994, Home for the Holidays, 1998, A Glen Campbell Christmas, 1999, Meet Glen Campbell, 2008, Ghost on the Canvas, 2011, See You There, 2013; author (autobiography) Rhinestone Cowboy, 1994. Mem. Nat. Reading Coun. Named Entertainer of Yr., 1968; Best Male Vocalist 1968, 69; TV Personality of Year 1969; Entertainer of Year, Gt. Britain Country Music Assn., 1974; recipient 8 Grammy awards, 3 Am. Music awards, 8 Acad. Country Music awards, Q Legend award, 2008; named Entertainer of Yr., Country Music Assn., 1968, Male Vocalist of Yr., 1968; named to Country Music Hall of Fame, 2005, Musician's Hall of Fame (as mem. of The Wrecking Crew), 2007; tribute performance in his honor, Country Music Assn. Awards, 2011. Office: Sandy Brokaw c/o The Brokaw Co Ste 804 9255 Sunset Blvd West Hollywood CA 90069 also: Capitol Records 3222 W End Ave Nashville TN 37203-1306 Home: 1888 Century Park E Fl 9th Los Angeles CA 90067-1735 Office Phone: 310-273-2060.

CAMPBELL, JEFFREY J., rail transportation executive; BS in Accountancy, U. Tenn., 1979; MBA, Embry Riddle Aero. U. With FedEx, 1981—99, sr. mgr., corp. procurement, 1990—95, mng. dir., ops. support, 1995—96, mng. dir., air ops. supply chain mgmt., 1996—99; v.p., chief sourcing officer Burlington Northern Santa Fe, Fort Worth, Tex., 1999—2002; v.p., tech. svcs., chief info. officer Burlington Northern Santa Fe Corp., Fort Worth, Tex., 2002—. Office: Burlington Northern Santa Fe Corp 2650 Lou Menk Dr Fort Worth TX 76131-2830 Office Fax: 817-352-7171.

CAMPBELL, JOHN MORGAN, retired chemical engineer; b. Virden, Ill., Mar. 24, 1922; S. John M. and Ione Marie (Whittler) C.; m. Gwendolyn Thompson, Aug. 27, 1945; children: John Morgan, Robert, Charles. BS in Chem. Engring, Iowa State U., 1943; MS, U. Okla., 1948, PhD, 1951. Devel. engr. and supr. E.I. duPont de Nemours & Co., Inc., 1943-46; spl. instr. chem. engring. U. Okla., 1946-50; tech. adviser to v.p. Black Sivalls and Bryson, Oklahoma City, 1951-54; mem. faculty U. Okla. Sch. Petroleum Engring., 1954-69, chmn. dept., 1956-63, Erle P. Halliburton prof., 1963-69, dir., 1969, Petroleum Research Center, 1964-69. Pres. John M. Campbell & Co. (engring. counselors, mgmt. consultants), 1968-82; chmn. bd. Petrotech Ltd., Petroleum Learning Programs Ltd. Author: Oil Property Evaluation, 1959, Effective Technical Communications, 1969, Decision Methods For Petroleum Investments, 1969, Gas Conditioning and Processing, 2 vols., 1970, 6th edit., 2000, The Professional - From Puberty to Senility, 1970, Effective Communication for the Technical Man, 1972, Petroleum Reservoir Property Evaluation, 1973, Mineral Property Economics (3 vols.), 1978, Petroleum Evaluation for Financial Disclosures, 1983, Analysis and Management of Petroleum Investments, 1987, Successful Communication Strategies and Practices, 2000, Analysis and Management of Risky Investments, 2001; also numerous articles, chpts. in books. Recipient Hanlon award Gas Processors Assn., 1987, Disting. Achievement award Iowa State U., 1988, Disting. Grad. award Okla. U. Mem. NAE, AIME (hon. mem. 1994, exec. com. coun. edn., mineral industries econs. award 1989), Soc. Petroleum Engrs. (hon. mem. 1994, J.F. Caril award 1978, Arps award 1989), Am. Arbitration Assn. (arbitration panel), Internat. Petroleum Inst. (pres. 1968-82), Sigma Alpha Epsilon, Phi Lambda Upsilon, Pi Epsilon Tau. Clubs: Lion. Home: 2531 S Berry Rd Norman OK 73072-6904

CAMPBELL, JOHN ROY, animal science professor, academic administrator; b. Goodman, Mo., June 14, 1933; s. Carl J. and Helen (Nicoletti) C.; m. Eunice Vieten, Aug. 7, 1954; children: Karen L., Kathy L., Keith L. BS, U. Mo., 1955; MS, U. Mo., Columbia, 1956, PhD, 1960, DSc (hon.), 2005; DLitt (hon.), Nat. Coll. Natural Medicine, 2013. Instr. dairy sci. U. Mo., Columbia, 1960-61, asst. prof., 1961-65, assoc. prof., 1965-68, prof., from 1968; assoc. dean, dir. resident instrn. Coll. Agr. U. Ill., Urbana-Champaign, 1977-83, dean Coll. Agr. Urbana, 1983-88; pres. Okla. State U., Stillwater, 1988-93. Author (with J.F. Lasley): The Science of Animals That Serve Mankind, 1969, The Science of Animals That Serve Humanity, 2nd edit., 1975, 3rd edit., 1985; author: In Touch with Students, 1972; author: (with R.T. Marshall) The Science of Providing Milk for Man, 1975; author: Reclaiming A Lost Heritage...Land-Grant and Other Higher Education Initiatives for the Twenty-First Century, 1998, Dry Rot in the Ivory Tower, 2000; author: (with M.D. Kenealy and K.L. Campbell) Animal Sciences...The Biology, Care and Production of Domestic Animals, 2004, rev. edit., 2010; author: (with K.L. Campbell) Companion Animals...Their Biology, Care, Health and Management, 2005, 2nd edit., 2009. Recipient Superior Tchg. award Gamma Sigma Delta, 1967, Internat. award for disting. svc. to agr., 1985, Disting. Svc. award Coll. Osteo. Medicine Okla. State U., 1992, 57th Ann. Disting. Svc. award, U. Mo. Alumni Assn., 2012, Inducted into Lincoln Cabinet, a Patriotic Society Dedicated to Abraham Lincoln, 2013. Fellow Am. Dairy Sci. Assn. (dir. 1975-78, 80-86, pres. 1980-81, Ralston Purina Disting. Tchg. award 1973, Award of Honor 1987); mem. Nat. Assn. Coll. Tchrs. Agr. (Ensminger Interstate Disting. Tchr. award 1973, Teaching fellow 1973, Disting. Educator award 1990, Nat. Assn. State and Univ. and Land-Grant Colls. (commns. on home econs. and vet. medicine, com. on water resources, coun. of presidents), Okla. Futures, Nat. Coll. Naturopathic Med-.(mem. bd. dirs. 1997-2013, disting. Svc. award 2012), Gamma Sigma Delta. Office: Okla State U 201AS Stillwater OK 74078-0001 Personal E-mail: jrcampbell.educator@gmail.com. Business E-Mail: benita.bale@okstate.edu.

CAMPBELL, KRISTIN ANN, lawyer; b. Salt Lake City, Utah, 1961; d. Robert S. and Karen H. Campbell; m. Robert James Samuelson, 2009. BA, Ariz. State U.; JD, Cornell U. Sch. Law, Ithaca, NY. Bar: Mass. 1987. Atty. Rackemann, Sawyer & Brewster, Boston, Goodwin Proctor LLP, Boston; real estate counsel Staples, Inc., 1993, head internat. legal matters Europe, Asia and S.Am., sr. v.p., dep. gen. counsel, 2005—07, sr. v.p., gen. counsel, sec., 2007—11; exec. v.p., gen. counsel Hilton Worldwide Inc., McLean, Va., 2011—. Bd. dirs. The Trustees of Reservation. Mem.: Mass. Bar Assn. Office: Hilton Worldwide Inc 7930 Jones Branch Dr Ste 1100 Mc Lean VA 22102 Office Phone: 508-253-5000.

CAMPBELL, MARIA BOUCHELLE, lawyer, consultant; b. Mullins, SC, Jan. 23, 1944; d. Colin Reid and Margaret Minor (Perry) C. Student, Agnes Scott Coll., 1961-63; AB, U. Ga., 1965, JD, 1967. Bar: Ga. 1967, Fla. 1968, Ala. 1969. Pvt. practice law, Birmingham, Ala., 1968-94; law clk. U.S. Cir. Ct. Appeals, Miami, Fla., 1967-68; assoc. Cabaniss, Johnston and Gardner, 1968-73; sec., counsel Ala. Bancorp., Birmingham, 1973-79; sr. v.p., sec., gen. counsel AmSouth Bancorp., 1979-84, exec. v.p., gen. counsel, 1984-94, AmSouth Bank, 1984-94; exec. asst. to rector Parish of Trinity Ch., NYC, 1994-99; lawyer, mediator Sirote & Permutt, 1999-2001; cabinet ofcl., supt. of banks State of Ala., Montgomery, 2001—03; chmn. fin. svcs. SC& B Strategic Solutions, Montgomery, 2003—; of counsel Steiner Crum & Byars, Montgomery, 2003—. Bd. trustees Ptnrship for Women's Health Columbia U., 1996-2000; bd. dirs. Leake and Watts Childrens Svcs., Inc., 1997-99; lectr. continuing legal edn. programs; cons. to charitable orgns. Exec. editor Ga. Law Rev, 1966-67. Bd. dirs. St. Anne's Home, Birmingham, 1969-74, chancellor, 1969-74; bd. dirs. Children's Aid Soc., Birmingham, 1970-94, 1st v.p., 1988-90, pres., 1990-92; trustee Canterbury Cathedral Trust in Am., 1992—, Discovery 2000 Children's Mus., 1991-94, Soc. for Propagation of Christian Knowledge, 1991-93; bd. dirs. NCCJ, 1985-94, 99-2002, state chair, 1990-93; bd. dirs. Positive Maturity, 1976-78, Mental Health Assn., 1978-81, YWCA, 1979-80, Op. New Birmingham, 1985-87, pers. com., 1987-90, v.p., 1990-94; bd. dirs. Soc. for the Fine Arts U. Ala., 1986-89, Baptist Hospital Found. of Birmingham Inc., 1994-95, Alliance for Downtown N.Y., 1995-99, chair affordable housing initiative region 2020, 2000-01, Habitat for Humanity of Birmingham, 2000-02; commr. Housing Authority, Birmingham Dist., 1980-85, Birmingham Partnership, 1985-86, Leadership Birmingham, 1986—, program com., 1989-90, co-chair program com., 1990-91, mem.'s coun., 1999-2002; mem. pres. adv. coun. Birmingham So. Coll, 1988-92, chair bd. overseers Masters Program, 1990-94; mem. pres.'s cabinet U. Ala., 1990-95; trustee Ala. Diocese Episcopal Ch., 1971-72, 74-75, mem. canonical revision com., 1973-75, 89-91, liturg. commn., 1976-78, treas., chmn. dept. fin., 1979-83, 2000-03; mem. coun., 1983-87, chancellor, 1987-91, cons. on stewardship edn., 1981-94, dep. to gen. conv., 1985, 88, 91; mem. Standing Commn. on Constn. and Canons, 1988-94, mem. investment com., 2000—, vice chmn., 2003—; vestryman St. Luke's Episcopal Ch., 1991-94; bd. advisors So. region of Am. Soc. Corp. Secs., pres., 1992-94; cmty. advisor Jr. League Birmingham, 1992-93; mem. adv. bd. Cahaba River Soc., 1991-94; trustee St. Andrew's Sewanee Sch., 1998—; commr. Ala. Securities Commn., 2001-03; bd. dirs. Ala. Agrl. Commn., 2001-03; bd. dirs. Ala. Housing Fin. Authority, 2001-03; bd. regents Univ. of the South, 2002—; bd. dirs. Housing Enterprise Ctrl. Ala., 2003—, Fin. Investors of South, 2003—04, Associated Long Term Care Ins. Co., 2004—. Named One of Top 10 Women in Birmingham, 1989, One of Top 5 Women in Bus., 1993. Mem. ABA, State Bar Ga., Fla. Bar, Ala. Bar Assn., Birmingham Bar Assn., Am. Corp. Counsel Assn. (bd. dirs. Ala. 1984-89), Assn. Bank Holding Cos. (chmn. lawyers com. 1986-87), Greater Birmingham C. of C. (bd. dirs. 1988-94, exec. com. 1992-94, vice chmn., gen. counsel 1993-94), Kiwanis, The Church Club N.Y., Order of St. John of Jerusalem, Summit Club. Office: PO Box 668 Montgomery AL 36101 Home Phone: 205-714-7766. Personal E-mail: mcampbell@scbstrategic.com.

CAMPBELL, MICHAEL H., lawyer, air transportation executive; Grad., U. Richmond, 1971; JD, U. Va., 1974. Ptnr. Ford & Harrison LLP, 1978—96, of counsel, 2005—06; sr. v.p., human resources and labor rels. Continental Airlines, Inc., 1997—2004; exec. v.p., human resources, labor rels. Delta Air Lines, Inc., 2006—07, exec. v.p., human resources, labor rels. & comm., 2007—08, exec. v.p. human resources & labor rels., 2008—. Mem.: Phi Beta Kappa. Office: Delta Air Lines Inc 1030 Delta Blvd Atlanta GA 30320-6001 Office Phone: 404-715-2600. Office Fax: 404-715-5042. Business E-Mail: michael.h.campbell@delta.com.

CAMPBELL, MICHAEL L., theatre company executive; Co-founder, CEO Premiere Cinemas Corp., 1982—89; founder, CEO Regal Cinemas, Inc., 1989; co-chmn., co-CEO Regal Entertainment Group, Knoxville, Tenn., 2002—05, CEO, 2005—09, chmn., 2005—, exec. chmn. Knoxville, Tenn., 2009. Bd. dirs. Nat. Assn. Theatre Owners, Fandango, Inc., Regal Entertainment Group, 2002—, National CineMedia, Inc., 2006—. Office: Regal Entertainment Group 7132 Regal Ln Knoxville TN 37918 Office Phone: 865-922-1123. Office Fax: 865-922-3188. Business E-Mail: michael.campbell@regmovies.com.

CAMPBELL, PAUL GLADSTONE, JR., state legislator, chemical engineer; b. West Jefferson, NC, July 10, 1946; s. Paul Gladstone and Edith Louise (Winkler) C.; m. Vicki Lee Garner, June 29, 1967; children: Christie M. Campbell Snipes, Jeremy Paul, Caroline Elizabeth. BS in Chem. Engring., Clemson U., 1968; MBA, Jacksonville State U., 1978. Process engr. Ormet Corp., Hannibal, Ohio, 1968-70; sr. process engr. Revere Copper & Brass Co., Scottsboro, Ala., 1970-76, carbon mgr., 1976-78, Alumax of SC, Goose Creek, 1978-86, casting mgr., 1986-89, dir. human resources, 1989, sr. v.p., gen. mgr., 1999—; mem. Dist. 44 SC State Senate, 2007—. Bd. dirs. 1st Fin. Holdings, Charleston, S.C.; authority mem. Charleston Naval Complex Redevel. Authority, 1994—; adv. bd. Coll. Charleston-Sch. of Bus. and Econs., Engring. adv. bd. Clemson U. Editor Light Metals, 1989; contbr. articles to profl. jours. Pres., bd. dirs. Trident United Way, Charleston, 1990—; chmn. bd. dirs. Leadership S.C., Columbia, 1993-95; pres., bd. dirs. Coastal Carolina Coun. Boy Scouts of Am. Recipient numerous awards. Mem. AIME (bd. dirs. 1995—), AIChE, The Minerals, Metals and Materials Soc. (bd. dirs. 1990-95, pres. 1995), Am. Soc. Materials, S.C. C. of C. (pres., bd. dirs. 1991-95), Berkeley County C. of C. (pres., bd. dirs. 1991-95). Republican. Presbyterian. Avocations: running, reading, computers. Mailing: 150 Loganberry Cir Goose Creek SC 29445-7240 Office: Alumax of SC PO Box 1000 Goose Creek SC 29445-1000 also: 604 Gressette Bldg Columbia SC 29201 Home Phone: 843-569-0089; Office Phone: 803-212-6016, 843-296-1001. Business E-Mail: PaulCampbell@scsenate.org.

CAMPBELL, RON, professional sports team executive; m. Mary Jane Campbell; children: Andrea, Holly, RJ. BBA cum laude, Ea. Mich. U., 1977; MS in Fin., Walsh Coll., 1990. CPA 1979. Joined Palace Sports & Entertainment, 1981, now exec. v.p.; joined Detroit Pistons, 1984, exec. v.p.; head The Palace of Auburn Hills, 1988; pres. Tampa Bay Lightning, 1999—; alt. gov. NHL Bd. Govs. Bd. dirs. Pistons-Palace Found., Tampa Sports Commn., Florida Sports Found., Tampa Bay Convention and Visitors Bur., H. Lee Moffitt Cancer Center & Rsch. Inst. Found.; mem. Outback Pro-Am Exec. Bd.d, Chrysler Championship Leadership Bd., The Champions Fund. Hon. chair SilverSpoons and Sandcastles, 2007; emeritus mem., former vice-chmn. Ea. Mich. U. Found. Named one of Top 40 under 40, Crain's Detroit Bus., 1995. Office: Tampa Bay Lightning St Pete Times Forum 401 Channelside Dr Tampa FL 33602

CAMPBELL, STEPHEN C., oil and gas company executive; Grad., Tex. A&M U. With Anadarko Petroleum Corp.; joined Newfield Exploration Co., 1999, mgr. investor rels., v.p. investor rels., 2005—. Mem.: Tex. Pub. Rels. Assn., Nat. Investor Rels. Inst., Pub. Rels. Soc. of America, Petroleum Investor Rels. Assn. Office: Newfield Exploration Co 363 N Sam Houston Pky E Ste 100 Houston TX 77060 Office Phone: 281-847-6000. Office Fax: 281-405-4242.

CAMPBELL, THOMAS W., state legislator; b. Staunton, Va., May 29, 1961; s. Newton W. and Alma Crosier Campbell; m. Susan Sharp. BA, BS, W.Va. U. Adminstrv. asst. City of Lewisburg, W.Va., 1984—85; CFO Greenbrier Respiratory and Rehab., 1984—98; mem. Dist. 28 W.Va. House of Delegates, 1996—, vice chair Fin. Com.; CFO Carson Assocs., Inc., 1998—. Vol. Read Aloud W.Va. Mem.: Im Inst. CPA, W.Va. Soc. CPA, Knights Golden Horseshoe, Lewisburg Rotary. Democrat. Presbyterian. Mailing: PO Box 1126 Lewisburg WV 24901 Office: State Capitol, Rm 203-E Charleston WV 25305 Office Phone: 304-340-3181, 304-645-5547. Business E-Mail: wvdeltc@mail.wvnet.edu.

CAMPBELL, TODD J., federal judge; b. Rockford, Ill., 1956; BA cum laude, Vanderbilt U., 1978; JD with high honors, U. Tenn., 1982. Bar: Tenn. 1982. With Gullett, Sanford, Robinson & Martin, Nashville, 1982-92; counsel to Vice Pres. of U.S., Washington, 1993-95; with Doramus & Trauger, Nashville, 1995; judge US Dist. Ct. (mid. dist.) Tenn., Nashville, 1995—2005, chief judge, 2005—. Democrat.

CAMPER, KAREN D., state legislator; b. Jan. 15, 1958; divorced; 1 child, Bruce Jr. AS, U. Albany, SUNY; attended, U. Tenn., Knoxville. Cert. Alcohol & Drug Abuse Team Course US Army, Equal Opportunity Leadership Course US Army, Primary, Basic & Advanced Leadership Devel. Courses US Army, Basic, Ops., & Advanced Mgmt. Courses US Army. Owner Key II Entertainment; substitute tchr. Memphis City Sch. Sys.; exec. dir. The Humble Hearts Found., Inc.; chmn./ CEO Joint Svcs. Black Heritage Com.; charter mem. Women in Mil. Svc. for Am.; mem. Dist. 87 Tenn. House of Reps., 2008—. Democrat. Baptist. Office: 20 Legislative Plaza Nashville TN 37243-0087 Home: PO Box 16966 Memphis TN 38186-0966 Office Phone: 901-315-8899, 615-741-1898. Business E-Mail: rep.karen.camper@capitol.tn.gov.

CAMPFIELD, STACEY, state legislator; b. June 8, 1968; AA in Mktg., Excelsior Coll.; AA, Broome CC; BS in Mgmt., Regents Coll. Mem. Dist. 18 Tenn. State Senate, 2005—, mem. Health and Welfare Com., Judiciary Com. & State and Local Govt. Com. Recipient award, Whip Leadership Team, Knox County Del. of Legislators; named Friend of Taxpayers, 2004. Mem.: West Knox Republican Club, College Republicans, Young Republicans, Knox Heritage, Citizens Police Acad., West Knox Rep. Club, Am. Red Cross, Westhills Homeowners Assn., American Red Cross, Norwood Homeowners Assn., Knoxville Traffic Calming Com., Concora Faragut Rep. Club. Republican. Office: 2011 Flagler Knoxville TN 37912 Office Phone: 615-741-1766. E-mail: sen.stacey.campfield@capitol.tn.gov.

CAMPION, EDMUND RONAN, orthopedist, educator; b. Hanover, NH, Feb. 17, 1954; BA, Harvard U.; MD, Dartmouth U., 1981. Cert. Am. Bd. Orthop. Surgery, 1993. Intern orthop. surgery St. Luke's Presbyn. Med. Ctr., Denver, 1981—82; resident U. NC, Chapel Hill, 1985—90; fellowship Alfred I. duPont Inst., Wilmington, Del., 1990—91; asst. prof. surgery U. NC Sch. Medicine, Chapel Hill, 1991—96, asst. prof. orthopaedics, 1996—98, dir., orthop. residency program, 1996—, assoc. prof., 1998—2005, prof. orthopaedics, 2006—; dir., dept. orthopaedics & orthop. residency program Wake Med. Ctr., Raleigh, 1991—96. Reviewer Jour. of Am. Acad. Orthopaedic Surgeons; contbr. articles to med. jours. Mem. Operation Smile, Panama, 1995, Colombia, 1996, Nicaragua, 1998, Mid. East, Asia, 1999. Office: Dept Orthopaedics CB #7055, Bioinformatics Bldg UNC Sch Medicine Chapel Hill NC 27599-7055 Office Phone: 919-966-9066, 919-968-3514. Office Fax: 919-843-5922. E-mail: ed_campion@med.unc.edu.

CAMPSEN, GEORGE E., III, state legislator; b. Charleston, SC, Mar. 30, 1959; s. George E. Campsen and Myrtle Snap; m. Lalla Lee Laffitte; children: George, Boyce. BS, Furman U., 1981; JD, U. SC, 1988, MS, 1989. Exec. v.p. Ft. Sumter Tours Inc., 1985—; ptnr. Campsen & Campsen Attorneys At Law, 1989—; co-chmn., gov. Mark Sanford's transition team, 2002—03; mem. Dist. 43 SC State Senate, 2005—. Recipient William Bentley Ball Life & Religious Liberty Def. award, Order of Palmetto, Gov. Mark Sanford; named Conservationist of Yr., SC Wildlife Fedn., Champion of SC Family, Palmetto Family Coun., Legislator of Yr., SC Assn. Conservation Dist. Mem.: Nat. Taxpayers Union, SC Policy Coun., Heritage Found., Am. Assn. Individual Investors, Hibernian Soc., Atlantic Coast Conservation Assn., SC Waterfowl Assn., Ducks Unlimited. Republican. Baptist. Mailing: 360 Concord St Ste 201 Charleston SC 29401 Office: 604 Gressette Bldg Columbia SC 29201 Home Phone: 843-886-8454; Office Phone: 843-722-0123, 803-212-6016.

CANADA, MARY WHITFIELD, retired librarian; b. Richmond, Va., June 13, 1919; d. Waverly Thomas and Ruth Bradshaw (Smith) C. BA magna cum laude, Emory and Henry Coll., 1940; MA in English, Duke U., 1942; BS in LS, U. NC, 1956. Asst. circulation dept. Duke U. Libr., 1942-45, undergrad. libr., 1945-55, reference libr., 1956-85, asst. head reference dept., 1967-79, head dept., 1979-85, ret., 1985. Contbr. articles to profl. jours. Duke U. grantee Can., 1979, 81. Mem. ALA (life; initiated performance evaluation discussion group), Southeastern Libr. Assn. (sec. coll. and univ. sect., chmn. nominating com. reference svcs. divsn., also chmn. divsn.), NC Libr. Assn. (chmn. nominating com., chmn. newspaper com., chmn. coll. and univ. sect.), Alumni Assn. Sch. Libr. Sci. U. NC (pres.), Va. Hist. Soc. (life), Va. Geneal. Soc., DAR (chpt. regent), Campus Club (Duke U.), Va. Mus. Fine Arts, Duke U. Hosp. Aux., Beta Phi Mu. Methodist. Home: 1312 Lancaster St Durham NC 27701-1132

CANADA, WILLIAM H., plastic surgeon; b. Huntington, W.Va., Sept. 5, 1930; MD, W.Va. U., 1956. Intern Meml. Hosp., Charleston, W.Va., 1956-57, gen. surgeon, 1957-59; plastic surgeon Baylor U. Med. Ctr., Houston, 1959-61; chief plastic surgeon Las Vegas Surgery Ctr., 1987—. Attending surgeon Univ. Med. Ctr., Las Vegas; clin. instr. plastic surgery Baylor U., Houston. Fellow ACS. Office: William H Canada Md 5656 Bee Cave Rd Ste E201 West Lake Hills TX 78746-5035

CANADY, ALEXA IRENE, pediatric neurosurgeon, educator; b. Lansing, Mich., Nov. 7, 1950; d. Clinton Jr. and Hortense (Golden) C.; m. George Davis, June 18, 1988. BS, U. Mich., 1971, MD cum laude, 1975; DHL (hon.), Marygrove Coll., 1994, U. Detroit, 1997; DSc (hon.), Ctrl. Mich. U., 1999, U. So. Conn., 1999, U. W. Fla., 2006. Diplomate Am. Bd. Neurol. Surgery. Intern in surgery Yale U., New Haven, 1975-76; resident in neurosurgery U. Minn., Mpls., 1976-81; fellow in pediatric neurosurgery Children's Hosp. Pa., Phila., 1981-82; instr. neurosurgery U. Pa., Phila., 1981-82; staff neurosurgeon, instr. neurosurgery Henry Ford Hosp., Detroit, 1982-83; asst. dir. neurosurgery Children's Hosp. Mich., Detroit, 1986-87, chief of neurosurgery, 1987-97; assoc. prof. neurosurgery Wayne State U., Detroit, 1988-91, vice chmn. neurosurgery, 1991—2001; prof. neurosurgery Sacred Heart Hosp., Pensacola, Fla., 1997—2001; prof. pediat. in neurosurgery Fla. State U., 2006—. Clin. instr. neurosurgery Wayne State U. Sch. Medicine, 1985, mem. internal rev. com. dept. anatomy, 1988, chmn. search com. dept. neurosurgery, 1989, internal rev. com. dept. neurology, 1991-92, 125th anniversary celebration com., 1992, internal rev. com. dept. pediat., 1993, chmn. search com. dept. ophthalmology, 1992-93, internal rev. com. dept. neurosurgery, 1994; chmn. neurobiol. devices panel, FDA, cons. neurol. devices panel Med. Devices Adv. Com., 1994—, chmn., 1998-2000, co-chair ctr. devices and regulatory health enhanced sci. rev., 2001; vis. prof. Med. Coll. S.C., 1990; clin. prof. dept. clin. scis., pediatric neurosurgery Fla. State Coll. Medicine, 2007-; mem. surg. com. Children's Hosp. Mich., chmn. operating room subcom. surg. com., intensive care unit com., med. record com., med. exec. com.; Detroit; presenter various profl confs. in U.S. and internat. Contbr. chpts. to books. Bd. dirs. Inst. Am. Bus., 1986-88. Recipient citation Women's Med. Assn., 1975, Candace award Nat. Coalition 100 Black Women, N.Y., 1986, Golden Heritage award, 1989, Leonard F. Sain Esteemed Alumni award U. Mich., 1990, Disting. Alumni award Everett H.S., Pres.'s award Am. Med. Women's Assn., 1993, Variety Heart award for Med., Sci. and Tech. Variety Club, 1994, Shining Star award Colgate-Palmolive Co./Starlight Found., 1994, Golden Apple award Roeper Sch., 1995, Athena award Alumni Assn. U. Mich., 1995, Golden Apple Faculty Tchg. award U. Fla. Pediat. Residents, 2004, Chmn. Recognition award Fla. Bd. Medicine, 2005; named Outstanding Young Woman in Am., 1977, Top 100 Bus. & Profl. Women of Am., 1985, Woman of Yr. Detroit Club Nat. Assn. Negro Bus. & Profl. Women's Club, Inc., 1986; named to Mich. Woman's Hall of Fame, 1989; grantee Am. Cancer Soc., 1979, Minn. Med. Found., 1979, Am. Cancer Soc., 1981-82, Widman Found. Early Intervention Treatment and Follow-Up of Infants with Post-hemorrhagic Hydrocephalus, 1984-85, Neuropsychol. Recovery and Family Adaptation to CHI Children's Hosp. Mich., 1987-88, Hydrocephalus Induced Endocrinopathies: Morphologic Correlates Children's Hosp. Mich., 1989, 91; finalist Inst. Medicine African Am. Portrait Gallery, 2006; poster placed in Nat. Acad. Medicine Gallery African Am. Physicians, 2006. Mem. AMA, ACS, Am. Assn. Neurol. Surgeons, Congress Neurol. Surgeons, Am. Soc. Pediatric Neurosurgery, Nat. Med. Assn. Detroit Med. Soc., Mich. Assn. Neurol. Surgeons (sec. 1992-93, v.p. 1994-95, pres. 1995-96), Transplantation Soc. Mich. (adv. bd. 1993-94), Mich. State Med. Soc. (child abuse and neglect divsn. 1986), Southeastern Mich. Surg. Soc. (sec. 1986-87), Soc. Crit. Care Medicine, Wayne County Med. Soc. (ethics com., pub. affairs com., law com.), U. Mich. Med. Ctr. Alumni Soc., Delta Sigma Theta. Office: 6064 Forest Green Rd Pensacola FL 32505 Office Phone: 850-416-7101. Personal E-mail: alexacanady@aol.com.

CANADY, CHARLES TERRENCE, state supreme court justice, former congressman; b. Lakeland, Fla., June 22, 1954; m. Jennifer Houghton, Oct. 1996; c. Julia Grace and Anna Elizabeth BA, Haverford Coll., 1976; JD, Yale U., 1979. Atty. Holland and Knight, Lakeland, 1979—82, Lane, Trohn, et al, 1983—92; mem. 44th dis. Fla. House of Reps., 1984-90, mem. Marketable Record Title Act Study Commn., 1985-86, majority whip, 1986-88, mem. crime prevention and law enforcement study com., 1987-88; mem. US Congress from 12th Fla. dist., 1993-2001; gen. counsel Gov. Jeb Bush, Fla., 2001—02; judge Ct. Appeals (2nd Dist.), Lakeland, 2002—08; justice Fla. Supreme Ct., Tallahassee, 2008—, chief justice, 2010—12. Mem. counsel Ctrl. Fla. Regional Coun., 1983-84. V.p. United Cerebral Palsy, Polk County, 1982-83; bd. dirs. Big Brothers & Big Sisters, 1984-85. Recipient Allen Morris award Fla. Ho. of Reps., 1986, Legislator of the Yr. Fla. Assn. Realtors, 1986, Spec Leadership award Save Our Home and Lands, 1986; named Most Valuable Legislator in Growth Mgmt. Fla. Regional Coun. Assn. Mem. ABA, Lakeland Bar Assn., Lakeland C. of C., Winter Haven C. of C. Republican. Presbyterian. Office: Fla Supreme Ct 500 S Duval St Tallahassee FL 32399-1925 Office Phone: 850-410-8092.*

CANARY, NANCY HALLIDAY, lawyer; b. Cleve., Apr. 21, 1941; d. Robert Fraser and Nanna (Hall) Halliday; m. Sumner Canary, Dec. 1975 (dec. Jan. 1979). BA, Case Western Res. U., 1963; JD, Cleve. State U., 1968. Bar: Ohio 1968, Fla. 1972, US Dist. Ct. (no. dist.) Ohio 1975, US Supreme Ct. 1974, US Dist. Ct. (so. dist.) Fla. 1994. Law clk. to presiding judge Ohio Ct. Appeals, Cleve., 1968—69; ptnr. McDonald, Hopkins & Hardy, Cleve., 1969—83; ptnr. managing Palm Beach office Thompson, Hine, LLP, Cleve., 1984—2002; sole practitioner Palm Beach, Fla., 2003—. Trustee Beck Ctr. for Cultural Arts, Lakewood, Ohio, 1980—90, Ohio Motorists Assn., 1989—95, Ohio Chamber Orch.; trustee, mem. devel. adv. com. Fairview Gen. Hosp., Cleve., 1980—96; chairperson Sumner Canary Lectureship com. Case Western Res. U. Law Sch.; sec. bd. govs. Churchill Ctr., Washington, 2000—02; bd. dirs. Comerica Bank & Trust Co., F.S.B., 1993—2000. Mem. Ohio State Bar Assn., Cleve. Bar Assn., Palm Beach County Bar Assn., Estate Planning Coun. Cleve., Estate Planning Coun. Palm Beach County, Gulf Stream (Fla.) Golf Club, Westwood Country Club (Cleve.). Republican. Avocations: horseback riding, collecting Churchill books, classical music. Home: 200 N Ocean Blvd Delray Beach FL 33483-7126 Office: 125 Worth Ave # 310 Palm Beach FL 33480 Home: 12500 Edgewater Dr # 1806 Cleveland OH 44107-1677 Office Phone: 216-226-7466, 561-833-5900.

CANCELMI, DANIEL J., controller; BS in Acctg., U. Duquesne, Pitts., 1985. CPA. With, audit Coopers & Lybrand, 1984—85, Allegheny Health Sys., 1994—98; CFO Hahnemann U. Hosp., Phila., 1998—99; v.p., asst. contr. Tenet Healthcare Corp., 1999—2004, v.p., contr., 2004—07, sr. v.p., prin., acctg. officer, 2007—. Mem.: AICPA, FICPA, PICPA. Office: Tenet Healthcare Corp 1445 Ross Ave Ste 1400 Dallas TX 75202 Office Phone: 469-893-2246. Office Fax: 469-893-3246.

CANCILLA, RUSSELL J., oil and gas industry company executive; B in Criminology, M in Ops. Mgmt.; grad., FBI Nat. Acad. Exec. Program, Quantico, Va. Mil. aide to pres. The White House, 1991; prin. dep. asst. sec., US & Fgn. comml. svc. US Dept. Commerce; v.p., real estate & mgmt. svcs. BP, v.p., resources & capabilities, health, safety, security & environment; v.p., chief security officer Innovene; chief security officer Baker Hughes, Inc., 2006—09, v.p., Health, Safety, Environment & Security, 2009—. Office: Baker Hughes Inc 2929 Allen Parkway Suite 2100 Houston TX 77019 Office Phone: 713-439-8600. Office Fax: 713-439-8699.

CANEGATA, JOHN MICHAEL, political organization administrator; b. Nov. 29, 1970; s. David and Carmen Canegata. Positions including energy specialist, hazardous materials team capt., energy team leader, and cmty. amb. Hovensa refinery, 1992—2012; co-owner D & J Shooting Gallery LLC; chmn. Rep. Party of the VI, 2012—. With 2nd Inf. Divsn. US Army, 1988—91, Ft. Sill, Okla., and Camp Stanley, South Korea. Republican. Office: Republican Party of the Virgin Islands PO Box 295 Christiansted VI 00821 Office Phone: 340-226-0315. E-mail: johncanegata@gmail.com.*

CANFIELD, GREG, state agency administrator, former state legislator; b. Birmingham, Ala. m. Rachel Coward; children: Rachel, John. BS in Fin., U. Ala., Birmingham, 1983. Gen. mgr., regional sales mgr. Emery Worldwide, 1983—89; brokerage rep. Provident Life & Accident, 1990—93; founder, pres., CEO Canfield Ins. & Fin. Services, 1991—2008; pres. Vestavia Hills City Coun., 2000—06; mem. Dist. 48 Ala. House of Reps., Montgomery, 2006—11; agent J.H. Berry Ins., Birmingham, 2008—11; dir. Ala. Devel. Office, 2011—. Former bd. mem. Ala. Gymnastics Edn. Found.; liaison Vestavia Hills Sr. Citizens Assn.; mem. Our Lady of Sorrows Cath. Ch., extraordinary min. of communion, lector; bd. dirs., pres. Vestavia Hills C. of C.; bd. dirs. Leadership Vestavia Hills, 1997—2001, pres., 1999—2000; mem. Leadership Birmingham Class of 2005. Republican. Roman Catholic. Office: Ala Devel Office 401 Adams Ave Sixth Fl PO Box 304106 Montgomery AL 36130

CANGEMI, JOSEPH PETER, psychologist, consultant, educator; b. Syracuse, NY, June 26, 1936; m. Amelia Elena Santaló, Oct. 6, 1962; children: Michelle, Lisa Ann. BS, SUNY, Oswego, 1959; MS, Syracuse U., 1965; EdD, Ind. U., 1974; LLD (hon.), William Woods U., 1996; DHC (hon.), Moscow State U., Russia, 2001. Diplomate Am. Bd. Vocat. Experts, Am. Bd. Forensic Examiners, Am. Coll. Counselors, in Profl. Counseling Internat. Acad. Behavioral Medicine, Counseling and Psychotherapy, cognitive behavior therapist, life cert. sch. psychologist, counselor NY. Instr. Syracuse Pub. Schs., 1959-60, vocat. rehab. coord., rsch. assoc., 1961-65; instr., asst. dir. Carol Morgan Sch., Santo Domingo, Dominican Republic, 1960-61; asst. head basketball coach SUNY C.C., Syracuse, 1962-63, lectr., chmn. dept. psychology evening-extension divsn., 1962-65, vis. lectr., 1966; supr. edn. Orinoco Mining divsn. US Steel Corp., Ciudad Piar, Venezuela, 1965—66; supr. tng. and devel. Orinoco Mining divsn. U.S. Steel Corp., Puerto Ordaz and Ciudad Piar, Venezuela, 1966-68; asst. prof. psychology Western Ky. U., Bowling Green, 1968—76, assoc. prof., 1976, prof., 1979—2006, prof. emeritus, 2001—; scholar in residence, 2010—; dir. Creative Leadership and Change, Inc., 1970—. Project dir. U. Los Andes, Merida, Venezuela, Inter-Am. Devel. Bank, Washington, Western Ky. U., 1975—77; cons., advisor R. R. Donnelley & Sons, Coca Cola; cons. Gould Corp., Eaton Corp., Firestone Tire & Rubber Co.(US, South America, Asia), Uniroyal/Goodrich Tire and Rubber Co., Gen. Tire and Rubber Co., Jefferson Smurfit, Std. Products, Tyson Foods, others, Govt. & U. Lanzhou, China, US Army, Sealy Corp., Siemans Nuc. Power Co. Host conversation program Wester Ky. U. divsn. Radio, TV Film, 1968—71; author: Higher Education and the Development of Self-Actualizing Personalities, 1977, La Administracion Participativa, 1983, Higher Education in the United States and Latin America, 1983; author: (with Mario Noronha) Marketing Y Venda, Portuguese edit., 1992; author: (with Carl Kreisler) Raymond C. Gibson-Distinguished Kentuckian, Renowned Educator and Statesman: An Anthology, 1996; author: (with Mario Noronha, Casimir Kowalski, George Guttschalk) Falhas Organizaciones, Protuguese edit., 1996; editor (with George Guttschalk): Effective Management, 1980; editor: (with Casimir Kowalski) Perspectives in Higher Education, 1983, Andersonville Prison, Lessons in Organizational Failure, 1993; editor: (with Casimir Kowalski and Jeffrey Claypool) Participative Management: Employee Management Cooperation, 1985, Chinese edit., 1990; editor: (with Casimir Kowalski and Habib Khan) Leadership Behavior, 1998; editor: (with Tatiana Ushakova and Casimir Kowalski) Leadership for the 21st Century, Russian edit., Russian Academy of Sciences, 1997, Psychology of Contemporary Leadership, Russian Edit., Russian Acad. Scis., 2007; editor: (with R. Miller, C. Kowalski, T. Hollopeter) Developing Trust in Organizations, 2005; editor: (with Joel Snell and Casimir Kowalski) Social Essays on Chaos Theory, 2008; editor: Educator's Svc. Bull., 1971—72, Psychology and Edn.: An Interdisciplinary Jour., 1977—, Jour. Human Behavior and Learning, 1983—89, Orgn. Devel. Jour., 1983—89; mem. editl. bd. Archivos Panamenos de Psicologia, 1968—88, Coll. Student Jour., 1973—2004, Edn., 1976—, Faculty Rsch. Bull. Western Ky. U., 1981—86, Jour. Instrnl. Psychology, 1977—90, Counseling and Values, 1979—84, Technol. Horizons Edn. Jour., 1979—92, Jour. Fgn. Psychology, Russia, 1996—2003, Forensic Examiner, 1998—2004; contbr. 300 artcles to profl. jours., chapters to books; co-editor (with casimir Kowalsky & Henry Czaplicki): Heroes of Solidarity, 2010. Past mem. House of Goa, Lisbon, 1996—97; trustee William Woods U., 1988—. Recipient certs. and awards, US Army Armor Sch., 1974, Eaton Corp., 1974, 1976, ICETEX, Colombia, 1977, Colombian Nat. Assn. Indsl. Engrs., 1977, Decreto City of Bucaramanga, Colombia, 1983, Quality Control Assn., 1979, Decreto, State of Santander, Colombia, 1977, Excellence in Productive Tchg. award, Western Ky. U. Coll. Edn., 1979, 1991, 1999, Fireston Tire and Rubber Co. award, 1978, 1981, 1991, Profl.-Tech. Socs. award, 1983, Coll. Student Jour. and Models of Excellence award, 1983, Disting. Pub. Svc. award, Western Ky. U., 1983, Excellence in Pub. Svc. award, Coll. Edn., 1983, Disting. Alumnus award, SUNY, Oswego, 1983, award, Uniroyal-Goodrich Tire and Rubber Co., 1986, Excellence in Rsch. and Creativity award, Coll. Edn., Wester Ky. U., 1987, United Rubber Workers/Internat. Brotherhood Elec. Workers award, 1991, Jour. Edn. award, Project Innovation, 1992, Bridgestone-Firestone award, Valencia, Venezuela, 1994, Outstanding Contbn. award, Southeastern divsn. Redman Industries, 1996—97, Summit Excellence Svc. award, Western Ky. U., Coll. Ednl. Behavioral Scis., 2008; nominee Prof. of Yr. Nat. award, Carnegie Found., WKU, 1999—2000. Mem.: APA, ACA (past regional chmn. com. internat. edn.), Nat. Bd. Visitor Sch. Edn. Syracuse (exec. com. mem.), Nat. Bd. Visitors Sch. Edn. Ind. U., Mensa, Soc. Psychology Mgmt., InterAm. Soc. Psychology, Intenrat. Registry Ogn. Devel. Profls., Nat. Assn. Gifted (past mem., bd. dirs.), Internat. Assn. Edn. and Vocat. Guidance, Assn. Specialists Group Work (charter), Internat. Coun. Psychologists (past area chmn. Ky.), Nat. Vocat. Guidance Assn. Profl., Colombian Nat. Soc. Indsl. Engrs. (hon.), Panamanian Psychol. Assn. (hon.), Ky. Acad. Arts and Scis. (life), Alumni Assn. SUNY, Oswego, Capitol Arts Assn., Ind. U. Alumni Assn. (life), Olde Stone Country Club, Eta Sigma Gamma (health educator), Gold Key, Phi Delta Kappa, Sigma Tau Delta, Sigma Delta Psi, Psi Chi, Pi Kappa Delta. Home: 1409 Mt Ayr Cir Bowling Green KY 42103-4708 Office: Western Ky U Dept Psychology Bowling Green KY 42101 Office Phone: 270-842-3436. Fax: 270-842-0432. Personal E-mail: joseph.cangemi@wku.edu. Business E-Mail: joseph.cangemi@creativeleadershipandchange.com.

CANNADAY, ED, state legislator; Mem. Dist. 15 Okla. House of Representatives, 2007—. Democrat. Address: RR 2 Box 4220 Porum OK 74455-9593 Office: Oklahoma House of Representatives 2300 N Lincoln Blvd Rm 539-B Oklahoma City OK 73105 Office Phone: 405-557-7375. E-mail: ed.cannaday@okhouse.gov.

CANNING, MARTIN S., information technology executive; B in Applied Sci., U. Mich.; MBA, U. Rochester. With Kodak (Office Imaging Divsn.); sr. v.p., sales & mktg. Danka Bus. Sys.; v.p., gen. mgr., worldwide mktg., v.p., gen. mgr., N. Am. Lexmark International, Inc., v.p., gen. mgr., Lexmark svcs., 1999, v.p., gen. mgr., PSSD Worldwide Mktg. & Lexmark Svcs. & PSSD North Am. Sales & Mktg., 2002—06, v.p., pres., Printing Solutions and Svcs. Divsn., 2007—. Office: Lexmark International Inc One Lexmark Ctr Dr 740 W New Cir Rd Lexington KY 40550 Office Phone: 859-232-2000. Business E-Mail: martin.canning@lexmark.co.uk.

CANNON, DEAN, state legislator; b. Bitburg US AFB, Germany, Aug. 2, 1968; m. Ellen Friedley; children: Dean III, Katherine, Sarah. BS, U. Fla., 1989, JD, 1992. Atty.; mem. Dist. 35 Fla. House of Reps., Tallahassee, 2004—, chair select policy coun. on strategic and econ. planning, mem. office of reapportionment, rules and calendar coun. Gen. counsel Orange County 2000 Charter Rev. Commn.; mem. redistricting adv. com. City of Orlando, 2000—02; sec. Orange County Del., 2004, vice chmn., 2005, chmn., 2006. Trustee Orlando Sci. Ctr., 1998—2004; chmn. of bd. Life for Kids Adoption Agency, 2004; coun. mem. ABA State and Local Govt. Sect. Republican. Baptist. Office: Fla House of Reps 420 The Capitol 402 S Monroe St Tallahassee FL 32399-2742 also: 301 S Bronough St Ste 500 Tallahassee FL 32301-1724 Office Phone: 407-623-5740, 850-488-2742.

CANNON, JONATHAN Z., law educator; b. 1945; m. Alice P. Cannon; children: Ariel, Maia A., Benjamin Z. BA summa cum laude, Williams Coll., 1967; postgrad., Oxford U., 1967-68; JD cum laude, U. Pa., 1974. Law clk. US Ct. Appeals (D.C. cir.), 1974-75; assoc. Beveridge & Diamond, P.C., 1975-80, ptnr., 1980-86, 1990-92; dep. gen. counsel, litigation and regional ops. EPA, Washington, 1987, dep. asst. adminstr. for enforcement & compliance, 1987-88, dep. asst. adminstr. for solid waste & emergency response, 1988-89, asst. adminstr. for solid waste & emergency response, 1989; dir. Gulf of Mexico Program U.S. EPA, Washington, 1992-93; acting asst. adminstr. for policy, planning & evaluation EPA, Washington, 1993, acting dep. adminstr., spl. advisor to adminstr., 1993, asst. adminstr. for adminstrn. & resource mgmt., CFO, 1993-95, gen. counsel, 1995-98; Blaine T. Phillips Disting. prof. environmental law U. Va. Sch. Law, Charlottesville, 1998—, dir. Environmental & Land Use Law Program, 1999—; mem. Barack Obama's Presdl Transition Team, 2008—09. Lectr. environ. law U. Va. Sch. Law, 1983-87, 97-98; adj. prof. environ. law Washington and Lee Law Sch., 1982-83. Office: U Va Sch Law 580 Massie Rd Charlottesville VA 22903-1738 Office Phone: 804-924-3819. E-mail: jzc8j@virginia.edu.

CANNON, ROBERT EUGENE, library director; b. Dec. 20, 1945; s. Wendell Eugene and Louise Marie (Bredehoeft) C.; m. Miriam Ruth Hillson, May 25, 1974; 1 child, Alexander. BA in Music, Calif. State U., LA, 1967; postgraduate student, Ariz. State U., 1967-68; MS in Libr. Sci., U. So. Calif., 1970; MPA, San Diego State U., 1978. Adult svcs. libr. Tucson Pub. Libr., 1969-70, Altadena Libr. Dist., 1970-71; head tech. processing, regional coord. San Diego County Libr., 1971-76; asst. dir. Tulare County Libr., Visalia, Calif., 1976-78; dir. Kern County Libr., Bakersfield, Calif., 1978-86; exec. dir. Pub. Libr. of Charlotte and Mecklenburg County, 1986—2003; dir. Broward County Libr., Ft. Lauderdale, Fla., 2003—; exec. bd. Southeast Libr. Info. Network, 2003—; bd. dirs. Broward County Libr. Found., 2003—. Sec., treas. Pub. Libr. Charlotte and Mecklenburg County, 1986-2003; sec. Mus. New South, 1991-93, bd. dirs., 1991-97, pres.'s coun. Fla. Atlantic U., 2003—. Founder Novello Festival of Reading, 1991—2003, Internat. Bus. Libr., 1994—2003, Virtual Libr., 1995—2000, Virtual Village Comm. Ctr., 2000—03, BizLink, 1998—2003; co-founder Charlotte's Web, 1995—2000, Cybrary, 2010; bd. visitors Sch. Info. and Libr. Sci. U. NC, Chapel Hill; bd. visitors Johnson C. Smith U., 2002—03; mem. Internat. Network Pub. Librs. Bertelsman Found., Germany, 1996—2003; co-founder Novello Festival Press, 2000—03; founder ImginOn.org, 2003; bd. dirs. Smart Start of Charlotte Mecklenburg, 2000—03. Recipient Pegasus award, Pub. Rels. Soc. Am., 1998, Bridge Builders award, Partnerships for Livable Cmtys., 2003; named NC Libr. Dir. of Yr., NC Pub. Libr. Dirs. Assn., 1995. Mem. ALA, Fla. Libr. Assn., Broward County Libr. Found. (exec.). Office: Broward County Libr 100 S Andrews Ave Fort Lauderdale FL 33301-1830

CANTERO, RAOUL G., III, lawyer, former state supreme court justice; b. Madrid, Aug. 1, 1960; m. Ana Maria Cantero; 3 children. BA in English and Bus., Fla. State U.; JD cum laude, Harvard U. Bd. cert. in appellate practice:. Law clk. to Hon. Edward B. Davis U.S. Dist. Ct. (so. dist.) Fla.; shareholder, head appellate divsn. Adorno & Yoss, Miami; justice Fla. Supreme Ct., Tallahassee, 2002—08; ptnr., appellate & litigation practice White & Case, Miami, Fla., 2008—. Lectr. in field. Contbr. articles to legal jours., short stories to anthologies; author: Non-Final Review of Insurance Coverage Issues: Wading through the Quagmire, 1995, Changes to the Florida Rules of Appellate Procedure, 1997, Discovery from Medical Experts: How Much is Too Much?, 1997, Certifying Questions to the Florida Supreme Court: What's So Important?, 2002. Mem. planning and zoning bd. City of Coral Gables, 1993—2001; mem. pastoral coun. St. Augustine Ch., 1990—97, chmn., 1997—2001, head Men's Retreat Ministry, 1994—2000; bd. dirs. Legal Svcs. of Greater Miami, Inc., 1991—95. Mem.: Dade County Bar Assn. (mem. appellate ct. com. 1998—99), Fla. Bar Assn. (mem. appellate rules com. 1993, sec. 1997—99, treas. appellate practice sect. 1999—2000, vice-chair 2001—02, sec. appellate practice sect. 2000—01, mem. 11th jud. cir. jud. nominating commn. 2001—02). Office: White & Case Ste 4900 Wachovia Fin Ctr 200 S Biscayne Blvd Miami FL 33131

CANTLIFFE, DANIEL JAMES, horticulture educator; b. NYC, Oct. 31, 1943; s. Sarah Lucretia Keesler C.; m. Elizabeth F. Lapetina, June 5, 1965; children: Christine, Deanna, Danielle, Cheri. BS, Delaware Valley Coll., Doylestown Pa., 1965; MS, Purdue U., West Lafayette, 1967, PhD, 1971. Asst. prof. horticulture U. Fla., Gainesville, 1974-76, assoc. prof., 1976-81, prof., 1981—2007, asst. chair dept., 1983-84, acting chair dept., 1984-85, chmn. dept., 1985-92, acting chair dept. fruit crops, 1991-92, chair dept. hort. scis., 1992—2011, prof. rsch. found., 2005, disting. prof., 2007—, county ext. dir., IFAS, SJC St. John County. Vis. prof. U. Hawaii, Honolulu, 1979-80; cons. Intota, Proctor and Gamble, Syngenta. Contbr. articles to profl. jours. and conf. procs., chpts. to books. Recipient rsch. award Fla. Fruit and Vegetable Assn., Orlando, 1986, Alumni Achievement award Delaware Valley Coll., Doylestown, 1990, Distinguished Agrl. Alumni award Purdue Univ., 1999, Group Hon. award USDA, 1997; fellow U. Fla., 2005, named Disting. Internat. Educator, 2005. Fellow: Crop Sci. Soc. Am. (pres. 1991—92, Seed Sci. award 1997), Am. Soc. Hort. Sci. (v.p. rsch. 1991—92, pres.-elect 1993—94, pres. 1994—95, chmn. 1995—96, mem. outstanding rsch. award selection com. 2003—06, chair outstanding rsch. award selection com. 2006, task force on the future hort. sci. 2004—, Outstanding Grad. Educator award 1991, Best Paper Vegetable Sect. 1992, Membership Recruitment award 1996, Outstanding Rsch. award 1997, vegetable publ. award 1997, So. Region Leadership and Adminstrn. award 2000), Internat. Soc. Hort. Sci. (hon.; chair sect. of vegetables 1998—, veg sect. chair 2002—06, coun. rep., nominations and award com. 2003—, Meritorious Svcs. medal, Chair Vegetable sect. 2006); mem.: Inst. Food and Agrl. Scis., Plasticulture Soc. Am., N. Am. Strawberry Growers Assn., Bot. Soc. Am., Fla. State Hort. Soc. (hon.; v.p. vegetable sect. 1984—85, pres. 1991—92, chmn. exec. com. 1992—93, best paper vegetable sect. 1991, 1993, Profl. Excellence Program award 1996, 1996, best paper vegetable sect. 1999, 2001, 2002, 2004, best paper garden and landscape sect. 2005, best paper vegetable sect. 2009, 2010), Internat. Soc. Tropical Horticulture, Am. Soc. Agronomy, Am. Soc. Plant Physiologists, Fla. Seed Assn., Crop Sci. Soc. Am., Phi Beta Delta, Gamma Sigma Delta (Disting. Leadership award 2003, Dist. Svc. Agr. award 2005), Phi Kappa Phi, Delta Tau Alpha, Sigma Xi. Office: 3125 Agricultural Center Dr Saint Augustine FL 32092-0572 Office Phone: 904-209-0430 203. Business E-Mail: djcant@ufl.edu.

CANTOR, ERIC IVAN, United States Representative from Virginia, lawyer; b. Richmond, Va., June 6, 1963; m. Diana Marcy Fine, 1989; children: Evan, Jenna, Michael. BA in Polit. Sci., George Washington U., 1985; JD, Coll. William & Mary, Williamsburg, Va., 1988; MS in Real Estate Devel., Columbia U., NYC, 1989. Mem. Dist. 73 Va. House of Delegates, 1992-2001; mem. US Congress from 7th Va. Dist., 2001—, chief dep. whip, 2003—09, asst. minority leader (minority whip), 2009—11, majority leader, 2011—; chmn. Congressional Task Force on Terrorism & Unconventional Warfare, 2001—. Co-author (with Kevin McCarthy & Paul Ryan): Young Guns: A New Generation of Conservative Leaders, 2010. Named one of The 50 Most Powerful People in DC, GQ mag., 2009. Republican. Jewish. Office: US House of Representatives 303 Cannon House Office Bldg Washington DC 20515 also: 4201 Dominion Blvd #110 Glen Allen VA 23060 Office Phone: 202-225-2815, 804-747-4073. Office Fax: 202-225-0011, 804-747-5308.*

CANTRELL, SCOTT, newspaper music critic; b. Ft. Smith, Ark., Nov. 14, 1949; s. Bert Thomas and Elizabeth Winstel (Scott) C. BFA, So. Meth. U., 1971; MS, Rensselaer Poly. Inst., 1974. Prodr., announcer Sta. WMHT, Schenectady, N.Y., 1973-86; music critic Times Union, Albany, N.Y., 1981-87, Rochester, N.Y., 1987-90; classical music editor Kansas City (Mo.) Star, 1990-99; music critic Dallas Morning News, 1999—. Freelance contbr. N.Y. Times, High Fidelity, Musical Am., Ovation, Classical and various other publs., 1973—; organist, choirmaster various chs., Albany, 1971-87. Recipient Deems Taylor award ASCAP, 1987, 89. Mem. Am. Guild of Organists, Music Critics Assn. N.Am. (exec. bd. 1989-2001, pres. 1993-97). Episcopalian. Avocations: travel, art, architecture, reading, cuisines. Office: The Dallas Morning News PO Box 655237 Dallas TX 75265-5237 E-mail: scantrell@dallasnews.com.

CANTRELL, WESLEY E., retired finance company executive; Grad. with highest honors, Southern Tech. Inst.; PhD (hon.), Southern Poly. State U. Pres. Lanier Worldwide Inc., 1977—87, pres., CEO, 1987—99, chmn., CEO, 1999—2001. Bd. dirs. AnnTaylor Stores Corp., 1998—2009, First Union Nat. Bank, Atlanta, REIT, Inc., Piedmont Office Realty Trust, Inc., 2007—. Office: Piedmont Office Realty Trust Inc Bd Directors 11695 Johns Creek Pky Ste 350 Johns Creek GA 30097 Office Phone: 770-418-8800. Business E-Mail: wesley.cantrell@annaly.com.

CANTRELL TRUSDELL, MARY LOUISE, retired academic administrator; b. Chandler, Okla., Oct. 24, 1921; d. George Herbert and Lois Elizabeth (Bruce) Cantrell; m. Robert William Trusdell, Jan. 7, 1943 (dec. Nov. 10, 2006); children: Timothy Lee(dec.), Laurence Michael. BA, Ga. So. Coll., 1965; MEd, U. Va., 1974. Dir. specific learning disabilities program Savannah Country Day Sch., Ga., 1960—65; learning disabilities tchr. Richmond Pub. Schs., Va., 1966—73; dir. New Cmty. Sch., Richmond, 1974—75, Fed. Learning Disabilities Project, Dept HEW, Mid. Peninsula, Va., 1975—76; supr. programs for learning disabled Va. Dept. Edn., Richmond, 1976—86; bd. dirs. Learning Disabilities Coun., Richmond, Very Spl. Arts- Va., 1986—91; mem. adv. com. Learning Disabilities Rsch. and Devel. Project, Woodrow Wilson Rehab. Ctr., Fisherville, Va., 1983. Bd. dirs. Savannah Assn. Retarded Children, 1957—60, Meml. Guidance Clinic, Richmond, 1966—69. Co-editor: Understanding Learning Disabilities: A Parent Guide and Workbook, 1989, 2002. Named Tchr. of Yr., Learning Disabilities Ctr., Richmond, 1972. Mem.: Alliance for the Mentally Ill. Cen. Va. (pres. 1990—93), Orton Dyslexia Soc. (pres. capital area br. 1968—70, nat. bd. dirs. 1970—72, Va. br. 1986—91). Presbyterian. Avocations: travel, theater, reading.

CANTRILL, THOMAS H., lawyer; b. Springfield, Ill., Apr. 5, 1948; BBA with honors, So. Meth. U., 1970; JD with honors, U. Tex., 1973. Bar: Tex. 1973. Shareholder Jenkens & Gilchrist, P.C., Dallas, firm leader estate planning practice group, firm pres. & chmn., 2004—07; ptnr. Hunton and Williams, LLP, 2007—. Fellow Tex. Bar Found.; mem. ABA, Am. Coll. Trusts and Estate Counsel, Tex. State Bar Assn., Dallas Bar Assn., Internat. Acad. Estate and Trust Law, Order Coif, Beta Alpha Psi, Beta Gamma Sigma. Office: Hunton and Williams 1445 Ross Ave Ste 3700 Dallas TX 75202-2799 Office Phone: 214-468-3311. Office Fax: 214-800-3011. Business E-Mail: tcantrill@hunton.com.

CANTÚ, OSCAR, bishop; b. Houston, Dec. 5, 1966; s. Ramiro and Maria de Jesus Cantú. BA, Univ. Dallas, 1989; MDiv, MA in Theol. Studies, Univ. St. Thomas, Houston, 1994; STL, Pontifical Gregorian Univ., Rome, 2000. Ordained priest Archdiocese of Galveston-Houston, Tex., 1994; parochial vicar St. Christopher parish, Houston, 1994—96, St. Cecilia parish, Houston, 1996—97, St. Francis Cabrini parish, Houston, 2002—03; pastor Holy Name parish, Houston, 2003—08; ordained bishop, 2008; aux. bishop Archdiocese of San Antonio, Tex., 2008—, apostolic adminstr., 2010. Theology instr. U. St. Thomas, Houston, 2003—05. Roman Catholic. Office: Archdiocese of San Antonio 2718 W Woodlawn Ave PO Box 28410 San Antonio TX 78228-0410 Office Phone: 210-734-2620. Office Fax: 210-734-0231.

CANTUS, CHARLES H., information technology executive; BA in History, Hampden-Sydney Coll., Va., 1985. Sr. exec. positions Profl. Svcs. Coun., v.p., govt. rels., 1996—2001; mng. dir., govt. rels. BearingPoint, Inc., v.p., govt. rels., 2001—09; v.p., govt. rels., N.Am. Pub. Sector Computer Sciences Corp., 2009—. Office: Computer Sciences Corp 3170 Fairview Park Dr Falls Church VA 22042 Office Phone: 703-876-1000. Business E-Mail: ccantus@csc.com.

CANTUS, H. HOLLISTER, marketing and government relations consultant; b. NYC, Nov. 16, 1937; s. Howard J. and Eleanor (Hollister) C.; m. Barbara Jane Park, Feb. 7, 1961; children: Charles Hollister, Jane-Scott. BA, Williams Coll., 1959. Mem. prof. staff Com. on Armed Services US House of Representatives, Washington, 1970-74; dep. asst. sec. def. U.S. Dept. Def., Washington, 1974-75; dir. congl. relations U.S. Energy Research and Devel. Adminstrn., Washington, 1975-77; group v.p. bldg. systems United Technologies Corp., Washington, 1977-87; assoc. adminstr. NASA, 1987-88; group v.p. missiles and space Lockheed Corp., Washington, 1988-94; sr. v.p. ICF Kaiser Internat., Inc., Fairfax, Va., 1994—97; CEO The ILEX Group, McLean, Va., 1997—. Capt. USNR, 1961-83. Fellow AIAA (assoc.); mem. Georgetown Club, Farmington (Va.) Country Club. Republican. Office: The ILEX Group 1600 Tysons Blvd Mc Lean VA 22102 Office Phone: 703-245-6721. Business E-Mail: hhcantus@theilexgroup.com.

CANTWELL, DON, artistic director; b. Charleston, SC, July 10, 1935; s. James Richard Jr. and Helen (Thompson) C.; m. Patricia Downs; children: Kimberly S., Dewey S. Jr., Joshua Paul. Grad. high sch., Charleston. Dir. Charleston Ballet Sch., 1969—; artistic dir. Charleston Ballet Theatre, 1969—. Mem. Southeastern Ballet Assn. (v.p. 1981-82, 85-86, pres. 1983-84, 86-87, chmn. bd. 1984-85, 87-88). Office: Charleston Ballet Theatre 217 Calhoun St Apt A Charleston SC 29401-1360 Home Phone: 843-720-8650; Office Phone: 843-723-7334.

CANTWELL, JOHN WALSH, advertising executive; b. Fall River, Mass., July 16, 1922; s. William J. and Esther (Walsh) C.; m. Evelyna Dyson; children from previous marriage: Sharon, Peter, Paul. BS in Econs., Holy Cross Coll., 1944; MA, Georgetown U., 1945; postgrad., Columbia U., 1949-50. Asst. sales mgr. Internat. Milling Co., 1947-48; v.p. mgmt. supr. Compton Advt., NYC, 1948-60; sr. v.p. mgmt. supr. Sullivan, Stauffer Colwell & Bayles, NYC, 1960-65; pres., CEO Pritchard, Wood (advt.), NYC, 1965-68, Parkson Advt. Agy., Inc., 1968-69; sr. v.p. J.B. Williams Co., Inc., 1968-69; pres. Jack Cantwell, Inc., 1970—; chmn., CEO Dolphin Med. Acoustics, Ltd., 1997-99; CEO Byrd Walsh Internat. LLP, 2004—. Home: 5500 NW 69th Ave Apt 302 Lauderhill FL 33319-7269 Personal E-mail: jaudecantwel@aol.com. Business E-Mail: jaudecantwel@comcast.net.

CAO, JOSEPH (ANH QUANG CAO), former United States Representative from Louisiana, lawyer; b. Saigon, South Vietnam, Mar. 13, 1967; s. My Quang Cao and Khang Thi Tran; m. Hieu Kate Hoang; children: Sophia, Betsy. BS in Physics, Baylor U., 1990; MA in Philosophy, Fordham U., 1995; JD, Loyola U., 2000. Assoc. Waltzer & Assoc.; in-house counsel Boat People S.O.S., Inc. (BPSOS); pvt. practice immigration law New Orleans, 2002—09; mem. US Congress from 2nd La. Dist., 2009—11, US House Homeland Security Com., 2009—11, US House Transp. & Infrastructure Com., 2009—11, US House Oversight & Govt. Reform Com., 2009—11. Tchr. philosophy and ethics Loyola U. Vol. Boat People S.O.S., Inc. (BPSOS), bd. mem., 1996—2002, MQVN Cmty. Devel. Corp.; mem. Bd. Elections for Orleans Parish, Rep. Parish Exec. Com., State Rep. Exec. Com.; at-large del. Rep. Nat. Convention, 2008; bd. mem. Mary Queen of Vietnam Cath. Ch.'s Cmty. Devel. Corp.; mem. Nat. Adv. Coun. to US Conf. of Cath. Bishops. Republican. Roman Catholic. Office Phone: 604-367-5001. Personal E-mail: acad@caolawfirm.com.

CAPEHART, BARNEY LEE, industrial and systems engineer, educator; b. Galena, Kans., Aug. 20, 1940; s. Samuel Alfred and Mary Jane (Bliss) Capehart; m. Lynne Carol Fowler, Sept. 2, 1961; children: Thomas David, Jeffrey Donald, Cynthia Diane. BSEE, U. Okla., 1961, MEE, 1962, PhD, 1967. Instr. elec. engring. U. Okla., Norman, 1965—67; mem. tech. staff Aerospace Corp., San Bernardino, Calif., 1967—68; asst. prof. indsl. and sys. engring. U. Fla., Gainesville, 1968—72; assoc. prof. indsl. engring. U. Tenn., 1972—73; assoc. prof. indsl. and sys. engring. U. Fla., Gainesville, 1973—79, prof., 1979—, asst. chmn., 1987—88. Cons. Martin Marietta Corp., U.S. Naval Tng. Device Ctr., State of Fla., Hicks and Assocs., Casazza, Schultz & Assocs., U.S. Dept. Energy, Dep. Ass. Sec. Bldg. Techs., Washington, 1989—90; nat. lectr. Assn. Energy Engrs.; expert witness in energy and safety cases; chmn. Regional Energy Action Com., 1977—79; mem. Region IV adv. group appropriate tech. Dept. Energy, 1978—80; mem. Local Energy Action Program, 1980—81. Author: books in field; editor: Internat. Jour. Energy Sys., 1985—88; contbr. articles to profl. jours. Pres. Fla. League Conservation Voters, 1984—86; dir. Energy Analysis and Diagnostic Center U. Fla., Fla., dir. Indsl. Assessment Ctr., 1995—99; grad. leadership Gainesville, 1984. Decorated USAF Commendation medal; recipient Palladium medal, Am. Assn. Engring. Socs., 1988; named May 26, 1987, Barney Capehart Day in his honor, Alachua County, Fla., Disting. Grad. award, Okla. U. Coll. Engring., 2012; named to Assn. Energy Engrs. Hall of Fame. Fellow: IEEE (mem. energy com. 1988—90), AAAS, Assn. Energy Engrs., Inst. Indsl. Engrs. (dir. energy mgmt. divsn. 1986—87); mem.: Assn. Energy Engring., ASHRAE, Disting. Grad. Soc. Coll. Engring. U. Okla., Fla. Conservation Found., Audubon Soc. (Fla. chpt. Conservationist of the Yr. 1987), Sigma Xi, Fla. Blue Key, Eta Kappa Nu, Tau Beta Pi, Alpha Pi Mu, Sigma Tau. Home: 1601 NW 35th Way Gainesville FL 32605-4846 Office: U Fla Dept Indsl & Systems Engring 303 Weil Hall Gainesville FL 32611-2083 Office Phone: 352-392-1464 ext. 2008. Personal E-mail: energydoc1@aol.com. Business E-Mail: capehart@ise.ufl.edu.

CAPEL, JEFF, III, men's college basketball coach; b. Fayetteville, NC, Feb. 12, 1975; s. Jeff Capel; m. Kanika Capel. BA, Duke U., Durham, NC, 1997. Basketball player France, CBA, 1997—2000; asst. coach Old Dominion U. Monarchs, 2000—01, Va. Commonwealth U. Rams, 2001—02, head coach, 2002—06, Okla. U. Sooners, 2006—11; asst. coach Duke U. Blue Devils, 2011—. Asst. coach US Men's World U. Games, 2005. Named Va. State Coach of Yr., CoSIDA, 2002, Coach of Yr., Richmond Times-Dispatch, 2004, VaSID, 2004. Achievements include at 27, becoming the youngest head coach in Division I men's basketball, 2002. Office: Duke University Basketball 118 Cameron Indoor Stadium PO Box 90555 Durham NC 27708 Office Phone: 919-613-7500.

CAPELLAS, MICHAEL D., information technology executive; b. Aug. 19, 1954; m. Marie Capellas; 2 children. BBA Kent St. U., 1976. With Republic Steel Corp., 1976—81; corp. dir. for info. systems, contr. and treas. of Asia Pacific ops. Schlumberger Ltd., 1981—96; founder, mng. ptnr. Benchmarking Partners, Cambridge, Mass., 1996; dir. supply chain mgmt. SAP Am., 1996—97; sr. v.p., gen. mgr. for global energy bus. Oracle Corp., 1997—98; chief info. officer Compaq Computer Corp., Houston, 1998-99, acting COO, 1999, pres., CEO, 1999—2000, chmn., CEO, 2000—02; pres. Hewlett-Packard Co., 2002; chmn., CEO WorldCom Inc., 2002—04; pres., CEO MCI, Inc., Ashburn, Va., 2004—06; acting pres & CEO Serena Software, Inc., 2006—07; sr. adv. Silver Lake Partners, 2006—07; chmn., CEO First Data Corp., Greenwood Village, Colo., 2007—10; sr. adv. Kohlberg Kravis Roberts & Co., 2010—; CEO Acadia Enterprises, LLC, Dallas, 2010—. Bd. dirs. Cisco Systems Inc., 2006—. Bd. govs. Boys & Girls Clubs Am.; bd. trustees Am. U., Washington. Recipient Hope Technology Award, ctr. for Missing and Exploited Children. Mem.: bd. of Trustees of American University in Wash. DC. Avocations: travel, golf, running, music. Office: Acadia Enterprises LLC 5050 Quorum Dr Ste 540 Dallas TX 75254 Office Phone: 972-980-8402.

CAPERS, LAYNGLYN M., delivery service executive; b. NYC; BS in Computer Sci., Pace U., NYC. Joined United Parcel Service of America, Inc. (UPS), 1976, various mgmt. positions, 1979—, customer automation applications devel. mgr., 1997—2002, portfolio mgr., customer tech., 2002—. Named one of Premier 100 IT Leaders, Computerworld, 2006. Office: United Parcel Service Inc 55 Glenlake Pky NE Atlanta GA 30328 Business E-Mail: lcapers@ups.com.

CAPILOUTO, ELI, academic administrator; b. Montgomery, Ala., Aug. 22, 1949; m. Mary Lynne Capilouto; 1 child, Emily. BS, U. Ala., 1971; DMD, U. Ala., Birmingham, 1975, MPH in Epidemiology, 1985; ScD in Health Policy Mgmt., Harvard U., 1991. Instr. Dept. Operative Dentistry Sch. of Dentistry, U. Ala., Birmingham, 1975—79, asst. prof., 1979—85; assoc. scholar Ctr. for Aging Sch. of Medicine, U. Ala., Birmingham, 1985—87, asst. prof. Dept. Cmty. and Pub. Health Dentistry, 1989—92, scientist Ctr. for Aging, 1993—; sr. rsch. fellow dental care adminstrn. Harvard Sch. Dental Medicine,

Boston, 1985—87, Robert Wood Johnson dental services rsch. scholar, 1985—87; rsch. fellow Nat. Ctr. Health Services Rsch. and Health Care Tech. Harvard Sch. Pub. Health, Boston, 1987—89; asst. prof. Sch. Pub. Health, U. Ala., Birmingham, 1989—92, assoc. scholar Lister Hill Ctr. for Health Policy, 1990—92, scholar, 1992—, assoc. prof. health care orgn. and policy, 1992—97, interim chair Dept. Health Care Orgn. & Policy, 1994, interim dean, 1994—96, dean, 1996—2001, charter faculty mem. Ctr. for Health Promotion, 1996—, prof., 1997—, sr. scholar John J. Sparkman Ctr. for Internat. Pub. Health Edn., 1999—; acting provost U. Ala., Birmingham, 2002—05, provost, 2005—11; pres. U. Ky., Lexington, 2011—. Contbr. articles to profl. jours. Mem.: ADA, Soc. Med. Decision Making, Internat. Assn. Dental Rsch., Assn. Health Services Rsch., American Soc. Geriatric Dentistry, American Assn. Pub. Health Dentistry, American Assn. Pub. Health, American Assn. Dental Schools, Ala. Dental Assn., Omicron Kappa Upsilon. Office: University of Kentucky Office of President 101 Main Building Lexington KY 40506-0032 Office Phone: 859-257-1701.*

CAPITAN, WILLIAM HARRY, university president emeritus; b. Owosso, Mich., Feb. 7, 1933; s. Harry and Anthe (Sarris) C.; m. Dolores Marie Randolph, Sept. 19, 1959; children: Rita, Edwin. BA, U. Mich., 1954; postgrad., Queens U.; postgrad. (Ulster Am. fellow), 1954-55; MA, U. Minn., 1958, PhD, 1960. Registered mediator 2001, lic. Capt. USCG, auxiliary USCG, 2001, comdr. flotilla, 2005, cert. auxiliary comdr. USCG, 2010. Instr. philosophy U. Minn., 1959-60, U. Md., 1960-62; asst. prof., assoc. prof., chmn. dept. Oberlin (Ohio) Coll., 1962-70; dean fine arts, v.p. acad. affairs, acting pres. Saginaw Valley State U., U. Ctr., Mich., 1970-74; v.p. acad. affairs, dean faculty, acting pres. W.Va. Wesleyan Coll., Buckhannon, 1974-79; pres. Ga. Southwestern U/, Americus, 1979-95; pres. emeritus Ga. Southwestern Coll., Americus, 1996—. Adj. prof. U. Ga., 1996. Author: Introduction to the Philosophy of Religion, 1972, Speak For Yourself, 1987; editor: (with D.D. Merrill) Metaphysics and Explanation, Art, Religion, and Mind, 1967, The Ethical Navigator, 2000. Adv. bd. mem. Hellenext, Arlington, Va.; trustee Charles L. Mix Meml. Fund, Inc., 1979—96; pres. Americus Sumter County C. of C., 1985; v.p. Hellenic-Am. C. of C., Atlanta; lay reader Episcopal Ch., Americus, Ga.; bd. dir. Saginaw Symphony Orch., 1970—74; Project Save; Buckhannon C. of C.; Sumter County United Way. Vice capt. USCG Aux., comdr. USCG Aux., 2004—06. Am. Council Lerned Socs. fellow Paris, 1967-68 Mem. Am. Soc. Aesthetics, Am. Philos. Assn., Rotary (pres. 1990-91), Beta Theta Phi, Omicron Delta Kappa, Phi Kappa Phi, Phi Delta Kappa. Episcopalian. Office: GA Southwestern State U Americus GA 31709

CAPITO, SHELLEY MOORE, United States Representative from West Virginia; b. Glen Dale, W.Va., Nov. 26, 1953; d. Arch A. Moore, Jr. and Shelley Riley; m. Charles L. Capito, Jr.; children: Charles, Moore, Shelley. BS in Zoology, Duke U., Durham, NC, 1975; MEd, U. Va., 1976. Career counselor W.Va. State Coll., 1976—78; dir. Ednl. Info. Ctr., W.Va. Bd. Regents, 1978—81; mem. Dist. 30 W.Va. House of Delegates, 1996—2000; mem. US Congress from 2nd W.Va. dist., 2001—. Republican. Presbyterian. Office: US House of Representatives 2366 Rayburn House Office Bldg Washington DC 20515 also: 4815 MacCorkle Ave SE Charleston WV 25304 Office Phone: 202-225-2711.*

CAPLOW, THEODORE, sociologist; b. NYC, May 1, 1920; s. Samuel Nathaniel and Florence (Israel) C.; m. Margaret Mary Pettit, 1981. AB, U. Chgo., 1939; PhD, U. Minn., 1946; LLD, Ball State U., 2003. Mem. faculty U. Minn., 1945—60; prof. sociology Columbia U., 1961—70; Commonwealth prof. U. Va., Charlottesville, 1973—2005, chmn. dept. sociology, 1970—78, 1984—86, prof. emeritus, 2005—. Vis. prof. U. Bordeaux, France, 1950, U. Aix-Marseille, France, 1951, U. Utrecht, Netherlands, 1954-55, Stanford, 1957, P.R., 1959, U. Bogota, Colombia, 1962, Sorbonne, Paris, France, 1968-69, Institut d'Etudes Politiques, Paris, 1983, U. Rome, 1984, U. Oslo, 1986; pres. Mendota Research Group Inc., 1957-65 Author: Sociology of Work, 1954, Principles of Organization, 1964, Two Against One, 1968, L'Enquête Sociologique, 1970, Toward Social Hope, 1975, Peace Games, 1989, American Social Trends, 1991, Perverse Incentives, 1994; sr. author: The Academic Marketplace, 1957, The Urban Ambience, 1964, Middletown Families, 1982, All Faithful People, 1983, Recent Social Trends in the United States, 1960-90, 1991, Systems of War and Peace, 1995, Sociologie Militaire, 2000, The First Measured Century, 2001, Leviathen Transformed, 2002, Forbidden Wars, 2007, Armageddon Postponed, 2010. With AUS, 1943-45, PTO. Decorated Purple Heart. Mem. Tocqueville Soc. (pres. 1979-83), Am. Sociol. Assn. (sec. 1983-86), Farmington Hunt Club, Albemarle Yacht Club,(Charlottesville), Century (N.Y.C.), Tarratine Club (Dark Harbor, Maine). E-mail: tc@virginia.edu.

CAPO, THOMAS P., automotive executive; BS in Acctg. & Fin., U. Detroit Mercy, MA in Economics, MBA in Fin. V.p., contr. Chrysler Fin. Corp.; treas. Chrysler Corp., 1991—93, v.p., treas., 1993—98; sr. v.p., treas. DaimlerChrysler Corp., 1998—2000; chmn. Dollar Thrifty Automotive Group, Inc., 2003—. Bd. dirs. JLG Industries, Inc., Sonic Automotive, Inc., Cooper Tire & Rubber Co., 2007—, Lear Corp., 2009—. Former trustee U. Detroit Mercy. Office: Dollar Thrifty Automotive Group Inc 5330 E 31st St Tulsa OK 74135 also: Lear Corp Bd Directors 21557 Telegraph Rd Southfield MI 48033 Office Phone: 918-660-7700, 248-447-1500. Office Fax: 918-669-2934. Business E-Mail: tcapo@dtag.com. E-mail: tcapo@lear.com.

CAPORELLA, NICK A., consumer products company executive; b. 1937; Pres. Caporella & Sons Inc., 1966—72; chmn. BSI Inc., 1972; exec. v.p. Burnup & Sims Inc., Ft. Lauderdale, Fla., 1972, chmn., pres. & CEO, 1976—94; with Corp. Mgmt. Advisors, Inc., 1992; pres. National Beverage Corp., 1985—2002, chmn., CEO, 1985—. Office: National Beverage Corp 8100 SW 10th St Ste 4000 Fort Lauderdale FL 33324 Office Phone: 954-581-0922. Office Fax: 954-473-4710. Business E-Mail: ncaporella@nationalbeverage.com.

CAPPER, JOSEPH H., medical products executive; BS in Acctg., West Chester U., Pa.; MBA in Internat. Fin., George Wash. U., Washington. Various positions including nat. sales dir. diabetes care divsn. Bayer Healthcare; pres., CEO CCS Med. Holdings, Inc., 2003—08; pres., CEO, bd. dirs. Home Diagnostics, Inc., 2009—. Officer USN. Office: Home Diagnostics Inc 2400 NW 55th Court Fort Lauderdale FL 33309 Office Phone: 954-677-9201. Office Fax: 954-739-8506. Business E-Mail: jcapper@homediagnostics.com.

CAPPETTA, PAMELA GUYLER, counselor; b. Huntington, Pa., May 16, 1949; d. Thomas Winslow and Lois Olene (Lukens) Guyler; m. Christopher John Boll, Aug. 16, 1969 (div. Aug. 1985); 1 child, Kirstin Boll Kochanek; m. Robert Christopher Cappetta, May 4, 1991 (div. Aug. 19, 2008). BS, Shippensburg U., 1971; MEd, Coll. William and Mary, 1980, EdD, 1990. Lic. profl. counselor, Va.; lic. marriage and family therapist, Va. Social worker York-Poquoson Social Svcs., Grafton, Va., 1981-84; coord. PACES family counseling ctr. Coll. William & Mary, Williamsburg, Va., 1984-87; family therapist TMJ rsch. ctr. Med. Coll. Va., Sch. Dentistry, 1984-88; clin. assoc., counselor Family Living Inst., Williamsburg, Va., 1985-88; clin. asst. prof. Med. Coll. Va., Sch. Dentistry, Richmond, Va., 1990-94; med. family therapist Norge Family Practice, Williamsburg, 1992-94; co-owner, counselor Family Living Inst., 1988-94; allied health prof. Williamsburg Place, 1993—; counselor pvt. practice, Williamsburg, 1995—. Dir. coord. Transitions, Williamsburg, 1992-94; holotropic breathwork practitioner, Williamsburg, 1996—; faculty Asheville (N.C.) Body-Mind Clinic, 1999-2003. Contbr. articles to profl. jours. Vol. Va. Breast Cancer Found., Williamsburg, 1995-2003; bd. dirs. Va. Cancer Pain Initiative, Richmond, 1996. Mem. Am. Acad. Pain Mgmt., Nat. Bd. of Cert. Counselors, Eye Movement Desentization and Reprocessing Internat. Assn. Democrat. Avocations: travel, reading, walking dogs, bicycling. Office: Ste 2 362 McLaws Cir Williamsburg VA 23185 Office Phone: 757-253-5708. Business E-Mail: drpamm@cox.net.*

CAPPS, THOMAS E., board member; b. 1935; B, JD, U. N.C., Chapel Hill. Chmn. Consolidated Natural Gas Co., Va. Electric and Power Co.; sr. counsel Carolina Power and Light Co., 1970; v.p., gen. counsel Boston Edison Co., 1974—75; atty. Steel Hector and Davis, 1975; v.p. Va. Power, 1984—86; pres. Dominion Resources, Inc., Richmond, Va., 1986—89, COO, 1989—90, CEO, 1990—2005, chmn. Richmond, Va., 1992—2007. Bd. dirs. Assoc. Electric and Gas Ins. Svc. Inc., Amerigroup Corp., 2005—, The Shaw Group Inc., 2007—. Office: The Shaw Group Inc Bd Directors 4171 Essen Ln Baton Rouge LA 70809 Office Phone: 225-932-2500. Office Fax: 225-987-3328. Business E-Mail: thomas.capps@shawgrp.com.

CARABIN, DANA A., lawyer; JD; attended, U. Tex., Austin, 1995. Gen. counsel, sec. Quanta Svcs. Inc., 2001—05, EGL Inc., 2005—, chief compliance officer, 2006—. Office: EGL Inc 15350 Vickery Dr Houston TX 77032 Office Phone: 281-618-3100. Office Fax: 281-618-3223. Business E-Mail: dana.carabin@eaglegl.com.

CARAM, DOROTHY FARRINGTON, educational consultant; b. McAllen, Tex., Jan. 14, 1933; d. Curtis Leon and Elena (Santander) Farrington; m. Pedro C. Caram, June 7, 1958 (dec. Aug. 2000); children: Pedro M., Juan D., Hector L., Jose M. BA, Rice U., 1955, MA, 1974; EdD, U. Houston, 1982; postgrad., U. Madrid, 1957. Tchr. Houston Ind. Sch. Dist., 1955-56, 56-60, St. Mark's Episcopal Ch., Houston, 1964-65; substitute tchr. St. Vincent De Paul Cath. Sch., Houston, 1965-68; mgr. med. office Houston, 1983; dir. Fed. Home Loan Bank, Little Rock, 1976-82; pres. Inst. Hispanic Culture, Houston, 1983, 93, chmn. bd. and pres., 1984; with Houston Ednl. Excellence Program, 1980. Mem. task force Tex. Edn. Agy., 1981-83; adv. coun. Nat. Inst. Neurol. and Communicative Disorders and Stroke, 1972-76; pres. IDM Satellite Comm. of Tex. Divsn., Inc., 1990, chmn. bd., 1998—99 asst. to pres. U. Houston, 1991-94, ret., 1994, cmty. adv. com. mem., U. Tex. Health Sci. Ctr. Houston, 1989-1991, Com. Protection & Human Subjects UTSCH Med. Sch., 1986-88. Prodr.: IHCH's Days of Hispanic World Miller-outdoor Theatre, 1983—2009, 2011, 2013. Mem. coun. Miller Theater, Houston, 1976—, adv. bd. emeritus, 2000-; adv. bd. Lighthouse For Blind, Houston, 1979-; bd. dir. Houston Pops, 1983-87, United Way Tex., 1991-94; mem. task force Quality Integrated Edn., Houston, 1972; bd. dirs. United Way Tex., Gulf Coast, 1989-95, exec. bd., sec.; mem. Civil Svc. Commn. Houston, 1983-85; bd. mgrs. Harris County Hosp. Dist., 1988-90; founder, mem. Houston Hispanic Forum, bd. dirs., 1985, 2006—, pres., 1989-90; chmn. bd. Teatro Bilingue de Houston, 1989-90; pres. Mexican Cultural Inst. Houston, Inc., 1997; bd. dirs. Southmain Ctr. Assn., 1998-2005, Harris County Hosp. Dist. Found., 1997-2005, emeritus mem., 2005—; bd. dirs. Houston Ind. Sch. Dist. Found., 1996-2002, chmn. peer com. magnet and vanguard schs., 1996-2002; adv. bd. Theater Under Stars, Career and Recovery, Jobs for Progress of Tex. Gulf Coast, Inc., AAMA; bd. dirs. Majestic Seas Aquarium, 1998-99; bd. dir., treas. Colonial Homes Found. for Youth, 1999; mem. Mil. and Hospitler Order of St. Lazarus of Jerusalem, 1982-; pres. Braes Rep. Women, 2002-03, precinct judge, 1998-2006; v.p. edn. bd. Houston Grand Opera, 2001-05; commr. Tex. Commn. on Arts, 2003-09; Rice alumni 50th graduation com., 2001-05, alumni coun. U. Houston, 2003; appointments chmn. Tex. Fedn. Rep. Women, 2003-05; advisor Amb. Internat. Ballet Folklorico, 2003—; trustee U. St. Thomas, Houston, 2005—10; bd. dirs. Houston C.C. Found., 2004-06, chair, U. Houston Alumni Adv. Coun., 2003-07, chair, Rice 1955 alumni class, 2005-13, chair adv. bd. Mexican Inst. Greater Houston, 2006-; co-chair Houston Celebrate Mex., 2010. Recipient, Savvy award, 1975, Willie Velasquez Outstanding Hispanic Citizenship award, 1994, Outstanding Alumni award, Dorothy F. Caram Leadership award Blueprint-United Way Tex., Greater Houston, 2000-, Woman of Vision award Delta Gamma Found., 2003; named Vol. of Yr., United Way Tex. Gulf Coast, 1992, Outstanding Alumnus, Coll. Edn. U. Houston, 2000, Rice Alumni award, 2005, Extraordinary Eucharistic Min., St. Vincent de Paul Cath. Ch., 2003—, Disting. Alumni award U. Houston, 2008, Mayor's Hispanic Heritage Lifetime Achievement award, 2009; decorated Lady in Court of Isabel La Catolica by King Carlos (Spain), 1984; Oustanding Sr. fellow Am. Leadership Forum, 2004, Outstanding Mex. Am. Woman award, Lulac Coun. 402, 2010, leadership award, 2010, Otlhi award Mexican Govt., 2009, Cmty. & Leadership award Lationo Learning Ctr., 2010, Hispanic Woman of Yr. award, 2012. Mem. Cedars Club (pres. 1978), Tex. Commn. Arts (treas. 2005—07), L.Am. Philharmonic Orch. (pres., chmn. bd. Houston, 2013). Roman Catholic. Home: 2603 Glen Haven Blvd Houston TX 77025-2132 Personal E-mail: dcaram@att.net.

CARAWAY, DWAINE R., councilman; Attended, Tex. Southern U. Owner Profile Group; councilman, Dist. 4 Dallas City Coun; dep. mayor pro tem City of Dallas, mayor pro tem, 2009—. Mem. Econ. Devel. com.; vice chmn. Pub. Safety com.; chmn., Mktg. Task Force Trinity River Corridor Project. Former v.p. Dallas Parks & Recreation Bd.; former chmn. South Dallas/Fair Park Trust Fund; former mem. Dallas Youth Commn., Roosevelt High Sch. Mentoring Program, Dallas/Ft. Worth Regional Sports Commn. Adv.; founder Grambling/Prairie View Football Classic. Mem.: Cedar Crest Neighborhood Assn. (bd. mem.), Dallas NAACP, Cotillion Idlewild Club, Pylon Salesmanship Club, Kappa Alpha Psi Frat. Office: City Hall 1500 Marilla St Rm 5EN Dallas TX 75201 Office Phone: 214-670-0781. Office Fax: 214-670-3409. Business E-Mail: dwaine.caraway@dallascityhall.com.

CARBONELL, ANA, legislative staff member; b. 1970; Aide to State Senator Lincoln Diaz-Balart Fla. Senate, Tallahassee; dist. dir. to Representative Lincoln Diaz-Balart US House of Representatives, Washington, 1993—2004, chief of staff to Representative Lincoln Diaz-Balart, 2004—. Campaign mgr. Lincoln Diaz-Balart for US Congress, 1992, 2000, 2008. Bd. dirs. Alliance of Young Cubans, Fla. Office: Office of Representative Lincoln Diaz-Balart 2244 Rayburn House Office Bldg Washington DC 20515-0921 also: Dist Office 8525 NW 53rd Terrace Ste 102 Miami FL 33166 E-mail: ana.carbonell@mail.house.gov.

CARBONELL, JOAQUIN R., III, telecommunications industry executive, lawyer; b. Camaguey, Cuba, 1952; arrived in US, 1961; BA summa cum laude, Boston Coll.; JD, Duke U.; MS in Mgmt., Stanford U., 1989. Bar: Fla. 1978. Joined BellSouth Enterprises Inc., 1980; gen. atty. BellSouth, Fla., 1986—90, gen. atty., DC office, 1990; v.p., Latin Am. BellSouth Internat., pres., Latin Am.; pres. BellSouth Europe; v.p., group counsel, wireless svcs. BellSouth Enterprises, Inc.; sr. v.p., gen. counsel, regulatory and legal Cingular Wireless LLC (merged with AT&T Wireless), 2001—04; exec. v.p., gen. counsel Cingular Wireless, LLC, 2004—. Alfred P. Sloan Fellow, 1989. Mem.: Phi Beta Kappa. Office: Cingular Wireless LLC Glenridge Highlands Two 5565 Glenridge Connector Atlanta GA 30342 Office Phone: 404-236-6000. Office Fax: 404-236-6005.

CARD, ANDY (ANDREW HILL CARD JR.), former White House chief of staff, former United States Secretary of Transportation; b. Brockton, Mass., May 10, 1947; s. Andrew Hill and Joyce Ann (Whitaker) C.; m. Kathleene Marie Bryan, 1967; children: Tabetha, Rachel, Drew. BS in Engring., U. SC, 1971; D in Pub. Svc. (hon.), U. Mass. Amherst, 2007. Structural design engr. Maurice Reidy Engrs., Inc., 1971-72, David M. Berg, Inc., 1972-75; mem. 8th Norfolk Dist. Mass. House of Reps., 1975—79, mem. 7th Plymouth Dist., 1979—83; v.p. CMIS Corp., Vienna, Va., 1983; N.H. campaign mgr. for George H.W. Bush, 1987-88; spl. asst. to for inter-govtl. affairs The White House, 1983-87, dep. asst. to Pres., dir. Office of Intergovernmental Affairs Washington, 1988, asst. to Pres. & dep. chief of staff, 1989-92; sec. US Dept. Transp., Washington, 1992—93; pres., CEO American Automobile Mfrs. Assn. (AAMA), Washington, 1992—98; v.p. govt. relations General Motors Co., Washington, 1999—2000; chief of staff to Pres. The White House, Washington, 2000—06; acting dean George Bush Sch. Govt. & Pub. Svc., Tex. A&M U., 2011—. Head of task force federal relief effort Hurricane Andrew Southern Fla., 1992; bd. dirs. Union Pacific Corp. 2006-, Lorillard, Inc., 2011- Candidate for gov., Mass., 1982. Served in US Merchant Marines, 1965—67. Named one of The Nation's Outstanding Legislators, Nat. Republican Legislators' Assn., 1982; recipient Edward Brooke award, Mass. Republican Party, 2006 Republican. Office: Bush School Government & Public Service 4220 TAMU College Station College Station TX 77843 Office Phone: 979-862-8007.

CARD, ORSON SCOTT, writer; b. Richland, Wash., Aug. 24, 1951; s. Willard Richards and Peggy Jane (Park) Card; m. Kristine Allen, May 17, 1977; children: Michael Geoffrey, Emily Janice, Charles Benjamin(dec.), Zina Margaret, Erin Louisa(dec.). BA in Theater, Brigham Young U., Provo, Utah, 1975; MA in English, U. Utah, 1981. Editor Brigham Young U. Press, 1974-76; assoc. editor Ensign mag., Salt Lake City, 1976-78; columnist Sci. Fiction Rev., 1979—86; sr. editor Compute! Publs., Greensboro, NC, 1983; game design cons. Lucasfilm Games, 1989-92; disting. prof. Southern Va. U., Buena Vista, 2005—. Dir. workshop Lit. Boot Camp, 2001—. Author: (novels) A Planet Called Treason, 1978, Songmaster, 1979 (Hamilton-Brackett Meml. award, 1981), Hart's Hope, 1983, Saints, 1983 (Book of Yr., Assn. Mormon Lette, 1984), Wyrms, 1987, Lost Boys, 1992, Treasure Box, 1996, Pastwatch: The Redemption of Christopher Columbus, 1996, Stone Tables, 1997, Homebody, 1998, Enchantment, 1999, Magic Street, 2005, Invasive Procedures, 2007, Stonefather, 2008, (Ender saga) Ender's Game, 1985 (Hugo award, World Sci. Fiction Soc., 1986, Nebula award, Sci. Fiction & Fantasy Writers America, 1986), Speaker for the Dead, 1986 (Hugo award, World Sci. Fiction Soc., 1987, Nebula award, Sci. Fiction & Fantasy Writers America, 1987), Xenocide, 1991, Children of the Mind, 1996, A War of Gifts: An Ender Story, 2007, Ender in Exile, 2008, (Shadow saga) Ender's Shadow, 1999, Shadow of the Hegemon, 2001, Shadow Puppets, 2002, Shadow of the Giant, 2005, (Tales of Alvin Maker) Seventh Son, 1987 (Mythopoeic Fantasy award, 1988), Red Prophet, 1988, Prentice Alvin, 1989, Alvin Journeyman, 1995, Heartfire, 1998, The Crystal City, 2003, (Homecoming Saga) The Memory of Earth, 1992, The Call of Earth, 1992, The Ships of Earth, 1994, Earthfall, 1995, Earthborn, 1995, (Women of Genesis series) Sarah, 2000, Rebekah, 2001, Rachel and Leah, 2004, (Worthing series) Capitol, 1978, Hot Sleep, 1978, The Worthing Chronicle, 1983, The Worthing Saga, 1990, (Empire series) Empire, 2006, Hidden Empire, 2009, (short story collections) Unaccompanied Sonata and Other Stories, 1980, Cardography, 1987, The Folk of the Fringe, 1989, Maps in a Mirror: The Short Fiction of Orson Scott Card, 1990, Keeper of Dreams, 2008, (non fiction) Characters and Viewpoint, 1988, How to Write Science Fiction and Fantasy, 1990, published works under various pseudonyms including Frederick Bliss, P.Q. Gump, Byron Walley, Brian Green, Dinah Kirkham, Noam D. Pellume; editor: (anthologies) Dragons of Light, 1980, Dragons of Darkness, 1981, Future on Fire, 1991, Future on Ice, 1998, Masterpieces, 2001, The Phobos Science Fiction Anthology Volume 1, 2002, The Phobos Science Fiction Anthology Volume 2, 2003, Orson Scott Card's InterGalactic Medicine Show, 2008. Recipient John W. Campbell award for Best New Writer, World Sci. Fiction Conv., 1978, Margaret A. Edwards award for Lifetime Contbn. to Young Adult Lit., Young Adult Libr. Svcs. Assn., 2008, Lifetime Achievement award, Whitney awards, 2008. Mem.: Sci. Fiction Writers America, Authors Guild. Democrat. Mem. Lds Ch. Address: c/o Tor Books 175 5th Ave Fl 14 New York NY 10010-7703 also: Barbara Bova Lit Agy PO Box 770365 Naples FL 34107

CARDEMIL, CRISTINA, epidemiologist, pediatrician; MD, U. Pa.; MPH, Johns Hopkins U. Cert. Am. Bd. Pediat., 2010. Med. epidemiologist Ctrs. Disease Control and Prevention, Atlanta, 2010—; pediatrician Internat. Med. Ctr., Atlanta, 2012—14. Major USPHS, 2010—14, Atlanta. Fellow: Am. Acad. Pediat. Office: Ctrs Disease Control and Prevention 1600 Clifton Rd NE Atlanta GA 30329*

CARDEN, CHARLES BUFORD, advertising executive; b. Tulsa, Nov. 28, 1944; s. Buford Walkley and Marian Ruth (Beck) C.; m. Donna Marie Sandmaier, July 11, 1970; children: Kristin, Mark. BA in Math., Westminster Coll., Fulton, Mo., 1967; MBA, Harvard U., 1969. Exec. v.p., CFO Mariner Post-Acute Network; mem., fin. staff Ford Motor Co., Dearborn, Mich., 1971-81; dir., investor rels. Leaseway Transp. Corp., Beachwood, Ohio, 1981-82, v.p., treas., 1982-88, v.p., fin., 1988—92, CFO, 1989-92, sr. v.p., fin. and adminstrn., CFO, 1992; sr. v.p., CFO John H. Harland Co., 1999—2007. Former bd. dirs. Goldleaf Fin. Solutions (acquired by Jack Henry and Assocs.), Netzee (acquired by Certegy); bd. dirs. Ivox Corp.; bd. advisor Dialog Med.; bd. dirs. SuperMedia Inc. (formerly Idearc Inc.), 2010—. Trustee Fairmount Theater of the Deaf, Cleve., 1989, Bellflower Ctr. for Prevention of Child Abuse, 1992. 1st lt. U.S. Army, 1969-71, Vietnam. Lt. US Army, 1969—71. Mem. Fin. Execs. Inst., Nat. Assn. Corp. Treasurers, Chagrin Valley Country Club (Chagrin Falls, Ohio). Office: SuperMedia Inc 2200 W Airfield Dr Dallas TX 75261 Office Phone: 972-453-7000. Office Fax: 972-453-3969. Business E-Mail: charles.carden@supermedia.com.

CARDENAS, ALBERTO R., lawyer, lobbyist; b. Havana, Cuba, 1948; m. Diana Cardenas; 6 children. BS, Fla. Atlantic U., 1969; JD, Seton Hall U., 1974. Bar: Fla. 1974, US Supreme Ct. 1980, US Dist. Ct. (southern dist.) Fla. 1992. Ptnr., chair Advocacy and Govt. Affairs Group Tew Cardenas LLP, Miami, Tallahassee, Washington; chmn. The American Conservative Union, 2011—. Dir. Performing Arts Ctr.; trustee The Wolfsonian Found; policy coord. Office of the Pres.-Elect, US Dept. of Commerce, 1980—81; chmn. Presdl. Adv. Com. on Small & Minority Bus. Affairs, 1981—84; mem. adv. com. on internat. trade US Senate, 1985—86; bd. dirs. Fed. Nat. Mortgage Assn., 1985—90; mem. Pres. Bush's Commn. on Trade Policy, 1991—93; bd. dirs. Dade County Commrs., City of Miami; chmn. Fla. Rep. Party, 1999—2003; bd. trustees Fla. Agrl. & Mech. U. Named one of The 100 Most Influential Hispanics, Hispanic Bus., 2007, The

Legal Impact Leaders, South Fla. Bus. Leaders, 2008. Republican. Office: Tew Cardenas LLP Four Seasons Tower, 15th Fl 1441 Brickell Ave Miami FL 33131-3407 also: 700 12th St NW, Ste 1150 Washington DC 20005 also: The American Conservative Union 1331 H St NW Ste 500 Washington DC 20005-4735 Office Phone: 305-536-1112, 703-836-8602. Office Fax: 305-536-1116, 703-836-8606. E-mail: ac@tewlaw.com.

CARDENOSA, GILDA, diagnostic radiologist, educator; MD, Columbia U., 1984. Diplomate Am. Bd. Radiology-diagnostic radiology, 1984. Resident diagnostic radiology Mass. Gen. Hosp., Boston, 1985—89, fellow; prof. radiology Med. Coll. of Va.; dir. breast imaging Nelson Clinic; hosp. affiliations include Va. Commonwealth Univ. Med. Ctr. Office: Virginia Commonwealth University Medical Ctr Radiology Department 9000 Stony Point Pkwy Richmond VA 23235 Office Phone: 804-560-8906 ext. 7862. Office Fax: 804-237-6663. E-mail: gcardenosa@vcu.edu.

CARDMAN, LAWRENCE SANTO, physics professor, researcher; b. Mt. Vernon, NY, Oct. 7, 1944; s. Michael L. and Alice (Willis) C.; m. Helen-Andrea Fox; children: Andrew Lawrence, Michael Allan, Zena Maria. BA, Yale U., 1966, PhD in Physics, 1972. Instr. physics Yale U., New Haven, 1971—72, rsch. assoc., 1972; NAS/NRC postdoctoral fellow Nat. Bur. Stds., 1972—73; asst. prof. U. Ill., Urbana, 1973—78, assoc. prof., 1978—82, prof., 1982—95, adj. prof., 1995—, co-prin. investigator nuc. physics lab. Champaign, 1982—89, 1992; dep. assoc. dir. physics Continuous Electron Beam Accelerator Facility, Newport News, Va., 1993—96; assoc. dir. for physics Thomas Jefferson Nat. Accelerator Facility, Newport News, Va., 1996—; prof. U. Va., Charlottesville, 2002—. Vis. scientist Centre D'Etudes Nucleaire Saclay, France, 1980-81, Continuous Electron Beam Accelerator Facility, Newport News, Va., 1989-90; adj. prof. Coll. William and Mary, Williamsburg, Va., 1995—. Contbr. over 95 articles to profl. jours. Nat. Acad. Scis.-NRC Postdoctoral Rsch. fellow, 1972-73. Fellow Am. Phys. Soc.; mem. Sigma Xi. Avocations: woodworking, electronics, computers, cooking. Office: Jefferson Lab 12000 Jefferson Ave Newport News VA 23606 Office Phone: 757-269-7032. Business E-Mail: cardman@jlab.org.

CARDONE, KATHLEEN, federal judge; b. Medina, NY, Dec. 25, 1953; d. Vincent Dominic and Rose Elizabeth (Burgio) Cardone; m. Eduardo Ariel Rodriguez, June 20, 1980 (div.). Student, U. Barcelona, 1973, Andean Ctr., 1975; BA, SUNY-Binghamton, 1976; JD, St. Mary's Law Sch., San Antonio, 1979. Bar: Tex. 1979, US Dist. Ct. (WE dist.) Tex. Legal cons. YWCA Women's Resource Ctr., El Paso, 1981; sole practice El Paso, 1982—; judge Mcpl. Ct. No. 5, El Paso, 1983—, US Dist. Ct. (we. dist.) Tex., 2003—. Bd. dirs. YWCA, El Paso, 1981—, El Paso del Norte Credit Union, 1983; steering com. mem. El Paso Cmty. Devel., 1981; bd. dirs. El Paso Women's Employment and Edn., 1981. Mem.: ABA, Tex. Bar Assn. Roman Catholic. Office: 525 Magoffin Ave El Paso TX 79901

CARDOZO, ARLENE ROSSEN, writer; b. Mpls., Jan. 12, 1938; d. Ralph and Beatrice (Cohen) Rossen; m. Richard Nunez Cardozo, June 29, 1959; children: Miriam, Rachel, Rebecca. BA, U. Minn., 1958, MA, 1982, PhD, 1990. Founder dir. Writers Unlimited, Mpls., 1972—76, Woman at Home Workshops, Mpls., 1976—81; lectr. U. Minn. Summer Arts Study Ctr., 1981—85; artist-in-residence Split Rock Arts Ctr., Duluth, Minn., 1984—85; adj. prof. Dept. Mass Comm. U. Minn., 1990—97, Augsburg Coll., 1994—96, St. Cloud State U., 1994, U. Miami, 1998—2000; cons. Sequencing Mothers, manuscript and pub. industry. Author: The Liberated Cookbook, 1972, Woman at Home, 1976, Jewish Family Celebrations, 1982, Sequencing, 1986, 1989, 1996, Journey on the Home Front, 2011; editor: pub. The Read-Aloud Rev.; contbr. essays, articles, reviews; prodr.: (radio) Once Upon a Time; prodr.: (radio) guest appearances Today Show, Phil Donahue Show, Dr. Ruth Show, CBS News Nightwatch, Attitudes, radio and TV, US and Can., featured in NY Times, Washington Post, Mpls. Star Tribune, Redbook Mag. Founder, Harvard Neighbors, Cambridge, 1963—64. Vol. Mpls. Pub. Schs., 1972—82; pres. Rachel Liba Cardozo Children's Found., 1992—; dir. Brownstone Distbg. Mem.: Nat. Book Critics Circle, Authors League Am., Authors Guild, Hadassah (life), Nat. Press Club. Jewish. Home: 1007 Pine Tree Trl Stillwater MN 55082 also: 452 SW 28th Rd Miami FL 33129-2619 E-mail: arcardozo@att.net.

CARDOZO, RICHARD NUNEZ, marketing professional, educator, entrepreneur; b. Mpls., Feb. 13, 1936; s. William Nunez and Miriam (Honig) C.; m. Arlene Rossen, June 29, 1959; children: Miriam, Rachel (dec.), Rebecca. AB, Carleton Coll., 1956; MBA, Harvard U., 1959; PhD, U. Minn., 1964. Asst. prof. bus. adminstrn. Harvard U., 1964-67; assoc. prof. mktg. U. Minn., 1967-71, prof., 1971—2000, Curtis L. Carlson chair in entrepreneurial studies, 1987-2000, prof. entrepreneurial studies, strategic mgmt., 2000—02, prof. emeritus, 2002—; dir. Ctr. for Exptl. Studies in Bus., 1969-73, chmn. dept. mktg., 1975-78; dir. Case Devel. Ctr., 1980-2000, Entrepreneurial Studies Ctr., 1987-2000. Dir. Nat. Presto Industries, Brownstone Distbg., Valspar Corp., 1976-96, Best Buy Co., 1985-92; Fulbright lectr. Hebrew U., Jerusalem, 1980; vis. prof. bus. adminstrn. Harvard U., Grad. Sch. Bus., 1982-83; adj. prof. U. Miami, 2003-07; cons. in field; mem. editl. bd. Jour. Mktg., 1976-93, Jour. Mktg. Rsch., 1976-82, Jour. Bus. Venturing, 1987-2002. Author: Product Policy: Cases and Concepts, 1979; co-author: (with others) Problems in Marketing, 4th edit, 1968, New Product Forecasting, 1981, Business Financing, 1999; contbr. articles to profl. jours. Dir. Kids, Inc., 1971—76, Rachel Cardozo Children's Found., 1992—. Fellow, Ford Found., Kaiser, 1961—63; Fulbright fellow, London Sch. Econ., 1956—57. Mem. Am. Mktg. Assn. (entrepreneurship rsch. award 2006), AAAS, Product Devel. and Mgmt. Assn., Acad. Mgmt. Jewish. Avocations: music, kayaking. Home: 452 SW 28th Rd Miami FL 33129-2619 Personal E-mail: dickcardozo@att.net.

CARDWELL, SUE POOLE, reclamation services company executive; b. Oct. 31, 1952; d. Robert Thomas Poole and Alice Katz Jost, Mary B. (Edwards) (stepmother) and Patricia Alice (Coleman) (stepmother) P.; m. Charles Howard Cardwell, Nov. 24, 1979; children: Jonathon Aaron, Jacqueline Leigh. Student, Western Ky. U., Bowling Green; BA, Transylvania U., Lexington, Ky., 1973; M in Constrn. Mgmt., Eastern U. Cert. level I and level II concrete technician, constrn. inspector. Clk.-typist Ky. Dept. Mines and Minerals, 1974; sr. reclamation insp. divsn. reclamation Ky. Dept. Natural Resources, Madisonville, 1974-77; pres. Reclamation Svcs. Unltd., Inc., Central City, Ky., 1977—. Chmn. West Ky. adv. group Office Surface Mining, Dept. Interior, 1979-84; adv. bd. U. Ky. Symposium on Surface Mining Reclamation and Hydrology, also mem. exec. adv. com.; mem. exec. bd. Ky. Task Force on Exploited and Missing Children; bd. dirs., sec. Ky. Alliance for Missing and Exploited Children; mem. Rep. Senatorial Inner Circle, 1984-94, Am. Concrete Inst. Contbg. editor Ky. Coal Jour. With WAC, 1972-73. Recipient Nat. Collegiate Engring. award, US Achievemnt Acad., 2003; named hon. Ky. Col.; named to W.Va. Ship of State. Mem. Ky. Ready Mix Assn. (mem. quality assurance/quality control com.), W.Va. Surface Mine Assn., Am. Concrete Inst., ASCE, Internat. Code Coun., Am. Concrete Inst., Internat. Bldg. Code Coun., Internat. Bldg. Code Group. Office: 701 Temple St Central City KY 42330-2130 Office Phone: 270-754-3976. Business E-Mail: scardwel@muhlon.com.

CAREK, DONALD J(OHN), child psychiatry educator; b. Sheboygan, Wis., Aug. 10, 1931; s. Peter and Rose (Gergisch) C.; m. Frances M. Schaefer, Jan. 28, 1956; children: Carla, Thomas, Therese, Peter, Mary Beth, Christopher MD, Marquette U., 1956. Diplomate Am. Bd. Psychiatry and Neurology (examiner in child psychiatry, psychiatry). Intern Walter Reed Army Hosp., 1956-57; resident U. Mich. Hosps., 1959-63; pediatrician Fort Meyer Dispensary, Arlington, Va., 1958-59; instr. psychiatry U. Mich., Ann Arbor, 1962-65, asst. prof., 1965-66; dir. day care Children's Psychiat. Hosp., Ann Arbor, 1965-66; assoc. prof. psychiatry and pediatrics Med. Coll. Wis., Milw., 1966-74, acting chmn. div. human behavior, 1970-73, prof. psychiatry, 1974-76; pres. med. staff Milw. Psychiat. Hosp., 1971-73; prof. psychiatry and pediatrics, chief youth divsn. Med. U. S.C., Charleston, 1976-96, emeritus prof. psychiatry, 1996—; staff psychiatrist Vols. in Medicine, Hilton Head, SC, 2004—. Co-author: Guide to Psychotherapy, 1966; author: Principles of Child Psychotherapy, 1972; mem. editorial bd. Am. Jour. Child & Adolscent Psychiatry, 1988-93; contbr. articles to profl. jours. Bd. dirs. Cedarcrest Girls Residential Treatment Ctr., 1969-71. Capt. USAR, 1956-59. Named Best Doctors in America Southeast Region, 1995. Fellow Am. Acad. Child Psychiatry (life, com. on adolscent psychiatry 1979-85, com. on psychotherapy 1986-90), Am. Psychiat. Assn., Am. Coll. Psychiatrists (membership com. 1991-98); mem. AMA, AAAS, Am. Orthopsychiatry Assn., Am. Psychosomatic Soc., Soc. Profs. Child Psychiatry, S.C. Med. Assn. (mental health com. 1992-93), S.C. Dist. Cr. Am. Psychiat. Assn., Charleston County Med. Soc., S.C. State Bd. Med. Examiners (med. disciplinary commn. 1992-95), Alpha Omega Alpha, Alpha Sigma Nu. Roman Catholic. Home: 97 Nightingale Ln Bluffton SC 29909 Office: Med Univ SC 171 Ashley Ave Charleston SC 29425-0001 Home Phone: 843-705-7343; Office Phone: 843-792-2436. Personal E-mail: dcarek@sc.rr.com.

CAREY, ALBERT P., food products executive; Grad., U. Md. With Procter & Gamble Co.; various positions with Del Monte and Frito Lay N.Am. PepsiCo, Inc., 1981—98, sr. v.p., sales and retailer strategies, 1998—2002; COO PepsiCo Beverages and Foods, 2002—03; v.p., sales PepsiCo, N.Am., 2002—03; pres., sales PepsiCo, Inc., 2003—06; COO Frito-Lay North America, Inc. (subs. of PepsiCo, Inc.), pres., CEO, 2006—12; CEO Americas Beverages PepsiCo, Inc., 2011—. Bd. dirs. The Home Depot, Inc., 2008—. Office: Frito-Lay North America Inc 7701 Legacy Dr Plano TX 75024 Office Phone: 972-334-7000. Office Fax: 972-334-2019. Business E-Mail: albert.carey@pepsico.com.

CAREY, GERALD JOHN, JR., research institute director emeritus, former air force officer; b. Bklyn., Oct. 1, 1930; s. Gerald John and Madeline (McNamara) C.; m. Joan Bennett, Apr. 24, 1954; children: Gerald John, III, Cathleen, John Kevin, Daniel. BS, U.S. Mil. Acad., 1952; MS in Aero. Engring, Tex. A&M U., 1961. Commd. 2d lt. USAF, 1952, advanced through grades to maj. gen., 1978; pilot trainee Victoria, Tex., 1953; flight instr. Laredo, Tex., 1954-56; asst. air attache Tokyo, 1958-61; aero. engr. Air Force Systems Command, Andrews AFB, Md., 1963-66; flight comdr. Seymour Johnson AFB, 1967; ops. officer Udorn, Thailand, 1969-70; wing comdr. 1st and 56th Tactical Fighter Wings, Tampa, Fla., 1973-75; asst. dep. chief of staff ops. Tactical Air Command Hdqrs., Langley AFB, Va., 1975-78; comdr. USAF Tactical Air Warfare Center, Eglin AFB, Fla., 1978-81; ret., 1981; emeritus assoc. dir. Rsch. Inst. Ga. Inst. Tech., Atlanta, 1981—. Mem. USAF Sci. Adv. Bd., 1995. Decorated Legion of Merit, D.S.M., D.F.C. with 2 oak leaf clusters. Mem. Air Forces Assn., Daedalians, Tau Beta Pi, Sigma Gamma Tau. Office: Ga Inst Tech Rsch Inst Atlanta GA 30332-0001 Personal E-mail: gjcarey@comast.net.

CAREY, MATTHEW, consumer products company executive; Mgmt. positions through sr. v.p., chief technology officer Wal-Mart, 1985—2006; chief tech. officer eBay Marketplaces through sr. v.p., chief tech. officer eBay, 2006—08; exec. v.p., CIO Home Depot, Inc., Atlanta, 2008—. Mem. adv. bd. Hewlett-Packard, Dell Computers, IBM. Office: The Home Depot 2455 Paces Ferry Rd NW Atlanta GA 30339-4024 Office Phone: 770-384-4488.

CAREY, ROBERT MUNSON, physician, educator; b. Lexington, Ky., Aug. 13, 1940; s. Henry Ames and Eleanor Day (Munson) C.; m. Theodora Vann Hereford, Aug. 24, 1963; children: Adonice Ames, Alicia Vann, Robert Josiah Hereford. BS, U. Ky., 1962; MD, Vanderbilt U., 1965; Doctor Honoris Causa, Fed. U. Ceara, Brazil, 1998. Diplomate Am. Bd. Internal Medicine, Am. Bd. Endocrinology and Metabolism, Nat. Bd. Med. Examiners. Intern in medicine U. Va. Hosp., Charlottesville, 1966; jr. asst. resident in medicine N.Y. Hosp.-Cornell Med. Ctr., NYC, 1968-69, sr. asst. resident, 1969-70; instr. endocrinology, dept. medicine Vanderbilt U. Sch. Medicine, Nashville, 1970-72; postdoctoral fellow in medicine St. Mary's Hosp. Med. Sch., London, 1972-73; asst. prof. internal medicine, endocrinology and metabolism U. Va. Sch. Medicine, Charlottesville, 1973-76, assoc. prof., 1976-80, prof., 1980—, James Carroll Flippin prof. medical sci. and dean, 1986—2002, prof. u., 2002—, David A. Harrison III disting. prof. medicine, 2002—, assoc. dir. Clin. Rsch. Ctr., 1975-86, prof., dean emeritus, 2002—, head. div. endocrinology and metabolism, dept. internal medicine, 1978-86, chmn. gen. faculty, chmn. med. adv. com., chmn. exec. com., 1986—. Attending staff U. Va. Hosp., Charlottesville, 1973—, pres. clin. staff, 1977-79, vice chmn. med. policy com., 1986—, adv. bd. 1986—; mem. study sect. on exptl. cardiovascular scis. NIH, 1982-85; mem. cardiovascular and renal adv. com. USDA, 1988—; vis. prof. div. nephrology, U. Miami Med. Sch., Fla., 1979, 83, 84, Hosp. das Clinicas da Univ., Fed. do Ceara, Forteleza, Brazil, 1981, hypertension div. Mt. Sinai Sch. Medicine, N.Y.C., 1981, div. pediatric endocrinology N.Y. Hosp.-Cornell Med. Ctr., 1981, dept. endocrinology St. Vincent's Hosp., Univ. Coll., Dublin, Ireland, 1982, depts. physiology and endocrinology Mayo Grad. Sch. Medicine, Rochester, Minn., 1984, div. rsch. Cleve. Clinic Found., 1984, Genentech, Inc., San Francisco, 1984, divs. endocrinology and metabolism U. Mass., U. Pa. Sch. Medicine, Boston U. Med. Sch., 1984, U. N.C. Sch. Medicine, 1985, Harvard Med. Sch., Boston, 1987, Jefferson Med. Coll., 1988; Bley Stein vis. prof. endocrinology U. So. Calif., 1987; Pfizer vis. prof. in pharmacology U. Chgo., 1988; co-organizer 3d Internat. Meeting on Peripheral Actions of Dopamine, Charlottesville, 1989; v.p. Va. Ambulatory Surgery, Inc., 1986—; speaker, presenter numerous nat. and internat. profl. meetings and congresses. Author: (with E.D. Vaughn) Adrenal Disorders, 1988; co-editor: Hypertension: An Endocrine Disease, 1985; mem. editorial bd. Jour. Clin. Endocrinology and Metabolism, 1981-84, Hypertension jour., 1983-84, 2002-08, Am. Jour. Physiology: Heart and Circulatory Physiology, 1987-89, Am. Jour. Hypertension, 1987—; author over 300 articles, revs., papers for profl. jours., contbr. 19 chpts. to books. Mem. exec. com. and fin. com. U. Va. Health Services Found., 1986—; bd. dirs. Va. Kidney Stone Found., Inc., 1986—, The Harrison Found., Inc. U. Va., 1986—, Dyslexia Ctr., Charlottesville, 1986—. Surgeon (lt. comdr.) USPHS, 1966-68, res., 1968—. Recipient Attending Physician of Yr. awrd dept. internal medicine U. Va. Med. Ctr., 1983-84, Disting. Alumnus award and Founder's medal Vanderbilt U.; USPHS fellow Vanderbilt U., 1970-72; recipient numerous NIH grants as co-prin. and prin. investigator, 1972—, Thomas Jefferson award, U. Va., 2003; named to Hall Disting. Alumni, U. Ky., 2000. Master ACP (program com. regional meeting 1987); fellow Coun. for High Blood Pressure Rsch. AHA (program com. 1984-86, exec. and long rang planning coms. 1992—; chair-elect 2002-04, chair 2004-06, past chair 2004-08); mem. Inst. Medicine of NAS, Am. Heart Assn. (established investigator 1975-80, chair, coun. ops. com., 2006-08), Va. affiliate Am. Heart Assn. (bd. dirs. 1977-83, pres. 1979-80, Disting. Service award), The Endocrine Soc. (fin. com. 1988—, chair devel. com. 1991-92, pres. elect 2007-08, pres. 2008-), Am. Fedn. Clin. Rsch. (so. sect. councilor 1978-81, nominating com. 1982), So. Soc. Clin. Investigation (nominating com. 1982, sec.-treas. 1985-86), Inter-Am. Soc. for Hypertension, Am. Soc. Clin. Investigation, Am. Clin. and Climatol. Assn., Am. Soc. Hypertension (intersocietal affairs com. 1986—), Internat. Soc. Hypertension, Assn. Am. Physicians, AMA, Albemarle County Med. Soc., Med. Soc. Va., Assn. Am. Med. Colls Coun. of Deans, Inst. of Medicine, Nat. Acad. of Scis., The Raven Soc., Alpha Omega Alpha (Disting. Med. Alumnus award Vanderbilt U. 1994). Home: 2805 Magnolia Dr Charlottesville VA 22901 Office: U Va Sch Medicine PO Box 801414 Charlottesville VA 22908-1414

CARGILL, JENNIFER S., library director, educator; MLS, La. State U. Dean librs., prof. libr. and info. scis. La. State U. Coun. mem. Online Computer Libr. Ctr.; chair mems. coun. del. Southeastern Libr. Network. Contbr. articles to profl. jours. Mem.: ALA (adv. com. Am. Librs. online 2006—08, mem. com. on accreditation), Assn. Southeastern Rsch. Librs. (bd. dirs.). Office: La State U Librs Baton Rouge LA 70803 Office Phone: 225-578-2217. E-mail: cargill@lsu.edu.

CARGILL, ROBERT MASON, lawyer; b. Atlanta, Nov. 15, 1948; s. George Slade Jr., and Emma Elizabeth (Matthews) C.; m. Sharon McEver, June 12, 1971; children: Ansley Lauren, Kristin Lucille. BS summa cum laude, Ga. Inst. Tech., 1970; JD magna cum laude, Harvard U., 1973. Bar: Ga. 1973, D.C. 1975. Assoc. atty. Hansell & Post, Atlanta, 1976-81, ptnr., 1981-89, Jones Day, Atlanta, 1989—. Lt. USNR 1973-76. Mem. Swedish Am. C. of C. Atlanta (bd. dirs.), Swiss Am. C. of C. (bd. dirs.), Cherokee Town Country Club. Methodist. Avocations: tennis, travel. Home: 230 Colewood Way NW Atlanta GA 30328-2923 Office: Jones Day Ste 800 1420 Peachtree St NE Atlanta GA 30309 Home Phone: 404-252-6869; Office Phone: 404-581-8909. Business E-Mail: rcargill@jonesday.com.

CARIUS, ROBERT WILHELM, mathematics professor, retired military officer; b. Peoria, Ill., Jan. 4, 1929; s. Henry Clarence and Mary Magdalen (Wilhelm) C.; m. Geraldine Mary Sullivan, Mar. 16, 1957; children: Patricia, Mary, Linda, Robert, Daniel, Sara. BS in Naval Sci, U.S. Naval Acad., 1951; BS in Aero. Engring, U.S. Naval Postgrad. Sch., 1958; MS in Nuclear Engring, Iowa State Coll., 1959. Commd. ensign USN, 1951, advanced through grades to rear adm., 1977, served with Fighter Squadron 74, 1953-56, served with U.S.S. Bennington, 1959-61, project mgr. U.S. AEC, 1964-65, served with Air Anti-Submarine Squadron 33, 1962-63, command officer Air Anti-Submarine Squardon 29, 1966-68, exec. officer U.S.S. Princeton, 1968-70, R & D br. head Dept. Navy, 1970-71, command officer U.S.S. New Orleans San Diego, 1971-73, mem. staff Anti-Submarine Wing Pacific, 1973-77, comdr. Anti-Submarine Wings Atlantic, Naval Air Sta. Jacksonville, Fla., 1977-79, with aviation programs Dept. Navy, from 1979; instr. physics Ark. Coll., Batesville, 1983-85, asst. prof. physics, 1986—. Bd. govs. USO, Jacksonville. Mem. exec. bd. United Way of Jacksonville, N.E. Fla. coun. Boy Scouts Am.; pres. Independence County United Way. Decorated Legion of Merit, Air medal, Meritorious Service medal; recipient Spl. award United Way of Jacksonville, 1979 Mem. U.S. Naval Acad. Alumni Assn., Assn. Naval Aviation, Ret. Officers Assn., Ark. Hist. Soc., Batesville Symphony Assn., Naval Helicopter Assn., U.S. Naval Inst., Jacksonville C. of C. (gov.) Clubs: Rotary. Roman Catholic. Home: 2630 Antioch Rd Cave City AR 72521-9249 Office: Lyon Coll Batesville AR 72501

CARL, PARKER LOREN, US marshal; b. 1950; Gen. bus. cert. Ky. Bus. Coll., 1971. Mgr. Ky. Fin. Co., 1973—77; dep. sheriff Woodford County Police Dep., Ky., 1978—79, detective Ky., 1980—85, sheriff Ky., 1986—96, chief of police Ky., 2003—04; dir. fin. integrity enforcement divsn. Office Ky. Atty. Gen., 1996—2003; dist. coord. for Rep. Ben Chandler US House of Representatives, 2004—10; US marshal (ea. dist.) Ky. US Dept. Justice, 2010—. Svc. with USAF, 1969—71. Office: US Marshal Federal Bldg Barr & Limestone St Rm 162 Lexington KY 40507 Office Phone: 859-233-2513.

CARLE, MATT, professional hockey player; b. Anchorage, Sept. 25, 1984; m. Clancey Kabella, 2010. Defenseman U. Denver Pioneers, 2003—06, San Jose Sharks, 2006—08, Tampa Bay Lightning, 2008, 2012—, Phila. Flyers, 2008—12. Recipient Hobey Baker Meml. Award, 2006; named NCAA Defenseman of Yr., Inside College Hockey.com. Achievements include being a member of NCAA National Championship Team, U. Denver, 2004, 2005. Avocations: hiking, fishing. Office: Tampa Bay Lightning Hockey Club St Pete Times Forum 401 Channelside Dr Tampa FL 33602

CARLETON, DON EDWARD, academic administrator, writer; b. Dallas, Jan. 22, 1947; s. Edward Preston and Wilma Jo (Smith) C.; m. Suzanne Marie Young, Jan. 2, 1974; children: Ian Alexander, Aunna Fleur. BS, U. Houston, 1969, MA, 1974, PhD, 1978. Tchr. Friendswood Ind. Sch. Dist., Tex., 1969-71; teaching fellow U. Houston, 1971-75; research asst. Southwest Ctr. for Urban Research, Houston, 1974-75; dir. Houston Met. Research Ctr., 1975-79, Barker History Ctr., Austin, 1979-91, Briscoe Ctr. for am. History, U. Tex., Austin, 1991—. Urban adv. editor Handbook of Tex., Austin, 1983—95; sr. lectr. dept. history U. Tex., Austin, 1985—, dept. journalism, 1997—; J.R. Parten chair in Archives Am. History, 1989—; cons. Amon Carter Mus., Ft. Worth, 1983, Birmingham (Ala.) Pub. Libr., 1978, Nat. Archives Romania, 1998, 1999, Brooklands New Media, Ltd., England, 2005—06, Houston Endowment, 2010. Editorial bd. Southwestern Hist. Quar., 1980-90; author: Who Shot the Bear?, 1984, Red Scare!, 1985, (Coral Tullis best book award Tex. Hist. Assn. 1986), A Breed So Rare: The Life of J.R. Parten, Liberal Texas Oilman, 1896-1992, 1998 (Tex. Inst. Letters Book award 1998), Being Rapoport: Capitalist With a Conscience, 2002; editor: UT Press, Focus on America Series, 1999-; oral hist., mem. bd. advs. Pioneers of Television Project, Acad. Television Arts and Scis., L.A., 1998-, Dolph Briscoe: My Life in Texas Ranching and Politics, 2008, Ross Sterling: Texan, 2007, Conversations with Cronkite, 2010, Big Red Memoirs of A Tex. Entrepreneur & Philanthropist, 2011, DEnton A. Cooley 100,000 Hearts: A Surgeons Memoir, 2012; contbr. articles to profl. jours. Recipient Presdl. Excellence award, U. Tex., Austin, 1982; grantee, Parten Found., 1982, O'Connor Found., 1982. Fellow: Tex. State Hist. Assn. (grantee 1983); mem.: Philos. Soc. Tex., Tex. Inst. Letters, Headliners Club Austin. Democrat. Avocations: reading, travel. Office Phone: 512-495-4527. Business E-Mail: d.carleton@austin.utexas.edu.

CARLISLE, ERVIN FREDERICK, university provost, educator; b. Delaware, Ohio, Mar. 20, 1935; s. Ervin Frederick C. and Winnifred (Lucas) Pope; children: Lindy, Rebecca, Ginna, Jana; m. Barbara, Sept. 28, 1973. BA, Ohio Wesleyan U., 1956; MA, Ohio State U., 1957; PhD, Ind. U., 1963. Mem. faculty Ohio U., Athens, 1962-63, DePauw U., Greencastle, Ind., 1963-66; asst. prof. dept. English Mich. State U., East Lansing, 1966-68, assoc. prof., assoc. chmn. dept. English, 1968-72, prof., 1972-79, chmn. dept. English, 1979-81, asst.

to pres., 1981-85; provost, exec. v.p. for acad. affairs Miami U., Oxford, Ohio, 1985-89; sr. v.p., provost Va. Poly. Inst. and State U., Blacksburg, 1989-94, William E. Lavery prof., 1995-2000, William E. Lavery prof., sr. v.p. and provost emeritus, 2000—; mem. bd. visitors Zayed U., United Arab Emirates, 2001—. Author: The Uncertain Self, 1973, Loren Eiseley, 1983, Searching for Ervin, 2006, Heartbreak Waltz, 2007, 09; editor: American Poetry and Prose, 1970. Served to 1st lt. USAF, 1957-60. NEH fellow, 1972-73; NEH grantee, 1978, 80 Home: 1227 N Lakeside Dr Lake Worth FL 33460 E-mail: efredcarlisle@bellsouth.net.

CARLISLE, RICK (RICHARD PRESTON CARLISLE), professional basketball coach, retired professional basketball player; b. Ogdensburg, NY, Oct. 27, 1959; m. Donna Carlisle; 1 child, Abigail Claire. Student, U. Maine; BA in Psych., U. Va., 1984. Profl. basketball player Boston Celtics, 1984—87, NY Knicks, 1987—88, NJ Nets, 1989, asst. coach, 1989—94, Portland Trail Blazers, 1994—97, Ind. Pacers, 1997—2000; head coach Detroit Pistons, 2001—03, Ind. Pacers, 2003—07, exec. v.p. basketball ops., 2006—07; head coach Dallas Mavericks, 2008—. Named Coach of Yr., NBA, 2002. Achievements include member of the NBA Finals Championship winning a Boston Celtics, 1986; head coach of the NBA Finals Championship winning Dallas Mavericks, 2011. Avocations: golf, piano. Office: Dallas Mavericks 2500 Victory Ave Dallas TX 75219

CARLOCK, JOHN BRUCE, JR., retired language educator; b. Pitts., Sept. 21, 1925; s. John Bruce and Sydney Jane (Whiteside) C.; m. Ruth Olive McCardle, Oct. 19, 1948; children: Elizabeth Kehl, Rebecca Riley, John Bruce III, David Matthew (dec.). BA, Wesleyan U., 1951; PhD, U. S.C., 1973. Prof. English, Erskine Coll., Due West, SC, 1973—2008, chmn. dept. English. Dir. theatre studies Erskine Coll., Due West, 1973-91. Editor: (jour.) Voice of Sanity, 1988—. Bd. dirs. Upstate S.C. chpt. ACLU, Abbeville (S.C.) Opera House, pres., 1995-96. Served USAF, 1943—46, Maj. USAF, 1951—69, Vietnam. Decorated Bronze Star USAF, Air Force Commendation medal. Mem. MLA, Beta Theta Pi. Democrat. Avocations: reading, writing, speaking, orcharding. Home: Burning Tree Farm 247 Arborville Rd Donalds SC 29638

CARLOCK, MARGO, museum association administrator; BA, MA, Southern Ill. U., Carbondale; MBA prog., U. Chgo. Student worker Southern Ill. U. Mus., 1971—74; adminstrn. intern Lincoln's New Salem Hist. Park, 1977; asst. to dir., Internat. Mktg. Divsn. Mo. Dept. Agr., 1978—81; first scholar mgmt. trainee First Nat. Bank of Chgo., 1981—82; fgn. svc. officer US Dept. State, 1982—87; cons. Mo. Dept. Edn., 1989; project dir. Mo. Divsn. Med. Svcs., 1989; asst. to dir. Mo. Divsn. Aging, 1989—93; dir. comm. Missourians for Higher Edn., 1991; exec. dir. Va. Assn. Museums, 1994—. Office: Va Assn Museums 200 S Third St Richmond VA 23219 Business E-Mail: mcarlock@vamuseums.org.

CARLSON, DAVID EMIL, physicist, researcher; b. Weymouth, Mass., Mar. 5, 1942; s. Emil Algot and Anne Alice (Salomaa) C.; m. Mary Ann Lewinski, June, 1966; children: Eric, Darcey. BS in Physics, Rensselaer Poly. Inst., 1963; PhD in Physics, Rutgers U., 1968. Research scientist U.S. Army Nuclear Effects Lab., Edgewood Arsenal, Md., 1968-69; head photovoltaic device research RCA Labs., Princeton, NJ, 1970-83; dep. gen. mgr., dir. research Solarex Thin Film Div., Newtown, Pa., 1983-86, gen. mgr., 1986-88, v.p., 1988-98; chief scientist BP Solar, 1999—. Contbr. articles to profl. jours.; patentee in field. Served to capt. Signal Corps U.S. Army, 1968-70, Vietnam. Decorated Bronze Star medal; recipient Ross Coffin Purdy award Am. Ceramic Soc., 1976, Outstanding Achievement award RCA Labs., 1973, 76, Walton Clark medal Franklin Inst., 1986, Karl W. Boer Solar Energy medal of merit U. Del. and Internat. Solar Energy Soc., 1995. Fellow IEEE (co-recipient Morris N. Liebmann award 1984, William R. Cherry award 1988); mem. Am. Phys. Soc., Am. Vacuum Soc., Sigma Xi. Achievements include inventor amorphous silicon solar cell, 1974. Home: 217 Yorkshire Dr Williamsburg VA 23185-3912 Office: BP Solar 630 Solarex Ct Frederick MD 21703 Office Phone: 301-698-4256. Business E-Mail: dave.carlson@bp.com.

CARLSON, DAVID HAROLD, library director, dean; b. New Haven, May 27, 1954; s. Harold E. and Marion R. (Bennett) C.; m. Sherry A. Murray, June 5, 1976; children: Karen A., Alison M. BA, U. Conn., 1977; MLS, U. Mich., 1979; MS, U. Evansville, 1983. Bibl. instr. libr. U. Evansville, Ind., 1979-84; systems analyst libr. U. RI, Kingston, 1984-87; dir. libr. systems U. Louisville, 1987-91; exec. dir. Triangle Rsch. Librs. Network, Chapel Hill, NC, 1991—94; dir. librs. Bridgewater State Coll., Mass., 1994—2001, acting asst. v.p. acad. info. resources Mass., 1995—97; prof., dean libr. affairs So. Ill. U., Carbondale, 2001—12; dean, Sterling C. Evans endowed chair in libr. adminstrn. Tex. A&M U. Libraries, 2012—. Chmn. Scholarly Pub. and Academic Resources Coun., 2009—12; bd. dirs. Ill. Libr. Assn., 2011—12; presenter in field. Contbr. articles to profl. jours. Named Ill. Academic Libr. of Yr., Ill. Assn. Coll. and Rsch. Libraries, 2010. Mem. ALA, Assn. Coll. and Rsch. Librs., Libr. and Info. Tech. Assn., Electronic Frontier Found. Office: Texas A&M University Provost and Executive Vice President 1248 TAMU College Station TX 77843-1248 Business E-Mail: davidhcarlson@tamu.edu.

CARLSON, GARY E., finance company executive; Grad., Western Mich. U., Kalamazoo, 1974. Cost acct. Sundstrand Data Control, Redmond, Wash., 1978—81; sr. cost acct. Advanced Tech. Lab, Bothell, Wash., 1981—83; gen. mgr. First Am. Mortgage, Kirkland, Wash., 1983—86; pres. Eagle Home Mortgage, Inc., 1986—, Colony Escrow, Inc., Bellevue, Wash., 1986—; v.p. Second Mortgage Sources, Inc., Bellevue, Wash., 1990—. Office: Lennar Corp 700 NW 107th Ave Miami FL 33172 Office Phone: 305-559-4000. Office Fax: 305-226-4158. Business E-Mail: carlsog@eagle-home.com.

CARLSON, GEORGE THEODORE, physics professor; b. Mitchel Field, NY, Dec. 16, 1951; s. Calva Laura Carlson. BS in Physics, Lowell Technol. Inst., Mass., 1974; MS in Physics, U. SC, Columbia, 1979; PhD in Physics, U. SC, 1979. Vis. asst. prof. physics U. Cin., 1979—80; asst. prof. physics W.Va. Inst. Tech., Montgomery, 1980—83, prof. physics, 1988—; asst. prof. physics State U. Coll., Buffalo, 1984—85, Fredonia, NY, 1986—87. Contbr. articles to profl. jours. Mem.: Am. Assn. Physics Tchrs. Home: 201 Hillside Dr Nitro WV 25143 Office: WVa Inst Tech 405 Fayette Pike Montgomery WV 25136 Business E-Mail: george.carlson@mail.wvu.edu.

CARLSON, JAMES G., healthcare services executive; Grad., Rider Univ. Mgmt. positions through pres. wc. group ops. Prudential Ins. Co.; CEO Workscape Inc.; exec. v.p., pres. United Healthcare UnitedHealth Group, Inc.; pres., COO Amerigroup Corp., Virginia Beach, Va., 2003—07, pres., CEO, 2007—08, chmn., pres., CEO, 2008—. Bd. dir. Nat. Kidney Found.; bd. mem. Va. Aquarium & Marine Sci. Ctr., Va. Beach Neptune Festival; mem. health sector adv. bd. Fuqua Sch. Bus. Duke Univ. Office: Amerigroup Corp 4425 Corp Ln Virginia Beach VA 23462

CARLSON, MARSHALL, professional sports team executive; m. Lynn Carlson; children: Kate, Hendrick. BSBA, U. NC, Chapel Hill, 1996. Team engr. NASCAR SuperTruck Series Hendrick Motorsports, 1996—98, dir. mktg. services, 1998—2000, project mgr., 2000—02, v.p. corp. fin. mgmt., 2002—04, exec. v.p., gen. mgr., 2005—. Named one of Forty Under 40, Street & Smith's SportsBus. Jour., 2009. Office: Hendrick Motorsports 4400 Papa Joe Hendrick Blvd Charlotte NC 28262

CARLSON, ROBERT CHARLES, financial planner, writer; BS in Fin. Mgmt. with high honor, Clemson U., 1979; MS in Acctg., U. Va., 1982, JD, 1982. CPA Md.; bar: DC 1982. Law clk. US Dept. Justice, Washington, 1982, US Dept. Edn., Washington, 1982-83; editor Tax Savs. Report, Balt., 1983-85, Fin. Independence, Balt., 1983-85, Tax Wise Money (formerly Tax Avoidance Digest), Balt., 1985—97, Bob Carlson's Retirement Watch, 1991—; prin. R.C. Carlson Adv., Fairfax, Va., 1988-94; pres. Ctr. for Retirement Security, Inc., Fairfax, 1992—; mng. mem. Carlson Wealth Advisors, LLC. Mem. Va. Fiscal Alternative Commn., Richmond, 1989-91; trustee Fairfax County, Va. Employees' Retirement System, 1992—, chmn. 1995—; commr., Fairfax County Housing and Redevel. Authority, 2008-; defined contribution plan adv. com. Va. Ret. Sys., 2011-; trustee Va. Retirement Sys., 2000-05 Author: Tax Savings Through Short-Term Trusts, 1985, 199 Loopholes That Survived Tax Reform, 1987, How to Handle and Win a Federal Tax Appeal, 1988, Retirement Tax Guide, 1989, rev. 4th edit. 1994, How to Slash Your Mutual Fund Taxes, 1990, 2d rev. edit. 1991, Tax Wise Money Strategies, 1995, Estate Planning Strategies, 2d edit., 1998, New Rules of Estate Planning, 2003, New Rules of Retirement, 2005, Invest Like a Fox...Not Like a Hedgehog, 2007, (with Eric Tyson) Personal Finance For Srs. For Dummies, 2010. Treas. Friends Michel Frey, 2011-, 10th Dist. Rep. Com., Fairfax, 1988-92; treas. No. Va. Rep. Bus. Forum, Alexandria, 1990—, Atoka Country Supper Com., Springfield, Va., 1989-92; chmn. Fairfax Area Young Reps., Annandale, Va., 1989-91; treas. Wahlquist for Senate, 1988-94, Butler for Congress, 1992-94; chmn. Sully Dist. Rep. Com., Fairfax County, Va., 2004—10, defined contribution plan adv. com. Va. Retirement Sys., 2011 Named one of Outstanding Young Men of Am., U.S. Jaycees, 1983. Mem. DC Bar Assn., Conservative Club, Sully Dist. Rep. Com. (chmn., 2004-10), Phi Kappa Phi, Phi Gamma Sigma. Home: PO Box 222070 Chantilly VA 20153-2070

CARLSON, ROBERT MARSHALL, health facility administrator; b. Jamestown, NY, Oct. 6, 1950; s. Marshall Lawrence and Alice (Christine) C.; m. Robin Shankey, May 29, 1987; children: Todd Marshall, Scott Thomas. BS, Bowling Green State U., Ohio, 1972; postgrad. in pub. health, U. Utah, 1972; ME in Health Edn., U. Toledo, 1977. Planning analyst, then found. dir. Riverside Hosp., Toledo, 1975-78; hosp. planning coord. Med. Coll. Ohio, Toledo, 1978-80, asst. hosp. dir. for ambulatory programs, 1980-81; cons. P.M.S. (Planning & Mgmt. Services) Inc., Bloomington, Minn., 1981-82; dir. health tech. mktg., sr. cons. Ellerbe Cons. Group, Bloomington, 1983-85; mktg. dir. Ellerbe Assocs. Inc., Mpls., 1986; v.p. Ellerbe Assocs., 1987-89, Export USA Publs., Mpls., 1989-91; dir. physician svcs. HealthEast, St. Paul, 1991-95; exec. adminstr. OSF Med. Group, OSF Healthcare Systems, Peoria, Ill., 1995-99; dir. clin. svcs. Phycor, Inc., Nashville, 1999-2000; sr. assoc. Progressive Healthcare, Inc., Nashville, 2000—02; adminstr. Medicine Patient Care Ctrs., Vanderbilt U. Med. Ctr., Nashville, 2003—06; v.p., exec. dir. ambulatory clinics Tulane U. Hosp. and Clinic, New Orleans, 2007—. Served to commdr., Med. Svc. Corps., USNR, 1972-98. Mem. Med. Group Mgmt. Assn., Am. Coll. Med. Practice Execs., Assn. Mil. Surgeons of U.S., Profl. Ski Instrs. Am., Res. Officers Assn., Phi Kappa Phi, Kappa Sigma. Lutheran. Office: Tulane U Hosp and Clinic 1415 Tulane Ave Ste 6122 New Orleans LA 70112 Business E-Mail: bob.carlson@unthsc.edu.

CARLSON, RONALD LEE, law educator; b. Davenport, Iowa, Dec. 10, 1934; s. Arthur A. and Louise (Sehmann) C.; m. Mary Murphy, Apr. 10, 1965; children: Michael, Andrew. BA, Augustana Coll., 1956; JD (Clarion DeWitt Hardy law scholar), Northwestern U., 1959; LL.M. (E. Barrett Prettyman law scholar), Georgetown U., 1961. Bar: Ill. 1959, Iowa 1959, D.C. 1960, U.S. Supreme Ct. 1966. Mem. firm Betty, Neuman, McMahon, Hellstrom & Bittner, Davenport, Iowa, 1961-65; U.S. commr. So. Dist. Iowa, 1964—65; prof. law U. Iowa, Iowa City, 1965-73, Washington U., St. Louis, 1973-84; John Byrd Martin prof. law U. Ga., 1984-95, Fuller E. Callaway prof. law, 1995—2002, Fuller E. Callaway prof. emeritus, 2002—. Vis. prof. Wayne State U., Detroit, 1974, Detroit, 1976—77, Detroit, 1979, U. Tex., 1978, St. Louis U., 1982—86, 1988, U. Iowa, 1986—87, 1996, Ohio State U., 2003, U. Tenn., Knoxville, 2006; cons. Legis. Com. Criminal Code Revision Iowa, 1969—73; moderator Robert Vance Forum on The Bill of Rights, 1990—96, 2002—03; Founder's Day lectr. U. Ga., 2005; interdisciplinary law lectr. Ohio State U., 2009. Author: Criminal Law Advocacy, 1982, rev. edit., 2014, Successful Techniques for Civil Trials, 1983, rev. edit., 1992, Pocket Proof of Facts, 1993, Trial Handbook for Georgia Lawyers, 2014, Student's Guide to Elements of Proof, 2011; co-author (with S. Moak): Criminal Justice Procedure, 2013; co-author: (with D. Brown and S. Crump) Adjudication of Criminal Justice, 2007; co-author: (with M. Ladd) Cases on Evidence, 1972; co-author: (with J. Yeager) Criminal Law and Procedure, 1979; co-author: (with M. Bright) Maine Objections at Trial, 1991, New Hampshire Objections at Trial, 1992, Oregon Objections at Trial, 1992; co-author: (with A. Montgomery and M. Bright) Minnesota Objections at Trial, 1992; co-author: (with R. Aronson and M. Bright) Washington Objections at Trial, 1992; co-author: (with J. Young, K. Curtis, and M. Bright) Virginia Objections at Trial, 1998; co-author: (with E. Imwinkelried) Dynamics of Trial Practice: Problems and Materials, 2010; co-author: (with E. Imwinkelried, J. Seaman and E. Beecher-Monas) Evidence Teaching Materials for an Age of Science and Statutes, 2012; co-author: (with M. Bright and E. Imwinkelried) Objections at Trial: A Concise Guide, 2013; co-author: (with M. Carlson) Carlson on Evidence, 2014. V.p. alumni bd. Augustana Coll., Rock Island, Ill., 1968; com. mem. Found. Freedom Commn. Ga. Bar. Recipient Roscoe Pound Found. Jacobson award, ATLA, 1987. Mem.: ABA (Harrison Tweed award 2000), UGA (Outstanding Tchg. Meigs award 1989), Ga. Trial Lawyers Assn. (Lifetime Achievement award 2005), Am. Inns. of Ct., Fed. Practice Inst. (dir. 1980—83, dean 1985—89), Fed. Bar Assn. (chmn. law sch. divsn. 1978—79, nat. coun. 1994—95, Earl W. Kintner award 1992), UGA Disting. Advocate Series (dir. 2006—10). Republican. Office: U Ga School of Law Sch of Law Athens GA 30602 Office Phone: 706-542-5186. Business E-Mail: leecar@uga.edu.

CARLSON, W. BERNARD, historian, educator; b. Neptune, NJ, Aug. 1, 1955; s. W. Bernard and Hildegard Kessler Carlson; m. Jane E. Fewster, Aug. 24, 2002; children: Julia Marion, Rachel Alexandra. BA in History, Holy Cross Coll., 1977; MA in History, U. Pa., 1981, PhD in History, 1984. Asst. prof. Mich. Technol. U., Houghton, 1983—86; prof. U. Va., Charlottesville, 1986—; postdoctoral fellow history Harvard Bus. Sch., 1988—89. Author: (book) Innovation as a Social Process: Elihu Thomson and the Rise of General Electric, 1870-1900, 1991, Technology in World History, 2005. Mem.: IEEE, Bus. History Conf., Am. Soc. Engring. Edn., Soc. History Tech. Presbyterian. Avocations: painting, cooking. Office: Univ Va Dept Sci Tech Soc Charlottesville VA 22904 Office Fax: 434-924-4306.

CARLTON, ALFRED PERSHING, JR., lawyer; b. Raleigh, NC, Aug. 27, 1947; s. Alfred P. and Katherine (Singleton) C.; m. Blair Creech Carlton, Apr. 21, 2001; children: Mary Elizabeth, Troy Eugene. BSBA, U. N.C., 1969, JD, 1975; MPA, U. Dayton, 1973; LLD, Stetson U., 2002, U. Denver, 2003. Bar: N.C. 1975, U.S. Dist. Ct. (ea. dist.) N.C. 1975, U.S. Ct. Appeals (4th cir.) 1976, U.S. Supreme Ct. 1993. Pvt. practice, Raleigh, 1975-77; counsel N.C. Bankers Assn., Raleigh, 1977-79; sec., gen. counsel Bancshares N.C., Inc., Raleigh, 1979-82; adj. prof. law Campbell U., Buies Creek, NC, 1979—82; ptnr. Allen and Pinnix, PA, Relaigh, NC. Active City of Raleigh Hist. Properties and Hist. Dists. Commn., 1978-82; exec. bd. Occoneechee coun. Boy Scouts Am., 1983-94; trustee U. N.C. at Wilmington, 1997-2005, chmn. 2004-05; bd. advisors Elon U. Law Sch., 2004—; mem. Chief Justice's Commn. on Professionalism, 1998-2001. 1st lt. Med. Svc. Corps, USAF, 1970-73 Fellow Am. Bar Found.; mem. ABA (ho. of dels. 1982-84, 1987—, chmn. of the house 1996-98, bd. govs. 1996-98, chmn. standing com. on jud. independence 1998-2001, pres.-elect 2001-02, pres. 2002-2003), N.C. Bar Assn. (bd. govs. 1981-82, 92-95), Am. Law Inst., N.C. Legis. Rsch. Commn. (study com. on pub. financing 1985-88). Democrat. Episcopalian. Avocations: tennis, gardening. Office: Allen and Pinnix PA PO Box 1270 Raleigh NC 27602 Home Phone: 919-755-6915; Office Phone: 919-755-0505. E-mail: apcarlton@allenpinnix.com.

CARLTON, BOB D., corporate financial executive; Attended, Le-Tourneau U., Hardin-Simmons U. Dir., tax North Am. Coal Corp. (NACoal, subs. NACCO Industries, Inc.), 2004—05, contr., 2004—06, v.p., fin. svcs., 2005—08; v.p., CFO North American Coal Corp., 2008—. Office: North American Coal Corp Ste 1100 5340 Legacy Dr Ste 300 Plano TX 75024-3141 Office Phone: 972-239-2625. Office Fax: 972-387-1328. Business E-Mail: bob.carlton@nacoal.com.

CARLTON, PAUL KENDALL, JR., physician; b. Roswell, N.Mex., May 13, 1947; s. Paul Kendall and Helen C. (Sweat) C.; m. Dorothea Janice Prichard, July 5, 1969; children: Paul Kendall III, Christianne Joy, Stephanie Jill, Luke Jeffrey. BS, USAF Acad., 1969; MD, U. Colo., 1973, DSc (hon.), 2003. Diplomate Am. Bd. Surgery, 1980, 1990, 2000. Commd. 2d lt. USAF, 1969, advanced through grades to lt. gen., 1999; resident in surgery Wilford Hall Med. Ctr., San Antonio, 1973-78; comdr. USAF Hosp. Torrejon, Madrid, 1985-88, Scott Med. Ctr., Scott AFB, Ill., 1988-91; command surgeon Air Edn. and Tng. Command, San Antonio, 1991-94; comdr. Wilford Hall Med. Ctr., San Antonio, 1994-99, surgeon gen., 1999—2002; prof., dir. Homeland Security Health Sci. Ctr. Tex. A&M, 2002—. Decorated Air medal, Legion of Merit (2), Def. Disting. Svc. medal, Airman's medal; recipient Hoekton Silver award AMA, 1978, Nathan Davis award, AMA, 2001. Fellow ACS (gov. 1992-96). Avocations: hunting, flying. Office: Tex A&M U Health Sci Ctr Office of Innovation and Preparedness College Station TX 77845 also: 7th Fl 301 Tarrow St College Station TX 77840-7896

CARMACK, JOHN, computer game company and aerospace transportation executive, game designer; b. Aug. 20, 1970; Attended, U. Mo., Kansas City. Software developer Softdisk, Shreveport, La.; co-founder, tech. dir. id Software, LLC, Mesquite, Tex., 1991—; founder, lead engr. Armadillo Aerospace, Mesquite. Developer or co-developer Wolfenstein 3D, Doom, Quake computer game series. Recipient lifetime achievement award, Walk of Games, San Francisco, 2006; named one of 50 most influential people in tech., Time Mag., 1999; named to Hall of Fame, Acad. Interactive Arts & Sciences. Office: id Software 3819 Towne Crossing 222 Mesquite TX 75150 also: Armadillo Aerospace 2455 Ridge Rd Rockwall TX 75087 Office Fax: 972-613-3589, 972-686-9288. Business E-Mail: johnc@idsoftware.com.

CARMACK, TERRY ALAN, legislative staff member; m. Mary Gabriel Harpring (dec.); 2 children. Chief of staff to Rep. Anne Northup US House of Representatives, Washington, 2000—07, asst. Appropriations Com., 2003—07, chief of staff to Gus Bilirakis, 2009—10; polit. dir. Nat. Rep. Congl. Com., 2007—08; state dir. to Senator Mitch McConnell US Senate, 2010—. Office: Office of Senator Mitch McConnell Gene Snyder US Courthouse 601 W Broadway, Room 630 Louisville KY 40202-2228 Office Phone: 502-582-6304. Office Fax: 502-582-5326.

CARMAN, JOSEPH B., healthcare services executive company; Grad., U. N.C., Chapel Hill. Acctg. Arthur Andersen; with Per-Se Technologies; pres., health care fin. svcs. Team Health Holdings, Inc., 2004, chief adminstrv. officer. Office: Team Health Holdings Inc 265 Brookview Town Centre Way Ste 400 Knoxville TN 37919 Office Phone: 865-693-1000. Office Fax: 865-539-3073. Business E-Mail: joseph_carman@teamhealth.com.

CARMICHAEL, DAVID M., energy executive; b. 1938; BA, MBA, LLB, U. Tex. Officer Welltech Inc., Houston, 1976—84; pres. Carcon Corp., Houston, 1984—86; vice chmn. Am. Oil & Gas Corp. (merged with KN Energy, Inc.), chmn., pres. & CEO, 1985—94; vice chmn. KN Energy, Inc., 1994—96; pvt. investor, 1996—. Bd. dirs. Ensco Internat. Inc., 2001—10, Natural Resource Ptnrs. LP, 2002—, Cabot Oil & Gas Corp., 2006—. Office: Cabot Oil & Gas Corp Bd Directors 840 Gessner Rd Ste 1400 Houston TX 77024-4152 Office Phone: 281-589-4600. Office Fax: 281-589-4828. Business E-Mail: david.carmichael@cabotog.com.

CARMICHAEL, VIDET, state legislator; b. Meridian, Miss., Feb. 26, 1950; m. Donna Smith; 2 children. BS, MEd, Miss. State U. Tchr., coach, prin.; mem. Dist. 33 Miss. State Senate, 2000—, chair edn. com., vice chair state libr. com., mem. appropriations com., bus. and fin. instns. com., corrections com., county affairs com., hwys. and transp. com., pub. utilities com., mem. vets. and mil. affairs com. Mem.: Mason. Republican. Baptist. Mailing: 5396 Springhill Loop Meridian MS 39301 Office: State Capitol Rm 404A PO Box 1018 Jackson MS 39215 Home Phone: 601-693-2750; Office Phone: 601-359-3244. E-mail: vcarmichael@senate.ms.gov.

CARMODY, EDMOND, bishop; b. Moyvane, Ireland, Jan. 12, 1934; s. Michael and Mary (Stack) Carmody. MEd, Our Lady of the Lake U., 1968, M in Social Work, 1973; LHD (hon.), U. of Incarnate Word, San Antonio. Cert. tchr. Tex., counselor Tex. Ordained priest Archdiocese of San Antonio, 1957, asst. archdiocesan chaplain of scouts, sec. archdiocesan tribunal, archdiocesan moderator Cath. youth orgn., vice chancellor, dir., family life program, dir., pastoral svcs., aux. bishop, 1988—92; assoc. pastor St. Mary's Ch., Victoria, Tex., St. Margaret Mary's Ch., San Antonio; pastor St. Henry's Ch., San Antonio; missionary to Latin Am. St. James Soc., Guayaquil, Ecuador, 1983—88; ordained bishop, 1988; bishop Diocese of Tyler, Tex., 1992—2000, Diocese of Corpus Christi, Tex., 2000—10, bishop emeritus, 2010—. Chaplain Tex. Army Nat. Guard; lectr. Incarnate Word Coll. Pastoral Inst., Oblate Coll. of Southwest. Mem. exec. bd. East Tex. area coun. Boy Scouts Am. Named a Prelate of Honor, His Holiness by Pope John Paul II, 1979. Mem.: KC (state chaplain), Nat.

Conf. Cath. Bishops (mem. com. for ch. in Latin Am., chmn. missions com., mem. marriage and family life com.). Roman Catholic. Office: Diocese of Corpus Christi PO Box 2620 Corpus Christi TX 78403-2620 Home Phone: 361-882-6191. Office Fax: 361-882-1018.

CARMODY, RICHARD PATRICK, lawyer; b. Chgo., June 2, 1942; s. Thomas Francis and Margaret (Tully) C.; m. Alison Pierce Cutter, Dec. 27, 1968; children: Elizabeth Carmody Gonzalez, Emily Pierce Carmody. BA, U. Ill., 1964; JD, Vanderbilt U., 1975. Bar: Ala. 1975, U.S. Dist. Ct. (no., mid. and so. dists.) Ala. 1975, U.S. Ct. Appeals (11th cir.) 1985, U.S. Supreme Ct. 1988. Assoc. Lange, Simpson, Robinson & Somerville, Birmingham, Ala., 1975-81, ptnr., 1981—2002; chmn. exec. com. Lange, Simpson Robinson & Somerville, Birmingham, Ala., 1987-93; ptnr. Adams and Reese, Birmingham, 2003—07; spl. counsel Adams and Reese, Lange Simpson LLP, 2008—. Mem. Am. Bankruptcy Inst., Washington, 1985—, co-chair ethics com. 1999-2005; bd. dirs. Am. Bd. Cert., 2000-05, 2010-, mem. exec. com., 2001-03, mem. faculty com., 2004-2005, mem. stds.com., 2005-; dir. Am. Coll. Bkcy Found., 2009-, mem. probonocoms 2009-Bd. dirs. Birmingham Coun. Campfire Boys and Girls Inc., 1978-90, pres., 1983-85; bd. dirs. Ala. region NCCJ, 1995—, state chair, 2000-02; bd. dirs. St. Vincent's Hosp. Foudn., 2002-10, chair, 2008-09; active Leadership Birmingham, 1998—. Fellow Am. Coll. Bankruptcy, 1999—. Mem. Ala. Bar Assn. (chmn. bankruptcy and comml. law sect. 1985, exec. com. 1986-93), Greystone Golf & Country Club, Kiwanis. Roman Catholic. Avocations: golf, sports, travel. Office: Adams & Reese LLP 2100 3d Ave N Ste 1100 Birmingham AL 35203 Office Phone: 205-250-5033. Business E-Mail: richard.carmody@arlaw.com.

CARMODY, THOMAS G., JR., state legislator; BFA, La. State U. Coll. Design, 1983. Real estate broker; mem. Dist. 6 La. House of Reps., 2008—, mem. commerce com., edn. com., mcpl., parochial and cultural affairs com. Republican. Office: State Capitol PO Box 44486 Baton Rouge LA 70804 Mailing: 5916 Fairfield Ave Shreveport LA 71106 Office Phone: 225-342-6945, 318-862-9956. Office Fax: 318-862-9958. Business E-Mail: carmodyt@legis.state.la.us.

CARMOLA, JOHN J., aerospace and defense parts manufacturing company executive; BS in Mech. & Aerospace Engring., U. Rochester, NY; MBA in Fin., Xavier U., Ohio. Various mgmt. positions, corp. mfg. mgmt. program General Electric Co., gen. mgr., marine bus.; various positions, mfg., engring., quality & svcs. GE Aircraft Engines; pres., Landing Gear Divsn. Goodrich Corp., 1996—2000, pres., Engine Sys. Divsn., 2000, v.p., group pres., engine & safety sys., 2000—02, v.p., group pres., electronic sys., 2002—03, v.p., segment pres., engine sys., 2003—05, v.p., segment pres., airframe sys., 2005—07, v.p., segment pres., actuation & landing sys., 2007—. Office: Goodrich Corp Four Coliseum Ctr 2730 W Tyvola Rd Charlotte NC 28217 Office Phone: 704-423-7000. Office Fax: 704-423-7002. Business E-Mail: jack.carmola@goodrich.com.

CARMON, DOMINIC, bishop emeritus; b. Opelousas, La., Dec. 13, 1930; Ordained priest Soc. of the Divine Word, 1960; ordained bishop, 1993; aux. bishop Archdiocese of New Orleans, 1993—2006, aux. bishop emeritus, 2006—. Missionary to Papua New Guinea, 1961—68. Roman Catholic. Home: 337 Bertolino Dr Kenner LA 70065-2532 Office Phone: 504-273-5863. Office Fax: 504-273-5747. E-mail: dcarmon@sprynet.com.

CARNAHAN, ROBERT PAUL, retired civil engineer, educator, researcher, consultant; b. Bradenton, Fla., July 22, 1936; s. Robert Dewey and Marion (Wilbur) C.; m. Geraldine Schott, July 30, 1938; children: Robert P. Jr., Christopher T., Sean P. BCE, U. Fla., 1959; MS in Sanitary Engring., U. N.C., 1964; PhD, Clemson U., 1973. Registered profl. engr., Fla., Va., Md. Commd. 2d lt. US Army, 1959, advanced through grades to lt. col., 1975; co. comdr. 92d Engring. Battalion, Ft. Bragg, NC, 1960-61; project officer US Environ. Hygiene Agy., Edgewood Arsenal, Md., 1961—63; instr. Med. Field Svc. Sch., San Antonio, 1966—68; sr. environ. engr. 20th Pvt. Med. Unit, Vietnam, 1968-69; project officer US Army Med. R&D Command, Washington, 1973—75; project devel. officer US Army Material Devel. and Rsch. Ctr., Ft. Belvoir, Va., 1975—79; divsn. chief EPA br. US Army Med. Bioengring. R&D Lab., Frederick, Md., 1979—80; asst. prof. dept. civil engring. and mechs. U. South Fla., Tampa, 1980—84, assoc. prof. dept. civil engring. and mechs., 1984—89, prof. dept. civil engring. and mechs., 1989—93, assoc. dean rsch., 1993—2007, prof. emeritus, 2007; prin. Enviroprogress, Inc., 2007—12. Adj. rsch. prof. dept. chemistry Am. U., 1976-77; adj. prof. dept. civil, mech. and environ. engring. George Washington U., 1979-80. Contbr. numerous articles to profl. jours. Decorated Legion of Merit, Bronze Star with oak leaf cluster, Meritorious Service Medal with oak leaf cluster, Army Commendation medal with oak leaf cluster; recipient Silver medal for research and devel. Am. Def. Preparedness Assn., Rsch. award U.S. Dept. of Army Rsch., Comdr.'s award for tech. Meradcom. Mem. ASCE, Nat. Soc. Profl. Engrs., Am. Inst. Chem. Engrs., Water Pollution Control Fedn., Membrane Soc., Internat. Desalination Assn., Am. Desalting Assn. (Hall of Fame 1998), Fla. Engring. Soc., Internat. Assn. Water Pollution Research, Am. Acad. Environ. Engrs. (cert.), Sigma Xi, Chi Epsilon, Tau Beta Pi. Democrat. Roman Catholic. Home: 506 Terrace Hill Dr Tampa FL 33617-3850

CARNALL, GEORGE HURSEY, II, lawyer; b. Ft. Smith, Ark., Feb. 19, 1947; s. George and Kathleen (Browne) C.; m. Janet Spaulding, Aug. 28, 1971; children: Clayton Wilson, Abigail Browne, Kevin Joseph. BS in Econs. and Bus. Adminstrn., Millikin U., Decatur, Ill., 1969; JD, Vanderbilt U., 1974. Bar: Tenn. 1974, U.S. Dist. Ct. (we. dist.) Tenn. 1974. Assoc. Arnoult & May, Memphis, 1974-76, Watson Cox & Arnoult, Memphis, 1976-79; gen. counsel S.M.R. Enterprises, Memphis, 1980-82, pres., 1982-87; pres. internat. divsn. Fantastic Sam's Internat., Inc., Memphis, 1987-91; pres. LP Svcs., Inc., Memphis, 1992-97, Mid South FS, Inc., Olive Branch, Miss., 1997—2008, Carnall Franchise Group, Memphis, 1991—. Sec. Lil Pals Pet Photography, Inc., 2005—10; dir. devel. Southern Bapt. Edn. Ctr. Sch., 2002—. Contbr. articles to legal jours., mags., newspapers. Bd. dirs. Teen Challenge, Memphis, 1982-87. Served with U.S. Army, 1969-71. Mem. Cornerstone Assembly of God Ch. Office: Carnall Franchise Group 6375 Nellwood Olive Branch MS 38654 Office Phone: 662-349-5003. E-mail: jcandgc@comcast.com.

CARNE, JOHN D., oil industry executive; Engring. & mgmt. positions through dir. ops. UK & Norway Cooper Energy Services subs. Cameron Internat. Corp., 1971—96, plant mgr. subsea systems Leeds, England, 1996—99, ops. dir., ea. hemisphere drilling & production systems, 1999—2002, v.p., pres. valves & measurement group Houston, 2002—07, pres. drilling & production systems, 2007—10, exec. v.p., COO, 2010—. Office: Cameron Internat 1333 W Loop St Houston TX 77027-9100 Office Phone: 713-939-2211. Business E-Mail: john.carne@c-a-m.com.

CARNES, EDWARD EARL, federal judge; b. Albertville, Ala., June 3, 1950; BS, U. Ala., Tuscaloosa, 1972; JD cum laude, Harvard Law Sch., 1975. Asst. atty. gen. State of Ala., Montgomery, 1975—92, chief capital punishment & post-conviction litigation divsn., 1981—92; judge US Ct. Appeals (11th cir.), 1992—2013, chief judge, 2013—. Mem.: Jud. Conference Adv. Com Criminal Rules (chmn. 2001—04). Office: Rm 403 1 Church St Montgomery AL 36104-4096*

CARNES, JAMES EDWARD, retired electronics executive; b. Cumberland, Md., Sept. 27, 1939; s. Roy Clifton and Alta C.; m. Nancy Louise Zolto, Nov. 26, 1977; 1 child, Gillian. BS in Engring. Sci., Pa. State U., 1961; MA in Elec. Engring., Princeton U., 1967, PhD in Elec. Engring., 1970; PhD (hon.), Thomas Edison State Coll., 1994, Kean U., 1998. Mem. tech. staff RCA Labs., Princeton, NJ, 1969-77; mgr. tech. application RCA Consumer Electronics, Indpls., 1977-80, dir. new products lab, 1980-82, div. v.p. engring., 1982-87; v.p. consumer electronics and info. scis. David Sarnoff Rsch. Ctr. (subs. SRI Internat.), Princeton, NJ, 1987-90, pres., COO, 1990-93, pres., CEO, 1993—2002, interim CEO, 2006—07, dir, 2007—10, sr. advisor, 2002—03; sr. v.p. SRI Internat., 1990-95; chmn. bd. Sensar, Inc., Princeton, NJ, 1992-2000, Orchid Biocomputer Inc., 1995-97, Sarnoff Digital Comm., Inc., 1996-97. Dir. Sarnoff Real Time Inc., Sarif, Inc., Delsys Pharm. Corp., Orchid Biocomputer, Inc., Sarnoff Digital Comms., Nova Corp., SRI Internat., C-Cor Inc., 2002-2007; Village at Pa. State, 2004—12; short course lectr. UCLA, 1973-81, Am. U. Washington, 1976, Ctrl. Poly. Inst., London, 1974. Contbr. articles to profl. jours. Campaign chmn. Princeton Area United Way, 1992, bd. dirs., 1992-94, 1st v.p., 1993-94; chmn. bd. trustees United Way Greater Mercer County, 1994-96; chmn. sci. adv. bd. Rider Coll., 1990-92; trustee Rider U., 1993-2002, Ind. Coll. Fund. N.J., 1990-96, Thomas Edison State Coll. Found., 1992—, Am. Boychoir Sch., 1995-2002, Regional Planning Partnership, 1997-2002; mem. bd. overseers N.J. Inst. Tech., 1993-98; co-chair Prosperity N.J., 2000-02; Lt. USN, 1961-65. Recipient David Sarnoff Outstanding Achievement award RCA, 1981, Engr. of Yr. award Ctrl. N.J. Engring. Coun., 1991, Humanitarian award NCCJ, 1994, Citizen of Yr. award Mercer County C. of C., 1996, N.J. Tech. Coun. High Tech. Hero award, 1999, N.J. Network Chmn.'s award, 2000; named to Jr. Achievement Bus. Hall of Fame, 1998, Am. Electronics Assn. N.J. High Tech Hall of Fame, 1999, Acad. Digital TV Pioneers, 2002. Fellow IEEE (Centennial medal 1984, Region I award 1993); mem. Am. Electronics Assn., Nat. Acad. Engring. (com. on mem., 2004-2006, nom. com., 2007), Pa. State U. Alumni Assn. (coun., exec. com.; Outanding Engr. Alumnus award 1992, Pres. and Exec. dir. award 1995, Disting. Alumnus award 1996, v.p. 1997-99, pres. 1999-2001, alumni fellow 2003, soc. disting. alum exec. bd, 2004-, v.p., 2009-11, pres., 2011-13, Leonhard bd., 2004-, Schreyer ext bd. advisors, 2010-). Achievements include inventor in field. Avocation: golf. Home: 7038 Kingsmill Ct Bradenton FL 34202 Home Phone: 941-907-1597. Personal E-mail: jim.carnes@psualum.com.

CARNES, JULIE ELIZABETH, federal judge; m. Stephen S. Cowen. AB summa cum laude, U. Ga., 1972, JD magna cum laude, 1975. Bar: Ga. 1975. Law clk. to Hon. Lewis R. Morgan US Ct. Appeals (5th cir.), 1975-77; asst. US atty. (northern dist.) Ga. US Dept. Justice, Atlanta, 1978—90, appellate chief criminal divsn., 1987—89; spl. counsel US Sentencing Commn., 1989, commr., 1990—96; judge US Dist. Ct. (northern dist.) Ga., Atlanta, 1992—2009, chief judge, 2009—. Mem. US Atty. General's Advisory Com. on Sentencing Guidelines, 1988—90. Office: US Courthouse 75 Spring St SW Ste 2167 Atlanta GA 30303-3309 Office Phone: 404-215-1510.*

CARNEY, BECKY, state legislator; b. Person Co, NC, Dec. 25, 1944; m. Gene Carney; 5 children. Commr. Merklenburg County, 1996—2002; state rep. Dist. 102 NC, 2002—. Mem. Edn. com., Edn. Subcom. on Presch., Elem. and Secondary Edn., Fin. com., Pub. Utilities com., Transp. com.; vice chmn. Fin. Instns. com. Democrat. Mailing: Dist Off PO Box 32873 Charlotte NC 28232 Office: North Carolina House of Representatives 16 W Jones St Rm 1221 Raleigh NC 27601-1096 Office Phone: 919-733-5827. E-mail: Becky.Carney@ncleg.net.

CARNEY, JOHN, state legislator; b. Sept. 30, 1969; m. Jennifer Martin; children: Chase, Ethan. BA in Hist., Berea Coll., 1991; MA in Instructional Leadership, Eastern Ky. U. Cert. teaching Campbellsville U. Former employee Campbellsville Mcpl. Water Co.; former social studies tchr. Washington County High Sch.; former spl. edn. tchr. Campbellsville High Sch.; social studies tchr. Taylour County High Sch.; mem. Dist. 51 Ky. House of Reps., 2009—. Republican. Office: 702 Capitol Ave Rm 413A Frankfort KY 40601 also: 340 Pembroke Way Campbellsville KY 42718 Office Phone: 502-564-8100 Ext. 708, 270-465-5400.

CARNEY, JOHN M., dermatologist; MD, Nothwestern U. Diplomate Am. Bd. Dermatology, 1984. Resident dermatology Univ. Hosp., Cleveland, Ohio, 1981—84; fellow physiology Harvard Med. Sch., Boston, 1984—85; fellow dermatologic surgery University Tenn. Med. Ctr., Memphis, 1985—86; hosp. affiliation include University of Ark. Med. Sciences. Office: SW Med Arts Bldg 11321 Interstate 30 Ste 201 Little Rock AR 72209 Office Phone: 501-455-4700.

CARNEY, RAY, JR., mining executive; BS in Acctg., Pa. State U. CPA. With Ernst & Young LLP; various fin. leadership positions Alcoa, Inc., 2002—08, group contr., global rolled products divsn., 2006; corp. contr. Dresser-Rand Group, Inc., 2008, v.p., contr., chief acctg. officer, 2008—. Office: Dresser Rand Group Inc West8 Tower 10205 Westheimer Rd Ste 1000 Houston TX 77042 Office Phone: 713-354-6100. Office Fax: 713-354-6110.

CARNINE, LESLIE V., state legislator, retired school system administrator; b. San Diego, July 25, 1941; s. Lester V. and Phylis L. (Ellwanger) C.; m. Linda J. Glispey, Aug. 14, 1965; Children: Wendy Jo, Thaddeus Alan. BA, Buena Vista Univ., 1963; MS, Ctrl. Mo. State Univ., 1965; EdD, Univ. Ark., 1969. High sch. prin. Harrison (Ark.) Sch. Dist., 1977—79; from asst. supt. to supt. of schools Texarkana (Ark.) Sch. Dist., 1979—87; supt. of schools Wichita Falls (Tex.) Ind. Sch. Dist., 1987—97, Little Rock Sch. Dist., Ark., 1997—2001; clin. asst. prof. & exec. in residence Univ. Ark. Coll. Edn. & Health Programs, 2001; mem. Dist. 94 Ark. House of Reps., 2009—. Mem. Ark. Assn. Ednl. Adminstrs. (bd. dirs.), Tex. Assn. Sch. Adminstrs. (mem. Profl. Devel. com.). Republican. Presbyterian. Mailing: PO Box 615 Rogers AR 72757 Office Phone: 479-636-2619. Business E-Mail: carninel@arkleg.state.ar.us.

CARNS, JIM, state legislator; m. Judy Carns; 3 children. Degree in engring., U. Ala. Businessman; mem. Dist. 48 Ala. House of Reps., Montgomery, 2011—. Republican. Office: PO Box 43797 Birmingham AL 35243 also: Ala House of Reps Rm 537-B 11 S Union St Montgomery AL 36130 Office Phone: 334-242-7600. Personal E-mail: jwcarns@yahoo.com.

CAROLAND, WILLIAM BOURNE, structural engineer; b. Clarksville, Tenn., July 9, 1929; s. Enoch Arden and Jennie Wimberly (Bourne) C.; m. Eloise Joyce Crickard, June 3, 1957; children: Richard Bradley, Jennifer Dorothy. Student, U. Tenn., 1947-52. Registered surveyor, Ky., 1967-2000; profl. engr., Ky., 1967-, Tenn., 1972-2004, Fla., 1972-2001, W.Va., 1972-2004, Mich., 1972-2004, Ind., 1974-2004. Survey party chief King & Clark Engrs., Clarksville, 1955-56, Michael Baker Jr., Inc., Jackson, Miss., 1956-57, asst. designer Charleston, W.Va., 1957-62, project supr. Louisville, 1962-63, designer Charleston, 1963-64; bridge designer Vogt, Ivers & Assocs., Cin., 1964-65; sr. structural engr. Brighton Engring., Frankfort, Ky., 1965-73; chief bridge engr. Beam, Longest & Neff, Indpls., 1973-79; with Am. Cons. Engrs., Lexington, Ky., 1979—2001, chief bridge engr., 1988—2001; ret., 2001; cons. Am. Cons. Engrs., 2001—03. Cons. in field; mem. Am. Cons. Engrs. Coun. Contbr. papers to profl. publs. With U.S. Army, 1952-55. Recipient Welded Steel Design award Lincoln Arc Welding Found., 1974, Welded Steel Design hon. mention, 1975, silver award 1999; Bridge Design award Prestressed Concrete Inst., 1977, 92, Grand Conceptor award Am. Consulting Engrs. Coun., 2001. Avocations: woodworking, photography. Home: 114 Christal Dr Georgetown KY 40324

CAROLIN, BRIAN, automotive executive; b. Eng., July 2, 1956; Joined Nissan Motor Mfg. Ltd. (UK), 1984; various leadership positions in human resources, purchasing, product planning, sales/mktg. Nissan Motor Mfg. Ltd./Nissan Europe; mng. dir. Nissan Motor Great Britain, 1998; sr. v.p. sales/mktg. Nissan Europe, 2005—08; chief N.Am. sales Nissan Motor Co. Ltd., 2008—; sr. v.p. sales/mktg. Nissan North America Inc., 2008—. Named a Power Player, Advt. Age, 2008. Office: Nissan North America Inc PO Box 685001 Franklin TN 37068-5001 Office Phone: 615-725-1000. Office Fax: 615-725-3343.

CARONA, JOHN, state legislator; b. Dec. 14, 1955; m. Debbie Carona; 5 children. BBA, U. Tex., Austin, 1978. Lic. real estate broker Tex., cert. mgr. cmty. associations. Profl. cmty. assn. mgr.; pres. Prin. Mgmt. Group, Inc.; founder, pres., CEO Associa; mem. Dist. 109 Tex. House of Representatives, 1991—92, mem. Dist. 108, 1993—96; mem. Dist. 16 Tex. State Senate, 1996—. Named Legislator of Yr., Cmty. Associations Inst., Tex. Chpt., 1999; named to Legis. Hall of Fame, Tex. Assn. Realtors, 1999, 2001. Mem.: YMCA, Kiwanis Club, Hist. Preservation, Friends Park. Republican. Baptist. Office: 8080 N Central Expressway Ste 1440 LB 44 Dallas TX 75206 also: PO Box 12068 Capitol Station Austin TX 78711 Office Phone: 214-378-5751, 512-463-0116.

CAROSELLA, DEBRA B., food products executive; BJ, U. Mo., Columbia. With Kraft, M&M Mars, Nestle Confections, Eagle Snacks, Anheuser-Busch, J. Walter Thompson, Monsanto Co.; v.p., gen. mgr., meals bus. unit ConAgra Foods Inc., 2001—02, exec. v.p., innovation, Grocery Product Divsn., 2003—04, sr. v.p., strategic mktg., innovation, 2005—07; joined WhiteWave Foods Co. (subs. Dean Foods Co.), 2007, sr. v.p., innovation, Dean Foods Co., 2007—. Office: Dean Foods Co 2515 McKinney Ave Ste 200 Dallas TX 75201-6915 Office Phone: 214-303-3400. Office Fax: 214-303-3499. Business E-Mail: debra_carosella@deanfoods.com.

CARP, DANIEL ALLEN, air transportation executive, former consumer products company executive; b. Wytheville, Va., May 4, 1948; BBA in Quantitative Methods, Ohio U., 1970; MBA, Rochester Inst. Tech., 1973; MS in Mgmt., MIT, 1988. Stats. analyst Eastman Kodak Co., Rochester, NY, various postions in market rsch. and mgmt., gen. mgr. sales Kodak Can., gen. mgr. consumer electronics divsn., asst. gen. mgr. Latin Am. region, 1986-88, v.p., gen. mgr., 1988-90, gen. mgr. European Mktg. Cos., 1990—95, exec. v.p., asst. COO, 1995-97, pres., COO, 1997-2000, pres., CEO, 2000, chmn., pres., CEO, 2000—01, chmn., CEO, 2001—05, chmn., 2005; non-exec. chmn. Delta Air Lines, Inc., Atlanta, 2007—. Bd. dirs. Eastman Kodak Co., 1997—2005, Tex. Instruments Inc., 1997—; bd. dir. Norfolk Southern Corp., 2006—, Delta Air Lines, Inc., Liz Claiborne Inc., 2006—; mem. Bus. Council; mem. bd. trustees George Eastman House; mem. adv. coun. MIT Sloan; mem. Alumni Hall of Distinction, N.Y. State Commn. on Ind. Colls. & Univs. Sloan fellow Sloan Sch. of Mgmt., MIT; recipient Leadership award, 2001, Person of the Yr. award, 2004, PhotoImaging Manufacturers & Distributors Assn., Corning award for Excellence, 2005, Diversity Best Practices CEO award, 2005. Office: Delta Air Lines Inc 1030 Delta Blvd Atlanta GA 30320-6001*

CARPENTER, ALVIN RAUSO, finance company executive; b. Berea, Ky., Jan. 24, 1942; s. Warren G. and Pauline E. Carpenter; m. Marilyn Rex; 1 child, Dana. BA in Polit. Sci., U. Cin., 1964. Joined Chessie Seaboard R.R., 1964; pres. CSX Rail Transport, Jacksonville, 1988—89, CSX Distbn. Svcs., Jacksonville, 1990—92; exec. v.p. sales & mktg. CSX Transp., Inc., 1989—92, pres., CEO, 1992—99; vice chmn. CSX Corp., 1999—2001. Bd. dirs. Fla. Rock Industries, Nations Bank, Barnett Bank, Inc., Am. Heritage Life Ins. Co., Blue Cross & Blue Shield, Fla., One Valley Bancorp, W.Va., Regency Centers Corp., 1993—, Stein Mart, Inc., 1996—, PSS World Med., Inc., 2005—, Lender Processing Svcs., Inc., 2009—. Bd. dirs. St. Vincent's Hosp., Meml. Hosp., Jacksonville, Jacksonville Symphony. Mem. Nat. Freight Traffic Assn., San Jose Country Club, Timuquana Country Club, Epping Forest Yacht Club, River Club, Laurel Valley Golf Club (Ligonier, Pa.). Avocations: tennis, golf. Office: Lender Processing Services Inc Bd Directors 601 Riverside Ave Jacksonville FL 32204 Office Phone: 904-854-5100. Office Fax: 904-854-4124. E-mail: alvin.carpenter@lpsvcs.com.

CARPENTER, DAVID E., rental company executive; V.p., investor rels. Rent-A-Center, Inc. Office: Rent A Center Inc 5501 Headquarters Dr Plano TX 75024 Office Phone: 972-801-1214. Office Fax: 972-943-0113. Business E-Mail: david.carpenter@rentacenter.com.

CARPENTER, DELBERT STANLEY, educational administration educator; b. Wichita Falls, Tex., May 18, 1950; s. Delbert Stanley Sr. and Nancy (Williams) S.; m. Noralyn Gray, July 13, 1973 (div. Mar. 1986); m. Janet Ann Stewart, July 15, 1989 (div. June 1993); m. Linda Jan Meerdink Evans, June 25, 1994; 1 child, Susanne Gray Carpenter; stepchildren: Robert Scott Evans, Peter Clark Evans. BS, Tarleton State U., 1972; MS, East Tex. State U., 1975; PhD, U. Ga., 1979. Actuarial technician A.S. Hansen, Inc., Dallas, 1972-74; grad. asst. ctrl. housing office East Tex. State U., Commerce, 1974-75; men's resident dir. Oglethorpe U., Atlanta, 1975-77; grad. asst. rsch., tchg., counseling and human devel. dept. U. Ga., Athens, 1977-79; dean students U. Ark., Monticello, 1979-81; asst. dir. devel. Tex. A&M U., College Station, 1982-84, from asst. prof. ednl. adminstrn. to assoc. prof., 1985-95, prof., 1995—2003; prof., chair counseling leadership adult edn. sch. psychology Tex. State U., San Marcos, 2003—10; interim dean Coll. Edn., 2010—11, dean, 2011—. Mem. editl. bds. various profl. jours.; contbr. articles to profl. jours. Named Outstanding Doctoral Alumnus, Students Affairs Administrn. U. Ga., 1995, Disting. Tchg. award Assn. Former Students Coll. of Edn., 1996. Mem. Assn. for the Study Higher Edn. (exec. dir. 1987-98, Disting. Svc. award 1996), Am. Coll. Pers. Assocs. (Annuit Coeptis award 1995, Sr. Scholar 2000, chair 2001-04, Esther Lloyd-Jones Profl. Svc. award 2004), Nat. Assn. Student Pers. Adminstrn. (mem.-at-large nat. bd. 2001-03, Pillar Prof. award 2010), South Assn. for Coll. Student Affairs (Melvene Hardee award 1997), Alpha Phi Omega (pres., bd. dirs. 1986-90, Nat. Disting. Svc. award 1990, trustee endowment fund 1996—2008, chair 1997—2005), Alpha Chi. Avocations: golf, reading, travel. Home: 10909 Olympia Fields Loop Austin TX 78747 Office Phone: 512-245-2150. Business E-Mail: stanc@txstate.edu.

CARPENTER, JARED K., state legislator; b. Apr. 26, 1977; m. Erica Carpenter; 1 child, Cole. BA in Comm., Ea. Ky. U., Richmond, 2000. Banker, bus. devel. officer First So. Nat. Bank, 2001—; mem. Dist. 34 Ky. State Senate, 2011—. Mem. Berea Utilities Adv. Bd. Mem.: Ky. Bankers Assn. Republican. Baptist. Office: Kentucky State Senate Annex Rm 203 702 Capitol Ave Frankfort KY 40601 Office Phone: 502-564-8100 ext. 730.

CARPENTER, JOANN DEAKIN, history professor; b. Bangor, Maine, Aug. 9, 1955; d. Donald Frederick and Sylvia Hanson Deakin; m. Bruce Michael Carpenter, June 15, 1984; 1 child, Michael Hanson. BA, Wofford Coll., 1977; MA, PhD, Emory U., 1987. Prof. history Fla. C.C., Jacksonville, Fla., 1988—. Author supplements Prentice-Hall, Upper Saddle, NJ, 1999—; faculty dir. NEH-Faces of America Fla. C.C., Jacksonville, 2001—02. Cons. Boys and Girls Club, Jacksonville, 2003—. Mem.: Orgn. American History, So. Hist. Assn. (recruiting officer 1988—), Am. Hist. Assn. Democrat. Luth. Avocations: reading, needlecrafts, cooking. Office: Florida Community Coll Jacksonville 11901 Beach Blvd Jacksonville FL 32246 Office Fax: 904-646-2315. Business E-Mail: jcarpent@fccj.edu.

CARPENTER, LESTER, state legislator; b. Sept. 1, 1970; m. Niesha Carpenter. Grad., Paramedic Sch., Wallace State CC; attended, Northeast Mississippi Cmty. Coll. Paramedic; mem. Dist. 1 Miss. House of Reps., 2008—, vice chair interstate cooperation com., mem. banking and fin. svcs. com., corrections com., county affairs com., Medicaid com., municipalities com., tourism com. Republican. Baptist. Home: 8 Carpenter Drive Burnsville MS 38833 Office: PO Box 1018 Jackson MS 39215 Home Phone: 662-427-8281. E-mail: lcarpenter@house.ms.gov.

CARPENTER, NANCY J., health science association administrator; Assoc. dir. H.A. Chapman Inst. Med. Genetics, Tulsa, Okla.; pres. Am. Bd. Med. Genetics, 2001—. Adj. prof. biochemistry Okla. State U. Office: H A Chapman Inst Med Genetics 4502 E 41st St Tulsa OK 74135-2553 Business E-Mail: ncarpenter@hillcrest.com.

CARPENTER, ROBERT C., retired banker, former state legislator; b. Franklin, NC, June 18, 1924; m. Helen Carpenter. Student, Ind. U., Kokomo, 1947, Purdue U., 1950, U. Va., 1964, Western Carolina U. V.p. bank, 32 yrs.; ret.; mem. N.C. Senate, Raleigh, 1988—2004. Ranking minority mem. appropriations com. on Dept. Transp., judiciary I com., mem. appropriations/base budget com., commerce com., pensions and retirement and aging com., vice chmn. transp. com. Mem. Am. Legis. Exch. Coun.; commr. Macon County, N.C., 1978-82. Pilot USN, 1943-45. Mem. Am. Legion, KC, Rotary. Republican. Roman Catholic.

CARPENTER, WILLIAM F., III, hospital management company executive, lawyer; BA, JD, Vanderbilt Univ. Ptnr. Waller Lansden Dortch & Davis, Nashville, 1983—98; gen. counsel Am. group HCA, Inc., 1998—99; sr. v.p. to exec. v.p., gen. counsel, corp. sec. LifePoint Hospitals, Inc., Brentwood, Tenn., 1999—2006, pres., CEO, 2006—. Bd. dir. Psychiatric Solutions Inc., 2004—, Fedn. Am. Hospitals. Office: Lifepoint Hospitals Inc Ste 200 103 Powell Ct Brentwood TN 37027

CARPENTER, WOODROW WILSON, retired manufacturing executive, ceramics engineer; b. Snyder, Ill., Sept. 11, 1915; s. Marion Ernest and Margaretta (Fawver) Carpenter; m. Fay D. Turner, Nov. 24, 1939 (div. 1959); 1 child, Gay M. Caldwell; m. Irmgard K. Toberg, Sept. 3, 1960. BS in Ceramic Engring., U. Ill., 1939. Rsch. engr. Ingram Richardson Mfg. Co., Frankfort, Ind., 1939-54; dir. rsch. Barrows Porcelain Enamel Co., Cin., 1954-58; chmn. bd. Ceramic Coating Co., Newport, Ky., 1958-97, Thompson Enamel, inc., Bellevue, Ky., 1997—2013; ret. Founder mag. Glass On Metal, 1982, W.W. Carpenter Enamel Found., 2003. Lt. col. AUS, 1941-46, PTO Mem. Enamelist Soc. (founder 1986). Avocations: magic, puzzles, golf. Home: 645 Colfax Ave Bellevue KY 41073-1621

CARPER, BARBARA ANNE, nursing educator; BSN, Tex. Women's U., 1959; clin. cert. in anesthesia, U. Mich., 1962; MEd, Columbia U., 1966, EdD, 1975. Instr. U. N.Mex. Coll. Nursing, Albuquerque, 1966-69; assoc. prof. Tex. Women's U. Coll. Nursing, Denton, 1976-80, prof., coord. doctoral program, 1980-82; prof. grad. program U. So. Maine Sch. Nursing, Portland, 1982-84; prof., chairperson dept. nursing Colby-Sawyer Coll., New London, 1984—89; prof. Regents Coll., SUNY, Albany, 1985-89; assoc. prof., coord. undergrad. program U. N.C. Coll. Nursing, Charlotte, 1989-91, interim dean, 1991-92, prof., assoc. dean for acad. affairs, 1992—99, prof., 1994—99, prof. emeritus. Vis. scholar Harvard U., 1981-82; mem. Nursing Theory Think Tank, 1982; mem. exec. bd., chmn. project com. New Eng. Orgn. Nursing, 1986-88; vis. prof. Marion A. Buckley Sch. Nursing, Adelphi U., 1989-90; Green Chair honor prof. Harris Coll. Nursing, Tex. Christian U., 1980-81; Margaret D. McLean lectr. Meml. U. Nfld., Can., 1990; numerous consultations, workshops, lectures, seminars and speeches in field. Mem. editorial bd. Jour. Advances in Nursing Sci., 1978-99, Asian Jour. Nursing Studies, 1993-95; contbr. articles to profl. jours. Bd. dirs., mem. exec. com., mem. patient and cmty. svcs. com. Nat. Kidney Found. N.H., 1987-89; bd. dirs. Hospice at Charlotte, 1991-97, co-chairperson ethics adv. com., 1995-97, vice chair at large 1996-97; bd. dirs. Cmty. Health Svcs., 1991-94. Fellow Am. Acad. Nursing (co-chair ethics/legal adv. com. 1983-86, mem. planning com. 1988, Ann. Sci. Sessions of Acad., mem. expert panel on ethics 1991—); mem. ANA (coun. nurse rschrs.), N.C. State Nursing Assn., Sigma Theta Tau (Disting. lectr. 1994-95), Phi Kappa Phi. Personal E-mail: drbcarper@gmail.com.

CARPI, JANICE E., insurance company executive, lawyer; b. Whittier, Calif., June 15, 1952; d. Leonard William and Elizabeth Louise (Severns) Carpi; m. Garland M. Harwood III, July 3, 1993; 1 child, Sarah Elizabeth. BA in Internat. Affairs, George Washington U., 1975; JD, Southern Meth. U., 1978. Bar: Nev. 1978, Tex. 1979, Va. 1994. Assoc. Wesner Wylie & Pleasant, Dallas, 1979—80; underwriting atty. Chgo. Title Ins. Corp., Dallas, 1980—83; underwriting counsel Lawyers Title Insurance Corp., Dallas, 1983—86, sr. v.p., 1983—, v.p., sr. underwriting counsel Richmond, Va., 1986—98, counsel, 1990—2009; spkr. Practicing Law Inst., NYC, 1998; v.p., sr. underwriting counsel LandAmerica Fin. Group, Richmond, 1998, counsel, 1998—2009, sr. v.p., 2007—08; nat. comml. underwriting counsel Fidelity National Title, 2009—; sr. v.p., nat. comml. underwriting counsel Fidelity National Financial Services, 2009—. Contbr. chpts. in books. Vol. Jr. League Dallas, 1983—85, Habitat for Humanity, Richmond, 1996—; eucharistic min. St. Martin's Episc. Ch., Richmond, 2001—. Fellow: Am. Coll. Real Estate Lawyers (chair meetings com. 2001—); mem.: ABA (chair Title Ins. com. 2001—), Coll. of State Bar Tex., Phi Delta Phi. Avocation: travel. Office: Fidelity National Financial Inc 601 Riverside Ave Jacksonville FL 32204 Office Phone: 904-854-8100. Office Fax: 904-357-1007.

CARR, BESSIE, retired elementary school educator; b. Nathalie, Va., Oct. 10, 1920; d. Henry C. and Sirlena (Ewell) Carr. BS, Elizabeth City Coll., NC, 1942; MA, Columbia U. Tchrs. Coll., 1948, PhD, 1950, EdD, 1952. Cert. adminstr., supr., tchr. Prin. pub. sch., Halifax, Va., 1942—47, Nathalie-Halifax County, Va., 1947—51; prof. edn. Southern U., Baton Rouge, 1952—53; supr. schs. Lackland Schs., Cin., 1953—54; prof. edn. Wilberforce U., Ohio, 1954—55; tchr. Leland Sch., Pittsfield, Mass., 1956—60; chair math. dept., tchr. Lakeland Mid. Sch., NY, 1961—83. Founder, organizer, sponsor 1st Math Bowl and Math Forum Area, 1970—76. Recipient Carr award, Halifax County Sr. High Sch., 1962. Mem.: AAUW (auditor 1970—85), Black Women Bus. & Profl. Assn. (charter mem. Senegal, Africa chpt.), Ret. Tchrs. Assn., Assn. Suprs. Math. (chair coordinating coun. 1976—80), Delta Kappa Gamma (auditor internat. 1970—76). Democrat. Avocations: travel, photography, souvenirs.

CARR, BONNIE JEAN, professional ice skater; b. Chgo., Sept. 29, 1947; d. Nicholas and Agnes Marie (Moran) Musashe; m. James Bradley Carr, Dec. 8, 1984; children: Brittany Jean, James Bradley II, Brooke Anderson. BS, Northwestern U., 1969; JD (hon.), Loyola U., Chgo., 1978. Skater Adventures on Ice, Mpls., 1961; prin. skater Jamboree on Ice, Chgo., 1961-68; society editor The Free Press, Colorado Springs, Colo., 1969; prin. skater, publicist on tour, asst. lighting dir., tour ednl. tutor Holiday on Ice Internat., 1970-74; skating dir. William McFetridge Sports Ctr., Chgo., 1975-86; choreographer, prin. skater Ice Time, USA, Mundelein, Ill., 1975—. Skating coach St. Bronislava Athletic Club, Chgo., 1967-69; publicity dir. Amateur Skating Assn. Ill., Chgo., 1968; founder, dir. skating programs for blind, hearing impaired and mentally handicapped, Chgo., 1975-85; phys. fitness advisor Exec. Health Seminars, Chgo., 1979; founder, dir. skating programs Fred Hutchinson Cancer Rsch. Ctr., Seattle, 1985-86; guest spkr. Am. Cancer Soc., Columbia, S.C., 1973; conditioning coach Riverside Wellness and Fitness Ctr., Richmond, Va., 1989-91, Southampton Rec. Assn., Richmond, 1991-94; figure & speed skating coach Va. Spl. Olympics, 1991—. Recipient Key to City, Mobile, Ala., 1973, Svc. Recognition award Spl. Olympics, Chgo., 1984. Mem. Am. Guild Variety Artists, Am. Coun. on Exercise (cert. 1990-96). Avocations: writing, dance. Home and Office: Ice Time USA 1110 Cresthill Ct Leland NC 28451 Personal E-mail: bonniejcarr@gmail.com.

CARR, CASSANDRA COLVIN, communications company executive; b. Champaign, Ill., Nov. 14, 1944; d. A.B. and Irene Colvin; m. Edward M. Carr, Nov. 27, 1970. BA, Vanderbilt U., 1966; MA, U. Tex., 1973. Mgr., revenue requirements Southwestern Bell Telephone Co., Austin, Tex., 1985, mgr., congl. asst. program Washington, 1986; dir., govt. rels. Southwestern Bell Corp., St. Louis, 1986-87, mng. dir., govt. rels., 1987-88, v.p. fin., treas., 1988, sr. v.p. fin., treas., 1988-90, v.p., revenues and pub. affairs Austin, Tex., 1990, sr. v.p., human resources San Antonio, 1994—98, sr. exec. v.p., external affairs, 1998—2002; sr. advisor Public Strategies, Inc., 2002—. Bd. dirs. YRC Worldwide Inc., 1997—2010, Temple-Inland Inc., 2004—. Commr. St. Louis Regional Conv. and Sports Complex Authority; bd. dirs. The Arch Funds, Inc., St. Louis, The Conf. Bd., N.Y.C., Found. Women's Resources, Austin. Recipient YWCA Leader award YWCA of St. Louis, 1988. Mem. Fin. Execs. Inst., Nat. Assn. Corp. Treasurers, St. Louis Club, Forest Hills Country Club. Office: SBC Communications Inc PO Box 2933 175 E Houston 6th Fl San Antonio TX 78299-2933 also: Public Strategies Inc 98 San Jacinto Blvd Austin TX 78701 Office Phone: 512-474-8848. Office Fax: 512-474-0120. Business E-Mail: cassandra.carr@pstrategies.com.

CARR, JOE, state legislator; b. Mar. 25, 1958; m. Ginny Carr; children: Erin, Maddie, Joe Jr. BS, Middle Tenn. State U., 1981. Owner Cedar Snag Farms, Virtual Edge, LLC.; pvt. pilot; mem. Dist. 48 Tenn. House of Reps., 2008—. Republican. Christian. Mailing: 3750 Overall Rd Lascassas TN 37085 Office: 205 War Memorial Bldg Nashville TN 37243 Office Phone: 615-741-2180. Business E-Mail: rep.joe.carr@capitol.tn.gov.

CARR, LEILA S., bank executive; b. 1961; 2 children. BA in History, U. Va., 1983. Banker First Union Nat. Bank, 1983—2000; sr. v.p., dir., sales, mktg. & product devel. Synovus Fin. Corp., Columbus, Ga., 2000—04, sr. v.p., retail banking, 2004—05; exec. v.p., retail banking Synovus Financial Corp., Columbus, Ga., 2005—. Active The Family Ctr., Columbus; bd. mem. St. Luke Early Learning Ctr., Girls, Inc., Columbus. Named one of 25 Women to Watch, US Banker, 2006, 25 Most Powerful Women in Banking, 2007. Mailing: Synovus Financial Corp PO Box 120 Columbus GA 31902 Office Phone: 706-649-2311. Business E-Mail: leilacarr@synovus.com.

CARR, NEVIN P., JR., federal agency administrator; BS in Naval Arch., US Naval Acad., 1979, MS in Ops. Rsch. Served Office Sec. Def.; served office chief naval ops. USN, exec. asst. to comdr., US Fleet Forces Command, dep. dir. surface warfare, combat systems and weapons, 2006, dep. asst. sec., internat. programs, dir. Navy internat. programs office; chief naval rsch., dir. test evaluation and tech. requirements Office Naval Rsch., Arlington, Va., 2008—. Served USN, served USN, Black Sea, comdr. USN, USS Arleigh Burke, comdr. USN, USS Cape St. George. Office: Office Naval Rsch One Liberty Ctr 875 N Randolph St Ste 1425 Arlington VA 22203-1995

CARR, OSCAR CLARK, III, lawyer; b. Memphis, Apr. 9, 1951; s. Oscar Clark Carr Jr. and Billie (Fisher) Carr Houghton; m. Mary Leatherman, Aug. 4, 1973; children: Camilla Fisher Carr Brinner, Oscar Clark IV. BA in English with distinction, U. Va., 1973; JD with distinction, Emory U., 1976. Bar: Tenn. 1976, US Dist. Ct. (we. dist.) Tenn. 1977, (no. dist.) Miss. 1977, US Ct. Appeals (6th cir.) 1985, (5th cir.) 1995, US Dist. Ct. (so. dist.) Miss. 2000; cert. mediator Tenn. 2007, US Supreme Ct. Assoc. Glankler Brown, PLLC (formerly Glankler, Brown, et al, Memphis, 1976-82, ptnr., 1982—, chief mgr., 1998-00; vestryman St. Johns Episcopal Ch., Memphis, 2011—. Mem. Emory Law Coun., 2004—08. Treas., vestryman St. John's Episcopal Ch., Memphis, 1988—91, sr. warden, 1991; mem. Commn. on Ministry Diocese of West Tenn., 1987—90; King of Carnival Memphis, 1994; bd. dirs. West Tenn. chpt. Juvenile Diabetes Found., 1998—2004, dir., 1998—2002; bd. dirs. Memphis Ballet Soc., 1980, Memphis-Shelby County Unit Am. Cancer Soc., Memphis Oral Sch. Deaf, 1988—91, Carnival Memphis. Recipient Living and Giving award, West Tenn. chpt. Juvenile Diabetes Rsch. Found., 2002; named Super Lawyer, 2006—10, Benchmark Litigation Star, Tenn.; named one of Best Lawyers in America, 1993—2010. Fellow Tenn. Bar Found., Litig. Counsel Am.; mem. ABA, Tenn. Bar Assn. (we. dist. coun. environ. law 1992-2000), Memphis-Shelby County Bar Assn. (bd. dirs. 1985-87), Memphis Country Club (atty. 2004-), Lawyers Jour. Club of Memphis. Episcopalian. Office: Glankler Brown PLLC Ste 400 6000 Poplar Ave Memphis TN 38119 Home Phone: 901-458-1155; Office Phone: 901-525-1322, 901-525-1322. Business E-Mail: ocarr@glankler.com.

CARR, ROBYN, writer; m. Jim Carr; 2 children. Author: Chelynne, 1980, The Blue Falcon, 1981, The Bellerose Bargain, 1982, The Braeswood Tapestry, 1984, The Troubadour's Romance, 1985, By Right of Armes, 1986, The Everlasting Covenant, 1987, Rogue's Lady, 1987, Tempted, 1987, Informed Risk, 1987, Woman's Own, 1990, Mind Tryst, 1992, The House on Olive Street, 1999, The Wedding Party, 2001, Blue Skies, 2004, Runaway Mistress, 2005, Never Too Late, 2006, A Summer in Sonoma, 2010, Four Friends, 2014, (anthologies) To Mother with Love, 1989, That Holiday Feeling, 2009, More Than Words, Volume 6, 2010, Midnight Kiss, 2010, (non-fiction) Practical Tips for Writing Popular Fiction, 1992, (Virgin River Series) Virgin River, 2007, Shelter Mountain, 2007, Whispering Rock, 2007, A Virgin River Christmas, 2008, Second Chance Pass, 2009, Temptation Ridge, 2009, Paradise Valley, 2009, Under the Christmas Tree (novella), 2009, Forbidden Falls, 2010, Angel's Peak, 2010, Moonlight Road, 2010, Midnight Confessions (novella), 2010, Promise Canyon, 2011, Wild Man Creek, 2011, Harvest Moon, 2011, Bring Me Home for Christmas, 2011, Hidden Summit, 2012, Redwood Bend, 2012, Sunrise Point, 2012, My Kind of Christmas, 2012, (Grace Valley Series) Deep in the Valley, 2000, Just Over the Mountain, 2002, Down by the River, 2003, (Thunder Point Series) The Wanderer, 2013, The Newcomer, 2013, The Hero, 2013. Avocation: travel. Address: Nancy Bertand Public Relations Inc 2816 NW 57th Ste Ste 101 Oklahoma City OK 73112

CARREKER, JAMES D., investment company executive; BS in Mktg., Okla. State U., MBA. With Federated Dept. Stores, 1972; pres., CEO Trammell Crow Co. (subs. CB Richard Ellis Group, Inc.), Trammell Crow Residential Co., Dallas, 1988—98; mng. gen. partner Wyndham Hotels; pres., CEO & bd. dirs. Wyndham Hotel Corp.; CEO Wyndham Internat., Inc., 1998—99, chmn., 1999—2000; bd. dir., non-exec. chmn. Bombay Co., Inc., Fort Worth, 2002—03, CEO, chmn. bd. dirs., 2003—06; owner, founder JDC Holdings, Inc., 2000—. Bd. dirs. Homegate Hospitality Inc., 1996—, Cracker Barrel Old Country Store Inc. (formerly, CBRL Group Inc.), 2002—09, Brown Jordan Internat. Inc. (formerly Winsloew Furniture Inc.), 2001—, Performing Brands, Inc., 2007—. Office: Performing Brands Inc Bd Directors 4951 Airport Pky Ste 600 Addison TX 75001 Office Phone: 972-818-3862.

CARRERAS, FRANCISCO JOSÉ, retired academic and foundation administrator; b. San Juan, May 13, 1932; s. Francisco and Antonia (Muriente) C.; m. Ana Elisa Carreras, Mar. 29, 1964; children: Inés María, María Soledad, Irene María, Marianne, Francisco José, María del Pilar. Student, Instituto Superior de Estudios Clásicos, Havana, Cuba, 1954-57; BA, Universidad Pontificia de Comillas, Santander, Spain, 1959; MA, Fordham U., Bronx, NY, 1960; PhD, Universidad Pontificia Gregoriana, Rome, 1966. Mem. faculty U. P.R., Rio Piedras Campus, 1962-69, acad. asst. to dir., 1967-69, dir. humanities dept., 1967-68; pres. Cath. U. P.R., Ponce, 1969-81; academician P.R. Acad. Arts and Scis., 1970; exec. dir. Angel Ramos Found., Inc., San Juan, 1984—; mem. P.R. State Commn. on Post-Secondary Edn., 1973. Dir. Banco Popular de P.R. Author: Filosofía de la Coordinación de José Vasconcelos, 1971, Incógnita y Revelación, 1981; also articles. Adv. Sociedad Puertorriqueña UNESCO, 1973; pres. P.R. Endowment for Humanities, 1977; bd. dirs. Angel Ramos Found., 1977; bd. dirs. Damas Hosp., 1978, P.R. Acad. Arts and Scis., 1980; adv. bd. dirs. Orgns. Universidades Católicas de América Latina, 1976. Recipient Pres.'s medal Ana G. Mendez Univ. Sys.-P.R., 2000; named Knight of St. Gregory the Great, 2007. Mem. Fundación Puertorriqueña Humanidades (pres. 1977), Ponce Sales and Mktg. Execs. Assn., Alpha Phi Omega, Phi Delta Kappa. Clubs: Rotary, Lions. Roman Catholic. Home: 1 St C-16 Villas Del Pilar San Juan PR 00926-5448 Office: Angel Ramos Found Inc PO Box 362408 San Juan PR 00936-2408 Office Phone: 787-763-3530. Business E-Mail: fcarreras@farpr.org.

CARRICK, FREDERICK ROBERT, neurologist, researcher; b. Toronto, Ont., Can., Feb. 26, 1952; s. Donald Thomas and June Madeline Carrick; m. Eve Diminture, Dec. 29, 1973; children: Tricia A. Carrick-Merlin, James E. DC, Can. Meml., Toronto, 1979; PhD, Walden U., Mpls., 1996. Diplomate in chiropractic neurology Am. Chiropractic Assn., 1985, diplomate Am. Acad. Chiropractic Neurology, Va., 1989, Am. Chiropractic Neurology Bd., Va., 1995, Am. Acad. Pain Mgmt., Va., 2000, cert. in childhood devel. disorders ABCN, Tex., 2004, vestibular rehab. ACNB, Tex., 2005, in electrodiagnostics 2005. Clin. neurologist Epsom Clinic, NH, 1979—90; prof. neurology Carrick Inst. Grad. Studies, Cape Canaveral, Fla., 1984—; disting. post grad. prof. clin. neurology Logan Coll., St. Louis, 1990—99; prof. emeritus neurology Parker Coll., Dallas, 1997—2000. Contbr. sci. articles to profl. publs. Cpl. Can. Army Commando, 1970—73, Cyprus, Middle East. Decorated Medal UNFICYP UN, Medal Svc. de la Paix Govt. Can. Fellow: ACA, Royal Coll. Physicians and Surgeons, Am. Coll. Clin. Neurology, European Acad. Chiropractic Neurology, Internat. Coll. Chiropractors. Avocations: aviation, boating, martial arts. Office: Carrick Inst Graduate Studies 203-8941 Lake Dr Cape Canaveral FL 32920 Office Fax: 321-868-6468. Business E-Mail: registrar@carrickinstitute.org.

CARRICO, CHARLES W., SR., (BILL CARRICO), state legislator; b. Marion, Va., Nov. 6, 1961; Treas. Grayson Republican Party; mem. Dist. 5 Va. House of Delegates, 2002—12; mem. Dist. 40 Va. State Senate, 2012—, mem. Transp. Com., Edn. and Health Com., Privileges and Elections Com. & Rehab. and Social Services Com. Mem. pastor coun. Ch. of God. Mem.: Va. State Police Assn. (youth leadership coun.). Republican. Pentecostal. Office: Senate of Virginia PO Box 396 Richmond VA 23218 also: PO Box 1100 Galax VA 24333 Office Phone: 804-698-7540. Office Fax: 804-698-7651. E-mail: district40@senate.virginia.gov.

CARRICO, PAUL D., chemical company executive; b. Louisville, 1950; MChE, U. Louisville, 1973; MMgmtS, MIT, 1993. Gen mgr. vinyl and olefins CONDEA Vista; bus. mgr. resin divsn. Georgia Gulf Corp., 1999—2005, v.p. polymers, 2005—06, v.p. chemicals and vinyls, 2006—08, pres., CEO, 2008—. Bd. dirs. Ga. Gulf Corp., 2008—. Office: Ga Gulf Corp 115 Perimeter Ctr Pl Ste 460 Atlanta GA 30346 Office Phone: 770-395-4500. Office Fax: 770-395-4529.

CARRIER, RONALD EDWIN, academic administrator, director; b. Bluff City, Tenn., Aug. 18, 1932; s. James Murphy and Melissa (Miller) C.; m. Edith Marie Johnson, Sept. 7, 1955; children: Michael Lavon, Linda Lois Carrier Frazee, Jennine Marie. BS, Ea. Tenn. State U., Johnson City, 1955; MS in Econs., U. Ill., Champagne-Urbana, 1957, PhD in Econs., 1960; Doctorate (hon.), William and Mary Coll., Williamsburg, Va., Bridgewater Coll., Va., Jacksonville State U., Ala., Francis Marion U., Florence, SC, Romanian Am. U., Bucharest. Assoc. prof. econs. U. Miss., Oxford, 1960-63; dir., prof. Bur. Bus. and Econ. Rsch., Memphis U., 1963-66, provost, v.p. acad. affairs, 1966-71; pres., chancellor James Madison U., Harrisonburg, Va., 1971—2002, pres. emeritus, 2002—; pres. Ctr. Innovative Tech., Herndon, Va., 1986-87. Chancellor Romanian Am. U.; vis. scholar LMI, 2008—09; bd. dirs. Project Meridian, US State, 2010. Author: Plant Locations: A Theory and Explanations, 1968; contbr. articles to profl. jours. Mem. White House Conf. Balance Econ. Growth, Va. Indsl. Facilities Study Commn., 1972—75; chmn. Va. Land Use Adv. Com., 1974—77, Va. Gov.'s Electricity Costs Commn., 1975—; mem. Va. Gov.'s Energy Resource Adv. Commn., 1975—76, Gov.'s Regulatory Reform Adv. Bd., 1983, Joint Subcom. to Study Coal Slurry Pipeline Feasibility 2002., 1983; chair ethics com. Senate Va., 1999; mem. Va. Higher Edn. Steering Commn., 2002; mem. bd. visitors Va. State U., 2002—04. Earheart fellow, 1958-60; recipient Ben Franklin award Memphis Printing Industry, 1966, Faculty award East Tenn. State U., 1955, Disting. Svc. award Jr. C. of C., 1965; named Outstanding alumni award East Tenn. State U., 1975, Disting. Alumnus in Higher Edn., 1999, Virginian of Yr. award Va. Assn. Broadcasters, 1982, cultural laureate Va., Outstanding Virginian FFA, 1991, Named Sports Hall of Fame, 2009 Mem.: Sigma Phi Epsilon, Omicron Delta Gamma, Omicron Delta Kappa. Methodist. Office:

James Madison U MSC 5730 Harrisonburg VA 22807 Home: 209 Divot Dr Harrisonburg VA 22802 Home Phone: 540-438-1582; Office Phone: 540-568-8181. Business E-Mail: carriere@jmu.edu.

CARRIG, KENNETH J., human resources specialist; m. Lisa Carrig; 3 children. BS in Labor Econs., Cornell U., 1981. With PepsiCo, Inc.; head human resources Continental Airlines, 1995—97; global practice leader human capital practice Andersen Cons.; v.p., chief adminstrv. officer Sysco Corp., Houston, 1998—99, sr. v.p. adminstrn., 1998—2004, exec. v.p., chief adminstrv. officer, 2004—09; exec. v.p. Human Resources Comcast Cable Comcast Corp., Phila., 2009—11; corp. exec. v.p., chief human resources officer SunTrust Banks, Inc., Atlanta, 2011—. Fellow: Nat. Acad. of Human Resources. Office: SunTrust Banks Inc 303 Peachtree St NE Atlanta GA 30308

CARRINGTON, PAUL DEWITT, lawyer, educator; b. Dallas, June 12, 1931; s. Paul and Frances Ellen (DeWitt) C.; m. Bessie Meek, Aug., 1952; children: Clark DeWitt, Mary Carrington Coults, William James, Emily Carrington. BA, U. Tex., 1952; LLB, Harvard U., 1955. Bar: Tex. 1955, Ohio 1962, Mich. 1967. Practice, Dallas, 1955; teaching fellow Harvard U., 1957-58; asst. prof. law U. Wyo., 1958-60, Ind. U., 1960-62; assoc. prof. Ohio State U., 1962-65; prof. U. Mich., 1965-78; dean Duke U. Sch. Law, Durham, NC, 1978-88, prof., 1978—2010. Reporter civil rules adv. com. Jud. Conf. of U.S., 1985-92. Author (with Meador and Rosenberg): Justice on Appeal, 1977, Appeals, 1994; author: (with Babcock) Civil Procedure, 1977, 3d edit., 1983; author: Stewards of Democracy, 1999, Spreading America's Word, 2005; author: (with Cramton) Reforming the Supreme Court, 2006; author: (with Jones) Law and Class in America, 2006. Trustee Ann Arbor (Mich.) Bd. Edn., 1970-73; pres. Pvt. Adjudication Ctr., Inc., 1988-94, chmn., 1995-2002. With US Army, 1955—57, with USAR, 1957—61. Guggenheim fellow, 1988-89. Fellow: Am. Acad. Appellate Lawyers, Am. Acad. Arts and Scis., Am. Bar Found.; mem.: ABA, Am. Law Inst. Office: Duke U Sch Law Durham NC 27708-0362 Home Phone: 919-489-8668; Office Phone: 919-613-7040. Business E-Mail: pdc@law.duke.edu.

CARRION, ARTURO, health products executive; BBA in Acctg., U. Puerto Rico. CPA. With KPMG LLP, 1978—87; v.p., fin. GA Life, 1987—98; pres. Triple-S Vida, Inc. (subs. of Triple-S Management Corp.), 1998—, Triple S Mgmt. Corp. Mem. Puerto Rico Soc. of CPAs. Office: Triple-S Management Corp 1441 F D Roosevelt Ave San Juan PR 00920 Office Phone: 787-749-4949. Business E-Mail: acarrion@ssspr.com.

CARRION, RICHARD L., bank executive; b. San Juan, PR, 1952; BS, U. Penn.; MS in Mgmt. Info. Systems, MIT. Pres. Popular Inc., 1991—2009, Popular, Inc., 2010—; chmn. Popular Inc., 1993; chmn., CEO Popular, Inc., 1994—. Bd. dirs. Nynex Corp., 1995—97, Verizon Comm., 1997—, Fed. Reserve Bank NY, 1999, 2008—. Mem. exec. bd. Internat. Olympic Com. (IOC), 2004—; chmn., CEO Fundacion Banco Popular & Banco Popular Found. Office: Popular Inc Popular Ctr Bldg 209 Munoz Rivera Ave San Juan PR 00918 Office Phone: 787-765-9800. Office Fax: 787-759-7803.

CARRIÓN MUÑOZ, ARTURO L., banker; b. Santurce, PR, Nov. 6, 1933; s. Arturo L. and Celia (Muñoz) Carrión; m. Mercedes Crespo (div.); children— Arturo Luis, Eduardo Enrique, Carlos Rafael, Jaime Miguel, Mercedes; m. Eva Silén, Apr. 27, 1978 BBA in Econs., U. P.R.; grad. Stonier Grad. Sch. Banking, Rutgers U. Asst. v.p. Banco Popular de P.R., San Juan, 1962-68, 2d v.p., 1968-69, v.p., 1969-73, sr. v.p., 1973-78, exec. v.p., 1978—. Pres. organizing com. 8th Pan Am. Games, San Juan, 1979 Recipient Salesman of Yr. award Sales and Mktg. Exec. Assn., 1979, Citizen of Yr. award P.R. Mfrs.'s Assn., 1979, Top Mgmt. award Sales and Mktg. Exec. Assn., 1980 Mem. Fin. Analyst Assn. (pres. 1980-81) Clubs: Bankers (P.R.) (bd. dirs.). Roman Catholic. Avocations: music; sports. Office: Banco Popular de Puerto Rico Banco Popular Ctr Hato Rey PO Box 2708 San Juan PR 00936

CARROLL, BARBARA A., drilling company executive; b. Va. BS in Biology, James Madison U.; BS in Civil Engring., La. Tech. U., Ruston, MS in Environ. Sci.; MBA in Fin., Houston Baptist U. Gen. mgr. corp. environ. protection and compliance Panhandle Eastern Corp.; pub. affairs mgr. ExxonMobil Corp., Baytown, procurement svcs. mgr., materials and svc. mgr., 1990; v.p. environ., health and safety TEPPCO Ptnrs., LLP, 2002; cons. Rowan Companies, Inc., 2006—07, v.p. environ. affairs, 2007—08, v.p. health and safety and environment, 2008—. Bd. dirs. Armand Bayou Nature Ctr., Galveston Bay Found., Tex. Nature Conservancy. Office: Rowan Companies Inc 2800 Post Oak Blvd Ste 5450 Houston TX 77056 Office Phone: 713-621-7800. Office Fax: 713-960-7560.

CARROLL, CHRIS, marketing executive; BS in Mgmt., Manhattan Coll., 1980. Area mktg. mgr. Burger King Corp., Miami, Fla., 1985—86, regional dir. mktg., 1986—87, nat. dir. advt./sales promotion, 1987—89, dir. mktg., 1989—91, v.p. advt./sales promotion, 1991—93, v.p. internat. mktg., 1993—94; dir. retail mktg. LensCrafters Inc., 1994—96; sr. v.p. mktg./merchandising Olin Mills Corp., 1996—97; acct. dir. TracyLocke, 1997—99; sr. v.p. global mktg. Subway Restaurants, 1999—2005; exec. v.p., chief mktg. officer Cosi, Inc., 2006—08; exec. v.p., chief client officer Zimmerman Advt., 2009—. Office: Zimmerman Advt Hdqs 2200 W Commercial Blvd Fort Lauderdale FL 33309 Office Phone: 954-644-4000.

CARROLL, CHUCK (CHARLES A. CARROLL), manufacturing executive; Joined Rubbermaid Inc., 1971, pres. Rubbermaid specialty products, 1988—90, pres., gen. mgr. housewares product divsn., 1990—94, pres., COO, 1993-99; pres., CEO Amana Appliances, 2000—01, Goodman Global, Inc., Houston, 2004—08, non-exec. chmn., 2008—. Bd. dirs. Rubbermaid Inc., 1993—99, Goodman Global, Inc., 2001—. Office: Goodman Global Inc 5151 San Felipe Blvd Ste 500 Houston TX 77056

CARROLL, FRANK EDWARD, JR., radiologist, researcher; b. Phila., Oct. 25, 1941; s. Frank Edward Sr. and Marie Elizabeth (Mullin) C.; m. Saramae Dorothy Dever, Sept. 4, 1965; children: Frank Leonard, Mark Edward. BS in Biology, St. Joseph's Coll., 1963; MD, Hahnemann Med. Coll., 1967. Diplomate Am. Bd. Radiology. Rsch. asst. Hahnemann Med. Coll. and Hosp., Phila., 1965-66; rotating intern U.S. Naval Regional Med. Ctr., Oakland, Calif., 1967-68; submarine med. officer U.S. Submarine Med. Sch., U.S. Naval Submarine Base, Gorton, Conn., 1968, SSBN 659 Will Rogers Polaris Nuclear Submarine, 1968-69; staff physician Armed Forces Staff Coll., Norfolk, Va., 1969-70; diagnostic radiology resident St. Mary's Hosp. and Med. Ctr., San Francisco, 1970-72; resident, fellow, rschr. U. Calif. San Francisco Sch. Medicine, 1972-73; asst. prof. diagnostic radiology Yale U. Sch. Medicine, New Haven, 1973-74; staff radiologist Broadway Hosp., Vallejo, Calif., 1974-75, Franklin (Pa.) Regional Med. Ctr., 1975-83; asst. prof. diagnostic radiology Vanderbilt U. Med. Ctr., Nashville, 1983-87, chief sect. pulmonary imaging, 1983—2000, assoc. dir. divsn. diagnostic radiology, 1984, dir. lab. radiologic rsch., 1984-85, assoc. prof. diagnostic radiology, 1987-94, dir. diagnostic radiology, 1985-89, assoc. prof. physics and astronomy, 1993-99, prof. diagnostic radiology, 1994—2004, emeritus prof. diagnostic radiology, 2004—, prof. physics and astronomy, 1999—; founder Mxisystems, Inc., Nashville. Adj. asst. prof. diagnostic radiology Duke U. Med. Ctr., Durham, N.C., 1981-83; cons. in field; referee jours. in field, including Investigative Radiology, Acad. Radiology, Radiology, Chest, Jour. Applied Physiology, Archives of Internal Medicine, Am. Jour. Neuroradiology, others; grant reviewer NIH, Washington. Contbr. articles to profl. jours., chpts. to books. Bd. dirs. Nashville Opera, 1988-94, Franklin Emergency Ambulance Svc., 1975-83, St. Patrick's Sch. Bd., 1975-83; asst. scoutmaster Boy Scouts Am., Franklin, 1975-83, physician and merit badge counselor, Nashville, 1983—; pres. Am. Cancer Soc., Franklin, 1975-83; design prodn. vol. Cheekwood Fine Arts Mus., Nashville, 1995—. Lt. comdr. USNR, 1963—73, submarine med. officer USNR, 1968—71, base physician Armed Forces Staff Coll., 1970—71. Fellow Am. Coll. Radiology, Am. Coll. Chest Physicians; mem. Am. Soc. Laser Medicine and Surgery, Soc. Photo-Optical Instrumentation Engrs., Soc. for Magnetic Resonance Imaging, Assn. Univ. Radiologists, Radiol. Soc. N.Am., Soc. thoracic Radiology, Tenn. Radiologic Soc., Mid. Tenn. Radiologic Soc. Achievements include production of pulsed, tunable, monochromatic X-rays by the free electron laser; designed and commissioned dedicated tabletop laser tunable, synchrotron source for monochromatic 3-D mammography without breast compression, k-edge imaging, auger cascade radiotherapy, phase contrast imaging, time-of flight imaging and protein crystallography; evaluation of lung water by magnetic resonance imaging. Home: 1216 Vintage Pl Nashville TN 37215-4707 Office: Vanderbilt U Med Ctr Emeritus Office 211 Oxford House Nashville TN 37232-4245 Office Phone: 615-322-0860. Business E-Mail: frank.carroll@vanderbilt.edu.

CARROLL, J. RANDALL, bank executive; b. Atlanta, 1945; BS in Indsl. Mgmt., Ga. Inst. Tech., 1968. Various positions Trust Co. of Ga., 1968—72, First Nat. Bank of Tucker, Ga., 1972—74, exec. v.p., br. coord. metro Atlanta area, 1974—86; founder, chmn., pres., CEO Mountain Nat. Bank, Tucker, 1988—2004; chmn., CEO Merit Holding Corp. (merged with Synovus Fin. Corp.), 1996—99; pres., COO Bank of North Georgia, Alpharetta, 2004—06, vice-chmn., 2006—; CEO Bank of Coweta, Ga., 2009—. Trustee Ga. Tech. Athletic Assn.; bd. trustees Georgia Tech Found., Inc., DeKalb Med. Found., Inc.; bd. dirs., treas. Emile T. Fisher Found. Dental Edn. in Ga., Inc.; bd. dirs., sec. HealthMPowers. Office: Bank of Coweta 110 Jefferson St Newnan GA 30263-1421 also: Bank of North Georgia Corp Hdqs 8025 Westside Pky Alpharetta GA 30009 Office Phone: 770-253-1340.

CARROLL, JAMES EDWIN, child neurologist, researcher; b. Joplin, Mo., May 15, 1945; s. George Henry and Sarah Frances (Montee) C.; m. Shirley Ann Carol Rohlander, July 1, 1967; children: John, Peter, Ruth, Rebecca, Timothy, Matthew, Lydia, Elizabeth. BS, U. Louisville, 1966, MD, 1969. Diplomate Nat. Bd. Med. Examiners, Am. Bd. Pediat., Am. Bd. Psychiatry and Neurology. Resident in pediat. Louisville (Ky.) Children's Hosp., 1969-71; resident in child neurology U. Colo., Denver, 1973-76; fellowship, faculty Washington U., St. Louis, 1976-84; chief child neurology, prof. Med. Coll. Ga., Augusta, 1984-88; prof., dir. pediat. tng. program Kuwait U., 1988-90; prof., dir. child neurology, vice chmn. neurology Med. Coll. Ga., Augusta, 1990—. Co-dir. Jerry Lewis Neuromuscular Rsch. Ctr., Washington. U., 1982-84; dir. Muscular Dystrophy Clinic, Med. Coll. Ga., 1991—; mem. Ga. Myasthenia Gravis Med. Adv. Bd., 1985-88. Author book chpts.; contbr. over 60 articles to profl. jours. Mem. exec. bd. United Cerebral Palsy of Ctrl. Savannah River Area, Augusta, 1985-88. Served to lt. comdr. USN, 1971-73. Recipient Investigator award NIH, 1979-83, grant NIH, 1986-89, Meritorious Honor award for scv. in Embassy in Kuwait, U.S. Dept. State, 1990. Fellow Am. Acad. Pediat., Am. Acad. Neurology; mem. Soc. for Pediat. Rsch., Am. Neurol. Assn. Republican. Presbyterian. Achievements include characterization of biochemical findings in a number of neuromuscular diseases. Home: 2711 Hunters Xing Augusta GA 30907-4710 Office: Med Coll Ga Child Neurology CJ2103 Augusta GA 30912 Office Phone: 706-721-3371. E-mail: jcarroll@mcg.edu.

CARROLL, JAMES VINCENT, III, lawyer; b. Houston, Sept. 21, 1940; s. James Vincent and Adoline (Easley) C.; children: Mary Latham, James Vincent IV, David Carter. BBA, U. Tex., 1962, JD, 1964. Bar: Tex. 1965, D.C. 1983. Mem. Andrews & Kurth L.L.P. and predecessors, 1965-95; mng. ptnr. Washington, 1981-83; mng. shareholder Houston office of Littler Mendelson P.C., 1995—98; mem., firm-wide mgmt. com. Littler Mendelson P.C., 1995—98, shareholder, 1995—2006; ret., 2006. Mem. U.S. del. 2d UN Conf. on Exploration and Peaceful Uses of Outer Space, 1982. Contbr. articles in field to profl. jours. Served with USCG, 1964-65, lt. comdr. USNR, 1965-69. Fellow Houston Bar Assn., ABA Found.; mem. NAM (labor law adv. com. 1983-93), ABA (vice-chmn. oil com. natural resources sect. 1980-85, chmn. energy and natural resources litigation com. 1985-86, coun. mem. 1986-89, chmn. technology com. 1988-89), Tex. Bar Assn. (dir. labor law sect. 1974-76, chmn. fed. and state agy. subcom., com. on coordination with other state and fed. groups 1975-77), Houston Bar Assn. (founder and first chmn. labor and employment law sect. 1995-96, coun. mem. 1996-99), Tex. Assn. of Bus. (bd. dirs. 1986-89), U.S. C. of C. (labor law adv. com. 1984-87), East Tex. C. of C. (bd. dirs. 1984-87), U. Tex. Law Sch. Assn. (dir. 1980-83), Greater Houston Partnership (mem. govt. affairs coun. 1994-99), Houston Country Club, Tex. Home: 5130 Holly Terrace Dr Houston TX 77056-2100 Business E-Mail: jcarroll@littler.com.

CARROLL, MILTON, oil industry executive; b. Houston, 1950; m. Cynthia Carroll; 3 children. BS in Indsl. Tech., Tex. So. Univ., 1973. Various positions Schlumberger Well Services; founder, chmn., CEO Instrument Products, Inc., Houston, 1977—; bd. dir. CenterPoint Energy, Inc., Houston, 1992—, chmn., 2002—. Commr. Port of Houston, 1987—93; former dir. Blue Cross and Blue Shield of Tex., 1994, Seagull Energy Corp., 1997, Texas Eastern Products Pipeline Co. (TEPPCO), 1997, Devon Energy Corp., 2003—05; bd. dirs. EGL Inc., 2003—, DCP Midstream Partners, 2005—. Dir. Houston Endowment Inc., Ocean Energy, Health Care Svcs. Corp. Mailing: CenterPoint Energy PO Box 1700 Houston TX 77251-1700

CARROLL, PHILIP JOSEPH, JR., board member; b. New Orleans, Sept. 24, 1937; s. Philip Joseph and Rosemary Agnes (McEntee) Carroll; m. Charlene Marie Phillips, Jan. 3, 1959; children: Phillip III, Kenneth, Bruce. BS in Physics, Loyola U., New Orleans, 1958; MS in Physics, Tulane U., 1961. Dir., energy conservation divsn. U.S. Dept. Commerce, Washington, 1973—74; exec. dir. Nat. Ind. Energy Conservation Coun., 1974; petroleum engr. Shell Oil Co., New Orleans, L.A., NYC and Midland, Tex., 1961—73, regional engr., mgr., Southern exploration and prodn., 1974—75, div. mgr., prodn., Western exploration and prodn., 1975—78, gen. mgr., prodn., Western ops., 1978—79, gen. mgr., plans and integration, 1979, v.p., pub. affairs, 1979—85; mng. dir. Shell Internat. Gas, Shell Internat. Petroleum Co., 1985—86; sr. v.p., adminstrn. Shell Oil Co., Houston, 1986—88, exec. v.p., adminstrn., 1988—93, pres., 1993—98, bd. dirs., 1990; chmn., CEO Fluor Corp., Irvine, Calif., 1998—2002. Bd. dirs. BAE Sys., Texas Med. Ctr., Envirofuels, LLC, Boise Cascade Corp., Vulcan Materials Co., 1999; head, policy planning adv. bd. Iraq Oil Ministry, 2003—. Trustee Com. for Econ. Devel., 1991—, Baylor Coll. Medicine, Boys & Girls Clubs of Am.; mem. Gov.'s Bus. Coun. (Tex.), Nat. Petroleum Coun., Conf. Bd., 1991—, Nat. Action Coun. for Minorities in Engring., 1993—; adv. bd. mem. Salvation Army; bd. adminstrs. adv. bd. mem. Ctr. Bioenviron. Rsch. Tulane U.; bd. dirs. Am. Petroleum Inst., Am. Air Mus., Cen. Houston, Tex. Med. Ctr., Nat. Action Coun. for Minorities in Engring. Master: 25 Yr. Club Petroleum Industry; mem.: Am. Petroleum Inst. (life), Champions Golf Club, River Oaks Country Club, Tchefuncta Country Club (Covington, La.). Avocation: golf. Office: Vulcan Materials Co Bd Directors 1200 Urban Ctr Dr Birmingham AL 35242 Office Phone: 205-298-3000. Office Fax: 205-298-2960. Business E-Mail: carrollp@vmcmail.com.

CARROLL, ROY, retired academic administrator; b. England, Ark., Dec. 8, 1929; m. Eleanor Kate Moorefield, 1953; children: Jane, Linda. BA cum laude, Ouachita Bapt. U., 1951; MA, Vanderbilt U., 1959, PhD, 1964. Math. tchr. Baker H.S., Columbus, Ga., 1955; asst. prof. history and polit. sci. Mercer U., Macon, Ga., 1959-65; prof. history, chmn. dept. history and polit. sci. Armstrong State Coll., Savannah, Ga., 1965-69; prof. history, chmn. dept. history Appalachian State U., Boone, NC, 1969-79; v.p. planning gen. adminstrn. U. NC Sys., 1979-90, 91-96, sr. v.p., v.p. acad. affairs, 1996-99, ret., 1999; interim chancellor U. NC, Asheville, 1990-91. Mem. NC Justice Edn. and Tng. Stds. Commn., 1979-90, chmn. planning com., 1981-88; mem. adv. bd. Inst. Transp. Rsch. and Edn., Rsch. Triangle Park, 1980—; bd. dirs. Western NC Devel. Assn., 1990-91, NC State Employees Credit Union, 1990-91, Rsch. Triangle Inst., 1996-2000; trustee Appalachian State U., 2000-05. Contbr. articles to profl. jours. Inf. officer U.S. Army, 1951-53, Japan, Korea. Fulbright scholar, Eng., 1958-59. Office: U NC Gen Adminstrn PO Box 2688 Chapel Hill NC 27515-2688 Home: 134 Carolina Meadows Villa Chapel Hill NC 27517 E-mail: rcl@ga.unc.edu.

CARROLL, SEAN, healthcare services company executive; BA in Profl. Writing, Miami U., Oxford, Ohio. Various sales and mgmt. positions, including dist. sales mgr., nat. and key account mgr. and sales rep. Lanier Bus. Products, 1987—91; co-founder TransQuick, Inc. (acquired by Rodeer Sys., Inc.), pres., CEO, 1990—97, gen. mgr., 1997—98; v.p., sales, COO Rodeer Sys., Inc. (acquired by Webmedx, Inc.), divsn. sales and svc. devel., 1998—99, CEO, former bd. dirs., 1999; pres., med. transcription divsn., CEO, sales and mktg. Webmedx, Inc., bd. dirs., CEO, 2004—. Bd. dirs. AHIMA Found., 2009—. Office: Webmedx Inc 3350 Riverwood Pkwy SE Ste 1850 Atlanta GA 30339-3300 Office Phone: 770-522-4881. Office Fax: 770-522-4889. Business E-Mail: scarroll@webmedx.com.

CARROLL, STEPHEN DOUGLAS, chemist, researcher; b. Clarendon, Ark., Nov. 2, 1943; s. Albert Genson and Wilma Mae (Hill) C.; m. Nonnie Lee Dyer, June 8, 1991; children: Geoffrey Genson, Raymond Loyd. BA, Hendrix Coll., 1965; MS, U. Ark., 1970. Del. chemist Chicopee Mfg. Co., North Little Rock, Ark., 1969-73, Mgr. Quality Assurance, 1973-80; cons. self employed, Clarendon, Ark., 1980-82; rsch. asst. U. Ark., Marianna, 1982-87, rsch. specialist, 1987-98, rsch. assoc., 1998—2004, program assoc. III, 2004—. Mem. Am. Chem. Soc. Democrat. Methodist. Avocations: photography, writing, painting. Office: U Ark Highway 1 Byp Marianna AR 72360 E-mail: dcarroll@uark.edu.

CARROZZA, VINCENT A., investment company executive; b. NYC, Jan. 15, 1925; s. Rocco Carrozza and Barbara DeLuca; m. Anne Reeves Carrozza, Jan. 10, 1954; children: Fay, Lynn, Robert. BA, Columbia U., NYC, 1949. Gen. mgr. Midnight Sun Broadcasting Co., Fairbanks, Alaska, 1954—56; dir. Alaska Statehood Campaign, Fairbanks, 1956; exec. v.p. Dallas Tex. Corp., 1958—69; real estate developer Ctr. City Inc., Dallas, 1969—90; chmn., CEO Carrozza Investments, Dallas, 1990—. Trustee Monyreit, NYC, 1986—90. Trustee, pres. Dallas Mus. Art, 1976—90; trustee, vice chmn. St. John's Coll., Santa Fe, 1984—89, Annapolis, Md., 1984—89; trustee Columbia U., NYC, 1990—93; trustee, exec. com. Am. Acad. Rome, NYC, 1984—90; trustee Italian Acad. Advanced Studies, NYC, 1992—95; world coun. mem. Internat. Ho., NYC; founding mem. Goals For Dallas; bd. dirs. Alzheimer's Disease and Related Disorders. Sgt. inf. US Army, 1942—45, Europe. Recipient Order Merit, Rep. Italy, 1987. Mem.: Nat. Inst. Aging (bd. dirs. 1970—), Century Assn., Idlewild. Avocation: tennis. Office: Carrozza Investments 2714 Routh St Dallas TX 75201

CARRUTHERS, THOMAS NEELY, lawyer; b. Columbia, Tenn., Oct. 11, 1928; s. Thomas Neely and Ellen Douglas (Everett) Carruthers; m. Dale Gilder Jones, Feb. 7, 1959; children: Thomas Neely III, Virginia Carruthers Smith, Catherine Everett. AB, Princeton U., 1950; LLB, Yale U., 1955. Assoc. Bradley, Arant, Rose & White, Birmingham, Ala., 1955-63, ptnr., 1963—2009, chair exec. com. and mng. ptnr., 1990-95, of counsel, 2010—. Mem. editl. bd. Yale Law Jour., 1953—55. Trustee Ala. Shakespeare Festival, Leadership Ala., pres., 1995—96, chmn., 1996—97; trustee Birmingham Mus. Art, chmn., 1995—2002; bd. dirs. 2020 Birmingham Com., Ala. Dept. Archives and History; bd. advisors Cumberland Law Sch., chmn., 1993—95, Constl. Reform Task Force; chmn. exec. com. Ala. Acad. Honor, 1999—2009; active Boy Scouts Am., Birmingham, exec. bd. Birmingham Coun., Lakeshore Found., 2005—, trustee, chmn., 2008—09; v.p., trustee Jefferson County Hist. Soc., 2009—; chancellor Episcopal Diocese Ala., 2003—06; trustee Children's Hosp., Ala., 1985—, chair, 1996—97. Recipient Silver Beaver award, Boy Scouts Am., Thurmond Arnold Appellate Competition prize, Yale U., 1954, Birmingham-So. Coll. medal Honor, 1992, Pub. Svc. award, Birmingham Bar, 1996, Brotherhood and Sisterhood award, NCCJ, 2000, Justice Pub. Svc. award, Ala. Appleseed Ctr. Law, 2007, commendations, State Ala., Ala. Commn. Higher Edn., Jacksonville State U.; named Humanitarian of Yr., 1997. Fellow: Ala. Bar Found.; mem.: ABA, Birmingham Bar Assn. (Outstanding Lawyer of Yr. award 2001), Ala. Bar Assn. (Multiple Sclerosis Legecy Leadership award 2008), Am. Law Inst., Am. Tax Policy Inst. (past trustee), Am. Coll. Tax Counsel, So. Fed. Tax Inst. (pres. 1993—94, trustee, past chmn.), Internat. Bar Assn., Mountain Brook Club, Rotary (pres. 1992—93, Spain-Hickman award 2003). Episcopalian. Office: Bradley Arant Boult Cummings LLP One Federal Pl 1819 5th Ave N Birmingham AL 35203 Office Phone: 205-521-8263. E-mail: tcarruthers@babc.com.

CARSON, CANDACE F., oil industry executive; BS in Fin., Miami U. CFO, energy service GE Co., 2007—08; v.p., energy service GE Co, 2007—08; v.p., fin (energy infrastructure) General Electric Co., 2008—. Office: General Electric Co 4200 Wildwood Pkwy Atlanta GA 30339 Business E-Mail: candace.carson@ge.com.

CARSON, CULLEY CLYDE, III, urologist, educator; b. Westerly, RI, Feb. 25, 1945; s. Culley Clyde Jr. and Dorothy (Scarborough) C.; m. Mary Jo McDonald, Aug. 10, 1970; children: Culley Clyde IV, Hilary. BS, Trinity Coll., 1967; MD, George Washington U., 1971. Diplomate Am. Bd. Urology. Intern Dartmouth Med. Ctr., 1971-72, resident surgery, 1971-73; fellow urology Mayo Clinic, Rochester, Minn., 1975-78; instr. urology U. Minn. Mayo Med. Sch., Rochester, 1978; asst. prof. urology Duke U. Med. Ctr., Durham, NC, 1978-84, assoc. prof., 1984-88, prof., 1988-93, Rhodes Disting. chair, 1993—; prof., chmn. urology U. N.C., Chapel Hill, 1993—, Rhoads disting. prof., 2000—. Chief urology Durham VA Hosp.; mem. new drug panel U.S. FDA; mem. exec. com. U.S. Pharmacopea. Author: Endourology, 1985, Atlas of Urologic Endoscopy, 1986, Impotence, 1992, 98, Complications of Invasive Procedures, 1995, Textbook of Erectile Dysfunction, 2009, Textbook of Men's Health 2nd edit., 3rd edit.,2009; editor-in-chief Mediguide to Urology, 1994—, Contemporary Urology, 1997—; contbr. chpts. to urol. texts. Maj. M.C., USAF, 1973-75. Named Command Flight Surgeon of Yr., USAF, 1974, Healthcare Hero, Rsch. Triangle, 2007; recipient Calvin Klopp Rsch. award, 1971, Friedman rsch. prize, 1971, Cristol Mayo Alumni award, 1992, Jesse H. Neal award, 2001; rsch. fellow Am. Heart Assn., 1969, O'Dea travel fellow, 1978, Book award, Royal Coll. Medicine, 1999, St. Paul's medal, Brit. Assn. Urol. Surgery, 2014. Fellow: ACS, Am. Surg. Assn.; mem.: AMA, AAAS, Am. Assn. Genitourinary Surgeons, Am. Urol. Assn. (pres. SE sect. 2006, Disting. Contbn. award 2011, Outstanding Contbn. award 2011), Sexual Medicine Soc. (pres. 2003), Internat. Soc. Urology, Am. Fertility Soc., Soc. Urol. Pros Surgery (pres. 2006, F. Brantly Scott award, 2012), Soc. U. Urol. (pres., 2013-), NY Acad. Scis., Mayo Alumni Assn., Soc. Univ. Urologists (pres. 2013), Gov.'s Club, Carolina Club, Trinity Club (Hartford), Sigma Xi, Psi Chi, Alpha Omega Alpha. Home: 10387 Holt Chapel Hill NC 27517-8542 Office: UNC 2113 Physicians Office Bldg Chapel Hill NC 27517 Office Phone: 919-966-2574. Personal E-mail: culleyccarson3@gmail.com. Business E-Mail: carson@med.unc.edu.

CARSON, JOHN, state legislator; m. Beverly Carson; 2 children. B in Acctg., Ga. State U., Atlanta; M in Fin., Kennesaw State U., Ga. CPA. With Home Depot, KPMG, GE Capital; with comml. real estate group SunTrust Bank; mem. Dist. 43 Ga. House of Reps., Atlanta, 2011—. Eagle scout Boy Scouts America; mem. Johnson Ferry Bapt. Ch. Mem.: Ga. Soc. CPA's, Comml. Fin. Assn., Cobb C. of C., NE Cobb Bus. Assn., Rotary Internat. Republican. Office: Office Dist 3605 Sandy Plains Rd Marietta GA 30066 also: Ga House of Reps 607-F Coverdell Legis Office Bldg Atlanta GA 30334 Office Phone: 404-575-2785, 404-656-0287. Business E-Mail: john.carson@house.ga.gov.

CARSON, JOHN C., JR., investment company executive; BA in Internat. Economics and History, Dartmouth Coll., 1979; MBA, Harvard U., 1984. With Chase Manhattan Bank, NYC, Caracas, Venezuela, Morgan Stanley & Co., Security Pacific; joined Morgan Keegan & Co., Inc., Memphis, 1994, pres. Fixed Income Capital Markets Divsn., exec. mng. dir., CEO, 2008—. Office: Morgan Keegan Morgan Keegan Tower 50 N Front St Memphis TN 38103 Office Phone: 901-524-4100. Office Fax: 901-524-4797.

CARSON, LEONARD ALLEN, lawyer; b. Lorain, Ohio, Nov. 6, 1940; s. Frank and Josephine (Sulewski) Guzewicz. BS in Bus. Adminstrn., U. Fla., 1963, JD, 1966. Bar: Fla. 1967. Staff acct. Peat, Marwick, Mitchell & Co., NYC, 1963-64; mem. firm Kates and Ress, P.A., Miami, Fla., 1967-70; corp. counsel, asst. to exec. v.p. and treas. Cordis Corp., Miami, 1970-73; judge Indsl. Claims Ct., Ft. Lauderdale, Fla., 1973; mem. Fla. Indsl. Rels. Commn., Tallahassee, 1973-74, chmn., 1974-76, Fla. Pub. Employees Rels. Commn., Tallahassee, 1976-80; of counsel Seyfarth, Shaw, Fairweather & Geraldson, Tallahassee and Miami, 1980-83; pres. Carson & Adkins, Tallahassee, 1983—. Mem. Fla. Law Revision Coun., 1976-77, Internat. Assn. Indsl. Accident Bds. and Commns., 1974-76 Served with USMCR, 1960-66. Mem. ABA, Am. Arbitration Assn. (nat. panel 1968-73), Capital Tiger Bay Club. Independent. Roman Catholic. Home: 233 Rose Hill Dr N Tallahassee FL 32312-9022 Office: Ste 201 2930 Wellington Cir Tallahassee FL 32309-6888 Home Phone: 850-893-8906; Office Phone: 850-894-1009. Business E-Mail: lacarson@carson-adkinslaw.com.

CARSON, SANDRA G., retail executive; b. Tex. m. Chip Carson; 5 children. Degree in Nursing, Amarillo Coll., 1988. Registered nurse; cert. occupl. and environ. health and safety profl. Dir., safety Sweetheart Cup Co., 1989—92; dir., safety and health svcs. Pioneer Frozen Foods, 1992—95; mgr., health svcs. Sysco Corp., Houston, 1995, sr. mgr., health and safety, 1997, dir., health and safety, 1999, dir., human resources, 2001, mem., ops. coun., 2003, dir., occupl. risk mgmt., 2003, asst. v.p., safety and crisis mgmt., 2007—08, v.p., safety and crisis mgmt., 2005—. Mem. Women's Foodservice Forum. Recipient Outstanding Nursing Majoraward. Office: Sysco Corp 1390 Enclave Pky Houston TX 77077-2099 Office Phone: 281-584-1390. Office Fax: 281-584-2721. Business E-Mail: carson.sandra@corp.sysco.com.

CARSTARPHEN, MERIA JOEL, school system administrator; b. Selma, Ala., 1970; married. BA in Polit. Sci. & Spanish, Tulane U., New Orleans, 1992; EdM in Adminstrn. Elem & Secondary Edn., Auburn U., Ala., 1997; EdM in Adminstrn., Harvard U., Cambridge, Mass., 1999, EdD in Adminstrn., Planning, and Social Policy, 2002. Tchr. Selma Mid. Sch., Ala., 1992—96; grad. rsch. asst. Auburn U. Truman Pierce Inst., 1996—97; freelance photographer Nat. Geographic Soc., Washington, 1997—99; spl. asst. to the supt. Columbus City Schools, Ohio, 1999—2001; ind. cons. Kingsport, Tenn., Boston, 2001—03; exec. dir. comprehensive sch. improvement and accountability Kingsport City Schools, Tenn., 2003—04; chief accountability officer DC Public Schools, 2004—06; supt. St. Paul Public Schools, Minn., 2006—09, Austin Ind. Sch. Dist., Tex., 2009—. Bd. mem. Coun. of Gt. City Schs., Ednl. Testing Svc., Austin Ptnrs. in Edn., Austin Ind. Sch. Dist. Pub. Edn. Found., Tex. Sch. Alliance, Tex. Coun. Urban Sch. Dists.; mem. Children's Hosp./Austin Ind. Sch. Dist. Health Svc. Adv. Bd. John E. Stevens fellow, Harvard Grad. Sch. Edn., 1998, Herold Hunt fellow, 2001. Office: Austin Independent School District 1111 W Sixth St Austin TX 78703 Office Phone: 512-414-2412.*

CARSWELL, JANE TRIPLETT, retired family physician; b. Raeford, NC, Feb. 26, 1932; d. Arthur Dula and Madeline Mapp (Warburton) C.; m. Kenmer A. Roberts, 2000. Student, Flora Macdonald Coll., 1950-52; AB in Chemistry, U. N.C., 1954; MD, Med. Coll. Va., 1958. Diplomate Am. Bd. Family Practice. Resident Med. Coll. Va., Richmond, 1958-61; practice medicine specializing in family medicine Harlan, Ky., 1961-62, Lenoir, NC, 1962—. Chmn. Lenoir Human Relations Com., N.C., 1962-64; vice-chmn. Caldwell County Council Status of Women, Lenoir, 1976-78 Mem. Caldwell County Med. Soc. (pres. 1965), N.C. Acad. Family Physicians (N.C. Family Physician of Yr. award 1983), N.C. Med. Soc., Am. Acad. Family Practice (Nat. Family Dr. of Yr. award 1984) Presbyterian. Avocations: hiking, backpacking, skiing, photography.

CARTER, AMY ALEXANDER, state legislator; b. Mar. 14; m. Doug Carter; 2 children. State rep. Dist. 175, Ga., 2007—; mem. Children and Youth, Edn., Higher Edn. and Budget and Fiscal Affairs Oversight Com., 2007—; house rep. Ga.; diversified coop. tng. coord. Lowndes HS. Recipient Ga's Outstanding New Career and Tech. EdN. Tchr. of the Year, 2002, Valdosta Woman of the Year, 2003, Leadership Ga.'s Dale Threadgill Cmty. Svc. award, 2004, Valdosta-North Rotary Club Most Outstanding Mem., 2004, Azalea City Kiwanis Club Citizen of the Year, 2005. Democrat. Home: PO Box 4930 Valdosta GA 31604-4930 Office Phone: 229-245-2733. Fax: 229-245-8890. E-mail: amy.carter@house.ga.gov.

CARTER, BARRY R., corporate financial executive; BA in Computer Sci., East Carolina U.; MBA in Orgns. & Mgmt., Syracuse U. Various sr. exec. info. tech. positions AMR, American Airlines, Inc., Electronic Data Sys. Corp., Sabre, United Healthcare; chief info. officer AirTran Airways, Inc., Capital One Auto Fin.; sr. v.p., shared svcs., chief info. officer Alliance Data Systems Corp., 2004—. Office: Alliance Data Systems Corp 7500 Dallas Pkwy Ste 700 Plano TX 75024-4006 Office Phone: 972-348-5100. Office Fax: 972-348-5335.

CARTER, BRUCE THOMAS, ophthalmologist; b. Front Royal, Va., Mar. 28, 1944; MD, U. Va., 1970. Cert. ophthalmology, 1977. Intern ophthalmology Ky. Med. Ctr., Lexington, 1970—71; resident pediat. ophthalmology U. Va. Hosp., Charlottesville, 1973—76; fellowship U. Pitts., 1976—77; staff mem. Martha Jefferson Hosp., Charlottesville, Va.; pediatric ophthalmologist U. Va. Health Sys.; pvt. practice. Clin. instr. ophthalmology U. Va. Sch. Med., 1977—78, clin. asst. prof., 1978—85, clin. assoc. prof., 1985—. Office: Albemarle Pediat Ophthalmology & Strabismus PC 1101 E Jefferson St Ste 3 Charlottesville VA 22902 also: U Va Health Sys Dept Ophthalmology PO Box 800715 Charlottesville VA 22908-0715 Office Phone: 434-295-5193. Office Fax: 804-977-0714. Business E-Mail: btcarter.md@gmail.com.

CARTER, DAVY, state legislator; b. Mar. 31, 1975; married; 3 children. BS in Corp. Fin., Ark. State U., 1997; grad., La. State U. Grad. Sch. Banking, 2003; JD, William H. Bowen Sch. Law, 2005. Mem. Dist. 48 Ark. House of Reps., 2009—. Republican. Office: State Capitol Rm 350 Little Rock AR 72201 also: PO Box 628 Cabot AR 72023 Office Phone: 501-682-6211, 501-682-7771, 501-605-1346. Business E-Mail: davy.carter@gmail.com.

CARTER, DONALD F., gas industry executive; m. Betty Carter; 1 child. Degree in Engring., Ga. Inst. Tech.; MBA, Brenau U., 1992. Registered profl. engr., Ga. Various positions AGL Resources, Inc.; joined Atlanta Gas Light Co., 1984; region mgr., Northwest Jersey Svc. Area Elizabethtown Gas, 2004—05, gen. mgr., v.p., 2005—. Mem. Gwinnett C. of C., Gwinnett Coun. for Quality Growth, Gwinnett United Way Campaign Cabinet, Cumming-Forsyth C. of C.; former bd. dirs. Greater North Fulton C. of C., Utilities Protection Ctr of Ga,; bd. dirs. NJ Utilities Assn., NJ C. of C. Office: AGL Resources Inc 10 Peachtree Pl NE Atlanta GA 30309 Office Phone: 404-584-4000. Office Fax: 404-584-3714.

CARTER, DOYLE, councilman; m. Trish Carter; children: Heather, Meagan, DJ. Owner Cycle Accessories West; mem. Jacksonville City Coun., Fla., 1999—2003, mem. Dist. 12 Fla., 2011—. Mem. Justice Coalition Bd. Mem.: Cattlemens Assn., Westside Republican Club, Hyde Park Masonic Lodge, Scottish Rites. Office: Jacksonville City Council 117 W Duval St Jacksonville FL 32202 Office Phone: 904-630-1380. E-mail: doylec@coj.net.

CARTER, DUDLEY ROCHELLE, lawyer; b. Franklinton, La., Sept. 10, 1950; s. James Cecil and Mildred Grace (Stennis) R. BA in Polit. Sci., La. State U., 1972; JD, Yale U., 1975. Bar: Ga. 1976, US Dist. Ct. (no. dist.) Ga. 1976, US Ct. Appeals (5th cir.) 1976, US Ct. Appeals (11th cir.) 1997. Vista atty. Atlanta Legal Aid Soc., 1975-76; law clk. to Hon. Joel J. Fryer Fulton County Superior Ct., Atlanta, 1976-77; trial atty. U.S. Dept. Labor, Atlanta, 1977-82; assoc. Hendrick Spanos & Phillips PC, Atlanta, 1982-88, shareholder (ptnr.), 1988-94, Spanos & Rochelle, P.C., Atlanta, 1994-97; shareholder Littler Mendelson, P.C., Atlanta, 1997—. Mem. adv. bd. Coverdell Leadership Inst., Atlanta, 1996—; mem. Ga. Commn. on Equal Opportunity; bd. dirs. Ga. Pub. Policy Found., 1996—, Ctr. Ethics & Corp. Responsibility, Ga. State U., J. Mack Robinson Coll. Bus., 2001—07, 2007—08, Midtown Alliance, Atlanta, 1982—92. Mem. State Bar Ga. (mem. labor sect.), Atlanta Bar Assn. (mem. labor/employment sect., chairperson alt. dispute resolution com. 1986-92, mem. bench and bar com. 1986-87), Christian Legal Soc., Federalist Soc. (mem. adv. bd. Atlanta Lawyers chpt.), Yale Club Ga. (bd. dirs. 1982-86), Ctr. Ethics Responsibility (bd. dirs.). Republican. Avocations: outdoor activity, music. Home: 2769 Brook Grove Ln Atlanta GA 30339-5331 Office: Littler Mendelson 3344 Peachtree Rd NE Ste 1500 Atlanta GA 30326-4803 Business E-Mail: DRochelle@littler.com.

CARTER, EARL (BUDDY CARTER), state legislator; b. Savannah, Ga. m. Amy Carter; children: Joel, Barret, Travis. Mayor, Pooler, 1996—2004; state rep. Dist. 159 Ga., 2004—09; mem. Appropriations, Economic Devel. & Tourism Coms.; sec. Health & Human Svcs. Com.; state senator Dist. 1 Ga., 2009—. Republican. Office: Capitol Office 301-A Coverdell Legislative Office Bldg Atlanta GA 30334 also: 406 Purple Finch Dr Pooler GA 31322 Office Phone: 404-656-5109, 912-748-1414. Office Fax: 404-656-5109, 912-748-4029. Personal E-mail: bcarter331@aol.com.

CARTER, FLETCHER FAIRWICK, university administrator, education educator retired; b. Bagdad, Fla., Feb. 12, 1930; s. Ollie Martin and Florence Lista (Owens) C.; m. Edith J. Houston, Apr. 2, 1961. BA in Polit. Sci., U. Fla., 1953; MA in Social Scis., Appalachian State U., 1960; PhD in Higher Edn. Adminstrn., Fla. State U., 1965. Tchr. Santa Rosa County Pub. Schs., Milton, Fla., 1955-61, jr. H.S. math. and sci. tchr., 1957-61; instr. in geography Appalachian State U., Boone, N.C., 1961; analyst Fla. State Dept. Edn., Tallahassee, 1961-62; registrar Mitchell Coll., Statesville, N.C., 1963-64; instr., student tchg. supr. Fla. State U., Tallahassee, 1964-65; prof. edn. Radford (Va.) U., 1965—, asst. dean Sch. Edn., 1967-72, dir. instnl. rsch. and analyses, 1968—2001, prof. ednl. studies, 2001—, asst. dir. assessment,accreditation and evaluation coll. edn. and human devel., 2006—; cons. dept. rsch., testing, assessment, data analyst Roanoke City Pub. Schs., 2009—. Tchg. fellow Appalachian State U., Boone, N.C., 1959-60; mem. com. on program costing State Coun. for Higher Edn. in Va., 1974, mem. com. on reporting practices, 1981, cons. on facilities, 1986, mem. com. on rsch. facilities, 1988-90 Chmn. bd. trustees Radford Pub. Libr., 1986-2002. 1st lt. U.S. Army, 1952-55, Korea. Kellogg fellow Fla. State U., 1961-63. Mem. Va. Assn. for Mgmt., Analysis and Planning (charter, bd. dirs. 1969—), So. Assn. Instnl. Rsch. (charter, nominating com.), Assn. Instnl. Rsch. (assoc. clubs com., paper com. 1997), Am. Ednl. Rsch. Assn., Masons (50 yr. cert. 2003), Lions (pres., sec., 25 Yr. cert. 1994), Phi Eta Sigma, Phi Delta Kappa (pres., sec.), Pi Gamma Mu. Methodist. Home: 305 Fairway Dr Radford VA 24141-3909 Office: Radford U PO Box 6924 Radford VA 24142-6924 Home Phone: 540-639-1263. Business E-Mail: fcarter@radford.edu.

CARTER, FRANCES TUNNELL (FRAN CARTER), fraternal organization administrator; b. Springville, Miss. d. David Atmond and Mary Annie (McCutcheon) Tunnell; m. John T. Carter; children: Wayne, Nell Branum. BS, U. So. Miss., 1946; MS, U. Tenn., 1948; EdD, U. Ill., 1954. Tchr. elem. sch., Thaxton, Miss., 1942—43, Cumberland, Miss., 1943—44; tchr. h.s. home econs. Randolph, Miss., 1944—45, Maben, Miss., 1946—47; instr. Wood Coll., Mathiston, Miss., 1947—48, East Ctrl. Jr. Coll., Decatur, Miss., 1948—49; prof. home econs. Clarke Coll., Newton, Miss., 1950—56; prof. Samford U., Birmingham, Ala., 1956—84; editor, children and youth products and resources Woman's Missionary Union, Birmingham, 1983—85; pres. CarterCraft, Inc., Birmingham, 1983—89, Carter and Carter Consultants, 1987—2004; nat. exec. dir. Kappa Delta Epsilon, Birmingham, 1987—2003; founder, exec. dir. Am. Rosie the Riveter Assn., 1998—. Vis. prof. Hong Kong Bapt. U., 1965-66, Anhui Normal U., People's Republic of China, 1987; medical/dental mission team mem. Honduras, Mex., 1983, 84, 89, 1994; tchr. workshops in China, 1988, 90, 92, 95, 97, 2000; tchr. workshops in Indonesia, 1993; lectr. in symposium at invitation of Russian Edn. Ministry, Moscow, 1994, U. Nanjing, People's Republic of China, 1997; curriculum writer Bapt. Brotherhood Commn., 1986-90; writer N.Am. Mission Bd., 1995-98. Author: Sammy in the Country, 1960, Tween-Age Ambassador, 1970, Ching Fu and Jim, 1978; co-author: Sharing Times Seven, 1977, also short stories, articles; feature writer: Crusader Mag., 1986-95, The Current, 1987-2003; editor 103 Rosie Stories, 2001. Tchr. Sunday Sch., Bapt. Ch., Birmingham, 1980—; mem., lt. col. CAP, 1968—1996, bd. dirs. Aerospace Edn. Ala. Wing, 1991-94, dir. pub. affairs regional S.E., 1994-95; v.p. Women's Civic Club of Birmingham, 1997-98, 2002-03; placement officer ESL Sch., 1995-98, pres., 1982-83, Test of English as a Fgn. Lang. tchr., 1998-2007; Silver rep. Dist. 6 Ala. Nat. Silver Haired Congress, 1991-96, Ala. Silver Haired Legislator Dist. 55 Jefferson County, 1996-2000; alt. Dist. 6, Nat. Silver Haired Congress, 2000-09. Recipient Career Achievement award Profl. Fraternity Assn., 1988, Outstanding Alumnae award Wood Coll., 1992, Outstanding award Kappa Delta Pi, 1992, Brewer award for Aerospace Edn. Southeast region CAP, 1994, Vol. of Yr. award Nat. Profl. Fraternity Assn., 1999, Lillian K. Keil award WWII Vets. Com., Washington, DC, 2004, cert. Rosie the Riveter reunion, Little White House, Warm Springs, Ga., 1997; named Birmingham's Woman of Yr., 1977, Birmingham's Vol. of Yr., 1980; named to Sr. Citizen Hall of Fame, 2002. Mem. AARP (local pres. 1988-89, asst. state dir. 1989-93, Nat. Cmty. award 1992), Birmingham's Women C. of C. (pres. 1975-76, 2003-04), Nat. League Am. Pen Women (3rd v.p. 1988-90, nat. pres. 1994-96), Ala. League Pen Women (pres. 1970-72), Birmingham League Am. Pen Women (pres. 1968-70, 76-78), Ala. Writers Conclave (pres. 1978-79), Ala. State Poetry Soc. (pres. 1979-82), Ala. Federated Women's Clubs (dist. dir. 1988-90, Outstanding Woman of Ala. Club award 1988, Eddie Gibson Internat. Min. award 2008, Remembrance Day award U. Montevallo Honoring Vets., Rosies, 2008), Freedoms Found. Valley Forge (pres. Birmingham area chpt. 1990-91), Nat. Fellowship Bapt. Educators (sec. 1987-93), Birmingham Bus. and Profl. Club (pres. 1986-87), Am. Rosie the Riveter Assn. Inc. (founder 1998, pres. 1998-2003, nat. exec. dir. 2003—), Kappa Delta Epsilon (nat. pres. 1980-85, exec. dir. 1987, 2003-, co-dir. ESL Sch. 1994-98), Alpha Delta Kappa, Delta Kappa Gamma, Phi Delta Kappa (Nat. Profl. Fraternity Assn. award 1999, cert. emeritus 2000), Birmingham Civic Club (pres. 1982-83, v.p. 2003-04, 06-07), Birmingham Women's C. of C. (pres. 2003-04), Samford U. Ret. Faculty Assn. (Sunday Sch. tchr. 1970-, pres. 2004-06, Spirit of 45 medal 2011). Home: 209 University Park Dr Birmingham AL 35209-6772 Personal E-mail: fran.carter@juno.com.

CARTER, HENRY MOORE, JR., retired foundation executive; b. Portsmouth, Va., Mar. 10, 1932; s. Henry and Debbie (McCoy) C.; m. Martha Rhea Greene, Aug. 21, 1954; 1 dau., Ann Clair. BA, Randolph-Macon Coll., 1953; MA, Vanderbilt U., 1954. Tchr. English, Norfolk County Public Schs., Portsmouth, 1954-59, head dept. English, 1957-59; headmaster Bollingbrook Sch., Petersburg, Va., 1959-66; dir. public relations Randolph-Macon Coll., Ashland, Va., 1966-68; dir. Randolph-Macon Fund, 1968-69, dir. devel., 1969-77; pres. Winston-Salem (N.C.) Found., 1977-97. Pastmem. adv. com. Kate B. Reynolds Trust for Poor and Needy; former chair bd. dirs. N.C. Ctr. for Nonprofits; former sec. Winston-Salem Campaign Coordinating Com. Past chmn., bd. dirs. coord. com. Winston-Salem Crime Stoppers; past chmn. Emergency Loan Fund, Southeastern Coun. Founds., N.C. Assn. Cmty. Founds., Forsyth Common Vision Coun., Old Salem Inc; past mem. adv. bd. Mary Baldwin Coll.; former sec.-treas. Twin City Devel. Corp; past bd. dirs. Crosby Scholars Cmty. Partnership, Hospice Found., Forsyth Tech. Coll. Found.; ret. pres. Waccamaw Cmty. Found. Carnegie fellow, 1953-54. Mem. Litchfield Country Club, Rotary. Republican. Methodist.

CARTER, HODDING, III, (WILLIAM), educator, retired foundation executive, retired journalist, commentator and public official; b. New Orleans, Apr. 7, 1935; s. William Hodding and Betty Brunhilde (Werlein) C.; m. Margaret A. Wolfe, June 21, 1957 (div. 1978); children: Catherine Ainsworth, Elizebeth Fearn, William Hodding IV, Margaret Lorraine; m. Patricia M. Derian, 1978. BA, Princeton U., 1957; LLD (hon.), Stetson Coll., 1980, Kenyon Coll., 1984; LittD (hon.), Tusculum Coll., 1983; LLD (hon.), George Washington U., 1986, N.Y. Inst. Tech., 1987; LHD (hon.), U. Maine, 1985, U. San Diego, 1991, Millsaps Coll., 1998, U. SC, 2004. Reporter Delta Democrat-Times, Greenville, Miss., 1959-62, mng. editor, 1962-66, editor, pub., 1966-77; asst. sec. state for pub. affairs, dept. spokesman US Dept. State, Washington, 1977-80; vis. prof. Am. U., 1980; anchorman and chief corr. Inside Story, PBS, 1981-84; chief corr., exec. editor Capitol Jour., PBS, 1985-86; pres. MainStreet TV Prodn. Co., 1985-95; Knight chair in pub. affairs journalism U. Md., 1995-98; pres., CEO John S. and James L. Knight Found., Miami, 1998—2005; prof. leadership and pub. policy U. NC, Chapel Hill, 2006—. Vis. prof. Duke U., 1991; op. ed. columnist Wall St. Jour., 1980-90. Author: The South Strikes Back, 1959, The Reagan Years, 1988; contbr. to books, newspapers and mags.; commentator on TV and radio; columnist Newspaper Enterprise Assn., 1992-95. Co-chmn. Young Dem. Clubs Miss., 1965-68; founding mem. Loyal Dems. of Miss., 1968; mem. Charter Commn. Dem. Party, 1973-74; del. Dem. Conv., 1968, 72, 76, Dem. Mini Conv., Kansas City, Mo., 1974; mem. campaign staff Johnson for Pres., 1964, Carter for Pres., 1976; mem. exec. com. So. Regional Coun., 1969-75, Miss. Dem. Party, 1976-79; trustee Princeton U., 1983-98; dir. Dreyfus Corp. Funds; bd. dirs. Enterprise Corp. of the Delta, Ctr. Pub. Integrity, Americans for Campaign Reform; mem. Knight Found. Commn. on Intercollegiate Athletics; former chmn. Action Coun. for Peace in the Balkans, Am. Com. for US-Soviet Rels. Recipient Editl. award, Soc. Profl. Journalists, 1961, 4 Emmy awards for pub. affairs TV, 1984—85, Edward R. Murrow award for best fgn. documentary, 1984; Nieman fellow, Harvard U., 1965—66. Mem.: Pen/Am., Nat. Press Club, Coun. Fgn. Rels., Princeton Club NY, Tarratine Club. Episcopalian. Business E-Mail: hoddingcarter@umc.edu.

CARTER, IAN R., hotel executive; b. Newcastle, England; Pres., Splty. Chemicals bus. General Electric Co., 1995—98; v.p. Black & Decker Corp. (merged with The Stanley Works), 1999—2000, pres., Europe, Power Tools and Accessories Group, 2000—04, pres., Europe, Mid. East, Africa & Asia, 2004—05; CEO Hilton International Co. (subs. of Hilton Hotels Corp.), 2005; exec. v.p., pres., Global Ops. Hilton Hotels Corp., 2006—08; exec. v.p. Hilton Internat. Co. (subs. of Hilton Hotels Corp.), 2006; pres., global ops. & devel. Hilton Worldwide, Inc., 2008—. Bd. dirs. Ladbrokes PLC (formerly Hilton Group PLC), 1998—99, 2005—06, Burberry Group plc, 2007—. Bd. dirs. Internat. Bus. Leaders Forum; chmn. Internat. Tourism Partnership. Avocations: squash, tennis. Office: Hilton Worldwide 7930 Jones Branch Dr Ste 1100 Mc Lean VA 22102 Office Phone: 703-883-1000. Business E-Mail: ian.carter@hilton.com.

CARTER, JAINE M(ARIE), human resources specialist, director; b. Chgo., Oct. 29, 1946; m. James Carter, Apr. 8, 1970; children: Paul, Todd. BS, Northwestern U., 1968; PhD, Walden U., 1988. Mgmt. cons. to bus., 1969; chmn. bd. Pers. Devel., Inc., Palatine, Ill., 1969—; dir. women's divsn. Lake Forest Coll. Advanced Mgmt. Inst., Ill., 1970—. Writer, lectr., tchr., cons. mgmt. devel. programs; faculty AMA; speaker weekly cable TV series Life Skills; pres. bd. dirs. Family Renewal Inst., 1991—96. Author: How to Train for Supervisors, 1969, Career Planning Workshop for Women, 1975, Training Techniques That Bring About Positive Behavioral Change, 1976, Assertive Management Role Plays, 1976, Understanding the Female Employee, 1976, Rx for Women in Business, 1976, New Directions Needed in Management Training Programs, 1980, The Burnout of Retirement, 1983, Successfully Working with People, 1984, Assertiveness Training for Supervisors, 1985, Successfully Managing People, 1986, The New Success, 1986, Employee Assistance Program Handbook, 1988, Stay Out of Your Own Way-And Get the Job You Want, 1989, He Works/She Works-Successful Strategies for Working Couples, 1996; columnist: Scripps- Howard News Svc., Balancing Work and Family, 1996—2004; columnist Scripps-Howard News Svc. He Works/She Works, 1996—2004; moderator, content expert (TV spl.) Commitment to Quality, Nat. Tech. U., 1989; author: (TV series) Executive Communications, 1988 prodr.: (TV series) Relationships, 1992; creator, prodr., host (TV series) Choices, 1992, 1993, host (radio talk show), 1992—96, co-host Your Own Business!, 1993—97. Mem.: Pres.'s Forum (exec. dir. 1998—).

CARTER, JASON, state legislator; b. Atlanta, Aug. 07; m. Kate Carter; 2 children. B, Duke U., Durham, NC; JD, U. Ga. Law clk. to the Hon. Frank Mays Hull US Ct. Appeals 11th Cir.; atty. Bondurant, Mixson & Elmore, LLP; mem. Dist. 42 Ga. State Senate, Atlanta, 2010—. Contbr. articles to profl. jours. Vol. Peace Corps, Lochiel, South Africa; bd. dirs. DeKalb Women's Resource Ctr. to End Domestic Violence, Ga. Afterschool Investment Coun., Carter Ctr. Democrat. Office: PO Box 573 Decatur GA 30030 also: Ga State Senate 327B Coverdell Legis Office Bldg Atlanta GA 30334 Office Phone: 404-881-4123, 404-463-1376. Business E-Mail: jason.carter@senate.ga.gov.

CARTER, JEAN GORDON, lawyer; b. Ft. Belvoir, Va., July 30, 1955; d. Thomas Laney and Cleone (Hunter) Gordon; m. Michael L. Carter, Sept. 17, 1977; children: Christina Jean, William Gordon. BS in Accountancy magna cum laude with honors, Wake Forest U., 1977; JD with high honors, Duke U., 1983. Bar: N.C. 1983; CPA; bd. cert. specialist in estates. Acct. Arthur Andersen & Co., Charlotte, NC, 1977-80; atty. Moore & Van Allen, Raleigh, NC, 1983-90; ptnr. Hunton & Williams, Raleigh, NC, 1990—. Mem. Am. Coll. Trusts and Estates Coun., N.C. Bar Assn., Wake County Estate Coun. (pres. 1991-92), Order of Coif, Phi Beta Kappa. Democrat. Presbyterian. Avocations: reading, travel, snorkeling. Home: 3913 Stratford Ct Raleigh NC 27609-6351 Office: Hunton & Williams One Bank of America Plz Raleigh NC 27601-2947 Home Phone: 919-510-0112; Office Phone: 919-899-3088. Business E-Mail: jcarter@hunton.com.

CARTER, JIMMY (JAMES EARL CARTER JR.), 39th President of the United States; b. Plains, Ga., Oct. 1, 1924; s. James Earl and Lillian (Gordy) Carter; m. Rosalynn Smith, July 7, 1946; children: John William, James Earl III, Donnel Jeffrey, Amy Lynn. Attended, Ga. Southwestern Coll., Ga. Inst. Tech.; BS, US Naval Acad., 1947; LLD (hon.), Morris Brown Coll., 1972, Morehouse Coll., 1972, U. Notre Dame, 1977, Emory U., 1979, Kwansei Gakuin U., Japan, 1981, Ga. Southwestern Coll., 1981, NY Law Sch., 1985, Bates Coll., 1985, Centre Coll., 1987, Creighton U., 1987; PhD (hon.), Weizmann Inst. Sci., 1980, Tel Aviv U., 1983, Haifa U., 1987; DHL (hon.), Ctrl. Conn. State U., 1985; DEng (hon.), Ga. Inst. Tech., 1979. Farmer, warehouseman, Plains, Ga., 1953-77; mem. Dist. 14 Ga. State Senate, 1963-67; gov. State of Ga., Atlanta, 1971-75; Pres. of the US Washington, 1977-81; Univ. Disting. prof., founder Carter Presdl. Ctr. Emory U., Atlanta, 1982—; founder Jimmy Carter Libr. & Mus., Atlanta. Chmn. congressional campaign com. Democratic Nat. Com., 1974. Author: Why Not the Best?, 1975, A Government as Good as Its People, 1977, Keeping Faith: Memoirs of a President, 1982, Negotiation: The Alternative to Hostility, 1984, The Blood of Abraham, 1985, Everything to Gain: Making the Most of the Rest of Your Life, 1987, An Outdoor Journal, 1988, Turning Point: A Candidate, a State, and a Nation Come of Age, 1992, Talking Peace: A Vision for the Next Generation, 1993, Always a Reckoning, 1995, Living Faith, 1996, Sources of Strength: Meditations on Scripture for a Living Faith, 1997, The Virtues of Aging, 1998, An Hour Before Daylight: Memories of a Rural Boyhood, 2001, Christmas in Plains: Memories, 2001, The Nobel Peace Prize Lecture, 2002, The Hornet's Nest: A Novel of the Revolutionary War, 2003, Sharing Good Times, 2004, Our Endangered Values: America's Moral Crisis, 2005, Palestine Peace Not Apartheid, 2006, Beyond the White House: Waging Peace, Fighting Disease, Building Hope, 2007, A Remarkable Mother, 2008, We Can Have Peace in the Holy Land: A Plan That Will Work, 2009, White House Diary, 2010, Through the Year with Jimmy Carter: 366 Daily Meditations from the 39th President, 2011, NIV Lessons from Life Bible: Personal Reflections with Jimmy Carter, 2012, A Call to Action: Women, Religion, Violence, and Power, 2014. Active vol. Habitat for Humanity, bd. dirs., 1984—87; mem. Sumter County Sch. Bd., Ga., 1955—62, chmn., 1960—62; mem. Sumter County Libr. Bd., 1961; founding mem. The Elders, 2007—; Sunday sch. tchr. Maranatha Bapt. Ch., Plains; trustee Mercer U., 2012—. Svc. to lt. USN, 1946—53. Recipient Silver Buffalo award, Boy Scouts America, 1978, Gold medal, Internat. Inst. Human Rights, 1979, International Mediation medal, American Arbitration Assn., 1979, Martin Luther King, Jr. Peace prize, 1979, Internat. Human Rights award, Synagogue Coun. America, 1979, Harry S. Truman Pub. Svc. award, 1981, Ansel Adams Conservation award, Wilderness Soc., 1982, Human Rights award, Internat. League Human Rights, 1983, World Meth. Peace award, 1985, Albert Schweitzer Prize for Humanitarianism, 1987, Edwin C. Whitehead award, Nat. Ctr. Health Edn., 1989, Jefferson award, American Inst. Pub. Svc., 1990, Liberty medal, Nat. Constn. Ctr., 1990, Spirit of America award, Nat. Coun. Social Studies, 1990, Physicians for Social Responsibility award, 1991, Aristotle prize, Alexander S. Onassis Found., 1991, W. Averell Harriman Democracy award, Nat. Dem. Inst. Internat. Affairs, 1992, Spark M. Matsunaga medal of peace, US Inst. Peace, 1993, Humanitarian award, CARE Internat., 1993, Conservationist of Yr. medal, Nat. Wildlife Fedn., 1993, Freedom award, Nat. Civil Rights Mus., 1994, Félix Houphouët-Boigny Peace prize, UNESCO, 1994, Bishop John T. Walker Disting. Humanitarian award, Africare, 1996, Indira Gandhi prize for peace, disarmament & Devel., 1997, UN Human Rights award, 1998, Hoover Medal, 1998, Internat. Child Survival award, UNICEF Atlanta, 1999, William Penn Mott, Jr., Park Leadership award, Nat. Parks Conservation Assn., 2000, Zayed Internat. prize for the environment, 2001, Herbert Hoover Humanitarian award, Boys & Girls Clubs America, 2001, Nobel Peace Prize, Norwegian Nobel Com., 2002, Berkeley medal, U. Calif., 2007, Mahatma Gandhi Global Nonviolence award, Mahatma Gandhi Ctr. Global Nonviolence, James Madison U., 2009, American Peace award, 2009, Internat. Catalonia award, 2010, Internat. Advocate for Peace award, Yeshiva U. Benjamin N. Cardozo Sch. Law, 2013; named Humanitarian of Yr., GQ mag., 1996. Democrat. Office: Carter Ctr 1 Copenhill 453 Freedom Pkwy NE Atlanta GA 30307-1406*

CARTER, JOHN LOYD, lawyer; b. Clayton, N.Mex., Oct. 2, 1948; s. John Allen and Ruth (Laughlin) C.; m. Dorel Susan Payne, Sept. 20, 1975; children: Matthew, Caroline, Susan. BA, So. Meth. U., 1970, JD cum laude, 1973. Bar: Tex. 1973, U.S. Ct. Appeals (5th and 11th cirs.) 1975, U.S. Ct. Appeals (D.C. cir.) 2004, U.S. Supreme Ct. 1976, U.S. Dist. Ct. (so. dist.) Tex. 1974, U.S. Dist. Ct. (no. dist.) Tex. 1978, U.S. Dist. Ct. (ea. dist.) Tex. 1985, U.S. Dist. Ct. (we. dist.) Tex. 1999. Assoc. Vinson & Elkins, Houston, 1973-80, ptnr., 1980—2012. Editor-in-chief: Southwestern Law Jour., 1972—73. Fellow Am. Coll. Trial Lawyers, Am. Bar Found., Tex. Bar Found. (life), Houston Bar Found.; mem. Order of the Coif, Barristers. Office: Vinson & Elkins 2500 First City Tower Houston TX 77002-6760 Home Phone: 713-627-1410; Office Phone: 713-758-2124. Business E-Mail: jcarter@velaw.com.

CARTER, JOHN RICE, United States Representative from Texas, lawyer; b. Houston, Nov. 6, 1941; s. John James and Elizabeth (Rice) Carter; m. Erika Theodora Van Bruegel, June 15, 1968; children: Gilianne, John, Theodore, Danielle. BA in History, Tex. Tech U., 1965; JD, U. Tex. Sch. Law, Austin, 1969. Bar: Tex. 1969. Counsel Tex. House of Reps., Austin, 1969—72; pvt. practice atty. Round Rock, Tex., 1973—81; mcpl. judge, 1978—80; judge 277th Dist. Ct. Williamson County, Tex., 1981—82, dist. judge, 1982—2002; mem. US Congress from 31st Tex. Dist., Washington, 2003—; sec. US House Republican Conf., Washington, 2007—13. Chmn. Round Rock Planning Com., 1975—78. Mem.: Williamson County Bar Assn. (pres. 1976), Round Rock Jaycees (pres. 1975, Jaycee of Yr. 1975). Republican. Office: US House of Representatives 409 Cannon House Office Bldg Washington DC 20515 also: One Fin Ctr 1717 N IH 35 Ste 303 Round Rock TX 78664 Office Phone: 202-225-3864.*

CARTER, KARL H., marketing executive; b. Washington DC, 1973; BA in Bus. Adminstrn., Electronic Media Mktg., George Wash. U. Founder Soul Underground, Wash., 1997, Atlanta; head creative mktg. dept. Burrell Comm.; co-founder, CEO GTM Inc., 2000—; co-founder Change The Game, 2001—. Music Editor: weekly newspaper Rolling Out; co-prodr.: (radio show) truth.FM. Human rights activist Black August Hip Hop Project. Recipient AdColor Innovator award. Achievements include development of the most successful youth-focused ant-tobacco campaign in history, receiving numerous awards including the Grand Effie award for achievement and diversity. Office: GTM 256 Walker St Ste 100 Atlanta GA 30313

CARTER, KATHLEEN SHARP, educational consultant, appraiser, shop owner; b. Pitts., Aug. 17, 1953; 1 child, Emily Rebecca Carter Cox. BA, Allegheny Coll., Meadville, Pa., 1975; MA, Duke U., Durham, NC, 1976, PhD, 1979. Vis. instr. Allegheny Coll., Meadville, Pa., 1979; instr. Duke U., 1979; vis. asst. prof. NC State U., Raleigh, 1979—80; lifestyles editor Suffolk News-Herald, Va., 1980—81; free-lance writer Va. Pilot and Ledger-Star, Norfolk, 1981—83; instr. Paul D. Camp CC, Franklin, Va., 1981—87, title iii grant coord., 1984—87; exec. dir. Hampton Rds. C. of C., Suffolk, 1986—87; instr. Greensboro Coll., NC, 1988—89; vis. lectr. U. NC, Greensboro, 1989—89; prof. history High Point U., NC, 1989—2008; owner Cat's Cradle Used, Rare and Out Print Books, High Point, 1999—; ednl. cons. Kathleen S. Carter, High Point, 2003—; pub. Deep River Press, High Point, 2008—12; mng. editor Joun. NC Assn. Historians, 2007—12; owner Cat's Cradle Antiques and Books, 2013—. Ednl. cons. Davidson County Schools, Lexington, NC, 2003—07; mng. editor Hist. Geography, An Ann. Jour., High Point, 2007—12; ednl. cons. Guilford County Sch., Greensboro, 2007—13. Contbr. articles to profl. jours. (Brewster award, Assn. Historians, NC). Chair, land use plan update com. City High Point, NC, 1996—97; mem. Guilford County Hist. Preservation Commn., Greensboro, 1997—2000; chair, hist. preservation commn. City High Point, 1997—2000, planning and zoning commr., 2008—; planning and zoning commn. chair Children's Ctr., 2009—10, chair Franklin, Va., 1983—85. Recipient Foster B. Doane prize, Allegheny Coll., 1975, Sears Tchg. and Svc. award, High Point U., 1990; NEH Summer Seminar fellow, Nat. Endowment Humanities, 1990, Tchr. Inst. grant, NC Humanities Coun., 1992. Mem.: Nat. Coun. History Edn., Ind. Online Booksellers Assn. Independent. Presbyterian. Avocations: gardening, travel, hiking, fishing, camping. Office: Cats Cradle Books and Antiques 811 Carrick St High Point NC 27262 Office Phone: 336-991-8740. Office Fax: 866-829-3983. Business E-Mail: info@catscradlebks.net.*

CARTER, ROBERT B., delivery service executive; b. Taiwan, 1959; B, U. Fla.; MBA, U. South Fla. Exec. v.p. FedEx Info. Svcs.; v.p. info. & telecomm. FedEx Corp., 1993—98, exec. v.p. info. services, CIO Memphis, 2000—. Bd. dir. Saks Inc.; bd. dirs. First Horizon Nat. Corp., 2007—. Named Chief Tech. Officer of Yr., Infoworld, 2000, Chief of Yr., Information Week, 2005. Office: FedEx Corp 942 S Shady Grove Rd Memphis TN 38120 also: First Horizon National Corp 165 Madison Memphis TN 38103 Office Phone: 901-818-7500, 901-523-4444. Office Fax: 901-395-2000. Business E-Mail: rcarter@fhnc.com.

CARTER, ROSALYNN SMITH (ELEANOR ROSALYNN SMITH CARTER), former First Lady of the United States; b. Plains, Ga., Aug. 18, 1927; d. Edgar and Allie (Murray) Smith; m. James Earl Carter, Jr., July 7, 1946; children: John William, James Earl III, Donnel Jeffrey, Amy Lynn. Attended, Ga. Southwestern Coll., 1944—46; DHL (hon.), Morehouse Coll., 1980; LLD (hon.), U. Notre Dame, 1987. First Lady of U.S., Washington, 1977—81; disting. centennial lectr. Agnes Scott Coll., Decatur, Ga., 1988—92; disting. fellow, Women's Studies Dept. Emory U., Atlanta, 1990—. Author: First Lady from Plains, 1984; co-author (with Jimmy Carter) Everything to Gain: Making the Most of the Rest of Your Life, 1987, (with Susan Golant) Helping Yourself Help Others: A Book for Caregivers, 1994, (with Susan Golant) Helping Someone With Mental Illness: A Compassionate Guide for Family, Friends and Caregivers, 1998, (with Susan Golant & Kathryn E. Cade) Within Our Reach: Ending the Mental Health Crisis, 2010; appeared in (documentaries) Jimmy Carter Man from Plains, 2007 Co-founder Every Child by Two Campaign for Early Immunization; co-founder (with Jimmy Carter) The Carter Ctr., 1982, trustee, creator and chair Mental Health Task Force; ann. host Rosalynn Carter Symposium on Mental Health Policy; founder Rosalynn Carter Fellowships for Mental Health Journalism, 1996; chair Internat. Com. of Women Leaders for Mental Health; adv. bd. mem. Habitat for Humanity; mem. Ga. Gov.'s Commn. to Improve Svcs. for Mentally and Emotionally Handicapped, 1971; pres. bd. dir., Rosalynn Carter Inst. for Caregiving Ga. Southwestern State U.; hon. chair Pres.'s Commn. on Mental Health, 1977—78; deacon Maranatha Bapt. Ch., Plains, Ga., 2006—. Recipient Vol. of Decade award Nat. Mental Health Assn., 1980, Presdl. Citation APA, 1982, Nathan S. Kline medal of merit Internat. Com. Against Mental Illness, 1984, Disting. Alumnus award Am. Assn. State Colls. and Univs., 1987, Dorothea Dix award Mental Illness Found., 1988, Dean's award Columbia U. Coll. Physicians and Surgeons, 1991, Notre Dame award for internat. humanitarian svc., 1992, Eleanor Roosevelt Living World award Peace Links, 1992, Nat. Caring award The Caring Inst., 1995, Kiwanis World Svc. medal Kiwanis Internat. Found., 1995, Jefferson award Am. Inst. for Pub. Svc., 1996, Ga. Woman of Yr. award Ga. Commn. Women, Rhoda and Bernard Sarnat Internat. prize in mental health, Inst. Medicine, US Surgeon General's Medallion, Presdl. Medal of Freedom, 1999; named to Nat. Women's Hall of Fame, 2001. Fellow: Am. Psychiat. Assn. (hon.). Democrat. Avocations: fly fishing, birdwatching, swimming, bicycling. Office: The Carter Ctr One Copenhill 453 Freedom Pkwy NE Atlanta GA 30307-1406*

CARTER, ROY, secondary school educator, coach; b. Mars Hill, NC, Dec. 2, 1943; s. Marion "Bill" and Jessie (Buckner) Carter; m. Patricia Burleson, 1965; children: Todd, Andrea Gimlin, Stacy. BS in Edn. and Sci., East Tenn. State U., Johnson City, 1968. Cert. in safety edn. Appalachian State U., 1978, in athletic adminstrn. Nat. Fedn. HS Athletic Administrators, 1995, in agr. NC Agrl. and Tech. State U., 2005. Tchr., football coach Andrews and Hendersonville HS, 1972—96, Madison HS, 1996—99, Wilkes Ctrl. HS, NC, 1999—2004, North Wilkes HS, NC, 2004—08. Vol. Habitat for Humanity; mem. First Bapt. Ch., West Jefferson, NC. Named Conf. Coach of Yr., 1993, Tchr. of Yr., Andrews HS, 1997. Mem.: NC HS Athletic Assn. (mem. re-alignment com. 1999, Merit award, Award of Achievement 1995), NC Coaches Assn. Democrat. Mailing: PO Box 166 Glendale Springs NC 28629

CARTER, SCOTT A., gas industry executive; b. Ga. m. Tanya Carter; children: Brooke Carter, Hannah Carter. BBA in Acctg., Valdosta State U., 1995. CPA. V.p. Atlanta Gas Light Co.; sr. acct. Conn & Company P.C., Deloitte & Touche, 1997—2001; v.p., regulatory affairs AGL Resources, Inc. Student mem. Assn. Cert. Fraud Examiners; v.p., hon. mem. acctg. orgn. Valdosta State U.; mem. Ga. Soc. CPAs. Mem. AICPA. Office: AGL Resources Inc Ten Peachtree Pl NE Atlanta GA 30309 Office Phone: 404-584-4000. Office Fax: 404-584-3945. Business E-Mail: SCarter@aglresources.com.

CARTER, STEPHEN F., state legislator; BA, La. State U. Former assoc. athletic dir. La. State U.; former pres. EBR Alumni Assn., U. Lab Sch. Found.; former bd. mem. Children's Charter Sch.; owner Steve Carter Enterprises; mem. Dist. 68 La. House of Reps., 2008—, mem. edn. com., mcpl., parochial and cultural affairs com., ways and means com., joint legis. com. on capital outlay. Capt. USAF, 1967—71. Republican. Presbyn. Office: 3115 Old Forge Baton Rouge LA 70808 also: Capitol Office State Capitol Post Office Box 44486 Baton Rouge LA 70804 Office Phone: 225-362-5305, 225-342-6945. Office Fax: 225-362-5306. E-mail: carters@legis.state.la.us.

CARTER, SUSAN K., construction executive; b. 1958; BS in Acctg., Ind. U., 1981; MBA in Strategic, Northern Ill. U., 1992. CPA. Dir. finance Honeywell Aerospace, 1996—99; v.p. Honeywell Transp. & Power, 1999—2002; v.p. fin., chief acctg. officer Cummins Inc., Columbus, Ind., 2002—04; exec. v.p., CFO Lennox Internat., Inc., Richardson, Tex., 2004—09; sr. v.p. to exec. v.p., CFO KBR, Inc., Houston, 2009—. Bd. dirs. Air Products & Chemicals Inc., 2011—. Office: KBR Inc 601 Jeffersson St Houston TX 77002

CARTER, SUSAN WEBBER (SUSAN WEBBER WRIGHT), federal judge; b. Texarkana, Ark., Aug. 22, 1948; d. Thomas Edward and Betty Jane (Gary) Webber; m. Robert Ross Wright, III, May 21, 1983 (dec. June 4, 2006); 1 child, Robin Elizabeth Wright. BA, Randolph-Macon Woman's Coll., 1970; MPA, U. Ark., Fayetteville, 1973, JD with high honors, 1975. Bar: Ark. 1975. Law clk. to Hon. J. Smith Henley US Ct. Appeals (8th Cir.), 1975-76; asst. prof. law, asst. dean U. Ark., Little Rock, 1976—78, assoc. prof., 1980—83, prof., 1983—90; judge US Dist. Ct. (western dist.) Ark., 1990, US Dist. Ct. (eastern dist.) Ark., Little Rock, 1990—2013, chief judge, 1998—2005, sr. judge, 2013—; judge Fgn. Intelligence Surveillance Ct. (FISC), Washington, 2009—. Vis. assoc. prof. Ohio State U., Columbus, 1981, La. State U., Baton Rouge, 1982—83; mem. adv. com. U.S. Ct. Appeals (8th cir.), St. Louis, 1983—88. Author (with R. Wright): Land Use in a Nutshell, 1978, Land Use in a Nutshell, 2d edit., 1985; editor-in-chief: Ark. Law Rev., 1975; contbr. articles to profl. jours. Mem.: American Law Inst., Pulaski County Bar Assn., Ark. Bar Assn., American Judicature Soc., Ark. Women's Forum. Anglican. Office: US Dist Ct Ea Dist Ark 500 W Capitol Ave Ste D157 Little Rock AR 72201-3397 Office Phone: 501-604-5100. Business E-Mail: susan_wright@ared.uscourts.gov.*

CARTER, TERRY, retail executive; Grad., Univ. Okla., 1971. With QuikTrip Corp., Tulsa, Okla., 1980—, CFO, dir. Bd. chmn. Tulsa Area United Way. Office: Quick Trip PO Box 3475 Tulsa OK 74101-3475

CARTER, THOMAS SMITH, JR., retired rail transportation executive; b. Dallas, June 6, 1921; s. Thomas S. and Mattie (Dowell) C.; m. Janet R. Hostetter, July 3, 1946 (dec. 1981); children: Diane Carter Petersen, Charles T., Carol Koehler. BSCE, So. Meth. U., 1944; MS in Engring. Mgmt., Kans. U., 1991. Registered profl. engr., Mo., Kans., Okla., Tex., La., Ark. With Mo. Kans. Tex. RR, 1946-54, chief engr., 1954-61, v.p. ops., 1961-66; v.p. Kansas City So. Rlwy. Co., La. and Ark. Rlwy. Co., 1966-74; pres. Kansas City So. Rlwy. Co., 1973-86, chmn. bd., 1981-91; pres. La. and Ark. Rlwy. Co., 1974-86, chmn. bd., 1981-91, CEO, 1981-91; ret., 1991. With U.S. Corps of Engrs., 1944-46. Fellow ASCE, Am. Rlwy. Engring. and Maintenance Assn. (life), Chi Epsilon, Kiwanis Internat., Hide-A-Way Lake Club.

CARTER, VINCE, professional basketball player; b. Daytona Beach, Fla., Jan. 26, 1977; BA in African Am. Studies, U. NC, 2001. Forward Toronto Raptors, 1998—2004, NJ Nets, 2004—09, Orlando Magic, 2009—10, Phoenix Suns, 2010—11, Dallas Mavericks, 2011—. Pres. Visions in Flight Inc.; mem. US nat. team Summer Olympic Games, Sydney, 2000. Goodwill amb. Big Bros./Big Sisters Am.; founder Embassy of Hope Found. Recipient Gold medal, men's basketball, Summer Olympic Games, Sydney, 2000; named NBA Rookie of Yr., 1999; named to NBA All-Rookie 1st Team, 1999, Ea. Conf. All-Star Team, NBA, 2000—07. Achievements include winning the NBA Slam Dunk Contest, 2000. Office: Dallas Mavericks 2909 Taylor St Dallas TX 75226

CARTER-MILLER, JOCELYN, educational services company executive, former retail executive; b. 1957; BSc in Acctg., U. Ill., Urbana-Champaign, 1979; MBA in Mktg. & Fin., U. Chgo., 1981. CPA. Various sr. level positions Mattel, Inc., 1984—91; corp. v.p., chief mktg. officer Motorola, Inc., 1992—2002; exec. v.p., chief mktg. officer Office Depot, Inc., 2002—04; pres. TechEdventures, Inc., Lauderdale Lakes, Fla., 2005—. Bd. dirs. Prin. Fin. Group, Inc, 2001—, The Interpublic Group of Companies Inc., 2007—, NETGEAR, Inc., 2009—. Co-author (with Melissa Giovagnoli): Networlding: Building Relationships and Opportunities for Success, 1998. Office: TechEdventures Inc 3020 NW 33rd Ave Fort Lauderdale FL 33311

CARTIAUX, XAVIER, wholesale distribution executive; b. Belgium, Feb. 12, 1969; Various positions including purchasing mgr. & sr. buyer Ingram Micro, Inc.; dir. mktg. & comm. IRIS Sorftware; merchandising dir. ScanSource Europe, 2002—04, mng. dir., 2004—09, pres., 2009—. Office: ScanSource Inc 6 Logue Ct Greenville SC 29615 Office Phone: 864-288-2432. Office Fax: 864-288-1165.

CARTLEDGE, RAYMOND EUGENE, retired paper company executive; b. Pensacola, Fla., June 12, 1929; s. Raymond H. and Meddie (Brookins) C.; m. Gale Perry, June 30, 1962; children: John R., Perri Ann, Susan R. BS, U. Ala., 1952; postgrad., Harvard Bus. Sch., 1970. With Procter & Gamble Co., 1955-56, Union Camp Corp., Wayne, NJ, 1956-70, 80-94, pres., COO, 1983—, chmn., pres., CEO, 1986-94; pres., CEO Clevepak Corp., White Plains, NY, 1971-79; chmn. Savannah Foods, 1996-97. Past chmn. Am. Paper Inst.; trustee Am. Enterprise Inst.; trustee, life councillor The Conf. Bd.; bd. dirs. Blount Internat.; past chmn. Inst. Paper Sci. and Tech.; ret. dir. Graftec Internat., Sunoco, Delta Airlines, Nations Bank. Served with U.S. Army Airborne Infantry, 1952-55., chmn. Graftec Internat., 2004-07, 1987-94 Office: 27 Seawatch Dr Savannah GA 31411-2913 Office Phone: 912-598-3214. Personal E-mail: recart1234@att.net.

CARTY, DONALD J., former computer company executive, former air transportation executive; b. Toronto, July 23, 1946; m. Ana Carty; 3 children. Grad., Queen's U., Kingston, Ont., 1968, Harvard U., 1971. With Air Canada, 1971—73, Canadian Pacific Rwy.; gen. mgr. Montcel Distbrs. unit Celanese Can. Ltd., Montreal, 1973—78; sr. v.p. fin. Americana Hotels, 1978—79; v.p., ops. rsch. American Airlines, 1979—80, v.p. profit improvement, 1980—81, v.p., controller, 1981—83, sr. v.p., controller, 1983—85, sr. v.p. airline planning, 1987-89; pres., CEO CP Air, 1985—87; exec. v.p. fin. and planning AMR and Am. Airlines, DFW Airport, Tex., 1989-95; pres. AMR Airline Group and Am. Airlines, Inc., DFW Airport, Tex., 1995-98; chmn., pres., CEO AMR Corp., Ft. Worth, 1998—2002, chmn., CEO, 2002—03; chmn. Virgin Am., Inc., VAI Partners, LLC, San Francisco, 2006; vice chmn., CFO Dell Inc., Round Rock, Tex., 2007—08. Bd. dirs. Dell Inc. (formerly Dell Computer Corp.), 1992-, Sears, Roebuck & Co., 2001-05.; mem. Nat. Infrastructure Adv. Coun., Office of Sec., US Dept. Homeland Security. Bd. trustees Queen's U.; gov. Dallas Symphony Assn., Inc.; trustee So. Methodist U. Recipient The Order of Canada, 2003.

CARTY, RITA MARY, dean, emerita; b. Pitts., Dec. 23, 1937; d. Ignatius and Frances (Brisini) Cardillo; m. Wayne Lee Carty, Aug. 20, 1966; 1 child, Gina Marie. Diploma in Nursing, Ohio Valley Gen. Hosp., McKees Rocks, Pa., 1958; BSN, Duquesne U., 1965, PhD (hon.), 1995; MSN, Cath. U., 1966, PhD, 1977. Sch. nurse South Fayette Twp. Sch. Dist., McDonald, Pa., 1958-60; charge nurse Ohio Valley Gen. Hosp., McKees Rocks, Pa., 1960-62, instr., 1962-65; asst. prof. Cath. U., Washington, 1966-72, lectr., 1972-74; dir. nursing div. univ. affiliated program Georgetown U., Washington, 1978-81; assoc. prof., grad. program coordinator George Mason U., Fairfax, Va., 1981-85, chmn. dept. nursing, 1985-93, dean and prof. sch. nursing, 1993—2002, dean, prof. Coll. Nursing and Health Sci., 1993—2000. Dir. WHO Collaborating Ctr., 1991-2006, vis. prof., u. alabama, 2006-. Contbr. articles to profl. jours. Mem. Luxmanor Citizens Assn., Rockville, Md., 1985—. Recipient Bice Lectureship award, sch. nursing U. Va., Charlottesville, 1984, Progress of Excellence award region III Nat. U. Continuing Edn., 1985, Chief Nurse Officer award, 1992. Fellow Am. Acad. Nursing, Salzburg fellow, Austria, 2002; mem. Va. Soc. Profl. Nursing (bd. dirs. 1985-87, Va. Pioneer Nurse award, 2000), Am. Assn. Coll. Nursing (bd. dirs. 1987-90, pres. 1990-92, Sister Bernadette Armiger award, 2002, Resident emerita, 2002), Nat. League Nursing (exec. com. 1987-89), Cath. U. Nurses Alumnae (pres. 1979-81), Golden Key Soc. (hon.), Sigma Theta Tau (1st v.p. 1970-73). Roman Catholic. Avocations: horse back riding, painting, drawing, emeritus. Office: George Mason U Coll Health and Human Svcs 4400 University Dr Fairfax VA 22030-4444 Business E-Mail: rcarty@gmu.edu.

CARUSO, NICK J., corporate financial executive; BA in Acctg., La. State U. Treas. Shell Energy Resources, Inc.; various positions, including contr., gen. auditor through v.p., fin., CFO Shell Oil Co., 1969—2001; CFO Dynegy Holdings, Inc. (subs. Dynegy Inc.), exec. v.p., bd. dirs.; exec. v.p., CFO Dynegy, Inc., 2002—05, AmerenIP (formerly Ill. Power Co.), 2003. Office: Dynegy Holdings Inc 1000 La St Ste 5800 Houston TX 77002 Office Phone: 713-507-6400. Business E-Mail: nick.caruso@dynegy.com.

CARVALHO, JULIE ANN, psychologist; b. Washington, Apr. 11, 1940; d. Daniel Henry and Elizabeth Cecilia (Gardiner) Schmidt; children: Alan R., Dennis M., Melanie D., Celeste A., Joshua E. BA with high honors, U. Md., 1962, postgrad., 1962-63, 68-73, Va. Poly. Inst., 1979-88, Argosy U., 2003—04; MA, George Washington U., 1966; PhD in Social Policy, Human Devel., Va. Tech. Walden U. Social sci. rsch. analyst Mental Health Study Ctr., NIMH, Adelphi, Md., 1963-67; edn. and tng. analyst Computer Applications, Inc., Silver Spring, Md., 1967-68; edn. program specialist, program analyst Nat. Ctr. for Edni. R&D, U.S. Office of Edn., Washington, 1969-73; equal opportunity specialist Office of Sec., HEW, Washington, 1973-77; legis. program, civil rights analyst Office for Civil Rights Dept. Health and Human Svcs., Washington, 1977-85; ind. cons. Adj. lectr. No. Va. C.C., George Mason U., Montgomery Coll., Strayer U., Park U., Shepherd Coll., Germanna Coll., U. Md. U. Coll., Va. Internat. U., Prince William Hosp., Fairfax County Pub. Schs., Fairfax County Dept. Social Svcs., all Washington area, 1986—; proposal evaluator, edn. dept. HUD, HHS Ed. Dept., 1989—; presenter in field. Contbr. articles to profl. jours. Bd. dirs. Child Care Ctrs., 1970—76, HEW Employees Assn., 1973—78; steering com. Alliance for Child Care, 1975—80. Mem.: ASPA (condr. panels 1975, 1991), APA (panel condr. 1969, 1975, editor Bull. of Peace Psychology 1991—97, divsn. 48), Soc. Psychol. Study of Social Issues (presenter, congl. bd. ednl. reform 2010), Unitarian Universalists for Social Justice (bd. dirs. Balt.-Washington region 2003—07), Federally Employed Women (nat. editor 1975—79), Psychologists Soc. Responsibility (cons., chair action com. on status of women), Capitol Area Social Psychologists Assn. (conf. chmn. 1985, 1993), Fairfax County Assn. for the Gifted (pres. 1980), Phi Alpha Theta, Psi Chi, Alpha Sigma Lambda (hon.).

CARVILLE, JAMES, JR., (CHESTER JAMES CARVILLE), political scientist, commentator; b. Fort Benning, Ga., Oct. 25, 1944; s. Lucille Carville; m. Mary Matalin, Nov. 25, 1993; 2 children. Grad., La. State Univ. Litigator, Baton Rouge, 1973—79; cons. Bob Casey's 1986 Penn. gubernatorial race, Sen. Harris Wofford's 1991 campaign; chief strategist, cons. Bill Clinton's 1992 presdl. campaign; cons. Gov. Jim Florio's 1993 re-election campaign, NJ, Ehud Barak's campaign for Prime Min. Israel, 1999. Co-host CNN's Crossfire; political contributor CNN; ptnr. Hawthorne Lane Restaurant, San Francisco; adj. prof. No. Va. CC, Alexandria, 2005—; co-host 60/20 Sports, XM Radio, 2008—; prof. practice Dept. Polit. Sci. Tulane U., 2009—; spkr. in field. Author: We're Right, They're Wrong: A Handbook for Spirited Progressives, 1996, ...And the Horse He Rode in on: The People vs. Kenneth Starr, 1998, Stickin': The Case for Loyalty, 2000; co-author (with Mary Matalin): All's Fair: Love, War and Running for President, 1994; (with Paul Begala) Buck Up, Suck Up... and Come Back When You Foul Up, 2003, Take It Back: Our Country, Our Party, Our Future, 2006, (with Jeff Nussbaum) Had Enough?, 2003, (with Patricia C. McKissack) Lu and the Swamp Ghost, 2004; co-author (with Rebecca Buckwalter-Poza): 40 More Years: How the Democrats Will Rule the Next Generation, 2009; actor: (films) The People vs. Larry Flynt, 1996, Old School, 2003, Wedding Crashers, 2005, Man of the Year, 2006; (TV series) Boston Common, 1996, Arli$$, 1997, (voice only) King of the Hill, 1997, Mad About You, 1998, Spin City, 1999, (voice only) Family Guy, 2000; appearance (documentaries) The War Room, 1993, The Hunting of the President, 2004, (TV-polit. series) K Street. Named Campaign Mgr. of the Year, Am. Assn. of Political Consultants, 1993. Democrat. Avocation: watching reruns of the andy griffith show. Office: Gaslight Inc 424 S Washington St Lower Level Alexandria VA 22314 also: Tulane U 316 Norman Mayer New Orleans LA 70118 Office Phone: 703-739-7777. Business E-Mail: james@carville.info. E-mail: carville@tulane.edu.

CASADA, GLEN, state legislator; b. Jeffersonville, Ind., Aug. 2, 1959; m. Jill Casada; children: Sarah, Rich, Emmaleigh, Clark. Mem. Consumer & Employee Affairs Coms., Children & Family Affairs Coms., Employee Affairs Subcom., Family Justice Subcom.; house rep. Tenn.; tchr. L & M HS, 1983; sales rep. Schering-Plough Health, 1984—; commr. Dist. 4 Williamson County, 1994—2001; ptnr. Tlc Med. Equipment County, 1998—99; state rep. Dist. 63 Tenn., 2002—; rep. whip. Mem.: Williamson County Habitat Humanity, C. of C., Brightstone, Franklin Noon Rotary. Republican. Baptist. Office: 4893 Bethesda-Duplex Rd College Grove TN 37046 also: 112 War Memorial Bldg Nashville TN 37243-0163 Office Phone: 615-595-8759, 615-741-4389. Business E-Mail: rep.glen.casada@capitol.tn.gov.

CASAREZ, RUEBEN CHARLES, lawyer; b. El Paso, Tex., Sept. 26, 1953; s. Ramon and Irene (Lucero) C.; m. Nicole J. Bremner, Nov. 13, 1982. AB in Psychology, Stanford U., 1975; JD, U. Tex., 1979. Bar: Tex. 1979. Assoc. Butler & Binion, Houston, 1979-87, ptnr., 1988-95; sr. counsel Wells Fargo & Co., Houston, 1995—2010, sr. co. counsel, 2010—. Pres. Houston Housing Fin. Corp., 1992-94. Mem. Houston Housing Authority, 2006—. Mem. ABA, Hispanic Bar Assn. Houston (pres. 1991-92), Mexican Am. Bar Assn. Houston, Assn. for Advancement Mexican Ams. (gen. counsel 1992-98), Am. Law Inst. Democrat. Roman Catholic. Office: Wells Fargo Bank PO Box 3326 MAC T0060-021 Houston TX 77253-3326

CASAS, DAVID, state legislator; b. Las Palmas, Canary Island, Sept. 18, 1971; m. Ann Casas. Former state rep. Dist. 68, Ga.; state rep. Dist. 103 Ga., 2004—; mem. Arts & Humanities Coms., Econ. Devel. & Tourism Coms.; campaign mgr. Ga. State House Race, 2000; tchr. Cobb County Schs., 1996—. Mem.: Soc. Hist. Preservation, Ga. Rep. Party. Republican. Mailing: PO Box 283 Lilburn GA 30048 Office Phone: 770-931-8033. Fax: 770-931-8033. Business E-Mail: dcasas@legis.state.ga.us.

CASAZZA, JOHN ANDREW, electrical engineer, energy executive; b. Bklyn., Jan. 3, 1924; s. John Andrew and Jane (Granata) C.; m. Madeline Russo, Apr. 24, 1949; children: John Anthony, Joan Bernadette Casazza Fram. Student, Cooper Union, 1941-43; BEE, Cornell U., 1945. Registered profl. engr., N.J. Successively system planning and devel. engr., gen. mgr. planning and rsch., v.p. planning and rsch. Pub. Svc. Electric & Gas Co., Newark, 1946-77; v.p. Stone & Webster Mgmt. Cons., NYC, 1977-79; pres. Casazza, Schultz & Assocs., Inc., Arlington, Va., 1979-90; chmn. bd. CSA Energy Cons., 1991-97; pres. Am. Edn. Inst., 1994—2008. Mem. energy engring. bd. NRC, 1988—94; mem. rsch. adv. com. Elec. Power Rsch. Inst., Palo Alto, Calif., 1976—77; mem. U.S. Energy Assn. World Energy Conf., 1983—92; bd. dirs. Ga. Sys. Ops. Co., 1996—2005; mem. Power Engineers Supporting Truth, 2003—. Contbr. numerous articles to profl. publs. Pub. trustee N.J. Marine Scis. Consortium, 1973-79; treas. N.J. Energy Rsch. Inst., 1977; mem. N.J. Gov.'s Panel on Solar Energy, 1975-77. Ensign USN, 1943-45. Fellow IEEE (life, chmn. energy policy com. 1981-82, chmn. environ. quality com. 1984-85, U.S. activities bd. citation of honor 1985, Herman Halperin award 1990, U.S. activities bd. dirs. VII profl. leadership award 1992); mem. Internat. Conf. on Large High Voltage Electric Sys. (Exec. com. U.S. nat. com. 1974-93, Atwood assoc. 1986—, spl. citation 1982, Philip Sporn award 1994), Springfield Golf and Country Club. Roman Catholic. Avocations: golf, writing. Personal E-mail: jackcasazza@aol.com.

CASCIANO, DANIEL ANTHONY, biologist, educator; b. Buffalo, Mar. 1, 1941; s. Frederick James and Rose Ann C.; m. Gertrude Ann Tara, Aug. 22, 1964; children: Anne, Jonathan. BS, Canisius Coll., 1962; PhD in Cell Biology, Purdue U., 1971. Rsch. asst. Roswell Park Meml. Inst., Buffalo, 1963—64; rsch. asst. dept. biol. scis. Purdue U., West Lafayette, Ind., 1965—66, tchg. asst., 1969, rsch. trainee, 1966—71; trainee NIH, 1966—71; postdoctoral investigator U. Tenn., Oak Ridge Nat. Labs., 1971—73; assoc. prof. dept. biochemistry and molecular biology U. Ark. for Med. Scis., Little Rock, 1974—90, prof. dept. biochemistry and molecular biology, 1990—, prof. dept pharmacology and toxicology, 1990—; rsch. biologist Nat. Ctr. Toxicological Rsch., Jefferson, Ark., 1973, program dir. divsn. mutagenesis rsch., 1976—78, dir. divsn. genetic toxicology, 1979—97, dir. divsn. genetic and reproductive toxicology, 1997—99, dep. dir. for rsch., 1999—2000, acting dir., 1999—2000, dir., 2000—06; pres. Dan Casciano and Assocs., 2006—; sr. sci. advisor, applied sci. U. Ark., Little Rock, 2008—. Contbr. articles to profl. jours. Mem. Tissue Culture Assn., Environ. Mutagen Soc., AAAS, Beta Beta Beta. Home and Office: 47 Marcella Dr Margeux Pl Little Rock AR 72223-9172 Office Phone: 501-837-2401. Business E-Mail: dcasciano@sbcglobal.net.

CASDEN, JASON, school librarian; BA in English & Linguistics, Ohio State U.; MLS, U. NC, Chapel Hill, 2006. Lead librarian, digital services devel. digital libr. initiatives NC State U., Raleigh, 2007—. Developer, technical lead Course Views Project, WolfWalk Project. Recipient Cutting-Edge Libr. Services award, ALA, 2009, Gertrude S. Carraway award, Preservation NC, 2009; named to Movers & Shakers, Libr. Jour., 2011. Office: NC State University Libraries 2 Broughton Dr Raleigh NC 27695-7111 Office Phone: 919-513-0701. Business E-Mail: jason_casden@ncsu.edu.

CASE, CHARLES DIXON, lawyer; b. Manning, SC, Mar. 23, 1952; s. James E. and Jennie (Stout) C.; m. Margie Toy, Aug. 28, 1982; children: J. Everett II, Elliot T. BS in Physics, N.C. State U., 1973; JD, Harvard U., 1977. Bar: N.C. 1977, U.S. Dist. Ct. (ea., mid. and we. dists.) N.C., U.S. Supreme Ct. Environ. atty., ptnr. Moore & Van Allen, 1977-92; ptnr. Hunton & Williams, Raleigh, NC, 1992—. Adj. prof. law Campbell U., Buies Creek, NC; hearing officer NC OSHA Safety and Health Rev. Bd., Raleigh, 1981-84; chmn. Wake County Bd. Adjustment, Raleigh, 1979-83; mem. NC Hazardous Waste Study Commn., 1982. Co-author: Toxic Tort and Hazardous Substance Litigation, 1995, Brownfields: A Comprehensive Guide to Remediating Contaminated Property, 2nd edit., 2002; contbr. articles to profl. jours. Pres. Coll. Phys. and Math. Scis. Found., N.C. State U. 1994-95, bd. dirs., 1991-98, 2000—; mem. bd. visitors N.C. State U., 1995—, chmn., 1999-2000. Home: 1540 Carr St Raleigh NC 27608-2302 Office: Hunton & Williams PO Box 109 Raleigh NC 27602-0109 Home Phone: 919-828-2199; Office Phone: 919-899-3045. E-mail: ccase@hunton.com.

CASE, RICHARD W., sports association executive; m. Barbara Case; two children. Sec. gen. USA Baseball (formerly U.S. Baseball Fedn.), 1980—. Bd. dirs. U.S. Olympic Com.; cons., advisor and dir. in field; producer instml. videotapes, books and brochures with a concentration in the areas of player and coach tng., vol. enlistment, accident prevention, juv. delinquency, and youth tournament operation in all sports. Recipient USA Baseball Pres.'s award, Am. Baseball Coaches Assn. award of honor, Centenary medal Juan Antonio Samaranch, Internat. Olympic Com. Pres., others; inducted into Nat. Jr. Coll. Athletic Assn. Hall of Fame, Nat. Assn. Intercollegiate Athletics Hall of Fame, Nat. Police Assn. Hall of Honor; recipient numerous hon. citizenship and commendation awards. Mem. Internat. Baseball Assn. (sec. gen.). Office: USA Baseball 403 Blackwell St Durham NC 27701-3972

CASEBIER, LINDY, state legislator; b. Dec. 27, 1960; Former state senator Dist. 7; del. Rep. Nat. Conv., 1984; state rep. Dist. 29 Ky., 1987—92; chmn. Jefferson County Rep. Party, 1991; mem. Edn. Com., Appropriations & Revenue Com.; tchr. Named Outstanding Young Man of America, 1990. Mem.: Ky. Music Edn. Assn., Am. Cancer Soc. (former bd. mem.), Ky. Edn. Assn., Jefferson County Tchrs. Assn., Valley Optimist Club. Republican. Baptist. Mailing: 3304 Hardwood Forest Louisville KY 40214 Home Phone: 502-935-4085.

CASELLAS, SALVADOR E., federal judge; b. San Juan, 1935; BS in Fgn. Svc. cum laude, Georgetown U., 1957; LLB magna cum laude, U. P.R., 1960; LLM, Harvard U., 1961. Ptnr. Fiddler, Gonzalez & Rodriguez, 1962-72, 77-94; judge US Dist. Ct. PR, San Juan, 1994—2005, sr. judge, 2005—. Mem. P.R. Acad. Jurisprudence, P.R. Commn. on Bicentennial of U.S. Constn., 1987-89; aide to Sec. of U.S. Army, 1985-89, emeritus, 1990—. Dir. Alliance for Drug Free P.R., 1993-94. 1st lt. U.S. Army, 1961-62, Res., JAGC, 1963-67. Recipient Comdrs. medal Second U.S. Army, 1990, P.R. Nat. Guard medal, 1990. Mem. Am. Bar Found., PR Bar Assn. Office: US Courthouse 300 Recinto Sur St Ste 342 San Juan PR 00901 Office Phone: 787-977-6060.

CASEY, BRIAN O., investment company executive; BS in Fin., Trinity U.; MBA, U. Tex., Dallas; grad., Securities Industry Assn. Inst. at U. Pa. Cert. fin. planner, Dallas, 1985—87; balanced portfolio mgr., v.p., bd. dirs. of pvt. trust co., 1987—92; v.p. mktg. and client services Westwood Management Corp., 1992—96, exec. v.p, 2000—02, COO, 2000—05, bd. dirs., 2000—, pres., 2002—, sec., 2003—, CEO, 2006—; chmn., pres., CEO Westwood Trust, 1996—; COO Westwood Holdings Group, Inc., 2001—05, pres., sec., bd. dirs., 2001—, CEO, 2006—. Vol. Big Brothers & Sisters Program Met. Dallas; active patron Habitat for Humanity; bd. dirs. Tartan, 2002-, Baylor Health Care System Found., 2008-; mem. Gov.'s Bus. Coun., Tex., 2006-. Mem.: Young Pres. Orgn. Office: Westwood Holdings Group Inc 200 Crescent Court Ste 1200 Dallas TX 75201 Office Phone: 214-756-6900. Office Fax: 214-756-6979. Business E-Mail: bcasey@westwoodgroup.com.

CASEY, DANIEL ARTHUR, lawyer; b. Pitts., May 8, 1956; s. Robert Louis and Rosemary (Doran) C.; m. Maria Cristina Pena, Aug. 1, 1981; children: Patricia, Robert, Andrew. BS, Wheeling Coll., 1978; JD, Georgetown U., 1981. Bar: Fla. 1981, U.S. Dist. Ct. (so. dist.) Fla. 1986, U.S. Ct. Appeals (11th cir.) 1986, U.S. Dist. Ct. (mid. dist.) Fla. 1989. Asst. State Atty. Dade County State Atty., Miami, Fla., 1981-86; assoc. K&L Gates LLP, Miami, 1986-89, ptnr., 1990—2004, adminstrv. ptnr. & mem. exec. com., 2005—. Adj. prof. law Nova U. Law Sch., 1989-96. Contbr. articles to profl. publs. Nat. bd. dir. YMCA of the USA; past pres. YMCA So. Broward County; mem. Ins. Info. Council; past pres. Greater Hollywood C. of C. Mem.: Dade County Bar Assn. (bd. dir.), Alpha Sigma Nu. Office: K&L Gates LLP Southeast Fin Ctr Ste 3900 200 S Biscayne Blvd Miami FL 33131-2399 Office Phone: 305-539-3324. Office Fax: 305-358-7095. Business E-Mail: dam.casey@klgates.com.

CASEY, GEORGE WILLIAM, JR., retired military officer; b. Sendai, Japan, July 22, 1948; s. George William Casey; m. Sheila Casey. BS in Internat. Rels., Georgetown U., 1970; MA in Internat. Rels., U. Denver. Commd. 2nd lt. US Army, 1970, advanced through grades to gen., 2003, various positions, 1970-82, exec. officer 1st Battalion, 10th Infantry, 4th Divsn. Ft. Carson, Colo., 1982-84, sec. gen. staff 4th Infantry Divsn., 1984-85, comdr. 1st Battalion, 10th Infantry, 4th Divsn., 1985-87; congl. program coord. Office of the Chief of Legis. Liaison, Washington, 1988-89; spl. asst. to chief of staff US Army, Washington, 1989-91, chief of staff 1st Cavalry Divsn. Ft. Hood, Tex., 1991-93, comdr. 3rd Brigade, 1st Cavalry Divsn., 1993-95; asst. chief of staff G-3 (ops.), V Corps. US Army Europe, 1995; chief of staff V Corps. US Army Europe & Seventh Army, Germany, 1995-96, asst. divsn. comdr. 1st Armored Divsn., 1996-97; asst. dep. dir. politico-mil. affairs J-5 The Joint Staff, The Pentagon, Washington, 1997-99; comdg. gen. US Army Europe, 1st Armored Divsn., 1999—2001; dir. for strategic plans & policy (J-5) The Joint Staff, The Pentagon, Washington, 2001—03, dir., 2003; vice chief of staff US Army, Washington, 2003—04, chief of staff, 2007—11; comdr. Multi-Nat. Force-Iraq, Baghdad, 2004—07. Decorated Legion of Merit with 2 Oak Leaf Clusters, Def. Meritorious Svc. medal, Meritorious Svc. medal, Army Commendation medal with Oak Leaf Cluster, Army Achievement medal with Oak Leaf Cluster, Disting. Svc. medal with Oak Leaf Cluster, Def. Disting. Svc. medal (2).

CASEY, H(ORACE) CRAIG, JR., electrical engineering educator; b. Houston, Dec. 4, 1934; s. H.C. and Mae (Walls) C.; m. Jean Anne Merritt, June 14, 1960 (div. 1983); children: Anne, Michael; m. Jacqueline Lucas, Jan. 22, 1983. BSEE, Okla. State U., 1957; MSEE, Stanford U., 1959, PhD, 1964. Devel. engr. Hewlett-Packard, Palo Alto, Calif., 1957-62; mem. tech. staff Bell Labs., Murray Hill, NJ, 1964-79; chmn. dept. elec. engring. Duke U., Durham, NC, 1979-94, prof. elec. engring., 1979—. Mem. Dept. of Def. Adv. Group Electron Devices, Washington, 1975-79; bd. dirs. Acme Elec., 1984-91. Author: Heterostructure Lasers, 1978, Devices for Integrated Circuits: Silicon and III-V Compounds, 1999. Fellow IEEE (pres. Electron Devices Soc. 1988-89, editor centennial issue Trans. on Electron Devices 1984); mem. Am. Phys. Soc. Office: Duke U Dept Elec Engring Durham NC 27706 Business E-Mail: hcc@ee.duke.edu.

CASEY, JOHN DUDLEY, writer, language educator; b. Worcester, Mass., Jan. 18, 1939; s. Joseph Edward and Constance (Dudley) C.; m. Jane Barnes, June 10, 1967 (div. 1980); children: Maud, Nell; m. Rosamond Pinchot Pittman, June 27, 1982; children: Clare, Julia. BA, Harvard U., 1962, LLB, 1965; MFA, U. Iowa, 1968. Prof. English U. Va., Charlottesville, 1972-92, U. Iowa, 1998, U. Va., 1999—. Lit. executor Estate of Breece D'J Pancake, 1979—; resident scholar Am. Acad. in Rome, 1990-91. Author: An American Romance, 1977 (runner up Ernest Hemingway award 1977), Testimony and Demeanor, 1979 (Friends Am. Lit. award 1980), Spartina, 1989 (Nat. Book award 1989), Supper at the Black Pearl, 1995, The Half-life of Happiness, 1998; co-translator: You're an Animal, Viskovitz (by A. Boffa), 2002, Enchantments (by L. Ferri), 2005, Compass Rose, 2010; contbr. stories (O. Henry award 1989), essays maj. nat. mags. including New Yorker, Esquire. With USAR, 1959-60. Guggenheim fellow, 1979-80, Nat. Endowment for Arts fellow, 1983, resident Am. Acad. in Rome, 1990-91; grantee Strauss living AAAL, 1992-97. Mem. PEN. Avocation: rowing. Office: U Va Dept English Bryan Hall Charlottesville VA 22903-3289: Michael Carlisle Inkwell 521 5th Ave New York NY 10175

CASEY, MICHAEL D., retail executive; Sr. mgr. Price Waterhouse LLP; v.p., fin. Carter's, Inc., 1993—97, sr. v.p., fin., 1997—98, sr. v.p., CFO, 1998—2003, exec. v.p., CFO, 2003—08, prin. acctg. officer, 2008, CEO, 2008—09, chmn., CEO, 2009—. Bd. dirs. Carter's, Inc., 2008. Office: Carter's Inc The Proscenium 1170 Peachtree St NE Ste 900 Atlanta GA 30309 Office Phone: 404-745-2700. Office Fax: 404-892-0968. Business E-Mail: mike.casey@carters.com.

CASEY, ROBERT REISCH, lawyer; b. New Orleans, May 19, 1946; s. Robert Taylor Casey and Merlyn Lucille (Reisch) Weilbaecher. BBA magna cum laude in Acctg., U. Notre Dame, 1968; JD, Tulane U., 1971; LLM in Taxation, NYU, 1973. Bar: La. 1971; cert. La. Bd. Legal Specialization (tax law). Ptnr. Jones, Walker, Waechter, Poitevent, Carrère & Denègre, LLP, Baton Rouge, 1971—. Mem. bd. editors Tulane Law Rev., 1970-71. Named one of Top 100 Attys., Worth mag., 2005—06, 2006—07. Mem. ABA (chmn. partnerships com. tax sect. 1982-84, mem. coun. 1985-88, sec. 1988-89, vice chmn. 1989-91), La. State Law Inst., Am. Coll. Tax Counsel, Order of Coif, Beta Gamma Sigma, Beta Alpha Psi, Phi Delta Phi. Avocations: golf, French horn. Office: Jones Walker Waechter Poitevent Carrere & Denegre LLP 4 United Plz 8555 United Plaza Blvd Ste 500 Baton Rouge LA 70809-7028 Office Phone: 225-248-2090. Office Fax: 225-248-3090. Business E-Mail: rcasey@joneswalker.com.

CASEY, THOMAS W., corporate financial executive; BS in Acctg., Kings Coll., Wilkes-Barre, Pa. Audit supr. Coopers & Lybrand, 1984—90; with Citicorp., 1990—92; from advisor/contr., to analyst GE Capital Corp., 1992—99, sr. v.p., CFO GE Fin., 1999—2002; exec. v.p., CFO Washington Mut., Inc., Seattle, 2002—08, Clear Channel Communications, Inc., San Antonio, 2010—. Mem. Pres.'s Coun. Washington Mut., Inc. Office: Clear Channel 200 E Basse Rd San Antonio TX 78209

CASON, JAMES CALDWELL, retired ambassador; s. Arthur and Marion C.; m. Carmen Aguiluz, Aug. 1972; children: James, William. BA in Internat. Rels., Dartmouth Coll., 1966; MA, Johns Hopkins U., 1968; grad. with distinction, Nat. War Coll., 1991; PhD (hon.), U. North Paraguay, 2008. With US Fgn. Svc., numerous locations, Portugal, 1969—2008; trade promotion officer US Trade Ctr., Milan, 1979-81; polit. counselor US Embassy, Montevideo, Uruguay, 1981-82, polit. officer Panama City, Panama, 1982-83; desk officer Guatemala US Dept. State, Washington, 1983-87; polit. counselor US Embassy, La Paz, Bolivia, 1987-90, dep. chief of mission Tegucigalpa, Honduras, 1991-95; polit. advisor, comdr.-in-chief US Atlantic Command/Supreme Allied Comdr. Atlantic NATO, 1995-97; dep. chief of mission US Embassy, Kingston, Jamaica; dir. policy, planning & coord., Bur. We. Hemisphere Affairs US Dept. State, Washington, chief of mission, US Interests Section Havana, Cuba, 2002—05, US amb. to Paraguay Asuncion, 2005—08. Pres. Ctr. Free Club, 2009; dir. Quincy Oil & Gas Co., Toronto, Canada, 2009; sr. insp. US State Dept., 2009; mayor, Coral Cables, Fla., 2011—. Fulbright scholar, 1968-70; Recipient Superior Honor award, US Dept. State, Dept. Disting. Honor award, Joint Chiefs of Staff Best Essay award, Def. Intelligence Agy. Writing award, Chmn. of the Joint Chiefs of Staff Joint Meritorious Svc. medal, Nat. Humint Intelligence award, 1991, Coast Guard's Disting. Pub. Svc. award, Presdl. Rank, award, 2006, Jose Falcon medal Govt. Paraguay, 2008.

CASON, NICA VIRGINIA, retired nursing educator; b. Edna, Tex. 1 child, Cynthia Diane. Diploma, Lillie Jolly Sch. Nursing, 1965; BSN, U. Tex. Med. Br., Galveston, 1967; MSN, U. So. Miss., 1981. RN Miss. Pub. health nurse Miss. State Dept. Health, Pascagoula, 1978; nursing instr. Miss. Gulf Coast Community Coll.-Jackson County Campus, Gautier, 1981-84, chair ADN program, 1984—2004, ADN divsn. chair, 2004—08. Col. USAFR, ret. Mem. NOADN, Nat. League Nursing, Sigma Theta Tau, Phi Kappa Phi.

CASPI, AVSHALOM, psychology professor, researcher; b. Jerusalem, May 5, 1960; BA, U. Calif., Santa Cruz, 1981; MA, Cornell U., 1983, PhD, 1986. Lic. Wis. Psychologist, 1987, registered Nat. Register of Health Svc. Providers in Psychology, 2002. Hosp. internship yr. UCLA Neuropsychiatric Inst. and Clinics Consultation, 1982—83; rsch. asst. Brentwood Veteran's Hosp. and UCLA Neuropsychology in geriatric medicine, 1983—84; with Neuroscience Associates, Inc., LA, 1983—84, Forensic Psych Consultants, Inc., San Diego, 1995—; rsch. assoc., Berlin Longitudinal Study on Youth Development Technical Univ. of Berlin, West Germany, 1985; rsch. assoc., Carolina Population Ctr. U. NC, Chapel Hill, 1986; asst. prof. psychology Harvard U., 1986—89; clin. supervisor U. Wis. Psychology Tng. Clinic, 1987—2007; asst. prof. psychology U. Wis., Madison, 1989—91, assoc. prof. psychology, 1991—95, prof. psychology, 1995—2007, faculty mem., Inst. for Rsch. on Poverty, 1995—2007; faculty mem., NSF Nat. Consortium on Violence Rsch. Carnegie-Mellon U., 1995—2007; Edward M. Arnett Prof. Psychology and Neuroscience, Dept. Psychology and Neuroscience, Dept. Psychiatry and Behavioral Sciences Inst. for Genome Science and Policy, Duke U., Durham, NC, 2007—; prof. personality develop., MRC Social, Genetic and Develop. Psychiatry Rsch. Centre Inst. of Psychiatry, King's Coll., London, 1997—. Vis. scholar, Inst. for Rsch. on Poverty U. Wis., Madison, 1991; adv. bd. mem. Zeitschrift fur Soziologie der Erziehung und Sozialisation, 2001—, Journal of Child Psychology and Psychiatry, 2004—; invited lectr. in field. Contbr. of several articles to profl. jours.; mem. editl. bd. for several publications, assoc. editor Journal of Personality, 1991—96, cons. editor American Journal of Sociology, 1996—98, Perspectives on Psychological Sci., 2006—07, ad hoc reviewer for journals, publishing houses and grants. Recipient Margaret Bernauer Rsch. award, Wis. Psychological Assn., 1994, Robert L. Fantz award, Am. Psychological Found., 1995, Disting. Scientific award for Early Career Contribution to Psychology (Develop. Psychology), Am. Psychological Assn., 1995, Royal Soc. Wolfson Rsch. Merit award, 2006, Mortimer D. Sackler MD prize for Disting. Achievement in Develop. Psychobiology, Sackler Inst. of Develop. Psychobiology at Columbia U. Med. Ctr. and Weill Cornell Med. Coll. of Cornell U.; co-recipient with T.E. Moffitt, John P. Hill Meml. award, Soc. for Rsch. in Adolescence, 2002, with T.E. Moffitt, Disting. Scientific Contribution award, Internat. Soc. for the Study of Behavioral Develop., 2008, with T.E. Moffitt, Epidemiology and Control of Mental Disorders, Am. Pub. Health Assn., 2008, with T.E. Moffitt, Rema Lapouse award for Significant Contributions to Scientific Understanding of Epidemiology and Control Mental Disorders, Am. Pub., 2008; named ISI Highly Cited Researcher, 2006; Found. for Child Develop. Pre-Doctoral Fellowship, 1983, Cornell U. Coll. of Human Ecology, Grad. Fellow, 1984, Nat. Acad. of Edn. Spencer Fellow, 1990—92, U. Wis. H.I. Romnes Faculty Fellow, 1993—98, U. Wis. Vilas Foundation Assoc., 1995—96, Ctr. for Advanced Study in the Behavioral Sciences Fellow, Palo Alto, 1998. Fellow: Assn. for Psychological Sci., British Acad., Am. Psychopathological Assn., Acad. Med. Sciences (UK). Avocations: travel, cooking, photography, basketball, hiking. Office: Duke U Box 104410 Grey House 2020 W Main St Ste 201 Durham NC 27708 Address: Institute of Psychiatry King's College London Box Number P080 Institure of Psychiatry De Crespign Park London SE5 8AF England Office Phone: 919-684-5835, 0044 207 848 0936. Office Fax: 919-684-6679, 0044 207 848 5262. Business E-Mail: avshalom.caspi@duke.edu, avshalom.caspi@kcl.ac.uk.

CASSEL, JOHN ELDEN, accountant; b. Apr. 24, 1934; s. Elbert Emry and Erma Ruth (McDowell) C.; m. Mary Lou Malcom, June 3, 1953; children: John Elden, James Edward, Jerald Eugene. Plant mgr., asst. gen. mgr. Baker and Taylor Co., Oklahoma City, 1966—71; paymaster, officer mgr. Robberson Steel Co., Oklahoma City, 1971—76; pvt. investor, 1976—. Methodist. Home: 2332 NW 118th St Oklahoma City OK 73120-7404 Office Phone: 405-755-0415. Personal E-mail: cassel5@hotmail.com.

CASSIDY, BILL (WILLIAM CASSIDY), United States Representative from Louisiana, former state senator; b. Highland Park, Ill., Sept. 28, 1957; m. Laura Layden; children: Will, Meg, Kate. BS in Biochemistry, La. State U., 1979, MD, 1983. Assoc. prof. medicine La. State U. Health Sci. Ctr.; mem. La. State Senate from Dist. 16, 2006—09, mem. edn. & environ. quality com., vice chair health and welfare com.; mem. US Congress from 6th La. Dist., 2009—. Sunday sch. tchr. Chapel on the Campus. Mem.: Am. Coll. Physicians, La. State Med. Soc. (bd. dirs.), East Baton Rouge Parish Med. Soc. (pres. 1998), Am. Assn. Study of Liver Diseases, Gastroenterology Soc., Rotary Club Baton Rouge. Republican. Office: US House of Representatives 1131 Longworth House Office Bldg Washington DC 20515 also: 5555 Hilton Ave Ste 100 Baton Rouge LA 70808 Office Phone: 202-225-3901, 225-929-7711. Office Fax: 202-225-7313, 225-929-7688.*

CASSIDY, JACK, academic administrator, educator; b. Phila., Mar. 12, 1941; married; 2 children. BA in English, Gettysburg Coll., Phila., 1962; MEd in Secondary Edn., Temple U., Phila., 1965, PhD in Ednl. Psychology, 1975. Tchr. Hawaii Dept. Pub. Instrn., Island Kauai, Lihue, 1965-69; instr. Temple U., 1970-71; reading supr. Newark Sch. Dist., Del., 1972—78; prof. Millersville U., Pa., 1998; assoc. dean Coll. Edn. Tex. A&M U., Corpus Christi, 1998—2011. Spl. cons. Ednl. Testing Svc., 1977-93. Sr. author: Basic Life Skills, Macmillan Lit. Series, Read-Reason-Write, Scribner Reading Series; contbr. articles to profl. jours. Coach Cmty. Swim Teams, Kapaa, Hawaii, 1967-68. Named to Elected Reading Hall of Fame, 2010. Mem. Internat. Reading Assn. (legis. com. 1975-76, dir. 1976-79, pres. 1982-83), Diamond State Reading Assn. (pres. 1974-75), Nat. Coun. Tchrs. English, Assn. for Supervision and Curriculum Devel., Nat. Coun. Accreditation Tchr. Edn. (exec. bd. 1986-88, chmn. 1988-89, 1997-2000), Coll. Reading Assn. (dir. 1994-97, pres. 1999-2000). Home: 8000 Donore Pl Apt 12 San Antonio TX 78229-2676 Office Phone: 361-825-5611. Personal E-mail: dr.jackcassidy@gmail.com.

CASSIS, TAMI BUSS, dermatologist, educator; BS in Psychology, U. Wis., 1995; MD, U. Louisville, 2001. Diplomate Am. Bd. Dermatology. Cosmetic dermatology intern The Dermatology and Aesthetic Ctr., Boca Raton, Fla., 2004; intern internal medicine Univ. of Louisville, Ky., 2002, resident divsn. dermatology Ky., 2005, asst. clin. prof., dept. dermatology Ky., 2005—; vol. faculty, dept. dermatology Veterans Adminstrn. Hosp., 2005—; hosp. affiliations include Advanced Dermatology and Dermaesthetics of Louisville, Ky., 2005—, Cassis Dermatology and Aesthetics Ctr., Ky., 2008—. Named one of 40 Under 40, Bus. First, 2006, Top Doc, Louisville Mag., 2009; grantee Wilds Found. Rsch. Fellowship, 1994, Golden Key Honor Soc., 1994, Psi Chi Psychology Nat. Honor Soc., 1994, Order of Omega Nat. Honor Soc., 1995, Hilldale Found. Fellowship, 1994, Alpha Omega Alpha Honor Soc., 2001. Mem.: Women's Dermatologic Soc. (bd. dirs. 2007, bus. interest group task force 2009, young physicians task force 2009, membership com. 2011), Am. Soc. of Dermatologic Surgery, Ky. Med. Assn. (legis. com. 2007, cancer com. 2007), Med. Dermatologic Soc. (edn. work grou 2006), Am. Chem. Soc., Am. Soc. of Laser Medicine, Gamma Phi Beta Alumni Assn. Office: Cassis Dermatology and Aesthetics Center Ste 100 9301 Dayflower St Prospect KY 40059 Office Phone: 502-326-8588. Office Fax: 502-326-8589.

CASSPI, OMRI, professional basketball player; b. Holon, Israel, June 22, 1988; s. Shimon and Ilana Casspi. Forward Maccabi Tel Aviv, Israeli Basketball Super League, 2005—06, 2007—09, Hapoel Galil Elyon, Israeli Basketball Super League, Israel, 2006—07, Sacramento Kings, 2009—11, Cleve. Cavaliers, 2011—13, Houston Rockets, 2013—. Named Sixth Man of Yr., Israeli Basketball Super League, 2008; named to All-Israeli Basketball Super League Team, 2009, NBA All-Rookie Team, 2010. Achievements include member of Israeli Basketball Super League championship winning Maccabi Tel Aviv, 2006, 2009; member of the Israeli Basketball Association State Cup winning Maccabi Tel Aviv, 2006; being the first Israeli born basketball player to play in the NBA, 2009. Office: Houston Rockets 1510 Polk St Houston TX 77002*

CASTAGNA, VANESSA J., apparel executive; b. Muncie, Ind., 1949; m. Neil Castagna. BS in Psychology & Speech Comm., Purdue U., 1971. Sr. v.p., & gen. mgr. Lazarus, 1972—85; v.p., Merchandising - Women's Target Stores, 1985—92; sr. v.p., gen. merchandising mgr., Women's & Jjr.'s Marshall's Stores, Mass., 1992—94; sr. v.p., gen. mdse. mgr., home decor, furniture, crafts, children's apparel Wal-Mart Stores, Bentonville, Ark., 1994—96, sr. v.p., gen. mdse. mgr., women's & children's accessories & apparel, 1996—99; exec. v.p. JC Penney Co., Inc., Plano, Tex., 1999—2004; COO, Merchandising, & Catalog JC Penney Stores, 1999—2001, pres., COO, Catalog, & Internet Plano, Tex., 2001—03, chmn., CEO, Catalog, & Internet, 2002—04; exec. chmn. Mervyns LLC, Hayward, Calif., 2005—07; sr. mem., Ops. Divsn. Cerberus Capital Management, LP, NYC, 2005—. Bd. dirs. Carter's Inc., Levi Strauss & Co, 2007—, SpeedFC, 2009—. Chair Women's Leadership Coun. United Way of Met. Dallas; bd. dirs. JC Penney Afterschool Fund, Nat. Minority Supplier Devel. Coun., Cox Sch. Bus. So. Methodist U. Recipient AMY award, Young Menswear Assn., 2006; named one of 50 Most Powerful Women in Bus., Fortune mag., 2000—04, Most Powerful Women, Forbes mag., 2004—05, Next 20 Female CEOs, Pink Mag. & Forté Found., 2006. Office: Levi Strauss & Co Bd Directors 1155 Battery St San Francisco CA 94111 Office Phone: 415-501-6000. Office Fax: 415-501-7112. E-mail: vcastagna@levi.com.

CASTAGNA, WILLIAM JOHN, federal judge; b. Phila., 1924; Student, U. Pa., 1941-43; LLB, U. Fla., 1949, JD, 1967. Bar: Fla. 1949. Pvt. practice atty., Miami, Fla., 1949—50, Clearwater, Fla., 1950—70; ptnr. MacKenzie, Castagna, Bennison & Gardner, Clearwater, 1970-79; judge US Dist. Judge (mid. dist.) Fla., Tampa, 1979—92, sr. judge, 1992—. Mem. USAF, 1943—45. Democrat. Office Phone: 813-301-5935.

CASTEEL, DIANN BROWN, education educator; d. Harold James Brown and Clara Ruth (Phillips) Johnston; m. Everette Kenneth Casteel, Oct. 7, 1972; children: Trisha DiAnn, Mary Camille, Cheyenne James. BS, East Tenn. State U., 1973, MA, 1976, EdD, 1994. Cert. tchr., Tenn. Tchr. Greene County Bd. Edn., Greeneville, 1973-90; dir. Project Choice, Greeneville-Greene County Ctr. for Tech., 1990-91; tchr. Doak Sch., Tusculum Sta., Tenn., 1992-2000; asst. prin. Chuckey Elem. Sch., Greene County Bd. Edn., Mohawk, Tenn., 2000—01, Tenn., 2001—03; prof. edn. in grad. and profl. studies Tusculum Coll., 2004—; asst. prin. Doak Elem. Sch., Greeneville, 2003—04; ret., 2004; prof. edn. Tusculum Coll., 2013—. Founder Iowa-Tenn. Student Exch. Program, Dayton and Greeneville, 1986—87; asst. prof. edn. Tusculum Coll., Greenville, Guidance and Assessment for Single Parent/Displaced Homemaker Program, 1989—90. Founder Hay Relief Program, Tenn., 1986-87; leader 4-H Club, Baileyton Elem. Sch., 1985-88; mem. Ottway United Meth. Ch., Greeneville, 1985-92; v.p. Ottway United Meth. Women, Greeneville, pres., 1976; mem. women's group study exch. to India, Rotary Internat., 1989; mem. 1st Christian Ch., Greenville, Tenn., 1992—. Recipient Horse of Yr. award Appalachian Horse Show Assn., 1967, Outstanding Citizen award Ruritan Nat., 1986, 4-H Emerald Club Leader award, 1987, DIANA award Epsilon Sigma Alpha, 1990, Book of Golden Deeds award Greeneville Exchange Club, Tenn., 1992. Mem. NEA, Greene County Edn. Assn., East Tenn. Edn. Assn., Tenn. Edn. Assn., Internat. Platform Assn., U.S.S. Greenville, Inc., Andrew Johnson Women's Club, Alpha Delta Kappa Tau Chpt., Kappa Delta Pi, Phi Delta Kappa. Independent. Methodist. Avocations: cooking, reading, swimming, horses. Home: 2545 Flatwoods Rd Greeneville TN 37745-8582 Office: Tusculum Coll 60 Shiloh Rd Greeneville TN 37743 Office Phone: 423-636-7300 ext. 5126. Business E-Mail: dcasteel@tusculum.edu.

CASTEEN, JOHN THOMAS, III, retired academic administrator; b. Portsmouth, Va., Dec. 11, 1943; s. John Thomas and Naomi Irene (Anderson) C.; m. Elizabeth Betsy Casteen; children: John Thomas IV, Elizabeth, Lars, Alex, Lily Foote. BA (hon.), U. Va., 1965, MA, 1966, PhD, 1970; LLD (hon.), Shenandoah Coll. Conservatory Music, 1984; DHL (hon.), Bentley Coll., 1992; degree (hon.), Piedmont CC, Va., 1992; DPA, Bridgewater Coll., 1993; degree (hon.), U. Athens, Greece, 1996; DHL (hon.), Transylvania U., 1999. Asst. prof. English U. Calif., Berkeley, 1970—75; assoc. prof., dean admissions U. Va., Charlottesville, 1975—82; adj. prof. Va. Commonwealth U., Richmond, 1982—85; pres., prof. English U. Conn., Storrs, 1985—90; George M. Kaufman presdl. prof. of English U. Va., 1990—2010, pres., 1990—2010. Bd. dirs. Wachovia, Inc.; dir. U. 21 LBC, 2001-, U21 Global Pte Ltd., 2008-; chair U. 21. Author: 16 Stories, 1981; contbr. articles to various publs.; mem. editl. adv. bd. The Presidency. Sec. edn. Commonwealth of Va., Richmond, 1982-85; trustee Mariner's Mus., 1990—, Coll. Entrance Exam Bd., N.Y.C., 1980-90, chmn. 1986-88; mem. So. Regional Edn. Bd., 1982-85. New Eng. Bd. of Higher Edn., 1986-90; mem. nat. adv. com. Nat. Domestic Violence Media Campaign, 1992—; dir. Am. Coun. on Edn., 1993-96. Recipient Outstanding Virginian award, 1993, Gold medal, Nat. Inst. Social Scis., 1998, Leadership award, Southern Assn. Colls. and Schs. Commn., 1999, Pres. Leadership Group award, Higher Edn. Ctr. Alcohol and Other Drug Prevention's, 2002, Architecture Svc. medal, Va. Soc. Am. Inst. Archs., 2004. Mem. Assn. Am. Univs. (exec. com.), So. Assn. Colls. and Schs. (chair commn. on colls. 1995-97, pres. 1998), Assn. Governing Bds. Colls. and Schs. (coun. pres. 1992—), Keswick Club, Farmington County Club, Commonwealth Club (Richmond), Phi Beta Kappa, Chesapeake Bay Found. (bd. trustees 2005-), Leifur Eiriksson Found. (bd. dirs. 2004-), Jefferson Sci. Assocs, LLC (chair, bd. dirs. 2006-). Episcopalian. Business E-Mail: jtc@virginia.edu.

CASTELLANOS, ALEX (ALEJANDRO CASTELLANOS), lobbyist, media consultant; b. Havana, Cuba, 1954; arrived in US, 1961; s. Jose and Olga Castellanos. Grad., U. NC, Chapel Hill, 1976. Creative mem. Bush-Cheney 2004 campaign; sr. strategist Romney for President Campaign; mem. John McCain for President Ad Coun.; chief media strategist Midnight Ride Media, Nat. Media Inc.; founding ptnr. Purple Strategies, LLC, Alexandria, Va., 2008—. Guest commentator (TV series) Crossfire, CNN, Head to Head, MSNBC. Named one of The 50 Most Powerful People in DC, GQ mag., 2007. Republican. Office: Purple Strategies, LLC 815 Slaters Ln Alexandria VA 22314 Office Phone: 703-548-7877.*

CASTLE, DARRELL, lawyer; b. Kingsport, Tenn., 1948; m. Joan Castle; 1 child, Joanna. BA in History and Polit. Sci., East Tenn. State U., Johnson City, 1970; JD, Memphis State U. Law Sch., 1979. Pvt. practice atty. The Law Offices of Darrell Castle and Associates, Memphis, 1984—. Founder Mia's Children Found., Inc., Bucharest, Romania, 1988—; state chmn. Constitution Party, Tenn., vice chmn. nat. com., platform chmn., nat. convention, US vice-presdl. candidate, 2008; bd. mem. Conservative Caucus, 2005—; chmn. Nat. Veterans Coalition, 2007. 1st lt. USMC, Far East. Constitution Party. Office: Darrell Castle & Associates 4515 Poplar Ave Ste 510 Memphis TN 38117-7513 Office Fax: 901-458-9443.

CASTON, MOANICA, electric power industry executive; b. Shreveport, La. BS, La. State U.; JD, Harvard U. Cert.: (sr. profl. in human resources). Mgr. Southern Co.; corp. sec. Southern Nuclear Oper. Co. Inc., gen. counsel, dir. human resources, v.p. external affairs; v.p. diversity Ga. Power, 2011—. Mem.: ABA, Am. Assn. of Blacks in Energy, Nat. Assn. of African Americans in Human Resources, Soc. for Human Resources Mgmt., Soc. of Corp. Secs. Governance Professionals, Energy Bar Assn. Office: Georgia Power 96 Annex Atlanta GA 30396 Office Phone: 888-660-5890.

CASTOR, BETTY (BETTY CASTOR), former academic administrator; b. Glassboro, NJ, May 11, 1941; d. Joseph L. and Gladys (Wright) Bowe; children: Katherine, Karen, Frank. BA, Glassboro State Coll., 1963; MEd, U. Miami, 1968. Commr. Hillsborough County Bd. Commissioners, 1972—76, chmn., 1975—76; mem. Fla. State Senate from Dist. 23, 1976—78, Fla. State Senate from Dist. 21, 1982—86, pres. pro tempore, 1985—86; commr. edn. State of Fla., Tampa, 1986—93; pres. U. South Fla., 1994—99, exec. dir. Dr. Kiran C. Patel Ctr. for Global Solutions, 2007—; pres. Nat. Bd. Profl. Tchg. Stds., San Antonio, 2000—07. Bd. dirs. NorthStar Bank, 2009—. Bd. mem. Hillsborough Hosp. & Welfare Bd., 1972—76, chmn., 1973—74; mem. Hillsborough County Environmental Protection Commn., 1972—76, chmn., 1973—74; bd. mem. Tampa Bay History Ctr., Hillsborough County Edn. Found., Collins Ctr. for Pub. Policy; mem. Tampa Bay Regional Planning Coun., 1972—76, Tampa Bay Area Com. on Fgn. Rels. Recipient Good Govt. award, Town 'N Country Jaycees, 1975, Outstanding Legislator of Yr. award, Fla. Edn. Assn. (FEA), 1977, Lifetime Achievement award, 2008; named to The Fla. Women's Hall of Fame, 1996. Mem.: League Women Voters (Hillsborough County pres. 1969—71). Democrat. Lutheran. Office: Dr Kiran C Patel Center for Global Solutions 4202 East Fowler Ave CPR 107 Tampa FL 33620 Office Phone: 813-974-2954. Office Fax: 813-974-2522. E-mail: bcastor@cas.usf.edu.

CASTOR, KATHY (KATHERINE ANNE CASTOR), United States Representative from Florida; b. Miami, Fla., Aug. 20, 1966; d. Don and Betty (Bowe) Castor; m. William Lewis; children: Julia, Chrissy. BA, Emory U., Atlanta, 1988; JD, Fla. State U. Coll. Law, 1991. Asst. gen. counsel Fla. Dept. Cmty. Affairs, 1991—94; practicing atty. Fla., 1994—2000; mem. Hillsborough County Bd. Commissioners, Fla., 2002—06, US Congress from 11th Fla. Dist., Washington, 2007—13, US Congress from 14th Fla. Dist., 2013—. Mem.: Fla. Assn. Women Lawyers (past pres.). Democrat. Presbyterian. Office: 4144 N Armenia Ave, Ste 300 Tampa FL 33607 also: US House of Representatives 205 Cannon House Office Bldg Washington DC 20515 Office Phone: 813-871-2817, 202-225-3376. Office Fax: 813-871-2864, 202-225-5652.*

CASTRO, ÁNGEL, accountant, author, educator; b. Matanzas, Cuba, Aug. 7, 1930; s. Dolores and Ángel (Martínez) Castro; m. Rula Lappas, Feb. 24, 1973; 1 child, Alexander. BA, Havana State U., 1949; MBA, Havana U., Cuba, 1955, LLD, 1961; LLD in Spanish Law, Norte Oriente U., Cuba, 1958, JD, 1961. CPA Havana U. Prof. José Martí Nat. U., Havana, 1954—60, dean, 1957—60; head Spanish dept. Rolfe HS, Iowa, 1965—66, tchr., 1965—66; asst. prof. Spanish lang. and lit. Carroll Coll., Waukesha, Wis., 1966—67, Hampton Inst., Va., 1967—68, Old Dominion U., Norfolk, Va., 1968—72; cons. Va CC, Thomas Nelson CC, Hampton, 1968; dir. retrain HS tchrs. French, German and Spanish fgn. lang. methodology Summer Insts., 1969—70; acct. Arthur Young & Co., NYC, 1973—; pres. Angel Castro & Co., North Miami Beach, Fla., 1977—83; sr. acct. Angel Castro Accts., 1982—; instr. Fla. Career Coll., 1983—. Instr. acctg. Coll. Author: JoséMartí: Páginas Literarias, 1969, Refugiados, 1970, Poemas del Destierro, 1971, Cuentos de New York, 1973, El Tirano & los Tiburones, 2002. Home: 1271 NE 179th St North Miami Beach FL 33162-1313 Home Phone: 305-949-7170.

CASTRO, JOAQUÍN, United States Representative from Texas, former state legislator; b. San Antonio, Sept. 16, 1974; s. Jesse Guzman and Maria Castro; m. Anna Flores, Nov. 2, 2013. BA in Comm. & Polit. Sci. with honors, Stanford U., Calif., 1996; JD, Harvard U. Law Sch., Mass., 2000. Atty., San Antonio; mem. Dist. 125 Tex. House of Representatives, 2003—13; mem. US Congress from 20th Tex. Dist., Washington, 2013—, US House Armed Services Com., 2013—, US House Fgn. Affairs Com., 2013—. Vis. prof. law St. Mary's U.; adj. prof. Trinity U., San Antonio. Democrat. Roman Catholic. Office: US House of Representatives 212 Cannon House Office Bldg Washington DC 20515 Office Phone: 202-225-3236, 210-348-8216. Office Fax: 210-979-0737.*

CASTRO, JULIÁN, Mayor, San Antonio, Texas; b. San Antonio, Sept. 16, 1974; s. Jessie Guzman and Maria Castro; m. Erica Lira Castro; 1 child, Carina. BA, Stanford U., 1996; JD, Harvard Law Sch., 2000. City councilman San Antonio City Coun., Tex., 2001—; founder Law Offices of Julián Casrto, PLLC, 2005—; mayor City of San Antonio, 2009—. Keynote spkr. Democratic Nat. Convention, 2012. Bd. mem. Family Services Assn.; San Antonio advisory bd. mem. Clear Channel; advisory bd. mem. San Antonio Nat. Bank. Named one of The Politics 40 Under 40, TIME Mag., 2010. Democrat. Roman Catholic. Office: Office of the Mayor PO Box 839966 San Antonio TX 78283 Business E-Mail: mayorjuliancastro@sanantonio.gov.*

CASTRONEVES, HÉLIO, race car driver; b. Sao Paulo, Brazil, May 10, 1975; 1 child, Mikaella. Race car driver IndyCar Series Penske Racing, 2001—; owner NasrCastroneves Racing. 1st pl. Indy 500 Indpls. Motor Speedway, 2001, 2002, 2009, 2nd pl. Indy 500, 2003; 1st pl. Bombardier ATV 200 Phoenix Internat. Raceway, 2002, 2nd pl. Purex Dial Indy 200, 2003, 2nd pl. XM Satellite Radio Indy 200, 2005; 2nd pl. Radisson Indy 225 Pikes Peak Internat. Raceway, 2002; 2nd pl. Gateway Indy 250 Gateway Internat. Raceway, 2002, 1st pl. Emerson Indy 250, 2003; 2nd pl. Chevy 500 Tex. Motor Speedway, 2002, 1st pl. Chevy 500, 2004, 1st pl. Bombardier Learjet 500, 2006; 2nd pl. SunTrust Indy Challenge Richmond Internat. Raceway, 2003, 1st pl. SunTrust Indy Challenge, 2005; 2nd pl. Kans. Indy 300 Kans. Speedway, 2003; 1st pl. Firestone Indy 225 Nazareth Speedway, 2003; 2nd pl. Toyota Indy 300 Homestead-Miami Speedway, 2004, 2006; 2nd pl. Peak Antifreeze Indy 300 Chicagoland Speedway, 2005, 1st pl. Peak Antifreeze Indy 300, 2008; 1st pl. Honda Grand Prix St. Petersburg, 2006, 2007; 1st pl. Indy Japan 300 Twin Ring Motegi, 2006; 1st pl. Firestone Indy 400 Mich. Internat. Speedway, 2006; 2nd pl. Motorola Indy 300 Infineon Raceway, 2007; 1st pl. Indy Grand Prix Sonoma County, Calif., 2008. Performer: Dancing with the Stars, 2007 (winner, 2007); featured in People, Cosmopolitan, Esquire and Sports Illustrated, interviewed by David Letterman and Regis and Kelly. Amb. Smile Found., 2004—. Recipient Key of Miami, Mayor Manual Diaz; named Next Hottest Race Car Driver, ESPN Mag., 2000. Achievements include becoming the fifth race car driver in history to win the Indianapolis 500 for two consecutive years. Avocations: tennis, running. Mailing: Penske Racing 200 Penske Way Mooresville NC 28115 Office Phone: 704-664-2300.

CATALFO, ALFRED, JR., (ALFIO CATALFO), lawyer; b. Lawrence, Mass., Jan. 31, 1920; s. Alfio and Vincenza (Amato) C.; m. Caroline Joanne Mosca (dec. Apr. 1968); children: Alfred Thomas, Carol Joanne, Gina Marie; m. Gail Varney, 1988. AB, U. Ala., 1941; BA, U. NH, 1945; attended, Harvard U., 1950, MA in History, 1952; LLB, Boston U., 1947, JD (hon.), 1969; postgrad., Suffolk U. Sch. Law, 1955-56, Am. Law Inst., NYC, 1959; attended, Nat. Inst. Criminal Trail Lawyer, 1980. Bar: NH 1947, US Dist. Ct. 1948, US Ct. Appeals 1978, US Supreme Ct. 1979. Pvt. practice, Dover, NH, 1948—2006; ptnr. Catalfo Law Firm, Dover, 1980—; county atty. Strafford County, Dover, NH, 1949-50, 55-56; bd. immigration appeals US Dept. Justice, 1953—; football coach Berwick Acad., South Berwick, Maine, 1944, Mission Catholic HS, Roxbury, Mass., 1945-46; with Tenn. Bar Course, 2006, Am. Trial Assn., 1952—. Judge advocate Dept. NH Disabled Am. Veterans, 1950—68, 1972—, comdr., 1956—57; life mem. Disabled Am. Vet., 1948—; chmn. Am. Legion Dept. Convension, 1967, 1977, 1984, Disabled Am. Vet. Dept., 1957, 1960, 1963, 1970, Dover Dem. City Com., 1961—66, Strafford County Dem. Com., 1964—68, Dem. State Com., 1956—58; elect. mem. pres. Pledge Del. Sen John F. Kennedy, 1960; com. elect mem. John F. Kennedy Pres. US, 1960. Author: Laws of Divorces, Marriages, and Separations in New Hampshire, 1962, History of the Town of Rollinsford, (1623-1973), 1973, High School Poetry, 1940. Pres. Young Dems. of Dover, 1953-55; 1st vice-chmn. Young Dems., NH, 1954-56; mem. Strafford County Dem. Com., 1948-75; vice-chmn. NH Dem. Com., 1954-56, 1st chmn., 1956-58, chmn. spl. activities, 1958-60; del. Dem. Nat. Conv., 1956-60, 76; chmn. NH Dem. Conv., 1958, conv. dir., 1960; mem. Dem. state exec. com., 1960-70; Dem. nominee for U.S. Senate, 1962; vice-chmn. Dover Cath. Sch. Com., 1969-71; mem. Dover Bd. Adjustment, 1960-65; apptd. lt. commdr. NH Govs. Mil. Staff. Pilot US Naval Air Corp., lt. commdr. USNR, 1942-44. Recipient keys to cities of Dover, Somersworth, Concord, Berlin, Manchester and Rochester NH, 6 nat. plaques DAV, 3 disting. svc. awards Am. Legion, Am. Legion Life Membership award, spl. recognition award Berwick Acad., 1985, nominee US Senator, 1962, Opposing US Senator Norris Cotton, Rep. Incumbent Attended Dem. Nat. Conv. NYC, 1976, 1980, Nat. Placques, Disabled Am. Vet., 1957, 60, 63, 70, 85, 95, Disting. Svc. Placques, Nat. Am. Legion, 1967, 77, 85, Lt. Commdr. award, US Naval Res. NH Govs. Mil. Staff. Mem. ABA, NH Bar Assn., Strafford County Bar Assn. (v.p. 1966-67, pres. 1968-69), Assn. Trial Lawyers Am., NY State Trial Lawyers Assn., Mass. Trial Lawyers Assn., NH Trial Lawyers Assn., Tex. Trial Lawyers Assn., Nat. Assn. Criminal Def. Lawyers, NH Assn. Criminal Def. Lawyers, Am. Judicature Soc., Phi Delta Phi, DAV (judge adv. NH dept. 1950-68, 72—; comdr. chpt. 1953-54, comdr. NH 1956-57), Am. Legion (life, chmn. state conv. 1967, 77, 84), Navy League, NH Hist. Soc., Dover Hist. Soc., Rollinsford Hist. Soc., Eagles Club, Sons of Italy, Lions, Elks, K.C. (grand knight 1975-77), Moose, Lebanese Club, Berwick Acad. Alumni Assn. (pres. 1974-76), Tenn. Bar Assn., NH Hist. Soc., Dover Hist. Soc. (Northam Colonist), Rollinsford Hist. Soc., Clubs: Eagles (Somersworth, NH), Sons of Italy (Portsmouth, NH). Lodges: Lions, Elks, K.C. (grand knight 1975-77), Moose, Lebanese (Dover). Office: 219 Jay Bird Dr Gatlinburg TN 37738 Home: 450 Central Ave Dover NH 03820-3425 Office Phone: 865-430-3228.

CATANESE, ANTHONY JAMES, academic administrator; b. New Brunswick, NJ, Oct. 18, 1942; s. Anthony James and Josephine Marlene (Barone) C.; m. Sara Jean Phillips, Oct. 23, 1968; children: Mark Anthony, Michael Scott, Mark Alexander. BA, Rutgers U., 1963; M in Urban Planning, NYU, 1965; PhD, U. Wis., 1968. Asst. prof. city planning Ga. Inst. Tech., Atlanta, 1967-78, assoc. prof., 1968-73, chmn. doctoral studies com., 1970-73; James A. Ryder prof. transp. and planning, dir. Ryder program in transp. U. Miami, Coral Gables, Fla., 1973-75; dean Sch. Architecture and Urban Planning U. Wis., Milw., 1975-82; prof. architecture and urban planning, provost Pratt Inst., NYC, 1982-84; dean Coll. Architecture, U. Fla., Gainesville, 1984-89; pres. Fla. Atlantic U., Boca Raton, 1989—2002, pres., prof., 1990—2002; pres. Fla. Inst. Tech., Melbourne, 2002—. Sr. Fulbright prof., Colombia, 1971-72; sr. cons. State of Wis., 1965-67, sr. planner State of N.J., 1963-67; pres. A. J. Catanese & Assocs., Inc., 1967—; mem. pres. commn. NCAA, 1991-93. Author: Scientific Methods of Urban Analysis, 1972, New Perspectives on Urban Transportatio Research, 1972, Systematic Planning-Theory and Applications, 1970, Planners and Local Politics: Impossible Dreams, 1973, Urban Transportation in South Florida, 1974, Personality, Politics and Planning, 1978, Introduction to Urban Planning, 1979, Introduction to Architecture, 1979, The Politics of Planning and Development, 1984, Uban Planning, 1988; contbr. articles to profl. jours. Chmn. Mid. DeKalb County Dem. Party, 1969-71, mem. 5th Congl. Dist. Dem. caucus, 1971; aide-de-camp Gov.'s Office, State of Ga., 1971-72; mem. Ga. Dunes Studies Commn., 1972-73; bd. dirs. Archtl. Rsch. Ctrs. Consortium, 1976—; mem. Urban Policy Task Force, Carter presdl. campaign, 1976, 80; pres. Park West Redevel. Corp., 1976-78; chmn. Milw. City Plan Commn., 1978-82; bd. dirs. Goals for Milw. 2000, 1978-82, Environ. Edn. Found. Fla.; chmn. Gainesville (Fla.) Planning Bd., 1986-89. With USAR, 1961-63. Recipient fellowships State of N.J. Act of 1927, 1962-63, Werner Hegemann Found., 1963-65, Wis. Alumni Rsch. Found., 1965-68, Richard King Mellon Trust, 1966-67, Ford Found., 1967, Nat. Endowment Arts, 1980. Mem. Am. Inst. Planners (bd. govs., v.p. 1971-74), Am. Inst. Cert. Planners (mem. exec. com. 1971-74), Am. Planning Assn., Transp. Rsch. Bd., Regional Sci. Assn., Am. Acad. Polit. and Social Scis., Assn. Coll. Schs. Planning, Heritage Club, Wycliff Club, Tower Club. Office: Fla Inst Tech 150 W University Blvd Melbourne FL 32901 Office Phone: 321-674-7232. Business E-Mail: catanese@fit.edu.

CATANIA, KENNETH C., neuroscientist, educator; BS in Zoology, U. Md., College Park, 1989; MS in Neuroscience, U. Calif., San Diego, 1992, PhD in Neuroscience, 1994. Rsch. asst. National Zoological Park, Washington, 1988—90; postdoctoral fellow, dept. psychology Vanderbilt U., Nashville, 1995—98, rsch. asst. prof., dept. psychology, 1998—2000, asst. prof., dept. biol. sciences, 2000, assoc. prof., dept. biol. sciences, 2006, prof. biological sciences, 2006—, Stevenson Prof. Biological Sciences, 2011—. Contbr. articles to Nature, Proceedings of NAS USA, Nature Neuroscience, and others, chapters to books. Recipient John F. Kennedy Ctr. Young Scientist award, 1997, Capranica Found. award in Neuroethology, 1998, Internat. Soc. of Neuroethologists Young Investigator award, 1998, Nat. Sci. Found. Career award, 2003, C.J. Herrick award in Neuroanatomy, 2005, Co-author on 2009 Cozzarelli Prize paper, PNAS, 2009, Pradel Research award, NAS, 2013; MacArthur Fellow, John D. and Catherine T. MacArthur Found., 2006, Searle Scholar, 2001. Office: Department of Biological Sciences Vanderbilt University Box 351634 Station B Nashville TN 37235-1634 also: Vanderbilt University Office Address U7231A MRB3 465 21st Ave S Nashville TN 37235 Office Phone: 615-936-8277. Office Fax: 615-343-6707. Business E-Mail: ken.catania@vanderbilt.edu.

CATANZARO, TONY, dancer; b. Bklyn. s. Archie Achilles and Elvira (Alessandra) C.; children: Maya Vanesa, Antonio; m. Mara Beatiz Betancourt, 1998; 1 child, Beatriz. Student, Performing Arts, NYC, 1961-64. Artistic dir. Bay Ballet Theatre, Tampa, Fla., 1994-95, City of Coral Gables, Fla., 1997—. Dance panel Mass. Coun. for Arts and Humanities, 1978-80; mem. Com. for Pub. Action for Arts; mem. blue ribbon com. for Mass. arts lottery bill Spl. Commn. on Performing Arts; mem. hon. com. Dance/New Eng.; coach Internat. Ballet Competition, Moscow, 1981; staged first Nutcracker in Medellin, Colombia, 1995 (first nutcracker ever in S.A.); artistic dir. dance dept. Youth Ctr., Coral Gables, 1997—. Appeared with modern dance cos. Paul Sanansardo Co., 1963-64, Pearl Lang Co., 1966-70, Norman Walker, 1963-70, Harkness Ballet Co. II, 1967, N.J. Ballet Co., 1968-69, Ala. Ballet Co., 1969, Boston Ballet Co., 1969-70, 73-76, Joffrey Ballet, 1970-73, Dennis Waynes Dancers, Boston, 1977-78, artistic dir., choreographer, Boston Ballet Ensemble, 1980-81; prin. dancer, Boston Ballet Co., 1980-82; artistic dir. Ballet Acad. of Miami, 1984—, Ballet Theatre of Miami, 1985-96, Ballet Theatre of Miami Ensemble, 1989-95; leading dance roles in (Broadway) Annie Get Your Gun, 1966, Golden Boy; London Palaedium, 1968. Team coach for Am. team Internat. Ballet Competition, Varna, Bulgaria, 1994. With USNG, 1967-70. Office: 8915 SW 207th St Cutler Bay FL 33189-3608

CATES, ANDREW F., recreational facility executive; b. Memphis; BBA in Fin., U. Tex., Austin. Analyst, Capital Markets Group Trammell Crow Co. (subs. CB Richard Ellis Group, Inc.), 1993—95; assoc. Crow Family Holdings, 1995—96; founding ptnr. Viceroy Investments, LLC, 1996; founder Value Acquisition Fund, 2004; pres. & founder RVC USA Mgmt., LLC. Bd. dirs. Pioneer Natural Resources Co., 2009—, Soulsville Charter Sch., Soulsville Found., Myelin Repair Found., Lambda Alpha Internat., Grizzlies Found., Grizzlies Acad.; project developer & chmn. Soulsville Revitalization Project; minority owner Memphis Grizzlies NBA. Office: RVC USA Management LLC 429 N Main St # 101 Memphis TN 38103-1525 Office Phone: 901-432-4744. Office Fax: 901-432-4664. Business E-Mail: acates@rvcusa.com.

CATHY, S. TRUETT, food products executive; m. Jeannette Cathy; children: Dan, Don, Trudy. Owner The Dwarf House, Atlanta, 1946; founder, chmn. Chick-fil-A, Inc., 1967—. Founder WinShape Ctr. Found., 1984—, WinShape Homes prog., WinShape Camps, 1985—. Author: It's Easier to Succeed Than to Fail, 1989, Eat Mor Chikin: Inspire More People, 2002, It's Better to Build Boys Than Mend Men, 2004; co-author: The Generosity Factor, 2002. Recipient Horatio Alger award, Horatio Alger Assn., 1989, Entrepreneur of Yr. - Lifetime Achievement award, Ernst & Young, 2000, Chmn. award, Georgia Sports Hall of Fame, 2003, Catalyst Lifetime Achievement award, Injoy/John Maxwell, 2003, Humanitarian award, Norman Vincent & Ruth Stafford Peale, 2003, Lifetime Achievement award, Nat. Poultry & Food Distributors Assn., 2005; named one of Forbes 400: Richest Americans, 2006—. Office: Chick-fil-A Inc 5200 Buffington Rd Atlanta GA 30349-2998

CATLETT, JOHN, state legislator; m. Cheri Catlett; 2 children. B in History, Ark. Tech U., B in Polit. Sci. Former mil. police officer USAF; former wildlife officer Ark. Game and Fish Commn.; mem. Dist. 61 Ark. House of Representatives, 2011—. Democrat. Office: 11732 W Hwy 28 Rover AR 72860 Office Phone: 479-495-9662. Office Fax: 479-299-4187. Business E-Mail: john.catlett@arkansashouse.org.

CATLIN, FRANCIS IRVING, physician; b. Hartford, Conn., Dec. 6, 1925; s. Robert Irving and Frances Rose (Maleski) C.; m. Rebecca Vaughan Graham, June 11, 1948; children: Robert, Andrew, Martha. AA, Princeton U., 1949; MD, Johns Hopkins U., 1948, DSc, 1959. Diplomate: Am. Bd. Otolaryngology. Intern Union Meml. Hosp., Balt., 1948-49; resident in otolaryngology Johns Hopkins Hosp., Balt., 1950, 52-54; from instr. to assoc. prof. Johns Hopkins U. Med. Sch., Balt., 1956-72; prof. otorhinolaryngology and communicative scis. Baylor U. Med. Sch., Houston, 1972-91, prof. emeritus, 1991—. Chief otolaryngology svc. Tex. Children's Hosp., 1972-91, emeritus staff, 1991—, mem. credentials com., 1989—. Contbr. articles to med. jours. Capt. M.C. USAF, 1950-52. Fellow Am. Otol. Soc.; mem. AMA, ASTM (F29 com. on anesthesia and respiratory equipment 1989-2004), Tex. Med. Soc., Am. Acad. Otolaryngology, Am. Coun. Otolaryngology, Am. Laryngological, Rhinological and Otol. Soc., Am. Speech and Hearing Assn. (life), Houston Philos. Soc., Am. Soc. Pediat. Otolaryngology (charter mem. 1985—, v.p. 1985-86, pres. 1986-87, guest hon. 2000, 07). Episcopalian. Home: 8580 Woodway Dr #1124 Houston TX 77063-2466

CATO, CARSON, manufacturing executive; m. Mary Margaret Mendenhall; 1 child, William. B, NC State U., Raleigh, 1981; MBA, Winthrop U., Rock Hill, SC, 1988. V.p. procurement and risk mgmt. CommScope, Inc., sr. v.p. global supply chain. Mayor Town of Cornelius, NC, 2001—03. Office: CommScope Inc 1100 CommScope Pl SE Hickory NC 28602 Office Phone: 828-324-2200. Office Fax: 828-982-1708. Business E-Mail: ccato@commscope.com.

CAUDILL, WILLIAM HOWARD, lawyer; b. Memphis, Mar. 18, 1951; m. Chris Looney, Sept. 2, 1978. BSBA, U. Ark., 1973; M in Pub. Acctg., U. Tex., 1977, JD, 1978. Bar: Tex. 1978, U.S. Dist. Ct. (so. dist.) Tex. 1978, U.S. Tax Ct. 1978, U.S. Claims Ct. 1978, U.S. Ct. Appeals (5th cir.) 1978; CPA, 1977. Ptnr. Fulbright & Jaworski, LLP, Houston, 1986—2013, Norton Rose Fulbright, 2013—. Mem. Tex. Quarter Dollar Coin Adv. Com., 2002-04; mem. vestry St. John the Divine Episc. Ch., Houston, 1982-86, 89-93; coun. del. Episcopal Diocese of Tex., 2003-06; bd. dirs., pres. St. John the Divine Meml. Endowment Fund, 1995-2007; bd. dirs. Sam Houston Area coun. Boy Scouts Am., 2004—. Mem.: ABA (chair CLE subcom. 1994—2000, chair spl. projects subcom., vice chair, chair partnership com. 1994—2006, coun. mem. 2008—11, vice chair, Sect. CLE 2011—14, tax sect., liason to AICPA 2014—), Am. Coll. Tax Counsel, State Bar Tex. (dir. tax course 1986—87, bd. dirs. taxation sect. 1987—92, chair-elect 1990, chair 1991—92). Avocations: fishing, music, golf, hunting. Office: Norton Rose Fulbright 1301 Mckinney St Ste 5100 Houston TX 77010-3031 Office Phone: 713-651-5292. E-mail: william.caudill@nortonrosefulbright.com.

CAULEY, MICHAEL A., prosecutor; b. 1948; BA, Bethany Coll.; JD, U. Pittsburgh. Former U.S. atty. mid. dist., Fla. Home: 2011 Pieris Ct Vienna VA 22182-3958

CAULFIELD, E. MICHAEL, board member; BA, Colby Coll., 1968; MBA, Dartmouth U., 1974. Ptnr. Greenwich Assocs.; various exec. positions Mellon Nat. Corp.; joined Prudential Ins. Co., Newark, 1989, v.p. fin. mgmt., 1998, exec. v.p., CEO, Prudential Investments Newark, 2001—02; COO Mercer Human Resource Consulting, 2005; pres. Mercer Human Resources Consulting, NYC, 2005—06. Bd. dirs. Unum Group, Mellon Nat. Corp, 2004—05. Office: Unum Group Bd Directors 1 Fountain Sq Chattanooga TN 37402 Office Phone: 423-294-1011. E-mail: ecaulfield@unum.com.

CAULFIELD, JAMES BENJAMIN, pathologist, educator; b. Mpls., Jan. 1, 1927; s. Linus Joseph and Olive Bell (Curtis) C.; m. Virginia Walsh, Jan. 28, 1950; children: Ann, John, Clare. BA, Miami U., Oxford, Ohio, 1947; BS, U. Ill., 1948, MD, 1950. Intern Henrotin Hosp., Chgo., 1950-51; resident U. N.C., Chapel Hill, 1951-52, U. Kans. Med. Ctr., Kansas City, 1954-55; vis. investigator Rockefeller Inst., NYC, 1955-56; instr. pathology Harvard U., 1959-64, asst. prof., 1964-70, assoc. prof., 1970-75; asst. pathologist Mass. Gen. Hosp., Boston, 1960-64, assoc. pathologist, 1964-75; prof., chmn. dept. pathology U. S.C., 1975-85; prof. pathology U. Ala., Birmingham, 1985—. Adj. prof. Med. U. S.C., Charleston, 1981-85; rsch. on collagen network of heart and changes associated with alterations in the network. Contbr. articles to profl. jours. Served with USN, 1944-46, 52-54. Mem. Am. Soc. Cell Biology, Am. Soc. Pathology, Internat. Acad. Pathology, Fedn. Exptl. Pathology, Electron Microscopy Soc., Internat. Study Group for Heart Research (treas. Am. sect. 1972-85), N.Y. Acad. Scis., Harvard Club, Boston Athenaeum Club, Sigma Xi, Phi Eta Sigma. Office: U Ala Dept Pathology 506 Kracke Bldg 619 19th St S Birmingham AL 35233-0001

CAULKINS, ANN, publishing executive; b. Shreveport, La., 1962; m. Kelley Anderson; 2 children. BA in Comm., Baylor U., Waco, Tex., 1984. Various positions including advt. dir., sr. v.p. sales & mktg. and retail advt. dir. Ft. Worth Star-Telegram, 1984—98; sales mgr. Cable Connection Mag., 1988—90; advt. dir., sr. v.p. sales & mktg. Lexington Herald-Leader, Ky., 1998—2002; pub. The State, Columbia, SC, 2002—05; pres., pub. Charlotte Observer, NC, 2006—. Methodist. Office: Charlotte Observer 600 S Tryon St Charlotte NC 28202-1880 Office Phone: 704-358-5000. E-mail: acaulkins@charlotteobserver.com.

CAUTHEN, CHARLES EDWARD, JR., retired retail executive, management consultant; b. Columbia, SC, Oct. 26, 1931; s. Charles Edward and Rachel (Macaulay) C.; m. Hazel Electa Peery, June 13, 1959; children: Portia Cauthen White, Rachel Cauthen Rohrer, Sara Cauthen Landfear, Sidney Cauthen Bullard. BA, Wofford Coll., Spartanburg, SC, 1952; cert. Charlotte Meml. Hosp., Sch. Hosp. Adminstrn., 1956; MS in Bus. Adminstrn. and Labor Mgmt., Kennedy-Western U., Aguoro Hills, Calif., 1986, PhD in Bus. Adminstrn., 1986; LLD, Montreat-Anderson Coll., NC, 1991. Asst. adminstr. Union Meml. Hosp., Monroe, NC, 1956-58; adminstr. Lowrance Hosp., Inc., Mooresville, NC, 1958-61; v.p., mgr. Va. Acme Market, Bluefield, W.Va., 1961-68; v.p. Acme Markets and A-Mart Stores (now Acme Markets of Tazewell, Va., Inc.), North Tazewell, Va., 1965-87; adminstr. Lowrance Hosp., Inc., Mooresville, NC, 1958-61; v.p., mgr. Va. Acme Market, Bluefield, W.Va., 1961-68; v.p. Acme Markets and A-Mart Stores (now Acme Markets of Tazewell, Va., Inc.), North Tazewell, Va., 1965-87, exec. v.p., 1968-71, pres., 1971-87; provost, pres. King Coll., Bristol, Tenn., 1987—92; pres. Doran Devel. Corp., 1971-87, Big A Market, Inc., 1981-87. Cons. in field, 1992—2000. Author: Evaluation of the Small Company for Strategic Planning, Merger or Acquisition, 1987, Cauthen Collection of Weapons and Artifacts, 2012. Elder Westminster Presbyn. Ch., Bluefield, W.Va., deacon, trustee; bd. dir. Internat. Inst. Christian Studies, 1993—97, Tenn. Inst. Pub. Policy, 1994—2001. To 1st lt. US Army, 1952—54. Mem. W.Va. Assn. Retail Grocers (v.p., dir. 1968-

82), Va. Food Dealers Assn. (dir. 1978), Bluefield Sales Exec. Club (dir. 1965-67), Rotary (bd. dirs. 1966). Republican. Home: 3654 Caddington Ter Midlothian VA 23113-2698 Home Phone: 804-464-2383.

CAUTHRON, ROBIN J., federal judge; b. Edmond, Okla., July 14, 1950; d. Austin W. and Mary Louise (Adamson) Johnson. BA, U. Okla., 1970, JD, 1977; MEd, Cen. State U., Edmond, Okla., 1974. Bar: Okla. 1977. Law clk to Hon. Ralph G. Thompson US Dist. Ct. (We. Dist.) Okla., 1977-81; staff atty. Legal Svcs. Ea. Okla., 1981-82; pvt. practice law, 1982-83; spl. judge 17th Jud. Dist. State Okla., 1983-86; magistrate US Dist. Ct. (we. dist.) Okla., Oklahoma City, 1986-91, judge, 1991—2001, 2008—, chief judge, 2001—08. Editor Okla. Law Rev. Bd. dirs. Juvenile Diabetes Found. Internat., 1989-92; mem. nominating com. Frontier Coun. Boy Scouts Am., 1987, Edmond Ednl. Endowment; trustee, sec. First United Meth. Ch., 1988-90. Mem. ABA, Okla. Bar Assn., Okla. County Bar Assn. (bd. dirs. 1990— bench and bar com.), McCurtain County Bar Assn. (pres. 1986), Am. Judicature Soc., Nat. Assn. Women Judges, Fed. Bar Assn., Nat. Coun. Women Magistrates (bd. dirs. 1990-91), Okla. Jud. Conf. (v.p. 1985), Am. Inns of Ct. (pres. 1991-92), Order of Coif, Phi Delta Phi. Office: US Courthouse 200 NW 4th St Ste 4001 Oklahoma City OK 73102-3029

CAVALIER, MICHAEL D., movie theater company executive, lawyer; JD, U. Ga., Athens, 1991. Assoc. atty. Akin, Gump, Strauss, Hauer, Feld, L.L.P.; assoc. gen. counsel Cinemark Holdings, Inc., 1993—97, gen. counsel, 1997—, v.p., 1999—2006, asst. sec., 2001—03, sec., 2003—, sr. v.p., 2006—. Office: Cinemark Holdings Inc 3900 Dallas Pky Ste 500 Plano TX 75093 Office Phone: 972-665-1000. Office Fax: 972-665-1004. Business E-Mail: mcavalier@cinemark.com.

CAVANAGH, HARRISON DWIGHT, ophthalmologist, educator; s. William Edwards and Marie Corrine (Logue) C.; m. Lynn Ayres Gantt, Dec. 27, 1964; 1 dau., Catherine DuVal. AB, Johns Hopkins U., 1962, MD (Joseph Collins scholar 1963-65), 1965; PhD in Biology, Harvard U., 1972. Life diplomate Am. Bd. Ophthalmology. Intern Johns Hopkins Hosp., 1965-66, resident in ophthalmology, 1969-73; fellow corneal surgery Mass. Eye and Ear Infirmary, Boston, 1973-75; instr. ophthalmology Johns Hopkins Med. Sch., 1969-73; asst. prof. Harvard U. Med. Sch., 1975-76; mem. faculty Emory U., 1976-87, F. Phinizy Calhoun prof. ophthalmology, chmn. dept., 1978-87; prof. Georgetown U., Washington, 1987-91; Disting. Univ. prof., vice chmn. dept. ophthalmology U. Tex. Southwestern Med. Ctr., Dallas, 1991-95, W. Maxwell Thomas chair prof., 1995—; med. dir., assoc. dean clin. svcs. Zale Lipsky U. Hosp./U. Tex. Southwestern Med. Ctr. Vis. prof. Georgetown U., 1986-87; cons., chmn. visual scis. study sect A NIH, 1980-84; Heed Found. scholar, 1973-74; sci. adv. panel Nat. Soc. Prevention Blindness, Knights Templar Found.; civilian cons. USAF, 1983-86, USN, Bethesda Naval Hosp., 1989-91; mem. neuroscis. behavior study sect. NIH, 1989-93; organizing com. 3rd-4th Internat. Conf. on Confocal Microscopy and 4th-5th Internat. Conf. on 3D Image Processing in Microscopy, 1991—. Editor-in-chief Jour. Cornea, 1989-96, Eye and Contact Lens Jour., 2002-2007; mem. editorial bd. Jour. Scanning, Bioimaging Jour.; contbr. articles to profl. jours. Recipient Heed Found. award, 1981, Gold medal for lifetime achievement, Brit. Contact Lens Assn., Sr. Sci. Investigators award, Rsch. to Prevent Blindness, Inc., 1996, 35th Castroviejo Gold medal, 2009; named 2d Joseph Koplowitz lectr., Georgetown U., 1983, 14th Waldert lectr., U. Rochester, 1987, 5th Morton B. Server lectr., U. Calif., Berkeley, 1991, George Nissal lectr., Brit. Contact Lens Assn., 1997, 21st James McDonald lectr, Loyola U. Chgo., 1998, 3d Maxwell Boschner lectr., U. Toronto, Top Ophthalmologists Consumer Res Coun. award, 2002; named one of Best Drs. in America, 1979, Best Drs. in Dallas, 2007, Tex. Super Drs., 2008, Castle Connolly Top Dr., 2008. Fellow: ACS, Internat. Coll. Surgeons, Royal Microscopy Soc., Am. Acad. Optometry (lectr. 2005, Max Shapiro award 2001, Hon. Fellowship award), Royal Soc. Medicine, Am. Acad. Ophthalmology (hon.; assoc. sect. govt. rels. and rsch. 1979—83, Honor Recognition award 1982, Whitney Sampson lectr. 1997, Sr. Achievement award 1999); mem.: Singapore Nat. Eye Ctr. (mem. sci. adv. bd. 2010—), Eye Bank Assn. Am. (bd. dirs. 1997—99, R. Townley Paton, M.D. award 2000, Bausch and Lomb Visionaries award 2005), South-Ctrl. Eyebank Assn. (pres. 1997), Assn. Rsch. in Vision and Opthalmology (exec. sec.-treas. 1981—86, Honor Recognition award 1987), New Eng. Ophthal. Soc., Internat. Soc. Contact Lens Rsch. (pres. 2009—11, Montague Ruben medal 2005, Brit. Contact Lens Assn. medal 2007), Internat. Eye Found. Eye Surgeons, Keratorefractive Soc. (bd. dirs.), Castroviejo Soc. Corneal Surgeons (pres. 1988—90, Honor Recognition award 1987, 1996), Contact Lens Assn. Ophthlamologists Am. (pres. 1987, Honor Recognition award 1988, 20th Conrad Behrens medal lectr. 1989, 7th Donald Korb award 2008, 31st World Ophthalmology Congress Hamano Gold medal 2008), Harvard Club (Dallas, N.Y.), Park Cities Club, Johns Hopkins Club (comdr.), Order of St. John (U.S., U.K.), Phi Beta Kappa. Republican. Episcopalian. Home: 27 Lakeside Park Dallas TX 75225-8110 Office: U Tex Southwestern Med Ctr Dept Ophthalmology 5323 Harry Hines Blvd Dallas TX 75390-9057 Office Phone: 214-648-8074, 214-645-2020. Business E-Mail: dwight.cavanagh@utsouthwestern.edu.

CAVANAUGH, LUCILLE J., oil industry executive; b. Phila. B, Immaculata Coll., Pa. Joined ExxonMobil Corp., 1977, former head Asia Divsn., gen. mgr. supply and engring., pres. credit corp., gen. mgr. west coast refining and mktg., v.p. global supply and distbn., v.p. human resources, 2002—. Bd. dirs. United Way Met. Dallas. Office: Exxon Mobil Corp 5959 Las Colinas Blvd Irving TX 75039-2298 Office Phone: 972-444-1000. Office Fax: 972-444-1198.

CAVANAUGH, WILLIAM D., aerospace and defense services company executive; BS in Mktg. & Economics, Miami U.; MBA, George Mason U. Sr. v.p. mktg. & bus. devel. Ogden Environ. and Energy Svcs.; v.p., bus. devel., fed. svcs. Fluor Corp., 1999—2002; COO Kelly, Andersen & Assocs., Inc., 2003—04; sr. v.p., bus. devel. DynCorp International, LLC, 2006—. Office: DynCorp International Inc 3190 Fairview Park Dr Ste 700 Falls Church VA 22042 Office Phone: 571-722-0210. Office Fax: 571-722-0252.

CAVE, STEVE, gas industry executive; Dir. investor rels. AGL Resources, Inc., v.p. fin., 2009—. Office: AGL Resources Inc 10 Peachtree Place NE Atlanta GA 30309 Office Phone: 404-584-3801. Office Fax: 404-584-3714. Business E-Mail: scave@aglresources.com.

CAVENDISH, KIM L. MAHER, museum administrator; b. Washington, Feb. 25, 1946; d. Joseph Wilson and Helen Elizabeth (Bell) Leverton; m. William Fredrick Maher, June 12, 1965 (div. 1980); 1 child, Lauren Robinson; m. Daryl Kent Cavendish, Feb. 26, 2000. Student, Duke U., 1963-65, George Washington U., 1966; BA in English, U. Fla., 1969. Social worker Fla. Health and Rehab. Svc., Gainesville, 1969-71, Delray Beach, 1972-74, fraud unit supr. West Palm Beach, 1974-76, direct svc. supr., 1977-78; ctr. dir. Palm Beach County Employment and Tng. Adminstrn., West Palm Beach, 1979-81; exec. dir. Discovery Ctyr., Inc., Ft. Lauderdale, Fla., 1981-92, Mus. Discovery & Sci., Ft. Lauderdale, 1992-94; CEO Va. Air and Space Ctr., Hampton, 1995-99; pres. Orlando Sci. Ctr., 2000—02, Mus. Discovery & Sci., Ft. Lauderdale, 2002—. Bd. dirs. Singing Pines Mus., Boca Raton, Fla., 1984-88, Broward Art Guild, Ft. Lauderdale, 1985-91, Va. Space Grant Consortium, Va. Aerospace Bus. Roundtable, Hampton, 1995—2000, Assn. Sci./Tech. Ctrs., 2002—, Giant Screen Cinema Assn., 2005-, South East Coastal Ocean Observing Regional Assn., 2007-; mem. Leaderhip Broward II, Ft. Lauderdale, 1983-84, faculty Inst. New Sci. Ctrs., 1992, Cultural Execs. Coun. Broward County. Recipient Cultural Arts award Broward Cultural Arts Found., 1985, Woman of Yr. award Women in Comm., 1990, Woman of Distinction award So. Fla. Mag., 1993; namedOutstanding Fundraiser, Fla. Assn. Nonprofit Orgns., 1994. Mem. Am. Assn. Mus., Assn. Sci. and Tech. Ctrs., Southeastern Mus. Conf., Va. Assn. Mus. (bd. dirs. 1999—), Fla. Sci. Tchrs. Assn. (bd. dirs.), Fla. Assn. Mus. (bd. dirs. 1989-95, pres. 1993-95), Leadership Broward Alumnae (curriculum com. 1984-86), Ft. Lauderdale Downtown Coun. (bd. dirs. 1992—95), Women's Exec. Club, Phi Kappa Phi. Democrat. Methodist. Avocations: scuba diving, piano, creative writing, collecting art and antiques, painting. Office: Mus Discovery & Sci 401 SW 2nd St Fort Lauderdale FL 33311

CAVENDISH, MICHAEL ROBERT, lawyer; b. Hollywood, Fla., Mar. 4, 1972; s. Thomas Hamilton and Cheryl Anne Cavendish; m. Michele Lynne Cavendish, June 5, 1994. BS, Fla. State U., Tallahassee, 1993; MA, U. Fla., Gainesville, 1995, JD, 1998. Bar: Fla. 1998. Assoc. McGuire Woods, LLP, Jacksonville, Fla., 1998—2003; shareholder Boyd & Jenerette, PA, Jacksonville, 2004—. Contbr. articles to profl. jours. Mem. Million Dollar Advocates Forum, 2006—; bd. dirs. Cmty. Connections Jacksonville, Inc., 2002—05; co-chmn. Challenge Capital Campaign, 2005; co-chmn. campaign Charlie Crist for Gov., Jacksonville, 2006; elder Riverside Presbyn. Ch., Jacksonville, 2002—. Named one of Legal Elite, Fla, Trend Mag., 2006; named to, Law Deacon 3000, 2006; Ralph R. Bailey scholar, U. Fla., 1996—98. Fellow: Fla. Bar Found.; mem.: ABA (chair ethics subcom. 2007, chair trial evidence com. 2007), Fla. Bar (mem. rules of civil procedure com. 2003—, Excellence in Legal Writing award 2000), Chester Bedell Am. Inn of Ct. Presbyterian. Office: Boyd & Jenerette PA 201 N Hogan St Ste 400 Jacksonville FL 32202

CAVITT, MARK A., child and adolescent psychiatrist, educator; MD, East Tenn. State U., Johnson City, 1989. Diplomate Am. Bd. Psychiatry and Neurology, 2004, Am. Bd. Psychiatry and Neurology-child and adolescent psychiatry, 2004. Intern Vanderbilt Univ. Sch. Medicine, Nashville, resident psychiatry, 1989—92, fellow child & adolescent psychiatry, 1992—94; med. dir. pediatric psychiatry svcs. All Children's Hosp., chair divsn. neurology, psychology & devel. pediat.; asst. clin. prof. Univ. S Fla. Coll. Medicine. Recipient Univ. S Fla. Dept. Psychiatry and Behavioral Sci. award of Appreciation for Clin. Faculty, 2008; named one of Top 100 Doctors of Tampa Bay, 2007—08, Best Doctors of Tampa Bay, 2007—10. Office: All Children's Hospital 880 6th St S Ste 110 Department 7970 Saint Petersburg FL 33701 Office Phone: 727-767-8477. Office Fax: 727-767-8244.

CAZAYOUX, DON (DONALD J. CAZAYOUX JR.), lawyer, former federal prosecutor, former United States Representative from Louisiana; b. New Roads, La., Jan. 17, 1964; m. Cherie Cazayoux, 1986; children: Michael, Chavanne, Katie. BS in Psychology, La. State U., 1985, MA in Clinnical Psychology, 1993; JD, Georgetown U.Law Ctr., 1991. Atty. Chaffe, McCall, Philips, Toler, & Sarpy L.L.P., Baton Rouge; prosecutor Pointe Coupee Parish; mem. Dist. 18 La. House of Reps., 2000—08; mem. US Congress from 6th La. Dist., Washington, 2008—09; mediator Perry Dampf Dispute Solutions, 2009—10; US atty. (middle dist.) La. US Dept. Justice, Baton Rouge, 2010—13; of counsel Long Law Firm, Baton Rouge, 2013—. Mem.: ABA, Baton Rouge Bar Assn., Fed. Bar Assn., La. Bar Assn. (mem. House of Delegates), Lions Club. Democrat. Roman Catholic. Office: Long Law Firm One United Plz Ste 500 4041 Essen Ln Baton Rouge LA 70809 Office Phone: 225-922-5110. Office Fax: 225-922-5105. E-mail: djc@longlaw.com.*

CEBULA, RICHARD JOHN, economics professor, writer; b. Bklyn., Mar. 24, 1944; s. Jerome Matthew and Miriam (Lyons) C.; m. Louise E. Bedrossian, June 2, 1965 (div. Dec. 1981); children: David, Christina. BA, Fordham Coll., 1966; MA, U. Ga., 1968; PhD, Ga. State U., 1971. Asst. prof. Ohio U., Athens, 1971-73; from assoc. to full prof. Emory U., Atlanta, 1973-92; prof. econs. Ga. Inst. Tech., Atlanta, 1992-99; Shirley and Philip Solomons Eminent Scholar Chair in Econs. Armstrong Atlantic State U., 1999—2010; Billy J. Walker/Wells Fargo endowed chair fin. Davis Coll. Bus., Jacksonville U., Fla., 2010—. Author: Determinants of Human Migration, 1979, The Deficit Problem in Perspective, 1987, Crisis in Commercial Banking, 1993, Geographic Living Cost Differentials, 1983, Economics of the Sports Industry, 1995, Savings and Loan Crisis, 1992, Microeconomics Alive!, 1997, Macroeconomics Alive!, 1997, Financial Economics, 1999; editor Jour. Econs. and Fin., 1995-98; assoc. editor Annals of Regional Sci., 1998—; co-editor Jour. Econs. and Fin. Edn.; regional editor Internat. Advances in Econ. Rsch., 1996—; mem. editl. bd. Am. Jour. Econs.; mem. editl. bd., adv. editor Pub. Fin. Rev., East Econ. Jour., Rev. Fin. Econ., Rev. Reg. Stud., Global Bus. Econ. Rev., Internat. Migration Rev., others; contbr. more than 2050 articles to profl. jours. Econ. advisor US Congressman Levitas, Washington, 1974—84, Fed. Res. Bank, Atlanta, 1984, US Senator Sam Nunn, Washington, 1995. Recipient citation of excellence, Anbar Electronic Intelligence, UK, 1996. Mem. Am. Econs. and Fin., Am. Econ. Assn., Acad. of Econs. and Fin. (v.p. 1999-2001, pres. 2001-03, rsch. fellow 2000, service fellow 2003). Achievements include research on effects of welfare on migration, determinants of geographic living-cost differentials, effects of budget deficits on interest rates, economic growth, causes of bank and thrift failures. Avocations: jogging, tennis. Office: Davis College of Business 2800 University Blvd N Jacksonville FL 32211 Office Phone: 904-256-7904. E-mail: cebulari@mail.armstrong.edu, rcebula@ju.edu.

CECIL, DAVID ROLF, mathematician, educator; b. Tulsa, July 12, 1935; s. Neil McKinley and Ola Ethel (Turner) C.; m. Betty Lou Poe, June 14, 1958; 1 child, Eric Alan. Student (Pitts. Plate Glass Co. scholar), Carnegie Inst. Tech., 1954-55; BA, U. Tulsa, 1958; postgrad (fellow), Tulane U., 1958-59; MS, Okla. State U., 1960, PhD, 1962. Grad. teaching asst. Okla. State U., 1959-62; sr. research mathematician Atlantic Refining Co., 1962; asst. prof., then assoc. prof. math. North Tex. State U., Denton, 1962-69; prof. math. Butler U., Indpls., 1969-70, Tex. A&M U., Kingsville, 1970—2006, chmn. dept., 1980-85, asst. dean coll. arts and scis., 2000—04; pres. Tex. Acad. Sci., 2001—02. Cons. Edn. Service Ctr. Region II, 1979-80, Air Force Office Sci. Rsch., Wilford Hall Med. Ctr., Tex., 1988-90. Author Debugging BASIC Programs, 1984, (in Spanish) Depuracion de Programas en BASIC, 1989, (with Stan Albert) Probability, 1993; contbr. articles to math. jours. Founder Kingsville Computer Club, 1980; mem. credit com. Kingsville Area Educators Fed. Credit Union, 1979-2006, bd. dirs., 2006-. Faculty fellow North Tex. State U., 1968-69; Faculty fellow Tex. A&I U., 1971-73; presidential grant, Tex. A&M U., 2005. Fellow Tex. Acad. Scis. (v.p. 1999, pres. 2001-2002); Sigma Xi. Methodist. Avocations: woodworking, paper engineering. Office Phone: 361-592-1839. Business E-Mail: kfdrc00@tamuk.edu.

CEDEL, MELINDA IRENE, music educator, violinist; b. Ft. Worth, July 31, 1957; d. Albert and Emilia Florence (Sylvester) C. Student, N.C. Sch. Arts, 1974-77; MusB Edn., U. S.C., 1979. Cert. tchr., S.C. Tchr. music Charleston (S.C.) County Pub. Schs., 1979—92. Pvt. tchr. music, 1983—, part-time violin tchr. Glynn County Pub. Schs., 2005-10; concertmaster Brunswick (Ga.) Civic Orch., 1993-97, pers. mgr., 1995-96 Performed with Florence Symphony, Columbia Philharm., S.C. Chamber Orch., Augusta Symphony, Jacksonville Symphony Orch., Savannah (Ga.) Symphony, Hilton Head (S.C.) Symphony, Jacksonville Summer Symphonetta, Valdosta (Ga.) Symphony Orch.; musician Charleston Symphony, 1979-92, Charleston Symphony Chamber Orch., Long Bay (S.C.) Symphony; musician, mgr. Charlestowne String Quartet, 1983-92; condr. Charleston County Prep. Orch., 1983-84; performer Piccolo Spoleto, 1980-91; co-dir. Charleston County Strolling Strings. Former bd. dirs. Brunswick Cmty. Concert Assn. Mem. Am. String Tchrs. Assn., Mensa, Kappa Phi Kappa. Avocations: sailing, water sports, reading, travel, tennis. Home: 220 Five Pounds Rd Saint Simons Island GA 31522-1903

CEIPS, CATHERINE C., state legislator; b. Berkeley County, SC, Feb. 16, 1955; d. Sidney and Virginia Black Crawford; m. Richard N. Ceips, May 17, 1986 (dec.). BS, U. S.C., 1976. Fed. rep. field dir. Congressman Joe Wilson, Congressman Floyd Spence; commn. svc. dir. Med. U. SC; tchr. Beaufort and Berkeley County Schs.; owner Sea Island Ophthalmology; mem. SC State Legis. from Dist. 124, 2003—06; mem. med., mil., pub. and mcpl. affairs com. SC State Legis.; mem. SC State Senate from Dist. 46, SC, 2007—. Commn. svc. dir. Med. U. SC; mem. Beaufort Hist. Found., Open Land Trust, Beaufort Little Theatre, Beaufort County GOP. Mem.: Women in the Outdoors, Beaufort County Rep. Women's Club. Republican. Lutheran. Office: State Capitol 326A Blatt Bldg Columbia SC 29211 Home: 1207 Bay St Beaufort SC 29902 E-mail: CeipsC@scstatehouse.net.

CELLA, JOHN PAUL, allergist, immunologist; MB, Bchir, Royal Coll. of Surgeons, Ireland, 1984, B in Obstetrics, 1984. Diplomate Am. Bd. Internal Medicine, 1987, Am. Bd. Allergy and Immunology, 2003, lic. Fla., 1995. Intern Umdnj-Univ. Hosp., 1984—85; resident internal medicine Columbia Univ. Overlook Hosp., 1985—87; fellow allergy and immunology Univ. of Calif. Irvine Med. Ctr., 1987—91; hosp. affiliations include Bayfront Med. Ctr., Blake Med. Ctr., Manatee Meml. Hosp. Office: Manatee Memorial Hospital 206 Second St E Bradenton FL 34208-1000 Office Phone: 941-746-5111.

CERA, SUSAN MARIE, colon and rectal surgeon, director; BS in Biology, Georgetown U., DC, 1994, MD, 1998. Diplomate Am. Bd. Surgery, 2004, Am. Bd. Colon and Rectal Surgery, 2005, lic. Fla., NC. Intern Carolinas Med. Ctr., Charlotte, NC, resident in surgery, 1999—2004; fellow in colon and rectal surgery Cleve. Clinic, Weston, 2004—05, clin. assoc. staff colorectal surgery dept., 2004—05, staff colorectal surgery divsn. Naples, 2005—06; hosp. affiliation includes Physicians Regional Med. Ctr.-Pine Ridge, Fla.; staff colorectal surgery divsn. Physicians Regional Med. Group, 2006—; chief endoscopy Physicians Regional Healthcare System, 2006—, dir. anorectal physiology, 2006—. Author: various publs. Mem. Crohn's and Colitis Found. of America. Named one of Southwest Fla.'s Top 40 Under 40, Gulfshore Life Mag., 2007, Consumer's Rsch. Coun. of America: Guide to America's Top Surgeons, 2008—09. Fellow: Am. Soc. of Colon and Rectal Surgeons, ACS (South Fla. chpt.); mem.: Cleve. Clinic (internal rev. bd. 2004—06, grad. med. edn. com. 2005—06, vice chair, rsch. and edn. 2005—06, chief, endoscopy 2006), Physicians Regional Healthcare System (operating rm. mgmt. com. 2006—, ethics com. 2006—, infection control com. 2006—), Physicians Regional Med. (vice chair, rsch. and edn. 2006—), Southeastern Surgical Congress, Soc. Laparoendoscopic Surgeons, Soc. Am. Gastrointestinal Endoscopic Surgeons, Lee County Med. Soc., Internat. Soc. Colon and Rectal Surgeons, Fla. Gastroenterologic Soc., Collier County Med. Soc., Assn. Women Surgeons, AMA, Am. Coll. Gastroenterology. Office: Physicians Regional Medical Group Desk 22 6101 Pine Ridge Rd Naples FL 34119 Office Phone: 239-348-4400. Office Fax: 239-348-4149.

CEREZO, CARMEN CONSUELO, federal judge; b. San Juan, 1940; BA, U. P.R., 1963, LLB, 1966. Pvt. practice, 1966-67; law clk. U.S. Dist. Ct., San Juan, 1967-72; judge Superior Ct., P.R., 1972-76, Ct. Intermediate Appeals, 1976-80, US Dist. Ct. PR, 1980—93, 1999—, chief judge, 1993—99. Office: Federico Degetau Fed Bldg Rm CH-131 150 Carlos Chardon Ave Hato Rey PR 00918-1761

CERF, VINTON GRAY, computer scientist, information technology executive; b. New Haven, June 23, 1943; s. Vinton Thruston and Muriel (Gray) Cerf; m. Sigrid L. Thorstenberg, Sept. 10, 1966; children: David, Bennett. BS in Math., Stanford U., Calif., 1965; MS in Computer Sci., UCLA, 1970, PhD in Computer Sci., 1972; PhD (hon.), Capitol Coll., Md., Gettysburg Coll., Pa., U. Balearic Islands, Palma, Lulea Inst. Tech., Sweden, Swiss Fed. Inst. Tech., Zurich, George Mason U., Va., U. Twente, The Netherlands, Rovira & Virgili U., Spain, U. Pisa, Tschingua U., U. Beijing, Rensselaer Poly. Inst., NY. Sys. engr. IBM Corp., 1965-67; prin. programmer UCLA, 1967-72; asst. prof. elec. engring. and computer sci. Stanford University, 1972-76; program mgr. info. processing techniques office, Def. Advanced Rsch. Projects Agy., US Dept. Def., Arlington, Va., 1976—81, prin. scientist, 1981-82; dir. sys. devel. MCI Comm. Corp., 1982-83, v.p. engring., MCI Digital Info. Svcs. Co. Washington, 1983-86, sr. v.p. architecture and tech., then sr. v.p. technology strategy, 1994—2005; v.p. Corp. Nat. Rsch. Initiatives, Reston, Va., 1986-94; v.p., chief internet evangelist Google, Inc., Mountain View, Calif., 2005—. Sr. programmer Jacobi Sys. Corp., Santa Monica, Calif., 1968—70; mem. US Presdl. Info. Tech. Adv. Com., 1997—2001; bd. dirs. Internet Corp. Assigned Names & Numbers (ICANN), 1999—2007, ClearSight Systems Corp., Avanex Corp.; vis. scientist NASA Jet Propulsion Lab., Pasadena, Calif. Recipient Kilby award, 1995, Silver medal, Internat. Telecomm. Union, 1995, Industry Legend award, Computer & Comm. Industries Assn., 1996, Computer & Comm. prize, NEC Found., Tokyo, 1996, Computerworld/Smithsonian Leadership award, 1996, Nat. Medal Tech., 1997, Living Legend medal, Libr. Congress, 2000, Prince of Asturias award, 2002, Presdl. Medal of Freedom, 2005, Japan prize, 2008, Webby Lifetime Achievement award, Internat. Acad. of Digital Arts and Sciences, 2010, Yuri Rubinsky Meml. award, Internat. World Wide Web Conf., Alexander Graham Bell award, Alexander Graham Bell Assn. for Deaf; named one of the 50 Most Important People on the Web, PC World, 2007; named to Nat. Inventors Hall of Fame, 2006; grantee Marconi Internat. Fellowship Found., 1998. Fellow: NAE (Charles Stark Draper award 2001), AAAS, IEEE (Koji Kobayashi award 1992, Alexander Graham Bell award 1997, Third Millennium medal), Assn. Women in Sci., Am. Acad. Arts & Scis., Assn. Computing Machinery (Software & Systems award, SIGCOMM award, Turing award 2004), Soc. Tech. Comm. (hon.); mem.: Internet Soc. (founding pres. 1992—95), Yale Polit. Union (hon.). Achievements include recognition as one of the 'fathers of the Internet' for design of the TCP/IP protocols and the architecture of the Internet; while working at MCI Comm. Corp., led the engineering of

MCI Mail, the first commercial email service to be connected to the Internet. Office: Google Inc 1600 Amphitheatre Pkwy Mountain View CA 94043 Home Phone: 703-448-0965; Office Phone: 703-234-1823. E-mail: vint@google.com.

CERNY, KEITH, performing arts association administrator; married; 4 children. BA in Music and Physics, U. Calif., Berkeley; MBA, Harvard Bus. Sch.; PhD, Open U., UK. Sr. engagement mgr. McKinsey & Co.; sr. mgr. to ptnr. Accenture; CEO Sheet Music Plus; exec. dir. Russel Reynolds Assoc.; exec. dir. & CFO San Fransisco Opera, 2004—07; gen. dir. & CEO Dallas Opera, 2010—. Panel Nat. Performing Arts Convention. Recipient Pacific Telesis Award, Calif. Mgmt. Rev., 1993; named Vol. of Yr., Harvard Bus. Sch Community Partners, 2000. Mem.: Strategy Cont. Opera Am., Phi Beta Kappa. Office: The Dallas Opera 2403 Flora St Ste 500 Dallas TX 75201

CERVANTES, CHARLES R., geriatrician; MD, Baylor U., 1979. Diplomate Am. Bd. Internal Medicine, 1983, Am. Bd. Internal Medicine-geriatric medicine, 2000. Resident internal medicine Baylor Hosp.; hosp. affiliations include Baptist Med. Ctr., Santa Rosa Hosp. Office: Baptist Medical Center 111 Dallas St San Antonio TX 78205-1230 Office Phone: 210-297-7000.

CHABERT, NORBY, state legislator; b. La. BA in Govt., Nicholls State U., Thibodaux, La., 2001. Founder Chabert Devel. LLC, 2006; mem. Dist. 20 La. State Senate, 2009—, interim mem. senate and govtl. affairs com., mem. ins. com., judiciary B com., natural resources com., select com. on coastal restoration and flood control, chair select com. on vocat. and tech. edn. Bd. mem. Nicholls Cols. Athletic Found., Friends of STHS, Leonard J. Chabert Med. Ctr. Found. Mem.: Maple St. Pk. Assn., KC Coun. 5013, The Krewer of Terranians, The Krewe of Hercules, Houma Rotary Club. Democrat. Office: State Capitol PO Box 94183 Baton Rouge LA 70804 also: PO Box 2417 Houma LA 70361 Office Phone: 225-342-2040, 985-858-2927. Office Fax: 985-858-2930. E-mail: chabertn@legis.state.la.us.

CHADEN, LEE A., apparel and former food products executive; BS in Indsl. Engring., Purdue U.; MBA, U. Calif., Berkeley. Brand mgr. Procter & Gamble Co., 1966—70; sr. product mgr. Playtex Apparel, Inc., 1970—74, pres., Playtex Can., 1974—76, area v.p., internat. divsn., 1976—77, v.p., gen. mgr., family products divsn., 1977—79; ptnr. Mktg. Corp. of Am., 1979—81; prin. Gen. Consumer Elecs., 1981—83; CEO Interac Corp., 1983—85; gen. ptnr. Marketcorp Ventures, 1985—91; pres., U.S. and Westfar divsns. of Playtex Sara Lee Corp., 1991—94, pres., CEO, Sara Lee Intimates, 1994—95, v.p., 1995—98, sr. v.p., 1998—99, CEO, Sara Lee Branded Apparel, 1999—2001, sr. v.p., human resources, 2001—03, exec. v.p., 2003—06, CEO, branded apparel unit, 2004—06, exec. chmn. branded apparel, 2006; exec. chmn. Hanesbrands, Inc., Winston Salem, NC, 2006—07, non-exec. chmn., 2007—09. Bd. dir. Hanesbrands, Inc., R.R. Donnelley & Sons Co. Office: Hanesbrands Inc 1000 E Hanes Mill Rd Winston Salem NC 27105

CHADWICK, GREGORY D., endodontist; DMD, UNC Chapel Hill Sch. Dentistry, 1973, MS in endodontics, 1976. Pvt. practice, Charlotte, NC; adj. faculty UNC Sch. Dentistry, Charlotte. Fellow: Pierre Fouchard Acad., Acad. of Dentistry Internat., Am. Coll. of Dentists; mem.: ADA (pres. 2001—02). Office: 130 Providence Rd Charlotte NC 28207

CHAFE, WILLIAM HENRY, history professor, historian; b. Boston, Jan. 28, 1942; s. William Robinson and Elsie (Crabtree) C.; m. Lorna Jane Waterhouse, July 12, 1964; children: Christopher Robert, Jennifer Elizabeth. AB, Harvard U., 1962; AM, Columbia U., 1966, PhD, 1971. Instr. Columbia Grammar Sch., NYC, 1963-65, Vassar Coll., Poughkeepsie, NY, 1970-71; from asst. prof. to prof. Duke U., Durham, NC, 1971—79, prof., 1979—, Alice Mary Baldwin Disting. prof., 1988—, dean Faculty Arts and Scis., 1995—2004, vice provost undergrad. edn., 1999—2004. Author: The American Woman, 1972, Women and Equality, 1977, Civilities and Civil Rights: Greenboro, North Carolina, and the Black Struggle for Freedom, 1980 (R.F. Kennedy book award 1981), The Unfinished Journey, 1986, A History of Our Time, 1986, The Paradox of Change:American Women in the 20th Century, 1991, Never Stop Running: Allard Lowenstein and the Struggle to Save American Liberalism, 1993(Sidney Hillman book award, 1994), The Road to Equality, 1994, Remembering Jim Crow, 2002 (Lillian Smith award, 2003), Private Lives/Public Consequences: Personality and Politics in Modern America, 2005, The Unfinished Journey: American Since World War II, 2006, The Rise and Fall of the American Century: The United States from 1890 to 2008, 2008, Bill and Hillary: The Politics of the Personal, 2012. NEH fellow, 1974-75, 84-85, Rockefeller Found. fellow, 1978, Guggenheim fellow, 1989-90; grantee Nat. Humanities Ctr., Rsch. Triangle Pk., N.C., 1981-82, Ctr. for Advanced Study, Palo Alto, Calif., 1989-90. Fellow Soc. Am. Historians; mem. Am. Hist. Assn. (chmn. nominating com., 1987-88), Orgn. Am. Historians (co-chmn. program com. 1981-82, chair nominating com. 1991, exec. bd. 1993-96, pres. 1998-99), Am. Studies Assn., So. Hist. Assn. Avocations: sailing, tennis. Office: Duke U 224 Carr Building Box 90719 Durham NC 27708 Office Phone: 919-684-5436. Business E-Mail: william.chafe@duke.edu.

CHAFEY, DAVID H., JR., bank holding company executive; BS in Fin., Fairfield U.; M in Fin., NYU. Supr., Retail Banking Group Banco Popular, 1996—2004, dir.; sr. exec. v.p. Popular Internat. Bank Inc., 1999, Popular N.Am. Inc., 2000; pres. Banco Popular de Puerto Rico, 2004; sr. exec. v.p. Popular Inc., 1997—2009; pres., COO Popular, Inc., 2009—. Bd. dirs. Popular Inc., 1996—2004, Visa Internat., L.Am., 2004—; chmn., pres. Puerto Rico Investors Tax-Free Fund Inc., I, II, III, IV, V, VI, 1999—, Puerto Rico Tax-Free Target Maturity Fund Inc., I, II, 1999—, Puerto Rico Investors Flexible Allocation Fund., 1999. Trustee Fundacion Banco Popular Inc., PR; mem. San Jorge Children's Rsch. Found. Inc., 1998—; mem. adv. com. Colegio San Ignacio, 2005—; trustee Fairfield U., 2006—. Mem.: Puerto Rico Bankers Assn. (past pres.), Nat. Assn. (bd. dirs.). Office: Popular Inc 209 Munoz Rivera Ave Popular Ctr Bldg San Juan PR 00918 Office Phone: 787-765-9800. Business E-Mail: dchafey@bppr.com.

CHAFFIN, VERNER FRANKLIN, lawyer, educator; b. Martin, Ga., Sept. 26, 1918; s. Emory Franklin and Mabel (Verner) C.; m. Corinne Ethel Tison, July 17, 1943; children— Ethel, Verner Franklin, Mary Davis, John Edwards. AB, U. Ga., LL.B., 1942; J.S.D., Yale, 1961. Bar: Ga. bar 1942, Ala. bar 1953, U.S. Supreme Ct. bar 1965. Atty. Dept. Justice, 1946-47; mem. faculty U. Ala., 1947—57; prof. law U. Ga., Athens, 1954-69, Fuller E. Callaway prof., 1969—89, Fuller E. Callaway prof. emeritus, 1989—; mem. nat. labor panel Am. Arbitration Assn., 1957—89, mem. pub. employment disputes settlement panel, 1969—89; mem. panel arbitrators Fed. Mediation and Conciliation Service, 1973—89. Trustee Inst. Continuing Legal Edn. Ga., 1969-76 Author: Georgia Annotations to the Restatement (Second) Trusts, 1970, Studies in the Georgia Law of Decedents' Estates and Future Interests, 1979, The Rule Against Perpetuities in Georgia, 1984; Contbr. numerous articles to legal jours. Mem. permanent jud. commn. Gen. Assembly, Presbyn. Ch. U.S.A., 1972-75; elder 1st Presbyn. Ch., Athens, 1966-71, 74-79, 96-98; pres. Athens chpt. Am. Cancer Soc., 1968-69, Athens Community Concert Assn., 1966-67; with USN; Lt. Cmdr. USNR. Sterling fellow Yale, 1950-51 Fellow Am. Coll. Trust & Estate Council (life), Lawyers Found. GA (life), ABA; mem. Am. Law Inst., Pres. Athens Historical Soc., Western Circuit, Ga., Am. bar assns., Ga. Hist. Soc., Athens-Clarke Heritage Found., Blue Key, Sphinx, Phi Beta Kappa, Phi Kappa Phi, Phi Delta Phi, Omicron Delta Kappa, Sigma Nu. Clubs: Athens City, Yale Club Ga. Office: University of Georgia Law School Athens GA 30602 Home: 689 St Ives Dr Athens GA 30606-3872 Business E-Mail: vfchaffin@bellsouth.net.

CHAFIN, H. TRUMAN, state legislator; b. July 10, 1945; s. Tom and Hazel Marie Chafin; m. Letitia Neese; children: Elizabeth Truman, Carah Catelyn, Carly Letitia. BBA, Marshall U., Huntington, W.Va.; attended, Detroit Coll. Law, Mich. State U., East Lansing; JD, Emory U., Ga. Atty.; judge City of Williamson, W.Va.; mem. Dist. 6 W. Va. State Senate, Charleston, 1983—, majority leader. Pres. Mingo County Commn., W.Va., 1981—82; former mem. Gov. Jud. Adv. Com., W.Va., State Dem. Exec. Com., W.Va. Mem.: ABA, Trial Lawyers America, W.Va. Bar Assn., Mingo County Bar Assn., LOOM, Beni Kedem Shriner, Scottish Rite Masons, BPOE, Pi Kappa Alpha. Democrat. Presbyterian. Office: State Capitol Complex Rm 223M Bldg 1 Charleston WV 25305 Office Phone: 304-357-7808, 304-235-2221. Business E-Mail: truman.chafin@wvsenate.gov.

CHAGNON, LUCILLE TESSIER, owner, literacy acceleration consultant; b. Gardner, Mass., June 1, 1936; d. Fred G. Tessier and Alfreda C. (Ross) Noel; m. Richard J. Chagnon, Sept. 16, 1978; children: Daniel, David. BMus, Rivier Coll., Nashua, NH; cert. in human resource mgmt. and cmty. devel., Inst. Cultural Affairs, Chgo., 1969; MEd, Boston Coll., 1972. Educator, N.H., 1960-73; internat. cons. Inst. Cultural Affairs, Chgo., 1973-79; staff tng. dir. CO-MHAR, Inc., Phila., 1979-81; pres., owner Chagnon Assocs., Collingswood, NJ, 1981—86; project cons. Right Mgmt. Cons., Phila., 1982—91, 2001—03; prin. Sacred Heart Sch., Camden, N.J., 1986-87; founder, dir. Lifeline Literacy Project, 1988-94; literacy and developmental learning specialist Rutgers U., Camden, 1989-99; coord. work readiness, Workforce Devel. Inst. Drexel U., Phila., 1999-2000. Adj. grad. faculty dept. counseling psychology Temple U. Sch. Edn., Phila., 1984—89; pres. Literacy Acceleration Cons., 2003—. Author (with Richard J. Chagnon): The Best is Yet to Be: A Pre-Retirement Program, 1985; author: Easy Reader, Learner, Writer, 1994, Voice Hidden, Voice Heard: A Reading and Writing Anthology, 1998, You, Yes YOU, Can Teach Someone to Read: A Step by Step How-To Book, 2005. Bd. dirs. Camden County Literacy Vols. of Am., 1987—91, Handicapped Advocates for Ind. Living, 1987—; mem. Collingswood (N.J.) Bd. Edn., 1985—89. Mem.: Nat. Coun. Tchrs. English, Internat. Reading Assn., Inst. Cultural Affairs. Home and Office: 4176 Vivian St PO Box 438 Chincoteague Island VA 23336-0438 Office Phone: 757-336-5047. Office Fax: 757-336-1391. E-mail: lifeline248@aol.com.

CHAHIN, NIZAR, neurologist, educator; MD, Damascus U., 1992. Diplomate American Bd. Psychiatry and Neurology-neurology, 2001, American Bd. Psychiatry and Neurology-clin. neurophysiology, 2009. Resident in neurology Univ. Mo. Affiliated Hosp., Columbia, 1997—2000; fellow in peripheral nerve disease Mayo Clinic, Rochester, Minn., fellow in neuromuscular disease, 2003—06, fellow in electromyography, 2006—07; clin. asst. prof. dept. neurology Univ. NC; physician Univ. NC Hosps. Office: University of North Carolina Hospitals 101 Manning Dr Chapel Hill NC 27514-4220 Office Phone: 919-966-4131.

CHAIKIN, HARRY LOUIS, internist; MD, Thomas Jefferson U., 1978. Diplomate Am. Bd. Internal Medicine, Am. Bd. Geriat. Medicine. Intern Wilmington Gen. Hosp., 1979; resident Christiana Care Health Sys., 1981; hosp. affiliation includes Atlantic City Med. Ctr., Bacharach Inst. for Rehab. Named one of the Top Doctor, NJ Monthly, 2005, Phila Mag., 2007, 2009—11. Office: AtlantiCare Regional Medical Center City Campus 1925 Pacific Ave Frederiksted VI 00840 Office Phone: 609-345-4000.

CHAIN, BOBBY LEE, electrical contractor, former mayor; b. Hattiesburg, Miss., Sept. 19, 1929; s. Zollie Lee and Grace (Sellers) Chain; m. Betty Sue Green, June 30, 1967; children: Robin Ann, Laura Grace, Bobby Lee, John Webster. BS, U. So. Miss., Hattiesburg, 1957; DBA (hon.), William Carey U., Hattiesburg, 1983. Chief electrician Miss. Power & Light Co., Natchez, 1950—53; asst. to gen. supt. atomic energy plant Allegany Electric Co., Oak Ridge, 1954—55; owner, chmn. bd. Chain Electric Co., Hattiesburg, 1955; owner, pres. Chainco, Two LLC, oil properties, Hattiesburg, 1974—2003; dir. Deposit Guaranty Nat. Bank, Jackson, Miss., 1965—2000; adv. dir. Am. South Bank, 2000—01; ret., 2003. Mem. Interstate Oil Compact Commn., 1972—; mem. nat. adv. coun. SBA, 1966—67; bd. dirs. Miss. Econ. Coun., 1991—93; dir. Fed. Home Loan Bank Dallas; past mem., past pres. Miss. Trustees Instns. Higher Learning. Nat. coord. Trent Lott Nat. Ctr. Excellence in Econ. Devel. and Entrepreneurship; past mem., pres. So. Regional Edn. Bd., Mississipians Quality Edn.; past chmn. Commn. Efficiency Govt., Miss. Econ. Coun.; mem. Miss. State Workforce Devel. Coun.; chmn. Pearl River County Dist. Workforce Coun.; past bd. dirs. Pub. Edn. Forum Miss.; mem. commissioning com. USS John C. Stennis CVN-74 Aircraft Carrier, 1995; bd. dirs., v.p. Armed Forces Mus., Camp Shelby, Miss.; mem. Friend of West Point Assn. Grads.; v.p. Friends Miss. Vets. Bd., Miss. Armed Forces Mus.; mayor City of Hattiesburg, 1980—85; chmn. Advanced Tech. Ctr. Pearl River Coll. With US Army, 1950—51, Korea. Recipient Disting. Svc. award, U. So. Miss., 1976, Hub award, 1979, Continuous Outstanding Svc. award, 1980, Liberty Bell award, Forrest County Bar Assn., 1980, Svc. to Edn. award, Phi Delta Kappa, 1980, Disting. Citizen award, Pine Burr Area Coun. Boy Scouts Am., 1995, Lifetime Achievement award, Pine Burr Area Coun. Boy Scouts America, 2008, Masonic Lifetime Achiever, 2008, Excellence award, Miss. Coll. Sch. Bus. Exec.; named Noble Patron, Hon. Order St. George 155th Separate Armored Brigade, Bobby L. Chain Tech. Ctr. in his honor, Bobby L. Chain Hattiesburg Mcpl. Airport in his honor; named to Miss. Bus. Hall of Fame, 1994, USM Constrn. Engring. Tech. Hall of Fame; Paul Harris fellow, Rotary Internat., 1990. Mem.: State Miss. Gov (Govs. Medal of Svc. award 2009, Disting. Svc. award Pearl River Coll. 2009, Hope award Nat. Multiple Sclerasis 2009), Miss. Bus. Roundtable, Newcomen Soc. N.Am., Hattiesburg C. of C., U. So. Miss. Alumni Assn. (Outstanding Svc. award 1972, Sales and Mktg. Man of the Yr. award 1981, named in Recognition of Gift of Land to City Chain Pk.), U. So. Miss. Century Club, Hattiesburg Country Club (past bd. dirs.), Shriners, Kiwanis, Beta Gamma Sigma, Omicron Delta Kappa. Presbyterian. Home: 312 6th Ave Hattiesburg MS 39401-4294 Office: PO Box 2058 Hattiesburg MS 39403-2058 E-mail: blc@bchain.com.

CHALK, JOHN ALLEN, SR., lawyer; b. Lexington, Tenn., Jan. 16, 1937; AA, Freed-Hardeman Coll., 1956; BS, Tenn. Tech. U., 1962, MA, 1967; JD, U. Tex., 1973. Bar: Tex. 1973, DC 1977. Pastor chs., Dayton, Ohio, 1956-60, Cookeville, Tenn., 1960-66, Abilene, Tex., 1966-71; assoc. Rhodes and Seamster, Abilene, 1973-74, Rhodes and Doscher, Abilene, 1974; ptnr. Rhodes, Doscher, Chalk and Heatherly, Abilene, 1975-78; gen. counsel La Jet, Inc., Abilene, 1978-84, also v.p., sec; exec. v.p. Dabney Corp., Dallas, 1984-86; pres. Dabney Capital, Dallas, 1984-86; assoc. Gandy, Michener, Swindle, Whitaker & Pratt, Ft. Worth, 1986, ptnr., 1987-93, Michener Larimore Swindle Whitaker Flowers Sawyer Reynolds & Chalk, Ft. Worth, 1993-2000, Whitaker Chalk Swindle & Schwartz LLP, Ft. Worth, 2000—. Mem., Am. Law Inst., 2009-, mem. strategic alliances edn. com. Nat. Ct. Reporters Assn., 1994-95; pres. Tarrant County Bar Assn., 2009-10, chair, State Bar Tex. ADR Sect., 2009-10; pres. Mahon Inn Ct., Ft. Worth, 2013-14; cert. master mediator Dispute Resolution Svcs. Tarrant County, Tex.; Tex. court-approved mediator, credentialed advanced mediatior Tex. Mediator Credentialing Assn.; mem. panel of neutrals Am. Arbitration Assn., 1992—; mem. CPR Internat. Inst. Dispute Resolution Panel of Neutrals, 2005—; contract mediator EEOC, Dallas, 1999-2001; mem. neutrals panel Internat. Ctr. Dispute Resolution, Dublin, 2003—; mem London Ct. Internat. Arbitration, 2003—, adj. prof., Lipscomb U., Nashville, Tenn., 2009, Pepperline U. Sch Law, Calif., 2011, 13. Author: Having Your Cake and Condemming It too: When Asserting the Power of Eminent Domain Constitutes Brench of an Oil And Gas Lease 17 Tex. Wesleyan LR 29, 2010, Arbitration White Paper, 2008, Eminent Domain Power Granted to Private Pipeline Companies, 2009; editor The Arbitration Newsletter, 2006—; conbtr. numerous articles on U.S. Dept. Edn. fed. student fin. assistance, domestic and internat. arbitration and mediation, also articles on religion; presenter in fields. Trustee Osteo. Health Care Found., Inc., Ft. Worth, 1987—96, sec.-treas., 1990—91, sr. v.p., pres.-elect, 1991—92, pres., 1992—93; mem. nat. adv. coun. Am. United Separation of Ch. and State, 1979—82, pres. bd. trustees, 1981—82; mem. Strategy for 2000, City of Ft. Worth, 1995—2000; featured spkr. radio and TV programs Herald of Truth, 1966—69; trustee, chmn. bd. Christian Scholarship Found., Inc., Atlanta, 1980—; co-chair capital gifts campaign All Church Home Children, Inc., 2004—06; trustee Abilene Regional Mental Health Retardation Ctr., 1978—80; chmn. Abilene Bicentennial Com., 1975—76; dir. Health Care of Tex., Inc., 1987—2003; bd. dir. Ft. Worth Symphony Orch. Assn., 2005—, mem. exec. com., 2008—. Recipient Power Attys., Ft. Worth Bus. Press, 2008; named Atty. of Excellence, 2003—13; fellow, Coll. Comml. Arbitrators. Fellow Am. Bar Found. (life), Tex. Bar Found. (life), Chartered Inst. Arbitrators London (fellow, panel mem.), Tarrant County Bar Found. (founding, life); mem. ABA (acting assoc. editor, mem. editl. bd. Family Adv. 1977-78), Fed. Bar Assn., Coll. State Bar Tex. (maintaining fellow) Tex. Bar Alternative Dispute Resolution Sect. Coun. (treas. 2007—08, chair, 2009-10), Am. Health Lawyers Assn. (dispute resolution svc. panel of neutrals, mem. ADR svc. coun.), Am. Arbitration Assn. (panel arbitrators and mediators), Internat. Ctrs. Arbitration (panel arbitrators and mediators), CPR Internat. Inst. for Conflict Resolution (Tex. at large panel of neutrals; S.W. region employment panel of neutrals), Internat. Ctr. Dispute Resolution (mem. panel arbitrators), Tex. Assn. Mediators, Tarrant County Assn. Mediators, State Bar Tex., Tarrant County Bar Assn. (pres. 2009-10; Blackstone award, 2013), Tex. Mediator Credentialing Assn., Coll. Comml. Arbitrators, ADR Svc. Coun. Home: 3601 Verde Vista Ct W Aledo TX 76008-3679 Office: Whitaker Chalk Swindle & Schwartz PLLC 3500 DR Horton Tower Fort Worth TX 76102-4186 Office Phone: 817-878-0575. Office Fax: 817-878-0501. Business E-Mail: jchalk@whitakerchalk.com.

CHALMERS, DAVID B., petroleum executive; b. Denver, Nov. 17, 1924; s. David Twiggs and Dorrit (Bay) C.; 1 child, David B. BA, Dartmouth Coll., Hanover, NH, 1947; A.M.P., Harvard U., Cambridge, Mass., 1966. Various positions Bay Petroleum Co., Denver, 1951-55; various positions Tenneco Oil Co., Houston, 1955-67; v.p. Occidental Petroleum Corp., Houston, 1967-68; pres. Can. Occidental Petroleum Ltd., 1968-73; pres., CEO Petrogas Processing Ltd., 1968-73; officer Cansulex Ltd., 1968-73; chmn., CEO, dir. Coral Petroleum, Inc. and subs., Houston, 1973—. Served to lt. USMC, 1943-45, 49-50, Korea Mem. Am. Petroleum Inst., Petroleum Club of Houston, Lochinvar Golf Club, Houston Racquet Club, Denver Country Club, Houston Club. Republican. Episcopalian. Home: 5600 San Felipe St Unit 4 Houston TX 77056 Home Phone: 713-961-7357. Personal E-mail: coraloil@aol.com.

CHAMBERLAIN, GLENDA JANE See FLANAGAN, GLENDA

CHAMBERS, ANNE COX, publishing executive, former diplomat; b. Dayton, Ohio; 3 children. Student, Finch Coll., NYC; D in Pub. Svc. (hon.), Wesleyan Coll., 1982; DHL (hon.), Spelman Coll., 1983, Brenau Coll., 1989; LLD (hon.), Oglethorpe U., 1983, Clark Atlanta U., 1989. Bd. dirs. Cox Enterprises, Inc.; Am. amb. to Belgium, 1977-81; dir. Bank of the South, 1977—82, Coca-Cola Co., 1981—91; chmn. bd. Atlanta Jour. Constn. Bd. mem. Fulton National Bank, 1973, Ctrl. Atlanta Progress, 1973; mem. Atlanta C. of C., 1973; dir. Am. Soc. of Fr. Leg. of Honor, Am. Adv. Bd. of Pasteur Found. Trustee, mem. internat. coun. Mus. Modern Art; trustee Carter Ctr.; mem. nat. com. Whitney Mus. Am. Art; bd. dirs. Atlanta Arts Alliance, High Mus. Art, Cmtys. in Schs., MacDowell Colony, Forward Arts Found., Emory Mus. Art & Archaeology, NY Bot. Garden, Coun. Am. Ambs., Chmn.'s Coun., Met. Mus. Art, French Am. Found. Decorated Légion d'honneur France, l'Order de la Couronne Belgium; recipient Women of Achvmt. award, YMCA, 1985; named one of Forbes 400: Richest Americans, 2006—, World's Richest People, Forbes Mag., 2007—. Mem.: Coun. Fgn. Rels. Office: 6205 Peachtree Dunwoody Rd Atlanta GA 30328

CHAMBERS, DWAYNE, food products executive, marketing professional; BA in Comm., Oklahoma City U., 1987. V.p., dir. McDonald's Restaurants account Moroch & Associates, Inc., 1987—99; v.p. mktg. Sonic Corp. (Sonic Drive Ins), Oklahoma City, 1999—2003, Red Robin Gourmet Burgers, Inc., Greenwood Village, Colo., 2003—05; chief mktg. officer Noodles & Co., Broomfield, Colo., 2005—09; sr. v.p. mktg. & brand devel. Fuddruckers/Koo Koo Roo restaurants (subs. Magic Brands LLC), 2009—10; v.p., chief mktg. officer Krispy Kreme Doughnuts, Inc., Winston-Salem, NC, 2010—. Office: Krispy Kreme Doughnut Corp PO Box 83 Winston Salem NC 27102

CHAMBERS, LAMAR M., chemical company executive; B in Bus. Adminstrn., U. West Ga., 1976. Staff auditor internal auditing Ashland, Inc., 1976, asst. controller, 1991, exec. asst. to CEO, 1994, auditor, 1998, v.p., controller, 2004—08, sr. v.p., CFO, 2008—; with Ashland Coal; controller Ashland Paving and Construction, Inc. (APAC), 1987, sr. v.p. fin. and adminstrn., 2001—03, v.p. regional ops., 2003—04; adminstrv. v.p. Ashland Petroleum Co., 1996; v.p. fin., controller Marathon Ashland Petroleum, LLC, 1998. Mem.: AICPA. Office: Ashland Inc 50 E RiverCenter Blvd PO Box 12391 50 E Rivercenter Blvd Covington KY 41012-0391 Office Phone: 859-815-3333. Office Fax: 859-815-3559.

CHAMBERS, NORMAN C., construction executive; B, Springfield Coll.; MBA, Boston Coll., 1982. Mgmt. positions through sr. v.p. Halliburton Co., 1985—2000; pres., CEO Petrocosm Corp., 2000—01; COO Capstone Turbine Corp., 2001—02; pres. Comfort Sys. USA, 2002—03, COO, 2003—04, NCI Bldg. Sys. Inc., Houston, 2004—06, bd. dirs., 2003—, pres., 2004—, CEO Houston, 2007—.

Office: NCI Building Systems Inc 10943 N Sam Houston Pky W Houston TX 77064 Office Phone: 281-897-7788. Office Fax: 281-477-9674. Business E-Mail: nchambers@ncilp.com.

CHAMBERS, RAY WAYNE, security and loss control consultant; b. Cascade, W.Va., June 22, 1931; s. Robert and Mildred Ethel (Starrett) C.; m. Joan Roberta Tilley, Apr. 7, 1952; children: Rebecca H. Frase, Bonita I. Knight, Diana L. Sobalvarro. Cert. protection profl., mgmt. cons. Enlisted U.S. Army, 1949, advanced through grades to lt. col., 1971, sgt.-maj. tank battalion Republic of Korea, 1952-53, Europe, 1956-60, 62-65, 67-70, intelligence battalion ops. officer Socialist Republic of Vietnam, 1966-67, dep. chief staff ops., intelligence command, ret., 1973; v.p. loss prevention Little Gen. Store div. Gen. Host Corp., Tampa, Fla., 1973-84; pres. Assets Protection Systems Assocs., Inc., Largo, Fla., 1985—. Loss control cons. JRB Investigations Inc., Largo, 1986-87. Contbr. articles to profl. jours. Bd. dirs. Del Prado Imperial Assn., Largo, chmn. neighborhood watch com., 1983-88. Decorated Bronze Star, Legion of Merit. Mem. Am. Soc. Indsl. Security (chmn. 1975-76, cert. 1976), Internat. Assn. Profl. Security Cons. (exec. dir. 1990-93), Retail Grocers Assn. Fla. (chmn. crime prevention 1983-85), Pinellas Assn. Pvt. Investigators (pres. 1986), Fla. Crime Prevention Officers Assn., Nat. Assn. Convenience Stores, Internat. Found. for Protection Officers, Assn. Counter Intelligence Corps Vets, Inst. Mgmt. Cons. Republican. Avocations: swimming, historial studies. Home and Office: Assets Protection Sys Assoc Inc 11113 Bella Loma Dr Largo FL 33774-4622

CHAMBERS, ROBERT CHARLES (CHUCK CHAMBERS), federal judge; b. Williamson, W.Va., Aug. 27, 1952; s. James Edgar and Geraldine (Kiser) Chambers; children: James Bryan, Lenna Rebecca, Elizabeth Nora. BA, Marshall U., Huntington, W.Va., 1974; JD, W.Va. U. Coll. Law, 1977. Legal counsel W.Va. State Senate, 1978; mem. W.Va. House of Delegates, 1978—97, speaker of the house, 1987—97; judge US Dist. Ct. (so. dist.) W.Va., 1997—. Mem. exec. com. Nat. Conf. State Legislatures. Mem.: W.Va. Trial Lawyers Assn. Democrat. Methodist. Office: Sidney L Christie Federal Bldg 2nd Fl 845 Fifth Ave Huntington WV 25701 Office Phone: 304-528-7583.

CHAMBERS, ROBERT HUNTER, III, academic administrator, consultant, historian, educator; b. Winston-Salem, NC, Oct. 24, 1939; s. Robert Hunter and Hildred (MacDonald) C.; m. Alice Louise Grant, Aug. 18, 1962 (div. 1995); children: Lisa, Grant. AB, Duke U., 1962; B.D., Yale U., 1965; PhD, Brown U., 1969. Asst. prof., dean Davenport Coll. Yale U., New Haven, 1969-74; vis. fellow Clare Coll., Cambridge U., Eng., 1972-73; prof., dean Coll. Arts and Scis. Bucknell U., Lewisburg, Pa., 1975-84; vis. scholar Doshisha U., Kyoto, 1982; pres., prof. English Western Md. Coll., Westminster, 1984—2000; sr. cons. Marts & Lundy, Inc., Gainesville, Fla., 2001—; provost, dean Trinity Coll., U. Melbourne, Australia, 2004—05. Founding dir. Wellway Ctrs., Inc., Ft. Worth, 1984—88, WMC Devel. Corp., 1985—88; presdl. chmn. Centennial Conf., Md. and Pa., 1986, 1998—99; mem. segmental adv. com. State Bd. Higher Edn., Annapolis, Md., 1985—88; mem. internat. adv. coun. U. Buckingham, England; mem. cmty. bd. Carroll Co. Health Svcs., Inc., 1988—2000; assoc. fellow Davenport Coll., Yale U. Author, editor: Twentieth Century Interpretations of All the King's Men, 1977. Contbr. articles to profl. jours. Bd. dirs. Ind. Coll. Fund of Md., Balt.,1984—; mem. coun. on grad. edn. Brown U., 1989; mem. City of Westminster Mayoral Task Force, 1990; co-chair spl. gifts Am. Heart Assn.; mem. task force on assessment Nat. Assn. Ind. Colls. and Univs., 1991-92, mem. commn. on state rels., 1992-95; mem. Gov.'s Edn. Policy Transition Team, 1994-95; mem. Md. Citizens for Arts; bd. dir. Coun. of Ind. Colls., 1997-2000. Rockefeller Brothers fellow, 1962-63; Nat. Endowment for the Humanities grantee, 1978, U.S.-Japan Friendship Commn. grantee, 1982; recipient Balt. Regional Coun. Govts. award, 1989. Mem.: NCAA (pres. coun. 1999—2000), MLA, Internat. Assn. Univ. Presidents, Coun. on Econ. Edn. in Md. (trustee 1), Am. Studies Assn., Md. Ind. Coll. and Univ. Assn. (bd. dirs. 1984—2000, exec. com. 1985—88, 1991—2000, budget com. 1985—89, 1991, chair 1994—98), Mid. States Assn. Colls. and Schs. (commr. 1985—91, exec. com. 1986—91, vice chair 1987—89, chair 1990), Higher Edn. Commn., The Japan Soc., Nat. Assn. Ind. Colls. and Univs. (policy com. 1998—2000), Melbourne Club, Center Club, Yale Club, Rotary (hon. 1990), Phi Beta Kappa Assocs., Phi Beta Kappa. Avocations: running, reading, travel. Office: Marts & Lundy Inc 10040 SW 52d Rd Gainesville FL 32608 Home Phone: 352-505-6097. Personal E-mail: rchambers22@cox.net.

CHAMBERS, SUSAN (MARY SUSAN CHAMBERS, M. SUSAN CHAMBERS), retail executive; b. 1957; BS in Sys. & Data Processing, William Jewell Coll., Liberty, Mo., 1990. Various tech. assignments Amoco Oil Corp.; with Hallmark Cards Inc., 1985—99; from store/club mgr. to v.p. applications devel. for merchandising Wal-Mart Stores Inc., Bentonville, Ark., 1999—2002, sr. v.p., benefits & ins. adminstrn., 2002—03, exec. v.p., risk mgmt., benefits & adminstrn., 2004—06; exec. v.p., global people divsn. Wal-Mart Stores, Inc., 2006—. Bd. trustees William Jewell Coll., 2010—; mem. bus. adv. bd. Kans. State U.; mem. adv. coun. Women Impacting Pub. Policy (WIPP); mem. leadership coun. New America Found.; bd. visitors Duke U. Fuqua Sch. Bus. Recipient Citation for Achievement, William Jewell Coll. Alumni Assn., 2010; named one of The 50 Most Powerful Women in Bus., Fortune mag., 2008—12, The 100 Most Powerful Women, Forbes mag., 2009. Office: Wal-Mart Stores Inc 702 SW 8th St Bentonville AR 72716-8611 Office Phone: 479-273-4000. Office Fax: 479-277-1830. E-mail: Susan.Chambers@wal-mart.com.

CHAMBERS, THOMAS P., energy executive; BSChemE, U. Notre Dame. With BP plc group of companies, 1981—92; with internat. bus. devel. group Pennzoil Exploration and Prodn.; dir. of planning Apache Corp., 1995—2001, v.p. corp. planning, 2001—09, v.p. planning and investor rels., 2009—10, CFO, 2010—, exec. v.p., 2010—. Mem. adv. bd. Houston Found. for Life. Mem.: Soc. of Petroleum Engrs. Office: Apache Corporation Ste 100 2000 Post Oak Blvd Houston TX 77056-4400 Office Phone: 713-296-6000.

CHAMBLISS, PRINCE CAESAR, JR., lawyer; b. Birmingham, Oct. 3, 1948; s. Prince Caesar and Marguerite (Pearson) Chambliss; m. Patricia Toney Chambliss, Dec. 26, 1971; 1 child, Patience Brandyn. Student, Wesleyan U., Middletown, Conn., 1966—68; BA, U. Ala., Birmingham, 1969—71; JD, Harvard U., 1974. Bar: Ala. 1974, Tenn. 1976. Spl. asst. to pres. U. Ala., Birmingham, 1974—75; law clk. to judge US Dist. Ct. (no. dist.) Ala., Birmingham, 1975—76; assoc. firm Armstrong, Allen, Braden, Goodman, McBride & Prewitt, Memphis, 1976—81, ptnr., 1981; mem. Stokes Bartholomew Evans & Petree, P.A.; sec., treas. Tenn. Bd. Law Examiners, 1988—92, v.p., 1992—; ptnr. Evans Petree PC, 2005—. Bd. dirs. ARC Memphis chpt., 1st vice chmn., 1988—89; trustee Miles Coll. Sch. Law, Birmingham, 1982—88. Recipient Comty.Svc. award, Jud. Coun. Nat. Bar Assn., 1982, Boss of Yr., Memphis Legal Secs. Assn., 1984; named one of Am.'s Top Black Lawyers, Black Enterprise Mag., 2003, Best Lawyers in Am., 2006, 150 Best Lawyers in Tenn., Bus. Tenn. Mag., 2006. Fellow: Am. Coll. Civil Trial Mediators; mem.: ABA, Memphis Coun. Internat. Visitors (bd. dirs. 1983—), Assoc. Atty.-Mediators, Ala. Bar Assn., Tenn. Bar Assn. (sec. 1995—97), Nat. Bar Assn., Fed. Bar Assn. (pres. Mid-South chpt. 1984—85), Memphis Bar Assn. (dir. 1983—85, pres. 1997—98). Office: Evans Petree PC 1000 Ridgeway Loop Rd Ste 200 Memphis TN 38120 Office Phone: 901-521-4590. Business E-Mail: pchambliss@evanspetree.com.

CHAMBLISS, SAXBY (CLARENCE SAXBY CHAMBLISS), United States Senator from Georgia; b. Warrenton, NC, Nov. 10, 1943; m. Julianne Frohbert; 2 children. BA in Bus. Adminstrn., U. Ga., 1966; JD, U. Tenn., 1968. Bar: Ga. 1969, US Supreme Ct. 1974, US Ct. Appeals (5th circuit) 1976. Atty. Moore, Chambliss & Warfel, Moultie, Ga.; state atty. Colquitt County, Ga., 1970—76; mem. US Congress from 8th Ga. Dist., 1995—2002; US Senator from Ga., 2003—. Mem. Moultrie-Colquitt Econ. Devel. Authority, Ga. Vol. basketball/baseball coach Recreation Dept., Moultrie, Ga., YMCA; bd. managers U. Ga. Alumni Assn. Recipient Friend of Farmer award, Ga. Farm Bur., 1995, Disting. Svc. award, Ga. Peanut Commn., 1997, W. Stuart Symington award, Air Force Assn., 1998, Fed. Legis. of Yr. award, Safari Club Internat., 1999, Lucite award, Rep. Nat. Lawyers Assn., 2003, Disting. Alumni award, U. Ga. Terry Coll. Bus., 2004, Cmty. Health Defender award, Nat. Assn. Cmty. Health Centers, Inc., 2005, Legis. of Yr. award, Biotechnology Industry Orgn., 2005, Taxpayer Hero award, Coun. Citizens Against Govt. Waste, 2005. Mem.: ABA, Southern Jud. Bar Assn., Moultrie Bar Assn. Republican. Episcopalian. Office: US Senate 416 Russell Senate Office Building Washington DC 20510 also: District Office Ste 1340 100 Galleria Parkway SE Atlanta GA 30339-3179 Office Phone: 202-224-3521, 770-763-9090. Office Fax: 202-224-0103, 770-226-8633.*

CHAMEIDES, WILLIAM L., earth science educator, atmospheric chemist; b. NYC, Nov. 21, 1949; m. Bonnie Green. BA, SUNY, Binghamton, NY, 1970; M in Physics, Yale U., 1973, PhD, 1974. Rsch. investigator space physics U. Mich., Ann Harbor, Mich., 1974-75, asst. rsch. scientist space physics, 1975-76; assoc. prof. physics U. Fla., Tallahassee, 1976-80; assoc. prof. geophysical scis. Ga. Tech., Atlanta, 1980-85, acting dir. earth and atmosphere sci., 1988-89, dir. earth and atmosphere sci., 1989-94, prof. earth and atmosphere sci., 1985-95, regents' prof. earth and atmosphere sci., 1995—; chief scientist Environmental Defense Fund, 2004—07; dean, Nicholas Prof. Sch. Environment and Earth Sciences Duke U., 2007—. Lecturer U. Mich.; editor: bd. trustees UCAR, Boulder, Colo., 1991-96, Ga. Conservancy, Atlanta, 1992-95; chair atmospheric chem. com. Nat. Rsch. Coun., Washington, D.C., 1993-96; vice chair, Com. on America's Climate Choices, Duke U. Editor: J. Geophys. Res. Am. Geophys. Union, Washington, D.C., 1984-87. Recipient James B. MacElwane award for outstanding young scientist, Am. Geophys. Union, 1983; fellow Am. Geophys. Union, 1983. Fellow Am. Geophys. Union (MacElwane award); mem. Am. Men and Women and Sci., AAAS, NAS Home: 3603 Barn View Pl Durham NC 27705-1343 Office: A246 LSRC Box 90329 Duke University Durham NC 27708-0329 Office Phone: 919-613-8004. Office Fax: 919-613-8061. Business E-Mail: bill.chameides@duke.edu.

CHAMITOFF, GREGORY ERROL, astronaut, aerospace engineer; b. Montreal, Aug. 6, 1962; came to U.S., 1974; s. Ashley Morton and Shari Janet (Wexler) C.; m. Alison Chantal Caviness; children Natasha and Dimitri. BS in Elec. Engring., Calif. Poly. State U., San Luis Obispo, 1984; MS in Aero. Engring., Calif. Inst. Tech., Pasadena, 1985; PhD in Aeronautics/Astronautics Engring., MIT, 1992; MS in Space Sci. (Planetary Geology), U. Houston, Clear Lake, 2002. Fellow, mem. tech. staff C.S. Draper Lab., Cambridge, Mass., 1985-93; vis. prof. dept. aeronautics U. Sydney, Australia, 1993-95; flight control engr. United Space Alliance, Houston, 1995-98; astronaut NASA, Johnson Space Ctr., Houston, 1998—. Pvt. pilot, 1995—; dive master PADI, 1993; assignments with astronaut office have included Space Station procedure and display develop., crew support for Internat. Space Station(ISS) Expedition 6, led CAPCOM for ISS Expedition 9 and Space Station Robotics; crew mem. Aquarius undersea rsch. habitat, NEEMO 3 mission (NASA Extreme Environment Mission Ops.), 2002; ISS flight engr., sci. officer Expedition 17 and 18, 2008; mission specialist, STS-124 Mission (Discovery), mission to Internat. Space Station to launch components to complete Japanese Kibo Lab., 2008; mission specialist STS-134 Mission-Final Flight of Endeavour, 2011. Contbr. to numerous technical publs. Mem. AIAA (sr. mem., Tech. Excellence award 1998), IEEE, Eta Kappa Nu (v.p. chpt. 1982-84), Tau Beta Pi. Achievements include research on autonomous flight control systems, spacecraft guidance, navigation, control, as well as resource utilization for human missions to Mars. Office: Astronaut Office/CB NASA Lyndon B Johnson Space Ctr 2101 NASA Pkwy Houston TX 77058

CHAMPAGNE, SIMONE, state legislator; b. Jeanerette, La. m. Gary P. Champagne; 5 children. Continuing edn. in Banking. Mem. South Lake Fausse Devel. Found., Jeanerette Hist. Preservation Found., Jeanerette, La.; pres. Jeanerette C. of C., Jeanerette, La.; mem. Dist. 49 La. House of Reps., 2008—, mem. appropriations com., mcpl., parochial and cultural affairs com., natural resources and environment com., house exec. com., mem. joint legis. com. on the budget. Office: District Office 1407 Main Street Jeanerette LA 70544 also: Capitol Office Post Office Box 44486 Baton Rouge LA 70804 Office Phone: 337-276-4916, 225-342-6945. Office Fax: 337-276-4918. E-mail: champags@legis.state.la.us.

CHAMPION, SAM (SAMUEL JAMES CHAMPION), weather anchor; b. Paducah, Ky., Aug. 13, 1961; s. James H. and Sylvia Champion; m. Rubem Robierb, Dec. 21, 2012. BA in Broadcast News, Eastern Ky. U. With WPSD-TV, Paducah, WCWJ-TV (formerly WJKS-TV), Jacksonville, Fla.; weather forecaster Eyewitness News, WABC-TV, NYC, 1988—2013, Good Morning America, NYC, 2012—13; mng. editor, weather anchor The Weather Channel, Atlanta, 2014—. Host (TV series) Sea Rescue, 2012—13. Vol. Multiple Sclerosis Soc., March of Dimes Found. Office: The Weather Channel 300 Interstate North Pky SE Atlanta GA 30339-2403*

CHAMPLIN, RICHARD EUGENE (DICK CHAMPLIN), hematologist, oncologist, medical educator; b. Milw., Feb. 13, 1949; BS in Engring. Scis., Purdue U., West Lafayette, Ind., 1971; MD, U. Chgo. Pritzker Sch. Medicine, 1975. Diplomate American Bd. Internal Medicine, cert. in hematology and med. oncology. Intern medicine LA County Harbor-UCLA Med. Ctr., 1975—76, resident hematologic oncology, 1976—78; fellowship UCLA Ctr. Health Scis., 1978—80, asst. prof. medicine, 1981—85, assoc. prof., 1985—90; prof. medicine U. Tex. MD Anderson Cancer Ctr., Houston, 1990—, chmn. dept. hematology, 1995—97, exec. com., divsn. cancer medicine, 1997—, Robert C. Hickey chair clin. cancer care, 1998, chmn. dept. stem cell transplantation & cellular therapy, 1998—. Exec. editor The Oncologist, 2005—, assoc. editor Biology of Blood & Marrow Transplantation, 1999—, Exptl. Hematology, 2002—, mem. editl. bd. Bone Marrow Transplantation, 2002—, Blood, 2002—; contbr. articles to profl. jours., chapters to books. Pres. Coun. Donor Collections & Transplant Centers, bd. dirs. Nat. Marrow Donor Program, Mpls., 1990—93; v.p. bd. dirs. Found. Accreditation Cellular Therapy, 1996—. Recipient New Investigator Rsch. award, Nat. Inst. Arthritis, Diabetes, Digestive & Kidney Diseases, 1982—84, Faculty Achievement award, U. Tex. MD Anderson Cancer Ctr., 2002, Waun Ki Hong award for Excellence in Team Sci., 2008, Lifetime Achievement award, American Soc. for Blood & Marrow Transplantation, 2011; Giannini Found. fellowship, 1979—81. Fellow: ACP; mem.: Transplantation Soc. (Lifetime Achievement award 2011), Internat. Soc. Cell Therapy, American Soc. Clin. Oncology, American Assn. Cancer Rsch., Internat. Soc. Exptl. Hematology, American Soc. Hematology, American Soc. Blood & Marrow Transplantation (pres. 1992—94, Thomas Lecture award 2004), Alpha Omega Alpha. Office: Univ Tex MD Anderson Cancer Center 1515 Holcombe Blvd PO Box 301402 Unit 423 Houston TX 77030

CHAN, CHIU M., information technology executive; BS in Pharmacy, U. Houston. Registered pharmacist. With Lifemark Corp., M.D. Anderson Cancer Ctr.; chmn., CEO Ambulatory Infusion Therapy Specialists (now Dynacq), 1986—; dir., pres., sec., COO Dynacq Healthcare, Inc., 1992—. Office: Ambulatory Infusion Therapy Specialist Inc 10304 I 10 E Ste 369 Houston TX 77029-5890 Office Phone: 713-673-2000. Office Fax: 713-378-6416.

CHAN, ELISA, councilwoman, engineering company executive; b. Taipei, Taiwan; m. Clifford Hew; 1 child, Nikola. MS in Computer Sci., U. Tex., San Antonio. Co-founder, pres. Unintech Consulting Engineers, Inc., 1992—; councilwoman, Dist. 9 San Antonio City Coun., 2009—. Com. chair China Steering Com., San Antonio; mem. City of San Antonio Planning Commn. Bd. govs. Cancer Therapy and Rsch. Ctr. Recipient Small Bus. Leaders Award in Career Achievement, North C. of C., 2008; named one of 40 Under Forty Rising Stars, San Antonio Bus. Jour., 2003. Office: Frost Bank Bldg 16500 San Pedro, Ste 290 San Antonio TX 78232 also: City Hall PO Box 839966 San Antonio TX 78283 Office Phone: 210-207-0955. Office Fax: 210-207-0956. E-mail: district9@sanantonio.gov.

CHAN, PHILIP, retired dermatologist, military officer; b. Oceanside, NY, Oct. 14, 1946; s. Walter O. and Anna (Yee) C. BA, Harvard U., 1968; MD, Columbia U., 1972. Diplomate Am. Bd. Dermatology. Commd. capt. U.S. Army, 1973, advanced through grades to col., 1987; dermatologist Martin Army Cmty. Hosp., Ft. Benning, Ga., 1995-98; ret. U.S. Army, 1998; tchr. Tai Chi, Reiki, blues harmonica, ballroom dancing Columbus, Ga., 1999—. Adj. asst. prof. Uniformed Svcs. U. Health Scis., 1995—97; part-time instr. Rankin Arts Ctr., Columbus State U., 2002—08. Editor (govt. pub.) Procs. of Vesicant Workshop, 1987; conbtr. articles to profl. jours. Fellow: Am. Acad. Dermatology; mem.: AMA, Assn. Mil. Dermatologists, Mensa. Home: 6300 Milgen Rd #1285 Columbus GA 31907-0962

CHAN, PHILIP S., corporate financial executive; Degree in Advanced Acctg., U. Houston. CPA Tex. V.p., fin., CFO, treas. & bd. dirs. Dynacq Healthcare, Inc., 1992—. Office: Dynacq Healthcare Inc 10304 Interstate 10 E Ste 369 Houston TX 77029 Office Phone: 713-378-2000. Office Fax: 713-673-6416. Business E-Mail: philipchan@dynacq.com.

CHANCE, GLORIA A., bank executive; m. Don Grady. BSBA in Decision Sciences, East Caolina U., Greenville, NC, 1988. IT team mgr. Wachovia Corp., Atlanta, western regional mktg. dir., dir. online customer svc., dir. e-commerce, sr. v.p., group exec., and chief e-commerce officer Charlotte, NC. Spkr. in field. Active GirlTalk, Charlotte, C.W. Williams Cmty. Health Ctr.; bd. dirs. Thurgood Marshall Coll. Fund, Inc.; bd. visitors East Carolina U.; bd. dirs. McColl Ctr. Visual Art. Named one of 25 Women to Watch, US Banker, 2007. Mem.: Phi Kappa Phi. Office: Wachovia Corp 1 Wachovia Ctr Charlotte NC 28288 Office Phone: 704-374-6565.

CHANCE, JANE, English literature scholar; b. Neosho, Mo., Oct. 26, 1945; d. Donald William and Julia (Mile) C.; m. Dennis Carl Nitzsche, June, 1966 (div. Mar. 1969); 1 child, Therese; m. Paolo Passaro, Apr. 30, 1981,(div. May 2002); children: Antony Damian, Joseph Sebastian. BA in English with honors and highest distinction, Purdue U., West Lafayette, Ind., 1967; AM in English, U. Ill., Urbana, 1968, PhD in English, 1971; LittD, Purdue U., 2013. Lectr. U. Sask., Canada, 1971—72, asst. prof., 1972—73; asst. prof. English, Rice U., Houston, 1973—77, assoc. prof., 1977—80, prof., 1980—2008, Andrew W. Mellon disting. chair English, 2008—11, Andrew W Mellon disting. prof. emerita English, 2011; hon. rsch. fellow U. Coll. U. London, 1977—78. Dir. NEH Summer Seminar for Coll. Tchrs. on Chaucer and Mythography, 1985, NEH Summer Inst. for Coll. Tchrs. on Medieval Women, 1997; pres., founder TEAMS, 1986-89, Tolkien at Kalamazoo, 2000-; founder, dir. medieval studies program Rice U., 1986-92, 2005-2008; founding mem. Rice U. Commn. on Women, 1986-88; resident Rockefeller Found., Bellagio, Italy, 1988; mem. Sch. Hist. Studies, Inst. for Advanced Study, Princeton, 1988-89; vis. rsch. fellow Inst. for Advanced Studies in Humanities, U. Edinburgh, 1994; Eccles fellow Humanities Ctr., U. Utah, 1994-95; vis. scholar Inst. Med. Humanities, U. Tex. Med. Br., Galveston, 2011-12; adv. bd. mem. PMLA, 2009-12; spkr., lectr. in field. Author: The Genius Figure in Antiquity and the Mid. Ages, 1975, Tolkien's Art: A Mythology for Eng., 1979, National Geographic Beyond the Movie - The Lord of the Rings, 2007, Ringers: Lord of the Fans; rev. edit. Tolkien's Art: A Mythology for Eng., 2001; author: Woman as Hero in Old English Literature, 1986, rev. edit., 2005, The Lord of the Rings: The Mythology of Power, 1992, rev. edit., 2001, Japanese trans., 2003, Medieval Mythography: From Roman North Africa to the Sch. of Chartres, AD 433-1177 (South Ctrl. MLA best book prize, 1994), The Mythographic Chaucer: The Fabulation of Sexual Politics, 1995, Medieval Mythography, vol. 2: From the Sch. of Chartres to the Ct. at Avignon, 1177-1350, 2000, The Literary Subversions of Medieval Women, 2007 (SCMLA Book prize, 2008); translator: Christine de Pizan's Letter of Othea to Hector, 1990; editor: The Mythographic Art: Classical Fable and the Rise of the Vernacular in Early France and Eng., 1990, Medievalism in the Twentieth Century, Studies in Medievalism, vol. 2:2, 1983, The Inklings and Others, vol. 3:3, 1990, Gender and Text in the Later Mid. Ages, 1986, The Assembly of Gods, 1999, Tolkien the Medievalist, 2002, 2008, Tolkien and the Invention of Myth, 2004, Women Medievalists and the Academy, 2005; co-editor: Approaches to Teaching Sir Gawain, 1986, Mapping the Cosmos, 1985, Tolkien's Modern Middle Ages, 2005, Issue on Cognitive Alterities/Neuromedievalism, Postmedieval, 2012; gen. editor: Focus Libr. of Medieval Women, 1988—, Boydell & Brewer Libr. of Medieval Women, 1997—, series editor: Greenwood Guides to Hist. Events in the Medieval World, 2001—08, Praeger Series on the Mid. Ages, 2003—13, mem. editl. bd.: Coll. Lit., 2002—, Postmedieval: A Journal of Medieval Cultural Studies, 2008—; contbr. numerous essays, reviews, poems. Bd. dirs. Rice U. Press, 1981-88, Internat. Chaucer Studio, 2003—. NEH fellow, 1977-78, Guggenheim fellow, 1980-81, Mellon leave Rice U., 1988, Disting. Faculty Tchg. fellow, 1995, Rice U., Ctr. for Study of Cultures fellow, 1998, NEH fellow St. Louis U. Ctr. for Med. Studies, 2003, Mellon fellow, Pope Pius Vatican Film Libr., 2003; Travel grant ACLS, 1982; recipient Women's Ctr. IMPACT award Rice U., 1998, Best Essay prize Soc. Medieval Feminist Scholarship, 2005. Mem. AAUP (Rice U. chpt. sec., treas. 1975-76), MLA (life; Roth Scaglione Prize Com., 2007-09, 11-, chair, 2008-09), SCMLA, Scientia (acting dir. 1983-84, sec. 1982-83), Tex. Faculty Assn. (exec. com. 1995-99, v.p. 1998-2000, Achievement award 1998), Medieval Acad. America (life), South Ctrl. Modern Assn. (life), Tex. Medieval Assn. (life), East End Hist. Dist. Assn. (bd. mem., 2013-). Avocations: photography, travel, writing. Home: 1207 Post Office St Galveston TX 77550-5040 Business E-Mail: jchance@rice.edu.

CHANCE, KENNETH BERNARD, SR., endodontist educator, humanitarian, philanthropist, academic administrator; b. NYC, Dec. 8, 1953; s. George E. and Janie L. (Bolles) Chance; m. Sharon Lee Lewis, July 11, 1981 (div.); children: Kenneth Bernard, Dana Marie, Christopher, Jacquelyn; m. Keli Green Chance, July 17, 2010. BS, Fordham U., Bronx, NY, 1975; DDS, Case Western Res. U., Cleve., 1979; Cert. in Endodontics, U. Medicine and Dentistry NJ, 1982; Cert. in Bus. Adminstrn., Internat Bus. & Mgmt. Ctr., U. Ky. Gatton Coll. Bus. and Econs., 2007. Asst. attending Jamaica Hosp., Queens, NY, 1981-87; chief endodontics Kings County Med. Ctr., Bklyn., 1982-91; assoc. prof. endodontics U. Medicine and Dentistry NJ, 1987; also dir. external affairs NJ Dental Sch.; asst. attending North Ctrl. Bronx Hosp., NY, 1983-91, Kingsbrook Jewish Med. Ctr., 1986-92; asst. dean external affairs and urban resource devel. NJ Dental Sch., 1989-97; cons. Harlem Hosp., NYC, 1982-90; health policy advisor to US Senator Frank Lautenberg of NJ, 1991—99; dir. health policy program The Joint Ctr. Polit. and Econ. Studies, 1993-94; acting chmn. dept. endodontics NJ Dental Sch., 1994-97; fed. rels. adv. com. U. Medicine and Dentistry NJ, 1994-97; dean, prof. endodontics Meharry Med. Coll. Sch. Dentistry, 1997-2000; prof., dir. divsn. endodontics U. Ky., Lexington, 2000—, prof.,grad. sch., 2008—. Commencement spkr. Case Western Res. U. Sch. Dental Medicine, 2005; spkr., presdl. leadership lecture series Megar Evers Coll., 2006; cons. commr. health dept. health, NJ, 1991—97; mentor Leadership Legacy Program Ctr. Interprofl. Healthcare Edn. Rsch. & Practice U. Ky., 2011; mem. 100 Black Men America Inc., 1998—, Inst. Medicine Robert Wood Johnson Health Policy Fellowships Adv. Bd., 2007—13, Nat. Campaign Exec. Com. Case Western Res. U. Sch. Dental Medicine, 2011—; faculty adv. Student Nat. Dental Assn. U. Ky., 2011—; elec. mem. adminstrn. Bd. Coun. Deans Am. Assn. Dental Schs., 1999. Sci. reviewer Jour. of Dental Edn., 2004—. Mem. healthcare task force Congl. Black Caucus, 1994—2001; trustee Case Western Res. U., 2005—, mem. alumni and univ. rels. com., 2005—06, mem. presdl. search com., 2006, vice chmn. academic affairs and student life com., 2006, mem. audit com., 2006; mem. nat. adv. com. Robert Wood Johnson Summer Med. and Dental Edn. Program, 2006; min. music, sr. organist Sharon Bapt. Ch., Bronx, 1983—91, Greater Zion Hill Bapt. Ch., NYC, 1972—81. Recipient Dr. Paul P. Sherwood award for excellence in endodontics Case Western Res. U. Dental Sch., 1979, Cmty. Svc. award U. Medicine and Dentistry NJ, 1997, Tenn. Outstanding Achievement award, 1998, Outstanding Academician award U. Medicine and Dentistry NJ, 1999, Disting. Alumnus of Yr. award, Case Western Res. U., 2004, Found. grant award U. Medicine and Dentistry NJ, 1984, Exceptional Merit award, 1985, Excellence award, 1990, Disting. Practioner award Nat. Acad. Practice Dentistry, 2001, Faculty award U. Ky., Sch. Dentistry, 2005, award Megar Evers Coll., 2006; fellow Nat. Dental Leadership Devel. PEW, 1991, Robert Wood Johnson Health Policy, 1991, Pierre Fauchard Acad., 1996; named to The Best Dentists in America Woodward/White, Inc., 2004, Top Dentists, 2011, Faculty award U. Ky. Sch. Dentistry, 2008, Appreciation & Recognition award, Case Western Res. U. Dental Sch., 2011, Discovering the Future of Dental Medicine Major Donor award, Case Western Res. U. Sch. Dental Medicine, 2012, Excellence Svc. award, Jamaica Hosp., 1981, fellow, Acad. Polit. Sci., 1995, Sci. Contbr. award, Nat. Dental Assn., 1995, Outstanding Svc. award, 1995, U. Medicine & Dentistry NJ, 1995, ADEA Gies AADR Acad. Dental Careers award, 2012. Fellow Am. Coll. Dentists, Internat. Coll. Dentists; mem. ADA, Internat. Assn. Dental Rsch., Am. Dental Edn. Assn. (chair minority affairs sect. 2003), Am. Assn. Dental Schs., Nat. Dental Assn., Am. Assn. Endodontists, Greater Met. Dental Soc. NY (pres.-elect 1986-87, v.p. 1984-86), Ky. Assn. Endodontists, Omicron Kappa Upsilon (pres.-elect 2006, pres. 2007). Home: 2140 Mangrove Dr Lexington KY 40513 Office Phone: 859-323-5891. Business E-Mail: kbchan2@uky.edu.

CHANCE, RONNIE, state legislator; m. Cressida Stevens; children: Ellia, Eva. BBA, Ga. State Univ. Pub. rels. exec.; mem. Dist. 16 Ga. State Senate, 2005—. Republican. Methodist. Office: 139 Regal Oak Tyrone GA 30290 Office Phone: 770-969-9155. Office Fax: 770-969-9755. Business E-Mail: ronnie.chance@senate.ga.gov.

CHANCELLOR, VAN, collegiate athletics administrator, former women's college basketball coach; b. Louisville, Miss., Sept. 27, 1943; m. Betty Chancellor; children: John, Renee. Student, East Ctrl. Jr. Coll., Decatur, Miss.; B Math. and Phys. Edn., Miss. State U., 1965, MEd, 1974. Head coach boys' basketball Noxapater HS, Miss.; head coach women's basketball U. Miss., Oxford, 1978—97; head coach, gen. mgr. Houston Comets, 1997—2007; head coach women's basketball La. State U., 2007—11, spl. asst. to the athletic dir., 2011—. Head coach West Team WNBA All-Star Game, 1999, 2000, 2001; head coach USA Basketball Women's World Championship Team, 2002, US Women's Olympic Basketball Team, Athens, Greece, 2004. Recipient Gold medal Olympic Games, Athens, 2004; named Southeastern Conf. Coach of Yr., 1987, 90, 92, Nat. Coach of Yr., Women's Basketball News Svc., 1992, WNBA Coach of Yr., 1997, 98, 99, USA Basketball Nat. Coach of Year, 2002; named to Women's Basketball Hall of Fame, 2001, Naismith Meml. Basketball Hall of Fame, 2007. Achievements include coaching the Houston Comets to four WNBA Championships, 1997-2000. Office: La State University Athletics Dept PO Box 25095 Baton Rouge LA 70894-5095

CHANCY, MARK A., bank executive; b. 1964; BBA in Finance, Southern Methodist U., Dallas; MBA, Northwestern U. With First Boston Corp., 1986; with corp. finance dept. Robinson-Humphrey Co., 1989, CFO, 1997—2001; sr. v.p., treas. SunTrust Banks, Inc., Atlanta, 2001—04, corporate exec. v.p., CFO, mem. policy com., 2004—11, wholesale banking exec., 2011—. Bd. dirs. Robinson-Humphrey Co., 1998—2001. Office: SunTrust Banks Inc PO Box 4418 Atlanta GA 30302-4418 Office Phone: 404-588-7711. Office Fax: 404-827-6173.

CHANDLER, ARTHUR BLEAKLEY, pathologist, educator; b. Augusta, Ga., Sept. 11, 1926; s. Clemmons Quillian and Mary Isabella (Bleakley) Chandler; m. Jane Stoughton Downing, Sept. 2, 1953; children: Arthur Bleakley, John Downing. Student, U. Ga., 1943-44; MD, Med. Coll. Ga., 1948. Diplomate Am. Bd. Pathology. Intern Baylor U. Hosp., Dallas, 1948-49; resident in pathology, NIH trainee in cancer dept. pathology Med. Coll. Ga., 1950-51, asst. in pathology, 1949-50, mem. faculty, 1949—, prof. pathology, 1962-2000, chmn. dept., 1975-2000, emeritus prof., emeritus chmn., 2001—. Com. mem. Nat. Heart, Lung and Blood Inst., 1969—93. Mem. editl. bd. Haemostasis, 1975—83, Pathology Rsch. and Practice, 1987—2001;, author papers in field; contbr. chapters to books. Trustee Young Mens Libr. Assn. Fund, 1962—72, Historic Augusta, Inc., 1966—69, Augusta-Richmond County Mus., 1965—87, Dan Printup Meml. Trust, 1985—2000, Acad. Richmond County, 1984—. Officer AUS Med. Corps, 1951—53. Fellow Commonwealth Fund, Thrombosis Rsch. Inst., Oslo, 1963—64. Mem.: AMA, Sch. Medicine Alumni Assn. Med. Coll. Ga. (pres. 1996—97), Richmond County Med. Soc. (trustee 1984—2002, sec. 1987, v.p. 1988), Med. Assn. Ga., Ga. Heart Assn., Ga. Assn. Pathologists (pres. 1984—85), Am. Heart Assn. (chmn. coun. on thrombosis 1978—80, chmn. com. on coronary lesions and myocardial infarctions 1980—82, fellow coun. arteriosclerosis), Am. Soc. Hematology, Am. Assn. Pathologists, Coll. Am. Pathologists, Am. Assn. History Medicine, Internat. Soc. for History of Medicine, Internat. Soc. Thrombosis and Haemostasis, Internat. Acad. Pathology, Alpha Omega Alpha. Episcopalian. Achievements include invention of the Chandler Loop method for producing a thrombus in vitro. Home: 803 Milledge Rd Augusta GA 30904-4351 Office: Med Coll Ga Dept Pathology Augusta GA 30912

CHANDLER, DAVID A., state supreme court justice; m. Glenda Chandler; 2 children. B in edn, M in edn, EdD, Miss. State Univ.; JD, Univ. Miss.; LLM, Univ. Va., 2004. Bar: Miss. 1994. Rsch. & curriculum specialist Miss. State Univ.; atty. private practice Tupelo, Miss.; mcpl. judge Weir, Miss., 1999—2001; judge Miss. Ct. Appeals, 2001—08; assoc. justice Miss. Supreme Ct., 2009—. Adj. prof. Miss. Coll. Sch. Law. Contbr. articles to profl. law jours. Mem.: ABA, Miss. Bar Assn., Tupelo Bar Assn., Lamar Order Univ. Miss. Sch. Law. Methodist. Office: Miss Supreme Ct 450 High St Jackson MS 39201 Office Phone: 601-359-2107.*

CHANDLER, ELIZABETH BRANNEN (BETH CHANDLER), lawyer; b. 1963; BBA magna cum laude, U. Ga., 1985; JD magna cum laude, U. Ga. Sch. Law, 1988. Bar: Ga. Ptnr. Troutman Sanders LLP, 1988—2000; v.p., asst. gen. counsel, corp. sec. Mirant Corp., 2000—06; city atty. legal dept. City of Atlanta, 2006—09; v.p., sec., gen. counsel Asbury Automotive Group, Inc., Duluth, Ga., 2009—12. Mem.: ABA, Ga. State Bar Assn. (mem. bd. govs.).

CHANDLER, HUBERT THOMAS, former army officer; b. Charleston, W.Va., Dec. 8, 1933; s. Hubert Paris and Eleanor Lee (Gay) C.; m. Mary Frances Ritter, June 4, 1955; 1 son, Thomas Ritter. Student, Morris Harvey Coll., Charleston, 1951-52, U. Louisville, 1952-53; D.D.S., Balt. Coll. Dental Surgery, 1957; grad., Army War Coll., 1974. Diplomate: Am. Bd. Prosthodontics. Commd. Dental Corps U.S. Army, 1957, advanced through grades to maj. gen., dep. to chief Dental Corps, 1975-78, dep. comdr. Med. Command, dental surgeon Europe, 1979-82, asst. surgeon gen., chief Dental Corps, 1982-86, dir. personnel Med. Dept., 1983-85; assoc. dean for profl. devel. Dental Sch., U. Md., Balt., 1988-92. Exec. com. Transatlantic council Boy Scouts Am., 1980-82; chmn. trust fund Girl Scouts Europe, 1981-82; pres. European Assn. Rod and Gun Clubs, 1981-82, Am. German Friendship Club, Heidelberg, W. Ger., 1981-82. Decorated D.S.M., Bronze Star, Meritorious Service medal, Army Commendation medal Fellow Am. Coll. Prosthodontists; mem. ADA. Office: 1714 Besley Rd Vienna VA 22182-2004 Personal E-mail: htchandler@earthlink.net.

CHANDLER, LAWRENCE BRADFORD, JR., lawyer; b. New Bedford, Mass., June 20, 1942; s. Lawrence Bradford and Anne (Crane) C.; m. Madeleine Bibeau, Sept. 7, 1963 (div. June 1984); children: Dawn, Colleen, Brad. BS in Bus. Adminstrn., Boston Coll., 1963; LLB, U. Va., 1966, JD, 1970. Bar: Mass. 1966, U.S. Supreme Ct. 1967, Va. 1970, W.Va. 1993, adv.: Am. Bd. Trial Advs. Ptnr. Chandler, Franklin & O'Bryan, Charlottesville, Va., 1971—2003, Chandler Law Group, Charlottesville, 2003—. Pres. Western Va. Chpt., 1992-93. Capt. U.S. Army, 1967-71. Named one of Va. Super 100 Lawyers, 2009—10. Mem.: ATLA (chair state dels. 1993—94, exec. com. 1993—94, bd. govs. 1995—2001), ABA, Am. Assn. Profl. Liability Attys., Am. Soc. on Law, Medicine and Ethics, Am. Coll. Legal Medicine, Charlottesville Bar Assn., Am. Bd. Trial Advs. (pres. Va. chpt.), Va. Trial Lawyers Assn. (pres. 1985—86), Assn. U.S. Army (pres. 1971—73). Roman Catholic. Office: Chandler Law Group PO Box 6747 Charlottesville VA 22906-6747 Home: 2200 Ballard Ridge Dr Charlottesville VA 22906 Office Phone: 434-971-7273. Personal E-mail: goofyc@mindspring.com.

CHANDRAHASA, USHA, allergist, immunologist; MD, U. Madras, India, 1992. Diplomate Am. Bd. Internal Medicine, 2000, Am. Bd. Allergy and Immunology, 2005, lic. Fla., 2002. Resident internal medicine Northeastern Pa. Hosp., 1998—2000; fellow allergy and immunology La. State Univ. Health Sci. Ctr., 2000—02; hosp. affiliations include Fawcett Meml. Hosp., Peace River Regional Med. Ctr., Charlotte Regional Med. Ctr. Office: Charlotte Regional Medical Center 809 E Marion Ave Punta Gorda FL 33950-3898 Office Phone: 941-639-3131.

CHANEY, CARL J., bank executive; B in Banking & Fin. with honors, U. Miss., JD; grad., Leadership Gulf Coast. Ptnr., bd. dirs. Watkins, Ludlam, Winter and Stennis, P.A., Jackson, Miss., 1995—98; exec. v.p., CFO Hancock Bank, Baton Rouge, 1998—2006, pres., 2008—, exec. v.p., CFO Gulfport, Miss., 1998—2006, pres., Gulfport, 2008—, sr. v.p., 1999—2001, CEO, bd. dirs., 2006—, pres., Tallahassee, 2008—, pres., Mobile Ala., 2008—; exec. v.p., CFO Hancock Holding Co., 1998—2006, sr. v.p., 1999—2001, co-CEO, 2006, CEO, bd. dirs., 2006—, pres., 2008—. Instr. Ala. Sch. Banking; bd. dirs. Miss. Power Co., Gulfport, Hancock Bank of Fla., 2003—, Hancock Bank of Ala., 2007—. Named one of South Miss. Outstanding Cmty. Leaders; recipient Disting. Faculty award, Miss. Sch. Banking, President's award, La. State U. Mem.: Miss. Gulf Coast C. of C. (past chmn.), Miss. Bankers Assn. (bd. dirs.). Office: Hancock Holding Co One Hancock Plz Gulfport MS 39501 Office Phone: 228-868-4727. Office Fax: 228-563-5673. Business E-Mail: carl_chaney@hancockbank.com.

CHANEY, CHARLES R., state legislator; BS, La. State U. Owner/mgr. Albert's Men's Wear; mem. Dist. 19 La. House of Reps., 2008—, mem. agr., forestry, aquaculture, and rural devel. com., civil law and procedure com., edn. com. Democrat. Office: State Capitol PO Box 44486 Baton Rouge LA 70804 Mailing: PO Box 8 Rayville LA 71269 Office Phone: 225-342-6945, 318-728-5875. Office Fax: 318-728-5876. Business E-Mail: chaneyb@legis.state.la.us.

CHANG, MARIAN S., filmmaker, composer; b. Atlanta, Aug. 19, 1958; d. C. H. Joseph and C. S. (Chun) Chang. MusB, Harvard U., Cambridge, Mass., 1981; MFA in Film Making, Columbia U., NYC, 1994. Composer, dir., choreographer Exptl. Theatre, Dance, Boston, 1981-88; composer for modern dance co. Performing Arts Ensemble, Boston, 1986-88; co-dir., choreographer, performer Theatre S., Boston, 1987-88; prodr., dir., writer, digital designer, composer NYC, 1991—. Founder, prodr. Shy Artists Prodns., Boston, NYC, 1988—94. Recipient 1st prize, Kansas City Music Scholarship Competition, 1976, Nino Cerruti Film award, 1995; grantee, NY Coun. Humanities, 1998; fellow, Mass. Artists' Fellowship Program in Choreography, 1987, Mass. Artists' Fellowship Program in Music Composition, 1988. Achievements include first artist in Mass. Artists' Fellowship Program to receive awards in both music and choreography. Home: PO Box 413005 PMB 147 Naples FL 34101-3005 Personal E-mail: m.chang3d@gmail.com.

CHANG, PHILLIP J., plastic surgeon; Attended, U. Rochester, 1992. Diplomate Am. Bd. Plastic Surgery, Am. Soc. of Plastic Surgeons. Resident Loma Linda Univ. Med. Ctr., 1996; fellow Univ. of Rochester, 2000; hosp. appointments include Inova Fair Oaks Hosp., Inova Loudoun Hosp.; tech. instr. Plastic Surgery Soc. Named Top Dr., Health and Beauty Mag., 2009—11. Office: c/o Aesthetica Cosmetic Surgery & Laser Center 19500 Sandridge Way Ste 350 Leesburg VA 20176-3693 Office Phone: 703-729-5553.

CHANG, SAM S., urologist, surgeon, educator; b. Seoul, Republic of Korea, Feb. 19, 1966; m. Michelle Chang; children: Grace, Rachel, Julia. AB, Princeton U., NJ, 1988; MD, Vanderbilt U., Nashville, 1992. Prof. urol. surgery Vanderbilt U. Med. Ctr., 2005—. Com. chair Am. Joint Com. Cancer, Chgo., 2003—; bd. Vanderbilt U. Med. Ctr. Alumni Assoc., 2004—; exec. com. Soc. Urol. Oncology, 2004; prostate bd. Am. Urol. Assn. Found., 2006—; exam com. Am. Bd. Urology, Am. Urol. Assn., 2008—. Recipient CaPCURE Young Investigator award, Prostate Cancer Found., 2001—04, Disting. Svc. award, Soc. Urol. Oncology, 2005; named to Best Doctors in Am., 2006—; fellow, Meml. Sloan-Kettering Cancer Ctr., NYC, 1999—2000, Am. Urol. Assn./European Assn. Urology, 2006. Mem.: AMA (assoc.), Tenn. Med. Assn. (alt. ho. of dels. 2003—05), Am. Urol. Assn. (assoc.; guidelines panel-treatment superficial bladder cancer 2004—, mem. prostate adv. coun. 2004—). Office: Vanderbilt University Medical Center A-1302 Medical Center North Nashville TN 37232-2765 Office Fax: 615-322-8990. Business E-Mail: sam.chang@vanderbilt.edu.

CHANG, YENHUI, immunogeneticist, director; arrived in US, 1985; d. Zhen-xiang Zhang and Qing-guo Zhou; m. Chiang Chang; 1 child, Jeffrey. MD, Shandong Med. U., Jinan, China, 1977; PhD in Molecular Biology, U. Edinburg, 1984. Cert. lab.dir. Fla. State, 1993, D. Abhi Am. Bd. Histocompatibility & Immunogenetics, 1998; lab. dir. NY State, 2003. Postdoc. fellow Columbia U., NYC, 1988—90; rsch. assoc. U. Toronto, Canada, 1990—92; bone marrow transplantation lab. dir. All Children's Hosp., St. Petersburg, 1993—2005, histocompatibility lab. dir., 2005—. Lab. dir. Medigen Biotech., Taipei, Taiwan, 2007—, HealthBanks Biotech., Taipei, 2011—12. Mem.: Clin. Immunology Soc., Am. Soc. Histocompatibility & Immunogenetics. Achievements include research in post-transplant cell lineage chimerism, bone marrow transplantation in lupus mice and discovery of new HLA alleles, DNA fragment exchange between phage and bacterial chromosome; diagnostic assessment of primary immunodefciency through genomic testing(NGS). Office: All Children's Hosp Pathology and Lab Medicine 501 6th Ave South Saint Petersburg FL 33701 Office Fax: 727-767-8367.*

CHANG-DIAZ, FRANKLIN R., astronaut; b. San José, Costa Rica, Apr. 5, 1950; s. Ramón A. Chang-Morales and Maria Eugenia Diaz De Chang; m. Peggy Marguerite Doncaster; 4 children. BSc in Mech. Engring., U. Conn., 1973; PhD in Applied Plasma Physics, MIT, 1977; PhD (hon.), U. National de Costa Rica; DSc (hon.), U. Santiago de Chile, U. Conn.; LLD (hon.), Babson Coll. Mem. technical staff Charles Stark Draper Lab. MIT, Mass., 1978—81; astronaut NASA, Houston, 1981—; founder Ad Astra Rocket Co., 2005, chmn., CEO. Vis. scientist plasma fusion ctr. MIT, Mass., 1983—93; adj. prof. physics Rice U., Houston, U. Houston, Houston; dir. advanced space propulsion lab. Johnson Space Ctr. NASA, Houston, 1993—2005; presenter in field; founder Astronaut Sci. Colloquium Program, 1987—; founder, dir. Astronaut Sci. Support Group, 1987—89; astronaut Space Shuttle Columbia, 1986, Space Shuttle Atlantis, 1989, 1992, Wake Shield Facility, Space Habitation Module 2, 1994, U.S. Microgravity Payload, 1996, Discovery Mission, 1998. Recipient Liberty medal, Pres. Ronald Reagan, 1986, Congl. Hispanic Caucus, 1987, Cross of Venezuelan AF, Pres. Jaime Lusinchi, 1988, Flight Achievement award, Am. Astronautical Soc., 1989, Wyld Propulsion award, AIAA, 2002, Exceptional Svc. medal, 1988, 1990, 1993, Disting. Svc. medals, 1995, 1997, Space Flight medals, NASA, 1986, 1989, 1992, 1994, Medal of Excellence; named Hon. Citizen, Govt. Costa Rica, 1995. Achievements include patents in field. Avocations: music, glider planes, soccer, scuba diving, hiking. Office: Astronaut Office CB NASA Johnson Space Center Houston TX 77058 also: Ad Astra Rocket Co 141 W Bay Area Blvd Webster TX 77598 Office Phone: 281-526-0500. Office Fax: 281-526-0599. Business E-Mail: franklin@adastrarocket.com.

CHANNELL, R. MICKEY, state legislator; b. Sept. 9, 1942; m. Carolyn DeVane; children: Sara Lynn, Laura, Mel, Carrie. Former state rep. Dist. 77, Ga.; former state rep. Dist. 116 Ga., 2004—; owner Channell Super Value, 1963—72; mem. Greene County Commn., 1972—80, Sch. Bd., 1980—92; organizer County Youth Baseball Program, First United Meth., 1982; chmn. Ga. Nonpub. Post Secondary Edn. Commn., 1992; state rep. Dist. 111 Ga., 1992—2002; house rep. Ga.; sec. Transp. Com.; mem.; Intra Govt. coord. Ways & Means & Appropriations Coms.; founder Corner Pantry Food Mart, Channell Enterprises & Factory Direct Homes Ga.; businessman, investor. Mem.: Greensboro C. of C. (pres. 1966—67), Green County Rotary Club (founding mem.). Democrat. Methodist. Address: 2811 Hwy 15 S Greensboro GA 30642 Mailing: 409 Legis Off Bldg Atlanta GA 30334-2823 Office Phone: 404-656-0213, 706-453-1230. Fax: 706-342-1902.

CHAO, ALBERT, chemicals executive; B, Brandeis U., Waltham, Mass.; MBA, Columbia U., NYC. Dep. mng. dir. plastics fabrication bus., Singapore; asst. to chmn. China Gen. Plastics Group; with plastics group Gulf Oil Corp.; with tech. dept. Hercules Inc.; with contr.'s group Mobil Oil Corp.; co-founder Westlake Chem. Corp., 1985, exec. v.p., 1985—96, pres., 1996—2004; bd. dirs. Westlake Chemical Corp., 2003—, pres., CEO, 2004—. Bd. dirs. Titan Group. Office: Westlake Chem Corp 2801 Post Oak Blvd Ste 600 Houston TX 77056 Office Phone: 713-960-9111.

CHAO, JAMES, chemicals executive; s. T. T. Chao. BS, MIT; MBA, Columbia U. Various fin., mgmt. and tech. positions Mattel, Inc., Devel. Bank of Singapore, Singapore Gulf Plastics Pte. Ltd., Gulf Oil Corp.; spl. asst. to chmn. China Gen. Plastics Group; pres. Westlake Chemical Corp., 1985—96, vice chmn., 1996—2004, chmn., 2004—; mng. dir. Titan Chemicals Corp. Bhd., Malaysia, chmn., 2003. Bd. dirs. Westlake Chem. Corp., 2003—. Office: Westlake Chemical Corp Ste 600 2801 Post Oak Blvd Houston TX 77056 Office Phone: 713-960-9111. Office Fax: 713-963-1590. Business E-Mail: JChao@westlake.com.*

CHAPIN, LLOYD WALTER, academic administrator; b. Atlanta, Jan. 7, 1937; s. Lloyd Walter and Carolina (McCall) C.; m. Louise Williams, June 21, 1958; children: Laura, Caroline, Lloyd, Anne. BA cum laude, Davidson Coll., 1958; MDiv cum laude, N.Y., 1961; PhD, Union Theol. Sem., NYC, 1967; LHD, Eckerd Coll., 2010. Ordained to ministry Meth. Ch., 1961. Asst. prof. Philosophy & Religion Colgate U., Hamilton, N.Y., 1965-70, asst. dean of faculty, 1968-70; assoc. dean Emory U., Atlanta, 1970—79; v.p., dean of faculty, prof. philosophy and religion Eckerd Coll., St. Petersburg, Fla., 1979—2010. Bd. dirs. Presbyn. Counseling Ctr., St. Petersburg, Fla., 1986-93. Editor symposium proceedings Future of Church Related Coll., 1986; contbr. articles to profl. jours. Pres. Sch. PTA, Atlanta, 1974; trustee St. Paul Sch., 1992-96, Canterbury Sch., 2005-11; bd. dirs. Fla. Humanities Coun., 1993-2000. Recipient Rockefeller and Kent fellow, 1962-65; U.S. Dept. Edn. grantee Eckerd Coll., 1983, Ford Found., 1986, 91, 2008, Knight Found., 1989, Coun. for the Advancement of Pvt. Higher Edn., 1989, Nat. Endowment for the Humanities, 1989, 91, 98, 2010, Howard Hughes Med. Inst., 1991. Mem. Am. Conference of Acad. Deans (bd. dirs.), Soc. for Values in Higher Edn., Omicron Delta Kappa, Phi Beta Kappa. Democrat. Avocations: reading, classical music. Home: 4737 Dolphin Cay Ln S Apt 207 Saint Petersburg FL 33711-4671

CHAPLIN, HARVEY R., wine and liquor wholesale executive; b. Bklyn., 1929; Chmn., CEO So. Wine Spirits of Am., Miami, 1994—. Named to Sky Ranch Found. Hall of Fame, 2006. Office: Southern Wine & Spirits 1600 NW 163rd St Miami FL 33169-5672

CHAPMAN, BETH KILLOUGH, political consultant, former state official; b. Greenville, Ala., Apr. 6, 1962; m. James Chapman, 1988 (dec. Apr. 4, 2011); children: Winston Taylor, William Thatcher. BS, U. Montevallo, Ala., 1984; MS magna cum laude, U. Ala., Birmingham. Dir. spl. events Cystic Fibrosis Found.; appointments sec. to Gov. Fob James State of Ala., Montgomery, 1995—96, press sec. to Gov. Steve Windom, 2000—01, state auditor, 2003—07, sec. of state, 2007—13; founder Beth Chapman & Associates, LLC, 1996; political cons. Ala. Farmers Fedn., Montgomery, 2013—. Author: The Power of Patriotism: The Speech Heard Around the World, 2003 (Freedoms Found. George Washington Honor Medal). Mem. Shelby County Child Advocacy Ctr., Shelby County Ct. Appointed Spl. Advocates Prog.; George W. Bush del. Republican Nat. Conv., 2000, 2004; mem. Republican Women's Leadership Coun., Lakeside Baptist Ch., Ala. Electoral Coll., 2004—. Republican. Baptist. Office: Alabama Farmers Fedn PO Box 11000 Montgomery AL 36191 Office Phone: 334-288-3900.*

CHAPMAN, DANIEL P., epidemiologist; b. St. Paul, Mar. 16, 1958; s. James and Joan Chapman. MA, PhD, U. Iowa, 1988. Postdoctoral fellow U. Iowa Coll. of Medicine dept. Psychiatry & Preventive Medicine, Iowa City, 1988—92; psychiat. epidemiologist Ctrs. Disease Control and Prevention, Atlanta, 1992—. Past pres. Ga. Assn. Physicians for Human Rights, Atlanta, 1998—2010. Mem.: Phi Beta Kappa. Republican. Mem. United Ch. Of Christ. Avocation: movies.*

CHAPMAN, GILBERT WHIPPLE, JR., publishing executive; b. NYC, July 1, 1933; s. Gilbert W. and Katherin (Bright) C.; m. Judith Coste, June 14, 1956; 1 child, Gilbert W. III BA, Yale U., 1956. Pub. McGraw-Hill, Inc., N.Y.C., 1958-72; exec. v.p., dir. Morgan Grampain, Inc., NYC, 1971-75; pres. Pub. Group Esquire Inc., NYC, 1975-78; pres., dir. Diversion Communications, Inc., NYC, 1978-85, Kalo Communications, Inc., NYC, 1985-91; chmn., CEO Cemark, Inc., 1991—. Trustee Village of Mill Neck, 1993—2000, Choate Sch., Wallingford, Conn., 1986—91, Pomfret Sch., 1980—86; bd. dirs. Planned Parenthood of Nassau County, 1985—2002, Planned Parenthood of Nassau County Found., 2000—11, Cmty. Hosp. of Glen Cove, 1986—90, North Shore U. Hosp., 1990—94. Mem.: Piping Rock Club (pres. 2000—06), Racquet and Tennis Club. Republican. Episcopalian. Home: 121 Factory Pond Rd Locust Valley NY 11560-1405 Office: 13531 E Boundary Rd Midlothian VA 23112-3953 Office Phone: 516-676-0277.

CHAPMAN, MARTHA CLOUD, bank executive; Grad. in Art, U. N.C., Greensboro, 1942. Bd. dirs. First Nat. Bancshares Inc. Former bd. dirs. Boys and Girls Home, Charles Lea Center Found.; chairperson Gov. Jim Edward's Inaugural Ball; former bd. dirs. Music Found., Queens Coll., Spartanburg County Found., Spartanburg Methodist Coll., The SC Devel. Bd., The SC Mining Council, YMCA, Walker Found. Office: First National Bancshares Inc Bd Directors 215 N Pine St Spartanburg SC 29302 Office Phone: 864-948-9001. Office Fax: 864-281-0830. Business E-Mail: mchapman@ebankfirstnational.com.

CHAPMAN, N. A., telecommunications industry executive; Pres. ExxonMobil Upstream Tech. Computing Co. (subs. Exxon Mobil Corp.), ExxonMobil Global Services Co. (subs. of ExxonMobil Corp.), 2009—. Office: Exxonmobil Global Services Co 3030 Irving Blvd Dallas TX 75247-6213 Office Phone: 214-951-2000. Business E-Mail: n.chapman@exxonmobil.com.

CHAPMAN, RICHARD E., healthcare services company executive; V.p. info. sys. Galen Healthcare and Humana, Inc.; sr. v.p., info. svcs. Columbia/HCA Healthcare Corp., 1993-97; chief info. officer, sr. v.p. Vencor, Inc., 1997—98; sr. v.p. Kindred Healthcare, Inc., 1998—2005, chief info. officer, 1998—, chief adminstrv. officer, 2001—, exec. v.p., 2005—. Ranked one of top ten chief info. officers in nation by PC Weekly, 1997. Office: Kindred Healthcare Inc 680 S 4th St Louisville KY 40202-2412 Office Fax: 502-596-4170. Business E-Mail: richard.chapman@kindredhealthcare.com.

CHAPMAN, ROBERT FOSTER, federal judge; b. Inman, SC, Apr. 24, 1926; s. James Alfred and Martha (Marshall) Chapman; m. Mary Winston Gwathmey, Dec. 21, 1951 (dec. Sept. 1998); children: Edward, Foster, Winston; m. Mary Vail St. Georges, Sept. 30, 2000. BS, U. SC, 1945, LLB, 1949, LLD (hon.), 1986, Coll. Charleston, 1999. Bar: S.C. 1949. Assoc. firm Butler & Moore, Spartanburg, 1949—51; partner firm Butler, Chapman & Morgan, Spartanburg, 1953—71; judge US Dist. Ct. S.C., 1971—81, US Ct. Appeals (4th Cir.), 1981—91, sr. judge, 1991—. Chmn. S.C. Rep. Party, 1961—63. Ensign USNR, 1943—46, lt. USNR, 1951—53. Recipient Nat. Patriot's award, Congl. Medal of Honor Soc., 1985. Fellow: Am. Coll. Trial Lawyers; mem.: Order of Palmetto. Presbyterian.

CHAPMAN-BANKS, IAN F., computer company executive; BSc in Applied Sci. & Computer Studies, Sheffield Hallam U., UK, 1984; MBA in Strategy, Economics & Fin., U. Chgo., 2002. Dir., sales & mktg. Xerox Corp., 1989—98; regional mktg. dir., Asia Pacific Apple Computer, Inc., 1998—2002; consumer mktg. dir., Asia Microsoft Corp., 2002—04, mktg. dir. Asia/Pacific home and entertainment divsn. Hong Kong, 2002—05; gen. mgr., mktg. & bus. devel., Motorola Mobile Devices, North Asia, corp. v.p. Motorola, Inc., 2005—09; sr. v.p., world wide sales, mktg. & bus. ops. Chartered Semiconductor, 2009—10; gen. mgr., Asia Pacific Dell, Inc., 2010—. Mem. Motorola WW Mktg. Coun. Office: Dell Inc 1 Dell Way Round Rock TX 78682-2222 Office Phone: 512-338-4400. Office Fax: 512-283-6161. Business E-Mail: ian_chapman-banks@dell.com.

CHAPPEL, DONALD R., petroleum pipeline company executive; b. Oct. 19, 1951; m. Erin Chappel. Grad., U. Ill. CPA, Ill. With Arthur Andersen & Co., Chgo., 1973—82, Beatrice Cos., Inc./Esmark, Inc., 1982—87, dir. N.Am. ops. analysis, dir. fin./ops. analysis and audit; joined Waste Management, Inc., 1987, v.p., contr. chem. waste mgmt. divsn., v.p., contr. West and Mountain groups, v.p., contr. N.Am. solid waste ops., 1995-97, v.p., acting CFO, 1997-2000; sr. v.p., CFO Williams Companies, Inc., Tulsa, 2003—. Office: One Williams Ctr Tulsa OK 74172

CHAPPELL, FRED DAVIS, language educator, poet; b. Canton, NC, May 28, 1936; s. James Taylor and Anne Mae (Davis) C.; m. Susan Nicholls, Aug. 2, 1959; 1 son, Christopher Heath. BA, Duke U., 1961, MA, 1964; LittD, U. NC, Asheville, 1989, Spring Hill Coll., 1991, LittD, 2008. Prof. English U. NC, Greensboro, 1964—2004, emeritus prof. English, 2004—. Adv. editor Skyhook, 1958-59, Red Clay Reader, 1964-65, Greensboro Rev., 1964—, Ga. Rev., 1990—. Author: It Is Time, Lord, 1963, The Inkling, 1965, Dagon, 1968, The World Between the Eyes, 1971, The Gaudy Place, 1972, Midquest, 1981, Moments of Light, 1982, Castle Tzingal, 1984, I Am One of You Forever, 1985, Source, 1985, The Fred Chappell Reader, 1988, First and Last Words, 1989, Brighten the Corner Where You Are, 1989, More Shapes Than One, 1992, C, 1993, Plow Naked, 1993, Spring Garden: New and Selected Poems, 1995, Farewell, I'm Bound To Leave You, 1996, A Way of Happening, 1998, Look Back All the Green Valley, 1999, Family Gathering, 2000, Backsass, 2004, Shadow Box, 2009, Ancestors And Others, 2009. Recipient Roanoke-Chowan Poetry prize, NC Lit. Assn., 1979, Prix de Meilleur des Lettres Etrangers, 1973, NC award in lit., State of NC, 1987, Bollingen prize for poetry, 1985, World Fantasy award, World Fantasy Assn., 1992, 1994, T.S. Eliot prize, Ingersoll Found., 1993, Aiken Taylor Poetry award, 1996, Irene Lenore Heasley prize, 1999, SEBA Novel award, 2000, Eminescu medal for poetry, 2001, Appalachian Heritage Writers award, 2004, Thomas Wolfe award, 2005, Caroliniana award, 2007; named NC Poet Laureate, 1997—2002, John Tyler Caldwell award, 2010; named to NC Lit. Hall of Fame, 2006; grantee Nat. Acad. Arts and Letters, 1968; NDEA fellow, 1961—63, Rockefeller grantee, 1967—68. Mem.: Order of the Longleaf Pine. Democrat. Avocations: books, wine. Home Phone: 336-275-8851.

CHAPPELL, MILES LINWOOD, JR., art historian, educator; b. Norfolk, Va., June 6, 1939; s. Miles Linwood Sr. and Melrose Clarice (Debnam) C.; m. Marcial Cassada, July 23, 1966; children: Ashley, Oliver, Picot. BS in Chemistry, Coll. William and Mary, 1960; PhD in Art History, U. N.C., 1971. Prof. art history Coll. William and Mary, Williamsburg, Va., 1971—2005, chair dept., Chancellor prof. art history, 1987, prof. emeritus, 2005—; elected to Accademia delle Arti del Disegno Florence, Italy, 2006. Mem. artistic adv. bd. Interlochen Ctr. for Arts. Author: Cristofano Allori, 1984, Lodovico Cigoli, Disegni, 1992, The Fine Art of Drawing, 1993; co-author: Disegni dei Toscani, 1979, Lodovico Cigoli, tra manierismo e barocco, 1992, Author: Renascence of the Florentine Baroque in "Dialoghi di storia dell'arte", 1998, The Artistic Education of Maria de'Medici, 2003, Cigoli's Treatise on Perspective in The Perspective Treatise, 2002; contbg. author: The Medici. Michelangelo and Late Renaissance Art, 2002; Colorire Nat. e Vero-Figline, Cigoli e I Suoi amici, 2008; Il Cannochiale e il Pennello= Galileo e le anti, 2009; formulator and co-author: Form, Function and Finesse: Drawings from the Herman Found., 1983; co-editor L'Arte, Collezionismo, Conservazione: scritti in onore di Marco Chiarini, 2004; asst. editor: Studies in Iconography, 1978-80; mem. adv. bd. Eighteenth-Century Life, 1980-84, 85—; contbr. more than 100 articles on Renaissance and Baroque art to profl. jours. Mem. internat. survey of Jewish monuments, U. Ill., 1978. Harvard U. Ctr. for Italian Renaissance Studies fellow, Florence, 1980; Cité Internat. des Arts, 1995; recipient numerous rsch. grants. Mem. Kunsthistorisches Institut Florence, Phi Beta Kappa (Alpha chpt. award for scholarship 1987, v.p. 1992-93, 2003-05, Thomas Ashley Graves, Jr. award for excellence in tchg. 2005). Avocations: drawing, painting, music. Home: 139 Ridings Cv Williamsburg VA 23185-3903 Office: Coll William and Mary Dept Art History Williamsburg VA 23187 Office Phone: 757-220-1433. E-mail: mlchap@wm.edu.

CHAPPELL, SHERI POLSTER, federal judge; b. Sheboygan, Wis., May 30, 1962; Attended, U. Wis.-Eau Claire, 1980—82; BA, U. Wis.-Madison, 1984; JD, Nova Southeastern U. Law Sch., 1987. Asst. state atty. Fla. 20th Judicial Cir., 1987—2000, cir. ct. judge, 2000—03; magistrate judge US Dist. Ct. (middle dist.) Fla., Ft. Myers, Fla., 2003—13, judge, 2013—. Mem.: Lee County Bar Assn., Fed. Bar Assn. Office: US District Court 2110 First St Fort Myers FL 33901 Office Phone: 239-461-2060. Office Fax: 239-461-2139.*

CHARAF, ANTHONY N., air transportation executive; BS in Engring, magna cum laude, Northrop U., LA, MS in Mgmt. Project engr. Pacific Airmotive Corp., Burbank, Calif., 1977; various positions Aviall, Inc., Dallas, 1979—89, v.p. ops. Ryder Airline Svcs. (subs.), 1989—93; v.p., gen. mgr. Pacific Airmotive, then v.p. internat. mktg. UNC, Inc., 1993—96; dir. power plant maintenance Delta Air Lines, Inc., 1996—97, mng. dir. power plant maintenance, 1997—98, v.p. power plant maintenance, 1998—2000, sr. v.p. Delta Air Logistics, 2000—04, sr. v.p. Delta TechOps divsn., 2004—05, pres. TechOps, 2008—. Office: Delta Air Lines Inc PO Box 20706 Atlanta GA 30320-6001 Office Phone: 404-715-2600. Office Fax: 404-715-5042. E-mail: tony.charaf@delta.com.

CHARANIA, BARKAT, real estate consultant; b. Ahmedabad, Gujrat, India, June 27, 1941; came to U.S., 1961; s. Ismail and Zenabai Charania; m. Jerilyn Lee Scott, Apr. 10, 1962 (div. May 1970); children: Sultana, Ramzan, Kalvin, Kevin, Stephen; m. Maher Kurani, Oct. 11, 1970; children: Munira, Rahim, Munira Moon. Student, Alpena CC, Mich., 1961-62, U. Calif., LA, 1962-63, U. Pa., 1965-68, Lincoln Tech. Sch., 1983. Cert. comml. investment mem.; cert. hotel adminstr. Pres. Eurindus, Inc., Cherry Hill, NJ, 1965-83, Airline Inn, Inc., Atlanta, 1980-83; owner B.C. Investments & Realty Co., Atlanta, 1985—; pres. Southern Inn, Inc., Chattanooga, 1987—; owner B.C. Hospitality Mgmt. Co., Atlanta, 1987—; pres. Trident Devel. Corp., Charleston, SC, 1989—, BJM Hospitality, Inc., 1993—, ICI Long Distance Inc., 1995—, Universal Connect Corp., 1995—; CEO CRM Ventures, LLC, 1997—, RBM Properties, LLC, 2000—10; sr. assocs. Marcus & Millichap, Atlanta, 1996-97; CEO Charania Bros., LLC, 1999—, 786 Investments, LLC, 2003—09, Small Axe, Inc., 2003—07; ptnr., CEO CQ Capital, 2005—10; CEO Creative Capital Inc., 2004—10, CQ Capital Ptnrs., 2006—10, CQ Constrns. LLC, 2006—10, Camp Geek Villas, LLC, 2007—, Charania Hospitality Group, 2007—, Charania Group Cos., 2007—; chmn. Am. Fueling Sys., 2011—. Cons. Pattni Holdings, Atlanta, 1984—, Esmail Internat., Inc., Atlanta, 1986—, Harbour Enterprise, Chattanooga, 1987—, Shin Inc., Chattanooga, 1987—, ABC Inc., Chattanooga, 1988—; CEO Charania Hospitality Group, 2007-, Charania Group Co., 2007-. Ga. coord. Agakhan Found. U.S.A., Atlanta, 1988; chmn. Southeastern Enterprising People's Assn., 1990, 91. Mem. Atlanta Bd. Realtors, Nat. Assn. Realtors, Realtor Nat. Mktg. Inst., Comml. Investment Real Estate Coun., Edn. Inst., Internat. Real Estate Inst., Ismaili Commerce Club (v.p. Atlanta chpt. 1982), S.E. Region (chmn. Agakhan econ. planning bd. for U.S.A.), Internat. Real Estate Fedn. Republican. Avocations: reading, travel, swimming, tennis. Home: 5855 Hershinger Close Duluth GA 30097-6433 Office: CGC Global 1 Glenlake Pky Ste 700 Atlanta GA 30328 Office Phone: 404-499-2247, 404-275-9514. Business E-Mail: bc@bcirealty.com.

CHARANJIVA, LAKSHMAN, electric power industry executive; Grad. in Sr. Exec. Program, U. Va.; MBA in Fin., Tulane U. chartered acct., Inst. of Chartered Accountants, India. Sr. positions Arthur Andersen, Mumbai, India; sr. mgr., mgr. and sr. cons. Cap Gemini Ernst and Young; v.p. Ernst and Young Consulting (acquired by Capgemini); v.p., ERP Packages Capgemini, NY; v.p., global bus. solutions AES Corp., chief info. officer, v.p., global bus. tech. solutions Washington; v.p., chief info. officer Fla. Power and Light Co. (subs. NextEra Energy Inc.). Mgmt. cons. World Bank Group; charter mem. TiE-DC. Office: Florida Power & Light Co 700 Universe Blvd Juno Beach FL 33408 Office Phone: 561-694-4000. Business E-Mail: lakshman_charanjiva@fpl.com.

CHARDON, MARC D'ESTOURNELLES, software company executive; b. Concord, NH, Nov. 1, 1955; s. Alain Jean and Phoebe Warren (Ashley) C.; m. Sallie Garrett Shepherd, May 24, 1986; 1 child, Robert d'Estournelles. BA magna cum laude, Harvard U., 1976. Secretaire-generale Groupe Dumay, Geneva, 1977—82; prin. Chardon Energy Sys., Westport, Mass., 1982—83; joined Digital France, 1984, gen. mgr.; gen. mgr., fin. Microsoft Corp., 1998, CFO, info. bus. worker, 2003—05; pres., CEO Blackbaud, Inc., 2005—. Bd. dirs. Blackbaud, Inc. Office: Blackbaud Inc 2000 Daniel Island Dr Charleston SC 29492-7541 Office Phone: 843-216-6200. Office Fax: 843-216-6100. Business E-Mail: marc.chardon@blackbaud.com.

CHARI, RAVI S., surgeon; s. Ranga S. and Rajiswari B. Chari; m. Sharon Elizabeth Albers, Mar. 20, 1993; children: Tristan Albers, Danielle Jean. MD, U. of Saskatoon, 1989. Asst. prof. of surgery and cell biology U. Mass med. Ctr., Worcester, 1998—2001; prof. of surgery and cancer biology Vanderbilt U. Med. Ctr., Nashville, 2001—. Mem. sci. com. Internat. Hepato-Pancreaitoc-Biliary Assn., Germany, 2004—06; sec. Soc. of U. Surgeons, Winter Park, Fla., 2006—; counselor Am. Hepato-Pancreatico-Biliary Assn., Winter Park, Fla., 2006—. Grant, NIH, 2005—. Fellow: ACS (ACS Faculty Fellowship award 1999—2001). Office: Vanderbilt Univ 1313 21st Avenue South Nashville TN 37232-4753 Business E-Mail: ravi.chari@vanderbilt.edu.

CHARITY, LINDA B., state banking agency administrator; B, U. Fla., Gainesville; MBA in Fin., Fla. State U., Tallahassee. Bank examiner Fla. Office Fin. Regulation (formerly Dept. Banking and Fin.), West Palm Beach, chief bur. rsch., planning, and staff devel. Tallahassee, dep. dir. fin. instns., chief bur. fin. instns., 2000—03, dir. divsn. fin. instns., 2003—, acting commr., 2009, 2012—. Office: Fla Office Fin Regulation 200 E Gaines St Tallahassee FL 32399-0371 Office Phone: 850-410-9800. Office Fax: 850-410-9548. E-mail: linda.charity@flofr.com.

CHARLESWORTH, ARTHUR THOMAS, mathematics professor; b. Gainesville, Fla., Nov. 8, 1944; s. Arthur Riggs and Martha Jean (Hamilton) C.; m. Josephine Ann Owenby, Sept. 10, 1966; 1 child, Jonathan David. BS in Math., Stetson U., 1966; AM in Math., Duke U., 1968, PhD in Math., 1974; MS in Computer Sci., U. Va., 1983. Trajectory analysis engr. Apollo support dept. GE, Daytona Bch., Fla., 1966-67; instr. Jacksonville (Fla.) U., 1968-69, Randolph-Macon Coll., Ashland, Va., 1969-71; asst. prof. Queens Coll., Charlotte, NC, 1974-76, U. Richmond, Va., 1976-82, assoc. prof. Va., 1982-89, prof. Va., 1989—. Sec. astronomy, math., physics sect. Va. Acad. Sci., 1977-78, chmn., 1978-79; treas. Md., D.C., Va. sect. Math. Assn. Am., 1980-82. Contbr. articles to maj. computer sci. jours. Chmn. Trinity Meth. Comsn. on Missions, Richmond, 1981. Research grantee NASA Langley Rsch. Ctr., Hampton, Va., 1987, 88, 89, 90, 91, 92. Mem. IEEE, Assn. Computing Machinery (sr.), Omicron Delta Kappa, Sigma Xi. Avocations: hiking, rock collecting. Office: U Richmond Dept Math/Computer Sci Richmond VA 23173 Business E-Mail: charlesworth@richmond.edu.

CHARLIP, RALPH BLAIR, military officer, health facility administrator; b. Detroit, July 16, 1952; s. Jack Edward and Dorothea (Steinman) Charlip; m. Cynthia Lanell Sallas, May 23, 1987. BA, U. Ariz., 1976, MPA, 1977. Commd. 2nd lt. USAF, 1978, advanced through grades to lt. col., 1994; squadron comdr. USAF Regional Hosp., Langley AFB, Va., 1978-79, dir. patient adminstrn., 1979-80, plant mgr., 1980-81; dir. med. resource mgmt. USAF Clinic Andersen, Andersen AFB, Guam, 1981-82; dir. patient adminstrn. Malcolm Grow USAF Med. Ctr., Andrews AFB, Md., 1983-84; intern Data Systems Design Ctr., Gunter AFB, Ala., 1984-85; health policy devel. officer USAF Hdqs., Bolling AFB, DC, 1985-89; dir. patient adminstrn. USAF Med. Ctr., Wright-Patterson AFB, Ohio, 1989-92; assoc. dir. med. svcs. Air Nat. Guard Hqrs., Andrews AFB, 1992-94; dir. plans integration and mktg. Dept. Def. Health Svcs. Region VII, Ft. Bliss, Tex., 1994-96; comdr. 423 Clinic, Upwood, England, 1996-97; adminstr. aerospace med. Armstrong Lab., Brooks AFB, Tex., 1997; dep. comdr. 59 Med. Support Group, Lackland AFB, Tex., 1997-99; assoc. adminstr. 59 Med. Wing, Lackland AFB, 1999-2000; dir. health adminstrn. ctr. VA, Denver, 2000—07; chief, Emergency SVCS VHA V19, 2008—10; dep. adminstr. mgmt, food and nutrition svc. US Dept. Agr., 2008—10; assoc. dir. Human Capital USGS, 2010—11; program exec. human resources strategic initiatives US Dept. Interior, 2011—. Chair U.S. Air Force Med. Svc. Corps. Career Devel. Com., 1995—2000; adj. faculty U. Md., St. Leo Coll., Air Nat. Guard Quality Ctr., Met. State Coll., Denver, Denver Fed. Exec. Bd., 2000—07; mem. Civil Air Patrol Nat. Health Svc. Group, 2005—06. Author: (book) Your Health Benefits, 1989; contbr. chapters to books; co-author (with Brig Gen Nancy R. Adams): Tricare Region 7 Prepares For Delivery of Services, 1996; co-author: (with Major David Estill, Capt Gretchen Lizza) Nightingale House: Home Away from Home, 1990. Recipient Ray Brown award, AMSUS, 2004. Fellow: Am. Acad. Med. Adminstrs. (state chairperson 2005—07), Am. Coll. Healthcare Execs. (regent's adv. coun. 1994—2008, credentials com. 1999, awards com. 2004—05, editl. bd. 2005—08); mem.: Air Force Assn., Air Force Med. Svc. Corps. Assn. (sec., v.p., pres.). Home: 2333 Dulles Station Blvd Herndon VA 20171

CHARNOVITZ, STEVE, law educator; b. Savannah, Ga., Sept. 15, 1953; s. Edward and Minnie H. Charnovitz. BA, Yale U., New Haven, 1975; MA of Pub. Policy, Kennedy Sch. Govt., Harvard U., 1983; JD, Yale Law Sch., 1998. Bar: NY, DC. Policy analyst, internat. rels. officer US Dept. Labor, Washington, 1975—86; legis. asst. to spkr. of House US House of Representatives, Washington, 1987—91; policy dir. Competitiveness Policy Coun., Washington, 1991—95; dir. Global Environment & Trade Study (GETS), Yale U., 1995—99; atty. Wilmer Cutler Pickering Hale & Dorr LLP, Washington, 1998—2004; assoc. prof. George Washington U. Law Sch., 2004—. Author: Trade Law & Global Governance, 2002; co-author: Global Warming and the World Trading System, 2009; co-editor: Law in the Service of Human Dignity, 2005; mem. editl. bd. Jour. Internat. Econ. Law, Jour. Environment & Devel., World Trade Rev.; contbr. articles to profl. jours., chapters to books. American Polit. Sci. Assn. Congl. fellow, 1984—85. Mem.: American Law Inst., Coun. Fgn. Rels., American Soc. Internat. Law, Cosmos Club. Office: George Washington U Law School 2000 H St NW Washington DC 20052 Office Phone: 202-350-9444. Office Fax: 202-706-6076. Business E-Mail: scharnovitz@law.gwu.edu.

CHASEN, JERRY SIMON, lawyer; BA summa cum laude, Tufts U., 1973; JD cum laude, NYU, 1976; LLM in Estate Planning, U. Miami Law Sch., 1994. Bar: NY 1976, Fla. 1977, N.Mex. 1987, Calif. 1988. Law clk. to Hon. Edward Weinfeld US Dist. Ct. (so. dist. NY), 1977—78; ptnr. Chasen & Assocs., P.A., Miami, Fla. Contbr. articles to profl. publs. Mem. friends bd. Bass Mus. Art, 2003—; chair gay and lesbian cmty. project fun adv. com. Dade Cmty. Found., 2005—; mem. steering com. Greater Miami Leave a Legacy Campaign; vice chair bd. dirs. Mus. Contemporary Art, North Miami, Fla., 1995—99; nat. bd. dirs. Lambda Legal Def. & Edn. Fund, 1998—2002. Named one of Top 100 Attys., Worth mag., 2005—06. Mem.: Planned Giving Coun. Miami-Dade County (past pres. bd. dirs. 1995—). Office: Chasen & Associates PA Apt 3809 900 Biscayne Blvd Miami FL 33132-1570 Office Phone: 305-377-0718. Office Fax: 305-377-1427. E-mail: jchasen@chasenlaw.com.

CHASSANIOL, LYDIA GRAVES, state legislator; b. Dec. 29, 1950; Mem. Dist. 14 Miss. House of Reps., 2007—, chair tourism com., mem. agr. com., appropriations com., corrections com., drug policy com., fees, salaries and adminstrn. com., investigate state offices com. Republican. Methodist. Mailing: PO Box 211 Winona MS 38967 Office Phone: 601-359-3226. Office Fax: 601-359-3938. E-mail: lchassaniol@senate.ms.gov.

CHASTEEN, JOHN CHARLES, history professor; b. Chapel Hill, NC, Dec. 12, 1955; s. Robert J. and Nina Chasteen; m. Carmen Torres, Nov. 30, 1979; children: Ana Ackerman, Erwin. PhD, U. NC, Chapel Hill, 1988. Asst. prof. Bates Coll., Lewiston, Maine, 1988—90; prof. U. NC, 1990—. Author: Both in Blood and Fire: A Concise History of Latin America; translator: The Lettered City (MLA Scaglione prize). Mem.: Latin Am. Studies Assn., Am. Hist. Assn. Office Fax: 919-962-1403. Business E-Mail: chasteen@unc.edu.

CHATARD, PETER RALPH NOEL, JR., retired plastic surgeon; b. New Orleans, June 25, 1936; s. Peter Ralph Sr. and Alberta Chatard; m. Patricia Myrl White, Jan. 31, 1963; children: Andrea Michelle, Faedra Noelle, Tahra Deonne. BS in Biology, Morehouse Coll., 1956; MD, U. Rochester, 1960. Diplomate Am. Bd. Plastic Surgery, Am. Bd. Otolaryngology. Intern Colo. Gen. Hosp., 1960-61; asst. resident in gen. surgery Highland Gen. Hosp., Rochester, NY, 1963-64; resident in otolaryngology Strong Meml. Hosp., Rochester, 1964-67; resident in plastic and reconstructive surgery U. Fla., 1980-82; staff otolaryngologist Group Health Corp. of Puget Sound, Seattle, 1967-68; practice medicine specializing in otolaryngology Seattle, 1968-80; practice medicine specializing in plastic surgery, 1982—; clin. asst. prof. otolaryngology, head and neck surgery U. Wash., Seattle, 1975—. Plastic surgery cons. western sec. Maxillofacial Rev. Bd. State of Wash., 1982-90, cons. Conservation of Hearing Program, 1968-80; trustee Physicians and Dentist Credit Bur., 1974-80, 84-87, pres. 1976-77, 84-85; active staff mem. Northwest Hosp., Seattle; courtesy staff Swedish Hosp., Overlake Hosp., Bellevue, Stevens Meml. Hosp., Edmond, Wash., Seattle, others. Capt. USAF, 1961-63. Fellow ACS, Am. Rhinologic Soc., Seattle Surg. Soc., Am. Acad. Facial Plastic and Reconstructive Surgery, Am. Acad. Otolaryngology-Head and Neck Surgery, Northwest Acad. Otolaryngology and Head and Neck Surgery, Soc. for Ear, Nose and Throat Advances in Children, Pacific Oto-Ophthalmological Soc.; mem. Am. Soc. Plastic Surgery, Am. Soc. for Aesthetic Plastic Surgery, Inc., Lipoplasty Soc. N. Am., Wash. Soc. Plastic Surgeons, Nat. Med. Assn., King County Med. Soc., Wash. State Med. Assn., N.W. Soc. of Plastic Surgeons. Avocations: photography, cynology, microcomputing, architecture. Home: 13211 Frazier Pl NW Seattle WA 98177-4132 Office: Peter Chatard 5002 Flagstone Dr Sarasota FL 34238-4439 Personal E-mail: chatard@aol.com.

CHATFIELD, MARY VAN ABSHOVEN, independent researcher; d. Cornelius and Elma Elizabeth (Sumner) van Abshoven; m. Robert W. Chatfield, June 22, 1963 (div. 1981); 1 child, Robert Warner Jr.; m. Alexander Watts, Jan. 6, 1996 (div. 2000). AB, Radcliffe Coll., 1958; SM, Columbia U., 1961; MBA, Harvard U., 1972. With library system Harvard U., Cambridge, Mass., 1961-92, librarian Bus. Sch., 1963-78, head libr., 1978-92; acting head libr. Countway Libr. Harvard Med. Sch., 1988-89; head libr. Angelo State U., San Angelo, Tex., 1992-95; collections care mgr. Fosterfields, Morristown, NJ, 1996-97; mgr. libr. svcs. Montclair (N.J.) Art Mus., 1997; exec. dir. Mendham (N.J.) Free Pub. Libr., 1997-99; coord. pub. and tech. svcs. Tom Green County Libr., San Angelo, Tex., 1999—2004; Concho Valley Master Gardener San Angelo Mus. Fine Arts, docent, rschr.; v.p., market rsch. Xerox Nano-coating Corp., 2005. Bd. dirs. Historic San Angelo, Friends Fairmount Cemetery. Democrat. Episcopalian. Avocations: reading, embroidery, collecting, museum studies, public art. Home: 115 N Jackson St San Angelo TX 76901-3215 Personal E-mail: marychat@suddenlink.net.

CHATTERJI, AARON (RONNIE CHATTERJI), economics professor; BA in Economics, Cornell U.; PhD, U. Calif., Berkeley. Assoc. prof. Faqua Sch. Bus. Duke U., Durham, NC, faculty affiliate Ctr. for Entrepreneurship and Innovation, faculty affiliate Ctr. for Energy, Devel. and Global Environment, advisor Program for Entrepreneurs. Sr. economist White House Coun. of Econ. Advisors (CEA), 2010—11. Contbr. Washington Times, Phila. Inquirer, Raleigh News & Observer; contbr. articles to profl. jours. Bd. mem. Durham Communities in Schools. Recipient Rising Star award, Aspen Inst.; grantee Jr. Faculty Fellowship, Kauffman Found.; fellow Ctr. for American Progress. Office: The Fuqua School of Business Duke University 100 Fuqua Dr, Box 90120 Durham NC 27708 Office Phone: 919-660-7903. E-mail: ronnie@duke.edu.

CHATTMAN, RAYMOND CHRISTOPHER, association executive; b. San Rafael, Calif., Apr. 11, 1956; s. Raymond Rene Chattman and Virginia Mae (Kirkland) Robinson; m. Patti Lyn Barnard Chattman, Feb. 14, 1975 (div. 1977); m. Dawn Irene Russell Kilpatrick, Aug. 21, 1993 (div. 1998); children: Christian Paige, Bradley Charles Kilpatrick. BS, Excelsior Coll., Albany, 1988; MBA, Averett Coll., Danville, Va., 1995. Dir. planning, ops. Comms. Media Group Inc., Alexandria, Va., 1981; comms. mgr. ANPA Found., Reston, Va., 1982-84; graphics editor Times-Herald Record, Middletown, NY, 1984-85; editor employee comms. Washington Gas Light Co., 1985-86; exec. dir., CEO Soc. Newspaper Design, Reston, 1986-96; dep. exec. dir. AIAA, Reston, 1996—2005; v.p. Am. Chiropractic Assn., Arlington, Va., 2005—06; mng. dir. Tagless Consulting Co., 2006—. Asst. coach Herndon Optimist Youth Football, Va., 1994, Herndon Youth Soccer, 1992. Served in US Army, 1974-81, Korea, Germany, USAR, 1981-90. Recipient Thomas Jefferson award Dept. Def., 1979, Keith L. Ware award Dept. Army, 1978, 83, 86, 87. Mem.: Am. Mgmt. Assn., Nat. Assn. Govt. Communicators (Blue Pencil award 1978), Am. Soc. Assn. Execs. (cert. assn. exec. 2005). Avocations: travel, reading, golf.

CHAU, PIN PIN, bank executive; b. Hong Kong; d. Waihing Wong; m. Raymond Chau; 1 child, Christine. Grad., Rutgers U.; BA magna cum laude, phi beta kappa, and phi kappa phi, Coe Coll., 1965; MA in Asian Hist., Yale U., 1967. With Nat. Westminster Bank (now Fleet), 1970—87; chief lending officer United Orient Bank, NYC, 1987—88, COO, 1988—89, pres., CEO, 1989—93, The Summit Nat. Bank (subs. Summit Bank Corp), 1993—2006; CEO Summit Bank Corp., Atlanta, 1999—; pres., CEO & bd. dirs. Trident Bancshares, Inc., 2008—; pres., CEO Touchmark Nat. Bank (subs. Touchmark Bancshares Inc.), 2010—, Touchmark Bancshares, Inc., 2010—. Bd. dirs. Consumer Credit Counseling Service, Turknett Leadership Group; exec. com. Ga. Dept. Industry, Trade and Tourism, 1999—; bd. dirs. UCBH Holdings Inc., 2007—08, United Comml. Bank (subs. UCBH Holdings Inc.), 2007—08. Bd. dirs. Atlanta Coll. Arts; bd. councilors Carter Ctr. Mem.: Internat. Women's Forum, Soc. Internat. Bus. Fellows (assoc.). Avocation: painting. Office: Touchmark Bancshares Inc 3651 Old Milton Pky Alpharetta GA 30005 Office Phone: 770-407-6700. Business E-Mail: pinpin.chau@touchmarknb.com.

CHAUVIN, KERRY J., energy executive; BS in Mech. Engring., La. State U., MBA. Mgr. new constrn., project mgr. Delta Shipyard, 1973—77; exec. v.p., gen. mgr., mgr. engring. Delta Fabrication, 1977—79, pres., 1979—84; COO Gulf Island Fabrication, Inc., 1989—90, pres., 1990—2009, CEO, 1990—, chmn., 2001—. Office: Gulf Island Fabrication Inc 567 Thompson Rd Houma LA 70363 Office Phone: 985-872-2100. Office Fax: 985-876-5414. Business E-Mail: kerry_chauvin@gulfisland.com.

CHAVEZ, J. ANTHONY, lawyer; b. Auburn, Calif., Oct. 5, 1955; s. Marco Antonio and Barbara Ann (Lawrence) Chavez-Rivas; m. Terry Leavitt-Chavez. BA, U. Calif., Santa Barbara, 1977; JD, Stanford U., 1981. Bar: Calif. 1981, Tex. 1982, US Dist. Ct. (so. and no. dists.) Calif. 1982, (cen. dist.) Calif. 1983, US Dist. Ct. (so. dist.) Tex. 1982, (we. dist.) Tex. 1983, (no. dist.) Tex. 1991, NY 1986, US Dist. Ct. (ea. and so. dists.) NY 1986, US Supreme Ct. 1986. With legal dept. Exxon Co. U.S.A., Houston, 1981-85, NYC, 1985-86; assoc. gen. counsel Sybron Corp., Saddlebrook, NJ, 1986-88, Crown Equipment Corp., New Bremen, Ohio, 1989-90; trial atty. Exxon Co. U.S.A., Houston, 1990-92; counsel complex litigation Exxon Chem. Co., Houston, 1992-95; counsel internat. oil and gas exploration Exxon Exploration Co., Houston, 1995-96; counsel antitrust, mergers and acquisitions Exxon Chem. Co., Houston, 1996-2000; counsel intellectual property licensing ExxonMobil Chem. Co., Baytown, Tex., 2000—04, Univation Technologies, 2004—09; counsel, info. tech. Exxon Mobil Corp., 2009—. Presenter numerous legal edn. seminars and programs. Contbr. articles to profl. jours. Mentor Ft. Bend Ind. Sch. Dist., 1998, Houston Bar Assn., 1998. Chancellor's scholar U. Calif., 1976; Outstanding Contribution award, Antitrust Law, U. Svc. award for dist. svc. to campus cmty. U. Calif., Santa Barbara, 1977. Fellow Houston Bar Found.; mem. ABA (antitrust sect., vice chair corp. counseling com. 1998-2000, vice chair intellectual property com. 2000-03, vice chair Sherman Act sect. 2 com. 2003-06, vice-chair Listserve 2006-07, mem. long range planning com. 2006-07, vice chair, tech. resources 2007-10, mem., competitiveness task force 2008-09; co-chair Tech. and Fin. Resources Task Force 2010-11, coun. mem., 2011-), Houston Bar Assn. (chair antitrust and trade regulation sect., 1997-98, vice-chair 1996-97, sec.-treas. 1995-96, coun. 1993-95). Republican. Avocations: hiking, theater, travel. Home: 4908 Cedar St Bellaire TX 77401 Office: Exxon Mobil Corp 800 Bell St # 1841K Houston TX 77002 Business E-Mail: j.anthony.chavez@exxonmobil.com.

CHAVEZ, JOHN RICHARD, historian, educator; b. Pasadena, Calif., Jan. 12, 1949; s. Manuel and Andrea (Quiroz) Chavez; m. Lorena Jeanne Poirier, Aug. 11, 1984; children: Monica Antonia, David Mario. BA in English, Calif. State. U., LA, 1971, MA in English, 1972, BA in Spanish, 1975; MA in Am. Culture, U. Mich., Ann Arbor, 1978, PhD in Am. Culture, 1980. Lectr. Calif. State U., LA, 1980-81, Long Beach, 1981-84; vis. asst. prof. program in Am. Culture U. Mich., Ann Arbor, 1984-86; asst. prof. dept. history Tex. A&M U., College Station, 1986-89; assoc. prof. history So. Meth. U., Dallas, 1989-97, prof., 1997—. Author: The Lost Land: The Chicano Image of the Southwest, 1984 (nominated Pulitzer prize, 1984), Eastside Landmark: A History fo the East LA Community Union, 1998, Beyond Nations: Evolving Homelands in the North Atlantic World, 2009 (World Hist. Book prize, 2010); co-author: Tchg. Mexican Am. History, 2002; co-editor: Memories and Migrations: Mapping Boricua and Chicana Histories, 2008; contbr. articles to profl. jours. Fullbright fellow, Spain, 2001. Mem.: World History Assn., Tex. State Hist. Assn., Am. Hist. Assn., Western History Assn., Nat. Assn. Chicano Studies. Democrat. Roman Catholic. Office: So Meth U Dept History Dallas TX 75275-0176 Business E-Mail: jchavez@smu.edu.

CHAVEZ, LINDA, think-tank executive, author, columnist; b. Albuquerque, June 17, 1947; m. Christopher Gersten Chavez, June 15, 1967; children: David, Pablo, Rudy. BA, U. Colo., 1970; attended, UCLA. Legis. staff mem. House Judiciary Subcom. Civil and Constl. Rights, Washington, 1972-74; asst. dir. legis. American Fedn. Teachers, 1975—77, asst. to pres., 1982—83; cons. civil rights sect. Office Mgmt. & Budget, Exec. Office of the Pres., Washington, 1977; asst. dir. legislation American Educator mag., 1975—77, editor, 1977-83, asst. to pres., 1982—83; staff dir. US Commn. on Civil Rights, 1983-85; dep. asst. to Pres., dir. Office Pub. Liaison The White House, 1985-86; chmn. Nat. Commn. on Migrant Edn., 1988—92; founder, pres. Ctr. Equal Opportunity, Washington, 1995—. Mem. Adminstrv. Conf. of the US, 1984—86; bd. dirs. Greyhound Lines, Inc., 1995—99, ABM Industries, Inc., 1997—, Pilgrim's Pride Corp., 2004—08, REO, 2012—, Research Electro-Optics Inc., 2012—; founder, chmn. Stop Union Polit. Abuse, 2004—, Republican Issues Campaign. Author: Out of the Barrio: Toward a New Politics of Hispanic Assimilation, 1991, An Unlikely Conservative: The Transformation of an Ex-Liberal, 2002, Betrayal: How Union Bosses Shake Down Their Members and Corrupt American Politics, 2004; polit. commentator, analyst FOX News Channel, nationally syndicated columnist, TV appearances include O'Reilly Factor, the Glen Beck Show, Hannity and Colmes, Rush Limbaugh Show, Good Morning America, Newshour with Jim Lehrer. Presdl. nomination for US Sec. of Labor, 2001; candidate for US Senate Md., 1986; bd. dirs. Campaign Prevent Teen Pregnancy, Found. Tchg. Economic. Recipient Living Legend award, Libr. of Congress, 2000. Mem.: Coun. Fgn. Rels. (co-chair com. on diversity 1998—2000). Republican. Roman Catholic. Office: Center for Equal Opportunity 7700 Leesburg Pike Ste 231 Falls Church VA 22043-2616 Office Phone: 703-442-0066. Office Fax: 703-442-0449. E-mail: Lchavez@ceousa.org.

CHAVIN, WALTER, biological sciences educator, researcher; b. NYC, Dec. 6, 1925; s. Isidor and Fanny (Kesch) C. BS, CCNY, 1946; MS, NYU, 1949, PhD, 1954. Rsch. asst. N.Y. Aquarium, NYC, 1947-48; instr. dept. zoology U. Ariz., Tucson, 1949-51; rsch. specialist dept. fishes Am. Mus. Natural History, NYC, 1951-53; prof. biol. scis. Wayne State U., Detroit, 1953-90, prof. emeritus, 1990—; prof. radiology Wayne State U. Med. Sch., Detroit, 1975-80; dir. Radiation Biology Inst. Wayne State U., Detroit, 1959-71; pres. Chavin Design and Fine Arts, Inc., 2007—. Research assoc. Argonne (Ill.) Nat. Lab., 1955-58. Contbr. 225 articles to profl. jours. NSF Sr. Postdoctoral fellow, 1960-61; Rsch. grantee NSF, AEC, NIH. Fellow AAAS (sec. 1978-85), N.Y. Acad. Scis.; mem. Nat. Assn. Photoshop Profls., Am. Physiol. Soc., Am. Soc. Zoologists (treas., sec.), Soc. Exptl. Biology and Medicine (com. 1986-90), Endocrine Soc., Am. Orchid Soc., South Fla. Orchid Soc., Pan Am Orchid Soc., Am. Bonsai Soc., Gold Coast Bonsai Soc., Lighthouse Bonsai Soc., Palm Beach Bonsai Soc., Sigma Xi (chpt. pres. 1974), Palm Beach Digital Imaging Group, Boca Raton Mus. Art, Art League. Independent. Home: 16484 Bridlewood Cir Delray Beach FL 33445-6678 E-mail: raja25@bellsouth.net.

CHEATHAM, EDDIE, state legislator; With UAM Coll. Tech.; ret.; mem. house of rep. Dist. 9 Ark., 2007—. Democrat. United Methodist. Address: 2814 Ashley 239 Crossett AR 71635 Office Phone: 870-364-5659. Business E-Mail: cheathame@arkleg.state.ar.us.

CHEATWOOD, CHRIS J., oil and gas company executive; BS, U. Okla.; MS in Geology, U. Tulsa. With Exxon Corp.; joined Pioneer Natural Resources Co., 1997, v.p. domestic exploration, 1998, sr. v.p. exploration, 2000, exec. v.p. worldwide exploration, 2002—07, exec. v.p. geoscience, 2007—10, exec. v.p. bus. devel. and tech., 2010—, Pioneer GP. Office: Pioneer Natural Resources Co Ste 200 5205 N O Connor Blvd Irving TX 75039 Office Phone: 972-444-9001. Office Fax: 972-969-3576.

CHEATWOOD, ROY CLIFTON, lawyer; b. Rome, Ga., Aug. 27, 1946; s. Herman Arthur and Dorothy Mary (Griffin) C.; m. Cynthia Morrison, June 27, 1969; children: Clifton, Scott, Dancy. BA, U. South Fla., 1968; JD, Tulane U., 1974. Bar: La. 1974, U.S. Dist. Ct. (ea. dist.) La. 1974, U.S. Dist. Ct. (mid. dist.) La. 1975, U.S. Ct. Appeals (5th cir.) 1975, U.S. Dist. Ct. (we. dist.) La. 1977, U.S. Supreme Ct. 1977, U.S. Ct. Appeals (11th cir.) 1981, U.S. Dist. Ct. (no. dist.) Tex. 1990. Assoc. Jones, Walker, Waechter, Poitevent, Carrere & Denegre, New Orleans, 1974-78, ptnr., 1978-91, Phelps Dunbar, New Orleans, 1991—2004, practice coord., comml. litigation practice group, 1992—2004, mem. mgmt. com., 1995—2002; shareholder Baker, Donelson, Bearman, Caldwell & Berkowitz, New Orleans, 2004—, Louisiana mgn. ptnr., 2004—, bd. dirs., 2005—. Adj. prof. La. State U., Baton Rouge, 1980, Loyola U., New Orleans, 1981, 84-86; faculty mem. Nat. Inst. Trial Advocacy, 1986-2003; master barrister Tulane Inn of Ct. Co-author: Louisiana Courtroom Evidence, 1993. Firm campaign rep. United Way, New Orleans, 1982, 98, recruiter, 1983-86, 88, acct. exec. area lawyers, 1989; bd. dirs. Children's Bur., New Orleans, 1988, 1st v.p., 1991, pres., 1993-95; mem. session St. Charles Presbyn. Ch., 1988-91, session New Covenant Presbyn. Ch., 2000—03, clk. of session, chair pastor-nominating com., 2000—02. 1st lt. U.S. Army, 1968-71, Vietnam. Mem. ABA (litigation sect./vice chmn. 5th cir. trial practice com. 1975-76, co-chmn. 1976-78, judge regional nat. appellate adv. com. 1978, co-chmn. ann. litigation meeting 1981, judge nat. appellate adv. competition 1978, membership chmn. litigation sect. 1983-86, mem., fed. practice task force 2008-2009), La. State Bar Assn. (bd. legal specialization 1998-2004, chmn. 2000-02, cont. legal edu. comm., 2005-). Office: 201 St Charles Ave Ste 3600 New Orleans LA 70170 Office Phone: 504-566-5200. Business E-Mail: rcheatwood@bakerdonelson.com.

CHEEK, ARTHUR LEE, construction executive, pilot; b. Raleigh, NC, Aug. 6, 1940; s. Arthur Lee Sr. and Margaret Louise (Bradburn) C.; m. Sandra Lee Tigges, July 21, 1958 (wid. Sept. 1971); children: Michael Sidney, Robert Bruce; m. Sheila Ann Waters, June 27, 1987. Comml. pilot. Capt. Air America, Inc., Far East, 1965-66; corp. pilot Am. Enka Corp., Asheville, N.C., 1966-68; capt. TWA/Saudi Arabian Airlines, Jidda, Saudia Arabia, 1968-71; owner Custom Homes, Inc., Asheville, 1971-80; contract adminstr. SEU Constrn., Inc., Cape Coral, Fla., 1985-89, corporate pilot, 1980-85, v.p. contract adminstrn and constrn. litigation support svcs., 1987—96; v.p., gen. mgr. Coral Rock, Inc., Punta Gorda, Fla., 1994-96, West Coast Industries, Ft. Myers, Fla., 1990-96, Advantage Transp., Punta Gorda, Fla., 1994-96; ins. sales, 1998-99, Gen. Elec. Fin. Assurance, 1999-2000, cons. in constrn. claims and litigation, 2000—11; pres. Cheek & Assocs. Constrn. Co., 2003—12; cons. Constrn. Claims, 2011—12. With USMC, 1957-60, U.S. Army, 1960-65, ETO. Mem.: Masons. Republican. Avocations: reading, fishing. Personal E-mail: alcheek@charter.net.

CHEEK, JIMMY GEARY, academic administrator, agricultural studies educator; b. Gorman, Tex., Sept. 7, 1946; s. Geary B. and Mayme (Wright) C.; m. Ileen Griffin, Aug. 23, 1969; children: Jennifer Leigh, Jeffrey Stewart. BS with high honors, Tex. A&M U., 1969, PhD, 1975; MEd, Lamar U., 1972. Agrl. edn. instr. Beaumont HS, Tex., 1969-73; supr. manpower tng. Beaumont Ind. Sch. Dist., 1971-73; grad. fellow Tex. A&M U., College Station, 1973-74, instr., 1974-75; asst. prof. U. Fla., Gainesville, 1975-80, assoc. prof., 1980-85, prof., 1985—2009, asst. dean for acad. programs Coll. Agr., 1992-99, dean Coll. Agrl. and Life Scis., 1999—2004, sr. v.p. for agr. and natural resources, 2005—09, head Inst. Food and Agrl. Scis.; chancellor U. Tenn., Knoxville, 2009—. Cons., seminar leader Pa. Coop. Extension Svc., 1985, Dept. Agrl. and Extension Edn., Pa. State U., 1985; cons. Gainesville (Fla.) Bd. Realty, Inc., 1988, 89, 90, 91, 92; review team mem. So. Assn. Colls. and Schs., 1977, 78; reviewer various books. Sr. author: (with others) Effective Oral Communication, 2d edit., 2000. Chair Rawlings Elem. Sch. Adv. Com., 1982-83, 85-86; pres. Rawlings Elem. Sch. PTA, 1985, v.p., 1984; mem. Ft. Clarke Sch. Adv. Com., 1987—; mem. Hidden Oak Elem. Sch. Adv. Com., 1988-90. Recipient Hon. Tex. State Future Farmers Am. degree, 1972, Hon. Fla. State Future Farmers Am. degree, 1978, Hon. Am. Future Farmers Am. degree, 1984, Outstanding Rsch. Paper award So. Agrl. Edn. Rsch. Conf., 1984, 88, 92; Merit award scholar Tex. A&M U., 1967-69; named of the 30 Notable Grads. Coll. Edn., Tex A&M U., 1999. Fellow N.Am. Colls. and Tchrs. Agr. (Ensminger-Interstate Disting. Teaching award 1990, Disting. Educator award 2005), Am. Assn. Agrl. Edn.(v.p. 1991-92, Disting. Svc. award 1998); mem. Am. Vocat. Ednl. Rsch. Assn. (pres. 1986), Fla. Vocat. Assn. (pres. 1992), Am. Vocat. Assn., Nat. Vocat. Agr. Tchrs. Assn. (Outstanding Svc. award so. region 1987), Fla. Vocat. Agr. Tchrs. Assn., Fla. Assn. Vocat. and Adult Tchr. Educators, Nat. Future Farmers Am. Alumni Assn., Assn. Internat. Agrl. Edn., U. Fla. Agrl. Alumni and Friends, Sigma Xi, Phi Kappa Phi (pres. 2003—), Gamma Sigma Delta, Alpha Zeta, Phi Delta Kappa, Iota Lambda Sigma, Alpha Gamma Rho (hon.). Office: University of Tennessee at Knoxville Office of Chancellor 527 Andy Holt Tower Knoxville TN 37996-0184 Office Phone: 865-974-3265. Office Fax: 865-974-4811. Business E-Mail: chancellor@utk.edu.*

CHEEK, SHERRI SMITH, state legislator; m. Jon Cheek. Legislature asst., Senator Ron Bean, 1992—2003; managing ptnr. Rental Business, 1988—; mem. Dist. 38 La. State Senate, 2004—, vice chair health and welfare com., select com. on women and children, mem. environ. quality com., fin. com., labor and indsl. rels. com., joint legis. com. on the budget. Mem.: Women in the Outdoors, Southern Hills Bus. Assn., Shreveport C. of C., DeSoto Parish C. of C., Nat. Wild Turkey Fedn., Leadership Shreveport. Republican. Baptist. Address: 9973 Mansfield Rd Keithville LA 71047 Office: PO Box 94183 Baton Rouge LA 70804 Office Phone: 225-342-2040. Business E-Mail: smithcheek@legis.state.la.us.

CHEESEWRIGHT, DAVE, retail executive; b. 1962; Joint Degree in Sports Sci. & Mathematics, Loughborough U. With Mars Confectionary; joined Asda, 1999; COO Walmart Canada, 2004—05, CEO, 2008—11; pres., CEO Walmart Europe, Middle East & Africa (EMEA) & Canada region, 2011—14, Wal-Mart International, 2014—. Bd. dirs. Yihaodian, Massamart Holdings Ltd., 2012—. Office: Wal-Mart Stores Inc 702 SW Eighth St Bentonville AR 72716*

CHELBERG, ROBERT DOUGLAS, military officer; b. Ironwood, Mich., Sept. 1, 1938; s. Raymond Rodahl and Marion Dora (Watson) C.; children: Robert, Kathryn. BS, U.S. Mil. Acad., West Point, NY, 1961; MBA, N.Mex. State U., 1973. Commd. 2d lt. U.S. Army, 1961, advanced through grades to lt. gen., 1991, ret., 1993; various assignments in U.S., Europe, Vietnam, 1961-78; student Nat. War Coll., Ft. McNair, Washington, 1978-79; asst. dir. pers. adminstrn. and svcs. Office Asst. Sec. Def. for Mil. Pers. Policy, Washington, 1979-80, staff dir., dep. to dep. asst. sec. def., 1980-81; comdr. 528th Arty. Group, U.S. Army So. Europe Task Force, 1981-83; chief of staff, dep. comdg. gen. Ft. Jackson, SC, 1983-86; asst. chief of staff, plans and policy Allied Forces So. Europe, 1986; exec. to supreme allied comdr. Europe, 1986-87; chief policy and programs br., policy div. Supreme Hdqrs., 1987-90; spl. asst. to supreme allied comdr. Europe for harmonization and verification Supreme Hdqrs., 1990; spl. advisor to sec.-gen. NATO, 1990-91; chief of staff U.S. European

Command, Stuttgart, Germany, 1991-93; dep. dir. George C. Marshall European Ctr. for Security Studies, Garmisch, Germany, 1994-95; mng. dir. European region CUBIC Applications Inc., Stuttgart, Germany, 1995-98; sr. cons. European region Cubic Applications, Inc., 1998—2003; sr. advisor European affairs Econ. Devel. Partnership, Aiken, SC, 1999—2011; sr. fellow Joint Forces Staff Coll., 2001—; program mgr. Def. Threat Reduction Agy., European Field Office, 2003—06; cons. Northrop Grumman, 2006—10, TASC, 2010—. Dist. commr. Transatlantic coun. Boy Scouts Am., Brussels, Belgium, 1987-90, v.p. membership, 2004-08. Recipient Def. Disting. Svc. medal, Def. Superior Svc. medal with oak leaf cluster, Army DSM, Legion of Merit, Bronze Star with four oak leaf clusters, 10 Air medals, Meritorious Svc. medal with oak leaf cluster; recipient Vet. of Yr. award VFW Post 3676, 1985, Outstanding Alumnus Svc. award Lake Superior State U., 1986, Army Exceptional Civilian Svc. award, 1995, Disting. Eagle Scout award, 1990; named to N.Mex. State U. Bus. Sch. Hall of Fame, 2001. Mem. Fedn. German-Am. Clubs (pres. 1994-96), Mil. Officers Assn. America (SC State v.p. 1999-2003), Wounded Warriors South Fla. (bd. mem.), Phi Eta Sigma, Phi Kappa Phi. Avocations: swimming, trap shooting. Home and Office: 10241 Heronwood Ln West Palm Beach FL 33412

CHELLGREN, PAUL WILBUR, energy industry executive; b. Tullahoma, Tenn., Jan. 18, 1943; s. Wilbur E. Chellgren and Kathryn L. (Berquist) Chellgen; children: Sarah, Matthew, Jane; m. Deborah Ann Cole, May 12, 2007. BS, U. Ky., 1964; MBA, Harvard U., 1966; diploma in devel. econ., Univ. Coll., Oxford, Eng., 1967. Assoc. McKinsey & Co., Washington and London, 1967—68; ops. analyst Office Sec. Def., Washington, 1968—70; adminstrv. asst. Boise Cascade Corp., Idaho, 1970—71, divsn. gen. mgr. LA, 1971—72; gen. mgr. Universal Capital Corp., Kansas City, Mo., 1972—74; exec. asst. to chmn. Ashland (Ky.) Inc., 1974—77; adminstrv. v.p. Ashland Chem. Co., Columbus, Ohio, 1977—78, group v.p., 1978—80; sr. v.p., group oper. officer Ashland Inc., Covington, Ky., 1980—88, sr. v.p., CFO, 1988—92, pres., COO, 1992—96, pres., CEO, 1996—97, chmn., CEO, 1997—2002; operating ptnr. Snow, Phipps LLC, NYC, 2005—. Bd. dirs. PNC Bank Corp., Centre Coll.; adj. prof. No. Ky. U. Dir. Am. Friends of Univ. Coll. Oxford, Inc.; dir., chmn. Taft Mus., Cin.; trustee No. Ky. U. Found., Ea. Ky. U. Found. 1st lt. US Army, 1968—70. Fellow: Univ. Coll. (Oxford, Eng.) (hon.); mem.: U. Ky. Fellows, Queen City Club (Cin.), Comml. Club, Met. Club. Office: 541 Buttermilk Pike # 207 Crescent Springs KY 41017 Home: 3100 N Ocean Blvd Unit 1103 Fort Lauderdale FL 33308 Office Phone: 859-341-1280.

CHEN, CHUN-HUNG, engineering educator; b. Kaohsiung, Taiwan, Taiwan, Oct. 27, 1964; came to U.S., 1991; s. Ping-Ho and Pao-Yu Chen; m. Mei-Mei Liu, June 15, 1991; 1 child, Valerie. PhD, Harvard U., 1994. Asst. prof. U. Pa., Phila., 1994-2000, acting grad. group chair, 1999-2000; prof. George Mason U., Fairfax, Va., 2000—. Cons. Computer Command and Control Co., Phila., 1997—. Recipient Grad. Assistance in Areas of Nat. Need award U.S. Dept. Edn., 1998; recipient Motion Planning and Simulation award U.S. Army Rsch. Office, 1997, Engring. Design award NSF, 1998, Robust Design Optimization award Sandia Nat. Labs., N.Mex., 1998, Small Aircraft Sys. Transportation Devel. award NASA, 2002, Info. Tech. Rsch. award NSF, 2003. Mem. IEEE (sr.; Best Paper in Automation award 2003), Inst. Ops. Rsch. and Mgmt. Scis. Achievements include development of simulation tool, 1992 (MasPar award); patents for optimal computing allocation, 1999 (Eliahu Jury award 1994). Avocations: trains, aircraft, weather forecasting. Office: George Mason U Dept Sys Engring & Ops Rsch 4400 University Dr MS 4A6 Fairfax VA 22030 Office Phone: 703-993-3572. Business E-Mail: cchen9@gmu.edu.

CHEN, JAMES MING, law educator; b. Taipei, Taiwan, Dec. 17, 1966; s. Hsien-Shih Chen, Shuang-Ling Chen; m. Heather Elaine Worland, May 22, 2010. BA, MA, Emory U., 1987; JD, Harvard U., 1991. Bar: Va. 1991, D.C. 1991. Law clk. to Hon. J. Michael Luttig US Ct. Appeals (4th cir.), McLean, Va., 1991—92; law clk. to Hon. Clarence Thomas US Supreme Ct., Washington, 1992—93; assoc. prof. law U. Minn. Law Sch., Mpls., 1993—99, prof. law, 1999—2001, James L. Krusemark prof. law, 2001—07, assoc. dean, 2004—07; dean, prof. law Louis D. Brandeis Sch. Law, U. Louisville, 2007—12, law prof., 2012—. Vis. prof. Université de Nantes, France, 1995, Heinrich-Heine-Universität, Düsseldorf, Germany, 1999, Slovak Agrl. U., Nitra, Slovakia, 2000. Contbr. articles to profl. jours. Office: University of Louisville Louis D Brandeis Sch Law Wilson W Wyatt Hall Louisville KY 40292 Office Phone: 502-852-6879. Office Fax: 502-852-0862. Business E-Mail: jim.chen@louisville.edu.

CHEN, WEI R., physics professor; b. Shanghai, People's Republic of China, July 5, 1958; arrived in US, 1982; m. Chinyun Lu, June 28, 1986; children: Jason Yunti, Vivian Antie. M Physics, U. Oreg., 1984, PhD in Physics, 1988. Lectr. in physics Parks Coll. St. Louis U., Cahokia, Ill., 1988-89; rsch. assoc. U. Oreg., Eugene, 1989; physics instr. Okla. Sch. Sci. and Math., Oklahoma City, 1989—99; assoc. prof. U. Ctrl. Okla., Edmond, 2001—05, prof., 2005—, asst. dean Coll. Math. and Sci., 2006—. Vis. rsch. assoc. U. Okla., Norman, 1991, adj. assoc. prof., 1996—. Recipient Tchr. Rsch. Assoc. award, US Dept. Energy, 1995, US Prof. of Yr. Award for Outstanding Master's Universities and Colleges Prof., Carnegie Found. for Advancement of Tchg. and Coun. for Advancement and Support of Edn., 2008, NHI Tchr. Rsch. fellow, 1993; vis. scholar NIH Tchr. Rsch. fellow, 1991. Fellow: Internat. Soc. Optical Engring.; mem.: Sigma Xi. Office: 221G Howell Hall 100 N University Dr Edmond OK 73034-5207 Office Phone: 405-974-5147. Business E-Mail: wchen@uco.edu.

CHEN, ZHIJIAN (JAMES), science educator, researcher; Degree in Biology, Fujian Normal U., China, 1985; PhD in Biochemistry, SUNY-Buffalo, 1991. Prof. molecular biology U. Tex. Southwestern Med. Ctr, 1997—, co-chair, genetics and develop. program, George L. MacGregor Disting. Chair dept. molecular biology. Investigator Howard Hughes Med. Inst., 2005—. Contbr. articles to several publications. Recipient Norman Hackerman award in Chem. Rsch., Welch Found., 2005, Edith and Peter O'Donnell award in Sci., Acad. of Medicine, Engring. and Sci. of Texas, 2007, NAS award in Molecular Biology, 2012; Anna Fuller Fellowship, Salk Inst., 1991—92, Searle Scholar, 1998, Leukemia and Lymphoma Soc. Scholar, 2002, Burroughs Wellcome Fund Investigator in Pathogens of Infectious Diseases, 2002, Am. Cancer Soc. Rsch Scholar, 2002. Office: U Tex Southwestern Med Ctr at Dallas 5323 Harry Hines Blvd Dallas TX 75390 Office Phone: 214-648-1145. Office Fax: 214-648-1675. Business E-Mail: zhijian.chen@utsouthwestern.edu.

CHENAULT, JAMES STOUFFER, judge; b. Richmond, Ky., May 1, 1923; s. Joe Prewitt and Russell (Stouffer) C.; m. Dorothy Neff, Apr. 21, 1960; children: Jean Russell. AB, Ea. Ky. U., 1949, LLD (hon.), 1975; LLB, U. Ky., 1949. Bar: Ky. 1949, U.S. Ct. Mil. Appeals 1956, U.S. Supreme Ct. 1960. Prosecuting atty. City of Richmond, Ky., 1950-57; commonwealth's atty. 25th Jud. Ct. of Ky., Clark, Jessamine and Madison Counties, 1964-66, cir. judge, 1966-80, chief cir. judge Clark and Madison Counties, 1980-93; chief regional judge Bluegrass Region of Ky., 1978-93; spl. judge Ky. Ct. of Appeals, 1973, Ky. Supreme Ct., 1984. Ky. rep. Nat. Ctr. State Cts., 1972-78; mem. Ky. Commn. on Corrections and Community Svc., 1973-77, Ky. Crime Commn. Cts. Sect., 1972-80, chmn., 1976-80, Task Force on Office for Pub. Advocacy, 1981-82, Gov.'s Jud. Adv. Coun., 1972-75, Ky. Jud. Coun., 1977-81, State and Fed. Jud. Coun., 1979-84; vol. faculty intensive trial seminar U. Ky., 1983, 85, 87, 90; lectr. So. Police Inst., 1970-80, Nat. Conf. Appellate Ct. Clks., 1985, Nat. Conf. U.S. Dist. Ct. Clks., 1988, Nat. Conf. on Tech. and the Cts., Chgo., 1984, Denver, 1988, 3rd Fed. Jud. Conc, 1987, Ala. Appellate Judges Conf., 1990; adj. faculty Sch. Law Enforcement Ea. Ky. U., 1967-73; lectr. numerous state jud. confs.; presenter 1st Nat. Jud. State of the Art Conf., Phoenix, 1987. Councilman City of Richmond, 1949-50. Lt. (j.g.) USN, 1943-46, PTO. Recipient Outstanding Contbn. award Ky. Coun. Crime and Delinquency, 1974, Outstanding Contbn. award City of Richmond, 1977, Disting. Svc. award Dept. Mass Comm. Ea. Ky. U., 1993, Outstanding Trial Judge award Ky. Acad. Trial Attys., 1993, Ky. Chief Justice Spl. award, 1994; named Outstanding Alumnus Ea. Ky. U., Richmond, 1982; inducted into U. Ky. Law Sch. Hall of Fame, 2000. Mem. ABA (lectr., presenter ann. meeting San Francisco chpt. 1987), Am. Judicature Soc., Internat. Acad. Trial Judges, Ky. Bar Assn. (pres. younger lawyers conf. 1956-57), Ky. Assn. Cir. Judges (pres. 1970-75, editor newsletter 1976-93, Outstanding Contbn. award 1978), Ky. Commonwealth's Attys. Assn. (pres. 1965-66), Richmond C. of C. (Outstanding Svc. award 1983, Outstanding Achievement award 1989), Exch. Club (pres. Richmond chpt. 1955, Outstanding Lifetime Achievement award 2003), Elks. Avocations: Kentucky history, gardening. Home and Office: 302 High St Richmond KY 40475-1344

CHENEY, FRANCES NEEL, librarian, educator; b. Washington, Aug. 19, 1906; d. Thomas Meeks and Carrie (Tucker) Neel; m. Brainard Cheney, June 21, 1928. BA, Vanderbilt U., 1928; BS in L.S, Peabody Library Sch., 1934; MS, Columbia, 1940; Litt.D., Marquette U., 1966. Librarian, chemistry library Vanderbilt U., 1928-29, circulation asst., 1929-30, reference librarian, 1930-37, Joint U. Libraries, 1937-43, head reference dept., 1945-46; asst. prof. Peabody Library Sch., Nashville, 1946-49, asso. prof., 1949-50, 52-67, prof., 1967-75, prof. emeritus, 1976—, also asso. dir. Asst. to chair of poetry Library of Congress, 1943-44, bibliographer gen. reference div., 1944-45; vis. faculty Japan Library Sch., Tokyo, 1951-52 Mem. Cath. Commn. on Intellectual and Cultural Affairs. Recipient Beta Phi Mu award for outstanding teaching, 1959, Mudge award for reference service, 1962; Constance Lindsay Skinner award, 1976; Mary U. Rothrock award, 1979; award Japan Library Assn., 1982 Mem. ALA (exec. bd., hon.), S.E. Library Assn. (pres. 1960-62), Tenn. Library Assn. (past pres.), Tenn. Hist. Assn., Tenn. Folklore Soc., Bibliog. Soc. Am., Assn. Am. Library Schs. (past pres.), Delta Delta Delta. Home: 2015 Richard Jones Rd # SE Nashville TN 37215-2801

CHENG, ALEXANDER HUNG-DARH, engineering educator, consultant; b. Taipei, Taiwan, May 25, 1952; came to U.S., 1976; m. Daisy T. Cheng, Nov. 23, 1979; children: Jacqueline, Julia. BS, Nat. Taiwan U., Taipei, 1974; MS, U. Mo., 1978; PhD, Cornell U., 1981. Asst. prof. Cornell U., Ithaca, 1981-82, Columbia U., NYC, 1982-85; assoc. prof. U. Del., Newark, 1985-93, prof., 1993—2001; dean engring. prof. U. Miss., Oxford, 2009—. Author: Multilayered Aquifer Systems, 2000, Trefftz & Collocation Methods, 2008, Modeling Groundwater Flow And Contaminant Transport; editor: Engineering Analysis with Boundary Elements, 1996—; editor 9 books; editor-in-chief Progress in Water Resources Series, 1998—; assoc. editor Jour. Engring. Mech., 1998—2004; contbr. over 100 articles to profl. jours. Recipient Basic Rsch. award U.S. Nat. Com. Rock Mechanics NRC, 1994, 99, Eminent Scientist award WIT. Mem. ASCE (chair, exec. com. engring. mech. divsn., Engring. Mechanics Inst. (v.p.), W.L. Huber Civil Engring. prize 1994), Am. Geophys. Union, Am. Inst. Hydrology (v.p. acad. affairs). Office: U Miss Sch Engring University MS 38677 Office Phone: 662-915-5362. E-mail: acheng@olemiss.edu.

CHEOKAS, MIKE, state legislator; Attended, Pierce Coll., Emory U. State rep. Dist. 134, Ga., 2004—. Bd. mem. New Horizons Habitat for Humanity; co-chair Rosalynn Carter Inst., 1999—. Mem.: Americus Kiwanis Club. Democrat. Mailing: 411 Legis Off Bldg Atlanta GA 30334

CHEPER, NICHOLAS J., biology educator; s. Nicholas and Frances Cheper; m. Nancy Cheper; 1 child, Laura. PhD, U. Tenn., Knoxville, 1979. Prof. biology East Ctrl. U., Ada, Okla., 1980—, chair biology, 1980—. Office: Dept Biology East Central Univ Ada OK 74820

CHER-KILLIGAN, BEATRICE M., history professor, art educator; d. Alfred and Katherine Cherkezian. BFA in painting and art history magna cum laude, Fla. Internat. U., Miami; MFA in Visual Arts cum laude, U. Miami, Coral Gables, 1997. Tchr. drawing and two-dimensional design U. Miami Coral Gables, 1996—97; tchr. arts and philosophy dept. Miami Dade Coll., 1997—2001; adj. prof. New World Sch. Arts, Miami, 1998—2000, Barry U., Miami, 1999—2001; adj. instr. U. Phoenix, Plantation, Fla., 1999—2001; prof. Am. Intercontinental U., Weston, Fla., 2001—. Dir. Sch. Ballet Dance Experience Coral Gables, 1978—82, Gables Art Gallery, 1978—82. Exhibitions include The New Gallery, Coral Gables, 1996, Lowe Mus., 1997, Arte Contemporaneo, Miami, 2000, Cornell Mus. Art, Fla., 2000, M-DCC Kendall Campus Art Gallery, Miami, 2000, Union Planters Bank, Coral Gables, 2001, Miura Mus. Art, Tokyo, 2003, R. Martin Gallery, Buenos Aires, 2005, Promo Arte Gallery, Tokyo, 2006. Apptd. vice chairperson City Coral Gables Cultural Affairs Bd., 1995—2001; mem. Coral Gables Cultural Coun., 1999—2001, vice chairperson, 2001—, Mozart Festival Coral Gables, 2001—, Bach Soc. Coral Gables, 2001—. Personal E-mail: bcher5@gmail.com.

CHERRY, ANDREW LAWRENCE, JR., social work educator, researcher; b. Dothan, Ala., Nov. 11, 1943; s. Andrew L. Cherry and Wyalene Cain; m. Mary Elizabeth Dillon, July 16, 1988. MSW, U. Ala., Tuscaloosa, 1974; D Social Work, Columbia U., 1986. Child welfare worker Escambia County Dept. Pensions and Securities, Brewton, Ala., 1968-72; psychiat. social worker Bryce State Hosp., Tuscaloosa, 1974-79; instr. Salisbury (Md.) State Coll., 1981-85; asst. prof. Marywood Coll. Sch. Social Work, Scranton, Pa., 1986-87; prof. Barry U. Sch. Social Work, Miami, Fla., 1987—2003; prof. mental health Sch. Social Work U. Okla., Tulsa, 2003—, endowed prof. mental health sch. social work, 2003—. Cons. Informed Families Dade County, Miami, 1990—98, Miami Coalition for Care to Homeless, 1991—93, NAACP Minority Media and Telecomm. Coun., 1992—2000; with drug abuse prevention program Cath. Charities, Miami, 1991—2000, Broward Children's Svc., Ft. Lauderdale, 1992—94, The Biscayne Inst., 1994—2004, St. Luke's Addiction Recovery Ctr., 1995—2000; interim dir. child welfare divsn. Cath. Charities, 1998—2000; project evaluator Substance Abuse and Mental Health Svcs. Adminstrn., Okla., 2004—09. Author: The Socializing Instinct: Individual, Family and Social Bonds, 1994, A Research Primer for the Helping Professions: Methods, Statistics, and Writing, 2000, Examining Global Social Welfare Issues Using MicroCase, 2002, 2d edit., 2004; co-author: Social Bonds and Teen Pregnancy, 1992; co-editor: Teenage Pregnancy: A Global View, 2001, Substance Abuse: A Global View, 2002, International Handbook of Adolescent Pregnancy, 2014; series advisor Greenwood Press World View of Social Issues, 1999, Cherry, A. & Dillon, M. E, 2010, Using The DSM-IV-TR in Social Work and The Helping Professions. Eddie Bowers Publishing Co., Inc.; contbr. articles to profl. jours. Bd. mem. Mental Health Assn. Tulsa, Okla. Scholar, NIMH, 1979. Fellow: Am. Orthopsychiat. Assn.; mem.: NASW, N.Y. Acad. Scis., Conf. Social Work Edn. Achievements include research in and devel. of the social bond theory; extensive work and rsch. among the mentally disabled, homeless, at-risk children and the addicted. Office: University Oklahoma Tulsa Campus 4502 E 41st St Ste 3J08 Tulsa OK 74135-2512 Office Phone: 918-660-3633. Business E-Mail: alcherry@ou.edu, alcherry11@cox.net.*

CHERRY, KENNETH JEROME, JR., surgeon; b. Richmond, Va., Oct. 22, 1947; s. Kenneth Jerome and Alice (Cottingham) Cherry; m. Robin Wheeler, Sept. 10, 1983; children: Katherine, Sarah, Kenneth III. Undergrad., Duke U., Durham, NC, 1970; MD, U. Va., Charlottesville, 1974. Diplomate Am. Bd. Surgery, Gen. Vascular Surgery. Intern, resident surgery U. Va., Charlottesville, 1974-80; resident vascular surgery U. Calif. San Francisco, 1980-81; instr. surgery Mayo Med. Sch., Rochester, Minn., 1981—84, asst. prof. of surgery, 1988—95, assoc. prof. of surgery, 1995—, prof. of surgery, 1995—2004; prof. of surgery, head divsn. vascular surgery U. Va. Health Sys., 2004—. Surgeon Rochester Meth. Hosp., St. Mary's Hosps., Rochester. Contbr. articles to profl. jour. Mem. ACS, Am. Surg. Assn, Midwestern Vascular Surg. Soc., Soc. Vascular Surgery (Disting. Fellow), Peripheral Vascular Soc., Soc. for Vascular Surgeons. Avocations: reading, history, outdoor activites. Home: 1010 Tanglewood Rd Charlottesville VA 22901 Office: Divsn Vascular Surgery Univ Va Health System PO Box 800679 Charlottesville VA 22908-0679 Office Phone: 434-243-7052. Business E-Mail: kjc5kh@virginia.edu.*

CHERRY, KIM, bank executive; b. Memphis, Feb. 16, 1962; d. Neal Cordell and Patsy Collins; m. Richard Cherry, Nov. 23, 1985. Grad. in Srategic Comm., U. Mo.; BA in Communication Arts, Rhodes Coll., 1984. Cert. pub. rels. Exec. v.p., corp. comm. First Horizon National Corp.; asst. pub. rels. Memphis in May, 1983-84; specialist comm. Memphis Light, Gas & Water, 1984-85; writer Guardsmark, Memphis, 1985-86; specialist media & comm. 1st Tenn. Bank, Memphis, 1986. Mem. Pub. Relations Soc. Am. Office: First Horizon National Corp 165 Madison Memphis TN 38103 Office Phone: 901-523-4444. Business E-Mail: kcherry@firsthorizon.com.

CHERRY, MIKE, state legislator; b. Feb. 6, 1943; Mem. Dist. 4 Ky. House of Reps., Ky., 1999—; mem. Agr. & Natural Resources Com., Edn. Com., State Govt. Com., 1999—, Caldwell Site Based Decision Making Coun., Labor Market 4 Sch.-to-Work Coun.; chmn. Princeton Tourism Commn.; bd. dir. Caldwell Free Clinic. Treas. Ctr. Presbyterian Ch. Recipient Outstanding Cmty. Svc. award, Princeton C of C. Mem.: Elks. Democrat. Presbyterian. Mailing: 803 S Jefferson St Princeton KY 42445 Office: Capitol Annex Rm 357E Frankfort KY 40601 Home Phone: 270-365-7801; Office Phone: 502-564-8100 ext 665. Fax: 502-365-7801.

CHERTOFF, MICHAEL, consulting firm executive, lawyer, former United States Secretary of Homeland Security; b. Elizabeth, NJ, Nov. 28, 1953; s. Gershon and Livia Chertoff; m. Meryl Justin; 2 children. AB magna cum laude, Harvard U., 1975, JD magna cum laude, 1978; LLD (hon.), Seton Hall Sch. Law, 2002. Bar: DC 1980, NY 1987, NJ 1990. Law clk. to Hon. Murray I. Gurfein US Ct. Appeals (2nd Cir.), NYC, 1978-79; law clk. to Justice William J. Brennan Jr. US Supreme Ct., Washington, 1979-80; assoc. Latham & Watkins LLP, Washington, 1980-83, ptnr., 1994—2001; asst. US atty. (southern dist.) NY US Dept. Justice, NYC, 1983-87, 1st asst. US atty. Dist. NJ Newark, 1987-90, US atty., 1990—94, asst. atty. gen. criminal divsn. Washington, 2001—03; judge US Ct. Appeals (3rd Cir.), Newark, 2003—05; sec. US Dept. Homeland Security, Washington, 2005—09; sr. of counsel Covington & Burling LLP, Washington, 2009—; co-founder, mng. prin. Chertoff Group, Washington, 2009—. Mem. Atty. General's Adv. Com. of US Attorneys, 1991—94; spl. counsel US Senate Whitewater Com., 1994—96, NJ State Senate Judiciary Com., 2000. Recipient John Marshall award for trial of litigation, US Dept. Justice, 1987, Henry E. Petersen Meml. award, 2006, Disting. Pub. Svc. award, Anti-Defamation League, 1992, Prosecutive Leadership award, US Dept. Health & Human Services, 1994, Benjamin L. Hooks award for disting. svc., NAACP, 2007, Transatlantic Leadership award, European Inst., 2008; named one of The 50 Most Powerful People in DC, GQ mag., 2007. Mem.: American Law Inst. Office: The Chertoff Group 1110 Vermont Ave NW Ste 1200 Washington DC 20005 also: Covington & Burling LLP 1201 Pennsylvania Ave Washington DC 20004 Office Phone: 202-662-5060, 202-649-4260. E-mail: mchertoff@cov.com.

CHESNEY, KENNY, musician; b. Knoxville, Tenn., Mar. 26, 1968; m. Renee Zellweger, May 9, 2005 (annulled Dec. 20, 2005). Degree in advt., E. Tenn. State U., 1991. Performer Chuckie's Trading Post and Quarterback's Barbecue, Johnson City, Tenn.; resident performer The Turf, Nashville; publ. deal with Acuff-Rose, 1992; record contract with Capricorn, Tenn., 1993; with RCA, Subsidiary BNA, Tenn.; creator, owner Blue Chair Bay Rum, 2013—. Musician: (albums) In My Wildest Dreams, 1993, All I Need To Know, 1995, Me & You, 1996, I Will Stand, 1997, Everywhere We Go, 1999, No Shirt, No Shoes, No Problem, 2002, All I Want For Christmas is a Real Good Tan, 2003, When the Sun Goes Down, 2004 (Album of Yr., Country Music. Assn., 2004), The Road & the Radio, 2005, Just Who I Am: Poets & Pirates, 2007, Lucky Old Sun, 2008, Hemingway's Whiskey, 2010, Welcome to the Fishbowl, 2012, Life on a Rock, 2013, (songs) The Good Stuff, 2002 (Single of Yr., Acad. Country Music, 2003), You Save Me, 2005 (Male Video of Yr., Country Music TV, 2007), I Go Back, 2004 (Male Video of Yr., Country Music TV, 2005), (with Tracy Lawrence & Tim McGraw) Find Out Who Your Friends Are, 2007 (Musical Event of Yr., Country Music Assn., 2007, Vocal Event of Yr., Acad. Country Music, 2008), (with Grace Potter) You and Tequila, 2011 (Music Video of Yr., Country Mussic Assn., 2011), (with Tim McGraw) Feel Like a Rock Star, 2012 (Musical Event of Yr., Country Music Assn. Awards, 2012); musician: (guest appearance with Willie Nelson and Leon Russell) Last Thing I Needed First Thing This Morning, 2003; prodr., co-dir. (TV films) Boys of Fall, 2010. Recipient Top New Male Vocalist award, Acad. Country Music, 1997, Top Male Vocalist award, 2002, Entertainer of Yr. award, 2005—08, Entertainer of Yr. award, Country Music Assn., 2004, 2006—08, Touring award, Billboard Music Awards, 2005—08, Country Songs Artist of Yr. award, 2006, Favorite Male Singer award, People's Choice Awards, 2007. Office: c/o Morris Management Group Inc 818 19th Avenue S Nashville TN 37203

CHESNEY, RUSSELL WALLACE, pediatrician, educator; b. Knoxville, Tenn., Aug. 25, 1941; s. Jack and Helen Wallace (McColl) C.; m. Patricia Joan Cook, June 8, 1968; children: Karen, Christopher, Gillian. AB, Harvard U., Cambridge, Mass., 1963; MD, U. Rochester, NYC, 1968. Diplomate Am. Bd. Pediatrics. Intern then resident Johns Hopkins U. Hosp., Balt., 1968-70, 72-73; renal fellow NIH, Balt., 1970-72, Montreal Childrens Hosp., Montreal, Que., Canada, 1973-75; asst. then prof. U. Wis., Madison, 1975-85; prof., vice chmn. U. Calif., Davis, 1985-88; Le Bonheur prof., chair Dept. Pediat. U. Tenn. Health Sci. Ctr., Memphis, 1988—. Mem. Rsch. Study Sect. NIH,

Washington, 1983—88, mem. Nat. Kidney and Urology Diseases Adv. Bd., 1988—91; sec.-treas., pediat. dept. chmn. Am. Med. Schs., 1993—99, pres., 2001—03; mem. coun. Am. Pediat. Soc., 1995—2004, v.p., 2001—02, pres., 2002—03; chmn. Fed. Pediat. Orgn., 1995—96; Birdsong lectr. U. Va., 1995; vice chair Task Force on Pediat. Edn., 1996—99; chair Am. Bd. Pediats., 2000—02; bd. trustees Assn. Children's Hosps., 2002—07. Contbr. articles to profl. jours., chpts. to text and med. books. Lt. comdr. USPHS, 1970-72, Balt. Recipient Founders award in Pediatric Rsch., So. Soc. Pediatric Rsch., 1993; Jour. Pediatrics lectr. U. Rochester, 1985, Paul Gaffney lectr. U. Pitts., 1988, Ira Greifer award, 2010 Mem. Am. Pediat. Soc. (mem. coun. 1995-, v.p. 2001-02, pres. 2002-03), Am. Acad. Pediats. (pres. Tenn. state chpt. 1995-98, E. Meade Johnson award 1985, Nutrition award 1996, St. Geme award 2001, Henry Barnett award 2004), Am. Soc. Pediat. Nephrology (Founders award 2005), Internat. Pediat. Nephrology Assoc. (Iragreifer award 2010), Soc. for Pediat. Rsch. (pres. 1986-87), Midwest Soc. for Pediat. Rsch. (pres. 1984-85), Am. Soc. for Pediat. Nephrology (pres. 1986-87), VA Merit Rev. Bd. (chmn. 1988-90). Office: U Tenn Dept Pediat Le Bonheur Childrens' Med Ctr 50 S Dunlap St, Rm 306 Memphis TN 38103-2893 Office Phone: 901-287-5036, 901-488-2070. Office Fax: 901-287-5036. Business E-Mail: rchesney@utmem.edu.

CHESSON, ANDREW LONG, JR., dean, neurology educator; b. Raleigh, NC, Nov. 29, 1948; s. Andrew L. C.; m. Linda Denise Illian, July 29, 1972; children: Andrew III, Lisa. BA, U. Tex., 1970; MD, U. Tex. Med. Sch., 1974. Lic. med. dr. Tex., La.; cert. Am. Bd. Psychiatry and Neurology, Am. Bd. Sleep Medicine; accredited Clin. Polysomnographer. Intern U. Tex. Med. Br., Galveston, 1974-75, resident in neurology, 1975-78; staff neurologist, dir. VA Hosp. neurology outpatient clinic VA Med. Ctr., Shreveport, 1978-85, cons., 1985—, clin. dir. dept. neurology Shreveport, 1993-95; instr. neurology La. State U. Med. Ctr., Shreveport, 1978-79, asst. prof. neurology, 1979-84, assoc. prof., 1984-93, dir. neurophysiology labs., 1988—2009, prof., 1993—, dean, 2009—. Assoc. dean for acad. affairs La. State U. Med. Ctr., Shreveport, 1994—, mem. various coms., 1978-94, acting chmn. dept. neurology, 1994-95; chief resident U. Tex. Med. Br. Dept. Neurology, 1977-78; reviewer in field; presenter in field. Contbr. chpts. to books and articles to profl. jours. Edward P. Stiles grantee, 1987. Fellow Am. Acad. Neurology (chmn. quality assurance subcom. sect. on sleep 1995—), Clin. Sleep Soc., Am. Sleep Disorders Assn. (chmn. stds. of practice com. 1995—); mem. AMA. Avocations: camping, backpacking, canoeing, wood working. Office: La State University Med Ctr Office of Dean 1501 Kings Hwy Shreveport LA 71130-3932

CHESTEEN, DONNIE, state legislator; m. Stephanie Chesteen; children: Roxanna, Christopher. Grad., Troy State U., Ala. Ret. pharm. sales rep. Bristol-Meyers Squibb; athletic dir., head football coach Samson HS, Ala.; mem. Dist. 87 Ala. House of Reps., Montgomery, 2011—. Mem. Choctawhatchee, Pea and Yellow Rivers Watershed Mgmt. Authority, First Bapt. Ch., Geneva. Mem.: Ala. Farmers Fedn., Ala. Cattleman's Assn. Republican. Office: PO Box 39 Geneva AL 36340 also: Ala Hosue of Reps Rm 630-E 11 S Union St Montgomery AL 36130 Office Phone: 334-242-7742. Personal E-mail: dchesteen@panhandle.rr.com.

CHESTERFIELD, LINDA PONDEXTER, state legislator; b. Hope, Ark. BS in History and Polit. Sci., Hendrix Coll., Conway, Ark.; MS in Edn., Ouachita Bapt. U., Arkadelphia, Ark. Retired social studies tchr. Fuller Jr. HS, Little Rock; mem. Dist. 36 Ark. House of Reps., 2003—08; mem. Dist. 34 Ark. State Senate, 2011—. Pres. Ark. Dem. Black Caucus; past pres. Little Rock Sch. Bd. Mem.: NEA (mem. exec. com., chair Black Caucus), Ark. Edn. Assn. Democrat. Mailing: Dist Address 12 Keo Dr Little Rock AR 72206 Office Phone: 501-888-1859. Personal E-mail: lchesterfield@comcast.net.

CHESTLER, CARL M., internist; MD, U. Miami, Coral Gables, Fla., 1966. Lic. Fla., 1973. Intern Jackson Meml. Hosp., 1967, resident internal medicine, 1968—72, fellow; hosp. affiliation includes Mt. Sinai Med. Ctr. Office: Mount Sinai Medical Center GRNE Ste 810 4300 Alton Rd Miami Beach FL 33140 Office Phone: 305-674-5925. Office Fax: 305-674-5927.*

CHESTNUT, ALFRED PAGE, biology professor; b. Port Norris, NJ, Sept. 24, 1946; s. Alphonse F. and Janet Wood Chestnut; m. Elizabeth McCord Chestnut, May 23, 1981; children: Elizabeth Page Callen, Mary Hamilton, Ann Claridge. BS in Biology, Wake Forest U., Winston-Salem, NC, 1968; MS in Biology, U. Richmond, Va., 1972; PhD in Biology, U. So. Miss., Hattiesburg, 1980. Prof. and chmn. Belhaven Coll., Jackson, Miss., 1980—. Bd. mem. Sigma Xi, Jackson, 1988—90; pres., officer Miss. Acad. Scis., Jackson, 1992—96; pres. Miss. Assn. Biologists, Jackson, Miss., 1994—95. Elder First Presbyn. Ch., Jackson, 1990—; bd. mem. Voice of Calvary Ministries, Jackson, 1996—2002. Recipient Dudly Peeler award, Miss. Acad. Scis., 2005, Tchr. of Yr., Belhaven Coll. Student Body, 1982, 1989, Headway award, Belhaven Coll. Faculty, 1990. Mem.: Miss. Acad. Scis. (pres. and bd. mem. 1993—96, Dudley Peeler award 2005), Sigma Xi. Conservative. Christian. Achievements include research in working with Trypanosoma lewisi; development of numerous cooperative programs between Belhaven College and UMMC. Avocations: bible study, gardening, music, tennis, travel. Office: Belhaven Coll 1500 Peachtree St Jackson MS 39202

CHESTNUT, CHARLES S., IV, state legislator; b. Gainesville, Fla., July 27, 1962; m. Tiffany Watts-Chestnut; children: Ashlei, Charlie. BBA with honors, Bethune-Cookman Coll., Daytona Beach, Fla.; AS in Mortuary Sci., Miami-Dade CC, Fla. Funeral dir.; commr. City of Gainesville, 2000—06, mayor pro tem, 2003—04, 2005—06; mem. Dist. 23 Fla. House of Reps., Tallahassee, 2006—, ranking mem. state univs. and pvt. colls. policy com., mem. edn. policy coun., health care appropriations com., select com. Seminole Indian compact rev., select policy coun. on strategic and econ. planning. Mem. Cmty. Redevelopment Agency, 2000—06, Met. Transp. Planning Orgn., 2000—06, Alachua County Poverty Reduction Adv. Bd., 2004—06, North Ctrl. Fla. Regional Planning Coun., 2000—03, 2004—06; mem. various coms. Florida League of Cities, 2002—05. Mem.: Alpha Sigma Lambda. Democrat. Methodist. Office: 3131 NW 13th St Ste 33 Gainesville FL 32609-2177 also: 1003 The Capitol 402 S Monroe St Tallahassee FL 32399-5794 Office Phone: 352-955-3083, 850-488-5794.

CHESTNUT, E. RANDALL, consumer product company executive; Pres. Std. Knitting Co., 1984-88, Beacon Mfg. Co., 1988-95; v.p. corp. devel. Crown Crafts, Inc., 1995, bd. mem., 1995—, pres., chmn., CEO, 2001—. Vice chmn. Wiscassett Mills Co., 1990—94. Office: Crown Crafts Inc PO Box 1028 Gonzales LA 70707-1028 Office Phone: 225-647-9100.

CHESTON, SHEILA CAROL, aerospace defense company executive, lawyer; b. Washington, Nov. 5, 1958; d. Theodore C. and Gabrielle Joan (Hellings) C. BA, Dartmouth Coll., 1980; JD, Columbia U., 1984. Bar: N.Y. 1986, D.C. 1986, U.S. Dist. Ct. D.C. 1987, U.S. Ct. Appeals (D.C. cir.) 1987, U.S. Dist. Ct. (so. and ea. dists.) N.Y. 1989, U.S. Ct. Appeals (2d cir.), U.S. Supreme Ct. 1989. Law clk. to judge US Ct. Appeals (9th Cir.), L.A., 1984-85; assoc. Wilmer, Cutler & Pickering LLP, Washington, 1985-92, ptnr., 1992-93; gen. counsel Def. Base Closure & Realignment Commn., US Dept. Def., 1993; spl. assoc. counsel to Pres. The White House, Washington, 1994; dep. gen. counsel Dept. Air Force, US Dept. Def., 1993-95, gen. counsel, 1995-98; ptnr. Wilmer, Cutler & Pickering LLP, Washington, 1998—2002; sr. v.p., gen. counsel, sec. BAE Systems, Inc., Rockville, Md., 2002—09, exec. v.p., 2009—10; corporate v.p., gen. counsel Northrop Grumman Corp., L.A., 2010—. Adj. prof. in internat. litig. Georgetown Law Sch., 1991-2003; bd. dirs., BAE Systems, Inc., 2002-2010 Mem. ABA, D.C. Bar Assn., Women's Bar Assn., American Bar Found., American Soc. Internat. Law, Coun. on Fgn. Rels. Democrat. Episcopalian. Office: Northrop Grumman Corp 2980 Fairview Park Dr Falls Church VA 22042-4511 Office Phone: 310-553-6262. Office Fax: 310-556-4561.

CHEVALIER, ROBERT LOUIS, nephrologist, educator, medical researcher; b. Chgo., Oct. 25, 1946; s. Frank Charles and Marion Helen (Jahnke) C.; m. Janis Julia Slezak, Dec. 23, 1970; 1 child, Juline Arianne. BS, U. Chgo., 1968, MD, 1972. Diplomate Am. Bd. Pediatrics, Bd. Pediatric Nephrology. Pediatric resident U. NC, Chapel Hill, 1972-75, postdoctoral fellow, 1975-77; nephrology fellow U. Colo., Denver, 1977-78; asst. prof. U. Va., Charlottesville, 1978-83, assoc. prof., 1983-88, prof., 1988—, chief pediatric nephrology, 1978-91, vice chmn. pediatrics, 1988-96, Genentech prof., 1993-97, acting chmn. pediat., 1996-97, chmn. pediat., 1997—, Shepherd prof., 1997—, dir. NIH Child Health Rsch. Ctr. Established investigator Am. Heart Assn., 1983-88. Mem. editl. bd. Renal Failure, 1988—, Pediatric Nephrology, 1995-97, Kidney Internat., 1998—; contbr. numerous articles to profl. jours., chpts. to books. Chmn. med. adv. bd. Nat. Kidney Found. Va., Richmond, 1986-89. Fellow Am. Acad. Pediatrics, Am. Heart Assn.; mem. Am. Pediatric Soc., Am. Physiol. Soc., Am. Soc. Nephrology, Am. Soc. Pediatric Nephrology (pres. 1991-92), Am. Bd. Pediatrics, Internat. Pediat. Nephrology Assn. (councillor 1999—), Soc. Pediatric Rsch., So. Soc. Pediatric Rsch. (pres. 1990-91, chair internat. workshop on devel. nephrology 2001). Office: U Va Dept Pediat / Divsn Nephrology PO Box 800386 Charlottesville VA 22908-0386 Office Phone: 434-924-5093. Office Fax: 434-982-3561. E-mail: rlc2m@virginia.edu.

CHEVALIER, ROGER ALAN, astronomy educator, consultant; b. Rome, Sept. 26, 1949; came to US, 1962; s. Frank Charles and Marion Helen (Janhke) C.; m. Margaret Mary With, July 27, 1974.; children: Chase Arthur, Max Toussaint. BS in Astronomy, Calif. Inst. Tech., 1970; PhD in Astronomy (Woodrow Wilson and NSF fellow), Princeton U., 1973. Asst. astronomer Kitt Peak Nat. Obs., Tucson, 1973-76, assoc. astronomer, 1976-79; assoc. prof. astronomy U. Va., Charlottesville, 1979-85, prof. astronomy, chmn. dept., 1985-92, W.H. Vanderbilt prof. astronomy, 1990—; dir. Leander McCormick Obs., 1985-92. Cons. Lawrence Livermore Nat. Lab., Livermore, Calif., 1981-90; bd. trustees U. Space Rsch. Assn., 2000-06. Contbr. numerous rsch. articles to Astrophys. Jour., other astronomy and physics jours. Recipient Heineman prize for astrophysics Am. Astron. Soc./Am. Inst. Physics, 1996; named Va. Outstanding Scientist, Sci. Mus. Va., 1991; Woodrow Wilson Found. fellow Princeton U., 1970-71, NSF fellow, 1970-73; elected to Nat. Acad. Scis., 1996. Mem. NAS, NRC (Astro 2010 Sci. Frontier Panel on Stars and Stellar Evolution chair 2008-10), Am. Astron. Soc. (councilor 1988-91), Internat. Astron. Union, Ill. Sci. Lectr. Assn. (v.p. 1975-85), US Nat. Com. for Internat. Astron. Union (vice chair 2005-07, chair 2008-). Home: 1891 Westview Rd Charlottesville VA 22903-1632 Office: U Va Dept Astronomy PO Box 400325 Charlottesville VA 22904-4325

CHEW, STEPHEN LINN, psychology professor; BA, U. Tex., Austin; PhD, U. Minn., Twin Cities. Prof., chair psychology Samford U., Birmingham, Ala., 1993—. Contbr. articles to profl. jours. Recipient Outstanding Masters Universities & Colleges Prof. of Yr. award, Carnegie Found. for Advancement of Tchg. & Coun. for Advancement & Support of Edn., 2011; Carnegie Scholar, Carnegie Acad. for Scholarship of Tchg. and Learning. Fellow: American Psychological Assn. (Robert S. Daniel Excellence in Tchg. Award, Soc. for Tchg. of Psychology 2005). Office: Howard College of Arts and Sciences Samford University, Burns 309 800 Lakeshore Dr Birmingham AL 35229 Office Phone: 205-726-2562. Office Fax: 205-726-2895. E-mail: slchew@samford.edu.

CHEWNING, THOMAS N., retired energy executive; m. Nancy Jones; 2 children. B in History, U. NC, 1967; MBA, U. Pa., 1969. CEO Air Van Lines, Inc., Seattle; v.p. adminstrn. Dominion Capital, v.p. and treas. Dominion Lands Dominion Resources, Inc., Richmond, Va., 1987—88, asst. treas., 1988—91, v.p., treas., 1991—92, v.p., 1992—94, exec. v.p., CFO, 1999—2009; treas. Dominion Energy, 1992—94, pres., CEO, 1994—99; exec. v.p., CFO Consol. Natural Gas Co., 2000—. Bd. dirs. U. NC Gen. Alumni Assn. Named Co-Richmonder of Yr., Richmond's Style Mag., CFO of the Yr., Utility Industry, 2005.

CHIANG, W.C.W (WILLIE CHIANG), oil industry executive; b. Corning, NY, 1960; BS in Mech. Engring., SD Sch. Mines and Tech., 1981; Completed Advanced Mgmt. Program, U. Pa. Wharton Sch., 2004. With Chevron Corp., Powerine Oil Co., Unocal/Tosco/Phillips; refinery mgr. ConocoPhillips, L.A., San Francisco, gen. mgr., v.p. western region refining, pres. downstream strategy, integration and specialty bus., 2003—05, pres. Americas supply and trading, 2005—07, sr. v.p. comml., 2007—08, sr. v.p. refining, mktg., & transp., 2008—10, sr. v.p. refining, mktg., transp. & comml., 2010—. Bd. dirs. Chevron Phillips Chemical Co. LLC. Mem. bd. dirs. Soc. Performing Arts; bd. mem. Leadership Edn. for Asia Pacifics (LEAP). Mem.: Nat. Petrochemical Refiners Assn. Office: ConocoPhillips 600 North Dairy Ashford Rd PO Box 2197 Houston TX 77079

CHIAO, LEROY, astronaut; b. Milw., Aug. 28, 1960; s. Tsu Tao and Cherry (Chu) Chiao; m. Karen Chiao, 2003. BS in Chemical Engring., U. Calif., Berkeley, 1983; MS, U. Calif., Santa Barbara, 1985, PhD in Chemical Engring., 1987. Postdoctoral researcher U. Calif., Santa Barbara, 1987; materials engr. Hexcel Corp., Dublin, Calif., 1987-89, Lawrence Livermore (Calif.) Nat. Lab., 1989-90; astronaut NASA, Houston, 1990—. Keynote commencement spkr. Dept. Engring., U. Calif., Berkeley, 1996, Santa Barbara, 1996; lectr. Beijing Inst. Aeronautical Materials, 1988, Changsha Inst. Tech., 5th Dept., Peoples Republic of China, 1988; mission specialist STS-65, 1994, STS-72, 1996, STS-92, 2000. Contbr. Internat. Encyclopedia Composite Materials, 1989. Recipient NASA Space Flight medal, 1994, 1996, 2000, NASA Exceptional Svc. award, 1996, 2000, NASA Individual Achievement award, 2001, 2002, 2003, 2004, NASA Group Achievement award, 1995, 1997, NASA Going the Extra Mile award, 2004, Komarov Diploma, Fedn. Aeronautique Internationale, 1996, De La Vaulx medal, 1994, Korolev Diploma, 2002, Excellence award in Sci. and Tech., US Pan Asian Am. C. of C., 2003, 100 Most Influential Asian Americans in the 1990's award, A-Magazine, 2000. Mem. ASTM, AIAA, Soc. Advancement Material and Process Engring. Broke a nearly 30 year tradition of having at least one crewman with previous experience in piloting the capsule. Comdr. and NASA Sci. Officer of Expedition-10 headed for the International Space Station with Russian-US crew (with Salizhan Sharipov and Yuri Shargin) in the Soyuz TMA-5 on October, 2004, landed in April, 2005 (with Salizhan Sharipov and Roberto Vittori). First Asian-Am. to perform a spacewalk. First Am. to vote in presidential election while in space, 2004. Office: NASA-JSC 2101 NASA Rd 1 Houston TX 77058-3691

CHICOLA, JEFFREY P. (JEFF CHICOLA), pediatric otolaryngologist; MD, La. State U., 1973. Lic. Fla., 1976, diplomate Am. Bd. Otolaryngology, 1977. Intern Charity Hosp. Med. Ctr. of La., resident otolaryngology, 1974—77; divsn. chief, divsn. of pediatric otolaryngology dept. of surgery Nemours Children's Clinic, Pensacola; hosp. affiliations include Sacred Heart Hosp., West Fla. Hosp. Office: 5153 N Ninth Ave Pensacola FL 32504 Office Phone: 850-505-4735. Office Fax: 850-505-4714.*

CHIEGO, WILLIAM J., museum director; b. Newark, Sept. 17, 1943; s. William Joseph and Rose Marie (Del Guercio) C.; m. Elizabeth Kimball Lee, July 3, 1971; children: Ruth Katharine, Rose Monica. BA in History with distinction, U. Va., 1965; MA in Art History, Case Western Reserve U., 1968, PhD in Art History, 1974. Asst. curator Toledo (Ohio) Mus. Art, 1973-74, assoc. curator European Paintings, 1974-76; curator Portland Art Mus., 1976-79, chief curator, 1979-82, N.C. Mus. Art, Raleigh, 1982-86; dir. Allen Meml. Art Mus. Oberlin (Ohio) Coll., 1986-91; dir. Marion Koogler McNay Art Mus., San Antonio, 1991—. Trustee Intermuseum Conservation Assn., Oberlin, 1986-91; mem., co-chmn. mus. liaison com. Midwest Art History Soc., 1987-91; mem. exhbn. adv. com. Am. Fedn. Arts, 1988-94; mem. conservation grant panel Inst. Mus. Svcs., 1991-93; chair membership com. Assn. Art Mus. Dirs., 1997-99, trustee, 2000-02; lectr. in field. Co-author, editor exhbn. catalog Sir David Wilkie of Scotland, 1987, An Eye for the Stage The Tobin Collection of Theatre Arts at McNay Art Mus., 2004; co-organizer, author intro. to French Paintings from The Chrysler Museum, 1986; coord. rsch. The N.C. Mus. Art Intro. to the Collections, 1983; author: Master Prints from the Gilkey Collection, 1980, From Oregon Private Collections, 1977; organizer, author: (with others) Oberlin Alumni Collect Modern and Contemporary Art, 1989, Reginald Rowe: A Retrospective, 1996, Carl Rice Embrey: A Retrospective, 1997, O'Keeffe and Texas, 1998, César A. Martinez: A Retrospective, 1999; author/editor: Modern Art at The McNay, 2001; contbr. articles to profl. jours. Resident fellow Yale Ctr. for British Art, New Haven, Conn., 1982, Bingham Travel fellow Art History Case Western Reserve U., 1970-71, Univ. fellow Art History, 1969-70, Nat. Defense Edn. Act fellow Latin Am. History, 1965; Mus. Mgmt. Inst. scholar, 1981. Mem. Phi Beta Kappa. Office: McNay Art Museum PO Box 6069 San Antonio TX 78209-0069 E-mail: william.chiego@mcnayart.org.

CHILD, JEFFREY B., investment company executive; BSChemE, U. Calif., Davis; MBA, U. Pa. Mng. dir., healthcare group Banc of America Securities LLC, mng. dir., US equity capital markets, 1999—2003. Bd. dirs. Amerigroup Corp., 2003—, ev3 Inc., 2007—. Trustee, bd. edn. Menlo Park City Sch. Dist. Office: Amerigroup Corp 4425 Corporation Ln Virginia Beach VA 23462 Office Phone: 757-490-6900. Office Fax: 757-518-3600. Business E-Mail: jchild@ev3.net.

CHILDERS, BOB EUGENE, educational association executive; b. Cleveland, Miss., Sept. 16, 1930; s. William Nick and Allie Jeanette (Doty) C.; m. Jo Ann Roberts, May 1, 1953; children: William Frank, Robert Clayton, John Murry, Julia Ann. BA, Union U., 1953; MA, Memphis State U., 1958; EdD, U. Tenn., 1964. Cert. tchr., adminstr., Tenn. Field engr. RCA, El Paso, Tex., 1955-57; instr. USN, Memphis, 1957-60; prin. Halls H.S., Knoxville, Tenn., 1960-61, McMinn County H.S., Athens, Tenn., 1961-64; asst. commr. Tenn. State Dept. Edn., Nashville, 1964-66; regional dir. USOE, Vocat.-Tech. and Adult Edn., Atlanta, 1966-69; exec. dir. Commn. Occupl. Edn., Atlanta, 1969-82, So. Assn. Colls. and Schs., Atlanta, 1982-92. Cons. U.S. Dept. Edn., Washington, 1963-79, Fla. State Legislature, Tallahassee, 1979, Md. Values Edn. Commn., Annapolis, 1979-80; founder, pres. Childers-Childress Family Assn., 1982-88, 90-96. Editor SACS Procs., 1982-92. Bd. dirs. Boy Scouts Am., Atlanta, 1980-87, Ctr. for Citizenship Edn., Washington, 1978-81; bd. trustees YMCA, Nashville, 1964-66; v.p. Religious Heritage of Am., St. Louis, 1979-86; active Rotary, Atlanta, 1981-92. With U.S. Army, 1953-55. Mem. Am. Vocat. Assn. (life 1966, cons.), Am. Tech. Edn. Assn. (life 1978, pres.1984, v.p. 1983), Am. Vocat. Rsch. Assn., Am. Soc. Assn. Execs., Phi Delta Kappa (past treas. 1960-61, sec. 1960-61), Iota Lambda Sigma, Sigma Alpha Epsilon (pres. 1952). Democrat. Baptist. Avocations: genealogy, vitaculture, gardening. Home and Office: 960 River Rd Woodruff SC 29388-9110

CHILDERS, D. BRADLEY, energy executive, lawyer; BA in Poitical Sci., Claremont McKenna Coll., 1982; JD, U. Southern Calif., 1986. Assoc. Sullivan & Cromwell LLP, 1989—94; various positions, including corp. counsel Occidental Petroleum Corp., 1994—2002; v.p. bus. devel. Occidental Oil and Gas Corp., 1999—2002; gen. counsel, sec. Universal, 2002—06, sr. v.p., 2002—07, sr. v.p. bus. devel., 2005; pres. internat. divsn. Universal Compression, Inc., 2006—07; sr. v.p. Exterran GP, LLC, 2006—11, pres. N.Am. ops., 2008—11, chmn., pres., CEO, 2011—; sr. v.p. corp. devel. Exterran Holdings, Inc., 2007—08, pres., CEO, 2011—. Bd. dirs. Exterran GP LLC, 2008—. Office: Exterran Holdings Inc 16666 Northchase Dr Houston TX 77060 Office Phone: 281-836-7000.

CHILDERS, GREG, state legislator; m. Melanie Hefty, 1993; children: Cameron, Connor, Cole. With Norman's Postal Tng. Ctr.; mem. Dist. 43 Okla. State Senate, 2011—. Republican. Office: 2300 N Lincoln Blvd Rm 520 Oklahoma City OK 73105 Home: 4756 Del Porte Dr Del City OK 73115-4356 Office Phone: 405-521-5522. Business E-Mail: childers@oksenate.gov.

CHILDRESS, RICHARD THOMAS, international business consultant, author; b. Huntington, W.Va., Nov. 22, 1942; s. Grover Burgess and Zenna Belle C.; m. Elli Lisbeth, June 13, 1962; 1 child, Tyrone Richard. BA in Psychology, U. Cin., 1964; MA in Asian Studies, U. Ariz., 1976. Commd. 2d lt. U.S. Army, 1964, advanced through grades to col., 1984; gen. staff officer Asian affairs, exec. officer Dept. of Army, 1978—81; dir. Asian and polit. mil. affairs White House, Nat. Security Coun., 1981—89; pres. Asian Investment Strategies, 1989—; pres., co-founder Asian Energy Corp., Tulsa, Okla., 1992—. Sr. adv. Sec. of State, 1982-88; US del. Assn. Southeast Asian Nations, 1982-88; leader, participant US Policy Del., Vietnam, Laos, 1982-89; designated White House Surrogate Spkr. Pres. US; NSC advisor to two presdl. envoys; Rep. Nat. Comm., adv. bd. US-ASEAN Bus. Coun., Inc.; policy adv. Nat. League Prisoners of War, Missing in Action families, mem. U.S.-Philippine Bus. Com.; exec. com. US-Thailand Bus. Coun.; co-chair adv. coun. Nat. Ctr. S.E. Asian Studies, Georgetown U.; Indochina forum Aspen Inst.; spkr. in field.nat Contbr. articles to profl. jours. Decorated Def. Disting. Svc. medal, Legion of Merit with Oak Leaf, Bronze Star, Vietnamese Cross of Gallantry, others; recipient Humanitarian awards Fgn. Govts., Nat. League Prisoners of War/Missing in Action Families, Svc. to Mankind, Pace award Dept. Army. Mem. Asia Soc., Thai-Am. Assn. Mailing: PO Box 104 Flat Rock NC 28731

CHILDRESS, STEVEN ALAN, law educator; b. Mobile, Ala., Feb. 9, 1959; s. Roy and Mary Helen Childress;children: Ani, Steven. BA, U. Ala., 1979; JD, Harvard U., 1982; PhD in Jurisprudence and Social Policy, U. Calif., Berkeley, 1995. Bar: Calif. 1983, U.S. Ct. Appeals (5th cir.) 1984, D.C. 1986, U.S. Ct. Appeals (9th cir.) 1986, U.S. Supreme Ct. 1987. Law clk. to judge U.S. Ct. Appeals (5th cir.), Shreveport, La., 1982-83; assoc. Morrison & Foerster, San Francisco, 1983-84; adj. lectr. law Golden Gate U. Sch. Law, San Francisco, 1984-86; grad. instr. U. Calif., Berkeley, 1985-86; assoc. Brobeck, Phleger & Harrison, San Francisco, 1986—88; assoc. prof. law Tulane U. Law Sch., New Orleans, 1988-96, prof. law, 1996—, Conrad Meyer III prof. law, 2007—. Co-author: Federal Standards of Review, 1986, 4th edit., 2010; contbr. articles to profl. jours. Regents fellow U. Calif. at Berkeley, 1985. Mem. Law and Soc. Assn., Phi Beta Kappa. Office: Tulane U School of Law New Orleans LA 70118 Office Phone: 504-865-5829. Business E-Mail: achildr@tulane.edu.

CHILDS, JULIANNA MICHELLE, federal judge; b. Detroit, Mar. 24, 1966; BS, U. South Fla., 1988; MA, U. SC Sch. Bus., 1991; JD, U. SC Sch. Law, 1991. Assoc. Nexsen Pruet, LLC, Columbia, SC, 1992—99, ptnr., 2000; dep. dir. divsn. labor SC Dept. Labor, Licensing & Regulation, 2000—02; commr. SC Workers' Compensation Commn., 2002—06; cir. ct. judge SC Jud. Dept., 2006—10; judge US Dist. Ct. SC, 2010—. Office: US Dist Ct 300 E Washington St Greenville SC 29601 Office Phone: 864-241-2190.

CHILDS, RAND HAMPTON, information technology executive, consultant; b. Charlotte, NC, Oct. 20, 1949; s. Wade Hampton and Francis Marion (Rand) C.; m. Anne Elizabeth Turner, Jan. 4, 1986; children: Ian Peter, Ryan Patrick. BS in Chemistry, Ga. Inst. Tech., 1971, MS in Chemistry, 1977; postgrad., Eidgenossische Technische Hochschule, Zurich, Switzerland, 1971-72. Sys. analyst computing svcs. dept. Ga. Inst. Tech., Atlanta, 1974-80, mgr. data processing computing svcs. dept., 1980-83, assoc. dir. office of computing svcs., 1983-87; v.p. software devel. Sirsi Corp., 1987-94, acting mgr. data conversion dept., 1995-97, v.p. R&D, 1994—2001; ind. software cons. RHChilds, LLC, 2002—12. Cons. in field. Contbr. articles to profl. jours.; compiler: (with Naugle and Sherry) A Concordance to the Poems of Samuel Johnson. World Student Fund scholar Ga. Inst. Tech. and Swiss Govt., 1971-72. Mem. AAAS, Am. Chem. Soc., Assn. Computing Machinery, Info. Industry Assn., VIM (6000) (Control Data Corp. User Group), Sigma Xi, Alpha Iota Delta of Chi Psi (Atlanta). Home: Rand H Childs 12451 N Shawdee Rd SE Huntsville AL 35803-3717 E-mail: randchilds@mac.com.

CHILES, STEPHEN MICHAEL, retired lawyer; b. July 15, 1942; s. Daniel Duncan and Helen Virginia (Hayes) C.; m. Deborah E. Nash, June 13, 1964; children: Stephen, Abigail. BA, Davidson Coll., 1964; JD, Duke U., 1967. Bar: N.Y. 1970, Pa. 1978, Wis. 1981, Ill. 1986, U.S. Dist. Ct. (ea. dist.) Pa. 1978, U.S. Tax Ct. 1978, U.S. Supreme Ct. 1978. Officer trust dept. Irving Trust Co., NYC, 1970-75, v.p., 1975-77; assoc. atty. Stassen Kostos & Mason, Phila., 1978-79, mem., shareholder, 1979-85; ptnr. McDermott, Will & Emery LLP, Chgo., 1986—2004, of counsel, 2005—06. Contbr. articles to profl. jours. Served to capt. U.S. Army, 1967-69. Decorated Bronze Star, Army Commendation medal. Mem.: State Bar Wis., Landings Club, (Savannah, Ga.). Republican. Episcopalian. Personal E-mail: stevec715@gmail.com.

CHILES, WILLIAM E., air transportation executive; BBA in Petroleum Land Mgmt., U. Tex., Austin; MBA, Southern Meth. U., Dallas. Various positions including v.p. domestic ops. Gulf Mex. Western Oceanic, Inc., 1972—77; founder, pres., CEO Chiles Offshore, Inc. (formerly Chiles Drilling Co.), 1977—2002, Southwestern Offshore Corp., 1992—96; sr. v.p. drilling ops. Cliffs Drilling Co., 1996—97; v.p. bus. devel. ENSCO International, Inc., 2002—03; exec. v.p., COO Grey Wolf, Inc., 2003—04; pres., CEO, bd. dirs. Bristow Group, Inc., 2004—, CFO, 2005—06. Bd. dirs. Norsk Helikopter AS, Basic Energy Svcs., Inc. (formerly Sierra Well Svc., Inc.), 2003—. Office: Bristow Group Inc 2103 Citywest Blvd Ste 400 Houston TX 77042-2835 Office Phone: 713-267-7600. Office Fax: 713-267-7620. Business E-Mail: william.chiles@bristowgroup.com.

CHILSON, JOHN A., lawyer, retired military officer; s. Kenneth N. and Jean Kay Chilson; m. Donna Carol Mays, May 2, 1992; children: Matthew A., Cara N. BS, US Naval Acad., 1991; JD, U. Mich., 1999; grad., Naval War Coll., Newport, RI, 2007. Bar: Mich. 1999, U.S. Ct. Appeals for the Armed Forces 1999, N.C. 2003, U.S. Dist. Ct. (ea. dist.) N.C. 2003, U.S. Dist. Ct. (mid. dist.) N.C. 2003, U.S. Dist. Ct. (we. dist.) N.C. 2003, U.S. Ct. Appeals (4th cir.) 2003. Commd. ensign USN, 1991, advanced through grades to lt. comdr., 2002, surface warfare officer, engr. Charleston, SC, 1992—95, instr. leadership Newport, RI, 1995—97, atty. JAG Corps Pensacola, Fla., 1999—2003; atty. Womble Carlyle Sandridge & Rice PLLC, Winston-Salem, NC, 2003—04; lt. comdr. USNR, 2003—; atty. Ellis & Winters LLP, Greensboro, NC, 2004—06, Comerford Britt, LLP, Winston-Salem, NC, 2006—; chair, profl. negligence sect. NC Advocate Justice, 2013—14; mem. com. NC Adv. Justice, 2012—13. Editor: Mich. Jour. Law Reform (Louis Honigman Meml. award, 1999, Dykema Meml. award, 1998), Adelphia Law Jour. Naval acad. info. officer Naval Acad. Admissions Office, Clemmons, NC, 2003—10; youth soccer coach YMCA, Clemmons, NC, 2003—08; baseball coach Little League, Clemmons, NC, 2005—; asst. v.p. baseball ops. S.W. Forsyth Little League, Clemmons, NC, 2007—11; nonresident dir. Navy Mut. Aid Assn., Arlington, Md., 1999—2003; softball coach Little League, 2009—; coach NC State Championship Little League Team, 2008. With Jag Corps USN, 2012. Recipient AV Superior Rating award, Martindale-Hubbell, 2013; named Rising Star, NC Super Lawyers Mag., 2009; named one of NC's Best Lawyer's Under 40, Bus. NC Mag., 2007. Mem.: ABA, Assn. Am. Justice, NC Advocates for Justice (bd. govs., chair, profl. negligence sect. 2013—14), NC Bar Assn. (young lawyer's divsn. mil. liaison com. 2003—04, lawyer effectiveness and quality life com. 2005—07, professionalism com. 2007—08). Avocations: sports, history. Office: Comerford & Britt LLP Ste 200 250 W First St Winston Salem NC 27101 Office Fax: 336-631-8228. Personal E-mail: chilsonj@comerfordbritt.com.

CHILTON, ELIZABETH EASLEY EARLY, newspaper executive; b. Williamson, W.Va., Dec. 9, 1928; d. Carl Brooks and Susie Mason (Easley) Early; m. William Edwin Chilton III, Apr. 5, 1952 (dec. Feb. 1987); 1 child, Susan Carroll Chilton Shumate Student, Hollins Coll., Va., 1946—48; AA Primary Edn., Marjorie Webster Coll., Washington, 1950; LLD (hon.), W.Va. State U., 2004; D (hon.), U. W.Va., 2004; LLD (hon.), U. Charleston, 2011. Pub. rels. staff Charleston Gazette, W.Va., 1952—87; v.p., treas. Daily Gazette Co., Charleston, 1987—91, pres., 1991—, pub., 2004—, also dir., chmn. bd. dirs., 1994—. Mgmt. com. The Charleston Newspapers, 1991-99; adv. bd. Eberly Coll. Arts and Scis., 1996; vice chair Am. Com. IPI. Mem. editl. bd. The Charleston Gazette, 1987— Chmn. W.Va. Gov.'s Mansion Preservation Found., Charleston, 1989—; bd. trustees U. Charleston, 1989-98, Marshall U.-Yeager Scholars, Huntington, W.Va., 1990-96, W.Va. State Coll. Found., 1988-96, WSWP-TV Pub. Broadcasting, 1980-94, Faculty Merit Scholars, 1991—, W.Va. Humanities Coun., 1994-00; bd. dirs. BIDCO, 1996-98, Advantage Valley, Charleston, 1996-98, Greater Kanawha Valley Found., 1980-86, adv. bd., 1986—; bd. dirs. W.Va. U., Sulgrave Manor Found., 2001, Childrens Express, Charleston Renaissance, Washington, Gunston Hall Plantation, 1977-92, pres., 1989-92; bd. dirs. Clay Ctr. Arts and Scis., Nat. Youth Sci. Found., 1998, Kid's Count; bd. dirs. Worth Bingham Prize Found., exec. com. 1987—; sec. bd. govs. W.Va. U., 2004—. Recipient John Marshall medal for civic responsibility, Marshall U., 1997, Pres. Disting. Svc. award, W.Va. U., 2000, Second Century award for excellence in leadership, W.Va. State Coll., 2003, Voice award, Nat. Alliance Mental Illness, 2006, Grad. Distinction, Edn. Alliance, 2007. Mem. So. Newspaper Pubs. (journalism edn. com. 1992-94, minority affairs com. 1994—), Nat. Soc. Colonial Dames W.Va. (pres.), Internat. Press Inst. (dir. Am. com. 1994—), Newspaper Assn. Am. (com. 1987—), Nat. Trust for Historic Preservation, Garden Club Am. (chmn. libr., bd. dirs. 1989-92), Jr. League Charleston, Edgewood Country Club Charleston, Yale Club N.Y.C., Sulgrave Club Washington, Briar Hills Garden Club, Kanawha Garden Club, Sea Pines Country Club Hilton Head Democrat. Presbyterian. Avocations: travel, reading, gardening. Home: 806 Cedar Rd Charleston WV 25314-1206 Office: The Charleston Gazette 1001 Virginia St E Charleston WV 25301-2895

CHIN, SIU AH, physicist; b. Kwangtung, China, Feb. 12, 1949; PhD, Stanford U., Calif., 1975. Assoc. prof. Tex. A&M U., College Station, 1990—92, prof., 1993—. Fellow: Am. Phys. Soc. Achievements include research in forward fourth-order symplectic algorithms. Business E-Mail: chin@physics.tamu.edu.

CHIN-LOR, DAISY, cosmetics executive; Grad., City U. New York Hunter Coll. Corp. v.p. Avon Taiwan, pres.; corp. v.p. Avon Thailand, pres.; area v.p. Avon Asia Pacific; pres. Chanel Thailand; exec. recruiter Russell Reynolds Assocs.; exec. v.p. Red Door Spas, chief mktg. officer; exec. v.p. Birks & Mayors Inc., chief mktg. officer; pres. Tupperware Korea, BeautiControl N. Am. Tupperware Corp., 2011—, mng. dir., 2011—. Office: Tupperware Corporation PO Box 2353 Orlando FL 32802 Office Phone: 800-366-3800.

CHIOU-TAN, FAYE, physician, educator; b. Hsin-Chu, Taiwan, Mar. 27, 1964; d. George and Tricia Chiou; m. Filemon Tan, Jr.; children: Filemon III, Michelle. AB, Princeton U., NJ, 1985; MD, Baylor Coll. of Med., Houston, 1990. Diplomate Am. Bd. Electrodiagnostic Medicine, Am. Bd. Phys. Med. Rehab. Asst. prof. Baylor Coll. Medicine, Houston, 1995—2002, assoc. prof., 2003—09, residency program dir., 2007, prof., 2009—. Contbr. articles to profl. jours. Chief svc. phys. medicine and rehab. Harris County Hosp. Dist., Houston, 2000—, dir. electrodiagnosis, 1995—, dir. Ctr. for Trauma Rehab. Rsch., 2000—; med. Harris County Hospital; Best Doctors in Am., 2007-. Recipient Excellence in Rsch. Writing award Assn. Acad. Physiatrists/Am. Jour. Phys. Medicine and Rehab., 1999, 2000, 2003; named one of Am's Top Physicians, Consumer's Rsch. Coun. Am., 2003, 04, Fulbright and Jaworski Tchng. award, 2002,2007, Fulbright and Jaworski Enduring Ednl. Materials award, 2008, Top 100 Health Profls., Internat. Biographical Ctr., 2008, Outstanding Scientist, 2010, Outstanding Coun. Svc. award, Am. Acad. PMR, 2011. Mem.: AAPMR Program Ctr., AmJ PMR (edlt. bd. mem. 2004—09), PMR (assoc. editor), Am. Bd. Electrodiagnostic Medicine (examiner 2006—09), Assn. Acad. Physiatrists (chair rsch. 2006—07, program com. 2007—08), Am. Assn. Neuromuscular Electrodiagnostic Medicine (rsch. com. chmn. 2005—08, nominating com. mem. 2010—, chair web cme ctr.). Avocations: cooking, hiking. Office: Baylor Coll Medicine Dept PM&R 3601 N MacGregor Way Ste 240 Houston TX 77004

CHIRON, HARLAN S., orthopedic surgeon, educator; b. NYC, Oct. 24, 1941; d. Albert Edward and Rose L. Chiron; m. Judy G. Chiron, Feb. 17, 1990; children: Stewart, Pamela, Diana. BA, Lafayette Coll., Easton, Pa., 1962; MD, Chg. Med. Sch., 1966. Intern Hosp. for Joint Disease, 1966—67, resident, 1967—68, 1970—72, fellow, 1972—73; ptnr. S. Fla. Orthopedic Assn., Miami, 1974—, pres., 1985—; prof. U. Miami, 1974—2006. Chief orthopedic surgery Victoria Hosp., Miami, 1978—80, S. Miami Hosp., 1993—96. Capt. USAF, 1970—72. Frauenthal fellowship, Hosp. for Joint Disease, NYC, 1972. Avocations: tennis, piano, reading, photography. Office: S Fla Orthopedic Assn Ste 203 4675 Ponce de Leon Blvd Miami FL 33146

CHISHOLM, MARTHA MARIA, dietitian; b. Havana, Cuba, Nov. 27, 1958; arrived in U.S., 1961; d. Robert Lester and Martha Clara (Latour) C. BS in Dietetics and Nutrition, Fla. Internat. U., 1983, MS in Dietetics and Nutrition magna cum laude, 1995. Lic. dietitian, Fla. Pediatric clin. dietitian Miami (Fla.) Children's Hosp., 1983-86, 92-96, pediatric gastroenterology dietitian, 1986-92, dietitian Ketogenic Diet Ctr., 1994-96, pediatric clin. dietitian, staff relief, 1997; dietitian Pediatric Cystic Fibrosis Ctr., 1993-96, dietitian feeding and swallowing disorder team, 1994-96; clin. dietitian Oncology and Hospice Mercy Cath. Hosp., 1997—2005, So. Miami Hosp., Miami, Fla., 2005—; supr. diet office South Miami Hosp. Cons. United Cerebral Palsy Assn. Miami, 1989-94, Roche Labs., Miami, 1991-95, Children's Rehab. Network, Miami, 1990-95. Mem. Homeless Ministry, St. Louis Cath. Ch., Miami, 1991-94, Eucharistic min., 1993-96, young adult ministry co-leader, 1994-96; mem. fgn. mission ministry Amor En Accion, 1995-2000, vol. South FL SPCA, 2009- Mem. Am. Dietetic Assn. (registered dietician), Fla. Dietetic Assn. (Disting. Dietitian 1997), Miami Dietetic Assn. (sec. 1988-89, Recognized Young Dietitian award 1988, Hurricane Andrew Relief Fund chair 1992-93, mem. nominating com. 1993-94, Disting. Dietitian 1996), Sierra Club (Miami chpt. cert. outings leader 1998-2000), South Fla. SPCA (horse rescue ranch vol. 2009-), Phi Kappa Phi. Republican. Roman Catholic. Avocations: backpacking, bicycling, horseback riding, photography, canoeing, rowing, backpacking. Home: 5935 Turin St Coral Gables FL 33146-3245 Office: S Miami Hosp Bapt Health Sys 6200 SW 73d St Miami FL 33143-4989

CHISM, GARY ALAN, state legislator; b. Columbus, Miss., Dec. 24, 1950; m. Barbara Digby. Former Dist. 3 Lowndes County Bd. Edn.; former bd. trustees East Miss. Cmty. Coll.; co-owner Columbus Ins. Svc. Inc.; mem. Dist. 37 Miss. House of Reps., 2000—. Mem.: Soc. Cert. Ins. Counselors, Miss. Assn. Life Underwriters, Nat. Assn. Ins. Fin. Advisor, Ind. Ins. Agts. Miss., Ind. Ins. Agts. America, Mason. Republican. Baptist. Mailing: PO Box 2343 Columbus MS 39704-2343 Office Phone: 662-327-0777, 601-359-2433. E-mail: gchism@house.ms.gov.

CHISUM, WARREN D., state legislator; b. July 4, 1938; m. Omega Chisum. Oil & gas prodr.; mem. Dist. 88 Tex. House of Representatives, 1988—. Republican. Office: Room CAP GW.15 Capitol PO Box 2910 Austin TX 78768 Home: PO Box 1512 Pampa TX 79066-1512 Office Phone: 806-665-3552, 512-463-0736.

CHIU, HARRY, information technology executive; COO Citrix Sys., Inc. Office: Citrix Systems Inc 851 W Cypress Creek Rd Fort Lauderdale FL 33309 Office Phone: 954-267-3000. Office Fax: 954-267-9319. Business E-Mail: harry.chiu@citrix.com.

CHIZNER, MICHAEL A., cardiologist, educator; MD, Cornell U. (Weill), 1974. Diplomate Am. Bd. Internal Medicine, 1977, Am. Bd. Internal Medicine-cardiovasc. disease, 1979. Resident internal medicine NY Hosp., NYC, 1974—77; fellow cardiovasc. disease Georgetown Affiliation Hosps., Washington, 1977—79; clin. prof. medicine Univ. of Fla. Coll. of Medicine, Univ. of Miami Sch. of Medicine, Nova Southeastern Univ., Barry Univ.; chief med. dir. The Heart Ctr. of Excellence Broward Health. Editl. adv. bd. The Am. Heart Hosp. Jour., Cardiovasc. Reviews and Reports. Author various articles and book chpts. Named one of Best Physicians in the US, Top Docs, Castle Connelly. Fellow: ACP, Am. Heart Assn., Am. Coll. of Cardiology. Office: Broward General Medical Center 1625 SE 3rd Ave Ste 300 Fort Lauderdale FL 33316 Office Phone: 954-355-5001. Business E-Mail: mchizner@browardhealth.org.

CHMIEL, MARK E., marketing professional; BA in Bus. Comm. and Micro-Econs., Mich. State U., 1978. Acct. supr. J. Walter Thompson, 1984—86; sr. v.p., acct. dir. Young & Rubicam, NY, 1986—99; gen. mgr., new bus. dir. Earle Palmer Brown, 1999—2000; chief mktg. officer Catalyst LLC, 2000—04; chief mktg. strategist Baja Fresh divsn. Fresh Enterprises Inc., 2005—06; sr. v.p. brand/concept innovation Denny's Corp., Spartanburg, SC, 2007—08, exec. v.p., chief mktg. & innovation officer, 2008—. Office: Dennys Corp Hdqs 203 E Main St Spartanburg SC 29319

CHO, RICHARD, professional sports team executive; b. Myanmar (formerly Burma), Aug. 10, 1965; arrived in US, 1968; married; 2 children. BS in Engring., Wash. State U., Pullman, 1990; JD, Pepperdine U., Malibu, Calif., 1997. Engr. Boeing Co., Seattle, 1990—95; intern to the pres. Seattle Supersonics, 1995—97, part-time cons., 1997, dir. basketball affairs, 1997—2000, asst. gen. mgr., assoc. legal counsel, 2000—05, asst. gen. mgr., v.p. legal, 2005—07; asst. gen. mgr. Oklahoma City Thunder, 2008—10; gen. mgr. Portland Trail Blazers, 2010—11, Charlotte Bobcats, 2011—. Office: Charlotte Bobcats 333 E Trade St Charlotte NC 28202

CHOATE, JERRY D., retired board member; married; 2 children. BS in Indsl. Mgmt., San Jose State U., 1961. Ops. supr. Allstate Corp., 1962-79, asst. v.p., Midwest Life Region, 1979-82, asst. v.p. mktg., 1982-83, v.p., sales, 1983-85, field exec. v.p., Western Territory, 1985-87, sr. v.p., field adminstrn., 1987-88, sr. v.p. product adminstrn., 1988-89, pres., personal property & casualty ops., 1989-95, chmn., CEO, 1995-98, Allstate Ins. Co., 1995—98. Bd. dirs. Amgen, Inc., Van Kampen Mut. Funds, Valero Energy Corp., 1999—. Chmn. Roadway Safety Found.; bd. dirs. Hwy. Users Fedn., Ins. Inst. Hwy. Safety, St. Francis Hosp., Evanston, Ill.; mem. adv. bd. J. L. Kelllogg Grad. Sch. Mgmt. Northwestern U.; bd. trustees AICPCU. Mem. Comml. Club. Chgo. Office: Valero Energy Corp Bd Directors 1 Valero Way San Antonio TX 78249-1112 Office Phone: 201-345-2000. Office Fax: 201-345-2646. Business E-Mail: jerry.choate@valero.com.

CHOBY, DAVID RAYMOND, bishop; b. Nashville, Jan. 17, 1947; s. Raymond and Rita Choby. Attended, St. Ambrose Coll., Davenport, Iowa, Cath. U. Am., Washington; degree in Canon Law, Angelicum Ch., Rome. Ordained priest Diocese of Nashville, 1974; assoc. pastor St. Joseph Parish, Madison, Tenn.; adminstr. St. Ann Parish; diocesan tribunal resident, Christ the King Parish; pastor St. John Vianney Parish, Gallatin, Tenn., 1989—2005; ordained bishop, 2006; bishop Diocese of Nashville, 2006—. Faculty mem. Pontifical Coll. Josephinum, Columbus, Ohio, 1984—89, bd. dirs.; mem. Presbyteral Coun., Coll. Consultors. Roman Catholic. Office: Diocese of Nashville 2400 Twenty-First Ave S Nashville TN 37212 Office Phone: 615-383-6393. Office Fax: 615-292-8411. Business E-Mail: bishop@dioceseofnashville.com.

CHOE, SONG-YUL, engineering educator; m. Marina Choe, May 25, 1981. PhD, Tech. U. Berlin, Germany, 1991. Dir. Hyundai Motor Co., Seoul, Republic of Korea, 1996—2001; rsch. prof. Miss. State U., Starkville, Miss., 2001—02; prof. Auburn U., Ala., 2002—. Arbitrator High Ct. Seoul, 1996—99. Office: Auburn Univ 201 Ross Hall Auburn University AL 36849-5341 Business E-Mail: choe@eng.auburn.edu, choe@auburn.edu.

CHOI, ALBERT H., law educator; s. James Hwajin and Margaret Dukrak Choi; m. Geeyoung Min, July 1, 2006. BA, Pomona Coll., Claremont, Calif., 1994; PhD, MIT, Cambridge, 2001; JD, Yale U., New Haven, Conn., 2001. Asst. prof. economics U. Va., Charlottesville, 2005, assoc. prof. law, 2005—. Dir. John M. Olin Program, Charlottesville, 2006—. Personal E-mail: alberthchoi@gmail.com.

CHOI, K.J. (KYUNG-JU CHOI), professional golfer; b. Wando, South Korea, May 19, 1970; m. Hyunjung Kim; children: David, Amanda; 1 child, Daniel. Mem. PGA Tour, 1994—. Mem. South Korean team World Cup, 2002, 2003, 2005; mem. internat. team Presidents Cup, 2003, 2007, 2011. Achievements include earning first PGA Tour Card for Korean Citizen, 1994; winner, PGA Tour events including Compaq Classic of New Orleans, Tampa Bay Classic presented by Buick, 2002; Chrysler Classic of Greensboro, 2005; Chrysler Championship, 2006; Memorial Tournament, AT&T National, 2007; Sony Open in Hawaii, 2008; THE PLAYERS Championship, 2011; winner, Kolon Cup Korean Open, 1999, SK Telecom Open, Korea, 2003, 05. Office: c/o PGA 100 Ave Champions Palm Beach Gardens FL 33410-9601

CHOI, WOON GYU, economist; s. Sookja Cha; m. Moon Hee Lee, Feb. 22, 1987; children: Jacho, Olivia Jeeyoon. BA, Seoul Nat. U., 1983, MA, 1985; PhD, UCLA, 1995. Economist Bank of Korea, Seoul, 1987—91; asst. prof. Hong Kong U. Sci. & Tech., 1995—2000; sr. economist Internat. Monetary Fund, Washington, 2000—, instr. macroecon. internat. fin. and related policy. Contbr. chapters to books, articles to profl. jours. Fellow U. Fellowship, U. of Calif., LA, 1991-1992; scholar Magna Cum Laude, Seoul Nat. U., 1983; Korean Air Line fellowship, 1981, Won-Yeong Lee Fellowship, 1982, U. Spl. scholarship, Grad. Sch. Seoul Nat. U., 1983—86, Rsch. grants, Coun. Hong Kong, China, 2000. Achievements include research in macroeconomic and financial policies, money demand, interest rates, international reserves and financial cycles. Office: Internat Monetary Fund 700 19th St NW Washington DC 20431 Business E-Mail: wchoi@imf.org.

CHOKSI, MARY CLAIRE, investment company executive; b. 1950; m. Armeane Choksi; children: Maaren, Tristen, Alexander Nicolas. BA in French, U. Minn.; MA in Internat. Affairs, John Hopkins U.; MA in Pub. Affairs, U. Minn. With, pension devel. divsn. World Bank, sr. program officer, South and S.E. Asia; mng. dir., founding ptnr. Strategic Investment Partners Inc., Arlington, Va., 1987—. Bd. dirs. Emerging Markets South Asia Fund, Emerging Markets Quantitative Portfolio, HJ Heinz Co., Avis Budget Group Inc. Trustee Nat. Mus. Women in the Arts; bd. dirs. Beauvoir-The Nat. Cathedral Elem. Sch. Office: Strategic Investment Partners Inc 16th Fl 1001 19th St N Arlington VA 22209-1722 Office Phone: 703-243-4433. Office Fax: 703-243-2266. Business E-Mail: mchoksi@strategicgroup.com.

CHOPIN, L. FRANK, lawyer; b. New Orleans, Apr. 29, 1942; s. Alton Francis and Floretta (Thensted) C.; children: Philip, Alexandra, Christopher. BBA, Loyola U., New Orleans, 1964, JD, 1966; diploma in mil. law, Judge Adv. Gen.'s Sch., U. Va. Sch. Law, 1966; postgrad., Nat. Law Ctr., George Wash. U., 1967-68; LLM in Taxation, U.

Miami, Fla., 1976; PhD in Law, Cambridge U., Eng., 1986. Bar: La. 1966, Fla. 1968, Iowa 1980, U.S. Dist. Ct. (so. dist.) Fla. 1968, U.S. Ct. Appeals (5th cir.) 1968. Ptnr. Chopin & Chopin, Miami, 1969—77; assoc. prof. law Drake U., Des Moines, 1979—80; ptnr. Cadwalader, Wickersham & Taft, Palm Beach, Fla., 1980—94, Chopin, Miller & Yudenfreund, Palm Beach, Fla., 1994—98, Chopin & Miller, Palm Beach, Fla., 1998—2005, L. Frank Chopin, PLC, Palm Beach, Fla., 2005—. Adj. prof. law U. Miami, 1982—96, U. Sherbrooke, Canada, 1982—94. Author: The New Residency Rules for Canadian Tax Considerations, 1985; also numerous articles in legal jours. Mem. Housing Fin. Authority; trustee Preservation Found., Palm Beach Community Chest, Inc. Served to capt. U.S. Army, 1966-68. Mem. Internat. Bar Assn., Fed. Bar Assn., Fla. Bar (tax sect.), Loyola U. Alumni Assn., U. Miami Alumni Assn., St. Thomas More Law Soc., Phi Alpha Delta (charter). Republican. Roman Catholic. Office: L Frank Chopin PLC PO Box 4297 West Palm Beach FL 33402 Office Phone: 561-655-9500.

CHOPPIN, GREGORY ROBERT, chemistry professor; b. Eagle Lake, Tex., Nov. 9, 1927; s. Gilbert P. and Nellie M. (Guidroz) C.; m. Ann M. Warner; children: Denise, Suzanne, Paul, Nadine. BS in Chemistry, Loyola U., New Orleans, 1949, DSc (hon.), 1969; PhD in Chemistry, U. Tex, 1953; DSc Tech. (hon.), Chalmers U., Göteborg, Sweden, 1985. Rsch. scientist Lawrence Radiation Lab., Berkeley, Calif., 1953-56; faculty Fla. State U., Tallahassee, 1956—, R.O. Lawton Disting. prof. chemistry, 1968—2001, prof. emeritus, 2001—. Vis. scientist Centre d'Etude Nucleaire, Mol, Belgium, 1962-63; vis. prof. Sci. U. Tokyo, 1978; vis. scientist European Transuranium Inst., Karlsruhe, Germany, 1979-80, 95; cons. Argonne Nat. Lab., Ill., Los Alamos Nat. Lab., N.Mex., Lawrence Livermore Nat. Lab., Calif., Brookhaven Nat. Lab., N.Y., Sandia Nat. Lab., N.Mex., Kaiser-Hill Co.; served on panels and commns. including NRC Chem. Sci. and Tech. Bd., NRC Radioactive Waste Mgmt. Bd. Co-author: Nuclear Chemistry: Theory and Applications, 1980, 2d edit., 1995, 3d edit., 2002; editor: Plutonium Chemistry, 1983, Actinide-Lanthanide Separations, 1985, Lanthanide Probes in Life, Chemical and Earth Sciences, 1989, Principles and Practice of Solvent Extraction, 1992, 2d edit., 2004, Separations of f-Elements, 1995, Chemical Separation Technologies and Related Methods of Nuclear Waste Management, 1999; mem. editl. bd. sci. jours. including Handbook on Physics and Chemistry of Rare Earths; co-discoverer of chemical element 101 Mendelevium; contbr. over 500 articles to sci. jours. Served to cpl. U.S. Army, 1946-48. Recipient Alexander von Humboldt Stiftung award, 1979, Chem. Mfrs. Assn. Edn. award, 1979, Seaborg Actinide Separations Sci. award, 1989, Presdl. citation, Am. Nuclear Soc., 1991, Scientist of Yr. award, Fla. Acad. Sci., 1992, Spedding award, N.Am. Rare Earth Rsch. Conf., 1996, Chem. Pioneer award, Am. Inst. Chemistry, 1997, Becquerel medal, Brit. Royal Soc. Chem., 2000, George Hevesy medal, Jour. Radiology and Nuc. Chem., 2005. Fellow AAAS; mem. Am. Chem. Soc. (award Fla. sect. 1973, So. Chemist award 1971, award in Nuclear Chemistry 1985, OESPER award Cin. sect. 1995), Royal Soc. Arts and Sci. (hon. fgn. mem.) (Sweden), Rare Earth Rsch. Conf. (pres. bd. 1981-83, chmn. 16th conf. 1983), Sigma Xi, Phi Beta Kappa. Avocations: sailing, racquetball. Home: 3290 Longleaf Rd Tallahassee FL 32310-6406 Business E-Mail: choppin@chem.fsu.edu.

CHOPRA, ANEESH PAUL, former federal official; b. Trenton, NJ, July 13, 1972; BA, Johns Hopkins U., 1994; MA in Pub. Policy, Harvard U., 1997. Mng. dir., head Financial Leadership Coun. and Working Coun. for Health Plan Execs. Adv. Bd. Co., Washington; sec. tech. State of Va., Richmond, 2005—09; chief tech. officer The White House, 2009—12; assoc. dir. for tech. Office Sci. & Tech. Policy (OSTP), Exec. Office of the Pres., 2009—12. Former chair Solutions Com., IT Investment Bd., Effectiveness and Efficiency Com., Coun. of Va.'s Future; former co-chair Heathcare IT Coun. Bd. mem. No. Va. Conservation Trust, Ctr. for Innovative Tech. Recipient State Leadership Advocacy Award, Healthcare Info. and Mgmt. Sys. Soc. (HIMSS), 2007; named one of The Top 25 in Doers, Dreamers, and Drivers issue, Govt. Tech. mag. Democrat.

CHOU, CHUNG-KWANG, bio-engineer; b. Chung-King, China, May 11, 1947; came to the U.S., 1969, naturalized, 1979; s. Chin-Chi and Yu-Lien (Hsiao) C.; m. Grace Wong, June 9, 1973; children: Jeffrey, Angela. BSEE, Nat. Taiwan U., 1968; MSEE, Washington U., 1971; PhD, U. Wash., 1975. Postdoctoral fellow U. Wash., Seattle, 1976-77, asst. prof., 1977-81, rsch. assoc. prof., 1981-85; rsch. scientist, head biomed. engring. sect. City of Hope Nat. Med. Ctr., Duarte, Calif., 1985-98, dir. dept. radiation rsch. divsn. radiation oncology, 1985-98; dir. Corp. RF Dosimetry Lab. Motorola, Inc., Plantation, Fla., 1998-2000; chief EME scientist, dir. Corp. EME Rsch. Lab. Motorola Inc., 2000—09, Enterprise Mobility Solutions Motorola Inc., 2009—10, Motorola Solutions, Inc., 2011—. Sci. adv. Mobile Mfrs. Forum, 2001—; sci. advisory bd. assoc. Motorola, 2005. Mem. editl. bd. IEEE EMC, MTT, 1999—; assoc. editor Jour. Bioelectromagnetics, 1987-2003; contbr. 200 articles to profl. jours. and chpts. to books. 2d lt. Army of Taiwan, 1968-69. Fellow: IEEE (life; subcoms. 1979—, ad hoc task force on health care reform 1993—97, vice chmn. 1994—95, mem. med. tech. policy com. 1995—98, chmn. 1996—98, chmn. internat. com. electromagnetic safety TC 95 2007—, std. coordinating com., mem., com. man and radiation 1990—2000, 2011—, Standards medallion 2005), Motorola Sci. Adv. Bd. Assn., Electromagnetic Acad., Am. Inst. for Med. and Biol. Engring.; mem.: Internat. Adv. Com., Progress Electromagnetic Rsch. Symposium, Internat. Radio Sci. Union, Radiation Rsch. Soc., Bioelectromagnetics Soc. (bd. dirs. 1981—84, Curtis Carl Johnson Meml. award 1995, d'Arsonval medal 2006), N.Am. Hyperthermia Soc., Internat. Microwave Power Inst. (1st Spl. Decade award 1981, Outstanding Paper award 1985), Nat. Coun. Radiation Protection and Measurements (subcom. vice chmn. 1995—2000, IEEE liaison 1997—99, coun. mem. 1998—2004), Commn. K., Tau Beta Pi, Sigma Xi. Office Phone: 954-723-5387. Personal E-mail: drckchou@gmail.com. Business E-Mail: ck.chou@motorolasolutions.com.

CHOU, WUSHOW, retired computer scientist; b. Shanghai, Kiangsu, China, Feb. 12, 1939; m. Lena Sun, Apr. 17, 1965; children: Warren, Wesley. BEE, Cheng Kung U., Tainan, Taiwan, 1961; MEE, U. N.Mex., 1965; PhD in Elec. Engring. and Computer Sci., U. Calif., Berkeley, 1968. Acting asst. prof. U. Calif., Berkeley, 1968-69; v.p. Network Analysis Corp., Glen Cove, NY, 1969-76; vis. prof. SUNY, Stony Brook, 1976; rsch. prof. George Washington U., Washington, 1975-76; prof. computer sci. dept. and elec. and computer engring. dept. NC State U., Raleigh, 1976—2003, prof. emeritus, 2003—, dir. computer studies, 1976-88; dep. asst. sec. for info. systems U.S. Dept. Treasury, Washington, 1994-97, chief info. officer, 1996-97; ret. Pres. ACK Computer Applications, Cary, NC, 1978—93; vis. prof. Poly. U., Bklyn., 1988—89; cons. AT&T, IBM, U.S. Govt., Singapore Govt., French Govt. Author, editor: Computer Communication, Vol. 1, 1984, Vol. 2, 1985, Advances in Telecommunications, 1985—86, editor-in-chief: Jour. Telecom., 1982—85, IT Profl., 1998—2001; chmn. adv. bd. IT Profl., 2002—; contbr. articles to profl. jours.; author: Fast Tracing Your carrier: Soft Skills for Engineering and IT Professionals, 2013. Recipient award, GSA, Washington, 1988, Treasury Dept., 1997; Rsch. grantee, NSF, 1978, Army Rsch. Office, 1982, AT&T, 1987. Fellow: IEEE (award 2001, 2002), Assn. Computing Machines. Office: NC State U Dept Computer Sci PO Box 8206 Raleigh NC 27695-0001 Business E-Mail: chou@ncsu.edu.

CHOW, RITA KATHLEEN, nursing consultant; b. San Francisco, Aug. 19, 1926; d. Peter and May (Chan) Chow. BS, Stanford U., 1950, nursing diploma, 1950; MS, Case Western Res. U., 1955; profl. diploma in nursing edn. adminstrn, Columbia U., 1961, EdD, 1968; B of Individualized Studies, George Mason U., 1983. Asst. in teaching Stanford U., Calif., 1951—52; instr., dir. student health Fresno Gen. Hosp. Sch. Nursing, Calif., 1952—54; instr. Wayne State U. Coll. Nursing, Detroit, 1957—58; rsch. assoc., project dir. cardiovasc. nursing rsch. Ohio State U., Columbus, 1965—68; commd. officer USPHS, 1968, advanced through grades to nurse dir. (capt.), 1974; spl. asst. to dep. dir. Nat. Ctr. Health Svcs. Rsch., Health Svcs. and Mental Health Adminstrn., HEW, Rockville, Md., 1969—73, dep. dir. manpower utilization br., 1970—73; dep. dir. Office Long Term Care; dep. chief nurse officer USPHS, Rockville, 1973—77; chief quality assurance br. div. long-term care Office Stds. and Certification, Health Standards and Quality Bur., Health Care Fin. Adminstrn., HHS, 1977—82; supervisory clin. nurse and spl. asst. to health systems adminstr. USPHS Indian Hosp., HRSA, HHS, Rosebud, SD, 1982—83; dir. patient edn., asst. dir. nursing G. W. Long Hansen's Disease Ctr., USPHS, Carville, La., 1984—89; dir. nursing Fed. Med. Ctr., Ft. Worth, 1989—95; pvt. cons., 1995—98; dir. Nat. Interfaith Coalition on Aging, Natl. Coun. on Aging, Washington, 1998—2010. Author: (book) Identifying Nursing Action with the Care of Cardiovascular Patients, 1967, Cardiosurgical Nursing Care: Understandings, Concepts and Principles for Practice, 1975; mem. editl. bd. Nursing and Health Care, 1983—95; contbr. articles to profl. jours. With Nurse Corps US Army, 1954—57, with USAR, 1954—68. Recipient Nursing Svc. award, Assn. Mil. Surgeons U.S., 1969, Commendation medal, USPHS, 1972, Meritorious Svc. medal, 1977, DSM, 1987, citation for outstanding contbn. to cardiovascular nursing, Am. Heart Assn., 1972—79, award for disting. achievement in nursing rsch., Nursing Edn. Alumni Assn., Columbia U. Tchrs. Coll., 1973, Disting. Alumnus award, Case Western Res. U. Sch. Nursing, 1979, Women's Honors in Pub. Svcs. award, ANA, 1988, USPHS Commendable Svc. medal, U.S. Dept. Justice, Bur. Prisons, 1995, Holistic Nurse of the Yr. award, Am. Holistic Nurses Assn., 2001, Artist of Life First prize, Internat. Womens Writing Guild, 1987, Chief Nurse Officer award, USPHS, 2003, Spirituality & Aging award, Nat. Interfaith Coalition Aging, Nat. Coun. Aging, 2009; grantee, Sigma Theta Tau, 1966. Fellow: Am. Assn. Advancement Sci., Am. Acad. Nursing, Gerontological Soc. Am., Nat. Gerontological Nursing Assn. (bd. dirs., Lifetime Achievement award 2010), Am. Assn. of Integrative Medicine (diplomate Coll. of Nursing 2003).

CHOWDHURI, PRITINDRA, retired electrical engineer, educator; b. Calcutta, India, July 12, 1927; arrived in US, 1949, naturalized, 1962; s. Ahindra and Sudhira (Mitra) C.; m. Sharon Elsie Hackebeil, Dec. 28, 1962; children: Naomi, Leslie, Robindro, Rajendro. B.Sc. in Physics with honors, Calcutta U., 1945, M.Sc., 1948; MS, Ill. Inst. Tech., 1951; D.Eng., Rensselaer Poly. Inst., 1966. Jr. engr. lightning arresters sect. Westinghouse Electric Corp., East Pittsburgh, Pa., 1951-52; elec. engr. high voltage lab. Maschinenfabrik Oerlikon, Zurich, 1952-53; research engr. High Voltage Rsch. Commn., Daeniken, Switzerland, 1953-56; devel. engr. high voltage lab. GE, Pittsfield, Mass., 1956-59, elec. engr. research and devel. ctr. Schenectady, NY, 1959-62, engr. elec. investigations transp. systems div. Erie, Pa., 1962-75; staff mem. Los Alamos Nat. Lab., N.Mex., 1975-86; prof. elec. engring. Ctr. Elec. Power Tenn. Technol. U., Cookeville, 1986—2005, emeritus prof., 2005—14. Lectr. Pa. State U. Behrend Grad. Ctr., Erie, 1969—75. Author: Electromagnetic Transients in Power Systems, 2d edit., 2004. Patentee in field. Fellow AAAS, IEEE, IET, UK, NY Acad. Scis. Democrat. Unitarian Universalist. Home: 690 Valley Forge Rd Cookeville TN 38501-1574 Personal E-mail: pchowdhuri@charter.net.

CHRISTENSEN, DONNA MARIE, Delegate to United States House Representative from Virgin Islands; b. Teaneck, NJ, Sept. 19, 1945; d. Almeric L. Christian and Virginia Sterling; m. Chris Christensen; children: Rabiah Green, Karida Green stepchildren: Lisa, Esther, Bryan, David. BS, St. Mary's Coll., Notre Dame, Ind., 1966; MD, George Washington U. Sch. Medicine, 1970; LLD (hon.), Moravian Coll., Bethlehem, Pa. Intern Calif. Pacific Med. Ctr., San Francisco; resident Howard U., Washington; cmty. health physician US VI Dept. Health; med. dir. Gov. Juan F. Luis Hosp., St. Croix; vice chairperson US VI Dem. Territorial Com., 1980; mem. US VI Bd. Edn., 1984, US VI Status Commn., 1988-92; del.-at-large US Congress from US VI, 1997—; 1st vice chair Congressional Black Caucus, 2011—. Mem. Congl. Caucus Women's Issues, Congl. Nat. Guard & Res. Caucus, Congl. Rural Caucus. Founding mem., trustee Caribbean Youth Orgn. Recipient Disting. Alumni award, George Washington U., Disting. Svc. award, Howard U. Sch. Medicine; named one of Most Influential Black Americans, Ebony mag., 2006; named to Power 150, 2008. Mem.: St. Croix Environ. Assn., St. Croix Women's Coalition, VI Med. Soc. (pres., sec.), VI Med. Inst., Caribbean Studies Assn., Nat. Med. Assn. (trustee). Democrat. Office: US House of Representatives 1510 Longworth House Office Bldg Washington DC 20515 also: Nisky Ctr Ste 207 St Thomas VI 00802 Office Phone: 202-225-1790. Office Fax: 202-225-5517. E-mail: donna.christensen@mail.house.gov.*

CHRISTENSEN, SUZANNE, investment company executive; BS with honors, U. Fla.; M in Acctg., Fla. Atlantic U. CPA. Sr. v.p. fin. Franklin Templeton Investments, chmn. enterprise risk mgmt. com.; head enterprise risk fin. planning & analysis Invesco Ltd., 2011—. Mem.: AICPA Exec. Com. Risk Assurance & Adv. Svcs. Task Force (vice chmn.). Office: Invesco Limited Two Peachtree Pointe 1555 Peachtree St NE Suite 1800 Atlanta GA 30309 Office Phone: 404-479-1095.

CHRISTIAN, CORA L.E, health facility administrator, physician; b. St. Thomas, VI, Sept. 11, 1947; d. Alphonso Augustine and Ruth Christian; m. Simon B. Jones-Hendrickson, Oct. 23, 1976; children: Nesha Christian-Hendrickson, Marcus Christian-Hendrickson. BS in Biology, Marquette U., 1967; MPH, Johns Hopkins U., 1975; MD, Jefferson Med. Coll., Phila., 1971. Diplomate Am. Coll. Forensic Examiners, Am. Bd. Quality Assurance and Utilization Rev., Am. Acad. Family Practice. Pvt. family-based practice, Frederiksted, VI, 1975—; asst. commr. Dept. Health, St. Croix, VI, 1977—91; educator, CEO, now med. dir. VI Med. Inst., Inc, St. Croix, 1978—; dir., prin. investigator US VI Household Survey, St. Croix, VI, 1988; chief med. cons., med. dir. Hovensa, LLC, St. Croix, 1990—; cons. VI AIDS Edn. and Tng., NYC, 1992—2005. Pres. Caribbean Studies Assn., 2000—01; pres., exec. sec., treas. VI Med. Soc., St. Croix, 1995—. Contbr. articles to profl. jours., chapters to books. Bd. dirs. Am. Cancer Soc., St. Croix, 1991—2005. Named to Trail Blazers for Women's History, Women's Bus. Ctr., 2000; Paul Harris fellow, Rotary, 1997. Mem.: AARP (nat. bd. dirs. 2004—10, vice chair ins. trust 2006—10), SGI (area leader 2010—), Interfaith Coalition (pres. 2010), Am. Acad. Family Physicians (pres. VI chpt. 1976—, com. mem. 1996—2005). Buddhist. Avocation: dance. Home: PO Box 1338 Frederiksted VI 00841 Office: VI Med Inst Inc PO Box 5989 Christiansted VI 00823-5989 Office Fax: 340-712-2449. Personal E-mail: corachristian@gmail.com.

CHRISTIAN, DAVID A., energy executive; BS in Mech. Engring., Va. Poly. Inst. & State U., 1976. CEO, generation Dominion Resources, Inc., v.p., nuc. ops., 1998—2000, sr. v.p., nuc. through sr. v.p., services & nuc. ops., 2000; pres., chief nuclear officer Dominion Nuclear, 2007—09; CEO Dominion Generation, 2010—. Mem. adv. bd. Ga. Inst. Tech. George W. Woodruff Sch. Mech. Engring. Office: Dominion Resources Inc 120 Tredegar St Richmond VA 23219 Office Phone: 804-819-2000. Office Fax: 804-819-2233. Business E-Mail: david.christian@dom.com.

CHRISTIAN, JAMES WAYNE, economist, writer; b. Ft. Worth, Oct. 7, 1934; s. Nap B. and Daphne (Wright) Christian; m. Jo June Maples, June 5, 1952; children: Amy Joella, Nicole Denise. BA, U. Tex., Austin, 1962, MA, 1964, PhD, 1965. Dir. internat. div. Fed. Home Loan Bank Bd., Washington, 1972—74; sr. v.p., chief economist Nat. Savs. and Loan League, Washington, 1974—80, U.S. League Savs. Inst., Chgo., 1980—91; pres. James Christian Assocs., Fair Oaks Ranch, Tex., 1991; dir. Real Estate Ctr. at Tex. A & M Univ., 1993—95. Prof. econs. Iowa State U., 1965—74; dir. Nat. Housing Conf., 1980—84; cons. 26 developing country govts., 1970—2001. Contbr. articles to profl. jour. Mem. Dem. Nat. Com. With USN, 1952—55, with USAF, 1955—59. Recipient Am. Legion award, 1949; univ. fellow, 1964, NSF fellow, 1965, Social Sci. Rsch. Coun. grant, 1968—69. Mem.: Cosmos, Phi Kappa Phi, Pi Sigma Alpha, Omicron Delta Epsilon, Phi Beta Kappa. Democrat. Methodist. Avocation: birdwatching.

CHRISTIAN, JOHN CATLETT, JR., lawyer; b. Springfield, Mo., Sept. 12, 1929; s. John Catlett and Alice Odelle (Milling) C.; m. Peggy Jeanne Cain, Apr. 12, 1953; children: Cathleen Marie, John Catlett, Alice Cain. AB, Drury Coll., 1951; LLB, Tulane U., New Orleans, 1956. Bar: La. 1956, Mo. 1956, US Supreme Ct. 1975. Assoc. Porter & Stewart, Lake Charles, La., 1956-58, Wilkinson, Lewis, Wilkinson & Madison, Shreveport, La., 1958-62, ptnr., 1962-64, Milling, Benson, Woodward, Hillyer, Pierson & Miller, New Orleans, 1964-92, of counsel, 1993-94. Pres. Sherburne Land Co., 1974-83, Pointe-Martin Mgmt., Inc., 1990-2000; dir. Emerald Land Corp. Pres. Kathleen Elizabeth O'Brien Found., 1963-. Served with USMC, 1951—53. Fellow Am. Coll. Trial Lawyers; mem. ABA, Fed. Bar Assn., Mo. Bar, La. Bar Assn., La. Landowners Assn. (bd. dirs. 1983-2001), Boston Club, Kappa Alpha Order, Omicron Delta Kappa, Phi Delta Phi. Home: 100 Christwood Blvd Apt 146 Covington LA 70433 Personal E-mail: jcchristiansr@aol.com.

CHRISTIAN, MIKE, state legislator; b. Jan. 13, 1970; Ret. state trooper, Okla.; mem. Dist. 93 Okla. House of Representatives, 2008—. Republican. Office: Oklahoma House of Representatives 2300 N Lincoln Blvd Rm 537-C Oklahoma City OK 73105 Mailing: 648 SW 41st Oklahoma City OK 73109 Office Phone: 405-557-7371. Business E-Mail: mike.christian@okhouse.gov.

CHRISTIAN, WAYNE, state legislator; m. Lisa Christian; 3 children. BBA, Stephen F. Austin State U., Nacogdoches, Tex. Investment advisor; mem. Dist. 9 Tex. House of Reps., 1997—2004, 2007—; mayor Graham, Tex., 2004—06. Republican. Mailing: 204 Houston St Center TX 75935 Address: Rm CAP GN.07 Capital PO Box 2910 Austin TX 78768 Office: 202 E Pillar Room 209 Nacogdoches TX 75961 Office Phone: 936-598-9966, 512-463-0556, 936-560-3982.

CHRISTIANSEN, JAMES EDWARD, agricultural educator; b. Douglas, Ariz., Sept. 1, 1930; s. Felix Lawrence and Ada Naomi (Squire) C.; m. Jean McInnes, Dec. 25, 1950; children: James Lawrence, Bruce John. BS, U. Ariz., 1951, M Agrl. Edn., 1957; PhD, Ohio State U., 1965. Tchr. vocat. agriculture Tolleson (Ariz.) Union High Sch., 1954-57, Snowflake (Ariz.) Union High Sch., 1957-58, Tempe (Ariz.) Union High Sch., 1958-61; project mgr. Near East Found., Resht, Iran, 1961-63; asst. instr. Ohio State U., Columbus, 1964; cons. ctr. for vocat.-tech. edn. Nat. Ctr. for Rsch. in Vocat.-Tech. Edn., Columbus, 1965; asst. prof. U. Fla., Gainesville, 1966-68; prof. Tex. A&M U., College Station, 1968—2004, prof. emeritus, 2005—. Cons. agrl. edn. US AID, San Jose, Costa Rica, 1967, San Jose, 1986, Asuncion, Paraguay, 1983, Belize, 1990, Malaysia, 1992, El Salvador, 1994, Mexico, 1999, 2000, 2002, 2004, Dominican Republic, 2005, Botswana, 2006, Internat. Inst. Cooperation in Agrl., San Jose, 2001; sr. scientist Norman Borlaug Inst. Internat. Agr., 2011. Author: Exploring Agriculture, 6th ed., 1984, 5th ed., 1979; contbr. articles to profl. jours. Elder A&M Presbyn. Ch., Covenant Presbyn. Ch., College Station, 1969-72, 81-83, 90-92, 2008-2010. Sgt. US Army, 1951-53. Recipient Coll. Disting. Tchg. award, Tex. A&M U., 1983, Internat. Excellence award, 1996, Bush Excellence award for faculty in internat. tchg., George Bush Presdl. Libr. Found., 2004; named Disting. Lectr., Am. Assn. Agrl. Edn., 2000. Mem. Am. Vocat. Assn. (resolutions com. 1988-91), Am. Assn. Tchr. Educators in Agr. (treas. 1977-80, chmn. editing-mng. bd. 1973-76, Disting. Svc. award 1985), Assn. for Internat. Agrl. and Extension Edn. (chmn. constn. and bylaws 1986-87, 96-99, scholarly activities 2000-03, Outstanding Svc. award 2000, Outstanding Leadership award 2003), Vocat. Agr. Tchrs. Assn. Tex. (Outstanding Tchr. Educator award 1979, Disting. Svc. award 1992, 2002), Kiwanis (sec. Snowflake chpt. 1957), Phi Beta Delta, Phi Delta Kappa (Norman Borlaug Internat. Rsch. and Svc. award, 2004), Phi Kappa Phi. Republican. Avocations: landscape and instructional photography, rifle target shooting, archaeology. Office: Tex A&M U Dept Agrl Leadership Edn and Comm 2116 TAMU College Station TX 77843-2116 Business E-Mail: j-christiansen@tamu.edu.

CHRISTIANSEN, MARK D., lawyer; b. Olney, Tex., June 10, 1955; s. Leon H. and Doris J. (Jennings) C. BA, U. Okla., 1977, JD, 1980. Bar: U.S. Dist. Ct. (we. dist.) Okla. 1984, U.S. Dist. Ct. (ea. dist.) Okla. 1993, U.S. Ct. Appeals (10th cir.) 1987. Assoc. Crowe & Dunlevy, Oklahoma City, 1980-85, mem., 1986—. Editor: The Oil and Gas Reporter. Bd. trustees Ctr. for Am. Internat. Law. Mem.: ABA (chmn. oil and natural gas exploration and prodn. com. 1999—2001, chmn. energy and natural resources litigation 2001—), Ctr. Am. and Internat. Law, Rocky Mountain Mineral Law Found. (mem. exec. com., mem. bd. trustees), Okla. Bar Assn., Oklahoma City Mineral Lawyers Soc. (pres. 1989—90). Home: 20 N Broadway Ave Ste 1800 Oklahoma City OK 73102-8296 Office: Crowe & Dunlevy Mid America Tower 20 N Broadway Ave Ste 1800 Oklahoma City OK 73102-8273

CHRISTIANSEN, PATRICK T., lawyer; b. Mpls., 1947; BSEE summa cum laude, U. Notre Dame, 1969; JD, Harvard U., 1972. Bar: Fla. 1972, Minn. 1974, U.S. Tax Ct. 1977, U.S. Supreme Ct. 1980. Mem. Akerman, Senterfitt & Eidson P.A., Orlando, Fla. Chmn. bd. Orlando Mus. Art; mem., bd. dirs. The Greater Orlando C. of C., Jobs and Edn. Partnership; chmn. Orange County Transp. Roundtable, BusinessForce, 2002--; mem. Orange County Blue Ribbon Commn., steering com., chmn. transp. com.; bd. dirs. United Arts Cen. Fla., Orlando Downtown Devel. Bd.; trustee, chmn. Orlando Repertory Theatre, 2002--, U. Ctrl. Fla. Found., 2001--; bd. trustees U. Ctrl. Fla.;

mem. Orange County Arts & Cultural Affairs Adv. Com., chmn. advancement com., 2001--. Mem. ABA (sects. on bus. law, taxation, real property), Fla. Bar (trial lawyers sect., co-chmn. land trust com. real property, probate and trust law sect. 1978-82, dir. real property divsn. 1982-84, vice chmn. 1984-85, chmn. 1985-86, vice-chmn. UCC subcom. corp., banking and bus. law sect. 1979-84, bd. govs. young lawyers sect. 1981-83), Am. Coll. Real Estate Lawyers, Minn. State Bar Assn., Orange County Bar Assn. Office: Akerman Senterfitt Ste 1200 PO Box 231 420 South Orange Ave Orlando FL 32801

CHRISTIANSON, GERYLD B., government agency administrator, consultant; b. Boyd, Minn., Dec. 31, 1934; m. Sue Singer, July 9, 1960; children: Stephen, Alexander. BA in Internat. Rels., U. Minn., 1957; postgrad., Johns Hopkins U., 1967-68. Fgn. svc. officer Dept. State, NATO Office, Bur. European Affairs, various fgn. locations, 1958-75; fgn. policy advisor Senator Claiborne Pell, Washington, 1975-81; dem. staff dir. Senate Fgn. Rels. Com., Washington, 1981-87, staff dir., 1987-95; sr. counselor The Evans Group, Ltd., Washington, 1995, 97—; v.p. Jefferson Waterman Internat., Washington, 1995-97. With USAR, 1957—63. Mem. Coun. on Fgn. Rels. Democrat. Episcopalian. Avocations: collecting political buttons, tennis. Home: 8716 Mary Lee Ln Annandale VA 22003-3659 Personal E-mail: geryld.christianson@verizon.net.

CHRISTIE, GEORGE CUSTIS, lawyer, educator, writer; b. NYC, Mar. 3, 1934; s. Custis and Sophie (Velimahitis) C.; m. Susan D. Monserud, Apr. 20, 1965 (div. July 1974); 1 child, Constantine George; m. Deborah D. Carnes, Dec. 20, 1974; children: Rebecca Sophia, Nicholas George. AB, Columbia U., 1955, JD, 1957; diploma in internat. law (Fulbright scholar), Cambridge U., Eng., 1962; SJD, Harvard U., 1966; Doctorate (hon.), U. Athens, 2007. Bar: NY 1957, DC 1958. Assoc. Covington & Burling, Washington, 1958-60; Ford Found. fellow in law teaching Harvard U., 1960-61; assoc. prof. law U. Minn., Mpls., 1962-65, prof. law, 1965-66; asst. gen. counsel for Near E. and S. Asia, AID, Dept. State, 1966-67; prof. law Duke U., 1967-79, James B. Duke prof. law, 1979—. Vis. lectr. U. Witwatersrand, South Africa, 1980, Fudan U., China, U. Otago, New Zealand, 1985; fellow Nat. Humanities Center, 1980-81; scholar-in-residence McGuire, Woods & Battle, Richmond, Va., 1983, vis. Freda Alverson prof. law George Washington U., spring 1988; vis. prof. law Northwestern U., 1991-92, U. Athens, Greece, 2000; vis. fellow Rsch. Sch. Social Scis., Australian Nat. U., 2002. Author: Jurisprudence: Text and Readings on the Philosophy of Law, 1973, 3rd edit. (with P. Martin), 2008, The Sum and Substance of the Law of Torts, 1980, Law, Norms & Authority, 1982, Cases and Materials on the Law of Torts, 1983, 2d edit. (with J. Meeks), 1990, 4th edit. (with others), 2004, The Notion of an Ideal Audience in Legal Argument, 2000, French edit., 2005, (with others) Cases and Materials on Advanced Torts, 2004, Philosopher Kings? The Adjudication of Conflicting Human Rights and Social Values, 2011. With US Army, 1957. Mem. ABA, Am. Law Inst., Am. Soc. Internat. Law, Phi Beta Kappa. Democrat. Greek Orthodox. Home: 5212 Twin Pines Ln Durham NC 27705-8599 Office: Duke U Sch Law PO Box 90360 Durham NC 27708-0360 Office Phone: 919-613-7052. Business E-Mail: gcc@law.duke.edu.

CHRISTIE, JACK, councilman, chiropractor; children: John, Katherine, Patrick. DC, Tex. Chiropractic Coll. With Army Reserves Med. Corps; councilman-at-large Position 5 Houston City Coun., 2012—. Chmn. Tex. State Bd. Edn., 1995—2000. Bd. dirs. Spring Branch-Meml. C. of C. Named to Tex. Sci. Hall of Fame, 2000. Office: City Hall Annex 900 Badby, First Floor Houston TX 77002 Office Phone: 832-393-3017. Office Fax: 832-393-3261. E-mail: atlarge5@houstontx.gov.

CHRISTISON, MURIEL BRANHAM, retired museum director, art history educator; b. Mpls. d. Harold D. and Helen (Ferguson) Branham; children: Evelyn, Carolyn. BA, U. Minn., 1933, MA, 1940; diploma, U. Paris, 1936, U. Brussels, 1938. Grad. asst. dept. fine arts U. Minn., Mpls., 1933-36; curatorial rsch. asst. Mpls. Inst. Arts, Mpls., 1936-42, head edn., 1944-47; assoc. dir. Va. Mus. Fine Arts, Richmond, 1948-61; oper. and assoc. dir. Krannert Art Mus. U. Ill., Champaign, 1962-74, dir. Krannert Art Mus., 1975-82; ret., 1982; interim dir. Muscarelle Mus. Coll. William and Mary, Williamsburg, Va., 1984-85, 94-96, mem. vis. com., 1982-96, vis. prof. fine arts, 1983-98. Head grad. program mus. studies U. Ill., 1974—82; cons. U. Tex., Austin, Washington U., St. Louis, 1972, St. Louis, 1978, Ill. Arts Coun., 1968—82; v.p. Midwest Mus. Conf. Am. Assn. Mus., regional rep., 1972—82; examiner S.C. Arts Coun., 1984, 1986, Ohio Arts Coun., 1986, Nat. Endowment for the Arts, 1973, 1983, NEH, 1980. Author: numerous exhbn. catalogs; contbr. articles to profl. jours. Carnegie scholar Inst. Internat. Edn., 1936; CRB fellow Belgian-Am. Edn. Found., 1938; recipient Disting. Svc. award Midwest Mus. Conf., 1982 Mem.: Colonial Williamsburg Fund, William and Mary Found., Coun. Va. Mus. Fine Arts, Assn. Preservation Va. Antiquities, Am. Assn. Museums (regional rep. 1972—82, bd. dirs. 1972—82, surveyor, examiner 1982—), Assn. Art Mus. Dirs. (emerita 1982, hon. 1982—). Home: 3907 Foxfield Terrace Richmond VA 23233 also: 3907 Foxfield Ter Henrico VA 23233-1018

CHRISTMAN, LISA P., food service executive; AA in Fashion Merchandising, Bauder Fashion Coll., 1980. Dist. mgr. Lane Bryant, 1985—91; retail dist. mgr. Limited Brands, 1985—95; dist. mgr. County Seat, 1991—95, Goody's Family Clothing, 1995—2001; regional v.p., retail ops. Cracker Barrel Old Country Store, Inc., 2001—. Office: Cracker Barrel Old Country Store Inc 305 Hartmann Dr Lebanon TN 37088-0787 Office Phone: 615-444-5533. Office Fax: 615-443-9476.

CHRISTNER, BRENT CRAIG, biology professor, researcher; b. July 31, 1970; BS in Molecular Biology and Biotechnology, Westminster Coll., New Wilmington, Pa., 1992; MS in Microbiology, U. Dayton, Ohio, 1996; PhD in Microbiology, Ohio State U., 2002. Tchg. asst., dept. biology U. Dayton, Ohio, 1994—95; tchg. and grad. rsch. asst., dept. microbiology Ohio State U., Columbus, 1997—2002; post-doctoral researcher Dept. Land Resources and Environmental Sciences, Montana State U., Bozeman, 2002—04, asst. rsch. prof., 2004—06; asst. prof., dept. biol. sciences La. State U., Baton Rouge, 2006—. Participant in several workshops and committees; invited cons. for NASA Johnson Space Ctr., Acquisition and Curation Team, 2001; US Rep. at the North Greenland Ice Core Project Basel Ice Meeting Niels Bohr Inst., Denmark, 2004; mem. US Ice Core Working Group, 2007—10; NASA Exobiology Panel Reviewer, Washington, 2009; participant in the PolarTREC during the 2009-2010 Antarctic Field Season. Referee for peer-reviewed journals and grant applications, research has been highlighted in Astrobiology Magazine, BBC Worldwide, Bloomberg News, Chemical and Engineering News, CBC Radio, CBS Sunday Morning. CBS Radio, Discovery Magazine, Environmental Research Web, Forum, Geotimes, Globe and Mail, La Presse, KDKA Radio, Live Science, Microbiology Today, Microscopy Today, National Geographic, Nature, Nature Reviews Microbiology, New Scientist, Science Magazine, Science Podcast, Science Friday (NPR), Science Daily, Scientific American, The Advocate, Astrobiology Web, Bozeman Chronicle, New York Times, Telegraph, Washington Post, Time, Wired and Yahoo News. Recipient Antarctic Svc. medal of the U.S.A., NSF for Scientific Exploration and Svc. in Antarctica, 2006, Rsch. named by Discover Mag. as one of the Top 100 Stories of 2008. Mem.: Am. Soc. Microbiology, Am. Soc. Limnology and Oceanography, Am. Geophysical Union. Office: Dept Biological Sciences 282 Life Sciences Building Louisiana State University Baton Rouge LA 70803 Home Phone: 225-218-4045; Office Phone: 225-578-1734. Business E-Mail: xner@lsu.edu.

CHRISTOPHER, ERIC, retail executive; BA in Modern Fgn. Language, U. Wash. Worked Nordstrom's; v.p., quality assurance, corp. ethics officer QVC, Inc., 1996—2008; v.p., quality assurance Zale Corp., 2008—. Office: Zale Corp 901 W Walnut Hill Ln Irving TX 75038-1003 Office Phone: 972-580-4000. Office Fax: 972-580-5547.

CHRISTOPHER, GREGORY L., metal products executive; Joined Mueller Industries, Inc., 1992, v.p., Sales Std. Products divsn., pres., Std. Products divsn., 2005—07, COO, 2007—08, CEO, 2008—, Mueller Copper Tube Co., Inc. Office: Mueller Industries Inc Ste 150 8285 Tournament Dr Memphis TN 38125 Office Phone: 901-753-3200. Office Fax: 901-753-3251. Business E-Mail: gchristopher@muellerindustries.com.

CHRISTOPHER, JOE RANDELL, retired language educator; b. Bartlesville, Okla., June 27, 1935; s. Ernest Randell and Blanche (Woods) C.; m. Mary Lynn Hayes, June 9, 1958; children: Saralinda Michelle Christopher-Evans, Vandy Maria, Randell Llewellyn-Hayes C. BA, U. Okla., 1957, MA, 1959, PhD, 1969. Instr. Tarleton State U., Stephenville, Tex., 1963-67, asst. prof., 1967-68; vis. prof. Western N.Mex. U., Silver City, summer 1970; assoc. prof. Tarleton State U., Stephenville, Tex., 1968-87, prof., 1987-2001, prof. emeritus, 2001—. Invited lecturer Abilene Christian U. Ctr. for Christian Writing, 1990; keynote spkr. C.S. Lewis for 20th Century conf., Oklahoma City U., 1998. Author: (with Dean W. Dickensheet, Robert E. Briney) A. Boucher Bibliography, 1969; (play) A Foretaste of Blood to Come, 1973; (with Joan K. Ostling) C.S. Lewis: An Annotated Checklist of Writings about Him and His Works, 1974; (book) C.S. Lewis, 1987; (chapbook) Musings beneath a Tree of Amalion, 2nd edit., 1993; editor: (book) Chad Walsh Reviews C.S. Lewis, 1998, Sayers on Holmes: Essays and Fiction on Sherlock Holmes by Dorothy L. Sayers, 2001; (Dark Fantasy issue) Niekas 45, 1998; assoc. editor: (with Jonathan B. Himes and Salwa Khoddam) Truths Breathed Through Silver: The Inklings' Moral and Mythopoeic Legacy, 2008; editor: The Casebook of Gregory Hood by Anthony Boucher and Denis Green, 2009; (book) Ars Poetica or The Variety of Poetic Genres: Ars Poetica, 2012; contbg. editor: The Lamp-Post of the Southern California C.S. Lewis Soc.; mem. editl. bd. Windhover: A Journal of Christian Literature, The Mythopoeic Press. Mem. exec. coun. Episcopal Diocese Ft. Worth (affiliated with Nat. Episcopal Ch.), 2011—13. Mythopoeic scholar for publ. books, 1976, 88; guest of honor Mythopoeic Conf., N.Y. C.S. Lewis Weekend, Tulsa C.S. Lewis Conf.; papers collected Western History Collections, U. Okla. Librs., Norman, Dick Smith Libr., Tarleton State U., Stephenville, Tex. Mem.: MLA (life), South Ctrl. MLA (life), Conf. on Christianity and Lit., Mythopoeic Soc., Dorothy L. Sayers Soc., Lewis Carroll Soc. N.Am., C. S. Lewis and Inklings Soc. (mem., exec. bd.), Praed St. Irregulars (hon.), West 87th St. Irregulars (hon.). Democrat. Episcopalian. Office: Tarleton State U Box T-0300 Stephenville TX 76402-0300 Office Phone: 254-968-1905. Business E-Mail: jchristopher@tarleton.edu.

CHRISTOPHER, ROBERT PAUL, retired physical medicine physician; b. Cleve., Apr. 27, 1932; s. Walter Matthews and Charity Marie (Roberts) C.; m. Doreen Mary O'Leary, Apr. 28, 1962; children: Robert Jr., Judith, Mark. BS, Northwestern U., 1954; MD, St. Louis U., 1959. Diplomate Am. Bd. Physical Medicine and Rehab. Chief rehab. medicine V.A. Hosp., Ann Arbor, Mich., 1963-67; asst. prof. rehab. medicine U. Mich., 1964-67; assoc. prof. rehab. medicine U. Tenn., Memphis, 1967-71, prof. rehab. medicine, 1971-2001, ret., 2001. Med. dirs. Les Passees Children's Rehab. Ctr., Memphis, 1976-98, Le Bonheur Hosp. Rehab. Svcs., Memphis, 1981-2001, Regional Med. Ctr. Rehab. Svcs., Memphis, 1967-2001, assoc. med. dir. St. Joseph Rehab. Ctr., Memphis, 1981-98. Contbg. author: Seating the Cerebral Palsey Child, 1983; author: sound/slide program Systems of Physical Therapy in Cerebral Palsy, 1971; contbr. articles to profl. jours. Pres. Mid-South Health Systems Agy., Memphis, 1980; mem. Mayor's Adv. Council for Disabled, Memphis, 1977-98. Recipient Disting. Svc. Commn. on Accredited Rehab. Facilities, 1982. Fellow Am. Acad. Phys. Medicine and Rehab. (sec. 1982-88, v.p. 1992—, pres. elect 1993, pres. 1994), Am. Acad. Cerebral Palsy (pres. 1987); mem. AMA, Am. Congress Rehab. Medicine, So. Soc. Phys. Medicine and Rehab. (sec. 1976-2000), Am. Bd. of Phys. Medicine and Rehab. (vice chmn. 1992-98), East Memphis Cath. Club (bd. dirs. 1969-80), K.C. (Grand Knight 1969-70). Avocations: travel, swimming. Home: 818 Island Club Sq Vero Beach FL 32963-5505 Personal E-mail: drbobchris1@bellsouth.net. Business E-Mail: drbobchris1@comcast.net.

CHRISTOPHER, RUSSELL LEWIS, baritone; b. Grand Rapids, Mich., Mar. 12, 1930; s. Russell Stewart and Violet (Jurewicz) C.; m. Gail B. Eldredge, Aug. 24, 1963 (div. 1985); 1 son, Russell Frederick. AA, Grand Rapids Jr. Coll., 1950; MusB, U. Mich., 1953, MusM, 1954. Music librarian NBC, NYC, 1955-58. Elected U. Mich. Sch. Music Alumni Bd. Govs., 1997-2003. Prin. artist, N.Y.C. Opera Co., 1958-60, San Francisco Opera Co., 1962, 63, Met. Opera Assn., N.Y.C., 1963-91, soloist, L.A., Montreal, Chgo., Richmond symphony orchs., 1963—; sang role Maecenas in: world premiere Antony and Cleopatra at new, Met. Opera House, 1966; recs.: Carmen (Deutsche Grammophon), 1973, La Traviata (Electra Records), 1982, (CD) I'll Take Romance, 2002; numerous TV prodns. Live from the Met (Emmy award 1985); Miami Beach Symphony, Hollywood Bowl, Balt. Civic Opera, Central City Opera, Dayton Opera Assn., Phila. Lyric Opera Assn., Met. opera tour, Japan, 1975, 86; concert soloist, Spoleto (Italy) Festival, 1977. Mem. U. Mich. Sch. Music Alumni Bd., 1997. Recipient award Martha Baird Rockefeller Fund for Music, 1961; auditions winner Am. Opera, 1962; auditions winner Met. Opera, 1963; Mrs. Frederick K. Weyerhaeuser award, 1963; Disting. Alumni award Grand Rapids Jr. Coll., 1964, Alumnus of Yr. award U. Mich. Club of N.Y., 1978; recipient citation of merit award for outstanding contbns. to field of music, Alumni Bd., Sch. of Music, U. Mich., 1995. Mem. Am. Guild Musical Artists (nat. bd. govs. 1985-91, 94-99, exec. com. 1994-99).

CHRISTY, JOHN RAYMOND, atmospheric scientist; b. Fresno, Calif., May 24, 1951; s. Clyde Roger and Georgia Lou (Prentice) C.; m. Alice Babette Joslin, Sept. 27, 1975; children Alison Ruth, Brian John. BA in Math, Calif. State U., Fresno, 1973; MDiv, Golden Gate Bapt. Sem., 1978; MS in Atmospheric Sciences, U. Ill., 1984, PhD in Atmospheric Sciences, 1987. Sci. master Nyeri (East Africa) Bapt. H.S., Kenya, 1973-75; instr. U. S.D., Vermillion, 1981-82; bivocational misson-pastor Grace Bapt. Ch., Vermillion, SD, 1978-82; rsch. scientist U. Ala., Huntsville, 1987-91, assoc. prof., 1991, disting. prof. atmospheric sci., 2008—, dir., Earth System Sci. Ctr.; climatologist Ala. State, 2000—. Contbr. Intergovtl. Panel on Climate Change, UN, 1992, 1994, 1996, and 2007, lead author 2001. Featured in Discover Mag., 2001, NPR Radio, 2004; contbr. articles to profl. jours. Pres. Grissom High PTSA, Huntsville, 1997-99; chmn. facilities com., Grisson High Sch. Recipient Medal for Exceptional Scientific Achievement NASA, 1991, Disting. Rsch. award U. Ala., Huntsville, 1993, Disting. Alumnus Calif. State U., Fresno, 2007. Fellow Am. Meterol. Soc. (Spl. award 1996); mem. Am. Geophys. Union (panel mem. official statement on climate change, 2003) Baptist. Achievements include co-developer of method to utilize satellite data for global temperature monitoring. Office: Earth System Science Ctr NSSTC U Alabama 320 Sparkman Dr NSSTC 4040 Huntsville AL 35805 Office Phone: 256-961-7763. Office Fax: 256-961-7751. Business E-Mail: john.christy@nssstc.uah.edu.

CHU, CHUNG KWANG, distinguished research professor emeritus; b. Seoul, Republic of Korea, May 18, 1941; s. Jee Young Huh; children: Susan, Jackie. BS, Seoul Nat. U., 1964; MS, Idaho State U., 1970; PhD, SUNY, Buffalo, 1974. Rsch. assoc. Sloan-Kettering Cancer Inst., NYC, 1974-80; asst. prof. Idaho State U., Pocatello, 1990-82; asst. prof. medicinal chemistry U. Ga., Athens, 1982-87, assoc. prof., 1987-89, prof., 1990-98, disting. rsch. prof., 1998—2007, disting. rsch. prof. emeritus, 2008—. Adv. bd. NIH, Pharmasset, Atlanta. Fellow: AAAS; mem.: Am. Chem. Soc. (Rsch. grant 1988), Am. Assn. for Cancer Rsch., Am. Assn. Colls. Pharmacy, Internat. Soc. Antiviral Rsch. Achievements include patents for drug discovery field. Office: U Ga Coll Pharmacy Athens GA 30602 Office Phone: 706-542-5379. Office Fax: 706-542-5381. Business E-Mail: dchu@uga.edu.

CHU, DAVID S.C., think-tank executive, former federal agency administrator; b. NYC, May 28, 1944; s. H. T. and Esther Chu; m. Laura L. Tosi. BA in Economics & Mathematics magna cum laude, Yale U., 1964, PhD in Economics, 1972. Asst. dir. nat. security and internat. affairs Congl. Budget Office (CBO), Washington, 1978—81; dir. then asst. sec. def. for program analysis and evaluation US Dept. Def., 1981—93; economist RAND Corp., Santa Monica, Calif., 1970—78, sr. fellow Washington, 1993—94, dir. Washington rsch. dept., 1994—96, dir. Washington office, assoc. chmn. of rsch. staff, 1996—98; v.p. army rsch. divsn., dir. Arroyo Ctr., 1998—2001; under sec. for pers. & readiness US Dept. Def., Washington, 2001—09; pres., CEO Inst. Def. Analyses, Alexandria, Va., 2009—. Capt. US Army, 1968—70, Vietnam. Decorated Bronze Star, Army commendation medal; recipient Medal for Disting. Pub. Svc., US Dept. Def., Nat. Pub. Svc. award. Fellow: Nat. Acad. Pub. Adminstrn. (chmn., bd. trustees 1999—2001); mem.: Phi Beta Kappa. Office: Institute for Defense Analyses 4850 Mark Ctr Dr Alexandria VA 22311 Office Phone: 703-845-2000.*

CHU, KATHY, reporter; BA in English, U. Calif., Berkeley, 1997; MA, Columbia U. Grad. Sch. Journalism, NYC, 1999. Pub. cons. Prentice Hall, San Francisco, 1988; features editor, asst. news editor, reporter The Daily Californian, 1995—97; writer Berkeley guides Fodor's Travel Guides, 1996; reporter Time Warner Inc., NYC, 1999; freelance reporter Newsday/Asian Wall St. Jour., 1999—2000; bus. reporter Dow Jones News Svc., Jersey City, 2000—05, USA Today, 2005—. Recipient Clarion award for Newspaper Feature Series, Assn. Women in Comm., 2008, Award for Consumer Reporting, NY Press Club, 2009, George Polk Award for Bus. Reporting, LI Univ., 2009; grantee Joseph E. Hughes Comm. Coun. Fellowship, Am. Bankers Ass. Stonier Grad. Sch. Banking, 2005. Mem.: Newswomen's Club NY (Front Page award for Bus. Reporting 2004, Award for Beat Reporting 2009). Mailing: USA Today Hdqs 7950 Jones Branch Dr Mc Lean VA 22108

CHU, PAUL CHING-WU, physicist, academic administrator, educator; b. Hunan, China, Dec. 2, 1941; arrived in U.S., 1963, naturalized, 1973; m. May P. Chern; children: Claire, Albert. BS, Cheng-Kung U., Taiwan, 1962; MS, Fordham U., 1965; PhD, U. Calif., San Diego, 1968; PhD (hon.), Fordham U., 1988, Northwestern U., 1988, Chinese U. of Hong Kong, 1988, Fla. Internat. U., 1989, SUNY, 1989, Whittier Coll., 1991, Hong Kong Bapt. U., 1999, Providence U., 2005, U. Macau, 2006, Loughborough U., 2007. Tchg. asst. Fordham U., Bronx, NY, 1963—65; rsch. asst. U. Calif., San Diego, 1965—68; tech. staff Bell Labs., Murray Hill, NJ, 1968—70; asst. prof. physics Cleve. State U., 1970—73, assoc. prof., 1973—75, prof., 1975—79; prof. physics U. Houston, 1979—, dir. magnetic info. rsch. lab., 1984—88, dir. Space Vacuum Epitaxy Ctr., 1986—88, T.L.L. Temple chair sci., 1987—, M.D. Anderson chair physics, 1987—89, dir. Tex. Ctr. for Superconductivity, 1987—2001; prin. investigator Lawrence Berkeley Nat. Lab., 1999—; dir. NSF/materials rsch. sci. and engring. ctr. U. Houston, 1996—97; convenor Heads of Univs. Com., Hong Kong, 2003—04; pres. Hong Kong U. Sci. and Tech., 2001—09; exec. dir. Tex. Ctr. Superconductivity, 2005—. Resident, rsch. assoc. Argonne Nat. Lab., Ill., 1972; vis. scientist Hansens Physics Lab., Stanford, 1973; mem. vis. staff Los Alamos Sci. Lab., 1975—80; hon. prof. Zhongshan U., 1988, Chinese Acad. Scis. Physics Inst., 1979, Nankai U., 1991, Chinese U. Sci. and Tech., 1991, Nanjing U., 1996, Dongnan U., 2003, Nat. Tsinghua U., 2009; bd. dirs. Coalition for the Comml. Application of Superconductors, 1989—; mem. White House ad hoc rev. panel on long-range plan for R & D of superconductivity, 1989; mem. rsch. adv. com. Inst. for Tech. and Strategic Rsch., 1989; vis. Miller rsch. prof. U. Calif., Berkeley, 1991; mem. adv. com. to redesign the space sta. The White House, Washington, 1993; mem. sch. adv. bd. Ctr. Nanoscale Sci. and Tech., Rice U., 1995—; internat. adv. com. Hong Kong Bapt. U., 1995—; internat. adv. bd. China-Am. Tech. Corp., 1995—; mem. adv. com. on rsch. planning Higher Edn. Coordinating Bd., State of Tex., 1997—2000; bd. dirs. S.S. Chern Found. Math. Rsch., 2000—, Applied Superconductivity Conf., 2000—02, pres., 2000—02; advisor Hong Kong Area of Excellence Project, 2001—06; mem. inst. physics acad. adv. com. Academia Sinica, 2001—, mem. ctrl. adv. com., 2002—, mem. coun., 2002—; chmn. ad hoc Com. on Future Nat. Energy, 2002—; dir. search com. Academia Sinica Ctr. Applied Sci. Engineering Rsch., 2002—; mem. rsch. adv. bd. U. Tex., Dallas, 2004—; mem. adv. bd. Ctr. for Nanomagnetic Systems U. Houston, 2004—, mem. pres.'s exec. adv. coun., 2004—; mem. founding governing bd. Acad. Medicine, Engring. and Sci. Tex., 2004—; mem. program adv. com. Inst. Advanced Studies, Nanyang Tech. U., 2005—; hon. pres. Jiaxing U., 2006; founding dir. Inst. Advanced Study, Hong Kong U. Sci. and Tech., 2006—; mem. univ. adv. com. Nat. Tsing Hua U., 2006—; mem. bus. and sci. adv. bd. Britton Chance Ctr. for Biomed. Protonics, Hunzhong U. Sci. and Tech., Wuhun, China, 2006—; cons. in field; mem. exec. com. Commn. on Strategic Devel., Hong Kong SAR Govt., 2006—; adv. bd. Chinese Assn Sci. and Tech.-Texas, 2006—07; mem. adv. bd. Aurora Imaging Tech. Inc., 2007—; internat. adv. coun. King Abdullah U. Sci. and Tech., 2008, mem. pres.'s inservation adv. coun., 2009; mem. panem on neutron rsch. Nat. Rsch. Coun., 2008; reviewer US Dept. Energy, mem. materials sci. review panel; mem. consultation com. Ministry of Edn., China, 2009—; hon. advisor Hong Kong Union Young Leaders, 2009—10; mem. Sci. & Tech. Adv. Group Bd., Exec. Yuan, Taiwan, 2009—11; dir., bd. dirs. Chiang Chen Indsl. Charity Found., 2010—; mem. acad. adv. com. Rsch. Ctr. Applied Sci., 2010; mem. com. rsch. univs. Nat. Rsch. Coun., 2010—; mem. Internat. Adv. Com. Japan Sci & Tech. Agy., 2010—; sr. mem. Shenzhen Mpcl. Sci. & Tech. Adv. Com., 2010—. Mem. editl. bd.: High Tech. Bus., 1988—, Modern Physics Letters B, 1988—, Applied Superconductivity, 1992—98, Indian Jour. Pure and Applied Physics, 1992—, News and Reviews of

Physics in China Today, 1992—, Internat. Jour. Modern Physics, 1988—, Brazilian Jour. Physics, 1995—, Sci. in China, 1997—, Chinese Sci. Bull., 1997—, Applied Physics Rev. (Korea), 1998—2000; contbr. articles to profl. jours. Internat. adv. com. World Lab. Pan Am. Ctr. for Collaboration in Sci. and Tech., 1998—; mem. Pres. Com. on the Nat. Medal Sci., 2007—; bd. dirs. Hong Kong Sci. and Tech. Pk., 2003—, T.S. Chang Scholarship Found., 1999—. 2d lt. Nationalist Chinese Air Forces, 1962—63. Recipient Phys. and Math. Sci. award, NY Acad. Sci., 1987, Leroy Randle Grumman medal, Grumman Corp., 1987, Achievement award, Chinese Am. Acad. and Profl. Assn., 1987, Disting. Alumnus award, U. Calif., San Diego, 1987, Faculty Rsch. award, U. Houston, 1987, Sigma Xi Rsch. Excellence award, 1987, Achievement award, NASA, 1987, Nat. Medal Sci., Pres. of US, 1988, Disting. Alumnus award, Cheng-Kung U., 1988, Medal of Sci. Merit, World Cultural Coun., 1989, Founders' prize, Texas Instruments, 1990, St. Martin de Porres award, 1990, Superconductivity Excellence award in sci. accomplishments, World Congress on Superconductivity, 1994, Bernd Matthias prize, 4th Internat. Conf. on Materials and Mechanisms of Superconductivity, High Temperature Superconductors, 1994, Disting. Sci. Achievement award, Washington Met. Assn. Chinese Am. Profls., 1998, Houston Hall of Fame award, George Bush Internat. Airport, 1999, Sharif U., 1999, Esther Farfel award, U. Houston, 2000, Houston Hall of Fame award, Greater Houston Conv. and Vis. Bur., 1988, John Fritz medal, United Engring. Found., 2001, Achievement award, Chinese Profl. Club, 2006, Disting. Chair award, Zhejiang U., 2006, Lifetime Achievement award, Chinese Inst. Engrs., 2008, Ettore Majorana prize, Ettore Majorana Found. and Ctr. Sci. Culture, 2007—08; named Hon. Citizen, State of Tex., 1987, City of Houston, 1987, Best Rschr. in US, US News and World Report, 1990, One of 20th Century's 100 Most Intellectual People in Gas and Electric, Century of Power, Heat Energy, 2000, Honoree, Alliance for Multicultural Cmty. Svcs., 2000; named to Hall of Fame, Hong Kong Inst., 2010. Fellow: Chinese Acad. Scis., Tex. Acad. Scis., Am. Phys. Soc. (teller divsn. Solid State Physics 1976, internat. prize com. 1988—89, selection com. Oliver E. Buckley Prize in condensed matter physics 2005—06, mem. selection com. 2009—, Internat. prize for new materials 1988, David Adler Lectureship award 2008—); mem.: NAS (mem. panel on High Temperature Superconductivity 1987, sect. co-chair 1992—95, condensed matter experiment screening com. 2003—, selection com., Comstock award 1988, John J. Carty award for advancement of sci. 2005), AAAS, Phi Kappa Phi, Russian Acad. Engring. (fgn. mem. 2005), Electromagnetic Acad., Third World Acad. Scis., Academia Sinica (mem. adv. com. Inst. Physics 1997—2000, 2007—), Am. Acad. Arts and Scis., Royal Soc. Encouragement of Arts Mfrs. and Commerce. Office: U Houston Texas Ctr Superconductivity 202 Houston Science Center Houston TX 77204-5002 Office Phone: 713-743-8222. Office Fax: 713-743-8201.

CHU, WEI-KAN, physicist, researcher, professor; b. Kunming, China, Apr. 1, 1940; arrived in US, 1963. s. Din Yuan and Y.C. (Wong) C.; m. Agnes Kuen, May 28, 1966; 1 child, Lawrence D. BS in Physics, Cheng-Kung U., 1962; MS, Baylor U., 1965, PhD, 1969. Postdoctoral fellow Baylor U., Waco, Tex., 1969-72; rsch. fellow, sr. rsch. fellow Calif. Inst. Tech., Pasadena, 1972-75; staff advisor, sr. engr. IBM, Hopewell Junction, NY, 1975-81; rsch. prof. physics U. N.C., Chapel Hill, 1981-88; disting. prof. physics U. Houston, 1989—2002, Robert A. Welsh prof. physics, 2002—08; prof. Cullen U. Panel mem. NSF, Washington, 1992, U.S. Dept. Energy, Washington, 1992, 93, 94, 97. Co-author: Backscattering Spectrometry, 1978; co-editor: HTS Materials, Bulk Processing and Bulk Applications, 1992, Procs. of the 6th U.S.-Japan Workshop on High Tc Superconductors, 1994, Procs. of the 10th Anniversary High Temperature Superconductors Workshop on Physics, Materials and Applications, 1996, Procs. of 6th Internat. Conf. Materials and Mechanisms of Superconductivity and High Temperature Superconductors, VI, 2000; contbr. chpts. to books and over 380 articles to profl. jours. Recipient Disting. Achievement award Baylor U., Waco, 1991, Assn. Am.-Chinese Profls., 1994, 2013, Superconductivity award of excellence for outstanding individual accomplishment World Congress on Superconductivity, 1994, Outstanding Alumni of Yr. Nat. Cheng-Kung U., 1997, 98. Fellow Am. Phys. Soc.; mem. Materials Rsch. Soc. Achievements include patents in field. Office: U Houston Tex Ctr Superconductivity Houston TX 77204-5002 Office Phone: 713-743-8252. Business E-Mail: wkchu@uh.edu.

CHUMLEY, WILLIAM ROB, state legislator; b. Greer, SC, Feb. 16, 1971; s. Rob; m. Tammy W. Chumley; children: William Sumter Chumley. BA, Clemson U., 1992; JD, Samford U., 1997. Bd. dirs. Friends of Ben's Creek, 1997—98; rep. Spartanburg County Landuse Com., 1997—98; candidate, Dist. 35 SC State House of Representatives, 2000, SC House of Representatives, 2002; mgr. Drainbox, LLC Mktg. Patented Products; mem. Reidville Hist. Soc.; prof., bus. law, pub. speaking, and marketings Spartanburg Tech. Coll.; rep. SC State House of Representatives, 2010—; mem. Dist. 35 SC House of Representatives, 2011—. Republican. Christian. Address: 3303 Greenpond Rd Woodruff SC 29388 Office: 304A Blatt Bldg Columbia SC 29201 Home Phone: 864-433-9150; Office Phone: 864-303-2726.

CHUNG, KYUNG WON, medical educator, biomedical researcher; b. Seoul, Republic of Korea, Aug. 15, 1938; s. Jin Rok Chung and Yoon Hee Kim; m. Young Hee Min, Aug. 20, 1966; children: Harold Mooinn, John Moojohn. MS in Biology, Yonsei U., Seoul, Republic of Korea, 1966; MS in Anatomy, St. Louis U., 1969; PhD in Anatomy and Cell Biology, U. Okla. Coll. Medicine, Okla. City, 1971. Asst. prof. SUNY, Bklyn., 1972—77, U. Okla. Coll. Medicine, 1977—79, assoc. prof., 1979—86, prof., vice chmn., 1986—, dir. human anatomy, 1988—2007. Chmn. State of Okla. Anat. Bd., Okla. City, 1993—2008; vis. prof. Oxford U., 2005. Author: (textbook) Gross Anatomy, Board Review Series, Temas Clave Anatomia, 2008, Anatomie Humaine, 1995. Recipient Aesculapian award, U. Okla. Coll. Medicine, 1979—80, 1983—84, 1986, 1988, Edger W. Young Lifetime Achievement award, 1990, Stanton L. Young Master Tchr. award, 1992, Lifetime Achievement award, Korean Cultural Ctr. Orange County, Calif., 2007, 2003; named David Ross Boyd Disting. Prof., U. Okla. Coll. Medicine, 1993. Mem.: Am. Assn. Clin. Anatomists, Endocrine Soc., Am. Assn. Anatomists. Home: 809 Hollowdale Edmond OK 73003 Office: University Okla Coll Medicine 940 Stanton L Young Blvd Oklahoma City OK 73104 Office Fax: 405-271-3548. Business E-Mail: kyung-chung@ouhsc.edu.*

CHUNG, PAUL W., lawyer, energy executive; BBA, JD, Univ. Tex., Austin. Bar: Tex. 1985. Various legal positions with different companies including Vinson & Elkins, LLP; v.p., asst. gen. counsel Tejas, 1996—99; exec. v.p., gen. counsel Coral Energy, LLC, 1999—2001, Coral, 1999—2004, Shell Trading North America, 2001—04; exec. v.p., gen. counsel, sec. Targa Resources, Inc., 2004—. Office: Targa Resources Inc 1000 Louisiana Ste 4300 Houston TX 77002 Office Phone: 713-584-1000. Office Fax: 713-584-1100.

CHUNG, WINGYAN, computer scientist, information scientist, educator; naturalized, US, 2010; s. Choi Chung and Yuk-ying Wu; m. Christina Hoiyin Leung, Dec. 22, 1996; children: Simon Tinlap children: Lydia Gimsin, Daniel Tinhang. BBA, Chinese U. Hong Kong, 1993; MS in Info. and Tech. Mgmt., The Chinese U. Hong Kong, 2000; PhD in Mgmt., U. Ariz., 2004. Network adminstr. Tucson Police Dept., 2003; registered tchr. Hong Kong Govt., 1998. Tchr. Ho Fung Coll., Hong Kong, 1993—94, CCC Tam Lee Lai Fun Meml. Secondary Sch., 1994—98; textbook rev. com. mem. commerce & bus. studies Curriculum Devel. Coun., Hong Kong Edn. Dept., 1997—99, com. mem. commerce & bus. studies, 1997—99; tchg. asst. Chinese U. Hong Kong, 1998—2000; grad. tchg. assoc. U. Ariz., Tucson, 2000—01, rsch. assoc. Artificial Intelligence Lab, 2001—04, instr., 2003—04, vis. scholar, 2013; asst. prof. computer info. systems U. Tex., El Paso, 2004—07; asst. prof. mgmt. info. sys. Santa Clara U., 2007—11; assoc. prof. UNC Fayattaville State U., 2011—13; dir. Knowledge Sys. lab. Sch. Bus. & Econs. UNC Fayetteville State U., 2011—13; editor info. sys. area ACM Competing Review; assoc. editor Jour. Info. Privacy & Security; assoc. editor knowledge mgmt. & bus. intelligence track Int. Conf. on Info. Sys., 2013; assoc. prof. Stetson U., 2013—; rsch. dir. Ctr. Bus. Intelligence and Analytics. Acad. conf. reviewer Eighth Internat. Conf. Info. Visualization, 2004—04, European Conf. Digital Libraries, 2002—03, Internat. Conf. Asian Digital Libraries, 2001—03, Workshop Info. Tech. and Systems, 2003—03, Hawaii Internat. Conf. Sys. Scis., 2002—02, Internat. Conf. Digital Libr., Beijing, 2002—02; chmn. commerce and bus. studies subjects panel CCC Tam Lee Lai Fun Meml. Secondary Sch., Hong Kong, 1996—98; acad. conf. reviewer Internat. Conf. Info. Systems, 2002—02; acad. jour. reviewer Jour. Mgmt. Info. Sys., ACM Transactions on Info. Sys., IEEE Transactions on Sys., Man and Cytometrics, ACM Transactions on Computing Educator, Decision, Support Sys., Internat. Am. Soc. Info. Sci. and Tech. Contbr. articles to profl. jours. Ch. deacon Christian and Missionary Alliance Tsing Yi Alliance Ch., Hong Kong, 1998—2000, bible class tchr., 1996—2000. Recipient Young Investigators Initiative award, U.S. Def. Advanced Rsch. Projects Agys. Info. Processing Tech. Office, 2003, Best Rsch. Paper award, U. Tex., El Paso, 2006; named Outstanding Prof./Rschr., U.S. Govt. Dept. Homeland Security, 2005; grantee, NSF KDD Program, 2002, NSF CPATH, Interactive CCF, Living on Knowledge Soc., Cmty. Bldg. Project, 2007—11, NSF Program for Rsch. Experience Undergrad., 2009—11, NSF TUES Program Computing, 2011—; fellow, U. Tex., El Paso, 2004; scholar, Rotary Internat. Found., Hong Kong, 1999, U. Ariz., Dept. MIS, 2000—04; Rsch. grant, U. Tex., El Paso, 2004—06. Mem.: IEEE, Decision Scis. Inst., Assn. Info. Systems, Assn. Computing Machinery. Achievements include development of an automatic text mining framework for knowledge discovery on the web; methodology on collecting and analyzing information of terrorist web sites; visual framework for knowledge discovery on the web. Mailing: Stetson University School of Business Administration 421 N Woodland Blvd Unit 8398 Deland FL 32723

CHURCH, DALE WALKER, lawyer; b. Portland, Oreg., Dec. 17, 1939; s. Floyd Walker and Lydia Belle (Barnette) C.; m. Mollie Ann Harper, Apr. 11, 1964; 1 child, Forrest Gregory. BS, Oreg. State U., 1961; JD, George Washington U., 1967. Bar: D.C. 1968, Calif. 1971. Contracting officer, exec. sec. contract rev. bd. CIA, Langley, Va., 1963-69; corp. gen. counsel, asst. sec. directory of contracts ESL, Inc., Sunnyvale, Calif., 1969-77; dep. under sec. rsch. and engring. U.S. Dept. Def., Washington, 1977-80; ptnr. Surrey and Morse, Washington, 1980-84, Seyfarth, Shaw, Fairweather & Geraldson, Washington, 1984-88, Pillsbury, Madison & Sutro, Washington, 1988-93, McDermott, Will & Emery, Washington, 1993-97; chmn., CEO Mech. Tech., Inc., 2002—05; founder & counsel Manitions Indstl. Base Task Force, 1995—; chmn. MTI Micro Fuel Cells, 2002; chmn., CEO Ventures & Solutions LLC, 1997—. Counsel def. mgmt. to pres.'s Blue Ribbon Commn.; cons. Def. Sci. Bd., Washington, 1980—; lectr. profl. orgns. and colls. Task force on Industry-to-Industry Coop., AMC Commander's Exec. Round Table.; active Ctr. Strategic and Internat. Studies Def. Orgn. Project; co-founder, counsel, treas. Youth Engaged in Svc. Am. Mem. ABA, Am. Electronics Assn. (former gen. counsel, chmn. def. conversion com.), Nat. Def. Indsl. Assn. (bd. dirs., exec. com. chmn. investments com., 97-, CASA vol., 2008-), Nat. Contracts Mgmt. Assn., Def. Sci. Bd. Acquisition Reform Task Force, Calif. Bar Assn., D.C. Bar Assn., Fed. Bar Assn., Soc. Logistics Engrs. (hon.), Delta Theta Phi, Sigma Phi Epsilon. Home: 9 Franklin St Alexandria VA 22314-3828 Office: Ventures & Solutions LLC 704 Fairfax Way Williamsburg VA 23185-8202 Office Phone: 703-519-0800. Personal E-mail: legaldale@aol.com.

CHURCH, ERIC (KENNETH ERIC CHURCH), musician; b. Granite Falls, NC, May 3, 1977; m. Katherine Blasingame, Jan. 8, 2008; 1 child, Boone McCoy. Degree in mktg., Appalachian State U., Boone, NC. Musician: (albums) Sinners Like Me, 2006, Carolina, 2009, Chief, 2011 (Album of Yr., Country Music Assn. Awards, 2012, Album of Yr., Acad. Country Music Awards, 2013), The Outsiders, 2014, (songs) The Only Way I Know (with Jason Aldean and Luke Bryan), 2012 (Vocal Event of Yr., Acad. Country Music Awards, 2013, Collaborative Video of Yr., CMT Music Awards, 2013). Recipient Top New Solo Vocalist award, Acad. Country Music, 2010. Office: c/o Q-Prime South 131 South 11th St Nashville TN 37206*

CHURCH, MARTHA ELEANOR, retired academic administrator; b. Pitts., Nov. 17, 1930; d. Walter Seward and Eleanor (Boyer) Church. BA, Wellesley Coll., Mass., 1952; MA, U. Pitts., 1954; PhD, U. Chgo., 1960; DSc (hon.), Lake Erie Coll., Painesville, Ohio, 1975; LittD (hon.), Houghton Coll., NY, 1980; LHD (hon.), Queens Coll., 1981, Ursinus Coll., 1981, St. Joseph Coll., 1982, Towson State U., 1983, Dickinson Coll., 1987, Coll. Notre Dame Md., 1995; LLD (hon.), Hood Coll., 1995; LHD (hon.), Ill. Coll., 2003. Instr. geography Mt. Holyoke Coll., South Hadley, Mass., 1953-57; lectr. geography Ind. U. Gary Ctr., 1958; instr., then asst. prof. geography Wellesley Coll., 1958—65; dean coll., prof. geography Wilson Coll., 1965-71; assoc. exec. sec. Commn. Higher Edn., Mid. States Assn. Coll. and Secondary Sch., 1971-75; pres. Hood Coll., Frederick, Md., 1975-95, pres. emerita, 1995—, chair bd. trustees, 2006—08, trustee emerita, 2008—, cons. to pres., 2012—; sr. scholar Carnegie Found. Advancement of Tchg., Princeton, 1995—97; interim pres. Ill. Coll., 2002—03; interim v.p. acad. affairs Holy Names U., Oakland, Calif., 2005—06. Vice chmn. bd. dirs. Am. Coun. on Edn., 1978—78, nat. identification panel, 1977—95; mem. Md. Humanities Coun., 1985—86; co-chmn. nat. adv. panel Nat. Ctr. Rsch. to Improve Postsecondary Tchg. and Learning U. Mich., 1985—90; trustee Carnegie Found. Advancement of Tchg., 1986—96, vice chair, 1990—92, chair, 1992—94; bd. visitors Def. Intelligence Coll., 1988—91; trustee Nat. Geog. Soc., 1989—2007, trustee emerita, 2007—, com. rsch. and exploration, 1998—2006, audit rev. com., 1993—98, chair membership, medals and awards com., 2000—07, exec., audit and compensation, mission programs com.; adv. bd. dirs. Automobile Club Md., 1991—2002; adv. bd. Boyer Ctr. Messiah Coll., Grantham, Pa., 1997—2005; trustee Internat. Partnership Svc. Learning, 1999—2002; dir. emerita Farmers and Mechanics Nat. Bank, 2000—; cons. Choice: Books Coll. Librs. Author: The Spatial Organization of Electric Power Territories in Massachusetts, 1960; Co-editor: A Basic Geographical Library: A Selected and Annotated Book List for Am. Colls, 1966; cons. editor, Change mag., 1980-01. Bd. dirs. Japan Internat. Christian U. Found., 1977-91, Nat. Rsch. Com., 1993-96; bd. advisors Fund Improvement of Postsecondary Edn., HEW, 1976-79; mem. Sec. of Navy's Adv. Bd. on Edn. and Tng., 1976-80; chmn. Md. Commn. on Civil Rights, 1981-82; trustee Bradford Coll., Mass., 1982-87, Peddie Sch., N.J., 1982-98, chair acad. affairs com., 1987, 96-97, adv. trustee, 1998-; trustee Nat. Geog. Soc. Edn. Found., 1989-97, 99-2010; chmn. bd. dir. Medici Found., Princeton, N.J., 1985-05; trustee United Bd. Christian Higher Edn. in Asia, 1995-04, sec. bd. trustees, 1998-2003, chmn. com. on trustees, 1997-04, chmn. East and Intra-Asia program subcom., 1996-97, exec. com., 1998-04; mem. Md. Jud. Disabilities Commn., 1985-94; commr. Edn. Commn. States, Md., 1981-99; exec. com. Campus Compact: Project Pub. and Cmty. Svc., 1986-89. Named Disting. fellow, Internat. Partnership for Svc.-Learning and Leadership, 2006—. Mem. John and Mable Ringling Mus. Art (Sarasota, Fla.), (vol., 2010-), Ch. Palms (Sarasota), Missions Com. (coord., 2013-), Legacy Soc., Legacy Giving Team. Avocation: photography. Home: 3029 Taywood Mdws Sarasota FL 34235-2030 Personal E-mail: trekkerchurch@gmail.com.

CHURCH, RANDOLPH WARNER, JR., lawyer; b. Richmond, Va., Nov. 6, 1934; s. Randolph Warner and Elizabeth Lewis (Gochnauer) C.; m. Lucy Ann Canary, July 4, 1970; children: Leslie R. Pennell, L. Weeks Kerr. BA with honors, U. Va., 1957, LLB, 1960. Bar: Va. 1960, US Dist. Ct. (ea. dist.) Va. 1962, US Ct. Appeals (4th cir.) 1981, US Supreme Ct. 1999. Assoc. McCandlish, Lillard & Marsh, Fairfax, Va., 1960-63; ptnr. McCandlish, Lillard & Church and successor partnerships., Fairfax, 1963-84; city atty. Fairfax, 1968-72; mng. ptnr. McCandlish, Lillard & Church and successor partnerships, Fairfax, 1975-83, Hunton & Williams, Fairfax, 1984-99, mem. exec. com., 1988-94, sr. counsel, 2000—. Bd. dirs. George Mason Bank, George Mason Bankshares, Inc., George Mason Mortgage Co., 1991-98, Va. Found. Rsch. and Econ. Edn., Inc., 1994-2000. Author: Appellate Civil Litigation, 1984; panelist: Lawyer Professionalism: Is Change in Order? 1988, Marketing Legal Services: What's Hot and What's Not, 1990, (with others) Equity Practice and Tips on Brief Writing. Active Fairfax Com. of 100, 1988—, bd. dirs., 1989-92; bd. visitors George Mason U., Fairfax, 1982-90, rector, 1983-86, chmn. adv. bd. Coll. Arts and Scis., 1999-2006, mem. adv. bd. Coll. Arts Humanities Social Scis., 2008-12; bd. dirs. Fairfax Symphony, 1991-02, gen. counsel, exec. com., 1996-02, 07; bd. dirs. Fairfax Symphony Orch. Found., Inc., 1999—, Va. Found. Humanities and Pub. Policy, 1993-99, 2007-10, vice chmn., 1997-99; mem. Va. Mus. Fine Arts Found., 2000-06, exec. com., 2005-06; pres. Fall for the Book, Inc., 2001-04, bd. dirs., 2001—, Parkinson Found. Nat. Capital Area, 2010-, treas. 2012-. Fellow Va. Law Found., Am. Bar Found.; mem. Va. Bar Assn. (v.p. 1975), Country Club of Fairfax, U. Va. Club, Phi Beta Kappa, Omicron Delta Kappa, Soc. Cin. Home: 5114 Forsgate Pl Fairfax VA 22030-4507 Office: Hunton & Williams 1751 Pinnacle Dr Ste 1700 Mc Lean VA 22102-3836 E-mail: rchurch@hunton.com.

CHURCHEY, RANDY L., real estate company executive; BS, U. Ala. Ptnr., Health Care Practice Coopers & Lybrand, LLP, chmn., Hospitality and Real Estate Practice; sr. v.p., CFO FelCor Lodging Trust, Inc.; pres., COO RFS Hotel Investors, Inc., 1999—2003, bd. dirs., 2000—03; pres. The Encore Companies, 2003—06; pres., CEO Beverly Enterprises, Inc. (BEI), 2006—07; interim CEO Great Wolf Resorts, Inc., 2008, bd. dirs.; founder, co-chmn. MCR Devel., LLC; pres., CEO & bd. dirs. Education Realty Trust, 2010—. Bd. dirs. Innkeepers USA Trust, 2004—. Office: Education Realty Trust 999 S Shady Grove Rd Ste 600 Memphis TN 38120-4130 Office Phone: 901-259-2500. Office Fax: 901-259-2594. Business E-Mail: rchurchey@edrtrust.com.

CHURCHILL, WARD LEROY, social sciences educator, advocate; b. Urbana, Ill., Oct. 2, 1947; s. Jack Churchill and Maralyn L. (Allen) Debo; m. Leah R. Kelly, Aug. 8, 1995 (div.); 1 child, Jasmine Ann; m. Natsu Saito AA, Ill. Ctrl. Coll., 1972; BA, Sangamon State U., 1974, MA, 1975; LHD (hon.), Alfred U., 1992. Program dir. Boulder Valley Sch. Dist., Boulder, 1977-78, U. Colo., Boulder, 1978-90, assoc. prof., 1991-97, prof., 1997—2007, chmn., Dept. Ethnic Studies, 1997—2005. Vis. prof. Alfred U., N.Y., 1990-91. Author: Pacifism as Pathology: Reflections on the Role of Armed Struggle, 1986, Struggle for the Land: Indigenous Resistance to Genocide, Ecocide and Expropriation in Contemporary North America, 1993, Indians Are Us?: Culture and Genocide in Native North America, 1994, Since Predator Came: Notes on the Struggle for American Indian Liberation, 1995, From a Native Son: Selected Essays in Indigenism, 1985-1995, 1996, A Little Matter of Genocide: Holocaust and Denial in the Americas 1492 to the Present, 1997, Fantasies of the Master Race: Literature, Cinema and the Colonization of American Indians, 1998, Struggle for the Land: North American Resistance to Genocide, Ecocide, and Colonization, 2002, Acts of Rebellion: The Ward Churchill Reader, 2002, Life in Occupied America, 2003, On the Justice of Roosting Chickens: Reflections on the Consequences on U.S. Imperial Arrogance and Criminality, 2003, Kill the Indian, Save the Man: The Genocidal Impact of American Indian Residential Schools, 2004; co-author (with Jim VanderWall) Agents of Repression: The FBI's Secret Wars Against the Black Panther Party and the American Indian Movement, 1988, The COINTELPRO Papers: Documents from the FBI's Secret War Against Domestic Dissent, 1991; editor: New Studies on the Left, 1987-94; contbg. editor: Z Magazine, 1987—, Issues in Radical Therapy, 1982-87, Dark Night Field Notes, 1992—. Mem. governing coun. Colo. AIM, Denver, 1993—, co-dir., 1982-93; comms. dir. Am. Indian Anti-Defamation Coun., Denver, 1992-94; mem. steering com. Yellow Thunder Camp, Rapid City, S.D., 1981-85. Recipient Gustavus Myers award in writing Gustavus Myers Ctr., 1984. Avocation: films.

CIARA, BARBARA, news anchor; Attended, U. Ariz., Tucson; BA summa cum laude, Hampton U., Va., 2000. Various prodn. positions KZAZ-TV, Tucson, 1976—81; various prodn. and anchor positions, Hampton Roads area NBC, ABC, Va.; mng. editor of partnership between WVEC-TV and WHRO pub. TV, 1996—2000; mng. editor, anchor WTKR News Channel 3, Norfolk, Va., 2000—. Mng. editor (partnership between commercial TV, cable and newspaper) L-N-C, 1997—99. Prodr.: (numerous documentaries including) Guilty Til Proven Innocent (Emmy award, 2000), Massive Resistance, Operation Haiti (Emmy nomination, 1997), Letters from the Hood (Emmy nomination, 1995), others. Vol. Tidewater AIDS Crisis Taskforce, Habitat for Humanity, Am. Cancer Soc., Children's Hosp. of Kings Daughters, Urban League of Hampton Roads, Joy Fund; bd. dirs. Va. Marine Sci. Mus.; adv. bd. mem. Foodbank of Southeastern Va. Inc., Va. Stage Co., Am. Red Cross, Am. Heart Assn. Recipient Edward R. Murrow award, Radio & TV News Dirs. Assn, 1997; named to Power 150, Ebony mag., 2008. Mem.: Nat. Assn. Black Journalists (past bd. dirs., pres. 2007—). Office: NewsChannel 3 720 Boush St Norfolk VA 23510 Office Phone: 757-446-1000.

CIAVARRA, CHRISTOPHER A., food service executive; b. 1971; Attended, Conn. Coll., New London. Account mgmt. with mktg. and advt. firms; account supr. Fidelity Investments; account dir. Common Sense; mktg. cons. Cracker Barrel Old Country Store, Inc., 2001—05; dir. mktg. ARAMARK, 2005—08; v.p. brand and menu strategy Cracker Barrel Old Country Store, Inc., 2008—10, sr. v.p. mktg., 2010—. Office: Cracker Barrel Old Country Store Inc 305 Hartmann Dr Lebanon TN 37088 Office Phone: 615-444-5533. Office Fax: 615-443-9476.

CICCONE, ALVIN J., family practice physician; MD, Va. Commonwealth U., 1964. Diplomate Am. Bd. Family Practice. Resident family medicine Norfolk Gen. Hosp., 1965—66; assoc. prof. family medicine

Eastern Va. Med. Sch.; pres. Va. Acad. of Family Physicians; 1st chairmen family practice dept. Eastern Va. Med. Sch.; hosp. affiliation includes Sentara Norfolk Gen. Hosp. Named Virginia Family Doctor of the Year, 1988. Office: Sentara Healthcare 6015 Poplar Hall Dr Norfolk VA 23502

CICET, DONALD JAMES, lawyer; b. New Orleans, May 24, 1940; s. Arthur Alphonse and Myrtle (Ress) C.; m. Iona Perry. BA, Nicholls State U., 1963; JD, Loyola U., New Orleans, 1969. Bar: La. 1969, US Dist. Ct. (ea. dist.) La. 1972, US Dist. Ct. (mid. dist.) La. 1978, US Dist. Ct. (we. dist.) La. 1979, US Ct. Appeals (5th cir.) 1972, US Supreme Ct. 1972. Pvt. practice, Reserve, La., 1969—88, LaPlace, La., 1988—; staff atty. La. Legis. Coun., 1972-73; legal counsel Nicholls State U. Alumni Fedn., 1974-76, 78-80; spl. counsel Pontchartrain Levee Dist., 1976—2001. Adminstrv. law judge La. Dept. Civil Svc., 1981—2006. Pres. Boys' State of La. Inc., 1990-92, bd. dirs., 1988-2007. With AUS, 1964, USNG, 1964-70. Recipient Am. Jurisprudence award Loyola U., 1968. Fellow La. Bar Found.; mem. La. Bar Assn. (ho. dels. 1973-77, 79-85), 40th Jud. Dist. Bar Assn. (pres. 1985-87), Nicholls State U. Alumni Fedn. (exec. coun. 1972-76, 77-85, pres. 1982, James Lynn Powell award 1980), Am. Legion (post cmdr. 1976-77, dist. judge adv. 1975-95, judge adv. La. dept. 1990-92, 93-96, mem. La. dept. commn. on nat. security and govtl. affairs 1974-89, chmn. 1977-78, 79-81, 85-89, M.C. Gehr blue cap award 1983). Roman Catholic. Home: 263 Central Ave Reserve LA 70084-6003 Office: 197 Belle Terre Blvd La Place LA 70069-0461

CICOLANI, ANGELO GEORGE, research and development company executive, operating engineer; b. Norwood, Mass., Mar. 4, 1933; s. Luigi and Maria (Fossa) Cicolani; m. Marilyn Adell Griffith, June 4, 1955 (div. Jan. 1968); children: George, Susanne, Diana; m. Patricia Anne Kirsch, Nov. 1, 1970 (dec. July 1995); m. Christine Elizabeth Blair, Apr. 1, 2001. Student, Northeastern U., 1950; BS, U.S. Naval Acad., Annapolis, Md., 1955, Naval Postgrad. Sch., 1969. Commd. ensign U.S. Navy, 1955, advanced through grades to lt. comdr., 1975, chief reactor operator, 1958-62, exec. officer, 1963-67, sys. analyst for Strategic Sys. Project Office Arlington, Va., 1969-75; cons. Arlington, 1975-77; sr. rschr. R&D Assocs., Arlington, 1977-82, program mgr., sr. scientist, 1982-87, chief staff, tech. dir. Springfield Rsch. Facility, 1988—2003. Underwriter music commns., 1987—; mission vulnerability cons., 2003—. Author: The Role of Systems Analysis, 1974; author, editor Mineral Minutes Jour., 1972—74; contbr. numerous reports on command and control survivability rsch., 1978-86, numerous reports on underground mil. facilities rsch., 1987. Pres. emeritus bd. dirs. Dumbarton Concerts, Washington, 1982—. Mem.: Mineral Soc. DC (pres. 1972—77), Ops. Rsch. Soc. Am., Nature Conservancy, Mil. Officers Assn., Naval Submarine League, Naval Inst. Achievements include development of installation and underground facilities vulnerability assessment techniques and courses of instruction. Home Phone: 703-329-9595. Personal E-mail: deadletterbox@verizon.net.

CIGARRAN, THOMAS G., healthcare services company executive, professional sports team executive; m. Connie Cigarran; 2 children. BS, Villanova U.; MBA, NYU. Pres. AmSurg Corp., 1993—96, CEO, 1993—97, advisor, 1997—99, chmn., 1992—2009; co-founder Healthways, Inc., pres., 1981—2001, CEO, 1988—2003, chmn., 1988—, Nashville Predators, 2010—. Former bd. dirs. Genderm, Inc., Meretek Diagnostics, Inc, Clintrials Rsch. Inc. (CCRO), Corp. Family Solutions, Inc. (CFAM), Internat. Clinical Labs. Inc. (ICL); bd. dirs. Nashville Capital Network, AmSurg Corp., 2009—. Office: Healthways Inc 701 Cool Springs Blvd Franklin TN 37067 Office Phone: 615-614-4929. Business E-Mail: thomas.cigarran@healthways.com.

CIGARROA, FRANCISCO GONZALEZ, academic administrator, pediatric surgeon; b. Laredo, Tex., Dec. 1, 1957; s. Joaquin and Barbara Cigarroa; m. Graciela Alarcon; children: Maria Cristina, Barbara Carisa. BS, Yale U., 1979; MD, U. Tex. S.W., 1983. Diplomate Am. Bd. Surgery, Am. Bd. Pediat. Surgery. Dir. pediat. surgery U. Tex. Health Sci. Ctr., San Antonio, 1994—2000, dir. pediat. abdominal organ transplantation, 1994—2000, pres., 2000—09; chancellor U. Tex. Sys., 2009—. Assoc. prof. U. Tex., San Antonio, 1994—2000; mem. Gov.'s Coun. Sci. and Biotech., Tex., 2002, Pres.'s Com. on Nat. Medal of Sci., 2003—; dir. adv. coun. pub. health U.S. Sec. of Health and Human Svcs., 2002—. Contbr. chapters to books; co-author: Abnormal Surgery in Infancy and Childhood, 1993, Hepatobiliary and Pancreatic Disease: the Team Approach, 1994, Surgical Correction of Laryngotraceo Esophageal Cleft. Recipient Brotherhood/Sisterhood award, Nat. Conf. for Cmty. and Justice, 2005; named Mr. S.Tex., Washington Birthday Assn., Larado, Tex., 2003; named a Person of Vision, Prevent Blindness, Tex., 2005. Avocations: guitar, hunting. Office: U Tex Sys Office of Chancellor 601 Colorado St, 4th Fl Austin TX 78701 Office Phone: 512-499-4201. E-mail: chancellor@utsystem.edu.

CIMINELLA, CHRISTINA CLAIRE See JUDD, WYNONNA

CINK, STEWART, professional golfer; b. Huntsville, Ala., May 21, 1973; m. Lisa Cink; children: Connor Stewart, Reagan Braswell. Degree in mgmt., Ga. Inst. Tech. Profl. golfer PGA Tour, 1995—; winner Mexican Open, 1996, 1999, Canon Greater Hartford Open, 1997, MCI Classic, 2000, MCI Heritage, 2004, WGC-NEC Invitational, 2004, Travelers Championship, 2008, British Open, 2009. Mem. US team Presidents Cup, 2000, 2005, 2007, 2009, Ryder Cup, 2002, 2004, 2006, 2008, 2010. Achievements include being a member of the Ryder Cup winning US team, 2008. Avocations: roller hockey, hiking. Office: c/o PGA Tour 112 PGA Tour Blvd Ponte Vedra Beach FL 32082

CINQUEMANI, MICHAEL A., motor and generator manufacturing company executive; BS in Mech. Engring., Case Western Res. U., 1982; MBA, U. Md., College Park, 1988. Various exec. and managerial positions, including v.p., global sales Reliance Electric Co.; gen. product mgr., AC motors Rockwell Automation, Inc., 2001—04, v.p., global sales, 2004—07; exec. v.p., dodge & internat. sales Baldor Electric Co., 2007—. Office: Baldor Electric Co 5711 R S Boreham Jr St Fort Smith AR 72901 Office Phone: 479-646-4711. Office Fax: 479-648-5792. Business E-Mail: mcinquemani@baldor.com.

CIOCON, JERRY O., geriatrician; MD, U. Philippines, 1980. Diplomate Am. Bd. Internal Medicine, 1985, Am. Bd. Internal Medicine-geriatric medicine, 2000. Intern Univ. Philippines Coll. of Medicine, 1981; intern internal medicine Mercy Hosp., 1983, resident internal medicine, 1985; fellow geriatric medicine Long Island Jewish Med. Ctr., 1987; dept. chair Cleve. Clinic Fla. Named Outstanding Alumni Educator of the Year, Univ. Philippines Alumni Assn., 2009, Cleve. Clinic Fla. Educator of the Year, 2009. Fellow: Am. Coll. of Angiology, Am. Geriat. Soc., Am. Coll. of Physicians; mem.: Internat. Psychogeriatrics Assn., Fla. Geriat. Soc. (pres. elect), Gerontol. Soc. of America. Office: Cleveland Clinic Florida 3100 Weston Rd Weston FL 33331-3602 Office Phone: 954-659-6001.

CIOLLI, KENNETH, family practice physician; MD, U. Tex., 1985. Diplomate Am. Bd. Family Practice. Resident family medicine Univ. Tex. Affil Hosp., 1987—90; hosp. affiliations include St. Luke's Baptist Hosp., Southwest Tex. Meth. Hosp., Christus Santa Rosa Med. Ctr. Office: Saint Lukes Baptist Hospital 7930 Floyd Curl Dr San Antonio TX 78229-3950 Office Phone: 210-297-5000.*

CIRCEO, LOUIS JOSEPH, JR., research scientist, civil engineer; b. Everett, Mass., Aug. 31, 1934; s. Louis Joseph and Matilda (Marotta) C.; m. Brigitta H. Rockstroh, Jan. 26, 1961 (dec. 1986); children: Renata B., Craig L. BS in Engring., U.S. Mil. Acad., West Point, 1957; MS in Soils Engring., 1961; PhD in Civil Engring., Iowa State U., 1963. Registered profl. civil engr., DC. Commd. 2d lt. U.S. Army, 1957, advanced through grades to col., 1987; rsch. assoc. Lawrence Radiation Lab., Livermore, Calif., 1962-64; civil engr. Bangkok Bypass Road, Thailand, 1965—66; instr. dept. engring. and mil. sci. U.S. Army Engr. Sch., Ft. Belvoir, Va., 1966—68; civil engr. advisor Vietnamese Nat. Mil. Acad., Dalat, Vietnam, 1968-69; rsch. tech. mgr. Def. Atomic Support Agy., Washington, 1969-72; comdr. 20th Engr. Bn., Ft. Campbell, Ky., 1973-75; ops. rsch. analyst nuclear activities br. SHAPE, NATO, Mons, Belgium, 1975-79; dir. U.S. Army Constrn. Engring. Rsch. Lab., Champaign, Ill., 1979-83; dir. Nuclear Survivability, Security and Safety Directorate, Hdqrs. Def. Nuclear Agy., Washington, 1983-87; ret., 1987; dir. Constrn. Rsch. Ctr., Ga. Inst. Tech., Atlanta, 1987—98; prin. rsch. scientist Ga. Tech Rsch. Inst., Atlanta, 1998—2010; prin. Applied Plasma Arc Techs., Atlanta, 2010—. Mem.: ASCE, Soc. Am. Mil. Engrs., Assn. U.S. Army, Sigma Xi. Roman Catholic. Achievements include patents for recovery of fuel products from carbonaceous matter using plasma arc; in-situ plasma soil stabilization method and apparatus; in-situ plasma remediation and vitrification of contaminated soils, deposits and buried materials. Avocations: reading, travel. Office: Applied Plasma Arc Techs 4245 Navajo Trail NE Atlanta GA 30319-1532 Office Phone: 770-314-4002. Business E-Mail: lou@plasmatech.us.

CISKOWSKI, MICHAEL S., energy executive; BBA in Fin., MBA in Fin., Ctrl. State U., Okla. Various fin. & planning positions Williams Exploration Co., Getty Oil Co.; various positions, including investor rels. dir., fin. planning dir. & mgr., fin. planning Valero Energy Corp., San Antonio, exec. v.p., CFO, 2003—. Office: Valero Energy Corp One Valero Way San Antonio TX 78269-6000 Office Phone: 210-345-2000. Office Fax: 210-345-2646. Business E-Mail: mike.ciskowski@valero.com.

CISNEROS, HENRY GABRIEL, construction executive, former United States Secretary of Housing and Urban Development; b. San Antonio, June 11, 1947; s. J. George and Elvira (Munguia) C.; m. Mary Alice Perez; children: Teresa Angelica, Mercedes Christina, John Paul. BA, Tex. A&M U., 1969, M. Urban and Regional Planning, 1970; MPA, Harvard U., 1973; D. Public Adminstrn., George Washington U., 1975. Adminstrv. asst. to city mgr., San Antonio, 1968, Bryan, Tex., 1969-70; asst. dir. dept. model cities San Antonio, 1969-70; asst. to exec. v.p. Nat. League Cities, Washington, 1970-71; White House fellow asst. US Dept. Health Edn. & Welfare, Washington, 1971-72; teaching asst. dept. urban studies and planning M.I.T., 1972; mem. City Coun., San Antonio, 1975-81; mayor City of San Antonio, 1981-89; chmn. Cisneros Asset Mgmt., 1989-93; sec. US Dept. Housing & Urban Devel., Washington, 1993-97; pres., COO, Univision Comm., Inc., LA, 1997-2000; chmn. City View, San Antonio, 2005—. Contbr. articles to profl. jours. Chmn. Nat. Civic League; vice chair New Am. Alliance. Recipient Jefferson Award, Am. Inst. Pub. Svc., 1982, Torch of Liberty Award, Anti-Defamation League B'nai B'rith, 1982, Nat. Recognition Award, Mexican Govt., 1985, President's Award, Nat. League of Cities, 1989, Hispanic Man of Yr., Vista Mag., 1991, Founder Award, Ptnrs. for Livable Places, 1992, Fourth Annual Legends & Fans Award, Boys & Girls Clubs Am., 1993, Hubert Humphrey Award, Leadership Conf. for Civil Rights, 1994, Hero of People, ACORN, 1994, Thomas Jefferson award for pub. architecture, AIA, 1995, Maestro award for Leadership, Latino Leaders Summit, 2007; grantee White House Fellow, 1971—72. Mem.: Police Found. Democrat. Office: City View 454 Soledad St Ste 300 San Antonio TX 78205-1555 Fax: 210-228-9906. E-mail: hcisneros@city-view.net.

CISNEROS, MARY ALICE P., not-for-profit executive, former councilwoman; m. Henry G. Cisneros; children: Teresa, Mercedes, John. Attended, San Antonio Coll., Our Lady of the Lake U. Pres. River City Mgmt.; co-founder American Sunrise, 2001, pres., 2011—; councilwoman Dist. 1 San Antonio City Coun., 2007—11. Del. Dem. Nat. Com., 1988; trustee San Antonio Ind. Sch. Bd.; chmn. Communities in Schools, Southland Coll. Scholarship Program; bd. mem. San Antonio Youth Literacy Bd., Mayor's Commn. for Children and Families. Chmn. J.C. Penney Golden Rule Awards; chmn. & founder Women's Employment Network Odyssey Awards; fin. coord. Jimenez Sr. Citizen Thanksgiving Dinner. Named Outstanding Dem. Woman of Yr., 1985; named to San Antonio Women's Hall of Fame, 2007. Mem.: Nat. League Cities (sec. Dem. Mcpl. Officials). Office: American Sunrise 454 Soledad, Suite 300 San Antonio TX 78205 Office Phone: 210-228-9693. Fax: 210-228-9906. E-mail: chocomeza@americansunrise-sa.org.

CITRO, YOLANDE, real estate agent; b. Grenoble, France; Former owner restaurants A Bientot du Soir, Le Christophe, NYC, Le Petit Cafe, Miami Beach, Fla.; formerly with SOL Sotheby's Internat. Realty, Miami, Wimbish-Riteway Realtors, Fla.; luxury real estate agent Triangle Properties, Inc., Miami Beach. Office Phone: 305-705-9105. Office Fax: 305-705-9122. Business E-Mail: yolande@yolandecitro.com.

CIVANTOS, FRANCISCO J., otolaryngologist, plastic surgeon, educator; Attended, Harvard U.; MD, Columbia U. Coll. of Physicians and Surgeons. Diplomate Am. Bd. Otolaryngology. Resident Univ. of Ill. Coll. of Medicine, Chgo.; fellow Vanderbilt Univ. Med. Ctr., Nashville; assoc. prof. otolaryngology Univ. of Miami Miller Sch. of Medicine; co-dir. divsn. of head and neck surgery Univ. of Miami Health System. Named one of the Top Doctors, 2011, the Best Doctors in America, 1996—. Fellow: ACS. Office: University of Miami Hospital and Clinics Department of Otolaryngology ENT 1475 NW 12th Ave Miami FL 33136 Office Phone: 305-243-5214.

CLAFLIN, JAMES ROBERT, pediatrician, allergist; b. Apr. 30, 1946; m. Marcee Claflin; children: James Sean (dec.), Brian Scott (dec.), Susan Nicole, Timothy Lynn. Student, Northwestern State Coll.; MD, U. Okla., 1971. Diplomate Am. Bd. Pediatrics, Am. Bd. Allergy Immunology. Intern U. Tex. Med. Br., Galveston, 1971-72; advanced through grades to lt. col. USAF, 1969-84, chief pediatric svcs. Goodfellow AFB, 1972-73, 75-77, chief pediatric svcs. and hosp. svcs. RAF Upper Heyford Eng., 1977-80, chief allergy and clin. immunology Carswell AFB, 1982-84; fellow allergy/immunology Willford Hall USAF Med. Ctr., Lackland AFB, Tex., 1980-82; ret. USAF, 1984. Clin. asst. prof. pediatrics, Oklahoma U.; presenter in field. Contbr. articles to profl. jours. Advisor child welfare com. Tom Green County, 1976-77; mem. child welfare com. RAF, Upper Heyford, Eng., 1978-80; mem. sch. and pub. health com. Tarrant County Med. Soc., 1984-85, chmn., 1986-87, publs. com., 1988-89, religion and meml. com., 1989; mem. quality assurance and infectious disease coms. Cook-Ft. Worth Children's Hosp., 1986-89; v.p. Brenham State Sch. Parent Assn., 1987-88; pres. Parents Assn. for the Retarded of Tex., 1987-88; chmn. cmty. conscience com. Wedgwood Bapt. Ch. Recipient Svc. award Am. Diabetes Assn., 1976. Fellow Am. Acad. Pediatrics, Am. Coll. Allergy (mem. com. on allergic rhinitis, mem. com. on adverse reactions to food 1991-96), Am. Acad. Allergy; mem. AMA (Am. Coll. Allergy, Asthma and Immunology (spkr. ho. of dels. 2001-03, bd.regent, 2005-08), Oklahoma County Med. Soc. (pres.-elect 2003-04, pres. 2004-05) Okla. State Med. Assn. (sec.-treas. 2003-05, v.p., 2005—06), Okla. Allergy and Asthma Soc. (pres. 1998-2000). Home: 750 NE 13th St Oklahoma City OK 73104-5051

CLAIR, WALTER K., cardiac electrophysiologist, educator; MPH, Harvard Coll. Diplomate Am. Bd. Internal Medicine, 1984, Am. Bd. Internal Medicine-cardiovasc. disease, 2000, Am. Bd. Internal Medicine-clin. cardiac electrophysiology, 2006. Resident internal medicine Brigham and Women's Hosp., 1982—84; fellow cardiovasc. disease Duke Univ. Med. Ctr., 1989—92, fellow cardiac electrophysiology, 1984—88; asst. prof. medicine Vanderbilt Univ.; hosp. affiliation includes Vanderbilt Univ. Med. Ctr., dir. arrhythmia consultation, med. dir. clin. electrophysiology. Office: Vanderbilt Heart Institute 1215 21st Ave S Ste 5209 Nashville TN 37232 Office Phone: 615-322-2318.

CLAITOR, DAN, state legislator; m. Sharmaine Claitor; 2 children. B in Finance, LSU; JD, Loyola U. Works in family business Claitor's Law Books; former prosecutor Orleans Parish Dist. Attorney's Office, legal counsel; mem. Dist. 16 La. State Senate, 2009—, interim com. fin. com., senate and govtl. affairs com., mem judiciary A com., local and mcpl. affairs com., retirement com. Republican. Office: PO Box 94183 Baton Rouge LA 70804 Mailing: 7520 Perkins Rd Ste 170 Baton Rouge LA 70808 Office: Claitor's Books 3165 South Acadian Baton Rouge LA 70808 Office Phone: 225-342-2040. Business E-Mail: claitord@legis.state.la.us.

CLANCY, DENYSE FINN, lawyer; BA magna cum laude, Yale U., 1989; MA in English, Columbia U., 1992; JD summa cum laude, So. Meth. U., 1999. Bar: Tex. 1999. Atty. Baron & Budd, P.C., Dallas. Editor: So. Meth. U. Sch. Law Rev. Named a Rising Star, Tex. Super Lawyers mag., 2006. Mem.: Tex. Trial Lawyers Assn., Assn. Trial Lawyers of Am. Office: Baron & Budd PC 3102 Oak Lawn Ave Ste 1100 Dallas TX 75219 Office Phone: 214-521-3605. E-mail: dclancy@baronbudd.com.

CLAPP, DAVID FOSTER, retired librarian; b. Birmingham, Ala., July 17, 1952; s. Merwin Bailey and Katherine Lorraine (Aderholt) C.; m. Sara Louise Stephan, Sept. 18, 1982. BA in Classical Langs., Tulane U., 1975; MS in LS, U. Ill., 1980; cert. advanced study in info. mgmt., U. Chgo., 1987. Asst. mgr. Kroch's & Brentano's Bookstore, Chgo., 1976-79; libr. I acquisitions dept. Chgo. Pub. Libr., 1980-82, libr. II, 1st asst. Walker br., 1982-83, libr. II, head Clearing br., 1983-84, libr. III, head Rogers Park br., 1984-89; asst. dir. for ext. svcs. Chattanooga-Hamilton County Bicentennial Libr., 1989—2002, dir., 2002—10. Recipient Outstanding Pub. Svc. award Friends Chgo. Pub. Libr., 1987; Josie B. Houchens fellow U. Ill., 1979. Mem. ALA, Pub. Libr. Assn., Libr. Adminstrn. and Mgmt. Assn., Tenn. Libr. Assn. (exec. bd. 1991-92), Chattanooga Area Libr. Assn. (pres. 1991-92), Mensa, Beta Phi Mu, Kiwanis of Chattanooga (v.p. 2009-2010), RE:START - The Ctr. Adult Edn. (bd. mem.). Avocations: genealogy, history, development and philosophy of religions, ancient history. Home: 944 Lower Mill Rd Hixson TN 37343-2890 Office Phone: 423-757-5320. Business E-Mail: clapp_david@lib.chattanooga.gov.

CLAPP, ROGER HOWLAND, retired publishing executive; b. Scarsdale, NY, May 11, 1928; s. Kenneth John and Louise (Allen) Clapp; m. Patricia Anne Townshend, June 26, 1954 (dec. Nov. 18, 1998); children: Roger Howland Jr.(dec.), Georgia Louise, Sarah Townshend. BA cum laude, Amherst Coll., 1954. V.p. Benton & Bowles, Inc., NYC, 1954-67, Rumrill-Hoyt, Inc., NYC, 1967-72; v.p., advt. dir. Richmond (Va.) Newspapers, Inc., 1972-93. Author: Through The Ages: An Abbreviated History of Our World, 2004. Counselor SCORE Naples Am. Small Bus.; bd. dirs. Richmond chpt. Better Bus. Bur., 1986—88, ARC, 1987—93. With USN, 1948—52, Korea. Recipient Silver medal, Am. Advt. Fedn., 1980. Mem.: Internat. Newspaper Advt. and Mktg. Execs. (pres. 1988). Home: 15470 Cedarwood Ln # 103 Naples FL 34110-8638

CLARK, ARTHUR WATTS, insurance company executive; b. Seattle, Nov. 28, 1922; s. Irving Marshall and Nell (Watts) C.; m. Mary Dick Cannon, Nov. 21, 1942; children: Arthur Watts, Claiborne Marshall, Johnston Jewell. AB, U. N.C., 1943; MA, U. Calif., 1948. With Home Security Life Ins. Co., Durham, NC, 1948-50, 52-85, pres., 1967-75, chmn., chief exec. officer, 1975-85, also dir.; chmn., chief exec. officer Peoples Life Ins. Co. of Washington, D.C., 1983-85; chmn., pres., chief exec. officer Peoples Security Life Ins. Co., 1985-86, chmn. bd., 1986-88. Mem. Res. Forces Policy Bd., Office Sec. Def., 1975-78. Treas. Research Triangle Regional Planning Commn., 1959-63; mem. N.C. Health Ins. Adv. Bd., 1966-70; chmn. bd. dirs. N.C. Ctrl. U. Found., Zool. Coun., 1994-96, chmn., 1996-2002; vice-chmn. bd. dirs. N.C. Med. Found.; chmn. Greater Triangle Cmty. Found., 1992-94, The Explorer's Club, 1999—. With USAAF, 1942-46, USAF, 1952, maj. gen. USAF, ret. Decorated D.S.M., Legion of Merit with oak leaf cluster, Bronze Star. Mem. Am. Life Conv. (dir. 1972), Am. Life Ins. Assn. (dir. 1973-75), Life Office Mgmt. Assn. (dir. 1973-76), Am. Council Life Ins. (dir. 1976), Life Insurers Conf. (exec. com. 1972-75, 1983-86), Assn. N.C. Life Ins. Cos. (chmn. 1986-87), Phi Beta Kappa, Sigma Xi. Office: 194 Finley Golf Course Rd Ste 100 Chapel Hill NC 27517 Home: 100 Cedar Berry Ln Chapel Hill NC 27517 Office Phone: 919-929-3399. Personal E-mail: artwclark@aol.com.

CLARK, BRIAN, geophysicist, oil industry executive; BS, Ohio State Univ., 1970; MA, Harvard Univ., PhD, 1977. Instr. to asst. prof. physics Brandeis Univ.; joined Schlumberger Companies, 1979; rsch. scientist Schlumberger-Doll Rsch., Ridgefield, Conn.; rsch. scientist and logging-while-drilling mgr. Schlumberger Houston Product Ctr.; v.p., dir. rsch. Schlumberger-Doll Rsch., 1994—97; v.p., tech. ctr. mgr. Schlumberger Product Ctr., Sugar Land, Tex., 1997; Schlumberger Fellow Schlumberger Tech. Ctr., Sugar Land, Tex. Bd. dir. Rsch. Partnership to Secure Energy for America; mem. US nat. com. World Petroleum Coun. Recipient Formation Evaluation award, Soc. Petroleum Engineers, 1996; named Texas Inventor of the Yr., Tex. State Bar Assn., 2002, Outstanding Inventor of the Yr., Houston Intellectual Property Law Assn., 2002. Mem.: Am. Inst. Physics (mem. gov. bd.), Nat. Acad. Engring., Acad. Med., Engring. & Sci. of Texas. Achievements include patents in field. Office: Schlumberger Tech Ctr 110 Schlumberger Dr Sugar Land TX 77478 Office Phone: 281-285-8000.

CLARK, BRYANT W., state legislator; b. Jackson, Miss., Oct. 31, 1974; Mem. Dist. 47 Miss. House of Reps., 2004—, vice chair rules com., mem. edn. com., judiciary A com., judiciary en banc com., pub. health & human svcs. com., select com. poverty, transp. com., mem. wildlife, fisheries & pks. com. Democrat. Baptist. Office: PO Box 1018 Jackson MS 39215-1018 Office Phone: 662-834-6133. Business E-Mail: bclark@house.ms.gov.

CLARK, CALEB MORGAN, political scientist, educator; b. Washington, June 6, 1945; s. Tanner Morgan and Grace Amanda (Kautzman) C.; m. Janet Morrissey Sentz, Sept. 28, 1968; children: Emily Claire, Grace Ellen, Evelyn Adair. BA, Beloit Coll., Wis., 1966; PhD, U. Ill., 1973. Lectr. N.Mex. State U., Las Cruces, 1972-75, asst. prof., 1975-78, assoc. prof. govt., 1978-81; assoc. prof. polit. sci. U. Wyo., Laramie, 1981-84, prof., 1984-92, U. Auburn, 1992—, prof., head polit. sci. Co-author: Comparative Patterns of Foreign Policy and Trade, 1976, Development's Influence on Yugoslav Political Values, 1976, Taiwan's Development, 1989, Women in Taiwan Politics, 1990, Foresight, Flexibility and Fortuna in Taiwan's Devel., 1992; mng. editor IS Notes, 1984-92; co-editor: North/South Relations, 1983, State and Development, 1988, Polit. Stability and Economic Development, 1988, Polit. Stability and Economic Development, 1991, The Evolving Pacific Basin, 1992, Technological Change and Rurdal Development in Poor Countries, 1994, Beyond the Developmental State, 1998, The ROC on the Threshold of the 21st Century, 1999, Democracy and the Status of Women in East Asia; cons., assoc. editor Soviet Union, 1974-77, World Affairs, 1975-84, Social Sci. Jour., 1978-80; contbr. articles to profl. jours. NDEA fellow, 1966-69; Woodrow Wilson dissertation fellow, 1969-70; grantee N.Mex. Humanities Coun., 1975, Wyo. Coun. for Humanities, 1982, U.S. Dept. Edn., 1983-85, Pacific Cultural Found., 1984-86, Am. Coun. Learned Socs., 1976, Met. Life Edn., 1978-80, NEH, 1978, NSF, 1981, Chiang Ching-Kuo Found., 1993-95. Mem. Am. Polit. Sci. Assn., Am. Assn. Chinese Studies (exec. coun. 1995-97), Western Polit. Sci. Assn., Assn. Asian Studies, Southern Polit. Sci. Assn., Internat. Studies Assn. (exec. dir. West 1981-84), Ala. Polit. Sci. Assn. (v.p. 1993-94, pres. 1994-95), Phi Beta Kappa (treas. 1983-91), Pi Eta Sigma, Phi Kappa Phi, Phi Beta Delta. Office Phone: 334-844-5371. Business E-Mail: clarkcm@auburn.edu.

CLARK, CHARLES T(ALIFERRO), retired statistician; b. Danville, Ill., Mar. 18, 1917; s. Charles A. and Kathryn S. C.; m. Pearl W. DuBose, Oct. 6, 1943; children: Charles A., Mary D., Robert S. BBA, U. Tex., 1938, MBA, 1939, PhD, 1956. Asst. mgr. Austin C. of C., Tex., 1940-41; dir. personnel U. Tex., Austin, 1946-59, asst. prof. bus. stats., 1959-60, assoc. prof., 1961-79, prof., 1979-91, Mary Lee Harkins Sweeney Centennial prof. emeritus in bus., 1991—. Bd. dirs. Tex. Student Publs., Austin, 1964-69, Tex. Union, Austin, 1969-83, Univ. Fed. Credit Union, Austin, 1976-84, Univ. Coop. Soc., Austin, 1980-84. Author numerous text books; (with L.L. Schkade) textbooks Statistical Analysis for Adminstrative Decision, 1969, 4th edit., 1983, (with John R. Stockton) Introduction to Business and Economic Statistics, 1971, 3d edit., 1980; contbr. articles to profl. jours. Served to 2d lt. USAAC, 1941-46, PTO. Recipient 11 teaching awards U. Tex., 1960-80 Mem. Coll. and Univ. Personnel Assn. (pres. 1959), Austin Personnel Assn. (pres. 1950), Austin Stat. Assn. (pres. 1975) Office: U Tex Dept Mgmt Sci & Info Systems Austin TX 78712 Home Phone: 512-345-0149.

CLARK, CORNELIA A., state supreme court chief justice; b. Franklin, Tenn., Sept. 15, 1950; BA, Vanderbilt U., Nashville, 1971; MA, Harvard U., 1972; JD, Vanderbilt Sch. of Law, 1979. Atty. Farris, Warfield & Kanaday (now Stites & Harbison PLLC), 1979—89; judge 21st Judicial Dist., Tenn., 1989—99; dir. Tenn. Administrative Office of Ct., 1999—2005; justice Tenn. Supreme Ct., 2005—, chief justice, 2010—. Former adjunct prof. Vanderbilt U. Sch. of Law; faculty Nat. Judicial Coll.; former faculty mem. Am. Academy of Judicial Ed.; former mem. Supreme Ct. Commissions on Rules of Civil Procedure and Tech. Mem.: ABA, Am. Judicature Soc., Tenn. Bar Assn., Williamson County Bar Assn. (Liberty Bell award 2005), Nashville Bar Assn. (second v.p.), Lawyers Assn. for Women (bd. dirs. Marion Griffin chapter). Office: Tenn Supreme Ct 318 Supreme Ct Bldg 401 7th Ave N Nashville TN 37219*

CLARK, DAYLE MERITT, civil engineer; b. Lubbock, Tex., Sept. 5, 1933; s. Frank Meritt and Mamie Jewel (Huff) C.; m. Betty Ann Maples, Apr. 11, 1968; 1 child, Alison. BS, Tex. Tech U., 1955; MS, So. Meth. U., 1967. Registered profl. engr.; registered profl. land surveyor. Field engr. Chgo. Bridge & Iron Co., 1955; mgr. L.K. Long Construction Co., 1958-64; prof. U. Tex. Arlington, 1964-99. Cons. AID, 1966, NSF, 1967-68; expert witness in court cases. Editor Tex. Civil Engr., 1967-71; contbr. articles to profl. jours. Served to capt. USAF, 1955-57. Fellow ASCE (pres. Dallas br. 1987, pres. Tex. sect. 1992-93, Profl. Svcs. award 1991, Award of Honor 1998), Tex. Soc. Profl. Engrs. (achievement award in civil engring. Dallas chpt. 1995), Rotary (pres. Arlington-West 1986, Paul Harris fellow, Rotarian of Yr. 1987). Office: PO Box 185 Arlington TX 76004-0185

CLARK, DONALD, JR., lawyer; BS, U. Southern Miss., 1971; JD, U. Miss., 1973. Bar: Miss. 1973, US Dist. Ct. (no. and so. dists.) Miss. Spl. asst. atty. gen. State of Miss., 1973—80; atty., chair Butler, Snow, O'Mara, Stevens and Cannada, PLLC, Ridgeland, Miss. Named one of America's Leading Lawyers for Bus., Chambers USA. Mem.: ABA, Capital Area Bar Assn., Miss. Assn. County Bd. Attorneys, Miss. Bar, Nat. Assn. Bond Lawyers. Office: Butler, Snow O'Mara Stevens & Cannada PLLC PO Box 6010 Ridgeland MS 39158 Office Phone: 601-985-4586. E-mail: don.clark@butlersnow.com.

CLARK, ELOISE ELIZABETH, biologist, educator; b. Grundy, Va., Jan. 20, 1931; d. J. Francis Emmett and Ava Clayton (Harris) C. BA, Mary Washington Coll., 1951; PhD Zoology, U. N.C., 1958; DSc, King Coll., 1976; postdoctoral rsch., Washington U., St. Louis, 1957—58, U. Calif. Berkeley, 1958—59. Rsch. asst., then instr. U. N.C., 1952—55; from instr. to asst. prof. Columbia U., 1959—65, assoc. prof. biol. sci., 1966—69; with NSF, Washington, 1969—71, head molecular biology, 1971—73, divsn. dir. biol. and med. scis., 1973—75, dep. asst. dir. biol., behavioral and social scis., 1975—76, asst. dir. biol., behavioral and social scis., 1976-83; prof. biol. sci. to trustee prof. emeritus Bowling Green State U., Ohio, 1983—2002, trustee prof. emeritus, 2002—, v.p. acad. affairs, 1983—96. Instr. Marine Biol. Lab., Woods Hole, Mass., 1958—63. Contbr. articles to profl. jours. and congl. hearings. Mem. alumnae bd. Mary Washington Coll., U. Va., 1967—70; bd. regents Nat. Libr. Medicine, 1973—83; mem. policy group competitive grants program U.S. Dept. Agr.; mem. White House Interdepartmental Task Force on Women, 1978—80, Task Force for Conf. on Families, 1980, Com. on Health and Medicine, 1976—80; vice chmn. Com. on Food and Renewable Resources, 1977—80; mem. selective excellence task force Ohio Bd. Regents, 1984—85; mem. Ohio Adv. Coun., Coll. Prep. Edn., 1983—84, Ohio Inter-Univ. Coun. for Provosts, 1983—96, chmn., 1984—85, 1995—96; nat. adv. rsch. resources coun. NIH, 1987—89; mem. informal sci. edn. panel NSF, 1986—88, adv. com., social, behavioral and econ. scis., 1997—2000; program adv. coun. sci., tech. and pub. policy Harvard U., 1988—90, mem. editl. bd. Forum, 1997—2001; mem. governing bd. OhioLink, 1990—96, vice chair, 1992, chair, 1993—94. Named Disting. Alumnus Mary Washington Coll., 1975; Wilson scholar, 1956; E.C. Drew scholar, 1956; USPHS postdoctoral fellow, 1957-59; recipient Disting. Svc. award NSF, 1978; fellow Assn. Women in Sci. Mem. AAAS (coun. 1969-71, bd. dirs. 1978-82, pres.-elect, 1992, pres., 1993, chmn. bd. 1994), Soc. Gen. Physiology (sec. 1965-67, coun. 1969-71), Biophys. Soc. (coun. 1975-76), Am. Soc. Cell Biology (coun. 1972-75), Marine Biol. Lab. (trustee 1993), Nat. Assn. State Univs. and Land Grant Colls. (higher edn. and tech. com. 1988-93, com. info. tech. 1994-96), Consortium Social Sci. Assn. (bd. dirs. 1993-96), Ohio Coun. Rsch. and Econ. Devel., Assn. Women Sci. (bd. dirs. 1998-2001), Phi Beta Kappa (com. qualifications 1985-2006, chair 1998-2004, senate 1996-2006, exec. com. 1997-2003), Sigma Xi, Omicron Delta Kappa Home Phone: 828-505-1244.

CLARK, EUGENIE, zoologist, educator; b. NYC, May 4, 1922; m. Hideo Umaki, 1942; m. Ilias Konstantinou, 1949; 4 children; m. Chandler Brossard, 1966; m. Igor Klatzo, 1969; m. Henry Yoshinobu Kon, 1997. BA, Hunter Coll., 1942; MA, NYU, 1946, PhD, 1950; DSc (hon.), U. Mass., Dartmouth, 1990, U. Guelph, 1995, U. South Hampton, 1995. Rsch. asst. ichthyology Scripps Instn. Oceanography, 1946-47; with NY Zool. Soc., 1947-48; rsch. asst. animal behavior Am. Mus. Nat. Hist., NYC, 1948-49, rsch. assoc., 1950-80; instr. Hunter Coll., 1954; exec. dir. Cape Haze Marine Lab., Sarasota, Fla., 1955-67; assoc. prof. biology CUNY, 1966-67; assoc. prof. zoology U. Md., 1968-73, prof. zoology, 1973-92, prof. emerita, sr. rsch. scientist, 1992—. Vis. prof. Hebrew U., 1972; sr. rsch. scientist, trustee emerita Mote Marine Lab., Sarasota, Fla., 1999—; sci. advisor Save Our Seas Found., 2010—. Author: Lady with a Spear, 1953, The Lady and the Sharks, 1969, Desert Beneath the Sea, 1991; subject of biographies Shark Lady (Ann McGovern), 1978, Adventures of the Shark Lady (Ann McGovern), 1998, Eugenie Clark, Adventures of a Shark Scientist (Ellen R. Butts, Joyce R. Schwartz), 2000, Fish Watching with Eugenie Clark (Michael E. Ross), 2000, America's Shark Lady (Ann McGovern), 2004, Eugenie Clark, Marine Biologist (Ronald A. Reis) 2005, Dr. Eugenie Clark Swimming with Sharks (Lisa Rao), 2006. Recipient Myrtle Wreath award in sci. Hadassah, 1964, Nogi award in art Underwater Soc. Am., 1965, Dugan award in aquatic sci. Am. Littoral Soc., 1969, Diver of Yr. award Boston Sea Rovers, 1978, David Stone medal, 1984, Stoneman Conservation award, 1982, Gov. of S. Sinai medal, 1985, Lowell Thomas award Explorers Club, 1986, Wildscreen Internat. Film Festival award, 1986, medal Gov. Red Sea, Egypt, 1988, Nogi award in Sci., 1988, Women's Hall of Fame award State of Md., 1989, Women Educators award, 1990, Alumnae award, Franklin Burr award Nat. Geog. Soc., 1993, Wyland Icon award, 2005, Henry Luce III Lifetime Achievement award, Wings WorldQuest Women of Discovery Awards, 2006, Conservation medal of Costa Rica, 2007, Sci. Diving Lifetime Achievement award, Am. Acad. Underwater Scis., 2007, Sci. Diving Lifetime medal of the Explorers Club, 2008, Bonaire's Lifetime Achievement award, 2010, Lifetime Making a Difference award, Nat. Marine Educators Assn., 2010, Nat. Coun. Jewish Woman award, 2010, Grand Cayman Internat. Scuba Diving Hall of Fame award, 2010, Beneath the Sea Women Divers Hall of Fame, 2010, Fla. Governor's award: Induction to Womens Hall of Fame, 2010; named to Hunter Coll. Hall of Fame, 1990, Diver's Equipment Mfg. Assn. Hall of Fame, 1993, Bermuda Underwater Explorers Inst. Hall of Fame, 2004, Hall of Fame Cmty. Video Archives, 2007, Fla. Women's Hall of Fame, 2010, Internat. Scuba Diving Hall of Fame, 2010, Beneath The Sea's Pioneer Diver of Yr., 2010; Fellow AEC, 1950; Saxton fellow, 1952; Breadloaf Writer's fellow; Fulbright scholar Egypt, 1951. Fellow: AAAS; mem.: Am. Elasmobranch Soc. (disting. fellow 1999), Am. Littoral Soc. (v.p. 1970—89), Nat. Pks. and Conservation Assn. (vice chmn. 1976), Internat. Soc. Profl. Diving Scientists, Soc. Woman Geographers (Gold medal 1975, U. Md. Pres.'s medal 1993), Israeli Zool. Soc. (hon.), Am. Soc. Ichthyology and Herpetology (life). Achievements include research in ecology and behavior of tropical sand and coral reef fishes; morphology and taxonomy marine fish; isolating mechanisms of poecillid fish; behavior of coral reef and deep sea sharks. Office: Ctr Shark Rsch Mote Marine Lab 1600 Ken Thompson Pkwy Sarasota FL 34236 Office Phone: 941-388-4441 Ext. 317. Business E-Mail: yoppe@mote.org.

CLARK, GARY CARL, lawyer; b. Flippin, Ark., Mar. 4, 1947; m. Jane W. Clark; children: Ross, Lauren. BS in Agrl. Edn., Okla. State U., 1969, MS, 1972; JD with honors, U. Tex., 1975. Bar: Okla. 1975, U.S. Dist. Ct. (no. dist.) Okla. 1975, U.S. Ct. Appeals (10th cir.) 1979. Tchr. Laverne H.S., Okla., 1969—70; assoc. Conner, Winters, Ballaine, Barry & McGowen, 1975—81, ptnr., 1981, Baker & Hoster, Tulsa, 1981—97; dir. Crowe & Dunlevy, PC, Tulsa, 1997—2004; v.p., gen. counsel Okla. State U. Found., Stillwater, 2004—08; v.p. rels. Okla. State U., 2008—. Lawyer-staffed Panel of Ct. Appeals, 1991; speaker in field. Vol. Legal Svcs. Ea. Okla., 1993—2004; trustee Okla. State Univ., Tulsa, 1999-2001; mem. bd. regents Okla. State Univ. and A&M Colls., 1993-2001, chmn., 1997-98; mem. Okla. Jud. Evaluation Com., 1999. Recipient Silver Beaver award Boy Scouts Am., 1996. Fellow Am. Coll. Trust and Estate Coun., Am. Bar Found., Okla. Bar Found.; mem. Okla. Bar Assn. (pres. 2002, bd. govs. 1997-99, 2001-2003, John Shipp Ethics award 1999, chair estate planning and probate sect. 1988-89, vice chair probate code com. 1991, bd. dirs. young lawyers divsn., mem. real property sect., co-chair tech. strategic planning task force, 2000, Golden Gavel award, 2003, Golden Quill award, 2003, chair awards com., 2007), Tulsa County Bar Assn. (pres. 1993-94, Golden Rule award 1993, Outstanding Sr. Lawyer 1996), Tulsa County Bar Found. (pres. 1994-95, treas. 1995-99, charter fellow), Tulsa Title and Probate Lawyers Assn. (pres. 1989-90), Okla. State U. Alumni Assn. (life), FFA Alumni Assn. (life), Order of Coif, Alpha Gamma Rho Alumni Assn. (Okla. chpt. dir., past pres.), Phi Delta Phi, Am. Law Inst. Home: 320 Eyler Ln Stillwater OK 74074-2819 Office: Okla State University 107 Whitehurst Stillwater OK 74078 Business E-Mail: gary.clark@okstate.edu.

CLARK, HANLEY C., state insurance commissioner; b. West Hamlin, W.Va. m. Holly Hoback; 3 children. BA in History, English, Bus., Marshall U., 1972; MA in History, U. W. Va., 1974. Spl. asst. to gov. State of W. Va., Charleston, 1980-81, asst. to ins. commr., 1981-85, dep. ins. commr., 1985-88, acting ins. commr., 1988-89, ins. commr., 1989—2001. Mem. Nat. Assn. Ins. Commrs. (former chmn s.e. zone). Office: WV Insurance Comm PO Box 50540 Charleston WV 25305-0540

CLARK, JACK, retired health facility administrator; b. Munford, Ala., Feb. 23, 1932; s. Raymond E. and Ora (Camp) C.; m. Louise Omega Lackey, Jan. 30, 1951; 1 son, Terry Wayne. BS, Springhill Coll., Mobile, Ala., 1960. Staff acct. Max E. Miller, C.P.A., Mobile, 1960-62; comptr. Mobile Gen. Hosp., 1962-67; assoc. adminstr. fin. Univ. Med. Ctr., Mobile, 1967-74; regional mgr. Humana Inc., Mobile, 1974-75, v.p., 1975-80, sr. v.p., 1980-84, exec. v.p., 1984-93, Galen Health Care, Mobile, 1993-94; ret. Columbia-HCA Healthcare, 1994. Trustee Mid-South region Humana hosps., 1974-87, Southwestern region, 1987-89, region IV, 1989-91, region 2, 1991-93, Regional Hosps., Columbia/HCA, 1994—. Bd. dirs. Agape S. Ala., Mobile, 1983, Rainbow Omega, 2000—; trustee Faulkner U., Montgomery, Ala., 1993—. Served in USAF, 1952-56, Korea. Mem. Hosp. Fin. Mgmt. Assn. (assoc.), Am. Hosp. Assn., Ala. Hosp. Assn., Ala. Hosp. Assn. Accts. (pres. so. council, dir. 1967-68), Mobile C. of C. Democrat. Mem. Ch. of Christ. Home: 6449 Canebrake Rd Mobile AL 36695-3817

CLARK, JAMES COVINGTON, journalist, historian; b. Washington, May 22, 1947; s. William Edward and Louise (Covington) C.; children: Randall Healy, Kevin Healy. BA, Lenoir-Rhyne Coll., 1975; MA, Stetson U., 1986; PhD, U. Fla., 1998. Reporter UPI, Washington, 1967, Columbia (S.C.) Record, 1968, AP, Charlotte, NC, 1969-70, Phila., 1972-73, Hickory (N.C.) Daily Record, 1974-75; regional editor Tampa (Fla.) Tribune, 1976-77; asst. exec. editor The Orlando (Fla.) Sentinel, 1977-98; syndicated columnist UP Syndicate, 1997-99; editor, pub. Orlando Mag., 2000—08; pres. Winter Pk. Mag., 2008—10. Lectr. U. Ctrl. Fla., Orlando, 1986-. Author: Last Train South, 1984, Faded Glory: Presidents Out of Power, 1985, The Murder of James Garfield, 1994, Trips Through Florida History, 2000, Red Pepper and Gorgeous George, 2011, Presidents in Florida, 2012, Pineapple Anthology of Florida Literature, 2013. Recipient George Polk award L.I. U., 1983, Gerald Loeb award, L.A., 1983, Arthur Thompson prize Fla. Hist. Soc., Gainesville, 1989. Mem. Authors Guild, Orgn. Am. Historians, Am. Hist. Assn., Am. Soc. Mag. Editors, Fla. Mag. Assn. (pres.). Personal E-mail: clarknews@aol.com.

CLARK, JAMES EDWARD, federal marshal; Formerly with Fed. Bur. Prisons, Morgantown, W.Va.; dep. marshal US Marshals Svc., US Dept. Justice, Louisville, 1996—2001, jud. security insp., 2001—09, acting chief dep. US marshal (we. dist.) Ky., 2009—10, US marshal (we. dist.) Ky., 2010—. Served with USAF. Office: US Courthouse 601 W Broadway Rm 162 Louisville KY 40202 Office Phone: 502-588-8000.

CLARK, JANET EILEEN, retired political science professor; b. Kansas City, Kans., June 5, 1940; d. Edward Francis and Mildred Lois (Mack) Morrissey; m. Caleb M. Clark, Sept. 28, 1968; children: Emily Claire, Grace Ellen, Evelyn Adair. AA, Kansas City Jr. Coll., 1960; AB, George Wash. U., Washington, DC, 1962, MA, 1964; PhD, U. Ill., 1973. Staff US Dept. Labor, Washington, 1962-64; instr. social sci. Kans. City Jr. Coll., Kans., 1964-67; instr. polit. sci. Parkland Coll., 1970-71; asst. prof. govt. N.Mex. State U., Las Cruces, 1971-77, assoc. prof., 1977-80; assoc. prof. polit. sci. U. Wyo., 1981-84, prof., 1984-94; prof. polit. sci., head dept. U. West Ga., Carrollton, 1994—2006; ret., 2006. Co-author: Women, Elections and Representation, 1987, The Equality State, 1988, Women in Taiwan Politics: Overcoming Barriers to Women's Participation in a Modernizing Society, 1990, Women at the Polls: Gender GAP, Cultural Politics and Contest Constuencies in the US, 2008; editor Women and Politics, 1991-2000; contbr. articles to profl. jours. Wolcott fellow, 1963-64, NDEA Title IV fellow, 1967-69. Mem. Internat. Soc. Polit. Psychology (gov. coun., 1987-89), NEA (pres. chpt. 1978-79), Am. Polit. Sci. Assn., We. Polit. Sci. Assn. (exec. coun. 1984-87), Western Social Sci. Assn. (exec. coun. 1978-81, v.p. 1982, pres. 1985), Women's Caucus for Polit. Sci. (treas. 1982, pres. 1987), LWV (exec. bd. 1980-83, 2002-2003, treas. 1986-90, pres. 1991-93, 2004-06), Women's Polit. Caucus, Beta Sigma Phi (v.p. chpt. 1978-79, sec. 1987-88, treas. 1988-89, v.p. 1989-90, pres. 1990-91), Phi Beta Kappa, Chi Omega (prize 1962), Phi Kappa Phi. Home: 2507 Waterford Rd Auburn AL 36832-4113 Personal E-mail: jclark@westga.edu.

CLARK, JANET F., oil industry executive; b. New Orleans, 1955; BA in Economics, Harvard U., 1977; MBA in Finance, U. Pa., 1982. CFO Santa Fe Energy Resources, 1997—99, sr. v.p., 1998—99, exec. v.p., corp. develop. & adminstrn., 1999—2001; sr. v.p., CFO Nuevo Energy, 2001—04; sr. v.p., treas., CFO Marathon Oil Corp., 2004—05, exec. v.p., treas., CFO, 2005—. Bd. dirs. Exterran Holdings Inc., 2003—, Dell Inc., 2011—. Bd. dir. New Hope Housing; trustee Joy Sch.; bd. mem. Houston Symphony, YES Prep Pub. Schools, Greater Houston Cmty. Found.; bd. overseers Rice U.-Jones Grad. Sch. Mgmt. Coun. Named Best CFO of Yr., Houston Bus. Journal, 2011; named one of The 100 Most Powerful Women, Forbes mag., 2009, The Most Influential Woman of 2010, Houston Woman's mag. Office: Marathon Oil Co 5555 San Felipe Rd Houston TX 77056-2723 Business E-Mail: jclark@marathonoil.com.

CLARK, JONATHAN C., finance company executive; BA in Econs., U. Va., Charlottesville; MBA, Harvard U., Boston. With Hewlett-Packard, Dean Witter, First Boston; pres., prin. SBG Industries, 1993—99; dir., COO Prudential Securities Inc., 1999—2000; mng. dir. Credit Suisse Securities, 2000—07; sr. v.p. corp. fin. SLM Corp. (Sallie Mae), Reston, Va., 2008—09, treas., 2008—09, exec. v.p., treas., 2009—11, exec. v.p., CFO, 2011—. Office: SLM Corp 12061 Bluemont Way Reston VA 20190 Office Phone: 703-810-3000.

CLARK, JOSH, state legislator; b. Atlanta, June 14; m. Chelsey Clark; children: Levi, Stephen, Moriah, Brianna. Nutraceutical distbn. co. owner; real estate investment and mgmt. co. owner; mem. Dist. 98 Ga. House of Representatives, 2011—. Mem. exec. com. Berea Sch. Ministry. Republican. Office: PO Box 303 Buford GA 30515 also: Georgia House of Reps 612 Coverdell Legis Office Bldg Atlanta GA 30334 Office Phone: 404-656-0325. Business E-Mail: josh.clark@house.ga.gov.

CLARK, KEITH F., otolaryngologist; MD, U. of Mich., Ann Arbor, 1978; PhD in Laryngeal Physiology, U. of Okla., 1999. Intern surg. William Beaumont Hosp., Detroit, 1979; resident otorhinolaryngology Univ. of Iowa, Iowa City, 1983; hosp. affiliations include Univ. Hosp. and Children's Hosp., Okla., The Okla. City Ear, Nose and Throat Clinic. Fellow: ACS, Triologic Soc., Am. Acad. of Otolaryngology, Head and Neck Surgery; mem.: Okla. County Med. Soc., Okla. Acad. of Otolaryngology. Office: The Oklahoma City Ear, Nose and Throat Clinic 535 NW 9th St 300 Oklahoma City OK 73102 Office Phone: 405-272-6027. Office Fax: 405-272-8315.

CLARK, KEVIN D., medical products executive; Pres. ImmunoVision, Inc., Springdale, Ark., 1987—95, COO, 1987—, IVAX Diagnostics, Inc., Miami, Fla., 2007—, acting CEO, 2008, pres., CEO, 2010—. Mem. adv. bd. Ark. BioVentures, 2000—03; mem. exec. com. U. Ark. Tech. Devel. Found., 2003—. Mem.: Ark. Biotech Assn. (exec. v.p. 1995—2004, pres. 2002). Office: IVAX Diagnostics Inc 2140 N Miami Ave Miami FL 33127 Office Phone: 305-324-2300. Office Fax: 305-324-2585.

CLARK, LARRY, state legislator; b. Louisville, Ky., July 24, 1945; Electrician; mem. Dist. 46 Ky. House of Reps., 1984—, spkr. pro tempore, 1993—; mem. Ky. State Labor Mgmt. Adv. Coun., Jefferson County Dem. Exec. Fin. Com., Econ. Adv. Coun. to Mayor Louisville, Ky., Appropriations & Revenue Com., Licensing & Occupations Com., State Govt. Com.; co-chmn. Gov.'s Task Force Unemployment Ins. Mem.: Pvt. Indsl. Fund Coun. (bd. dir.), Bellarmine Coll. (bd. overseers), Nat. Elec. Code Com., Jefferson County Elec. Bd. Control, Am. Cancer Soc. (bd. dir.), Commn. Louisville & Jefferson County Cultural Complex Task Force (mem., fine arts ctr.), Okolona Dem. Club. Democrat. Roman Catholic. Home: 5913 Whispering Hills Blvd Louisville KY 40219 Office: 702 Capitol Ave Annex Rm 304A Frankfort KY 40601 also: 700 Capitol Ave Capitol Rm 305 Frankfort KY 40601 Home Phone: 502-968-3456; Office Phone: 502-564-7520, 800-372-7181. Business E-Mail: Larry.Clark@lrc.ky.gov.

CLARK, LEIF MICHAEL, federal judge; b. Washington, Nov. 12, 1947; s. Charles G. and Gertrude Lyda (Zimmer) C. BA cum laude, U. Md., 1968; MDiv, Trinity Luth. Sem., Columbus, Ohio, 1972; JD cum laude, U. Houston, 1980. Bar: Tex. 1980, U.S. Dist. Ct. (we. dist.) Tex. 1981, U.S. Dist. Ct. (so. dist.) Tex. 1983, U.S. Ct. Appeals (5th cir.) 1984. Dir. Housing for Exceptional People, Detroit, 1974-75; ptnr. Cox & Smith, Inc., San Antonio, 1980-87; judge for western dist. Tex.

U.S. Bankruptcy Ct., San Antonio, 1987—. Prof. McGeorge Internat. Law Program, Salzburg, Austria, 1989-99; mem. adv. group US Del. Working Group UNCITRAL, 1995-96, 2008-; mem. adv. bd. ALI-ABA Cross Border Insolvency Project, 1995-96, USAID Jud. Tng. Project, 1995-98, Arbitrazh Ct. Judges Russian Fedn. Adv. bd. Insol Internat. Project, 1995, Quadrennial-plenary Session, 2009. Mem. ABA, Am. Coll. Bankruptcy, Nat. Banker Conf. (exec. com. 2008-), Am. Bankruptcy Inst. (dir. 1991—, exec. com. 1995—, v.p. rsch. 1998—), Nat. Conf. Bankruptcy Judges (planning com. 1992 ann. meeting, endowment com. 2006-09), Comml. Law League, State Bar Tex. Lutheran. Avocations: photography, choral singing, running, travel. Office: US Bankruptcy Ct 615 E Houston St San Antonio TX 78205 Office Phone: 210-472-5181. Office Fax: 210-472-5160. Business E-Mail: judge_leif_clark@txwb.uscourts.gov.

CLARK, MARCUS R., state supreme court justice; b. Sulphur, La., Feb. 24, 1956; s. Hilda W. and Charles Gerald Clark; m. Allyson Ayers Clark, 1990; children: Nicole, Cooper. Grad., NE La. U., Monroe, 1978; JD, La. State U., Baton Rouge, 1985. Det. Ouachita Parish Sheriff's Office, Monroe, 1978—82, Metro Narcotics, Monroe, 1981—82; asst. dist. atty. 4th Jud. Dist. Atty.'s Office, La., 1985—96, chief felony drug prosecutor, 1990—96; judge Sect. 2 4th Jud. Dist. Ct., 1997—2009, chief judge, 2004—06; assoc. justice 4th dist. La. Supreme Ct., New Orleans, 2009—. Mem. Supreme Ct. Uniform Rules Com.; mem. new judgeship com., ad hoc NCSC study com., criminal judges com., salary and pers. com., ct. tech. com. 4th Jud. Dist. Ct.; mem. Post-Conviction DNA Testing Adv. Commn., YWCA S.A.F.E. Task Force. Treas. NE Baptist Sch. PTO; bd. mem. Alzheimer's Assn. Mem.: La. Coun. Juvenile and Family Ct. Judges, Nat. Coun. Juvenile and Family Ct. Judges, 2nd Cir. Judges' Assn., 4th Jud. Dist. Ct. Bar Assn., La. Bar Assn., Judge Fred Fudicker Am. Inns of Ct., La. Dist. Judges Assn. (mem. exec. com.). Office: La Supreme Ct 400 Royal St New Orleans LA 70130 Office Phone: 504-310-2300.*

CLARK, PAT ENGLISH, lawyer; b. Austin, Tex., Feb. 26, 1940; s. Pat Wheeler and Jennie Bell (Lagrone) C.; m. Peggy Arnold Gray, March 16, 2002; 1 child, Susan Louise Beisert. BA, U. Tex., JD, 1963. Bar: Tex. 1963, U.S. Ct. Mil. Appeals 1964, U.S. Dist. Ct. (so. and no. dists.) Tex. Staff atty. Phillips Petroleum Co., Houston, 1967-69; atty. Amoco Production Co., Houston, 1969-75; ptnr. Vinson & Elkins, Houston, 1975-95, Borrego & Clark, 1996-99; of counsel Lorance & Thompson PC, Houston, 2012—. Capt. JAGC, U.S. Army, 1964-67. Methodist. Office: Lorance & Thompson PC 2900 N LoopWest Ste 500 Houston TX 77092 Business E-Mail: pclark8@austin.rr.com.

CLARK, PERRY B., state legislator; b. Sept. 30, 1957; Former mem. Econ. Devel. & Tourism Com., Judiciary Com., State Govt. & Vet. Affairs; house rep. Ky.; state rep. Dist. 37 Ky., 1995—2006; state senator Dist. 37, 2006—; quality trainer. Democrat. Christian. Mailing: 5716 New Cut Rd Louisville KY 40214-5606 Office: Capitol Annex Rm 229 Frankfort KY 40601 Home Phone: 502-366-1247; Office Phone: 502-564-8100 715. Business E-Mail: perry.clark@lrc.state.ky.us.

CLARK, RICHARD, councilman; m. D'Atra Pruett; children: McKenzie, Keegan. Grad., U. Fla. Pres. Supreme Janitorial; councilman, Dist.3 Jacksonville City Coun., Fla. Mem. Peyton Subcommittee Transition Team, Small Bus. Com. for JEDC Restructuring, Recreation & Cmty. Devel., Transp., Energy & Utilities Coms., Election Canvassing Bd.; alt. Jacksonville Waterways Commn.; vice chmn. Personnel Com. Bd. mem. River Garden, JaxCare; mem. Gator Bowl Com.; asst. chmn. Ecology Tournament Players Clubs, 2004. Mem.: Nat. Fedn. Ind. Businesses, Bldg. Operators & Mgrs. Assn., Internat. Facility Mgmt. Assn. (former pres.). Republican. Office: 117 W Duval St Ste 425 Jacksonville FL 32202 Office Phone: 904-630-1386. Business E-Mail: rclark@coj.net.

CLARK, RON, federal judge; b. Venezuela, 1953; BA in Econs. with high honors, U. Conn., 1973, MA, 1974; JD, U. Tex., 1979. Bar: Tex. 1980, U.S. Ct. Appeals (5th and 11th cirs.) 1981, U.S. Supreme Ct. 1982, U.S. Dist. Ct. (ea. dist.) Tex. 1983; cert. in civil trial law and civil appellate law, Tex. Bd. Legal Specialization. Trial atty. City of Abilene, Tex., 1979-82; ptnr. Henderson, Bryant & Wolfe, Sherman, Tex., 1983-93, Wolfe, Clark, Henderson & Tidwell, Sherman, 1993—2002; judge US Dist. Ct. (ea. dist.) Tex., Beaumont, 2002—. Chmn. Fed. Civil Justice Reform Act com. for Eastern Dist. Tex., 1994-95. Author: Texas Municipal Law and Procedure Manual, 1989, 3d edit., 1995; editor-in-chief Am. Jour. Criminal Law, 1978-79. Mem. Tex. House of Reps., 1997—2002. 2nd lt. US Army, 1974-76. Roman Catholic. Office: US Dist Ct Fed Bldg and US Courthouse 300 Willow St Ste 221 Beaumont TX 77701

CLARK, TIM (TIMOTHY HENRY CLARK), professional golfer; b. Durban, South Africa, Dec. 17, 1975; Student, NC State U., Raleigh, 1996—97. Profl. golfer, 1998—; mem. PGA Tour, 2001—; mem. South African team World Golf Championships - World Cup, 2002, 2005; mem. Internat. team Presidents Cup, 2003, 2005. Recipient Order of Merit, South African Tour, 2001—02. Achievements include winner Nationwide Tour events: Buy.com Fort Smith Classic, 2000, Buy.com Boise Open, 2000; winner European Tour events: Bell's South African Open, 2002, South African Airways Open, 2005, Barclays Scottish Open, 2005; winner, CVS Charity Classic (with Nick Price), 2006, Australian Open, 2008; winner PGA Tour events: The Players Championship, 2010. Office: PGA Tour 100 PGA TOUR Blvd Ponte Vedra Beach FL 32082

CLARK, VALERIE, state legislator; b. Oct. 05; m. Bob Clark; children: Pearson, Barrett. Attended, Harvard Principals Inst.; grad., SUNY, Plattsburgh; MEd, U. NC, Chapel Hill; PhD, U. Ga. Tchr. Gwinnett County; prin. Duluth Mid. Sch., Shiloh Mid. Sch., Ctrl. Gwinnett HS; mem. Dist. 104 Ga. House of Representatives, 2011—. Republican. Office: 252 Regal Dr Lawrenceville GA 30046-4771 also: Georgia House of Reps 507 Coverdell Legis Office Bldg Atlanta GA 30334 Office Phone: 404-656-0202. Business E-Mail: valerie.clark@house.ga.gov.

CLARK, WENDY, advertising executive; b. England, 1970; m. Jeff Clark; 3 children. BA in English and Creative Writing, Fla. State U., 1991. Dir. advt. Cingular Wireless LLC (formerly BellSouth Mobility), Atlanta; sr. v.p., dir. client svcs. GSD&M, Austin, Tex., 2001—04; sr. v.p. advt. AT&T Inc. (merger of SBC Communications & AT&T Corp.), San Antonio, 2004—08; sr. v.p. integrated mktg. comm. & capabilities Coca-Cola Co., Atlanta, 2008—. Mem. adv. bd. Canoe Ventures, 2010—. Bd. dirs. Jack & Jill Late Stage Cancer Found., Atlanta. Recipient POW! award, Womenetics.com, Inc., 2010; named a Woman to Watch, Advt. Age, 2007, Fortune mag., 2009; named one of 40 Under 40, 2009, 2010; named to Advt. Hall of Achievement, Am. Advt. Fedn., 2007. Mem.: Assn. Nat. Advertisers (bd. dirs.). Office: Coca Cola Co Hdqs 1 Coca Cola Plaza Atlanta GA 30313 Home Phone: 404-676-2121.

CLARK, WILLIAM A., political scientist, educator; b. Phila., Feb. 3, 1958; s. William A. Clark and Joan A. Thackrah; m. Jana E. Ihrig, Sept. 27, 1986; children: Phoebe N., Griffin McL. BA, Pa. State U., University Park, 1980; MA, Drew U., Madison, NJ, 1981; PhD, U. SC, Columbia, 1987. Prof., Polit. Sci. Hillsdale Coll., Mich., 1987—88, La. State U., Baton Rouge, 1991—; assoc. dir. James F. Byrnes Internat. Ctr., Columbia, SC, 1988—91. Office: La State Univ Dept Polit Sci Baton Rouge LA 70803-5433 Office Fax: 225-578-2540. Business E-Mail: poclark@lsu.edu.

CLARKE, ALYCE GRIFFIN, state legislator; b. Yazoo City, Miss. m. Lee William Clarke; 1 child. BS, Alcorn State U.; MS, Tuskegee Inst.; postgrad., Jackson State U., Miss. Coll. Nutritionist; mem. Dist. 69 Miss. House of Reps., 1985—. Vice chmn. Interstate Coop com. Active Econ. Devel. Com., Exec. Dem. Commn., New Hope Found. Mem. Nat. Assn. Cmty. Health Ctrs., Pub. Health Assn., Jack & Jill Am., Alcorn Alumni, Alpha Kappa Alpha. Democrat. Baptist. Office: PO Box 1018 Rm 119A-NC Jackson MS 39215 Office Phone: 601-359-3096. Business E-Mail: aclarke@house.ms.gov.

CLARKE, EUGENE (BUCK) S., state legislator; b. Greenville AFB, Apr. 4, 1956; m. Paula Clark; children: Anne Read, Carlisle, Ellen. CPA. Mem. Dist. 22 Miss. State Senate, 2004—. Mem.: AICPA, MSCPA, Rotary Club. Republican. Methodist. Address: PO Box 373 Hollandale MS 38748 Home Phone: 662-827-5685; Office Phone: 662-827-7261, 601-359-3172. Fax: 662-827-7264; Office Fax: 601-359-5957. Business E-Mail: bclarke@senate.ms.gov.

CLARKE, JANET MORRISON, marketing executive; d. Morton and Shirley (Harkinson) Morrison, m. Frederick G.E. Clarke, Oct. 4, 1980. BA in Architecture, Princeton U., 1976. Sales rep. Sci. Press, Ephrata, Pa., 1977-78, R.R. Donnelley & Sons Co., Chgo., 1978, various positions including sr. v.p. Information Technol. and dir. venture capital fund, 1978—97; mng. dir., global database mktg. Citibank, 1997—2000; chmn., CEO KnowledgeBase Marketing, Inc., 2000—01; exec. v.p. Young & Rubicam, Inc, 2000—01; chief mktg. officer DealerTrack, Inc., 2002—03; founder Clarke Littlefield LLC, 2001—, pres., 2001—02, 2003—. Bd. dirs. Cox Communications, 1995—2004, Asbury Automotive Group, ExpressJet Holdings Inc., 2002—, eFunds Corp., 2000—, Forbes.com Inc., Gateway Computers, 2005—, Cox Enterprises, 2007—; mem. sch. bd. Harvard Bus. Sch. Charter trustee, Princeton U.; bd. dirs. YWCA, Westbrook, Conn., 1984—; mem., regional chmn. Nat. Ann. Giving Com. Princeton (N.J.) U., 1985—. Mem.: York Golf & Tennis Club, Landmark (Stamford, Conn.), Princeton (N.Y.C.). Republican.

CLARKE, JEFFREY W., computer company executive; b. 1963; m. Loretta Clarke; 2 children. BS in Elec. Engring., U. Tex., San Antonio, 1986. Reliability/product engr. Motorola, Inc., Austin, Tex.; quality engr. Dell, Inc., 1987, various engring. and mgmt. positions, then dir. product devel., 1989—95, dir. desktop devel., 1995—2001, v.p., gen. mgr. relationship product group, 2001—03, sr. v.p. bus. client product group, 2003—, vice-chmn. global ops. & end user computing solutions, 2009—. Launched Dell Precision Workstation product line, 1997; delivered keynote speech Nat. Instruments NIWeek 2005, Austin. Office: Dell Inc Hdqs 1 Dell Way Round Rock TX 78682 Office Phone: 512-338-4400. Office Fax: 512-728-3653. Business E-Mail: jeffrey_clarke@dell.com.

CLARKE, LEWIS JAMES, landscape architect; b. Eng., Mar. 10, 1927; s. Roland and May (Pringle) C.; children: Lewis Nigel, Jennifer Kay, Rachel May, Lisa Elaine. Dip. Arch., Sch. Architecture, Leicester, Eng., 1950; Dip. L.D., Kings Coll, U. Durham, 1951; M.L.A., Harvard U., 1952. Prof. Sch. Design N.C. State Univ., Raleigh, 1952-68; sr. partner Lewis Clarke Assos., Raleigh, 1952—. Served with Corps Royal Engrs., 1946-49. Smith Mundt fellow, Fulbright fellow, 1951-52. Fellow Inst. Landscape Architects, Am. Soc. Landscape Architects; mem. Royal Inst. Brit. Architects. Home and Office: Lewis Clarke Assocs 1701 Glen Eden Dr Raleigh NC 27612-4335

CLARKE, RICHARD ALAN, risk management firm executive, former federal official; b. Mass., Oct. 27, 1950; BA, U. Pa., 1972; MS, MIT, 1978. Nuclear weapons & European security analyst US Dept. Def., 1973-77; sr. analyst Pacific Sierra Rsch. Corp., 1978-79; sr. analyst Bur. Politico-Mil. Affairs US Dept. State, Washington, 1979-85, dep. asst. sec. for intelligence, 1985-89, asst. sec. for politico-mil. affairs, 1989-92; spl. asst. to Pres. for global affairs Nat. Security Coun., Washington, 1992—98, nat. coord. for security, infrastructure protection, & counter-terrorism, 1998—2001, spl. adviser for cyberspace security, 2001—03; chmn. Good Harbor Consulting, LLC, Arlington, Va., 2003—. Chair Critical Infrastructure Protection Bd., 2001—03; adj. faculty Harvard U., Cambridge, Mass., 2003—; security cons. ABC News, Washington, 2003. Author: (non-fiction) Against All Enemies: Inside America's War on Terror, 2004, Your Government Failed You: Breaking the Cycle of National Security Disasters, 2008; co-author (with Robert K. Knacke): Cyber War: The Next Threat to National Security and What to Do About It, 2010; author: (novels) The Scorpion's Gate, 2005, Breakpoint, 2007. Office: Good Harbor Consulting LLC 2101 Wilson Blvd 10th Fl Ste 1000 Arlington VA 22201

CLARKE, ROBERT LOGAN, lawyer; b. Tulsa, Okla., June 29, 1942; s. Ralph Logan and Faye Louise (Todd) C.; m. Jean (Puddin) Barrow Talbert, Sept. 23, 1967; 1 child, Robert Logan Jr. BA Econs., Rice U., 1963; LLB, Harvard U., 1966. Bar: N.Mex. 1966, Tex. 1967. Legis. asst. to U.S. Senator Edwin L. Mechem, Washington, 1964; assoc. Hinkle, Bondurant, Cox, Eaton & Hensley, Roswell, N.Mex., 1966, Bracewell & Giuliani, LLP (formerly Bracewell & Patterson), Houston, 1968-73, ptnr., 1973-85, ptnr., head fin. svcs. sect., 1992—; comptr. of currency Washington, 1985-92; dir. FDIC, Washington, 1985-92, Resolution Trust Corp., Washington, 1989-92; sr. ptnr. Bracewell & Giuliani, LLP (formerly Bracewell & Patterson), 1992—. Bd. dirs. Cmty. Bancorp. N.Mex., Inc., Cmty. Bank, Eagle Materials, Inc.,1994-, First Investors Fin. Svcs., Inc., Stewart Info. Svcs. Corp., Mutual Omaha Ins., Dubai Fin. Svcs. Authority, sr. advisor to pres. Nat. Bank Poland, 1992-2000; advisor to bank suprs. in Ea. Europe, Mexico, Argentina, Brazil and Kazakhstan. Precinct chmn. Harris County Reps., 1970-74, 76-85, legal counsel, 1984-85; trustee Mus. N.Mex. Found., 1992-, Internat. Folk Art Found., 1995-02, Rice U., 2006-; dir. Santa Fe Chamber Music Festival, 2003—; founding dir. Houston Rep. Club, 1982-85; bd. dirs. Houston Polit. Action Com., 1983-85; trustee Trout Unltd., 1997-05; mem. adv. com. Harris County Reagan-Bush campaign, 1984; asst. scoutmaster Boy Scouts Am., Houston, 1980-85; deacon 1st Presbyn. Ch. Houston. Capt. U.S. Army, 1966-68, Rice U., 2006-2010. Recipient Disting. Svc. medal U.S. Treasury Dept., 1992, Banking Leadership award Western States Sch. Banking, Albuquerque, 1993. Mem. Houston Bar Assn., Houston Bar Found., State Bar Tex., State Bar N.Mex., Rice U. Alumni Assn. (chmn. area club com. 1984-85, mem. exec. bd. dirs. 1987-89, Disting. Alumnus award 1992), River Oaks Country Club, Houston Club, Coronado Club, Houston City Club, Rotary (trustee student's ednl. fund). Avocations: tennis, fishing, hiking. Office: Bracewell & Giuliani LLP Pennzoil South Tower 711 Louisiana St Ste 2300 Houston TX 77002-2781 Office Phone: 713-221-1180. Business E-Mail: robert.clarke@bgllp.com.

CLARKE, THOMAS HAL, lawyer; b. Atlanta, Aug. 10, 1914; s. James Caleb and Mary Cox (DeSaussure) C.; m. Mary Louise Hastings, July 12, 1951; children: Thomas Hal Jr., Katie Clarke Hamilton, Rebecca DeSaussure Clarke Morrison. LLB, Washington and Lee U., 1938. Bar: Ga. 1939, U.S. Dist. Ct. (no. dist.) Ga., U.S. Ct. Appeals (5th cir.), U.S. Supreme Ct., 1973. Ptnr. Clarke & Anderson, Atlanta, 1948-60, Mitchell, Clarke, Pate & Anderson, Atlanta, 1960-69, 73-85; of counsel Gambrell, Clarke, Anderson & Stolz, Atlanta, 1985-92. Copyright trustee Gone With the Wind and sequels, 1983—2002. Mem. Fed. Home Loan Bank Bd., Washington, 1969-73; past pres., bd. dirs. Atlanta Hist. Soc.; past bd. visitors Emory U.; trustee emeritus Washington and Lee U. Served with USNR, 1942-46, ETO, PTO. Mem. Internat. Bar Assn. (past chmn. savs. and bldg. socs. com.), ABA (chmn. savs. and loan com. 1970-73, chmn. corp. banking and bus. law sect. 1973-74, mem. ho. of dels. 1974-80, editor The Business Lawyer 1972), Ga. Bar Assn., Atlanta Bar Assn., Am. Law Inst., Atlanta Lawyers Club (past pres.), Selden Soc., English Speaking Union (past pres., chmn. bd.), Metropolitan Club (Washington D.C.), Commerce Club, Piedmont Driving Club (Atlanta). Presbyterian. Home: 186 15th St NE Atlanta GA 30309-3511

CLARKE-REED, GWYNDOLEN, state legislator; b. Delray Beach, Fla., Oct. 24, 1940; children: Vincent, Veronica. AA, NYC Cmty. Coll., 1968; BS, Brooklyn Coll., 1973; MS, Adelphi U., 1979. Tchr. NYC Schs., 1979—85; commr. City of Deerfield Beach, Fla., 1993—2005; mem. Dist. 92 Fla. House of Reps., 2008—, ranking mem. health and family svcs. policy coun., mem. elder and family svcs. policy com., preK-12 appropriations com., roads, bridges and ports policy com. Mem. Dist. 18 NYC Sch. Bd., 1980—83. Bd. mem. C.J. Nixon Mango Festival, Inc., 1986—; mem. Broward County Planning Coun., 2000—05, Broward County Cmty. Devel. Com., North Broward Hosp. Cmty. Primary Care, 2003, Deerfield C. of C. Mem.: Common Highlands Homeowners Assn. (charter mem. 1987—), Am. Assn. U. Women (Fla. Women's Issues chmn.), Nat. League of Cities (bd. dirs. 1996), Broward League of Cities (pres. 2002—03), Fla. Black Caucus Local Elected Officials, Fla. League of Cities (bd. dirs. 1999—2005), Kiwanis of Deerfield West, Am. Cancer Soc., J.M. Unit Boys & Girls Club (bd. mem.), Delta Sigma Theta Sorority. Democrat. Office: 402 S Monroe St Rm 1402 Tallahassee FL 32399-1300 also: Pompano Beach City Hall 100 W Atlantic Blvd Pompano Beach FL 33060-6099 Office Phone: 850-488-0880, 954-786-4848. Business E-Mail: gwyn.clarke-reed@myfloridahouse.gov.

CLARKSON, CHARLES ANDREW, real estate investment executive; b. Grove City, Pa., Sept. 1, 1945; s. Harold William and Jean Henrietta (Jaxtheimer) C.; m. Patricia Holt, June 14, 1969; children: Thomas Byerly, Blair Elizabeth, John Holt. AB, Princeton U., 1967; JD, George Washington U., 1972. With N.Y. Urban League, 1967—68; real estate negotiator Safeway Stores, Washington, 1968-69; mortgage banker J.W. Rouse Co., Washington, 1970-73; pres. Alex Brown Realty, Balt., 1973-76; founder, pres. The Clarkson Group, Jacksonville, Fla., 1976—. Bd. dirs. Ramgow, Inc.; chmn. mem. adv. com. arts JCCI, 2010; chmn. Ixreveal. Hon. trustee UNF Found.; mem. Environ. Land Mgmt. Study Com III, Fla.; chmn. bd. trustees WJCT-TV; mem. Commn. on Future of the South; chmn. bd. govs. FCCJ Found.; bd. Jacksonville Symphony, The Clarkson Group. Mem.: The Lodge at Ponte Vedra, Sawgrass Club. Office: The Clarkson Group Ste 200 3100 University Blvd S Jacksonville FL 32216-2727

CLARKSON, JOHN G., ophthalmologist, educator, medical association administrator; m. Diana Teasdale; children: Paige, David. BS, Princeton U.; MD, Miami Sch. Medicine, 1968. Intern U. Hosp., Boston; resident ophthalmology U. Miami/Jackson Meml. Med. Ctr., Fla.; ophthalmic pathology, retinal and vitreous surgery fellow Johns Hopkins U., Balt.; chmn. dept. ophthalmology, dir. Bascom Palmer Eye Inst., 1991—96; sr. v.p. med. affairs, dean Sch. Medicine U. Miami, 1995—2006, dean emeritus, prof. ophthalmology, 2006—; exec. dir. Am. Bd. Ophthalmology, 2006—. Recipient Nat. Physician of Yr. Lifetime Achievement award, Castle Connolly Med. Ltd., 2012. Mem.: Macula Soc., Retina Soc., Am. Ophthalmol. Soc., Am. Acad. Ophthalmology, Am. Bd. Ophthalmology (bd. dirs.), Club Jules Gonin. Office: University Miami Miller Sch Medicine Suite 1560 1120 NW 14th St Miami FL 33136 Office Phone: 305-243-7878. Business E-Mail: jclarkson@miami.edu.

CLARKSON, KELLY BRIANNE, singer, songwriter; b. Ft. Worth, Tex., Apr. 24, 1982; d. Stephen Michael Clarkson and Jeanne Rose, Jimmy Taylor (Stepfather); m. Brandon Blackstock, Oct. 20, 2013; stepchildren: Seth, Savannah. Winner inaugural American Idol contest, 2002; 2d place World Idol contest, 2004. Singer: (albums) Thankful, 2003, Breakaway, 2004 (Choice Album, Teen Choice Awards, 2005, Best Pop Vocal Album, Grammy Awards, 2006), My December, 2007, All I Ever Wanted, 2010, Stronger, 2011 (Best Pop Vocal Album, Grammy Awards, 2013), Greatest Hits - Chapter 1, 2012, Wrapped in Red, 2013, (songs) A Moment Like This, 2002 (Best Selling Single of Yr., Billboard Music Awards, 2002), Miss Independent, 2003 (ASCAP Song Writer award, American Soc. Composers, Authors & Publishers, 2004), Breakaway, 2004, Since U Been Gone, 2004 (Choice Single, Teen Choice Awards, 2005, Best Female Video, Best Pop Video, MTV Video Music Awards, 2005, Best Female Pop Vocal Performance, Grammy Awards, 2006), Because of You, 2005 (Best Female Video, MTV Video Music Awards, 2006, Song of Yr., American Soc. Composers, Authors & Publishers, 2007), Behind These Hazel Eyes, 2005, Walk Away, 2006, My Life Would Suck Without You, 2009, I Do Not Hook Up, 2009, (songs with Jason Aldean) Don't You Wanna Stay, 2011 (Best Single by a Vocal Collaboration, Best Music Video by a Duo or Group Collaboration, Am. Country Awards, 2011, Musical Event of Yr., Country Music Assn. Awards, 2011, Single of Yr., Acad. Country Music Awards, 2012); actress (films) From Justin to Kelly, 2003, (TV appearances) MADtv, 2002, American Dreams, 2003, King of the Hill, 2004, Reba, 2007, mentor (reality TV competition) Duets, 2012. Named Choice Female Artist, Teen Choice Awards, 2003, 2005, 2006, Favorite Female Performer, People's Choice Awards, 2005, 2006, Artist of Yr., American Music Awards, 2005, Favorite Adult Contemporary Artist, 2005, 2006, Favorite Pop/Rock Female Artist, 2006, Favorite Female Singer, Nickelodeon Kids' Choice Awards, 2006. Office: c/o Starstruck Entertainment Inc 40 Music Square West Nashville TN 37203 Office Phone: 615-259-5200.*

CLARY, DEBBIE A., state legislator; b. Shelby, NC, Aug. 29, 1959; Attended, Gardner Webb U. State rep. Dist. 48, NC, 1995—2002; state rep. Dist. 110 NC, 2003—08; state senator Dist. 46 NC, 2008—; broadcaster; pres. Millennium Mktg. Group Inc. Republican. Baptist. Address: 214 S Lafayette St Shelby NC 28150 Office: NC Senate 300 N Salisbury St Rm 314 Raleigh NC 27603-5925 Office Phone: 919-715-3038. E-mail: Debbie.Clary@ncleg.net.

CLAURE, R. MARCELO, telecommunications industry executive; BS in Economics & Fin., Bentley Coll., 1993, PhD (hon.) in Comml. Sci., 2004. Co-founder, gen. mgr. USA Wireless, 1993—95; various exec. positions Unplugged Comm., Inc., 1995—97, pres., Small World Comm., pres., Unplugged Internat.; chmn., pres. & CEO Brightstar Corp., Miami, 1997—. Mem. Coun. on Fgn. Rels.; bd. adv. World Econ. Forum; bd. trustees Fla. Internat. U., Bentley Coll.; bd. dirs., L.Am. Georgetown U.; founder, bd. dirs. One Laptop Per Child; bd. dirs. Bolvian-Am. C. of C.; bd. trustees Bentley Coll. Recipient PODER-BCG Bus. award, PODER Mag., award of excellence, América Economía; named Entrepreneur of Yr., Ernst & Young, 2001,

USA Today, 2001, Hispanic Entrepreneur of Yr., Hispanic Bus. Mag., 2003, Entrepreneur of Yr., Bus. Leader Mag., CEO of Yr., LISTA; named one of 50 Most Important Hispanics in Tech. and Bus., Hispanic Engr. & Info. Tech. mag., 2005. Office: Brightstar Corp 9725 NW 117th Ave Ste 300 Miami FL 33178 Office Phone: 305-421-6000. Business E-Mail: r.claure@brightstarcorp.com.

CLAVELL-RODRIGUEZ, LUIS A., healthcare company executive; BS, Catholic U. PR; MD, U. PR. Cert. Nat. Bd. Med. Examiners, Am. Bd. Pediatrics, Sub-Bd. Pediatric Hematology/Oncology. Fellowships tng., Pediatric Hematology & Oncology Harvard Medical Sch., Children's Hosp. Med. Ctr., Boston, Sidney Farber Cancer Inst., Boston; prin. investigator, Children's Oncology Group & Dana Farber Acute Lymphoblastic Leukemia Consortium San Jorge Children's Hosp., chief med. officer, pres., Profl. Bd. San Juan; prof., pediatrics and pathology U. PR Sch. of Med., 1980—94, dir., pediatric hematology oncology, 1984—94; chmn. Triple-S Management Corp., 2008—. Mem. Am. Soc. Clin. Oncology, Am. Soc. Hematology. Office: Triple-S Management Corp 1441 F D Roosevelt Ave San Juan PR 00920 Office Phone: 787-749-4949. Office Fax: 787-749-4191. Business E-Mail: lclavell-rodriguez@ssspr.com.

CLAWSON, CURTIS JAY, retired manufacturing executive; b. Sept. 28, 1959; s. Jack and Cherie Clawson. BA in Spanish, Purdue U., 1984; BS, Purdue U. Krannert Sch. Mgmt., 1984; MBA, Harvard Bus. Sch., 1990. Various positions Arvin Industries, Inc., 1986—95, Allied Signal, 1995—97; pres. Beverage Cans American Bus. Unit American Nat. Can Group Inc., 1998—99, pres., COO Chgo., 1999—2000; chmn., pres., CEO Hayes Lemmerz Internat., Northville, Mich., 2001—09; chmn., CEO Hayes Lemmerz International, Inc., Northville, Mich., 2009—12. Bd. dirs. Lear Corp., 2009—12. Named to The Ind. Basketball Hall of Fame, 2003. Republican.*

CLAWSON, DAVID KAY, orthopedic surgeon; b. Salt Lake City, Aug. 8, 1927; s. David J. and Elva (Gundry) C.; m. Janet Dorothy Smith, June 1, 1952; children: Kim Debra, David Roger. Student, U. Utah, 1944-45, 47-48; MD, Harvard U., 1952. Diplomate: Am. Bd. Orthopedic Surgery. Intern Stanford U. Hosp., 1952-53, resident gen. surgery, 1953-54; resident orthopedic surgery Stanford U. Hosp., also San Francisco City and County Hosp., 1954-57; fellow in orthopedics Nat. Found. Infantile Paralysis, 1955-58; hon. sr. registrar Royal Nat. Orthopedic Hosp., London, Eng., 1957-58; asst. prof. UCLA Med. Sch., 1958; asst. prof. surgery, head div. orthopedic surgery U. Wash. Med. Sch., 1958-61, assoc. prof. surgery, head div. orthopedic surgery, 1961-65, prof., 1964-83, chmn. dept. orthopedics, 1964-75; dean Coll. Medicine, U. Ky., 1975-83, vice chancellor for clin. profl. services, 1982-83; exec. vice chancellor U. Kans. Med. Ctr., Kansas City, 1983-94, cons. to chancellor, 1994; prof. orthopaedic surgery U. Ky., 1994—, cons. to dean, 1994—. Mem. Accreditation Coun. for Grad. Med. Edn., 1977-88; chmn. residency rev. com. on structure and functions, 1987-88; chmn. coun. of deans Assn. Am. Med. Coll., 1985-86, chmn. of the assembly, 1988-89, immediate past chmn., 1989-90, disting. svc. rep. to exec. coun., 1992-95; active Am. Orthopaedic Soc. for Sports Medicine, 1972-87, founder, 1972; active Assn. Orthopaedic Chmn., 1971-73, founder, 1971. Contbr. med. jours.; mem. editorial bd.: Clin. Orthopedics and Related Research, 1964—. Mem. Heart of Am. coun. Boy Scouts Am., 1989—, mem. adv. bd., 1989-92, Regional Task Force and Edn. Found., 1972—. With USNR, 1945-46. Exchange fellow Am. Orthopedic Assn., 1967 Mem. AMA (coun. for med. affairs 1988—), Am. Acad. Ortho. Surgeons (coun. on health policy 1990-95), Am. Orthopaedic Assn., Assn. Acad. Health Ctrs., Assn. Am. Univs., Assn. Bone and Joint Surgeons (pres. 1977), Harvard Med. Sch. Alumni Assn. (pres. 1984-85), Henry Clay Meml. Found. (pres. 2007-09). Home: 3785 Jamaica Ct Lexington KY 40509-9506 also: 10 E Roanoke St Seattle WA 98102-3257

CLAWSON, ROXANN ELOISE, retired college administrator, computer company executive; b. Dallas, Tex., Oct. 15, 1945; d. Robert Wellington Clawson and Jeannette Irene (Rodenhauser) Clawson Clayton. BFA, Mich. State U., 1968. Libr. asst. Cooper Union, NYC, 1970—75, asst. libr., 1976—82; assoc. to dean, 1985—2008; computer cons., 1986—2008. Actor: The Dragon's Nest, 1989. Mem.: NAFE, NY Per. Computer Group. Democrat. Lutheran.

CLAXTON, PHILIP A., brokerage house executive; BA in Econs. and Computer Sci., NYU, MBA. CFO SureTrade; v.p. strategy Quick & Reilly Group; v.p. global internet strategy FleetBoston Fin.; sr. mgr. fin. planning and analysis E*TRADE Fin.; CFO TradeKing, Charlotte, NC. Office: TradeKing PO Box 49050 Charlotte NC 28277-3432 E-mail: pclaxton@tradeking.com.

CLAY, DISKIN, classical studies educator; b. Fresno, Calif., Nov. 2, 1938; s. Norman and Florence Patricia (Diskin) C.; m. Jenny Strauss, June 21, 1963 (div. 1977); 1 child, Andreia; m. Sara Christine Clark, Oct. 28, 1978 (div. 1999); children: Hilary, Christine; m. Andrea Purvis, 2000. BA, Reed Coll., 1960; MA, U. Wash., 1963, PhD, 1967. Asst. prof. Reed Coll., Portland, Oreg., 1966-70; from asst. prof. to assoc. prof. Haverford Coll., Pa., 1970—76; prof., Francis White prof. Greek Johns Hopkins U., Balt., 1976-88; Disting. prof. Grad. Ctr. CUNY, NYC, 1988-90; RJR Nabisco prof. classical studies Duke U., Durham, NC, 1990—2008; ret., 2008. Elizabeth Whitehead prof. Am. Sch. Classical Studies in Athens, 1988-89; Blegen rsch. prof. Vassar Coll., Poughkeepsie, NY, 1985-86. Author: Oxychynchan Poems, 1973, Sophocles, Oedipus the King, 1978, Lucretius and Epicurus, 1983, John Locke: Questions Concerning the Law of Nature, 1990, Paradosis and Survival: Three Chapters in the History of Eipcurean Philosophy, 1997, Platonic Questions: Dialogues with the Silent Philosopher, 2000, Sophocles: Philoctetes, 2003, Archilochos Heros: the Cult of Poets in The Greek States, 2004, Euripides: the Trojan Women, 2004. Fulbright fellow, Univs. Montpellier and Poitiers, France, 1960-61; Woodrow Wilson fellow, 1961-62; Am. Coun. Learned Socs., Turkey, 1975; NEH fellow, 1974-75. Fellow The Lorenzo Valla Found; mem., Dante Soc. Am., Soc. for Ancient Greek Philosophy (pres. 1991-92). Home: 2543 Sevier St Durham NC 27705 Home Phone: 919-419-8675. Business E-Mail: dclay@duke.edu.

CLAY, EDWIN S., III, library director; m. Debra Clay; 1 child, Maggie. Grad., Randolph Macon Coll., 1966; MLS, U. NC, 1967. Dir. Va. Wesleyan Coll. Libr., Va. Beach Pub. Libr. and Info. Office, Fairfax County Pub. Libr., Va., 1982—. Asst. to city mgr., Virginia Beach; mem. Nat. Mgmt. and Planning Adv. Com., Libr. of Congress; adj. faculty mem. Cath. U. Sch. of Libr. & Info. Sci. Past. pres. Virginians for the Arts; chmn. Va. Commn. for Arts; bd. dirs. FCPL Found. Recipient Managerial Excellence award, 2000. Mem.: Va. Pub. Libr. Dir.'s Assn. (past pres., Named Outstanding Libr. Dir. 2002), Va. Libr. Assn. (bd. dirs.). Office: Fairfax County Pub Libr Ste 324 12000 Government Center Pky Fairfax VA 22035-0012 Office Phone: 703-324-3100. Office Fax: 703-324-8365.

CLAY, JERRELL G., insurance company executive; CLU; registered securities prin. Mem., mgmt. adv. com. ING Southland Life Ins. Co.; bd. advisor, Ind. Mktg. Orgn. Protective Life Ins. Co., Birmingham, Ala.; pres. Protective Financial Services, Inc., 1985—; chmn., CEO, co-founder 3 Mark Finance, Inc., 1997—; bd. dirs. aVinci Media Corp., 1990—; CEO aVinci Media Corp. (formerly Secure Alliance Holdings Corp.), 2006—09. Past pres., Houston Chpt. Soc. Fin. Svc. Professionals. Mem.: Soc. of Fin. Svc. Professionals (former pres., Houston chpt.). Office: 3 Mark Financial Inc 1600 Hwy 6 Ste 400 Sugar Land TX 77478 Office Phone: 281-269-2300. Office Fax: 281-269-2347. Business E-Mail: jerrellc@3mark.com.

CLAY, ROBERT N., thoroughbred breeder; b. Lexington, Ky., Sept. 17, 1946; s. Albert Green and Lorraine Case (Newlin) C.; m. Blythe Baldwin, Aug. 10, 1968; children: Heather Newlin, Case Baldwin. BA, Coll. William & Mary, 1968; SCMP, Harvard Bus. Sch., 1980. Pres. Top Yield Industries Inc., Lexington, Ky., 1978-84; owner Three Chimneys Farm, Midway, Ky., 1984—. Bd. dirs. PNC Bank, Pitts., Citizens Fidelity Corp. Trustee Blood-Horse Mag., U. Ky.; bd. dirs. U. Ky. Equine Rsch. Found., Midway (Ky.) Coll., Coll. William & Mary Endowment Assn.; co-chmn. Bluegrass Tomorrow; past chmn. The Lexington Sch. Lt. USN, 1969-71. Mem. Thoroughbred Owners and Breeders Assn. (pres.), Keeneland Assn. (bd. dirs.), The Breeders' Cup Ltd. (bd. dirs.), Am. Horse Coun. (mem. exec. com.), Am. Horse Fed. (dir.), Ky. Thoroughbred Assn. (bd. dirs.), Thoroughbred Club Am. (past pres.), The Jockey Club. Office: Three Chimneys Farm PO Box 114 Midway KY 40347-0114

CLAYCOMB, HUGH MURRAY, lawyer, writer; b. Joplin, Mo., May 19, 1931; s. Hugh and Fern (Murray) C.; m. Jeanne Cavin, May 5, 1956; children: Stephen H., Scott C. BS in Bus., U. Mo., 1953, JD, 1955; LLM, U. Miss., 1969. Bar: Mo. 1955, Ark. 1957, US Dist. Ct. (ea. dist.) Ark. 1957, US Supreme Ct. 1979. Asst. staff judge advocate USAF, 1955-57; law clk. Ark. Supreme Ct., Little Rock, 1957—58; ptnr. Gregory & Claycomb, Pine Bluff, Ark., 1958-69; partner Haley, Claycomb, Roper & Anderson, Warren, Ark., 1969—. Dir. The Strong Co., Inc., Pine Bluff, Ark., bd. dirs. Ark. Cmty. Found. Author: Arkansas Corporations, 1967, 82, 92. Pres. Jefferson County Bar Assn., Pine Bluff, 1969, Warren YMCA, 1973-75, SE Ark. Legal Inst., 1980-81, Ctrl. Ark. Estate Planning Coun., 1963-64, pres. Bradley County YMCA Found.; spl. assoc. justice Ark. Supreme Ct., 1978, 87, Civil Practice Com., 2003-13, Profl. Practicum Com., 2006-. Lt. USAF, 1955-57. Recipient Pres.'s award Ark. Trial Lawyers Assn., 1985. Fellow Am. Bar Found.; mem. Ark. Bar Found. (pres. 1990), Ark. Bar Assn. (sec.-treas. 1998-2000, pres. 2002-03, C.E. Ransick award 1996), Warren Rotary (pres. 1972, Paul Harris fellow). Episcopalian. Home: 619 E Cedar St Warren AR 71671-3001 Office Phone: 870-226-2681. Business E-Mail: hmclaycomb@sbcglobal.net.

CLAYTON, BENJAMIN J., oil industry executive; Gen. tax officer ConocoPhillips, Houston. Mem. bd. dirs. Internat. Tax and Investment Ctr. Office: ConocoPhillips PO Box 2197 Houston TX 77252-2197

CLAYTON, DAVID A., lab administrator; m. Lauretta Swanson, 1965; children: Lindsay, Ryan, Megan. BS, Northern Ill. U., DeKalb, 1965; PhD, Calif. Inst. Tech., Pasadena, 1970. Prof. Stanford U., Calif., 1970—96, program dir., med. scientist tng. program, 1978—96; sr. sci. officer Howard Hughes Med. Inst., Chevy Chase, Md., 1996—99, v.p. sci. devel., 2000—01, v.p., chief sci. officer, 2001—07, v.p. rsch. ops., 2007—08, lab. head Ashburn, Va., 2008—. Mem. adv. com. nucleic acids and protein synthesis, Am. Cancer Soc., 1976-80; mem. molecular biology study sect., NIH, 1982-86, chmn., 1984-86; mem. sci. rev. bd. Howard Hughes Med. Inst., 1993-96; mem. nat. adv. bd. Gen. Med. Sci. Coun., 1996-99; Fisher lectr. So. Ill. U., 1989. Contbr. scientific papers to profl. publs. Active Howard Hughes Med. Inst. Sci. Rev. Bd., Chevy Chase, Md., 1993—96, Nat. Adv. Gen. Med. Scis. Coun., Bethesda, Md., 1996—99; active and chair, adv. bd. academic coun. Stanford U., 1989—92; active U. Md., College Park, 2003—06. Recipient Warner-Lambert/Parke Davis award, 1982. Mem. Inst. Medicine Nat. Acad. Sci., Am. Soc. Biochemistry and Molecular Biology. Episcopalian. Office: Howard Hughes Med Inst 19700 Helix Dr Ashburn VA 20147-2408

CLAYTON, EVA M., consulting firm executive, former United States Representative from North Carolina; b. Savannah, Ga., Sept. 16, 1934; m. Theaoseus T. Clayton; children: Theaoseus Jr., Martin, Reuben, Joanne. BS, Johnson C. Smith U., 1955; MS, NC Central U., 1965. Asst. sec. for cmty. development NC Dept. Natural Resources & Cmty. Development, Raleigh, 1977—81; mem. bd. commissioners Warren County, NC, 1982—92; founder, pres. Tech. Resources Internat., NC, 1981—92; mem. US Congress from 1st N.C. Dist., Washington, 1993—2002; asst. dir. gen., spl. adv. to dir. gen. UN Food & Agrl. Org. (FAO), NYC, 2003—06; sr. counselor The Livingston Group, L.L.C., Washington; founder Eva Clayton Associates Internat., Raleigh, NC. Mem. Warren County NC Bd. Commrs., 1982—92, chair, 1982—90. Named Legislator of Yr., American Planning Assn., 2002. Democrat. Presbyterian. Office: The Livingston Group LLC 499 South Capitol St SW Ste 600 Washington DC 20003 also: Eva Clayton Associates International 3100 Smoketree Court Ste 420 Raleigh NC 27604 Office Phone: 202-289-9881. Office Fax: 919-981-0440.

CLEARY, RAYMOND E., III, state legislator; b. Cin., Aug. 13, 1948; m. A. Lisa Cleary; children: Dodge, Sonya, Ryan, Jenny, Besty, Leslie. BA, Ohio State U., 1970, DDS, 1973. Dentist, 1975—; mem. Dist. 34 SC State Senate, 2004—. Capt. USAF, 1973—75. Republican. Office: 501 Gressette Bldg Columbia SC 29201 Mailing: 3577 Marion Ln Murrells Inlet SC 29576 Home Phone: 843-357-2234; Office Phone: 803-212-6100. Office Fax: 843-650-5100. Business E-Mail: CLEARYR@scsenate.org.

CLEAVELAND, WILLIAM H. (BILL CLEAVELAND), lawyer, former state legislator; b. St. Mary's, Pa., Dec. 14, 1950; m. Deborah Overstreet; 1 child, William Corbin. BS in Ceramic Engring., Alfred U., NY, 1972; JD, Western New Eng. Coll., Springfield, Mass., 1978. Pvt. practice atty. William H. Cleaveland PLC, Roanoke, Va.; mem. Dist. 17 Va. House of Delegates, Richmond, 2010—12. Mem.: Va. Trial Lawyers Assn. Republican. Office: William H Cleaveland PLC 40 British Woods Dr Ste 101 Roanoke VA 24019 Office Phone: 540-992-4041. Office Fax: 540-992-4546.

CLEGG, ROGER BURTON, lawyer; b. Odessa, Tex., Apr. 18, 1955; s. Joe Dunn and Margaret Elisabeth (Blau) C.; m. Joann Ruth Catalfamo, June 15, 1985; 1 child, Paul. BA magna cum laude, Rice U., 1977; JD, Yale U., 1981. Bar: DC 1981. Grad. fellow Office Gen. Counsel, CIA, Langley, Va.; mem. staff editorial and research div. Republican Nat. Com., Washington, 1980; law clk. to presiding judge US Ct. Appeals, Washington, 1981-82; atty.- adviser office of legal policy US Dept. Justice, Washington, 1982, spl. asst. to atty. gen., 1982-83, dep. asst. atty. gen., 1983-84, acting asst. atty. gen., office legal policy, 1984, assoc. dep. atty. gen., 1984-85, spl. litigation counsel, civil div., 1985, asst. to solicitor gen., 1985-87, dep. asst. atty. gen. civil rights div., 1987-91, dep. asst. atty. gen. env. div., 1991-93; v.p., gen. counsel Nat. Legal Ctr. for Pub. Interest, Washington, 1993-97, Ctr. for Equal Opportunity, Washington, 1997—2005, pres. Falls Church, Va., 2006—. Editor-in-chief Yale Studies in World Public Order, 1979-80. Mem.: D.C. Bar, Federalist Soc., Phi Beta Kappa. Republican. Methodist. Office: 7700 Leesburg Pike Ste 231 Falls Church VA 22043 Home: 10328 Sager Ave Unit 122 Fairfax VA 22030-3568 Office Phone: 703-442-0066.

CLELAND, SHERRILL, college president; b. Galion, Ohio, Sept. 21, 1924; s. Fred Burr and Doris Louise (Gregg) C.; m. Betty Irene Chorpenning, July 6, 1946 (dec. June 1986); children: Ann Denise Cleland Feldmeier, Douglas Stewart Cleland, Sarah McDermott Cleland Allen, Scott Cameron Cleland; m. Diana Ashley Drake, Sept. 3, 1988; stepchildren: Cynthia Rush, Allison Abizaid, Linda Wiener, Carol Abizaid, Amanda Abizaid, Richard Abizaid. AB, Oberlin Coll., Ohio, 1949; MA, Princeton U., NJ, 1951, PhD in Econs., 1957; LLD (hon.), Marietta Coll., Ohio, 1989. Instr. econs. Princeton U., 1951-55; asst. prof. U. Richmond, 1955-56; mem. faculty Kalamazoo Coll., 1956-73, acad. v.p., 1964-67; prof. econs., pres. Marietta Coll., Ohio, 1973—89, now prof. emeritus Ohio, 1989—. Econs. adviser Hashemite Kingdom Jordan, 1963-64; Ford Found. vis. prof. econs. and devel. adminstrn. Am. U. Beirut, Lebanon, 1967-69, lectr. China, 1985, 89, hon. prof. Southwestern U. Fin. and Econs., Chengdu Peoples Republic China, 1985; cons. examiner North Ctrl. Assn. Colls., 1960-90; dir. Cleve. Fed. Res. Bank, Cin. br., 1980-85. Co-editor, author: Continuity and Change in the World Oil Industry, 1970; contbg. author: Linear Programming and Theory of Firm, 1962; contbr. to profl. jours. Pres. Kalamazoo chpt. Human Rels. Coun., 1958-60; bd. dirs. Tuition Exch., Inc., 1975—; chmn. Student Loan Funding Corp., 1991-97; bd. dirs. AHEAD Corp., Amideast, Inc.; past pres. Ohio Coll. Assn.; chmn. East Ctrl. Coll. Consortium, Ind. Colls., Univs. Ohio; trustee Oberlin Coll., 1976-82, Mt. Vernon Coll., 1992-97; dir. Knowledge Works Found., Cin., 1997—2013, dir. emeritus; mem. Sarasota Coun. of the Blind, 2005-. With AUS, 1944-46. Decorated Bronze Star, Purple Heart.; recipient Kazanjian Found. teaching award econs., 1971; Leadership tng. fellow N. Central Assn. Colls., 1959 Fellow Middle East Studies Assn.; mem. Am. Econ. Assn., Ivy League Sarasola, Princeton Club, Sarasota, UN Assn. (past pres. Kalamazoo chpt.), Ohio Assn. for Freedom to Die. Presbyterian. Home: 4489 Highland Oaks Cir Sarasota FL 34235-5175 Home (Summer): 67 Birch Tree Ln Waitsfield VT 05673 E-mail: dadcleland@yahoo.com.

CLEM, ALEXANDER MURPHREE, lawyer; b. Vero Beach, Fla., Nov. 6, 1963; s. Chester Earl and Tilley (Murphree) Clem; m. Carmen Maria Chinchilla, May 18, 1996; children: Cristina, Isabella, Alexander II. BA in Polit. Sci., Furman U., Greenville, SC, 1986; JD cum laude, Stetson U., St. Petersburg, Fla., 1990. Bar: Fla., Tenn. Assoc. Maguire, Voorhis & Welle, 1991—97; ptnr. Morgan & Morgan PA, Orlando, Fla., 1997—. Bd. overseers Stetson U. Coll. Law, 2007—; lectr. in field. Named Disting. Alumnus, Stetson U. Coll. Law, 2005, Lawyer of Distinction, Orlando Mag., 2006; named one of Fla's. Legal Elite, Fla. Trend mag., 2006, Best of the Bar, Orlando Bus. Jour., 2006, Top 5% Attys., Fla. Super Lawyers mag., 2007; scholar, Rotary, 1986. Mem.: ABA, Orange County Bar Assn. (legis. com., fed., state trial practice com., chmn. courtroom tech. subcom.), Acad. Fla. Trial Lawyers (pres. 2004—05, exec. com., bd. dirs.). Republican. Roman Catholic. Office: Morgan & Morgan PA 20 N Orange Ave Ste 160 Orlando FL 32801

CLEM, RALPH S., career officer, educator; BA in Geography with honors, San Diego State Coll., 1965; MA in Geography and Soviet Studies, Columbia U., 1972, PhD in Geography and Soviet Studies with distinction, 1976; student, Air Command and Staff Coll., 1987, Air War Coll., 1989. Commd. 2d lt. USAF, 1965, advanced through grades to maj. gen., 2000; spl. agt. detachment 101 Off. Spl. Investigations, Hartford, 1965-68, spl. agt. dist. 51 Bangkok, 1968-69, supervising case officer hdqs. Washington, 1969-70; chief intelligence 915th Airborne Early Warning and Control Group, Homestead AFB, Fla., 1976-78, 93rd Tactical Fighter Squadron, Homestead AFB, 1978-83, 482d Tactical Fighter Wing, Homestead AFB, 1983-90; intelligence staff officer, sr. strategic air ops. analyst Off. Mil. Forces, Nat. Security Agy., Ft. George G. Meade, Md., 1990-93; mobilization asst. to asst. dep. dir. ops. Nat. Security Agy., Ft. George G. Meade, 1993-96; mobilization asst. to comdr. Hdqs. Air Intelligence Agy., Kelly AFB, Tex., 1996-98; dep. chief Air Force Res. Hdqs. USAF, Washington, 1998-2000; aide to chief of Air Force Res. 482nd Tactical Fighter Wing, Homestead AFB, Fla., 2000—; prof., internat. rels. Fla. Internat. Univ., Miami, Fla., and dir., Ctr. for Transnat. and Comparative Studies. Contbr. articles to profl. jours. Decorated Rep. Vietnam Campaign medal. Office: Dept Internat Relations DM 367A Florida Internat Univ 11200 SW 8th St Miami FL 33199

CLEMA, JOE KOTOUC, computer scientist; b. Omaha, Sept. 23, 1938; s. Joseph Arthur and Sylva Marie (Kotouc) C.; m. Maria Estela Cobos, Apr. 1, 1960; children: Jennifer Arta. Student, U.S. Mil. Acad., 1957—60; BS, U. Nebr., 1963; MS, U. Miami, 1969; PhD, Colo. State U., 1973. Systems analyst Gen. Electric, Louisville, 1969-70; head sci. applications Colo. State U., Ft. Collins, 1970-73; project engr. Gen. Dynamics, Ft. Worth, 1973-77; sr. mgr. Simulation Tech., Inc., Dayton, Ohio, 1977-79; program mgr. Pratt and Whitney, West Palm Beach, Fla., 1979-82; dept. mgr. CACI, Dayton, 1982-83; dir. spl. projects Systems and Applied Scis., Vienna, Va., 1983-85; chief software engr. IIT Rsch. Inst., Annapolis, Md., 1985-90; cons. to IBM with, pres. Neurosystems, Inc., Bethesda, Md., 1991-98; cons. on IRS tax system modernization TRW, Merriefield, Va., 1993-95, cons. simplified tax & wage sys., 1995-96; mgr. Sys. Resources Corp., 1997-98, Houston Assocs., Inc., Arlington, Va., 1998—2002; dir. Nat. Tech., Inc., McLean, Va., 2002—04; sr. scientist 1st IO Commd., Ft. Belvoir, 2004—. Contbr. articles to profl. jours. Sustaining mem. Rep. Nat. Com., Washington, 1983—. Served to capt. U.S. Army, 1963-67. First Ann. Simulation Symposium Rsch. grantee, 1972; recipient Outstanding Svc. award Ann. Simulation Symposium Bd. Dirs., 1980. Mem.: ACM (nat. lectr. 1978—83), IEEE (sr.), Internat. Platform Assn., Ann. Simulation Symposium (chmn. bd. dirs. 1979), Spl. Interest Group on Simulation (chmn. 1979—81), Mid Atlantic Electronic Commerce Network (bd. dirs. 1995—98), Soc. Computer Simulation (bd. dirs., program chmn. 1988—96), Nat. Def. Indsl. Assn., Herndon C. of C., Toastmasters, No. Va. Tech. Coun., Armed Forces Comm. and Elec. Assn., Worldgate Athletic Club, Hidden Creek Country Club. Republican. Avocations: bridge, tennis. Home: 301 Missouri Ave Herndon VA 20170-5426 Office: 1st Info Ops Commd Fort Belvoir VA 22060 Personal E-mail: joeclema2@cs.com. Business E-Mail: joe.clema@us.army.mil.

CLEMENS, JEFF, state legislator; b. Detroit, Sept. 8, 1970; BA, Michigan State U., East Lansing. Energy contractor; mayor City of Lake Worth, Fla., 2007—09; mem. Dist. 89 Fla. House of Representatives, 2011—. Bd. mem. United Arts Coun., 1999—2000; vice chmn. Lake Worth Civil Svc. Bd., 2003; chmn. Lake Worth Cmty. Redevelopment Agency, 2004—06; mem. exec. bd. Palm Beach County League of Cities, 2007—09; mem. Met. Planning Orgn., 2007—09. Mem.: Coll. Pk. Neighborhood Assn. (pres. 2004), Lake Worth Kiwanis Club (pres. 2005), Fla. Kiwanis Club (lt. gov. divsn. 21 2006). Democrat. Office: 508 Lake Ave Ste C Lake Worth FL 33460-3809 also: Fla House of Reps 1401 The Capitol 402 South Monroe St Tallahassee FL 32399-1300 Office Phone: 561-540-1140, 850-488-0260.

CLEMENS, ROGER (WILLIAM ROGER CLEMENS), retired professional baseball player; b. Dayton, Ohio, Aug. 4, 1962; s. Bess Clemens and Woody Booher (Stepfather); m. Debra Lynn Godfrey, Nov. 24, 1984; children: Koby Aaron, Kory Allen, Kacy Austin, Kody Alec. Attended, San Jacinto Jr. Coll., Pasadena, Tex., 1981, U. Tex.,

Austin, 1982—83. Pitcher Boston Red Sox, 1984—96, Toronto Blue Jays, 1997—98, NY Yankees, 1999—2003, 2007, Houston Astros, 2004—06, Sugar Land Skeeters, Atlantic League, Tex., 2012. Pitcher Team USA, World Baseball Classic, 2006. Co-founder Roger Clemens Found., 1992. Recipient Thomas A. Yawkey award, Boston Red Sox, 1986, Cy Young award, Am. League, 1986—87, 1991, 1997—98, 2001, Cy Young Award, Nat. League, 2004; named Boston Red Sox Rookie of Yr., 1984, Am. League MVP, 1986, All-Star Game MVP, 1986, Maj. League Player of Yr., Sporting News, 1986, Pitcher of Yr., 1986, 1991, 1997—98, 2001, Sportsman of Yr., March of Dimes, 2001; named to Am. League All-Star Team, 1986, 1988, 1990—92, 1997—98, 2001, 2003, Nat. League All-Star Team, 2004—05, MLB All-Century Team, 1999. Achievements include holds MLB record for strikeouts in a single game (20); recorded 300th career win and 4,000 career strikeouts, June 13, 2003; being a member of World Series Champion New York Yankees, 1999, 2000; holds MLB record for Cy Young Awards (7), 2004; holds MLB record for oldest player to win Cy Young Award (age 42), 2004; became 8th pitcher to reach 350 career wins, July 2, 2007. Office: Roger Clemens Foundation 8572 Katy Fwy Ste 106 Houston TX 77024-1821*

CLEMENT, EDITH BROWN, federal judge; b. Birmingham, Ala., Apr. 29, 1948; d. Erskine John and Edith (Burrus) Brown; m. Rutledge Carter Clement Jr., Sept. 3, 1972; children: Rutledge Carter III, Catherine Lanier. BA, U. Ala., 1969; JD, Tulane U., 1972. Bar: La. 1973. Law clk. to Hon. Herbert W. Christenberry US Dist. Ct., New Orleans, 1973-75; ptnr. Jones, Walker, Waechter, Poitevent, Carrere & Denegre, New Orleans, 1975-91; judge US Dist. Ct. (ea. dist.) La., New Orleans, 1991—2001, US Ct. Appeals (5th cir.), New Orleans, 2001—. Fellow La. Bar Found. (life); mem. Am. Law Inst., La. Bar Assn., Federalist Soc. Advisory Bd. Louisiana Chpt., Maritime Law Assn. US, Fed. Bar Assn., Am Inn Ct., Com. Admin. Office of the Judicial Conference of the US, 5th Cir. Judicial Coun, Tulane Law Sch. Inn of Ct. Office: US Ct Appeals 5th Cir 600 Camp Street Rm 200 New Orleans LA 70130-3313

CLEMENT-HOLMES, LINDA W., consumer products company executive; b. Chgo., Mar. 31, 1962; d. Thestal Tyndal and Fanny Ida (Turner) Clement. BS in Indsl. Mgmt. & Computer Sci., Purdue U., 1982. Communications svc. rep. Ind. Bell, Indpls., 1981-82; various positions The Procter & Gamble Co., Cin., 1982—2009, sr. v.p. global diversity & global bus. services, 2010—. Bd. dirs. Cin. Financial Corp., 2010—. Mem. Nat. Tech. Assn., Assn. Computational Linguistics, Am. Assn. Artifical Intelligence, Delta Sigma Theta. Democrat. Avocations: dance, aerobics, jazz music, silk flower arranging, mug collecting. Office: The Procter & Gamble Co 1 Procter And Gamble Plz Cincinnati OH 45202-3315

CLEMENTS, GLENN H., insurance company executive; BBA, MBA, U. Houston. Group pres., eastern ops. Stewart Title Co. (subs. of Stewart info. Svcs. Corp.). Bd. dirs. World Pres. Orgn. Houston Chpt., Tex. Land Title Assn., PropertyInfo Corp., Inc.; adv. dir. BBVA Compass Bank-Houston; chmn. U. Houston Hobby Ctr. Public Policy, Houston Achievement Place. Mem. Mortgage Bankers Assn.; mem., dist. coun. Urban Land Institute; bd. dirs., ctr. for public policy U. Houston; bd. dirs. World Presidents Organization, Houston. With USN. Mem.: World Pres. Orgn. Avocations: golf, skiing, hunting. Office: Stewart Information Services Corp 1980 Post Oak Blvd Ste 800 Houston TX 77056 Office Phone: 713-625-8100. Office Fax: 713-629-2244. Business E-Mail: gclements@stewart.com.

CLEMENTS, JAMES P. (JIM CLEMENTS), academic administrator; b. 1964; m. Beth Clements; children: Tyler, Hannah, Maggie, Grace. BS in Computer Sci., U. Md., Balt., 1985, MS, 1991, PhD in Ops. Analysis, 1993. Bus. analyst, software engr. G.P. Taurio Corp., 1986—89; vis. asst. prof. Dept. Computer and Info. Scis. Towson U., Md., 1989, asst. prof., 1993—95, assoc. prof., 1995, chair Dept. Computer and Info. Scis., 1997—99, prof., 2000—09, Robert W. Deutsch Disting. prof. info. tech., 2002, v.p. econ. & cmty. outreach, 2004—07, provost, v.p. academic affairs, 2007—09; pres. W.Va. U., Morgantown, 2009—13, Clemson U., 2013—. Adj. prof. mgmt. Loyola Coll., Md., 1992—93; adj. prof. info. sys. & tech. Whiting Sch. Engring., Johns Hopkins U., 1993—99; spkr. in field. Co-author: Successful Project Management, 1999; contbr. articles to profl. jours. Office: Clemson University 201 Sikes Hall Clemson SC 29634 Office Phone: 864-656-3413. E-mail: president@clemson.edu.*

CLEMENTS, JERRY K., lawyer; b. Ft. Worth, Feb. 2, 1954; BS magna cum laude, Tex. Christian U., 1975; JD cum laude, Baylor U., 1981. Bar: Tex. 1981, US Ct. Appeals (5th cir.) 1981, US Dist. Ct. (all dists. Tex.) 1981, US Supreme Ct. 1981. Chair litig. dept., mem. mgmt. com. Locke Lord Bissell & Liddell LLP (formerly Locke, Liddell & Sapp, LLC), Dallas, 2002—06, mng. ptnr., 2007, chair. Contbr. articles to profl. publs.; editor-in-chief: Baylor Law Rev., 1981. Bd. mem. Tex. State Bd. Physician Asst. Examiners, 1997—2000. Named one of Top Ten Litigators, Dallas Bus. Jour., Top 50 Female Trial Lawyers in Tex., Tex. Monthly Mag., The 50 Most Influential Women Lawyers in Am., Nat. Law Jour., 2007. Fellow: Dallas Bar Found., Tex. Bar Found., Internat. Soc. Barristers, Am. Coll. Trial Lawyers, Am. Bar Found.; mem.: Tex. Assn. Def. Counsel, Dallas Bar Assn., ABA, Am. Bd. Trial Advs. Office: Locke Lord Bissell & Liddell 100 Congress Ave, Ste 300 Austin TX 78701 also: 2200 Ross Ave, Ste 2200 Dallas TX 75201 Office Phone: 214-740-8799. Office Fax: 214-740-8800. E-mail: jclements@lockelord.com.

CLEMENTS, MARK ANDREW, electrical and computer engineering professor, entrepreneur; m. Melinda Perry Perry, Aug. 13, 1977; children: Isaac Perry, Christina Melissia, Andrea Elaine. ScD, Mass. Tech., Cambridge, 1981. Prof. Ga. Inst. Tech., Atlanta, 1982—. Founder, dir. Nexidia, Inc., Atlanta, 2000—. Achievements include patents for speech related technology. Office: Georgia Inst Tech Sch 777 Atlantic Dr Atlanta GA 30332-0250

CLEMENTS, STEPHEN D., JR., cardiologist, educator; MD, Med. Coll. Ga., Atlanta, 1966. Diplomate Am. Bd. Internal Medicine, 1971, Am. Bd. Internal Medicine-cardiovasc. disease, 1975. Intern Grady Meml. Hosp., Atlanta, 1967, resident, 1969, fellow, 1971; prof. medicine cardiology The Emory Clinic, Atlanta; hosp. affiliation includes Emory Univ. Hosp. Named one of the Top Doctors in Atlanta, 1999, 2001, 2005. Mem.: Am. Soc. of Echocardiography, Am. Heart Assn., Am. Coll. of Cardiology. Office: Emory Clinic NE A Bldg Ste 2200 1365 Clifton Rd Atlanta GA 30322 Office Phone: 404-778-3468.

CLEMMER, ANN V., state legislator; b. Aug. 10, 1958; m. Jamie Clemmer; 3 children. Polit. sci. prof. U. Ark., Little Rock; mem. Dist. 29 Ark. House of Reps., 2009—. Republican. Office: State Capitol Rm 350 Little Rock AR 72201 also: 7415 Camille Dr Benton AR 72015 Office Phone: 501-682-6211, 501-682-7771, 501-316-0364. Business E-Mail: avclemmer@sbcglobal.net.

CLEMMONS, ALAN D., state legislator; b. Myrtle Beach, SC, Dec. 6, 1958; s. Carl Lee and Geraldine Owens Clemmons; m. Laura Ann Fipps Clemmons, May 3, 1985; children: Laura Alayne, Kelly Leigh. BS, Coastal Carolina U., Conway, SC, 1982; JD, Hamline U. Sch. Law, St. Paul, 1989. Real estate atty.; mem. Dist. 107 SC House of Reps., 2003—. Mem.: Christian Missionary Maya Indians Southern Mex., Horry County Bar Assn., SC Bar Assn., Rotary Club Myrtle Beach, Lions Club (dir. 1994). Republican. Office: 522B Blatt Bldg Columbia SC 29201 Mailing: 1800 A N Oak St Myrtle Beach SC 29577 Office Phone: 803-734-2994, 843-448-4246. E-mail: clemmonsa@scatatehouse.net.

CLERICO, JOHN ANTHONY, oil industry executive, investment company executive; b. Bartlesville, Okla., July 17, 1941; s. Ralph E. and Lorraine G. (O'Connell) C.; m. Beverly A. Smith; 1 child, Diane A. BS, Okla. State U., 1963; postgraduate, U. Mo., 1964, U. Colo., 1972. With treasury dept., CFO Phillips Petroleum, 1964-66, Conoco, Inc., 1966-83; asst. treas. Union Carbide Corp., Danbury, Conn., 1983-86, treas., CFO, 1984—92; exec. v.p., CFO Praxair, Inc., 1992—2000; co-founder, chmn. and investment advisor ChartMark Investments, Inc., Tulsa, Okla., 2000—; CEO Global Industries Ltd., 2008—10; chmn. Global Industries, Ltd., 2010—. Mem. bd. dirs, chmn. audit com. MacroSolve, Inc.; mem. bd. dirs. Cmty. Health Sys., 2003—, Ednl. Devel. Corp., 2004—; bd. dirs. Global Industries, Ltd., 2006—08. Mem. bd. trustees Okla. State U. Found., chmn. investment com. Office: ChartMark Investments Inc 2200 S Utica Pl Ste 525 Tulsa OK 74114-7052 also: Global Industries Ltd 8000 Global Dr Carlyss LA 70665 Office Phone: 337-583-5000. Office Fax: 337-583-5100. Business E-Mail: john@ChartMark.com.

CLEVELAND, CRAWFORD HARALSON, allergist, immunologist; BA, U. Va.; MD, Tulane U., 1975. Diplomate Am. Bd. Internal Medicine, 1979, Am. Bd. Allergy and Immunology, 1993, lic. Fla., 1982. Intern U. Louisville, 1975—76, resident internal medicine, 1975—77, U. South Ala., 1977—79; fellow allergy and immunology East Carolina U., 1990—92; chmn. dept. medicine Sacred Heart Hosp., with exec. com.; hosp. affiliations include West Fla. Cmty. Care Ctr., Baptist Hosp. Mem.: Escambia County Med. Soc., Fla. Med. Assn., AMA, Am. Thoracic Soc., Ala. Soc. Allergy, Asthma and Immunology, Fla. Allergy, Asthma and Immunology Soc., Am. Lung Assn. (bd. northwest Fla. region, pres. 1996—98). Office: West Florida Community Care Center 5500 Stewart St Milton FL 32570-4304 Office Phone: 850-983-5500.

CLEVELAND, GEORGE G., state legislator; m. Nancy Cleveland; 4 children. State rep. Dist. 14, NC, 2005—. Mem.: VFW, NRA, NC Rifle & Pistol Assn., NCOA, Am. Vets., Am. Legion. Republican. Office: North Carolina House of Representatives 300 N Salisbury St Rm 417A Raleigh NC 27603-5925 Office Phone: 919-715-6707. Business E-Mail: George.Cleveland@ncleg.net.

CLEVELAND, HERSCHEL, state representative; b. Paris, Ark., Apr. 7, 1946; m. Leona Cleveland. BSBA, JD, U. Ark. Mcpl. judge Ho. of Reps., 1999, 2001; Ark. State Rep., Dist. 26 Ark. Ho. of Reps., 1999—2001, Ark. State Rep., Dist. 84, 2001. Chmn. ALC/JBC Parks and Tourism Subcom., ALC/Performance-Based Budgeting Subcom., Legis. Facilities; mem. ALC-Adminstrv. Rules and Regulations, ALC-JBC Budget Hearings, ALC-Peer, others. Served USAR, 1968—76. Democrat. Baptist. Office: Hixon and Cleveland Law Office PO Box 588 Paris AR 72855

CLEVELAND, RALPH, gas industry company executive; b. Macon, Ga. B in Mech. Engring., Ga. Tech., 1981—86; postgrad. in Mech. Engring., Rice U., 1988—90; MBA, Tulane U. Engr., various positions Mobil Oil Co., 1986—96, plant supt., 1996—98, fin. analyst, bus. analyst, 1997—98; tech. supr. ExxonMobil, 1999; worked in oil & gas prodn., rsch. & devel., natural gas processing and petrochemicals) AGL Resources, Inc.; mgr., SE Ga. ops. AGL Resources Inc. (Atlanta Gas Light Co.), 2000—01; v.p., ops., Va. Natural Gas AGL Resources, Inc., 2001—02, v.p., engring. & constrn., chief engr., Atlanta Gas Light, 2003—05, sr. v.p., engring. & ops., 2005—08, exec. v.p., engring. & ops., 2008—. Chmn., CEO N.Am. Energy Standards Bd., Houston. Bd. dirs. Am.Inst. Mng. Diversity; regional bd. mem. Jr. Achievement, Teach America; founder, pres. Capital and Enterprise Develop. Group. Recipient Outstanding Ga. Citizen, Sec. State Ga.; named one of Atlanta's Men of Distinction,,Atlanta Bus. League & Who's Who Black Atlanta, Top 100 Most Influential Blacks in Corp. America, SaVoy Mag. Mem.: 100 Black Men, South Metro, American Assn. Blacks Energy, Nat. Soc. Black Engrs. (life), Nat. Black MBA Assn. (life), Kappa Alpha Psi. Home: PO Box 78441 Atlanta GA 30357-2441 Office Phone: 404-584-4000. Office Fax: 404-584-3945.

CLEVENGER, REX T., utilities executive; BBA, U. Mo. CPA. With Koch Industries; sr. v.p., fin. Reliant Resources, Inc., Houston, 2000—. Office: Reliant Resources Inc 5221 N Ocnnor Blvd 290 Connor Irving TX 75039 Office Phone: 972-831-7350. Office Fax: 972-831-7399.

CLEYS, RICHARD P., wholesale distribution executive; b. 1951; BA in Bus. Adminstrn., Loyola U. Chgo., 1973. CPA. Auditor Ernst & Young LLP; supr. fin. reporting, then dir. corp. acctg. Gould Inc., 1977—85, asst. contr., corp. contr., then v.p. & group contr., 1985—93; v.p. fin., CFO AB Dick Inc., 1993—96; v.p., contr. Lanier Worldwide, Inc., Atlanta, 1996—98; v.p. fin., treas. Lanier Worldwide Inc., 1999—2001; v.p., CFO ScanSource, Inc., Greenville, SC, 2002—. Office: ScanSource Inc 6 Logue Ct Greenville SC 29615 Office Phone: 864-288-2432. Office Fax: 864-288-1165.

CLICK, DAVID FORREST, lawyer, investment advisor; b. Miami Beach, Fla., Dec. 17, 1947; s. David Gorman and Helen Margaret (McPhail) C.; m. Helaine London, June 2, 1974; children: Kenneth Randall, Adam Elliott. BA, Yale U., 1969, JD, 1973, MA, 1974. Bar: Conn. 1973, Md. 1983, U.S. Supreme Ct. 1983, Fla. 1984, Maine 1984; bd. cert. wills, trusts, estates. Asst. prof. Western New England Sch. Law, Springfield, Mass., 1974-77; assoc. prof. Ind. U., 1977-78, U. Md., Balt., 1978-84; assoc. Nixon, Hargrave, Devans and Doyle, Jupiter, Fla., 1984-86; pvt. practice, Jupiter, 1986—. Pres. Click Capital Mgmt., LLC. Contbr. articles to profl. jours. Mem. Christmas Cove (Maine) Improvement Assn., Palm Beach County Estate Planning Coun., pres. 1988-89; participant Leadership Palm Beach County, 1991-92. Mem. ABA, Fla. Bar Assn., Palm Beach County Bar Assn. (cultural activities award 1992, named a Fla. Super Lawyer), Yale Club of Palm Beaches (pres.), Kiwanis (chmn. scholarship com.). Presbyterian. Home: 19216 Pinetree Dr Jupiter FL 33469-2002 Office: 810 Saturn St Ste 15 Jupiter FL 33477-4456 Office Phone: 561-747-7077.

CLIFFORD, STEVE, professional basketball coach; B in Spl. Edn., U. Maine, Farmington, 1983. Tchr., basketball coach Woodland Jr.-Sr. HS (Dragons), Baileyville, Maine, 1983—85; asst. basketball coach St. Anselm Coll. Hawks, NH, 1985—89, Fairfield U. Stags, Conn., 1989—90, Boston U. Eagles, Mass., 1990—94, Siena Coll. Saints, NY, 1994—95; head basketball coach Adelphi U. Panthers, NY, 1995—99; asst. basketball coach East Carolina U. Pirates, NC, 1999—2000; advance scout NY Knicks, 2000—01, asst. coach, 2001—03, Houston Rockets, 2003—07, Orlando Magic, 2007—12, LA Lakers, 2012—13; head coach Charlotte Bobcats, 2013—. Office: Charlotte Bobcats 333 E Trade St Charlotte NC 28202*

CLIFFORD, STEWART BURNETT, banker, director; b. Boston, Feb. 17, 1929; s. Stewart Hilton and Ellinor (Burnett) C.; m. Cornelia Park Woolley, Apr. 26, 1952; children: Cornelia Lee Wareham, Rebecca Lyn Mailer-Howat, Jennifer Leggett Danner, Stewart Burnett Jr. AB, Harvard U., Cambridge, Mass., 1951, MBA, 1956. Asst. cashier Citibank, N.A., NYC, 1958-60, asst. v.p., 1960-63; exec. v.p., gen. mgr. Merc Bank, Montreal, Que., Canada, 1963-67, v.p. planning Overseas div., 1967-68; v.p., adminstr. comml. banking group Citibank, NYC, 1969-72, v.p. head world corp. dept. London, 1973-75, sr. v.p. domestic energy, 1975-80, sr. v.p., head pvt. banking and investment divsn., 1981-87, div. exec., head investment divsn., 1987-93; sr. banker Pvt. Bank US, 1993-94; cons. MB Investment Ptnrs., NYC, 1995—2008. Trustee Spence Sch., NYC, 1976—88, chair bd. trustees, 1984—86; elder Brick Ch., NYC; trustee Presbyn. Ch. Found., 1996—2001, Auburn Seminary, NYC; bd. dirs. Nat. Inst. Social Scis., NYC; trustee emeritus Princeton Theol. Sem.; com. univ. resources Harvard Coll.; bd. dirs. Monumental Corp., Balt., 1974—89, Harvard Alumni Assn., 1989—91; pres. Woolley-Clifford Found.; bd. mem. Asphalt Green. 1st lt. US Army, 1951—54. Mem.: Hurlingham Club (London), Soc. Colonial Wars, Harvard Club (NYC), Union Club (NYC, former pres.), Bath and Tennis Club (Palm Beach), Duxbury Yacht Club (Mass.), Pilgrims (NYC). Republican. Home: 330 S Ocean Blvd Apt 3A Palm Beach FL 33480

CLIFTON, MATTHEW P., petroleum refining company executive; b. 1951; V.p. econ. engring. & legal affairs Holly Corp., Dallas, 1988—91, sr. v.p., 1991—95; chmn., CEO Holly Logistic Svcs. LLC; pres. Holly Refining & Marketing Co., Holly Corp., Dallas, 1995—2005, CEO, 2005—07, chmn., CEO, 2007—11; exec. chmn. HollyFrontier Corp., Dallas, 2011—. Office: HollyFrontier Corp Ste 1300 2828 N Harwood Dallas TX 75201 Office Phone: 214-871-3555.

CLIFTON, RUSSELL B., retired mortgage company executive, consultant; b. Maroa, Ill., Jan. 16, 1930; s. Russell Thomas and Clara Leoda (Luckenbill) C.; m. Mary Joyce Hartline, Oct. 10, 1948; 1 son, Steven Shawn. BA, Mich. State U., 1957. Bank auditor Arthur Andersen & Co., Detroit, 1957-59; v.p. Mich. Nat. Bank, Lansing, 1959-65; sr. v.p. Assoc. Mortgages Co., Kansas City, Mo., 1965-69; v.p. Fed. Nat. Mortgage Assn., Washington, 1969-85, ret., 1985; pres., chief exec. officer First Chesapeake Mortgage, Inc., Beltsville, Md., 1985-86, also bd. dirs.; cons. banking and mortgage lending, 1986—. Mem. adv. com. Home Owner's Warranty Corp., Washington, 1978-81; bd. dirs., mem. exec. com., treas. Nat. Acad. Conciliators, Washington, 1979-91; bd. dirs. Lincoln Savs. & Loan (now Seasons Savs. Bank), Richmond, Va., 1987-89; bd. dirs., treas. Nat. Ctr. for Dispute Settlements, Washington, 1987-91. Served with U.S. Army, 1952-54. Named disting. fellow Nat. Assn. Cert. Mortgages Bankers, 1975 Mem. Phi Kappa Phi, Beta Alpha Psi, Beta Gamma Sigma, Tau Sigma. Methodist.

CLINE, BENJAMIN L., state legislator; b. Stillwater, Okla., Feb. 29, 1972; m. Elizabeth Cline. BA, Bates Coll., Lewiston, Maine; degree in law, U. Richmond, Va. From policy advisor to chief of staff to Bib Goodlatte US House of Representatives, Washington, 1994—2002; pres. NDS Corp., Va., 2002—07; mem. Dist 24 Va. House of Delegates, Va., 2002—; asst. commonwealth atty. Rockingham County and City of Harrisburg, Va. Republican. Roman Catholic. Office: PO Box 1405 Amherst VA 24521 also: Capitol Office Gen Assembly Bldg Rm 722 PO Box 406 Richmond VA 23218 Office Phone: 434-946-9908, 804-698-1024. Business E-Mail: DelBCline@house.virginia.gov.

CLINE, BOBBY JAMES, insurance company executive; b. Floydada, Tex., Mar. 12, 1932; s. Howard O. and Carrie (Tomlinson) C.; m. Martha Nolen, May 29, 1954; children: Carolyn, Pamela, Millie, Robert, Sean. BBA, U. Tex., 1954. Casualty underwriter Ins. Co. N.Am., Dallas, 1956-59; account exec./ptnr. Munger-Moore & Assocs., Dallas, 1959-68; ptnr. Harris-Moore & Assocs., Dallas, 1968-70; sr. v.p. Alexander & Alexander Inc., Dallas, 1970-72, exec. v.p., 1972-77, pres., 1977-96, vice chmn. bd.; exec. v.p. Aon Risk Svcs. Tex., Dallas, 1997-2000; chmn. bd. Tex. Banc Ptnr., Inc., Tex., 2000—05; ptnr. Tex Cap Ins.-Concord Ins., Dallas, 2005—. Bd. dirs. Vision Bank. Served with USN, 1954-56. Mem. Soc. CPCUs (dir.), U. Tex. Ex-Students Assn. (past pres.), Salesmanship Club, Preston Trail Golf Club, Dallas Club, Dallas Athletic Club, Garland Toastmasters, Riverhill Country Club. Baptist. Avocations: golf, hunting. Office: Tex Cap Ins 13465 Midway Ste 200 Dallas TX 75244 Home: 1305 Colonel Dr Apt 604 Garland TX 75043-1366 Office Phone: 972-720-5363. Personal E-mail: bcline@texcap-concord.com.

CLINE, ROBERT THOMAS, retired land developer; b. McClave, Colo., May 31, 1925; s. John Howard and Goldie Gladys (Hiltabidel) C.; m. Martha Carolyn Erwin, Mar. 6, 1946; children: Carolyn Cline Price, Roberta Cline Colquitt. Student, Pueblo CC, Colo., 1943, Wofford Coll., 1944. Real estate salesperson George H. Williams Co., Arlington, Va., 1946; real estate broker Lyon Pk. Realty Co., Arlington, 1946-48; cartographic rep. Hearne Bros. Map Co., Detroit, 1949-58; owner Aero Surveys Map Co., Marietta, Ga., 1958-65, Imperial Builders, Marietta, 1965-69; sec., treas. Personality Homes, Landmark Realty, Smyrna, Ga., 1969-78, Landmark Bldg. & Devel., Inc./Landmark Realty Co., Smyrna, 1978-96; ret., 1996. State sec. Christian Men's Fellowship Christian Ch., Ga., 1962-64; bd. dirs. Campbellstone Apts. for Elderly, Atlanta, 1980-86. With USAF, 1943-46. Republican. Avocation: collecting and flying radio controlled aircraft. Home: 2129 Ellis Farm Dr Marietta GA 30064-2879

CLINE, SARA MCLAUGHLIN, state banking agency administrator; BBA, W.Va. U., Morgantown; grad., Grad. Sch. Banking, Baton Rouge, La., 1991. Comml. loan portfolio mgr. Huntington Nat. Bank, W.Va.; joined W.Va. Divsn. Banking, Charleston, 1984, bank examiner, dir. depository instns., dep. commr., acting commr., 2008—09, commr., 2009—. Chair W.Va. Bd. Banking and Fin. Instns. Office: West Virginia Division Banking One Players Club Dr Ste 300 Charleston WV 25311-1638 Office Phone: 304-558-2294. Office Fax: 304-558-0442. E-mail: scline@wvdob.org.

CLINE, TERRY LEE, state agency administrator, public health service officer; b. Ardmore, Okla., July 31, 1958; BS in Psychology, U. Okla., 1980; MS in Clin. Psychology, Okla. State U., PhD. Clin. instr. dept. psychiatry Harvard Med. Sch., Boston; staff psychologist McLean Hosp., Belmont, Maine; clin. dir. cmty. health ctr. Cambridge, Mass.; commr. Okla. Dept. Mental Health & Substance Abuse Services, Oklahoma City, 2001—04; sec. health State of Okla., Oklahoma City, 2004—06; adminstr. Substance Abuse and Mental Health Services Adminstrn. (SAMSHA), US Dept. Health & Human Services, Rockville, Md., 2006—08, health attache, US Embassy Baghdad, Iraq, 2008—09; commr. health State of Okla., Oklahoma City, 2009—. Office: Okla Dept Health 1000 NE 10th Oklahoma City OK 73117 Office Phone: 405-271-5600.

CLINEBURG, BERNARD H., bank executive; Attended, Robert Morris Coll. Chmn., pres., CEO United Bank (formerly George Mason Bankshares); pres., CEO George Mason Bank; pres. Cardinal Financial Corp., 2001—06, chmn., CEO, 2001—, Cardinal Bank, 2006—. Mem. INOVA Health System Found.; bd. dirs., MEM. exec. com. Va. Bankers Assn.; former bd. trustee Va. Bankers Assn. Sch.

Bank Mgmt., George Mason U. Found.; bd. dirs. Va. Bankers Assn. Edn. Found. Office: Cardinal Financial Corp 8270 Greensboro Dr Ste 500 Mc Lean VA 22102 Office Phone: 703-584-3400. Office Fax: 703-584-3410. Business E-Mail: bernardh.clineburg@cardinalbank.com.

CLINGMAN, RACHEL GIESBER, lawyer; BA, Rice U., 1989; JD, U. Tex., 1992. Bar: Tex. Ptnr. Sutherland Asbill & Brennan, Houston. Dir. Houston Downtown Alliance; mem. corp. guild Dress for Success Houston; mem. adv. coun., pres. Women's Energy Network Houston; mem. adv. bd. World Oil Women's Global Leadership Conf. in Energy and Tech., 2005—09; mem. United Way Tex. Gulf Coast Alexis de Tocqueville Soc., 2006—; mem. steering com. women's initiative United Way Tex. Gulf Coast, 2007—10; mem. economic adv. bd. Greater Houston Partnership, 2009, 2010; co-founder legal adv. bd. Children at Risk, 2006—07; bd. dirs. Houston Area Women's Ctr., 2007—. Recipient Client Svc. award, BTI Consulting Group, 2007, 2011; named a Tex. Super Lawyer, 2010, Tex. Local Litigation Star, Benchmark Litigation, 2010—11; named one of 25 Extraordinary Women in the Law, Tex. Lawyer, 2008; named to The Top 5 Women in Energy, Energy Law, 2007, The Best Lawyers in America, 2007—11, Chambers USA: Guide to Leading Bus. Lawyers, 2008—10, The 45 Under 45, The American Lawyer, 2011. Fellow: Litigation Counsel America; mem.: American Bd. Trial Advocates. Office: Sutherland Asbill & Brennan 1001 Fannin St Ste 3700 Houston TX 77002-6760 Office Phone: 713-470-6189. Office Fax: 713-654-1301. Business E-Mail: rachel.clingman@sutherland.com.

CLODFELTER, DANIEL GRAY, Mayor, Charlotte, former state legislator, lawyer; b. Thomasville, NC, June 2, 1950; s. Billy G. and Marie Lorene (Wells) C.; m. Elizabeth Kay Bevan, Aug. 20, 1974; children: Julia Elizabeth, Catherine Gray. BA, Davidson Coll., 1972; AB, Oxford U., 1974; JD, Yale U., 1977. Bar: N.C. 1977, U.S. Dist. Ct. (we. dist.) N.C. 1977, U.S. Dist. Ct. (ea. dist.) N.C. 1979, U.S. Ct. Appeals (4th cir.) 1984, U.S. Dist. Ct. (mid. dist.) N.C. 1985. Law clk. to presiding judge US Dist. Ct., Charlotte, NC, 1977—78; assoc. Moore & Van Allen, Charlotte, 1978—82, ptnr., 1983—; mem. Dist 37 NC State Senate, 1999—2014; mayor City of Charlotte, NC, 2014—. Mem. Charlotte City Coun., 1987-93, Charlotte-Mecklenburg Planning Commn., 1984-87, chmn., 1986-87; state sec. Rhodes Scholarship Trust, N.C., 1986-97; trustee Z. Smith Reynolds Found., Inc., Winston-Salem, N.C., 1983—; bd. dirs. N.C. Ctr. for Pub. Policy Rsch., 1994-96. Rhodes scholar, 1972. Mem. N.C. Bar Assn. (antitrust law com., bankruptcy sect. coun.). Democrat. Office: Office of Mayor 600 E 4th St Charlotte NC 28202 also: Moore & Van Allen 100 N Tryon St 4700 Charlotte NC 28202-4003 Office Phone: 704-331-1041, 704-336-7600. E-mail: clodfelterd@mvalaw.com.*

CLORE, LAWRENCE HUBERT, lawyer; b. Tulsa, July 31, 1944; s. Hubert Charles and Jessie Louada (Fowler) Clore; m. Carol Jean Roegelein, June 3, 1967 (div. 1981); children: Robert William, James Lawrence; m. Martha Jo Lawyer; children: Kathryn Denise, Michael Hubert. BBA, Tex. Christian U., 1966; JD, U. Tex., 1969. Bar: Tex. 1969, cert.: Tex. Bd. Legal Specialization (specialist in labor and employment law). Assoc. Fulbright & Jaworski, Houston, 1971-77, ptnr., 1977—. Capt. US Army, 1969—71, Vietnam. Mem.: ABA, Houston Mgmt. Lawyers Forum (chmn. 1976—77), Indsl. Rels. Rsch. Assn., Tex. Bar Assn. (labor and employment sect., coun. 1990—93, vice chair 1993—94, chair 1994—95). Republican. Methodist. Avocations: hunting, fishing, golf. Office: Fulbright & Jaworski 1301 Mckinney St Ste 5100 Houston TX 77010-3031 Home Phone: 713-465-1660; Office Phone: 713-651-5403. Business E-Mail: lclore@fulbright.com.

CLOSE, MICHAEL JOHN, property manager, lawyer; b. Sandusky, Ohio, Jan. 24, 1943; s. Robert J. and Mary Lee (Graefe) C.; m. Nancy L. Schelp, June 18, 1995; children: Christina C., Karen L. AB in History, Lafayette Coll., Easton, Pa., 1965; JD cum laude, U. Mich., 1968. Assoc. Dewey, Ballantine, Bushby, Palmer & Wood, NYC, 1968-76; ptnr. Dewey Ballantine, NYC, 1976-96; pres., CEO Balmer Parc LLC, NYC, 2003—. Chmn. Tax Rev., N.Y.C. Author: Tax Aspects of Oil and Gas Drilling Funds, 1972, Drilling Funds: The 1977 Perspective, 1977, Special Allocations in Oil and Gas Ventures, 1982, The Final Section 704 (b) Regulations: Special Allocations Reach New Heights of Complexity, 1986, Fringe Benefit Regulation and the New York Law Firm Culture: A New Era, 1989, Off Balance Sheet Financings, 1994; contbr. articles to profl. jours. Bd. dirs., adminstrv. vice-chmn. Conn. Swimming, Inc., 1992-99; chmn. ad-hoc com. on by-laws USA Swimming, Inc., 1995-96; bd. dirs. Sharks Swim Team, Inc., 1991-94, pres., 1992-94; trustee Asolo Theatre Repertory Endowment Fund, 2005—; bd. dirs. Asolo Repertory Theatre, Inc., 2006—, mem. exec. com., 2006-, mem. corp. governance com., 2007-, dir. emeritus, First Citizens Banc Corp., Sandusky, Ohio, 2011- Mem. ABA, Assn. of Bar of City of N.Y., N.Y. Law Inst. (life mem.), N.Y. State Bar Assn., Ohio State Bar Assn., Real Estate Bd. N.Y.(assoc.), India House (N.Y.C.), Burning Tree Country Club (Greenwich, Conn.), Meadows Country Club (Sarasota, Fla.), Phi Delta Phi, Theta Chi. Republican. Home: 4951 Windsor Park Sarasota FL 34235-2610 Office: Balmer Parc LLC 18th Fl 445 Park Ave New York NY 10022 Office Phone: 212-486-8500. Personal E-mail: thecloses@comcast.net. Business E-Mail: mclose@dakotarealtyny.com.

CLOUSE, JAMES STEVEN (STEVE CLOUSE), state legislator; b. Ozark, Ala., Feb. 7, 1956; s. James C. and Ruth C. Clouse; m. Diane H. Clouse, 1988; children: Todd, Anne Myree. V.p. Clouse Oil & Market, 1978—; mem. Dist. 93 Ala. House of Reps., 1994—. Mem.: Ozark Rotary Club (Paul Harris award 1991), Boys & Girls Club (dir. 1994—95). Republican. Methodist. Mailing: PO Box 818 Ozark AL 36361-0818 Office: State House Repr 11 S Union St Rm 526-A Montgomery AL 36130 Home Phone: 334-774-7384; Office Phone: 334-774-9122.

CLOUTIER, C. R., bank executive; Mem. adv. com. SEC; pres., CEO, bd. dirs. MidSouth Bank, N.A. (subs. of MidSouth Bancorp, Inc.), 1984—, MidSouth Bancorp, Inc., 1984—. Bd. dirs. ICBA Bancard Inc. Mem., exec. com. Ind. Cmty. Bankers of America. Office: MidSouth Bancorp Inc 102 Versailles Blvd Lafayette LA 70501 Office Phone: 337-237-8343. Office Fax: 337-267-4434.

CLUCK, ROBERT, Mayor, Arlington, Texas; Med. tng. U. Tex. Southwestern Med. Sch.; pvt. practice, ob-gyn. Arlington, Tex., 1971—94; former med. dir. Arlington Meml. Hosp., v.p., med. affairs, 2002—; former med. dir. Harris Methodist Health Plan; councilman, dist. 4 Arlington, Tex., 1999—2003; mayor City of Arlington, Tex., 2003—. Mem. Workforce Solutions Workforce Governing Bd.; bd. dirs. Arlington C. of C., Tex. Mcpl. League, U. Tex. Metroplex Coun. General medical officer USAF, Clark Air Force Base, Philippines, Vietnam War. Mailing: Office of Mayor 101 W Abram St Arlington TX 76004-0231 Office Phone: 817-459-6122. Business E-Mail: robert.cluck@arlingtontx.gov.*

CLUCK, TERRY WAYNE, biology professor, geneticist; b. Sentinel, Okla., May 21, 1950; s. Joe Alton and Ruby Bishop Cluck; m. Jane C. Coleman; children: Sam J., James W. PhD in Genetics, Tex. A&M U., College Station, 1985. Tchr. So. Bapt. Mission, Nyeri, Central Province, Kenya, 1972—74; registered sanitarian Sweetwater-Nolan County Health Dept., Tex., 1977—80; rsch. geneticist USDA - Agr. Rsch. Svc., Weslaco, 1985—87; biology prof. Campbell U., Buies Creek, 1987—90; prof. biology East Ctrl. U., Ada, 1990—. Grantee Bridges to Baccalaureate, NIH - Nat. Gen. Med. Scis., 1995—. Mem.: Beta Beta Beta Biol. Honor Soc. (dist. dir. 1996—, Yokley Faculty Svc. award 2006). Conservative. Avocation: reading. Office: East Central Univ 1100 E 14th Ada OK 74820 Business E-Mail: tcluck@ecok.edu.

CLURMAN, SALLY, tax specialist; B in Acctg., U. Miss. With Arthur Andersen & Co., 1984—89; mgr., tax compliance & planning Gannett Co., Inc., 1989—2002, dir., taxes, 2002—08, v.p., taxes, 2008—. Mem., tax com. Newspaper Assn. of America. Office: Gannett Co Inc 7950 Jones Branch Dr Mc Lean VA 22107-0150 Office Phone: 703-854-6000. Office Fax: 703-854-2053. Business E-Mail: sclurman@gannett.com.

CLUTE, ROBERT EUGENE, political science professor; b. Earlville, Iowa, July 12, 1924; s. Henry and Leta (Allen) C.; m. Doris Reams, 1947; children: Robert Eugene, Andrea Reams. BA, U. Ala., 1947; MA, George Washington U., 1948; PhD, Duke U., 1957. Selector U.S. Displaced Persons Commn., Frankfurt, Fed. Republic Germany, 1948-50; analyst USAF, Austria, 1950-54; rsch. assoc. Duke U., Durham, N.C., 1957-58; vis. asst. prof. Tulane U. La., New Orleans, 1958-59; asst. prof. U. Nev., 1959-62; assoc. prof. U. Ga., Athens, 1962-68, prof. polit. sci., 1968—, head dept. polit. sci., 1972-75, grad. coord., 1975-88, chmn. social scis. div., 1982-93, prof. emeritus, 1993—. Am. specialist to Anglophone Africa, Cultural Affairs div. U.S. Dept. State, 1977. Author: The International Legal Status of Austria, 1962; (with others) The International Law Standard and Commonwealth Developments, 1966, De lege pactorum, 1970, Law and Justice, 1970; contbr. articles to profl. jours. With U.S. Army, 1943-46. Fulbright scholar 1967-68; Danforth assoc. 1972. Mem. Am. Soc. Internat. Law, Am. Polit. Sci. Assn., Ga. Polit. Sci. Assn., So. Polit. Sci. Assn., Internat. Studies Assn., African Studies Assn., Phi Kappa Phi, Phi Alpha Theta, Pi Sigma Alpha, Phi Beta Delta. Democrat. Episcopalian. Home: Ste 214 Arbor Terr 3736 Atlanta Hwy Athens GA 30606-3159 Office: U Ga Dept Polit Sci Athens GA 30602

CLYBURN, JAMES ENOS (JIM CLYBURN), United States Representative from South Carolina; b. Sumter, SC, July 21, 1940; s. Enos Lloyd and Almeta (Dizzley) Clyburn; m. Emily England; children: Mignon, Jennifer, Angela. BA in History, SC State Coll., Orangeburg, 1962; LHD (hon.), Winthrop Coll., 1987; DSc (hon.), Coll. Charleston, 1992, Med. U. SC, 1993; LHD (hon.), St. Augustine Coll., 1994; LLD (hon.), Claflin Coll., 1995; LHD (hon.), SC State U., 1995; LLD (hon.), Voorhees Coll., 1996. Tchr. Charleston County Pub. Sch. Sys., SC; employment counselor SC Employment Security Commn., 1965—66; dir. Charleston County Neighborhood Youth Corps/New Careers Projects, 1966—68; exec. dir. SC Commn. Farmworkers Inc., 1968—71; staff mem. Gov. John C. West, Charleston, 1971-74; commr. SC Human Affairs Commn., 1974-92; mem. US Congress from 6th SC dist., 1993—; asst. majority leader (majority whip) US Congress from 6th SC Dist., 2007—11, asst. minority leader (minority whip), 2011—; chmn. US House Democratic Caucus, 2006—07; mem. Joint Select Com. on Deficit Reduction, 2011. Pres. Nat. Assn. Human Rights Workers, 1980—81, Internat. Assn. Ofcl. Human Rights Agencies, 1985—87; bd. dirs. James R. Clark Sickle Cell Anemia Found., SC Literacy Assn. Recipient Pub. Adminstr. of Yr. award, Am. Soc. Pub. Adminstrn.; named one of the Most Influential Black Americans, Ebony mag., 2006. Mem.: NAACP (life), Shriners, Masons, Omega Psi Phi. Democrat. Office: US House of Representatives 242 Cannon House Office Bldg Washington DC 20515 also: 1225 Lady St Ste 200 Columbia SC 29201 Office Phone: 202-225-3315. Office Fax: 202-225-2313. E-mail: jclyburn@mail.house.gov.*

CLYBURN, WILLIAM, SR., state legislator; b. Camden, SC, May 19, 1941; s. Charlie and Hettie Clyburn; m. Beverly Laverne Dozier, 1964; children: William Jr., Wilson Anthony, Courtney Lavenne. BS in Physical Edn., Allen U., 1964; MEd, U. SC, 1975. Mem. Aiken County Coun., 1981—86, Aiken City Coun., 1973—80; prin. Aiken Elem. Sch., SC, 1975, Aiken HS, 1983—86; pub. rels. cons.; mem. Dist. 82 SC House of Reps., 1995—, mem. Ways and Means Com., Subcommittee on Health, Human Svcs. and Medicaid & Subcommittee on Property Tax. Commr. SC Workers' Compensation. Named Citizen of Yr., Omega Psi, Aiken Coll. Christian Fellow. Mem.: Greater Aiken C. of C. (bd. mem. 1974—76, 1996—). Democrat. Mailing: 664 Edrie St Aiken SC 29801 Office: 416C Blatt Bldg Columbia SC 29201 Home Phone: 803-649-6167, 803-771-8711; Office Phone: 803-734-3033, 803-643-4833. Business E-Mail: WC@schouse.org.

CO, ANGELA, architect, educator; M. in Arch., Columbia U.; BA in Arch., U. Pa, BS in Computer Sci. Prof. arch. U. Kentucky Coll Design; founder Studio Co. Instr. Columbia U., U. Pa. Recipient Hon. Design Award, Columbia U., Loewenfish Mem. Prize for Design Excellence, Arnold W. Brunner Rome Prize, Am. Acad. in Rome, 2011; grantee MacDowell Colony Fel Arch., MacDowell Colony, 2010. Achievements include research in collaboration with Aeolab on Weather-Making Balloon media installation and nomadic pavilion. Office: University of Kentucky Coll Design 117 Pence Hall Lexington KY 40506

COAKLEY, PAUL STAGG, archbishop; b. Norfolk, June 3, 1955; s. John A. Coakley, Jr. and Mary Coakley, Stella (Bisbee) (Stepmother). BA in English, U. Kans., 1977; grad. in Pre-Theology, St. Pius X Sem., Erlanger, Ky., 1979; MDiv in Theology, Mount St. Mary's Sem., Emmitsburg, Md., 1983; STL in Christian Spirituality, Pontifical Gregorian U., Rome, 1987. Ordained deacon Diocese of Wichita, 1982, ordained priest, 1983; assoc. pastor St. Mary's Ch., Derby, Kans., 1983—85; chaplain Kans. Newman Coll., Wichita, 1987—89; dir., Office of Youth and Young Adult Ministry Diocese of Wichita, 1987—91; pastor Our Lady of Guadalupe Ch., Wichita, 1989—90; assoc. dir. Spiritual Life Ctr., Wichita, 1990—95; pastor Ch. of the Resurrection, Wichita, 1995—98; dir., spiritual formation Mount St. Mary's Sem., 1998—2002; dir. Spiritual Life Ctr., Wichita, 2002—04; ordained bishop, 2004; bishop Diocese of Salina, Kans., 2004—10; archbishop Archdiocese of Okla. City, Okla., 2010—. Adj. spiritual dir. Inst. Priestly Formation, Omaha, 2000—04; vice chancellor Diocese of Wichita, 2004. Bd. trustees Newman U., 2003—05; mem. adv. bd. Coronado Area Coun. of Boy Scout. Mem.: Equestrian Order of the Holy Sepulchre of Jerusalem, Rotary Club, KC (Fourth degree). Roman Catholic. Office: Archdiocese of Okla City 7501 NW Expressway Oklahoma City OK 73132-2180 Office Phone: 405-721-5651. Office Fax: 405-721-5210.

COALE, SHERRI, women's college basketball coach; b. Healdton, Okla., Jan. 19, 1965; m. Dane Coale; children: Colton, Chandler. B in Edn. summa cum laude, Okla. Christian U., Oklahoma City, 1987. Asst. coach Edmond Meml. HS, 1987-89; head varisty coach Norman HS, 1989-96; head coach women's basketball U. Okla. Sooners, Norman, 1996—. Bd. mem. USA Basketball, 2005—08, WBCA, v.p., 2006—. Bd. dirs. Am. Cancer Soc.; mem. Coaches vs. Cancer, Westside Ch. of Christ, Norman; vol. Children's Miracle Network. Named All-State Coach, 1993, Regional Coach of Yr., 1993, Big All-City Coach of Yr., 1993. Mem. NEA, Women's Basketball Coaches Assn., Okla. Girls Basketball Coaches Assn., Okal. Coaches Assn., Fellowship of Christian Athletes, Norman Optimists, Okla. Edn. Assn., Profl. Educators of Norman. Office: Univ Okla Athletics Dept 180 W Brooks St Rm 235 Norman OK 73019-6049 Fax: 405-325-7623.

COALTER, MILTON J., JR., library director, educator; b. Memphis, July 5, 1949; s. Milton J. and Jewel (Mitchel) C.; children: Martha Claire, Siram Jacob. BA, Davidson Coll., 1971; MDiv, Princeton Theol. Sem., 1975, ThM, 1977; PhD in Religion, Princeton U., 1982. Asst. prof. Am. religion N.C. State U., Raleigh, 1981-82; pub. svcs. libr. The Iliff Sch. Theology, Denver, 1982-84, acting libr. dir., 1984-85; libr. dir., prof. bibliography and rsch. Louisville Presbyn. Theol. Sem., 1985—2004, Union Presbyn. Sem., Richmond, Va., 2004—; acting pres. Louisville Presbyn. Theol. Sem., 2002—03. Bd. dirs. Louisville Inst., Scholars Press; gen. assembly coun. task force on ch. membership growth Presbyn. Ch., Louisville, 1989-91. Author: (with John M. Mulder) The Letters of David Avery, 1979, Gilbert Tennent, Son of Thunder, 1986; (with John M. Mulder and Louis B. Weeks) The Presbyterian Presence in the Twentieth Century, 7 vols., 1989-92, Vital Signs, 1996, Resources for American Christianity, 2002, website for religion divsn. Lilly Endowment, 2000--; editor: (with Virgil Cruz) How Shall We Witness?, 1995; contbr. articles to profl. jours. Mem. Gen. Assembly Theol. Task Force on Peace, Unity and Purity of the Ch., 2001—06. Recipient Jonathan Edwards award Princeton U., 1977-80, Tchg. award Assn. Princeton Grad. Alumni, 1979-80, Francis Makemie award Presbyn. Ch. Dept. History; Lilly Endowment grantee, 1987-90, 99—, N.J. Hist. Commn. grantee, 1979-80, Pew Charitable Trust grantee, 1990-93; Princeton U. Whiting fellow, 1980-81. Mem. Am. Theol. Libr. Assn. (bd. dirs. 1997-03, pres. 1998-00). Presbyterian. Office: William Smith Morton Libr Union Presbyn Sem 3401 Brook Rd Richmond VA 23227 Office Phone: 804-278-4311.

COAR, RICHARD JOHN, mechanical engineer, aerospace transportation executive, consultant; b. Hanover, NH, May 2, 1921; s. Herbert Greenleaf and Anne (Langille) C.; m. Cecilie Berle, 1942 (dec. 1971); children— Gregory, Candace, Andrea, Kenneth; m. Lucille Hicks, 1972. BS in Mech. Engring., Tufts U., 1942. Engr. Pratt & Whitney Aircraft, East Hartford, Conn., 1942-56; chief engr. Fla. Research and Devel. Ctr., 1956-70, asst. gen. mgr., 1970—72; v.p. engring. Pratt & Whitney Aircraft, East Hartford, 1972—76, exec. v.p., 1976-83, pres., 1983-84; sr. v.p. United Techs., Hartford, 1983-84, exec. v.p., 1984-86. Patentee aircraft engines and controls Corporator Hartford Hosp., 1983; bd. dirs. Hartford Symphony, 1985-87. Recipient Franklin W. Kolk Air Transp. Progress award Soc. Automotive Engrs., 1985, Daniel Guggenheim medal for contbns. to aeronautic and space propulsion sys., 1998. Mem. ASME (George Westinghouse Gold medal 1986), NAE, Am. Soc. Metals (disting. life mem.), Tau Beta Pi.

COATES, HARRY E., state legislator; b. Seminole, Okla., 1950; m. Betty Coates; children: Jeremy, Heather, Eddie, Brandon. Owner Harry E. Coates, Inc.; mem. Dist. 28 Okla. State Senate, 2002—. Mem.: Jasmine Moran Children's Mus., Seminole Indsl. Found. (past pres.), Seminole C. of C., Prof. Construction Estimators Assn., Construction Specifiers Inst., Nat. Roofing Contractors Assn., Roof Cons. Inst., Aircraft Owners and Pilots Assn., Okla. Rifle Assn., NRA. Republican. Baptist. Office: 2300 N Lincoln Blvd Rm 531 Oklahoma City OK 73105 Mailing: US 377 N Seminole OK 74868 Office Phone: 405-382-7660. Business E-Mail: coates@oksenate.gov.

COATES, SHIRLEY JEAN, finance educator; b. Nashville, Oct. 9, 1944; d. Jerry Baxter Springer and Cora Louise Green; m. Arthur Andrew Coates; children: Andrea, John. BS, Mid. Tenn. State U., 1968; MS, Brigham Young U., 1971. Lic. profl. tchr., cert. tchr. Tenn. career level III. Instr. Young Harris Coll., Young Harris, Ga., 1968—70, U. of Miss., Oxford, Miss., 1971—72; tchr. Dickson County Jr. H.S., Dickson, Tenn., 1972—73, Hickman County H.S., Centerville, Tenn., 1973—. Bus. dept. chmn. Hickman County H.S., Centerville, Tenn., 1994—. Sponsor, Hickman County - Tenn. type-a-thon Leukemia Soc. of Am., BPA Chpt., Nashville, 1989—99; sec. Hickman County H.S. Band Boosters, Centerville, Tenn., 1988—94, Hickman County H.S. Athletic Booster Club, Centerville, Tenn., 1995—96; pageant chmn. Hickman County 4-H Vol. Leaders, Centerville, Tenn., 1990—94; project dir. (head start book dr.) South Ctrl. Human Resources Agy., Centerville, Tenn., 1988—89. Recipient Most Disting. H.S. Tchr., Hickman County Tenn. Edn. Assn., 2003; named Tchr. of Yr., Hickman County HS Bd. of Edn., 1990, Bus. Dept. Tchr. of Yr., Hickman County H.S., 2000, Most Disting. H.S. Tchr., Hickman County Tenn. Edn. Assn., 2002. Mem.: Bus. Profls. Am. (honor adv. 1991, star advisor 1992), Assn. for Career and Tech. Edn., DAR (asst. registrar, treas. 1998—2002).

COATS, ANDREW MONTGOMERY, law educator, trial and appellate lawyer, former dean, mayor; b. Oklahoma City, Okla., Jan. 19, 1935; s. Sanford Clarence and Mary Ola (Young) C.; m. Linda M. Zimmerman; children: Andrew, Michael, Jennifer, Sanford BA, U. Okla., 1957, JD, 1963. Assoc. Crowe and Dunlevy, Oklahoma City, 1963-67, ptnr., 1967-76, sr. trial ptnr., 1980—96; dist. atty. Oklahoma County, Oklahoma City, 1976-80; mayor City of Oklahoma City, 1983-87; dean U. Okla. Coll. Law, 1996—2010, dean emeritus, 2010—, Samuel Roberts Nobel Found. presdl. prof., Arch B. & Joanne Gilbert prof. law. Pres. Okla. Young Lawyers Conf., 1968—69; dir. Local Okla. Bank, Oklahoma City; bd. dirs. IBC Bank Okla., 2004—. Democratic nominee US Senate, 1980; pres. Oklahoma County Legal Aid Soc., 1972-73. Served to lt. USN, 1960-63 Named Outstanding Lawyer in Okla., Oklahoma City U., 1977, Phi Beta Kappa of Yr., 2003, U. Okla. Coll. Law bldg. named in honor of Andrew M. Coats, 2005, Okla. Hall of Fame, 2006. Fellow Am. Coll. Trial Lawyers (pres. 1996-97, 10th Cir. regent 1992-96), Am. Bar Found., Internat. Acad. Trial Lawyers; mem. ABA, US Supreme Ct. Hist. Soc. (trustee), Okla. Bar Assn. (pres. 1992-93), Okla. County Bar Assn. (pres. 1976-77), Am. Bd. Trial Advs. (charter pres. Okla. Chap.) Order of Coif, Oklahoma City Golf and Country Club (bd. dirs. 1977-80, 93-96), Petroleum Club (pres. 1995), Phi Beta Kappa (pres. 1975), Pi Kappa Alpha (pres. 1956), Phi Delta Phi (pres. 1962). Clubs: Oklahoma City Golf and Country, Petroleum. Democrat. Episcopalian. Avocations: music, golf. Office: Univeristy of Oklahoma College Law 300 Timberdell Rd Norman OK 73019-5081 Office Phone: 405-325-4720. Business E-Mail: acoats@ou.edu.

COATS, JANET S. (JANET WEAVER), media consultant, former editor; b. 1964; m. Mark Weaver, 1993 (div. Jan. 2007); children: Sam, Rachel, Luke; m. Rusty Coats, Apr. 2007; stepchildren: Carly, Casidy. B in journalism, U. Mo., 1984. Reporter Irving Daily News, Irving, Tex., 1984—86; reporter, asst. city editor Stuart News, 1986—89; from reporter to dep. mng. editor/features and sports Virginian-Pilot, Norfolk, Va., 1989—94; mng. editor The Wichita Eagle, 1994—97, Sarasota Herald-Tribune, 1997—99, exec. editor, 1999—2003; dean faculty Poynter Inst., St. Petersburg, Fla., 2003—04; mng. editor Tampa Tribune, 2004—05, exec. editor, v.p., 2006—09; media cons. Coats2Coats; new media journalism initiative mgr. The Patterson Found., Sarasota, Fla. Juror Pulitzer Prize; Reynolds fellow U. Mo. Donald W. Reynolds Journalism Inst.,

2011—12; spkr. in field. Mem.: Am. Soc. Newspaper Editors (bd. dirs.). Office: The Patterson Foundation 2 N Tamiami Trail Ste 206 Sarasota FL 34236 Business E-Mail: jcoats@thepattersonfoundation.org.

COATS, MICHAEL L., retired science administrator, retired astronaut; b. Sacramento, Jan. 16, 1946; m. Diane Eileen Carson; 2 children. BS, US Naval Acad., 1968; MS in Adminstrn. Sci. and Tech., George Washington U., 1977; MS in Aeronautical Engring., US Naval Postgraduate Sch., 1979. Designated naval aviator USAF, 1969, mem. Attack Squadron 192, USS KITTYHAWK, 1970—72; flight instr. A-7E Readiness Training Squadron, Naval Air Station, Lemoore, Calif., 1972—73; project officer, test pilot A-7 and A-4 Aircraft Strike Aircraft Test Directorate, 1974; flight instr. US Naval Test Pilot Sch., Patuxent River, 1976—77; astronaut NASA, 1979—91, Capcom in Mission Control for STS-4 and STS-5, 1982, pilot STS 41D (Discovery), 1984, acting chief Astronaut Office, 1989—90, comdr. STS-29, STS-39, 1989—91; v.p. Avionics and Comm. Ops. Loral Space Info. Sys., 1991—96; v.p. Civil Space Programs Lockheed Martin Missiles and Space, Sunnyvale, Calif., 1996—98; v.p. Advanced Space Transp. Lockheed Martin Space Systems Co., Denver, 1998—2005; dir. Johnson Space Ctr., NASA, Houston, 2005—12. Decorated Defense Superior Svc. Medal, 3 Disting. Flying Crosses, 32 Strike Flight Air Medals, 3 Individual Action Air Medals, 9 Navy Commendation Medals with Combat V.; recipient NASA Space Flight medal, 1984, 1989, 1991, Special Act or Service award, 1989, NASA Medal for Outstanding Leadership, 1990, NASA Disting. Svc. Medal, 1992, FAI Gold Space medal, 2006, Meritorious Executive award, 2009, Johnson Space Ctr. Presidential rank award, 2009, Nat. Space Trophy, Rotary Nat. award for Space Achievement Found., 2012; named to The Astronaut Hall of Fame, 2007. Fellow: AIAA (assoc.); mem.: Assn. Space Explorers, Soc. Experimental Test Pilots.

COATS, SANFORD CHARLES (SANDY COATS), federal prosecutor; b. Okla. City, 1971; married; 3 children. BA in History, Tulane U., New Orleans, 1994; JD, U. Okla. Coll. Law, 1998. Advt. sales Okla. Gazette, 1994—95; law clk. McKinney & Stringer P.C., Oklahoma City; gen. counsel American Ctrl. Gas Co., 1998; legal intern US Dist. Ct. (western dist.) Okla., 1998; assoc. Fellers, Snider, Blankenship, Bailey & Tippens, 1999—2003; asst. US atty. (western dist.) Okla. US Dept. Justice, 2004—09, US atty., 2010—. Recipient Directors award, Dir. Exec. Office US Attorneys, 2007. Office: US Attorneys Office 210 Park Ave Ste 400 Oklahoma City OK 73102*

COBB, CURT, former state legislator; b. Dec. 28, 1971; m. Margaret Anne Cobb; children: Nina Bryce, Ella Grace. Mem. Dist. 62 Tenn. House of Reps., Tenn., 2003—09; mem. Commerce Com., Joint Bus. Tax Com., Transp. Com., Utilities & Banking Com.; entrepreneur Cobb Realty & Auction, Llc. Mem.: Nat. Wild Turkey Fedn., Mason Lodge, Ducks Unlimited, Farm Bur. Bedford County, Fayetteville-Lincoln County C. of C., Shelbyville-Bedford County C. of C., Mid Tenn. Assn. Realtors. Democrat. Methodist. Home: 1928 Wartrace Pike Shelbyville TN 37160-5222

COBB, JIM, state legislator; m. Suzanne Cobb. Mem. Govt. Ops. Com., Health & Human Resources Com., Health Care Facilities Subcom.; state rep. Dist. 31 Tenn., 2007—. Mem.: Hamilton County C. of C., Dayton & Spring City C. of C., Rhea County Rep. Party (former treas.), Am. Legion Post 0100 (Dayton), Rhea County Rep. HQ Commerce (chmn.), Hamilton County Pachyderm Club. Republican. Office: 169 East Ridge Rd Spring City TN 37381 also: 110 A War Memorial Bldg Nashville TN 37243-0131 Office Phone: 615-741-1450, 423-365-4848. Office Fax: 615-741-4917. Business E-Mail: rep.jim.cobb@capitol.tn.gov.

COBB, STEPHEN A., lawyer; b. Moline, Ill., Jan. 27, 1944; s. Archibald William and Lucile Bates C.; m. Nancy L. Hendrix, Dec. 18, 1971. AB cum laude, Harvard U., 1966; MA in Sociology, Vanderbilt U., 1968, PhD in Sociology, 1971, JD, 1977. Bar: Tenn. 1978, U.S. Dist. Ct. (mid. dist.) Tenn. 1978, US Supreme Ct. 2011. Asst. prof. Tenn. State U., Nashville, 1970-74, dept. head, 1972-74; mem. edn. com. Tenn. Ho. Reps., Nashville, 1974—86, chair edn. oversight com., 1985—86; pvt, practice law Nashville, 1978-86; with Waller Lansden Dortch & Davis, Nashville, 1986-90, ptnr., 1990—2005. Fulbright Jr. lectr. U. Caen, France, 1977—78; lectr. dept. sociology Fisk U., 1981—86. Former pres. Sister Cities of Nashville, Inc.; former mem. So. Regional Edn. Bd., former vice chmn commn. ednl. quality; mem. Task Force Readig Mid. Grades. Decorated officer Ordre des Palmes Academiques (France); recipient Paul Simon Internat. award, 1990, Edwin Cudeki Internat. Bus. award, 1992; NDEA fellow, NIMH fellow, 1966-70, Pres. award, Tenn. Bar Assn., 2010. Mem. ABA, Tenn Fgn. Lang. Inst., Tenn. Bar Assn., Nashville Bar Assn., (former pres.), Fedn. Alliances Francaises (former pres.), Order of Coif. Home: 1929 Castleman Dr Nashville TN 37215-3901

COBB, TERRI REAMER (CECI COBB), film and video producer; b. NYC, Feb. 18, 1934; d. Leo Odell and Jean (Wister) Gruber; m. Ira Reamer, July 4, 1954 (div. May 1975); children: Jeff, David, Ellen; m. David G. Cobb, Aug. 2, 1975; children: Bart, Melissa, Brian (dec.). Student, U. Miami, 1953-54, Miami Dade C.C., 1970-72. Vocalist The Girlfriends, NYC, 1952-53; dental asst. Miami, Fla., 1953-56; med. asst., 1956-58; prodr., host TV talk show People and Places, Tampa, Fla., 1981-95; freelance film and video prodr., prodn. coord. mgr. pres. Encore Film & Video Prodn., Tampa, 1984—. Freelance model, actress, Fla.; seminar leader Tom Kirby Assocs., Fla., 1986—; cons. U. South Fla. Dept. Edn., Tampa, 1980—; location scout, coord. films and commls.; freelance TV prodr., tech. dir. Co-prodr., host: (TV show) Insights (Telly award 2003). Health educator, fund raiser, speaker Fla. March of Dimes, 1964—91; chair planning com. Tampa/Hillsborough; bd. dirs. Fla. Healthy Mother-Healthy Baby Coalition; mem. Hillsborough River Tech. Adv. Coun.; co.-prodr., host Live Healthy (TV Show). Recipient Jone Intercable Golden Cassette award, 1989, Crystal Reel award Fla. Motion Picture & TV Assn., 1990, award Alliance for Cmty. Media, 2001. Mem. Fl. Cattlemans Assn., Emilys list, Parkinsons Disease Assn. Screen Actors Guild. Avocations: tennis, boating, walking, reading. Home: 8155 C 476B Bushnell FL 33513-8920 Personal E-mail: terricobb@aol.com.

COBB, TYRUS RAYMOND, JR., (TY COBB), retired engineer, retired military officer; b. Duncan, Okla., June 23, 1940; s. Tyrus R. and Mary Elizabeth (Bagby) Cobb; m. Beverly Joan York, June 7, 1962; children: Christine E., Tyrus R. III. BS in Mil. Engring., US Mil Acad., West Point, NY, 1962; MA in Geography, Earth Scis., U. Tex., Austin, 1970; MBA, Fla. Inst. Tech., Melbourne, 1984. Cert. lifeguard Red Cross. Inf. officer through the grades to lt. col. US Army, 1962—83; ret., 1983; pres., co-owner Ty Cobb's Sport Locker, Sparta, NJ, 1983—93; R&D engr. US Army Weapons R&D Command, 1985—2005; ret., 2005. Youth football, soccer, basketball and baseball coach, 1972—; pres. Sparta Babe Ruth Baseball; vol. lifeguard East Rowan County YMCA, NC; ordained elder Presbyn. Ch., 1972—; mem. First Presbyn. Ch., Salisbury, NC. Decorated Combat Infantryman's Badge, Three Bronze Stars, Purple Heart. Mem.: NARFE, AMVETS Post 845, Assn. US Army, Kiwanis Internat. (life Hickson award). Republican. Mailing: Cobb For Congress 1025 Faye Ln Salisbury NC 28146-7178 Office Phone: 980-234-0803.

COBB-HUNTER, GILDA, state legislator; b. Orangeburg, SC, Nov. 5, 1952; d. Selvin and Nina Walker Cobb; m. Terry Keith Hunter. BS, Fla. A&M U., 1973, MA, 1978. Mem. Dist. 66 SC House of Reps., 1993—, mem. Ways and Means Com. Recipient Disting. Alumni award, NAFEO. Mem.: NAACP, SC Am. Civil Liberties Union, SC Fair Share (bd. dir.), Nat. Assn. Social Workers, SC Libr. Found., SC Low Income Housing Coalition, Safe Kids, SC Planned Parenthood. Democrat. Baptist. Address: 112 Estate Court Orangeburg SC 29115 Mailing: 309C Blatt Bldg Columbia SC 29201 Office: 4188 Five Chop Rd Orangeburg SC 29115 Office Phone: 803-534-2448, 803-734-2809. Fax: 803-734-8711. Business E-Mail: gch@legis.lpitr.state.sc.us.

COBBS, JAMES HAROLD, engineer, retired engineering consultant; b. Bristow, Okla., Aug. 25, 1928; s. Harold Martin and Ella A. (Rountree) C.; m. Charlotte Marie Fisher, Aug. 16, 1953 (dec. June 1990); m. Mary J. Armer, May 28, 1994; children: James Harold, David Charles, Gregory Lee, Matthew Louis. BS in Petroleum Engring., U. Okla., 1949, postgrad., 1949—51, U. Tulsa, 1955—68. Registered profl. engr. 8 states; cert. of qualification Nat. Coun. Engring. Examiners. Assoc. engr. Tidewater Oil Co., Midland, Tex., 1951-52, reservoir engr. Houston, 1952-55, divsn. reservoir engr. Tulsa, 1955—59; pvt. practice cons. engr., 1959-63; sr. engr. Fenix & Scisson Inc., Tulsa, 1963-69; pres. Cobbs Engring., Inc., cons. engrs., Tulsa, 1969—2011. Faculty U. Wis. Ext. Contbr. articles to profl. jours.; patentee in field. Various positions including scoutmaster Indian Nations coun. Boy Scouts Am., 1962-81; instr. first aid ARC, 1969-81; active Vols. in Tech. Assistance, 1978-. Mem. NSPE, Am. Underground Constrn. Assn., Petroleum Engrs., Nat. Acad. Forensic Engrs., World Rock Boring Assn., Okla. Soc. Profl. Engrs. Republican. Mem. Christian Ch. (elder, chmn. bd. elders 1971, 79). Personal E-mail: james_cobbs@yahoo.com, cobbseng@sbcglobal.net.

COBLE, JOHN HOWARD, United States Representative from North Carolina, lawyer; b. Greensboro, NC, Mar. 18, 1931; s. Joseph Howard and Johnnie (Holt) Coble Student, Appalachian State U., Boone, NC, 1949-50; BA in Hist., Guilford Coll., Greensboro, NC, 1958; JD, U. NC Sch. Law, Chapel Hill, 1962. Bar: NC 1966. Field claim rep., supt. State Farm Mut. Automobile Ins. Co., 1961-67; asst. county atty. Guilford County, NC, 1967-69; asst. US atty. Mid. Dist. NC, 1969—73; mem. NC Ho. Reps., 1969, 1979—84; sec. NC Dept. Revenue, 1973—77; atty. Turner, Enochs & Sparrow, Greensboro, NC, 1979—83; mem. US Congress from 6th NC dist., 1985—, mem. transp. and infrastructure com., mem. judiciary com., ranking mem. cts. the Internet and intellectual property subcommittee. Served to capt. USCG, 1952-56, commdg. officer USCGR. Mem. NC Bar Assn., Greensboro Bar Assn., Masons (33 degree; master Mason), Am. Legion, VFW, Lions, SAR. Republican. Presbyterian. Office: US House of Representatives 2188 Rayburn House Office Bldg Washington DC 20515 Office Phone: 202-225-3065. Office Fax: 202-225-8611.*

COBOS, EVERARDO, hematologist, educator; BS, U. Tex., El Paso, 1977; MD, U. Tex., San Antonio, 1981. Diplomate Am. Bd. Internal Medicine, 1985, Am. Bd. Internal Medicine-med. oncology, 1987, Am. Bd. Internal Medicine-hematology, 1988, lic. Tex., 1988. Resident internal medicine Letterman Army Med. Ctr., San Francisco, 1983—85, fellow hematology and oncology, 1985—88; prof. medicine Tex. Tech Univ., assoc. dean for oncology programs, divsn. chief oncology/hematology; hosp. affiliation includes Univ. Med. Ctr. Author: (publs.) Plasma Cell Granuloma: A Case Report of Multiple Lesions in the Lung and Review of the Literature, 2007, Acquired Hemophilia: A Case Report of 2 Patients with Acquired Factor VIII Inhibitor Treated with Rituximab Plus a Short Course of Steroid and Review of the Literature, 2007, Biological Treatment for Liver Tumor and New Potential Biomarkers, 2007, The Role of Radiofrequency Ablation in Multiple Liver Metastases to Debulk the Tumor: A Pilot Study Before Alternative Therapies, 2007, Advances in Immunotherapy of Multiple Myeloma: From the Discovery of Tumor-associated Antigens to Clinical Trials, 2007, and numerous others. Office: Southwest Cancer and Research Center 602 Indiana Ave Lubbock TX 79430 Office Phone: 806-775-8600. E-mail: everardo.cobos@ttuhsc.edu.

COBURN, TOM (THOMAS ALLEN COBURN), United States Senator from Oklahoma; b. Casper, Wyo., Mar. 14, 1948; m. Carolyn Denton; 3 children. BS in Acctg., Okla. State U., 1970; MD, U. Okla., 1983. Mfg. mgr. ophthalmic divsn. Coburn Optical Industries, 1970-78; resident surgery St. Anthony's Hosp., 1983-84; resident in family practice U. Ark. Area Health & Edn. Ctr., 1984-86; pvt. practice family physician, obstetrician, 1986—94; mem. US Congress from 2nd Okla. Dist., 1995-2001; US Senator from Okla., 2005—; mem. US Senate Judiciary Com., 2005—. Bd. dirs Optical Mfrs. Assn., 1973—74, Better Vision Inst., 1976—77, Saxon Publishing Co., Norman, Okla., Family Rsch. Coun.; co-chmn. President's Advisory Coun. on HIV/AIDS, 2001—. Author (with John Hart): Breach of Trust: How Washington Turns Outsiders Into Insiders, 2003. Recipient Spl. Legislative award, Okla. Psychol. Assn., 1999; named one of The 50 Most Powerful People in DC, GQ mag., 2009, The 100 Most Influential People in the World, TIME mag., 2013. Mem.: AMA, Pan American Allergy Soc., Southern Med. Assn., East Ctrl. County Med. Soc., Ark. Med. Soc., Okla. Med. Assn., American Acad. Otolaryngic Allergy, American Acad. Family Practice. Republican. Baptist. Office: US Senate 172 Russell Senate Office Building Washington DC 20510 Home: 1800 S Baltimore Ave Tulsa OK 74119-5216 Office Phone: 202-224-5754, 918-581-7651. Office Fax: 202-224-6008, 918-581-7195.*

COCANOUGHER, ARTHUR BENTON, retired academic administrator; b. Lubbock, Tex., July 6, 1938; s. Arthur Clifton and Bonnie Odell (Ford) C.; m. Dianne Esther Reisenauer, May 27, 1967; children: Carolyn, David. Mgr. Gen. Electric Co., NYC, 1962-67; asst. prof. U. So. Calif., Los Angeles, 1970-72; assoc. prof. So. Meth. U., Dallas, 1972-73; prof. mktg. U. Houston, 1973-75, chmn. dept., 1975-76, dean Coll. Bus., 1976-85, sr. v.p., provost, 1985-87; dean Tex. A&M U. Coll. Bus., College Station, 1987-2001, emeritus, disting. prof., 2001—; interim chancellor Texas A&M U. System, 2003—04. Trustee fixed income mutual funds Legg Mason Ptnrs.; cons. in field. Contbr. articles to profl. jours. Bd. dirs. Better Bus. Bur., Houston, 1979-87, West Houston Assn., 1984-87. Served to 1st lt. U.S. Army, 1960-62. Recipient Nicholas Salgo award So. Meth. U., 1973, Outstanding Service award U. Houston Alumni Assn., 1982, Disting. Alumnus award Coll. Bus. U. Tex.-Austin, 1981. Mem. Am. Mktg. Assn., Acad. Mktg. Sci. Home: 4409 Nottingham Ln Bryan TX 77802-5904 Office: Tex A&M U Coll Bus Coll Bus 4112 Tamu College Station TX 77843-4112

COCHRAN, GEORGE MOFFETT, retired judge; b. Staunton, Va., Apr. 20, 1912; s. Peyton and Susie (Robertson) C.; m. Marion Lee Stuart, May 1, 1948; children— George Moffett, Harry Carter Stuart. BA, U. Va., 1934, LLB, 1936; LLD (hon.), James Madison U., 1991. Bar: Va. 1935, Md. 1936. Asso. law firm, Balt., 1936-38; partner firm Peyton Cochran and George M. Cochran, Staunton, 1938-64, Cochran, Lotz & Black, Staunton, 1964-69; justice Supreme Ct., Richmond, Va., 1969-87. Pres. Planters Bank & Trust Co., Staunton, 1963-69 Chmn. Woodrow Wilson Centennial Commn. Va., 1952-58, Va. Cultural Devel. Study Commn., 1966-68, Frontier Culture Mus. Va., 1986-98; mem. Va. Commn. Constl. Revisi on, 1968-69, Jud. Coun. Va., 1963-69, Va. Ho. Dels., 1948-66, Va. Senate, 1966-68; chmn. bd. dirs. Stuart Hall, 1971-86; mem. bd. visitors Va. Poly. Inst., 1960-68; trustee Mary Baldwin Coll., 1967-81, U. Va. Law Sch. Found., 1975-89, Woodrow Wilson Birthplace Found., 1955-93, to Lt. comdr. USNR, 1942-46. Recipient Algernon Sydney Sullivan award Mary Baldwin Coll., 1981. Mem. ABA, Va. Bar Assn. (pres. 1965-66), Raven Soc., Soc. of Cin., Phi Beta Kappa, Phi Delta Phi, Beta Theta Pi. Episcopalian. Home and Office: 24 Ridgewood Dr Staunton VA 24401-2424

COCHRAN, JOHN EUELL, JR., aerospace engineer, lawyer, educator; b. Dawson, Ala., May 22, 1944; s. John Euell and Beatrice Ann (Raley) Cochran; m. Gladys Carol Holdbrooks, Dec. 26, 1965; children: Christopher, Jonathan. BAE., Auburn U., 1966, MS, 1967; PhD, U. Tex.-Austin, 1970; JD, Jones Law Sch., 1976. Registered profl. engr., Ala.; bar: Ala. 1977. Asst. prof. aerospace engring. Auburn (Ala.) U., 1970-75, assoc. prof., 1975-78, alumni assoc. prof., 1978-80, alumni prof., 1980-81, prof., 1981—, assoc. athletic dir., 1981-84, interim head aerospace engring., 1992-93, head aerospace engring., 1993—2013, expert witness engring. patents, prof. emeritus, 2013—. Cons. Northrup Svcs., Huntsville, Ala., 1970—71, U.S. Army Missile Command, Redstone Arsenal, Ala., 1975—82, SRS Tech., Huntsville, 1984—89, Dept. Justice, 1996—97, Boeing Co., 1998, others; pres. Eaglemark, Inc.; legal cons. Sigmatech, Inc. Assoc. editor: Jour. Guidance Control and Dynamics, 1989—91; contbr. articles to profl. jours. Recipient Walter Gilbert award, 2012; Tau Beta Pi fellow, 1965, Nat. Coll. Athletic Assn. fellow, 1965, NSF fellow, 1968. Fellow: AIAA, Am. Astronautical Soc.; mem.: NSPE, ABA, Auburn United Meth. Ch. (pres. 2007—08), Ala. Soc. Profl. Engrs. (v.p. Auburn chpt. 1985, pres. 1986, Young Engr. of the Yr. 1980), Am. Helicopter Soc., Auburn Rotary Club, U. Club (pres. 2006—08). Methodist. Achievements include analysis, simulation and reconstruction of aircraft accidents; research in areas of dynamics and control, orbital mechanics, spacecraft attitude dynamics and control; stability and control of aircraft including towed vehicles; missile launcher dynamics; simulation using hardware-in-the-loop (HWIL); simulation of aerospace and transportation systems; short courses/seminars on engineering topics and engineering law and ethics. Home: 1887 Prim Dr Auburn AL 36830-7545 Office: Auburn U 211 Davis Hall Auburn AL 36849 Business E-Mail: cochrjo@auburn.edu.

COCHRAN, KELVIN JAMES, fire chief, former federal agency administrator; b. 1960; m. Carolyn Marshall Cochran; 3 children. B in Orgnl. Mgmt., Wiley Coll., 1999; M in Indsl./Orgnl. Psychology, La. Tech U., Ruston, 2004. Firefighter Shreveport Fire Dept., La., 1981—85, fire tng. officer, 1985—90, asst. chief tng. officer, 1990—99, fire chief, 1999—2008, City of Atlanta Dept. Fire Rescue, 2008—09, 2010—; adminstr. US Fire Adminstrn. Fed. Emergency Mgmt. Agy. (FEMA), US Dept. Homeland Security, Washington, 2009—10. Bd. dirs. Salvation Army, Boy Scouts of America, Vols. of America, Rotary Internat. Mem.: Internat. Assn. Fire Chiefs (IAFC) (2nd v.p. 2006, 1st v.p. 2007). Office: Atlanta Dept Fire Rescue 226 Peachtree St SW Atlanta GA 30303 Office Phone: 404-546-7000. Office Fax: 404-546-7245. E-mail: kjcochran@atlantaga.gov.

COCHRAN, SANDRA BROPHY, restaurant chain company executive; b. Columbus, Ga., Aug. 25, 1958; d. Jeremiah J. and Jane G. Brophy; m. Donald Q. Cochran, May 25, 1991; children: Katherine Jane, Donald Quinton III. BSChemE, Vanderbilt U., Nashville, 1980; MBA, Pacific Luth. U., Tacoma, Wash., 1985. V.p. Sun Trust Banks, Atlanta, 1985-92; v.p., asst. sec. Books-A-Million, Inc., Birmingham, Ala., 1992—93, CFO, 1993—96, exec. v.p., CFO, 1996—99, pres., 1999—2004, pres., CEO, 2004—09; exec. v.p., CFO Cracker Barrel Old Country Store, Inc., Lebanon, Tenn., 2009—10, pres., COO, 2010—11, pres., CEO, 2011—. Bd. dirs. Books-A-Million, Inc., 2006—09, Cracker Barrel Old Country Store, Inc., 2011—, Dollar General Corp., 2012—. Capt. 9th Inf. Divsn. US Army, 1980—85. Office: Cracker Barrel Old Country Store Inc 305 Hartmann Dr Lebanon TN 37087 Office Phone: 615-443-5533. Office Fax: 615-443-9818.

COCHRAN, THAD (WILLIAM THAD COCHRAN), United States Senator from Mississippi; b. Pontotoc, Miss., Dec. 7, 1937; s. William Holmes and Emma Grace (Berry) Cochran; m. Rose Clayton, June 6, 1964; children: Thaddeus Clayton, Katherine Holmes. BA in Psychology, U. Miss., 1959, JD cum laude, 1965. Bar: Miss. 1965. Atty., Jackson, Miss., 1965-72; assoc. Watkins & Eager, 1965-72; mem. US Congress from 4th Miss. Dist., 1973—78; US Senator from Miss., 1978—; chmn. US Senate Agrl. Com., 2003—05, ranking mem., 2013—; chmn. US Senate Appropriations Com., 2005—07; vice chmn. US Senate Republican Conf., 1985—91, chmn., 1991—97. Served as lt. USNR, 1959—61. Recipient Congressional Leadership award, Airports Coun. Internat. North America, 2004, Conservation Achievement award, Nat. Wildlife Fedn.; named Outstanding Young Man of Jackson, 1971, Conservationist of Yr., Dicks Unlimited, 1994; named one of Three Outstanding Young Men of Miss., 1971. Mem.: ABA, Miss. Bar Assn. (pres. young lawyers sect. 1972—73), Rotary, Pi Kappa Alpha, Phi Kappa Phi, Omicron Delta Kappa. Republican. Baptist. Office: US Senate 113 Dirksen Senate Office Building Washington DC 20510-0001 also: District Office Ste 614 188 East Capitol St Jackson MS 39201-2137 Office Phone: 202-224-5054, 601-965-4459. Office Fax: 202-224-9450, 601-965-4919. E-mail: senator@cochran.senate.gov.*

COCHRANE, BETSY LANE, former state senator; b. Asheboro, NC; d. William Jennings and Bobbie (Campbell) Lane; m. Joe Kenneth Cochrane, 1958; children: Lisa, Craig. BA cum laude, Meredith Coll., Raleigh, 1958. Tchr. Winston-Salem Sch. Sys., NC, Highland Presbyn. Ch. Sch.; mem. NC Ho. of Reps., Raleigh, 1980-88, house minority leader, 1985-88; mem. NC Senate, 1988—2000, chmn. Commn. on Aging, 1989-99, vice chmn. higher edn. com., 1991-92, senate minority whip, 1993-94, senate minority leader, 1995-96, vice chmn. senate appropriations, 1995—2000, vice chmn. senate commerce commn., 1995—2000, ranking minority mem. senate agr., 1995—2000; bd. advisors BRCC, 2012—14. Mem. comm. on Future of South, 1985—86, Nat. Rep. Platform Com., Joint Legis. Ethics Com., 1989—2000, chmn., 1989—90; mem. NC Parks Commn., 1989—96, Retail Mchts. Adv. Bd., 1989—2000, Govtl. Ops., 1989—97, Gov.'s Advocacy Coun. on Children and Youth, 1990—2000, Select Com. on Redistricting, 1991, 1992, 1994, Revenue Law, 1992—2000, Order of LongLeaf Pine, 1992, Environ. Rev. Com., 1997—2000, Utility Rev. Com., 1997—2000, Gov.'s Blue Ribbon Task Force Environ. Indicators, 1989—91; spkr. in field. Trustee Davie County Hosp.; bd. advisors Z. Smith Reynolds Found., 1996—99, Meredith Coll., chmn. pres.'s adv. coun., 1999—2001, govs. adv. budget com., 1989—93, pub. sch. forum, 1985—99, mem. Meredith Challenge Bd., 2005—, year book editor, 1958—, mem. student govt., 1955—58; mem. Davie County Schs. Task Force on Facilities, 2001—02, So. Regional Edn. Bd., 1987—2001, Meredith May Ct., 1957, 1958, Stephen's Ministry, 2008—; chmn. NC Kids

Voting Davie Co., 2008; bd. mem. Garden Club Chaplin, 2008—10, v.p., 2010—13; with United Daughters of Confederacy, 2010—; del. GOP Nat. Conv., 1976, 1988, 1992, 1996; trustee CUMC, 2006—12, trustee sec., 2007—; mem. Bible Study Fellowship, discussion leader, 2003—09; mem. Faith Works Task Force, 2005—, chaplin, v.p., 2010—; gov. candidate NC Lt. Gov., 2000; bd. dir. Davie County Sch. Mebane Challenge, 2004—07, Forks Yadkin Mus., 2002—, vice chmn., 2004—. Recipient Woman in Govt. award, NC Jaycees, 1985, Myers-Honeycutt award for excellence in pub. svc., 1996, Dr. Ewald W. Busse award, Aging Advocates of N.C., 1997, Women Achievement award, FWC NC, 2002, Trail Blazer award, 2013; named Disting. Citizen of Yr., NC Libr. Dirs., 1991, Legislator of Yr., NC Divsn. Aging, 1991, NC Assn. for Home Care, 1992, NC Health Facilities Assn., 1993, NC Wildlife Fedn., 1995, Autism Found., 1995, Disting. Alumnae of the Yr., Meredith Coll., 1996; named one of 10 Outstanding Legislators in Nation, 1987, 100 Outstanding Graduates, Meredith Coll.; named to NC GOP Hall of Fame, 2001, GOP Hall of Fame, Davie County, 2003. Mem.: United Daughters Confederacy, Kappa Nu Sigma, Garden Club (chaplin 2008—10, v.p. 2010—13), Bermuda Run Adv. Bd. (sec. 2012), Seekers Book Club, Stephen Ministry. Baptist. Home and Office: 331 Orchard Pk Dr Advance NC 27006-9582 Personal E-mail: betsycochrane@triad.rr.com. Business E-Mail: betsyc@ncleg.net.

COCHRANE, EUGENE W., JR., foundation administrator; BA in History, Erskine Coll., 1970; MA in Econ. and Bus. Admin., Appalachian State U., 1972. Residency Charlotte Memorial Hospital; former hospital administrator; admin., hospital div. Duke Endowment, 1980—91, dir. health care div., 1991—96, v.p., dir. health care div., 1996—2003, exec. v.p., dir. health care div., 2003—05, pres., 2005—. Bd. dirs. Southeastern Council of Found., Grantmakers in Health; mem. N.C. Inst. of Medicine, N.C. Med. Care Commn.; adv. bd. mem. Kate B. Reynolds Health Trust. Bd. of visitors Davidson Coll. Fellow: Am. Coll. of Healthcare Executives. Office: Duke Endowment 100 N Tryon St Ste 3500 Charlotte NC 28202*

COCHRANE, ROBERT LOWE, biologist; b. Morgantown, W.Va., Feb. 10, 1931; s. Thomas Joseph and Isabelle Durston (Lowe) C. BA, W.Va. U., 1953; MS, U. Wis., 1954, PhD, 1961. Rsch. asst. genetics U. Wis., Madison, 1953—55, rsch. asst. zoology, 1957—60; with Fur Animal Exptl. Sta., Petersburg, Alaska, 1955; agt. in animal husbandry USDA, Madison, Wis., 1955—61; biologist FDA, Washington, 1961—62; sr. research fellow dept. anatomy U. Birmingham (Eng.), 1962—65; project assoc. dept. physiology U. Pitts., 1965—66; sr. endocrinologist Eli Lilly & Co., Indpls., 1966—80; rsch. assoc. G.D. Searle & Co., Skokie, Ill., 1980—81; with Short's Fur Farm, Granton, Wis., 1981—83; rsch. assoc. Marshfield (Wis.) Med. Found., 1983—84; biologist Northwood Fur Farms, Inc., Cary, Ill., 1984. Participant Internat. Mink Show, Wis., 1976—2006, W.Va. Fox Show, Morgantown, 1989; FAO cons. Wildlife Inst. India, Dehra Dun, 1985; adj prof. divsn. animal and vet. sci. W.Va. U., Morgantown, 1987—; ad hoc reviewer competitive rsch. grants U.S. Dept. Agr. Ad hoc reviewer (various sci. jours.). Recipient Knight of Golden Horse Shoe award W.Va. Pub. Sch. System, 1945, W.Va. Boy's State, 1948; U. Birmingham (Eng.) sr. rsch. fellow, 1962-65. Mem. AAAS, Am. Inst. Biol. Scis., Soc. Exptl. Biology and Medicine, Soc. Reprodn. and Fertility, Soc. Study Reprodn., Am. Soc. Animal Sci., Endocrine Soc., N.Y. Acad. Sci., Soc. Endocrinology, Coun. Agrl. Sci. and Tech., Internat. Platform Assn., NRA (life), Sigma Xi, Pi Kappa Alpha, Gamma Sigma Delta. Presbyterian. Achievements include discovery of the ovarian hormonal requirements for ova-implantation and embryonic diapause in the rat, the elucidation of the role played by prostaglandins in corpus luteum function, parturition and ductus arteriosus closure in the rat; discovery of timing, duration and pattern of reproductive cycles in martens; development of steroid synthesis inhibitors for controlling reproduction in mammals; rsch. in the successful raising of ruffed grouse in captivity, dissemination of scientific information on fur farming and raising ruffed grouse to the commercial trade and public. Home: 404 Junior Ave Morgantown WV 26505-2208 Office Phone: 304-293-1966. Business E-Mail: rcochra2@wvu.edu.

COCKE, WILLIAM MARVIN, JR., plastic surgeon, educator; b. Balt., Aug. 2, 1934; s. William M. and Clara E. (Bosley) C.; m. Sue Ann Harris, Apr. 25, 1981; children: Gregory William, Laura Marie, Julie Ann; children by previous marriage: William Marvin III, Catherine Lynn, Deborah Kay, Brian Thomas. BS with honors in Biology, Tex. A&M U., 1956; MD, Baylor U., 1960. Diplomate: Am. Bd. Plastic Surgery (guest examiner 1978). Intern surgery Vanderbilt U. Hosp., Nashville, 1960-61; fellow gen. surgery Ochsner Clinic and Found. Hosp., New Orleans, 1961-64; chief resident surgery Monroe (La.) Charity Hosp., 1963-64; resident reconstructive surgery Roswell Park Meml. Inst., Buffalo, 1965-66; chief resident plastic surgery VA Hosp., Bronx, NY, 1966; practice medicine specializing in plastic surgery Nashville, 1968-75, Sacramento, 1976-79; pvt. practice medicine specializing in plastic surgery Bryan, Tex., 1980-92; prof. surgery, head div. plastic/reconstructive surgery Marshall U. Sch. of Medicine, Huntington, W.Va., 1992—. Mem. staff Cabell-Huntington Hosp., Huntington Vets. Med. Ctr.; asst. prof. plastic surgery Vanderbilt U. Sch. Medicine, Nashville, 1968-69, asst. clin. prof. plastic surgery, 1969-75; assoc. prof. plastic surgery Ind. U. Sch. Medicine, Indpls., 1975-76; chief plastic surgery service Wishard Meml. Hosp., Ind. U., 1975-76; assoc. prof. surgery U. Calif. Sch. Medicine, Davis, 1976-79, chmn. dept. plastic surgery, 1976-79; prof. surgery, chief div. plastic surgery Tex. Tech. U. Sch. Medicine, Lubbock, 1979-80, dir. Microsurg. Research Lab., 1979-80; clin. prof. surgery Tex. A&M U. Sch. Medicine, 1983-92; prof. plastic surgery, 1986-89; chief plastic surgery svc., dept. surgery, Olin Teague VA Med. Ctr., Temple, Tex., 1986-92; prof. Marshall U. Sch. Medicine, 1992—. Author textbooks on plastic surgery; contbr. articles to profl. jours. Served with M.C. USAF, 1966-68. Recipient Dean Echols award Ochsner Hosp. Found., 1963 Mem. ACS, Am. Assn. Plastic Surgeons, Soc. Head and Neck Surgeons, Assn. Acad. Surgery, Alton Ochsner Surg. Soc., Alpha Omega Alpha. Episcopalian. Home: 45 Olde Farm Rd Ona WV 25545-9747 Office: VA Med Ctr 1540 Spriing Valley Road Huntington WV 25704

COCKERHAM, ANGELA, state legislator; b. Jackson, Miss., Aug. 20; Atty.; mem. Dist. 96 Miss. House of Reps., 2005—, vice chair judiciary A com. Mem.: Miss. & La. Bar Asns, Alpha Kappa Alpha. Democrat. Baptist. Home: 2518 Pilgrim Rest Rd Magnolia MS 39652 Home Phone: 601-783-4979; Office Phone: 601-783-6600. Business E-Mail: acockerham@house.ms.gov.

COCKERHAM, SIDNEY JOE, professional society administrator; b. Waxahachie, Tex., Aug. 17, 1951; s. Sidney Julius and Joan (Barlow) C. BS in Biology, U. Tex., Arlington, 1973. Cert. tchr., Tex. Tchr. Tex. Pub. Schs., Waxahachie, 1973-77; dir., founder U.S. Nat. Tennis Acad., Dallas, 1982—. Lt. USN, 1977-82. Avocation: tennis. Home and Office: 3523 McKinney Ave # 208 Dallas TX 75204 Office Phone: 903-654-6387. E-mail: sjcntx_sohw@yahoo.com.

COCKLIN, KIM ROLAND, gas industry executive, lawyer; b. Massillon, Ohio, Apr. 13, 1951; s. Roland and Jacqueline Lou (Cope) C.; m. Crystal Elaine Chandler; children: Ross, Toben, Brooke. BS, Wichita State U., 1973, M in Adminstrn. Justice, 1975; JD, Washburn U., 1981. Bar: Colo. 1981, D.C. 1984, U.S. Appeals Ct. (5th, 8th and 10th cirs.) 1984. Instr. Wichita (Kans.) State U., 1974-81; atty. Colo. Interstate Gas Co., Colorado Springs, 1981-84, Tex. Gas Transmission Corp., Owensboro, Ky., 1984-85, gen. counsel, 1985-87, v.p., gen. counsel, 1987-89, sr. v.p., gen. counsel, 1989; sr. v.p. Planning, Rates and Regulatory, and Bus. Devel. Williams Gas Pipeline, Owensboro, Ky.; sr. v.p., gen. counsel, chief compliance officer Piedmont Natural Gas, Charlotte, NC, 2003—06; pres., COO Atmos Energy Corp., 2006—08, bd. dirs., 2009—, pres., CEO, 2010—. Bd. dirs. Big Brothers and Big Sisters of Greater Charlotte. Mem. ABA, Fed. Energy Bar Assn., Colo. Bar Assn., Ky. Bar Assn., D.C. Bar Assn., Daviess Bar Assn., Am. Gas Assn. (legal com.), Phi Kappa Phi. Avocations: fishing, golf. Mailing: Atmos Energy Corp PO Box 650205 Dallas TX 75265-0205

COCKWELL, IAN G., real estate company executive; B in commerce with honours. chartered acct. Investor and exec. in the real estate industry; joined Brookfield Homes Corp., 1994, various sr. exec. positions, 1994—2002, pres., CEO, bd. dirs., 2002—; sr. exec. Brookfield Residential Group, 1994—2002; vice chmn., pres. Brookfield Properties Corp., chmn., CEO, 1998—2002; residential chmn., pres., CEO, sr. mng. dir., bd. dirs. Brookfield Asset Mgmt. Inc.; chmn. Brookfield Mgmt. Svcs. Ltd. Former bd. dirs. Norbord Inc., Falconbridge Ltd.; bd. dirs. Wilmington Capital Mgmt., Inc., 1988—, chmn.; bd. dirs. Carma Corp.; bd. dirs Lincorp Holdings, Inc., 1994—; bd. dirs. Parkbridge Lifestyle Cmtys., Inc., 2004—, chmn. Office: Brookfield Homes Corp 8500 Executive Park Ave Ste 300 Fairfax VA 22031 Office Phone: 703-270-1700. Business E-Mail: icockwell@brookfieldhomes.com.

CODINA, ARMANDO M., board member; b. Cuba; US, 1960; m. Margarita Codina; children: Ana, Ali, Andri, Amanda. Attended, Jacksonville U. Clk Am. Nat. Bank; bank officer Republic Bank, Miami, Fla.; founder, pres. Profl. Automated Svcs., Inc., 1970—78; founder, chmn. & CEO Codina Group (formerly InterAmerica Investments Inc.), Coral Gables, Fla., 1979—2006; CEO, pres. Flagler Devel. Group, 2006—08, chmn., 2008. Bd. dirs. BellSouth Corp., 1989—2006, GM Corp., 2002—09, Merrill Lynch & Co., Inc., 2005—09, Burger King Holdings, Inc., 2005—07; former bd. dirs. Fla. East Coast Industries, Inc., 2006—07; bd. dirs. AMR Corp., 1995—, The Home Depot, Inc, 2007—. Home: 2855 S Le Jeune Rd Miami FL 33134-6612 Office: Home Depot Inc Bd Directors 2455 Paces Ferry Rd NW Atlanta GA 30339-4024 Office Phone: 770-433-8211. Office Fax: 770-384-2356. Business E-Mail: armando_codina@homedepot.com.

CODNER, MARK ALLEN, plastic surgeon; b. Atlanta, Oct. 9, 1961; BA summa cum laude, Emory U., 1982; MD, Emory Sch. Medicine, 1987. Cert. Am. Bd. Surgery, 1993, Am. Bd. Plastic Surgery, 1997. Resident in gen. surgery NY Hosp.-Cornell Med. Ctr. and Meml. Sloan-Kettering Cancer Ctr., 1987—92; resident in plastic surgery Emory U., 1992—94; fellow in oculoplastic surgery Southeastern Oculoplastic Ctr., Atlanta, 1994—95; fellow in aesthetic surgery Baker, Gordon & Stuzin Plastic Surgers Assocs., Miami, 1995; pvt. practice Paces Plastic Surgery, Atlanta, fellowship dir., 1994—; asst. clin. prof. plastic surgery Emory U. Co-chmn. Atlanta Breast Surgery Symposium, 1998—2004, chmn., 2005; assoc. editor Plastic and Reconstructive Surgery, 2001—08; chmn. Atlanta Oculoplastic Surgery Symposium, 2008. Recipient Best Presentation award, Royal Can. Soc. Plastic Surgery, 2003, Pathways to Leadership award, 2006. Fellow: Am. Coll. Surgeons; mem.: AMA, Am. Fedn. Clin. Rsch., Ga. Med. Assn., Southeastern Soc. Plastic and Reconstructive Surgeons (Best Paper 1995, 1996), Am. Soc. Aesthetic Plastic Surgery (Best Journal article 1997, Sherrel Aston award 2001, 2006), Am. Soc. Plastic and Reconstructive Surgeons, Am. Assn. Plastic Surgeons, John Gordon Stipe Soc. Scholars, Sigma Xi, Phi Beta Kappa, Alpha Omega Alpha. Office: Paces Plastic Surgery Ste 640 1411 Grayson Pt Buckhead GA 30625-2237 Office Phone: 404-351-0051. Office Fax: 404-351-0632.

CODY, RICHARD ARTHUR, communications executive, retired military officer; b. Montpelier, Vt., Aug. 20, 1950; m. Vicki Lyn Cody; children: Clint, Tyler. BS, US Mil. Acad., 1972. Master army aviator. Commd. 2d lt. U.S. Army, 1972, advanced through grades to gen., 2004, ret., 2008; comdr. 1st bn., 101st aviation regt. 101st Airborne Divsn., Operation Desert Storm; bn. exec. officer, co. comdr. Attack Helicopter Bns.; asst. divsn. comdr. for maneuver 4th Inf. Divsn. (Mechanized), Ft. Hood, Tex., 1998—2000; comdr. 101st Airborne Divsn., Ft. Campbell, Ky., 2000—02; dep. chief of staff, G-3 US Army, Washington, 2002—04, vice chief of staff, 2004—08; sr. v.p. Washington ops. L-3 Communications Inc., 2008—. Decorated Disting. Svc. medal, Legion of Merit with 4 oak leaf clusters, DFC, Bronze Star medal, Meritorious Svc. medal with 4 oak leaf clusters, Air medal, Army Commendation medal with 2 oak leaf clusters, Army Achievement medal, Southwest Asia Svc. medal, Humanitarian Svc. medal, NATO medal, Southwest Asia Kuwait Liberation medal Avocation: golf.

CODY, THOMAS GERALD, retired retail executive, lawyer; b. NYC, Nov. 4, 1941; s. Thomas J. Cody and Esther Mary Courtney; m. Mary Ellen Palmer, Nov. 26, 1966; children: Thomas Jr., Mark, Amy, Anne. BA in Philosophy, Maryknoll Coll., 1963; JD, St. John's U., 1967; LLD (hon.), Cen. State U., Wilberforce, Ohio, 1985. Bar: N.Y. 1967. Assoc. Simpson Thacher & Bartlett, LLP, N.Y., 1967-72; asst. prof. law sch. St. John's U., N.Y., 1972-76; sr. v.p., gen. counsel, sec. Pan Am. Airways, N.Y., 1976-82; sr. v.p. law and pub. affairs Macy's, Inc. (formerly Federated Dept. Stores Inc.), Cin., 1982-88, exec. v.p. legal & human resources, 1988—2003, vice chmn. legal, human resources and external affairs, 2003—10. Trustee Xavier U., Cin., Children's Hosp. Med. Ctr., Cin; bd. dirs. Cin. USA Regional Chamber Mem. ABA, Bankers Club, Queen City Club, Hyde Park Country Club, Commonwealth Club of Cin. Roman Catholic.

CODY, WILLIAM BERMOND, political science professor; b. Brunswick, Ga., Jan. 15, 1949; s. Bermond Hamp and Dorothy Jane (Satterfield) C.; m. Mildred Ann McInnis, Sept. 5, 1970; children: Margaret Jae, Elizabeth Joelle. AB, U. Ga., 1971, MA, 1973, JD, 1986; PhD, New Sch. Social Rsch., 1980. Bar: Ga. 1986. Student advisor New Sch. Social Rsch., NYC, 1978-79; asst. to pres. Robeal Mgmt. Co., Charleston, SC, 1983-85; assoc. Carr, Tabb & Pope, Atlanta, 1987; legal asst. Ga. Ct. Appeals, Atlanta, 1987-89; asst. prof. polit. sci. U. Ga., Athens, 1989-90; asst. prof. Oxford (Ga.) Coll. Emory U., 1990-93; assoc. prof. Oxford (Ga.) Coll. Emory U., 1993—2009; prof. Oxford Coll. Emory U., 2009—. Adj. instr. Coll. New Rochelle, N.Y., 1978-79; vis. asst. prof. Clemson (S.C.) U., 1980-83; mem. Emory U. Senate, 1995-97, pres.-elect, 1996-97, pres., 1997-98. Vestryman St. Bede's Episcopal Ch., Atlanta, 1988-92, jr. warden, 1990, sr. warden, 1991; bd. dirs. Interfaith, Inc., Atlanta, 1989-90. Mem. ABA, Am. Polit. Sci. Assn., Ga. Polit. Sci. Assn., So. Polit. Sci. Assn., Am. Hist. Assn., Acad. Polit. Sci., Ga. Bar Assn., Am. Assn. U. Profs., Assn. Am. Colls. U. (assoc.). Democrat. Office: Polit Sci Dept Oxford Coll Emory U Oxford GA 30054 E-mail: bcody@emory.edu.

CODY, WILMER ST. CLAIR, educational policy consultant; b. Mobile, Ala., Jan. 1, 1937; s. Wilmer St. Clair and Madeline (Maygarden) C.; m. Caroline Marie Burns, Aug. 16, 1958; children: David Marshall, Alison Marie. AB, Harvard U., 1959, EdM, 1960, EdD, 1968. Tchr. Newton (Mass.) Schs., 1960, Mobile County Schs., 1960-62, prin., 1962-64; dir. tchr. edn. Atlanta Schs., 1966-67; supt. Chapel Hill (N.C.) Schs., 1967-71; sr. rsch. assoc. Nat. Inst. Edn., 1971-73; supt. Birmingham (Ala.) City Schs., 1973-83, Montgomery County Schs., Rockville, Md., 1983-87; dir. nat. assessment project Council Chief State Sch. Officers, 1987-88; supt. edn. State of La., 1988-92; exec. dir. Nat. Edn. Goals Panel, Washington, 1992-93; dir. Nat. Faculty/So. Region, New Orleans, 1993-95; commr. edn. State of Ky., Frankfort, 1995-99; pres. Cody Assocs., Inc., 1999—. Cons. in field; mem. Nat. Assessment Governing Bd., 1998—2002, Smithsonian Nat. Bd., 2005—11, Orleans Pub. Edn. Network, 2000—. Mem. Nat. Adv. Com. on Juvenile Justice and Delinquency Prevention, 1976-78; bd. dirs. Comty. Chest, Campfire Girls; trustee Nat. Coun. Econ. Edn., So. Assn. Colls. and Schs., 1990-92; chmn. Nat. Assessment Edn. Policy Com., 1983-87; dir. S.W. Edn. Devel. Lab., 1988-92; steering com. Edn. Commn. of the States, 1990-92, So. Region Edn. Bd., 1990-92, 96-99; exec. bd. Nat. Coun. for Accreditation of Tchr. Edn., 1990-92, 96-98, chair 1998; pres. Coun. Chief State Officers, 1997-98; pres. Harvard Club La., 2006. Named Educator of Yr. ALA, 1977. Mem.: Am. Assn. Sch. Adminstrs. Methodist. Home: 1535 Eleonore St New Orleans LA 70115-4242 Business E-Mail: wscody@bellsouth.net.

COE, DOUG, religious organization administrator; b. 1930; m. Janice Coe; 6 children. BS, Williamette U. Asst. to assoc. exec. dir. Internat. Christian Leadership, 1959—65, sr. assoc. exec. dir., 1965—69; head, assoc. dir. Fellowship Found., Inc. (formerly Internat. Christian Leadership), Arlington, Va., 1969—. Mem. planning com. Nat. Student Leadership Forum on Faith and Values. Named one of 25 Most Influential Evangelicals in America, TIME mag., 2005. Office: Fellowship Found 2145 N 24th St Arlington VA 22207 Office Phone: 703-536-6591.

COELHO, ANTHONY LEE, healthcare products and services company executive; b. Los Banos, Calif., June 15, 1942; m. Phyllis Coelho; children: Kristin Coelho, Nicole Coelho. BA in Polit. Sci., Loyola U., LA, 1964. Congl. staff for rep, B. F. Sisk, 1965—78; mem. US House Rep., 1978—89; US congressman Calif., 1979—89; mng. dir. Wertheim Schroder & Co., 1989—95; pres., CEO Wertheim Schroder Investment Svcs., 1990—95; founder, pres. ETC, 1995—97; chmn., president's com. Employment of People with Disabilities, 1994—2001; gen. chmn., to former v.p. Al Gore, 1999—2000. Former bd. dirs. Pinnacle Global Group, Inc., Cyberonics, Inc., Circus, Inc., Cadiz, Inc.; bd. dirs. Svc. Corp. Internat., 1991—. Chmn. Epilepsy Found. Democrat. Roman Catholic. Office: Service Corp International 1929 Allen Pky Houston TX 77019 Office Phone: 713-522-5141. Office Fax: 713-525-5586.

COEYTAUX, REMY RENE, physician, researcher; s. Paul Alfred and Sylvia Nelly Coeytaux; m. Kristen DiMambro Coeytaux, June 30, 1990; children: Alex Arthur, Ethan Arthur. AB, Brown U., Providence, RI, 1986; MD, Stanford U., Calif., 1992—96; PhD, U. N.C., Chapel Hill, 2004. Lic. physician NC Med. Bd., 1999. Asst. prof. family medicine U. N.C. Sch. of Medicine, Chapel Hill, 2001—; founder Integrated Health Ctr., Chapel Hill. Dir. clin. trials program U. N.C. Dept. of Family Medicine, 2003—.

COFER, JAMES ERWIN, SR., academic administrator; s. Erwin Davis and Marjorie Pearl Cofer; m. Deborah Ann Jones, Aug. 22, 1970; children: James E. Jr., Katherine Leigh. BS in Bus. Adminstrn., Miss. State U., Starkville, 1971, MBA, 1975; EdD, U. of Ark., 1998. V.p. fin. and adminstrn. U. Ark. Sys., Little Rock, 1995—98, U. Mo. Sys., Columbia, 1998—2002; pres. U. La., Monroe, 2002—10, Mo. State U., Springfield, 2010—. Mem., bd. of directors St. Francis Med. Ctr., Monroe, La., 2005—, Ouachita Econ. Devel. Corp., Monroe, La., 2002—, Monroe Chamber of Commerce, Monroe, La., 2002—. 2nd lt. USAF, 1971—73. Recipient Eisenhower Exch. fellowship, Eisenhower Found., 1995—96. Office: Missouri State University Carrington Hall, Rm 201 901 S National Ave Springfield MO 65897 Office Phone: 417-836-5000. Office Fax: 318-342-1019, 417-836-7669. Business E-Mail: cofer@ulm.edu. E-mail: president@missouristate.edu.

COFFEY, KENDALL BRINDLEY, lawyer; b. Merced, Calif., Dec. 5, 1952; s. John Brindley and Valerie Althea (Kendall) C.; m. Joni Beth Armstrong, Jan. 28, 1984; 1 child, Meredith Armstrong. BS in Broadcasting, U. Fla., 1975, JD, 1978. Bar: Fla. 1978, U.S. Ct. Appeals (9th and 11th cirs.) 1982. Law clk. U.S. Ct. Appeals (5th cir.), Newnan, Ga., 1978; assoc., bd. dirs. Greenberg, Traurig, Askew, Hoffman, Lipoff, Rosen & Quentel, P.A., Miami, Fla., 1978-88; founding mem. Coffey, Aragon, Martin & Burlington, P.A., Miami, 1988-93, also bd. dirs.; U.S. atty. U.S. Dept. of Justice, Miami, Fla., 1993-96; ptnr. Coffey Burlington PL, 2007—. Lectr. in field. Contbr. articles to profl. jours. Named Outstanding Young Dem. in Fla., Fla. Dem. Women's Clubs, 1975. Mem. Dade County Bar Assn. (pres. 1990-91), U. Fla. Law Rev. Alumni Assn. (pres. 1986-88, Most Productive Young Lawyer in Fla.). Office: Coffey Burlington Office in the Grove Penthouse 2699 S Bayshore Dr Miami FL 33133 Office Phone: 305-858-2900. Business E-Mail: kcoffey@coffeyburlington.com.

COFFEY, THOMAS FRANCIS, JR., retired writer; b. Walthourville, Ga., Feb. 14, 1923; s. Thomas Francis and Julian (Bacon) Coffey; m. Mary Corley, Apr. 6, 1946 (dec. July 1988); 1 child, Mary Cynthia Smith; m. Marjorie Kinsner Guice, Nov. 11, 1989. Student Am. Press Inst., Columbia U., 1964; student program for urban execs., MIT, 1970. Reporter Savannah Eve. Press, Ga., 1940-42, asst. city editor, sports editor, 1945-55, city editor, 1960-64, mng. editor, 1964-67; dir. civilian pub. rels. US Army, Camp Stewart, Ga., 1942; news dir. Sta. WSAV-TV, Savannah, 1955-57; sports editor Savannah Morning News, 1957-60, mng. editor, 1967-69, assoc. editor, 1974-87, editor, 1987-89, columnist, 1989-98; ret., 1998. Commnetator Sta. WJCL-TV, Savannah, 1990—99. Author: Working for God, 1992, Only in Savannah, 1995, Savannah Lore and More, 1997. Bd. dirs. United Way Savannah; asst. city mgr. City of Savannah, 1969—74; lay leader Episc. Ch. With US Army, 1943—45. Decorated Bronze Star, Purple Heart. Mem.: Midway Soc. Ga. (pres. 1985), Nat. Soc. Newspaper Columnists, Nat. Conf. Edit. Writers, Internat. City Mgmt. Assn., Ga. A.P. News Coun., Greater Savannah Hall of Fame Assn. (pres. 1969), Am. Bus. Club (past pres. Savannah chpt.), Am. Legion, SR (pres. Ga.), Sigma Delta Chi. Home: 6401 Habersham St Unit 1B Savannah GA 31405-5632 Office: Savannah News Bldg 1375 Chatham Pkwy Savannah GA 31405

COFFIELD, SHIRLEY ANN, lawyer, educator; b. Portland, Oreg., Mar. 31, 1945; BA, Willamette U., 1967; MA, U. Wisc.-Madison, 1969; JD, George Washington U., 1974. Bar: D.C. 1975. Clk. Stitt, Hemmendinger and Kennedy, Washington, 1973-74; asst. gen. counsel Office U.S. Trade Rep., Washington, 1975-79; ptnr. Reaves & Coffield, Washington, 1979-82; sr. counsel to dep. asst. sect. textiles and apparel U.S. Dept. Commerce, Washington, 1982-85; spl. counsel Skadden, Arps, Slate, Meagher and Flom, Washington, 1985-87; ptnr.

Piper & Marbury, Washington and Balt., 1987-90, Baker & Hostetler, Washington, 1990-94, Keller and Heckman, L.L.P., Washington, 1994-98, Duane, Morris & Heckscher, 1998-2000, Coffield Law, Washington, 2000—. Adj. prof. internat. econ. law Georgetown U. Law Sch., 1982—. Mem. Fed. Bar Assn., Am. Soc. Internat. Law, D.C. Bar, Pi Gamma Mu, Phi Delta Phi. Office: Coffield Law STE 520 445 Clayton Ln Alexandria VA 22304-7157 Office Phone: 202-331-8220. Personal E-mail: coffieldlaw@yahoo.com.

COFFMAN, EDWARD MCKENZIE, retired history professor; b. Hopkinsville, Ky., Jan. 27, 1929; s. Howard Beverly and Mada (Wright) C.; m. Anne Nelson Rouse, June 30, 1955; children: Anne Wright, Lucia Page, Edward McKenzie. AB, U. Ky., 1951, MA, 1955, PhD (So. Faculty fellow), 1959. Army inf. officer, 1951—53; Instr., asst. prof. Memphis State U., 1957-61; research asso. George C. Marshall Research Found., 1960-61; asst. prof., assoc. prof., prof. history U. Wis., Madison, 1961-92, prof. emeritus, 1992—. Dwight D. Eisenhower vis. prof. Kans. State U., 1969-70; vis. prof. mil. history U.S. Mil. Acad., 1977-78; disting. vis. prof. USAF Acad., 1982-83; Harold K. Johnson vis. prof. U.S. Army Mil. History Inst., 1986-87; mem. adv. com. Dept. Army Mil. History Program, 1971-76, 87-89, chair, 1989-93; mem. Nat. Hist. Publs. and Records Commn., 1972-76; John F. Morrison vis. prof. U.S. Army Command and Gen. Staff Coll., 1990-91. Author: The Hilt of the Sword: The Career of Peyton C. March, 1966, The War to End All Wars: The American Military Experience in World War I, 1968, The Old Army: A Portrait of the American Army in Peacetime, 1784-1898, 1986, The Regulars: The American Army, 1898-1941, 2004, The Embattled Past: Reflections on Military History, 2013; adv. com. Arno Press series The American Military Experience and The George C. Marshall Papers; chmn. editl. bd. Jour. Mil. History, 1995-99. Recipient Outstanding Civilian Svc. medal Dept. Army, 1978, Comdr.'s Pub. Svc. award, 1987, Disting. Civilian Svc. medal, 1991; Guggenheim fellow, 1973-74; Harmon Lectr. USAF Acad., 1976; Am. Philos. Soc. grantee, 1960; named U. Ky. Disting. Alumnus, 1995. Mem. Soc. for Mil. History (pres. 1983-85, Samuel Eliot Morison prize 1990, Moncado prize 1995, Disting. Book award, 2005, ABC-CLIO Spencer Tucker award), So. Hist. Soc., Phi Beta Kappa. Democrat. Home: 1089 Lakewood Dr Lexington KY 40502-2523

COFFMAN, JENNIFER BURCHAM, federal judge; b. Union City, Tenn., 1948; BA, U. Ky., 1969, MA, 1971, JD, 1978. Ref. libr. Newport News (Va.) Pub. Libr., 1972-74, U. Ky. Libr., 1974-76; atty. Law Offices Arthur L. Brooks., Lexington, Ky., 1978-82; ptnr. Brooks, Coffman and Fitzpatrick, Lexington, 1982-92, Newberry, Hargrove & Rambicure, Lexington, 1992-93; judge US Dist. Ct. (we. and ea. dist.) Ky., 1993—; chief judge US Dist. Ct. (ea. dist.) Ky., 2007—. Adj. prof. Coll. Law, U. Ky., 1979-81. Bd. dirs. YWCA Lexington, 1986—92, Shepherd Ctr., 2000—05. Mem. Ky. Bar Assn., Fayette County Bar Assn., U. Ky. Law Sch. Alumni Assn. Office: US Dist Ct 101 Barr St Ste 219 Lexington KY 40507-1313 Office Phone: 859-233-2453.

COFFMAN, MICHAEL S., international organization official, ecologist; b. 1943; m. Susan Coffman; children: Jonathan, Tamera. BS in Forestry, No. Ariz. U., 1966, MS in Biology, 1967; PhD in Forest Sci., U. Idaho, Moscow, 1970. Instr., rschr. Mich. Tech. U.; former mgr. Champion Internat. (now Internat. Paper), Stamford, Conn.; founder, pres. Environmental Perspectives, Inc. (EPI), Bangor, Maine, 1992—; exec. dir., CEO Sovereignty Internat. Author: Saviors of the Earth? The Politics and Religion of Environmentalism, 1994; pub.: monthly newsletter Discerning the Times Digest, 1999. Bd. mem. Nazarene Ch. Nazarene. Office: Sovereignty Internat PO Box 191 Hollow Rock TN 38342 also: EPI 6 Heather Rd Bangor ME 04401 Office Phone: 731-986-0099.

COFONI, PAUL MICHAEL, former information technology executive; b. Westerly, RI, Oct. 14, 1948; s. Sylvester James and Sarah Eleanor (Castagna) Cofoni; m. Karen Sue Tapley, May 31, 1970; 2 children. BS in Math., U. R.I., 1970; student in Sr. Exec. Program, MIT, 1989. With General Dynamics, 1974—91; v.p., Tech. Mgmt. Group Eastern Region, pres., Tech. Mgmt. Group Computer Sciences Corp., El Segundo, Calif., 1991—2001, pres., Fed. Sector, 2001—05; pres. U.S. Ops. CACI Internat., Inc., Arlington, Va., 2005—07, pres., CEO, 2007—12, chief advisor to the bd., 2012—. Mem. Am. Inst. of Aeronautics and Astronautics, Profl. Svcs. Coun.; chmn. Am. Heart Assn., 2009—, Armed Forces Comm. & Electronics Assn. With US Army, 1970—74. Mem.: AIAA, Info. Tech. Assn. Am. (bd. dirs.), Armed Forces Comms. and Electronics Assn. (bd. dirs.), Nat. Def. Indsl. Assn. (bd. dirs.), The Bus. Roundtable. Office: CACI Internat Inc 1100 N Glebe Road Arlington VA 22201

COGBILL, JOHN VALENTINE, III, lawyer; b. Munich, Jan. 30, 1948; m. Janet Mary Cogbill; children: John, Jamie, Chrissy. BS in Engring., USMA, 1970; JD, U. Richmond, 1979. Bar: Va. 1979, admitted to practice: US Fed. Ct. 1979. Joined McGuireWoods LLP, Richmond, Va., 1987, ptnr., land use & environ. dept., mng. ptnr. Richmond office. Mem. Commonwealth Transp. Bd., 1995—99, Richmond Met. Authority Bd., 1995—99; chmn. Nat. Capital Planning Commn., 2001—09; bd. trustees The Henricus Found., 2001—. Vice-chair Va. War Meml. Ednl. Found., 2008. Served US Army, 1970—76. Fellow: Va. Law Found.; mem.: Chesterfield-Colonial Heights Bar Assn., Am. Coll. Real Estate Lawyers, Richmond Bar Assn. (Hill-Tucker Svc. award 2007), Va. Bar Assn., Greater Richmond C. of C. (bd. dirs. 1998—2002, Bernard L. Savage Cmty. Svc. Award 2003). Office: McGuireWoods LLP One James Ctr 901 E Cary St Richmond VA 23219-4030 Office Phone: 804-775-4383. Office Fax: 804-698-2031. Business E-Mail: jcogbill@mcguirewoods.com.

COGBURN, MAX OLIVER, JR., federal judge; b. Cambridge, Mass., Apr. 1951; s. Max Oliver Sr. and Mary (Heidt) Cogburn. BA, U. NC, Chapel Hill, 1973; JD, Samford U. Cumberland Sch. Law, Birmingham, Ala., 1976. Bar: NC 1976. Atty. Roberts, Cogburn & Williams, Asheville, NC, 1976—80; asst. US atty. (western dist.) NC US Dept. Justice, Asheville, 1980—92, lead atty. Organized Crime & Drug Enforcement Task Force, 1982—86, 1988—91, chief asst. US atty., 1986—88; pvt. practice Charlotte, NC, 1992—95; magistrate judge US Dist. Ct. (western dist.) NC, 1995—2004, judge, 2011—; ptnr. Cogburn & Brazil, P.A., Asheville, 2004—11. Mem.: NC Bar Assn., NC Acad. Trial Lawyers, 28th Jud. Dist. Bar. Office: US Courthouse 100 Otis St Asheville NC 28801 also: US Courthouse Rm 212 401 W Trade St Charlotte NC 28202

COGEN, JEFFREY DAVID, professional sports team executive; b. 1957; m. Jill S. Cogen. Grad., Old Dominion U. Mktg. dir. Ringling Bros., Barnum & Bailey Circus; mktg. asst. Detroit Red Wings, 1985; dir. mktg. Olympia Arena, Inc.; v.p. mktg. and promotion Dallas Stars, 1993—2001, pres., 2007—; exec. v.p. mktg. and comms. S.W. Sports Group, 1998—2001; COO Fla. Panthers, 2001—04, Tex. Rangers, 2004, pres., 2004—07. Office: Dallas Stars 2601 Avenue of the Stars Frisco TX 75034 Office Phone: 214-387-5500.

COGGINS, PAUL EDWARD, JR., lawyer; b. Hugo, Okla., May 21, 1951; s. Paul E. and Rebecca (Cates) C.; m. Regina T. Montoya, June 12, 1976; 1 child, Jessica Chandler. BA summa cum laude in Polit. Sci., Yale U., New Haven, Conn., 1973; BA with 1st class honors, Oxford U., 1975; JD cum laude, Harvard U., Cambridge, Mass., 1978. Bar: Tex. 1978. Tchr. Project New Gate N.Mex. State Penitentiary, 1973; law clk. Mass. Ct. Appeals, 1978-79; fed. prosecutor US Atty.'s Office, Dallas, 1980-83; assoc. Johnson & Swanson, Dallas, 1979-80, ptnr., 1983-86, Meadows, Owens, Collier, Reed & Coggins, Dallas, 1986-93; US atty. US Dept. Justice, Dallas, 1993-2001; prin. Fish & Richardson, P.C., Dallas, 2001—. Mem. adv. com. Magnet Sch. in Dallas, 1984—. Author: The Lady is the Tiger, 1987; co-author: Out of Bounds, 1992. Pres. bd. dirs. Dem. Forum, Dallas, 1985—; mem. North Tex. Crime Commn., chair, 2004. Named a Rhodes scholar, 1973—76; named one of Best Lawyers in Dallas, D Mag., 2005. Mem. ABA, CASA (pres. 2005), Dallas Bar Assn. (mem. pro bono panel), Dallas County Hist. Found., Town and Gown (pres., 2003-04). Office: Fish & Richardson PC 5000 Bank One Ctr 1717 Main St Dallas TX 75201-4612 Office Phone: 214-292-4003. Fax: 214-747-2091. Business E-Mail: coggins@fr.com.

COGHLAN, CHRIS (CHRISTOPHER B. COGHLAN), professional baseball player; b. Gaithersburg, Md., June 18, 1985; s. Tim and Heather Coghlan. Attended, U. Miss., University, 2003—06. Outfielder Miami Marlins, 2009—. Named Nat. League Rookie of Yr., Baseball Writers' Assn. America, 2009. Office: Miami Marlins 501 Marlins Way Miami FL 33125

COGHLAN, KELLY JACK, lawyer; b. Longview, Tex., Sept. 3, 1952; s. Howard and Peggy Coghlan. BBA with honors, So. Meth. U., 1975, JD cum laude, 1978. Bar: Tex. 1978, U.S. Dist. Ct. (so. dist.) Tex. 1979, U.S. Tax Ct. 1981, U.S. Ct. Appeals (5th cir.) 1981, U.S. Supreme Ct. 1984. Law clk. to presiding judge Finis E. Cowan U.S. Dist. Ct. (so. dist.) Tex., 1978-79; assoc. Vinson & Elkins, Houston, 1979-84; equity ptnr. Dotson, Babcock & Scofield, Houston, 1984-88, chmn. risk mgmt. com., head gen. litigation group, 1987-88; with Coghlan & Assoc., Houston, 1988—. Bd. dirs. Sta. KSBJ, Houston, sec., 1988-2006, chmn. long range planning com., 1989-93, mem. exec. com., 1990-97, v.p., 1994-97. Mem. So. Meth. U. Law Sch. Southwestern Law Jour. Mem. steering com. Palmer Drug Abuse Program, Houston, 1980-82; bd. mem. adv. bd. Salvation Army Boys and Girls Club, 2009-; vol. jr. high and H.S. youth programs, 1990—, 2d Bapt. Ch., Houston, 1990—; mem. 1st Meth. Ch., Longview, Tex., 1962—; youth min., Wesley United Meth. Ch., Longview, 1972-77. Recipient So. Meth. U. M award, 1975, Russell Baker Moot Ct. 1st pl. award So. Meth. U. Law Sch., 1976, Honor Guard Alliance Def. Fund, 2007-, Silver SVc. award, 2010, Faith in Action award Houston Area Pastor Coun., 2007, Family Adv. of Yr. award CWA Concerned Women America, 2009; named Impact Player of 1999, Tex. Lawyer. Fellow: Pro Bono Coll. State Bar Tex., Coll. State Bar Tex., Houston Bar Found. (life), Tex. Bar Found. (life); mem.: ABA, Houston Young Lawyers Assn. (chmn. com. on consumer rights 1981—82), Houston Bar Assn., Tex. Bar Assn., Gulf Coast Mensa, Nat. Eagle Scout Assn. (life), Am. Mensa, So. Meth. U. Student Found. (hon.), Lambda Chi Alpha, Phi Delta Phi (hon.), Beta Gamma Sigma (hon.), Blue Key Soc. (hon.; pres. 1974—75), Order of Coif (hon.). Avocations: youth work, drums. Office: 505 Lanecrest Ln Ste 1 Houston TX 77024-6716 Office Phone: 713-973-7475.

COHEN, BERNARD H., dermatologist, educator; MD, Columbia U., 1967. Diplomate Am. Bd. Dermatology, 1972, cert. hair restoration surgery. Resident dermatology NYU Med. Ctr., NYC, 1968—71; clin. prof. dermatology and cutaneous surgery dept. Univ. of Miami Sch. Med., dir. surg. tng. dermatology and cutaneous surgery dept., voluntary prof.; hosp. affiliation include Univ. of Miami Jackson Meml. Hosp. Office: Cole Instruments Ste 230 4425 Ponce De Leon Blvd Miami FL 33146 Office Phone: 305-476-9544.

COHEN, ELLEN, councilwoman, former state legislator; b. Aug. 28, 1940; m. Lyon Cohen (dec.); children: Marcie, Eric. BBA, Northwood U. Former exec. dir. American Jewish Com.; pres., CEO Houston Area Women's Ctr., 1989—2008; mem. Dist. 134 Tex. House of Reps., 2007—11; councilwoman Dist. C Houston City Coun., 2012—. Democrat. Jewish. Office: City Hall Annex 900 Bagby, First Floor Houston TX 77002 Office Phone: 832-393-3004. Office Fax: 832-393-3239. E-mail: districtc@houstontx.gov.

COHEN, EZRA HARRY, lawyer; b. Macon, Ga., Mar. 13, 1942; s. Harry M. and Rena C. Cohen; m. Bonnie E. Cohen, Feb. 1, 1969 (div. Mar. 1988); children: Aaron M., Eileen R.; m. Katherine C. Meyers, June 18, 1989. BA, Columbia U., 1964; JD, Emory U., 1969. Bar: Ga. 1969. Ptnr. Troutman, Sanders, Lockerman & Ashmore, Atlanta, 1969-76, 79—; judge U.S. Bankruptcy Ct., U.S. Dist. Ct. (no. dist.) Ga., Atlanta, 1976-79. Dir. S.E. Bankruptcy Law Inst., Atlanta. Contbg. author: Cowan's Bankruptcy Laws & Practices, 1979. Mem. Emory U. Law Sch. Coun., Atlanta, 1988—. With U.S. Army, 1964-66, ETO. Fellow Am. Coll. Bankruptcy; mem. Ga. Bar Assn. (chmn. bankruptcy law sect.), Assn. Former Bankruptcy Judges (bd. dirs.), Nat. Assn. Bank Judges (assoc.), Atlanta Bar Assn. (bd. dirs. 1988-90), Lawyers Club of Atlanta. Home: 546 W Wesley Rd Atlanta GA 30305-3534 Office: Troutman Sanders 600 Peachtree St NE Ste 5200 Atlanta GA 30308-2216 E-mail: ezra.cohen@troutmansanders.com.

COHEN, HARRIS L., diagnostic radiologist, consultant; b. Bklyn., Sept. 18, 1951; s. Samuel G. and Lola Estera (Altman) C.; m. Sandra Wilensky, Oct. 18, 1979; children: David Matthew, Lauren Elizabeth, Benjamin Adam. BA cum laude in Chemistry, CUNY, Bklyn., 1969—73; MD in Medicine, SUNY, Bklyn., 1972—76. Diplomate Am. Bd. Radiology, Nat. Bd. Med. Examiners; cert. added qualifications in pediatric radiology Am. Bd. Radiology. Asst. prof. radiology SUNY Health Sci. Ctr., Bklyn., 1981-88; asst. chief of imaging Brookdale Hosp. Med. Ctr., Bklyn., 1983-85; med. dir. diagnostic med. imaging program Coll. Health Related Professions, SUNY Health Sci. Ctr., Bklyn., 1985—88, 1994—; assoc. prof. radiology Cornell U. Med. Coll., NYC, 1988-93; chief pediatric CT and ultrasound North Shore U. Hosp.-Cornell, Manhasset, NY, 1988-93, assoc. dir. divsn. CT/ultrasound/magnetic resonance imaging, 1988-93; assoc. dir. radiology Kings County Hosp., Bklyn., 1993-2000; prof. radiology SUNY Health Sci. Ctr., Bklyn., 1993-2000, assoc. chmn. acad. affair and clin. rsch., 1998-2000; vis. prof. radiology, dir. divsn. pediat. imaging Johns Hopkins U., Balt., 2000—02; prof. radiology, vice chmn. dept. radiology, dir. divsn., body imaging, chief pediatric body imaging SUNY, Stony Brook, 2002—08, dir. abdominal imaging fellow program, 2003—08; med. dir. radiology LeBonheur Children's Hosp., Memphis, 2008—; exec. vice chmn. radiology, prof. radiology, ob-gyn. and pediat. U. Tenn. Sch. Medicine, 2008—09, radiologist-in-chief, 2012—; chmn., dept. radiology U. Tenn. Health Sci. Ctr., 2009—; bd. dir. LeBonheur ULPS. Dir. divsn. ultrasound U. and Kings County Hosps., Bklyn., 1985-88, 93-2000, dir. divsn. pediat. radiology, 1999-2000; cons. ultrasound and pediatric imaging Brookdale Hosp. Med. Ctr., Bklyn., 1988-2009; RSNA internat. vis. prof., India, 2005, Kenya, 2013; RSNA Eyler editl. fellow, 2004-05; editor-in-chief, continuous profl. improvement program Am. Coll. Radiology, editor-in-chief ACR PSE Series Author, editor, co-editor: Ultrasonography of the Prenatal and Neonatal Brain, 1996, 2d edit., 2002, Spanish transl., 2002, Obstetrics & Gynecology (Ultrasound), 1997, Fetal and Pediatric Ultrasound, 2001, Chinese Transl., 2003, Spanish Transl., Ecografia Fetal y Pediatrica, 2004, Gastrointestinal Disease VI, 2004, Ultrasound III, 2005, Neuroradiology III, 2006, Chest Disease VI, 2007; author, editor, co-editor Bone Disease, 2010; mem. editl. bd.: Jour. Diagnostic Med. Sonography, 1985—2000, Jour. Ultrasound in Medicine, 2002—, Ultrasound Quarterly, 2002—, Radiographics, 2012, reviewer:, 1991— (Editors cert. recognition, 1990-2003); contbr. chapters to books, articles to profl. jours., ednl. CDs and videos. Recipient Master Tchr. award in radiology, SUNY Health Sci. Ctr. at Bklyn. Alumni Assn., 1996, Tchr. of Yr. award, SUNY Stony Brook Radiology, 2006; named one of Best Drs. in NY, Castle Connoly, 2003—, Radiology Editors Forum, 2006—, NY Mag., 2003—08, Best Drs. in Am., Castle County, 2007—, Best Drs. in Memphis, Memphis Mag., 2010—, America's Top Radiologist, Consumer's Rsch. Coun. America, 2007. Fellow: Am. Inst. Ultrasound in Medicine (chmn. pediat. sect. 1994—95, chmn. ctrl. program com. 1995—97, bd. dirs. 1999—2002, bd. govs. 1999—2002, co-chair emergency ultrasound 2001—04, chmn. pediat. sect. 2013—), Am. Acad. Pediat. (chmn. radiology sect. 1992—94, exec. svc. sec. 2008—12, exec. coun. sect. radiology 2008—, grand round contbg. editor radiology), Soc. Radiologists in Ultrasound (chmn. constn. com. 1996—98, program com. 2004—07, mem. program com. 2013—), Am. Coll. Radiology (stds. and accreditation com. 1992—98, commn. ultrasound edn. com. 1998—, task force on disaster planning 2001—05, assoc. editor, ACR Case in Point 2010—, editl. bd. pediats. radiographics, disting. com. svc. award 1998, 2004); mem.: TN Radiol. Soc. (alt. councilor to ACR), Radiologic Soc. N.Am. (audiovisual com. 1992—96, exhibits com. 2002—04, coord. ultrasound cases of day 2004—06, exhibits com. 2007—12, Eyler editl. fellow 2004—05, internat. vis. prof., India 2006), Soc. Pediat. Radiology (liaison to Am. Acad. Pediat. 1993—94, liaison to Am. Inst. Ultrasound in Medicine 1995, program com. 2004—08, nom. com. 2007—09, chmn., SRU futures ultrasound com. 2008—09, bd. dirs. 2009—10, bd. govs. 2010—12, mem. ultrasound com. 2013—, mem. cardiac com. 2013—), SUNY-Downstate Alumni Assn. (councillor, bd. mgrs. 1998—2001), Alpha Omega Alpha. Avocations: basketball, baseball. Home: 5639 Ashley Sq S Memphis TN 38120-2470 Personal E-mail: hcohenmb@optonline.net.

COHEN, HARVEY JAY, geriatrician, hematologist, oncologist, educator; b. Bklyn., Oct. 21, 1940; s. Joseph and Anne (Margolin) C.; m. Sandra Helen Levine, June 1964; children: Ian Mitchell, Pamela Robin. BS, Bklyn. Coll., 1961; MD, Downstate Med. Coll., Bklyn., 1965. Diplomate Am. Bd. Internal Medicine, Am. Bd. Hematology. Intern, then resident internal medicine Duke U. Med. Ctr., Durham, NC, 1965-67, fellow hematology and oncology, 1969-71; chief hematology-oncology VA Med. Ctr., Durham, NC, 1975-76, chief med. svc., 1976-82, assoc. chief staff-edn., 1982—2007, geriatric rsch., edn. and clin. ctr.; assoc. prof. medicine Duke U. Med. Ctr., Durham, 1976-80, Walter Kempner prof. medicine, 2007—, also dir. Ctr. for Study of Aging, 1982—, chair dept. medicine, 2006—10, prof. med., 1980—2007. Chair bd. sci. counselors Nat. Inst. Aging, 1999—2003; chair Women's Health Initiative, Observational Study Monitoring Bd., 2005—. Author: Medical Immunology, 1977; co-author: (with H.G. Koenig) The Link Between Religion and Health: Psychoneuroimmunology and the Faith Factor, 2002, Taking Care After 50, 2000, Practical Geratric Oncology, 2010; editor: Cancer I and II, 1987, Jour. Gerontology: Med. Scis., 1988-92, Geriatric Medicine, 1997; contbr. 300 articles to profl. jours. Served as surgeon USPHS, 1967-69. Fellow ACP, Am. Geriat. Soc. (bd. dirs. 1987-96, chair bd. dirs. 1995-96, sec. 1991-93, ethics com. 1992-96, pres. 1994-95, Dennis W. Jahnigen Meml. award 2005), Gerontology Soc. Am. (clin. sec., rsch. com. 1987-92, chair publs. com. 1996-98, program chair 1994, pres. 2000, Joseph Freeman award, 1998, Donald P. Kent award, 2005); mem. Am. Soc. Clin. Oncology, BJ Kennedy award, 2010, Am. Soc. Hematology, Am. Assn. Cancer Rsch., Alliance Clin. Trials Oncology Group B (chair, Cancer in Elderly Com.), Assn. Am. Physicians, Internat. Soc. Geriat. Oncology (bd. dirs. 2000-06, pres. 2004-06, Paul Calabresi award, 2009), Am. Fedn. Aging Rsch. (bd. dirs. 2004-, pres. 2014-). Home: 2811 Friendship Cir Durham NC 27705-5521 Office: Duke U Med Ctr for Study Aging & Human Devel Box 3003 Durham NC 27710-0001 Business E-Mail: cohen015@mc.duke.edu.

COHEN, JEFF, publishing executive, newspaper editor; b. Cheyenne, Wyo. m. Kathryn M. Kase. BA in Journalism, U. Tex., Austin, 1976. Sports and feature writer San Antonio Light, 1976—89, mng. editor, 1989—93; spl. projects editor new media, newspaper divsn. Hearst Corp., NYC, 1993—94; editor Times Union, Albany, NY, 1994—2002; exec. v.p., editor Houston Chronicle, 2002—. Pulitzer Prize juror, 1999—2000. Pres. U. Tex. Coll. Comm. Adv. Coun. Recipient Benjamin Bradlee Editor of Yr. award, Nat. Press Found., 2007; fellow Multicultural Mgmt. Program, U. Mo. Sch. Journalism, 1987, Newspaper Mgmt. Ctr., Kellogg Grad. Sch. Mgmt., Northwestern U., 1990. Office: Houston Chronicle 801 Texas Ave Houston TX 77002

COHEN, KENNETH P., oil industry executive, lawyer; BA, Northwestern U.; JD, Baylor U. Law Sch.; LLM, Yale Law Sch. Law dept. Exxon USA, 1977, pub. affairs; law dept. Exxon Co. Internat.; asst. gen. counsel Exxon Chem. Co., gen. counsel, 1995—99; v.p. pub. affairs ExxonMobil Corp., 1999—. Editor-in-chief Baylor Law Rev.; spkr. in field. Office: Exxon Mobil Corp 5959 Las Colinas Blvd Irving TX 75039-2298

COHEN, LORI G., lawyer; b. Boston, May 18, 1965; BA cum laude, Duke U., 1987; JD with distinction, Emory U., 1990. Bar: Georgia, Am. Bar Assoc. Ptnr., products liability, medical malpractice def. litig. Alston & Bird LLP, Atlanta, 1990—2005; ptnr., litig. products liability, life scis. Greenberg Traurig LLP, Atlanta, 2005—. Editor Medical Malpractice & Strategy, Product Liability Law & Strategy, Pharmaceutical and Medical Device Law Bulletin. Recipient Top Defense Wins Award, Top 10 Under 40, Nat. Law Jour., 1999—2000; named one of The 50 Most Influential Women Lawyers in America, 2007, The Nation's Top Litigators, 2008. Mem.: Product Liability Advisory Council, Defense Research Institute. Office: Greenberg Traurig LLP Ste 400 The Forum 3290 Northside Pkwy Atlanta GA 30327 Home Phone: 404-355-3781; Office Phone: 678-553-2385. Office Fax: 678-553-2386. Business E-Mail: cohenl@gtlaw.com.

COHEN, N. JEROLD, lawyer; b. Pine Bluff, Ark., June 13, 1935; s. Maurice and Gertrude L. Cohen; children: Pamela, Lindsey L., Giles T. BBA, Tulane U., 1957; LLB magna cum laude, Harvard U., 1961. Bar: N.Y. 1962, Ga. 1966, D.C. 1966. Assoc. Cleary, Gottlieb, Steen and Hamilton, NYC, 1961-65, Sutherland, Asbill, and Brennan, Atlanta, Washington, 1965, ptnr., 1968-79, 81—; chief counsel IRS, 1979-81, adv. coun., 1999-2000, chmn. Former pres., former mem. nat. bd. dirs. ACLU Ga.; chmn. Atlanta Cmty. Rels. Commn., 1976-79. 1st lt. US Army, 1958. Recipient Gen. Counsel's award U.S. Dept. Treasury, Commrs. award IRS. Fellow Am. Bar Found.; mem. ABA (past chair tax sect., diet svc. awards tax sect., 2011), FBA, Am. Law Inst., Am. Tax Policy Inst. (mem. bd.), Am. Coll. Tax Counsel (regent, former chair). Office: Sutherland Asbill & Brennan 999 Peachtree St NE Ste 2300 Atlanta GA 30309-3996 Office Phone: 404-853-8038. Business E-Mail: jerry.cohen@sutherland.com.

COHEN, PHILIP HERMAN, accountant; b. Bklyn., Dec. 4, 1936; s. David J. and Toby (Jaeger) C.; m. Susan Rudd; children: Davina Ellen, Tobias Samuel Dory. BS, NYU, 1957. From acct. to ptnr.

Touche Ross & Co., NYC, 1957-81; exec. v.p. fin., CFO Integrated Resources, Inc., NYC, 1981-86, sr. exec. v.p. fin., CFO, 1986-90; fin. and real estate cons. Philip H. Cohen & Co., 1990—. Chmn. bd. dirs., pres., CEO FRMT Ltd. (A Bermuda Mut. Ins. Co.), 1996—99; bd. dirs. FMRT Ltd. (A Bermuda Mut. Ins. Co.); chmn. exec. com. FRMT Ltd. (A Bermuda Mut. Ins. Co.), 1999—2001; pres. Mitcor Corp.; bd. dirs. Odin Mgmt. Corp., Sy Sims Sch. Bus. Yeshiva U., 1991—2010; chmn. bd. dirs. Fraternity Risk Mgmt. Trust, 1994—99, chmn. exec. com., 1999—2000; -. Bd. dirs. Alpha Epsilon Pi Found., Inc., 1976—2005, 2013-, Nat. Interfrat. Conf., 1975-86, Nat. Interfrat. Found., 1996-2004, State of Israel Bonds, N.Y.; bd. dirs. Sutton Pl. Synagogue, 1984-99, v.p., 1993-99; bd. dirs. joint purchasing com. Fedn. Jewish Philanthropies, 1977-78; mem. Cmty. Bd. Manhattan, N.Y., 1992-2006; internat. bd. dirs. Hillel Found. for Jewish Student Campus Life, 1999—2011, mem. exec. com. of bd. dirs., 2005—, chair audit com.; adv. bd. U. Miami Med. Sch's. Inst. Stem Cell Rsch., 2008-. Recipient State of Israel Bond Peace award 1983, Accts. Bankers and Fin. award Am. Jewish Congress, 1984, Gold medal Nat. Interfraternity Conf., 1994, Disting. Svc. award Fraternity Exec. Assn., 1999. Mem. Found. Acctg. Edn., Am. Inst. CPA's (real estate com. 1987-90), N.Y. State Soc. CPA's (admissions com. 1968-69, chmn. fin. and leasing com. 1972-74, com. on rels. with the bar 1974-76, com. on real estate acctg. 1976-79, com. ins. 1980-81, fin. acctg. standards com. 1983-86, chmn. mem.-in-industry com. 1981-83, chief fin. officers com. 1984-86, furtherance com. 1986, annual conf. com. 1985-87, com. on ops. 1987-88, bd. dirs. 1983-86, v.p. 1985-86, Outstanding CPA in Industry award 1986), Fin. Execs. Inst., Am. Acctg. Assn., Nat. Assn. Accts., Soc. Ins. Accts., Alpha Epsilon Pi (supreme gov. 1966-73, nat. pres. 1974-76, mem. fiscal control bd. 1977-81, vice chmn. 1981-92, chmn. 1992-2005, chmn. emiritus 2008-, exec. com. Miami-Dade county, Am. Israel polit. action com. mem.), Beta Alpha Psi, Areopagus Clubs: South Fla. Alumni Alpha Epsilon Pi. Lodges: Masons(chair. bd. gen. welfare of lodge, 1998), AIPAC(Nat. Coun. mem.) Jewish. Home: 1500 Ocean Dr Ste 903 Miami Beach FL 33139 Office Phone: 305-532-5872.

COHEN, SHELDON IRWIN, lawyer; BS in Ceramic Engring., Rutgers U., 1959, AB in Humanities, 1959; LLB, Georgetown U., 1964. Bar: Va. 1964, D.C. 1964, U.S. Ct. Appeals (D.C. and 4th cirs.) 1964, U.S. Supreme Ct. 1967. Assoc. Chapman, Disalle & Friedman, Washington, 1964-70; pvt. practice law Washington, Arlington, Va., 1970—. Author: Security Clearances and the Protection of National Security Information, Law and Procedure, 2000. Vice chmn. Arlington Dem. Com., 1968-70; mem. Va. Dem. Cen. Com., 1969-70. Capt. USAR, 1959-67. Mem. ABA (chmn. govt. pers. com. 1986-89, chmn. nat. security interests com. 1990-95), D.C. Bar Assn. (chmn. civil svc. law com. 1984-86), Cosmos Club. Democrat. Office: PO Box 4068 Oakton VA 22124-8468 Office Phone: 703-522-1200. E-mail: sicohen@sheldoncohen.com.

COHEN, STANLEY, retired biochemistry educator; b. Bklyn., Nov. 17, 1922; s. Louis and Fannie (Feitel) Cohen; m. Olivia Larson, 1951 (div.); children: Burt, Kenneth, Cary; m. Jan Elizabeth Jordan, 1981. BA in Chemistry and Zoology, Bklyn. Coll., 1943; MA in Zoology, Oberlin Coll., Ohio, 1945; PhD in Biochemistry, U. Mich., 1948; PhD (hon.), U. Chgo., 1985, Oberlin Coll., 1989, Washington U., 1993. Instr. dept. biochemistry and pediat. U. Colo., Denver, 1948-52; Am. Cancer Soc. fellow in radiology Washington U., St. Louis, 1952-53, assoc. prof. dept. zoology, 1953-59; asst. prof. biochemistry Vanderbilt U. Sch. Medicine, Nashville, 1959-62, assoc. prof., 1962-67, prof. biochemistry, 1967-86, disting. prof., 1986-2000, disting. prof. emeritus biochemistry, 2000—. Charles B. Smith vis. rsch. prof. Meml. Sloan-Kettering Cancer Ctr., 1984; Feodor Lynen lectr. U. Miami, Fla., 1986; Steenbock lectr. U. Wis., 1986. Contbr. articles to profl. jours. Recipient William Thomson Wakeman award, Nat. Paraplegia Found., 1974, Earl Sutherland rsch. prize for achievement in rsch., Vanderbilt U., 1977, Albion O. Bernstein, MD award, NY State Med. Soc., 1978, Lewis S. Rosenstiel award, Brandeis U., 1982, Alfred P. Sloan award, GM Cancer Rsch. Found., 1982, Louisa Gross Horwitz prize, Columbia U., 1983, Disting. Achievement award, Lab. Biomed. & Environ. Scis., UCLA, 1983, Lila Gruber Meml. Cancer Rsch. award, Am. Acad. Dermatology, 1983, Bertner award, M.D. Anderson Hosp./U.Tex., 1983, Gairdner Found. Internat. award, 1985, Nat. Med. Sci., 1986, Fred Conrad Koch award, Endocrine Soc., 1986, Nobel prize in physiology/medicine, 1986, Albert Lasker award for basic med. rsch., 1986; named to Hall of Honor, Nat. Inst. Child Health & Human Devel., NIH, 2007. Fellow: Jewish Acad. Arts & Scis.; mem.: NAS (H.P. Robertson Meml. award 1981), Internat. Inst. Embryology, Am. Chem. Soc., Internat. Acad. Sci. (hon.), Am. Acad. Arts & Scis., Am. Soc. Biol. Chemists.

COHEN, STEPHEN MARK, colon and rectal surgeon, educator; MD, UCLA, LA, 1987. Diplomate Am. Bd. Surgery, 2001, Am. Bd. Colon and Rectal Surgery, 2007. Resident in surgery Boston Univ. Med. Ctr. Hosp., Mass., 1988—92; fellow in colon and rectal surgery Cleve. Clinic Fla., Ft. Lauderdale, 1992—94; assoc. clin. prof. surgery Emory Univ.; hosp. affiliations include Emory Univ. Hosp. Midtown, Southern Regional Med. Ctr.; pvt. practice Atlanta Colon and Rectal Surgery, P.A., Ga. Office: Atlanta Colon and Rectal Surgery PA 33 SW Upper Riverdale Rd Ste 127 Riverdale GA 30274 Office Phone: 770-997-1975. Office Fax: 770-997-1966.

COHEN, STEVE (STEPHEN IRA COHEN), United States Representative from Tennessee, former state legislator; b. Memphis, May 24, 1949; s. Morris David and Genevieve (Goldsand) Cohen. BA, Vanderbilt U., Nashville, 1971; JD, U. Memphis, 1973. Bar: Tenn. 1974. Legal advisor Memphis Police Dept., 1975-78; commr. Shelby County Bd. Commissioners, 1978-80; mem. Dist. 30 Tenn. State Senate, 1983—2007, dep. spkr., 2000—07; mem. US Congress from 9th Tenn. dist., 2007—. Interim judge Shelby County Gen. Sessions Ct., 1980; mem. Shelby County Charter Commn., 1984; mem. exec. com. Nat. Conf. State Legislatures, 1998—2005. Bd. trustees Memphis Coll. Art, 1988—2002; del. Dem. Nat. Conv., 1980, 1992, 2004, 2008, Am. Coun. Young Political Leaders USA/Japan Study Mission, 1986; v.p. Tenn. Constl. Conv., 1977; chmn. Shelby County Legis. Del., 1988—90. Recipient Legislator of the Year, Boys & Girls Clubs of Tenn., 2003, Pub. Leadership award, Tenn. Human Rights Campaign, 2002. Mem.: Memphis Bar Assn. Democrat. Jewish. Office: US House of Representatives 2404 Rayburn House Office Bldg Washington DC 20515 also: Clifford Davis Fed Bldg Ste 369 167 N Main St Memphis TN 38103*

COHEN, WILLIAM MARK, lawyer; b. NYC, May 22, 1951; s. Martin and Annabelle (Turner) C.; m. Melinda Pauline Salomon, Aug. 3, 1975; children: Jessica, Adam. AB, Rutgers U., 1973; JD, Georgetown U., 1976. Bar: Tenn. 1976, U.S. Dist. Ct. (mid. dist.) Tenn. 1976, U.S. Ct. Appeals (6th cir.) 1977, U.S. Supreme Ct. 1980. Law clk. to chief judge U.S. Dist. Ct. (mid. dist.) Tenn., Nashville, 1976-78; asst. U.S. atty. U.S. Atty.'s Office, 1978—83, 1st asst. U.S. atty., 1983—92, chief criminal divsn., 1992—98, asst. U.S. atty., 1998—2002, 2003—05; sr. litigation counsel US Atty.'s Office, 2002—03, 2005—07; adj. prof. law Vanderbilt U. Law Sch., 2003—; instr. Nashville Sch. Law, 2007—. Home: 6021 Foxland Dr Brentwood TN 37027-5733

COHN, ISIDORE, JR., surgeon, educator; b. New Orleans, Sept. 25, 1921; s. Isidore and Elsie (Waldhorn) C.; m. Jacqueline Heymann, July 4, 1944 (div. Aug. 1971); children: Ian Jeffrey, Lauren Kerry; m. Marianne Winter Miller, Jan. 3, 1976. BS in Chemistry with honors, Tulane U., New Orleans, 1942; MD, U. Pa., Phila., 1945; M.Med. Sci. in Surgery, U. Pa., 1952, DMS in Surgery, 1955; LHD (hon.), U. SC, 1995. Diplomate Am. Bd. Surgery (bd. dirs. 1969-75). Intern Grad. Hosp. U. Pa., 1945-46, resident in surgery, 1949-52; fellow dept. surg. rsch. U. Pa., 1947-48; vis. surgeon Charity Hosp., New Orleans, 1952-62, sr. vis. surgeon, 1962-2000, hon. sr. vis. surgeon, 2000—; surgeon in chief La. State U. Svc., Charity Hosp., New Orleans, 1962-89; prof. surgery La. State U. Sch. Medicine, New Orleans, 1959-2000, emeritus chmn., emeritus prof. surgery, 2000—. Cons. surgeon VA Hosp., New Orleans, Touro Infirmary, New Orleans; instr. surgery La. State U. Sch. Medicine, New Orleans, 1952-53, asst. prof., 1953-56, assoc. prof., 1956-59, prof., 1959-2000, chmn. dept. surgery, 1962-89; mem. surg. rsch. rev. com. VA, Washington, 1967-68; dir. Nat. Pancreatic Cancer Project, 1975-84; mem. Soc. Surg. Chairmen, 1962-89. Mem. editl. bd. Am. Surgeon, 1963-87, Current Surgery, 1964-90, Am. Jour. Surgery, 1968-96, emeritus, 1997—, Digestive Diseases and Scis., 1978-82, Surg. Gastroenterology, 1982—, Cancer, 1992—2002, Digestive Surgery, 1995—. Bd. dirs. New Orleans Met. Conv. and Visitors Bur., 1998-2000, New Orleans Mus. Art, 2004-2009, hon. life mem., 2010-, Jewish Endowment Found., 2006-2012. Served to capt. M.C., AUS, 1946-47. Isidore Cohn, Jr. Professorship named in his honor at La. State U., 1987, Isidore Cohn, Jr., M.D. Student Learning Ctr. at La. State U. Health Sci. Ctr. Sch. Medicine dedicated in his honor, 2002, Spirit of Charity award Med. Ctr. La., 2003; named Outstanding Alumnus, Isidore Newman Sch., New Orleans, La., 2003, Role Model, Young Leadership Coun. New Orleans, 2006, Tzedakah award, Jewish Endowment Found, 2009, Isaac Delgado Meml. award, New Orleans Mus. Art, 2012, Chmn.'s award Arts Coun. New Orleans, 2012, Chmn. award, Arts Coun. New Orleans (jt. mem. 2012). Fellow ACS (exec. com., bd. govs. 1987-91, vice-chmn. 1989-90, chmn. 1990-91, 1st v.p. 1993-94), Southern Surg. Assn. (1st v.p. 1979-80, treas.-recorder 1981-82, pres. 1982-83, hon. mem. 2009-); mem. AMA, Am. Surg. Assn., La. Surg. Assn. (pres. 1968), So. Med. Assn., La., Orleans Parish med. socs., Soc. Univ. Surgeons, Southeastern Surg. Congress (chmn. forum on progress in surgery 1967-69, councillor for La. 1967-73, pres. 1972), Surg. Biology Club II, Assn. Acad. Surgery, Isidore Cohn, Jr.-James D. Rives Surg. Soc., Internat. Surg. Soc., Am. Gastroenterol. Assn., Bockus Soc. Gastroenterology, Soc. Surgery Alimentary Tract (trustee 1969-80, recorder 1973-76, pres. 1976-77, chmn. bd. 1977-78, Founders medal 2004), Am. Soc. Microbiologists, Soc. Surg. Oncology, NY Acad. Scis., Am. Assn. Cancer Research, Southeastern Cancer Research Assn. (pres. 1975), Collegium Internationale Chirurgiae Digestivae, Am. Cancer Soc. (vice chmn. clin. investigation adv. com. 1969, chmn. clin. investigation adv. com. 1969-73), Tex. Surg. Soc. (hon.), Sigma Xi, Phi Beta Kappa, Alpha Omega Alpha, Omicron Delta Kappa. Home: 510 Iona St Metairie LA 70005-4430 Office: La State U Med Sch New Orleans LA 70112 Home Phone: 504-835-6135. Personal E-mail: drdrdrjr@gmail.com.

COHN, JAMES I., federal judge; b. Montgomery, Ala., 1948; BS, U. Ala., 1971; JD, Samford U., 1974. Asst. pub. defender Broward County Pub. Defender's Office, 1975; asst. state atty. Broward County State Atty.'s Office, 1975—78; pvt. practice atty. Ft. Lauderdale, Fla., 1978—95; cir. judge 17th Jud. Circ. Ct. Fla., 1995—2003; judge US Dist. Ct. (so. dist.) Fla., Ft. Lauderdale, 2003—. Mem. Ala. Nat. Guard US Army, 1970—72, mem. Fla. Army Nat. Guard US Army, 1975—76, mem. USAR, 1972—75. Office: US Dist Ct US Courthouse 299 E Broward Blvd Rm 203 Fort Lauderdale FL 33301 Office Phone: 954-769-5490.

COHN, RICHARD A., gastroenterologist; MD, U. of Tex., 1977. Diplomate American Bd. Internal Medicine, 1980, American Bd. Internal Medicine-gastroenterology, 1983. Resident internal medicine Univ. of Conn. Health ctr., 1978—80, fellow gastroenterology, 1980—82; hosp. affiliation includes Mercy Med. Ctr. St. Mary's. Office: Mercy Medical Center St Mary's 900 E Oak Hill Ave Knoxville TN 37917-4556 Office Phone: 865-545-8000.*

COIL, JAMES H., III, lawyer; b. Mobile, Ala., July 14, 1945; AB, Duke U., 1967; JD, Harvard U., 1970. Bar: Ga. 1971, US Supreme Ct., US Cts of Appeals (4th, 5th, 9th, 11th) & Dis. Columbia Cir., Supreme Ct. Ga., Ga. Ct of Appeals. Mem. Kilpatrick & Cody, Atlanta, 1974; ptnr. Kilpatrick Townsend & Stockton LLP, Atlanta, 1980—. Mem. editorial bd.: The Trademark Reporter, 1979, author New Supervisor's EEO Handbook, contbr. articles to profl. jours. Capt. USMC, 1971—74. Named one of Best Lawyers in America, 2001—, Super Lawyers, 2004—. Mem. ABA, State Bar Ga., Atlanta Bar Assn. Office: Kilpatrick Townsend & Stockton LLP 1100 Peachtree St Ste 2800 Atlanta GA 30309-4530 Office Phone: 404-815-6500, 404-815-6348. Business E-Mail: jcoil@kilpatricktownsend.com.*

COKER, DONALD WILLIAM, bank management, expert witness, business valuation and economic consultant; s. William Mack and Gloria Antoinette C.; m. Linda Carol Sandlin, July 12, 1969; children: Caroline Tiffany, Brittany Blaire. BA, postgrad., U. Ala., 1968, U. Houston, 1973, Spring Hill Coll., 1995—96, Harvard Bus. Sch., 2005; degree in Real Estate Fin., Securities, Construction Fin., Southern Meth. U., Tex., 1984. Trust mgr., real estate mortgage officer Regions Fin. (formerly AmSouth Bank), Mobile, 1968—72; sr. loan officer, lending mgr. Bank of America (formerly Gibraltar Savs.), Houston, 1972—73; mortgage officer, asst. regional mgr., asst. treas. Citicorp Real Estate, Houston, 1973—74; comml. loan officer JPMorgan Chase Bank (formerly SW Bancshares and M Bank-Houston and Bank of SW), 1974—77; regional mgr. Citigroup (formerly Comml. Credit Co.), Houston, 1977—83, Ford Motor Credit, Houston, 1983-84; sr. v.p., mgr. lending and mortgage banking BBVA (formerly First Fed. Savs.), San Antonio, 1984—85; exec. v.p., bd. dirs. Home Savs. (now Citigroup), Houston, 1985-86; Don Coker banking, mgmt. valuation, economic, and expert witness consulting Woodstock, 1986—. Cons. Prentice-Hall Pub., IRS, FDIC, USAID, Internat. Acctg. Stds. Bd., Resolution Trust Corp., World Bank; cons. to over 90 banks worldwide, attys., corps. and govt. agys.; nat. healthcare and profl. practice valuation cons.; expert witness on bus. and intangible asset valuation, econ., fin., real estate and banking. Author: Complete Guide to Income Property Financing & Loan Packaging, 1984; tech. editor: Complete Real Estate Computer Workbook, 1986; contbr. over 100 articles to profl. jours. Trustee Katy Sch. Dist., Houston, 1987; treas. Nottingham Country Civic Club, Houston; precinct leader, del. and dep. voters registrar Rep. party. With USAR, 1966—68. Named Expert Witness Cons., DRI & AAJ. Mem. Nat. Hosp. Assn., Am. Bankruptcy Inst., Nat. Assn. State Savs. and Loan Suprs., Am. Mortgage Bankers Assn., Tex. Mortgage Bankers' Assn., Am. Bankers Assn., Greater Grady Meml. Hosp. Task Force, Internat. Coun. Shopping Ctrs., U.S. Savs. and Loan League, Houston C. of C. (bus. devel. com.), Fulton Dekalb Hosp. Authority, Sweetwater Country Club. Republican. Episcopalian. Achievements include development of a patented check fraud prevention system. Office Phone: 770-852-2286. Business E-Mail: bankexpert@cs.com.

COKER, HOWARD COLEMAN, lawyer; b. Jacksonville, Fla., Apr. 30, 1947; BS in Journalism, U. Fla., 1969, JD, 1971. Bar: Fla. 1972, cert.: Fla. (in civil trial practice) 1985, Nat. Bd. Trial Advocacy (civil trial specialist) 1987. Asst. state atty. Fourth Jud. Cir., 1972; assoc. Howell, Kirby, Montgomery, D'Aiuto & Dean, P.A., 1973-76; pres., dir. Coker, Schickel, Sorenson & Posgay, P.A., Jacksonville, Fla., 1976—; learn to read Kiss Pig for Literacy, 2007. Guest lectr. more than 40 CLE seminars on litig. and trial matters throughout Fla., for Fla. Bar Assn., Fla Justice Assn. (formerly Acad. Fla. Trial Lawyers); advisor mock trial team U. Fla. Law Sch., 1991-98; adj. prof. U. North Fla.; mem. Nat. Conf. Bar Pres., 1997-2003, co-leader US & Russia Joint Conf. Rule of Law - People to People Ambassador Program, 2007- Chair ednl. adv. coun. U. North Fla., 1992-94, chair adv. bd. for paralegals, 1990-92; bd. dir. Jacksonville Zool. Gardens, 2000-, chair, 2006-07; mem. adv. bd. Parks, Recreation, Entertainment & Conservation, Jacksonville, 2006-; bd. dir. Spina Bifida Assn. Jacksonville, 2000-. Named Lawyer of Yr., The Daily Record, 2007, Flabota Plaintiff Trial Lawyer Of Yr., 2007; named one of Best Lawyers in Am., Million Dollar Advocates Forum, 1999—2000, Top Lawyers in Fla., Fla. Monthly, 2003—08, Fla. Legal Elite, 2005—08, Jacksonville Best Lawyers, 2006—08, Fla. Super Lawyers, Top 100, Lawyers Fla., 2006—10. Fellow Am. Bar Found., Internat. Soc. Barristers; mem. ABA (ho. of dels., jud. qualifications commn.), ATLA, Am. Arbitration Assn. (panel arbitrators 1983—), Fla. Bar Assn. (pres. 1998-99, bd. govs. 1994-99, exec. com. 1995-97, all bar fconf. del. 1990-92, 94, 96, 97, budget com. 1995-97, bd. rev. coml. on profl. ethics chair 1995-96, disciplinary rev. com. 1994-95, jud. qualification screen com. 1994-95, legis. com. 1994-95, profl. retreat chair 1996, program evaluation com. chair 1996-97, 4th jud. cir. grievance com. reviewer 1994-97, coun. sects. 1991-94, chair 1993-94, sect. leadership conf. chair 1995, trial lawyers sect. exec. coun. 1987-94, bd. govs. liaison 1996, chair 1992-93, exec. co. 1989-93, legis. com. 1988-93, supreme ct. jud. nominating commn. 2007-), Am. Bd. Trial Advocates (pres. Jacksonville chpt. 1988—, media rep. 1988, exec. com. 1988—, diplomate; Jacksonville chpt. Trial Lawyer of Yr. 2003), Am. Judicature Soc., Chester Bedell Meml. Found. (trustee 1996-2001), First Coast Trial Lawyers Assn. (Pres. award 1996), Fla. Justice Assn. (formerly Acad. Fla. Trial Lawyers; bd. dirs. 1995—, pres. 2002-2003, Eagle sponsor 1990—; Silver Eagle award 1996, 1997, 2004, Legislative Shoe Leather award 1998, 2000, Golden Eagle award 1998, Eagle Workhorse award 1999, Wings of Justice award 2000, Staff Appreciation award 1999, B. J. Masterson award 2005, Perry Nichols award 2006, M. McKinley Smiley award 2006, Ai. J. Cone Lifetime Achievement award, 2009, Tiger in the Bush award 2007), Fla. Lawyers Assn. for Maintenance of Excellence (bd. dirs. 1995-97), So. Trial Lawyers, Fla. Supreme Ct. Hist. Soc., Jacksonville Bar Assn., Roscoe Pound Found., U.S. Supreme Ct. Hist. Soc., Internat. Acad. Trial Lawyers, Fla. Conservation Assn. (pres. 1993-94), Fla. Ducks Unltd. — (chmn. 1991-93; Sportsman of Yr. 1994), Fla. Wildlife Fedn., Seminole Club (bd. dirs. 1988, pres., 1989), U. Fla. Nat. Alumni Assn. (pres.'s coun. 1992-2001), Sigma Alpha Epsilon, Phi Delta Phi. Office: PO Box 1860 136 E Bay St Jacksonville FL 32201 Home: 4931 River Point Rd Jacksonville FL 32207 Office Phone: 904-356-6071. Office Fax: 904-353-2425. Business E-Mail: hcoker@cokerlaw.com.

COKER, LARRY E., college football coach; b. June 23, 1948; m. Dianna Bryant; 1 child, Lara. BS in History, Northeastern St. Univ., Tahlequah, Okla., 1970; MS in Guidance Counseling and Phys. Edn., Northeastern St. Univ., 1973. Offensive backfield coach Tulsa U., 1979—82; offensive coord. Okla. St. U., 1983—88, U. Okla., 1990—92; defensive backfield coach Ohio State U., 1993—94; quarterbacks coach, offensive coord. U. Miami, 1995—2000, head coach, 2001—06; head coach start up program 2011 U. Texas San Antonio, 2009—. Recipient Paul "Bear" Bryant award, Nat. Sportscasters & Sportswriters Assn., 2001. Achievements include coaching U. Miami to the 2001 BCS Nat. Championship. Office: U Texas San Antonio PE 2 01 02 San Antonio TX 78249 Office Phone: 210-458-4161. Office Fax: 210-458-4813.

COLAN, JOANNE, video blogger, television personality; b. Lancashire, UK, Mar. 20; Rschr., host, writer, prodn. coord. BBC TV, BBC Radio; Europe VJ MTV, 2000—04; music/DJ curator Table 50 club, Manhattan; travel adventure series host, Any Given Latitude Fine Living Network; host, co-prodr. Rocketboom.com, 2006—09; co-host, new correspondent of Planet Green show Dean of Invention, 2010—. Moderator of edn. program for student in the US, Gaza, and Iraq with global tchg. organization Global Nomads Group Health and Sustainability; journalist, on-camera reporter, Human Rights Watch Orgn. WITNESS; works as a AADP Cert. Integrative Nutrionist. Recipient Best European Satellite Music Programme award, What Satellite UK & Europe TV Poll, 2001; named one of Top 10 Savvy Women in Podcasting, Podonomics, 2006. Business E-Mail: hi@rocketboom.com.

COLANERO, STEPHEN A., marketing professional; BS in Acctg., Villanova U., Pa., 1988; MBA, U. Pa. Wharton Sch., 1992. Various positions to sr. v.p. strategic mktg. Blockbuster, Inc., 1994—2006; sr. v.p. retail mktg. Washington Mutual, Inc., 2006—07; v.p. mktg. RadioShack Corp., 2008—09; exec. v.p., chief mktg. officer AMC Theatres, AMC Entertainment, Inc., 2009—. Office: AMC Entertainment Inc PO Box 725489 Atlanta GA 31139

COLASURDO, GIUSEPPE N., dean, pulmonologist, educator; b. Morrone Del Sannio, Italy; arrived in USA, 1988, naturalized; B, Liceo Scientifico Galileo Galilei, Pescara, Italy; MD summa cum laude, G. D'Annunzio Sch. Medicine, Chieti, Italy. Cert. in pediatric pulmonology, lic. Italy, Tex., Colo. Residency U. Tex. Med. Br., Galveston; fellowship U. Colo. Health Sci. Ctr., Nat. Jewish Med. and Rsch. Ctr., Denver; lab. asst. to Dr. Gary L. Larson Denver; clin. pulmonologist; joined as asst. prof. pediat. in the divsn. pulmonary medicine U. Tex. Med. Sch. at Houston, 1995, head divsn. pulmonary medicine, 1997—2001, dir. fellowship tng. program in pediatric pulmonary medicine, 2001—05, chmn. dept. pediat., 2005—07, dean, H. Wayne Hightower disting. prof. in the med. sciences, 2007—; interim pres. U. Tex. Health Sci Ctr. at Houston, 2011—; CEO UT Physicians; physician-in-chief Children's Meml. Hermann Hosp., Houston. Editl. reviewer: American Jour. Physiology, American Jour. Respiratory and Critical Care Medicine, Pediatric Pulmonology; contbr. articles to profl. jours., chapters to books. Decorated Knight of Order of Merit of Italian Republic Consul Gen. Italy; recipient David W. Smith Trainee award, We. Soc. Pediatric Rsch., Basic Scientist Devel. award, NIH, Facolta di Medicinee Chirurgia award, G. D'Annunzio Sch. Medicine, Exec. communicator of Yr. award, Houston, Internat. Assn. Bus. Communicators, 2008; grantee, NIH, Children's Miracle Network, Cystic Fibrosis Found. Mem.: American Thoracic Soc., Soc. Pediatric Rsch., Alpha Omega Alpha, Houston Delta Chpt. Office: University Tex Med Sch Houston Office of Dean 6431 Fannin MSB G150 Houston TX 77030 Office Phone: 713-500-5010. Office Fax: 713-500-0602. Business E-Mail: med.dean@uth.tmc.edu.

COLBERT, ALICE TAYLOR, history professor; b. Atlanta, May 11, 1955; d. Codie Artez and Fay (Waits) Taylor; m. James Early Colbert Jr., May 18, 1991. BA, Shorter Coll., 1977; MA, Emory U., 1983, PhD, 1988. Adminstrv. asst. Atlanta Hist. Soc., 1980-81, mus.

asst., 1981-83; contract curator Gulf Islands Nat. Seashore, Nat. Pk. Svc., Fla. and Miss., 1983-84; prof. history, dir. mus. Shorter Coll., Rome, Ga., 1984—2005, dean Sch. Edn. and Social Scis., 2002—05; chair dept. history, geography, polit. sci., philosophy & religious studies U. Ark., Ft. Smith, 2005—10; co-chair Am. Democracy Project, 2007—10; adviser Hardwood Mus., 2009—; dean, Coll. Arts & Humanities Lander U., Greenwood, SC, 2010—12, assoc. v.p., academic affairs, 2012—13; regional campus dean U. SC Union, 2013—. Mus. cons. Chieftains Mus., Rome, 1986-2005; project dir. Ga. Women Meeting Challenges symposium; mem. Southeastern Mus. Conf., editorial bd. mem. Jour. Cherokee Studies, 2008- Editor Jour. Cherokee Studies, 1988-2005, Jour. Ga. Assn. Historians, 1995-2002; regional coord. New Ga. Guide, 1993-96; contbr. articles to profl. jours. Mem. Ga. Rev. Bd. Nat. Register of Historic Places, 1995—98, Ga. Hist. Records Adv. Bd., 2001—05. Exhibit and program grantee Ga. Humanities Coun., 1987, 88, 93, grant Ark. Heritage Resources. Mem.: Nat. Coun. on Pub. History, Am. Hist. Assn., Orgn. Am. Historians, So. Hist. Assn., Pi Gamma Mu (sec. 1985—2005). Avocations: public speaking, historical research. Home: 109 Brookfield Ave Greenwood SC 29646 Office: University SC Union PO Drawer 729 Union SC 29379 Office Phone: 864-427-3681 7719. Business E-Mail: acolbert@mailbox.sc.edu.

COLBERT, TOM, state supreme court chief justice; b. Oklahoma City, Okla., Dec. 30, 1949; Grad., Ea. Okla. State Coll., 1970; BS, Ky. State U., 1972, EdM, 1976; JD, U. Okla. Coll. Law, 1982. Asst. dean Marquette U. Law Sch., 1982—84; asst. dist. atty. Okla. County, 1984—86; atty. Miles-LaGrange & Colbert, 1986—89, Colbert & Associates, 1989—2000, Okla. Dept. Human Services, 1988—89, 1999—2000; judge Okla. Ct. Civil Appeals, 1999—2004, chief judge, 2004; justice Okla. Supreme Ct., 2004—, vice chief justice, 2011—12, chief justice, 2013—. Served in criminal investigation divsn. US Army, 1973—75. Mem.: ABA, Nat. Bar Assn., Tulsa County Bar Assn., Okla. Bar Assn. Office: Oklahoma Supreme Ct Okla Judicial Ctr 2100 N Lincoln Blvd Ste 4 Oklahoma City OK 73105-4907*

COLBORN, GENE LOUIS, anatomy educator, researcher; b. Springfield, Ill., Nov. 23, 1935; s. Adin Levi and Grace Downey (Tucker) C.; divorced; children: Robert Mark, Adrian Thomas, Lara Lee Colborn Russell; m. Sarah Ellen Crockett, Aug. 14, 1976; children: Jason Matthew, Nathan Tucker. BA with honors, Ky. Christian Coll., Grayson, 1957; BS with honors, Milligan Coll., Tenn., 1962; MS in Anatomy, Wake Forest U., Winston-Salem, NC, 1964, PhD in Anatomy, 1967. Postdoctoral fellow U. N.Mex. Sch. Medicine, Albuquerque, 1967—68; asst. prof. U. Tex. Health Sci. Ctr., San Antonio, 1968—72, assoc. prof., 1972—75; assoc. prof. anatomy Med. Coll. Ga., Augusta, 1975—88, prof. anatomy, 1988—2000, prof. surgery, 1993—2000, emeritus prof. anatomy and surgery, 2000—, dir. Ctr. for Clin. Anatomy, 1987—2000, dir. med. gross anatomy, 1975—2000, cons. dept. surgery, 1977—2000; clin. prof. surgery Emory U. Sch. Medicine, Atlanta, 1996—; chmn. divsn. anat. scis. Ross U. Sch. Medicine, Dominica, 2000—01; prof. Am. U. Caribbean Sch. Medicine, St. Maarten, Netherlands Antilles, 2002—04, chmn. anatomy, 2002—04. Pres. Ga. State Anat. Bd., 1983-93; cons. Eisenhower Army Med. Ctr., 1990-96; founder, pres. Gelco Med. Pub. Co., 2004-. Author: Practical Gross Anatomy, 1982, Surgical Anatomy, 1987, Hernias, 1988, Musculoskeletal Anatomy, 1989, Workbook of Surgical Anatomy, 1990, Clinical Gross Anatomy, 1993, Modern Hernia Repair, 1996, The Embryological and Anatomical Basis of Surgery, 2002, Benchmark Questions in Clinical Anatomy, 2008, Gray's Anatomy for Students- A Study Guide, 2008; mem. editl. bd.: Clin. Anatomy Jour.; contbr. numerous articles on cardiac conduction, nervous sys., primate anatomy, cell culture and clin. and surg. anatomy to profl. jours. Active San Antonio Symphony Mastersingers, 1970-75, Augusta Opera, 1975—2011, Augusta Choral Soc., 1975-95, Augusta Opera Guild, 2009-; judge Regional Sci. Fairs, Augusta, 1978-90, elder, Presbyn. Ch., 2008-. Recipient Golden Apple award, U. Tex. Health Sci. Ctr., 1975, Outstanding Med. Educator award, Med. Coll. Ga., 1976, 1977, 1978, 1982, 1987, 1988, 1990, 1991, 1997, Disting. Faculty award, 1978, 2000, Excellence in Tchg. award, 1997, 1999, Regents' award in tchg., 1998, others. Mem. AAUP, Am. Assn. Clin. Anatomists (membership chmn. 1982-86, mem. editl. bd. Jour. Clin. Anatomy 1994—), Am. Assn. Anatomists, Columbia County Choral Soc. (founding mem.), KC (4th degree). Republican. Avocations: opera, chess, tennis, camping. Address: Med Coll Ga 178 Creekview Ct Martinez GA 30907 Office Phone: 706-868-9290. Personal E-mail: glcolb@yahoo.com.

COLBOURN, TREVOR, retired academic administrator, historian; b. Armidale, NSW, Australia, Feb. 24, 1927; came to U.S., 1948; s. Harold Arthur and Ella Mary (Henderson) C.; m. Beryl Richards Evans, Jan. 10, 1949; children: Katherine Elizabeth, Lisa Sian Elinor. BA with honors, U. London, 1948; MA, Coll. William and Mary, 1949, Johns Hopkins, 1951, PhD, 1953. From instr. to asst. prof. Pa. State U., 1952-59; from asst. prof. to prof. Am. history Ind. U., 1959-67; dean Grad. Sch., prof. history U. N.H., 1967-73; v.p. for acad. affairs San Diego State U., 1973-77, acting pres., 1977-78; pres. U. Central Fla., Orlando, 1978-89. Author: The Lamp of Experience, 1965, 2d edit., 1998, The Colonial Experience, 1966, (with others) The Americans: A Brief History, 1972, 4th edit., 1985; co-editor: (with others) The American Past in Perspective, 1970; editor: (with others) Fame and the Founding Fathers, 1974, 2d edit., 1998. Mem. Orgn. Am. Historians, Am. Assn. State Colls. and Univs. Office: U Cen Fla Office Pres Emeritus Orlando FL 32816-1110 Office Phone: 407-823-2373. Business E-Mail: colbourn@mail.ucf.edu.

COLBY, IRA, dean, educator; b. Pittsfield, Mass., Aug. 17, 1949; s. Ira S. Colby and L. Mary; m. Deborah Judith Norton, May 7, 1970; 1 child, Lisa. BS, Springfield Coll., Mass., 2019, HHD (hon.), 2010; MSW, Va. Commonwealth U., Richmond, 1975; D in Social Work, U. Pa., Phila., 1984. LCSW Tex. State Bd. Social Worker Examiners, 1986. Dir. BSW program Ferrum Coll., Va., 1975—80; asst. to assoc. prof. social work U. Tex., Arlington, 1982—93; dir. Sch. Social Work U. Ctrl. Fla., Orlando, 1993—99; vis. scholar U. Wales Sch. Applied Scis. and Internat. Devel., Ctr. Applied Social Studies, Swansea, 1998; dean, prof. social work Grad. Coll. Social Work U. Houston, 1999—. Co-convener, co-chair Action Network Social Work Edn. and Rsch., Washington, 2000—03, bd. mem., 2007—10; hon. prof. East China U. Sci. and Tech., Shanghai, 2007—. Author: (textbook) Introduction to Social Work 4th edit.; contbr. articles to profl. jours. Treas. Nat. Assn. Deans and Dirs. Schs. Social Work, 2003—05. Recipient Gertrude Golliday Meml. Tchg. Excellence award, U. Tex.-Arlington, 1988, Fernando G. Torgerson Tchg. award, 1991—92, Disting. Alumni award, Va. Commonwealth U., 2005; named Social Worker of Yr., Tex. NASW, 1984, 1997. Fellow: Phi Alpha, Phi Kappa (2008), Nat. Acad. Practice; mem.: Coun. on Social Work Edn. (site visitor 1986—2014, pres. 2007—10, co-convener 2012—14, chair congl. fellows com. 1999—2001). Democrat. Avocations: reading, running, snowboarding. Office: University Houston Grad Coll Social Work 110HA Social Work Bldg Houston TX 77204-4013 Office Fax: 713-743-3267. Business E-Mail: icolby@uh.edu.*

COLE, DERHAM, JR., state legislator; b. Columbia, SC, Mar. 12, 1977; s. J. Derham and Candace Carlson Cole; m. Suzanne Boulware, Jan. 5, 2008. BS, U. SC, 1999, MA in Internat. Bus. Studies, 2003, JD, 2003. Atty. Parker Poe Adams & Bernstein LLP; mem. Dist. 32 SC House of Reps., 2008—. Republican. Office: Dist/Home Office PO Box 1467 Spartanburg SC 29304 also: Capitol Office 402B Blatt Bldg Columbia SC 29201 Home Phone: 864-285-4732; Office Phone: 864-591-2030, 803-212-6790. E-mail: derhamcole@schouse.org.

COLE, ERIK, professional hockey player; b. Oswego, NY, Nov. 6, 1978; m. Emily Cole; children: Bella, Landon. Attended, Clarkson U. Left wing Carolina Hurricanes, 2001—08, 2009—11, Edmonton Oilers, 2008—09, Montreal Canadiens, 2011—13, Dallas Stars, 2013—. Mem. USA Olympic Hockey Team, Torino, Italy, 2006. Achievements include being a member of Stanley Cup Champion Carolina Hurricanes, 2006. Office: Dallas Stars American Airlines Ctr 2500 Victory Ave Dallas TX 75201

COLE, JAMES OTIS, lawyer; b. Florence, Ala., Feb. 6, 1941; s. Calloway and Eula (Reynolds) Cole; m. Ada Dolores Cole, Dec. 16, 1961; children: James Otis Jr., Lerone Barrington. BA, Talladega Coll., 1963; JD, Harvard U., 1971. Bar: Ill. 1971, Calif. 1977, admitted to practice: US Dist. Ct. (no. dist.) Ill. 1971, US Supreme Ct. 1981. Assoc. Kirkland & Ellis, Chgo., 1971-73; assoc. gen. counsel The Clorox Co., Oakland, Calif., 1973—93, v.p. corp. affairs, 1993—97; sr. v.p., gen. counsel, sec. AutoNation, Inc., Ft. Lauderdale; of counsel Ruden, McClosky, Smith, Schuster & Russell, 2002—. Arbitrator Contra Costa County Superior Ct., Martinez, Calif., 1980. Counsel East Oakland Youth Devel. Ctr.; bd. dir. Oakland Ballet, Bay Area Urban League, Oakland, Black Filmmakers Hall of Fame, Oakland, pres., 1980—83. Mem.: Calif. Bar Jud. Nominees Evaluation Commn. (commr. 1985), Charles Houston Bar Assn. (pres. 1985), Calif. Assn. Black Lawyers, Nat. Bar Assn. (bd. gov. 1981), ABA, Oakland Athletic Club. Office: Ruden McClosky Smith Schuster & Russell 200 E Broward Blvd Fort Lauderdale FL 33302

COLE, JAMES S., dean, dental educator; b. Mpls. m. Barbara Cole. BS, Stephen F. Austin State U., 1967; DDS, Baylor Coll. Dentistry, 1975. Instr., restorative sciences Baylor Coll. Dentistry, Texas A&M U., Dallas, 1977—81, v.p., dir. computer services, 1981—92, prof., restorative sciences, 1992—, interim pres. and dean, 1990, exec. v.p., assoc. dean, CFO, COO, vice dean, interim dean, 1999—2000, dean, 2000—; pres., treas. Baylor Oral Health Found., 1997—99; interim pres. Tex. A&M U. Sys. Health Sci. Ctr., 2000—01. Bd. mem. Friends of the Nat. Inst. of Dental and Craniofacial Rsch., 2005—. Lt. USN, 1967—71. Recipient Dentist of Yr., Dallas County Dental Soc., 2000. Fellow: Internat. Coll. Dentists, Am. Coll. Dentists. Office: 3302 Gaston Ave Dallas TX 75246 Office Phone: 214-828-8300. Office Fax: 214-828-8496. Business E-Mail: JCole@bcd.tamhsc.edu.

COLE, MARK L., state legislator, systems analyst; b. Lousiville, June 6, 1958; m. Eugenia Ann Fairchild; 4 children. BS, We. Ky. U., 1980; AAS, Germanna C.C., 1990; BLS, Mary Washington Coll., Va., 1993. Sys. analyst; state del. dist. 88 Va. House of Dels., Va., 2002—. Elected mem. Spotsylvania County Bd. Suprs.; mem. Rappahannock River Basin Comm., Quantico Civilian-Mil. Coun., Fredericksburg Met. Planning Org., 2000—02, High Growth Coalition, 2000—02. With USN, 1980—85, with USNR, 1985—. Republican. Baptist. Office: Gen Assembly Bldg Rm 808 PO Box 406 Richmond VA 23218 Address: Dist Offict PO Box 6046 Fredericksburg VA 22403 E-mail: Del_Cole@house.state.va.us.

COLE, MICHAEL H., food products executive, lawyer; BS, Univ. Va.; JD, Univ. Va., Charlottesville, 1985. Bar: Va. 1985. With McGuireWoods LLP; Joined Smithfield Foods, Inc., Va., 1996, sec., 1999—, v.p., dep. gen. counsel, v.p., chief legal officer, sec. Bd. dirs. Pennexx Foods, Inc., 2001. Office: Smithfield Foods Inc 200 Commerce St Smithfield VA 23430 Office Phone: 757-365-3000. Office Fax: 757-365-3017.*

COLE, RICHARD CARGILL, language educator; b. Kansas City, Kans., Apr. 16, 1926; s. Horace Richard and Iris Verner (Cargill) C.; m. Florence Adaline Mason, June 27, 1956; children: Celia Elizabeth Cole Shaw, Paul Richard. BA, Hamilton Coll., 1950; MA, Yale U., 1951, PhD in English, 1955. English tchr. Manlius (N.Y.) Sch., 1951-52; asst. to dean of freshmen Yale U., New Haven, 1953-54; instr. English U. Tex., Austin, 1954-57; assoc. prof. Radford Va. Coll. (now Univ.), 1957-59, prof. English, 1959-61, Davidson (N.C.) Coll., 1961-93, prof. emeritus, 1993—. Author: Irish Booksellers and English Writers, 1740-1800, 1986; author, editor: Robert Colvill's Atalanta and Savannah, 1987, John Singleton's Grand Tour, 1815-1817, 1988, The General Correspondence of James Boswell, 1766-1767, 1993, Thomas Mante, Writer, Soldier, Adventurer, 1993, The General Correspondence of James Boswell, 1768-1769, 1997; contbr. articles to profl. jours. Sgt. USAAF, 1944-46, ETO. Robert Warnock Rsch. fellow Yale U., 1975-76, Rsch. fellow Yale U. Div. Sch., 1978; rsch. grantee Bd. Higher Edn., Presbyn. Ch., 1968, Piedmont U. Ctr. NC, 1968; grantee Am. Coun. Learned Socs., 1976, Nat. Endowment for the Humanities, 1985, 89. Mem. Phi Beta Kappa. Republican. Presbyterian. Home: 100 Cynthia Dr Chapel Hill NC 27514-6613

COLE, RICHARD RAY, communications educator, former dean; b. Forney, Tex., Apr. 20, 1942; s. Richard W. and G. Gladys C.; m. Lynda F. Painter, May 31, 1968. BJ, U. Tex., 1964, MA, 1966; PhD, U. Minn., 1971. Asst. city editor The News, Mexico City, 1966-67; freelance writer, 1966-67; reporter Harrow Observer, Harrow-on-the-Hill, England, 1968; asst. prof. W.Va. U., 1967-68; instr. U. Minn., 1968-71; mem. faculty U. NC, Chapel Hill, 1971—, prof. journalism, 1979—, John T. Kerr Jr. disting. prof., 2002—, dean Sch. Journalism and Mass Comm., 1979—2005; mem., bd. dirs. Lee Enterprises, 2006—, NC Press Found., 2010—. Nat. scholarship com. Freedom Forum, 1980-86, chmn., 1987-93; chief judge H.L. Mencken Nat. Writing Award Competition, 1983-90; mem. journalism awards program steering com. William Randolph Hearst Found., 1981-2005, chmn., 1991-2005; chmn. accrediting teams US journalism schs.; mem. faculty adv. com. World Press Inst.; mem. Nat. Accrediting Coun. on Edn. in Journalism and Mass Comm., 1987-96, v.p., 1989-95; cons. in field; creator cooperative programs with univs. in Mexico City, Santiago, Chile, Brazil, State of Parana, Havana, Cuba, United Arab Emirates China; apptd. adh., coun. facultad comunicaciones Pontificial Cath. U. Chile, 1999—. Co-author: Gathering and Writing The News: Selected Readings, 1975; editor: Communication in Latin America: Journalism, Mass Communication, and Society, 1996; asst. editor Journalism Quar., 1973-85; contbr. articles to profl. jours. Chmn. U. NC Bicentennial Observance Planning Com., 1986-87; mem. Bicentennial Policy Com., 1988-94. Recipient Excellence award in undergrad. tchg. Amoco Found., 1978, Freedom Forum medal for lifetime accomplishments in journalism-mass comm. adminstrn., 1992, Earl Gluck award for disting. svc. to broadcasting, 2004, Dist. Svc. medal UNC-Chapel Hill General Alumni Assn., 2005; named to NC Journalism Hall of Fame, 2005, Order of Long Leaf Pine award NC Gov., 2005; grantee U. Minn., U. NC Dept. State, Internat. Comm. Agy., Internat. Media Fund, US AID, others; Fulbright fellow, Brazil, 2001. Mem. Assn. Edn. Journalism and Mass Comm. (exec. com. 1977-79, 81-84, chmn. coms. 1974-75, 77-79, pres. 1982-83, nat. task force on future mass comm. of edn. 1983-84), Internat. Assn. Mass Comm. Rsch. (coun. 1980-88, v.p. 1984-88), Assn. Schs. Journalism and Mass Comm. (exec. com. 1983-88, 1992-93, pres. 1986-87, mem. nat. steering com. to select 1st journalist in space NASA 1985-86), Inter Am. Press Assn., Order of Golden Fleece, Sigma Delta Chi, Kappa Tau Alpha. Office: U NC Sch Journalism & Mass Communication PO Box 3365 Chapel Hill NC 27599-0001 Home Phone: 919-929-2436; Office Phone: 919-843-8289. Business E-Mail: richard_cole@unc.edu.

COLE, RICKEY L., political organization administrator; b. Ovett, Miss., 1966; Chmn. Miss. Dem. Party, 2001—04, 2012—, exec. dir., 2011—12. Past com. mem. Miss. Dem. Nat. Com.; past chmn. Miss. Young Dem. Democrat. Office: Mississippi Democratic Party Miss State University 832 N Congress St Jackson MS 39215 Office Phone: 601-969-2913. E-mail: rcole@mississippidemocrats.org.

COLE, SUE W., investment company executive; m. Gordon Cole; 2 children. BSBA, U. NC, Greensboro, 1972, MBA in Fin., 1977. Sr. v.p. NCNB; exec. v.p. NC Trust Co., 1987—97, pres., 1997—2003, CEO, bd. dirs., 2001—03; pres. US Trust Co. of NC, 1997—2003, CEO, bd. dirs., 2001—03; regional CEO Mid-Atlantic region US Trust Co., N.A., 2003—06; prin. Granville Capital, Inc., 2006—. Bd. dirs. Unifi Inc., 2001—07, NC Citizens for Bus. and Industry, Martin Marietta Materials, Inc., 2002—, chair Mgmt. Devel. and Compensation Com., mem. Nominating and Corp. Governance Com. Mem. exec. com. NC Ctr. for Pub. Policy Rsch.; bd. dirs. Marion Covington Found., Tannenbaum-Sternberger Found., Cmty. Found. of Greensboro, Moses Cone Wesley Long Cmty. Health Found.; chmn. NC Biotechnology Ctr.; co-chmn. Bryan Sch. Bus. and Economics, U. NC, Greensboro. Mem.: NC Citizens for Bus. and Industry (hon. chairwoman). Office: Granville Capital Inc 300 N Greene St Ste 1750 Greensboro NC 27401 Office Phone: 336-273-8544. Office Fax: 336-217-4128.

COLE, SUSAN STOCKBRIDGE, retired theater educator; b. San Francisco, Jan. 26, 1939; d. Elmer Leroy Stockbridge and Martha Louise Rosenauer; m. John Michael Day, June 28, 1965 (div. May 1968); m. Willie Robert Cole, June 12, 1976. AB, Stanford U., Calif., 1960, MA, 1961; PhD, U. Oreg., 1972. Asst. prof. theatre Bakersfield (Calif.) Coll., 1962-69; grad. tchg. fellow U. Oreg., Eugene, 1969-72; asst. prof. theatre Keuka Coll., Keuka Park, NY, 1972-75; prof. Appalachian State U., Boone, NC, 1975—2005, dept. chair theatre and dance, 1989—2005; ret., 2005. Cons. Dept. Pub. Instrn., Raleigh, N.C., 1980—2005, N.C. Arts Coun., Raleigh, 1989-93. Author: American National Biography, 1999, Notable Women in American Theatre, 1990; designer more than 100 play prodns., 1962-2005; dir. more than 60 play prodns. Recipient Outstanding Svc. award, Coll. Fine and Applied Arts, Appalachian State U., 2005, NC Order of Long Leaf Pine, 2011. Mem.: Am. Soc. for Theatre Rsch., Assn. for Theatre in Higher Edn., N.C. Theatre Conf. (pres. 1991—92, Svc. award 1997, Disting. Career award 2005), Southeastern Theatre Conf. (pres. 1998—99, Suzanne Davis award 2002), Lions Club Internat. (dist. officer 1997—, treas. 1999—2004, past pres., sec. 2007—), Alpha Psi Omega (pres. 1997—2002). Democrat. Episcopalian. Avocation: reading. Home: PO Box 220 Todd NC 28684-0220 Personal E-mail: coless@appstate.edu.

COLE, THOMAS WINSTON, JR., retired academic administrator, chemistry professor; b. Vernon, Tex., Jan. 11, 1941; s. Thomas Winston and Eva Mae (Sharp) C.; m. Brenda S. Hill, June 14, 1964; children: Kelley S., Thomas III. BS, Wiley Coll., Marshall, Tex., 1961; PhD, U. Chgo., 1966; PhD (hon.), W.Va. State Coll., U. Charleston, Allegheny Coll., Wiley Coll. Mem. faculty Atlanta U., 1966-82, prof. chemistry, chmn. dept., 1971-82, Fuller E. Callaway prof., 1969-80, project dir. Resource Ctr. Sci. and Engring., 1978-82, univ. provost, v.p. acad. affairs, 1979-82; pres. W.Va. State Coll., Institute, 1982-86; chancellor W.Va. Bd. of Regents, 1986-88; pres. Clark Atlanta U., 1989—2002, pres. emeritus, 2002—; pres., CEO Great Schs. Atlanta, 2004—06; interim chancellor U. Mass., Amherst, 2007—08. Vis. prof. U. Ill., summer 1972, MIT, 1973-74; summer chemist Miami Valley Lab. Procter and Gamble co., 1967; Celanese Corp., Charlotte, N.C., 1974, UNCF lectr., 1975-84; bd. dirs. C&P Telephone Co., Nat. Pub. TV Stas., United Nat. Bank, Thomas Meml. Hosp. Mem. Leadership Atlanta. So. Regional fellow, summer 1961; Woodrow Wilson fellow, 1961-62; Allied Chem. fellow, 1963; Danforth scholar, 1971-82. Mem. Am. Chem. Soc., AAAS, Nat. Inst. Sci., Nat. Orgn. Profl. Advancement Black Chemists and Chem. Engrs., Sigma Xi, Sigma Pi Phi, Alpha Phi Alpha Lodges: Rotary. Office: Sta WCLK-FM 111 James P Brawley Dr SW Atlanta GA 30314-4207 Office Phone: 413-545-2211.

COLE, TODD GODWIN, management consultant transportation; b. Coushatta, La., Mar. 5, 1921; s. Ira and Lucie (Triche) C.; m. Inez Hamilton, Feb. 9, 1953 (div. 1974); children: Michael H., Diane Cole Janusz (dec. 1994); m. Josephine Giovanetti, Oct. 1974 (dec. 1985); m. Pamela Wilds, Mar., 1987. Student, La. State U., 1935—37; LLB, Woodrow Wilson Coll., 1947. CPA, Ga. With Delta Airlines, 1940-63, dir., exec. v.p. adminstrn., 1955-63; sr. v.p. fin. and adminstrn., dir. Ea. Airlines, 1963-67, vice chmn., chmn. fin. com., dir., 1967-69; v.p., asst. to pres., dir. C.I.T. Fin. Corp., NYC, 1969, v.p. fin., 1969-71, mem. exec. com., 1970-86, exec. v.p., 1971-73, pres., chief adminstrv. officer, 1973-80, pres., COO, 1980-83, pres., CEO, 1984-86; CEO, bd. dirs. Frontier Air Lines D.I.P., 1987-89; vice chmn., dir. Ea. Air Lines D.I.P., 1989-91; mng. dir. Simat, Hellesen & Eichrer, Inc., 1992-96; pres. Cole & Wilds Assocs., Miami, 1996—; vice chmn. Hawaiian Airlines, Inc., 2002—03; founding dir. Coral Gables Trust Co., 2004. Chmn. Arrow Air, Inc., 1997-98; bd. dirs. Kaiser Ventures, LLC. Mem. Ga. Bar Assn. Office: Todd G Cole 60 Edgewater Dr #14E Coral Gables FL 33133-6975 Office Phone: 305-666-8136. Personal E-mail: coletg@bellsouth.net.

COLE, TOM (THOMAS JEFFREY COLE), United States Representative from Oklahoma; b. Shreveport, La., Apr. 28, 1949; s. John D. and Helen Gale Cole; m. Ellen Decker; 1 child, Mason. BA in History, Grinnell Coll., Iowa, 1971; MA in Brit. History, Yale U., New Haven, 1974; PhD in Brit. History, U. Okla., Norman, 1984. Instr. U. Okla., 1975-78; lectr. Grinnell Coll., 1977—79; instr. Okla. Bapt. U., 1981; mem. Okla. State Senate, 1988—91; founding ptnr., pres. Cole, Hargrave, Snodgrass & Associates, Oklahoma City, 1989—; sec. of state State of Okla., Oklahoma City, 1995-99; mem. US Congress from 4th Okla. Dist., 2003—. Exec. dir. Nat. Rep. Congl. Com., 1999—2000, chmn., 2006—08. Exec. dir. Okla. Rep. Com., 1980—81, Reagan-Bush Presdl. campaign, Okla., 1984; chmn. Okla. Rep. Party, 1985—89; mem. nat. bd. dirs. Fulbright Assn.; enrolled mem. Chickasaw Nation, Okla. Recipient Congl. Lifetime Achievement award, Nat. Ctr. Am. Indian Enterprise Devel., 2009, Robert A. Taft award, Okla. Rep. Party, Guardian Small Bus. award, Nat. Fedn. Ind. Bus.; named to Chickasaw Nation Hall of Fame, 2004; Fulbright Fellow, 1977—78, Thomas J. Watson Fellow. Mem.: Okla. C. of C., Soc. Study Labor Hist., Am. Hist. Assn., Inst. Hist. Rsch., Phi Alpha Theta. Republican. Methodist. Office: US House of Representatives 2458 Rayburn House Office Bldg Washington DC 20515 also: 2420 Springer Dr Ste 120 Norman OK 73069 Office Phone: 202-225-6165. Office Fax: 202-225-3512.*

COLEMAN, BRITTIN TURNER, lawyer; b. Tuscaloosa, Ala., Dec. 12, 1942; s. Jefferson Jackson and Rose Wallace (Turner) C.; m. Johanna M. Nicol, June 1963 (div. 1967); 1 child, Anna M. Shields; m. Jane M. Kirkman, June 27, 1970; children: Mary Elizabeth, Emily

Jane. BA in Am. Studies, U. Ala., 1964, LLB, 1967. Bar: Ala. 1967, U.S. Dist. Ct. (no. dist.) Ala. 1972, U.S. Ct. Appeals (5th cir.) 1975, U.S. Ct. Appeals (11th cir.) 1981, U.S. Dist. Ct. (mid. and so. dists.) Ala. 1986. With Bradley, Arant, Rose & White, Birmingham, Ala., 1971—, ptnr., 1976—2012, of counsel, 2012—. Adj. prof. law, coach Nat. Mock Trial teams Cumberland Sch. Law, 1979-84 (2 Nat. Championships); former mem. faculty Ala. Def. Lawyers Assn. Trial Acad., 1992, 2009; former mem. Ala. Pattern Jury Instructions Com.; mem. ct.'s adv. group No. Dist. Ala., 1997; former mem. Product Liability Adv. Coun. Bd. dirs. Downtown YMCA, 1993-99; active Canterbury United Meth. Ch. Capt. JAGC, U.S. Army, 1967-71. Decorated Two Bronze Star, Two Army Commendation medals, Vietnam Svc. medal, Vietnam Campaign medal, Vietnam Civil Action Honor medal; recipient Sam W. Pipes Disting. Alumnus award, U. Ala. Sch. Law, 2009. Master: Birmingham Inn of Am. Inns of Ct.; fellow: Birmingham Bar Found. (bd. dirs. 2000—02), Ala. Law Found., Am. Bar Found.; mem.: ABA, Farrah Law Soc., Def. Rsch. Inst., Ala. Def. Lawyers Assn., Am. Bd. Trial Advocates, Ala. Law Inst., Birmingham Bar Assn. (chmn. grievance com. 1989, exec. com. 1992—94, pres.-elect 1998, pres. 1999, past chmn. civil cts. com., past chmn. CLE com., past chmn. ins. com., past Liberty Bell award com., past chmn. election com., past exec. com. young lawyers sect., past chmn. long range planning com., chmn. nominating com. 2008), Am. Judicature Soc., Ala. Law Sch. Found. (pres. 1994—96, exec. com. 1997—), The Club, Ala. Alumni of Order of Coif (pres. 1992—94). Office: Bradley Arant Boult Cummings LLP One Federal Pl 1819 5th Ave N Birmingham AL 35203 Business E-Mail: bcoleman@babc.com.*

COLEMAN, BROOKS P., state legislator; b. Oct. 11, 1939; m. Mary Clair Coleman; 1 child. Former state rep. Dist. 65, Ga.; state rep. Dist. 80, Ga., 1992—2002, Dist. 97, 2004—; house rep. Natural Resources & Environ. & Retirement Coms., Ga., mem. edn.; asst. supt. Gwinnett County Schs.; motivational spkr. Republican. Baptist. Address: 3919 Hillside Dr Duluth GA 30136-2714 Mailing: 501 Legis Off Bldg Atlanta GA 30334 Office Phone: 404-656-0177, 770-822-6500.

COLEMAN, CREIGHTON B., state legislator; b. Winnsboro, SC, May 12, 1956; s. George F. and Lucy Davis Coleman; m. Marian Walker McNair, 1990; children: Creighton B. Jr., Chandler McNair, Marion Walker. BA, The Citadel, 1979; JD, U. SC, 1985. Prosecutor 5th Jud. Cir., 1985—90, 6th Jud. Cir., 1990—92; atty. Coleman and Tolen, LLC; mem. Dist. 41 SC House of Reps., 2000—09; mem. Dist. 17 SC State Senate, 2009—. Mem.: Pub. Defenders Bd. Chester & Fairfield Counties, SC Bar Assn. (former mem. com. disciplinary procedures). Democrat. Episcopalian. Office: 513 Gressette Bldg Columbia SC 29201 Home: 125 Garden St Winnsboro SC 29180 Address: PO Box 1006 Winnsboro SC 29180 Home Phone: 803-635-7066; Office Phone: 803-212-6180, 803-635-6884. E-mail: CBC@scstatehouse.net.

COLEMAN, GARNET F., state legislator; b. Sept. 8, 1961; m. Angelique Coleman; children: Austin, Evan. Attended, Howard U., Washington; BA, U. St. Thomas; completed sr. exec. state and local govt. program, Harvard U. John F. Kennedy Sch. Govt., Mass. Bus. counselor; bank mktg. specialist; small bus. owner; mem. Dist. 147 Tex. House of Representatives, 1991—. Founder S.M.A.R.T. Kids; CEO Apartments for America, Inc. Recipient of several awards and honors. Democrat. Office: 5445 Alameda Ste 501 Houston TX 77004 also: Room CAP GW.17 Capitol PO Box 2910 Austin TX 78768 Address: PO Box 88140 Houston TX 77288 Office Phone: 713-520-5355, 512-463-0524, 713-520-5355.

COLEMAN, GARY L., insurance company executive; BBA, U. Texas. With KPMG; joined Torchmark Corp., 1981, v.p., chief acctg. officer Birmingham, Ala., 1994—99, exec. v.p., CFO, 1999—2012, co-CEO, 2012—. Office: Torchmark Corp 3700 S Stonebridge Dr PO Box 8080 Mc Kinney TX 75070-8080*

COLEMAN, HENRY EDWIN, artist, educator; b. Charlottesville, Va., Oct. 26, 1938; s. Albin Clayton and Mary Louise (Nay) C.; m. Charlotte Heyne, Dec. 29, 1962 (dec. 1984); children: Edwin Randolph, Mary Clayton; m. Leslie W. Rose, Jan. 4, 1993; 1 stepson, John A. Rose. AB in Fine Arts, Coll. William and Mary, 1961; MA, U. Iowa, 1963. Instr. art Lawrence Coll., Appleton, Wis., 1963-64; mem. faculty Coll. William and Mary, Williamsburg, Va., 1964-99, prof. fine arts, 1989—91, chair dept. fine arts, 1987—91. Cons. for purchasing CSX Corp. Art Collection, Richmond, Va., 1985. Illustrator: Oscar Wilde's Remarkable Rocket, 1974; one-man shows include Radford Coll., Va., 1975, Gallery II West, St. George, Utah, 1984, U. Maine, Presque Isle, 1989, Andrew & Laura McLain Mus., Florenceville, N.B., Can., 1989, Muscarelle Mus. Art William & Mary Coll., Williamsburg, Va., 1999, exhibited in group shows at Patio Show, Iowa City, 1962—63, Des Moines Art Ctr., 1963, Lawrence Coll., Appleton, 1964, 20th Century Gallery, Williamsburg, 1964—66, Chrysler Mus., Norfolk, Va., 1972, So. Ill. U., Carbondale, 1975, Peninsula Art Ctr., Newport News, Va., 1980, Nat. Small Image Exhbn., Spokane, Wash., 1984, Am. Drawing Biennial Muscarelle Mus. of Art, Coll. William and Mary, Williamsburg, 1988, 1990 (Honorable Mention award), 1992, Internat. Cultural Exch. Art Exhibit, Neyagawa, Japan, 1988, Bowery Gallery, N.Y.C., 1988, Invitational D'Art Ctr., Norfolk, 1991, Peninsula Fine Arts Mus., Newport News, 1995—96, 2001, The Charles H. Taylor Art Ctr., Hampton, Va., 2006. Commr. Williamsburg Arts Commn., 1985-91; bd. dirs. Yorktown (Va.) Arts Found., 1989-93; juror Occasion for the Arts, Williamsburg, 1988, 27th Regional Art Exhbn., W.C. Rawls Libr. & Mus., Courtland, Va., 1990; commr. archtl. rev. bd., City Williamsburg, 1994-2000. Summer Rsch. grantee Coll. William & Mary, 1976, Semester Faculty grantee, 1985, Faculty Rsch. grantee, 1991-92. Office: Coll William and Mary Andrews Hall Williamsburg VA 23185 Personal E-mail: henryandleslie@gmail.com.

COLEMAN, JACK ANDREW, JR., otolaryngologist; b. Mpls., Oct. 17, 1951; s. Jack Andrew and Patricia Marie Coleman; m. Margaret Overton, June 14, 1987; children: Kelley Anne, Jennifer Allison, Jack Andrew Christian. BA, U. Va., 1973; postgrad., U. Autonoma Guadalajara, Mex., 1973-77; MD, U. Cin., 1979. Diplomate Am. Bd. Gen. Otolaryngology, Nat. Bd. Med. Examiners, cert. Am. Acad. Facial Plastic and Reconstructive Surgery. Intern, surgery U. Cin. Gen. Hosp., 1979—80, resident in surgery, 1980—81; resident in otolaryngology U. Pitts. Eye and Ear Hosp., 1981-84; staff physician Southside Cmty. Hosp., Farmville, Va., 1984-85, Univ. Med. Ctr., Lebanon, 1985-88; instr. Vanderbilt U. Med. Ctr., Nashville, 1988-93, asst. prof., 1993-96; chief otolaryngology Nashville Gen. Hosp., 1988-93; staff physician Centennial Med. Ctr., St. Thomas Hosp., Nashville, 1996-2000, Chesapeake Gen. Hosp., 2000-01, Sentera Bayside Hosp., 2000—; asst. clin. prof. otolaryngology Eastern Va. Med. Sch., 2000-01; facial plastic surgeon Franklin Surgical Assn., Tenn., 2008—, practice limited to cosmetic surgery. Mem. edn. com. Laser Inst. Am., Cin., 1991—96; cons. InFLUENT, San Francisco, 1998—99, 2000—03, Ethicon Endo-Surgery, 2001—03; mem. med. adv. bd. Pj Med., 2000—03; physician Police S.W.A.T. Team, Chesapeake, Va. Editor: Management of Lower Airway Stenosis, 1995, Sleep Apnea Vols. 1 and 2, 1998—99. Cubscout leader Boy Scouts Am., 1998—99; hon. chmn. physician adv. bd. Nat. Rep. Congl. Com., 2001. Comdr. USNR. Grantee, Laserscope Co., 1988, Karl Storz Instruments, 1989, Vanderbilt U. Rsch. Coun., 1994. Fellow: ACS (mem. history and archives com. 1988—93), Am. Acad. Facial Plastic and Reconstructive Surgery, Am. Acad. Otolaryngology and Head and Neck Surgery (mem. relative value scale com. 1988—90, chmn., mem. com. sleep disorders 1990—98, mem. com. on infectious diseases 1990—98, mem. polit. contact network 1991—96, mem. self-instructional packages subcommittee 1991—96, mem. allergy and immunology com. 1991—96, mem. subcommittee on core edn. 1992—93, chmn. sleep disorders com. 1995—96); mem.: Am. Rhinologic Soc., Laser Inst. Am. (sr.; mem. edn. com. 1991), Assn. Military Surgeons US (life), Am. Acad. Sleep Medicine (mem. clin. practice review com. 1999—2001), H. William Scott, Jr. Soc., Amateur Athletic Union (coach, ofcl. Tae Kwon Do program 1998—2001), Rotary. Avocations: military history, military awards, military miniatures, skydiving. Home: 2832 Sulphur Springs Rd Murfreesboro TN 37129

COLEMAN, JEAN BLACK, nurse, physician assistant; b. Sharon, Pa., Jan. 11, 1925; d. Charles B. and Sue E. (Dougherty) Black; m. Donald A. Coleman, July 3, 1946; children: Sue Ann Lopez, Donald Ashley. Grad., Spencer Hosp. Sch. Nursing, Meadville, Pa., 1945; student, Vanderbilt U., 1952-54. RN, Ga. Nurse, dir. nursing Bulloch Meml. Hosp., Statesboro, Ga, 1948-51, nurse supr. surgery, 1954-67, dir. nursing, 1967-71; physician's asst., nurse anesthetist Office Dr. Robert H. Swint, Statesboro, 1971-96; physician asst. Office Dr. Earl L. Alderman, Statesboro, 1996-98, Dr. Swaroop Reddy, Statesboro, 1998—. Mem. physician's asst. adv. com. Ga. Med. Bd., 1989-97; mem. physician assts. adv. com. Ga. Bd. Med. Examiners, 1987-97, ex-officio mem., 1994-95. Recipient Dean Day Smith Svc. to Mankind award, 1995; named Woman of Yr. in med. field Bus. and Profl. Women, 1980; Paul Harris fellow Rotary Club. Mem. ANA, Am. Acad. Physician Assts., Ga. Nurses Assn., Ga. Assn. Physician Assts. (bd. dirs. 1975-79, v.p. 1979-80, pres. 1980-81). Republican. Roman Catholic.

COLEMAN, JOSIAH DENNIS, state supreme court justice; s. Thomas Coleman; m. Ashleigh Burke Coleman; 1 child. BA cum laude in history and philosophy, U. Miss., Oxford, 1995; JD, U. Miss., 1999. Policy rsch. intern Office of the Sec. of State; summer law clk. Tupelo, Miss.; law clk. to US Magistrate Judge S. Allan Alexander Oxford, Miss.; atty. Holland, Ray, Upchurch & Hillen, Tupelo, Dunbar Davis, Oxford, 2005—07, Hickman Goza & Spragins, Oxford, 2007—12; assoc. justice Miss. Supreme Ct., Jackson, 2013—. Vol. firefighter Toccopola Vol. Fire Dept., Pontotoc County, Miss.; mem. bd. deacons Coll. Hill Presbyn. Ch., Oxford; bd. dirs. Internat. Guest House, Oxford. Office: Mississippi Supreme Ct 450 High St Jackson MS 39201

COLEMAN, LINDA, former state legislator; Former dem. freshman chairwoman; house rep. NC; state rep. Dist. 39 NC, 2005—09. Democrat. Office Phone: 919-733-5934. E-mail: lindac@ncleg.net.

COLEMAN, LINDA F., state legislator; b. Mound, Miss., Sept. 27, 1961; m. Nelson Brenson Coleman. Mem. Dist. 29 Miss. House of Reps., 1992—; atty. Supt. Pleasant Green MB Ch. Sunday Sch. Mem.: Nat. Magnolia Bar Assn., Nat. Miss. Bar Assn. Democrat. Baptist. Mailing: 1389 Cedar Rd Mound Bayou MS 38762 Fax: 601-741-3472. Business E-Mail: lcoleman@house.ms.gov.

COLEMAN, LINDA F., state legislator; b. Birmingham, Ala. BA, Ala. A&M U., Normal, 1971; MA, U. Ala., Birmingham, 1976. Tchr. Birmingham Pub. Sch. Sys., 1972—82; councilwoman Birmingham City Coun., 1985—87; recruitment specialist Am. Red Cross; realtor ReMAX Realty Consultants; mktg. profl. Birmingham-Jefferson County Transit Authority; compliance officer Americans with Disabilities; mem. Dist. 60 Ala. House of Reps., Montgomery, 2003—06; mem. Dist. 20 Ala. State Senate, Montgomery, 2006—, chair health com. Mem. Jefferson County Positive Maturity Bd., St. Mary's Cath. Ch., Fairfield, Ala.; state dir. Nat. Found. Women Legislators; bd. mem. Am. Red Cross, Birmingham Area Chpt., cmty. volunteers. Mem.: Ala. Realtors Assn. Democrat. Roman Catholic. Office: Ala State Senate Ala State House 11 S Union St Rm 732 Montgomery AL 36130 Office Phone: 205-254-2079, 334-242-7864. Office Fax: 205-254-2505. Business E-Mail: lindacoleman60@bellsouth.net.

COLEMAN, MARY H., state legislator; b. Noxapater, Miss., Sept. 25, 1946; m. Cayle Casey; children: Marcus, Crystal, Arqullas. Exec. asst. to state auditor, 1987—92; mem. Dist. 65 Miss. House of Reps., 1995—. Mem.: Nat. Orgn. Women, Women Govt., Southern Conf. State Legislators, NAACP, United Way, Rotary. Democrat. Baptist. Mailing: 308 Lynnwood Lane Jackson MS 39206 Home Phone: 601-982-0496; Office Phone: 601-362-8105, 601-359-3336. Business E-Mail: mcoleman@house.ms.gov.

COLEMAN, MERIKA, state legislator; b. Lakenheath, Eng., Nov. 6, 1973; m. Edward Coleman; children: Elexia, Xaviar. BA in Mass Comm., U. Ala., Birmingham, MPA. Instr. Miles Coll., 1997—99, asst. prof. polit. sci.; policy analyst Ala. Arise, 1999; econ. justice strategist Greater Birmingham Ministries; dir. cmty. and econ. devel. Lawson State CC, adj. prof. govt.; dir. econ. and cmty. devel. City of Bessemer; mem. Dist. 57 Ala. House of Reps., Montgomery, 2002—. Mem. women's caucus and Southern caucus Ctr. on Policy Alternatives; mem. steering com. Mayor's Roundtable on Housing; mem. adv. com. Wider Opportunities for Women-Self Sufficiency Stds., Ala. Citizens Policy Project. Exec. bd. mem. Midfield Neighborhood Assn.; del. Am. Coun. Young Polit. Leaders, Japan, 2003; bd. mem. Greater Birmingham Ministries, Women Legislators' Lobby. Fleming fellow, Ctr. Policy Alternatives, 2004. Mem.: Midfield Voter's League, Delta Sigma Theta. Democrat. Baptist. Office: PO Box 28888 Birmingham AL 35228 also: Ala House of Reps Ala State House 11 S Union St Rm 539-B Montgomery AL 36130 Office Phone: 205-325-5308, 334-242-7755.

COLEMAN, ROBERT L., obstetrician, gynecologic oncologist; b. San Diego, Nov. 3, 1961; s. Gary A. and Marlene Beatty; m. Fay K. Leiting, July 23, 1982; children: Kay, Joe, Mary, Theresa children: Jay, Christina. BS in Math., Creighton U., Omaha, 1983; MD, Creighton U. Sch. Medicine, 1987. Diplomate Am. Bd. Med. Examiners, Am. Bd. Ob-Gyn., cert. in gynecologic oncology; ob-gyn. gyn. oncologist. Ob-gyn. residency Northwestern U. Med. Ctr., Chgo., 1987—91; gynecologic oncology fellowship U. Tex. MD Anderson Cancer Ctr., Houston, 1991—93, assoc. prof. dept. gynecologic ogy, 2004—06, prof., dir. clin. rsch., dept. gynecologic oncology, 2006—; asst. prof., dir. dept. ob-gyn. Creighton U. Sch. Medicine, 1993—96; asst. prof. ob-gyn. U. Tex. Southwestern Med. Ctr., Dallas, 1996—2000, assoc. prof. dept. ob-gyn., 2000—04, Patricia Duniven Fletcher prof. gynecologic oncology & ob.-gyn., vice chmn. gynecologic svcs. Dallas, 2001—04. Examiner Am. Bd. Ob-Gyn., 2001—, examiner divsn. gynecologic oncology, 2006—; bd. dirs. Gynecologic Cancer Found., Chgo., 2006—, Ann Rife Cox chair gynecology, 2010—. Author: Handbook of Gynecologic Oncology, 2001; contbr. articles to profl. jours., chapters to books. Fellow: ACS, Am. Gynecol. & Obstetrical Soc., Am. Coll. Obstetricians & Gynecologists; mem.: Western Assn. Gynecologic Oncologists, Soc. Gynecologic Oncologists, Internat. Gynecologic Cancer Soc., Assn. Professors Gynecology & Obstetrics, Am. Soc. Clin. Oncology (mem. grants selection com. 2006—), Am. Assn. Cancer Researchers, Am. Assn. Cancer Rsch., Felix Rutledge Soc. (program chmn. 2003). Office: U Tex MD Anderson Cancer Ctr 1155 Herman Pressler Dr Unit # 1362 Rm CPB6 3244 Houston TX 77030 Office Phone: 713-792-6810. Office Fax: 713-792-7586. Business E-Mail: rcoleman@mdanderson.org.

COLEMAN, ROBERT WINSTON, lawyer; b. Oklahoma City, Mar. 1, 1942; s. Clint Sheridan and Genevieve (Ross) C.; m. Judith Moore, Sept. 7, 1963; children: Robert Winston, Jr., Claire Elizabeth. BA, Abilene Christian Coll., 1964; JD with hons., U. Tex., 1968. Bar: Tex. 1968, Ga. 1970. Law clk. to presiding justice U.S. Ct. Appeals (5th cir.), Montgomery, Ala., 1968-69; assoc. Kilpatrick, Cody, Rogers, McClatchey & Regenstein, Atlanta, 1969-75; ptnr. Meyers, Miller, Middleton, Weiner & Warren and predecessor, Dallas, 1975-80, Jones, Day, Reavis & Pogue, Dallas, 1981-85; dir. Baker, Glast and Middleton, P.C., Dallas, 1985-92; ptnr. Vial, Hamilton, Koch & Knox, LLP, Dallas, 1992-2000, Brown McCarroll LLP, Dallas, 2000—09; of counsel Wilson Elser Moskowitz Edelman & Dicker LLP, 2009—. Mem. exec. com. Dallas County Dem. Com., 1980-87. Mem. ABA, Dallas Bar Found., Dallas Bar Assn., Tex. Bar Assn., Ga. Bar Assn., Am. Judicature Soc. Office Phone: 214-698-8048. Personal E-mail: rwclawyer@sbcglobal.net, robert.coleman@wilsonelser.com.

COLEY, BETTY See FREDEMAN, BETTY

COLEY, JIM, state legislator; b. Houston, Feb. 11, 1951; m. Paula Coley; 2 children. Tchr. Bolton HS; state rep. Dist. 97 Tenn., 2007—. Recipient Lincoln award, Grassroots award, Shelby County Rep. Party. Mem.: Shelby County Edn. Assn., Memphis Bridges, Friends of Orpheum (co-founder), Exch. Club, Bartlett & Northeast Rep. Club (co-founder), Phi Alpha Theta, Pi Sigma Alpha, Omicron Delta Kappa. Republican. Church Of Christ. Office: 2498 Kenwood Ln Bartlett TN 38134 also: 207 War Memorial Bldg Nashville TN 37243-0197 Office Phone: 615-741-8201. Office Fax: 615-253-0267. Business E-Mail: rep.jim.coley@capitol.tn.gov.

COLEY, MARTI, state legislator; b. Blountstown, Fla., Mar. 15, 1961; m. David Coley (dec. Mar. 2005); children: Kristin, Vance, Hunter. Attended, Chipola Jr. Coll., Marianna, Fla., 1980—81; degree in English edn., Fla. State U., Tallahassee, 1984. Tchr., Thomasville, Ga., Malone HS, Jackson County, Fla., 1985—89; English tchr. Chipola Coll.; mem. Dist. 7 Fla. House of Reps., Tallahassee, 2005—, dep. majority whip, 2006—08, alternating chair joint adminstrv. procedures com., vice chair edn. policy coun., mem. joint select com. on collective bargaining, preK-12 appropriations com., preK-12 policy com., select com. on Seminole Indian compact rev. Bd. dirs. Stopover House; mem. Golson Sch. Adv. Bd. Republican. Assembly Of God. Office: Chipola Coll Bldg L Rm 108 3094 Indian Cir Youngstown FL 32466-1701 also: 319 The Capitol 402 S Monroe St Tallahassee FL 32399-1300 Office Phone: 850-718-0047, 850-488-2873.

COLEY, RANDOLPH C., lawyer; b. Atlanta, Feb. 20, 1947; BA, Vanderbilt U., 1969, JD, 1978. Bar: Ga. 1978, Tenn. 1997, Tex. 1999. Ptnr. King & Spalding LLP, Atlanta, 1978—96; exec. dir. Morgan Keegan & Co., Memphis, 1996—99; ptnr. King & Spalding LLP, Houston, 1999—2004, mng. ptnr. Houston office & mem. Oper. Com., 1999—2005, mem. policy com., 2001—04; dir. Deltic Timber Corp., 2007—, Gastar, Ltd., 2009—. Exec. student writing editor: Vanderbilt Law Review 1977-78. Bd. dir. Jung Ctr., The Alley Theatre. Mem. ABA, Order of the Coif., State Bar Tex. Office: King & Spalding LLP 1100 Louisiana Houston TX 77002 Office Phone: 713-751-3256. Office Fax: 713-751-3290. Business E-Mail: rcoley@kslaw.com.

COLGAN, CHARLES JOSEPH, state legislator; b. Frostburg, Md., Sept. 25, 1926; s. Raymond Joseph and Ruth Amelia Deibler Colgan; m. Agnes Loretta Footen, 1948; children: Charles J., Ruth A. Willis, Michael J., Raymond T., Dorothy R. Chaplin, Timothy C., Patrick S., Mary A. Finnigan. A&P mechanic Capital Airlines Inc., Washington, 1951—53; 1st officer Lubrizol Corp., Wickliffe, Ohio, 1953—59; chief pilot Adams Properties, Washington, 1959—64; v.p. & airport mgr. Parkwood Airways, Manassas, Va., 1964—65; pres., dir. & chmn. bd. Colgan Airways Corp., 1965—86; mem. bd. suprs. Gainesville Magisterial Dist., Prince William County, Va., 1971—75; mem., bd. dir. Washington Met. Coun. Govt., 1972—75, vice chmn., 1975—; chmn. Prince William County Bd. Suprs., 1974; mem. Dist. 29 Va. State Senate, 1976—, pres. pro tempore, 2008—12; mem. Fin., Gen. Laws, Local Govt. & Rules Coms. Recipient Outstanding Pub. Servant award, Greater Manassas Jaycees, 1970, 1974, Outstanding Pub. Office award, Prince William County Soil Conservation Svc., 1973, Outstanding Citizen award, Stonewall Jackson HS Varsity Club, 1974; named Boss of Yr., Greater Manassas Jaycees, 1974, Man of Yr., Mannassas Jour. Messenger Newspaper, 1975; named to Hall of Fame, Va. Aviation, 1980. Mem.: Northern Va. CC, Aviation Advisor Com., Greater Manassas C. of C., KofC (4 Degree), Lions Club. Democrat. Roman Cath. Address: 7805 Strasburg St Manassas VA 22110 Mailing: 10677 Aviation Ln Manassas VA 20110-2701 Office: Capitol Office Senate of Virginia Rm 626 PO Box 396 Richmond VA 23218 Office Phone: 703-368-0300, 804-698-7529. Office Fax: 703-257-2856, 804-698-7651. Business E-Mail: district29@sov.state.va.us.

COLGATE, DORIS ELEANOR, sailing school owner, administrator; b. Washington, May 12, 1941; d. Bernard Leonard and Frances Lillian (Goldstein) Horecker; m. Richard G. Buchanan, Sept. 6, 1959 (div. Aug. 1967); m. Stephen Colgate, Dec. 17, 1969. Student, Antioch Coll., 1958-60, NYU, 1960-62. Rsch. supr. Geyer Moyer Ballard, NYC, 1962-64; adminstrv. asst. Yachting Mag., NYC, 1964-68; v.p. Offshore Sailing Sch. Ltd., Inc., NYC, 1968-78, pres. Ft. Myers, Fla., 1978—2001; pres., CEO On and Offshore, Inc., Ft. Myers, 1984-2001; v.p. Offshore Travel, Inc., City Island, 1978-88; pres., CEO Offshore Sailing Sch. Ltd., Inc., Ft. Myers, 2001—. Pres. bd. dirs. Women's Sailing Found., 1998-2000, chair 2000-02, adv. coun., 2002—; chair US Sailing Comml. Sailing Schs., 2005-07. Author: The Bareboat Gourmet, 1983, Sailing: A Woman's Guide, 1999; co-author: Fast Track to Cruising, 2005, Fast Track to Sailing, 2009; contbr. articles to profl. jours. Bd. dirs. Fla. Repertory Theatre, 2001—07, 2011—13. Recipient Betty Cook Meml. Lifetime Achievement award, 1994, Sail Industry Leadership award, 1996, Timothea Larr award, US Sailing, 2003, Visitor and Conv. Bur. Junonia and Chrysalis award, Lee Co., 2010, 2013. Mem. Royal Ocean Racing Club (London chpt.), Nat. Women's Sailing Assn. (founder, chair nat. women's adv. bd. 1990-94, pres. 1994-00, chair 2000-02, Leadership in Women's Sailing award 2004), Am. Women's Econ. Devel. Corp. (adv. bd. 1980-86), Boat US (nat. adv. coun. 1995—), Sail Am. (bd. dirs. 2000-06, chair mktg. com. 2005-06), Internat. Sailing Summit (exec. com. 2000—10, chair comml. sailing com. US Sailing 2005-07). Avocations: piano, sailing, photography, writing, cooking. Office: Offshore Sailing Sch Ltd Inc 16731 McGregor Blvd Fort Myers FL 33908-3843 Office Phone: 239-985-7511. Business E-Mail: doris@offshoresailing.com.

COLKER, MARVIN LEONARD, classics educator; b. Pitts., Mar. 19, 1927; s. Philip Marcus and Sarah (Grodner) C.; m. Hazel Robinson, Nov. 28, 1959; 1 son, Philip Ian. BA summa cum laude, U.

Pitts., 1948; PhD, Harvard U., 1951; LittD (hon.), U. Dublin, 1987. Sheldon fellow Harvard U., 1951-52; Fulbright fellow U. Paris, 1951-52; Instr. classics U. Va., 1953-56, asst. prof., 1956-59, asso. prof., 1959-68, prof., 1967-98, chmn. dept. classics, 1963-68, prof. emeritus, 1998—. Cataloguer Mediaeval manuscripts U. Dublin, Ireland, 1958-2009, lectr. patristics, Mediaeval Latin, 1962-63; co-dir. Mediaeval manuscripts course standing conf. Nat. and Univ. Librarians, Dublin, 1968. Author: Fulcoii Belvacensis Epistolae, 1954, Henrici Augustensis Planctus Evae, 1956, Richard of S. Victor and the Anonymous of Bridlington, 1962, Analecta Dublinensia: Three Medieval Latin Texts in the Library of Trinity College, Dublin, 1975, Galteri De Castellione Alexandreis, 1978, America Rediscovered in the Thirteenth Century, 1979, Trinity Coll. Dublin Library: Descriptive Catalogue of the Mediaeval and Renaissance Latin Manuscripts, 2 vols., 1991, A Previously Unpublished Hist. of the Trojans, 1998, Previously Unpublished Letters Ascribed to Saint Jerome, 2000, Michael of Belluno and His Speculum Conscientie: the Unique Manuscript Recently Discovered, 2003, Petronius Rediuiuus et Helias Tripolanensis, 2007, Trinity Coll., Libr. Dublin, Descriptive Catalogue of the Mediaeval and Renaissance Latin manuscripts Supplement One, 2008, Constitutiones quae vocantur ordinis Praemonstratensis, 2008; mem. editl. bd. Medievalia et Humanistica; assoc. editor Retiarius. Grantee Am. Philos. Soc., Trinity Trust, NEH, U. Dublin Fund; ACLS fellow, 1962-63, Sesquicentennial Rsch. Assn. fellow U. Va., 1973-74, Ctr. Advanced Studies rsch. assoc. U. Va., 1992-93, Guggenheim fellow, 1973-74, Fulbright fellow to London and Dublin, 1987-88, Bibliog. Soc. Am. fellow, 1996. Mem. Mediaeval Acad. Am. (former councillor) Assn. for Manuscripts and Archives in Rsch. Collections, Classical Assn. Mid. West and South, Phi Beta Kappa. Home: 105 Westminster Rd Charlottesville VA 22901-2229 Personal E-mail: mlcolker@cstone.net.

COLL, EDWARD GIRARD, JR., university president; b. Pitts., Aug. 9, 1934; s. Edward G. and Alive V. (Ebeling) C.; m. Carole Hulse, Feb. 3, 1958; children— Thomas, Jean Coll Mendenhall, Peter, Karen, Kelly. BA, Duquesne U., 1960, LHD (hon.), 1983, Alfred U., 2000. Div. dir. United Fund Allegheny County, Pitts., 1959-61; asst. to exec. v.p. United Fund Dade County, 1961-63; asst. to v.p. for devel. affairs U. Miami, 1963-66, dir. corp. and found. relations, 1966-67, dir. devel., 1967-72, sec. univ. corp., 1972-73, v.p. for devel. affairs, 1973-82; pres. Alfred U., NY, 1982-2000; ret., 2000. Bd. dirs. Steuben Trust Co.; lectr. in field. Contbr. articles to profl. jours. Chmn. zoning bd. appeals Dade County, 1973-82; bd. dirs. Nat. Ctr. Child Abuse and Neglect, 1985-90; pres. com. NCAA, 1988-92, coun. mem. 1993-97, vice-chair divsn. III, 1990, v.p., 1994-96; trustee Coun. for Support and Advancement Edn., Washington, 1981-82, 87-89, chair, 1991-92. With U.S. Army, 1953-56. Univ. Adminstr. Fulbright fellow U. Warwick, Coventry, Eng., 1985. Mem. Ind. Colls. and Univs. N.Y. (bd. dirs. 1982-86), Duquesne Univ. Alumni Assn., Am. Mktg. Assn. (hon.), Miami Club, University Club, Genesee Valley Club, Wellsville Country Club, Delta Mu Delta, Phi Kappa Phi, Beta Gamma Sigma. Roman Catholic. Home: 4202 Dunham Pk Flowery Branch GA 30542 Office: 4202 Dunham Park Flowery Branch GA 30542 Personal E-mail: edcarolecoll@bellsouth.net.

COLLAR, GARY L., industrial manufacturing executive; BSBA, Calif. State U., 1980. With Caterpillar, Inc.; pres., CEO ZF-Unisia Autoparts, Inc., 1994—2001; v.p., bus. devel., N.Am. ZF Friedrichshaven A.G., 2001—02; v.p., market devel., challenger divsn. AGCO Corp., 2002—04, sr. v.p., gen. mgr., EAPAC, 2004—08, sr. v.p., gen. mgr., Europe, Africa, Middle East, 2004—, sr. v.p., gen. mgr., Australia, 2009—, sr. v.p., gen. mgr., New Zealand, 2009—. Office: AGCO Corp 4205 River Green Pky Duluth GA 30096 Office Phone: 770-813-9200. Office Fax: 770-813-6118. Business E-Mail: Gary.Collar@agcocorp.com.

COLLARD, CRAIG A., pharmaceutical executive; BS in Engring., Southern Coll. Tech., Marietta, Ga. Sales and mktg. positions including field sales rep. Dura Pharmaceuticals, Inc., 1992—98; dir. nat. accounts DJ Pharma, Inc., 1998—2002; v.p. sales Verum Pharmaceuticals, Inc., Rsch. Triangle Pk., NC, 2002—03; founder, pres., CEO Carolina Pharmaceuticals, Inc., 2003—04; founder, pres., CEO, bd dirs. Cornerstone BioPharma Holdings, Ltd., 2004—08; pres., CEO, chmn. Cornerstone Therapeutics, Inc (merged with BioPharma), 2008—. Bd. dirs. Auriga Labs. Inc.; chmn. Critical Therapeutics Inc. Bd. dirs. Hilltop Home Found., Raleigh, NC. Office: Cornerstone Therapeutics Inc 1255 Crescent Green Dr Ste 250 Cary NC 27518 Office Phone: 919-678-6611. Business E-Mail: ccollard@cornerstonebiopharma.com.

COLLEN, TOM, women's college basketball coach; b. Dec. 21, 1953; m. Nicki Taggert; children: Connor David, Reese Elizabeth. B in Phys. Edn., Bowling Green State U., 1977; M in Recreation Edn., Miami U., Ohio, 1983. Asst. coach Miami U., Ohio, 1982-84, U. Utah, 1984-86, Purdue U., 1986—93, U. Ark., 1993—95, assoc. head coach, 1995—97, head coach, 2007—, Colo. State U., Ft. Collins, 1997—2002, U. Louisville, 2003—07. Named Western Athletic Conf. Coach of Yr., 1999, Dist. VII Coach of Yr., Women's Basketball Coaches Assn., 1999, Nat. Coach of Yr., Women's Basketball Jour., 1999, Women's Basketball News Svc., 1999, Southeastern Conf. Coach of Yr., 2012. Office: University Ark Womens Basketball Program Athletics Dept 131 Barnhill Arena Fayetteville AR 72701 Office Phone: 479-575-3000. Business E-Mail: tcollen@uark.edu.

COLLETTE, FRANCES MADELYN, retired tax specialist, lawyer, consultant, advocate; b. Yonkers, NY, Aug. 5, 1947; d. Morris Aaron and Esther (Gang) Volbert; m. Roger Warren Collette, Dec. 25, 1971; children: Darren Roger, Bonnie Frances. BEd summa cum laude, SUNY, Buffalo, 1969; JD cum laude, U. Miami, 1980. Bar: Fla. 1980. Employment counselor Fla. Bur. Employment Security, Miami, Fla., 1969-73; unemployment claims adjudicator Fla. Bur. Unemployment, Miami, 1973-77; owner Unemployment Svcs. Fla., Inc., Miami, 1977-93. Cons. Fla. unemployment tax and personnel; lectr. in field. Mem. ad hoc comm. students with Asperger's Syndrome Dade County Pub. Schs., 1998-2000; vol. child advocate Exceptional Student Edn., 1993-2010; 1st v.p. BBB South Fla., 1980-81, bd. govs., 2d vice chair, 1990-91; mem. Supt.'s Dist. Adv. Panel for Students with Disabilities, Miami-Dade County Pub. Schs., 2003-10; mem. adv. panel Fla. Diagnostic and Learning Resources System/South, 05-07. Recipient Outstanding Cmty. Svc. award, UM-NSU CARD, 2007. Jewish.

COLLEY, GERALD (JERRY) E., retail executive; Pres. Rose Auto Parts; sr. v.p., stores & customer satisfaction Auto Zone, Inc., 1997—2001; pres., N.Am. stores Office Depot, Inc., Delray Beach, Fla., 2001, CEO. Office: Office Depot Inc 6600 N Military Trlal Boca Raton FL 33496-2434 Office Phone: 561-438-4800. Office Fax: 561-438-4001. Business E-Mail: Jerry.Colley@officedepot.com.

COLLEY, JOHN LEONARD, JR., management consultant, educator, writer; b. Wilmington, NC, Feb. 17, 1930; s. John L. and Icie (Hall) C.; m. Tommie Lancaster, Dec. 14, 1950; children: John Lawrence, Claire Ellen, Thomas Michael. BS, N.C. State U., 1957; MS, Yale U., 1959; DBA, U. So. Calif., 1964. Planning engr. ops. and systems analysis Western Electric Co., 1959-62; chief ops. analysis Hughes Aircraft Co., 1962-65; group leader Research Triangle Inst., Durham, N.C., 1965-67; also lectr. U. So. Calif., 1963-65; adj. prof. indsl. engring. N.C. State U., 1965-67; prof. bus. adminstrn. Darden Grad. Sch. Bus., U. Va., 1967—, Almand R. Coleman prof. bus. adminstrn., 1979—, dir. div. research, 1973-74; Sesquicentennial asso. of Center for Advanced Studies, 1974-75; pres. Southeastern Cons. Group, Ltd., 1969-92. Bd. dirs. Blue Cross/Blue Shield of Va., 1981-97, chmn. bd., 1985-86, Worldwide Cryogenics Ltd., Hillcrest Group, Dominion Holdings, LLC, Avid Med. Co-author: Operations Planning and Control-Text and Cases, 1977, Operations Planning and Control, 1978, Corporate Strategy, 2002, Corporate Governance, 2003, What is Corporate Governance?, 2005, How to Plan and Implement Strategy, 2005; author: Corporate and Divisional Planning, 1984, Case Studies in Service Operations, 1996, How to Play and Execute Strategy, 2005, Principles of General Management, 2006. Served with USAF, 1952-56. Recipient Disting. Prof. award U. Va. Alumni Assn., 1987, Disting. Faculty award The Z Soc., 1996, Raven award Raven Soc., 1998, IMP Faculty award, 1999, Frederick S. Morton Leadership award Darden Sch./U. Va., 2000, 06. Mem. Ops. Research Soc. Am., Inst. Mgmt. Sci., Am. Inst. Decision Scis., Raven Soc., Sigma Xi, Tau Kappa Epsilon, Tau Beta Pi, Alpha Pi Mu, Beta Gamma Sigma, Phi Kappa Phi, Omicron Delta Kappa. Clubs: Farmington (Charlottesville); Yale (N.Y.C.). Home: 1423 Foxbrook Ln Charlottesville VA 22901-3119 also: 1423 Foxbrook Ln Charlottesvle VA 22901-3119 E-mail: colley@virginia.edu.

COLLIER, ALBERT M., pediatrician, educator, director; b. Elba, Ala., May 3, 1937; s. Milford William and Ida Ruth C.; m. Mary Gaynell Wehler, July 17, 1960; children: Albert Mark, Dennis Murray, Jonathan Lee. BS, U. Miami, 1959, MD, 1963. Pediatric resident U. Miami, Coral Gables, Fla., 1963-66; fellow infectious diseases U. NC, Chapel Hill, 1968-70, from asst. prof. to assoc. prof., 1971-80, prof., 1980—, chief divsn. infectious disease, 1980—2004, assoc. dir. Ctr. Environ. Med. Lung Bio, 1980—2004, acting dir. Frank Porter Graham Child Devel. Ctr., 1990-92, assoc. chmn. pediat. rsch., 1997—2003, med. sch. res. integrity officer, 2000—. Contbr. over 100 articles to profl. jours. Recipient Louis Dienes award Internat. Orgn. Mycoplasmology, Vienna, Austria, 1988. Mem. Gideons (zone leader 1990-93). Baptist. Office: U NC Chapel Hill Dept Pediatrics Sch Medicine 413 Mac Nider Blvd CB 7231 Chapel Hill NC 27599 E-mail: uncacl@med.unc.edu.

COLLIER, BOYD DEAN, finance educator, management consultant; b. Waco, Tex., Jan. 16, 1938; s. Denis Lee and Anne Alice (Berry) C.; m. Barbara Nell Joseph, June 20, 1966; children: Diedra Michelle, Christopher Boyd. BBA, Baylor U., 1963, MS, 1965; PhD, U. Tex., 1970. CPA, Tex. Asst. prof. U. N.C., Greensboro, 1969—72, asst. dean, 1970—72; assoc. prof. U. Houston, 1972—73; chief ops. auditor Glastron Boat Co., Austin, Tex., 1979; prof. bus. econs., dean Ctr. for Bus. Adminstrn. St. Edward's U., Austin, 1974—83; prof. fin., head dept. acctg. and fin. Tarleton State U., Stephenville, Tex., 1983—96, exec. dir. office planning, evaluation and instrnl. rsch., accreditation liaison officer, 1996—2003. Co-owner Vranich, Collier Co., CPA's, Austin, 1974-83; v.p. fin. Execucom Sys., Austin, 1979; sr. lectr. U. Tex., Austin, 1980-83; compliance officer Tex. A&M U.; bd. dirs. Acctg. Info. Sys., Houston, 1974-78; advisor Office of Atty. Gen., State of Tex., Austin, 1986, Office of Comptr., State of Tex., Austin, 1986, mem. editl. bd. Internat. Rsch. Jour, Pub. Mpcl. Fin. Author: Measurement and Environmental Deterioration, 1971; editl. advisor Jour. Accountancy, NYC, 1982—; contbr. articles to profl. jours. Faculty advisor Coll. Reps. of Tex., Stephenville, 1984-1988. With USN, 1955-59. Fellow Earhart Found., Ann Arbor, Mich., 1963, 68, NSF, Washington, 1966, Am. Coll. Forensic Examiners, 2007; O.A. grant, 2009; commd. hon. Surgeon Gen. State Tex., 2004., O.A. Grant Tchg. Execellence award, 2009, Outstanding Faculty Svc. award Coll. Bus., Tarleton State U., 2012, award Tex. A&M U. Sys. Bd. Regents Bestowed Title Prof. Emeritus, 2012. Fellow Am. Bd. Forensic Acctg.; mem. AICPA, Nat. Acctg. Assn. (v.p. 1978-83, Outstanding Svc. award 1983, Sargent Americanism award 1989), Am. Acctg. Assn., Tex. Soc. CPA, Southwestern Fin. Assn., U. Tex. Austin Ex-Students Assn. (life), Sigma Xi (pres. Tarleton chpt. 2005-06). Libertarian. Avocations: tennis, hiking, collecting coins and walking canes. Home: 930 N Charlotte Ave Stephenville TX 76401-2004 Office: Tarleton State U 1603 W Washington PO Box 505T Stephenville TX 76401-0505 Business E-Mail: collier@tarleton.edu.

COLLIER, CURTIS LYNN, federal judge; b. Marianna, Ark., Oct. 4, 1949; s. Lenzora and Lucille (Edwards) C.; m. Cheryl Elaine Hollingshed, July 17, 1975; children: Galen, Cayanna, Christian. BS, Tenn. State U., 1971; JD, Duke U., 1974. Bar: Ark., Tenn., U.S. Dist. Ct. (ea. dist.) Tenn. 1995. Asst. U.S. atty. for ea. dist. La., Dept. Justice, New Orleans, 1979-87, supervisory asst. U.S. atty. for ea. dist. Tenn. Chattanooga, 1987-95; judge US Dist. Ct. (ea. dist.) Tenn., Chattanooga, 1995—2005, chief judge, 2005—. Dir. A.I.M. Ctr., Chattanooga, 1988-93. Bd. dirs. Children's ADvocaty Ctr., 1990—. Capt. JAGC, USAF, 1974-79. Mem. Chattanooga Bar Assn. (com. mem. 1988—), Tenn. State U. Alumni Assn. (treas. 1990—), Omega Psi Phi. Baptist. Avocations: reading, jogging, kiting, stereo. Office: US Dist Ct 900 Georgia Ave Rm 317 Chattanooga TN 37402

COLLIER, LACEY ALEXANDER, federal judge; b. Demopolis, Ala., June 23, 1935; s. James Porter and Virginia Slade (Lacey) C.; m. Beverly Anne Brady, Sept. 1, 1956; children: Lorrie Collier Berry, Teri Collier Siebert, Frank. Student, U. Ala., 1953-55; BA in Govt. and Internat. Rels., US Naval Postgrad. Sch., 1970; MA in Polit. Sci., U. West Fla., 1972, BA in Acctg., 1975; JD with honors, Fla. State U., 1977. Bar: Fla. 1978, U.S. Dist. Ct. (no. dist.) Fla. 1978, U.S. Ct. Appeals (5th cir.) 1978, U.S. Ct. Appeals (11th cir.) 1981. Commd. USN, 1955, advanced through grades to lt. comdr., ret., 1975; asst. state atty. Office of State Atty. 1st. Jud. Cir. of Fla., 1977-84; cir. judge 1st Jud. Cir., 1984-91; judge US Dist. Ct. (no. dist.) Fla., Pensacola, 1991—2003, sr. judge, 2003—. Adj. prof. polit. sci. U. West Fla., 1973; adv. grand juries 1st Jud. Cir., 1978-84; lectr. La. Judges Conf., 1986, Robert A. Taft Inst. Govt., 1989—; faculty Fla. New Judges' Coll., 1989-92. Pres. St. Paul's Cath. Ch. Men's Club, 1972; chmn. leadership in action program Pensacola Jaycees, 1971-72; divsn. leader CFC/United Way, 1973; mem. public safety task force Action '76, 1974; vice chmn. Escambia County charter com., 1978-79; bd. dirs. Fla. State Law Sch. Alumni Assn., 1980-81; pres. city-county Drug Abuse Commn., 1982-83; chmn. City Pensacola Revenue Study Com., 1985-86; official adv. Escambia Govtl. Study Commn., 1986-87; mem. Presdl. Search Com. U. W. Fla., 1987; chmn. Edn. Conf. subcom. Fla. Conf. Crct. Judges, 1987-89; trustee, pres.U. W. Fla. Found., 1988—; mem. adv. bd. students in free enterprise U. W. Fla., 1989—; trustee Pensacola Little Theater/Cultural Ctr., 1989—; lectr., mem. adv. bd., chmn. Nativity Cath. Ch., 1990—; chmn. Pensacola com. Nat. Mus. Naval Aviation Found., 1990—; bd. dirs. Big Brother/Big Sister of NW Fla., sec., 1990-92; mem. adv. bd. African-Am. Heritage Soc., 1990—; mem. adv. bd. Sacred Heart Hosp., 1991—. Recipient 11 air medals; named Disting. Alumni U. W. Fla., 1988, Pensacola BIP Profl. Leader of Yr., 1989. Mem. ABA, Fla. Bar (standard jury instrns. com. civil 1989—), Okalossa-Walton Bar Assn., Escambia-Santa Rosa Bar Assn., Am. Inns of Court (exec. bd. Pensacola chpt., founding mem.), Assn. Naval Aviation, Gulf Coast Econs. Club (v.p. 1990-92, pres. 1993—), Fla. State Law Sch. Alumni Assn. (bd. dirs. 1981-81), Fla. Conf. Cir. Judges, C. of C. (chmn. Com. 100 1987-89, task force on port/airport devel., chmn. bldg. and sites task force 1989—). Office: US Courthouse 1 N Palafox St Pensacola FL 32501-5665

COLLIER, SPENCER, state agency administrator, former state legislator; m. Melissa Collier; children: Christopher, Connor, Colby, Caroline. BS, Troy State U., Ala. State trooper Ala. Dept. Pub. Safety; legal investigator Cunningham and Bounds LLC; mem. Dist. 105 Ala. House of Reps., Montgomery, 2006—10; dir. Ala. Dept. Homeland Security, 2010—. Ala. rep. Nat. Conf. State Legislatures Criminal Justice Com.; mem. Mobile County Rep. Exec. Com., Mobile Christian Ctr., Ala. Working Waterfront Commn., Gulf States Marine Fisheries Coun.; bd. dirs. Vol. Mobile and Bayou Health Clinic. Republican. Office: Ala Dept Homeland Security PO Box 304115 Montgomery AL 36130-4115 Office Phone: 334-353-3050.

COLLINGS, CHRIS D., lawyer; b. McAllen, Tex., July 2, 1970; B of Social Work with honors, U. Tex., Austin, 1997; JD, South Tex. Coll. Law, 2001. Bar: Tex. 2002, US Dist. Ct. (so. dist. Tex.) 2002, US Dist. Ct. (we. dist. Tex.) 2003, US Dist. Ct. (ea. dist. Tex.) 2004. Former outside gen. counsel Storage Investment Advisors, LLP; jud. intern First Dist. Ct. Appeals, 1999; assoc. Brown Sims P.C., 2003—08; mng. mem. Collings Law Firm, PLLC, 2008—. Cpl. USMC, 1989—94, vet., Persian Gulf War. Named a Tex. Super Lawyers Rising Star, Tex. Monthly Mag., 2006, Profl. on Fast Track, Houston Tex. Mag., 2006. Mem.: Am. Inns of Ct., Vets. Fgn. Wars, U. Tex. Football Team. Office: Collings Law Firm, PLLC 440 Louisiana St Ste 1450 Houston TX 77002 Office Phone: 713-337-1180. Office Fax: 713-337-1179. E-mail: chris@collings-law.com.

COLLINS, CHARLES S., state legislator; b. Detroit, Mich., Nov. 30, 1962; m. Leeann Whalen Collins; children: Jamie Collins, Andrew Collins, Austin Collins, Jordan Collins. BS in Economics, US Naval Acad., 1985; MA in Quantitative Economics, George Wash. U., 1986. Soviet mil. capabilities instr. Navy & Marine Corps Intelligence Ctr.; with Procter & Gamble, Cin., Ohio, assoc. dir., Wal-Mart Beauty Care Sales; v.p., Wal-Mart sales team leader Eastman Kodak; v.p., mng. Heinz; mem. elder. trustee & sunday sch. tchr. First Christian Ch., Fayetteville, chmn.; pres. Property Owners Assn.; chmn. Selective Svc. Appeals Bd.; co-owner Crown Ptnrs.; mem. Am. Legion, US Naval Acad. Alumni Assn., Wash. County Rep. Com., USNA Nomination Interview Com., Nat. Rifle Assn.; with Procter & Gamble (Wal-Mart Global Customer team), Fayetteville, Ark., 1996; mem. Dist. 89 Ark. House of Representatives, 2011—. Naval Intelligence officer USN; with aircraft carrier USS America CV-66, USN; navy reservist, lt. comdr. USN. Republican. Office: 3225 Piper Glen Fayetteville AR 72703 Office Phone: 479-283-9303. Business E-Mail: clcollins6@cox.net.

COLLINS, DAVID BROWNING, religious institution administrator; b. Hot Springs, Ark., Dec. 18, 1922; s. Charles Frederick and Agnes Elizabeth (George) C.; m. Maryon Virginia Moise, Oct. 14, 1945; children: Melissa, Christopher, Matthew, Geoffrey. BA, U. of the South, 1943, BD, 1948, STM, 1962, DD, 1974. Ordained to ministry Episcopal Ch. as deacon, 1948, as priest, 1949. Rector St. Andrew's Episc. Ch., Marianna, Ark., 1948-53; priest-in-charge Holy Cross Episc. Ch., West Memphis, Ark., 1949-53; chaplain and assoc. prof. of religion U. of the South, Sewanee, Tenn., 1953-66; dean Cathedral of St. Philip, Atlanta, 1966-84; exec. dir. Windsong Ministries, Inc., 1984—2010; pres. House of Deps. Episcopal Ch., 1985-91. Trustee Ch. Pension Fund, N.Y.C., 1976-88; mem. Bd. of Clergy Deployment, N.Y.C., 1971-76. Contbr. articles to profl. jours. Pres. Christian Council of Met. Atlanta, 1977-78; chaplain Atlanta Braves Booster Club, 1966-84. Served to lt. (j.g.) USNR, 1943-46. Episcopalian. Avocation: baseball. Home: 13000 Avonlea Pl Apt 108 Woodstock GA 30189-4909 E-mail: davidbrev@bellsouth.net.

COLLINS, DOUG (DOUGLAS A. COLLINS), United States Representative from Georgia, former state legislator; b. Gainesville, Ga., Aug. 16, 1966; m. Lisa Collins; children: Jordan, Copelan, Cameron. BA in Polit. Sci. & Criminal Law, North Ga. Coll. & State U., 1988; MDiv, New Orleans Baptist Theological Seminary, 1996; JD, John Marshall Law Sch., 2007; Grad., Ga. Legislative Leadership Inst. Sr. pastor Chicopee Baptist Church, 1994—2005; mng. ptnr. Collins & Csider Law Firm, 2010—; mem. Dist. 27 Ga. House of Reps., 2007—13; mem. US Congress from 9th Ga Dist., Washington, 2013—, US House Fgn. Affairs Com., 2013—, US House Judiciary Com., 2013—, US House Oversight & Govt. Reform Com., 2013—. Chaplain USN, major-chaplain 94th Airlift Wing USAFR, 2002—, Iraq War. Named one of Georgia's Most Influential Citizens, James mag. Republican. Southern Baptist. Office: US House of Representatives 513 Cannon House Office Bldg Washington DC 20515 also: 11 Green St SE Gainesville GA 30501 Office Phone: 202-225-9893, 770-297-3388. Office Fax: 202-226-1224, 770-297-3390.*

COLLINS, EILEEN MARIE, astronaut; b. Elmira, NY, Nov. 19, 1956; d. James Edward and Rose Marie (O'Hara) C.; m. James Patrick Youngs, Aug. 1, 1987; 2 children. AS in Math., Sci., Corning C.C., 1976; BA in Math., Econs., Syracuse U., 1978; grad., USAF Undergrad. Pilot Tng., Vance AFB, Okla., 1979, USAF Test Pilot Sch., Edwards AFB, Calif., 1990; MS in Ops. Rsch., Stanford U., 1986; MA in Space Systems Mgmt., Webster U., 1989; student, Air Force Inst. Techology, 1986; grad., Air Force Test Pilot Sch., Edwards AFB, Calif., 1990. Commd. 2d lt. USAF, 1978, advanced through grades to col., 1993, T-38 instr. pilot 71st flight tng. wing Vance AFB, 1979-82, C-141 aircraft comdr. and instructor pilot, 86th mil. airlift squadron Travis AFB, Calif., 1983-85, ret., 2005; asst. prof. math., T-41 instr. pilot USAF Acad., Colorado Springs, Colo., 1986-89; astronaut Johnson Space Ctr. NASA, Houston, 1991—2006. Served on astronaut support team responsible for Orbiter prelaunch check-out, final launch configuration, crew ingress/egress, landing/recovery; spacecraft communicator, CAPCOM, also served as the astronaut office spacecraft systems branch chief, chief information officer, shuttle branch chief, astronaut safety branch chief; pilot, space shuttle Discovery (STS-63), 1995 (first women pilot of space shuttle), space shuttle Atlantis (STS-84), 1997; comdr. space shuttle, Columbia (STS-93), 1999 (first women shuttle comdr.); crew comdr. space shuttle, (STS-114) Discovery; during this Return To Flight mission, the crew tested and evaluated new procedures for flight safety, shuttle inspections and repair techniques, 2005. Col. USAF. Decorated Air Force Commendation medal with one oak leaf cluster, Air Force Meritorious svc. medal with one oak leaf cluster, Armed Forces Expeditionary medal for svc. in Grenada (Operation Urgent Fury, 1983), Def. Superior Svc. medal, Def. Meritorious Svc. medal, Disting. Flying Cross, French Legion Honor, Disting. Flying Cross, NASA Outstanding Leadership medal, NASA Space Flight medals; recipient Harmon Trophy, 1995, Free Spirit award, 2006. Mem.: Am. Inst. Aeronautics and Astronautics, US Space Found., Order of Daedalians, Air Force Assn., The Ninety-Nines, Women Military Avaitors. Avocations: running, golf, hiking, camping, reading, photography, astronomy.

COLLINS, HUBERT C, state legislator; b. Riceville, Ky., Aug. 19, 1936; s. Johnnie W. and Nola Spradlin Collins; m. Beatrice Daniel, 1959. Mem. Johnson Co. Exec. Com., Ky., 1965—87, chmn. Ky.,

1982—87; ret. tchr. Johnson Co.; car dealer, real estate broker, auctioneer; mem. Dist. 97 Ky. House of Reps., 1991—. Mem.: Ky. HS Athletic Assn., Johnson Co. Edn. Assn. (former pres.), Ky. Automobile Dealer's Assn., Ky. Col., Ky. Edn. Assn., Nat. Rifle Assn., Odd Fellow, DAV. Democrat. Baptist. Mailing: 72 Collins Dr Wittensville KY 41274 Office: Ky Legislature Annex Rm 329H 702 Capitol Ave Frankfort KY 40601 Office Phone: 502-564-8100 ext. 654.

COLLINS, JAMES WILLIAM, health science association administrator, epidemiologist, mechanical engineer; b. Atlanta, Oct. 19, 1962; s. Thomas Allen and Mary Frank Collins; m. Maria Joao Ponte, Oct. 25, 1992; children: Karina Maria, James Seth. B of Mech. Engring., Ga. Inst. Tech., 1984; MSME, W.Va. U., 1989; PhD in Health Policy and Mgmt., Johns Hopkins U., 1998. Rsch. mech. engr. Ctrs. Disease Control and Prevention, Nat. Inst. Occupl. Safety and Health, Morgantown, W.Va., 1984—90, rsch. epidemiologist, 1992—2004; assoc. dir. sci. Ctrs. Disease Control and Prevention, Nat. Inst. Occupl. Safety and Health, Divsn. Safety Rsch., 2004—. Bd. editors Jour. Injury Control and Safety Promotion, Amsterdam, 2004—; guest lectr. occupational epidemiology Johns Hopkins U; guest lectr. occupational safety and health W.Va. U. Pres. Exch. Club, Fairchance, Pa., 2000—06; fin. com. Mt. Moriah Bapt. Ch., Smithfield, 2004—06. Capt. USPHS, 1984—2005. Recipient Spl. Assignment award, USPHS, 1991, Surgeon Gen Exemplary Svc. medal, 1992, Achievement medal, 1996, Pub. Health Svc. citation, 1996, Crisis Response Ribbon, 2002, Outstanding Unit citation, 2002, U. S. Pub. Health Svc. Engring. Lit. award, Chief Engr. USPHS, 2000, Partnering award Worker Safety and Health, Nat. Inst. Occupl. Safety and Health, 2003, 2006, Alice Hamilton Excellence in Occupl. Safety and Health Human Studies Rsch. award, 2005. Mem.: Commd. Officers Assn. USPHS (pres., v.p., treas. 1984—2005, Mem. of Yr. 1988). Conservative. Baptist. Achievements include research in intervention trials demonstrating highly effective programs to prevent back and other musculoskeletal injuries among health care workers due to patient lifting and slips and falls. Avocations: travel, hunting, fishing, softball, coaching. Office: Ctrs Disease Control & Prevention 1095 Willowdale Rd Mail stop 1900 Morgantown WV 26505 Home: 3415 Halleck Rd Morgantown WV 26508-3643 Business E-Mail: jcollins1@cdc.gov.

COLLINS, JANET L., psychiatrist; B in Clin. Psychology, San Diego State U., 1975, M in Clin. Psychology, 1977; PhD in Ednl. Psychology, Stanford U. Recruited Centers for Disease Control and Prevention, 1990, acting dir. Nat. Ctr. for HIV, Sexually Transmitted Diseases and Tuberculosis Prevention, acting dir. Adolescent and Sch. Health Divsn., dep. dir. Nat. Ctr. Chronic Disease Prevention and Health Promotion, dir. Nat. Ctr. Chronic Disease Prevention and Health Promotion, 2005—09, assoc. dir. for program, 2009—. Named a Disting. Alumnus (Monty award), San Diego State U., 2009. Office: Centers for Disease Control & Prevention Office of Assoc Dir for Program 1600 Clifton Rd Mail Stop D14 Atlanta GA 30333

COLLINS, JEFFREY LYNN, state legislator; b. Rocky Mount, NC, Dec. 9, 1955; m. Beanie Cavenaugh Collins; children: Jonathan Collins, Rachel Collins, Charles Collins. Grad. in Journalism, U. NC, Chapel Hill, 1978. Chmn., polit. action com., v.p., Northeast Area Nat. Assn. of Ins. & Fin. Advisors (NAIFA), NC, pres. Rocky Mount; founder, bd. dirs. Faith Christian Sch.; interim pastor, founder Rocky Mount Bible Ch.; mem. Rocky Mount Human Rels. Commn.; tchr., math, coach, basketball & baseball Falls Rd. Bapt. Sch., 1979—92; fin. cons. AXA Advisors, LLC, 1992—; mem. Dist. 25 NC House of Representatives, 2011—. Named Advisor of the Yr., Nat. Assn. of Ins. & Fin. Advisors (NAIFA), 2002; scholar Morehead Scholar, U. NC, 1978 Republican. Office: 1109 Culpepper Dr Rocky Mount NC 27803 Address: North Carolina House of Representatives 16 W Jones St Room 1006 Raleigh NC 27601-1096 Office Phone: 252-443-1441, 919-733-5802. Personal E-mail: jeffcollins4nchouse@gmail.com. Business E-Mail: Jeff.Collins@ncleg.net.

COLLINS, JENNIFER, academic administrator, law educator; BA with Distinction in History, cum laude, Yale U., 1987; JD magna cum laude, Harvard Law Sch., 1991. Law clerk to Honorable Dorothy W. Nelson US Ct. of Appeals, 9th Dist., Pasadena, Calif., 1991—92; assoc. Miller, Cassidy, Larocca & Lewin, Washington, 1992—93; atty.-advisor Office of Legal Counsel, US Dept. of Justice, Washington, 1993—94; asst. US atty. US Atty.'s Office for DC, 1994—2002, asst. US atty., homicide sect., 1997—2002; counsel Sidley Austin Brown & Wood, Washington, 2002—03; asst. to prof. of law Wake Forest U. Sch. of Law, 2003—, assoc. provost for academic and strategic initiatives, 2010—13, vice provost, 2013—. Adj. prof. George Washington U. Sch. of Law, 2003; presenter in the field. Co-author (with Dan Markel and Ethan Leib): Privilege or Punish? Criminal Justice and The Challenge of Family Ties, 2009; contbr. of articles to peer-reviewed publications. Office: Wake Forest University Reynolda 204 1834 Wake Forest Rd Winston Salem NC 27109 Office Phone: 336-758-3852. Business E-Mail: collinjm@wfu.edu.*

COLLINS, NANCY ADAMS, state legislator; b. Memphis, Nov. 10, 1947; m. Jim Collins; children: Adam, Amy, Connor, Josh. Attended, Itawamba CC, Fulton, Miss., Miss. U. for Women, Columbus. RN. OB sonographer; speech therapist; mem. Dist. 6 Miss. State Senate, 2011—. Republican. Methodist. Office: Miss State Senate PO Box 1018 Jackson MS 39215 Office Phone: 601-359-3221. Business E-Mail: ncollins@senate.ms.gov.

COLLINS, PATRICK B., retired corporate financial executive; CPA. Ptnr. PricewaterhouseCoopers LLP (formerly Coopers & Lybrand LLP), Houston, 1967—91; ind. bus. cons., 1991—. Bd. dirs. TransCoastal Marine Svcs., Inc., 1997—; adv. mem. bd. dirs. HCC Ins. Holdings, Inc., 2009—. Mem.: AICPA. Office: HCC Insurance Holdings Inc Bd Directors 13403 NW Freeway Houston TX 77040 Office Phone: 713-690-7300. Office Fax: 713-462-2401.

COLLINS, T. JAY, retired energy executive; m. Maxann Simpson; 2 children. BA, Rice Univ., M in Engring.; MBA, Harvard Univ. Sr. v.p., CFO Oceaneering International, Inc., 1993—95, exec. v.p., oilfield marine svcs., 1995—98, COO, 1998—2006, pres., 1998—2011, CEO, 2006—11. Bd. dirs. Oceaneering Internat., Inc., 2002—, Nat. Ocean Industries Assn., Am. Productivity & Quality Ctr. Bd. dir. CanCare, Houston. Office: Oceaneering International Inc 11911 FM 529 Houston TX 77041

COLLINS, TERRI, state legislator; m. Tom Collins; 3 children. With First Am. Bank; founder, cons. TLC Solutions; mem. Dist. 8 Ala. House of Reps., 2011—. Mem. Decatur-Morgan County C. of C.; mem., Bible study leader Wesley Meml. United Meth. Ch.; bd. dirs. Vol. Ctr. Morgan County. Republican. Office: Ala House of Reps Rm 522-D 11 S Union St Montgomery AL 36130 also: 2128 6th Ave Ste 504 Decatur AL 35601 Office Phone: 334-242-7693, 256-260-2146. Business E-Mail: terri.collins@alhouse.gov.

COLLINS, WALLACE, political organization administrator, former state legislator; b. Norman, Okla., Apr. 11, 1941; s. Clarence A. and Lois Sargent Collins; m. Pat Womack Collins; children: Eddy, David, Greg, Mike, Ryan, John. Machinist Collins Auto Machine; mem. Dist. 45 Okla. House Reps., 1997—2001, 2007—11, asst. minority floor leader; chair Okla. Dem. Party, 2011—. Chair Cleveland County Democratic Party, 2001. Democrat. Roman Catholic. Office: Oklahoma Democratic Party 4100 N Lincoln Blvd Oklahoma City OK 73105 Office Phone: 405-427-3366. Office Fax: 405-427-1310.*

COLLINS, WALTER LLOYD GEORGE, editor; b. Broken Arrow, Okla., Dec. 6, 1917; s. Dow Otho and Myrtle Hester (Campbell) C.; m. Ruth Leona Hamilton, Sept. 3, 1935; children: Mary, Walter, Alvin, Shirley. BA, Pan Am. U., 1966; MA, U. Tulsa, 1975. Aviation cadet USAAF, 1942; advanced through grades to maj. USAF, 1962; exec. in charge C-E Installation Project NATO, Europe, North Africa, Mid. East, 1956-57; sr. editor radar and missiles project USAFE, 1957-58; ops. officer C-E divsn. Def. Atomic Support Agy., Alburquerque, 1959-63; dir. comm.-elec., spacetrack NORAD, Colorado Springs, 1963-64; ret., 1964; gen. mgr. Desert Lodge, Moab, Utah, 1967-68; design engr. planner Beech Aircraft Corp., Wichita, Kans., 1968-72; dir. internat. student affairs Spartan Sch. Aeronautics, Tulsa, 1979-83; pres. R&W Internat., Tulsa, 1984-88, Alpha-Omega Press, Tulsa, Ponca City, Okla., 1990—. Adv. bd. edn. com. Okla. Acad. State Goals, 1977—95. Author: On the Razor's Edge, 1990, Manner of Man, 2001, Into Fields of Fire, 2004. Active Kay County Rep. Com., 1993—, Okla., Ponca City Traffic Commn., 1997-2000. Mem. Acad. Am. Poets, Nat. Order Battlefield Commns., Am. Air Mus. in Great Britain, Air Force Assn., Mil. Officers Assn. Am. Avocations: writing, photography. Home: 1601 Acadamy Rd Ponca City OK 74604 Personal E-mail: wgcollins@cableone.net.

COLLINS, WILLIAM EDWARD, JR., aeromedical administrator, psychologist, researcher; b. Bklyn., May 16, 1932; s. William Edward and Loretta Agnes (Brasier) C.; m. Corliss Jean Barnes, June 20, 1970; 1 child, Corliss Adora. BS, St. Peter's Coll., Jersey City, 1954; MA, Fordham U., Bronx, NY, 1956, PhD, 1959. Lic. psychologist, Okla. Psychol. rsch. asst. Fordham U., 1954-56, tchg. fellow, 1958, grad. instr., 1958-59, rsch. asst., 1958-59; rsch. psychologist US Army Med. Rsch. Lab., Ft. Knox, Ky., 1959-61; rsch. psychologist Aviation Psychology Lab. FAA Civil Aeromed. Inst., Oklahoma City, 1961-63, chief sensory integration sect., 1963-65, lab. supr., 1965-86, human resources rsch. br. mgr., 1986-88, inst. dep. dir., 1988—89, dir., 1989-2001; tech. profl. Chickasaw Nation Industries-Aviation, 2002—11; with FAA Rsch., Engring. & Devel. Adv. Com.'s, Subcom. Aircraft Safety, 2008—12; adj. assoc. prof. psychology U. Okla., Norman, 1963-70, adj. prof., 1970-89; adj. assoc. prof. rsch. psychology dept. psychiatry and behavioral scis. U. Okla. Health Scis. Ctr., Oklahoma City, 1965-71, adj. prof., 1971—. Mem. Nat. Acad. Sci.-NRC Com. on Vision, 1963-82, mem. exec. coun., 1973-81; mem. Nat. Acad. Sci.-NRC Com. on Hearing, Bioacoustics and Biomechanics, 1963-87; appearances before House Sub-Com. on Pub. Health and Environ., 1971, House Sub-Com. on Investigations and Oversight, 1983, House Sub-Com. on Transp., Aviation and Materials, 1987, 88; judge Okla. State Sci. and Engring. Fair, Ada, 1980, 81, 82; mem. Okla. Bd. Examiners Psychologists, 1981-84, chmn., 1982-84; evaluator proposals NSF, 1968-82, HEW, 1971-80; presenter, lectr. in field. Contbr. articles to profl. jours., chapters to books. Served to res. capt. Med. Services Corps, US Army, 1959-61. Recipient Outstanding Achievement award Okla. City Federally Employed Women, 1986, Dept. Transportation Sec. award, 1986, citation for svc. to aviation medicine Okla. State Legislature, 1999, Disting. Career Svc. award FAA, 2001; named to Okla. Aviation and Space Hall of Fame, 2004; named Fed. Employee of Yr. Okla. City Fed. Exec. Coun., 1985, named in his honor Ann. award Most Outstanding Scientific, Tech. FAA Pub. Aerospace Medicine, 2003. Fellow AAAS, APA (abstractor Psychol. Abstracts 1962-2002, citation 1973), NY Acad. Scis., Aerospace Med. Assn. (Raymond F. Longacre award 1971, presdl. exec. com. 1982-84, exec. coun. 1982-85, editl. bd. Aviation, Space and Environ. Medicine 1974-2000, assoc. editor 1980-2000, Pres.'s Citation 1993, Harry G. Moseley award 1998, Life Scis. and Biomed. Engring. Profl. Excellence award 1989, Pres.'s award 1999, Louis H. Bauer Founders award 2007), Am. Psychol. Soc. (charter), Aerospace Human Factors Assn. (charter, Paul T. Hansen award 1998, William E. Collins award publ. excellence in human factors named in his honor 2002); mem. Assn. Aviation Psychologists (pres. 1974-75), Okla. Psychol. Assn. (Disting. Psychologist award 1984), South African Soc. Aerospace and Environ. Medicine (Silver Medal award 1998), Nat. Mus. Am. Indian (charter, cert. of appreciation 1995), US Holocaust Meml. Mus. (charter mem.), Nat. Mus. African Am. History & Culture (charter mem.). Home: 8900 Sheringham Dr Oklahoma City OK 73132-4764 Office: Dept Psychiat Behavior Sci Okla U Health Sci Ctr Williams Pavillion Oklahoma City OK 73190-3048

COLLINSON, JUDY, apparel executive; With Urban Outfitters Inc.; exec. v.p. and gen. merchandising mgr. Barneys NY Inc.; exec. dir. women's apparel Anthropologie. Named top women's mcht., Barney's NY Inc. Office: Anthropologie Incorporated 30 Industrial Park Blvd Trenton SC 29847 Office Phone: 800-309-2500.

COLLINS-SMITH, LINDA, state legislator; Mem. 8-State Econ. Task Force, Ark. C. of C.; pres. Ark. Lodging Assn.; commr. Ark. Ethics Commn.; mem. Ark. Strategic Planning Com. for Developing Agri-Tourism, Ark. Small Bus. Coun.; pres. Ark. State U. Regional Leaders Grad. and Alumni; bd. dirs. Days Inn Corp.; mem. Lower Miss. Delta Devel. Coun., Nat. Rifle Assn.; founder, pres. Randolph County Tourism; bd. dirs. Rotary Club; mem. Sutton Free Will Baptist Ch., Women In Lodging; mem. Dist. 80 Ark. House of Representatives, 2011—. Democrat. Office: PO Box 90 Pocahontas AR 72455 Office Phone: 870-378-1434. Business E-Mail: Linda.Collins-Smith@arkansashouse.org.

COLLMER, ROBERT GEORGE, retired language educator; b. Guatemala, Nov. 28, 1926; (parents Am. citizens); s. G. Russell and Constance Ethel (Cravener) Collmer; m. Linnie Maffett Burney, Jan. 5, 1948 (dec. 1979); children: Carol Linda Collmer McLaren, Mark Wesley; m. Alys Edney, July 4, 1981. BA, Baylor U., Waco, Tex., 1948, MA, 1949; PhD, U. Pa., Phila., 1953. Asst. instr. U. Pa., Phila., 1949—52; instr. Phila. Bibl. U., 1952—54; from assoc. prof. to prof., chmn. dept. English Hardin-Simmons U., Abilene, Tex., 1954-58, 61; Smith-Mundt vis. prof. Inst. Tecnologico, Monterrey, Mexico, 1958—60; ind. rschr. U. Leiden, Netherlands, 1960; acad. dean, prof. Wayland Bapt. U., Plainview, Tex., 1961—66; Fulbright vis. prof. Universidad Nacional, Asuncion, Paraguay, 1966—67; prof. English Tex. Tech U., Lubbock, 1967—73; prof., chmn. dept. English Baylor U., Waco, Tex., 1973—80, disting. English prof., 1992—97, emeritus disting. English prof., 1997—, dean grad. studies and rsch., 1979—92. Vis. English prof. U. Jordan, 1997. Editor (with others): Am. Bypaths, 1980, The English Journals of Lodewijck Huygens, 1982, Bunyan in Our Time, 1989; contbr. articles to profl. jours. With US Army, 1945—46. Grantee, Am. Philos. Soc., 1976, Dutch Ministry Edn. Scis., 1981; fellow, Rockefeller Found., 1958, Smith-Mundt, 1958—60, Fulbright-Hays, 1966—76; Hon. Rsch. fellow, U. Glasgow, 1994, Sr. Rsch. grantee, Fulbright-Hays, 1982. Mem.: Conf. Coll. Tchrs. English (pres. 1983—84), Conf. Christianity and Lit. (pres. 1982—85), Assn. Tex. Grad. Schs. (pres. 1982—83), S. Ctrl. Renaissance Conf. (pres. 1970—71), Deans Conf. So. Assn. Bapt. Schs. (pres. 1963—64). Democrat. Avocations: traveling to Latin America and Europe, book collecting. Office Phone: 254-772-1897. Personal E-mail: rcol1017@aol.com.

COLLYER, ROBERT B., retired trade association administrator; b. Decatur, Ill., Oct. 16, 1932; s. Murray Gordon and Frances Mary (Evans) C.; m. Margaret Mary Hebel, Feb. 27, 1960; 1 son, Bryan. BA, Humboldt Coll., 1956. Cons. DeLeuw Cather & Co., 1957-59; claims and mgr. govt. relations Indsl. Indemnity Co. Calif., San Francisco, San Jose, Sacramento, 1960-73; exec. asst. UBA Inc., Washington, 1974-81; dep. under sec. Employment Standards Adminstrn. U.S. Dept. Labor, Washington, 1981-84; pres. The Collyer Co., 1984—2007; exec. dir. Internat. Assn. Indsl. Accident Bds. and Commns., 1990-96; exec. dir., sec.-treas. Internat. Workers' Compensation Found., 1990—2007; dean Internat. Workers' Compensation Coll., 1990-96; ret., 2007. Co-founder, dir. Nat. Symposium Workers Compensation U. Maine, 1976-80; dir. Western States Self-Ins. Colloquim, Inc., Nat. Employers' Adv. Council on Workers Compensation; cons. Nat. Indsl. Council; mem. Nat. Adv. Commn. on State Workers Compensation Law Compliance U.S. Dept. Labor; mem. Nat. Adv. Commn. on Indsl. Rehab. Research and Tng. Program U. N.C.; mem. steering com. Nat. Workers Compensation Info. Exchange Group; mem. steering com. Permanent Disability Study Adv. Commn. NSF; mem. steering com. U.S. Longshoremen and Harbor Workers' Reform Group Pres. Marin county Republican Council, (Calif.), 1973; mem. Calif. Rep. Central Com., 1970-73; asst. county chmn. Com. to Re-elect Pres., 1972. Named Republican of Yr. Marin County, 1972 Home and Office: Spruce Creek Fly In 25 Lazy Eight Dr Port Orange FL 32128

COLODNY, EDWIN IRVING, lawyer, retired air transportation executive; b. Burlington, Vt., June 7, 1926; s. Myer and Lena (Yett) Colodny; m. Nancy Dessoff, Dec. 11, 1965; children: Elizabeth, Mark, David. AB with distinction, U. Rochester, 1948; LLB, Harvard U., 1951; D in Comml. Sci. (hon.), Robert Morris Coll., 1985; LLD (hon.), Middlebury Coll., 1986; HHD (hon.), Kings Coll., 1988; LLD (hon.), U. Vt., 2004. Bar: N.Y. 1951, DC 1958. With CAB, 1954-57, USAirways Inc. (formerly Allegheny Airlines Inc.), 1957-91; exec. v.p. mktg. and legal affairs USAirways, Inc. (formerly Allegheny Airlines Inc.), 1969-75, pres., 1975-90, CEO, 1975-91, chmn. bd. dirs., 1978-92; also chmn. USAirways Group, Inc., 1978-92; ret., 1992; of counsel Paul, Hastings, Janofsky and Walker, Washington, 1991—2002; chmn. Comsat Corp., 1997-2000; of counsel Dinse, Knapp & McAndrew, Burlington, Vt., 2004—. Interim pres. U. Vt., 2001—02; interim pres., CEO Fletcher Allen Health Care, Burlington, 2002—03. Trustee Vt. Law Sch., Vt. Symphony. Lt. US Army, 1952—54. Recipient James D. McGill Meml. award, U. Rochester, Wright Bros. Meml. award, 1990, Tony Jannus award, 1990. Mem.: ABA, U. Rochester (bd. trustees). Personal E-mail: eic8225@aol.com.

COLOMBO, MICHAEL ALLEN, lawyer; b. Lumberton, NC, Sept. 2, 1948; BS, NC State Univ., 1970; JD, Univ. SC, 1979. Bar: NC, SC, US Ct. of Appeals, US Dist. Ct., US Tax Ct. Ptnr. Colombo Kitchin Attys., Greenville, NC. Capt. fighter pilot USAF, 1970—75. Mem.: ABA (ho. of delegates 2007—), Am. Coll. of Trust and Estate Counsel, Pitt County Bar Assn. (pres. 1988—89), NC Bar Assn. (pres. 2005—06). Office: Colombo Kitchin Attys 1698 E Arlington Blvd Greenville NC 27858 Office Phone: 252-321-2020.

COLON, ENNIO M., pediatrician; b. Mar. 16, 1962; BS in Biology, U. PR Ctrl., 1983; MD, Universidad Central del Caribe Med. Sch., Bayamon, PR, 1987. Cert. Am. Bd. Pediat. Resident, pediat. Miami Children's Hosp.; fellow, pediat. infectious diseases Tulane Med. Sch., New Orleans, 1990—92; staff mem. South Fla. Pediat. Partners, Miami, Fla. Contbr. several articles to profl. jours.; TV appearance focusing on Autism Awardness. Fellow: Am. Acad. Pediat.; mem.: Nat. Alliance for Autistic Rsch., AMA, Medico Americano Acad. Inter-American Doctors. Avocations: soccer, bicycling, swimming. Office: South Fla Pediat Partners 7800 SW 87th Ave #C-350 Miami FL 33173 Office Phone: 305-271-4711. Office Fax: 305-271-8732.

COLON, GUSTAVO ALBERTO, plastic surgeon; b. Ponce, PR, June 14, 1938; s. Gustavo Enrique and Araceli (de Ramery) Colon; m. Nairda Muniz, June 23, 1962 (dec. June 16, 1997); children: Gene, Albert, Lisa, Nairda; m. Carvea Colon, Dec. 31, 2005. BA, Johns Hopkins U., 1960; MD, U. Md., 1964. Diplomate Am. Bd. Plastic Surgery. Intern USPHS Hosp., Balt., 1964—65, resident in surgery New Orleans, 1965—69, chief plastic surgery, 1971—72; resident in surgery Tulane U., New Orleans, 1969—71, clin. prof. plastic surgery, 1972—. Mem. staff East Jefferson Gen. Hosp., Touro Infirmary, Lakeside Hosp., Drs. Hosp. Jefferson, chmn. bd., 1982—85. Served with USPHS, 1964—71. Decorated USCG commendation ribbon. Fellow: ACS; mem.: ACS, AMA, New Orleans Surg. Soc., Am. Cleft Palate Assn., Am. Soc. Aesthetic Surgery, Am. Burn Assn., Am. Soc. Plastic & Reconstructive Surgery. Roman Catholic. Home: 321 Rue Saint Peter Metairie LA 70005-3473 Office: 4224 Houma Blvd Ste 120 Metairie LA 70006 Office Phone: 504-888-4297. E-mail: gacolon@bellsouth.net.

COLONEY, WAYNE HERNDON, civil engineer; b. Bradenton, Fla., Mar. 15, 1925; s. Herndon Percival and Mary Adore (Cramer) C.; m. Anne Elizabeth Benedict, June 21, 1950; 1 child, Mary Adore. B.C.E. summa cum laude, Ga. Inst. Tech., 1950. Registered profl. engr. and surveyor, Fla., Ga., Ala., N.C. Project engr. Constructora Gen. S.A., Venezuela, 1948-49, Fla. Rd. Dept., 1950-55; hwy. engr. Gibbs & Hill, Inc., Guatemala, 1955-57, project mgr. Tampa, Fla., 1957-59; project engr., then assoc. J.E. Greiner Co., Tampa, 1959-63; ptnr. Barrett, Daffin & Coloney, Tallahassee, 1963-70; pres. Wayne H. Coloney Co., Inc., Tallahassee, 1970-78, chmn., bd. chief exec. officer, 1978-85; pres., sec. Tesseract Corp., 1975-85; dep. chmn. Howden Airdynamics Am., Tallahassee, 1985-90; pres. Coloney Co. Cons. Engrs., Inc., 1978—96; v.p., dir. Howden Coloney Inc., Tallahassee, 1985-90; prin. Coloney-Von Soosten & Assocs. Inc., Tallahassee, 1990—2002, Aurora Mgmt. Ptnrs., Tallahassee, 2002—03; prin. engr. Coloney Bell Engring., 1996—. Chmn. adv. com. Area Vocat. Tech. Sch., 1965-78; pres. Retro Tech. Corp., 1983-93, Profl. Mgmt. Con. Group, 1983-87; pres., bd. dirs. Internat. Enterprises Inc., 1967-73; bd. dirs., exec. com. GTO, Inc., 1990-2006. Patentee roof framing system, dense packing external aircraft fuel tank, tile mounting structure, curler rotating device, bracket system for roof framing; contbr. articles to profl. jours. Pres. United Fund Leon County, 1971-72; bd. dirs. Springtime Tallahassee, 1970-72, pres., 1981-82; bd. dirs. Heritage Found., 1965-71, pres., 1967; mem. Pres.'s Adv. Council on Indsl. Innovation, 1978-79; bd. dirs. LeMoyne Art Found., 1973, v.p., 1974-75; bd. dirs. Goodwill Industries, 1972-73, Tallahassee-Popoyan Friendship Commn., 1968-73; mem. Adv. Com. for Hist. and Cultural Preservation, 1969-71; vice chmn. Govs. Commn. for Purchase from the Blind, 1980-2002. Served with AUS, 1943-46. Fellow ASCE, Nat. Acad. Forensic Engrs. (pres.); mem. NSPE, Am. Def. Industries Assn., Fla. Engring. Soc. (sr.), Fla. Inst. Cons. Engrs., Fla. Surveying and Mapping Soc., ANAK, Koseme Soc., Fla. Small Bus. Assn. (pres. 1981), Gov.'s Club, Phi Kappa Phi, Omicron Delta Kappa, Sigma Alpha Epsilon, Tau Beta Pi. Anglican. Home: 1304 Hollow Oak Cir Tallahassee FL 32308 Home Phone: 850-222-5798. Personal E-mail: whcoloney@yahoo.com.

COLPO, CHARLES C., healthcare industry executive; m. Debra Colpo; 2 children. Grad., Va. Poly. Inst., State U. Joined Owens & Minor, Inc., 1981, sr. v.p., ops., 1999—2008, sr. v.p., tech., 2005—06, exec. v.p., adminstrn., 2008—10, exec. v.p., COO, 2010—. Office: Owens & Minor Inc 9120 Lockwood Blvd Mechanicsville VA 23116 Office Phone: 804-723-7000. Office Fax: 804-723-7100. Business E-Mail: charlie.colpo@owens-minor.com.

COLSON, JOHN R., electric power industry executive; With PAR Elec. Contractors Inc. (subs. of Quanta Svcs.), 1971—97, pres., 1997—97; CEO Quanta Services, Inc., Houston, 1997—2011, chmn., 2002—. Bd. dir. Quanta Svcs., 1998—, US Concrete Inc., 1999—. Mem.: Mo. Valley Chpt. Nat. Elec. Contractors Assn. (bd. dir.). Office: Quanta Svcs 2800 Post Oak Blvd Ste 2600 Houston TX 77056-6175 Office Phone: 713-629-7600.

COLSON, RANDALL ELWIN, lawyer; s. Elwin and Joanne Colson; m. Valerie Colson, Aug. 13; children: Catherine, Christopher. BA in Liberal Arts, Wheaton Coll., Ill., 1986; BSEE, U. Ill., 1986; JD, Northwestern U., 1991. Lic.: U.S. Patent and Trademark Office 1995, bar: Ill. 1991, Tex. 1995. Engr. Data Gen. Corp., Westboro, Mass., 1986—88; atty. D'Ancona & Pflaum, Chgo., 1991—94, Haynes and Boone LLP, Dallas, 1994—. Bd. dirs. Turtle Creek Manor, Dallas, 2004—, pres., 2007, 2008. Named Tex. Super Lawyer, Tex. Monthly Mag. Mem.: Dallas (Tex.) Bar Assn. Office: Haynes and Boone LLC 2323 Victory Ave Dallas TX 75219-7657

COLSTON, DAVID BERNARD, state legislator; m. Zandra Colston; children: Da'Yandra, David. Mem. Dist. 69 Ala. House of Representatives, 2011—. Mem. deacon and choir & usher boards Mount Olive Missionary Bapt. Ch. Democrat. Office: Ala House of Reps Rm 525-D 11 S Union St Montgomery AL 36130 Office Phone: 334-242-7535.

COLSTON, FREDDIE CHARLES, political science professor; b. Gretna, Fla., Mar. 28, 1936; s. Henry Bill and Willie Mae (Taylor) C.; m. Clarice L. Walker, Dec. 24, 1960; 1 child, Deirdre Colston Graddick; m. Doris Marie Suggs, Mar. 13, 1976 BA, Morehouse Coll., 1959; MA, Atlanta U., 1966; PhD, Ohio State U., 1972. Chmn. dept. social studies Attucks HS, Hollywood, Fla., 1960—64, swimming coach, 1962—65; instr. social sci. Ft. Valley State Coll., Ga., 1966-68; assoc. prof. polit. sci. So. U., Baton Rouge, 1972-73, U. Detroit, 1973-76; assoc. prof., chmn. div. social sci. Dillard U., New Orleans, 1976-78; asst. prof. polit. sci. Delta Coll., University Center, Mich., 1978-79; assoc. dir. Exec. Seminar Ctr. U.S. Office Pers. Mgmt., Oak Ridge, 1980-87; prof. Inst. of Govt. Tenn. State U., Nashville, 1987-88; prof., dir. pub. adminstrn. program N.C. Ctrl. U., Durham, 1988-91; prof. dept. history and polit. sci. Ga. Southwestern State U., Americus, 1992-97. Pres. Broward County (Fla.) Social Studies Coun., 1961-62; mem. constn. com. Fla. State Tchrs. Assn., 1963-64; chmn. human rels. coun. Ga. Southwestern State U., 1997; dir. Gen. Roll of Honor, Internat. Biog. Ctr., Cambridge, 2010. Author: Dr. Benjamin E. Mays Speaks: Representative Speeches of a Great American Orator, 2002, A Long Journey: Dr. Benjamin E. Mays Speaks on the Struggle for Social Justice in America, 2011; contbr. articles to profl. jours. Mem. bd. mgmt. Northwestern Br. YMCA, Detroit, 1976; mem. govt. subcom. Task Force 2000, City of Midland, Mich., 1979; mem. City of Oak Ridge Convention & Visitors Bur. Bd., 2001-02. Recipient Mr. Psi award Psi chpt., Omegi Psi Phi, 1959, 50 Yr. Svc. award, 2006, Outstanding Faculty award Kappa Delta Sorority, Ga. Southwestern State U., 1995, Outstanding Faculty award Sabu orgn. Ga. Southwestern State U., 1997, Outstanding Svc. award, Attucks HS Alumni Assn., 2007, The World Congress of Arts, Scis. and Comm., Lifetime Achievement award, Internat. Biog. Ctr., Chambridgeshire, Eng., 2010, named Hon. Dir. Gen., IBC, Cambridge, Eng., 2011, Am. Biog. Inst., Raleigh, NC, 2011, Lifetime Achievement award, 2011, named to Profl. Hall of Fame, ABI, 2011, Dir. Gen.'s Roll Honor, IBC, 2010, Order of Internat. fellowship, 2010; grantee C-Span, 1994, 95, 96; fellow Ford Found., 1967, So. Fellowships Fund, 1968-71; scholar Morehouse Coll., 1955, Atlanta U., 1965, Nat. Def. Edn. Act, 1964. Mem. Am. Polit. Sci. Assn. (com. on the status of blacks in the profession 1977-80), Ctr. Study Presidency, Assn. Study Afro-Am. Life, Pi Sigma Alpha, Alpha Phi Gamma. Avocations: reading, photography, sports. Home: 116 Downing Dr Oak Ridge TN 37830-8790 Personal E-mail: freddie12@comcast.net.

COLSTON, MARQUES, professional football player; b. Harrisburg, Pa., June 5, 1983; s. James and Josie Colston. BA, Hofstra U., Hempstead, NY, 2006. Wide receiver New Orleans Saints, 2007—. Co-owner Harrisburg Stampede, Am. Indoor Football Assn., 2008—. Founder Colston Charities, 2006—. Achievements include member of Super Bowl XLIV championship winning New Orleans Saints, 2010. Office: New Orleans Saints 5800 Airline Dr Metairie LA 70003

COLTON, W. M., energy executive; BSChemE, Mich. Technol. U. Asst. treas. ExxonMobil Corp., v.p., strategic planning. Office: Exxon Mobil Corp 5959 Las Colinas Blvd Irving TX 75039-2298 Office Phone: 972-444-1000, 972-444-1350. Business E-Mail: w.colton@exxonmobil.com.

COLVIN, O. MICHAEL, medical association administrator, educator; b. Princeton, Ind., June 15, 1936; s. Jack Gene and and Evelyn Mae (Satkamp) C.; m. Arline Mae Lockerbie, Aug. 23, 1959; children: Michael Eric, Jennifer Susan, Kimberly Anne, Christopher Andrew. BA in Chemistry, Ind. U., 1957; MD, Washington U., St. Louis, 1961. Intern, resident Johns Hopkins Hosp., Balt., 1961-64; clin. assoc. Nat. Cancer Inst., Bethesda, Md., 1964-66; fellow in pharmacology Johns Hopkins U., Balt., 1966-68, physician, 1968-95, from asst. prof. to prof. medicine, 1968-95; dir. Duke Comprehensive Cancer Ctr. Duke U. Med. Ctr., Durham, NC, 1995—2002; Wm. Shingleton prof. cancer rsch. Duke U. Sch. Medicine, Durham, 2002—. Grant rev. study sect. Nat. Cancer Inst., Bethesda, 1968—. Recipient Career Devel. award Nat. Cancer Inst., 1975-80. Mem. AAAS, Am. Soc. Clin. Oncology, Am. Soc. Bone Marrow Transplantation, Am. Assn. Cancer Rsch. Home: 208 Arcadia Ln Chapel Hill NC 27514-1472 Office: Duke U Med Ctr 419 Jones Bldg PO Box 3843 Durham NC 27702-3843 Office Phone: 919-684-4167. Business E-Mail: colvio03@mc.duke.edu.

COLWELL, GENE THOMAS, engineering educator; b. Chattanooga, Aug. 3, 1937; s. William Clarence and Mary Virginia (Smith) Colwell; m. Peggy Ann Fletcher, June 1, 1973. BSME, U. Tenn., 1959, MSME, 1962, PhD, 1966. Rsch. engr. Oak Ridge Nat. Lab., Tenn., 1959—62, 1965—68; instr. U. Tenn., Knoxville, 1962—65; asst. prof. Ga. Inst. Tech., Atlanta, 1966—71, assoc. prof., 1971—77, prof., 1977—95, prof. emeritus, 1995—, assoc. dir. Atlanta, 1984—87. Vis. prof. U. Carabobo, Venezuela, 1971; cons. in field. Contbr. articles to profl. jours. Numerous rsch. grants. Fellow: ASME (life); mem.: Sigma Xi, Pi Tau Sigma. Achievements include patents in field. Avocations: tennis, golf, hiking. Home: 9145 Prestwick Club Dr Duluth GA 30097-2442

COLWELL, JOHN AMORY, physician; b. Boston, Nov. 4, 1928; s. Arthur Ralph and Jeane (Haskins) C.; m. Jane Kuebler, June 19, 1954(deceased); children: John Clayton, Ann Kimbell, Karen Elizabeth, James Lewis; m.Georgia Van Cleve February 14,2010. AB, Princeton U., 1950; MD, Northwestern U., 1954, MS in Medicine, 1957, PhD in Physiology, 1968. Intern Univ. Hosps., Cleve., 1954-55; resident in internal medicine Passavant Meml. Hosp., Chgo., 1955-57, VA Research Hosp., Chgo., 1959-60; from instr. to assoc. prof. medicine Northwestern U. Med. Sch., 1960-71; fellow in endocrinology and diabetes Northwestern U. Med. Ctr., Chgo., 1960-63; clin. investigator, then chief metabolic sect. VA Research Hosp., 1961-71; prof. medicine Med. U. S.C., Charleston, 1971—2008, emeritus prof. medicine, 2009, dir. endocrinology-metabolism-diabetes div., dept. medicine, 1972-94, dir. diabetes ctr. Charleston, 1994—, rsch. coord., 1973-79; assoc. chief staff rsch. and devel. VA Med. Center, Charleston, 1971-93. Bd. dirs. Am. Diabetes Assn., 1982-88, v.p. 1985, pres. elect 1986, pres., 1987; bd. dirs. S.C. Dabetes Assn., 1971-80/ Author: Clinical Recognition and Treatment of Diabetic Vascular Disease, 1975; co-author: Diabetes and Metabolic Disorders, 1975, 82, Diabetes, Endocrinology and Metabolic Disorders, 1981, Diabetes, 2003; contbr. articles med. jours. Served to capt. M.C. USAF, 1957-59. Grantee: NiH, VA, 1962-94. Master ACP; mem. AAAS, Am. Diabetes Assn., Am. Fedn. Clin. Rsch., Am. Physiol. Soc., Ctrl. Soc. Clin. Rsch., Endocrine Soc., So. Soc. Clin. Investigation. Clubs: Skokie Country (Glencoe, Ill.), Carolina Yacht (Charleston), Yeamans Hall (Charleston), Cloister Inn (Princeton U.). Republican. Episcopalian. Home: 182 Broad St Charleston SC 29401-2429 Business E-Mail: colwelja@musc.edu.

COLYER, DALE KEITH, agricultural economics professor; b. Albion, Ill., Dec. 22, 1931; s. Wallace C. and Louella (Walker) C.; m. Norma L. DeWind, Sept. 18, 1959; children: Claudia R., Wallace C. BS, U. Ill., 1954, MS, 1955; PhD, U. Wis., 1963. Rsch. asst. Fed. Res. Bank of Kansas City, Mo., 1958-60; asst. prof. U. Mo., Columbia 1963-65, assoc. prof., 1965-70; prof. W.Va. U., Morgantown, 1970—2001, prof. emeritus, 2002—; interim assoc. dir. W.Va. Agrl. Exp. Sta., 2000. Fulbright lectr., Rosario, Argentina, 1968; dir. resource mgmt. divsn. W.Va. U., 1978-83; agrl. economist U.S. AID, Quito, Ecuador, 1984-87, cons., 1983, 88, 89, 90, 91, 93. Assoc. editor Rev. Agrl. Econs., 1991-93; author, editor of 4 books; contbr. articles to profl. jours. With U.S. Army, 1956-58. Benedum Disting. scholar W.Va. U., 1994. Mem. Am. Agrl. Econ. Assn. (Best Pub. Rsch. award 1968), N.E. Agrl. Econ. Coun. (editor 1977-81, pres. 1979-80, disting. mem. 1984), Davis Coll., W.Va. (Dean's Recognition award, 2011), Internat. Assn. Agrl. Economists, Fulbright Assn, Am. Agrl. Econ. Assoc. (dir. 2006-08). Home: 936 Riverview Dr Morgantown WV 26505-4634 Office: West Va U Agrl Scis PO Box 6108 Morgantown WV 26506-6108 Office Phone: 304-293-5487, 304-293-4832. Business E-Mail: dcolyer@wvu.edu.

COMBE, JOHN CLIFFORD, JR., lawyer; b. New Orleans, Jan. 5, 1939; s. John Clifford and Gladys Ann (Reine) C.; m. Lynne Wendel Watson, July 11, 1964; children: John, Wendy, Holly. BBA, Tulane U., 1960, LLB, 1965. Bar: La. 1965, US Dist. Ct. (ea. and mid. dists.) La. 1965, US Ct. Appeals (5th cir.) 1965, US Supreme Ct. 1971, US Ct. Appeals (11th cir.) 1981, US Dist. Ct. (we. dist.) La. 1986. Assoc. Jones, Walker, Waechter, Poitevent, Carrere & Denegre, New Orleans, 1965—, ptnr., 1970—, sr. ptnr., 1989—. Editor: La. Bar Jour., 1975-77; contbr. articles to legal jours. Organizer, mem. Crestmont Pk. Improvement Assn.; organizer Greater New Orleans Law Explorer program Boy Scouts Am., 1974; mem. St. Catherine of Siena Parish Sch. Bd., 1976-89; trustee Acad. of Sacred Heart, 1993-96. Lt. (j.g.) USN, 1960-62. Recipient Monte M. Lemann award, La. Civil Svc. League, 1990. Fellow: ABA (mem. ho. of dels. 1982—88), La. State Bar Found., Am. Bar Found., Am. Coll. Trial Lawyers (state chair 1999—2000); mem.: La. Bar Assn. (mem. bd. govs. 1973—74, sec.-treas. 1975, mem. bd. govs. 1975—76, 1977—78, 1978—80, pres. 1979—80, Outstanding Young Lawyer award 1978, pres. award 1989), So. Regional Conf. Bar Pres., Nat. Conf. Bar Pres., Def. Rsch. Inst., Am. Judicature Soc. (mem. bd. govs. 1982—86), La. Assn. Def. Counsel (bd. dirs. 1969—75, faculty trial acad. 2000—02), Internat. Assn. Def. Counsel (speaker 1989, mem. faculty trial acad. 1991), Stratford Club (pres. 1993—95), Boston Club. Republican. Roman Catholic. Office: Jones Walker Waechter Poitevent Carrere & Denegre 201 St Charles Ave New Orleans LA 70170-5100 Office Phone: 504-582-8144. Business E-Mail: jcombe@joneswalker.com.

COMBS, DOUGLAS L., state supreme court justice; b. Shawnee, Okla., Oct. 17, 1951; m. Janet Lea Combs; children: Christopher, Eric. BA in Polit. Sci., U. Okla., 1973; JD, Oklahoma City U., 1976. Bar: Okla. 1976. Law clk. Okla. Supreme Ct.; asst. state atty. gen. State of Okla., spl. dist. judge, 1995—2003; judge 23rd Dist. Ct., Pottawatomie County, Okla., 2003—11; justice Okla. Supreme Ct., 2011—. Bd. mem. Okla. Judicial Conf., 2006—10, pres., 2009. Office: Oklahoma Supreme Ct Okla Judicial Ctr 2100 N Lincoln Blvd Ste 4 Oklahoma City OK 73105-4907 Office Phone: 405-521-3847.*

COMBS, LESLIE A., state legislator; b. Aug. 1, 1958; BBA in Acctg. Chief acct. Ky. Dept. Agr., 1981—84; special asst. to pres. Pikeville Coll., 1984—2007; v.p. regional services Southeast Telephone, 2007—09; mem. Dist. 94 Ky. House of Reps., 2007—. Former pres., dir. Pike County HS Site Based Decision Making Coun. Mem.: Ctrl. Ky. Planned Giving Coun., ARH Hosp. Bd. Democrat. Presby. Mailing: 245 E Cedar Dr Pikeville KY 41501 Office: Ky Legislature Annex Rm 373 702 Capitol Ave Frankfort KY 40601 Office Phone: 502-564-8100 ext. 669. Business E-Mail: Leslie.Combs@lrc.ky.gov.

COMER, EVAN PHILIP, manufacturing executive; b. Cumberland Gap, Tenn., May 29, 1927; s. Evan Mitchell and Margaret Nola (Estep) C.; m. Mary Blanc, Aug. 28, 1948; children: Vivian, Jane. BA, Carson-Newman Coll., Jefferson City, Tenn., 1948; MA, Columbia U., NYC, 1949. Asst. prof. psychology, dir. student personnel and placement Furman U., Greensville, SC, 1949-52; self-employed writer, 1952-53; supervisory conf. leader Union Carbide Nuclear Co., Oak Ridge, 1953-55; instr. in-plant tng. U. Tenn., Knoxville, 1955-56; with Foote Mineral Co., 1956-67, 69-84, v.p., gen. mgr. chems. and minerals div., 1970-80, pres., chief exec. officer Exton, Pa., 1980-84, also bd. dirs.; pres., chief exec. officer, chmn. bd. Ashram Farm, Inc., Rutledge, Tenn., 1984-98. Mem. Pa. adv. bd. Liberty Mut. Ins. Co.; chmn. exec. com., dir. Phila. Mfrs. Mut. Ins. Co. Pres. Southeastern C.C., Whiteville, NC, 1967-69; mem. adv. bd. Carson-Newman Coll.; bd. dirs. Pa. Sci. and Engring. Found.; mem. Pa. Gov's Sci. Adv. Com.; mem. adv. coun. Pa. Tech. Assistance Program, Pa. State U.; chmn. bd. Chester County Pvt. Industry Coun., 1983-84; mem. Jefferson County Planning Commn., Tenn., 1998—, Jefferson County Zoning Appeals Bd., 1998—; mem. regional resource stewardship coun. TVA, 2000—07; pres. Jefferson County Hist. Soc., 2003-06, bd. dir., treas. Dandridge Mcpl. Pub. Libr., 2006—08, treas., Regency Ret. Cmty. Ch., 2009-; With USNR, 1945-46. Mem.: AIME, Am. Mining Congress, Ferroalloys Assn. (chmn. bd. dirs. 1983—84), Mining Club (NYC). Baptist. Home: 739 E 2nd North St Apt 380 Morristown TN 37814 Personal E-mail: comerevan@bellsouth.net.

COMER, JAMES R., state agency administrator, former state legislator; b. Aug. 19, 1972; m. Tamara Jo Comer; children: Reagan, Harlan, Aniston. BA in Agrl. magna cum laude, Western Ky. U., Bowling Green. Founder, owner James Comer, Jr. Farms, Monroe County, Ky.; co-owner Land & Cattle Co., Ky.; dir. South Ctrl. Bank, Monroe County, Ky.; mem. Dist. 53 Ky. House of Reps., 2001—12; commr. Ky. Dept. Agrl., 2012—. Pres. Monroe County C. of C., 1999—2000. Mem.: Monroe County Farm Bureau, Monroe County C. of C. (former pres.). Republican. Baptist. Office: Ky Dept Agriculture 111 Corporate Dr Frankfort KY 40601 Office Phone: 502-564-4696. Office Fax: 502-573-0046. Business E-Mail: james.comer@ky.gov.

COMINI, ALESSANDRA, art historian, educator, musicologist; b. Winona, Minn., Nov. 24, 1934; d. Raiberto and Megan (Laird) C. BA, Barnard Coll., NYC, 1956; MA, U. Calif., Berkeley, 1964; PhD with distinction, Columbia U., NYC, 1969. Tchg. asst. U. Calif., Berkeley, 1964, vis. instr., 1967; preceptor Columbia U., 1965-66, 67-68, instr., 1968-69, asst. prof., 1969-74; vis. asst. prof. So. Methodist U., summers 1970, 72, assoc. prof. art history, 1974-75, prof., 1975—, univ. disting. prof., 1983—2005. Alfred Hodder resident humanist Princeton U., 1972-73; disting. vis. lectr. Oxford U., 1996; vis. asst. prof. Yale U., 1973; vis. humanist various univs.; lectr. in English, German and Italian; keynote spkr. Gewandhaus Symposia, Leipzig, Germany, 1983, 85, 87, 89, Mahler Internat Congress, Amsterdam, 1988, 95, Hamburg, 1989, Oxford, 1996, Montpellier, 1996, Internat. Mahler Fest, Boulder, Colo., 1998; featured spkr. Purchase, NY, 1989, Leningrad, 1990, Stockholm, 1991, Berlin, 1993, Bethoven Extravaganza, Milw., 1994, Schiele Symposium, Indpls., 1994, Helsinki, 1996, Schubertiads at Curtis Inst., Phila., Reed Coll., Oreg. and So. Meth. U., 1997, Santa Fe Opera, 1997-02, 06, Dallas Symphony Orch., 1998-2006, Indpls. Symphony Orch., 2007, Brahmsfest of So. Meth. U., 2005, Mozart Internat. Symposium U. Dublin, Ireland, 1999, San Diego Mus., 1999-2005, Giacometti Symposium, Nasher Sculpture Ctr., Dallas, 2005, 06, Neue Galerie, 2005, 06, 07, 08, 09, 10, 11, 12, Mozartfest of So. Meth. U., 2006, Klimt Atelier, Vienna, 2006; panelist NEH Mus. and Pub. Programs, 1978—79; vis. scholar Kalamazoo Coll., 1999, assoc. producer KLIMT MUSIK CD, 2007, curator Egon Schiele Portraits, Neue Galerie, NY, 2014. Author: Schiele in Prison, 1973, Egon Schiele's Portraits, 1974 (Nat. Book award nominee 1975, reissued 1990, Charles Rufus Morey Book award 1974), Gustav Klimt, 1975, reissued 1986, 90, 93, 01, also German, French and Dutch edit., Egon Schiele, 1976, reissued 1986, 94, 01, 09, also German, French and Dutch edits., The Fantastic Art of Vienna, 1978, The Changing Image of Beethoven, 1987, reissued, 2008, Egon Schiele: Nudes, 1995, In Passionate Pursuit: A Memoir, 2004; contbg. author: World Impressionism, 1990, Käthe Kollwitz, 1992, Egon Schiele, 1994, Violetta and her Sisters, 1994, Salome, 1996, By a Finnish Fireside: An Evening with Akseli Gallen-Kallela and Gustav Mahler, 1997, The Visual Wagner, 1997, Irony and Gustav Mahler, 2000, Toys in Friend's Attic, 2001, Beethoven and His World, 2000, Pilgrimage to Schiele, 2005, The Two Gustavs: Klimt, Mahler, and Vienna's Golden Decade, 1897-1907, The Decisive Decade, 1987-1907, 2009, Ferdinand Hodler and Austrian Art, 2012, Remembering Serga Sabarsky; contbr. numerous articles to Stagebill, Arts Mag., English Nat. Opera, Chgo. Lyric Opera; also author various catalogue and book introductions, also book revs. for NY Times, Women's Art Jour. Awarded Grand Decoration of Honor for svcs. to Republic of Austria, 1990; recipient Charles Rufus Morey Book award Coll. Art Assn. Am., 1974, Laural award AAUW, 1979; named Outstanding Prof., 1977, 79, 83, 85, 86, 87, 88, 90, 98, 99, 2000, 01, 02, 03, 04, Laurence Perrine prize Phi Beta Kappa Gamma of Tex., 2003, award Vet. Feminists America, 2010; AAUW travel fellow, 1966-87; NEH grantee, 1975; named Meadows Disting. Tchg. Prof., 1986-87, Tchr./Scholar of Yr., United Meth. Ch., 1996; Comini Lectr. Series in Art History named in her honor So. Meth. U., 2005, Vet. Feminists America award, 2010, Disting. ALumna award Barnard Coll., 2011. Mem. ASCAP, Nat. Mus. for Women in the Arts (nat. bd. 1997—), Coll. Art Assn. Am. (bd. dirs. 1980-84), Women's Caucus for Art (bd. dirs. 1974-78, Life Achievement award 1995, Tex. Women's Hall of Fame 2002), Tex. Inst. Letters. Democrat. Avocations: piano, flute. Home: 2900 McFarlin Blvd Dallas TX 75205-1920 Office: So Meth U Divsn Art History Dallas TX 75275 Office Phone: 214-369-8523. Business E-Mail: acomini@smu.edu.

COMMANDER, CHARLES EDWARD, lawyer, real estate consultant; b. Jacksonville, Fla., Aug. 17, 1940; s. Charles Edward Jr. and Eleanor (Wood) C.; m. Victoria Coxe, Aug. 10, 1963; children: Eleanor, Charles IV, Christopher. BS in Commerce, Washington & Lee U., 1962; JD, U. Fla., 1965. Bar: Fla. 1966. Atty., assoc. ptnr. Mahoney, Hadlow, Chambers and Adams, Jacksonville, 1966-73; pres. Barnett Winston Properties, Jacksonville, 1973-74; founding ptnr. Commander, Legler, Werber, Dawes, Sadler & Howell, Jacksonville, 1974-91; ptnr., mgmt. com. Foley & Lardner, 1991—2003. Cons. First Union Nat. Bank Fla., Jacksonville, 1990-95; chmn. bd. dirs. First Nat. Bank, Jacksonville, 1979-84; chmn. Property Investment Svcs., Inc., Jacksonville, 1974—; bd. Everbank Fin. Corp., 1994-, Everbank FSB, 2002-; trustee Builders Investment Group, King of Prussia, Pa. and Fullerton, Calif., 1977-80; dir. Koger Equity Inc., 1993-95, Computer Power, 1974-79, 86-92; bd. dirs. U. Fla. Law Ctr. Assn., 2002-, Patriot Transp. Holding Co., 2004-; mem. bd. advisors Lanier Upshaw, Inc. Editor Law Review U. Fla., 1964-65; reporter Fla. Law Revision Comm., 1975-76. Trustee The Bolles Sch., Jacksonville, 1980-90, U. Fla. Law Ctr. Assn., 2004-, Delta Waterfowl Found., 2005—; pres. U. No. Fla. Found., 1994-97, Cummer Gallery of Art, 1993—2002; bd. dirs. Jacksonville Housing Authority, 1995—2003; vice chmn. Mus. Sci. and History, Jacksonville, 1968-73, Jacksonville Zool. Soc., 1972-76, Jacksonville Housing Commn., 2006—; pres. bd. dirs. The River Club, Jacksonville, 1977-84. Episcopalian. Avocations: fishing, hunting, boating, farming. Office: Foley & Lardner Ste 1300 One Independent Dr Jacksonville FL 32202-5017 E-mail: ccommander@foley.com.

COMMEYRAS, MICHELLE, literature and language professor; b. Paris, June 15, 1953; d. Elizabeth Donaldson and Andre Francois Commeyras. BA, U. Mass., Boston, 1979, MA, 1986; PhD, U. Ill., Champaign, 1991. Prof. lang. and literacy edn. U. Ga., Athens, 1991—. Editor: (book) Teachers as Readers: Readers as Teachers, 2003; author: No Deposit, No Return Enriching Literacy Teaching and Learning Through Critical Inquiry Pedagogy, 2006. Liberal. Avocation: reading. Office: Univ Ga 309 Aderhold Hall Athens GA 30602

COMMODORE, MIKE, professional hockey player; b. Fort Saskatchewan, Alta., Canada, Nov. 7, 1979; Attended, U. ND, 1997—2000. Defenseman NJ Devils, 2000—02, Calgary Flames, 2003—05, Carolina Hurricanes, 2005—08, Ottawa Senators, 2008, Columbus Blue Jackets, 2008—11, Detroit Red Wings, 2011—12, Tampa Bay Lightning, 2012—. Achievements include being a member of NCAA National Championship Team, University of North Dakota, 2000; being a member of Stanely Cup Champion Carolina Hurricanes, 2006; being a member of the IIHF World Championship Gold Medalists, Team Canada, 2007. Office: Tampa Bay Lightning Hockey Club Tampa Bay Times Forum 401 Channelside Dr Tampa FL 33602

COMP, PHILIP CINNAMON, medical researcher; b. Kewanee, Ill., Feb. 28, 1945; s. Franklin Howard and Alberta (Cinnamon) C.; m. Carol Lee Winter, May 11, 1974; children: Vanessa Cinnamon, Justin Philip, Aubrie Elizabeth. BA, Reed Coll., 1967; MD, U. Wash., 1971; PhD, U. Okla., 1978. Intern, then resident U. Pa. Hosp., Phila., 1971-74; fellow allergy sect. U. Okla. Health Sci. Ctr., Oklahoma City, 1974-76, asst. prof. medicine, 1976-82, assoc. prof. medicine, 1982-88, prof. medicine, 1988—, dir. thrombosis/coagulant lab., 1979—99, dir. gen. clin. rsch. ctr., 2000—04; attending physician med. svc. VA Med. Ctr., Oklahoma City, 1976—, assoc. chief of staff rsch., 1992—; dir. adult sect. Okla. Comprehensive Hemophilia Treatment Ctr., Oklahoma City, 1980—. Affiliated mem. cardiovasc. biology rsch. program Okla. Med. Resident Found., Oklahoma City, 1988—; program dir. Gen. Clin. Rsch. Ctr., 2000—04. Avocation: compost making. Office: VA Med Ctr 921 NE 13th St (151) Oklahoma City OK 73104 Home Phone: 405-720-9326; Office Phone: 405-271-6466.

COMPER, TONY (F. ANTHONY), retired bank executive; b. Toronto, Ont., Can., Apr. 24, 1945; m. Elizabeth Comper. BA in English, U. Toronto, 1966, LLD (hon.); LHD (hon.), Mt. St. Vincent; D.Litt (hon.), U. New Brunswick. Joined BMO Fin. Group (Bank of Montreal), 1967, various positions, 1967—78, v.p. sys. devel., 1978—82, sr. v.p. personal banking, 1982, sr. v.p., sr. ops. officer treasury group, 1982-84, sr. v.p., mgr. London br., 1984-86, sr. v.p., sr. mktg. officer corp. and govt. banking, 1986-87, exec. v.p. ops., 1987-89, chief gen. mgr., COO, 1989-90, pres., COO, 1990-99, chmn., 1999—2004, pres., CEO, 1999—2007. Bd. dirs. BMO Fin. Group and its subs. Harris Fin. Corp., BMO Nesbitt Burns Corp. Ltd., Internat. Monetary Conf., 2004—, Spectra Energy Corp., 2007—. Vice chair C.D. Howe Inst.; dir. C.D. Howe Meml. Found., Catalyst, NY; chair Catalyst's Can. Bd. Advisors; chair corp. adv. bd. Learning Partnership; past chair Capital campaign U. Toronto, governing coun.; former vice-chair St. Michael's Hosp.; mem. U. New Brunswick's Forging Our Futures Campaign; hon. chair bd. govs. Yee Hong Ctr. Geriatric Care; founder FAST, 2005; bd. governors Jr. Achievement of Can. Recipient Human Rels. award Can. Coun. Christians and Jews, 1998, Award of Merit B'Nai Brith, Can., 2003. Mem. Women in Capital Markets Adv. Cun., N.Am Policy Com., Can. Coun. Chief Execs., Internat. Bus. Leaders Adv. Coun. Mayor Bejing, Internat. Bus. Coun. World Econ. Forum, Harris Nat. Assn. (chmn. 1999-2004). Avocations: golf, classical music, theater, art. Office: Spectra Energy Corp Bd Directors 5400 Westheimer Ct Houston TX 77056 Office Phone: 713-627-5400. Office Fax: 713-627-4607. Business E-Mail: tony.comper@bmo.com.

COMPTON, JOHN JOSEPH, philosophy educator; b. Chgo., May 17, 1928; s. Arthur Holly and Betty Charity (McCloskey) C.; m. Marjorie Ann Yaple, July 8, 1950; children: Elizabeth Holly, Catherine Marchus, John Arthur. BA, Coll. of Wooster, 1949; MA, Yale U., 1951, PhD, 1953. Asst. prof. philosophy Vanderbilt U., Nashville, 1952-55, assoc. prof., 1955-68, prof., 1968-98, prof. emeritus, 1998—, chmn. or acting chmn. dept., 1966-73, 84-85, 88-89, 93-95. Vis. prof. Colo. Coll., Colorado Springs, 1977, Wesleyan U., Middletown, Conn., 1984. Contbr. articles to profl. jours. and chpts. in books. Mem. bd. advisers Matchette Found., 1968—; trustee Coll. of Wooster, Ohio, 1975—. Recipient Harbison award for disting. teaching Danforth Found., 1966; fellow Belgian-Am. Edn. Found., 1956-57, sr. fellow NEH, 1974-75, fellow Ctr. for Humanities, Wesleyan U., 1974-75. Mem. AAAS, AAUP, Am. Philos. Assn. (sec. ea. div. 1970-73, v.p. 1974), Metaphys. Soc. Am. (pres. 1979), Soc. for Phenomenology and Existential Philosophy, So. Soc. for Philosophy and Psychology, Philosophy of Sci. Assn., Soc. for Values in Higher Edn. (Kent fellow 1951), Phi Beta Kappa. Democrat. Avocations: hiking, camping, gardening, choral singing, cooking. Home: 3708 Whitland Ave Nashville TN 37205-2430 Personal E-mail: jjcompton@aol.com.

COMPTON, WALTER KNOX, oil industry executive, lawyer; b. 1962; BBA, Southern Meth. U., 1983; JD, U. Ark., 1987. Bar: Ark. 1987. Assoc. Compton, Prewett, Thomas & Hickey, PA, El Dorado, Ark., 1987—88; corp. atty. Murphy Oil Corp., 1988—96, mgr., Law Dept., corp. sec., 1996—2009, v.p., Law Dept., corp. sec., 2009—11, sr. v.p., gen. counsel, 2011—. Office: Murphy Oil Corp 200 Peach St PO Box 7000 El Dorado AR 71731-7000 Office Phone: 870-862-6411. Office Fax: 870-864-6371. Business E-Mail: WCompton@murphyoilcorp.com.*

COMSTOCK, BARBARA J., state legislator, lawyer; b. Springfield, Mass., June 30, 1959; m. Elwyn Charles; children: Daniel, Peter, Catherine. BA, Middlebury Coll., Vt., 1981; JD, Georgetown U. Law Ctr., Washington, 1986. Sr. aide to Rep. Frank Wolf US House of Representatives, Washington; chief investigative counsel, chief counsel US House of Reps. Com. on Govt. Reform and Oversight, Washington; dir. rsch. & strategic planning Rep. Nat. Com., 1999—2001; chief spokesperson, comm. strategist to Atty. Gen. john Ashcroft US Dept. Justice, Washington, 2002—03; ptnr., sr. prin. govt. rels. Blank Rome, LLP, 2003—07; owner, ptnr. pub. affairs firm. Corallo Comstock, Alexandria, Va.; mem. Dist. 34 Va. House of Dels., Richmond, 2010—. Sr. cons. Romney for Pres., 2006—08; legal & polit. commentator CNN, FOX News, MSNBC. Mem. McLean Cmty. Ctr. Governing Bd., 1993—96; bd. mem. Support Our Aging Religious, Childhelp. Mem.: Northern Va. Tech. Coun., Fairfax County C. of C., Federalist Soc. Republican. Roman Catholic. Office: Corallo Comstock 520 N Washington St Alexandria VA 22314 also: Va House of Dels Gen Assembly Bldg Rm 407 PO Box 406 Richmond VA 23218 also: PO Box 6156 Mc Lean VA 22106 Office Phone: 804-698-1034, 703-209-3787. Office Fax: 804-698-6734. Business E-Mail: delbcomstock@house.virginia.gov.

CONANT, ALLAH B., JR., lawyer, entrepreneur, small business owner; b. Waco, Tex., July 24, 1939; s. Allah B. and Frances Louise (James) C.; children: Heather Lee Arsham, Lisa Lynn, Leslie Marie Thorne; stepchild, Thomas R. Bone II. BA, N. Tex. State Coll., Denton, 1961; JD cum laude, Baylor U., 1963. Bar: Tex. 1963, US Tax Ct. 1963, US Dist. Ct. (no. dist.) Tex. 1964, US Dist. Ct. (so. dist.) Tex. 1969, US Ct. Appeals (5th cir.) 1970, US Supreme Ct. 1971, US Ct. Appeals (8th cir.) 1975, US Ct. Appeals (4th and 7th cirs.) 1978, US Ct. Appeals (3d and 11th cirs.) 1981, US Dist. Ct. (ea. dist.) Tex. 1986, US Dist. Ct. (we. dist.) Tex. 1986, US Ct. Appeals (10th cir.) 1987, US Ct. Appeals (2d cir.), 2004; bd. cert. Tex. Trial Law, Tex. Bd. Legal Specialization. Since practiced in, Dallas; ptnr. Shank, Irwin, Conant, Lipshy & Casterline, 1964-90; owner ABC Ranch, 1981-89; of counsel Whittenburg Whittenburg and Schachter, 1990; mem. Conant Whittenburg French & Schachter, Dallas, 1991-99; ptnr. Conant French & Chaney, LLP, Dallas, 1999—2005; ret., 2006; owner AAA Storage, Gun Barrel City, Tex. Contbr. to legal jours. Trustee St. John's Episcopal Sch., 1987-90; bd. dirs. The Libr. at Cedar Creek, 2007-10, 2011-. With USMC Res., 1957—63. Fellow Am. Bar Found. (life), Tex. Bar Found. (life), Dallas Bar Found. (life); mem. ABA (coun. gen. practice sect. 1977-80, chmn. 1982-83, del. 1983-86), Dallas Bar Assn., State Bar Tex., Trial Attys. Am., Baylor Law Sch. Counsellors, Baylor Law Alumni Assn. (dir. 1979-82), Baylor Law Rev. Ex-Editors Assn., N.Tex. State U. Alumni Assn. (dir., v.p.), Henderson County Bar Assn., Sigma Phi Epsilon, Omicron Delta Kappa, Phi Delta Phi (historian 1962). Clubs: Petroleum (Dallas). Avocations: reading, travel, boating, target shooting. Home Phone: 214-538-1065. Personal E-mail: abconant@hotmail.com.

CONAWAY, MIKE (KENNETH MICHAEL CONAWAY), United States Representative from Texas; b. Borger, Tex., June 11, 1948; m. Suzanne Conaway; 4 children. BBA, Tex. A&M U., 1970. CPA. Acct. Price Waterhouse, Midland, Tex.; CFO Arbusto Energy Inc., Midland, 1981—86; mem. US Congress from 11th Tex. Dist., 2005—, US House Ethics Com. (formerly House Standards of Official Conduct Com.), 2009—, chmn., 2013—. Mem. Midland Ind. Sch. Dist., 1985—88, Tex. State Bd. Pub. Accountancy, 1995—2002, chmn., 1997—2005. Served in US Army, 1970—72. Named Vol. of Decade, Midland YMCA, 1990. Republican. Baptist. Office: US House of Representatives 2430 Rayburn House Office Bldg Washington DC 20515 also: 6 Desta Dr Ste 2000 Midland TX 79705 Office Phone: 202-225-3605.*

CONCHA, MARIO, management consultant; b. Bogota, Colombia; BSChemE, Cornell U., 1964; sr. exec. program, U. Va. With Union Carbide Corp.; internat. v.p. Occidental Chem., 1985—92; pres.-internat. GS Industries, 1992—98; v.p., chemicals and resins Ga. Pacific, 1998—2000, pres., chem. divsn., 2000—05; pres., founder Mario Concha and Assocs., LLC. Fin. com. mem. Atlanta Opera, bd. mem. Named one of 50 Most Important Hispanics in Tech. & Bus., Hispanic Engr. & Info. Tech. mag., 2005. Mem.: Founders Club Chem. Industry, Am. Chem. Soc., Am. Inst. Chem. Engr. Office: Mario Concha and Associates LLC 669 W Paces Ferry Rd Atlanta GA 30327 Office Phone: 404-949-9300. Business E-Mail: mconcha@conchaconsulting.com.

CONDIT, K.C., information technology executive; Store mgr. Rent-A-Center Inc, 1997—98, mgmt. positions through sr. dir. info. security & support services Plano, Tex., 1998—. Named one of Premier 100 IT Leaders, Computerworld, 2007. Office: Rent A Center 5501 Headquarters Dr Plano TX 75024-5837 Office Phone: 972-801-1186.

CONDIT, LINDA FAULKNER, retired economist; b. Denver, May 30, 1947; d. Claude Winston and Nancy Isabel (McCallum) Faulkner; m. John Michael Condit, Dec. 20, 1970; 1 child, David Devin. BA, U. Ark., 1969; MA, U. Wis., 1970; postgrad., U. Minn., 1974-77. Rsch. asst. U. Wis., Madison, 1969—70; economist St. Louis Fed. Res. Bank, 1971—73; ops. analyst No. States Power co., Mpls., 1973-76; energy economist, 1976—78; from ecoomist to v.p. Pennzoil Co., Houston, 1978—95, v.p., 1995—98; v.p., corp. sec. Pennzoil-Quaker State Co., Houston, 1998—2002. Econ. cons. Jr. Achievement, 1983. Recipient Alumni award, U. Ark., 1969. Mem. Internat. Assn. Energy Economists (pres., v.p., treas.), Nat. Assn. Bus. Economists, Internat. Bus. Coun. (v.p.), Am. Econ. Assn., N.Am. Soc. Corp. Planners, Am. Soc. Corp. Secs. (membership chmn.), Hits Theatre (bd. dirs.), Corp. Alliance To Eliminate Ptnr. Violence (bd. dirs.), Leadership Am., Harvard Discussion Group Indsl. Economists, Nat. Soc. Colonial Dames America, Forst Club, River Oaks Women's Breakfast Club (v.p., pres.), Mortar Bd., Phi Beta Kappa, Kappa Alpha Theta. Home: 11822 Village Park Cir Houston TX 77024-4418

CONDON, KATHRYN A., civilian military employee; BA, U. Rochester, NY; MBA, Syracuse U., NY. Revenue officer Internal Revenue Office, Poughkeepsie, NY, 1983—86; mgmt. analyst, chief info. support officer US Mil. Acad., West Point, NY, 1986—88; program analyst US Army Engring. & Housing Support Ctr., Ft. Belvoir, Va., 1988; mgmt. analyst Base Realignment & Closure Commn., Washington, 1988—89; program & mgmt. analyst, Office Chief of Staff, Dept. Army, US Dept. Def., Washington, 1989—93, program analyst, Office Asst. Chief of Staff for Installation Mgmt., 1993—94, asst. for program analysis, acting dep. for program analysis & installation assistance, Office Asst. Sec. for Installations, Logistics & Environment, 1994—97, spl. asst. resources & mil. support, 1997—2000, interagency coord. mil. support to civil authorities, Office Sec. of Army, 2000—03, asst. dep. chief of staff for ops. G-3/5/7, 2003—06, civilian dep. to commdg. gen., Army Materiel Command, 2006—09, spl. asst. to under sec. of Army, 2009—10, exec. dir. Army Nat. Cemeteries Program Arlington, Va., 2010—. Recipient Presdl. Rank award, 2005, 2009, General Brehon B. Somervell Medal of Excellence, 2009, Meritorious Civilian Svc. award, Army Achievement Medal for Civilian Svc., Commander's award for civilian svc. Mem.: American Soc. Mil. Comptrs., Assn. US Army. Office: Arlington National Cemetery Fort Myer VA 22211

CONDOS, BARBARA SEALE, real estate broker, developer, investor; b. Kenedy, Tex., Feb. 24, 1925; d. John Edgar and Bess Rochelle (Ainsworth) Seale; m. George James Condos, Dec. 24, 1955 (dec.); 1 child, James Alexander. MusB magna cum laude, U. Incarnate Word, San Antonio, 1946. Lic. real estate broker, Tex. Ptnr., CEO Mountain Top-V.I. Devel. Properties, V.I., 1977-85; ret. pres. Investment Realty Co., L.C., San Antonio, 1978—2010. Choreographer, dancer San Antonio Symphony's Youth Concerts and Opera Festival; actress San Antonio Little Theatre-Patio-Players 1948—. Trustee San Antonio Little Theatre, 1953-76; mem. coun. McNay Mus., 1986—, chmn. coun., 1987—, chair coun., 1988—, trustee, 1989-97, trustee emerita, 1997—; bd. dirs. San Antonio Performing Arts Assn., 1978—; mng. trustee Russell Hill Rogers Fund for Arts. Mem. Internat. Real Estate Fedn., Internat. Real Estate Inst., Nat. Assn. Realtors, Tex. Assn. Realtors, San Antonio Bd. Realtors, Tex. Watercolor Soc. (signature mem.), The Argyle Club, FIABCI(life). Avocation: painting. Home: 217 Geneseo Rd San Antonio TX 78209-5913 Office: 16350 Bcanco San Antonio TX 78230 Office Phone: 210-828-9261. Personal E-mail: bscondos@gmail.com. Business E-Mail: bsc@investmentrealty.com.

CONE, ROBERT W., career military officer; b. Manchester, NH, 1957; m. Jill Cone. BS, US Mil. Acad., 1979; MA in Sociology, U. Tex., Austin, 1987; MA in Nat. Security and Strategic Studies with distinction, Naval War Coll., 1998. Commd. 2d. lt. US Army, 1979, advanced through grades to commdg. gen., 2011; platoon leader B Troop then exec. officer A Troop 2nd Squadron, 1st Cavalry, 2nd Armored Divsn., Fort Hood, Tex., 1979—81; aide-de-camp to asst. divsn. comdr. 2nd Armored Divsn., Fort Hood, Tex., 1981—82; battalion maintenance officer 1st Battalion, 67th Armor, 2nd Armored Divsn., Fort Hood, Tex., 1982, comdr. D Co., 1982—85; instr. then asst. prof. Dept. Behavioral Sci. and Leadership US Mil. Acad., West Point, NY, 1987—90; ops. officer then exec. officer 11th Armored Cavalry Regiment, V Corps US Army Europe and Seventh Army, Germany, 1991—94; exec. officer 3rd Armored Cavalry Regiment, III Corps, Fort Bliss, Tex., 1994; comdr. 1st Squadron, 3rd Armored Cavalry Regiment, III Corps, Fort Bliss, Tex., Fort Carson, Colo., 1994—96; spl. asst. to commdg. gen. Fort Carson, Colo., 1996—97; comdr. 2nd Brigade, 4th Infantry Divsn., Fort Hood, Tex., 1999—2001; dir. Joint Advanced Warfighting Program Inst. Def. Analysis, Alexandria, Va., 2001—03; dir. Joint Lessons Learned Collection Team US Ctrl. Command, Operation Iraqi Freedom, Qatar, 2003; dir. Joint Ctr. for Lessons Learned US Joint Forces Command, Suffolk, Va., 2003—04; comdr. gen. Nat. Training Ctr. and Fort Irwin, Fort Irwin, Calif., 2004—07; commdg. gen. Combined Security Transition Command Operation Enduring Freedom, Afghanistan, 2007—08; spl. asst. to chief staff US Army, Washington, 2008—09; spl. asst. to commdg. gen. US Army Training & Doctrine Command (TRADOC), Fort Monroe, Va., 2009, commdg. gen., 2011—, III Corps and Fort Hood, Fort Hood, Tex., 2009—11; dep. commdg. gen. ops. US Forces-Iraq, 2010—11. Decorated Def. Disting. Svc. Medal, Def. Superior Svc. Medal with oak leaf cluster, Legion of Merit with two oak leaf clusters, Bronze Star Medal, Meritorious Svc. Medal with two oak leaf clusters, Army Commendation Medal with two oak leaf clusters, Army Achievement Medal, Parachutist Badge, Ranger Tab, Joint Chiefs of Staff Identification Badge, Ghazi Wazir Mohammad Akbar Kahn State Medal Islamic Republic of Afghanistan; fellow Seminar XXI Program, MIT. Mem.: Phi Kappa Phi. Office: TRADOC Building 27 66 Ingalls Rd Fort Monroe VA 23651

CONE, ROGER D., biophysics professor; BA in Biochemistry summa cum laude, Princeton U., NJ; PhD in Biology, Mass. Inst. Tech., Cambridge, Mass. Asst. prof. cell and devel biology Oreg. Health and Sci. U., dir. Ctr. for Study Weight Regulation, sr. scientist Vollum Inst.; co-founder, lead rschr. Northwest Neurologic, Inc.; co-founder, pres., chief scientific officer, dir. ZNOMICS, Inc.; prof. molecular physiology and biophysics Vanderbilt U. Sch. Medicine, Nashville, 2008—, chmn. dept. molecular physiology and biophysics, 2008—. Former mem. sci. bd. Neurocrine Biosciences, Lexicon Genetics, Trega Biosciences; sci. advisor Mankind Corp. Mem.: NAS, The Endocrine Soc., Phi Beta Kappa. Office: Vanderbilt University Sch Medicine Office 8425C MRB IV 702 Light Hall Nashville TN 37232-0615 Office Phone: 615-936-7085. Business E-Mail: roger.cone@vanderbilt.edu.

CONEWAY, PETER RICHARD, private equity firm executive, former ambassador; b. Cleve., Apr. 13, 1944; s. Albert Earl and Clara Laroux (Durham) C.; m. Marsella Lynn Martin, July 29, 1967; children: Natalie, Cecile. BBA, U. Tex., 1966; postgrad., U. Hong Kong, 1967; MBA, Stanford U., 1969. Advisory dir. Goldman, Sachs & Co., Dallas, 1969—75, in instl. sales, 1969-75, v.p., resident mgr. Houston, 1975-78, ptnr., 1978—92, mng. dir. equity divsn. Tokyo, 1987—88; US amb. to Switzerland & Liechtenstein US Dept. State, Bern, 2006—09; mng. dir. Riverstone Holdings LLC, Houston, 2009—. Chmn. Stanford Bus. Sch. Trust, 1983—; trustee Houston Ballet Found., 1983—, Mus. Fine Arts, 1983—; bd. dirs, chmn., bd. visitors U. Tex M.D. Anderson Cancer Ctr. Outstanding Young Tex. Ex award, 1983, U. Tex. Bd. Regents, Disting. Alumnus award, U. Tex., 2003. Allied mem. N.Y. Stock Exchange; mem. Houston C. of C. (bd. dirs.); Clubs: River Oaks (Houston), Coronado (Houston). Baptist. Office: Riverstone Holdings LLC, 1000 Louisiana Ste 1000 Houston TX 77002 Office Phone: 713-357-1400. Office Fax: 713-357-1399.

CONFER, ANTHONY WAYNE, veterinary pathologist, educator; b. Hot Springs, Ark., July 29, 1947; s. Edwin M. and Gloria V. (Parker) C.; m. Carolyn Gay Pope, Aug. 15, 1970; children: Andrew W., Aaron J., Michael E., Christina A. DVM, Okla. State U., 1972; MS, Ohio State U., 1974; PhD, U. Mo., 1978. Diplomate Am. Coll. Vet. Pathologists. Assoc. prof. La. State U., Baton Rouge, 1978-81, Okla. State U., Stillwater, 1981-85, prof., 1985—, dept. head, 1986-99, 2004—08, assoc. dean for rsch. Coll. Vet. Medicine, 1999-2001, Sitlington endowed chair food animal rsch., 1995—, regents prof., 2003—. Vis. prof. U. BC, Vancouver, 1990-91; cons. Ft. Dodge Lab., Iowa, 1987-92, 2003—05, Baxter Healthcare Corp., Round Lake, Ill., 1988-89, Vet. Reference Lab., Dallas, 1988-89, Smith Kline Beechan Ltd., Lincoln, Nebr., 1990; mem. Conf. Rsch. Workers-Animal Diseases, 1981—2008; cons. Diamond Animal Health, Des Moines, 1994-98, Pfizer Animal Health, Kalamazoo, Mich., 1997—, Acad. Vet. Cons., 2009-. Mem. editl. bd. Am. Jour. Vet. Rsch., 1993-2004, 2006—09, Vet. Pathology, 1995-97, 2005—08; contrb. over 200 sci. publs. in field. V.p. Stillwater Soccer Assn., 1987-91, pres., 1992-93; pub. rels. specialist Stillwater H.S. Soccer Club, 1990-96; cub master Cub Scout pack 22, Stillwater, 1987-89; panel mgr. USDA-NRI, 2006-08. Capt. USAF, 69-77. Recipient Beecham award for rsch., SmithKline Beecham Lab., 1985, Norden Disting. Tchr. award, Pfizer, Inc., 1987, 2002, Eminent Faculty award, Okla. State U., 2003, Pfizer Rsch. award, 2011; named Disting. Alumna, Okla. State Vet. Med. Alumni Assn., 2009. Mem. AVMA (Vet. Rsch. award 1992), Am. Coll. Vet. Pathologists (chair standing edn. com. 1994-96, program chair 1995), Morris Animal Found. (sci. advisor 1991-95), Am. Soc. Microbiology, Sigma Xi (chpt. lectr. 1993). Mem. Lds Ch. Avocations: physical fitness, guitar, cooking. Home: 2817 W 28th Ave Stillwater OK 74074-2212 Office: Okla State U Dept Vet Pathobiology Stillwater OK 74078-2007 Office Phone: 405-744-4542. Business E-Mail: anthony.confer@okstate.edu.

CONGDON, DAVID S., transportation executive; s. Earl E. Congdon. BS in Bus. Adminstrn., U. NC, Wilmington. Various positions including dir. employee rels., dir. safety & pers., v.p. maintenance and equipment, v.p. quality mgmt., v.p. transp., others Old Dominion Freight Line, Inc., 1978—97, pres., COO, 1997—2007, pres., CEO, 2008—. Bd. dirs. Old Dominion Freight Line, Inc., 1998—, NC Trucking Assn., Am. Trucking Assn., Piedmont Triad Partnership. Bd. mem. Communities in Schools, High Point, NC; chmn. leadership giving United Way Greater High Point. Office: Old Dominion Freight Line Inc 500 Old Dominion Way Thomasville NC 27360 Office Phone: 336-889-5000. Office Fax: 336-822-5229. Business E-Mail: david.congdon@odfl.com.

CONGDON, JOHN RHODES, transportation executive; b. Balt., Feb. 17, 1933; s. Earl Everett and Lillian Francis (Herbert) C.; m. Barbara Natalie Neblett, June 17, 1952; children: Susan Lee, John Rhodes, Jeffrey Whitefield. Student, U. Richmond, 1952-53. Driver Old Dominion Freight Line, 1951; founder, chmn. Old Dominion Truck Leasing, 1963—; vice chmn. Old Dominion Freight Line. Deacon River Rd. Ch., 1981; pres. Dorset Woods Civic Assn., 1973-74. With U.S. Army, 1953-55. Mem. Va. Hwy. Users Assn. (pres. 1976-78), River Rd. Citizens, Country Club of Va., Masons, Shriners. Home: Randolph Sq 112 W Square Dr Richmond VA 23238 Office: 7511 White Pine Rd Chesterfield VA 23832 Home Phone: 804-784-4034; Office Phone: 804-275-7832.

CONINE, ERNEST, columnist; b. Dallas, Dec. 31, 1925; s. Ernest and Myrtle Conine; m. Phyllis Joan Hoyland, Nov. 28, 1953 (dec.); m. Ulla Fisher, Jan. 10, 1981. BS, So. Methodist U., 1948. Staff writer UPI, Dallas, 1948-51; Washington corr. Dallas Times Herald, 1952-55; successively Washington corr., Moscow corr., New Eng. mgr. Bus. Week mag., 1955-63; fgn. corr. L.A. Times, Vienna, 1963-64, public affairs columnist, mem. editorial bd., 1964-87, contbr., 1988-92. Mem. Ctr. Internat. and Strategic Affairs, UCLA, 1975-90, Internat. Inst. for Strategic Studies, 1984-98; mem. Calif. Seminar Internat. Security and Fgn. Affairs, 1970-93, L.A. Com. Fgn. Affairs, 1973-93. Contbr. articles to popular mags. and bus. jours. Served with Army Air Corps, 1944-46, AUS, 1951-52. Mem. Soc. Profl. Journalists. Home and Office: 12501 Longhorn Pkwy #319 Austin TX 78732

CONINE, JEFFREY GUY, professional sports team executive, retired professional baseball player; b. Tacoma, June 27, 1966; Student, UCLA. Infielder, outfielder Kansas City Royals, 1992, 1998, Miami Marlins (formerly Fla. Marlins), 1993-97, 2003—05, spl. asst., 2008—; infielder, outfielder Balt. Orioles, 1999—2003, 2006, Phila. Phillies, 2006, Cin. Reds, 2007, NY Mets, 2007. Named So. League Most Valuable Player, 1990, Nat. League All-Star Team, 1994, 1995, All-Star Game Most Valuable Player, 1995. Achievements include member of Major League Baseball's World Series championship winning Florida Marlins, 1997, 2003. Office: Miami Marlins 501 Marlins Way Miami FL 33125

CONKEL, ROBERT DALE, lawyer, consultant; b. Oct. 13, 1936; s. Chester William and Marian Matilda (Ashton) Conkel; m. Elizabeth A. Cargill, June 15, 1958; children: Debra Lynn, Dale William,

Douglas Alan; m. Brenda Jo Myers, Aug. 2, 1980; 1 child, Chelsea Ashton. BA, Mt. Union Coll., 1958; JD cum laude, Cleve. Marshall Law Sch., 1965; LLM, Case Western Res. U., 1972. Bar: Ohio 1965, U.S. Ct. Appeals (5th cir.) 1979, U.S. Tax Ct. 1974, U.S. Supreme Ct. 1974, Tex. 1978. Supr. Social Security Adminstrn., Cleve., 1958—65; trust officer Harter Bank & Trust Co., Canton, Ohio, 1965—70; exec. v.p. Am. Actuaries, Inc., Grand Rapids, Mich., 1970—73; mgr. plans and rsch. A.S. Hansen, Inc., Dallas, 1973—74; pvt. practice Dallas, 1973—; pension cons., southwest regional dir. Am. Actuaries, Inc., Dallas, 1974—88. Sr. cons. Coopers & Lybrand, Dallas, 1989; pres. Robert D. Conkel, Inc., 1989—; mem. devel. bd. Met. Nat. Bank, Richardson, Tex.; instr. Am. Mgmt. Assn., 1975, Am. Coll. Advanced Pension Planning, 1975—76; enrolled actuary Joint Bd. Enrollment U.S. Depts. Labor and Treasury. Contbr. articles to legal publs.; mem. editl. adv. bd.: jour. Jour. Pension Planning and Compliance, 1974—83. Sustaining mem. Rep. Nat. Com., 1980—; chmn. Zoning Bd. Adjustments, Richardson, Tex., 2005—10, Bldg. & Stds. Com., Richardson, Tex., 2008—10. Mem.: ABA (employee benefit com. sect. taxation), Am. Acad. Actuaries, Am. Soc. Pension Profl. & Actuaries (dir. 1973—81), Dallas Bar Assn., Tex. Bar Assn., Ohio State Bar Assn. Office: 100 N Central Expy # 519 Richardson TX 75080-5332 Home Phone: 972-644-0410; Office Phone: 972-997-8211.

CONKLIN, HOWARD LAWRENCE, lawyer; b. NYC, Apr. 16, 1943; s. Weldon F. and Gladys (Meyer) C. BS, Fairleigh Dickinson U., 1961; MBA, Syracuse U., 1969; JD, Fordham U., 1974. Bar: Fla. 1974, U.S. Dist. Ct. (so. dist.) 1976, U.S. Supreme Ct. 1978, U.S. Dist. Ct. (mid. dist.) Fla. 1980; lic. pilot FAA; lic. capt. USCG. Mktg. planning specialist Trans World Airlines, NYC, 1969-71; sr. transp. analyst Paine Webber, NYC, 1971-74; ptnr. Tripp, Scott, Conklin & Smith, Ft. Lauderdale, Fla., 1974-97; v.p. govt. and airport rels. Alamo Rent-a-Car, Inc., Ft. Lauderdale, 1997; v.p. govt. rels. AutoNation, Inc., Ft. Lauderdale, 1997—. Chmn. Ft. Pierce Area Coun. C. of C., Ft. Pierce Harbor Adv. Com., St. Lucie County, Investment Adv. Com. St. Lucie County; bd. dirs. ARC; elected del. Dem. Party Nat. Conv., 2004. Col. USAF, 1964—68, Vietnam. Decorated Bronze Star, Legion of Merit. Mem. ABA, Air Force Assn., Res. Officers Assn., St. Lucie County Bar Assn., Indian River County Bar Assn., Mil. Officers Assn., Army Navy Club (Washington), Pelican Yacht Club, Sons of Norway. Avocations: flying, sailing. Office: Howard L Conklin Atty 1101 N US Hwy 1 PNB 214 Fort Pierce FL 34950 Business E-Mail: hlconklin@gmail.com.

CONKLYN, ELIZABETH D., insurance company executive; PhD. Sr. v.p. human resources and orgn. Mobile Telecom. Techs. Corp., Jackson, Miss.; sr. v.p. human resources USAA (United Svcs. Automobile Assn.), exec. v.p. people svcs. Mem. Conf. Bd. Adv. Coun. Human Resource Mgmt., 2000. Bd. trustees United Way San Antonio. Office: USAA 9800 Fredericksburg Rd San Antonio TX 78288 Office Phone: 210-498-8222.

CONLEY, CLAY, chef; Attended, Tulane U., Fla. State U., Tallahassee. Chef Canoe, Atlanta, Horseradish Grille, Atlanta, Wellesley Figs; chef tournant Olives restaurant, 1996, chef de cuisine Las Vegas; culinary dir. Olives Group; chef de cuisine Azul, Mandarin Oriental, Miami, 2005—. Guest chef James Beard House, 2002. Named one of Fla.'s Rising Stars, StarChefs.com, 2008. Office: Azul Mandarin Oriental 500 Brickell Key Dr Miami FL 33131

CONLEY, RENAE, energy executive; BS in Accountancy, Ball State U., MBA. Pres. Cincinnati Gas and Electric Co.; pres. and CEO Cadence; v.p. sales dept. and gen. mgr. corp. comm. and investor rels. Cinergy; with PSI Energy; pres. and CEO Entergy La. Ltd. Liability Co., 2000—10, dir., 2000—10; pres. and CEO Entergy Gulf States, 2000—10, dir., 2000—10; chief diversity and inclusion officer Entergy Corp., v.p. investor rels., 1999, exec. v.p. human resources and adminstrn. La., 2011—. Bd. dirs. Fed. Res. Bank of Atlanta, New Orleans; bd. trustees Ball State Univ.; bd. trustees dean's adv. coun. La. State Univ. Bd. dirs. La. Disaster Recovery Found. Named Key Woman in Energy in the Americas, 2004. Office: Entergy Corporation 639 Loyola Ave New Orleans LA 70113 Office Phone: 504-576-4000. Office Fax: 504-576-4428.

CONN, MARGARET ELBOW, human resources specialist; b. Albany, NY, Jan. 5, 1951; d. Matthew H. and Margaret A.B. Elbow; m. Richard E. Conn, Apr. 3, 1982. BA, Tufts U., Medford, Mass., 1972; MBA, Columbia U. Grad. Sch. Bus., NYC, 1977. Cert. arbitrator BBB. Asst. to provost Simmons Coll., Boston, 1972—75; human resources mgmt. Ford Motor Co., Dearborn, Mich., 1977—90. Charter mem. Women in Philanthropy, Hilton Head Island, SC, 2005—; bd. mem. Commodore HOA, First Presbyn. Ch., Hilton Head Island, 1993—; mem. Prayer Shawl Ministry, Hilton Head Island, 2005—. Presbyterian. Avocation: travel. Home: 2 Village N Dr #7 Hilton Head Island SC 29926

CONNAUGHTON, SEAN THOMAS, lobbyist, former federal agency administrator; b. Mar. 23, 1966; s. Eugene and Patricia Connaughton; m. Teresa Voda, 1984; children: Courtney, Sean Jr. BS, US Merchant Marine Acad., 1983; MS, George Washington U., 1988; JD, George Mason U., 1992; Grad., US Naval War Coll., 1998; D in Pub. Adminstrn. (hon.), Mass. Maritime Acad., 2007. Bar: Va. 1992. Def. contractor, Arlington, Va.; civil servant Office Maritime Safety, Security, and Environ. Protection US Coast Guard, Washington; of counsel Troutman Sanders LLP, 2000; maritime adminstr. US Dept. Transp., Washington, 2006—09; corp. v.p. for govt. affairs Am. Bur. Shipping (ABS), Washington, 2009—. Chmn. at large Prince William Bd. County Supervisors, 1999—2006; bd. dirs. Met. Washington Council of Govts.; chief elected official No. Va. Workforce Investment Bd., bd. dirs. Skillsource Group; mem. No. Va. Transp. Authority; mem. steering com. large urban county caucus Nat. Assn. of Counties; mem. U.S. Merchant Marine Adv. Bd. Mem. Prince William County adv. bd. George Mason U., mem. com. for performing arts ctr.; mem. Woodbridge Campus adv. bd. No. Va. CC; chmn. 9/11 Meml. Fund, Potomac Hosp. Capital Campaign; bd. dirs. Homeland Protection Inst., Ltd., No. Va. Sci. Ctr. Belmont Bay, Conservation Leaders Network; mem. Prince William C. of C., Prince William-Greater Manassas C. of C., Prince William County Rep. Com., Nat. Conf. Rep. County Officials. With U.S. Coast Guard, 1983—86, comdr. USNR. Recipient Disting. Svc. award, Nat. Assn. Counties, 2004; named Maritime Person of Yr., Propeller Club US, 2007, Govt. Man of Yr., Maritime Port Coun. Greater NY and Vicinity, 2007. Mem.: Propeller Club of U.S., Reserve Officers Assn., Naval Reserve Assn., Veterans Pro Bono Consortium, Maritime Law Assn., DC Bar Assn., Va. Bar Assn. Office: American Bureau Shipping (ABS) 1421 Prince St Alexandria VA 22314 Office Phone: 703-519-9985. E-mail: SConnaughton@eagle.org.

CONNELL, ALASTAIR MCCRAE, physician; b. Glasgow, Scotland, Dec. 21, 1929; came to U.S., 1970; s. Alex McCrae and Maud (Crawford) C.; m. Joyce Dethlefs, 1983; children: Stewart, Fiona, Alison, Iain, Andrew. BS, U. Glasgow, 1951, MB, ChB, 1954, MD, 1969. Intern Western Infirmary, Glasgow, 1954-55; resident in gastroenterology Cen. Middlesex and St. Mark's Hosp., London, 1957-60; practice medicine specializing in gastroenterology, 1960—91; mem. med. staff Med. Rsch. Coun., 1960-64; sr. lectr. clin. sci. Queen's U., Belfast, No. Ireland, 1964-70; Mark Brown prof. medicine Med. Ctr., U. Cin., 1970-79, dir. div. digestive diseases, 1970-79, prof. physiology, 1972-79, assoc. dean, 1975-77; dir. Office Clin. Affairs, 1975-77; dean Coll. Medicine, U. Nebr. Med. Ctr., 1979-84, prof. internal medicine, 1979-84; v.p. health scis. Va. Commonwealth U., Richmond, 1984-88; scholar-in-residence Inst. Medicine, 1988-89; vice chancellor health scis. Ea. Carolina U., 1990—91; dir. Office Healthcare Inspections, Dept. Vets. Affairs, Washington, 1991-96; adj. prof. med. George Washington U., 1992-97; prof. kinesiology and health scis. Coll. William and Mary, 2005—. Vis. prof. dept. moral philosophy U. St. Andrews, Scotland, 1984-86; mem. sci. adv. bd. Nat. Found. for Ileitis and Colitis, 1974-80, chmn. rsch. devel. com., 1974-78; mem. Personal Health Com. Ohio, 1974-76; trustee Medco Peer Rev., 1974-79; adj. prof. health adminstrn. Va. Commonwealth U., 1996-2000; med. dir. Williamsburg Landing, 1999-02; chair Sr. Svcs. Coalition, Williamsburg, Va., 2005-06. Author: Clinical Tests of Gastric Function, 1973; author: (with T. Wan) Monitoring the Quality of Health Care, 2002; author: How The Scots Created America, 2008, Dust in the Veterans Eyes, 2009; assoc. editor Am. Jour. Digestive Diseases; contbr. articles to profl. jours. Served with M.C. Royal Army, 1955-57. Fellow Royal Coll. Physicians (Edinburgh), ACP; mem. Brit. Soc. Gastroenterology, Internat. Group for Study Intestinal Motility (past pres.). Avocations: stamp collecting/philately, painting, piano. Address: 6728 Tarpleys Tavern Rd Williamsburg VA 23188 Business E-Mail: amconn@wm.edu.

CONNELLY, GAIL, educational association administrator; Exec. dir. NAESP, Alexandria, Va., 2007—. Office: NAESP 1615 Duke St Alexandria VA 22314 Office Phone: 703-684-3345. Office Fax: 800-396-2377. E-mail: naesp@naesp.org.

CONNELLY, SHARON RUDOLPH, lawyer, financier and real estate investor; b. Kingwood, W.Va. d. John E. and Lorene E. Rudolph; 1 child, John. BS, W.Va. State U., 1966; MBA, Ind. U., 1968; JD, Cath. Univ., 1976; LLM in Taxation, Georgetown U., 1995. Mgr. IRS, Washington, 1969-76; asst. contr. Mfrs. Hanover, NYC, 1976-77; compliance chief D.C. Dept. Labor, Washington, 1977-79; dir. compliance U.S. Dept. Commerce, Washington, 1979-82; asst. insp. gen. NASA, Washington, 1982-84; dir. insp. office Nuc. Regulatory Commn., Washington, 1984-89, sr. exec. US Govt., 1982—98. Contbr. articles to profl. jours. Mem.: Va. State Bar.

CONNELLY, TERRENCE JOHN, SR., broadcast executive; b. Chgo., Aug. 23, 1947; s. Charles Bernard, Jr. and Margaret Agnes (Gilmore) C.; m. Andrea Susan Hahn, Feb. 12, 1972; children: Terrence John, Jr., Bridget Colleen. BS in Comms., U. Ill., 1970. Reporter WITI-TV, Milw., 1970-73, WRGB-TV, Schenectady, N.Y., 1973-74; news dir. WNYT-TV, Albany, N.Y., 1974-76, WDAF-TV, Kansas City, Mo., 1976-78; exec. news producer WMAQ-TV, Chgo., 1978-80; v.p. TV news Taft Broadcasting, Cin., 1980-86; v.p., gen. mgr. WCPO-TV, Cin., 1986-88, WKRC-TV, Cin., 1988-92, WSYX-TV, Columbus, Ohio, 1992-95; pres., gen. mgr. WJLA-TV, Washington, 1995-98; sr. v.p., gen. mgr. The Weather Channel, Atlanta, 1999—2008; pres. Owner Connelly Productions, Atlanta, 2008—. Dir. teletext, Taft Broadcasting, Cin., 1981-86; mem. broadcast adv. bd. UPI, N.Y.C., 1983-85. Editor/gen. mgr.: WCPO TV news, 1987 (Peabody award for investigative report 1987). Bd. dirs. United Way, Washington, 1995-99, Easter Seals Bd., Washington, 1995-97, Muscular Distrophy Assn., Columbus, 1992-95; chmn. Neediest Kids, Inc., Washington, 1995-99. With U.S. Army, 1970-76. Mem. Soc. Profl. Journalists, Radio-TV News Dirs. Assn., Nat. Assn. TV Program Execs., Rotary. Roman Catholic. Office: The Weather Channel 300 Interstate North Pkwy SE Atlanta GA 30339-2403

CONNER, CHUCK (CHARLES F. CONNER), trade association administrator, former federal agency administrator; b. Lafayette, Ind., Dec. 30, 1957; m. Druscilla Conner; children: Katie, Benjamin, Andrew, Emily. BS in Agrl. Economics, Purdue U., 1980. Agrl. aide to Senator Richard Lugar US Senate, 1980—87; minority staff dir. US Senate Agrl., Nutrition & Forestry Com., 1987—95, majority staff dir., 1995—97; pres. Corn Refiners Assn., 1997—2001; spl. asst. to the Pres. for Agrl., Trade, & Food Assistance Nat. Econ. Coun., 2001—05; dep. sec. USDA, Washington, 2005—09, acting sec., 2007—08; pres., CEO Nat. Council of Farmer Cooperatives (NCFC), Washington, 2009—. Republican. Office: National Council of Farmer Cooperatives (NCFC) 50 F St NW Ste 900 Washington DC 20001 Office Phone: 202-626-8700. Office Fax: 202-626-8722.

CONNER, LEWIS HOMER, JR., lawyer; b. Chattanooga, Mar. 21, 1938; s. Lewis H. Sr. and Cleo (Johnson) C.; m. Ashley Whitsitt, June 1, 1960; children: Holland Ashley, Lewis Forrest. BA, Vanderbilt U., 1960, JD, 1963. Bar: Tenn. 1963, U.S. Dist. Ct. (all dists.) Tenn. 1963, U.S. Ct. Appeals (6th cir.) 1963, U.S. Ct. Mil. Appeals 1964, U.S. Supreme Ct. 1990; cert. mediator, Tenn. Founding ptnr., atty. Dearborn & Ewing, Nashville, 1972-80; judge Ct. Appeals Middle Dist., Nashville, 1980-84; sr. ptnr., atty. Waller Lansden Dortch & Davis, Nashville, 1985-89, 2005—, Boult, Cummings, Conners & Berry, Nashville, 1989-96; of counsel Stokes & Bartholomew, Nashville, 1997—2005. Chmn. Willis Coroon, Tenn., 1996—99; spl. chief justice Supreme Ct. Tenn., 1980—81; lectr. law Vanderbilt U. Sch. Law, Nashville, 1984—93; life del. Sixth Cir. Ct. Appeals Jud. Conf. Mng. editor Vanderbilt Law Rev. Elder Westminster Presbyn. Ch.; bd. dirs. Tenn. Golf Assn., Nashville, 1965—, pres., 1985; chmn. Tenn. Golf Found., 1992-93, 96-97, 2000-01; fin. co-chmn. Alexander for Gov., 1974-78; chmn. Tenn. Rep. Fin. Com., 1975, Tenn. Corrections Overcrowding Commn., 1985-86; bd. dirs. Boys & Girls Club Middle Tenn., 1980—, pres., 1991-92; bd. govs., chmn. Tenn. State Mus., 1987-91; bd. govs. Gaylord Music City Bowl, 1998-, chmn., 2002—. Recipient Tennesseean of Yr. award, Tenn. Golf Found., 2001, Nat. Lifetime Achievement award, Boys & Girls Club Mid. Tenn., 2003, Hope award, Multiple Sclerosis Soc., 2006. Fellow Am. Acad. Matrimonial Lawyers, Am. Coll. Civil Trial Mediators, Am. Bar Found., Tenn. Bar Found., Nashville Bar Found.; mem. ABA, Am. Arbitration Assn. (bd. dirs. 1990-96, chmn. Tenn. large complex case panel 1992—, panel of arbitrators 1975—, panel of mediators 1995—), Tenn. Bar Assn., Tenn. Jud. Conf., Nashville Bar Assn. (pres. 1986-87, bd. dirs., 1984-87), Commn. on the FutuAm. re of the Cts. in Tenn., Order of the Coif, PGA of Am. (hon. Tenn. sect.), The Golf Club Tenn. (founder, exec. com. 1991-2009), Richland Country Club (bd. dirs. 1976-79, pres. 1978-79), Belle Meade Country Club, The Honors Course, Naples Grande Golf Club, Royal Poinciana Golf & Country Club, Nashville City Club, Nashville Cumberland Club, Nashville Stadium Club, Tenn. Golf Assn. (pres. 1985, bd. dirs. 1965-2008, amateur player of yr., Tenn., 1973, Tenn. Golf Hall of Fame, 2010), Tenn. Golf Found. (founding bd. mem. 1992-2010, chmn. 1993-99) Republican. Avocations: golf, basketball, softball, politics. Office: Waller Lansden Dortch and Davis PO Box 150039 Nashville TN 37215-0039 Home: 101 Abbottsford Nashville TN 37215-2437 Office Phone: 615-850-8497. Business E-Mail: lew.conner@wallerlaw.com.

CONNER, STEWART EDMUND, lawyer; b. Louisville, Oct. 7, 1941; s. James Pleasant and Lucille (Winter) C.; m. Joan E. Fish, May 20, 1989; children: Shannon Lynn, Erin Eileen, Margaret Eisele; stepchildren: Hunt Rounsavall, Gibbs Rounsavall, Christine Rounsavall. BS, U. Louisville, 1963, JD cum laude, 1966. Bar: Ky. 1966, U.S. Dist. Ct. (ea. and we. dists.) Ky. 1966, U.S. Tax Ct. 1967. Assoc. Wyatt, Tarrant & Combs, Louisville, 1966-72, ptnr., 1972—88, chmn. gen. corp. sect., 1980-90, mng. ptnr., 1988-2001, chmn. exec. com., 1988—2004. Bd. dirs. DNP Select Income Fund, 2004—, Louisville Water Co., 1990—2007, chmn., 2004—07; adj. prof. U. Louisville, 2000—03, U. Ky., 2009—11. Author, editor: Kentucky Business Practice Handbook, 1988; editor Kentucky Legal Forms, 1988; contbr. to U. Ky. Law Rev. Bd. dirs. Coun. on Higher Edn., 1992-95, Lincoln Heritage coun. Boy Scouts Am., 1989—, chair, 2005-07, dePaul Sch., 1996-2004. With U.S. Army, 1968-69, Vietnam. Fellow Am. Bar Found., Ky. Bar Found.; mem. ABA (banking com. 1983), Ky. Bar Assn., Louisville Bar Assn. (chmn. ethics com. 1980), Ky. C. of C. (bd. dirs. 1992-96), Greater Louisville Inc. (bd. dirs. 1996-2001), Law Club, Lawyers Club, Harmony Landing Country Club. Republican. Office: Wyatt Tarrant & Combs LLP 2800 PNC Plz Louisville KY 40202 Home Phone: 502-228-4795; Office Phone: 502-562-7223. Business E-Mail: sconner@wyattfirm.com.

CONNER, TERRY W., lawyer; b. Houston, Feb. 27, 1951; BA, U. Tex., 1972, JD with honors, 1975. Bar: Tex. 1975. Ptnr. Haynes and Boone LLP, Dallas, mng. ptnr., mem. bd. dirs. Adj. prof. So. Meth. U. Sch. Law, 1987-92, co-dir. ann. comml. lending inst. Note and comment editor Tex. Law Rev., 1974-75; spl. contbg. editor: Comml. Loan Documentation Guide, 1988. Mem. adv. coun. U. Tex. Dallas Sch. Mgmt., mem. exec. edn. adv. coun.; mem. Dallas Citizens Coun.; mem. bd. dirs., health care adv. coun. Dallas Regional Chamber; mem. exec. bd. So. Meth. U-in-Taos; mem. bd. dirs. Dallas AfterSch. Network. Mem. ABA (mem. corp., banking and bus. law sect.), State Bar Tex. (mem. fin. instns. com., mem. CLE com.), Tex. Assn. Bank Counsel (bd. dirs. 1987-91), Dallas Bar Assn. Office: Haynes & Boone LLP 3100 Nationsbank Plz 2323 Victory Ave Dallas TX 75219-7657 Office Phone: 214-651-5604. Office Fax: 214-200-0408. Business E-Mail: terry.conner@haynesboone.com.

CONNICK, PATRICK, state legislator; b. New Orleans, La., Feb. 4, 1963; BA, U. New Orleans, 1983; JD, Loyola U. Law Sch., 1993. Atty.; mem. Dist. 84 La. House of Reps., 2008—, mem. appropriations com., house and govtl. affairs com., judiciary com., house exec. com., joint legis. com. on the budget. Republican. Cath. Office: Capitol Office PO Box 44486 Baton Rouge LA 70804 also: 5201 Westbank Expy Ste 100 Marrero LA 70072-2901 Office Phone: 504-371-0240, 225-342-6945. Office Fax: 504-371-0242. E-mail: connickp@legis.state.la.us.

CONNOLLY, GERALD E., United States Representative from Virginia; b. Boston, Oct. 20, 1950; m. Cathy Connolly; 1 child, Emily Rose. BA in Lit., Maryknoll Coll., Glen Ellyn, Ill., 1971; MPA, Harvard U., 1979. Devel. assoc. Heifer Project Internat., Little Rock, 1971-72; assoc. exec. dir. American Freedom From Hunger Found., 1972-74; exec. dir. US Com. Refugees, Arlington, Va., 1975-78; sr. profl. staff mem. US Senate Com. Fgn. Rels., Washington, 1979-89; v.p. SRI Internat., Washington, 1989—97; dir. cmty. rels. Sci. Applications Internat. Corp. (SAIC); mem. US Congress from 11th Va. dist., 2009—. Chmn. Fairfax County Bd. Supervisors, 2003—08. Bd. trustees Greater Washington Initiative; past pres. Fairfax County Fedn. Citizens Associations, Mantua Citizens Assn.; mem. US del. to World Population Conf., Bucharest, Romania, 1974; Congl. advisor UN Conf. New and Renewable Energy Resources, 1981; del. Dem. Nat. Conv., 1984, 1988; mem. US del. to 14th Ann. Conf. Soviet Acad. Sci., Moscow, 1990, Fairfax County Dem. Com., 1984; bd. dirs. Fairfax Partnership for Youth, ARC Nat. Capital Area, Fairfax County C. of C., Medical Care for Children Partnership, Inst. Regional Excellence, Va. Inst. Govt. Mem.: Va. Assn. Counties, Washington Trade Assn. Democrat. Office: US House of Representatives 424 Cannon House Office Bldg Washington DC 20515 also: 4115 Annandale Rd Ste 103 Annandale VA 22003 Office Phone: 202-225-1492, 703-256-3071. Office Fax: 202-225-3071, 703-354-1284.*

CONNOR, JOHN THOMAS, JR., portfolio manager; b. NYC, June 16, 1941; s. John Thomas and Mary (O'Boyle) Connor; m. Susan Scholle, Dec. 18, 1965; children: Seanna, Marin, John. BA cum laude, Williams Coll., 1963; JD, Harvard U., 1967. Bar: N.Y. 1968, DC 1980. Assoc. Cravath, Swaine & Moore, NYC, 1967-71; dep. dir. Office Econ. Policy and Case Analysis, Pay Bd., Washington, 1971-72, Bur. East-West Trade, U.S. Dept. Commerce, Washington, 1972-73; sr. v.p. U.S.-USSR Trade and Econ. Coun., Moscow, 1973-76; assoc. Milbank, Tweed, Hadley & McCloy, NYC, 1976-79; ptnr. Curtis, Mallet-Prevost, Colt and Mosle, Washington, 1980-82; v.p., gen. counsel, sec. PHH Corp., 1982-88; v.p., asst. gen. counsel Prudential Ins. Co. Am., Newark, 1988-90; ptnr. Sills Cummis, Newark, 1990-94; counsel Chadbourne & Parke, NYC, 1994-96, Patterson, Belknap, Webb & Tyler, LLP, 1996-98; portfolio mgr. Third Millennium Russia Fund, 1998—2012. Bd. dirs., chmn. audit com. Micros Sys. Inc., 1983—93. Author: Out of the Red: Investment and Capitalism in Russia, 2008. Pres., trustee Newark Boys Chorus Sch.; Fulbright tutor Ferguson Coll., Poona, India, 1963—64; chmn. Coun. Econ. Priorities; mem. Am. Law Inst., 1984—2004; exec. dir. N.J. Dems., 1969—70; del. Dem. Nat. Convention, Denver, 2008. Mem.: Coun. Fgn. Rels., DC Bar Assn., N.Y. State Bar Assn., Everglades Club (Fla.), Union Club (N.Y.C.), Baltusrol Golf Club N.J., Chevy Chase Club (Md.), Wianno Club (Cape Cod) (bd. govs. 2008—), Phi Beta Kappa.

CONNOR, TERENCE GREGORY, lawyer; b. Chelsea, Mass., Dec. 28, 1942; s. Joseph Gerard Sr. and Rosalie Cecilia (Ryan) C.; m. Julie Kaye Berry, Dec. 18, 1971; children: Cormac, Kristin, Etain, Brendan. AB, Georgetown U., 1964, LLM, 1975; JD, Seton Hall U., 1967. Bar: D.C. 1968, U.S. Supreme Ct. 1976, Fla. 1980. Trial atty. U.S. Dept. Justice, Washington, 1973-76; labor counsel Nat. Airlines Inc., Miami, Fla., 1976-79; practicing atty. Morgan, Lewis & Bockius, Miami, 1979—2006, mem. firm wide governing bd., 1996—2000, mng. ptnr., 1996—2002; co-team head labor and employment Hunton and Williams, Miami, 2006—. Chmn.: Dade citizen com. for Observance Bicentennial of U.S. Constitution, 1986. Served to capt. JAG, USAF, 1968-73. Mem. Fla. Bar Assn. (chair labor and employment law sect. 1994-95, mem. exec. coun. 1986-93), Miami C. of C. (co-chair pers. and Labor mgmt. com. 1993-94) Office: Hunton & Williams LLP 1111 Brickell Ave Ste 2500 Miami FL 33131 Home: 1517 San Rafael Ave Miami FL 33134-6241 Home Phone: 305-665-8719.

CONOVER, PAMELA C., recreational facility executive; married. Gen. mgr., N.Am. Shipping Fin. Divsn. Citibank; cashier Wells Fargo Bank, London, with NYC, 1979—81; asst. treas. US Line, 1981—85; various positions including mng. dir., N. Am. Ship Financing Divsn. Citicorp., 1985—94; CEO Epirotiki Cruise Line, Athens, Greece, 1985—94, pres., 1994—; pres., COO Cunard Line Ltd. (merged with Carnival Corp.), 2001—04; v.p., Strategic Planning Carnival Corp., 1994—98, pres., CEO, Seabourn Cruise Line, 2006—. Achievements include only female pres. major cruise line; Cunard Line Ltd. launched Queen Mary II in 2004, largest transatlantic cruise ship to date. Office: Carnival Corp 3655 N W 87 Ave Miami FL 33178-2428 Office Phone: 305-599-2600. Office Fax: 305-406-4700. E-mail: pconover@carnival.com.

CONOVER, WILLIAM JAY, statistics educator; b. Hays, Kans., Dec. 6, 1936; s. William Joseph Conover and Viola Marie (Herman) Beishline; m. Patricia Louise Solomon, June 11, 1960 (div. Apr. 1994); children: Christopher Michael, Robert Andrew, Judith Ann, Therese Marie, William Joseph; m. Susan Theresa Mole, Dec. 27, 1996; 1 child, Chloe Theresa. BS, Iowa State U., 1958; MA, Cath. U., 1962, PhD, 1964. Asst. prof. stats. Kans. State U., Manhattan, 1964-67, assoc. prof. stats., 1967-73; vis. prof. stats. U. Zürich, Switzerland, 1970-71; prof. stats. Tex. Tech U., Lubbock, 1973-81, Horn prof., 1981—, area coord. of info. systems/quantitative scis., assoc. dean, 1978-88. Vis. prof. U. Calif., Davis, 1976-77; vis. staff mem. Los Alamos (N.Mex.) Sci. Lab., 1976—; cons. Sandia Lab., Albuquerque, 1979—. Author: Practical Nonparametric Statistics, 1971, 3rd edit., 1999, Modern Bus. Stat., 1983, 2d edit., 1989; co-author 9 textbooks on statistics; contbr. articles to profl. jours. Lt. (j.g.) USN, 1958-61. Recipient Rushing Faculty Rsch. award Tex. Tech Dad's Assn., 1983, Samuel Wilks award US Army, 1997. Fellow Am. Statis. Assn. (Don Owen award San Antonio chpt. 1986); mem. Inst. Math. Stats., Biometric Soc., Inst. Decision Scis. Roman Catholic. Avocations: chess, basketball. Office: Tex Tech U Coll Bus Adminstrn Lubbock TX 79409 Business E-Mail: jay.conover@ttu.edu.

CONRAD, ANDREW J., microbiologist, medical products executive; m. Courtney Thorne-Smith, 2000 (div.). BS in Neurobiology, UCLA, PhD in Cell Biology. Co-founder, chief sci. officer National Genetics Institute, Inc., 1992—; global head, clin. trials Lab. Corp. of America of Holdings, exec. v.p.; chief sci. officer Laboratory Corp. of America Holdings, 2009—. Co-founder, lab. dir. Calif. Health & Longevity Inst., 2006—; bd. dir. Dole Food, Castle & Cook, Inc., NovaRx Inc., David H. Murdock Rsch. Inst. Contbr. numerous articles to profl. scientific & medical journals. Bd. dir. Autism Speaks. Office: Laboratory Corp of America Holdings 358 S Main St Burlington NC 27215 Office Phone: 336-229-1127. Office Fax: 336-513-4510. Business E-Mail: andrew.conrad@labcorp.com.

CONRAD, DAVID PAUL, business broker, real estate developer, retired food service executive; b. Greensboro, NC, Jan. 11, 1946; s. Lucas Lee and Elizabeth Gertrude (Kincaid) Conrad; 1 child, Lucas Wilfong. BSBA, East Carolina U., 1970; cert. in Real Estate, Forsyth Tech. Coll., 1979. From cashier to cook Libby Hill Seafood, Greensboro, 1962—64; plant mgr. Libby Hill Seafood Restaurants, Inc., Greensboro, 1970—76, mgr. Winston-Salem, NC, 1976—85, v.p., dir. ops. Greensboro, 1985—93, also bd. dirs., 1985—93; comml. real estate broker Allied Comml. Real Estate, Kernersville, NC, 1993; franchise owner Swisher Maids of West Greensboro, NC, 1994—99, regional dir. NC, 1996—98; broker-in-charge VR Bus. Brokers, 1998—2000; founder, former owner Triad Bus. Brokerage, Greensboro, 2002—04, Star Video Games, Greensboro, High Point and Wilkesboro, NC, 2002—05; founder, owner CedarMountain Log Homes, Beech Mountain, NC, 2005—, Blue Ridge Bus. Brokerage Co., Boone, NC, 2005—; founder Grand Coastal Bus. Brokerage, Myrtle Beach, SC, 2008, Blue Ridge Comml. Real Estate, 2010—. Pvt. pilot; founder, owner Halfway to You, 2011. Mem. Greensboro Jaycees, 1973—81; vol. Wesley Long Hosp.; founder owner halfwaytoyou.com, 2011; mem. Alliance Merger and Acquisition Ads. Staff sgt. NC N.G., 1968—74. Mem.: Inst. Cert. Bus. Counselors, Masons. Republican. Methodist. Home: 127 Hilltop Dr Bristol VA 24202 Business E-Mail: david@blueridgebrokerage.com.

CONRAD, GLEN E., federal judge; b. 1949; BA in Govt., Coll. William and Mary, 1971, JD, 1974. US magistrate judge US Dist. Ct. (we. dist.) Va., Roanoke, 1976—2003, judge, 2003—10, chief judge, 2010—. Mem.: ABA, Va. Trial Lawyers Assn., Nat. Coun. U.S. Magistrate Judges, Roanoke City Bar Assn., Va. Bar Assn., Am. Inns. Ct. (Ted Dalton chpt.), Phi Alpha Delta. Office: US Dist Ct We Dist Va PO Box 2822 Roanoke VA 24001

CONRAD, HAROLD THEODORE, psychiatrist; b. Milw., Jan. 25, 1934; s. Theodore Herman and Alyce Barbara Conrad; m. Elaine Marie Blaine, Sept. 1, 1962 (dec.); children: Blaine, Carl, David, Erich, Rachel. AB, U. Chgo., 1954, BS, 1955, MD, 1958. Diplomate Am. Bd. Psychiatry. Intern USPHS Hosp., San Francisco, 1958-59, commd. sr. asst. surgeon, 1958, advanced through grades to med. dir., 1967, resident psychiatry Lexington, Ky., 1959-61, Charity Hosp., New Orleans, 1961-62; chief of psychiatry USPHS Hosp., New Orleans, 1962-67, clin. dir., 1967; dep. dir. divsn. field investigation NIMH, Chevy Chase, Md., 1968; chief NIMH Clin. Rsch. Ctr., Lexington, 1969-73; cons. psychiatry region IX USPHS, HEW, San Francisco, 1973-79; dir. adolescent unit Alaska Psychiat. Inst., Anchorage, 1979-81, supt., 1981-85; clin. assoc. prof. psychiatry U. Wash. Med. Sch., 1981-85; psychiatrist pvt. practice, Houma, La., 1985—2004; ret., 2005. Contbr. articles to profl. jours. Recipient cmty. awards for contbns. in field of drug abuse and equal employment opportunity for minorities. Fellow: Am. Psychiat. Assn. (Disting. life), Royal Soc. Medicine; mem.: AMA, Alpha Delta Phi, Alpha Omega Alpha. Home: 100 La Rosa RD Long Beach MS 39560

CONRAD, PAUL ERNEST, transportation consultant; b. Hartford, Conn., June 11, 1927; s. Ernest and Agnes Anita (Eis) C.; m. Audrey Grace Lindner, June 17, 1947; children: Cynthia Dale, Robin Sue, Kristen Diane. BS, U. Conn., 1949. Hwy. engr. Fed. Hwy. Adminstrn., Southeast U.S., Conn. and N.Y., 1949-55; prin. assoc. Wilbur Smith & Assocs., Columbia, S.C., 1955-69, sr. v.p., 1969-72, exec. v.p., 1972-91, also bd. dirs. Bd. dirs. Spring Valley Homeowners Assn., 1976-77, 97-98, Enclave Comty. Assn., 1999-2004, 09-. With USN, 1945-46. Mem. NSPE, ASCE, Inst. Transp. Engrs., Am. Cons. Engrs. Coun. Lutheran. Home: 103 Enclave Loop Columbia SC 29223-3260 Home Phone: 803-788-3906. Personal E-mail: pauleconrad@aol.com.

CONRAD, ROBERT JAMES, JR., federal judge; b. Chgo., May 17, 1958; BA Clemson U., 1980, JD U. Va., 1983. Law clk. Michie, Hamlett, Donato and Lowry, 1981—83, assoc., 1983—86; ptnr. Horn and Conrad, 1986—87; sole practice Robert J. Conrad Jr., PA, 1987—88; ptnr. Bush, Thurman and Conrad, 1988—89; asst. US atty. (we. dist.) NC US Dept. Justice, 1989—2001, US atty. (we. dist. NC), 2001—04; ptnr. Mayer, Brown, Rowe & Maw LLP, Charlotte, NC, 2004—05; judge US Dist. Ct. (we. dist.) NC, 2005—06, chief judge, 2006—; adj. prof. Wake Forest Law Sch., 2009—; instr. Trial Advocacy Coll. U. Va. Office: US Dist Ct 235 Charles R Jonas Fed Bldg 401 W Trade St Charlotte NC 28202 Home Phone: 704-352-7460. Business E-Mail: robert_conrad@ncwd.uscourts.gov, robert_conrad@nwwd.uscourts.gov.

CONRAD, STEVEN ALLEN, critical care and emergency physician, biomedical engineer, educator; b. St. Martinville, La., Aug. 23, 1953; s. Karl Donovan and Dolores Beatrice (Bienvenu) C.; m. Mona Theresa Hollier, Aug. 9, 1974; children: David, Lesley, Taylor. BS, U. S.W. La., 1974; MD, La. State U., Shreveport, 1978; MS, Case Western Reserve U., Cleve., 1980, PhD, 1985; MS in Engring., La. Tech. U., 1981; MBA, La. State U., 2001, MS in Info. Sys. Tech., 2003; MSc in Bioinformatics, U. Manchester, 2006. Diplomate Am. Bd. Internal Medicine, Critical Care Medicine, Am. Bd. Emergency Medicine; cert. nutritional support physician; cert. clin. rsch. investigator Assn. Clin. Rsch. Investigators, 2004. Postdoctoral trainee in biomed. computing Case Western Res. U., 1979—80; resident internal medicine La. State U., Shreveport, 1981-84; fellow in critical care medicine Mayo Grad. Sch. Medicine, Rochester, Minn., 1984-86; from asst. prof. medicine to prof. bioinformatics and computational biology La. State U. Med. Ctr., Shreveport, La., 1986—2003, prof. medicine, emergency medicine, pediatrics, anesthesiology, bioinformatics and computational biology, 2003—, dir. critical care medicine tng. program, 1987—2007; instr. computer sci. Winona State U., 1985—86, prof. neurosurgery, 2009—. Cons. physician critical care VA Med. Ctr., 1986—2003, dir. extracorporeal life support program, 1993—, co-dir. nutritional support svc., 1994—2007, transplant intensivist Willis Knighton Regional Heart Transplant Program, 1994—2004, attending physician in pediat. ICU, 1994—; mem. emergency med. svcs. task force Shreveport Fire Dept., 1992—; prin. investigator in multiple device and drug trials. Editor: Pulmonary Function Testing: Principles and Practice, 1984; mem. editl. bd. Internat. Jour. Electronic Healthcare, 2003—, ASAIO Jour., 2004—; manuscript reviewer ASAIO Jour., 2004-, Artificial Organs, Intensive Care Medicine, Critical Care Chest Medicine, Chest; abstract reviewer Critical Care Medicine; contbr. chpts. to books and articles to profl. jours. Grantee, Am. Heart Assn., NHLBI. Fellow ACP, Am. Coll. Critical Care Med., Am. Coll. Chest Physicians, Am. Coll. Emergency Physicians, Am. Acad. Emergency Physicians; mem. IEEE (sr.), Biomed. Engring. Soc., Shock Soc., Am. Soc. Artificial Internal Organs, Internat. Soc. for Artificial Organs, Soc. for Acad. Emergency Medicine, Am. Soc. for Parenteral and Enteral Nutrition, Internat. Soc. for Computational Biology, Alpha Omega Alpha, Sigma Xi, Phi Kappa Phi, Beta Gamma Sigma, Sigma Iota Epsilon. Office: La State U Health Scis Ctr 1501 Kings Hwy Shreveport LA 71103-4228 Office Phone: 318-675-6885. Business E-Mail: sconrad@lsuhsc.edu.

CONRAD-ENGLAND, ROBERTA LEE, pathologist; b. Meriden, Conn., Aug. 25, 1950; d. Hans and Emma Ann (Bort) Conrad; m. Gary Thomas England, June 6, 1976; children: Eric Bryan, Christopher Ryan. BS in Microbiology, U. Ky., 1972, MD, 1976. Diplomate Nat. Bd. Med. Examiners, Bd. Am. Pathologists. Resident anatomic and clin. pathology Emory U. Affiliated Hosps., Atlanta, 1976-80; pathologist Western Bapt. Hosp., Paducah, Ky., 1980—2005. Cons. Marshall County Hosp., Benton, Ky., 1985-2005, chair infection control com., 1985-2005 Mem., com. chairperson PTA, Poducah, Ky., 1993-94; mother's asst. Boy Scouts Am., Poducah, 1991-94. Fellow Coll. Am. Pathologists, Am. Soc. Clin. Pathologists; mem. Ky. Med. Assn., Ky. Soc. Pathologists, Ky. Women Mentors in Sci., Alpha Omega Alpha, Phi Beta Kappa. Avocations: swimming, snorkeling, interior decorating.

CONROY, PAT (DONALD PATRICK CONROY), writer; b. Atlanta, Oct. 26, 1945; s. Donald and Frances Dorothy (Peck) Conroy; m. Barbara Bolling, Oct. 10, 1969 (div. 1977); 1 child, Megan stepchildren: Jessica, Melissa; m. Lenore Fleischer, 1981 (div. Oct. 25, 1995); 1 child, Susannah stepchildren: Gregory, Emily; m. Cassandra King, 1997. BA in English, The Citadel, Charleston, SC, 1967, LittD (hon.), 2000. Former English tchr., Beaufort, SC, Daufuskie Island, SC. Author: (novels) The Boo, 1970, The Water Is Wide, 1972 (Anisfield-Wolf Book award, Cleve. Found., 1972), The Great Santini, 1976, The Lords of Discipline, 1980 (Lillian Smith Book award, So. Regional Coun./U. Ga., 1981), The Prince of Tides, 1986, Beach Music, 1995, South of Broad, 2009 (#1 Publishers Weekly bestseller), The Death of Santini, 2013, (nonfiction) The Pat Conroy Cookbook: Recipes of My Life, 1999, My Losing Season, 2002, My Reading Life, 2010, (screenplays) Conrack, 1974, The Great Santini, 1979, The Lords of Discipline, 1983, Invictus, 1988, The Water Is Wide, 2006; co-author (with Becky Johnston) The Prince of Tides, 1991. Recipient Achievement in Edn. award, NEA, 1974, Governor's award for Arts, State of Ga., 1978, Golden Plate award, American Acad. Achievement, 1992, Lit. award, U. SC Thomas Cooper Libr. Soc., 1995, Gov.'s award in the Humanities for disting. achievement, State of SC, 1996, Humanitarian award, Ga. Commn. on Holocaust, 1996, Medal of Merit for outstanding lit. achievement, Lotos Club NYC, 1996; named to The SC Hall of Fame, 2009; grantee Ford Found., 1971. Mem.: PEN, Writers Guild, Authors Guild America. Democrat. Address: c/o Claudia Rinaldi Marly Rusoff & Associates Inc PO Box 524 Bronxville NY 10708*

CONSER, WALTER HURLEY, JR., religion and philosophy educator; b. Riverside, Calif., Apr. 4, 1949; s. Walter Hurley and Barbara Healy C.; m. Janet Gunter, June 7, 1986; 1 child, Emily. BA, U. Calif., Irvine, 1971; MA, Brown U., Providence, 1974, PhD, 1981. From vis. asst. prof. to prof. U. N.C., Wilmington, 1985—. Author: Church and Confession, 1984, God and the Natural World, 1993, Sacred Spaces, 1999, A Coat of Many Colors, 2005, Presbyterians in North Carolina, 2012; editor: Southern Crossroads, 2008, Experience of the Sacred, 1992, Religious Diversity and American Religious History, 1997; mem. adv. bd. Jour. So. Religion, 1997—. Mem. Am. Hist. Assn. Mem. Am. Acad. Religion. Office: Dept Philosophy and Religion U NC 601 S College Rd Wilmington NC 28403-5601

CONSTANT, GUY J., corporate financial executive; BA in Polit. Sci. and Economics, U. Manitoba; MBA in Fin., The U. Western Ont., 1993. Dir., exec. compensation American Airlines, Inc., 1995—2004; sr. dir. compensation Brinker International Inc., 2004—05, v.p. strategic planning and analysis and investor relations, 2005—08, sr. v.p. fin., 2008—10, prin. accounting officer, exec. v.p., CFO, 2010—; CFO Chili's Grill & Bar, 2010—. Office: Brinker International Inc 6820 LBJ Freeway Dallas TX 75240 Office Phone: 972-980-9917. Office Fax: 972-770-9593. Business E-Mail: guy.constant@brinker.com.*

CONSTANTINE, PAUL J., wholesale distribution executive; Grad., Furman U., Greenville, SC. Staff acct. KPMG LLP, Elliott Davis LLC; account exec. Prudential Securities Inc.; dir. merchandising Gates/Arrow Distbg. Inc.; dir., v.p. merchandising POS & barcoding sales unit ScanSource, Inc., 1999—2004, v.p. solutions & svcs., 2005—08, v.p. merchandising ScanSource Security Distbn. (subs.), 2008—. Office: ScanSource Inc 6 Logue Ct Greenville SC 29615 Office Phone: 864-288-2432. Office Fax: 864-288-1165.

CONWAY, ANNE CALLAGHAN, federal judge; b. Cleve., July 30, 1950; BA, John Carroll U., 1972; JD, U. Fla., 1975. Bar: Fla. 1975, U.S. Ct. Appeals (5th and 11th cirs.), U.S. Dist. Ct. (mid., no. and so. dists.) Fla., U.S. Supreme Ct. 1981. Law clk. to Hon. John A. Reed Jr. US Dist. Ct. (mid. dist.) Fla., Orlando, Fla., 1975-77; from assoc. to ptnr. Wells, Gattis & Hallowes, Orlando, 1978-81; assoc. Carlton, Fields, Ward, Emmanuel, Smith & Cutler, P.A., Orlando, 1982-85, ptnr., 1985-91; judge US Dist. (mid. dist.) Fla., Orlando, 1991—2008, chief judge, 2008—. Mem. adv. com. on local rules U.S. Dist. Ct., Orlando, 1990-91, grievance com. Orlando divsn., mid. dist., 1986-91. Bd. dirs. So. Ballet Theatre, Winter Park, Fla., 1985-89, adv. bd., 1985-89; bd. dirs. Greater Orlando Area Legal Svcs., 1978-85. Mem. ABA, Orange County Bar Assn. (chairperson state and fed. trial practice com. 1989-90). Office: George C Young US Courthouse & Fed Bldg 401 W Ctrl Blvd Ste 6750 Orlando FL 32801 E-mail: anne_conway@flmd.uscourts.gov.

CONWAY, EARL CRANSTON, business educator, retired manufacturing company executive, educator; b. Asbury Pk., NJ, Nov. 14, 1931; s. Earl Cranston and Alda Evelyn (Hendrickson) C.; m. Nancy Lou Schucker, Oct. 23, 1954; children: Karen Marie, Anne Margaret, Earl Edward, Nancy Maureen. BA in Polit. Sci. and Internat. Rels., U. Pa., Phila., 1954. Sales-mktg. rep. Procter & Gamble, Phila., 1957-59, unit mgr. Balt. and Chgo., 1960-64, dist. mgr. Minn., Pa., 1964-69, divsn. mgr., nat. sales mgr. Cin., 1970-81, gen. sales mgr. Europe Brussels, 1981-85, corp. dir. world-wide quality Cin., 1985-92. Co-chmn. U.S. Quality Coun. of Conf. Bd., N.Y.C., 1989-92; adj. prof. U. Cin., 1990-2005; adj. faculty Indian River C.C., Indian River County, Fla., 1996-99; lectr. quality and strategic planning Ministry of Light Industry, Hong Kong, Shanghai, Guangzhou and Wuxi, Peoples Republic of China, 1992—, Moscow and Kirov, Russia, 1994—; vis. lectr. bus. and engring. schs.; advisor quality mgmt. V.P. Gore, U.S. and Gov. Jim Hunt, N.C., 1992-93, 93-94. Vice chmn. nat. bd. dirs. Vols. of Am., New Orleans, 1991-96; mem., bd. trustees Ursuline Acad., Cin., 1992-93; mem. planning and zoning bd. City of Vero Beach, Fla., 1995-99, Charter Review Commn., Fla., 2005-; bd. dirs., v.p. Civic Assn., Indian River County, Fla., Vero Beach, Fla., 1995—; vice chmn., bd. dirs. Indian River Meml. Hosp., Indian River County, 1999-2004. 1st lt., inf. US Army, 1955-56. Recipient Taguchi Quality Engring. award Am. Supplier Inst., 1989, Recognition by Ministry of Light Industry, People's Republic of China, Guangzhou and Wuxi, 1992-93. Mem. Am. Soc. Quality. Republican. Roman Catholic. Home: 1020 Olde Doubloon Dr Vero Beach FL 32963-2449

CONWAY, JACK (JOHN WILLIAM CONWAY), state attorney general; b. Louisville, Ky., July 5, 1969; s. Tom and Barbara Conway; m. Elizabeth Davenport Conway. BA in Pub. Policy, Duke U., Durham, NC, 1991; JD with honors, George Washington U. Law Sch., 1995. Legis. aide US House Banking Com., Washington, 1991—92; atty. US Dept. Justice, Washington; legal counsel, dep. cabinet sec. Office Gov. Paul Patton, Ky., 1995—2001; atty. Conliffe Sandman Sullivan, 2001—08; atty. gen. State of Ky., 2008—. Bd. mem. Muhammad Ali Ctr., 1999—2001, African Am. Heritage Ctr., 2000—01; bd. dirs. Louisville Library Found., 2001—07. Mem.: Leadership Louisville Found., Louisville Bar Assn., Ky. Bar Assn. Democrat. Roman Catholic. Office: Office of the Attorney General 700 Capitol Ave Ste 118 Frankfort KY 40601 Office Phone: 502-696-5300. E-mail: Attorney.General@ag.ky.gov.*

CONWAY, JAMES TERRY, retired military officer; b. Walnut Ridge, Ark., Dec. 26, 1947; m. Annette Drury; children: Brandon, Scott, Samantha. BS in Psychology, Southeast Mo. State U., 1969; grad. with honors, Basic Sch., U.S. Army Inf. Officers' Advan, Marine Corps Command and Staff, Air War Coll. Commd. 2nd lt. USMC, 1970, advanced through grades to gen., 2006; rifle platoon comdr., 106mm recoilless-rifle platoon comdr. 3rd Bn. 1st Marines, Camp Pendleton; weapons platoon comdr. Basic Inf. Tng. Sch., Camp Pendleton; co. comdr. Inf. Tng. Regiment, Camp Pendleton; exec. officer of marine detachment USS Kitty Hawk; series and co. comdr. in Recruit Tng. Regiment Marine Corps Recruit Depot, San Diego; aide to comdg. gen., dir. Sea Sch.; regiment's asst. 3rd Bn. 2nd Marines 2nd Marine Divsn., Camp Lejeune; sect. head tactics group Basic Sch.; ops. officer 31st MAU; with ops. divsn. Hdqs. Marine Corps.; sr. aide to Chmn. Joint Chiefs of Staff The Pentagon; divsn. G-3 ops. officer 2nd Marine Divsn.; comdr. 3rd Bn. 2nd Marines, 1990; pres. Marine Corps U., Quantico, Va., 1998—2000; commdr 1st Marine Divsn., 2000—02; commdr. I Marine Expeditionary Force, 2002—04; dir. ops. (J-3), The Joint Staff US Dept. Def., Washington, 2004—06; comdt. USMC, Washington, 2006—10. Decorated Def. Disting. Svc. medal (3), Disting. Svc. medal, Legion of Merit, Def. Meritorious Svc. medal, Meritorious Svc. Medal, Navy Commendation medal, Navy Achievement medal, Combat Action Ribbon

CONWAY, M. MARGARET, political science professor, consultant; b. Terre Haute, Ind., May 14, 1935; d. Frank J. and Mary K. Conway. BS in Econs., Purdue U., 1957; MA in Polit. Sci., U. Calif., Berkeley, 1960; PhD in Polit. Sci., Ind. U., 1965. From lectr. to prof. U. Md., College Park, 1963—89; prof. U. Fla., Gainesville, 1989—98, disting. prof., 1998—2000, disting. prof. emeritus, 2000—. Mem. Am. Polit. Sci. Assn. (v.p. 1991-92, pres. women's caucus sect. 1991-92, pres. polit. orgns. and parties sect. 1989-91), So. Polit. Sci. Assn. (pres. 1986-87).

CONWAY, RICHARD ASHLEY, environmental engineer; BS, U. Mass., 1953; MS, MIT, 1957. Registered profl engr., W.Va. Sr. corp. fellow Union Carbide Corp., South Charleston, W.Va., 1957-97; pvt. cons., 1997—. Cons. sci. adv. bd. EPA, chmn. environ. engring. com., 1988-93; sci. adv. bd. DOD Strategic Environ. R&D Program, 1992-98; mem. report rev. com. NAS. Author: Industrial Waste Disposal, 1980; editor: Hazardous Solid Waste Testing, 5 vols., 1981-87, Environmental Risk Analysis, 1982; patentee in field. Served to 1st lt. U.S. Army, 1954-56. Recipient Personal Achievement award in Chem. Engring., Chem. Engring. mag., N.Y.C., 1986. Fellow ASCE (chmn. environ. engring. divsn. 1975, Hering medal 1974), Am. Acad. Environ. Engrs. (diplomate, trustee 1994-97, Kappe award 1999, Fair award 2004), Internat. Water Quality Assn. (governing bd. 1978-88), Soc. Environ. Chemistry and Toxicology (bd. dirs. 1983-86, Rachel Carson award 1997); mem. NAE, ASTM (Dudley medal 1984), Water Environ. Fedn. (Gascoigne medal 1967, Rudolfs medal 1974, 83). Avocations: tennis, history. Personal E-mail: conwayenv@aol.com.

CONWELL, HALFORD ROGER, physician; b. Cin., Jan. 28, 1924; s. Halford Fredrick and Erma Pearl (Cornelius) C.; m. Margaret Ann King, Dec. 15, 1965; children: Mark A., Sherri L., John H. BA, U. Wooster, 1948; MA, U. Louisville, 1950; MD, U. Cin., 1955. ATP; diplomate crew coordination tng. Continental Airlines. Lt. USNR, 1943—54; practice in aviation medicine Huntsville, Tex., 1959—; mem. staff Huntsville Meml. Hosp., chief of staff, 1974-75, chief medicine, 1976-80, bd. trustees, 1991—2005. Locomotive fireman, Pa. RR, 1940-41, sr. U.S. med. officer Brit. Caledonian Airways, 1977-89; cons. Aeromexico; chief flight surgeon Continental Airlines, 1996—; mem. Walker County Hosp. Dist., 1975-79, chmn., 1976-79; asst. dean of men, instr. psychology Heidelberg U., Tiffin, Ohio, 1950-51; instr. psychology Cin. Coll. Pharmacy; sr. med. examiner FAA; cons. C.A.A. (U.K.), C.A.A. (Australia); newspaper columnist, 1992-. Capt. (hon.) Tex. Internat. Airline, Continental Airlines Golden Eagles, 2007; founder Bomber Command Mus. (R.A.F.). Recipient safe pilot award Nat. Pilots Assn., Pilot Proficiency award FAA, Profl. Svc. Citation. Fellow Aerospace Med. Assn., Civil Aviation Assn. (John A. Tamisiea award 2000, Bernice Audie Davis award 2005), Civil Aviation Med. Assn. (v.p. 1968-80, dir. 1968—, pres. 1980-81, award of merit 1994, 97), Airline Pilos Assn.(Lifetime Achievement award 2008); mem. Brit. Assn. Aerospace Medicine, Latin Am. Aviation Med. Assn., Scottish Assn. Aviation Med. Examiners, Airline Med. Dirs. Assn., Mitchell Pediatric Soc., Academie Internationale de Medicine Aeronatque et Spatiale, Aircraft Owners and Pilots Assn. (med. adv. panel), Confederate Air Force (founding mem.), Air Transp. Assn. (med. com.), Order Ky. Cols., Quiet Birdmen, Masons, Psi Chi, Alpha Psi Omega. Office: 27230 Paula Ln Conroe TX 77385-9052 Office Phone: 936-295-5222.

COODY, ANN, state legislator; m. Dale Coody; children: Jeff, Nina. BA in Speech and Drama, Hardin-Simmon Univ.; MEd, Univ. Okla. Former prin. Lawton's Macarthur HS; mem. Dist. 64 Okla. House of Representative, 2005—. Republican. Mailing: 104 S State Hwy 65 Lawton OK 73501 Office: 2300 N Lincoln Blvd Rm 439 Oklahoma City OK 73105 Office Phone: 405-557-7398. E-mail: anncoody@okhouse.gov.

COOEY, WILLIAM RANDOLPH, retired economics professor; b. Wheeling, W.Va., Feb. 23, 1942; s. William Earl and Marguerite Ruth (Potts) C.; m. Linda Faye Whiteman, Aug. 11, 1973; children: William Justin, Crissa Kaye. BA, Bethany Coll., 1964; MS, W.Va. U., 1966; postgrad., Miss. State U., 1973-74. Prof. Bethany (W.Va.) Coll., 1966—2011, adminstrv. chair econs. dept., 2002—11, John F. and Evelyn Cassey Steen chair in econs., 2002—11. V.p., bd. dirs. Cooey-Bentz Co., Wheeling, 1980-90; part-time assoc. prof. Ohio U., St. Clairsville, 1967-86, W.Va. U., West Liberty, 1976-84; pvt. practice legal cons., Bethany, 1975—95. Contbr. articles to publs. West Va. Commn. Higher Edn. Advisor Boy Scouts Am., Bethany, 1986-90; asst. coach Little League Baseball, Bethany, 1986-90. Recipient James E. Allison Award for Tchg. Excellence, 2004. Mem. Midwestern Econs. Assn., Beta Beta Beta, Omicron Delta Epsilon, Gamma Sigma Kappa. Achievements include Bethany College W. Randolph Cooey Value Added awared in economics (endowed by anonymous donor), Cooey-Davis Internship award (endowed by anonymous donor). Avocations: woodworking, making videos, computers. Home: 102 Pt Breeze Dr Bethany WV 26032

COOGAN, PHILIP SHIELDS, pathologist; b. Peoria, Ill., Feb. 13, 1938; s. Paul Mathew and Elizabeth Ann (Shields) C.; m. Carol Jean Gerlach, June 18, 1960 (div. 1985); children: Mary Brighid, Philip Gerlach, Joseph Baker, Clare Ann; m. Joan C. Storozynski, Dec. 24, 1987. Student, U. Notre Dame, 1955—58; MD, St. Louis U., 1962. Diplomate: Am. Bd. Pathology. USPHS summer rsch. trainee pathology St. Louis U. Med. Sch., 1958—61; intern Presbyn.-St. Luke's Hosp., Chgo., 1962—63, resident, 1963—67; rsch. pathologist, chief histopathology U.S. Air Force Sch. Aerospace Medicine, 1967—69; asst. prof. pathology Rush Med. Coll., Chgo., 1971—73, assoc. prof., 1972—75; assoc. prof. pathology Northwestern U., Chgo., 1974—78; dir. anatomic pathology Northwestern Meml. Hosp., Chgo., 1974—78; prof. pathology James H. Quillen Coll. Medicine, East Tenn. State U., Johnson City, 1978—2004. Cons. FDA, 1972-81, USPHS, 1962-67 Assoc. editor: Year Book Pathology and Clinical Pathology, 1978-80. Served with USAF, 1967-69. Recipient Hektoen award Chgo. Path. Soc., 1969; named Outstanding Tchr. East Tenn. State U. Coll. Medicine, 1980, 81, 83, 84, 85 Mem. AMA, AAAS, U.S. and Can. Acad. Pathology, Am. Soc. Exptl. Pathology, Am. Soc. Clin. Pathology, Coll. Am. Pathology, Am. Soc. Investigative Pathology, Alpha Omega Alpha. Roman Catholic. Home Phone: 423-282-6770. E-mail: coogan@etsu.edu.

COOGLER, L. SCOTT, federal judge; b. Nantucket, Mass., 1959; BA, U. Ala., 1981, JD, 1984. Law clk. to Hon. Paul Conger 6th Jud. Cir. Ct. Ala., 1984, judge, 1996—2003; pvt. practice atty. Ala., 1984—99; adj. prof. U. Ala. Sch. Law, 2000—03; judge US Dist. Ct. (no. dist. Ala.), 2003—. Mem. Nat. Guard US Army, 1988—91. Office: US Dist Ct No Dist Ala Hugo Black Courthouse 1729 5th Ave N Birmingham AL 35203

COOK, ANN JENNALIE, literature educator, cultural organization administrator; b. Wewoka, Okla., Oct. 19, 1934; d. Arthur Holly and Bertha Mable (Stafford) C.; children: Lee Ann Merrick, Amy Ceil Leonard; m. Gerald George Calhoun, Apr. 1994. BA, U. Okla., 1956, MA, 1959; PhD, Vanderbilt U., 1972. Instr. English U. Okla., 1956-57; tchr. English NC, 1958—61, Conn., 1958—61; instr. So. Conn. State Coll., 1962-64; asst. prof. U. SC, 1972—74; adj. asst. prof. Vanderbilt U., Nashville, 1977-82, assoc. prof., 1982-89, prof., 1990-98, prof. emerita, 1999—. Exec. sec. Shakespeare Assn. Am., 1975-87; chmn. Internat. Shakespeare Assn., 1988-96, v.p. 1996—. Author: Privileged Playgoers of Shakespeare's London, 1981, Making a Match: Courtship in Shakespeare and His Society, 1991; assoc. editor Shakespeare Studies, 1973-80; contbr. articles to profl. jours. Trustee Folger Shakespeare Libr., 1985—90, Shakespeare Birthplace Trust (life), Friends of the Shakespeare Birthplace Trust, Nashville Symphony, 2000—06, Univ. Sch. Nashvillle, 2000—04, Nashville Opera Guild, 2000—03, Nashville Shakespeare Festival, 2002—, Shakespeare League of Nashville; pres. English-Speaking Union, 2003—07, nat. bd. dirs., 2004—. Recipient Letseizer award, 1956, Nat. Leadership award Delta Delta Delta, 1956; Danforth fellow, 1968-72, Folger summer fellow, 1973, Donelson fellow, 1974-75, fellow Rockefeller Found., 1984, Guggenheim Found., 1984-85; grantee Folger seminar NEH, 1992-93. Mem. MLA, AAUP, Shakespeare Assn. Am., Shakespeare Inst., Vanderbilt Libr. Heard Soc. (pres. 2004-06), Phi Beta Kappa. Episcopalian. Office: Vanderbilt U Dept English Nashville TN 37235 Home: 6666 Brookmont Terr Apt 207 Nashville TN 37205 Office Phone: 615-322-2541. Personal E-mail: gercalhoun@aol.com.

COOK, BYRON, state legislator; b. Bryan, Tex., 1954; m. Kay Cook; 2 children. AS, Navarro Coll., Corsicana, Tex., 1974. Businessman; rancher; mem. Dist. 8 Tex. House of Representatives, 2002—. Republican. Baptist. Avocations: tennis, hunting, fishing, skiing, riding. Office: Room E2.214 Capital Extension PO Box 2910 Austin TX 78768 Mailing: PO Box 1397 Corsicana TX 75151 Office Phone: 512-463-0730. Office Fax: 512-463-2506.

COOK, CAMILLE WRIGHT, retired law educator; b. Tuscaloosa, Ala. d. Reuben Hall and Camille Tunstall (Searcy) Wright; children: Sydney, Reuben, Cade, Camille. AB, U. Ala., 1945, JD, 1948. Bar: Ala. 1948. Asst. prof. law, Law Sch. Auburn (Ala.) U., 1968; mem. faculty Sch. Law U. Ala., 1968-93, assoc. dean, dir. continuing legal edn., prof. law, Law Sch., 1975-93, asst. acad. v.p., 1984-85; prof. emeritus, 1993—. Bd. dirs. U. Ala. Law Sch. Found., Am/South. Mem. Smithsonian Coun., Washington, 1972-78, Ala. Air Pollution Commn., 1971-81; vestry Christ Episcopal Ch. Recipient outstanding commitment to tchg. award U. Ala., 1990, disting. alumni award, 1996, Algernon Sydney Sullivan award, 1999. Fellow Am. Bar Found., Ala. Bar Assn. (award merit 1973); mem. ABA (Rawles Spl. Merit award 1983), Farrah Law Soc. (trustee 1972—, disting. alumnae award 1992), Am. law Inst. (coun., Rawles Spl. Merit award 1983). Episcopalian. Home: 32 Ridgeland Tuscaloosa AL 35406-1607 Personal E-mail: camillewcook1@comcast.net.

COOK, CHARLES CLINTON, energy executive; b. 1964; B in Archtl. Engring., U. Tex., M in Fin. Joined Destec Energy, Inc. (acquired by Dynegy Inc.), 1991, v.p., 2002; v.p., asst. treas. Dynegy Inc., Houston, sr. v.p., treas., 2005—07, sr. v.p., strategic planning and corp. bus. devel., treas., 2008; exec. v.p., comml. & market analytics Dynegy, Inc., 2008—, interim CFO, 2011—. Office: Dynegy Inc Ste 5800 601 Travis St Ste 1400 Houston TX 77002-3253 Office Phone: 713-507-6400. Business E-Mail: charles.cook@dynegy.com.

COOK, CHARLES WILKERSON, JR., retired bank executive, municipal official; b. Nashville, Sept. 10, 1934; s. Charles Wilkerson and Virginia (Jones) C.; m. Sally Randolph Frierson, June 24, 1961 (dec. May 2001); children: Charles Wilkerson III, John Stephenson Frierson; m. Mary Hawkins, Jan. 18, 2003. BS, Yale U., 1956; postgrad., Rutgers U., 1964-66. With Third Nat. Bank, Nashville, 1959-85, pres., 1979-83, chmn., 1983-85, also dir.; with Third Nat. Corp., Nashville, 1985-89, pres., chief exec. officer, 1985-87, chmn. bd. dirs., chief exec. officer, 1987-89, dir., 1983-90; exec. v.p. Sun Trust Banks, Inc., 1989-90; dir. fin. Met. Govt. of Nashville-Davidson County (Tenn.), Nashville, 1991-93; pres., CEO, dir. Union Planters Bank of Mid. Tenn., N.A., Nashville, 1993-99, chmn., bd. dirs., 2000—01; ret., 2001; vice chmn. Nashville Bank and Trust Co., 2004—07, dir., 2004—; mem. Met. Govt. Bd. Equalization, 2004—08. Bd. dirs. Nashville Electric Power, chmn. bd. dirs., 1997-2003; bd. dirs. Quality Industries, Inc., Richland Place, Inc. Author: History of a Bank Merger, 1969. Active Metro Nashville-Davidson County Govt. Social Svcs. Commn., 1970-85; sr. warden Christ Episcopal Ch., Nashville, 1970-71; pres. Episc. Churchmen of Tenn., 1974; mem. bishop and coun. Episc. Diocese of Tenn., 1979-81; chmn., bd. dirs. United Way Nashville, 1984-85; chmn. Project PENCIL, 1988-89, Jr. Achievement of Nashville, Bill Wilkerson Hearing and Speech Ctr., Nashville, 1970-80, Ensworth Sch., 1978-81, Better Bus. Bur. Nashville, 1980-83, Nashville Meml. Hosp., 1974-89, Tenn. Performing Arts Mgmt. Corp., 1985-89, vice-chmn., 1987-89, v.p., Tenn. State Mus. Found., 1986-89; adv. bd. Salvation Army, Nashville, 1976-79; bd. dirs. Episcopal Ch. Found., 1991-92, St. Luke's Cmty. House, 1999-2004, chmn., 2002-03; bd. dirs. Nashville Pub. TV Corp., 1998—, chmn., 2006—, Nashville Cmty. Found., 2000—, Tenn. Hist. Soc., 2000—, pres., 2008-; campaign chmn. United Way Mid. Tenn., 1994. With USN, 1956-59; capt. Res., 1977-84. Mem. Nashville C. of C. (bd. govs. 1982-84, 95-2000), Belle Meade Country Club (bd. dirs. 1996-2000, pres. 1999-2000), Army-Navy Club (Washington), Yale Club NYC, Univ. Club (Nashville). Home Phone: 615-292-0011.

COOK, E. GARY, manufacturing executive; BS, Univ. Va., 1966; PhD in Chemistry, Va. Polytechnic Inst., 1970. Sr. mgmt. positions, including v.p., printing, pub., v.p., med. products, v.p., corp. plans E.I. DuPont de Nemours & Co., 1969—92; sr. v.p., pres.-chem., bd. dir. Ethyl Corp., 1992—94; pres., COO Albemarle Corp., 1994—96; chmn., pres., CEO Witco Corp. (merged with Crompton Knowles to become CK Witco), 1996—99; chmn. Louisiana Pacific Corp., 2000—, Integrated Environ. Tech. LLC, 2002—. Bd. dir. Trimeris Corp. Office: Louisiana Pacific Corp 414 Union St Ste 2000 Nashville TN 37219-1711 Office Phone: 615-986-5600. Office Fax: 615-986-5666.

COOK, GARY RAYMOND, academic administrator, minister; b. Little Rock, Ark., Sept. 27, 1950; s. Raymond C. and Vada (James) C.; m. Sheila Gayle Raymer, Dec. 28, 1974; children: David Daniel, Mark Andrew. BA, Baylor U., 1972; MDiv, So. Sem., Louisville, 1975; MA, U. North Tex., 1977; D in Ministry, Southwestern Sem., 1977. Pastor 1st Bapt. Ch., McGregor, Tex., 1976-78; dir. denomination and community rels. Baylor U., Waco, Tex., 1978-88; pres. Dallas Bapt. U., 1988—. Author: Retirees in Mission, 1977; co-editor: Abner McCall: One Man's Journey, 1981. Mayor pro tem City of Waco, 1983-84, mem. city coun., 1981-84; past bd. dirs. Tex. Dept. on Aging; past internat. bd. dirs. Habitat for Humanity. Recipient Humanitarian award Waco Conf. Christians and Jews, 1986, Disting. Alumnus award Southwestern Sem., 2000, Baylor U., 2003. Mem. Rotary (sustaining). Home and Office: 3000 Mountain Creek Pkwy Dallas TX 75211-6700

COOK, GERALD, electrical engineering educator; b. Hazard, Ky., Oct. 31, 1937; s. Rudolph H. and Rose I. (Boyer) C.; m. Nancy Anne Gillespie, June 9, 1962; children: Gerald Boyer, Allan Binford. BS, Va. Poly. Inst., 1961; MS, MIT, 1962, ScD, 1965. Registered profl. engr., Va. Lectr. U. Colo., Colorado Springs, 1966—68; asst. prof. U.S. Air Force Acd., Colorado Springs, 1966—68; assoc. prof. U. Va., Charlottesville, 1968—73, prof., 1973—81; prof., chmn. dept. Vanderbilt U., Nashville, 1981—85; Earle C. Williams prof. elec. engring. George Mason U., Fairfax, Va., 1985—, chmn. dept. elec. and computer engring., 1990—98. Vis. prof. Tech. U. Denmark, 1979-80; vis. rschr. Night Vision Lab., Ft. Belvoir, 1998-99. Author: Mobile Robots: Navigation, Control and Remote Sensing, 2011; editor-in-chief IEEE Trans. on Indsl. Electronics, 1984-91. Recipient Outstanding Rsch. award USAF Office Aerospace Rsch., 1968, Cert. of Achievement, U.S. Army, 1981; NSF fellow, 1961-64. Fellow IEEE (life, pres. Indsl. Electronics Soc. 1981-83, Centennial medal 1984, Eugene Mittelmann Achievement award 1989), Am. Soc. Engring. Edn. (Outstanding Rsch. awrd S.E. sect. 1971), Sigma Xi, Eta Kappa Nu, Phi Kappa Phi, Tau Beta Pi. Home: 4821 Fox Chapel Rd Fairfax VA 22030-4508 Office: George Mason U Dept Elec Engring Fairfax VA 22030 Office Phone: 703-993-1699. Business E-Mail: gcook@gmu.edu.

COOK, J. MONTGOMERY (MONTY COOK), communications educator; BA, U. NC Chapel Hill, 1986. Various editing positions Myrtle Beach Sun News, Akron Beacon Jour.; sect. designer Washington Post, 1996—97, asst. sports editor, 1997—2000; assoc. mng. editor presentation Orlando Sentinel, 2000—04; dep. mng. editor The Balt. Sun, 2004—07, dir. content devel., 2007—08, editor, sr. v.p., 2008—10; exec. prodr. Reese Felts Digital Newsroom U. NC, Chapel Hill, 2010—. Office: University NC Sch Journalism and Mass Comm Carroll Hall 19 Chapel Hill NC 27599 Office Phone: 919-843-4734. Business E-Mail: monty_cook@unc.com.

COOK, J. VINCENT, lawyer; JD, U. Ga., 1962. Founder, mng. ptnr. Cook Noell Tolley & Bates LLP, Athens, Ga. Adj. prof. law U. Ga. Sch. Law. Mem.: Athens-Western Cir. Bar Assn. (past pres.), Ga. Civil Justice Found. (past pres.), Am. Bd. Trial Advocates (past pres. Ga. chpt.), Ga. Trial Lawyers Assn. (past pres.), State Bar Ga. (pres. 2007, treas.). Office: Cook Noell Tolley & Bates LLP 304 E Washington St Athens GA 30601 Office Phone: 706-549-6111.

COOK, JONATHAN L., dermatologist, educator; MD, U. SC, 1999. Diplomate Am. Bd. Dermatology, 2005. Resident internal medicine Harvard Sch. of Medicine, Mass., 1992—93; resident dermatology Emory Univ. Hosp., Ga., 1993—96; fellow mohs and dermatologic surgery Univ. of Pa., 1996—97; prof. dermatology dept. Duke Univ.; hosp. affiliation include Duke Univ. Med. Ctr. Office: Duke Medicine Ste 400 5324 McFarland Drive Durham NC 27707 Office Phone: 919-419-4945. Office Fax: 919-419-4930.

COOK, KENNETH RAY, radiologist; b. Sublette, Kans., Sept. 16, 1953; s. Curtis Carl and Carmen Madonna (Countryman) Cook; m. Paula Rose Petryszyn, July 22, 1978; children: Erin Michelle, Leah Nicole, Tara Rachelle. AA, Hutchinson CC, Kans., 1976; BA, U. Kans., 1979, MD, 1983. Diplomate Am. Coll. Radiology; lic. pvt. pilot. Resident in diagnostic radiology U. Kans. Med. Ctr., 1983-87; pvt. practice, Corpus Christi, Tex., 1987—; chmn. mgmt. com. Radiology Assocs., Corpus Christi, 1997—2002. Staff radiologist Spohn Meml. Med. Ctr., Columbia N.W., Corpus Christi, 1987-99; chief radiology Bay Area Med. Ctr., 1993-99, vice chmn., trustee, 1993-94, chmn., 1994-96, chmn. mgmt. commn., 1997-2013; chief radiology Rehab. Hosp. South Tex., 1989-91; asst. clin. prof. family practice U. Tex., San Antonio; med. dir. Del Mar Coll. Ultrasound Technol. Sch.; chief Corpus Christi Med. Ctr., 1998-99 Recipient Resident Tchg. award U. Kans. Dept. Radiology, Kansas City, 1985-86, Resident Tchg. award, Med. Ctr. Kans. U., 1986-87 Mem. AMA, Am. Coll. Radiology, Radiologic Soc. N. Am., Tex. Med. Soc., Tex. Radiologic Soc., Am. Inst. Ultrasound in Medicine, Nueces County Med. Soc. Republican. Roman Catholic. Avocations: fishing, hunting, camping, flying. Office: Radiology Assocs PO Box 5608 Corpus Christi TX 78465-5608 Home Phone: 361-850-9151; Office Phone: 361-561-3100. Personal E-mail: kcook963@msn.com. Business E-Mail: kcook@xraydocs.com.

COOK, MAURICE GAYLE, soil science educator, consultant; b. Frankfort, Ky., Dec. 26, 1931; s. Price Cash and Evelyn (Moore) C.; m. Eva Nancy Blalock, Aug. 27, 1966; 1 child, Stephen Price. BS, U. Ky., 1957, MS, 1959; PhD, Va. Poly. Inst., 1961. From asst. prof. to prof. N.C. State U., Raleigh, 1961-92, Alumni Disting. prof., 1975; ret., 1992. Spl. advisor Gov. N.C., 1999-2000. Author: Concepts in Soil Science, 1973; contbr. numerous articles to profl. jours. With U.S. Army, 1957; col. USAR, 1962-90. Named to Hall of Disting. Alumni, U. Ky., 2000, Hall of Fame, NC Assn. Soil and Water Conservation Dists., 2006, Coll. Agr. Hall of Disting. Alumni, U. Ky., 2012. Fellow Soil Sci. Soc. Am., Am. Soc. Agronomy, Soil and Water Conservation Soc. (bd. dirs. 1979-88, pres. 1986-87, Hugh Hammond Bennett award 2006), Nat. Assn. Colls. and Tchrs. Agr. (Disting. Tchr. award); mem. Soil Sci. Soc. N.C. (Achievement award 1991), N.C. Divsn. Soil and Water Conservation (exec. dir. 1982-84), Internat. Erosion Control Assn., Gamma Sigma Delta (Merit award 1986), Epsilon Sigma Phi, Alpha Zeta (pres. 1976-85). Baptist. Home: 3458 Leonard St Raleigh NC 27607-6827 Personal E-mail: mgcook@mindspring.com.

COOK, PHILIP CARTER, lawyer; b. Atlanta, Nov. 4, 1946; BS, Ga. Inst. Tech., 1968; JD cum laude, Harvard U., 1971. Bar: Ga. 1972. Law clk. to Hon. Lewis R. Morgan U.S. Ct. Appeals (5th cir.), 1971-72; mem. Alston & Bird, Atlanta, dep. mng. ptnr. Atlanta & Washington. Pres. Harvard Journal of Legislation 1970-71. Fellow Am. Coll. Tax Counsel; mem. ABA (chmn. sect. taxation, com. on banking and savs. instns. 1995), D.C. Bar, State Bar Ga. (chmn. taxation sect.), Am. Law Inst., Atlanta Tax Forum (trustee 1986-91, pres. 1991), Phi Kappa Phi, Omicron Delta Kappa. Office: Alston & Bird 1 Atlantic Ctr 1201 W Peachtree St NW Atlanta GA 30309-3424 Office Phone: 404-881-7491. Office Fax: 404-881-7777. Business E-Mail: pcook@alston.com.

COOK, PHILIP JACKSON, economist, educator; b. Buffalo, Oct. 15, 1946; s. Gerhard Albert and Lura (Lincoln) C.; m. Judith Walmsley, June 27, 1966; children; Elizabeth Camden, Brian Lincoln. BA, U. Mich., 1968; PhD, U. Calif., Berkeley, 1973. Prof. Duke U., Durham, NC, 1973—, dir. Inst. Policy Scis., 1985—89, dir. Sanford Inst. Pub. Policy, 1997—99. Vis. scholar Inst. Rsch. in Social Sci. U. NC, Chapel Hill, 1980, mem. adv. bd. Injury Prevention Rsch. Ctr., 1990—; expert Office Poly. and Mgmt. Analysis, criminal divsn. U.S. Dept. Justice, 1982; mem. rsch. adv. com. U.S. Sentencing Commn., 1986—91, chair rsch. adv. com., 1986; mem. adv. bd. H. John Heinz III Sch. Pub. Policy and Mgmt. Carnegie Mellon U., 1992—; mem. Ctr. Gun Policy Rsch. Johns Hopkins U., 1995—2003; cons. enforcement divsn. U.S. Dept. Treasury, 1999—2000; rsch. assoc. Nat. Bur. Econ. Rsch., 1996—; mem. adv. com. Harvard Injury Control Ctr. Author: Selling Hope, 1989, The Winner-Take All Society, 1995, Gun Violence, 2000, Evaluating Gun Policy, 2003, Paying the Tab: The Economics of Alcohol Policy, 2007, The Gun Debate, 2014 Recipient Sims Award, Economics Dept., U. Mich., 1967, Kenneth J. Arrow award for best paper published in health econ., 1994, Vernon Meml. prize, Jour. Policy Analysis & Mgmt., 1997, 2008, Nat. Sci. Found. fellowship, 1968—70, Richard A. Stubbing Tchr. Mentor Award, Duke U., 2008. Fellow: Am. Soc. Criminology; mem.: Inst. Medicine of NAS, Nat. Rsch. Coun. Com. on Law and Justice (vice chair 2008—), Am. Econ. Assn., Assn. Pub. Policy and Mgmt. (treas. 1985—93, v.p. 2007—09), Phi Beta Kappa. Office: Duke University Sch Pub Policy PO Box 90245 Durham NC 27708-0245 Business E-Mail: pcook@duke.edu.

COOK, RICHARD T., gifted and talented educator; b. Glendale, Calif., Jan. 27, 1959; m. Sandra Cook; children: Matthew, Justin. BA in Secondary Edn. and History, Southeastern Coll. of Assemblies of God, 1981. Tchr. Southside Christian Sch., 1988—93, Peeples Middle Sch., Jackson Pub. Sch. Sys., Miss., 1993—. Mem.: Miss. Ednl. Computing Assn. (bd. mem. 2007—08), Miss. Assn. Gifted Children. Republican. Office: Richard Cook for Congress PO Box 720962 Byram MS 39272 Office Phone: 601-255-4062. E-mail: richard@richardcookforcongress.com.

COOK, ROBERT D., allergist, immunologist; MD, U. Tex., 1977. Diplomate Am. Bd. Internal Medicine, 1980, Am. Bd. Allergy and Immunology, 1983, lic. Tex., 1977. Intern Barnes Jewish Hosp., 1977—78, resident internal medicine, 1978—80; fellow allergy and immunology Univ. of Colo. Med. Ctr., 1980—82; hosp. affiliations include Brackenridge Hosp., Dell Children's Med. Ctr., Heart Hosp. of Austin, North Austin Med. Ctr., Seton Northwest Hosp., Seton Med. Ctr., St. David's Med. Ctr. Named Super Dr., Tex. Monthly Mag.; named one of Best Doctors, Austin Monthly Mag., Best Doctors in America, America's Top Physicians. Fellow: Am. Acad. of Allergy, Asthma, and Immunology, Am. Coll. of Asthma, Allergy & Immunology. Office: Seton Medical Center 1201 W 38th St Austin TX 78705-1006 Office Phone: 512-324-1000.

COOK, RONALD D., diversified financial services company executive, lawyer; BBA, U. Fla.; JD, Stetson U. Asst. v.p., assoc. group counsel Equifax, Inc., 1993—98; atty., pvt. practice Tampa, Fla., 1998—2003, 2006; sr. v.p., assoc. gen. counsel Certegy, 2002—06; gen. counsel Fidelity National Information Services, Inc., 2006—, exec. v.p., 2006—08, corp. exec. v.p., 2008—, corp. sec., 2008—. Contbr. articles to profl. jours. Mem. Am. Arbitration Assn. Mem.: Fla. Bar Assn. Office: Fidelity National Information Services Inc 601 Riverside Ave Jacksonville FL 32204 Office Phone: 904-854-5000. Office Fax: 904-357-1105. Business E-Mail: ronald.cook@fnis.com.

COOK, SHARLA J., career officer; BS in Edn. with honors, Brigham Young U., 1971; disting. grad., Officer Tng. Sch., 1972; aircraft maintenance officer course, Chanute AFB, Ill., 1973; M in Logistics Mgmt., Air Force Inst. of Tech., 1977; grad., Air Command and Staff Coll., 1985; disting. grad., Indsl. Coll. of Armed Forces, 1993. Commd. 2d lt. USAF, 1972, advanced through grades to brigadier gen., 1998; wing job control officer U-Tapao Air Base, Thailand, 1975-76; aide-de-camp air logistics ctr. comdr. Sacramento Air Logistics Ctr., McClellan AFB, Calif., 1981-82, dep. br. chief inventory and scheduling br., 1982-84; comdr. 374th Orgnl. Maintenance Squadron, Clark Air Base, The Philippines, 1985-87; maintenance ops. officer 58th Tactical Tng. Wing, Luke AFB, Ariz., 1988-90, asst. dep. comdr. for maintenance, 1990-91; dep. comdr. 58th Support Group, Luke AFB, 1991-92; comdr. 8th Logistics Group, Kunsan Air Base, South Korea, 1993-94; chief maintenance engring. Hdqs. Pacific Air Forces, Hickam AFB, Hawaii, 1994-95, asst. dir. logistics, 1995-96; dir. aircraft directorate Ogden Air Logistics Ctr., Hill AFB, Utah, 1996-97; dir. logistics Hdqs. Air Edn. and Tng. Command,

Randolph AFB, Tex., 1997—; comdr. 82d tng. wing Air Edn. and Tng. Command, Sheppards AFB, Tex., 1999—. Decorated Legion of Merit, Meritorious Svc. medal with 4 oak leaf clusters. Address: 82 TRW/CC Sheppard AFB TX 76311

COOK, VICTOR JOSEPH, JR., business educator, consultant; b. Durant, Okla., June 25, 1938; s. Victor Joseph and Athelene Ann (Arduser) C.; m. Linda Lee Potter, June 6, 1960 (div. 1971); children: Victor Joseph III, William Randall, Christopher Phelps; m. barbara Brainard, Dec. 29, 1989 (div. 1997). BA, Fla. State U., 1960; MS, La. State U., 1962; PhD, U. Mich., 1965. Rsch. assoc. Mktg. Sci. Inst., Phila., 1965-68; assoc. rsch. dir. Boston, 1968-69; asst. prof. U. Chgo., 1969-75; pres., dir. Mgmt. & Design, New Orleans, 1975-78; prof. Freeman Sch. Bus. Tulane U., 1978—. Pres. Styjl Furniture, 1998—; cons. Ford Motor Co., Dearborn, Mich., 1964-67, IBM, NYC, 1968-72, Sears, Roebuck & Co., Chgo., 1975-77, Internat. Computers Ltd., ICL, London, 1982-91, DuPont Co., Wilmington, 1986-95, Bases Group, Cin., 1986-89. Author: Brand Policy Determination, 1967, Readings in Marketing Strategy, 1989, Competing for Customers and Capital, 2006. Mem. Am. Mktg. Assn., Am. Econ. Assn., Inst. for Ops. Rsch. and The Mgmt. Scis., Beta Gamma Sigma, Phi Beta Kappa. Republican. Achievements include patents for furniture The Style. Office: Tulane U AB Freeman Sch Bus New Orleans LA 70118 Home: 930 Poydras St Apt 2020 New Orleans LA 70112-2045 Home Phone: 561-779-5577; Office Phone: 504-865-5476. Personal E-mail: v2@thestyle.com. Business E-Mail: victor.cook@tulane.edu, vcookj@tulane.edu.

COOK, WILLIAM, state legislator; b. Washington, Aug. 12, 1945; children: Kerri Cook, Billy Cook. BS in Bus. Adminstrn., U. Md. Bd. dirs. HOA; commr. Mid-East Regional Housing Authority; chmn. Cypress Landing Tennis Com.; fin. dir. Beaufort County Rep. Party; treas. Down East Rep. Club; pres. Falls Ch. Va. Home Owners Assoc.; with Potomac Electric Power Co.; state rep. Dist. 6 NC, 2011—. Republican. Office: 75 Cape Fear Dr Chocowinity NC 27817 also: North Carolina House of Representatives 16 W Jones St Rm 1303 Raleigh NC 27601-1096 Office Phone: 919-733-5406, 252-946-5876. Business E-Mail: bill@cookinthehouse.com, Bill.Cook@ncleg.net.

COOK, WILLIAM JOHN, industrial and systems engineering educator; b. NJ, Oct. 18, 1957; BA in Math., Rutgers U., 1979; MS in Ops. Rsch., Stanford U., 1980; PhD in Combinatorics and Optimization, U. Waterloo, Canada, 1983. Alexander von Humboldt rsch. fellow, Institut für Okonometrie und Ops. Rsch. Universität Bonn, Germany, 1983—85, John von Neumann prof., Rsch. Inst. for Discrete Math., 1994—95; asst. prof., Sch. of Ops. Rsch. and Indsl. Engring. Cornell Univ., NY, 1985—87; assoc. prof., Indsl. Engring. and Ops. Rsrch. and the Mgmt. Sci. Divsn. of the Grad. Sch.of Bus. Columbia Univ., NY, 1987—88; mem. tech. staff, Combinatorics and Optimization Rsrch. Group Bell Comm. Rsch., 1988—94; Noah Harding prof., Computational and Applied Math. Rice Univ., Tex., 1996—2001; Chandler family chair prof., Indsl. and Sys. Engring. Georgia Tech., 2002—. Vis. assoc. prof., Institut für Okonometrie und Ops. Rsch. Universität Bonn, Germany, 1986—87; vis. prof., Program for Applied and Computational Math. Princeton Univ., NJ, 2000—02; adj. prof., sch. Math. Georgia Tech., 2002—. Editor: (jours.) SIAM Jour. on Discrete Math., 1992—2009, Math. Programming, Series B, 1999—2003, Math. Programming, Series A, 2003—07, Mathematical Programming Soc. and Springer Verlag, 2008—; co-editor: INFORMS Jour. on Computing, 1992—2003; editor: SIAM Jour. on Optimization, 2006—; co-author: (books) Combinatorial Optimization, 1998, The Traveling Salesman Problem: A Computational Study, 2006; author: Research Trends in Combinatorial Optimization, 2009, In Pursuit of the Traveling Salesman: Mathematics at the Limits of Computation, 2011. Recipient Beale-Orchard-Hays prize, Math. Programming Soc., 2000, Frederick W. Lanchester prize, INFORMS, 2007, Faculty of Math. Alumni Achievement medal, Univ. of Waterloo, 2011; fellow, INFORMS, 2010, Alexander von Humboldt Rsch., 1983, SIAM, 2009. Mem.: NAE. Office: Georgia Institute of Technology 765 Ferst Dr Atlanta GA 30332 Home: 35 Governors Lane Princeton NJ 08540 E-mail: bico@isye.gatech.edu.

COOK-DEEGAN, ROBERT MULLAN, physician, educator; s. William Raymond Cook and Merry (Mullan) Low. BA in Chemistry, Harvard Coll., 1975; MD, U. Colo., 1979. Intern U. Colo., Denver, 1979-80, postdoctoral fellow, rsch. pathologist, 1980-82; sr. assoc. Office Tech. Assessment, U.S. Congress, Washington, 1982-88; acting exec. dir. biomed. ethics adv. com. U.S. Congress, Washington, 1988-89; expert Nat. Ctr. Human Genome Rsch., Bethesda, Md., 1989-90; dir. div. bio-behavioral scis. and mental disorders Inst. Medicine, NAS, Washington, 1991-94; sr. program officer NAS, 1994-96; Cecil and Ida Green fellow U. Tex., Dallas, 1996; dir. Nat. Cancer Policy Bd., 1996-2000, Robert Wood Johnson Health Policy Fellowship Program, 2001—02, Ctr. Genome Ethics Law and Policy, Duke U., 2002—. Author: The Gene Wars: Science, Politics, and the Human Genome, 1994; contbr. articles and chpts. in field. Bd. dirs. Physicians for Human Rights, Boston, 1987-96; dir. ctr. excellence Ethical, Legal & Social Implications Rsch., NIH, 2004—. Recipient Robert Johnson Health Policy Rsch. Investigator award, 1999—2002; grantee Alfred P. Sloan Found., Georgetown U., 1988—91, NSF, 1990—91, Nat. Cancer Inst. and Robert Wood Johnson, 1992—2000, Burroughs Wellcome Fund, 2000—01. Fellow AAAS. Achievements include research in history of human genome project, public policy in cancer, health policy, tobacco control, neurology, psychiatry, behavioral medicine, neuroscience and addiction; U.S. federal policy on Alzheimer's disease and other dementing disorders, public policy on human gene therapy and bioethics. Office: Duke Univ Box 90141 Durham NC 27708-0141 Office Phone: 919-668-0793.

COOKE, CARLTON LEE, JR., mayor; b. Marion, Ala., July 12, 1944; s. Carlton Lee and Willie (Rinehart) Cooke; divorced; 1 child, Kimberly Ann. Student, U. Hawaii, Honolulu, 1963; BA in History, English, La. Tech. U., Ruston, 1966; postgrad., U. Tex., Austin, 1972. Mfg. engr. Tex. Instruments, Austin, 1972-75, site personnel mgr., 1975-81, mktg. mgr., 1981-83; pres., CEO Greater Austin C. of C., 1983-87; mayor City of Austin, Austin, 1988—91. CEO, pres. good2CU.com, Inc., 1999—2000; chmn., CEO Habitek Internat., Inc., 1991—, Tanisys Tech. Corp., 2002—03; pres., CEO U.S. Med. Sys., Inc., 1992—, The Life Store Med. Group, LLC, 2004—06; bd. dirs. New Century Equity Holdings Corp., Bill Concepts Corp., U.S. Long Distance Corp., Sharps Compliance Corp., Med. Polymers Tech., Inc., ProActive Med. Techs., Inc., CUville.com, Inc., FIData.com, Inc., Staubach Co., Tanisys Tech. Corp., Stewart Title, Reliability, Inc., Sr. Quality Lifestyle Corp., 2008—, Bluedoorway Dot Com; participant U.S. Conf. Mayors, Washington, 1991; mem. Anthony Commn., U.S. Congress; ptnr. 290/71 LLC, PHC Investments L.L.C., Angelon Econs., 2012—. Contbg. editor: to mags. Co-chmn. Jerry Lewis Telethon, Austin, 1986—87; chmn. United Negro Telethon, 1991, Tex. Housing Fin. Corp., 1992—94, Austin Charter Com., 1993—94, Tex. Walk of Stars, 1991—2003; chair Texas 4000 Gala, 2008; co-chair SaveKUTAustin Dot Com, 2009; hon. chair Huston Tillotson U. Gala, 2012; bd. trustees Huston Tillotson, 2013—; mem. Austin City Coun., 1977—91, mayor pro tem, 1979; mem. adv. bd. U. Miami Rosenstiel Sch. Ctr. Sustainable Fisheries, 2001—02. Capt. USAF, 1966—72, Vietnam. Decorated Bronze Star; recipient Carl Burnett Cmty. award, 1981, Disting. Austin Citizen's award, 1992, Excellence award, Real Estate Coun. Austin, 1992, Hon. award, Austin History Ctr. Assn., 2012; named Jaycee of the Yr., Austin Jaycees, 1976, Hall of Leadership, US Jaycee Found., 2008; named one of Five Outstanding Young Texans, Tex. Jaycees, 1979. Mem.: VFW (life), ACE Acad. (bd. mem.), Querencia Barton Creek Angelon Econs. (mem. bd. advisors), Austin-San Antonio Corridor Coun. (pres. 1988, 1991), Tex. Mcpl. League (pres. 1991), Headliners Club, Town and Gown Club, Tex. 4000 Club (mem. bd. dirs.), Austin Jaycees (mem. bd. advisors, pres. 1975). Baptist. Avocations: travel, reading, civic work, movies, art. Home: PO Box 50442 Austin TX 78763-0442 Office Phone: 512-347-8800. Personal E-mail: usmedsys@sbcglobal.net.

COOKE, KEVIN, state legislator; b. Carrollton, Ga., Feb. 1, 1980; m. Crystal Cooke. BS in Edn. & Sports Studies, U. Ga., 2003. Former law enforcement official; real estate appraiser Duffy Appraisals Inc., 2005—; mem. Dist. 18 Ga. House of Representatives, 2011—. Republican. Office: Georgia House of Representatives 612 Coverdell Legis Office Bldg Atlanta GA 30334 Office Phone: 404-656-0325. Business E-Mail: kevin.cooke@house.ga.gov.

COOKE, MARCIA GAIL, federal judge; b. Sumter, SC, Oct. 16, 1954; d. Heyward and Ella (Randolph) C. BS in Fgn. Svcs., Georgetown U., 1975; JD, Wayne State U., 1977. Bar: Mich. 1978, U.S. Dist. Ct. (ea. dist.) Mich. 1978, U.S. Ct. Appeals (6th cir.) 1983, Fla. 2001. Staff atty. Wayne County Legal Svcs., Detroit, 1978-79; asst. defender Detroit Defender's Office, 1979-80; asst. atty. US Atty.'s Office, Detroit, 1980-83; assoc. Miro, Miro & Weiner, Bloomfield Hills, Mich., 1983-84; magistrate judge US Dist. Ct. (ea. dist.) Mich., Detroit, 1984—92; dir. profl. devel. & tng. US Atty.'s Office (so. dist) Fla., 1992, 1994—99, exec. asst. US atty., 1992—94, acting adminstr. atty., 1996—97; chief insp. gen., Exec. Office of the Gov. State of Fla., 1999—2002; asst. county atty. Miami-Dade County, 2002—04; judge US Dist. Ct. (so. dist) Fla., Miami, 2004—. Mem. ABA, Fed. Bar Assn. (bd. dirs. 1986), Nat. Bar Assn., Wolverine Bar Assn., Order of Barristers, NCCJ (Pathfinder award 1986), Women's Econ. Club. Roman Catholic. Avocations: film, lit., tennis. Office: US Dist Ct Ferguson US Courthouse 400 N Miami Ave Rm 11-2 Miami FL 33128 Office Phone: 305-523-5150.

COOKE, WALTA PIPPEN, automobile dealership owner; b. Shreveport, La., Oct. 18, 1940; d. Billy Burt and Eula (Heaton) Pippen; m. John William Cooke II, Dec. 20, 1958; children: Cheryl Cooke Williams, John William III. BA, Baylor U., Waco, Tex., 1963. Co-owner, sec.-treas. Pippen Motor Co., Carthage, Tex., 1972-80, owner, sec.-treas., 1980—. Bd. dirs. Sabine River Authority of Tex., 1993-99, pres. bd., 1996-97; past dir. Toledo Bend Joint Project; chmn. lower basin project com. Sabine River Authority Tex., 1999, mem. by-laws com., chmn. 50th ann. com., 1999. Pianist for sanctuary choir Ctrl. Bapt. Ch., Carthage, 1986—; chmn. 50th anniversary celebration com. Sabine River Authority of Tex., 1999; mem. Panola Co. Heritage Found., 2000—, patron mem.; mem. task force Groundwater Conservation, East Tex. Area.; bd. mem. Panola County Appraisal Dist., sec.; founding dir. Carthage Ind. Sch. Dist. Edn. Found.; mem. Panola County Rep. Adv. Com., 2004—, Panola County Groundwater Mgmt. Study Com.; active Tex. Forestry Svc. Recipient Outstanding Forestry Conservationist award, 2005; named Tex. Zone Outstanding Tree Farmer of Yr., Tex. Forestry Assn, 2006, Outstanding Tree Farmer of Yr., State of Tex. - Tex. Forestry Assn., 2007, Outstanding Citizen of Yr., Panola County, 2010; named to Disting. Alumni Hall of Fame, CISD, 2008. Mem. Carthage Book Club (rec. sec. 1995-97, 1st v.p. 2009-, pres., 2010-2012), Carthage Club (dir., 2006-), Century Club (chmn.), C.I.S.D. Edn. Found., NE Tex. Regional Mobility Authority (bd. mem. 2007-). Avocations: reading, gardening, travel, music. Home: 200 Timberlane Dr Carthage TX 75633-2231 Office: Pippen Motor Co 1300 W Panola St Carthage TX 75633-2346 Office Phone: 903-693-6691.

COOKSEY, JOHN CHARLES, ophthalmologist, former United States Representative from Louisiana; b. Alexandria, La., Aug. 20, 1941; s. Henry Oscar and Ruth (Lee) C.; m. Dorothy Ann Grabill, Dec. 30, 1969; children: Karen, Carol Ann, Catherine. MD, La. State U., New Orleans, 1966; MBA, U. Tex., Austin, 1994. Mem. US Congress from 5th La. Dist., 1996—2002; ophthalmologist Cooksey Vision & Cosmetic Ctr., Monroe, La., 1972—; assoc. clin. prof. La. State U. Sch. Medicine, New Orleans, 1982—90, clin. prof., 1990—. Mem. teaching staff E.A. Conway Hosp., Monroe, 1972—; vis. lectr. Alton Ochsner Med. Found., New Orleans, 1978—; asst. clin. prof. La. State U. Med. Sch., New Orleans, 1979-82. Served in USAF, 1967—69 USAFR, 1969—72. Republican. Methodist. Address: Cooksey Vision & Cosmetic Ctr 1310 N 19th St Monroe LA 71201 Office Phone: 318-388-2020. Business E-Mail: jcooksey@cookseymd.com.*

COOKSEY, MARIAN, state legislator; b. Ada, Okla., Nov. 6, 1943; m. Ada Cooksey; 1 child, Ronnie Anne. Attended, Univ. Ctrl. Okla. Former staff mem. to Lt. Gov. Mary Fallin, former dep. chief to, former purchasing agt. to; realtor; mem. Dist. 39 Okla. House of Representatives, 2005—. Republican. Baptist. Mailing: 1105 Columbia Court Edmond OK 73003 Office: 2300 N Lincoln Blvd Rm 409 Oklahoma City OK 73105 Office Phone: 405-557-7342. E-mail: mariancooksey@okhouse.gov.

COOL, BRENDA L., food service executive; Attended, St. Cloud State U., Minn., 1982—87. Structure dist. mgr. Limited Brands, Atlanta, 1993—2003; dist. mgr. The Children's Place, 1999—2003; regional v.p. retail ops. Cracker Barrel Old Country Store, Inc. Office: Cracker Barrel Old Country Store Inc 305 Hartmann Dr Lebanon TN 37088-0787 Office Phone: 615-444-5533. Office Fax: 615-443-9476.

COOLEY, DENTON ARTHUR, surgeon, educator; b. Houston, Aug. 22, 1920; s. Ralph C. and Mary (Fraley) C.; m. Louise Goldsborough Thomas, Jan. 15, 1949; children: Mary, Susan, Louise, Florence, Helen. BA, U. Tex., 1941; MD, Johns Hopkins U., 1944; Doctorem Medicinae (hon.), U. Turin, Italy, 1969; HHD (hon.), Hellenic Coll., 1984, Holy Cross Greek Orthodox Sch. of Theology, 1984; DSc honoris causa, Coll. of William and Mary, 1987. Diplomate: Am. Bd. Surgery, Am. Bd. Thoracic Surgery. Intern Johns Hopkins Sch. Medicine, Balt., 1944-45, resident surgery, 1945-50; sr. surg. registrar thoracic surgery Brompton Hosp. for Chest Diseases, London, 1950-51; assoc. prof. surgery Baylor U. Coll. Medicine, Houston, 1951—62, prof. surgery, 1962-69; clin. prof. surgery U. Tex. Med. Sch., Houston, 1975—; founder, pres. Tex. Heart Inst., 1962—2004, pres. emeritus, 2004—, surgeon-in-chief, 1962—. Chief cardiovascular surgery St. Luke's Episcopal Hosp.; cons., cardiovascular surgery Tex. Children's Hosp. Contbr. articles to profl. jours. Served as capt., M.C., 1946-48. Named one of ten Outstanding Young Men in U.S., U.S. C. of C., 1955, Man of the Yr. award Kappa Sigma, 1964; named Disting. Alumnus U. Tex, John Hopkins U.; recipient Rene Leriche prize Internat. Surg. Soc., 1967, Billings Gold medal Am. Surg. Soc., 1967, Vishnevsky medal Vishnevsky Inst., USSR, 1971, Theodore Roosevelt Award, 1980, Presdl. Medal of Freedom, presented by Pres. Reagan, 1984, Gifted Tchr. award Am. Coll. Cardiology, 1987, Disting. Svc. award AMA, 1997, Nat. Medal of Tech., U.S. Dept Commerce, 1998 Hon. fellow Royal Coll. Physicians and Surgeons of Glasgow, Royal Coll. Surgeons of Ireland, Royal Australasian Coll. Surgeons, Royal Coll. Surgeons of Eng.; mem. ACS, Am. Surg. Assn., Internat. Cardiovascular Soc., Am. Assn. Thoracic Surgery, Soc. Thoracic Surgery, Soc. Univ. Surgeons, Am. Coll. Cardiology, Am. Coll. Chest Physicians, Soc. Clin. Surgery, Soc. Vascular Surgery, Western Surg. Assn., Tex. Surg. Soc., Halsted Soc. Achievements include performance of numerous heart transplants; implanted 1st artificial heart, 1969; first surgeon to successfully remove pulmonary embolisms, squeezing the lungs flat to remove the inaccessible blood clots. Office Phone: 832-355-4932. Business E-Mail: dcooley@heart.thi.tmc.edu.

COOLEY, FANNIE RICHARDSON, counselor, educator; b. Tunnel Springs, Ala., July 4, 1924; d. Willie C. Richardson and Emma Jean (McCorvey) Stallworth. BS, Tuskegee Inst., Ala., 1947, MS, 1951; PhD, U. Wis., 1969. Cert. counselor. Asst. inst. Tuskegee Inst., 1947-48, prof. counseling, 1969-2000, prof. emeritus, 2000—. Instr. Alcorn A&M Coll., Lorman, Miss., 1948-51; asst. prof. Ala. A&M Coll., Normal, 1951-62, assoc. prof., 1964-65; grad. fellow Purdue U., West Lafayette, Ind., 1962-64; house fellow U. Wis., Madison, 1965-69; cons. VA Med. Ctr. Tuskegee, 1969—. Mem. AAUW, AAUP, ASCD (bd. dirs., Disting. Svc. award 1985), Ala. Assn. Counseling and Devel. (pres. 1976-77, Svc. award 1978-79), Ala. Assn. for Counselor Edn. (pres. 1985-86), Aassn. Specialists in Group Work (pres. 1989-90, Career award 1998), Internat. Platford Assn., Chi Sigma Iota. Episcopalian. Office: Tuskegee Inst Coll Liberal Arts and Edn Bioethics Ctr Tuskegee Institute AL 36088 Home: 185 Mountain Oak Dr Wetumpka AL 36093-3907 Business E-Mail: fannie@tuskegee.edu.

COOLIDGE, EDWIN CHANNING, chemistry professor; b. Mt. Vernon, Ohio, Jan. 30, 1925; s. Walter Hatheral and Sarah Helen (Fay) C.; m. Bonita Mae Warner, May 1, 1953; 1 son, Edwin Channing. AB in Chemistry, Kenyon Coll., 1944; PhD, Johns Hopkins, 1949. Research chemist Procter & Gamble Co., Cin., 1949-54; asst. prof. chemistry Hamilton Coll., Clinton, N.Y., 1954-58; asst. prof. N.Mex. Inst. Mining and Tech., Socorro, 1958-61; asso. prof. Stetson U., Deland, Fla., 1961-64, prof. chemistry, 1965-95, prof. emeritus, 1995—; dir. NSF Undergrad. Research Program, Stetson U., 1964-67. Dir. Mid-Fla. Colls. Year Abroad Program, Inc., 1968-69, German dir., 1969-70; Fulbright lectr. Paedagogische Hochschule, Freiburg, Germany, 1982-83 Contbr. articles to profl. jours. Served with AUS, 1950-52. Mem. Am. Chem. Soc., Royal Soc. Chemistry, Phi Beta Kappa, Sigma Xi, Gamma Sigma Epsilon, Omicron Delta Kappa. Episcopalian. Home: 450 N McDonald Ave Apt 16 Deland FL 32724 E-mail: ecoolidg@stetson.edu.

COOLMAN, C. DOUGLAS, landscape architectural firm executive; BS in Landscape Architecture, Mich. State U. With Edward D. Stone, Jr. & Assocs., 1968—, prin., 1974—. Mem.: Am. Soc. Landscape Architecture. Address: 1512 E Broward Blvd Ste 110 Fort Lauderdale FL 33301-2126

COOMER, CHRISTIAN, state legislator; b. Oct. 31; m. Heidi Coomer; children: Christian, Collin. B, Lee U., Cleve., Tenn.; JD, U. Ga. Pvt. practice atty., Bartow County, Ga.; mem. Dist. 14 Ga. House of Representatives, 2011—. JAG USAF, reservist USAFR. Republican. Office: 14 Claire Cove Cartersville GA 30120 also: Georgia House of Reps 404 Coverdel Legis Office Bldg Atlanta GA 30334 Office Phone: 770-383-9171, 404-656-0109. Business E-Mail: christian.coomer@house.ga.gov.

COONS, BARBARA LYNN, public relations executive, librarian; b. Peoria, Ill., June 1, 1948; d. Harold Leroy and Norma (Brauer) C. BA, Stephens Coll., Columbia, Mo., 1970; MA, U. N.C., 1972; MLS, Cath. U., 1982. Rsch. asst. Am. Revolution Bicentennical Office Libr. of Congress, Washington, 1974-76, editl. asst., office of the Asst. Librarian, 1976-78; ednl. liaison specialist Libr. of Congress, Washington, 1978-82; dir. rsch. svc. Gray and Co., Washington, 1982-85, v.p., 1985-86; from v.p., dir. rsch. svcs. to sr. mng. dir. Hill and Knowlton Pub. Affairs Worldwide, Washington, 1986—96; U.S. dir. rsch. svcs. Hill and Knowlton USA, 1996—2004; sr. v.p. media analysis and competitive intelligence Strategy One, Washington, 2004—12; sr. v.p Edelman Berland, 2012—. Pres. Library of Congress Profl. Assn., 1982, adj. prof. Georgetown U. Sch. Continuing Studies, 2008-. Mem. Spl. Libraries Assn., Stephens Coll. Alumnae Club of Greater Washington (pres. 1987). Presbyterian. Home: 709 Arch Hall Ln Alexandria VA 22314-6208 Office Phone: 202-326-1733. E-mail: barbara.coons@edelmanberland.com.

COOPER, ARTHUR WELLS, retired ecologist, educator; b. Washington, Aug. 15, 1931; s. Gustav Arthur and Josephine (Wells) C.; m. Jean Farnsworth, Aug. 30, 1953; children: Paul Arthur, Roy Alan. BA, Colgate U., 1953, MA, 1955; PhD, U. Mich., 1958. Asst. prof. botany N.C. State U., Raleigh, 1958-63, assoc. prof., 1963-68, prof., 1968-71, prof. forestry, 1976—2001, prof. emeritus, 2001—, head dept. forestry, 1980-94, faculty athletics rep., 1990-2001. Asst. sec. N.C. Dept. Natural and Econ. Resources, Raleigh, 1971-76; mem. N.C. Coastal Resources Commn., Raleigh, 1976-89, N.C. Environ. Mgmt. Commn., Raleigh, 1989-91; chmn. Com. Scientists for Nat. Forest Mgmt. Act, Washington, 1977-79, 82, Govs. Task Force on Forest Sustainability, 1995-96; bd. dirs. N.C. Environ. Def. Fund, 1987-90, So. Environ. Law Ctr., 1987-90; pres. Assn. Ret. Faculty, 2009-10, NC State U. Trustee N.C. Nature Conservancy, Chapel Hill, 1977-87; mem. coun. NCAA, 1995-96, mem. Divsn. I mgmt. coun., 1996-2001. Recipient Am. Motors Conservation award, 1972, Sol Feinstone award SUNY Coll. Environ. Sci. and Forestry, Syracuse, 1982, Outstanding Svc. to Forestry award N.C. Forestry Assn., 2002; named Conservationist of Yr., N.C. Wildlife Fedn., 1982. Fellow AAAS, Soc. Am. Foresters (chmn. N.C. divsn. 1984, Appalachian Soc. 1990, Gifford Pinchot medal 1999); mem. Ecol. Soc. Am. (cert. sr. ecologist 1982-2005, v.p. 1974-75, pres. 1980-81, Disting. Svc. award 1984), N.C. Acad. Sci. (pres. 1979). Democrat. Office: NC State U Dept Forestry Raleigh NC 27695-8008 Home: 130 Wee Loch Dr Cary NC 27511-3885 Personal E-mail: awcooper@earthlink.net. Business E-Mail: awcooper@ncsu.edu.

COOPER, AUSTIN MORRIS, chemist, engineer, researcher, consultant; b. Long Beach, Calif., Feb. 1, 1959; s. Merril Morris and Charlotte Madeline (Wittmer) C. BS in Chemistry with honors, Baylor U., 1981; BSChemE with honors, Tex. Tech U., 1983, MSChemE with honors, 1985. Solar energy researcher U.S. Dept. Energy, Lubbock, Tex., 1983-85; advanced mfg. and process engring. mgr. McDonnell Douglas Space Systems Co., Huntington Beach, Calif., 1986-87, chem.-process line mgr., 1987-89, prin. material and process engr., 1999—. Contbr. articles to profl. jours. Mem. AIChE, Am. Chem. Soc., Soc. Advancement of Materials and Process Engrs., SCV, SAR, Sigma Xi, Omega Chi Epsilon, Kappa Mu Epsilon, Beta Beta Beta.

COOPER, BARBARA LEE WARD, state legislator; b. Memphis, Aug. 4, 1929; d. Elisha and Mattie Belle Rogers Ward; m. John David Cooper, 1951; children: Carl, Joan, Wallace Burnett, Tanya. Former prodr. Parents Want To Know, Wqox TV, Channel 30; house rep. Tenn.; elem sch. tchr. Memphis City Sch., 1950—94; dir. SW Area Cmty. Rels., 1970—80; supr. compensory edn., 1980—86; parent coord., 1980—86; instr. study skills Shelby State CC, 1986—88, St. Augustine Sch., 1988—94; instr. Adult Basic Edn. & Ged, 1994—; state rep. Dist. 86 Tenn., 1997—; mem. Edn. Com., Govt. Opers

Com., Higher Edn. & Consumer Affairs Subcom.; writer, advisor Cmty. Dist. 86 Newspaper. Recipient Svc. award, Urban League, 1980, Regional Conf. award, Chpt. 1, 1988, Svc. award, St. Augustine Sch., 1990, Manasses HS, 1997; named one of Tchr. of Yr., Memphis City Sch., 1969. Mem.: NAACP (co-gov. 1986), Tenn. State U. Alumni Orgn., Universal African America People's Orgn. (program chmn. 1986). Democrat. Roman Catholic. Office: 99 North Main St, #2105 Memphis TN 38103 also: 38 Legislative Plz Nashville TN 37243-0186 Office Phone: 901-578-7002, 615-741-4295. Office Fax: 615-253-0327. Business E-Mail: rep.barbara.cooper@capitol.tn.gov.

COOPER, CARL WADE, lawyer; b. Huntsville, Ala., June 1, 1957; s. Erwin E. and Margery A. (Waters) C.; m. Catherine Ann Farlow, Sept. 17, 1983; children: Caroline, Ryan, Brooke, Marshall. BA in Polit. Sci., BS in Econs., So. Meth. U., 1978; JD, U. Tex., Austin, 1981. Bar: Tex. 1981, US Dist. Ct. (no. dist.) Tex. 1981, US Dist. Ct. (we. dist.) Tex. 1986, US Dist. Ct. (so. dist.) Tex. 1987, US Ct. Appeals (5th cir.) 1992, US Dist. Ct. (ea. dist.) Tex. 1994. Joined Jackson Walker, LLP, Dallas, 1981, mng. ptnr. Austin office, 2006—10, mng. ptnr. of firm, 2010—. Bd. mem. capitol area coun. Boy Scouts America, chmn. Bee Cave dist.; bd. dirs. Downtown Austin Alliance, 2002—03, past chmn., mem. adv. bd.; bd. dirs. Envision Ctrl. Tex., chair, 2002—04; mem. CAMPO Transit Working Group. Recipient Individual IMPACT award, Downtown Austin Alliance, 2008; named a Super Lawyer, Thomson Reuters, 2003—04, 2008—10; named one of Best Lawyers in America, Bankruptcy and Creditor-Debtor Rights Law, 2008—11. Fellow: Tex. Bar Found. (life); mem.: ABA, State Bar Tex., Travis County Bar Assn., Am. Bankruptcy Inst. Republican. Office: Jackson Walker LLP Ste 1100 100 Congress Ave Austin TX 78701-4042 Office Phone: 512-236-2220. Office Fax: 512-391-2108. Business E-Mail: wcooper@jw.com.

COOPER, CARLOTTA ARLENE, writer, animal breeder; b. Jasper, Tenn., Feb. 21, 1962; d. Carl Otis and Betty Charlsie MacNabb Cooper; life ptnr. Desterie Shane Grimes; 1 child, Orion Hunter Grimes. B, U. South, Sewanee, 1984. Programming dir. Miller Plz., Chattanooga, 1987—89, exec. dir., 1989—91; writer Blue Cross and Blue Shield Tenn., Chattanooga, 1993—95; writer, columnist Dog News and other nat. mag., NYC, 1996—; writer TriCities.com, Media Gen., Bristol, Va., 2004—06. Showdog owner, breeder, handler Hever English Setters, Kingsport, Tenn., 1987—; adj. prof. Va. Intermont Coll., Bristol, 2004—. Author: (making your home safe from puppies) Puppy-Proofing Your Home; contbr. articles to profl. jours. Recipient Guerryaward, U. South, 1984; fellow, U. Va., 1985—87; scholar, U. South, 1983; Wilkins scholar, 1991—94. Mem.: English Setter Assn. Am. (Previous awards for my dogs include awards as best bred by exhibitor, best puppy 1997, 1998, 1999), Ctrl. Carolina English Setter Club, Phi Beta Kappa. D-Liberal. Episcopalian. Avocations: dogs, horses, history, literature, photography. Office: Virginia Intermont Coll 1013 Moore St Bristol VA 24201 Home: 1902 W Main St Greeneville TN 37743-4421 E-mail: carlottacooper@vic.edu.

COOPER, CARRIE, library director; B in Elem. Edn., Fla. State U., Tallahassee, 1992; MA in Libr. and Informational Svcs., U. So. Miss., Hattiesburg, 1997. Former 4th & 5th grade tchr. and HS libr., Fla.; team leader of Learning Resources Ea. Ky. U. Crabbe Libr., 1998—2002, coord. of rsch. and instrn., 2002—05, interim dean libraries, 2005—06, dean, 2006—11; dean univ. libraries William and Mary U., 2011—. Grantee HW Wilson Profl. Devel. Grant, ALA, 2000. Office: College of William and Mary Swem Library PO Box 8795 Williamsburg VA 23187-8795 Office Phone: 757-221-3055. Business E-Mail: clcooper@wm.edu.

COOPER, CHARLES G., state banking agency administrator; married; 2 children. BBA in Fin. and Econs., Baylor U., Waco, Tex.; grad. degree in Banking, Southern Meth. U., Dallas. Cert. advanced peace officer. With FDIC, 1970—82, bank examiner Houston, 1970, rev. examiner, field office supr. Houston NE Field Office; sr. v.p. Allied Bancshares, Houston; exec. v.p. Team Bank, Ft. Worth; chief credit officer Bank North Tex., Hurst; sr. v.p. loan adminstrn. Compass Bank, Dallas; exec. v.p., chief credit officer Lone Star Bank, Dallas; chief credit officer to pres., CEO Bay View Bank and Bay View Capital Corp., San Mateo, Calif., 2001; mem. bd., mem. exec. com. Gt. Lakes Bancorp (after merger with Bay View), Buffalo, 2006—08; sr. adviser strategic transitions Diamond A - Ford Corp., Dallas, 2008; commr. Tex. Dept. Banking, Austin, 2008—. Bd. mem. Ft. Worth Stock Show Syndicate, 1990; mem. Youth Livestock Auction Com. State Fair Tex., 2005. Office: Texas Department of Banking 2601 N Lamar Blvd Austin TX 78705-4294 Office Phone: 877-276-5554. Office Fax: 512-475-1313. E-mail: charles.cooper@banking.state.tx.us.

COOPER, CHARLES HOWARD, retired photojournalist, publishing executive; b. Clinton, NC, July 17, 1920; s. John Howard and Ella Jane (Bass) C.; m. Nell Elizabeth Slaughter, Jan. 2, 1943; children: Charles Howard II, John Phillip. Grad., U.S. Air Force Sch. Photography, 1943. Chief photographer, mgr. photo dept. Durham Herald Co. (N.C.), 1945-85; pub. Durham Morning Herald, 1945, Durham Sun, 1945-85. Chmn. Miss Nat. Press Photographer Pageant, 1952, 53, 55 Mem. Citizens Safety Com., Durham, 1961-71. Served with USAAF, 1942-45, ETO. Mem. Nat. Press Photographers Assn. (life, exec. dir. 1963-2000, exec. dir. emeritus 2001—, Fellowship award, Joseph A. Sprague award 1961, Pres.'s medal 1964, 67, 2001, Merit award 1965, Joseph Costa award 1977, exec. dir. emeritus 1998, interim exec. dir. 2001), Carolinas Press Photographers Assn. (life, pres. 1952-54) Democrat. Baptist. Home Phone: 919-489-3700. Personal E-mail: chcscoop@verizon.net. Business E-Mail: chc@verizon.net.

COOPER, CLARENCE, federal judge; b. Decatur, Ga., 1942; BA, Clark Coll., 1964; JD, Emory U., 1967; MPA, Harvard U., 1978. Atty. Atlanta Legal Aid Soc., 1967; asst. dist. atty. Fulton County, 1968-75; judge City of Atlanta Mcpl. Ct., 1975-80, Fulton County Superior Ct., 1980-90, Ga. Ct. Appeals, 1990-93, US Dist. Ct. (no. dist.) Ga., Atlanta, 1994—2009, sr. judge, 2009—. Co-chair Supreme Ct. Commn. Racial & Ethnic Bias in Ct. Sys. Mem. adv. com. Internat. Friendship Force; active Butler St. YMCA, Atlanta Conv. and Visitors Bur., 100 Black Men of Atlanta, Ga. Health Decisions. With U.S. Army, 1968-70. Decorated Bronze Star; recipient Al Thompson Award for Cmty. Svc., Thurgood Marshall award, Outstanding Jurist, 1974. Mem. ABA, NAACP, Nat. Bar Assn., State Bar Ga., Atlanta Bar Assn., Fed. Bar Assn., Gate City Bar Assn., Omega Phi Psi (Omega Man of Yr. award 1991), Kappa Boule, Lawyers Club Atlanta, Old Warhorse Lawyer's Club. Office: Richard B Russell Fed Bldg 1701 US Courthouse 75 Spring St SW Atlanta GA 30303-3309

COOPER, CYNTHIA F., consulting firm executive, accountant; b. Clinton, Miss., 1964; m. Lance L. Cooper; 2 children. BS in Acctg., Miss. State U.; MS, U. Ala. CPA, cert. Info. Sys. Auditor, Fraud Examiner. Accountant PricewaterhouseCoopers, Deloitte & Touche; v.p. internal audit WorldCom (now MCI), chief audit exec.; pres. Cynthia Cooper Consulting, LLC, 2004—. Past mem. accounting adv. bd. U. Ala.; mem. internal auditing adv. bd. La. State U. Author: Extraordinary Circumstances: The Journey of a Corporate Whistleblower, 2008. Recipient Accounting Exemplar Award, 2003, Maria & Sidney E. Rolfe Award, Women's Econ. Round Table, 2003; named one of The People of Yr., TIME mag., 2002; named to Am. Inst. Certified Pub. Acct. Hall of Fame, 2004. Mem.: Assn. of Certified Fraud Examiners, Inst. Internal Auditors, Info. Sys. Audit and Control Assn., Am. Inst. CPAs. Office Phone: 601-919-0916.

COOPER, DONALD LEE, physician; b. Columbus, Kans., Aug. 11, 1928; s. Calvin M. and J. Pearl (Mullen) C.; m. Dona Faye Maddux, June 4, 1950; children: Donald Lee, Catherine Susan, Cheryl Lyn, Tad Houston. AB, Pittsburg State U., 1949; MD, U. Kans., 1953. Intern St. Mary's and Childrens Mercy hosps., Kansas City, Mo., 1953-54; pvt. practice medicine Manhattan, Kans., 1956-57; team physician, asst. dir. Health Center Kans. State U., 1957-60; dir. health service, team physician Okla. State U. Hosp. and Clinic, Stillwater, 1960-90, dir. athletic medicine, 1990-98, emeritus dir., 1998—. Vis. lectr. divsn. sportsmedicine, dept. orthopedic surgery Coll. Medicine U. Okla. Health Scis. Ctr., 1974—; liaison officer Am. Coll. Health Assn. to Nat. Athletic Trainers Assn., 1963—; Am. chmn. 1st Am.-Soviet Conf. on Student Health, Moscow, Russia, 1967; team physician U.S. Olympic Team, 1967-68; mem. Pres.'s Coun. Phys. Fitness and Sports, 1981-92, del. to Moscow to rev. phys. culture and olympic tng. sites in Russia, 1989; team physician U.S. Deaf Olympic Team, LA, 1985; elected chmn. Joint Commn. on Competitive Safeguards and Med. Aspects of Sports, 1986. Author: (with others) Standard Nomenclature of Athletic Injuries, 1966; Contbr. (with others) articles med. jours. Served to capt. USAF, 1954-56. Recipient Pres.'s Challenge Sportsmedicine award Nat. Athletic Trainers Assn., 1974, Bill Coltrin Meml. award Western Athletic Conf. Sports Writers Assn., 1974, Edward Hitchcock award Am. Coll. Health Assn., 1975; named among 10 healthy American fitness leaders Nat. Jaycees, Pres.'s Coun. on Physical Fitness and Sports, Allstate Ins. Co., 1995; inductee Okla. Hall of Fame, 1998. Mem. AMA (chmn. com. med. aspects sports 1971-76, chmn. 1976-77, mem. coun. sci. affairs 1976-79), Nat. Collegiate Athletic Assn. (med. cons. to football rules com. 1969-75), Am. Coll. Health Assn. (past pres., exec. com.), Southwestern Coll. Health Assn. (past pres.), Nat. Athletic Trainers Assn., Alpha Omega Alpha, Nu Sigma Nu. Presbyterian (elder 1971—). Club: Lion. Office: Okla State U Hosp & Clinic 1202 Farm Rd Stillwater OK 74078-0001 Home: 5505 W 19th Ave # 212 Stillwater OK 74074-1323 Office Phone: 405-744-7031. Office Fax: 405-744-6556.

COOPER, EUGENE BRUCE, speech pathology/audiology services professional, educator; b. Utica, NY, Dec. 20, 1933; s. Clements Everett and Beulah (Wetzel) C.; m. Crystal Silverman, Sept. 12, 1965; children: Philip Adam, Ivan Bruce. BS, SUNY, Geneseo, 1955; MEd, Pa. State U., 1957, DEd, 1962. Pathologist speech and lang. Franklin County Schs., Chambersburg, Pa., 1957-59; asst. prof. Ohio U., 1962-64, Pa. State U., 1964-66; program specialist U.S. Office Edn., 1966; exec. sec. sensory study sect., rsch. and demonstrations Rehab. Services Adminstrn., HEW, Washington, 1966-67; faculty U. Ala., Tuscaloosa, 1967-96, prof. speech-lang. pathology, 1969-96, chmn. dept. communicative disorders, dir. Speech and Hearing Ctr., 1967-96, prof., chair emeritus, 1996—; Disting. prof. comm. scis. and disorders Nova Southeastern U., 1997—2009. Chmn. Ala. Bd. Examiners Speech Pathology and Audiology, 1979; cons.-at-large Nat. Student Speech-Lang.-Hearing Assn., 1983-88. Author: Personalized Fluency Control Therapy, 1976, Understanding Stuttering: Information for Parents, 1979, revised edit., 1990; (with Crystal Cooper) The Cooper Personalized Fluency Control Therapy Program, 1985, 2d edit., 2003, Cooper Assessment for Stuttering Syndromes, 1995; contbr. articles to profl. jours. Fellow Am. Speech, Lang. and Hearing Assn. (legis. coun. 1971-72, 85-97), Divsn. Fluency and Fluency Disorders (steering com. 1993-99, divsn. coord. 1994-99), Am. Speech, Lang. and Hearing Found. (chmn. adv. and devel. bd. 1988-89, trustee 1989-94); mem. Coun. Exceptional Children (pres. divsn. children comm. disorders 1975-76), Nat. Coun. Grad. Programs in Speech, Lang. Pathology and Audiology (pres. 1978-80), Nat. Coun. State Bds. Examiners Speech-Lang. Pathology and Audiology (pres. 1980, 91, mem. exec. bd. 1988-91), Nat. Coun. Comm. Disorders (chmn. 1982), Nat. Alliance Prevention and Treatment on Stuttering (pres. 1985-86), Internat. Fluency Assn. (bd. dirs. 1991-96, pres. 2d world congress on fluency disorders 1997, chmn. specialty commn. on fluency disorders 1997-99). Office Phone: 954-385-1422. Personal E-mail: ebcooper@aol.com.

COOPER, GRANT, composer, conductor, educator; b. Wellington, New Zealand; Degree in Pure Math., U. Auckland; fellow in trumpet study with Gerard Schwarz. Artistic dir. 2 summer festivals Bach and Beyond Festival, Anchorage Festival of Music in Alaska; commd. composer Cayuga Chamber Orch., Coloratura Soprano, Rap Singer; music dir. Fredonia Chamber Players, 1983—89, Penfield Symphony Orch., 1993—99; assoc. conductor Syracuse Symphony Orch., 1997, resident conductor, 2001—; artistic dir., composer, conductor W.Va. Symphony Orch., 2001—. Guest conductor Cayuga Chamber Orch., Philharmonic Orchs. Buffalo and Rochester, XIVth Commonwealth Games closing ceremonies, Mozart Wochen Heidelberger Schlossfestspiele; prof. music, dir. orchs. Ithaca Coll. Sch. Music, 1993—2003. Conductor (appearances) Syracuse Symphony Orch., conductor Skaneateles Fest., Spokane Symphony, Erie Philharmonic, Kansas City Symphony, millenium celebration with Auckland Philharmonia, (recordings) Delos Internat., Atoll, Ode, Mark, Kiwi Pacific, conductor (CD) premier recordings string music New Zealand composer, Douglas Lilburn, Points in a Changing Circle. Fellow Fund for Arts, Chautauqua County. Office: WV Symphony Orch PO Box 2292 Charleston WV 25328

COOPER, JAMES HAYES SHOFNER (JIM COOPER), United States Representative from Tennessee, lawyer; b. Nashville, June 19, 1954; s. William Prentice Jr. and Hortense (Powell) Cooper; m. Martha Bryan Hays, 1985; children: Mary Argentine Adams, John James Audubon, Hayes Hightower. BA in History and Economics, U. NC, Chapel Hill, 1975; BA, MA in Politics and Economics, Oxford U., 1977; JD, Harvard Law Sch., 1980. Atty. Waller, Lansden, Dortch & Davis, Nashville, 1980-82; mem. US Congress from 4th Tenn. dist., 1983—95; mng. dir. Equitable Securities Corp., Nashville, 1995-99; co-founder, ptnr., chmn. bd. dirs. Brentwood Capital Advs. LLC, Nashville, 1999—2002; mem. US Congress from 5th Tenn. dist., 2003—. Adj. prof. Vanderbilt U. Owen Sch. Mgmt., Nashville, 1995—. Morehead-Cain scholar, 1972, Rhodes scholar, 1975. Mem.: Phi Beta Kappa. Democrat. Episcopalian. Mailing: US House of Representatives 1536 Longworth House Office Bldg Washington DC 20515-1535 Office: Congressman Jim Cooper 1536 Longworth Hob Washington DC 20515-4205 Office Phone: 202-225-4311. E-mail: jim.cooper@owen.vanderbilt.edu.*

COOPER, JAMES MICHAEL, education educator; b. Steubenville, Ohio, July 29, 1939; s. James Stanley and Regina Marie (Coen) C.; m. Susan Callaway, Sept. 1, 1962 (div. June 1978); children: Jeffrey, Craig, Cynthia; m. Shamim Sisson, June 13, 1987. AB in History with distinction, Stanford U., 1961, AM in Edn., 1962, AM in History, 1966, PhD in Edn., 1967. Tchr. Jordan Jr. High Sch. of Palo Alto (Calif.) Unified Sch. Sys., 1961-63, Palo Alto High Sch., 1963-65; lectr. Stanford U. Sch. Edn., 1967; asst. prof. edn. U. Mass., Amherst, 1968-71; assoc. prof. U. Houston, 1971-74, prof., 1974-84; Commonwealth prof. U. Va. Curry Sch. Edn., Charlottesville, 1984—2004, dean, 1984-94, prof. emeritus, 2004—. Chmn. U. Houston faculty senate, 1982; exec. bd. dirs. Holmes Group, East Lansing, Mich., 1985-94; unit accreditation bd. Nat. Coun. Accreditation of Tchr. Edn., Washington, 1986-90 Co-author: Those Who Can, Teach, 11th edit., 2007; editor: Developing Skills for Instructional Supervision, 1984, Classroom Teaching Skills, 8th edit., 2006; co-editor: Kaleidoscope: Readings in Education, 11th edit., 2007. Recipient Florence B. Stratemeyer award Assn. for Student Teaching, Washington, 1967, Fulbright-Hays award Portugal Coun. Internat. Exch. Scholars, Washington, 1980, Outstanding Leader in Tchr. Edn. award Assn. Tchr. Educators, 1990. Mem.: ASCD, Raven Soc. (The Raven award 2001), Am. Assn. Colls. for Tchr. Edn. (bd. dirs. 1990—93), Am. Edml. Rsch. Assn., Omicron Delta Kappa, Phi Delta Kappa. Democrat. Roman Catholic. Avocations: golf, travel. Office Phone: 434-977-5216. Business E-Mail: jimcooper@virginia.edu.

COOPER, JAMES NELSON, medical educator; b. SI, Aug. 6, 1938; s. Charles Sylvester and Ella (Sabine) C.; m. Carolyn Olverson; children: John Emerson, Charles Key, James Ashley, Catherine Quesenberry. BA, Columbia U., 1959; MD, NYU, 1963. Diplomate Am. Bd. Internal Medicine and Gastroenterology. Intern Georgetown U., Washington, 1963-65; resident Boston City Hosp., 1965-66; fellow gastroenterology U. Chgo., 1966-68; clin. assoc. prof. medicine Georgetown U., Washington, 1977-83, prof. medicine, 1983—2007, asst. dean Sch. Medicine, 1985—2005, dir. transitional residency program, 1985—2001; pres. med. staff Fairfax Hosp., Falls Church, Va., 1975-77, chief gastroenterology, 1971—82, chmn. dept. medicine, 1982—2005; prof. George Mason U., Fairfax, 2006—, dir. med. rsch. devel., 2006—; prof. medicine Va. Commonwealth U. Sch. Medicine, Richmond, 2003—05. Cons. State Dept., Washington, 1970—74; dir. Inova Instn. Rsch. and Edn., 1991—2005; chmn. bd. dirs. Theranostics Health, Rockville, Md., 2007—, CEO, 2007—08. Editor: Gastointestinal and Hepatic Complications In Pregnancy, 1986. Served to maj. USAR, 1964-71. Fellow ACP (Laureate award 1997), ACG; mem. Am. Gastroent. Assn., Am. Assn. Study Liver Diseases, No. Va. Acad. Internal Medicine (pres. 1975), Cosmos Club, Sigma Xi. Office: 10900 University Blvd MS6E3 Manassas VA 22010 Business E-Mail: jcoopera@gmu.edu.

COOPER, JAMES RUSSELL, retired law educator; b. New Kensington, Pa., July 21, 1928; s. John Edward and Isabella Bird (Bowen) C.; m. Carolyn Hocker, Sept. 21, 1953 (div. Dec. 1975); children: L. Rachel, Julia Anderoni, Evan Lloyd, Jennifer Meyer; m. Leigh Ann Brian, Feb. 25, 1995 (div. Nov. 1999). BS in Econs., U. Pa., Phila., 1952, JD, 1955. Bar: D.C., 1955, U.S. Supreme Ct., 1964; ordained to ministry Universal Brotherhood Movement, Inc., Founder Pastor Meeting House for Aspiring Spirits, ARC Internet Ch. Pres., chmn. Radio WKPA-AM, WYDD-FM, New Kensington, 1959-64; urban renewal dir. Redevelopment Authority, New Kensington, 1964-68; assoc. prof. U. Ill., Champaign-Urbana, 1968-74; prof. legal studies Ga. State U., Atlanta, 1974-94, emeritus prof., 1994—. Author: Twilights Last Gleaming, 1992, Real Estate Investments, 3d edit. 1992, Meeting House for Aspiring Spirits, 2008, Modern Codex of Meeting House for Aspiring Spirits-Heirloom edit., 2009, Connect with Occupy wall Street Ows. Org Now Pamphlet, 2012. Sgt. U.S. Army, 1946-48. Mem. Fed. Bar Assn., D.C. Bar Assn., Am. Real Estate Soc. (founder, dir.). Achievements include creator of website, www.spiritsmeetinghouse. Office Phone: 828-707-7705, 838-283-1511. Personal E-mail: jrc@spiritsmeetinghouse.com.

COOPER, JERRY W., state legislator; b. McMinnville, Tenn., Aug. 6, 1948; m. Lisa Cooper; children: Elisa Lee, Sally Denice, Faith Rae, Holly. Mem. Mfg. Mgmt. Program Gen. Electric, 1970—73; co-founder Cooper Mfg. Inc.; state senator Dist. 14 Tenn., 2005—. Named Outstanding Young Man of Tenn., 1977, Young Man of Yr., McMinnville, 1981, Tenn. Small Businessman of Yr., US Small Bus. Adminstrn., 1983, Outstanding Senator of Yr., Tenn. Forestry Assn., 1992, Tenn. Assn. Home Care, 1997. Mem.: Jaycees (McMinnville) (former pres.), Tenn. Tech. Found., Nat. Assn. Mfrs., Nat. Fed. Ind. Bus., Jaycees (Tenn.) (pres. 1980—81). Democrat. Baptist. Mailing: PO Box 137 Smartt TN 37378 Home: 175 Faith Rae Blvd Morrison TN 37357-6515 Office Phone: 615-741-6694. E-mail: sen.jerry.cooper@legislature.state.tn.us.

COOPER, JON, professional hockey coach; b. Prince George, BC, Canada, Aug. 23, 1967; m. Jessie Cooper; children: Julia, Josephine, Jonathan. Degree in business adminstrn., Hofstra U. Head coach, gen. mgr. St. Louis Bandits (formerly Texarkana Bandits) (NAHL), 2003—08; head coach Green Bay Gamblers (USHL), 2008—10, Norfolk Admirals (AHL), 2010—12, Syracuse Crunch (AHL), 2012—13, Tampa Bay Lightning, 2013—. Recipient Louis A.R. Pieri Meml. award for Outstanding Head Coach, AHL, 2012. Achievements include winning the Robertson Cup Championship as coach of the St. Louis Bandits, 2007, 2008, named Coach of Yr. 2 times; winning 2 Anderson Cup Championships as coach of the Green Bay Gamblers, 2008-10; winning the Calder Cup as coach of the Norfolk Admirals, 2011-12. Office: Tampa Bay Lightning Hockey Club St Pete Times Forum 401 Channelside Dr Tampa FL 33602

COOPER, JUDITH KASE, retired theater educator, playwright; b. Wilmington, Del., Dec. 13, 1932; d. Charles Robert and Elizabeth Edna (Baker) Kase; stepchildren: James, Elizabeth, John, Katherine, Ann, Patty, Doreen, Jeff. BA, U. Del., 1955; MA, Case Western Res. U., 1956. Tchr., dir. theatre Agnes Scott Coll., 1956, U. Tenn., 1957, U. Md., Germany, 1958—60, Denver Civic Theatre, Denver U., Kent Sch., 1960—61; dir. children's theatre U. N.H., Durham, 1962-69; dir. theatre resources for youth Somersworth, NH, 1966-69; assoc. prof. theatre U. South Fla., Tampa, 1969-74, assoc. prof. edn., 1975-83, prof., 1984—99, artistic dir. ednl. theatre, 1976—99, ret., 1999. Project dir. Hillsborough County Artists-in-Schs. Evaluation and Inservice Project, 1980—82; dir. Internat. Ctr. for Studies in Theatre Edn.; mem. Nat. Theatre Conf., Coll. Fellows Am. Theatre. Author: The Creative Drama Book: Three Approaches, other books; editor: Creative Drama in a Developmental Context; Children's Theatre, Creative Drama and Learning, Drama as a Meaning Maker, Introduction to Drama Teacher Resource Guide, Interconnecting Pathways to Human Experience, Teaching the Arts Across the Disciplines; contbr. articles to profl. jours.; pub. (plays) Snow White and The Seven Dwarfs, 1960, The Emperor's New Clothes, 1966, Southern Fried Cracker Tales, 1995. Bd. dirs. Fla. Alliance for Arts Edn., sec., 1976-77, vice-chmn., 1979-82, chmn., 1982-84; chmn. Wingspread Conf. on Theatre Edn., 1977; drama adjudicator Nat. Arts Festival, Ministry of Edn., Bahamas, 1975, 76, 79, 80; regional chmn. Alliance for Arts Edn., chmn. nat. adv. coun., mem. edn. adv. com., 1986—; trustee Children's Theatre Found.; bd. dirs. Coll. Fellows Am. Theatre of J.F. Kennedy Ctr. for Performing Arts, 1991-93, Fla. Assoc. Theatre Ed., exec. dir. 1995-99, Coll. Bus., 1993—; cons. S.E. Ctr. for Edn. in Theatre, 1995, Fla. Dept. Edn., 1994-96; cons. theatre edn. and prodn.; steering com. Arts for a Complete Edn., 1991-92; mem. curriculum writing com. Fla. Dept. Edn., 1994-96; active St. Marks Episcopal Parish, Tampa; lector, Bridge Club, Tampa Coterie, 2010-, Inter AAUW, 2012 Recipient Disting. Book of Yr. award, Am. Alliance for Theatre and Edn., 1989, Arts Recognition award, Arts Coun. Hillsborough County, 1995, Judith Kase Cooper Sr. Rsch. award, Am. Alliance for Theatre & Edn. Mem. Children's Theatre Assn. Am. (pres.-elect 1975-77, pres. 1977-79, chmn. symposia 1981-85, spl. recognition citation 1984), Am. Theatre Assn. (chief divsn. pres.'s coordinating coun. 1977-78, commn. on theatre edn. 1982—, elected), Am. Alliance for Theatre and Edn. (dir. and project dir. theatre literacy collaborative study Internat. Ctr. for Studies in Theatre Edn., Presdl. award 1992), Speech Comm. Assn. (membership dir. 1961), Southeastern Theatre Confs. (Sara Spencer award 1980), Fla. Theatre Confs. (Disting. Career award), Nat. Theatre Conf., Internat. Assn. Theatres for Children and Youth, Internat. Amateur Theatre Assn. (N.Am. bd. dirs.), Fla. Assn. for Theater Edn. (Theatre Edn. of Yr. award 1986, exec. dir. 1994-99), Arts Coun. Hillsborough County (Arts Recognition award), Children's Theatre Found. Am. (trustee 1977-), Tampa Mus., Coterie Club. Republican. Episcopalian.

COOPER, KATHLEEN BELL, senior fellow, dean, former federal agency administrator; b. Dallas, Feb. 3, 1945; d. Patrick Joseph and Ferne Elizabeth (McDougle) Bell; m. Ronald James Cooper, Feb. 6, 1965; children: Michael, Christopher. BA in Math. with honors, U. Tex., Arlington, 1970, MA in Econs, 1971; PhD in Econs, U. Colo., 1980. Research asst. econs. dept. U. Tex., Arlington, 1970-71; corp. economist United Banks of Colo., Denver, 1971-79, chief economist, 1980-81; v.p., sr. fin. economist Security Pacific Nat. Bank, Los Angeles, 1981-83, 1st v.p., sr. economist, 1983-85, sr. v.p., economist, 1985-86, sr. v.p., chief economist, 1986-87, exec. v.p., chief economist, 1988-90; chief economist Exxon Corp., Irving, Tex., 1990-99, chief economist, mgr. econs. & energy divsn. corp. planning, 1999-2001; under sec. for econ. affairs & statistics adminstrn. US Dept. Commerce, Washington, 2001—05; dean Coll. Bus. Adminstrn. U. N. Tex., Denton, 2005—07; sr. fellow, pub. policy John G. Tower Ctr., Southern Methodist U., 2007—. Bd. dirs. The Williams Companies, Inc., 2006—, Texas Security Bank, 2008—10. Trustee Scripps Coll., 1987-1999, 2006-, Com. for Econ. Devel.1993-2001, 2006-10; mem. Coun. on Fgn. Rels., Internat. Women's Forum. Mem. Nat. Assn. Bus. Economics (past pres. Denver and L.A. chpts.; bd. dirs. 1975-78, pres. 1985-86), Nat. Bur. Econ. Rsch. (bd. dirs. 1987-2001, 05-, vice chair 2008-10), Am. Bankers Assn. (econ. adv. com. 1979-81, 86-90, chmn. 1989-90), U.S. Assn. Energy Econs. (pres. 1996), Am. Econ. Assn., Conf. Bus. Economists.

COOPER, KEITH D., computer science and engineering educator; BS, Rice U., Houston, 1978, MA, 1982, PhD, 1983. Faculty Rice U., 1983—, chmn. dept. computer sci., 2002—08, L. John & Ann H. Doerr chair computational engring., prof. computer sci., elec. and computer engring. Mem. acad. planning and coordination com. Los Alamos Computer Sci. Inst., Houston. Co-author (with Linda Torczon): Engineering Compiler, 2003; contbr. articles to numerous profl. jours. Fellow: Assn. Computing Machinery. Office: Rice U Dept Computer Sci Duncan Hall 2065 6100 S Main St Houston TX 77251-1892 Office Phone: 713-348-6013. Business E-Mail: keith@rice.edu.

COOPER, LAWRENCE ALLEN, lawyer; b. San Antonio, Feb. 1, 1948; s. Elmer E. and Sally (Tempkin) C.; 1 child, Jonathan Alexander. BA, Tulane U., 1970; JD, St. Mary's U., San Antonio, 1974; LLM, Emory U., 1980. Bar: Ga. 1975, Tex. 1975. Atty. pvt. practice, Atlanta, 1975—. Freelance arbitrator and meditator. Named one of Ga. Super Lawyers, 2009—13. Mem.: ABA, Atlanta Bar Assn., Cobb County Bar Assn., Ga. Trial Lawyers Assn., Southern Trial Lawyers Assn., Ga. Bar Assn., Tex. Bar Assn. Home: 660 Willow Knoll Dr Marietta GA 30067-4682 Office: Cohen Cooper Estep & Allen LLC Ste 600 3330 Cumberland Blvd Atlanta GA 30339 Office Phone: 404-814-0000 206. Personal E-mail: lacooperatty@mindspring.com.*

COOPER, N. LEE, lawyer; m. Joy Clark; children: Clark, Catherine. BS, U. Ala., 1963, LLB, 1964. Pvt. practice, Birmingham, Ala., 1966—; founder Maynard, Cooper & Gale, P.C., Birmingham. Vice chair U.S. Congl. Commn. on Structural Alternatives for the Fed. Cts. of Appeals; dir. Lawyers Com. for Civil Rights. Articles and Notes editor Ala. Law Rev., 1962-64. Nat. bd. dirs. U. Ala.; trustee Ala. Law Sch. Found.; bd. overseers Rand Inst. for Civil Justice. 1st lt. U.S. Army, 1964-66, capt. USAR. Fellow Am. Bar Found.; mem. ABA (chair, litig. sect. 1985-86, sec. litig. sect. 1976-78, Birmingham bar del. to ho. of deps. 1979-80, Ala. del. to ho. of dels. 1980-89, mem. drafting com. on model rules of profl. conduct 1982-84, mem. commn. on professionalism 1985-87, chair select com. on ho. of dels. 1989-90, chair ho. of dels. 1990-92, pres.-elect 1995-96, pres. 1996-97, chair Katrina task force 2005-06), Am. Judicature Soc. (dir.), Am. Bar Endowment (dir.), Am. Law Inst. (coun., advisor project on restatement of law governing lawyers), Ala. Bar Assn. (pres. young lawyers sect. 1974-75, Merit award 1976), Birmingham Bar Assn. (sec.-treas. 1972). Office: Regions Harbert Plz 1901 6th Ave N Ste 2400 Birmingham AL 35203-4604

COOPER, ROBERT ELBERT, state supreme court justice; b. Chattanooga, Oct. 14, 1920; s. John Thurman and Susie Inez (Hollingsworth) C.; m. Catherine Pauline Kelly, Nov. 24, 1949; children: Susan Florence Cooper Hodges, Bobbie Cooper Martin, Kelly Ann Smith, Robert Elbert Jr. BA, U. N.C., 1946; JD, Vanderbilt U., 1949. Bar: Tenn. 1948. Assoc. Kolwyck and Clark, 1949-51; ptnr. Cooper and Barger, 1951-53; asst. atty. gen. 6th Jud. Ct. Tenn., 1951-53; judge 6th Jud. Circuit Tenn., 1953-60, Tenn. Ct. Appeals, 1960-70, presiding judge Eastern divsn., 1970-74; justice Tenn. Supreme Ct., 1974-90, chief justice, 1976-77, 84-85. Chmn. Tenn. Jud. Coun., 1967-90; chmn. Tenn. Code Commn., 1976-77, 84-85; mem. Tenn. Jud. Standards Commn., 1971-77. Mem. exec. bd. Cherokee coun. Boy Scouts Am., 1960-64; bd. dirs. Met. YMCA, 1956-65, St. Barnabas Nursing Home and Apts. for Aged, 1966-69. With USNR, 1941-46. Recipient Nat. Heritage award Downtown Sertoma Club, Chattanooga, 1989. Mem. Am., Tenn., Chattanooga bar assns., Conf. Chief Justices, Phi Beta Kappa, Order of Coif, Kappa Sigma, Phi Alpha Delta. Clubs: Signal Mountain Golf and Country, Masons (33 deg.), Shriners. Democrat. Presbyterian. Home and Office: 196 Woodcliff Cir Signal Mountain TN 37377-3147

COOPER, ROBERT ELBERT, JR., state attorney general; b. Chattanooga, Jan. 19, 1957; s. Robert Elbert and Catherine (Kelly) Cooper. BA in Economics, magna cum laude, Princeton U., NJ, 1979; JD, Yale Law Sch., New Haven, 1983. Reporter Raleigh Times, NC, 1979—80; law clk. to hon. Louis F. Oberdorfer US Dist. Ct., Washington, 1983—84; assoc. Bass, Berry & Sims, PLC, Nashville, 1984—90, ptnr., 1990—2003; legal counsel to gov. Phil Bredesen State of Tenn., Nashville, 2003—06, atty. gen., 2006—. Adj. prof. Vanderbilt U. Law Sch., Nashville. Recipient Pres. award, Nashville Bar Assn., 1992. Mem.: ABA, Nashville Bar Assn., Tenn. Bar Assn. Democrat. Office: Office of Atty Gen PO Box 20207 Nashville TN 37202-0207 Office Phone: 615-741-3491. Office Fax: 615-741-2009. Business E-Mail: bob.cooper@ag.tn.gv.*

COOPER, ROY ASBERRY, III, state attorney general; b. Rocky Mount, NC, June 13, 1957; s. Roy Asberry Jr. and Beverly (Batchelor) Cooper; m. Kristin Bernhardt, Mar. 28, 1992; children: Hilary Godette, Natalie Rose, Claire Kristin. BA, U. NC, Chapel Hill, 1979; JD, U. NC Sch. Law, 1982. Bar: NC 1982. Ptnr. Fields and Cooper, Rocky Mount, 1982—2001; mem. NC House of Reps., 1987—91, chmn. jud. com., 1989—91; mem. NC Senate, 1991—2001, Dem. majority leader, 1997—2001; atty. gen. State of NC, 2001—. Recipient Morehead scholar, U. NC, 1975—79. Mem.: Nat. Assn. Attorneys Gen. (pres. 2010—11, Kelley-Wyman award 2013). Democrat. Presbyterian. Office: Office of Attorney General Department of Justice 9001 Mail Service Ctr Raleigh NC 27699-9001 Office Phone: 919-716-6400. Office Fax: 919-716-6750.*

COOPER, SHARON MEYER, state legislator; m. Tom Cooper. Registered nurse, administrator. Former state rep. Dist. 31, Ga.; former state rep. Dist. 30 Ga.; mem. Indsl. Com., Natural Resources & Environ. & U. Sys. Com., Ga.; house rep. Ga.; state rep. Dist. 41 Ga., 2004—; majority caucus chairwoman; house rep. Ga. Republican. Mailing: 4028 River Ridge Chase Marietta GA 30067 Office: 611 Legislative Office Bldg Atlanta GA 30301 Office Phone: 770-952-7681. Fax: 770-952-8688.

COOPER, SIMON F., hotel executive; M, U. Toronto. Exec. v.p. OMNI Hotels USA; pres., COO Delta Hotels & Resorts, Toronto, Ont., Canada; sr. v.p. Marriott Lodging Internat., Etobicoke, Canada, 1998; pres. Marriott Lodging Can., Etobicoke, Canada, 1998, sr. v.p., New Eng. Region, 2000; pres., COO Ritz-Carlton Hotel Co., 2001—10; pres., mng. dir., Asia Pacific Marriott International, Inc. (formerly Marriott Corp.), 2010—. Bd. dirs. First Horizon Nat. Corp., 2005—. Bd. dirs. Woodrow Wilson Internat. Ctr. for Scholar; bd. adv. Can. Inst.; chmn. U. Guelph; mem. The Royal & Ancient Golf Club of St. Andrews, Scotland. Mem.: Am. Hotel and Motel Assn. (fellow bd. trustees Ednl. Inst.). Office: Marriott International Inc 10400 Fernwood Rd Bethesda MD 20817-1102 also: First Horizon National Corp Bd Directors 165 Madison Memphis TN 38103 Office Phone: 301-380-3000, 901-523-4444. Office Fax: 301-380-3969. Business E-Mail: simon.cooper@marriott.com.

COOPER, THOMAS ASTLEY, bank executive; b. Phila., July 19, 1936; s. Thomas Astley and Elmira (Betts) C.; m. Anita June Danenberger, Sept. 7, 1957; children: Aleta Cooper Bossert, Anita Cooper Barbato, Alane Cooper Inacker, Allison Cooper Cardona, Anne Cooper Fleming, Thomas Astley III. BA, Haverford Coll., 1957; BD, Drew U., 1960; postgrad., Pa. U., Wharton, 1972; Program for Mgmt. Devel., Harvard U., 1976. Pres. Girard Bank, Phila., 1978; vice chmn. Mellon Bank, Mellon Nat. Corp., Pitts., 1982; pres. Bank of Am., Bank Am. Corp., San Francisco, 1984; chmn. Investment Svcs. for America, Tampa, Fla., 1986-90; pres., CEO Goldome, Buffalo, 1986-90; prin. TAC Assocs., Buffalo, 1992-95; CEO Chase Fed. Bank, Miami, Fla., 1993-96; chmn. Flatiron Credit, Denver, 1997—2003. Dir. Dela. No. Cos., Buffalo, Renaissance Reins., Bermuda; CEO, TAC Assocs. Inc. Pres. Marco Luth. Ch. Mem. Island Country Club (Fla.), Brant Beach Yacht Club (NJ). Office: 1291 Laurel Ct Marco Island FL 34145-2351

COOPER, WALTER W., insurance company executive; BS in Mech. Engring., Gannon U., MBA. Gen. mgr., internat. ops. Bausch and Lomb; mktg. postions Jostens, Canada, mktg. positions, N.Am., various postions, including gen. mgr., interna. ops. Nuevo Laredo, Mexico; sr. positions, including v.p., mktg. and product, specialized care svcs., sr. v.p., United Retiree Solutions UnitedHealth Group, Inc., v.p., strategic initiatives, 2004—06; sr. v.p., sales and mktg., interim sr. v.p., health svcs. WellCare Health Plans, Inc., corp. leader, health svcs. and human resources, sr. v.p., strategic initiatives, 2006, sr. v.p., chief mktg. officer and pres., Splty. Bus. Unit, 2010, chief adminstrv. officer, 2010—. Office: WellCare Health Plans Inc 8725 Henderson Rd Renaissance 1 Tampa FL 33634 Office Phone: 813-290-6200. Office Fax: 813-262-2802. Business E-Mail: walt.cooper@wellcare.com.

COOPER, WILLIAM EDWIN, professor, former academic administrator; b. Balt., Mar. 20, 1951; s. William Daniel and Mildred (Hively) C.; m. Clarissa Holmes, July 5, 1984; children: Ashley, Courtney. AB magna cum laude, Brown U., 1973, AM, 1973; PhD, MIT, 1976. NIH postdoctoral fellow speech comm. group MIT Rsch. Lab. Electronics, Cambridge, 1976—78, rsch. affiliate, 1978—83; asst. prof. psychology Harvard U., Cambridge, 1978—81, assoc. prof. psychology, 1981—83; prof. psychology U. Iowa, Iowa City, 1983—89, assoc. dean R&D Coll. Liberal Arts, 1987—89; prof. psychology Tulane U., New Orleans, 1989—96, dean Coll. Arts and Scis., 1989—91, dean faculty liberal arts and sci., 1991—96; prof. linguistics and psychology Georgetown U., Washington, 1996—98, exec. v.p. main campus, 1996—98; pres. U. Richmond, Va., 1998—2007, prof., pres. emeritus, 2007—. Fellow Newcomb Coll., 1989-96. Author: Speech Perception and Production: Studies in Selective Adaptation, 1979, Wisdom of the Grottoes, 2008, Flashpoint China, 2009, Buchanan's Reach, 2009, The Dance of Her Napkin, 2012, Overtones, 2014; co-author: Syntax and Speech, 1980, Fundamental Frequency in Sentence Production, 1981; editor: Cognitive Aspects of Skilled Typewriting, 1983; co-editor: Sentence Processing: Psycholinguistic Studies Presented to Merrill Garrett, 1979; contbr. articles to profl. jours. Recipient Harold Schlosberg Meml. award in psychology, 1973, Acoustical Soc. Am. Biennial award, 1986; NSF grad. fellow, 1973, John Simon Guggenheim fellow, 1983; Fulbright Sr. scholar, U. Fed. de Minas Gerais, Belo Horizonte, Brazil, 1984. Mem. Phi Beta Kappa, Sigma Xi. Office: U Richmond 211 Weinstein Hall Richmond VA 23173 Business E-Mail: bcooper@richmond.edu.

COOPER, WILLIAM JAMES, JR., history professor; b. Kingstree, SC, Oct. 22, 1940; s. William James and Mamie (Mayes) C.; m. Patricia Holmes, Sept. 1, 1962; children: William James III, Michael Holmes. AB, Princeton U., 1962; PhD, Johns Hopkins U., 1966. Asst. prof. history La. State U., Baton Rouge, 1968-70, assoc. prof., 1970-78, prof., 1978—, dean Grad. Sch., 1982-89, Boyd prof., 1989—. Douglas Southall Freeman prof. U. Richmond, 2000. Author: The Conservative Regime: South Carolina 1877-1890, 1968, The South and the Politics of Slavery 1828-1856, 1978, Liberty and Slavery: Southern Politics to 1860, 1983, Jefferson Davis, American, 2000, Jefferson Davis and the Civil War Era, 2008, We Have the War Upon Us: The Onset of the Civil War, November 1860-April 1861, 2012; co-author: The American South: A History, 1990, 4th edit., 2008; editor: Jefferson Davis, The Essential Writings, 2003, co-editor: A Master's Due: Essays in Honor of David Herbert Donald, 1985, Writing the Civil War: The Quest to Understand, 1998, In the Cause of Liberty: How the Civil War Redifined American Ideals, 2009; editor: Social Relations in Our Southern States (Daniel Hundley), 1979, So. Biography Series, 1979-93; also articles. Served to capt. U.S. Army, 1966-68. Recipient Prize for Biography L.A. Times, 2001, Jefferson Davis award Mus. of Confederacy, 2000, 12; sr. fellow Inst. So. History, Johns Hopkins U., 1971-72, rsch. fellow Charles Warren Ctr. Studies in Am. History, Harvard U., 1975-76, Guggenheim fellow, 1980-81, NEH fellow, 1988-89; named Disting. Rsch. Master La. State U., 1980. Fellow Soc. Am. Historians; mem. Am. Hist. Assn., Orgn. Am. Historians, Southern Hist. Assn. (pres., 2010). Presbyterian. Home: 250 Amherst Ave Baton Rouge LA 70808-4603 Office: La State U Dept History Baton Rouge LA 70803-0001 Home Phone: 225-766-3871; Office Phone: 225-578-4495. Business E-Mail: wcooper@lsu.edu.

COOPER, WILLIAM S., retired state supreme court justice; b. Sept. 15, 1941; BA, U. Ky., 1963, JD with high distinction, 1970; attended, Nat. Jud. Coll., 1980, attended, 1983, attended, 1993. Law clerk Faurest, Collier, Arnett, Hensley & Coleman, 1968; ptnr. Collier, Arnett, Coleman & Cooper, 1970—79; judge Ky. 9th Judicial Cir., Div. 1, 1979—96; vice-regional judge Ky. Central Region, 1981—83, Ky. Green River Region, 1983—92, chief regional judge, 1992—96; assoc. justice Ky. Supreme Ct., Frankfort, 1996—2006; ret., 2006. Mem. Council for Higher Education Subcom. for Legal Education, 1983—85, U. Ky. Coll. of Law Visiting Com., 1986—, Ky. Evidence Rules Review Commn., 1995—2006, chair., 2000—06; chair Ky. Supreme Ct. Criminal Rules Com., 1997—2006; mem. Am. Law Inst., 2003—; CLE lecturer U. Ky., 1983—2004; lecturer U. Louisville, 1977—85, Murray State U., 1978, Northern Ky. U., 1986, Circuit Judges Jud. Coll., 1981—93, Dist. Judges Jud. Coll., 1992. Editor: Ky. Law Jour., 1969—70. Captain USAF, 1963—67. Recipient Community Service award, Knights of Columbus, 1991, Hall of Fame award, Elizabethtown-Hardin County Chamber of Commerce, 1997. Fellow: Ky. Bar Found. (life; bd. dirs. 1992—96, 2002—06); mem.: Circuit Judges Assn. (continuing education com. 1980—84, chair 1982—84), Ky. Bar Assn. (evidence rules com. 1987—92, chmn. com. jury instrns. 1991—93, mem. com. jury instrns. 1991—97, Publications com. 2007—, Ky. Bar Center award 1992, Outstanding Judge award 2004).

COOPER, WILLIAM WAGER, economics, accounting and finance professor, dean; b. Birmingham, Ala., July 23, 1914; s. William Wager and Rae (Rossman) C.; m. Ruth Fay West, Sept. 11, 1944. AB, U. Chgo., 1938; postgrad., Columbia U., NYC, 1940—42; DSc (hon.), Ohio State U., Columbus, 1970; MA (hon.), Harvard U., Cambridge, Mass, 1976; DSc (hon.), Carnegie Mellon U., Pitts., 1982; D (hon.), U. Alicante, Spain, 1995. Asst. to comptroller TVA, 1938-40; prin. economist Bur. Budget, 1942-44; asst. prof. econs. U. Chgo., 1944-46; asst. prof. to prof. Carnegie-Mellon U., 1946-68; dean Carnegie-Mellon U. (Sch. Urban and Pub. Affairs), 1968-75, univ. prof. mgmt. sci. and pub. affairs, 1975-76, research prof. mgmt. sci. and pub. policy, 1976—; Arthur Lowes Dickinson prof. accounting Grad. Sch. Bus. Adminstrn., Harvard U., 1976-80; prof. mgmt. and FWANCE, mgmt. scis. and info. sys. info. risk & dieratious mgmt. dgpartment U. Tex., Austin, 1980; Foster Parker prof. fin. and mgmt. emeritus Red McCombs Sch. Bus., Austin, 1994—; chmn. mgmt. sci. and info. systems dept. U. Tex., 1986-88. Vis. disting. internat. lectr. acctg. Am. Acctg. Assn., 1986, dir. pubs., chmn., pubs. com., exec. com., 1987-89; disting. IBM vis. prof. Aoyama Gakuin U., Tokyo, 1993. Author 27 books including; co-author (with A. Charnes): Management Models and Industrial Applications of Linear Programming; co-author: (with H. Leavitt, M.W. Shelly) New Perspectives in Organization Research; co-author: (with others) Studies in Budgeting; co-author: (with A. Charnes and R. Niehaus) Studies in Manpower Planning; co-author: (with Y. Ijiri) Eric Louis Kohler: Accounting's Man of Principles; co-author: (with A. Charnes, A. Lewin and L. Seiford) Data Envelopment Analysis: Theory, Methodology, Applications; co-author: (with A. Whinston) New Directions in Computational Economics; co-author: (with R.G. Thompson and R.M. Thrall) Extensions and New Developments in DEA: The Annals of Operations Research; co-author: (with L.M. Seiford and Kaoru Tone) Data Envelopment Analysis: A Comprehensive Text, 2000; co-author: (with L.M. Seiford and J. Zhu) Handbook of Data Envelopment Analysis, 2004; co-author: (with L.M. Seiford and Kaoru Tone) Introduction to Data Envelopment Analysis, 2005, 2nd edit., 2007; co-author: (with Piyu Yue) The Challenge of Muslim Countries: Present, Future and Past, 2008; editor: Auditing: A Jour. Practice and Theory, 1978—81; co-editor (with Y. Ijiri): Kohler's Dictionary for Accountants, 6th edit.; mem. editl. bd. Mgmt. Sci., 1954—74, Naval Rsch. Logistics Quar., 1957—74; contbr. over 500 articles to profl. jours. Co-recipient John Von Neumann theory prize, 1982; recipient award Am. Inst. Accts., 1945, Profl. Achievement citation U. Chgo. Alumni Assn., 1986, Outstanding Contbr. to Auditing award Am. Acctg. Assn., 1988, Outstanding Acctg. Educator award, 1990, Notable Contbns. to Lit. award in govtl. and non-profit acctg., 1991, Lifetime Contbns. to Mgmt. Acct. award, 2002, Gold medal award Soc. Multi-Criteria Decision Making, 2004; named to U. Tex. Coll. Bus. Adminstrn. Hall of Fame, 1990, Acctg. Hall of Fame, 1996, Internat. Operational Rsch. Hall Fame, 2006; Erskine fellow, U. Canterbury, New Zealand, 1991, fellow Inst. Ops. Rsch. and Mgmt. Sci., 2002 (Impact award, 2006). Fellow Econometric Soc., AAAS, INFORMS; mem. Inst. Mgmt. Sci. (1st pres.), Ops. Research Soc. Am. (editorial bd. 1957-68), Inst. of Operational Rsch. and Mgmt. Scis., presdl. citation achievements U. Tex., 2009 Office: U Tex Austin Red McCombs Sch Bus 1 Univ Station 6B6500 Austin TX 78712-0212 Home: Apt 331 1034A Liberty Park Dr Austin TX 78746-6853 Home Phone: 512-327-4749; Office Phone: 512-471-1822. Business E-Mail: cooperw@mail.utexas.edu.

COOPER-DYKE, CYNTHIA, women's college basketball coach, retired professional basketball player; b. Chgo., Apr. 14, 1963; m. Brian Dyke; children: Brian, Cyan. BS in Phys. Edn., U. So. Calif., LA, 1986. Guard Segovia, Spain, 1986—87, Parma, Italy, 1987—94, 1996—97, Alcamo, Italy, 1994—96, Houston Comets, 1997—2000; ret. WNBA, 2000; head coach Phoenix Mercury, 2001—02; guard Houston Comets, 2003—04; ret. WNBA, 2004; head basketball coach Prairie View A&M U. Lady Panthers, 2005—10, U. NC-Wilmington Seahawks, 2010—. Mem. US nat. team US Goodwill Games, 1986, 1990, World Championships, 1986, 1990, Pan Am. Games, 1987, Summer Olympic Games, Seoul, 1988, Barcelona, 1992. Recipient Gold medal, women's basketball, Pan Am Games, 1987, Seoul Olympic Games, 1988, Bronze medal, women's basketball, Barcelona Olympic Games, 1992; named MVP, WNBA, 1997, 1998, WNBA Finals MVP, 1997—2000; named to Women's Basketball Hall of Fame, 2009, Naismith Meml. Basketball Hall of Fame, 2010. Achievements include member of NCAA women's basketball national championship winning University of Southern California Trojans, 1983-1984; member of WNBA Finals championship winning Houston Comets, 1997-2000. Office: University NC Wilmington Womens Basketball 601 S College Rd Wilmington NC 28403 Office Phone: 910-962-3418. Business E-Mail: coop@uncw.edu.

COOPERMAN, SAUL, retired educational administrator; b. Newark, Dec. 18, 1934; s. Louis Frank and Lucille (Swarthberg) C.; m. Paulette Beth Koch, Aug. 17, 1958; children: Suzanne, Deborah, David. BS, Lafayette Coll., 1956; MEd, Rutgers U., 1964, EdD, 1969; DHL (hon.), Drew U., 1984. Tchr. North Plainfield H.S., NJ, 1960-64; prin. Belvidere H.S., NJ, 1964-68; rsch. asst. Rutgers U., New Brunswick, NJ, 1968-69; supt. schs. Montgomery Twp., NJ, 1969-74, City of Madison, NJ, 1974-82; commr. N.J. State Dept. Edn., Trenton, 1982-90. Pres. Educate Am., 1990—2000, 10,000 Mentors, Newark, 1996—2000; chmn. edn. adv. panel New Am. Sch. Devel. Corp., 1990—97; sec., treas. New Am. Schs., 2000—05; founder, chmn. bd. dirs. Acad. for Tchg. and Leadership, 2004—11; started mentoring program NJIT, 2013—. Author: How Schools Really Work: Practical Advice to Parents from an Insider, Eddie and Me: A Story of Friendship; contbr. 67 articles to ednl. jours.; prodr.: (documentaries) Sex Over Sixty, 2007; columnist (newspaper) Star Ledger, 1998—2003. Served to rank of comdr. USNR, 1956—82. Avocations: reading, athletics, travel. Address: 4061 Bayhead Dr Bonita Springs FL 34134 Home: 181 Roundtop Rd Bernardsville NJ 07924-2106

COOPER-RUSPOLI, ANNIE NATAF, psychiatrist, director; d. Victor and Arlette Nataf; m. Stephane Frank Ruspoli, June 9, 1997; 1 child, Jonathan Cooper. MD, U. Paris, 1975. Resident psychiatry Emory U. Sch. Medicine, Atlanta, 1975—78, fellow child psychiatry, 1978—79; med. dir. child and adolescent unit Ga. Regional Hosp.

Atlanta, 1980—91; psychiatrist Piedmont Psychiat. Clinic, Atlanta, 1996—. Mem. Counseil Nat. de l'Ordre des Medecins, Paris, 1991—; sci. adv. bd. mem. Skyland Trails Ctr., Atlanta, 2008—11. Trustee Atlanta Internat. Sch., 1985—97, bd. dirs., 1997—2005; trustee Alliance Francaise d'Atlanta, 1992—95, Ga Casa, Atlanta, 1992—2001. Mem.: AMA, Atlanta Med. Assn., Ga. Med. Assn., Ga. Psychiat. Assn., Am. Psychiat. Assn. Independent. Office: Piedmont Psychiatric Clinic 35 Collier Rd Ste M-275 Atlanta GA 30309 Office Fax: 404-355-2917. Personal E-mail: acooperrus@aol.com.*

COPE, DONALD GENE, transportation company executive, controller; b. Superior, Nebr., Mar. 1, 1950; s. Ray E. and Fern L. (Bailey) C.; m. Cynthia J. Ball, May 29, 1976; children: Jeffrey S., Melissa A. BS in Acctg., Nebr. Wesleyan U., Lincoln, 1972; MBA, U. Wis., Oshkosh, 1982. CPA, Wis., Ind. Sr. auditor KPMG-Peat Marwick, Lincoln, Nebr., 1972-74; controller, v.p. Schneider National, Inc., Green Bay, Wis., 1974-87; v.p. controller Whiteford Sys., So. Bend, Ind., 1987-90; v.p., fin., contr. Crete Carrier, Lincoln, Nebr., 1990-91; v.p., fin. J.B. Hunt Transport Services, Inc., Lowell, Ark., 1991, sr. v.p., contr. & chief acctg. officer. Bd. dirs. Salvation Army, Green Bay, Wis., 1977-82, Family Violence Ctr., Green Bay, 1977-82. Avocations: flying, scuba diving, skiing. Home: 2769 E Weston Pl Fayetteville AR 72703-6580 Office: JB Hunt Transport Services Inc 615 JB Hunt Corp Dr Lowell AR 72745-0130 Office Phone: 479-820-0000. Office Fax: 479-820-3418. Business E-Mail: donald_cope@jbhunt.com.

COPELAND, EDWARD MEADORS, III, surgeon, educator; b. Augusta, Ga., Oct. 6, 1937; s. Edward Meadors Jr. and Louise (Leggitt) C.; m. Martha Patterson, Ar. 24, 1964; children: Edward Meadors IV, Catherine Leggitt. BA, Duke U., 1959; MD, Cornell U., 1963. Diplomate Am. Bd. Surgery (bd. dir. 1983-91, chmn. 1990-91). Intern in surgery U. Pa. Hosp., Phila., 1963-64, resident in gen. surgery, 1964-69; resident surg. oncology Anderson Hosp., Houston, 1971-72; asst. prof. to prof. U. Tex. Med. Sch., Houston, 1972-82, U. Tex. M.D. Anderson Hosp. and Tumor Inst., Houston, 1972-82; prof. U. Fla. Coll. Medicine, Gainesville, 1982—, chmn. dept., 1982—2003, disting. prof., 2004—08; disting. prof. emeritus, 2008—. Project dir. Nat. Large Bowel Cancer Project, Nat. Cancer Inst., Houston, 1981-82; bd. dirs. Sun Bank North Ctrl. Fla. Maj. US Army, 1969-71, Vietnam. Decorated Bronze Star Rep. Vietnam; recipient Seale Harris award So. Med. Assn., 1984, Disting. Alumnus award M.D. Anderson Hosp. and Tumor Inst., 1987, Lifetime Achievement award, 2008. Fellow Am. Surg. Assn., So. Surg. Assn. (pres. 1998-99), Texas Surg. Soc., Soc. of Black Academic Surgeons, Royal Acad. of Surgeons, Ireland; mem. ACS (chmn. bd. govs. 1995-96, bd. regents 1997-2007, vice chmn. 2002-03, chmn. 2004-05, pres.-elect 2005-06, pres. 2006-07), Assn. Acad. Surgery (pres. 1978-79), Soc. Surg. Oncology (pres. 1998-99), Soc. Surg. Chmn. (pres. 1996-98), Halsted Soc. (pres. 1993), Southeastern Surg. Congress (pres. 2000-01), Soc. Univ. Surgeons, Gainesville Country Club. Avocations: fishing, golf, tennis. Home: 2605 NW 7th Rd Gainesville FL 32607-2600 Office: Univ Fla Coll Medicine Dept Surgery PO Box 100286 Gainesville FL 32610-0286 Office Phone: 352-265-0169. Business E-Mail: copelem@surgery.ufl.edu.

COPELAND, FLOYD DEAN, insurance company executive, lawyer; b. Jackson, Miss., Apr. 11, 1939; s. Clyde Xenephon and Dorothy Russell (Dean) C.; m. Linda Gail Langston, Dec. 22, 1965; children: Albion Ehlers, Russell Braden. BA in history, U. Miss., 1961; BA in jurisprudence, U. Oxford, Eng., 1963; LLB, Yale U., 1965. Bar: Ga. 1967, Tenn. 1998. Assoc. Alston, Miller & Gaines, Atlanta, 1967-71; ptnr. Alston & Bird, Atlanta, 1972-97; exec. v.p., gen. counsel Provident Companies, Inc., Chattanooga, 1997-99; exec. v.p. legal and adminstrv. affairs, gen. counsel UnumProvident Corp., Chattanooga, 1999—2002, sr. exec. v.p., gen. counsel, 2002—, chief adminstrv. officer, 2003—. Bd. dirs. Atlanta Metro Boys and Girls Clubs, 1986-97; sec. State and Dist. Rhodes Scholarship Selection Committees, Atlanta, 1976-97. Capt. US Army, 1965—67. Rhodes scholar, 1961, Carrier scholar, 1957. Mem. Am. Law Inst. Presbyterian. Avocations: bicycling, reading, travel.

COPELAND, HENRY JEFFERSON, JR., former college president; b. Griffin, Ga., June 13, 1936; s. Henry Jefferson and Emory (Drake) C.; m. Laura Harper, Dec. 21, 1958; children: Henry Drake, Eleanor Harper. BA, Baylor U., 1958; PhD, Cornell U., 1966. Instr. Cornell U., Ithaca, NY, 1965-66; asst. prof. history Coll. Wooster, Ohio, 1966-69, assoc. dean, 1969-74, dean, 1974-77, pres., 1977-95, prof. history, 1995-98. Woodrow Wilson fellow, 1960 Presbyterian.

COPELAND, LEWIS, principal; BS in Elem. Edn., U. South Ala., 1967, MA in Elem. Edn., 1971; AA in Edn. Adminstrn. Supervision, Auburn U., 1975. Prin. W.P. Davidson H.S., Mobile, Ala., 1982—. Recipient Blue Ribbon Sch. award U.S. Dept. Edn., 1990-91, 95-96; named Secondary Prin. of Yr., Ala. State PTA, 1993-94, Outstanding Sch. Adminstr., Ala. Music Educators Assn., 1997. Office: WP Davidson HS 3900 Pleasant Valley Rd Mobile AL 36609-2022

COPELAND, ROBERT BODINE, internist, cardiologist; b. Arab, Ala., Jan. 24, 1938; s. Haden Paul and Jimmie Alice (Bodine) Copeland; m. Virginia (Jenny) Ruth Trammell, June 26, 1960; children: Robert Theodore, Haden McTieyre. BS, Auburn U., 1960; MD, U. Ala., Birmingham, 1963. Diplomate Am. Bd. Internal Medicine, cert. internal medicine, cardiovasc. diseases and geriatrics. Intern then resident, clin. rsch. fellow in cardiology Mass. Gen. Hosp., Harvard Med. Sch., Boston, 1963-67; physician Clark Holder Clinic, LaGrange, Ga., 1967-77; founder, dir. Ga. Heart Clinic, LaGrange, 1972—2006; founder, pres. So. Cardiopulmonary Assocs., LaGrange, 1977—2003; clin. prof. med. U. Ala., Birmingham, 1980—2005, Emory U., Atlanta, 1980—2012. Bd. govs. Joint Commn. on Accreditation of Healthcare Orgns., Chgo., 1991—97, Am. Bd. Internal Medicine, Phila., 1980—86; trustee West Ga. Med. Sys., LaGrange; co-founder, med. dir. Troup Care Free Med. Clin., LaGrange, 2008—. Contbr. Trustee LaGrange Coll.; chmn. bd. trustees ACP-ASIM Found., 1999—2002. Recipient Disting. Alumni award, U. Ala., Birmingham, 1985. Fellow: ACP (gov. Ga. chpt. 1987—91, Master 1993, regent 1993—99, chair bd. regents 1998—99), NAS Inst. Medicine, Am. Coll. Cardiology, Royal Coll. Physicians; mem.: Am. Clin. and Climatological Assn., Am. Heart Assn. (pres. Ga. affiliate 1985—86). Office: 1551 Doctors Dr Lagrange GA 30240-4139 Personal E-mail: rbcopeland1101@gmail.com.

COPENHAVER, DEKE, mayor, Augusta-Richmond, Georgia; b. Montreal, Can. m. Malisa Copenhaver. Attended, U. Ga.; BA in Polit. Sci., Augusta Coll. Former assoc. Nations Bank Securities, Atlanta; former prin. Huffines, Dukes, and Copenhaver LLC; former sales rep. Blanchard and Calhoun Real Estate; former exec. dir. Ctrl. Savannah River Land Trust, 2001—06; mayor City of Augusta-Richmond, 2007—. Mem. Partnering & Leveraging com. Ga. Land Conservation Partnership Adv. Coun.; bd. mem. Ga. Dept. Cmty. Affairs; former chmn. Environ. Issues Com.; grad. Leadership Ga., 2004. Former bd. mem. Augusta Symphony, Hist. Augusta, Young at Art, Main St. Augusta, Metro Augusta Family YMCA, Ga. Alliance Land Trusts, St. Joseph's Hosp. Found.; bd. mem. Ga. Mcpl. Assn. Legis. Policy Coun., Cmty. Found. for Ctrl. Savannah River Area, Augusta State U. Found., Ga. Conservancy, Augusta Hist. Mus., CSRA Regional Devel. Ctr., Richmond-Burke County Job Training Authority; editl. com. Leadership Augusta's Destination 2020 Initiative; deacon Reid Meml. Presbyterian Ch. Recipient Linda H. Walter Leadership award, Metro Augusta Family YMCA, 2003, Top Forty Under Forty, Ga. Trend Mag., 2003; named a Notable Georgian, 2006; named one of the 100 Most Influential Georgians, 2007. Mem.: Kiwanis Club of Augusta. Independent. Avocations: golf, hunting, running, writing. Office: 530 Greene St Rm 806 Augusta GA 30901 Home: 75 Conifer Cir Augusta GA 30909-4508 Office Phone: 706-821-1831. Fax: 706-821-1835. E-mail: mayordeke@augustaga.gov.*

COPENHAVER, JOHN BARNS, not-for-profit executive, lawyer; b. Pearisburg, Va., Aug. 18, 1953; s. William Pierce and Jane Farrier Copenhaver; m. Diana Lynn Thompson, Dec. 10, 1994. BSc, Brown U., Providence, RI, 1975; JD, U. Ga., Athens, Ga., 1979. Bar: Ga. 1979; cert. bus. continuity profl. Disaster Recovery Inst., 1993. Geologist Texasgulf Inc., Houston, 1975—76; law clk. Ga. Ct. Appeals, Atlanta, 1980—81; regional dir. FEMA, Atlanta, 1981; pres. Disaster Recovery Inst. Internat., Atlanta, CEO. Bd. advisors Can. Ctr. Emergency Preparedness, Toronto, Ont., Canada, 2005—; bd. dir. Bus. Continuity Advancement Orgn., Tokyo. Co-author: A Legal Guide to Homeland Security and Emergency Preparedness for State and Local Governments; editor: Jane's Guide to Citizen Safety. Mem. Capital Campaign Com. U. Ga., Athens, 2005—06; founder, pres. Global Partnership Preparedness Found., Washington, 2004—; mem. Law Sch. Bd. Visitors U. Ga., 2002—05. Mem.: Buckhead Club, Commerce Club, Capital City Club, Kiwanis Club. Meth. Avocations: golf, travel, scuba diving. Office: Disaster Recovery Institute 1200 Abernathy Rd Suite 1700 Atlanta GA 30328 Business E-Mail: john.copenhaver@worleyparsons.com.

COPENHAVER, JOHN THOMAS, JR., federal judge; b. Charleston, W.Va., Sept. 29, 1925; s. John Thomas and Ruth Cherrington (Roberts) Copenhaver; m. Camille Ruth Smith, Sept. 7, 1950; children: John Thomas III, James Smith, Brent Paul. AB, W.Va. U., 1947; LLB, W.Va. U. Coll. Law, 1950. Bar: W.Va. 1950. Law clerk to Hon. Ben Moore US Dist. Ct. (so. dist.) W.Va., 1950-51, judge, 1976—; ptnr. Copenhaver & Copenhaver, Charleston, 1951-58; referee in bankruptcy US Bankruptcy Ct. (so. dist.) W.Va., 1958—73, US bankruptcy judge, 1973—76. Adj. prof. W.Va. U. Coll. Law, 1970—76; faculty Fed. Jud. Ctr., 1970—76; mem. adv. com. bankruptcy rules Jud. Conf. US, 1978—84. Pres. Legal Aid. Soc. Charleston, 1985; chmn. Charleston Mcpl. Planning Commn., 1964; chmn., pres. W.Va. Housing Devel. Fund, 1969—72; chmn. vis. com. W.Va. U. Coll. Law, 1980—83. Served with US Army, 1944—46. Recipient Gavel award, W.Va. U. Coll. Law, 1971, Outstanding Judge award, W. Va. Trial Lawyers Assn., 1983. Fellow: American Bar Found.; mem.: ABA, Nat. Conf. Bankruptcy Judges, Kanawha County Bar Assn., W.Va. Bar Assn., Beta Theta Pi, Phi Delta Phi. Republican. Presbyterian. Office: US Courthouse PO Box 2546 Charleston WV 25329-2546 Office Phone: 304-347-3146.

COPES, MARVIN LEE, academic administrator; b. Connersville, Ind., Sept. 19, 1938; s. Kenneth Edward and Frances Gertrude (Bean) C.; m. Luretta Ann Grenard, Aug. 26, 1961; children: Bradley Alan, Brian Keith, Brent Lee, Shelby County Yellow Dot Program (coord.). BS, Purdue U., 1961, MS, 1962, PhD, 1975; postgrad., Ind. State U., Terre Haute, 1967—68, Ind. U. Southeast, 1967—68. Cert. pub. mgr., Ky. Grad. asst. agrl. edn. Purdue U., West Lafayette, Ind., 1961—62, grad. instr., 1968—69; tchr. vocat. agriculture Tri-County Sch. Corp., Walcott, Ind., 1964—65; vocat. dir. Met. Sch. Dist. Vernon Twp., Crothersville, Ind., 1965—68; also dir. Ind. Vocat. Agr. Demonstration Ctr., 1965—68; asst. exec. sec. Kappa Delta Pi Hdqrs., West Lafayette, 1969—70; dir. Blue River Vocat.-Tech. Ctr., Shelbyville, Ind., 1970—79; nat. curriculum devel. coord. ITT Ednl. Svcs., Indpls., 1979—80, nat. dir. edn., 1980—82; dir. ITT Tech. Inst., Ft. Wayne, Ind., 1982—83, Indpls., 1983—86, Am. Coll., Mobile, Ala., 1986—89; nat. dir. edn. Am. Career Educators, Charlotte, NC, 1989, v.p. ednl. resources, 1989—91; pres. Treasure Wheel, Inc., Mobile, 1991—93; dean acad. affairs Phillips Jr. Coll., Mobile, 1992—96; v.p. acad. affairs Am. Inst. Commerce, Davenport, Iowa, 1993—96; dir. Ky. Tech. Jefferson State Campus, Louisville, 1996—98, Jefferson Cmty. & Tech. Coll., 1998—2000, exec. dir. of occupl., tech. and apprenticeship programs, 2000—02, CEO Spl. Programs, 2001—02; dir. Heritage Inst., Falls Church, Va., 2002—03; edn., cmty. svc. AARP, Maylene, Ala., 2004—12; ctr. mgr. Jefferson County WIA Career Ctr., Birmingham, 2004—05; asst. outreach coord. Employer Support the Guard and Reserve, Ala., 2004—; prin., owner Corp. Online Profile Employment Solutions, 2006—12; job developer Jefferson County Office of Sr. Citizen Svcs., 2007; job counselor aware program positive maturity Jefferson County Office Sr. Citizen Svcs., 2008—09; curriculum developer Shop Rat, Orgn., 2008—09; coord. Shelby County RSVP Program Positive Maturity, 2008—. Chmn. profl. devel. com. Ky. Postsecondary Tchr. Credentialing Adv. Bd.; mem. Welfare Reform Task Force, Ky.; bd. dirs. Pvt. Ind. Coun., Future Connections Sch. to Work; organizer Advanced Tech. Skills Acad., Advanced Welding Tech. Ctr.; pres. CopeSkills Cons., Power Ptnrs. cons.; columnist, Shelby County Reporter Newspaper, Sr. Living Newspaper; Shelby County retired sr. vol. program coord., Positive Maturity, 2008-. Author: A Curriculum Guide for Training in Agricultural Supply, 1968, Student Handbook for Cooperative Progress in Agricultural Occupations, 1968, A Predictability of Career Choices of High School Seniors, 1975, Personal Awareness Handbook, 1989, Retention Handbook, 1989, Placement Handbook, 1990, Vocational Adjustment Handbook, 1990, Train The Trainer Handbook, 1990, Instructor Certification Handbook, 1990, Administrative Certification Handbook, 1990, Master Teacher, 1990, Wheel of Fortune Enterprise Training Manual, 1991, Instructor Training Manual, 1993, Faculty Inservice Training Manual, 1993, Disaster Plan, 1993, Contract Training, 1994, School-to-Work Training, 1994, Assessment Planning, 1995, Welfare Reform, 1996, Guidelines for Apprenticeship Training, 2002, Guidelines for Corporate College, 2002, A Guide for Boomer and Business, 2007; mem. editl. bd. AARP/Ala.; columnist AgeTimes.com, Moments Newspaper. Ops. coun. Met. Coll.; pres. Loper PTO, 1974-76; leader 4-H, 1964-68; advisor Future Farmers Am., 1964-70; cubmaster Boy Scouts Am., 1976-80, commr., bd. dirs. Shelby County, 1978-92; mem. vocat. gng. com., chair Futuring Project, NY State Dept. Edn.; bd. dirs. N.E. India Christian Mission, 1974, Kentuckiana Works; chmn. Shelby County Youth for Christ; mem. Nat. Curriculum Focus Group, 1993-96; bd. dirs., treas. Accrediting Coun. for Ind. Colls. and Schs., 1994; deacon area So. Bapt. Ch., 1995; mem. Kentukiana Edn. and Workforce Inst., Louisville Area Workforce Devel. Coun., School-to-Work Partnership Coun., Louisville/Jefferson County Redevel. Authority; bd. dirs. Career Resources One Stop Shop/Job Link, Pvt. Ind. Coun.; Louisville/Jefferson County Workforce investment bd., North Ctrl. Ky. Workforce Investment Bd.; mem. Louisville/Jefferson County Youth Coun., North Ctrl. Ky. Youth Coun., chmn.; mem. Immigrant/Refugee Task Force, Kentuckiana Works Skilled Trades Roundtable; mem. Leadership Louisville, 2000, Leadership Shelby County, 2005; chair, bd. dirs. Econ. and Indsl. Devel. Authority, Shelby County, 2006, edn. focus group, sr. vol. program, 2006; mem. Shelby County Transp. Task Force; mem. Ala. Silver Haired Legislature, 2007—08; Nat. Com. Employer Support Guard & Res. Outreach Subcom., 2009-12; 1st lt. US Army, 1962-64. Recipient US Congrl. award, Dist. 6 Ala., Ala. Golden Eagle Journalism award, 2007, South Shelby County Citizen of the Yr., 2011, Res. Employer Outreach of Yr. award, ESGR Seven Seals award, 2008, 2011, Hon. Col., Ala. State Militia, 2012, Pres. Vol. Svc. award, Bronze, Silver, Gold, Lifetime awards; named to Ala. Sr. Citizens Hall of Fame, 2007, Ala. Sr. Hall of Fame, Permanent Mem., 2012. Mem. ASCD, Am. Vocat. Assn., Ind. Vocat. Assn., Nat. Coun. Local Adminstrs., Ind. Coun. Local Adminstrs., Bus. Profls. Am., Nat. Bus. Edn. Assn., Soc. Mfg. Engrs., Ky. Vocat. Assn. (pres. region 13), Robotics Internat., Network Iowa Svc. Learning, Ind. Assn. Pvt. Career Schs. (bd. dirs.), Future Farmers Am. Alumni Assn., Greater Shelby County C. of C., South Shelby County C. of C. (amb.), Prichard C. of C. (bd. dirs.), Pershing Rifles, Gideons Internat., Metro Scholars, Davenport C. of C., Masons, Kiwanis, Order Ea. Star, Alpha Tau Alpha, Kappa Delta Pi, Phi Delta Kappa, Delta Pi Epsilon. Home: 170 Sunset Trail Alabaster AL 35007 Office Phone: 205-669-3837. Personal E-mail: mlcopes@charter.net. Business E-Mail: marvine@positivematurity.org.

COPLEY, EDWARD ALVIN, lawyer; b. Memphis, Jan. 17, 1936; m. Connie James Patterson, Nov. 17, 1990; children: Julie, Ward, Drew, Kelly, Zeke. BA in English, Southern Meth. U., 1957, JD, 1960. Bar: DC, Tex., US Dist. Ct. (no. dist.) Tex., US Ct. Fed. Claims 1962, US Tax Ct. 1966, US Ct. Appeals (5th cir.) 1968, US Supreme Ct. 1963. Atty. antitrust divsn. US Dept. Justice, Washington, 1960—62, atty. tax divsn. Ft. Worth, 1962—66; assoc. Akin, Gump, Strauss, Hauer & Feld, Dallas, 1966-67, ptnr., 1968—2001, sr. counsel, 2001—. Adj. prof. taxation Southern Meth. U., 1966—79. Named one of Top 100 Wealth Advisors in the US, Citywealth Mag., 2006, 2011. Fellow Am. Coll. Probate Counsel, Am. Coll. Trust and Estate Counsel; mem. ABA, Internat. Acad. Estate Trust Law, Dallas Bar Assn. (tax sect.), Dallas Estate Coun. (pres. 1975-76), Southern Meth. U. Law Sch. Alumni Assn. (pres. 1978-79), Salesmanship Club, Order of Woolsac, Barristers, Dallas Country Club, Phi Alpha Delta. Avocations: racquetball, photography, hunting, fishing, reading. Home: 3711 Shenandoah St Dallas TX 75205-2120 Office: Akin Gump Strauss Hauer & Feld Ste 4100 1700 Pacific Ave Dallas TX 75201-4624 Office Phone: 214-969-2709. Office Fax: 214-969-4343. E-mail: ecopley@akingump.com.

COPLIN, MARK DAVID, lawyer; b. Balt., Dec. 1, 1928; m. Judith Charlotte Levinson, Jan. 27, 1991. BA, U. Md., 1949, LLB, 1952. Bar: Md. 1952. Law clk. presiding justice U.S. Ct. Appeals (4th cir.), 1952-53; assoc. Weinberg and Green, Balt., 1953—60, mem., 1960—98; sr. ptnr. Saul Ewing, Balt., 1998-2001. Pres. Md. chpt., Am. Jewish Congress, 1971-74, Balt. Jewish Coun., 1976-78; pres. HIAS of Balt., Inc., 1972-74; mem. adv. com. Md. Blue Sky, 1968-92; bd. dirs. Jewish Family Svc., 1992-98; chmn. bd. trustees Balt. Hebrew U., 1987-89; mem. bd. visitors Balt. City Coll., 1990-97, sec., 1992-97. Mem. ABA, Md. Bar Assn., Balt. City Bar Assn., Balt. Bar Found. (pres. 1991-93), Order of Coif, Omicron Delta Kappa, Jewish. Personal E-mail: mdc12128@aol.com.

COPPRIDGE, ALTON JAMES, urological surgeon; b. Roanoke, Va., Dec. 8, 1926; s. William Maurice Coppridge and Ferrie (Patterson) Choate; m. Helen Allen Burnett, June 24, 1950; children: William Allen, Virginia Choate BA, U. N.C., 1949; MD, U. Va., 1953. Diplomate Am. Bd. Urology. Intern N.C. Meml. Hosp., Chapel Hill, 1953—54; surg. resident State U. Iowa, Iowa City, 1954—56; urology resident U. Mich., Ann Arbor, 1956—59; mem. Coppridge Urol. Group, P.A., Durham, NC, 1959—89; ret., 1989. Chmn. dept. Durham County Gen. Hosp., 1978—84; asst. clin. prof. Duke Med. Ctr., Durham, 1970—89; clin. instr. U. N.C. Med. Sch., Chapel Hill, 1960—75. Contbr. articles to urologic lit Served with U.S. Army, 1944-46, Japan Mem.: ACS, NRA, Carolina Urol. Soc. (pres. 1985), N.C. Med. Soc. (pres. sect. urology 1978), Am. Urol. Assn. (exec. com. S.E. sect. 1983—86), Safari Internat. Club (Tucson) (pres. N.C. chpt. 1979—80), Durham Pistol and Rifle Club. Democrat. Presbyterian. Avocation: hunting. Home: A213 - 2600 Croasdaile Farm Pky Durham NC 27705 Office Phone: 919-384-2783.

CORBEIL, STEPHEN E., healthcare services company executive; b. Dec. 6, 1959; m. Mary Kay; children: Michael Kay, Mark Kay, John Kay. B in Economics & Polit. Sci., U. Mich.; M in Hosp. & Health Adminstrn., U. Iowa. Joined Nat. Med. Enterprises, 1984; asst. adminstr. Lutheran Med. Ctr., St. Louis, 1985; CEO Green Oaks Hosp., Tex., North Tex. Hosp. for Children, Med. City Dallas Hosp., Harton Regional Med. Ctr., Tullahoma, Tenn.; sr. v.p., ops., tenets ctrl. NE southern states region Tenet Healthcare Corp., sr. v.p., tenets outpatient svcs. divsn., head, outpatient strategic devel. group, 2006—; pres., midwest divsn. HCA, Inc., Kansas City, 2007—, Holland Colours, Kansas City, 2007—. Office: HCA Inc One Park Plz Nashville TN 37203 Office Phone: 615-344-9551. Office Fax: 615-344-2266. Business E-Mail: steve.corbeil@hcahealthcare.com.

CORBETT, JEFFREY A., electric power industry executive; b. New Bern, NC; BSEE, U. NC, Charlotte. Registered profl. engr., Va., NC, Fla. Various engring and leadership positions Va. Power; supr., distbn. stds. Carolina Power & Light Co. (subs. of Progress Energy, Inc.), 1999, v.p., distbn., 2005—06, sr. v.p., 2008—; joined Progress Energy, Inc., 1999; gen. mgr., eastern region, dir., distbn., power quaility and reliabilty Progress Energy Carolinas (subs. of Progress Energy, Inc.), pres., CEO and v.p., distbn., v.p., eastern region Wilmington, NC, 2002—05; v.p., distbn. Fla. Power Corp. (subs. of Progress Energy, Inc.), 2005—06, sr. v.p., 2006—07, sr. v.p., energy delivery, 2006—08; sr. v.p., energy delivery carolinas Progress Energy, Inc., 2008—. Bd. dirs. Fla. Power Corp., Carolina Power & Light Co. Office: Progress Energy Inc 410 S Wilmington St Raleigh NC 27601 Office Phone: 919-508-5400. Office Fax: 919-546-2920. Business E-Mail: jeffrey.corbett@pgnmail.com.

CORBETT, LUKE R., energy executive; b. Feb. 11, 1947; m. Becky Corbett; 1 child, Carrie. Grad., U. Ga., 1969. Geophysicist Amoco Prodn. Co., Mitchell Energy, Aminoil; with Kerr-McGee Corp., 1985, group v.p., 1992—95, pres., COO, 1995—97, chmn., CEO, 1997—2006. Bd. dirs. Domestic Petroleum Coun., BOK Fin. Corp., Noble Corp., Integris Health, Inc., OGE Energy Corp., 1996—, OG&E, 1996—, Anadarko Petroleum Corp. (acquired by Kerr-McGee Corp.), 2006—. Mem. Nat. Petroleum Coun.; trustee Okla. United Meth. Ch.; bd. dirs. Allied Arts Found., United Way. Mem.: Okla. Bus. Roundtable, Soc. Exploration Geologists, Am. Assn. Petroleum Geologists, Oklahoma City C. of C. (bd. dirs.). Office: Anadarko Petroleum Corp Bd Directors 1201 Lake Robbins Dr The Woodlands TX 77380 also: OGE Energy Corp Bd Directors 321 N Harvey Oklahoma City OK 73101 Office Phone: 832-636-1000, 405-553-3000. Office Fax: 405-553-3567. Business E-Mail: corbettl@oge.com.

CORBIN, DONALD L., state supreme court justice; b. Hot Springs, Ark., Mar. 29, 1938; BA, U. Ark., 1964, JD, 1966. Bar: Ark. 1966, U.S. Dist. Ct. (we. dist.) Ark. 1966. Atty. pvt. practice, DeQueen, Ark., 1966—67; lawyer Lewisville and Stamps, 1967-80; judge Ark. Ct. Appeals, 1981-87, chief judge, 1987-90; assoc. justice Ark. Supreme Ct., Little Rock, 1991—. State rep. Ark. Gen. Assembly, 1971-80. Served with USMC, 1955-59. Mem. ABA, Ark. Bar Assn., SW Ark.

Bar Assn., Sigma Alpha Epsilon. Democrat. Avocation: duck hunting. Office: Supreme Ct Justice Bldg 625 Marshall St 120 Justice Bldg Little Rock AR 72201-1054 Office Phone: 501-682-6837. Business E-Mail: dcorbs@aol.com.*

CORBIN, THOMAS D., state legislator; b. Greenville, SC, 1965; s. Barbee and Gail McCarty Corbin; m. Leann Robertson, Dec. 12, 1993; children: Elliott Corbin, William Corbin. BS, Clemson U., 1987. Mem., deacon and sunday sch. tchr. Clearview Bapt. Ch.; v.p. Burban Creek Res., 2009, pres., 2010; mem. Dist. 17 SC House of Representatives, 2011—. Republican. Address: 1139 Bailey Mill Rd Travelers Rest SC 29690 Office: 522B Blatt Bldg Columbia SC 29201 Office Phone: 864-834-9915. E-mail: info@votecorbin.com.

CORBY, FRANCIS MICHAEL, JR., business executive; b. Chgo., Feb. 2, 1944; s. Francis M. and Jean (Wolf) C.; m. Diane S. Orselli, Aug. 5, 1972; children: Francis Michael III, Brian A., Christopher S. BA, St. Mary of the Lake, 1966; MBA, Columbia U., 1969. With Chrysler Corp., 1969-80; treasury mgr. Chrysler Peru S.A., Lima, 1973-74; fin. dir. Chrysler Wholesale Ltd., London, 1974-76; mng. dir. Chrysler Comml. S.A. de C.V., Mexico City, 1976-77; v.p., treas. Chrysler Fin. Corp., Troy, Mich., 1977-80; treas. Joy Mfg. Co., Pitts., 1980-83, contr., 1983-86, v.p., 1984-86; sr. v.p. fin., CFO Harnischfeger Industries, Inc., Milw., 1986-94, exec. v.p. fin. and adminstrn., 1994-99; exec. v.p. Frederick & Co., 2000-2001; exec. v.p., CFO Guide Corp., Pendleton, Ind., 2001—04; sr. v.p., CFO GST Autoleather Inc., Hagerstown, Md., 2004—05; exec. v.p., CFO, Exide Techs., Alpharetta, Ga., 2005—. Bd. dirs. Magnasphere Corp. Mem.: Country Club of Naples. Office: 13000 Deerfield Pkwy Bldg 200 Alpharetta GA 30004 Business E-Mail: fran.corby@exide.com.

CORCORAN, RICHARD, state legislator; b. Mar. 16, 1965; m. Anne Corcoran. BA, St. Leo U., Fla., 1989; JD, Regent U., 1996. Atty.; mem. Dist. 45 Fla. House of Representatives, 2011—. Republican. Office: Fla House of Reps 1101 The Capitol 402 S Monroe St Tallahassee FL 32399-1300 Home: 17953 Hunting Bow Cir Ste 101 Lutz FL 33558-5375 Office Phone: 727-816-1580, 850-488-8528.

CORDELL, F. THOMAS, lawyer; JD, U. Idaho, Moscow. Bar: Okla. 1979, US Dist. Ct. (Western Dist.), Okla. 1979, US Dist. Ct. (Eastern Dist.), Okla. 1979, US Dist. Ct. (Northern Dist.), Okla., US Ct. Appeals (10th Cir.). Ptnr. Frailey, Chaffin, Cordell, Perryman, Sterkel, McCalla & Brown LLP, Chickasha, Okla. Mem.: Fedn. Def. & Corp. Counsel (pres. 2010—11). Office: Frailey Chaffin Cordell Perryman Sterkel McCalla & Brown LLP 201 N 4th St PO Box 533 Chickasha OK 73018 Office Phone: 405-224-0237. Office Fax: 405-222-2231. Business E-Mail: tcordell@fccpsm.com.*

CORDEN, PAUL H., retired college program director, food service executive; b. Chattanooga, Sept. 28, 1947; s. Henry and Iris Cordon; m. Lori Corden, July 1968; 2 children. Degree, Xavier U., Cin., 1970, Ohio and Chase Coll. Law, Northern Ky. U. Mgr. plant ops. in comml. beverage industry; v.p. global equipment supplier in food svc. industry; pres. med. tech. co.; dir. profl. devel. for bus. and industry Spartanburg Cmty. Coll. Enlisted, med. corpsman USN, 1968. Decorated Bronze Star. Democrat. Home: 102 Montgomery Cir Spartanburg SC 29302-3437 Office Phone: 864-236-8260, 864-576-3660. Business E-Mail: volunteerforcordon@yahoo.com.

CORDERO, JOSE FERNANDO, pediatrician, dean; b. Camuy, PR, July 25, 1948; s. Fernando and Ana T. Cordero; m. Milagros J. Garcia, June 18, 1970; children: Jose F., Ana M., Joann M., Maria M. BS in Biology, U. P.R., Rio Piedras, 1969; MD, U. P.R., San Juan, 1973; MPH, Harvard U., 1979. Diplomate Nat. Bd. Med. Examiners, Am. Bd. Med. Genetics, Am. Bd. Pediatrics; lic. physician, Ga. Intern Boston City Hosp., 1973-74, jr. asst. resident dept. pediatrics, 1974-75; clin. and rsch. fellow pediatrics Mass. Gen. Hosp., 1975-77; pediatrician South End Cmty. Health Ctr., Boston, 1977-79; epidemiology intelligence svc. officer Bur. Epidemiology Ctrs. for Disease Control & Prevention, Atlanta, 1979-81, dep. chief birth defects and genetic diseases br., 1985-88, acting chief birth defects and genetic diseases bd., 1988-89, asst. dir. sci. divsn. birth defects and devel. disabilities, 1989-94, dep. dir. nat. immunization program, 1994—2001, dir. Nat. Ctr. on Birth Defects and Devel. Disabilities, 2001—06; asst. surgeon gen. USPHS, 1998—2006; dean U. P.R. Grad. Sch. Pub. Health, San Juan, 2006—. Clin. instr. pediatrics Children's Hosp., Boston, 1978-79; clin. asst. prof. pediatrics Emory U., 1982—. Co-editor jour. Teratology, 1983-86; mem. editl. bd. Birth Defects Ency., 1988; reviewer jours.; contbr. numerous articles and abstracts to publs. Mem. working group cancer chemotherapy Internat. Agy. Cancer Rsch., 1980; mem. task force on child health and related issues FDA, 1980-83; mem. rev. coms. NIH; coord. U.S. Govt. Task Force Premature Thelarche in P.R., 1982-85; trustee Calif. Birth Defects Monitoring Program, 1983-89; mem. adv. bd. TERIS, Seattle, 1986—, Fla. Teratogen Info. System, 1986-90; cons. WHO, Guatemala, 1990, 91, 92, Copenhagen, 1991; founding mem. Emmaus Community, 1992—; mem. troop 547 com. Boy Scouts Am., 1983-94. Recipient Arthur S. Flemming award, 1988, Physician's Recognition award AMA, 1980, 84, 88. Mem. APHA, Am. Soc. Human Genetics, Am. Bd. Med. Genetics, Am. Acad. Pediatrics (nutrition com. 1980, com. on drugs 1988-93, genetic com. 1985), Am. Epidemiology Soc., Mass. Med. Soc., Genetics Soc. Ga., Coalition of Spanish Speaking Mental Health and Human Svcs. Orgn., Teratology Soc., Soc. Pediatric Rsch. Roman Catholic. Avocations: bird watching, flying, painting, travel. Office: U PR Grad Sch Pub Health PO Box 365067 San Juan PR 00936-5067 Business E-Mail: jcordero@rcm.upr.edu.

CORDES, JOSEPH JOHN, economics professor; b. San Francisco, Apr. 16, 1949; s. Joseph John and Elisabeth (Kaiser) Cordes; m. Ann Elizabeth Knippel, June 22, 1974; children: Paul Joseph, Sarah Anne. BA, Stanford U., 1971; MS in Econs., U. Wis., 1975, PhD in Econs., 1977. Asst. prof. George Washington U., 1975—80, assoc. prof., 1980—85, prof. econs., 1985—2003, assoc. dean Coll. Arts and Scis., 1985—88, chair Dept. Econs., 1991—97, dir. PhD program in pub. policy and adminstrn., 1993—2006; assoc. dir. Trachtenberg Sch. Pub. Policy and Pub. Adminstrn., George Washington U., 2003—07, dir., 2007—09. Social sci. analyst US Dept. Labor, 1971, 1972; fin. economist Office of Tax Analysis, US Treas. Dept., 1980—81, 1984; dep. asst. dir. for tax analysis Congl. Budget Office, 1989—91. Author: The Impact of Tax and Financial Policy on Industrial Innovation, 1980; co-editor: Democracy, Social Values and Pub. Policy, 1998; contbr. articles to profl. jours. Ford Found. fellow, U. Wis., 1972—74. Mem.: Assn. for Rsch. on Nonprofit Orgn. and Voluntary Action, Assn. Pub. Policy Analysis and Mgmt., Eastern Econ. Assn., Internat. Inst. Pub. Fin., Nat. Tax Assn., Am. Econ. Assn. Democrat. Roman Catholic. Office: Sch Pub Policy and Adminstrn George Washington U 805 21st St Washington DC 20052 Office Phone: 202-994-5826. Office Fax: 202-994-8913.

CORDNER, HAROLD, pain management specialist; MD, St. George's U., Grenada, 1987. Diplomate American Bd. Anesthesiology, 1994, American Bd. Anesthesiology-pain medicine, 2007. Intern Monmouth Med. Ctr., Long Br., 1988—89, resident anesthesiology, 1989—92; fellow St. Christopher's Hosp. for Children, Phila., 1991; hosp. affiliations include Holmes Regional Med. Ctr., Melbourne, Palm Bay Cmty. Hosp.; assoc. surg. care Vero Beach Outpatient Surg. Ctr.; physician pain mgmt. Sebastian River Med. Ctr. Office: Sebastian River Medical Center 13695 North U S Hwy 1 Sebastian FL 32958-3230 Office Phone: 772-388-9999.*

CORDOBA, RICARDO, energy executive; B in Electro-Chem. Engring., M in Electro-Chem. Engring., Institut Nat. Polytechnique de Grenoble, France. Joined Alstom, 1982, GE Co., 1999, gen. mgr., GE Power Sys. Energy Products, Europe and Ctrl. Asia, gen. mgr., global sales, region exec., GE Energy, Europe, sales region exec., GE Power Sys., Europe, 2003, v.p., Energy Sales, region exec., Western Europe and North Africa, 2007—08, v.p., Energy Sales, Western Europe, 2008; pres., GE Energy Western Europe and North Africa General Electric Co., 2008—. Office: GE Energy 4200 Wildwood Pkwy Atlanta GA 30339 Office Phone: 678-844-6000. Office Fax: 678-844-6690. Business E-Mail: ricardo.cordoba@ge.com.

CÓRDOVA, FRANCE ANNE-DOMINIC, federal official, astrophysicist; b. Paris, Aug. 5, 1947; came to U.S., 1953; d. Frederick Ben Jr. and Joan Francis (McGuinness) C.; m. Christian John Foster, Jan. 4, 1985; children: Anne-Catherine Cordova Foster, Stephen Cordova Foster. BA in English with distinction, Stanford U., 1969; PhD in Physics, Calif. Inst. Tech., 1979; PhD (hon.), Loyola Marymount U., 1997, Ben Gurion U., 2011, Purdue U., 2012. Staff scientist earth and space sci. div. Los Alamos Nat. Lab., 1979-89, dep. group leader space astronomy and astrophysics group, 1989; prof., head dept. astronomy and astrophysics Pa. State U., University Park, 1989—96; chief scientist NASA, Washington, 1993-96; vice chancellor for rsch., prof. physics U. Calif., Santa Barbara, 1996—2002, chancellor, disting. prof. physics & astronomy Riverside, 2002—07; pres. Purdue U., West Lafayette, Ind., 2007—12, pres. emeritus, 2012—; dir. NSF, Arlington, Va., 2014—. Mem. Nat. Com. on Medal of Sci., 1991-94; adv. com. for astron. scis. NSF, 1990-93, external adv. com. Particle Astrophysics Ctr., 1989-93; bd. dirs. Assn. Univs. for Rsch. in Astronomy, 1989-93; mem. Space Telescope Inst. Coun., 1990-93; mem. com. space astronomy & astrophysics Space Sci. Bd., 1987-90, internat. users com. Roentgen X-ray Obs., 1985-90, extreme ultraviolet explorer guest observer working group NASA, 1988-93, com. Space Sci. and Applications Group, NASA, 1991-93; mem. Hubble Telescope Adv. Camera Team, 1993; chair Hubble Fellow Selection Com., 1992; bd. dirs. BioCrossroads, 2007-, SAIC Inc., 2008-; trustee Mayo Clinic, 2008-; mem. Nat. Sci. Bd., NSF, 2008-; bd. regents Smithsonian Instn., 2009-, chair, 2012- Guest editor Mademoiselle mag., 1969; editor: Multiwavelength Astrophysics, 1988, The Spectroscopic Survey Telescope, 1990; contbr. articles to profl. jours. including Astrophysics Jour., Nature, Astrophysics and Space Scis., Advanced Space Rsch., Astron. Astrophysics, Mon. Nat. Royal Astron. Soc., chpts. to books. Named one of America's 100 Brightest Scientists under 40, Sci. Digest, 1984; grantee NASA, 1979; recipient Distinguished Svc. medal, NASA, Kilby Laureate, 2000. Fellow American Acad. Arts & Scis., Assn. for Women in Sci. (AWIS); mem. Internat. Astron. Union (US nat. com. 1990-93), American Astron. Soc. (v.p. 1993-96, chair high energy astrophysics divsn. 1990, vice chair 1989). Achievements include research in analysis of ultra-soft x-ray emission from active galactic nuclei; observations and modeling of the winds from accretion disks; studies of the interstellar medium using ultraviolet spectroscopy of nearby hot binary stars; observations and modeling of extended x-ray emitting regions in close binary systems; understanding the accretion geometry of magnetic binaries with accreting white dwarfs; coordinating radio and x-ray observations of x-ray binaries in an effort to find a unified model for correlated behavior; search for evidence of galactic magnetic monopoles by identifying a class of ultrasoft x-ray emitters; studying the multispectial emission from neutron stars; making observations of x-ray emitting pulsars and their associated supernova remnants in the radio and infrared; conceiving space instruments and data systems for imaging detectors (co-principal investigator for optical/UV Telescope launched 1999 on ESA's X-Ray Multi-Mirror mission); making multifrequency observations of high-energy sources. Office: National Science Foundation 4201 Wilson Blvd Rm 1225 N Arlington VA 22230 Office Phone: 703-292-7000. Office Fax: 703-292-9232.*

CORDOVA, RUBEN CHARLES, art historian, curator, photographer; s. Ruben Cordova and Rose (Martinez) Vollmer. BA in Semiotics, Brown U., Providence, 1980; PhD in Art History, U. Calif., Berkeley, 1998. Pub. rels. assoc. Am. Craft Coun. and Am. Craft Mus., 1986—87; curator Hershel B. Chipp collection, 1990—91; instr. of record U. Calif., Berkeley, 1994, 1995, 1996; curator Mexican Mus., San Francisco, 1996—97; asst. prof. U. Tex. Pan Am., Edinburg, 1998—99, U. Tex., San Antonio, 1999—2007; guest prof. Sarah Lawrence Coll., Bronxville, NY, 2007—08; vis. scholar U. Houston, 2009—10. Cons. Arts and Entertainment Network, 1997; mem. art selection univ. libr. U. Tex Pan Am., 1998—99, mem. art exhbns. com., 1998—99; mem. faculty senate U. Tex., San Antonio, 2000—02, mem. univ. assembly, 2000—02; mem. adv. bd. NEH Rev. Com. San Antonio Mus. Art, 2000, A Ver: Revisioning Art History, UCLA, 2002; juror Henry Bonilla Congressional Art Competition, 2005. Author: (exhbn. catalogue) Arte Caliente: Selections from the Joe. A. Diaz Collection, 2004, Con Safo: The Chicano Art Group and the Politics of South Texas, 2009, (exhbn. catalogue editor) La Lengua Muerta, 2010; exhibitions include Francisco Zúñiga, Mexican Mus., San Francisco, 1996—97, Trees of Life, 1996—97, Community Collects, 1997, Day of Dead, 1997—98, Fantastic Creatures, 1997—98, Arte Contemporaneo, Aztlán Cultural Ctr., San Antonio, 2004, Mestizaje, Arte Reyes, San Antonio, 2005, César Chávez, Inst. Tex. Cultures, 2006, Barrio Dogs, Arte Reyes, 2006, Jesse Almazan, 2007, Enrique Martinez, One 4 Zero 6 Gallery, 2007, Counterculture x3, Vtrue Art Space, 2007; contbr. chapters to books, articles to catalogues and profl. jours.; one-man shows include Inst. Texan Cultures, 2006, exhibited in group shows at Stella Haus Gallery Blue Star Art Complex, San Antonio, 2005, Ctrl. Libr. Art Gallery, 2005 (1st Pl. award, 07), 2007, Alameda Nat. Ctr. Latino Arts and Culture, 2005, i2i Gallery, 2005, 2006, Gallista Gallery, 2005, Aztlán Cultural Ctr., 2005, 2006, 2007, Casa Margarita Gallery, 2005, 2006, Finesilver Art Gallery, 2006, Bihl Haus Arts, 2006, 2007, exhibited in group shows, Dia de los Muertos, Arte Reyes, 2009, Jesse Trevino, Museo Alameda, San Antonio, 2009—10, Blue Star Contemporary Art Center, 2006, San Anto Cultural Arts, San Antonio, 2006, Guadalupe Cultural Arts Center, 2007, Say Si, 2006, 2007, Willo North Gallery, Phoenix, 2011, Church, Treviso, Italy, 2011; author: Dia De Muertos and Jesse Trevino From Offer Page go have. Recipient Extending the Reach Instl. award, NEH, U. Tex.-San Antonio, 2001—02, rsch. award, U. Tex. San Antonio, 2000, 2003—04, 2005; grantee, U. Calif., Berkeley, 1996—97, Dean's Rsch. Asst. award, 1993—94, Tinker Found., 1994, Vice Chancellor Rsch. Fund award, U. Calif., Berkeley, 1994—95, McEnerny Fellowship for Innovation in Tchg., 1995—96, U. Calif., Berkeley, 1996, Judith Rothschild Found., Mexican Mus., 1997, William and Flora Hewlwtt Found., 1997; fellow, Samuel H. Kress Found., 1995—96, U. Calif., Berkeley, 1998; vis. scholar, U. Houston, 2009—10; Katz Grad. fellow, U. Calif., Berkeley, 1995, Marian Hahn Simpson fellow, 1995. Mem.: MASA, Nat. Assn. Chicano Scholars, Am. Assn. Museums (mem. curators' com., mem. Latino network pub. interest com., mem. Native Am. and mus. collaboration network), Coll. Art Assn. (mem. assn. L.Am. art, mem. Am. soc. Hispanic art hist. studies). Avocations: art collecting, movie memorabilia, photography. Home: 40 Silverhorn Dr San Antonio TX 78216

COREY, ANGELA B., prosecutor; b. Jacksonville, Fla. d. Thomas and Lorraine Corey. BS, Fla. State Univ.; JD, Univ. Fla. Bar: Fla. 1980, cert.: (in criminal trial law). Assoc. Howell & Howell, Jacksonville Beach, Fla., 1980—81; asst. state atty. 4th Judicial Circuit, Jacksonville, Fla., 1981—2007, 7th Judicial Circuit, St. Augustine, Fla., 2007—09; state atty. 4th Judicial Circuit, Jacksonville, Fla., 2009—. Republican. Episcopalian. Office: Office of State Atty Duval County Courthouse Annex 220 E Bay St Jacksonville FL 32202 Office Phone: 904-630-2400.

COREY, KAY JANIS, small business owner, apparel designer, nurse; b. Detroit, Aug. 22, 1942; d. Alexander Michael Corey and Lillian Emiline (Stanley) Kilborn; divorced; children: Tonya Kay, William James, Jason Ronald. Student, C.S. Mott Community Coll., 1960-62, Mich. State U., 1962-64; AA, AS in Nursing, St. Petersburg Jr. Coll., 1978; student, U. South Fla., 1985-86. RN; cert. perioperative nurse; cert. varitypist. Mgr. display Lerner Shops, Flint, Mich., 1960-62; layout artist Abdulla Advt., Flint, 1966-67; varitypist, artist City Hall Print Shop, Flint, 1967-70; nurse Suncoast Hosp., Largo, Fla., 1976-78; nurse, coord. plastic surgery svc., perioperative staff nurse Largo Med. Ctr. Hosp., 1978-81, 84-90; assoc. dir. nursing Roberts Home Health Svc., Pinellas Park, Fla., 1982-84; co-owner Sand Castle Resort, White Bay, Jost Van Dyke, Brit. Virgin Island, 1990-95; perioperative nurse HCA Gulf Coast Surgery Ctr., 1995-99; perioperative nurse, surg. nurse Blake Med. Ctr. Hosp., 2000—07, Cmty. Hosp., 2007—. Designer, artist K.J. Originals clothing line, 1990-95, The Magic Needle clothing line, 1998; insvc. edn. instr., dir. video edn., team leader oncology dept. Largo Med. Ctr. Hosp., 1980-81; designer, mfr. Haelan Jewelers--Fine Custom Jewelry, 1999. Editor, illustrator: (book) Some Questions and Answers About Chemotherapy, 1981, Thoughts for Today, 1981; illustrator (cookbooks) Spices and Spoons, 1982, Yom Tov Essen n' Fressen, 1983; various brochures and catalogues; art work in permanent collection of C.S. Mott Jr. Coll., Flint, 1962; artist, designer of casual and hand painted clothing for children and adults. Historian Am. Businesswomen's Assn., Flint, 1968-73 (scholarship 1976); outreach chmn. Temple B'nai Israel, Clearwater, Fla., 1981-85; regional outreach coord. Union of Am. Hebrew Congregations, N.Y.C., 1983-85. Mem. Assn. of Oper. Rm. Nurses, Phi Theta Kappa. Republican. Jewish. Avocations: sailing, scuba diving, tennis, original teddy bear making, golf. Address: 905 Victoria Dr Dunedin FL 34698 Personal E-mail: kaysemail@tampabay.rr.com.

COREY, LINDA ANN, medical educator, researcher; b. Latrobe, Pa., June 7, 1948; d. John Stephen and Anna Lucy Corey. PhD, NC State U., Raleigh, 1974. Postdoc. fellow Ind. U. Purdue U., Indpls., 1974—76; prof. Va. Commonwealth U., Richmond, 1976—. Chartered mem. EDC1 study sect. NIH, Washington, 1997—2001, 2002—06. Mem. bd. Action Prevention Devel. Disabilities, Richmond, Va., 1979—82. Postdoc. fellow, NIH, 1974—76. Mem.: AAUP (campus rep. 2006—), AAAS, Internat. Biometrics Soc., Internat. Soc. Twin Rsch., Internat. Genetic Epidemiology Soc., Am. Soc. Human Genetics, Am. Epilepsy Soc. Independent. Roman Catholic. Achievements include research in genetic effects on prolonged seizures. Avocations: travel, dog breeding, art, crafts. Office: Virginia Commonwealth Univ PO Box 980033 Richmond VA 23298-0033 Office Fax: 804-827-1124. Business E-Mail: corey@vcu.edu.

COREY, ORLIN RUSSELL, publishing executive; b. Nowata, Okla., May 4, 1926; s. Lue A. and Nada Gladys (Patton) C.; m. Irene Lockridge, Aug. 25, 1949 (div. 1974); m. Shirley Trusty, Nov. 27, 1975. BA, Baylor U., 1950, MA, 1952; cert. of directing and acting, Ctrl. Sch. Speech and Drama, London, 1956. Drama dir., asst. prof. Georgetown (Ky.) Coll., 1952-59; drama dir., assoc. prof. Centenary Coll., Shreveport, La., 1960-68; dir. touring repertory theatre of classics Everyman Players, Pineville, Ky., 1958-80; pub., editor Anchorage Press, Inc., New Orleans, 1977-2000, editl. advisor, 2000—. Guest dir. U. N.H., Durham, 1968; lectr. Ohio State U., also other univs., 1968—75; prodr. John F. Kennedy Ctr., Washington, 1973—75; pres. Children's Theatre Found., Inc., Greensboro, NC, 1977—2001; mem. exec. com. Nat. Theater Conf., 1985. Author: Theatre for Children, 1973, Towers of the Brazos, Theatre for Children—Kid-Stuff or Theatre?, 1974, An Odyssey of Masquers: The Everyman Plwyers, 1990, Religious Drama: A Classic Quartet, 1999; adapter, dir. drama of book of Job, 1960; prodr. La. World Expo, World Theatre Festival, New Orleans, 1984. Bd. dirs. New Orleans Ctr. Creative Arts, 1975—, Nat. Theatre Conf. With USN, 1944-46, PTO. Recipient religious drama award Nat. Cath. Theater Assn., 1968, Radius, London, 1974. Fellow Am. Theatre (dean Coll. Fellows 1994-96, Jennie Heiden award 1970); mem. Children's Theater Assn. Am. (pres. 1971-73), Am. Alliance for Theatre and Edn. Avocations: photography, cooking, reading.

CORKEN, HEATHER MARIE, lawyer; b. Kalamazoo, May 12, 1969; d. Michael Rhodes and Karen Marie Fitzgerald; m. Kevin Robert Corken, May 14, 1994; children: Katherine Marie, Brittany Michelle, Margaret Alice, Elizabeth Ashley. BA, Rhodes Coll., Memphis, 1991; JD, Vanderbilt U. Sch. Law, Nashville, 1994. Bar: Tex. 1994. Assoc. Fulbright & Jaworski LLP, Houston, 1994—2005, ptnr., 2006—. Mem. United Way of Tex. Gulf Coast, mem. women's initiative steering com.; mem. Alexis de Tocqueville Soc.; mem. adv. coun. Houston Zoo. Mem.: ABA, Houston Bar Assn., DRI, State Bar Tex. Office: Fulbright & Jaworski LLP Fulbright Tower 1301 McKinney Ste 5100 Houston TX 77010 Office Fax: 713-651-5246. Business E-Mail: hcorken@fulbright.com.

CORKER, BOB (ROBERT PHILLIPS CORKER JR.), United States Senator from Tennessee; b. Orangeburg, SC, Aug. 24, 1952; s. Robert Phillips Corker; m. Elizabeth Corker, 1987; children: Julia, Emily. BS in Indsl. Mgmt., U. Tenn., 1974. Founder Bencor Corp., 1978—2001, Chattanooga Neighborhood Enterprise, 1986—; finance & adminstrn. commr. State of Tenn., 1995—96; owner Osborne Bldg. Corp. & Stone Fort Land Co., 1999—; mayor City of Chattanooga, Tenn., 2001—05; US Senator from Tenn., 2007—. Bd. dirs. U. Chattanooga Found., Chattanooga Housing Authority, Creative Discovery Mus., Southside Devel. Corp.; mem. exec. com. United Way. Mem.: Urban League, Rotary Club. Republican. Episcopalian. Office: US Senate 425 Dirksen Senate Office Building Washington DC 20510 also: 3322 West End Ave Ste 610 Nashville TN 37203 Office Phone: 202-224-3344, 615-279-8125. Office Fax: 202-228-0566, 615-279-9488.*

CORLESS, GARY A., wholesale distribution executive; BS in Fin., Fla. State U., 1985. Various leadership positions Physician Bus., 1990—96, regional v.p., sales & ops., 1996—97; v.p., Southern Region Diagnostic Imaging, 1997—98, sr. v.p., Eastern Region, 1998—99; pres., Elder Care Bus., Gulf South Med. Supply PSS World Medical, Inc., 1999—2002, pres., Physician Bus., Physician Sales & Svc., 2002—05, exec. v.p., 2002—10, COO, 2005—10, pres., CEO, 2010—. Office: PSS World Medical Inc 4345 Southpoint Blvd Jacksonville FL 32216 Office Phone: 904-332-3000. Office Fax: 904-332-3213. Business E-Mail: gcorless@pssd.com.

CORLEW, JOHN GORDON, lawyer; b. Dyersburg, Tenn., July 13, 1943; s. Emmett Atkins and Margaret Elizabeth (Swann) C.; m. Elizabeth Lee Scott, July 8, 1967; children: John Scott, William

Heath, Carey Elizabeth. BA, U. Miss., 1965; JD, Vanderbilt U., 1968. Bar: Miss. 1968. Clk. to judge U.S. Dist. Ct. (so. dist.) Miss., 1968-69; assoc., then ptnr. Megehee, Brown, Williams & Corlew, Pascagoula, Miss., 1969-74; sole practice Pascagoula, 1975-78; ptnr. Corlew, Krebs & Hammond, Pascagoula, 1978-84, Watkins & Eager, Jackson, Miss., 1984—2009, Corlew, Munford & Smith, Jackson, 2009—. Mem. Miss. State Senate, 1974-80, chmn. appropriations com., 1979, chmn. constn. com., 1975-79, chmn. legis. audit com., 1978; chmn. Miss. State Bd. Pub. Welfare, 1980-84. Mem. ABA, Am. Coll. Trial Lawyers, Am. Bd. Trial Advs., Miss. Bar Assn., Hinds County Bar Assn., Miss. Bar Found., Order of Coif, Phi Delta Phi. Democrat. Methodist. Home: 2124 Eastover Dr Jackson MS 39211-6719 Office: 4450 Old Canton Rd Ste 111 Jackson MS 39211 Office Phone: 601-366-1106.

CORN, MORTON, environmental engineer, educator; b. NYC, Oct. 18, 1933; s. Julius and Sophie (Haber) C.; m. Jacqueline Karnell, Aug. 21, 1955; children: Matthew Irwin, Frederick Eliot. BS in Chem. Engring., Cooper Union, 1955; MS, Harvard U., 1956, PhD, 1961. Asst. san. engr. USPHS, Cin., 1956-58; rsch. assoc. Harvard, 1960-61; asst. prof. U. Pitts., 1962-65, assoc. prof., 1965-66, prof. Grad. Sch. Pub. Health and Sch. Engring., 1967-79; prof. and divsn. head environ. health engring. Sch. Hygiene and Public Health, Johns Hopkins U., Balt., 1980-97; prof. emeritus Johns Hopkins U., Balt., 1997—; pres. Morton Corn; Assocs., Cons. Engrs., 1977—. Cons. divsn. biology and medicine AEC, 1965—74; chmn. air pollution rsch. grants com. EPA, 1968—71, mem. sci. adv. bd., 1978—84; mem. com. no biol. effects air pollution NAS, 1971, mem. com. risk assessment, 1982—83; mem. expert panel occupl. health WHO, 1973—98; asst. sec. labor for occupl. safety and health U.S. Dept. Labor, 1975—77; mem. Allegheny County Air Pollution Adv. Com., 1967—72; mem. nat. adv. com. health vital stats. Dept. HHS, 1979—81; mine health rsch. adv. com. Nat. Inst. Occupl. Safety and Health, 1986—89, GM/UAW joint health and safety adv. com., 1988—92; chmn. OTA Commn. Preventing Injury and Illness in the Workplace, 1982—84; chmn. tech. adv. bd. Clean Sites, Inc., Alexandria, Va., 1984—87; trustee Assoc. Univ., Inc., 1991—93; mem. Hanford tank adv. panel DOE, 1993—99; cons. Health, Safety and Environment, 1993. Chmn. Gov. of Md.'s Toxic Coun., 1986-89. NSF postdoctoral fellow U. London, 1961-62; WHO fellow, 1970; Guggenheim fellow, 1972 Fellow APHA, Argentine Acad. Engring.; mem. Argentine Acad. Scis., Am. Soc. Safety Engrs., Am. Indsl. Hygiene Assn. (bd. dirs. 2000-03), Am. Conf. Govt. Indsl. Hygienists (chmn. 1983-84). Home: 7425 Pelican Bay Blvd Apt 1701 Naples FL 34108-5504 Office Phone: 410-827-7305. Personal E-mail: mjcorn.com@gmail.com.

CORNELISON, ALBERT OTTO, JR., (BERT CORNELISON), lawyer, oil industry executive; b. NYC, Apr. 22, 1949; s. Albert O. and Margaret E. (Adams) C.; children: Adam Snow, Brendan Stover, Morgan Adams. BS cum laude, U. Santa Clara, 1971; JD, U. Calif., Davis, 1974. Bar: Calif. 1975, DC 1975, US Dist. Ct. (dist. DC) 1975, US Ct. Appeals (DC cir.) 1976, Md. 1989, Tex. 1992. Assoc. Howrey & Simon, Washington, 1974—82, ptnr., 1983—84; sr. assoc. counsel litig. Ogden Corp., NYC, 1984—86; v.p., gen. counsel Ogden Fin. Svcs., NYC, 1987—89; dep. gen. counsel Electronic Data Systems (EDS), 1990—93; staff v.p., assoc. gen. counsel litig. Dresser Industries, 1994—98; v.p., assoc. gen. counsel Halliburton Co., Houston, 1998—2002, v.p., gen. counsel, 2002, exec. v.p., gen. counsel, 2002—. Mem.: ABA, Assn. Gen. Counsels, State Bar of NY. Office: PO Box 42807 Houston TX 77242-2807*

CORNELL, DEWEY GENE, psychologist; b. Louisville, June 22, 1956; m. Nancy Emily Trinka, Aug. 19, 1978; children: Cristina, Allison, Erin. AB, Transylvania U., 1977; MA, U. Mich., 1979, PhD, 1981. Lic. clinical psychologist. Intern U. Mich. Psychol. Clinic, Ann Arbor, 1979-81; postdoctoral scholar dept. psychiatry U. Mich., Ann Arbor, 1981-83; clin. psychologist Ctr. Forensic Psychiatry, Ann Arbor, 1983-86; asst. prof. Sch. Edn., U. Va., Charlottesville, 1986-91, assoc. prof., 1991-99, prof., 1999—, faculty assoc. Inst. Law, Psychiatry and Pub. Policy, 1986—. Dir. Va. Youth Violence Project, 1996—; asst. prof. psychology Mich. State U., East Lansing, 1985-86; pvt. practice, Charlottesville, 1986—. Author: Families of Gifted Children, 1984, Designing Safer Schools for Virginia, 1998; co-editor: Juvenile Homicide, 1989, Issues in School Violence Research, 2004; co-author: Recommended Practices in Gifted Education, 1991, Guidelines for Responding to Student Threats of Violence, 2006, School Violence: Fears versus Facts, 2006; contbr. articles to profl. jours. Fellow Internat. Soc. Rsch. Aggression; mem. APA, Am. Psychology Law Soc., Va. Psychol. Assn., Am. Edni. Rsch. Assn., Nat. Assn. Sch. Psychologists Achievements include development of threat assessment guidelines for schools and colleges. Avocations: Go, basketball, tennis. Office: University Va Sch Edn 417 Emmet St PO Box 400267 Charlottesville VA 22904-4267 Home Phone: 434-973-3943; Office Phone: 434-924-0793. Business E-Mail: dcornell@virginia.edu.

CORNELSON, GEORGE HENRY, IV, retired textile company executive; b. Spartanburg, SC, July 12, 1931; s. George Henry Cornelson III and Elizabeth Marshall (Woodward) Cornelson; m. Ann Martin Shaw, Oct. 6, 1956; children: George Henry Cornelson V, Martin Shaw, Scott Montgomery, Elizabeth Woodward. Student, Davidson Coll., NC, 1949-51; BS in Textiles, NC State U., Raleigh, 1953; postgrad. in Bus. Adminstrn., Harvard U., Cambridge, Mass., 1953—54; DHL (hon.), Presbyn. Coll., Clinton, SC, 2003. With indsl. engring. dept. Clinton Mills, Inc., SC, 1954-55, 57-58, from v.p. to pres., 1958—86, CEO, 1985—86; v.p. Clinton Mills Sales Corp., NYC, 1958—86. Bd. dirs. Elastic Fabrics of Am., NC Textile Found., exec. com.; pres. Clinton Investment Co., 1985—86; bd. dirs. Clinton Mills of Geneva, past pres., dir.; vice chmn. bd. dirs. Bailey Fin. Corp., 1996—99; bd. dirs. Anchor Bank, Myrtle Beach, SC, 1999—2000, Carolina First Bank, Greenville, SC, 2000—03; mem. SC Gov.'s Trade Mission to Far East, Hong Kong, Singapore, 1979, Kuala Lumpur, 1979, Taiwan, 1979, Malaysia, 1979. Trustee Presbyn. Coll., Clinton, 1959—68, 1994—2005, trustee emeritus, 2006—; trustee Davidson Coll., 1992—95, bd. visitors, 1986—91; trustee Ind. Coll. and Univs. S.C., 1971—92, life trustee, 1993—; trustee Thornwell Home for Children, Clinton, 1968—76, exec. com., 1973—74, sec. bd. trustees, 1974; organizing chmn. Greater Clinton Planning Commn., 1967—68; pres. Cmty. Chest and United Fund, 1963—64; chmn. Laurens County dist. Boy Scouts Am., 1973, exec. bd. Blue Ridge coun., 1974; chair adv. com. Bailey Found., 1969—; dir. SC State Mus. Found., 1986—89; expansion com. mem. Carolina's NFL, 1988—92; bd. dirs. Columbia Theol. Sem., Decatur, Ga., 1990—93; trustee Laurens County Health Care Sys., 1996—2000, chmn., 1997—99; deacon 1st Presbyn. Ch., Clinton, 1959—67, elder, 1967—73, 1976—81, 1983—87, 1988—93, elder emeritus, 2006. Officer USAF, 1955—57. Recipient Disting. Svc. award, Clinton Jr. C. of C., 1962, Outstanding Young Alumnus award, NC State U., 1965, Disting. Alumnus award, 1999, McCallie Sch., 1989, Order of Palmetto, SC, 2009. Mem.: SC Textile Mfrs. Assn. (bd. dirs. 1973—82, pres. 1979—80), Am. Textile Mfrs. Inst. (rsch. and tech. svcs. com. 1964—71, vice chmn. Crafted With Pride in USA com. 1985—87, vice chmn. edn. com. 1975—76, cotton com. 1981—82, safety amd health com. 1981—82), Clinton C. of C. (bd. dirs. 1959—61, 1966, v.p. 1968, pres. 1969), SC C. of C. (bd. dirs., exec. com. 1975—79), Musgrove Mill Golf Club (founder, bd. dirs.), Lions Club, Kappa Alpha, Phi Psi. Home: Merrie Oaks 1644 Hwy 56 S Clinton SC 29325

CORNETT, MICK, mayor, Oklahoma City; b. Oklahoma City, 1958; m. Lisa Cornett; 3 children. Degree in journalism television news, Univ. of Oklahoma. Sportscaster and news anchor KOCO-5, 1981—97, city hall news anchor, 1997—99; pres. Mick Cornett Video Productions Inc., 1999—; ward 1 council mem. Oklahoma City Council, 2001—04; mayor Oklahoma City, 2004—. Chair urban econ. policy com. U.S. Conf. Mayors, trustee, 2007—. Office: 200 N Walker 3rd Floor Oklahoma City OK 73102 Business E-Mail: mayor@okc.gov.*

CORNETTE, ROBERT E., pediatric nurse practitioner, educator; s. Robert E. and Betty M. Cornette; m. Kandis C. Lowe; children: M. Blake Gibson, Emily K. Gibson. Cert. practitioner, Pediatric Nursing Certification Bd., 1999, DNP, U Ky., Lexington, 2008. Assoc. dean nursing Tenn. Wesleyan Coll.; assoc. prof. Berea Coll., Ky., 2002—12; pnp Family Care Ctr., Lexington, Ky., 2003—12; asst. prof. U. Ky., 2009. Contbr. articles to profl. jour. Fellow: Nat. Assn. PNP; mem.: Nat. Scholars Honor Soc., Delta Epsilon Iota, Sigma Theta Tau. Avocations: motorcycling, jogging. Office: 6233 Apache Trail Knoxville TN 37920 also: 9845 Cogdill Rd Knoxville TN 37932 Office Fax: 865-777-5114. Business E-Mail: rcornette@twcnet.edu.*

CORNFIELD, DANIEL BENJAMIN, sociology educator; b. Washington, Nov. 5, 1952; s. Melvin and Edith (Haas) Cornfield; m. Hedy Merrill Weinberg, June 30, 1985. AB, U. Chgo., 1974, AM, 1977, PhD, 1980. Assoc. prof. sociology Vanderbilt U., Nashville, 1980—. Contbr. articles to profl. jours. Appearances various TV and radio programs. Russell Sage Found., 1985, Nat. Coun. Employment Policy, 1980. Mem.: Indsl. Rels. Rsch. Assn., Southern Sociol. Soc., Am. Sociol. Assn. Democrat. Jewish. Avocations: guitar, clarinet, saxophone, piano, labor union. Office: Dept Sociology Vanderbilt U Nashville TN 37203

CORNISH, RICHARD POOL, lawyer; b. Evanston, Ill., Sept. 9, 1942; s. William A. and Rita (Pool) C.; children: William Darby, Richard Gordon. BS, Okla. State U., 1964; LLB, U. Okla., 1966. Bar: Okla. 1966, U.S. Dist. Ct. (ea. dist.) Okla. 1969, U.S. Supreme Ct. 1979. Ptnr. Baumert & Cornish, McAlester, Okla., 1967-71, Cornish & Cornish, Inc., McAlester, 1971-77; magistrate U.S. Dist. Ct. for Ea. Dist. Okla., McAlester, 1976—2000; prin. Richard P. Cornish, Inc., McAlester, 1977—. Bd. dirs. McAlester Boys Club, 1970-80, pres., 1974. Capt. JAGC, USAR, 1966-78. Mem. Okla. Bar Assn. (legal aid to servicemen com., legal specialization com.), Pittsburg County Bar Assn., McAlester C. of C. (bd. dirs. 1973-75). Roman Catholic. Home: 611 E Creek Ave Mcalester OK 74501-6929 Office: PO Box 1106 Mcalester OK 74502-1106 Office Phone: 918-423-5070. Business E-Mail: cornishrp@yahoo.com.

CORNIS-POPE, MARCEL HORATIU, literature educator, literary critic, program director; b. Arad, Romania, Feb. 14, 1946; came to U.S., 1983; s. Gheorghe and Sidonia (Bogdan) Cornis-Pop; m. Doina Damian, July 31, 1967 (div. Nov. 1975); m. Micaela V. Lungu, May 27, 1976; children: Laura A., Anca L., Oana R. BA in English, Babes-Boyai U., 1967; MA in English Lit., Babes-Bolyai U., Cluj-Napoca, Romania, 1968; PhD in Am. and Comparative Lit., U. Timisoara, Romania, 1977. Cert. tchr. English. Asst. prof. English U. Timisoara, Timis County, Romania, 1968—77, assoc. prof. English, 1977—83; Fulbright vis. prof. U. Northern Iowa, Cedar Falls, 1983—87; Mellon faculty fellow Harvard U., Cambridge, Mass., 1987—88; assoc. prof. Va. Commonwealth U., Richmond, 1988—91, prof. English, 1991—. English dept. chair Va. Commonwealth U., Richmond, 2000—06, dir. interdisciplinary PhD program, 2006—10, English co-chair, 2010—11. Author: Anatomy of the White Whale, 1982 (Romanian writers award 1983), Hermeneutic Desire and Critical Rewriting, 1992, The Unfinished Battles: Romanian Postmodernism Before and After 1989, 1996, Narrative Innovation and Cultural Rewriting in the Cold War Era and After, 2000; co-editor: Violence and Mediation in Contemporary Culture, 1995, History of the Literacy Cultures of East-Central Europe, 4 vols., 2004-10; translator novels, poetry from and into English; assoc. editor European Studies Jour., 1984; mng. editor Micromegas, 1984-87; editor The Comparatist, 1990-98; contbr. articles to profl. jours. Lt. Romanian Inf., 1975, Zalau, Romania. Fulbright Rsch. and Teaching grantee, 1983-85; Mellon Faculty fellow Harvard U., 1987-88, fellow The Netherlands Inst. Advanced Studies in the Humanities and Social Scis., 1999-2000; recipient Romanian Writers' awards for best book criticism, Bucharest, Romania, 1983, for best poetry transl. into English, 1976, Disting. Scholarship award Va. Commonwealth U., 1991, Disting. Lectr. award Va. Commonwealth U., 1994, Phoenix award for disting. editl. achievement, 1996, Univ. Overall award, 2006. Mem. MLA (pres. Romanian Studies Assn. Am. 1991-94, bibliographer MLA Internat. Bibliography 1985-95), Soc. for the Study of Narrative Lit., Soc. for Critical Exch., South Alantic MLA, Internat. Comparative Lit. Assn. (v.p. coordinating publ. com. 2009-13, pres. coord. pub. com. 2013-), Internat. Assn. Philosophy and Literature. Ea. Orthodox. Avocations: tennis, travel. Home: 1504 Sunset Ln Richmond VA 23221 Office: Va Commonwealth Univ Dept English PO Box 842005 Richmond VA 23284-2005 Office Fax: 804-828-8684. Business E-Mail: mcornis@vcu.edu.

CORNWELL, DAVID (WILLIAM DAVID CORNWELL SR.), lawyer; b. Washington, Sept. 28, 1960; s. Edward E. and Shirley (Nims) C.; m. Kimberly Hargrave, Aug. 10, 1991; children: Taylor Alexis, William David Jr. BA, Tufts U., 1982; JD, Georgetown U., 1985. Bar: NY 1986, Calif. 1995, Ga. Assoc. Whitman & Ransom (now Whitman, Breed, Abbott & Morgan), NYC, 1985-87; asst. counsel, dir. equal employment NFL, NYC, 1987-92; assoc. Steinberg & Moorad, Newport Beach, Calif., 1992-93, of counsel, 1997; joined The Upper Deck Co., LLC, Carlsbad, Calif., 1993, v.p., gen. counsel, 1994—97; gen. counsel, sec. Upper Deck Authenticated, Ltd., Carlsbad, Calif., 1993-97; pvt. practice Newport Beach, Calif., 1997—2012; pres. DNK Cornwell, LLC; ptnr. sports, media and entertainment Gordon & Rees LLP, 2012—. Bd. dirs. Internet Extra, San Francisco; expert witness, litigation cons. in sports-related cases; guest lectr. Wharton Bus. Sch. Mem. ABA (minority in-house counsel), Calif. Bar Assn., NY Bar Assn., Sports Lawyers Assn. (bd. dir.), Nat. Football League Coaches Assn. (exec. dir., 2012-) Avocation: basketball. Office: Gordon & Rees LLP 3455 Peachtree Rd Ste 1500 Atlanta GA 30326 Office Phone: 404-869-9054. Office Fax: 678-389-8475.*

CORNYN, JOHN, III, United States Senator from Texas; b. Houston, Feb. 2, 1952; s. John and Gale Cornyn; m. Sandra Hansen; children: Danley, Haley. BA in Journalism, Trinity U., San Antonio, 1973; JD, St. Mary's U., 1977; LLM, U. Va., 1995. Bar: Tex. 1977, US Dist. Ct. We. Dist. Tex. 1980, cert.: Tex. Bd. Legal Specialization (in personal injury trial law). Atty. Groce, Locke & Hebdon, San Antonio, 1977—84; judge 37th Dist. Ct., Bexer County, 1985—90; presiding judge 4th Adminstrv. Jud. Region, 1989—92; justice Supreme Ct. Tex., Austin, 1991—97; ptnr. Thompson & Knight, 1997—99; atty. gen. State of Tex., Austin, 1999—2002; US Senator from Tex., 2002—; asst. minority leader (minority whip), 2013—; mem. US Senate Finance Com., 2009—, US Senate Agrl., Nutrition & Forestry Com., 2009—11, US Senate Armed Services Com., 2011—13; vice chmn. US Senate Select Com. on Ethics, 2007—09, US Senate Republican Conf., 2007—09; chmn. Nat. Republican Senatorial Com. (NRSC), 2009—13. Tex. Supreme Ct. liaison Gender Bias Task Force, 1993—95; chmn. James Madison Meml. Found., 2009—. Recipient Outstanding Tex. Leader award, John Ben Shepperd Pub. Leadership Forum, 2000, James Madison award, Freedom Info. Found. Tex., 2001, Disting. Alumnus award, Trinity U., 2001, Mfg. Legis. Excellence award, Nat. Assn. Manufacturers, 2004, Congl. Partnership award, Nat. Assn. Devel. Orgn., 2004, Friend of Farm Bur. award, American Farm Bur. Fedn., 2004, Friend of Rural Water award, Tex. Rural Water Assn., 2004, Hero of Taxpayer award, American Tax Reform, 2004, Statesman of Yr. award, Tex. Asian Rep. Conf., 2004, Border Texan of Yr. award, 2005, Children's Champion award, Nat. Child Support Enforcement Assn., Fighter of Free Enterprise award, Tex. Assn. Bus., Guardian of Small Bus. award, Nat. Fedn. Independent Bus., Latino Leadership award, Nat. Coalition Latino Clergy & Christian, Internat. Leadership Legislative award, Mex. American Chamber of Commerce; named a Champion for Healthcare in Rio Grande Valley, Valley Baptist Med. Ctr., Tex., 2004. Fellow: San Antonio Bar Found., Tex. Bar Found.; mem.: ABA, Tex. Bar Assn., Robert W. Calvent Inn of Ct. (pres. 1994—95), William Sessions Inn of Ct. (master bencher 1988—90, pres. 1989—90), American Law Inst. Republican. Church Of Christ. Office: US Senate 517 Hart Senate Office Bldg Washington DC 20510 also: District Office Ste 1530 221 West Sixth St Austin TX 78701-3403 Office Phone: 202-224-2934, 512-469-6034. Office Fax: 202-228-2856, 512-469-6020.*

CORONADO, WILLIAM J., tobacco company executive; Various mgmt. positions Universal Corp., Richmond, Va., 1981—89, contr., 1989—2000, mgmt. positions, 2000—02; sr. v.p. Universal Leaf Tobacco Co. (subs. Universal Corp.), Richmond, Va., 2002—03; v.p., strategic planning Universal Corp., Richmond, Va., 2003—. Mailing: Universal Corp PO Box 25099 Richmond VA 23260-5099 Office Phone: 804-359-9311. Office Fax: 804-254-3584. Business E-Mail: william.coronado@universalcorp.com.

CORR, EDWIN GHARST, ambassador; b. Edmond, Okla., Aug. 6, 1934; s. E.L. and Rowena C.; m. Susanne Springer, Nov. 24, 1957; children: Michelle Ruth, Jennifer Jean, Phoebe Rowena. BS, U. Okla., 1957, MA, 1961, U. Tex., 1969. Fgn. svc. officer Dept. State, Wash., 1961-62; assigned to Mex., 1962-66; Peace Corps dir. Cali, Colombia, 1966-68; Panama desk officer Dept. State, 1969-71; program officer Inter Am. Found., 1971; exec. asst. to amb. Am. Embassy, Bangkok, 1972-75, counselor polit. affairs Quito, Ecuador, 1976, dep. chief of mission, 1977-78; dep. asst. sec. internat. narcotics matters Dept. State, 1978-80; U.S. Amb. to Peru Lima, 1980-81; U.S. Amb. to Bolivia La Paz, 1981-85; U.S. Amb. to El Salvador San Salvador, 1985-88; Dept. State diplomat-in-residence U. Okla., Norman, Okla., 1988—90, prof. polit. sci., 1990—96; dir. Energy Inst. Ams. U. Okla., 1996—2002; assoc. dir. Internat. Programs Ctr. U. Okla., 1996—2007, sr. rsch. fellow, 2007—; cons., contractor Okla. U. Author: The Political Process in Colombia, 1971; co-editor: Low-Intensity Conflict: Old Threats in a New World, 1992, The Middle East Peace Process: Vision vs. Reality, 2002, The Search for Israeli-Arab Peace, 2007; co-author: The Search for Security: The U.S. Grand Strategy in the 21st Century, 2003; contbr. to books and profl. jours. Mem. bd. dirs., vice chair Bd. Med. Assistance Programs Internat., Smile Colombia With USMC, 1957—60, capt. USMC. Mem. Am. Fgn. Service Assn. Home: 1617 Jenkins Ave Norman OK 73072-6508 E-mail: ecorr@ou.edu.

CORR, JAMES VANIS, furniture manufacturing executive, accountant; b. Selma, Ala., June 28, 1922; s. Mark Stroud and Julia (Dozier) C.; m. Judith Ann Hackney, Feb. 3, 1971; children by previous marriage: James Jr., William V., Emily S., Julia D. BS, U. Ala., 1948, LLB, 1951. CPA, Ala., Ga. Ptnr. Dent & Corr, CPA's, Birmingham, Ala., 1954-61; exec. v.p. Buck Creek Industries, Inc., Atlanta, 1961-70, pres., 1970-77, also bd. dirs.; v.p. Sperry & Hutchinson Co., NYC, 1976-78, group v.p. furnishings divsn. Atlanta, 1976-78. Pres. JVC Enterprises, Inc., Atlanta, 1978—; speaker tax clinic U. Ala., 1954—. Bd. dirs. Met. YMCA, Birmingham. With AC, USMCR, 1944-46 Decorated D.F.C., Air medal with 2 oak leaf clusters. Mem. Ala. Soc. CPAs (past chmn. Birmingham chpt.), Ga. Soc. CPAs, ABA, Ala. Bar Assn., Am. Inst. CPAs, Ala. Textile Assn., Ga. Textile Assn., Exch. Club (Birmingham), Mountain Brook (Ala., past pres.). Home: 545 River Chase Pt NW Atlanta GA 30328-3555 Office Phone: 770-859-0900.

CORRADA DEL RIO, ALVARO, bishop; b. Santurce, PR, May 13, 1942; Ordained priest Soc. of Jesus, 1974; pastoral coord. Northeast Cath. Hispanic Ctr., NYC, 1982-85; aux. bishop Archdiocese of Washington, Md., 1985; ordained bishop, 1985; bishop Diocese of Tyler, Tex., 2001—. Roman Catholic. Office: Bishop of Tyler 1015 ESE Loop 323 Tyler TX 75701-9663 Office Phone: 903-534-1077. Office Fax: 903-939-1037. E-mail: bishopoffice@dioceseoftyler.org.

CORRADO, MICHAEL LOUIS, law educator; b. Altoona, Pa., Feb. 12, 1940; s. Alfred Ernest and Isolina Dorothy (Marinella) C.; m. Gail Ann Byer, Nov. 1966; children: Crispin Allyn, Gianmichael David. BA, Pa. State U., 1965, BS, 1966; MA, Brown U., 1968, PhD, 1970; JD, U. Chgo., 1984. Bar: Ill. 1985, U.S. Ct. Appeals (7th cir.) 1985, U.S. Ct. Appeals (4th cir.) 1989, U.S. Dist. Ct. (no. dist.) Ill. 1987. Prof. philosophy Ohio U., Athens, 1970-81; jud. clk. U.S. Ct. Appeals (7th cir.), Chgo., 1984-85; atty. Mayer Brown & Platt, Chgo., 1985-88; from assoc. prof. to prof. law U. N.C., Chapel Hill, 1988—, Arch Allen prof. law, 1999—, prof. philosophy, 2001—, assoc. dean, 1996—. Author: Analytic Tradition in Philosophy, 1975, Justification and Excuse, 1994, Comparative Constitutional Review, 2005; editor Law and Philosophy, 1996-2001, carolina Series in Comparative Law, 2000-. Sgt. U.S. Army, 1961-64. Mem. ABA, Am. Philos. Assn., Am. Soc. Polit. and Legal Philosophy. Office: U NC Law Sch Cb 3380 Chapel Hill NC 27599-0001

CORRELL, DONALD L., healthcare industry executive; m. Chris Correll. BS in Acctg., Pa. State U.; MBA in Fin., NYU. CPA NY. Various positions, including sr. v.p., CFO, chmn., pres., CEO United Water Resources, Harrington Park, NJ, 1978—2003; pres., CEO, bd. dirs. Pennichuck Corp., Merrimack, NH, 2003—06, American Water Works Co., Vorhees, NJ, 2006—10. Mem., environ. fin. adv. bd. U.S. EPA; commr. NJ Water Supply Authority; pres. Nat. Assn. Water Companies; bd. dirs. HealthSouth Corp., 2005—, NJ Resources Corp., 2008—. Bd. mem. U.S. C. of C. Office: HealthSouth Corp 3660 Grandview Pkwy Ste 200 Birmingham AL 35243 Office Phone: 205-967-7116. Office Fax: 205-969-3543. Business E-Mail: donald.correll@healthsouth.com.

CORRIERE, JOSEPH N., JR., urologist, educator; b. Apr. 3, 1937; m. Evelyn Pavia Mossey, June 25, 1960 (div. July 1984); children: Joseph N., Christopher John, Gregory James, Evelyn Anne; m. Eileen Doyle Brewer, Oct. 17, 1987. BA, U. Pa., 1959; MD, Seton Hall Coll. Medicine, 1963. Diplomate Am. Bd. Urology (trustee). Intern Pa. Hosp., Phila., 1963—64; asst. instr. surgery, fellow Harrison Dept.

Surgery Rsch. Hosp. U. Pa., Phila., 1964—65, asst. instr. urology, 1965—68, USPHS urol. rsch. trainee, 1967—68, instr. urology, 1968—69, assoc. in urology, 1969—71, asst. prof. urology, 1971—74; veneral disease trainee Phila. Dept. Pub. Health, 1965; radioisotope trainee William H. Donner Ctr. for Radiology, Phila., 1965—66; prof., dir. divsn. urology, dept. surgery U. Tex. Med. Sch., Houston, 0974—1993, interim chmn. dept. surgery, 1980—82, assoc. chmn. dept. surgery, 1984—86; chief urology svc. Hermann Hosp., 1974—93, Tex. Med. Ctr., Houston. Cons. residency rev. com. in urology Lyndon Baines Johnson Hosp., 1993—99, M.D. Anderson Cancer Ctr.; cons. NASA. Contbr. numerous articles to profl. jours. Maj. USAF, 1969—71. Mem.: ACS, Am. Assn. for Surgery of Trauma, Am. Assn. Genitourol. Surgery, Soc. Univ. Urologists, Soc. Univ. Surgeons (sec.-treas. 1984—86, pres. 1987—88, 1987—88), Am. Urol. Assn. (dir. edn. 1993—2002). Roman Catholic. Home: 7511 Morningside Dr Houston TX 77030-3619 Office: MD Anderson Cancer Ctr Unit 1274 1220 Holcombe Blvd Houston TX 77030-4004

CORRIGAN, MICHAEL, county official, former councilman; m. Edna DeAngelis; children: Chelsea, Emily, Connor. AA, Fla. Jr. Coll.; attended, U. North Fla.; grad., Leadership Fla., 1996, Leadership Jacksonville, 1997. Councilman Dist. 14 Jacksonville City Coun., Fla., 2003—11, pres. Fla., 2006—07, Nu-Trend Plastics; Duval County tax collector City of Jacksonville, 2011—. Chmn. Fin. Com.; mem. Recreation, Cmty. Devel. & Personnel Coms. Chmn. 1000 in 1000, Fla. First Coast Workforce Devel. Consortium, Spl. Com. on City Pension Reform; co-chmn. Jacksonville Children's Commn. Rev. Com.; mem. North Fla. Transp. Planning Org., Tourist Devel. Coun., Jacksonville Children's Zone Com., Duval County Tourist Devel. Coun., Spl. Com. on Group Health Benefits. Recipient Cmty. Connections Tribute Honoree, 2004, Delores Kesler Cmty. Mentor award, TELEmachus, 2008, Nat. Family Week Adv. award, Family Foundations, 2008. Mem.: First Coast Manufacturing Assn. (bd. mem.), Gator Bowl Assn., Big Brothers & Big Sisters (pres. 1993—94), Riverside Avondale Preservation (chmn. 1996—98, Neighborhood Adv. award 2009), Rotary Club of West Jacksonville (pres. 2002—03, J.J. McCranie award 1999, Robert T. Shircliff award 2007). Republican. Roman Catholic. Office: Duval County Tax Collector 231 E Forsyth St Jacksonville FL 32202 Office Phone: 904-630-1916. E-mail: taxcollector@coj.net.

CORRIGAN, TIMOTHY J., federal judge; b. Jacksonville, Fla., 1956; BA, U. Notre Dame, 1978; JD, Duke U., 1981. Law clk. to Hon. Gerald B. Tjoflat US Ct. Appeals (11th cir.), 1981—82; pvt. practice atty. Fla., 1982—96; magistrate judge US Dist. Ct. (mid. dist.) Fla., 1996—2002, judge Jacksonville, 2002—. Office: US Dist Ct Simpson US Courthouse 300 N Hogan St Rm 11-100 Jacksonville FL 32202 Office Phone: 904-549-1300.

CORRIGAN, VICTOR E., cardiologist; Grad. summa cum laude, U. Ga.; MD, Med. Coll. Ga., 1983. Diplomate Am. Bd. Internal Medicine, 1986, Am. Bd. Internal Medicine-cardiovasc. disease, 1989, Am. Bd. Internal Medicine-inteventional medicine, 1999. Resident internal medicine Emory Univ. Hosp., Atlanta, 1983—86, fellow cardiovasc. disease, 1986—88; hosp. affiliation includes Piedmont Heart Inst., Atlanta. Fellow: Am. Coll. of Cardiology; mem.: Am. Heart Assn., Atlanta Cardiology Group. Office: Piedmont Heart Institute Ste 300 275 Collier Rd NW Atlanta GA 30309 Office Phone: 404-605-2800.

CORRIVEAU, DAVID O., recreational facility executive; Co-founder D&B Holding, 1989—95; pres., co-CEO Dave & Buster's, Dallas, 1995—, dir., 1995—, co-chmn. bd., 1996—. Office: Dave and Busters 2481 Monana Dallas TX 75220

CORROTHERS, HELEN GLADYS, criminal justice official; b. Montrose, Ark., Mar. 19, 1937; d. Thomas and Christene (Farley) Curl; m. Edward Corrothers, Dec. 17, 1968 (div. Sept. 1983); 1 child, Michael Edward. AA in Liberal Arts magna cum laude, Ark. Bapt. Coll., 1955; BS in Bus. Adminstrn. Mgmt., Roosevelt U., 1965; grad. officer leadership sch., WAC Sch., 1965; grad, Inst. Criminal Justice, Exec. Ctr. Continuing Edn., U. Chgo., 1973; postgrad., Calif. Coast U., 1981—. Enlisted U.S. Army, 1956, advanced through grades to capt., 1969, chief mil. pers. Ft. Meyer, Va., 1965-67; dir. for housing Giessen Support Ctr., Germany, 1967-69; resigned, 1969; social interviewer Ark. Dept. Corrections, Grady, 1970-71, supt. women's unit Pine Bluff, 1971-83; commr. U.S. Parole Commn., Burlingame, Calif., 1983-85, U.S. Sentencing Commn., Washington, 1985-91; fellow U.S. Dept. Justice, Washington, 1992-95; criminal justice cons., 1996—. Instr. women and crime U. Md., College Park, 1994; instr. corrections U. Ark.-Pine Bluff, 1976-79; mem. bd. visitation Jefferson County Juvenile Ct., Pine Bluff, 1978-81; bd. dirs. Vols. in Cts., 1979-83, Vols. Am., 1985-94; mem. Am./Can. study team Mex. penal system Am. Correctional Assn., Islas Marias, Mex., 1981; mem. Ark. Commn. Crimes and Law Enforcement, 1975-78; mem. U.S. Atty. Gen.'s Correctional Policy Study Team, 1987. Mem. Ark. Commn. on Status of Women, 1976-78; bd. dirs. Com. Against Spouse Abuse, 1982-83; mem. nat. adv. bd. dept. criminal justice Xavier U., Cin., 1993-97; bd. dirs. Bapt. Mission Found. of Md./Del., Columbia, Md., 1993-98. Recipient Ark, Woman of Achievement award Ark. Press Women's Assn., 1980, Human Rels. award Ark. Edn. Assn., 1980, Outstanding Woman of Achievement award Sta. KATV-TV, Little Rock, 1981, Correctional Svc. award Vols. Am., 1984, William H. Hastie award Nat. Assn. Blacks in Criminal Justice, 1986, Outstanding Victim Advocacy award Nat. Victim Ctr., 1991, Appreciation cert. Dept. Justice Office for Victims of Crime, 1994; recipient testimonial for svc. to fed. judiciary Adminstrv. Office of Cts., 1991 Excellence award Am. Chaplains Assn., 2009. Mem.: NAFE, Nat. Orgn. Hispanics in Criminal Justice, Am. Soc. Criminology, Nat. Coun. on Crime and Delinquency, Ark. Law Enforcement Assn., N.Am. Assn. Wardens and Supts., Am. Correctional Assn. (treas. 1980—86, v.p. 1986—88, pres. 1990—92, mem. Del. Assembly 1993—, chmn. rsch. coun. 1997—2000, mem. past pres. coun. 1998—, chmn. Correctional awards com. 2001—05, chmn. retirees com. 2005—07, mem. pres.'s field adv. task force 2005—07, mem. ethics com. 2003—, E.R. Cass Correctional Achievement award 1993), Ark. Sheriff's Assn. (hon.), Delta Sigma Theta (local sec. 1976—79, local parliamentarian 1983). Baptist. Avocations: reading, music. Office: Am Correctional Assn 206 N Wash St Ste 200 Alexandria VA 22314

CORSIGLIA, NANCY, bank executive; AB, Smith Coll.; MBA, Dartmouth Coll. Mgr. in treas. office Gen. Motors Corp.; CFO Fedn. Agrl. Mortgage Corp.; v.p. fed. govt. fin. Paine Webber Inc.; advisor Bank of Va., contbr., interim CFO, 2010, CFO, 2011—, exec. v.p., 2011—. Mem.: Pvt. Nat. Mortgage Acceptance Co. Mortgage Opportunity Funds (bd. dirs.), Stoneleigh-Burnham Sch. (bd. trustees). Office: Bank of Virginia PO Box 5658 Midlothian VA 23112 Office Phone: 804-744-7576.

CORTES, JORGE, oncologist; b. Mexico; MD, U. Nat. Autónoma Méx. Dep. chair dept. leukemia U. Tex. MD Anderson Cancer Ctr., Houston, 2002—. Recipient Young Investigator award, Celgene, 2005, Dr. John J. Kenny award, Leukemia & Lymphoma Soc., 2006, Svc. to Mankind award, 2007, Faculty Achievement award in clin. rsch., U. Tex. MD Anderson Cancer Ctr., 2007; fellow Hematology, Oncology, 1991—95. Mem.: Am. Assn. Cancer Rsch., Am. Soc. Clin. Oncology, Am. Soc. Hematology. Office: MD Anderson Cancer Ctr 1515 Holcombe Blvd Unit 428 Houston TX 77030 Business E-Mail: jcortes@mdanderson.org.

CORTEZ, PATRICK PAGE, state legislator; BA Edn. & Gen. Studies, U. La, Lafayette. Co-owner & operator La-Z-Boy Furniture Gallery, Stoma's Furniture; mem. Dist. 43 La. House of Reps., 2008—12; mem. Dist. 23 La. State Senate, 2012—. Republican. Office: 101 W Farrell Rd Bldg 5 Ste 100 Lafayette LA 70508 also: La State Senate State Capitol 900 N 3rd St Baton Rouge LA 70804 Office Phone: 337-993-7430. Business E-Mail: cortezp@legis.la.us.

CORTY, ANDREW P., publishing executive; b. Wilmington, Del., June 16, 1952; s. Claude and Susanne Corty; m. Betty L. Wallace, Apr. 30, 1983; children: Robert Wallace, Edward Wallace. AB, Harvard U., 1974; MBA, Stanford U., 1978. Copy editor The Morning News, Wilmington, 1974—75; reporter The Record, Havre de Grace, Md., 1975—76; asst. to pub. The St. Petersburg (Fla.) Times, 1978—80; pub. Fla. Trend mag., St. Petersburg, 1981—85; gen. mgr. Washington Post mag., 1985—89; mktg. dir. St. Petersburg Times, 1989—91; v.p., sec., bd. dirs. Times Pub. Co., St. Petersburg, 1991—; vice chmn. Congrl. Quar., Inc., Washington, 1991—2009; pres. Fla. Trend, St. Petersburg, 1991—. Trustee and exec. com. Salvador Dali Mus., St. Petersburg, Fla; mem. Leadership Fla.; mem., bd. trustees Enterprise Fla., 2009-. Office: Times Publishing Co PO Box 1121 Saint Petersburg FL 33731-1121

CORZINE, JENNIFER JEAN, music educator; b. Evanston, Ill., Apr. 2, 1946; d. Raymond Alfred and Majorie Palmer; children: Christopher, Lindsay, Erin. MusB with hon., Wis. State U., 1968; MA, U. Hawaii, 1970; MS, Fla. State U., 1991, MSW, 1994. Cert. tchr. NY, Fla. Vocal music tchr. Tomorrow River Sch., Amherst, Wis., 1968—69, Greece Ctrl. Sch. Dist., Rochester, NY, 1970—71; instrumental music tchr. Pittsford Ctrl. Sch., NY, 1971—72; gen. music tchr. Evansville-Vanderburgh Sch. Corp., Ind., 1972—73; instrumental music tchr. Maclay Sch., Tallahassee, 1973—. Vol. choir mem. various ch., 1970—85; vol. family counselor Family Living Ctr., Tallahassee, 1986; vol. Am. Heart Assn., 1999—2005; vol. supr. social work interns Maclay Sch., 2002—06. Mem.: Fla. Bandmasters Assn., Fla. Music Educators Assn., Music Educators Nat. Conf. Achievements include established instrumental music program at Maclay School. Avocations: travel, reading, gardening. Office: Maclay Sch 3737 N Meridian Rd Tallahassee FL 32312 Office Phone: 850-893-2138. Business E-Mail: jcorzine@maclay.org.*

COSGROVE, JOHN A., state legislator; b. Montgomery, Ala., June 7, 1954; m. Sue Ann Culpepper; children: Michael, Brian. Elected mem. Chesapeake City Coun., 1998—2000; Chesapeake vice-mayor, 2000—01; state del. Dist. 78 Va., 2002—. Mem.: Chesapeake Crimeline, Sorensen Inst., Fraternal Order Police, South Norfolk Ruritan, Fourth Congressional Dist. GOP Com. (chmn.), Chesapeake Rotary. Republican. Baptist. Mailing: Dist Off PO Box 15843 Chesapeake VA 23328 Office Phone: 757-547-3422. Fax: 757-548-4795. Business E-Mail: Del_Cosgrove@house.state.va.us.

COSKEY, WILLIAM A., engineering company executive; BSEE, Tex. A&M U., 1975. Registered profl. engr. Founder, bd. dirs. ENGlobal Corp., 1985, pres., CEO, chmn., 1985—2001, COO, 2001—03, pres., 2001—05, chmn., 2005—, pres., CEO, 2007—. Bd. dirs. Petrocon FSC Ltd. Mem. Tex. A&M U. Elec. Engring. Dept. Adv. Coun., 1999—, chmn., 2006—. Named an Entrepreneur of Yr., Ernst & Young, 2009. Mem.: Instrument Soc. America. Office: ENGlobal Corp 654 N Sam Houston Pky E Ste 400 Houston TX 77060-5914 Office Phone: 281-878-1000. Office Fax: 281-878-1010. Business E-Mail: william.coskey@englobal.com.

COSLET, JONATHAN, investment company executive; BS in Economics summa cum laude, Univ. Pa.; MBA, Harvard U. Investment mgmt. positions Drexel Burnham Lambert, 1987—89, Donaldson, Lufkin & Jenrette, 1991—93; sr. ptnr. TPG Capital, LP, 1993—. Bd. dirs. Burger King Corp., Petco Animal Supplies, Inc., Quintiles Transnational Corp., IASIS Healthcare Corp., Fidelity Nat. Info. Svcs., J.Crew Group, Inc., Harrah's Entertainment, Inc., Biomet, Inc., Neiman Marcus, Inc., 2005—. Named Baker Scholar, Loeb Fellow, Gordon Fellow, Steur Fellow. Office: TPG Capital LP Ste 3300 301 Commerce St Fort Worth TX 76102 Office Phone: 817-871-4000. Office Fax: 817-871-4010.

COSPOLICH, JAMES DONALD, electrical electronics executive, consultant; b. New Orleans, Dec. 19, 1944; s. Clarence James and Olga Marie C.; m. Shirley Patricia Knipper, Feb. 4, 1967; children: Brian James, Jeffery Donald, Stephen William. BEE, La. State U., 1967, MEE, 1972. Registered profl. engr., La., Calif., Tex. Geophysicist Pan Am. Petroleum Corp. subs. AMOCO, New Orleans, 1967; elec. engr. Waldemar S. Nelson & Co., New Orleans, 1967, asst. v.p., mgr. elec. engring., 1974—83, v.p., mgr. elec. engring., 1983—85, sr. v.p. ops., 1985—91, exec. v.p., 1991—2008, sr. cons., 2009—; with USCG Res., 1964—72. Mem. API RP 500,RP 505, RP 14F, & RP 14FZ Task Groups; ex-Mem. Nat. Elec. Code Panel 14. Past mem. Rep. Nat. Com., Washington, 1988; v.p. Ormond Civic Assn., Destrehan, La., 1985, pres., 1986; past mem. representing St. Charles Parish, New Orleans Internat. Airport Noise Abatement Com. Mem. NFPA (nat. elec. code com.), IEEE, NSPE, Instrument Soc. Am. (sr., com. mem. 1975—), Am. Petroleum Inst. (com. recommended practice stds.), Gas Processors Assn., La. Engring. Soc., Ormond Country Club, The Am. Legion. Republican. Roman Catholic. Avocations: fishing, tennis, golf, skiing, boating, woodworking. Home: 61 Rosedown Dr Destrehan LA 70047-2529 Office: Waldemar S Nelson & Co Inc 1200 Saint Charles Ave New Orleans LA 70130-4334 Personal E-mail: jim.cospolich@wsnelson.com.

COSS, STEPHEN K., lawyer; b. 1969; m. Jennifer Coss; children: Lucas, Kevin, Erin. BA, Duke U., 1991; JD, U. Va. Sch. Law, 1994. Assoc. Parker Poe Adams & Bernstein LLP, 1994—99; gen. counsel Sonic Automotive Inc., Charlotte, NC, 2000—04, sr. v.p., gen. counsel, 2004—. Mem.: ABA, 1994. Office: Sonic Automotive 4401 Colwick Rd Charlotte NC 28211-2311 Office Phone: 704-566-2420. Fax: 704-927-3412. E-mail: steve.coss@sonicautomotive.com.

COSSÉ, STEVEN A., lawyer, retired oil industry executive; b. Dec. 2, 1947; m. Andree D. Cossé. BA in Polit. Sci., Southeastern La. U., Hammond; JD, Loyola U. Bar: La. 1975. Jr. acct. trainee Ocean Drilling & Exploration Company, New Orleans, 1969, several positions with accounting and land departments, 1969—74, atty., 1974—83, gen. counsel, 1983—91, Murphy Oil Corp., El Dorado, Ark., 1991—2011, v.p., 1993—94, sr. v.p., 1994—2005, exec. v.p., 2005—11, pres., CEO, 2012—13. Dir. Simmons First Nat. Corp., 2004—; bd. dirs. Murphy Oil Corp., 2011—. Chmn. Southern Arkansas Chapter of the American Red Cross. Mem.: Union County Bar Assn., La. Bar Assn., American Corp. Counsel Assn., Nat. Assn. of Manufacturers. Office: Murphy Oil Corp 200 Peach St PO Box 7000 El Dorado AR 71731-7000 Office Phone: 870-862-6411. Office Fax: 870-864-6373. E-mail: steve_cosse@murphyoilcorp.com.*

COST, MIKE, telecommunications industry executive; BS in Law, Middle Tenn. State U., 1982; postgrad., Belmont U., 1992. Various positions BellSouth; v.p., device supplier mgmt. Cingular Wireless, 2000—07; COO Pantech Wireless, Inc., 2006—07; pres., COO Brightstar US, 2007—09; global COO Brightstar Corp., 2009—. Bd. dirs. Curing Kids Cancer Found.; treas. Pi Kappa Alpha. Office: Brightstar Corp Ste 300 9725 NW 117th Ave Miami FL 33178 Office Phone: 305-421-6000. Business E-Mail: michael.cost@brightstarcorp.com.

COSTA, GREGG JEFFREY, federal judge; b. Baltimore, 1972; BA, Dartmouth Coll., 1994; JD, U. Tex. Sch. Law, 1999. Elementary sch. tchr., Sunflower, Miss., 1994—96; law clk. to Hon. A. Raymond Randolph US Ct. Appeals (DC Cir.), Washington, 1999—2000; Bristow Fellow, Office Solicitor Gen. US Dept. Justice, Washington, 2000—01; law clk. to Chief Justice William Rehnquist US Supreme Ct., Washington, 2001—02; assoc. Weil, Gotshal & Manges, Houston, 2002—05; asst. US atty. (southern dist.) Tex. US Dept. Justice, Houston, 2005—12; judge US Dist. Ct. (southern dist.) Tex., Galveston, Tex., 2012—. Office: US District Court 601 Rosenberg Rm 411 Galveston TX 77550 Office Phone: 409-766-3530.*

COSTA, MARY, soprano; b. Knoxville, Tenn., Apr. 5, 1930; Student, L.A. Conservatory of Music; PhD (hon.), Hardin-Simmons U., 1973; D in Fine Arts (hon.), Carson-Newman Coll., Jefferson City, Tenn., 2007. Film voice of Aurora Disney's Sleeping Beauty, 1959; appeared TV commls., 1955—57; debut LA Opera, 1958; appeared Glyndebourne Opera House, 1958; v.p. Calif. Inst. Arts; in La Boheme, San Francisco Opera, 1959; recorded "La Boheme" for RCA Victor from the stage of Rome Opera Ho., 1961; soloist John F. Kennedy Meml. Svc. at Sports Arena, LA, 1963; as Violetta in La Traviata Met. Opera, NYC, 1964; appeared Royal Opera House Covent Garden, Teatro Nacional de San Carlos, Grand Theatre de Geneve, Vancouver, Lisbon, Kiev, Leningrad, Tbilisi, Boston, Cin., Hartford, Newark, Phila., San Antonio, Seattle; toured US with Bernstein's Candide; appeared English prodn. Candide; tour Soviet Union, 1970; Bolshoi debut in La Traviatta, 1970; revival Bernstein's Candide at John F. Kennedy Ctr. for Performing Arts, 1971; starring role motion picture The Great Waltz, 1972; v.p. Hawaiian Fragrances, Honolulu, 1972; appeared internat. recitals, orchs.; command performance at the White House, 1974; Met. Opera hist. tour of Japan as Musetta in La Boheme, 1975. Recipient DAR Honor medal, 1974, Tenn. Hall of Fame award, 1987, Women of Achievement award, Northwood Inst., Palm Beach, Fla., 1991, So. Birmingham Coll., 1993, Tenn. Achievement award, Gov. of Tenn., 1998, Disney Legends award, 1999, Disting. Verdi performances of 20th Century, Met. Opera Guild, 2001, Hon. award, LA Guild Opera, 2009; named Woman of Yr., LA, 1959, Tenn. Woman of Distinction, Am. Lung Assn., 2000; named to Hall of Fame, Knoxville Opera, 2007; Mary Costa Scholarship established at U. Tenn., 1979. Achievements include apptd. by Pres. to serve on Nat. Coun. on the Arts, 2003; featured artist at Hollywood Bowl tribute to "Walt Disney: 75 Years of Music", 2004.

COSTELLO, FREDRICK W., state legislator; b. Orlando, Fla., Feb. 9, 1950; m. Linda Gail Ditzig Costello; children: Lucas Jacob, Angela, Eric David. BS, Graceland U., 1970; DDS, U. Iowa, 1974. Dentist; mayor City of Ormond Beach, Fla., 2002—10; mem. Dist. 26 Fla. House of Representatives, 2011—. Capt. USAF, 1974—77. Republican. Office: Fla House of Representatives 1101 The Capitol 402 S Monroe St Tallahassee FL 32399-1300 Office Phone: 850-488-9873.

COSTELLO, STEPHEN C., councilman, engineering company executive; m. Debra Costello; children: Stephen, Christopher. BS in Civil Engring., SUNY, Buffalo; MBA, U. Houston. Civilian US Army Corps of Engrs., Galveston, Tex.; co-founder, pres. Costello, Inc.; councilman-at-large, Position 1 Houston City Coun., 2010—. Chair, bd. mem. Meml. Park Conservancy. Mem.: Am. Coun. Engring. Companies, Tex. Coun. Engring. Companies (bd. mem.), Houston Coun. Engring. Companies (past pres.), Houston Area Road Runners Assn. (pres. 1995—97). Avocation: running. Office: City Hall Annex 900 Bagby, 1st Fl Houston TX 77002 Office Phone: 832-393-3014. Office Fax: 832-393-3347. E-mail: atlarge1@cityofhouston.net.

COSTELLO, WILLIAM F., broadcast executive; Ptnr. KPMG LLP; CFO, COO & bd. dirs. Best Products; pres. QVC Internat., 2001; CFO QVC Inc., West Chester, Pa., 1989, COO, 2002. Bd. dirs. HSN Inc. Office: QVC 1363 Enterprise Dr West Chester PA 19380-5959 also: HSN Inc Bd Directors 1 Hsn Dr Saint Petersburg FL 33729-0001 Office Phone: 272-872-1000. E-mail: william.costello@hsn.net.

COSTER, JOHN M., retail executive, health science association administrator; BS in Pharmacy, St. John's U., NY, 1984; MS in Health Policy, U. Md., Balt., 1988, PhD in Health Policy, 1989. Staff mem. Am. Soc. Hosp. Pharmacists, 1984—87; policy fellow Ctr. Drugs & Pub. Policy, U. Md. Grad. Sch., 1988—90; health analyst US Congress Office Tech. Assessment, 1989—90; profl staff mem. US Senate Spl. Com. on Aging, 1990—94; v.p. policy & programs Nat. Assn. Chain Drug Stores, Alexandria, Va., 2000—07; v.p. fed. affairs & pub. policy Rite Aid Corp., 2007—09; sr. v.p. govt. affairs National Community Pharmacists Association, 2009—. Recipient Alumni Outstanding Achievement award, St. John's U., 2009. Office: NCPA 100 Daingerfield Rd Alexandria VA 22314 E-mail: john.coster@ncpanet.org.

COSTLEY, GARY EDWARD, chemicals executive; b. Caldwell, Idaho, Oct. 26, 1943; s. Donald Clifford and Verna C.; m. Cheryl J. Zesiger, Dec. 21, 1963; children: Angela I., Chad D. BS, Oreg. State U., MS in Nutrition-Biochemistry, PhD in Nutrition-Biochemistry, Oreg. State U. Dir. nutrition, dir. public affairs, v.p. public affairs, v.p. & asst. to pres. Kellogg Co., sr. v.p. corp. devel., sr. v.p. sci. and quality, exec. v.p., sci. and tech., exec. v.p.; pres. Kellogg USA Inc.; area dir. Kellogg N.Am., to 1994; chmn., pres. & CEO Internat. Multifoods, 1997—2004; dean, Grad Sch. Mgmt. Wake Forest U., 1995—97; chmn., CEO International Multifoods Corp., 1997—2004, pres., 1997—2001; co-founder, mng. dir. C&G Capital and Mgmt., LLC. Bd. dirs. Candlewood Inc., Tiffany & Co., Prestige Brands Holdings, Inc., 2004—, Covance Inc., 2007—. Trustee Miller Found, Battle Creek, Youth for Understanding Internat. Exch., Am. Health Found., Sarah W. Stedman Ctr.-Duke U. Med. Sch. Mem. Am. Inst. Nutrition. Lutheran. Home: 257 Barefoot Beach Blvd 404-202 Bonita Springs FL 34134-8594 Office: Covance Inc Bd Directors 210 Carnegie Ctr Princeton NJ 08540 Office Phone: 609-452-4440. Office Fax: 609-452-9375. Business E-Mail: gary.costley@covance.com.

COSTONIS, JOHN J., law educator, former academic administrator; b. 1937; AB, Harvard U., 1959; LLB, Columbia U. Bar: D.C. 1967, Ill. 1968. Asst. prof. U. Pa., 1965-69; assoc. Ross, Hardies, O'Keefe, Babcock & Parsons, Chgo., 1968-70; dean law sch. Vanderbilt U., Nashville, 1985—98, prof. environtl. law, 1998; pres. Quantum Found., Fla., 1996—97; chancellor La. State U. Law Sch., Baton Rouge, 1998—2007, Judge Albert Tate, Jr. and Rosemary Neal Hawkland prof. Vis. lectr. internat. law U. Chgo., 1968; vis. assoc. prof. U. Ill.-Chgo., 1970, prof., 1972—77; vis. prof U. Calif.-Berkeley, 1975—76; prof. NYC, 1978; advisor to pres. Adv. Coun. of Hist. Preservation, Nat. Endowment for Arts, NSF, Sec. Interior, Nat. Trust for Hist. Preservation. Past articles editor: Columbia Law Rev.

Served to 1st lt. I.C. U.S. Army, 1960-62. Mem. Am. Law Inst., Am. Planning Assn. Office: La State U Sch Law Office of Chancellor 400 Law Ctr E Campus Dr Baton Rouge LA 70803-0001 Office Phone: 225-388-8491.

COSTRELL, ROBERT MICHAEL, economist; b. Washington, Apr. 10, 1950; s. Louis and Esther (Klaiman) C.; m. Rochelle Myrna Ryman, Dec. 17, 1983 (dec. Nov. 26, 2013); children: Sarah Anne, Benjamin David. BA, U. Mich., 1972; PhD, Harvard U., 1978. Asst. prof. U. Mass., Amherst, 1978—85, assoc. prof., 1985—92, prof., 1992—2006; prof. edn. reform and econs., endowed chair edn. accountability U. Ark., Fayetteville, 2006—; fellow George W. Bush Inst., Southern Meth. U., 2011—13. Vis. asst. prof. U. Toronto, 1982-84; adj. assoc. prof. Brandeis U., Waltham, Mass., 1986; cons. panel on tech. and employment NAS, Washington, 1986, joint econ. com. U.S. Congress, 1987-88; vis. scholar Boston U., 1993-94; dir. R&D Mass. Exec. Office for Adminstrn. and Fin., 1999-2002, chief economist, Commonwealth of Mass., 2003-06; edn. advisor Mass. Gov. Mitt Romney, 2005-06; steering com. Econ. Framework and Specifications, Nat. Assessment of Ednl. Progress, 2001-02, govs. designee Pub. Employee Retirement Adminstrn. Commn. 2001-2003, Mass. Sch. Bldg. Authority, 2005-06. Contbr. articles to profl. jours. Pres. Brookline Com. for Quality Edn., 1990-95; gov. appointee Mass. Tax Alternatives Commn., 1997-98; adv. coun. on edn. stats. US Dept. Edn., 2001-02; mem. Nat. Tech. Adv. Coun. US Dept. Edn., 2008-09. Mem. Am. Econ. Assn., Assn. Edn. Fin. & Policy, Phi Beta Kappa. Jewish. Home: 3683 W Howard Nickell Rd Fayetteville AR 72704 Office: U Ark 201 Grad Edn Bldg Fayetteville AR 72701 Office Phone: 479-575-5332. Business E-Mail: costrell@uark.edu.

COTE, RICHARD JAMES, pathologist, researcher; b. LA, May 10, 1954; s. Richard Patrick and Katherine C.; m. Anne L. Foxen, Feb. 8, 1992; children: Nicholas Foxen, Juliet Anne, Grace Elizabeth. BS in Biology, U. Calif., Irvine, 1976, BA in Chemistry, 1976; MD, U. Chgo., 1980. Diplomate Am. Bd. Pathology. Intern in surgery U. Mich. Hosp., Ann Arbor, 1980-81; rsch. fellow, immunology Meml. Sloan-Kettering Cancer Ctr., NYC, 1981-83; rsch. assoc., immunology Meml. Sloan-Kettering Hosp., NYC, 1983-85, fellow, pathology, 1987-88, chief fellow, pathology, 1988-90; resident, pathology Cornell U. Med. Ctr., NYC, 1985-87; asst. prof., pathology Keck Sch. Medicine, U. So. Calif., LA, 1990-95, assoc. prof., 1995-99, prof., 1999—2009; dir. genitourinary program Keck Sch. Medicine, U. So. Calif./Norris Cancer Ctr., 1997—2009; chair biomed. nanosci. initiative U. So. Calif., 2005—09; attending pathologist Kenneth Norris Cancer Ctr., 1990—2005, dir. lab. immuno and molecular pathology, 1991—2005; prof., Joseph R. Coulter jr. chair pathology Miller Sch. Medicine U. Miami, 2009—, dir. Dr. John T. McDonald Found., Biomed. Nanotech. Inst., 2009—, dir., Genitourinary Cancer Program, Sylvester Comprehensive Cancer Ctr., 2009—. Founder, dir. IMPATH, Inc., NYC, 1988—2003; chief med. officer Chromavision Med. Sys. (now Clarient Inc.), 2004—05; mem. numerous nat. and internat. adv. bds.; sci. cons. MD Anderson Cancer Ctr., Houston, 2002—; founder Filtini Inc., 2008. Author: Immunomicroscopy, 1994, 2006; editor Modern Surg. Pathology; assoc. editor Applied Immunohistochemistry; mem. editl. bd. Jour. Clin. Oncology, 2007—; contbr. articles to profl. jours., book chpts. Patentee in field. Am. Cancer Soc. fellow, 1988; named one of Best Doctor's in Am., 2005—, Am's. Top Doctor's, 2001—, South Fla. Super Drs., 2011; recipient rsch. grants, awards NIH, ACS, others, 1981—. Mem.: Assn. Am. Physicians, Am. Assn. Cancer Rsch., Alpha Omega Alpha Med. Honor Soc., Phi Beta Kappa. Home: 4050 Battersea Rd Miami FL 33133 Office: University Miami Miller Sch Medicine Dept Patholgy R-5 1120 NW 14th St Ste 1416 Miami FL 33136 Office Phone: 305-243-2683. Business E-Mail: rcote@med.miami.edu.

COTHAM, TRICIA ANN, state legislator; Former social studies tchr. Northeast Mid. Sch.; former tchr. Independence HS; asst. prin East Mecklenburg HS; bd. trustee NC Tchrs. Acad., 2005—07; state rep. Dist. 100 NC, 2007—. Named Charlotte-Mecklenburg Tchr. of Yr., 2001, Mint Hill Tchr. of Yr., 2003. Democrat. Office: NC House of Reps 300 N Salisbury St Rm 403 Raleigh NC 27603-5925 Address: 107 Sardis Grove Ln Matthews NC 28105 Office Phone: 919-715-0706. E-mail: Tricia.Cotham@ncleg.net.

COTON, CARLOS DAVID, finance manager; b. Havana, Cuba, Dec. 29, 1950; arrived in US, 1960; s. Jose Manuel Coton and Guillermina (Guitian) Coton Lopez; m. Susana M. Muriel, May 18, 1997; children: Alexandra Beatriz, David Alexander, Sean Stephen. AA, Miami Dade C.C., 1971; BA, Fla. Internat. U., 1973, MS, 1983; PhD in Internat. Bus., Nova U., 1992; diploma, U. Dayton, 2012, diploma in Lay Ministry Program, 2012. Supr. trainee Richards Dept. Store, Miami, Fla., 1967-68, supr., 1968-73, mgr. distbn., 1973-76; dir. ops. Bassett Furniture Mfg., 1976-79; asst. dir. Fla. Internat. U., Miami, 1979-82; dir. Luth. Ministries Projects, Miami, 1982-84; fin. mgr. Emery Worldwide, Miami, 1984-90; v.p. fin. Transworld Computers, Miami, 1989—; v.p. Carinter Miami, 1991-95; v.p. ops. Internat. Sys. and Electronics, Miami, 1995—; adj. prof. Nova SE U., 2013; doctoral dissertation com. chair Humbolt Internat. U., 2013—. Substitute tchr. Dade County Pub. Schs., Miami, 1973—; adj. prof. Fla. Internat. U., 1980—, Miami-Dade Coll., 1980-, Archdiocese of Miami, Virtus Tng.; tchr. CCD Curriculum at Archdiocese Miami, archdiocesan lay min., 2012-, youth ministries dir.; chair St. Brendan Sch. Bd., 2012-; pres. CDC Cons.; cons. Internat. Bus. Income Tax Resolutions Property Mgmt., cons. in field. Author: (poetry book) ...And Other Poems, 1973, Wilm Life Writing English for the World of Work, In My Life; contbr. articles to profl. jours. Mem. Council on Laraza, Calif., 1980; mem. Dade County United Way. Mem.: Nat. Soc. Tax Profls., Am. Inst. Profl. Bookkeepers, Ecuadorian Inter-Am. C. of C., Nat. Coun. Tchrs. English, Acad. Internat. Bus., Am. Mgmt. Assn., Miami=Santiago Sister Cities Program, Am. C. of C., Cuban-Am. Orgn., Fla. HS Activities Assn. (ofcl.), Greater Miami Football Ofcls. Assn., Greater Miami C. of C. (mentor STAR/HOPE, hispanic com. mem., S.Am. com. mem.W. Dade com. mem.), Greater Miami Basketbal Ofcls.Assn., Miami Ofcls. club, Phi Delta Kappa. Democrat. Roman Catholic. Avocations: football referee, basketball referee. Home: 1320 SW 91st Ave Miami FL 33174-3130 E-mail: cdcoton@gmail.com.

COTTAM, GENE LARRY, retired biochemistry educator; b. Coffeeville, Kans., Nov. 3, 1940; s. Paul Clifford and Juanita Serene (Carver) C.; m. Melanie Lou Poor, June 8, 1963; children: Laura Ann, Janell Sue, Melinda Kay. BA in Chemistry, U. Kans., 1962; MS in Organic Chemistry, U. Mich., 1963, MA in Biochemistry, 1965, PhD in Biochemistry, 1967. Postdoctoral fellow Southwestern Med. Ctr./U. Tex., Dallas, 1967-68, asst. prof. biochemistry, 1968-73, assoc. prof. biochemistry, 1973-79, prof. biochemistry, 1979-99.

COTTEN, ANNIE LAURA, psychologist, educator; b. Oxford, NC, Nov. 18, 1923; d. Leonard F. and Laura Estelle (Spencer) Cotten; children: Hollis W., Rebecca Ann, Laura Cotten. Diploma, Hardbarger Bus. Coll., 1944; AB, Duke U., 1945; MEd, U. Hartford, Conn., 1965; PhD, The Union Inst., 1979. Diplomate Am. Bd. Sexology, lic. Am. Assn. Marriage & Family Therapists, 1987. Asst. to pres. So. Meth. U., 1953; rsch. asst. Duke U., 1947-49; exec. sec. Ohio Wesleyan U., 1955-56, Conn. Coun. Chs., 1958-60; adj. prof. U. Hartford, 1976-78, 1976-78; clin. pastoral counselor Hartford Hosp., 1962-65; asst., then assoc. dir. social svcs. Hartford Conf. Chs., 1965-67; tchg. fellow U. NC, 1970-71; assoc. prof. Ctrl. Conn. State U., New Britain, 1967-93, adj. prof., 1994—2002. Adj. prof. St. Joseph Coll., 1986-96; clin. intern Montefiore Med. Ctr., 1995; dir. elderhostel programs Ctrl. Conn. State U., 1989-93, organizer ctr. adult learners, 1991-93; cons. Somers Correctional Ctr., Conn., 1980-81, instr./rschr., 1980-81; cons. Conn. Life Ins. Mktg. Rsch., 1981-1982; amb. to China, spring, 1986; presenter 3d Internat. Interdisciplinary Cong. on Women, 1987; vis. prof., scholar Duke U., 1989; adj. prof. health and human svcs. Ctrl. Ch. St. U., 1995-2002; vis. prof. Conn. Coll., New London, 1990; mem. clin. faculty, Am. Bd. Sexology, 1994; land developer NC Triangle, 1995—, presenter World Assn. Svc. Health SWeden, 2009, dept. com. AASECT, 2009-; presenter WHS, Sweden, 2009. Author: Comparisons of Gender Differences in Sexuality 1970s/1990s; cons. editor: Jour. Feminist Family Therapy, 2000—, reviewer: Contemporary Sexuality, 2003, Sexual and Relationship Jour., 2005. Fellow: Am. Acad. Clin. Sexologists (clin. faculty 1994—, founder), Nat. Coun. Family Rels.; mem.: APA (chair divsn. 1987—91), AASECT, Devel. Com., AASECT (devel. com. 2008—, pres., the sexual self and cancer 2012), Soc. Sci. Study of Sexuality (presenter ann. meeting 2003), Conn. Assn. Marital and Family Therapists (clin.) (bd. dirs. 2000—02, 2007), Sex Info. and Edn. Coun. of Conn. (bd. dirs. 1994—2002, Human Sexuality Leader of Yr. 1997), Conn. Psychol. Assn., Am. Assn. Sex Educators Counselors and Therapists (sex therapy cert. com. 2005, Disting. Svc. award 1998, diplomate sex therapy 2005—), Hartford Women's Network. Personal E-mail: anniecotten@nc.rr.com.

COTTER, MICHAEL WILLIAM, retired ambassador; b. Madison, Wis., Aug. 1, 1943; s. Patrick William and Lois Katherine (Schaus) Cotter; m. Joanne Marie Miller, Aug. 30, 1974. BSFS, Georgetown U., 1965; JD, U. Mich., 1968; MS, Stanford U., 1976. Polit.-mil. affairs officer Am. Embassy, Ankara, Turkey, 1980-82; sr. Turkish desk officer U.S. Dept. State, Washington, 1982-84; polit. officer Am. Embassy, Kinshasa, Zaire, 1984-86, polit. counselor, 1986-88; mgmt. analyst sec. of mgmt. U.S. Dept. State, 1988-90, office dir. politico-military affairs, 1990-92; dep. chief of mission Am. Embassy, Santiago, Chile, 1992-95; U.S. amb. to Turkmenistan, 1995-98; internat. cons. Washington, 1999-2001; lectr. Chapel Hill, NC, 2001—. Publisher Am. Diplomacy Publs., Chapel Hill, NC, 2001—. Mem.: Am. Fgn. Svc. Assn. (secy 1989—91, bd govs 1988—89). Home and Office: 685 Fearrington Post Pittsboro NC 27312-8523 E-mail: mwcotter@hotmail.com.

COTTER-SMITH, CATHLEEN MARIE, artist, educator; b. Dallas, 1950; d. Robert Jay and Betty Ann Cotter; 1 child, Ryan Patrick Holt; m. Jack Glendon Smith, Jr., 1991. BS, East Tex. State U., 1974; MS, Tex. A&M U., Commerce, 1977. Freelance artist, Garland and Plano, Tex., 1976—; assoc. prof. art Grayson County Coll., Dennison, Tex., 1981-85; prof. art Collin County C.C., Plano, Tex., 1986—, coord. art dept., 1986-97. Cons. on book Equine Images, 1992. One-woman shows include Cultural Art Ctr., Plano, 1990, Collin County CC Gallery, Plano, 1994, Biblical Arts Ctr.; exhibited in group show S.W. Watercolor Soc., Dallas, 1990, juried show Southwestern Watercolor Soc. (signature status), 2000, Invitational Water Media Show, 2001, Western Fedn. Watercolor Exhbn., 2003, Rotunda of Russell Senate Bldg, The Mall at the Lincoln Meml., Hillcrest Gallery, Dallas, 2004, Hillcrest Gallery, Dallas, 2005, Wilshire Linten Art Show, 2005, Dallas, Southwestern Watercolor Soc., 2005, Murray State Coll., 2006, juried art festival, Park City Presbyn., 2007, Mill Country Arts Found., 2007, juried arts festival, Gables Villa Rosa, Dallas, 2008, Watermarks II, Group Experimental Watermedia Show, Collin Coll., Plano, Tex., 2008, Beginnings PCPC Juried Art Festival at Gables Villa Rosa, Dallas, 2008, Expressions in Watercolor, 14th St. Gallery, Plano, 2008, On-Location Paintings, Isreal, 2008, Western Fedn. Watercolor Socs. Exhbn., 2009, Southwestern Watercolor Soc., 2010, Commn. Watercolor Paintingsof Old and New Plano, Med. Ctr. Plano, 2011; represented in permanent collection Farmerville C. of C., 2004, Webb Chapel Ch. of Christ, Cross Timbers Small Works Exhbn., Murray State Coll., Tishomingo, Okla.; illustrator: nat. card line, 1997-2000. Mentor Boles Children's Home, Quinlan, Tex., 1996—2003. Recipient award S.W. Watercolor Soc. Mem.: Southwestern Watercolor Soc. (signature mem., award in group 1999). Republican. Avocation: nature lover. Office: Collin County CC 2800 E Spring Creek Pky Plano TX 75074-3300 Office Phone: 972-881-5817.

COTTON, JOHN G., career military officer; m. Cindy Cotton; children: Jennifer, Charles, Christine. Grad., US Naval Acad., 1973. Commd. 2d lt. USN, 1973, advanced through ranks to vice adm., 2003; comdr. Light attack Wing, US Pacific Fleet, Lemoore, Calif., 1978—80, VFA-204 "River Rattlers", 1993—94; commdg. officer NAS Keflavik 1066, 1994-96; commanding officer Navy Command Ctr. 106, 1996—97; dep./vice comdr. Naval Air Force, U.S. Atlantic Fleet, Norfolk, Va., 1997—99; dep. dir. Naval Reserve N095B USNR, 1999—2000; mem. Reserve Forces Policy Bd., 2000—03; asst. dep. chief of naval ops. (warfare requirements & programs N6/N7R) USNR, 2000—03, chief, 2003—; comdr. USNR Force, 2003—. Decorated Meritorious Svc. awards (2 times), Navy Commendation medals (2 times), Navy Achievement medals; Adm. Stanley David Griggs Excellence in Leadership Mem. award, 1995. Office: 4400 Dauphine St New Orleans LA 70146-5000

COTTON, TOM (THOMAS BRYANT COTTON), United States Representative from Arkansas; b. Russellville, Ark., May 13, 1977; s. Thomas Leonard and Avis (Bryant) Cotton; m. Anna Peckham. BA in Govt., Harvard Coll., 1999; JD, Harvard Law Sch., 2002. Law clk. to Hon. Jerry Edwin Smith US Ct. Appeals (5th Cir.), 2002—03; assoc. Gibson Dunn & Crutcher LLP, 2003—05; mgmt. cons. McKinsey & Co., 2010—11; mem. US Congress from 4th Ark. Dist., Washington, 2013—, US House Financial Services Com., 2013—, US House Fgn. Services Com., 2013—. Served in 101st Airborne Divsn. US Army, 2005—09, Iraq, Afghanistan. Decorated Bronze star, Ranger Tab, Combat Infantryman Badge, Army Commendation medal. Republican. Methodist. Office: US House of Representatives 415 Cannon House Office Bldg Washington DC 20515 also: 215 W Main St Rm 300 Clarksville AR 72830 Office Phone: 202-225-3772, 479-754-2120.*

COTTRELL, JAMES RAY, lawyer; b. Norton, Va., Aug. 9, 1952; BA in English, Va. Mil. Inst., Lexington, 1974; JD, T.C. Williams Sch. Law, U. Richmond, 1976. Bar: Va. 1977, DC 1979. Ptnr. Cottrell Fletcher Schinstock Bartol & Cottrell, PC (formerly Gannon & Cottrell), Alexandria, Va., 1977—. Co-author: Virginia Family Law, Theory and Practice, with Forms; contbr. articles to profl. jours. Named one of Top Family Lawyers in Washington Met. Area, Washingtonian Mag./Va. Bus. Mag. Mem.: ATLA, ABA (mem. family law sect.), Arlington Bar Assn., Fairfax Bar Assn., Alexandria Bar Assn., DC Bar, Va. Trial Lawyers Assn., Va. State Bar (sec. 1987—88, vice chmn. 1988—89, chmn. 1989—90, bd. govs. family law sect., Disting. Svc. award), Phi Delta Phi. Office: Cottrell Fletcher Schinstock Bartol & Cottrell 801 N Fairfax St Ste 404 Alexandria VA 22314-1774 Office Phone: 703-836-2770. Office Fax: 703-836-9086.

COTTY, NEIL A., bank executive; b. 1954; BBA in Acctg., Hofstra U., 1976. CPA 1981. Various position including CFO J.P. Morgan Europe J.P. Morgan Chase & Co., 1983—96; contr. capital markets NationsBank, 1996—98; contr. Bank of America Corp., 1998—99, fin. support exec. Global Corporate & Investment Bank, 1999—2002, sr. fin. exec. for consumer products, 2003—04, prin. acctg. officer, 2004—08, CFO global banking, securities & wealth mgmt., 2008—09, chief acctg. officer, 2009—, interim CFO, 2010—. Office: Bank of America Corp 100 N Tryon St Charlotte NC 28255 Office Phone: 704-386-5681. Office Fax: 704-386-6699. Business E-Mail: neil.cotty@bankofamerica.com.

COUCH, JAMES RUSSELL, JR., neurology educator; b. Bryan, Tex., Oct. 25, 1939; married; 2 children. BS, Texas A&M U., 1961; MD, Baylor U., 1965, PhD in Physiology, 1966; fellow, Lab of Neuropharmacology, NIMH, 1967-69; postgrad., Nat. Inst. Neurol. Diseases and Stroke, 1969-72. Diplomate Am. Bd. Psychiatry and Neurology, subspeciality clin. neurophysiology, 1992, recert., 2002; lic. physician, Tex., Md., Kans., Mo., Ill., Okla.; cert. Headache Medicine, United Coun. Neurologic subspecialties, 2006. Intern Barnes Hosp., St. Louis, 1966-67; resident in neurology Washington U. Sch. Medicine, St. Louis, 1969-72; mem. staff Kans. U. Med. Ctr., Kansas City, asst. prof. div. neurology, 1972-76, assoc. prof., 1976-79; prof., chief divsn. neurology So. Ill. U. Sch. Medicine, Springfield, 1979-92, acting chmn. dept. medicine, 1988-89; staff VA Hosp., Kansas City, Mo., Marion, Ill., Oklahoma City, St. Joseph (Mo.) Hosp., Kansas U. Med. Ctr., Atchison (Kans.) Hosp., Kansas City Gen. Hosp., Meml. Med. Ctr., Springfield, dir. EEG lab., muscular dystrophy clinic, cons. speech and hearing lab., 1979-92; staff St. John's Hosp., Springfield; prof., chmn. dept. neurology Okla. U. Coll. Med. and Health Sci. Ctr., Oklahoma City, 1992—2006, prof. neurology, 2006—; staff Presbyn. Hosp., Oklahoma City, Univ. Hosp., Oklahoma City, Childrens Hosp. of Okla., Okla. Med. Ctr. Investigator Mental Retardation Rsch. Ctr. Kans. U. Med. Ctr., Kansas City, 1972—79; bd. dirs. postgrad. neurology course Continuing Med. Edn. Kans. U. Med. Ctr., Southern Ill U. Med. Sch., U. Okla Med. Sch.; examiner Am. Bd. Psychiatry and Neurology, 1975—77, 1979, 1984—85, 1989—98, 2000—01, 2005, 2008, Am. Bd. Neurosurgery, 1977; cons. Richland Meml. Hosp., Olney, Ill., 1981—85, Abraham Lincoln Meml. Hosp., Lincoln, Ill., 1981—92; staff cons. Lincoln Devel. Ctr., Outpatient Clinics, Lincoln, 1981—92; vis. prof. Northwestern U., Chgo., 1982, Chgo., 1993, U. Nebr., 1992, Wayne State U. Med. Sch., 1992, Ind. U. Med. Sch., 1992, U. Rochester, 1992, U. Ala., Birmingham, 1994, U. W.Va., Morgantown, 1995, U. Mo., Columbia, Med. Sch. Kans. U., 1996, 2001, R.I. Hosp., Providence, 1996, Med. Coll. S.C., 1996, U. So. Fla., 1996, 1999, Med. Sch. Brown U., 1996, U. Md., 1997, U. Minn., 1997, U. North Tex., 1997, L.I. Jewish Hosp., 1998, So. Ill. U. Med. Sch., 1999, com. mem. med. sch., 2003, 2004, 2006; vis. prof. U. Calif., Irvine, 2000; com. mem. med. sch. Kans. U., 1972—79, So. Ill. U., 1980—92, 1997, U. Nebr., Omaha, 1999, Washington U., St. Louis, 2001, Henry Ford Hosp., Detroit, 2001, Penn State Med. Sch., 2003, Mayo Clinic Scottsdale, 2003, U. Utah, 2003, St. Louis U., 2004, U. Ill., Chgo., 2003; vis. prof. neurology Albert Einstein Med. Sch., 2006. Mem. editl. bd. Headache, 1979-92, Jour. Stroke & Cerebrovascular Disease, 1995-2008; sect. editor, Headache Current Treatment Options Neurology, 2003-; contbr. articles to profl. jours. Med. adv. bd. Lincoln Land Epilepsy Assn., 1980-92; exec. bd., chmn. edn. com. Am. Soc. Neurorehab., 1990-95. Fellow Nat. Heart Inst., 1965-66, NIH, NIMH, 1967-69; recipient numerous grants for neurology rsch., 1969—. Fellow Am. Acad. Neurology (bd. dirs. asst. sec.-treas. 1984-86, sec.-treas. 1986-88, chmn. sect. neurorehab. 1996-98, mem. headache sect. Am. Acad. Neurol.(chair 2003-05), program dir. Consortium of Neurology program Am. Acad Neurol.(chair 2003-05), chair 2003—,chair headache sect., 2003-05, chmn. section of headache and facial pain 2003—05), Stroke Coun. of Am. Heart Assn.; mem. AMA, Am. Neurol. Assn. (elected 1989), Am. Headache Soc. (exec. com. ad hoc 1983-85, winter headache course, membership com. 1983-85, chmn., 1994-96, faculty continuing med. edn. courses 1982—2007, edn. com. 1983—1985, chair,1996-98, achievement recognition com., publs. com. 1986—, bd. dirs. 1983-92, treas. 1992-94, sec. 1994-96, pres.-elect 1996-98, pres. 1998-2000),Nominating Com.Am. Headacche Soc. 2001-08,Clin. Action Team Am. Headacche Soc. 2008-, Am. Geriatric Soc., Am. Assn. Univ. Profs. Neurology (chmn. undergrad. edn. com, sec.-treas. 1992-96, chmn. VAMC com. 1997-2001) Am. Soc. Neurorehab. (chmn. edn. com. 1989-95, bd. dirs. 1990-98), Neurosci. Soc. (sec. Kansas City chpt. 1976-77, pres. 1977-78, pres. Sangamon County chptr. of Neurosci. 1982-92, pres. 1986-87), Consortium of Neurology (program dir., chair 2003—2005), FDA(mem. peripheral Ctrl. Nervous sys. adv. comm.2004-08); Ill. Med. Soc., Sangamon County Med. Soc., Okla. State Med. Soc., Okla. County Med. Soc., Baylor U. Med. Alumni Assn., Washington U. Med. Alumni Assn., Sigma Xi, Alpha Omega Alpha, Phi Eta Sigma, Phi Kappi Phi. Home: 1616 Queenstown Rd Oklahoma City OK 73116-5523 Office: U Okla Health Sci Ctr Dept of Neurology PPOB209 PO Box 26901 Oklahoma City OK 73190-0001 Office Phone: 405-271-4113. Business E-Mail: james-couch@ouhsc.edu.

COUCH, JESSE WADSWORTH, retired insurance company executive; b. Atlanta, Mar. 2, 1921; s. Jesse Newton and Laura (Day) W.; m. Charlotte Lucretia Collins, Jan. 13, 1945 (dec.); children: Robert Collins (dec.), Laura W.; m. Charlotte H. Gran, Oct. 17, 1997. AB, Princeton, 1947. With 1st Nat. Bank Houston, 1947-51; assoc. Wray Assocs., Houston, 1951-60; ptnr. Wray, Couch & Elder, Houston, 1960-69; v.p. Marsh & McLennan, Inc., 1969-83; pvt. cons., 1983-95. Mem. exec. bd. Episcopal Diocese of Tex., 1965-67, 68-71; trustee St. Luke's Episcopal Hosp., 1971-76; bd. dirs. Houston-Harris County YMCA, 1969-74, Houston Soc. Prevention Cruelty to Animals, 1974—2004; Bd. dirs. Tex. divsn. Am. Cancer Soc., mem. exec. com., 1982-91; chmn. Am. Cancer Soc. Greater Houston, 1981-83; trustee Mus. Fine Arts, Houston, 1970-74. Served to capt. USAAF, 1943-46. Mem.: Houston C. of C. (aviation com. 1965—75), Allegro Club, Bayou Club, Houston Country Club, Rod & Gun Club, Eagle Lake. Home: 6015 Pine Forest Rd Houston TX 77057-1431 Personal E-mail: jcouch@pdq.net.

COUCH, ROBERT BARNARD, physician, scientist, microbiologist, educator; b. Guntersville, Ala., Sept. 25, 1930; s. Ezekiel Harvey and Frances Jane (Barnard) C.; m. Katherine Frances Klein, Apr. 23, 1955; children: Robert Steven, Leslie Ann, Colleen Frances, Elizabeth Lee. BA, Vanderbilt U., 1952, MD, 1956. Diplomate Am. Bd. Internal Medicine. Intern Vanderbilt U. Hosp., Nashville, 1956—57, resident in medicine, 1959—60, chief resident in medicine, 1960—61; clin. assoc. NIH, Washington, 1957—59, sr. investigator, 1961—65, head clin. virology sect., 1965—66; assoc. prof. Baylor Coll. Medicine, Houston, 1966—71, prof. microbiology, immunology and medicine, 1971—2000, Disting. prof., 1995—2012, head infectious diseases sect. medicine, 1987—92, chmn. dept. microbiology and immunology, 1989—2000, dir. influenza rsch. ctr., 1974—91, dir. acute viral respiratory diseases unit, 1991—96, dir. respiratory pathogens rsch. unit, 1996—2012, dir. Ctr. for Infection and Immunity Rsch., 1999—2012, prof. molecular virology, microbiology and medicine, 2000—12, prof. emeritus, 2012—; adj. prof. Internal Medicine, U. Tex. Med. Branch, Galveston, Tex., 2013—. Mem. rsch. rev. panels infectious diseases; cons. NIH, Dept. Def., FDA, various others. Contbr. articles to profl. jours. Served to sr. surgeon USPHS, 1957-66.

Mem. ACP, AAAS, Soc. Exptl. Biology and Medicine, Am. Soc. Microbiology, Infectious Diseases Soc. Am., Am. Assn. Immunologists, Am. Fedn. Clin. Rsch., Am. Soc. Clin. Investigation, So. Soc. Clin. Investigation, Am. Assn. Physicians, Am. Soc. Epidemiology, Am. Soc. Virology.

COUCH, ROBERT M., real estate company executive; b. Apr. 3, 1957; m. Anne E. Couch; children: Mary Stuart, Frances. BS, Washington & Lee U., 1978, JD, 1982. Bar: 1984. Law clk. to Hon. John F. Wisdom US Ct. Appeals (5th Cir.); law clk. to Hon. Lewis F. Powell, Jr. US Supreme Ct.; gen. counsel, CFO First Comml. Bancshares, Inc., Birmingham, Ala.; chmn. Mortgage Bankers Assn., 2003—04, mem. blue ribbon task force; pres., CEO New South Fed. Savings Bank, Birmingham, Ala.; mng. dir. Collateral Mortgage, Ltd.; pres. Govt. Nat. Mortgage Assn. (Ginnie Mae), Washington, 2006—07; gen. counsel, chief legal officer US Dept. Housing & Urban Devel. (HUD), Washington, 2007—09; founding ptnr., CEO ARK Real Estate Strategies, LLC, Birmigham, Ala., 2009—. Past pres. Mortgage Bankers Assn. Ala.; mem. thrift industry adv. coun. Fed. Reserve. Office: ARK Real Estate Strategies LLC 421 Office Pk Dr Birmingham AL 35223 Office Phone: 205-776-8860.

COUCH, TIM, state legislator; b. 1961; Self-employed Hyden Grocery/Couch's Shell; mem. Dist. 90 Ky. House of Reps., 2003—. Mem.: NRA, Nat. Fedn. Ind. Bus. Owners, Nat. Wild Turkey Fedn., Ky. Retail Fedn., Hyden C. of C. Republican. Church Of God. Mailing: PO Box 710 Hyden KY 41749 Office: Capitol Annex Rm 432B 702 Capitol Ave Frankfort KY 40601 Office Phone: 502-564-8100 ext. 632.

COUDERT, DALE HOKIN, real estate executive, marketing consultant; b. Chgo., Nov. 29, 1941; d. Sidney and Ruth (Brower) Manowitz; m. Frederic R. Coudert (div.); children Dana, Alexandra. BA, Northwester U., 1964. V.p. Cross & Brown, NYC, 1975-86; dir., sec. First Women's Bank, NYC, 1980-87; head bus. devel., office of pres. 1st N.Y. Bank for Bus., 1988-91; mktg. dir. Lafer Mgmt., NYC, 1993-94; pres., CEO Coudert Assocs. Ltd., NYC, 1991—; broker Brown Harris Stevens Palm Beach Real Estate, Pal, 1999—; founder, pres. Coudert Inst., 2001—. Dir. Hosp. Tak Co., LI, NY, 1979—98; creator, chmn., CEO Coudert Inst. at Villa Dei Fiori, Palm Beach, Fla., 2001—. Pub., editor: (book) Business and Pleasure, 1986-87. Bd. dirs. Women's Rep. Club, N.Y.C., 1994, N.Y. Drama League, N.Y.C., 1975—; mem. nat. bd. dirs. Aspen Art Mus., Kennedy Ctr., 1996-98; trustee, treas. Zoo of the Palm Beaches at Dreker Park, 1996-98, bd. dirs., 1996—; regent St. John the Divine, N.Y.C., 1988. Fellow Aspen Inst. (life); mem. Internat. Womens Forum, Met. Opera Club, Women's Forum Fla. Avocations: piano, voice, dance, golf, tennis. also: Brown Harris Stevens Palm Beach Real Estate Ste 329 340 Royal Poinciana Plz Palm Beach FL 33480-4048 E-mail: dal1129@aol.com.

COUGHLIN, CATHERINE M., telecommunications industry executive; b. St. Louis, 1958; BA in Econs., Northwestern U., Evanston, Ill.; MBA in Fin., St. Louis U. With Southwestern Bell Telephone Co., St. Louis, 1979; sr. v.p. mktg. Southwestern Bell Yellow Pages; v.p. consumer mktg. SBC Ops., sr. v.p. bus. comm. svcs., global markets; pres., CEO AT&T Midwest; sr. exec. v.p., global mktg. officer AT&T Inc. (merger of SBC Communications & AT&T Corp.), 2007—. Bd. dirs. Northwestern U. Mem. Chgo. 2016 Olympic Com.; bd. dirs. Northwestern U., The Chgo. Network, After School Matters. Named a Power Player, Advt. Age, 2008, 2009. Mem.: The Commercial Club and The Chgo. Network, The Civic Com., Econ. Club of Chgo. Mailing: AT&T Inc Global Hdqs 175 E Houston San Antonio TX 78205 Business E-Mail: catherine.coughlin@att.com.

COULTER, JAMES G., investment company executive; b. 1959; 3 children. BA in Engring. Sciences summa cum laude, Dartmouth Coll.; MBA, Stanford Grad. Sch. Bus., 1986. Prin. Air Ptnrs., L.P; ptnr., former bd. dirs. Colony Advisors, Inc; fin. analyst Lehman Bros. Kuhn Leob Inc.; assoc. SPO Ptnrs., 1986—88; v.p. Keystone, Inc., 1986—92; co-chmn. Beringer Wine Estates Holdings, Inc., 1996—97, bd. dirs., 1996—; co-founder Tex. Pacific Group, 1993, founding ptnr.; mng. gen. ptnr. Texas Pacific Group, 1997—; founder Newbridge Asia; fin. analyst Kuhn, Loeb & Co.; founder Colony Capital, TPG Ventures. Former bd. dirs. Genesis Health Ventures, Inc., Oxford Health Plans Inc., Northwest Airlines, Inc., America West Holdings Corp., NeighborCare, Inc.; bd. dirs. J. Crew Intermediate Llc, 1997, GlobespanVirata Inc., 1998—2003, Conexant, Inc., 1998—2003, Zhone Technologies, Inc., 1999—2008, eVolution Global Ptnrs., L.L.C, Am. Savings Bank, Continental Airlines, Seagate Software Holdings Corp., New SAC, Gate Gourmet Switzerland Gmbh, Virgin Entertainment Group, Ltd., Allied Waste Industries, Genesis Eldercare, Inc., J. Crew Operating Corp., 1997—, J.Crew Group, Inc., 1997—, Veritas Software Tech. Corp., 2000—, Seagate Tech. Holdings, 2000—, MEMC Electronic Materials Inc., 2001—, Neiman Marcus, Inc., 2005—, Lenovo Group Ltd., 2005—, Alltel Corp., 2007—. Trustee Stanford U., 2007-. Recipient Phi Beta Kappa, Dartmouth Coll.; named one of Forbes 400: Richest Americans, 2009. Office: Texas Pacific Group Ste 3300 301 Commerce St Fort Worth TX 76102 Office Phone: 817-871-4000. Office Fax: 817-871-4010. Business E-Mail: james.coulter@alltel.com.

COULTER, LISA JUNE, art educator; b. Hoxie, Kans., May 7, 1963; d. Howard Eugene and June Lillian Cressler; m. Charles Edward Coulter, Jan. 13, 1958; children: Christopher James, Michael Logan. AA, Colby CC, Kans., 1983; BS, Ft. Hays State U., Kans., 1985; MA, Kans. State U., Manhattan, 1991. Asst. prof., theatre dir. Murray State Coll., Tishomingo, Okla., 1991—, head lang. arts, fine arts, 2006—. Dir.(with Woodie King): (plays) Oklahoma Fall Arts Inst., 1992, (with Ted Herstand), 1997. Recipient Tchr. of Yr., Murray State Coll., 1999, 2004—05; named Educator of Yr., 1995. Mem.: Phi Theta Kappa, Delta Psi Omega (rep. 2003—07), Theta Alpha Pi (life). Liberal. Avocations: theater, travel, swimming, antiques. Office: Murray State Coll One Murray Campus Str Tishomingo OK 73460 Business E-Mail: lcoulter@mscok.edu.

COUNSELMAN, KENNETH, family practice physician, educator; MD, Tulane U., 1976. Diplomate Am. Bd. Family Practice. Resident family medicine Naval Hosp., Charleston, SC, 1976; physycian VA Gulf Coast Veterans Health Care System; prof. family and rural health dept. Fla. State Univ.; hosp. affiliation includes West Fla. Cmty. Care Ctr. Office: West Florida Community Care Center 5500 Stewart St Milton FL 32570-4304 Office Phone: 850-983-5500.

COUPLES, FREDERICK STEVEN, professional golfer; b. Seattle, Oct. 3, 1959; m. Thais; 2 children: Gigi, Oliver. Student, U. Houston. Mem. US team USA vs. Japan, 1984, Ryder Cup, 1989, 91, 93, 95, 97, Asahi Glass Four Tours World Championship of Golf, 1990, 91, Dunhill Cup, 1991, 92, 93, 94, World Cup, 1992, 93, 94, 95, Presidents Cup, 1994, 96, 98, capt. 2009. Founder Millie Medin Violet Sobich Couples Fund. Named All-Am., 1978, 79; winner numerous skins games, golf tournaments and internat. tournaments (and more than 15 PGA events) including Kemper Open, 1983, Tournament Players Championship, 1984, Byron Nelson Golf Classic, 1987, French PGA, 1988, Nissan L.A. Open, 1990, 92, Tournoi Perrier de Paris, 1991, B.C. Open, 1991, Federal Express St. Jude Classic, 1991, Johnnie Walker World Championship, 1991, Nestle Invitational, 1992, The Masters, 1992, (with Jan Stephenson) J.C. Penney Classic, 1983, (with Mike Donald) Sazale Classic, 1990, (with Raymond Floyd) RMCC Invitational, 1990, Buick Open, 1994, World Cup, 1994, Dubai Desert Classic, 1995, Johnnie Walker Classic, 1995, The Player's Championship, 1996, Bob Hope chrysler Classic, 1998, Memorial Tournament, 1998, Shell Houston Open, 2003, ACE Group Classic, 2010, Toshiba Classic, 2010; recipient Vardon trophy, 1991, 92; named PGA Player of Yr. Golf World Mag., 1991, 92, Golf Writers Assn., 1991, 92, PGA Tour Player of Yr, 1993, 94. Achievements include being the leading money winner PGA, 1992. Address: c/o PGA Tour 100 Ave of The Champions PO Box 109601 Palm Beach Gardens FL 33410

COURSEN, SAM, telecommunications industry executive, electronics executive; 4 children. BSEE, Auburn U. Student engr. AT&T Inc. (merger of SBC Communications & AT&T Corp.), Atlanta, 1973; tech. position Bell Labs. (subs. AT&T), Naperville, Ill., 1974, dist. mgr. Bedminster, NJ, 1979; dist. mgr., unix std. oper. environment AT&T Inc. (merged with SBC Comm. & AT&T Corp.), 1985, divsn. mgr., internal data ctr., networking computing svcs., 1987; joined NCR Corp., 1993, v.p., svcs., 1995, v.p., global applications, 1997, v.p., chief info. officer, 1998, Freescale Semiconductor, Inc., 2005—. Office: Freescale Semiconductor Inc 6501 William Cannon Dr W Austin TX 78735 Office Phone: 512-895-2000. Business E-Mail: sam.coursen@freescale.com.

COURSEY, WILL, state legislator; b. Oct. 22, 1978; BA in Polit. Sci., U. Ky. Assoc. v.p. Fin. Svcs. Bank; mem. Dist. 6 Ky. House of Reps., 2009—. Democrat. Baptist. Office: 702 Capitol Ave Rm 332F Frankfort KY 40601 also: PO Box 467 Benton KY 42025 Office Phone: 502-564-8100 Ext. 659, 270-527-4610.

COURSON, JOHN EDWARD, state legislator, insurance company executive; b. Nov. 21, 1944; s. James W. and Mary C. (Harris) C.; m. Elizabeth Poinsett Exum, Apr. 1973; children: James Poinsett, Elizabeth Boykin, Harris Russell. BA, U. SC, 1968, LLD (hon.), 2007; PhD in Pub. Adminstrn. (hon.), Citadel; PhD in Humane Letters (hon.), Coll. Charleston, 2007. Sr. v.p. Keenan & Suggs; mem. Dist. 20 SC State Senate, 1985—, chair Edn. Com. Field dir. S.C. Republican Party, 1969—75, sec., 1976—80; nat. committeeman for S.C. Rep. Nat. Committee, 1980—88; chmn. campaign '80 for S.C.; Presdl. elector Rep., 1980, 1984; chmn. edn. com. SC State Senate; co-chmn., treas. Re-elect Thurmond Com., 1990—95. With USMCR, 1968—74. Recipient Mounted Gold Elephant, S.C. Republican Party, 1975, 1980, 1982, Order of Palmetto; named Young Agt. of Yr., Ind. Ins. Agts. S.C., 1981. Mem.: Am. Legion, Marine Corps League, Palmetto Club, Columbia Ball Club, Forest Lake Club, Tarantella Club, Sigma Chi. Republican. Episcopalian. Avocations: tennis, politics. Office: 412 Gressette Senate Office Bldg PO Box 142 Columbia SC 29202 also: 2934 Wheat St Columbia SC 29205 also: PO Box 142 Columbia SC 29202 Home Phone: 803-256-7853; Office Phone: 803-212-6250, 803-799-5533. Business E-Mail: edu@scsenate.org.

COURT, LEONARD, lawyer, educator; b. Ardmore, Okla., Jan. 11, 1947; s. Leonard and Margaret Janet (Harvey) C.; m. JoAnn Dilleshaw, Sept. 2, 1967; children: Chris, Todd, Brooke. BA, Okla. State U., 1969; JD, Harvard U., 1972. Bar: Okla. 1973, US Dist. Ct. (we. dist.) Okla. 1973, US Dist. Ct. (no. dist.) Okla., 1978, US Dist. Ct. (ea. dist.) Okla. 1983, US Ct. Appeals (10th cir.) 1980, US Ct. Mil. Appeals 1973, Am. Law Inst., 2009. Assoc. Crowe & Dunlevy, Oklahoma City, 1977-81, shareholder, dir., 1981—. Adj. prof. Okla. U. Law Sch., Norman, 1984-85, 88-89, 99-00, Okla. City U. Law Sch., 1998-2008; planning com. Ann. Inst. Labor Law, SW Legal Found., Dallas, 1984-2004. Contbg. author: (supplement book) The Developing Labor Law, 1978, Corporate Counsel's Annual, 1974, Labor Law Developments, 1993, Employment Discrimination Law, Supplement, 1998, 2000, Winning Legal Strategies for Employment Law, 2005. Chmn. bd. elders Meml. Christian Ch., Oklahoma City, 1980, 98-2000; cubmaster Last Frontier coun. Boy Scouts Am., 1984, co-chmn. sustaining fund raising drive Oklahoma City Downtown YMCA, 1989, mem. bd. mgmt., 1994-96; participant Leadership Oklahoma City, 1987-88, bd. govs. Okla. State U. Found., 1990-2002, 2010-; Oklahoma City Ronald McDonald House, 1990-93, mem. exec. com. 1991-93; co-chmn. ann. teleparty fundraising drive Am. Heart Assn., Okla. City, 1996-98, bd. dirs., 1996-98. Capt. USAF, 1973-77. Recipient Leadership in Law award, Okla. Jour. Record, 2007. Fellow Am. Coll. Labor and Employment Lawyer; mem. Am. Employment Law Coun., US C. of C. (mem. labor rels. com. 1997—, chmn., wages hour and legal 1999—, mem. steering com. 1999—), Am. Law Inst., Oklahoma City C. of C. (mem. sports and recreation com. 1982-85, indsl. devel. com. 1986), Okla. State U. Alumni Assn. (nat. bd. dirs. 1989—, nat. exec. com., 1992-97, pres. 1995-96, chmn. alumni ctr. task force 1998—, Disting. Alumni award 1998, Hall Fame 2006), Okla. County Alumni Assn. (bd. sec. 1987-88, treas. 1988-89, v.p. 1989-90, pres. 1990-91), Harvard Law Sch. Assn., ABA (labor and employment law sect. com. on devel. of law under Nat. Labor Rels. Act, com. on EEO law, lititgation sect./employment and labor rels. law com.), Okla. Bar Assn. (labor and employment law sect. coun. 1978-83, 85-87, chmn. 1986), Okla. County Bar Assn., Fed. Bar Assn., US Tennis Assn. (life). Office: Crowe & Dunlevy Mid America Tower 20 N Broadway Ave Ste 1800 Oklahoma City OK 73102-8273 Office Phone: 405-235-7700. E-mail: courtl@crowedunlevy.com.

COURTNEY, EDWARD, retired classics educator; b. Belfast, Northern Ireland, Mar. 22, 1932; came to U.S., 1982; s. George and Kathleen (Nicholson) C.; m. Brenda Virginia Meek, Dec. 18, 1962; children: Richard Marcus, Adam Matthew. BA, Trinity Coll., Dublin, Ireland, 1954; MA, Oxford U., 1957. Research lectr. Christ Ch., Oxford, 1955-59; lectr. in classics King's Coll., London, 1959-70, reader in classics, 1970-77, prof. Latin, 1977-82; prof. classics Stanford U., Calif., 1982-93, Ely prof. humanities Calif., 1986-93; Gildersleeve prof. classics U. Va., Charlottesville, Va., 1993—2002, prof. emeritus, 2002—. Author: Commentary on the Satires of Juvenal, 1980, The Poems of Petronius, 1991, The Fragmentary Latin Poets, 1993, 2d edit., 2003, Musa Lapidaria, A Selection of Latin Verse Inscriptions, 1995, Archaic Latin Prose, 1999, A Companion to Petronius, 2002; editor: Valerius Flaccus, Argonautica, 1970, Juvenal, The Satires, A Critical Text, 1985, Statius, Silvae, 1990; joint editor: Ovid, Fasti, 1978, 4th edit., 1997. Mem. Am. Philol. Assn. Avocation: chess. Personal E-mail: edcourt2@cs.com.

COURTNEY, WILLIAM HARRISON, IT firm executive; b. Balt., July 18, 1944; s. Wilbur Harry Courtney and Mary Lee (Mitchell) Fleming; m. Laryssa Lapychak; children: William Jr., Mary Alison. BA in Econs., W.Va. U., 1966; PhD in Econs., Brown U., 1980. Fgn. svc. officer Dept. State, Washington, 1972-99; dep. exec. sec. NSC, The White House, Washington, 1987-88; dep. U.S. negotiator U.S.-Soviet Def. and Space Talks, Geneva, 1988-91; amb. Nuc. Testing and Nuc. Weapons Safety, Security, and Dismantlement, ACDA, Washington, 1991-92, Kazakhstan, 1992-95, Georgia, 1995-97; spl. asst. to Pres. for Russia, Ukraine and Eurasia, White House, Washington, 1997-98; sr. advisor Fgn. Affairs Reorgn. U.S. Dept. State, Washington, 1998-99; sr. advisor U.S. Commn. Security & Coop. Europe, 1999; sr. v.p. nat. security programs DynCorp, Alexandria, Va., 2000—04; dir. strategy and devel. Computer Scis. Corp., Falls Church, Va., 2004—. Mem.: Am. Acad. Diplomacy, Coun. Fgn. Rels. Episcopalian. Office: 3110 Fairview Park Dr Falls Church VA 22042 Home: 3730 48th St NW Washington DC 20016-3213 Office Phone: 202-215-4243. Personal E-mail: courtneywmh@gmail.com. Business E-Mail: wcourtney@csc.com.

COURTWAY, THOMAS C., academic administrator, former state legislator; b. Wynne, Ark., Dec. 30, 1952; s. Bob and Betty Courtway; m. Melissa Courtway; children: Brad, Corey, Drew, Ryan. BA in Econs., Hendrix Coll., 1974; JD with honors, U. Ark., 1978; MLT, Georgetown U., 1983. Legis. aide to US Senator Dale Bumpers, 1979—82, US Senator David Pryor, 1983—86; atty. Wright, Lindsey & Jennings, Little Rock, 1986—93; pvt. practice Conway, Ark., 1993—95; atty. Brazil Law Firm, Conway, 1995—2000; mem. Ark. Ho. of Reps. from Dist. 45, 1995—2001, chmn. Revenue & Taxation Com., mem. Econ. & Tax Policy, Insurance & Commerce & Joint Budget Coms.; founder Courtway & Osment, Conway, 2000—02; gen. counsel U. Ctrl. Ark., 2002—03, 2004—05, v.p., gen. counsel, 2006—, interim pres., 2008—; interim dir. Ark. Dept. Edn., 2002—04; v.p. planning and ops. Hendrix Coll., 2005—06. Democrat. Methodist. Office: U Ctrl Ark / Office of Pres Wingo Hall, Ste 207 201 Donaghey Ave Conway AR 72035 Office Phone: 501-852-2659. E-mail: Tcourtway@uca.edu.

COUSINS, ROBERT JOHN, nutritional biochemist, educator; b. NYC, Apr. 5, 1941; s. Charles Robert and Doris Elizabeth (Sifferlen) C.; m. Elizabeth Anne Ward, Jan. 25, 1969; children: Sarah, Jonathan, Allison. BA, U. Vt., 1963; PhD, U. Conn., 1968. NIH postdoctoral fellow biochemistry U. Wis., 1968-70; asst. prof. nutrition Rutgers U., 1971-74, assoc. prof., 1974-77, prof. nutritional biochemistry, 1977-79, prof. II (disting. Prof.), 1979-82, dir. grad. program in nutrition, 1976-82, mem. grad. programs in biochemistry, nutrition and toxicology; Boston family prof. human nutrition and biochemistry U. Fla., Gainesville, 1982—, eminent scholar chair, 1982—; dir. Nutritional Sci. Ctr., U. Fla., 1987—, grad. coun., 1990-93. Mem. nutrition study sect. NIH, 1980-84; mem. USDA Expt. Sta., dir. subcom. on human nutrition, 1987-01; J.L. Pratt vis. prof. Va. Poly. Inst. and State U., 1980; Wellcome vis. prof. Auburn U., 1986; C. Malcolm Trout vis. scholar Mich. State U., 2003; mem. NAS, 2000-, Inst. of Med. Commn. on opportunities in nutrition and food scis., 1991-93, Food and Nutrition Bd., 1997-02, Dietary Reference Intakes Sci. Evaluation Commn., 1999-01, Ad Hoc Bionutrition Commn., NIH, 1993; Mary Short lectr. U. Md., 1989, James Waddell lectr. U. Wis., Madison, 1989, Stars in Nutrition lectr. Pa. State U., 1990, Hans Fisher lectr. Rutgers U., 1995, Lucille Hurley lectr. U. Calif., Davis, 1997, Eric Underwood lectr. Evian, France, 1999; Disting. spkr. biochemistry U. Wis., Milw., 1989; Mary Shoub lectr. U. Md., 1989; James Waddell Meml. lectr. U Wis., Madison, 1989, Eric Underwood lectr., Evian, France, other lectureships. Assoc. editor Jour. Nutrition, 1990-96; mem. editl. com. Ann. Revs. Nutrition, 1985-90, 96-99, assoc. editor, 1999-04, editor, 2005-; contbg. editor Nutrition Revs., 1980-88; mem. editl. bd. FASEB Jour., 1994-99, Biol. Trace Element Rsch. 1982-03; contbr. articles in nutritional biochemistry to profl. jours., chpts. to books Recipient Mead Johnson award in nutrition, 1979, Osborne and Mendel award for basic rsch. in nutrition, 1989, U. Conn. Disting. Alumnus award, 1991, Merit award NIH, 1992, USDA Sec.'s Honor award, 2000, Am. Coll. Nutrition Rsch. award, 2003, Bristol-Myers Squibb/Mead Johnson award for disting. achievement in biomed. rsch., 2003; Future Leader grantee Nutrition Found., Inc., 1973, NIH grantee, 1972—, Am. Coll. Nutrition Rsch. award, 2003, Dannon Inst. Mem. award, 2010, W.O. Atwnter lectrship., USDA, ARS, 2011 Mem. AAAS, NAS (elected mem. 2000), Am. Soc. Biochem. and Molecular Biology, Am. Soc. Nutrition Sci. (chmn. nominating com. elected officers 1983, coun. 1986-89, pres.-elect 1995-96, pres. 1996-97), Soc. Exptl. Biology and Medicine (edit. bd. Proc. 1980-86), Am. Chem. Soc., Soc. Toxicology, Fedn. Am. Socs. Exptl. Biology (vice chmn. summer conf. 1985, chmn. summer conf. 1989, bd. dirs. 1989—, v.p. 1990-92, pres., chmn. bd. 1991-92, chmn. subcom. consensus conf. biomed. funding 1991-94, chmn. pub. affairs exec. com. 1992-93), Albron Labs. (sci. adv. bd. mem. 2013-), Sigma Xi, Phi Kappa Phi, Gamma Sigma Delta (U. Conn. Disting. Alumni). Office: U Fla Ctr for Nutritional Sciences 201 Food Sci & Human Nutr Bldg Gainesville FL 32611 Home: 4714 NW 57th Dr Gainesville FL 32606-4369 Business E-Mail: cousins@ufl.edu.

COUVILLION, DAVID IRVIN, retired federal judge; b. Simmesport, La., Oct. 27, 1934; s. J. Forest Couvillion and Leontine Rabalais. BS, La. State U., 1956, JD, 1959; LLM, Georgetown U., 1973. Bar: La. 1959. Pvt. practice, Marksville, La., 1959-67; adminstrv. asst. US Congressman Speedy O. Long, Washington, 1967-72; assoc. McCollister, McCleary, Fazio and Holliday, Baton Rouge, 1974-85; spl. trial judge US Tax Ct., Washington, 1985—2008. Mem. ABA, La. State Bar Assn. Personal E-mail: irvincouvillion@att.net.

COUVILLION, P. DOUG, food service executive; 2 children. CPA. Dir. fin., contr. Landry's Restaurants; v.p. fin. Cracker Barrel Old Country Store, Inc., 2001—05, sr. v.p. fin., 2005—. Office: Cracker Barrel Old Country Store Inc 307 Hartmann Dr Lebanon TN 37087 Office Phone: 615-444-5533. Office Fax: 615-443-9818.

COVER, ELLEN CATHERINE, biology professor, researcher; b. Beaumont, Tex., Feb. 8, 1954; d. John Alfred and Josephine Elizabeth McGill Cover. BS in Chemistry, Lamar U., Beaumont, 1974, BS in Biology, 1974, MS, 1977; PhD, Okla. State U., Stillwater, 1980. Asst. prof. Fla. Keys CC, Key West, 1980—83; prof. Manatee CC, Bradenton, Fla., 1983—2000; dean, western scis. East West Coll. Natural Medicine, Sarasota, Fla., 1995—2005; asst. prof. Lamar U., 2006—. Editor: (newsletter) Gator Tales. Bd. dirs. Clean Air and Water Inc., Beaumont, 2007—, Friends Anahuac Refuge, Tex., 2007—. Recipient Tchg. Excellence award, NISOD. Mem.: Alliance McFaddin and Tex. Point Refuges, Native Plant Soc. Tex., Audubon Soc., Tex. Acad. Sci., Am. Soc. Microbiology, Lamar U. Student Clubs (faculty sponsor). Office: Lamar Univ PO Box 10037 Dept Biology Beaumont TX 77710 Business E-Mail: eccover@my.lamar.edu.

COVEY, CYCLONE, history professor; b. Guthrie, Okla., May 21, 1922; s. Cyclone Davis and Lola (Best) C.; m. Bonnie Mae Bagby Hansen, June 12, 1949; children: Christopher Cyclone, Mark Nicholas, Julie Kristiana, Jonathan Baldridge, Timothy Nathaniel. BA, Stanford U., 1944, PhD, 1949; postgrad., U. Chgo., 1944-45, U. Okla., 1945-46; postdoctoral, Harvard U., 1953-54. Instr. history and humanities Reed Coll., Portland, Oreg., 1947-50; instr. humanities and music Okla. A.&M, Stillwater, 1950-51; from asst. prof. to prof. Okla. State U., Stillwater, 1957-68; prof. govt., history and fgn. langs. McKendree Coll., Lebanon, Ill., 1951-53, 54-56; faculty fellow Harvard U., Cambridge, Mass., 1953-54; vis. asst. prof. Am. studies Amherst (Mass.) Coll., 1956-57; prof. history Wake Forest U., Winston-Salem, N.C., 1968-88, prof. emeritus, 1988—. Ford postdoctoral fellow, 1953, Carnegie vis. asst. prof., 1956, Oak Ridge seminarian, 1964, Danforth asso., 1962; dir. Wake Forest in Venice, 1972. Author: The Wow Boys, 1957, The American Pilgrimage, 1960, A Cyclical Return to the Timeless Three-Clock Revolution, 1966, The Gentle Radical, 1966, Calalus, 1975, Homeric Troy and the Sea Peoples, 1987, Power & Epistemology in the State of Oklahoma and Oklahoma State University, 1991, The Primeval Middle East & Greece Pleistocene to Bronze, 1992, Admiral Piri, Amerigo Vespucci,

& Utopia, 1994, Emily Dickinson's Terror and the Swarthy Fellow, 1995, The Big Frame, 1995, Sui Chan Chan?, 1996, Xia to Xi-Xia, 1996, Origin of English America, 1997, 2d edit., 2006, Gateway Essays, 1998, America's Classical Blossoming 1847-1852, 1998, A Critical Reprise of Aboriginal American History 8th edit., 2008, Fate & Will, 3d edit., 2005, Mallarmé the Dice-Thrower, 2006, Psychosis of an Authoritarian Texan, 2005, Government and Gangster Assassination 1931-1977, 2005, 4th edit., 2005, 6th edit., 2008, Aegean Vs. Asia Minor: 16th-9th Century B.C., 2008, A Critical Reflection on the Kennedy Assassination, 2013; trans. editor: Cabeza de Vaca's Adventures in the Unknown Interior of America, 1961. Recipient Root Cutler award, Inst. for Study of Am. Cultures, Columbus, Ga., 1990, Fell & Burrows Cave awards, Midwestern Epigraphic Soc., 1997. Democrat. Home: 4071 Tangle Ln Winston Salem NC 27106-2931 Home Phone: 336-722-0437.

COVINGTON, ROBERT NEWMAN, retired law educator; b. Evansville, Ind., Sept. 9, 1936; s. George Milburn and Roberta (Newman) C.; m. Paula Anne Hattox, July 29, 1972. BA, Yale U., 1958; JD, Vanderbilt U., 1961. Bar: Tenn. 1961. Asst. prof. law Vanderbilt U., Nashville, 1961-64, assoc. prof., 1964-69, prof., 1969—2008, prof. emeritus, 2008—. Chair faculty senate Vanderbilt U., 1988-89; vis. prof. U. Mich., 1971, U. Calif., Davis, 1975-76, U. Tex., 1983; adminstrv. law officer Calif. Agrl. Labor Rels. Bd., 1975-76; cons. Tenn. Dept. Labor, 1972, Tenn. Law Libr. Commn., 1965-75; pres. OLLI at Vanderbilt, 2013-14. Author works in field. Mem. ABA, Tenn. Bar Assn., Am. Arbitration Assn., Tenn. Employment Rels. Rsch. Assn. (pres.-elect 2000-01, pres. 2001-02), Order of Coif, Univ. Club (Nashville), Phi Beta Kappa. Democrat. Episcopalian. Home: 907 Estes Rd Nashville TN 37215-1008 Office Phone: 615-390-6216. Business E-Mail: robert.covington@vanderbilt.edu.

COVINGTON, VIRGINIA MARIA HERNANDEZ, federal judge; b. Tampa, Fla., 1955; BS, U. Tampa, 1976, MBA, 1977; JD, Georgetown U., 1980. Trial atty. FTC, 1980—81; asst. state atty. 13th Jud. Cir., Fla., 1982—83; asst. US atty. civil divsn. Mid. Dist. Fla., 1983—88, asst. US atty., chief asset forfeiture sect. criminal divsn., 1989—2001; judge 2nd Dist. Ct. Appeal, Fla., 2001—04, US Dist. Ct. (mid. dist.) Fla., Tampa, 2004—. Office: US Dist Ct Gibbons US Courthouse 801 N Florida Ave 14th Fl Tampa FL 33602 Office Phone: 813-301-5340. Office Fax: 813-301-5630.

COWAN, BRYAN D., medical educator, department chairman; b. Brush, Colo., Jan. 19, 1949; m. Harriette L. Hampton. MD, U. Colo. Sch. Medicine, Denver, 1971—75. Cert. Reproductive Endocrinology Sub-Specialty Am. Bd. Ob-Gyn., 1983. Prof., chmn. U. Miss. Med. Ctr., Jackson, 2002—06. Lt. comdr. USN, 1975—83. Office: Univ Miss Med Ctr 2500 N State St Jackson MS 39216-4505 Office Fax: 601-984-6904.

COWAN, FREDERIC JOSEPH, judge; b. NYC, Oct. 11, 1945; s. Frederic Joseph Sr. and Mary Virginia (Wesley) C.; m. Linda Marshall Scholle, Apr. 28, 1974; children: Elizabeth, Caroline, Allison. AB, Dartmouth Coll., 1967; JD, Harvard U., 1978. Bar: Ky. 1978, U.S. Dist. Ct. (we. dist.) Ky. 1979, U.S. Ct. Appeals (6th cir.) 1984, U.S. Supreme Ct. 1989. Vol. Peace Corps, Ethiopia, 1967-69; assoc. Brown, Todd & Heyburn, Louisville, 1979-83; ptnr. Rice, Porter, Seiller & Price, Louisville, 1983-87; atty. gen. Commonwealth of Ky., 1988-92; counsel Lynch, Cox, Gilman & Mahan P.S.C., 1992—2006; judge Jefferson Cir. Ct., Ky., 2007—. Ky. State Rep., 32d legis. dist., 1982-87; chair Ky. Child Support Enforcement Commn., 1988-91, Ky. Sexual Abuse and Exploitation Prevention Bd., 1988-91; bd. dirs. Ky. Job Tng. Coordinating Coun., Frankfort, Louisville Bar Found., 1986; chmn. bd. dirs. The Family Pl., 2005-06; mem. Jud. Divsn. Am. Bar. Assn.,del. 2010, Conf. State and Local Trial Judges, 2009-. Vice chmn. judiciary criminal com. Ky. Ho. of Reps., 1985-87; chmn. budget com. on justice Judiciary and Corrections Ky. Ho. of Reps., 1985-87, Leadership Ky., 1985; U.S. del. election mission to Namibia Nat. Dem. Inst. for Internat. Affairs, 1989; U.S. del. dem. instns. seminar Nat. Dem. Inst. for Internat. Affairs, Slovenia, 1992; electoral supr. Orgn. for Security and Cooperation in Europe, Bosnia and Herzogovina, 1996; adv. com. Samara Oblast, Russia, 2001. Mem. ABA (del. 2008-), Nat. Conf. State Trial Judges, Am. Bar Found., fellow, Ky. Bar Assn., Louisville Bar Assn., Ky. Cir. Judges Assn. Methodist. Home: 1747 Sulgrave Rd Louisville KY 40205-1643 Office: Jefferson Cir Ct Jud Ctr 700 W Jefferson St Louisville KY 40202 Office Phone: 502-595-3011.

COWAN, JOHN JAMES, physicist, astronomer, educator; b. Washington, Apr. 3, 1948; s. John Robert and Anna V. Cowan; m. Linda Elaine Demetry, May 29, 1971. BA, George Washington U., 1970; MS, Case Inst. Tech., 1972; PhD, U. Md., 1976. Postdoctoral fellow Harvard U., Cambridge, Mass., 1976—79; asst. prof. U. Okla., Norman, 1979—84, assoc. prof., 1984—89, prof. physics and astronomy, 1989—, S.R. Noble Presdl. prof., 1998—2002, David Ross Boyd prof., 2002—; rsch. fellow U. Tex., 2002—11, David Ross Boyd emeritus prof., 2011—. Mem. rev. panel NASA, Washington, 1987; vis. rsch. assoc. Harvard U., Cambridge, 1987—88; vis. prof. Columbia U., NYC, 1991—92; mem. com. visitors NSF, Washington, 2002; lectr. in field. Reviewer: Astrophys. Jour., 1976—; contbr. articles to profl. jours. Recipient Kinney-Sugg Outstanding Prof. award, U. Okla., 2004; grantee, NASA, 1994—2007, 2010—, NSF, 1997—2011. Mem.: Am. Astron. Soc., Phi Beta Kappa. Achievements include co-discoverer of gold in one of the oldest stars in the universe. Avocations: racquetball, physical fitness. Office: Univ Okla 440 W Brooks St Norman OK 73019 Business E-Mail: cowan@nhn.ou.edu.

COWAN, KEITH O., telecommunications industry executive; b. Hartford, Conn., 1956; BA, Univ. NC, Chapel Hill, 1978; JD, U. Va., 1982. Assoc. Alston & Bird LLP, 1982—90, ptnr., 1990—96; from exec. officer to pres. mktg. and product mgmt. BellSouth Corp., Atlanta, 1996—2005, pres. mktg. & product devel., 2005—07; exec. v.p. Genuine Parts Co., 2007; pres. strategy & corp. initiatives Sprint Nextel Corp., Reston, Va., 2007—, acting pres. CDMA bus. unit, 2008. Former mem. adminstrv. com., chmn. securities practice group, chmn. continuing legal edn. com. Alston & Bird; bd. dirs. Atlanta Landmarks, Inc. Mem. bd. dirs. Metro Atlanta YMCA, VSA Arts of Ga. Mem.: Atlanta Bar Assn. (former bd. dirs., chmn. bus. and fin. law sect., chmn. continuing legal edn. com.). Office: Sprint Nextel Corp 20001 Edmund Halley Dr Reston VA 20191

COWART, JIM CASH, investment company executive; b. Hereford, Tex., July 1, 1951; s. Orville P. and Rosa Stratton (Cash) C.; m. Janet Carol Bergman, Aug. 24, 1973; 1 child, Jefferson Cash. BA in Computer Sci., Pomona Coll., 1973; MBA with honors, Harvard U., 1977. Prin., ind. investor EOS Capital, Inc., Cowart & Co. LLC; with Lehman Brothers; computer analyst US House of Reps., 1973—74; asst. v.p., mktg. Amtrak, 1974—75; v.p., investment banking Kidder, Peabody & Co., 1977—82; sr. v.p., investment banking Shearson Lehman, 1982—87; with, investment banking & venture capital Shearson Venture Capital, pres., 1983—87; founding gen. ptnr. Capital Resource Ptnrs., 1987—91; gen. ptnr. Aurora Ptnrs., Laguna Niguel, Calif., 1991; chmn., CEO Aurora Electronics, Inc., Irvine, Calif., 1992—97, Auriga Medical Products GmbH, 2004—. Bd. dirs. BE Aerospace, Inc., 1989—. Avocations: politics, travel, technology, philosophy. Office: BE Aerospace Inc Bd Directors 1400 Corporate Ctr Way Wellington FL 33414 Office Phone: 561-791-5000. Office Fax: 561-791-7900. Business E-Mail: jim_cowart@beaerospace.com.

COWART, RICHARD G., lawyer; b. Bourne, Mass., 1954; BSBA magna cum laude, U. Southern Miss., 1975; JD with honors, U. Miss., 1978. Ptnr., chmn. health law pub. policy dept. Baker Donelson Bearman Caldwell & Berkowitz PC, Nashville. Editor: (articles) Miss. Law Jour., 1977—78; law columnist The Tennessean. Mem.: ABA, Miss. Bar, Tenn. Bar Assn., Am. Health Lawyers Assn. (pres. 2004—05, bd. dir.), Phi Delta Phi, Omicrom Delta Kappa, Phi Kappa Phi. Office: Baker Donelson Bearman PC Commerce Ctr Ste 1000 211 Commerce St Ste 800 Nashville TN 37201-1817 Office Fax: 615-726-5660. Business E-Mail: dcowart@bakerdonelson.com.

COWART, T(HOMAS) DAVID, lawyer; b. San Benito, Tex., June 12, 1953; s. Thomas W. Jr. and Glenda Claire (Miller) C.; children: Thomas Kevin, Lauren Michelle, Megan Leigh; m. Greta E. Gerberding, Aug. 12, 1995. BBA, U. Miss., 1975, JD, 1978; LLM in Taxation, NYU, 1979. CPA Tex., Miss.; bar: Miss. 1978, Tex. 1979. Assoc. Dossett, Magruder & Montgomery, Jackson, Miss., 1978; ptnr., assoc. Strasburger & Price, Dallas, 1979-87; shareholder Johnson & Gibbs, Dallas, 1988-90, Jenkens & Gilchrist, Dallas, 1991—2007; ptnr. Sonnenschein Nath & Rosenthal, Dallas, 2007—. Adj. prof. law So. Meth. U. Sch. Law, 1988; mem. key dist. adv. coun. IRS, Dallas, 1989—95, chmn., 1990—93; mem. Coll. State Bar Tex.; lectr. in field. Mem. editl. bd.: Flexible Benefits, 1993—, 401k Advisor, 1994—, COBRA, 1996—. Mem. adv. com. Goals for Dallas, 1984-85; vol. Children's Med. Ctr., 1992-96. Recipient Best Lawyer award, Corp. Coun., 2003; named Best Lawyer in Am., 2001—, Best Lawyer in Dallas, 2003—10, Tex. Super Lawyer, 2003—10. Mem.: ABA (health care task force 1991—98, sect. 83 issues task force, chmn. health plan designs issues subcom. 1992—95, sect. taxation, employee benefit com., vice-chmn. 1995—98, chmn.-designate joint com. on employee benefits 1997—98, chmn. 1998—99, chmn. joint com. employee benefits 1999—2000), Am. Bar Found., Dallas Bar Found., Am. Law Inst., Phi Alpha Phi, Dallas Benefits Soc. (co-moderator 1991—92, bd. dirs. 1991—93), S.W. Benefits Assn. (bd. dirs. 1994—97), Dallas Bar Assn. (lectr. 1985—, coun. mem. employee benefits sect. 1989—92, treas. 1992, sec. 1993, v.p. 1994, pres. 1995), State Bar Tex. (fed. legislation, regulations and revenue rulings subcom. 1986—87, chmn. fiduciary stds. for trustees subcom. 1987—88, sect. taxation, com. compensation and employee benefits), Am. Coll. Employee Benefits Counsel (bd. govs. 2000—07, 1st chair, charter mem., pres. 2002—03), Beta Alpha Psi, Omicron Delta Kappa. Office: Sonnenschein Nath & Rosenthal LLP 2000 McKinney Ave Ste 1900 Dallas TX 75201-1957 Office Phone: 214-259-0906. Business E-Mail: dcowart@sonnenschein.com.

COWEN, SCOTT S., academic administrator; m. Marjorie Cowen; 4 children. BS, U. Conn., 1968; MBA, George Washington U., 1972, DBA in Fin., 1975; PhD (hon.), Hebrew Union Coll. Jewish Inst. Religion, 2009. Asst. prof. mgmt. Bucknell U., 1974—76; faculty Case Western Res. U., Cleve., 1976—98, dean, Albert J. Weatherhead III prof. mgmt., 1984—98; Seymour S Goodman Meml. prof. bus. A.B. Freeman Sch. Bus. Tulane University, 1998—, prof. econs. Faculty of Liberal Arts and Scis., 1998—, pres., 1998—. Eleanor F. and Philip G. Rust vis. prof. Colgate Darden Grad. Sch. Bus. Adminstrn., U. Va., 1982—83; bd. dirs. Newell Rubbermaid Inc., 1997—, Am. Greetings Corp., 1989—, Jo-Ann Stores Inc., 1989—, Forest City Ent. Inc., 1987—; cons. in field. Co-author: Introduction to Business: Concepts and Applications, 1981, Information Requirements of Corporate Boards of Directors, 1983, Accounting Today: Principles and Applications, Innovation in Professional Education: Steps on a Journey From Teaching to Learning, 1995; contbr. articles to profl. jours. Bd. dirs. Nat. Merit Scholarship Corp., 2006—, Nat. Collesiate Athletic Assn., 2003—, New Orleans Redevel. Authority, 2006—; chmn. SE Regional Airport Authority, 2008—. With US Army, 1968—71. Recipient Torch of Learning, Hebrew U., Torch of Liberty, Anti-Defamation League, Leadership Cleve. award, Greater Cleve. Growth Assn., 1987—88, Shofor award, Ctrl. Synagogue NY, 2006, CASE Chief Exe. Leadership award, 2007; co-recipient Wward of Achievement in Edn., No. Ohio Live Mag., 1991; named Disting. Alumni, George Washington U., 1998—99; named one of The 10 Best Coll. Presidents, TIME mag., 2009; named to, Sch. Bus. Adminstrn. Hall of Fame U. Conn.; fellow, Ernst & Whitney, Cleve., 1978, 1979. Mem.: Nat. Assn. Ind. Colls. and Univs., Am. Coun. Edn. (bd. dirs. 1999—2003), Am. Assembly of Collegiate Schs. Bus. (pres. 1995—96). Office: Tulane University Tech Srvcs 1555 Poydras St Ste 1400 New Orleans LA 70112-5406 Office Phone: 504-865-5201. Office Fax: 504-865-5202. Business E-Mail: scowen@tulane.edu.*

COWEN, TYLER, economics professor, writer; b. Jan. 21, 1962; m. Natasha Cowen. BS in Economics, George Mason U., 1983; PhD in Economics, Harvard U., 1987. Asst. to assoc. prof. econ. U. Calif., Irvine, 1987—89; prof. econ. George Mason U., 1989—, Holbert C. Harris Chair of Economics, 2000—. Gen. dir. Mercatus Ctr., George Mason U., 1998—, James M. Buchanan Ctr. for Polit. Econ., 1998—; co-owner Marginal Revolution Economics Blog. Editor: (novels) The Theory of Market Failure: A Critical Examination, 1988, Public Goods and Market Failures: A Critical Examination, 1991; co-author Explorations in the New Monetary Economics, 1994; author Risk and Business Cycles: New and Old Austrian Perspectives, 1998, In Praise of Commercial Culture, 1998, What Price Fame?, 2000, Creative Destruction: How Globalization is Changing the World's Cultures, 2002, Markets and Culture Voices: Liberty vs. Power in the Lives of the Mexican Amate Painters, 2005, Good & Plenty: The Creative Successes of American Arts Funding, 2006, Discover Your Inner Economist: Use Incentives to Fall in Love, Survive Your Next Meeting, and Motivate Your Dentist, 2007, Create Your Own Economy: The Path to Prosperity in a Disordered World (re-released with new title The Age of Infovore: Succeeding in the Information Economy, 2010), 2009, An Economist Gets Lunch-New Rules for Everyday Foodies, 2012, (Kindle Edition) The Great Stagnation: How America Ate All the Low-Hanging Fruit of Modern History, Got Sick, and Will (Eventually) Feel Better, 2011; editor: Economic Welfare, 2000, co-editor Southern Economic Journal, (novels) New Theories of Market Failure, 2002; contbr. articles to profl. publications including The New Republic, The Wall Street Journal, Forbes, Newsweek & The Wilson Quarterly, Economic Scene column, NY Times; co-author (with Alex Tabarrok): Modern Principles: Macroeconomics, 2009, (economics blog) Marginal Revolution; author: (dining guide) Tyler Cowen's Ethnic Dining Guide; referee for several journals and publications. Named one of Influential Thinkers of 2011, Foreign Policy Mag. Office: MSN 1D3 Carow Hall George Mason University Fairfax VA 22030 Office Phone: 703-993-2312. Office Fax: 703-993-4910. E-mail: tcowen@gmu.edu.

COWHER, BILL (WILLIAM LAIRD COWHER), sportscaster, former professional football coach; b. Pitts., May 8, 1957; s. Laird and Dorothy Cowher; m. Kaye Cowher, 1981 (dec. July 23, 2010); children: Meagan Lyn, Lauren Marie, Lindsay Morgan. BS in Edn., N.C. State, 1979. Profl. football player Phila. Eagles, 1979, 1983-84, Cleve. Browns, 1980-82, spl. teams coach, 1985-86, secondary coach, 1987-88; def. coord. Kans. City Chiefs, 1988-91; head coach Pitts. Steelers, 1992—2007; studio analyst, The NFL Today CBS Sports, 2007—. Named NFL Coach of Yr., AP, 1992, Sporting News, 1992, 2004, Pitts. Man of the Yr., Dapper Dan Club, Best Coach, Espy award, 2006. Achievements include being the youngest head coach to lead his team to the Super Bowl, 1995; head coach for the Super Bowl XL champions, 2006. Office: c/o CBS Sports 51 W 52nd St New York NY 10019

COWHIG, MICHAEL T., consumer products company executive; b. Boston, Mass., Jan. 23, 1947; BS in Indsl. Mgmt. magna cum laude, Boston Coll., 1968; MBA, Bobson Coll., 1972. V.p., mfg., N.Am. Gillette Co., 1984—91, sr. v.p., global mfg. and tech. ops., stationery products, 1996—97, sr. v.p., mfg. and tech. ops., grooming, 1997—2000, sr. v.p., global supply chain and bus. devel., 2000—02, sr. v.p., global mfg. and tech. ops., 2002—04, pres., tech. and mfg., 2004—06, pres., global tech. and mfg., 2004—05; pres., global tech. and mfg., Gillette Global Bus. Unit Procter & Gamble Co., 2005—06; chmn. Newell Rubbermaid Inc., 2010—. Bd. dirs. Wilsons The Leather Experts, 2002—, Newell Rubbermaid Inc., 2005—, CCL Industries, 2007—. Office: Newell Rubbermaid Inc 3 Glenlake Pky Atlanta GA 30328 Office Phone: 770-418-7000. Office Fax: 770-407-3970.

COWHILL, WILLIAM JOSEPH, retired naval officer, consultant; b. Bklyn., May 29, 1928; s. Joseph Henry and Lucy Rose (Foppiano) C.; m. Jennifer Jackson, Apr. 16, 1955; children Robin, Joseph, Beth, Michael, Douglas. BS, Northwestern U., 1950. Commd. ensign USN, 1950, advanced through grades to vice adm., 1979, comdg. officer USS Dace and USS Will Rogers, 1965-68, PCO instr., div. Naval Reactors, AEC, 1968-70, comdg. officer USS Holland, Rota, Spain, 1970-72, nuclear power program mgr. Bur. Naval Personnel, 1972, comdr. tng. command, U.S. Atlantic Fleet, 1973-75, asst. dep. chief naval ops. for submarine warfare, Office Chief Naval Ops., Washington, 1975-77, comdr. submarine force, U.S. Pacific Fleet, 1977-79, dep. chief ops. for logistics, office chief naval ops., 1979-83, dir. logistics, joint chiefs of staff, 1983-85, ret.; pvt. cons. Washington, 1985—. Decorated Def. D.S.M., Navy D.S.M., Legion of Merit. Home and Office: 9428 Vernon Dr Great Falls VA 22066

COWLES, JIM E., lawyer; b. Wichita Falls, Tex., Mar. 3, 1934; BBA, U. Tex., 1958, LLB, 1961. Bar: Tex. 1961, US Supreme Ct., US Dist. Ct. (we. and no. dists. Tex.) 1962, US Dist. Ct. (ea. dist. Tex.) 1964, US Ct. Appeals (5th cir.) 1968, US Dist. Ct. (so. dist. Tex.) 1979. Founder to shareholder Cowles & Thompson, P.C., Dallas, 1978—. Served in JAG USNR. Named a True Tex. Legend, State Bar Tex., 2010; named one of Best Lawyers in Am., Am. Lawyer, 1993—2013, Best Lawyers in Dallas, D mag., 1997—2013, Top 100 Super Lawyers in Tex., Tex. Monthly and Law & Politics mag., 2003—13, Top 10 Lawyers in Tex., 2005, Top 15 Bus.-Def. Lawyers in Dallas/Ft. Worth, Dallas Bus. Jour., 500 Leading Lawyers in Am., Lawdragon, Tex.25 Greatest Lawyers Last Quarter Century. Mem.: Patrick E. Higginbotham Am. Inn Ct., Am. Bd. Trial Advs., Def. Rsch. Inst., Coll. State Bar Tex., Intern. Assn. Def. Coun., Tex. Assn. Def. Coun. (Pres.'s award 1993), Dallas Assn. Def. Coun., State Bar Tex., Dallas Bar Assn. (Trial Lawyer of Yr. Award 2005), ABA. Office: Cowles & Thompson PC 901 Main St Ste 3900 Dallas TX 75202-3793 Office Phone: 214-672-2101. Office Fax: 214-672-2301. E-mail: jcowles@cowlesthompson.com.

COWLEY, ALAN HERBERT, chemist, educator; b. Manchester, Eng., Jan. 29, 1934; came to U.S., 1958; s. Herbert and Dora (Smalley) C.; m. Deborah Elaine Cole, Jan. 26, 1977; 1 dau., Emily Margaret McLaughlin; children by previous marriage: Peter, David, Alison Jane. B.Sc. with honors in Chemistry, U. Manchester, 1955, M.Sc., 1956, PhD, 1958; PhD (hon.), U. Bordeaux I, 2003. Postdoctoral fellow, instr. U. Fla., 1958-60; tech. officer with Exploratory Group, Billingham Divsn. Imperial Chem. Industries, Ltd., England, 1960—61; mem. faculty U. Tex., Austin, 1962—88, asst. prof. chemistry, 1962—67, assoc. prof. chemistry, 1967—70, prof. chemistry, 1970—84, George W. Watt Centennial prof. chemistry, 1984—88, Robert A. We;ch Chair in Chemistry, 1989—; Sir Edward Frankland Prof. of Inorganic Chemistry Imperial Coll., London, 1988—89. Co-chmn. Gordon Rsch. Conf. on Sci. Edn., 1992, bd. trustee vice chair, 1993, bd. trustee chair, 1994—95; pres. Internat. Coun. on Main Group Chemistry, 1997—98; mem. Internat. adv. bd. Dalton Transactions, 1997—2000; Institut Universitaire de France Prof., 1999; mem. scientific adv. bd. Materia, Inc., 2004; mem. sci. and engring. adv. bd. Orfid, Inc., 2004; Gauss Professorship Gottingen Acad. Sciences, 2005. Author: Compounds Containing Phosphorus-Phosphorus Bonds, 1973; also tech. papers; editorial bd.: Inorganic Chemistry, 1979-83, Chem. Revs., 1984-88, Polyhedron, 1984-98, Jour. Am. Chem. Soc., 1986-91, Jour. of Organmetallic Chemistry, 1987-, Organometallics, 1988-91, Progress in Inorganic Chemistry, 1988-, Heteroatom Chemistry, 1988-96, Advances in Inorganic Chemistry, 1989-; mem. internat. adv. bd. Jordanian Jour. of Chemistry, 2004. Mem. exec. bd. Tex. Sci. and Math. Renaissance Centers, 1991—93. Dalton Chem. scholar, 1955-58; Guggenheim fellow, 1976-77; Chemical Pioneer award, Am. Inst. of Chemists, 1994, von Humboldt prize, 1996; decorated Chevalier dans l'Ordre des Palmes Academiques, French Govt., 1997 Mem. Am. Chem. Soc.(Southwest Regional award, 1986, award for Distinguished Svc. in the Advancement of Inorganic Chemistry, 2009), Royal Soc. Chemistry (award for Main-Group Element Chemistry, 1980, Centenary medal and lectureship); corres. mem. Mexican Acad. Sciences; fellow Royal Soc. Home: 2501 Woodmont Ave Austin TX 78703-3258 Office: Dept Chemistry & Biochemistry Univ Texas at Austin WEL 4-330 1 University Station A5300 Austin TX 78712-0165 Office Phone: 512-471-7484. Business E-Mail: cowley@mail.utexas.edu.

COWLEY, CLARK, advertising executive; Ptnr. SuperMedia Inc. (formerly Idearc Search Mktg.). Office: SuperMedia Inc 2200 W Airfield Dr Dallas TX 75261 Office Phone: 972-453-7000. Office Fax: 972-453-3969. Business E-Mail: clark.cowley@supermedia.com.

COWLING, LARRY, state legislator; Farmer; owner Cowling Farm & Trucking, Foreman, Ark.; mem. Dist. 2 Ark. House of Reps., 2007—. Democrat. Episcopal. Address: PO Box 427 Foreman AR 71836 Office Phone: 870-542-7452. Fax: 870-542-7743. Business E-Mail: cowlingl@arkleg.state.ark.us.

COWSERT, WILLIAM S. (BILL), state legislator, lawyer; b. Jackson, Miss., May 31, 1963; m. Amy Cowsert; children: Bob, Caty, Will. BS, Presbyn. Coll.; JD, U. Ga. Law Sch. Bar: Ga. 1983. Ptnr. Cowsert & Avery, Athens, Ga.; mem. Dist. 46 Ga. State Senate, 2007—, apptd. adminstrn. fl. leader, 2008—. Vol. Athens Little League; active First Presbyn. Ch. Athens. Mem.: Clarke County Heart Assn. (past pres.), Athens Touchdown Club (bd. dirs.), Athens Sertoma Club (past pres.). Republican. Presbyterian. Office: PO Box 512 Athens GA 30603 Office Phone: 706-543-7700. Office Fax: 706-202-3211. Business E-Mail: bill.cowsert@senate.ga.gov.

COX, ALBERT HARRINGTON, JR., retired economist; b. St. Louis, Oct. 13, 1932; s. Albert Harrington and Hildegarde (Raab) C.; m. Frances Marie French, Apr. 12, 1960; children: Cynthia, Bruce Harrington. BBA, U. Tex., 1954, MBA, 1956; PhD, U. Mich., 1965. Asst. prof. finance So. Meth. U., Dallas, 1959; economist First Nat. City Bank, NYC, 1960-61; sec. research com. Am. Bankers Assn.,

NYC, 1962-64; v.p., economist First Nat. Bank, Dallas, 1965-68; spl. asst. to chmn. Pres.'s Council Econ. Advs., Washington, 1969-70; exec. v.p., chief economist, dir. Lionel D. Edie & Co., NYC, 1970-75; sr. econ. adv. Merrill Lynch, Pierce, Fenner & Smith, Inc., NYC, 1970-75; pres. Merrill Lynch Econs., Inc., NYC, 1976-81, chmn., 1982-84; chief economist Merrill Lynch & Co., 1976-81; ret., 1984. Mng. dir. Merrill Lynch Capital Markets Group, Merrill Lynch Capital Fund; mem. econ. adv. bd. Dept. Commerce, 1974-76; dir., sr. econ. adviser BIL Trainer, Wortham Inc. (Bank in Liechtenstein, A.G.), 1985-90; sr. econ. adviser Trainer Wortham, Inc., 1991; portfolio cons. Seibels Bruce Ins. Cos., Columbia, SC, 1993-94, dir., 1994-97; mem. Pres.'s Inflation Policy Task Force, 1980; disting. lectr. bus. and econs. U. SC, Hilton Head, 1988-90; dir. Nestor, Inc., 2003-06. Author: Regulation of Interest Rates on Bank Deposits, 1966; contbg. economist Coast Business, 1997-99, Bankers Monthly mag., 1970-88; bus. columnist Hilton Head News, 1990-98; contbr. articles to profl. jours. Mem. Nat. Assn. Bus. Economists (past dir.), Securities Industries Assn. (chmn. econ. adv. com. 1979-80), Am. Econ. Assn., Beta Gamma Sigma, Beta Theta Pi, Phi Eta Sigma. Republican. Mem. Reformed Ch. Home and Office: 5485 Villa Springs Ct Suwanee GA 30024 Office Phone: 678-513-0626. Personal E-mail: albertfrances@bellsouth.net.

COX, BRYAN KEITH, professional football coach; b. St. Louis, Feb. 17, 1968; m. Kim Cox; children: Lavonda, Brittani, Chiquita, Bryan Jr. BS in Mass. Comm., Western Ill. U., Macomb, 1991. Linebacker Miami Dolphins, 1991-95, Chgo. Bears, 1996-98, NY Jets, 1998—2000, New England Patriots, 2001, New Orleans Saints, 2002; defensive line coach NY Jets, 2006—08, Cleve. Browns, 2009—10, Miami Dolphins, 2011, Tampa Bay Buccaneers, 2012—. Named to The American Football Conf. Pro Bowl Team, NFL, 1992, 1994, 1995. Office: Tampa Bay Buccaneers One Buccaneer Pl Tampa FL 33607

COX, CARRIE S., pharmaceutical executive; b. 1957; m. Ken Cox; 2 children. BS, Mass. Coll. Pharmacy & Health Sci., 1981. With Sandoz Pharm. (now Novartis), 1982—92; v.p. women's healthcare Wyeth-Ayerst, 1990—97; sr. v.p. & head global bus. mgmt. Pharmacia & Upjohn, 1997—99, exec. v.p., 1999—2002; exec. v.p., pres. global prescription bus. Pharmacia Corp., 2002—03; exec. v.p., pres. global pharm. Schering-Plough Corp., 2003—09; CEO Humacyte, Inc., 2010—. Bd. dirs. Texas Instruments Inc., 2004—, Cardinal Health, Inc., 2009—, Celgene Corp., 2009—. Mem. health coun. & mgmt. exec. coun. Harvard Sch. Pub. Health. Named Healthcare Businesswoman of Yr., Healthcare Businesswomen's Assn., 2001; named one of The 50 Most Powerful Women in Bus., Fortune mag., 2005—09, The 10 Most Powerful Women in NJ Bus., Star-Ledger, 2006. Office: Humacyte Inc 7020 Kit Creek Rd Morrisville NC 27560

COX, CHAPMAN BEECHER, retired lawyer, charitable organization and aerospace executive; b. Dayton, Ohio, July 31, 1940; s. Charles Benjamin and Jewel Lorene (Nicholson) C.; m. Jeannette Gail Korody, Aug. 28, 1964; children: Charles Benjamin, Andrew David. BA, U. So. Calif., 1962; JD, Harvard U., 1965. Bar: Calif. 1966, Colo. 1972, U.S. Ct. Mil. Appeals 1966, U.S. Supreme Ct. 1986. Res. affiliation US Marine Corps, 1960—93, commd. officer, 1965—68, ret. as col.; assoc. Adams, Duque & Hazeltine, Los Angeles, 1968-72, Sherman & Howard, Denver, 1972-74, ptnr., 1974-80, mng. ptnr., 1980-81, ptnr., 1987-90; dep. asst. sec. U.S. Dept. Navy, Washington, 1981-83, asst. sec., 1983-84; gen. counsel Dept. Def., Washington, 1984-85, asst. sec., 1985-87; pres., CEO United Svc. Orgns., Inc., 1990-96; sr. v.p. Lockheed Martin IMS, 1996-2000; ret., 2000. Vis. lectr. U. Colo. Sch. Law, Boulder, 1977-78; def. policy bd. US Dept. Def., 1988-90; comml. space transp. adv. com. US Dept. Transp., 1989-91; chmn. Colo. Commn. Space Sci. and Industry, 1988-90. Gen. counsel Colo. Reps., Denver, 1977-81; del. U.S. Dept. State cultural exch. mission to Syria and Jordan, 1979; ruling elder Presbyn. Ch., 1976—; bd. dirs. United Svc. Orgns., 1985-96, Colorado Springs Symphony Orch., 1988-90, MicroLithics Corp., 1989-91, Presbyn. Ch. U.S.A. Found., 1990-99, Freedoms Found., 1994-99, Fund for Am. Studies, 1995-00, New Covenant Trust Co., 1996-99, Presbyn. Lay Com., 1997-00, Alliance Def. Freedom, 2002-, chmn., 2007-, Manhattan Initiative, Inc., 2005-11, Army-Navy Club Washington, 1998-2000. Decorated Navy Achievement medal, Marine Corps Unit Commendation medal, Marine Corps Meritorious Commendation medal, Nat. Def. Svc. medal, Vietnam Svc. medal, Armed Forces Res. medal, Cross of Gallantry Unit Citation, Vietnam Campaign medal, Def. Disting. Pub. Svc. medal, Navy Disting. Pub. Svc. medal. Fellow: Am. Coll. Trust and Estate Counsel; mem.: ABA (standing com. law and nat. security 1988—2002), Colo. Bar Assn. (bd. govs. 1977—79, chmn. probate and trust law sect. 1978—79), Calif. Bar Assn., Army-Navy Club of Washington. Republican. Presbyterian. Office Phone: 704-655-8768.

COX, CHRIS W., lobbyist; BA in History, Rhodes Coll., Memphis. Various sr. positions including dep. dir. fed. affairs divsn. NRA Inst. Legis. Action (NRA-ILA), 1995—2002, exec. dir., chief lobbyist, 2002—. Chmn. NRA Polit. Victory Fund. Office: NRA ILA 11250 Waples Mill Rd Fairfax VA 22030 E-mail: ccox@nrahq.org.

COX, CLAIR EDWARD, II, urologist, medical educator; b. Lawrenceville, Ill., Sept. 2, 1933; s. Clair Edward and May E. (Judy) C.; m. Clarice Wicks, Aug. 23, 1958; children— Clair Edward III, Daniel Paul, Kevin Christopher, Kenneth Harold. Student, U. Mich., 1951-54, MD, 1958. Diplomate Am. Bd. Urology. Intern U. Colo. Med. Center, Denver, 1958-59, surg. resident, 1959-60; resident urology U. Cal. Med. Center at San Francisco, 1960-63; mem. faculty Bowman Gray Sch. Medicine, Wake Forest U., Winston Salem, NC, 1963-72, assoc. prof., 1967-70, prof. urology, 1970-72; prof., chmn. dept. urology U. Tenn. Med. Sch., Memphis, 1972—99, prof., 1999—2009, prof. emeritus, 2009—. Contbr. profl. jours. Fellow ACS; mem. AMA, Am. Assn. Genito-Urinary Surgeons, Am. Urol. Assn., Internat. Soc. Urology, N.Y. Acad. Scis., Infectious Disease Soc. Am., Soc. Univ. Urologists, Am. Assn. Med. Colls., Am. Soc. Microbiology. Achievements include research in urinary tract infectious disease. Home: 6011 Sweetbriar Cv Memphis TN 38120-2514 Office Phone: 901-490-1690. E-mail: icox@uthsc.edu.

COX, DOUG, state legislator, physician; b. Aug. 9, 1952; m. Drenda Cox; children: Matt, Cassie, Scott. B, Okla. State Univ., 1974; MD, Univ. Okla., 1978. Cert. Am. Bd. Family Practice, Am. Bd. Emergency Med. Residency in family practice Tulsa Med. Coll. Univ. Okla., 1978—81; past chief of staff Integris Grove Gen. Hosp.; med. dir. Grove EMS; mem. Dist. 5 Okla. House of Representatives, 2005—. Mem.: Okla. State Med. Assn., Am. Coll. Emergency Physicians, Am. Acad. Family Practice. Republican. Office: Oklahoma House of Representatives 2300 N Lincoln Blvd Rm 410 Oklahoma City OK 73105 also: 33471 S 595 Road Grove OK 74344 Office Phone: 405-557-7415. E-mail: dougcox@okhouse.gov.

COX, EMMETT RIPLEY, federal judge; b. Cottonwood, Ala., Feb. 13, 1935; s. Emmett M. Jr. Cox and Myra E. (Ripley) Stewart; m. Ann MacKay Haas, May 16, 1964; children: John Haas, Catherine MacKay. BA, U. Ala., 1957, JD, 1959. Bar: Ala. 1959, US Ct. Appeals (5th, 8th and 11th cirs.), US Supreme Ct. Assoc. Mead, Norman & Fitzpatrick, Birmingham, Ala., 1959—64; assoc. then ptnr. Gaillard, Wilkins, Smith & Cox, Mobile, Ala., 1964—69; ptnr. Nettles, Cox & Barker, 1969—81; judge US Dist. Ct. (so. dist.) Ala., Mobile, 1981—88, US Ct. Appeals (11th cir.), Mobile, 1988—2000, sr. judge, 2000—. Mem. def. svcs. com. Jud. Conf. US, 1992—98, chair, 1995—98, mem. jud. br. com., 2001—05. Mem.: Maritime Law Assn. US, Fed. Bar Assn., Mobile Bar Assn., Ala. Bar Assn., Alpha Tau Omega (past pres.), Phi Delta Phi, Omicron Delta Kappa. Office: US Courthouse 11th Circuit 113 Saint Joseph St Ste 433 Mobile AL 36602-3624 also: 56 Forsyth St NW Atlanta GA 30303

COX, GLENN ANDREW, JR., retired energy executive; b. Sedalia, Mo., Aug. 6, 1929; s. Glenn Andrew and Ruth Lonsdale (Atkinson) C.; m. Veronica Cecelia Martin, Jan. 3, 1953; children: Martin Stuart, Grant Andrew, Cecelia Ruth. BBA, Southern Meth. U., 1951. Joined Phillips Petroleum Co., Bartlesville, Okla., 1956, asst. to chmn., oper. com., 1973-74, v.p., mgmt. info. and control, 1974-80, exec. v.p., 1980-85, dir., 1982-91, pres., COO, 1985-91. Bd. dirs. BOK Fin. Corp., Bank of Okla., The Williams Co.'s, Inc., Helmerich and Payne, Tulsa, Union Tex. Petroleum Holdings, Houston, Thermon Industries, Inc., San Marcos, Tex., Cimarex Energy, Inc., Denver. Pres. Cherokee Area coun. Boy Scouts Am., 1977-82, South Ctrl. region, 1987-90, mem. nat. exec. bd., 1987-94; mem. bd. curators Ctrl. Meth. Coll., Fayette, Mo., 1984-88, 1997—; trustee Philbrook Mus. Art, 1987-92, So. Meth. U., Dallas, 1988-96; bd. dirs. Okla. United Meth. Found.; mem. Okla. State Regents for Higher Edn., 1990-96. Mem. Am. Petroleum Inst. (bd. dirs. 1982-91), Nat. Assn. Mfrs. (bd. dirs. 1985-91), Bartlesville Area C. of C. (pres. 1978), Hillcrest Country Club. Methodist.

COX, HEADLEY MORRIS, JR., lawyer, educator; b. Mt. Olive, NC, July 25, 1916; s. Headley Morris and Frank (English) C.; m. Irene Todd, June 26, 1940; children: John Morris, Deborah English, Thomas Headley; m. Elizabeth Shelton Smith, Dec. 30, 1994. AB, Duke, 1937, AM, 1939; postgrad., U. Colo., 1944-45; PhD, U. Pa., 1958; JD, U. S.C., 1984. Successively instr., asst. prof., assoc. prof., prof. English Clemson (S.C.) U., 1939-82, head dept., 1950-69, dean Coll. Liberal Arts, 1969-80; of counsel Olson, Smith, Jordan & Cox, P.A., 1984—2004; ret., 2010. Sr. Fulbright lectr. in Am. lit. Universitat Graz, Austria, 1958-59 Served with USNR, 1944-46. Mem. Phi Beta Kappa. Methodist. Address: 211 Riggs Dr Clemson SC 29631-1427

COX, HEATHER, finance company executive; B in Economics, U. Ill., Urbana-Champaign. Fin. services and banking positions Household Internat., New Century Mortgage, Advanta Fin. Corp.; various operational leadership roles including sr. v.p. ops. E*Trade, 1999—2008; sr. v.p. US card ops., bus. chief risk officer US card Capital One Fin., 2008—. Chmn. Gov. Commn. on Govt. Reform & Restructuring, Va. Named one of The 25 Women to Watch, American Banker, 2011. Office: Capital One Financial 1680 Capital One Dr Mc Lean VA 22102

COX, HENRY, engineer, researcher; b. Phila., Mar. 7, 1935; s. Henry Robert and Helen (Kane) C.; m. Mary Ann Shaw, Sept. 3, 1960 (dec.), m. Andrea Fos, Nov. 24, 2012; children: James, Daniel, Michael, Diane, step: Annik Fos. BS, Coll. Holy Cross, 1956; ScD, MIT, 1963. Analyst Office Sec. of Def., 1970-72; research assoc. Scripps Instn. Oceanography, LaJolla, Calif., 1972-73; officer in charge Naval Underwater Systems Ctr., New London, Conn., 1973-76; div. dir. Def. Advanced Research Projects Agy., 1976-78; project mgr. Naval Electronic Systems Command, Arlington, Va., 1978-81; divisional v.p. BBN Systems and Tech. Corp., Arlington, 1981-91; chief tech. officer, sr. v.p. Orincon Corp., Arlington, 1991—2003; chief tech. officer Lockheed Martin Orincon Def., Arlington, 2003—05; sr. fellow Lockheed Martin, Arlington, 2005—. Contbr. articles to tech. jours. Served to capt. USN, 1956-81. Decorated Legion of Merit; decorated Meritorious Svc. medal, Navy Commendation medal; recipient Def. Superior Svc. medal, Dept. Def., 1978, NDIA Martell-Bushnell award, 2007. Fellow Acoustical Soc. Am., IEEE (Disting. Tech. Achievement award Oceanic Engring. Soc. 1991); mem. Am. Soc. Naval Engrs. (hon. Gold medal), Nat. Acad. Engring., US Naval Inst. Roman Catholic. Home: 6513 Waterway Dr Falls Church VA 22044-1328 Office: Lockheed Martin 4350 Fairfax Dr Arlington VA 22203-1695 Home Phone: 703-354-7684; Office Phone: 571-357-6437. Business E-Mail: harry.cox@lmco.com.

COX, JAMES D., law educator; b. 1943; JD, U. Calif. Hastings Sch. Law, 1969; LL.M., Harvard U., 1971; D in Mercature (hon.), U. South Denmark, 2001. Bar: Calif. 1970. Atty.-adv. Office Gen. Counsel FTC, Washington, 1969-70; teaching fellow Boston U., 1970-71; asst. prof. U. San Francisco, 1971-74; assoc. prof. U. Calif. Hastings Sch. Law, 1974-75; vis. assoc. prof. Stanford U., 1976-77; prof. U. Calif. Hastings Sch. Law, 1977-79; vis. prof. Duke U. Sch. Law, spring 1979, prof., 1979-2000, Brainerd Currie prof. law, 2000—. Com. on corps. State Bar Calif., NC bus. corp. act. draft com., NC nonprofit corp. draft com.; E.T. Bost rsch. prof., 1980, 96; legal adv. com. NY Stock Exch., 1995—; legal adv. bd. NASD, 1999—; mem. ABA com. corporate laws, 2006-. Author: Financial Information, Accounting and the Law, 1980, Quick Review of Corporations, 4th edit., 2004, (with Hillman and Langevoort) Securities Regulation: Cases and Materials, 5th edit., 2006; (with Hazen) Corporations, 2d edit., 2003. Sr. Fulbright Rsch. fellow, Australia, 1989. Mem. Am. Law Inst., Order of Coif, Phi Kappa Phi Office: Duke U Sch Law Durham NC 27708-0360 Office Phone: 919-613-7056. Business E-Mail: cox@law.duke.edu.

COX, JAMES SIDNEY, physician; b. Homer, La., Nov. 17, 1950; s. Sidney and Rita (Haynes) C.; m. Judy Katherine Vickers, Oct. 21, 1984; children: Shannon Ruth, Sarah Anne, Megan Elizabeth. Student, La. State U., 1968-71; MD, Tulane U., 1971-75. Diplomate Am. Bd. Family Practice, Am. Bd. of Emergency Medicine. Intern, resident in family practice John Peter Smith Hosp., Ft. Worth, 1975-78; city health officer family practice City of Athens, Tex., 1978-84; pvt. practice Athens, 1978-84, Ft. Worth, 1984—; mem. staff Henderson County Meml. Hosp., Athens, vice chief med. staff, 1981-82; mem. staff Lakeland Med. Ctr., Athens, chief med. staff, dir., 1983-84; vice chief emergency medicine dept. Harris Meth. Hosp., Ft. Worth, 1988-91, dir. occupational medicine, 1989—2008, chief emergency dept. Ft. Worth, 1992-93, 98-2000, sec. med. staff, 1994-95, sec. emergency medicine divsn., 1996-97. Pres., chmn. bd. dirs. Occuhealth Physicians Group, P.A., 1989-2009, Ft. Worth; mem. faculty U. Tex. Health Sci. Ctr.-Dallas Cmty. Medicine Dept., John Peter Smith Hosp., Ft. Worth, 1978-96, course dir. ACLS, 1989-1998, mem. affiliate faculty ACLS, 1991-95, med. rev. officer for urine drug testing, 1992-2009; med. bd. Harris Meth. Hosp., 1992-95, 98-2000; team chmn. emergency dept. redesign Rochester Inst. Tech. Coll. Bus., 1996; v.p. for physician affairs Emergency Medicine Cons., 1998-2005, exec. dir., 2005-06, chief adminstrv. officer, 2006—2011, exec. v.p., 2011-; assoc. med. dir. Harris Meth., Ft. Worth, 2000-2007; med. dir. ACLS, Campbell Health Sys., 1997-98; bd. dirs. North Tex. Accountable Healthcare Partnership, 2012-; bd. dirs. MD Polit. Action Com., 2011-, Tex. Alliance Patient Access, 2013-. Author: Intestinal Obstruction: A Programmed Text, 1975. Recipient Quality Cup award of Excellence, USA Today, 1996, Health Care Hero Ft. Worth Bus. Press, 2014. Fellow Am. Acad. Family Physicians, Am. Coll. Emergency Physicians (bd. govs. Emergency Medicine Action Fund, 2012-); mem. AMA (Physician's Recognition award), Tex. Med. Assn. (alt. del. 1994-96, 2003-05, del. 2005-), Tarrant County Med. Soc. (bd. dirs. 1994-96, 2003—, sec. treas. 2008-, v.p. 2008-09, pres. elect 2009-10, pres., 2010-11), Rotary (bd. dirs. Athens chpt. 1983-84), Alpha Epsilon Delta., Tex. Med. Assn.(vice-chair., Physicians Health and Rehab. Comm., 2008-, com. emergency med. svc. & truma, 2010-, pres., med. dir. project access Tarrant County, 2011-), Tarrant County Med. Soc. (bd. trustee, 2011-, Humanitarian award, 2012, chmn. bd. trustees 2013-) Presbyterian. Avocations: reading, skiing, bonsai, horticulture, astronomy. Home: 3458 Lantern Holw Fort Worth TX 76109-2411 Office: Emergency Medicine Cons 6451 Brentwood Stair Rd Ste 200 Fort Worth TX 76112-3200 Office Phone: 817-496-9700, 817-507-1757. Business E-Mail: jcox@emdocs.com.

COX, JOHN A., state legislator, transportation executive; b. Wilmington, NC, Aug. 13, 1944; m. Dottie Cox; children: Holly Norwood, Natalie Marie. Cert. transp. broker Transp. Intermediaries Assn. Founder, chmn. Cox Transp. Services, Inc., 1982—, Cox Truck Brokerage, Inc.; mem. Dist. 55 Va. House of Delegates, Richmond, 2010—. Bd. dirs. Traffic Ins., Ltd. Ordained deacon First Bapt. Ch., Ashland, Va.; former bd. mem. Hanover Edn. Found.; bd. mem. Ashland Vol. Rescue Squad; mem. Hanover County Sheriff's Bus. Adv. Bd.; pres. Hanover Sheriff's Found. Served with USAR, 1966—72. Mem.: Truckload Carriers Assn. (bd. dirs.), Va. Trucking Assn. (past pres.), The Fed. Club, Richmond Transp. Club (former pres.). Republican. Office: Va House of Delegates Gen Assembly Bldg Rm 821 PO Box 406 Richmond VA 23218 also: 10451 Dow-Gil Rd Ashland VA 23005 Office Phone: 804-698-1055, 804-365-9000. Office Fax: 804-698-6755, 804-798-5282. Business E-Mail: deljcox@house.virginia.gov.

COX, KENNY R., state legislator; b. La., Oct. 2, 1957; s. Mary Cox; m. Candie Cox; 4 children. BS, Northwestern State U., Natchitoches, La.; MA, US Army Command Gen. Staff Coll.; attended, US Comptr. Sch. on Planning, Program, Budget & Execution. Ret. lt. col. US Army; mem. Dist. 23 La. House of Reps., Baton Rogue, 2012—. Democrat. Office: La House of Reps 900 N 3rd St PO Box 94062 Baton Rouge LA 70804 Business E-Mail: coxk@legis.la.gov.

COX, KERMITT L., former insurance company executive; B in Math., Iowa State U., Ames, 1965; grad. in Actuarial Sci., U. Nebr., 1975. Actuary Mutual of Omaha Insurance Co., 1973—85, asst. v.p., 1985—87; v.p., internat. actuary ALFAC Inc., 1987—98, dep. corp. actuary, 1998—2000, sr. v.p., 1998—2007, corp. actuary, 2000—07, sr. advisor, actuarial, 2007—08. Served in USAF. Mem.: Southeastern Actuarial Club, Internat. Actuarial Assn., Am. Acad. Actuaries, Soc. Actuaries.

COX, MARVIN KIRKLAND, state legislator; b. Petersburg, Va., Aug. 17, 1957; m. Julie Kirkendall; children: Lane, Blake, Carter. Tchr. Manchester HS, 1980—; state del. Dist. 66 Va., 1990—; chmn. Agr. Com., Chesapeake and Natural Resource Com.; mem. Appropriations Com., Gen. Laws Com. Recipient Leadership & Orgn. award, Time-Life Mag. Fellow: Christian Men's (chmn.); mem.: Colonial Heights Hist. Cmty., Colonial Heights Jaycees, Colonial Heights Rotary. Republican. Baptist. Home: 131 Old Brickhouse Ln Colonial Heights VA 23834-2179 Home Phone: 504-520-2797; Office Phone: 804-698-1066. Fax: 804-526-3020. E-mail: del_cox@house.state.va.us.

COX, NANCY JANE, microbiologist; b. Emmetsburg, Iowa, July 21, 1948; d. Emmett Stanley and Verna Lucille (Olson) Cox; m. Evan Lindsay Cox, Apr. 11, 1981; 1 child, Julia Claire Lindsay. BS with honors, Iowa State U., 1970; PhD, Cambridge U., Eng., 1975. Postdoctoral fellow Muscular Dystrophy Assn., Balt., 1975—77; staff fellow Ctrs. for Disease Control, Atlanta, 1978—80, rsch. chemist, 1980—, now dir. influenza divsn. Contbr. articles to profl. jours. and books. Named one of 100 Most Influential People, Time mag., 2006; Marshall scholarship, 1970. Mem.: AAAS, Am. Soc. microbiology, Am. Soc. Virology, Sigma Xi. Methodist. Office: Div Viral Diseases 7-111 Centers for Disease Control 1 600 Clifton Rd Atlanta GA 30316-2228

COX, RODY POWELL, internist, educator; b. New Brighton, Pa., June 24, 1926; s. Raymond James and Hazel (Powell) C.; m. Jane Beverly Birks, Sept. 5, 1953 (dec. Apr. 1995); children: Shelley Lea, Rody Powell, Sue Ellen; m. LaVaun Jeanne Sears, Mar. 1, 1997. Student, Franklin and Marshall Coll., 1946-48; MD, U. Pa., 1952. Diplomate Am. Bd. Internal Medicine. Intern U. Mich., 1952-53, resident in medicine, 1953-54, U. Pa., Phila., 1953-57, asst. prof. medicine, 1957-60; rsch. assoc. U. Glasgow, Scotland, 1960-61; prof. medicine NYU, NYC, 1961-79, prof. pharmacology, 1972-79, chief div. human genetics, 1972-79; prof., vice chmn. dept. medicine Case-Western Res. U., Cleve., 1979-88; chief med. svc. VA Med. Ctr., Cleve., 1979-88; dean Med. Sch. U. Tex. Southwestern Med. Ctr., Dallas, 1988-89, prof. internal medicine, 1988—. Mem. metabolism study sect. NIH, 1970-74, chmn. genetics study sect., 1978-79, chmn. mammalian genetics study sect., 1979-81; mem. panel on clin. scis. NRC, 1976-86. Editor: Cell Communication, 1974; co-editor: Epithelial Cell Culture, 1981; contbr. articles to profl. publs. Sgt. U.S. Army, 1944-46, NATOUSA. Fellow Royal Soc. Medicine (Eng.); Master ACP; mem. Am. Soc. Clin. Investigation (emeritus), Assn. Am. Physicians, Ctrl. Soc. Clin. Rsch., John Morgan Soc. U. Pa., Harvey Soc., Am. Clin. Climatol. Assn., Am. Soc. Human Genetics, Interurban Clin. Club, Alpha Omega Alpha (councillor NYU chpt. 1970-76). Home: 5 Connaught Ct Dallas TX 75225-2459 Office: U Tex Southwestern Med Ctr 5323 Harry Hines Blvd Dallas TX 75390-8889 Home Phone: 214-363-4329; Office Phone: 214-648-7805. Business E-Mail: rcox@mednet.swmed.edu, rody.cox@utsouthwestern.edu.

COX, STEPHEN A., consumer agency administrator; BA in Criminal Justice, U. Tenn-Chattanooga; MS in Mktg., U. Md., MBA; Disting. Grad., US Dept. Def. Info Sch. Strategic comm. cons. Booz, Allen, Hamilton, 2005—06; v.p. comm. Council Better Business Bureaus (CBBB), Arlington, Va., 2006—09, pres., CEO, 2009—. Served in USMC, 1982—2005. Decorated Bronze Star. Office: Council Better Business Bureaus (CBBB) 3033 Wilson Blvd Ste 600 Arlington VA 22201-3863 Office Phone: 703-276-0100.

COX, WALTER THOMPSON, III, lawyer, federal judge, educator; b. Anderson, SC, Aug. 13, 1942; s. Walter Thompson and Mary (Johnson) C.; m. Victoria Grubbs, Feb. 8, 1963; children: Lisa, Walter. BS, Clemson U., 1964; JD, U. S.C., 1967. Bar: S.C., 1967, U.S. Dist. Ct. S.C., 1967, U.S. Ct. Appeals (4th cir.), 1976, U.S. Ct. Appeals for Armed Forces, 1984, U.S. Supreme Ct., 1987. Commn. capt. U.S. Army, 1964, atty., 1964-73; ptnr. Jones, McIntosh, Threlkeld, Newman & Cox, Anderson, SC, 1973-78; trial judge 10th cir. State S.C., Anderson, 1978-84; judge US Ct. Appeals for the Armed Forces, Washington, 1984—2000, chief judge, 1995-99, sr. judge, 2000—; sr. lecturing fellow Duke U. Law Sch., Durham, NC; of counsel Nelson Mullins Riley & Scarborough, LLP, Charleston, SC, 2003—. Adj. prof. Charleston Sch. Law, 2005. Mem. ABA, FBA, Judge Adv.'s Assn., S.C. Bar Assn. (del.), Wild Dune Golf and Racquet Club. Episcopalian. Office: Nelson Mullins Riley & Scarborough LLP 151 Meeting St St 600 Charleston SC 29401 Office Phone: 843-853-5200. Business E-Mail: walter.cox@nelsonmullins.com.

COXE, HENRY M., III, lawyer; b. 1948; m. Mary Coxe; children: Katie, Matson, Anne English. BA in Polit. Sci., U. of South, Tenn., 1969; JD, Washington and Lee U., 1972. Bar: Va. 1972, Fla. 1973, US Supreme Ct. 1995, US Ct. Appeals (5th Cir.) 1975, US Ct. Appeals (11th Cir.) 1981, US Dist. Ct. (Mid. Dist. Fla.) 1975, Jud. Qualifications Commn., Fla. Supreme Ct. Innocence Commn. Dir. felony divisions & spl. prosecution divsn. Fla. State Atty. Office, 1973; mgr. pvt. law firm, 1981—96; ptnr. Bedell Dittmar DeVault Pillar & Coxe PA, Jacksonville, Fla., 1996—. Bd. dirs. Jacksonville Area Legal Aid; chmn. disciplinary grievance com. US Dist. Ct. (Jacksonville); mem. judicial nom. commn. Fourth Judicial Cir., 1987—91, First Dist. Ct. Appeal, 1994—96; charter mem. Fla. Bench/Bar Commn. Recipient Justice for All award, Jacksonville Area Legal Aid, 2004, Pro Bono award, City of Jacksonville, Pres. award, Am. Bd. Trial Advocates, 2004; named Lawyer of Yr., Financial Daily News. Master: Chester Bedell Inn of Ct.; fellow: Am. Coll. Trial Lawyers; mem.: Va. State Bar, Fla. Bar (bd. gov. 1995—, pres. 2006—07, Pres. Pro Bono Svc. award, Pres. Award of Merit), Jacksonville Bar Assn. (pres. 1995—96, bd. gov. 1992—96). Office: Bedell Dittmar DeVault Pillans & Coxe PA The Bedell Bldg 101 E Adams St Jacksonville FL 32202-3303 Office Phone: 904-353-0211. Office Fax: 904-353-9307. Business E-Mail: hmc@bedellfirm.com.

COYLE, FRANK A., healthcare company executive, lawyer; b. Tenn. BA in English, Carson Newman Coll.; JD, Vanderbilt U. Atty. Baker, Worthington, Crossley, Stansberry & Woolf, 1990—95; asst. v.p. devel. of physician svcs., in-house devel. counsel Columbia/HCA, 1995—98; sec., gen. counsel Iasis Healthcare Corp., 1998—99; sec. IASIS Healthcare Holdings Inc.; sec., gen. counsel IASIS Healthcare, LLC, 1999—. Office: IASIS Healthcare LLC Bldg E 117 Seaboard Ln Franklin TN 37067 Office Phone: 615-844-2747. Office Fax: 615-846-3006.

COZART, BRUCE, state legislator; m. Deborah Cozart; 2 children. Owner, gen. contractor Bruce Cozart Constrn., Inc., Ark.; mem. Dist. 24 Ark. House of Reps., 2011—. Active Habitat for Humanity; mem. First Assembly God Ch., Hot Springs, Ark.; former mem. Lake Hamilton Sch. Bd. Mem.: Ark. Home Builders Assn. (pres.), Hot Springs Home Builders Assn. (past pres.). Office: 420 Rock Creek Rd Hot Springs AR 71913 Office Phone: 501-627-3232. Office Fax: 501-760-2578. Business E-Mail: bruce.cozart@arkansashouse.org.

CRACKEL, THEODORE JOSEPH, historian; b. Urbana, Ill., Sept. 10, 1938; s. Orville Loy and Aleta (Smith) C.; m. Kay Knight, Sept. 2, 1961 (div. 1972); children: Todd, Dana; m. Mai Thi Nguyen, Oct. 14, 1972 (div. 1991); children: John, Robert; m. Mary-Jo Kline, May 23, 1998. BA, U. Ill., 1962; MA, Rutgers U., 1971, PhD, 1985. Commd. 2nd lt. U.S. Army, 1962, advanced through grades to lt. col., 1978, tank unit comdr. Germany, 1963-66, advisor Vietnam, 1966-67, 71-72; weapons sys. analyst Combat Devels. Command, Ft. Knox, Ky., 1968—69; asst. prof. history U.S. Mil. Acad., West Point, NY, 1972-75, 78-81; instr. Dept. Strategy U.S. Army Command and Gen. Staff Coll., 1975-77; dir. mil. history and strategy studies U.S. Army War Coll., Carlisle Barracks, Pa., 1981-83, ret., 1983; sr. fellow The Heritage Found., Washington, 1983-85; sr. cons. GE Co., Washington, 1985-87; exec. dir. Papers of the Comdg. Gens., 1988-93; dir., editor Papers of the War Dept. 1784-1800, 1993—2004; vis. prof. history dept. US Mil. Acad., West Point, NY, 2001—02; prof. U. Va., Charlottesville, Va., 2004—10, editor-in-chief The Papers of George Washington, 2004—10; ret., 2010; dir. Occoquan Group, 2010—. Author: The Army Additional Duty Guide, 1970, Mr. Jefferson's Army, 1987, The Illustrated History of West Point, 1991, History of the Civil Reserve Air Fleet, 1993, West Point: A Bicentennial History, 2002; contbr. chapters to books, articles to profl. jours. Mem. Assn. Documentary Editing, Orgn. Am. Historians, Soc. Historians of Early Am. Republic, Army and Navy Club (Washington), Chi Psi.

CRADDICK, THOMAS RUSSELL, state legislator; b. Beloit, Wis., Sept. 19, 1943; s. Russell Francis Craddick and Beatrice Eleanor Kowalick C.; m. Nadine Nayfa, 1969; children: Christi Leigh, Thomas Russell. BBA, MBA, Tex. Tech. U. Sales rep. Mustang Mud/Newpark Resources; owner, pres. Craddick, Inc.; mem. Dist. 82 Tex. House of Representatives, 1969—; spkr. of house Tex. House of Reps., 2003—09. Mem.: Jr. C. of C., Midland Country Club, Lions (former dir.). Republican. Roman Catholic. Office: 500 West Texas Ste 880 Midland TX 79701 also: Room CAP 1W.09 Capitol PO Box 2910 Austin TX 78768 Office Phone: 432-682-3000. Office Fax: 512-463-0500, 432-684-4864.

CRADDOCK, DELBERT L., energy executive; BS in Petroleum Engring., U. of Tulsa, 1978. Captain Civil Air Patrol; with Santa Fe Minerals, Inc., Sun Gas; joined XTO Energy, Inc., 1995, v.p. ops. San Juan divsn. Bd. dirs. San Juan Coll. Found. Office: XTO Energy Inc 810 Houston St Fort Worth TX 76102-6298 Office Phone: 817-870-2800. Office Fax: 817-870-1671. Business E-Mail: delbert_craddack@xtoenergy.com.

CRAFT, EDMUND COLEMAN, retired manufacturing executive; b. Plainfield, NJ, Dec. 23, 1939; s. Edmund Coleman and Ruth Irene (Morrell) C.; m. Gail Christensen; children: Edmund Coleman III, Elisabeth Gordon, William Todd. BS, Lycoming Coll., 1963; post-grad., Syracuse U., 1963-64; grad. exec. program, U. Minn., 1984. With Borg-Warner Corp., Detroit, adminstrv. asst. to chmn. Chgo., 1969-70; with Borg-Warner Ltd., Letchworth, Hertfordshire, Eng., 1970-75; v.p. hydraulics div. Borg-Warner, Wooster, Ohio, 1975-79; dir. hydraulics div. Donaldson Co. Inc., Mpls., 1979-83, v.p., 1983-2000; sr. advisor Global Aftermarket, 2000-2001; ret., 2001. Bd. dirs. Jr. Achievement of Upper Midwest Inc., 1993-2000, mem. exec. com., 1994-2000; divsn. chmn. United Way, Wooster, 1974. Mem.: Automotive Filter Mfrs. Coun. (vice chmn. 1985-89, chmn. 1989-91, bd. dirs. 1991-2000), Dataw Island Club, Dataw Island Yacht Club., Beaufort Rowing Club (bd. mem. 2012, v.p. 2012-14). Republican. Presbyterian. Avocation: golf. E-mail: craft@islc.net.

CRAFT, KAY STARK, real estate company executive; b. Yoakum, Tex., Oct. 15, 1945; d. Jesse James and Leona Charlotte (Manchen) Stark; m. Michael Joseph Grogan IV, May 31, 1969 (div. June 1974); 1 child, Michael Joseph V; m. Roger Dale Craft, Apr. 1, 1983. AA, Victoria Coll., Tex., 1964; BS, S.W. Tex. State U., 1966, Broadway Sch. Real Estate, Hot Springs, Ark., 1985. Lic. real estate broker, Ark. Tchr. Victoria Ind. Sch. Dist., 1966-68, Pasadena (Tex.) Ind. Sch. Dist., 1968-85; real estate agt. Coldwell Banker, Hot Springs Village, Ark., 1985-88; prin. broker-owner Cross Roads Realty, Inc., Hot Springs Village, Ark., 1988—, pres., bd. dirs., 1991—, v.p., 1988-91; sec., bd. dirs. Craft Classic Homes, Inc., Hot Springs Village, Ark., 1987—2002. Recipient Congressional Order of Merit, NRCC, 2003, Nat. Leadership award, 2003, Bus. Person of the Yr., 2003, 2004, Ronald Reagan Gold medal, 2004, 2005. Mem. DAR, Colonial Dames of 17th Century, Nat. Soc. Magna Carta Dames, Nat. Assn. Realtors, Ark. Realtors Assn. (Million Dollar Club 1991—, Lifetime Million Dollar Prodr. award 1997, 2002-04, Multi Million Dollar Prodr. award 1993-94, 96-2003, cert. Grad. Realtors Inst. 1992, Silver award 2003, 2007, Gold award 2004, 2006, Platinum award 2005), N.W. Garland Bd. Realtors (treas. 1992, Million Dollar Prodr. award 1990-98), Woman's Coun. Realtors, Residential Sales Coun. (cert. residential specialist 1993). Republican. Methodist. Avocations: genealogy, travel, reading. Home: 45 Gerona Way Hot Springs National Park AR 71909-2762 Office: Cross Roads Realty Inc 4136 N Highway 7 Hot Springs National Park AR 71909-9564

CRAFT, MARY FAYE, public relations executive, consultant, television producer; b. Glennville, Ga., Jan. 20, 1936; d. James Levy Durrence and Mary Frances Thompson; widow; children: James P. Craft, Joseph A. Craft. DD, Calvary Grace Bible Inst., Rillton, Pa., 1975; cert. of journalism arts, CNS Internat., Willow Springs, Mo., 1991; D of Phil. in Film and Video, LaSalle U., Mandeville, La., 1995. Cert. tchr., Protocol Sch. of Washington, D.C., 1993. Dist. mgr. Family Record Plan, Honolulu, 1963-64; acct. exec. Heirloom Inc., Honolulu, 1964-65; pres. Durracraft Advt. and Photography, Cocoa Beach, Orlando, Fla., 1965-71; CEO Western American Corp., Orlando, 1971-73; pres. Mary Faye Craft & Assocs., Washington, 1977—; prodr., host FCAC Ch. 10, Fairfax, Va., 1990—; editor MFDC Rev., Springfield, Va., 1992—94; pres. Facets, Inc., Savannah, Ga., 2003—08, MF Craft & Assoc. Travel, Orlando, 1972-73. Owner, mgr. Gallery Unique, Alexandria, Va., 1974-75. Author: Poems of Perception, 1984, Gifts of Poetry, 1986, Poems by Mary Faye Craft, 1988, Poems A to Z, 1997, MFDC Rev. Millennium edit., 1999, Christmas Poems and Songs, 2000, The Legend of Tattnall Count and other Poems, 2001, MFDC Rev. edit., 2002, True to the Red White and Blue, Facets of Life, 2003, Life is a Poem, 2005, Facets, 2008, (book) Facets Change, Change, Change, 2009, Facets of Mary Faye, 2011; composer, performer music album Facets of Music, 1989 (Mid Atlantic Contest winner 1990), CD Facets of Music, 2007, Facets of Mary Faye, 2009. Bd. dirs. Jacksonville Sister's City Assn., 1996—; active Nursing Home Ministries, 1985—, Homeless Ministries, 1989—. Recipient Paul E. Garber award, Grover Loening award, Gill Robb Wilson award Civil Air Patrol, Maxwell AFB, Ala., 1982, 83, Golden Poets award, World of Poetry, Las Vegas, 1987, Tattnal County Bicentennial Poet Laureate, 2001. Mem. AAUW, Nat. Press Club (Silver Owl), Garden Club, Mil. Officers Assn., Air Force Assn., Marine Corps Assn., Rotary Internat. (Paul Harris fellowship), Toastmasters Internat. (Competent Communicator award), Phi Theta Kappa. Republican. Roman Catholic. Avocations: photography, television production. Home: PO Box 23577 Jacksonville FL 32241-3577 Office Phone: 202-737-2249. Personal E-mail: mfctv@aol.com.

CRAFT, PHILLIP R., plastic surgeon; BS, U. Ala., 1985—89; post-grad., U. Ala., 1989—90; MD, U. Tenn., 1990—94. Lic. Fla. Resident gen. surgery U. Tenn., 1994—97, burn fellow, 1997—98, resident in plastic surgery, 1998—2000; hyperbaryc oxygen tng. cours Columbia, SC, 1997; microsurgery tng. course, 1999; plastic surgeon. Author: (publs.) Traumatic and Pseudocyst of the Spleen, 1996, Steriotactic and Ultrasound Core Needle Breast Biopsy Performed by Surgeons, 1997. Mem.: Fla. Med. Assn., Am. Soc. of Plastic Surgeons. Office: 1441 Brickell Ave 3rd Fl Sky Lobby Miami FL 33131 Office Phone: 305-624-0009. Office Fax: 305-373-1175.

CRAGG, CHRISTOPHER EUGENE, oil industry executive; b. Gilmer, Tex., Mar. 27, 1961; s. H. Eugene and Jean (Cammack) C.; m. Lauren Elaine Jones, May 22, 1982. BBA cum laude, Southwestern U., Georgetown, Tex., 1983. CPA, Tex. V.p. Tubular Svcs.; exec. v.p., CFO & pres. Sooner Inc.; v.p., contr. Ocean Energy; mgr., internal audit Cooper Industries; sr. mgr. Price Waterhouse, mgr., 1983-87, sr. acct., 1987; joined Oil States International, Inc., 2006, sr. v.p., ops. Bd. dirs. Powell Industries. Trustee Southwestern U., Georgetown, 1983-85; counselor Meth. Youth Fellowship, Dallas, 1984-87. Named one of Outstanding Young Men of Am. 1985. Mem. AICPAs, Tex. State Soc. CPAs, Petroleum Accts. Soc. (internat. com.), Pi Kappa Alpha (v.p., sec., exec. coun. 1981-83). Avocations: bicycling, basketball, racquetball, reading. Office: Oil States International Inc Three Allen Ctr 333 Clay St Ste 4620 Houston TX 77002 Office Phone: 713-652-0582. Office Fax: 713-652-0499. Business E-Mail: christopher.cragg@oilstatesintl.com.

CRAGG, CLINTON H., aerospace engineer, retired military officer; b. 1955; married; 3 children. BS, US Naval Acad., 1978; MA in Strategic Studies and Internat. Rels., Naval War Coll. With USS Sand Lance, Bremerton, Wash.; asst. engr. USS Trepang, New London, Conn., 1984; engr. USS Alabama; exec. officer USS Tunny; commdg. officer USS Ohio, 1996; chief current ops. US European Command; prin. engr. NASA Engring. and Safety Ctr. (NESC), Hampton, Va., 2003—. Contbr. articles to profl. jours. Officer USN, 1978—2003. Avocations: skiing, photography. Office: NASA Engineering and Safety Center NASA Langley Research Center Mail Stop 118 Hampton VA 23681 E-mail: clinton.h.cragg@nasa.gov.

CRAIB, KENNETH BRYDEN, research and development company executive, physicist, economist; b. Milford, Mass., Oct. 13, 1938; s. William Pirie and Virginia Louise (Bryden) C.; m. Gloria Faye Lisano, June 25, 1960; children: Kenneth Bryden, Judith Diane, Lori Elaine, Melissa Suzanne, Brandi Lynn. BS in Physics, U. Houston, 1967; MA in Econs., Calif. State U., 1982; postgrad., Harvard U., 1989. Aerospace technologist NASA, Houston, 1962-68; staff physicist Mark Sys., Inc., Cupertino, Calif., 1968-69; v.p. World Resources Corp., Cupertino, 1969-71; dir. resources devel. divsn. Aero Svc. Corp., Phila., 1971-72; dir. ops. Resources Devel. Assocs., Los Altos, Calif., 1972-80, pres., CEO Diamond Springs, Calif., 1980-85; owner Sand Ridge Arabians, 1980-98; chmn., dir. Resources Devel. Assocs., Inc., 1982-86, Devel. Support Internat. Inc., Placerville, Calif., 1981-86; pres., chn., dir. RDA Internat., Inc., 1985-96, chmn., CEO, dir., 1995—2000; mgr. acad. affairs U. Phoenix, Sacramento, 2001—02, chmn. Coll. Undergrad. Bus. and Mgmt. Ft. Lauderdale, Fla., 2002—, prof., 2002—06; prof., dir. acad. affairs, chief acad. officer U. Phoenix, Savannah, Ga., 2006—12; adj. prof. Midlands Tech. Coll., Columbia, SC, 2013—, Webster U., Columbia, 2013—. Adj. prof. Sacramento City Coll., 1996—2001; prof. U. Phoenix, Sacramento, 1997—2002. Contbr. articles to profl. jours. Served with USAF, 1957-61. Recipient Sustained Superior Performance award NASA, 1966; NASA grantee, 1968. Mem. Am. Soc. Photogrammetry, Soc. Internat. Devel., Agrl. Rsch. Inst., Calif. Select Com. Remote Sensing, Internat. Assn. Natural Resources Pilots, Remote Sensing Soc. (coun.), Am. Soc. Oceanography (charter), Aircraft Owners and Pilots Assn., Gulf and Cribbean Fisheries Inst., Placerville C. of C., Harvard Alumni Assn., Exptl. Aircraft Assn., Asian Fisheries Soc., Savannah Coun. on World Affairs. Mailing: 3712 Beacon Dr Sumter SC 29154 Personal E-mail: kencraib@gmail.com.

CRAIG, GEORGE DENNIS, economics professor, consultant; b. Sept. 14, 1936; s. George S. and Alice H. (Childs) C.; m. Lelah Price, Aug. 21, 1984; children: R. Price Coyle, R. Nolan Coyle, Deborah L. Craig, W. Sean Coyle. BA, Wheaton Coll., 1960; MS, U. Ill., 1962, PhD, 1968. Asst. prof. econs. La. State U., Baton Rouge, 1965-69; assoc. prof. sch. bus. No. Ill. U., DeKalb, 1969-82; prof. econs., chmn. Oklahoma City U., 1982—. Cons. AT&T, Oklahoma City, 1984—. Contbr. articles to profl. jours. Mem. Am. Econs. Assn., So. Econs. Assn., Nat. Assn. Bus. Economists, Internat. Inst. Forecasting. Avocations: tennis, bridge. Home: 6915 Avondale Ct Oklahoma City OK 73116-5008 Office: 6421 Avondale Dr Ste 208 Oklahoma City OK 73116-6429 Home Phone: 405-842-6724; Office Phone: 405-842-8925. Personal E-mail: craigg784@aol.com.

CRAIG, HAROLD KENT, mechanical contracting executive, systems analyst; b. Columbus, Ohio, Nov. 21, 1956; s. Harold Harding and Mildred Annie (King) C.; m. Cathy M. Preslar, Nov. 19, 1979 (div. Sept. 2000); 1 child, Brian Scagel; m. Liann Craig Tabor, Oct. 24, 2000 (div. Dec. 2004); m. Kristi Linn Servies Craig, May 14, 2005 (div. 2009). Student, Goddard Coll., 1979. Lic. plumbing, boiler making, air conditioning, forced warm air heating; cert. exam proctor. V.p., project mgr. Craig Plumbing Co., Inc., Raleigh, N.C., 1972-95; v.p., project mgmt., sys. analyst Confluence Tech., Raleigh, NC, 1976—2008; sr. sys. analyst Datasonix Inc., Smithfield, NC, 1980—83; heating, ventilation, air cond., plumbing and mech. cons. Valley Constrn. Co., Inc., Koslusco, Miss., 1985-86; chief, sr. project mgr., estimator Sneeden Mechanical Contractors, Inc., Wilmington, NC, 1986-88; U.S. bus. agent The Circle Group, Arusha, Tanzania, 1974—; sr. estimator, sr. project mgr. Bay Mech. Inc., Raleigh, 1996—97; sr. project mgr., estimator Atlantic Coast Mech., Inc., Raleigh, 1997-98; sr. estimator, project mgr. Superior Plumbing & Mech., Inc., Wilson, NC, 1998—2003; sr. project mgr., estimator Raleigh office Goldstar Mech., Charlotte, NC, 2003—06; mgr. comm. divsn. Goldstar Mech. Svcs., Inc., 2003—06; project mgr. and sr. estimator 1st Class Heating AIV, Waxhaw, NC, 2007—09. Sys. cons. Consulting, Tech., and Design, Inc., Research Triangle Park, NC, 1988-94; bd. dirs. NC Bldrs. Inst., Durham, NC. Author: Yes, the Sun Will Rise, 1979, Kent's Carolina Barbecue Book, 2010; editor Joe's Bozart mag., 1978; mem. editl. bd. In the Steps, 1976-81; contbr. articles to profl. jours.; contbg. editor, Contractor mag., 1998—2012, Sacred Fire, 2011, Poor Maris Words. Mem. bd. adjustments Town of Cary (N.C.), 1981; mem. bd. Raleigh Artists' Cmty., 1974-79 1st Covenant Spiritual fellowship, 2008. Mem.: Am. Humanists Assn. (Humanists N.C. chpt. bd. dirs. 1974—81, editor The Tarheel Humanist newsletter 1975—78, named Humanist Adv. 1979). Mailing: PO Box 10814 Midwest City OK 73140 Business E-Mail: kent@hkentcraig.com.

CRAIGEN, WILLIAM JAMES, clinical geneticist, educator; BS, BA, U. Tex., 1981; PhD, Baylor Coll., 1987, MD, 1988. Lic. Tex., 1991, cert. Am. Bd. Clin. Genetics-Med. Genetics, 2010, Am. Bd. Clin. Biochemical Genetics-Med. Genetics, 2010. Resident pediat. Baylor Coll. Medicine, 1988—92, fellow clin. genetics, 1988—90, assoc. prof. clin. genetics, asst. prof. molecular and human genetics and pediat. depts.; hosp. affiliation includes St. Luke's Hosp., Woman's Hosp., Tex., Harris Couonty Hosp. Dist.; staff physician genetics ctr. Tex. Children's Hosp. Office: Texas Children's Hospital Clinical Care Center 6701 Fannin St 16th Fl Houston TX 77030 Office Phone: 832-822-4280. Office Fax: 832-825-4294.

CRAIGHEAD, MARTIN S., energy executive; BS in Petroleum & Natural Gas Engring., Pa. State U.; MBA, Vanderbilt U. Joined Baker Atlas (subs. of Baker Hughes Inc.), 1986, region mgr., L.Am., Asia, region mgr., E&P solutions, 1995—2001, v.p., mktg. & bus. devel., 2001—03, v.p., worldwide ops., 2003—05, pres., 2005, INTEQ (acquired by Baker Hughes Inc.), 2005—07; v.p. Baker Hughes, Inc., 2005—09, group pres., drilling and evaluation, 2007—09, sr. v.p., COO, 2009—10, pres., COO, 2010—11, pres., CEO, 2011—. Bd. dirs. Jr. Achievement. Office: Baker Hughes Inc 2929 Allen Pky Ste 2100 Houston TX 77019-2118 Office Phone: 713-439-8600. Office Fax: 713-439-8699. Business E-Mail: martin.craighead@bakerhughes.com.

CRAIGHEAD, SARAH L., parks director; m. John F. Shireman. BA, Transylvania U., Lexington, Ky.; grad. student, George Mason U., Fairfax, Va., Cath. U., Washington. Park ranger Independence Nat. Hist. Pk. US Nat. Pak. Svc., Phila., park ranger Ocmulgee Nat. Monument Ga., park ranger Acadia Nat. Pk. Maine, park ranger Mammoth Cave Nat. Pk. Ky., park ranger Carlsbad Caverns Nat. Pk. N.Mex., park ranger Grand Canyon Nat. Pk. Ariz., mgmt. position at Manassas Nat. Battlefield Pk. Va., mgmt. position with the nat. capitol regional office Washington, mgmt. position at Mesa Verde Nat. Pk. Colo., supt. Chickasaw Nat. Recreation Area Okla., supt. Washita Battlefield Nat. Hist. Site Okla., supt. Saguaro Nat. Pk. Ariz., supt. Death Valley Nat. Pk. Calif., 2009—12, supt. Mammoth Cave Nat. Pk. Ky., 2012—. Office: Mammoth Cave National Park 1 Mammoth Cave Pky PO Box 7 Mammoth Cave KY 42259 Office Phone: 270-758-2183. Office Fax: 270-758-2349.*

CRAIN, BRIAN A., state legislator, lawyer; b. Andrews AFB, Md. s. Harold and Joan Crain; m. Lori Crain, 1990; children: Sarah, Catherine. BBA, Univ. Okla., 1983; JD, Univ. Tulsa, 1991. Asst. dist. atty., Tulsa, Okla., 1996—99; atty. Hanson & Holmes PLC, Tulsa; mem. Dist. 39 Okla. State Senate, 2004—. Mem. Tulsa Lawyers Helping Children. Mem.: Tulsa County Bar Assn., Tulsa Title & Probate Lawyers, Tulsa Rotary. Republican. Baptist. Office: 2300 N Lincoln Blvd Rm 417B Oklahoma City OK 73105 Home: 5515 E 86th St Tulsa OK 74137-2954 Office Phone: 405-521-5620. Business E-Mail: crain@oksenate.gov.

CRAIN, JOHN WALTER, historian, educator; b. Amarillo, Tex., July 11, 1944; s. John Clyde and Roma (McDowell) C. BA, U. Tex., Austin, 1966; MA, S.W. Tex. State U., 1970; cert. arts adminstrn., Harvard U., 1975; cert. mus. mgmt., U. Calif.-Berkeley, 1979. Dir. Star of the Republic Museum, Washington-on-the-Brazos, Tex., 1971-76, Dallas Hist. Soc., 1976-90; chmn. Dallas County Hist. Commn., 1993-95; commn. Tex. Hist. Commn., 2007—. Cons. in field. Exec. dir. Summerlee Commn. on Tex. History, 1990-91; v.p., bd. dirs. program History Summerlee Found., Tex., 1990—, pres., 2004-; bd. dirs. Dallas County Hist. Found., Friends of Gov.'s Mansion; mem. adv. bd. Clements Ctr., So. Meth. U., pres. Friends of Govs. Mansion; adv. trustee Tex. State History Mus. Found., 2012. Mem. Tex. State Hist. Assn. (hon., coun. 1994, exec. com., pres.), Conf. of S.W. Founds. (bd. dirs.), Tex. Map Soc. (bd. dirs., pres.), Philos. Soc. Tex. Methodist. Office: 5556 Caruth Haven Ln Dallas TX 75225-8146

CRAMER, DALE LEWIS, retired economics professor; b. Dixon, Ill., June 25, 1924; s. Ray C. and Rebecca (Levan) C.; m. Hula Jean Bond, Aug. 30, 1946; children: Becky Cramer McCarn, Craig Alan, Randall Scott. BS, Bradley U., 1949, MA, 1951; PhD, La. State U., 1958. Asst. prof. econs. La. State U., 1953-54, U. Tex.-El Paso, 1955-57, assoc. prof., 1957-58; assoc. prof. econs. U. Ala., 1958-63, prof., 1963-88, prof. emeritus econs., 1988—, head dept., 1968-72, acting head dept., 1981-82. Contbr. articles to profl. jours., books. Served with AUS, 1943-46. Earhart Found. fellow, 1954-55 Mem. Am., So. econ. assns., AAUP, Omicron Delta Epsilon, Beta Gamma Sigma. Home: 800 Rice Valley Rd N Apt F29 Tuscaloosa AL 35406-2750

CRAMER, GAIL, economist; b. Walla Walla, Wash., Sept. 27, 1941; s. Lawrence Theodore and Myrtle Pauline (Latimer) C.; m. Marilyn Jean Karlenberg, Aug. 31, 1963; children: Karilee, Bruce. BS, Wash. State U., Pullman, 1963; MS, Mich. State U., East Lansing, 1964; PhD, Oreg. State U., Corvallis, 1968. Asst. prof. Mont. State U., Bozeman, 1967-72, assoc. prof., 1972-76, prof., 1976-86; L.C. Carter prof. U. Ark., Fayetteville, 1987-2000; prof., dept. head La. State U., 2000—. Vis. prof. Harvard U., Cambridge, 1974-75, Winrock Internat., Morrilton, Ark., 1980-81, U. Calif. Berkeley, 1993, Ohio State U., Columbus, 1994; bd. dirs. Internat. Agrl. Mgmt. Assn. Co-author: Grain Marketing, 1993, Agricultural, Economics and Agribusiness,

1997; editor Am. Agrl. Econs. Assn. Jour., 1999-2002, Agrl. Econs., Critical Concepts Econs., vol. I-IV, 2011. Bd. dirs. ARC, Bozeman, 1982-83, Bozeman Kiwanis Club, 1972-86 (Disting. Pres. 1983); mem. White House Agrl. commn. Washington. Recipient E.G. Nourse award, Am. Inst. Coop., Washington, 1968, Communication award, Am. Agrl. Econs. Assn., 1980, Rice Rsch. award, Tech. Workers, Little Rock, 1992, 1998, SAEA Lifetime Achievement award, 2002, Alumni Achievement award, Wash. State U., 2013. Fellow: IAMA; mem.: Nat. Assn. Agrl. Econ. Administrators (pres. 2004—), Gamma Sigma Delta Internat. (Dist. Achievement Agrl. award). Avocations: basketball, running, writing. Office: La State U Dept Agrl Econs Baton Rouge LA 70808 Home: 13735 Clarendon Dr Baton Rouge LA 70810-3584 Business E-Mail: gcramer@agcenter.lsu.edu.

CRAMER, H. R. (HAL CRAMER), oil industry executive; BS in Indsl. Engring., Syracuse U., NYC; MBA, SUNY, Albany. With Mobil Oil, 1973; pres. Mobil South Inc.; v.p., Pacific Rim Mobil Corp., v.p. Europe Africa Mid. East mktg. and refining divsn., 1996—98; exec. v.p. and CFO Mobil Corp. (merged with Exxon), 1998—2000; v.p. ExxonMobil Corp., 2000—; pres. ExxonMobil Fuels Marketing Co., 2000—. Mem. exec. com. Mobil Oil. Office: Exxon Mobil Fuels Mktg 3225 Gallows Rd Fairfax VA 22037

CRAMER, JAMES PERRY, management strategist, author, educator; b. Aberdeen, SD, Aug. 7, 1947; s. Harry John and Carol B. (Bickel) C.; m. Corinne M. Aaker, Dec. 21, 1969; children: Ryan James, Austin Michael. BS, Northern State U., Aberdeen, 1969; MA, St. Thomas U., St. Paul, 1974; planning cert., U. Minn., Mpls., 1976; bus. mgmt. cert., Wharton Sch. Bus., U. Pa., 1987. Dir., teaching faculty U. Minn., Mpls., 1974-76; dir. St. Louis Park Community Svcs., Minn., 1976-78; exec. v.p. Minn. Soc. Architects, Mpls., 1978-82; pres., chief exec. officer AIA Svc. Corp., Washington, 1982-86, also bd. regents; pres. Greenway Comms. Inc., 1994—. Pres. Am. Archtl. Found. and Octagon Mus., Washington, 1986-89; CEO AIA, Washington, 1989-94; group pub. Architecture Mag., 1982-88, pub. chmn., 1990-94; with Archtl. Tech. Mag., 1983-89; chmn. The Greenway Group; pres. Greenway Comm. Inc., 1994—; adj. prof. U. Hawaii Sch. Arch., 1999—. Pres. Coun. Archtl. Components, Washington, 1980-81; pres. Greenway Civic Assn., McLean, Va., 1986-88; trustee Nat. Bldg. Mus., Washington, 1989-94; chmn. Washington div. United Way Assn., 1992; White House liaison, 1988-95. Recipient Disting. Alumnus award No. State U., 1992, medal of Distinction, U. Minn., 1994; Richard Upjohn fellow; leadership fellow Western Behavioral Scis. Inst., 1998-. Mem. AIA (hon.; chmn. 1981-82, CEO 1989—, Spl. award 1982), Am. Soc. Assn. Execs. (cert. assn. exec.), Mag. Pubs. Am., Octagon Soc. (life hon.), Am. Archtl. Found. (life; pres. 1986-89, regent 1981-82, 86—), Am. Design Coun. (founder, bd. dirs. 1988-95), Soc. Archtl. Historians (bd. dirs. 1994-97), Design Futures Coun. (chmn. 1994—). Avocations: gardening, tennis, antiquarian books, design. Home: 2320 Littlebrooke Dr Dunwoody GA 30338-3156

CRAMER, MARK CLIFTON, lawyer; b. St. Petersburg, Fla., July 20, 1954; s. William Cato and Alice J. Cramer; m. Carol Blankenship, Aug. 6, 1977; children: Ryan Albert, Philip Rogers. BA, U. N.C., 1976; JD, U. Va., 1979. Bar: DC, 1979, Fla. 1982, NC 1986. Assoc. Cramer & Lipsen, 1979-80; ptnr. Cramer & Cramer, 1980-81; dir. congl. rels. US Govt. Printing Office, Washington, 1981, dep. gen counsel, 1981-83; gen. counsel, 1983-85; vice pres., gen. counsel Blankenship-Cramer Devel. Corp., Charlotte, NC, 1985—2003; legis. cons. NC Drug Cabinet, 1990; pvt. practice, 1991—. Sec. fed. liaison NC Global TransPark Authority, 1991-03; vice pres. Found. for Transp. Trade and Commerce, 1998-03, v.p. Counsel Inst. for Defense and Bus., 2003-07; pres. Inst. for Defense and Bus., 2007-; exec. dir. Real Estate and Bldg. Industry Coalition, 1995-2006; program counsel Ctr. of Excellence in Logistics and Tech., 2000-03; assoc. dir. Ctr. of Excellence in Logistics and Tech., 2003-07, exec. dir., 2007-, sec. Ctr. for Air Commerce Studies, 2001-02, sec., treas. Piedmont Pub. Policy Inst., 2003-06, exec. dir., 2006-07, Adj. faculty, Kenan-Flagler Bus. Sch., U. North Carolina, Chapel Hill, 2007-. Editor: Legislative Histories of the Laws Affecting the US Govt. Printing Office as Codified in Title 44 of the US Code. Liaison mem. Adminstrv. Conf. US, 1984-85; mem. Mecklenburg County Zoning Bd. of Adjustment, 1986-92, chair, 1991-92; commr. NC Gen Statutes Commn., 1988-93; mem. East Mecklenburg Planning Dist., 1989, Charlotte Mecklenburg Consolidation Charter Study Commn., 1990, Mecklenburg County Redistricting Com., 1991; Transp. Commn. of 100, 1994; Charlotte Mecklenburg Citizens Transit Advisory Group, 1999-2003; Surface Water Improvement & Mgmt. Task Force, 1997-99; Charlotte Mecklenburg Smart Growth Task Force, 1999-2001; mem. blue ribbon com. NC Transp. Needs, 2004-05; vice chmn. Mecklenburg County Reps., 1989-93; mem. Post-Constrn. ordinance Stakeholder's Group, 2004-05; founder, moderator Rep issues Forum; co-chmn. Mecklenburg County Com. to re-elect Gov. Jim Martin, 1988; elector US Presdl. Electoral Coll., 1992; bd. dir., exec. com. Nat. Chamber Found., 2007-, Nat. Defense Industry Assn., 2007-, Bus. Exec. Nat. Security, 2007-. Recipient Pub. Printer's Gold medal for disting. svc., US Govt. Printing Office, Long Leaf Pine award, Gov. State of NC. Mem. NC Bar Assn., Fla. Bar Assn. DC Bar. Assn., Mecklenburg County Bar Assn., NC C. of C., Phi Beta Kappa, Sigma Nu (recipient Sr. Scholarship award 1976). Business E-Mail: cramer@idb.org. E-mail: cramer@usa.com.

CRAMER, ROBERT W., lawyer; b. Monticello, Ind., Nov. 10, 1957; s. James Robert and Doris Pace Cramer; m. Ann Ashley Hollowell, May 30, 1981; children: Ashley Pace, Robert Wayne Jr., David McKinnie. BA, U. NC, 1980, MBA, JD, U. NC, 1984. Bar: NC 1984, U.S. Dist. Ct. (we. dist.) NC 1984, U.S. Supreme Ct. 2001. Atty. Mc Guire Woods LLC (and predecessor firms), Charlotte, NC, 1984—. Bd. dirs. U. NC Law Found., Inc., Chapel Hill, 2001—10; mem. bd. advisors Harvest Ctr., 2005—, Sports Friends Internat., 2006—. Office: McGuire Woods LLC 201 N Tryon St Charlotte NC 28202

CRANDALL, CHAUNCEY WARREN, IV, cardiologist, director; b. Fairfax, Va., July 4, 1954; s. Chauncey Warren and Ruth Wills Crandall; m. Deborah Newell Crandall, Mar. 13, 1978; children: Christian P., Chadwick B. BS, Va. Commonwealth U., Richmond, 1976; MD, Va., Fla., 1983. Diplomate American Bd. of Internal Medicine, American Bd. of Cardiovascular Disease. Intern, medicine Yale U. St. Marys Hosp., New Haven, 1983—84, resident, medicine, 1984—86; fellow, cardiology Mt. Sinai Med. Ctr. and Beth Israel Hosp., NYC, 1986—88; fellow, interventional cardiology Va. Commonwealth U., Richmond, Va., 1988—89, dir., heart transplantation, 1989—93; chief of the Heart Transplant Program, dir. coronary critical care and dir. med. edn. Med. Coll. of Va. and VA Med. Ctr.; dir., heart transplantation Palm Beach Cardiovascular Clinic, Jupiter, Fla., 1998—2008, dir., preventive cardiology and clin. medicine, 2000—, assoc. dir. interventional cardiology; chief, cardiology St. Marys Hosp., Palm Beach, Fla., 1995—99; dir., interventional cardiology Good Samaritan Med. Ctr., Palm Beach, 2010—; staff mem. Palm Beach Gardens Med. Ctr., Jupiter Med. Ctr. Faculty mem. Duke U., 1993; dir., founder, bd. chmn. Chadwick Found., Palm Beach, 2004, dir., med. missions, 2004—; med. dir. health services Palm Beach Atlantic U.; dir. echocardiology Tenet Health Services, Palm Beach County. Author: (book) Raising the Dead: A Doctor Encounters the Supernatural, 2010; prodr.: (radio) Doctor on Call with Dr Chauncey Crandall; contbr. several articles in medical journals; dir., med. editor Heart Health Report, NewsMax Magazine, dir., editor Crandell Health Book Series. Bd. trustee Palm Beach Atlantic U.; bd. dirs. Christ for All Nations, Regent U., Palm Beach Cardiovascular Clinic, Salvation Army. Recipient Best Doctors award, Castle Connolly Guide Fla., 2005; named one of Palm Beach Elite Top 100, Palm Beach Daily News, 2008, Top Cardiologist, Leading Physicians of World, 2010; named to Palm Beach A List, 2010. Fellow: Soc. for Cardiac Angiography and Intervention, American Soc. of Cardiovascular Interventionists, American Coll. of Chest Physicians, American Coll. Cardiology; mem.: Internat. Soc. for Heart and Lung Transplantation, Beta Beta Beta Honor Soc., Alpha Kappa Delta. Office: Palm Beach Cardiovasc Clinic 600 University Blvd Ste 200 Jupiter FL 33458*

CRANDALL, GRANT, lawyer, labor union administrator; b. Columbus, Ohio, Aug. 22, 1947; s. Vaughn Joseph and Virginia C. C.; m. Penelope Anne Caldwell, June 23, 1971; children: Jesse Scott, Andrew Ross. BS, Grinnell Coll., 1969; PhD, Oxford U., Eng., 1972; JD, UCLA, 1975. Bar: W.Va. 1975, U.S. Dist. Ct. (so. dist.) W.Va. 1975, U.S. Ct. Appeals (4th cir.) 1979, U.S. Dist. Co. (no. dist.) W.Va. 1986, U.S. Supreme Ct. 1987, U.S. Ct. Appeals (3d cir.) 1990. Ptnr. Crandall, Pyles, Havilland and Turner (and predecessors), Charleston, W.Va., 1975—2004. Gen. counsel United Mine Workers Am., Fairfax, Va., 1996. Rhodes scholar, 1970-72. Mem. Mountain State Bar Assn., Legal Aid Soc. (v.p. 1979-84), W.Va. State Bar (chmn. employment law com. 1988-90). Democrat. Avocation: athletics. Office: Crandall Pyles Ste 300 122 Capitol St Charleston WV 25301 also: UMW 8315 Lee Hwy Fairfax VA 22031-2215 Home: 3105 Ellenwood Dr Fairfax VA 22031 Office Phone: 304-345-3080. Business E-Mail: gcrandall@umwa.org.

CRANE, BENJAMIN MCCULLY, professional golfer; b. Portland, OR, Mar. 6, 1976; married; 1 child. BA in Sociology, U. Ore., 1999. Mem. PGA Tour, 2006—. Achievements include Nationwide Tour wins: Buy.com Wichita Open, 2000, Gila River Classic, 2001; PGA Tour wins: BellSouth Classic, 2003, US Bank Championship, 2005, Farmers Insurance Open, 2010. Mailing: 100 PGA TOUR Blvd Ponte Vedra Beach FL 32082

CRANE, JAMES R. (JIM CRANE), delivery service executive, professional sports team owner; m. Franci Neely. BS in Indsl. Safety, Ctrl. Mo. State U., 1976. Founder, chmn., CEO Eagle Global Logistics, Inc., Houston, 1984—2007; chmn., CEO Crane Capital Group; chmn. Crane Worldwide Logistics, 2008—; owner Houston Astros, 2011—. Former bd. dirs. HCC Ins. Holdings; bd. dirs. We. Gas Holdings LLC, Ft. Dearborn Life Ins. Co. Bd. dir. Houston Mus. Natural Sci.; pres. The Crane Found. Named Houston Entrepreneur of Yr., 1996, Outstanding Industry Profl., Internat. Transp. Mgmt. Assn., #1 CEO Golfer, Golf Digest, 2006. Mem.: World Presidents' Orgn. Office: Houston Astros 501 Crawford St Houston TX 77002 also: Crane Worldwide 1500 Rankin Rd Houston TX 77073-4800

CRANE, MIKE, state legislator; m. Tracey Crane; children: Caitlin, Alden, Ethan. B in Indsl. Mgmt., Ga. Inst. Tech., Atlanta. Lic. gen. contractor Ga., builder Fla. Constrn. co. owner; mem. Dist. 28 Ga. State Senate, Atlanta, 2011—. Patron Gospel for Asia. Mem.: Nat. Assn. Homebuilders. Republican. Office: PO Box 700 Newnan GA 30265 also: Ga State Senate Coverdell Legis Office Bldg Atlanta GA 30334

CRANE, RANDY, federal judge; b. Houston, 1965; BA, U. Tex., 1985, JD, 1987. Pvt. practice atty., McAllen, Tex., 1988—2002; judge US Dist. Ct. (so. dist.) Tex., McAllen, 2002—. Office: US Dist Ct Bentsen Tower 1701 W Bus Hwy 83 Ste 1011 Mcallen TX 78501 Office Phone: 956-618-8083.

CRANSTON, PHILIP EDWARD, foreign language professional; b. Pittsfield, Mass., Mar. 22, 1929; s. Julius Byron and Ruth Runnells (Pepin) C.; m. Mechthild Grieser-Fuerst, Oct. 12, 1938. BA, U. Ariz., 1951; MA, U. Calif., Berkeley, 1958, PhD, 1972. Asst. prof. fgn. lang. Calif. State U., Hayward, 1964-69, Western Carolina U., Cullowhee, N.C., 1971-72; from asst. prof. to prof. French U. N.C., Asheville, 1972—95; prof. emeritus, 1995. Vis. assoc. prof. French Clemson (S.C.) U., 1984. Author: (poetry) Time of the Sun, 1968, Before Time, 1979; translator (poetry of J. Supervielle) Naissances/Births, 1992, Les Amis Inconnus/ Unknown Friends, 2008, (Latin, Italian, French, Spanish, and German poetry) Tones/Countertones, 2002; contbr. articles to profl. jours. Seaman recruit to Lt. USNR, 1951-55. Grantee Ministry of Edn., Paris, 1962-64, NEH, 1976, 81. Mem. MLA, Am. Literary Translators Assn., Phi Beta Kappa, Phi Kappa Phi. Democrat. Avocation: writing verse. Home: 113 Houston St Clemson SC 29631-1311

CRANWELL, C. RICHARD, lawyer, former political organization administrator; b. Ceredo-Kenova, W.Va., July 26, 1942; s. James Edward and Mary Elizabeth (Peters) Cranwell; married; 6 children. BS, Va. Polytech. Inst., Blacksburg, 1965; JD, U. Richmond T.C. Williams Sch. Law, 1968. Bar: Va. 1968, US Dist. Ct. (we. dist.) Va. 1968, US Dist. Ct. (ea. dist.) Va. 1980, US Ct. Appeals DC 1982, US Ct. Appeals (6th cir.) 1996. Assoc. Tilley & Pedigo, Roanoke, Va., 1968-70; ptnr. Pedigo & Cranwell, Roanoke, 1970-78, Cranwell, Flora, Selbe & Barbe, Roanoke, 1978-80, Gardner, Rocovich & Cranwell, Roanoke, 1980-82, Cranwell, Flora & Moore, Vinton, Va., 1982, Cranwell, Moore & Emick PLC, Roanoke, 1982—; chmn. Dem. Party of Va., 2005—10. Mem. Dist. 14 Va. House of Delegates, 1972—2002, Dem. leader, 1992—2002. Legal advisor Vinton Rescue Squad, Mt. Pleasant Rescue Squad, Montvale Rescue Squad; bd. dirs. Vinton Ann. Dogwood Festival, 1973—75, Roanoke Valley Juvenile Diabetes Found. Named an Influential Young Mem. of Gen. Assembly, Capital Press Corps, 1975, 1977; named one of Outstanding Young Men in America, US Jaycees, 1970, 1972. Mem.: ABA, Roanoke County-Salem Bar Assn., Va. Trial Lawyers Assn., Million Dollar Advocates Forum, Acad. Rail Labor Attorneys, Assn. Trial Lawyers of America, Va. State Bar Assn., Phi Delta Phi. Democrat. Methodist. Avocations: reading, golf, tennis, politics. Office: Cranwell, Moore & Emick 111 Virginia Ave W Roanoke VA 24022 Office Phone: 540-904-1621. Office Fax: 540-344-7073.

CRAPOL, EDWARD P., history professor; b. Buffalo, Sept. 29, 1936; s. Paul H. and Emmi H. (Klinger) C.; m. Jeanne Zeidler, Aug. 1, 1973; children: Heidi, Jennifer, Paul, Andrew. BA, SUNY, Buffalo, 1960; MS, Univ. Wis., 1964, PhD, 1968. Tchr. Amherst Ctrl. Jr. High Sch., Amherst, NY, 1961-63; instr. history Wis. State Univ., Eau Claire, Wis., 1966-67; asst. prof. history Coll. William and Mary, Williamsburg, Va., 1967-71, assoc. prof. history, 1971-77; exchange prof. history Univ. Exeter, Exeter, England, 1976-77; prof. history dept. Coll. William and Mary, Williamsburg, Va., 1978—, chmn. history dept., 1981-84, acting chmn. history dept., 1986-87, prof. history, 1994—2004, prof. emeritus, 2004—. Vis. faculty Utah State U., summer, 1972; reviewer grant proposals NEH, 1983—95; lectr. in field. Author: America for Americans: Economic Nationalism and Anglophobia in the Late Nineteenth Century, 1973, James G. Blaine: Architect of Empire, 1999, John Tyler, The Accidental President, 2006; editor: Women and American Foreign Policy: Lobbyists, Critics, and Insiders, 1987, 1992; reviewer manuscripts for Diplomatic History, Journal of the Early Republic, Alfred A. Knopf, Scholary Recources, Greenwood Press, Kent State Univ. Press, D.C. Health, Univ. N.C. Press; paperback editor jours., 2012. Va. Found. for Humanities and Pub. Policy grant, 1983, NEH grant, 1984, 1986, Internat. Studies Curriculum Devel. grant Coll of William and Mary, 1987; U. Humanities fellow Coll. William and Mary, 1988; recipient Thomas A. Graves Jr. award William and Mary Coll., 1991, Thomas Jefferson award Coll. William and Mary, 1992 Mem. Soc. Historians Am. Fgn. Rels., Orgn. Am. Historians, Am. Hist. Assn. Home: 148 Mimosa Dr Williamsburg VA 23185-4004 E-mail: edpcal@wm.edu.

CRAVINS, DONALD R., JR., state legislator; s. Donald Cravins and Patricia Arceneaux; m. Yvette Puckett; children: Dominique Claire, Donald III. Mem. La. State Ho. of Reps. from Dist. 40, 2005—06, mem. Adminstrn. of Criminal Justice, Environ., Labor & Indsl. Rels. Coms.; mem. La. State Senate from Dist. 24, 2006—; atty. McGlinchey Stafford PLLC, Baton Rouge, Domengeaux, Wright, Roy & Edwards, Lafayette. Mem.: Baton Rouge Bar Assn., La. Bar Assn., Fed. Bar Assn. Democrat. Office: Domengeaux Wright Roy & Edwards 556 Jefferson St Ste 500 Lafayette LA 70501 Office Phone: 337-233-3033. Fax: 337-943-2406. E-mail: cravinsd@legis.state.la.us.

CRAWFORD, CAROL TALLMAN, law educator; b. Mt. Holly, NJ, Feb. 25, 1943; m. Ronald Crawford; children: Timothy, Jeffrey, Richard. BA, Mt. Holyoke Coll., 1965; JD magna cum laude, Washington Coll. Law, Am. U., 1978. Bar: Va. 1978, DC 1979. Legis. asst. to Senator Bob Packwood, Washington, 1969-75; assoc. firm Collier, Shannon, Rill & Scott, Washington, 1979-81; exec. asst. to chmn. FTC, Washington, 1981-83, dir. bur. consumer protection, 1983-85; assoc. dir. Office of Mgmt. & Budget, Washington, 1985-89; asst. atty. gen. legis. affairs U.S. Dept. Justice, Washington, 1989-90; commr. U.S. Internat. Trade Commn., 1991-2000; disting. vis. prof. law George Mason U., Arlington, Va., 2000-01. Bd. dirs. Smithfield Foods, Inc., 2000—, Ind. Women's Forum, 2002—. Trustee Barry Goldwater Chair of Am. Instns., Ariz. State U., Phoenix, 1983—; chair internat. trade and investment subcom. Federalist Soc., 1998—99, chair internat. and nat. security sect., 1999—2003; adv. com. NAFTA Labor Agreement, 2002—08; bd. trustees Torray Fund, 2006—. Republican.

CRAWFORD, CAROLYN, state legislator; d. William Smith; m. Mike Crawford; children: Marly, Emily, Jackson. B in Sociology, U. South Ala., Mobile. Child case mgr. Gulf Coast Mental Health Clinic; lic. social worker South Miss. Regional Ctr.; mem. Dist. 121 Miss. House of Reps., Jackson, 2012—. Active L.B. Youth Recreation League; registered mem. Saginaw Chippewa Indian Tribe Mich. Mem.: Harrison County Rep. Women, Harrison County Rep. Club. Republican. Roman Catholic. Office: Miss House of Reps PO Box 1018 Jackson MS 39215 Business E-Mail: ccrawford@house.ms.gov.

CRAWFORD, DAVID J., insurance company executive; BS, Iowa State U. Pres., Midwest Svcs. ERA; pres. AmeriSpec; sr. v.p., sales, v.p., real estate sales, Southern Region, Eastern Divsn. American Home Shield Corp., joined, 1987, pres., COO, 2006—. V.p. Nat. Home Warranty Assn., 1994-95, pres., 1995-97. Office: American Home Shield Corp 889 Ridgelake Blvd Memphis TN 38120 Office Phone: 901-537-8000. Business E-Mail: dcrawford@americanhomeshield.com.

CRAWFORD, FRED ALLEN, JR., cardiothoracic surgeon, educator; b. Columbia, SC, Oct. 17, 1942; s. Fred Allen and Susan Valery Floyd C.; m. Mary Jane Dantzler, June 11, 1966; children: Fred Allen III, Mary Elizabeth. MD, Duke U., 1967. Diplomate Am. Bd. Surgery, Am. Bd. Thoracic Surgery. Intern Duke U. Med. Ctr., Durham, NC, 1967-68, resident in surgery, 1971-76, instr. surgery, 1975-76; asst. prof. surgery, chief divsn. cardiac surgery U. Miss., Med. Ctr., Jackson, 1976-79; prof. surgery pediat., chief divsn. cardiothoracic surgery Med. U. of S.C., Charleston, 1979—, chmn. dept. surgery, 1988—. Contbr. numerous articles to profl. jours. Maj. U.S. Army, 1969-71. Decorated Bronze Star. Mem. ACS, Am. Surg. Assn., Charleston County Med. Soc., S.C. State Med. Assn., Soc. Thoracic Surgeons, So. Surg. Assn., So. Thoracic Surg. Assn., Am. Heart Assn., Am. Assn. Thoracic Surgery (pres. 2003), Am. Bd. Thoracic Surgery (bd. dirs. 1991-2002, chmn., 2001), Am. Coll. Cardiology, Phi Beta Kappa, Alpha Omega Alpha. Presbyterian. Office: 25 Courtney Dr Ste 7018 MSC 295 Charleston SC 29425-2950 Home Phone: 843-884-0361; Office Phone: 843-876-4840. Business E-Mail: crawfrdf@musc.edu.

CRAWFORD, JAMES W., JR., state legislator; b. Oct. 4, 1937; m. Harriet Cannon; 3 children. Mem. coun., Oxford City, 1964—68; developer; state rep. Dist. 22 NC, 1995—2002; state rep. Dist. 32, 2003—. With USN, 1960—62. Recipient Carroll V. Singleton award, Bd Realtors, Valand award, Appreciation & Recognition award, NC Psychol. Assn., Outstanding Legislator award, NC Alliance Mentally Ill, Guardian of Small Bus. award, Nat. Fedn. Ind. Bus., NC, 1998. Mem.: NC Mental Health Assn. (former pres.), Roanoke Island Hist. Assn., Oxford Zoning Adjustment Bd., C. of C., Nat. Fed. Ind. Bus., NC Mchts. Assn., Lakeland Art Ctr., St. Andrews Presbyn. Coll. Bd., Jaycees (Disting. Svc. award). Democrat. Methodist. Office: NC House of Reps 16 W Jones St Rm 1326 Raleigh NC 27601-1096 Address: PO Box 5144 Henderson NC 27536 Office Phone: 919-733-5824. Business E-Mail: Jim.Crawford@ncleg.net.

CRAWFORD, JULIE, nonprofit arts administrator; d. Priscilla and Clinton Althaus; BA, U. North Tex., Denton, 1973. Exec. dir. Denton Cmty. Theatre, Tex., 1988—94, Am. Assn. of Cmty. Theatre, 1994—. Bd. mem. Stage West Theatre, 2012—; pres. Live Theatre League of Tarrant County, 2009—; bd. mem./treas. SW Theatre Assn., 1988—2000; bd. mem., v.p. planning and devel. Am. Assn. Cmty. Theatre, 1988—94; bd. mem. Denton Cmty. Theatre, Tex., 1987—88; bd. mem., pres., treas. Lago Vista C. of C., Tex., 2002—07. Recipient Lifetime Achievement award, Denton Cmty. Theatre, 1994, Vol. of Yr. award, SW Theatre Assn., 1996, Disting. Svc. award, 1996; fellow, Am. Assn. of Cmty. Theatre, 1996, SW Theatre Assn., 1997. Mem.: Tex. Nonprofit Theatres. Office: Am Assn Cmty Theatre 1300 Gendy St Fort Worth TX 76107 Office Phone: 817-732-3177. Office Fax: 817-732-3178. Business E-Mail: julie@aact.org.*

CRAWFORD, KRISTOPHER R., state legislator; b. Anderson, Nov. 12, 1969; s. Robert Donald and Karen Sue Crawford; m. Rebecca Crawford; children: Madeline, Jessica, Abigail, Lillian. BS, The Citadel, 1992; MD, Med. U. SC, 2001. Chief resident Mcleod Family Practice; mem. Dist. 63 SC House of Reps., 2007—, mem. Labor, Commerce, and Industry Com. & Rules Com. Trustee SC Med. Assn. Mem.: SC Med. Assn. (trustee). Republican. Home: 217 Dozier Blvd Ste 105 Florence SC 29501 Office: 327D Blatt Building Columbia SC 29201 Home Phone: 843-673-0703; Office Phone: 803-734-2992, 843-656-0778. Business E-Mail: CrawfordK@schouse.org.

CRAWFORD, PATTI CYNTHAI (CYNDA), veterinarian, educator; BS in Animal Sci. (hon.), NC State U., Raleigh, 1975, MS in Animal Sci., 1978; PhD in Immunology/infectious Disease, U. Fla., Gainesville, 1984, DVM in Veterinary Medicine, 1989. Maddie's clin.

asst. prof. shelter medicine, Maddie's Shelter Medicine Program, Dept. Small Animal Clin. Sciences U. Fla. Coll. Veterinary Medicine. Contbr. of several articles to profl. publications. Recipient Fla. Assn. of kennel Clubs award for Outstanding Clin. Investigation, 2004. Achievements include patents pending in field. Office: U Fla College of Veterinary Medicine PO Box 100126 2015 SW 16th Ave Gainesville FL 32610-0138 Office Phone: 352-273-8723. Office Fax: 352-392-6125. Business E-Mail: CrawfordC@vetmed.ufl.edu.

CRAWFORD, RICK, state legislator; b. Cedartown, Ga., Apr. 02; m. Susan Crawford; children: Janae, Parker. State rep. Dist. 16, Ga., 2007—; mem. Intergovernmental Coordination Com., 2007—, State Planning and Cmty. Affairs and Code Revision Com., 2007—. Mem.: Polk County C. of C., Exchange Club Cedartown, Kiwanis Club Cedartown. Democrat. Baptist. Office: PO Box C Cedartown GA 30125 Office Phone: 770-748-4090. E-mail: rick.crawford@house.ga.gov.

CRAWFORD, RICK (ERIC ALAN CRAWFORD), United States Representative from Arkansas; b. Homestead AFB, Fla., Jan. 22, 1966; m. Stacy Crawford; children: Will, Delaney. BA in Agr. Bus. & Economics, Ark. State U., Jonesboro, 1996. Agri-reporter, news anchor Sta. WKAIT, Jonesboro; farm dir. Sta. KFIN-FM, Jonesboro; syndicated prodr., anchor Delta Farm Roundup TV, Cape Girardeau, Mo., Jonesboro, Greenville, Miss.; John Deere dealer group mktg. mgr.; owner, operator AgWatch Network, Ark.; mem. US Congress from 1st Ark. Dist., 2011—, US House Agrl. Com., 2011—, US House Transp. & Infrastructure Com., 2011—. Features columnist NE Ark. Bus. Today. First vice-chmn. Craighead County GOP Com.; mem. 4-H Found. Bd. Ark. Served in US Army, 1985—89. Named Announcer of Yr., Nat. Fedn. Profl. Bullriders, 1996—98. Mem.: Nat. Assn. Farm Broadcasting (Newscast award 2006, 2008). Republican. Office: US House of Representatives 1711 Longworth House Office Bldg Washington DC 20515 Office Phone: 202-225-4076. Office Fax: 202-225-5602.*

CRAYTON, SANDRA AUSTIN, management consultant; B in Nursing, Case Western Res. U., Cleve.; MPH, U. Mich.; JD, Cleve. State U. Cert. in fin. course for sr. execs. Harvard U. Bus. Sch. Pres. Huron Rd. Hosp.; sr. v.p., gen. mgr. med., surg. & psychiatry mgmt. ctrs. Univ. Hosps. Cleve., 1988—90; exec. v.p., COO The U. Chgo. Hosps., 1990—94; various sr. mgmt. positions including pres. clin. mgmt. svcs., Caremark Rx, Inc. and pres. physician svcs. Caremark, Inc., 1994—97; pres., CEO Sedona Health Care Group, Inc., 1997—99, PhyServ, LLC, 1999—2001; ind. cons. Met. Atlanta Rapid Transit Authority; mng. dir. Alvarez & Marsal, 2006—; project leader USC Care U. So. Calif. Keck Sch. Med.; project leader, chief restructuring officer Grady Health Sys. Bd. dirs. NCCI Holdings, Inc., Gambro AB, Cancer Treatment Centers America, Nat. City Corp., Ferro Corp., 1994—. Office: Alvarez & Marsal 3424 Peachtree Rd NE Ste 1500 Atlanta GA 30326-1139 Office Phone: 404-260-4040. Office Fax: 404-260-4090.

CRAYTON, WILLIAM H., food service executive; BA in Bus. & Acctg., Point Loma Nazarene U., 1982; MS in Mgmt., Baker U., Baldwin City, Kans., 1997; attended, Belmont U. Scarlett Leadership Inst., Nashville, 2008—09. Positions in buying, mdse. planning & systems devel., allocation and store ops. Mervyn's, County Seat Stores, JC Penny's, 1981—89; various positions in mdse., merchandise sys. devel. and store ops. Payless ShoeSource Inc, 1989—2001; dir. info. tech. bus. devel. Hallmark Cards, 2001—03; v.p. account engagement Planalytics Inc., 2003—05; prin. Columbus Consulting Inc., 2005—06; pres. Crayton Consulting LLC, 2005—06; v.p. mdse. planning and allocation Cracker Barrel Old Country Store, Inc., 2006—. Office: Cracker Barrel Old Country Store Inc 305 Hartmann Dr Lebanon TN 37088-0787 Office Phone: 615-444-5533. Office Fax: 615-443-9476.

CREAMER, PAULA, professional golfer; b. Mountain View, Calif., Aug. 5, 1986; Profl. golfer LPGA Tour, 2004—. Recipient Louise Suggs Rolex Rookie of the Year award, 2005; named Amateur of the Yr., Golf Digest, 2004, Golfweek, 2004, Player of the Yr., Am. Junior Golf Assoc., 2003. Achievements include being the first amateur to win the LPGA Final Qualifying Tournament, 2004; being youngest person to win the LPGA Final Qualifying Tournament, 2004; winning three career LPGA tour events; winning 19 national championships, 11 American Junior Golf Association tournaments. Office: Ladies Professional Golf Association 100 International Golf Drive Daytona Beach FL 32124

CREASIA, JOAN CATHERINE, dean, nursing educator; b. Burlington, Vt., Aug. 14, 1941; d. Ramon J. and Marjorie E. (Rising) LaBelle; m. Donald A. Creasia, June 29, 1963; children: Karen, Tracey. BSN, U. Vt., Burlington, 1964; MSN, U. Tenn., 1978; PhD, U. Md., 1987. Staff nurse psychiat. unit Mass. Mental Health Ctr., Boston, 1964-65; instr. D'Youville Sch. Nursing, Cambridge, Mass., 1965-66; staff nurse Boston Lying-In Hosp., 1966-67; staff nurse med. surg. units Norwood Hosp., Mass., 1967-70; staff nurse, nursing supr. Oak Ridge Hosp., Tenn., 1971-74; staff nurse, supr. Frederick Meml. Hosp., Md., 1977-78, 86-92; instr. in nursing U. Tenn., Knoxville, 1974-77; rsch. asst. U. Md., Balt., 1980-83; instr., coord., asst. prof. med. surg. nursing Frederick (Md.) C.C., 1978-80, 81-83; asst. prof., coord. RN-BSN program U. Md. Sch. Nursing, Balt., 1983-90, assoc. prof., chair RN-BSN/MS programs, 1990-94, dir. statewide programs, 1991-94; assoc. dean for acad. programs and interim dean Med. U. SC Coll. Nursing, Charleston, 1994-95; dean, Coll. Nursing, U. Tenn., Knoxville, 1995—. Cons. in field. Author: Conceptual Foundations of Professional Nursing Practice, 1991, 96 (Book of Yr. award Am. Jour. Nursing 1992), Conceptual Foundations: The Bridge to Professional Nursing Practice, 2001, 4th edit., 2006, 5th edit., 2010; contbr. articles to profl. jours. and books. Bd. dirs. Tenn. Ctr. for Nursing. Recipient Outstanding Achievement in Indirect Nursing Rsch. award, 1987, Nat. Rsch. Svc. award, 1982, 83, Profl. Nurse Traineeship award, 1981, Outstanding Leadership award Md. Nurses Assn., 1990, Excellence in Nursing Leadership award Tenn. Orgn. Nurse Execs., Knoxville Coun., 2006, Excellence in Edn. award Sigma Theta Tau, Gamma Chi chpt., 2010. Mem.: ANA, Am. Assn. Colls. Nursing, Nat. League Nursing, Phi Kappa Phi, Sigma Theta Tau (award 2010). Home: 605 Scotswood Cir Knoxville TN 37919-7457 Office Phone: 865-974-7583. Personal E-mail: joan.creasia@comcast.net. Business E-Mail: jcreasia@utk.edu.

CREASMAN, WILLIAM THOMAS, obstetrician-gynecologist, educator; b. Miami, Ariz., Sept. 3, 1934; s. George Dewey and Pauline (Cate) C.; m. Erble Jeannie Garrett, Aug. 29, 1958; children: Valrie Kay, William Scott. BA, Baylor U., 1956, MD, 1960. Intern Jefferson Davis Hosp., Houston, 1960-61; resident U. Rochester, N.Y., 1963-67; asst. prof. M.D. Anderson Hosp., Houston, 1969-70; asst. prof. dept. ob-gyn Duke Med. Ctr., Durham, N.C., 1970-74, assoc. prof., 1974-78, prof., 1978—, James Ingram prof., 1982—; Sims-Hester prof., chmn. dept. ob-gyn Med. U. S.C., Charleston, 1986, disting. prof., 2010. Key investigator Duke Comprehensive Cancer Ctr., 1971-86; trustee N.C. Cancer Inst., 1976-86. Author: Gynecologic Oncology, 1981; contbr. articles to profl. jours. Recipient Pres's award Am. Coll. Obstetricians and Gynecologists, 1973; recipient First Prize paper Am. Coll. Obstetricians and Gynecologists, 1980; Robertson Meml. lectr. Dundee, Scotland, 1976 Fellow Am. Coll. Obstetricians and Gynecologists, Am. Gynecol. and Obstetrical Soc.; mem. Soc. Gynecologic Oncologists (sec-treas. 1975-78, pres. 1988), Am. Radium Soc., Soc. Pelvic Surgeons Republican. Baptist. Home: 906 Red Coat Run Mount Pleasant SC 29464-9220 Office: OBGYN Dept Med Univ SC Charleston SC 29425

CREECH, CLARENCE BUDDY, pediatric epidemiologist, educator; b. July 16, 1973; Grad. cum laude, MPH, Vanderbilt U.; MD, U. Tenn. Coll. Medicine, 1999. Cert. Pediatrics. Pediatric staff mem. Vanderbilt Children's Hosp., 1999, chief resident, pediatrics, 2002, pediatric infectious disease fellow, asst. prof., pediatric infectious diseases, 2006—. Contbr. articles to profl. jours. Office: Monroe Carell Jr Childrens Hosp at Vanderbilt 2200 Childrens Way Nashville TN 37232 Office Phone: 615-936-6772. Business E-Mail: buddy.creech@vanderbilt.edu.

CREEL, MICHAEL ALLEN, energy executive; b. Lake Charles, La., Dec. 27, 1953; s. Harold Lee and Reba (Harkens) Creel; m. Kathy Roberts, Nov. 26, 1977; children: Michael Andrew, Matthew Robert. BS in Acctg., McNeese State U., 1975. CPA Tex. Contr. Guaranty Fed. Savs. Loan Assn., Lake Charles, 1973-76, Houston 1st Am. Savs., 1976-80; mgr. cash adminstrn. Coastal Corp., Houston, 1980—81, mgr. cash control, 1981-82, project leader corp. fin., 1982-84, mgr. fin. planning, 1984-86, dir. fin. planning, 1986-91; dir. corp. fin. Enron Corp., Houston, 1991-93, gen. mgr. corp. fin., 1994-95; v.p., treas. NorAm Energy Corp., Houston, 1995-97; sr. v.p. fin. Tejas Energy LLC, Houston, 1997, sr. v.p., CFO, 1998-99; sr. v.p. Enterprise Products Co. Partners, LP, Houston, 1999—2001, CFO, 2000—01, exec. v.p., CFO, 2001—07, dir., pres., CEO, 2007—10; pres., CEO Enterprise Products Holdings LLC, Houston, 2010—. CFO EPCO, 2000—05, COO, 2005—07, group vice chmn., CFO, 2007—; pres., CEO EPE Holdings, 2005—07; dir. Enterprise Products GP, 2005—, Edge Petroleum Corp., 2005—, DEP GP, 2006—. Mem.: AICPA, Fin. Execs. Internat., Tex. Soc. CPAs, Nat. Eagle Scout Assn. Office: Enterprise Products Holdings LLC 1100 Louisiana St Houston TX 77002 E-mail: mcreel@eprod.com.*

CREGG, ROGER A., board member, retired construction executive; b. Peabody, Mass., Apr. 5, 1956; BS in Acctg., Northwestern U., M in Mgmt. CFO Sweetheart Cup Co.; exec. v.p., fin., CFO Zenith Electronics Corp.; sr. v.p. PulteGroup, Inc. (formerly Pulte Homes Corp.), Bloomfield Hills, Mich., 1998—2003, CFO, 1998—2011, exec. v.p., 2003—11. Bd. dirs. Fed. Res. Bank Chgo., 2004—, Comerica Inc., 2006—. Mem.: Fin. Execs. Internat. Office: c/o Comerica Corp Hdqs Comerica Bank Tower 1717 Main St Dallas TX 75201 Business E-Mail: racregg@comerica.com.

CREHAN, JOSEPH EDWARD, lawyer; b. Detroit, Dec. 8, 1938; s. Owen Thomas and Marguerite (Dunn) C.; m. Sheila Anderson, Nov. 6, 1965; children: Kerry Marie, Christa Ellen. AB, Wayne State U., Detroit, 1961; JD, Ind. U., 1965. Bar: Ind. 1965, Mich. 1966, U.S. Supreme Ct. 1984. Pvt. practice, Detroit, 1966-68; assoc. Louisell & Barris (P.C.), 1968-72; ptnr. Fenton, Nederlander, Dodge, Barris & Crehan (P.C.), 1972-74, Barris & Crehan (P.C.), 1975-88; pvt. practice Bloomfield Hills, Mich. and Naples, Fla., 1977—. Mem. Am. Trial Lawyers Assn. Roman Catholic. Home and Office: 827 Bentwood Dr Naples FL 34108-8204

CREIGHTON, CHARLES BRANDON (BRANDON CREIGHTON), state legislator; b. Montgomery County, Tex. m. Fawn Creighton; 2 children. BA in Govt., U. Tex.; JD, Okla. City U. Former mem. child support divsn. Office Tex. Atty. Gen.; former brief writer criminal appellate divsn. Office Okla. Atty. Gen.; vice chmn. Lone Star Groundwater Conservation Dist., 2001—06; v.p., gen. counsel The Signorelli Co., Developers and Builders; mem. Dist. 16 Tex. House of Representatives, 2006—. Mem.: Mont. County Rep. Party (chmn. fin. com.), State Bar Tex. Republican. Avocations: hunting, fishing. Office: 326 1/2 Main St Ste 110 Conroe TX 77301 also: Room EXT E2.210 Capitol Extension PO Box 2910 Austin TX 78768 Home Phone: 936-539-0028.

CRENSHAW, ANDER, United States Representative from Florida, lawyer; b. Jacksonville, Fla., Sept. 1, 1944; m. Kitty Crenshaw, 1971; children: Sarah, Alex. BA in Polit. Sci., U. Ga., 1966; JD, U. Fla., 1970. Mem. Fla. Ho. of Reps., 1972—78, Fla. State Senate, 1986—94, Rep. leader, 1990—92, pres., 1993; sr. v.p. Donaldson, Lufkin & Jenrette, 1990—95, William R. Hough & Co., St. Petersburg, 1995—; mem. US Congress from 4th Fla. Dist., 2000—, dep. majority whip, mem. appropriations com., corrections day com. Commr. State Ethics Commn., 1983—85, Constl. Revision Com., 1998; mem. Nat. Rep. Congl. Com., Ho. Rep. Policy Com., Rep. Prescription Drug Task Force. Mem. Grace Episcopal Ch., Ocala, Fla. Republican. Episcopalian. Office: US House of Representatives 440 Cannon House Office Bldg Washington DC 20515*

CRENSHAW, JESSE, state legislator; b. Sept. 23, 1946; BA, Ky. State U.; JD, U. Ky. Atty.; mem. Dist. 77 Ky. House of Reps., 1993—. Democrat. Mailing: 121 Constitution St Lexington KY 40507 Office: Capitol Annex Rm 332D 702 Capitol St Frankfort KY 40601 Office Phone: 859-259-1402, 502-564-8100 ext. 620. Office Fax: 859-259-1441.

CRENSHAW, RANDALL W., communications executive; BS in Chemistry, Miss. Coll., 1974; MBA in Bus. Various mgmt. positions CommScope, Inc., Hickory, NC, 1985—2000, exec. v.p., procurement & gen. mgr., network products group, 2000—04, exec. v.p., gen. mgr., enterprise solutions, 2004—10, exec. v.p. procurement, chief supply officer, 2010—11, exec. v.p., COO, 2011—. Office: CommScope Inc 1100 CommScope Pl SE Hickory NC 28602 Office Phone: 828-324-2200. Office Fax: 828-982-1708. Business E-Mail: rcrenshaw@commscope.com.

CRENSHAW, REGGIE, diversified service company executive; BS in Sys. Engring., US Mil. Acad., West Point. Strategy and mgmt. positions Ford Credit, General Electric Capital; sr. v.p. Bank of America Corp.; sr. v.p., process quality and innovation Wachovia; sr. v.p., innovation and process improvement Servicemaster Co., Servicemaster Global Holdings, 2009—. Office: The ServiceMaster Co 860 Ridge Lake Blvd Memphis TN 38120 Office Phone: 901-597-1400. Office Fax: 630-663-2001. Business E-Mail: reggie.crenshaw@servicemaster.com.

CRERAN, HEATHER, diagnostic laboratory executive; BA in Polit. Sci., Economics, Duke U., Durham. V.p. of ops. IMPATH, 1989—2003; COO ChromaVision Med. Sys. Inc., 2004—07; exec. v.p. and COO Clarient Inc., 2004—07; pres. CSI Labs., 2008—, COO, 2008—11, CEO, 2011—. Mem.: Virtual Sci. Inc., Duke Univ. Alumni Network, Exec. War Coll. Discussion Group. Office: CSI Laboratories 2580 Westside Pkwy Ste 400 Alpharetta GA 30004-8948 Office Phone: 770-817-0817. Office Fax: 678-205-4668.

CRESCIMBENI, JOHN R., councilman; Grad., Fla. Cmty. Coll; BS in Mgmt., Econ., Mktg., Jacksonville U. Councilman-at-large, Group 2 Jacksonville City Coun., 1991—99, 2008—; franchisee Hickory Farms; exec. dir. Scenic Fla., Inc. Mem. Rules, Fin., Pub. Health & Safety Coms. Bd. mem. Tree Hill Nature Ctr. Mem.: Jacksonville Humane Soc. Democrat. Office: 117 W Duval St Ste 425 Jacksonville FL 32202 Office Phone: 904-630-1381. Business E-Mail: jrc@coj.net.

CRESSLER, JOHN DAVID, electrical engineering educator; b. Chattanooga, Sept. 18, 1961; s. Charles W. and Elizabeth (Bolling) C.; married; children: Matthew J., Christina E., Joanna M. BS in Physics, Ga. Inst. Tech., 1984; MS in Applied Physics, Columbia U., 1987, PhD in Applied Physics, 1990. Mem. staff rsch. divsn. IBM Thomas J. Watson Rsch. Ctr., Yorktown Heights, NY, 1984-92; prof. Auburn U., Ala., 1992—2002; Byers prof. elec. and computer engring. Ga. Inst. Tech., 2002—. Co-author (with Guofu Niu) Silicon-Germanium Heterojunction Bipolar Transistors, 2003; author Reinventing Teenagers: the Gentle Art of Instilling Character in Our Young People, 2004; editor (book) Silicon Heterostructure Handbook: Materials, Fabrication, Devices, Circuits, and Applications of SiGe and Si Strained-Layer Epitaxy, 2006; contbr. articles to profl. jours. Recipient Auburn U. Alumni Engring. Coun. Rsch. award, 1996, Auburn U. Birdsong Merit Testing award, 1998, Auburn U. Alumni Undergraduate Tchg. Excellence award, 1999. Fellow IEEE (sr. mem., assoc. editor Jour. of Solid-State Circuits 1998-2001, guest editor for Transactions on Nuclear Sci. 2002-05, assoc. editor Transactions on Electron Deveices, 2005-; mem. tech. program com. Internat. Solid-State Circuits Conf., 1992-98, 1999-2001, Bipolar/BiCMOS Circuits and Tech. Mtg., 1995-99, Internat. Electron Devices Mtg., 1996-97, Nuclear and Space Radiation Effects Conf., 2000, 2002-06, Internat. Reliability Physics Symposium, 2005; tech. program chair, Internat. Solid-State Circuits Conf., 1998; conf. co-chair 2004 Topical Mtg. on Silicon Monolithic Integrated Circuits in RF Systems, Internat. advisor European Workshop on Low Temperature Electronics; mem. technical program com. Internat. SiGe Tech. and Device Mtg.; mem. exec. com. ECS Symposium on SiGe: Materials, Processing, and Devices; IEEE Electron Device Soc. Disting. Lectr., 1994-; recipient Millennium medal, 2000); mem. Eta Kappa Nu (C. Holmes MacDonald award 1996). Office: Ga Inst Tech Sch Elec and Computer Engring 777 Atlantic Dr NW Atlanta GA 30332-0250 Office Phone: 404-894-5161. Office Fax: 404-894-4641. Business E-Mail: cressler@ece.gatech.edu.

CRICHTON, FLORA CAMERON, volunteer, foundation administrator; b. Waco, Tex. d. William Waldo and Helen Emelyn (Miller) Cameron; m. John H. Crichton, 1989 (dec.); children: Ike Simpson Kampmann III(dec.), Megan Cameron Kampmann, Helen Miller Kampmann(dec.). Dir., mem. exec. com. Certain-Teed Corp., 1971—78; exec. com. San Antonio World's Fair, 1968. Mem. Pres.'s Mission to Latin Am., 1969; U.S. del. Inter-Am. Commn. Women, 1969—72; mem. nat. adv. coun. Georgia O'Keefe Mus.; mem. citizens stamp adv. commn. U.S. Postal Svc., 1969—71; cons. Bur. Inter-Am. Affairs, Dept. State, 1972—75; pres. Flora Cameron Found.; trustee Trinity U., San Antonio, 1965—2005, chmn., 1976—78; trustee Sweet Briar Coll., 1969—78; mem. Pres.'s Commn. German-Am. Tricentennial, 1983—84; bd. govs. East-West Ctr., Honolulu, 1989—92; vice chmn. Rep. Party Tex., 1958—60; mem. Tex. Rep. Nat. Com., 1960—65; del. Rep. Nat. Conv., 1960, 1964, alt. del., 1968, sec. platform com., 1960; former mem. Rep. Nat. Fin. Com., 1965—; vice chmn. nat. fin. com. George Bush for Pres., 1987—88; former mem. bd. dirs. San Antonio Art Inst., Sch. Am. Rsch., Santa Fe; former mem. nat. coun. Met. Opera. Mem.: San Antonio Jr. League, Colonial Dames Am. Home: 315 Westover Rd San Antonio TX 78209-5653 Office: 5701 Broadway St San Antonio TX 78209-5722

CRICHTON, THOMAS, IV, lawyer; b. Shreveport, La., Dec. 2, 1947; BS, La. State U., 1969, JD, 1972. Bar: Tex. 1972, La. 1972, D.C. 1988. Mem. Vinson & Elkins, LLP, Dallas, co-head Tax Law Sect., 2005—08. Adj. prof. sch. law U. Houston, 1978-86. Mem. Order of Coif, Beta Alpha Psi, Beta Gamma Sigma, Omicron Delta Kappa, Phi Kappa Phi. Office: Vinson & Elkins LLP 3700 Trammell Crow Ctr Dallas TX 75201-2975 also: Vinson & Elkins LLP 2500 First City Tower 1001 Fannin St Ste 3300 Houston TX 77002-6706 also: Vinson & Elkins LLP 2200 Pennsylvania Ave NW Ste 500 W Washington DC 20037-1701 Office Phone: 214-220-7984. Business E-Mail: tcrichton@velaw.com.

CRIGLER, B. WAUGH, federal judge; b. Charlottesville, Va., July 17, 1948; s. Bernard Weaver and Jayne (Waugh) C.; m. Anne (Kendall), June 20, 1970; children: C. Kendall, Jason C., and Anne Stuart. BA in history, Washington and Lee U., 1970; JD, U. Tenn., 1973. Bar: Tenn., 1973, US Dist. Ct. (ea. dist.) Tenn., 1973, Va., 1974, DC, 1974, US Dist. Ct. (we. and ea. dists.) Va., 1975, US Ct. Appeals (4th cir.) 1978, US Supreme Ct., 1979. Law clk. to presiding judge U.S. Dist. Ct. Tenn., Knoxville, Tenn., 1973-74; ptnr. Lea and Crigler, Culpeper, Va., 1974-75, Lea, Davies, Crigler, and Barrell, Culpeper, Va., 1975-79, Davies, Crigler, Barrell, and Will, PC, Culpeper, Va., 1979-81; magistrate judge U.S. Dist. Ct., Charlottesville, Va., 1981—. Instr. Sch. Law, U. Va., 1986—,; mem. criminal rules adv. com. Jud. Conf. U.S., 1992-97; mem. Fed. and State Jud. Coun., Va., 1992-2001. Mem.: ABA (criminal law com. young lawyers divsn. 1974—80), Tenn. Bar Assn., Va. Bar Assn. (chmn. criminal law corrections young lawyers divsn. 1979—80), Va. State Bar (standing com. on professionalism 1997—2003, chmn. and moderator VSB Professionalism for Law Students. 2000—03), Thomas Jefferson Inn of Ct. (pres. 1991—92), Order of Coif, Phi Kappa Phi. Avocations: landscaping, swimming, biblical studies. Office: US Magistrate Judge 255 W Main St Rm 328 Charlottesville VA 22902-5058

CRIM, RANDALL W., colon and rectal surgeon, educator; m. Ellen Crim; children: Emily, Patrick, Andrew, Charlotte Rose. BA, U. Tex.; MD, U. Tex., Dallas, 1984. Diplomate Am. Bd. Surgery, 2009, Am. Bd. Colon and Rectal Surgery, 2010. Resident in gen. surgery St. Paul Med. Ctr., Dallas, 1984—89; fellow in colon and rectal surgery Cleve. Clinic Found., Ohio, 1989—90; clin. asst. prof. surgery Univ. Tex. Southwestern Med. Ctr.; hosp. affiliations include Baylor Med. Ctr., Irving, Las Colinas Med. Ctr.; pvt. practice Tex. Colon and Rectal Specialists, 1990—. Featured lectr. Author: various publs. Mem. Crohn's and Colitis Found. of America. Named one of Best Doctors in America, 1996—2008, 2011—12, Best Doctors in Dallas, D Mag., 2001, 2003—10, Tex. Super Doctors, Tex. Monthly, 2006—10. Mem.: United Ostomy Assn., Tex. Soc. Colon and Rectal Surgeons, Tex. Med. Assn., Dallas Soc. Gen. Surgeons, Dallas County Med. Assn., Am. Soc. of Colon and Rectal Surgeons, AMA, ACS. Avocations: baseball, baseball caps collecting. Office: Texas Colon and Rectal Specialists Tuscan Professional Bldg 701 Tuscan Dr Ste 125 Irving TX 75039 Office Phone: 972-759-2040.

CRIMM, RONALD (RON) E., state legislator; b. Mar. 11, 1935; m. Phyllis Crimm. Ins. agency owner; former mem. Dist. 47 Ky. House of Reps., Ky., mem. Dist. 33, 1997—; trustee Suburban Hosp.; adv. bd. Methodist Children's Home, Nortons Hosp.; bd. mem. Good Samaratan Home LLC. Treas. Jeff City GOP, 1991—93, chmn., 1993—95. Mem.: Shriners, JeffERstown C. of C., Masons (33 degree), Middletown C. of C. (bd. dir.). Republican. Methodist. Mailing: PO Box 43244 Louisville KY 40253-0244 Office: Capitol Annex Rm 424F Frankfort KY 40601 Home Phone: 502-245-8905; Office Phone: 502-245-2118, 502-564-8100 ext 706. Fax: 502-244-1015. E-mail: repcrimm@roncrimm.net.

CRIPPEN, TIMOTHY ALAN, sociology educator; b. Ft. Wayne, Ind., June 1, 1952; s. Raymond R. and Wilda E. Crippen; m. Pamela A. Crippen, Mar. 3, 1973. AB, Ind. U., 1974; MA, U. Tex., 1976, PhD, 1982. Asst. prof. sociology U. Mary Washington, Fredericksburg, Va., 1982—88, assoc. prof. sociology, 1988—94, prof. sociology, 1994—. Mem. editl. bd. Evolutionary Behavioral Scis., 2013—. Author: Crisis in Sociology, 1999; contbr. articles to profl. jours. Mem. Social Forces (editl. bd. 2009-), Evolutionary Behavioral Scis. (editl. bd. mem., 2013-), AAAS, Am. Sociol. Assn. (co-chair elect, sect. on evolution, biology and soc. 2012-), Assn. for Politics and Life Scis., Human Behavior and Evolution Soc., Southern Sociol. Soc., Phi Kappa Phi. Office: U Mary Washington Dept Sociology and Anthropology 1301 College Ave Fredericksburg VA 22401 Office Phone: 540-654-1503. Business E-Mail: tcrippen@umw.edu.

CRISAFULLI, STEVE, state legislator; b. Rockledge, Fla., July 26, 1971; m. Kristen Crisafulli; children: Carly, Kennedy. AA, Brevard Cmty. Coll.; BA, U. Central Fla. Supr. Brevard County Soil & Water Consveration, 1998—2002; mem. Dist. 32 Fla. House of Reps., 2008—, vice chair natural resources appropriations com., mem. agr. and natural resources policy com., econ. devel. policy com., gen. govt. policy coun. Dir. Brevard County Farm Bur., 1996—2004, 2006—; grad. Leadership Brevard, 1998, former program com. mem., 1999—2000. Recipient Pres. award, Fla. Farm Bureau, 2005. Republican. Office: House Office Bldg 402 S Monroe St Rm 317 Tallahassee FL 32399-1300 also: 2460 N Courtenay Pkwy Ste 108 Merritt Island FL 32953-4193 Office Phone: 850-488-4669, 321-449-5111. Business E-Mail: steve.crisafulli@myfloridahouse.gov.

CRISER, MARSHALL M., lawyer, retired academic administrator; b. Rumson, NJ, Sept. 4, 1928; s. Marshall and Louise (Johnson) C.; m. Paula Porcher, Apr. 27, 1957; children: Marshall III, Edward, Mary, Glenn, Kimberly, Mark. BSBA, U. Fla., 1951, LLB, 1951 (replaced by J.D., 1967). Bar: Fla. 1951. Pvt. practice, Palm Beach, 1953-84; ptnr. Gunster, Yoakley, Criser & Stewart, 1955-84; atty. Palm Beach County Sch. Bd., 1958-64; pres. U. Fla., Gainesville, 1984-89, pres. emeritus, 1989—; shareholder Mahoney, Adams & Criser, Jacksonville, Fla., 1989-97; of counsel McGuire Woods, LLP, Jacksonville, 1998-2000, ret. ptnr., 2000—. Dep. chmn. Rinker Group Ltd., 2003-07; chmn. bd. dirs. Rinker Materials, Corp., 1989-2002; mem. pres.'s coun. NCAA, 1986-87; chmn. Installment Land Sales Bd., 1963-64, chmn. Acad. Task Force rev. tort and ins. law, Fla., 1986-88, The Emerald Funds; chmn. bd. trustees Emerald Fund, 1997-98; mem. Scripps Fla. Funding Corp., 2004-06, chmn., 2004-06. Bd. dirs. Univ. Med. Ctr., Jacksonville, 1989-96, Shands at Jacksonville Hosp., 1999-2002, M.E. Rinker, Sr. Found., 1998—; bd. dirs. Shands Tchg. Hosp., Gainesville, Fla., pres., 1984-89, bd. dirs., 1996-2001; bd. govs. Good Samaritan Hosp., West Palm Beach, pres., 1979-84; mem. Fla. Bd. Regents, 1965, 71-81, chmn., 1974-77, Bus.-Higher Edn. Forum, 1987-89; trustee Collins Ctr., 1989-99; chmn. Alliance for World Class Edn., Duval County, 1998-2001; chmn. Fed. Crt. Adv. Group Mid. Dist. of Fla., 1991-96; bd. dirs. Flagler System, Inc., 1975-; trustee U. Fla., 2001-03, chmn., 2001-03; mem. Fla. Fed. Jud. Nominating Com., 2001-05; mem. Gov.'s Med. Malpractice Task Force, 2002—03. With U.S. Army, 1951-53. Fellow Am. Bar Found.; mem. Fla. Coun. 100 (chmn. 1979-80, Govs. Bus. Leadership award, 2009, Shands Healthcare Lifetime Achievement award, 2009, U. Fla. Found. Lifetime Vol. award, 2010), ABA (ho. dels. 1968-72), Fla. Bar (gov. 1960-68, pres. 1968-69), former dir. Bell South Corp., FPL Group, Perini Corp., Barnett Banks, Inc., Fla. Blue Key, Phi Delta Phi, Sigma Nu. Office: 100 NW 20th St Gainesville FL 32603 Office Phone: 352-392-5977. Business E-Mail: mcriser@uff.ufl.edu.

CRISMON, MILES LYNN, clinical psychopharmacologist, dean, educator; b. Tulsa, Feb. 13, 1951; s. Isaac Edward and Geneva Angeline (Pate) Crismon; children: Teresa Lynne, Anthony Edward, Olya Grace, Sensey Alexander. BS in Pharmacy, U. Okla., 1974; PharmD, U. Tex. Health Sci. Ctr., San Antonio, 1979. Diplomate Am. Bd. Clin. Pharmacology, lic. pharmacist Tex., N.Mex. Resident hosp. pharmacy USPHS Gallup Indian Med. Ctr., 1974-75; resident psychopharmacology U. Tex. Health Sci. Ctr., 1979; asst. prof. U. Tex. Coll. Pharmacy, Austin, 1979-85, assoc. prof., 1985—91, prof., 1991—, asst. dean, 1984-85, head clin. divsn., 1985-96, assoc. dean. clin. programs, 2004—07, dean Coll. Pharmacy, 2007—. Clin. pharmacologist Austin State Hosp., 1979—2004, Healthcare Rehab. Ctr., Austin, 1985—98; cons. Tex. Dept. Mental Health, 1983—91, 1996—2006, Healthcare Financing Adminstrn., Balt., 1986—98, Okla. Dept. Mental Health, 1988; vis. prof. Coll. Arts Sci. & Tech., Kingston, Jamaica, 1989, 1991, Nat. Mental Health Inst., Singapore, 2007; co-dir. Tex. Medication Algorithm Project, 1996—2006; dir. Children's Medication Algorithm Project, 1998—2006. Contbr. articles to profl. jours., chapters to books. Lt. sgt. USPHS, 1974—76. Recipient Janssen Pharmaceutica Partnering Rsch. award for mental health, 1998; named Tchr. of Yr., Child Psychiatry Presidency Program, UTSCUMC, Austin, 2010; grantee NEH, 1981, Robert Wood Johnson Found., 1997, Meadows Found., 1997, 1999, Hogg Found., 1999, Houston Endowment, 1999. Fellow: Am. Coll. Clin. Pharmacy Rsch. Inst. (bd. regents 2002—05, bd. trustee 2010—, CNS Rsch. award 1989); mem.: Acad. Pharm. Rsch. & Sci., Tex. Soc. Health-Sys. Pharmacists (bd. dirs. 1981—84, 1986—89, treas. 1987—89, bd. dirs. 1992—95, pres. 1993—94), Coll. Psychiat. & Neurologic Pharmacists (founding mem.), Am. Soc. Health-System Pharmacists (chmn. psychopharmacy splty. practice group 1991). Democrat. Roman Catholic. Avocations: hiking, camping, scuba. Office: U Tex Coll Pharmacy 1 University Sta MC A 1900 Austin TX 78712 Office Phone: 512-471-3718.

CRISMOND, LINDA FRY, public relations executive; b. Burbank, Calif., Mar. 1, 1943; d. Billy Chapin and Lois (Harding) Fry; m. Donald Burleigh Crismond, 1965 (dec.); m. Peter G.A. Lecog, Feb. 2009. BS, U. Calif.-Santa Barbara, 1964; M.L.S., U. Calif.-Berkeley, 1965. Cert. county libr., Calif., assn. exec. Reference libr., EDP coordinator San Francisco Pub. Library, 1965—72; head acquisition San Francisco Pub. Libr., 1972-74; asst. univ. libr. U. So. Calif., LA, 1974-80; chief dep. county libr. L.A. County Pub. Libr., LA, 1980-81, county libr. Downey, 1981-89; exec. dir ALA, Chgo., 1989-92; v.p. public rels. Profl. Media Svc. Corp., Chgo., 1992-98; v.p. pub. rels. Follett Media Distbn., Crystal Lake, Ill., 1999—2003; nat. media cons. BWI, Lexington, Ky., 2003—07; pres. Frugal Dougal's Golf Cart Accessories, Tarpon Springs, Fla., 2007—, Discount Doug's Golf Course Products, 2009—. Western rep. quality control council Ohio Coll. Libr. Ctr., Columbus, 1977-80; mem. Am. Nat. Standards Inst., N.Y.C., 1978-80; bd. councillors U. So. Calif. Sch. Libr. and Info. Mgmt., 1980-83; adv. bd. mem. UCLA Libr. Sch., 1981-89; chmn. bd. dirs. L.A. County Pub. Libr. Found., 1982-85; mem. OCLC Users Coun., 1988-89; mem. exec. com. L.A. County Mgmt. Coun., 1986-88, pres., 1988; cons. libr. Trinity Coll., 1995-99; prin. The Charleston Group, Inc., 1996—. Author: Directory of San Francisco Bay Area, 1968, Against All Odds, 1994; editor: Urban Librs. Coun. Exch., 1994-2005, The Charleston Report, 1996-99 Bd. dirs. So. Meth. U. Libr., 1992-98. Named Staff Mem. of Year San Francisco Pub. Libr., 1968 Mem. ALA, Calif. Libr. Assn. (council 1980-82), Calif. County Libr. Assn. (pres. 1984), L.A. County Mgmt. Assn. (pres. 1988). Home: 303 Mariner Dr Tarpon Springs FL 34689-5840

CRISP, CHARLES R., retired gas industry executive, board member; Mgmt. Devel. Program, Harvard U.; BSChemE, Tex. Tech U. Joined Houston Industries, 1996, pres., domestic power generation group, 1997—98; COO Shell Oil Co. (Coral Energy LLC), 1998—99, pres., 1998—2000, CEO, 1999—2000; pres., COO Tejas Gas Corp., 1988—96. Bd. dirs. Shell Oil Co. (Coral Energy LLC), 1998—2000, EOG Resources Inc., 2002—, IntercontinentalExchange Inc., 2002—, AGL Resources Inc., 2003—. Office: AGL Resources Inc Ten Peachtree Place Atlanta GA 30309 Office Phone: 404-584-4000. Office Fax: 404-584-3945. Business E-Mail: ccharles@aglresources.com.

CRISPELL, BRIAN LEWIS, history professor, dean of students; b. Rochester, NY, Apr. 5, 1964; s. Elmer Lyle and Florence Louise Crispell; m. Jean Ann Thomas, Feb. 3, 1990; children: Thomas Riley, Conner Francis, Sarah Katherine. BS in Social Studies Edn., Fla. State U., Tallahassee, 1990, MA in History, 1993, PhD in History, 1996. Tchr. Thomas County Schs., Thomasville, Ga., 1990—2000; adj. prof. U. South Fla., Tampa/Sarasota, 2000—08; prof. Fla. Coll., Temple Terrace, 2000—. Author: (book) Testing the Limits-George Smathers and Cold War America, 1999. Sgt. USAF, 1982—87. Recipient Top Lecturing Prof. award, Fla. Coll., 2001—07; nominee Bancroft prize, Columbia U., 1999—2000. Mem.: Hist. Soc., So. Hist. Assn. Republican. Mem. Ch. Of Christ. Avocations: hiking, baseball, travel. Office: Fla Coll 119 N Glen Arven Ave Temple Terrace FL 33617 Office Phone: 813-899-6745. Business E-Mail: crispellb@floridacollege.edu.

CRISPENS, MARTA ANN, gynecologic oncologist, educator; MD, U. Ala., 1991. Diplomate Am. Bd. Ob-Gyn, Am. Bd. Ob-Gyn-gynecologic oncology, lic. Tenn. Intern Univ. Ala. Med. Ctr., 1992, resident, 1992, 1994; fellow Univ. Tex. MD Anderson Cancer Ctr., 1996; asst. prof. ob-gyn. dept. Vanderbilt Univ., assoc. prof. ob-gyn. dept.; gynecologic oncologist Ingram Cancer Ctr. Vanderbilt Univ. Med. Ctr. Co-author: numerous publs. Named Recognized Dr., HealthGrades. Mem.: ACOG, ACS, Am. Assn. for Cancer Rsch., Soc. of Gynecologic Oncology, Am. Soc. of Clin. Oncology. Office: Vanderbilt University Medical Center 1211 Medicial Center Dr Nashville TN 37232 E-mail: marta.crispens@vanderbilt.edu.*

CRISPIN, ANDRE ARTHUR, diversified financial services company executive; b. Brussels, Aug. 23, 1923; came to U.S., 1947; naturalized Am. citizen; m. Sylvia Clevenger; 5 children. Student, U. Louvain, Belgium, 1943. V.p. Am. Supply and Equipment Co., Houston, 1947-48; chmn. Crispin Co., Houston, 1949—; hon. consul-gen. Belgium; ret. hon. consul-gen. Past chmn. bd. trustees so. region Inst. Internat. Edn.; mem. Citizens Environ. Coalition; past pres. Music Guild Houston; past chmn. bd. trustees Awty Internat. Sch. With Belgian Army, 1940, 44-46; chmn. emeritus Houston Counsular Ball, mem. Senate of Internat. Jr. C. of C. Decorated officier Ordre de Leopold II, Civic Cross 1st class, officier Ordre de Leopold Ier (Belgium); chevalier Legion d'Honneur (France), Commdr.'s Cross Order of the Crown (Belgium), 1997; named one of 5 Outstanding Young Texans, 1953; recipient Houston Internat. Svc. award, 1986, medal of City of Bordeaux, Disting. Consul award Pres. George H. Bush. Mem. Nat. Assn. Steel Pipe Distbrs. (past pres., bd. dirs.), Academie Internationale du Vin, Alliance Française de Houston (past pres., dir., exec. com.), Commanderie de Bordeaux d'Amerique (grand maitre emeritus, gov.), Commanderie de Bordeaux du Texas à Houston (founder, past maitre, commandeur), Commanderie du Bontemps, de Medoc et de Graves (France, commandeur d'honneur), German Wine Soc., Prodhomme, Jurade de St. Emilion Stylobate, Piliers Chablisiens, Compagnon de Loupiac, Echevin, Lussac Puisseguin St. Emilion, Lalande de Pomerol, Hospitaliers de Pomerol, Downtown Houston Assn., Belgian-Am. C. of C. (past bd. dirs.), French-Am. C. of C. (past pres. Houston chpt., dir.), Houston C. of C. (now named Greater Houston Partnership, bd. dirs. world trade divsn., internat. bus. com., past chmn.), Jr. C. of C. (internat. senator 2001), World Trade Assn. (past pres., dir.), Petroleum Club of Houston (past dir., past 1st v.p.). Home: One Crestwood Dr Houston TX 77007 Office Phone: 713-224-8000. E-mail: andrecris@crispinco.com.

CRISTESCU, NICOLAIE DAN, engineering educator; b. Chelmenti, Romania, Feb. 17, 1929; married (dec.); 1 child. Diplomat, Bucharest U., Romania, 1951, docent, 1967; PhD, Romanian Acad., 1955. Asst. prof. U. Bucharest, Romania, 1951-55, lectr., 1955-57, assoc. prof., 1957-66, prof., 1966-92, dept. chmn., 1982-90, pres., 1990-92; vis. grad. rsch. prof. U. Fla., 1970-76, grad. rsch. prof. dept. aerospace engring. mechanics and engring. sci. Gainesville, 1992—. Vis. prof. Johns Hopkins U., Balt., 1968-69, Drexel U., Phila., 1969; lectr. in field. Author: Dynamic Problems in Theory of Plasticity, 1958, The Mechanics of Extensible Strings, 1964, Dynamic Plasticity, 1967, 70 (in Japanese), Introduction to Rate-Dependent Plasticity (A Dynamic Approach), 1971, Rock Mechanics, 1983, 2d edit., 1984, supplemental 1988, Mechanics of Composite Materials, 1983, Rock Rheology, 1989, Rock Mechanics-Rheology Aspects, 1990, Rock Viscoplasticity, 1992, Viscoplasticity of Geomaterials, 1994, (with I. Suliciu) Viscoplasticity, 1976, 82, (with S. Cleja-Tigoiu) Theory of Plasticity with Application to Metal Working, 1985, (with U. Hunsche) Time Effects in Rock Mechanics, 1998, (with E.M. Craciun and E. Soos) Mechanics of Elastic Composites, 2004, (with H.R. Hardy, Jr. and R.O. Simionescu) Basic and Applied Salt Mechanics, 2002, Dynamic Plasticity, 2007; contbr. articles to profl. jours.; sr. editor: Internat. Jour. Plasticity; mem. editl. bd. Internat. Jour. Mechanical Sci., Mechanics Rsch. Comm., Mechanics of Cohesive-Frictional Materials and Structures, others. Fellow Romanian Acad., Acad. Europaea; mem. ASME (Arpad L. Nadai award 1995), Soc. Scholars, Internat. Soc. Interaction of Mechanics and Maths. (founder), Am. Rock Mechanics Assn. (founder), Am. Acad. Mechanics, Soc. Exptl. Stress Analysis, Group Français de Rheology, Internat. Assn. Computer Methods and Advances in Geomechanics, Internat. Soc. Rock Mechanics, Tau Beta Pi, Sigma Xi. Achievements include research in mechanics of solid deformable bodies, theory of plasticity, rheology, rock and soil mechanics, mechanics of powder-like materials. Office: U Fla 231 Aerospace Bldg PO Box 116250 Gainesville FL 32611-6250 Office Phone: 352-392-6747. Office Fax: 352-392-7303. Business E-Mail: cristesc@ufl.edu.

CRISTOL, A. JAY, federal judge; b. Fountain Hill, Pa., Feb. 25, 1929; s. Samuel and Mae (Stein) C.; m. Eleanor Rubin; children: Stephen Michael, David Alan. BA, U. Miami, 1958, LLB, 1959, PhD, 1997. Bar: Fla. 1959. Spl. asst. to Atty. Gen. of Fla., Tallahassee, 1959-65; sr. ptnr. Cristol, Mishan, Sloto, Miami, 1959-85; judge U.S. Bankruptcy Ct., Miami, 1985-93, chief judge, 1994-99, chief judge emeritus, 1999—. Adj. prof. U. Miami Law Sch.; bd. govs. 11th cir. Nat. Conf. Bankruptcy Judges; bankruptcy rules adv. com. Jud. Conf. of U.S., 1995-2001; bankruptcy com. U.S. Ct. Appeals (11th cir.), 1996-2002; tchr. bankruptcy law to judges in Czech Republic, Slovenia, Thailand, Russia, Ukraine, India, Malaysia, Hong Kong, South Africa, Egypt. Bd. trustees U. Miami, 1988-90, Coral Gables; bd. dirs. ARC, Miami, 1989—, Wings Over Miami Aviation Mus., 2001—. Capt. USNR, 1951-89. Fellow Am. Coll. Bankruptcy; mem. ABA, Am. Bankruptcy Inst., Nat. Conf. Bankruptcy Judges, Bankruptcy Bar Assn. (so. dist. of Fla.), Fla. Bar Assn., Dade County Bar Assn. Avocations: water-skiing, windsurfing, flying, reading. Office: US Bankruptcy Ct 1412 Fed Bldg 51 SW 1st Ave Miami FL 33130-1669 Office Phone: 305-714-1772, 305-714-1770. Business E-Mail: a_jay_cristol@flsb.uscourts.gov.

CRITTENDEN, JOHN CHARLES, engineering educator; b. Nov. 12, 1949; BS in Chem. Engring., U. Mich., 1971, MS in Civil and Environ. Engring., 1972, PhD in Civil and Environ. Engring., 1976. Sr. v.p. Limno-Tech, Inc., Ann Arbor, Mich., 1975-77; asst. prof. civil and environ. engring. Wash. State U., Pullman, 1977-78; asst. prof. civil engring., environ. engring. sect. U. Ill., Urbana, 1978-79, Mich. Tech. U., Houghton, 1979-81, assoc. prof. civil engring., environ. engring. sect., 1981-84, adj. prof. chem. engring., 1981-84, prof. civil and environ. engring., 1984—. Dir. Ctr. for Clean Indsl. and Treatment Techs., Houghton, 1992—; presdl. prof. civil engring. CenCITT Mich. Tech. U., 1988—. Mem. AIChE, ASCE (Rudolph Hering award 1980, Walter L. Huber rsch. prize 1991), Am. Acad. Environ. Engrs., Water Pollution Control Fedn., Internat. Soc. Humic Substances, Assn. Environ. Engring. Profs., Am. Water Works Assn. (publs. award 1989), Am. Chem. Soc. Achievements include patents in field. Office: Georgia Inst Tech 800 W Peachtree St Ste 400 A-H Atlanta GA 30332-0595

CROCKER, BILL (WILLIAM R. CROCKER), lawyer; b. 1936; m. Donna Crocker; children: Cindy Crocker Asche, Will. BBA, Baylor U., 1958, LLB, 1960. Bar: Tex. 1961, US Dist. Ct. (northern dist.) Tex. 1961, US Dist. Ct. (eastern dist.) Tex. 1963. Pvt. practice atty., Austin, Tex.; nat. committeeman for Tex. Republican Nat. Com. (RNC), 2004—13, mem. Rules Com. and Resolutions Com., 2004—13, gen. counsel, 2011—13. Chief counsel Tex. Office Consumer Credit Commr., 1967—69; exec. dir. Tex. Motor Vehicle Commn., 1971—74. Chmn. Eastland County Republican Party, 1961—62; pres. Smith County Young Republicans, 1963—64; chmn. Resolutions Com. 14th Senatorial Dist. Conv., 1996; vice chmn. Travis County Republican Party, 1996; precinct chmn., election judge Travis County Precinct 256, 1998, 2000, 2002, 2004; chmn. Audit Com. Republican Party of Tex., 2003; del. Republican Nat. Conv., 2004; pres. Baylor U. Alumni Assn., 1976, 1981, v.p., 1978—80. Mem.: NRA (life), Federalist Soc., Travis County Bar Assn., State Bar Tex. (chmn. Comsumer Credit Law Sect.). Republican. Avocations: hunting, fishing, birdwatching, photography, travel, reading. Office: 807 Brazos St # 1014 Austin TX 78701-2508*

CROCKER, RYAN CLARK, dean, former ambassador; b. Spokane, Wash., June 19, 1949; m. Christine Barnes. BA in English, Whitman Coll., 1971; postgraduate student, Univ. Coll., Dublin, Ireland; LLD (hon.), Gonzaga U., 2009; PhD in Nat. Security Affairs (hon.), Nat. Def. U., 2010; LLD (hon.), Seton Hall U., 2012; LHD (hon.), American U. Afghanistan, 2013. Fgn. svc. officer US Consulate, Khorramshahr, Iran, 1972—74; econ. comml. officer US Embassy, Doha, 1974—76, chief econ./comml. sect. US interests sect. Baghdad, 1978—80, chief polit. sect. Beirut, 1981-84, polit. counselor Cairo, 1987-90; dep. dir. Office Israel & Arab-Israeli Affairs US Dept. State, Washington, 1985-87, US amb. to Lebanon Beirut, 1990-93, US amb. to Kuwait Kuwait City, 1994-97, US amb. to Syria Damascus, 1998—2001, interim envoy to Afghanistan Kabul, Afghanistan, 2002, dep. asst. sec. for Near Eastern Affairs Washington, 2001—03; dir. governance Coalition Provisional Authority, Baghdad, Iraq, 2003; internat. affairs adv. Nat. War Coll., 2003—04; US amb. to Pakistan US Dept. State, Islamabad, 2004—07, US amb. to Iraq Baghdad, 2007—09; dean, exec. prof. George Bush Sch. Govt. & Public Svc. Tex. A&M U., College Station, Tex., 2010—11, 2012—; US amb. to Afghanistan US Dept. State, Kabul, 2011—12. Mem. US Advisory Commn. on Diplomacy, 2010—, Broadcasting Bd. Govs., 2013—, Spl. Com. on the Future of Shortwave Broadcasting, 2013—; Kissinger sr. fellow Yale U., 2012—13; James Schlesinger Disting. Vis. prof. U. Va., 2013—; bd. dirs. Mercy Corps., 2013—. Trustee Whitman Coll. Recipient Presdl. Disting. Svc. award, 1994, Disting. Civilian Svc. award, US Dept. Def., 1997, 2008, Secretary's Disting. Svc. award, US Dept. State, 2008, 2012, Presdl. Medal of Freedom, The White House, 2009, Donovan award, Nat. Clandestine Svc., 2009, Marshall medal, Assn. US Army, 2011, Dir. Ctrl. Intelligence's Director's award, 2012, Allama Sayed Jamaluddin medal, Govt. of Afghanistan, 2012, Robert C. Frasure Meml. award for Exceptional Courage & Leadership, Rivkin award, American Fgn. Svc. Assn., Disting. Honor award, US Dept. State, Superior Honor awards (3); named an Honorary Marine, USMC, 2012. Mem.: Assn. American Ambassadors, American Acad. Diplomacy, Coun. Fgn. Relations. Office: Bush School Government & Public Service Texas A&M U 4220 TAMU Allen 2132A College Station TX 77843 Office Phone: 979-862-8007. Office Fax: 979-845-4155. E-mail: rcrocker@tamu.edu.*

CROCKETT, DODEE FROST, brokerage house executive; b. Oklahoma City, Oct. 19, 1956; d. Carl S. Frost and Mikki (Matheny) Marcus; m. Billy Crockett. M in Theol. Studies, So. Meth. U., Dallas, 2003. Chartered advisor in philantropy 2005, cert. divorce fin. analyst 2006. M.D., mng. dir., wealth mgmt. advisor Merrill Lynch Global Wealth Mgmt., Dallas, 1980—. Bd. dirs. Ronald McDonald House of Dallas, 1992—2002, Dallas Social Venture Ptnrs., 2003—, chair of bd., 2005; trustee Dallas Opera, 1991—2004, vice-chmn., 2012-13; vice-chair, exec. bd. Perkins Sch. Theology, So. Meth. U., Dallas, 2003- centennial campaign co-chair; adv. bd. Dallas Found.; pres. Cir. Shared Housing Ctr., Dallas; adv. bd. Ctr. Family Compass, Dallas, 1994-. Recipient Spirit of Compassion award, 2008, Merrill Lynch David Brady award, 2009, Dallas Womens Found. Power Purse Advisor award, 2011; named one of The Top 100 Women Fin. Advisors, Barron's, 2006—13, Top Ten Advisor North Tex., Dallas Bus. Jour., 2009—13, Barron's Top 1000 Advisors, 2009—14. Mem. Nat. Assn. Securities Dealers (gen. securities prin., mcpl. securities rulemaking bd. prin., registered options prin., bd. arbitrators), NYSE (com. mem.), Merrill Lynch Cir. of Champions. Office: Merrill Lynch Pierce Fenner and Smith 2000 Premier Pl 5910 N Central Expy Ste 2000 Dallas TX 75206-5152 Home: 333 Loneman Overlook Wimberley TX 78676

CROCKETT, JOHN R., III, lawyer; BA, U. NC, 1986; JD, U. Ky., 1990. Bar: Ky. 1980, Ky. State Ct., Fed. Ct. Ky., US Dist. Ct. (so. dist.) Ind. Ptnr. Frost Brown Todd LLC, Louisville, chmn. of firm. Former bd. mem. Bingham Child Guidance Ctr.; bd. dirs. Harmony Landing Country Club, 1998—2001, 2004—08, pres., 2000—01; bd. dirs. Family and Children's Pl., 2003—, pres., 2006—09; bd. dirs. Greater Louisville, Inc., 2009—; mem. steering com. 21st Century Parks, 2009—. Named one of The Best Lawyers in America, 2008—11; named to Ky. Super Lawyers, Personal Injury Def.: Products, 2010. Mem.: ABA, Ky. Bar Assn., Louisville Bar Assn. Office: Frost Brown Todd LLC 400 W Market St Ste 3200 Louisville KY 40202-3363 Office Phone: 502-568-0258. Office Fax: 502-581-1087. Business E-Mail: jcrockett@fbtlaw.com.

CROCKETT-STARK, ANNE B., state legislator; b. Wytheville, Va., Dec. 12, 1942; m. Carl E. Stark; children: Anne C. Carney, Susan C. Aker. BS in English/Pub. Speaking, Radford U., 1969, MS Communication/Coll. Guidance, 1979; post grad. studies, Va. Poly Inst. & State U. Ret. tchr. and guidance counselor Wythe County Schools, Wytheville, Va.; councilwoman Wytheville Town Coun., 1978—82; counselor, Title III student orgns. liaison, instr. Wytheville

CC, 1980-83; chmn. town sect. VML State Bd., 1980—82; with Wythe County Bd. Suprs., 1999—2005, chmn., 2003, VACO State Bd. Dirs., 2003—05; mem. Dist. 6 Va. House of Dels., 2006—; mem. Edn. Com., Counties Com., Cities & Towns Com., Sci. & Tech. Com., 2006—. Co-chair Wythe County Jamestown 2001 Cmty. Com.; lay minister Holy Trinity Lutheran Ch. Recipient Nat. Jaycette's Woman in Govt. award, 1981. Mem.: Wythe-Bland C. of C., Wythe County Hist. Soc., Wilderness Road DAR, Wythe County Genealogical Soc., Quota Club Internat. (past pres.), Order of Eastern Star, Alpha Delta Kappa (past pres.). Republican. Office: PO Box 628 Wytheville VA 24382 Office Phone: 276-227-0247. Office Fax: 276-227-0248. Business E-Mail: DelACrockett-Stark@house.virginia.gov.

CROFT, CHARLES, cardiologist; MD, U. Cape Town, 1973. Diplomate Am. Bd. Internal Medicine, 1982, Am. Bd. Internal Medicine-cardiovasc. disease, 1983, Am. Bd. Internal Medicine-interventional cardiology, lic. Fla. Physician Holmes Regional Ctr. Office: Holmes Regional Medical Ctr 1350 S Hickory St Melbourne FL 32901-3276 Office Phone: 321-434-7000.

CROFT, GEORGE T., physicist; b. Washington, Sept. 29, 1926; s. William Thomas and Georgietta (Lyon) C.; m. Geraldine Frizzel (div. Feb. 1995); children: Linda Marie, David Thomas, John Frizzell Croft; m. Nancy Mitchell, Aug. 14, 1996. BS in Physics, Western Md. Coll., Westminster, 1948; PhD in Physics, U. Pa., 1953. Rsch. physicist McGraw-Edison, West Orange, N.J., 1953-58; dir. R&D and staff engring. Pitney Bowes, Stamford, Conn., 1958-70; v.p. corp. R&D and staff engring. Addressograph-Multigraph, Cleve., 1970-76; v.p. R&D Am. Optical, Southbridge, Mass., 1976-80; pres. Technol. Resources Mgmt. Group, Hilton Head Island, S.C., 1980-87; dir. Coll. of Hilton Head U. S.C., Hilton Head Island, 1983-85; instr. physics and math. Savannah (Ga.) Tech. Inst., 1987-95; asst. adj. prof. physics U. S.C., Beaufort, 1995—. Pres. Intellectual Resources Group, Inc., 1992—; mem. adv. coun. to dean engring. U. Mass., Amherst, 1978-83; mem. R&D coun. Am. Mgmt. Assn., 1975-1980; mem. corp. assoc. adv. com. Am. Phys. Soc., 1977-80. Author: Three Dimensional Analytic Geometry, 2000, Applications of Three Dimensional Analytic Geometry, 2002, An Alternative Theory of Global Warming & Cooling, 2009; contbr. articles to profl. jours. Served with USNR, 1945-46, PTO. Mem. IEEE, Am. Phys. Soc. Achievements include staffing and organizing 3 research and development labs and establishing product development and related research programs in them; product development in office equipment and optical equipment industries; patents on safe hand gun locks. Home: 22 Coventry Ct Bluffton SC 29910-5706

CROFT, HARRY ALLEN, psychiatrist; b. Houston, July 2, 1943; s. Louis and Ida (Kaplan) C.; m. Benay Bleacher, Dec. 27, 1964; children: Jamie Sue, Bradley Lane, Chasen Ashley. BS, So. Meth. U., 1964; MD, U. Tex. at Galveston, 1968. Intern Brackenridge Hosp., Austin, 1968-69; resident in obstetrics and gynecology U. Tex. Med. Br., 1969-70, resident in psychiatry, 1970-73; dir. methadone program Galveston County, Tex.; dir. sex therapy program U. Tex., Galveston, 1972-73; commd. capt. U.S. Army, 1973, advanced through grades to maj., 1975; chief (Mental Hygiene Service, Brooke Army Med. Center), Houston, 1973-76; pvt. practice, 1976—; med. dir. San Antonio Psychiat. Rsch. Ctr., 1988—. Clin. asst. prof. psychiatry and ob-gyn. Med. Sch. San Antonio, 1973-75; columnist San Antonio Express-News, 1975-76; weekly contbr. Sta. KMOL-TV (NBC) newscast, also KENS TV, 1988-90, KMOL TV, 1990-92; dir. rsch. and edn. Covenant Behavioral Health; med. dir. Healthy Pl.; host Healthy Pl. TV Show 2007-. Contbr. articles to profl. jours. Recipient physician's recognition award AMA, 1974, awards for med. TV work Nat. Healthcare Assn., 1988, Women in Comm., 1988; Meritorious Svc. medal U.S. Army, 1976, Ware 1st place audio-visual award Dept. Army, 1976, Gov.'s award State of Tex., 1991, award City of San Antonio, award Acad. Radio and TV Health Comm., Jules Bergman award-Broadcaster of Yr. award, 1995, Best Radio Show In U.S., Nat. Mental Health Assn., 1996; named Honoree, Am. Heart Assn., 2003. Mem. Am. Psychiat. Assn. (award 1991), Tex. Med. Assn. (award 1988), Am. Soc. Sex Educators, Counselors and Therapists, Am. Soc. Addiction Medince (cert. addictionist). Home: 12738 Hunters Chase St San Antonio TX 78230-1930 Office: 8038 Wurzbach Rd Ste 570 San Antonio TX 78229-3815 Home Phone: 210-602-9418; Office Phone: 210-692-1222. Personal E-mail: hacmd@aol.com.

CROFT, TERRENCE LEE, lawyer, mediator, arbitrator; b. St. Louis, Apr. 13, 1940; s. Thomas L. and Anita Belle Croft; m. Merry Patton, July 9, 1977; children: Michael, Shannon, Kimberly, Kristin, Benjamin, Katherine. AB, Yale U., 1962; JD with distinction, U. Mich. Law Sch., 1965. Bar: Mo. 1965, Ga. 1970, Fla. 1970, US Ct. Appeals (5th, 8th and 11th cirs.), US Supreme Ct. Assoc. Coburn, Croft & Kohn, St. Louis, 1965—69, Hansell, Post, Brandon & Dorsey, Atlanta, 1969—73; ptnr. Huie, Sterne & Ide, Atlanta, 1973—78, Kutak, Rock & Huie, Atlanta, 1978—83; shareholder Griffin, Cochrane & Marshall, Atlanta, 1983—93; ptnr. King & Croft LLP, Atlanta, 1994—2012. Mediator & arbitrator, resolution expert JAMS, 2009—; owner Croft ADR, Atlanta, 2013—. Named one of Top 100 Lawyers Ga., Ga. Super Lawyers., Best Lawyers ADR. Fellow: Am. Coll. Civil Trial Mediators, Internat. Acad. Mediators (disting. fellow); mem.: ABA (ho. of dels. 1993-99), State Bar Ga. (bd. govs. 2002-, chair alt. dispute resolution sect.), Atlanta Bar Assn. (pres., sec., treas. bd. dirs. 1986-99, chmn., bd. dirs. litig. sect. 1982-86, 2010-, pres. Alt. Dispute Resolution Lawyers sect. 1996-97, Charles Watkins award 1996, Distinguished Svc. award 2007), Atlanta Bar Found. (pres. 1998-2003), Ga. Trial Lawyers Assn., Atlanta Internat. Arbitration Soc., Lawyers Club Atlanta, Old War Horse Lawyers Club. Episcopalian. Avocations: walking, shooting, motorcycling, reading. Home: 2580 Westminster Heath NW Atlanta GA 30327-1449 Office: Croft ADR 707 The Candler Bldg 127 Peachtree St NE Atlanta GA 30303-1810 Home Phone: 404-609-9011; Office Phone: 404-577-8400. Office Fax: 404-577-8401. Business E-Mail: tlc@croftadr.com.

CROMBIE, NICHOLAS E., retail executive; Dir., sales and mktg., gen. merchandising mgr. Lechmere, Inc., 1988—96; regional v.p. Caldor, Inc., 1996—99; area v.p., Mid-South CVS, 1999—2002; zone v.p., stores Michaels Stores, Inc, 2002—07; exec. v.p., Store Ops. Michaels Stores, Inc., 2007—. Office: Michaels Stores Inc 8000 Bent Branch Dr Irving TX 75063 Office Phone: 972-409-1300. Office Fax: 972-409-1556. Business E-Mail: CrombieN@michaels.com.

CROMER, GEORGE GREGORY, state legislator; BS in Indsl. Mgmt. Tech., Southeastern La. U., 1981. Employee Lockheed Martin, NASA Michoud Assembly Facility, New Orleans; mem. Dist. 90 La. House of Reps., 2008—, mem. civil law and procedure com., house and govtl. affairs com., house exec. com. Republican. Office: PO Box 2088 Slidell LA 70459 also: Capitol Office PO Box 44486 Baton Rouge LA 70804 Office Phone: 985-645-3592, 225-342-6945. Office Fax: 985-645-3594. E-mail: cromerg@legis.state.la.us.

CROMER, RONNIE W., state legislator; b. Newberry, SC, Dec. 1, 1947; m. Linda Cromer; children: Candice, Heather. BS in Pharmacy, U. SC, 1973. Pharmacist, 1973—; mem. Dist. 18 SC State Senate, 2004—, chair Fish, Game and Forestry Com., mem. Banking and Ins. Com., Fin. Com., Gen. Com., Invitations Com. & Rules Com. Republican. Lutheran. Office: 305 Gressette Bldg Columbia SC 29201 Mailing: PO Box 378 Prosperity SC 29127 Home Phone: 803-364-3950; Office Phone: 803-212-6330. Business E-Mail: CROMERR@scsenate.org.

CRONCE, PAUL CALVIN, retired dermatologist; b. Trenton, NJ, Dec. 25, 1931; s. Paul I. and Rachie Cathryn (Allen) C.; m. Nancy Elizabeth Dorrien, Aug. 27, 1960 (div. Aug. 1979); children: Paul Allen, Charles Scott, Thomas Taylor. BA summa cum laude, Duke U., Durham, NC, 1954; postgrad., Duke U. Grad. Sch. Arts & Scis., Durham, NC, 1954—55; MD, Duke U. Sch. Medicine, Durham, NC, 1960. Diplomate Am. Bd. Dermatology, 1965. Rotating med. intern USPHS Hosp., Boston, 1960-61; acting dermatology resident USPHS Hosp., Staten Island, 1961—62, dermatology resident, 1962—65, asst. chief dermatology, 1965—66; vis. fellow in dermatology Columbia-Presbyn. Med. Ctr., NYC, 1964-65; ptnr. Alden & Cronce Dermatology, Atlanta, 1966-73; pres. and treas. Alden Dermatology Assocs., P.A., Atlanta, 1973-99; ret., 1999. Instr. medicine, dermatology Emory U. Sch. Medicine, 1967-71, asst. clin. prof. dermatology, 1971-78, assoc. clin. prof. dermatology, 1978-89, clin. prof. dermatology, 1989-2001, prof. emeritus dermatology, 2001-. Contbr. articles to profl. jours. Fellow Am. Acad. Dermatology; mem. Southeastern Dermatological Assn., Ga. Soc. Dermatologists (vice chmn. 1971), Med. Assn. Ga., Internat. Soc. Dermatologic Surgery, Atlanta Dermatological Assn. (sec.-treas. 1967, pres. 1968), Med. Assn. Atlanta, Phi Beta Kappa, Alpha Omega Alpha. Republican. Presbyterian. Avocations: travel, gardening.

CRONE, MARCIA ANN, federal judge; b. Dallas, Dec. 12, 1952; d. Dan Moody and Marian Louise (Stewart) Cain; m. W. Seth Crone, Jr., Aug. 30, 1986; children: Kimball Montclair, Kirby Armitage. BA summa cum laude, Univ. of Tex., Austin, 1973; JD summa cum laude, Univ. of Houston, 1978. Bar: Tex. 1979, D.C. 1982. With Andrews Kurth LLP, 1978-92; magistrate judge So. Dist. Tex., Houston, 1992—2003; US dist. judge Ea. Dist. Tex., Beaumont, 2003—. Methodist. Office: US Dist Ct 300 Willow St Ste 239 Beaumont TX 77701-2200

CRONENWETT, LINDA R., dean, educator, hospital administrator; BSN, U. Mich., 1966, PhD in Nursing, 1983; MSN in Maternal-Child Nursing, U. Washington, 1970. Dir. profl. nursing, dir. nursing rsch. and edn. Mary Hitchcock Meml. Hosp., Lebanon, NH, Dartmouth-Hitchcock Med. Ctr., Lebanon; mem. faculty U. Mich., U. NH, Dartmouth U.; Sarah Frances Russell disting. prof. nursing systems U. NC Sch. Nursing, 1998—99, prof., dean, 1999—; chief nursing officer academic affairs U. NC Chapel Hill Hospitals, 2003—. Bd. dirs. Inst. Healthcare Improvement, NC Inst. Medicine; nat. adv. com., Transforming Care at the Bedside Project Robert Wood Johnson-IHI; pres. NC Deans and Dirs. Baccalaureate and Higher Degree Nursing Programs, NH Nurses Assn.; mem. NIH Nat. Adv. Coun. Nursing Rsch.; chair ANA Congress Nursing Practice. Mem. editl. bd. Jour. Nursing Measurement; contbr. articles to profl. hours. Served with USN Nurse Corps. Recipient Disting. Profl. Svc. award Assn. Women's Health, Obstetric and Neonatal Nurses, 1993, Disting. Scholar Nursing award NYU, 1997, NH Nursing Leadership award, Disting. Contbn. to Nursing Rsch. award Eastern Nursing Rsch. Soc., Dissemination award Sigma Theta Tau. Fellow Am. Acad. Nursing (sec.), Nat. Academies of Practice. Office: Univ NC Sch Nursing Carrington Hall CB 7460 Chapel Hill NC 27599-7460 Office Phone: 919-966-3731. Business E-Mail: lincron@email.unc.edu.

CRONIN, CAROLINE, information technology executive; BS in Acctg., Florida State U., MBA. CPA. CFO Optio Software, corp. contr.; asst. corp. contr. Med. Mgr. Corp.; sr. acct. Coopers and Lybrand; v.p. fin. Jacada, 2008, CFO, 2011—. Office: Jacada Incorporated 400 Perimeter Center Terrace Suite 100 Atlanta GA 30346 Office Phone: 770-352-1300. Office Fax: 770-352-1313.

CRONIN, JUSTIN, writer, English professor; b. 1962; BA in English and Am. Lit., Harvard U., 1984; MFA, U. Iowa Writers' Workshop, 1989. Creative writing prof., author in-residence La Salle U., Phila., 1992—2005; prof. English Rice U., Houston. Author: (novels) Mary and O'Neil, 2001 (PEN/Hemingway award, 2002, Stephen Crane prize), The Summer Guest, 2005, The Passage, 2010, The Twelve, 2012. Recipient Whiting Writers' award, 2002; grantee Pew Fellowship in the Arts, 2001, Nat. Endowment Arts Fellowship in Fiction, 2004. Office: Rice U Herring Hall 324 6100 Main St Houston TX 77005 Office Phone: 713-348-4582. E-mail: jccronin@rice.edu.

CROOM, FREDERICK HAILEY, academic administrator, mathematician, educator; b. Lumberton, NC, Aug. 6, 1941; s. Robert DeVane and Anna Rosalyn (Currie) Croom; m. Henrietta Brown, Aug. 17, 1963 (div. May 2000); children: Elizabeth Bonner, Frederick Hailey; m. Nancy Mishoe Brennecke, June 1, 2002; children: Alexander McMillan, Augustus Brennecke. BS, U. N.C., 1963, PhD, 1967. Asst. prof. math. U. Ky., Lexington, 1967-71, U. of the South, Sewanee, Tenn., 1971-74, assoc. prof., 1974-81, prof., 1981—, dir. Summer Sch., 1980-88, assoc. dean, 1984-88, provost, 1989-2001. Author: (book) Basic Concepts of Algebraic Topology, 1978, Principles of Topology, 1989. Pres. Tenn. Coll. Assn., 1999—2000; bd. dirs. St. Andrews-Sewanee Sch., 1981—86, Tenn. Found. Ind. Colls., 1996—99; trustee U. of the South, 1983—85. Fellow Woodrow Wilson, 1963, NSF, 1963—67. Mem.: AAUP, Mat. Assn. Am., Am. Math. Soc., Sigma Xi. Episcopalian. Office: U South University Ave Sewanee TN 37383-0001 Office Phone: 931-598-3385. Business E-Mail: fcroom@sewanee.edu.

CROOM, HENRIETTA BROWN, retired biology professor; b. Burlington, NC, Sept. 23, 1940; d. Grady Anderson and Emma Mabel (Cheek) Brown; children: Elizabeth Bonner, Frederick H. Jr. AB in Chemistry, U. NC, 1962, PhD in Biochemistry, 1968. Rsch. assoc. U. Ky., Lexington, 1969-70; asst. prof. U. of the South, Sewanee, Tenn., 1972-82, assoc. prof., 1982-88, prof. biology, 1988—2008, chair, 1993—96, co-chair, biochemistry, 2003—05. Vis. prof. microbiology La. State U., Baton Rouge, 1977-78; vis. scholar Vanderbilt U., Nashville, 1981-82, U. Hawaii-Manoa, Honolulu, 1989-90, U. Ky., Lexington, 1989. Dist. commr. U.S. Pony Clubs, Sewanee, 1973-76; bd. advisers St. Andrews-Sewanee Sch., 1986—; leader Girl Scouts US, Sewanee, 1971-72; rsch. assoc. Bishop Mus., Honolulu, 2005-07. Recipient Sci. Tng. Program award NSF, 1973-77, Faculty Devel. award Mellon Found., 1981-82, Rsch. Opportunity award NSF, 1989, rsch. grant Bishop Rsch. Inst., Honolulu, 1990, rsch. grant NSF, 1991—; named Pew fellow Faculty Scholars Program, Lexington, 1988, 90. Mem. Am. Soc. Cell Biology, Soc. Study Evolution, Phi Beta Kappa, Sigma Xi. Democrat. Episcopalian. Avocations: horseback riding, hiking. Home: 247 Hales Wood Rd Chapel Hill NC 27517 Home Phone: 919-537-8601.

CROOM, SYLVESTER, professional football coach; b. Tuscaloosa, Ala., Sept. 25, 1954; m. Jeri Croom; 1 child, Jennifer. BA in History, U. Ala., 1975, MA in Ednl. Adminstrn., 1977. Ctr. New Orleans Saints, 1975; grad. asst. U. Ala. Crimson Tide, 1976, linebackers coach, 1977—86; running backs coach Tampa Bay Buccaneers, 1987—90, Indpls. Colts, 1991, San Diego Chargers, 1992—96; offensive coord. Detroit Lions, 1997—2000; running backs coach Green Bay Packers, 2001—03; head football coach Miss. State U. Bulldogs, 2003—08; running backs coach St. Louis Rams, 2009—11, Jacksonville Jaguars, 2012—. Named Southeastern Conf. Coach of Yr., 2007. Office: Jacksonville Jaguars One Stadium Pl Jacksonville FL 32202

CROSBY, JOHN DICKEY, state legislator; b. Nov. 30; m. Rose Crosby; 2 children. Atty., 1963—80; Tifton Co. Commr., 1971—78; judge State Ct., 1971—78, Tift Superior Ct., Ga., 1980—2000; mem. Dist. 13 Ga. State Senate, 2008—; sec. Ethics. Com. Republican. Office: 302-A Coverdell Legislative Office Bldg Atlanta GA 30334 also: PO Box 891 Tifton GA 31793 Office Phone: 404-463-5258. Office Fax: 404-657-0459. Business E-Mail: John.Crosby@senate.ga.gov.

CROSBY, WILLIAM E., state legislator; b. Charleston, SC, Nov. 29; s. Miner and Maude Crosby; m. Marvel Jean Crosby, Apr. 12, 1958; children: Kenny Crosby, Kevin Crosby, Kim Ahl Crosby. Attended, Inst. Comm. Studies, 1962; grad., Trident Tech. Coll., 1967. Mem. Assn. of Met. Planning Orgns. (AMPO); vice chmn. Berkeley County Election Commn.; mem. Berkeley County Sch. Strategic Planning Team; chmn. Charleston Area Transp. Study (CHATS), Com. on Justice and Pub. Safety; mem. Elks; pres. Goose Creek Civic Club; dir., trustees Goose Creek Exch. Club; chmn. Goose Creek Recreation Commn., Regional Special Purpose Dist. Commn.; mem. SC Assn. of Counties (SCAC); bd. dirs. St. Timothy Luth. Ch.; mem. Task Force of Trident 2000; bd. dirs. YMCA; vice chmn. Berkeley County Coun., 1997—2009; mem. Dist. 117 SC House of Representatives, 2011—. Republican. Office: South Carolina House of Representatives District 117 310D Blatt Bldg Columbia SC 29201 Address: 2680 Hanford Mills Ln North Charleston SC 29406 Office Phone: 803-212-6879.

CROSIER, GERALD L., state legislator; b. Union, W.Va., Dec. 11, 1933; married; 3 children. Former sheriff Monroe County, W.Va.; mem. Dist.26 W.Va. House of Delegates, 2002—, vice chmn. Natural Resources Com. With US Army. Democrat. Presbyterian. Office: 1900 Kanawha Blvd E, Rm 230E Charleston WV 25305 Mailing: PO Box 52 Union WV 24983 E-mail: gcrosier@mail.wvnet.edu.

CROSS, ALVIN MILLER (AL CROSS), journalist; b. Knoxville, Tenn, Apr. 24, 1954; s. Perry Martin and Winnie Cook Miller C.; m. Patricia Hodges, June 19, 1976. BA in Mass Comm., Western Ky. U., 1978; postgrad., Poynter Inst. Media Studies, 1999. Sports reporter Clinton County News, Albany, Ky., 1965—71; announcer WANY Radio, Albany, 1968-75; advt. mgr., reporter, editor College Heights Herald, Bowling Green, Ky., 1973-74; editor and gen. mgr. The Reporter, Monticello, Ky., 1974-75; asst. mng. editor Logan Leader & News-Democrat, Russellville, Ky., 1975-77; editor Leitchfield Gazette, Grayson County News-Gazette, Ky., 1977-78; reporter Courier-Journal, Louisville, 1978-88, polit. writer, 1989—2004, polit. columnist, 1999—; dir. Inst. for Rural Journalism and Cmty. Issues U. Ky., Lexington, 2004—. Contbg. author: Campaigns and Elections: Contemporary Case Studies, 2002, Kentucky Governors, 2004, Kentucky 24/7, 2004. Rep. acad. coun. Associated Student Govt. We. Ky. U., 1972-73; bd. dirs. Sigma Delta Chi Found, 2001—. Recipient Founder's award Foothills Festival Inc., Albany, 1989, Outstanding Print Journalist in Ky. and Adjoining States award journalism dept. Western Ky. U., 1995, Deadline Reporting award Metro Louisville Journalism, 1989, 92, Column Writing award, 1989, 2004, Continuing Coverage award, 1992, 95, East Ky. Leadership Found. Media award, 2009, First Amendment award, Ky. Coun. Tchrs. English, 2006; Named to Ky. Journalism hall of Fame, 2010 Mem. Soc. Profl. Journalists (regional dir. 1987-89, v.p. Louisville chpt. 1983-84, pres. 1984-85, chmn. nat. com. Project Watchdog 1995-99, nat. sec.-treas. 1999-2000, pres.-elect 2000-01, pres. 2001-02, Outstanding Newspaper in Region 5 award 1974, Outstanding Ky. Journalist 2005), Ky. Hist. Soc., Appalachian Studies Assn., Filson Hist. Soc, Com. Concerned Journalists, Internat. Soc. Weekly Newspaper Editors, Assn. for Edn. in Journalism and Mass. Comm., Nat. Newspaper Assn., Western Ky. U. Alumni Assn. Baptist. Avocations: reading, gardening, boating, touring, political memorabilia collecting. Home: 123 W Todd St Frankfort KY 40601-2825 Office: U Ky 122 Grehan Bldg Lexington KY 40506-0042 Office Phone: 859-257-3744. E-mail: al.cross@uky.edu.

CROSS, EASON, JR., architect; b. Bisbee, Ariz., Nov. 14, 1925; s. Eason and Olive (Hardwick) C.; m. Diana Johnson, June 17, 1950; children: Ben, Becca, Amy, Susan. BA, Harvard U., 1949, MArch, 1951. Assoc. Charles M. Goodman, Washington, 1952-59, Keyes, Lethbridge & Condon, 1959-61; ptnr. Cross & Adreon, Arlington, Va., 1961-87; pres. Va. Architects Accord P.C., Alexandria, 1989—2009; prin. Cross Assocs., Alexandria, Va., 1987—2012. Author: The Boy Boy and Me, 2008. Pres. Hollin Hills Cmty. Assn., 1978; chmn. Fairfax County Appeals Bd., 1970-80; pres. Old Dominion DESA, 1997-98, Purysburg Preservation Found., 1998-2007. QM 3/C USNR, 1943—46, WWII. Recipient Ware prize, 1950, Washington Bd. Trade design award, 1965, Bethesda-Chevy Chase C. of C. design awards, 1966, 67; House and Home awards AIA, 1965-66; Mid-Atlantic Region design awards, 1967, 69; Nat. Honor award, 1968; Nat. Honor award Am. inst. Steel Constrn., 1967; 4 awards HUD-Washington Ctr. Urban Studies furniture competition, 1971; Frameworks Home Design Merit award, 1995; Fairfax County Exceptional Design award 1985, 87, N.V. CAA Design award 1999. Fellow AIA, Housing Competition ADPSR winner 1993; mem. Va. Soc. AIA (Energy award 1979, Design award 1986, Noland medal 1994), Fox Club, Ga. Salzburger Soc. Purysburg Found. Episcopalian. Achievements include patents for fastenings and furniture.

CROSS, J. BRUCE, lawyer; b. Sharon, Pa., Oct. 6, 1949; s. John Lantz and Agnes (Bruce) C.; m. Joy Cross; children: Lantz Davis, Heather Lynn. BA, U. Notre Dame, Ind., 1971; JD, U. Ark., Fayetteville, 1974. Bar: Ark. 1974, US Ct. Appeals (8th cir.) 1979, US Supreme Ct. 1980. Ptnr. House, Holmes and Jewell, Little Rock, 1974-90, Cross and Gunter, P.A., Little Rock, 1990, McGlinchey Stafford Lang, Little Rock, 1991-97, Cross, Gunter, Witherspoon & Galchus, P.C., Little Rock, 1997—. Chpt. atty. Ark. Subcontractors Assn., Little Rock, 1987-90; mem. young execs. coun. Associated Gen. Contractors, 1989. Contbr. to profl. publs. Active Big Bros. Ark., Little Rock, 1976-87; pres., bd. dirs. Ark. divsn. Nat. Soc. to Prevent Blindness, 1987-90; bd. dirs. Urban League Ark., 1989, Ark. Constrn. Edn. Found., Boy Scouts Am., 2004-08, Single Parent Scholarship Fund of Pulaski County, 2004-08, pres., 2007; nat. bd. dirs. Associated Builders and Contractors Am., 1999-;chmn. Nat. Legis. Com., 2008; active Leadership Hot Springs, Habitat for Humanity, Youth Home; bd. dirs. Single Parent Scholarship Fund, 2005-06, Mus. of Discovery, 2005-08, exec. com., Jr. Achievement Ark., 2005-08, exec. com. Recipient Pres.'s award Nat. Soc. to Prevent Blindness, Am. Hospitality Assn., 2003. Mem. Ark. Hospitality Assn. (bd. dirs. 1988-89), Ark. Subcontractors Assn., Assoc. Bldrs. and Contrs. Ark. (pres. 1999-2000, bd. dir. 1999-2007), Ark. Bar Assn. (past chmn. labor sect.), Ark. Ready Mixed Concrete Assn., Little Rock C. of C. (ptnrs. in edn. com. 1989-90), ABA (sect. labor and employment law com. on labor arbitration and the law of collective bargaining agreements 1981-99, com. on devel. of the law under the NLRA 2000—), Greater Hot Springs C. of C., Leadership Hot Springs, Notre Dame Club Ark.

(pres.). Roman Catholic. Office: Cross, Gunter, Witherspoon & Galchus PC 500 President Clinton Ave Ste 200 Little Rock AR 72201-1747 Business E-Mail: bcross@cgwg.com.

CROSSNO, RONALD J., health services company executive, physician; BS in Zoology, Tex. A&M U., 1977; MD, U. Tex. Med. Sch., San Antonio, 1981. Part-time med. dir. cmty-based hospice, Tex.; regional med. dir. VistaCare, 2002—08; nat. med. dir. Odyssey Healthcare, 2008—11; sr. nat. med. dir. hospice divsn. Gentiva Health Services, Austin, 2011—. Mem. speaker's bur. American Med. Dir. Assn. Inst. Long-Term Care; mem. ethics com., bd. mem. Tex. Pain and Advocacy Info. Network. Fellow: American Acad. Hospice and Palliative Medicine (mem. edn. com. 2004—06, mem. hospice med. dir. course planning com. 2005, co-chmn. rural spl. interest group steering com. 2005—, mem. hospice-based physician edn. task force 2006, chmn. pub. policy com. 2006—07, co-chmn. long-term care spl. interest group steering com. 2006—07, dir.-at-large 2006—08, alt. del. to the AMA 2006—10, mem. pub. policy com. 2006—, treas. bd. dirs. 2008—09, pres. 2011—), American Acad. Physicians; mem.: Nat. Hospice and Palliative Care Orgn. (bd. dirs.), Tex. Med. Dir. Assn. (mem. pub. policy com.), American Med. Dir. Assn. (mem. pub. policy com.), Tex. Acad. Palliative Medicine (bd. dirs., chmn. edn. com.). Office: Gentiva Health Services Hospice Divsn 4201 W Parmer Ln Bldg C Ste 100 Austin TX 78727-4161 Office Fax: 512-310-9328.*

CROSSWHITE, MARK A., utilities executive; b. Decatur, Ala. Grad., Leadership Ala.; B, U. Ala., Huntsville, 1984; JD, U. Ala., 1987. Ptnr. Balch & Bingham LLP, Birmingham, Ala.; gen. counsel Southern Co., 2004, sr. v.p., 2004, counsel Ala. Power Co., 2006—08, sr. v.p. Ala. Power Co., 2006—08, exec. v.p. external affairs Ala. Power Co., 2008—10, CEO Gulf Power Co. Ala., 2011—, pres. Gulf Power Co., 2011—. Bd. dirs. U. Ala. Law Sch. Found., Laps for Cystic Fibrosis Found. Mem.: ABA (vice chair, electricity com. of pub. utility, comm. and transp. sect.), Fla. C. of C. (bd. dirs.), James Madison Inst. (bd. dirs.), Enterprise Fla. (bd. dirs.), Fla. Coun. of 100 (bd. dirs.), Edison Electric Inst. Legal Com. Office: Southern Company Gulf Power Company PO Box 830660 Birmingham AL 35283-0660 Office Phone: 800-225-5797.

CROTTY, JOHN T., investment advisor; BA in Econs., Grinnell Coll.; MBA, U. Chgo. V.p. planning and bus. devel. Am. Hosp. Supply Corp.; co-founder CroBern, Inc., 1986, former pres., CEO; mng. ptnr. CroBern Management Partnership LLP, 1986—. Bd. dirs. Owens & Minor, Inc., 1999—, Omnicare Inc., 2004—, non-exec. chmn., 2008—10. Office: Omnicare Inc 100 E Rivercenter Blvd Covington KY 41011

CROTTY, ROBERT BELL, minister; b. Dallas, Aug. 16, 1951; s. Willard and Betty (Bell) C.; m. Sarah (Smith), Mar. 8, 1980; children: Robert Edwin, Rebecca Bell. BA, Va. Mil. Inst., 1973; JD, U. Tex., 1976. Bar: Tex., 1976; US Dist. Ct. (no., so. and ea. dists.) Tex., 1977; US Ct. Appeals (5th cir.), 1978. Assoc. Akin, Gump, Strauss, Hauer, and Feld, Dallas, 1976-82, ptnr., 1983-92, hiring ptnr., 1988-91; prin. McKool Smith, P.C., Dallas, 1992-94; ptnr. Crotty & Johansen, LLP, Dallas, 1995—2005; pvt. practice Crotty Law Firm, Dallas, 2006—07; men's equipping dir. Watermark Cmty. Ch., Dallas, 2007—. Vis. bd. Va. Mil. Inst., 1995-99. Mem. Leadership Dallas, 1981; dir. Salesmanship Club, 1989—90, 1994—95, 2001—02, 2005—07, 2011—12, pres., 2005—06; dir. Va. Mil. Inst. Alumni Assn., 1991—95, Highland Pk. Ind. Sch. Dist. Edn. Found., 1991—97, 2004—, pres., 1997—2000; chmn. bd. dir. Salesmanship Club Youth & Family Ctr., Inc., 2001—02; chmn. G.T.E. Byron Nelson Classic, 1995; bd. dir. Goodwill Industries of Dallas, Inc., 2002—08; pres. Dallas Bus. League, 1983, Big Bros. Big Sisters Met. Dallas, 1987—88. First lt. US Army, 1976, first lt. USAR, 1973—81. Fellow Tex. Bar Found. (sustaining life), Dallas Bar Found. (sustaining life, pres. fellows 1999-2000); mem. Tex. Law Rev. Assn. (life), State Bar Tex. Avocations: reading, hunting, golf, bicycling. Office: Watermark Cmty Ch 7540 LBJ Freeway Dallas TX 75251 Personal E-mail: robertbcrotty@gmail.com.

CROUTHAMEL, THOMAS GROVER, SR., editor, consultant; b. Berkeley, Calif., Sept. 10, 1930; s. Martin Luther and Elizabeth (Grover) C.; m. Madalene Donati, Sept. 6, 1954; children: Thomas Grover Jr., Annalise. BS, Thiel Coll., 1953. Sr. drug investigator FDA, L.A. and Edison, N.J., 1958-81; pres. Thomas G. Crouthamel, Inc., Bradenton, Fla., 1981—; ptnr. Crouthamel & Crouthamel, Bradenton, 1983-93; treas. Crouthamel Enterprises, Inc., Liberty Hill, Tex., 1986-92; sr. editor Keystone Press, Bradenton, 1982—2008. Author: Auditing EtO, 1982, It's OK, 1986, A History of Trailer Estates, 1987; When the Unthinkable Happens, 1995; contbr. articles to profl. jours. Cubmaster Boy Scouts Am., Pomona, Calif., 1963, committeeman, Spotswood, N.J., 1968-76, adult adviser Explorer Post, 1976-79; trustee Spotswood Libr. Bd., 1970-79; co-leader Compassionate Friends, Sarasota, Fla., 1984-90, chpt. advisor, facilitator, Englewood, Fla., 1989-91. With U.S. Army, 1953-55. Mem. Internat. Narcotics Officers Assn., The Authors Guild, Toastmasters (pres. 1969-71), Masons (high priest local chpt. 1967), FDA Alumni Assn., T.E. Masonic Square Club (pres. 2002, 03), Am. Legion, VFW. Avocations: travel, reading, fishing. Office: PO Box 6163 Bradenton FL 34281-6163

CROW, HAROLD EUGENE, physician, educator; b. Farber, Mo., Jan. 17, 1933; s. Leslie J. and Laura L. (Sparks) C.; m. Mary Kay Krenke, July 5, 1974; children: Janet L., Jason P. BA in Chemistry, Park Coll., Parkville, 1955; MD, U. Mo., 1963. Diplomate Am. Bd. Family Practice, Am. Bd. Med. Examiners. Intern E.W. Sparrow Hosp., Lansing, Mich., 1963-64; pvt. practice medicine specializing in family practice Lansing, 1964-70; dir. family practice residency E.W. Sparrow Hosp., Lansing, Mich., 1970-82; chmn. dept. family and community medicine Sch. Medicine, U. Nev., Reno, 1982-87, dir. office Rural Health Sch. Medicine, 1984-87; med. dir. S.W. Med. Assocs., Reno, 1987-88; dir. Lynchburg (Va.) Family Practice Residency Program, 1988-96; patient advocate Cons. for Caring, Sun City Center, Fla., 1996—98; dir. Outer Banks Edn. and Program Devel. Project, East Carolina U. Sch. Medicine, Nags Head, NC, 1999—2004; tchr. and cmty. activist Sr. Cmty. Sun City Ctr. Dir. Outer Banks Edn. and Program Devel. Project. Developer non-rotational residency model for family practice tng., tng. model for rural med. practice; innovator computerized health info. systems for family physicians. Numerous civic activities. With US Army, 1955—57. Named to Hall of Fame, Sparrow Hosp. Sys., 2006. Mem.: MI Acad. Family Physicians, Am. Coll. Physician Exec. Presbyterian. Home: 408 Stoneham Dr Sun City Center FL 33573-5841 Office Phone: 813-634-7980. Personal E-mail: hecrow7@gmail.com.

CROW, MARY KURTZ, hematologist; MD, Baylor U., Waco, Tex., 1989. Lic. Tex., 1990, diplomate Am. Bd. Internal Medicine, 2002, Am. Bd. Internal Medicine-med. oncology, 2005, Am. Bd. Internal Medicine-hematology, 2006. Resident internal medicine coll. medicine Baylor Univ., Houston, 1989—92, fellow hematology and oncology coll. medicine, 1994—95; hosp. affiliations include Cypress Fairbanks Med. Ctr., Houston, Houston NW Med. Ctr. Office: Houston Northwest Medical Center 710 FM 1960 W Houston TX 77090 Office Phone: 281-586-0200.

CROW, TIMOTHY M., consumer products company executive; B, Calif. State Univ., Northridge. Retail mgmt. positions through v.p. human resources automotive group Sears Roebuck; sr. v.p. human resources K-Mart Corp., 1999—2002; v.p. performance systems Home Depot, Inc., Atlanta, 2002—05, sr. v.p. talent, org. & performance systems, 2005—07, exec. v.p. HR, 2007—. Bd. dir. Human Resources Policy Assn. Office: Home Depot 2455 Paces Ferry Rd Atlanta GA 30339-4024

CROWDER, MARJORIE BRIGGS, lawyer; 2 children. BA, Carson-Newman Coll., 1968; MA, Ohio State U., 1969, JD, 1975. Bar: Ohio 1975, US Dist. Ct. (so. dist. Ohio) 1975, US Ct. Appeals (6th cir.) 1983, US Ct. Claims 1992, US Supreme Ct. 2001. Asst. dean of women Albion Coll., Mich., 1969-70; dir. residence hall Ohio State U., Columbus, 1970-71, acad. counselor, 1971-72; assoc. Porter, Wright, Morris, Arthur, Columbus, 1975—83, ptnr., 1983-2000; AmeriCorps atty. Southeastern Ohio Legal Svs., Portsmouth, Ohio, 2000—02, staff atty., 2002—03; domestic violence team leader Legal Aid Soc. Columbus, 2003—04; supr. legal rsch. Franklin Co. Mcpl. Ct., 2005—07; program mgr. children, families and cts. Supreme Ct. Ohio, 2007—. Legal aide Cmty. Law Office, Columbus, 1973—74. Co-author: (book) Going to Trial, A Step-By-Step Guide to Trial Practice and Procedure, 1989. Trustee, pres. Epilepsy Assn. Ctrl. Ohio, Columbus, 1977—84; bd. dirs. Scioto County Domestic Violence Task Force, 2001—03, v.p., 2001—03; bd. dirs. Action Ohio Coalition Battered Women, 2002—07, Columbus Speech & Hearing, 1977—82. Fellow: Columbus Bar Found. (trustee 1993—95); mem.: Scioto County Bar Assn., Columbus Bar Assn. (com. chmn. 1979—83, docket control task force 1989—91, editor 1981—83), ABA (mem. gavel awards com. 1989—96, gen. practice sect. 1983—, chair litig. com. 1987—89, mem. exec. coun. 1989—93, dir. bus. com. group 1990—91, chair program com. 1991—93, torts and ins. practice sect. 1993—, vice chair health ins. law com. 1993—96), Ohio Bar Assn. (mem. joint task force gender fairness 1991—93), Scioto County Bar Assn. Home: 13602 Goswick Ridge Pl Midlothian VA 23114-5504 Office Phone: 614-387-9385. Business E-Mail: crowderm@sconet.state.oh.us.

CROWDER, RICHARD THOMAS (DICK CROWDER), economics professor, former ambassador; b. Baskerville, Va., Aug. 3, 1939; s. George Thomas and Estelle (Morgan) C.; m. Margaret Rainey, Sept. 4, 1960; children: Richard, Matthew. BS, Va. Poly. Inst. and State U., 1960, MS, 1962; PhD, Okla. State U., 1967. Staff economist Exxon USA, Houston, 1966-68; dir. econ. analysis Wilson & Co., Inc., Oklahoma City, 1968-75; sr. v.p. The Pillsbury Co., Mpls., 1975-89; under sec. for internat. affairs and commodity programs USDA, Washington, 1989—92; exec. v.p., gen. mgr. Armour Swift-Eckrich (divsn. of ConAgra), 1992—94; sr. v.p., internat DEKALB Genetics Corp., 1994—99; ind. cons., 1999—2002; pres., CEO American Sneed Trade Assn., Alexandria, Va., 2002—05; chief agrl. negotiator Office US Trade Rep., Exec. Office of the Pres., Washington, 2005—07; prof. internat. trade Va. Tech. U. Coll. Agrl. & Life Sciences, Blacksburg, Va., 2007—. Sr. advisor Office Spl. Trade Representation, Washington, Office of Tech. Assessment, 2007-08; exec. v.p. Pillsbury Restaurant Group, 1987-89; bd. dirs. Smithfield Foods, Inc., 2011- Rep. precinct vice chmn. Hennepin County. Capt. U.S. Army, 1962-64. Mem. American Agrl. Economics Assn. (bd. dirs. 1975-78, assoc. editor 1983-86). Methodist. Avocations: running, tennis, bridge, reading. Office: Va Tech U Coll Agrl & Life Sciences 210 A Hutcheson Hall Blacksburg VA 24061 Office Phone: 540-231-6301. E-mail: rcrowder@vt.edu.

CROWE, A. G., state legislator; Mem. Dist. 76 La. House of Reps., 2000—07; mem. Dist. 1 La. State Senate, 2008—, vice chair commerce, consumer protection and internat. affairs com., interim mem. natural resources com., mem. judiciary C com., local and mcpl. affairs com., retirement com.; owner Express Imaging. Republican. Office: Capitol Office PO Box 94183 Baton Rouge LA 70804 also: 646 Carnation St Slidell LA 70460-1812 Office Phone: 985-643-3600, 225-342-2040. Fax: 985-645-3566. E-mail: crowea@legis.state.la.us.

CROWE, DEWEY (RUSTY) E., II, state legislator; b. Apr. 2, 1947; m. Sarah Barron; children: Catherine Barron, John Barron. State senator Dist. 3, Tenn., 1991—; rep. Gov.'s Coun. Health & Physical Fitness, 1991—; mem. Vets. Affairs Com., 1991—, Senate Comm. & Info. Com., 1991—; sec. Govt. Ops. Com.; vice chmn. Senate Majority Caucus, Judiciary Subcom., Law Enforcement & Criminal Justice Subcom.; mem. Energy & Natural Resources Com., State Govt. Com., Local Govt. Com., Adminstr. Higher Edn. Mem.: 1st Tenn. Human Devel. Agy., Am. Legion Post No 24, Lions Club (Johnson City). Republican. Methodist. Office: 808 East Eighth Ave Johnson City TN 37601 also: 8 Legislative Plz Nashville TN 37243 Office Phone: 615-741-2468, 423-926-8288. Business E-Mail: sen.rusty.crowe@capitol.tn.gov.

CROWELL, CRAVEN H., JR., retired federal agency administrator; b. Nashville, Aug. 27, 1943; s. Craven H. and Addie Ailene (Cooper) Crowell; m. Fredricka Friedli, Nov. 27, 1970; 1 child, Stephanie Kaye. BA, Lipscomb U., 1965. Reporter, city editor Nashville Tennessean, 1964-77; press sec. Senator Jim Sasser, 1977-80, chief of staff, 1989-93; dir. info. Tenn. Valley Authority, Knoxville, 1980-87, v.p. govtl. and pub. affairs Nashville, 1987-89, chmn. bd. dirs., 1993-2001; ret., 2001. Mem. exec. com. Nuc. Energy Inst.; past chmn. bd. dirs., mem. exec. com., mem. bd. adv. coun. Electric Power Rsch. Inst.; bd. dirs. EPRI Worldwide. Hon. pres. Hohai U., China, 1997. With USMC, with USNR. Recipient Nat. Headliner award, 1969; named Alumnus of the Yr., Lipscomb U., 1995. Mem.: Econ. Club N.Y., Pi Delta Epsilon. Democrat. Mem. Ch. Of Christ. Office Phone: 865-671-3398. Personal E-mail: cravencrowell@aol.com.

CROWLEY, JOHN FRANCIS, III, professor, consultant; b. New Haven, Jan. 29, 1945; s. John Francis Jr. and Anna Cecil (Elliott) C.; m. Alice Ann Kennedy, Dec. 26, 1970; children: John Francis IV, Sarah Ann. MA in Regional and City Planning, U. Okla., 1973, PhD in Urban Geography, 1977. Dir. planning Seminole, Okla.; chief planner Okla. State Parks, 1973—74; asst. prof. environ. design U. Ga., Athens, 1974—78, prof., dean Coll. Environ. and Design, 1996—; exec. dir. Tulsa Metro Area Planning Commn., 1978—80; v.p., devel. Williams Realty Corp., Tulsa, 1980—87; pres. Urbantech Inc., Tulsa, 1987—; dir. Okla. Dept. of Transp., Oklahoma City, 1993—95. Bd. dirs. Athens Classic Ctr. Authority, 1983-89; chmn. Sales Tax Overview Com., Tulsa, 1988-90; sec. bd. trustees Tulsa County Pub. Facilities Authority, 1983-96. Mem. bd. dir., Zamorano U., Honduras. Interpreter US Army Security Agency, 1965—67, dir. Foreign Mil. Tng., 1967—69, Ft. Sill. Sara Moss faculty fellow U. Ga., 1976. Fellow Am. Inst. Cert. Planners, Am. Soc. Landscape Arch.; mem. Am. Soc. Landscape Architects, Am. Planning Assn., Nature Conservancy, Urban Land Inst., Transp. Rsch. Bd. Democrat. Roman Catholic. Avocations: art, sports, travel. Home: 335 Crystal Ct Athens GA 30606-3245 Business E-Mail: jcrowley@uga.edu.

CROWLEY, JOHN WILLIAM, literature and language professor; b. New Haven, Dec. 27, 1945; s. John Adam and Mary T. (McKenna) C.; m. Sheila A. Myers, Mar. 17, 1967 (div. 1977); children: Matthew, Anne; m. Susan Wolstenholme, May 27, 1978 (div. 2001); children: Raphael, Mary; m. Emily T. Smith, Nov. 23, 2001. BA, Yale U., 1967; MA, Ind. U., 1969, PhD, 1970. Asst. prof. English Syracuse (N.Y.) U., 1970-74, assoc. prof., 1974-79, prof., 1979—2002, dir. humanities doctoral program, 1985—88, 1996—2002, dir. grad. studies, 1986-89, chair, 1989—92; ret., 2002. Author: George Cabot Lodge, 1976, The Black Heart's Truth, 1985, The Mask of Fiction, 1989, The White Logic, 1994, The Dean of American Letters, 1999, Bill W. and Mr. Wilson, 2000; co-author: Drunkard's Refuge, 2004; editor: New Essays on Winesburg, Ohio, 1990, Chinese edit., 2006, Genteel Pagan, 1991, The Sunnier Side, 1996, The Rise of Silas Lapham, 1996, Drunkard's Progress, 1999; co-editor: The Haunted Dusk, 1983. Hon. Woodrow Wilson fellow, 1967; NDEA fellow, 1967-70; Nat. Endowment for Humanities summer stipend, 1975 Mem.: Phi Beta Kappa. Democrat. Home: 663 High Field Rd Tuscaloosa AL 35405 Business E-Mail: jcrowley@english.as.ua.edu.

CROWLEY, WILLIAM C., board member, investment company executive; BS in Psychology, Yale U., 1979. Mem. staff to mng. dir. mergers and acquisitions dept. Goldman Sachs, 1986—99; pres., COO ESL Investments, Inc., 1999—2003, 2011—12; sr. v.p. fin., bd. dirs. Kmart Corp., 2003—05; exec. v.p., chief adminstrv. officer Sears Holdings Corp., 2005—11. Bd. dirs. AutoNation, Inc., 2002—. Mailing: AutoNation Inc Bd Directors 200 SW 1st Ave Fort Lauderdale FL 33301

CROWNOVER, JAMES W., retired management consultant, board member; b. 1943; m. Molly Crownover. BSChemE, Rice U., 1966; MBA, Stanford U., 1968. Ptnr. McKinsey & Co., 1968—98, mng. dir., head, southwest practice, 1998—94; non-exec. chmn. Republic Services, Inc., 2011—. Former bd. dirs. Xpedior Inc.; bd. dirs. Unocal, 1998—2007, McKinsey & Co., 1990—98, Great Lakes Chemical Corp., 2002—05, Republic Svcs., Inc., Weingarten Realty Investors, 2001—, Allied Waste Industries, 2002—, Chemtura Corp., 2005—, FTI Consulting, 2007—. Mem. DeMint for Senate Com., Nat. Rep. Senatorial Com.; trustee St. John''s Sch., Houston, Tex., Houston Zoo; bd. dirs. Houston Grand Opera; trustee, Rice Univ., 1999-, chmn., 2005-. Republican. Office: Rice U 6100 Main Houston TX 77005-1827 Office Phone: 713-348-0000. Office Fax: 713-348-5479. Business E-Mail: jcrownover@weingarten.com.

CROWNOVER, MIKE, energy executive; BBA in Acctg., U. Tex., Arlington. With Halliburton Energy Svcs., 1977—97; corp. compensation mgr. to corp. human resources mgr. to corp. human resources dir. to exec. dir. employee rels. and retail human resources Valero Energy Corp., 1997—2002, v.p. human resources, 2002—08, sr. v.p. human resources, 2008—, officer, 2005—. Bd. mem. S.W. Mental Health Ctr. Office: Valero Energy Corpn 1 Valero Way San Antonio TX 78292-0500

CROWNOVER, MYRA, state legislator; m. Ronny Crownover (dec.); children: Scott, Luke, John, Dan. BEd, So. Meth. U.; MEd, Tex. A&M U. Former pub. sch. tchr.; co-owner Robinson Drilling Co.; pres. Crownover, Inc.; mem. Dist. 64 Tex. House of Representatives, Tex., 2000—. Dir. Northstar Bank; mem., treas. Southern States Energy Bd., 2005—. Republican. Office: PO Box 535 Lake Dallas TX 75065 also: Room CAP 4S.02 Capitol PO Box 2910 Austin TX 78701 Office Phone: 512-463-0582, 940-321-0013. Office Fax: 940-497-0121.

CRUM, JOHN KISTLER, management consultant; b. Brownsville, Tex., July 28, 1936; s. John Mears and Mary Louise (Kistler) C. BS, U. Tex., 1960, PhD, 1964; grad. Advanced Mgmt. Program, Harvard U., 1975. Research fellow Robert A. Welch Found., 1962-64; asst. editor Am. Chem. Soc., Washington, 1964-65, assoc. editor, 1966-68, mng. editor, 1969-70, group mgr. jours., 1970, dir. books and jours. div., 1971-75, treas., chief fin. officer, 1975-80, dep. exec. dir. and chief operating officer, 1981-82, exec. dir., 1983—2003, CEO; pres., CEO Quinta Assocs., LLC, 2004—. Chmn. bd. Centcom Ltd., 1983-2003, Sci. Info. Internat., Ltd., 1995-2003; chmn. governing bd. Chem. Abstracts Svc., 1991-1996, ACS publs., 1997-2003; mem. U.S. nat. com. Internat. Union Pure and Applied Chemistry; sr. mem. Con. Bd.; mem. Bretton Woods Com., 2002—; bd. dirs. Consumers Union of U.S., 1991-93. Contbr. articles to profl. jours. Fellow Washington Acad. Scis.; mem. Royal Chem. Soc. (London), Am. Chem. Soc., Am. Soc. Assn. Execs., Coun. Engring. and Sci., Soc. Execs., Assn. Sci. Soc. Editors, N.Y. Acad. Scis., Chem. Soc. Washington, Cosmos Club, City Club, Univ. Club (Washington), Chemists Club (N.Y.), Sigma Xi, Phi Theta Kappa. Republican. Home: PO Box 780 Cobbs Creek VA 23035 Business E-Mail: johnkcrum@mpwifi.com.

CRUM, RICHARD, air transportation executive; married; 4 children. Degree, George Mason U., 1993. Electronic pub. supr. Air Transport Assn. America, 1995—96; sys. and planning mgr. Universal Air Travel Plan, 1996, ops. and svcs. dir., 1996—99, pres., chmn., 1999—2003; pres., CEO AirPlus Internat., 2003—. Named one of Top 100 Rising Stars in Travel Industry, Travel Agent Mag., 2000. Mem.: Nat. Bus. Travel Assn., Assn. Corp. Travel Execs. (pres. 2007—). Avocations: reading, running, music, sports. Office: AirPlus Internat 225 Reinekers Ln Ste 500 Alexandria VA 22314-2878 Office Phone: 703-373-0940. Office Fax: 703-373-0941.

CRUMBLEY, DONALD LARRY, accounting educator, writer; b. Kannapolis, NC, Jan. 18, 1941; s. Carl Donald and Velvia (Kelly) C.; m. Donna Darlene Loflin, Aug. 31, 1963; children: Stacey Lynn, Dana Lea, Heather Ann. BS cum laude, Pfeiffer U., 1963; MS, La. State U., 1965, PhD, 1967. CPA NC, cert. forensic acct.; diplomate Am. Bd. Forensic Accts.; cert. fraud deterrence CFF. Grad rsch. asst. La. State U., Baton Rouge, 1963-65, tchg. asst., 1965-66; asst. prof. acctg. Pa. State U., State College, 1967-69; staff acct. Arthur Andersen & Co., NYC, 1969-70; adj. asst. prof. NYU Grad. Sch. Bus., 1970; faculty resident Laventhol & Horwath, 1972; assoc. prof., dir. M. Bus. Taxation program U. So. Calif., LA, 1973-74, U. Fla., Gainesville, 1970-73, 74-75; prof. Tex. A&M U., College Station, 1975-97, Shelton prof. taxation, 1984-97; KPMG endowed prof. La. State U., Baton Rouge, 1997—. Newspaper and mag. columnist; creator Soc. for a Return to Acad. Stds., 1993—. Author: Financial Management of Your Coin-Stamp Estate, 1978, Practical Guide to Preparing a Federal Gift Tax Return, 1981, Readings in Selected Tax Problems of the Oil Industry, 1982, Handbook of Accounting for Natural Resources, 1986, Handbook of Estate Planning, 1988, Handbook of Governmental Accounting and Finance, 1988, 1992, Handbook of Financial Management for Banks, 1988, The Ultimate Rip-off: A Taxing Tale, 2005, Accosting the Golden Spire, 1989, Handbook on Financial Aspect of Divorce and Separation, 1989, Keys to Understanding the Financial News, 2000, Keys to Estate Planning and Trusts, 1989, Keys to Personal Financial Planning, 1991, Keys to Surviving a Tax Audit, 1991, Handbook of Natural Gas Accounting, 1991, Keys to Understanding Social Security Benefits, 1992; co-author: Donate Less to the IRS, 1981, Readings in Oil Industry Accounting, 1980, Estate Planning: A Guide for Advisers and Their Clients, West's Federal Taxation, 4 vols., Trap Doors and Trojan Horses, 1991, Financial Analysis, 1994, How To Manage Corporate Cash, 1994, Costly Reflections in a Midas Mirror, 1995, Barron's Guide to Tax Terms, 1995, Activity Based Costing, 1995, Deadly Art Puzzle: Accounting for Murder, 1996, The Bottom Line is Betrayal, 1995, Non-profit Sleuths: Follow the Money, 1997, Simon the Incredible: A Novel, 1998, Chemistry in Whispering Caves, 1998, Computer Encryptions in Whispering Caves, 1999, The Big R: An Internal Auditing Action Adventure, 2000, The Big R: A Forensic Accounting Action Adventure, 2008, U.S. Master Auditing Guide, 2d edit., Forensic and Investigating Accounting, 2003, 2d edit., 2005; contbr. chpts. to books, articles to profl. jours.; editor Oil, Gas & Energy Quar., 1977—, Jour. Forensic Acctg., 1999—2008; co-editor Tex. Tax Services, 1983—; cons. editor Lawyers and Judges Pub. Co., Tucson; contbg. editor Hard Facts and Tax Angles; mem. editl. bd. Jour. Petroleum Acctg., Jour. Managerial Issues, Jour. East-West Bus., Forensic Examiner, Acctg. Educators' Jour., Acctg. Rev.; mem. editl. adv. bd. Advances in Acctg. Named to Alumni Hall of Fame, A.L. Brown H.S., 1972; recipient Contbn. to Cmty. award Sta. WRUF, 1972; Coll. Bus. Adminstrn. Rsch. award Tex. A&M U., 1982; Ford Found. grantee, 1966-67; Disting. Alumni award Pfeiffer Coll., 1972; Arthur Young Rsch. grant, 1984-85. Mem. Am. Taxation Assn. (pres. 1974-75, trustee 1975-77, founder), Am. Inst. CPA's, Am. Acctg. Assn., Nat. Taxation Assn., Am. Tax Assn. (founding pres.), Govt. Fin. Officers' Assn., Tex. Soc. CPA's, La. Soc. CPA's, Numis. Lit. Guild, Order of Sundial, Phi Kappa Phi, Beta Gamma Sigma, Beta Alpha Psi. Methodist. Office: La State U Dept Acctg 3101 Patrick Taylor Baton Rouge LA 70803-0001 Office Phone: 225-578-6231. Business E-Mail: dcrumbl@lsu.edu.

CRUMBLY, JACK, state legislator; Educator Earle Sch. Dist., Ark.; mem. Dist. 16 Ark. State Senate, 2007—. Chmn. subcommittee on minority health Ark. State Senate; mem. St. Francis County Quorum Ct. Democrat. Address: 1823 SFC 414 Widener AR 72394 Office Phone: 870-633-7338. Business E-Mail: crumblyj@arkleg.state.ar.us.

CRUMP, CHARLES METCALF, lawyer; b. Memphis, Oct. 9, 1913; s. Dabney Hull and Mary Hadden (Metcalf) Crump; m. Diana Temple Wallace, July 20, 1940; children: Charles Metcalf, Philip Hugh Wallace, Stephen Beard. BA, Rhodes Coll. (formerly Southwestern at Memphis), 1934; LLB, U. Va., 1937; D in Canon Law with honors, Seabury-Western Theol. Sem., 1983; DCL with honors, U. of South, 1991; DCL, St. Augustine's Coll., 1994; LLD with honors, St. Paul's Coll., 1997; D in Canon Law with honors, Voorhees Coll., 1992. Bar: Tenn. 1936, US Supreme Ct. 1946. Assoc. Metcalf, Metcalf & Apperson, Memphis, 1937—40; ptnr. Apperson, Crump & Maxwell, & Successors, 1940—. Sec. adv., adv. dir. Bank of Am. (formerly Commerce Union Bank of Memphis; former bd. dirs. Ripley Industries, Inc.; former bd. dirs., sec. Elmwood Cemetery. Contbr. articles to profl. jours. Pres. Chickasaw Boy Scouts Am. Coun., 1953; v.p. United Fund, Memphis, 1955; pres. Sheltered Occupl. Shop, 1963, Memphis Cmty. Leadership Tng., 1968—69; v.p. tours US Peoples Friendship Assn., 1981—95; founding mem. Diversity Memphis, 2005—; mem. Tenn. Gen. Assembly, 1939—43; sec. Shelby County Dem. Exec. Com., 1939—50; v.p. House Deps. Gen. Conv., 1964—95, 1967—70; chancellor Diocese of W. Tenn., 1982—; mem. nat. exec. coun. Episcopal Ch., 1964—70; mem. Nat. Assn. Christians & Jews, 1971—2005. With USNR, 1944—46, PTO. Recipient Outstanding Citizen award, Memphis Jaycees, 1943, Human Rels. award, NCCJ, 1985. Mem.: Tenn. Bar Assn. (award of merit 1964), Memphis Roundtable (sr. chmn.), Am. Coll. Trust & Estate Planning Coun., Memphis Bar Assn. (dir., treas., sec. 1971—73), ABA, Rotary (pres. 1977—78), Memphis Country Club. Office: 6000 Poplar Ave Ste 400 Memphis TN 38119-3972 Home Phone: 901-682-3522; Office Phone: 901-756-6300. Business E-Mail: appersoncrump@aol.com.

CRUNDWELL, DUNCAN JAMES, electronics executive; b. Maidstone, Kent, Eng., Mar. 18, 1957; arrived in US, 1995; s. James Stanley and June Crundwell; m. Bridgette Grieve, Dec. 24, 1983 (div. Jan. 1995); 1 child, Ben; m. Natasha Shankova, May 12, 1995. BSME, Brunel U., London, 1979; MBA, Henley Mgmt. Coll., Eng., 1996. Charterd engr. Student engr. Dowty Group, Cheltenham, Eng., 1975-79; chief engr. Yamco, London, 1979-80; tech. mgr. Bandive, London, 1980-84; custom projects mgr. Solid State Logic, Oxford, Eng., 1984-86, systems mgr., 1986-88, product group mgr., 1988-90; mng. dir. Solid State Logic Organ Systems, Brandon, Eng., 1990-95, CEO, pres. Detroit, 1995—2002, 1602 Group LLC, Alexandria, Va., 2002—; founding ptnr. People Going Global LLC, 2000—. Tchr. Opening Windows Engring., Oxford Schs., 1988—91; client, project mgr. new hdqs. bldg. Solid State Logic. Prodr.: (radio program) Glad to Be Gay or Not?, 1977 (UK Local Radio award, 1977). Recipient award, Royal Inst. Brit. Archs., 1989, Dir. Gen.'s cert., Engring. Coun., London, 1990. Mem.: Instn. Mech. Engrs. (chmn. YM panel 1988—89, sec. 1987—88, Outstanding Project Work award 1979). Anglican. Achievements include inventor in field. Avocations: photography, architecture, music, fine art. Home: 1602 Group 5600 General Washington Dr # B211 Alexandria VA 22312-2415

CRUSE, JULIUS MAJOR, JR., pathologist, educator; b. New Albany, Miss., Feb. 15, 1937; s. Julius Major and Effie (Davis) C. BA, BS with honors, U. Miss., 1958; DMS with honors, U. Graz, Austria, 1960; MD, U. Tenn., 1964, PhD in Pathology (USPHS fellow), 1966, USPHS postdoctoral fellow, 1964-67; DD (hon.), Gen. Theol. Sem., NYC, 1999. Prof. immunology and biology Grad. Sch. U. Miss., 1967—74, prof. pathology, 1974—, assoc. prof. microbiology, 1974—, dir. grad. studies program in pathology, 1974—, dir. clin. immunopathology, 1978—, dir. immunopathology sect., 1978—, dir. tissue typing lab., 1980—, assoc. prof. medicine, 1989—, prof. medicine, disting. prof. history medicine Med. Sch., 2003—, Guyton disting prof., 2004—09, 2010—, prof. microbiology, 2010, vice chair pathology, dir. anatomic pathology. Lectr. pathology U. Tenn. Coll. Medicine, 1967-74; adj. prof. immunology Miss. Coll., 1977-92; mem. NIH study section on transplantation immunology, 1992; mem. sci. adv. bd. Immuno Tech. Corp., LA; active FDA Expert Panel on Alternatives to Silicone Breast Implants, 1994—, mem. Keller Libr. Author: Immunology Examination Review Book, 1971, rev. edit., 1975, Introduction to Immunology, 1977, Principles of Immunopathology, 1979; editor-in-chief Immunologic Rsch., 1981—, Pathology and Immunopathology Rsch., 1982-90, Concepts in Immunopathology, 1985—, The Year in Immunology, 1984—, Pathobiology: Jour. Immunopathology, Molecular and Cellular Biology, 1990-98, Exptl. & Molecular Pathology, 1999—, Transgenics: Biological Analysis Through DNA Transfer, 1992-; immunology cons.: Dorland's Illustrated Medical Dictionary, 1967-1994; contbns. to Microbiology and Immunology; editor Immunomodulation of Neoplasia, Antigenic Variation: Molecular and Genetic Mechanisms of Relapsing Disease, 1987, Autoimmunoregulation and Autoimmune Disease, 1987; The Year in Immunology, vol. 1, 1984-85, vol. 2, 1985-86, The Year in Immunology, vol. 3, 1987, The Year in Immunology, vols. 4, 5, 1988, vol. 6, 1989-90, Genetic Basis of Autoimmune Disease, 1988, Cellular Aspects of Autoimmunity, 1988, Therapy of Autoimmune Diseases, 1989, B Lymphocytes: Function and Regulation, Conjugate Vaccines, 1989, Molecules and Cells of Immunity, 1990, Immunoregulation and Autoimmunity, 1986, Organ-Based Autoimmune Diseases, 1985, Autoimmunity: Basic Concepts, Systemic and Selected Organ-Specific Diseases, 1985, Clinical and Molecular Aspects of Autoimmune Diseases, 1990, Immunoregulatory Cytokines and Cell Growth, 1989, Complement Profiles, 1992; co-editor: Self-Nonself Discrimination in the Immune System, 1992, Complement Profiles, vol. 1, 1992, Illustrated Dictionary of Immunology, 1995, 2d edit., 2003, 3d edit., 2009, 10, Atlas of Immunology, 1998, 2d edit., 2003, 3rd edit., 2010, Immunology Guidebook, 2004, Historical Atlas of Immunology, 2005, T.S. Eliot Bibliography, 2003, Historical Atlas of Immunology, 2005; editor-in-chief: Experimental and Molecular Pathology, 1999—; mem. editl. bd. Human Immunology, 2007-; contbr. chpts. to books and articles to profl. jours. Recipient Pathologists award in continuing edn. Coll. Am. Pathologists-Am. Soc. Clin. Pathologists, 1976; Julius M. Cruse collection in immunology established in his honor Middleton Med. Libr., U. Wis., Madison, 1979, Julius M. Cruse collection of T.S. Eliot's works, St. Mark's Libr.,Julius M Cruse Rare Book Reading Room Hon. award, Keller Libr., Gen. Theol. Sem. (Episcopal), NYC, Julius M. Cruse collection in history of immunology Rowland Med. Libr., U. Miss. Med. Ctr., 2004, Julius M Cruse Collection of T.S. Eliot, Emory U. Woodruff Libr., Atlanta, 2008; Wilson Found. grantee, 1990-95, 93-94, 95-98, 99-2003; B.S. Guyton lectr. on history of medicine, 1998; Fulbright scholar U. Graz, Austria, 1958-60. Fellow AAAS, Royal Soc. Medicine, Royal Soc. Promotion Health, Am. Acad. Microbiology, Am. Soc. for Histocompatibility and Immunogenetics (chmn. publs. com. 1987-95, councillor 1997-99, historian 2000—), Intercontinental Biog. Assn.; mem. AMA (Physicians Recognition award 196-75), Clin. Immunology Soc., Am. Inst. Biol. Scis., Am. Soc. Clin. Pathologists, Can. Soc. Microbiologists, NY Acad. Scis. Exptl. Biology and Medicine, Am. Diabetes Assn., Soc. Francaise d'Immunologie, Reticuloendothelial Soc., Transplantation Soc., Electron Microscopy Soc. Am., Am. Assn. History Medicine, The Paul Ehrlich Soc., Am. Soc. Investigative Pathology, Am. Assn. Pathologists, Am. Chem. Soc., Brit. Soc. Immunology, Can. Soc. Immunology, Am. Soc. Microbiology, Internat. Acad. Pathology, Am. Assn. Immunologists (historian 1990—), T.S. Eliot Soc., Soc. of Mary, Mariological Soc. Am., Sigma Xi, Phi Kappa Phi, Phi Eta Sigma, Alpha Epsilon Delta, Gamma Sigma Epsilon, Phi Chi. Anglican Catholic. Office: U Miss Med Ctr Dept Pathology 2500 N State St Jackson MS 39216-4500 Office Phone: 601-984-1565. Business E-Mail: jcruse@umc.edu.

CRUSTO, MITCHELL FERDINAND, lawyer, educator; b. New Orleans, Apr. 22, 1953; BA magna cum laude, Yale U., 1975; BA, Oxford U., Eng., 1980, MA, 1985; JD, Yale U., 1981. Bar: La. 1982, Mo. 1984, Ill. 1985. Law clk. to Hon. John M. Wisdom U.S. Ct. Appeals (5th cir.), New Orleans, 1981-82; assoc. Jones, Walker, Waechter, Pointevent, Carrere & Denegre, New Orleans, 1982-84; sr. v.p., gen. counsel, asst. corp. sec. Stifel, Nicolaus & Co., Inc., St. Louis, 1984-88; CEO Crusto Capital Resources, Inc., St. Louis, 1988-89; assoc. dep. adminstr. for fin., investment and procurement U.S. Small Bus. Adminstrn., Washington, 1989-91; dir. corp. environ. policy Monsanto Co., St. Louis, 1991-93; sr. mgr. Arthur Andersen Environ. Svcs., Chgo., 1993-95; prof. Loyola Sch. Law, New Orleans, 1995—. Vis. prof. Vt. Law Sch., summers 2000-2003, Washington U. Sch. Law, summer 1999; mem. faculty Washington U., St. Louis, 1985-89, St. Louis U. Law Sch., 1987-88, Webster U., St. Louis, 1986; securities advisor to sec. of state State of Mo., 1986-89; lectr. legal divsn. Securities Industry Assn., 1986-88; mem. Pres. Clinton transition team natural resource cluster EPA, 1992; owner Angelic Asset Mgmt., 1998—. Contbr. articles in newspapers, mags., jours. Mem. ABA, La. Bar Assn., Mo. Bar Assn., Ill. Bar Assn., Middle Temple (London). Office: Loyola U Sch Law 7214 Saint Charles Ave # 901 New Orleans LA 70118-3538 Home: PO Box 410648 Saint Louis MO 63141-0648 Office Phone: 314-323-9307. Business E-Mail: mfcrusto@loyno.edu.

CRUTCHER, MICHAEL BAYARD, lawyer, retired consumer products company executive; b. Seattle, Apr. 7, 1944; s. M. Bayard and Marjorie (Sandstrom) C.; m. Judith Johnston, Aug 26, 1967; children: Alexandra, Andrew, Charles. BA, Yale U., 1966; JD, Harvard U., 1969. Bar: Wash. 1969, Ky. 1990. Assoc. Preston, Thorgrimson, Ellis & Holman, Seattle, 1969-73, ptnr., 1974-89; sr. v.p., gen. counsel, sec. Brown-Forman Corp., Louisville, 1989—2003, vice chmn., gen. counsel, sec., 2003—07. Bd. dirs. Distilled Spirits Coun. U.S., 1991-99, chmn., 1992-94; chmn. Internat. Ctr. Info. on Beverage Alcohol, 1994-95, Internat. Ctr. Alchohol Policy, 1996-97, Louisville Fund for Arts, 2004-07; trustee Bellarmine U., 2003-. Republican. Home: 4801 Bonita Bay Blvd Apt 1204 Bonita Springs FL 34134 Home Phone: 239-992-0811. Personal E-mail: michaelcrutcher@cmbargmail.com.

CRUTCHFIELD, KEVIN S., mining executive; BS in Mining Minerals Engring., Va. Poly Inst. & State U.; completed Business Executive Program, U. Va. Various exec. mgmt. positions, including v.p., ops. Pittston Coal Co., Pittston, 1986—95; chmn., pres., CEO Cyprus Australia Coal Co.; various exec. positions, including pres., CEO AEI Resources, Inc.; pres., CEO AMVEST Corp.; v.p. El Paso Corp., 2001—03; pres. Coastal Coal Co., 2003; v.p. ANR Holdings, LLC, 2003, exec. v.p., 2003—05, Alpha Natural Resources, Inc., 2004—07, pres., 2007—09, CEO, 2009—, chmn., 2012—. Bd. dirs. Alpha Natural Resources, Inc., 2007—, King Pharmaceuticals Inc., 2010—. Office: Alpha Natural Resources Inc One Alpha Pl PO Box 2345 Abingdon VA 24212 Office Phone: 276-619-4410. Business E-Mail: KCrutchfield@alphanr.com.

CRUZ, JANET, state legislator; b. Tampa, Fla., July 7, 1956; m. Stephen Rifkin; children: Ana, Raymond. Grad. in opticianry dispensing, Hillsborough CC, Tampa, 1977. Owner, optician Pearle Vision Ctr.; dir. optical ops. CIGNA Healthcare, regional dir. seniors group sales; nat. fin. account mgr. Aetna Healthcare; mem. Dist. 58 Fla. House of Reps., Tallahassee, 2010—. Mem. West Tampa C. of C., Tampa Latin C. of C. Past chair Hillsborough County Dem. Hispanic Caucus; past corp. chair United Way Campaign CIGNA Healthcare; past bd. mem. Paint Your Heart Out Tampa. Mem.: NAACP, Nat. Assn. Latino Elected Officials, Hillsborough CC Alumni Found. Democrat. Roman Catholic. Office: 2221 N Himes Ave Ste B Tampa FL 33607-3139 also: Fla House of Reps 1401 The Capitol 402 S Monroe St Tallahassee FL 32399-1300 Office Phone: 813-673-4673, 850-488-9460.

CRUZ, NELSON RAMON, professional baseball player; b. Monte Cristi, Dominican Republic, July 1, 1980; Outfielder Milw. Brewers, 2005, Tex. Rangers, Arlington, 2006—. Named Pacific Coast League MVP, 2008, American League Championship Series MVP, Maj. League Baseball, 2011; named to American League All-Star Team, 2009, 2013. Office: Tex Rangers 1000 Ballpark Way Arlington TX 76011*

CRUZ, TED (RAFAEL EDWARD CRUZ), United States Senator from Texas, lawyer; s. Rafael Bienvenido and Eleanor Elizabeth (Darragh) Cruz; m. Heidi Suzanne Nelson, May 27, 2001. AB cum laude, Princeton U., Princeton, NJ, 1992; JD magna cum laude, Havard Law Sch., Cambridge, Mass., 1995. Bar: Tex. 1997, DC 1998, US Supreme Ct., US Ct. Appeals (4th, 5th, DC, Fed. cirs.), US Dist. Ct. (Tex.). Law clk. to Hon. J. Michael Luttig US Ct. Appeals (4th Cir.), Washington, 1995—96; law clk. to Justice William Rehnquist US Supreme Ct., Washington, 1996—97; assoc. Cooper, Carvin, & Rosenthal PLLC, Washington, 1997—99; domestic policy advisor Bush-Cheney 2000, Austin, Tex., 1999—2000; assoc. dep. atty. gen. US Dept. Justice, Washington, 2001; dir. Office Policy Planning FTC, Washington, 2001—03; solicitor gen. State of Tex., Austin, 2003—08; ptnr. Morgan, Lewis & Bockius LLP, Houston, 2008—12; US Senator from Tex., 2013—; mem. US Senate Armed Services Com., 2013—, US Senate Commerce, Sci. & Transp. Com., 2013—, US Senate Rules & Adminstrn. Com., 2013—, US Senate Judiciary Com., 2013—, US Senate Spl. Com. on Aging, 2013—; vice chmn. grass roots outreach Nat. Republican Senatorial Com. (NRSC), 2013—. Team mem. Bush-Cheney 2000, Inc., 1999—2000; US Dept. Justice coord. Bush-Cheney Transition Advisory Com., 2000—01; adj. prof. US Supreme Ct. litig. U. Tex. Sch. Law, 2004—09. Editor: (primary) Harvard Law Rev., 1995, (exec.) Harvard Jour. of Law and Pub. Policy, 1995, (co founding) Harvard Latino Law Rev. Atty. Bush-Cheney Presdl. Recount, Fla., 2000; US Dept. Justice coord. Bush-Cheney Transition Team, Washington, 2001; found. dir. Tex. Mavericks; bd. advisors Tex. Rev. Law & Politics, Hispanic Alliance for Progress. Recipient Best US Supreme Ct. Merits Brief award, Nat. Assn. Atty. Generals, 2003—07; named Traphagen Disting. Alumnus, Harvard Law Sch.; named one of The 20 Young Hispanics to Watch, Newsweek mag., 1999, The 100 Most Influential Hispanics, Hispanic Bus. mag., 1999, Hispanic Bus. Mag., 2000, The 50 Most Influential People in Politics, George mag., 2001, Litigation's Rising Stars, The American Lawyer, 2007, The 50 Most Influential Minority Lawyers in America, The Nat. Law Jour., 2008, The 25 Greatest Tex. Lawyers of the Past Quarter Century, Tex. Lawyer, 2010, America's Leading Lawyers for Bus., Chambers USA, 2009, 2010; named to The Appellate Hot List, The Nat. Law Jour., 2010; John M. Olin fellow, Harvard Law Sch. Mem.: American Law Inst., Tex. Philos. Soc., Tex. Lyceum (past v.p., dir.). Republican. Baptist. Office: US Senate 185 Dirksen Senate Office Building B40B Washington DC 20510 Office Phone: 202-224-5922. Office Fax: 202-228-0755.*

CRUZ SOTO, CARMEN YULIN, mayor, San Juan, Puerto Rico, former territorial legislator; b. PR, Feb. 25, 1963; d. Pedro Cruz and Carmen Irene Soto Molina; married; 1 child. B in Polit. Sci., magna cum laude, Boston U.; M, Carnegie Mellon U., Pitts. Human resources dir. to various companies; advisor to Sila Maria Calderon Office of Mayor, San Juan; advisor to the pres. PR Legislature, San Juan, at-large rep., 2009—12, pres., 2012; mayor City of San Juan, 2013—. Pres. Popular Women's Orgn., 2005—. Popular Democratic Party. Office: Office of the Mayor City Hall San Francisco St San Juan PR 00902-4100*

CUBAN, MARK, professional sports team owner, Internet company executive; b. Pitts., July 31, 1958; m. Tiffany Stewart, Sept. 21, 2002; children: Alexis Sofia, Alyssa. BA in Bus. Adminstrn., Ind. U., 1981. Founder MicroSolutions (sold to CompuServe), 1983-90; pres. Radical Computing; co-founder Audionet (became broadcast.com in 1998 (acquired by Yahoo!), 1995—99; owner, mng. ptnr. Dallas Mavericks, 2000—; co-founder, pres., chmn. HDNet and HDTV Cable Network, 2001—; chmn., co-owner Magnolia Pictures, Landmark Theaters; chmn., majority owner Rysher Entertainment; co-owner 2929 Entertainment. Owner IceRocket; ptnr. RedSwoosh; investor Weblogs, Inc., Brondell, Inc., Goowy Media Inc.; spkr. in field. Exec. prodr.: (films) Godsend, 2004; exec. prodr.: (films) Criminal, 2004, The War Within, 2005, One Last Thing..., 2005, Bubble, 2005, Good Night and Good Luck, 2005, The Jacket, 2005, Akeelah and the Bee, 2006, The Architect, 2006, Diggers, 2006, Fay Grim, 2006, Turistas, 2006, Black Christmas, 2006, Fast Track, 2006; exec. prodr.: (films) Broken English, 2007; exec. prodr.: (films) We Own the Night, 2007, Redacted, 2007, The Life Before Her Eyes, 2007, What Just Happened, 2008, Quid Pro Quo, 2008, Two Lovers, 2008, The Burning Plain, 2008, The Girlfriend Experience, 2009, The Road, 2009, Rejoice and Shout, 2010, Tim and Eric's Billion Dollar Movie, 2012; (documentaries) Searching for Debra Winger, 2002, Enron: The Smartest Guys in the Room, 2005, Herbie Hancock: Possibilities, 2006, Gonzo: The Life and Work of Dr. Hunter S. Thompson, 2008, Conquering Kilimanjaro with Angie Everhart, 2009, Casino Jack and the United States of Money, 2010; (TV series) The Mark Cuban Show, 2002; exec. prodr.: (TV series) Geek to Freek with Dennis Rodman, 2007; co-exec. prodr. (TV series) Star Search, 2002—04; actor: (films) Talkin About Sex, 1994, Lost at Sea, 1995; (TV series) Walker, Texas Ranger, 2000, Entourage (3 episodes), 2010, (video) Like Mike 2: Streetball, 2006; (TV films) 20 on 20, 2007; host, prodr.: (TV series) The Benefactor, 2004; panel mem. (TV series) Shark Tank, 2011—, maintains (blog site, Blogmaverick.com); performer: Dancing With the Stars, 2007. Founder Mark Cuban Found., The Fallen Patriot Fund, 2003—. Recipient Webby Entrepreneur of Yr., Internat. Acad. Digital Arts and Scis., 2006; named a WIRED Renegade, WIRED Rave Awards, 2006; named one of Forbes 400: Richest Americans, 2000—, 50 Most Influential People in Sports Bus., Street & Smith's SportsBus. Jour., 2007, 2008, The Most Influential People in the World of Sports, Bus. Week, 2007, 2008; nominee WIRED Rave award-Blogs, 2005. Office: Dallas Mavericks The Pavillion 2909 Taylor St Dallas TX 75226

CUBIÑÁ, SILVIA KARMAN, museum director, curator; b. Miami; 2 children. BA in art history, Boston Coll., 1987. With Cuban Mus. Art, Miami, Mex. Mus., San Francisco; adj. curator inova Inst. Visual Arts, U. Wis., Milw.; independent curator, 1997—2002; founding dir. Moore Space, Miami, 2002—08; exec. dir., chief cur. Bass Mus. Art, Miami, 2008—. Puerto Rico commr. Bienal de Sao Paolo, 1997; juror Hugo Boss Award, Guggenheim Mus., 2006. Curator (exhibitions) French Kissing in the USA, Moore Space, Miami, 2007. Fellow Ctr. Curatorial Leadership, 2007. Office: Bass Mus Art 2121 Park Ave Miami Beach FL 33139 Office Phone: 305-673-7530 ext. 9-2002. Office Fax: 305-674-5475. E-mail: scubina@bassmuseum.org.

CUCIN, ROBERT LOUIS, plastic surgeon, lawyer; b. NYC, Apr. 17, 1946; s. Robert and Julia C. BA magna cum laude, Cornell U., 1967, MD, 1971; JD, Fordham U., 1985; MBA, Columbia U., 2003. Bar: N.Y. 1983, NJ State Supreme Ct., Washington Ct. of Appeals; bd. cert. legal medicine, diplomate Am. Bd. Surgery, Am. Bd. Plastic Surgery, lic. physician NJ, N.Y. State, Calif., Va., gen. socs. prin.; securities license series 4, 7, 24, 27, 63, 79, 86, 87 and 99. Intern Cornell-N.Y. Hosp., NYC, 1971-72, resident in gen. surgery, 1972-76, resident in plastic surgery, 1977-79; fellow in surgery Meml.-Sloan Kettering Found., 1972-76, 77-79; practice medicine specializing in plastic surgery Columbia MBA, NYC, 1979—; instr. surgery Cornell U. Med. Coll., 1980—; asst. attending plastic surgeon Beth Israel North, N.Y. Downtown Hosp., 1979—, N.Y. Hosp., 1980—, Drs. Hosp., 1987—. Pres. Esquire Cadillac Limousine Svc. Inc., 1977—93, Beaux Arts Holdings, 1979—, Rocin Labs., Inc., 1981—; pres., CEO Biosculpture Tech., Inc., 2001—. Author: The Kindest Cut, Keeping Face, Medical Malpractice: Handling Plastic Surgical Cases; contbr. articles to profl, jours. Mem. N.Y. County Health Svc. Rev. Orgn., 1976—; founder, dir Rocin Found. for Plastic Surg. Rsch., 1979—; Maj. M.C., USAF, 1976-77; Japan. Fellow: ACS, Am. Coll. Legal Medicine, Internat. Coll. Surgeons; mem.: ABA, ATLA, AMA (Physicians Recognition award 1978, 1981), N.Y. Acad. Scis., N.Y. County Med. Soc. (health systems, pub. rels., peer rev. coms.), N.Y. State Med. Soc., Royal Soc. Medicine, Am. Soc. Plastic and Reconstructive Surgery, Am. Mensa, Cornell Club, N.Y. Athletic Club, Phi Beta Kappa. Republican. Home: 1701 S Flagler Dr Apt 607 West Palm Beach FL 33401-7341 Office Phone: 212-586-9500.

CUDNIK, BRIAN, astronomer, educator; s. Paul and Irene Cudnik; m. Susan Vogel, June 3, 1995. BS in Physics and Astronomy, No. Ariz. U., Flagstaff, 1994; MS in Astronomy, San Diego State U., 1998. Outreach technician Rice U., Houston, 1998—99; rsch. asst. Prairie

View Solar Obs., Tex., 1999—2001; physics lab. specialist Prairie View A&M U., 2001—; adj. prof. U. St. Thomas, Houston, 2005—. Contbr. articles to profl. jours. Worship projectionist and elder Houston First Ch. God, 2001—. Mem.: Am. Astron. Soc., Houston Astron. Soc. (sec. 2001—05). Conservative. Evangelical. Office: Prairie View A&M Univ Dept Physics PO Box 519 MS 2230 Prairie View TX 77446 Office Fax: 936-261-3149. Business E-Mail: bmcudnik@pvamu.edu.

CUELLAR, HENRY ROBERTO, United States Representative from Texas, lawyer; b. Laredo, Tex., Sept. 19, 1955; s. Martin and Odilia (Perez) Cuellar; m. Imelda Rios; children: Christina Alexandra, Catherine Ann. AA, Laredo Cmty. Coll., 1976; BS in Fgn. Svc., cum laude, Georgetown U., Washington, 1978; JD, U. Tex., Austin, 1981, PhD in Govt., 1998; MA in Internat. Trade, Tex. A&M Internat. U., Laredo, 1982. Bar: Tex., US Dist. Ct. (so. dist.) Tex., US Ct. Appeals (5th cir.), US Ct. Internat. Trade; lic. customs broker 1983. Pvt. practice atty., Laredo; mem. Dist. 43 Tex. House of Reps., 1987—93, mem. Dist. 42, 1993—2001; sec. of state Tex., 2001; mem. US Congress from 28th Tex. dist., 2005—. Instr. Laredo Cmty. Coll., 1982—86; adj. prof. internat. comml. law Tex. A&M Internat. U., 1984—86. State legal advisor Am. GI Forum Tex., 1986—88; bd. dirs., treas. Stop Child Abuse & Neglect (SCAN), 1982—83; pres. bd. dirs. Laredo Vol. Lawyers Program Inc., 1982—83, Laredo Legal Aid Soc. Inc., 1982—84, Internat. Good Neighbor Coun., 1984—85. Named Laredo Pro Bono Atty. of Yr., 1985. Mem.: ABA, Inter-Am. Bar Assn., Tex. Bar Assn., Laredo Young Lawyers Assn. (pres. 1982—83), Kiwanis (bd. dirs. 1982—83). Democrat. Roman Catholic. Office: US House of Representatives 2431 Rayburn House Office Bldg Washington DC 20515 also: 602 E Calton Rd Ste 2 Laredo TX 78041 Office Phone: 202-225-1640.*

CUI, ZHENG, oncologist, educator; PhD, U. Mass., Amherst, 1988. Prof. Wake Forest U. Sch Medicine, Winston-Salem, NC, 1996—. Achievements include invention of new cancer therapy. Home: 2522 Lullington Dr Winston Salem NC 27103 Office: Pathology Wake Forest Univ Medical Center Blvd Winston Salem NC 27157 Personal E-mail: zhengcu@yahoo.com.

CULBERSON, JOHN ABNEY, United States Representative from Texas, lawyer; b. Houston, June 24, 1956; m. Belinda Burney, Dec. 1989; 1 child, Caroline Virginia. BA in History, So. Meth. U., Dallas, 1981; JD, South Tex. Coll. Law, 1988. Oil rig mud logger, 1978—81; polit. advt. agy. employee, 1981—85; sr. assoc. civil def. atty. Lorance & Thompson, Houston, 1985; mem. from Dist. 125 Tex. House of Reps., 1987—93, mem. from Dist. 130, 1993—2001, minority whip, 1999—2001; mem. US Congress from 7th Tex. dist., 2001—. Recipient Leader of Excellence award, Free Market Assn., 1993, Outstanding Young Houstonian award, Houston Jaycees, 1994, Friend of Taxpayer award, Tex. Citizens for Sound Economy, 2000, Hero of Taxpayer award, Americans for Tax Reform, 2002, Spirit of Enterprise award, US C. of C., 2002, Mfg. Legis. Excellence award, Nat. Assn Manufacturers, 2005, Brighter Vision award, Seniors Coalition, 2005. Republican. Office: US House of Representatives 2352 Rayburn House Office Bldg Washington DC 20515 also: 10000 Memorial Dr Ste 620 Houston TX 77024 Office Phone: 202-225-2571.*

CULBERTSON, RICHARD ALLEN, healthcare educator, health facility administrator; b. Fremont, Ohio, Aug. 13, 1946; s. Raymond Clark and Ruth Elizabeth Culbertson; m. Linnea VanDyne, July 11, 1970 (div. Dec. 1981); m. Susan Mary Leary, May 3, 1986. BA, Lawrence U., 1967; MDiv, Harvard U., 1970; M in Health Adminstrn., U. Minn., 1973; PhD, U. Calif., San Francisco, 1993. Cert. healthcare exec. Am. Coll. Health Execs. Asst. prof. U. Minn., Mpls., 1976—78; dep. dir. and COO St. Paul-Ramsey Med. Ctr., 1978—84; hosp. dir. and CEO Kaiser Found. Hosp., LA, 1984—87; dir. adminstrn. U. Calif. San Francisco Med. Group, 1987—92; assoc. dean and vice chancellor U. Wis., Madison, 1992—95; assoc. prof. and dir. Ind. U., Indpls., 1995—97; assoc. prof. Tulane U., New Orleans, 1997—2009, prof., 2009—12; prof., dir. La. State U., Sch. Pub. Health, New Orleans, 2012—, interim dean, 2013—. Chmn. bd. dirs. Aurora HealthCare Inc., Milw., 1994—2007; spl. asst. to pres. for NCAA cert. Tulane U., New Orleans, 1999—2008, 2008—, chair senate com. on intercollegiate athletics, 2002—05; cvc cvc, 2010—; chair sch. pub. health and tropical medicine faculty Tulane U., 2005—07; cert. site reviewer NCAA, Indpls., 2001—; mem. governing bd. Touro Infirmary, New Orleans, 2004—09. Contbg. author The Nation's Health, 6th edit., 2001; contbr. articles to profl. jours. Mem. Mardi Gras Krewe of Mid-City, Krewe of Ancient Druids; pres. Humane Soc. Ramsey County, St. Paul, 1981—84; bd. dirs. Touro Found., New Orleans, 2004—07, Wis. Profl. Rev., Madison, 1994—95, Eldercare Dane County, Madison, 1994—95. Recipient Spurgeon award for cmty. svc., Explorer Scouts, St. Paul, 1983; named Emerging Leader in Healthcare, Healthcare Forum, San Francisco, 1986; Nat. Leader fellow, W.K. Kellogg Found., 1985—88. Mem.: Am. Hosp. Assn. Chgo. (regional policy bd. 2006—09, governance com. 2006—09, leadership devel. coun. 2009—12), U. Minn. Pres. Club, Harvard Club (La.), Delta Omega Soc. (Eta chpt.), Phi Beta Kappa (La. Alpha chpt.), Beta Theta Pi. Avocations: swimming, Tae Kwon Do, sports. Office: La State University Sch Pub Health 20 Gravier St 3rd Fl New Orleans LA 70112 Office Phone: 504-568-5960. Business E-Mail: rculbe@lsuhsc.edu.

CULKIN, CHARLES WALKER, JR., certified Government financial manager, retired trade association administrator; b. Aug. 22, 1947; s. Charles Walker and Helen Elizabeth (Wilson) C.; m. Carolyn DeWayne Franklin, Apr. 5, 1974; children: David Laurence Franklin, Kimberly Anne Franklin A in Bus. Adminstrn., Benjamin Franklin U., Washington, 1968, BA in Comml. Sci., 1970. Asst. auditor United Va. Bank, Vienna, 1967—70; sr. asst. dir. US GAO, Washington, 1970—97; exec. dir. Assn. Gov. Accts., Washington, 1997—2003; ret., 2003. Chmn. Pacific Emerging Issues Conf., Honolulu, 1982; spkr. confs. and seminars; founder, incorporator Reston Commuter Bus., Inc., 1971, treas., dir., 1971-78 Pub. The Jour. Govt. Fin. Mgmt., 1997-2003; contbr. articles to profl. jours Recipient RCB Bd. Dirs. award 1978, Outstanding Achievement award Fairfax County Bd. Suprs., Va., 1978, Nat. Pres. award Am. Soc. of Mil. Comptr., 1999, 2003 Mem. Am. Assn. for Budget Program Analysis, Inst. Internal Auditors (sec. no. Va. chpt. 1984-86), Assn. Govt. Accts. (dir. Hawaii chpt. 1981-84, conf. mgr. fed. leadership conf. 1994, No. Va. chpt. 1991—, Nat. AGA Spl. Recognition award 1988, 90, 93, Pres.'s award 1992, 95-96, Outstanding Mem. award 1983, nat. treas.-elect, 1995-96, nat. treas. 1996-97, Edn. award 1994, Robert W. King Meml. award 2006), Nat. Assn. Accts. (no. Va. chpt. dir. 1977-78, v.p. 1979-80), Benjamin Franklin U. Alumni Assn. (pres. 1988-92, Outstanding Leadership award 1991, Bd. Govs. Svc. award 1992, Disting. Alumni award, 1995), George Washington U. Gen. Alumni Assn. (dir. 1991-92, Vol. of Yr. award 1992), KC (Coun. #3358 dep. grand knight 2004-2005, grand knight 2005-07, Knight Yr., 2004-2005, 2007-08, assembly #0167 faithful comptroller 2007-10, faithful capt. 2010-2011, Sr Knight of The Yr. award, 2010-11, coun. #15332, fin. sec., 2011-13, Knight of Yr., 2011-12, family of Yr., 2012-13), Fla. State Coun., State Basketball Free Throw Chair (dist. warden #48, 2012-13, dist. dep. #50, 2013-). Roman Catholic. Home: 5351 Fox Run Rd Sarasota FL 34231-7348 Personal E-mail: cinandchas@verizon.net.

CULKIN, DANIEL JOSEPH, urologist, educator, department chairman; s. Lawrence Francis and Madeline Culkin; m. Jane Marie Graham, July 10, 1981; children: Matthew Lawrence, Daniel James. BS, Creighton U., Omaha, Nebr., 1968—72, MD, 1975—79; MS, Loyola U., Chgo., 1972—75; MBA/HCM, U. Phoenix, 2003—05. Lic. dr. Okla. State Bd. Med. Licensure, 2009, La. State Med. Licensure Bd., 2009, Ill. State Med. Bd., 2009. Fellow endourology and neurourology Loyola U. Med. Ctr., Maywood, Ill., 1982—85, urology instr., 1985—87; asst. prof. urology La. State U. Med. Ctr., Shreveport, La., 1987—88, assoc. prof. urology, 1988—91, prof. urology, 1991—94; chief urology Shreveport Va. Med. Ctr., 1987—88; prof., chair dept. urology Okla. U. Health Sci Ctr., Okla. City, 1994—, Pres.'s Assoc. Presdl. prof., 2006. Mem. SW Oncology Group, San Antonio, 1991—. Mem.: AMA (assoc.), Soc. U. Urology (pres. 2003—04), Am. Paraplegic Soc. (dir. 1988—91). Catholic. Avocations: water sports, golf, fishing. Home: 6104 LaQuinta Dr Edmond OK 73025 Office: Univ Okla Health Sci Ctr PO Box 26901 Oklahoma City OK 73190 Office Fax: 405-271-3118. Business E-Mail: daniel-culkin@ouhsc.edu.

CULLIGAN, THOMAS M., electronics executive; b. Aug. 1951; BS, MS, Fla. State U. Legis. dir. Fla. Congressman Earl Hutto, Fla.; chief of staff Fla. Sec. of State; exec. McDonnell Douglas; pres. govt. ops. Allied Signal, 1994—96, v.p. mktg., sales and svc., 1996—99; v.p., gen. mgr. def. and space Honeywell Internat., Inc., 1999—2001; CEO Raytheon International, Inc., 2001—; sr. v.p., bus. develop. Raytheon Co., Arlington, Va., 2001—. Office: Raytheon Co 1100 Wilson Blvd Arlington VA 22209-3978

CULPEPPER, GUY LEE, physician; b. Dallas, June 14, 1957; s. Pat McPherson; m. Deborah Mills, Oct. 4, 1986; children: Dillon, Justin, Logan. BS in Biology, SMU, 1980, BA in Psychology, 1980; MD, U. Tex., Houston, 1984. Lic. dr. Am. Bd. Family Medicine, 1984. Pres. Bent Tree Family Physicians, Dallas, 1987—; CEO Jefferson Physician Grp., Dallas, 1995—. Found. bd. Dallas County Cmty. Coll., 2003—07. Fellow: AAFP. Home: 5353 Spanish Oaks Dr Frisco TX 75034 Office: Bent Tree Family Physicians 3550 Parkwood Blvd #600 Frisco TX 75034 Office Fax: 972-377-8808. Personal E-mail: glcdlc@aol.com.

CUMMINGS, ALEXANDER B., JR., food products executive; b. Liberia; BS in Fin. and Economics, Northern Ill. U.; MBA in Fin., Atlanta U. Joined The Pillsbury Co., 1982, v.p., fin., 1993—97; dep. region mgr., Nigeria Coca-Cola Co., 1997, region mgr., Nigeria, 1998, pres., North and West Africa divsn., 2000, pres., COO, Africa Group, 2001—, exec. v.p., chief adminstrv. officer, 2002—. Chmn. The Coca-Cola Africa Found.; mem. Ctr. for Global Devel. Commn. on U.S. Policy toward Low-Income Poorly Performing States; bd. dirs. Africa-Am. Inst., Corp. Coun. on Africa, U.S.-Egypt Bus. Coun.; past bd. dirs. Sabathani Cmty. Ctr., Mpls. Office: The Coca-Cola Co 1 Coca-Cola Plz Atlanta GA 30301-2499 Office Phone: 404-676-2121. Business E-Mail: acummings@na.ko.com.

CUMMINGS, CANDACE S., lawyer; b. New London, Conn., Apr. 11, 1947; m. Roger Cummings; children: Carolyn, Julia. BA in Economics, Middlebury Coll., 1969; MD, U. Va., 1972. Bar: Pa. 1972. Assoc. Dechert, Price & Rhoads, Phila., 1972—85, ptnr., 1980—95; v.p., gen. counsel VF Corp., Greensboro, NC, 1994-96, v.p. adminstrn., gen. counsel, 1996—97, v.p. adminstrn., gen. counsel, sec., 1997—2012. Mem.: NC Bar Assn., Pa. Bar Assn. Avocation: golf.

CUMMINGS, SAM R., federal judge; b. 1944; BBA with high honors, Tex. Tech. U., 1967; JD cum laude, Baylor U., 1970. With Culton, Morgan, Britain & White, Amarillo, Tex., 1970-87; judge US Dist. Ct. (no. dist.) Tex., 1987—. Com. chmn. Troop 86, Boy Scouts Am., Amarillo; trustee Presbyn. Children's Home, Amarillo, Howard Payne U., Brownwood, Tex. Recipient Wall St. Jour. award, Am. Jurisprudence award; Judge Hunter D. Barrow Meml. scholar Baylor U. Sch. Law. Mem. Kiwanis (v.p. South Amarillo club). Office: US Dist Ct 1205 Texas Ave Rm 210C Lubbock TX 79401

CUMMINGS, STEPHEN EMERY, investment banking executive; b. Atlanta, May 27, 1955; s. Robert Emery and Catherine Brierly (Longyear) C.; m. Karen Lee Ludwick, Feb. 21, 1981; children: William Ludwick, Stephen Clifton, Caroline Margret, Russell Ludwick, Lee Wyman. BA in Adminstrv. Sci., Colby Coll., Waterville, Maine, 1977; MBA, Columbia U., NYC, 1979. V.p. Kidder, Peabody & Co., Inc., NYC, 1979-85; with Bowles Hollowell Conner & Co. (merged with First Union), Charlotte, 1985—98, chmn., CEO, 1993—98; Managing Director and Head of Mergers and Acquisitions First Union Corp. (now Wachovia Corp.), 1998—99, Managing Director, Co-Head Investment Banking Group, 1999—2000; sr. exec. v.p., co- head Corporate and Investment Banking division Wachovia Corp., 2000—04, sr. exec. v.p., head Corporate and Investment Banking division, 2004—. George F. Baker scholar Colby Coll., 1977. Mem. Beta Gamma Sigma. Republican. Episcopalian. Office: Wachovia Corp 1 Wachovia Ctr Charlotte NC 28288

CUNNINGHAM, ALEC R., health products executive; B, Okla. St. Univ.; MBA, Univ. So. Calif. Mgmt. positions Okla. Health Care Authority, 1994—96; mgmt. positions through v.p. bus. develop. & compliance WellPoint Health Networks, 1996—2004; v.p. bus. develop., sr. v.p. govt. rels., divsn. pres. Fla. & Hawaii WellCare Health Plans, Tampa, Fla., 2005—09; CEO WellCare Health Plans, Inc., Tampa, Fla., 2009—. Office: WellCare Health Plans 8725 Henderson Rd Tampa FL 33634 Mailing: WellCare Health Plans PO Box 31372 Tampa FL 33631-3372

CUNNINGHAM, ALICE JEANNE, chemistry educator, author, consultant; b. Walnut Ridge, Ark., Sept. 23, 1937; d. Percy Smith and Barbara Beryl (Fry) C. Student, Vanderbilt U., 1955-57; BA in Chemistry, U. Ark., 1959; PhD in Chemistry, Emory U., 1966. Chemist Layne Rsch., Memphis, 1959; instr. Secondary Schs., Gainesville, Atlanta, Ga., 1959-62; postdoctoral rsch. assoc. U. Tex., Austin, 1967-68; asst., assoc. prof. Agnes Scott Coll., Decatur, Ga., 1968-79, chair dept. chemistry, 1978-90; prof. W.R. Kenan Jr., 1979-92; prof. emerita, 1992. Vis. asst. prof. Agnes Scott Coll., Decatur, 1966-67; vis. scholar Emory U., Atlanta, 1984-85; vis. prof., 1985-86. Contbr. articles to profl. jours. Active Hazardous Waste Mgmt. Authority, Ga., 1991-94. Fellow AAAS; mem. Am. Chem. Soc. (com. on profl. tng. mem. 1979-88, chair 1983-88, cons., com. profl. tng. 1989-93), Sigma Xi, Iota Sigma Pi, Sigma Delta Epsilon (Hon. Mem. award 1990). Avocations: walking, reading, fishing.

CUNNINGHAM, ATLEE MARION, JR., aeronautical engineer; b. Corpus Christi, Tex., Aug. 17, 1938; s. Atlee Marion and Carlos Dean (Shepherd) Cunningham; m. Diana Wahl Bonelli, July 17, 1976; children from previous marriage: Christopher Atlee Acie, Scott Patrick, Sean Michael. BSME, MSME, U. Tex., 1961, PhD, 1966. Rsch. scientist Def. Rsch. Lab., Austin, Tex., 1965; engring. staff specialist Gen. Dynamics Corp., Ft. Worth, 1965—93, Lockheed Corp., Ft. Worth, 1993—95, Lockheed Martin, 1995—, sr. prin. rsch. engr., sr. LM fellow, 2002—. Vis. indsl. prof. So. Meth. U. Inst. Tech., Dallas, 1969—70; vis. assoc. prof. aero. engring. U. Tex., 1978—; lectr. in aeroelasticity Nat. Cheng Kung U., Taiwan, 1984, U. Tex., Arlington, 1990—; mem. tech. teams NATO-RTO; cons. NASA, USAF, USN, U. Tex.; cons. on aeroelastic and vibration issues for Lockheed Martin F-16, C-130J, F-22 and F-35 aircraft. Contbr. articles to profl. jours. V.p. Tex. Fine Arts Assn., Ft. Worth, 1972. With USN, 1962—64. Recipient NASA Cert. of Recognition for tech. publ., 1980, Achievement award, Gen. Dynamics, 1980, 1983, 1989, Meml. Rsch. award, Found. Tex. A & M U.; Welding Rsch. Assn. fellow, 1961—62. Fellow: AIAA (assoc.; tech. reviewer jours.); mem.: Sigma Xi. Achievements include innovations in subsonic, transonic and supersonic steady and oscillatory aerodynamics method; major contributions to aeroelastic developments and improvements for Gen. Dynamics/Lockheed Martin F-16 and F-111 aircraft, F-22 and F-35 aircraft; development of new methods for predicting high angle of attack aerodynamics in subsonic and supersonic flows; steady and unsteady force testing techniques for aerodynamic investigations using water tunnels, new concepts and methods for nonlinear aeroelasticity; pioneered new technology development for unsteady separated flows and buffeting on aircraft maneuvering at high angle of attack involving support of Air Force; Navy; NASA; Nat. Aerospace Lab. (Netherlands); Lockheed Martin; U. Tex., Austin; patents in field. Home: 4932 Black Oak Ln Fort Worth TX 76114-2936

CUNNINGHAM, BILL, state supreme court justice; b. Ky. m. Paula Cunningham; 5 children. BA, Murray State U., 1962; JD, U. Ky. Coll. Law. City atty., Eddyville, Ky., 1974—91; pub. defender Ky. State Penitentiary, 1974—76; commonwealth atty. 56th Jud. Dist., 1976—88; hearing officer Ky. Bd. Claims, 1981—85; trial commr. Lyon County Dist. Ct., 1989—92; cir. ct. judge 56th Jud. Cir., Ky., 1991—2007; assoc. justice Ky. Supreme Ct., 2007—. US Army, Vietnam, Korea, Germany. Recipient Outstanding Commonwealth Atty. of Ky. Office: Ky Supreme Ct 700 Capitol Ave Rm 235 Frankfort KY 40601 Office Phone: 502-564-5444.*

CUNNINGHAM, JAMES BLAIR, United States ambassador to Afghanistan; b. Allentown, Pa., Sept. 2, 1952; s. Blair and Julia Katherine Cunningham; m. Leslie Ann Genier, Aug. 9, 1975; children: Emma Julianne, Abigail Kathleen. BS in Polit. Sci. & Psychology cum laude, Syracuse U., 1974. Staff asst. to the amb., polit. officer fgn. svc. US Embassy, Stockholm, 1975-77, polit.-mil. affairs officer Rome, 1981-85; dep. Spanish affairs officer US Dept. State, Washington, 1977-79, sec. affairs, 1979-81, US mission to NATO Brussels, 1985-88, dir. pvt. office of NATO sec. gen. Manfred Woerner, 1988-90, dep. polit. counselor U.S. mission to UN Washington, 1990-92, dep. dir. Office European Security & Polit. Affairs, 1992-93, dir. Office European Security & Polit. Affairs, 1993-95; dep. chief of mission US Embassy, Rome, 1996—99; dep. US rep. to UN US Dept. State, NYC, 2001—05, acting permanent rep. to UN, 2001, consul gen. Hong Kong & Macau Spl. Adminstrv. Regions, 2005—08, US amb. to Israel Tel Aviv, 2008—11, dep. amb. to Afghanistan for Kabul Kabul, 2011—12, US amb. to Afghanistan, 2012—. Recipient President's Meritorious Svc. award, Nat. Performance Review Hammer award. Mem.: Asia Soc., Coun. Fgn. Rels. Office: US Embassy 6180 Kabul Pl Dulles VA 20189*

CUNNINGHAM, JASON, dentist; m. Angela R. Cameron; children: Andrew, Alexis. Dentist, Erwin, Tenn.; part time assoc. dentist Sophisticated Smiles, Johnson City, Tenn., 2004—. Mem.: Am. Acad. of Dental Sleep Medicine, Acad. of Gen. Dentistry, Am. Acad. of Cosmetic Dentistry, Tenn. Dental Assn., ADA. Office: Sophisticated Smiles 189 Corporate Dr Ste 20 Johnson City TN 37601 Office Phone: 423-928-8359. Office Fax: 423-282-6018.

CUNNINGHAM, JOEL LUTHER, mathematics professor, former academic administrator; b. Mooresville, NC, Jan. 11, 1944; s. Elbert Claxton and Ruth Morton (Journey) Cunningham; m. Trudy Bender, June 12, 1965; children: Nancy Elizabeth, Susan Ruth. BA, U. Tenn., Chattanooga, 1965; MA, U. Oreg., 1967, PhD, 1969. Asst. prof. math. U. Ky., Lexington, 1969—74; dean continuing edn. U. Tenn., Chattanooga, 1974—79; acad. v.p. Susquehanna U., Selinsgrove, Pa., 1979—84, pres., 1984—2000; vice-chancellor U. South, Sewanee, Tenn., 2000—10, prof. math. Chmn. Tenn. Ind. Coll. Assn., 2006—08, Appalachian Coll. Assn., 2007—09; trustee Assn. of Episcopal Coll., 2000—, chair, 2002—06; bd. dirs. Sunbury (Pa.) Hosp., 1992—2000; mem. nat. adv. com. Woodrow Wilson Fedn., 1995—2007; pres. Sunbury (Pa.) Hosp., 1998—2000, Coll. and U. Anglican Commn., 2001—, treas., 2002—; mem. St. Mary's Conf. Ctr., 2000—. Woodrow Wilson fellow, 1965, Am. Coun. on Edn. fellow, 1976—77. Mem.: Soc. for Values in Higher Edn. (bd. dirs. 1992—99, v.p. 1994—95, pres. 1995—99), Math. Assn. Am., Am. Math. Soc., Sigma Chi (chmn. bd. leadership tng. 1977—87, treas. 1987—89, v.p. 1989—91, pres. 1991—93, Internat. Balfour award 1965), Sigma Xi. Episcopalian. Home: PO Box 3326 Sewanee TN 37375 Office: University of the South 735 University Ave Sewanee TN 37383 Office Phone: 931-598-1101. E-mail: jcunning@sewanee.edu.

CUNNINGHAM, MICHAEL, lawyer; b. 1961; m. Jane Whittendale; children: Spencer, Austin. BS in Applied Math. & Statistics, SUNY Stony Brook, 1983; JD magna cum laude, Order of the Coif, U. Pa. Law Sch., 1988. Engr. Sperry Def. Electronics (now Unisys Corp.), 1983—85; with Dechert LLP, 1988—94; ptnr. & assoc. gen. counsel PricewaterhouseCoopers, 1994—2002; assoc. gen. counsel IBM Bus. Consulting Svc. Divsn., 2002—04; sr. v.p. Red Hat, Inc., 2004—07, gen. counsel Raleigh, NC, 2004—, exec. v.p., 2007—. Mem.: ABA (Bus. Law sect.), Computer Law Assn., Order of the Coif. Office: Red Hat Inc 100 E Davie St Raleigh NC 27601-2088 Office Phone: 919-754-3700. Office Fax: 919-547-0024. Business E-Mail: mcunningham@redhat.com.

CUNNINGHAM, RALPH SANFORD, energy executive; b. Albany, Ohio, Oct. 16, 1940; s. Harold Sanford and Julia Marie (Lasch) C.; m. Deborah Elaine Brookshire, Dec. 23, 1976; children: Ralph Sanford, Susan Ellen, Stephen Earl, Jennifer Marie. BS in Chem. Engring., Auburn U., Ala., 1962; MS, Ohio State U., 1962, PhD, 1966. With Exxon Co. U.S.A., Benicia, Calif., 1966-80, mgr. refinery, 1977-80; exec. v.p. Tenneco Oil Processing and Mktg., Houston, 1980-81, pres., 1982-89, also bd. dirs.; formerly exec. v.p. Tenneco Oil Co., pres.; dir. EPCO, Inc., 1987—97; chmn., CEO Clark Oil & Refining Corp., Clayton, Mo., 1989; pres., CEO CITGO Petroleum Corp., 1995—97; dir. Enterprise Products Partners L.P., 1998—2005, CEO; chmn., dir. TEPPCO Partners, L.P., 2005; pres., CEO Enterprise GP, LLC, 2007—10; dir. Enterprise Holdings, LP, 2007—; chmn. Enterprise Products Holdings LLC, 2010—13. Bd. dirs. IT Corp. Chmn. United Way Solano-Napa Counties, Calif., 1979; exec. council, v.p. Silverado council Boy Scouts Am., 1978-79. Mem. Am. Inst. Chem. Engrs., Am. Petroleum Inst., Sigma Xi. Republican. Presbyterian. Office: Enterprise Products Holdings LLC 1100 Louisiana St Houston TX 77002*

CUNNINGHAM, RONNIE WALTER, venture capitalist; b. Creston, Iowa, Mar. 16, 1932; s. Walter Wilfred and Gladys (Backen) C.; m. Dorothy League, Dec. 27, 1997; children: Brian Keith, Kimberly Ann. BS in Physics, UCLA, 1960, MA, 1961; advanced mgmt. program, Harvard Grad. Sch. Bus., 1974. Rsch. asst. Planning Rsch. Corp., Westwood, Calif., 1959-60; physicist RAND Corp., Santa Monica, Calif., 1960-64; astronaut NASA, 1964-71; crew member of first manned Apollo spacecraft Apollo 7; chief, Skylab br., 1968-71; sr. v.p. Century Devel., 1971-74; pres. Hydrotech Devel. Co., Houston, 1974-76; sr. v.p. 3D/Internat., Houston, 1976-79; founder The Capital Group, Houston, 1979-86; mng. ptnr. Genesis Fund, 1986-98. Bd. dirs. numerous tech. based cos.; mem. adv. bd. Nat. Renewable Energy Lab.; lectr. in field. Author: The All American Boys, 1977; host radio talk show Lift-Off to Logic, 1998—. Judge Rolex awards for enterprise, 1984. With USNR, 1951-52, fighter pilot USMCR, 1952-74, col. ret. Recipient Disting. Exceptional Svc. medals, NASA, Disting. Svc. medal, also; Haley Astronautics award; Profl. Achievement award UCLA Alumni, 1969; Spl. Trustee award Nat. Acad. Television Arts and Scis., 1969; medal of valor Am. Legion, 1975; Outstanding Am. award Am. Conservative Union, 1975, George Haddaway award, 2000; named to Internat. Space Hall of Fame, Houston Hall of Fame, Astronaut Hall of Fame, 1997. Fellow Am. Astronautical Soc.; mem. Soc. Exptl. Test Pilots, Am. Inst. Aeros. and Astronautics, Assn. Space Explorers-U.S.A., Am. Geophys. Union, Sigma Pi Sigma.

CUNNINGHAM, TOM ALAN, lawyer; b. Houston, Nov. 5, 1946; s. Warren Peek and Ellen Ardelle (Benner) Cunningham; m. Jeanne Adrienne Moran, July 21, 1972; 1 child, Christopher Alan. BA, U. Tex., 1968, JD, 1974. Bar: Tex. 1974, U.S. Dist. Ct. (so. dist.) Tex. 1976, U.S. Dist. Ct. (no. dist.) Tex. 1982, U.S. Dist. Ct. (we. dist.) Tex. 1984, U.S. Ct. Appeals (5th and 11th cirs.) 1981, U.S. Ct. Appeals (8th cir.) 1991, U.S. Supreme Ct. 2007. Ptnr. Fulbright & Jaworski L.L.P., Houston, 1974—98; founding ptnr. Cunningham Darlow, LLP, Houston, 1998—. Contbr. articles to jours. Bd. trustee Children's Charity Fund, Houston, 1983—88; active South Tex. Ctr. Legal Responsibility; mem. exec. com., bd. dirs. Assn. for Cmty. TV. Lt. (j.g.) USNR, 1969—72. Recipient Pres. award, State Bar of Tex., 1983, Houston Bar Assn., 1988. Fellow: Houston Bar Found., Am. Bd. Trial Advs., Am. Bar Found., Am. Coll. Trial Lawyers (Tex. state chair 2010—12), Tex. Bar Found. (life; chmn. bd. trustees, adv. bd., chair 1995—, chair bd. trustees 1995—, chair Lola Wright com., adv. bd., new fellows com., awards com., pub. com., bd. dirs., ct. ruels com.); mem.: ABA (arbitration com. 1995—, litigation sect., discovery com., forum com. constrn. industry, alternate dispute resolution com.), Tex. State Jud. Conduct Commn. (chair 2012—13), CPR Inst. for Dispute Resolution, Resolution Forum, Inc. (pres.), Tex. Empowerment Network (bd. dirs.), Tex. Ctr. Legal Ethics and Professionalism, Tex. Bd. Legal Specialization, State Bar Tex. (chmn. spl. com. on lawyer adt. and solicitation 1982, chmn. dist.4H grievance com. 1982—88, bd. dirs. 1989—92, chair bd. dirs. exec. com. 1991—92, chair com. for lawyer discipline 1992—94, chair gen. counsel adv. com., ct. rules com., exec. com., Pres.'s award 1983, Pres.'s citation for meritorious svc. 1991, Pres.'s spl. recognition for meritorious svc. 1993, 1994, nominee Outstanding Young Lawyer 1981), Houston Bar Assn. (professionalism com., chmn. constn. bicentennial com., membership com., arbitration com., Pres.'s award 1988), Am. Arbitration Assn. (panel of arbitrators), Houston Club, Coronado Club, Phi Delta Phi. Home: 10811 Pine Bayou St Houston TX 77024-3018 Office: Cunningham & Darlow LLP 919 Milam St Ste 575 Houston TX 77002-5430 Office Phone: 713-255-5500. Business E-Mail: tcunningham@cunninghamdarlow.com.

CUNNINGHAM, WILLIAM HENRY, retired food products executive; b. Oxnard, Calif., Dec. 2, 1930; s. William Henry and Carrie Edna (Wilson) C.; m. Carmen Nelson Alden, Jan. 19, 1957; children: Nelson, Clifford, Cynthia. BA, U. Calif., Santa Barbara, 1952; B of Foreign Trade, Am Grad. Sch. Internat. Mgmt., 1958. With Colgate-Palmolive Internat., NY and Colombia, El Salvador, 1958-63; mktg. cons. Anderson, Clayton Co., Mexico City, Buenos Aires and Lima, 1963-66; mgr. consumer divsn. Cyanamid, Buenos Aires, 1966-69; dir. mktg. and sales Alimentos Kraft, Caracas, Venezuela, 1969-74; gen. mgr. Panama and Cen. Am. Panama and Ctrl. Am. Kraft Foods, Inc., 1974-80; pres. Alimentos Kraft Alimentos Kraft Foods, Inc., Venezuela, 1980-86; v.p., dir. Kraft Foods, Inc. Kraft Gen. Foods, Walt Disney World, Fla., 1986-92. V.p., dir. The Land, Epcot Ctr., Walt Disney World, Fla. Stewareship chmn. St. Lukes Meth. Ch., Windermere, Fla., 1991-92; vol. Inter Exec. Svc. Corp. for assignment in L.Am. to help local industry, 1993, assignment to Bogota Colombia, 1994, Ctrl. Russia, 1996; vol. Second Helping; Spanish transl. Free Clinic, Deep Well; pres. Hosp. Aux., Hilton Head, S.C. 2002-03. Recipient Tribute Appreciation award U.S. State Dept., 1980, Order of Vasco Nunez de Balboa, Govt. Panama, 1980, First Class Work Merit award Govt. Venezuela, 1985, Jonas Mayer Disting. Alumni award Thunderbird Grad. Sch. for Internat. Mgmt., 1997, Friendship award US-Panimian Bus. Coun., 2006, Citizen's Honor award Hilton Head, 2003. Mem. Am. C. of C. (pres., founder Panama City chpt. 1979, sec. Caracas 1986), Am. Soc. (pres. Panama City chpt. 1977), Walt Disney World Participant Assn. (pres. 1990-91), U. Calif. Alumni Assn. (bd. dirs. Santa Barbara 1992-98, chair awards, Lifetime Achievement award 2006, Friendship award 2006, Panama-US Bus. Coun.), Hilton Head, Translator & Patient Access Hosp. Volunteers Medicine. Democrat. Methodist. Avocation: reading. Home: 11 Bear Creek Dr Hilton Head Island SC 29926-1904 Personal E-mail: carmenac@havgrey.com.

CUNNINGHAM, WILLIAM HUGHES, retired academic administrator, marketing professional, educator; b. Detroit, Jan. 5, 1944; married; 1 child BA, Mich. State U., 1966, MBA, 1967, PhD, 1971, LLD (hon.), 1993. Mem. faculty University of Texas, Austin, 1971—, assoc. prof. mktg., 1973-79, prof., 1979—, assoc. dean grad. programs, 1976-82, Foley/Sanger Harris prof. retail merchandising, 1982-83, acting dean Coll. Bus. Adminstrn. and Grad. Sch. Bus., 1982-83, dean, 1983-85, pres., 1985-92, Centennial Chair Bus. Edn. Leadership, 1983-85, Regents Chair Higher Edn. Leadership, 1985-92, Lee Hage and Joseph D. Jamail Regents Chair Higher Edn. Leadership, 1992-2000, James L. Bayless Chair for Free Enterprise, 1988—; chancellor U. Tex. Sys., Austin, 1992-2000. Bd. dirs. Lincoln Nat. Corp. (formerly Jefferson-Pilot Corp.), John Hancock Funds, S.W. Airlines Co., LIN TV Corp., Hicks Acquisitions Co. I Inc.; mem. corp. Conf. Bd. Author: (with W.J.E. Crissy and I.C.M. Cunningham) Selling: The Personal Force in Marketing, 1977, 2d edit. (with D.W. Jackson and Cunningham), 1988, Effective Selling, 1977, Spanish edit., 1980, (with S. Lopreato) Consumers' Energy Attitudes and Behavior, 1977, (with Cunningham) Marketing: A Managerial Approach, 1981, 2d edit. (with Cunningham and C. Swift), 1988, (with R. Aldag and C. Swift) Introduction to Business, 1984, 3d edit. (with R. Aldag and S. Block), 1992, 4th edit. (with R. Aldag and M. Stone), 1995, (with B. Verhage and Cunningham) Grondslagen van het Marketing Management, 1984, (with R. Aldag and S. Block) Business in a Changing World, 1992, also monographs and articles; editor Jour. Mktg., 1981-84. Bd. dirs. Houston Area Rsch. Coun., 1984; mem. Mental Health/Mental Retardation Legis. Oversight Com., 1984; mem. adv. bd. Found. for Cultural Exch./The Netherlands-U.S.A.; bd. dirs. Lyndon Baines Johnson Found. Recipient Tchg. Excellence award U. Tex. Coll. Bus. Adminstrn., 1972, Alpha Kappa Psi, 1975, Hank and Mary Harkins Found., 1978, Disting. Scholastic Contbn. award Coll. Bus. Adminstrn. Found. Adv. Coun., 1982, Disting. Alumnus award Coll. and Grad. Sch. Bus., Mich. State U., 1983, 93, Tree of Life award Jewish Nat. Fund, 1992, U. Tex. Austin Presdl. citation, 2005; named among top 20 profs. Utmost Mag., 1982; Rsch. grant Univ. Rsch. Inst., 1971-73, Latin Am. Inst., 1972, So. Union Gas Energy, 1975-76, ERDA, 1976 Mem. Am. Inst. for Decision Scis., Am. Mktg. Assn., Assn. Consumer Rsch., So. Mktg. Assn., S.W. Social Sci. Assn., Phi Kappa Phi, Omicron Delta Kappa Office: Univ Tex PO Box E Austin TX 78713 Office Phone: 512-232-7540.

CUOMO, PAUL C., lawyer; b. Syosset, NY, Aug. 3, 1970; BA in Polit. Sci., Villanova U., Pa., 1992; JD cum laude, American U. Washington Coll. Law, 1995. Bar: Md. 1995, DC 1998, US Dist. Ct. DC, US Dist. Ct. (ea. dist.) Wis. Trial atty., health care services & products divsn. FTC; assoc. antitrust & trade regulation practice group Collier, Shannon, Rill & Scott, PLLC; ptnr. antitrust practice Howrey LLP, Washington, 2000—. Antitrust compliance officer Nat. Assn. Music Merchants. Contbr. articles to profl. jours. Named one of 40 Under 40 Leading Antitrust Lawyers, Global Competition Rev., 2008, Washington's 40 Under 40 Rising Stars, The Nat. Law Jour., 2009. Mem.: ABA. Office: Howrey LLP 909 Fannin St FL 15 Houston TX 77010-1026 Office Phone: 202-383-6547. Office Fax: 202-383-6610. E-mail: CuomoP@howrey.com.

CUPP, HORACE BALLARD, surgeon, educator; b. Bristol, Va., Nov. 30, 1930; s. Horace Ballard and Laura Reece Cupp; m. Ann Miller, Dec. 3, 1958; children: Robert Ballard, Laura Cupp Oliva. BA, U. Tenn., 1951; MD, Duke U., 1955. Diplomate Am. Bd. Neurol. Surgery. Resident neurosurgery Duke U., Durham, NC, 1958—64; pvt. practice Johnson City, Tenn., 1964—2000; clin. prof. surgery Coll. Medicine East Tenn. State U., Johnson City, 1980—2000. Bd. dirs. Johnson City Med. Ctr. Hosp., 1990—2000. Past comdr. Johnson City Power Squadron, 1965—. Lt. comdr. USNR, 1956—58. Fellow: ACS; mem.: So. Neurol. Soc., Assn. Neurol. Surgeons, Congress Neurol. Surgeons, Johnson City Rotary, Coral Lodge #142. Seventh-Day Adventist. Avocations: travel, photography, fly fishing. Home: 604 E Holston Ave Johnson City TN 37601-4014 Personal E-mail: horacebcupp@embarqmail.com.

CURD, HOWARD R., financial consultant, textiles executive; Grad., NY Inst. Fin. Founding ptnr. New Centurion Capital Ptnrs., LLC; chmn., CEO, bd. dirs. Jamesway Corp.; chmn., CEO, ind. dir. US Playing Cards; chmn., CEO, bd. dirs. Polycast Tech. Corp., Cmty. Nat. Bank, Fourier Spain, The Jesup Group, Jesup Lamont, Sterling Plastics, Rome Plastics, Ensolite, Uniroyal Tech. Corp., 1992—2003, Uniroyal Engineered Products, LLC, 2003—. Ind. dir. KeySpan Corp., Cin. Fan & Ventilator, Inc., AGP Plastics; ind. dir., trustee Brothers Gourmet Coffees, Inc., DeGeorgio Constrn. co.; bd. dirs. Poughkeepsie NY Savings & Loan, A. Schulman Inc., 2006—. Office: New Centurion Capital Partners LLC 888 7th Ave Ste 1701 New York NY 10019 also: Uniroyal Engineered Products LLC 1800 2nd St Ste 970 Sarasota FL 34236 Office Phone: 212-561-5151, 941-906-8580.

CURL, GREGORY L., bank executive; b. 1948; BA in Polit. Sci., S.W. Mo. State U., 1970; MA in Govt., U. Va. Comml. bank officer Boatmen's Bancshares, St. Louis, 1974, vice chmn., COO; spl. asst. to Senator John C. Danforth US Senate, Washington, 1976—78; joined Bank of America Corp., Charlotte, NC, 1996, vice chmn. corp. devel., pres. specialized lending, 1997—98, dir. corp. planning and strategy, 1998, global corp. strategic devel. and planning exec., chief risk officer, 2009—10. Bd. dirs. Enstar Group, Inc., Grupo Financiero Santander Serfin, China Construction Bank, 2005—. Bd. dirs. Jefferson Scholars Found., U. Va. Officer USN, 1970—74. Woodrow Wilson Fellow, 1970, Philip Dupont Scholar, U. Va., McIntire Fellow. Office: Bank of America Corp 100 N Tryon St, 18th Fl Charlotte NC 28255

CURL, ROBERT FLOYD, JR., chemistry professor; b. Alice, Tex., Aug. 23, 1933; s. Robert Floyd and Lessie (Merritt) Curl; m. Jonel Whipple, Dec. 21, 1955; children: Michael, David. BA, Rice U., 1954; PhD, U. Calif., Berkeley, 1957; D (hon.), U. Buenos Aires, 1997, U. Littoral, 2002. Rsch. fellow Harvard U., Cambridge, Mass., 1957—58; from asst. prof. to prof. chemistry Rice U., Houston, 1958—2003, Kenneth S. Pitzer-Schlumberger prof. natural scis., 2003—05, Kenneth S. Pitzer-Schlumberger prof. natural scis. emeritus, 2005—, Univ. prof. Lovett Coll., 2003—05, Univ. prof. emeritus, 2005—. Vis. rsch. officer NRC Can., 1972—73; vis. prof. Inst. Molecular Sci., Okazaki, Japan, 1977, U. Bonn, 1985; Erskine fellow U. Canterbury, 1999; hon. prof. Univ. Sci. & Tech. China, 2002—, Xiamen U., 2006—. Contbr. articles to profl. jours. Recipient Clayton prize, Instn. Mech. Engineers London, 1958, Internat. New Materials prize, Am. Phys. Soc., 1992, Sr. US Scientist award, Alexander von Humboldt Found., 1984, Nobel prize in chemistry, 1996, Order of Golden Plate, 1997, Achievement award, Am. Carbon Soc., 1997, Tex. Disting. Scientist award, 1997, Johannes Marcus Marci award in spectroscopy, 1998, Madison Marshall award, 1998, Space Act award, 1998, Centenary medal, Royal Soc. Chemistry, 1999, Presdl. Gold Medal, Indian Sci. Congress, 2008; named to, Tex. Sci. Hall of Fame; Alfred P. Sloan Fellow, 1961—63. Fellow: Am. Acad. Arts and Scis., Am. Optical Soc., Royal Soc. of New Zealand (hon.); mem.: NAS, European Acad. Scis., Arts and Letters (titulaire mem.), Am. Chem. Soc., Sigma Xi, Phi Beta Kappa. Methodist. Home: 1824 Bolsover Rd Houston TX 77005-1728 Office: Rice University PO Box 1892 6100 Main St Houston TX 77005-1892 Office Phone: 713-348-4816. E-mail: rfcurl@rice.edu.

CURL, SAMUEL EVERETT, retired dean, agriculturist, consultant; b. Ft. Worth, Dec. 26, 1937; s. Henry Clay and Mary Elva (Watson) C.; m. Betty Doris Savage, June 6, 1957 (div.); children: Jane Ellen, Julia Kathleen, Karen Elizabeth; m. Mary Behrends Reeves, Sept. 11, 1993; stepchildren: Ryan Andrew, Shelly Lyn. Student, Tarleton State Coll., 1955-57; BS, Sam Houston State U., 1959; MS, U. Mo., 1961; PhD, Tex. A&M U., 1963. Mem. faculty Tex. Tech U., Lubbock, 1961, 63-76, 79-97, tchr., rschr. animal physiology and genetics, 1963-76, asst., assoc. and interim dean Coll. Agrl. Sci., 1968-73, assoc. v.p. acad. affairs, prof., 1973-76, dean Coll. Agrl. Scis. and Natural Resources, prof., 1979-97; pres. Phillips U., Enid, Okla., 1976-79; agrl. cons., 1964-76, 2004—; dean and dir. divsn. agrl. scis. and natural resources Okla. State U., Stillwater, 1997—2004, ret., 2004; past pres. So. Assn. Agrl. Scientists. Bd. dirs. Am. Distance Edn. Consortium, Okla. Sci. and Tech. R&D Bd., Food and Agr. Ednl. Info. Sys., Okla. Youth Expo.; past chmn. So. Region Adminstrv. Heads, So. Region Adminstrv. Heads Liaison to Coun. on Agrl. Rsch., Ext. and Tchg.; mem. adminstrv. com. Okla. State U. Sch. Internat. Studies; former bd. dirs. Mid Am. Internat. Agrl. Consortium, 1997—2002, past chmn., 1998—99, 2001—02; mem. Gov.'s Task Force on Agrl. Devel. in Tex., 1982—83, 1988, Tex. Crop and Livestock Adv. Com., 1985—91, Tex. Agrl. Resources Protection Authority, 1989—97, Tex. Agribus. Rsch. Promotion Coun., 1995—97, Okla. State Com., Exptl. Program to Stimulate Competitive Rsch.; del. Eisenhower Consortium for Western Environ. Forestry Rsch., 1979—84; mgmt. com. S.W. Consortium on Plant Genetics and Water Resources, 1984—97, chmn., 1989—95; mem. USDA Nat. Planning Com. on Hispanic Minority Recruitment, 1988—93; trustee Consortium for Internat. Devel., 1979—97, mem. exec. com., 1981—84, 1986—87, 1989—90; former mem. High Plains Rsch. Coord. Bd., So. Regional Coun., U.S. Joint Coun. Food and Agrl. Scis.; former trustee Water Inc.; chmn. agrl. and natural resources program rev. task force Sam Houston State U., 1982—83; mem. adv. com. Sch. Agr. Angelo State U., 1989—95; mem. 1995 farm bill task force Tex. Dept. Agr., 1994—95; chair agrl. team Okla. Govs. EDGE project; adj. faculty mem., outreach coord. Tarleton State U., Stephenville, Tex., 2005—06, exec. asst. to provost, 2006—11; spl. asst. to Dean Agrl. and Human Sci. Rsch. and Devel., 2006—10, spl. asst. to dean Agrl. & Environ. Scis., 2010—11; cons. in field. Author: (with others) Progress and Change in the Agricultural Industry, 1974, Food and Fiber for a Changing World, 1976, 2d edit., 1982; contbr. 95 articles to profl. jours. Pres. Lubbock Econ. Coun., 1982; bd. dirs. Market Lubbock Econ. Devel. Corp., 1995-97; former mem. bd. overseers Ranching Heritage Assn.; mem. Goals for Lubbock: A Vision into the 21st Century Com., 1995-96; elder Westminster Presbyn. Ch., Lubbock, 1994-97; mem. First United Meth. Ch., Stillwater, 1997-2005; mem. adminstrv. coun. First United Meth. Ch., Acton, Tex., 2005—08; 2d lt. U.S. Army, 1959, capt. USAR. Danforth Assn. fellow, 1964-76, Am. Coun. Edn. fellow, 1972-73; recipient Faculty-Alumni Gold medal U. Mo., 1975, Outstanding Agr. Alumnus award Sam Houston State U., 1986, Disting. Alumnus award, 1993, Tex. Citation for Outstanding Svc. award Tex. 4-H Found., 1987, Tex. 4-H Alumni award, 1993, Gerald W. Thomas Outstanding Agriculturist award Tex. Tech. U., 2008, Tarleton State U. Academic Forum, 2007; Disting. Svc. award Vocational Agrl. Tchrs. Assn. Tex., 1987, Blue and Gold Meritorious Svc. award Tex. Future Farmers of Am., 1988, Tex. State degree Future Farmers Am., 1988, Area Disting. Svc. award Vocat. Agr. Tchrs., 1987, Okla. Hon. State degree Future Farmers Am., 2002. Mem.: Profl. Agrl. Workers Tex. (bd. dirs., Disting. Svc. to Tex. Agr. award 1984), Coun. Adminstrv. Heads of Agr., Nat. Assn. State Univs. and Land-Grant Colls. (exec. com. bd. agr. 1994—97, 1998—2001), Assn. U.S. Univ. Dirs. Internat. Agrl. Programs, Am. Assn. Univ. Agrl. Adminstrs., Am. Soc. Animal Sci. (program com. Biennial Symposium on Animal Reprodn. 1972—76, reviewer Jour. Animal Sci.), Lubbock C. of C. (chmn. agr. task force, chmn. rsch. com. 1981—86, bd. dirs. 1988—92, water com., legis. affairs com., agr. com., gubernatorial appointments task force), West Tex. C. of C. (former bd. dirs., chmn. agrl. and ranching com.), Century Club, Tex. Tech. U. Centennial Rotary (hon.), Okla. State U. Alumni Assn., Lubbock Rotary Club (bd. dirs., 1st v.p.), Sirloin Club Okla., Sigma Xi, Gamma Sigma Delta, Phi Kappa Phi, Omicron Delta Kappa, Farmhouse Frat. (assoc.). Methodist. Home: 2615 Waters Edge Dr Granbury TX 76048 Office Phone: 817-776-1285. Personal E-mail: samcurl@charter.net.

CURL, WALTON W., orthopedic surgeon, educator; BS, US Mil. Acad., 1968; MD, Duke U., 1973. Cert. American Bd. Orthop. Surgery, American Bd. Orthop. Surgery-orthop. sports medicine. Intern orthop. surgery Letterman Army Med. Ctr., 1975, resident orthop. surgery, 1978; fellow Keller Army Hosp. US Mil. Acad., 1979; prof. orthopaedics Wake Forest Univ.; orthop. surgeon Wake Forest Bapt. Med. Ctr. Contbr. numerous articles to profl. publs. Served Vietnam, served in operation desert storm Saudi Arabia, served Med. Corps US Army, ret. col., US Army Reserves. Recipient two Bronze Stars award; named one of the Best Doctors in America. Mem.: Hughston Sports Medicine Soc., Herodicus Soc., Assn. Mil. Surgeons of US, American Orthop. Soc. of Sports Medicine, American Coll. Sports Medicine, Nat. Athletic Trainer's Assn., American Acad. of Orthop. Surgeons. Office: Wake Forest Baptist Medical Center Medical Center Blvd Winston Salem NC 27157 Office Phone: 336-716-2011.*

CURLEY, THOMAS (TOM CURLEY), former publishing executive; b. Easton, Pa., July 6, 1948; s. John Joseph and Emily Dixon (Sprague) Curley; m. Marsha Stanley, Sept. 14, 1974; children: Laura Stanley, Melinda Burke. BA in Polit. Sci., La Salle U., 1970; MBA, Rochester Inst. Tech., 1977. Reporter The News Tribune, Woodbridge, NJ, 1967, 1968, reporter, copy editor, 1970—72; night city/suburban editor The Times-Tribune, Rochester, NY, 1972—76; dir. info. Gannett Co., Inc., Rochester, 1976—80, dir. rsch., 1980—82; editor Norwich (Conn.) Bulletin, 1982—83; pub. The Courier-News, Bridgewater, NJ, 1983—85; exec. v.p. USA Today, Washington, 1985—86, pres., 1986—89, pres., COO, 1989—91, pres., pub., 1991—2003; sr. v.p. Gannett Co., Inc., 1998—2003; pres., CEO The Associated Press (AP), NYC, 2003—12. Trustee LaSalle U., Phila., 1987—, Rochester Inst. Tech., Ronald McDonald House Charities; mem. exec. bd. Ad Council. Pres. Ctrl. Jersey C. of C., Plainfield, NJ, 1984—85; exec. v.p. United Way Somerset Valley, Bridgewater, 1985; bd. dirs. Assn. for Retarded Citizens, Manville, NJ, 1983—85. Recipient Alumnus of Yr. award, Rochester Inst. Tech., 1986; Pub. Opinion Rsch. fellow, Northwestern U., 1976.

CURLIN, WILLIAM GEORGE, bishop emeritus; b. Portsmouth, Va., Aug. 30, 1927; Attended, Georgetown U., St. Mary's Sem., Balt. Ordained priest Archdiocese of Washington, DC, 1957, aux. bishop DC, 1988—94; ordained bishop, 1988; bishop Diocese of Charlotte, NC, 1994—2002, bishop emeritus, 2002—. Roman Catholic. Office: 3005 Markworth Ave Charlotte NC 28210-6432

CURNOCK, ROBERT J., communications executive; b. Chgo., Dec. 14, 1957; m. Karen Curnock. BA in Comm., Baylor U., Waco, 1981. Gen. assignment reporter KWTX-TV, Waco, weekend sports anchor; owner Dub-L Tape, Waco, 1985—. Pub. rels. dir. McLennan County Rep. Party; county del. GOP Conv., state del.; election judge; mem. state panel on small bus. Republican. Avocations: tennis, skiing, softball, chess, golf. Office: PO Box 8800 Waco TX 76714

CURRAN, CHARLES EDWARD, theology studies educator, priest; b. Rochester, NY, Mar. 30, 1934; s. John F. and Gertrude (Beisner) C. BA, St. Bernard's Coll., 1955; Licentiate in Sacred Theology, Pontifical Gregorian U., Rome, 1959, STD, 1961, Acad. Alfonsiana, 1961; PhD (hon.), U. Charleston, 1987, Concordia Coll., Portland, 1992. Ordained priest Roman Cath. Ch., 1958. Prof. moral theology St. Bernard's Sem., Rochester, 1961-65; from asst. prof. to prof. Cath. U. Am., Washington, 1965-87; vis. Kaneb prof. Cath. studies Cornell U., Ithaca, NY, 1987-88; vis. Brooks prof. Religion U. So. Calif., LA, 1988-89, vis. Firestone prof. Religion, 1989-90; vis. Goodwin-Philpott eminent scholar in Religion Auburn (Ala.) U., 1990-91; Elizabth Scurlock U. prof. of human values So. Meth. U., Dallas, 1991—. External examiner in Christian ethics U. W.I., 1982-86; lectr. in field. Author: Christian Morality Today, 1966, A New Look at Christian Morality, 1968, Contemporary Problems in Moral Theology, 1970, Catholic Moral Theology in Dialogue, 1972, The Crisis in Priestly Ministry, 1972, Politics, Medicine and Christian Ethics: A Dialogue with Paul Ramsey, 1973, New Perspectives in Moral Theology, 1974, Ongoing Revision: Studies in Moral Theology, 1976, Themes in Fundamental Moral Theology, 1977, Issues in Sexual and Medical Ethics, 1978, Transition and Tradition in Moral Theology, 1979, Moral Theology: A Continuing Journey, 1982, American Catholic Social Ethics: Twentieth Century Approaches, 1982, Critical Concerns in Moral Theology, 1984, Directions in Catholic Social Ethics, 1985, Directions in Fundamental Moral Theology, 1985, Faithful Dissent, 1986, Toward an American Catholic Moral Theology, 1988, Sexualitat und Ethik, 1988, Tensions in Moral Theology, 1988, Catholic Higher Education, Theology, and Academic Freedom, 1990, The Living Tradition of Moral Theology, 1992, The Church and Morality: An Ecumenical and Catholic Approach, 1993, History and Contemporary Issues: Studies in Moral Theology, 1996, The Origins of Moral Theology in the U.S.: Three Different Approaches, 1997, Moral Theology at the End of the Century, 1999, The Catholic Moral Tradition Today: A Synthesis, 1999, Catholic Social Teaching 1891-Present: A Historical, Theological, and Ethical Analysis, 2002, The

Moral Theology of Pope John Paul II, 2005, Loyal Dissent: Memoir of a Catholic Theologian, 2006, Catholic Moral Theology in the US: A History, 2008, The Social Mission of the US Catholic Church: A Theologien Perpective, 2011; also articles; (with others) Dissent In and For the Church: Theologians and Humanae Vitae, 1969, The Responsibility of Dissent: The Church and Academic Freedom, 1969; editor: Absolutes in Moral Theology?, 1968, Contraception: Authority and Dissent, 1969, Moral Theology: Challenges for the Future, 1990; co-editor book series: (with Richard A. McCormick) 1st 11 vols. Readings in Moral Theology: No. 1: Moral Norms and Catholic Tradition, 1979, No. 2: The Distinctiveness of Christian Ethics, 1980, No. 3: The Magisterium and Morality, 1982, No. 4: The Use of Scripture in Moral Theology, 1984, No. 5: Official Catholic Social Teaching, 1986, No. 6: Dissent in the Church, 1988, No. 7: Natural Law and Theology, 1991, No. 8: Dialogue About Catholic Sexual Teaching, 1993, Feminist Ethics and the Catholic Moral Tradition: Readings in Moral Theology No. 9, 1996, John Paul II and Moral Theology: Readings in Moral Theology No. 10, 1998, The Historical Development of Fundamental Moral Theology in The United States: Readings in Moral Theology No. 11, 1999, The Catholic Church, Morality, and Politics: Readings in Moral Theology No. 12, 2001, Change in Official Catholic Moral Teachings: Readings in Moral Theology No. 13, 2003, Conscience Readings in Moral Theology No. 14, 2004, Marriage: Readings in Moral Theology No. 15., 2009, Virtue: Readings in Moral Theology No 16, 2011. Am. Assn. Theol. Schs. fellow, 1971; Georgetown U. Kennedy Ctr. for Bioethics scholar, 1972, Am. Pubs. award, PROSE award, 2009, award Am. Acad. Arts & Socs., 2010; named ABC-TV person week, 1986. Mem. Cath. Theol. Soc. Am. (pres. 1969-70, John Courtney Murray award 1972), Soc. Christian Ethics (pres. 1971-72, mem. editorial bd. Ann. 1991—), Am. Theol. Soc. (pres. 1989-90), Coll. Theology Soc. (Pres. award, 2003). Avocations: golf, swimming, reading. Home: 4125 Woodcreek Dr Dallas TX 75220-5074 Home Phone: 214-352-8974. Business E-Mail: ccurran@smu.edu.

CURRAN, CHRISTOPHER, economics professor; b. Washington, Nov. 5, 1943; s. Charles Daniel and Virginia (Wray) C.; m. Nannette Carter, June 10, 1978; children: John Fredrick, Christianne Michelle. BA in History, Rice U., 1967; MS in Econs., Purdue U., 1969, PhD in Econs., 1972. Grad. instr. econs. Purdue U., 1967-70; asst. prof. econs. Emory U., Atlanta, 1970-77, sr. acad. assoc. Law and Econs. Ctr., 1983-86, sr. acad. assoc. law and econs., 1986—, assoc. prof. econs., 1977—, dir. undergrad. studies, 1994-96. Fulbright lectr., Peru, 1976; adj. assoc. prof. Fuqua Sch. Bus., Duke U., 2000. Contbr. articles and book revs. to profl. jours. Bd. mem. Lullwater Sch., Atlanta, 1975; v.p. Virginia Hill Condo Assn., Atlanta, 1993, pres. 1994, treas. 1995. Krannert rsch. grantee, 1969-70, grantee Emory U., 1972, 75, 79, Emory Bus. Sch., 1978-80, 82. Mem. Am. Econ. Assn., So. Econ. Assn., Am. Law and Econs. Assn., European Assn. Law and Econs. (assoc.), Therapy Dogs Internat., Inc. (assoc.), Belgian Sheepdog Club Am. (2nd v.p 2009-11), Rabun County Hist. Soc. (bd. mem. 2010-). Avocation: tennis. Home: 500 Ledford Rd Dillard GA 30537-1752 Office: Emory U Dept of Economics 1602 Fishburne Atlanta GA 30322-0001 Office Phone: 404-727-6355.

CURRENCE, JOHN, chef; b. New Orleans; m. Bess Currence. Degree, U. NC. Asst. to resident pasta chef Aurora, Chapel Hill, NC; sous chef Gautreau's, New Orleans, 1989; exec.-sous chef Bacco; owner, chef City Grocery, Oxford, Miss., 1992—, Bouré, Oxford, 2002—, Big Bad Breakfast, Oxford, 2008—, Snackbar, Oxford, 2009—. Vol. farmers' coop. and market. Named Best Chef: South, James Beard Found., 2009. Mem.: Miss. Restaurant Assn. (pres., chmn. bd. dirs. 2000—01, mem. bd. dirs.). Office: City Grocery 152 Courthouse Sq Oxford MS 38655 Office Phone: 662-232-8080.

CURRENT, WILLIAM A., SR., state legislator; b. Gastonia, NC, May 4, 1933; Dentist; state rep. Dist. 109 NC, 2005—. With Dental Corps USN, 1958—60. Mem.: Gaston County Health Dept., Gaston Family Health Svc., NC Dental Found., NC Dental Soc. Republican. Address: Dist Off 224 S New Hope Rd Gastonia NC 28054 Office: North Carolina House of Representatives 300 N Salisbury St Rm 418B Raleigh NC 27603-5925 Office Phone: 919-733-5809. Business E-Mail: Bill.Current@ncleg.net.

CURRERI, PETER WILLIAM, health facility administrator, consultant; b. Milw., Sept. 2, 1936; s. Anthony Rudolph and Dorothea Christiana (Heubsch) C.; m. Patricia Ann Egry, Aug. 14, 1958 (div. 1975); children: Charles Anthony, James Bradley, Regina Dawn. BA, Swarthmore Coll., 1958; MD, U. Pa., 1962. Intern Hosp. of U. Pa., 1962-63, resident in surgery, 1963-68; asst. prof. surgery U. Tex., Southwestern Med. Ctr., Dallas, 1971-74; assoc. prof. surgery U. Wash. Med. Sch., Seattle, 1974-77; prof. surgery Cornell U. Med. Ctr., NYC, 1977-81; prof., chmn. surgery U. South Ala. Med. Sch., Mobile, Ala., 1981—88; chmn. Strategem of Ala., Inc., Daphne, 1988—. Mem. surgery anesthesiology and trauma study sect. NIH, Washington, 1980-84, chmn., 1986-88; commr. Physician Payment Rev. Commn., Washington, 1988-97; mem. Medicare Payment Adv. Com., 1997-99. Contbr. articles to profl. jours. Lt. col. U.S. Army, 1968-71. Decorated Meritorious Svc. medal; recipient Rsch. Career Devel. award NIH, 1972, Curtis P. Artz award Am. Trauma Soc., 1989. Mem. Am. Assn. for Surgery of Trauma (pres. 1989-90), Am. Burn Assn. (pres. 1983-84), Am. Coll. Surgeons (sec. bd. govs. 1987-89), Halstead Surg. Soc. (pres. 1988-89), Soc. Univ. Surgeons (pres. 1980-81), Assn. Acad. Surgery (recorder 1972-74). Avocations: golf, walking. Office: Strategem Inc 26064 Capital Dr Ste A Daphne AL 36526-6166 Office Phone: 251-625-2205.

CURREY, RUSSELL M., packaging company executive; Joined Rock-Tenn Co., 1983, exec. v.p., gen. mgr., recycled fiber divsn., 1992—94, sr. v.p., mktg., planning, 1994—2001, exec. v.p., gen. mgr., corrugated packaging divsn., 2001—08. Bd. dirs. Rock-Tenn Co., 2003—. Mailing: Rock Tenn Co P O Box 4098 Norcross GA 30091 Office: Rock Tenn Co 504 Thrasher St Norcross GA 30071 Office Phone: 770-448-2193. Office Fax: 678-291-7666. Business E-Mail: rcurrey@rocktenn.com.

CURREY, THOMAS ARTHUR, ophthalmologist; b. Itawamba County, Miss., July 9, 1933; s. Charles Edward Currey and Anna L. (Williams) C; m. Carol Ann Clabough, Nov. 7, 1959; children: Thomas A. Jr., C. Russell. Degree, U. Miss., 1955; MD, U. Tenn., 1958. Diplomate Am. Bd. Ophthalmology. Intern City of Memphis Hosps., 1958-59; resident in ophthalmology U. Tenn., Memphis, 1962-65; pvt. practice Memphis, 1965—; mem. staff St. Francis Hosp., 1965—, pres. med. staff, 1985. Assoc. instr. ophthalmology dept. family practice, 1990—, asst. clin. instr. ophthalmology U. Tenn., 1965—. Fellow ACS; mem. Tenn. Med. Assn. (v.p. 1987), Tenn. Acad. Ophthalmology (pres. 1975), Memphis & Shelby County Med. Soc. (treas. 1983-86). Avocations: photography, travel, sports. Office: Eye Specialists Assoc PC 1900 Kirby Pky Memphis TN 38138-3690 Office Phone: 901-754-0930. Personal E-mail: tcurrey901@aol.com.

CURRIE, BECKY, state legislator; b. May 2, 1957; m. Bruce Currie. AS, S W CC.; attended, U. Southern Miss. Registered nurse; mem. Dist. 92 Miss. House of Reps., 2008—, mem. juvenile justice com., Medicaid com., pub. health and human svcs. com., univs. and colls. com. Republican. Episcopalian. Home: 407 Oliver Dr Brookhaven MS 39601 Office: PO Box 1018 Jackson MS 39215 Home Phone: 601-833-5953. E-mail: bcurrie@house.ms.gov.

CURRIE, CAMERON MCGOWAN, federal judge; b. Florence, SC, 1948; BA, U. S.C., 1970; JD with honors, George Washington U., 1975. Tchr. Moultrie H.S., Mt. Pleasant; law intern to magistrate judge Hon. Arthur L. Burnett U.S. Dist. Ct. D.C., 1973-74; atty. Arent, Fox, Kintner, Plotkin & Kahn, Washington, 1975-78; asst. U.S. Atty. Office U.S. Atty., Washington, 1978-80, Columbia, S.C., 1980-84; magistrate judge US Dist. Ct. SC, Columbia, 1984-86, judge, 1994—; pvt. practice Columbia, 1986-89; chief dep. atty. gen. Office Atty. Gen., State of S.C., Columbia, 1989-94. Adj. prof. in trial advocacy Sch. Law U. S.C., 1986-89. Assoc. editor SEC No Action Letters Index, 1972-73. Bd. dirs. Wings, Inc., 1986-94, sec., 1992-94. Mem. S.C. Bar, D.C. Bar, S.C. Women Lawyers Assn., Fed. Judges Assn., John Belton O'Neall Inn of Ct. Office: US Dist Ct 901 Richland St Columbia SC 29201

CURRIE, JOHN L., gynecologic oncologist; MD, U. NC, 1967. Diplomate Am. Bd. Ob-Gyn-gynecologic oncology, 1982, Am. Bd. Ob-Gyn, 1991, lic. Conn. Resident gynecologic oncology Hosp. Univ. Pa., Phila., 1968—72; fellow gynecologic oncology Duke Univ. Med. Ctr., Durham, 1978—80; hosp. affiliations include Mary Hitchcock Meml. Hosp., Med. Ctr.; dir. women's health and gynecologic oncology dept. John B. Amos Cancer Ctr.; gynecologic oncologist. Office: c/o John B Amos Cancer Center 1831 5th Ave Columbus GA 31904 Office Phone: 860-545-4341.

CURRIE, JOHN THORNTON (JACK CURRIE), retired investment banker; b. Houston, Aug. 4, 1928; s. John Felix and Irma Lillian (Haxthausen) C.; m. Dorothy Lee Peek, May 30, 1959; children: Harriss Thornton, Laura Graef. BA, U. Tex., 1949, BBA, 1950. Salesman Harris, Upham & Co., NYC and Houston, 1950-52; ptnr. Moreland, Brandenberger & Currie, Galveston, Tex., 1955-60; pres., bd. dirs. Moroney, Beissner & Co., Inc., Houston, 1960-74; sr. v.p., bd. dirs. Rotan Mosle Inc., Houston, 1974-81, chmn., 1981-83; vice chmn. Rotan Mosle Fin. Corp., Houston, 1984; mng. dir. Mason Best Co., Houston, 1984-86. Bd. dirs. family mut. funds managed by Am. Nat. Ins. Co., Galveston, Artspace Inc., Mpls., Minn., Internat. Exec. Svc. Corps.; rep. Muslim Comml. Bank, Karachi, Pakistan, 1992, Govt. of Lithuania, Vilnius, 1993, Capital Ptnrs., Bratislava, Slovakia, 1997. Trustee Holly Hall, Houston, 1968-73, Harris and Eliza Kempner Fund, Galveston, Tex., 1975—03; mem. devel. bd. U. Tex. Health Sci. Ctr., Houston, 1978-89, U. Tex. Med. Br., Galveston, 1992—; mem. Chancellor's Coun. U. Tex. System; established Mary Tucker Currie Professorship, Tex. A&M U.; 1st lt. U.S. Army, 1952-54. Mem.: Krewe of Momus Galveston, Galveston Artillery Club, Houston Country Club. Republican. Episcopalian. Avocations: sailing, hunting, history. Office: 520 Post Oak Blvd Ste 125 Houston TX 77027-9495 Home: 6218 Cedar Creek Houston TX 77057

CURRIER, MARY MARGARET, public health service officer; b. Ann Arbor, Mich., 1956; Attended, Trinity Coll., 1977—78; BA, Rice U., 1978; MD, U. Miss. Sch. Medicine, 1983; MPH, Johns Hopkins Sch. Hygeine & Pub. Health, 1987. Cert. gen. preventive medicine and pub. health. Resident pub. health Johns Hopkins U.; served various capacities Miss. Dept. Health, Jackson, 1984—, staff physician prenatal care, family planning, sexually transmitted disease and pediat. program, state epidemiologist, 1993—2003, 2007—09, state health officer, 2010—. Mem.: APHA, AMA, Miss. Ctrl. Med. Soc. Office: Mississippi Department of Health 570 East Woodrow Wilson Dr Jackson MS 39216 Office Phone: 601-576-7634. Office Fax: 601-576-7931.

CURRY, BILL (WILLIAM ALEXANDER CURRY), college football coach, retired professional football player; b. College Park, Ga., Oct. 21, 1942; s. Bill and Eleanor Curry; m. Carolyn Newton; children: Billy, Kristin. Bs in Indsl. Mgmt., Ga. Inst. Tech., Atlanta, 1965. Ctr. Green Bay Packers, 1965—66, Balt. Colts, 1967—72, Houston Oilers, 1973, LA Rams, 1974; offensive line coach Ga. Inst. Tech. Yellow Jackets, 1976, head football coach, 1980—86; asst. coach Green Bay Packers, 1977—79; head football coach U. Ala. Crimson Tide, 1987—89, U. Ky. Wildcats, 1990—96; NCAA football analyst, contbg. writer ESPN, 1997—2007; dir. Leadership Baylor Baylor Sch., Chattanooga, 2006—08; head football coach Ga. State U. Panthers, Atlanta, 2008—. Pres. NFL Players Assn., 1973—75. Author: Ten Men You Meet in the Huddle: Lesson from a Football Life, 2008. Recipient Bobby Dodd Nat. Coach of Yr. award, 1989, Amos Alonzo Stagg award, AFCA, 2007, Pres. Gerald R. Ford Legends Ctr. award, 2008; named Atlantic Coast Conf. Coach of Yr., 1985, Southeastern Conf. Coach of Yr., 1989; named to Am. Football Conf. Pro Bowl Team, NFL, 1971, 1972, Ga. Tech. Athletic Hall of Fame, State of Ga. Sports Hall of Fame, Atlanta Sports Hall of Fame, 2010; Disting. Exec. fellow, Robinson Coll. Bus. at Ga. State Univ., 2008—. Achievements include member of NFL championship winning Green Bay Packers, 1966, 1967 (Super Bowl I); Balt. Colts, 1969 (Super Bowl III), 1971 (Super Bowl V). Office: Ga State University Football c/o Intercollegiate Athletics PO Box 3975 Atlanta GA 30302-3975 Office Phone: 404-413-4110.

CURRY, DALE BLAIR, retired journalist; b. Memphis, May 30, 1941; d. Hamilton Minter and Doris (Terry) Blair; m. Douglas Hester Curry, Dec. 21, 1963; children: Jennifer, Elizabeth. BA, U. Miss., 1963. Reporter The Commerical-Appeal, Memphis, 1962-63, Atlanta Constn., 1963-65, The States-Item, New Orleans, 1969-72, The Morning Advocate, Baton Rouge, 1974-76, 82-84; food editor The Times-Picayune, New Orleans, 1984—2004; columnist New Orleans Mag.; food and travel freelance writer. Author: New Orleans Home Cooking. Elder St. Charles Ave. Presbyn. Ch., New Orleans, 1984-87, 91-94. Recipient award AP, UPI, New Orleans Press Club; named among Top 50 alumni 50th Anniversary U. Miss. Sch. Journalism, 1998. Mem. Assn. Food Journalists (pres. 1994-96), Theta Sigma Phi (Alumni of Yr. U. Miss. chpt.). E-mail: dalecurry2004@yahoo.com.

CURRY, JOHN MICHAEL, investment banker; b. Buffalo, Dec. 30, 1942; s. John Vincent and June (Eisele) C.; m. Thea Adrian Kirk, July 12, 1969 (div. 1982); children: John Adrian, James Prescott; m. Margaretta Buckley, Mar. 17, 1990; 1 child, Michael Jeremiah. BA, U. San Francisco, 1968; MBA, Harvard U., Cambridge, Mass., 1970; postgrad., Suffolk U., Boston, 1971. Cert. property mgr.; registered rep. and gen. securities rep.; registered fiduciary and investment adviser, registered securities prin. Developer Devel. Corp. Am., Boston, 1970-73; founder, chmn. APT Mgmt. Group, Inc., Boston, 1977—, Am. Securities Team, Inc., Boston, 1992—, Am. Properties Team, APT Asset, Boston, 1987—; chmn. Am. Devel. Team, 1985-92, Am. Realty Team, Fla., 1994—, Infrastructure Repair Technologies, 1998—, APT Mgmt. Group Inc. Bd. dirs. six corps.; Boston rep. Taylor Woodrow PLC, London, 1983-85. Vol. various fed., state, local polit. orgns. and campaigns. Sgt. US Army, 1961-64. Recipient Modernization award Building Mag., 1980-81, Outstanding Restoration award Lowell C. of C., 1981, Nat. Jewish Life award, 1987. Mem. Harvard Club (Boston), Soc. Colonial Wars, Sons Am. Revolution (Palm Beach chpt.). Personal E-mail: jcurry1@gmail.com. Business E-Mail: jcurry@aptfin.com.

CURRY, KELLY EDWIN, hospital administrator; b. Owensboro, Ky., Jan. 19, 1955; s. Martha (Fogle) C.; m. Susan Marie Miller, July 23, 1977; children: Natalie Marie, Leah Sloane. BS in Acctg., U. Ky., 1977. CPA, Ky. Sr. auditor Touche Ross & Co. CPA's, 1977-79, Humana, Inc., 1979-82; chmn., pres., founder Found. in Christ Ministries Ltd., Ireland, 1995—2007; dir., internal audit Health Management Associates, Inc., Naples, Fla., 1982, dir., reimbursement, 1983-84, hosp. ops. cons., 1985-87, v.p., fin. ops., 1987-92, CFO, 1987—94, sr. v.p., fin., CFO Naples, 1992—94, COO, 2007—08, chief adminstrv. officer, 2008—10, exec. v.p., CFO, 2010—. Mem. AICPA, Ky. Soc. CPAs, Fla. Soc. CPAs. Republican. Baptist. Avocations: golf, fishing, running. Office: Health Management Associates Inc 5811 Pelican Bay Blvd Naples FL 34108-2710 Office Phone: 239-598-3131. Office Fax: 239-598-2705. Business E-Mail: kelly.curry@hma.com.

CURRY, LEONARD B., political organization administrator, management consultant; b. Key West, Fla. married; 3 children. BS in Acctg., summa cum laude, U. Fla., Gainesville. CPA. Sr. mgr. PricewaterhouseCoopers, 1995—2002; co-founder, mng. dir. ICX Group, Inc., 2003—; vice chmn. Rep. Party of Fla., 2011, chmn., 2011—. Treas. Duval County Rep. Exec. Com., 2007, chmn., 2008—; mem. Southside United Meth. Ch.; bd. mem. Jacksonville Symphony Assn., Jacksonville Housing Commn.; commr. Fla. State Boxing Commn., 2010—. Mem.: South Jacksonville Rotary. Republican. Office: ICX Group Inc SunTrust Tower 76 S Laura St Ste 1700 Jacksonville FL 32202 also: Republican Party of Fla 420 E Jefferson St Tallahassee FL 32301 Office Phone: 904-208-2200, 850-222-7920. Office Fax: 904-208-2201, 850-681-0184.*

CURRY, R. CHARLES, JR., cardiologist; MD, U. Fla., 1969. Diplomate American Bd. Internal Medicine, 1972, American Bd. Internal Medicine-cardiovasc. disease, 1975. Resident internal medicine Univ. of Fla.; fellow cardiovasc. disease Univ. of Fla. Affiliated Hosp., Gainseville, 1972—74; physician Fla. Hosp. Office: Florida Hospital 601 E Rollins St Orlando FL 32803-1489 Office Phone: 407-894-4474.

CURTIN, DAVID YARROW, chemist, educator; b. Phila., Aug. 22, 1920; s. Ellsworth Ferris and Margeretta (Cope) C.; m. Constance O'Hara, July 1, 1950; children— Susan McLean, David Ferris, Jane Yarrow. AB, Swarthmore Coll., 1943; PhD, U. Ill., 1945. Pvt. asst. Harvard, 1945-46; instr., then asst. prof. chemistry Columbia U., 1946-51; mem. faculty U. Ill., Urbana, 1951—, prof. chemistry, 1954-86, Fuson prof. emeritus, 1988—, head div. organic chemistry, 1963-65. Vis. lectr. Inst. de Quimica, Mexico, summer 1955, U. Tex., 1959; Reilly lectr. U. Notre Dame, 1960 Mem. editorial bd.: Organic Reactions, 1954- 64; adv. bd., 1965—; mem. bd. editors: Jour. Organic Chemistry, 1962-66. Einstein fellow Israel, 1982. Mem. Am., Brit., Swiss chem. socs., Nat. Acad. Sci., Am. Crystallographic Assn. Achievements include special research organic reaction mechanisms, stereochemistry, exploratory organic chemistry, reactions in solid state. Home: 15010 Shell Point Blvd Fort Myers FL 33908-1637

CURTIN, LAWRENCE N., lawyer; b. Glen Ridge, NJ, Apr. 29, 1950; BS with honors, Fla. State U., 1972; JD with honors, Fla. State U. Coll. Law, 1976. Bar: Fla. 1976, US Dist. Ct. (no. dist.) Fla., US Ct. Appeals (4th, 5th, 11th and DC cirs.). Law clerk to Hon. William Stafford U.S. Dist. Ct. (No. dist.) Fla., 1976-78; exec. ptnr. Holland & Knight, Tallahassee. Mem. Law Review, 1975-76; co-author: Surface Water Pollution Control, vol. 1, 1986-96; contbr. articles to profl. jours. Mem. ABA (litig., corp., bus. and banking sects.), Fla. Bar (chmn. energy law com. 1983-84, mem. administrv. and environ. and land use law sect., natural resources law), Tallahassee Bar Assn., Beta Gamma Sigma, Sigma Iota Epsilon. Office: Holland & Knight LLP PO Drawer 810 315 S Calhoun St Ste 600 Tallahassee FL 32301-1897 Office Phone: 850-224-7000, 850-425-5678. E-mail: larry.curtin@hklaw.com.

CURTIS, JOYCE MAE, retired physical education educator; b. Cleburne, Tex., Aug. 27, 1937; d. Robert Joyce and Maudie Mae C. BS, North Tex. State U., 1959, MS in Phys. Edn., 1960; D of Phys. Edn., Ind. U., 1970. Prof. Abilene (Tex.) Christian U., 1959—2004; grad. asst. Ind. U., 1967-70; ret., 2004. Treas. Tex. Assn. Intercollegiate Athletics for Women, 1971-79. Co-editor: (book) Physical Education Activities Handbook, 1971; author: (manual) Manual for Bowling Teachers at Abilene Christian University, 1982, Manual for Badminton Teachers at Abilene Christian University, 1985; author: (text) Pickle-Ball for Player and Teacher, 3d edit., 1999, Intermediate Bowling Notebook, 1993;contbr. articles to profl. jours. Vol. Vera West Women's Ctr., Hope Fund Com., Hendrick Med. Ctr. Named Bowler of Yr. Abilene Women's Bowling Assn., 1967, Outstanding Educator of Am., 1975; recipient Disting. Svc. award Tex. Assn. for Intercollegiate Athletics for Women, 1982, Faculty Devel. award Abilene Christian U., 1991; inducted into ACU Sports Hall of Fame, 2003, Pathfinder award, Tex. Assoc. Health, Phy. Ed., 2008, Pathfinder award Nat. Assn. Girls & Woman's Sports-AAHPERD, 2009. Mem. AAHPERD (life), Tex. Assn. for Health, Phys. Edn., Recreation and Dance, Abilene Women's Bowling Assn. (life), Delta Psi Kappa (life), Phi Lambda Theta. Mem. Ch. of Christ. Avocations: travel, golf, gardening. Personal E-mail: jmc37C@suddenlink.net.

CURTIS, PHILIP KERRY, executive recruiter, lawyer; b. Mineola, NY, Nov. 6, 1945; s. William Kerry and Cherry (Smith) C.; m. Janet (McDowell), Sept. 9, 1970; 1 child, Kerry Bowen. BA, Dartmouth Coll., 1967; JD, Harvard Law Sch., 1971; MBA, Harvard U., 1974. Bar: N.Y., 1971; Ga., 1976. Assoc. White and Case, NYC, 1971-72, Hansell and Post, Atlanta, 1975-76; counsel, asst. to pres. Wiggins and Assoc., Atlanta, 1976-82; exec. v.p. Coers, Steinemann, and Co., Atlanta, 1982-84; exec. v.p., ptnr. Western Devel. SE, Atlanta, 1984-87; ptnr., sr. v.p. Charter Properties, Inc., Atlanta, 1987-93; exec. v.p. JDN Realty Corp., Atlanta, 1994-96; pres. Habersham Ptnr., Atlanta, 1996—2002; ptnr. Matteson Ptnr., Atlanta, 2002—10, Olmstead Lynch, Kreutz, 2010—. Adj. prof. GA State U., 2009—; hon. real estate bd. mem. Robinson Coll. Bus., 2009—. Elder Peachtree Presbyn. Ch., Atlanta, 1983-86; dir. Met. Arts Found., Atlanta, 1983-87; 1st lt., USAR, 1970-78. Mem.: SAR (pres. Atlanta chpt. 2005—06), St. George Soc. (pres. Atlanta chpt. 2007—), Soc. War of 1812, Mil. Order World Wars (sr. vice cmdr., Atlanta Chpt. 2008—09), Gen. Soc. SR, Old Guard (col., past comdt.), Mil. Order Stars and Bars, Civil War Roundtable, Venerable Order St. John, Nat. Meml. Day Assn. Ga. (pres. 2006—08), Soc. Colonial Wars, Burge Plantation Club, Buckhead Fifty Club (pres. 2008—09), Sigma Chi Club Atlanta (bd. dirs. 1985—86), Atlanta Forum, Harvard Bus. Sch. Club of Atlanta (pres. 1982—83), Dartmouth Club of Ga. (pres. 1982—84), Buckhead Rotary Club (dir. 2009—11), Cherokee Town and Country Club, Harvard Club of Ga., German Club (pres. 1986—87). Republican. Home: 3111 Arden Rd NW Atlanta GA 30305-1916 Office: 3060 Peachtree Rd NW Ste 1570 Atlanta GA 30305 Office Phone: 404-266-9981.

CURTISS, CHARLES, state legislator; b. Feb. 9, 1947; married, 1966; 1 child, Nichole. Fire chief Cassville Fire Dept., 1980; commr. White Co., Tenn., 1982, exec., 1986; house rep. Environ. Commerce Com., Tenn.; state rep. Dist. 43 Tenn., 1995—; mem. Conservation Com., Environ. Commerce Com.; with Mfg. Com.; clerk; treas.;

sunday sch. tchr. Plainview Freewill Baptist Ch. Mem.: Eastern Star, Shriner, York & Scottish Rite Mason, Sparta Lodge No 99 F&AM, White County Farm Bur., Nat. Rifle Assn., America Legion. Democrat. Freewill Baptist. Office: 120 General Jones Rd Sparta TN 38583 also: 34 Legislative Plz Nashville TN 37243-0143 Office Phone: 931-761-2765, 615-741-1963. Business E-Mail: rep.charles.curtiss@capitol.tn.gov.

CURY, BRUCE PAUL, lawyer, magistrate, educator; b. Englewood, NJ, Mar. 19, 1942; s. Beddy Galib and Violet (Maloof) C.; m. Orahdella Elizabeth Green, Oct. 14, 1972; 1 child, Lauren Elaine. BS, U. Ky., 1965; JD, U. Louisville, 1972. Bar: Fla. 1972, U.S. Dist. Ct. (mid. dist.) Fla. 1974, U.S. Ct. Appeals (5th cir.) 1980, U.S. Ct. Appeals (11th cir.) 1982, U.S. Supreme Ct. 1976. Assoc. George McDowell P.A., Tampa, Fla., 1972-73; sole practice Tampa, 1973-76; adj. prof. bus. law U. Tampa, 1977-85; adj. prof. criminal law U. South Fla., 1984-85; chief asst. pub. defender Office of Pub. Defender, Tampa, 1974-85; sole practice Tampa, 1985-90; gen. counsel Fla. Dept. Transportation, Bartow, 1990—2008; sole practice Tampa, 2008—. Magistrate traffic ct., Tampa, 1993—, hearing officer, Parking Ct. Tampa, 2013-2014; chmn. Hills County Zoning Bd. Tampa, 1989-97; pres., dir. Bay Area Legal Svcs., Inc., Tampa, 1980-92; chmn. Hills County Land Use Appeals Bd. Tampa, 1997-1999. Legal counsel Big Bros./Big Sisters Greater Tampa, Inc., 1983-95; pres, bd. dirs. Rape Crisis Ctr., Tampa, 1982-86; bd. dirs. Hillsborough Edn. Found., Tampa, 1999—2009; chmn. Hillsborough County City-County Planning Commn., Tampa, 1999-2003, 2005-2013. 1st lt. US Army, 1966—69. Recipient Indigent Accused award Fla. Pub. Defender, 1985, Dirs. award Sexual Abuse Treatment Ctr. Tampa, 1986, Pres. and Dirs. award Bay Area Legal Svcs. Tampa, 1992, Sec. of Transp. Leadership award Fla. Dept. Transp., 2000, Bd of County Commn. award Outstanding Contribution and Svcs. to Hillsborough County, 2003, Hillsborough County City-County Planning Commn. Vision, Leadership and Exemplary Svc. award, 2013. Mem. Criminal Def. Lawyers Assn. Hillsborough County, Fla. Bar Assn. (mem. several sects., chmn. 13th Jud. Circuit grievance com.), Hillsborough County Bar Assn. (mem. several coms., dir., exec. counsel trial lawyers sect.), Fla. Leadership 2000, Am. Inn Cts. (master). Republican. Methodist. Office: 1301 Bayshore Blvd Tampa FL 33606 Office Phone: 813-258-2610. Business E-Mail: bcury@tampabay.rr.com.

CURZER, HOWARD JAY, philosophy professor; b. Pitts., Aug. 15, 1952; s. Abraham and Ruth Tracht Curzer; m. Anne C. Epstein, May 31, 1981; 1 child, Mirah Epstein. BA in Math., Wesleyan U., Middletown, Conn., 1974, MA in Math., 1975; PhD in Philosphy, U. Tex., Austin, 1985. Vis. asst. prof. U. Houston, 1980—82; prof. Tex. Tech U., Lubbock, 1983—. Author: Ethical Theory and Moral Problems, editor anthologies; contbr. articles to profl. jours. Grantee Clark Scholar Mentoring grant, 2002, Arts and Humanities award, Tex. Tech U., 2007, Faculty Devel. Leave grant, 2006—07. Office: Texas Tech Univ Philosophy Dept Lubbock TX 79409-3092 Business E-Mail: howard.curzer@ttu.edu.

CUSCHIERI, JOSEPH M., acoustical engineer, professional society administrator; b. Malta, 1957; BS in Mech. Engring., U. Malta; PhD, U. Southampton Inst. Sound and Vibration Rsch., UK, 1976. Joined faculty ocean engring. Fla. Atlantic U., 1983; engring. profl. Lockheed Martin Corp.-Perry Technologies, Lockheed Martin Corp.-MS2 Underseas Systems; from acting exec. dir. to exec. dir. Inst. Noise Control Engring.-USA, Indpls., 2005—. Contbr. articles to profl. jours. Recipient R. Bruce Lindsay award, Acoustical Soc. America, 1991. Mem.: Inst. Noise Control Engring. (bd. dirs. 2005). Office: Lockheed Martin Undeseas Systems 100 E 17th St Riviera Beach FL 33404 also: Inst Noise Control Engring USA 9100 Purdue Rd Ste 200 Indianapolis IN 46268 Office Phone: 571-494-2557. Office Fax: 561-494-2591. Business E-Mail: ed@inceusa.org.

CUSHING, BRIAN, professional football player; b. Park Ridge, NJ, Jan. 24, 1987; s. Frank and Antoinette Cushing. B, U. So. Calif., LA, 2009. Linebacker Houston Texans, 2009—. Recipient John McKay award, Univ. So. Calif., 2006; named 1st Team All-Am., Sports Illus., 2008, 1st Team All-Pac-10 Conf., 2008, NFL Defensive Rookie of Yr., AP, 2009; named to Am. Football Conf. Pro Bowl. Team, NFL, 2009; finalist Butkus award, Butkus Found., 2008. Office: The Houston Texans Two Reliant Pk Houston TX 77054

CUTBIRTH, JASON, communications executive; BS in Mgmt., U. Phoenix, 2004. V.p., corp. sponsorships, nat. promotions Six Flags Theme Parks, 1991—98; dir., sales AIM Tech., 1999—2000; mng. dir., mktg., corp. comm. Administaff, Inc., 2000—. Office: Administaff Inc 19001 Crescent Springs Dr Kingwood TX 77339 Office Phone: 281-358-8986. Office Fax: 281-348-3718. Business E-Mail: jason_cutbirth@administaff.com.

CUTCHINS, MALCOLM ARMSTRONG, aerospace engineer, educator, researcher; b. Franklin, Va., Mar. 27, 1935; s. Samuel. B. Sr. and Lavita (MacLean) C.; m. Margaret Virginia Garwood, Oct. 9, 1954 (dec.); children: Malcolm, Jr., Kelly, Leigh Ann; m. Luanne McKnight Mount, Sept. 25, 1999 (dec.); m. June Pavelec Paterson, Mar. 18, 2012. BSCE, Va. Tech., 1956, MS in Engring. Mech., 1964, PhD in Engring. Mech., 1967. Various positions to sr. mech. engr. Lockheed-Ga. Co., 1956-66; from assoc. prof. to prof. Auburn (Ala.) U., 1966—99, emeritus, 1999—. Contbr. articles to profl. jours.; patentee in field, chapter to books. Officer USAF, 1956-59. Recipient Engr. of Yr. award Ala. Soc. Profl. Engrs., 1985, Birdsong Merit Tchg. award, 1997. Fellow AIAA (assoc.; chmn. structural dynamics tech. com. 1985-87, chmn. 30th SDM Nat. Conf. 1989), Sigma Gamma Tau (nat. pres. 1982-85, nat. v.p. 1979-82), Omicron Delta Kappa (faculty sec. Auburn chpt. 1988-99, Province faculty dir., gen. nat. coun. and bd. dirs. 1996-2002, Meritorious Svc. award 2000, Five Star Soc. 2005-), Opelika-Auburn News (weekly commentator, 1992-2009). Avocation: basketball. Office: Auburn U Aerospace Engring Dept Auburn AL 36849-5338

CUTCLIFFE, DAVID, college football coach; b. Birmingham, Ala., Sept. 16, 1954; m. Karen Oran; children: Chris, Marcus, Katie, Emily. B, U. Ala., Tuscaloosa, 1976. Asst. coach Banks HS Jets, Birmingham, 1976—80, head football coach, 1980—82; asst. coach U. Tenn. Volunteers, 1982—93, 2006—07, offensive coord., 1993—98; head football coach U. Miss. Rebels, 1998—2005; asst. coach U. Notre Dame Fighting Irish, Ind., 2005; head football coach Duke U. Blue Devils, Durham, NC, 2007—. Recipient Frank Broyles award, 1998, Walter Camp Coach of Yr. award, Walter Camp Football Found., 2013; named Coach of Yr., Southeastern Conf., 2003, Atlantic Coast Conf., 2013. Office: Duke Univ Athletic Dept 118 Cameron Indoor Stadium PO Box 90555 Durham NC 27708 Office Phone: 919-684-2635. Business E-Mail: dukefootball@duaa.duke.edu.*

CUTRIGHT, PHILLIPS, sociologist, educator; b. Wooster, Ohio, Mar. 1, 1930; s. Clifford R. and Eva N. (Goddin) C.; m. Karen L. Bowles, Oct. 31, 1965; children: Anuschka, Jennifer. AB, Coll. Wooster, 1955; PhD, U. Chgo., 1960. Mem. faculty Wash. State U., Pullman, 1960-61, Dartmouth, 1961-62; with Social Security Adminstrn., 1962-65; mem. faculty Vanderbilt U., Nashville, 1965-67, Washington U., St. Louis, 1967-68, Harvard-MIT, 1968-70; prof. sociology Ind. U., Bloomington, 1970—94. Cons. in field, 1971—. Contbr. articles to profl. jours. Served with USAF, 1951-53. Home: 28 Clubside Dr Asheville NC 28804 Home Phone: 828-232-9936. Personal E-mail: cutrightkandp@att.net.

CUTSHAW, KENNETH ANDREW, lawyer; b. Knoxville, Tenn., Sept. 2, 1953; s. Harvey Audley and Frankie Janelle (Temple) C.; m. Diane Dracos. BA, U. Tenn., 1975, JD, 1978; LLM, Am. U., 1987. Bar: Tenn. 1978, D.C. 1987, U.S. Dist. Ct. (mid. dist.) 1978, Tenn., (ea. dist.) 1978, Tenn. Supreme Ct. 1978, U.S. Supreme Ct. 1987, U.S. Fed. cir., 1991. Sr. atty. State of Tenn. Legis., Nashville, 1979-80, The 1982 World's Affair, Knoxville, 1980-83, cons., 1984; campaign mgr. for candidate U.S. Senate, 1983-84; asst. dep., asst. sec. import adminstrn. Dept. Commerce, Washington, 1985-87, chief of staff export adminstrn., 1987-89, dep. asst. sec. export enforcement, 1989-91; ptnr. Miller & Steuart, Washington, 1991-93; pres. Global Trading Ptnrs., Inc., Washington, 1991-93; of counsel Troutman Sanders, LLP, Atlanta, 1993-95, Smith Gambrell & Russell, LLP, 1995-99; ptnr. Holland & Knight, LLP, Atlanta, 1999—2006; exec. v.p., gen. coun. Cajun Open Co. dba Church's Chicken, Atlanta, 2006—12; provost Am. U., Tbilisi, Ga., 2012—. Mem. U.S. Govt. Industry Adv. Com. on Customs and Trade, 1994-96; adj. prof. Ga. State U., 1997—, Emory U., 2002—, Ga. Tech., 2005—; hon. counsul Govt. of India; bd. dir. India, China Am. Inst.; Georgia; ptnr. KBS India. Co-author: Doing Business in China, 1995, Doing Business in Russia, 1999, Doing Business in India, 2001; contbr. articles to profl. jours. Vice chmn., exec. com. Tenn. Rep. Party, 1982-85; internat. chmn. Boy Scouts Am., Atlanta; co-chmn. Awakening Weekend. Roddy Acad. scholar U. Tenn., 1971-72. Mem. ABA, Internat. Bar Assn., Ga. Bar Assn., Atlanta Bar Assn., Tenn. Bar Assn. (com. chmn. 1983-84), D.C. Bar Assn., Am. Coun. Young Polit. Leaders (bd. dirs., co-chmn.), Coun. on Fgn. Rels., Atlanta Round Table (chmn.), World Trade Ctr. (bd. dirs.), Sigma Chi. Baptist. Avocations: flying, skiing, hiking, cultural events, golf. Home: 5560 Whitner Dr Nw Atlanta GA 30327-4745 Office: P O Box 51155 Durham NC 27717 Office Phone: 404-312-5544, 770-350-3882. Office Fax: 770-512-3966. Personal E-mail: kencutshaw@gmail.com.

CYRUS, CYNTHIA J., provost, music educator; b. Seattle, Sept. 2, 1963; d. John D. and Virginia J. Cyrus; m. Thomas B. Dowling; children: Amelia Berle, Nathaniel Berle, Nissa Berle. BA, Pomona Coll., 1984; MA, U. N.C., 1987, PhD, 1990. Vis. asst. prof. U. Rochester, NY, 1991—92, SUNY, Stony Brook, NY, 1992—94; asst. prof. Blair Sch. Music Vanderbilt U., Nashville, 1994—2001, assoc. prof., 2001—, assoc. dean Blair Sch. Music, 2004—11. Session organizer Internat. Medieval Congress, Kalamazoo, 2001—04; mem. adv. bd. rsch. jour. Vanderbilt U., 2004—07; lectr. in field. Author: (book) Scribes for Women's Converts in Late Medieval Germany, 2009; editor: Online Reference Book for Medieval Studies, 1997—2007, De tous biens plaine: 28 Settings of Hayne, 2000; contbr. articles to profl. jours.; editor: Music Education in the Middle Ages and the Reneaissance, 2010, Music Dance and Society: Mediaval & Rennaissus Studies in Memory, 2011. Organizer Bellevue Project-Oriented Unschoolers, Nashville, 2002—06. Recipient Friends of Libr. award, Pontifical Inst. Mediaeval Studies, Toronto, Can., 2000, Faculty Excellence award, Blain Sch., 2009; grantee, Univ. Rsch. Coun., 1995—96, Vanderbilt U., 1996, NEH Summer Inst., 2003, NEH Collaborative, 2004—05; fellow, The Ohio State U., 1990—91; Joseph E. Pogue fellowship, U. N.C., 1984—88. Mem.: Internat. Machaut Soc. (webmaster 2002—03, bd. dirs. 2002—05), Coll. Music Soc. (campus rep. 2002—04), Am. Musicol. Soc. (chmn. program com. S.C. chpt. 1995—96, mem. com. moderated elec. discussion list 2002—06, bd. com. on comm. 2005—08, chair local arrangements com. 2008), Medieval Acad. Am. Office: Blair School Music Vanderbilt Univ 2400 Blakemore Ave Nashville TN 37212 also: Vanderbilt University PMB 4070823 2301 Vanderbilt Pl Nashville TN 37240 Office Phone: 615-322-7693.

CZARNECKI, GERALD MILTON, investment banker, venture capitalist; s. Casimir M. and Rose-Mary (Grajek) C.; m. Lois Rae DiJoseph, July 9, 1965; 1 dau., Robyn Alexandra. BS, Temple U., 1965; MA, Mich. State U., 1967; LHD (hon.), Nat. U., 1994. C.P.A., Ill., Tex. With Continental Bank, Chgo., 1968-79, v.p., operating gen. mgr. trust ops. and gen. mgr. corp. svcs., 1971-78; pres. Fla. Computing Svcs., 1979; exec. v.p. Houston Nat. Bank, 1979-82; sr. v.p. fin. Republic Bank Corp., 1982-83, exec. v.p., 1983-84; pres., CEO Altus Bank, 1984-87; chmn., chief exec. officer Bank of Am. Hawaii, Honolulu, 1987-93; sr. v.p. human resources and adminstrn. IBM Corp., Armonk, NY, 1993-94; pres. UNC Inc., Annapolis, Md., 1994-95; chmn., CEO Deltennium Group, Inc., Boca Raton, Fla., 1995—, Renaissance, Inc., 1999—2001; pres., CEO, bd. dirs. Jr. Achievement Worldwide, 2007—08; pres., CEO O2Media Inc., 2007—12. Mem. faculty DePaul U., Chgo., 1975-78, Bank Adminstrn. Inst., 1978-85, Grad. Sch. Banking, U. Wis., 1979-86, Inroads Inc., Chgo. 1977-79 (chmn. bd. dir.), Inroads Inc. Houston, 1981; vis. prof. Jones Sch. Bus., Rice U., 1980; adj. prof. econs. Houston Bapt. U., 1980-82, policy and strategy So. Meth. U., 1983-84; mem. adv. com. Banking Ctr., Tex. So. U., 1980-82; chmn. securities processing sub-com. Am. Nat. Standards Inst., 1974-79; mem. Tuskegee Inst. State Adv. Coun., 1984-87; mem. treas., mem. exec. com., bd. dirs. Nat. Coun. Savs. Instns., 1984-90; pres. thrift adv. coun. Fed. Res. Bd., 1986-90; chmn. bd. dir. Great Clips Mid-Atlantic, Inc., 1997-2004, Deltennium Corp., 1996-, Renaissance Inc., 1999-2004; bd. dirs. State Farm Ins. Cos., State Farm Banks, ATM Nat. Inc., 2003-06, Software Internat. Inc. (chmn. bd., chair governance com.); chmn. audit com., mgr. bd. dirs., Del Global Techs. Inc., 2001—; mem. bd. dirs., chmn. May Software Group, Inc. Author: Your in Charge.What Now?, Your a Non-Profit Director.What Now?, Success Principles for Leaders?, Lead with Love, Take Two and Call Me in the Morning; contbr. articles to profl. publs. Bd. dirs., treas. Hawaii Theatre Ctr., 1988-93; bd. dirs. Honolulu Econ. Devel. Corp., 1988-93, Nature Conservancy Hawaii, 1988-93, U. Hawaii Pres.' Coun., 1988-93, Aloha United Way, 1988-93; mem. Bus. Roundtable of Hawaii, 1989-93; chmn. Mil. Affairs Coun., 1992-93; mem. exec. and policy coms. Bus. Coun. N.Y. State, 1993-94; mem. adv. bd. Corp. Leadership Coun., 1993-94; nat. bd. dirs. Jr. Achievement, 1993—; trustee, founder & chmn. Nat. U., 1994—, chair Nat. Leadership Inst, 2005—, InPractice, Inc., 2004—; bd. dirs. Jr. Achievement Worldwide, 1994—. Capt. US Army, 1960—63. Mem. AICPA, Am. Bankers Assn. (chmn. securities processing com. 1974-77, trust ops. com. 1978, mem. exec. com. ops. and automation div. 1980-83, rsch. com.), Am. Econ. Assn., Nat. Assn. Corp. Dirs. (bd. dirs. D.C. chpt. 1999—), Tex. Soc. CPAs, Fin. Execs. Inst., Consumer Bankers Assn. (bd. dirs. 1986-89), N. Am. Soc. Corp. Planners (bd. dirs. Dallas Chpt. 1982-83), Assn. for Corp. Growth, Orgn. Resource Counselors, Inc., Hawaii C. of C. (bd. dirs. 1988-89, chmn. bd. 1990-92), Omicron Delta Epsilon, Alpha Delta Phi. Office Phone: 561-293-3743. Business E-Mail: gmc@deltennium.com.

CZARNECKI, KAREN M., legislative staff member, former federal agency administrator; b. Phila., 1966; BA in World Politics, Cath. U. America, Washington, 1988; JD, Cath. U. Columbus Sch. Law; Grad. Inst. Comparative Polit. & Econ. Sys., Georgetown U., 1987. Domestic policy adv. to v.p. The White House, Washington, 1989—91; various positions including dir. lctrs./seminars Heritage Found., Washington; dir. Civil Justice and Health & Human Svc. task forces American Legis. Exchange Coun., Washington; joined US Dept. Labor, Washington, 2001, dep. asst. sec. for intergovernmental affairs, 2003—09, dir. Office 21st Century Workforce, 2003—09; chief of staff to Rep. Mike Kelly US House of Representatives, Washington, 2011—. Tchr. pub. policy internship seminar Fund for American Studies, Georgetown U., 2008—. Regular contbr. (all women news-analysis prog.) To the Contrary, PBS, 1997—. Republican. Office: US House of Representatives 515 Cannon House Office Bldg Washington DC 20515 Office Phone: 202-225-5406. E-mail: karen.czarnecki@mail.house.gov.

DAANE, JAMES DEWEY, banker; b. Grand Rapids, Mich., July 6, 1918; s. Gilbert L. and Mamie (Blocksma) D.; m. Blanche M. Tichenor, Apr. 28, 1941 (div. 1952); 1 dau., Elizabeth Marie Daane Mallek; m. Onnie B. Selby, Jan. 23, 1953 (dec. Dec. 1961); m. Barbara W. McMann, Feb. 16, 1963; children: Elizabeth Whitney, Olivia Quartel. AB magna cum laude, Duke U., 1939; MPA, Harvard U., 1946, D in Pub. Adminstrn. (Littauer fellow), 1949. With Fed. Res. Bank, Richmond, Va., 1939-60, asst. v.p., 1953-57, v.p., 1957-60, also cons. to pres. bank, adviser to pres. Mpls., 1960; asst. to sec. treasury, 1960-61; dep. undersec. treasury for monetary affairs, 1961-63; mem. bd. govs. Fed. Reserve System, Washington, 1963-74; vice chmn. bd. dirs. Commerce Union Bank, Sovran Bank/Cen. South, Nashville, 1974-78; chmn. internat. policy com. Commerce Union Corp., 1978-87; dir. Nat. Futures Assn., Ill., 1983—2002; chmn. internat. policy com Sovran Fin. Corp., Nashville, 1988; chmn. money market com. Commerce Union Bank, 1974-87; chmn. money market com. cen. S. Sovran Bank, 1988-90. Assoc. economist Fed. Open Market Com., 1955-56, 58-59; chief IMF Fiscal Mission to Paraquay, 1950-51; vice chmn. Tennessee Valley Bancorp. Inc., 1975-78; Frank K. Houston prof. banking and fin. Owen Grad. Sch. Mgmt., Vanderbilt U., 1974-85, Valere Blair Potter prof. banking and fin., 1985-89, Frank K. Houston prof. emeritus, 1989—, Alan R. Holmes prof. econs. Middlebury Coll., 1991-93; bd. dirs. Chgo. Bd. of Trade, 1979-82; prof. fin. Vanderbilt U. Editor: (with David C. Colander) The Art of Monetary Policy. Bd. advisers Patterson Sch. Diplomacy and Internat. Commerce, U. Ky. Mem. J.F. Kennedy Sch. Govt. Assn. of Harvard U., Am. Econ. Assn., Am. Finance Assn. Home: 102 Westhampton Pl Nashville TN 37205-3439 Office: Vanderbilt U Owen Grad Sch Mgmt 401 21st Ave N Nashville TN 37203 E-mail: dewey.daane@owen.vanderbilt.edu.

DACH, LESLIE ALAN, retail executive, former public relations company executive; b. NYC, Apr. 17, 1954; s. Joseph and Edith (Lipsyzc) D.; m. Mary Ann Dickie, Nov. 19, 1983; children: Jonathan Alexander, Eliza May. BS in Biology, Yale U., 1975; MPA, Harvard U., 1981. Staff scientist Environ. Def. Fund., Washington, 1977-79; assoc. dir. Nat. Audubon Soc., Washington, 1981-84, legis. dir., 1984-87; dir. scheduling Mondale-Ferraro campaign, Washington, 1984; spl. asst. to chmn. U.S. Senate Agr. Com., Washington, 1987; dir. comm. Dukakis for Pres., Boston, 1987-88; sr. v.p. Edelman Pub. Rels., Washington, 1989-90, exec. v.p., 1990-96, vice chmn., 1996—2006; exec. v.p. corp. affairs & govt. rels. Wal-Mart Stores, Inc., Bentonville, Ark., 2006—. Office: WalMart Stores Inc 702 SW 8th St Bentonville AR 72716

DADERKO, DEAN, curator, critic; BFA in Sculpture, Tyler Sch. Art, 1997. Curator The Americas In Residence, Fonderie Darling, Montreal, Canada; dir. Parlour Projects, Williamsburg, Bklyn., 2000—05; vis. curator Centro de Investigaciones Artisticas, Buenos Aires, Cooper Union Sch of Arts, NYC, MIT, Cambridge, Mass.; critic painting/printmaking Yale U., 2010; curator Contemporary Arts Mus. Houston, 2011—. Curator SIDE X SIDE, Visual AIDS, 50 Artists Photography The Future and Piece de Resistance. Recipient Curatorial Rsch. Fellowship, French American Cultural Exchange, 2008—09. Office: Contemporary Arts Museum Houston 5216 Montrose Blvd Houston TX 77006-6547 Office Phone: 713-284-8258. Business E-Mail: ddaderko@camh.org.*

DADY, ROBERT EDWARD, lawyer; b. NYC, Nov. 11, 1936; s. Edward Joseph and Florence (Scheidt) D.; m. Mollie D. Richman; children: Michael, Andrew, Rachel. BA, Queens Coll., 1958; LLB, Fordham Law, 1961. Bar: N.Y. 1962, Fla. 1974. Asst. gen. counsel The Equity Corp., NYC, 1962-66; gen. atty. ITT_Levitt and Sons, Inc., Washington, Lake Success, NY, 1966-70; sr. v.p.-legal First Realty Investment Corp., Miami Beach, Fla., 1970-71; v.p.-legal, sec. Cavanagh Cmtys. Corp., Miami, Fla., 1971-75; ptnr. Mann & Dady, P.A., Miami, 1975-80, Mann, Dady, Corrigan & Zelman, P.A., Miami, 1980-83, Dady, Siegfried & Kipnis, P.A., Miami, 1984-85; pvt. practice Miami, 1985-87; ptnr. Kimbrell and Hamann, P.A., 1987-89; shareholder Popham, Haik, Schnobrich & Kaufman, Ltd., 1990-96; of counsel Fieldstone, Lester, Shear & Denberg, Coral Gables, Fla., 1996—2009; counsel Brod Goldfarb, Pa., 2009—10; of counsel Siegfried, Rivera, Lerner, De La Torre & Sobel, 2011—13; pres. Robert E. Dady PA, 2013—. Past adj. prof. law U. Miami Sch. Law.; bd. dirs. Spectrum Programs, Inc., pres., 1984-86, Spectrum Found., Inc., pres. 1988—. Author: Land Acquistion and Development, 1975. Bd. dirs., exec. comm. Miami Coalition for a Safe and Drug Free Cmty., 1992-99; vice-chmn. Childrens Home Soc. Found. Miami, 1993-96, bd. dirs., 1993-2004; appointed to (by gov.) Fla. Jud. Nom. Com., 1995-98; bd. dirs. Wellness Cmty., Greater Miami, 2001-06. Mem. Nat. Land Coun. (pres. 1974-81, vice chmn. bd. dirs. 1973—2008, chmn. bd. dirs. 2008-), Builders Assn. So. Fla. (life dir., gen. counsel 1982-2001), ABA (environ. law com., timesharing and recreation law com., vice chmn. 2004, lectr. practicing law inst., interstate land sales dept.), Elite Atty. Fla., Fla. and NY Bar Assn. Democrat. Home: 8440 SW 143rd St Village of Palmetto Bay FL 33158-1457 Office: Robert E Dady Pa 8440 SW 143 St Palmetto Bay FL 33158-1457 Office Phone: 305-233-9757. Business E-Mail: Robertdadylaw@gmail.com.

DAFFRON, MARYELLEN, retired librarian; b. Richmond, Va., Nov. 12, 1946; d. William Charles and Ellen (Ahern) D.; m. Newton J. Frank. BA, Coll. Mt. St. Joseph on Ohio, Cin., 1968; MLS, Drexel U., 1970. Libr. Richmond Pub. Libr., 1969-73, FMC, Washington, 1973—93; with U.S. Immigration and Naturalization Svc. Office of Gen. Counsel, Washington, 1993—2003; law libr. Office of Prin. Legal Advisor, U.S. Immigration and Customs Enforcement, Washington, 2003—05, ret., 2005. Vol. No. Va. Hotline, Arlington, 1974-79. City of Richmond fellow, 1968. Mem.: Beta Phi Mu. Roman Catholic.

D'AGNESE, JOHN JOSEPH, sanitation, public health and pest management consultant; b. NYC, Apr. 2, 1920; s. Michele and Liberata (Cucolo) D'A.; m. Helen DeSantis, Oct. 29, 1942; children: John Jr., Linda, Diane, Michele, Helen, Gina, Paul. BS, CCNY, 1946; student, U. San Francisco, 1953-54. Lic. pest mgmt., Fla., Ga.; cert. food safety mgr.; lic. chief purser USCG. Chief purser U.S. Merchant Marine, 1942-46; quarantine officer USPHS, Staten Island, N.Y., 1946-53, supervisory quarantine officer San Francisco, 1953-62, Mexican border supervisory quarantine officer El Paso, Tex., 1962-68, chief program ops. quarantine div. Ctr. Disease Control Atlanta, 1968-80, dir. quarantine div., 1980-81, ret., 1981; dir. Cruise Ship Consultation Svc., Fernandina Beach, Fla., 1981—. Dir. D'Agnese Studio Fine Art Gallery; adminstr., trainer Chartered Inst. Environ. Health/Nat. Registry of Food Svc. Profls. Contbr. sci. and health-related articles to nat. mags. and jours. including Pest Control Tech.,

Jour. Environ. Health, Jour. Milk Food Tech., Pest Control Jour. Mag. Bd. dirs. Nat. Coun. Aging, 1986-90; bd. dirs. Amelia Island Film Festival, Coalition for Reduction-Elimination Ethnic Disparities Health. Recipient United Fund Leadership award El Paso Tex., 1966-67. Fellow Nat. Sanitation Found.; mem. APHA, Fla. Pest Control Assn., Ga. Pest Control Assn., Nat. Assn. Fed. Ret. Employees. Democrat. Roman Catholic. Avocations: music, tennis, fencing, chess, fishing, cooking. Home: 3240 S Fletcher Ave Fernandina Beach FL 32034-4378 Fax: 904-321-1518. E-mail: jjdcscs@yahoo.com.

DAHLBURG, JOHN-THOR THEODORE, news correspondent; b. Orange, NJ, Apr. 30, 1953; s. Donald Russell and Madeline (Blackadore) D.; m. Yvonne Michelle Bastien, Nov. 18, 1980; children: Cecile, Charlotte. BA summa cum laude, Wash. and Lee U., Lexington, Va., 1975; LLD with highest honors, U. Toulouse, France, 1980. Reporter, pub. affairs dir. Sta. WLUR-FM, Lexington, Va., 1971-75; stringer Lynchburg News, Va., 1974-75; news clk., intern Time Mag., Paris, 1974; reporter, editor Boca Raton News, Fla., 1980-81; newsman AP, Miami, Paris, 1981-83, editor, fgn. desk NYC, 1984-86, corr. Moscow, 1986-90, LA Times, Moscow, 1990—93, bur. chief New Delhi, 1993—96, Paris, 1996—2001, Miami, 2001—06; state and investigations editor South Fla. Sun-Sentinel, 2006—. Journalistes en Europe fellow, 1983-84; recipient George Polk award L.I. U., 1993, Excellence citation Overseas Press Club Am., 1993, Hal Boyle award, 1996, Cert. of Merit AP News Execs. Coun., 1993, Robert F. Kennedy Journalism award, 1996, Soc. Profl. Journalists award for internat. reporting, 1997; named finalist Pulitzer Prize in internat. reporting, 1992, 93. Mem.: Soc. Profl. Journalists (bd. dirs. South Fla. chpt.). Avocations: Model T Ford restoration, rowing, Salsa dancing. Personal E-mail: jdahlburg@sun-sentinel.com.

DAHN, CONNEY COLLEY, special education educator; m. Larry Dahn; 3 children. BA, Univ. Ala. Spl. edn. tchr., 1974—, South Fork H.S., 1990—93, Martin County H.S., 1993—2004, Jensen Beach (Fla.) H.S., 2004—. Founder Friends Chorus for mentally and physically challenged students, 1989; coach Spl. Olympics. Named Christa McAuliffe Ambassador for Edn., Fla. Dept. Edn., Fla. Tchr. of Yr., 2007, Sch. Tchr. of Yr., Martin County Sch. Dist. (twice). Mem.: Kappa Delta. Avocation: running. Office: Jensen Beach High Sch 2876 NW Goldenrod Rd Jensen Beach FL 34957 E-mail: ccdahn@comcast.net.

DAIL, JOSEPH GARNER, JR., retired judge; b. Elloree, SC, June 15, 1932; s. Joseph Garner and Esther Vernette (Harbort) D.; m. Martha E. MacReynolds; children: Mary Holyoke. BS, U. N.C., 1953, JD with honors, 1955. Bar: N.C. 1955, Va. 1976. Pvt. practice, Washington, 1959-76; ptnr. Croft, Dail & Vance (and predecessor), 1966-76; sole practitioner McLean, Va., 1976—83; counsel Gabeler, Ward & Griggs, 1983-87; judge U.S. adminstrv. law Fresno, Calif., 1987-94, San Francisco, 1994-97, Tampa, 1997-99; sr. U.S. adminstrv. law judge, 1999—2005; ret., 2005. Assoc. editor: N.C. Law Rev, 1954-55. Lt. USNR, 1955-59; capt. Res. (ret.). Mem. N.C. Bar Assn., Va. Bar Assn., Transp. Lawyers Assn. (Disting. Svc. award 1976), Order of Coif, Phi Beta Kappa. Republican. Home: 4737 Dolphin Cay Ln S #304 Saint Petersburg FL 33711 Personal E-mail: macdail@aol.com.

DAJANI, LORRAINE HOLLINGSWORTH, endocrinologist; MD, Universidad Nacional de la Plata, Argentina, 1982. Diplomate Am. Bd. Internal Medicine, 1986, Am. Bd. Internal Medicine-endocrinology, diabetes and metabolism, 1989. Resident internal medicine Wayne State Univ., Detroit, 1984—86, fellow endocrinology, diabetes and metabolism, 1986—87, Univ. Med. Ctr., Jacksonville, Fla., 1987—88; physician St. Vincent's HealthCare, Jacksonville, Fla. Office: NE FL Endocrine and Diabetes Associates Ste 200 915 W Monroe St Jacksonville FL 32204 Office Phone: 904-384-2240.*

DAKE, MARCIA ALLENE, retired nursing educator, dean; b. Bemus Point, NY, May 22, 1923; d. Earl B. and Bernice DeLeo (Haskin) D. Diploma, Crouse Irving Hosp., 1944; BS, Syracuse U., 1951; MA, Columbia U., 1955, EdD, 1958. RN. Tchr., sch. nurse various locations, 1946—48; chmn. health dept. SUNY, Oneonta, 1952—56; dean coll. nursing U. Ky., Lexington, 1958—72; dir. dept. nursing edn. ANA, Kansas City, 1972—74; project dir. program devel. nursing ARC, Washington, 1975—79; dir. nursing edn. James Madison U. Coll. Nursing, 1979—81; prof. dean Coll. Nursing, 1981—88; ret., 1988. Editor, resident photographer: Greenspring Village Photo Directories, 2000—; programmer, host Closed Circuit TV Studio, 2000. Mem. Ky. Bd. Nursing Edn. Nurse Registration, 1969-72, pres., 1970-72; pres. Va. Coun. Deans of Baccalaureate Nursing Programs, 1981-84; nurse officer Civil Def. Otsego County, N.Y., 1953-56; mem. Def. Adv. Com. on Women in Svcs., 1963-65; mem. Ky. Comprehensive Health Planning Coun., 1968-71; pres. Ky. League for Nursing, 1961-65; bd. dir. Cmty. Ch. Coll., Sun City Ctr., Fla., 1989-92, Sun City Ctr. Guardianship Found., 1990-98; trustee United Cmty. Ch., Sun City Ctr., 1993-96, chmn. pers. com., 1994-96, fin. com., 1994-95, vice chmn. bd. trustees, 1995-96, stewardship com., 1996-98, mem. pastoral rels. com., 1996-98, mem. long range planning com., 1996-97, chmn. pastoral rels. com., 1998—; sec. Caloosa Women's Golf Assn., Sun City Ctr., 1991-92; treas. Greater Sun City Ctr. Disaster Coun., 1992-94; mem., vice chmn. resident adv. com. Greenspring Village, Springfield, Va., 1999-2000, corr. sec. resident adv. com., 2001; prodr., host Channel 6 T.V Greenspring Village, 2001; prodr., pub. resident/staff photo directories, 2000-11. 1st lt. U.S. Army Nurse Corps., 1945—46. Recipient 4th Gold award, Pres.'s Coun. Svc. and Civic Participation, 2008, Lifetime award, 2009, 5th Gold award, Pres. Coun. Civic Participation, 2011. Fellow Nat. League Nursing; mem. ANA, Va. Nurses Assn. (pres. dist. 9 1983-85), Va. Soc. Profl. Nurses (treas. 1983-88), Va. Assn. Colls. Nursing (sec. 1980-82, pres. 1982-85), Alliance Nursing Orgns. (chmn. Va. 1985-88), LWV, Delta Kappa Gamma, Kappa Delta Pi, Pu Lambda Theta. Address: 222 7442 Spring Village Dr Springfield VA 22150-4444

DALE, GEORGE, former state commissioner; m. Yvette Bosarge; 5 children. Grad., Pearl River Jr. Coll., Poplarville, Miss.; student, Millsaps Coll.; grad., Miss. Coll., Master's Degree; postgrad., U. So. Miss., Auburn U. Tchr., coach, prin., adminstr. Moss Point (Miss.) Pub. Schs.; adminstrv. asst. Gov. Bill Waller; commr. ins. State of Miss., 1975—2008; sr. govt. advisor Adams & Reese LLP, Jackson, Miss., 2008—. Active Miss. Coll., YMCA, Miss. Heart Assn. Office: Adams & Reese LLP Ste 350 1018 Highland Colony Pkwy Ste 800 Ridgeland MS 39157-2057

DALE, ROBERT E., state legislator; Mem. Dist. 70 Ark. House of Reps., 2009—. Republican. Baptist. Office: State Capitol Rm 350 Little Rock AR 72201 also: 90 Claud Hottinger Rd Dover AR 72837 Office Phone: 501-682-6211, 501-682-7771, 479-498-2467. Business E-Mail: redale70@yahoo.com.

DALEMBERT, SAMUEL DAVIS, professional basketball player; b. Port-Au-Prince, Haiti, May 10, 1981; Student, Seton Hall U., South Orange, NJ, 1999—2001. Ctr. Phila. 76ers, 2001—10, Sacramento Kings, 2010—11, Houston Rockets, 2011—12, Milw. Bucks, 2012—13, Dallas Mavericks, 2013—. Hon. commr. La Liga del Barrio, Phila. Recipient Global Leadership in Humanitarianism award, Consular Corps Assn. Phila., 2006, J. Walter Kennedy Citizenship award, NBA, 2010. Avocations: reading, video games. Office: Dallas Mavericks 2909 Taylor St Dallas TX 75226*

DALEO, ROBERT, corporate financial executive; Undergraduate, Fordham U.; MBA in Fin., CUNY. Various fin. & operational positions Automatic Data Processing, McGraw-Hils; chmn., policy-owners examining com. Northwestern Mut. Insu. Co.; COO Thomson Newspapers, sr. v.p., CFO, 1994; exec. v.p., bus. ops. & planning Thomson Corp., sr. v.p., fin. & bus. devel. Stanford, Conn., 1998, exec. v.p., 1998—, CFO, 1997—, bd. dirs., 2001—. Bd. dirs. Equifax Inc. Vice chmn. NJ Cmty. Devel. Corp.; mem., President's Coun., bd. trustee Fordham U.; bd. adv., Prudential Ctr. for Bus. Ethics Rutgers U. Office: Thompson Reuters Corp 3 Times Sq New York NY 10036 also: Equifax Inc Bd Directors 1550 Peachtree St NW Atlanta GA Office Phone: 643-223-4000, 403-885-8000. Office Fax: 403-885-8988. Business E-Mail: robert.daleo@thomsonreuters.com.

DALEY, SHARON R., human resources specialist; BS in Indsl. & Labor Rels., Rutgers U., 1983. Sr. human resources mgr., indsl. contr. sys. General Electric Consumer & Indsl., 1997—99; mgr., orgn. & staffing GE Infrastructure Energy, 1999; sr. human resources mgr. GE Global Rsch., Niskayuna; v.p, human resources General Electric Co., Atlanta, 2005—. Office: GE Infrastructure Energy 4200 Wildwood Pkwy Atlanta GA 30339 Office Phone: 678-844-6000. Office Fax: 678-844-6690. Business E-Mail: Sharon.Daley@ge.com.

DALEY, TOM, not-for-profit foundation executive; b. Phoenix, Ariz., Jan. 29, 1964; m. Ava Daley, 1987; 1 child, Marissa. BA in Econs. and Bus., Hendrix Coll., 1986; JD, Tex. Wesleyan U. Sch. Law, 2007. Founder Daley Info. Svcs., 1986; mgr., trading floor tech. Chgo. Stock Exch., 1991—94; founder, dir. Fin. Svcs. Practice SEI, Inc., 1994—98; co-founder, pres. TSI Holdings, LLC, Evanston, Ill., 1998—2002; v.p. software devel. Cantor Fitzgerald, 2002—07; exec. dir. Thomas J. and Ava P. Daley Found., 2007—. Democrat. Office: 3001 S Hardin Blvd Ste 110-211 Mc Kinney TX 75070 Office Phone: 214-234-1611, 224-673-8867.

DALKE, GARY R., oil industry executive; Treas., v.p., CFO Phoenix Fuel, 1997—98; contr., chief info. officer Giant Ariz. (subs. Giant Industries, Inc.), 1998, v.p., asst. sec., 1998; v.p., contr., asst. sec. Giant Industries, Inc., 1998; chief acctg. officer Giant Industries, Inc. and Giant Ariz., 2002, Western Refining, Inc. Affiliate Co., 2003—05; prin. acctg. officer Western Refining, Inc., El Paso, Tex., 2003—07, treas., 2005—07, CFO, 2005—. Office: Western Refining 123 W Mills Ave El Paso TX 79901

DALKIN, ALAN C., endocrinologist, educator; MD, U. Mich., 1984. Diplomate Am. Bd. Internal Medicine, 1987, Am. Bd. Internal Medicine-endocrinology, diabetes and metabolism, 1990, lic. Va. Intern internal medicine Univ. of Chgo. Hosps., 1984—85, resident internal medicine, 1985—87; fellow endocrinology and metabolism Univ. of Mich. Med. Ctr., Ann Arbor, 1987—90, asst. prof. internal medicine, 1990—91, Univ. of Va. Health Sciences Ctr., Charlottesville, 1991—97, assoc. prof. internal medicine, 1997—2007, interim chief, divsn. clin. rheumatology, 1991—, prof. internal medicine, 2007—. Co-author: (publs.) Pituitary follistatin gene expression in female rats: Evidence that inhibin regulates transcription, 2004, Testosterone stimulates FSH beta transcription via activation of extracellular signal-regulated kinase (ERK) in rat pituitary cells, 2005, The sensitivity of Fibroblast Growth Factor 23 measurements in tumor induced osteomalacia, 2006, Hypercalcemia: A practical approach to a surprising condition, 2007, Combination therapy for treatment of osteoporosis: A review, 2007. Mem.: ACP, Soc. for the Study of Reproduction, The Pituitary Soc., Endocrine Soc. Office: University of Virginia Fontaine Research Pk 450 Ray C Hunt Dr PO Box 801412 Charlottesville VA 22908 Office Phone: 434-243-2603. Office Fax: 434-243-9143. E-mail: acd6v@virginia.edu.

DALLAS, TERRY G., electric power industry executive; b. Fulton, Ky. BS in Civil Engring., Ga. Inst. Tech., 1973; MBA in Fin., U. Calif., LA, Calif., 1979. With Civil Engr. Corp. USN; from mgr. fin. control and planning to sr. v.p. ARCO Brit., Ltd., 1988—96, sr. v.p., 1996—2000; exec. v.p., CFO Unocal (acquired by Chevron), El Segundo, Calif., 2000—05. Bd. dirs. Mirant Corp., GenOn Energy, Inc., 2010—. Office: GenOn Energy Inc Bd directors 1000 Main St Houston TX 77002 Office Phone: 832-357-3000. Office Fax: 832-357-0140. Business E-Mail: terry.dallas@genon.com.

DALLAS, WENDELL, gas industry executive; b. Opelika, Ala. 3 children. Degree in Mech. Engring., Auburn U.; grad. Leadership Savannah, 2004, grad. Leadership Ga., 2006. Ops. supvr. El Paso Energy, Macon; region mgr., Southeast Ga. Atlanta Gas Light (subs. of AGL Resources Inc.), Savannah, svc. area mgr. Macon, 2000, v.p., gen. mgr., 2006—. Bd. dirs. Atlanta Neighborhood Devel. Partnership, Cmtys. in Schs. Ga., Gwinnett Tech. Coll.; mem., Engring Alumni Coun. Auburn U.; vice chmn., Workforce Investment Bd. State of Ga. Office: AGL Resources Inc 10 Peachtree Pl NE Atlanta GA 30309 Office Phone: 404-584-4000. Office Fax: 404-584-3714. Business E-Mail: wdallas@aglresources.com.

DALLY, JAMES WILLIAM, mechanical engineering educator, consultant; b. Sardis, Ohio, Aug. 2, 1929; s. William Hiram and Martha (Siebert) D.; m. Anne Evangeline Tziritas, Dec. 22, 1955; children: Lisa, William, Michelle. BSME, Carnegie Mellon U., 1951, MSME, 1953; PhD, Ill. Inst. Tech., 1958. Registered profl. engr., Md. Asst. dir. rsch. Armour Research Found., Chgo., 1961-64; prof. Ill. Inst. Tech., Chgo., 1964-71; prof., chmn. dept. U. Md., College Park, 1971-79; dean Coll. Engring. U. R.I., Kingston, 1979-82; mgr. mech. devel. IBM, Manassas, Va., 1982-84; prof. mech. engring. U. Md., College Park, 1984-97. Disting. vis. prof. USAF Acad., 1995-96; mem. tech. assessment bd. Army Rsch. Lab., 1997-2000; pres. College House Enterprises, LLC, 1998-, engring. cons. James W. Dally Assn. Author: Photoelastic Coatings, 1977, Engineering Measurements, 1984, 2nd edit., 1993, Packaging Electronic Systems, 1990, Product Engineering and Manufacturing, 1998, Design Analysis of Structural Elements, 3rd edit., 2003, 4th edit., 2004, Experimental Stress Analysis, 2005, Introduction to Engineering Design, Book 9, 2006, 3nd edit., 2008; engineer: Mech. Design of Electronic Sys., 2008, Experimental Solid Mechanics, 2010; contbr. articles. Recipient Boeing Outstanding Educator award, 1996. Fellow ASME (Daniel C. Drucker medal 2012), Am. Acad. Mechanics (bd. dirs. 1984-88, pres. 1990-91, Disting. Svc. award 2004), Soc. Exptl. Mechanics (hon., pres. 1970-71, Murray lectureship 1979, Past Pres. award 1971, M.M. Frocht award 1976, Hetenyi award 1995, F.G. Tatnall award 2001, Charles E. Taylor award 2002, Outstanding Alumni award Ill. Inst. Tech., 2009); mem. Nat. Acad. Engring., U.S. Nat. Com. Theoretical and Applied Mechanics (chmn. 1982-84, vice-chmn., 1984-86). Achievements include patents in field. Office Phone: 865-558-6111. Personal E-mail: jdally0829@comcast.net.

DALLY, TROY J., consumer products company executive; Joined Lowe's Companies, Inc., 1999, v.p. merchandising millwork, sr. v.p., gen. mgr. hardlines/bldg. products, 2011—. Office: Lowe's Companies Inc 1000 Lowe's Blvd Mooresville NC 28117

D'ALOIA, G(IAMBATTISTA) PETER, manufacturing executive; b. Sao Paulo, Brazil, Jan. 10, 1945; s. John and Rosali (Picarelli) D'Aloia; m. Marguerite Ann Fuccello, Aug. 3, 1946; children: Jonelle, Tara. BS in Acctg., NYU, 1966, LLM in Taxation, 1976; JD, St. John's U., 1969. Bar: NY 1969. Tax atty. Arthur Young and Co., NYC, 1969-72, Allied Chem. Co., Morristown, NJ, 1972-79; chief tax counsel Allied Corp., Morristown, NJ, 1979-81, dir. taxes, 1981-83; v.p. taxes Allied-Signal Inc., Morristown, NJ, 1983-88, v.p., treas., 1988-92, v.p., contr., 1992-95, v.p. devel., CFO, 1995-2000; sr. v.p., CFO American Standard Companies, Inc., Piscataway, NJ, 2000—. Bd. dirs. FMC Corp., 2002—, AirTran Airways, 2004—. Mem. Bd. Edn., Mendham, NJ, 1977—80. Mem.: NY State Bar Assn., Assn. of Bar City of NY, ABA. Roman Catholic. Avocations: jogging, sailing, gardening. Office: AirTran Airways Bd Directors 2702 Love Field Dr Dallas TX 75235-1908 Office Phone: 407-318-5600. Office Fax: 407-318-5900. Business E-Mail: g.daloia@airtran.com.

DALTON, CLAUDETTE ELLIS HARLOE, anesthesiologist, educator, dean; b. Roanoke, Va., Jan. 18, 1947; d. John Pinckney and Dorothy Anne (Ellis) Harloe; m. Henry Tucker Dalton, May 17, 1973 (div. 1979); 1 child, Gordon Tucker; m. H. Christopher Alexander, III, Apr. 29, 2000 (div. 2010). BA, Sweet Briar Coll., Va., 1969; MD, U. Va., Charlottesville, 1974. Resident anesthesiology U. N.C., Chapel Hill, 1974—77; med. edn. Lenoir County Meml Hosp./East Carolina U., Kinston, 1978—80; med. edn. intensive care Presbyn Hosp., Charlotte, NC, 1981—82; practice anesthesiology Charlotte Eye, Ear, Nose and Throat Hosp., 1982—85, Medivision Charlotte and Orthop. Hosp. Charlotte, 1985—89; asst. prof. U. Va. Health Scis. Ctr., Charlottesville, Va., 1992—2006; dir. Office Cmty. Based Med. Edn., Charlottesville, 1994—2006; asst. dean cmty. based med. edn. U. Va., Charlottesville, 1996—2006, med. dir. Pre-Anesthesia Clinic, 1996—2006, asst. prof. anesthesiology and med. edn., 1996—2006; med. dir. perioperative svcs. Rockingham Meml. Hosp., 2006—10, cons. in surg. efficiency, 2010—11; founder med. team for the remote area med. clinic in Wise Cmty. Svc./Outreach, 1999—; cons. Intermittent Domestic Joint Commn. Resources, 2011—. Adv. bd. Nat. Bd. Med. Examiners, 2004—10; exec. com. Accreditation Coun. Continuing Med. Edn., 2004—09; mem. Va. Bd. Medicine, 2005—, chair credentials com., 2008—10, chair competency com., 2008—, v.p., 2010—, pres., 2011—, chair, legis. com., 2010; spkr. in field; elected AMA Coun. Med. Edn., 2004—11, chair, 2008—09, past chair, 2009—10, chair nominating com., 2006; chair Subcom. on Continuing Med. Edn., 2005—07, Task Force on Rules & Regulations, 2006, Reentry Task Force, 2007—08, MOC/MOL Task Force, 2008—11, cons., surg. efficiency & productivity, 2010—. Author: emergency med. svc. tng. program, 1981, patient edn. materials for illiterate patients, 1979—. Bd. dirs. Charlottesville Family Svcs., Family Svcs. Albemarle County, 1992—93, Coun. Aging, Am. Cancer Soc.; exec. dir. Cmty. Involvement Coun. Lenoir County, Kinston, 1979; county coord. Internat. Yr. of Child, Kinston, 1979; bd. dirs. U. Va. Women's Ctr., Lenoir County CC; mem. sch. medicine com. women U. Va. Med. Sch. Recipient Gov.'s award, State of NC, 1980, Outstanding Tchg. award, U. Va. Sch. Medicine, 1993, Sharon L. Hostler U. Va. Outstanding Woman in Medicine award, 2002, Svc. to Disadvantaged Populations award, AMA-Hosp. Rsch. and Edn. Trust, 2005, Pres.'s award, Va. Acad. Family Physicians, 2006. Mem.: AMA (Coun. on Med. Edn.), Rockingham Med. Soc., Va. Soc. Anesthesiology, Albemarle County Med. Soc., Med. Soc. Va. (bd. dirs. Va. Health Quality Coun. 1995—97, chair ad hoc com. on telemedicine 1996—99, 2d v.p. 1998—99, chair scope of practice com. 1999—2002, dist. dir. 1999—2005, editor med. news Va. Med. Quar., legis. com., health access com., strategic planning and implementation com., women's com., med. affairs com., bd. medicine adv. com., Cmty. Svc award 2003), Alpha Omega Alpha, U. Va. Med. Alumni Assn. (assoc. bd. dirs. 1989—92, chair women in medicine leadership conf. 1998—99). Avocations: dance, writing, gardening, history.

DALTON, JAMES EDGAR, JR., health facility administrator; b. Gretna, Va., Sept. 17, 1942; married. Bachelors degree, Randolph-Macon Coll., 1964; Masters degree, Va. Commonwealth U., 1966. Adminstrv. resident Lynchburg (Va.) Gen. Hosp., 1965-66, adminstrv. asst., 1966-69, asst. adminstr., 1969-70; adminstr. Princeton (W.Va.) Cmty. Hosp., 1970-72; regional adminstr. Humana, Inc., Dallas, 1972-73, regional v.p. Tampa, Fla., 1973-76; dir. hosp. svcs. Am. Medicorp Inc., Atlanta, 1976-77, Dallas, 1977-78; v.p. Hosp. Corp. Am., Nashville, 1978-79, Arlington, Tex., 1979-87, HealthTrust, Inc., Arlington, 1987-89, Nashville, 1989-90; pres., CEO Quorum Health Group, Inc., Brentwood, Tenn., 1990-2001; pres. Edinburgh Assocs., Inc., 2001—07. Chmn. Signature Hosp. Corp., 2006—. Home and Office: 6505 Edinburgh Dr Nashville TN 37221-3707 Home Phone: 615-661-9790. Personal E-mail: jdalton561@aol.com.

DALTON, JOHN JOSEPH, lawyer; b. NYC, Feb. 7, 1943; s. John Henry and Anna Veronica D.; m. Martha Warren Egan, Feb. 24, 1968; children: Martha G., J. Michael, W. Brian. BBA, Fairfield U., 1964; JD, Northwestern U., 1967. Bar: Ill. 1967, Ga. 1970, US Dist. Ct. (no. and mid. dists.) Ga., US Dist. Ct. (no. dist.) Ill., US Ct. Appeals (2d, 4th, 5th, 7th, 10th and 11th cirs.), US Tax Ct., US Supreme Ct. Atty. Clausen, Miller, Chgo., 1967-69; ptnr. Troutman Sanders (formerly Troutman, Sanders, Lockerman & Ashmore), Atlanta, 1970—. Chmn. adv. bd. Atlanta Vol. Lawyers Found., 1993. With US Army, 1968—69. Fellow: Am. Bar Found., Am. Coll. Trial Lawyers (regent 2001—05, sec. 2005—06, treas. 2006—07, pres. 2008—09); mem.: Atlanta Bar Assn. (chmn. bd. Ga. Justice Project 2003—04, bd. dirs.), Highlands Country Club, Peachtree Golf Club, Piedmont Driving Club. Office: Troutman Sanders 600 Peachtree St NE Ste 5200 Atlanta GA 30308-2216 Office Phone: 404-885-3120. Office Fax: 404-962-6539. Business E-Mail: john.dalton@troutmansanders.com.

DALTON, ROY BALE, JR., federal judge; b. Jacksonville, Fla., July 9, 1952; BA with high honors, U. Fla., 1974, JD, 1976. Bar: Fla. 1977, US Dist. Ct. (northern dist. middle dist. and southern dist.) Fla., US Ct. Appeals (5th cir. and 11th cir.), US Ct. Fed. Claims, US Supreme Ct. Pvt. practice, Lakeland, Fla., 1977, Orlando, Fla., 1977—2003; mem. Dalton & Carpenter, PA, Orlando, Fla., 2003—11; of counsel Carlyle Appellate Law Firm, The Villages, Fla., 2004—11; judge US Dist. Ct. (middle dist.) Fla., 2011—. Counsel to Senator Mel Martinez US Senate, Washington, 2005—06. Fellow: American Coll. Trial Lawyers; mem.: ABA, American Bd. Trial Advocates, Acad. Fla. Trial Lawyers, Assn. Trial Lawyers of America, Orange County Bar Assn., Phi Delta Phi. Office: US District Court Bryan Simpson United States Courthouse 300 N Hogan St Jacksonville FL 32202 Office Phone: 904-549-1900.

DALTON, WILLIAM STEVEN, hospital administrator, oncologist, educator; b. Ft. Worth, 1949; BA in Chemistry/Philosophy, U. N.Mex., 1971; MD, Ind. U., 1980, PhD in Toxicology/Med. Life Scis., 1976. Diplomate Am. Bd. Internal Medicine, Am. Bd. Oncology. Intern Ind. U., Indpls., 1980-81; resident in internal medicine U. Ariz., Tucson, 1981-83, fellow in oncology, 1983—; assoc. dir. clin. investigations H. Lee Moffitt Cancer Ctr., Tampa, Fla., 1997—99, dep. dir., 1999—2001, pres., CEO, dir., 2002—. Faculty medicine, pharmacology U. Ariz. Coll. Medicine, 1985—96, prof., 1993—96, dean, 2001—02; prof. oncology, medicine, and biochemistry U. South Fla.,

1997—99, prof., chmn. Dept. Interdisciplinary Oncology, 1999—2001. Mem. ACP, Am. Osteo. Assn., Sigma Xi. Office: H Lee Moffitt Cancer Ctr 12902 Magnolia Dr Tampa FL 33612-9416 E-mail: dalton@moffitt.usf.edu.

DALY, CHARLES ULICK, foundation executive; b. Dublin, May 29, 1927; came to US, 1934, naturalized, 1940; s. Ulick deBurgh and Violet (Sealy-King) D.; m. Mary Larmonth, June 11, 1949 (dec.); children: Michael, Douglas; m. Christine Sullivan, Nov. 5, 1988; children: Charles, Kevin. BA in Internat. Rels., Yale U., 1949; MS in Journalism, Columbia U., 1959. Mgr. then v.p. Mexican subs. Pacific Molasses Co., San Francisco, 1949-50, 52-58; congl. fellow Am. Polit. Sci. Assn., 1959-60; editor Stanford U., Calif., 1961; staff asst. Pres. Kennedy and Pres. Johnson, 1962-64; v.p. U. Chgo., 1964-71; v.p. govt. and cmty. affairs Harvard U., Cambridge, Mass., 1971-76; editor Media and the Cities, The Quality of Inequality, Urban Violence; pres. Joyce Found., Chgo., 1978-86; dir. John F. Kennedy Found., Boston, 1988-2001, dir. emeritus, 2001—. Mem. Lloyd's of London, 1976—; freelance writer, 1958—. Mem. Commn. on Adminstrv. Rev., US Ho. of Reps.; chmn. Donor's Forum, Chgo., 1980; bd. dirs. American Ireland Fund; vice. chmn. Joyce Fedn. With USNR, 1945-46; USMCR, 1950-52. Decorated Silver Star, Purple Heart. Mem. Bantry Sailing Club (Ireland). Home: 2155 Ibis Isle Rd No. 17 Palm Beach FL 33480 Office Phone: 617-794-7610. Personal E-mail: daly4charlesu@aol.com.

DALY, GAIL M., law librarian, educator, dean; b. Detroit; BA in Edn., U. Mich., 1968, MA in Library Sci., 1969; JD, U. Minn., 1989. Assoc. dir. U. Minn. Law Sch. Libr.; assoc. dean for library and tech., assoc. prof. law, dir. Underwood Law Library So. Meth. U. Dedman Sch. Law, Dallas. Former mng. editor Minn. Law Rev.; vis. assoc. law Rsch. Librs. Group Stanford U., Mountain View, Calif.; mem. Nat. Mus. and Libr. Svcs. Bd., Washington, 2004—. Mem.: ABA, Am. Assn. Law Librs., Assn. Am. Law Schs. Office: Southern Methodist University Underwood Law Library 6550 Hillcrest Ave Dallas TX 75275 Office Phone: 214-768-1873. Business E-Mail: gdaly@mail.smu.edu.

DAMERIS, THAD THANO, lawyer; b. Houston, Feb. 27, 1960; BBA, Southern Meth. U., 1982; JD with honors, U. Tex., 1986. Bar: Tex. 1986, US Dist. Ct. (no., so., ea., we. dist. Tex., Ariz., so., no. dist. Calif., DC, so., ea. dist. NY, we. dist. Ark.), US Ct. Appeals (5th, 8th, 9th cir.), US Supreme Ct. Mng. ptnr. Houston office, co-chair transp. sector team Hogan Lovells (formerly Hogan & Hartson), Houston. Contbr. articles to profl. jours. Fellow: Tex. Bar Found., Houston Bar Found.; mem.: ABA (chmn. Aviation & Space Law com., vice chmn. Aviation Litigation com., co-chmn. mfg. div. Forum on Air & Space Law), Am. Bd. Trial Advocates, Internat. Bar Assn., Am. Soc. Internat. Law, NTSB Bar Assn., Def. Rsch. Inst., Lawyer Pilot Bar Assn., Tex. Assn. Def. Counsel, State Bar Tex. Office: Hogan Lovells US LLP 700 Louisiana St Ste 4300 Houston TX 77002-2782 Office Phone: 713-632-1410. Office Fax: 713-583-6297. Business E-Mail: thad.dameris@hoganlovells.com.

DAMRON, RICK D., retail executive; Joined Lowe's Companies, Inc., 1981, various positions including store mgr., dist. mgr. and regional v.p., sr. v.p., ops., North East Divsn., 2004, sr. v.p., ops., North Ctrl. Divsn., 2008, sr. v.p., logistics, 2009—11, exec. v.p. store ops., 2011—. Office: Lowe's Companies Inc 1000 Lowe's Blvd Mooresville NC 28117 Office Phone: 704-758-1000. Business E-Mail: ricky.damron@lowes.com.

DAMRON, ROBERT R., state legislator, investment banker; b. Danville, Ky., June 20, 1954; s. Ben R. and Jane Raney Damron; m. Paula L. Berke; 1 child, Robert Paul. BS in Acctg., U. Ky., 1976, MBA, 1984. Investment banker, 1992—; v.p. Ctrl. Ky. Ag Credit, 1976—91; mem. Dist. 39 Ky. House of Reps., 1993—; majority caucus chmn. Recipient Defending Freedom award, NRA, 1996; named Citizen of Yr., Ky. Mental Health Assn., 1998. Mem.: Jessamine County Beef Cattle Assn., Jessamine C. of C., Nicholasville Rotary, Lone Oak Country Club (treas. 1987—88, 1992—93, pres. 1989—91), Masonic Lodge. Democrat. Disciples Of Christ. Home: 231 Fairway W Nicholasville KY 40356 Office: 702 Capitol Ave Annex Rm 313A Frankfort KY 40601 also: 700 Capitol Ave Rm 312 Frankfort KY 40601 Home Phone: 859-887-1744; Office Phone: 502-564-2217, 800-372-7181. Business E-Mail: Robert.Damron@lrc.ky.gov.

DAN, MICHAEL T., retired security firm executive; Exec. v.p. Brink's, Inc., 1985—92, pres. No. Am. ops., 1992—93, CEO, 1993—2011, pres., 2002—04; pres., CEO Brink's Holding Co., 1995—2011, Brink's Co. (formerly Pittston Co.), Richmond, Va., 1998—2011, chmn., 1999—2011, BAX Global Inc., 1998—2006. Bd. dirs. The Brink's Co., 1998—, Prin. Fin. Group, Prin. Life Ins. Co. Office: Brink's Co 1801 Bayberry Ct PO Box 18100 Richmond VA 23226-8100 Business E-Mail: mdan@pittston.com.

DANAHAY, MICHAEL E., state legislator; BS in Bus. Admin., McNeese State U. Sales rep. Lake Charles Office Supply; mem. Dist. 33 La. House of Reps., 2008—, mem. house and govtl. affairs com., mcpl., parochial and cultural affairs com., ways and means com., joint legis. com. on capital outlay. Democrat. Office: State Capitol PO Box 44486 Baton Rouge LA 70804 Mailing: 1625 Beglis Pkwy Sulphur LA 70663 Office Phone: 225-342-6945, 337-527-5581. Office Fax: 337-527-5803. Business E-Mail: danahaym@legis.state.la.us.

DANBURG, JEROME SAMUEL, retired oil industry executive; b. Houston, Dec. 21, 1940; s. August and Rosalie (Bornstein) D.; m. Gudrun Ella Ernestine Scholz, Sept. 8, 1965; children: Aron Ralf, Andrea Leda, Sylvia Freia, Sonja Rebecca. BS in Physics, MIT, 1962; Diplom in Physics, Freie Universität Berlin, 1964; PhD in Physics, U. Calif., Berkeley, 1969. Assoc. physicist Brookhaven Nat. Lab., Upton, N.Y., 1969-72; sr. rsch. geophysicist Shell Devel. Co., Houston, 1973-81, rsch. mgr., 1981-86, rsch. dir., 1992-93; mgr. Shell Oil Co., Houston, 1986-92, 93-94, Shell EP Tech Co, Houston, 1994-99, Shell Internat. EP Inc., Houston, 1999—2003, Shell E&P Co., Houston, 2004—10. Physics dept. vis. com. mem. U. Tex., Austin, 1990-2001. Contbr. articles to profl. jours. Fulbright scholar, Freie Universität Berlin. Mem. Am. Phys. Soc., Fulbright Alumni Assn. Home: 5315 Huisache St Bellaire TX 77401-4933

DANCE, ROSALYN, state legislator; b. Chesterfield County, Va., Feb. 10, 1948; m. Nathaniel A. Dance; children: Nathaniel A. III, Tanya Dance Kelly. A in Nursing, John Tyler CC, Chester, Va., 1975; BS in Nursing, Va. State U., Petersburg, 1986; MPA, Va. Commonwealth U., 1994. RN. Ret. registered nurse; former dep. dir. Southside Tng. Ctr., Va.; councilwoman Petersburg City Coun., Va.; former mayor City of Petersburg; mem. Dist. 63 Va. House of Delegates, 2005—. Former chmn., bd. managers Southside YMCA, Va.; bd. dirs. John Tyler CC Coll. Found.; former chmn., bd. mem. United Way, Southside Ops. Mem.: Tri-City Univ. Women's Club (hon.), Petersburg Breakfast Rotary (former pres.), Phi Kappa Phi, Delta Sigma Theta, Petersburg Alumnae Chpt. Democrat. Baptist. Office: PO Box 2584 Petersburg VA 23804 also: Capitol Office Gen Assembly Bldg Rm 813 PO Box 406 Richmond VA 23218 Office Phone: 804-698-1063. Office Fax: 804-698-6763. Business E-Mail: delrdance@house.virginia.gov.

DANDY, ROSCOE GREER, author, psychotherapist, educator, retired public health service analyst; b. LA, Dec. 20, 1946; s. Roscoe Conkling and Doris L. (Edwards) D.; m. Lesley A. Dandy, Oct.,2007. BA, Calif. State U., 1970; MSW, U. So. Calif., 1973; MPH, U. Pitts., 1974, MPA, 1975, DPH, 1981; cert., Harvard U., 1981. Lic. clin. social worker. Youth counselor Calif. State Youth Authority, Ontario, Calif., 1971; pub. health intern Colo. State Dept. Health, Denver, 1974; health planning intern Green Engring Corp., Pitts., 1975; adminstrv. health intern Kane Hosp., Pitts., 1979; assoc. dir. U.S. Pub. Health Clinic, Washington, 1980-81; asst. chief trainee VA Hosp., Washington, 1981-83, asst. chief med. adminstrn. svc. Ft. Howard, Md., 1983-85, clinical social worker, 1985-93; psychotherapist Columbia Inst. of Psychotherapy, Inc., 1989-91, D.A. Wynne & Assocs. Inc., 1991-94; pub. health analyst USPHS, 1993—2007; program dir. and asst. prof. health care mgmt. Indian River State Coll., Ft. Pierce, Fla., 2012—. Instr. U. Pitts., 1977-80, Grad. Sch. Washington ext. campus Cen. Mich. U., 1980—, Columbia Pacific U., San Rafael, Calif., 1990—, Nova U., Ft. Lauderdale, Fla., 1991—; vis. instr. Andrews AFB, Washington, Walter Reed Army Med. Ctr. Hosp., Washington, Aberdeen Proving Ground, Md., Ft. Meade, Md., Ft. Hamilton, N.Y.; mem. Nat. Review Panel for Substance Abuse Contracts, 1991-93; adj. prof., pub. health Nova Southeastern U., 2010-. Author: (book) Board and Care Homes in Los Angeles County, 1976. Police cmty. liaison Howard County Police Dept., 1989-93; vol. deployment, Emergency Response Team, Hurricane Katrina, Gulfport, Miss., 2005. Recipient cash award, Dept. Health and Human Svc., 2005, Outstanding Performance evaluation, USPHS, 2005, 2006, Spl. Adminstr. award, 2007, Special Citation award, Sec. award, HHS, 2006; named Project Officer of Yr., Inst. Coll. Rsch. Devel. and Support, 1999; nominee Expert Peer Review panelist, Dept. Health and Human Svc., 2009—11. Mem. APHA, NASW, AAUP, Am. Assn. Healthcare Execs. Avocations: reading, poetry, music, track. Home: 23 Reybury Ln Palm Coast FL 32164

DANG, KIMBERLY ALLEN, energy executive; B in Acctg., Tex. A&M U., College Station; MBA, Northwestern U. With venture capital firm, Austin, Tex.; legis. asst. US Congressman Jack Fields, Washington; with real estate investment area Goldman Sachs; dir. investor rels. Kinder Morgan, Inc., Houston, 2001—02, v.p. investor rels., 2002—09, treas., 2004—05, v.p., CFO, 2005—. Office: Kinder Morgan 500 Dallas St Ste 1000 Houston TX 77002 Office Phone: 713-369-9000.

DANIEL, CATHY BROOKS, educational consultant; b. Nashville, Sept. 1, 1946; d. Conway William and Alliene Marie (Gilliam) B.; m. James Newton Daniel Jr., Dec. 29, 1967 (div. July 1988; children: Laura Marie, James Newton III. Student, Memphis State U., 1964—66; BS, George Peabody Coll., 1968, MA, 1971. Cert. elem. tchr., special edn. tchr., learning disabilities and behavior disorders. Tchr. Fairview (Tenn.) Elem. Sch., 1968-69; special edn. tchr. Ross Elem. Sch., Nashville, 1969-70, Rosebank Elem. Sch., Nashville, 1970-71, Graymar Elem. Sch., Nashville, 1971-73, Norman Binkley Elem. Sch., Nashville, 1973-74; cons. ednl. and family counseling, ednl. testing Franklin, Tenn., 1975—. Methodist. Avocation: tennis. Home and Office: 2203 Springdale Dr Franklin TN 37064-4962 Office Phone: 615-794-0705.

DANIEL, DAVID EDWIN, academic administrator, civil engineer; b. Newport News, Va., Dec. 20, 1949; s. David Edwin and Betty Ruth (Aschenback) D.; m. Frances Louise Locker, June 12, 1971 (div.); children: Katherine Ruth, William Monroe; m. Susan Nielsen Brady, May 12, 1989; 1 child, Alexander David. BS, U. Tex., 1972, MS, 1974, PhD, 1980. Staff engr. Woodward-Clyde, San Francisco, 1974-77; asst. prof. U. Tex., Austin, 1981-85, assoc. prof., 1985-91, prof., 1991-96; prof., head dept. civil engring. U. Ill., Urbana, 1996-2001, dean, Coll. Engring., Gutgsell prof. civil engring., 2001—05; pres. U. Tex., Dallas, 2005—. Mem. ASCE (Norman medal 1975, Cross medal 1984, 2000, Middlebrooks award 1995, Richard R. Torrens award 1995), NAE. Office: University of Texas Dallas Office of President PO Box 830688 Richardson TX 75083-0688 Business E-Mail: dedaniel@utdallas.edu.*

DANIEL, MARILYN S., lawyer; b. Tulsa, Okla., July 30, 1940; d. Basil M. and Kathryne (Shannon) Stewart; m. John A. Daniel, June 15, 1962; 1 child, John S. BA, Rhodes Coll., 1962; JD, U. Ky. Coll. of Law, 1976. Bar: Ky. Sec. math. tchr., Ky, NJ, 1962—71; legal clerk U.S. Dist. Judge, Lexington, Ky., 1977; asst. U.S. atty. U.S. Dept. Justice, Lexington, 1978—81; gen. counsel Mason & Hanger Corp., Lexington, 1982—92, v.p. adminstrn., 1992—96, sr. v.p., 1996—99. Dir. The Mason Co., Lexington, 1990—99, Ky. Bar Assn. for Women, 1991—93; vol. dir. Maxwell St. Legal Clinic, 1999—2007. Mem. Fayette County Bd. Edn., 1985—88; vol. atty. Maxwell St. Legal Clinic, 1999—; trustee Transylvania Presbytery, 1985—98; elder Maxwell St. Presbyn. Ch., 1993—. Recipient Women of Achievement award YWCA, 1993; named to Hall of Fame U. Ky. Coll. Law, 2009. Mem. Am. Immigration Lawyers Assn., KBA (CLE chair ann. conv. 1992), Fayette County Bar Assn. (Henry T. Duncan award 1994, Lawyer Citizen award 2005). Avocations: gardening, cooking, hiking, quilting, handwork.

DANIEL, NICOLE C., chemicals executive; BA in Govt., The Coll. of William and Mary, 1990; Wash. Semester Program, American U., 1988; JD, Ind. U., Bloomington, 1997. Assoc. Woods Rogers P.L.C., Roanoake, Va., Hunton & Williams LLP, Richmond, Va.; head, legal affairs, polymer additives segment and Asia- Pacific regional ops. Albemarle Corp., dir., investor rels., 2005—08, asst. gen. counsel, asst. sec., 2008—10, v.p., chief compliance officer, corp. sec., 2010—. Office: Albemarle Corp 451 Florida St Baton Rouge LA 70801 Office Phone: 225-388-8011. Office Fax: 225-388-8924. Business E-Mail: Nicole.Daniel@albemarle.com.

DANIEL, WARREN TODD, state legislator; m. Lydia Daniel; 3 children. BS in Nat. Security Pub. Affairs, US Mil. Acad., West Point, 1991. Lic., NC. Mem. NRA, Mil. Adv. Com. for Cong. McHenry; leader AWANA; mem. Eagle Scout; atty. Daniel Law Firm, P.A., Morganton, NC, 2000—; mem. Dist. 44 NC State Senate, 2011—. 2nd lt. US Army; capt. US Army, 1991-97. Republican. Bapt. Office: 309 W Union St Morganton NC 28655 Address: NC Senate 300 N Salisbury St Room 411 Raleigh NC 27603-5925 Office Phone: 919-715-7823, 828-439-8075. Business E-Mail: Warren.Daniel@ncleg.net.

DANIEL, WILLIAM BUCHANAN, IV, state legislator; b. Nov. 6, 1955; m. Lynda Hiltz Daniel. House rep., La.; petroleum engr. Oil & Gas Prodn. Co., 1979—81; dist. engr. Oil & Gas Resources Co., 1981—85; pres. Oil & Gas Operation Co., 1985—91; state rep. Dist. 68 La., 1996—; mem. Natural Resources Com., Retirement Com., Ways & Means Com., Joint Com. Capital Outlay, 1996—; engr. rsch. analyst. Mem.: La. Engring. Soc., Soc. Petroleum Engr. Democrat. Episcopal. Address: 6728 Pikes Lane Baton Rouge LA 70808 also: 17170 Perkins Rd Baton Rouge LA 70810 Office Phone: 504-767-4090. Fax: 504-769-3050, 225-219-4356.

DANIELL, HERMAN BURCH, pharmacologist; b. Cadwell, Ga., May 25, 1929; s. Walter and Ruby Florence (Burch) Daniell; m. Mickey Marucheau, May 24, 1952 (dec.); m. Lorraine Smith, June 30, 1957 (dec.); children: Kimberley Ann, Anthony Burch, Walter Herman. BS in Pharmacy, U. Ga., 1951, MS in Pharmacology, 1964; PhD in Pharmacology, Med. U. S.C., 1966. Owner-operator retail pharmacies, Savannah, Ga., 1953-62; instr. U. Ga., 1962-64; USPHS trainee Med. Coll. S.C., Charleston, 1964—66; mem. faculty Med. U. S.C., 1966-92, prof. pharmacology, 1978-92, prof. emeritus, 1992—. Contbr. articles to profl. jours. Served to capt. M.S.C. US Army, 1951—53. Grantee, USPHS, 1966—85, S.C. Heart Assn., 1966—73. Mem.: Am. Soc. Pharmacology and Exptl. Therapeutics, Sigma Xi, Kappa Sigma, Rho Chi. Episcopalian. Home: 1549 Burningtree Rd Charleston SC 29412-2630

DANIELS, JENNIFER M., lawyer; b. 1963; BA, U. Penn., 1985; JD, Harvard Law Sch., 1988. Bar: NY 1989. Joined IBM Corp., 1990; v.p., gen. counsel IBM Americas; v.p., asst. gen. counsel, chief trust and compliance officer IBM Internat.; v.p., gen. counsel, sec. Barnes & Noble, Inc., 2007—10; sr. v.p., gen. counsel, corp. sec. NCR Corp., Duluth, Ga., 2010—. Office: NCR Corp 2651 Satellite Blvd Duluth GA 30096 Office Phone: 937-445-1936. Office Fax: 937-445-5541.

DANIELS, JON, professional sports team executive; b. NYC, Aug. 24, 1977; s. Mark and Mindy Daniels; m. Robyn Daniels, Nov. 2003; 1 child, Lincoln. Grad. in applied economics and mgmt., Cornell U., Ithaca, NY, 1999. With Allied Domecq, Boston, 1999—2001; intern, baseball ops. dept. Colo. Rockies, 2001; baseball ops. asst. Tex. Rangers, 2002—03, dir. baseball ops., 2003—05, asst. gen. mgr., 2004—05, gen. mgr., 2005—. Office: Tex Rangers Rangers Ballpark in Arlington 1000 Ballpark Way Arlington TX 76011

DANIELS, KIMBERLY, councilwoman; m. Ardell Daniels; 6 children. BS in Criminology, Fla. State U., MA in Christian Edn., PhD in Christian Psychology. Founder Operation Boomerang; councilwoman-at-large Group 1 Jacksonville City Coun., 2011—. Office: Jacksonville City Council 117 W Duval St Jacksonville FL 32202 also: PO Box 28007 Jacksonville FL 32226-0278 Office Phone: 904-630-1393. E-mail: KimDaniels@coj.net.

DANIELSEN, ALBERT LEROY, economics professor, energy and utilities consultant; b. Council Bluffs, Iowa, May 26, 1934; s. Moroni Lloyd and Geneva Gale (Williford) Danielsen; m. Eleanor Jean Gibson, June 7, 1958; children: Bartley Roland, Lea Anne, Albert William. BS, Clemson U., 1960; PhD, Duke U., 1966. From asst. prof. to prof. econs. U. Ga., Athens, 1963—97, prof. emeritus, 1997—; dir. Office Internat. Market Analysis, U.S. Dept. Energy, Washington, 1976—78, James C. Bonbright Utilities Ctr., U. Ga., 1991—; pres. Nat. Bus. and Econ. Edn. Assocs. Inc., 1988—2007; exec. dir. Vertically Integrated Elec. Utilities Ctr., 2007—. Econ. cons. on pvt. contracts, regulation, elec. restructuring and privitization Czech Republic, Egypt, India, Malaysia, Panama and U.S.; testified before numerous regulatory agys.; dir. nat. utility confs., 1980—; assoc. Repeal Laws; bd. dirs. Electric Markets Rsch. Found., 2012—. Author: Evolution of OPEC, 1982, Principles of Public Utility Rates, 1988, OPEC, Encyclopedia Britannica, 2002, The Global Warming Mass Movement, 2013; contbr. articles to profl. jours.; author: documents in field. Grantee, Social Sci. Rsch. Coun., 1982. Mem.: Am. Econs. Assn., Internat. Assn. Energy Economists. Baptist. Avocations: swimming, golf. Office Phone: 706-202-2534. Personal E-mail: danielsen@bellsouth.net. Business E-Mail: bonbright@terry.uga.edu, danielsen@repeallaws.org.

DANIELSON, GILBERT LAWRENCE, consumer products company executive; b. Monmouth, Ill., Aug. 22, 1946; BS, Drake U., 1968. With Arthur Andersen & Co., Chgo.; v.p. fin., CFO Aaron's, Inc., Atlanta, 1990-98, CFO, bd. dirs., 1990—, exec. v.p., 1998—. Bd. dirs. Abrams Industries, Inc., Servidyne, Inc., 2000—. 1st lt. U.S. Army, Vietnam. Office: Aaron's Inc 309 E Paces Ferry Rd NE Atlanta GA 30305-2377 Office Phone: 404-231-0011. Office Fax: 404-240-6583. Business E-Mail: Gil.Danielson@aaronrents.com.

DANIELSON, PAUL E., state supreme court justice; m. Elizabeth "Betsy" Danielson; 1 child, Erik. BA, Fla. State U., Tallahassee; JD with honors, U. Ark., Fayetteville, 1975. Bar: Ark. 1975. Law clk. to Assoc. Justice Frank Holt Ark. Supreme Ct., assoc. justice position 5, 2007—; pvt. practice atty.; dep. pros. atty. 6th and 15th jud. dists. State of Ark.; city atty. City of Booneville, Ark.; cir. judge 15th jud. cir. Ark. Cir. Ct., 1994—2007. Instr. U. Ark. Sch. Law. Named Outstanding Trial Judge of Yr., Ark. Trial Lawyer Assn., 2003. Fellow: Ark. Bar Found.; mem.: Ark. Jud. Coun., Ark. Bar Assn. Office: Ark Supreme Ct Justice Bldg 625 Marshall St Little Rock AR 72201*

DANING, JOSEPH, state legislator; b. Phila., Pa., Dec. 12, 1942; s. Sofronio and Mary (Martin) Daning; m. Brenda Joyce Daning, Sept. 21, 1964; children: Michael, Timothy. BA, Trident Tech Coll., Charleston, SC, 1992; BS, Southern Ill U., 1995; MA, Webster U., St. Louis, 1999. Councilman Goose Creek City Coun., SC, 1978—86, 1992—, mayor pro tem., 2008; mem. Dist. 92 SC House of Reps., 2008—. Bd. dirs. Coun. Mil. Educators SC, 2004—. Mem. USAF, 1960—64. Republican. Cath. Office: 118 Queensbury Cir Goose Creek SC 29445 also: Capitol Office 310B Blatt Bldg Columbia SC 29201 Office Phone: 843-553-9288, 803-734-2951. E-mail: joedaning@schouse.org.

DANK, DAVID, state legislator; b. Pittsburgh, Pa., July 14, 1938; m. Odilia Dank; 1 child, Trina. Attended, U. Okla. Former newspaper publisher Moore Monitor, Okla. Conservative Rev.; former polit. commentator & analyst KTOK, Okla. News Network, OETA TV; former exec. vice pres. Okla. Retail Mchts. Assn.; pres. Dank Consulting; mem. Dist. 85 Okla. House of Representatives, 2008—. Republican. Catholic. Office: 2300 N Lincoln Blvd Rm 433 Oklahoma City OK 73105 also: 6705 Reed Dr Oklahoma City OK 73116 Office Phone: 405-557-7392, 405-843-4586. Business E-Mail: david.dank@okhouse.gov.

DANNELLY, CHARLIE SMITH, state legislator; b. Bishopville, SC; m. Rose Dannelly; 1 child, Charlie II. BA, Johnson C. Smith U., 1962; MEd, U. NC Chapel Hill, 1966. Ret. educator; state senator Dist. 38 NC, 1995—; dep. pres. Pro Tempore, 2003—10. 1st lt. 82nd Airborne US Army, Republic of Korea. Recipient Appreciation award; named Legislator of Yr., Disting. Legislator. Democrat. Baptist. Office: NC Senate 16 W Jones St Rm 1127 Raleigh NC 27601-2808 Office Phone: 919-733-5955. Business E-Mail: Charlied@ncleg.net.

DANSBY, WALTER, school system administrator; m. Sharon Dansby; children: Marsha, Leigh Ann. BA, U. Tex., Arlington; MA in Edn., Tarleton State U. History tchr., coach Rosemont Middle Sch., Tex., 1974; head HS basketball coach Paschal HS, asst. prin.; prin. O.D. Wyatt HS; exec. dir. instruction South Quadrant; assoc. supt. Instrnl. Team for Area 1 Fort Worth Independent Sch. Dist., dep. supt.

operational mgmt. and human resources, interim supt., 2011—12, supt., 2012—. Recipient Excellence in Edn. Award, Multi-Ethnic C. of C., Men of Distinction Award, Alpha Theta Sigma Fraternity, Disting. Svc. Award, Greater Fort Worth Area Negro Bus. and Profl. Women's Club, Pub. Sector Advocate Award, Black Contractors Assn., Marion J. Brooks Living Legend Award in Edn. Office: Fort Worth Independent School District Administration Building 100 N University Dr Fort Worth TX 76107 Office Phone: 817-871-2000. E-mail: Walter.Dansby@fwisd.org.*

DANTICAT, EDWIDGE, writer, educator; b. Port-au-Prince, Haiti, Jan. 19, 1969; arrived in US, 1981; d. Andre Miracin and Rose Souvenance Danticat. BA in French Lit., Barnard Coll., NYC, 1990; MFA in Creative Writing, Brown U., Providence, 1993. Prodn., rsch. asst. Clinica Estetico, 1993—94; adj. prof. NYU, 1996—97; vis. prof. creative writing U. Miami, 2000, 2008. Author: (novels) Breath, Eyes, Memory, 1994, Krik? Krak!, 1995, The Farming of Bones, 1998 (Super Flaiano prize, Italy, 1999), Behind the Mountains, 2002, The Dew Breaker, 2004 (The Story prize ann. book award, 2005), Anacaona: Golden Flower, Haiti, 1490, 2005, Brother, I'm Dying, 2007 (Nat. Book Critics Cir. award for autobiography, 2007, Dayton Lit. Peace prize, 2008), Claire of the Sea Light, 2013; co-author (with Jonathan Demme) Island on Fire: Chronicla of Haitian Art, 1997, Odillon Pierre, Artist of Haiti, 2000; editor: (books) The Beacon Best of 2000: Great Writing by Men and Women of All Colors, 2001, After the Dance, 2002, (anthology) The Butterfly's Way: Voices from the Haitian Dyaspora in the United States, 2002; contbr. articles short stories to various pubs. and anthologies. Recipient Woman of Achievement award, Barnard Coll., 1995, Internat. Flaiano prize for lit., Italy, 1999, Pushcart Short Story prize; named a MacArthur Fellow, John T. & Catherine MacArthur Found., 2009. Mem.: Alpha Kappa Alpha.*

DANTZLER, DERYL DAUGHERTY, lawyer, educator, dean; b. Macon, Ga., Jan. 26, 1944; d. Marshall Harrison and Gertrude Earle (Baker) Daugherty; m. L. Keitt Dantzler, June, 1968 (div. 1975); 1 child, Kennon Otis. BA, Mercer U., Macon, Ga., 1964, JD, 1970. Bar: Ga. 1970, U.S. Dist. Ct. (mid. dist.) Ga. 1970, U.S. Ct. Appeals (5th and 11th cirs.) 1970, U.S. Supreme Ct. 1973. Assoc. Mincey, Kenmore & Bennett, Macon, 1970-73; ptnr. Bennett, Mobley & Dantzler, 1973-78; pvt. practice, 1978-79; asst. prof. Law Sch., Mercer U., 1979-84, prof., 1984—, dir. trial practice, 1985—, apptd. Tommy Malone disting. chair in trial advocacy, 2007; dean Nat. Criminal Def. Coll., Inc., 1985—. Mem. Nat. Assn. Criminal Def. Lawyers (Presdl. Commendation 1985, 89, Lifetime Achievement award 1996, Champion of Liberty award, 2011), Assn. Continuing Legal Edn. Adminstrs., Ga. Bar Assn. Office: Mercer U Law Sch Macon GA 31207-0001 Office Phone: 478-746-4151. E-mail: dean@ncdc.net.

DANZEISEN, MARCIA, corporate financial executive; Worked in corp. mktg. & comm. Xerox; sr v.p., assoc. dir. Macquarie Mortgages USA; worked in corp. mktg. & comm. IBM Corp.; comm. cons. Freddie Mac, 1992—93; sr v.p., strategic planning exec. Bank America, 1993—2000; sr v.p., mktg. dir. JP Morgan Chase, 2000—05; assoc. dir., head, mktg. Macquarie, 2005—08; sr v.p. global mktg. & comm. Fidelity National Information Services, Inc., 2008—. Office: Fidelity National Information Services Inc 601 Riverside Ave Jacksonville FL 32204 Office Fax: 904-854-4124.

DANZIGER, RAPHAEL, political scientist, researcher; b. Haifa, Israel, June 26, 1944; came to U.S., 1968; s. Norbert and Hanna Danziger; m. Carla Danziger, June 12, 1970; children: Elon, Tamar. BA in Polit. Sci. and History Islamic Countries, Hebrew U., Jerusalem, 1965; MA in Near Ea. Studies, U. Wash., 1970; MA in European and Near Ea. History, Princeton U., 1972, PhD in Near Ea. Studies, 1974. Rschr. Shiloah Ctr. for Mid. Ea. Studies Tel Aviv (Israel) U., 1975-76; dep. dir. Inst. Mid. Ea. Studies U. Haifa (Israel), 1976-77; policy analyst commn. on internat. affairs Am. Jewish Congress, NYC, 1981-86, asst. dir. commn. on internat. affairs, 1986-90; dir. rsch. and info. Am. Israel Pub. Affairs Com., Washington, 1990—2010, sr. rsch. advisor, 2010—. Cons. Hudson Inst., Croton-on-Hudson, N.Y., 1974-75; vis. rsch. fellow dept. history U. Bergen, Norway, 1980; vis. fellow dept. Near Ea. studies Princeton (N.J.) U., 1981; lectr. dept. Mid. East history U. Haifa, 1975-81; vis. asst. prof. dept. history U. Wash., Seattle, 1980-81; lectr. in field. Author: Abd al-Qadir and the Algerians: Resistance to the French and Internal Consolidation, 1977; editor Near East Report, 1992—2010, editor-in-chief emeritus, 2010-; contbr. articles to profl. jours. Lt. Israeli Army, 1965-68. Mem. Mid. East Studies Assn., Mid. East Inst. Office: Am Israel Pub Affairs Com 251 H St NW Washington DC 20001-2017 Office Phone: 202-639-5268. Business E-Mail: rdanziger@aipac.org.

DANZL, DANIEL FRANK, emergency physician; b. Cin., Apr. 2, 1950; s. Frank Bernard and Mary Ellen (Doerger) D.; m. Joanna Colosimo Danzl, Nov. 25, 1978; children: Maggie, Julia. BS magna cum laude, U. Cin., 1972; MD, Ohio State U., 1976. Diplomate Am. Bd. Emergency Medicine. Intern St. Francis Med. Ctr., Peoria, Ill., 1976-77; resident in emergency medicine U. Louisville, 1977-79, asst. prof. emergency medicine, 1979-83, assoc. prof. emergency medicine, 1983-89, prof. emergency medicine, 1989-91, prof., chair, 1991—. Bd. dirs., councilman-at-large Univ. Assn. for Emergency Medicine, 1988-89, indsl./govtl. rels. com., 1984-85, nominating com., 1987-88; bd. dirs. Soc. for Acad. Emergency Medicine, 1989, mem. annals of emergency meidcine task force, 1989; bd. dirs. Am. Bd. Emergency Medicine, sec.-treas., 1995-96, pres.-elect, 1996-97, pres. 1997—, mem. ad hoc com., oral examiner, 1982—; mem. Com. to Advise the Nat. ARC, 1984-87; reviewer for various med. jours. Author book chpts., monographs and textbooks including Airway Management in the Trauma Patient in the Clinical Practice of Emergency Medicine, 1991; editl. bd. Jour. Emergency Medicine, 1983—, Poisindex-Emergindex, 1982—, Jour. Wilderness Medicine, 1991—; contbr. more than 70 articles to Jour. Wilderness Medicine, Jour. Emergency Medicine, Annals of Emergency Medicine, Am. Jour. Emergency Medicine, others. Mem. Water Safety Com. Nat. Safety Coun.-Pub. Safety Div., 1981-84; alternate med. dir. Jefferson Vocat. Edn.-Louisville EMS Paramedic Tng. Program, 1989-90, 90-91. Recipient Silver Tongue Orator award Soc. Tchrs. of Emergency Medicine, 1986, 88; grantee Office of Naval Resources, 1983-85, Key Pharmaceuticals, 1985, Hoffman-LaRoche, Inc., 1988, 89. Fellow Am. Coll. Emergency Physicians (nat. coun. mem. 1981-93, reference com. mem. 1981, 85, 89, rsch. com. mem. 1982-83, 83-84); mem. AMA (Physician's Recognition awards), NAS, Am. Soc. Circumpolar Health, Soc. for Acad. Emergency Medicine (bd. dirs. 1989, task force 1989), Nat. Rsch. Coun., Undersea and Hyperbaric Oxygen Med. Soc., Ky. Chpt. Am. Coll. Emergency Physicians (councillor 1981-93, sec.-treas. 1983-84, pres.-elect 1984-85, pres. 1985-86), Wilderness Med. Soc., Phi Beta Kappa, Beta Theta Pi, Alpha Omega Alpha, Phi Eta Sigma. Roman Catholic. Achievements include research on hypothermia. Home: 4804 Smith Rd Floyds Knobs IN 47119-9238 Office: U Louisville Dept Emergency Med 530 S Jackson St Louisville KY 40202-1675

DAOUST, DONALD ROGER, pharmaceutical executive, microbiologist, cosmetics executive; b. Worcester, Mass., Aug. 13, 1935; s. G. Arthur and Alice Anne (Lavalee) D.; m. Johanna K. Kalinoski, May 30, 1959 (div. 2003); children: Donna Jean, Stephen Michael, Sandra Marie; m. Barbara Neubert, 2005. BA, U. Conn., 1957; MS, U. Mass., 1959, PhD, 1962. Sr. rsch. microbiologist Merck Sharp & Dohme, Rahway, NJ, 1962-70, rsch. fellow, 1970-72, mgr. biol. quality control West Point, Pa., 1972-75; dir. quality control Armour Pharm. Co., Kankakee, Ill., 1975-76, v.p. quality assurance and regulatory compliance Phoenix, 1976-78; v.p., quality control Carter-Wallace, Inc., Cranbury, NJ, 1978—2001. Contbr. articles o profl. jours., chapters to books. Mem. Borough Coun., South Plainfield, N.J., 1970-72; treas. George Washington coun. Boy Scouts Am., 1981-84, pres., 1984-87, area v.p., bd.dirs. NE region U.S., 1987—2004. Recipient Disting. Svc. award South Plainfield Jaycees, 1969, silver Beaver award Boy Scouts Am., 1988, Silver Antelope award N.E. region, 1992; named Outstanding Young Man, N.J. Jaycees, 1970. Mem.: AAAS, Pharm. Mfrs. Assn. (quality control adminstrn. 1979—82, adv. bd. 1982—94, vice chmn 1988—90, chmn. 1990—92), Am. Soc. for Quality Control, Am. Soc. Microbiology, Laurel Oak Country Club (Sarasota, Fla.) (bd. govs. 2009—, pres. 2010—12). Achievements include patents in field. Avocations: golf, reading, gardening. Home: 3254 Chas MacDonald Dr Sarasota FL 34240 Personal E-mail: dondaoust@comcast.net.

D'APPOLONIA, MICHAEL R., construction executive; BA in Economics, Pa. State U. COO Edrei Comm. Corp.; pres., CEO Environmental Transp. Svc. Inc.; exec. officer Ametech, Inc., Halston Borghese, Inc., McCulloch Corp., Simmons Upholstered Furniture Inc.; pres. Nightingale & Assocs., LLC, 1986—2006, Moll Industries, Inc., 2002—03, Cone Mills Corp., chief restructuring officer, 2003—05; pres., CEO Kinetic Systems, Inc., Durham, 2006—. Bd. dirs. The Wash. Group Internat., Inc., 2001—07, Moll Industries Inc., 2002—03, Exide Technologies Inc., 2004—, Kinetic Sys., Inc., 2006—, Westmoreland Coal Co., 2008—. Office: Kinetic Systems Inc Ste 500 6517 Hilburn Dr Raleigh NC 27613-1908 Office Phone: 919-474-4600. Office Fax: 919-474-8214. Business E-Mail: mdappolonia@kineticsgroup.com.

DARBY, DREW, state legislator; b. San Angelo, Tex. m. Clarisa Fisher Darby; children: Derek, Devon, Taylor, Ashley, Regan. BBA in Fin., U. Tex., JD; grad. emerging polit. leaders program, U. Va. Founder W. Drew Darby and Associates Law Firm; owner Surety Title Co., Double D. Title, Inc.; former mem. San Angelo City Coun.; mem. Dist. 72 Tex. House of Representatives, 2006—. Former chmn. Lake Nasworthy Adv. Bd., San Angelo Adv. Bd. Mem.: NRA, Tex. Sheep and Goat Raiser's Assn. Republican. Presbyterian. Office: 36 W Beauregard Ste 517 San Angelo TX 76901-4648 also: Rm EXT E1.508 Capitol Extension PO Box 2910 Austin TX 78768 Office Phone: 325-658-7313, 512-463-0331.

DARBY, KAREN SUE, law educator; b. Columbus, Ohio, Sept. 15, 1947; d. Emerson Curtis and Kathryn Elizabeth (Bowers) Dum; m. R. Russell Darby, Dec. 21, 1974; children: David Randolph, Michael Emerson. BA magna cum laude, Capital U., Columbus, 1969; JD, Ohio State U., 1980. Bar: Ohio 1980, Pa. 1998, U.S. Dist. Ct. (so. dist.) Ohio 1981. High sch. English tchr. Columbus Pub. Schs., 1969-72; employee rels. specialist GE, Circleville, Ohio, 1972-74, mgr. EEO and manpower programs chem. met. div. Worthington, Ohio, 1974-77; atty. Ohio Legal Rights Svc., Columbus, 1980-81; pvt. practice Columbus, 1981-90; assoc. dir. Ohio Continuing Legal Edn. Inst., Columbus, 1989-95; dir. Phila. Bar Edn. Ctr., 1995-97; assoc. dir. Pa. Bar Inst., Phila., 1997—2002; exec. dir. Ill. Inst. for Continuing Legal Edn., 2002—07, cons., continuing legal edn., curriculum devel., 2007—. Mem. rules adv. com. Supreme Ct. Ohio, Columbus, 1989-94. Author, editor: Civil Commitment in Ohio - A Manual for Respondents' Attorneys, 1980. Mem. divorce mediation panel Ohio State U. Commn. on Interprofl. Edn., Columbus, 1988-91; vol. Boy Scouts Am., Columbus, 1988-92, Columbus Pub. Schs., 1984-95. Mem.: ABA. Lutheran. Avocations: organ, piano, gardening. Home: 300 Skyline Rd Georgetown TX 78628 Personal E-mail: kdarby@alicle.org.

D'ARCY, GERALD PAUL, engineering executive, consultant; b. Jackson, Mich., June 6, 1933; s. Merlin Wellington and Jessie Elizabeth (Sober) D.; m. Dorothy Lee Cordell, Nov. 27, 1953; children: Sherry, Janet, Nancy, Deborah, Helen. BSMechE, U. Tex., 1956; MSMechE, U. Colo., 1962; PhD, U. Tex., 1973. Registered profl. engr., Tex. Commd. 2d lt. USAF, 1956, advanced through grades to col., ret., 1986; asst. chief soil and rock mechanics group Air Force Weapons Lab., Kirtland AFB, N.Mex., 1962-67; rsch. assoc. Lawrence Radiation Lab., Livermore, Calif., 1967-70; chief phys. & engring. scis. divsn. Air Force Systems Command, Andrews AFB, Md., 1973-74; chief guns, rockets & explosives divsn. Air Force Armament Lab., Eglin AFB, Fla., 1975-79; vice comdr., later comdr. Air Force Geophysics, Hanscom AFB, Mass., 1979-84; comdr., dir. Air Force Office of Sci. Rsch., Bolling AFB, 1984-86; v.p. Applied Rsch. Assocs. Inc., Albuquerque, 1986-94; ret., 1994. Mech. engring. vis. com. U. Tex., Austin, 1976-79. Inventor soil stress gage; author more than 20 articles. Decorated Legion of Merit; recipient Meritorious Svc. award for nuclear weapons devel. U. Calif., Livermore, 1970; named Disting. Engring. Grad. U. Tex., Austin, 1985. Mem.: U. Tex. Mech. Engring. Acad. Dist. Alumni, Phi Kappa Phi. Democrat. Methodist. Avocation: woodworking. Home: 808 Plantation Way Panama City FL 32404-8603 Personal E-mail: utdeg@comcast.net.

DARCY, ROBERT EMMETT, political science and statistics professor; b. Elizabeth, NJ, Feb. 25, 1942; s. John William and Jane (Alton) D.; m. Susan Wylie, 1964 (div. 1965), m. Lynne C. Murnane, Aug. 30, 1975; children: Mary Frances, Catherine Rose. BA, U. Wis., Madison, 1965; MA, U. Ky., Lexington, 1970, PhD, 1971. Asst. prof. George Washington U., Washington, 1971—77, Okla. State U., Stillwater, 1977—80, assoc. prof. polit. sci. and stats., 1980—85, prof., 1985—90, Regents prof., 1991—2010, emeritus, 2010—. Expert witness on racial disparities, ballot and election procedures Atty. Gen., State of Okla., Oklahoma City, 1984-86, 91-95, 98, 2002, Ohio, 1991, NH, 1995, 2004-05, NC, 1998, NY, 1999, Fed. Dist. Ct., 2002, 03, 04, 05; vis. prof. U. Conn., 1984, U. New Orleans, 1985, Queen's U., Belfast, 1987, Nat. U. Ireland, Galway, 1988, Australian Def. Force Acad., 1991, U. NSW, 1991, Trinity Coll., Dublin, 1993, U. Tel Aviv, 2007, Liaoning Normal U., Dalian, China, 2010; mem. Okla. Commn. on Status Women, 1997-2010, co-chmn. summit 1997, 99; mem. Okla. Jud. Evaluation Commn., 1997-2001, Legis. Task Force on Jud. Selection, 1999-2000; vice chmn. gen. faculty Okla. State U., 2004-05, faculty coun., 2004-05, chair gen. faculty, 2005-06, faculty coun., 2005-06; lectr. in field. Author: Women, Elections and Representation, 1987, 90, 94, Guide to Quantitative History, 1995, Okla. Women's Almanac, 2005; co-editor Jour. Okla. Politics, 1991-99, 2005, Social Sci. Jour., 1983-85, Korean Jour. Pub. Policy, 2005; contbr. articles to profl. jours. With US Army, 1966—68. Recipient Liberty Bell award Okla. Bar Assn., 1999, Commendation, Okla. Ho. of Reps., 2000; Bruce fellow Keele U., Eng., 1998, Outstanding Achievement award, Nat. Assn. Commns. Women, 2006, 08; vis. rsch. scholar Acad. Korean Studies, Seoul, 1983. Mem. Polit. Studies Assn. Ireland, Am. Polit. Sci. Assn., Okla. Polit. Sci. Assn. (pres. 1992, Outstanding Okla. Polit. Scientist award 1993, Lifetime Achievement award 2013), Rotary. Republican. Home: 2215 W 5th Ave Stillwater OK 74074-2818 Business E-Mail: bob.darcy@okstate.edu.

DARDEN, CLAIBOURNE HENRY, JR., marketing research professional; b. Greensboro, NC, June 26, 1943; s. Claibourne Henry and Gerry (Bonkemeyer); m. Anita McMurry; children: Claibourne III, Prentiss. BS, Washington & Lee U., 1966; MBA, Emory U., 1968. Pres. Darden Rsch. Corp., Atlanta, 1968—. TV commentator, spkr. in field. Bd. dirs. Nat. Wild Turkey Fedn., Edgefield, SC, 1985—2000, Quality Deer Mgmt. Assn., Bogart, Ga., 2001—06, Ga. Conservancy, 1985—91, Washington & Lee Alumni Assn., Atlanta, 1986—87. Mem. Am. Mktg. Assn. (bd. dirs. Atlanta chpt. 1970-75, Mktg. Profl. of Yr. 1976), N.Y. Yacht Club, Druid Hills Golf Club. Presbyterian. Avocations: hunting, sailing, fishing. Office: Darden Rsch Corporation 1534 N Decatur Rd NE Atlanta GA 30307-1022

DARDENNE, JAY (JOHN LEIGH DARDENNE JR.), Lieutenant Governor of Louisiana; b. Baton Rouge, Feb. 6, 1954; s. John Leigh Sr. and Janet Lucille (Abramson) Dardenne; m. Catherine Eloise McDonald, Aug. 20, 1983; children: John Leigh III, Matthew Michael. BA in Journalism, La. State U., 1976; JD, La. State U. Law Ctr., 1979. Bar: La. 1979. Law clk. to hon. Frank J. Polozala US Dist. Ct. La., Baton Rouge, 1979-81; ptnr. Kennon, Odom & Dardenne, LLC, Baton Rouge, 1981—; mem. Baton Rouge Met. Coun., 1989—91; mem. Dist. 16 La. State Senate, 1992—2006; sec. of state State of La., 2006—10, lt. gov., 2010—. Pres. Muscular Dystrophy Assn., Baton Rouge, 1981—84, mem. nat. bd., 1993—; pres. Cerebral Palsy Assn., Baton Rouge, 1985—86, River City Festivals Assn., Baton Rouge, 1986—87; chmn. Leadership Greater Baton Rouge Alumni, Inc., 1986—87, Baton Rouge Sports Commn., 1989—92. Recipient Disting. Leader award, Nat. Assn. Cmty. Leadership Organizations, 1986. Mem.: ABA, Baton Rouge Bar Assn., La. State Bar Assn. (Outstanding Young Lawyer 1986), Rotary, Sigma Chi. Republican. Jewish. Office: Office of the Lieutenant Governor Capitol Annex Building 1051 N 3rd St PO Box 44243 Baton Rouge LA 70804 Office Phone: 225-342-2279, 225-342-7009. Office Fax: 225-342-5577, 225-342-1949. E-mail: admin@sos.louisiana.gov.*

DARIOTIS, TERRENCE THEODORE, lawyer; BA in Philosophy, St. Joseph's Coll., Rensselaer, Ind., 1969; JD, Loyola U., Chgo., 1973; LL M. in Taxation, U. Fla., 2003. Bar: Ill. 1973, Fla. 1975, US Tax Ct. 1993, US Supreme Ct., 1978; bd. cert. in wills, trust and estates law Fla. Bar, 2001-. Law clk. to presiding justice Appellate Ct. of Ill. (2d dist.), Waukegan, 1973-74; assoc. Keith Kinderman, Tallahassee, 1975-76; sole practitioner Tallahassee, 1976—82, 2000—; ptnr. Kahn and Dariotis, P.A., Tallahassee, 1982-96, Warfel, Goldberg, Dariotis, Waldoch & Olive, P.A., Tallahassee, 1996-00. Adj. prof. Fla. State U. Coll. Bus., 1987-93. Office: 1695 Metropolitan Cir Ste 6 Tallahassee FL 32308-3731 Office Phone: 850-523-9300. E-mail: tdariotis@nettally.com.

DARLING, JOHN ROTHBURN, business educator; b. Holton, Kans., Mar. 30, 1937; s. John Rothburn and Beatrice Noel (Deaver) D.; m. Melva Jean Fears, Aug. 20, 1958; children: Stephen, Cynthia, Gregory. BS, U. Ala., 1959, MS, 1960; PhD, U. Ill., 1967; PhD (hon.), Chung Yuan Christian U., Taiwan, 1998; D in Econs. (hon.), Helsinki Sch. Econs., 2001. Divisional mgr. J.C. Penney Co., 1960-63; grad. teaching asst. U. Ill., Urbana, 1965-66; asst. prof. mktg. U. Ala., Tuscaloosa, 1966-68; assoc. prof. mktg. U. Mo., Columbia, 1968-71; prof. adminstrn., coord. mktg. Wichita State U., 1971-76; dean, prof. mktg. Coll. Bus. Adminstrn. So. Ill. U., Carbondale, 1976-81; v.p. acad. affairs and rsch., prof. internat. bus. Tex. Tech U., Lubbock, 1981-86; provost, v.p. acad. affairs, prof. mktg. and internat. bus. Miss. State U., Mississippi State, 1986-90; chancellor, disting. prof. internat. bus. La. State U., Shreveport, 1990-95; pres. Pittsburg State U., Kans., 1995-99, prof. mktg. and internat. bus., 1995-2000; vis. disting. prof. mktg. Rockhurst U., 2000—03; disting. prof. mgmt. Tex. State U., San Marcos, 2003—07; disting. vis. prof. U. Tex., San Antonio, 2007—. Mktg. rsch. cons. Southwestern Bell, 1970; sr. v.p. Boothe Advt. Wichita, 1972; pres. Bus. Rsch. Assocs., 1972-76; cons. Bus. Rsch. Assocs., 1976-82; spl. cons. FTC, Washington, 1972-75, U.S. Dept. Justice, 1973-74, Atty. Gen., State of Kans., 1972-76, Dist. Atty. 18th Jud. Dist., Wichita, 1972-76, Maya Internat. Inc., Houston, 1995—2000, Morrison and Assocs., Inc., Shreveport, 1995-97; vis. disting. prof. internat. mktg. Helsinki Sch. Econs. and Bus. Adminstrn., 1993—. Author: (with Harry A. Lipson) Marketing Fundamentals, Text and Cases, 1980, (with Raimo Nurmi) International Management Leadership: The Primary Competitive Advantage, 1997; mem. bd. cons. editors Jour. Advt., 1984—97; mem. editl. rev. bd. Jour. Internat. Bus. Studies, 1991—96, Jour. Entrepreneurship, 1997—; contbr. articles to profl. jours. Bd. dirs. Outreach Found., 1973-79, v.p., 1975-77; trustee Graceland Coll., Lamoni, Iowa, 1976-82; mem. mgmt. com. Park Coll., Kansas City, 1976-79. With USAR, 1954—62. Decorated Comdr. Order of the Lion of Finland Republic of Finland; recipient Disting. Eagle Scout award, Boy Scouts Am., 1997. Mem. Internat. Coun. Small Bus., Am. Mktg. Assn., Am. Mgmt. Assn., Acad. Internat. Bus., Am. Econs. Assn., Am. Arbitration Assn., (mem. nat. panel arbitrators and mediators 1993-99), Nat. Assn. Intercollegiate Athletics (mem. governing bd. 1994-95), So. Bus. Adminstrn. Assn., So. Mktg. Assn., So. Econs. Assn., So. Assn. Colls. and Schs. (chair reaccreditation com. 1982-95, chair faculty qualifications criteria com. 1989-90, com. to rev. criteria for accreditation 1990-92, commr. 1992-95), Nat. Assn. State Univs. and Land-Grant Colls. (chair regional accreditation rev. com. 1989-90), Sales and Mktg. Execs. Internat., Beta Gamma Sigma, Phi Kappa Phi, Omicorn Delta Kappa, Phi Delta Kappa, Kappa Delta Phi, Mu Kappa Tau, Pi Sigma Epsilon, Alpha Kappa Psi, Chi Alpha Phi, Alpha Phi Omega, Phi Eta Sigma, Delta Mu Delta, Alpha Mu Gamma. Avocations: golf, tennis. Home: 29622 Terra Bella Fair Oaks Ranch TX 78015 Office: U Tex Dept Mgmt One UTSA Cir San Antonio TX 78249 Home Phone: 830-755-5421. Personal E-mail: jrd@gvtc.com.

DARNELL, DAVID CLARK, bank executive; b. 1953; B in Bus., Wake Forest U., Winston-Salem, NC, 1975; MBA, U. NC. Credit analyst Bank of America Corp., Greensboro, NC, 1979, exec. v.p. comml. divsn. Fla., pres. NationsBank-Midwest St. Louis, 1996, pres. global comml. banking Charlotte, NC, 2005—11, co-COO, 2011—. Mem., bd. visitors Wake Forest U. Trustee St. Louis U.; nat. bd. dirs. Mus. of Sci. & Industry Found.; bd. dirs. St. Louis Regional Commerce & Growth Assn., St. Louis Downtown Partnership, Inc., St. Louis Sci. Ctr., United Way Greater St. Louis. Mem.: Charlotte Chamber of Commerce (chmn. 2010). Office: Bank of America Corp Hdqs 100 N Tryon St Ste 220 Charlotte NC 28255 Office Phone: 704-386-5681. Office Fax: 704-386-6699. Business E-Mail: david.darnell@bankofamerica.com.

DARNELL, RILEY CARLISLE, lawyer, former state official; b. Clarksville, Tenn., May 13, 1940; s. Elliott Sinclair and Mary Anita (Whitefield) D.; m. Mary Penelope Crockarell, June 2, 1963; children: Neil Whitefield, Duncan Edward, Mary Eve, Penelope Joy, Dawson Riley. BS, Austin Peay State U., 1962; JD, Vanderbilt U., 1965. Bar: Tenn. 1965. Gen. practice, Clarksville, 1965-66, 69—; mem. Tenn. House Reps. from 67th dist., 1971—80, treas. house-senate caucus, 1971—86, sec. house com. ways & means, chmn. joint ho. -senatefiscal rev. com., 1975—80; men. Tenn. State Senate from 22nd dist., 1980—92, chmn. transp. com., 1982—86, chmn. joint com. children & youth, 1987—89, majority leader, 1988—92; sec. state State of Tenn., Nashville, 1993—2009. Served to Capt. JAGC, USAF, 1966-69. Fellow Tenn. Bar Found.; mem. ABA, Montgomery County

Bar Assn., Tenn. Trial Lawyers, Tenn. Bar Assn., Nat. Conf. State Legislators (jud. task force), So. Lesig. Conf. (mem. fiscal affairs com.) Democrat. Mem. Ch. Of Christ. Personal E-mail: rileycdarnell@yahoo.com.

DARROW, DAVID H., pediatric otolaryngologist, educator; MD, Duke U. Diplomate Am. Bd. Otolaryngology, 1994. Resident otolaryngology Univ. of Calif. San Diego Med. Ctr.; fellow pediatric otolaryngology Children's Meml. Ctr., Chgo.; hosp. affiliations include Children's Hosp. of The King's Daughter, Sentara Leigh Hosp., Sentara Norfolk Gen. Hosp.; assoc. prof. otolaryngology Eastern Va Med. Sch. Office: Childrens Hospital of The Kings Daughters 601 Childrens Ln Norfolk VA 23507 Office Phone: 757-668-7000.

DARVISH, YU, professional baseball player; b. Osaka, Japan, Aug. 16, 1986; s. Farsad and Ikuyo Darvish; m. Saeko Dokyu (div.); 2 children. Pitcher Hokkaido Nippon Ham Fighters, Japan Pacific League, 2005—11, Tex. Rangers, 2012—. Mem. Japanese nat. team Asian Baseball Championship, 2007, Summer Olympic Games, 2008, World Baseball Classic, 2009. Founder Yu Darvish Water Fund, 2007—. Recipient Eiji Sawamura award, Nippon Profl. Baseball, 2007, Mitsui Golden Glove award, 2007, 2008, Gold medal, Asian Baseball Championship, 2007, World Baseball Classic, 2009; named Pacific League MVP, 2007, 2009; named to Pacific League All-Star Team, Nippon Profl. Baseball, 2007—11, American League All-Star Team, Maj. League Baseball, 2012, 2013. Achievements include leading the Nippon Professional Baseball's Pacific League in: strike-outs, 2007, 2010, 2011; earned run average, 2009, 2010; leading the American League in: strikeouts, 2013. Office: Tex Rangers 1000 Ballpark Way Arlington TX 76011*

DAS, SUMAN KUMAR, plastic surgeon, researcher; b. Calcutta, India; came to U.S., 1980; s. Bisweswar and Devi Rani (Ghosh) D.; m. Carole Ellen Simmons, July 10, 1976 (div. Apr. 1984); children: Louise Angelique, Natalie Krishna; m. Rosyln Tanner, Mar. 22, 1991. B of Medicine and Surgery, Calcutta U., India, 1967; MD, Ednl. Commn. Fgn. Med. Grad., 1981. Diplomate Am. Bd. Plastic Surgery. Intern R.G. Kar Med. Coll. and Hosp., Calcatta, 1966-67, resident in gen. surgery, house officer, 1967-68; sr. house officer in accident and emergency, orthopaedics Royal Infirmary, Bolton, Lancs, Eng., 1968-69, house surgeon in gen. surgery, 1969-70; sr. house officer in gen. surgery Royal United Hosp., St. Martins's Hosp., Bath, Eng., 1970-72; house officer in medicine Whiston Hosp., Prescot, Liverpool, Eng., 1970; registrar in gen. surgery Frenchay Hosp., Bristol, Eng., 1972-73, sr. house officer in plastic surgery, 1973-74; registrar in plastic surgery Frenchay Hosp., Bristol, Eng., 1974, Royal Victoria Infirmary, Fleming Meml. Children's Hosp., Newcastle-Upon-Tyne, Eng., 1974-77; fellow in plastic and reconstructive surgery Hosp. for Sick Children, Toronto, Ont., Can., 1978; fellow in micro and hand surgery St. Vincent's Hosp., Melbourne, Australia, 1979-80, asst. plastic surgeon, 1979-80; rsch. assoc. in plastic surgery UCLA Med. Ctr., 1980-82; co-dir. microsurgery tng. program Harbor/UCLA Med. Ctr., 1980-82; dir. plastic surgery rsch. VA Wadsworth Med. Ctr., LA, 1980-82; resident in plastic surgery U. Miss. Med. Ctr., Jackson, 1982-83, sr. and chief resident in plastic surgery, 1983-84; pvt. practice Jackson, 1984-86; chief and asst. prof. div. plastic surgery U. Miss. Med. Ctr., Jackson, 1986-87, chief and assoc. prof. div. plastic surgery, 1987-90, prof. plastic surgery, chief div. plastic surgery, chief, 1990-95, clin. prof. plastic surgery, 1995—. Cons. plastic surgery Miss. Bapt. Med. Ctr., River Oaks Hosp.; attending Meth. Rehab. Ctr., U. Miss. Med. Ctr., River Oaks East Hosp., St. Dominiso Hosp.; vis. prof. dept. surgery divsn. plastic surgery U. Calif., San Francisco, 1981, U. Ala., 1992; mem. patient care com. U. Miss., Jackson, 1990—92; pres. internet co. Nxmed.com. Inc., 1999—2003; dir. St. Dominic Ambulatory Surgery Ctr., 1999—2004; med. dir. St. Dominic's Ambulatory Surgery Ctr., 1999—2004, pres., 2003—04; dir. outreach program St. Dominic Hosp.; presenter and exhibitor in field at numerous profl. meetings. Author: (with others) Manual of Operative Plastic and Reconstructive Surgery, 1980, Textbook of Surgery, 2nd edit., 1988, Ency. of Flaps, 1990; mem. editorial bd. So. Med. Jour., 1993-1999; contbr. articles to Brit. Jour. Surgery, Brit. Jour. Plastic Surgery, Indian Jour. Dermatology, Hand, Plastic Surgery Forum, Jour. Singapore Acad. Sci., Jour. Oral Surgery, Plastic Reconstrn. Surgery, Acta Anatomica, Jour. Clin. Pathology, others; inventor turmeric on wound healing. Pres. NxMed.com Internet Distant Edn., 2000—. Recipient prize North Eng. Surg. Soc., 1977, Plastic Surgery Ednl. Found. Rsch. grant 1983-84, other grants Eli Lilly 1989, Tyra, 1989, Collagen Corp. 1989, 90-91, NIH, 1989, Am. Soc. Aesthetic Plastic Surgery, 1990, 91. Fellow ACS, Royal Coll. Surgeons London, Royal Coll. Surgeons Edinburgh (traveling scholarship 1976); mem. AMA, AAAS, Am. Fedn. for Clin. Rsch., Am. Assn. Hand Surgery (rsch. grant com. 1990-91, chmn. rsch. grant com. 1992), Am. Assn. Acad. Plastic Surgeons (fellowship com. 1990), Am. Soc. Plastic and Reconstructive Surgeons, Am. Assn. Plastic Surgeons, Internat. Soc. Burn Injuries, Internat. Soc. Reconstructive Microsurgery, Internat. Soc. Surgery, Internat. Soc. Emergency Medicine and Critical Care (charter), Brit. Assn. Plastic Surgeons (best prize and cert. 1967), Brit. Soc. Surgery of Hands (European traveling scholarship 1977), Soc. N.Am. Skull Base Surgery (founding), Miss. State Med. Assn., Plastic Surgery Rsch. Coun., N.Y. Acad. Sci., S.E. Soc. Plastic and Reconstructive Surgeons (program com. 1990—, trustee 1997-2000, historian 2000-01, chmn. CME com. 1999—, asst. sec. 2001—, v.p. 2005-06, pres. elect 2006-07, pres. 2007—), Miss. Acad. Scis. (chmn. 1992), Acad. Surg. Rsch., Assn. for Acad. Surgery, Southeastern Surg. Congress, Internat. Fedn. Surg. Colls., So. Med. Assn. (chmn. 1992), Cmty. Outreach Prof. St. Dosh Hosp.(bd. mem. 2003-), Miss. Children's Mus. (ptnrs. adivsory bd. mem.) 2007, Cmty. Found. of Greater Jackson (trustee 2007-, Smile Train ptnr. 2008-), Miss. Symphony (bd. mem. 09-), Lions Club (Flora), Sigma Xi. Achievements include discovery that silicone does not elicit any change in T cell population; that capsular contracture with silicone implant is not an immunological effect; rsch. on best treatment for finger tip amputation in children, size and lengthening of human omentum, muscle transplantation by microvascular technique fatigue like normal muscle. Home: 242 Highland Hills Ln Flora MS 39071-9613 Office: 2629 Ct House Cir Flowood MS 39232 Office Phone: 601-362-0611. Office Fax: 601-362-0192. Personal E-mail: Sushrata@aol.com.

DASBURG, JOHN HAROLD, air cargo and freight services executive; b. Queens, NY, Jan. 7, 1943; s. Jean Henry and Alice Etta Dasburg; m. Mary Lois Diaz, July 16, 1968; children: John Peter, Kathryn. AA, U. Miami, 1963; BS in Indsl. Engring., U. Fla., 1966, MBA, 1971, JD, 1973. Various positions KPMG Peat Marwick, Jacksonville, Fla., 1973-78, tax ptnr., 1978-80; v.p. tax Marriott Corp., Washington, 1980-82, v.p. fin., 1982-84, sr. v.p., 1984-85, exec. v.p., CFO, chief real estate officer, 1985-88, pres. lodging group, 1988-89; exec. v.p. Northwest Airlines, Inc., 1989, pres., CEO, 1989—2001; chmn. Burger King Corp., Miami, Fla., 2001—03, pres., CEO, 2001—02; chmn., CEO, pres. Astar Air Cargo, Inc., Miami, 2003—. Bd. dirs. Travelers Companies, Inc., 1994—, Genuity Inc., 2000—, Winn-Dixie Stores, Inc., 2002—05, Ryder System, Inc., 2002—, WCI Communities Inc., 2004—07, Riverwood Internat. Corp.; mem. adv. bd. Trilantic Capital Ptnrs. Bd. governers Fla. State U.; bd. dirs. Mercy Hosp., Mercy Found., Mayo Found. Lt. USN, 1966—69, Vietnam. Recipient Comml. Air Transport Laureate award, 2001, Horatio Alger award, Horatio Alger Found. Disting. Americans, 2001; named Airline Industry Man of Yr., Travel Agent mag., 1994. Republican. Roman Catholic. Office: ASTAR Air Cargo Inc Hdqs 1200 Brickell Ave16th Fl Miami FL 33131 Office Phone: 305-982-0500. Office Fax: 305-416-9564. Business E-Mail: john.dasburg@astaraircargo.us.

DASCHER, PAUL EDWARD, dean, accounting educator; b. Oct. 1, 1942; s. Albert Jacob abd Ruth (Mountney) D.; m. Nancy Patricia Byrne; children: Mitchell Paul, Heidi Beth. BS, Pa. State U., 1964, MS, 1966, PhD, 1969. Instr. acctg. Pa. State U., 1968-69; asst. prof. acctg. Va. Poly. Inst., Blacksburg, 1969-71, assoc. prof. acctg., 1971-73; prof. acctg. Drexel U., Phila., 1973-93, dept. head, 1974-77, dean Coll. of Bus. and Adminstrn., 1977-93; dean Sch. Bus. Adminstrn. Stetson U., Deland, Fla., 1993—2004, prof. acctg., 1993—, M.E. Rinker, Sr. dist. prof., 2002—. Vis. prof. Northeastern U., Boston, 1976; cons. Price Waterhouse and Co., N.Y.C., 1974-75; lectr. in field. Co-author: Financial Accounting, 1980, 4th edit., 1995, Accounting Readings, 1982, Managerial Accounting, 1985, 11th edit., 2002; contbr. numerous articles to profl. jours. Fellow Price Waterhouse & Co., Armstrong Cork Co.; recipient Socio-Econ. Disting. Svc. award Nat. Assn. Accts., 1973, 75, 81, Faculty Appreciation award Drexel U., 1977, Commendation medal Phila. chpt. Pa. Inst CPAs, 1977, Meritorious Svc. award Cmty. Accts., 1981; named one of Outstanding Young Men of Am., 1979 Mem. Am. Acctg. Assn., Fin. Execs. Inst., Inst. Mgmt. Accts. (nat. v.p. 1989-90), Accts. for Pub. Interest (pres. 1986-89), Alpha Kappa Psi, Beta Alpha Psi, Beta Gamma Sigma. Republican. Lutheran. Avocations: tennis, reading. Office: Stetson U Sch Bus Adm Deland FL 32723 Office Phone: 386-822-7404. Business E-Mail: pdascher@stetson.edu.

DASSO, JEROME JOSEPH, real estate educator; b. Neillsville, Wis., Jan. 12, 1929; s. Henry J. and Frances (Schweickert) D.; m. Patricia Mary Conger, June 13, 1959 (div. 1978); children: James Daniel, Mary Cecilia, Nancy Ann, Wendy Jo. BS, Purdue U., 1951; MBA, U. Mich., 1952; MS, U. Wis., 1960, PhD, 1964. Ptnr. Dasso Constrn. Co., Dubuque, Iowa, 1956-58; planner Franklin County, Columbus, Ohio, 1960-61; asst. prof. U. Ill., Urbana, 1964-66; vis. chairholder U. Hawaii, Honolulu, 1982-83; mem. faculty U. Oreg., Eugene, 1966-95, H.T. Miner chair in real estate, 1978-95, H.T. Miner chair emeritus, 1995—. Vis. prof. U. Wis., Madison, 1984; cons. Internat. Assn. Assessing Officers, Chgo., 1972-75; ednl. cons. Hawaii Real Estate Commn., Honolulu, 1982-83, life mem., Purdue U. Pres. Coun. Co-author: (S. Kahn, R. Nesslinger et al.)l Principle of Right of Way Acquisition, 1972, (with G. Kuhn) Real Estate Finance, 1983, (with A.A. Ring) Real Estate Principles and Practices, 8th edit., 1977, 9th edit., 1981, 10th edit., 1985, 11th edit., 1989, (with Jim Shilling) 12th edit., 1995, Computerized Assessment Adminstration, 1973; contbr. numerous articles to various publs. Lt. USNR, 1952—60. Vivian Stewart vis. scholar Cambridge U., spring, 1987. Fellow Am. Inst. Corp. Asset Mgmt. (bd. govs. 1988-91), Homer Hoyt Inst. Adv. Studies Real Estate & Urban Land Econs.; mem. Real Estate Educators Assn. (pres. 1980-81, Outstanding Svc. award 1981, Disting. Career award 1989), Am. Real Estate and Urban Econs. Assn. (bd. dirs. 1974-77, 80-83), Real Estate Ctr. Dirs. Chairholders Assn. (pres. 1987-88), Am. Real Estate Soc. (life, bd. dirs. 1985-86, v.p. 1988-89, pres. elect 1989-90, pres. 1990-91, Pioneer award, 2009), Am. Fin. Assn. (life), Nat. Assn. Realtors (edn. com. 1970-76), Internat. Real Estate Soc. (pres. 1994-95), VFW. Roman Catholic. Avocations: golf, skiing, hiking, photography. Home Phone: 512-864-9825.

DASTUGUE, MICHAEL P., corporate financial executive; BBA in Fin. & Acctg., Texas A&M U.; MBA in Fin. & Acctg., U. Tex., Austin. Lic. CPA, Tex. Sr. acct. Arthur Andersen & Co.; chmn., CEO Penney J.C. Funding Corp.; treas. JCPenney Co., Inc., fin. analyst, 1991, asst. treas., 1999, dir., corp. fin., 2004—06, sr. v.p., 2004—10, dir., property devel., 2006—10, sr. v.p., fin., 2010—11, exec. v.p., CFO, 2011—. Office: JC Penney Co Inc 6501 Legacy Dr Plano TX 75024 Office Phone: 972-431-1000. Office Fax: 972-431-1362.

DATTILO, THOMAS A., retired manufacturing executive; b. June 12, 1951; BA, OH State U.; JD, U. Toledo; graduate of Advanced Mgmt. Program, Harvard Bus. Sch. Mem., corporate legal staff Dana Corp., 1977-82, with ins. operations dvsn., 1982-85, v.p. then gen. mgr., Precision Control Divsn., and other sr. mgmt. positions Laurinburg, NC, 1985—98; pres., CEO Hayes-Dana Inc., St. Cahtarines, Ont., Canada; pres. Victor Reinz Products, N. Am., Lisle, Ill.; pres., sealing products group Dana Corp., Toledo, 1997—99; pres., COO Cooper Tire and Rubber Co., Findlay, Ohio, 1999—2000, chmn., pres., CEO, 2000—06; sr. advisor Cerberus Ops. and Adv. Co., LLC, 2007—09; non-exec. chmn. Harris Corp., 2012—. Bd. dirs. Cooper Tire & Rubber Co., 1999—2006, Harris Corp., 2001—, Alberto-Culver Co., 2006—11, Hayworth, Inc. Mem.: Mfr. Alliance (vice chmn.), Rubber Mfr. Assn. (chmn.), Automotive Parts Manufacturer's Assn., Young President's Orgn. Office: Harris Corporation 1025 W NASA Blvd Melbourne FL 32919-0001

DAUBECHIES, INGRID, mathematics educator; b. Houthalen, Limburg, Belgium, Aug. 17, 1954; came to U.S, 1987; naturalized, 1996; d. Marcel and Simmone (Duran) D.; m. A. Robert Calderbank, May 9, 1987; children: Michael, Carolyn. BS in Physics, Vrije U., Brussels, Belgium, 1975, PhD in Physics, 1980; Doctor Honoris Causa, U. Libre de Bruxelles, Belgium, 2000, Ecole Polytechnique Fédérale, Lausanne, Switzerland, 2001, U. Pierre et Marie Curie, Paris, France, 2005, U. degli Studi di Genova, Italy, 2006, U. Hasselt, Belgium, 2008. Rsch. asst. dept. theoretical physics Vrije U., Brussels, 1975-84, rsch. prof. dept. theoretical physics, 1984-87; tech. staff mem. Mathematics Rsch. Ctr. AT&T Bell Labs., Murray Hill, NJ, 1987—94; prof. mathematics dept. Rutgers U., New Brunswick, NJ, 1991—93; prof. mathematics dept. and Program in Applied and Computational Mathematics Princeton U., NJ, 1994—, dir. program in applied and computational math. NJ, 1997—2001, William R. Kenan, Jr. professorship NJ, 2004, prof. Ctr. for the Study of Brain, Mind and Behavior NJ, 2005—11, dir. grad. studies Program in Applied and Computational Mathematics NJ, 2007—11; prof. dept. math. and program in applied and computational mathematics Duke U., NC, 2011—. Vis. lectr. Princeton U., N.J., 1981-83; vis. prof. NYU, 1986-87; mem. bd. trustees Princeton U. Press, 2004-08. Author: Ten Lectures on Wavelets, 1992; contbr. rsch. articles to profl. jours; mem. of several editl. bds. MacArthur Found. fellow, 1992-97; recipient Louis Empain prize for Physics Belgium NSF, 1984, Internat. Soc. for Optical Engring. Recognition of Outstanding Achievement, 1998, Eduard Rhein Found. Basic Rsch. award, 2000, Gold medal (Gouden Penning) Flemish Royal Acad. of Arts and Sciences, Belgium, 2005, Internat. Congress for Indsl. and Applied Mathematics (ICIAM) Pioneer prize, 2008, Francqui medal and chair, Belgium, 2010, Benjamin Franklin medal in Electrical Engineering, Franklin Inst., 2011. Fellow IEEE(Information Theory Soc. for Golden Jubilee award for Technological Innovation, 1998); mem. American Acad. of Arts and Sciences, NAS (medal in math. 2000), American Mathematical Soc. (v.p. 2001-03, editor-in-chief for journal, 2003-06, Ruth Lytle Satter prize 1997, Leroy P. Steele prize for Exposition, 1994, Leroy P. Steele prize for Seminal Contribution to Rsch., 2011), American Women Mathematicians, Math. Assn. America, Royal Netherlands Acad. of Arts and Sciences (fgn. mem.), American Philosophical Soc., London Mathematical Soc. (hon.), Académie des Sciences, Paris, France (fgn. mem.), Royal Acad. of Arts and Sciences, Belgium (fgn. mem.), Internat. Math. Union (pres. 2011- (first woman to hold this position) Office: Duke U 111 Physics Box 90320 Durham NC 27708-0320 Office Phone: 609-258-2262, 919-660-2805. Office Fax: 609-258-1735, 919-660-2821. Business E-Mail: icd@princeton.edu, ingrid@math.duke.edu.

DAUGHERTY, JOHN A., JR., realtor; Grad., U. St. Thomas. Founder, pres., CEO John Daugherty, Realtors, Houston, 1967—. Mem. exec. bd. Luxury Real Estate Bd. Regents, 2008—. Involved with Target Hunter, St. Joseph's Hosp. Found. Bd., Tex. Children's Hosp. Devel. Bd., United Way, U. St. Thomas. Recipient Luxury Real Estate Lifetime Achievement award, 2008, Spirit of Giving award, Nancy Owens Meml. Found., 2008. Mem.: World Presidents Org., Houston Assn. Realtors. Office: John Daugherty Realtors 520 Post Oak Blvd 6th Fl Houston TX 77027-9477 Office Phone: 713-626-3930. Business E-Mail: jad@johndaugherty.com.

DAUGHERTY, LEO, literature and language educator; b. Louisville, May 16, 1939; s. F.S. and Mollie Repass (Brown) D.; m. Virginia Upton; 1 child, Mollie Virginia; m. Lee Graham. AB in Fine Arts and Lit., Western Ky. U., 1961; MA in English, U. Ark., 1963; PhD in Am. Lit., Tex. A&M U., 1970; postgrad., Harvard U., 1970-71. Cert. fine arts tchr. Asst. prof. lit. U. Wis., Superior, 1962-63; teaching fellow East Tex. State U., Commerce, 1963-65; asst. prof. lit. Frederick Coll., Portsmouth, Va., 1965-66, Va. State U., Norfolk, 1966-68; prof. lit. and linguistics Evergreen State Coll., Olympia, Wash., 1972—96, prof. emeritus, 1996—; lectr. interdisciplinary studies U. Va., Charlottesville, 2000—. Acad. dean Evergreen State Coll., Olympia, 1975-76, founding dir. Ctr. Study of Sci. and Human Values, 1990—; past grant evaluator NEH. Author: The Teaching of Writing at Evergreen, 1984, William Shakespeare, Richard Barnfield, and Sixth Eacl of Derby, 2010, The Assassination of Shakespeare's Patron, 2011, rev. edit., 2013, editor. (with Richard Barnfield)Greenes Funerals & Orpheus, 2009; contbr. short stories, articles to profl. and literary jours. Active Friends of Bodleian Libr., Oxford, Eng., 1983—; assocs. Alderman Libr., U. Va., 1996—. Recipient NEH award, 1973, 78, 83. Mem.: MLA (life), Soc. Lit. and Sci., Shakespeare Assn. Am., Active Malone Soc. Avocations: painting, aerobics, travel, piano. Office: Univ Va Zehmer Hall Charlottesville VA 22903 Business E-Mail: ld8t@virginia.edu.

DAUGHTREY, MARTHA CRAIG, federal judge; b. Covington, Ky., July 21, 1942; d. Spence E. Kerkow and Martha E. (Craig) Piatt; m. Larry G. Daughtrey, Dec. 28, 1962; 1 child, Carran. BA cum laude, Vanderbilt U., 1964, JD, 1968. Bar: Tenn. 1968. Pvt. practice, Nashville, 1968; asst. US atty. US Dept. Justice, Nashville, 1968—69; asst. dist. atty. Nashville, 1969—72; asst. prof. law Vanderbilt U., Nashville, 1972—75; judge Tenn. Ct. Appeals, Nashville, 1975—90; assoc. justice Tenn. Supreme Ct., Nashville, 1990—93; judge US Ct. Appeals (6th cir.), Nashville, 1993—2009, sr. judge, 2009—. Lectr. law Vanderbilt Law Sch., Nashville, 1975—82, adj. prof., 1988—90; mem. faculty NYU Appellate Judges Seminar, NYC, 1977—90, NYC, 1994—. Contbr. articles to profl. jours. Pres. Women Judges Fund for Justice, 1984—85, 1986—87; active various civic orgns. Recipient Athena award, Nat. Athena Program, 1991; named Woman of the Yr., Women Prof. Internat., 1976. Mem.: ABA (chmn. appellate judges conf. 1985—86, ho. of dels. 1988—91, chmn. jud. divsn. 1989—90, standing com. on continuing edn. of bar 1992—94, commn. on women in the profession 1994—97, bd. editors ABA Jour. 1995—2001, Margaret Brent award 2003), past mem., bd. visitors, Memphis State Sch. of Law, past mem., ed. bd., Judge's Journal, Lawyers Assn. for Women (pres. Nashville 1986—87), Nat. Assn. Women Judges (pres. 1985—86), Am. Judicature Soc. (bd. dirs. 1988—92), Nashville Bar Assn. (bd. dirs. 1988—90), Tenn. Bar Assn. Office: US Ct Appeals 300 Customs House 701 Broadway Nashville TN 37203-3944

DAUGHTRY, NAMON LEO, state legislator; b. Sampson County, NC, Dec. 3, 1940; s. Namon Lutrell and Annie Catholeen Thornton Daughtry; m. Helen Finch; children: Majorie Dana, Kelly Kathleen. Atty. Daughtry, Woodard, Lawrence & Starling; ptnr. Johnston County Hams & Farmers Tobacco Warehouse; state senator NC, 1989—92; state rep. Dist. 95 NC, 1993—2002; state rep. Dist. 26 NC, 2003—. With USAF, 1966—70. Recipient Guardian of Small Bus. award, Nat. Fedn. Ind. Bus., 1998; named Man of Yr., Boy Scouts, 1996, Rep. Leader of Yr., Nat. Rep. Legislators Assn., 1998. Mem.: Eastern Warehouse Assn. (former pres.), NC Acad. Trial Lawyers, Johnston County & NC Bar Assns., Selma-Smithfield C. of C. (former mem., bd. dir., Disting. Citizen award 1994), Bright Belt Assn. (former chmn., bd. dir.). Republican. Episcopalian. Address: 405 E Market St PO Drawer 1960 Smithfield NC 27577-1960 Office: North Carolina House of Representatives 16 W Jones St Rm 2207 Raleigh NC 27601-1096 Office Phone: 919-733-5605. Business E-Mail: Leo.Daughtry@ncleg.net.

DAVENPORT, GAIL, state legislator; b. Atlanta, Mar. 01; d. Nathaniel and Helen Dixon Davenport. BA, Spelman Coll., Atlanta. Real estate profl. Coldwell Banker Success 2000 Realty Inc.; mem. Dist. 44 Ga. State Senate, 2007—. Founder, pres. Concerned Black Citizens Coalition Clayton County. Chair United Negro Coll. Fund; founder Clayton County Black History Ctr., Metro South Youth Assn., Clayton County Sojourner Truth Verse Speaking Choir; del. Dem. Nat. Conv., 1988, 2004. Recipient Cmty. Leader of Century award, Women in the NAACP, 1999, Mayor's Masked award, United Negro Coll. Fund, 2000, Disting. Leadership award, Star Vol. award, Pinnacle Leadership award, Delta Sigma Theta Sorority, 2003. Mem.: NAACP (Image award for disting. svc., Clayton County br. 1989, 1996), American Bus. Women's Assn. (past pres. Greenbriar chpt., Woman of Yr. 1992, Mem. Choice award), Ga. Assn. Realtors (Hall of Fame award), Atlanta Bd. Realtors, Nat. Assn. Realtors, Nat. Alumnae Assn. Spelman Coll. (life), Nat. Coun. Negro Women (life Outstanding Cmty. Leader of Yr., Clayton County sect. 1997). Democrat. Methodist. Office: PO Box 1074 Jonesboro GA 30237 also: Ga State Senate 304A Coverdell Legis Office Bldg Atlanta GA 30334 Office Phone: 678-215-9974. Office Fax: 404-463-5260. Business E-Mail: gail.davenport@senate.ga.gov.

DAVENPORT, JAMES ROBERT, vice mayor, city council, retired utilities executive; b. Roanoke, Va., Jan. 8, 1930; s. Henry Ashby and Mary Bruce (Doss) D.; m. Catherine Lee Wright, July 14, 1956; children: James Robert Jr., Catherine D. BA in Econs., Roanoke Coll., Salem, Va., 1952; MBA, U. N.C., 1955. Adminstrv. asst. Appalachian Power Co. (now Am. Elec. Power), Roanoke, 1955-63, area devel. cons., 1963-69, area mgr. Martinsville, Va., 1969-77, divsn. mgr. Lynchburg, Va., 1977-91; ret. Mem. City Coun., Lynchburg, 1980-88, vice mayor, 1995-98, chmn. fin. and planning com., 1995-98; bd. dirs. Region 2000, Lynchburg, 1994-98; dir. CentraHealth, Inc., Lynchburg, 1987—2004, chmn. bd. trustees 1990-93; dir. Va. Bapt. Hosp., Lynchburg, 1982-87, treas., 1985-86; mem. Indsl. Devel. Authority, City of Lynchburg, 1982-93, 98—, chmn., 1985-93; dir. Lynchburg Area Devel. Corp., 1977—, Ctrl. Va. Industries, Lynchburg, 1979-83, chmn. bd., 1980; dir. Presbyn. Home, Inc., Lynchburg, 1980-83, vice chmn. bd., 1983; mem. Lynchburg Rep. City Com., 1993—; bd. dirs. United Way of Ctrl. Va., Lynchburg, 1980-83, Daily Bread, Lynchburg, 1988-92, Ctrl. Lynchburg, Inc., 1980-82, Jr. Achievement, Lynchburg, 1980-83; mem. econ. and tech. devel. adv. com. Ctrl. Va.

C.C., Lynchburg, 1988; chmn. Downtown Action Commn., Lynchburg, 1979-82; pres. Southeastern Cmty. Devel. Assn., Roanoke, 1976; chmn. United Way of Martinsville and Henry County, Va., 1976; mem. Va. Gov.'s Commn. on Transp. Policy, 1999-2000; elder Rivermont Presbyn. Ch. 1st Lt. U.S. Army, 1952-55. Recipient Outstanding Citizen award NCCJ, 1990. Mem. Greater Lynchburg C. of C. (pres. 1980-81, econ. devel. dept. head 1979-80, exec. adv. coun. 1982-86, Team 2000 1985-88, named Pro-Opera Civica 1988), Rotary Club of Lynchburg (v.p. 1983-84), Boonsboro Country Club. Avocations: tennis, church activities, travel. Home: 130 Westminster Way Lynchburg VA 24503-1259 E-mail: kitybobdavenport@gmail.com.

DAVEY, CHARLES BINGHAM, soil scientist, educator; b. Bklyn., Apr. 7, 1928; s. Francis Joseph and Mary Elizabeth (Bingham) Davey; m. Elizabeth Anne Thompson, July 11, 1952; children: Douglas Alan, Barbara Lynn, Andrew Martin. BS, Syracuse U., 1950; MS, U. Wis., 1952, PhD, 1955. Soil scientist Rsch. Svc. Dept. Agr., Beltsville, Md., 1957-62; assoc. prof. N.C. State U., Raleigh, 1962-65, prof., 1965—, Carl Alwin Schenck Disting. prof., 1978—, Alumni Disting. prof., 1989, head dept., 1970-78. Editor: Tree Growth and Forest Soils, 1970; assoc. editor: Soil Sci. Soc. Am. proc., 1967—72; contbr. articles to profl. jours. With US Army, 1955—57. Fellow: AAAS, Soc. Am. Foresters (Barrington Moore Rsch. award), Soil Sci. Soc. Am. (pres. 1975—76, Disting. Svc. award), Am. Soc. Agronomy; mem.: Internat. Soc. Tropical Foresters, Sigma Xi (Rsch. award), Xi Sigma Pi, Gamma Sigma Delta, Phi Kappa Phi. Achievements include patents in field. Office: Forestry Dept 3113 Faucette Dr Raleigh NC 27695-8008 Home: 2210 Fernglen Pl Cary NC 27511-3890 Office Phone: 919-515-7787. Personal E-mail: charl168@bellsouth.net. Business E-Mail: cdavey@unity.ncsu.edu.

DAVID, CATHERINE ANNE, retail executive; b. NYC, Sept. 18, 1963; d. James Hayes and Patricia Kathleen (Lombard) D. BBA, U. Notre Dame, 1985; M Mgmt, Northwestern U., 1991. Mgr. Irish Gardens Flower Shop, Notre Dame, Ind., 1983-85; sales rep. Gallo Wine Co., LA, 1985-86, sales trainer, 1986-87, mgr. tng., 1987; mktg. mgr. E&J Gallo Winery, Modesto, Calif., 1987-89, systems cons. Lisle, Ill., 1989-90, field mktg. mgr., 1990; e-commerce merchandise mgr. Target Stores, Mpls., 1991; v.p., gen. mgr., target.direct Target Corp.; v.p., gen. mgr. The Great Indoors, Sears Grand; pres., COO Kirkland's, Inc., Jackson, Tenn.; pres. Burnes Group; exec. v.p., Merchandising Pier 1 Imports, Inc., 2009—. Trustee U. Notre Dame, 1992—; mem. adv. coun. U. Notre Dame Coll. Bus. Adminstrn., 1987-90; bd. dirs. Notre Dame Club Orange County, Calif., 1986-87, Josephinum Sch. Recipient Rev. Lester E. Collins Leadership award, 1985; LILCO Athlete scholar, Little League scholar Plainview Little League, N.Y., 1981. Mem. Notre Dame Club Mpls. Roman Catholic. Avocations: sports, travel, reading. Office: Pier 1 Imports Inc 100 Pier 1 Pl Fort Worth TX 76102 Office Phone: 817-252-8000. Office Fax: 817-878-7881. Business E-Mail: cdavid@pier1.com.

DAVID, GELDMACHER STEPHEN, medical educator; s. John Frederick Geldmacher and Joan Elizabeth Meyer; married. BA, U. Rochester, NY, 1982; MD, SUNY, Syracuse, 1986. Diplomate Am. Bd. Psychiatry and Neurology, 1992. Asst. prof. neurology Robert Wood Johnson Med. Sch., 1991—92, Case Western Res. U., 1993—2002, U. Va., 2002—11; neurology prof. U. Ala., Birmingham, 2011—. Fellow: ACP. Business E-Mail: dgeldmacher@uab.edu.*

DAVID, GEORGE ALFRED LAWRENCE, retired manufacturing executive, board member; b. Bryn Mawr, Pa., Apr. 7, 1942; s. Charles Wendell and Margaret (Simpson) David; m. Barbara Osborn, Sept. 4, 1965 (div. 1997); children: Eliza Pell, Hannah Lawrence, Henry Gibb; m. Marie Douglas, Aug. 2003 (separated). BA, Harvard U., 1965; MBA, U. Va., 1967. Asst. prof. fin. & acctg. U. Va., Charlottesville, 1967—68; v.p. Boston Consulting Group, Inc., 1968—75; sr. v.p. corp. planning & devel. Otis Elevator Co., NYC, 1975—77, sr. v.p., gen. mgr. L.Am. ops. West Palm Beach, Fla., 1977—81, pres. N.Am. ops. Farmington, Conn., 1981—85, exec. v.p., COO, 1985—89; exec. v.p., pres. comml./indsl. bus. United Technologies Corp., Hartford, Conn., 1989—92, COO, 1992—94, pres., 1992—99, CEO, 1994—2008, chmn., 1997—2009, pres., 2002—06. Bd. dirs. Citigroup Inc., 2002—08, BP plc, 2008—. Chmn. Greater Hartford chpt. ARC, 1985—87; vice chmn. Peterson Inst. Internat. Economics, Washington; past bd. dirs. Nat. Minority Supplier Devel. Coun., US-ASEAN Bus. Coun.; past bd. trustees Wadsworth Atheneum Mus. Art, Hartford. Recipient Order of Friendship, Russian Fedn., 1999, John R. Alison award, Air Force Assn., 2001, Legion of Honor, Govt. of France, 2002; named CEO of Yr., Industry Week mag., 2003, Chief Exec. mag., 2005; named one of America's Most Powerful People, Forbes mag., 2000. Republican. Episcopalian. Mailing: BP Americas Hdqs Bd Directors 501 Westlake Park Blvd Houston TX 77079

DAVID, PHILLIP J., biotechnology company executive; PhD Genetics. CEO Sygen Internat. plc, Berkeley, Calif., 1982—. Office: Sygen International 100 Bluegrass Commons Blvd Ste 2200 Hendersonville TN 37075-2739

DAVID, RUTH A., public service research institute executive; BSEE, Wichita State U., 1975; MSEE, Stanford U., 1976, PhD in Elec. Engring., 1981. With Sandia Nat. Lab., 1975—94, dir., develop. testing ctr. to dir. advanced info. technologies, 1991—94; dep. dir. for Sci. and Tech. CIA, 1995—98; pres., CEO Analytic Services, Inc., 1998—. Adj. prof. U. N.Mex.; mem. Dept. Homeland Security Adv. Coun., vice-chair, sr. adv. com. academia and policy rsch.; former pres. President's Homeland Security Adv. Coun.; mem. Corp. for the Charles Stark Draper Lab. Inc.; chair, com. on tech. insight-gauge, evaluate and review NRC, mem. com. on scientific communication and nat. secutiry, mem. com. on info. for terrorism prevention, mem. naval studies bd.; mem. adv. bd. Nat. Security Agy.; mem. adv. bd., tech. divsn. Jet Propulsion Lab.; mem. external adv. com Purdue U. Homeland Security Inst.; mem. Def. Sci. Bd., Dept. Energy Nonproliferation and Nat. Security Adv. Com., Senate Select Com. on Intelligence Tech. Adv. Group, Securities and Exchange Commn. Tech. Adv. Group; frequently provided speeches, interviews, lectures, briefings and articles on many aspects of homeland security. Coauthor of three books on signal processing algorithms; contbr. scientific papers. Mem. nat. adv. com. Wichita State U. Found. Named to Women in Technology Internat. Hall of Fame, 2010. Fellow: AIAA (assoc.); mem.: AAAS (mem. com. on scientific freedom & responsibility), Armed Forces Communications and Electronics Assn. (mem. internat. bd. dir.), NAE (councillor 2007—, com. on engring. edn.), Eta Kappa Nu, Tau Beta Pi. Office: Analytic Services Inc 5275 Leesburg Pike Falls Church VA 22041-3803 Office Phone: 703-416-2000.

DAVIDSON, ANN D., defense industry executive, lawyer; b. Upper Montclair, NJ, 1952; Attended, Georgetown U.; BA, Ohio U., 1974; JD, U. Dayton, 1979. Bar: 1979. Assoc. Coolidge, Wall, Womsley & Lombard, Dayton, Ohio, 1979—80; atty. US Dept. of Navy, 1980—83; asst. gen. counsel Honeywell Internat., 1983—90; dep. gen. counsel Alliant Techsystems, Inc., 1990—93; v.p., gen. counsel, corp. sec. Power Control Technologies, Inc., 1993—98; assoc. gen. counsel, asst. sec. Parker Hannifin Corp., Cleveland, 1998—2001; v.p. Alliant Techsystems, Inc., 2001—04, gen. counsel, 2001—05, corp. sec., 2001—05, sr. v.p., 2004—05; v.p., gen. counsel Thales N.Am., 2005—07; v.p., chief ethics and compliance officer ITT Def. & Info. Solutions, 2007—09, v.p., corp. responsibility, 2009—11; sr. v.p., chief legal officer, corp. sec. ITT Exelis, Inc., McLean, Va., 2011—. Office: ITT Exelis Inc 1650 Tysons Blvd Ste 1700 Mc Lean VA 22102*

DAVIDSON, C. SIMON, lawyer, columnist; b. London, Eng., 1974; BA with honors, U. Va., 1996, JD, 1999. Bar: DC, Va., Mass., Conn., US Dist. Ct., Conn., US Dist. Ct., Dist. Mass., US Dist. Ct., DC, US Dist. Ct. (ea. dist.) Va. Ptnr. McGuireWoods LLP, Washington. Contbg. writer Roll Call. Author: A Question of Ethics; contbr. articles to law jours. Office: McGuireWoods LLP One James Ctr 901 E Cary St Richmond VA 23219-4030 Office Phone: 804-775-1059. Office Fax: 804-698-2256. E-mail: cdavidson@mcguirewoods.com.

DAVIDSON, CHARLES D., energy executive; m. Nancy Davidson. BSChE, Purdue Univ., 1972; MS, Univ. Tex., Dallas, 1980. With ARCO Oil & Gas, 1972—93, sr. vice-pres., Eastern District, 1992—93; sr. v.p. Vastar Resources, Inc., 1993—97, pres., CEO, 1997—2000, Noble Energy Inc., 2000—01, chmn., pres., CEO, 2001—09; chmn., CEO Noble Energy, Inc., 2009—. Chmn. offshore com. Independent Petroleum Ass. Am. Mem. adv. bd. Univ. Tex., Dallas. Mem.: Am. Inst. Chem. Engineers, Soc. Petroleum Engineers. Office: Noble Energy Ste 100 100 Glenborough Houston TX 77067 Office Phone: 281-872-3100. Office Fax: 281-872-3111.

DAVIDSON, F. CHANDLER, sociologist, educator; b. May 13, 1936; m. Sharon Lavon Plummer, Nov. 1, 1986. BA, U. Tex., 1961; PhD, Princeton U., 1969. Prof. sociology Rice U., Houston, 1966—2003, prof. polit. sci., 1997—2003, rsch. prof. emeritus, 2003—, Radoslav Tsanoff prof. pub. affairs, 2000—03, chair dept. sociology, 1979-83, 86-89, 1995—2003. Co-prin. investigator NSF, 1988-92, Rockefeller Found., 1990. Author: Biracial Politics, 1972, Race and Class in Texas Politics, 1990, Protecting Minority Voters, 2006; editor: Minority Vote Dilution, 1984, (with Bernard Grofman) Controversies in Minority Voting, 1992, (with Grofman) Quiet Revolution in the South, 1994. Mem. Nat. Commn. on the Voting Rights Act, 2005. Hon. discharge USN, 1962. Fulbright scholar, 1961-62; Woodrow Wilson fellow, 1963-64, rsch. fellow Nat. Endowment for Humanities, 1976-77; recipient Gustavus Myers Ctr. Human Rights award for outstanding book on human rights, 1993, Ally award Ctr. for the Healing of Racism, 1996, Brown award for superior tchg., Rice U., 1997, 99, 2000, 2002, Brown award for excellence in tchg. Rice U., 1998. Mem. Am. Polit. Sci. Assn. (Fenno prize 1995), Phi Beta Kappa. Office: Rice U Dept Sociology 6100 S Main St Houston TX 77251-1892 Business E-Mail: fcd@rice.edu.

DAVIDSON, GLEN HARRIS, federal judge; b. Pontotoc, Miss., Nov. 20, 1941; s. M. Glen and Lora (Harris) D.; m. Bonnie Payne, Apr. 25, 1973; children: Glen III, Gregory P. BA, U. Miss, 1962, JD, 1965. Bar: Miss. 1965, admitted to practice: US Ct. Appeals (5th Cir.) 1965, US Supreme Ct. 1971. Asst. dist. atty. First Jud. Dist., Tupelo, Miss., 1969-74, dist. atty., 1975; US atty. (no. dist.) Miss. US Dept. Justice, Oxford, 1981-85; judge US Dist. Ct. (no. dist.) Miss., Aberdeen, Miss., 1985—2000, chief judge, 2000—07, sr. judge, 2007—; chief judge Jud. Conf. U.S., 2004. Atty. Lee County Sch. Bd., Miss., 1974—81. Bd. dirs. Cmty. Devel. Found., Tupelo, 1976-81; exec. bd. Yocona Coun. Boy Scouts Am., 1972—. Maj. USAF, 1966-69. Mem.: Kiwanis (pres. Tupelo 1978), Miss. Prosecutors Assn., ATLA, Lee County Bar Assn. (pres. 1974), Miss. Bar Found., Fed. Bar Assn. (v.p. 1984). Presbyterian. Office: US Dist Courthouse 301 W Commerce St Ste 342 301 W Commerce St # 13 Aberdeen MS 39730-2520 Office Phone: 662-369-6486. Office Fax: 662-369-8339. Business E-Mail: Glen_Davidson@msnd.uscourts.gov.

DAVIDSON, JACK LEROY, academic administrator; b. Indpls., July 14, 1927; s. Lawrence L. and Emma (Jones) D.; m. Ina Stanfill, June 20, 1948; children: William (dec.), Nancy, Evan. BA, Franklin Coll., 1949; MA, Ind. U., 1955, Ed. Adminstrn., 1961, PhD, 1967. Tchr., guidance counselor, coach Mitchell (Ind.) Pub. Schs., 1949-57; elem. prin., supervising prin. Vincennes (Ind.) Pub. Schs., 1957-59; supt. Worthington (Ind.) Pub. Schs., 1959-61, Salem (Ind.) Pub. Schs., 1961-65, Oak Ridge (Tenn.) Pub. Schs., 1965-68, Manatee County (Fla.) Pub. Schs., 1968-70, Austin (Tex.) Pub. Schs., 1970-80, Tyler (Tex.) Public Schs., 1980-91; spl. asst. to pres. U. Tex., Tyler, 1991-96. Vis. prof. U. Tex.; chmn. Tex. Adv. Com. on Ednl. Improvement. Schs.; cons. Tex. Edn. Agy. Author: Effective School Board Meetings, 1970, The Superintendency & Leadership for Effective Schools, 1987, Live Each Moment, 2009; Contbr. articles to ednl. jours. Bd. dirs., pres. Southwest Ednl. Devel. Lab.; charter mem. Tex. Commn. on Inter-Govtl. Rels.; bd. dirs. Austin Jr. Achievement; pres. bd. dirs. Salvation Army, pres. adv. bd., 2005-07. With USNR, 1945-47. Recipient Super Supt. award Tex. PTA, 1982, award of honor Nat. Sch. Pub. Rels. Assn., 1990, Disting. Svc. award AASA, 1992, Founders award Tyler Ind. Sch. Dist. Found., 2005; named one of 100 Top Exec. Educators Exec. Educator mag., 1984, 89; Dr. Jack L. Davidson Conf. Ctr. named in his honor, 2004. Mem. Am. Assn. Suprs. Curriculum Devel., Am. Assn. Sch. Adminstrs., Tex. Assn. Sch. Adminstrs., Rotary (pres. Tyler club), Phi Delta Kappa (outstanding educator award 1992). Methodist (deacon, dir.). Home: 1807 Picadilly Pl Tyler TX 75703-2409 Personal E-mail: davidsonji@suddenlink.net.

DAVIDSON, JAMES JOSEPH, III, lawyer; b. Lafayette, La., July 27, 1940; s. James Joseph and Virginia Lee (Dunham) Davidson; m. Kay Cecile Holloway, Aug. 7, 1962; children: Kimberly Kay, James Joseph IV, Lynda Leigh, Virginia Holland. BA, U. SW La., 1963; JD, Tulane U., 1964. Bar: La. 1964, US Dist. Ct. (we. dist.) La. 1965, US Ct. Appeals (5th cir.) 1972, US Supreme Ct. 1975, US Dist. Ct. (ea. dist.) La. 1979, US Ct. Appeals (11th cir.) 1981, US Dist. Ct. (mid. dist.) La. 1986. Ptnr. Davidson, Meaux, Sonnier & McElligott, Lafayette, La., 1964—. Mem. exec. bd. Evangeline area coun. Boy Scouts Am., 1969—80; trustee U. La. Lafayette Found., 1980—2010, pres., 1988—91. Fellow: Am. Bar Found. (life); mem.: ABA (ho. dels. 2002—04, 2006—08, 2010—12), Assn. Transp. Practitioners, Assn. Def. Trial Attys., Internat. Assn. Def. Counsel, Am. Counsel Assn., Am. Bd. Trial Advs., Nat. Assn. RR Trial Counsel, La. Assn. Def. Counsel (dir. 1975—77), La. State Law Inst. (coun. 2002—), La. Bar Found., La. State Bar Assn. (del. 1970—80, bd. gov. 2007—09, pres. 2011—12). Republican. Baptist. Home: 539 Girard Park Dr Lafayette LA 70503-2601 Office: PO Box 2908 Lafayette LA 70502-2908 Office Phone: 337-237-1660.

DAVIDSON, JOHN KENNETH, SR., sociologist, educator, researcher, writer, consultant; b. Augusta, Ga., Oct. 25, 1939; s. Larcie Charles and Betty (Corley) D.; m. Josephine Frazier, Apr. 11, 1964; children: John Kenneth Jr., Stephen Wood. Student, Augusta Coll., 1956-58; BS in Edn., U. Ga., 1961, MA, 1963; PhD, U. Fla., 1974. Asst. prof. dept. psychology and sociology Armstrong State Coll., Savannah, Ga., 1963-67; asst. prof. sociology Augusta Coll., 1967-74; acting chmn., asst. prof. dept. sociology Ind. U., South Bend, 1974-76; assoc. prof. sociology U. Wis., Eau Claire, Wis., 1976-78, prof., 1978—2004, prof. emeritus, 2004—, chmn. dept. sociology, 1976-80, asst. spl. projects to dean grad. studies and univ. rsch., 1987-91, coord. family studies, 1990—2004, acting chmn., dept. sociology (summer), 2003—05. Rsch. cons. dept. ob-gyn. Med. Coll. Ga., Augusta, 1969-74, pediatrics, 1972-73, assoc. dir. health care project, 1971-73, rsch. instr., 1971, rsch. assoc., 1972-73, rsch. cons. dept. community dentistry, 1974-79; program coord. Community Devel. in Process Phase II and III, Title I Higher Edn. Act of, 1965, 1970; sociology and anthropology com. Univ. System Ga., 1970-74, chmn. curriculum sub-com., 1970-72; dir. Sex Edn., The Pub. Schs. and You project Ind. Com. on Humanities, 1975. Co-author: Marriage and Family, 1992, Marriage and Family: Change and Continuity, 1996; co-editor: Speaking of Sexuality: Interdisciplinary Readings, 2001, 2005, 2010, Cultural Diversity and Families, 1992; editor (assoc.): Jour. Marriage and the Family, 1975—85, Sociol. Inquiry, 1986—92, Sociol. Imagination, 1993—2004; editor: (cons.) Jour. Sex Rsch., 1991—95; editor: (cons) Sociol. Inquiry, 2001—05; reviewer: Jour. Deviant Behavior, 1979—90, Sociol. Spectrum, 1985—2005, Jour. Family Issues, 1995—2004, Jour. Sex Rsch., 1996—2005; contbr. articles to profl. jours. Past state chmn. pub. affairs Ind. Assn. Planned Parenthood Affiliates, 1975-76; past bd. dirs. Planned Parenthood North Cen. Ind., chmn. pub. affairs com., 1975-76; past bd. dirs., 1st v.p., resources allocation com. Wis. Family Planning Coordinating Council; past bd. dirs., exec., info., internat. and edn. coms., chmn. social sci. rsch. com. Assn. for Vol. Sterilization; past pres. citizens adv. bd. Eau Claire and Chippewa Falls Planned Parenthood Clinics; past mem. dirs. Planned Parenthood of Wis., Inc.; past mem. Eau Claire Coord. Coun., Eau Claire County Adv. Health Forum, Eau Claire County Task Force on Family Planning, Eau Claire Task Force on Teen Pregnancy. Fellow Nat. Coun. Family Rels. (past chmn. com. stds. and criteria for cert., former mem. devel. com. and cert. com., Ernest G. Osborne award); mem. Am. Sociol. Assn., So. Sociol. Soc., Mid-South Sociol. Assn. (pres.-elect 1998-99, pres. 1999-2000, past pres. 2000-01, hotel negotiator, 2003-06), Midwest Sociol. Soc., Groves Conf., Wis. Coun. Family Rels. (bd. dirs., exec. com., past pres.), Soc. Sci. Study Sex., Tex. Coun. Family Rels., Augusta Coll. Alumni Soc., U. Fla. Alumni Soc., U. Ga. Alumni Soc., Pres. Club. U. Wis.-Eau Claire, Kappa Delta Pi, Phi Kappa Phi (chpt. pres. 1991-92, Nat. Forum editl. com. 1992-99), Phi Theta Kappa, Alpha Kappa Delta (editor nat. newsletter 1979-83, nat. v,p. 1992-94, nat. pres.-elect 1994-96, nat. pres. 1996-98, nat. past pres. 1998-2000, exec. coun. 1992-2000) Episcopalian. Office Phone: 512-246-1093. Business E-Mail: davidsj@uwec.edu.

DAVIDSON, MITCH, utilities executive; married; 3 children. BA in Indsl. Tech., SW Tex. State U.; MBA, U. Houston. Sr. v.p., exec. v.p. Entergy and Entergy-Koch LP; sr. v.p. Duke Energy N.Am.; joined NextEra Energy Resources LLC, 2004, v.p., 2004—06, CEO, 2004, sr. v.p., 2006, pres., 2006—. Office: NextEra Energy Resources LLC PO Box 14000 North Palm Beach FL 33408-0420 Office Phone: 905-335-4904.

DAVIES, MARK G., vascular surgeon, scientist; MS in Biol. Scis., Trinity Coll., Dublin, 1989, MD, 1986, PhD, 1994; MBA, U. Rochester, NY, 2008; CPE in Med. Mgmt., ACPE, Tampa, Fla., 2012. Resident, gen. surgery, rsch. fellow vascular biology Duke U., Durham, NC, 1991—; fellow endovascular surgery U. Wash., Seattle, 1997—99; asst. prof. surgeon U. Rochester Vascular, Endovascular Surgery Dept., 1999—2004, assoc. prof., surgeon, 2004—08; vice chmn., surgeon, vascular, endovascular surgery Meth. Hosp., Houston, 2008. Prof. surgery Weill Cornell Med. Sch., NYC, 2008—; sr. investigator Meth. Hosp. Rsch. Inst., 2008—. Recipient Mentored Scientist award, Am. Vascular Assn. Von Liebig Found.; grant, NIH. Fellow: RCS (Eng.), ACS, Soc. Vascular Surgery; mem.: RCS (Ireland), Soc. U. Surgeons, Am. Surg. Assn. Office: 6550 Fannin Smith Tower Ste 1401 Houston TX 77030 Business E-Mail: mdavies@tmhs.org.*

DAVIES, PAMELA L., academic administrator; BS, U. Fla.; MS, Mo. State U.; PhD in Internat. Bus., U. Tenn., PhD in Strategic Planning. Prof. mgmt., dean LeBow Coll. Bus. Drexel Univ., 1997—2000; prof. mgmt., dean McColl Sch. Bus. Queens University, Charlotte, NC, 2000—01, COO, 2001—02, pres., 2002—. Bd. dirs. Charming Shoppes Inc., 1998—, C&D Technologies Inc., 1998—, Family Dollar Stores Inc., 2009—, Sonoco Products Co. Co-author: Management: Challenges for the 21st Century; contbr. articles to profl. jours. Bd. dir. YMCA Greater Charlotte, Charlotte C. of C., Charlotte Regional Partnership, Presbyterian Hosp.; bd. mem. Assn. Presbyterian Colleges & Universities. Recipient Women in Bus. Achievement award, Charlotte Bus. jour., 2003, Servant in Leadership award, YMCA Greater Charlotte, 2008; named one of 50 Most Influential Women, Mecklenburg Times, 2009. Office: Queens U of Charlotte 1900 Selwyn Ave Charlotte NC 28274 Office Phone: 704-337-2200. Business E-Mail: pdavies@cdtechno.com.

DAVILA, MARTA LIGIA, gastroenterologist, educator; MD, Harvard U., 1988. Lic. Calif., 1989, Tex., 2005, diplomate American Bd. Internal Medicine, 2001, American Bd. Internal Medicine-gastroenterology, 2003. Resident internal medicine Univ. of Calif. San Francisco Affiliated Hosp., 1989—91, fellow gastroenterology, 1991—93, fellow endoscopy, 1993—94; prof. Univ. of Tex.; hosp. affiliation includes Univ. of Tex. M.D. Anderson Cancer Ctr. Office: University of Texas MD Anderson Cancer Center 1515 Holcombe Blvd Box 91 Houston TX 77030-4095 Office Phone: 713-792-2121.*

DAVIS, ANTHONY, JR., professional basketball player; b. Chgo., Mar. 11, 1993; s. Anthony and Erainer Davis. Student, U. Ky., Lexington, 2011—12. Forward, ctr. New Orleans Pelicans (formerly New Orleans Hornets), 2012—. Mem. US nat. team Summer Olympic Games, London, 2012. Recipient Naismith trophy, Atlanta Tipoff Club, 2012, Adolph R. Rupp trophy, Commonwealth Athletic Club Ky., 2012, John R. Wooden award, LA Athletic Club, 2012, Oscar Robertson trophy, US Basketball Writers Assn., 2012, Pete Newell Big Man award, Nat. Assn. Basketball Coaches, 2012, Gold medal, men's basketball, Summer Olympic Games, 2012; named Southeastern Conf. Freshman of Yr., 2012, Southeastern Conf. Defensive Player of Yr., 2012, Southeastern Conf. Player of Yr., 2012, Nat. Freshman of Yr., US Basketball Writers Assn., 2012, Defensive Player of Yr., Nat. Assn. Basketball Coaches, 2012, Coll. Basketball Player of Yr., The Sporting News, 2012, AP, 2012, NCAA Final Four Most Outstanding Player, 2012; named a Unanimous 1st Team All-American, AP, US Basketball Writers Assn., The Sporting News, Nat. Assn. Basketball Coaches, 2012. Achievements include second freshman in NCAA Division I history named college basketball player of the year by the Associated Press, 2012; member of NCAA Final Four Division I National Championship winning University of Kentucky Wildcats, 2012; first overall pick in the NBA Draft, 2012. Office: New Orleans Pelicans 5800 Airline Dr Metairie LA 70003*

DAVIS, BARRY, critical care specialist; MD, Tufts U., 1974. Diplomate Am. Bd. Internal Medicne, 1977, Am. Bd. Internal Medicne- pulmonary disease, 1980, Am. Bd. Internal Medicne-critical care medicine, 2009. Intern Jackson Meml. Hosp., Miami, Fla., 1975, resident in internal medicine, 1975—77; fellow in pulmonary disease Mass. Gen. Hosp., Boston, 1977—79; critical care specialist Bora Raton Cmmty. Hosp. Office: Bora Raton Community Hospital 951 NW 13th St Ste 2A Boca Raton FL 33486 Office Phone: 561-391-1666.

DAVIS, BARRY E., energy executive; BA in. fin., Tex. Christian U. V.p., marketing & development Endevco, Inc.; founder Ventana Natural Gas Company (now Crosstex Engergy), 1992; pres., CEO Comstock Natural Gas, Inc., Crosstex Energy, Inc., 1996—. Office: Crosstex Energy Services 2501 Cedar Springs Rd Ste 100 Dallas TX 75201*

DAVIS, BENJAMIN ALANDO, lawyer; s. Carolyn Davis; m. Aysha Khan, July 13, 2004; children: Nadia Carolyn, Alexander Barock children: Benjamin Sikander. AS, U. Md., 1991; BS, Columbus U., 1993; JD, U. Ga., 1996. Bar: Ga. 1996. Assoc. Scott, Quarterman and Wells, Athens, Ga., 1995—96; prin. Davis Law Firm, P.C., Atlanta, 1997—. Law clk. to Hon. Steve Jones, Athens, 1994—96. Judge Nat. H.S. Mock Trial, Atlanta, 1996—2004. Cpl. US Army, 1987—91. Scholar, U. Ga. Sch. Law, 1991. Mem.: Ga. Assn. Criminal Def. Lawyers (assoc.). Office: Davis Law Firm PC Ste 200 1201 Peachtree St Atlanta GA 30361 Business E-Mail: davislawfirm@msn.com.

DAVIS, BONNIE CHRISTELL, judge; b. Petersburg, Va., July 13, 1949; d. Robert Madison and Margaret Elizabeth (Collier) Davis. BA, Longwood Coll., Farmville, Va., 1971; JD, U. Richmond, 1980. Bar: Va. 1980, US Dist. Ct. (ea. dist.) Va. 1980, US Ct. Appeals (4th cir.) 1982. Tchr. Chesterfield County Schs., Chesterfield, Va., 1971-77; pvt. practice Chesterfield, 1980-83; asst. commonwealth atty. Chesterfield County, 1983-93; judge Juvenile and Domestic Rels. Ct. for 12th Jud. Dist. Va., 1993—. Adviser Youth Svcs. Commn., Chesterfield, 1983-93; cons. Task Force on Child Abuse, 1983-93, Met. Richmond Multi-Discipline Team on Spouse Abuse, 1983-93, Va. Dept. of Children for handbook Step by Step Through the Juvenile Justice System in Virginia, 1988; nat. adv. com. for prodn. on missing and runaway children Theatre IV; adv. group to set stds. and tng. for Guardians Ad Litem, Supreme Ct. Va., 1994; chmn. jud. adminstrn. com. Jud. Conf. Va. for Dist. Cts., 1995-97, 2001-03; state adv. com. for CASA and children's Justice Act, 1998-2002. Co-author: Juvenile Law and Practice in Virginia, 1994. Task force on core values Chesterfield County Pub. Schs., 1999. Mem.: Va. Assn. Dist. Ct. Judges (bd. dirs. 2013—), Chestfield Pub. Edn. Found. (Bravo award 2009), Chesterfield-Colonial Heights Bar Assn., Met. Richmond Women's Bar Assn., Va. Trial Lawyers Assn., Va. Bar Assn., Va. State Bar (bd. govs. family law sect. 1997—2001, bd. govs. sr. lawyers conf. 2005—09, bd. govs. gen. practice sect. 2005—), State-Fed. Jud. Coun. Va. Office: Chesterfield Juvenile and Domestic Rels Dist Ct 7000 Lucy Corr Blvd Chesterfield VA 23832-6717 Home: 3242 Jersey Ct Colonial Heights VA 23834 Office Phone: 804-751-4115.

DAVIS, BRIAN JORDAN, federal judge; b. Jacksonville, Jan. 23, 1953; BA, Princeton U., 1974; JD, U. Fla. Coll. Law, 1980. Atty. Mahoney, Hadlow & Adams, P.A., Jacksonville, Fla., 1980—82, Brown, Terrell, Hogan, Ellis & McClamma & Yegelwel, Jacksonville, Fla., 1988—91; asst state's atty State of Fla., 1982—88, chief asst. state's atty. 4th Judicial Dist., 1991—94; cir. judge 4th Judicial Cir. Fla., 1994—2013; judge US Dist. Ct. (middle dist.) Fla., Tampa, 2013—. Office: US District Court 300 North Hogan St Jacksonville FL 32202 Office Phone: 904-549-1900.*

DAVIS, BUTCH (PAUL HILTON DAVIS), former college football coach; b. Tahlequah, Okla., Nov. 17, 1951; m. Tammy Davis; 1 child, Andrew. BS in Biology & Life Sci., U. Ark., 1974. Head coach Rodgers HS, Tulsa, 1978; asst. Okla. State U. Cowboys, 1979—83; defensive line coach U. Miami Hurricanes, 1984—88, Dallas Cowboys, 1989—93, defensive coord., 1993—94; head coach U. Miami Hurricanes, 1995—2001, Cleve. Browns, 2001—04, U. N.C. Tar Heels, Chapel Hill, 2006—11; spl. asst. to head coach Tampa Bay Buccaneers, 2012—. Office: Tampa Bay Buccaneers One Buccaneers Pl Tampa FL 33607

DAVIS, CALVIN DE ARMOND, historian, educator; b. Westport, Ind., Dec. 3, 1927; s. Harry Russell and Abbie Jane (Moncrief) Davis. AB, Franklin Coll., Ind., 1949; MA, Ind. U., 1956, PhD, 1961. Tchr. Wilson Sch., Columbus, Ind., 1949-51, 53-54; asst. prof. history Ind. Central Coll., Indpls., 1956-57; teaching assoc. Ind. U., 1958-59; asst. prof. history U. Denver, 1959-62, Duke U., Durham, NC, 1962-64, assoc. prof., 1964-76, prof., 1976-96, prof. emeritus, 1996—. Cons. NEH, 1974. Contbr. articles to profl. jours.; author: (essays) Ency. U.S. Fgn. Rels., 1997, Oxford Companion to American Military History, 1999, Scribner's Ency. Am. Fgn. Policy, 2002, The United States and the First Hague Peace Conference, 1962 (Albert J. Beveridge award, 1961), The United States and the Second Hague Peace Conference, 1976; contbg. author: American Statesmen Secretaries of State from John Jay to Colin Powell, 2004; editor: The Civil War Begins: Recollections of Three Soldiers of the Seventh Indiana Volunteer Infantry Regiment, 2011. With US Army, 1951—53. Mem.: Soc. Historians Am. Fgn. Rels., Orgn. Am. Historians, Am. Hist. Assn. Home: 511 E Nightingale Dr Greensburg IN 47240-8589 Office: Duke U Dept History Durham NC 27708

DAVIS, CAROL, educational association administrator, educator; English tchr.; curriculum specialist Terrebonne Parish Pub. Sch.; pres. La. Assn. Educators, Baton Rouge, 2000—. Trainer instrn. and profl. devel. La. Assn. Educators; field site coord. Nicholls State U. Mem.: Terrebonne Assn. Educators (pres.), La. Assn. Educators (v.p., bd. dirs., chair program and budget com., co-chair strategic planning com.). Office: Louisiana Association of Educators 8322 One Calais Ave Baton Rouge LA 70809-3412

DAVIS, CAROLYN R., councilwoman; Councilwoman, Dist. 7 Dallas City Coun., 2007—. Vice chmn. Housing com.; mem. Quality Life & Govt. Svcs. com., Trinity River Corridor Project com., Transp. & Environ. com. Pres. Queen City Neighbors in Action/Crime Watch, Pearl C. Anderson Middle Learning Ctr. PTA; former bd. mem. Cmty. Devel. Commn., North Tex. Housing Coalition, Urban Rehabilitation Standards Bd., Preservation Dallas; bd. mem. African-Am. Mus. Arts; task force mem. Single Family Housing Standards; rep. DISD Area 2 Dist. 9; adv. com. "Forward Dallas" Comprehensive Plan Vision. Recipient Cmty. Svc. award, Allstate; named one of 50 Who Make Dallas Work, D Mag. Office: City Hall 1500 Marilla St Rm 5FS Dallas TX 75201 Office Phone: 214-670-4689. Office Fax: 214-670-5115. Business E-Mail: carolyn.davis@dallascityhall.com.

DAVIS, CINDY, retail executive; BBA, Coll. William and Mary; M in Internat. Mktg., Am. Grad. Sch. Internat. Mgmt. (Thunderbird). Sr. v.p., group acct. dir. TracyLocke/DDB; v.p. brand mgmt. Starwood Vacation Ownership; sr. v.p. brand mgmt. Promus Hotel Corp.; with Harrah's Entertainment; v.p. brand mktg. Pizza Hut; pres. global devel. and comm. Rapp Collins Worldwide; sr. v.p., Sam's club membership and mktg. Wal-Mart Stores, Inc., 2007, exec.v.p. of membership, mktg. and eCommerce, 2008, exec. v.p. of global customer insights, 2011—. Named a Woman to Watch, Advertising Age, 2011. Office: Wal-Mart Stores, Incorporated 702 SW 8th St Bentonville AR 72716 Office Phone: 479-273-4000. Office Fax: 479-273-4053.

DAVIS, CLARENCE CLINTON, JR., lawyer; b. Alexandria, La., Sept. 24, 1956; s. Clarence Clinton Sr. and Julia Isabel (Pace) D.; m. Lisa Cheryl Russell, Aug. 6, 1977 (div. Aug. 1978). BS with hons., Northwestern State U., 1977; JD cum laude, So. Meth. U., 1980. Bar: Fla. 1980, U.S. Tax Ct. 1981, U.S. Ct. Appeals (5th cir.) 1981, Tex. 1982; cert. tax law Tex. Bd. Legal Specialization; CPA, Tex. Assoc. Trenam, Simmons, Kemker, Scharf, Barkin, Frye & O'Neill, Tampa, Fla., 1980-81, Moore & Peterson, Dallas, 1981-85, mem., 1986-89; ptnr. Krage & Jarvey, LLP, Dallas, 1989—. Author: Partnership Taxation in Theory and Practice, 1991-95, Advanced Problems in Partnership Taxation, 1992—2008, Fundamentals of LLC and Partnership Taxation, 1996—2008, Understanding LLC and Partnership Allocations and Basis, 1996—2008, Real Estate and Tax Deferred Exchanges, 1996-99, Tax Advice for Real Estate and Small Business, 2004—07, LLCs & Partnerships the Sophisticated Practitioner, 2009-14, LLC & Partnership Principles: An Introduction to Subchapter K, 2009-11, Navigating the LLC and Partnership Allocation and Basis Minefield, 2009-13. Mem. ABA (taxation sect.), Tex. Bar Assn. (tax exempt orgn. subcom. taxation sect. 1986-87), Fla. Bar Assn., Dallas Bar Assn., Coll. State Bar Tex., Tex. Soc. CPAs, Order of Coif, Phi Kappa Phi. Republican. Episcopalian. Office Phone: 214-397-1919. Business E-Mail: ccdavis@kjllp.com.

DAVIS, CLARICE MCDONALD, lawyer; b. New Orleans, Jan. 20, 1941; d. James A. and Helen J. (Ross) McDonald. BA cum laude, U. Tex., Austin, 1962, MA, 1964; JD magna cum laude, Southern Meth. U., 1968. Bar: Tex. 1969, US Dist. Ct. (no. dist.) Tex. 1970, US Ct. Appeals (5th and 11th cirs.), US Supreme Ct. 1973. Instr. law Southern Meth. U. Sch. Law, 1968—69; law clk. to Hon. Irving L. Goldberg US Ct. Appeals (5th cir.), Dallas, 1969-71; assoc. Akin, Gump, Strauss, Hauer & Feld LLP, Dallas, 1971—79, ptnr., 1979, gen. counsel, 1984—2004, sr. counsel, mem. ethics com. Comments editor Southwestern Law Jour., 1967-68; instr. Southern Meth. U. Sch. Law, 1968-69. Bd. visitors Southern Meth. U., Dallas, 1979-82, v.p. Law Sch. Alumni Adv. Coun., 1992, pres. 1993-94, mem. bd. govs., 1995-98. Mem.: ABA, Dallas Bar Assn., Phi Beta Kappa. Avocations: photography, swimming, running, golf. Office: Akin Gump Strauss Hauer & Feld LLP 1700 Pacific Ave Ste 4100 Dallas TX 75201-4624 Office Phone: 214-969-2711. Office Fax: 214-969-4343. Business E-Mail: cdavis@akingump.com.

DAVIS, D. SCOTT (D. SCOTT DAVIS), delivery service executive; b. Oreg., 1952; BS in Fin., Portland State U., 1974; advanced mgmt. program, Wharton Sch. Bus., U. Pa. CPA. CFO, then CEO II Morrow, 1986—91; mgmt. positions UPS, 1986—98; CEO Overseas Ptnrs., Ltd., Bermuda, 1998—2000; v.p. fin. United Parcel Service, Inc. (UPS), Atlanta, 2000—01, sr. v.p., CFO, treas., 2001—06, vice chmn., CFO, treas., 2006—07, chmn., CEO, 2008—. Bd. dirs. Honeywell Internat., 2005—, UPS, Inc., 2006—; dep. chmn. Fed. Res. Bank, Atlanta. Mem. fin. coun. Ga. Coun. Econ. Edn.; bd. trustees Annie E. Casey Found. Office: UPS Inc 55 Glenlake Pkwy NE Atlanta GA 30328

DAVIS, DAISY SIDNEY, history professor; b. Matagorda County, Tex., Nov. 7, 1944; d. Alex C. and Alice M. (Edison) Sidney; m. John Dee Davis, Apr. 17, 1968; children: Anaca Michelle, Lowell Kent. BS, Bishop Coll., Dallas, 1966; MS, East Tex. State U., Commerce, 1971; MEd, Prairie View A&M U., Tex., 1980; postgrad., U. Tex., Austin, Tex. A&M U., Commerce. Cert. profl. lifetime secondary tchr., Tex.; mid-mgmt. adminstr. Tchr. Dallas Pub. Schs., 1966—2004, history dept chairperson, 1998—2004, substitute tchr., 2004—. Instr. Am. History El Centro Coll., 1991-98; scorer SAT and Tex. Assessment of Knowledge Skills; adv. Am. history telecourse Dallas Coumty C.C. dist. Coord. Get Out the Vote campaign, Dallas, 1972, 80, 84, 88, 92, 94, 96, 98, 2000, 02, 04, 08, 12; sec., bd. trustees St. John Bapt. Ch., 1995-98; pres. The Amazons. Recipient Outstanding Tchr. award Dallas pub. schs., 1980, Jack Lowe award for ednl. excellence, 1982; Free Enterprise scholar So. Meth. U., 1987; Constl. fellow U. Dallas, 1988; named to Hall of Fame, Holmes Acad., 1979. Mem. NEA, Tex. State Tchrs. Assn., Classroom Tchrs. Dallas (faculty rep. 1971-77, 95—), Dallas County History Tchrs., Afro-Am. Daus. Republic of Tex. (founder), Top Ladies of Distinction (named Top Ladies of Yr., 2012), Zeta Phi Beta. Clubs: Jack & Jill America Inc., (Dallas) (rec. sec., v.p., chair Beautillion Ball, pres., Disting. Mother award, Nat. Committment award 1997). Democrat. Baptist. Home: 1302 Mill Stream Dr Dallas TX 75232-4604

DAVIS, DANIEL, state legislator; m. Rebekah Davis; 2 children. Councilman, Dist. 12 Jacksonville City Coun., Fla., 2003—10, pres. Fla., 2007—08; mem. Dist. 13 Fla. House of Reps., 2011—. Former chmn. Fin. Com., vice chmn.; mem. Rules Com.; former mem. Growth Mgmt. Com., Value Adjustment Bd.; appointed mem. State Impact Fee Com.; chmn. Personnel Com. Mem. Duval County Tourist Devel. Coun., Seaport & Airport Spl. Com. Recipient Charles D. Webb award, Jacksonville City Coun., 2004. Mem.: Northeast Fla. Builders Assn. (assoc. dir.). Republican. Office: Unit 3 8465 Merchants Way Jacksonville FL 32222-2852 also: Fla House of Reps 1102 The Capital 402 South Monroe St Tallahassee FL 32399-1300 Office Phone: 904-573-4994, 850-488-5102.

DAVIS, DARRELL L., retired automotive executive; b. Sharon, Pa., Aug. 8, 1939; s. Paul Darrell and Dorothy Jane (Snyder) D.; m. Jacqueline Donna Pain, July 18, 1986; children: Paul Darrell II, Robert Tod. BS, Youngstown State U., 1963; cert. Stanford Exec. Program, Stanford U., 1987; cert. Global Leadership Program, U. Mich., 1993. Svc. rep., warranty mgr., dist. mgr., asst. zone mgr. Chrysler Motors Corp., Orlando, Fla., 1966-77, zone mgr. Omaha, 1977-78, Troy, Mich., 1978-79, nat. distbn. mgr., regional mgr., gen. mgr. import export ops., gen. sales mgr. Detroit, 1979-88; pres., chief exec. officer Alfa Romeo Distbrs. N. Am., Orlando, 1988-91; gen. sales mgr. Chrysler Corp., Orange, Calif., 1991-93; v.p. Chrysler Internat. Corp., Detroit, 1993-95; gen. mgr. Europe Chrysler Corp., Detroit, 1993-95; pres., COO Chrysler Fin. Corp., Southfield, Mich., 1995-97, chmn., CEO, 1997-98; v.p. Chrysler Corp., 1997—98; sr. v.p. Daimler Chrysler Corp., 1998—2001; bd. mgmt. Daimler Chrysler Svcs. AG, 1999—2000; CEO Daimler Chrysler Fin. Svcs. N.Am., LLC, 1999-2000; sr. v.p., gen. mgr. global svc. and parts divsn. Daimler Chrysler Corp., 2000—01, ret., 2001—. Author automotive profl. materials, 15 books on Chrysler high performance vehicles. Hon. judge Pebble Beach Concours d'Elegance, 1999—2007; bd. dirs. Boys and Girls Clubs of S.E. Mich., 1998—2001, Walter P. Chrysler Mus., 2001—12; bd. advisors Beeghly Coll. Edn., Youngstown State U., Ohio, 2004—07. Lt. US Army, 1963—65. Mem.: Classic Car Club Am. (treas. Fla. region 2001—06), Antique Auto Club Am. (pres. Fla. region 2007). Avocation: American history. Office: 100 Tech Dr Sanford FL 32771 Office Phone: 407-330-9100. Personal E-mail: ddavis8839@aol.com.

DAVIS, DAVID SCOTT, academic administrator, chemistry professor; b. Danville, Va., July 26, 1963; s. Jerry O'Neil and Patricia Ann Davis; m. Cathy Louise Daniel, July 18, 1998; children: Ryan Matthew Glisson, Miller Ann, Layne Elizabeth. BS, Erskine Coll., SC, 1985; PhD, Emory U., Atlanta, 1990. Asst. prof. Mercer U., Macon, Ga., 1991—96, assoc. prof., 1996—2004, prof., 2004—, vice provost, 2004—07, sr. vice provost for rsch., 2007—, dean grad. studies, 2007—. Author numerous scientific articles in scientific jours. Pres. Huguenin Heights Neighborhood Assn., Macon, Ga., 1998—99; mem. nominating com. Ga. Sports Hall of Fame; adminstrv. bd. Mulberry St. United Meth. Ch., Macon, Ga., 2003—06; bd. mem. Flying Fleet Club of Erskine Coll., Due West, SC, 2002—05, Intown Macon (Ga.), 1997—2000. Recipient ILI Program award, NSF, 1997—99, CCLI Program, 2002—04; Fellowship, Coun. on Undergraduate Rsch., 1994, Athletic scholarship, Erskine Coll., 1981—85. Mem.: Am. Conf. of Academic Deans, Am. Assn. of Higher Edn., Coun. of Colls. of Arts and Scis., Coun. on Undergraduate Rsch., Ga. Acad. of Sci., The Am. Chem. Soc., Omicron Delta Kappa, Sigma Xi, Phi Kappa Phi, Pi Alpha. Methodist. Avocations: golf, reading, woodworking. Home: 624 Bellgrove Pointe Macon GA 31220 Office: Mercer Univ 1400 Coleman Ave Macon GA 31207 Office Fax: 478-301-5576; Home Fax: 478-301-5576. Business E-Mail: davis_ds@mercer.edu.

DAVIS, EDDIE JOE, foundation administrator; b. Wichita Falls, Tex., Jan. 20, 1945; s. Dennis Drapper and Ruby Mae (Callaway) D.; m. Jo Ann Meuse, June 8, 1968; children: Phillip Michael, Jennifer Ann. BS in Journalism, Tex. A&M U., 1967, MEd in Adminstrn., 1974, PhD in Higher Edn., 1980; student, Harvard Grad Sch. Bus., 1971. Dir. mgmt. svcs. Tex. A&M U., College Station, 1972-78, assoc. v.p. bus., 1978-80, v.p. fiscal affairs, 1983-87, prof. ednl. adminstrn., dep. chancellor fin. and adminstrn., 1987-91, dep. chancellor, 1991-93, interim pres., 2006—08; pres. Tex. A&M Found., College Station, 1993—; v.p. fiscal affairs, treas. North Tex. State U., Denton, 1980-83. Bd. dirs. Coun. Govtl. Rels., Washington, chmn. costing policies com., 1992-93. Pres., Brazos County A&M Club, 1978; bd. dirs. Brazos County United Way, Tex., 1980; mem. formula adv. com. State Coord. Bd., 1981—, chair formula study com., 1992-93. Col. AUS, 1967-90, Vietnam. Mem. Tex. Assn. State Sr. Coll. and Univ. Bus. Officers (pres. 1985-86), Southern Assn. Coll. and Univ. Bus. Officers (chmn. 1984-85), Endowed Diamond Century Club, 12th Man Found. Adv. Bd., A&M Legacy Soc. Roman Catholic. Home: 6004 Augusta Cir College Station TX 77845-8984 Office: Tex A&M Found 401 George Bush Dr College Station TX 77840-2811 Office Phone: 409-845-8161. E-mail: edavis@tamu.edu.

DAVIS, EDGAR GLENN, healthcare executive, educator; b. Indpls., May 12, 1931; s. Thomas Carroll and Florence Isabelle (Watson) Davis; m. Margaret Louise Alandt, June 20, 1953 (dec. Sept. 2008); children: Anne-Elizabeth, Amy Alandt, Edgar Glenn Davis Jr.; m. Joanne Warvel Davis, Apr. 4, 2009. AB, Kenyon Coll., 1953; MBA, Harvard U., 1955. With Eli Lilly & Co., Indpls., 1958—63, mgr. budgeting and profit planning, 1963—66, mgr. econ. studies, 1966—67, mgr. Atlanta sales dist., 1967—68, dir. market rsch. and sales manpower planning, 1968—69, dir. mktg. plans, 1969—74, exec. dir. pharm. mktg. planning, 1974—75, exec. dir. corp. affairs, 1975—76, v.p. corp. affairs, 1976—90, v.p. health care policy, 1990; pres., chmn. bd. dirs. Centre for Health Sci. Info., Boston, 1990—; fellow Ctr. for Bus. and Govt. Kennedy Sch. of Govt. Harvard U., 1991—95; adj. prof. Butler U., Indpls., 1995—. Exec. in residence Butler U. Coll. Bus., 1995—2009; mem. Inst. Ednl. Mgmt., Harvard U. Grad. Sch. Edn., 1987; chmn. staff Bus. Roundtable Task Force on Health, 1981—85; U.S. rep. UN Indsl. Devel. Orgn. Conf., Lisbon, 1980, Casablanca, 1981, Budapest, 1983, Madrid, 1987; participant meeting of experts on pharms UNIDO, 1981; rep. to UN Commn. on Narcotic Drugs, Vienna, 1981, UN Econ. and Social Coun., NYC, 1981, UN Indsl. Devel. Orgn. Conf.; Ctr. for Bus. and Govt. fellow Kennedy Sch. Govt., Harvard U.; co-chmn. Harvard Conf. on Govt. Role in Civilian Tech., 1992, Harvard Conf. Pharmaceutical Rsch., Innovation and Pub. Policy, 1993, Harvard Biotech. Roundtable, 1991—96; vis. scholar, advisor Health and Welfare Unit, Inst. for Econ. Affairs, London; vis. scholar Green Coll. Oxford (Eng.) U., 1994—; chmn. Nat. Fund for Med. Edn., 1994—; dir. English Speaking Union, Indpls.; gov. Soc. Indiana Pioneers; lectr. in field; mem. bd. visitor Jordon Coll. Fine Arts Buttee U., 2012—. Contbr. articles to profl. jours. Pres. Eli Lilly and Co. Found., 1976—88; trustee Indpls. Symphony Orch., 2010—, life trustee; bd. trustees Indpls. Symphony Ochestra, 2013—; mem., bd. dirs. Ivy Tech. CC Found., 2014—; pres., chmn. bd. Indpls. Health Inst., 1988—91; trustee Kenyon Coll., Gambier, Ohio, Ind. Hist. Soc., 2000—10; pres. bd. trustees Boston Biomed. Rsch. Inst., 1991—95, trustee emeritus; chmn. Nat. Fund for Med. Edn., 1996—; bd. dirs. Carnegie Coun. on Ethics and Internat. Affairs, 1985—92; accredited nongovtl. observer rep. to UN Goodwill Found. Ind. Inc., 1987—95; bd. dirs. Sta. WFYI Pub. TV, Indpls., 1983—91, Am. Symphony Orch. League, 1987—92, mem. dirs. coun., 1987—; bd. dirs. Nat. Health Coun., 1984—91, Pub. Affairs Coun., Washington, 1984—92, Nat. Fund for Med. Edn.; bd. advisors Christian Theol. Sem., Bishops Sch., LaJolla, Calif.; chmn. bd. dirs. Ind. Repertory Theatre, 1979—85; mem., bd. dir. The Nature Conservancy, Ind. Chpt.; vice chmn., exec. com., bd. dirs. Indpls. Symphony Orch. and Ind. State Symphony Soc., 1977—91; chmn. task force on fine arts Commn. for Future of Butler U.; chmn. exec. com. Pan Am. Econ. Leadership Conf. 10th Pan Am. Games, Indpls.; bd. govs. Soc. Ind. Pioneers; mem. bd. visitors Coll. Fine Arts, Butler U., 2012—. Mem.: NAM (vice-chmn. health policy com. 1987—91, bd. dirs.), Am. Symphony Orch. League N.Y. (mem. dir. coun.), Inst. Medicine NAS, Ind. Soc. Pioneers (bd. govs.), Indian Lake Yacht Club (Mich.), Svc. Club Indpls., Dramatic Club of Indpls., Univ. Club (Indpls.) (bd. dirs.), Literary Club Indpls., Reform Club London, Edgartown Golf Club, Contemporary Club, Woodstock Club, Naples Yacht Club, Edgartown Yacht Club (Martha's Vineyard). Home: 7941 Clearwater Pkwy Indianapolis IN 46240-4902

DAVIS, EDWARD R., III, consumer products company executive; Treas. Tupperware Brands Corp., 2002—, v.p., 2004—. Office: Tupperware Brands Corp 14901 S Orange Blossom Trail Orlando FL 32837 Office Phone: 407-826-5050. Office Fax: 407-826-8268.

DAVIS, EGBERT LAWRENCE, III, lawyer; b. Winston-Salem, NC, Dec. 30, 1937; s. Egbert Lawrence Jr. and Eleanor (Layfield) D.; m. Alexandra Holderness, Aug. 25, 1962; children: Alexandra Davis Hipps, Egbert L. IV, Lucinda Davis, Pamela Davis. AB, Princeton U., 1960; LLB, Duke U., 1963; MBA, George Washington U., 1966. Bar: NC 1963. Assoc. Womble, Carlyle, Sandridge & Rice, Winston-Salem, NC, 1965-70, ptnr., 1970-82, Raleigh, NC, 1982-97, of counsel, 1997—. Sec. Wachovia Realty Investments, Winston-Salem, 1979—82; co-chair Young Life Winston-Salem; discussion group leader Bible Study Fellowship, 1983—90. Mem. editl. bd. Duke U. Law Jour., 1963. Chmn. N.W. Environ. Preservation Com., Inc., Winston-Salem, 1980; co-chair Winston-Salem Young Life Com., 1980—81; mem. N.C. Courts Com., 1972—74; chmn. bd. trustees N.C. Bapt. Hosp., Winston-Salem, 1981—82; chmn. N.C. Family Bus. Forum, 1993—94; co-chmn. Raleigh Wake Leadership Found., 2002—04; mem. state coun. N.C. Prison Fellowship, 1994—97; bd. dirs. NC Found. for Econ. Edn., 1996—2006; exec. com. Ea. Ctr. for Regional Devel., 1996—97; sunday sch. tchr. and stephen minister; bd. dirs. Haven House Svcs. Inc., 1983—98; rep. N.C. Ho. of Reps., 1970—74; senator N.C. Senate, 1974—78; chmn. N.C. Dem. Party, 1989—91; elder White Meml. Presbyn. Ch.; bd. dirs. Ctr. for Citizenship, Enterprise and Govt., 2003—05. Capt. US Army, 1963—65. Named Citizen of Yr. Winston-Salem Mayor's Com. on Employment of the Handicapped, 1971, Young Man. of Yr. Winston-Salem Jaycees, 1972; recipient Freedom Guard award N.C. Jaycees, 1973, U.S. Jaycees, 1973. Mem. N.C. Bar Assn. (bd. govs. 1979-82), Duke U. Law Sch. Alumni Assn. (bd. dirs. 2006—12), Coastal Conservation Assn. (bd. dirs. 1997-2006), Raleigh Rotary Club (pres. 1986-87), George A. Coburn Found. Inc. (bd. dirs. 1998-). Republican. Avocations: history, writing, biking, swimming, spending time with family. Office: Womble Carlyle Sandridge PO Box 831 Raleigh NC 27602-0831 Office Phone: 919-755-2103. Business E-Mail: ldavis@wcsr.com.

DAVIS, ERROLL BROWN, JR., school system administrator, former academic administrator; b. Pitts., Aug. 5, 1944; s. Erroll Brown and Eleanor Margaret (Boykin) D.; m. Elaine E. Casey, July 13, 1968; children: Christopher, Whitney BS in Elec. Engring., Carnegie-Mellon U., 1965; MBA in Finance, U. Chgo., 1967. Corporate finance staff Ford Motor Co., Detroit, 1969-73, Xerox Corp., Rochester, 1973-78; v.p. finance Wis. Power & Light Co., Madison, 1978-82, v.p. finance & pub. affairs, 1982-84, exec. v.p., 1984-87, pres., 1987—98, pres., CEO, 1988-98; pres. WPL Holdings, Inc., 1990—98, Alliant Energy Corp., Madison, 1998—2003, CEO, 1990—2005, chmn., 2000—06; chmn., CEO Interstate Power & Light Co., 2000—05; chancellor U. Sys. Ga., Atlanta, 2006—11; supt. Atlanta Public Schools (APS), 2011—. Bd. dirs. Alliant Energy Corp., 1982—2006, Wisconsin Power & Light, 1984—2006, Amoco, 1991—98, BP plc, 1998—2010, Union Pacific Corp., 2004—, Gen. Motors Corp., 2007—. Mem. bd. regents U. Wis., 1987-94; bd. dirs. United Way Dane County, 1984-89, chmn., 1987; life trustee Carnegie Mellon U., chmn. bd. trustees, 2000-03; mem. bd. trustees U. Chgo., 2005—. Recipient Black Engineer of Yr. award, US Black Engineer, 1988, Bronze medal, Financial World, 1993, Disting. Alumnus award, U. Chgo. Grad. Sch. Bus., 1993, Ellis Island Medal of Honor, 2001, Dr. Martin Luther King Jr. Award, City of Madison, 2001, Carnegie-Mellon Alumni Disting. Svc. award, 2004, James E Steward award, American Assn. of Blacks in Energy, 2005; named one of The 100 Most Influential Georgians, Ga. Trend mag., 2008, The 100 Influential Atlantans, Atlanta Bus. Chron., 2006, 2007, The 75 Most Powerful Blacks in Corporate America, Black Enterprise mag., 2005, The 50 Most Powerful Black Executives in America, Fortune mag., 2002. Mem. American Soc. Corp. Execs., Electric Power Rsch. Inst. (bd. dirs. 1990-2006), Assn. Edison Illuminating Cos. (bd. dirs. 1993-2006), Edison Electric Inst. (bd. dirs. 1995-2006, chmn. 2002-03), US Olympic Com. (bd. dirs. 2004-08). Avocations: biking, golf. Office: Atlanta Public Schools 130 Trinity Ave Atlanta GA 30303 Office Phone: 404-802-2820.*

DAVIS, FERD LEARY, JR., law educator, consultant; b. Zebulon, NC, Dec. 4, 1941; s. Ferd L. and Selma Ann (Harris) D.; m. Joy Baker Davis, Jan. 25, 1963; children: Ferd Leary III, James Benjamin, Elizabeth Joy. BA, Wake Forest U., 1964, JD, 1967; LLM, Columbia U., 1984. Bar: NC 1967. Editor Zebulon Record, NC, 1958; tchr. Davidson County Schs., Wallburg, NC, 1966; ptnr. Davis & Davis and related law firms, Zebulon and Raleigh, NC, 1967—76; asst. pros. Wake County Dist. Ct., Raleigh, 1968—69; town atty. Town of Zebulon, 1969—76; founding dean Campbell U. Sch. Law, Buies Creek, NC, 1975—86, prof. law, 1975—2005; founding dean, prof. law Elon U. Sch. Law, Greensboro, NC, 2005—08, founding dean emeritus & prof. law emeritus, 2008—; vis. sr. legal fellow Ctr. Creative Leadership, 2009; acting exec. dir. Karamah Muslim Women Lawyers Human Rights, 2010. Dir. Inst. to Study Practice of Law and Socioecon. Devel., 1985-2005; chmn. The Davis Cons. Group, Inc., Greensboro, 1987-2005; pres. LAWLEAD/NIELLP, 1998—; cons. U. Charleston, W.Va., 1979; vis. scholar Ctr. for Creative Leadership, 1993. Assoc. editor Wake Forest U. Law Rev. Trustee Wake County Pub. Librs., 1971-75, Olivia Raney Trust, 1969-71; mem. NC State Dem. Exec. Com., 1970-72, NC Gen. Statutes Commn., 1977-79, Commn. on the Future of NC, 1980-83; dir., Howard Meml. Christian Edn. Fund, NC BarCares, 2000-06, Karamah, 2009-10. 1st Lt. USAR, 1959-66. Babcock scholar Wake Forest U., 1963-67; Dayton Hudson fellow Columbia U., 1982-83. Fellow Am. Bar Found., Coll. Law Practice Mgmt.; mem. ABA, NC Bar Assn., NC State Bar, Am. Judicature Soc. (nat. adv. com. 2005—), Rotary, Phi Delta Phi, Delta Theta Phi, Omicron Delta Kappa, Am. Law Inst. Democrat. Office: Elon U Sch Law 201 N Greene St Greensboro NC 27401 Home: 1729 Davistown Rd Wendell NC 27591 Office Phone: 336-278-9201. E-mail: davislaw@elon.edu.

DAVIS, FRANK TRADEWELL, JR., lawyer; b. Atlanta, Feb. 2, 1938; s. Frank T. and Sue (Burnett) D.; m. Winifred Storey, June 23, 1961; children: Frank, Frederick, Gordon. AB, Princeton U., 1960; JD, George Washington U., 1963; LLM, Harvard U., 1964. Bar: Ga. 1963, U.S. Ct. Appeals (5th cir.) 1963, D.C. 1966, U.S. Supreme Ct. 1968, U.S. Ct. Appeals (11th cir.) 1982, U.S. Ct. Appeals (10th cir.) 2003, NY, 2012, Cert. Mediator. Assoc. Hansell, Post Brandon & Dorsey, Atlanta, 1964-67; ptnr. Hansell & Post, Atlanta, 1968-77, 79-86, Long, Aldridge & Norman, Atlanta, 1986—2002, McKenna, Long & Aldridge, Atlanta, 2002—. Ptnr. Am. Arbitration Assn., Nat. Roster Arbitrator, 1995-, gen. counsel Pres.'s Reorgn. Project Office of Pres., 1977-79; vis. instr. U. Ga. Law Sch., 1964-66, Ga. State U. Law Sch., 1988-90; vis. prof. Emory U. Law Sch., 1992-2008; dir. Red and Black Newspaper U. Ga., 2005-09. Author: Business Acquisitions, 1977, (2d edit.), 1982, Leading 21st Century Non-Profit Boards, 2013; contbr. articles to legal jours. Bd. dirs. Nat. Inst. Justice, 1980—81; mem. steering com. Nat. Transp. Inst., 2011—, mem. bd., 2011—, chmn., 2012—; bd. dirs. Westminster Schs., 1969—98, emeritus mem., 1998—, chmn. bd. dirs., 1984—89; bd. dirs. Va. Sem., 1980—94, exec. com., 1985—89; mem. Atlanta Charter Commn.; chmn. Atlanta Crime Commn., 1977; mem. bd. councilors Carter Presdl. Ctr., 1988—; chmn. Rotary Ednl. Found. Atlanta, 1998—2010; commr. Atlanta Regional Commn., 1999—; bd. dirs, Ga. First Amendment Found., 1996—; mem. bd. gen. Theol. Sem., 2011—, vice chair, 2012—; sr. warden All Saints' Episcopal Ch., 1982, 2002, vestry, 2000—03. Lt. USNR, 1960—62. Fellow Am. Bar Found. (life); mem. Am. Law Inst. (life), Atlanta C. of C. (bd. dirs. 1975-77), Piedmont Driving Club (Atlanta), Capital City Club (Atlanta), Cedar Creek Racquet Club (Cashiers, N.C.), The Army and Navy Club (Washington), Rotary (pres. Atlanta chpt. 1990-91, bd. dirs., sec. 1988-89, chmn. bd., 1991-92, chmn. Ednl. Found. 1997—). Home: 2525 Peachtree Rd 15 Atlanta GA 30305 Office: 303 Peachtree St NE Ste 5300 Atlanta GA 30308-3264 Office Phone: 404-527-4080. Personal E-mail: ftd@mckennalong.com.

DAVIS, FRANK WAYNE, lawyer; b. Ada, Okla., Aug. 24, 1936; s. Roscoe Gladstone and Neva Dell (Peck) Davis; m. Kay Diane Higginbotham, Aug. 12, 1961; children: David, Paul. Student, U. Ill., Urbana, 1956-57; BA, East Cen. U., 1958; LLB, U. Okla., Norman, 1959. Bar: Okla. 1959, U.S. Dist. Ct. (we. dist.) Okla. 1965, U.S. Ct. Appeals (10th cir.) 1976. Acting postmaster U.S. Postal Service, Ada, 1959-61; assoc. Denny W. Falkenburg, Medford, Okla., 1961; county atty. Logan County, Guthrie, Okla., 1961-65; sole practice Guthrie, 1965—83, 1988—; ptnr. Davis and Hudson, Guthrie, 1983—88. Mcpl. judge City of Guthrie, 1974—78; rep. State of Okla., Oklahoma City, 1978—2004; vice chmn. judiciary com. Okla. Ho. of Reps., 1981—82, 1989, 1991—2004, minority fl. leader, 1982—86, asst. minority fl. leader, 1986—90. Scoutmaster Troop # 850 Boy Scouts Am., Guthrie, 1961—2000; del. Rep. Nat. Convs., 1984, 1996, alt. del., 2000; chmn. Logan County Reps., Guthrie, 1964—69; del. gen. conf. United Meth. Ch., Portland, Oreg., 1976; trustee Okla. United Meth. Found. Recipient Silver Beaver award, Boy Scouts Am., 1978. Mem.: Logan County Bar Assn. (pres. 1972—73), Okla. Bar Assn., Am. Legion, Masons 32 degree KCCH, Lions (v.p. 2004—05, pres. 2005—06, zone chmn. 2007—08, vice dist. gov. 2008—09, dist. gov. 2009—10, coun. chair. 2010—11), Gideons. Methodist. Avocations: fishing, stamp collecting/philately, farming, oil and gas production. Office: 115 N Division St Guthrie OK 73044-3240 Home: 2121 N Walnut Guthrie OK 73044 Home Phone: 405-282-1478; Office Phone: 405-282-1420. Personal E-mail: repfwdavis@wmconnect.com, fdavisatt@yahoo.com.

DAVIS, GARY L., gastroenterologist, educator; b. Sharon, Pa., Oct. 27, 1950; Attended, Iowa State U.; MD, U. of Minn. Med. Sch., 1976. Diplomate Am. Bd. Internal Medicine, 1979, Am. Bd. Internal Medicine-gastroenterology, 1983. Resident internal medicine Mayo Clinic, 1977—79, fellow gastroenterology, 1979—81; fellow hepatology Nat. Insts. of Health Clin. Ctr., 1982—84; med. staff assoc. liver diseases sect. Nat. Inst. of Arthritis, Diabetes, Digestive, and Kidney Diseases; asst. prof. gastroenterology, hepatology and nutrition divsn. Univ. of Fla. Coll. of Medicine, med. dir. adult liver transplantation, dir. hepatobiliary diseases sect., 1991, prof., 1993; with Baylor Univ. Med. Ctr.; prof. Baylor Coll. of Medicine. Mem.: Am. Ass. for the Advancement of Sci., Internat. Liver Transplantation Soc., Am. Soc. of Transplantation, European Assn. for the Study of the Liver, Am. Assn. for the Study of Liver Diseases, Am. Gastroent. Assn. Office: Baylor Health Care System 3410 Worth Ste 860 Dallas TX 75246 Office Phone: 214-820-8500. Office Fax: 817-820-0993.

DAVIS, GEORGE A., pharmacist, researcher; Pharmacy intern Kroger Pharmacy, Little Rock, 1990-93; pharmaceutics lab asst. Clin. Pharmacokinetics Lab. U. Ark., 1991-93; clin. staff pharmacist Med. Ctr. U. Ky., Lexington, 1993-97, lectr., 1995—, asst. prof. dept. pharm. practice and sci., 1997—. Mem. resident recruitment com., resident survey com. U. Ky. Med. Ctr., 1993-95; presenter in field. Jour. referee Pharmacotherapy, Annals of Pharmacotherapy, Am. Jour. Health Sys. Pharmacy; contbr. articles to profl. jours. Psychiat. Drug Therapy fellow Am. Soc. Hosp. Pharmacists, 1995, Geriatric Drug Therapy fellow, 1996. Mem. Am. Soc. Health Sys. Pharmacists, Am. Coll. Clin. Pharmacy, Kappa Psi.

DAVIS, GREG (CHARLES G. DAVIS), mayor; m. Suzann Davis; 3 children. BS in Civil Engring., Miss. State U. Mem. Miss. State Ho. of Reps., 1991—97; mayor City of Southaven, Miss., 1997—. Del. Am. Coun. Young Polit. Leaders, 2004; mem. Joint Civilian Orientation Conf. US Dept. Defense, 2007. Vol. Make-a-Wish Found., Saint Jude Children's Rsch. Hosp.; chmn. DeSoto County Bush-Cheney Reelection Campaign, 2004; adv. bd. U. Miss. Sch. Bus. Named one of Top 40 Under 40, Miss. Bus. Jour. Mem.: NRA. Republican. Home: 3094 Loganberry Cv Southaven MS 38672-6043

DAVIS, GREGORY KEITH, federal prosecutor; b. 1962; BS in Chemical Engring., Miss. State U., 1984; JD, Tulane U. Sch. Law, 1987. Assoc. Stamps & Stamps, Jackson, Miss., 1987—89; co-founder Davis, Goss & Williams PLLC, Jackson, 1989—2012; US atty. (southern dist.) Miss. US Dept. Justice, Jackson, 2012—. Mem.: ABA, Magnolia Bar Assn., Nat. Bar Assn., Miss. State Bar Assn., Alpha Phi Alpha Fraternity, Inc. Office: US Attorney's Office 188 East Capitol St #500 Jackson MS 39201 Office Phone: 601-965-4480.*

DAVIS, HALL L., IV, funeral director; b. La., 1951; s. Hall Davis III and Elsie Harrington Davis; m. Cecile Clayton Davis; children: Erica, Pamela, Felicia, Hall V. Attended, Southern U., Knoxville Coll.; degree in Mortuary Sci., Commonwealth Coll. Mortuary Sci., 1975. Cert. Funeral Svc. Practioner. State death investigator West Baton Rouge and Iberville Parish; dep. sheriff Iberville Parish; funeral dir., embalmer Hall Davis & Son Funeral Svc., Baton Rouge; owner The Honderosa Ranch. Century mem. Boy Scouts of America; founder Hall's We Care Kids, S.A.V. (Sharing a Vision); mentor Cohn Elem. Sch.; vol. 100 Black Men Metro Baton Rouge; mem. C. of C., Baton Rouge, West Baton Rouge, Greater Baton Rouge Port Comm., West Baton Rouge Devel. Corp., Union Bapt. Ch., Brusly, La., deacon, usher; mem. bd. dirs. United Way, Better Bus. Bur. Recipient Appreciation award, Port Allen Middle Sch., Mentoring award, Cohn Elem. Sch., Cmty. Svc. award to Fight Drug Abuse, Where Svc. Matters award, Vol. Baton Rouge, La. Best award, Israelite Bapt. Ch., Corp. Vol award, Above and Beyond award, Law Enforcement, Disting. Svc. award, LA Recreation and Parks Assn., Meritorious and Faithful Svc. to People and Churches of West Baton Rouge award, Man of Yr. award, Union Bapt. Ch., Mem. of Month award, Outstanding and Dedicatory award, Citizenship award for Cmty. Svc.; named to Power 150, Ebony mag., 2008. Mem.: Baton Rouge Funeral Dirs. Assn. (pres. 1987—94), Baton Rouge Consistory, La. State Coroner's Assn., Nat. Funeral Dirs. and Morticians Assn. (pres. 2007—, ednl. chair, sect. 2004—07), Nat. Funeral Dir.'s Assn., La. Funeral Dirs. Assn., La. State Bd. Embalmers and Funeral Dirs. (pres. 1994—2000), Baton Rouge Shriner's, Port Allen Rotary Club, Masons, Stone Sq. Lodge No. 8 (Humanitarian award), Pi Sigma Eta Nat. Morticians Frat. Office: Hall Davis & Sons Funeral Svcs LTD 9348 Scenic Hwy Baton Rouge LA 70807 Office Phone: 225-778-1612. Office Fax: 225-778-1613. Business E-Mail: hall@hallsinc.net.

DAVIS, HARDIE, state legislator; b. Macon, Ga., Dec. 05; m. Evett Davis; 1 child, Benjamin Joshua. Sr. pastor Abundant Life Worship Ctr.; state rep. Dist. 122 Ga., 2007—10; state senator Dist. 22, 2010—. Mem.: IEEE, Nat. Soc. Black Engrs., Bd Zoning Appeals (Augusta Richmond County), Child Enrichment, Leadership Augusta, U. Health Care Found. Democrat. Office: Ga State Senate 327-A Coverdell Legis Office Bldg Atlanta GA 30334 Home: PO Box 6389 Augusta GA 30916-6389 Office Phone: 706-434-8553, 404-656-0340. Office Fax: 866-390-7894, 404-657-7853. Business E-Mail: hardie.davis@senate.ga.gov.

DAVIS, HELEN GORDON, retired state senator; b. NYC, 1926; m. Gene Davis; children: Stephanie, Karen, Gordon. BA, Bklyn. Coll.; postgrad., U. South Fla., 1967—70. Tchr. High Sch. Commerce, NYC, Hillsborough High Sch., Tampa, Fla.; grad. asst. U. South Fla., 1968; mem. Fla. Ho. of Reps. (1st woman to be elected in 1974 from Hills Co., 1st woman to chair the legis. del.), 1974-88; state senator Fla., 1988-92; mem. Fla. Supreme Ct. Commn. on Gender Bias in the Cts., 1988-90, Fla. Supreme Ct. Commn. on Mediation and Arbitration, 1987—. Chmn. senate appropriations subcom. human svcs., mem. rules com., internat. trade and econ. devel. com., health and rehab. svcs. com. Jud. chmn. Local Govt. Study Commn. Hillsborough County (Fla.), 1964; mem. Tampa Commn. on Juvenile Delinquency, 1966-69, Mayor's Citizens Adv. Com., 1966-69, Quality Edn. Commn., 1966-68, Gov.'s Citizen Com. for Ct. Reform, 1972, Hillsborough County Planning commn., 1973-74; mem. Gov.'s Commn. on Jud. Reform, 1976; mem. employment com. Commn. Cmty. Rels., 1966-69; by-laws chmn. Arts Coun. Tampa, 1971-74; 1st v.p. Tampa Symphony Guild, 1974; bd. dirs. U. South Fla. Found., 1968-74, Stop Rape, 1973-74; past pres. PTA; active adv. commn. Nat. Child Care Action Campaign, Nat. Ctr. for Crime and Delinquency; chair Hillsborough Dem. Exec. Com., also pres.; active Fla. Com. on the Status of Women, 2001. Recipient U. South Fla. Young Dems. Humanitarian award, 1974, Diana award NOW, 1975, Woman of Achievement in Arts award Tampa, 1975, Tampa Human Rels. award, 1976, Hannah G. Solomon Citizen of Yr., 1980, St. Petersburg Times/Fla. Civil Liberties award, 1980, Friend of Edn. award, 1981, Fla. Alliance for Responsible Parenting award, 1981, Humanitarian award Judeo-Christian Clinic, 1984, Fla. Network of Runaway Youth award, 1985, Ctr. for Women Leader-adv. Friend award, 1985, Nat. Assn. Juvenile Ct. Judges Appreciation award, 1987, AAUW Leadership award, 1987, Hillsborough County Halfway House appreciation award, 1988, Martin Luther King award City of Tampa, 1988, Appreciation award Nat. Fedn. Dem. Women, 1989, Dept. Legal Affairs appreciation, 1990, Superwoman award Mus. Sci. and Industry, 1990, Nat. Childcare Merit award NASP, 1992, Am. Judicature award Am. Judicature Assn., 1993, Woman of Courage award City of Tampa, 2000, Liberty Bell award, Hillsborough Bar Assn., 2005, Lifetime Achievement award Brklyn. Coll., 2009; named Fla. Motion Picture and TV Outstanding Legislator, 1990; named to Fla. Women's Hall Fame, 1998, Fla. Displaced Home Makers award, 2008, Womens Hall of Fame, 2011. Mem. LWV (pres. Hillsborough County 1966-69, Fla. adminstrn. of justice chmn. 1969-74, First Leadership Achievement award 2004, Highest Achievement award 2006), Am. Arbitration Assn., Hills County Bar Assn. (Liberty Bell award 2005), Hills County Expy. Authority, Fla. Supreme Ct. Commn. Arbitration. Democrat. Home: 4902 Bayshore Blvd Apt 713 Tampa FL 33611-3866

DAVIS, HERBERT OWEN, lawyer; b. Washington, June 11, 1935; s. Owen Stier and Claudie Lea (Pointer) D.; children: Herbert O. Jr., Ann P., Paul B. BA, U. N.C., 1957; JD, Duke U., 1960. Bar: N.C. 1960, U.S. Dist. Ct. (mid. dist.) N.C. 1960. Assoc. Smith Moore Smith Schell & Hunter, Greensboro, NC, 1960—66, ptnr., 1966—86, Smith Helms Mulliss & Moore, Greensboro, 1986—2002, Smith Moore LLP, Greensboro, 2002—06, of counsel, 2006—08, Smith Moore Leatherwood LLP, Greensboro, 2008—. Editor in chief Duke Law Jour., 1959—60. Mem. ABA, NC Bar Assn., Greensboro Country Club, Phi Beta Kappa. Home: 2303 Danbury Rd Greensboro NC 27408-5123 Office: Smith Moore Leatherwood LLP 300 N Greene St Ste 1400 Greensboro NC 27401-2171 Business E-Mail: bert.davis@smithmoorelaw.com.

DAVIS, JAMES LEE, lawyer; b. High Point, NC, May 2, 1940; AB with high honors, Guilford Coll., 1968; JD with honors, U. N.C., 1971. Bar: N.C. 1971. With Ward and Smith P.A., New Bern, NC. Charles A. Dana scholar. Mem. N.C. State Bar, N.C. Bar Assn. (chmn. real property sect. coun. 1981-82), Craven County Bar Assn. (pres. 1978-79), Order of Coif. Office: Ward and Smith PA PO Box 867 New Bern NC 28563-0867 Home Phone: 252-633-3358; Office Phone: 252-672-5404. E-mail: jld@wardandsmith.com.

DAVIS, JARET L., lawyer; BA in Economics, cum laude, U. Miami, Fla., 1996, JD magna cum laude, 1999. Bar: Fla. Intern to Bob Graham US Senate, Miami, 1995; law clk. to SE regional office enforcement and market regulation divisions US Securities and Exchanges Commn., 1997; co-mng. shareholder Greenberg Traurig LLP, Miami. Contbr. articles to profl. jours. Bd. trustees Miami Children's Initiative; bd. dirs. Miami Coalition Christian and Jews, City Year, Friends of Little River, Miami Children's Hosp., U. Miami Sch. Law Alumni Assn., v.p. fundraising; vice chmn. bd. dirs. American Diabetes Assn.; mem. impact cir. Big Brothers Big Sisters Greater Miami; mem. coun. elders Iron Arrow Honor Soc.; mem. adv. bd. U. Miami Law Rev., U. Miami Sch. Law Moot Ct. Recipient Ruth Shack Cmty. Leadership award, Leave a Legacy and the Miami Found., 2011, M. Minnette Massey Moot Ct. award, U. Miami Sch. Law Charles C. Papy, Jr. Moot Ct. Bd., 2011; named Top Dealmaker of Yr., Corp. Fin. Category, Daily Bus. Rev., 2010; named one of Top 20 Professionals Under Forty, Brickell Mag., 2009, 40 Under 40, South Fla. Bus. Jour., 2009, The M&A Advisor, 2011, 100 Most Accomplished Blacks in Law, ICABA, 2009, South Fla. 50 Most Powerful Black Professionals, Success South Fla. mag., 2010, Top 20 Under 40, The Miami Herald, 2010, Minority 40 Under 40, The Nat. Law Jour., 2011, 40 Under 40 Outstanding Lawyers Miami-Dade County, Cystic Fibrosis Found., 2011; named to SuperLawyers, 2009, 2011. Mem.: ABA, Bus. Law Sect., Fla. Muslim Bar Assn., Dade County Bar Assn., Wilkie D. Ferguson Bar Assn., Fla. Regional Minority Bus. Coun., Beacon Coun., Greater Miami C. of C., Miami-Dade C. of C. Office: Greenberg Traurig LLP 333 SE 2nd Ave Ste 4400 Miami FL 33131 Office Phone: 305-579-0676. Business E-Mail: davisj@gtlaw.com.

DAVIS, JAY M., wholesale distribution executive; Joined Nat. Distbg. Co., 1970, COO, 1991—97, pres., 1991—2003, CEO, 1997—, chmn., 2003—. Bd. dirs. Acuity Brands, Inc., 2003. Office: National Distributing Company Inc 1 National Dr SW Atlanta GA 30336 Office Phone: 404-696-9440. Office Fax: 404-505-1013.

DAVIS, JEAN E., bank executive; b. Durham, NC, Dec. 9, 1955; BS in Polit. Sci. & Indsl. Rels., U. NC; MBA, Duke U. Joined Wachovia Corp. (now Wells Fargo & Co.), Charlotte, NC, 1985, regional v.p., Piedmont Triad Region, 1996—98, merger coord., Va. ops., 1998, exec. v.p., dir., human resources, 1998—99, sr. exec. v.p., dir., human resources, 1999—2000, sr. exec. v.p., chief tech. & ops. officer, 2000—01, sr. exec. v.p., divsn. head, info. tech., e-commerce and ops., 2001—. Mem. Fin. Svcs. Roundtable; bd. trustees U. NC, bd. visitors. YMCA of Greater Charlotte. Named one of 25 Women to Watch, US Banker Mag., 2003. Office: Wachovia Corp 300 S Brevard St Charlotte NC 28202-2350 Office Phone: 704-590-0000. Office Fax: 704-374-3425. Business E-Mail: davisj@wachovia.com.

DAVIS, JEFFREY A., retail company executive; BS in Acctg., Pa. State U.; MBA, U. Pitts. CPA. Audit supervisor KPMG Pete Marwick; with Hillman Co.; CFO McKesson Gen. Med.; CEO Lakeland Tours, LLC; v.p. fin. health and wellness merchandise unit Walmart US Wal-Mart Stores, Inc., Bentonville, Ark., 2006—07, v.p. fin. US store ops., 2007—09, sr. v.p. fin. & strategy, 2009—10, sr. v.p., treasurer, 2010—. Recipient Sam M. Walton Entrepreneur of Yr. Award. Mem.: Nat. Assn. Black Accountants. Office: Wal-Mart Stores Inc 702 SW 8th St Bentonville AR 72716-6299

DAVIS, JERRY, councilman; m. Rachel Andress; children: Dean, Rylie, Ryan. BA in History & Polit. Sci., Washington Coll., 1995; MA in Edn. Adminstrn., Prairie View A&M U., 1999. Ptnr. Breakfast Klub, 2003—; CEO Making It Better, 2006—; founder EIH Investments, LLC; councilman Dist. B Houston City Coun., 2012—. Office: City Hall Annex 900 Bagby, First Floor Houston TX 77002 Office Phone: 832-393-3009. Office Fax: 832-393-3291. E-mail: districtb@houstontx.gov.

DAVIS, JIM, state legislator; Orthodontist; state senator Dist. 50 NC, 2011—. Republican. Mailing: 37 Georgia Rd Franklin NC 28734 Office: NC Senate 16 W Jones St Room 2111 Raleigh NC 27601-2808 Office Phone: 919-733-5875, 828-342-4483. Business E-Mail: Jim.Davis@ncleg.net.

DAVIS, JOAN CARROLL, retired museum director; b. Sept. 20, 1931; d. Homer Leslie and Ruby Isabelle (Stone) G.; m. Frederic E. Davis, Aug. 22, 1953; children: Timothy, Terri, Tami, Traci, Todd, Tricia. Student, Bob Jones U., 1949-52. Supr. Day Care Ctr. Bob Jones U., Greenville, SC, 1953-63; docent Univ. Art Gallery, Greenville, 1964-73, dir., 1974—; ret., 1999. Republican. Baptist. Office: 217 Stadium View Dr Greenville SC 29609 Personal E-mail: fedjed@juno.com.

DAVIS, JOE A., lawyer; b. Alexandria, La., Apr. 1, 1960; married. BS, Univ. Tex., Dallas, 1982; JD, Baylor Univ. Law Sch., Waco, 1985. Ptnr. Hunton & Williams LLP, Dallas, 1985—2005; exec. v.p., gen. counsel Crosstex Energy LP, Dallas, 2005—. Mem.: Natural Gas & Electric Power Soc., N. Tex. (past pres.), N. Tex. Chapter, Gas Processors Assn., Texas State Bar. Office: Crosstex Energy LP 2501 Cedar Springs Ste 100 Dallas TX 75201 Office Phone: 214-721-9246. Business E-Mail: joe.davis@crosstexenergy.com.

DAVIS, JOHN, state legislator; m. Jayne Davis. Grad., Baylor U., 1982, U. Houston-Clear Lake, 1987. Past pres. Oates Industries; ind. mfr. rep. RPM; mem. Dist. 129 Tex. House of Representatives, 1999—. Republican. Office: 1350 NASA Pkwy Ste 212 Houston TX 77058 also: Room CAP 4S.03 Capitol PO Box 2910 Austin TX 78768 Office Phone: 281-333-1350, 512-463-0734.

DAVIS, KOLAN LEON, legislative staff member; b. Franklin, Ind., Feb. 17, 1958; married; 1 child. BA in History cum laude, U. Dallas, 1980; JD, Ind. U., 1984. Bar: Ind. 1984. Staff atty. Ctr. Jud. Studies, Washington, 1984-85; counsel, subcommittee on adminstrv. practice and procedure US Senate Judiciary Com., Washington, 1985-87, chief counsel, subcommittee on adminstrv. oversight and the courts, 1995—2000; counsel to Senator Charles E. Grassley, Washington, 1987-91, fgn. policy advisor, tax counsel, 1998—2000, chief counsel, legis. dir., 2000; Rep. staff dir., chief counsel US Senate Fin. Com., Washington, 2001—. Cand. Ind. Dist. 58 House seat, 1988, precinct committeeman, 1982-84. With USAR, 1980-83. Named one of The Fabulous 50, Roll Call, 2009. Mem. Phi Alpha Theta, Phi Delta Phi. Methodist. Office: US Senate Com on Finance 219 Senate Dirksen Office Bldg Washington DC 20510-6200 Office Phone: 202-224-4515, 202-224-5315. Business E-Mail: kolan_davis@finance-rep.senate.gov.

DAVIS, LANCE ALAN, foundation administrator, research and development executive, metallurgical engineer; b. Ridley Park, Pa., Nov. 19, 1939; s. Earl W. and Ruth Naomi (Lentz) D.; m. Susan Ruth Kroesser, July 28, 1962; children: Susan, Virginia, Lance Jr. BS in Metall. Engring., Lafayette Coll., 1961; M in Engring., Yale U., 1963, PhD, 1966. Applied scientist research staff Yale U., New Haven, 1966-68; staff physicist Allied Chem. Corp., Morristown, NJ, 1968-74, mgr. strength physics, 1974-78, mgr. Metglas Devel. sect., 1978-80; dir. materials lab. Allied Corp., 1980-84; v.p. R&D, Allied-Signal, Inc., 1984-94; dir. Office of Tech. Transition US Dept. Defense, Washington, 1994-99; exec. officer Nat. Acad. Engring., Washington, 1999—. Contbr. numerous articles to profl. jours., chpts. to books; co-inventor 6 patents. Mem. AIME, NAE, Am. Soc. for Metals, Am. Phys. Soc., Materials Research Soc., Sigma Xi, Phi Beta Kappa, Tau Beta Pi. Home: 4006 Ellicott St Alexandria VA 22304-1012 Office: 500 Fifth St, NW Washington DC 20001 Office Phone: 202-334-3677. E-mail: ldavis@nae.edu.

DAVIS, LAWRENCE A., JR., academic administrator; BS in Math., AM&N Coll.; PhD in Mechanics, Iowa State Univ. Chancellor U. Ark., Pine Bluff, 1991—. Office: U Ark Office of Chancellor PO Box 4982 Pine Bluff AR 71611-4982

DAVIS, LAWRENCE WILLIAM, radiation oncologist; b. North Braddock, Pa., Sept. 5, 1935; s. William Paul Davis and Julia Helen Zukas; children: James G., Karen E. BS, Juniata Coll., Huntington, Pa., 1957; MA, U. Pa., 1969; MBA, Temple U., 1984; MD, Georgetown U., 1961. Diplomate Am. Bd. Radiology, lic. physician Pa., Md., 1, NY, Ga. Asst. instr. radiology U. Pa., Phila., 1962-66, instr. radiology, 1966, 68-69, asst. prof. radiology, 1969-72, assoc. prof. radiology, 1972-75; prof. radiation therapy Thomas Jefferson Sch. Medicine, 1975-84; prof. and chmn. radiation oncology Albert Einstein Coll. Medicine, Bronx, 1984-91, Emory U., Atlanta, 1991—2009, prof. radio-oncology, 2009—11, prof. emeritus, 2011—. Cons. Armed Forces Radiobiology Rsch. Inst., Bethesda, 1968-70; exec. com. of med. staff Montefiore Med. Ctr., 1984-87, 1990-91, div. coun., 1988-89; prof. svc. com. Phila. div. Am. Cancer Soc., 1970-75; trustee 1981-95, asst. exec. dir. radiation oncology 1994-09, assoc. exec. dir. radiation oncology, Am. Bd. Radiology, 2004-11. Assoc. editor Internat. Jour. Radiation Oncology, 1986—2011, mem. editl. bd. Neuro Oncology, 1989—99, assoc. editor, 1991—2003, mem. editl. bd. Am. Jour. Clin. Oncology, 1991—2003; contbr. numerous articles to profl. jours. Capt. USAF, 1966—68. Recipient Gold medal Am. Coll. Radiology, 2008; fellow Am. Cancer Soc., Phila., 1963-64, NIH, 1964-66, Am. Cancer Soc. traineeship, 1968-71. Fellow Am. Coll. Radiology; mem. AAAS, Am. Assn. Cancer Rsch., Am. Coll. Radiology (commn. on radiation oncology 1981-90, bd. chancellors 1993-99), Am. Soc. Therapeutic Radiology and Oncology (chmn. bd. 1988-89, pres. 1987-88), Am. Radium Soc. (pres. 1992-93), Radiol. Soc. N.Am., Alpha Omega Alpha. Office Phone: 404-281-7841. Personal E-mail: larry@lwdavis.com. Business E-Mail: lawrence.davis@emory.edu.

DAVIS, LEONARD, federal judge; BA, U. Tex., Arlington, 1970; MS, Tex. Christian U., 1974; JD cum laude, Baylor U., 1976. Judge US Distict, 2002—; chief justice Twelftu Ct Appeals, 2000—02; pvt. practise, 1976—2002. Office: US Dist Ct Fed Bldg and US Courthouse 211 W Ferguson Third Fl Tyler TX 75702 Office Phone: 903-590-1084.

DAVIS, LINDA B., wholesale distribution executive; b. Mar. 4, 1953; V.p., treas. ScanSource, Inc. Office: ScanSource Inc 6 Logue Ct Greenville SC 29615 Office Phone: 864-288-2432. Office Fax: 864-288-1165.

DAVIS, LOUIS J., lawyer; BA, Southwestern U., Georgetown, TX, 1974; JD Order of the Barons, U. Houston, 1976. Bar: Tex. 1976; cert. in oil, gas and mineral law Tex. Bd. Legal Specialization. Ptnr. Baker and McKenzie LLP, Houston. Spkr. Various Confs., Baker & McKenzie Global Oil & Gas Steering Com. Co-author: (article) Common Legal Issues in US Shale Plays, The Landman Magazine, December 2009 and Texas Natural Resources Section Newsletter, 2009. Recipient Legal Media Group, Euromoney Worlds Co. Energy & Resource Lawyers, 2013; named Tex. Super Lawyer, Super Lawyers, the Best Lawyer in America, H Tex. Magazine, 2010—14; named one of the Best Lawyers in Houston, Who's Who in Energy, Houston Business Jour., 2013. Office: Baker and McKenzie LLP Partner Oil Gas 700 Louisiana St Ste 3000 Houston TX 77002 Business E-Mail: Louis.Davis@bakermckenzie.com.*

DAVIS, LULA JOHNSON, retired legislative staff member; b. La., 1949; BS in Office Adminstrn., Southern U., Baton Rouge, MEd in Guidance Counseling. Legis. corr. to Senator Russell B. Long US Senate, Washington, mem. Democratic floor staff, 1993—95, chief floor asst., 1995—97, asst. sec., 1997—2008, sec. for majority, 2008—10; office asst. for floor staff US Senate Democratic Policy Com. Named one of The Fabulous 50, Roll Call, 2009. Democrat.

DAVIS, MARGARET BERGAN, foundation administrator; b. Chgo., Nov. 22, 1958; d. John Jerome and Carolyn Elizabeth (Widener) Bergan; m. Andrew Bashaw Davis; children: Caroline Bashaw, Katharine Elizabeth. AB in Art History, Mount Holyoke Coll., 1980. Asst. dir. devel. Northwestern U., Evanston, Ill., 1980-82; exec. dir. The Corporate Project, Chgo., 1982-84; asst. v.p., cons. Charles R. Feldstein & Co., Chgo., 1986-91; dir. devel. Ravinia Festival Assn., Highland Park, Ill., 1991—98; mng. dir. MBD Consulting Group; pres., CEO US Marine Corps Scholarship Found. (MCSF), Alexandria, Va., 2009—. Mem. adj. faculty Columbia Coll., Chgo., 1995—; panelist Evanston Arts Coun., 1995—. Bd. dirs. Chgo. Children's Mus., 1981—, Milton (Mass.) Acad., 1989—, Family Focus, Chgo., 1995—. Recipient Superior Pub. Svc. award, Dept. Navy, US Dept. Def., 2008. Mem. Nat. Soc. Fund Raising Execs., Chgo. Yacht Club. Office: Marine Corps Scholarship Foundation 121 S Asaph St Alexandria VA 22314

DAVIS, MARK S., federal judge; b. Portsmouth, Va., 1962; BA, U. Va., 1984; JD, Washington & Lee U., 1988. Bar: Va. 1988. Law clk to Hon. John A. MacKenzie US Dist. Ct. (ea. dist.) Va., 1988—89; assoc. McGuire Woods LLP, 1989—96, ptnr., 1996—98, Carr & Porter LLC, 1998—2003; judge Portsmouth Cir. Ct. (3rd judicial cir.) Va., 2003—08, US Dist. Ct. (ea. dist.) Va., 2008—. Office: Walter E Hoffman US Courthouse 600 Granby St Norfolk VA 23501

DAVIS, MERRILL, public relations executive; Attended, U. Tex., Austin, Rice U. Dir. tng. programs for new policy initiatives within the elec.-utility industry, Tex.; energy policy cons. Governor's Energy Office; pub. outreach specialist Texas Ratepayers' Orgn. to Save Energy; instr. The Princeton Rev.; v.p., comm. Tenet Healthcare Corp.; joined Public Strategies, Inc., Austin, 1994, bd. dirs., assoc., prin. & sr. assoc., mng. dir. Austin, 2009—. Contbr., rsch. project Nat. Sci. Found. Office: Public Strategies Inc 98 San Jacinto Blvd Ste 1200 Austin TX 78701 Office Fax: 512-474-0120. Business E-Mail: mdavis@pstrategies.com.

DAVIS, MIKE, men's college basketball coach; b. Fayette, Ala., Sept. 15, 1960; m. Tamilya Floyd; children: Lateesha, Mike Jr., Antoine. Attended, U. Ala., Tuscaloosa; B in Telecomm., Thomas Edison State Coll., Trenton, NJ, 2000. Draft pick Milw. Bucks, 1983; profl. basketball player Switzerland, 1983—85, Italy, Topeka Sizzlers, Continental Basketball Assn., 1988—89; asst. coach Miles Coll. Golden Bears, Birmingham, Ala., 1989—90; basketball coach Venezuelan nat. team, profl. club teams; asst. coach Wichita Falls Texans, Continental Basketball Assn., 1990—94; player-coach Chgo. Rockers, Continental Basketball Assn., 1994—95; asst. coach U. Ala. Crimson Tide, 1995—97, Ind. U. Hoosiers, 1997—2000, head basketball coach, 2000—06, U. Ala.-Birmingham Blazers, 2006—12, Tex. So. U. Tigers, 2012—. Named Nat. Coach of Yr., Charlotte Observer, 2002, Conf. USA Coach of Yr., 2011. Office: Texas Southern University Basketball Program 3100 Cleburne St Houston TX 77004 Office Phone: 713-313-1997.*

DAVIS, MORRIS, lawyer; BA in Economics, Rice U., 1964; JD, U. Tex., 1967. Ptnr. McGinnis, Lochridge & Kilgore, LLP, Austin, Tex., 1967—2006; gen. counsel Temple-Inland, Inc., Austin, Tex., 2006—. Office: Temple Inland Inc 1300 S Mo Pac Expy Fl 3 Austin TX 78746-6933 Office Phone: 512-434-5800. Office Fax: 512-434-8001. Business E-Mail: information@templeinland.com.

DAVIS, NATHANIEL (NATE) A., broadcast executive; BE, Stevens Inst. Tech., NJ, 1976; Masters in Engring. Computer Sci., Moore Sch. at Pa.; MBA, Wharton Sch., U. Pa., 1982. Sr. v.p., network ops., COO, sr. v.p., fin. & v.p. sys. develop. MCImetro; various sr. engring. and fin. roles MCI Comm., 1986—98; CFO MCI Telecommunications, 1996—98; exec. v.p., network and technical services Nextel Comm., 1998—99; pres., COO XO Comm. (formerly Nextlink Comm. Inc.), 2000—03; exec. in residence Columbia Capitol, 2003—06; pres., COO XM Satellite Holdings, Inc., Washington, 2006—07, pres., CEO, 2007, also bd. dir., 1999—. Mng. dir., owner RANND Advisory Group, Oakton, Va., 2003—06; bd. dir. Mutual of Am. Capitol Mgmt. Corp., Charter Comm., 2005—, XO Comm. (formerly Nextlink Comm. Inc.), 2000—03; bd. dirs. K12 Inc., 2009—. Office: K12 Inc 2300 Corp Park Dr Herndon VA 20171 Office Phone: 703-483-7000. Business E-Mail: nathaniel.davis@xmradio.com.

DAVIS, RANDY, state legislator; m. Martha Lindsey; 1 child, Judson. BM, MM, U. So. Miss., Hattiesburg; degree in edn., Ala. State U., Montgomery. Tchr., adminstr., exec. to the supt. Mobile County Pub. Schools; pub. rels. coord. Baldwin County Pub. Schools; mem. Dist. 96 Ala. House of Reps., Montgomery, 2002—; asst. prof. music U. Mobile. Performer: Mobile Opera, Mobile Symphony; resident conductor: Baldwin County Pops Band, founder: North Mobile Cmty. Chamber Symphony. Mem. Chickasaw United Meth. Ch.; bd. mem. Mobile Arts Coun., Boys and Girls Club, Bounds YMCA, US Sports Acad., Daphne-Spanish Fort Rotary. Republican. Office: Ala House of Reps Ala State House 11 S Union St Montgomery AL 36130 Office Phone: 334-242-7724, 251-442-2552.

DAVIS, RAY C., energy executive; Chmn., CEO Cornerstone Natural Gas Inc., 1993—96; dir. Crosstex Energy, Inc., 1996—2000; v.p. of gen. ptnr. ET Co. 1, 1996—; co-CEO, co-chmn. bd. of gen. ptnr. LaGrange Energy, 2002—; co-CEO of gen. ptnr. LaGrange Acquisition, 2002—; co-CEO, co-chmn. bd. of gen. ptnr. Energy Transfer Partners, Dallas, 2004—07. Named one of Forbes 400: Richest Americans, 2009. Office: Energy Transfer Company 3738 Oak Lawn Ave Dallas TX 75219-4333

DAVIS, REBECCA C., insurance company executive; Student, Auburn U., Ala.; BBA, Columbus State U., Ga. With AFLAC, 1973—, asst. v.p. policyholder svc. dept., 1978, v.p. mktg. adminstrn. and ops., 1984, v.p. client svcs. and adminstrn., 1987, sr. v.p., asst. dir. mktg., 1992, sr. v.p., chief adminstrv. officer, 1999, exec. v.p., chief adminstrv. officer, 2004—. Office: AFLAC 1932 Wynnton Rd Columbus GA 31999 Office Phone: 706-323-3431.

DAVIS, ROBERT D., retail executive; BBA, So. Meth. U., 1993. Acct. Rent-A-Ctr., Inc., Tex., 1993—97, treas., 1997—99, v.p., fin., 1998—99, sr. v.p., fin., 1999—2008, CFO, 1999—, exec. v.p., fin., 2008—. Office: Rent-A-Center Inc 5501 Headquarters Dr Plano TX 75024-3556 Office Phone: 972-801-1100. Business E-Mail: robertdavis@rentacenter.com.

DAVIS, ROBERT EDWIN, lawyer; b. New Orleans, July 2, 1934; BA, JD, So. Meth. U., Dallas, 1958. Bar: Tex. 1958. Ptnr. Hughes & Luce, LLP, Dallas; ptnr., litigation practice K&L Gates LLP, Dallas, 2008—. Mem. adv. com. Tex. Supreme Ct. Named a Tex. Super Lawyer, Tex. Monthly, 2003—06; named one of Best Lawyers in Dallas, D Mag., 2005. Mem.: Am. Coll. Tax Counsel, Dallas Bar Assn. (chair Sect. Taxation 1977, chair 1977, pres. 1980), ABA, Tex. Bar Found., State Bar Tex. (chair Sect. Taxation 1976—77, dir. 1981—82). Office: K&L Gates LLP Ste 2800 1717 Main St Dallas TX 75201 Office Phone: 214-939-5447. Office Fax: 214-939-5849. Business E-Mail: robert.davis@klgates.com.

DAVIS, ROBERT LARRY, lawyer; b. Lubbock, Tex., June 6, 1942; s. R. H. and Bernice (Pray) Davis; m. Peggy Saunders, Jan. 23, 1965; children: Lee Michael, Melissa Lynn. BA, Rice U., 1964; LLB with honors, U. Tex., 1967. Bar: Tex. 1967, U.S. Dist. Ct. (we. dist.) Tex. 1969, U.S. Dist. Ct. (so. dist.) Tex. 1989. Assoc. Royston Rayzor & Cook, Houston, 1967-68; from assoc. to ptnr. Brown McCarroll, Austin, Tex., 1968—. Bus. sect. coord., mem. m tarian, mem. exec. com. Downtown Revitalizati 1978—80; mem., past pres. Boys Club, Au 1981—; trustee Eanes Ind. Sch. Dist., Aus 1990—93. Methodist. Avocations: sports, m 3607-3 Pinnacle Rd Austin TX 78746 Office: B One Congress Plz III Congress Austin TX 574-327-1806; Office Phone: 512- rdavis@mailbmc.com.

DAVIS, ROBIN JEAN, state supreme court c County, W.Va., Apr. 6, 1956; m. Scott Segal W.Va. Wesleyan Coll., 1978; MA in Indsl. Rel 1982. With Segal & Davis L.C., 1982-96; justi of Appeals, 1996—, chief justice, 1998, 2002, 2014—. Mem. W.Va. U. Law Inst., W.Va. B 1991-96. Contbr. articles to W.Va. Law Rev. Handbook on West Virginia Rules of Civil Pro West Virginian award, 2000. Mem. ABA, Ass Am., Kanawha County Bar Assn., Am. Acad. Office: Supreme Ct of Appeals Bldg 1 Rm Charleston WV 25305 Office Phone: 304-558- robin.davis@courtswv.gov.*

DAVIS, ROY WALTON, JR., lawyer; b. Mar s. Roy Walton and Mildred Gertrude (Wilson) Combs, Sept. 10, 1955; children: R. Walto Rebekah Wilson, Sally Fielding. BS, Davidso honors, U. N.C., 1955. Bar: N.C. 1955, U.S. D 1960, U.S. Ct. Appeals (4th cir.) 1963. Ptnr. D 1959-60; from assoc. to ptnr. and pres. Va Starnes & Davis, Asheville, N.C., 1960—. articles to profl. publs. Chancellor Episc. Di 1980—. With U.S. Army, 1956-59. Recipien sionalism award, NC Supreme Ct., 2009. Barristers, Am. Coll. Trial Lawyers (state cha Found.; mem.: ABA (Ho. of Dels. 1989—92, sects.), N.C. Assn. Def. Attys., N.C. State Bar (IOLTA 1987—93, bd. law examiners 2002—), young lawyers divsn. 1965—66, chair adminsi 1999—2002, v.p. 2004—06, Gen. Practice Ha Home: 359 Country Club Rd Asheville NC 2 Winkle Buck Wall Starnes & Davis 11 N M 28801-2932 Home Phone: 828-253-5983; 2991. Business E-Mail: rdavis@vwlawfirm.c

DAVIS, SAMUEL MARION, law educator, b. Pascagoula, Miss., Nov. 24, 1944; s. Mari (Butler) D.; m. Carolyn Mary Peele, Au Samantha Carrie, Sarah Ellen. BA, U. So. Mi 1969; LLM, U. Va., 1970. Bar: Miss. 1969, Miss. 1969, US Supreme Ct. 1978, US Ct. A US Ct. Appeals (5th cir.) 1992. From asst. pro Law Sch., Athens, 1970-78, asst. dean, 1973-7 dean, 1986-92, assoc. v.p. for acad., 1994-97; Oxford, 1997—2010, Jamie L. Whitten chair 1998—. Vis. assoc. prof. Wash. and Lee U. La 1975-76. Author: Rights of Juveniles, 2009; co Legal System, 1983, 4th edit., 2009, Children 1987. Fellow: Miss. Bar Found.; mem.: AB Inst. Democrat. Methodist. Avocations: sailing, University of Mississippi School Law PO Box Law Center University MS 38677 Office Business E-Mail: smdavis@olemiss.edu.

DAVIS, STEVE, state legislator; m. Melissa Kelli, Ashli. Realtor; mem. Dist 109 Ga. Hou chmn. state planning & cmty. affairs com., m property, transp. committees. Republican. Offi Atlanta GA 30334 Mailing: 1109 Green Riv 30252

DAVIS, THOMAS PINKNEY, secondary sc ment chairman; b. Seminole, Okla., Oct. 10, 19 and Flora Elizabeth (Bollinger) D.; m. Leslie A 1990; children: Brianna Elizabeth, Mary Kath Robert McKenzie, Victoria Anne; stepchildr Jennifer Dawn, Matthew Joseph, Daniel Jacob BS with honors, East Ctrl. U., Ada, Okla., 1 1979; MS, Tex. A&M U., Coll. Sta., 2006. Di U., 1991-92; tchr., chair math. dept. Roosev math., chair math. dept. Keota HS, 1993-2000; Spade Ind. Sch. Dist., Tex., 2000—06, Buck 2006—09, Blackwell Ind. Sch. Dist., 2009—. Assn. of Lunar and Planetary Observers/The adj. instr. Connors State Coll., 1998-99; rsc Accelerator Lab., 1999; adj. instr. Western Tex. Sci. Books and Films, 1986—, The Math. T Grand Lodge Tex. Mirabeau B. Lamar award, Brit. Interplanetary Soc., Soc. Antiquaries of S IEEE, Am. Astronautical Soc., Am. Astron. S Planetary Observers, Nat. Coun. Tchrs. Math., Math., Okla. Acad. Sci., Alpha Chi, Pi Gam Episcopalian. Avocations: chess, gardening, astr well Ind Sch Dist 100 Hornet Dr Blackwell E-mail: tp_davis@yahoo.com.

DAVIS, TINE WAYNE, JR., retail grocery Miami, Fla., Sept. 16, 1946; s. Tine Wayne an Davis; m. Mary Katherine Owen, Dec. 1, 1967; Rebecca, Elizabeth Ashley, Katherine Chase. B 1971. Bar:. Counsel Winn-Dixie Stores, v.p. pub. mem. Winn-Dixie Stores Inc., Jacksonville, Fla Barnett Bank of Jacksonville, Jacksonville, Fl Mgmt., Inc.; chmn. Agribus Inst. Fla., 1982; chm Inc., Fla., 1989—2002; dir. Enstar Grp. Inc., M Fla. Tax Watch, Inc., 1981—82; trustee Jackso Sch.; chmn. Retail Industry Polit. Action Com., trustees Jacksonville County Day Sch.; bd. dirs. Children's Hosp., Jacksonville Art Mus., Lead trustee Bolles Sch.; mem. Pres.'s Cabinet U. Commn. Unity Tax, 1984. With US Army, 1971. Mktg. Inst. (govt. rels. com.), Ala. Bar Assn., Fla. 1983—85), Fla. Bar Assn., Fla. Supermarket Ass Assn. Industries Fla. (chmn. 1981—83), Phi De Episcopalian. Office: Winn-Dixie Stores Inc 5 Jacksonville FL 32254-3601 Office Fax: 904-783

DAVIS, TOM (THOMAS MILBURN DAVIS I executive, former United States Representative Minot, ND, Jan. 5, 1949; m. Peggy Rantz, 1973 (d Carlton, Pamela, Shelley; m. Jeannemarie A. 1 stepchildren. BA in Polit. Sci., Amherst Coll., 1971 Legislative asst. Va. House of Delegates, 1964-67 1975-79; v.p., gen. counsel Advanced Technologi Fairfax County Bd. Supervisors, Fairfax, Va., 19

94; v.p., gen. counsel then corporate counsel, chair PRC, Inc., , Va., 1990-94; mem. US Congress from 11th Va. Dist., 2008; chmn. US House Govt. Reform & Oversight Com., 07, Nat. Republican Congressional Com. (NRCC), 2003; pres., CEO Republican Main Street Partnership), 2009—13; dir. govt. rels. Deloitte Consulting, Washington, . Mem. Metropolitan Washington Airports Authority, 2010—. dv. bd. Afghanistan-American Found.; bd. dirs. Boys & Girls artnership for Public Svc.; mem. advisory bd. Women in Govt. eader; chair adv. bd. Va. Legal Services; mem. Fairfax County, ant-Landlord Assn., Nat. Capitol Planning Commn., Northern nsp. Commn., Va. Assn. Cities, Gen. Govt. Steering Com.; lective Govtl. Policy Com. Va. Mcpl. League; pres. Washing- t. Coun. Governments. Served in US Army, 1971, 1st lt. served in Va. N.G. Recipient Congressional Tech. Policy Electronic Industry Alliance, 1999, Friend of the Shareholder American Shareholders Assn., 2002, Guardian of Small Bus. Nat. Fedn. of Ind. Bus., 2002, Hero of Taxpayer award, ans for Tax Reform, 2002, Jefferson award, Citizens for a Economy, 2002, RSA Conf. award for Public Policy, RSA , 2002, Sr. Guardian Medal of Honor, Seniors Coalition, 2002, hampion award, Nat. Assn. State Chief Info. Officers, 2003, h award, Chief Info. Officers Coun., 2004; named to The n Electronics Assn. High Tech Hall of Fame, 2000. Mem.: Crossroads Rotary Club (charter mem., past pres.). Republi- ristian Science. Office: Deloitte Consulting 1001 G St NW gton DC 20001 Office Phone: 202-220-2080, 202-513-8131. todavis@deloitte.com.*

TOM, state legislator; b. New Brunswick, NJ, May 31, 1960; omas and Yvonne C. Davis; m. Reid Lawrence Davis, Jan. 5, hildren: Elizabeth, Grace, Claire. BA, Furman U., 1982; JD, U. . Law, 1985. Atty. Harvey & Battey, P.A., 1985—; former d. of Dirs. for Hist. Beaufort Found., Greater Beaufort C. of ufort County Planning Bd., Lowcountry Coun. of Govts., t-Jasper Water & Sewer Authority, SC States Ports Authority; Mark Sanford's 2002 & 2006 Gubernatorial Campaigns; sr. dvisor Gov. Sanford's Adminstrn., co chief of staff, dep. chief chief of staff; chmn. Bi-State Jasper Port Negotiating Com.; Dist. 46 SC State Senate, 2008—. Republican. Office: PO 1107 Beaufort SC 29901 also: Capitol Office 602 Gressette olumbia SC 29201 Office Phone: 843-252-8583, 803-212- -mail: tomdavis@scsenate.org.

WENDY JEAN RUSSELL, state legislator, lawyer; b. West k, May 16, 1963; d. Jerry Russell and Virginia (Cornstubble); k Underwood, 1982 (div. 1984); 1 child, Amber; m. Jeff Davis, iv. 2005); 1 child, Dru. Attended, Tarrant County Coll., Tex., 86; BA, Tex. Christian U., Ft. Worth, 1990; JD with honors, U. Law Sch., Mass., 1993. Bar: Tex. 1993. Law clk. to Hon. uchwald US Dist. Ct. (northern dist.) Tex., 1993—94; atty. & Boone, Ft. Worth, 1994—99; part-owner Safeco Tile, 2004; CEO Ft. Worth divsn. Republic Title, Ft. Worth, 09; city councilwoman Dist. 9 Fort Worth City Coun., Tex., 2008; mem. Dist 10 Tex. State Senate, Austin, 2009—; of Cantey Hangar LLP, Ft. Worth, 2010—; founding ptnr. Davis PLLC, Ft. Worth, 2013—. Chair Regional Transp. 2005—06. Recipient Tex. Women's Health Champion Tex. Assn. of OB-GYNs, 2012, Meritorious Svc. award, Tex. on Family Rels., 2013, Camelot award, Child Protection able, 2013, Legislative Champion, Mothers Against Drunk (MADD), 2013, Legislator of Excellence award, Tex. State ing Coun., 2013, Silver Star award, Tex. Coun. Administrators n. (TCASE), 2013, Women Who Dared Award, Nat. Coun. Women, 2013, Champion for Social Change award, Tex. Assn. Sexual Assault, 2013, Judy Coyle Tex. Liberty award, Assn. nl. Educators, Horizon award, Christian Life Commn.; named of Yr., Tex. Monthly, 2009, Legislative Crime Fighter of the mbined Law Enforcement Associations of Tex. (CLEAT), amed one of 12 State Legislators to Watch in 2012, Governing 012. Democrat. Avocations: rugby, bicycling. Office: Newby LLC 600 W 6th St Ste 300 Fort Worth TX 76102 also: PO Box Capitol Station Austin TX 78711 also: 707 W Vickery Blvd Ste rt Worth TX 76104-1197 Office Phone: 817-332-3338, 512- 0, 817-878-2900. Office Fax: 512-475-3745, 817-332-1230, 3-2950.*

, WILLIAM ALLISON, II, retired lawyer; b. High Point, y 2, 1942; s. Robert Dorsey and Frances Elizabeth (Taylor) D.; abeth Gray Heefner, June 18, 1966; children: Sarah Scott, th Taylor. AB in Econs., U. N.C., 1964; LLB, Duke U., 1967; Taxation, NYU, 1968; M in Landscape Architecture, NC . Sch. Design, 2007—. Bar: N.C. 1967. Assoc. Womble Sandridge & Rice, Winston-Salem, NC, 1968-72, ptnr., 2005; landscape architecture technician Stimmel Assocs. PA, . Trustee NC Sch. Arts, Winston-Salem, vice chmn., 1990, 1992—96, NC Film Coun., 1994—95, Winston-Salem Pied- riad Film Commn., 1993—96; trustee The Penland (NC) Sch., 2005, vice chmn., 2000, chmn., 2001—02; trustee Winston ate Univ. Found., 2001—04, NC Audubon, 2003—04, Piemdut Conservancy, 2008—. Democrat. Avocations: hiking, travel, , Office Phone: 336-464-0067 ext. 138.

, WILLIAM EUGENE, federal judge; b. Winfield, Ala., Aug. 6; s. A. L. and Addie Lee (Lenahan) Davis; m. Celia Chalaron, 1963. JD, Tulane U., 1960; BS, Samford U., 2006. Bar: La. Assoc. Phelps Dunbar Marks Claverie & Sims, New Orleans, 64; ptnr. Caffery Duhe & Davis, New Iberia, La., 1964—76; US Dist. Ct., Lafayette, La., 1976—83, US Ct. Appeals (5th afayette, 1983—. Recipient Order of the Coif. Mem.: ABA, ne Assn. US, La. Bar Assn. Republican. Office: US Ct Appeals fayette St Ste 5100 Lafayette LA 70501-6883 Office Phone: 3-5280.

S, WILLIAM W., SR., computer company executive; BS, Southern U., Baton Rouge, La. Founder, CEO Pulsar Data Sys., n, Md., 1983—99; chmn. Spectrum Solutions Group, Inc. SRA International Inc 4300 Fair Lakes Ct Fairfax VA 22033

S, YVONNE, state legislator; b. Odessa, Tex., Feb. 4, 1955; d. and Ida Mae (Spivey) Davis. BS, U. Houston. Pers. clk. Shell ., Houston, 1974—77; vol. coord. to rep. Dick Slack Tex. of Reps., Odessa, Tex., 1977; rschr. to senator E. L. Short Tex. Senate, Austin, 1978—79; legis. asst. to Rep. Jim Mattox US of Representatives, Dallas, 1979—82, asst. to Rep. John Bryant DC, 1983—86; adminstrn. asst. Dallas County Commr. Ct., -86; campaign cons. to mayor Annette Strauss Office of Mayor, , 1986; Dallas coord. Mike Dukakis for Pres., 1987—88; ign cons. to councilman Charles Tardy, 1988; polit. dir. gen. n Dallas County Dem. Com., 1988; committeewoman Tex. Dem. Exec. Com., 1986—; polit. cons. YD Assoc., 1986—; bus. owner; mem. Dist. 111 Tex. House of Representatives, -. Recipient Precinct award, Progressive Voters League, 1986, award, Bus. & Profl. Women, 1987. Mem.: Dallas County Dem. n (auditor), West Dallas Cmty. Ctrs. (bd. dir.), Met. Bus. & Women Clubs (co-chmn.govt. affairs 1985), NAACP Dallas Chpt. (bd. mem.). Democrat. Office: 5787 S Hampton Rd Ste 447 Dallas TX 75232 also: Room CAP 1N.08 Capitol PO Box 2910 Austin TX 78768 Office Phone: 214-941-3895, 512-463-0598.

DAWES, ALAN S., automotive company executive; B in Applied Math., Harvard U., 1977, MBA, 1981. Asst. treas. Chase Manhattan Bank, 1977-80; fin. analyst GM, NYC, 1981-83, mgr. overseas borrowings, 1984, dir. overseas fin. analysis, 1985, dir. financing, investments and fin. planning, 1986, gen. dir. Treasurer's Office, 1987, asst. treas., 1988-91, asst. comptr. Detroit, 1991; fin. dir. Automotive Components Group, 1992; GM v.p., gen. mgr. Delphi Chassis Systems (formerly Delco Chassis Systems); CFO Delphi Chassis Systems, 1998; CFO, exec. v.p. Delphi Automotive Systems Corp., Troy, Mich., 1998—2005. Dir. AutoNation Inc., 2003—. Named Fin. Exec. of Yr. Automotive News Industry All Stars, 1999. Mem. Harvard Bus. Club. Office: AutoNation Inc 110 Southeast 6th St Fort Lauderdale FL 33301

DAWES, ROBERT LEO, mathematician, consultant; b. Big Spring, Tex., Mar. 5, 1945; s. William Robert and Josephine Melloo (Duflot) D.; m. Rosemary Mae Nelson, Oct. 10, 1970; children: Sara Michelle, Karen Melissa. BS in Math., Tex. Tech U., 1966, MS in Math., 1968; PhD in Math., U. Tex., 1977. Mem. tech. staff Tex. Instruments, Inc., Dallas, 1975-81; sr. specialist E-Systems, Inc., Garland, Tex., 1981-85; pres. Martingale Rsch. Corp., Allen, Tex., 1985-94; asst. prof. math. Hampton (Va.) U., 2002—04; pres. QED Corp., Bedford, Tex., 1995—2006; co-founder, chief scientist Advanced Receiver Techs. LLC, Dallas, 2006—. Founder, chair Metroplex Inst. Neural Dynamics, Dallas, 1986-90. Mem. city coun. City of Parker (Tex.), 1987-99. Lt. USNR, 1968-71. Mem. (sr.) IEEE (chmn. Dallas chpt. Acoustics, Speech and Signal Processing Soc. 1988), Internat. Neural Network Soc. (chair math. and theory spl. interest group 1990-92). Avocation: quantum mechanics. Home: 2217 Bedford Cir Bedford TX 76021

DAWKINS, DEBORAH JEANNE, state legislator; m. Craig Dawkins; 3 children. Mem. Dist. 48 Miss. State Senate, 2000—. Mem.: Am. Assn. U. Women, Miss. Heritage Assn., U. Southern Miss. Alumni Assn., League Women Voters, Miss. Fedn. Dem. Women, Miss. Wildlife Fedn., Coast Conservation Assn., Gulf Restoration Network (chair steering com.), Eagle Club. Democrat. Episcopalian. Mailing: Senate 442-RB PO Box 1018 Jackson MS 39215-1018 Home: 111 Lang Ave #3 Pass Christian MS 39571 Home Phone: 228-452-5182; Office Phone: 601-359-2936, 601-359-3237. Office Fax: 601-359-2879. Business E-Mail: ddawkins@senate.ms.gov.

DAWKINS-HAIGLER, DEE, state legislator; b. Jan. 31; m. David H. Haigler; children: Christopher, Christyn, Hannah, Joshua. Attending Ph.D. program, Clark Atlanta U. Pres./owner DDH & Assoc.; mgr. GOTV programs in Southeast for Clinton/Gore presdl. team; instr., grad. tchg. asst. & adj. prof. Clark Atlanta U., 1999—2001; state field/polit. dir. for Dem. Nat. Com. chmn. Howard Dean presdl. team SC, 2004; lead advance coord. in Southeast for Kerry/Edwards team, 2004; mem. Dist. 93 Ga. House of Reps., 2008—. Former pres. PTA & chmn. Academic Com. Martin Luther King Jr. High Sch.; vol. PTA mem. Salem Middle Sch., Murphey Candler Elem. Sch.; min. African Meth. Episcopal Ch. Democrat. Office: 6050 Kingston Wood Way Lithonia GA 30038 also: Ga House of Reps 607 Coverdell Legis Office Bldg Atlanta GA 30334 Office Phone: 404-656-0287. Business E-Mail: dee.dawkins-haigler@house.ga.gov.

DAWSON, ANDRE NOLAN, professional sports team executive, retired professional baseball player; b. Miami, Fla., July 10, 1954; m. Vanessa Turner, Dec. 16, 1978; children: Darius, Amber. Grad., Fla. A&M U., Tallahassee. Outfielder Montreal Expos, 1975-87, Chgo. Cubs, 1987-92, Boston Red Sox, 1992-94, Miami Marlins (formerly Fla. Marlins), 1994—96, spl. asst., 2000—. Recipient Gold Glove award, 1980-85, 87, 88, Silver Slugger award, 1980, 81, 83, 87, Hutch award, 1994; named Nat. League Rookie of Yr., 1977, Nat. League MVP, 1987; named to Nat. League All-Star Team, Maj. League Baseball, 1981-83, 87-91, Nat. Baseball Hall of Fame, Baseball Writers Assn. America, 2010. Achievements include leading the National League in: extra base hits, 1982, 1983; hits, 1983; home runs, runs batted in, 1987; intentional walks, 1990. Office: Miami Marlins 501 Marlins Way Miami FL 33125

DAWSON, CARI K., lawyer; AB, Princeton U., NJ, 1990; JD, Harvard U., Mass., 1993. Bar: Ga. Law clk. to hon Emmet G Sullivan US Ct. of Appeals (DC cir.); ptnr. Alston & Bird LLP, Atlanta, mem. diversity com., past mem. hiring, pro bono and associates com., chair class action practice team for litig. & trial practice group. Contbr. articles to profl. jours. Bd. dirs. Atlanta Symphony Orch.; bd. trustees Woodruff Arts Ctr. Named a Ga. Super Lawyer, Atlanta mag., 2004, Ga. Rising Star, Super Lawers, 2005—07; named one of 16 Lawyers Under 40 on the Rise, Fulton County Daily Report, 2003, Top 50 Up and Comers Under 40, Atlanta Bus. Chronicle, 2004, Best Lawyers in America, 2009, 2011; named to People on the Move, Multicultural mag., 2006, The 45 Under 45, The American Lawyer, 2011. Mem.: ABA, Nat. Bar Assn., Atlanta Bar Assn., Leadership Atlanta. Office: Alston & Bird LLP One Atlantic Ctr 1201 W Peachtree St Atlanta GA 30309-3449 Office Phone: 404-881-3449. Office Fax: 404-253-8567. Business E-Mail: cari.dawson@alston.com.

DAWSON, CARROLL R., retired professional sports team executive; b. Alba, Tex., May 3, 1938; Student, Paris Jr. Coll.; grad., Baylor U., Waco, Tex., 1960. Asst. coach Baylor U., head coach, 1973—77; asst. coach Houston Rockets, 1980—96, gen. mgr., 1996—2007; exec. v.p. basketball Houston Comets. Named to Paris Jr. Coll. Hall of Fame, Baylor U. Hall of Fame, Tex. Assn. Basketball Coaches Hall of Fame, Tex. Sports Hall of Fame, 2003.

DAWSON, EDWARD JOSEPH, diversified financial services company executive; b. Rochester, Pa., Apr. 1, 1944; s. Ralph Edward and Evelyn May (Riggle) Dawson; m. Lynda Sue Weir, 1975; 5 children. BS in Indsl. Mgmt., Carnegie Mellon U., Pitts., 1966; MBA in Fin., U. Chgo., 1968. Lic. securities broker/dealer, real estate broker. Computer sys. & corp. fin. analyst Tex. Instruments Corp., Dallas, 1968-70, product planning mgr., digital systems divsn., 1970-72, mgr. comml. equipment bus. objective, 1972-74, mktg. mgr., electronic watch divsn., 1975-76, mktg. mgr., home video systems, 1976-77; sr. v.p. ops. & mktg. Capital Alliance Corp., Dallas, 1977-80, exec. v.p. merger & acquisitions, 1980-81, chmn., pres., CEO, 1981—. Instr. Bus. Leadership Ctr., So. Meth. U. Cox Grad. Sch. Bus., 1999—. Author: (books on mergers & acquisitions) How to Successfully Sell Your Corporation, Trust in Business and Other Transactions:Who and When, Classes Taught at SMU: Deals 101, Deals 301, Power Negotiating in Merger and Acquisition Transactions. Mem. entrepreneurship adv. coun. Carnegie Mellon U., 1998—. Mem.: M&A Internat. Inc. (sec. 1988—89, v.p. 1989-90, 1996-97, pres. 1990-91, 1997-98), Beta Theta Pi, Omicron Delta Kappa. Office: Capital Alliance Corp 2777 N Stemmons Fwy Ste 1220 Dallas TX 75207-2293 Home: 685 Knob Hill Ct Argyle TX 76226 Office Phone: 214-638-8280. Office Fax: 214-638-8009. Business E-Mail: ed.dawson@cadallas.com.

DAWSON, KATON EDWARDS, former political organization administrator; b. Columbia, SC, Feb. 29, 1956; m. Candy Dawson; children: Anna, Katon Jr. Grad., U. SC. Pres., gen. mgr. Burns Auto Parts and Supply, Inc.; precinct committeeman Richland County Rep. Party, 1991, vice chmn., 1993; chmn. SC Rep. Party, 2002—09. Vol. Harnett for Lt. Gov., 1986, Glese for Solicitor, 1994, Osborne for Lt. Gov., 1998; mem. statewide steering com. Peeler for Lt. Gov., 1994; statewide fin. chmn. Harnett for Gov., 1994; mem. Richland County steering com. Beasley for Gov., 1998. Mem. Trenholm Rd. United Meth. Ch.; mem. Ten Yr. Planning Commn. Richland Sch. Dist. 1, parents rep., elected chairperson, Gifted Talented Prog. Republican.

DAWSON, MURIEL AMANDA (MANDY DAWSON), state legislator; b. Ft. Lauderdale, Fla., July 18, 1956; d. Clifford and Altemease (Laws) Hardy; divorced; children: Shatereas (Tibby), Colongie, Ashley. Student, Fla. A&M U., 1975—80; degree in liberal arts, Barry U. Legis. asst. Fla. Ho. of Reps., Ft. Lauderdale, 1988-92, state legislator Dist. 93, 1992-98; Fla. State Senator, Dist. 30 Fla. State Senate, 1998—2002, Fla. State Senator, Dist. 29, 2003—. Mem. budget subcom. on transp. and econ. devel., commerce and econ. opportunities, health, aging and long-term care, regulated industries, apportionment and redistricting coms. Chairperson Fla. Commn. Minority Health, 1993-95; mem. children, families and health com. Nat. Conf. State Legis., 1995-96; co-vice chair Fla. Women's Legis. Caucus, 1995-96, mem. select com. on telecom., 1994-95; assoc. trustee Bethune-Cookman Coll., 1994; mem. north area adv. bd. Sch. Bd. Broward County, 1992—; mem. health care task force Nat. Black Caucus of State Legislators, 1993—; mem. Fla. Conf. Black State Legislators, 1992—; bd. dirs. Broward County Urban League, Ft. Lauderdale, 1994—, Friends of Children, Youth and Families, Ft. Lauderdale, 1994, Voice of Choice Adv. Bd., 1995, Ft. Lauderdale Children's Theatre, 1994-96, Healthy Mothers/Healthy Babies Coalition of Broward County, 1993—, Minority Bus. Enterprise, 1991-92, Child Care Connection; mem. exec. adv. bd. Nat. Black Police Assn., 1994; adv. bd. Child Care Connection, 1992—; founding mem. Multicultural Women's Issues Group, 1993; mem. Broward Healthy Start Coalition, 1993—, Women's Polit. Caucus, Gwen Cherry chpt., 1990—, Ctrl. Broward Dem. Club, 1990—, Boisey Waiters Black Caucus Dem. Club of Broward County, 1990—, Young Dems. of Broward County, 1990—, Greater Ft. Lauderdale Dem. Club; founder Positive Images, 1996—; vice chair Broward County Legis. Del.; chmn. Nat. Task Force on Health Care Reform, Nat. Conf. Black State Legislators, 1999. Recipient Merit award M.A.D.D., 1991, Woman of the Yr. award Fla. Fedn. Bus. and Profl. Women, 1992, Competitive Edge Program award Broward C.C., 1991-92, 92-93, Trailblazer of Yr. award Broward County Young Dems., 1993, Margaret Roach Leadership award Broward County Urban League, 1993, Hon. McKnight Achiever award, 1993, Outstanding Svc. award Sickle Cell Disease Found. of Broward County, 1993, 94, With the Multitude of Her Being tribute African Am. Women of South Fla., 1993, Ashanti Cultural Arts Cmty. Svc. award, 1994, Woman of Distinction award Women's Polit. Caucus Gwen Cherry chpt., 1994, Impact award New Rep. Club of Broward County, 1994, Legis. Advocate award Fla. Assn. Cmty. Health Ctrs., Inc., 1994, Humanitarian of the Yr. award Sunshine Health Ctr., 1994, Legis. Roll Call award Fla. C. of C., 1993, 94, Legis. award Fla. Assn. C.C.'s, 1994, Legislator of the Yr. award Fla. Coll. Emergency Physicians, 1995, Commendation for Svc. award Ft. Lauderdale Mayor Jim Naugle and City Commrs., 1995, Advocate Appreciation award Broward County Walk a Mile for Edn., 1996, Advocate award Broward Pediat. Soc., 1996, Elderly Advocate award N.W. Federated Women's Club, 1996, Criminal Justice Image award Cmty. Reconstrn. Inst., 1998, Govt. award Family Ctrl., Inc., 1998, Alpha award Alpha Phi Alpha, 1999, African-Am. Achievers award JM Family Enterprises, Inc., 1999, Women and Children Advocacy award Greater Fla. region B'nai B'rith Internat., 1999, Trailblazer award Palm Beach County Urban League, 1999, Lifesaver award First Call for Help of Broward County, 1999, award of excellence Nostalgia in Gold, 1999, Elaine Gordon Lifetime Achievement award Bus. & Profl. Women of Fla., 1999, Disting. Legislator award Fla. Legal Svcs. Inc., 1999, Senator of Yr. award Fla. Assn. Rehabilitative Facilities, 1999, Great Svc. award Women's Pastoral Alliance, 2000, Outstanding Cmty. Svc. award North Broward NAACP, 2000. Mem. NOW, NAACP (subscribing life mem.), Bus. and Profl. Women (Woman of the Yr. 1995), Broward Assn. Black Social Workers (founding mem.), Optimists, Kiwanis, Order of Ea. Star., Democrat. Baptist. Avocations: reading, writing short stories for children, travel. Office: 419 NW 17th Ave Fort Lauderdale FL 33311

DAWSON, ROBERT TOOMBS, federal judge; b. El Dorado, Ark., 1938; BA, U. Ark., 1960, LLB, 1965. Pvt. practice atty., Fort Smith, Ark., 1965—98; judge US Dist. Ct. (western dist.) Ark., 1998—2009, sr. judge, 2009—. Mem. US Army, 1961—62, mem. Ark. Nat. Guard US Army, 1962—65. Office: PO Box 1624 Fort Smith AR 72902-1624 Office Phone: 479-783-2898.

DAY, JASON, professional golfer; b. Beaudesert, Australia, Nov. 12, 1987; m. Ellie Harvey, 2009. Profl. golfer PGA Tour, 2006—, PGA Tour Australasia. Mem. internat. team Presidents Cup, 2011. Achievements include Nationwide Tour wins: Legend Financial Group Classic, 2007; PGA Tour wins: HP Byron Nelson Championship, 2010. Office: c/o PGA Tour 100 PGA Tour Blvd Ponte Vedra Beach FL 32082

DAY, JOHN H., physicist; b. Savannah, Ga., June 5, 1952; s. John H. and Elsie M. (Gilliard) D.; m. Agnes A. Lasiter, Mar. 10, 1973 (div.); 1 child, Teresa D.; m. Yardyne Jackson, Feb. 25, 2006; 1 child (step), Gregory Proctor. BS in Physics, Bethune-Cookman Coll., Daytona Beach, Fla., 1973; MS in Physics, Howard U., Washington, 1976, PhD in Physics, 1982. Engr. Martin Marietta Aerospace Corp., Orlando, Fla., 1973; physicist Nat. Bur. Stds., Gaithersburg, Md., 1974—78, U.S. Geol. Survey, Reston, Va., 1979—82; engr. energy conversion sect. NASA/Goddard Space Flight Ctr., Greenbelt, Md., 1982—88, sect. head, 1988—90, asst. br. head space power br., 1990—92, br. head, 1992—98, chief technologist applied engring. and tech. directorate, 1998—99, chief elec. engring. divsn., 1999—2010, acting chief engr. Engring. & Safety Ctr., 2010—12; physics instr. Ga. Perimeter Coll., 2012—. Mem. Interagy. Advanced Power Group, Washington, 1983-97; mem. NASA Historically Black Colls. Working Group, Washington, 1991-92; adv. coun. Auburn U. Ctr. Space Power & Advanced Electronics, 1996-98; adv. bd. Tex. A&M Ctr. for Space power, 1994-98, NASA rep. Dept. Def. Space Experiment Review Bd., 1998-99; engring. dept. adv. bd. Capitol Coll., 1999-2011. Mem. Pub. Schs. Math. Task Force, Prince George's County, Md., 1991-92. Grad. fellow Howard U., 1973, 74, 75, 79, NSF fellow, 1976, 77, 78; recipient Outstanding Performance cert. NASA, 1984-85, 87, 92-96, Internat. Cometary Explorer Group award NASA, 1985, Internat. Sun-Earth Explorer Group award NASA, 1987, NASA Performance Mgmt. and Recognition System awards 1989, 90, 91, 92, 93, Cosmic Background Explorer Group Achievement award NASA, 1990, Roentgen Satellite Group Achievement award NASA, 1991, Gamma Ray Observatory Group award NASA, 1992, Upper Atmosphere Rsch. Satellite Team award NASA, 1992, Goddard Exceptional Achievement award, 1993, Hubble Space Telescope Power System Anomaly Investigation Team award, 1994, Hubble Space Telescope Servicing Mission Sys. Rev. Team award, 1994, GGS Power Electronics Rev. Team award 1994, Landsat 7 Design Rev. Team Stream-

lining award, 1995, GOES-J NASA-Industry Team award, 1995, Xray Timing Explorer Power Sys. Team award, 1996, Exceptional Svc. medal, NASA, 1998, Corp. Recruitment award, 2005, Minority Univs. Program Disting. Svc. award, 2008, Tropical Rainfall Measuring Mission Group Achievement award, 1998, Engring. Directorate Mentoring Program award, 2001, Presdl. Meritorious Exec. award, 2003, Goddard Diversity and Equal Opportunity Honor award, 2010, NASA Small Bus. Program award, 2011. Mem. AAAS, IEEE Power Engring. Soc., AIAA, Am. Phys. Soc. Forum on Physics and Soc., Nat. Soc. Black Physicists, Am. Assn. Physics Tchrs., Sigma Pi Sigma, Alpha Kappa Mu, Phi Beta Sigma. Achievements include design and development of solar electric power systems for numerous NASA sci. satellites. Home: 2655 Almont Way Roswell GA 30076-3466 E-mail: john.day@gpc.edu.

DAY, JOHN T., academic administrator, dean; b. Poughkeepsie, NY, Mar. 1, 1948; s. John T. and Catherine M. Day; m. Sharon R. MacFarland, July 4, 1970; children: Caitlin A., Laura E., Nathaniel A. BA summa cum laude, Coll. of the Holy Cross, 1970; MA, Harvard U., 1971, PhD, 1977. Allston Burr sr. tutor Harvard U., Cambridge, Mass., 1976—79; from asst. to full prof. English St. Olaf Coll., Northfield, Minn., 1979—2002, assoc. dean for interdisciplinary studies, 1999—2002, asst. v.p. for acad. affairs, 2000—02; English prof. Roanoke Coll., Salem, Va., 2002, v.p. acad. affairs, dean, 2002—. Trustee Roanoke Higher Edn. Authority, 2002—. Editor: (collection of essays) Word, Church, and State: Tyndale Quincentenary Essays; book reviewer: Sixteenth Century Jour., author essays. Office: Roanoke College 221 College Ln Salem VA 24153

DAY, LAWRENCE C., auto parts executive; V.p., Auto Express Div. Montgomery Ward; pres., CEO Monro Muffler Brake, Inc., 1995—98; pres. TBC Corp., 1998—; exec. v.p., COO TBC Corp., 1998; CEO TBC Corp., 1999—, chmn., 2005—. Bd. dirs. Lund Internat., Inc. Home: 4300 Tbc Way Palm Beach Gardens FL 33410-4281 Office: TBC Corp 7111 Fairway Dr Ste 201 Palm Beach Gardens FL 33418 Office Phone: 561-227-0955. Office Fax: 901-541-3625.

DAY, TERRENCE A., otolaryngologist, educator; MD, U. of Okla., Okla. City, 1989. Resident otolaryngology La. State Univ. Med. Ctr., Shreveport, 1990—95; fellow craniomaxillofacial surgery Univ. Hosp., Bern, Switzerland, 1994; fellow head and neck oncologic surgery Univ. of Calif. Davis Med. Ctr., Davis, Calif., 1995—96; prof. otolaryngology - head and neck surgery College of Medicine Med. Univ. of SC, vice chair for clin. affairs dept. of otolaryngology - head and neck surgery. Co-author: (publs.) Head and neck cancer disparities in South Carolina: descriptive epidemiology, early detection, and special programs, 2006, Driving performance in patients with cancer in the head and neck region: a pilot study, 2007, Effect of body mass index on chemoradiation outcomes in head and neck cancer, 2008, Effectiveness of calcium hydroxylapatite paste in vocal rehabilitation, 2009, Use of alpha,25-dihydroxyvitamin D3 treatment to stimulate immune infiltration into head and neck squamous cell carcinoma, 2010, and numerous others. Office: Medical University of South Carolina Hollings Cancer Center 86 Jonathan Lucas St Charleston SC 29425 Office Phone: 843-792-0700.

DAYHOFF, DIANE, retail executive; BA in Polit. Sci., Northwestern U., 1977, MBA in Fin. & Acctg., 1979. CFO Birraporitti's Restaurant Inc.; staff v.p., fin. Continental Airlines, 1989—2003; v.p., investor rels. Home Depot, Inc., 2003, sr. v.p., investor rels., 2003—. Office: The Home Depot Inc 2455 Paces Ferry Rd NW Atlanta GA 30339-4024 Office Phone: 770-433-8211. Office Fax: 770-384-2356. E-mail: diane_dayhoff@homedepot.com.

DAYLEY, DARREN, air transportation executive; BBA, U. North Tex., 1989. V.p., tech., customer experience portfolio Sabre Holdings Corp., 1989—2001, American Airlines, Inc., 2001—03, Southwest Airlines Co., 2003—; various tech. leadership positions, including dir., data architecture, dir., reservations & ticketing sys. SW Airlines Co., sr. dir., reservations & ticketing sys., sr. dir., eCustomer Technologies. Office: Southwest Airlines Co 2702 Love Field Dr Dallas TX 75235 Office Phone: 214-792-4000. Office Fax: 214-792-5015. Business E-Mail: darren.dayley@wnco.com.

DAYTON, EVERETT BRITT, consumer products company executive; Joined Lowe's Companies, Inc., 2003, v.p. store delivery fleet ops., sr. v.p. info. tech. bus. mgmt., 2011—. Office: Lowe's Companies Inc 1000 Lowe's Blvd Mooresville NC 28117

DEACON, JOHN C., lawyer; b. Newport, Ark., Sept. 26, 1920; BA, U. Ark., 1941, JD, 1948. Bar: Ark. 1948. Ptnr. Barrett & Deacon, Jonesboro, Ark. Commr. from Ark. to Nat. Conf. Commrs. on Uniform State Laws, 1966—, chmn. exec. com., 1977-79, pres. 1979-81. Recipient Ark. Outstanding Lawyer-Citizen award, 1973. Fellow Am. Coll. Trial Lawyers, Internat. Acad. Trial Lawyers (bd. dir. 1978-84), Southwestern Legal Found. (trustee 1975-95, chmn. Research Fellows 1983-85); mem. ABA (chmn. sect. bar activities 1967-68, Ark. del. 1967-79, bd. govs. 1980-83, 92-93, chair sr. lawyers divsn. 1994-95), Craighead County Bar Assn. (pres. 1968-69), N.E. Ark. Bar Assn. (pres. 1966-68), Ark. Bar Assn. (pres. 1970-71, Legacy award 2006), Am. Counsel Assn. (pres. 1974-75), Am. Bar Found. (pres. 1994-96), Internat. Assn. Def. Counsel, Nat. Assn. R.R. Trial Lawyers, Delta Theta Phi. Office: PO Box 1700 Jonesboro AR 72403-1700 also: Barrett & Deacon PA 300 S Church St Jonesboro AR 72401-2911 Office Phone: 870-931-1700. E-mail: jdeacon@barrettdeacon.com.

DEAL, NATHAN (JOHN NATHAN DEAL), Governor of Georgia, former United States Representative from Georgia, lawyer; b. Millen, Ga., Aug. 25, 1942; m. Sandra Dunagan; children: Jason, Mary Emily, Carrie, Katie. BA, Mercer U., 1964, JD, 1966. Pvt. law practice, 1979—82; asst. dist. atty. N.E. cir. Hall County, Ga., 1970—71, judge, juvenile court Ga., 1971-72, atty., 1977—79; mem. Dist. 10 Ga. State Senate, 1981—93, pres. pro tempore, 1991—93; mem. US Congress from 9th Ga. Dist., 1993—2003, 2007—10, US Congress from 10th Ga. Dist., 2003—07, mem. US House Energy & Commerce Com., 2007—10; gov. State of Ga., 2011—. Mem. Congressional Boating Caucus, Congressional Caucus on Unfunded Mandates, Congressional Travel and Tourism Caucus, Congressional Vietnam-Era Veterans Caucus, Rural Health Care Coalition, Speaker's Immigration Task Force. Bd. trustees Mercer U.; adv. bd. mem. of honors programs N. Ga. Coll. and U. Capt. JAGC US Army, 1966—68. Republican. Office: Office of the Governor 206 Washington St Suite 203 State Capitol Atlanta GA 30334 Office Phone: 404-656-1776.*

DEALY, RICHARD P., oil and gas company executive; BBA in Acctg. & Fin. with honors, Ea. N.Mex. U., 1987. CPA. With KPMG LLP; joined Parker & Parsley, 1992, v.p., contr., 1995—97; contr. Pioneer Natural Resources Co., 1997—98, v.p., 1997—2004, chief acctg. officer, 1998—2004, exec. v.p., CFO, 2004—; exec. v.p., CFO, treas. Pioneer S.W. Energy Partners, LP, 2007—. Bd. dirs. Pioneer Natural Resources GP LLC, 2007—. Office: Pioneer Natural Resources Co Ste 200 5205 N O'Connor Blvd Irving TX 75039 Office Phone: 972-444-9001. Office Fax: 972-402-7023.

DEAN, BEALE, lawyer; b. Ft. Worth, Feb. 26, 1922; s. Ben J. and Helen (Beale) Dean; m. Margaret Ann Webster, Sept. 3, 1948; children: Webster Beale, Giselle Liseanne. BA, U. Tex., Austin, 1943, LLB, 1947. Bar: Tex. 1946, U.S. Dist. Ct. (no., we. and ea. dists.) Tex., U.S. Cir. Ct. (5th and 11th cirs.) 1952, U.S. Supreme Ct. 1954. Asst. dist. atty., Dallas, 1947-48; assoc. Martin, Moore & Brewster, Ft. Worth, 1948-50; mem. Martin, Moore, Brewster & Dean, 1950-51, Pannell, Dean, Pannell & Kerry (and predecessor firms), 1951-65; ptnr. Brown, Herman, Scott, Young & Dean, Ft. Worth, 1965-71, Brown, Herman, Scott, Dean & Miles, Ft. Worth, 1971-98, Brown, Herman, Dean, Wiseman, Liser & Hart, LLP, Ft. Worth, 1998—2003; sr. counsel Brown, Dean, Wiseman, Liser, Proctor & Hart, LLP, Ft. Worth, 2003—06, Brown, Dean, Wiseman, Proctor, Hart & Howell, LLP, Ft. Worth, 2007—. Spl. asst. Atty. Gen., Tex., 1959—61. With USAAF, 1942—45, ETO. Named Best Lawyers America, 1987—2009, Tex. Super Lawyer, Law and Polit., Tex. Monthly, 2003—09. Mem.: AAJ, ABA, Sgt. Inn, Eldon Mahon Inn Ct., Nat. Coll. Dist. Attys. (regent 1985—2005), Tex. Bar Found. (charter mem.), Am. Bar Found., State Bar Tex. (bd. dirs. 1973—75), Am. Coll. Trial Lawyers, Ft. Worth-Tarrant County Bar Assn. (past pres. 1971—72, Blackstone award 1991), Bar Assn. 5th Fed. Cir. and 11th Fed. Cir., Ft. Worth Club, Ridglea Country Club, Ft. Worth Boat Club. Presbyterian. Office: 200 Fort Worth Club Bldg 306 W 7th St Fort Worth TX 76102-4905

DEAN, CHARLES S., SR., state legislator; b. Jacksonville, Fla., May 31, 1939; s. Charles S. and Rema Y. Dean; m. Judy Baxter; children: Shannon Wright, Charles S. AA, Ctrl. Fla. CC., 1962; BS in Criminology-Police Adminstrn., Fla. State U., 1963; MS in Criminal Justice, Rollins Coll., 1976. Intern City of Tampa, Fla., 1963; investigator Fla. Installment Land Sales, 1964; dir. gen. services Citrus County Sch. Bd., Fla., 1965—80; juvenile counselor Citrus County Juvenile Ct., Fla., 1972—75; sheriff Citrus County, Fla., 1981—96; cattleman; mem. Dist. 43 Fla. House of Reps., Tallahassee, 2002—07; mem. Dist. 3 Fla. State Senate, Tallahassee, 2007—, majority whip, 2008—10, chair agr. com., mem. criminal justice com., gen. govt. appropriations com., govtl. oversight and accountability com., reapportionment com., regulated industries com. Mem. Inverness Elks #2522, Citrus Lodge Masons (past master), Tampa and Citrus Shrine Club, Egypt Temple Shrine, Ocala Scottish Rite Bodies, Marine Corps League, Citrus Detachment #819. Republican. Baptist. Office: 415 Tompkins St Inverness FL 34450 also: 311 Senate Office Bldg 402 S Monroe St Tallahassee FL 32399-1100 Office Phone: 352-860-5175, 850-487-5017. Business E-Mail: dean.charles.web@flsenate.gov.

DEAN, EDWIN BECTON, entrepreneur; b. Danville, Va., Feb. 7, 1940; s. Edwin Becton and Lois (Campbell) D.; m. Deirdre Anne Jacovides, Aug. 16, 1964; children: Jennifer E., Kristin R., Brian N. BS in Physics, Va. Poly. Inst. and State U., 1963, MS in Math., 1965; postgrad., George Washington U., 1974-77; cert. profl. study engring. mgmt., Old Dominion U., 1998. Technician, assoc. engr. Johns Hopkins U. Applied Physics Lab., Laurel, Md., 1959-64; physicist, mathematician, electronic engr., and ops. rsch. analyst Naval Surface Warfare Ctr., Silver Spring, Md., 1964-79; owner, mgr. Gen. Bus. Svcs. and Beta Systems, Virginia Beach, Va., 1979-84, Virginia Beach Communique Inc., Virginia Beach, Va., 1980-81; registered rep. First Investors Corp., Arlington, Va., 1971-85; dir. Tips Club of Virginia Beach, Inc., 1980-82; computer specialist Naval Supply Systems Command, Norfolk, Va., 1982-83; head cost estimating office NASA Langley Rsch. Ctr., Hampton, Va., 1983-90, tech. resource mgr. Space Exploration Initiative Office, 1990-94, sr. rsch. engr. multidisciplinary optimization br., 1994-98; owner DFV Group, Inc., Va. Beach, 1996—98, pres., 1999—2002, cons., 2006—. Presenter in field; distbr. Shaklee, 1999—. Contbr. articles to profl. jours. Recipient Lifetime Achievement award, NASA, 2008, fellow, 1963-65. Mem. IEEE, Assn. for Computing Machinery, Am. Soc. for Quality Control, Am. Assn. Cost Engrs., Internat. Neural Network Soc., Internat. Coun. Sys. Engring., Internat. Cost Estimating & Analysis Assn., Sigma Pi Sigma, Pi Mu Epsilon, Phi Kappa Phi.

DEAN, KARL, Mayor, Nashville; b. Sioux Falls, SD, Sept. 20, 1955; m. Anne Davis; children: Rascoe, Frances, Wallen. BA, Columbia U., 1978; JD, Vanderbilt U., 1981; grad. sr. execs. in state and local govt., Harvard U. John F. Kennedy Sch. Govt., 1999. Asst. pub. defender Govt. Nashville, Davidson County, Tenn., 1983-90, pub. defender, 1990-99; metro law dir. City of Nashville, 1999—2007, mayor, 2007—. Adj. prof., law Vanderbilt U. Office: Mayor's Office 100 Metro Courthouse Nashville TN 37201 Office Phone: 615-862-6000. Office Fax: 615-862-6040. Business E-Mail: mayor@nashville.gov.*

DEAN, RICHARD HENRY, surgeon, educator; b. Radford, Va., June 16, 1942; s. Howard Lee and Minnie Yates (Crowder) D.; children: Richard Lancaster, Harrison Blaylock, Howard Lee Alexander, Williams Cabler. BA, Va. Mil. Inst., 1964; MD, Med. Coll. Va., 1968. Diplomate Am. Bd. Surgery (bd. dirs. 1993—), Am. Bd. Gen. Vascular Surgery, Am. Bd. Plastic Surgery. Surg. intern Vanderbilt U. Hosp., 1968-69, surg. asst. resident, 1969-73, chief. surg. resident, 1973-74, asst. prof. surgery sch. medicine, 1975-77, assoc. prof. surgery, 1977-81, prof. surgery, 1981-86, head divsn. vascular surgery sch. medicine, 1978-86; vascular rsch. fellow, instr. surgery Northwestern U. Hosp, 1974-75; Richard T. Meyers prof. and chmn. surgery Bowman Gray Sch. Medicine Wake Forest U., Winston-Salem, NC, 1987-89, dir. divsn. surg. scis., chmn. dept. gen. surgery Bowman Gray Sch. Medicine, 1989-97, sr. v.p. health affairs, 1997—2001; dir. Wake Forest U. Baptist Med. Ctr., 1997—; pres. Wake Forest U. Health Scis., 2001—. Vis. prof. U. Vienna, Austria, 1980, U. NSW, Sydney, Australia, 1982, U. Queensland, Brisbane, Australia, 1984, U. Rochester (N.Y.) Med. Ctr., 1986, 2nd Internat. Symposium on Ischemia, Madrid, 1986, U. Health Scis., Bethesda, Md., 1987, East Carolina U., Greenville, N.C., 1987, Ga. Bapt. Med. Ctr., Atlanta, 1988, Roanoke (Va.) Meml. Hosp., 1988, Ea. Va. Med. Sch., Norfolk, 1988 (two lectures), Mayo Clinic, Rochester, Minn., 1989, Med. Coll. Va., Richmond, 1990, W.Va. U. Health Sci. Ctr., Charleston, 1990, Va. Vascular Soc., Hot Spring, 1990, First All-Union Congress Cardiovascular Surgery, Moscow, 1990, Carolinas Heart Inst., Charlotte, 1991, U. Miami Sch. Medicine, 1991, Allegheny Gen. Hosp., Pitts., 1992, Northwestern U. Med. Sch., Chgo., 1992, U. Minn., Mpls., 1992, Nat. Naval Med. Ctr., Bethesda, 1992, Emory U. Sch. Medicine/Emory Hosp., Atlanta, 1992, Internat. Symposium Hosp. Universitario, Madrid, 1993, Ruprect-Karls-Universitat Heidelberg, Germany, 1993, La. State U. Med. Ctr., Shreveport, 1993, U. N.C., Chapel Hill, 1993, U. Man., Winnipeg, Can., 1993, U. Cin. Med. Ctr., 1993; Paul Dudley White vis. prof. U. Sao Paulo and Campinas, Brazil, 1982; Deryl Hart lectr. Duke U. Med. Sch., 1991; mem. Coun. on Cardio-Thoracic and Vascular Surgery, 1990-91; dir. Am. Bd. Plastic Surgery, 1995—; guest lectr. in field. Editor: (with J.A. O'Neill Jr.) Vascular Disorders of Childhood, 1983, (with W.P. Ritchie and G. Strele Sr.) General Surgery, 1994, (with J.S.T. Jao and D.C. Brewster) Current Diagnosis and Treatment in Vascular Surgery, 1995; mem. editl. bd. Jour. Vascular Surgery, Annals of Vascular Surgery; contbr. numerous chpts. to books and articles to sci. and profl. jours. Recipient Superior Performance award, 1997. Fellow: ACS (N.C. chpt., cardiovascular com. 1987), Am. Heart Assn. (stroke coun., coun. high blood pressure rsch.); mem.: AMA, Nat. Libr. Medicine (bd. regents 2001—), H. William Scott, Jr. Soc. (sec. 1982—87, pres. 1988—89), S.E. Surg. Congress, So. Surg. Assn. (v.p. 1997—98), So. Med. Assn., Forsyth-Stokes-Davie County Med. Assn., So. Assn. Vascular Surgery (program com. 1982—85, exec. coun. 1985—88, pres.-elect 1988—89, pres. 1990—91), Va. Surg. Assn. (hon.), So. Calif. Vascular Surgery Soc. (hon.), Assn. Acad. Surgery (exec. coun. 1978—80, nominating com. 1980), Soc. Vascular Surgery (publs. com. 1992—, recorder), Soc. Univ. Surgeons, Internat. Soc. Surgery, Internat. Soc. Cardiovascular Surgery (vis. prof. First Sci. Congress 1992), Am. Surg. Assn. (adv. membership com. 1991—), Am. Bd. Surgery (cons. com. on vascular surgery 1986—92, dir. 1993—). Office: Wake Forest Univ Sch Medicine Medical Center Blvd Winston Salem NC 27157-0001 Home: 2551 Warwick Rd Winston Salem NC 27104-1943

DEAN, VINCE, state legislator; b. Jan. 7, 1959; children: Sallie Kate, Olivia. State rep. Dist. 30, Tenn., 2007—. Mem.: East Ridge Ministerial Assn., Tenn. Mcpl. League (pub. safety policy com.), East Ridge Edn. Com., Alhambra Shrine, East Ridge Masonic Lodge 755. Republican. Baptist. Office: 1633 John Ross Rd Chattanooga TN 37412-1476 also: 107 War Memorial Bldg Nashville TN 37243-0130 Office Phone: 615-741-1934. Office Fax: 615-253-0271. Business E-Mail: rep.vince.dean@capitol.tn.gov.

DEANE, RICHARD HUNTER, JR., (RICK DEANE), lawyer, former prosecutor; b. Oct. 18, 1952; BA cum laude, U. Ga., 1974, JD, 1977; LLM, U. Mich., 1979. Bar: Ga. 1977. Asst. US atty. (no. dist.) Ga. US Dept. Justice, Atlanta, 1980-88, chief gen. crimes sect., 1988-91, chief criminal divsn., 1991-94, US atty. (no. dist.) Ga., 1998—2002; magistrate judge US Dist. Ct. (no. dist.) Ga., Atlanta, 1994-98; ptnr. Jones Day, Atlanta, 2002—, co-chair Corp. Criminal Investigations practice. Named one of America's Leading Lawyers for Bus., Chambers USA, Legal Elite, Ga. Trend mag.; named to TIME mag.'s 100 List of Innovators, 2001. Mem.: American Coll. Trial Lawyers. Office: Jones Day 1420 Peachtree St NE Ste 800 Atlanta GA 30309-3053 Office Phone: 404-581-8502. Office Fax: 404-581-8330. Business E-Mail: rhdeane@jonesday.com.

DEANGELO, JOSEPH J., consumer products company executive; B in Acctg. and Econs., SUNY, Albany. Fin. and operating positions CL Marvin, PLC; fin. and operating position Ga. Pacific; with aerospace GE, with power generation, with plastics, with elec. distbn. and control, appliances COO, pres., CEO capital transport internat. pool and modular space; exec. v.p. Stanley Works, 2003—04; sr. v.p. PRO Bus. and Tool Rental Home Depot, Atlanta, 2004—05, sr. v.p. Home Depot Supply and PRO Bus. and Tool Rental, 2005, exec. v.p. Home Depot Supply, 2005—07, COO, 2007; CEO HD Supply, 2007—. Office: HD Supply 2455 Paces Ferry Rd Atlanta GA 30399

DEANO, EDWARD JOSEPH, JR., lawyer, state legislator; b. New Orleans, Jan. 17, 1952; s. Edward Joseph and Alice Evelyn (Lanusse) D.; m. Susan Kathleen Bailey, Mar. 17, 1990. BS, U. Southwestern La., 1973; JD, La. State U., 1976. Atty. City of Mandeville, La., 1980—83, 2010—; former prosecutor Mandeville Misdemeanor Ct.; ptnr. Deano & Deano, Mandeville; state rep. La. Ho. of Reps., Baton Rouge, 1984—96; town atty. Town of Abita Springs, 1996—. Mem. civil law com., 1984-88, mcpl. and parochial affairs com., 1984-88, commerce com., 1988-92, ways and means com., 1992—, ins. com., 1992-96; chmn. house sub-com. on recreation, 1984-88, subcom. econ. devel., 1988-92; bd. dir. Area Health Edn. Coun., Mandeville Trail Head; pres. Cultural Alliance Americas 2008-, Green Fund; v.p. Friends Dew Drop Jazz Hall. Past pres. St. Tammany Humane Soc., St. Tammany Taxpayer's Assn., Mandeville Horizons; charter mem. Habitat for Humanity; past mem. Mandeville Vol. Fire Dept.; past coord. asst. St. Tammany dist. Boy Scouts Am.; mem. Mandeville City Charter Commn.; founder Krewe of the Emerald Trapazoid, pres. Cultural Alliance America, 2008-; v.p. Friends of Dew Drop, 2008-09; mem. 1st Mandeville Charter Commn., 1986, 2nd Mandeville Charter Commn., 2008-. Named La. Conservationist of Yr. St. Tammany Sportsmen's League, 1985, La. Wildlife Fedn., 1995, Legislator of Yr. La. Preservation Alliance, 1988, Alliance for Good Govt., 1988, 89, La. Alliance for Mentally Ill, 1989, La. Assn. Justices of the Peace and Constables, 1989, 94; named to 25 Mem. Cmty. Hall Fame of Century, St. Tammany News Banner, 1999; recipient Gov.'s award. Mem. US Supreme Ct. Bar Assn., La. Bar Assn., Covington Bar Assn., Krewe of the Emerald Trapazoid. Democrat. Roman Catholic. Avocations: outdoors, historical research, travel, crabbing. Office: Deano & Deano 895 Park Ave Mandeville LA 70448-4920 Office Phone: 985-626-1001. Personal E-mail: deanoanddeano@bellsouth.net. Business E-Mail: eddeano@bellsouth.net.*

DEARING, REINHARD JOSEF, curator, retired city official; b. Bamberg, Fed. Republic of Germany, May 1, 1947; m. Michele Jack, Feb. 14, 1967 (div. Oct. 1980); 1 child, Lauren; m. Patricia Lee Pollack, Jan. 2, 1982; 1 child, Bradford. AA, La. State U., Baton Rouge, 1968, BA, 1975, MA, 1977, postgrad., 1979; PhD, Northwestern Interventional U., 2003. CPM, Tulane U., 1989. Adminstrv. officer La. Nat. Bank, Baton Rouge, 1972-75; tchg. asst. La. State U., 1975-79; adj. asst. prof. U. So. Miss., Natchez, 1977-79; chief of staff, chief adminstrv. officer City of Slidell, La., 1979—2007; ret., 2007; curator City of Slidell, 2007—. Cons. La. Mcpl. Assn., Baton Rouge, 1985-87. Author: The Waffen-SS: A Representative Study, 1977, General James Dearing and the Cause of the Confederacy, 2001, SS General Karl Wolff and his Italian Odyssey, 2003; contbr. articles to profl. jours. Mem. Gov.'s Mcpl. Policy Task Force, PJPHS sch. bd. Col. La. State Guard, 1984—96, col., 2003—07, ret., 2007. Named Hon. State Senator, La. Mem. La. Mcpl. Assn., Nat. League Cities, St. Tammany Mcpl. Assn., Am. Pub. Works Assn., La. State U. Alumni Assn. (dir. 1985-87), Assn. US Army, Am. Legion, VFW, Internat. City Mgrs. Assn., Mil. Order of Stars and Bars, Order of So. Cross, SCV. Independent. Avocations: historic research, fencing, racquetball, jogging. Office: City of Slidell PO Box 828 Slidell LA 70459-0828

DEARMAN, ANDREW J., III, utilities executive; b. 1953; Jr. engr. Ala. Power Southern Co., 1975, various exec. positions in power generation and delivery, divsn. v.p. Ala. Power, sr. v.p., chief tech. officer Southern Energy (now Mirant Corp.), exec. v.p., chief transmission officer, 2001. Office: Southern Co 30 Ivan Allen Jr Blvd NW Atlanta GA 30308

DE ARMENDI, FERNANDO J., cardiologist; MD, Miami U., 1972. Diplomate American Bd. Internal Medicine, 1976, American Bd. Internal Medicine-cardiovasc. disease, 1979, lic. Fla. Intern Univ. of Miami/Jackson Meml. Veterans Affair Hosp., Miami, 1973, resident internal medicine, 1975, fellow cardiovasc. disease, 1975—77; hosp. affiliation includes Mercy Hosp. Office: Mercy Hospital 3663 S Miami Ave Miami FL 33133-4237 Office Phone: 305-858-8550.*

DEAS, DEBORAH V., child and adolescent psychiatrist, educator; BS, Coll. Charleston, 1978; MPH, U. SC, 1979; MD, Med. U. SC, 1989. Diplomate Am. Bd. Psychiatry and Neurology- addiction psychiatry cert. number 1128, 1997, Am. Bd. Psychiatry and Neurology- adult psychiatry cert. number 40618, 1995, Am. Bd. Psychiatry and Neurology- adult psychiatry cert. number 40618, 2005, Am. Bd. Psychiatry and Neurology- child and adolescent psychiatry cert. number 3894, 1995, Am. Bd. Psychiatry and Neurology- child and adolescent psychiatry cert. number 3894, 2007. Lab specialist

Med. Univ. SC, Charleston, SC, 1977—79; adminstrv. resident/planner Sea Island Comprehensive Health Care Corp., John Island, SC, 1979; rsch. assoc. Univ. Iowa, 1979—81; fellow exec. leadership acad. medicine Drexel Univ., 2005—06, nat. adv. com. exec. leadership acad. medicine, 2006—; on-call physician dept. behavioral medicine St. Francis Xavier Hosp., 1990—92; cons. physician Therapeutic Divsn. Municipal Probate Ct., Charleston, SC, 1989—93; staff physician Fenwick Hall Alcohol and Drug Treatment Ctr., John Island, SC, 1990—94, physician coord./liaison, 1992—94; rsch. specialist II Med. Univ. SC, 1981—85, intern, 1989—90, resident psychiatry, 1990—92, fellow chidl and adolescent psychiatry, 1992—94, fellow substance abuse rsch., 1993—94, physician vol. emergency psychiatry mobile crisis, 1990—94, clin. instr. dept. psychiatry and behavioral sciences, 1993—94, dir. adolescent substance abuse/dual diagnosis inpatient svcs., 1994—97, asst. prof. psychiatry, 1994—2000, dir. adolescent substance abuse/dual diagnosis program, 1994—, assoc. prof. psychiatry, 2000—05, clin. adv. coll. medicine, 2000—, dir. post baccalaureate remedial edn. program coll. medicine, 2001—, assoc. dean coll. medicine admissions, 2001—, diversity officer coll. medicine, 2002—, prof. psychiatry, 2005—, sr. assoc. dean for diversity coll. medicine, 2007—. Reviewer drug abuse and addiction for med. students Am. Acad. Child and Adolescent Psychiatry Rsch. Fellowship, 1995—; examiner Am. Bd. Psychiatry and Neurology, 1996—. Editl. bd. The Am. Jour. Addictions, 2003—, Jour. Psychiatric Practice, 2003—. Recipient Assn. for Academic Psychiatry Jr. Faculty Devel. award, 1996, Psychaitry Golden Apple award for Outstanding Tchg. in Child/ Adolescent Psychiatry Fellowship Program, 1996—97; named Travel awardee Mentor, Am. Coll. Neuropsychopharmacology, 2003—04, Black Women of Excellence, Coll. Medicine Student Govt. Assn. and Office of Student Diversity, 2006, Outstanding Mentor award, Am. Acad. Child and Adolescent Psychiatry, 2005—07; named one of America's Top Doctors, 2006, Best Doctors in America, 2007. Mem.: Internat. Soc. for Biomedical Rsch. on Alcoholism, Nat. Med. Assn., Am. Acad. of Addiction Psychiatry, Am. Coll. Psychiatrists, Am. Acad. of Child and Adolescent Psychiatry (co-chair Jeanne Spurlock Substance Abuse Fellowship 2004—, ad hoc com. on editorship and publs.), Am. Coll. Neuropsychopharmacology, Am. Psychiatric Assn. (Diagnostic Statis. Manual IV task force, substance use disorder sect. 2005—, coun. on addiction). Office: Medical University of South Carolina 67 President St PO Box 250861 Charleston SC 29425-0742 Office Fax: 843-792-7353.

DEATHERAGE, JAMES, agricultural products executive; Gen. mgr. Prodrs. Coop. Assn., Bryan, Tex. Bd. dirs. Land O'Lakes, Inc., 2009—; chmn. legis. and govtl. affairs com. Tex. Agrl. Coop. Coun., sec., 2004—05, v.p., 2005—06. Recipient Torch Award, BBB, 2007. Office: Producers Cooperative Association 1800 N Texas Ave Bryan TX 77803 Office Phone: 979-778-6000. Office Fax: 979-778-0243. Business E-Mail: James_Deatherage@landolakes.com.

DEATON, CHAD C., oil and gas industry executive; married; 3 children. BS in Geology, U. Wyo. With Schlumberger Oilfield Svcs., 1976—99, exec. v.p., 1998—99, sr. adv., 1999—2001; pres., CEO Hanover Compressor Co., 2002—04; chmn., CEO Baker Hughes, Inc., Houston, 2004—08, chmn., pres., CEO, 2008—10, chmn., CEO, 2010—11, exec. chmn., 2011—. Bd. dirs. Baker Hughes Inc., 2004—, Carbo Ceramics, Ariel Corp. Mem.: Petroleum Equip. Suppliers Assn. Office: Baker Hughes Inc 3900 Essex Lane Houston TX 77027 Mailing: Baker Hughes Inc PO Box 4740 Houston TX 77210-4740

DEAVENPORT, EARNEST W., JR., retired chemicals executive; b. Macon, Miss., 1938; m. Mary Ann Deavenport; children: Lisa, Scott. BS in Chem. Engring., Miss. State U., 1960; MA in Mgmt., MIT, 1985. Chem. engr. Eastman Chemical Co., 1960, pres. Carolina divsn. S.C., 1982, asst. gen. mgr., 1985, chmn., CEO Kingsport, Tenn., 1994—2002; v.p. Kodak, 1985—89, pres., group v.p., 1989—94; non-exec. chmn. Regions Financial Corp., Birmingham, Ala., 2010—. Bd. dir. AmSouth Bancorp, 1999-2006, King Pharmaceuticals, Inc., 2000-, Acuity Brands, Inc., 2002-, Regions Financial Corp., 2006-Alfred P. Sloan fellow MIT; recipient Exec. Excellence award Chem. Mgmt. and Resources Assn., 1995. Mem. Chem. Mfg. Assn. (bd. dir. 1994—), Soc. Chem. Industry (exec. com. Am. sect., Chem. Industry medal Am. sect. 2002), NAE. Office: Regions Financial Corp 1900 Fifth Ave N Birmingham AL 35203

DEBAKEY, LOIS, science administrator, educator; b. Lake Charles, La. d. S. M. and Raheeja (Zorba) DeBakey. BA in Math., Tulane U., MA in Lit. and Linguistics, 1959, PhD in Lit. and Linguistics, 1963. Asst. prof. English Tulane U., 1963—64; asst. prof. sci. communication Tulane U. Med. Sch., 1963-65, assoc. prof. sci. communication, 1965-67, prof. sci. comm., 1967-68, lectr., 1968-80, adj. prof., 1981-92; prof. sci. comm. Baylor Coll. Medicine, Houston, 1968—. Mem. biomed. libr. rev. com. Nat. Libr. Medicine, Bethesda, Md., 1973-77, bd. regents, 1981-86, cons., 1986-, co-chmn. permanent paper task force, 1987-, lit. selection tech. rev. com., 1988-93, chmn., 1992-93, outreach planning panel, 1988-89; dir. courses in med. comm. ACS and other orgns.; trustee DeBakey Med. Found., 1995-; mem. exec. coun. Commn. on Colls. So. Assn. Colls. and Schs., 1975-80; mem. nat. adv. coun. U. So. Calif. Ctr. Continuing Med. Edn., 1981; mem. steering com. Plain English Forum, 1984; mem. founding bd. dirs. Friends Nat. Libr. Medicine, 1985-, chmn. med. media award of excellence com., 1992-, bd. dirs., 2009, Friends Tex. med. Ctr. Libr. Adv. Com., 2008-; with cmty. coun. Methodist DeBakey Heart & Vascular Ctr., 2008-; mem. adv. com. Soc. for Preservation English Lang. Lit., 1986; mem. nat. adv. bd. John Muir Med. Film Festival, 1990-92; mem. The Internat. Health and Med. Film Festival, Acad. of Judges, 1992-93; mem. adv. bd. U. Tex. at Austin Sch. Nursing Found., 1993-; cons. legal writing com. ABA, 1983-, Ency. Brit. Biomed. and Health Database, 1999-; former cons. Nat. Assn. Std. Med. Vocabulary; pioneered instrn. in sci. comm. in med. sch.; mem. editl. bd. Meth. DeBaker Cardiovasc. Jour., 2008-. Sr. author: The Scientific Journal: Editorial Policies and Practices, 1976; co-author: Medicine: Preserving the Passion, 1987; Medicine: Preserving the Passion in the 21st Century, 2004; mem editl. bd.: Tulane Studies in English, 1966-68, Cardiovasc. Rsch. Ctr. Bull., 1971-83, Health Comms. and Informatics, 1975-80, Forum on Medicine, 1977-80, Grants Mag., 1978-81, Internat. Jour. Cardiology, 1981-86, Excerpta Medica's Core Jours. in Cardiology, 1981—, Health Comm. and Biopsychosocial Health, 1981-82, Internat. Angiology, 1985—, Jour. AMA, 1988-2002. CV Network, 2003-; editl. bd. mem. Meth. Debakey Cardiovasc. Jour., 2008-; mem. usage panel Am. Heritage Dictionary, 1980—; cons. Webster's Med. Desk Dictionary, 1986; editl. advisor Ency. Brit.; contbr. articles on biomed. comm. and sci. writing, literacy, also other subjects to profl. jours., books, encys., and pub. press. With Found. for Advanced Edn. in Sci., 1977—. Recipient Harold Swanberg Disting. Svc. award, Am. Med. Writers Assn., 1970, Bausch & Lomb Sci. award, 1st John P. McGovern award, Med. Libr. Assn., 1983, 50 Outstanding Women, Houston Ctr. for Humanities, 1990—91, Outstanding Alumna award, Newcomb Coll., 1994, Svc. Recognition award for 40 yrs., Baylor Coll. Medicine, 2008, Proclamation award, Lois & Selma DeBakey Family Day, Houston, 2008, Selma & Lois DeBakey Lectrs. award, Meth. DeBakey Heart & Vascular Ctr., 2009; Endowed Med. Humanities scholarship, Baylor U. Waco, 2009. Fellow Am. Coll. Med. Informatics, Royal Soc. for Encouragement of Arts, Mfrs., and Commerce; mem. Internat. Soc. Gen. Semantics, Med. Libr. Assn. (hon.), Coun. Biology Editors (dir. 1973-77, chmn. com. on editl. policy 1971-75), Coun. Basic Edn. (spl. com. writing 1977-79), Assn. Tchrs. Tech. Writing, Dictionary Soc. N.Am., Nat. Assn. Sci. Writers, Soc. for Health and Human Values, Com. of Thousand for Better Health Regulations, Golden Key, Phi Beta Kappa.

DEBAR, DENNIS, state legislator; m. Kelley Porter; children: Nathan, Leilani. B, U. Ctrl. Fla., Orlando; JD, Miss. Coll., Clinton. Atty.; mem. Dist. 105 Miss. House of Reps., Jackson, 2012—. Mem.: NRA, Res. Officers Assn., Rotary Internat. Republican. Methodist. Office: Miss House of Reps PO Box 1018 Jackson MS 39215 Business E-Mail: ddebar@house.ms.gov.

DE BARBIERI, MARY ANN, not-for-profit management consultant; b. Winston-Salem, NC, May 1, 1945; d. Robert Carroll and Annie Louise (Neal) Hutcherson; m. Alfredo Emanuelle De B.; children: Maria Luisa, Riccardo Roberto. BA in Theatre Arts, Mary Washington Coll., 1967; student, Herbert Berghof Studio, 1967—69. With J. Walter Thompson, NYC, 1967-68; asst. to prodr. Norman Twain Prodns., NYC, 1968-69, Contemporary Theatre Co., NYC, 1971-74; co. mgr. Folger Theatre Group, Washington, 1974-77, bus. mgr., 1977-80; mng. dir. Shakespeare Theatre at the Folger, Washington, 1980-90; performing arts cons. Alexandria, Va., 1990-92; dir. The Found. Ctr., Washington, 1992-94; pres. De Barbieri and Assocs., 1994—. Adj. prof. arts mgmt. grad. program Am. U., 1994-99; treas. League of Washington Theatres, 1983-86; chair selection com. The Washington Post/Ctr. Non Profit Advancement Award for Excellence in Nonprofit Mgmt., 1997, 98, 99, mem. selection com. 1996-99, The Washington Post Grants in the Arts, 1997—; curriculum design cons., core faculty Choral Mgmt. Inst. of Chorus Am., 2002—; presenter in field. Bd. dirs. Washington Area Lawyers for Arts, 1984-94; bd. dirs. Cultural Alliance Greater Washington, 1986-96, v.p., 1990-96; bd. dirs. Nat. Soc. Fundraising Execs., 1993-96, v.p. edn., 1995, treas., 1996; bd. dirs. Ctr. for Nonprofit Advancement, 2000-06, pres., 2004, 05; chair Performing Arts Coun., Alexandria, Va., 1981-84; founder, first chair Alexandria Commn. for Arts, 1984-88, theater commr., 1984-94; contbr. to study of downtown stages for new theater in Washington, 1985; mem. panel Va. Commn. for the Arts, 1990-96, 2005—08, 2010-. Recipient Outstanding Svc. to Theatre Cmty. award League of Washington Theatres, 1990. Office: 525 Beauregard Dr SE Leesburg VA 20175 Office Phone: 703-777-3585. Business E-Mail: debarasso@aol.com.

DEBARTOLO, EDWARD JOHN, JR., real estate developer, former professional football team owner; b. Youngstown, Ohio, Nov. 6, 1946; s. Edward J. and Marie Patricia DeBartolo; m. Cynthia Ruth Papalia, Sept. 27, 1968; children: Lisa Marie, Tiffanye Lynne, Nicole Anne. Student, U. Notre Dame, 1964—68. With Edward J. DeBartolo Corp., Youngstown, Ohio, 1960—, v.p., 1972—76, exec. v.p., 1976—79, chief adminstrv. officer, 1979—94, pres., CEO, 1995—; owner San Francisco 49ers, 1977—97; chmn. bd. DeBartolo Realty Corp., 1994—; chmn., CEO DeBartolo Entertainment, Inc. Mem. Nat. Cambodia Crisis Com., 1980—; adv. coun. Nat. Assn. People with AIDS, 1992; trustee Youngstown State U., 1974—77; nat. adv. coun. St. Jude Children's Rsch. Hosp., 1978—, local chmn., 1979—80; chmn. local fund drive Am. Cancer Soc., 1975—; chmn. 19th Ann. Victor Warner award, 1985, City of Hope's Spirit of Life Banquet, 1986; apptd. adv. coun. Coll. Bus. Adminstrn. U. Notre Dame, 1988; bd. dirs. Cleve. Clinic Found., 1991; lifetime mem. Italian Scholarship League. With US Army, 1969. Recipient Man of Yr. award, St. Jude Children's Hosp., 1979, Boy's Town of Italy in San Francisco, 1985, Sportsman of Yr. award, Nat. Italian Am. Sports Hall of Fame, 1991, Cert. of Merit, Salvation Army, 1982, Warner award, 1986, Silver Cable Car award, San Francisco Conv. and Visitors Bur., 1988, NFL Man of Yr. award, Football News, 1989, Svc. to Youth award, Cath. Youth Orgn., 1990, Hall of Fame award, Cardinal Mooney High Sch., 1993; named one of Forbes 400: Richest Americans, 2006—. Mem.: Internat. Coun. Shopping Ctrs., Dapper Dan Club (bd. dirs. 1980—), Fonderlac Country Club, Tippecanoe Country Club. Office: Debartolo Corp 7620 Market St Youngstown OH 44512-6076 also: Debartolo Holdings 15436 N Florida Ave Ste 200 Tampa FL 33613-1226

DEBEAUBIEN, HUGO H., lawyer; b. Detroit, Sept. 20, 1948; s. Phillip Frances and June (Hesse) deB.; m. Mary Lazenby, Apr. 30, 1977; 1 child, Hugo Samuel. BS in Bus., Fla. State U., 1970; JD, Stetson U., 1973. Bar: Fla. 1973, U.S. Dist. Ct. (mid. dist.) Fla. 1974, U.S. Supreme Ct. 1978, U.S. Ct. Appeals (11th cir.) 1981. Asst. state atty. Fla. 9th Jud. Cir. Ct., Orlando, 1973-76; ptnr. Drage, deBeaubien, Orlando, 1976-79; ptnr., pres. Drage, deBeaubien, Knight & Simmons, Orlando, 1980-87, Drage, deBeaubien, Knight, Simmons, Romano and Neal, Orlando, 1987-98; ptnr. Drage, deBeaubien, Knight, Simmons, Mantzaris and Neal, Orlando, 1999—; pres. deBeaubien, Knight, Simmons, Mantzaris and Neal LLP, 2002—. Lectr. Fla. Bar Assn., 1981-83; bd. dir. Fla. Citrus Sports Assn., 1996—; dir. Workforce Advantage Acad., 2004-. Mem. Nat. Assn. Criminal Def. Lawyers, Fla. State U. Alumni Assn. (bd. dirs. 1986-93, sec. 1993-94, treas. 1995-96, v.p. 1996-97, chmn.-elect 1997-98, chmn. 1998-99), Univ. Center Club Tallahassee, Country Club Orlando. Republican. Methodist. Avocations: golf, tennis. Home: 1125 Belleaire Cir Orlando FL 32804-6703 Office: deBeaubien Knight Simmons Mantzaris & Neal LLP 322 N Magnolia Ave Orlando FL 32801-1609 Office Phone: 407-422-2454. E-mail: hhb66@dbksmn.com.*

DE BEDOUT, JUAN ERNESTO, paper company executive; b. Medellin, Colombia, 1945; children: Juan Manuel De Bedout, Nicolas De Bedout. BS in Indsl. Engring., Purdue U., 1967, MS in Indsl. Engring., 1968. Mng. dir. Kimberly-Clark Corp., 1981, mng. dir., Ctrl. America, 1988—91, gen. mgr., Latin Am. Ops., 1992—94, v.p., Latin Am. Ops., 1994—98, group pres., L.Am. Ops., 1999—. Bd. adv. Penn State Enterprise Integration Industry; bd. dirs. The North Face, Wrangler, V.F. Corp., 2000—. Mem., engring. adv. coun. Purdue U. Recipient Outstanding Indsl. Engr., Purdue U., 1998, Disting. Engring. Alumnus, 2000, Engring. Alumni Assn., 2002. Office: Kimberly Clark Corp 351 Phelps Dr Irving TX 75038 Office Phone: 972-281-1200. Office Fax: 972-281-1490. Business E-Mail: juan.debedout@kimberly-clark.com.

DE BEER, FREDERICK C., dean, internist, educator; arrived in USA, 1989; MD, U. Pretoria, South Africa; attended, Royal Postgraduate Med. Sch., London. Prof. medicine U. Stellenbosch, South Africa; prof. internal medicine U. Ky. Coll. Medicine, Lexington, positions including chief divsn. endocrinology and molecular medicine, vice chmn. dept. internal medicine, dir. grad. ctr. nutritional svcs., 1993—2003, chmn. dept. internal medicine, 2003—, Jack M. Gill prof. medicine, 2003—, v.p. clin. academic affairs, 2011—, dean, 2011—; chief of medicine Vets. Affairs Med. Ctr., Lexington. Contbr. articles to profl. jours., chapters to books. Office: University Ky Coll Medicine Office of Dean 138 Leader Ave Lexington KY 40506-9963 Office Phone: 859-323-6582. Business E-Mail: fcdebe1@uky.edu.

DEBERRY, JOHN J., state legislator; b. Feb. 5, 1952; m. Georgia DeBerry; children: Chevida, Victoria. State rep. Dist. 90, Tenn., 1995—; mktg. advertising exec. Mem.: NAACP, Boy Scouts America. Democrat. Church Of Christ. Office: 1207 Sledge St Memphis TN 38104 also: 26 Legislative Plaza Nashville TN 37243-0190 Office Phone: 615-741-2239, 901-725-0130. Office Fax: 615-253-0294. Business E-Mail: rep.john.deberry@capitol.tn.gov.

DEBNEY, GEORGE C., mathematical physicist; b. Beaumont, Tex., Feb. 19, 1939; BA, Rice U., 1961; PhD, U. Tex., 1967. Analyst TRW, Houston, 1966-68; prof. math. Va. Tech., Blacksburg, 1968-85; sr. mathematician ANSER, Arlington, Va., 1985-87; sr. scientist Schafer Corp., Arlington, Va., 1987-89; sr. scientist, chief sys. engr. SAIC, Arlington, Va., 1989—2010; pvt. cons., 2010—. Contbr. more than 25 articles on relativity and gravitation to profl. jours. Rsch. fellow Soc. for Engring. Edn., 1975, 76. Mem. AIAA, Am. Phys. Soc., Math. Assn. Am. Achievements include research in defense techniques, performance, architecture, technology, and systems engineering. Personal E-mail: debneyg@gmail.com.

DEBRECHT, SUSAN J., librarian; b. St. Louis, Aug. 10, 1951; d. Edward August and Edith (Keeney) DeB.; children: Brian, Katherine. BA in History, U. Ky., 1973; MLS, U. Mo., 1976. Children's libr. Louisville Free Pub. Libr., 1974-76, talking book libr. head, 1976-83; lower/mid. sch. libr. Ky. Country Day Sch., Louisville, 1983-84; children's libr. Emmet O'Neal Libr., Mountain Brook, Ala., 1984-86, asst. dir., 1986-89, dir., 1989—. Active, chair Jefferson County Pub. Libr.; mem. admissions com. United Way; exec. bd. Jefferson County Libr. Bd.; bd. dirs. Mountain Brook Libr. Found., 1993—, Ala. Ctr. for Book. Mem. ALA, Ala. Libr. Assn. (mem. publicity com. 1992-93, pub. libr. chair 1995-96, eminent libr. 2012), Rotary Internat. Roman Catholic. Office: Emmet O'Neal Libr 50 Oak St Birmingham AL 35213-4295 Office Phone: 205-879-0492.

DE BREMAECKER, JEAN-CLAUDE, geophysics educator; b. Antwerp, Belgium, Sept. 2, 1923; came to U.S., 1948, naturalized, 1963; s. Paul J.C. and Berthe (Bouché) De B.; m. Arlene Ann Parker, Nov. 29, 1952 (dec.); m. Ruth F. Baer, July 6, 1998 (dec.); children—Christine, Suzanne. MS in Mining Engring, U. Louvain, Belgium, 1948; MS in Geology, La. State U., 1950; PhD in Geophysics, U. Cal. at Berkeley, 1952. Research scientist, sr. research scientist Inst. pour la Recherche Sci. en Afrique Centrale, Bukavu, Congo, 1952-58; Boese postdoctoral fellow Columbia, 1955-56; postdoctoral fellow Harvard, 1958-59; faculty Rice U., Houston, 1959—, prof. geophysics, 1965-94, prof. emeritus, 1994. Research asso. U. Calif., Berkeley, 1966; vis. mem. Tex. Inst. for Computational Mechanics, U. Tex., Austin, 1977; vis. prof. U. Paris, 1980-81 Author: Geophysics, the Earth's Interior, 1985. Chmn. Citizens for McCarthy, Houston, 1968. Served with Belgian Army, 1944-45. Mem. Am. Geophys. Union, Fedn. Am. Scientists, Internat. Assn. Seismology and Physics of Earth's Interior (assoc. sec. gen. 1963-71, sec. gen. 1971-79). Home: 3115 Broadmead Dr Houston TX 77025-3819 Office: Rice U Dept Earth Sci Box 1892 Houston TX 77251 Office Phone: 713-348-4886. Business E-Mail: jcldebre@gmail.com.

DECAMPLI, WILLIAM MICHAEL, surgeon, researcher; b. Allentown, Pa., Dec. 7, 1951; s. William John and Bernadine Louise (Diehl) DeCampli; m. Kristi Lynn Peterson, May 29, 1989; children: Elissa Cale, William Grant. BS in Physics, MIT, 1973; MA in Astrophysics, PhD in Astrophysics, Harvard U., 1978; MD, U. Miami, 1982; surg. residency, Stanford U., 1982—92. Diplomate Am. Bd. Thoracic Surgery, 1993, Am. Bd. Surgery, 1989, Am. Bd. Med. Examiners, 1983. Attending surgeon Children's Hosp., Oakland, Calif., 1992—95, The Children's Hosp. of Phila., 1996—2004, The Children's Cardiac Ctr., Newark, N.J., 1996—2004; asst. prof. of surgery U. of Pa. Sch. of Medicine, Phila., 1997—2003; co-dir. Ctr. for Adult Congenital Heart Disease, Newark, 1997—2004; rsch. scientist Stokes Rsch. Inst., The Children's Hosp. of Phila., 1998—; assoc. prof. of surgery U. of Pa., Phila., 2003—; attending surgeon The Congenital Heart Inst., Orlando, Fla., 2004—; prof. surgery Coll. Medicine, U. Ctrl. Fla.; dept. surgery Arnold Palmer Hosp. Children. Mem. strategic planning U.S. space program NASA, Mass., 1982—84, mem. space life sciences strategic planning subcom., 1984—87, mem. radiation biology rev. team, 1987—88; mem. performance subcom. cardiovasc. health adv. panel N.J. Dept. of Health and Sr. Svs., Trenton, 2002—04; guest reviewer Jour. of Thoracic and Cardiovasc. Surgery, Annals of Thoracic Surgery, Circulation, Anesthesia and Analgesia. Author: (peer-reviewed publs.) Journal of Thoracic and Cardiovascular Surgery, Annals of Thoracic Surgery, Circulation, Annals of Surgery, and others, Astrophysical Jour., Icarus, Moon & Planets, and others, (book chpts.) Gardner and Spray's Operative Cardiac Surgery, Current Pediatric Therapy, Pediatric Cardiac Surgery Annual, Yearbook of Medicine 1996, Endovascular Surgery, The Human Quest of Space, and others; contbr. Surgeon internat. vol. med. orgn. Heart to Heart, Inc. Fellow Paul Harris, Rotary Internat., 2000, Carl and Leah McConnell Surg. Rsch. fellow, Stanford U., 1986, Chaim Weismann Rsch. fellow, Calif. Inst. of Tech., 1979-80, ACS, 1996—, Am. Coll. Chest Physicians, 1996—, Am. Coll. Cardiology, 2001—; scholar Lee A. Loomis scholar, Harvard U., 1973. Mem.: Congenital Heart Surgeons Soc., Norman E. Shumway Surg. Soc., Internat. Soc. Adult Congenital Cardiac Disease, Soc. Thoracic Surgeons, Am. Assn. Thoracic Surgery. Achievements include patents for #5571127, scalpel handle having retractable blade support and method of use; #5797879 adjustable vascular shunt for control of pulmonary blood flow and method of use; #6053891 apparatus and methods for providing selectively adjustable blood flow through a vascular graft; participation in the greatest distance land-to-sea rescue mission in the history of the U.S. Air Force, 1987; primary authored the first paper analyzing ten year followup of survivors of heart transplantation, reprinted in the 1996 Year Book of Medicine. Home: 314 Salvadore Square Orlando FL 32789 Office: Congenital Heart Institute 50 Sturtevant St Orlando FL 32806 E-mail: wdecampli@orhs.org.

DECARO, THOMAS C., retail executive; Various positions, mdse. planning, allocation, fin. Sanger Harris Dept. Stores, May Dept. Stores, The Ltd. Stores, The Disney Store; sr. v.p., mdse. planning, allocation Kohl's Dept. Stores, 1996—98; v.p., mdse. Walt Disney Co., 1998—2000; sr. v.p., inventory mgmt. Michaels Store, Inc., 2000—05; exec. v.p., supply chain Michaels Stores, Inc., 2005—. Office: Michaels Store Inc 8000 Bent Branch Dr Irving TX 75063 Office Phone: 972-409-1300. Office Fax: 972-409-1556. Business E-Mail: tdecaro@michaels.com.

DECENZO, DAVID A., academic administrator; m. Terri DeCenzo; 4 children. B in Economics, U. Md., College Park; M, PhD, West Va. U. Dir., partnership devel., coll., bus., economics Towson U., Md., 1992—2002; dean, E. Craig Wall, Sr., Wall Coll, Bus. Adminstrn. Coastal Carolina University, sr. v.p., academic affairs, provost, 2006—07, pres., 2007—. Bd. dirs. AVX Corp., 2007—. Office: AVX Corp Myrtle Beach SC 29578 Mailing: AVX Corp Box 867 Myrtle Beach SC 29578 Office Phone: 843-448-9411. Office Fax: 843-916-7751. Business E-Mail: ddecenzo@coastal.edu.

DECESARE, JIM, state legislator; b. July 10, 1966; m. Amy Bingham DeCesare; children: Brooke, Justin. Mem. Dist. 21 Ky. House of Reps., Ky., 2005—; founding mem. Gen. Assembly Sportsman Caucus; bd. dir. Bowling Green Warren County Jaycees, 1994—95, Big Brothers Big Sisters Of South Ctrl. Kent, 1999—2003; mem. Leadership Bowling Green Alumni Assn., 2003—, Prime Time

Events, 2003—, Warren March Of Dimes Walk America, 2002, Bowling Green Area Chamber Golf Challenge, 2002, Arthritis Found Jingle Bell Run, 2002—03; chmn. Barren County March Of Dimes Walk America, 2001. Mem.: Acad Country Music, Country Music Assn., Citizen's Police Acad, Leadership Bowling Green, Warren Co. Young Repubs. Republican. Methodist. Address: 136 Cedar Trail Ave Bowling Green KY 42101 Office: 424 G Capitol Annex Frankfort KY 40601 Office Phone: 502-564-8100 ext 660, 270-792-5779. E-mail: jim.decesare@lrc.ky.gov.

DE CESPEDES, JORGE L., pharmaceutical executive; b. Cuba; arrived in US, 1961; m. Yvonne M. de Cespedes; 3 children. BBA, Fla. Internat. U. Sales positions Smith Kline Labs., Miami; co-founder, pres. & COO Pharmed Group Corp., Miami, 2005—; co-founder, mng. ptnr. Astri Group, Miami, 2005—. Minority owner Bobcats Basketball Holdings LLC, 2004—. Office: Pharmed Group Corp 1201 W Peachtree St NW Ste 500 Atlanta GA 30309-3471 Office Phone: 305-592-2324. Office Fax: 305-591-9643.

DECHURCH, STEPHANIE J., pediatrician; b. Mt. Clemens, Mich., Mar. 31, 1974; m. James DeChurch. MD, U. Fla. Coll. Medicine, Gainesville, 2000. Resident, pediat. Miami Children's Hosp., Fla.; staff mem. South Fla. Pediat. Partners, 2000—, Baptist Children's Hosp., Miami, 2003—, South Miami Hosp., 2003. Office: South Fla Pediat Partners 7800 SW 87th Ave #C-350 Miami FL 33173 Office Phone: 305-271-4711. Office Fax: 305-271-8732.

DECKELMAN, WILLIAM L., JR., lawyer; b. Crossett, Ark., Aug. 19, 1957; s. William and Marion Deckelman; m. Lisa Deckelman. BA, Ark. State U., 1978, MBA, 1979; JD, U. Ark., 1981. Bar: Tex. 1982. Assoc. Winstead Sechrest & Minick, Dallas, 1981—85; with MTech Corp. (acquired by Electronic Data Systems Corp. in 1988), 1985—88; sr. v.p., gen. counsel, sec. Affiliated Computer Services Inc., Dallas, 1989—93, exec. v.p., gen. counsel, sec., 1993—95; mng. shareholder Munsch Hardt Kopf & Harr PC, Austin, Tex., 1996—2000; exec. v.p., gen. counsel, sec. Affiliated Computer Services Inc., Dallas, 2000—07, dir., 2000—03; corp. v.p., sec., gen. counsel Computer Sciences Corp., Falls Church, Va., 2008—. Mem.: State Bar Tex. Office: Computer Sciences Corp 3170 Fairview Park Dr Falls Church VA 22042

DECKER, MYRA ANNE, accounting professor; AS, Okla. City CC; BS, MS, Okla. State U. Pub. and pvt. sector acct.; prof. bus./acctg. Okla. City CC, 1981—. Participant U. Ctrl. Okla. Educators' Leadership Acad., Edmond, 2000. Recipient President's Excellence in Tchg. award, Okla. City CC, 2008; named Okla. Prof. of Yr., Carnegie Found. for Advancement of Tchg. and Coun. for Advancement and Support of Edn., 2009. Office: Okla City CC Divsn Bus Rm 2R2 7777 S May Ave Oklahoma City OK 73199-4444 Office Phone: 405-682-1611 ext. 7332. Business E-Mail: mdecker@occc.edu.

DECKER, NICOLE FRIEDEL, consumer products company executive; Attended, U. NC, Chapel Hill. Auditor KPMG Peat Marwick; internal auditor Tupperware Brands Corp., mgr., consolidation acctg., sr. mgr., strategy & bus. devel., v.p., investor rels. Office: Tupperware Brands Corp 14901 S Orange Blossom Trail Orlando FL 32837 Office Phone: 407-826-5050. Office Fax: 407-826-8874.

DECLUE, TERRY JOE, pediatric endocrinologist; MD, U. South Fla., 1982. Diplomate Am. Bd. Pediatrics-pediatric endocrinology, 2004. Resident pediat. Univ. of South Fla., Tampa, 1983—85, fellow pediatric endocrinology, 1985—87; hosp. affiliations include St. Joseph's Hosp., St. Joseph's Children's Hosp. Office: St Joseph's Children's Hospital Third Fl MAB 3001 W Martin Luther King Blvd Tampa FL 33607 Office Phone: 813-554-8420.*

DE COCK, KEVIN, public health service officer; b. Belgium; B in Surgery, U. Bristol, UK, MD; diploma in tropical medicine and hygiene, Liverpool U., UK. Lic. in medicine UK, Calif., registered specialist in infectious and tropical diseases UK. Svc. in various positions and med. schools in the UK, US and sub-Sahara Africa; dir. divsn. HIV/AIDS prevention surveillance and epidemiology Centers Disease Control and Prevention, Atlanta, dir. Kenya, 2000—06, 2009—10, dir. Ctr. Global Health Atlanta, 2010—; dir. dept. HIV/AIDS WHO, 2006—09. Vis. prof. medicine and internat. health London Sch. Hygiene and Tropical Medicine; ex-officio mem. adv. bd. NIH Fogarty Internat. Ctr. Co-editor: AIDS in Africa, Second Edit., 1997; mem. editl. bd.: AIDS, The Lancet, The New Eng. Jour. Medicine; contbr. articles to profl. jours., chapters to books. Decorated Comdr. of Order Pub. Health Côte d'Ivoire; recipient Chalmers medal, Royal Soc. Tropical Medicine and Hygiene, Internat. Health Honor award, CDC, ATSDR, Mackel award, CDC, William C. Watson Jr. medal. Fellow: Royal Coll. Physicians, UK. Office: Centers Disease Control and Prevention Ctr Global Health 1600 Clifton Rd Atlanta GA 30333

DECOSTER, GRETCHEN, controller; Degree in Acctg., U. Wis., Oshkosh; MBA, DePaul U.; selected Exec. Mgmt. Program, Emory U., 2005. Mgr., fin. reporting Pepsi-Cola Gen. Bottlers, Inc.; dist. contr. Browning-Ferris Industries; contr., N.Am. parts divsn. AGCO Corp., 1999, dir., fin., N.Am., v.p., N.Am. customer support, 2006—. Office: AGCO Corp 4205 River Green Pkwy Duluth GA 30096 Office Phone: 770-813-9200. Office Fax: 770-813-6118. Business E-Mail: decoster.gretchen@agcocorp.com.

DE DATTA, SURAJIT KUMAR, soil scientist, agronomist, educator; b. Shwebo, Upper Burma, Burma, Aug. 1, 1936; s. Dinanath and Birahini De Datta; m. Vijayalakshmi L., April 20, 1967; 1 son, Raj Kumar De Datta. BS in Agr., Banaras Hindu U., 1956; MS Soil Sci. and Agrl. Chemistry, Indian Agrl. Rsch. Inst., New Delhi, 1958; PhD in Soil Sci., U. Hawaii, 1962. Postdoctoral agrl. expt. sta. Ohio State U., Columbus, 1962-63; prof. agronomy and soil sci. U. Philippines, Los Banos, Philippines, 1964-91; assoc. agronomist Internat. Rice Rsch. Inst., Manila, Philippines, 1964-69, agronomist, 1969-85, radiol. safety officer, 1967-78, acting head dept. soil chemistry, 1975-76, dept. head, agronomy, 1967-89, prin. scientist, 1986-91; assoc. dean internat. agr. Va. Tech., Blacksburg, 1993—2003, dir. office internat. rsch. edn. and devel., 1991—, prof. crop and soil environ. scis., 1991—, chair, 1996-97, assoc. v.p. internat. affairs, 2003—. Bd. dirs. S.E. Consrotium for Internat. Devel., Washington; prin. investigator IPM CRSP Project (USAID), Va. Tech., 1993; vis. prof. Purdue U., 1971-72, Kasetsart U., Thailand, 1984-91; vis. scientist U. Calif., Davis, 1978-79; hon. prof. Dniepropetrovsk State Agrarian U., Ukraine, USSR, 1998. Author: Principles and Practices of Rice Production, 1981; consulting editor: Fertilizer Rsch. Jour. 1978-96; contbr. over 366 articles to profl. jours. Recipient Internat. Soil Sci. award Soil Sci. Soc. Am., 1986, Best Paper award Weed Sci. Pest Control Coun. Philippines, 1986, Eminence award Bureau of Plant Industry, Philippines, 1987, Best Paper award Asian-Pacific Weed Sci. Soc., Taiwan, 1987, Second Best Paper award Asian-Pacific Weed Sci. Soc., Korea, 1989, Agronomic Rsch. award Am. Soc. Agronomy, 1990, Norman Borlaug award, New Delhi, India, 1992, Outstanding Alumnus award Coll. Tropical Agr. Human Resources, U. Hawaii, 1998, citation for contribution to the Filipino people, Pres. Rep. Philippines, 2004. Fellow Am. Soc. Agronomy, Soil Sci. Soc. Am., Crop Sci. Soc., Indian Soc. Soil Sci., Internat. Svc. in Agronomy, Internat. Svc. in Crop Sci., Nat. Acad. Agrl. Scis. (India). Hindu. Home: 512 Floyd St Blacksburg VA 24060 Office: Va Tech Office Internat Rsch Edn & Devel 526 Prices Fork Rd Blacksburg VA 24061-0378

DEDERICH-PEJOVICH, SUSAN, musician, educator; d. Robert Marwood and Martha Annette (Geffs) D.; m. Svetozar Pejovich; 1 child, Mira Zorina. MusB in Harp Performance, Cleve. Inst. Music, 1972; MBA in Acctg., U. Phoenix, Dallas, 2005. Prin. harp Okla. Symphony, 1973, New Orleans Symphony, 1974—76, Dallas Symphony Orch., Dallas, 1977—. Mem. contemporary music ensemble Voices of Change; founder Flute, Viola, Harp Trio Triptych; condr. So. Meth. U. Harp Ensemble; co-dir. Adriatric harp workshop, Krk, Yugoslavia, Summer Festival, Purgatory, Colo., Killington (Vt.) Music Festival; founder, mem. October Trio, 2002—. Musician: (consortium premier with Sir James Galway) Lieberman Concerto for Flute and Harp, 1995. Episcopalian. Office: Dallas Symphony 2301 Flora Suite 300 Dallas TX 75201

DEEB, LARRY CHARLES, pediatric endocrinologist, epidemiologist; b. Tallahassee, Fla., July 2, 1947; s. Charles Hobeica and Carol Anna (Goll) D.; m. Josephine Marie Sutter, Oct. 7, 1978; children: Michael Larry, Laura Elzabeth. BA in History, Emory U., 1969, MD, 1973. Diplomate Am. Bd. Pediatrics. Pediatric resident U. Minn., Mpls., 1973-75, pediatric endocrine fellow, 1975-77; epidemic intelligence svc. officer, diabetes control activity Ctrs. for Disease Control, Atlanta, 1977—79, head, epidemiology and statistics group, diabetes control activity, 1979—80; ckin. asst. prof., dept. pediatrics Coll. Medicine, U. Fla., 1981—88, assoc. clin. prof., dept. pediatrics, 1988—93, clin. prof., dept. pediatrics, 1993—; pediatric endocrinology Childrens Clinic, Tallahassee, 1980—; rsch. assoc. Ctr. for Study of Populations, Fla. State U., 1987—; assoc. in medicine Fla. State U., 1993—. Epidemiologist cons. State of Fla., Tallahassee, 1980-, Internat. Diabetes Fedn.; clin. prof. pediatrics U. Fla., Gainesville, 1980-; med. dir. Diabetes Ctr. at Tallahassee Meml. Hosp.; epidemiologist NIH, Bethesda, Md., 1988-93; bd. dirs. Fla. Camp for Children and Youth with Diabetes; assoc. in medicine Fla. State U. Coll. Medicine, 1993-, courtesy assoc. prof. behavioral and social medicine, 2004-, courtesy asst. prof., pediatrics, 2004-. Mem. editl. bd. practical Diabetes, 1987—, Clin. Diabetes, 1988-92, 96—, Meml. Hosp. 1992-, Diabetes Spectra, 1992; contbr. articles to profl. jours. Lt. comdr. USPHS, 1965-77. Recipient Frederick Clifton Moor award, Tallahassee Rotary Club, 2006. Fellow Am. Acad. Pediatrics, Lawson Wilkins Pediatric Endocrinology Soc., Internat. Soc. Pediatric and Adolescent Diabetes, Am. Assn. Clin. Endocrinologists; mem. Am. Diabetes Assn. (mem. programs com., 1984-85, chair, coun. on health care delivery and pub. health, 1986-87, chair, com. on affiliate edn. and program services, 1986-87, mem task force on epidemiology and statistics, 1988-, mem. publications com., 1989-91, bd. dir., 1990-93, chair, non-periodicals review panel, 1991-93, chair elect coun. on clin. endocrinology, 1992-94, mem. nominating com., 1993-95, chair coun. on clin. endocrinology and metabolism, 1994-96, chair coun. on diabetes in youth, 1996-97, publications policy com., 1996-97, chair publications policy com., 1997-97, mem. diabetes quality improvement com., 1998-2000, provider recognition com., 2000-2001, fin. com., 2002-2004, v.p., 2004-2005, pres.-elect, medicine and sci., 2005-2006, pres. medicine & sci., 2006-07), Safe at Schs. (co-chair 2008-) Internat. Diabetes Fedn. (chair task force insulin & other diabetes supplies, 2006-09), Rotary (Paul Harris fellow). Episcopalian. Home: 2307 Trescott Dr Tallahassee FL 32308-0929 Office: Children's Clinic 2416 E Plaza Dr Tallahassee FL 32308-5384 Address: Diabetes Ctr at Tallahassee Meml Hosp 1221 Hodges Dr Tallahassee FL 32308 Office: 2804 Remination Green Cir Tallahassee FL 32308 Office Phone: 850-878-0184. Office Fax: 850-216-1537. E-mail: lcdeeb@attglobal.net, lcdeeb@deeb.org.

DEEB, ZIAD L., neuroradiologist; MD, Am. U., Beirut, 1969. Diplomate Am. Bd. Radiology-diagnostic radiology, 1974, Am. Bd. Radiology-neuroradiology, 2004, lic. Ohio. Intern Am. Univ. Med. Ctr., Beirut, 1969, resident diagnostic radiology, 1969—71, Univ. Ariz. Med. Ctr., Tuczon, 1971—72; fellow neurol. radiology Peter Bent Brigham Hosp., 1972—73; hosp. affiliations include Cleveland Clinic, Ohio, Physicians Regional Med. Ctr.-Pine Ridge, Naples. Named Recognized Dr., HealthGrades. Mem.: Am. Soc. Neuroradiology, Am. Coll. Radiology. Office: Physicians Regional Medical Center 6101 Pine Ridge Rd Naples FL 34119 Office Fax: 239-348-4439.

DEEDS, CREIGH (ROBERT CREIGH DEEDS), state legislator; b. Richmond, Va., Jan. 4, 1958; s. Robert Livingston and Emma Tyree Deeds; m. Pamela Kay Miller; children: Amanda Jane, Rebecca Lewis, Susannah Kemper, Austin Creigh(dec.). Assoc. Carter, Craig & Bass, 1984—85, John C. Singleton, 1985—87; ptnr. Singleton & Deeds, 1988—99, R. Creigh Deeds, 2000—07, Hirschler Fleischer; Commonwealth atty. Bath Co., Va., 1988—92; mem. Dist 18 Va. House of Delegates, Va., 1992—2001; chmn. Va. Dem. Conf., 2000—01; mem. Dist 25 Va. State Senate, Va., 2001—. Author: Atty.-client Privilege, The Right to Coun. for the Party Under Grand Jury Investigation, 19 WF L Rev 487, 1983, Probable Cause Based on Hearsay, The Supreme Ct. Punts on Third Down, 20 WF L Rev 193, 1984. Recipient America Coun. Young Polit Leaders, 1992, Warren Stambaugh award, 1998, Leader in pub. policy, The Natural Conservancy, 1999, Legislature Hero, People of Conservative Votes, 2003—04. Mem.: Millboro Lodge 28 AF&AM, Va. State & America Bar Assn., Va. Trial Lawyers Assn., Millboro Ruritan Club (dir. 1990—92). Democrat. Presbyterian. Address: PO Box 266 Millboro VA 24460 Mailing: PO Box 396 Richmond VA 23218 Office: Dist Off PO Box 5462 Charlottesville VA 22905-5462 Office Phone: 434-296-5491, 804-698-7525. E-mail: district25@sov.state.va.us.

DEEL, FRANCES QUINN, retired librarian; b. Pottsville, Pa., Mar. 9, 1939; d. Charles Joseph and Carrie Miriam (Ketner) Q.; m. Ronald Eugene Deel, Feb. 5, 1983. BS, Millersville State Coll., 1960; M.L.S., Rutgers U., 1964; M.P.A., U. West Fla., 1981. Post librarian U.S. Army Armor (Desert Tng. Ctr.), Ft. Irwin, Calif., 1964-66; staff librarian Mil. Dist. of Washington, 1966-67; supervisory librarian 1st Logistical Command, APO San Francisco, 1967-68; tech. process specialist Naval Edn. and Tng. Supervisory Command, Washington, 1968-77, Pensacola, Fla., 1968-77; chief tech. library USAF Armament Lab., Eglin AFB, Fla., 1977-81; dir. command libraries Air Force Systems Command (Andrews AFB), Washington, 1981-92; mem. exec. adv. council Fed. Library and Info. Network, Washington, 1983-86; libr. Air Force Dist. of Washington (Bolling AFB), Washington, 1992-94; dir. Navy Dept. Libr., Washington, 1994; ret., 1994. Mem. ALA (dir.-at-large armed forces libraries sect. Chgo. 1983-86), Spl. Libraries Assn., D.C. Library Assn. Roman Catholic. Home: 99 Country Club Dr W Destin FL 32541-4433

DEEN, BOBBY, chef, restaurateur, television personality; b. Albany, Ga., Apr. 28, 1970; Sandwich delivery svc. The Bag Lady, Albany, 1989—91; restaurant mgr. The Lady, Savannah, Ga., 1991—96, The Lady & Sons, Savannah, 1996—. Co-founder, editor-in-chief Deen Bros. Good Cooking mag., Hoffman Media, 2010—; launched a line of spices, barbecue sauces and t-shirts; judge Beringer Great Steak Challenge. Co-author, with Jamie Deen (cookbooks) The Deen Bros. Cookbook-Recipes from the Road, 2007, The Deen Bros. Y'all Come Eat, 2008, The Deen Bros. Take It Easy: Quick and Affortable Meals the Whole Family Will Love, 2009, The Deen Bros. Get Fired Up: Grilling, Tailgating, Picnicking, and More, 2011, co-author, with Melissa Clark From Mama's Table to Mine: Everybody's Favorite Comfort Foods at 350 Calories or Less, 2013; author: Bobby Deen's Everyday Eats: 120 All-New Recipes, All Under 350 Calories, All Under 30 Minutes, 2014; published foru stand allone magazines with Jamie Deen, 2010, co-host Road Tasted, Food Network, 2006, regular TV appearances Paula's Home Cooking, Paula's Party, host (Cooking Channel show) Not My Mama's Meals. Named one of 50 Most Eligible Bachelors, People Mag., 2006. Avocation: guitar. Mailing: c/o The Lady & Sons 102 W Congress St Savannah GA 31401*

DEEN, JAMIE, chef, restaurateur, television personality; b. Albany, Ga., June 29, 1967; s. Paula Deen; m. Brooke Terry Deen, Mar. 5, 2005; children: Jack Linton, Matthew James. Grad., Valdosta State U., Ga. Sandwich delivery svc. The Bag Lady, Albany, 1989—91; restaurant mgr. The Lady, Savannah, Ga., 1991—96, The Lady & Sons, Savannah, 1996—. Co-founder, editor-in-chief Deen Bros. Good Cooking mag., Hoffman Media, 2010—; launched a line of barbeque sauces and t-shirts; judge Beringer Great Steak Challenge; invited spkr. in field. Co-author, with Bobby Deen (cookbooks) The Deen Bros. Cookbook-Recipes from the Road, 2007, The Deen Bros. Y'all Come Eat, 2008, The Deen Bros. Take It Easy: Quick and Affordable Meals the Whole Family Will Love, 2009, The Deen Bros. Get Fired Up: Grilling, Tailgating, Picnicking, and More, 2011, co-author, with John Kernick Jaime Deen's Good Food: Cooking Up a Storm with Delicious, Family-Friendly Recipes, 2013, published four stand alone magazines with Bobby Deen, 2010, co-host Road Tasted, Food Network, 2006, regular TV appearances include Paula's Home Cooking, CNN, Fox News, Today Show, host (Food Network Cooking Show) Home for Dinner. Bd. mem. Bethesda Home for Boys, Coastal America's Second Harvest. Mailing: c/o The Lady & Sons 102 W Congress St Savannah GA 31401*

DEEN, PAULA H., television personality, restaurant owner, chef; b. Albany, Ga., Jan. 19, 1947; m. Michael Groover, Mar. 2004; 2 stepchildren;children from previous marriage: Bobby, Jamie. Owner catering bus. The Bag Lady; owner The Lady and Sons restaurant, Savannah, Ga., 1990—. Host (TV series) Paula's Home Cooking, Food Network, 2002—13, Paula's Party; author: (cookbooks) The Lady and Sons Too!, 2001, 2008, The Lady and Sons Just Desserts, 2002, The Lady and Sons Savannah Country Cookbook, 2005, 2008, Christmas with Paula Deen: Recipes and Stories from My Favorite Holiday, 2007, Paula Deen's My First Cookbook; co-author: (with Martha Nesbit) Paula Deen & Friends: Living It Up, Southern Style, 2005, Paula Deen Celebrates!: Best Dishes and Best Wishes for the Best Times of Your Life, 2006, (with Sherry Sulb Cohen) Paula Deen: It Ain't All About the Cookin', 2007, (with Melissa Clark) Paula Deen's The Deen's Family Cookbook, 2009, Paula Deen's Southern Cooking Bible: The New Classic Guide to Delicious Dishes with More Than 300 Recipes, 2011, (with Brandon Branch) Paula Deen's Savannah Style, 2010; author: (mag.) Cooking with Paula Deen, 2006—; actor: (films) Elizabethtown, 2005. Provided sponsorships and donations of money, cookbooks and other services to cmty. groups and causes. Recipient Ga. Women Entrepreneurs (GWEN) award, Ga. Small Bus. Devel. Ctr., 2003; named Most Memorable Meal Yr. at The Lady and Sons restaurant, USA Today, 1999, Small Bus. Person Yr. in Ga., US Small Bus. Adminstrn., 2003; named one of The 100 Most Powerful Celebrities, Forbes.com, 2008. Office: Lady & Sons Restaurant 102 W Congress St Savannah GA 31401

DEERING, RONALD FRANKLIN, librarian, minister; b. Paxton, Ill., Oct. 6, 1929; s. Minor Franklin and Grace Gilmour (Perkins) D.; m. Geraldine Gibbons, June 27, 1953 (dec. Jan. 1965); m. Edith Ann Proctor, June 12, 1966; children: Mark David, Daniel Timothy. BA summa cum laude, Georgetown Coll., Ky., 1951; MDiv, So. Bapt. Theol. Sem., 1955, PhD, 1962; MLS, Columbia U., 1967. Ordained to ministry So. Bapt. Conv., 1950. Pastor 1st Hilltop Bapt. Ch., North College Hill, Ohio, 1949-50; instr. in Bible Georgeton (Ky.) Coll., 1950-51; pastor Blue River Bapt. Ch., Salem, Ind., 1954-59; instr. Greek, N.T. So. Bapt. Theol. Sem., Louisville, 1958-61, theol. libr., 1962-95, assoc. v.p. for acad. resources, 1995—. Chmn. So. Bapt. Hist. Commn., Nashville, 1987-90; interim pastor 31 chs. in Ind., Ky., 1961-90; del. Bapt. World Alliance, Miami, Fla., Toronto, Ont., Can., L.A., 1965, 80, 85. Contbr. articles to profl. jours. Eli Lilly Theol. Librarianship grantee, 1967. Mem. AAUP, ALA, Southeastern Libr. Assn., Am. Theol. Libr. Assn. (nat. pres. 1984-85), Ky. Libr. Assn., Phi Alpha Theta, Beta Phi Mu, Sigma Tau Delta. Democrat. Home: 3111 Dunlieth Ct Louisville KY 40241-2937 Personal E-mail: ron739@yahoo.com.

DEES, JERRY L., retired oil industry executive; Joined as geophysicist Atlantic Refining Co. (subs.) ARCO Oil & Gas Co., Dallas, 1962, mgr. exploration geophysics Cox Oil & Gas Producers, 1980—85, ctrl. dist exploration mgr. Midland, Tex., 1985—87, v.p. exploration & land ARCO Alaska, Inc. Anchorage, 1987—91; sr. v.p., mgr. exploration & land Vastar Resources, Inc. (formerly ARCO Oil & Gas Co.), Dallas, 1991—96, ret., 1996. Bd. dirs. Plains Resources Co., 1997—2002, Plains Exploration & Prodn. Co., 2002—, Geotrace Technologies, Inc., 2005—, Arguello Inc. Office: Plains Exploration and Production Co 700 Milam St Ste 3100 Houston TX 77002 Office Phone: 713-579-6000. Office Fax: 713-579-6611.

DEES, TOM MOORE, II, retired internist; b. Dallas, Mar. 4, 1931; s. Tom Hawkins and Maida Elizabeth (Board) D.; m. Suzanne Settle, Feb. 20, 1971; children: Tom Moore III, David Walsh. BA, Johns Hopkins U., 1952; MD, Southwestern Med. Sch., 1956. Intern Bellevue Hosp., NYC, 1957, resident, 1958-59; rsch. fellow in cardiology Southwestern Med. Sch., Dallas, 1961; internist, ptnr. pvt. practice medicine MedProvider, Dallas, 1962—2007; ret., 2007. Dir. and mng. ptnr. Swiss Ave. Med. Bldg., Dallas, 1984—2004; clin. asst. prof. medicine Southwestern Med. Sch., Dallas, 1962—; attending physician Baylor Med. Ctr., Dallas, 1962—. Mem. dist. commn. Boy Scouts Am., Dallas, 1963-72; mem. ofcl. bd. Highland Park Meth. Ch., Dallas, 1963-72. Capt. USAF, 1959-61. Mem. ACP (life), AMA, Am. Soc. Internal Medicine, Johns Hopkins U. Alumni Assn. (pres. North Tex. chpt 1964-68), Tex. Club of Internists (pres. 1992-93). Republican. Avocations: hunting, fishing, gardening. Home: 3649 Stratford Ave Dallas TX 75205-2810

DEESE, GEORGE E., food products company executive; With Flowers Foods, Inc. (formerly Flowers Industries, Inc.), Thomasville, Ga., 1964; pres., COO Flowers Bakeries, 1983—2002, Flowers Foods, Inc. (formerly Flowers Industries, Inc.), 2002—04, pres., CEO, 2004—06, chmn., pres., CEO, 2006—09, chmn., CEO, 2009—. Mem.: Quality Bakers Am. (vice chmn.), Grocery Manufacturers Am. (bd. dir.), Am. Bakers Assn. (chmn.). Office: Flowers Foods 1919 Flowers Cir Thomasville GA 31757

DEFFENBAUGH, GARY, state legislator; Mem. Dist. 66 Ark. House of Representatives, 2011—. Republican. Office: 1424 N 9th St Van Buren AR 72956 Office Phone: 479-719-8197. Business E-Mail: Gary.Deffenbaugh@arkansashouse.org.

DEFILIPPI, GEORGE, retired air force officer; b. Mobile, Ala., Sept. 6, 1947; s. George and Margaret Josephine (Lazzari) DeF.; m. Patricia Naismith McAdam, July 21, 1969; children: Jocelyn, Gwendolyn, Geoffrey, James. BS, USAF Acad., Colorado Springs, 1969; MS, Air Force Inst. Technology, Dayton, Ohio, 1977; cert. in bus. adminstrn., Georgetown Ctr. for. Profl. Devel., 2005. Enlisted USAF, 1969, advanced through ranks to col., exec. sec., program mgr. Scientific Adv. Bd. HQ USAF, Washington, 1984-86, chief tng. divsn. 602d Tactical Air Control Wing Davis Mountain AFB, Ariz., 1986-88, cmdr. 22d Tactical Air Support Tng. Squadron, 1988-89, cmdr. 23d Tactical Air Support Squadron, 1989-90, cmdr. Air Liaison Office XVIII Airborne Corps Ft. Bragg, NC, 1991-93, cmdr. Air Liaison Office to 3d Rep. Korea Army Uijongbu, Korea, 1992-93, mil. staff specialist Undersec. Def. Acquisition & Tech. Washington, 1993-96, mil. asst. to dir. strategic tactical systems, 1996-99; ret., 1999; field dir. mil. requirements Carlton Life Support Systems, Inc., Arlington, Va., 1999—2007; dir. Govt. Rels.-Air Programs Cobham N.Am., Arlington, Va., 2008—. Vol. Arlington Emergency Winter Shelter, 1993-99; active Arlington Com. of 100, 1994-2006; vestryman St. George's Episcopal Ch., 1996-99, Stephen min., leader, 1999—2005; abbot St. George's Urban Abbey, 2003-06; treas. St. George's Ch., 2005-. Mem. Assn. Unmanned Vehicle Sys. (bd. dirs. Capitol chpt. 1993-97), Air Force Assn. (Steele chpt. v.p. aerospace edn. 2006—, pres. 2004-06, v.p. ops. 2002-04, newsletter editor 1999—), Hist. Soc. Episcopal Ch. (bd. mem., treas. 2009-). Episcopal. Avocations: jogging, swimming, gardening. Office: Cobham N Am 2121 Crystal Dr Ste 625 Arlington VA 22202 Office Phone: 703-414-5302. Business E-Mail: george.defilippi@cobham.com.

DE FOREST, SHERWOOD SEARLE, agricultural engineer, products executive; b. Ames, Iowa, Sept. 20, 1921; s. Frank Ray and Clara Maud (Searle) De F.; m. Virginia Mary Flynn, June 20, 1947; children: David, Debra, Denise, Kimberly. Student, U. Cin., 1939-40; BS, Iowa State U., 1943, MS, 1947. Instr. agrl. engring. Iowa State U., 1946-47, extension agrl. engr., 1947-52; engring. editor Successful Farming mag., Des Moines, 1952-59; with US Steel, Pitts., 1959—77, mgr. agrl. equipment mktg., 1964—70, indsl. rep., 1970—77; v.p., assoc. The Montgomery Group, Inc., Tallahassee, 1977-96; pollution prevention engr. Fla. Dept. Environ. Protection, Tallahassee, 1996-99; owner De Forest Agri-Svcs., Tallahassee, 1977-99. Pres. Ginande Corp., 1986-91; tech. transfer project leader No. Agrl. Energy Center, Sci. and Edn. Adminstrn., U.S. Dept. Agr., Peoria, Ill., 1980-81; cons. Pakistan, 1984, Portugal, 1985, 86; mem. indsl. and profl. adv. com. Coll. Engring. Pa. State U., 1966-71; mem. NE Regional Agrl. Research Planning Com., 1970-72; mem. Fla. Gov.'s Continuing Care Adv. Coun., 1996-2000. Author: The Vision That Cut Druggery From Farming Forever, 2007;contbg. author: Power to Produce, U.S. Dept. Agr. Yearbook, 1969, Steel in Agriculture, 1966; pub. TravelHost of Pitts. mag., 1982-83; tech. editor Soc. Automotive Engrs. Internat., 1987-89; editor: Memories of Dr. J. Brownlee Davidson, Father of Agricultural Engineering 2005, Alcohol and Vegetable Oil as Alternative Fuels, Proceedings of Regional Workshops, 1981; contbr. numerous articles to Successful Farming Mag. Served to 1st lt. USAAF, 1942-46. Recipient Am. Soc. Agrl. Engrs.-Metal Bldg. Mfrs. Assn. award for disting. work in advancing knowledge and sci. of farm bldgs., 1964 Fellow: Am. Soc. Agrl. and Biol. Engrs. (pres. 1975—76); mem.: Fla. Life Care Residents Assn., Inc. (chpt. pres. 1999—2003, state bd. dirs. 2001—04, state treas. 2003—04). Presbyterian. Achievements include patents in field. Home and Office: 4173 Covenant Ln Tallahassee FL 32308-5766

DEGABRIELLE, DONALD J., JR., former prosecutor; b. Lake Charles, La., 1953; s. Donald J. DeGabrielle and Jackie Rosenthal. BA, McNeese State U., 1975; JD, La State U., 1978. Spl. agent FBI, New Orleans and NYC, 1979—82; asst. dist. atty. to chief of trials Orleans Parish Dist. Atty.'s Office, New Orleans, 1982—85; pvt. law practice, 1985; asst. US atty. (so. dist.) Tex. US Dept. Justice, Houston, 1986—2002, first asst. US atty. (so. dist.) Tex., 2002—06, US atty. (so. dist.) Tex., 2006—08; ptnr. Fulbright & Jaworski LLP, 2008—. Resident legal advisor So. African Nat. Directorate of Pub. Prosecutors, 2001. Business E-Mail: d_degabrielle@fullbright.com.

DE GENNARO, RICHARD, retired library director; b. New Haven, Mar. 2, 1926; s. Ralph and Acquilina (Pedicini) De G.; m. Birgit M. Erikson, June 12, 1953; children: Ralph, George, Christina. BA, Wesleyan U., 1951, MA, 1960; MS in LS, Columbia U., 1956; postgrad., Univs. Paris, Madrid and Perugia, 1951-55; grad. Advanced Mgmt. Program, Harvard U., 1971; DHL (hon.), Wabash Coll., 1991. Jr. acct. Atlas Constructors, Morocco, 1952-53; reference librarian N.Y. Pub. Libr., 1956-58, dir., 1987-90; successively reference librarian, asst. dir., assoc. univ. librarian systems devel., sr. assoc. univ. librarian Harvard U. Libr., 1958-70; dir. librs. U. Pa., 1970-86, adj. prof. English, 1979-86; libr. Harvard Coll., 1990-96. Vis. prof. Grad. Libr. Sch., U. So. Calif., 1968-69; cons. libr. bldgs., tech. and mgmt.; mem. overseers com. to visit libr., Harvard U.; cons. MIT, Johns Hopkins U.; mem. adv. bd. Chem. Abstracts Svc., 1967-70; mem. Palinet bd. Union Libr. Catalogue, 1970—; mem. com. internat. sci. and tech. info. programs NAS-NRC, 1977-79; mem. Mellon Found. JSTOR Bd., 1995—; sr. libr. advisor JSTOR; mem. governing bd. Rsch. Librs. Group, 1979-89, sr. vis. fellow, 1980-81, chmn., 1984-95; Bowker lectr., 1979; Lazerow lectr., 1984. Author: Shifting Gears, Information Technology and the Academic Library, 1984, Libraries, Technology, and the Information Marketplace, Selected Papers, 1987; contbr. articles to profl. jours. Bd. dirs. Ctr. for Rsch. Librs., 1977-81; trustee U. Pa. Press, 1978-82. With USN, 1942-46. Recipient Disting. Alumnus award Wesleyan U., 1991; Hugh Atkinson award, 1993; named Acad. Rsch. Libr. of Yr., 1991; Coun. Libr. Resources fellow, 1971; Rockefeller Found. Ctr. fellow, Bellagio, Italy, 1981; info. tech. fellow U. Edinburgh, 1984. Mem. Assn. Rsch. Librs. (pres. 1975, dir. 1973-76), ALA (pres. info. sci. and automation div. 1975), Am. Soc. Info. Soc. (Melvil Dewey medal 1986), Century Assn. Club, Grolier Club, Harvard Club. Home: Apt 1414 988 Blvd Of The Arts Sarasota FL 34236-4838

DEGIOVANNI-DONNELLY, ROSALIE FRANCES, biologist, educator; b. Bklyn., Nov. 22, 1926; d. Frank and Rose (Quartuccio) DeGiovanni; m. Edward Francis Donnelly, Sept. 23, 1961; children: Edward F. Jr., Francis M. BA, Bklyn. Coll., 1947, MA, 1953; PhD, Columbia U., 1961. Adj. prof. microbiology, genetics George Washington U., Washington, 1968—; rsch. biologist FDA, Washington, 1968-88. Contbr. articles to profl. jours. Recipient Merit award FDA, 1970. Mem. AAAS, AAUW, Italian Cultural Soc., Environ. Mutagen Soc., NY Acad. Scis., Am. Soc. Microbiology, McLean Indoor Club, Women's Club McLean, Sigma Xi, Sigma Delta Epsilon. Democrat. Roman Catholic. Avocations: theater, swimming, tennis, travel, photography. Home: George Washington University 1712 Strine Dr Mc Lean VA 22101-4744 Personal E-mail: edndol@gmail.com.

DEGIUSTI, TIMOTHY D., federal judge; b. Oklahoma City, 1962; BA, U. Okla., 1985, JD, 1988. Bar: Okla. 1988. Assoc. Andrews Davis Law Firm, Oklahoma City, 1988—90, 1993—95, ptnr., 1995—2000; trial counsel US Army JAGC, 1990—93; ptnr. Holladay, Chilton & DeGiusti, PLLC, 2000—07; judge US. Dist. Ct. (we. dist.) Okla., 2007—. Adj. prof. U. Okla. Coll. Law, 1998—2003. Mem. USAR, 1981—2003. Office: US Courthouse Rm 4301, Courtroom 502, Fifth Fl 200 NW Fourth St Oklahoma City OK 73102 Office Phone: 405-609-5120. Office Fax: 405-609-5131.

DEGREGORY, LANE, journalist, features writer; m. Dan DeGregory; children: Ryland, Tucker. MA in Rhetoric and Comm. Studies, U. Va. Staff writer Virginian-Pilot, Norfolk, 1990—2000, St. Petersburg Times, Fla., 2000—. Stories featured in Best Newspaper Writing edit., 2000, 2004, 2006, 2008. Recipient Ernie Pyle award for human interest writing, Scripps Howard Found., 2007, Am. Soc. Newspaper Editors award for non-deadline writing, 2008, Pulitzer prize for feature writing, 2009. Office: St Petersburg Times 490 First Ave S Saint Petersburg FL 33701 Business E-Mail: degregory@sptimes.com.

DEGUERIN, DICK, lawyer; b. Austin, Tex., Feb. 16, 1941; s. E. Mack and Marguerite S. DeGuerin; m. Janie Mitchell, Apr. 11, 1986; children from previous marriage: Anna Michele, Ann Carlin. BA, U. Tex., Austin, 1963; LLB, U. Tex. Sch. Law, 1965. Bar: Tex. 1965, US Dist. Ct. (so. dist.) Tex. 1968, US Ct. Appeals (5th cir.) 1971, US Supreme Ct. 1971, US Dist. Ct. (ea. dist.) Tex. 1973, US Ct. Appeals (8th cir.) 1974, US Dist. Ct. (no. dist.) Tex. 1979, US Ct. Appeals (11th cir.) 1981, US Dist. Ct. (ea. dist.) Mich. 1982, US Ct. Appeals (6th cir.) 1982, US Dist. Ct. (we. dist.) Tex. 1983, US Ct. Appeals (10th cir.) 1984, US Ct. Appeals (4th cir.) 1985. Asst. dist. atty. Harris County, Tex., 1965-68; trial assoc. Butler, Binion, Rice, Cook & Knapp, Houston, 1968-71; ptnr. Foreman & DeGuerin, Houston, 1971-82; sr. ptnr. DeGuerin & Dickson (formerly DeGuerin Dickson, & Hennessy), Houston, 1982—. Assoc. prof. criminal law South Tex. Coll. Law, 1969—70; adj. prof. criminal law U. Tex. Sch. Law, 1994; spkr. in field. Mem. Houston Jr. Bar Assn., 1965—76; charter mem., dir. Tex. Criminal Def. Lawyers Assn., 1973—76. Recipient Bum Steer award, Tex. Monthly, 1994, Award in recognition of efforts on behalf of muneer deeb, Tex. Justice Alliance, 2003, Hall of Fame award, Tex. Criminal Def. Lawyers Assn., 2004; named Houston's Most Famous Def. Atty., RO Mag., 1995, Lexis Nexis AV Rated for Thirty Years, Martindale-Hubbell, 1980—2010; named one of Top Ten Lawyers, Houston Chronicle, 1999, Texas' Top 100 Super Lawyers, Tex. Monthly, 2003, Top Attorneys in Tex., 2007, 2008, Tex. Super Lawyers, Law & Politics, 2003—10, Nation's Ten Top Litigators, The Nat. Law Jour., 2004, Houston's Top Lawyers for the People, H-Tex. mag., 2008—10, The Best Lawyers in America, 2009, The 25 Greatest Lawyers of the Past Quarter-Century, Texas Lawyer, Corp. Counsel Top Lawyers, Ann. Guide to Criminal Def. Law, 2010; named to Bar Register of Preeminent Lawyers, 2006—09. Fellow: Internat. Soc. Barristers, American Bar Found., American Coll. Trial Lawyers, Tex. Bar Found.; mem.: ABA, American Trial Lawyers Assn. (Top 100 Trial Lawyers 2007—09), American Bd. Trial Advocates, American Bd. Criminal Lawyers, American Judicature Soc. (charter mem.), American Assn. Justice (Top 100 Trial Lawyers 2007—08), Bar Assn. Fifth Fed. Cir., Calif. Attorneys for Criminal Justice, Harris County Criminal Lawyers Assn. (charter mem., past pres., former dir., Atty. of Yr. 1999, Lifetime Achievement award 2008), Houston Bar Assn., Nat. Assn. Criminal Def. Lawyers (life), Houston Trial Lawyers Assn., Internat. Acad. Trial Lawyers, State Bar Tex. (Outstanding Criminal Def. Lawyer of Yr. 1994), Tex. Bd. Trial Advocates, Tex. Trial Lawyer's Assn., Coll. Master Advocates of Barristers, Coll. State Bar Tex., Delta Theta Phi. Office: DeGuerin & Dickson 7th Fl The Republic Bldg 1018 Preston Ave Houston TX 77002-1818 Office Phone: 713-223-5959. Office Fax: 713-223-9231. E-mail: ddeguerin@aol.com.

DEGUTIS, LINDA CHRISTINE, public health service officer, epidemiologist, researcher; b. Chgo., Dec. 16, 1953; d. William Joseph and Genevieve (Karons) D.; m. Robert F. Miller, Aug. 16, 1975 (div. Mar. 1983); m. Bruce Fenton Carmichael, Mar. 26, 1988. BS, DePaul U., 1975; MSN, Yale Sch. of Nursing, 1982; DrPH, Yale Sch. of Medicine, 1994. Cert. RN Conn., Ill. Staff nurse Rush-Presbyn. St. Luke's Med. Ctr., Chgo., 1975-78, Yale-New Haven Hosp., Conn., 1978-81; trauma program coord. Yale Sch. Medicine, New Haven, 1982-91, 92-95, lectr. in surgery, 1984-95, asst. prof. sect. of emergency medicine, 1995—2003, assoc. prof. emergency medicine, pub. health, 2003—10; trauma coord. Bridgeport Hosp., Conn., 1991-92; Robert Wood Johnson Health Policy fellow Office of Senator Paul Wellstone, Washington, 1996-97; dir. Nat. Ctr. Injury Prevention and Control Centers Disease Control and Prevention, Atlanta, 2010—. Adv. mem. Conn. State com. on trauma; exec. com. mem. Conn. Adv. for Highway Safety, Hartford, Conn., 1995—. Contbr. articles to profl. jours. Founding mem. MADD-New Haven Chpt., 1983; vol. Conn. Spl. Olympic Games, New Haven, 1990-94, Internat. Spl. Olympic Games, New Haven, 1995; pres. Lake Point Condominium Assn. Bd., 1991. Mem. ACS, AAAS, Am. Pub. Health Assn. (exec. bd., chmn. injury control and emergency health svcs. sect.), Am. Trauma Soc., Nat. Assn. for Pub. Health Policy, Soc. Acad. Emergency Medicine. Office: Centers Disease Control and Prevention Nat Ctr Injury Prevention and Control 1600 Clifton Rd Atlanta GA 30333

DEHART, MARK DAVID, nuclear engineer, researcher; b. Waco, Tex., July 17, 1960; s. Donald Dean and Judy Marlene DeHart; m. Leigh Ellen Utley, Aug. 23, 1986; children: Kaitlyn Tyler, Kyle Travis. BS in Nuc. Engring., Tex. A&M U., College Station, 1984, MS, 1986, PhD, 1992. Sr. engr. Savannah River Lab., Aiken, SC, 1989—93; sr. R&D staff Oak Ridge Nat. Lab., Tenn., 1993—. US rep. OECD, NEA Expert Group on Burnup Credit, Paris, 1993—2005, IAEA Consultancy for Burnup Credit, Vienna, 2004—06; program com. chair, nuc. criticality safety divsn. Am. Nuc. Soc., La Grange Park, Ill., 1999—2002; adj. faculty U. Tenn., Knoxville, 2003—, Purdue U., West Lafayette, Ind., 2004—06. Contbr. scientific papers to profl. publs. Team organizer Odyssey of Mind, Knoxville, 2000—01; cub scout den leader Boy Scouts Am., Knoxville, 2000—01; dist. tech. bd. Mid. South Dist. Luth. Ch., Mo. Synod, Memphis, 2000—04, lay rep. to dist. conv., 2004—04; mem. chair East Tenn. Regional Youth Bd., 2001—; tech. bd. chmn. Grace Luth. Ch., Knoxville, 1996—2000, youth bd. chmn., 2001—05, youth worship leader, 2001—05, pres., 2006—06, elder, 2008—. Recipient George Westinghouse Signature award, 1991—92, President's Vol. Svc. award, Pres. US, 2007; Nuc. Engring. fellowship, US Dept. Energy, 1984—88. Mem.: Am. Nuc. Soc. (Disting. Svc. award 2005, Outstanding Svc. award 2001), Tau Beta Pi. Lutheran. Achievements include development of TRITON control module for high-fidelity multidimensional lattice physics and depletion. Office: Oak Ridge Nat Lab PO Box 2008 M/S 6170 Oak Ridge TN 37831-6170 Personal E-mail: markdehart@aggienetwork.com. Business E-Mail: dehartmd@ornl.gov.

DEHAY, JERRY MARVIN, business educator, small business owner; b. Brownwood, Tex., Nov. 21, 1939; s. Marvin Edward and Willie Marie (Daniell) DeHay; m. Dana Lea Laxson, May 29, 1960 (div. June 30, 1973); children: David, Deanna; m. Marilyn Ann Lethco, July 28, 1973; children: Colin, Beva, Sue. BBA, A&M Coll. Tex., 1962; MBA, Tex. A&M U, 1966; PhD, North Tex. State U., 1978. Sales mgr. Procter and Gamble, Corpus Christi, Tex., 1962-65; instr. mktg. Tex. A&M U., College Station, 1966-69; asst. prof. bus. Howard Payne U., Brownwood, Tex., 1969-73; coord. food mktg. Tarrant County Jr. Coll. N.E., Hurst, Tex., 1973-75; instr. math. Brownwood State Sch., 1976-77; asst. prof. mktg. E. Tex. State U., Commerce, 1977-78, prof., 1979-83, dir. Small Bus. Inst., 1979—83; assoc. prof. bus. Hardin Simmons U., Abilene, Tex., 1978-79; dean Coll. Bus. Adminstrn. Tarleton State U., Stephenville, Tex., 1983-94, dir. Small Bus. Inst., 1983—87, dir. Small Bus. Devel. Ctr., 1987—89, mem. dean's coun. Coll. Bus. Adminstrn., 2011—; CEO JMD Cons., Brownwood, Tex., 1994—; co-owner Recollections Antiques and Collectibles, Brownwood, Tex., 1996—; prof. bus. adminstrn. Howard Payne U., 2001—04, dir. continuing edn., 1971—73. Mem. adv. bd. Small Bus. Devel. Ctr. Co-author: Supervision, 1984; contbr. poems to anthologies; author, presenter (TV series) PBS Business File, 1985. Sec. bd. trustees Brownwood Ind. Sch. Dist., 1972; trustee Mullin (Tex.) Ind. Sch. Dist., 1979; chmn. regional adv. bd. SBA, Dallas; vice-chmn. Brownwood Bldg. Stds. Commn., 1997—2007; bd. dirs. Brown County Hist. Mus., pres., 1999, Brownwood City Coun., 2007—, mem., 2007—, Brownwood Tourism Bd., 2009—, Brownwood Retail Adv. Com., 2010—; bd. dirs. Brownwood Heritage Assn., 2006; mem. bd. trustees Douglas McArthur Acad. Freedom, 2007—. Named Outstanding Educator of Am., 1973, 1974, 1975, Outstanding Am. of Bi-Centennial Era, 1976. Mem.: Nat. Button Soc. (bd. dirs. 2009—12), West Ctr. Tex. Coun. Govts. (sec., treas. 2011—, v.p. 2012—), Sales and Mktg. Execs. Ft. Worth (educator mem.), Tex. State Button Soc. (pres. 2007—08), Pi Sigma Epsilon (educator v.p. 1984—85, adminstrv. v.p. 1985—86, nat. pres. 1987, Top Faculty Advisor award 1983), Mu Kappa Tau, Delta Sigma Pi. Baptist. Avocations: writing, singing. Home and Office: 801 Quail Run Brownwood TX 76801-6314 Business E-Mail: dehay@bwoodtx.com.

DE HEER, SARAH, online editor; BS in Bus. Mgmt., Ramapo Coll. Grassroots intern NJ Restaurant Assn., 2007; home and food editl. intern Meredith, 2008; home intern AOL, 2008, social mgr., 2008—11, online editor, 2008—11, Scripps Networks, 2011—. Author: (pub.) How to Cook Ham, 2009, The White House Honey Harvest, 2010, A Month of Brunch Menus, 2010, Shelf Life of Kitchen Staples, 2010, 10 Common Turkey Blunders and Solutions, 2010, Easy Marinades and Rubs, 2010. Office: Scripps Networks PO Box 51850 Knoxville TN 37950

DE HEER, WALTER A., physics professor; b. 1949; PhD, U. Calif., Berkeley, 1985. Prof. Ecole Polytechnique, Lausanne, Switzerland, 1987—96; Regents prof. Ga. Inst. Tech. Sch. Physics, Atlanta, 1996—. Contbr. articles to sci. jours. Recipient ACSIN Nanoscience Prize, 2009; named one of The Scientific American 50, 2006. Achievements include refining techniques to grow graphene out of silicon carbide, potentially changing the way electronics are made in the future. Office: Sch Physics Ga Inst Tech 837 State St Atlanta GA 30332-0430 Office Phone: 404-894-7879. E-mail: deheer@electra.physics.gatech.edu.

DEHMER, GREGORY JOSEPH, cardiologist; s. Joseph Anton and Bernadine Elizabeth (Bloom) D.; m. Sue Jane Vencil, Jan. 21, 1977; children: Jeffrey, Laura. BS, Carroll Coll., 1971; MD, U. Wis., 1975. Diplomate Am. Bd. Internal Medicine; cert in medicine, cardiology, and interventional cardiology. Dir. cardiac catheterization lab., asst. prof. medicine U. Tex. Health Sci. Ctr., Dallas, 1984-88; assoc. prof. medicine U. NC, 1988—2001; dir. cardiac catheterization lab U. NC Hosp., 1988—2001; prof. medicine, dir. cardiology divsn. Scott & White Clinic Tex. A&M U. Coll. Medicine, 2001—. Pres. Soc. Cardiovasc. Angiography and Interventions, 2006—07; trustee Am. Coll. Cardiology, 2009—. Mem. editl. bd. Am. Jour. Cardiology, 1990—, Jour. Am. Coll. Cardiology, 1999-2003, Circulation, 1993-2004. Maj. USAF, 1981—83. Fellow ACP, Am. Coll. Cardiology, Am. Heart Assn. (past pres.), Soc. Cardiovascular Angiography and Interventions; mem. Med CAC, Am. Coll. Cardiology(bd. trustees 2009-), ABIM (ICARD Test com., cons FDA Device com.) Avocation: skiing. Office: 2401 South 31st St Temple TX 76508

DEHOMBRE, MARIA CRISTINA, accountant; b. Havana, Cuba, Apr. 17, 1962; came to U.S., 1965; d. Ernesto Mario and Emelina (Miranda) Alvarez; m. Jose Enrique DeHombre, Aug. 27, 1982. BBA magna cum laude, U. Miami, Coral Gables, Fla., 1982. CPA, Fla. Sr. acct. Ernst and Whinney, Miami, 1982-86; payroll mgr. Burger King Corp., Miami, 1986—. Mem. Am. Inst. CPA's, Fla. Soc. CPA's, Cuban-Am. Inst. CPA's, Leadership Miami, Greater Miami C. of C. Republican. Roman Catholic. Avocations: bicycling, reading, travel, aerobics. Home: 5515 SW 89th Ct Miami FL 33165-6617 Office: Burger King Corp 17777 Old Cutler Rd Miami FL 33157-6347

DEISENHOFER, JOHANN, biochemistry professor, researcher; b. Zusamaltheim, Bavaria, Germany, Sept. 30, 1943; arrived in US, 1988, naturalized, 2001; s. Johann and Thekla (Magg) Deisenhofer; m. Kirsten Fischer-Lindahl, June 19, 1989. Degree in Physics, Tech. Univ. Munich, 1971, PhD, 1974. Postdoc. fellow Max-Planck Inst. Biochemistry, Martinsried, Germany, 1974-76, staff scientist, 1976-88; investigator Howard Hughes Med. Inst., Dallas, 1988—; prof. biochemistry U. Tex., Dallas, 1988—, regental prof., Virginia & Edward Linthicum disting. chair biomolecular sci. Contbr. articles to profl. jours. Recipient Biol. Physics prize, Am. Phys. Soc., 1986, Otto Bayer award, 1988, Nobel prize for chemistry, 1988. Mem.: AAAS, NAS, Academia Europaea, Am. Crystallographic Assn., Biophys. Soc., Fedn. Am. Scientists, German Soc. Biol. Chemistry, Scientists & Engineers America (mem. bd. advisors), Sigma Xi. Office: Howard Hughes Med Inst Univ Tex Southwestern Med Ctr 6001 Forest Park Rd Dallas TX 75390-9050 Business E-Mail: Johann.Deisenhofer@UTSouthwestern.edu.

DEITEMEYER, MICHAEL J., hotel executive; B in Bus., Fitchburg State Coll. Joined Interstate Hotels Corp., 1985; controller TRT Devel. Co., 1992, Shoreline Oper. Co., 1992; sr. v.p. fin. Omni Hotels Mgmt. Corp., COO, 1999—2004, pres., 2004—. Office: Omni Hotels 420 Decker Dr Ste 200 Irving TX 75062

DE JONGH, JOHN PERCY, JR., Governor of the United States Virgin Islands, real estate company executive; b. VI, Nov. 13, 1957; s. John P. and Delores (Webb) de Jongh; m. Cecile Rene Galiber, 1986; 3 children. BA in Economics, Antioch Coll., Yellow Springs, Ohio, 1981. With Tri-Island Econ. Devel. Coun; consumer mgr. Chase Manhattan Bank; commr. of fin. US VI, Charlotte Amalie, 1987—90, exec. asst. to commr. of fin., 1990—92; sr. mng. cons. Pub. Fin. Mgmt., Inc., 1993—96; pres., CEO, dir. Lockhart Companies, Inc., Charlotte Amalie, 1996—; gov. US VI, Charlotte Amalie, 2007—. Chmn. US VI Water & Power Authority, 1987—92; exec. dir. US VI Pub. Fin. Authority, 1988—90; chmn. US VI Tax Rev. Bd., 1987—90; sec. US VI Banking Bd., 1987—90; mem. US VI Small Bus. Devel. Agy., 1987—90; co-founder Chilmark Partners, LLC, 2003—. Pres. Karen Ingeborg Lockhart Found. Cmty. Found. US VI, St. Thomas/St. John C. of C.; trustee Antilles Sch. Named Person of Yr., Rotary II, 2000. Democrat. Office: Office of the Governor Govt House 21 22 Kongens Gade, Charlotte Amalie St Thomas VI 00802 Office Phone: 340-774-0001. Office Fax: 340-693-4374.*

DEKOSKY, STEVEN TRENT, neurologist; b. Camden, NJ, Mar. 23, 1947; s. Aaron and Evelyn (Gorlen) DeK.; m. Beverly Nelson; children: Allison. Lauren. AB in Psychology, Bucknell U., 1968; MD, U. Fla. Coll. Medicine, 1974. Diplomate in neurology Am. Bd.

Psychiatry and Neurology; recertified in neurology 2014. Resident in internal medicine John Hopkins Hosp., 1974—75; resident, neurology U. Fla., 1975—78; postdoctoral fellow, instr. neurology, neurochemistry U. Va. Sch. Medicine, Charlottesville, 1978-79; asst. prof. neurology, anatomy U. Ky. Coll. Medicine, Lexington, 1979-85, assoc. prof. anatomy and neurology, 1985-90, interim chmn. dept. neurology, 1985-87; grad. faculty U. Ky. Grad. Sch., Lexington, 1981-90; prof. psychiatry U. Pitts. Sch. Medicine, 1990—2008, prof. neurology, neurobiology, 1990—2008, grad. faculty, 1991—2008, interim chair dept. neurology, 2000—01, chair dept. neurology, 2002—08; v.p., dean U. Va. Sch. Medicine, 2008—13, prof., neurology, psychiatry & neurobehavioral scis., 2008—. Vis. prof. psychology U. Calif., Irvine, 1983; co-dir. Alzheimer's Disease Rsch. Ctr. U. Pitts. Med. Ctr., 1990-94, dir., 1994-2008, U. Ky. Med. Ctr., 1985-90; task force on Alzheimer's disease State of Ohio, Columbus, 1986-92; head, divsn. geriatrics and neuropsychiatry, dept. psychiatry, U. Pitts and Western Psychiatric Inst. and Clinc and Inst.: chair med. sci. adv. bd. Alzheimer's Assn., 1997-2002, nat. bd. dirs., vice-chair bd. dirs.; dir. behavioral neurology of aging tng. program U. Pitts., 1990-2008; bd. dirs. Alzheimer's Disease Internat., chair med. sci. adv. panel, 2002-; chair profl. adv. bd., Greater Pitts. Chpt. Alzheimer's Assn.; founding mem. Lexington-Blue Grass Chpt. Alzheimer's Assn.; vis. prof., dept. medical ethics and health policy, U. Pa. Perelman Sch. Medicine, 2013-14. Mem. editl. bd. of several leading neurology and Alzheimer's clin. publications, Ad Hoc reviewer for several clin. jours.; contbr. chapters to books, several articles to profl. jours. Named Best Doctors in America. Fellow ACP, Am. Neurol. Assn. (Presd. award 1988), Am. Acad. Neurology (chair, sect. on geriatrics, chair practice parameters com. for early detection, diagnosis and mgmt. of dementia); mem. Am. Soc. Neurochemistry, Am. Heart Assn. (stroke coun.), N.Y. Acad. Scis., Soc. Neurosci., Soc. Exptl. Neuropathology (councillor 1990-92), Behavioral Neurology Soc., Am. Bd. of Psychiatry and Neurology (chair strategic planning com., examiner in neurology, mem. Part I (written) Examination Com, mem. neurology coun. 2002), Am. Coll. Neuropsychopharmacology, Am. Neurological Assn., Am. Soc. Neurological Investigation, Behavioral Neurology Soc., Internat. Soc. Neurochemistry, Internat. Soc. Neuropathology, Nat. Neurotrama Soc. Office: U Va Sch Medicine PO Box 800793 Charlottesville VA 22908 Office Phone: 434-924-5118. Business E-Mail: dekosky@virginia.edu.

DE LA CRUZ, CARLOS, wholesale distribution executive; b. Havana, Cuba; arrived in Miami, 1975; m. Rosa de la Cruz; 5 children. BS, U. Pa., 1962, MBA in fin., 1963; JD, U. Miami Sch. Law, Fla., 1972. Car dealership exec.; chmn. Eagle Brands, Coca-cola Bottlers, PR, Trinidad and Tobago; co-founder De La Cruz Collection Contemp. Art Space, Miami, Fla. Co-founder Cuba Study Group; co-chmn. Mesa Redonda. Recipient Silver Medallion Brotherhood Award, Nat. Conf. of Christians & Jews, Distinguished Svc. Award, Fla. Internat. U., Social Responsibility Award, Urban League, Alexis de Tocqueville Award for outstanding philanthropy, United Way, 1997, Simon Weisenthal Ctr. Nat. Cmty. Svc. Award, 1998; named one of top 200 art collectors, ARTnews Mag., 2004—12. Achievements include becoming first hispanic chmn. United Way (1990) & U. Miami Bd. Trustees (1999). Avocation: collector of contemporary art, especially Latin Am.

DELAGI, GREG, electronics executive; BSBA, Nichols Coll., Dudley, Mass., 1984. With Materials & Controls bus. Texas Instruments, Inc., Attleboro, Mass., 1984, sales and mktg. position Semiconductor Group Austin, Tex. and Phoenix, mgr. sales ops. US Western region, with DSP ops., 1996, v.p., mgr. worldwide DSP Systems Bus. Unit, 2000, sr. v.p., gen. mgr. Wireless Terminals Bus. Unit, 2007—. Office: Tex Instruments Inc PO Box 660199 Dallas TX 75266-0199 Office Phone: 972-995-2011. Office Fax: 972-995-4360.

DELAHANTY, REBECCA ANN, school system administrator; b. South Bend, Ind., Oct. 18, 1941; d. Raymond F. and Ann Marie (Batsleer) Paczesny; m. Edward Delahanty, June 22, 1963; children: David, Debbie. BA, Coll. of St. Catherine, Minn., 1977; MA, Coll. St. Thomas, Minn., 1983; PhD, Ga. State U., 1994. Cert. in adminstrn. and supervision Ga. Initiator, tchr. gifted kindergarten Dist. 284 Sch., Wayzata, Minn., 1977-83; gifted kindergarten coord. St. Barts Sch., Wayzata, 1983-85; prin. Dabbs Loomis Sch., Dunwoody, Ga., 1987-91; asst. to supt. Buford (Ga.) City Schs., 1993-98, supt., 1998-99; prof. Ga. State U., 1999-2000; ednl. cons., 2000—; adv. coun. mem. U. Norte Dame, 2010—. Mem. adv. bd. Coll. Applied Profl. Studies U. St. Thomas, 2001—; mem., sci. adv. coun. U. Notre Dame, 2010—. Mem.: Kappa Delta Pi, Phi Delta Kappa.

DE LAMA, ALBERTO, artist; b. Havana; Tchr. Am. Acad. Art, Chgo.; pres. Graphic Direction, Tampa, Fla., 1982—. Works including Galeria Sans Souci, Caracas, Venezuela, Talisman Gallery, Bartlesville, Okla., LeBlanc's Wildlife Gallery, Minocqua, Wis., Univ. Club Tampa, Fla., Galeria Vanidades, Miami, Tampa Yacht Club, Fla., Tampa Bay History Ctr., 2010; represented in permanent collections Pullman Bank, Chgo., Talman Home Fed. Savs., Chgo., Jim Walter Corp., Tampa, Delta Airlines, Atlanta, Galeria Vanidades, Miami, Mahos, Tampa. Recipient Diamond medal, Gold medal, Palette and Chisel Acad. Chgo. Home: 3005 W Horatio St Tampa FL 33609-4121 Office Phone: 813-873-2363.

DELANEY, JOHN ADRIAN, academic administrator; b. Lansing, Mich., June 29, 1956; s. James Edward and Mary Ann (Langius) D.; m. Gena Barrett, Sept. 6, 1980; children: William Langius, Adrian Anne, Marye Margaret, James Barrett. BA in History, U. Fla., 1977, JD, 1981. Bar: Fla. 1981. With State Atty.'s Office, Jacksonville, Fla., 1981-91; chief asst. state atty. Jacksonville, Fla., 1986-91; gen. counsel City of Jacksonville, 1991-92, 94-95, chief of staff, mayor, 1992-94, mayor, 1995—2003; pres. U. North Fla., Jacksonville, 2003—; interim chancellor State Univ. Sys. of Fla., 2008—. Mem. Leadership Jacksonville, 1986, Leadership Fla.-13; chmn. bd. St. Paul's Episcopal Sch. Mem. Inns of Ct., Fla. Blue Key (pres. 1980), Rotary, Delta Upsilon. Roman Catholic. Avocation: camping. Home: 110 Bowles St Jacksonville FL 32266-4917 Office: Office of the Pres U North Fla Jacksonville FL 32224-2648 Office Phone: 904-620-2500. Business E-Mail: jdelaney@unf.edu.

DELANEY, KEVIN FRANCIS, retired military officer, consultant; b. Wolcott, Conn., Sept. 23, 1946; s. John and Mildred Delaney; m. Patricia Delaney, June 8, 1968; children: Kelly, Diana, Seana. BS in Engring., U.S. Naval Acad., Annapolis, Md., 1968; M in Bus., George Washington U., 1977; postgrad., MIT, 1984, Harvard U., 1993. Advanced through grades to rear admiral USN, 1980—82; comdg. officer Heli Anti-Sub Squadron 32, Norfolk, Va., 1980—82; air boss USS Guadalcanal, 1984-86; commdg. officer HSL-31, wing comdr. Helo Sea Control Wing 3, Mayport, Fla., 1987—89; commdg. officer Naval Air Sta., Jacksonville, Fla., 1989-91; comdr. shore activities U.S. Atlantic Fleet, Norfolk, Va., 1993-94; dir. shore installation mgmt. Chief Naval Ops., Washington, 1994-95; comdr. Navy Region S.E. Jacksonville, 1995-98; ret. USN; exec. v.p. Coggin Automotive Group, Jacksonville, Fla., 1998-2000; exec. v.p., COO HealthScreen Am., Jacksonville, Fla., 2000—02; pres., CEO Delaney & Assocs. Consulting, 2002—. Vol. Jax, Inc., Jacksonville, 1995-98, Childrens' Haven, Orange Park, Fla., 1995-98; chmn. Navy/Marine Corp. Relief Soc., Jacksonville, 1995-98; bd. dirs. Salvation Army, United Way, USO, YMCA, Jr. Achievement, World Affairs Coun., Freedoms Found.; vice chmn. Toyota Gator Bowl; past chair United Way Campaign N.E. Fla.; pres. Ronald McDonald House; bd. govs., pres. Fla. State Coll. Jacksonville Found; bd. trustees Jacksonville U., Fla. State Coll. Jacksonville; bd. dirs. Jacksonville C. of C.; chmn. Jacksonville Beaches C. of C, with Fla. Coun. Military Bases & Mission Suport Mem. Fla. C. of C., Rotary (pres. 2000), N.E. Fla. Safety Coun. (chmn.), Nat. Bd. Wounded Warrior Project, SBA Nat. Adv. Coun. Home: 4551 Swilcan Bridge Ln N Jacksonville FL 32224-5618 Office: Delaney and Assocs 8505 Baycenter Rd Ste 300 Jacksonville FL 32256 Office Phone: 904-733-7336 1453. E-mail: kdelaney@baywoodtech.com.

DELANEY, PETER B., energy executive; b. 1953; m. Karen R. Delaney. BA, U. Va.; MBA, Tulane U. CEO Enogex Inc. (subs. OGE Energy Corp.), 2002—04; chmn., pres. & CEO Enogex LLC (subs. OGE Energy Corp.); exec. v.p. fin. & strategic planning OGE Energy Corp., 2002—04, exec. v.p., 2004—07, COO, 2004—07, chmn., pres., CEO, 2007—10, chmn., CEO, 2010—. Office: OGE Energy Corp 321 N Harvey Oklahoma City OK 73101 Office Phone: 405-553-3000. Office Fax: 405-553-3567. Business E-Mail: peter.delaney@oge.com.

DELANEY, RAIGHNE C., lawyer; b. Phila., Apr. 25, 1967; s. Arthur J. and Maria B. D.; m. Sherry A Kuczynski Delaney, Jan. 12, 1991; 1 child, Eleana Alice. BA in Econ. cum laude, Temple U., Phila., 1989; JD with honors, George Washington U., 1995. Bar: Va. 1995, DC 1996, US Supreme Ct. 1999, US Cts. Appeals (4th cir., fed. cir., DC cir.) 1995, Supreme Ct. Va., DC Ct. Appeals, Md. Ct. Appeals, US Dist. Cts. (ea. dist.) Va., US Dist. Cts. (ea. dist.) DC, US Dist. Cts. (ea. dist.) Md, US Ct. Fed. Claims, US Bankruptcy Ct. (ea. dist.) Va., 1996. Assoc. Murray & Jacobs, Alexandria, Va., 1995-97; mem. Pompan, Murray, Ruffner & Werfel PLC, Alexandria, Va., 1997—. Mem. Fairfax, Va., 1996—, inst. Employment Law DC Bar Pub. Svc. Activities Corpn., 1997. Mem. Alexandria C. of C. Legis. Com., 1996—, Alexandria Red Cross Waterfront Festival (exec. com. 2002—). Decorated Army Commendation medal with Bronze Oak Leaf Cluster, Armed Forces Expeditionary medal, Parachutists Badge. Mem. Alexandria Bar Assn., Am. Legion, VFW, Disabled Am. Vets., No. Va. Dental Soc. (rep. peer rev. com. 1996-2001), Arlington Bar Assn., Va. State Bar (4th dist. Disciplinary Com. 2004—), The Dist. Columbia Bar, Veterans Fgn. Wars (Post 3876), Am. Legion Post 24, City of Alexandria (cmty. criminal justice bd., 2005—). Roman Catholic. Achievements include articles editor, The Environ. Lawyer 1994-1995; Mem. Peer Rev.Com., No. Va. Dental Soc., 1996-2001; 1st lt. US Army, 1989-92. Office: Bean, Kinney & Korman 2300 Wilson Blvd Ste 700 Arlington VA 22201-5424 Office Phone: 703-525-4000. Office Fax: 703-525-2207. Business E-Mail: rdelaney@beankinney.com.

DELANEY, WILLIAM J., III, food products executive; m. Debbie Delaney; 3 children. BBA, U. Notre Dame, South Bend, Ind., 1977; MBA, U. Pa., 1982. Asst. treas. Sysco Corp., 1987—91, treas., 1991—93, v.p., 1993—94; CFO Sysco Food Services LLC, Syracuse, NY, 1996—98, sr. v.p., 1998—2002, exec. v.p., 2002—04, pres., CEO Charlotte, NC, 2004—06; sr. v.p. fin. reporting Sysco Corp., Houston, 2007, exec. v.p., CFO, 2007—09, CEO, CFO, 2009, pres., CEO, 2010—. Office: Sysco Corp 1390 Enclave Pkwy Houston TX 77077*

DELANO, SCOTT, state legislator; b. Hendersonville, N.C., Sept. 20, 1971; m. Robin DeLano; children: Matthew, Emily. BA in Acctg., U. Southern Miss. Comml. real estate developer; mem. Dist. 117 Miss. House of Reps., 2010—, mem. county affairs com., juvenile justice com., ports, harbors and airports com., select com. on poverty. Republican. Presbyterian. Mailing: PO Box 4524 Biloxi MS 39535 Office: State Capitol PO Box 1018 Jackson MS 39215 Home Phone: 228-388-8087; Office Phone: 228-806-7418. E-mail: sdelano@house.ms.gov.

DE LARIA, DONALD A., theatre company executive; B in Entrepreneurial Studies & Mktg. and Economics, Babson Coll., Mass. Various positions in equity capital markets including corporate fin. analyst, dir. equity syndicate and v.p. instl. sales; founder Deephaven Fin. Group; v.p. investor rels. Regal Entertainment Group. Bd. dirs. Nat. Investor Rels. Inst., 2007-. Avocations: golf, skiing, boating, in-line skating, home remodeling. Office: Regal Entertainment Group 7132 Regal Ln Knoxville TN 37918 Office Phone: 865-925-9685. Office Fax: 865-922-3188. Business E-Mail: don.delaria@REGmovies.com.

DE LAS HERAS, GONZALO, board member, banker; b. Madrid, Jan. 16, 1940; came to U.S., 1984; s. Antonio and Mary (Milla) de Las H.; m. Kathleen Anne Devitt; children: Elizabeth, Stephen, James. BA, Cambridge U., 1960; LLD Del Amo Scholar, Madrid U., Spain, 1965; postgrad in Bus. Adminstrn. & Economics, U. So. Calif. Exec. dir. B.V.H.A. Ltd., London, 1971-76; exec. v.p. Banco Urquijo, Madrid, 1976-77; v.p., gen. mgr. Morgan Guaranty Trust Co. N.Y., Madrid, 1978-84, sr. v.p., mng. dir. NYC, 1984-90; pres. Emerging Mexico Fund, Inc., 1990—; exec. v.p., N.Am. bus. Santander BanCorp, NYC, 1990—, chmn., 2002—. Mem. N.Y. State Banking Bd., 1993-1997; trustee Inst. Internat. Bankers., bd. dirs., Santander BanCorp, 1998-2000, Sovereign BanCorp, Santander Holdings USA, Inc., 2006-. Contbr. articles on internat. econs., fin. to London, Madrid jours. Bd. dirs. Fgn. Policy Assn.; trustee, chmn. Inst. of Internat. Bankers; bd. dirs. Spanish Inst., Spain-US C. of C. Office: Santander BanCorp 207 Ponce de Leon Ave Hato Rey PR 00917 Office Phone: 787-777-4100. Office Fax: 787-766-1437. Business E-Mail: gonzalo.delasheras@santandernet.com.

DELATORE, RICHARD C., hotel executive; BSBA, Franciscan U., Steubenville, Ohio, 1970. V.p. Schiappa & Co., Wintersville, Ohio, 2002—; mem. Ohio State Racing Commn., 1995—99; bd. commr. Jefferson County, Ohio, 2000—04; coal and timber cons. Steubenville, Ohio, 1970—; v.p. Ohio-Rail Corp., Ohio, 2005—. Bd. dirs. MTR Gaming Group, Inc., 2004—. Mem. Steubenville City Sch. Bd. of Edn., 1993—2000, Jefferson County Joint Vocat.Sch. Bd. of Edn., 1995—98. Recipient Italian Am. of the Yr., Upper Ohio Italian Heritage Festival, 2006. Office: MTR Gaming Group Inc Bd Directors State Rt 2 Chester WV 26034 Office Phone: 304-387-5712. Office Fax: 304-387-2167.

DELAUP, MICKEY STEPHENS, lawyer; b. Monroe, La., Oct. 13, 1957; d. Norman Ray and Carolyn (Parker) Stephens; m. Stephen Guy deLaup, July 25, 1981; children: Carolyn Michelle, Stephen Louis. BA, La. Tech. U., 1978; JD, La. State U., 1981. Bar: La. 1981, U.S. Ct. Appeals (5th cir.) 1983, U.S. Dist. (ea. dist.) La. 1982, U.S. Dist. Ct. (mid. dist.) La. 1988, U.S. Dist. Ct. (we. dist.) La. 1991. Law clk. La. Supreme Ct., New Orleans, 1981-82; assoc. Bernard Cassisa Saporito & Elliot, Metairie, La., 1982-90; ptnr. Bernard, Cassisa & Elliott, Metairie, 1990-95; dir., shareholder LeBlanc, Miranda & deLaup, P.C., Metairie, 1995—2000, mng. ptnr., 1996; ptnr. deLaup & Enright LLC, 2006—12, Neuner Pate, 2013—. Bd. dirs. New Orleans Legal Assistance Corp., 1991, sec., 1992, 94-95; bd. dirs. New Orleans Pro Bono Project, 1989-95, sec., 1991, vice chair, 1992, chair, 1993; bd. dirs. La. Crime Victim's Svcs., 2005-09; mem. La. Atty. Disciplinary Bd. Hearing Com., 2002-06. Fellow: La. Bar Found.; mem. ABA, La. Assn. Def. Counsel (bd. dirs. 1995-96, 2012-), La. Bar Assn. (bd. govs. 1991-93, 97-98, 2013-, asst. bar examiner Torts 1993—2009, examiner, Torts, 2009-12, nominating com. 1998, 99, 2009-, house liaison to bd. govs. 1997-98), Jefferson Bar Assn. Aux. (Outstanding Pro Bono vol. 1992), Jefferson Bar Assn. (treas. 2012, sec. 2013), Def. Rsch. Inst., LSU Law Sch. Alumni Assn. (bd. dirs. 1993-94, treas. 1996-97, sec. 1997-98, v.p. 1998-99), Am. Bd. Trial Advs. (superlawyer, 2012, 2013). Office: Neuner Pate 2701 Metairie Rd Metairie LA 70001 Home Phone: 504-831-3442; Office Phone: 504-828-2277. Business E-Mail: mdelaup@LN-law.com.

DE LA VEGA, RALPH, telecommunications industry executive; b. Cuba, 1951; BSME, Fla. Atlantic U.; MBA, No. Ill. U.; grad. Exec. Program, U. Va. Mgmt. asst. BellSouth (then Southern Bell), Atlanta, 1974, positions of increasing responsibility to pres. Broadband and Internet Svcs.; pres. BellSouth Latin America; COO Cingular Wireless, LLC, 2004—07; group pres. regional telecommunications & entertainment AT&T Inc. (merger of SBC Communications & AT&T Corp.), 2007; pres., CEO AT&T Mobility, 2007—08, AT&T Mobility, LLC, 2008—. Bd. dirs. NY Life Insurance Co., 2009—. Author: Obstacles Welcome: Turn Adversity into Advantage in Business and Life, 2009. Chmn. Jr. Achievement Worldwide, 2009—; bd. dirs. Boy Scouts America, Ga. chpt., Atlanta Symphony Orchestra, Jr. Achievement Worldwide, 2005—. Named Exec. of Yr., Assn. Latino Profl. in Fin. & Acctg., 2004; named one of 50 Most Important Hispanics in Tech., Bus., Hispanic Engineer and Info. Tech. mag., 2003, 2005, Top 100 Hispanics, Hispanic Bus. mag., 2004. Office: AT&T Mobility Glenridge Highlands Two 5565 Glenridge Connector Atlanta GA 30342

DELEN, DANIEL M. (DAAN DELEN), tobacco company executive; b. Netherlands, 1965; BBA in Internat. Bus., Wash. State U. With Sara Lee Corp., England; pres. British American Tobacco Ltd., Japan, brand mgr. Guatemala, 1989, internat. brand mgr. England, 1992, mktg. dir. Singapore, 1994, Chile, 1995, Argentina, 1996, pres., Bus. Unit Japan, 2004; sr. v.p., mktg. & sales Brown & Williamson Tobacco Corp. (subs. British American Tobacco Ltd.), 2001; pres., CEO R.J. Reynolds Tobacco Co., Winston-Salem, NC, 2007—08, chmn., pres., CEO, 2008—10; pres., CEO Reynolds American, Inc., Winston-Salem, NC, 2011—. Bd. dirs. Reynolds American Inc., 2011—. Bd. dirs. Winston Salem Alliance. Office: Reynolds American Inc 401 N Main St Winston Salem NC 27101-2990

DELEON, CHARLES, lawyer; married; 3 children. BA in Govt. & Polit. Sci., George Mason U., 1988; JD, George Washington U., 1995. Senate intern US Senate, 1987—88; rsch. asst. Control Data Corp., 1988—89; intelligence analyst Army Intelligence and Security Command, 1990—94; legal intern Wilkinson, 1994—95; fed. counsel Electronic Data Sys. Corp., 1995—97; sr. legal counsel PSINet, 1997—2000; gen. counsel, corp. sec. CyBiz, Inc., 2000—01; dep. gen. counsel GTSI Corp., Chantilly, Va., 2001—04, sr. v.p., gen. counsel & corp. sec., 2001—. Former military intelligence officer US Army. Mem.: ABA, Va. State Bar. Office: GTSI Corp 2553 Dulles View Dr Ste 100 Herndon VA 20171-5219 Office Phone: 703-502-2000. Office Fax: 703-222-5204. Business E-Mail: charles.deleon@gtsi.com.

DE LEON, LIDIA MARIA, magazine editor; b. Havana, Cuba, Sept. 10, 1957; d. Leon J. and Lydia (Diaz Cruz) de L. BA in Communications cum laude, U. Miami, Coral Gables, Fla., 1979. Staff writer Miami Herald, Fla., 1978-79; editorial asst. Halsey Pub. Co., Miami, 1980-81, assoc. editor, 1981, editor, 1981—, editor Delta Sky mag., 1983-95. Mem. Am. Soc. Mag. Editors, Am. Assn. Travel Editors, Golden Key, Sigma Delta Chi. Roman Catholic. Avocation: tennis.

DELFINO, JOSEPH JOHN, environmental engineering sciences educator; b. Port Chester, NY, 1941; s. John J. and Frances C. Delfino; m. Dorothy Delfino; children: Janelle, Justin. BS in Chemistry, Holy Cross Coll., 1963; MS in Chemistry, U. Idaho, 1965; PhD in Civil and Environ. Engring. & Water Chemistry, U. Wis., 1968. From instr. to assoc. prof. chemistry USAF Acad., Colorado Springs, Colo., 1968-72; sect. head, tech. mgr. IBT & Nalco Environ. Sci., Northbrook, Ill., 1972-74; sect. head environ. scis. Wis. State Lab. Hygiene, Madison, 1974-82; from asst. prof. to assoc. prof. U. Wis., Madison, 1974-80, assoc. dir. water resources ctr., 1977-78, prof. civil and environ. engring., 1980-82; prof. environ. engring. sci. U. Fla., Gainesville, 1982—, affiliate prof. chemistry, 1990—, chmn. dept. environ. engring. sci., 1990—99, interim chmn., 2002—03, affiliate prof. natural resources and environment, 1994—, interim dir. Ctr. for Wetlands and Water Resources, 1995. Com. mem., std. methods exam. of water and wastewater Am. Water Works Assn., 1982—2008, part coord., 1987—90; regional v.p. North America Com. Tech., World Fedn. Engring. Orgns., 1998—2002. Writer, co-originator, chief tech. advisor documentary Fla. Water Story, Sta. WEDU-TV, Tampa, Fla.; assoc. editor Jour. Am. Water Resources Assn., 2004—; contbr. articles on water chemistry, environ. scis. and engring. to profl. publs. Mem. Citizens Environ. Quality Coun., Northbrook, Ill., 1972-74; mem. Mercury Tech. Adv. Com., State of Fla., 1991-93; mem. Alachua County Air Quality Commn., Fla., 1999; mem. T.M.D.L. tech. adv. com. Fla. Dept. Environ. Protection, 1999-00; mem. Water Mgmt. Com., Gainesville, 2006-08. Capt. USAF, 1968-72. Fellow AAAS, Am. Water Resources Assn.; mem. Am. Chem. Soc. (exec. com. environ. chem. divsn. 1973-76, editor Envirofacs environ. chem. divsn. 1973-76, student awards com. environ. chem. divsn. 1995-97, com. on environ. improvement 1998-01, Cert. of Merit environ. chem. divsn. 1991), Nat. Assn. State U. and Land Grant Colls. (ecology sect., exec. com. 1998-01), Assn. Environ. Engring. and Sci. Profs., Univs. Coun. on Water Resources (bd. dirs. 2009-; Pub. Svc. award 1990). Office: U Fla Dept Environ Engring Scis PO Box 116450 Gainesville FL 32611-6450

DELGADO-COLON, AIDA M., federal judge; b. Lares, PR, 1955; BA cum laude, U. PR, 1977; JD cum laude, Pontifical Cath. U. PR, 1980. Bar: PR 1980. Dir. investigations PR Governor's Advisory Bd. on Labor Policy, 1980-82; asst. fed. public defender, 1982—93; 1st asst. fed. public defender San Juan, 1992—93; magistrate judge US Dist. Ct. PR, San Juan, 1994—2006, judge, 2006—, chief judge, 2011—. Mem. Fed. Bar Exam. Com., 1986—; mem. local rules com. US Dist. Ct. PR 1991—; chmn. interpreters & ct. reports com., 1994-96, mem. criminal justice act com., 1994-96, EEO coord., 1995-99, EDR coord., 1999—; adj. prof. Pontifical Cath. U. PR Sch. Law, 2003-04. Mem. Fed. Magistrate Judges Assn., Women Judges Assn., PR Bar Assn., Cath. U. PR Law Sch. Alumni Assn., Nat. Hispanic Bar Assn. Office: Clemente Ruiz-Nazario US Courthouse Office 470 150 Carlos Chardon St San Juan PR 00918-1703 Office Phone: 787-772-3196.*

DELGADO HERNÁNDEZ, PEDRO ALBERTO, federal judge; b. San Juan, 1956; BS, U. Puerto Rico, 1979; JD, U. Puerto Rico Sch. Law, 1983. Law clk. Puerto Rican Inst. Judicial Studies, 1983—84; law clk. to Hon. Juan Torruella US Dist. Ct. PR, 1984, US Ct. Appeals (1st Cir.), 1984—86; ptnr. O'Neill & Borges LLC, 1986—93, 1996—2014; solicitor gen. Commonwealth of PR, San Juan, 1993—95; judge PR Cir. Ct. Appeals, 1995—96, US Dist. Ct. PR, San Juan, 2014—. Served in USAR, 1979—85. Office: US District Court 150 Ave Carlos Chardón St San Juan PR 00918*

D'ELIA, CHRISTOPHER FRANCIS, marine biologist, educator, academic administrator; s. Francis G. and Marian Frances (Wakeman) D'Elia; m. Jennifer Anne Hunnicutt, June 10, 1973; 1 child, Tallmadge Wakeman. AB, Middlebury Coll., 1968; PhD, U. Ga., 1974. Postdoctoral scholar UCLA, 1974; vis. asst. prof. U. So. Calif., LA, 1975; Noyes postdoctoral fellow Woods Hole (Mass.) Oceanog. Inst., 1975-77; from asst. prof. to assoc. prof. Chesapeake Biol. Lab. U. Md., Solomons, 1977—88, prof., 1988-99, SUNY, Albany, 1999—2004; dir. biol. oceanog. program NSF, Washington, 1987—89; dir. Md. Sea Grant Coll., 1989—98; v.p. rsch. SUNY, Albany, 1999—2002, prof. biology and pub. adminstrn. and policy, 2002—04; regional assoc. vice chancellor for rsch. and grad. studies, prof. environ. sci. and policy U. South Fla., St. Petersburg, 2004—09, prof. marine science, dir. Center Sci. Pol. Applic. Coastal Environments, 2004—09; dean and prof. Sch. Coast & Environ. La. State U., 2009—. Chair tech. adv. group Patuxent 208 Basin Plan, 1980—82; mem. adv. panel ocean scis. divsn. NSF, Washington, 1982—84, mem. fleet rev. com., 1999; chmn. Mid-Atlantic Regional Marine Rsch. Bd., 1991—96; mem. rsch. planning adv. group, priorities workgroup Chesapeake Bay Program, 1989—91, mem. sci. and tech. adv. com., 1993—98; cons. to govt. and industry, 1976—; regional rep. coastal resources adv. com., Md., 1982—83; mem. adv. com. Md. Sea Grant program, 1980—86; mem. sci. adv. bd. ecol. processes and effects com., marine monitoring com. EPA, 1991; mem. Leadership Md., 1997; mem. sea grant program assessment team NOAA, 2004, 2006; mem. Nat. Ctr. for Environ. Rsch. panel, 2004, Leadership St. Petersburg, 2005, US Nat. Com. for Intergovtl. Oceanog. Commn., 2006—. Mem. editl. bd. Limnology and Oceanography, 1983—86; contbr. 65 articles in profl. jours. and books. Bd. dirs. Hudson River Found., 1998—; acad. adv. com. Indsl. Rsch. Inst., 2001—03; mem. exec. inst. Albany-Colonie C. of C., 2000; mem. Com. Water Leadership Program, 2004—, US Nat. Com. Intergovtl. Oceanographic Commn., 2006—; bd. dirs. Astrolabe, Inc., 1991—99, v.p., 1994—99; bd. dirs. Sci. Ctr. of Pinellas, 2004—, vice chair, 2005—06, chair, 2006—. Recipient Outstanding Service cert., Tri-County Coun., Meritorious Svc. award, Chesapeake Bay Program, Md., Gov.'s Salute to Excellence award, 1994; grantee, ERDA, 1976, EPA, 1978—82, Dept. Energy, 1979, NOAA, 1989—98, NSF, 1979—; Disting. Patrick scholar, Acad. Natural Scis., 1982—83. Fellow: AAAS (mem. exptl. program to stimulate competitive rsch. rev. teams 2005); mem.: Great Lakes Rsch. Consortium (bd. gov. 1999—2004), Indsl. Rsch. Inst. (mem. acad. advancment com. 2001—04), Coun. Soc. Pres. (sec. 1993—96, treas. 1997, chmn.-elect 1998, chmn. 1999, past chmn. 2000, chmn. emeritus 2001—), Coun. Sea Grant Dirs. (chmn.-elect, chmn. budget com. 1994), Sea Grant Assn. (pres. 1991—92, chmn. fed. rels. com. 1992—93, pres. 1999, President's award), N.Y. Acad. Sci., Nat. Assn. State Univs. and Land Grant Colls. (co-chmn. bd. dirs. 1994—95, coun. grad. rsch. and grad. edn. exec. com. 2000—01, bd. oceans and atmosphere, mem. exec. com., chmn. edn. com., chmn. spl. task force reorganization), Nat. Assn. Environ. Profs. (bd. dirs. Md. 1985—86), Internat. Soc. Reef Studies, Estuarine Rsch. Fedn. (v.p. 1989—91, pres. 1991—93, past pres. 1993—95), Ecol. Soc. Am. (chmn. pub. affairs com. 1989—91, vice chmn. 1991—92), Am. Soc. Limnology and Oceanography, Am. Chem. Soc., Oceanog. Soc. (life), Vinoy Club, Cosmos Club, Sigma Xi. Avocations: sailing, skiing, private pilot. Office: School of the Coast & Environment Louisiana State University 1002Q Energy, Coast & Environment Bldg Baton Rouge LA 70803 Office Phone: 225-578-8574. Business E-Mail: cdelia@lsu.edu.

DELL, MICHAEL SAUL, computer company executive; b. Houston, Feb. 23, 1965; s. Alexander and Lorraine Dell; m. Susan Lieberman, Oct. 23, 1989; 4 children. Attended, U. Tex.; D in Econ. Sci. (hon.), U. Limerick, 2002. Founder Dell Computer Corp. (formerly PC's Ltd.), Austin, 1984; chmn. Dell, Inc., Round Rock, Tex., 1984—, CEO, 1984—2004, 2007—. Bd. dirs. Dell Inc., 1984—; founder MSD Capital, LP., NYC, 1998—; IT Governor, mem. found. bd. World Econ. Forum; mem. exec. com. Internat. Bus. Coun.; mem. US Bus. Coun., President's Coun. of Advisors on Sci. & Tech.; mem. gov. bd. Indian Sch. of Bus., Hyderabad, India; investor ValleyCrest, 2006—. Author: Direct From Dell: Strategies that Revolutionized an Industry, 1999; guest appearance with wife (films) The Sno Cone Stand, Inc., 2008. Co-founder Michael & Susan Dell Found., Austin, 1999—. Recipient Customer Satisfaction award, JD Power, 1991, 1993, Bower award for Business Leadership, Franklin Inst., 2013; named Entrepreneur of Yr., Inc. Mag., 1990, CEO of Yr., Fin. World Mag., 1993, Chief Exec. of Yr., Chief Exec. Mag., 2001; named one of Top 10 Most Powerful People in Bus., Fortune Mag., 2003, 2004, Forbes 400: Richest Americans, 2005—, 50 Who Matter Now, CNNMoney.com Bus. 2.0, 2006, World's Richest People, Forbes Mag., 2007—. Fellow: AAAS. Republican. Jewish. Achievements include donating a collection of materials to the Smithsonian in 2007, including his employee badge, one of the company's newest computers and a PC Limited computer from 1985. Office: Dell Inc 1 Dell Way Round Rock TX 78682-0001*

DELLACROCE, FRANK J., plastic surgeon, entrepreneur; b. West Monroe, La., Mar. 16, 1967; s. Frank T. and Glenda Gayle DellaCroce; m. Janet Davis DellaCroce, June 15, 1992. MD, LSU, Shreveport, 1994. Diplomate Am. Bd. Plastic Surgery, 2002. Founder, dir. Ctr. Restorative Breast Surgery, New Orleans, 2003—. Contbr. to profl. med. publs. Hon. bd. mem. Komen Found., 2011—14; force adv. bd. FORCE, Orlando, 2010—14. Recipient Spirit award, Am. Cancer Soc., 2009, Hope Lodge Hero award, 2010; named Innovator of Yr., New Orleans City Bus. Mag., 2009; named one of Best Drs. in America, 2009—14. Fellow: ACS, Am. Acad. Otolaryngology, Head & Neck Surgery; mem.: Am. Soc. Reconstructive Microsurgery, Am. Acad. Facial Plastic and Reconstructive Surgery, Am. Soc. Plastic Surgeons. Independent. Achievements include development of the body lift perforator flap for breast reconstruction; stacked DIEP flap for breast reconstruction. Avocations: artist, entrepreneur, philanthropist. Office: Ctr Restorative Breast Surgery 1717 St Charles Ave New Orleans LA 70130 Personal E-mail: drd@breastcenter.com.*

DELLENEY, FRANCIS GREGORY, state legislator; b. Chester, SC, Feb. 9, 1952; s. Francis Gregory and Ruby Wright Delleney; m. Rebecca Carolina Williams, 1983; children: Caroline Caldwell, Francis Gregory III. BA, The Citadel, 1974; JD, Samford U., 1981. Ptnr. Hamilton, Delleney & Hemlepp; mem. Dist. 43 SC House of Reps., 1991—, chair Subcommittee on Constl. Laws, mem. Judiciary Com. Comdr. USNR. Mem.: Am. Legion, Gideons Internat., Shrine Club, Masonic Lodge. Republican. Presbyterian. Office: 532C Blatt Bldg Columbia SC 29201 Mailing: PO Drawer 808 Chester SC 29706 Office Phone: 803-581-2211, 803-734-3074. E-mail: fgd@schouse.org.

DELLINGER, WALTER ESTES, III, lawyer, law educator; b. Charlotte, NC, May 15, 1941; s. Walter Estes and Grace Phelan (Lawing) D.; m. Anne Elizabeth Maxwell, June 12, 1965; children: Hampton, Andrew. AB with honors, U. N.C., at Chapel Hill, 1963; LLB, Yale U., 1966. Bar: N.C. 1970, DC, 1998. Assoc. prof. law U. Miss., 1966-68; law clk. to Justice Hugo L. Black US Supreme Ct., 1968-69; assoc. prof. law Duke U. Law Sch., 1969-72, Douglas B. Maggs prof. law, 1972—93, 1998—, assoc. dean, 1974-76, acting dean, 1976-78; prof. in residence US Dept. Justice, Washington, 1980-81, adv. to Pres., 1993, asst. atty. gen., Office Legal Counsel, 1993-96, acting solicitor gen., 1996-97; ptnr. O'Melveny & Myers LLP, Washington. Cons., draftsman N.C. Criminal Code Commn., 1970-78; vis. prof. U. Southern Calif. Law Ctr., 1973-74, U. Mich. Law Sch., 1977, Cath. U. Leuven, 1985 Mem. bd. editors Yale Law Jour., 1965-66, American Prospect; contbr. articles to profl. jours. Rockefeller Found. Humanities fellow, 1981-82; Nat. Humanities Ctr. Fellow, 1988-89; recipient Lifetime Achievement award The American Lawyer mag., 2013; named one of The 100 Most Influential Lawyers in America The Nat. Law Journal, 2013 Mem. ABA, N.C. State Bar.; mem. exec. com. Yale Law Sch. Assn. Democrat. Office: O'Melveny & Myers LLP 1625 Eye St NW Washington DC 20006 also: Duke University School Law Box 90389 Science Dr & Towerview Rd Durham NC 27708 Office Phone: 919-613-7187, 202-383-5319. Office Fax: 202-383-5414. Business E-Mail: wdellinger@law.duke.edu. E-mail: wdellinger@omm.com.*

DELL'OSSO, NICK (DOMENIC J. DELL'OSSO JR.), energy company executive; married; 2 children. BS in Economics, Boston Coll., 1998; MBA, U. Tex., Austin, 2003. Cons. Deloitte Cons.; assoc. Ernst & Young Corporate Finance; investment banker Banc of America Securities, 2004—06, Jefferies & Co., 2006—08; v.p. finance, CFO Chesapeake Midstream Devel., L.P., Oklahoma City, 2008—10; sr. v.p., CFO Chesapeake Energy Corp., Oklahoma City, 2010—. Office: Chesapeake Energy Corporation PO Box 18496 Oklahoma City OK 73154-0496 Office Phone: 405-935-8000.*

DELLY, GAYLA J., electronics executive; b. 1960; BS in Acctg., Samford U. CPA. Sr. mgr., audit group KPMG, 1984—95; contr. Benchmark Electronics, Inc., 1996—2002, treas., 1996—2006, v.p., fin., 2000—04, exec.v.p., 2004—06, CFO, 2001—06, pres., 2006—11, pres., CEO, 2011—. Bd. dirs. Power One, Inc., 2005, Flowserve Corp., 2008—. Office: Benchmark Electronics Inc 3000 Technology Dr Angleton TX 77515 Office Phone: 979-849-6550. Office Fax: 979-848-5270. Business E-Mail: gayla_delly@bench.com.*

DELOACH, HARRIS E.(EUGENE), JR., consumer products company executive, lawyer; b. Aug. 7, 1944; s. Harris Eugene and Julia (Murdock) Del; m. Louise Hawes, June 12, 1969; children: Harris Eigene III, John Wilson Malloy, Jeanette Hawes. BBA, U. SC, 1966; JD, 1969. Bar: SC 1969, US Dist. Ct. SC 1969, US Ct. Appeals (4th cir.) 1974. Ptnr. Wilmeth & DeLoach, Hartsville, SC, 1972-85; v.p., gen. counsel Sonoco Products Co., Hartsville, SC, 1986-90, exec. v.p., 1966-98, sr. exec. v.p., 2000, pres., CEO, 2002—05, chmn., pres., CEO, 2005—10, chmn., CEO, 2010—. V.p. HDFP, 1990-92; bd. dirsBank of Hartsville, Coker's Pedigreed Seed Co., Har tsville, Sonoco Products Co. Trustee Coker Coll., Hartsville, 1974-79, vice chmn., 1979; chmn. bd. trustees Byerly Hosp., Hartsville, 1976-79, chmn. 1997; chmn. bd. dirs. Thomas Hart Acad., Hartsville, 1984. Served to capt. USAF, 1969-72. Recipient Algernon Sydney Sullivan award Coker Coll., 1985, Disting. Alumnus award U. SC, 1998. Mem. ABA, SC Bar Assn., 4th Jud. Cir. Assn., SC (v.p. 1974-78), Darlington County Bar Assn. (pres. 1984), Hartsville C. of C. (pres. 1977), Rotary (pres. Hartsville club 1977, Citizen of Yr. Hartsville club 1980). Presbyterian. Home: 620 W Home Ave Hartsville SC 29550-4430 Office: Sonoco Products Co North Second St Hartsville SC 29550-3305

DELONG, BRAD (JAMES BRADFORD DELONG), economics professor; b. Boston, June 24, 1960; s. James V. DeLong and Fonya Usher (Lord) Helm; m. Ann Marie Marciarille, June 7, 1986; children: Michael M., Gianna D. Marciarille. BA, Harvard U., 1982, MA, 1985, PhD, 1987. Instr. MIT, Cambridge, Mass., 1980-87; asst. prof. economics Boston U., 1987-88, Harvard U., Cambridge, 1988-91, Danzinger assoc. prof. economics, 1991-93; assoc. prof. economics U. Calif., Berkeley, 1993—97, prof., 1997—; dep. asst. sec. for econ. policy US Dept. Treasury, Washington, 1993—95; rsch. assoc. Nat. Bur. Econ. Rsch., 1995—. Vis. scholar Fed. Res. Bank San Francisco, 1996—. Democrat. Office: U Calif Berkeley Dept Economics 601 Evans Hall Berkeley CA 94720 Office Phone: 510-643-4027. Office Fax: 510-642-6615. E-mail: delong@econ.berkeley.edu.

DELONG, MAHLON R., neurologist, educator; b. Des Moines, Iowa, Mar. 17, 1938; MD cum laude, Harvard U., 1966. Lic. Am. Bd. Psychiatry and Neurology, Nat. Bd. Med. Examiners. Asst. resident, intern Harvard Svc./Boston City Hosp., 1966—68; rsch. assoc. NIMH/Clin. Sci. Lab., Bethesda, Md., 1968—70, sr. staff fellow, 1970—71, NIMH/Neurophysiology Lab., Bethesda, Md., 1971—73; resident neurology Johns Hopkins U., Balt., 1973—76, asst. prof. neurology and physiology, 1975—80; chief neurology svc. Columbia (Md.) Med. Plan, 1976—80; dir. phys. diagnosis course Johns Hopkins Hosp., Balt., 1977—80; chief dept. neurology Baltimore City Hosps., 1980—85; assoc. prof. neurology and neurosci. Johns Hopkins Sch. Medicine, 1980—85, prof. neurology and neurosci., 1986—90; chmn. dept. neurology Emory U. Sch. Medicine, Atlanta, 2001—, prof. dept. neurology, 2001—, William Timmie Professor, dept. neurology; sect. chief dept. neurology Emory Clinic, Atlanta, 2001—. Mem. editl. bd.: Critical Revs. in Neurobiology, 1997—, Archives of Neurology, 1996—, mem. manuscript rev. com.: Sci., Jour. Neurophysiology, Annals of Neurology, others. Recipient Tchr.-Investigator award, Nat. Inst. Neurol. and Communicative Disorders and Stroke, 1974—79, Javitz Neuroscis. Investigator award, 1986, Fred Springer award, Am. Parkinson Disease Found., 1997, Disting. Leadership award, Huntington's Disease Soc. Am., 1998; named William Patterson Timmie chair neurology, 1993—, Ga. Biomed. Rsch. scientist, 1995; named to Soc. Scholars, Johns Hopkins U., 1998. Mem.: AAAS, Am. Acad. Arts & Sciences, Inst. Medicine, Assn. Univ. Profs. Neurology, Soc. for Neurosci., Am. Parkinson's Disease Assn. (sci. adv. bd. 1990—), Nat. Inst. Neurol. Disorders and Stroke (counselor 1993—99), Dystonia Med. Rsch. Found. (mem. grant rev. 1990—), Am. Neurol. Assn. (chmn. fin. com. 1995—96, 1994—96, councilor 1994—95, mem. fin. com. 1993—), Internat. Basal Ganglia Soc. (sec. 1995—98), Movement Disorder Soc. (mem. internat. exec. com. 1997—). Achievements include research in structure and focus of basal ganglia, motor functions of the basal ganglia; motor system physiology, movement disorders in man, pathophysiology of movement disorders, basal forebrain cholinergic system, and Alzheimer's Disease and related dementia. Office: Emory U Dept Neurology Ste 6000 1639 Pierce Dr Atlanta GA 30322

DELOTTO, JEFFREY DANIEL, language educator, writer; b. Nassawadox, Va., Dec. 23, 1949; s. Mayo Andrew and Emalyn Crouch DeLotto. BA, U. Fla., Gainesville, 1973; MA, Fla. State U., Tallahassee, 1974, PhD, 1980. Vis. lectr. Tex. Wesleyan U., Lubbock, 1977—80; lectr. in English Yarmouk U., Irbid, Jordan, 1980—82; prof. English Tex. Wesleyan U., Ft. Worth, 1983—, interim dean, sci. and humanities, 1997—99; Fulbright lectr. in English U. Plovdiv, Bulgaria, 1992—93. Gen. editor Tex. Wesleyan U. Press. Editor: AmarilloBay, 1995; author: Voices at the Door, 1995 (First pl. SW Poets Series, 1994), Days of a Chameleon Collected Poems, 2007. Fellow Fulbright Lectureship in Am. Lit., Coun. for Internat. Exch. of Scholars, 1992—93; NEH fellow, 1984, 1989. Mem.: Tex. Coll. English Assn. (pres. 2004—05), Conf. of Coll. Teachers of English (pres. 1999—2000, Best Paper award 1990, 2004, 2007), Coll. English Assn., Tex. Coun.Tchrs. English Lang. Arts (life; pres. 1990—91, Outstanding English Educator Post Secondary 1992), Ft. Worth Poetry Soc. Avocations: writing, poetry, sailing, painting. Home: 2415 Sandy Ln Fort Worth TX 76112 Office: Texas Wesleyan Univ 1201 Wesleyan St Fort Worth TX 76105 Business E-Mail: jdelotto@txwes.edu.

DELP, ROY EDWARD, music educator, singer; b. Newark, Oct. 14, 1943; s. Roy John and Jane Molenska Delp; m. Maryellen Butin, Apr. 16, 1966; children: George Edward, Roy Jonathan. MusB, Oberlin Coll. Conservatory Music, Ohio, 1965; MusM, New Eng. Conservatory, Boston, 1967. Asst. prof. music Augusta Coll., Ga., 1967—72; asst. prof. dept. music U. Wyo., Laramie, 1972—76; Walter S. James prof. voice coll. music Fla. State U., Tallahassee, 1976—, coord. voice and opera area faculty, 1982—. On-site reporter opera, musical theater program grant proposals NEA, Washington, 1991—93. Singer: Nat. Pub. Radio, (Operas) Lake George Opera Company, Orlando Opera Company, Orquesta Sinfonica de Chile; contbr. articles to profl. jours. Mem.: Music Tchrs. Nat. Assn., Nat. Assn. Tchrs. Singing (nat. pres. 1999—2004). Home: 1312 Lemond St Tallahassee FL 32308-0720 Office: Florida State Univ College Music Tallahassee FL 32306-1180

DELUCA, ANTHONY J., civilian military employee; b. NYC, Apr. 29, 1946; s. Joseph Anthony and Jean (Trentalange) DeL.; m. Mary Alaimo, June 18, 1967; children: Renee, Joseph, Regina. B in Econs., Fordham U., 1967; M in Pub. Adminstrn., Troy State U., 1976. Cert. Acquisition Profl. Level III. USAF procurement officer Eglin AFB, Fla., 1967-72, civil svc. various positions with the deputy for procurement and mfg. Fla., 1972-78; procurement analyst, USAF mem. Fed. Acquistion Regulation Project Office, 1978-79; supervisory procurement analyst Hdqs. Air Force Syss. Command, Andrews AFB, Md., 1979-82, advanced from first command competition advocate to deputy Air Force competition advocate gen., 1984-87; first civilian competition advocate gen. Office of the Asst. Sec. of the Air Force (Acquistion), Washington, 1987; dir. Air Force Office Small and Disadvantaged Bus. Utilization, Washington, 1990-2001; pres. INTECS Internat., Alexandria, Va., 2001—. Ira Eaker fellow Air Force Assn.; recipient Meritorious Civilian Svc. award, Exceptional Civilian Svc. award, Presdl. Disting. Rank award, Presdl. Meritorious Rank award, Minority Participation Program award Latin Am. Mgmt. Assn., Fed. Advocate award SBA, Frances Perkins award, Applause award; named Advocate of Yr., Small Disadvantaged Bus. Mem. Sr. Exec. Assn., Air Force Assn. Roman Catholic. Avocations: biking, music.

DELUCA, PATRICK PHILLIP, pharmacist, pharmaceutical educator, humanitarian scientist; b. Scranton, Pa., Sept. 7, 1935; m. Judy Beitzel, June 16, 1956; children: Paul, Thomas, Patrick, Donald, Michelle, Michael. BS in Pharmacy, Temple U., 1957, MS in Pharmacy, 1960, PhD in Pharmacy (SKF W.G. Karr fellow), 1963; Doctorate (hon.), U. Perugia, Italy, 2006. Analytical chemist SKF Co., 1957-59; sr. rsch. pharmacist CIBA Co., Summit, NJ, 1963-66, plant mgr., 1966-69, dir., 1969-70, Cormedics Corp., Somerville, NJ; faculty U. Ky. Coll. Pharmacy, 1970—, prof., assoc. dean, 1972-87, dir. ctr. for pharmaceutical sci. and tech., 1987-88, chmn. faculty pharm. scis., 1998-2000, emeritus prof., 2010—. Pharm. sci. adv. com. FDA, 2003-06; cons. to pharm. industry and FDA., editor-in-chief AAPS Pharm Sci. Tech., 1999-2007 Editor-in-chief: Jour. Pharm. Devel. and Tech., 1995—99; contbr. more than 240 articles to sci. and profl. jours. Co-founder Faith Pharmacy, 2000. Recipient Leo G. Penn award Temple U., 1957, Lunsford-Richardson Pharmacy Rsch. awards Richardson Merrell Co., 1960, 62, Best Paper Toward Advancement Indsl. Pharmacy award N.J. Pharmacy Discussion Group, 1965, Outstanding Educator award in U.S., 1974, Disting. Alumni award Temple U., 1989, Sturgill Rsch. award U. Ky., 1995, Advisory Com. Svc. award FDA, 2005, William Lyon award U. Ky., 2011, Joseph Sprowls award Temple U. Sch. Pharmacy, 2012; also numerous grants. Fellow: Am. Assn. Indian Pharm. Scientists, Inst. for Advanced Biotech., Am. Assn. Pharm. Scientists (bd. dirs. 1986—88, 2005—10, pres. 2008—09, Rsch. Achievement award 1988, Outstanding Manuscript award in pharm. devel. and technology 1998, Outstanding Educator award 2000, Sullivan medallist at UK 2001, Ky Pharmacist of Yr. 2002, Outstanding Manuscript award in pharm. devel. and technology 2002, Swintosky Disting. lectr. 2003, Outstanding Manuscript award in pharm. devel. and technology 2006, Dale Wurster Rsch. Achievement award 2006), Acad. Pharm. Sci. (pres. 1979—80); mem.: N.Y. Acad. Sci., Am. Soc. Hosp. Pharmacists (Rsch. award 1975), Parenteral Drug Assn. (Rsch. Achievement award 1975), Am. Pharm. Assn., Rho Chi, Sigma Chi. Achievements include research in pharmaceutical technology and novel drug delivery; co-founder Faith Pharmacy, Lexington. Home: 3292 Nantucket Dr Lexington KY 40502-3269 Office: U Ky Coll Pharmacy Limestone St Lexington KY 40536-0001 Business E-Mail: ppdelu1@uky.edu.

DELUCIA, GENE ANTHONY, government administrator, computer company executive; b. Methuen, Mass., Feb. 20, 1952; s. Antonio Gitano and Carmen Theresa (Carpenito) DeL. BS, Boston Coll., 1973; MBA, Northeastern U., 1980. Project mgr. Delphi div. Arthur D. Little Inc., Lowell, Mass., 1975-78, gen. mgr. eastern region, 1978-80; systems devel. mgr. Wang Labs. Inc., Lowell, 1980-83; pres., CEO Computer Innovations Inc., Lowell, 1983-86; pres. Corp. Investment Bus. Brokers, North Andover, Mass., 1986-88; v.p. Maximus Inc., Falls Church, Va., 1988-90, div. pres., 1990-96; pres. Strategic Visions Inc., Indian Rocks Beach, Fla., 1996—2001; prin. Capital Assocs., Inc., Indian Rocks Beach, 2001—. Mem. AOPA. Avocations: flying, golf, tennis. Home and Office: 518 Harbor Dr N Indian Rocks Beach FL 33785-3117 Personal E-mail: genedelucia@gmail.com.

DELURGIO, DAVID, cardiac electrophysiologist, educator; MD, U. Calif., 1990. Diplomate AM. Bd. Internal Medicine-cardiovasc. disease, 2007, AM. Bd. Internal Medicine-clin. cardiac electrophysiology. Intern UCLA Med. Ctr., 1991, fellow cardiovasc. disease Calif., 1993—95; resident internal medicine Emory Univ. Med. Ctr., Ga., 1991—93; joined Emory Univ., 1996, assoc. prof. medicine; hosp. affiliations include Emory Univ. Hosp., Emory Univ. Hosp Midtown. Mem.: ACP, Heart Rhythm Soc., Heart Failure Soc., Am. Coll. of Cardiology. Office: Emory University Hospital Midtown 550 Peachtree St NE Fl 6 Atlanta GA 30308 Office Phone: 404-686-2504.

DEMARA, RONALD FRANCIS, computer engineer, educator; BS, Lehigh U., 1987; MS, U. Md., College Park, 1989; PhD, U. So. Calif., 1992. Registered profl. engr., Calif., 1992. Assoc. engr. IBM Corp., Manassas, Va., 1986—89; assoc. prof., prof. U. Ctrl. Fla., Orlando, Fla., 1992—. Contbr. articles to profl. jours. Mem.: IEEE (sr.; assoc. editor Trans. VLSI), Assn. Computing Machinery. Office: University of Central Florida 4000 Central Florida Blvd Orlando FL 32816-2450 Business E-Mail: demara@mail.ucf.edu.

DEMARCO, PAUL J., state legislator; b. Birmingham, Ala., July 20, 1967; BA, Auburn U., Ala., 1990; JD, U. Ala. Sch. Law, 1993. Ptnr. Parsons Lee & Juliano PC; mem. Dist. 46 Ala. House of Reps., Montgomery, 2005—. Mem. adv. bd. Ala. Bar Inst. Continuing Legal Edn., Ala. Def. Lawyers Assn., Def. Rsch. Inst., Ala. State Bar. Active mem. Homewood C. of C., Hoover C. of C., Mountain Brook C. of C., Vestavia Hills C. of C.; past pres. Birmingham Bar Found. Republican. Office: Ala House of Reps Ala State House 11 S Union St Rm

537-F Montgomery AL 36130 also: Parsons Lee & Juliano PC 300 Protective Ctr 2801 Hwy 280 S Birmingham AL 35223 Office Phone: 334-242-7740, 205-314-7909. Business E-Mail: paul@pljpc.com.

DEMARCO, ROBERT, information technology manager; b. Newport, RI, Oct. 15, 1968; s. Robert Michael and Christine Ruth DeMarco; m. Lisa Marie Giangregorio, Oct. 1, 1988; children: Alicia Nicole, Bethany Ruth, Grace Antoinette, Jonah Robert. BS, Fitchburg State Coll., Mass., 1997; MS, Temple U. Sch.Pharmacy, Phila., 2007. Sr. compliance engr. Genzyme Corp., Framingham, Mass., 2004—05; dir. global it compliance Stiefel Labs., Research Triangle Park, NC, 2005—. Mem.: Internat. Soc. Pharm. Engrs. Republican. Avocations: hunting, restoring antique properties. Office: Stiefel Labs 20 TW Alexander Dr Research Triangle Park NC 27709 Business E-Mail: rdemarco@stiefel.com.

DE MARS, SUSAN S., lawyer, health products executive; BA, Claremont McKenna Coll., Calif.; JD, Harvard U., Cambridge, Mass. Ptnr. Sacks, Tierney, Phoenix, 1993—95; asst. gen. counsel PCS Health Systems, Irving, Tex., 1995—97, v.p., corp. accounts, 1997—99; v.p., gen counsel Advance PCS Health Systems, Irving, Tex., 1999—2000; sr. v.p., gen. counsel Advance PCS, Irving, Tex., 2000—. Office: Advance PCS Inc Ste 1200 750 W John Carpenter Fwy Irving TX 75039 Office Phone: 469-524-4700. Office Fax: 469-524-4702.

DEMARY, JO LYNNE, academic administrator, retired school system administrator; b. 1946; BEd, Coll. of William and Mary, 1968, DEd; MEd, U. Va. Commonwealth, 1972. Tchr. Fairfax County Schs., Va., Henrico County Schs., Va., from tchr. to asst. supt. Va.; asst. supt. pub. instruction Commonwealth of Va., 1994—99, acting supt. pub. instruction, 1999—2000, supt. of pub. instruction, 2000—06; dir. Ctr. for School Improvement Va. Commonwealth U.; assoc. Cross & Joftus. Bd. trustee Va. Ctr. for Tchg. Internat. Studies. Recipient Va. Assn. Elementary Sch. Principals 2000-2001 Pathfinders award, Breaking the Glass Ceiling award, Assn. Va. Women Educators, 2000, Outstanding Ednl. Leadership Alumni award, Coll. William and Mary Sch. Edn., 2001, Alumni Star award, Va. Commonwealth U., 2001, State Leadership award, Nat. Assn. Fed. Edn. Prog. Adminstr., 2002, Disting. Svc. award, Va. Art Edn. Assn., 2003, Va. Assn. Test Dir. Excellence in Assessment award, 2003, Pace Humanitarian award, Nat. Assn. State Directors Spl. Edn., 2004, Frank E. Flora Lamp of Knowledge award, Va. Assn. Secondary Sch. Principals, 2005, Disting. Alumni award, Henrico Ednl. Found., 2005, YWCA Outstanding Women's Award in Edn., 2006; named a Flame Bearer of Edn., United Negro Coll. Fund, 2007. Mem.: Edn. Commn. States, Nat. Coun. for Accreditation Tchr. Edn. (mem. task force on sch. health and safety, mem. internat. com., mem. state partnership bd.), Coun. Chief State Sch. Officers, Va. Commonwealth U. Alumni Assn. Office: Va Commonwealth U School of Education 1015 W Main St Richmond VA 23284 Office Phone: 804-828-1788. Office Fax: 804-827-0771.

DEMATTEO, DANIEL A., computer game company executive; Exec. and mgmt. positions B. Dalton Booksellers, 1987, Software Etc.; pres., COO GameStop Corp., Grapevine, Tex., 1996—2000, vice chmn., COO, 2000—08, CEO, 2008—10, exec. chmn., 2010—. Recipient Champion award, Entertainment Software Assn. Found., 2006. Office: GameStop Corp 625 Westport Pky Grapevine TX 76051 Office Phone: 817-424-2000. Office Fax: 817-424-2002.

DE MENT, IRA, federal judge; b. Birmingham, Ala., Dec. 21, 1931; s. Ira J. and Helen (Sparks) De M.; m. Ruth Lester Posey; 1 child, Charles Posey. AS, Marion Mil. Inst., 1951; AB, U. Ala., 1953, LLB, 1958, JD, 1969. Bar: Ala. 1958, U.S. Dist. Ct. (mid. dist.) Ala. 1958, U.S. Ct. Appeals (5th cir.) 1958, U.S. Supreme Ct. 1966, U.S. Dist. Ct. (so. dist.) Ala. 1967, U.S. Dist. Ct. D.C. 1972, U.S. Ct. Appeals (D.C.) 1972, U.S. Tax Ct. 1972, U.S. Customs and Patents Appeals 1976, U.S. Dist. Ct. (no. dist.) Ala. 1977, U.S. Ct. Appeals (11th cir.) 1981, U.S. Ct. Mil. Appeals 1972. Law clk. Sup. Ct. Ala., 1958-59; asst. atty. gen. State of Ala., 1959, spl. assty. atty. gen., 1966-69, 81-92; asst. US atty. Montgomery, Ala., 1959-61; pvt. practice, 1961-69, 77-92; judge US Dist. Ct. (mid. dist.) Ala., 1992—2002, sr. judge, 2002—. Acting U.S. atty. Mid. Dist. Ala. 1969, U.S. atty., 1969-77; asst. atty., legal advisor to police and fire depts. City of Montgomery, 1965-69; inst. Jones Law Sch., 1962-64; instr. Montgomery Police Acad., 1964-77; lect. constl. Ala. Police Acad., 1971-75; instr. law enforcement U. Ala., 1967, mem. adj. faculty New Coll., 1974-75, adj. prof. psychology, 1975-92; spl. counsel to Gov. State Ala., 1980-88, gen. counsel Commn. on Aging, 1980-82. Lt. col. USAR, 1953-74; maj. gen. USAFR ret. Decorated Legion of Merit, DSM, others; recipient Disting. Svc. award Internat. Assn. Firefighters, 1975, Rockefeller Pub. Svc. award Woodrow Wilson Sch. Pub. and Internat. Affairs Princeton U., 1976; named Alumnus of Yr. Marion Mil. Inst., 1988, Significant Sig award Sigma Chi Fraternity, 1998, Judicial Award of Merit Ala. State Bar, 1998, Marion Mil. Inst. Disting. Alumnus award, 2003. Mem. ABA, Fed. Bar Assn., D.C. Bar Assn., Ala. Bar Assn. (mem. editl. adv. bd. The Alabama Lawyer 1966-72), Am. Judicature Soc., Nat. Assn. Former U.S. Attys., Phi Alpha Delta. Republican. United Methodist. Clubs: Masons, Shriners. Address: US Dist Ct PO Box 2149 Montgomery AL 36102-2149 also: 1 Church St Montgomery AL 36104 E-mail: Ira_DeMent@almd.uscourts.gov.

DEMENT, JAMES ALDERSON, JR., lawyer; b. Clinton, Okla., Sept. 11, 1947; s. James Alderson and Ruby (Weaver) DeM.; m. Sally Anne Wylder, June 6, 1970; children: Stephen, Suzanne, Jonathan. BA summa cum laude, Tex. Christian U., 1969; JD in Internat. Affairs, Cornell U., 1972. Bar: N.Y. 1973, Tex. 1974. Assoc. Alexander & Green, NYC, 1972-73, Baker Botts, LLP, Houston, 1977-85, ptnr., 1998—; ptnr., chmn. corp. tax and internat. sect. Butler & Binion, LLP, Houston, 1985-97. Adj. prof. U. Houston, 1987-88; dir. Houston World Affairs Coun. 2002-06. Mem. editl. rev. bd. The Internat. Lawyer, 1987-94. Trustee Houston Ballet Found., 1989-96, Brazos Presbyn. Homes, Inc., 1990-96. Capt. USAF, 1973-77. Fellow Tex. Bar Found.; mem. State Bar Tex. (internat. law sect., chmn. 1989-90), Internat. and Comparative Law Ctr. Southwestern Legal Found. (adv. coun. 1986—), Houston Bar Assn. (internat. law sect., pres. 1989-90). Presbyterian. Office: Baker Botts LLP 910 Louisiana St Houston TX 77002-4995 Business E-Mail: james.dement@bakerbotts.com.

DEMENTIEVA, ELENA VYACHESLAVOVNA (YELENA DEMENTYEVA), professional tennis player; b. Moscow, Oct. 15, 1981; d. Viatcheslav and Vera Dementieva. Grad., European Grad. Sch., 1998. Profl. tennis player WTA Tour, 1998—. Recipient Female of Yr. Award, Russia, 2001, Women's Single's Silver medal, Sydney Olympics, 2000; named WTA Tour Most Improved Player, 2000. Achievements include winner 16 career singles titles, 6 career doubles titles, WTA; winner 3 career singles titles, 3 career doubles titles, ITF; Mem. Russian Fed Cupt Team, 1999, 2001-03, Russian Olympic Team, 2000, 2004, 2008; women's singles gold medal winner, Beijing Olympics, 2008. Avocations: chess, skiing. Office: c/o WTA Tour Corp Hdqs One Progress Plz Ste 1500 Saint Petersburg FL 33701

DEMERE, ROBERT H., JR., energy executive; b. Savannah, Ga., Feb. 15, 1924; s. Raymond McAllister and Josephine Elizabeth (Mobley) D.; m. Mary Elizabeth Bullock, Sept. 21, 1946; children—Robert H., John B., Raymond S., Sims B., Anne E. Econs. student, Yale U. Chmn. St. Joseph's/Candler Health Sys, Inc.; pres., CEO Colonial Group, Inc., 1986—. Bd. dirs. 1st Union Bank Savannah, 1st Union Corp. Ga. Bd. dirs. YMCA of Savannah, Mighty Eighth Air Force Mus., 1999—. Served to lt. (j.g.) USN, 1942-45. Named Indsl. Man of Yr., Internat. Mgmt. Coun., Savannah, 1972. Mem. Ind. Fuel Terminal Operators Assn. (v.p. 1986—), Ind. Liquid Terminal Operators Assn., Nat. Oil Jobbers Assn., S.C. Petroleum Marketers Assn., N.C. Oil Jobbers Assn., Ga. Oilmen's Assn., World Bus. Council, Sea Edn. Assn. (trustee 1982—), Ga. C. of C., Savannah (Ga.) Yacht Club, Century Club, Chatham Club, Cotillion Club, Oglethorpe Club. Avocations: sailing, fishing, swimming. Office: Colonial Group Inc 101 North Lathrop Ave Savannah GA 31415 Office Phone: 912-236-1331. Office Fax: 912-235-3881. Business E-Mail: bdemere@colonialgroupinc.com.

DE MERITT, JOHN, retail executive; BA in Polit. Sci., U. Houston; JD, South Tex. Coll. of Law. V.p., dir. leasing Eastern US Weingarten Realty Investors, 2001—06; co-founder Francescas Holding Corp., Houston, pres., CEO, mem. bd. dirs., 2007—. Named one of America's 20 Most Powerful CEOs 40 and Under, Forbes mag., 2012. Office: Francescas Holding Corp 3480 W 12th St Houston TX 77008 Office Phone: 713-864-1358. Office Fax: 713-426-2751.

DEMILLO, RICHARD ALLAN, computer scientist, educator, former dean; b. Hibbing, Minn., Jan. 26, 1947; s. Herman and Lorraine Kathryn (Edman) DeMillo; m. Diane Hanson, Dec. 26, 1969 (div. Apr. 1984); children: Allan, Gina, Andrew; m. Rhonda Martin, May 21, 1988; 1 child, Cara. BA in Math., Coll. St. Thomas, St. Paul, 1969; PhD in Info. and Computer Sci., Ga. Inst. Tech., Atlanta, 1972. Rsch. asst. Los Alamos Nat. Lab., N.Mex., 1969—71; asst. prof. dept. elec. engring. and computer sci. U. Wis., Milw., 1972-76; assoc. prof. info. and computer sci. Ga. Inst. Tech., 1976—81, prof., 1981—87, asst. dir. rsch., Sch. Info. & Computer Sci., 1984—87, dir. Software Engring. Rsch. Ctr., 1985—87, disting. prof. computing and mgmt., 2002—, John P. Imlay Jr. dean computing, 2002—08; prof. computer sci., dir. Software Engring. Rsch. Ctr. Purdue U., West Lafayette, Ind., 1987—96; v.p., gen. mgr. info. and computer scis. rsch. Telcordia Technologies (Formerly Bellcore), Morristown, NJ, 1994—2000, gen. mgr. Internet systems group, 2000—; v.p., chief tech. officer Hewlett-Packard Co., Palo Alto, Calif., 2000—02. Dir. computer and computation rsch. divsn. NSF, Washington, 1989—91; vis. prof. U. Padua, Italy, 1994; bd. dirs. Microelectronics Rsch. Corp., Austin, Tex., 1997—2000, Software Productivity Consortium, Reston, Va., 1998—2000, Telelogue Systems, Red Bank, NJ, 2000—03, San Francisco Exploratorium, 2001—02, Elity Systems, Somerville, NJ, 2001—04, RSA Security, Bedford, Mass., 2002—06, Computing Rsch. Assn., 2005—. Co-author: Foundations of Secure Computation, 1978, Applied Cryptology, Cryptographic Protocols and Computer Security, 1984, Software Testing and Evaluation, 1986; co-editor: Studies in Computer Science, 1994; mem. editl. bd. Transactions on Math. Software, 1982—85, Info. & Control, 1985—87, Transactions on Software Engring., 1989—96, series editor Software Sci. & Systems, 1990—96; contbr. articles to profl. jours. Fellow: AAAS, Assn. Computing Machinery; mem.: IEEE, Assn. Symbolic Logic, Soc. Indsl. & Applied Math., Math. Assn. America, Am. Math. Soc. Office: Ga Tech Coll Computing KACB Office 3136 801 Atlantic Dr Atlanta GA 30332-0280 Business E-Mail: rad@cc.gatech.edu. E-mail: rich@demillo.com.

DEMING, CLAIBORNE PAYNE, oil industry executive; BA, Tulane U., New Orleans, 1976, JD, 1979. Staff atty. and various positions in law, prodn., exploration and mktg. Murphy Oil Corp., El Dorado, Ark., 1979—88, v.p. petroleum ops., 1988—89, pres. Murphy Oil USA, Inc., 1989—92, exec. v.p., COO, 1992—93, bd. dirs., 1993—, pres., CEO, 1994—2008, chmn. of bd., 2012—. Office: Murphy Oil 200 Peach St El Dorado AR 71730 Office Phone: 870-862-6411. E-mail: claiborne.deming@murphyoilcorp.com.*

DEMLEITNER, NORA VERENA, dean, law educator; b. Schwabach, Bavaria, Germany, Dec. 11, 1966; d. K. Alfred and Walburga F. (Plank) Demleitner. BA summa cum laude, Bates Coll., Lewiston, Maine, 1989; JD, Yale Law Sch., New Haven, 1992; LLM with distinction, Georgetown U. Law Ctr., Washington, 1994. Bar: Mass. 1993, NY 1993, US Ct. Appeals (3rd cir.) 1993. Jud. clk. to Hon. Samuel A. Alito, Jr. US Ct. Appeals (3rd cir.), Newark, 1992—93; asst. prof. St. Mary's U. Sch. Law, San Antonio, 1994—97, dir. LLM programs, 1994—2001, assoc. prof., 1997—98, prof., 1998—2003, Hofstra U. Sch. Law, Hempstead, NY, 2001—12, vice dean academic affairs, 2006—07, interim dean, 2007, dean, 2008—12; dean, Roy L. Steinheimer prof. law Wash. & Lee U. Sch. Law, Lexington, Va., 2012—. Vis. prof. law U. Freiburg, Germany, 1997, 1999, U. Mich. Law Sch., Ann Arbor, 1999, Scuola Superiore di Santa Ana, Pisa, Italy, 2000, 2005, St. Thomas U. Sch. Law, Miami, Fla., 2002. Co-author: Sentencing Law and Policy: Cases, Statutes, and Guidelines, 2nd edit., 2007; mng. editor Federal Sentencing Reporter, 2001—, mem. exec. editl. bd. American Jour. Comparative Law, 2006—; contbr. articles to law jours. Named one of Top 50 Most Influential Women in Bus., LI Bus. News; named to Hall of Fame. Fellow: American Bar Found.; mem.: ABA, American Law Inst., Assn. American Law Schools (exec. com. mem. Immigration Law Sect. 2008—10, chair 2011—), Internat. Soc. Comparative Law, American Soc. Comparative Law (mem. exec. com. 2004—06), Phi Beta Kappa. Roman Catholic. Avocations: skiing, movies and theater, travel. Office: Washington & Lee University School of Law Sydney Lewis Hall Lexington VA 24450*

DEMME, JAMES, retail executive; b. 1941; Pres., CEO Shaws Supermarkets, 1988-91; exec. v.p. retail ops. Scrivner, Inc., 1992-94; pres., CEO and dir. Homeland Stores, Oklahoma City, 1994-97; Chmn. & CEO Bruno's Supermarkets Inc., Birmingham, Ala., 1997—. Office: Bruno's Supermarkets Inc 800 Lakeshore Pkwy Birmingham AL 35211-4447

DEMOND, WALTER EUGENE, lawyer; b. Sacramento, Oct. 15, 1947; s. Walter G. and Laura (Bartlett) D.; m. Kari; 1 child, William. BA, U. Tex., 1969, JD with honors, 1976. Bar: Tex. 1976, Nebr. 2004. With Clark, Thomas & Winters, Austin, 1976—, sr. ptnr. energy and telecomm. sect. Mem. mgmt. com. Clark, Thomas & Winters, 1984-94, 97-99, 2002-04. Capt. USAF, 1970-74. Fellow: Austin Bar Found. (founding mem.), Tex. Bar Found. (life), Am. Bar Found. (life); mem.: ABA (vice chmn. gas com. 1986—91, chmn. gas com. 1991—93, long-range planning com. 1995—, vice chmn. corp. governance com. 2003—07, chmn. program com. 2006—07, sect. vice chmn. 2007—08, pub. utility comm. and transp. law sect., chair elect 2008—), State Bar of Tex. (adminstrv. law com. 1984—87). Office: Clark Thomas & Winters Box 1148 Austin TX 78767 Office Phone: 512-472-8800. Business E-Mail: wed@ctw.com.

DEMONG, RICHARD FRANCIS, finance and investments educator; b. Freeport, Ill., May 2, 1944; s. Maurice Dale and Ruth Jane (Kidwell) DeM.; m. Sue Ann Liddle, June 17, 1967 (div. Dec. 1983); children: Cheryl Ann, Lynn Ann; m. Linda H. Krongaard, May 15, 1988. AA, Orange Coast Coll., Costa Mesa, Calif., 1964; BA, Calif. State U., 1966; MBA, Coll. of William & Mary, 1974; PhD, U. Colo., 1977. Cert. cost analyst; chartered fin. analyst. Time keeper Douglas Aircraft Co., Long Beach, Calif., 1966; instr. U. Colo., Boulder, 1974-77; Va. Bankers prof. bank mgmt., McIntire Sch. Commerce U. Va., Charlottesville, 1977—, dir. Ctr. for Fin. Studies, 1991—97; rsch. dir. Fin. Analyst Rsch. Found., Charlottesville, 1982-85; registered investment adv. rep. Va., 1996—. Cons. Fin. Forecasting & Svc., 1978—; fin. coord. Dalkon Shield Claimants Trust, 1989-1999. Author: (with others) 1998 Home Equity Loan Study, 1998, Principles of Financial Management, 2d edit., 1988; editor (with others) The Technology Industry: The Impact of the Internet, 2002; contbr. articles to profl. jours. Mem. Va. Small Bus. Coun., Richmond, 1981-82; chmn. U. Va. ROTC com., Charlottesville, 1981-84, 2001-05; co-chmn. Central Va. Score and Ace chpt., Charlottesville, 1981; dir. McIntire Small Bus. Inst., Charlottesville, 1978-82, Innisfree Village, 1995-98, 2002—, Charlottesville Cath. Sch. Bd., 2002-05. Capt. USAF, 1966-72, Vietnam, Col. USAFR, ret. Decorated DFC; named outstanding Air Force Mobilization Augmentee (reservist), Air Tng. Comman, 1980. Mem. Fin. Mgmt. Assn., Am. Fin. Assn., CFA Inst. Roman Catholic. Avocation: gardening. Office: U Va McIntire Sch of Commerce PO Box 400173 Charlottesville VA 22904 Office Phone: 434-924-3227. Business E-Mail: rfd@virginia.edu.

DEMONSABERT, WINSTON RUSSEL, chemist, consultant; b. New Orleans, June 12, 1915; s. Joseph Francis and Davida Elizabeth (Gullett) deM.; m. Eleanor Ray Ranson, Aug. 8, 1955; 1 child, Winston Russel. BS in Chemistry, Loyola U., New Orleans, 1937; MA in Edn., Tulane U., 1945, PhD in Chemistry, 1952. Asst. prof. Loyola U., New Orleans, 1948-49, assoc. prof., 1949-55, prof., 1955-66; chief chemist Nat. Ctr. for Disease Control, Dept. Health and Human Svcs., Atlanta, 1966-69; chief contract liason br. Nat. Ctr. for Health Svcs. Rsch., 1969-73; chief extramural programs Bur. Drugs FDA, Rockville, Md., 1973-79; scientist adminstr. office of interagy. sci. coordination Office of Commr., FDA, after 1979; now cons., govt. liaison environ. chemistry and toxicology. Assoc. prof. Tulane U., 1957-58; research chemist Am. Cyanamid Co., 1957-58; vice-chmn. Interagy. Testing Com., 1982. Contbr. to Ency. Americana, Ency. Chemistry, also profl. jours. Committeeman Boys Scouts Am., New Orleans and Atlanta; mem. curriculum coms. New Orleans Pub. Sch. Bd., 1965. Fellow AAAS, Am. Inst. Chemists (chmn. La. chpt. 1958-60, chmn. Ga. chpt. 1968-69, pres. D.C. chpt. 1982-83); mem. Am. Chem. Soc. (past chmn. La. sect.). Roman Catholic. Achievements include research in environmental effects (detection, prevention and treatment) of toxic wastes, pesticides and air pollution, and zirconium chemistry. Home and Office: 5006 Flint Rock Ct Chantilly VA 20151-4100 Office Phone: 703-631-7439. Business E-Mail: doctorate@verizon.net.

DEMOSS, HAROLD RAYMOND, JR., federal judge; b. Houston, Dec. 30, 1930; s. Harold R. and Jessy May (Cox) DeMoss; m. Judith Phelps; children: Harold R. III, Louise Holland. BA, Rice U., 1952; LLB, U. Tex., 1955. Bar: Tex. Assoc. Bracewell & Patterson LLP, Houston, 1957—61, ptnr., 1961—91; judge US Ct. Appeals (5th Cir.), Houston, 1991—2007, sr. judge, 2007—. Dir. Panama Canal Co., 1976—77; coun. mem. Admin. Conference of US, 1990—91. Chmn. bd. Tex. Bill of Rights Found., Houston, 1969—70; pres. Tanglewood Homeowners Assn., 1987; area chmn. Bush Congl. Campaign, 1968; mem. platform group Bush for Pres., Washington, 1988; rsch. analyst Bush/Quayle campaign, 1988; dist. del.-at-large Rep. Nat. Conv., Houston, 1980, alt. del.-at-large, 1984, 1988; Harris County vice chmn. Tower Senate campaign, Houston, 1972, Ford/Dale campaign, 1976; Harris County chmn. Loeffler for Gov. Primary, 1986; Harris County co-chair Regan/Bush campaign, 1980, 1984; Tex. state chmn. Bush for Pres. Primary, 1979—80, Tex. vice chmn., 1988; del. Rep. State Conv., Houston, 1968; vestryman St. Martin's Episcopal Ch., Houston, 1968—72; mem. exec. bd. Episcopal Diocese Tex., 1983—86, chmn. planning com., 1985—88, del. Diocesan Conv., 1976—88; bd. dirs. Amigos de las Americas, 1974—76. Sgt. US Army, 1955—57. Recipient Disting. Alumni award, Rice U., 2004, George Washington Disting. Svc. award, SAR, 2006. Fellow: Tex. Bar Assn. (life); mem.: ABA, N.Mex. Trial Lawyers Assn., Tex. Assn. Def. Counsel (bd. dirs. 1972—74), Houston Bar Assn. (bd. dirs. 1969—71, 1st v.p. 1972—73), Maritime Law Assn. US, Am. Judicature Soc., Internat. Bar Assn., The Houston Club. Avocations: fishing, waterskiing. Office: Bob Casey US Courthouse 515 Rusk St Ste 12015 Houston TX 77002-2605

DEMOTT, DEBORAH ANN, law educator; b. Collingswood, NJ, July 21, 1948; d. Lyle J. and Frances F. (Cummings) DeM. BA, Swarthmore Coll., 1970; JD, NYU, 1973. Bar: N.Y. 1974. Law clk. U.S. Dist. Ct. (so. dist.) N.Y., 1973; assoc. Simpson, Thacher & Bartlett, NYC, 1974-75; from asst. prof. to assoc. prof. Duke U., Durham, NC, 1975-80, prof. law, 1980—, David F. Cavers prof. law, 2000—. Vis. asst. prof. U. Tex., Austin, 1977-78; Bost rsch. prof. law, 1981; vis. prof. U. Calif. Hastings Coll. Law, 1986, U. Colo., 1989, U. San Diego, 1991; James L. Lewtas vis. prof. law Osgoode Hall Law Sch., Toronto, Ont., Can., 1991; vis. fellow U. Melbourne, 1993, 95, 98; Huber C. Hurst Eminent vis. scholar U. Fla. Coll. Law, 1996; Frances Lewis Scholar-in-Residence Washington and Lee Law Sch., 1998; centennial vis. prof. law dept. London Sch. Econs., 2000-02; vis. prof. internat. faculty U. Sydney Faculty of Law, 2004, McWilliams vis. prof., 2006, 2009, Ctrl. European U., 2009. Author: Shareholder Derivative Actions, 1987, Fiduciary Obligation Agency and Partnership, 1991; editor: Corporations at the Crossroads: Governance and Reform; contbr. articles to profl. jours.; bd. advisors Jour. Legal Edn., 1983-86. Trustee Law Sch. Admission Coun., 1984-88; mem. N.C. Gen. Statutes Commn., 1990-98; mem. selection com. Coif Book Award, 1988-90. Recipient Pomeroy prize NYU Sch. Law, 1971-73; AAUW fellow, 1972-73; Fulbright Sr. scholar Sydney U. and Monash (Australia) U., 1986. Mem. ABA, Am. Law Inst. (reporter restatement of agy.), The Assn. Am. Law Schs. (chmn. sect. bus. assocs. 2006). Office: Duke U Law Sch PO Box 90360 Durham NC 27708-0360 Office Phone: 919-613-7082. Business E-Mail: demott@law.duke.edu.

DEMPS, DELL, professional sports team executive; b. Long Beach, Calif., Feb. 12, 1970; m. Anita Demps; children: Jourdan, Tre, Riley. B, U. of Pacific, Stockton, Calif., 1992, MBA, 1998. Guard Golden State Warriors, 1992, 1993, San Antonio Spurs, 1995—96, Orlando Magic, 1996—97, Philippines, France, Greece, Turkey, Croatia; asst. coach NBA Devel. League, 2001—03; scout NY Knicks, 2001—05, dir. pro player pers., 2005, San Antonio Spurs, 2005—10; gen. mgr. Austin Toros, 2005—10, New Orleans Pelicans (formerly New Orleans Hornets), 2010—. Mem. adv. bd. U. of Pacific Eberhardt Sch. Bus., 2009—. Office: New Orleans Pelicans 5800 Airline Dr Metairie LA 70003*

DEMPSEY, BERNARD HAYDEN, JR., lawyer; b. Evanston, Ill., Mar. 29, 1942; s. Bernard H. and Margaret C. (Gallagher) D.; m. Cynthia T. Dempsey; children: Bernard H. III, Matthew B., Kathleen N., Rose Maureen G., Alexandra C., Anastasia M. BS, Coll. Holy Cross, Worcester, Mass., 1964; JD, Georgetown U., Washington, DC, 1967. Bar: Fla. 1968, DC 1979. Law clk. to chief judge Joseph P. Lieb US Dist. Ct. (mid. dist.) Fla., 1967-69; asst. US Atty. Mid. Dist. Fla., 1969-73; pvt. practice Orlando, Fla., 1973—; spl. asst. to US Atty. Mid. Dist. Fla., 1974. Lectr. in field. Contbr. articles to profl. jours. Recipient John Marshall award US Dept. Justice, 1972, US Atty's Outstanding Performance award 1969, 70, 71, 72, 73, 74. Mem.: ATLA, ABA, Am. Acad. Trial Counsel, Orange County Bar Assn., Am. Arbitration Assn., Fed. Bar Assn., Fla. Bar Found., Am. Judicature Soc., Fla. Bar Assn., Nat. Employment Lawyers Assn., US Attys. Assn. for Mid. Dist. Fla., Fla. Assn. Criminal Def. Lawyers, Nat. Assn. Criminal Def. Lawyers, Winter Park Racquet Club (Fla.), Delta Theta Phi. Republican. Roman Catholic. Office: Dempsey & Assocs PA 1560 Orange Ave Ste 200 Winter Park FL 32789-5544 Home Phone: 407-629-0383; Office Phone: 407-422-5166. Business E-Mail: bhd@dempsey-law.com.

DEMPSEY, JAMES RAYMON, manufacturing executive; b. Red Bay, Ala., Oct. 4, 1921; s. Newman W. and Maude (Berry) D.; m. Dolores Barnes, Jan. 19, 1943 (dec. Sept. 1997); children: Susan, David Barnes, Anne. Student, U. Ala., 1937—39; BS, U.S. Mil. Acad., 1943; MS, U. Mich., 1947, D (hon.) of Engring., 1964. Commd. 2d lt. U.S. Army, 1943; advanced through grades to lt. col. USAF, 1951; with photo reconnaissance squadron Eng., France, World War II; squadron comdr., 1945; guided missiles project officer, then chief guided missile projects (Research and Devel. Directorate, Air Force Hdqrs.), 1948- 49; exec. officer to (Dep. Chief Staff for Devel.), 1950-51; chief project sect. (Air Force Missile Test Center), Patrick AFB, Fla., then operations officer missile test range, 1951-53, resigned, 1953; asst. to v.p. planning Convair div. Gen. Dynamics Corp., 1953-54; dir. Gen. Dynamics Corp. (Atlas program), 1954-57; mgr. Gen. Dynamics Corp. (Convair-Astronautics div.), 1957-58; v.p. Gen. Dynamics Corp. (Convair div.), 1958-61; sr. v.p. Gen. Dynamics Corp.; pres. Gen. Dynamics Astronautics, 1961-65, Gen. Dynamics Convair, 1965-66; v.p. missiles, space and electronics group Avco Corp., 1966-68, v.p., group exec. govt. products group, 1968-75; pres. Digital Broadcasting Corp., 1978-79; mng. partner J.J. Finnigan Industries, Duluth, Ga., 1978-85; pres. Southeastern Rail Car Co., 1986-89; pvt. investor, 1990—. Trustee Phoenix Series Fund, 1968-91, Big Edge Series Fund, 1985-91, Phoenix Multi-Portfolio Fund, 1989-91, Precious Metal Holdings, 1980-93, Keystone Internat., 1987-93; chmn. bd. Transatlantic Capital Corp., Transatlantic Investment Corp., 1984-86; spl. com. on space tech. NASA Decorated Air medal with clusters, D.F.C.; Croix de Guerre (France); recipient Disting. Grad. award U.S. Mil. Acad., 2002 Fellow AIAA, Am. Astronaut. Soc.; mem. Air Force Assn. (bd. dirs. 1958-59), Burning Tree Club, Congl. Country Club. Home and Office: 6251 Old Dominion Dr No 057 Mc Lean VA 22101-4803

DEMPSEY, KATIE M., state legislator; b. Sept. 11; m. Lynn Dempsey. B in Early Childhood Edn., U. Ga. Mem. Dist. 13 Ga. House of Reps., Atlanta, 2007—. Commr. Rome City Commn., Ga. Mem. First United Meth. Ch., Rome; bd. mem. Exch. Club Family Resource Ctr.; trustee Floyd Med. Ctr.; pres. Floyd Healthcare Found. Mem.: Nat. League Cities, Ga. Mcpl. Assn., Assn. County Commissioners Ga., Ga. Econ. Developers Assn. Republican. Office: 811 Highland Ave Rome GA 30161 also: Ga House of Reps 508 Coverdell Legis Office Bldg Atlanta GA 30334 Office Phone: 706-506-9648, 404-656-0213. Business E-Mail: katie.dempsey@house.ga.gov.

DEMURO, GERARD J, information technology executive; B in commn., U. Pitts., 1977; MBA, Farleigh Dickinson U. V.p., gen. mgr. GTE Govt. Systems Commn. Systems Divsn., 1997—99; pres. General Dynamics Commn. Systems, 1999—2001; v.p. General Dynamics Systems Corp., 1999—2003; pres. General Dynamics C4 Systems, Inc., 2001—; exec. v.p., group. exec., info. sys. and tech. General Dynamics Corp., 2003—. Mem.: Nat. Contracts Mgmt. Assn., Assn. of the U.S. Army, AFCEA. Office: General Dynamics Corp Ste 100 2941 Fairview Park Dr Falls Church VA 22042

DENAULT, LEO P., energy executive; BS in Econs. and Acctg., Ball State U., Muncie, Ind., 1982; MBA, Ind. U., Bloomington, 1991. Staff acct. Cinergy Corp., Cin., 1982, various positions in tax acctg., budget and fin. analysis and strategic planning, mgr. corp. devel., 1991, v.p. corp. devel., Entergy Corp., New Orleans, 1999—2002, v.p. corp. devel. and strategic planning, 2002—04, exec. v.p., CFO, 2004—. Office: Entergy Corp 1340 Echelon Pkwy Ste 100 Jackson MS 39213-8210 Office Phone: 504-576-4000.

DENBURG, DORIAN SUE, lawyer; b. Newark, Nov. 29, 1954; d. Sheldon Marvin Denburg and Sybil Marjorie (Adlerstein) Scott; m. Alan Roy Niederhoffer, Apr. 12, 1986; children: Eren Kyle, Noah Jordan, Rachel Leigh. BA, U. Rochester, 1976; JD, U. Miami, 1982. Bar: Fla. 1982, U.S. Dist. Ct. (so. dist.) Fla. 1983, N.J. 1984, U.S. Dist. Ct. N.J. 1984. Legis. asst. Am. Israel Pub. Affairs Com., Washington, 1976-78; campaign coord. State Sen. Campaign for Elaine Bloom, Miami, Fla., 1978; editor Fla.-Israel C. of C. newsletter, Miami, 1978-79; fed. jud. intern Hon. Wm. Hoeveler, Miami, 1981-82; assoc. Shutts & Bowen, Miami, 1982-89; chief rights-of-way counsel Bell South Corp., Miami, 1987—2007; gen. atty. AT&T (formerly BellSouth), Atlanta, 2008—. Treas., exec. bd. Am. Jewish Com., Miami, 1985-91; steering com. Greater Miami Jewish Fedn., 1987—, chair bus. and profl. women, 1991—. Mem. ABA, Fla. Bar Assn., Dade County Bar Assn., Nat. Assn. Women Lawyers (pres.-elect 2009, pres. 2010-2011), Greater Miami C. of C. (Leadership award 1986). Democrat. Jewish. Avocations: ballet, neighborhood improvement, travel, reading. Office: AT&T 675 W Peachtree St 43d Fl Atlanta GA 30375-0001*

DENHAM, MITCHEL B., state legislator; b. Apr. 4, 1950; Banker Bank Maysville; mem. Dist. 70 Ky. House of Reps., Ky., 2001—. Served with USAR. Mem.: Underground Railroad Assn., Mason County Industry Devel. Authority (Maysville), Mason County C. of C. (Maysville) (trustee, asst. treas.), Rotary. Democrat. Presbyterian. Mailing: 306 Old Hill City Rd Maysville KY 41056 Office: Capitol Annex Rm 329G 702 Capitol Ave Frankfort KY 40601 Office Phone: 502-564-8100 ext. 696.

DENHAM, ROBERT DAYTON, language educator; b. Mooresville, NC, Oct. 20, 1938; s. Chester Dayton and Louise (Lowrance) D.; m. Rachel Deal Kanipe, Aug. 26, 1961; children: Scott Dayton, Kristin Elizabeth. BA, Davidson Coll., 1961; MA, U. Chgo., 1964, PhD, 1972. Prof. English Emory & Henry Coll., Va., 1966—86, 1988—89; dir. English programs, dir. Assn. Depts. of English MLA, NYC, 1986—88; John P. Fishwick prof. emeritus, dir. honors program Roanoke Coll., Salem, Va., 1989—2004; Hooker disting. vis. prof. McMaster U., 2000. Author: Northrop Frye and Critical Method, 1978, Northrop Frye: An Annotated Bibliography, 1987, Northrop Frye: A Bibliography of His Published Writings, 1931-2004, 2004, Northrop Frye: Religious Visionary and Architect of the Spiritual World, 2004; editor: Northrop Frye on Culture and Literature, 1978, Myth and Metaphor, 1990, Reading the World, 1991, A World in a Grain of Sand, 1991, Visionary Poetics, 1991, The Eternal Act of Creation, 1992, The Legacy of Northrop Frye, 1994, The Correspondence of Northrop Frye and Helen Kemp, 1996, Northrop Frye's Student Essays, 1997, Northrop Frye's Late Notebooks: Architecture of the Spiritual World, 1999, Northrop Frye's Diaries, 1942-1955, 2001, Northrop Frye on Literature and Society: Unpublished Papers, 2002, Northrop Frye's Notebooks and Lectures on the Bible and Other Religious Texts, 2003, Northrop Frye Unbuttoned: Wit and Wisdom from Frye's Notebooks and Diaries, 2004, Northrop Frye: Religious Visionary, 2004, Northrop Frye's Anatomy of Criticism, 2006, Charles Wright: A Companion to His Late Poetry, 2007, Charles Wright in Conversation: 1979-2006 Interviews, 2008, The Early Poetry of Charles Wright: A Companion 1960-1990, 2009, Poets on Paintings, 2011, Remembering Northrop Frye, 2010, Northrop Frye: Selected Letters, 1934-1991, 2011, The Northrop Frye Handbook, 2012. Capt. U.S. Army, 1964-66. James Still fellow U. Ky., 1982, NEH fellow for coll. tchrs., 1995-96, 2002-03; summer stipends and summer seminar awards NEH, 1973-74, 77-78, 84; grantee Can. Embassy, 1983, 85. Mem. MLA (del. assembly 1986-87), Nat. Coun. Tchrs. English, Nat. Collegiate Honors Assn., Assn. Depts. English, South Atlantic MLA (chmn. comparative lit. sect. 1984). Methodist. Avocations: letterpress printing, tennis, basketball, book collecting. Home: PO Box 197 Emory VA 24327 Office Phone: 276-356-5182. Business E-Mail: denham@roanoke.edu.

DENICOLA, T. KEVIN, corporate financial executive; b. 1954; BS in Chemistry, High Point U., 1976; MS in Chem. Engring., U. Va., 1979; MBA in Acctg.& Fin., Rice U., 1987. CPA. Auditor, acct. Ernst & Young LLP, 1987—90; assoc. Criterion Venture Ptnrs., 1990; analyst Lyondell Chem. Co., 1990—92, asst. treas., 1992—93, ethylene product mgr., 1993—96, dir., investor rels., 1996—98, v.p., corp. devel., 1998—2002, sr. v.p., CFO, 2002—08, Millenium Chemicals Inc. (subs. Lyondell Chem. Co.), 2002—08, Equistar Chemicals, LP (subs. Lyondell Chem. Co.), 2002—08, KBR, Inc., 2008—09. Bd. dirs. Comerica Inc., 2006—, Georgia Gulf Corp., 2009—; adjunct prof. Rice U., 2008—. Mem. Tom Delay Congl. Com., Nat. Rep. Congl. Com. Office: KBR Inc 601 Jefferson St Houston TX 77002 Office Phone: 713-753-3011. Office Fax: 713-753-5353.

DENISI, ANGELO S., professor; b. Bronx, NY, Aug. 4, 1951; m. Adrienne Colella; children: Jessica, Rebecca. B in Psychology, CUNY, 1973; PhD in Indsl. and Orgnl. Psychology, Purdue U., 1977. Asst. prof. Kent State U.; prof. U. SC, 1979—89, Rutgers U., 1989—97, Texas A&M U May Bus. Sch., 1997—2005, head dept. mgmt., Paul M. and Rosalie Robertson chair in bus. adminstrn., U. Disting. prof. dean; dean Tulane U. A.B. Freeman Sch. Bus., New Orleans, 2005—10, Albert H. Cohen chair bus., 2007—, prof. orgnl. behavior, 2010—; pres. Acad. Mgmt., 2008—09. Co-editor Managing Knowledge for Sustained Competitive Advantage; editl. bd. mem. Acad. Mgmt. Jour., Acad. Mgmt. Rev., Jour. Applied Psychology, Jour. Mgmt., Jour. Orgnl. Behavior; editor Acad. F Mgmt. Jour. Co-author (with Ricky Griffin): A Cognitive Approach to Performance Appraisal: A Program of Research and Human Resource Management; co-editor: Managing Knowledge for Sustained Competitive Advantage, Performance Management Systems: A Global Perspective; co-author: Managing Human Resources. Bus. Partnership Found. fellow, U. SC, 1987, Disting. fellow, 1988. Fellow: APA (pres. 1999—2000, Disting. Sci. Contbn. award 2005), Southern Mgmt. Assn., Soc. Indsl. and Orgnl. Psychology (Disting. Sci. Contbn. award 2005, William Owens award 1998), Acad. Mgmt. (pres. 2008—09, past pres. 2009—10, Orgnl. Behavior Outstanding Publ. award 1996). Democrat. Office: AB Freeman Sch Bus Goldring/Woldenberg Hall 7 McAlister Dr New Orleans LA 70118 Office Phone: 504-865-5414. Business E-Mail: adenisi@tulane.edu.*

DENNARD, THOMAS S., mortgage company executive; BA in Bus., Catawba Coll., Salisbury, NC. With Wachovia Mortgage, 1978; ptnr. Fleet Funding/Mid-Atlantic, 1982—94; co-founder, pres., CEO Laureate Capital LLC, Charlotte, NC, 1994—2007; CEO Grandbridge Real Estate Capital, LLC (subs. of BB&T Corp.), 2007—. Mem.: Mortgage Bankers Assn. America. Office: Grandbridge Real Estate Capital LLC 227 W Trade St Ste 400 Charlotte NC 28202 Office Phone: 704-332-4454. Office Fax: 704-332-5810. Business E-Mail: tdennard@gbrecap.com.

DENNEY, LEE, state legislator, veterinarian; m. Frank Denney; children: Will, Kate. BS in Agricultural Economics, Okla. State Univ., 1976, DVM, 1978. Co-owner Veterinary Med. Associates. Inc., Cushing, Okla., 1979—; city commission, mayor, vice mayor, 1994—2003; mem. Dist. 33 Okla. House of Representatives, 2005—. Taught at Central Tech, Drumright, 2004—05. Named one of 50 Women Making a Difference, Jour. Record, 1997, 2003. Mem.: Okla. Veterinary Med. Assn. Republican. Mailing: 834 E Sixth St Cushing OK 74023 Office: 2300 N Lincoln Blvd Rm 436 Oklahoma City OK 73105 Office Phone: 405-557-7304. E-mail: leedenney@okhouse.gov.

DENNIS, BRADLEY M., surgeon, educator; b. Atlanta, June 24, 1979; m. Kristen Morgan. BS in Biology, U. Ga., Athens, 2001; MD, Med. Coll. Ga., Augusta, 2005. Asst. prof., surgery Vanderbilt U., Nashville, 2013—.*

DENNIS, BRADY, journalist; Intern St. Petersburg Times, Fla., 1999—2000, staff writer, 2001—. Recipient Ernie Pyle award for human interest writing, Scripps Howard Found., 2006. Office: St Petersburg Times 490 1st Ave S Saint Petersburg FL 33701 Office Phone: 813-226-3386. E-mail: dennis@sptimes.com.

DENNIS, JAMES LEON, federal judge; b. Monroe, La., Jan. 9, 1936; s. Jenner Leon and Hope (Taylo) Dennis; children: Stephen James, Gregory Leon, Mark Taylo, John Timothy. BS in Bus. Adminstrn, La. Tech. U., Ruston, 1959; JD, La. State U., 1962; LLM, U. Va., 1984. Bar: La. 1962. Assoc. firm Hudson, Potts & Bernstein, Monroe, 1962—65, ptnr., 1965—72; judge 4th Dist. Ct. La. for Morehouse and Ouachita Parishes, 1972—74, La. 2d Circuit Ct. Appeals, 1974—75; assoc. justice La. Supreme Ct., 1975—95; coord. La. Constnl. Revision Commn., 1970—72; del., chmn. judiciary com. La. Constnl. Conv., 1973; judge US Ct. Appeals (5th cir.), New Orleans, 1995—; visiting prof. Tulane Law School, 2003. Chmn. La. Commn. on Bicentennial U.S. Constn.; mem. La. Ho. of Reps., 1968—72. With US Army, 1955—57. Mem.: ABA (com. on appellate practice), 4th Jud. Bar Assn., La. Bar Assn., Rotary. Methodist. Office: US Courthouse 600 Camp St Rm 219 New Orleans LA 70130-3425

DENNIS, JEFFREY S., cardiologist; MD, Boston U., 1974. Diplomate American Bd. Internal Medicine, 1978, American Bd. Internal Medicine-cardiovasc. disease, 1979. Resident internal medicine Emory Affiliated Hosp., Atlanta, 1975—77; fellow cardiovasc. disease Emory Univ., Atlanta, 1977—80; pvt. practice Greater Fort Lauderdale Heart Group; hosp. privileges include Broward Gen. Med. Ctr., North Broward Med. Ctr., Imperial Point Med. Ctr. Fellow: Clin. Coun. of Cardiology, American Coll. of Cardiology; mem.: ACP, AMA, Fla. Med. Assn., Broward County Med. Assn., Fla. Heart Assn., American Heart Assn. Office: Broward Health Ste 204 One W Sample Rd Pompano Beach FL 33064 Office Fax: 954-785-0229.

DENNIS, ROBERT J., footwear retail company executive; MBA with Distinction, Harvard Bus. Sch.; Bachelors and Masters Degrees in Biochemical Engring. and Organic Chemistry with honors, Rensselaer Polytechnic Inst. With McKinsey and Co., 1984—97, pntr., 1990—97; employed in sr. mgmt. roles Asbury Automotive, 1997—99; joined Hat World Corp., 2001, CEO, 2004; sr. v.p. Genesco, Inc., 2004, exec. v.p., COO, 2005—06, pres., 2006—, CEO, 2008—, chmn., 2010—. Bd. dirs. Genesco, Inc., 2006—. Office: Genesco Inc Genesco Park 1415 Murfreesboro Rd Nashville TN 37202 Office Phone: 615-367-7000.

DENNIS, RUTLEDGE M., sociologist, educator; b. Charleston, SC, Aug. 16, 1939; s. David and Ora Jane (Porcher) D.; children: Shay T., Imaro Marlin Aki, Kimya Nuru, Zuri Sanyika. BS, S.C. State U., Orangeburg, 1966; MA, Wash. State U., Pullman, 1969, PhD, 1975. Dir. Black studies program Va. Commonwealth U., Richmond, 1971—78, assoc. prof. dept. sociology, 1978—89; Commonwealth prof. dept. sociology George Mason U., Fairfax, Va., 1989—90, prof. dept. sociology, 1992—, enterim dir. African Am. studies, 2006—07. Mem. exec. com. African Am. Studies Program George Mason U., Fairfax, 2004—, co.-dir. sociology grad. program, 1993—2001, creator of Dennis-Weathers Award for intergroup rels., 2004, Va. Commonwealth U., 2010—; co coord. Southeastern Regional African Seminar, Richmond-Charlottesville, 1973—76; del. Ea. Va. Internat. Consortium, 1972—77; pres. Assn. Black Sociologists, 1981—83; founder Rutledge Dennis Found. for Human Devel., Ctr. for African Am. Culture and Leadership; co-founder African-Am. Acad.; co-investigator Black Middletown Project, 1980—81; co-editor Encyclopedia of Race, Ethnicity and Nationalism, 2010—; mem. editl. bd. Issues Race & Security, 2012—. Author: Finding the African America that Middletown Left Out: The Field Notes of a Sociologist, 2012; co-author: The Politics of Annexation, 1982; editor: Elsevier Sci. Ltd. Series in Race and Ethnic Rels., 1990—2009, Racial and Ethnic Politics, 1994, The Black Middle Class, 1995, W.E.B. Du Bois: The Scholar as Activist, 1996, Black Intellectuals, 1997, Marginality, Power and Social Structure: Issues in Race, Class and Gender Analysis, 2005; co-editor: The Afro-Americans, 1976, Race and Ethnicity in Rsch. Methods, 1993, Race and Ethnicity: Comparative and Theoretical Approaches, 2003, The Racial Politics of Booker T. Washington, 2006, The New Black: New Paradigms and Perspectives for the 21st Century, 2007, Biculturalism, Self Identity and Social Transformation, 2008. Housing commr. Richmond Redevel. and Housing Authority, 1977-80; bd. dirs. Housing Opportunities Made Equal, Richmond, 1976-80; participant Sea Island Voter Edn. Project, Charleston, SC, 1964. With U.S. Army, 1960-63, mem. publs. com. Assn. Black Sociologists, 2008- Fellow Fgn. Affairs scholar, 1965; recipient Cmty. Svc. award Boys Clubs Am., 1976; named Outstanding Educator of Am., 1975; Fenwick fellow George Mason U., 2005—; recipient Reise-Melton Cultural award, 1980, Disting. Leadership award Afro-Am. Studies Program, 1991, Nat. Black Monitor Family and Cmty. award 1985, Va. Commonwealth U., 1991, Sigma Rho Sigma Rsch. award, 1965, Pres.'s award S.C. State U., 1966, Jewish Educators award, 1998, Joseph Himes award for Disting. scholar, 2001, Ba'Alay Keriyah Soc., 2003, DuBois-Johnson-Frazier award for Disting. Scholarship, Tchg., and Svc., Am. Sociol. Assn., 2006, others; grantee Ford Found., 1970, NEH, 1978, NIMH, 1980-81; 25th Ann. lectr. African-Am. studies program Va. Commonwealth U., 1996, Faculty Devel. grantee Coll. Humanities and Social Sci. George Mason U., 2007, others. Mem. AAAS, AAUP (v.p. George Mason U. chpt. 2005—, pres. GMU chpt., 2008), NAACP (life, Faculty Excellence award George Mason U. chpt. 2007), Am. Sociol. Assn. (Cox-Johnson Frazier Com. award 2007-10), Ea. Sociol. Soc. (chmn. minorities com. 1992-94, mem. editl. bd. Race and Soc. 1998-2005), Assn. Black Sociologists (life; pres. 1981-82, 82-83, chmn. hist. and archives com., 2002-07, Leadership award 1995), Nat. Soc. collegiate Scholars (elected hon. mem.), Sigma Xi, Omicron Delta Kappa, Alpha Phi Alpha (Acad. Excellence award 1985), Alpha Kappa Mu, Alpha Kappa Delta. Office: George Mason U Dept Sociology Anthrop Fairfax VA 22030 Business E-Mail: rdenni1@gmu.edu.

DENNIS, VANCE W., state legislator; b. Dec. 9, 1975; m. Ashley Dennis; children: Walker, William. BS in Agr., U. Tenn., Knoxville; JD, U. Tenn. Coll. Law. Atty.; former bd. mem. & chmn. Hardin Co. Skills, Inc.; former bd. mem. C of C Hardin Co.; mem. Dist. 71 Tenn. House of Reps., 2008—. Republican. Baptist. Mailing: 545 Cedar Cove Ln Savannah TN 38372 Office: 105 War Memorial Bldg Nashville TN 37243

DENNISON, CORLEY FRANCIS, III, dean; b. Sutton, W.Va., Dec. 6, 1953; s. Corley Francis Dennison Jr. and Margel Colleen Dennison; m. Betty June Hawker, July 15, 1978; children: Cory, Brandon, Kevin. PhD, W.Va. U., Morgantown, 1992. Announcer, prodr. WMRA-FM, Harrisonburg, Va., 1975—76; news dir. WLLL, WGOL-FM, Lynchburg, Va.; program dir. WKYY, Amherst, Va.; prof. Marshall U., Huntington, W.Va., 1985—97, asst. dean journalism, 1999—2004, dean, sch. journalism and mass comm., 2004—, faculty senate pres.; ops. mgr., sta. mgr. NW Mo. State U., Maryville. Fellow: ASJMC Leadership Inst.; mem.: W.Va. Press Assn., Broadcast Edn. Assn., Assn. Edn. Journalism and Mass Comm. Avocations: Tae Kwon Do, hiking, fishing. Home: 42 Mourning Dove Ln Ona WV 25545 Office: Marshall Univ One John Marshall Dr Huntington WV 25755

DENNISON, RAMONA POLLAN, special education educator; b. Floydada, Tex., Jan. 19, 1938; d. William C. and Anne M. (Tivis) Pollan; m. Bob Dennison, Oct. 12, 1956; 1 child, Tajquah. BS, MEd, E. Cen. U., 1972, cert. in psychometry, 1974, lic. in profl. counseling, 1975. Lic. psychometrist, profl. counselor. Tchr. Konawa (Okla.) Pub. Sch., 1972—. Mem. NEA, DAR, PEO, Okla. Edn. Assn., Okla. Assn. Children of Learning Disabilities, Konana Edn. Assn., Lic. Profl. Counselor Assn., Nat. Assn. Children Learning Disabilities, E. Cen. Alumni Assn., Tanti Study Club, Oak Hills Country Club, Delta Kappa Gamma, Phi Delta Kappa. Democrat. Baptist. Avocations: tennis, bridge, walking, cooking, gardening. Home: 2922 Broken Spoke Ln Rockwall TX 75087

DENNY, RICHARD ALDEN, JR., retired lawyer; b. Atlanta, Oct. 13, 1931; s. Richard Alden and Maybeth Sullivan (Graham) D.; m. Margaret Hunt, Aug. 1954; children: Margaret Denny Dozier, Richard Alden III, Dallas Hunt, Lee Denny Griffith. BA, Washington and Lee U., 1952; LLB, Emory U., 1954. Bar: Ga. 1954. Assoc. King & Spalding, Atlanta, 1954-60, ptnr., 1960-92. Chmn. bd. Met. Atlanta Crime Commn., 1972-73; bd. dirs. Woodruff Arts Ctr., 1991-97, life trustee, 1997—; bd. dirs. High Mus. Art, Atlanta, 1971-2007, chmn., 1991-94, life trustee, 2007—; bd. dirs. Lovett Sch., Atlanta, 1969—, chmn., 1980-83, emeritus trustee, 1999—; founder High Mus. Atlanta Wine Auction, 1993, chief taster, 1998—. Recipient Disting. Alumnus award, 2012. Mem. Lawyers Club Atlanta (pres. 1972-73), Atlanta Lawyers Found. (chmn. 1976-77), Washington and Lee Alumni Assn. (pres. 1980-81), Piedmont Driving Club (pres. 1982-84), Carter Ctr. Bd. Councilors, Peachtree Golf Club, Omicron Delta Kappa. Episcopalian. Office: King & Spalding Ste 3100 1180 Peachtree St Atlanta GA 30309-3531

DENNY, WILLIAM (BILL) C., state legislator; b. Washington, Aug. 22, 1930; m. Sue Johnsey; children: Anne Piazza, Kitty Howell, William C. III, Sally Dobbs. Mem. Dist. 64 Miss. House of Reps., 1988—; mem. Nat. Conf. State Legislators, Miss. Rep. Exec. Com., Denny Devel. Inc. Multi. Nat. Banking. Mem.: Nat. Rep. Legislators Assn., Am. Legislature Exchange Coun., Miss. Flood Assn., Miss. Assn. Petroleum Landmen, Am. Assn. Petroleum Landmen, Miss. Track Club. Republican. Roman Catholic. Mailing: PO Box 12185 Jackson MS 39236-2185 Home Phone: 601-956-6807; Office Phone: 601-956-6807, 601-359-2431. E-mail: bdenny@house.ms.gov.

DENSON, WILLIAM FRANK, III, lawyer; b. Birmingham, Ala., Aug. 1, 1943; s. William Frank Jr. and Martha Jane (Wilson) D.; m. Deborah Lynn Davis, July 6, 1974; 1 child, Patricia Lynn Pyle. BA, U. Montevallo, 1965; JD, Emory U., 1968. Bar: Ala. 1968. Atty. Spain, Gillon, Riley, Tate & Ansley, Birmingham, 1969-73; atty., asst. sec.,

sec. Vulcan Materials Co., Birmingham, 1973-88, sec., asst. gen. counsel, 1988-92, v.p., sec., asst. gen. counsel, 1992-94, v.p. law, sec., 1994-98, sr. v.p. law, sec., 1998-99, sr. v.p., gen. counsel, sec., 1999—. Trustee U. Montevallo, 1987-99; bd. dirs. Glenwood Mental Health Svcs., 1990-96. Mem. ABA, Ala. State Bar, Country Club of Birmingham, Willow Point Country Club (Alexander City, Ala.), Kiwanis Club Birmingham. Republican. Episcopalian. Avocations: golf, reading, travel. Office: Vulcan Materials Co 1200 Urban Center Dr Birmingham AL 35242-2545 Home: 3891 Lockerbie Dr Birmingham AL 35223-2910

DENT, FREDERICK BAILY, retired textiles executive, former United States Secretary of Commerce; b. Cape May, NJ, Aug. 17, 1922; s. Magruder and Edith (Baily) D.; m. Mildred C. Harrison, Mar. 11, 1944 (dec.); children: Frederick Baily, Mildred Hutcheson, Pauline Harrison, Diana Gwynn, Magruder Harrison. BA, Yale U., 1944. With Joshua L. Baily & Co., Inc., NYC, 1946-47; joined Mayfair Mills, Arcadia, SC, 1947, pres., 1958—88, treas., 1977—2001, chmn., 1998—2001; sec. US Dept. Commerce, Washington, 1973—75, amb., spl. rep. for trade negotiations, 1975—77. Bd. dirs. Joshua L. Baily & Co. Chmn. Spartanburg County Planning and Devel. Commn., 1960-72; trustee emeritus Spartanburg Day Sch., Brevard Music Ctr.; past mem. corp. Yale U.; mem. Pres.'s Commn. on an All-Vol. Army, 1969-70; mem. Pres.'s Commn. on Indsl. Competitiveness, 1982. Lt. USNR, 1943-46, PTO. Named laureate, S.C. Bus. Hall of Fame, Textile Hall of Fame. Mem. Spartanburg Area C. of C. (chmn. 1991). Episcopalian. E-mail: dentf@bellsouth.net.

DENTON, JULIE CARMAN ROSE, state legislator; b. Louisville, Ky., June 9, 1960; d. Curtis and Patricia Rhae Loyd Carman; m. Thomas Glenn Rose, 1983; children: Thomas Jr., Taylor, Caroline; m. Barry Dixon Denton, 2000. State senate, Ky.; owner & sr. v.p. Coin Phone Mgmt. Co., 1986—; state senator Dist. 36 Ky., 1995—; mem. Health & Welfare Com., Banking & Ins. Com., Econ. Devel. Com., Labor & Tourism Com. Recipient Better Life award, Ky. Assn. Health Care Facil, 1997. Mem.: Nat. Assn. Women Bus. Owners, Coun. State Govts., Nat. Conf. State Legislators, Am. Legislature Exch. Coun. (Legislator of Yr. 1998), C. of C., Better Bus. Bur., Assn. Profl. Businesswomen, Nat. Fedn. Ind. Bus., Am. Pub. Comm. Coun. Republican. Christian. Address: 8708 Twin Ridge Ct Louisville KY 40242 Mailing: 1708 Golden Leaf Way Louisville KY 40245 Office: Capitol Annex Rm 230 Frankfort KY 40601 Home Phone: 502-489-9058; Office Phone: 502-564-8100 646. Fax: 502-489-9058.

DEO, NARSINGH, computer scientist, educator; b. Raniganj, Bihar, India, Jan. 2, 1936; s. Bihari Lal and Durga (Modi) Jee; m. Karen Ruth Baier, June 29, 1968. BS, Patna U., India, 1956; Dip. I.I.Sc., Indian Inst. Sci., 1959; MS, Calif. Inst. Tech., 1960; PhD, Northwestern U., 1965. Assoc. electronic engr. Burroughs Electro Data divsn., 1960-62; sr. engr. Jet Propulsion Lab., Pasadena, 1966-69, mem. tech. staff, 1969-71; v.p. Britt Electronics Corp., Santa Monica, Calif., 1968-69; asst. prof. elec. engring. Calif. State Coll., 1971; assoc. prof. elec. engring. Indian Inst. Tech., Kanpur, 1971-74, prof., head computer ctr., 1975-77; prof. Wash. State U., Pullman, 1977-87, chmn. dept. computer sci., 1980-84; Millican chair prof. U. Ctrl. Fla., Orlando, 1986—; dir. Ctr. Parallel Computation, 1989—. Electronics design cons. Ctr. Behavior Therapy, Beverly Hills, Calif., 1967—71; mem. faculty engring. ext. UCLA, 1965—68; vis. assoc. prof. U. Ill., Urbana; vis. prof. Wash. State U., Pullman, 1974—75, ETH, Zurich, Switzerland, 1993, Australian Nat. U., Canberra, 1996, Chuo U., Tokyo, 2002; vis. faculty IBM Thomas J. Watson Rsch., Yorktown Heights, NY, 1984, Oak Ridge Nat. Lab., 1994; pres. Forum Interdisciplinary Math., 2007—11. Author: Graph Theory with Application to Engineering and Computer Science, 1974, Simulation with Digital Computers, 1979; co-author (wih E.M. Reingold and J. Nievergelt): Combinatorial Algorithms: Theory and Practice, 1977; co-author: (with M.M. Syslo and J.S. Kowalik) Discrete Optimization Algorithms: With Pascal Programs, 1983; contbr. scientific papers to profl. jours. Recipient Fla. Gov.'s award, 1989; grantee, NSF, U.S. Dept. Transp., Army Rsch. Office, U.S. Army's PM-TRADE, Fla. High Tech. and Industry Coun. Fellow: IEEE, Assn. Computing Machinery; mem.: Inst. Combinatorics and Its Applications, Am. Assn. Advancement Sci. Achievements include patents in field. Home: 3901 Orange Lake Dr Orlando FL 32817-1637

DEPALMA, RALPH GEORGE, surgeon, educator, medical administrator; m. Maleva Tankard, Sept. 17, 1955; children: Ralph L., Edward F., Maleva B., Malinda G. AB, Columbia U, 1953; MD, NYU, 1956. Diplomate Am. Bd. Surgery, Am. Bd. Vascular Surgery. Resident in surgery Univ. Hosps., Cleve., 1962-64; from instr. to prof. surgery Case Western Res. U., Cleve., 1964-80; prof., chmn. surgery U. Nev., Reno, 1980-82, George Washington U. Sch. Medicine, Washington, 1982-92; Lewis B. Saltz prof. of surgery George Washington U. Med. Ctr., Washington, 1992-94; prof. surgery, vice-chmn. dept. surgery, assoc. dean U. Nev., Reno, 1994-2000; nat. dir. surgery US Dept. Vets. Affairs, Washington, 2000—08, Nat. Dir. Transplantation, 2007—10; prof. surgery Uniformed Svsc. U. Health Scis., Bethesda, Md., 2000—; spl. operations officer Va. Office R & D, 2010—. Chair nat. surg. quality program Dept. Vet. Affairs, 2005—08; faculty surg. complications collaborative Inst. for Health Care Improvement, 2007—08. Author: Practicing and Other Stories, 2005, Xlibris: Lives and Loves in Cars, 2006, Xlibris: Saeta for a Son, 2008; editor: (with J.M. Giordano) Reoperative Vascular Surgery, 1987, Chief Complaints Surgery and Dilemmas in Health Care, 2009, Basic Science of Vascular Surgery, 1988; assoc. editor: Haimovici Vascular Surgery: Principles and Techniques, 1989; co-editor: Basic Science in Vascular Disease, 1997, Vascular Surgery, Internat. Jour. Impotence Rsch.; mem. editl. bd. Vascular and Endovascular Surgery, 2003; contbr. 289 chapters to books; articles to profl. jours. Bd. dirs. Reno Opera, 1980-83, Reno Chamber Orch., 1999-00; stroke liaison nat. chpt. Am. Heart Assn., 1992-94; tech adv. group Nat. Quality Found., 2004, steering com. Surg. Complications Improvement Project, 2004-06, tech. adv. group Venous Thromboembolism, DOD Expert Panel Brain Injury, 2009-2012; mem. traumatic brain injury com., Dept. Vets. Affairs, 2013-. Capt. aviation med. examiner USAF, 1957—60, with USAFR, 1960—63. Recipient Founder's Honor award Am. Venous Forum, 2008, Alumni award NYU Coll. Medicine; name to Best Doctors in Am., 1994, named lectureship and surg. svc. GWU Hosp.; grantee USPHS, 1974-82, Lifetime Achievement award award, Assn. VA Surgeons, 2010 Fellow ACS (mem. com. trauma 2007-, expert panel DOD brain injury modeling 2009-12); mem. Cleve. Vascular Soc. (pres. 1977-78, registry 1978-80), Rocky Mt. Vascular Soc. (pres. 1981-82), Am. Surg. Assn., Soc. Vascular Surgery, Washington Acad. Surgery (sec. 1991-92, v.p. 1992-93, pres. 1993-94), Am. Venous Forum (sec. 1991-94, bd. dirs. found. 1992-95), Am. Coll. Healthcare Execs. (assoc.), 1996, Cosmos Club (admissions com. 1992-94, chair awards com. 1998, awards com. 2001, chair 2003—), Western Vascular Soc., Surgical Soc. Inst. Health Care Improvement (faculty 2006-2013), Cochrane Group, Interventional Bioiron Assn., Prospectors Club Reno, Phi Beta Kappa, Alpha Omega Alpha. Episcopalian. Achievements include research in atherosclerotic plaque dynamics, observations on regression of atherosclerosis in animal models and in men with PAD; effect of cigarette smoking on patency of vascular grafts; definition of cellular and subcellular changes in shock; altered mitochondrial metabolism; diagnosis and treatment of vasculogenic erectile dysfunction; treatment of limb ulceration due to advanced chronic venous disease; role of iron storage, inflammatory cytokines and survival in atherosclerosis; surgical quality improvement and reduction of surgical complications; injury due to exlosions and blasts. Avocations: sailing, literature, writing. Office Phone: 202-433-5612, 202-595-4511. Personal E-mail: docdepalma@msn.com. Business E-Mail: ralph.depalma@va.gov.

DEPAOLI, LOU, former professional sports team executive; m. Kathy DePaoli; children: Ryan, Emily. BA in Mgmt. of Profl. Sports Orgns., U. Mass. With Prudential Ins. Co. Am., Auburn, Mass.; owner ins. agy., Worcester, Mass.; v.p. sales Am. Hockey League Worcester IceCats, 1994—96; positions up to v.p. sales and mktg. Maj. League Baseball Fla. Marlins, 1996—2000; positions up to v.p. team mktg. and bus. devel. Team Mktg. and Bus. Ops. dept. NBA, 2000—05; exec. v.p., chief mktg. officer Atlanta Spirit, LLC (parent co. of NBA Atlanta Hawks, NHL Atlanta Thrashers and Philips Arena), 2005—08.

DEPASS-CREQUE, LINDA ANN, educational consultant, association executive, former education commissioner; b. NYC; d. Noel and Enid Louise (Schloss) DePass; m. Leonard J. Creque, July 29, 1967; children: Leah Michelle, Michael Gregory. BS, CUNY-Queens, 1963, MS, 1969; PhD, U. Ill., 1986. Tchr. 2d grade Bd. Edn., NYC, 1963, tchr. demonstrations, team tchr., 1964-65, master tchr., 1965-66; elem. tchr. P.S. 69, Jackson Hgts., N.Y., 1963-67; tchr. English Cath. U., Ponce, P.R., 1967; cmty. exch. elem. tchr. grades K-6 Ponce, 1966-67; tchr. 4th grade Dept. Edn., Virgin Islands, 1967—69, tchr. remedial reading, master tchr. Virgin Islands, 1968—69; program coord. Project HeadStart, Virgin Islands, 1969—73, coord. Inst. Developmental Studies Virgin Islands, 1970—71, acting dir. Virgin Islands, 1972—73; prin. Thomas Jefferson Annex Primary Sch., St. Thomas, Virgin Islands, 1973—80, Joseph Sibilly Elem. Sch., St. Thomas, 1980—87; commr. edn. Dept. Edn., St. Thomas, 1987—94; founder, pres. V.I. Inst. for Tchg. and Learning, St. Thomas, 1995—; pres. LCe Cons. Cons. Edn. Devel. Ctr., Mass. Nat. SSI Project, 1992-93, Coll. V.I., 1978; mem. exec. com., bd. overseers Regional Lab. Ednl. Improvement NE and Islands, Andover, Mass., 1988-92; bd. dirs. V.I. Pub. TV; mem. exec. bd. Leadership in Edn. Adminstrv. Devel., V.I., 1989—; op-ed columnist V.I. Daily News; presenter, keynote spkr. confs. in field. Contbr. articles to profl. publs. Trustee U. V.I., 1989—; mem. V.I. Residential Task Force for Human Svcs., 1989-94, V.I. Labor Coun.; bd. dirs. Nat. Urban Alliance for Effective Edn. Tchrs. Coll. Columbia U., N.Y.C., 1993—, Cultural Inst. V.I., 1989-94; mem. cultural endowment bd., V.I., 1989-94; mem. governing bd. East End Health Ctr., 1979-80; mem. Gov.'s Conf. Librs., 1978. Grantee V.I. Coun. on Arts Ceramics for Primary Children, 1974-78, Comprehensive Employment and Tng. Act, 1977, NSF, 1989-93, Carnegie Found., 1988-90; recipient award NASA, award St. Thomas-St. John Counselors Assn., 1988, Ednl. Excellence award Harvard U. Prins. Ctr., Ill. Edn. Svc. Ctr., 1975, Outstanding Leadership award FEMA, 1990, Disting. Svc. award Edn. Commn. of U.S., 1991, Outstanding Svc. award Coun. of Chief State Sch. Officers, 1995. Mem. LWV, St. Thomas Reading Coun., Nat. Assn. Tchrs. Math., Edn. Commn. of States (commr. 1987-93, steering com. 1988-92, internal audit com. 1988, policies priority com. 1991, exec. com. 1992, alt. steering com. 1991-94), Coun. Chief of State Sch. Officers (chair extra jurisdictions com., bd. dirs., task force early childhood edn., ednl. equity com., restructuring edn. com.), Phi Kappa Phi, Kappa Delta Pi, Phi Delta Kappa. Office: 1-1 Tabor Harmony PO Box 301954 St Thomas VI 00803-1954

DEPINHO, RONALD A., health facility administrator, research scientist, medical educator; s. Alvaro DePinho; m. Lynda Chin. MD, Albert Einstein Med. Coll., 1981. Feinberg scholar Albert Einstein Med. Coll.; prof. medicine (genetics) Harvard Med. Sch., Boston, 1998—2011, American Cancer Soc. rsch. prof.; mem. Dept. Adult Oncology Dana-Farber Cancer Inst., Boston, 1998—2011, dir. Belfer Inst. for Applied Cancer Sci.; pres. U. Tex. MD Anderson Cancer Ctr., 2011—. Co-founder, scientific adv. bd. AVEO Pharm. Inc., Cambridge, Mass.; bd. dirs. American Assn. Cancer Rsch. Bd. dirs. Am. Assn. Cancer Rsch., 2001. Recipient American Soc. Clin. Investigation award, 2000, Steven and Michele Kirsch Found. Investigator award, 2000, AACR-GHA Clowes award, 2003, Albert Szent-Gyrgyi Prize for Progress in Cancer Rsch., 2009. Mem.: Inst. Medicine. Office: University of Texas MD Anderson Cancer Center Office of President 1515 Holcombe Blvd Houston TX 77030 Office Phone: 713-792-2121. E-mail: rdepinho@mdanderson.org.

DEPPERSCHMIDT, THOMAS ORLANDO, retired economist, consultant; b. St. Louis, Dec. 3, 1935; s. Robert O. and Marcella C. (Meier) D.; m. Bertha Marie Waldman, Nov. 28, 1957; children: Susan D. Vescovo, Mark, Joel, Andrew, Amy D. Hester, Joan D. Benedict. AB, Ft. Hays State U., Kans., 1958; PhD, U. Tex., 1965. Asst. prof., then assoc. prof. W. Tex. State U., Canyon, 1961-66; prof. econs. Memphis State U., 1966—2001, prof. emeritus, 2001—, chmn. dept., 1977-83. Rssch. assoc. study NYC elevator industry, 1996, 2004. Author over 40 tech. treatises; co-author: Encyclopedia of Economics, 1974, Assessing Family Loss in Wrongful Death Litigation, 1999, Detritus: The SIP Initiative to Stalk Hitler, 2006, The Last Gray Line: Senior Citizens at War in Afghanistan, 2011, People Who Irritate the Hell Out of Us and How We Deal with Them, 2011, Halfway There: Dialogues on God and Man, 2012; editor: Financial Policies in Transition, 1968; author over 40 tech. treatises. With AUS, 1954-56. Mem.: Nat. Assn. Forensic Economists. Home: 1957 Mt Repose Germantown TN 38139-3443 Personal E-mail: todepperschmidt@yahoo.com.

DEPRIEST, PAUL D., gynecologic oncologist, educator; MD, U. Ky., 1985. Diplomate Am. Bd. Ob-Gyn, 1992, Am. Bd. Ob-Gyn-gynecologic oncology, 1994, lic. Ky. Intern Univ. Ky. Med. Ctr., Lexington, 1986, resident, 1988, fellow, 1991, chief med. officer; prof. gynecologic oncology dept. Univ. Ky.; hosp. affiliations include Univ. Hosp., Univ. Ky. Good Samaritan Hosp., Univ. Ky. Albert B. Chandler Hosp. Named Recognized Dr., HealthGrades. Mem.: Soc. Gynecologic Oncologists. Office: University of Kentucky Albert B Chandler Hospital Pavilion H 800 Rose St Lexington KY 40536 Office Phone: 859-323-5000.

DERBY, DAVID, state legislator; Mem. Dist. 74 Okla. House of Representatives, 2007—. Republican. Office: Oklahoma House of Representatives 2300 N Lincoln Blvd Rm 337 Oklahoma City OK 73105 Address: PO Box 2150 Owasso OK 74055 Home Phone: 918-260-6970; Office Phone: 405-557-7377. Business E-Mail: derbydavid@sbcglobal.net, david.derby@okhouse.gov.

DE REVERE, DAVID WILSEN, retired professional society administrator; b. Englewood, NJ, Nov. 13, 1937; s. Wilbur L. and Ethel M. (Gilchrist) De R.; m. Ellen B. Tompkins, June 7, 1958; children: Mark S., Roger T BA, Colgate U., Hamilton, NY, 1959; MDiv, Yale U., New Haven, Conn., 1963. Cert. master chaplain Internat. Conf. Police Chaplains. Sr. pastor 1st Ch. of Christ in Saybrook, Old Saybrook, Conn., 1963-85; exec. dir. Internat. Conf. Police Chaplains, Destin, Fla., 1985—2003. Author, editor: Chaplaincy in Law Enforcement, 1989. Chaplain Old Saybrook (Conn.) Dept. Police Svcs., 1964-85, FBI, 1991-2007. Home: 110 Sussex Ln Fayetteville GA 30215 Personal E-mail: davede@comcast.net.

DER-HOUSSIKIAN, HAIG, retired linguist, educator; b. Cairo, Aug. 16, 1938; s. Vagharsh and Adrine (Karalian) Der-H.; m. Gaylynne Hall, Aug. 27, 1961. Student, Am. U., Cairo, 1957-59; BA, Am. U., Beirut, 1961, MA, 1962; PhD, U. Tex., 1969. Research assoc. U. Dar-es-Salaam, Tanzania, 1966-67; asst. prof. linguistics U. Fla., Gainesville, 1967-72; dir. linguistics, 1971-72, 84-85; assoc. prof. U. Fla., Gainesville, 1972-77, dir. Ctr. for African Studies, 1973-79, prof., 1977—2003, chmn. dept. African and Asian langs. and lits., 1982-91, prof. emeritus, 2003—. Mem. grad. council U. Fla., 1988-91; sr. Fulbright lectr. Universidade de Luanda, Angola, 1972-73, Universite du Benin, Lome, Togo, 1979-81; vis. prof. African linguistics U. Zimbabwe, Harare, 1989; panelist, grant proposal reviewer U.S. Dept. Edn., Washington, 1976—2010; USIA Acad. Specialist Grant cons. to U. De Ouagadougou, Burkina Faso, 1981; USIA Acad. Specialist Grant lectr. U. Marien Ngouabi, Brazzaville, Congo, May-Aug. 1988; occasional grant proposal evaluator Social Sci. and Humanities Coun. Can. Author: TEM, Grammar Handbook, 1980, TEM, Communication and Culture, 1980, TEM, Special Skills, 1980; co-editor: Language and Linguistics Problems in Africa, 1977; compiler: A Bibliography of African Linguistics, 1972, reviewer: African Book Publ. Rev., 1996—; contbr. chapters to books. ACTION grantee, 1980-81. Mem. MLA (African Linguistics bibliographer 1967-74), Linguistics Soc. Am., African Studies Assn., Southeastern Conf. on Linguistics, Phi Kappa Phi. Armenian Apostolic. Avocations: reading, hiking, travel. Personal E-mail: haig@ufl.edu.

DE ROSA, CHRISTOPHER THOMAS, biomedical researcher; b. Cin., June 18, 1949; s. Frank P. and Mary Lorean De Rosa; children: Brian, Erin, Phillip, Joel. BA, Ohio Weslyan U., 1971; MS Ecology, Miami U., Oxford, Ohio, 1974, PhD Biology, 1977. From instr. to asst. prof. biology U. Va., Charlottesville, 1976—80; sr. scientist U.S. EPA, Cin., 1980—82, br. chief, 1984—88, dir. Nat. Ctr. Environ. Assessment, 1988—91; asst. prof. botany and zoology U. Maine, Orono, 1982—84; dep. assoc. adminstr. sci. Ctr. Disease Control and Prevention, Atlanta, 1991—92, dir. divsn. toxicology, 1991—2004, dir. divsn. toxicology and environ. medicine, 2005—07, asst. dir. toxicology and risk analysis Agy. Toxic Substances and Diseases Registry. Tchr. St. Bernard's Parish Sch., Cin., 1986—88; mem. steering com. risk assessment WHO, Geneva, 1992—2008, cons., State Dept., NASA, Dept. Energy, Dept. Def., NATO, Pan Am. Health Orgn.; reader, contbr. Ednl. Testing Svc., Princeton, NJ, mem. test devel. com.; presenter in field; credentialed mem. Sr. Biomed. Rsch. Svc.; pres., CEO Seven Lazy D Acres Inc., Mt. Gilead, Ohio, 2012—. Editor: Toxicology Letters, 1995; reviewer: Jour. Ambulatory Pediat., Quar. Rev. Biology, Oxford U. Press.; contbr. articles to profl. jours.; mem. editl. bd. Environ. Rsch., Environ. Health Perspectives, Toxicology and Indsl. Health, Environ. Rsch., Human and Ecological Risk Assessment. Mem. bd. edn. Hampden Sch. Dist., Maine, 1982—84. Recipient Bronze medal, U.S. EPA, 1981, 1986, 1988, 1998, Disting. Cons. Publ. award, Ctr. Disease Control, 1998, Hammer award, U.S. V.P. Al Gore, 2000; grantee, Am. Philos. Soc., 1977, Exxon Found., 1983, U.S. EPA, 1989, NSF, 1975, 1978; fellow, 1975; Faculty Rsch. grantee, U. Maine, 1982, Faculty Equipment grantee, 1983. Fellow: Collegium Ramazzini; mem.: AAAS, Assn. Environ. Health Sci. Found. (Lifetime Achievement award 2010), Alliance Pub. Health and Assocs., Inc. (founder and CEO 2009—), Soc. Occupl. and Environ. Health, N.Y. Acad. Scis., Animal Behavior Soc., Rsch. Soc. N.Am., Soc. Integrative and Comparative Biology, Ecol. Soc. Am., Soc. Risk Analysis, Am. Coll. Toxicology, Sigma Xi (grantee 1975). Avocations: landscape design, fly fishing, natural history, agriculture. Home: 5305 Burdock Creek Acworth GA 30101

DE ROSA, GUY PAUL, retired orthopedic surgery educator; b. Napoleon, Ohio, Oct. 25, 1939; married. BS, Notre Dame U., 1961; MD, Ind. U., 1965. Diplomate Am. Bd. Orthopedic Surgery. Resident in gen. surgery Sch. Medicine, Ind. U., Indpls., 1965—66, resident in orthopedic surgery, 1966—70; fellow in pediat. orthopedics Hosp. for Sick Children, London, 1969—70; asst. prof. orthopedic surgery Sch. Medicine, Ind. U., Indpls., 1970—76, assoc. prof., 1976—82, dir. undergrad. edn. dept. orthopedic surgery, 1972—, chief neuromuscular disease, 1972—, coord. Garceau-Wayu Lectureships dept. orthopedic surgery, 1975—, dir. Cerebral Palsy Clinic, 1978—88, orthopedic cons. Hemophilia Clinic, 1978—91, prof. orthopedic surgery, 1981—95, orthopedic cons. Rheumato-Orthopedic Clinic, 1984—95, chmn. dept. orthopedic surgery, 1986—95; exec. dir. Am. Bd. Orthopaedic Surgery, Chapel Hill, 1995; prof. orthopaedic surgery Duke U., 1995—2005. Attending physician Wishard Meml. Hosp., Indpls., 1970—95, Ind. U. Med. Ctr., Indpls., 1970—95, James Whitcomb Riley Hosp. for Children, Indpls., 1970—95; coord. Ctrl. Ind. and So. Ind. State Bd. Health Programs, Scoliosis and Sch. Screening, 1977; mem. orthop. surgery steering com. Children's Cancer Study Group, 1990; mem. residency rev. com. for orthop. surgery Accreditation Coun. for Grad. Med. Edn., 1990—; vis. prof. Children's Hosp., Columbus, Ohio, 1977, St. Joseph Hosp., Ft. Wayne, Ind., 1977, Miami Valley Hosp., Dayton, Ohio, 1978, Dayton, 1982, Dayton, 1985, Dayton, 1986, Deaconess Hosp., Evansville, Ind., 1980, Bloomington (Ind.) Hosp., 1982, U. Tex., Galveston, 1982, U. Mo. Med. Ctr., Columbia, 1983, Southwestern Mich. Area Health Edn. Ctr., Kalamazoo, 1985, Newington (Conn.) Children's Hosp., 1988, Children's Hosp. Med. Ctr., Akron, Ohio, 1992; and numerous others; active Hemophilia Med. Adv. Coun., 1978—; presenter in field. Contbr. articles to profl. jours. Bd. dirs. United Cerebral Palsy, 1973—85, Hemophilia Found., 1978—, New Hope of Ind., 1984—86, mem. long range planning com., 1984—85, mem. task force on serving brain injured, 1988; bd. dirs. Ind. Found. Hand Surg. Rsch. and Edn., 1989—95; mem. adv. bd. Head Injury Found., 1995, Children's Limb Found., 1992—; mem. pub. rels. and promotion com. Ind. Gov.'s Coun. on Phys. Fitness and Sports Medicine, 1986—92, mem. promotion com., 1988—92; dir. State of Ind. Orthop. Rsch. and Edn. Found., 1993, bd. trustees, 1994. Maj. USAF, 1970—72. Recipient Ensminger award for rsch. in trauma, 1967, Willis Gatch award, 1968; grantee grantee in field. Mem.: 20th Century Orthop. Assn., Internat. Soc. Orthop. Surgery and Traumatology, Scoliosis Rsch. Soc. (mem. edn. com. 1985—), Russell Hibbs Soc., Pediat. Orthop. Soc. N.Am. (mem. com. on fellowships 1986—92, bd. dirs. 1990—92, 2d v.p. 1994, 1st v.p. 1995, pres. 1996), Mid-Am. Orthop. Assn. (chmn. program com. 1986—87, bd. dirs. 1986—, sec. 1990—93, 2d v.p. 1993—94, 1st v.p. 1994—), Marion County Med. Soc., Acad. Orthop. Soc. (mem. undergrad. edn. com. 1983—87), Clin. Orthop. Soc., Assn. Orthop. Chmn., Ind. State Med. Soc., Ind. Orthop. Soc. (mem. exec. com. 1986—95), Am. Orthop. Foot and Ankle Soc. (mem. com. biomechanics 1982—84, mem. program com. 1985—), Am. Acad. Cerebral Palsy and Devel. Medicine, Am. Acad. Orthop. Surgeons (mem. com. undergrad. edn. 1976—83, chmn. 1979—83, mem. com. pediat. orthopedics 1988—94, mem. subcom. on spine 1990, mem. subcom. on pediats. program com. 1992, mem. coun. clin. resources 1993—94), Am. Acad. Pediats., Am. Fracture Assn. (Wellmerling award 1982), Am. Orthop. Assn. (mem. nominating com. 1988—89, del.-at-large exec. com. 1988—89, mem. com. on N.Am. traveling fellowship 1989—93, mem. com. planning and devel. 1991—, 2d pres.-elect 1994—), AMA, Am. Bd. Orthopedic Surgery (oral examiner 1983—, site investigator residency rev. com. 1983—, mem. credentials com. 1990—93, bd. dirs. 1990—, mem. oral examinations com. 1990—, mem. grad. edn. com. 1990—, mem. oral recert. examination com. 1992—93, mem. practice audit com. 1992—93, rep. alt. 1992—93, ACS adv. coun. 1992—94, sec. 1993—94, mem.

cert. renewal com. 1993—94, mem. fin. com. 1993—94, mem. exec. com. 1993—94, vice chmn. residency rev. com. 1994—, chmn. 1995—97, exec. dir), Spectators Orthop. Letters Club, Little Orthop. Club, Orthop. Letters Club, Alpha Epsilon Delta, Alpha Omega Alpha.

DERRICKSON, WILLIAM BORDEN, manufacturing executive; b. Milford, Del., May 30, 1940; m. Patricia Jean Hayes, Feb. 1, 1964; children: Stephen Russel, Michael Scot BSEE, U. Del., 1964; diploma, Harvard Bus. Sch., 1979. Registered profl. engr. Supr. elec. maintenance Delmarva Power, Salisbury, Md., 1964-68; instrumentation engr. Hercules, Inc., Wilmington, Del., 1968-69, Sun Shipbldg., Chester, Pa., 1969-70; dir. project Fla. Power & Light Co., Juno Beach, Fla., 1970-84; sr. v.p. Pub. Svc. Co. N.H., Manchester, 1984-85; pres. New Hampshire Yankee Electric Co., Seabrook, 1985-87; pres., COO Quadrex Corp., Campbell, Calif., 1988-89, chmn. bd., CEO, 1989-93; also chmn. bd. dirs.; chmn. bd., CEO QES Inc., Palm City, Fla., 1994—95, IBEX Engring. Svcs., Palm City, 1995—2006; pres. WPD Assoc., 2006—. Nuclear advisor Tenn. Valley Authority Bd. Dirs., 1987. Contbr. articles to profl. publs. Named Constrn. Man of Yr. ENR/McGraw-Hill Publs., 1984 Mem. NSPE, Am. Nuclear Soc., Project Mgmt. Inst., N.H. Soc. Profl. Engrs., Internat. Platform Assn., Rep. Senatorial Inner Circle. Republican. Avocations: golf, travel, coin collecting/numismatics, piano. Home: 1813 Eagles Glen Cove Austin TX 78732 Office Phone: 772-285-0774. Personal E-mail: bderricksn@aol.com.

DERTHICK, ALAN WENDELL, architect, firm executive; b. Johnson City, Tenn., July 6, 1931; s. Lawrence Gridley and Helda Lee (Hannah) Derthick; m. Jane Bailey, Dec. 22, 1958; children: Mark Alan, Steven John. BArch, Auburn U., 1954. Registered arch., Tenn., Ga., Ala. Ptnr. Derthick, Henley & Wilkerson Archs., Chattanooga, 1960—. Prin. works include Miller Pl., 1989 (Honor award), Hunter Mus. Art, 1977 (Honor awards), 1994, 2004, 2005, Chattanooga Pub. Libr., 1977 (Honor award), 1992, Hamilton County Cts. Bldg., 1992, Alexian Village, 1993, 2003, 2005, 2007, Covenant Transport Nat. Hdqrs., 1997, 2000, 2005, 2006, Chattanoooga Conv. Ctr., 2003, 2005, EPB Garage, 2003, 2005, 2006, 2009, TVPPA, 2002, Hardy Sch., 2001. Chmn. Chattanooga Codes Rev. Bd., 1975—95, Mayor's Better Schs. Task Force, Chattanooga, 1984—85, Hamilton County Codes Appeals Bd., 1999—2009; pres. 1st Christian Ch., 1978, 1984, 1998, 1999, 2000. With USAF, 1954—56. Recipient Honor award, Nat. Concrete Reinforcing Steel Inst., 1977. Mem.: AIA (pres. Chattanooga chpt. 1966, 1972, Gulf States Regional and Nat. Honor award 1961, 1977, 1978, 1989), Tenn. Soc. Archs. (pres. 1991), Mountain City Club. Home: 602 Marr Dr Signal Mountain TN 37377-2228 Office: Derthick Henley Wilkerson 1001 Carter St Chattanooga TN 37402-5014 Office Phone: 423-266-4816. Business E-Mail: alan@dhw-architects.com.

DERTING, TERRY L., biology professor, researcher; d. John Franklin and Edith Morelock Derting. BA, Mt. Holyoke Coll., South Hadley, Mass., 1978; MS, Va. Poly. Inst. State U., Blacksburg, 1981; PhD, Ind. U., Bloomington, 1986. Cert. evaluator Therapy Dogs Internat., AKC Canine Good Citizen Evaluator, Bat Species Survey Permit, Instl. Rsch. Human Subjects, Pet First Aid, Basic Wildlife Rehab. Asst. prof., biology Hollins Coll., Hollins, Va., 1989—91; vis. asst. prof., tchg. fellow biology Beloit Coll., Wis., 1991—93; prof. Murray State U., Ky., 1993—. Contbr. articles to profl. jours., chapters to books. Dir. PetSafe Program Humane Soc., Murray, 2004—; pres. Humane Soc. Calloway County, Murray, 2013—. Recipient Regent's award Tchg. Excellence, Murray State U., 1998, Max Carmen Outstanding Tchr. award, 2000, Undergrad. Disting. Mentor award, 2007, Editors' Citation Excellence Manuscript Rev., Jour. Natural Resources Environ. Edn., 2004, Disting. U. Tchr. Superlative award, Ky. Acad. Sci., 2006, Neil Weber award, 2009, Outstanding Biology Prof. award, 2009; grantee Tchg. Initiative Higher Edn. Leadership, Hewlett Packard, 2004—06, NSF, 2001—. Mem.: AAAS, Ky. Chpt. of The Wildlife Soc., Ky. Acad. Sci., Coun. on Undergrad. Rsch., Am. Soc. Mammalogists (grants-in-aid com., Joseph Grinnell award Cmmt. 1996—2007), Assn. Coll. and U. Biology Educators (pres. 2002—04), Sigma Xi (pres., v.p. 1996—98). Avocations: gardening, pet training. Office: Murray State University 16th St Biology 2112 Murray KY 42071 Office Phone: 270-809-6327. Office Fax: 270-809-2788.

DESAI, PRATIBHA KIRIT, hematologist; MD, U. Bombay, 1985. Lic. Fla., 1994, diplomate Am. Bd. Internal Medicine-hematology, 1994, Am. Bd. Internal Medicine-med. oncology, 1995. Resident internal medicine Cook County Hosp., Chgo., 1987—90; fellow hematology Univ. Ill. Hosp., 1991; physician hematology/oncology St. Petersburg Gen. Hosp., Fla.; hosp. affiliations include Bayfront Med. Ctr. Inc., Edward White Hosp., Largo Med. Ctr., Morton Plant Hosp., Northside Hosp., Palms of Pasadena Hosp., St. Anthony's Hosp. Office: St Petersburg General Hospital 6500 38th Ave N Saint Petersburg FL 33710 Office Phone: 727-344-6569.*

DESAI, SANJAY S., hand surgeon, educator; AB magna cum laude, Brown U., 1980; MD, George Wash. U., 1984. Diplomate Am. Bd. Orthopedic Surgery, 2003, cert. hand surgery 2003. Resident in orthopedic surgery Univ. Mass. Meml. Med. Ctr., Worchester, 1985—90; fellow in hand and microvascular surgery Duke Univ. Med. Ctr., Durham, NC, 1993—94; asst. prof. surgery Va. Commonwealth Univ.; hosp. affiliations include Henrico Doctor's Hosp., Bon Socours St. Mary's Hosp. Major Med. Corps US Army, Landstuhl Army Med. Ctr.,Germany. Recipient Alec Horowitz prize, George Wash. Univ., Meritorious Svc. medal, Army Achievement medal. Mem.: Southeastern Hand Club (v.p.), Richmond Acad. Medicine, Med. Soc. Va., Piedmont Orthopaedic Soc., Am. Soc. for Peripheral Nerve, Am. Assn. for Hand Surgery, Va. Orthopaedic Soc., Duke Hand Club, Am. Acad. of Orthopaedic Surgeons, Am. Soc. for Surgery of the Hand. Office: Bon Secours St Mary's Hospital 5801 Bremo Rd Richmond VA 23226-1907 Office Phone: 804-285-2011.*

DE SAINT PHALLE, THIBAUT, investment banker, consultant; b. Tuxedo Pk., NY, July 23, 1918; s. Fal and Marie (Duryee) de Saint P.; m. Rosamond (Frame), Jan. 12, 1946 (dec. 1960); children: Fal, Pierre, Thérèse; m. Elene Canrobert (Isles), June 21, 1965 (div. 1983); children: Marc, Diane; m. Mariana M. (Smith), April 24, 1983. Student, Harvard U., 1935—37; BA, Columbia U., 1939, JD, 1941. Bar: N.Y. 1942, U.S. Supreme Ct., 1945, D.C. 1984. Assoc. Chadbourne, Wallace, Parke, and Whiteside, NYC, 1941—50; ptnr., head corp. law dept. Lewis 1950and McDonald, NYC, 1950—58; v.p., treas. Becton, Dickinson, and Co., Rutherford, NJ, 1958—62, dir., 1958—67; sr. ptnr. Coudert Bros., NYC, 1962—66, counsel, 1966—77; of counsel Vorys, Sater, Seymour, and Pease, Washington, 1983—86. Ltd. ptnr. Dean Witter and Co., pres. Dean Witter Overseas Fin. Corp., N.Y.C., 1967-68; investment banker Stralem, Saint Phalle and Co., Inc., N.Y.C., 1968-70, vice chmn. bd. dir., 1968-70; mem. faculty, prof. internat. fin. and law Ctr. d'Etudes Industrielles, Geneva, 1971-76; dir. Export Import Bank U.S., Washington, 1977-81; Scholl chair internat. bus. Georgetown U. Ctr. Strategic and Internat. Studies, 1981-83; chmn. Saint Phalle Internat. Group, 1985-2009. Author: The Dollar Crisis, 1963; Multi Nat. Corporations, 1976; U.S. Productivity and Competitiveness in Internat. Trade, 1980; Trade Inflation and the Dollar, 1981, (rev. edit., 1984), The Federal Reserve, an Intentional Mystery, 1985; Saints, Sinners and Scalawags, 2004; contbg. numerous articles on internat. fin. and trade to profl. journals. Lt. comdr. USNR, 1942—46. Decorated Navy Commendation medal, Bronze Star, Legion of Honor, (France). Mem.: ABA, Jockey Club, Met. Club. Roman Catholic. Home and Office: 144 Moorings Pk Dr Apt M302 Naples FL 34105 Personal E-mail: thibaut@embarqmail.com.

DESANTIS, RON (RONALD DION DESANTIS), United States Representative from Florida, former federal prosecutor; b. Jacksonville, Sept. 14, 1978; m. Casey Black. BA in History, Yale U., 2001; JD, Harvard Law Sch., 2005; Grad., US Naval Justice Sch., 2005. Mil. prosecutor Trial Svc. Office Command South East, Naval Station Mayport, Fla., Joint Task Force-Guantanamo Comdr. (JTF-GTMO), Cuba; legal adv. to comdr. SEAL Team Spl. Ops. Task Force-West, Fallujah, Iraq; prosecutor US Attorney's Office (middle dist.) Fla. US Dept. Justice; mem. US Congress from 6th Fla. Dist., Washington, 2013—, US House Fgn. Affairs Com., 2013—, US House Judiciary Com., 2013—, US House Oversight & Govt. Reform Com., 2013—. Instr. US mil. law Fla. Coastal Sch. Law. Author: Dreams From Our Founding Fathers: First Principles in the Age of Obama, 2011. Served in USN, 2004—10, lt., JAG Corps. USNR, 2010—. Decorated Bronze star, Iraq Campaign medal. Mem.: VFW, American Legion. Republican. Roman Catholic. Office: US House of Representatives 427 Cannon House Office Bldg Washington DC 20515 also: 1000 City Ctr Circle Port Orange FL 32129 Office Phone: 202-225-2706, 386-756-9798. Office Fax: 202-226-6299, 386-756-9903.*

DESBIENS, NORMAN A., medical educator, researcher; b. Fall River, Mass., Nov. 24, 1946; s. J. Arthur and Cecile R. D.; m. Sarah F. Desbiens; children: Meaghan, Nicholas. BA, Providence Coll., 1968; MBS, Dartmouth Med. Coll., 1970; MD, Harvard Med. Sch., 1972. With Nat. Health Svc. Corps., Ladysmith, Wis., 1975-77; staff physician, internal medicine residency Marshfield (Wis.) Clinic, 1991-97, transitional residency, program dir., 1995-97; chmn. of medicine U. Tenn., Chattanooga, 1997—2007; med. cons. Program All-Inclusive Care Elderly, Chattanooga, 1998—. Vis. prof. U. South Sewanee, Tenn., 2011; med. dir. Program All-Inclusive Care Elderly, Chattanooga, 2011—. Contbg. author: Critica Cre Symposium, 1996; contbr. articles to profl. jours. Mem. Chattanooga Coalition for Improving End of Life Care, 1998-2003; Lt. comdr. USPHS, 1975-77. Recipient Gwen Sebold Rsch. award Marshfield Clinic, 195, Disting. Tchg. award U. Wis., Madison, 1993, George Magnin Tchg. award Marshfield Clinic, 1992, 84. Fellow ACP.

DE SELDING, EDWARD BERTRAND, retired bank executive; b. Summit, NJ, June 15, 1926; s. Edward Fitzgerald and Alene (Rockwell) deS.; m. Joan Bulkley, Oct. 21, 1950; children: Peter, Ann, Edward Bertrand. BA, Yale, 1950. With Spencer Trask & Co., Inc., NYC, 1950-77, ptnr., 1962-68, sr. v.p., dir., 1968-77, Hornblower, Weeks, Noyes & Trask, Inc., NYC, 1977-78; 1st v.p. Loeb Rhoades, Hornblower & Co., 1978-79; v.p. Bruns, Nordeman, Rea & Co., NYC, 1979-81, Bache Halsey Stuart, Inc., 1981-82, Conn. Nat. Bank, 1982-91, ret. Served with USAAF, 1944-46, Com. on trust funds Protestant Episcopal Ch., 1969-80, Trustee Episcopal funds of Conn., 1991-94. Mem.: NASD (chmn. dist. 12 com. 1971, gov. 1972), Town Darien Ct. Employees Pension Plan (chmn.), Tokeneke Club (pres. 1974—75), Sawgrass Country Club (pres. 2001, gov.). Republican. Episcopalian (vestryman 1961-63, 67-69, 77-79, warden 1984-87). Home: 1000 Vicars Landing Way F-303 Ponte Vedra Beach FL 32082-3118

DE SERRES, FREDERICK JOSEPH, JR., geneticist, toxicologist; b. Dobbs Ferry, NY, Sept. 24, 1929; s. Frederick J. and Helen Marie (Henshaw) de S.; m. Christine Marie Covone, Sept. 18, 1954; children: Mark, John, Paul, David, Jonathan, Lianne. BS in Biology, Tufts U., Medford, Mass., 1951; MS in Botany, Yale U., 1953, PhD, 1955; Doctorate (honoris causa), Cath. U. of Louvain, 1987. Research assoc. biology div. Oak Ridge Nat. Lab., 1955-57, sr. staff biologist, 1957-72; experimenters rep. NASA biosatellite program, 1964-68; coord. environ. mutagenesis program Oak Ridge Nat. Lab., 1969-72; lectr. U. Tenn., 1971-73; adj. prof. dept. pathology U. N.C., Chapel Hill, 1973-90; chief environ. mutagenesis br. Nat. Inst. Environ. Health Scis., Research Triangle Park, N.C., 1972-76, assoc. dir. genetics, 1976-86, guest rschr., 1994-98; rsch. dir. Ctr. for Life Scis. and Toxicology Rsch. Triangle Inst., Research Triangle Park, N.C., 1986-93, prin. sci., 1993-94; guest rschr. Nat. Toxicology program Nat. Inst. Environ. Health Scis., Research Triangle Park, N.C., 1994—; sr. cons. Tech. Planning & Mgmt. Corp., 1996—97, program mgr., 1998. U.S. coord. biol. and genetic consequences project U.S.-USSR Environ. Protection Agreement, 1972-78; chmn. panel mutagenesis and carcinogenesis U.S.-Japan Coop. Med. Sci. Program, 1972-87; chmn. subcom. environ. mutagenesis, com. to coordinate toxicology and related programs Dept. Health and Human Svcs., 1972-85; mem. com. on assessment nitrate accumulation in environ., divsn. biology and agr. NAS/Nat. Rsch. Coun., 1970-72; mem. com. chem. toxicity and aging, commn. on life scis. Nat. Rsch. Coun., 1986-87; cons. in govt., chmn. workshops on environ. pollutants and mutagenesis, 1961-86; vis. prof. U. Zagazig, Egypt, Ain-Shams U., Cairo, 1982, Case We. Res. U., 1983. Mem. editl. bd. Radiation Botany, 1965-74, Mutation Rsch., 1969-72, Jour. Toxicology and Environ. Health, 1975-78, Carcinogenesis, 1979-85; editor Jour. Environ. and Exptl. Botany, 1975-77, Mutation Rsch., 1973-98; sect. editor: Jour. Environ. Pathology and Toxicology, 1979, Jour. Toxicology and Indsl. Health, 1984-88; co-editor: Chemical Mutagens, Vol. 5, 1978, Vol. 6, 1980, Vol. 7, 1982, editor Vol. 8, 1983, vol. 9, 1985, vol. 10, 1986; cons. editor: Environmental Research, 1981-86; contbg. editor: Environmental Mutagenesis, 1979-81; contbr. over 500 articles to profl. jours. Recipient Dir.'s award NIH, 1976; Univ. Scholar Yale U., 1951-52, Wadsworth fellow, 1954-55; Nat. Cancer Inst. predoctoral fellow, 1952-54. Mem. AAAS, Genetic Soc. Am. (rep. to NRC 1970-73), Internat. Assn. Environ. Mutagen Socs. (v.p. 1985-89), Radiation Rsch. Soc., Am. Soc. Cancer Rsch., Environ. Mutagen Soc. (coun. 1969-72, v.p., 1972-73, pres. 1973-76, editor newsletter 1969-72, ann. award 1979, contbg. editor jour. 1979), Internat. Commn. Protection Against Environ. Mutagens and Carcinogensis (vice-chmn. 1976-84, commn. 1985-89), Environ. Mutagen Soc. (pres. 1991-93), European Environ. Mutagen Soc., Japanese Environ. Mutagen Soc., Alpha-1 Nat. Assn. (bd. dirs. 1998-2000), Alpha One Found. (med. and sci. adv. com. 1999-2002, bd. dirs. 1999-2004). Democrat. Roman Catholic. Avocations: photography, gardening, genealogy, genetic epidemiology. Home: 632 Rock Creek Rd Chapel Hill NC 27514-6716 Office Phone: 919-967-2963.

DESHAZO, RICHARD DENSON, medical educator, academic administrator, public broadcasting health producer, anchor; b. Birmingham, Ala., Apr. 4, 1945; s. Hyman Denson and Agnes L. (Carr) de S.; m. Gloria L. Jenkins, June 4, 1967; children: Melanie, Mollie, Matthew. BA in Chemistry, Religion, Birmingham So. Coll., 1967; MD, U. Ala., 1971. Diplomate Am. Bd. Internal Medicine, Am. Bd. Allergy and Immunology, Am. Bd. Rheumatology, Am. Bd. Geriatrics, Nat. Bd. Med. Examiners. Lt. col. U.S. Army Med. Corp., 1972-80; intern in pediat. Children's and Univ. Hosp., Birmingham, 1971-72; resident in internal medicine Walter Reed Army Med. Ctr., Washington, 1972-74, fellow in immunology, microbiology, 1974-75, fellow in clin. immunology, 1975-77; clin. asst. prof. medicine U. Colo. Sch. Med., Denver, 1977-78; asst. prof. medicine and pediatrics Uniformed Svcs. Univ. Health Scis., Bethesda, Md., 1978-80; assoc. prof. medicine and pediat. Tulane U. Sch. Medicine, New Orleans, 1980—89, prof. medicine and pediat., 1985-89, vice chair, clin. ops., 1986—89; prof., chmn. dept. medicine U. South Ala. Coll. Medicine, Mobile, 1989-97; prof. medicine and pediat., chmn. dept. medicine U. Miss. Med. Ctr., Jackson, 1997—2010, Billy Guyton disting. prof. medicine and pediat., 2004—; exec. prodr. health programming Miss. Pub. Broadcasting, 2010—. Clin. immunologist Fitzsimmons Army Med. Ctr., Denver, 1977-78; staff attending internal medicine, asst. chief, clin. immunologist, dir. lab. exptl. immunology, allergy, clin. immunology Svc. Walter Reed Army Med. Ctr., Washington, 1978-80; staff internist S.E. Cmty. Hosp., Washington, 1978-80; chief allergy and rheumatology dept. pediat. Tulane U. Sch. Med., New Orleans, 1980-89, adj. assoc. prof. microbiology, 1983-85, vice chair clin. ops. dept. medicine, 1985-89, dir. immunology program AIDS clin. trials unit, 1987-89; attending physician VA and U. Hosps., New Orleans, 1980-89, St. Jude Hosp., Kenner, La., 1987-89; mem. Nat. Sci. Adv. Com. on AIDS, NIH, 1987-91, study sect. on epidemiology of AIDS, 1987-91, AIDS clin. trials group, 1987-89, reviewers res., 1990-94; chief clin. immunology and allergy VA med. Ctr. New Orleans, 1985-89, assoc. chief staff edn., 1988-89; dir. tng. program internal medicine, v.p. health svcs. found., chief divsn. allergy depts. medicine and pediat., mem. various com. U. South Ala. Hosps. and Clinics, Mobile, 1989-97; chief clin. immunology, allergy and rheumatology dept. medicine VA Med. Ctr., Biloxi, Miss., 1989-97; mem. expert panel allergenic products FDA, 1991-96; asst. clin. coord. Health Care Financing Agy. coop. cardiovasc. project Ala. Quality Assurance Found, Birmingham, 1993-94, bd. dirs., 1994-95, fin. and planning com., 1995-96; pres. UMC Faculty Practice Plan, 2001-; guest prof. Children's Hosp. Kansas City, St. Louis U. Med. Sch., Walter Reed and Brooke Army Med. Ctr., Nat. Jewish Hosp., U. South Fla., U. Tex. Med. Br. at Galveston, Houston, Boston U., assoc. editor, Jour. Miss. State Med. Assoc., others; presenter in field. Assoc. editor, editl. bd. So. Med. Jour., 1995—2013, Am. J. Med., 2005-; mem. editl. bd. Jour. Allergy and Clin. Immunology, 1986-89, Postgrad. Medicine, 1986-94, Jour. Investigational Allergology and Clin. Immunology, 1987-93, Am. Jour. Med. Scis., 1989—, Annals of Allergy, 1991-96, Clin. Immunotherapeutics, 1993-99; host: (med. lit. project) Miss. Pub. Broadcasting-Weekly Statewide Audio Program, Southern Remedy, 2007-, prodr., Southern Remedy Radio & Television Miss. Pub. Broadcasting, Jackson, Miss.; contbr. 25 chpts. to books, over 175 articles to profl. jours. Elder Cumberland Presbyn. Ch., 1986-89; mem. adminstrv. bd. Christ United Meth. Ch., Mobile, 1990-97, chmn., 1993-96, chmn. coun. on ministries 1993-95; bd. dirs. Leadership Mobile, 1994-97; bd. stewards Galloway United Meth. Ch., 1999-2002, Mission MS, 1999-; bd. adv. Millsaps Coll. Sch. Bus., 1999-. Optimist Club scholar, 1963-67; Caduceus Club Travel fellow St. George Hosp. Med. Sch., London, 1970; grantee NIH, 1981-89, NIAID, 1985-88, Cancer Assn. New Orleans, 1982, 83, La. Lung Trust, 1982, 83, others; recipient Armed Forces Meritorious Svc. medal, 1980, Cert. Merit Cmty. Svc., City New Orleans, 1983, Martha Meyers Physician Role Model award U. Ala., Sch. Medicine, Birmingham, 2011, Miss. State Med. award, 2010, Miss. Humanities Comml. Media award, 2013, Am. Assoc. Med. Coll. Media award, 2012, 13. Fellow: ACP (program com. 1993-95, Laurate, 2011, 2012), Am. Coll. Rheumatology, Am. Coll. Chest Physicians, Am. Acad. Allergy, Asthma and Immunology (program and workshop com. 1985, chmn. 1986, grad. edn. com. 1988-89, allergy and immunology program dirs. assn. 1989-2005, standing com. fellowship programs 1990-97, standing com. immunology in med. schs. 1993, chmn. primer adv. com. 1992-93, co-chair com. on allergy in VA Med. Ctr. 1995-96, chair com. med. sch. 1994, Young Investigators award, 1979, Special Svc. award, 1993, 1996, 2006), Am. Coll. Allergy, Asthma, Immunology (editl. bd. 1995, Bernard Burman Lectureship 2002, Harold Nelson Leadership 2009), Am. Thoracic Soc. (program and workshop com. 1986-87, sec.-treas. 1987, nat. program com. 1988-90, vice-chmn. 1989, chmn. 1989, chair sect. immunology 1992), So. Med. Assn. (Morton Rsch. medal, 2004); mem.: AMA (editor Primer on Allergy 1994), Am. Assn. Immunology, Clin. Immunology Soc. So. Med. Assn., Am. Assn. Med. Colls. (coun. acad. socs. 1994—, coun. academic specialists 1997-, adminstrv. specialist 2010-), Am. Fedn. Clin. Rsch. (coun. so. sect. 1984-87, 93), Assn. Profs. Medicine (bd. dirs. 1995—2004, nat. manpower com. 1994-96, pres. 2001, fin. com. 2009, diversity com. 2010), Am. Bd. Med. Specialists (coun. bd. reps. and adminstrn. 1996-99), 2 Carnival Orgns., Am. Bd. Internal Medicine (bd. dirs. 2000-04), So. Soc. Clin. Investigation (coun. 1998—, pres. 2001, adv. council 2001-, Founder's medal 2004), Am. Bd. Allergy-Immunology (bd. dirs. 1995-2004, sec., 2003); Am. Clin. and Climatol. Assn., Miss. State Med. Assn. Avocations: gardening, swimming, youth work, writing. Office: U Miss Med Ctr Dept Internal Medicine 2500 N State St Jackson MS 39216-4105 Office Phone: 601-815-3865, 601-984-5600. Business E-Mail: rdeshazo@umc.edu.

DESHOTEL, JOE D., state legislator; b. Beaumont, Tex., Dec. 3, 1951; m. Claudia Deshotel; 1 child. BS in Polit. Sci., Lamar U., Beaumont, Tex., 1974; JD, Tex. So. U., Houston, 1978. Atty.; small business owner; mem. Ward 3, mem.-at-large Beaumont City Coun.; served on Job Training Coordinating Coun.; bd. regent Lamar U., v.p. for adminstrn., legal counsel Beaumont; mem. Dist. 22 Tex. House of Representatives, 1998—. Served with USAFR. Democrat. Roman Catholic. Office: One Plaza Sq Suite 203 Port Arthur TX 77642 also: Room GN.08 Capitol PO Box 2910 Austin TX 78768 Office Phone: 409-724-0788, 512-463-0662. Office Fax: 409-724-0750. Business E-Mail: joe.deshotel@house.state.tx.us.

DESHOTEL, JOHN DOUGLAS, bishop; b. Basile, La., Jan. 6, 1952; s. Welfoot Paul and Luna Marie (Manuel) Deshotel. BA, Holy Trinity Sem., Irving, Tex.; MDiv, Univ. of Dallas. Ordained priest Diocese of Dallas, Tex., 1978; assoc. pastor St. Patrick parish, Dallas, 1978—80, St. Anthony parish, Longview, Tex., 1980—82, St. Elizabeth of Hungary parish, Dallas, 1982—83, St. Thomas Aquinas parish, Dallas, 1983—88; pastor St. William parish, Greenville, Tex., 1988—92, Our Lady of Fatima parish, Quinlan, Tex., 1988—92, St. John Nepomucene parish, Ennis, Tex., 1995—2001; vice rector Holy Trinity Sem., Irving, Tex., 2001—06; pastor St. Monica parish, Dallas, 2006—08, San Juan Diego parish, Dallas, 2006—08; vicar gen. Diocese of Dallas, 2008—; ordained bishop, 2010; aux. bishop Diocese of Dallas, 2010—. Roman Catholic. Office: Diocese of Dallas 3725 Blackburn St PO Box 190507 Dallas TX 75219 Office Phone: 214-528-2240. Office Fax: 214-528-0287.

DESIDERIO, DOMINIC MORSE, JR., chemistry and neurochemistry professor; b. McKees Rocks, Pa., Jan. 11, 1941; s. Dominic Morse and Jewell Aline (Hull) D.; m. Julie Marie Thomas, Oct. 9, 1965; children— Annette Marie, Dominic Michael. BA, U. Pitts., 1961; MS, MIT, 1964, PhD, 1965. Organic control chemist Pitts. Coke and Chem. Co., 1958-60; research chemist U. Pitts., 1960-61; teaching asst. MIT, Cambridge, 1961-62, research asst., 1962-65; research chemist Am. Cyanamid Co., Stamford, Conn., 1966-67; asst. prof. chemistry Baylor Coll. Medicine, Houston, 1967-71, assoc. prof. chemistry and biochemistry, 1971-78; prof. neurology (chemistry) and molecular scis., dir. U. Tenn., Memphis, 1978—. Exch. student Internat. Assn. Exch. Students for Tech. Experience; polymer chemist Badische Anilin and Sodafabrik, Germany, summer 1962. Author and editor of books, chpts. in books and articles including Analysis of Neuropeptides by Liquid Chromatography and Mass Spectrometry,

1984, Mass Spectrometry of Peptides, 1990, Mass Spectrometry: Clinical and Biomedical Applications, vol. I, 1992, vol. II, 1994; co-editor (book series) Mass Spectrometry, 1997-; co-editor Mass. Spectrometry Rev., 1993-. Recipient 1st Ann. Internat. award Mass Spectrometry in Biochemistry and Medicine, Alghero, Italy, 1975; Intra-Sci. Research Found. fellow, 1971-75 Mem. Am. Soc. Biol. Chemistry, Am. Chem. Soc., Am. Soc. Mass Spectrometry, AAAS, Soc. for Neurosci., Memphis Neurosci. Soc. (pres. 1984-85), NIH (Metallobiochemistry study sect. 1985-89). Avocations: reading, amateur radio, fishing, travel. Office: U Tenn Health Sci Ctr Stout Neurosci Mass Spectrom Lab 847 Madison Ave Rm 117 Memphis TN 38163-0001 Office Phone: 901-448-5488. Business E-Mail: ddesiderio@uthsc.edu.

DESJARDINS, DANIEL D., poet, composer, translator, playwright; b. Miami, Fla., May 27, 1954; s. Ulysses John-Joseph (Pete) and Regine Madelaine (Copus) D. BS in Chemistry, Fla. State U., 1977; BSEE, U. N.Mex., 1984; student, Am. Coll. Paris, 1973-74, Boston U., 1975-76; MA in Playwriting, Queen Margaret U. Coll., Edinburgh, 2001. Chemist Fla. Dept. Agr., Ft. Lauderdale, 1978; commd. 2nd lt. USAF, 1982; advanced through grades to capt. USAFR, 1995, maj., 1996, lt. col., 2003; air liaison officer Kabul, Afghanistan, 2006—07; ret., 2010. Poet: Ode to Stoicism (World Poetry Golden Poet award 1992), Love's Tragedy (World Poetry Golden Poet award 1993), To Lord Acton and His Democratic Consorts, The Condensed Tale of Beowolf and Grendel in Modern English Prosody (semi finalist 1995, North Am. Open Poetry contest, Nat. Libr. Poetry), By The Wiskers of William Wallace (pub. in Best Poems of 1996, Nat. Libr. Poetry), To A Tender Gaoler, The New India, Quintus Horatius Flaccus, 2001, Let Them Have It, 2005; (tech. papers) Oil-Seal Compatibilities, 2001, Military Display Market Segment: Wearable and Portable, 2003, Military Display Market Segment: Ground Vehicles, 2003, Military Display Market Segment: Helicopter Displays, 2004, Mil. Cockpit Displays, 2004, Mil. Display Market Segment: Avionics, 2005, Military Display Market: Fourth Comprehensive Edit., 2006, Air Vehicle Displays in the Operational Environment, 2007, Displays for Intermediate UAV, 2008, Display Commarolity for Air Transport Cookpits, 2009, Military Display Performance Parameters, 2012; composer: The Beacon of Havana, It's a Shame, The New Girl in Our Town, Allegretto (cert. of achievement Unisong Internat. Song Contest, 1997), In a Garden Green, 2004; translator: A View of Hitler and the 1935 Reichsparteitag by a Member of the Académie Française, 1992, pub. 2007 via Authorhouse, The Notin Affair, 1996, A Few Reflections on the Abbé Pierre/Garaudy Affair, 1996, The Founding Myths of Israeli Politics, 1998; playwright: Der Anschluss, 1994, Young Man of Promise, 1995, Lazarro Spallanzani, 1998, Spectulations on the Nature of Heaven and Hell, 1999, A Few Greek Poets, 1999, rev. as a 2-act play and produced, Dayton, Ohio, 2004, The Sudeten Crisis, 2000, The Difference a Day Makes, 2002, Eye of the Needle, 2003, It Takes A Village, 2005, Till We Meet Again, 2006, No Time Like Yesterday, 2006, Lilacs in Summer, 2006, Athos' Wife, 2007, Marcus Aurelius, 2-act play, 2007, Lord Rumciman's Dinner Party, 2008, The Temptation of Jesus, 2008, prodr. Dayton, Ohio, Ha, Ha Hortense 2010, Monsieur le Président; prodr. French Cultural Ctr., Bujumbura, Burundi, 2011, 12, Oscar Wilde & The Art of Lying, 2011, Galatea Pygmalion Polyphemus, 2012, Socratas at Les Dialogues de Platon, 2014. Mem. Internat. Soc. Optical Engring., Soc. for Info. Display, Am. Assn. Stads., Toastmasters Internat., Phi Alpha Theta. Independent. Roman Catholic. Avocations: writing, collecting old records & books, scale model making.

DESJARDINS, RAOUL, medical association administrator, financial consultant; b. Montreal, Que., Can., Oct. 8, 1933; came to U.S., 1962; s. Elso and Blanche (Lemieux) D.; m. Regina Turgeon, Oct. 10, 1961; children: Bryan-Claude, John Andrew. BA, U. Montreal, 1953, MD, 1958; MS, Baylor U., 1964, PhD, 1966; MBA, Rutgers U., 1990. Diplomate Am. Bd. Medicine. Chief intern, resident St. Joan of Arc Hosp., Montreal, 1958-59; med. dir. Candiac (Can.) Med. Clinic, 1953-62, Ortho Research Found., Raritan, NJ, 1966-72; pres. Raoul Desjardins Assocs. Inc., Mendham, NJ, 1972-83, Research Cons. Inc., Mendham, 1983—, APG Internat., Inc., 1991—. Med. dirs. Iroquois Class Co., Candiac, 1959-62; asst. prof. Hahnemann Hosp. and U., Phila., 1976-80; bd. govs. Internat. Medicines Exch. and Devel., Georgetown, Ga., 1986—; chmn. bd. advisors Fed. Inst. Health, 1991—; chmn. bd. govs. Grand Masters Found., 1989—. Prodr. video: The Apgram: A New Tool to Measure Cardiovascular Performance, 1995. Recipient physician's recognition award AMA, 1969. Fellow: N.Y. Acad. Medicine, Am. Coll. Clin. Pharmacology, The Royal Soc. Health, Am. Coll. Angiology; mem.: Petroleum Club Houston, Doctors Club, Met. Club (membership com. 1991—), Med. Execs. Club, Beta Gamma Omega, Sigma Xi. Roman Catholic. Avocations: safaris, history. Office: Fed Inst Health 2001 Cone Creek Dr Houston TX 77090-1005 Office Phone: 281-710-8724. E-mail: doctord@fih.ky.

DESJARLAIS, SCOTT EUGENE, United States Representative from Tennessee, physician; b. Des Moines, Iowa, Feb. 21, 1964; s. Joe and Sylvia DesJarlais; m. Amy DesJarlais; children: Tyler, Ryan, Maggie. BS in Chemistry & Psychology, U. SD, 1987; MD, U SD Sch. Medicine, 1991. Physician, gen. practitioner Grand View Med. Ctr., Jasper, Tenn.; mem. US Congress from 4th Tenn. Dist., Washington, 2011—, US House Agrl. Com., Washington, 2011—, US House Edn. & the Workforce, Washington, 2011—, US House Oversight & Govt. Reform Com., Washington, 2011—. Republican. Episcopalian. Office: US House of Representatives 413 Cannon House Office Bldg Washington DC 20515 Office Phone: 202-225-6831. Office Fax: 202-226-5172.*

DESKIN, WILLIAM C., healthcare educator; b. Des Moines, Sept. 9, 1947; s. Jack L. and Iris E. Deskin; m. Patricia L. Snyder, Feb. 2, 1970; children: William C. Jr., Catherine D. Deskin-Constantine. BS in Health Planning, U. of Minn., 1976; MS in Health Svcs. Adminstrn., U. of St. Francis, Joliet, Ill, 1989; Exec. MBA, U. of Iowa, 1992; PhD, Walden U., Mpls., 2001. Cert. FACHE. V.p. Ottumwa (Iowa) Regional Health Ctr., 1989—96; dir. quality mgmt., utilization and planning Bay Med. Ctr., Bay City, Mich., 1997—2001; educator Cen. Mich. U. Coll. of Extended Learning, Lansing, Mich., 1998—, Delta Coll., University Center, Mich., 1998—, Bay City, 1998—, Spring Arbor U., Flint, Mich., 2001—, Walden U., Kaplan U., Grad. Courses Bus., Healthcare, Mgmt. & Doctoral Studies. Sculptures in stone and hard wood, various. Long range planning YMCA, Bay City, 1998—2002. Sgt. USMC, 1966—70. Fellow: Am. Coll. of Healthcare Execs. (profl. exam. com. 2000—, rep. Health Leadership Alliance 2004—05, product planning com. 2004—); mem.: Nat. Coun. Quality Assurance (cert. profl. healthcare quality, cert. profl. in healthcare). Methodist. Avocations: racquetball, guitar, sculpting. Office: 4724 Tolley Creek Dr Winston Salem NC 27106 Office Phone: 336-923-8134. Personal E-mail: w_deskin@hotmail.com.*

DESMARTEAU, DARRYL DWAYNE, chemistry professor; b. Garden City, Kans., May 25, 1940; s. Arthur L. and Esther P. (Deines) DesM.; m. Genie L. Hardy, Sept. 16, 1962; children: Scott (dec.), Noel, Chad. BS in Chemistry, Wash. State U., Pullman, 1963; PhD, U. Wash, 1966. Acting asst. prof. U. Wash., 1966-67; asst. prof. Northeastern U., Boston, 1967-71, Kans. State U., Manhattan, 1971-73, assoc. prof., 1973-77, prof., 1977-82; prof., chmn. dept. chemistry and geology Clemson U., SC, 1982-89, Tobey-Beaudrot prof. chemistry, 1989—; cons. Monsanto Chem. Co., St. Louis, 1976-78, Hooker Chem. Co., Grand Island, NY, 1978-80, Ausimont, Milan, 1985—2008, DuPont Co., Wilmington, Del., 1986-93. Bd. editors: Jour. Flourine Chemistry, 1981-2005; contbr. articles on fluorine chemistry to profl. jours. Served with USMCR, 1960-66. Recipient award for outstanding research Clemson U. Alumni Assn., 1985, award for Contbrn. to Sci. in S.C. Drug Sci. Found., 1988, Wash. State U. Alumni Achievement award, 1995, Sr. U.S. Scientist award (Humboldt-Preis) Alexander von Humboldt Found., 1988—, Internat. Moissn Prize in Fluorine Chemistry, 2006; Sloan Found fellow, 1975-77, Alexander von Humboldt Found. Research fellow Bonn., W.Ger., 1979-80; numerous research grants Fellow Am. Chem. Soc. (chmn. div. fluorine chemistry 1979, sec.-treas. 1976-78, exec. council 1973-80, award for Creative Work in Fluorine Chemistry 1983, Charles H. Stone award 1994); mem. Sigma Xi, Phi Lambda Upsilon, Alpha Chi Sigma Republican. Roman Catholic. Office: Clemson Univ Dept Chemistry Clemson SC 29634-0001 Home: 106 Fox Trail Ln Seneca SC 29672-8023 Business E-Mail: fluorin@clemson.edu.

DESMOND, THOMAS A., brokerage house executive; BA cum laude, U. Notre Dame, Ind.; MA with high honors, Mich. State U.; MBA with distinction, Northwestern U. Assoc. investment banking divsn. Lehman Brothers Holdings, Inc.; sr. product mgr., sr. analyst Morningstar Inc.; v.p. investment banking group Robert W. Baird & Co.; co-founder, ptnr., mng. dir. Baird Venture Ptnrs. LLC, Chgo.; chief growth officer TradeKing, Charlotte, NC. Office: TradeKing PO Box 49050 Charlotte NC 28277-3432 E-mail: tdesmond@tradeking.com.

DESOTELLE, JAMES, publishing executive; Chief info. officer Dex One Corp. (formerly R.H. Donnelley Corp.). Office: Dex One Corp 1001 Winstead Dr Cary NC 27513 Office Phone: 919-297-1600. Office Fax: 866-527-4550. Business E-Mail: james.desotelle@dexone.com.

DESSAU, NIGEL, computer company executive; b. Nottingham, Eng. Various sales, mktg. and exec. mgmt. positions in US & Europe IBM Corp., including head mktg. programs S/390 brand & Server Group worldwide and v.p. v.p. virtualization solutions; chief mktg. officer StorageTek, Louisville, Colo., 2005—06; sr. v.p. storage mktg. & bus. ops. Sun Microsystems, Inc., 2006—08; sr. v.p., chief mktg. officer Advanced Micro Devices, Inc., Austin, Tex., 2008—. Named one of The 25 Best Marketers, BtoB Mag., 2009. Office: AMD Austin Lone Star Advanced Micro Devices 7171 Southwest Pkwy Austin TX 78735 Business E-Mail: nigel.dessau@amd.com.

DESSLER, ALEXANDER JACK, astrophysicist, educator; b. San Francisco, Oct. 21, 1928; s. David Alexander and Julia (Shapiro) D.; m. Lorraine Hudek, Apr. 18, 1952; children: Pauline Karen, David Alexander, Valerie Jan, Andrew Emory. BS, Calif. Inst. Tech., 1952; PhD, Duke U., 1956. Sect. head Lockheed Missiles & Space Co., 1956-62; prof. Grad. Rsch. Ctr., Dallas, 1962-63, prof. space physics and astronomy, 1963-82, 86-93; chmn. dept. Rice U., Houston, 1963-69, 79-82, 87-92, campus bus. mgr., 1974-76; dir. space sci. lab. MSFC NASA, Huntsville, Ala., 1982-86; sr. rsch. scientist Lunar and Planetary Lab. U. Ariz., Tucson, 1993—2004. Sci. adviser Nat. Aeros. and Space Coun., 1969-70; pres. Univs. Space Rsch. Assn., 1975-81; adj. prof. dept. atmospheric scis. Texas A&M U., 2004-. Editor Jour. Geophys. Rsch., 1965-69, Revs. of Geophysics, 1969-74, The John Wiley Space Sci. Text Series, 1968-76, Geophys. Rsch. Letters, 1986-89, Atmospheric and Space Sci. Series, 1986—; adv. bd.: Planetary and Space Sci., 1963-92; assoc. editor Space Solar Power Rev., 1980-85. Served with USN, 1946-48. Recipient Outstanding Young Scientist award Tex. Wing Air Force Assn., 1964, medal for contbns. to internat. geophysics Soviet Geophys. Com., 1984, Stellar award for acad. devel., Rotary Nat., 1988. Fellow AAAS, Am. Geophys. Union (Macelwane award 1963, John Adam Fleming medal 1993, William Kaula award for publs. 2003); mem. Am. Astron. Soc., Internat. Assn. Geomagnetism and Aeronomy (v.p. 1979-83), Royal Swedish Acad. Scis. (fgn.), Cosmos Club (Washington). Office: Tex A& M Univ Dept Atmospheric Sci College Station TX 77843-3150 Home: 4780 Stonebriar Cir College Station TX 77845 Business E-Mail: alex.dessler@tamu.edu.

DETERT, NANCY C., state legislator; b. Chicago, Ill, Oct. 22, 1944; children: Mark, Bryan, Jamie. Attended, Sienna Heights Coll. Mortgage broker & owner Osprey Mortgage Co.; mktg. rep. Chapman & Assocs.; mem. Dist. 23 Fla. State Senate, 2008—, majority whip, 2008—10, chair edn. preK-12 com., mem. policy and steering com. on energy, environment and land use, policy and steering com. on social responsibility, commerce com., mem. children, families and elder affairs com., edn. preK-12 appropriations com., environ. preservation and conservation com., mem. Fla. legis. com. on intergovernmental rels. Mem. Sarasota County Sch. Bd., 1988—92, Venice Area C. of C. Edn. Com., 1998, Enterprise Fla. Bd. Dirs., 2009; ex-officio mem. Fla. Commn. on Tourism, 2009; bd. mem. NCSL Fin. Svcs.; v.p. NCSL Women's Legis. Network. Recipient Small Bus. of Yr. award, Venice Area C. of C, 1993, Fin. award, Women of Distinction, 1998, "She Knows Where She's Going" award, Girls Inc., 2000, Recognition of Svc., Fla. Boys & Girls Club, 2002, Leadership award, Fla. Bankers Assn., 2003, Music Svc. award, Fla. Assn. Mus., 2003, Fla. Heroes award, Nat. Acad. Recording Arts & Sci., 2004; named Legislator of Yr., Fla. Assn. Sch. Soc. Workers, 1999, Big Brothers Big Sisters, Fla. Assn. Sch. Adminstrs., Gulf Coast Marine Inst., Sarasota Classified Tchrs. Assn., 2000, Fla. Assn. Tech. Educators, 2001, Fla. Funeral Dirs., Fla. Sch. Bds. Assn., 2002, Fla. Assn. Conventions & Visitors Bur., Fla. Econ. Devel. Coun., Fla. Housing Coalition, 2004, Top 25 Legislators, Miami Herald, Outstanding Legislator of Yr., Funeral & Cemetery Alliance Fla., 2002. Mem.: Fla. Assn. Mortgage Brokers (legis. chmn. 1998, Legislator of Yr. 2001), Fla. Assn. Mortgage Brokers Suncoast Chpt. (pres. 1996), Venice-Nokomis Federated Women's Club (v.p. 1998), Sarasota Rep. Women's Club (pres. 1996). Republican. Catholic. Office: Senate Office Bldg 404 S Monroe St Rm 318 Tallahassee FL 32399-1100 also: 417 Commercial Ct Ste D Venice FL 34292 Office Phone: 850-487-5081, 941-480-3547. Office Fax: 941-480-3549. Business E-Mail: detert.nancy.web@flsenate.gov.

DETHLOFF, HENRY CLAY, historian, educator; b. New Orleans, Aug. 10, 1934; s. Carl Curt and Camelia (Jordan) Dethloff; m. Myrtle Anne Elliott, Aug. 27, 1961; children: Clay, Carl. BA, U. Tex., Austin, 1956; MA, Northwestern State U., Natchitoches, La., 1960; PhD, U. Mo., Columbia, 1964. From instr. to assoc. prof. history U. So. La., 1962—66, assoc. prof., 1966—69; from mem. faculty to prof. emeritus Tex. A&M U., College Station, 1969—99, prof. emeritus history, 1999—. Author: (book) Our Louisiana Legacy, 1968, The Centennial History of Texas A&M University, 1976-1976, 1975, Americans and Free Enterprise, 1979, A History of the American Rice Industry 1685-1985, 1988, Suddenly, Tomorrow Came: A History of Johnson Space Center, 1993, The U.S. and the Global Economy, 1945-1995, 1997, A Bookmark: The Texas A&M University Press, 1999; co-author: A History of American Business, 1983, Timeless Heritage, A History of the Forest Service in the Southwest, 1988, Pattillo Higgins and the Search for Texas Oil, 1989, A Special Kind of Doctor: A History of Veterinary Medicine in Texas, 1991, Louisiana: A Study of Diversity, 1998, Voyager's Grand Tour: To the Outer Planets and Beyond, 2003, Texas Aggies Go To War: In Service of Their Country, 2005, Texas AgriLife: The Land Grant Legacy in the Lone Star State, 2012; co-editor: (book) American Business History: Case Studies, 1987, Aerial Navigation, 1783-1903, 2003. Served to lt. (j.g.) USNR, 1956—58. Mem.: La. Hist. Assn., Tex. Hist. Assn., So. Hist. Assn., Econ. History Assn., Agrl. History Assn., Sigma Chi, Phi Alpha Theta, Phi Kappa Phi. Republican. Methodist. Home: 8709 Bent Tree Dr College Station TX 77845-5561

DETMER, DON EUGENE, health informatics, management and policy researcher; b. Winfield, Kans., Feb. 3, 1939; s. Lawrence Oscar and Esther Beulah (McCormick) Detmer; m. Mary Helen McFerson, Aug. 26, 1961; children: Mary Catherine, Emily Anne. Student, U. Kans., Lawrence, 1957—59, U. Durham, NC, 1959—60; MD, U. Kans., Kansas City, 1965; MA, U. Cambridge, Eng., 2002. Intern, then resident in surgery Johns Hopkins U., Balt., 1965—67; clin. assoc. surg. br. Nat. Heart Inst. NIH, Bethesda, Md., 1967—69; resident in surgery Duke U., Durham, NC, 1969—72; Global Cmty. Health fellow Dept. HEW, Inst. Medicine/NAS, Washington DC, 1972—73; prof. preventive medicine and surgery U. Wis., Madison, 1973—84; v.p. health scis., prof. surgery and med. info. U. Utah, Salt Lake City, 1984—88; univ. prof. health policy, prof. surgery and health evaluation scis. U. Va., Charlottesville, 1988—93, v.p., provost for health scis., 1988—96, sr. v.p., 1996—98, Louise Nurancy prof. health scis. policy, 1996—99, prof. emeritus, prof. med. edn., 1999—; Dennis Gillings prof. health mgmt. Cambridge U., 1999—2003; dir. Cambridge U. Health, 1999—2003; sr. assoc. judge bus. sch. Cambridge U., 2004—07; pres. and CEO Am. Med. Informatics Assn., Bethesda, Md., 2004—09, sr. advisor, 2009—11; med. dir. Advocacy and Health Policy, Am. Coll. Surgeons, 2011—13; dir. Advanced Interprofl. Informatics Certification, 2014—, Am. Med. Informatics, Bethesda. Mem. commn. on systemic interoperability US Dept. HHS, Washington DC, 2004—05, mem. Am. health info. cmty. workgroup confidentiality, privacy and security, 2006—08; bd. sci. counselors Nat. Ctr. Pub. Health Informatics, 2008—10; chmn. bd. dirs. Med-Biquitious, 2006—13; vice chmn. China Med. Bd. NY, Inc., 2002—04; chmn. bd. healthcare svcs. Inst. Medicine, Washington DC, 1994—2000; chmn. nat. com. vital health stats. HHS, Washington DC, 1996—99; chmn. Blue Ridge Acad. Health Grp., 1997—2001, co-chmn., 2002—, sr. mem., 2013—; regent Nat. Libr. Medicine, NIH, Bethesda, Md., 1987—91; trustee Nuffield Trust, 2000—06; bd. dirs., developer adminstrv. medicine U. Wis., Madison; membership com. chmn. sect. 12 Inst. Medicine, Washington DC, 2002—04, 2009—, chair IOM Membership com., 2009—12; chair Nat. Libr. Medicine NIH, Bethesda, 1989—91; assoc. Nat. Acads., 2002; vis. prof. Chime U. Coll. London, 2005—; health IT steering com. Agy. Healthcare Rsch. and Quality Nat. Resource Ctr., Rockville, Md., 2005—07; healthcare IT adv. panel Joint Commn. Accreditation Healthcare Orgns., Oakbrook, Ill., 2005—08; cons. in field; vice chmn. Friends of Nat. Libr. Medicine, Bethesda, Md., 2006—09; dir. Corp. Nat. Rsch. Initiative, 2008—, IBM Healthcare & Life Scis. Adv. Coun., 2006—09; mem. governing bd. Colonnade Club, 2014—. Contbr. articles on nat. health info. sys., compartment syndromes, health svcs. rsch. and policy to profl. jours. Chmn. pub. svc. com. bd. dir. United Way, Salt Lake City, 1986—88, Charlottesville, 1992—97; active USPHS, 1967—69; pres. Peace Luth. Ch., 1996—99, Browns Cove Meth. Ch., 2007—. Surgeon US Army, 1967—69, US Pub. Health Svc., surgeon US Army, 1972—73, US Pub. Health Svc. Recipient Global Cmty. Health fellowship, HEW, 1972—73, Don Eugene Detmer AIMA Signature award, 2008, Walsh McDermott medal, Inst. Medicine, Washington, 2009, Morris Collen medal, Am. Coll. Med. Informatics, 2010; fellow, Clare Hall, Cambridge U., 2000—05; Hon. fellow, 2012, Am. Acad. Nursing, 2012. Fellow: ACS (vice chmn. com. allied health pers. 1989—90, chmn. 1990—94, internat. health com. 1996—2002, web portal com. 2004—14, informatics com. 2004—), AAAS; mem.: HHS (bd. mem. 2008—11), NAS Inst. Medicine (chmn. Cecil awards com. 2004—06, Walsh McDermott medal 2009), Am. Coll. Med. Informatics, Sci. Counselors Nat. Ctr. (bd. mem. 2008—10), Coun. Med. Splty. Socs., Lake Bluff (treas. 2007—09), Royal Soc. Medicine, Soc. Med. Adminstrs. (treas. 1997—2000), Am. Hosp. Assn. (chmn. coun. hosp. med. staffs 1984—87), Assn. Acad. Health Ctrs. (bd. dir. 1996—98), Am. Med. Informatics Assn. (bd. dir. 1996—98, chair internat. com. 2004), Am. Acad. Physician Assts. (hon.), Clare Hall Cambridge U. (life), Alpha Omega Alpha. Methodist. Avocations: fly fishing, painting, horseback riding, crafts, art. Home: 5245 Browns Gap Tpke Crozet VA 22932-1613 Business E-Mail: detmer@virginia.edu.

DE TONNANCOUR, PAUL ROGER GODEFROY, library administrator; b. Fall River, Mass., May 22, 1926; s. R. Godefroy and Emilie (St. Germain) de T.; m. Mary E. Fenno, Apr. 9, 1955; children— Paul Godefroy, Camille Marie. AB cum laude, Providence Coll., 1952; MS, Simmons Coll., 1953; postgrad., Western Res. U., U. So. Cal. Asst. librarian Enoch Pratt Library, Balt., 1953-54; chief librarian, tech. analyst Armco Steel Corp., Balt., 1954-56; dir. rsch. library Gen. Dynamics (Ft. Worth div.), 1956—, dir. tech. information programs, 1964-87, with Proposal Devel. Ctr., 1987—. Cons. MLA, U.S. Office Edn. on sci. info. pers.; John Cotton Dana lectr., 1966 Singer, Ft. Worth Opera Assn. Chorus; Author: The Exploitation of Technical Information, 1966; co-author: Science Information Personnel, 1963; Contbr. articles to profl. jours. Active United Fund and Community Council; mem. exec. com. Big Bros. Tarrant County.; Trustee Cosmopolitan Internat., 1961-63. Served with USNR, 1943-46. Named Boss of Year Am. Bus. Women's Assn., 1965 Mem. ALA, AAAS, Am., Nat. mgmt. assns., Ft. Worth Art Assn., Spl. Libraries Assn., Am. Soc. Information Sci., Delta Epsilon Sigma. Clubs: Mason, Fort Worth Boat. Episcopalian. Office: PO Box 748 Fort Worth TX 76101-0748

DETTE, FRANZ JOSEF, electrical industry company executive; Advanced Diploma Engring. in Electronics, Tech. High Sch. Lippe Germany. Field test engr., broadcasting equipment Robert Bosch Fernseh GmbH, Darmstadt, Germany, 1977; with Piller Power Sys. GmbH, Osterode, Germany, 1979—94, sales dir., Power Supplies, sales mgr., sales engr.; mng. dir. DETA Akkumulatorenwerk GmbH, Bad Lauterberg, Germany, sales dir., Network Power Batteries; v.p., sales, Exide Motive Power Europe Exide Technologies, Manchester, held mng. dir. positions, Germany, Austria, 1998, dir., logistics, Exide Indsl. Energy Europe Manchester, 2003, dir., ops., Exide Indsl. Energy Europe, 2006—07, v.p., ops., Exide Indsl. Energy Europe Budingen, Germany, 2007, pres., Indsl. Energy Europe, 2008—. Office: Exide Technologies Bldg 200 13000 Deerfield Pky Milton GA 30004 Office Phone: 678-566-9000. Office Fax: 678-566-9188. Business E-Mail: franz.dette@exide.com.

DETZNER, KENNETH WILLIAM, state official; b. Chgo., 1952; BS in Polit. Sci., Fla. State U., Tallahassee, 1979. Dir. legislative & policy affairs Office Atty. Gen. State of Fla., Tallahassee, 1979—85; finance dir. Jim Smith for Gov. Campaign, 1985—87; exec. dir. Fla. Beer Wholesalers Assn., 1987—2000; chief of staff to the sec., acting sec. of state State of Fla., Tallahassee, 2002—03, sec. of state, 2012—; govtl. affairs and mgmt. cons., 2003—12. Republican. Office: Office of the Secretary of State 500 S Bronough St Tallahassee FL 32399 Office Phone: 850-245-6524. Office Fax: 850-245-6125. Business E-Mail: dos.secretaryofstate@dos.myflorida.com.*

DEUELL, ROBERT (BOB) F., state legislator; b. Mar. 11, 1950; m. Marilyn Deuell; 3 children. BS in Biology, George Mason U.; MD, Med. Coll. Va. Cert. family physician. Former med. missionary; med. dir. Hunt County Dept. Health, Greenville, Tex.; ptnr. Primary Care Assocs.; mem. Dist. 2 Tex. State Senate, 2003—. Chmn. Hunt County Mental Health & Retardation Ctr.; bd. dir. Hunt County Rape Crisis Ctr. Mem.: AMA, Hunt, Rains & Rockwall Counties Med. Soc., Tex. Physicians Rsch. Coun., Tex. Med. Assn., Rockwall Counties Med. Soc., America Heart Assn. Republican. Avocations: spending tim outdoors, music. Office: 18601 LBJ Freeway Ste 400 Mesquite TX 75150 also: PO Box 12068 Capitol Station Austin TX 78711 also: 2500 Stonewall St Greenville TX 75401 Office Phone: 972-279-1800, 512-463-0102, 972-279-1800, 903-450-9797.

DEUTCH, TED (THEODORE ELIOT DEUTCH), United States Representative from Florida, former state legislator; b. Bethlehem, Pa., May 7, 1966; s. Bernard and Jean Deutch; m. Jill Weinstock; children: Gabrielle, Serena, Cole. BA, U. Mich., 1988; JD, U. Mich. Law Sch., 1990. Atty.; mem. Dist. 30 Fla. State Senate, Tallahassee, 2006—10; mem. US Congress from 19th Fla. Dist., Washington, 2010—13, US Congress from 21st Fla. Dist., 2013—. Mem. ABA, Fla. Bar Assn., Century Village Democratic Club, Lake Worth West Democratic Club, Greater Boynton Beach Democratic Club, United South County Dem. Club, Deerfield Democratic Club, League of Women Voters, Women's Found. Palm Beach County, Nat. Safety Coun., U. Mich. Alumni Assn. United Jewish Communities, Jewish Fedn. South Palm Beach County (James & Marjorie Baer Leadership award), Voter's Coalition, Forum Club, Nat. Conf. State Legislatures. Democrat. Jewish. Office: US House of Representatives 1024 Longworth House Office Bldg Washington DC 20515 also: 8177 Glades Rd Ste 211 Boca Raton FL 33434 Office Phone: 202-225-3001, 561-470-5440.*

DEVANEY, CHRIS, political organization administrator; BA in Polit. Sci., U. Okla. Former journalist NBC Radio News, Washington; various media rels. positions US Senate Rep. Conf.; staff mem. to candidate Fred Thompson for US Senate Nashville, 1994; staff mem. to senator Thompson Tenn., Washington; exec. dir. Tenn. Rep. Party, 2005—06, chmn., 2009—; state dir. to senator Bob Corker Tenn., 2006—09. Republican. Office: Tenn Republican Party 2424 21st Ave Ste 200 Nashville TN 37212 Office Phone: 615-269-4260.*

DEVARO, JOHN MICHAEL, ophthalmologist; b. Rochester, NY, Feb. 23, 1962; m. Josepha Bueno, Oct. 7, 1990. AB, Dartmouth Coll., 1984; MD, U. Pa., 1988. Diplomate Am. Bd. Ophthalmology, Nat. Bd. Med. Examiners. Intern Pa. Hosp., Phila., 1988-89; resident in ophthalmology U. Pitts., 1989—92, chief resident, 1991; gen. ophthalmologist Danville Eye Ctr., Va., 1992-94; fellow pediat. Ophth. & Strabismus Duke U. Eye Ctr., Durham, NC, 1994-95; assoc. in pediat. and neuro-ophthalmology Nevyas Eye Associates, Bala Cynwyd, Pa., 1995—97; ophthalmologist Meml. U. Med. Ctr. Ga. Eye Inst., Savannah, Ga., 1997—2008; faculty, pediat. Mercer U. Sch. Medicine, Savannah, Children's Eye Inst., 2008—. Instr. Wills Eye Hosp., Phila. Contbr. chpt. to book Ophthalmology: A Comprehensive Text, 1995; contbr. articles to profl. jours. including Archives of Ophthalmology, Jour. of Pediat. Ophthalmology. Rufus Choate scholar Dartmouth Coll., 1984; short-term experimental rsch. fellow NIH, 1987. Fellow Am. Acad. Ophthalmology, Am. Acad. Pediat.; mem. Am. Assn. Pediatric Ophthalmology and Strabismus. Avocations: skiing, ice skating, scuba diving, piano, trumpet. Office: Children's Eye Inst 836 E 65th St Ste 36A Savannah GA 31405 Office Phone: 912-353-1001. Office Fax: 912-353-1026.

DEVAULT, JOHN LEE, oil industry executive, geophysicist; b. Kansas City, Mo., Aug. 4, 1937; s. Isaac Henderson and Evelyn Margaret (Rowell) DeVault; m. Janet Ann Miller, Sept. 11, 1968; children: Bryan Charles, Chris Lee. BSChE, Case Inst. Tech., 1959; BS, MacMurray Coll., 1961; MS, U. Houston, 1975. Lic. geophysicist Calif., Tex., Am. Assn. Petroleum Geologists, Soc. Ind. Profl. Earth Scientists. Geophysicist United Geophys., Europe, Africa, Middle East, Australia-Asia, Alaska, Houston, 1961—74; pres. Sercel Inc., Houston, 1974—88; chmn. bd. dirs. Jade Corp., Houston, 1988—. Contbr. articles to profl. jours. Trustee Culver Legion-Culver Academies; downstate v.p. Young Rep. Club, Springfield, 1960; bd. dirs. Jaycees, Springfield, Ill., 1960; dir. Houston Club; v.p. bd. dirs. Honors Coll., U. Houston, 1990—; bd. dirs. McMurray Coll. Mem.: Am. Inst. Profl. Geologists (pres. Tex. sect., lic. geophysicist), Soc. Exploration Goephysics, Geophys. Soc. Houston (hon.; pres. 1987), Culver Club Greater Houston (pres.). Mem. Disciples Of Christ. Office: Jade Corp PO Box 218567 Houston TX 77218-8567

DEVER, JAMES COLUMCILLE, III, federal judge; b. Lake Charles, La., May 25, 1962; s. James C. and Kathleen Marie (Donohue) D.; m. Amy Carole Nichols, June 1, 1985; children: Colum, Patrick, Mary Margaret. BBA, U. Notre Dame, 1984; JD, Duke U., 1987. Bar: NC 1987. Law clk. to Hon. Clifford Wallace U.S. Ct. Appeals (9th cir.), San Diego, 1987-88; commd. 1st lt. USAF, Washington, 1988; counsel Honors Program Office of the Air Force Gen. Counsel, Washington, 1988-92; atty. Maupin Taylor P.A., Raleigh, 1992—2004; judge US Dist. Ct. (ea. dist.) NC, 2005—. Editor-in-chief Duke Law Jour., 1986-87. Recipient Kent Fin. award U. Notre Dame, 1984. Mem. Order of Coif, Beta Gamma Sigma. Office: US Dist Ct Sanford Fed Bldg and Courthouse 310 New Bern Ave Raleigh NC 27601

DEVINE, JOHN PHILLIP, state supreme court justice; m. Nubia Piedad Gomez, 1989; 6 children. BS in bus. adminstrn. and mktg., Ball State U., 1980; JD, South Tex. Coll. Law, 1986. Analyst Shell Oil Co., Tex.; with Brown & Root Inc., 1988; dist. judge 190th Jud. Dist. Ct., Harris County, Tex., 1995—2002; spl. judge Harris County Justice of the Peace Cts., 2002—11; justice Tex. Supreme Ct., Austin, 2013—. Named Tex. Size Hero, Focus on the Family mag. Office: Texas Supreme Ct PO Box 12248 Austin TX 78711

DEVINEY, MARVIN LEE, JR., science administrator, director; b. Kingsville, Tex., Dec. 5, 1929; s. Marvin Lee and Esther Lee (Gambrell) D.; m. Marie Carole Massey, June 7, 1975; children: Marvin Lee III, John H., Ann-Marie K. Deviney Bowen. BS in Chemistry and Math., S.W. Tex. State U., San Marcos, 1949; MA in Phys. Chemistry, U. Tex., Austin, 1952, PhD in Phys. Chemistry, 1956. Cert. profl. chemist. Devel. chemist Celanese Chem. Co., Bishop, Tex., 1956-58; rsch. chemist Shell Chem. Co., Deer Park, Tex., 1958-66; sr. scientist, head group phys. and radio-chemistry Ashland Chem. Co., Houston, 1966-68, mgr. sect. phys. and analytical chemistry, 1968-71, mgr. sect. phys. chemistry div. rsch. and devel. Columbus, Ohio, 1971-78; rsch. assoc., supr. applied surface chemistry Ashland Ventures Rsch. and Devel., Columbus, 1978-84, supr. electron microscopy, advanced aerospace composites, govt. contracts, 1984-90; inst. scientist, mem. internal R & D com. SW Rsch. Inst., San Antonio, 1990-97; pres. MLD Polymers/Composites, Inc., 1997—; R&D dir. Nuresco Polymers, 1998—; cons. polymer divsn. Tex. State U., San Marcos, 1998—. Adj. prof. U. Tex., San Antonio, 1973-75, Ohio State U., 1990-91; mem. sci. adv. bd. Am. Petroleum Inst. Rsch. Project 60, 1968-74. Contbr. numerous articles to profl. jours.; patentee in field. Mem. ednl. adv. com. Columbus Tech. Inst., 1974-84, Cen. Ohio Tech. Coll., 1975-82, Hocking Tech. Coll., 1989-91. Lt. col., USAR, retired. Humble Oil Rsch. fellow, 1954. Fellow Am. Inst. Chemists (pres. Ohio Inst. 1978-82); mem. Tex. Acad. Sci., Am. Def. Preparedness Assn., Electron Microscopy Soc. Am., Materials Rsch. Soc., SAMPE Composites Soc., N.Am. Catalysis Soc., Am. Soc. Composites, Soc. Plastics Engrs., Soc. Automotive Engrs., Am. Chem. Soc. (chmn. chpt. exec. bd. 1969, bus. mgr. nat. div. Petroleum Chemistry, 1986-90, Best Paper award rubber div. 1967, 70, Honorable Mention awards 1968, 69, 73, symposia co-chmn., co-editor books on catalysis-surface chemistry 1985, carbon-graphite chemistry 1975), Engrs.' Coun. Houston (sr. councilor 1970-71), Sigma Xi, Phi Lambda Upsilon, Alpha Chi, Sigma Pi Sigma. Methodist. Home: 2048 Brabant Dr Plano TX 75025-3327 Office Phone: 512-864-1518. E-mail: deviney_marvin@hotmail.com.

DEVOGT, JOHN FREDERICK, management science and business ethics educator, consultant; b. Detroit, Oct. 20, 1930; s. Leo Henry and Dorothy Helen (Gibbs) D.; m. Ann Marie Berby, Aug. 29, 1959; children— Joanne Elise, Linda Christine. BS, U. N.C., 1957, PhD, 1966. Instr. Washington and Lee U., Lexington, Va., 1962-66, asst. prof., 1966-67, assoc. prof., 1967-70, prof., 1970-2000, head dept., 1968-90, prof. emeritus, 2000—; acad. dir. Washington and Lee Family Bus. Inst., 1987—89. State judge Blue Chip Enterprise Initiative, 1991-96; acad. Jonah A.Y. Goldratt Inst., 1991—; chmn. adv. bd. Lexington office CorEast Savs. Bank, Richmond, 1976-90. Chmn. Lexington City Sch. Bd., 1973; pres. Va. Sch. Bds. Assn., Charlottesville, 1974; v.p. Henry St. Playhouse, Lexington, 1985, Friends Rockbridge Choral Soc., 2000—04; deacon, elder Lexington Presbyterian Ch.; bd. dirs. Lexington Indsl. Devel., 2004—. Served to staff sgt. USAF, 1951—55. Vis. fellow, Univ. Coll., Oxford, Eng., 1983. Mem. Southern Mgmt. Assn. (pres. 1975-76), Rotary (Dist. 7570 Scholarship chair, 2013-2014, Multiple Paul Harris fellow), Lexington Golf and Country Club (bd. dirs. 2004-06), Phi Beta Kappa, Phi Eta Sigma, Beta Gamma Sigma. Presbyterian. Avocations: golf, singing. Home: 617 Stonewall St Lexington VA 24450-1947 Office: Washington and Lee Univ Lexington VA 24450 Personal E-mail: jdevogt@embarqmail.com. Business E-Mail: devogtj@wlu.edu.

DEVOLITES-DAVIS, JEANNEMARIE ARAGONA, state legislator; b. Swindon, Eng., Feb. 28, 1956; m. John Arthur Devolites; children: Nichole, Ashley, Cassandra, Alexandra. State del. Dist. 35, Va., 1999—2004; mem. Privileges & Elections Com., Health, Welfare & Inst. Com., Militia & Police Com., Claims Com., 1999—2004; house del. Va.; state senator Dist. 34 Va., 2005—; chmn. Providence Dist. Fairfax County Rep. Com.; bd. mem. Oakton High Sch. PTA. Named Outstanding Leader, Girl Scout Coun. Nation's Capital, 1994, Outstanding Vol., 1997. Mem.: Girl Scout Coun. Nation's Capital (troop leader), Greater Merrifield Bus. Assn. (bd. dir.), New Providence Rep. Women's Club (bd. dir.), Tysons Corner Rotary (dir. cmty. svc.). Republican. Roman Catholic. Office: Senate of Virginia PO Box 396 Richmond VA 23218 Office Phone: 703-938-7972. Business E-Mail: district34@sov.state.va.us.

DEVONSHIRE, DAVID W., board member; b. May 22, 1945; BS in Acctg., Widener U., Pa.; MBA, Northwestern U., Chgo. With Am. Hosp. Supply Corp., 1974—85; v.p., fin., controller Baxter International, Inc., 1985—87; corp. contr. Mead Corp., 1987—90; corp. v.p., controller Honeywell, 1990—92, v.p., fin., 1992—93; sr. v.p., CFO Owens Corning, Inc., 1993—98; exec. v.p., CFO Ingersoll-Rand Co., 1998—2002, Motorola, Inc., Schaumburg, Ill., 2002—07. Bd. dirs. Arbitron Inc., Career Edn. Corp., Roper Industries, Inc., 2002—, ArvinMeritor Inc., 2004—. Office: Roper Industries Inc Bd Directors 6901 Professional Pky E Ste 200 Sarasota FL 34240 Office Phone: 941-556-2601. Office Fax: 941-556-2670. Business E-Mail: ddevonshire@roperind.com.

DEVRIES, JAMES D., insurance company executive; Grad., Loyola U., Chgo., Northwestern U. Kellogg Sch. Mgmt., Ill. Sr. human resources assoc. The Quaker Oats Co.; v.p. human resources and corp. services Ameritech Monitoring Services; v.p. human resources SBC Telecom, Inc.; v.p. to sr. v.p. human resources Prin. Fin. Group, 2000—08; sr. v.p. human resources to exec. v.p., chief adminstrv. officer Allstate Ins. Co., 2008—. Office: Allstate Ins Co PO Box 12055 1819 Electric Rd SW Roanoke VA 24018

DE WAAL, FRANS B.M., biologist, psychology professor; b. Netherlands, 1948; B in Biology, U. Nijmegen, Netherlands, 1970; D in Biology, U. Groeningen, Netherlands, 1973; PhD in Biology, U. Utrecht, Netherlands, 1977. Rsch. assoc., lab. comparative physiology U. Utrecht, 1973—81; vis. asst. scientist Wis. Nat. Primate Rsch. Ctr., 1981—82, asst. scientist, 1982—85, assoc. scientist, 1985—91, affiliate scientist, 1991—; assoc. prof. psychology Emory U., 1991—93, prof, psychology, 1993—96, dir. grad. studies: Program in Population Biology, Ecology, & Evolution, 1996—2000, Charles Howard Candler prof. primate behavior, dept. psychology, 1996—; affiliate scientist Yerkes Nat. Primate Rsch. Ctr., 1989—91, rsch. prof. psychobiology, 1991—, dir. Living Links Ctr., 1997—. Adj. assoc. prof., biol. sciences U. Wis., Milw., 1988—91; spkr. in field. Author: Chimpanzee Politics: Power and Sex Among Apes, 1982, Peacemaking Among Primates, 1989 (LA Times Book award, 1989), Good Natured: The Origins of Right and Wrong in Humans and Other Animals, 1996, Bonobo: The Forgotten Ape, 1997, The Ape and the Sushi Master: Cultural Reflections by a primologist, 2001, My Family Album: Thirty Years of Photgraphy, 2003, Our Inner Ape: A Leading Primatologist Explains Why We are Who We Are, 2005, Primates and Philosophers: How Morality Evolved, 2006; consulting editor Zoo Biology, 1988—93; consulting editor: Jour. of Comparative Psychology; mem. editl. nd. Jour. of Comparative Psychology, 1993—, assoc. editor Am. Jour. Primatology, 1997—2003, mem. editl. bd. De Levende Natuur (Dutch), 1980—82, Animal Behavior, 1985—88; mem. editl. bd.: Primatologie, 1987; mem. editl. bd. Politics and the Life Sciences, 1991—; mem. editl. bd.: Primates, 1998—, Evolutionary Psychology, 2001—, PloS Biology, 2003—, Internat. Jour. of Primatology, Politics, and the Life Sciences; mem. editl. bd. Internat. Jour. of Primatology, Politics, and the Life Sciences, 1995—; contbr. articles to peer-reviewed jours., chapters to books. Recipient Presdl. Citation, APA, 2001, Arthur W. Staats award, 2005; named Carl Friedrich von Siemens Stiftung fellow, 1995; named one of The World's Most Influential People, TIME mag., 2007. Fellow: Am. Acad. Arts & Scis., Carl Friedrich von Siemens Stiftung (Germany), Japan Soc. for the Promotion of Sci.; mem.: Am. Philos. Soc., NAS (fgn. assoc.), Royal Dutch Acad. Scis. (corr.). Office: Living Links Ctr Yerkes Nat Primate Ctr 954 N Gatewood Rd Atlanta GA 30329 also: Dept Psychology Emory Univ Atlanta GA 30322 Office Phone: 404-727-3695, 404-727-7898. Office Fax: 404-727-3270, 404-727-0372.

DEWANE, FRANK JOSEPH, bishop; b. Green Bay, Wis., Mar. 9, 1950; s. Ben and Eleanor Dewane. BA in Social Scis., U. Wis., 1972; MA in Internat. Adminstrn., Am. U., Washington, 1975; STB, Pontifical Gregorian Univ., Rome, 1987; JCL, Pontifical Univ. St. Thomas Aquinas, Rome, 1989. Ordained priest Diocese of Green Bay, 1988; asst. pastor St. Peter and Paul Parish, Green Bay, 1988—91; mem. Permanent Observer Mission, Holy See to the United Nations, NYC, 1991—95; mem., Cor Unum Pontifical Coun., 1995—2001; under sec. Pontifical Council for Justice and Peace, 2001—06; ordained bishop, 2006; coadjutor bishop Diocese of Venice, Fla., 2006—07, bishop, 2007—. Roman Catholic. Office: Diocese of Venice PO Box 2006 1000 Pinebrook Rd Venice FL 34284 Office Phone: 941-484-9543. Office Fax: 941-488-2561.

DEWEESE, BOB M., state legislator, retired surgeon; b. Nov. 8, 1934; BS, U. Ky.; MD, U. Louisville. Ret. gen. surgeon; mem. Dist. 48 Ky. House of Reps., 1993—, minority caucus chmn., 2002—; mem. Appropriations & Revenue Com., Energy Com., Health & Welfare & Local Govt. Com. Mem.: Downtown Rotary Club, Louisville, Jefferson County Med. Soc., Louisville Surgical Soc. (former pres.), AMA. Republican. Home: 6206 Glen Hill Rd Louisville KY 40222 Mailing: 702 Capitol Ave Annex Rm 416 Frankfort KY 40601 Office: 700 Capitol Ave Capitol Rm 316A Frankfort KY 40601 Home Phone: 502-426-5565; Office Phone: 800-372-7181, 502-564-5391. E-mail: Bob.Deweese@lrc.state.ky.us.

DEWEY-BALZHISER, ANNE ELIZABETH MARIE, lawyer; b. Balt., Mar. 16, 1951; d. George Daniel and Elizabeth Patricia (Mohan) Dewey; m. Richard J. Balzhiser; children: Brendan M. Barnett, Andrew P. Barnett, Meghan E. Barnett. BA, Mich. State U., 1972; JD, U. Chgo., 1975; grad., Stonier Grad. Sch. Banking, East Brunswick, NJ, 1983. Bar: DC 1976. Legal clk. and atty. FTC, Washington, 1975—78; atty., sr. atty. Comptr. of Currency, Dallas and Washington, 1978—86; assoc. gen. counsel, gen. counsel, spl. counsel Farm Credit Adminstrn., McLean, Va., 1986—92; counsel, closed bank litig. and policy sect. FDIC, Washington, 1993—94; gen. counsel, spl. advisor Office of Fed. Housing Enterprise Oversight, HUD, Washington, 1994—2004; pres. Women Lead LLC, 2003—; adj. prof. legal studies Strayer U., 2009—. Chair, govt. rels. com., Parent Tchr. Student Assn. Thomas Jefferson HS Sci. and Tech., 2005—10. Mem.: FBA (bd. dirs. D.C. chpt. 1988—91, banking law com. exec. coun. 1995—2001), ABA (coun. 2002—07, govt. and pub. sect. law divsn., bus. law sect., banking law com., liaison to com. on women in the profession, adminstrv. law and regulatory practice sect.), D.C. Bar Assn., Women in Housing and Fin. (bd. dirs. 1982—83, gen. counsel 1991—93, co-chair profl. devel. com. 2002—06), Exchequer Club. Roman Catholic. Home: 104 Chardonnay Dr Stephens City VA 22655 Office: Women Lead LLC PO Box 3145 Winchester VA 22604 E-mail: womenlead@comcast.net.

DEWHURST, DAVID, Lieutenant Governor of Texas; b. Houston, Aug. 18, 1945; m. Tammy Jo Dewhurst, 1995 (div. 2000); m. Patricia Hamilton Dewhurst, 2009; 1 child, Carolyn. BA, U. Ariz., Tucson. Agent CIA; formerly with US Dept. State; founder Falcon Seaboard, 1981; ptnr. Falcon Seabord Diversified Energy & Investments Co.; commr. Gen. Land Office Tex., 1998—2002; lt. gov. State of Tex., 2003—; pres. Tex. State Senate, 2003—. Chmn. Gov.'s Task Force on Homeland Security, 2001—03, State Product Devel. Bd.; mem. Gov.'s Bus. Coun., Pres.'s Commn. on Capabilities US Intelligence Cmty. Officer USAF. Named to Tex. Rodeo Cowboy Hall of Fame, 2009. Mem.: Am. Quarter Horse Assn. (hon. v.p.), Nat. Cutting Horse Assn. Republican. Presbyterian. Avocation: horseback riding. Office: Office of the Lieutenant Governor Capitol Station PO Box 12068 Austin TX 78711 Office Phone: 512-463-0001. Office Fax: 512-463-0677.*

DEWHURST, MORAY P., utilities executive; BS in Naval Architecture and Marine Engring., MIT, Cambridge, MBA. Sr. ptnr. Mercer Mgmt. Consulting; co-founder, sr. ptnr., dir. Dean & Co., 1993—2001; sr. v.p. fin., CFO Florida Power & Light Co., 2001—08; v.p. fin., CFO FPL Group, Inc., Juno Beach, Fla., 2001—08, vice chmn., chief of staff, 2009—. Office: FPL Group Inc 700 Universe Blvd North Palm Beach FL 33408 Office Phone: 561-694-4000. Office Fax: 561-694-4999. Business E-Mail: m.dewhurst@fpl.com.

DEWITT, CHARLES W (CHARLIE), state legislator; b. Feb. 4, 1947; m. Patricia Dale Riddick; children: Renee, Chance. V. p. La Police Jury, 1976—78; state rep. Dist. 25, 1980—; spkr. house; chmn. Labor & Indsl. Rels. Com.; mem. Appropriations Com. & Joint Com. on Budget, House Legislature Svc. Coun.; La House Rep. Mem.: Small Bus. Assn., Cattleman's Assn., Rapides Parish Farm Bur., S Rapides Svc. Club, Belgian Am. Club, Amicus Club. Democrat. Roman Cath. Mailing: 5106 S Macarthur Dr Alexandria LA 71302-2908 Office Phone: 318-442-1513. Office Fax: 318-776-5495.

DEWITT, DALE, state legislator; b. Blackwell, Okla., Jan. 17, 1950; s. Ed and Ramona DeWitt; m. Carol Grell DeWitt; children: Garrett, Camille. A, No. Okla. Coll., 1970; BS, Okla. State Univ., 1973. Hog buyer for John Morrell; agriculture edn. instr. Braman Sch., 1973—2001, Helena-Goltry Schools; mem. Dist. 38 Okla. House of Representatives, 2002—. Mem.: Okla. State U. Extension Advisory Com., Pete Gailey Plan (former chmn. & developer), Kay Electric Coop., Okla. Cattleman's Assn., Kay Cattleman's Assn. Republican. Mailing: 2300 N Lincoln Blvd Rm 433 Oklahoma City OK 73105 also: 14235 W Stateline Rd Braman OK 74632 Office Phone: 405-557-7332. Business E-Mail: daledewitt@okhouse.gov.

DEWITT-MORETTE, CÉCILE, physicist; b. Paris, Dec. 21, 1922; came to US, 1948; d. André and Marie Louise (Ravaudet) Morette; m. Bryce S. DeWitt, Apr. 26, 1951; children: Nicolette, Jan, Chris, Abigail. BS, U. Caen, 1943; PhD, U. Paris, 1947. With Centre Nat. de la Recherche Sci., 1944-65, Maitre de Confs. prof., 1965-88. Mem. Inst. Advanced Studies, Dublin, 1946—47, Copenhagen, 1947—48, Princeton, 1948—50; founder, dir. Ecole d'ete de Physique Theorique, Les Houches, France, 1951—72; lectr. U. Calif., Berkeley, 1952—55, U. NC, Chapel Hill, 1956—71; prof. U. Tex., 1972—93, Jane and Roland Blumberg Centennial prof. physics, 1993—2000, prof. emeritus, 2000—. Author: Particules Elementaires, 1951, (with Y. Choquet-Bruhat and M. Dillard-Bleick) Analysis, Manifolds and Physics, 1977, rev. edit., 1982, 1996, (with A. Maheshwari, B. Nelson) Path Integration in Non Relativistic Quantum Mechanics, 1979, (with Y. Choquet Bruhat) Analysis, Manifolds and Physics, Part II, 92 Applications, 1989, rev. edit., 2000, (with P. Cartier) Functional Integration, Action and Symmetries, 2006, The Pursuit of Quantums Gravity, Memoris of Bryce Dewitt from 1946 to 2004, 2010, also articles. Decorated officier Ordre Nat. du Mērite, Officier Ordre des Palmes Acadēmiques; chevalier Ordre Nat. Legion d'Honneur; Rask-Oersted fellow, 1947-48, Prix des Sciences Physiques et Mathematiques (Comite du Rayonnement Français, 1992); recipient (with Bryce DeWitt) Marcel Grossman award, 2000, Disting. Achievement medal, American Soc. French Legion of Honor, 2007. Fellow American Phys. Soc.; mem. Internat. Astron. Union, European Phys. Soc., Inst. Hautes Etudes Scientific (trustee), French Soc. Physics (Membre d'honneur). Home: 2411 Vista Ln Austin TX 78703-2343 Office: University Texas Austin Department Physics 1 University Station C1600 Austin TX 78712-0268 Office Phone: 512-471-1052.

DEWSBURY, DONALD ALLEN, psychologist; b. Bklyn., Aug. 11, 1939; s. Edwin Leroy and Carol Wieler (Neil) D.; m.; children: Bryan Bradley, Laura Alison. AB, Bucknell U., 1961; PhD, U. Mich., 1965. NSF postdoctoral fellow U. Calif., Berkeley, 1965-66; mem. faculty dept. psychology U. Fla., Gainesville, 1966—, prof., 1973—2007, ret. prof. emeritus, 2007—. Author: Comparative Animal Behavior, 1978, Comparative Psychology in the Twentieth Century, 1984, Monkey Farm: A history of Yerkes Laboratories of Primate Biology, 1930-

1965, 2006; editor (with D. Rethlinghshafer): Comparative Psychology: A Modern Survey, 1973; editor: (with T. McGill, B. Sachs) Sex and Behavior: Status and Prospectus, 1978; editor: Mammalian Sexual Behavior, 1981, Foundations of Comparative Psychology, 1984, Leaders in the Study of Animal Behavior, 1985, Studying Animal Behavior, 1989, Contemporary Issues in Comparative Psychology, 1990, Unification Through Division: Histories of the Divisions of the American Psychological Association, vol. 1, 1996, vol. 2, 1997, vol. 3, 1998, vol. 4, 1999, vol. 5, 2000; editor: (with W. Pickren) Evolving Perspectives on the History of Psychology, 2002; editor: (with L.T. Benjamin, Jr. and M. Wertheimer) Portraits of Pioneers in Psychology, vol. 6, 2006; editor: (with L C Drickamer) Leaders in Animal Behavior, The Second Generation, 2010; editor: (with W. E. Pickre & M. Wertheimer) Portraits of pioneers in Development Psychology, 2012. Recipient Wainwright D. Blake prize in Psychology, Bucknell U., 1961, Phi Sigma award Biological Sci., U. Mich., 1962, Lifetime Achievement award, Soc. History of Psychology, 2008. Fellow: APA (pres. divsn. 6 1992-93, pres. divsn. 26 1997-98, 2008-, Clifford T. Morgan Disting. Svc. to divsn. 6 award, 1998, pres. divsn. 1 2008-09), AAAS, Animal Behavior Soc. (pres. 1978-79, Exemplar award, 1998, Exceptional Svc. award, 2003); mem.: Assn. Psychol. Sci., Cheiron Soc., Phi Beta Kappa, Psi Chi, Phi Eta Sigma, Sigma Xi (U. Fla. Sr. Rsch. award 1997). Avocations: opera, baseball, photography, jazz. Home: 4004 NW 59th Ave Gainesville FL 32653-8358 Office: Univ Fla Dept Psychology Gainesville FL 32611-2250

DHILLON, JANET L., lawyer, retail executive; b. 1962; Grad., Occidental Coll., 1984; JD, UCLA Law Sch., 1991. With Skadden, Arps, Slate, Meagher & Flom LLP, LA, Washington, 1991—2004; mng. dir. legal dept. U.S. Airways Group, Inc., Tempe, Ariz., 2004—05; dep. gen. counsel US Airways Group, Inc., 2005—06; sr. v.p., gen. counsel U.S. Airways Group, Inc., 2006—09; exec. v.p., gen. counsel, sec. JCPenney Co., Inc., Plano, Tex., 2009—; chmn. Retail Lit. Ctr. Recipient Order of Coif. Office Phone: 972-431-1916. Business E-Mail: jdhillon@jcpenney.com.*

DIAL, GERALD, state legislator; b. Delta, Ala., Nov. 17, 1937; m. Faye Dial; children: Melanie, Jason. BS, Livingston State U.; ED, Jacksonville State U.; postgrad., Auburn U. Mem. Lineville City Coun., Ala., 1972—74, Ala. House of Reps., Montgomery, 1974—82, Ala. State Senate, Montgomery, mem. Dist. 13, 2011—. Exec. dir. Ala. Rural Action Commn., 2007—10. Bd. trustees Troy State U. Brig. gen. Ala. Nat. Guard. Republican. Baptist. Avocations: hunting, fishing, working. Home: PO Box 248 Lineville AL 36266-0248 Office: State House Seventh Floor 11 S Union St Montgomery AL 36130 Office Phone: 334-242-7800. E-mail: geralddial@dialex.com.

DIAMOND, FRANK B., pediatric endocrinologist, educator; BA, Yale U., 1970; MD, Pa. State U., 1974. Diplomate Am. Bd. Pediatrics, 1979, Am. Bd. Pediatrics-pediatric endocrinolgy, 1980. Resident pediatrics Children's Hosp.-Univ. Ala., Birmingham, 1975—76; fellow pediatric endocrinology Children's Hosp.-Univ. Pa., 1976—78; pvt. practice Diagnostic Clinic, Largo, Fla.; asst. med. dir. Children Med. Svcs., Pasco County, Fla.; prof. pediatric endocrinology Universidad de San Francisco de Quito, Av Pampite, Ecuador; med. dir. All Children's Hosp. Weight Mgmt. and Fitness Program (Kidshapers); prof. pediatrics Univ. South. Fla., 1988—; hosp. affiliations include Tampa Gen. Hosp., All Children's Hosp., St. Petersburg, Fla. Mem.: Fla. Camp for Children and Youth with Diabetes (pres.), Human Growth Found. (pres.), Lawson Wilkins Pediatric Endocrine Soc. (dir.), Genentech Endowment for Growth Disorders (pres.). Office: All Children's Hospital Dept 6900 501 6th Ave S Saint Petersburg FL 33701 Office Phone: 727-767-4233. Office Fax: 727-767-3275.

DIAMOND, ROBERT MICHAEL, lawyer; b. NYC, Dec. 23, 1948; s. Meyer and Libby (Leventhal) Diamond; m. Amy B. Pullman, July 5, 1987; children: Michael Israel, Philip Brenner, Julia Rose. Student, Vassar Coll., 1969—70; AB, Colgate U., 1970; JD, Columbia U., 1974. Bar: DC 1974, Va. 1976, Md. 1982. Assoc. Fried, Frank, Harris, Shriver & Kampelman, Washington, 1974-75; from assoc. to ptnr. Reed Smith, LLP, Falls Church, Va., 1975—. Contbr. articles to profl. jours. and industry publs. Trustee Cmty. Assns. Inst., Alexandria, Va., sec., 1993, treas., 1994, pres.-elect, 1995, pres., 1996; liaison to joint editl. bd. Uniform Real Estate Acts, 1997—. Recipient Oustanding Leadership award, Cmty. Assns. Inst., 1989, Pres.'s award for outstanding leadership, 1989—90, others; named Superlawyer, Va., 2006—14, Washington, 2006—14; named one of America's Leading Lawyers, Real Estate, Northern Va., 2008—09. Mem.: Coll. Cmty. Assn. Lawyers, Urban Land Inst. Avocations: scuba diving, classic automobiles. Office: Reed Smith LLP 3110 Fairview Park Dr Ste 1400 Falls Church VA 22042-4536 Home Phone: 703-790-0222; Office Phone: 703-641-4273. Business E-Mail: rdiamond@reedsmith.com.

DIANA, JOHN NICHOLAS, physiologist; b. Lake Placid, NY, Dec. 19, 1930; s. Alphonse Walton and Dolores (Mirto) D.; m. Anita Louise Harris, May 8, 1966; children: Gina Sue, Lisa Ann, John Nicholas. BA, Norwich U., 1952; PhD, U. Louisville, 1965. Asst. prof. physiology Mich. State U. Med. Sch., 1966-68; assoc. prof., then prof. U. Iowa Med. Sch., 1969-78; prof. physiology, chmn. dept. La. State U. Med. Ctr., Shreveport, 1978-85; dir. cardiovasc. rsch. ctr. U. Ky., 1985-87, assoc. dean rsch. and basic sci., 1987-88, prof. emeritus, 1997—. Dir. T&H Rsch. Inst., 1988—; cons. Nat. Inst. Neurol. Diseases and Stroke, 1973-75, Nat. Heart, Lung and Blood Inst., 1974—, mem. cardiovasc. and renal study sect., 1980-85, mem. clin. scis. study sect., 1986-91, chmn. 1989-91; rsch. com. Iowa Heart Assn., 1974-77, bd. dirs., 1977-79; mem. cardiovasc. study sect. Am. Heart Assn., 1981-84. Author papers, abstracts in field. Served with AUS, 1952-54; Served with USAR, 1961-62. NIH postdoctoral fellow, 1965-67 Mem. Am. Fedn. Clin. Research, Am. Physiol. Soc. (editorial bd. jour. 1974-78), Microcirculation Soc. (pres. 1977-78, editorial bd. jour. 1979-85), Am. Heart Assn. (fellow council circulation), N.Y. Acad. Scis., La. Heart Assn. (dir. 1979-81, research com. 1978-82), Sigma Xi. Democrat. Achievements include patent for coronary vasodilator. Home: 7332 Saint Georges Way Bradenton FL 34201-2353

DIAW, BORIS (BORIS DIAW-RIFFIOD), professional basketball player; b. Cormeille-en-Parisis, France, Apr. 16, 1982; s. Issa Diaw and Elizabeth Riffiod. Forward, ctr. Centre Federal, Pau Orthez, France, 2000—03, Atlanta Hawks, 2003—05, Phoenix Suns, 2005—08, Charlotte Bobcats, 2008—12, JSA Bordeaux, France, 2011, San Antonio Spurs, 2012—. Mem. French nat. team FIBA European Championships, Serbia and Montenegro, 2005, Lithuania, 2011, FIBA World Championships, Japan, 2006, Summer Olympic Games, London, 2012. Co-founder Babac'Ards, 2005. Recipient Bronze medal, FIBA European Championship, 2005, Silver medal, 2011; named Most Improved Player, NBA, 2006. Achievements include member of French League Championship winning Pau Orthez, 2001, 03. Office: San Antonio Spurs 1 AT&T Center Pky San Antonio TX 78219

DIAZ, ALBERT, federal judge; b. Bklyn., 1960; BS in Economics, U. Pa., 1983; JD, NYU, 1988; MS in Bus. Adminstrn., Boston U., 1993. Bar: NY 1989, DC 1990, NC 1995. Trial and review atty. Marine Corps Base, Camp Lejeune, NC, 1988—91; appellate govt. counsel Office of JAG, Washington, 1991—95, reserve appellate def. counsel, 1995—2000; trial atty. Hunton & Williams, Charlotte and Raleigh, NC, 1995—2001; judge NC Superior Ct., Charlotte, NC, 2001—10, NC Bus. Ct., Charlotte, NC, 2005—10, US Ct. Appeals (4th Cir.), Richmond, Va., 2010—. Reserve mil. judge USN-Marine Corps Trial Judiciary, Piedmont Judicial Cir., Camp Lejeune, NC, 2000—05; reserve appellate judge USN-Marine Corps Ct. Criminal Appeals, Washington Navy Yard, Washington, 2005—06; presiding judge Mecklenburg County Drug Treatment Ct., 2002—10, Nat. HS Mock Trial Championships, 2005, Charlotte Mecklenburg Schs. Truancy Ct., 2005—10; adj. faculty Ctrl. Piedmont CC, 2006—; spkr. in field. Lt. col. USMC Reserve, 1995—2006. Mem.: ABA (mem. Conf. of State Trial Judges 2001—), Nat. Bar Assn., Mecklenburg County Bar, NC Bar Assn. (mem. Minorities in the Profession Com. & Hispanic-Latino Lawyers Com. 1998—), American Coll. of Bus. Ct. Judges, Justice Bobbitt Inn of Ct. (sec. 2004—), Hispanic Nat. Bar Assn. Office: US Court of Appeals Lewis F Powell, Jr US Courthouse 1100 E Main St Richmond VA 23219 Office Phone: 804-916-2700.

DIAZ, FRED M., JR., automotive executive; b. San Antonio, Tex., 1965; BA in Bus. Mgmt. & Psychology Minor, Tex. Luth. U., Seguine, 1988; MBA, Ctrl. Mich. U., 1995. Customer rels. mgr., external affairs Chrysler Corp., 1997—98; trainee Chrysler Group, LLC, 1989—90, zone svc. dist. mgr., B, 1990—92, zone svc. dist. mgr., A, 1992—94, customer rels. supr., 1994—95, customer rels. supr., nat. corr., 1995—97, field ops. mgr., 1998—2000, sr. mgr., sales, Caribbean PR, 2000—02, sr. mgr., sales & svc., 2002—03, sr. mgr., mktg., SW Bus. Ctr., 2003—04, dir., Dodge Brand Comm., 2004—06, regional dir., Denver Bus. Ctr., 2006—09, pres., CEO, Ram Truck Brand, 2009—13, pres., CEO Chrysler de Mexico, 2011—13; v.p. sales & mktg. Nissan USA, 2013—. Recipient Chairman's award, HENAAC/STEM, 2010; named Exec. of Yr., On Wheels Magazine Hispanic, Top 25 Corporate Elite Dynamic Leaders, 2011. Mem.: STEM (adv. bd. 2011). Office: Nissan USA One Nissan Way Franklin TN 37067*

DIAZ, HERIBERTO, medical products executive; BSEE, U. PR. With Prime Computer, Inc., 1981—90, Guidant Corp., 1990; gen. mgr., v.p., ops. Guidant del Caribe, Ltd., PR, 2003—06; v.p., ops., gen. mgr. Boston Sci., 2000—06; v.p., ops., L.Am. MedTech Plastics PR, Inc. Recipient Mfg. Exec. Yr., PR Mfg. Assn., 2003; named one of 50 Most Important Hispanics in Tech. & Bus., Hispanic Engr. & Info. Tech. mag., 2005. Office: MedTech Plastics PR Inc Cabo Caribe Industrial Ctr Bldg 1093 Vega Baja PR 00694 Office Phone: 787-858-6884. Office Fax: 787-858-0328.

DIAZ, JOSE FELIX, state legislator; b. Miami, Fla., Jan. 16, 1980; m. Therese Marie Diaz; 1 child, Dominick Jose. BA in English & Polit. Sci., U. Miami; JD, Columbia U., NYC, 2005. Atty. Akerman Senterfitt, 2006—; mem. Dist. 115 Fla. House of Representatives, 2011—. Republican. Office: 7901 SW 24th St Miami FL 33155-6524 also: Fla House of Reps 1101 The Capitol 402 S Monroe St Tallahassee FL 32399-1300 Office Phone: 305-442-6800, 850-488-3616.

DIAZ, PAUL J., health products executive; BS in Finance & Acctg., American U. Kogod Sch. Bus., 1984; JD, Georgetown U. Law Ctr., 1988. With Arthur Andersen LLC; CFO, gen. counsel Allegis Health Services, Inc., 1991—94, CEO, 1995—96; exec. v.p., COO Mariner Health Group, Inc., 1996—98; chmn., CEO Capella Sr. Living, LLC; mng. mem. Falcon Capital Partners, LLC; pres., COO Kindred Healthcare, Inc., 2002—03, pres., CEO Louisville, 2004—. Bd. dirs. Kindred Healthcare Inc., 2002—, DaVita, 2007—, PharMerica Corp., 2007—08. Named one of The 100 Most Influential People in Healthcare, Modern Healthcare mag., The Top 25 Minority Executives in Healthcare, 2008, 2010, The 25 Nest Latinos in Bus., Hispanic mag., 2008, 2009. Mem.: Johns Hopkins Bloomberg Sch. Pub. Health. Office: Kindred Healthcare 680 S Fourth St Louisville KY 40202

DIAZ-BALART, MARIO, United States Representative from Florida; b. Ft. Lauderdale, Fla., Sept. 25, 1961; m. Tia Diaz-Balart; 2 children. Student, U. South Fla. Pres. Gordeon Sloan Diaz-Balart, Boca Raton, Miami; adminstrv. asst. to Mayor Xavier Suarez City of Miami, 1985-88; mem. Dist. 115 Fla. House of Reps., Tallahassee, 1989—92, mem. Dist. 112, 2001—02; mem. Dist. 37 Fla. State Senate, Tallahassee, 1993—2000; mem. US Congress from 25th Fla. Dist., Washington, 2003—11, 2013—, US Congress from 21st Fla. Dist., 2011—13. Recipient Public Svc. award, American League Against Discrimination, 1992, Leadership award, Fla. Assn. State Troopers, 1993, 1996, Furtherance of Justice award, Fla. Attys. Assn., 1994, Legis. Courage award, Labor Coun. Latin American Advancement, 1996, Top Forty award, Fla. Chamber of Commerce, 1996, 2000, Govt. Recognition award, American Assn. Poison Control Centers, 1996, Disting. Leadership award, Fla. Police Benevolent Assn., 1996, Nat. Alliance Mentally Ill, 1997, Claude Pepper Meml. award, United Homecare Svcs., 2000, Golden Shovel award, Miami River Marine Grp., 2000, Legis. Distinction award, MADD, 2000, Lifetime Legis. Achievement award, Fla. Assn. CC's, 2000, Top Pillar award, Fla. Internat. U., 2000; named Senator of Yr., Fla. Assn. Life Underwriters, 1998, Conservationist of Yr., Biscayne Bay Found., 1999, Legis. of Yr., Fla. Assn. Realtors, 2000, Fla. Optometrics Assn., 2000. Mem.: Spanish American League Against Discrimination, Nat. Assn. Latino Elected Officials, Westchester Lions Club. Republican. Roman Catholic. Avocations: reading, biking, diving. Office: US House of Representatives 436 Cannon House Office Bldg Washington DC 20515-0925 also: 4715 Golden Gate Pkwy Ste 1 Naples FL 34116 Office Phone: 239-348-1620. Office Fax: 239-348-3569.*

DIAZ DE LA PORTILLA, MIGUEL A., state legislator; b. Miami, Fla., Jan. 30; m. Mari; hildren: Michael Alexander, Jon-Christian, Mary Ester. BA in Philosophy and English Lit. cum laude, U. Miami, 1984, JD, 1987. Bar: US Dist. Ct. (so. dist.) Fla., Supreme Ct. Fla. Atty. in govt. and adminstrv. law, Fla.; former commr. & chmn. Miami-Dade County Commn.; mem. Dist. 36 Fla. State Senate, 2011—. Mem. Governor's Commn. for Sustainable Fla., 1993—94; bd. dirs. Tri-Rail Commuter Rail Authority, 1993—97, chmn., 1996; bd. mem. South Regional Planning Coun., 1994—98; mem. adv. bd. Miami-Dade County Pub. Schools Facilities and Maintenance Adv. Bd., 2004—06. Mem.: ABA, NRA, Builders Assn. South Fla. (bd. dirs.). Republican. Office: 2100 Coral Way Ste 505 Miami FL 33145 also: Fla State Senate 312 Senate Office Bldg 404 S Monroe St Tallahassee FL 32399-1100 Office Phone: 305-643-7200, 850-487-5109. Business E-Mail: portilla.miguel.web@flsenate.gov.

DIAZ-DENNIS, PATRICIA, lawyer, communications executive; b. Santa Rita, N.Mex., 1946; d. Porfirio Madrid and Mary (Romero) Diaz; m. Michael John Dennis, Aug. 3, 1968; children: Ashley Elizabeth, Geoffrey, Alicia Sarah. BA in English, UCLA, 1970; JD, Loyola U. Sch. Law, LA, 1973. Bar: Calif. 1973, DC 1984, Tex. 1998. Law clk. Calif. Rural Legal Asst., McFarland, 1971; assoc. Paul, Hastings, Janofsky & Walker, LA, 1973—76; atty. Pacific Lighting Corp., LA, 1976—78; atty., asst. gen. atty. ABC, Hollywood, 1978—83; mem. NLRB, Washington, 1983—86; commr. FCC, 1986—89; ptnr., head comm. Jones, Day, Reavis & Pogue, 1989—91; v.p. govt. affairs US Sprint/United Telecom, 1991—92; asst. sec. for human rights & humanitarian affairs US Dept. State, Washington, 1992; spl. coun. comm. Sullivan & Cromwell LLP, 1993—95; sr. v.p., asst. gen. counsel SBC Comm. Inc., San Antonio, 1995—98, sr. v.p. regulatory and pub. affairs, 1998—2002, sr. v.p., gen. counsel, sec. SBC West, 2002—04; sr. v.p., asst. gen. counsel AT&T (formerly known as SBC), 2004—. Chmn., US del. Internat. Telecomm. Union Region 2 Broadcasting Conf., Rio de Janeiro, 1988; mem. adv. bd. Ctr. Telecom. Info. Studies, Columbia U., 1999—2005; bd. dirs. Telemundo Grp. Inc., 1989—92, Nat. Pub. Radio, 1993—99, Mass. Mut. Life Ins. Co., UST Inc. Exec. editor Loyola Law Rev., 1972—73. Com. mem. Hispanic leadership prog. Coro Found., LA, 1981—82; US del. UN Commn. Status of Women, Econ. and Social Coun., Vienna, 1984, World Conf. UN Decade Women, Nairobi, Kenya, 1985; bd. dirs. Nat. Network Hispanic Women, LA, 1983—92, Reading is Fundamental, 1991—98, Hispanic Scholarship Fund, 1997—2000, Mexican Am. Legal Defense and Ednl. Fund, 1999—2001, Found. for Women's Resources, 1982—2002, Bexar County Women's Bar Assn., 1998—2002; trustee Tomás Rivera Policy Inst., 1991—2005, Radio and TV News Dirs. Found., 1993—2005; nat. sec. Girl Scouts USA, 1999—2002, first vice chair, 2002—05, chair bd. dirs., 2005—. Recipient Outstanding Achievement award, Nat. Coun. Hispanic Women, 1986, Achievement award, City Club Cleve., 1986, Belva Lockwood Outstanding Lawyer award, Bexar County Women's Bar Assn., 2000, Pub. Endeavor award, Assn. Women in Comm., 2001, Leadership award, Cuban Am. Nat. Coun., 2002, Corp. Responsibility Svc. award, MALDEF, 2003, Fortune Dir. award, Hispanic Assn. Corp. Responsibility, 2004, Legacy of Leadership award, Spelman Coll., 2006; named Woman of Yr., Mex. Am. Opportunity Found., 1984, Hispanic Women's Coun., Inc., 1989, Hispanic Woman of Yr., Houston YWCA, 1992, Alumna of Yr., UCLA Latino Alumni Assn., 1999, Corp. Exec. of Yr., San Antonio Women's C. of C., 1999, Exec. of Yr., Nat. Hispanic Employee Assn., 1999; named one of 100 Influentials, Hispanic Mag., 1987, 1988, 1990, 1996, 80 Elite, Hispanic Women Directory, 2002, Top 100 Latinas, Hispanic Mag., 2003, Top 25 Elite Women, 2004, Top 100 Latinas, 2004, 25 Bets Latinos in Bus., 2008; named to Hall of Fame, San Antonio Women, 2002. Mem.: ABA, Fed. Comm. Bar Assn., Women's Forum Wash., Hispanic Bar Assn., LA County Bar Assn., Mexican Am. Bar Assn. (sec. 1980—81, trustee 1979—82). Democrat. Roman Catholic. Office: AT&T Rm 11 A 50 175 E Houston St San Antonio TX 78205 Office Phone: 210-351-3439. Business E-Mail: pdennis.1@att.com.

DICE, BRUCE BURTON, gas industry executive; b. Grand Rapids, Mich., Dec. 24, 1926; s. William and Wilma (Rose) D.; children: Karen, Kevin, Kirk. BS in Geology, U. Mich., 1950; MS in Geology, Mich. State U., 1956. With El Paso Natural Gas, 1956—62, Drilling and Exploration Co., 1962—63, Ocean Drilling and Exploration, New Orleans, 1963—75, Transco Exploration Co., Houston, 1975—82, pres., 1979—82, Dice Exploration Co., Inc., Houston, 1982—95, Wadi Petroleum, Inc., Houston, 1992—. Cons. in field. Mem.: Houston Geol. Soc., Am. Assn. Petroleum Geologists. Office: Wadi Petroleum Inc 4355 Sylvanfield Ste 200 Houston TX 77014 Home: 9505 Northpointe 9303 B Spring TX 77379 Business E-Mail: sgc@wadipetroleum.com.

DICHARRY, RICHARD N., lawyer; b. New Orleans, Sept. 12, 1951; BA magna cum laude, Loyola U., 1972, JD, 1975; LLM, Boston U., 1978. Bar: La. 1975. Atty. Phelps Dunbar, New Orleans, 1978—, mng. ptnr., chmn. mgmt. com. Mem.: ABA, La. State Bar Assn., Maritime Law Assn. of US, Internat. Assn. Claim Professionals (adjunct mem.). Office: Phelps Dunbar Canal Pl 365 Canal St Ste 2000 New Orleans LA 70130-6534 Office Phone: 504-584-9232. Office Fax: 504-568-9130. Business E-Mail: richard.dicharry@phelps.com.

DICIANNI, JOE, electronics executive; b. Chgo., July 13, 1946; s. Dominick and Annette (Schiavone) Di C.; m. Marlene Beth Chisholm, Dec. 31, 1969; children: Gina M., Robyn E. AA, Coll. DuPage, 1977; BGS in Bus., Northern Ill. U., 1982; MS in Bus. Mgmt., Aurora U., 1986. Computer operator Western Electric Co., Cicero, Ill., 1964-68; ops. supr. Allis Chalmers Co., Carol Stream, Ill., 1968-71, mgr., data ctr. Fiat-Allis divsn., 1971-78; asst. MIS mgr. Boise Cascade Co., Itasca, Ill., 1978-87; v.p., MIS and svcs., dir., MIS Ideal Industries, Inc., Sycamore, Ill., 1987; v.p., info. tech. Thomas & Betts Corp., 1996—. MIS advisor Kishwaukee Coll., Malta, Ill., 1988—; cons. of Foun., No. Ill. U., DeKalb, 1988—, cons. Sch. Bus., 1988—; cons. Resource Bank, Sycamore, 1988—. Bd. dirs. Sycamore United Way, 1988-89. Sgt. U.S. Army, 1966-68, Korea. Mem. Data Processing Mgmt. Assn., Share Users Group, Common Users Group, Guide Internat., Kishwaukee Sunrise Rotary Club (charter mem.). Republican. Roman Catholic. Avocations: golf, tennis, reading, softball, swimming. Home: 76 Iron Creek Ct N Apt 103 Collierville TN 38017-6972 Office: Thomas & Betts Corp 8155 T&B Blvd Memphis TN 38125 Office Phone: 901-252-8000. Office Fax: 901-252-1354. Business E-Mail: joe_dicianni@tnb.com.

DICINTIO, MICHELLE S., lawyer; BA in Polit. Sci. & Bus. Adminstrn. magna cum laude, U. Redlands, 1990; JD, U. Va., 1993. Bar: Va. 1993, DC 1994. Assoc., corp. & securities group Dechert Price & Rhoads, 1993—95, Dickstein Shapiro Morin & Oshinsky, 1995—2000; counsel, corp. & securities group Jenner & Block, 2000—01; dir., sr. counsel General Dynamics Corp., Falls Church, Va., 2001—03, v.p., assoc. gen. counsel, 2003—07; sr. v.p., gen. counsel Serco, Inc., 2007—09; CEO Corp. Counsel Consulting, 2009—; prin. Zell Law, 2009—. Mentor Everybody Wins, Washington, 2001—05. Mem.: ABA, Va. State Bar Assn., DC Bar Assn., Compliance and Ethics Leadership Counsel, Am. Corp. Counsel Assn., Phi Beta Kappa. Office: Zell Law 10105 Sanders Ct Great Falls VA 22066-2526 Office Phone: 571-203-9355. Office Fax: 571-323-5266.

DICK, BARRY LEE, surgeon; b. Cin., Feb. 23, 1954; MD, U. Cin., 1987. Diplomate Am. Bd. Surgery with added qualifications in vascular surgery. Intern U. Cin., 1987-88, resident in gen. surgery, 1988-92; fellow in vasc. surgery St. Louis U., 1992-93; attending Good Samaritan Hosp., Cin., 1993—2011; attending, v.p. med. staff St. Elizabeth Hosps., Edgewood, Ky., 1993-95, bd. trustees, 2000—11. Chmn. surgery St. Luke's Hosps., Florence, Ky., 1997-99. Fellow ACS; mem. Ohio Med. Assn., No. Ky. Med. Assn., Ky. Med. Assn., Mid West Vascular Surg. Soc. Office: St Elizabeth Physicians Vascular Surgery Edgewood 580 S Loop Rd Ste 201 Edgewood KY 41017 Office Phone: 859-578-0442.

DICK, MELVIN A., wholesale distribution executive; b. Bklyn., 1936; m. Bobbi Dick Sales exec. E. and J. Gallo Winery; with Gallo Wine Distbrs. of NJ, 1958; pres., wine divsn. Southern Wine and Spirits Of SC; gen. sales mgr., wine Southern Wine & Spirits of America, Inc., 1969, v.p., wine, 1972—76, pres., wine divsn., 1976—, owner, 1984—, sr. v.p., 1991—. Recipient Wine Star Man of the Yr. award, Wine Enthusiast Mag., 2004. Office: Southern Wine & Spirits of America Inc 1600 NW 163rd St Miami FL 33169 Office Phone: 305-625-4171. Office Fax: 305-625-4720. Business E-Mail: mdick@southernwine.com.

DICK, SHELLY DECKERT (RACHELLE LYNNE DECKERT DICK), federal judge; b. El Paso, Tex., 1960; BS, U. Tex., 1981; JD, La. State U. Paul M. Herbert Law Ctr., 1988. Ptnr. Gary, Field, Landry

& Dornier, Baton Rouge, 1988—94, Forrester, Dick & Clark, 1994—2013; judge US Dist. Ct. (middle dist.) La., 2013—. Ad hoc hearing officer La. Workforce Commn., 2008—13. Office: US District Court 777 Florida St Ste 139 Baton Rouge LA 70801 Office Phone: 225-389-3500.*

DICKENS, CHARLES HENDERSON, advocate, retired social sciences educator; b. Thomasville, NC, Nov. 22, 1934; s. Argie Marshall and Edna (Sullivan) D.; m. Jane McClung, Aug. 27, 1965; children: Martha Jane, Anne Elizabeth. BS, Duke U., 1957, MEd, 1964, ED, 1966. Asst. prof. Wake Forest U., Winston-Salem, NC, 1965-67; planning specialist NSF, Washington, 1967-69, assoc. program dir. undergrad. instrnl. program, 1969-73, study dir. sci. edn. studies group, 1973-83, sect. head scientific and tech. pers. studies sect., 1983-86, sect. head surveys and analysis sect., 1986-90; sr. policy analyst Fed. Coordinating Coun. for Sci., Engring., and Tech., Washington, 1990-92, exec. sec., 1992-93, ret., 1993. Mem. adv. bd. Am. Men and Women of Sci., New Providence, NJ, 1991—, C.C. Cameron Applied Rsch. Ctr. U. NC, Charlotte, 1994—99; cons. Stanford Rsch. Internat., 2002—14, Sr. Tar Heel Legis., 2005—, chair, Credentials and Elections Com., 2005—07, spkr., 2007—09; chair Rules and Bylaws Com., 2011—14; mem. bd. dirs. Western Carolina chpt. Alzheimer's Assn., 2009—10. Adv. bd. Buncombe County Coun. on Aging, 2000—06; active Buncombe County Aging Coordinating Consortium, 2005—, co-chmn., 2006—07; mem. adv. coun. Aging Land-of-Sky Regional Coun., 2005—, vice chmn., 2007—09, chmn., 2010—; active Friends of NC Sr. Tar Heels, Inc., 2005—11, v.p., 2007—09; mem. Land-of-Sky, Regional Coun., 2010—; vol. counselor Sr. Health Ins. Info. Program, 1996—. With US Army, 1958—59. Recipient Angier B. Duke prize Duke U., 1953-57, Mickey Hanula award, 1998, Margaret Hart Hardee Excellence award, NC Assn. Area Agys. on Aging, 2008, Appreciation award, NC, 2009, Kathleen Goodwin Cole award Land-of-Sky Regional Coun., 2010; Woodrow Wilson fellow Woodrow Wilson Fellowship Found., 1963, James B. Duke fellow Duke U., 1963-64. Fellow: AAAS; mem.: Nat. Active and Ret. Fed. Employees Assn. (v.p. chpt. 156 1995—96, pres. 1996—97, v.p. N.C. area I 1997—2001), Phi Beta Kappa. Republican. Presbyterian. Avocations: reading, computers, birdwatching, history. Home: 4 Arrow Pl Asheville NC 28805-9748 Personal E-mail: chas34@juno.com.

DICKERSON, DENNIS CLARK, SR., historian, educator; b. McKeesport, Pa., Aug. 12, 1949; s. Carl O'Neal and Oswanna (Wheeler) D.; m. Mary Anne Eubanks, Aug. 6, 1977; children: Nicole Denise, Valerie Anne, Christina Marie, Dennis Clark Jr. BA, Lincoln U., 1971; MA, Washington U., Mo., 1974, PhD, 1978; LHD (hon.), Morris Brown Coll., 1990; postgrad., Hartford Sem., Memphis Theol. Seminary; M.Div, Vanderbilt U., 2007. Instr. history Forest Park C.C., St. Louis, 1974, Pa. State U. Ogontz, Abington, 1975-76; from asst. to assoc. prof. history Williams Coll., Williamstown, Mass., 1976-85, assoc. prof., 1987-88, prof., 1988-99, Stanfield prof. history, 1992-99; assoc. prof. history Rhodes Coll., Memphis, 1985—87; James M. Lawson Jr. prof. history Vanderbilt U., Nashville, 1999—. Mem. com. examiners GRE History test Ednl. Testing Svc., Princeton, 1990-96; corporator Williamstown Savs. Bank, 1992-99; vis. prof. Payne Theol. Sem., Wilberforce, Ohio, 1992, 96, 98, 2002, 04; vis. prof. Am. religious history Yale Div. Sch., 1995. Author: Out of the Crucible, 1986, Religion, Race and Region: Research Notes on A.M.E. Church History, 1995, Militant Mediator: Whitney M. Young, Jr., 1998, A Liberated Past: Explorations in A.M.E. Church History, 2003, African Methodism and Its Wesleyan Heritage: Reflections on A.M.E. Church History, 2009, African American Preachers and Politics: The Careys of Chicago, 2010; historiographer, exec. dir. rsch. and scholarship, editor A.M.E. Ch. Rev., 2000—; contbr. articles to profl. jours. Historiographer, African Meth. Episcopal Ch., 1988—, min. 1977—; trustee Mass. Coll. Liberal Arts, 1992-95. Rockefeller Found. fellow U. Va., 1987-88. Mem. Am. Bible Soc. (chmn. bd. trustees 2006—), Am. Soc. Ch. History (pres. 2004), NAACP, Elks, Alpha Phi Alpha. Office: Vanderbilt U Dept History Nashville TN 37235-0001 Office Phone: 615-343-4329. Business E-Mail: dennis.c.dickerson@vanderbilt.edu.

DICKERSON, LAWRENCE RICHARD, oil industry executive; b. Cambridge, Eng., Dec. 11, 1952; s. Lamar Ronsell and Nancy Jane (Lawrence) Dickerson; m. Marcela E. Donadio, Feb. 17, 1981. BBA with honors, U. Tex., 1976. CPA Tex. Staff auditor Arthur Young & Co., Houston, 1976, sr. auditor, 1977—79; asst. contr. Diamond M. Co., 1979—80, mgr., planning, 1980—81, contr., 1981—82, v.p., 1983—85, v.p., adminstrn., 1986—; pres., bd. dirs. Diamond Offshore Drilling, Inc., 1998—, CEO, 2008—. With US Army, 1972—74. Mem.: AICPA, Internat. Assn. Drilling Contractors (chmn. fin. com.). Episcopalian. Office: Diamond Offshore Drilling Inc 15415 Katy Freeway Houston TX 77094 Office Phone: 281-492-5300. Office Fax: 281-492-5378. Business E-Mail: ldickerson@dodi.com.

DICKERSON, LON RICHARD, retired library administrator; b. Ypsilanti, Mich., Dec. 16, 1941; s. Lon E. and Maxine A. (Merryfield) D.; m. Anne Elizabeth Bryan, Aug. 24, 1968; children: Robert Lon, Sarah Elizabeth, Peter Bryan. AB, Albion Coll., 1964; MLS, U. Pitts., 1968. Dir. U. Liberia Librs., Monrovia, 1968-72, Lake Agassiz Regional Libr., Moorhead, Minn., 1972-85, Timberland Regional Libr., Olympia, Wash., 1985-92, Omaha Pub. Libr., 1993—96, Chatham-Effingham-Liberty Regional Libr., Savannah, Ga., 1996—2000, Jefferson Parish Libr., Metairie, La., 2004—12. Pres. Adv. Coun. State Libr., Minn., 1977-78, Minn. Regional Pub. Libr. Sys. Adminstrs., 1980, No. Lights Libr. Network Adv. Coun., Minn., 1981-82; v.p. Ga. Coun. Pub. Librs., 1998-00, pres., 2000. Contbr. articles to profl. jours. Libr. vol. Peace Corps Sierra Leone Libr. Bd., Freetown, 1964-67; mem. planning commn. City of Lacey, Wash.,1985-93; vice-chair planning commn. City of Lacey, 1991-93, mem. various sch. dist. coms.; bd. dir. Clay-Wilkin Opportunity Coun., Moorhead, Minn., 1982-85; mem. steering com. Omaha 2000, 1993-96, Omaha Free-Net, 1994-96, United Way of the Midlands Com., Omaha, 1996. Mem. ALA (internat. rels. com. 1974-75), Wash. Libr. Assn. (co-chmn. legis. planning com. 1987-92, Pres.'s award 1988), La. Libr. Assn., Pub. Libr. Assn. (nominating com. 1989-90), Tau Kappa Epsilon. Democrat. Congregationalist. Office Phone: 504-838-1133. Business E-Mail: ldickerson@jefferson.lib.la.us.

DICKERSON, PAMELA A., state legislator; b. New Orleans, Jan. 14, 1953; BS, So. U., New Orleans, 1975. Flight attendant Delta Air Lines, 1976—; small bus. owner; mem. Dist. 95 Ga. House of Representatives, 2011—. Democrat. Office: PO Box 1016 Conyers GA 30013 also: Georgia house of Reps 611 Coverdell Legis Office Bldg Atlanta GA 30334 Office Phone: 404-656-0314. Business E-Mail: pam.dickerson@house.ga.gov.

DICKEY, BURTON F., critical care specialist, educator; MD, U. Conn., 1980. Diplomate Am. Bd. Internal Medicine, 1983, Am. Bd. Internal Medicine- pulmonary disease, 1988, Am. Bd. Internal Medicine- critical care medicine, 1999. Resident in internal medicine Temple Univ. Hosp., Phila.; fellow in pulmonary disease Univ. Conn. Health Ctr., Farmington; prof. in medicine Case West Res. Univ.; hosp. affiliation include Univ. Tex. MD Anderson Cancer Ctr. Office: University of Texas MD Anderson Cancer Center 1515 Holcombe Blvd Houston TX 77030-4000 Office Phone: 713-792-6161.

DICKEY, DAVID HERSCHEL, lawyer, accountant; b. Savannah, Ga., Dec. 31, 1951; s. Grady Lee and Sara (Leon) D.; children: David Bradford, Carolyn Amanda. BBA in Acctg. and Fin., Armstrong Atlantic State U., 1974; M in Accountancy, U. Ga., 1977, JD, 1977. CPA; bar: Ga. 1978, U.S. Dist. Ct. (no. dist.) Ga. 1980, U.S. Ct. Claims 1978, U.S. Tax Ct. 1978, U.S. Ct. Appeals (5th and 11th cirs.) 1978, U.S. Supreme Ct. 1981. Assoc., acct. Thompson and Benken, Attys., Savannah, 1977-79; pub. acct. Arthur Andersen & Co., Atlanta, 1979-81; assoc. Oliver Maner LLP, Savannah, 1981—, ptnr., 1982—. Pres. Savannah Estate Planning Coun., 1986-87, chmn. bd., 1987-88; bd. dirs. Chatham-Savannah Citizen's Advocacy; mem. legal adv. bd. Small Bus. Coun. Am., Inc., 1989—; pres. Seminar Group, Inc., 1989—, Hist. Investment Properties, Inc., 1991—. Pres. L'Alliance Francaise de Savannah, 2001—03; bd. dirs. Savannah Theatre Co., 1984, Savannah chpt. Am. Cancer Soc., 1986—91, Hist. Savannah Found., Inc., 1988—94, Candler Hosp. Found., 2003; chmn., trustee Armstrong State Coll. Alumni Endowment Fund, Inc., 1991; chmn. lawyers divsn. Chatham County United Way, 1992; dir., v.p. Armstrong Atlantic State U. Found., 2001—03; bd. trustees The Candler Found., 2001—03. Recipient Outstanding Svc. award Am. Cancer Soc., 1987, Outstanding Alumni Svc. award Armstrong Atlantic State U., 1992; named to Leadership Savannah, Savannah C. of C., 1984-86. Fellow: Am. Coll. Trust and Estate Counsel (chair com.); mem.: S.R. (pres. Ga. chpt. 2001—03), SAR (pres. Ga. 1999), ABA (estate and gift tax com. taxation sect. 1990—), Mil. Order of the Stars and Bars (Lafayette McLaws chpt. comdr. 2005—07, 2011—12), Savannah Bar Assn., Ga. Bar Assn., St. Andrew's Soc., Soc. Colonial Wars, Sons Confederate Vets (comdr. Francis S. Bartow camp no. 93 1997—98), Chatham Club, First City Club (bd. dirs. Savannah 1987—90). Avocations: history, genealogy, music, computers. Home: 4 Springfield Pl Savannah GA 31411 Office: Oliver Maner LLP 218 W State St Savannah GA 31401-3232 Home Phone: 912-598-0275; Office Phone: 912-236-3311. Business E-Mail: ddickey@olivermaner.com.*

DICKEY, JAMES ALLEN, men's college basketball coach; b. Valley Springs, Ark., Apr. 2, 1954; m. Bettye Fiscus; children: Lauren, Jared. BEd, U. Ctrl. Ark., Conway, 1976; MEd, Harding U., Searcy, Ark., 1977. Asst. coach Harding U. Bison, 1976—77; head basketball coach Harding Acad. Wildcats, 1977—79; asst. coach U. Ctrl. Ark. Bears, 1979—81, U. Ark. Razorbacks, 1981—85, U. Ky. Wildcats, 1985—89, Tex. Tech. U. Red Raiders, 1990—91, head basketball coach, 1991—2001; asst. coach Okla. State U. Cowboys, 2002—08; head basketball coach U. Houston Cougars, 2010—. Named Dist. 7 Coach of Yr., Nat. Assn. Basketball Coaches, 1992, 1995—97, Southwest Conf. Coach of Yr., 1992, 1996. Office: University Houston Basketball Program c/o Athletics Dept 3100 Cullen Blvd Houston TX 77204-6002 Office Phone: 713-743-9430.

DICKEY, NANCY WILSON, chancellor, physician; b. Watertown, SD, Sept. 10, 1950; m. Franklin Champ; children: Danielle, Wilson, Elizabeth. BA, Stephen F. Austin State U.; MD, U. Tex., 1976. Diplomate Am. Bd. Family Practice. Resident family medicine Meml. Hosp. System, Houston, 1976-79; pres., vice chancellor health affairs TAMUS Health Sci. Ctr.; prof. family medicine TAMUS Coll. Med., College Station, Tex., 1996—, pres., 2006—. Hon. staff Polly Ryon Meml. Hosp., Richmond; active staff Coll. Sta. (Tex.) Med. Ctr., St. Josephs Hosp., Bryan, Tex. Reviewer Jour. of AMA; editl. adv. bd. Patient Care, Med. World News, Med. Ethics Advisor, Archives of Family Medicine. Coach youth soccer, 1986-88; sponsor United Meth. Youth Fellowship, 1991-95; bd. dirs. Hastings Ctr., Office of Early Childhood Devel., Am. Heart Assn.; mem. Christ United Meth. Ch., College Station. Recipient Disting. Alumni award U. Tex. Med. Sch., Citation of Merit Tex. Soc. of Pathologists, 1995. Mem. AMA (pres. elect 1997, pres. 1998, chair bd. trustees 1995-97, vice chair 1994-95, bd. trustees 1989-97, sec. treas. 1993-94, exec. com. 1991, other coms.), Inst. Medicine, Tex. Acad. of Family Physicians, Tex. Med. Assn., Alpha Omega Alpha. Office: 301 Tarrow St #7th Flr College Station TX 77840-7896

DICKEY, ROBERT, state legislator; b. Nov. 26; m. Cynde Dickey; children: Robert Lee IV, Marjie. BBA, U. Ga., 1976; MBA, Ga. Coll., 1989. Owner Dickey Farms; mem. Dist. 136 Ga. House of Reps., Atlanta, 2011—. Bd. mem. Crawford County Farm Bur.; bd. mem., past pres. Ga. Peach Coun.; founding bd. mem. Ga. Agri-Leaders Forum; bd. dirs. Flint Energies, 1994—2011, SunTrust Bank; mem. Crawford County Indsl. Authority, Crawford County C. of C., Mid. Ocmulgee Regional Water Planning Coun., Governor's Agrl. Adv. Bd., Ga., 2002—10. Mem., deacon, Sunday sch. tchr. Musella Bapt. Ch., Ga. Republican. Office: 3440 Old Hwy 341 N PO Box 10 Musella GA 31066 also: Ga House of Reps 607-H Coverdell Legis Office Bldg Atlanta GA 30334 Office Phone: 478-836-3136, 404-656-0287. Business E-Mail: robert.dickey@house.ga.gov.

DICKEY, ROBERT J., publishing executive; m. Lori Dickey; 1 child, Megan. With Daily Tidings, Ashland, Oreg., 1981; retail advt. mgr., advt. dir. Reno Gazette-Jour., Nev., 1989—93; pres., pub. The Desert Sun, Palm Springs, Calif., 1993—2005; v.p., Pacific Newspaper Group Gannett Co., Inc., 1997—2005, sr. group pres., Pacific Newspaper Group, chmn., Phoenix Newspapers, 2005—08, pres., US Cmty. Pub., 2008—. Bd. dir. Downtown Phoenix Partnership, Agua Caliente Devel. Authtority, Desert Health Care Dist., United Way of the Desert, Palm Springs Art Mus., Coachella Valley Econ. Partnership, Palm Springs Internat. Film Festival. Office: Gannett Co Inc 7950 Jones Branch Dr Mc Lean VA 22107-0910 Office Phone: 703-854-6000. Office Fax: 703-854-2053. Business E-Mail: gcishare@gannett.com.

DICKIE, MARTHA S., lawyer; b. July 14, 1956; m. James Rader; children: Clark, Joey. BA in Economics with spl. honors, U. Tex., Austin, 1977, JD, 1980. Bar: Tex. 1980, US Ct. Appeals (5th Cir.), US Dist. Ct. (So. Dist. Tex.), US Dist. Ct. (We. Dist. Tex.). Law clk. to Hon. Jack Roberts US Dist. Ct., 1980—82; atty. Minton Burton Foster and Collins PC, Austin, 1982—2004; of counsel Akin & Almanza, Austin, Tex., 2004, ptnr., 2005—09, Almanza, Blackburn & Dickie LLP, 2010—. Bd. mem. Tex. Alcoholic Beverage Commn., 1994—2000; mem. Tex. Bd. Legal Specialization, 1995—2001. Fellow: Tex. Bar Found. (trustee 1992—95, fellows chair 2003—04); mem.: State Bar Tex. (dir. 1989—92, pres. 2006—07, Pres. Citation 1997, 1998, Outstanding Third Yr. Dir. 1992), Travis County Bar Assn. (pres. criminal law and procedure sect. 1985—86, pres. 1988—89). Office: Almanza Blackburn & Dickie LLP Building H 2301 S Capital Texas Highway Austin TX 78746 Office Phone: 512-474-9486. Office Fax: 512-478-7151. Business E-Mail: mdickie@abdlawfirm.com.

DICKINSON, JESS H., state supreme court justice; b. Charleston, Miss., 1947; m. Janet Holiman; 5 children. BS, Miss. State U., 1978; JD cum laude, U. Miss. Sch. of Law, 1982. Bar: Miss. 1982. Atty. priv. practice, Jackson, Miss., 1982—83, Gulfport, Miss., 1984—2003; judge Forrest and Perry County Circuit Ct.; justice Miss. Supreme Ct., 2004—11, presiding justice, 2011—. Ed. bd. mem. Miss. Law Jour. Mem.: Miss. Bar Assn. (Ethics Com., Professionalism Com.). Office: Miss Supreme Ct PO Box 117 Jackson MS 39205 Office Phone: 601-359-2184. Business E-Mail: jdickinson@mssc.state.ms.us.*

DICKINSON, JODY, state legislator; m. Tommy Dickinson. Mem. Dist. 58 Ark. House of Reps., 2009—. Democrat. Baptist. Mailing: 711 Hodges St Newport AR 72112 Office Phone: 870-523-8222. E-mail: dickinsonj@arkleg.state.ar.us.

DICKINSON, ROBERT EARL, atmospheric scientist, educator, retired science administrator; b. Millersburg, Ohio, Mar. 26, 1940; s. Leonard Earl and Carmen L. (Ostby) D. AB in Chemistry and Physics, Harvard U., 1961; MS in Meteorology, MIT, 1962, PhD in Meteorology, 1966. Rsch. assoc. MIT, Cambridge, 1966-68; scientist Nat. Ctr. Atmospheric Rsch., Boulder, Colo., 1968-73, sr. scientist, 1973-90, head climate sect., 1975-81, dep. dir. A.A.P. divsn., 1981-86, acting dir., 1986-87; prof. atmospheric physics U. Ariz., 1990-93, regents prof., 1993-99; prof. earth and atmospheric scis. Ga. Inst. Tech., Atlanta, 1999—2008; chair Ga. Power/Ga. Rsch. Alliance; prof. U. Tex., Dept. Geologycal Sci., Austin, 2008—. Mem. climate rsch. com. NRC, Washington, 1985-90, chmn., 1987-90, com. earth sci., 1985-88, global change com., 1985-92; mem. WCRP sci. steering group GEWEX, 1988-92; UNU steering com. Climatic, Biotic and Human Interactions in Humid Tropics, 1984-88, steering com. Internat. Satellite Land Surface Climatology project, 1984-89. Editor: The Geophysiology of Amazonia, 1986; contbr. articles to profl. jours. Recipient G. Unger Vetlesen prize, 1996. Fellow AAAS, Am. Meteorol. Soc. (chmn. com. biometeorol. and aerobiol. 1987-89, Meisinger award 1973, Editors award 1976, Jule Charney award 1989, Walter Orr Roberts lectr. in interdisciplinary sci. 1995, Carl-Gustaf Rossby award 1997), Am. Geophys. Union (atmospheric sci. sect. 1986-88, pres.-elect 1988-90, pres. 1990-92, pres.-elect 2000-02, pres. 2002-04, Revelle medal 1996); mem. NAS, NAE, European Geoscis. Union (hon.), Chinese Acad. Scis. (fgn.). Democrat. Office: Ga Inst Tech EAS 311 Ferst Dr Atlanta GA 30332-0340 Home: 2001 S Mo Pac Expy Apt 1024 Austin TX 78746-7000

DICKISON, ALEXANDER KANE, physical science educator; b. Jamaica, NY, Oct. 16, 1943; s. William and Eileen S. (Kane) D.; m. Lois Jean Tansley, Mar. 21, 1967; children: Stephen William, Jonathan Harry. BS, Western Ill. U., Macomb, 1965; MS, Mont. State U., Bozeman, 1968, EdD, 1972. Instr. U. Wis., Green Bay, 1969-72, Mont. State U., Bozeman, 1972-73, Seminole State Coll., Sanford, Fla., 1973—; dept. chmn. phys. scis. Seminole C.C., Sanford, Fla., 1986—2012. Adj. prof. U. Ctrl. Fla., Orlando, 1972-83; del. US-Japan-China Confs. on Physics Tchg., 1989, 91, 93; mem. Fla. Statewide Com. on Common Course Numbering, 1981—2012; reader, table leader Advance Placement Test Readings, 1988-2001; mem. com. on career planning Am. Inst. Physics, 1991-95. Chair Seminole County Hist. Commn., Sanford, 1982—; mem. Citizen com., Expressway Authority, Seminole County, 1989-93; county liason St. John's Water Mgmt. Dist., Seminole County, 1981-91; energy com. East Fla. Regional Planning Com., Seminole county, 1976-82. Mem. NSTA, Am. Physics Soc., Am. Assn. Physics Tchrs. (exec. bd. 1991-95, treas. 1996-2002, v.p. 2007-08, pres. 2009, past pres., 2010, Outstanding Physics Tchr. of Yr. award Fla. sect. 1990, Disting. Svc. award 2003), Fla. Assn. Physics Tchrs. (chmn. 1975-76), Fla. Acad. Scis. (exec. sec. 1986-91, Disting. Svc. award 1993), Fla. Assn. Sci. Tchrs., Sigma Pi Sigma. Avocations: history, outdoors, travel, reading, golf. Office: Seminole State Coll 100 Weldon Blvd Sanford FL 32773-6132 Home: 368 Crystal Ridge Way Lake Mary FL 32746-2726 Business E-Mail: dickisoa@seminolestate.edu.

DICKSON, MARGARET HIGHSMITH, state legislator; b. Fayetteville, NC; m. John Dickson; children: Wyatt, Bright, Seavy. BA, U. NC Chapel Hill, 1971, MA. Owner Cape Fear Broadcasting Co.; former state rep. Dist. 41 NC; state rep. Dist. 44 NC, 2003—09; state senator Dist. 19, 2010—. Democrat. Office: NC State Senate 300 N Salisbury St Rm 300-C Raleigh NC 27603-5925 Office Phone: 919-733-5776. E-mail: Margaret.Dickson@ncleg.net.

DICKSON, REECY L., state legislator; m. Billie C. Dickson; children: Billy C. Jr., Dirk T., Ron H., Roxie J. Former county supt. edn.; mem. Dist. 42 Miss. House of Reps., 1993—, chair select com. on poverty; entrepreneur Glass House Fashions. Mem.: Eastern Star, NAACP. Democrat. Baptist. Mailing: PO Box 293 Macon MS 39341 Office Phone: 662-352-6582, 601-359-9473. Business E-Mail: rdickson@house.ms.gov.

DICKSON, THOMAS WALTER, supermarket chain executive; b. Charlotte, NC, Aug. 17, 1955; s. Rush Stuart and Joanne (Shoemaker) D.; m. Billie Cecelia Seddinger, Sept. 22, 1984; children: William Thomas, Michael Alan. BA in Econs., U. Va., 1977, MBA, 1980. Project mgr. spinning div. American & Efird, Inc., Mount Holly, N.C., 1980-81, project mgr. internat. Manchester, Eng., 1981-82, plant mgr. spinning div. Gastonia, N.C., 1982-84, mgr. Far East ops. Hong Kong, 1984-87, v.p. internat. ops. Mount Holly, 1987—91, exec. v.p., 1991—94, pres., 1994—96; exec. v.p. Ruddick Corp., Charlotte, NC, 1996—97, pres., CEO, 1997—2006, chmn., pres., CEO, 2006—12; chmn., CEO Harris Teeter Supermarkets, Inc. (formerly Ruddick Corp.), Matthews, NC, 2012—. Bd. dirs. Harris Teeter Supermarkets, Inc. (formerly Ruddick Corp.), 1997—. Bd. dirs. Dickson Found., Charlotte, 1983—. Mem. Charlotte Country Club, Linville Golf Club. Republican. Baptist. Office: Harris Teeter Supermarkets Inc 701 Crestdale St Matthews NC 28105 Office Phone: 704-372-5404. Office Fax: 704-372-6409.

DICKSON, TOM S., state legislator; b. Paradise, Pa., Sept. 22, 1945; m. Sherry White; children: James, Matt. BA, Maryville Coll.; M in Edn., Univ. Tenn., Chattanooga; edn. specialist degree, State Univ. We. Ga. Tchr through dep. supt. Whitfield Co. Schs., 1967—98, sch. supt., 1998—2003; mem. Dist. 6 Ga. House Reps., 2005—. Bd. dir. Ga. Fed. Credit Union, Ga. Project, Northwest Ga. United Way; past bd. mem. Ga. Sch. Supt. Assn., Jr. Achievement, Northwest Ga. Healthcare Partnership, Whitfield County Bd. Health. Mem.: Dalton Rotary Club. Republican. Methodist. Office: 5043 Village Dr Cohutta GA 30710 also: Ga House of Reps 245 State Capitol Atlanta GA 30334 Office Phone: 706-694-3908, 404-463-2247. Business E-Mail: tom.dickson@house.ga.gov.

DIDRIKSEN, CALEB H., III, lawyer; b. Cleve., Nov. 3, 1955; s. Caleb H. Jr. and Eleanore Ann (Hoepfl) D.; m. Sondra L. Brown, Apr. 21, 1993; children: Severin, Spencer, Luke, Eliza. BS in Engring., U. Ill., 1977; JD, Tulane U., 1982. Bar: La. 1982, Tex. 1995, US Dist. Ct. (ea., mid. and we. dists.) La. 1982, US Ct. Appeals (5th cir.) 1982, US Supreme Ct. 1987, lic. La. gen. contractor 2009. Assoc. McGlinchey, Stafford, New Orleans, 1982-84, Monroe & Lemann, New Orleans, 1984-88; pvt. practice New Orleans, 1988-89; sr. ptnr. Didriksen & Carbo, New Orleans, 1989—98, Didriksen Law Firm, 1998—. Mem. Boy Scouts-Eagle; scout leader, bd. trustees Munholland United Meth. Ch. Mem. ABA, La. Bar Assn. (asst. grader), New Orleans Bar Assn., Lic. La. Gen. Contractor, Tau Beta Pi, Gamma Epsilon. Avocations: flying, skiing. Home: 231 Garden Rd River Ridge LA 70123 Office Phone: 504-586-1600, 225-644-0444. Business E-Mail: caleb@didriksenlaw.com.*

DIEDRICH, RICHARD JOSEPH, architect; b. South Bend, Ind., May 8, 1936; s. Arthur Joseph and Lucille D.; m. Francyne L. Diedrich (div. 1980); children: Dawn Marie, Lisa Lee, Andrea Lynn; m. Linda P. Diedrich. BArch, U. Ill., 1961, MArch, 1962. Archtl.

designer Richardson Severns Scheeler & Assocs., Champaign, Ill., 1961-62; design critic U. Ill. Sch. Architecture, Champaign, 1961-62; archtl. designer Swensson & Kott, Nashville, 1963-64; architect, v.p. Miller Waltz Diedrich, Architects, Milw., 1965-77; pres. MWD Archs., Atlanta, 1978-80, Diedrich Archs., Atlanta, 1980-97; pres., exec. v.p. Diedrich/NBA, Atlanta, 1997—2002; pres. Diedrich LLC, Atlanta, 2002—. Instr. profl. devel. course Harvard Grad. Sch. Design, 1990-2004, 06. Author: Building Type Basics for Recreational Facilities, 2005, The 19th Hole: Architecture of the Golf Club House, 2008, Legendary Golf Clubhouses of the US and Great Britain, 2012; co-author: Golf Course Development and Real Estate; archtl. works include: Avondale Sta., Med. Ctr. Sta., Atlanta Rapid Transit, S. Miami Sta. of Miami Rapid Transit, Vt. Sunset Sta., L.A. Rapid Transit, Student Ctr., U. Ga., Bloomingdale's Stores, Boca Raton, Palm Beach Gardens, Mall of Am., Neiman Marcus Stores, Scottsdale, Ariz., Troy, Mich., Honolulu, Short Hills, N.J., King of Prussia, Pa., Paramus, N.J., Tampa, Fla., Coral Gables, Fla., Plano, Tex., Orlando, Fla., Grand Cypress Clubhouse, Orlando, English Turn Clubhouse, New Orelans, Golf Club Ga., Atlanta, Country Club North, Dayton, Old Overton Club House, Birmingham, Cherokee Country Club, Atlanta, Naples Nat. Golf Club, Sun City Hilton Head amenity facilities, Aerial Tram, Stone Mountain Park, Atlanta, Village Clubhouse, Kapaulua, Maui, Hawaii. Mem. Whitefish Bay Bd. Appeals, 1968-71; v.p. North Decatur Youth Assn., 1975-76; bd. dirs. Lake Burton Civic Assn., 2002-05; bd. govs. Urban Land Inst. Found., 2006. Margaret T. Biddle scholar, 1960. Fellow: Am. Inst. Arch.; mem. AIA (past pres. Milw. chpt., six design awards, two S.E. regional awards, four Ga. AIA awards), Wis. Architect (past pres.), Urban Land Inst. (gov.) Home and Office: 8 Brookhaven Dr Atlanta GA 30319

DIEHL, LOUIS F., hematologist; b. Trenton, NJ, Apr. 8, 1948; s. Louis and Anna D.; m. Anna Mae, Dec. 3, 1973; children: Megan, Erin. BS, Georgetown U., 1970, MD, 1975. Oncologist Johns Hopkins Oncology Ctr., Balt., 1999—2004, Duke U. Med. Ctr., 2004—.

DIEHL, STEPHEN ANTHONY, government representative; s. Anthony Stephen and Paula (Kula) D.; m. Barbara Lynn Marschman, Aug. 3, 1968. BS, LI U., 1963; postgrad. in bus., NYU, 1967-73. V.p. mktg. dir. Green Point Savs. Bank, Bklyn., 1969—77; sr. v.p., human resources dir. Green Point Bank, NYC, 1977—95. Dir. Human Resources NY Road Runners Club (NY City Marathon), 1996-2001; officer, dir. Soc. for Human Resources Mgmt., NY chpt., 1995-2001; human resources cons., 1997-; town coun. mem., Morrisville, NC, 2009-. Mem. Savs. Banks Mktg. Forum NY State (chmn. 1973-74), NYC Mktg. Forum (chmn. 1975-76), Human Resources Officers Forum (chmn. 1980-81), Savs. Banks Officers Forum (pres. 1986-87). Democrat. Roman Catholic. Avocations: photography, video, stereo. Personal E-mail: sadiehl@aol.com.

DIEHR, BEVERLY HUNT, lawyer; d. Carl William Jr. and Helen Fern (Rouse) Hunt; children: Erin Elizabeth, Sara Katherine, Dana Marie. BA with high honors, U. So. Fla., 1975; JD with high honors, U. Fla., 1978. Bar: Fla. 1978, U.S. Dist. Ct. (mid. dist.) Fla. 1979. Staff atty. Three Rivers Legal Svcs. Inc., Gainesville, Fla., 1979-82; assoc. Sessums and McCall, Tampa, 1982-83; asst. dist. legal counsel dist. 6 Fla. Dept. Health and Rehab. Svcs., Tampa, 1983-84; pvt. practice law Tampa, 1984—2004; sr. atty. Fla. Dept. Children and Families, 2004—10; chief legal counsel Fla. dept. health Hillsboraugh, Nonatee, Pinellas & Pasco County Health Dept., 2010—. Mem. Parents Adv. Bd., 1996—98, Beach Pk. Homeowners' Assn.; troop leader Girl Scouts US, 1993—97; bd. mem. Acad. Holy Names' Mothers' Assn., 1995—2001, v.p., 1996—97, pres., 1997—98. Mem. Fla. Bar Assn., Hillsborough County Bar Assn., Fla. Assn. Women Lawyers, Hillsborough Assn. Women Lawyers, Order of Coif. Democrat. Roman Catholic. Home: 4301 W Cleveland St Tampa FL 33609-3867

DIENER, BETTY JANE, business educator; b. Washington, Sept. 15, 1940; d. Edward George and Minnie (Feild) Diener; m. Robert D. Bell, 1987 (dec. 1993). AB, Wellesley Coll., 1962; MBA, Harvard U., 1964, DBA, 1974. Account exec. Young & Rubicam, Inc., NYC, 1964-70; product mgr. Am. Cyanamid Co., Wayne, NJ, 1970-72; asst. dean Sch. Bus. Case Western Res. U., Cleve., 1974-79; dean Sch. Bus. Adminstrn. Old Dominion U., Norfolk, Va., 1986-87; provost, vice-chancellor acad. affairs U. Mass., Boston, 1987-88, prof. mktg., 1987—2002, spl. asst. to chancellor econ. devel., 1993-94; prof., mgmt. Barry U., Miami Shores, Fla., 2002—. Pres. Environ. Bus. Coun. New Eng., Inc., 1995—97. Contbr. articles to profl. publs. Mem. Citizens Coun. Chesapeake Bay, 1986—87; adviser Jr. League, 1963—64, Plans for Progress, 1968—70, Leadership Met. Richmond, 1980—82; mem. Mass. Gov.'s Adv. Com. Sci. and Tech., 1988—90, Mayor's Task Force Empowerment Zones, 1994; mem. cmty. working group Mass. Mil. Reservation, 1997—2000; pres. Provincetown (Mass.) Repertory Theater, 2002, bd. dirs., 2001—03; commr. Norfolk Indsl. Devel. Authority, 1979—82; bd. dirs. Norfolk Conv. and Visitors Bur., 1979—82, Norfolk C. of C., 1979—82, Greater Norfolk Corp., 1986—87, Va. Orch. Group, 1982—87, Va. Stage Co., 1986—87, Karamu Ho., 1975—79, Woodruff Hosp., 1975—79, Women's City Club Cleve., 1976—79, Coun. Sustainable Fla., 2003—07, Bainbridge Grad. Inst., 2003—05; mem. adv. com. state and local govt. programs John F. Kennedy Sch. Govt., Harvard U., 1986—88. Recipient Honor award, Soil Conservation Soc., 1984; named Outstanding Working Woman, Glamour Mag., 1979; named one of 10 Outstanding Career Women of Decade, 1984; Fulbright scholar, China, 2001, India, 2009. Democrat. Office: Barry Univ Andreas Sch of Business Miami Shores FL 33161 Home: 4000 Towerside Ter Apt 1108 Miami FL 33138-2238 Personal E-mail: bejade@aol.com.

DIETEL, WILLIAM MOORE, former foundation executive; b. Islip, NY, Aug. 14, 1927; s. Frederick William and Zillah Yolanda (Vannuccini) D.; m. Linda Remington, June 16, 1951; children: Elizabeth Lynn, Cynthia Lyon, Lisa Remington, John Frederick, Victoria Moore. AB, Princeton U., 1950; MA, Yale U., 1952, PhD, 1959; postgrad., London U. Inst. Hist. Research, 1953-54. Instr. history U. Mass., Amherst, 1954-59; asst. dean of coll., asst. prof. humanities Amherst Coll., 1959-61; prin. Emma Willard Sch., Troy, NY, 1961-70; pres. Rockefeller Bros. Fund, NYC, 1975-87; sr. ptnr. Dietel Ptnrs. LLC, Fruit Hill. With Brain Mapping Med. Rsch. Ctr., LA; chmn.; adv. counsel Inst. for Philanthropy, London; internat. adv. com. Johns Hopkins UN Project; sr. counselor Mayday Fund; trustee F.B. Heron Found., mem. Am. Adv. Com., Courtauld Inst. Patron, Darlington Trust. Mem. Univ. Club (N.Y.C.), Cosmos Club (Washington). Office: PO Box 309 Flint Hill VA 22627-0309

DIETHELM, ARNOLD GILLESPIE, surgeon; b. Balt., Jan. 13, 1932; s. Oskar Arnold and Grace (Gillespie) D.; m. Nancy Lee Lane, June 21, 1951; children: Nancy Elizabeth, Linda Lane, Eugene Arnold (dec.), Ellen Jeanette, Richard Gillespie. AB, Wash. State U., 1953; MD, Cornell U., 1958; DSc (hon.), U. Ala., 1993. Intern, then resident in surgery NY Hosp., 1958-65; asst. in surgery, research fellow Peter Bent Brigham Hosp., Boston, 1965-66; research fellow surgery Harvard U. Med. Sch., 1966-67; instr. Cornell U. Med. Sch., 1964-65; mem. faculty U. Ala. Med. Center, Birmingham, 1967—, prof. surgery, 1973—, vice chmn. dept., 1973-82, chmn. dept. surgery, 1982-2000; prof. emeritus dept. surgery U. Ala. Sch. Medicine. Mem. residency rev. com. for surgery Accreditation Coun. for Grad. Med. Edn., 1994—, chmn., 1997-99. Contbr. articles med. jours. Mem. AAAS, ACS., AMA, Am. Soc. Nephrology, Am. Soc. Transplant Surgeons (pres. 1991-92), Am. Surg. Assn., Am. Bd. Surgery (dir. 1987-93), Assn. Acad. Surgery, Transplantation Soc., So. Surg. Assn. (pres. 1989). Home: 3248 Sterling Rd Birmingham AL 35213-3508 Office: U Ala Hosp Dept Surgery 619 19th St S Birmingham AL 35233-0001

DIETZ, DAVID W., elementary school educator; Tchr. Gainsville Jr. HS, 1975—. Recipient Tchr. Excellence award Internat. Tech. Edn. Assn., 1992. Office: Gainesville Jr HS 1201 S Lindsay St Gainesville TX 76240-5661

DIETZ, WILLIAM HARRY, pediatrician; b. Phila., Oct. 6, 1944; s. William H. and Margaret (Shoemaker) Dietz; m. Nancy Fenn, May 6, 1966. BA, Wesleyan U., 1966; MD, U. Pa., 1970; PhD, MIT, 1981. Diplomate Am. Bd. Pediatrics. Intern Children's Hosp. Phila., 1970-71; resident Upstate Med. Ctr., Syracuse, NY, 1974-76; rsch. assoc. NIH, 1971-74, MIT, Cambridge, 1976-81; assoc. prof. Tufts U. Sch. Medicine, Boston, 1986-96, prof., 1996-98; dir. clin. nutrition New England Med. Ctr., Boston, 1983-97. Adj. prof. Tufts U. Sch. Medicine, Boston, 1998—. Fellow: Am. Acad. Pediat. (chmn. task force on children and TV, Elk Grove Village, Ill. 1984—87); mem.: Nat. Acad. Scis., Inst. Medicine, Am. Dietetic Assn. (hon.), N.Am. Assn. Study Obesity (pres. 1993—94), Am. Soc. Clin. Nutrition (v.p. 1998—99, pres. 1999—2000, counselor). Office: CDC Divsn Nutrition Phys Act Obesity 4770 Buford Hwy NE # MS-K24 Atlanta GA 30341-3717 Office Phone: 770-488-6042. Business E-Mail: wcd4@cdc.gov.

DIGNAC, GENY (EUGENIA M. BERMUDEZ), sculptor; b. Buenos Aires, June 8, 1932; came to U.S., 1954; d. Jose Victor Marenco and Margarita Eugenia D.; m. Jose Y. Bermudez, Apr. 7, 1958; children— Alexander, Melanie. Student, U. Buenos Aires, 1952-54. Lectr. in field. Exhibited in one-woman shows at Galeria 22, Caracas, Venezuela, 1967, Michael Berger Gallery, Pitts., 1969, Cinema 2, Caracas, 1971, Pyramid Gallery, Washington, 1971; exhibited in numerous group shows including Corcoran Gallery of Art, Washington, 1958, 59, Inst. Contemporary Arts, Washington, 1967, Bklyn. Mus., 1968, Mus. Modern Art, Buenos Aires, 1971, Mus. Fine Arts, Boston, 1971, Palais des Beaux Arts, Brussels, 1974, Inst. Contemporary Arts, London, 1974; represented in permanent collections including Fundacio Joan Miro, Barcelona, Spain, Palazzo Dei Diamanti, Ferrara, Italy, Museo La Tertulia, Cali, Colombia, Galeria del Banco Central, Guayaquil, Ecuador, The Latinoamerican Art Found., San Juan, P.R., and others in Argentina, Chile, Germany, Italy, Ireland, Spain, U.S. and Venezuela; works include 30 Fire Gestures-, 1970-2008; radio and TV interviews, U.S. and abroad; works with lights, fire and temperatures; subject of profl. articles, films. Recipient prize for light sculpture IX Festival of Art, 1969 Home: 4109 E Via Estrella Phoenix AZ 85028-4515 Office: Alejandra Von Hartz Gallery 2630 NW 2nd Ave Miami FL 33127 also: Osuna Art 7200 Wisconsin Ave Bethesda MD 20814 E-mail: gdignac@aol.com.

DILCHER, DAVID LEONARD, paleobotany educator, researcher; b. Cedar Falls, Iowa, July 10, 1936; m. Katherine Swanson, 1961; children: Peter, Ann. BS in Natural History, U. Minn., 1958, MS in Botany, Geology and Zoology, 1960; postgrad., U. Ill., 1960-62; PhD in Biology, Geology, Yale U., 1964; participant OTS course field dendrology, Costa Rica, 1968; D honoris causa (hon.), Lyon U. 1, France, 2007. Teaching asst. U. Minn., Mpls., 1958-60, U. Ill., Urbana, 1960-62, Yale U., New Haven, Conn., 1962-63, Cullman-Univ. fellow, 1963-64, instr. biology, 1965-66; NSF postdoctoral fellow Senckenberg Mus., Frankfurt am Main, Fed. Republic of Germany, 1964-65; asst. prof. botany Ind. U., Bloomington, 1966-70, assoc. prof., 1970-76; Guggenheim fellow Imperial Coll., Univ. London, 1972-73; assoc. prof. geology Ind. U., Bloomington, 1975-77, prof. paleobotany, 1977-90, adj. prof. biology, adj. prof. geology, 1990—; grad. rsch. prof. Fla. Mus. Natural History, U. Fla., Gainesville, 1990—. Panel mem. for systematic biology program, NSF, 1977-79, panel mem. for selecting NATO postdoctoral fellow, 1982, mem. adv. com. Earth Sys. History, 1997-2000, bd. mem. on earth scis. and resources NRC, 2001-04; vis. lectr. to People's Republic of China Nat. Acad. Sci. com. on scholarly communications with China, 1986; corr. mem. Senckenberg Mus., Frankfurt, Fed. Republic Germany, 1989; hon. prof. Nanjing Inst. Geology and Paleontology, Acad. Sinica, China, 1998—, Jilin U., Changchau, China, 2001—; adj. prof. biology U. Tenn., Martin, 2000—; hon. prof., vice chmn. sci. com. rsch. ctr. paleontoloty and stratigraphy Jilin U., Changchun, China, 2001—; bd. dirs. Smithsonian Inst., 1998-2006; prof. Rsch. Found. Univ. Fla., 2004—. Author: (with D. Redmon, M. Tansey and D. Whitehead) Plant Biology Laboratory Manual, 1973, 2d edit., 1975; editor: (with Tom Taylor and Theodore Delevoryas) Plant Reproduction in the Fossil Record, symposium vol., 1979; (with T. Taylor) Biostratigraphy of Fossil Plants: Successional and Paleoecological Analysis, 1980; (with William L. Crepet) Origin and Evolution of Flowering Plants, Symposium Volume, 1984; (with Michael S. Zavada) Phylogeny of the Hamamedidae, symposium vol., 1986; (with Patrick S. Herendeen) Advances in Legume Systematics Part 4, The Fossil Record, 1992; mem. edilt. bd. Taxon, 2004—; contbr. over 200 articles to profl. jours. Mem. utilities bd. City of Bloomington, 1974-76; ruling elder First Presbyn. Ch. Bloomington, 1975-77; bd. dirs. United Campus Ministries, 1971-72, Smithsonian Mus. Natural History, 1998—; mem. coun. Monroe County United Ministries, 1975-77. Dist. Vis. Rsch. scholar U. Adelaide, Australia, 1981, 88; Vis. Rsch. scholar Birbal Sahni Palaeonbot. Inst., Lucknow, India, 1992; grantee Sigma Xi, 1961-62, 66, Ind. U., 1967-68, Orgn. Tropical Studies, 1971, Travel grantee Ind. U., 1968, 71, 77, 80, Rsch. grantee NSF, 1966-89, 96—, Amax Coal Found., 1980-81, NATO Coop, 1991-93; Eaton-Hooker fellow, 1963, Cullman-Univ. fellow, 1963-64, Guggenheim fellow, Giessen, Fed. Republic of Germany, 1972-73, Ind. U., 1972-73, Brit. Mus. Natural History, London, 1988-89; recipient Tracey M. Sonneborn award for disting. rsch. and excellenc in tchg. Ind. U., 1978-88, Bot. Soc. Am. Merit award, 1991, Birbal Sahni Found. award, 1998, U. Fla. Rsch. Found. Professorship award, 2004-06, Outstanding Palaeobotanist award Indian Palaeontological Soc., 2005, Mt. Changbai Friendship cup, Jilin Province China, 2006; hon. prof. Honzhou U., China, 2007; Doctorats Hon. Causa 2, U. Claude Bernard Lyon 1, France. Fellow Ind. Acad. Sci.; mem. NAS, AAAS, Bot. Soc. Am. (chmn. paleobot. sect. 1974, sec.-treas. 1975-77, rep. to jour. editl. bd. 1978-79, jour. editl. bd. 1981-82, conservation com. 1978-81, chmn. conservation com. 1981, 82, program dir. 1982-84, exec. bd. 1982-91, sec. 1984-88, pres.-elect 1988-89, pres. 1989-90), Paleontol. Soc., Paleontol. Assn., Internat. Orgn. Paleobotany (N.Am. rep. 1975-81, v.p. 1987-93), Assn. Tropical Biology, Am. Inst. Biol. Scis., Am. Assn. Stratigraphic Palynologists, Internat. Assn. Angiosperm Paleobotany (pres. 1977-80), Geol. Soc. Am. (com. on collection and collecting 1978-85), Ky. Acad. Scis., Senckenberg Natur Mus. und Forschungsgeshellshaft Frankfurt am Main (corr. mem. 1990), Sigma Xi (pres.-elect Ind. chpt. 1985-86, pres. 1986-87). Office: 2260 E Cape Cod Dr Bloomington IN 47401

DILG, JOSEPH CARL, lawyer; b. Dallas, Apr. 1, 1951; s. Millard John and Helen Mary (Gill) D.; m. Alexandra Gregg, Aug. 5, 1972; children: Helen Lane, Mary Saunders. BA in Economics, So. Meth. U., Dallas, 1973; JD with high honors, U. Tex. Sch. Law, 1976. Bar: Tex. 1976. Assoc. Vinson & Elkins, Houston, 1976—83, ptnr., 1983—2002, mng. ptnr., 2002—. Editor: U. Tex. Law Rev., 1976 (Outstanding Editor award, 1976). Trustee U. Tex. Law Sch. Found.; bd. dirs. Greater Houston Partnership, Houston Arts Alliance; chmn. exec. com. Bus. Com. for Arts, Inc. Named one of The Best Lawyers in America in Corp., M&A and Securities Law, 1993—2011, The Best Lawyers in America in Corp., Internat. Trade and Fin. Law, 2003—11, The Best Lawyers in America in Corp., Energy Law, 2007—11, The World's Leading Lawyers for Bus. in Corp./M&A Law, Chambers Global, 2002—05, The World's Leading Lawyers for Bus. in Energy Law, 2002—07, 2009, 2010, America's Leading Bus. Lawyers in Corp., Energy & Natural Resources Law, Chambers USA, 2003—09. Office: Vinson & Elkins LLP 3401 First City Tower 1001 Fannin St Ste 2500 Houston TX 77002-6760 Business E-Mail: jdilg@velaw.com.

DILL, DAVID M., hospital administrator; Exec. v.p., N.Am. Fresenius Med. Care Svcs. (subs. Fresenius Medical Care AG & Co. KGaA.); various fin., acctg. positions Renal Care Group, Inc. (acquired by Fresenius Med. Care Svcs.), 1996—2003, exec. v.p., CFO & treas., 2003—06; CEO, East Divsn. Fresenius Med. Care Svcs. (subs. Fresenius Medical Care AG & Co. KGaA.), 2006—07; CFO LifePoint Hosps., Inc., 2007—09; exec. v.p. LifePoint Hospitals, Inc., 2007—11, COO, 2009—, pres., 2011—. Bd. dirs. Psychiatric Solutions, Inc, 2005. Office: LifePoint Hospitals Inc 103 Powell Ct Ste 200 Brentwood TN 37027 Office Phone: 615-372-8500. Office Fax: 615-372-8575. Business E-Mail: david.dill@lpnt.net.

DILLARD, ALEX, retail executive; BA, Univ. Ark., 1971; JD, Univ. Tex., 1974. Bd. dir. Dillard's, Inc., Little Rock, 1975—, mgmt. positions through exec. v.p., pres., 1998—. Bd. dir. First Nat. Bank, Ft. Worth, Union Bank, Worthen Bank, Little Rock. Bd. dir. Med. Sciences Found. Fund, Univ. Ark., Philander Smith Coll. Office: Dillard's Inc 1600 Cantrell Rd Little Rock AR 72201-1110

DILLARD, CHANDRA ELISA, state legislator; b. Greenville, SC, Mar. 10, 1965; d. Moses C. and Vera H. Dillard. BS, Winthrop U., 1987; MA in Pub. Policy, Walden U., 2008. Bd. mem. Greenville County Libr. Bd., Greenville, SC, 1997—99, Phyllis Wheatley Assn., 1999—, The U. Ctr., 2003—; mem. Alliance for Quality Edn., 2000—03, Greenville Housing Fund, Greenville, SC, 2007—, Genesis Homes CDC, 2007—, Greenville City Coun., Greenville, SC, 1999—2008, Generations Group Homes, 2000—04, Mcpl. Assn. of SC, SC, 2006—08, United Way of Greenville Co., Greenville, SC, 2005—, Greenville Forward, Greenville, SC, 2007—; pres. Conf. of Black Mcpl. Elected Officals, 2006—08; adv. bd. mem. Bank of Travelers Rest, 2007—; dir. of cmty. rels. Furman U.; mem. Dist. 23 SC House of Reps., SC, 2008—. Democrat. Meth. Home: Home Office 5 Alleta Ave Greenville SC 29607 Office: PO Box 2207 Greenville SC 29602 also: Capitol Office 414D Blatt Bldg Columbia SC 29201 Home Phone: 864-233-6549; Office Phone: 864-294-2503, 864-467-4431, 803-212-6791. Office Fax: 864-467-5725. E-mail: dillarc@greatergreenville.com, chandradillard@schouse.org.

DILLARD, STEPHEN C., lawyer; b. Tyler, Tex., Nov. 1, 1946; BA, Baylor U., 1968, JD, 1971. Bar: Tex. 1971. Ptnr. Fulbright & Jaworski LLP, Houston, 1978—, chair, global litig. dept., 2004—11, mem. exec. com. Named a Tex. Super Lawyer, Tex. Monthly Mag., 2003, 2004, 2005, 2006, 2007—13. Fellow: Am. Bd. Trial Advs. (adv.), Internat. Assn. Def. Counsel, Am. Coll. Trial Lawyers (life), Tex. Bar Found. (life); mem.: ABA, Internat. Acad. Trial Lawyers, Houston Bar Assn., Tex. Assn. Def. Counsel, State Bar Tex., Phi Alpha Delta (v.p. 1984—87). Office: Fulbright & Jaworski LLP 1301 McKinney St Ste 5100 Houston TX 77010-3031 Office Phone: 713-651-5507, 713-651-5507. Office Fax: 713-651-5246.

DILLARD, WILLIAM, II, retail executive; b. 1945; married. Grad., U. Ark.; MBA, Harvard U. With Dillard Department Stores, Little Rock, 1967—, dir., 1968—, exec. v.p., 1973-77, pres. and COO, 1977—98, CEO, 1998—, chmn., 2002—. Nat. adv. bd. JPMorgan-Chase & Co., Dallas Region adv. bd.; dir. Acxiom Corp. Office: Dillard Dept Stores Inc 1600 Cantrell Rd Little Rock AR 72201-1110

DILLE, JOHN ROBERT, retired physician; b. Waynesbur, Pa., Sept. 2, 1931; s. Charles Emanuel and Ruth Emma (South) D.; m. Joan Marie Sirtosky, Dec. 17, 1955 (wid. Mar. 1996); children: Paul Andrew, John Alan. BS, Waynesburg Coll., Pa., 1952; MD, U. Pitts., 1956; M in Indsl. Health, Harvard U., Cambridge, Mass., 1960. Diplomate Am. Bd. Preventive Medicine. Intern Akron City Hosp., 1956-57; resident in aerospace medicine USAF Sch. Aerospace Medicine, San Antonio, 1960-62; program adv. officer FAA Civil Aeromed. Rsch. Inst., Oklahoma City, 1961-64; western region flight surgeon FAA, LA, 1965; chief FAA Civil Aeromed. Inst., US Dept. Transp., Oklahoma City, 1966-87, ret., 1987; med. dir. Okla. Dept. Corrections, Oklahoma City, 1990-93. Assoc. prof. U. Okla., 1961-98, dir. tng. residency in aerospace medicine, 1967-72; state surgeon Okla. Army N.G., 1990-91; surveyor Nat. Commn. on Correctional Health Care, 2000-04. Assoc. editor: Ag Pilot Internat. mag., 1980-98, Conservation Aeronautics mag., 1989-92, Above All mag., 1992; mem. editorial bd. Aviation, Space and Environ. Medicine, 1987-94; contbr. chpts. to textbooks and articles to profl. jours. With USAF, 1957-59; col. M.C., US Army N.G., 1976-91. Recipient Meritorious award William A. Jump Found., 1968; named Army N.G. Flight Surgeon of Yr. 1987, Master Flight Surgeon, 1987. Fellow: Am. Coll. Preventive Medicine (regent 1974—77), Aerospace Med. Assn. (mem. exec. coun. 1978—81, chmn. history and archives com. 1982—90, chmn. sci. program com. 1985, 1st v.p. 1990—91, pres. 1992—93, mem. exec. coun. 1993—98, chmn. nominating com. 1997—98, Theodore C. Lyster award 1978, Harry G. Moseley award 1987, Armstrong lectr. 1997, Marie Marvingt award 2008); mem.: Descendants Founders NJ, Am. Soc. Aerospace Medicine Specialists, Res. Officers Assn. (state surgeon Okla. dept. 2002—07, 2009, 2011—), Am. Air Mail Soc. (bd. dir. 1990—92, sec. 2012—), Soc. US Army Flight Surgeons (bd. govs. 1990—92, Order Aeromed. Merit), Internat. Acad. Aviation and Space Medicine, Mil. and Hospitaller Order St. Lazarus of Jerusalem commandary of Midwest (knight, hospitaller), Sigma Xi, Nu Sigma Nu. Presbyterian. Home: 335 Merkle Dr Norman OK 73069-6429 Personal E-mail: jrobtdille1@aol.com.

DILLER, KENNETH RAY, mechanical and biomedical engineer, educator; b. Wooster, Ohio, Nov. 20, 1942; married, 1967; 3 children. BME, Ohio State U., 1966, MSc, 1967; ScD, MIT, 1972. Rsch. assoc. biomed. engring. MIT, 1972-73; from asst. prof. to assoc. prof. mech. engring. U. Tex., Austin, 1973-84, prof. mech. & biomed. engring., 1984—. Alexander Von Humboldt fellow, Germany, 1983-84. Mem. AAAS, ASME (heat transfer mem. award 1994), Soc. Cryobiol. (treas. 1974-75, pres. 1994-95), Microcirculation Soc. Achievements include research in study of energy processes in living systems involving transport of heat and mass; applications include microscopic evaluation of burn injury process and frozen preservation of living tissues and organs; computer modelling and computerized analysis of biomedical images. Office: U Tex Dept Mech Engring Austin TX 78712-1063

DILLEY, KATHLEEN A., food service executive; V.p. retail ops. Cracker Barrel Old Country Store, Inc. Office: Cracker Barrel Old Country Store Inc 305 Hartmann Dr Lebanon TN 37087 Office Phone: 615-444-5533. Office Fax: 615-443-9476.

DILLIN, JOHN WOODWARD, JR., retired editor, reporter; b. Miami, Fla., July 6, 1936; s. John Woodward and Alberta (Thompson) D.; m. Gay Andrews, Oct. 1, 1966 (div. 1988); 1 child, Katherine. BSJ. with honors, U. Fla., 1958, postgrad. in U.S. history, 1961-63. Reporter St. Augustine Record, Fla., 1958, Tampa Tribune, Fla., 1960-61; with Christian Sci. Monitor, 1964—, reporter Boston, 1964-66, corr. Saigon, Vietnam, 1966-67, city editor Boston, 1967-71, corr. Atlanta and Washington, 1971-79, mng. editor for news Boston, 1979-83, nat. polit. corr. Washington, 1983-94, mng. editor Boston, 1994-99, assoc. editor, Washington bur. chief Washington, 1999—, ret., 2001. Served with AUS, 1958-59 Recipient Sigma Delta Chi award for Washington Corr., 1993; named Alumnus of Distinction, Coll. Journalism and Comms., U. Fla., 2002. Christian Scientist. Home: 5525 15th St N Arlington VA 22205-2712 Personal E-mail: rotag36@gmail.com.

DILLINGHAM, WILLIAM BYRON, literature educator, author; b. Atlanta, Mar. 7, 1930; s. Cornelius Howard and Emerald (Storey) D.; m. Marion Elizabeth Joiner, July 3, 1952; children: Rebecca Lynn, Judith Ann, Paul Christopher. BA, Emory U., 1955, MA, 1956; PhD, U. Pa., 1961. Instr. Emory U., Atlanta, 1956-62, asst. prof., 1962-66, assoc. prof., 1966-68, prof., 1968-84, chair. dept. English, 1979-82, 85-86, 90-91, Charles Howard Candler prof. Am. lit., 1984-96; prof. emeritus, 1996—. Author: Frank Norris: Instinct and Art, 1969, An Artist in the Rigging, 1972, Melville's Short Fiction, 1977, Melville's Later Novels, 1986, Melville and His Circle: The Last Years, 1996, Rudyard Kipling: Hell and Heroism, 2005, Being Kipling, 2008; co-author: Humor of the Old Southwest, 1964, 3d edit., 1994, Practical English Handbook, 10th edit., 1996, Rudyard Kipling: Life Love & Art, 2013; mem. editl. bd. Nineteenth-Century Lit., 1990-97, South Atlantic Rev., 1986-89, Frank Norris Studies, 1986-94. With US Army, 1950—52. Recipient Fulbright award, U.S. Govt., 1964—65, award of distinction, Emory U., 2000, Disting. Emeritus award, 2004, Choice award, 2005, 2007, 2013; fellow, Guggenheim Found., 1982—83; Sr. fellow, NEH, 1978—79, Heilbrun Disting. Emeritus fellow, 2002—03. Mem. MLA (mem. adv. coun. Am. lit. sect. 1988-90), Nat. Assn. Scholars, Soc. Lit. Scholars and Critics, Frank Norris Soc., Melville Soc. (pres. 1987), Kipling Soc., Phi Beta Kappa, Omicron Delta Kappa. Home: 1416 Vista Leaf Dr Decatur GA 30033-2012 Business E-Mail: wdillin@emory.edu.

DILLON, DAVID ANTHONY, editor, educator; b. Fitchburg, Mass., Aug. 24, 1947; s. John Joseph and Lauretta Irene (Morris) D.; m. Sally Ann Hall, June 5, 1971; children: Christopher, Catherine. BA, Boston Coll., 1963; MA, Harvard U., 1965, PhD, 1972. Asst. prof. So. Meth. U., Dallas, 1970-77; mag. editor D Mag., Dallas, 1978-81; archtl. editor Dallas Morning News, 1983—. Author: Experience and Expression, 1976, Dallas Architecture, 1986, Extending the Legacy: Planning America's Capital in the 21st Century, 1997, The Architecture of O'Neil Ford, 1999; contbg. editor Texas Architect, Landscape Architecture, 1990—, Archtl. Record, 1996—. Loeb fellow Harvard U., 1986-87; NEA Critic's grantee, 1980; recipient AP award for criticism, 1988, 90, 91, 2002. Democrat. Roman Catholic. Home: PO Box 3323 Amherst MA 01004-3323 Office: The Dallas Morning News 508 Young St Dallas TX 75202-4828 Office Phone: 207-522-4392. Business E-Mail: ddillon@dallasnews.com. E-mail: davidadillon@verzon.net.

DILLON, DONALD WARD, management consultant; b. Wichita, Kans., Jan. 31, 1936; s. Maurice B. and Helen M. (Ward) D.; m. Jacquelyn A. Hicks, Dec. 28, 1958; m. Brenda Marie Rager, July 9, 1983. B.Music Edn., Wichita State U., 1959, M.Music Edn., 1961; D.Music. Edn., U. Okla., 1970. Tchr. music Derby (Kans.) public schs., 1959-66; mem. faculty Southeastern La. U., Hammond, 1968-69; exec. dir. Okla. Arts and Humanities Council, 1969-73; asst. dir. fed.-state partnership Nat. Endowment Arts, Washington, 1973-79, dir. grants office, 1979; exec. dir. Music Educators Nat. Conf., Reston, Va., 1979-83; pres. Don Dillon Assocs. Inc., Dallas, 1983—2006, Dillon Exec. Svcs. LLC, 2006—09; ret., 2009—; pub. and ednl. cons. Sebilius Music, 2009—. Exec. mgmt. cons., bd.dirs. Fund Advancement Music Edn., 1979—83 Exec. editor: Music Educators Jour, 1979—83, Design for Arts Edn, 1980—83; Contbr. articles profl. jours. Bd. dirs. Nat. Com. Arts for Handicapped, 1980—83. Recipient Svc. award, NAMM Music Industry, 2010. Mem. Am. Soc. Assn. Execs., Inst. Assn. Mgmt. Cos., Meeting Planners Internat. Statis. Analyst, Piano Mfrs. Assn. Internat., Major Orch. Librs.' Assn. (bookkeeper), North American Saxophone Alliance (bookkeeper). Home: 6805 Lebanon Rd Apt 1522 Frisco TX 75034 Personal E-mail: don@dondillon.com.

DILLON, ROBERT SHERWOOD, retired diplomat; b. Chgo., Jan. 7, 1929; s. Dale Crowell and Viola May (Sherwood)D.; m. Caroline Sue Burch, June 16, 1951 (dec. Jan. 16, 2013); children: Dale, Robert Jr., John, Elizabeth, Thomas. BA, Duke U., 1951; postgrad., Princeton U., 1958-59. Ops. officer CIA, 1951-56; officer US Consulate, Puerto La Cruz, Venezuela, 1956—58, econ. officer Izmir, Turkey, 1960—62; polit. officer US Embassy, Ankara, Turkey, 1962—66; spl. asst. to under sec. for polit. affairs US Dept. State, Washington, 1968—69, dir. Turkish affairs, 1971—74; dep. prin. officer US Consulate Gen., Istanbul, Turkey, 1970—71; dep. chief of mission US Embassy, Kuala Lumpur, Malaysia, 1974—77, Ankara, Turkey, 1977—80, Cairo, 1980—81; US amb. to Lebanon US Dept. State, Lebanon, 1981—83; asst. sec. gen. UN, Vienna, 1984-88; pres. American-Middle East Ednl. & Tng. Services, Washington, 1988-95; officer US Dept. State, 1956—83. UN spl. humanitarian envoy for Rwanda & Burundi, 1994; advisor US Dept. State, 1995-96. Author: One of the Very Best Men, 2004, An American Soldier in World War I, 2005. Cpl. U.S. Army, 1947-48. Recipient Presdl. Honor award, White House, 1983.

DILORENZO, FRANCIS X., bishop; b. Phila., Apr. 15, 1942; s. Samuel and Anna (Porrino) DiLorenzo. STL, Pontifical U. of St. Thomas Aquinas, STD, 1975. Ordained priest Archdiocese of Phila., 1968; chaplain & instr. theology St. Pius X H.S., Pottstown, Pa., 1975—77; chaplain & assoc. prof. moral theology Immaculata Coll., Pa., 1977—83; vice rector St. Charles Borromeo Sem., Wynnewood, Pa., 1983—85, rector, 1985—88; ordained bishop, 1988; aux. bishop Diocese of Scranton, Pa., 1988—93; apostolic adminstr. Diocese of Honolulu, Hawaii, 1993-94, bishop, 1994—2004, Diocese of Richmond, Va., 2004—. Mem.: US Conf. Cath. Bishops (mem. adminstrv. com., chmn. com. on sci. & human values). Roman Catholic. Office: Catholic Diocese Of Richmond 7800 Carousel Ln Henrico VA 23294-4201 Office Phone: 804-359-5661. Office Fax: 804-358-9159. E-mail: bishopdilorenzo@richmonddiocese.org.

DIMICCO, DANIEL R., manufacturing executive; BS in Engring., Metallurgy and Materials Sci., Brown U., Providence, 1972; MS in Metallurgy and Materials Sci., U. Pa., Phila., 1975. Rsch. metallurgist, project leader Republic Steel, Cleve., 1975—82; plant metallurgist, mgr. quality control Nucor Steel, Plymouth, Utah, 1982—88, mgr. melting and casting Utah divsn., 1988—91; gen. mgr. Nucor-Yamato, Blytheville, Ark., 1991—92, v.p., 1992—99, exec. v.p., 1999—2000; pres., CEO Nucor Corp., Charlotte, NC, 2000—06, vice chmn., 2001—06, chmn., pres., CEO, 2006—11, chmn., CEO, 2011—. Office: Nucor Corp 1915 Rexford Rd Charlotte NC 28211 Office Phone: 704-366-7000. Office Fax: 704-362-4208.

DIMINO, JOSEPH C., lawyer; b. Rochester, NY, 1952; BA summa cum laude, U. Rochester, 1973; JD, U. Va., 1976. Aty. Norfolk Southern Corp., Va., corp. gen. counsel, 2000—02, sr. gen. counsel, 2002—05, v.p., corp. counsel, 2005—; v.p. Compliance, 2007, Audit & Compliance, 2008. ABA Office: Norfolk Southern Corp 3 Commerical Pl Norfolk VA 23510-2191 Office Phone: 757-629-2816.

DIMITROFF, THOMAS G., JR., professional sports team executive; b. Barbeton, Ohio, July 14, 1966; s. Thomas Dimitroff; m. Angeline Dimitroff, 2005. Attended, Guelph Coll., Can. Scouting coord. Saskatchewan Roughriders; part-time scout Kans. City Chiefs, 1993; area scout Detroit Lions, 1994—97; with scouting dept. Cleve. Browns, 1998—2001; nat. scout New Eng. Patriots, 2002—03, dir., coll. scouting, 2003—08; gen. mgr. Atlanta Falcons, 2008—. Named NFL Exec. of Yr., The Sporting News, 2009. Office: Atlanta Falcons Georgia Dome One Georgia Dome Dr NW Atlanta GA 30313

DIMITROULEAS, WILLIAM PETER, federal judge; b. Lynn, Mass., Mar. 28, 1951; s. Leo Peter and Mary (Kakatolis) Dimitrouleas; m. Linda Ruth Loughlin, Feb. 25, 1982 (div. Sept. 1982); m. Natalie Laine Barone, Mar. 26, 1985; 1 child, Scott. BA, Furman U., 1973; JD, U. Fla., 1975. Bar: Fla. 1976, U.S. Dist. Ct. (so. dist.) Fla. 1976. Asst. pub. defender Office Pub. Defender, Ft. Lauderdale, Fla., 1976-77; asst. state atty. State Atty.'s Office, Ft. Lauderdale, 1977-89; cir. ct. judge 17th Jud. Cir. Ct. Fla., Ft. Lauderdale, 1989-98; judge US Dist. Ct. (so. dist.) Fla., Fort Lauderdale, 1998—. Mem. Broward County Criminal Justice Planning Coun., Fla., 1983-89. Author: Sentencing Guidelines, 1987. Mem. Fla. Bar Assn. (criminal rules com., criminal cert. com., chmn. grievance com. 1987-88). Republican. Greek Orthodox. Avocation: track and field. Office: 299 E Broward Blvd # 203F Fort Lauderdale FL 33301-1944

DIMOND, ROBERT EDWARD, publisher, general manager; b. Washington, Dec. 12, 1936; s. James Robert and Helen Marie (Murphy) D.; m. Patricia Berger (div.); children: Mark Edward, Michele Lynn Keating, Melinda Ann, Hendrickson; m. Carol Mantia, 2012 BA in Journalism, George Washington U., 1961. Mng. editor Nat. Automobile Dealers Assn. Mag., Washington, 1955-63; editor, pub. Bus. Products Mag., Washington, 1963-69; v.p. Hitchcock Pub. Co.; pub. Infosystems Mag., Office Products Mag., Wheaton, Ill., 1969-81; pres. R.E. Dimond & Assocs., Hinsdale, Ill., 1981-83; pub. Networking Mgmt. Mag., Westford, Mass., 1983-89, Home Improvement Ctr. Mag., Lincolnshire, Ill., 1989-90; v.p., pub. dir. mining and constrn. group Intertec; pub. Coal, Rock Products, Internat. Construction, Concrete Products, Engring. and Mining Jour., C&D Materials Recycling and Keystone Directory, 1990-96; group v.p. Intertec Pub. Co., 1996-99; pres. R.E. Dimond & Assocs., 1999—; sr. v.p. CVI Capital. Keynote spkr. COMDEX, 1979. Served with USAF, 1961-62, info. officer fighter wing. Democrat. Roman Catholic. E-mail: dimondre@comcast.net.

DIMOPOULOS, LINDA J., food service executive; b. 1951; Attended, Fla. State U. With Darden Restaurants, Inc., 1982, sr. v.p., fin. ops., Red Lobster, 1993—98, sr. v.p., corp. contr., bus info. sys., 1998—99, sr. v.p., chief info. officer, 1999—2002, CFO, 2002—. Office: Darden Restaurants Inc 1000 Darden Ctr Dr Orlando FL 32837 Office Phone: 407-245-4000. Office Fax: 407-245-5296. Business E-Mail: linda.dimopoulos@darden.com.

DIMOS, JIMMY, state representative; b. Oct. 18, 1938; m. Dale Guilkey. BA, Northeastern La. U.; JD, Tulane U. Mem. La. Ho. of Reps., Baton Rouge, La., 1976—, speaker of house, 1988-92; also atty.; judge 4th Dist. Ct., Monroe, La. With USAR, 1963-69. Mem. Optimist (former v.p.), N.E. La. Univ. Alumni Assn. (past pres.), Jaycees Internat. Episcopalian. Address: 1216 Stubbs Ave Monroe LA 71201-5622 Office: 4th Dist Ct Ste 100 130 De Saird St Monroe LA 71201

DIMPERIO, JULIE, retail executive; Merchandising positions Givenchy Sport, Lloyd Williams; sr. v.p., internat. women's apparel Hartmarx Corp.; pres., crazy horse, first issue & curve Liz Claiborne, Inc., 2000—06; pres., Nautica women's sportswear & Kipling N.Am. wholesale V.F. Corp., 2006—. Office: V F Corp 105 Corporate Ctr Blvd Greensboro NC 27408 Office Phone: 336-424-6000. Office Fax: 336-424-7631. Business E-Mail: julie_dimperio@vfc.com.

DINAN, CURTIS L., gas industry executive; BA in Acctg. and Bus. Adminstrn., Drury U., Springfield, Mo., 1989. CPA. Assurance and bus. adv. ptnr. Arthur Andersen LLP, 2001—02; ptnr. audit practice Grant Thornton LLP, Tulsa, Okla., 2002—04; sr. v.p., chief acctg. officer ONEOK, Inc., Tulsa, 2004—06, sr. v.p., CFO., treas., 2007—11, ONEOK Partners, LP, 2007—11, pres. natural gas, 2011—. Bd. dirs. ONEOK Ptnrs., LP, 2007—. Past. pres., treas., dir. Tulsa Court Appointed Spl. Advocates; past. treas., dir. Child Abuse Network; mem. adv. bd. Breech Sch. Bus. Drury U. Mem.: AICPA, Okla. Soc. CPA's. Office: ONEOK Inc 100 W Fifth St Tulsa OK 74103

DINARDO, DANIEL NICHOLAS CARDINAL, cardinal, archbishop; b. Steubenville, Ohio, May 23, 1949; s. Nicholas and Jane (Green) DiNardo. BA, Cath. U. America, 1969, MA in Philosophy, 1969; BST, Pontifical Gregorian U., 1975, LTh; Licentiate in Patristics, Augustinianum. Ordained priest of Pitts., 1977, asst. chancellor, 1981—93, asst. sec. edn.; parochial vicar Saint Pius X Ch., Pitts.; part time prof., also spiritual dir. to the seminarians Saint Paul's Seminary, 1981; staff mem. Pontifical Congregation of Bishops, Rome, 1984—90; dir. of Villa Stritch Residence for American Priests working for the Holy See, Rome, 1986—89; co-administrator of Madonna del Castello Church, Swissvale, Pa., 1991; founding pastor Saint John and Saint Paul Church, Franklin Park, 1994; co-adjutor bishop of Sioux City, Iowa, 1997—98, ordained Iowa, 1997, bishop Iowa, 1998—2005; coadjutor archbishop of Galveston-Houston, 2004—06, archbishop, 2006—; elevated to cardinal, 2007; cardinal-priest Sant' Eusebio (Saint Eusebius), 2008—. V.p. US Conf. Catholic Bishops (USCCB), 2013—; mem. Pontifical Coun. for Culture, 2009—, Pontifical Coun. for Pastoral Care of Migrants and Itinerant People; chair United States Bishops' Com. on Pro-Life Activities, 2009—; bd. mem. Nat. Catholic Partnership for Persons with Disabilities; bd. trustee Catholic U. of America; advisor Nat. Assn. of Pastoral Musicians; mem. Ad Hoc Com. to Oversee the Use of the Catechism for the United States Conference of Catholic Bishops. Recipient Knight Grand Cross of the Order of Merit of the Italian Republic, 2008. Roman Catholic. Office: Archdiocese of Galveston Houston 1700 San Jacinto St PO Box 907 Houston TX 77001-0907*

DINCULEANU, NICOLAE, mathematician, educator; b. Padea, Romania, Feb. 26, 1925; came to U.S., 1976. s. Nicolae and Frusina (Lusca) Dobrescu; m. Elena Constantinescu, Feb. 9, 1959. Engr., Poly. Inst., Bucharest, 1950; licencie math., U. Bucharest, 1951; PhD in Math, U. Bucarest, 1957; Doctor honoris causa, U. Craiova, 1995, U. Bucharest, 2001. Prof. math. U. Bucharest, 1950-77; vis. prof. Queen's U., Kingston, Ont., Canada, 1966-67, U. Rennes, France, U. Erlangen, Germany, 1970; Disting. vis. prof. U. Pitts., 1970-71; vis. research prof. U. Fla., Gainesville, 1972-77, prof. math., 1977—2003. Author: Vector Measures, 1967, Integration on Locally Compact Spaces, 1974, Textbook of Mathematical Analysis, 2 vols, 1962, Vector Integration and Stochastic Integration in Banach Spaces, 2000; also articles. Recipient Knight of Order award, Steava Romaniei, 2011. Mem.: Romanian Acad. (hon.). Office: U Fla Math Dept Little Hall # 450A Gainesville FL 32611-2082 Office Phone: 352-392-0281. Personal E-mail: dinculeanunicola@bellsouth.net. Business E-Mail: nd@ufl.edu.

DIN-DZIETHAM, REBECCA L.P., cardiologist, educator; d. Pierre and Pauline Dzietham; m. Edouard Din; children: James T.E. Din, Dora T.M. Din, Emma H. Din. MD in Cardiology, residency in Cardiology, U. Paris Vi, 1979; MPH, Chapel Hill, 1992; PhD, UNC, Chapel Hill, 2000. Head divsn. cardiology Ctrl. Hosp., Yaounde, Cameroon, 1981—91; faculty, dept. medicine Sch. Medicine, Yaounde, 1983—91; GRA, TA UNC, Sch. Pub. Health, Chapel Hill, NC, 1991—2000; assoc. prof. Morehouse Sch. Medicine, Atlanta, 2001—. Office: Morehouse Sch Medicine 720 Westview Dr SW Atlanta GA 30310-1495 Home: 980 Forest Overlook Trl SW Atlanta GA 30331-8307 Office Fax: 404-752-1074. Business E-Mail: rdin@msm.edu.*

DINGLEDINE, RAYMOND J., JR., pharmacologist, educator; BS in Biochemistry, Mich. State U., 1971; PhD in Pharmacology, Stanford U., Calif., 1975. Postdoc. fellow U. Cambridge, England, 1975—77, U. Oslo, Norway, 1977—78; rsch. assoc. dept. physiology Duke U., Durham, NC, 1978; asst., assoc., then full prof. dept. pharmacology U. NC, Chapel Hill, 1978—92; prof., chmn. dept. pharmacology Emory U. Sch. Medicine, Atlanta, 1992—, exec. assoc. dean. rsch., 2008—. Vis. scientist Salk Inst. Biol. Studies, La Jolla, Calif., 1990—91; co-founder, mem. sci. adv. bd. NeurOp Inc., Atlanta, 2002—; apptd. sci. coun. Nat. Inst. Neurol. Disorders & Stroke, NIH. Mem. editl. bd. Neuropharmacology, Jour. Molecular Neurosci., Epilepsy Rsch., NeuroMolecular Medicine, former editor Molecular Pharmacology; contbr. articles to profl. jours. Recipient PhRMA Found. Career award in excellence, 1999, John A. Boezi Disting. Alumnus award, Michigan State U., Jacob Javits award in neurosciences, NIH, Bristol-Myers Squibb Neuroscience award; Alfred P. Sloan Fellowship, Klingenstein Fellowship. Fellow: AAAS; mem.: American Soc. Pharmacology & Exptl. Therapeutics, American Epilepsy Soc. (Basic Rsch. award 1995), Soc. Neuroscience, Inst. Medicine. Achievements include research in the pharmacology of neurotransmitter receptors, including glutamate, which are responsible for communication between neurons in the brain; contributions to the current understanding of seizure development in brain cells which has laid the foundation for new approaches to drug therapy for epilepsy. Office: Emory U Sch Medicine Dept Pharmacology 1510 Clifton Rd Atlanta GA 30322 Office Phone: 404-727-5983. Office Fax: 404-727-0365. E-mail: rdingledine@pharm.emory.edu.

DINGUS, DAVID H., manufacturing executive; BS, Ind. U. Various internat. operational and fin. positions Dresser Industries; pres. pvt. consulting firm; dir. fin. and adminstrn. Reedrill Corp., 1986—88, exec. v.p., 1988—89, pres., CEO, 1989—98; pres. AZZ, Inc., 1998—, COO, 1998—2001, bd. dirs., 1999—, CEO, 2001—, CGIT Westboro, Inc. Office: AZZ Inc 1 Museum Pl 3100 W Seventh St Ste 500 Fort Worth TX 76107 Office Phone: 817-810-0095. Office Fax: 817-336-5354.

DINKINS, CAROL EGGERT, lawyer; b. Corpus Christi, Tex., Nov. 9, 1945; d. Edgar H. Jr. and Evelyn S. (Scheel) Eggert; m. Bob Brown; children: Anne, Amy. BS, U. Tex., 1968; JD, U. Houston, 1971. Bar: Tex. 1971. Prin. assoc. Tex. Law Inst. Coastal and Marine Resources, Coll. Law U. Houston, Tex., 1971-73; assoc., ptnr. Vinson & Elkins LLP, Houston, 1973-81, 83-84, 85—, mem. mgmt. com., 1991-96, chair Adminstrv. and Environ. Law practice; asst. atty. gen. environ. & natural resources US Dept. Justice, Washington, 1981-83, dep. atty. gen., 1984-85. Chmn. Pres.'s Task Force on Legal Equity for Women, 1981-83; mem. Hawaiian Native Study Commn., 1981-83; dir. Nat. Consumer Coop. Banks Bd., 1981; chair Pres. Oversight Bd. on Privacy and Civil Liberties, 2006-08 Contbr. articles to profl. jours. Chmn. Gov.'s Conservation Task Force, 2000, Tex. Gov.'s Flood Control Action Group 1980-81; commr. Tex. Parks and Wildlife Dept., 1997-2001; bd. govs. The Nature Conservancy, 1996—, chmn. 2003-04; dir. Oryx Energy Co., 1990-95, U. Houston Law Ctr. Found., 1985-89, 96-98, Environ. and Energy Study Inst., 1986-98, Houston Mus. Natural Sci., 1986-98, 2000—; mem. exec. com., bd. dirs. Tex. Nature Conservancy, 1985—, chmn., 1996-99, 2003. Mem. ABA (house dels., past chmn. state and local govt. sect., past chair sect. nat. resources, energy, and environ. law, standing com. on fed. judiciary 1997-98, chair 2002-03, bd. editors ABA Jour., chair 2003-07, bd. govs. 2005—2008), Fed. Bar Assn. (bd. dirs. Houston chpt. 1986), State Bar Tex., Houston Bar Assn., Tex. Water Conservation Assn., Houston Law Rev. Assn. (bd. dirs. 1978). Republican. Lutheran. Office: Vinson & Elkins LLP 2300 First City Tower 1001 Fannin St Houston TX 77002-6706 Office Phone: 713-758-2528. Office Fax: 713-758-5311. Business E-Mail: cdinkins@velaw.com.

DINNEY, COLIN P., surgeon, urologist; m. Barbara Dinney. MD, U. Man., Winnipeg, 1982. Cert. in urology Royal Coll. Physicians & Surgeons, 1989. Prof., chmn. MD Anderson Cancer Ctr., Houston, 1991—. Office: Univ Texas MD Anderson Cancer Ctr 1515 Holcombe Blvd Unit 1373 Houston TX 77030 Office Fax: 713-794-5293. Business E-Mail: cdinney@mdanderson.org.

DIPENTIMA, RENATO ANTHONY, information technology executive; m. Patricia Ellen Gillespie, July 24, 1965; children: Margaret Ellen, Katherine Alice. BA, NYU, 1963; MA, George Washington U., 1979; PhD, U. Md., 1984. With Social Security Adminstrn., 1963—95, exec. officer Nat. Commn. Social Security Reform Balt., 1979—82, dep. commr. sys., 1990—95; v.p., chief info. officer Sys. Rsch. and Applications Corp., Arlington, Va., 1995-97; pres. SRA Fed. Sys., 1997-98, SRA Govt. Sector, 1999—2000, SRA Cons. and Sys. Integration, 2001—03, pres., COO, 2003—05, pres., CEO, 2005—07; sr. advisor Providence Equity Ptnrs. Bd. dirs. Brocade Corp., Capgemini Robot Solutions, Redhat (Adv. Bd.), ASI Govt., UMBC Poly Sci. Mem. Ptnr. Pub. Svc., Nat. Acad. Social Ins. Recipient Presdl. Meritorious Rank award, 1989, Presdl. Disting. Rank award, 1990. Business E-Mail: renny_dipentima@sra.com.

DIPERNA, FRANK PAUL, photographer, educator; b. Pitts., Feb. 4, 1947; s. Frank Paul and Virginia Carmella (DeRenna) DiP. BS in Mech. Engring., Va.Polytech. Inst., 1970; student, Visual Studies Workshop, 1971-72; MA in Photography, Goddard Coll., 1977. Assoc. prof. art and photography Corcoran Coll. Art and Design, Washington, 1974-94, prof., 1994—, chmn. photography dept., 1978—81, 1984—87, 1999—2002; prof. photography Ruesch Family, 2008.

Instr. photography No. Va. C.C., Alexandria, 1973-78, George Washington U., Washington, summer 1974; lectrs. and workshops Smithsonian Inst., 1976, Maine Photog. Inst. Rockport, 1977, Am. U., Washington, 1977, 78, 79, Internat. Ctr. Photography, N.Y.C., 1979, U. Del., 1981, James Madison U., Harrisonburg, Va., 1982, Rice U., Houston, No. Va. C.C., Sterling, 1991; resident Vt. Studio Ctr., Johnson, Vt., 2002; vis. prof. U. Ga, Study Abroad Program, Cortona, Italy, 2005, 08. Solo exhbns. include Kathleen Ewing Gallery, Washington, 1982, 84, 89, 95, 98, 2000, 06, Diane Brown Gallery, Washington, 1977, 78, 80, Bird in Hand Gallery, Alexandria, 1973, Corcoran Gallery Art, 1974, 77, Recontres Internationales de la Photographie, Arles, France, 1981, Rice U., Houston, 1986; group exhbns. include Athenaeum Mus., Alexandria, 1972, Photo Impressions Gallery, Washington, 1974, Va. Mus. Fine Arts, Richmond, 1973, 75, 80, The Franklin Inst., Phila., 1978, Susan Spiritus Gallery, Newport Beach, Calif., 1979, Mus. Fine Arts, Houston, 1979, Decordova Mus., Lincoln, Mass., 1979, Mpls. Inst. Arts, 1979, L.A. Inst. Contemporary Art, 1979, Denver Art Mus., 1979, Art Inst. Chgo., 1979, Phila. Coll. Art, 1980, Brown U., Providence, 1980, Arlington (Va.) Arts Ctr., 1981, Everson Mus. Art, Syracuse, N.Y., 1985, Comfort Gallery Haverford (Pa.) Coll., 1986, Washington Ctr. Photography, 1992, Nat. Mus. Am. Art, 1992, Smithsonian Inst., 1992, Carnegie Mus. Art, 1992, New Orleans Mus. Art, 1992, Corcoran Gallery Art, 1994, 96, 98, Virginia's Photographers, Longwood Ctr. for the Visual Arts, Farmville, Va., 1997, Kathleen Ewing Gallery, Washington, 1999, Art Mus. Western Va., Roanoke, 2002, Smithsonian Am. Art Mus., 2003, 1708 Gallery, Richmond, Va., 2003, Room Full of Mirrors, U. Md., 2004, Images of Italy, Kathleen Ewing Gallery, 2004, Road Trip Gallery, Smithsonian Mus. Am. Art, many others; represented in permanent collections Chrysler Mus., Norfolk, Va., Recontres Internationale de la Photographie, Arles, France, Bibliotheque Nationale, Paris, Libr. Cong., Washington, Polaroid (Euopa) Amsterdam, The Netherlands, Corcoran Gallery Art, Va. Mus. Fine Arts, Smithsonian Inst., Balt. Mus. Art, Nat. Mus. Am. Art, Washington, Met. Mus. Art, N.Y., Ctr. for Creative Photography, U. Ariz., Kathleen Ewimy Gallery, 2008, Am. U., 2008, Mostra Cortona, Italy, 2008, Katzen Arts Ctr., Am. U., 2009, 10, Catalyst, 2010, One Hour Photo, 2010, U. Ga., 2009, Deep Element: Photograph at the Beach: Corcoram Gallery Art, Washington, 2012, Covcovan Five, La Avorn Gallery Inc., San Mipuel Allende, Mex., 2012, Found I Wages, Civilian Art Projects, Washington, 2013. Artist-in-Residence Lightwork, Syracuse, N.Y., 1982, Camargo Found., Cassis, France, 1980, Vt. Studio Ctr., Johnson, 2002, Corcoren Coll. Art & Design San Maquel de Allender, Mex., 2011; Grad. fellow Va. Mus. Fine Arts, 1975. Avocations: tennis, fishing, playing guitar, birdwatching, furniture making. Office: Corcoran Coll Art & Design 500 17th St NW Washington DC 20006-4804 E-mail: bluebirdfd@aol.com.

DIPIETRO, JOSEPH A., academic administrator, medical educator; BS, U. Ill., Urbana, 1974, DVM, 1976, MS, 1980. Assoc. veterinarian Peotone Animal Hosp., Ill., 1976—78; instr. veterinary clin. medicine Coll. Veterinary Medicine, U. Ill., Urbana, 1976—80, asst. prof., 1980—84, assoc. prof., 1984—90, prof. Dept. Veterinary Pathobiology, 1990—97, acting assoc. dean rsch., 1990—91, asst. dean rsch., 1991—92, acting assoc. dean rsch., 1993—94, assoc. dean rsch., 1994—97; acting asst. dir. Agr. Experiment Station Coll. Agr., U. Ill., Urbana, 1993—94, asst. dir., 1994—97; dean Coll. Veterinary Medicine, U. Fla., Gainesville, 1997—2006, prof. Dept. Pathobiology, 1997—2006; prof. Comparative Medicine Dept., Coll. Veterinary Medicine U. Tenn., Knoxville, 2006—, chancellor Inst. Agr., 2006—10, pres., 2011—. Mem. bd. vet. medicine US Pharmacopia; equine adv. com. Fla. Farm Bur.; mem. organizing com. Internat. Cyathostome Workshop; commr. Ill. Racing Bd.; bd. dirs., fin. com. U. Fla. Found.; chmn. coun. on affirmative action U. Fla.; chmn. bd. dir. Vet. Med. Faculty Assn.; mem. Nat. Agrl. Rsch., Edn. and Economics Adv. Bd. Mem.: Tenn. Veterinary Med. Assn., American Veterinary Med. Assn., Assn. American Veterinary Med. Colleges (chmn. rsch. deans and directorss com., sec., bd.dirs., accreditation task force, comparative data com., pres.), Nat. Rsch. Coun. (bd. agr. & natural resources com. future role of pesticides in US agr.), American Assn. Equine Practitioners (biologic and therapeutic com., rsch. com.). Office: University of Tennessee Office of President 831 Andy Holt Tower Knoxville TN 37996-0180 Office Phone: 865-974-2241. Office Fax: 865-974-3753.*

DIRICO, TONY, aggregate and chemical products company executive; Pres., Southeast divsn. Martin Marietta Materials, Inc., Augusta, Ga. Office: Martin Marietta Materials 3019 Riverwatch Pky Augusta GA 30907 Office Phone: 706-860-1762. Business E-Mail: tonydirico@martinmarietta.com.

DI RITA, LARRY (LAWRENCE T.), bank executive, former federal agency administrator; b. Detroit; BS in Economics, US Naval Acad., 1980; MA in Latin Am. Studies, Johns Hopkins U., 1987. Dep. dir., fgn. policy & def. studies Heritage Found., 1993—95; policy dir. Presdl. Campaign for Sen. Phil Gramm, 1996; legis. dir., chief staff to Sen. Kay Bailey Hutchison US Senate, 1996—2001; spl. asst., chief spokesman US Dept. Def., 2001—06, prin. dep. asst. sec., 2001—06; sr. v.p. Bank of America Corp., comm. exec., 2006—. Former officer USN. Office: Bank of America Corp 100 N Tryon St 18th Fl Charlotte NC 28255 Office Phone: 704-386-5681. Office Fax: 704-386-6699.

DIRVIN, GERALD VINCENT, retired consumer products company executive; b. Phila., Mar. 28, 1937; s. Vincent A. and Mary (Fitch) D.; m. Polly Burnett, June 27, 1959; children: John, David, Barbara. BA, Hamilton Coll., Clinton, NY, 1959. With Procter & Gamble Co., 1959-94, sales mgt., then v.p. coffee divsn., 1975-80, group v.p. Cin., 1980-89, exec. v.p., 1990-94, dir., 1981-94. Bd. trustees Hamilton Coll. Mem. Comml. Club, Plantation Golf Club, Commonwealth Club, Camargo Club, Pine Valley Golf Club, Confrerie des Chevaliers du Tastevin, Pablo Creek Golf Club, Kingsley Golf Club. Republican. Roman Catholic.

DI SESSA, THOMAS GERALD, medical educator; b. Mount Vernon, NY, Aug. 10, 1944; s. Fred Peter and Rose Nancyann Di Sessa; m. Patricia Lynn Pantera, June 5, 1971; children: Thomas Gerald Jr., John Christopher, Peter Richard. MD, SUNY, 1971. Asst. prof. pediat. UCLA Med. Ctr., LA, 1979—85; prof. pediat. U. Tenn. Med Ctr., Memphis, 1985—2003, U. Ky., Lexington, 2003—. Mem. Internat. Children's Heart Found., Memphis, 1996—2007, Am. Heart Assn., Lexington, 2003—07, Boy Scouts Am. Blue Grass Coun., Lexington, 2003—07. Maj. USAF, 1974—76, Nellis Air Force Base. Recipient Best Book award, New Eng. Book Show, 1983, Franklin Moosenick Svc. award, Am. Heart Assn., 2006. Fellow: Am. Acad. Pediat., Am. Coll. Cardiology. Office Fax: 859-323-3499; Home Fax: 859-323-3499. Business E-Mail: tdise2@uky.edu.

DISMANG, JONATHAN, state legislator; b. Maynard, Ark., July 30, 1979; s. Paul and Nancy Dismang; m. Mandy Staggs; 1 child, Cade. BBA in Economics and Accounting, Harding U., Searcy, Ark., 2001. Owner Dismang Land & Cattle LLC, El Paso, Ark.; CFO Checklaw Recovery Sys. Inc., North Little Rock, Whitwell & Ryles Real Estate Investments, North Little Rock; mem. Dist. 49 Ark. House of Reps., 2008—11; mem. Dist. 29 Ark. State Senate, 2011—. Mem. adv. bd. Students in Free Enterprise. Mem.: NRA, Nat. Assn. Royalty Owners (chmn. exploratory bd.), Nat. Wild Turkey Fedn., Ducks Unlimited. Republican. Office: Dismang Land & Cattle 550 El Paso Rd El Paso AR 72045 Mailing: PO Box 475 Beebe AR 72012-0475 Office Phone: 501-766-8220. Business E-Mail: jonathan.dismang@senate.ar.gov.

DITKOWSKY, WILLIAM A., otolaryngologist; b. Chgo., Ill., Nov. 24, 1948; m. Joanie Ditkowsky; children: Rosie, Ellie. BS magna cum laude, U. Miami, MD, 1974. Diplomate Am. Bd. Otolaryngology, 1981. Intern surgery Jackson Meml. Hosp., resident otolaryngology, 1976—79, hosp. affiliations include, Bapt. Hosp., South Miami Hosp., Jackson South Cmty. Hosp.; chief med. staff; vol. clin. faculty dept. of otolaryngology head and neck surgery Univ. of Miami; physician Ear Nose Throat Miami, South Fla. Ear Nose Throat Assocs. Named one of Top Physicians, South Fla. Fellow: ACS, Am. Acad. of Otolaryngology Head and Neck Surgery (Achievement award), Am. Acad. of Otolaryngologic Allergy; mem.: AMA. Avocations: golf, travel. Office: 9275 SW 152 ST Suite 212 Miami FL 33157 Office Phone: 305-255-5995. Office Fax: 305-255-3018. E-mail: drditkowsky@aol.com.

DITTENHAFER, BRIAN DOUGLAS, banker, economist; b. York, Pa., Aug. 15, 1942; s. Nathaniel Webster and Evelyn Romaine (Myers) D.; m. Miriam Marcy, Aug. 22, 1964; 1 child. BA, Ursinus Coll., 1964; MA, Temple U., 1966, postgrad., 1967—71. Pers. asst. Philco Corp., Phila., 1965—66; tchg. asst. Temple U., Phila., 1966—67, rsch. assoc., 1968—69; bus. economist Fed. Res. Bank of Atlanta, 1971—76; v.p., chief economist Fed. Home Loan Bank of N.Y., NYC, 1976—79, sr. v.p., CFO, 1979—80, exec. v.p., 1980—85, pres., 1985—92, Collective Fed. Savs. Bank, 1992—94, Collective Bancorp, 1992—94; chmn. MBD Mgmt. Co., 1994—2008. Vice chmn. Fin. Instns. Thrift Plan, 1991-92, chmn., 1992; trustee Fin. Instns. Retirement Fund, 1985-92, vice chmn., 1991, chmn., 1992; bd. dirs. Investors Savs. Bank, 1997—, bd. dir. Investors Bancorp, 1997-, lead dir., 2012-. Bd. dirs. Social Compact, 1990-99, sec., 1995-99; mem. FNMA Found. Adv. Group, 1994; deacon Ctrl. Presbyn. Ch., 1981-84; bd. dirs. N.Y. Coun. Econ. Edn., 1983-89; chmn. Resolution Funding Corp., 1989-92. Temple U. fellow, G.E. Found. fellow Temple U. Mem. Forecaster's Club N.Y. (sec.-treas. 1982-84), Suntree Country Club (dir., treas. 2000-03), Nat. Assn. Corp. Dir.(mem. Governance fellow), Omicron Delta Epsilon.

DIVEN, DAYNA, dermatologist, educator; BA, U. Ariz., Tucson, 1982; MD, U. Tex., Galveston, TX, 1986; attended tng. course, US HHS; cert. bus. adminstrn. for physician execs., U. Houston. Diplomate Am. Bd. Dermatology, 1990, lic. ID, Tex. Intern internal medicine Univ. of Tex. Med. Branch, Galveston, Tex., 1986—87, resident dermatology, 1987—90, assoc. prof dermatology, 1990—2000, dir. dermatologic laser svc., 1990—2000, med. dir. dermatology clinic svcs., 1990—2000, telemedicine dermatology cons. Tex. Dept. of Corrections and Jurisprudence, 1997—2000, clin. prof. dermatology; hosp. affiliations include Univ. of Tex. Med. Br., Galveston, Tex., Univ. Med. Ctr. Brackenridge; employee health screening, tuberculosis exposure and fgn. travel physician Univ. Health Svc., 1987—88; chief dermatology sect. Ctrl. Tex. Veteran's Health Care Clinic, Austin, Tex. Brit. Assn. of Dermatology Fellowship. Mem.: Alpha Omega Alpha Honor Soc., Phi Kappa Phi, Phi Beta Kappa. Office: University of TX Medical Branch 301 University Blvd Galveston TX 77555-0144 Office Fax: 409-772-1943.

DIVERTIE, GAVIN D., critical care specialist; MD, Mayo Med. Sch., 1983. Diplomate Am. Bd. Anesthesiology, 1990, Am. Bd. Internal Medicine, 1987, Am. Bd. Internal Medicine- critical care medicine, 2001. Intern Pacific Med. Ctr., San Francisco; resident in internal medicine Mayo Grad. Sch. Medicine, Jacksonville, Fla., 1986—89, fellow in rsch., 1989—90; hosp. affiliation include Mayo Clinic. Co-author: Lack of effect of hyperglycemia on lipolysis in humans, 1990, Stimulation of lipolysis in humans by physiological hypercortisolemia, 1991, Insulin-like growth factor-binding protein-1 response to insulin during suppression of endogenous insulin secretion, 1993, Cortisol increases plasma insulin-like growth factor binding protein-1 in humans, 1993, Dynamic left ventricular outflow tract obstruction. Diagnosis by transesophageal echocardiography in a critically ill patient, 1993, Lipolytic responsiveness to epinephrine in nondiabetic and diabetic humans, 1997, Clinical relevance of time of onset, duration, and type of pulmonary edema after liver transplantation, 2003, A comparison of intensive care unit physician staffing costs at the 3 Mayo Clinic sites, 2006, Brain injury after cardiopulmonary arrest and its assessment with diffusion-weighted magnetic resonance imaging, 2007, Predictors of poor neurologic outcome after induced mild hypothermia following cardiac arrest, 2009, Safety and efficacy of levetiracetam for critically ill patients with seizures, 2009, Perspectives of Physicians and Nurses Regarding End-of-Life Care in the Intensive Care Unit, 2011. Office: Mayo Clinic 4500 San Pablo Rd S Jacksonville FL 32224-1865 Office Phone: 904-296-5287.

DIVINE, ROBERT ALEXANDER, history professor; b. Bklyn., May 10, 1929; s. Walter E. and Emily (Mable) D.; m. Barbara C. Renick, Aug. 6, 1955 (dec.); children: J. Douglas, Elisabeth T., Richard L., Kirk M.; m. Darlene S. Harris, June 1, 1996 (dec.); m. Joan Burdick, May 10, 2007. BA, Yale U., 1951, MA, 1952, PhD, 1954. Instr. U. Tex., Austin, 1954-57, asst. prof., 1957-61, assoc. prof., 1961-63, prof. history, 1963-96, chmn. dept. history, 1963-68, Piper prof., 1972, George W. Littlefield prof. Am. history, 1981-96, prof. emeritus, 1996—. Fellow Center for Advanced Study in Behavioral Scis. Stanford, Calif., 1962-63; Albert Shaw lectr. in diplomatic history, Johns Hopkins, 1968 Author: American Immigration Policy, 1924-52, 1957, The Illusion of Neutrality, 1962, The Reluctant Belligerent, 1965, Second Chance, 1967, Roosevelt and World War II, 1969, Foreign Policy and U.S. Presidential Elections, 1940-60, 2 vols., 1974, Since 1945: Politics and Diplomacy in Recent American History, 1975, Blowing on the Wind, 1978, Eisenhower and the Cold War, 1981, The Sputnik Challenge, 1993, Perpetual War for Perpetual Peace, 2000; co-author: America Past and Present, 1984, 9th edit., 2010. Recipient Eugene E. Emme Astronautical Lit. award, 1995. Mem. Orgn. Am. Historians, Soc. for Historians of Am. Fgn. Rels. Lutheran. Home: 10617 Sans Souci Pl Austin TX 78759-6185

DIVLJAKOVIC, VOJISLAV, manufacturing executive; b. Zagreb, Croatia; BSEE, MSEE, U. Zagreb, Croatia, PhD in Elect. Engring.; MBA, Washington U., St. Louis, 1998. Pres. BNT Comml. Group Brunswick Corp., pres. Navman; v.p. rsch. and devel. Mercury Marine (subs of Brunswick Corp.); assoc. prof. Ruder Boskovic Inst., Zagreb, Croatia; dir. new product devel. US Elect. Motors; sr. v.p. integrated ops. Life Fitness, 2002—05; pres. Titus d.o.o, Split, Croatia; v.p., gen. mgr. Electronic Solutions Divsn. 3M Corp., Austin, Tex., 2009—. Mem. Inst. of Elect. and Electronics Engr., Soc. of Automotive Engrs. Office: 3M Electronic Solutions Division 6801 River Place Blvd Austin TX 78726-4530 Business E-Mail: vdivljakovic@mmm.com.

DIX, SCOTT, state legislator; BBA, JD, U. Ga. Atty.; rep. 76th dist. Ga. House Reps., 1992—. Mem. house jud. com., house legis. and congl. reapportionment com., house rules com. Legis. aide U.S. Senator Mack Mattingly, 1984-86. Mem. Kiwanis. Republican. Baptist. Office: Legis Office Bldg Rm 411 Atlanta GA 30334

DIXIT, AJIT SURESH, chemicals executive, research scientist; b. Nadiad, India, Sept. 30, 1950; naturalized, 1981; s. Suresh Chaturlal and Narendra Suresh (Yajnik) D.; m. Darshana J. Desai, Oct. 27, 1981. MS, U. Maine, 1976; PhD, U. Miss., 1980. Rsch. assoc. U. Kans., 1980-81; sr. rsch. chemist Olin Corp., Pisgah Forest, N.C., 1981-85; rsch. assoc., mgr. pilot plant Ecusta divsn. P.H. Glatfelter Co., Pisgah Forest, 1985—2004; faculty & dept. head Wake Tech. CC, Raleigh, NC, 2004—. Nat. Sci. Talent scholar, 1967-72. Mem. Am. Chem. Soc., Royal Chem. Soc., TAPPI, Sigma Xi. Hindu. Home: 405 Magnolia Birch Ct Cary NC 27519 Office: 6600 Louisburg Rd Raleigh NC 27616 Office Phone: 919-532-5612. Personal E-mail: asddad1@live.com. Business E-Mail: asdixit@waketech.edu.

DIXON, DAVID ADAMS, chemistry professor, researcher; b. Houston, Dec. 3, 1949; s. John Wilburn Dixon and Nancy Eddy Wilder; m. Christine Diane Powless-Dixon, June 2, 1983; children: Michelle Dawes, Nicole Dawes, Jessica Dawes. BS in Chemistry, Calif. Inst. Tech., 1971; PhD in Phys. Chemistry, Harvard U., 1976. Asst. prof. chemistry dept. U. Minn., Mpls., 1977—83; mem. rsch. staff ctrl. rsch. and devel. dept. E.I. du Pont de Nemours and Co., Inc., Wilmington, Del., 1983—95, rsch. leader, 1990—95; assoc. dir. theory, modeling & simulation Environ. Molecular Sci. Lab., Pacific Northwest Nat. Lab., 1995—2002; prof. chemistry U. Ala., Tuscaloosa, 2004—, Robert Ramsay chair dept. chemistry, 2004—. Vis. assoc. chemistry Calif. Inst. Tech., Pasadena, 1977; adj. faculty chemistry dept. U. Pa., Phila., 1986; adj. prof. chemistry dept. U. Del., Newark, 1989—99, U. Utah, Salt Lake City, 1997—2003. Contbr. articles to profl. jours. Recipient ACS award for Creative Work in Fluorine Chemistry, 2003, Outstanding Contbn. award, DOE Hydrogen Program, 2010, Barnum award, U. Ala., 2011, SEC Faculty Achievement award, 2012; fellow, DuPont Ctrl. Sci. and Engring. Labs., Exptl. Sta., Wilmington, 1992—95; scholar, Autonomous Met. U., Mexico City, 1997; Jr. fellow, Harvard U., 1975—77, Alfred P. Sloan Rsch. fellow, 1977—81, Battelle fellow, Pacific Northwest Nat. Lab., 2002—03, Camille and Henry Dreyfus Tchr. scholar, 1978—83. Fellow: AAAS, Am. Phys. Soc., Am. Chem. Soc. (Leo Hendrik Baekeland award 1989); mem.: European Acad. Scis., Mat. Assn. Am., Soc. Indsl. & Applied Math., Assn. Computing Machinery. Avocations: swimming, reading, surfing, guitar. Office: U Ala Chemistry Dept Shelby Hall Box 870336 Tuscaloosa AL 35487-0336 Office Phone: 205-348-8441. Business E-Mail: dadixon@bama.ua.edu.

DIXON, DEBORAH BUTLER, state legislator; b. Bolton, Miss. m. Loviett Dixon; children: Camika, Consuela, Roderick, Broderick, Loviett III. Attended, Hinds CC, Raymond, Miss. Ret. Delphi Packard Electric; businesswoman; mem. Dist. 63 Miss. House of Reps., Jackson, 2012—. Mem.: NAACP, IUE-CWA, Miss. Fire Chiefs Assn., Miss. Farm Bur., Miss. Poultry Assn., Women and Men for Justice, Rotary, Masons. Democrat. Baptist. Office: Miss House of Reps PO Box 1018 Jackson MS 39215 Business E-Mail: ddixon@house.ms.gov.

DIXON, FREDERICK DAIL, architect; b. Raleigh, NC, Dec. 18, 1942; s. Frederick Dail (dec.) and Mary Isabel (Richbourg) D. (dec.); m. Artemis Markatos, July 7, 1968; children: Frederick Markatos. BArch, Clemson U., SC, 1966; MFA in Sculpture, UNC, Chapel Hill, 1970. Intern arch. Leslie Boney Archs., Wilmington, NC, 1966—68; project arch. John D. Latimer & Assocs., Durham, NC, 1968—72, Cogswell/Hausler Assocs., Chapel Hill, NC, 1972—74; founding ptnr. Designworks, Carrboro, NC, 1974—82, Dixon Weinstein Archs. PA, Chapel Hill, 1982—2009, Dail Dixon FAIA, Chapel Hill, 2009—. Instr. Boston Archtl. Ctr., 1970-71; vis. prof. arch. NC State U. Coll. Design, Raleigh, 1983-2005; studio instr. Penland Sch. of Crafts, 2007. Exhibitions include NC Mus. of Art, Duke Mus. of Art, Penland Gallery, Art Light, Design Gallery, GreenHill Gallery. Recipient Alpha Rho Chi medal, Clemson U.; co-recipient 1st Pl. award (with sculptor Patrick Dougherty), Pines Portico Competition Penland Sch. Crafts, 2005; HUD grantee. Fellow: Am. Inst. Archs. (NC & South Atlantic Chpt.). Democrat. Office: 310 1/2 West Franklin St Chapel Hill NC 27516 Office Phone: 919-259-5469. Business E-Mail: daildixon@gmail.com.

DIXON, GEORGETTE (GIGI), bank executive; Grad., Tenn. State U. Mktg. exec. Procter & Gamble Co., Brown & Williamson Tobacco Corp.; sr. v.p., dir. emerging markets Wachovia Corp., Charlotte, NC, 2002; sr. v.p., dir. nat. partnerships Wachovia Corp. (now Wells Fargo & Co.), Charlotte, NC, 2004—. Office: Wachovia Corp 301 South College St Ste 4000 Charlotte NC 28288-0143 Office Phone: 704-715-8579. Office Fax: 704-374-3425. E-mail: georgette.dixon@wachovia.com.

DIXON, GREGORY B., wholesale distribution executive; Attended, DeVry U. V.p., chief tech. office ScanSource, Inc., 1992—. Office: ScanSource Inc 6 Logue Ct Greenville SC 29615 Office Phone: 864-288-2432. Office Fax: 864-288-1165.

DIXON, HERBERT B., state legislator; b. Alexandria, La., July 29, 1949; m. Janet Dixon; children: Herbert Jr., Temika, Clayton, Rydell, Britanny. BS, Southern U., Baton Rouge, 1971; EdM, Southern U., 1975; EdM plus 30, Northwestern State U., Natchitoches, 1979; further studies, George Washington U. Field rep., 1980—2000; mem. Rapides Parish Sch. Bd., 1992—; vice chmn. Rapides Dem. Ctrl. Com., 1999—; sales rep. Nat. Motor Club, Inc.; mem. Dist. 26 La. House of Reps., 2008—, mem. edn. com., labor and indsl. rels. com., transp., hwys. and pub. works com. USN, 1972—78. Democrat. Protestant. Office: State Capitol PO Box 44486 Baton Rouge LA 70804 Mailing: 804 Broadway Ave Alexandria LA 71302 Office Phone: 225-342-6945, 318-487-5661. Office Fax: 318-487-5506. Business E-Mail: dixonh@legis.state.la.us.

DIXON, JIMMY, state legislator; Mem. Dist. 4 NC House of Representatives, 2011—. Republican. Office: PO Box 222 Warsaw NC 28398 Address: North Carolina House of Representatives 16 W Jones St Rm 1002 Raleigh NC 27601-1096 Office Phone: 910-590-1740, 919-715-3021. Business E-Mail: Jimmy.Dixon@ncleg.net.

DIXON, JOHN SPENCER, performing arts association administrator; b. London, Apr. 23, 1957; s. Richard Kennedy and Elizabeth Ann (Flaxman) D.; m. Karen Beth Swanson, Aug. 18, 1984; children: Katherine Elizabeth, John Spencer Jr. BA with honors, Oxford U., 1979, MA, 1985; MBA, Harvard U., 1982. Supply exec. Hi-Tec Sports Ltd., Essex, England, 1982-86; pres. Hi-Tec Internat. Ltd., Taichung, Taiwan, 1983-84; founder, ptnr. Transatlantic Mktg. Co., Essex, England, 1985-2000; exec. v.p. Decipher, Inc., Norfolk, Va., 1988-90; pres. Waller Whittemore & Co., Virginia Beach, Va., 1992—, PH Internat., Virginia Beach, Va., 1997—2001; organist, composer-in-residence Providence Presbyn. Ch., Virginia Beach, Va., 1998—; exec. dir. Acad. of Music, Norfolk, Va., 2003—. Mem.: Am. Guild Organists. Presbyterian. Avocations: music, sports. Home: 4829 Berrywood Rd Virginia Beach VA 23464-5874 Office: 5497 Providence Rd Virginia Beach VA 23464

DIXON, STEVEN C., energy company executive, geologist; b. 1958; BS in Geology, U. Kans., 1980. Geologist Beren Corp., Wichita, Kans., 1980—83; geological cons. Wichita, 1983—90; sr. v.p. exploration Chesapeake Energy Corp., 1991—95, sr. v.p. prodn.,

1995—2006, exec. v.p. ops., COO, 2006—, acting CEO, mem. Office of Chmn., 2013. Bd. dirs. Bronco Drilling Co., Inc., 2011—. Office: Chesapeake Energy Corp PO Box 18496 Oklahoma City OK 73154-0496*

DJEREJIAN, EDWARD PETER, academic administrator, retired ambassador; b. NYC, Mar. 6, 1939; s. Peter Minas and Mary (Yazudjian) D.; m. Francoise Andrée Haelters, July 31, 1971; children: Gregory, Francesca. BS in Fgn. Svc., Georgetown U., 1960, doctorate (hon.), 1992; LLD (hon.), Middlebury Coll., 2004. Staff asst. to sec. US Dept. State, 1963-64; Political officer Am. Embassy, Beirut, 1965-69; political/labor officer Am. Consulate Gen., Casablanca, Morocco, 1969-72; spl. asst. to under sec. US Dept. State, Washington, 1973-75; prin. officer Am. Consulate Gen., Bordeaux, France, 1975-77; political counselor Am. Embassy, Moscow, USSR, 1979-81, dep. chief of mission Amman, Jordan, 1981-84; dep. spokesman & dep. asst. sec. US Dept. State, Washington, 1984-85; spl. asst. to the Pres., dep. press sec. The White House, Washington, 1985-86; prin. dep. asst. sec. for Near East/South Asia US Dept. State, Washington, 1987-88, US amb. to Syria Damascus, Syria, 1988-91, asst. sec. Bur. Near Eastern & South Asian Affairs Washington, 1991-93, US amb. to Israel Tel Aviv, 1993-94; dir. James A. Baker III Inst. for Pub. Policy Rice University, Houston, 1994—; chmn. adv. group Pub. Diplomacy for the Arab and Muslim World, 2003; sr. advisor Iraq Study Group, 2006; mng. ptnr. Djerejian Global Consultants, LLP. Bd. dirs. Occidental Petroleum Corp., Global Industries, Ltd., Baker Hughes. Author: Danger and Opportunity: An American Ambassador's Journey Through the Middle East, 2008. 1st Lt. U.S. Army, 1961-62 (Korea). Recipient Presdl. award, Presdl. Meritorious Svc. award, 1988, Superior Honor award Dept. State, 1984, Disting. Honor award, 1993, Presdl. Disting. Svc. award, 1994, Ellis Island medal of honor, Moral Statesman award ADL, 1994. Mem. Coun. on Fgn. Rels. Armenian Apostolic. Avocations: writing, skiing. Office: Baker Inst Pub Policy Rice Univ - MS40 6100 Main St Houston TX 77005-1827 Office Phone: 713-348-4981. Business E-Mail: epd@rice.edu.

DJOKOVIC, NOVAK, professional tennis player; b. Belgrade, Serbia, May 22, 1987; s. Srdjan and Dijana Djokovic. Profl. tennis player ATP Tennis, 2003—. Recipient Order of St. Sava, Patriarch Irinej of Serbia, 2011, Order of Serbian Nat. Def. in America, 2011; named Most Improved Player, 2006 ATP Awards; named one of The 100 Most Influential People in the World, TIME mag., 2012. Achievements include winning 30 career singles titles, ATP; winner, Amersfoort, 2006, Metz, 2006, Adelaide, 2007, Sony Ericsson Open, 2007, 2011, 2012, Estoril Open, 2007, Rogers Masters, 2007, BA-CA Tennis Trophy, 2007; BNP Paribas Open, Indian Wells, 2008, 2011, Italian Open, 2008, 2011, Masters Cup, 2008, Barclays ATP World Tour Finals London, 2008, Dubai Tennis Championships, 2009, 2010, 2011; Serbia Open, 2009, 2011, Mutua Madrid Open, 2011; winning Grand Slam singles events: Australian Open, 2008, 2011, 2012, 2013; Wimbledon, 2011; US Open, 2011. Office: ATP 201 ATP Blvd Ponte Vedra Beach FL 32082 Office Phone: 904-285-8000. Office Fax: 904-285-5966.

DMOCHOWSKI, ROGER, urologist, educator; s. Sheila Dmochowski and Leon; m. Suzanne Sykora, Nov. 10, 1986; children: Colin Edward, Nicolas Roman. MD, U. Tex., Galveston, 1983. Diplomate Am. Bd. Urology. Staff urologist Naval hosp. U.S. Navy, Portsmouth, Va., 1989—93; dir. of resident edn. Ea. Va. Med. Sch., Norfolk, 1990—93; clin. instr. in surgery Uniformed Svcs. U. of Health Scis., Bethesda, Md., 1990—91, clin. asst. prof. in surgery, 1991—2006; asst. prof. dept. of urology U. Tenn., Memphis, 1994—95, assoc. prof. depts. of urology/gynecology, dir. divsn. of neurourology, 1996—98; med. dir. North Tex. Ctr. for Urinary Control, 1998—2001; prof. dept. of urology Vanderbilt U. Med. Ctr., Nashville, 2001—. Admissions com. Vanderbilt U. Sch. of Medicine, Nashville, 2004—; vis. prof. Walter Reed Army Med. Ctr., Tulane U. Med. Ctr., Kans. Med. Ctr.; lectr. in field. Contbr. chapters to books, articles to profl. jours. Recipient Zimskind award, Urodynamics Soc., 1999. Fellow: ACS; mem.: Internat. Continence Soc. (sci. com. 2003—06, edn. com. 2003—06), Am. Urogynecologic Soc., Societe' Internationale d'Urologie, Soc. of Genitourinary Reconstructive Surgeons, Urodynamicc Soc., Soc. of Govt. Svcs. Urologists, Southeastern Sect. Am. Urologic Assn., Soc. of Female Urology and Urodynamics (v.p. 2003—06, pres. 2006—), Am. Urologic Assn. (safety com. 2003—, Blue Ribbon com. 2005—06, chair practice parameters and guidelines com. 2005—06, pub. rels. com. 2005—06). Office: Vanderbilt Univ Med Ctr A-1302 Medical Ctr N Nashville TN 37232-2765

DOBBS, ELLY, state legislator; b. May 31; m. Ed Dobbs; 3 children. BA in Econ., U. Fla., 1972; JD, Fla. State. U. Former admin. rev. analyst Dept. Family Svcs.; former assoc. v.p. Sun Bank; former atty. Dade County, Miami, Fla.; former asst. atty. gen. Fla. Dept. Justice; atty. Parker, Hudson & Rainer; mem. Dist. 53 Ga. House of Reps., 2009—. Democrat. Presbyterian. Office: Ga House of Reps 512 Coverdell Legislative Office Bldg Atlanta GA 30334 Home: 10 Riverly Pl NW Atlanta GA 30327-2500 Office Phone: 404-419-6832, 404-656-7859. Business E-Mail: elly.dobbs@house.ga.gov.

DOBBS, GEORGE ALBERT, retired researcher; b. Atlanta, Oct. 16, 1943; s. Albert F. and Ruby Lee (Haynes) D. Student in Ministry and Theology, Fla. Bapt. Theol. Coll., 1963-67; BA, Cornell U., 1974; AA in Mortuary Sci. and Adminstrn., John A. Gupton Coll., 1990; PhD, Sacred Heart Theol. Sem., Nashville, Tenn., 2010. Cert. funeral svc. practitioner, ordained baptist minister, Oakhurt Baptist Ch. Deactour, Ga., 1965. Retail store mgr. Alterman Foods, Atlanta, 1962-74; ind. mng. agt. George A. Dobbs & Assocs., Decatur, Ga., 1974-78, motivational spkr., Hermitage, Tenn., 1992—; retail mgr. K-Mart Corp., Decatur, 1978-91; funeral dir., embalmer SCI Nashville Group, 1991-97, coord. svc. ctr. Nashville Family Funeral Homes, 1997—2001; funeral dir., embalmer Stewart Enterprises, Nashville, 2001—04, Phillips-Robinson, Nashville, 2004—11; wedding and funeral celebrant, 2003—; Ky. license embalmer, funeral dir., 2012—. Named Small Bus. Man of Yr., Dekalb Businessman's Assn., 1974, 76. Mem. Capital City Club, Order Ky. Cols., Masons (past master Ga. and Tenn.), Scottish Rite Mason (32d degree), Shriners, Philalethes Soc., York Rite, Tex, Lodge of Rsch., Ga. Lodge Rsch., Grand Coun. Ga., N.Am. Soc. Pipe Collectors, Universal Coterie of Pipe Smokers, Soc. of Pipe Collectors, Pipe Club London, Ky. Bourbon Cir., Khorasoan MOUPER (Tex., Calif. and Mo. grand lodges, past Lt. govs.), Internat. Optimist Club, J. Barleycorn Club, Knights of Mecca, Tenn. Yellow Dogs (life), Quatuor Coronati Lodge, Galilee Lodge State of Israel, Notary Pub., The True Gentelmans Club North America. Baptist. Independent.

DOBBS, JOHNNIE C., JR., retail executive; BBA, East Tex. State U., Texarkana, Tex. Distbn. ctr. gen. mgr. Svc. Merchandise; various civilian logistic related positions US Army, 1978; gen. mgr., regional mgr., dir., distbn. and logistics, v.p., membership and sales, Sam's Club, v.p., splty. distbn. and transp. Wal-Mart Stores, Inc., 1990, divisional v.p., sr. v.p., logistics, exec. v.p., logistics and supply chain, US, 2006—. Mem.: Retail Industry Leaders Assn. (chmn. logistics steering com.). Office: Wal-Mart Stores Inc 702 SW 8th St Bentonville AR 72716 Office Phone: 479-277-4000. Office Fax: 479-277-1830. Business E-Mail: johnnie.dobbs@walmartstores.com.

DOBES, WILLIAM LAMAR, JR., dermatologist, educator; b. Atlanta, Apr. 16, 1943; s. William Lamar and Sara (Wilson) Dobes; m. Martha Husmann, June 16, 1966; children: Margaret Alison Key, William Shane. BA, Emory U., 1965, MD, 1969. Diplomate Am. Bd. Dermatology. Intern Grady Meml. Hosp., Atlanta, 1969-70; fellow in dermatology Mayo Clinic, 1970-71; fellow U. Miami, 1971-73; clin. instr. Emory U. Sch. Medicine, Atlanta, 1973-77, asst. prof. dermatology, 1977-83, assoc. prof., 1983—. Dir. immunofluorescense lab., 1978-85; mem. staff Crawford Long, Grady Meml., Piedmont hosps., Atlanta; dir. Skin Cancer Project, Emory U., 1981-89; chmn. profl. edn. unit Atlanta chpt. Am. Cancer Soc., 1980-86, also bd. dirs., pres., 1986-87, chmn. bd. dirs., 1987-88; pres. Carter's Atlanta, project chmn. Physicians Com., 1992-95. Contbr. articles to profl. jours. and texts. Chmn. Ga. med. bd. Lupus Found., 1988, bd. dirs. Whitney Rsch. Lab., U. Fla., 1998-2002; Emory Yerkes Rsch. Ctr., 2004—, bd. dirs, v.p., 2006-. Dermatology Found. Rsch. award, 1979; named to best Doctors in Am., 2003-08. Fellow Am. Dermatol. Assn.; mem. AMA, ACP, Am. Soc. Cosmetic and Aesthetic Surgery, Soc. Investigative Dermatology, Am. Acad. Dermatology (chmn. com. quality assurance 1982-84, adv. coun. 1985-95, ad coun. exec. com. 1991-95, com. on stds. of care 1987-91, chmn. CLIA task force 1993-97), So. Med. Assn. (vice chmn. 1983), Pan Am. Med. Assn., Am. Soc. Dermatologic Surgery, Ga. Dermatol. Assn. (pres. 1986-87), Atlanta Dermatol. Assn. (pres. 1979), N.Am. Clin. Dermatologic Soc., Soc. Tropical Dermatology, Med. Assn. Atlanta (bd. dirs. 1985-92, chmn. comm. com. 1985-90, sec. 1988-89, pres.-elect 1989-90, pres. 1990-91), Med. Assn. Ga. (Intersplty. Coun. 1984-97, com. on cancer 1988-93, pub. rels. com. 1988-94, del. to Ga. Med. Assn. 1985—, Outstanding Svc. award 1993), Atlanta Clin. Soc., Atlanta Olympic Med. Com. (chmn. dermatology sect. 1996), Emory U. Med. Alumni Assn. (pres. 1980, 86, exec. com. 1992-97), Phi Delta Theta (past pres.), Phi Chi (past pres.), Cherokee Town & Country Club (Atlanta). Office: 2045 Peachtree St NE Ste 200 Atlanta GA 30309-1414 also: Emory U Sch Medicine Dept Dermatology Atlanta GA 30308 Home Phone: 404-261-1379; Office Phone: 404-351-7546.

DOBRANSKI, BERNARD, dean, law educator; b. Sept. 3, 1939; s. Walter John and Helen Dolores (Rudnick) Dobranski; m. Caroll Sue Wood, Aug. 31, 1963; children: Stephanie, Andrea, Christopher. BBA in Fin., U. Notre Dame, 1961; JD, U. Va., 1964; LLD, Ave Maria Sch Law, 2010. Bar: Va. 64, U.S. Supreme Ct. 68, U.S. Ct. Appeals (DC cir.) 71. Legal advisor to bd. Nat. Labor Rels. Bd., 1964—67; profl. staff mem. Pres.'s Adv. Commn. on Civil Disorders, 1967—68; adminstrv. asst. US House of Representatives, 1968—71; gen. counsel Washington Met. Area Transit Commn., 1971—72; mem. faculty Creighton U. Sch. of Law, Omaha, 1972—77, U. Notre Dame, 1977—83; prof., dean U. Detroit Sch. of Law, 1983—95, Cath. U. Am. Sch. of Law, 1995—99; prof., pres., dean Ave Maria Sch. Law, Ann Arbor, Mich., 1999—, Naples, Fla. Contbr. articles to profl. jours. Mem.: ABA, Hurlingham Club, Frank Murphy Honor Soc. Roman Catholic. Home Phone: 239-431-7446; Office Phone: 239-687-5321. Business E-Mail: bdobranski@avemarialaw.edu.

DOBSON, DONALD ALFRED, retired electrical engineer; b. Evanston, Ill., Feb. 19, 1928; s. Alfred Topping and Agnes Lucille (Park) D. BSEE, Northwestern U., 1950, PhD, 1955; MSEE, MIT, 1951. Research assoc. Northwestern U., Evanston, 1951-54; engr. Indsl. Research Products, Franklin Park, Ill., 1952; sr. engr. Sperry Gyroscope Co., Great Neck, NY, 1954-59; sr. tech. specialist N.Am. Aviation, Columbus, Ohio, 1959-63; research staff mem. Inst. for Def. Analyses, Arlington, Va., 1963-90, adj. staff mem., 1990-98, ret., 1998. Instr. physics Adelphi Coll., Garden City, N.Y., 1956 Mem. IEEE, Sigma Xi, Tau Beta Pi, Eta Kappa Mu, Pi Mu Epsilon

DOBSON, RICHARD LAWRENCE, dermatologist, educator; b. Boston, Apr. 12, 1928; s. Joseph William and Celia Beatrice (Siegler) D.; m. Marie C. Mollomo, 1950; children: Richard Lawrence, Pamela Blair, Lisa Marie, Karen Jill, David Scott; m. Rhoda H. Freda, Feb. 14, 2004. MD, U. Chgo., 1953; BS, U. N.H., 1981. Diplomate Am. Bd. Dermatology (v.p. 1987-88, pres. 1988-89). Intern Cin. Gen. Hosp., 1953-54; resident Hitchcock Clinic, Hanover, NH, 1954-57; asst. prof. dermatology U. NC, Chapel Hill, 1957-61; prof. U. Oreg., Portland, 1961-72, SUNY-Buffalo, 1972-79, Med. U. SC, Charleston, 1980-98, acting dean, 1985-86, chmn. dept. anatomy and cell biology, 1991-92; prof. emeritus Med. U. S.C., Charleston, 1998—. Vis. prof. U. Nijmegen, The Netherlands, 1969-70; hon. prof. Shanghai 2d Med. U.; hon. cons. Royal Prince Alfred Hosp., Sydney, Australia. Editor: Year Book of Dermatology, 1979-82, Clinical Dermatology, 1972-82, Contemporary Review, 1973-87; asst. editor: Jour. Am. Acad. Dermatology, 1979-87, editor, 1988-98; mng. editor Arch. Dermatol. Research, 1982-87. Served with USN, 1946-47. Fellow ACP, Am. Acad. Dermatology (pres. 1983-84); mem. Am. Dermatologic Assn. (treas. 1977-82), Soc. Investigative Dermatology (pres. 1975-76), Oreg. Dermatol. Soc. (pres. 1971-72); hon. mem. Brit. Assn. Dermatology, Spanish Assn. Dermatology, French Dermatology Soc., Polish Dermatology Soc., Finnish Dermatology Soc., Dutch Dermatology Soc., German Dermatology Soc., N.Am. Dermatology Soc., Ga. Dermatology Soc., Iowa Dermatology Soc. Republican. Roman Catholic.

DOBSON, RICK, energy executive; BS in bus. admin., U. Wis.; MBA in fin., U. Nebr. Cert. CPA. Audit mgr. Arthur Andersen, 1981—89; v.p., contr. Aquila Merchant Svcs., 1989—95; v.p., risk mgmt. acctg. Aquila, Kans. City, Mo., 1997, interim CFO, 2002—03, CFO, 2003—06; CFO, sr. v.p. Novelis, Inc., Atlanta, 2006—07; exec. v.p., CFO Reliant Energy, Inc., Houston, 2007—. Office: Reliant Energy Inc 1000 Main St PO Box 148 Houston TX 77201-0148

DO CANTO, LICY M., lobbyist; BA in Polit. Sci., Internat. Affairs, & Spanish Studies, Duke U., Durham, NC, 1995. Profl. cert. in pub. health leadership U. NC Sch. Pub. Health and Kenan-Flagler Bus. Sch., Chapel Hill, 2004. Cultural studies American Field Service, Istanbul, Turkey, 1990; aide to Barney Frank US House of Representatives, Washington; aide to Edward Kennedy US Senate, Washington, 1991; internat. relations, pub. affairs studies Ctr. for Internat. Studies, Madrid, 1993—94; dir. Cape Verdean Cmty. Outreach, US Senator Edward Kennedy, 1994; staff asst. Senate Judiciary Subcommittee on Immigration and Refugee Affairs to US Senator Edward Kennedy, 1995; sr. legis. asst. for domestic policy to US Congressman Barney Frank US Congress, 1996—2001; sr. mgr. fed. affairs, Fed. Govt. Relations Dept. American Cancer Soc., 2001—03; dir. fed. affairs Nat. Assn. Cmty. Health Centers, 2003—08; staff mem. US Dept. of Health and Human Services Nat. Medicaid Adv. Commission, 2005—06; CEO AIDS Alliance Children, Youth and Families, 2008; prin., co-dir. health & edn. practice group The Raben Group, Washington, 2008—10; founder, pres. The Do Canto Group, LLC, 2010—. Founder, chmn. Partnership for Medicaid. Quoted in media, including Politico, The Hill, Roll Call, and Inside Health Policy. Named one of Washington's Top Lobbyists, The Hill, 2010, 2011. Office: The Do Canto Group LLC 22575 Leanne Terrace Ashburn VA 20148 Office Phone: 202-997-5963. Business E-Mail: info@docantogroup.com.

DOCKERY, J. LEE, retired medical school administrator; b. Amity, Ark., 1932; MD, U. Ark., 1957. Rotating intern Jackson Meml. Hosp., Miami, Fla., 1957—58; resident in ob-gyn. U. Miami, 1958—61; active attending staff Jackson Meml. Hosp., Miami, Fla., 1963—75; active staff Doctor's Hosp. Miami, 1963—75; active staff, chmn. dept. ob-gyn. Bapt. Hosp. Miami, 1972—73; staff Shands Hosp., Gainesville, Fla., 1975—91; prof. ob-gyn. U. Fla., Gainesville, 1980—92, assoc. dean, 1980—86, exec. assoc. dean, 1986—88, interim dean, assoc. v.p. clin. affairs, 1988—91; exec. v.p. Am. Bd. Med. Specialties, 1991—97. Clin. adj. prof. dept. ob-gyn. Northwestern U. Med. Sch., 1992—; clin. prof. dept. ob-gyn. U. Fla. Coll. Medicine, 1992—2000; trustee McKnight Brain Rsch. Found., 1999—; prof. emeritus U. Fla. Coll. Medicine, 2000—; mem. Accreditation Coun. for Grad. Med. Edn., 1984—89, Liaison Com. for Med. Edn., 1989—91, Fla. Bd. Medicine, 1988—92; mem. exam. bd. Fed. State Med. Bds., 1991—94; mem. U.S. Med. Licensing Exam. Composite Com., 1996—2002, Nat. Com. on Fgn. Med. Edn. and Accreditation, 2001—04, chair, 2006—09. Mem.: AMA (mem. coun. med. edn. 1983—92, chmn. 1987—88), Fla. Med. Assn. (pres. 1983—84), So. Med. Assn. (pres. 1987—88), Alpha Omega Alpha.

DOCKERY, PAULA, state legislator; b. Queens, NY, June 6, 1961; m. C.C. Dockery. BA in Polit. Sci., U. Fla., 1983, MA in Mass. Comm., 1987. Dir. Polk County Family Caregivers, Inc.; v.p. Dockery Mgmt.; mem. Dist. 64 Fla. House of Reps., Tallahassee, 1994—2000; mem. Dist. 15 Fla. State Senate, Tallahassee, 2002—, chair criminal justice com., mem. environ. preservation and conservation com., transp. com., transp. and econ. devel. appropriations com., joint com. on pub. counsel oversight. Chairwoman Lakeland Civil Svc.; mem. Lakeland Pension Bd., Fla. Coun. Edn. Mgmt. Vice chmn. Polk County Edn. Found., Lakeland YMCA; bd. mem. Found. Florida's Future, Lakeland C. of C.; mem. Greater Lakeland Jr. League. Republican. Roman Catholic. Office: 302 Senate Office Bldg 404 S Monroe St Tallahassee FL 32399-1100 also: PO Box 2646 Lakeland FL 33806-2646 Office Phone: 863-413-2900, 850-487-5040. Business E-Mail: dockery.paula.web@flsenate.gov.

DOCKHAM, JERRY C., state legislator; m. Luise Dockham. State rep. Dist. 94, NC, 1988—2002; state rep. Dist. 80 NC, 2003—. Mem. Appropriations com., Appropriations Subcom. on Transp., Edn. com., Edn. Subcom. on Cmty. Colleges, Ethics com., Fin. Instns. com.; vice chmn. Ins. com. Republican. Mailing: PO Box 265 Denton NC 27239 Office: North Carolina House of Representatives 16 W Jones St Rm 2204 Raleigh NC 27601-1096 Office Phone: 919-715-2526, 336-250-7336. E-mail: Jerry.Dockham@ncleg.net.

DODANI, SUNITA, physician, educator; MD, MSc, U. Pitts., PhD, 2006. Diplomate. Asst. prof. Aga Khan U., Karachi, Sindh, Pakistan, 2000—02, U. Pitts., 2003—. Achievements include research in heart diseases in young population. Home: Gerogia Health Sciences University 4503 Health Science Bldg 997 San Sabastian Way Augusta GA 30912 Home Fax: 412-383-1974. Personal E-mail: sud9@pitt.edu.

DODD, EMMELINE IRWIN, retired biology educator; b. Nacogdoches, Tex., Aug. 30, 1939; d. Grady Scott and Addie Mae (Chambers) Irwin; m. Gene Dodd, Jan. 28, 1961 (div. 1967); 1 child, Catherine Denise. BA, Stephen F. Austin State U., Nacogdoches, 1961, MA, 1965; postgrad., Tex. A&M U., 1967-74; MS, U. Houston, 1982. CPA, lic. real estate broker, Tex.; cert. master naturalist. Biology tchr. Pasadena (Tex.) Ind. Sch. Dist., 1961-65; prof. of biology San Jacinto Coll., Pasadena, 1965-69; rsch. biologist NASA, Clear Lake, Tex., 1969-71; biology tchr. Houston Community Coll., 1971-72; prof. biology Coll. of Mainland, Texas City, Tex., 1973—2004; Piper prof. State of Tex., 1998; ret., 2004. Chmn. Houston Livestock Show and Rodeo, Clear Lake, 1991-94; staff advisor Lunar Rendezvous, Clear Lake, 1991; mem. com. Tex. Higher Edn. Coord. Bd., Austin, 1989—; founder Red Hats, Clear Lake. Recipient Outstanding Friend Arts award, 2011; named Lunar Rendezvous Vol. of Yr., 1995, Disting. Alumnus U. Houston Clear Lake and Stephen F. Austin U., 2003, Woman of Heart vol. work. Mem. Nat. Assn. Biology Tchrs. (planning com. 1990 conv.), Tex. Cmty. Coll. Tchrs. Assn. (pres. 1989-90, state social chmn. 1991-92), Clear Lake Panhellenic Soc., Tex. C.C. Tchrs. Assn. (state membership com. 1999), Stephen F. Austin Alumni Assn. (life), Chi Omega. Lutheran. Avocations: insect and bromeliad collecting, travel, reading. Personal E-mail: txdodd@aol.com.

DODD, GERALD DEWEY, JR., radiologist, educator; b. Oaklyn, NJ, Nov. 18, 1922; s. Gerald Dewey and Anne Aloysius (Keveney) D.; m. Helen Carolyn Glenzing, Apr. 5, 1946; children: Patricia, Michael, Barbara, Gerald Dewey III, Anne, Susan, Thomas. AB, Lafayette Coll., 1945; MD, Jefferson Med. Coll., 1947; DSc (hon.), Lafayette Coll., 1991. Diplomate Am. Bd. Radiology. Intern Fitzgerald Mercy Hosp., Darby, Pa., 1947; resident Jefferson Med. Coll., Phila., 1948—50; asst. radiologist, asst. in radiology Thomas Jefferson Med. Coll. and Hosp., Phila., 1952—54, assoc. in radiology, 1954—55; asst. radiologist, clin. prof. radiology Thomas Jefferson Med. Coll., 1961—66; assoc. radiologist, assoc. prof. radiology U. Tex. M.D. Anderson Cancer Ctr., Houston, 1955—61, prof., 1966—89, chmn. dept. diagnostic radiology, 1966—89, prof., head divsn. diagnostic imaging, 1984—92, Robert D. Moreton Chair Diagnostic Radiology, 1988—93, chair emeritus, 1996—; prof. radiology U. Tex. Med. Sch., Houston, 1971—, chmn. dept. radiology, 1971—74, prof. radiology Sch. Allied Health Scis., 1971—94. Cons. radiologist St. Luke's Hosp., Tex. Children's Hosp., Houston, 1966—, Singleton Prof. Radiology, 1995-99; vis. mem. grad. faculty Tex. A&M U., College Station, 1969-93; adj. prof. radiology Baylor Coll. Medicine, 1983—. Cons. to editor Radiology, 1977—86, cons. editor The Cancer Bull., 1979—89, assoc. editor Cancer, 1991—2000; editor: Breast Diseases, 1993—2004; referee CRC Critical Revs. in Radiol. Scis., 1969—95; contbr. articles to profl. jours. Dir.-at-large Am. Cancer Soc., 1977-90, pres., 1990-91, past officer dir.; mem. coun. Nat. Coun. Radiation Protection and Measurement, 1979-91, bd. dirs., 1981-91. Fellow Am. Coll. Radiology (bd. chancellors, 1971-80, pres. 1984-85, Gold medal 1989); mem. Radiol. Soc. N.Am. (Gold medal 1986), Am. Roentgen Ray Soc. (Gold medal 1992), Soc. Gastrointestinal Radiologists (Cannon medal 1995), Assn. Univ. Radiologists, Tex. Med. Assn., Tex. Radiol. Soc. (Gold medal 1988), Soc. Breast Imaging (Gold medal 1995), Harris County Med. Soc., Houston Radiol. Soc., Phila. Roentgen Ray Soc. (hon.), Gilbert H. Fletcher Soc. (Gold medal 2008), Alpha Omega Alpha, Phi Delta Theta, Phi Chi. Republican. Roman Catholic. Office: M D Anderson Hosp 1515 Holcombe Blvd Houston TX 77030-4009

DODD, ROGER J., lawyer; b. Sewickley, Pa., Sept. 15, 1951; s. Carl Roger and Dorothy Maude (Barley) Dodd; children: Matthew A., Andrew J. BA in Econs., Bucknell U., 1973; JD, U. Pitts., 1976, Ga., 1976, Fla., 1977. Ptnr. Blackburn, Bright, Edwards Dodd & Joseph, Valdosta, Ga., 1976-87; prin. Dodd & Burnham, P.C., Valdosta, 1987—; spl. asst. atty. gen. State of Ga., 1979-85; mem. faculty Ga. Inst. Trial Advocacy, 1986—92, chmn. of bd., 1988—91; mem. faculty Nat. Coll. Criminal Def., 1986—. Mem. faculty Nat. Coll. Criminal Def., 1986—, Advance Cross Exam., Advance Trial Inst.; adj. prof. Valdosta State Coll.; guest lectr. sch. law Mercer U. Ga. State U.; mem. family law sect. exec. com., 1985-88, criminal law sect., mem. family law sect., exec. com. 1985-88; mem. ABA family law sect., criminal law sect. exec. coms., 1992—; internat. lectr. in field. Co-author: Cross Examination: Science and Techniques, 1993; guest commentator on Court TV; peer rev. lawyer Trial Mag., 1991—; contbr. articles to profl. jours., newspapers; videos: Killer Cross-Examination (6 hrs. of audio & video tapes) The Art and Science of Cross Examination, 2 parts, 1990, How to Dominate a Courtroom on Cross Examination, 4 parts, 1994, co-author: Media Skills: The Lawyer as Spokes Bd. dirs. Lowndes Country Assn. Retarded Citizens, Valdosta, 1977, Valwood Sch., Valdosta, 1984-86, Nat. Bd. Trial Advocacy, 1989, civil trial specialist, criminal trial specialist, 1990; peer rev. lawyer Trial Mag., 1991; mem. Boy Scouts Am., sustaining mem. Alapaha Coun. Mem.: Am. Acad. Matrimonial Lawyers, Internat. Acad. Matrimonial Lawyers. Libertarian. Presbyterian. Office: PO Box 1066 613 N Patterson St Valdosta GA 31601-4609 also: Spohrer Dodd 701 W Adams St Jacksonville FL 32204 also: Dodd Law PO Box 684079 Park City UT 84068 Office Phone: 229-242-4470. Office Fax: 229-245-7731. E-mail: doddlaw@doddlaw.com.*

DODGE, WILLIAM DOUGLAS, risk management consultant; b. Savannah, Ga., Sept. 26, 1937; s. Kenneth Douglas and Bettie Wilbur (Sadler) D.; m. Susan Penny, Dec. 27, 1958 (div. 1976); children: Gregory D., Phillip C., Warren D., Andrew L.; m. Marian Elizabeth Monroe, Apr. 2, 1983. BS, Ga. Inst. Tech., 1959; MBA, Ga. State U., 1966. CPCU, ARM. Underwriter Liberty Mutual Ins. Co., Atlanta, 1960-66; ins. adminstr. Lockheed Corp., Marietta, Ga., 1966-78; risk mgr. Schlumberger Ltd., Atlanta, 1978-79; v.p. ins. Fuqua Industries, Inc., Atlanta, 1979-90, v.p. ins. and benefits, 1991-92; pres. Fuqua Ins. Co. Ltd., Hamilton, Bermuda, 1978-92, Fuqua Risk Retention Group, Atlanta, 1989-92; ind. risk mgmt. cons. Atlanta, 1992-95. Adv. bd. Risk Mgmt. Inc., N.Y.C., 1978-92; chmn. bd., mem. investment com. J&H WF Syndicate B., N.Y. Ins. Exch., N.Y.C., 1984-88. Co-author: The Hold Harmless Agreement, 1968. Mem. Exec. Com. Reorgn. and Mgmt. Improvement State of Ga., 1971, Agts. Licensing Exam. Revision Bd. State Ga., 1970; bd. dirs. Ga. State U. Ednl. Found., 1980-88; lt. comdr. USPS/Tybee Light Power Squadron, 1999, comdr., 2000—. Republican. Methodist. Avocations: gardening, boating. Office: Mickey Dodge & Assocs Inc 12 Pipers Pond Ln Savannah GA 31404-1122 Personal E-mail: savdodges@aol.com.

DODSON, J. MARSHALL (JOHN MARSHALL DODSON), energy company executive; b. 1971; BBA, U. Tex., 1993. CPA. Acctg. positions through sr. mgr. Arthur Andersen LLP, 1993—2002; fin. mgmt. positions Dynegy Inc., 2002—03, mng. dir., contr., Dynegy Generation, 2003—05; v.p., chief acctg. officer Key Energy Services, Inc., 2005—09, interim prin. fin. officer, 2009, v.p., treas., 2009—. Office: Key Energy Services Inc 1301 McKinney St Ste 1800 Houston TX 77010 Office Phone: 713-651-4300. Office Fax: 713-652-4005.

DODSON, SAMUEL ROBINETTE, III, retired investment banker; b. Nashville, Feb. 24, 1943; s. Samuel Robinette and Helen Elizabeth (Maiden) D.; m. Marsha Robertson Moody, Aug. 2, 1969; children—Bradley John, Andrew Caldwell. Student, Yale U., 1961-63; BS, Vanderbilt U., 1966; MBA, U. Chgo., 1968; MS, London Sch. Econs., 1968. Various fin. and planning positions Exxon Corp. and Affiliates, Houston, 1968-81; v.p. First Boston Corp., 1981-84, mng. dir., 1984-93, Merrill Lynch, Houston, 1993—2004; ret., 2004. Served to 1st lt. U.S. Army, 1963-64 Home Phone: 713-468-5353.

DOENECKE, JUSTUS DREW, historian; b. Bklyn., Mar. 5, 1938; s. Justus Christian and Eleanore Howard (Smith) Doenecke; m. Carol Anne Soukup, Mar. 21, 1970. BA magna cum laude, Colgate U., 1960; MA in History, Princeton U., 1962, PhD in History, 1966. Instr. history Colgate U., Hamilton, NY, 1963—64, Ohio Wesleyan U., Delaware, 1965—66, asst. prof. history, 1966—69; from asst. prof. history to prof. New Coll. Fla., Sarasota, 1969—2005, prof. emeritus, 2005—. Author: Not to the Swift: The Old Isolationists in the Cold War Era, 1979, The Diplomacy of Frustration: The Manchurian Crisis of 1931-1933 as Revealed in the Papers of Stanley K. Hornbeck, 1981, The Presidencies of James A. Garfield and Chester A. Arthur, 1981, When the Wicked Rise: American Opinion-Makers and the Manchurian Crisis of 1931-33, 1984, Anti-Intervention: A Bibliographical Introduction to Isolationism and Pacifism from World War I to the Early Cold War, 1987, In Danger Undaunted: The Anti-Interventionist Movement of 1940-41 as Revealed in the Papers of the America First Committee, 1990, (with J. Wilz) From Isolation to War, 1931-1941, 2003 (3rd edit.), The Battle Against Intervention, 1939-41, 1997, Storm on the Horizon: The Challenge to American Intervention, 1939-1941, 2000, The New Deal, 2003, (with M. Stoler) Debating Franklin D. Roosevelt's Foreign Policies, 1933-1945, 2005, Nothing Less Than War: A New History of American Entry into World War I, 2011, Selection of History and Military Book Clubs; contbr. articles to profl. jours. Recipient Herbert Hoover Book award Herbert Hoover Presdl. Libr. Assn., 2001, Woodrow Wilson Nat. fellow, 1960, Danforth fellow, 1960, Non-resident summer fellow Inst. for Humane Studies, 1970, 71, resident summer fellow Inst. for Humane Studies, 1975, 76, 78, 81, sr. rsch. fellow acad. yr. Inst. for Humane Studies, 1977-78, summer fellow NEH, 1971, fellow John Anton Kittridge Ednl. Fund, 1973, 80, Harry S. Truman Libr., 1973, Earhart Found., 1995, vis. fellow New Coll., Oxford, 1991. Mem. Soc. for Historians Am. Fgn. Rels. (Arthur S. Link prize for documentary editing 1991), Am. Hist. Assn., Orgn. Am. Historians, Hist. Soc. Episcopal Ch. (Burr Prize Com. mem. 2011), Phi Beta Kappa, Sarasota Assn. Campus Ministry (bd. mem. 2005-2011, 2013-, v.p. 2008-11, 2013-, mem. adv. bd., 2011-12). Episcopalian. Office: New Coll of Fla Sarasota FL 34243-2197 Business E-Mail: doenecke@ncf.edu.

DOERR, HARVEY, oil industry executive; With Hudson's Bay Oil & Gas (formerly Dome Petroleum Ltd., Calgary, Alta., Husky Oil Ops. Ltd., Lloydminster, Alta., Murphy Oil Co. Ltd., 1989—2006, various positions including mgr. dist. ops., sr. engr., mgr. fgn. ops. and gen. mgr. fgn. ops. & spl. projects, pres., 1997—2006; exec. v.p. Murphy Oil Corp., 2007—09, cons. Canada, 2009—. Former chair bd. dirs. C-Core; former bd. mem. Syncrude Can. Mem.: Assn. Profl. Engrs., Geologists and Geophysicists Alta. Office: Murphy Oil Corp PO Box 7000 El Dorado AR 71731-7000 Office Phone: 870-862-6411.

DOERRIE, BOBETTE, science educator; b. Albuquerque, June 22, 1944; d. Neill and Dorothy Madelyn (Jones) Patterson; m. Edward Lewis Horton, Aug. 21, 1966 (div. 1990); children: Leah, James, Carol, Neill; m. Jerome Lee Doerrie, July 28, 1991; children: Jennifer, Elena. BA, McMurry Coll., 1966; MEd, DePaul U., 1977. Cert. sec. broadfield sci. Tchr. Summit Sch., Dundee, Ill., 1974-77, Lamesa Mid. Sch., 1980—85, Lamesa HS, 1968—69, 1985—91, Perryton HS, 1991—2005; dir. ednl. svcs. Frank Phillips CC, 2006—08; primary prevention coord. Panhandle Crisis Ctr., 2008—10; physical science instr. Northwestern Okla. State U., 2010—. Co-dir. Dawson County Sci. Fair, 1981-91; coach Odyssey of the Mind, 1988-91; mem. McMurry U. Ednl. Adv. Bd., 1991-97, engring. team faculty advisor, 1993-2004, sci. olympiad coach, 1998-2000, sci. bowl advisor, 2001-05; instr. astronomy Frank Phillips Coll., 2006—08. Bd. dirs. Mus.Dawson County, 1983—90, Libr. Ochiltree County, 1993—95, v.p., 1993—95; bd. dirs. Perrytown Crisis Ctr., 2005—07, Crime Stoppers; Panhandle profl. writers, newsletter editor, 2007—; v.p. Bus. and Profsl. Women, 2008—. Recipient Excellence in Teaching award Tex. State Assn. for Physics Tchrs., 1992, Nat. Tchg. award RadioShack, 2001; NSF/Tex. Edn. Assn. Christa McAuliffe grantee, 1993, Outstanding Sci. Educator, Tex. Acad. Sci., 2002, Nat. Tchg. award Health Physics Soc., 2002; named Tchr. of Yr., Region XVI Gifted and Talented Tchrs., 1994, Perryton H.S., 2004. Mem.: Sci. Tchrs. of Tex. (treas. 1998—2001), Panhandle Profl. Writers, Delta Kamma Gamma (v.p. 2008—10, pres. 2000—02). Avocations: amateur radio, painting, astronomy, reading, writing. Home: 13925 County Rd B Booker TX 79005-4125 Office Phone: 806-435-5008. Personal E-mail: prevcoor@yahoo.com.

DOERY, MICHELLE, corporate financial executive; B in Acctg., Merrimack Coll., North Andover. CPA NH. CFO, N.Am. ABB Optical; CFO Infusion Svcs. Inc, MedChoice Pharmacy; CFO, corp. contr. Lennar Homes, South Fla., Ameripath Inc., South Fla.; auditor Grant Thornton LLP; regional v.p., fin. Lennar Homes LLC, Palm Beach, Fla., 2003—07; worked Jefferson Wells, 2007—08; cons. Point Blank Solutions, Inc., 2007, dir., fin. reporting, v.p., corp. contr., 2008, interim CFO, 2009, CFO, 2009—. Office: Point Blank Solutions Inc 2102 SW 2nd St Pompano Beach FL 33069 Office Phone: 954-630-0900. Office Fax: 954-630-9225. Business E-Mail: mdoery@pointblankarmor.com.

DOGGETT, LLOYD ALTON, II, United States Representative from Texas, retired judge; b. Austin, Tex., Oct. 6, 1946; s. Lloyd Alton and Alyce (Freydenfeldt) Doggett; m. Elizabeth Belk, 1969; children: Lisa, Catherine. BBA in Bus., U. Tex., Austin, 1967; JD with honors, U. Tex. Sch. Law, 1970. Bar: Tex. 1971, US Dist. Ct. (western dist.) Tex. 1972, US Ct. Appeals (5th cir.) 1972. Mem. Dist. 14 Tex. State Senate, 1973-85; ptnr. Doggett & Jacks, Austin, Tex., 1975-88; justice Tex. Supreme Ct., Austin, 1989-94; mem. US Congress from 10th Tex. Dist., 1995—2005, US Congress from 25th Tex. Dist., 2005—13, US Congress from 35th Tex. Dist., 2013—. Adj. prof. U. Tex. Sch. Law, 1989—94; chair Task Force on Jud. Ethics Tex. Supreme Ct., 1992—94. Bd. dirs. Consumers Union US, 1976—81, 1986—89. Recipient James Madison award, Freedom of Info. Found. Tex., 1990, First Amendment award, Nat. Soc. Profl. Journalists, 1990, Environ. Champion award, Tex. League Conservation Voters, 2006, Legis. Achievement award, American Assn. Retired Persons, 2008, Arthur B. DeWitty award for outstanding achievement in human rights, Austin chpt. NAACP; named Bus. Advocate of Yr., Tex. Assn. Mex.-American Chamber of Commerce, 2006, Best Elected Ofcl., Austin Chronicle, 2010; named an Outstanding State Senator, Common Cause, 1980, Outstanding Jurist in Tex., Mex. American Bar Assn., 1993; named one of The Five Outstanding Young Texans, Tex. Jaycees, 1977, The Best Legislators, Tex. Monthly mag., 1979, 1981. Mem.: Tex. Consumer Assn. (pres. 1973). Democrat. Methodist. Office: US House of Representatives 201 Cannon House Office Bldg Washington DC 20515-4310 also: PO Box 5843 Austin TX 78763 Office Phone: 202-225-4865, 210-998-0160. Office Fax: 512-487-9983.*

DOHERTY, KATE, editor; Sr. assoc. home editor Family Circle Mag.; home market editor HGTV mag. Home and Garden TV (HGTV). Office: Home & Garden Television 9721 Sherrill Blvd Knoxville TN 37932 Office Phone: 865-694-2700. Office Fax: 865-531-1588.

DOHERTY, PETER CHARLES, immunologist; b. Brisbane, Australia, Oct. 15, 1940; s. Eric C. and Linda Doherty; m. Penelope Stephens, 1965; children: James, Michael. B of Vet. Sci., U. Queensland, Australia, 1963, M of Vet. Sci., 1966; PhD, U. Edinburgh, Scotland, 1970; DSc (hon.), Australian Nat. U., 1996, U. Edinburgh, 1997, Tufts U., 1997, Warsaw Agrl. U., 1998, Latrobe U., 1999, Imperial Coll., U. London, 2000, Autonomous U. Barcelona, 2000, NC State U., 2000, U. Guelph, 2001, U. Pa., 2001, Mich. State U., 2002, U. Ill., 2002. Vet. officer Animal Rsch. Inst., Brisbane, 1963—67; sci. officer, dept. exptl. pathology Moredun Rsch. Inst., Edinburgh, 1967—71; rsch. fellow, dept. microbiology John Curtin Sch. Med. Rsch., Australian Nat. U., Canberra, 1972—75, prof., head dept. exptl. pathology, 1982—88; assoc. prof., prof. Wistar Inst., Phila., 1975—82; chmn. dept. immunology St. Jude Children's Rsch. Hosp., Memphis, 1988—2001, Michael F. Tamer Chair of biomed. rsch., 1988—; laureate prof. dept. microbiology and immunology U. Melbourne, Australia, 2002—. Mem. exptl. virology study sect. NIH, 1982—83, 1990—; bd. dirs. Internat. Lab. Animal Diseases, Nairobi, 1986—92; hon. prof. U. Tenn. Contbr. articles to profl. jours., chapters to books. Recipient Paul Ehrlich prize, Germany, 1983, Gairdner Found. Internat. award, 1986, Albert Lasker award for basic med. rsch., 1995, Nobel prize for medicine/physiology, 1996, Humanitarian award, Memphis City Coun., 1997, Peter Doherty Young Scientist award, Internat. Livestock Rsch. Inst., Kenya, 1998, Gregor Mendel medal, Villanova U., 2000, Vocational Svc. award, Rotary Club Melbourne, 2003, Centenary Medal, 2003, Curtin Medal, 2003; named Australian of Yr., Nat. Australia Day Coun., 1997, Living Nat. Treasure of Australia, 1998. Fellow: AAAS, Am. Soc. Microbiology, Royal Coll. Vet. Surgeons, Australian Soc. Immunology, Am. Coll. Vet. Pathologists, Am. Assn. Vet. Immunologists, Am. Soc. Med. Rsch., Australian Coll. Vet. Sci. (hon.), Scandinavian Soc. Immunology (hon.), Royal Soc. London; mem.: NAS (fgn. assoc.), Neuroimmunology Soc., Am. Assn. Pathologists, Paris Acad. Medicine (assoc.), Inst. Medicine, Internat. Union Immunological Societies (pres. 2008—10), Golden Key Nat. Honor Soc. (hon. life). Avocations: walking, reading. Office: St Jude Childrens Rsch Hosp MS 351 Rm E7062 262 Danny Thomas Pl Memphis TN 38105 also: U Melbourne Dept Microbiology and Immunology 3010 Melbourne VIC Australia Office Phone: 901-495-3470. Business E-Mail: peter.doherty@stjude.org. E-mail: pcd@unimelb.edu.au.

DOHERTY, REBECCA FEENEY, federal judge; b. Ft. Worth, Tex., June 3, 1952; d. Charles Edwin Feeney and Annabelle (Knight) Smith; divorced; 1 child, George Jason. BA, Northwestern State U., 1973, MA, 1975; JD, La. State U., 1981. Bar: La. 1981, U.S. Dist. Ct. (mid., ea. and we. dists.) La. 1981, U.S. Ct. Appeals (5th cir.) 1981, U.S. Dist. Ct. (so. dist.) Tex. 1986, U.S. Dist. Ct. (ea. dist.) Tex. 1989. Assoc. Onebane, Donohoe, Bernard, Torian, Diaz, McNamara & Abell, Lafayette, La., 1981-84, ptnr., 1985-91; judge US Dist. Ct. (we. dist.) La., Lafayette, 1991—. Adj. instr. Northwestern State U., Natchitoches, La., 1975; co-dir. secondary level gifted and talented program Webster Parish, La., 1978. Contbr. articles to profl. jours.; mem. La. Law Rev., 1980, 81. Recipient Am. Jurisprudence award Lawyers Coop. Pub. Co., 1980, Career Achievement award 1991; inducted into La. State U. Law Ctr. Hall of Fame, 1987. Mem. ABA, La. Bar Assn., La. Assn. Def. Counsel, La. Assn. Trial Lawyers, Acadian Assn. Women Attys., Order of Coif. Office: US Dist Ct 800 Lafayette St Ste 4900 Lafayette LA 70501-6879

DOHERTY, WILLIAM HENRY, writer, marketing executive; b. Fall River, Mass., Jan. 31, 1942; s. William Henry and Madeline Doherty; m. Sharon Ann Smith, May 20, 1970; children: Erin R., Sarah B. Grad. Fla. Inst. Tech. Sch. Bus. Adminstrn., 1982. Pres. internat. assn. profl. Terradacktils William H. Doherty Associates, Inc., William H. Doherty Productions, Inc., William H. Doherty Communications Corp., Palm Beach Gardens, Fla., 1968—; asst. prof. Pa. State U., 1980—82. Pres., CEO Am. Inst. Mgmt., 1985—; seminar leader bus. topics. Served USMC, 1960—63. Recipient Presdl. Sports award, 1970. Mem. Internat. Platform Assn. (winner Internat. Speakers Competition, 1983), Fla. Speakers Assn. (past pres.), Hotel Sales Mktg. Assn. (bd. dirs.), No. Palm Beach C. of C., Palm Beach Roundtable, No. Palm Beach Club, Rotary Club. Office: 11586 US Hwy 1 PO Box 79 North Palm Beach FL 33408

DOHNAL, DENNIS WILLIAM, judge; b. Cleve., Oct. 4, 1945; s. William Edward and Alta Louella Dohnal; m. Alecia Faye Woofter, Dec. 20, 1986; 1 child, Kelly Elizabeth;children from previous marriage: Todd Andrew, Mark Alan. BA, Bucknell U., Lewisburg, Pa., 1967; JD, George Washington U., 1970. Bar: Va. 1971. Asst. US atty. US Dept. Justice, Richmond, Va., 1971—74; ptnr. Bremner, Baber & Janus, Richmond, 1974—96, Brenner, Dohnal, Evans & Yoffy, Richmond, 1996—2000; US magistrate judge US Dist. Ct., Richmond, 2000—. Bd. dirs. Hanover Assn. Retarded Citizens, Va., 1995—2000, Cmty. Based Svcs., Hanover, 1999—2005. Fellow: Va. Law Found.; mem.: John Marshall Inn Ct., Richmond City Bar Assn. (pres. 1988—89), Va. State Bar Assn. (chmn. criminal law sect. 1983—84, Harry L. Carrico Professionalism award 1999). Avocations: gardening, fishing, boating, reading. Office: 701 E Broad St Richmond VA 23219

DOI, TAKAO, astronaut; b. Minamitama, Tokyo, Sept. 18, 1954; m. Abe Hitomi. B in Engring., U. Tokyo, 1978, M in Engring., 1980, PhD in Aerospace Engring., 1983; PhD in Astronomy, Rice U., 2004. Rsch. student Inst. of Space & Astronautical Sci., Japan, 1983—85; NRC rsch. assoc. NASA, Lewis Rsch. Ctr., Houston, 1985; astronaut Nat. Space Develop. Agy. Japan (merged with Ist. Space & Astronautic Sci. and Nat. Aerospace Lab. Japan, renamed JAXA-Japan Aerospace Exploration Agy. in 2003), 1985—; payload specialist tng. NASA, 1990—92, reported to Johnson Space Ctr., 1995. Rschr. conducting rsch. on microgravity fluid dynamics U. Colo., 1987—88; vis. scientist conducting rsch. on microgravity fluid dynamics Nat. Aerospace Lab., Japan, 1989; backup payload specialist Spacelab Japan mission (STS-47), 1992; project scientist Internat. Microgravity Lab. 2 mission (STS-65), 1994; mission specialist, performed 2 Extra Vehicular Activity spacewalks STS-87, US Microgravity Payload Flight, 1997; crew mem., mission to deliver the Japanese Logistics Module and the Canadian Spl. Purpose Dexterous Manipulator to the Internat. Space Station (ISS) STS-123 Mission (Endeavour), 2008. Contbr. articles several articles to profl. jours. Recipient Commendation award, Min. of State for Sci. & Tech., Spl. citation, Sci. Coun. Japan, Outstanding Svc. award, Nat. Space Devel. Agy. of Japan, 1992. Mem.: AIAA, Japan Soc. Aeronautical & Space Sci., Japan Soc. Microgravity Application. Achievements include First Japanese astronaut to perform a Extra Vehicular Activity spacewalk. Avocations: flying, soaring, tennis, jogging, soccer. Office: Astronaut Office CB NASA Johnson Space Center Houston TX 77058

DOKE, MARSHALL J., JR., lawyer; b. Wichita Falls, Tex., June 9, 1934; s. Marshall J. and Mary Jane (Johnson) D.; m. Betty Marie Orsini, June 2, 1956; children: Gregory J., Michael J., Laetitia Marie. BA magna cum laude, Hardin-Simmons U., 1956; LLB magna cum laude, So. Meth. U., 1959. Bar: Tex. 1959. Founding ptnr. Rain Harrell Emery Young & Doke, Dallas, 1965-87; assoc. Thompson, Knight, Wright & Simmons, Dallas, 1959, 62-65; founding ptnr. Doke & Riley, Dallas, 1987-92; ptnr. McKenna & Cuneo, 1993-96, Gardere Wynne Sewell L.L.P., Dallas, 1996—. Gen. counsel Tex. Rep. Party, 1976-77; mem. adv. coun. U.S. Ct. Fed. Claims, 1982—; mem. fed. acquisitions adv. panel U.S. OMB, 2005-06. Author: Ann. Procurement Rev., Govt. Contractor Briefing Papers, Contract Changes, Fed. Contract Mgmt., 1982—, also articles; editor-in-chief: Southwestern Law Jour., 1958-59. Pres. Hope Cottage-Children's Bur., Inc., 1969-70, Hope Cottage Found., 1997-2002, pres., 1998-2002; bd. visitors Law Sch., So. Meth. U., 1966-69, McDonald Obs., U. Tex., 1990—; dir. Tex. Hist. Found., 1993—, v.p., 1996-98, pres. 2000-2004, chmn., 2004—; law com., bd. trustees So. Meth. U., 1977-78; bd. dirs., pres. World Trade Assn., Dallas-Ft. Worth, 1979-80; chmn. bd. dirs. Internat. Trade Assn. Dallas/Ft. Worth, 1993-94; bd. dirs., sec. Mayor's Internat. Com., City of Dallas, 1984-87, mem. Judicial Nominating Commn., Dallas, 1997-2005, vice chair, 1998-2000, chair, 2000-2005. 1st lt. JAGC, U.S. Army, 1959-62. Fellow Am. Bar Found., Tex. Bar Found.; mem. ABA (chmn. sect. pub. contract law 1969-70, ho. of dels. 1970-72, 74-2003, bd. govs. 1980-82, nominating com. 1988-91, 2000-2003, chmn. conf. sect. dels. 1991-2003, standing com. on audit 2003—), Tex. Bar Assn., U.S. Ct. of Fed. Claims Bar Assn. (bd. govs. 1987-2001, pres. 1996, adv. com. 2006-), Bd. of Contract Appeals Bar Assn. (pres. 1988-90, bd. govs. 1988—), Am. Bar Retirement Assn. (bd. dirs., trustee 1980-84, pres 1982-84), Nat. Conf. Lawyers and CPAs (co-chmn. 1983-85), Nat. Contract Mgmt. Assn. (nat. bd. advisors 1983—), Dallas C. of C. (chmn. internat. com. 1979-83). Home: 11 Glenmeadow Ct Dallas TX 75225 Office: Gardere Wynne Sewell LLP Thanksgiving Tower 1601 Elm Ste 3000 Dallas TX 75201-7254 Office Fax: 214-999-3733. Business E-Mail: mdoke@gardere.com.

DOLAN, MICHAEL J., oil industry executive; BS in chem. engring., Worcester Polytechnic Inst.; MBA, Drexel Univ. Mgmt. positions Mobil Oil Corp., Houston, 1993—98, v.p., gen. mgr. petrochemicals Americas, 1998—2000; regional dir. Middle East & Africa ExxonMobil Chem. Co., Brussels, 2000—01; exec. v.p. ExxonMobil Saudi Arabia, 2001—03; dep. to pres. ExxonMobil Refining & Supply Co., Fairfax, Va., 2003—04; pres. ExxonMobil Chem. Co., Irving, Tex., 2004—08; v.p. ExxonMobil Corp., Irving, Tex., 2004—08, sr. v.p., 2008—. Dir. Am. Chemistry Council, Soc. of Chem. Industry. Dir. U.S.-Saudi Arabian Bus. Council; trustee Worcester Polytechnic Inst.; vice-chmn. develop. Sam Houston Area Council, Boy Scout Am.; active in Barbara Bush Found. for Family Literacy Celebration of Reading Program; mem. leadership team United Way of Tex. Gulf Coast Campaign, 2005—06. Office: Exxon-Mobil Corp 5959 Las Colinas Blvd Irving TX 75039

DOLAN, TERESA A., dean, educator, researcher; MPH, UCLA; BA in Zoology, Rutgers U., 1979; DDS, U. Tex., 1983; cert. gen. practice, L.I. Jewish Med. Ctr., 1985; cert. geriatric dentistry, Vets. Adminstrn., 1989; cert. dental pub. health, U. Fla., 1991; grad., Pub. Health Leadership Inst. Fla., 1998; grad. cert., U. Fla., 2001. Diplomate Am. Bd. Dental Pub. Health, 1994. Resident in gen. dentistry dept. dentistry L.I. Jewish Med. Ctr., 1983—84, chief resident in gen. dentistry dept. dentistry, 1984—85; fellow geriatric dentistry Vets. Adminstrn. Med. Ctr., Sepulveda, Calif., 1987—89; asst. prof. U. Fla. Coll. Dentistry, 1989—93, assoc. prof. with tenure, 1993—98, acting assoc. dean acad. affairs, 1996—97, assoc. dean acad. affairs, 1997—2001, prof. with tenure, 1998—, assoc. dean edn., 2001—03, interim dean, 2002—03, dean, 2003—. Rschr., tchr., spkr. in field, lectr. various seminars; vis. asst. prof. U. Calif., 1985—87, adj. asst. prof., 1987—89; faculty discipline com. Fla. Dept. Edn., Statewide Course Numbering Sys., 1998—; reviewer grants in field; participant NIH Summer Inst. Rsh. on Minority Aging, 1991; pres. Am. Bd. of Dental Pub. Health, 2005—06. Contbr. articles to profl. jours.; exec. prodr.: (ednl. satellite videoconf.) Dental Care for the Developmentally Disabled Patient, 1991, Challenges in Geriatrics: Moving on-Rehabilitation After Stroke, 1991, How Much is Enough? Dental Tretament Decisions for Older Adults, 1992; author (dir.): Five Steps to Improving the Oral Health of Your Older Patients: A Guide for Non-dental Health Professionals, 1994. Adv., treating dentist cmty.

nursing homes, 1989—96; dentist to low income elderly participants U. Fla. Geriatric Dental Demonstration Project, Jacksonville, 1990—92; dir. dental svcs. to older and medically compromised patients U. Fla. Geriatric Dental Group, 1990—95. Recipient numerous grants and awards; named honorable mention AARP Healthy Order Adults, 2000 Recognition Programs Exemplary Contbns. to Healthy Aging, 1992; fellow Vets. Adminstrn. Geriatric Dentistry; scholar Rsch., Robert Wood Johnson Found. Dental Health Svcs., 1985—87, L.I. U., 1984—85. Mem.: APHA, Am. Coll. Dentists, Phi Beta Kappa, Am. Soc. Geriatric Dentistry (ad hoc reviewer Spl. Care in Dentistry 1992—93, judge Saul Kamen Sci. Report award competition 1993—, chmn. ann. sci. session 1996), Fla. Coun. Aging, Fla. Pub. Health Assn., Am. Assn. Pub. Health Dentistry (abstract reviewer 1987, co-chmn. local arrangements ann. meeting 1992, ad hoc reviewer Jour. Pub. Health Dentistry 1994, session co-chmn. ann. meeting 1996, judge grad. student merit award projects 1997, mem. at large exec. coun. 1997—2000, mem. awards and nominations com. 2000, Pres.'s award 1999), Am. Dental Assn. (com. G Coun. Dental Edn. and Licensure 1999—, Geriatric Dental Care award 1991), Internat. Assn. Dental Rsch. (v.p. abstract reviewer geriat. oral rsch. sect. 1992—93, dir. behavioral sci. and health svcs. rsch. sect. 1992—95, pres.-elect program chmn. geriat. oral rsch. sect. 1993—94, pres. symposium organizer geriat. oral rsch. sect. 1994—95), Am. Assn. Women Dentists (chmn. com. student and component chpts. 1986—88, trustee dist. XIII Calif. 1986—89, contbg. editor Chronicle 1986—91), Acorn Clinic (v.p., acting pres. 1996—97, pres. 1997—99, past pres. 1999—2000), Fla. Coun. Aging (bd. trustees 1993—95), U. Health Sci. Ctr., Edn. Task Force, U. Curriculum Com., Geriatric Rsch., Edn. and Clin. Ctr., ACORN Clinic, Internat. Assn. Dental Rsch. (session co-chmn., abstract reviewer geriat. oral rsch. sect. 1991—92, immediate past-pres., chmn. nominations com. geriat. oral rsch. sect. 1995—96, mem. awards com. geriat. oral rsch. sect. 1996—97, constn. and bylaws com. 1996—), Am. Bd. Dental Pub. Health (dir.-elect 2000—01, pres. 2005—), Am. Dental Edn. Assn. (chair-elect spl. interest group in geriatric dentistry 1991—92, editl. rev. bd. Jour. Dental Edn. 1991—94, chmn. spl. intertest group in geriatric dentistry 1992—93, immediate past chmn. sect. on gerontology and geriat. edn. 1993—94, abstract reviewer ann. session 1998—2000, ann. session planning com. 2002—), Beta Beta Beta, Omicron Kappa Upsilon (Xi Omicron chpt. 1998), Phi Beta Kappa. Office: U Fla Coll Dentistry 1600 SW Archer Rd D 4-6B Box 100405 JHMH Gainesville FL 32610-0405 Office Phone: 352-392-2911. Office Fax: 352-392-3070. E-mail: tdolan@dental.ufl.edu.

DOLARA, PETER J., air transportation executive; b. Uruguay, Dec. 22, 1937; married; 3 children. BS, Coll. Alfonso Espinola, 1959. Mgr., internat. passenger sales American Airlines, Inc., 1971—73, mgr., Caribbean sales, 1973—75, mgr., passenger sales, N.Y., 1975—82, mgr., passenger sales, ea. divsn., 1982—84, v.p., Atlantic/Caribbean & N.Y. sales, 1984—89, sr. v.p., field svcs., Miami/Caribbean/L.Am., 1989—; mgmt. positions Trans Caribbean Airways, 1984—85. Bd. dirs. SunTrust Bank. Bd. dirs. Easter Seals Soc. of Dade County. Office: AMR Corp 4333 Amon Carter Blvd Fort Worth TX 76155

DOLCE, CARL JOHN, education administration educator; b. New Orleans, June 3, 1928; s. John and Nina (Puglia) D.; m. Nancy Lockwood, July 27, 1955; children: Carla, John. BA, Tulane U., 1947; MEd, Loyola U., New Orleans, 1955; EdD, Harvard U., 1963. Elem. sch. tchr. New Orleans Pub. Schs., 1948-54, secondary sch. tchr., 1954-55, jr. high sch. prin., 1955-63, supt. schs., 1965-69; rsch. assoc., lectr. Harvard Grad. Sch. Edn., Cambridge, Mass., 1963-65; dean Coll. Edn. and Psychology, N.C. State U., Raleigh, 1969-88, dean emeritus, prof. edn. adminstrn., 1989—. Chair adv. com. aesthetic edn. Cen. Midwest Regulatory Lab., St. Louis, 1968-71; chair exptl. schs. selection com. Office Edn., Washington, 1971-72; pres. Coun. Basic Edn., Washington, 1972-79; vice chmn. nat. assn. Elem. and Secondary Edn. Act Title IV state adv. councs., 1978-79 Editorial bd. Ednl. Forum, 1988; author book chpts., monograph, articles. Chmn. Wake County (N.C.) Sch. Study Com., Raleigh, 1978-79; chmn. tech. advisors Durham City/County Merger Task Force, 1988. Sgt. U.S. Army, 1950-52. Grantee U.S Office Edn. grantee, 1981—82, 1986—87;, 1971—78. Mem. Raleigh Chamber Music Guild (pres. 1978-1980, Phi Kappa Phi (pres. N.C. State U. chpt. 1982-83). Avocations: gardening, reading, mysteries, puzzles. Home: 801 Macon Pl Raleigh NC 27609-5552

DOLINER, NATHANIEL LEE, lawyer; b. Daytona Beach, Fla., June 28, 1949; s. Joseph and Asia (Shaffer) D.; m. Debra Lynn Simon, June 5, 1983. BA, George Washington U., 1970; JD, Vanderbilt U., 1973; LLM in Taxation, U. Fla., 1977. Bar: Fla. 1973. Assoc. Smalbein, Eubank, Johnson, Rosier & Bussey, PA, Daytona Beach, Fla., 1973-76; vis. asst. prof. law U. Fla. Law Sch., Gainesville, 1977-78; assoc. Carlton, Fields, Ward, Emmanuel, Smith & Cutler, PA, Tampa, Fla., 1978-82; shareholder Carlton Fields, P.A., Tampa, 1982—, chair bus. trans. practice group, 1984—2006, mng. shareholder, Tampa office, 2006—. Spkr. in field. Adv. bd. Mergers and Acquisitions Law Report, pub. Bur. Nat. Affairs. Dist. commr. Gulf Ridge coun. Boy Scouts Am., 1983—84; bd. dirs. Kol Ami Synagogue, Tampa, 2003—04, Big Bros./Big Sisters Greater Tampa, Inc., 1980—82, Child Abuse Coun., Inc., 1986—95, asst. treas., 1987—88, treas., 1988—89, pres.-elect, 1989—90, pres., 1990—91; bd. dirs. Tampa Jewish Fedn., 1988—91, Mus. Sci. and Industry, Tampa, 1994—2002, exec. com., 1994—2002, sec., 1995—97, first vice-chmn., 1997—99, chair, 1999—2001; mem. alumni bd. Vanderbilt Law Sch., 1999—2000; bd. dirs. Hillel Sch., Tampa, 1998—2004, first v.p., 1999—2000, pres., 2001—03; mem. bd. dirs. Fla. Holocaust Mus., 2006—, Fla. Coun. Economic Edn., 2010—. Fellow: Am. Coll. Tax Counsel, Am. Bar Found.; mem.: ABA (chmn. task force preliminary and ancillary agreements 1992—95, acquisition rev. task force 1992—95, chmn. programs subcom. 1995—98, vice-chmn. 1997—98, chmn. 1998—2002, sec. 2006—07, vice chair 2007—08, chair elect 2008—09, chair 2009—, panelist confs., mem. bus. law sect., M&A Com., bus. loan sect., M&A com.), Tampa C. of C. (chmn. Ambassadors Target Task Force of Com. of 100 1984—85, 1987—88, vice-chmn. govt. fin. and taxation coun. 1987—88, chmn. 1988—89, chair geographic task force 1989—90, bd. govs. 1991—93, exec. com. 1992, chmn. govtl. affairs com. 1992), Fla. Bar Assn. (exec. coun. tax sect. 1980—82, tax cert. com. 1987—88, vice-chmn. 1988—89, chmn. 1989—90), Am. Law Inst., Anti-Defamation League (regional bd. dirs. 1986—90, exec. com. 1987—90), Tampa Club (sec. 1987—89, bd. dirs. 1987—92, pres. 1990—91). Home: 13341 Golf Crest Cir Tampa FL 33624-4648 Office: Carlton Fields PA 4221 W Boy Scout Blvd Tampa FL 33607-5736 Office Phone: 813-229-4208. Business E-Mail: ndoliner@carltonfields.com.

DOLLAR, CREFLO A., minister, religious organization administrator; b. Coll. Park, Ga., Jan. 15, 1962; s. Creflo A. and Emma Dollar; m. Taffi Bolton; 5 children. BS in Edn., West Ga. Coll., Carrollton, 1984; DD (hon.), Oral Roberts U., 1998. With Brawner Psychiatric Inst.; founder, minister World Changers Ministries Christian Ctr., 1986—91, World Changers Ch. Internat. (previously World Changers Ministries Christian Ctr.), Coll. Park, Ga., 1991—; founder Creflo Dollar Ministries; co-founder Arrow Records, 1998—. Founder, pres. Creflo Dollar Ministerial Assn. Author: The Anointing to Live, Understanding God's Purpose for the Anointing, No More Debt, Live Without Fear, Divine Order of Faith, Claim Your Victory Today, 2006, 8 Steps to Create the Life You Want: The Anatomy of a Successful Life, 2008, and many others; co-author: The Successful Family; pub. CHANGE mag., The Max, host, minister (TV series) Changing Your World. Named to Power 150, Ebony mag., 2008. Office: World Changers Ch Internat 2500 Burdett Rd College Park GA 30349 Office Phone: 770-210-5700.

DOLLAR, MATT, state legislator; b. Atlanta, Nov. 30; BA in Polit. Sci., U. Ga. Comml. real estate broker; mem. Dist 45 Ga. House of Reps., Atlanta, 2003—. Republican. Office: Ga Hose of Reps 601 Coverdell Legis Office Bldg Atlanta GA 30334 Office Phone: 404-656-0254. Business E-Mail: matt.dollar@house.ga.gov.

DOLLAR, NELSON, state legislator; b. Burlington, NC; m. Lorrie Dollar; 1 child, Ian. Spl. asst. NC Gov. Office, 1985—89; pers. dir. NC Dept. Commerce, 1989—92; elector US Electoral Coll., 1996; instr. Wake Tech. CC, 1993—95; SN Dollar & Assoc., 1994—; media & pub relations cons.; state rep. Dist. 36 NC, 2005—. Republican. Office: NC House of Reps 16 W Jonese St Rm 307B1 Raleigh NC 27601-1096 Office Phone: 919-715-0795. E-mail: Nelson.Dollar@ncleg.net.

DOLLENS, RONALD W., medical products executive; b. Ind., Dec. 17, 1946; s. William Franklin and Louise Anna (Davis) D.; m. Susan Stanley, Aug. 30, 1969; children: Stephanie, Grant. BS, Purdue U., 1970; MBA, Ind. U., 1972. Sales rep., dir., Bus. Devel. Eli Lilly & Co., Indpls., 1972—85, pres., Med. Devices Divsn., 1991—94; sr. v.p. Advanced Cardiovasc. Sys., Santa Clara, 1985—88, pres., CEO, 1988—94, Guidant Corp., Indpls., 1994—2005; chmn. Kinetic Concepts, Inc. Bd. dirs. Ind. Health Industry Forum, Beckman Coulter Corp. Bd. dirs. Butler U., Indpls., Eiteljorg Mus., Indpls., St. Vincent Hosp. Found.; mem., Adv. Com., Regulatory Health US Dept. Health & Human Svcs., 2002—. Mem.: AdvaMed, Alliance for Aging Rsch., Healthcare Leadership Coun. (chmn. 2003—05, bd. trustees). Office: Kinetic Concepts Inc 8023 Vantage Dr San Antonio TX 78230-4726 Office Phone: 210-255-4726. E-mail: ronald.dollens@kci1.com.

DOLUISIO, JAMES THOMAS, dean, pharmacy educator; b. Bethlehem, Pa., Sept. 28, 1935; s. Dominic and Sue (Powell) D.; m. Phyllis M. Sabolski, June 20, 1959; children— Thomas, James, Rebecca. BS in Pharmacy, Temple U., 1957, MS, 1959; PhD, Purdue U., 1962; DSc, Phila. Coll. Pharmacy and Sci., 1983; DSc (hon.), Purdue U., 1995, Wilkes U., 2000. From asst. prof. to assoc. prof. pharmacy Phila. Coll. Pharmacy and Sci., 1961-67, also assoc. dir. dept., 1965-67; prof., chmn. dept. pharmacy U. Ky., Lexington, 1967-73; prof., dean U. Tex., Austin, 1973-98. Bd. dirs. Eckerd Corp., 1986-96, COR Therapeutics, 1994-02; cons. Smith Kline & French Labs., Phila., 1962-67, McNeil Labs., Ft. Washington, Pa., 1967-72, Hoechst Labs., Somerville, N.J., 1973-93, Nat. Inst. Drug Abuse, 1976-78, HEW, U.S. Surgeon Gen., 1975-83; cons. Merck-Medco, Franklin Lakes, N.J., 2000-2001. Contbr. to profl. and sci. jours. Active Pharmacists Against Drug Abuse Found, 1984; chmn. U.S. Pharmacopeial Conv., Inc., 1990-95; v.p. Fedn. Internat. Pharmaceutique, 1994-98. NSF fellow, 1959-61; Am. Found. Pharm. Edn. fellow, 1957-59 Mem. Am. Pharm. Assn. (pres. 1982, Remington Honor medal 1995), Am. Assn. Colls. Pharmacy, Am. Soc. Hosp. Pharmacy, Am. Assn. Pharm. Scientists (pres. 1988), Fed. Internat. Pharmacists (Lifetime Achievement award 2000), Rho Chi. Office: U Texas College of Pharmacy Austin TX 78712 Business E-Mail: doluisio.jt@mail.utexas.edu.

DOMBECK, HAROLD ARTHUR, insurance company executive; b. Bronx, NY, Mar. 23, 1941; s. Max J. and Rose R. (Schefren) D.; m. Cynthia E. Kofoed, May 14, 1983; children: Mark J., Glenn D., David S. BCE, NYU, 1962, MCE, 1963. Profl. engr., N.Y., N.J., Conn., Ga. Instr. San Antonio Coll., 1964-65, SUNY, Farmingdale, 1965-68; project mgr. H2M Group, Melville, NY, 1965-74, dir. environ. engring., 1971-81, dir. mktg., 1982-85, exec. v.p., 1986-88, pres., 1989-91, pres., CEO, chmn., 1991-94; CEO Dombeck Assocs. Inc., Duluth, Ga., 1995—. CEO Archs. and Engrs. Ins. Co., Naperville, Ill., 1987-2007, chmn. 1987—; v.p., CFO, Dod/Pritchard Comms. Inc., Norcross, Ga., 1998-2001; dir., Perceptive Solutions, Inc., Norcross, 2001-03; chmn. bd. dirs. Am. Cons. Engrs. Pension Trust, St. Louis, 1991-94; chmn. ACEC Bus. Inst. Trust, St. Louis, 1994-96. Pres. High Woods Civic Assn., St. James, N.Y., 1971-73, River Plantation Homeowners Assn., 1999-2001. 1st lt. USAF, 1963-65. Fellow ASCE, Am. Cons. Engrs. Coun. (pres. L.I. 1982-84); mem. Am. Acad. Environ. Engrs. (diplomate), NSPE (dir. 1982-85), N.Y. State Water Pollution Control Assn. (dir. 1980-83), N.Y. State Soc. Profl. Engrs. (pres. 1983-84, pres. Suffolk County chpt. 1978-80, Engr. of Yr. 1989, 90, Outstanding Svc. awards 1988, 89). Avocations: reading, golf, history. Office: Aelc Incorporated 2056 Westings Ave Ste 20 Naperville IL 60563-2495

DOMINGUEZ, DANIEL R., federal judge; b. San Juan, 1945; BA, Boston U., 1967; LLB cum laude, U. P.R., 1970. Bar: P.R. Atty. Hector M. Laffitte Law Offices, 1970—72; ptnr. Laffitte, Dominguez & Totti, 1973—84, Dominguez & Totti, 1983—94; judge US Dist. Ct. PR, San Juan, 1994—2011, sr. judge, 2011—. Gov. Adv. Com. on Labor Policy, 1984; mem. bd. Fed. Bar Examiners U.S. Dist. Ct. P.R., 1989—94; mem. Civil Justice Reform Act Adv. Group, 1991—94; mem. merit selection com. Appointment of U.S. Magistrate Judge, 1993; mem. com. for jud. reform Gov. P.R., 1993—94. With USAR, 1967. Mem.: Hyatt Dorado Beach Country Club, Berwind Country Club. Office: US Dist Ct PR US Courthouse CH-129 150 Ave Carlos Chardon San Juan PR 00918-1703*

DONAHUE, JACK, state legislator; Co-chair, Tax Competitiveness Task Force GNO, Inc.; Mem. Pub. Policy Com. St. Tammany W C. of C.; co-chmn., mem. Southpac (LABI); co-founder Bus. Congress for La.; v.p. Donahue-Asher Contractors, 1967—71; pres., v.p. Spartan Bldg. Corp., 1971—79; pres., chmn., CEO DonahueFavret Contractors, Inc., 2007—; mem. Dist. 11 La. State Senate, 2008—, vice chair judiciary A com., mem. edn. com., fin. com., senate and govtl. affairs com. Republican. Address: Capitol Office PO Box 94183 Baton Rouge LA 70804 Office: PO Box 896 Mandeville LA 70470 Fax: 985-727-9904. E-mail: donahuej@legis.state.la.us.

DONAHUE, TIMOTHY M., retired construction executive; b. 1949; BA in English Lit., John Carroll U., 1971. Pres., Paging Divsn. McCaw Cellular Comm. (now AT&T Wireless), 1986—89, pres., U.S. Ctrl. Region, 1989—91; regional pres., NorthEast, gen. mgr. AT&T Wireless, 1991-96; COO Nextel Comms. Inc. (now Sprint Nextel Corp.), Reston, Va., 1996—99, pres., 1996—2005, CEO, 1999—2005; exec. chmn. Sprint Nextel Corp., Reston, Va., 2005—06. Bd. dirs. NII Holdings, Nextel Ptnrs., Eastman Kodak Co., NVR Inc., 2006—. Bd. dir. John Carroll U. Recipient Networking and Communications Entrepreneur of the Yr., Ernst & Young, 2003, Greater Washington Master Entrepreneur of the Yr., 2003. Mem.: Cellular Telecommunications & Internet Assoc. (past chmn.). Office: NVR Inc Bd Directors 11700 Plz America Dr Ste 500 Reston VA 20190 Office Phone: 703-956-4000. Office Fax: 703-956-4750. Business E-Mail: tdonahue@nvrinc.com.

DONALD, ALEXANDER GRANT, psychiatrist, educator; b. Darlington, SC, Jan. 24, 1928; s. Raymond George and Chesnut Evans (McIntosh) Donald; m. Emma Louise Coggeshall, Oct. 25, 1958; children: Sandy, Mary Chesnut, Marion Lide. BS, Davidson Coll., 1948; MD, Med. U. S.C., 1952. Diplomate Am. Bd. Psychiatry and Neurology. Intern Jefferson Med. Coll., 1952-53; resident in psychiatry Walter Reed Hosp., 1956-59; dir. Mental Health Clinic, Florence, SC, 1962-66; dept. commr. S.C. Dept. Mental Health, 1966-67; dir. William S Hall Psychiat. Inst., Columbia, 1967-90; prof., chmn. dept. neuropsychiatry and behavioral scis. Sch. Medicine, U. S.C., Columbia, 1975-90, Disting. prof. neuropsychiatry, assoc. dean ednl. planning, 1990-91, Disting. prof. emeritus, 1991—. Bd. dirs. Health Resource Found.; trustee Richland Meml. Hosp., 1993—2002, vice-chmn., 1997, chmn., 1999; bd. dirs. S.C. Inst. Med. Edn. and Rsch., pres., 1992—96; trustee Palmetto Health Alliance, 1999—2004, vice-chmn., 2003; steward United Way of Midlands, 2003—08. Fellow: Am. Psychiat. Assn. (pres. S.C. chpt. 1967), Am. Coll. Psychiatrists; mem.: AMA, So. Psychiat. Assn. (v.p.), Columbia Med. Soc. (v.p. 1981, del. 1981, pres. 1989—90), Evening Music Club, Alpha Omega Alpha. Presbyterian. Office: U SC Sch Medicine 3555 Harden St Ext Ste 104 Columbia SC 29203-6894 Personal E-mail: grantd@bellsouth.net.

DONALD, ARNOLD W., cruise line company executive, former manufacturing executive; b. New Orleans, 1954; BA in Economics, Carleton Coll., Northfield, Minn., 1976; BS in Mech. Engring., Washington U., St. Louis, 1977; MBA, U. Chgo., 1980. Numerous positions of increasing responsibility Monsanto Co., St. Louis, 1977—95, pres. agrl. sector, 1995—98, sr. v.p., pres. nutrition and consumer sector, 1998—2000; chmn., CEO Merisant Co., 2000—03, chmn., 2003—05; pres., CEO Juvenile Diabetes Rsch. Found. Internat., 2005—08; CEO Carnival Corp., Miami, 2013—. Bd. dirs. Oil-Dri Corp. America, 1997—2013, Crown Holdings Inc., 1999—, Scotts Miracle-Gro Co., 2000—09, Carnival Corp., 2001—, Laclede Group, 2003—, Russell Brands, LLC, 2004—, Harris Financial Corp., 2009—, BMO Financial Corp., 2009—, Bank of America Corp., 2013—. Bd. dirs. United Way Greater St. Louis; bd. trustees Carleton Coll., Dillard U., Washington U., St. Louis Art Mus., Mo. Botanical Garden, St. Louis Sci. Ctr., Opera Theatre St. Louis. Recipient Exec. of Yr. award, Black Enterprise mag., 1997, Disting. Alumni award, Washington U., 1998, Eagle award, Nat. Eagle Leadership Inst., 1999, Black Engineers President's award, 2000; named one of The 50 Most Powerful Black Executives in America, Fortune mag., 2002. Office: Carnival Corp 3655 NW 87th Ave Miami FL 33178*

DONALD, BERNICE BOUIE, federal judge, legal association administrator; b. Desoto County, Miss., Sept. 17, 1951; d. Perry and Willie Bell (Hall) Bowie; m. W. L. Donald, Oct. 9, 1973. BA in Sociology, U. Memphis, 1974, JD, 1979; student, Nat. Jud. Coll., 1983-84. Bar: Tenn. 1979, US Fed. Ct. 1979, US Supreme Ct. 1989. Clk. South Ctrl. Bell Tel. Co., 1971-75, mgr., 1975-80; staff atty. Memphis Area Legal Svcs., 1980, Shelby County Public Defenders Office, 1980-82; judge Gen. Sessions Criminal Ct. of Shelby County, Tenn., 1982-88, US Bankruptcy Ct. (western dist.) Tenn., Memphis, 1988-96, US Dist. Ct. (western dist.) Tenn., Memphis, 1995—2011, US Ct. Appeals (6th Cir.), Memphis, 2011—. Mem. adv. com. on bankruptcy rules Jud. Conf., 1996—; faculty mem. Fed. Jud. Ctr., 1991—, Nat. Jud. Coll., 1992—; adj. prof. Shelby State CC, 1980-84, Cecil C. Humphreys Sch. of Law, 1985-88; judge in residence, Washington U., Mo., 2014, American U. Sch. of Law, Washington, DC, 2014; lectr., presenter in field. Featured in Essence mag., Ebony mag., Jet mag., Memphis mag., Dollars and Sense mag., Black Enterprise mag.; bd. editor American Bar Journal, 2003-11 Bd. dirs. Midtown Mental Health, 1990-92, 94-96, Memphis in May, 1994-97, Leadership Memphis, Inc., 1993-96, U. Memphis Alumni Bd., 1994—, Memphis Race Rels. and Diversity Inst., 1994—, Fed. Jud. Ctr., Stax Mus. of American Soul, Stax Acad. Charter Sch.; former bd. dirs. numerous religious and civic orgns. including Calvary St. Ministry, Memphis Literacy Coun., YWCA; co-founder 4-Life Recipient Cmty. Svcs. award Nat. Conf. Christians and Jews, 1986, Martin Luther King Cmty. Svc. award, Young Careerist award State of Tenn. Raleigh Bur. Profl. Women, plaques and certs., William Brennan award, U. Va., 2014; named Citizen of Yr. Excelsior Chpt. of Eastern Star, Woman of Yr. Pentecostal Ch. of God in Christ. Mem. ABA (mem. standing com. on Gavel awards 1989-95, mem. adv. com. Ctrl. and Eastern European Law Initiative 1999—, mem. house of delegates 1993-95, 99—, chair, commission on racial and ethnic diversity in the profession, 1994-97, bd. govs. 1999—, liason labor and employment law sect. 1999—, Law Libr. Congress 1999—, Appellate Judges Conf. 1999-2000, Africa Legal Tech. Assistance Project 2000—, mem. legal opportunity scholarship com. 2000—, Mus.'s bd. dirs. 2000—, numerous jud. adminstrn. divsn. coms., sec. 2008-11, Spirit of Excellence award, 2011 (also founder)), American Bar Found. (pres. 2012-), Nat. Assn. Women Judges (treas. 1986-87, sec. 1987-88, v.p. 1988-89, pres. elect 1989-90, pres. 1990-91), American Judges Assn., Nat. Ctr. State Cts., Nat. Bar Assn. (co-chair, program com. judicial coun. 2011-14, William H. Hastie award, 2013), Tenn. Bar Assn. (bd. dirs. 1997-98), Memphis County Bar Assn., Shelby County Bar Assn., American Trial Lawyers Assn., Assn. of Women Attys. (pres. 1991, bd. dirs.), Nat. Conf. Bankruptcy Judges (bd. dirs. 1993-96), Nat. Conf. of Women's Bar Assn. (bd. mem.), Nat. Conf. of Spl. Ct. Judges (sec.), Leadership Memphis (pres. 1987, bd. dirs.), Internat. Women's Forum, Memphis Bar Assn. (bd. dirs. 1993), American Judicature Soc. (bd. dirs., 2013-), Zeta Phi Beta (Alpha Eta Zeta chpt.). Avocations: reading, crossword puzzles, music, bicycling, walking. Office: Federal Building 167 N Main St Ste 951 Memphis TN 38103-1831*

DONALD, LUKE, professional golfer; b. Hemel Hempstead, England, Dec. 7, 1977; Grad. in Art Theory and Practice, Northwestern U. Profl. golfer, 2001—; mem. PGA Tour, 2002—. Mem. English team World Cup, 2004, 2005; mem. European team Ryder Cup, 2004, 2006, 2010, 2012. Achievements include winner PGA Tour events: Southern Farm Bureau Classic, 2002; Honda Classic, 2006; World Golf Championship-Accenture Match Play Championship, 2011, Children's Miracle Network Hospitals Classic, 2011; Transitions Championship, 2012; winner PGA European Tour events: Omega European Masters, Scandinavian Masters by Carlsberg, 2004; Madrid Masters, 2010; BMW PGA Championship, 2011, Barclays Scottish Open, 2011; member of Ryder Cup winning Team Europe, 2002, 2006, 2010. Mailing: c/o PGA Tour 112 PGA TOUR Blvd Ponte Vedra Beach FL 32082

DONALDSON, ROBERT HERSCHEL, university administrator, educator; b. Houston, June 14, 1943; s. Herschel Arthur and Vera Edith (True) D.; m. Judy Carol Johnston, June 27, 1964 (div. Apr. 30, 1984); children: Jennifer Gwynne, John Andrew; m. Sally Susan Abravanel, Mar. 31, 1985; children: Mark Elliot, Ryan Scott. AB, Harvard U., 1964, A.M., 1966, PhD, 1969. Prof. polit. sci. Vanderbilt U., 1968-81, assoc. dean Coll. Arts and Sci., 1975-81; provost, v.p. acad. affairs, prof. polit. sci. Herbert H. Lehman Coll. CUNY, 1981-84; pres. Fairleigh Dickinson U., Rutherford, NJ, 1984-90, U. Tulsa, 1990-96, trustees prof. polit. sci., 1996—. Vis. research prof. U.S. Army War Coll., 1978-79; pres. Am. coms. fgn. rels., 2002-05. Author: Stasis and Change in Revolutionary Elites, 1971, Soviet Policy toward India, 1974, The Soviet-Indian Alliance: Quest for

Influence, 1979, The Soviet Union in the Third World: Successes and Failures, 1981, Soviet Foreign Policy since World War II, 1981, 85, 88, 92, The Foreign Policy of Russia: Changing Systems, Enduring Interests, 1998, 2002, 05, 09. Council Fgn. Relations fellow, 1973-74 Mem. Coun. on Fgn. Rels., Phi Beta Kappa. Methodist. Home: 6449 S Richmond Ave Tulsa OK 74136-1669 Office: University Tulsa 800 S Tucker Dr Tulsa OK 74104-3126 Office Phone: 918-631-2409. Business E-Mail: robert-donaldson@utulsa.edu.

DONAWAY, CARL D., messenger service executive; BA, Calif. State U., Northridge; MBA, U. Minn. Ops. supr. Airborne, LA, 1977—78, sales rep., 1978—79, ops. mgr., 1979—80, L.A. sta. mgr., 1980, dist. ops. mgr., Midwest, dist. sales mgr., Midwest region, 1985, mktg. devel. dir. Seattle, 1987—88, customer support dir., 1988—90, v.p., customer support, 1990—92, v.p., bus. analysis, 1992, pres., ABX Air, 1992—99, sr. exec. v.p., field and air svcs., 1999—2002, pres., CEO, 2002—, chmn., 2002—; exec. chmn. DHL Holdings (USA), Plantation, Fla., 2003—. Office: DHL Holdings USA 1200 S Pine Island Rd Ste 600 Plantation FL 33324 Office Phone: 954-888-7000. Office Fax: 954-888-7310.

DONELAN, MARK ANTHONY, physicist; b. Grenada, West Indies, Mar. 27, 1942; arrived in Can., 1960, naturalized, 1969; s. William Gregory and Ivy (Payne) Donelan; m. June Lynch Donelan, June 10, 1967; children: Laura Maxwell, Laura, Maxwell. BEngring., McGill U., 1964; PhD, U. BC, 1970. Project engr. Procter & Gamble, Hamilton, Ont., Canada, 1964—66; Killam postdoctoral fellow Cambridge (Eng.) U., 1970—71; rsch. scientist Environ. Can., Burlington, Ont., 1971—96; prof. Rosenstiel Sch. Marine & Atmospheric Sci. U. Miami, 1996—. Assoc. prof. civil engring. McMaster U., Hamilton, Ont., 1979—85, prof. civil engring., 1985—93; adj. prof. Waterloo (Ont.) U., 1979—, Laval U., Que., 1990—94, U. Miami, Fla., 1992—96; emeritus scientist Environ. Can., Burlington, Ont., 1997—; Humboldt research fellow Max-Planck-Institut fur Meteorologie, Germany, 1984. Fellow: Royal Soc. Can., Am. Meteorol. Soc. (Sverdrup Gold medal 1994); mem.: AAAS, The Oceanography Soc., Am. Geophys. Union, Can. Meteorol. & Oceanographic Soc. Office: U Miami Rosenstiel Sch Marine/Sci 4600 Rickenbacker Cswy Miami FL 33149-1031

DONIE, SCOTT, Olympic athlete; b. Vicenza, Italy, Oct. 10, 1968; BA in Comm., Advt., Southern Meth. U., 1990. Olympic platform diver, Barcelona, Spain, 1992; Olympic springboard diver Atlanta, 1996. Recipient Silver medal platform diving Olympics, Barcelona, 1992, 4th place medal springboard diving Olympics, Atlanta, 1996. Home: 13315 Apple Tree Rd Houston TX 77079-7107 Office Phone: 212-998-2064. E-mail: scott.donie@nyu.edu.

DONLAN, THOMAS GARRETT, journalist; b. NYC, Mar. 31, 1945; s. Thomas Garrett and Elizabeth May (Beard) D.; m. Carol Knopes Donlan, Feb. 5, 1972; children: Nicholas G., Alice E. AB, Hamilton Coll., 1967; MA, Ind. U., 1968. Reporter The Record, Hackensack, N.J., 1969-74; newsman AP, Trenton, N.J., 1974-79; assoc. editor Barron's Mag., NYC, 1979-81, Washington editor Washington, 1981-91, editor editorial page, 1992—. Author: Supertech: How America Can Win the Technology Race, 1991, Don't Count On It: Why Your Pension May Be In Jeopardy and How to Protect Yourself, 1994, A World of Wealth: How Capitalism Turns Profit into Progress. Mem. Nat. Press Club, Severn Sailing Assn., Sailing Club of the Chesapeake, Annapolis Yacht Club. Avocations: sailing, squash. Home: 6516 Jay Miller Dr Falls Church VA 22041-1135 Office: Barron's Mag 1025 Connecticut Ave NW Ste 800 Washington DC 20036-5419 Home Phone: 703-941-0112. Business E-Mail: tg.donlan@barrons.com.

DONLON, WILLIAM JAMES, retired lawyer; b. Colo. Springs, Apr. 22, 1924; s. John Andrew and Kathleen M. D; m. Josephine A. Janssen, July 19, 1946; children: William James, Gregory A., Michele, Dru Ann Gazelle. Student, Colo. Coll., 1941-43; BS, U. Denver, 1949, JD, 1950. Bar: Colo. 1950, Ohio 1964, Ill. 1969, US Dist. Ct. Colo. 1956, US Dist. Ct. (no. dist.) Ill. 1974, US Ct. Appeals (10th cir.) 1957, US Ct. Appeals (5th cir.) 1970, US Ct. Appeals (7th cir.) 1974, US Ct. Appeals DC 1979, US Supreme Ct. 1965. Dep. clk. Dist. Ct., Denver, 1949-50; pvt. practice Denver, 1953-63; gen. counsel Brotherhood Ry. Airline & S.S. Clks., Freight Handlers, Express & Sta. Empl., Rosemont, Ill., 1963-84, Rockville, Md., 1963-86; ret., 1985. Instr. labor U. Ill., 1972-78. With USAAF, 1942-45. Decorated Air medal with 2 oak leaf clusters; named Ky. Col. Mem. ABA (coun. sect. labor and employment law 1977-86, co-chmn. railroad and airline com., 1974-76, co-chmn. equl employment com., 1976-77), Ill. Bar Assn., DC Bar Assn., Am. Legion, VFW, KC (Grand Knight coun. 10329, 1991-93, 2005-06), 34th Bomb Group Assn., Phi Alpha Delta, Phi Delta Theta. Democrat. Roman Catholic. Personal E-mail: donlonw@comcast.net.

DONNELLY, MICHAEL JOSEPH, management consultant; m. Barbara Lynne Webb. BA in Commerce, Simon Fraser U., 1976. Chartered acct. Acct. Campbell, Sharp, Chartered Accts. (now Grant Thornton), Victoria, Canada, 1973-76, KPMG, Victoria, 1976-79; controller Park Pacific Group of Cos., Victoria, 1979-80; gen. mgr. Indsl. Plastics (A subs. of the Park Pacific Group of Cos.), Victoria, 1980-83; chief fin. officer Action Group of Cos., Ft. Lauderdale, 1984-85; pres. Beacon Mgmt. Group, Inc., Pompano Beach, Fla., 1985—. Contbr. articles to profl. publs. Trustee, mem. bd. trade PAC Inc., 1990-95; dir. Enterprise Amb. Program, 1991-98, chmn. adv. bd., 1995-98; dir. NatBank, 1996-97., chmn. adv. bd. Fla. Atlantic U. Small Bus. Devel. Ctr., 1993-96; exec. adv. bd. Fla. Atlantic U. Coll. Bus., 1996-98; bd. dirs. Broward Alliance, 2001-02; dir. Nat. Assn. Accts., Ft. Lauderdale chpt., 1988-90; pres. Can. Am. C. of C., 1989-95, dir. 1989-; dir. Assn. for Corp. Growth, South Fla. chpt., 1998-2013; adv. bd. Fla. Small Bus. Devel. Ctr. Network, 1990-, chmn. 1995-2013; pres. Uptown Bus. Assn., 1989-90, chmn., CEO adv. coun., 1991-94; bd. govs. Greater Ft. Lauderdale C. of C., 1995-96, chmn. Uptown Bus. Coun., 1996, bd. govs. 1998-2006, bd. dirs., 1996, 1999-2004, vice chmn., Govt. Affairs, 1999-2000, chair of bd. 2001; bd. dirs. Gold Coast Venture Capital Club, 1986-2004, pres., 1989-91. Mem. Inst. Chartered Accts. B.C., Canadian Inst. Chartered Accts., Can. Am. C. of C., Assn. for Corporate Growth, Greater Fort Lauderdale C. of C. Avocations: bicycling, walking, golf. Office: Beacon Mgmt Group Inc 1000 W McNab Rd Pompano Beach FL 33069-4719

DONNEM, SARAH LUND, financial analyst, non-profit and political organization consultant; b. St. Louis, Apr. 10, 1936; d. Joel Y. and Erle Hall (Harsh) Lund; m. Roland W. Donnem, Feb. 18, 1961; children: Elizabeth Prince Donnem Sigety, Sarah Madison Ashe-Donnem. BA, Vassar Coll., 1958. Tech. aide, computer programmer Bell Labs, Whippany, NJ, 1959-60; chmn. placement vol. opportunities NY Jr. League, 1972-73, asst. treas., 1974-75, chmn. urban problems relating to mental health, 1967-69, mem. project rsch. com., 1967-70, chmn., 1973-74, mem. bd. mgrs., 1973-74. Chmn. cmty. rsch. Washington Jr. League, 1970-71, mem. bd. mgrs., 1970-71; mem. Stratford Hall (NY) Com., 1970—; bd. dirs. East Side Settlement House, Bronx, NY, 1972-04, hon., 2005—, v.p., 1975-76, chmn. Nat. Horse Show Benefit, 1976, winter antiques show com., 1994—, co-chmn. adv. com., 1991-94, chmn. VIP Day, 1999, Chasteston Exhibit NY Antigen Show, 2011, mem. nominating com., 1990-2000, mem. investment com., 1993-2003, mem. fin. com., 2004-05; bd. dirs. Stanley M. Isaacs Neighborhood Ctr., NYC, 1973-76, v.p., 1975-76; bd. dirs. Presbyn. Home for Aged Women, NYC, 1974-76, v.p., 1976; mem. exec. bd. NY Aux. of Blue Ridge Sch., 1971-75, sec. 1965-67, pres., 1973-75; budget and benevolence com. Brick Presbyn. Ch., NYC, 1973-76, mem. social svc. com., 1973-74, chmn. fgn. students com., 1963-64; bd. dirs. Search and Care, NYC, 1973-76, Project LEARN, Cleve., 1990-96, 2000—, trustee, 2000-06; chmn. Literacy Fund, 1991-95, mem., 1995—2005; mem. Friends of Project LEARN, 1986—2006, mem. Fedn. Cmty. Planning, Cleve., coun. on Older Persons, 1978-82, mem. future Planning task Force, 1980-81, commn. on social concerns, 1982-84; trustee Golden Age Ctrs. Greatr cleve., 1979-92, investment com., 1993, 1st v.p., 1980-81, pres. 1981-85, chmn. Western Res. Antiques show, 1979, 80; chmn. cleve. antiques Show Silver Anniv., 2000; mem. women's adv. coun. Westrn Res. Hist. Soc., 1977—2000, coord. sec., 1978; mem. women's com. Cleve. Orch., 1979-85, Vassar Coll. Cleve. sec. 1980-82, v.p., 1983, pres. 1984-86, leadership gift chair 50th reunion, 2008; mem. AAVC Club Liaison com., 1986-89, chmn. Chgo. regional program com., 1987-89; bd. dirs. Cleve. Ballet, 1980-01, exec. com. 1981, fin. com. 1982-88, 95-98, nominating com., 1988-90, 95-00, co-chmn. 1997-99; co-chmn. Yale Ball, 1983; bd. advisors Ret. Sr. Vol. Program, 1982, trustee, 1983-90, chmn. long range planning comm., 1986, sec. 1987-89; mem. Family Friends Adv. Coun., 1987-89; trustee Fairmount Presbyn. Ch., 1985-88; mem. long range planning com. United Way, Cleve., 1985-87; coord. Friends of Voinovich, 1987-89; womens adv. com. Voinovich for Gov., 1990, Voinovich for Senate, 1997-98, chmn. Voinovich Task Force on Aging, 1990-91, Ohio Adv. Coun. on Aging, 1991-02, legis. com., 1994-00; chmn. legis. com., Cuyahoga County Rep. Party, 1994, mem. policy com., mem. fin. com., 1999—, Plain Dealer adv. counsel for elderly coverage, 1991-93; chmn. Johns Hopkins Parents Fund, 1986-88, Project LEARN 15th Anniversary celebration (with Barbara Bush, hon. chmn.), 1989-90; coord. Decorative Arts Trust Cleve. Symposium, 1996; mem. Leadership Cleve. Class 1992, Historic Charleston Found. Nat. Adv. Coun., 2007-, Collection Com.; bd. mem., Hist. Charlecton Found., 2009-, Com. Hist. Charleston Internat. Antigue Show, 2009-, hon. chmn., 2011, chair philanthropy commn., 2012-, bd. trustees Gibbes Mus. Art, 2007-; bd. trustee, Charlecton Horticultural Soc., 2010-, co-chair benefit luncheon, 2012, del. White House Conf. on Aging, 1995; chmn. adv. com. Charleston Art and Antiques Forum, 2008-12. Named Vol. of Yr. NY Jr. League, 1975; recipient Sustainer Svc. award Jr. League Cleve., 1990. Mem. Nat. Inst. Social Scis. (membership com. 1972-92, trustee 1984-96), Nat. Soc. Colonial Dames (com. regional conf. Ill 2007), Colony Club (NYC), Union Club (NYC), Chevy Chase Club (Washington), Vassar Club, Kirtland Club (Cleve.), Carolina Yatch Club (Charleston), Met. Club (DC). Home (Winter): 1 King St Apt 307 Charleston SC 29401 Home: 2945 Fontenay Rd Shaker Heights OH 44120-1726

DONOFRIO, JOHN, lawyer; BSChemE, Rutgers U.; JD, George Washington U., 1987, LLM. Law clk. US Ct. Appeals (fed. cir.); ptnr. Kirkland & Ellis, LLP; assoc. gen. counsel Honeywell Internat., 1996—98, dep. gen. counsel, 1998—2000, v.p., gen. counsel Honeywell Aerospace Phoenix, 2000—05; sr. v.p., gen. counsel Visteon Corp., Van Buren Twp., Mich., 2005—09; exec. v.p., sec., gen. counsel Shaw Group, Inc., Baton Rouge, 2009—. Adj. prof. Seton Hall U. Sch. Law. Contbr. articles to profl. publs. Office: Shaw Group Inc 4171 Essen Ln Baton Rouge LA 70809

DONOVAN, BILLY (WILLIAM JOHN), men's college basketball coach; b. Rockville Centre, NY, May 30, 1965; m. Christine D'Auria; children: William, Hasbrouck, Bryan, Connor. BA in Gen. Social Studies, Providence Coll., 1987. Profl. basketball player Wyo. Wildcatters, Continental Basketball Assn., 1987, NY Knicks, NBA, 1987-88; grad. asst. coach U. Ky., Lexington, 1989-90, asst. coach, 1990-93, assoc. coach, 1993-94; head coach Marshall U., 1994-96, U. Fla., Gainesville, 1996—2007, 2007—, Orlando Magic, 2007. Named Hon. Mention All-Am., UPI, 1987, All-East, 1987, NABC All-Dist., 1986 (second team), 1987 (first team), All-Big East, 1986 (third team), 1987 (first team), New Eng. Player of Yr., 1987, Providence Male Athlete of Yr., 1986, 1987, Providence MVP, 1986, 1987, NCAA S.E. Region Most Outstanding Player, 1987; Nat. Rookie Coach of Yr., Basketball Times, 1994, W.Va. Coll. Coach of Yr., 1994, So. Conf. Coach of Yr., 1994, Gainesville Sun Sportsperson of Yr., 1999, Dist. VI Coach of Yr., 2000, 2003, Nat. Assn. Basketball Coaches, ESPN.com Nat. Coach of Yr., 2001, Southeastern Conf. Coach of Yr., 2011, 2013, Dist. IV Coach of Yr. US Basketball Writers Assn., 2011; named to Big East All-Tournament Team, 1987, All-Time Providence Civic Ctr. Team, 1999, Providence Hall of Fame, 1999. Achievements include head coach of NCAA Final Four men's basketball national championship winning University of Florida Gators, 2006, 2007. Office: U Fla Basketball Office PO Box 14485 Gainesville FL 32604-2485

DONOVAN, DONALD T., otolaryngologist, educator; Attended, Harvard U.; MD, Baylor Coll. of Medicine, 1976. Diplomate Am. Bd. Otolaryngology, 1981. Resident surgery Baylor Coll. of Medicine, Houston, 1977—78, resident otolaryngology, 1978—81, prof. Bobby R. Alford Dept. of Otolaryngology - Head and Neck Surgery; fellow head and neck surgery Columbia-Presbyn. Med. Ctr., 1981—82, St. Vincent's Hosp. and Med. Ctr., NY; interim dept. chair, dep. chief otolaryngology svc. Meth. Hosp.; hosp. affiliation includes St. Luke's Episcopal Hosp. Office: The Bobby R. Alford Department of Otolaryngology-Head and Neck Surgery One Baylor Plz Mail Stop NA-102 Houston TX 77030 Office Phone: 713-798-5906. Office Fax: 713-798-3520.

DONOVAN, JOHN, telecommunications industry executive; BSEE, U. Notre Dame; MBA in Fin., U. Minn. Ptnr., dir. industry practices telecom and media Deloitte Consulting; chmn., CEO inCode Telecom Group; exec. v.p. product, sales, mktg. and ops. Verisign; chief tech. officer AT&T Inc. (merger of SBC Communications & AT&T Corp.), San Antonio, 2008—. Bd. dirs. 2Wire, NII Holdings; chmn. bd. dirs. Amp'd mobile; spkr. in field. Author: The Value Enterprise, 1998, Value Creating Growth, 1999. Office: AT&T 175 E Houston San Antonio TX 78205

DONOVAN, ROBERTO E., brokerage house executive; BA, Boston U.; postgrad. degree, Universita degli Studi, Italy. Dir. ops. SureTrade, 1997; oper. officer Merrill Lynch Direct; co-founder, CEO SIM Monitor; mktg. dir. optionsXpress; chief compliance officer TradeKing, Charlotte, NC. Office: TradeKing PO Box 49050 Charlotte NC 28277-3432 E-mail: rdonovan@tradeking.com.

DOODY, LOUIS CLARENCE, JR., retired accountant; b. New Orleans, Feb. 5, 1940; s. Louis Clarence and Elsie Clair (Connors) D.; m. Barbara Virginia Pettett, Oct. 9, 1982; children by previous marriage: Dana Lori, Mary Lyn, Kathleen Louise. BCS, Tulane U., 1963. CPA, La. Acct. Louis C. Doody, CPA, 1963-68; ptnr. Doody and Doody, CPA's, Metairie, La., 1969—2005. Mem. AICPA, La. Soc. CPA's. Home: 36 Cypress Rd Covington LA 70433-4306

DOODY, RACHELLE, neurologist, educator, researcher; b. Pitts., Aug. 12, 1956; children: Clare, Robin, Justin, Aleah. BA, Rice U., Houston, 1978, PhD, 1992; MD, Baylor Coll. Medicine, Houston, 1983. Diplomate American Bd. Psychology & Neurology. Intern neurology McGill U., Montreal, Canada, 1983—84; resident neurology Baylor Coll. Medicine, 1984-87, asst. prof. neurology, 1987-96, founding dir. Alzheimer's Disease & Memory Disorders Ctr., 1989—, assoc. prof. neurology, 1996—2003, Effie Marie Cain chair Alzheimer's disease rsch., 2000—, prof. neurology, 2003—. Recipient Disting. Alumni award, Assn. Rice Alumni, 2009, Zenith award, Nat. Alzheimer's Assn., Disting. Faculty award, Baylor Coll. Medicine, 2011. Mem.: Alzheimer's Assn. (bd. dirs. Houston/Southwest chpt., Harry E. Walker award). Achievements include research in cognitive aspects of Alzheimer's disease, dementia, and aphasia; development of treatments for memory disorder and Alzheimer's disease. Avocations: fine arts, tennis, literature. Office: Baylor Coll Medicine Dept Neurology 1977 Butler Blvd Suite E5 101 Houston TX 77030-2744 Office Phone: 713-798-4734. Office Fax: 713-798-5326. E-mail: rdoody@bcm.edu.

DOOLAN, VICTOR H., retired automotive executive, board member; b. Kings Langley, England, Nov. 7, 1940; BA, Watford Coll., England. Chmn. Courland Automotive Practice USA; with BMW, 1976—93, pres. N.Am., 1993—99; exec. dir. Premier Automotive Group, 1999—2002; CEO, pres. Volvo Cars of N.Am., Inc., 2002—05. Bd. dirs. Fisker Automotive, Inc., Sonic Automotive, Inc., 2005—, Zag.com Inc., 2006—, BlueFire Ethanol Fuels, Inc., 2007—. Recipient Good Scout award, Boy Scouts of America, 1996, Marjorie Guthrie Leadership award, Huntington Disease Assn., 1998. Office: Sonic Automotive Inc Bd Directors 4401 Colwick Rd Charlotte NC 28211-2311 Office Phone: 704-566-2400. Office Fax: 704-536-4665. Business E-Mail: Victor.Doolan@sonicautomotive.com.

DOOLEY, MICHAEL P., law educator; b. Iowa City, 1939; BA, U. Iowa, 1960, JD, 1963. Bar: Iowa 1963, N.Y. 1964, Ill. 1971, Va. 1979. Assoc. Dewey, Ballantine, Bushby, Palmer & Wood, 1963-68; assoc. prof. U. Ill., 1968-71, prof., 1971-72; vis. prof. U. Va., 1971-72, prof., 1972-80, Doherty prof., 1980-90, William S. Potter prof. and dir. grad. studies, 1990—. Mem. Saltzburg Seminar in Am. Studies, 1986; mem. legal adv. com. N.Y. Stock Exch. Author: Fundamentals of Corporation Law, 1995, A Practical Guide for Corporate Directors, 1996, Model Business Corporation Act Annotated, 4th ed., 2009—10, Supplement. Named Ruby R. Vale Disting. Academic, Widener U. Sch. Law, 1996. Mem.: Am. Assn. Law Sch. (chmn. bus. sect., formerly), ALI, ABA (com. corp. laws 1983—91, corp. practice com. 1995—, com. corp. laws 1996—, reporter Model Bus. Corp. Act 1996—). Office: U Va Sch Law 580 Massie Rd Charlottesville VA 22903-1738 Office Phone: 434-924-3864. E-mail: mpd@virginia.edu.

DOOLEY, VINCENT JOSEPH, college athletics administrator, retired college football coach; b. Mobile, Ala., Sept. 4, 1932; s. William Vincent and Nellie Agnes (Stauter) D.; m. Barbara Anne Meshad, Mar. 19, 1960; children: Deanna, Daniel, Denise, Derek. BS in Bus. Adminstrn., Auburn U., 1954, MA in History, 1963. Asst. football coach Auburn U. Tigers, 1960, head freshman football coach, 1961-63; head football coach U. Ga. Bulldogs, Athens, 1964—88; athletic dir. U. Ga., Athens, 1979—2004; chmn. football exploratory com. Kennesaw State U., Ga., 2009—. Chmn. Ga. State Easter Seals Soc. Served to 2d lt. USMC, 1954-56, capt. res. Recipient James Corbett Meml. award, Nat. Assn. Collegiate Dirs. Athletics, 2004, John L. Toner award, Nat. Football Found. and Hall of Fame, 2004, Contbns. to Coll. Football award, Nat. Coll. Footbal Awards Assn. and ESPN2004, 2004, Francis J. "Reds" Bagnell award, Maxwell Club, 2005, Paul "Bear" Bryant Lifetime Achievement award, Nat. Sportscasters & Sportswriters Assn., 2010; named Coach of Yr., Southeastern Conf., 1966, 1968, 1976, 1978, 1980, NCAA Coach of Yr., 1980, Georgian of Yr., Ga. Assn. Broadcasters, 1984, Sports Adminstr. of Yr., Ga. Sports Hall of Fame, 1984, Divsn. 1-A S.E. Region Athletic Dir. of Yr., Nat. Assn. Collegiate Dirs. Athletics, 2001; named one of Top 100 Georgians of Century, Ga. Trend Mag., 2000; named to Ga. Sports Hall of Fame, 1978, Ala. Sports Hall of Fame, 1984, Coll. Football Hall of Fame, Nat. Football Found., 1994, Ga. Trend Mag. Hall of Fame, 2004. Mem. Am. Football Coaches Assn. (trustee, past chmn. ethics com., past pres.). Achievements include head coach of NCAA football National Championship winning University of Georgia Bulldogs, 1980. Office: c/o Athletic Dept Kennesaw State University 1000 Chastain Rd Kennesaw GA 30144

DOPPELT, AVA K., lawyer; b. Pitts., July 8, 1950; d. Morris Behr and Sylvia Joy Kirshenbaum; m. Art Doppelt. AB, Northwestern U., Ill., 1972; JD, NYU, 1976. Counsel Prentice-Hall, Inc., Englewood, NJ, 1976—78, Reader's Digest Assn., Pleasantville, NY, 1979—82; shareholder Allen, Dyer, Doppelt, Milbrath, & Gilchrist, P.A., Orlando, Fla., 1983—. Bd. mem. Orlando Ballet, Preserve the Eatonville Cmty., Fla. Mem.: ABA, Orange County Bar Assn. (William Trickel Jr. Professionalism award 2002), Fla. Exec. Women, Ctrl. Fla. Assn. for Women Lawyers (Golden Star award 2001), Internat. Trademark Assn., Copyright Soc. U.S., Fla. Bar, Phi Beta Kappa. Office: Allen Dyer Doppelt Milbrath & Gilchr 255 S Orange Ave Orlando FL 32801 Office Fax: 407-841-2343. Business E-Mail: adoppelt@addmg.com.

DORAN, MARY ANN, human resources specialist; b. 1955; BS in Mktg., Northeastern U., 1978. V.p., orgnl. devel. Jordan Marsh Co., 1979—93; v.p., human resources The Bombay Co., 1993—95; exec. search cons. Kenzer Corp., 1995—96; v.p., pers. devel. & staffing Zale Corp., 1996, v.p., orgnl. devel., 1996—2005, sr. v.p., human resources, 2005—10; sr. v.p. human resources RadioShack Corp., Ft. Worth, 2010—. Office: RadioShack Corp 300 RadioShack Cir Fort Worth TX 76102 Office Phone: 817-415-3011. Office Fax: 817-415-2647.

DORF, LAWRENCE E., family practice physician; Diplomate Am. Bd. Family Practice, Am. Bd. Family Practice-geriatric medicine, Am. Bd. Family Practice-hospice & palliative medicine. Resident family medicine Brookhaven Memorial Hosp., Patchogue, NY, 1982—85; hosp. affiliation includes Holy Cross Hosp. Office: 4981 NW 102nd Dr Coral Springs FL 33076-1704 Office Phone: 954-785-1640.*

DORFMAN, ALLEN B., international management consultant; b. NYC, Mar. 30, 1930; s. Harry and Jean (Schreiber) Dorfman; m. Elaine Turbé, Jan. 9, 1955; children: Nancy Ann, Jeffrey David. BBA summa cum laude, 1952; postgrad. mgmt. studies, Harvard Bus. Sch. From mem. exec. tng. squad to sr. mgmt. R.H. Macy's, NYC, 1954-67; asst. gen. mdse. mgr., v.p., mem. mgmt. com. NY div. Allied Stores Corp., NYC, 1967-69; v.p., gen. mdse. mgr. hard and soft goods, mem. exec. com. Town & Country Full Line Discount Stores div. Lane Bryant Corp., NYC, 1969-71; pres., dir. Nat. Bellas Hess Inc., Kansas City, Mo., 1971-73; corp. sr. v.p. and pres., CEO retail div. Jewelcor, Inc., NYC, 1973-77; corp. sr. v.p., dir. corp. ops., mem. exec. com. Vornado, Inc., Garfield, NJ, 1977-78; chmn. bd. dirs., CEO Allen B. Dorfman, Mgmt. Consulting Co., 1978—. Prof. Grad. Sch., LI U., NY. Bd. dirs., exec. v.p. Am. Cancer Soc., LI; bd. dirs. Kings Point Civic Assn., LI. With US Army, 1952—54. Recipient award, Advt. Club NY, Torch of Liberty award, Nat. Anti-Defamation League. Mem.: Nat. Assn. Catalog Showroom Merchandisers, Nat. Retail Mchts. Assn., Mass. Retailing Inst., Police Athletic League,

Philharmonics Assn., Boys Club, Boy Scouts Am., Adelphi Coll. Found., Wildwood Country Club Kings Point, LI (pres., bd. dirs.), Polo Club Boca Raton (bd. govs.-exec. com., chmn. coun. pres., chmn. emeritus coun. pres.), Sigma Alpha, Eta Mu Pi, Beta Gamma Sigma. Achievements include patents pending for zippered ice and roller skates. Office: Allen B Dorfman Mgmt Consulting Co, Polo Club-Penthouse Villa 17588 Ashbourne Ln Ste C Boca Raton FL 33496-4434 Office Phone: 561-241-4642. Business E-Mail: AllenDorfman@comcast.net.

DORIO, MARTIN MATTHEW, JR., real estate company executive, investor; b. Bklyn., Nov. 12, 1945; s. Martin M. and Josephine V. (Marsala) D.; m. Gayle M. Morris, June 16, 1968; children: Paul, Jay. BS, SUNY, Stony Brook, 1967; PhD, U. Mass., 1975. Rsch. chemist Diamond Shamrock Corp., Painesville, Ohio, 1975-76, group leader, 1977-79; venture mgr. Gen. Electric Lighting Bus., Cleve., 1979-81, quality and mfg. tech. mgr., 1981-87; dir. quality and productivity FMC Corp., Chgo., 1987-90; v.p. worldwide product mgmt. and market strategy Case Corp., Racine, Wis., 1990-91; v.p. corp. planning and devel. J.I. Case Corp., Racine, Wis., 1992-95; pres., CEO, dir. CLARK Material Handling Co., Lexington, Ky., 1995-99, chmn., CEO, dir., 1999—2001. Mem. adv. com. Dept. Energy, Washington, 1977-79, Am. Productivity and Quality Ctr., Houston, 1988-90; mem. adv. com. on quality Ency. Brit., 1988-90; mem. bd. examiners Malcolm Baldrige Nat. Quality Award, 1988-90; mem. adv. bd. Bioblend Lubricants Internat., Inc., 2001-03, Forintell Inc., 2002—; counselor Sr. Corps of Ret. Execs., 2002-03. Author: Multiple Electron Resonance Spectroscopy, 1979; contbr. articles to profl. jours.; patentee in field. Adv. bd. dirs. Mus. Culture and Diversity, 1997-99; bd. dirs. Lexington Arts & Cultural Coun., 1996-99; co-chair advanced divsn. Lexington: Strides Ahead, 1998-99, counselor SCORE chpt. 573, 2002-2003; chmn. endowment com. Temple Shalom, 2003-05. Capt. USAF, 1968-71. Recipient Nat. Svc. award Nat. Inst. Sci. and Tech., 1988-90. Mem. Am. Soc. Quality Control (exec. com. 1984-85), Am. Mgmt. Assn. Avocations: tennis, raquetball, photography, reading, writing. Home and Office: 1472 Palma Blanca Ct Naples FL 34119-3368 Office Phone: 239-272-2279. Business E-Mail: Marty@MartyDorio.com.

DORMAN, DAVID W., private equity firm executive, former telecommunications industry executive; b. Atlanta, 1954; m. Susan P. Dorman, 1971; 3 children. BS in Indsl. Mgmt., Ga. Inst. Tech., 1975. Pres. Sprint Bus. Services, 1990—94; chmn., pres., CEO Pacific Bell, 1994—97; exec. v.p. SBC Comm., 1997; chmn., pres., CEO PointCast Inc., 1997—98; CEO Concert Comm. Co., 1998—2000; pres. AT&T Corp., 2000—02, chmn., CEO, 2002—05; pres. AT&T Inc. (merger of SBC Communications & AT&T Corp.), San Antonio, 2005—06; mng. dir., sr. adv. Warburg Pincus, LLC, San Francisco, 2006—08; non-exec. chmn. Motorola, Inc., Schaumburg, Ill., 2008—10, Motorola Solutions, Inc., Schaumburg, Ill., 2011, CVS Caremark Corp., Woonsocket, RI, 2011—. Bd. dirs. AT&T Corp., 2002—05, AT&T Inc. (merger of SBC Comm. & AT&T Corp.), 2005—06, YUM! Brands, Inc., 2005—, CVS Corp., 2006—07, CVS Caremark Corp., 2007—, Motorola Inc., 2006—10, Motorola Solutions, Inc., 2011, lead dir., 2011—. Bd. dirs. Episcopal H.S., Alexandria, Va.; Ga. Tech. Found. Office: CVS Caremark Corp 1 CVS Dr Woonsocket RI 02895

DORMAN, JOE, state legislator; b. Burbank, Calif., 1970; s. Bill and Jan Dorman. BA in Polit. Sci., Okla. State Univ. Mail clerk, runner Okla. House of Representatives, 1994, several staff positions, including asst. to the exec. dir. of the House Stand, former spl. projects coordinator, former instr. of page mock legislature, mem. Dist. 65, 2002—, asst. Democrat Floor Leader, 2003—09. Mem.: OSU Alumni Assn., Capitol City Soc., America Inst. Parliamentarians, 4-H Alum, Farmers Union, Nat. Rifle Assn., Bricktown Rotary, Rush Springs' Lion Club. Democrat. Avocations: golf, hunting. Office: 2300 N Lincoln Blvd Rm 507 Oklahoma City OK 73105 Mailing: PO Box 559 Rush Springs OK 73082 Office Phone: 405-557-7305. Business E-Mail: dormanjo@lsb.state.ok.us, joedorman@okhouse.gov.

DORMINEY, HENRY CLAYTON, JR., allergist; b. Tifton, Ga., May 15, 1949; s. Henry Clayton and Virgina (Petty) D. BS, Davidson Coll., 1971; MD, U. Iowa, 1975. Diplomate Am. Bd. Internal Medicine, Am. Bd. Allergy and Immunology; lic. physician, Ga. Med. intern U. Iowa Hosps. and Clinics, Iowa City, 1975-76, med. resident, 1976-78, allergy and immunology fellow, 1978-80; practice medicine specializing allergy and clin. immunology Allergy & Dermatology Assocs. of Tifton, Ga., 1981—99, Allergy, Asthma and Sinus Clinic of Tifton, 1999—. Mem. staff Tift Regional Med. Ctr., 1982-2011; bd. dirs. Brumby's Crossing, Dorminey Enterprises; chmn. and founder Tifton Mus. Arts and Heritage, 1991; mem. Allergy, Asthma & Sinus Clinic of Tifton; pres. ZapAds, Inc., 2006—. Assoc. editor, contbg. author Vital Signs, 1969-71. Bd. dirs. Tift County Found. Ednl. Excellence, 1996—08, chmn. investment com., 1998—, v.p., 2004-05, pres., 2005-06; bd. dirs. Tifton Heritage Found., pres., 1992; bd. dirs. Tifton Mus. Arts and Heritage, 1991—2006, chmn. & pres., 1991-2002. Recipient Physician's Recognition award AMA, 1979, 85, Lee Willingham III trophy Davidson Coll., 1987, Tifton Main Street Program award, 1989, Best Adaptive Re-Use Project, Tifton Historic District, The Coca Cola Bldg., 1993; grantee Am. Coll. Allergy, 1980. Mem. Am. Acad. Allergy (travel grantee 1980), Tift County Med. Soc. (sec., treas. 1983-84, v.p., 1984-85, pres. 1985-86), Med. Assn. Ga., Am. Numismatic Soc., Forward Tifton, Tifton C. of C. Lodges: Rotary (Spl. Merit award, founder Tifton Directory, bd. dirs. 1988-93, 2006-07, pres.-elect 1989-90, pres. 1990-91, Paul Harris fellow 1993). Independent. Home: 21 Duck Dr Tifton GA 31794-3953 Office: 820 Love Ave Tifton GA 31794-4071 Office Phone: 229-382-3720. Personal E-mail: dorminey@friendlycity.net.

DORMINEY, O. LEONARD, bank executive; Divsn. mgr. South Ga. SunTrust Bank, Albany; pres., CEO First Nat. Bank of South Ga., 1999—2001; exec. v.p. comml. lending divsn. HeritageBank of South (subs. Heritage Fin. Group), 2001—03; bd. dirs. HeritageBank of South, 2001—, CEO, 2003—; bd. dirs. Heritage Financial Group, 2002—, pres., CEO, 2003—. Office: Heritage Financial Group 721 N Westover Blvd Albany GA 31707 Office Phone: 229-420-0000. Office Fax: 229-878-2054. Business E-Mail: ldorminey@eheritagebank.com.

DORN, JENNIFER LYNN, medical association administrator, former federal agency administrator; b. Grand Island, Nebr., Dec. 7, 1950; d. Harold Clarence and Ethel Agnes D.; 2 children BA, Oreg. State U., 1973; MPA, U. Conn., 1977. Legis. asst. to Senator M. Hatfield US Senate, Washington, 1977-81; com. staff Senate Appropriations, Washington, 1981-83; spl. asst. to sec. US Dept. Labor, Washington, 1983-84; dir. Comml. Space Transp., Washington, 1984-85; assoc. dep. sec. US Dept. Transp., Washington, 1985-87; asst. sec. for policy US Dept. Labor, Washington, 1989-91; sr. v.p. pub. support ARC, Washington, 1991-98; pres. Nat. Health Mus., 1998—2001; adminstr. Fed. Transit Adminstrn. (FTA) US Dept. Transp., Washington, 2001—05; alt. exec. dir. The World Bank (Internat. Bank for Reconstruction & Devel.), Washington, 2005—06; pres., CEO Nat. Acad. Pub. Adminstrn., Washington, 2007—10; sr. fellow Potomac Rsch. Group, 2010—11; CEO American Acad. Physician Assistants, 2011—. Mem. Washington Women's Forum, Cosmos Club. Republican. Lutheran. Office: American Acad Physician Assistants 2318 Mill Rd Ste 1300 Alexandria VA 22314 Office Phone: 571-319-4303. Business E-Mail: jdorn@aapa.org.

DORNING, JOHN JOSEPH, nuclear engineering, applied physics and applied mathematics educator; b. Bronx, NY, Apr. 17, 1938; s. John Joseph and Sarrah Cathrine (McCormack) D.; m. Helen Marie Driscoll, July 27, 1963; children: Michael, James, Denise. BS in Marine Engring., US Mcht. Marine Acad., 1959; MS in Nuc. Sci. and Engring., Columbia U., NYC, 1963, PhD in Nuc. Sci. and Engring., 1967. Marine engr. US Mcht. Marine, 1960-62; asst. physicist Brookhaven Nat. Lab., Upton, NY, 1967-69, assoc. physicist, grp. leader, 1969-70; assoc. prof. nuc. engring. U. Ill., Urbana, 1970-75, prof., 1975-84; Whitney Stone prof. nuc. engring., engring. physics and applied math. U. Va., Charlottesville, 1984—. NRC vis. prof. math. physics U. Bologna, Italy, 1975-76, 81, 85, 87; internat. prof. nuc. engring. Italian Ministry of Edn., 1983, 84, 86; physicist plasma theory grp., divsn. magnetic fusion energy Lawrence Livermore Nat. Lab., Calif., 1977-78; cons. to US nat. labs. and indsl. rsch. labs., 1970—. Contbr. articles to various publs. Served as ensign USN, 1959-60. Recipient Ernest O. Lawrence award US Dept. Energy, 1990, NAE, 2007. Fellow AAAS, Am. Phys. Soc., Am. Nuc. Soc. (Mark Mills award 1967, Arthur Holly Compton award 1998, Eugene P. Wigner award 1999, Glenn T. Seaborg medal 2002); mem. Am. Soc. Engring. Edn., (Glenn Murphy award 1988), Soc. Indsl. and Applied Math., NY Acad. Scis., NAE, Sigma Xi. Office: Univ Va Engring Physics Program PO Box 400745 116 Engineer's Way Charlottesville VA 22904-4745

DORRELL, KARL JAMES, professional football coach, former college football coach; b. Alameda, Calif., Dec. 18, 1963; s. John Dorrell; m. Kim L. Dorrell; children: Chandler, Lauren. BA, UCLA, 1986. Asst. coach UCLA Bruins, 1988, head football coach, 2003—07; receivers coach U. Ctrl. Fla. Golden Knights, 1989; offensive coord., receivers coach No. Ariz. U. Lumberjacks, 1990—91; wide receivers coach U. Colo. Buffaloes, 1992—93, offensive coord., 1995—98; wide receivers coach Ariz. State U. Sun Devils, 1994; offensive coord., receivers coach U. Wash. Huskies, 1999; wide receivers coach Denver Broncos, 2000—02, Miami Dolphins, 2008—10, quarterbacks coach, 2011, Houston Texans, 2012—. NFL Minority Coaching fellow, 1993, 1999. Office: The Houston Texans Two Reliant Park Houston TX 77054

DORRILL, WILLIAM FRANKLIN, political scientist, educator; b. Dallas, July 25, 1931; s. William Cumbie and Ruth (Esther Webb) D.; m. Martha Jeanne Brawley, Mar. 3, 1951; children: Jennifer Ruth, William Sidney, Rebecca Jeanne, Lisa Kathryn. BA, Baylor U., 1952; MA, U. Va., 1954; postgrad., Australian Nat. U., Canberra, 1954; PhD, Harvard U., 1972. Fgn. affairs analyst U.S. Govt., Washington, 1961-63; polit. scientist RAND Corp., Santa Monica, Calif., 1963-67; project chmn., sr. staff mem. Rsch. Analysis Corp., McLean, Va., 1967-68; dir. Asian Studies Ctr., assoc. prof. polit. sci. U. Pitts., 1969-77, chmn. dept. East Asian langs. and lits., 1972-77; dean Coll. Arts and Sci., prof. polit. sci. Ohio U., Athens, 1977-84; provost, prof. polit. sci. U. Louisville, 1984-88; pres. Longwood U., Farmville, Va., 1988-96, pres. emeritus, 1996—, prof. polit. sci. and history, 1988-96, bd. visitors, disting. prof., 1996—. Mem. faculty coll. mgmt. program Carnegie-Mellon U. and Nat. Ctr. for Higher Edn. Mgmt. Systems, summer, 1980; mem. com. on internat. edn. Am. Coun. on Edn., 1990, U.S. AID Univ. Ctr. Program Adv. Group, 1991; lectr. in field; higher edn. cons. U.S. Dept of State, China, 2000—01, Libya, 2004. Contbr. articles on East Asian politics and internat. relations to profl. jours., chpts. on Chinese politics and history to scholarly books. Mem. Athens County Bd. Mental Retardation and Devel. Disabilities, Ohio, 1982-84; chmn. bd. dirs. Kentuckiana Metroversity, 1986-88. Recipient Disting. Achievement medal Baylor U., 1980; Fulbright scholar, 1954; Soc. for Values in Higher Edn. Kent fellow, 1957-58; Ford Found. fgn. area fellow Taiwan, Hong Kong, 1959-61; Longwood U. Dorrill Dining Hall named in his honor, 2004. Fellow: Soc. for Values in Higher Edn.; mem.: Coun. on Postsecondary Edn. Environ. Task Force, Coun. for Internat. Exch. of Scholars (bd. dirs. 1992—96), Gov.'s Bus. Edn. Commn., Nat. Assn. State Univs. and Land Grant Colls. (acad. coun., exec. com. 1987—88), Southside Va. Bus. and Edn. Com. (exec. coun. 1992—2000), So. Assn. Colls. and Schs. (commn. on colls. 1986—88, chair vis. coms. 1990—, commn. on colls. 1991—96), Am. Assn. State Colls. and Univs. (com. on accreditation and instl. assessment 1989—96, chmn. 1990—96, gov.'s commn. econ. devel. in Southside Region Commonwealth Va. 1990—96, nominating com. 1993—94), Nat. Com. on U.S.-China Rels., Asia Soc. (adv. com. performing arts 1977—85), Assn. Asian Studies, Am. Conf. Acad. Deans (bd. dirs. 1980—84, vice chmn. 1981—82, chmn. 1982—83), Va. C. of C. (Va. emissary 1993—96), Rotary Internat. (gov.-elect dist. 7600 2002—03, gov. 2003—04). Democrat. Presbyterian. Achievements include Longwood U. building, Dorrill Dining Hall, named in honor of, 2004. Home: 1007 Fayette St Farmville VA 23901-2029 Office: Longwood U Dept History and Polit Sci Farmville VA 23909-0001 Personal E-mail: wdorrill@kinex.net.

DORRIS, WILLIAM E., lawyer; b. Dublin, Ga., Apr. 10, 1955; BA with high distinction, U. Ky., 1976, JD with high distinction, 1979. Bar: Ga. 1979, Ky. 1979. Mem. Smith, Currie & Hancock, Atlanta; ptnr. constrn. and pub. contracts grp. Kilpatrick Stockton, LLP, Atlanta, co-mng. ptnr., 2007—11, Kilpatrick Townsend & Stockton, LLP, Atlanta, 2011—. Contbr. articles to profl. jours.; co-author: Construction Disputes: Practice Guide with Forms. Mem. ABA, Ky. Bar Assn., State Bar Ga., Atlanta Bar Assn., Order of Coif, Phi Beta Kappa. Office: Kilpatrick Townsend & Stockton LLP Ste 2800 1100 Peachtree St NE Atlanta GA 30309-4530 Office Phone: 404-815-6104. Office Fax: 404-541-3183. E-mail: bdorris@kilpatrickstockton.com.

DORSA, PAUL T., healthcare executive; V.p., mergers, acquisition DaVita, Inc., ElSegundo, Calif., 2004—08; sr. v.p., devel. Vanguard Health Systems, Inc., 2008—. Bd. dirs. Nat. Kidney Found. of Middle Tenn., Inc. Office: Vanguard Health Systems Inc Ste 100 20 Burton Hills Blvd Nashville TN 37215 Office Phone: 615-665-6000. Office Fax: 615-665-6099. Business E-Mail: pdorsa@vanguardhealth.com.

DORSEY, YVONNE, state legislator; b. Aug. 19, 1952; Bank teller, 1971—74; travel counselor, 1974—76; exec. adminstr. & paralegal, 1976—91; exec. dir. La. Dept. Labor, 1992—93; mem. Dist. 67 La. House of Reps., 1993—2007; mem. Dist. 14 La. State Senate, 2008—, chair judiciary C com., mem. edn. com., health and welfare com., revenue and fiscal affairs com. Mem.: YMCA, NAACP, Nat. Conf. State Legislators, NCBSL. Democrat. Baptist. Office: Dist Off 1520 Thomas Delpit Dr Baton Rouge LA 70802 Fax: 504-342-9070. Business E-Mail: dorseyy@legis.state.la.us.

D'ORSI, CARL JOSEPH, medical educator, radiologist, researcher; b. Bklyn., Apr. 16, 1941; s. Anthony and Florence D'Orsi; m. Ellen Margaret Liberty, May 24, 2003; children: Michael Scott, Jonathin Liberty, Jenifer Liberty. BS, Downstate Med. Ctr. SUNY, Bklyn., 1964, MD, 1966. Cert. diagnostic radiology Am. Bd. Radiology, 1971. Asst. prof. radiology Harvard Med. Sch., Boston, 1970—80; prof. radiology and vice chair dept. radiology U. Mass. Med. Ctr., Worcester, 1980—2002; prof. radiology and hematology-oncology Emory U., Atlanta, 2002—. Vice chair breast cancer com. Am. Coll. Radiology, Reston, Va.; rev. editor RSNA, Chgo.; contbg. editor Breast Diseases, Phila.; pres. Soc. Breast Imaging, Reston, Va.; cons. Hologic Corp., Bedford, Mass., 2004—; com. mem. tech. assessment panel FDA, Washington, 2005—; lectr. in field; chair Bi-Rads Com. ACR. Contbr. articles to profl. jours. Lt. USNR, 1967—74. Recipient Radiology Editor's Recognition award with Distinction, Radiological Soc. N.Am., 1989, 1990, 1993, 1994, 2003, 2004, 2005, Disting. Svc. award, Am. Bd. Radiology, 2003; named Alumnus of Yr., Harvard Med. Sch., 2002. Fellow: Am. Coll. Radiology (Disting. Com. Svc. award 2003), Soc. of Breast Imaging (life; pres. 1989—90). Independent. Achievements include founder Soc. of Breast Imaging; author of BI-RADS method for reporting mammographic findings. Avocations: golf, woodworking, target shooting, travel. Home: 2271 Valley Brook way Atlanta GA 30319 Office: Emory Univ Winship Cancer Ctr 1701 Uppergate Dr Atlanta GA 30322 Business E-Mail: carl_dorsi@emoryhealthcare.org.

DORSMAN, PETER A., self service technologies company executive; BS, Syracuse U., NY, 1977. Various sr. mktg., strategic planning and sales mgmt. positions NCR Corp., 1978-96, v.p., gen. mgr. Systemedia bus., 2006—07, sr. v.p. global ops., 2008—; sr. v.p., gen. mgr. document systems divsn. Standard Register Co., 1996—98, sr. v.p., gen. mgr. document mgmt. & systems divsn., 1998—99, sr. v.p., gen. mgr. mfg. ops., 1999—2000, exec. v.p., COO, 2000—04. Bd. dirs. Applied Indsl. Technologies, Inc., 2002—. Office: NCR World Hdqs 3097 Satellite Blvd Duluth GA 30096 Mailing: Applied Industrial Technologies Inc Bd Directors 1 Applied Plz Cleveland OH 44115-5014 Business E-Mail: peter.dorsman@ncr.com.

DORWORTH, CHRISTOPHER E., state legislator; b. Ft. Lauderdale, Fla., July 17, 1976; m. Elizabeth Dorworth; children: Madison, Christopher Jr. BA, U. Fla., 1998; MBA, Duke U., 2006. Mem. Dist. 34 Fla. House of Reps., 2007—, vice chair mil. and local affairs policy com., mem. econ. devel. and cmty. affairs policy coun., fin. and tax coun., health care svcs. policy com., state univs. and pvt. colls. appropriations com. Chmn. Seminole Cmty. Coll. Dist. Bd. Trustees, Seminole Soil & Water Conservation Dist., Seminole County Bush/Cheney Campaign, 2004; vice chmn. Seminole County Planning & Zoning Commn., 2004; bd. dirs. Seminole County Regional C. of C., former vice chmn. Issues Com. Mem.: Seminole County Young Republicans (pres. 2003), Fla. Student Assn. Inc. (chmn. 1997—98). Republican. Presbyn. Office: House Office Bldg 402 S Monroe St Rm 200 Tallahassee FL 32399-1300 also: 1055 AAA Dr Ste 205 Heathrow FL 32746-5072 Office Phone: 850-488-5843, 407-333-1815. Business E-Mail: chris.dorworth@myfloridahouse.gov.

DOSSETT, MYRON B., state legislator; b. Jan. 9, 1961; Former magistrate Christian County Fiscal Ct.; mem. Dist. 9 Ky. House of Reps., 2007—; mem. econ. devel. & tourism com.; mem. labor & industry com. Mem.: Ruritan Club. Republican. Home: 491 E Nashville St Pembroke KY 42266-9792 Home Phone: 270-475-9503; Office Phone: 502-564-8100 ext. 657. Business E-Mail: Myron.Dossett@lrc.ky.gov.

DOSWALD, HERMAN KENNETH, language educator, retired academic administrator; b. Oakland, Calif., Mar. 24, 1932; s. Herman and Caroline Josephine (Mello) D.; m. Ruth Eugenie Hannes, Dec. 21, 1956; children: Caroline Susan, Stephanie Ann. AA, U. Calif., Berkeley, 1952, BA, 1955; MA, U. Wash., 1959, PhD, 1965. Instr., dept. German and Russian Oberlin (Ohio) Coll., 1959-60; instr., dept. German U. Wash., Seattle, 1960-61; instr., dept. fgn. langs. Seattle U., 1961-62; asst. prof. German U. Kans., Lawrence, 1964-67; asst., then assoc. prof., dept. fgn. langs. Fresno (Calif.) State U., 1967-72; prof., chmn. dept. German and Russian Kent (Ohio) State U., 1972-79; head dept. fgn. langs. Va. Poly. Inst. and State U., Blacksburg, 1979-84, assoc. dean adminstrn., Coll. Arts & Scis., 1984-86, interim dean Coll. Arts & Scis., 1986-87, dean, 1987-93, prof. German, 1993-96, prof. German, dean Coll. Arts & Scis. emeritus, 1996—. Adj. lectr. in German Cmty. HS, Roanoke, Va., 2006—07. Contbr. articles to profl. jours. Served to 1st lt. U.S. Army, 1962-64. Adenauer scholar, Munich, Fed. Republic Germany, 1953-54; Fulbright fellow, Vienna, Austria, 1958-59. Mem. Phi Beta Kappa, Phi Kappa Phi, Omicron Delta Kappa. Home: 906 Vista Ter Blacksburg VA 24060-3677 Personal E-mail: doswald@vt.edu.

DOSWELL, MARY CUMMINGS, energy executive; b. Atlanta, June 9, 1958; d. Robert Emery Cummings and Catherine Brierly Longyear; m. John Cabell Doswell II, July 3, 1982; children: Lindsay Cummings, Catherine Carter. BA in Physics cum laude, Mt. Holyoke Coll., South Hadley, Mass., 1980; MS in Engring., MIT, 1982. Sr. staff adminstrn. sr. coord. regulation, dir. demand-side analysis Va. Power Dominion Resources, Inc., Richmond, dir. market rsch. Va. Power, v.p. billing and credit Dominion Delivery, sr. v.p., chief adminstrv. officer, 2003—04, pres. and CEO Dominion Resources Svcs., 2004—07, sr. v.p. regulation & integrated planning, 2007—09, sr. v.p. alternative energy solutions, 2009—. Contbr. articles to profl. jours. Regional dir. admissions Mt. Holyoke Coll. Mem. Soc. Women Engrs., Elec. Utility Mkt. Rsch. Coun., Richmond C. of C. (chmn. bus. rsch. advisors), Women's Club, Tuckahoe Woman's Club, Sigma Xi. Office: Dominion PO Box 26532 Richmond VA 23261-6532

DOTSON, ALBERT, not-for-profit fundraiser; b. Detroit; m. Gail Ash Dotson; children: Ashley, Albert. BS econ., Dartmouth Coll.; JD, Vanderbilt Univ. Bar: Fla. With 100 Black Men of America, Inc., 1994—, vice-pres., chmn., 2004—; ptnr. Bizlin Sumberg Baena Price & Axelrod LLP. Lectr. Nat. Law Inst.; chmn. bd. trustees Miami Dade Coll. Found.; pres. Orange Bowl Com. Recipient Cmty. Excellence in Real Estate award, March of Dimes, 2002; named one of Cmty. Leader Award, Wilke D. Ferguson, Jr. Bar Assn., 1999, corporate elite in practice of law in So. Fla., Fla. Bus. Jour., 1999, So. Fla. Top Lawyers, Miami Metro, 2001, 100 Most Influential Black Americans, Ebony mag., 2006; named to Power 150, 2008. Office: 100 Black Men of America 141 Auburn Ave Atlanta GA 30303

DOTSON, DONALD L., lawyer; b. Rutherford County, NC, Oct. 8, 1938; s. Herman A. and Lottie E. (Hardin) D. AB, U. NC, 1960; JD, Wake Forest U., 1968. Bar: NC, Pa., DC, US Supreme Ct. Atty. NLRB, 1968-73, chmn., 1983-87; labor counsel Westinghouse Electric Corp., 1973-75; labor atty. Western Electric Co., 1975-76; chief labor counsel Wheeling-Pitts. Steel Corp., 1976-81; asst. sec. labor, 1981-83, 2001—; pvt. practice law, Washington, 1987-91; sr. v.p. Beverly Enterprises, 1991—2001; pvt. practice, 2001—. Served with USN, 1960-65. Episcopalian. Office: PO Box 4905 Charlottesville VA 22905 Office Phone: 800-227-7140.

DOTSON, GEORGE STEPHEN, retired oil industry executive; b. Okemah, Okla., Dec. 25, 1940; s. Hilmer C. and Alma Lucille (McGee) D.; m. Phyllis A. Nickerson, Aug. 17, 1963; children: Sarah, Grant. BS, M.I.T., 1963; MBA, Harvard U., 1970. Asst. to pres. Helmerich & Payne, Inc., Tulsa, 1970-73; v.p. Helmerich & Payne (Peru) Drilling Co., 1974-75, Helmerich & Payne Internat. Drilling Co., 1976-77, pres., COO, 1977—2006; v.p. drilling Helmerich & Payne, Inc., 1977—2006, ret. bd. dirs., 2006, Varco, Inc. Bd. dirs.

Atwood Oceanics, Inc.; chmn. Internat. Assn. Drilling Contractors, 1995. Served to capt. U.S. Army, 1964-68. Decorated Bronze Star. Office: 1918 E 30th Pl Tulsa OK 74114-5414

DOTY, DONALD D., retired bank executive; b. Independence, Kans., June 30, 1928; s. Laton L. and Dorothy (Russell) D.; m. Cheri F. Montgomery, June 14, 1952; children: John Scott, Susan Dorothy, Mark Montgomery. BS, Okla. State U., 1950; postgrad., U. Wis. Grad. Sch. Banking, 1963. Rancher, nr. Bartlesville, Okla., 1950-94; asst. cashier First Nat. Bank, Bartlesville, 1956-58, asst. v.p., 1958-60, v.p., 1964-69, exec. v.p., 1969-74; pres. WestStar Bank, n.a. (formerly First Nat. Bank), Bartlesville, 1974-93; also bd. dirs.; retired, 1993. Pres. First Bancshares, Inc., Bartlesville, 1974-93, bd. dirs.; chmn. S.W. Cattlemen's Credit Corp., 1979-90; pres. Bartlesville Credit Bur., 1972—; pres. Bartlesville-Area Indsl. Devel. Co., 1970—; chmn. First Okla. Life Ins. Co., Oklahoma City, 1990-95; chmn. Coll. Bus. Assocs., Okla. State U., 1991-92. Chmn., trustees Jane Phillips Episcopal Meml. Med. Ctr., 1970—; trustee Washington County Indsl. Devel. Trust Authority, 1973-80; chmn. Frank Phillips Found., Bartlesville, 1975—2003; trustee St. John Hosp., Tulsa, 1995-2004; bd. dirs. St. John Health Sys., 2004. Capt. USAF, 1953-55. Named to Okla. State U., Coll. of Bus. Hall of Fame, 1994; recipient Disting. S c. award Bartlesville, 1957, Disting. Alumni award Okla. State U., 2000. Mem. Am. Bankers Assn., Okla. Bankers Assn. (pres. 1984-85), Bartlesville C. of C. (v.p., bd. dirs. 1965-81, pres. 1981-82), Jaycees (Outstanding Young Man Bartlesville 1957, Okla. 1958), Masons, Shriners, Rotary, Sigma Alpha Epsilon. Republican. Episcopalian. Avocations: skiing, hunting, golf. Home: 2407 Kyle Ct Bartlesville OK 74006-6340 Office Phone: 918-337-3461. E-mail: dotyd@cableone.net.

DOTY, DUANE HAROLD, business educator; b. Wichita, Kans., July 5, 1960; s. David H. and Martha (Parker) D.; m. Susan Michal Smith, Dec. 30, 1991; children: Lindsey, Michala, Zachary, David. BA with honors, Tex. State U., San Marcos, 1982; MBA, U. Tex., Austin, 1987, PhD, 1990. Asst. prof. U. Ark., Fayetteville, 1990—95; chair dept. strategy and human resources Syracuse U. Sch. Mgmt., 1995; dean Coll. Bus. U. So. Miss., Hattiesburg, 2003—07, prof., 2003—09; dean Coll. Bus. & Tech. U. Tex., Tyler, 2009—13; asst. v.p. Strategic Initiatives, 2013—. Contbr. articles. Mem.: Acad. Mgmt. (Best Article award 1993, Scholarly Achievement award human resouces divsn. 1997). Avocations: fishing, hunting. Office: Univ Tex 3900 University Blvd Tyler TX 75799 Office Phone: 903-561-7360, 903-566-7101. Business E-Mail: harold_doty@uttyler.edu.

DOTY, GRESDNA ANN, theatre historian, educator; b. Oelwein, Iowa, Feb. 22, 1931; d. James William and Gresdna (Wood) D.; m. James G. Traynham, Nov. 28, 1980. AA, Monticello Coll., Alton, Ill., 1951; BA, Iowa State Tchrs. Coll., 1953; MA, U. Fla., 1957; PhD, Ind. U., 1967. Instr. S.W. Tex. State U., San Marcos, 1957—61, asst. prof., 1964—65, La. State U., Baton Rouge, 1967-73, assoc. prof., 1973-79, dir. theatre, 1973-77, 81-91, prof., 1979-84, Alumni prof., 1984—, Alumni prof. emeritus, 1996—, chair dept. theatre, 1991-93. Author: Anne Brunton Merry in the American Theatre, 1971; co-editor: (with Billy J. Harbin) Inside the Royal Court Theatre, 1956-81: Artists Talk, 1990; contbr. articles to profl. jours. Bd. dirs. Arts Coun. Greater Baton Rouge, 1987-92, pres., 1990-91, Leadership Greater Baton Rouge, 1993; bd. trustees La. Arts and Sci. Mus., 1996-2005, sec., 1997-2002, Planetarium Committee, 1998-2002. Rsch. grantee Nat. Endowment Humanities, 1981, Exxon Edn. Found., 1981, YWCA Woman Achievement, Arts and Humanities, 1995. Fellow S.W. Theatre Assn.; mem. Am. Theatre Assn. (bd. dirs. 1977-80), Am. Coll. Theatre Festival (nat. chmn. 1976-79), Am. Soc. Theatre Rsch. (mem. exec. com. 1988-91, v.p. 1994-97), Swine Palace Prodns. (founding bd. mem. 1991, mem. exec. bd. 1991-98), Nat. Theatre Conf. (sec. 1999-02), Coll. Fellows of Am. Theatre (dean-elect 2003-04, dean 2004-06). Home: 122 Highland Trace Baton Rouge LA 70810-5061 Home Phone: 225-766-2163. Business E-Mail: gresdna@msn.com.

DOTY, SALLY BURCHFIELD, state legislator; b. Kosciusko, Miss., Dec. 22, 1966; d. Charles Edward and Betty Prewitt Burchfield; m. W. Don Doty, June 4, 1988; children: Mary Eleanor, Sarah Caroline, Benjamin Gray. BA, Miss. U. for Women, 1988; JD, Miss. Coll., 1991. Bar: Miss. 1991, U.S. Dist. Ct. (no. and so. dists.) Miss. 1991, U.S. Ct. Appeals (5th cir.) 1991. Assoc. Wells, Moore, Simmons & Neal, Jackson, Miss., 1991-93; dir. legal writing Miss. Coll. Sch. Law, Jackson, 1994—97; atty. Allen, Allen, Boerner & Breeland, Brookhaven, Miss., 1997—2005; owner, developer Doty Family Rentals, LLC, Brookhaven, 2009—, Blue Heaven, LLC, Gulf Breeze, Fla., 2010—, Beach Heaven, LLC, Gulf Breeze, 2011—; mem. Dist. 39 Miss. State Senate, Jackson, 2012—. Author chpt.: Mississippi Civil Procedure, 1995. Mem. ABA, Miss. Bar Assn., Lincoln County Bar Assn. Republican. Methodist. Office: Miss State Senate PO Box 1018 Jackson MS 39215 Business E-Mail: sdoty@senate.ms.gov.

DOUBLES, MALCOLM CARROLL, college administrator; b. Richmond, Va., Aug. 14, 1932; s. Malcolm Ray and Catherine Clifford (Carroll) D.; m. Jacqueline Elizabeth McLeod, Dec. 21, 1956; children: Malcolm McLeod, John Carroll, Mary Blake. AB, Davidson Coll., NC, 1953; BD, Union Theol. Sem., Richmond, Va., 1957; PhD, St. Andrews U., Scotland, 1962. Ordained to ministry Presbyn. Ch., 1956. Minister Lebanon and Castlewood Presbyn. Chs., Va., 1960—65; asst. then assoc. prof. St. Andrews Presbyn. Coll., Laurinburg, NC, 1965—76, vis. prof., 2009—; provost Coker Coll., Hartsville, SC, 1976—97, disting. prof., 1997—2008; prof. SC Lay Sch. Theology, 1992—. Re-affirmation com. So. Assn. Colls. and Schs., Atlanta, 1985—97; prof. Shanghai Internat. Studies U., 1997—99. Author: The Sources of the Pentatench Displayed, 2000, A Century Plus: A History of Sonoco Products Company, 2006, In Quest of Excellence: A History of coker College on its Centennial, 2008, The Seduction of the Church, 2010; translator/reviser: Schurer's History of the Jews, 1980; contbr. articles and book revs. to profl. jours. Bd. mem. Darlington County Youth Home, Darlington, S.C., 1981-86. Younger humanist fellow NEH, Washington, 1971; Fulbright summer fellow U.S. Govt., Washington, 1983, 88. Mem. Am. Assn. Higher Edn., Soc. Bibl. Lit. (assoc. coun. 1967-78), Assn. Targumic Studies (chmn. 1974-83). Democrat. Home and Office: 1007 Scotia Village 2200Elm Ave Laurinburg NC 28352 Home Phone: 910-277-7512. Personal E-mail: mdoubles@aol.com.

DOUGAN, WILLIAM RICHMOND, alumni distinguished professor; BA, U. Va., Charlottesville, 1971; PhD, U. Chgo., 1979. Instr. Colgate U., Hamilton, NY; rsch. assoc. Nat. Planning Assn., Washington, 1972—73; rsch. cons. Urban Inst., Washington, 1973—74; asst. prof. Dartmouth Coll., Hanover, NH, 1980—85; vis. asst. prof. U. Chgo., 1985—88; prof. economics Clemson U., SC, 1988—2012, alumni disting. prof., 2012—. Cons. World Bank, Washington, 1982—84. Recipient Douglas W. Bradbury award, Calhoun Honors Coll., Clemson U., 2009; named Outstanding Grad. Tchr., Coll. Bus. and Behavioral Sci., Clemson U., 2005. Mem.: Am. Econ. Assn. Office: John E Walker Dept Economics 222 Sirrine Hall Clemson SC 29634-1309 Office Fax: 864-656-4192. Business E-Mail: douganw@clemson.edu.*

DOUGHERTY, F(RANCIS) KELLY, application developer; b. Lubbock, Tex., May 15, 1953; s. Francis Kelly and Mary Ann (Odell) D.; m. Bonnie Lee Burch, June 14, 1975; children: Anne Katherine, Margaret Erin, Mary Bridget, Kerry Meaghan, Frances Cara. BA in Math. and Physics summa cum laude, U. Dallas, 1975; MS in Computer Sci., U. Tex., Dallas, 1998; cert. assoc. customer svc., Life Office Mgmt. Inst., 1992. CLU; cert. computing profl.; chartered fin. cons.; Microsoft cert. programmer. Actuarial trainee Ranger Nat. Life Ins., Houston, 1976-77; mgr. time sharing svcs. Phila. Life Ins. Co., Houston, 1977-81; sys. engr. Electronic Data Sys., Dallas, 1981-85; IT analyst Transamerica Life and Protection, Plano, Tex., 1985—2013. Pres. St. Elizabeth Seton Parish Bd. Edn., 1989-92. U. Dallas scholar, 1971-75; Rice U. fellow, 1975-76. Fellow Life Mgmt. Inst. (master); mem. Assn. Computing Machinery, KC Roman Catholic. Home: 2713 S Cypress Cir Plano TX 75075-3154 Personal E-mail: fdougher1@verizon.net.

DOUGHERTY, MOLLY IRELAND, organization executive; b. Austin, Tex., Oct. 3, 1949; d. John Chrysostom and Mary Ireland (Graves) D.; m. Richard Pells, Oct. 2, 1999. Student, Stanford U., 1968—71, Grad. Theol. Union, Berkeley, 1976; BA, Antioch U., 1980. Tchr., fundraiser Oakland Cmty. Sch., Calif., 1973-77; assoc. prodr., asst. editor film Nicaragua: These Same Hands, Palo Alto, Calif., 1980; freelance journalist, translator Nicaragua, 1981; exec. dir. Vecinos, Austin, 1984—; ind. distbr. Univera, 2006—, LifeVantage, 2010—; English, French and Spanish lang. tutor St. Stephen's Episcopal Sch., Austin, 2003—07. Bd. dirs. Nat. Immigration Refugee and Citizenship Forum, Washington, 1985-88; spkr., fundraiser Salvadoran Assn. for Rural Health, 1986—; lectr. St. Stephen's Episcopal Sch., 1989. Office: Vecinos PO Box 4562 Austin TX 78765-4562 Office Phone: 512-476-1608. Personal E-mail: mollydougherty7@gmail.com.

DOUGLAS, DAVISON MCDOWELL, dean, law educator; b. Charlotte, NC, Sept. 16, 1956; s. John Munroe and Marjorie Elizabeth (Lutz) Douglas. AB, Princeton U., 1978; MA, Yale U., 1980, JD, 1983, MPhil, 1983, PhD in History, 1992; MAR, Yale Divinity Sch., 1983. Bar: NC 1984, US Dist. Ct. (middle and eastern dists.) NC, US Ct. Appeals (4th cir.). Jud. law clk. for Hon. Walter R. Mansfield US Ct. Appeals for 2nd Cir., NYC, 1983-84; assoc. Smith, Patterson, Follin, Curtis, James & Harkavy & Lawrence, Raleigh and Greensboro, NC, 1984-87, ptnr., 1987—90; asst. prof. law William and Mary Sch. Law, Williamsburg, Va., 1990—94, assoc. prof. law, 1994—96, prof. law, 1996—2001, Arthur B. Hanson prof. law, 2001—, dean, 2009—. Vis. prof. U. Iowa Coll. Law, 1989, Emory U. Sch. Law, 1996, U. Auckland Faculty Law, 2004, U. Melbourne Law Sch., 2007; dir. William & Mary Inst. Bill of Rights law, 1997—2004, William & Mary Election Law Program, 2005—08; vis. scholar Tohoku U., Grad. Sch. of Internat. Cultural Studies, 2002; Marc and Beth Goldberg disting. vis. prof. Cornell Law Sch., 2007. Editor: The Public Debate Over Busing and Attempts to Restrict Its Use, 1994, The Development of School Busing as a Desegregation Remedy, 1995; author: Reading, Writing and Race: The Desegregation of the Charlotte Schools, 1995, Jim Crow Moves North: The Battle Over Northern School Segregation, 1865-1954, 2005; co-editor (with N. Devins): Redefining Equality, 1998, A Year at the Supreme Court, 2004; co-author (with M. Curtis, P. Finkleman, W. Parker): Constitutional Law in Context, 2003; contbr. articles to legal jours., chapters to books. Bd. dirs. Wake County Civil Liberties Union, Raleigh, 1987—. Mem.: ABA, NC Acad. Trial Lawyers, NC Bar Assn. Democrat. Episcopalian. Avocations: bicycling, backpacking, church activities. Office: William and Mary School Law Room 108 PO Box 8795 Williamsburg VA 23187-8795 Office Phone: 757-221-3790. Office Fax: 757-221-3261. Business E-Mail: dmdoug@wm.edu.*

DOUGLAS, DONITA BOURNS, legal association administrator; BFA in Journalism (cum laude), Southern Methodist U.; JD, Okla. U. Coll. Law. Dir. educational programs Okla. Bar. Assn., 2000—12; v.p. profl. services InReach, Oreg., 2012—. Recipient Partners in Excellence award, 2012. Fellow: Okla. Bar Assn. (mem. civil procedure com., Earl Sneed award 2012, Mona Salyer Lambird Spotlight award 2007, President's award 2003); mem.: Assn. for Continuing Legal Edn. (pres. 2013—, co-chair state and provincial bar spl. interest group), Ruth Bader Ginsburg Inn of Court (emeritus mem.). Office: InReach 2506 NW 55th Terrace Oklahoma City OK 73112 Address: Association for Continuing Legal Education 1000 Westgate Dr Ste 252 Saint Paul MN 55114 Office Phone: 405-418-7591. Business E-Mail: ddouglas@inreachce.com.*

DOUGLAS, J. WILLIAM, JR., bank executive; b. Columbia, SC; Grad., U. SC, U. Del. Stonier Grad. Sch. Banking. Joined as sr. v.p br. ops. Athens First Bank & Trust Co., Ga., 1986; pres., CEO Athens First Bank & Trust, 2002—, chmn., 2009—. Vice chair Athens Area Cmty. Found.; bd. dirs. Athens Regional Health Svcs.; bd. dirs., past pres. Athens YMCA. Office: AFB&T Main Office Hdqs 150 W Hancock Ave Athens GA 30601 Mailing: Synovus Financial Corp 1111 Bay Ave Ste 500 Columbus GA 31901 Office Phone: 706-649-2311. Office Fax: 706-641-6555.

DOUGLAS, JAMES MATTHEW, law educator, dean; BA in Math., Tex. Southern U., 1966, JD, 1970; MS Law, Stanford U., 1971. Bar: Tex. 1970. Programmer analyst Singer Gen. Precision Co., Houston, 1966-70, 71-72; asst. prof. law Tex. Southern U., Houston, 1972—74, dean, prof. law, 1981—95, provost, v.p. acad. affairs, 1995, pres., 1995—99, prof., 1995—99, disting. prof., 1999—2005, disting. prof. law, 2007—, exec. vice pres. Houston, 2008—, provost, 2008—; asst. prof. Cleve.-Marshall Coll. Law, Cleve. State U., 1974—75, asst. prof., asst. dean student affairs, 1974-75; assoc. prof., assoc. dean Coll. Law Syracuse U., NY, 1975-80; prof. Northeastern U. Sch. Law, Boston, 1980-81; dean, prof. coll. law Fla. A&M U., Orlando, 2005—07; exec. v.p. Tex. Southern U., 2008—. Contbr. articles to profl. jours. Mem. steering com. Houston Campaign Homeless, 1988—89; bd. dirs. Sickle Cell Found. Tex., 1988—94, pres., 1990—91; bd. dirs. Boy Scouts Am., 1993—, Greater Houston Partnership, 1996—99. Mem.: Nat. Bar Assn., Houston Bar Assn. (chair law practice mgmt. sect. 1995—), Tex. Supreme Ct. Hist. Soc. (trustee 1990—), State Bar Tex., ABA, Houston C. of C. Home: 5318 Calhoun Rd Houston TX 77021-1714 Office: Tex So U 3100 Cleburne St Houston TX 77004-4501 Office Phone: 713-313-7352, 713-313-1122. Business E-Mail: jdouglas@tmslaw.tsu.edu, douglas.j@tsu.edu.

DOUGLAS, JERRY, bluegrass musician, dobro player; b. Warren, OH, May 28, 1956; Band mem. Country Gentlemen, 1973, J.D. Crowe & the New South, 1974, The Whites, 1979—85, Alison Krauss & Union Station, 1998—; co-founder band Boone Creek, 1976, band Strength in Numbers, 1989. Musician (session artist): appears on over 1500 albums, (albums include) The Great Dobro Sessions, 1994 (Grammy, Best Bluegrass Album, 1994); musician: (albums) (with J.D. Crowe & the New South) J.D. Crowe & the New South, 1975, Holiday in Japan, 1975, New South Live, 1975, (with Boone Creek) Boone Creek, 1977, One Way Track, 1977, (with The Whites) That Down Home Feeling, 1977, Buck & Family Live, 1979, More Pretty Girls Than One, 1979, (with Alison Krauss & Union Station) New Favorite, 2001 (Grammy, Best Bluegrass Album, 2001), Live, 2002 (Grammy, Best Bluegrass Album, 2003), Lonely Runs Both Ways, 2004 (3 Grammy awards: Best Country Group Performance, Best Country Instrumental Performance, Best Country Album, 2006), songs in O Brother, Where Art Thou?, 2000 (Grammy, Album of Yr., 2001); solo albums include Fluxology, 1979, Fluxedo, 1982, Under the Wire, 1986, Changing Channels, 1987, Everything is Going to Work Out Fine, 1987, Plant Early, 1989, Slide Rule, 1992, Restless on the Farm, 1998, Lookout for Hope, 2002, The Best Kept Secret, 2005, Best of the Sugar Hill Years, 2007. Recipient Musician of Yr. award, Country Music Assn., 2002, 2005, 2007, 12 Grammy awards, Top Specialty Instrument Player of Yr., Acad. Country Music, 2008; named Musician of Yr., Americana Music Assn., 2002, 2003, Best Musician, Nashville Scene Critic's Poll, 2004; Nat. Heritage Fellowship, Nat. Endowment for the Arts, 2004. Mailing: PO Box 58034 Nashville TN 37205 Office: Keith Case Fl 2 1025 17th Ave Nashville TN 37212 Office Phone: 615-327-4646. E-mail: info@jerrydouglas.com, keith@keithcase.com.

DOUGLAS, J(OCELYN) FIELDING, toxicologist, consultant; b. Delta, Utah, Jan. 25, 1927; s. Benjamin and Amelia (Fielding) D.; m. Rose Mary Terrazzino, Sept. 16, 1951; children: David Benjamin, Pamela Susan, Jason Terrell. BS with high honors, U. Ill., 1948; MA, Columbia U., 1950, PhD, 1953. Project leader Johnson & Johnson, New Brunswick, N.J., 1952-58; dir. biochemistry Carter-Wallace, Cranbury, N.J., 1958-74; dep. dir. carcinogenesis testing program Nat. Cancer Inst., Bethesda, Md., 1976-80; chief ops. Nat. Toxicology Program, Bethesda, 1980-84; pres. Sci. Svcs., Inc., Front Royal, Va., 1984—. Expert cons. NIH, Bethesda, 1976-81; cons. in field; pres. High Knob Owners Assn. Inc., 1999—; bd. dirs. High Knob Utilities Inc., Front Royal, Va. Author, editor: Carcinogenesis and Mutagenesis Testing, 1984; contbr. numerous articles to profl. jours. Pvt. U.S. Army, 1944-46. Recipient Richard Neff award Richard Neff Soc., 1966, Dir. award Nat. Cancer Inst., 1979; USPHS fellow, 1950-52. Fellow AAAS; mem. Soc. Toxicology, Am. Soc. Pharmacology and Exptl. Therapeutics, Am. Chem. Soc. (chmn. biochem. sect. 1954). Avocations: gardening, reading, meditation. Home and Office: Sci Svcs Inc PO Box 533 Front Royal VA 22630-0533

DOUGLAS, JOHN LEWIS, lawyer; b. Atlanta, Sept. 23, 1950; s. Charles Lewis Jr. and Bettye Lee (Phelps) D.; m. Rebecca Ann Peterson, Aug. 16, 1974; children: Amber Lynne, Dianna Michelle, John Lewis Jr., Scott Foster, Charles Tillman, Alexander Peterson, Michael Lawrence, Jolanta Kuuzik, Tomas Kuuzik. BA in Econs., Davidson Coll., NC, 1972; JD, U. Ga., 1977. Bar: Ga. 1977. Assoc. Alston and Bird, Atlanta, 1977-83, ptnr., fin. inst. regulation, mergers, acquistions Atlanta and Washington, 1990—; gen. counsel FDIC, Washington, 1987-89. Mem. bd. dirs. Fin. Svcs. Vol. Corp., Providian Fin. Corp., 2003-05. Contbr. articles to profl. jours. Republican. Mem. Lds Ch. Office: Paul, Hastings, Janofsky & Walker LLP 600 Peachtree St Ste 2400 Atlanta GA 30308-2222 Office Phone: 404-815-2214. Business E-Mail: johndouglas@paulhastings.com.

DOUGLAS, JOHN SIMONTON, JR., cardiologist, educator; b. Tuscumbia, Ala., Apr. 18, 1941; Grad., U. South; MD, Washington U. Sch. Medicine, St. Louis, 1967. Diplomate Am. Bd. Internal Medicine, Am. Bd. Cardiovascular Diseases, Am. Bd. Interventional Cardiology. Intern, medicine NC Meml. Hosp., Chapel Hill, 1967-68, resident, internal medicine, 1968-69; resident, cardiology Grady Meml. Hosp., Atlanta, 1971-72; fellow, cardiology Emory Affiliated Hosps., Atlanta, 1972-74; mem. staff Emory U. Hosp., Atlanta, 1972—, dir., cardiac catheterization lab., 2001—, dir., interventional cardiology, 2001—; assoc. prof. Emory U. Sch. Medicine, prof., medicine. Dir., Emory Practical Intervention Course Emory U. Contbr. several articles to profl. jours. Lt. comdr. US Navy Med. Corps, Camp Lejeune Marine Corps Base and in An Hoa, S. Vietnam. Named to Castle Connolly Guide to America's Top Doctors, Atlanta's Top Doctors, The Best Doctors in Am. Fellow: Am. Coll. Cardiology (former bd. mem.); mem.: Soc. for Cardiac Angiography and Intervention. Achievements include being the member of the team that performed the first coronary angioplasty at Emory University Hospital and in 1987 the first coronary stent in the US. Office: Emory U Hosp Ste F606 1364 Clifton Rd NE Atlanta GA 30322 Office Phone: 404-727-7040. Business E-Mail: john.douglas@emoryhealthcare.org.

DOUGLAS, LAURIE ZEITLIN, food products executive, information technology executive; BA in Economics, Duke U., 1984; MBA in Fin., U. Pa., 1989. Rsch. asst. Touche Ross & Co., 1985—87; sr. mng. consulting Deloitte & Touche LLP, 1989—95; dir., info. tech., sr. mgr., application devel. & v.p., info. tech. Home Depot, Inc., 1995—2003; sr. v.p., chief info. officer Kinko's Inc., 2003, Print Center, Inc., 2006; sr. v.p., chief information officer Publix Super Markets, Inc., 2006—. Adv. bd. mem. InformationWeek. Named one of Premier 100 IT Leaders, Computerworld, 2006. Office: Publix Supermarkets Inc 3300 Publix Corporate Parkway Lakeland FL 33811 Office Phone: 214-550-7020, 863-688-1188. Office Fax: 863-616-9649. Business E-Mail: laurie.douglas@publix.com. E-mail: laurie.zeitlin@fedexkinkos.com.

DOUGLAS, PAMELA SUSAN, physician, researcher, educator; b. New Brunswick, NJ, Dec. 2, 1954; d. Jocelyn Fielding and Rose Maria (Terrazzino) D.; m. Geoffrey Steven Ginsburg. AB, Princeton U., NJ, 1974; MD, Med. Coll. Va., 1978. Cert. Nat. Bd. Med. Examiners, Am. Bd. Internal Medicine (subspecialty in cardiovasc. disease), Nat. Bd. Echocardiography. Resident, internal medicine Hosp. U. Pa., Phila., 1978—81, clin. and rsch. fellow, cardiology, 1981—84, physician, 1984—90; asst. instr. medicine U. Pa. Sch. Medicine, Phila., 1979—81, asst. prof. medicine, 1984—90; physician Phila. VA Hosp., 1984—90; assoc. prof. medicine Harvard Med. Sch., Boston, 1990—2000; physician Beth Israel Deaconess Med. Ctr., 1990—2000; Dr. Herman and Ailene Tuchman prof. cardiovasc. medicine, head dept. U. Wis., Madison, 2000—04, assoc. dir. Cardiovasc. Rsch. Ctr., 2000—04; physician U. Wis. Hosp. and Clinics, Madison, 2000—04, William S. Middleton VA Hosp., 2000—; chief, divsn. cardiology Duke U. Med. Ctr., 2004—, Ursula Geller prof. for Rsch. in Cardiovascular Diseases, 2004—, dir., cardiovascular rsch. strategies, 2004—. Adv. bd. Mallinckrodt, 1997—2001, DuPont Pharm., 1998—2001, Premier Innovation Inst., 1999—2001, Nat. Women's Health Report Card, 1998—, Boston Women's Health, 1998—2001, Cardiology Domain, 2000—; mem. sci. adv. coun. Soc. Women's Health Rsch., 2001—. Mem. editl. bd. Am. Jour. Cardiology, 1986—, Jour. Sports Medicine and Physical Fitness, 1991—, Internat. Jour. Sports Cardiology, 1991—, Jour. Women's Health, 1991—, Am. Jour. Geriatric Cardiology, 1992—, Am. Heart Jour., 1996—, Jour. Clin. and Exptl. Cardiology, 1997—, Jour. Clin. and Basic Cardiology, —, Cardiology, 2000—; manuscript reviewer: numerous pubs. in field; contbr. numerous articles to profl. jours., chapters to books; editor: Heart Disease in Women, 1989, Cardiovascular Health and Disease in Women, 1993, 2d edit., 2002. Mem. med. com. USA Triathlon, 1988—, chmn. med. control. com., 1989—; chmn. antidoping control com. Internat. Triathlon Union, 1989—92, mem. med. com., 1989—92; physician, finish line med. team Hawaii Ironman Triathlon, 1984—99; dir. elite med. tent Boston Marathon, 1991—96. Named Best of Boston cardiologist, 1997—2000; nominee IOC Olympic prize for Med. Sci., 2000—; grantee, Commonwealth Pa., 1984—90, A.H. Robins, 1985—87, Echocardiography Rsch. Found., 1986—88, 1990—96, 1993, 1995—97, 1996—98, 1996—, Syntex, 1987—93, SOCAR, 1991—94, Gensia, 1992—93, Merck, 1992—93, 1993—97, St. Jude Med. Ctr., 1993, Women's Aid to Heart

Rsch., 1993, 1995, Hewlett-Packard, 1991—96, 1995—98, NIH, 1995—2000, 1999—2000, 2000—, Molecular Biosys. Inc., 1997—99, Nat. Ctr. Excellence in Women's Health, 1998—2000, Nat. Rsch. Consortium Women's Health, 1999—, Agilent Tech., 2000—, Inovise Med., 2000—; fellow, NIH, 1978, Am. Coll. Cardiology/European Soc. Cardiology/Merck, 1992. Fellow: Am. Coll. Sports Medicine, Am. Heart Assn. (session chair and structured sessions spkr. 1988—, bd. dirs. 1991—92, program com. 1993—95, exec. com. 1994—98, nominations com. coun. clin. cardiology 1995—2000, fellowship award 1982—83, 1983—84, grant 1985—86, 1986—87, 1987—88, 1988—89), Am. Coll. Cardiology (com. on women in cardiology 1994—2000, asst. sec. bd. trustees 1995—97, bd. trustees 1995—, audit com. 1996—97, nominating com. 1997—99, chair nominating com. 1998—99, com. expert consensus documents 1998—2001, mem. task force mem. rels. 1999—2000, forum for future writing group 1999—2000, task force for 21st century 1999—2000, chair tax status restructuring task force 2000—01, writing com. to develop clin. competence echocardiography statement 2000—, mem. echocardiography com. 2001—, budget fin. and investment com. 2001—, other coms., mem. editl. bd. 1993—97); mem.: Assn. Profs. Cardiology, Ctrl. Soc. Clin. Rsch., Am. Soc. Echocardiography (bd. dirs. 1993—96, session chair and structured sessions spkr. 1993—, sci. session program com. 1994—, judge young investigator rsch. awards 1995—2000, chair outcomes rsch. awards com. 1996—2001, devel. com. 1996—, sect. editor jour. 1998—, v.p. 1999—2001, strategic planning process co-chair 1999—2001, bd. dirs. 1999—, exec. com. 1999—, pres. 2001—, chair women's health adv. group 2001—, mem. editl. bd. 1993—, rsch. award 1992), Alpha Sigma Chi. Office: Duke U Med Ctr PO Box 17969 7022 N Pavillion DUMC Durham NC 27715 Office Phone: 919-681-2690. Office Fax: 919-668-7059.

DOUGLAS, SANDY (J. ALEXANDER M. DOUGLAS), beverage company executive; BA, U. Va., 1983. Dist. sales mgr. Coca-Cola Fountain, 1988—94; v.p. sales mktg. group Coca-Cola Enterprises, Inc., 1994—2000; exec. v.p., COO Coca-Cola N. Am. divsn., pres., 2000—03; sr. v.p., chief customer officer Coca-Cola Co., 2003—06, pres. N.Am. Group, 2006—. Bd. dirs. The Coca-Cola Co., 2004—, Radiant Systems, Transora. Bd. dirs. Atlanta YMCA; mem. Anglican studies advisory bd. Candler Sch. Emory U. Office: The Coca Cola Co One Coca Cola Plaza Atlanta GA 30313

DOUGLAS, WILLIAM ERNEST, retired commissioner; b. Charleston, SC, Nov. 26, 1930; s. William Ernest and Helen A. (Fortune) D.; m. Nancy Anne (Gibson), July 18, 1980. BA cum laude, The Citadel, 1956; postgrad., U. SC, 1956—59. With IRS, 1959—80, divsn. chief Newark dist., 1970—72, asst. dir. Jackson (Miss.) dist., 1972-73, asst. dir. Atlanta dist., 1973-74, asst. commr. S.E. region, 1974-78, dir. Regional Svc. Ctr. S.E. region, 1978-80; commr. fin. mgmt. svc. US Treasury Dept., Washington, 1980—91. Served in U.S. Army, 1948-52, Korean War, 1950-51. Recipient Exec. Excellence award Fed. Interagency Com. on Info. Resources Mgmt., 1985; Exec. Achievement award Sr. Exec. Svc., 1985; Am. Univ. Roger W. Jones Fed. Exec. Leadership award, 1986; Sec. of Treasury's Disting. Svc. award, 1991; Presdl. Exec. Disting. award, 1991. Home: 2040 Warm Springs Rd Columbus GA 31904

DOUGLAS, WILLIAM W., food products executive; m. Lisa Douglas; 2 children. BBA, Univ. Ga., 1983. With Ernst & Whinney, 1983—85; Joined Coca Cola Enterprises, Atlanta, 1985; corp. controller Coca Cola Beverages plc, London; CFO Coca Cola HBC, Greece, 2000—04; v.p., controller, chief acctg. officer Coca Cola Enterprises, Atlanta, 2004—05, sr. v.p. to exec. v.p., CFO, 2005—. Office: Coca Cola Enterprises Ste 900 2500 Windy Ridge Pkwy Atlanta GA 30339 Mailing: Coca Cola Enterprises PO Box 723040 Atlanta GA 31139-0040

DOUGLASS, JOHN G., law educator; BA in History, Dartmouth Coll., Hanover, NH, 1977; JD, Harvard U., 1980. Bar: Supreme Ct. Va. (Mediator) 1997, Va., DC, US Ct. Appeals 4th Cir., US Ct. Appeals DC Cir., US Dist. Ct. (Ea. Dist.) Va., US Dist. Ct. (We. Dist.) Va., US Dist. Ct. (Ea. Dist.) DC, US Dist. Ct. (We. Dist.) DC, US Dist. Ct. (Ea. Dist.) Md., US Dist. Ct. (We. Dist.) Md. Law clk. to Hon. Harrison L. Winter US Ct. Appeals (4th cir.), 1980—81; assoc. McGuire, Woods & Battle, Richmond, Va., 1981—83; asst. US atty. US Dept. Justice, Baltimore, 1983—86; assoc. counsel Office Ind. Counsel for Iran/Contra Investigation, 1987—90; assoc. Wright, Robinson, McCammon, Osthimer & Tatum, Richmond, 1986—91, ptnr., 1988—91; asst. US atty., chief criminal sect. US Dept. Justice, Richmond, Va., 1992—96; mediator McCammon Group, 1996—; asst. prof. law U. Richmond Sch. Law, 1996—99, assoc. prof. law, 1999—2002, prof. law, 2002—, acting assoc. dean, 2002, dean, 2008—11. Mem. Commn. on Va. Courts in the 21st Century. Founding dir., mem. bd. dirs. Interfaith Housing Corp. Mem.: Va. State Bar, Nat. Inst. Trial Advocacy. Office: University of Richmond School of Law 315 Carole Weinstein International Ctr 28 Westhampton Way Richmond VA 23173 Office Phone: 804-289-8198. Office Fax: 804-289-8683. Business E-Mail: jdougla2@richmond.edu.

DOUGLASS, JOHN JAY, lawyer, educator; b. Lincoln, Nebr., Mar. 9, 1922; s. Edward Lyman and Edna Marie (Ball) D.; m. Margaret Casteel Pickering, Aug. 31, 1946; children: Carrie Bess, Timothy Pickering, Margaret Marie. AB with distinction, U. Nebr., 1943; JD with distinction, U. Mich., 1952; MA, George Washington U., 1963; LLM, U. Va., 1973; postgrad., Army War Coll., 1963. Bar: Nebr. 1952, Mich. 1952, Tex. 1975. Inf. officer U.S. Army, 1943-52, advanced through grades to col., 1966, judge adv., 1952-74, Vietnam, 1968-69, mil. judge Ft. Riley, Kans., 1969-70; comdt. U.S. Army JAG Sch., Charlottesville, Va., 1970-74; ret. U.S. Army, 1974; dean Nat. Coll. Dist. Attys., Houston, 1974-94; prof. U. Houston, 1975—2011, emeritus prof., 2011—. Advisor on criminal law to Albania, 1991; advisor on elections to Ukraine, 1993; advisor Russian procuracy, 1994, Ukraine procuracy, 1995; named dist. mem. JAGC, 1994. Author: Ethical Concerns in Prosecution, 1988, 93; contbr. articles to profl. jours. Judge Harris County Absentee Voting, Houston, 1980-92; apptd. mem. Houston Ethics Commn., 2006. Decorated D.S.M., Legion of Merit, Bronze Star, Army Commendation medal; recipient U. Nebr. Alumni Achievement award, 2003. Fellow Am. Bar Found. (life); mem. ABA (ho. of dels. 1980-96, chmn. standing com. on law and electoral process 1987-90, Nelson award 2001), Tex. Bar Assn. (penal code and criminal process com. 1988-90), Houston City Club, Army and Navy Club, Order of Coif, Eagle Scout, Alpha Tau Omega. Avocation: tennis. Home: 25 T 14 E Greenway Plz Houston TX 77046-1406 Home Phone: 713-871-0696; Office Phone: 713-743-1831.

DOUMAR, ROBERT GEORGE, judge; b. Feb. 17, 1930; m. Dorothy Ann Mundy; children: Robert G., Charles C. BA, U. Va., 1951, LLB, 1953, LLM, 1988. Assoc. Venable, Parsons, Kyle & Hylton, 1955-58; sr. ptnr. Doumar, Pincus, Knight & Harlan, 1958-81; judge U.S. Dist. Ct. (ea. dist.) Va., Norfolk, 1981—96, sr. judge, 1996—. Lt. USAF. Mem. ATLA, Am. Judicature Soc., Def. Rsch. Inst., Internat. Soc. Barristers, Va. Conf. of Local Bar Assns., Va. Assn. Trial Lawyers. Roman Catholic. Office: US Dist Ct US Courthouse 600 Granby St Ste 344 Norfolk VA 23510-1923

DOVE, GORDON E., SR., state legislator; Mem. Dist. 52 La. House of Reps., 2004—, chair natural resources and environment com., mem. Acadiana del., La. Rep. legis. del., La. rural caucus. Republican. Office: Capitol Off 900 N Third St, PO Box 94062 Baton Rouge LA 70804 Address: PO Box 629 Houma LA 70361 Office Phone: 225-342-7263. Fax: 985-873-2077.

DOVE, RITA FRANCES, poet, language educator; b. Akron, Ohio, Aug. 28, 1952; d. Ray A. and Elvira E. (Hord) Dove; m. Fred Viebahn, Mar. 23, 1979; 1 child, Aviva Chantal Tamu Dove-Viebahn. BA summa cum laude, Miami U., Oxford, Ohio, 1973; postgrad., Universität Tübingen, Fed. Republic Germany, 1974-75; MFA, U. Iowa, 1977; LLD (hon.), Miami U., Oxford, Ohio, 1988, Knox Coll., 1989, Tuskegee U., 1994, U. Miami, Fla., 1994, Washington U., St. Louis, 1994, Case Western Res. U., 1994, U. Akron, 1994, Ariz. State U., 1995, Boston Coll., 1995, Dartmouth Coll., 1995, Spelman Coll., 1996, U. Pa., 1996, U. NC, 1997, U. Notre Dame, 1997, Northeastern U., 1997, Columbia U., 1998, Washington & Lee U., 1999, SUNY, Brockport, 1999, Pratt Inst., 2001, Howard U., 2001, Skidmore Coll., 2004. Asst. prof. English Ariz. State U., Tempe, 1981-84, assoc. prof., 1984-87, prof., 1987-89, U. Va., Charlottesville, 1989-93, Commonwealth prof. English, 1993—; U.S. poet laureate, cons. in poetry Libr. of Congress, Washington, 1993-95, spl. cons. in poetry, 1999-2000; columnist Washington Post, 2000—02. Writer-in-residence Tuskegee Inst., Ala., 1982; lit. panelist Nat. Endowment Arts, Washington, 1984-86, chmn. poetry grants panel, 1985; judge Walt Whitman award Acad. Am. Poets, 1990, Pulitzer prize in poetry, 1991, Ruth Lilly prize 1991, Nat. Book award in poetry 1991, 98, Anisfield-Wolf Book awards, 1992—, Shelley Meml. award, 1997, Amy Lowell fellowship, 1997; poetry panel chmn. Pulitzer prize, 1997; final judge Brittingham and Pollack prizes, 1997; juror Christopher Columbus Fellowship Found., 1998-02, Duke Ellington awards, 1999; bd. dir. Poetry Daily, 2002; chancellor Acad. Am. Poets, 2006-. Author: (poetry) Ten Poems, 1977, The Only Dark Spot in the Sky, 1980, The Yellow House on the Corner, 1980, Mandolin, 1982, Museum, 1983, Thomas and Beulah, 1986 (Pulitzer Prize in poetry 1987), The Other Side of the House, 1988, Grace Notes, 1989 (Ohioana award 1990), Selected Poems, 1993 (Ohioana award 1994), Lady Freedom Among Us, 1994, Mother Love, 1995, Evening Primrose, 1998, On the Bus with Rosa Parks, 1999 (Ohioana award 2000), Sonata Mulattica, 2009, American Smooth, 2004; (verse drama) The Darker Face of the Earth, 1994 (W. Alton Jones Found. grant 1994, Kennedy Ctr. Fund for New Am. Plays award 1995, Geraldine Dodge Found. grant, 1997), completely rev. 2d edit., 1996, expanded 3d edit., 2000 (first performance Oreg. Shakespeare Festival 1996); (novel) Through the Ivory Gate, 1992 (Va. Coll. Stores Book award 1993); (short stories) Fifth Sunday, 1985 (Callaloo award 1986); (essays) The Poet's World, 1995, (song cycle) Seven for Luck (music by John Williams), 1st performance Boston Symphony Orch., Tanglewood, 1998; mem. editl. bd. Nat. Forum, 1984-89, Iris, 1989—; mem. adv. bd. Ploughshares, 1992—, NC Writers Network, 1992-99, Civilization, 1994-97, Am. Poetry Rev., 2005-; assoc. editor Callaloo, 1986-98; adv. and contbg. editor Gettysburg Rev., 1987—, TriQuarterly, 1988—, Ga. Review, 1994—, Bellingham Rev., 1996—, Internat. Quarterly, 1997—, Callaloo, 1998—, Mid-Am. Rev., 1998—; editor Best Am. Poetry, 2000. Commr. The Schomburg Ctr. Rsch. in Black Culture, NY Pub. Libr., 1987—; mem. Renaissance Forum Folger Shakespeare Libr., 1993-95, Coun. Scholars Libr. of Congress, 1994—; mem. nat. launch com. AmeriCorps, 1994; mem. awards coun. Am. Acad. Achievement, 1994-2001; mem. adv. bd. Thomas Jefferson Ctr. Freedom of Expression, 1994—, US Civil War Ctr., 1995-99, Va. Ctr. Creative Arts, 1995—, Student Achievement and Advocacy Svcs., 2002—, DuBois Ctr. Am. History and Culture, 2005-, The Givens Found. African Am. Lit., 2005-; The Poets Corner elector Cathedral Ch. St. John the Divine, NYC, 1991-2002; bd. govs. Humanities Rsch. Inst. U. Calif., 1996-99; bd. dir. Poetry Daily, 2004—; chancellor Acad. Am. Poets, 2006—. Presdl. scholar, 1970, Nat. Achievement scholar, 1970-73; Fulbright/Hays fellow, 1974-75, rsch. fellow U. Iowa, 1975, teaching/writing fellow U. Iowa, 1976-77, Guggenheim Found. fellow, 1983-84, Mellon sr. fellow Nat. Humanities Ctr., 1988-89, fellow Ctr. Advanced Studies, U. Va., 1989-92, fellow Shannon Ctr. for Advanced Studies, U. Va., 1995—; grantee NEA, 1977, 89; recipient Lavan Younger Poet award Acad. Am. Poets, 1986, GE Found. award, 1987, Bellagio residency Rockefeller Found., Italy, 1988, Ohio Gov.'s award 1988, Literary Lion citation NY Pub. Libr., 1991, Women of Yr. award Glamour Mag., 1993, NAACP Great Am. Artist award, 1993, Golden Plate award Am. Acad. Achievement, 1994, Disting. Achievement medal Miami U. Alumni Assn., 1994, Renaissance Forum award leadership in the literary arts Folger Shakespeare Libr., 1994, Carl Sandburg award Internat. Platform Assn., 1994, Heinz award in arts and humanities, 1996, Charles Frankel prize/Nat. Humanities medal Pres. of US and NEH, 1996; inducted Ohio Women's Hall of Fame, 1991, Nat. Assn. Women in Edn. Disting. Woman award, 1997, Sara Lee Frontrunner award, 1997, Barnes & Noble Writers Writers award, 1997, Levinson prize Poetry mag., 1998, John Frederick Nims Translation prize, 1999, Libr. Lion award NY Pub. Libr., 2000, Duke Ellington Lifetime Achievement award, 2001, Emily Couric Women's Leadership award, 2003, Common Wealth award, 2006, Writing Today Grand Master award, 2006; Chubb fellowship, Yale, 2007; named Phi Beta Kappa poet Harvard U., 1993, Poet Laureate of Commonwealth of Va., 2004-06, Libr. of Va. Lifetime Achievement award 2008, Fulbright Lifetime Achievement medal, 2009, Premio Capri award, 2009, Ohoana Book award Essence Mags., 2010, Pushcart prize Best of Small Presses, 10. Fellow Am. Acad. Arts & Scis.; mem. PEN, ASCAP, Am. Philos. Soc., Poetry Soc. Am., Associated Writing Programs (bd. dir. 1985-88, pres. 1986-87), Am. Acad. Achievement (mem. golden plate awards coun. 1994—2001), Phi Beta Kappa (senator 1994-2001), Phi Kappa Phi. Office: U Va Dept English 219 Bryan Hall PO Box 400121 Charlottesville VA 22904-4121 Business E-Mail: rfd4b@virginia.edu.

DOVE, TIMOTHY L., oil and gas company executive; BS in Mech. Engring., MIT, 1979; MBA, U. Chgo., 1981. With Diamond Shamrock Corp., Maxus Energy Corp.; v.p. internat. Parker & Parsley, 1994—96, sr. v.p. bus. devel., 1996—97; exec. v.p. bus. devel. Pioneer Natural Resources Co., 1997—2000, exec. v.p., CFO, 2000—04, pres., COO, 2004—, Pioneer Southwest Energy Partners, LP, 2007—. Office: Pioneer Natural Resources Co Ste 200 5205 N O Connor Blvd Irving TX 75039 Office Phone: 972-444-9001. Office Fax: 972-969-3576.

DOW, DAVID SONTAG, retired ophthalmologist; b. Ann Arbor, Mich., Feb. 15, 1934; s. William Gould and Edna Lois (Sontag) Dow; m. Gail Anita Bade, Feb. 11, 1961 (dec. Feb. 2000); children: Steven Michael, Bonnie Jean, William Herbert, James Patrick; m. Figes Flaherty, Mar. 17, 2001. BS with distinction, U. Mich., 1956, MD, 1958, MS in Ophthalmology, 1964. Diplomate Am. Bd. Ophthalmology. Intern Denver Gen. Comm. Hosp., 1958-59; psychiatrist USAF Med. Svc., Wichita Falls, Tex., 1959-61; resident in ophthalmology U. Mich. Med. Ctr., Ann Arbor, 1961-64; pvt. practice ophthalmology Scruggs, Dow, and Kannwischer ptnr., Waco, Tex., 1964-88, Cen. Tex. Eye Clinic, Waco, 1988-97; pres. Woodway Found., 2006—09. Contbg. editor: Waco Tribune Herald, 1983—2010; author: pamphlets in field. Mem. Waco City Coun., 1977—81; mayor City of Waco, 1980—81; mem. Woodway City Coun., 1997—2001; bd. dir. Waco Symphony Assn., 1970—89, 1994—2001, 2006—09, pres., 1982—83; bd. dir. Tex. Med. Polit. Action Com., Austin, 1973—82; founding bd. dirs., chmn. Greater Waco Arts Coun., 1986—2010, chmn., 1992, 1994—2000, 2007—10. Capt. USAF, 1959—61. Mem.: Tex. Med. Assn., Am. Acad. Ophthalmology, Ridgewood Country Club, Rotary. Presbyterian. Avocations: politics, gardening, singing, golf.

DOWD, KENNETH ROBERT, elementary school educator; b. NYC, July 12, 1949; s. Robert Emmett and Mary (Rosko) D. AB magna cum laude, SUNY, Fredonia, 1971, MSEd, 1973; MLS, Syracuse U., NY, 1975; CAS, SUNY, Oswego, 1978, MS, 1986; AS magna cum laude, Onondaga C.C., 1986; BS summa cum laude, USNY, Regents Coll., 1988; postgrad., Gesell Inst., 1982, Sheldon Inst. for Gifted, 1982, Chautauqua Inst., 1983, postgrad., 1986—2003, Omega Inst. Holistic Studies, 1987, postgrad., 1989, Saybrook Inst., 1999, Coll. St. Rose, Albany, NY, 1990-99, U. Alaska, 1991-92, George Wash. U., Washington, DC, 1993, Drake U., Des Moines, Iowa, 1994, Utah State U., Logan, 1994-96, LI U., 1993, 95-97, 99, Tex. Tech. U., 1995-97, Ind. Wesleyan U., Marion, 1995-99, Alfred U., 1997, Adelphi U., Garden City, NY, 1999, U. Mo., 1999, Atlantic U., 2005—06, OASIS Inst., 2006. Cert. tchr. N-6, NY; cert. math. tchr. 7-12, NY; cert. sch. counselor, NY; cert. sch. media specialist, NY, pub. libr., NY; nat. cert. counselor. Tchr. Auburn City Schs., NY, 1971-72; tchr., curriculum developer, adminstrv. liaison West Genesee Ctrl. Sch., Camillus, NY, 1972-79; crisis counselor Contact-Syracuse, Inc., 1973-76; sch. counselor, substitute tchr., libr., computer club advisor, choral accompanist, human rels. cons. Oswego City Schs., NY, 1978—, leader, parent effectiveness workshops, pupil retention study, NY State Instrumental Music Accompanist; mem. staff student svcs. SUNY, Cayuga C.C., 2001—03. Cons. Syracuse City Schs., Fulton City Schs., Oswego County Bd. Coop. Edn. Svcs., Oswego Meth.Ch., Fulton Parents Anonymous, Syracuse rep. Sufi Order of West Holistic Health Conf., Washington, 1985, Assn. Humanist Psychol. Conf., Oakland, Calif., 1987, San Diego, 1990; US rep. Internat. Transpersonal Assn. Conf., Prague, Czech Republic, 1992. Author: Changes: Managing Child Behavior, 1981, Computer Literacy, 1985, Social Problems Impacting on School Achievement: Bibliotherapy Guide, 1988, Gifted and Growing: A Guide for Parents of Able Children, 1996; editor CNYALD News newsletter, 1980-82. Bd. dirs. Ctrl. NY Assn. for Learning Disabled, 1979-92, 1979-82; leader Parents Anonymous, Fulton, 1980-81, LI Ballet Piano Accompanist, LI dance pianist; mem. choir St. Joseph's Roman Cath. Ch., Camillus, Our Lady of Solace Ch., Syracuse, May Meml. Unitarian-Universalist Soc., Syracuse, St. Francis Xavier Ch., Marcellus; mem. Masterworks Chorale, Marcellus, SUNY, Fredonia Festival Chorus, Oswego Festival Chorus, Marcellus Chorale, Syracuse U. Oratorio Soc., Syracuse U. Chorus, vocal study, SUNY Oswego.; organist 1st Ch. of Christ Sci., Fulton; vocal soloist 1st Presby. Ch., Oswego, State St. Meth. Ch., Fulton, 1st Ch. Christ Sci., Fulton, Unity Ch., Syracuse, Keyboard Accompanist Our Lady Pompeii Ch., Liverpool, May Meml. Unitarian-Universalist Soc., Syracuse Blessed Sacrament Ch. NY State Regents' scholar, 1967, SUNY Coll. President's scholar, 1972; grantee GE and Bristol-Myers Squibb Co., 1981; baccalaureate Chautauqua Inst. Literary Program, 2000, Guild of Seven Seals, 2008, Chautauqua Parnassian Laureate, 2010, Olympian Laureate, 2011. Mem. NEA, ACA, NY Acad. Scis., Am. Fedn. Tchrs., NY State United Tchrs., Am. Sch. Counselor Assn., NY Counseling Assn., Assn. transpersonal Psych, Assn. Humanlistic psych. Inst. Noetic Scis., Assn. Rsch. and Enlightenment, NY State Sch. Counseling Assn., Assn. Humanistic Psychology (Syracuse) (newsletter editor 1985-90), Transpersonal Psychology Assn.(Syracuse) (founder, newsletter editor 1991-94, pres. 1995-), Assn. for Children with Learning Disabilities, Chautauqua Inst. Lit. and Sci. Circle, Food Bank Ctrl. NY, Habitat for Humanity, Feeding America, Nature Conservancy, Hospice Found. of Ctrl. NY, Oswego Co. Hospice, Syracuse Soc. for New Music, Syracuse Vocal Ensemble Guild, Schola Cantorum of Syracuse, NYS Early Music Assn., Syracuse Civic Morning Musicals, NYS Baroque, Syracuse Symphony Guild, May Meml. Unitarian-U. Soc., Syracuse Opera Guild, Oswego Opera Guild, Emerald Crest Country Club, Pine Grove Country Club, Prosperity Plus Investment Club, Sta. WCNY-TV Studio Club, WRVO Pub. Radio Guild, Oasis Sr. Learning Ctr., Kappa Delta Pi, Phi Delta Kappa. Home: 14 Trafalgar Cir Asheville NC 28805-0003 Personal E-mail: kendowd@windstream.net.

DOWD, MATTHEW JOHN, communications executive, political consultant; b. Detroit, May 29, 1961; m. Tammy Edgerly (div.); 3 children; m. Nicole Baines (div.); 2 children. Grad., Cardinal Newman Coll., St. Louis, 1983. Pres., founding ptnr. Pub. Strategies, Inc.; founder HotSoup.com; founder, pres. Dowd Strategic Consulting; founding ptnr. ViaNovo, Austin, Tex., 2005—. Former mem. campaign staff US senator Lloyd Bentsen; sr. strategist presdl. campaign Geroge W. Bush, 2000; sr. adv. Rep. Nat. Com., 2002; chief strategist re-election campaign Pres. Bush, 2004, Calif. Gov. Arnold Schwarzenegger, 2006; vis. prof. U. Tex. LBJ Sch. Pub. Affairs, Austin, 2005—. Co-author: Applebee's America: How Successful Political, Business, and Religious Leaders Connect With the New American Community, 2006 (NY Times bestseller); polit. contbr. (ABC) Good Morning America, 2007—, This Week with George Stephanopoulos. Named Pollster of Yr., Am. Assn. Polit. Consultants, 2004. Republican. Office: ViaNovo 327 Congress Ste 450 Austin TX 78701 Office Phone: 512-744-0044. Office Fax: 512-744-1477.

DOWDELL, JOHN EDWARD, federal judge; b. Tulsa, Okla., 1955; BA, Wake Forest U., 1978; JD, U. Tulsa Sch. Law, 1981. Law clk. to William J. Holloway US Ct. Appeals (10th Cir.), 1981—83; assoc. Norman, Wohlgemuth, Chandler & Dowdell, P.C., Tulsa, 1983—87, ptnr., 1987—2012; judge US Dist. Ct. (northern dist.) Okla., Tulsa, 2012—. Adj. settlement judge US Dist. Ct. (northern dist.) Okla., 1999—2012. Office: US District Court 333 W 4th St Rm 411 Tulsa OK 74103 Office Phone: 918-699-4700.

DOWDELL, MICHAEL FRANCIS, retired anesthesia nurse practitioner; b. Cleve., June 5, 1949; 1 child, Michael Patrick. BSN, Ohio State U., 1975; MA in Counseling, Nat. U., San Diego, 1981; MSN, Calif. State U., Long Beach, 1991; diploma in nursing anesthesia, Kaiser Sch. Anesthesia, LA, 1991; postgrad., Case Western Res. U., Cleve., 1996—. CRNA, ARNP; cert. c.c. instr. Calif. Enlisted USN, 1968, commd. ensign, 1974, advanced through grades to lt. comdr., 1984, ret., 1988; resident nurse anesthesist Kaiser Sch. Anesthesia for Nurses, 1989-91; staff nurse anesthetist Kaiser Hosp., Panorama City, Calif., 1991-92, HCA Med. Ctr., Largo, Fla., 1992-93, Meml. Mission Hosp., Asheville, N.C., 1993-97; owner Anesthesia Nursing Svcs. P.A., 1998—2013; ret., 2013. Vis. lectr. dept. anesthesia Makerere U., Kampala, Uganda, 1995. Mem.: VFW, NRA, Fleet Res. Assn., Assn. Mil. Surgeons U.S., Am. Assn. Nurse Anesthetists, Single Action Shooting Soc., Ret. Officers Assn., Am. Legion, Sigma Theta Tau. Republican. Avocations: fishing, shooting sports, travel. Personal E-mail: mfdpatexas@yahoo.com.

DOWE, ALISON, finance company executive; Dir. corp. comm. Synovus Fin. Corp. Office: Synovus Financial Corp Ste 500 1111 Bay Ave Columbus GA 31901 Office Phone: 706-641-3781. Office Fax: 706-641-6555.

DOWELL, CONNIE VINITA, library director; m. Steve Miller. B in Mass Comm. and Social Work, Mid. Tenn. State U., 1977; MLS, Peabody Coll., 1979. Reference asst. ctrl. and sci. libraries Vanderbilt U., 1978—79, dean libraries, 2009—; libr. asst. dir., head pub. svcs., faculty senate exec. mem. St. Mary's Coll., Md., 1980—84; libr. U. North Tex., U. Calif., Santa Barbara, Morgan State U.; libr., dean Conn. Coll., 1993—98, v.p., chief info. officer, 1998—99; dean libr. and info. access San Diego State U., 1999—2009. Presentor (libr. sci. alumni lecture) Libraries: Rapid Change, Enduring Values, Peabody, 2006. Recipient SirsiDynix-Am. Libr. Assn.-Allied Profl. Assn. award, 2006—07, John Cotton Dana Pub. Rels. award, Am. Libr. Assn.'s Lib. Adminstrn. and Mgmt. Assn. Mem.: Grolier Club of NY, Zamorano Club. Office: Vanderbilt University Jean and Alexander Heard Library 419 21st Ave S Nashville TN 37203-2427 Office Phone: 615-322-7100. Office Fax: 615-343-8279.

DOWELL, DAVID RAY, genealogist, ethicist, author, lecturer, library administrator; b. Trenton, Mo., Nov. 14, 1942; s. Clarence Ray and Ruth Lucille (Adams) D.; m. Arlene Grace Taylor, May 9, 1964 (div. 1983); children: Deborah Ruth, Jonathan Ray; m. Denise Jaye Christie, Aug. 19, 1983; stepchildren: David Lee Smithey, Jason Alan Smithey. BA in History, Okla. Bapt. U., Shawnee, 1964; AM in Latin Am. History, U. Ill., Urbana-Champaign, 1965—66, MLS in Libr. Sci., 1971—72; PhD in Libr. Sci., U. NC, Chapel Hill, 1977—86. Tchr. Wilson Jr. High Sch., Tulsa, 1964-65; head library adminstrv. services Iowa State U., Ames, 1972-75; asst. univ. librarian Duke U., Durham, N.C., 1975-81; dir. libraries Ill. Inst. Tech., Chgo., 1981—90; libr. dir. & asst. dean Pasadena City Coll., Calif., 1991—95; dir. libr./learning resources Cuesta Coll., San Luis Obispo, Calif., 1995—2007, instr., 1998—2011. Cons. County Commr.'s Library Planning Com., Durham, 1976, Gov.'s Conf. on Libraries and Info. Services, Raleigh, NC, 1978, Biblioteca do Centro Batista, Goiania, Brazil, 1978, chair Genealogy Com., 2008-2012, libr. support staff Nat. Certification 2007-2010. Author: Arturo Alessandri and the Widening of Political Participation in Chile, 1966, Relationship of Sex to Salary in a Female Dominated Profession, 1986, Libraries in the Information Age, 2002, 2009, It's All About Student Learning 2006, Crash Course in Genealogy 2011; Contbr. articles to profl. jours. Trustee Glenwood-Lynwood Pub. Library Dist., Ill., 1985-87, Treas. Chgo. Academic Libr. Coun., 1982-1989, bd. mem., Natural History Assn. Ctrl. Coast, 1995-1999, site vis. team mem. Western Assn. of Schs. and Colls., 2000-2007, Nat. adv. bd. Future Librs. Workforce Study, 2005-2008, Adminstr. Dowell Surname DNA Project, Smothers Tribe DNA Project, Dowell One-Name Study and Haplogroup Q DNA study, visitor Am. Coun. Edn., 2012-. Served to capt. USAF, 1967—71. Recipient Pub. Rels. Spl. award, John Cotton Dana Libr., 1995, Leadership award, EBSCO Cmty. Coll. Learning Resources and Libr., 2007. Mem. ALA (chmn. profl. ethics com. 1977-78, chmn. election com. 1982-83, chmn. libr. personnel adv. com. 1979-80, career pathways task force, 2000-02, awards com. 2001-05, Libr. of Future award jury, 2002-03, chmn. 2003-04, edn. com., 2003-04, scholarship taskforce, 2004-05), Assn. Coll. and Research Libraries (nominat ing com. 1979-80, libr. tech. asst. training com., 1992-2005, chair 1993-95, academic status com., 1993-97, instnl. priorities & faculty rewards task force, 1997, profl. devel. com, 1997-2001, Learning Resources Leadership award, 2007), Libr. Adminstrn. & Mgmt. Assn. (bd. dirs. 1981-83, membership com.& govtl. affairs task force, 1983-84, alternative finance task force, 1984-85, orientation com., 1985-87), Internat. Soc. Genetic Genealogists, Nat. Geneal. Soc., New Eng. Geneal. Soc., Southern Calif. Geneal. Soc., Middle Tenn. Geneal. Soc. Democrat. Baptist. Avocations: tennis, sports, genealogy. Home: 500 Elmington Ave Apt 509 Nashville TN 37205-2532

DOWELL, EARL HUGH, aerospace and mechanical engineering educator; s. Earl S. and Edna Bernice (Dean) D.; m. Lynn Cowell; children: Marla Lorraine, Janice Lynelle, Michael Hugh. BS, U. Ill., 1959; SM, MIT, 1961, ScD, 1964. Rsch. engr. Boeing Co., 1962-63; rsch. asst. MIT, 1963-64, rsch. engr., 1964, asst. prof., 1964-65; asst. prof. aerospace and mech. engring. Princeton U., 1964-68, assoc. prof., 1968-72, prof., 1972-83, assoc. chmn., 1975-77, acting chmn., 1979; William Holland Hall prof. mech. engring. and materials sci. Duke U., Durham, NC, 1983—, dean, 1983-99, chair, mech. engring. and materials sci., 2010—. Cons. to industry and govt. Author: Aeroelasticity of Plates and Shells, 1974, A Modern Course in Aeroelasticity, 1978, 4th edit., 2004, Nonlinear Studies in Aeroelasticity, 1988, Dynamics of Very High Dimensional Systems, 2003; editl. bd.: AIAA Jour., 2000-, Jour. Fluids and Structures, 1987—, Jour. Nonlinear Dynamics, 1990—; contbr. articles to profl. jours. Chmn. NJ Noise Control Coun., 1972-76. Named outstanding young alumnus U. Ill. Sch. Aero. and Astronautical Engring., 1973, disting. alumnus, 1975; recipient Alumni Honor award Coll. Engring. U. Ill. Fellow: ASME, AIAA (hon.; v.p. publs. 1981—83, Structures, Structural Dynamics and Material award 1980, Theodore Von Karman lectr. 2002, Walter J. and Angeline H. Crichlow Trust prize 2007), Am. Acad. Mechanics (pres. 1991, Disting. Svc. award 1994); mem.: NAE, Acoustical Soc. Am., Am. Helicopter Soc. Office: Dept Mech Engring and Materials Sci Duke U Box 90300 Hudson Hall Durham NC 27708-0300 Office Phone: 919-660-5302. Business E-Mail: dowell@ee.duke.edu.

DOWLING, RODERICK ANTHONY, investment banker; b. NYC, Dec. 29, 1940; s. John Joseph and Anne (Chisholm) D.; m. Lavinia Seibels, May 6, 1977; children: Lavinia Crosby, Roderick A.; children by previous marriage: Anne Chisholm, Katherine Burke. BS, Fairfield U., 1962; JD, Fordham U., 1965. Bar: N.Y. 1965, Ga. 1974. Assoc. Cahill, Gordon & Reindel, NYC, 1965-72; v.p., gen. counsel U.S. Industries N.E. Corp., NYC, 1972-73, Fugua Industries, Inc., Atlanta, 1973-81; chmn. Sun Trust-Robinson Humphrey Inc., Atlanta, 1981—, also bd. dirs. Mem. ABA, Bar Assn. City NY, Ga. Bar Assn., Atlanta Bar Assn., S.R., Piedmont Driving Club (Ga.), University Club (NY), Union Club (NY), Capitol City Club, Buckhead Club, Golf Club Ga., Palmetto Club (SC), Seabrook Island Club (SC), Kiawah Club. Home: 3038 Bakers Mdws SE Atlanta GA 30339-4813 Office Phone: 404-926-5074.

DOWLUT, ROBERT, lawyer; b. 1945; BS, Ind. U.; JD, Howard U., Washington, 1979. Bar: DC 1980, Va. Corp. Counsel. Gen. counsel NRA. Sec. NRA Civil Rights Def. Fund. Contbr. articles to prof. legal jours. Sec. NRA Civil Rights Def. Fund. Staff sgt. US Army, 82nd Airborne Divsn. and 12th Spl. Forces. Office: NRA South Tower 6N 11250 Waples Mill Rd Fairfax VA 22030-7400 Office Phone: 703-267-1250. Office Fax: 703-267-3985.

DOWNES, CYNTHIA A., construction executive; BS, Purdue U.; MBA, Northwestern U., 2002. CPA Illinois. V.p. and CFO Environ. Design Internat., Tatra Tech EM Inc.; exec. v.p. Versar Inc., 2011—, CFO, 2011—, treas., 2011—. Office: Versar Incorporated 6850 Versar Center Springfield VA 22151 Office Phone: 703-750-3000. Office Fax: 703-642-6807.

DOWNEY, LAURENCE, retired pharmaceutical executive; b. UK; MD, U. Manchester, UK; diploma, Royal Coll. Physicians; grad. Adv. Mgmt. Program, Harvard Bus. Sch., 1996. Joined Solvay Pharm. Inc., 1981; med. adv. Solvay Healthcare Ltd., Southampton, UK, 1979—86; v.p. med. svcs. to sr. v.p., comml. ops., interim pres., CEO Solvay Pharm. Inc., Marietta, Ga., 1986—2006, pres., CEO, 2006—08; and CEO, chmn. Organics LLC (Solvay subs.), Marietta, Ga., 2006; pres. Berkshire Pharma Consulting, 2008—; CEO Ketal Biomed. Inc. Home: 1124 Berkshire Rd NE Atlanta GA 30306 Home Phone: 404-892-1242.

DOWNEY, MORTIMER LEO, III, consulting firm executive, former transportation executive; b. Springfield, Mass., Aug. 9, 1936; s. Mortimer L. and Elizabeth (Carlin) D.; m. Joyce Vander Meyden, Oct. 21, 1961(dec. 2012); children: Stephen Michael, Christopher Sean. BA, Yale U., 1958; MPA, NYU, 1966; grad. Advanced Mgmt. Program, Harvard U., 1988. Various positions Port Authority of NY & NJ, 1958—73, supr. rail pub. services, 1973-75; budget analyst Com. on Budget US House of Representatives, 1975-76; dep. under sec. US Dept. Transp., Washington, 1977, asst. sec. for budget & programs, 1977-81; asst. exec. dir. NY Met. Transp. Authority (MTA), NYC, 1981-83, dep. exec. dir., 1983-85, CFO, 1985-86, exec. dir., CFO, 1986-93; dep. sec., COO US Dept. Transp., Washington, 1993-2001, acting sec., 2001; prin. cons. PB Consult, Inc., NYC, 2001—04, chmn., 2005—09; sr. advisor Parsons Brinckerhoff, 2009—; prin. Mort Downey Consulting LLC, 2005—. Bd. dirs. first vice chair, Washington Met. Area Transit Authority, Eno Found., sec.; mem. Comptr. Gen.'s adv. com., mem. industry leader coun. Am. Soc. Civil. Engrs., dir. Obama Transportation Transition Team, 2008, founding chmn., Coalition Americas Gateways & Trade Corridors; trustee Mineta Transp. Inst.: co-chair, US Dept of Transp. Nat. Freight Adv. Com. Lt. comdr. USCG, 1959—71. Recipient Res. Officers award for Top Acad. Standing, Coast Guard Officers Candidate Sch., Frank Turner medal for Disting. Career Svc., Transp. Rsch. Bd., Lifetime Achievement award, Am. Pub. Transp. Assn., Leadership award, Intelligent Transp. Soc. America, Claiborne Pell award, Nat. Corridors Initiative, NYU Wagner Sch. Alumni Torch award; named Mem. of Yr., Women's Transp. Seminar, 1999; named one of The Fed. 100 Info. Tech. Executives. Fellow Nat. Acad. Pub. Adminstrn.; mem. Am. Soc. Pub. Adminstrn., Yale Club (N.Y.), Women's Transp. Seminar, Yale Sailing Club, Pi Sigma Alpha. Democrat. Roman Catholic. Business E-Mail: mortdowney@verizon.net.

DOWNING, KEN, retail executive; Grad., Seattle Central Coll., Fashion Inst. Tech. Visual merchandising positions I. Magnin & Co.; dir., visual planning and presentation Neiman Marcus Stores, visual dept. positions Beverly Hills, Calif., 1990—92, visual mgr. Beverly Hills store to visual mgr. all stores & dir. pub. rels., 1992—97, v.p., pub. rels., 1997—2006, sr. v.p., dir., fashion, 2006—. Office: The Neiman Marcus Group Inc 1618 Main St Dallas TX 75201 Office Phone: 214-743-7600. Office Fax: 214-573-5320. Business E-Mail: ken_downing@neimanmarcus.com.

DOWNING, MARGARET MARY, newspaper editor; b. Altoona, Pa., June 3, 1952; d. Irvine William and Iva Ann (Regan) D.; m. Gary Beaver; children: Ian Downing-Beaver, Timothy Downing-Beaver, Abby Downing-Beaver. BA magna cum laude, Tex. Christian U., 1974. Reporting intern Corpus Christi Caller Times, 1973; reporter, bur. chief Beaumont (Tex.) Enterprise & Jour., 1974-76, Dallas Times Herald, 1976-80; reporter, asst. city editor, asst. bus., met. editor, mng. editor Houston Post, 1980—93; mng. editor Jackson (Miss.) Clarion-Ledger, 1993-97; editor-in-chief The Houston Press, 1998—. Jurist Pulitzer Prize Awards, 1992, 93; bd. dirs. News Media Credit Union, 1993, Santa's Helpers, 1992-93, Assn. Alternative Newspapers, 2009-; mem. membership com. Assn. Alternative Newspapers, 2000-. Respite foster parent vol. Harris County Children's Protective Svcs., 1993; chmn. landscape com. Windsor Hills Homeowners Assn.; active Madison Sta. Elem. PTA, 1993—98; coach South Madison County Soccer Orgn., 1997—98, First Colony Soccer Club, 2002—06; mem. runners club YMCA, 1994, mem. activities adv. bd., 1994, youth soccer and t-ball coach; coach Quail Valley Soccer Assn., 1999—2005; vol. Houston Taping for the Blind, 2000—02; vestry Grace Episcopal Ch., 2002—05, children's edn. bd., 2003, worship com., 2005—06; bd. dirs. Alvin-Manvel Helping Hands Fund, 2001, Leadership Jackson, 1996—98. Recipient Rick Nelson soccer coaching award, 2001. Mem.: Nat. Soc. Newspaper Columnists, Investigative Reporters and Editors, Inc., Nat. Edn. Writers Assn., Nat. Youth Sports Assn. (cert. coach), Press Club Houston (bd. dirs. 1982—85, pres. 1984, bd. dirs. 2000—04), AP Mng. Editors Assn. (2d v.p. La./Miss. chpt. 1995—96, 1st v.p. 1996—97, pres. 1997—98), Quota Club (bd. dirs. 1996—97). Episcopalian. Home: 3215 Breckenridge Ct Missouri City TX 77459-4907 Office: The Houston Press 1621 Milam St Ste 100 Houston TX 77002-8017 Home Phone: 281-416-1819; Office Phone: 713-280-2470. Personal E-mail: downingmargaret@yahoo.com. Business E-Mail: margaret.downing@houstonpress.com.

DOWNS, HARTLEY H., III, chemist; b. Ridgewood, NJ, Oct. 21, 1949; s. Hartley Harrison and Jennie Mae (Smith) D.; m. Cindy Marie Millen, June 19, 1976; children: Kathryn Marie, Jennifer Anne, Susanna Jayne. BS, Grove City Coll., 1971; MS, Indiana U. of Pa., 1973; PhD, W. Va. U., 1978; postgrad., U. Colo., 1976-77. Postdoctoral rsch. assoc. chemistry dept. U. So. Calif., LA, 1977-78; staff chemist corp. rsch. labs. Exxon Rsch. and Engring. Co., Linden, NJ, 1978-81, Houston, 1981-83, Annandale, NJ, 1983-86; rsch. scientist, surface chemistry and corrosion sci. group supr. Baker Hughes, Houston, 1986-91, tech. dir. fluids conditioning tech., 1997—2004; rsch. mgr. Baker Performance Chems., Houston, 1991-92, tech. dir., 1992-97; dir. tech. worldwide oilfield ops. Baker Petrolite, Houston, 2004—05, dir. R&D, 2005—07, sr. advisor, 2008; tech. fellow Baker Hughes, 2009—; apptd. to US Dept. Energy Ultra-Deepwater Ad. Com., 2010—. Contbr. articles to profl. jours., chpt. to book Recipient Award for Grad. Rsch., Sigma Xi, 1973, Union Carbide award W.Va. U., 1975, Stan Gillman award U. Colo., 1977, Tech. Merit award Baker-Hughes, 1989, 91, 93. Mem. Am. Chem. Soc., Soc. Petroleum Engrs., Offshore Operators Com. (task force on environ. sci.), NACE Internat. (chmn. task force on oil industry biocides 1996—2011, symposium chmn. mineral scale deposit control in oilfield ops. 1994, 98, chmn. corrosion/94 and corrosion/98 symposia, vice-chmn. microbiol. control in oil industry ops. corrosion/2000 symposium), SPE, Organising Com. & Session (chmn. delivery emerging tech., 2009, chmn. nanotech., 2010, chmn. water mgmt., 2011, chmn. designer materials, 2012, chmn. internat. symposium on oilfield chemistry, 2013, chmn. R&D workshop, 2013). Achievements include patents in field.

DOWNS, MAYANNE, lawyer; b. Orlando, Fla., Oct. 23, 1956; BA, U. Fla., Gainesville, 1979, JD, 1987. Bar: Fla. 1988, US Dist. Ct. (middle dist.) Fla., US Ct. Appeals (11th cir.), US Supreme Ct. Shareholder King, Blackwell, Downs & Zehnder, PA, Orlando, Fla.; city atty. Orlando, Fla., 2007—. Adv. com. Local Rules for Middle Dist., 1998—2001; mem. Fla. Supreme Ct. Tech. Commn., 1998—2000. Mem.: ABA, Ctrl. Fla. Assn. for Women Lawyers, The Fla. Bar (bd. govs. 2002—, pres. 2010—11), Orange County Bar Assn. (exec. coun. 1992—98, pres. 1997—98). Office: King, Blackwell, Downs & Zehnder, PA PO Box 1631 Orlando FL 32802-1631 Office Phone: 407-422-2472. Office Fax: 407-648-0161. E-mail: mdowns@kbdzlaw.com.

DOYLE, DELORES MARIE, retired principal; b. Madison, SD, July 24, 1939; d. Martin N. and Pearl M. (Anderson) Berkelo; m. Patrick J. Doyle; children: Kathleen, Shawn, Tamara, Timothy. AS, Dakota State Coll., Madison, 1959; BS, Mid. Tenn. State U., 1966, MEd, 1968, EdS, 1975; PhD, Peabody/Vanderbilt U., 1980. Cert. career ladder III tchr. Tchr. 4th grade Meriden-Cleghorn Schs., Meriden, Iowa, 1960-62; tchr. 1st grade Hanover (Ill.) Sch., 1963-66; tchr. 2d grade Hobgood Sch., Murfreesboro, Tenn., 1969-70; tchr. 1st grade Reeves-Rogers Sch., Murfreesboro, 1972-80, tchr. 2d grade, 1981-97, prin., 1997-2000; ret., 2000. Cooperating tchr. Mid. Tenn. State U. Student Tchrs., Murfreesboro, 1972—97, mem. task force edn., 1992—93; summer sch. dir. Murfreesboro City Schs., 1986—98; lead project tutor Reeves-Rogers Sch., Murfreesboro, 1987—90. Active Edn. 2000 Com., Murfreesboro C. of C., 1993; trustee Mid Tenn State U. Found., 1995—2001; bd. dirs. Grace Luth. Ch., Murfreesboro, 1991—93, 2001—03, mem. choir, 1975—. Recipient Tenn. Tchr. of the Yr. award, Dept. Edn., Nashville, 1992, Murfreesboro City Tchr. of the Yr. award, Murfreesboro City Schs., 1991, Mid-Cumberland Dist. Tchr. of the Yr. award, Dist. Dept. Edn., 1991, Trailblazer award, 1995; named Career Ladder III Tchr., Dept. Edn., Nashville, 1984; named to Tenn. Tchrs. Hall of Fame, 2001; Creative Tchg. grantee, State Dept. Edn., 1992, 1993. Mem.: Murfreesboro Edn. Assn. (pres. 1981—82), Tenn. Edn. Assn. (Disting. Classroom Tchr. award 1992, Disting. Adminstr. award 2000), Tenn. State Tchr. of Yr. Orgn. (v.p. 2000—), Nat. State Tchr. of Yr. Orgn., Delta Kappa Gamma. Democrat. Avocations: bridge, travel, reading, ballroom dancing. Home: 1710 Sutton Pl Murfreesboro TN 37129-6513 Personal E-mail: pandddoyle@comcast.net.

DOYLE, JOHN M., corporate financial executive; Sr. mgr. KPMG LLP, 1994—97, Ernst & Young LLP, 1997—2002; v.p., treas. IASIS Healthcare, LLC, 2002—06, chief acctg. officer, 2006, CFO. Office: IASIS Healthcare LLC 117 Seaboard Ln Bldg E Franklin TN 37067 Office Phone: 615-844-2747. Office Fax: 615-846-3006. Business E-Mail: jdoyle@iasishealthcare.com.

DOYLE, MICHAEL PATRICK, microbiologist, educator, director; b. Madison, Wis., Oct. 3, 1949; s. Donald Vincent and Evelyn (Bauer) Doyle; m. Annette Marie Ripple, Dec. 27, 1971; children: Michael Patrick, Patrick Matthew, Kristen Anne. BS in Bacteriology, U. Wis., 1973, MS in Food Microbiology, 1975, PhD in Food Microbiology, 1977. Sr. project leader Ralston Purina Co., St. Louis, 1977-80; asst. prof. U. Wis., Madison, 1980-84, assoc. prof., 1984-88, prof., 1988-91; prof., dir. U. Ga., Griffin, 1991—, dept. head Athens, 1993-99. Mem. sci. bd. U.S. FDA, 2000—03; regents prof. Bd. Regents Ga. U. Sys., 1997—; nat. adv. com. on microbiol. criteria for foods USA, Washington, 1988—90, 1994—2000; trustee Internat. Life Scis. Inst.-N.Am., Washington, 1992—, sci. advisor, 1987—96; mem. Internat. Commn. on Microbiol. Specifications for Foods, 1989—2000; Wis. Disting. prof. bd. regents U. Wis., Madison, 1988—91; James M. Craig Meml. lectr. Oreg. State U., Corvallis, 1990; sci. lectr. Am. Soc. Microbiology Found., 1991—93, 1999—2001; Peter J. Shields lectr. U. Calif., Davis, 1993; G. Malcolm Trout vis. scholar Mich. State U., Lansing, 1994; sci. adv. coun. Refrigeration Rsch. and Edn. Found., 1997—2002; York Disting. lectr. Auburn U., 1999. Editor: Food Microbiology: Fundamentals and Frontiers, 1997, 3rd edit., 2007, Foodborne Bacterial Pathogens, 1989, Emerging Issues in Food Safety, 2004—; contbr. articles to profl. jours. Recipient award for Profl. Excellence, Am. Agrl. Econs. Assn., 1992, Silver Plow Honor award, USDA, 1998, Ptnrs. in Pub. Health award, Ctrs. Disease Control and Prevention, 2001, Commrs. citation, FDA, 2006; named one of Top 100 Most Cited Rschrs. Agrl. Scis., Inst. Sci. Info., 2002. Fellow: AAAS, World Innovation Found., Am. Acad. Microbiology, Inst. of Food Technologists (Fred W. Tanner lectr. 1986, sci. lectr. 1987—90, exec. com. 2000—03, Samuel Cate Prescott award for rsch. 1987, Nicholas Appert award for preeminence in and contbns. to field of food tech. 1996), Internat. Assn. Food Protection (pres. 1992—93, Norbert F. Sherman article excellence award 1993, NFPA food safety award for outstanding contbn. to food safety rsch. and edn. 1999); mem.: NAS (assoc.), Inst. Medicine NAS (food and nutrition bd. 1991—97, com. to ensure safe food from prodn. to consumption 1998, chmn. rev. com. USDA E. coli O157:H7 in ground beef risk assessment 2001—02, chmn. food forum 2003—, com. nat. needs rsch. in vet. scis. 2004—05, vice chmn. food and nutrition bd. 2005—), Am. Soc. for Microbiology (chmn. food microbiology divsn. 1987—89, pub. and sci. affairs bd. 2003—, P.R. Edwards award for outstanding career achievements 1994), Gamma Sigma Delta, Phi Kappa Phi. Roman Catholic. Achievements include patents for for monoclonal antibody to enterohemorrhagic E. coli; competitive exclusion bacteria to reduce carriage of enterohemorrhagic E. coli by cattle and Listeria in floor drains; development of methods to control and detect foodborne pathogens. Office: U Ga Ctr Food Safety 1109 Experiment St Griffin GA 30223-1797 Business E-Mail: mdoyle@uga.edu.

DOYLE, ROBERT F., food service executive; married. BA in Chemistry, Ill. Inst. Tech., Chgo., 1978; MBA in Bus., Ind. U. Purdue U., Ft. Wayne, 1982. Sr. food technologist Ctrl. Soya Co., 1975—82; v.p. quality & stds. Metromedia Restaurant Group, Inc., 1982—2001; v.p. product devel. and quality assurance Cracker Barrel Old Country Store, Inc. Office: Cracker Barrel Old Country Store Inc 305 Hartmann Dr Lebanon TN 37088-0787 Office Phone: 615-444-5533. Office Fax: 615-443-9818.

DOZIER, ALVIN M., food service executive; Joined Cracker Barrel Old Country Store, Inc., 1990, regional v.p. restaurant ops. Named Regional V.P. of Yr., 2003. Office: Cracker Barrel Old Country Store Inc 305 Hartmann Dr Lebanon TN 37087 Office Phone: 615-444-5533. Office Fax: 615-443-9476.

DOZIER, DAVID CHARLES, JR., advertising and public relations executive; b. Santa Fe, Dec. 4, 1938; s. David Charles Sr. and Zelma (Martin) D.; m. Dianne Flusche, June 1, 1960; children: Deborah, Mary Rebecca, Michael, Constance. BA, U. Dallas, 1960. Editor sports Tex. Cath., Dallas, 1960-70, gen. sales mgr., 1964-70; dir. classified advt. Dallas Times Herald, 1970-74; chmn. DBG&H Unltd. Inc., Dallas, 1974—88, Dozier Co., Dallas, 1989—. Innovator, ptnr. Navi Pesanda Indian Blanket Creations, 1992. Author: A Compendium of Endurance, 1989. Mem. Am. Indian, Santa Clara Pueblo Tribe, N.Mex.; cert. athletic trainer Downtown YMCA, 1990-2003. Recipient Disting. Svc. award Pres. U.S. and HUD, 1984. Republican. Roman Catholic. Achievements include completed more than 165 marathons. Home and Office: The Dozier Co 7102 Wabash Cir Dallas TX 75214 Office Phone: 214-744-2800. Business E-Mail: david@thedoziercompany.com.

DOZIER, GLENN JOSEPH, diversified financial services company executive; b. Lexington, Ky., Apr. 7, 1950; s. Emmitt and Henrietta Elsie (Geisler) Dozier; m. Paula Jean Cook, June 3, 1974; children: Laura Jean, Diana Leigh. BS in Indsl. Engring. and Ops. Rsch., Va. Poly. Inst., 1972; MBA, U. Va., 1975. Mfg. engr. Tex. Instruments, Dallas, 1972-73; fin. analyst Dravo Corp., Pitts., 1975-76, mgr. corp. fin. analysis, 1976-79, dir. corp. devel., 1980-82, dir. corp. planning and devel., 1982-83; v.p. fin. Dravo Constructors, Inc., Pitts., 1983-87; CFO, treas., asst. sec. AMF Bowling Internat. Inc. and AMF Bowling, Inc., Richmond, Va., 1987-90; v.p., CFO, treas. Owens and Minor,

Inc., Richmond, 1990-93, sr. v.p. ops. and systems, CFO, 1991-92, sr. v.p. fin., CFO, 1992-96; CFO Displaytech, Inc., 1997-98; sr. v.p., CFO Hagler Bailly Inc., 1998-99, 1999-2000, This End Up Furniture Co., 2001—05; exec. v.p., CFO Upstate Group Inc.; exec. v.p. & GM Kiawah Island Golf Resort, 2005—07, Riverstone Properties LLC, 2007—. Author: (book) Economic Development Finance, 1986, CFO Handbook, 1996, Financial Executives Handbook. Mem. Colonies Civic Assn. Mem.: Colonies Swim and Tennis Club, Tau Beta Pi, Phi Kappa Phi, Alpha Pi Mu, Phi Eta Sigma. Republican. Methodist. Avocations: golf, travel, gardening.

DOZIER, THERESE KNECHT, government agency consultant, former education association administrator; BA in Social Studies Edn., U. Fla., 1974, MEd in Secondary Social Studies, 1976; EdD in Curriculum and Instrn., U. S.C., 1995; LHD (hon.), Winthrop Coll., 1985, U. S.C., 1985. Tchr. Lincoln Mid. Sch., Gainesville, Fla., 1974—76, Miami Edison Mid. Sch., Fla., 1976—77, Singapore Am. Sch., Singapore, 1986—89, Irmo HS, Columbia, SC, 1977—85, 1989—90, 1992—93; instr. and coord. profl. devel. schs. U. SC, Columbia, 1991—92; spl. advisor on tchg. to US Sec. Edn. Richard W. Riley US Dept. Edn., Washington, 1993—97, sr. advisor on tchg. to US Sec. Edn. Richard W. Riley, 1997—2001, sr. adv. on tchg. to US Sec. Edn.; assoc. prof., dir. Ctr. Tchr. Leadership Sch. Edn. Va. Commonwealth U., Richmond, 2001. Mem. Nat. Conf. State Legislatures Taskforce on Sch. Leadership, Nat. Com. on Tchr. Mobility, Com. to Enhance K-12 Tchg. Profession in Va., Va. State Action for Ednl. Leadership Consortium; mem. adv. bd. Nat. Tchr. Recruitment Clearinghouse; mem. adv. panel SRI Internat.'s Study of Alt. Cert. of Tchrs.; mem. meritorious new tchr. com. Mid-Atlantic Regional Tchr. Project; advisor rural initiative Nat. Bd. Profl. Tchg. Stds.; mem. policy and planning coun. Met. Ednl. Rsch. Consortium; advisor DeWitt-Wallace Reader's Digest Found. Tchr. Leadership Initiative; mem. acad. coun. Nat. Inst. Cmty. Innovations Internat. Grad. Ctr.; sr. counsel on tchr. quality issues Widmeyer Comm.; cons. N. Ctrl. Regional Lab. Profl. Devel. Ctr., Asian-Pacific Econ. Coun. Tchr. Devel. Web Portal Project, NBPTS Prin.'s Initiative; presenter in field; bd. dirs. Coun. Basic Edn. Named Nat. Tchr. of Yr., 1985, S. Carolinian of Yr., 1985, Alumna of Outstanding Achievement, U. Fla., 1997; recipient Disting. Alumnus award U. Fla., 1985, Nat. Jefferson award for outstanding pub. svc. benefiting local communities, 1986, Hammer award for helping to make govt. more efficient and effective V.P. Gore, 1995; named to the Order of the Palmetto, 1985; Fulbright-Hays fellow to China, 1985; Holmes scholar U. S.C., 1991-93. Office: Va Commonwealth Univ 1015 West Main St PO Box 842020 Richmond VA 23284 Office Phone: 804-827-0102. Office Fax: 804-827-0676.

DRAELOS, ZOE DIANA, dermatologist, consultant; b. Milw., Oct. 13, 1958; d. Dimitri Basil and Lorene June (Legan) Kececioglu; m. Michael Draelos, June 14, 1980; children: Mark, Matthew. BSME, U. Ariz., 1979, MD, 1983. Diplomate Am. Bd. Dermatology. Physician in solo dermatology practice, High Point, NC, 1988—. Cons., owner Dermatology Cons. Svcs., High Point, 1990—. Author: Cosmetics in Dermatology, 1995, Atlas of Cosmetic Dermatology, 2000. Rhodes scholar, Oxford, Eng., 1979. Office: Zoe Diana Draelos MD PA 2444 N Main St High Point NC 27262-7833 Office Phone: 336-841-2040.

DRAGICS, DAVID LEE, information technology executive; b. Newark, Ohio, Nov. 7, 1945; s. Nicholas Absolom and Cecile Mae (Provin) D. BSBA in Fin., Ohio State U., 1974; MBA in Fin. & Mktg., U. Pitts., 1980. Teller Bank One of Columbus, Ohio, 1965—68, fin. cons. Ohio, 1971—74; market rsch. officer Pittsburgh National Bank, 1974—81; corp. planning analyst Ryan Homes, Inc., Pitts., 1981—83, dir., investor relations, 1981—83; dir. strategic planning Landmark Savs. Assn., Pitts., 1984—87; dir., investor rels. UNC, Inc., Annapolis, Md., 1987—; dir. investor rels. Microdyne Corp.; joined CACI International, Inc., 1998, sr. v.p., investor rels. Cons. Accent Travel, Inc., Troy, Mich., 1984-88. Mem. Pitts. Symphony Soc., 1977-88, com. United Way of Allegheny County, 1981-87, World Affairs Council, Pitts., 1983-88, Washington, 1988—, com. United Way Cen. Md., 1988—; mem. partnership bd. United Way of Anne Arundel County, Md., 1988—, Naval Acad. Sailing Squadron, 1989—. Served to 1st lt. U.S. Army, 1968-71, Vietnam, col. USAR, Ohio State U. Athletic Com., Nat. Investor Rels.Inst., Naval Acad. Sailing Squadron. Decorated Bronze Star. Mem. Assn. of the U.S. Army, U.S. Naval Inst., Nat. Investor Relations Inst., Ohio State Alumni (pres. 1984-87). Avocations: sailing, downhill skiing, photography, reading. Office: CACI International Inc Bd Directors 1100 N Glebe Rd Arlington VA 22201 also: UNC Inc 175 Admiral Cochrane Dr Annapolis MD 21401-7316 Home: 2817 Durmont Ct Annapolis MD 21401-7825 Office Phone: 703-841-7800. Office Fax: 703-841-7882. E-mail: ddragics@caci.com.

DRAGO, DANA A., bank executive; BA in Bus. Adminstrn. and Fin., U. Mississippi; grad., Univ. Virginia CBA Grad. Sch. of Retail Banking. Sr. v.p. mid. market comml. ins. area Liberty Mut.l Ins.; with Bank of America; exec. v.p. Comerica Bank, 2011—, nat. retail bank dir., 2011—. Recipient Charlotte Women in Business Achievement award, Charlotte Bus. Journal's. Mem.: Am. Heart Assn. Office: Comerica Bank 1717 Main St Dallas TX 75201 Office Phone: 214-462-4000.

DRAGOVIC, DUSAN M., nephrologist; MD, Yugoslavia, 1993. Diplomate Am. Bd. Internal Medicine, 2002, Am. Bd. Internal Medicine-nephrology, 2004. Resident in internal medicine Lenox Hill Hosp., NY, 1999—2002, fellow in nephrology, 2002—04; hosp. affiliation includes Holy Cross Hosp.; physician Broward Gen. Med. Ctr.; pvt. practice Kidney Group of South Fla. Office: Kidney Group of South Florida 2001 NE 48th Ct No 4-5 Fort Lauderdale FL 33308 Office Fax: 954-771-2393.*

DRAKE, AMELIA F., otolaryngologist; b. Nov. 13, 1955; m. Craig Drake; children: Connor, Cliff. B in Biology, Cornell U., Ithaca, NY; MD, U. NC, Chapel Hill, 1981. Cert. in otolaryngology 1987. Residency, dept. surgery U. Mich. Med. Ctr., 1981—83, residency, dept. otolaryngology/head and neck surgery, 1983—87, adj. prof. vocal pedagogy Ann Arbor, 1986—87; fellowship Children's Hosp., Cin., 1987—88; asst. prof. surgery/otolarynogology U. Mich. Sch. Music, Ann Arbor, 1988—94; asst. prof. U. NC Dept. Pediat., 1989—94, assoc. prof., 1994—2001, prof., 2001—; assoc. prof. U. NC Dept. Otolaryngology/Head and Neck Surgery, 1994—2001, Newton D. Fischer disting. prof. surgery, 1999—, prof., 2001—, chief, divsn. pediatric otolaryngology, 2001—; dir. craniofacial ctr. U. NC Sch. Dentistry, 2001—. Dir. residency program, otolaryngology/head and neck surgery U. NC. Contbr. articles to profl. jours. Recipient Gabriel F. Tucker award, Am. Laryngol. Assn., 2006; named to Top Doctors in America, Castle Connolly Med. Ltd., 2002—07, Best Doctors, Bus. NC mag., 2006. Fellow: ACS; mem.: NC Soc. Otolaryngology and Head and Neck Surgery (past pres.), Carolina Masters Crew Club. Avocation: crew. Office: U NC Sch Medicine Dept Otolaryngology 1114 Bioinformatics Bldg CB 7070 Chapel Hill NC 27599-7405 Office Phone: 919-966-8926. Office Fax: 919-966-7656. Business E-Mail: amelia_drake@med.unc.edu.

DRAKE, BRAD, state legislator; b. Fort Walton Beach, Fla., Feb. 7, 1975; s. David Earl. AA, Okaloosa-Walton Cmty. Coll., Niceville; BSBA in Econ., U. Fla. Warrington Coll. Bus., Gainesville, 2000. Mktg. exec. Infinite Energy Inc.; pres. & owner Southern Mktg. Co.; legal asst. Fla. House of Reps., 2001—07, mem. Dist. 5, 2008—, mem. govt. accountability act coun., joint legis. sunset com., pub. safety and domestic security policy com., mem. state univs. and pvt. colls. appropriations com. Instr. Walton County Schs. Bd. mem. Hearts of Hope Ministries. Mem.: NRA, Ducks Unlimited, Walton County Taxpayers Assn., Crimestoppers of Walton County Inc. (chmn.), Athletes in Action Baseball, Kiwanis Club, Alpha Gamma Rho. Republican. Baptist. Office: House Office Bldg 402 S Monroe St Rm 313 Tallahassee FL 32399-1300 also: NWFL State College 908 US Hwy 90 Chautauqua Campus #205 Defuniak Springs FL 32433-1436 Office Phone: 850-488-4726, 850-892-8431.

DRAKE, JOSHUA, lawyer; b. Bad Tolz, Germany, Nov. 5, 1968; m. Cheryl Drake; children: Grace, Gideon, Hope. BA in Internat. Rels. and Polit. Sci., Rhodes Coll., 1991; JD, U. Ga., 1994. Bar: Ark. Law clk. Kopecky & Roberts, Washington, Ga., 1992—94; staff atty. Ctr. Ark. Legal Svcs., 1994—2003; ptnr. Hobbs, Garnett, Naramore and Drake, P.A., Hot Springs, Ark., 2003—. Pres. Ark. Legal Svc. Workers Union, 1996—2003. Bd. stewards First United Meth. Ch. of Hot Springs, 2004—; bd. mem. Garland County Law Libr. Com., 1998—, Pocket Theatre of Hot Springs, 2006—. Mem.: Ark. Bar Assn., Garland County Bar Assn., Soc. Am. Baseball Rsch. Green Party. Methodist. Office: 185 Hillside Place Hot Springs AR 71901 Office Phone: 501-262-2136. Office Fax: 501-624-5407. E-mail: josh@hobbsfirm.com, joshua@drake08.com.

DRAKE, MIRIAM ANNA, retired librarian, educator, journalist consultant; b. Boston, Dec. 20, 1936; d. Max Frederick and Beatrice Celia (Mitnick) Engleman; m. John Warren Drake, Dec. 19, 1960 (div. Dec. 1985); 1 child, Robert Warren. BS, Simmons Coll., Boston, 1958, MLS, 1971, DLS (hon.), 1997; postgrad., Harvard U., Cambridge, Mass., 1959—60; LHD (hon.), Ind. U., 1994. Assoc. United Rsch., Cambridge, Mass., 1958-61; with mktg. svcs. Kenyon & Eckhardt, Boston, 1963-65; cons. Boston, 1965-72; head rsch. unit libraries Purdue U., West Lafayette, Ind., 1972-76, asst. dir. libraries, prof. library sci., 1976-84; dean, dir. libraries, prof. Ga. Inst. Tech., Atlanta, 1984-2001, prof. emerita, 2001—; ret., 2001. Trustee Online Computer Libr. Ctr., Inc., 1978-84, chair, 1980-83; trustee Corp. for Rsch. and Edn. Networking, 1991-94, U.S. Depository Libr. Coun., 1991-94, Simmons Coll., 1999-2004; trustee, corporator adv. bd. Engring. Info., 1997-2001; hon. trustee Simmons Coll., 2004—; bd. dirs. Women's Commerce Club, 2005—09. Author: User Fees: A Practical Perspective, 1981, Information Today, 2002; co-author: (with James Matarazzo) Information for Management, 1994; editor: Ency. Libr. Info. Sci., 2nd edit.; mem. editl. bd. Coll. and Rsch. Librs. Jour., 1985-90, Librs. and Microcomputers Jour., 1983-93, Sci. and Tech. Librs., 1989-98, Database, 1989-97; contbr. chpts. to books, articles to profl. jours. and trade mags. Recipient Alumni Achievement award Simmons Coll. Sch. Libr. and Info. Sci., 1985, Kent Meckler Media award U. Pitts., 1994. Fellow: Nat. Fedn. Advanced Info. Svs. (hon.); mem.: ALA (councilor at large 1985—89, Hugh Atkinson Meml. award 1992), Assn. Info. and Dissemination Ctrs. (pres. 2001—03), Spl. Librs. Assn. (pres.-elect 1992—93, pres. 1993—94, H.W. Wilson award 1983, John Cotton Dana award 2002), Am. Soc. Info. Sci., Am. Mgmt. Assn. Office Phone: 404-636-0154. Business E-Mail: mdrake@bellsouth.net.

DRAKE, R. GLENN, consumer products company executive; Goup pres., N.Am. Tupperware Brands Corp., 2002—06, group pres., Europe, Africa, Middle East, 2002—. Office: Tupperware Brands Corp 14901 S Orange Blossom Trail Orlando FL 32837 Office Phone: 407-826-5050. Office Fax: 407-826-8874.

DRAKE, STEPHEN DOUGLAS, psychologist, health facility administrator; b. Iola, Kans., Sept. 8, 1947; s. Harry Francis and Emojean (Price) Drake; m. Rebecca Gonzalez, June 1, 1968; 1 child, Michael Paul. BA, U. Tex., 1970; PhD, U. North Tex., 1987. Diplomate Am. Bd. Forensic Examiners, lic. psychologist. Mental health worker Austin (Tex.) State Hosp., 1970-73; claims rep. Social Security Adminstrn., Galveston, Tex., 1974-77, ops. supr. Dallas, 1977-79, staff asst., 1979-80; clin. psychologist Terrell (Tex.) State Hosp., 1987-89, Austin State Hosp., 1989-90, program dir., 1990-92; cons. Tex. Rehab. Commn., 1992-98, chief mental med. cons., 1998—2003, med. adminstr., 2003—13. Contbr. articles to profl. jours. Vice-chmn. bd. dirs. Galveston Island Mental Health/Mental Retardation Ctr., 1977. Recipient award, Nat. Assn. Disability Examiners, 2001, Commr.'s citation, Social Security Adminstrn., 2005. Mem.: APA, Tex. Psychol. Assn., Mensa, Phi Kappa Phi. Avocations: Tae Kwon Do, weightlifting, eastern philosophy, languages, travel. Office: DARS 6101 E Oltorf St Austin TX 08741 Business E-Mail: drakestephen@sbcglobal.net.

DRAKE, THELMA DAY, former United States Representative from Virginia; b. Elyria, Ohio, Nov. 20, 1949; m. Ted Drake; 2 children. Grad. high sch. Realtor William E Wood Assoc. Re/ TNS, Hampton Roads, Va.; mem. Va. State House Dels. from 87th dist., 1995—2004; chair Va. Housing Commn.; mem. Chesapeake Bay Commn., US Congress from 2nd Va. Dist., 2005—08, mem. edn. and the workforce com., mem. resources com., mem. armed svcs. com.; cons. Future Law LLC. Bd. mem. Va. Zool. Soc. Recipient John Marshall award, Va. Property Rights Coalition; named Citizen of Yr., Va. Crime Prevention Assn., Legislator of Yr., YMCA, Commrs. of the Revenue, Va. Cable & Telecom. Assn.; named one of Outstanding Profl. Women of Hampton Roads. Republican. United Church Of Christ. Office Phone: 757-480-1120. Business E-Mail: thelmadrake@future.law.net.

DRAKE, VAUGHN PARIS, JR., electrical engineer; b. Winchester, Ky., Nov. 6, 1918; s. Vaughn Paris and Margaret Turney (Willis) D.; m. Lina Louise Wilson, May 5, 1946; 1 child, Samuel Willis. Student, U. Ky., Lexington, 1936—41. Registered profl. engr., Ky. From asst. engr. to gen. valuation and cost engr. Gen. Tel. Co. Ky., Lexington, 1945-81; ret., 1981. Author: (manual) Conduit Engineering for Telephone Engineers, 1958. Profl. adv. bd. Zoning Commn., Lexington and Fayette County, Ky., 1955-57. Comm. chief, combat engr. group AUS, 1941—45. Decorated Pearl Harbor Commemorative medal; recipient 10-Yr. Svc. award, Boy Scouts Am. Mem. IEEE (sr., chmn. Lexington sect. 1956-57), NSPE, Am. Mil. Engrs., Ky. Soc. Profl. Engrs. (pres. Bluegrass chpt. 1961-62, chmn. engrs. in industry sect. 1967-68, Outstanding Engr. in Industry award 1979), Ind. Tel. Pioneer Assn. (life), Ky. Hist. Soc., Vets. Fgn. Wars, Pearl Harbor Survivors Assn. Home and Office: 633 Portland Dr Lexington KY 40503-2161

DRAKE, W. HOMER, JR., federal judge; b. 1932; AB, Mercer U., Macon, Ga., 1954, LLB, 1956. Law clk. to Hon. Lewis R. Morgan U.S. Dist. Ct. Ga., 1961-64; ptnr. Swift, Currie, McGhee & Hiers, 1976-79; judge US Bankruptcy Ct., 1964-76, chief judge, 1968-76; bankruptcy judge US Bankruptcy Ct. (no. dist.) Ga., 1979—. Adj. prof. U. Ga. Law Sch., 1971-72, Emory U. Law Sch., Atlanta, 1973-75; chair in bankruptcy law Drake and Southeastern Bankruptcy Law Inst., Mercer U. Law Sch., 1996, endowed chair bankruptcy law, 2007; chair bd. trustees Mercer U., 2009- Author: Bankruptcy Practice for the General Practitioner, 3d edit., 1995; co-author: Chapter 13 Practice & Procedure, 1983, Chapter 11 Reorganizations, 2d edit., 1998. 1st lt. JAGC, US Army, 1956-59. Recipient David W. Pollard Achievement award Atlanta Bar Assn., 1994, Leadership award, 2007, Outstanding Alumnus award Mercer U. Sch. Law, 2003, Dist. Svc. award for Lifetime Achievement Emory Bankruptcy Devel. Jour., 2007, Atlanta Bar Assn. Leadership award, 2007; mem. com. on Administrn. Bankruptcy Sys., Judicial Conf., 1989-95. Fellow: Am. Coll. Bankruptcy; mem.: Nat. Conf. Bankruptcy Judges (pres. 1972—73), Southeastern Bankruptcy Law Inst. (founder, advisor). Address: US Bankruptcy Ct PO Box 1408 Newnan GA 30264-1408 Office: Lewis R Morgan Fed Bldg US Courthouse 18 Greenville St Newnan GA 30263-2602

DRAKEMAN, DONALD LEE, venture capitalist, educator; b. Camden, NJ, Oct. 21, 1953; s. Fred J. and Jean (Faucett) D.; m. Lisa Natale Drakeman, Aug. 23, 1975; children: Cynthia and Amy. BA magna cum laude, Dartmouth Coll., 1975; JD, Columbia U., 1979; MA, Princeton U., 1984, PhD, 1988. Bar: NJ 1979; US Dist. Ct. NJ 1979, NY 1980; US Supreme Ct. 1984. Assoc. Milbank, Tweed, Hadley and McCloy, NYC, 1979-82; gen. counsel Essex Chem. Corp., Clifton, NJ, 1982-89, v.p., 1987-89; pres. Essex Med. Products, Clifton, NJ, 1988-89; pres., CEO Medarex, Inc., Annandale, NJ, 1987—2006; venture ptnr. Advent Venture Ptnrs., London, 2007—. Adj. prof. polit. sci. Montclair State Coll., NJ, 1984; rsch. cons. Lilly Found., Inc., 1989—90; lectr. politics dept. Princeton U., 1990—93, 1995—2009, co-chair adv. coun. religion dept., 2001—08; chmn. adv. coun. James Madison Program in Am. Ideals and Instn., Princeton Univ., 2000—; mem. adv. coun. Index Ventures, Geneva, 2002—03; chmn. NJ Commn. Sci. and Tech., 2004—06; bd. advs. ETHICA, Asti, Italy, 2008—, St. John's U. Ctr. Law and Religion, 2013—; fellow Royal Hist. Soc., 2013—, Burgon Soc., 2009—; fellow health mgmt. Judge Bus. Sch. U. Cambridge, 2010—; vis. fellow program ch., state & soc. Notre Dame Law Sch., 2014—. Author: Church-State Constitutional Issues, 1990, Church State & Original Intent, 2009; co-editor Church-State in Am. History, 2d edit., 1986, 3d edit., 2003; contbg. articles to profl. jours. Chmn. Montclair bd. adjustment, 1984; trustee, chair Biotech. Coun. NJ, 1996-98; trustee, U. Charleston, 1999-2003, Drew U., 2002—; adv. coun. Rutgers Bus. Sch., 2002—07; trustee, Woodrow Wilson Nat. Fellowship Found., 2003-06, Am. Coun. Sci. & Health, 2010-2013. Harlan Fiske Stone Scholar, Columbia Univ., 1976-79; Alumni Svc. award, Princeton U. Alumni Assn., 1999, inducted NJ High Tech. Hall of Fame, 2000, fellow, Soc. Biology, 2012-. Mem.: John Maclean Soc., Yale Club, Princeton Club, Princeton Alumni Coun. Home Phone: 843-682-3771.

DRAPER, EDGAR, psychiatrist; b. St. Louis, Feb. 5, 1926; s. Neal McLain and Florence Mabel (Meyers) D.; m. Norma Jane Alexander, Mar. 16, 1949; children: Sue Draper, Anne Draper Klevay, Neal Edgar. AB, Washington U., 1946, Duke Div. Sch., Garrett Bibl. Inst., 1946—47, BD, 1949; MD, Washington U. Med. Sch., 1953; grad., Inst. for Psychoanalysis, Chgo., 1966. Diplomate Am. Bd. Psychiatry and Neurology; ordained deacon, elder Meth. Ch., 1946. Asst. pastor Edenton St. Meth. Ch., Raleigh, 1947, Grace Meth. Ch., Rockford, Ill.; pastor Garden Prarie, Ill., 1949; intern Washington U. Svc. City Hosp., St. Louis, 1953-54; resident in psychiatry U. Cin., 1954-55, 57-59; sr. asst. surgeon USPHS, Ft. Worth, 1955-57; from instr. to assoc. prof. U. Chgo., 1959-68; co-dir. psychiat. outpatient dept., prof. psychiatry U. Mich., Ann Arbor, 1968, dir. psychiat. resident edn., 1968-74, prof. postgrad edn., 1970-75; prof., chmn. dept. psychiatry U. Miss. Med. Ctr., Jackson, 1975-93; prof. psychiatry U. Miss., Jackson, 1993-94; prof. emeritus, 1994—. Cons. in field. Contbr. numerous articles to profl. jours. Bd. dirs. Friends Libr. U. Miss. Named Vis. scholar U. Chgo., 1987, Fellow Soc. for Sci. Study of Religion, 1987, Man of Month Pastoral Psychology, 1970; recipient Physicians Recognition award, 1982-85, Cert. Appreciation Mental Health Assn. Hinds County, 1983, Plaque of Commendation Chgo. Acad. Religion and Mental Health, 1966-67. Fellow Am. Psychiat. Assn. (disting. life fellow), Am. Coll. Psychiatry (life), Am. Soc. Psychoanalytic Physicians, Soc. for Sci. Study of Religion (life), Am. Coll. Psychoanalysts (life, program chmn., bd. regents), So. Psychiat. Assn. (parlimentarian 1980—), Soc. for Study of Psychiatry and Culture; mem. Miss. Psychiat. Assn. (past pres., Disting. Svc. award 2001), Miss. State Med. Soc., Mich. Psychiat. Soc., Washtenaw County Med. Soc., Mich. State Med. Soc., So. Psychiat. Assn., Mich. Psychoanalytic Soc., Mental Health Assn. (bd. dirs. Jackson, Spl. Svc. award, 2006, 07). Office Phone: 601-982-2176. Business E-Mail: purpledoced@aol.com.

DRAPER, E(RNEST) LINN, JR., retired electric utility executive; b. Houston, Feb. 6, 1942; s. Ernest Linn and Marcia L. (Saylor) D.; m. Mary Deborah Doyle, June 9, 1962; children: Susan Elizabeth, Robert Linn, Barbara Ann, David Doyle. Student, Williams Coll., 1960-62; BS Chem. Edn., Rice U., 1964, BS Chem. Edn., 1965; PhD in Nuclear Engring., Cornell U., 1970. Asst. prof. nuclear engring. University of Texas, Austin, 1969-72, assoc. prof., 1972-79; tech. asst. to CEO Gulf States Utilities Co., Beaumont, Tex., 1979, v.p. nuclear tech., 1980-81, sr. v.p. engring, tech. svcs., 1981-82, sr. v.p. external affairs, 1982-84, sr. v.p. external affairs and prodn., 1984-85, exec. v.p. external affairs and prodn., 1985-86, vice chmn., 1985-87, COO, 1986, pres., CEO, 1986-92, chmn. bd. dirs., 1987-92; pres. Am. Electric Power, Inc.; pres., COO American Electric Power Service Corp., Columbus, Ohio, 1992-93; chmn., pres., CEO Am. Electric Power Co. and Svc. Corp., Columbus, 1993—2004. Bd. dirs. Temple Inland Corp., Alpha Natural Resources, NorthWestern Corp., Alliance Data Sys., TransCan., Resources for the Future. Fellow NSF, 1965-66, AEC, 1967-68. Mem. NAE, Am. Nuclear Soc. (pres. 1984-85), Nuclear Energy Inst. (chmn. 1993-95), Edison Electric Inst. (chmn. 1996-97). E-mail: eldraper@aep.com.

DRAPKIN, DENNIS B., lawyer; b. NYC, Feb. 17, 1948; s. Eli and Ruth Drapkin; m. Adrienne Miller, June 30, 1974; children: Benjamin, Jennifer, Rebecca. AB summa cum laude, Dartmouth Coll., 1968, BE, 1969; JD, Yale U., 1972; LLM, London Sch. Econs., 1973. Bar: NY 1975, DC 1978, Tex. 1985. Assoc. Paul, Weiss, Rifkind, Wharton & Garrison, NYC, 1974—77; atty.-adv. to Tax Legis. Counsel, spl. asst. to asst. sec. tax policy Office of Tax Policy, U.S. Treasury Dept., 1977—80; assoc., ptnr. Cohen & Uretz, Washington, 1980—83; ptnr. Jones Day, Dallas, 1984—2011; adj. prof. SMU, Dedman Sch. Law, 2013—, U. Tex. Sch. Law, 2014—. Former mem. alumni coun. Dartmouth Coll., Hanover, NH, former mem. nominating and alumni trustee search com., former mem. joint com. alumni governance and trustee nominations, former mem. com. trustees; mem. Exec. Com. Dartmouth Club of Dallas. Named one of the Top Tax Lawyers in US, Euromoney/Internat. Tax Rev., 1997—, Best Lawyers in Am., 1999—, Tex. Super Lawyers, 2003—. Mem.: ABA (former vice-chair profl. svcs., former rep. to Nat. Conf. of Lawyers and CPAs, former chmn. sect. of taxation, chair tax sect. task force patenting tax strategies), Am. Coll. Employee Benefits Counsel, Am. Tax Policy Inst. (trustee), Am. Coll. Tax Counsel, Am. Law Inst. (life).

DRAY, MARK STANLEY, lawyer; b. Alliance, Ohio, Feb. 8, 1943; s. Dwight Leroy and N. Pauline (Clark) Dray; m. Jonadell Pascoe, June 5, 1965; children: Melisa Hudson, Justin Clark. BA, Mount Union Coll., Alliance, Ohio, 1965; JD, Coll. William and Mary, 1968, M in Law and Taxation, 1969. Bar: Va. 1968, U.S. Dist. Ct. (ea. dist.)

Va. 1970, U.S. Tax Ct. 1971. Tax sr. Price Waterhouse, Washington, 1969—70; assoc. Hunton & Williams LLP, Richmond, Va., 1970—77, ptnr., 1977—. Mem. So. Employee Benefits Conf., 1974—2009; mem. adv. coun. William and Mary Tax Conf., 1980—88; trustee So. Fed. Tax Inst., 1989—, chair, 1997; citizen lawyer William and Mary Law Sch., 2010; spkr. in field; citizen lawyer Mary Law Sch., 2010. Contbr. articles to profl. jours. Fellow: Am. Bar Found., Va. Law Found., Am. Coll. Tax Counsel, Am. Coll. Employee Benefits Counsel (bd. govs. 2004—07, officer 2005—07, charter, mem. chambers rateil 2006—, named Best Lawyers in America 1989—, Va. Super Lawyers 2006—); mem.: ABA (com. employee benefits 1975—, mem. joint com. employee benefits 1988—91, chmn. 1989—90, 1990—91), Order of Coif, Richmond Bar Assn., Va. Bar Assn., Blue Key, Country Club Va. Episcopalian. Avocation: golf. Office: Hunton & Williams LLP Riverfront Plz East Tower 951 E Byrd St Richmond VA 23219-4074 Office Phone: 804-788-8408. Business E-Mail: mdray@hunton.com.

DRAYTON, BILL (WILLIAM DRAYTON), social entrepreneur, lawyer, management consultant; b. NYC, June 15, 1943; s. William A. and Joan (Bergere) D. BA, Harvard U., Cambridge, Mass., 1965; MA, Oxford U., Eng., 1967; JD, Yale U., New Haven, 1970; LLD (hon.), Polytechnic U., 2006; PhD in Human Letters (hon.), Yale U., 2009; LHD (hon.), NYU, 2010, Babson Coll., 2011; LLD (hon.), Marquette U., 2011, U. San Diego, 2012, Hamline U., 2013. Bar: NY 1971, DC 1976. Cons. McKinsey and Co., Inc., NYC, 1970-77, of counsel, 1981-87; vis. assoc. prof. law Stanford U., 1975-76; lectr. John F. Kennedy Sch. Govt. Harvard U.; also dir. Harvard Regulatory and Mgmt. Group, 1976-77; cons. White House Domestic Policy Coun., 1977; asst. adminstr. for planning and mgmt. EPA, 1977-81; pres. Environ. Safety, Washington, 1981-89, chair, 1989—; pres., founder Ashoka: Innovators for the Pub., Arlington, Va., 1980-2001, chmn., CEO, 2001—. Nat. staff Hubert H. Humphrey Presdl. Campaign, Washington, 1968; dir. Corp. for Fiscal Policy, 1971-75; founder, chmn. Yale Legis. Svcs.; adv. coun. Carnegie Commn. Sci., Tech. and Govt., 1990-96. Contbr. articles to profl. jours. Pres. Ams. in India for McGovern, 1972; mem. Carter-Mondale Policy Planning, 1976, Carter-Mondale Govt. Reorgn. Transition Group, 1976-77; dep. dir. for issues Mondale-Ferraro campaign, 1984; energy and environment com. Dem. Nat. Com., 1982-86; bd. dirs. Oxfam Am., 1985-89, Appropriate Tech. Internat., 1988-97, chmn. bd. dirs., 1989-97; trustee Black Rock Forest (formerly Harvard Forest 1985-2011), NY; chmn. bd. dirs. Youth Venture, 1994—; founder, chair Get Am. Working!, 1997—; pres. Save EPA, Washington, 1981-83; chair Cmty. Greens, 2000—, chair environ. safety, 1984-; founder, dir. Social Entrepreneur Assocs., 1998—. Hon. fellow Balliol Coll. Oxford U., Eng., 2008; recipient Entrepreneurial Excellence award Yale U. Sch. Mgmt., 1987, Nat. Pub. Svc. award Nat. Acad. Pub. Adminstrn. and Am. Soc. Pub. Adminstrn., 1995, Pub. Svc. Achievement award Common Cause, 1999, Vanguard Nonprofit Lawyers award ABA, 2002, Edward A. Smith award for excellence in nonprofit leadership, 2002, Fast Co. Fast 50 award, 2004, Nat. Conservation award Nat. Wildlife Fedn., 2005, Social Entrepreneur award Skoll Found., 2005, Merit award Yale Law Sch., 2005, Goi Peace award, Japan, 2007, John Gardner Leadership award (Ind. Sector) 2011, Prince Asturias award for internat. cooperation (Spain) 2011, others; named an Hon. fellow U. Pa. Sch. Law, 2007, Hon. Dr. Human Letters Yale U., 2009; named one of America's Best Leaders US News and World Report and Harvard U., 2005; Henry fellow, 1965-67, MacArthur Prize fellow, 1984-89, Social Entrepreneur Lifetime Achievement award NY U., 2008, Prince Asturias award, Spanish Royal Family, 2011, John Gardener award, Independent Sector, 2011, Annual Creativity award, Smithsonian Inst. & Creativity Found., 2013. Mem. AAAS (com. on sci. pub. policy 1973-76), Assn. Bar City NY, Friends of India Soc. (chmn. 1974-75), Coun. Fgn. Rels., Pacific Coun. Internat. Policy, Nat. Acad. Pub. Adminstrn., Am. Acad. Arts and Scis., Asia Soc. (contemporary affairs com. 1987-2000), India Internat. Ctr. (New Delhi), Yale Law Sch. Assn. (exec. com. 2005—), Yale Club NY, Harvard Club NY, Phi Beta Kappa. Home: 1200 N Nash St Arlington VA 22209-3616 Office: 1700 N Moore St Ste 2000 Arlington VA 22209-1921 Office Phone: 703-527-8300.

DREES, BASTIAAN MEIJER, entomologist; b. Amsterdam, June 28, 1952; s. Jan Meijer and Jacoba Meijer Drees; m. Carol Frost, Oct. 30, 1953; children: Carly Jobes, Erin Lien. BA in Biology, W.Va. U., 1974, MSc in Entomology, 1976; PhD in Entomology, Ohio State U., 1980. Diplomate Am. Bd. Entomology. Ext. entomologist Tex. Agrl. Ext. Svc., Coll. Sta., Tex., 1980—; prof. dept. entomology Tex. A&M U., Coll. Sta., 1993—, coord. Tex. imported fire ant rsch. and mgmt. project dept. entomology, 1997—2002, dir. Tex. imported fire ant rsch. and mgmt. project dept. entomology, 2002—03. Author: (book) A Field Guide to Common Tex. Insects, 1998 (Tex. Reference Source award, Tex. Libr. Assn., 2001); contbr. articles to profl. jour. Recipient Faculty Disting. Achievement award in ext., Assn. Former Students of Tex. A&M U., 1996, Disting. Achievement award in ext., Entomol. Soc. Am., 1997, award for rsch. excellence, Orkin, 2001; Regents fellow, Tex. A&M U., 1000. Mem.: Southwestern Entomol. Soc. (pres. 2002), Entomol. Soc. Am. (pres. S.W. br. 2005—06, governing bd. mem. 2010—). Avocations: photography, music, art. Office: Texas A&M U RM 412 Dept Entomology College Station TX 77843-2475 E-mail: b-drees@tamu.edu, bart.drees@suddenlink.net.

DREILING, RICHARD W. (RICK DREILING), retail executive; b. 1953; BA in Industrial Relations, Rockhurst U., Mo. Various mgmt. positions Safeway, Inc., 1969—97; pres. The Vons Companies, Inc. (divsn. Safeway, Inc.), 1998—99; exec. v.p. mfg. & distbn. Safeway, Inc., 2000—03; chief ops. officer, exec. v.p. Longs Drug Stores Corp., 2003—05, COO, 2005; pres., CEO Duane Reade Holdings, Inc., NYC, 2005—07, chmn., pres., CEO, 2007—08; CEO Dollar General Corp., Goodlettsville, Tenn., 2008, chmn., CEO, 2008—. Office: Dollar General 100 Mission Ridge Goodlettsville TN 37072

DREIMANN, LEONHARD, manufacturing executive; b. Riga, Latvia; D in Mktg., Melbourne U., Australia. Officer, bd. dirs. Glacier Holdings, Inc.; pres. Salton, Inc. (subsidiary of SEVKO, Inc.), 1987—88; mng. dir. Salton Australia Pty. Ltd., 1988—93; founder Salton, Inc., Lake Forest, Ill., 1988—, pres., 1988—98, CEO, bd. dirs., 1988—; officer, bd. dirs. Salton Time, 1989—93. Dir. Glacier Water Systems, 1987—93. Recipient Ernst & Young Entrepreneur Of The Year for Ill./North West Ind., 1999. Achievements include the successful mktg. of The George Foreman Grill, Breadman, Juiceman, Ingraham, Farberware and Toastmaster - growing the co. from $8 million to $1 billion in sales. Office: Salton Inc 3633 S Flamingo Rd Miramar FL 33027-2936 Office Phone: 954-883-1000.

DRELL, DEE D., federal judge; b. New Orleans, 1947; BA, Tulane U., New Orleans, 1968, JD, 1971. Pvt. practice atty., La., 1975—2003; judge US Dist. Ct. (we. dist.) La., Alexandria, 2003—. Mem. JAG Corps US Army, 1971—75. Office: US Dist Ct PO Box 1071 Alexandria LA 71309 Office Phone: 318-473-7420.

DRENDEL, FRANK MATTHEW, cable company executive; b. Paxton, Ill., Jan. 16, 1945; s. Nora and Odell (Drendel); m. Marilyn Beste, 1968; 1 son. BS, No. Ill. U., 1970; postgrad., St. Louis U., 1973. Vice-pres., corp. mgr. Continental Transmission, St. Louis, 1969-72; v.p. ops. Cypress Communications, Los Angeles, 1972-73; CEO Commscope NC Gen. Instrument Corp., 1976—86, chmn., CEO CommScope NC, 1986—97; chmn., CEO CommScope, Inc., Hickory, NC, 1997—2011, chmn., 2011—. Bd. dir. Sprint Nextel Comm., Nat. Cable Telecommunications Assn. Served with U.S. Army, 1968-74. Named to Cable TV Hall of Fame, 2002. Mem. Calif. Cable TV Assn. (past dir., asso. dir.), Nat. Cable TV Assn. (past dir.), C. of C. Clubs: Lake Hickory Country. Presbyterian. Office: CommScope 1100 CommScope Pl SE Hickory NC 28603

DRENNEN, WILLIAM MILLER, JR., cultural organization administrator, film producer, writer; b. Charleston, W.Va., Nov. 5, 1942; s. William Miller and Margaret (Morton) D.; m. Sarah Polk Wilson, Nov. 27, 1969; children: Zachary Polk, Samuel Boyd. BArch., Yale U., 1964; postgrad., George Washington U., 1977, U. Charleston, 1978, W.Va. Grad. Coll., 1989-92, MA in Humanities, 1993. Freelance writer, film maker, 1967-69; v.p. Communication Corps, Inc., Washington, 1969-79; pres. Briar Mountain Coal and Coke Co., Charleston, 1980-89; founder, pres. Max Media, Inc., Charleston, 1984-89; commr. W.Va. Culture and History Div., 1989—97; instr. history W.Va. State Coll., 1997—2001; freelance writer, prodr., cons., 2001—. Mng. gen. ptnr. C&D Enterprises, 1979—; pres. Cox Morton Co., 1980-89; past pres., founder W.Va. Internat. Film Festival, Charleston, 1986-89; owner, sec., real estate agt. Greg Didden Assocs., Shepherdstown, W.Va., 2003-. Author: One Kanawha Valley Bank, 2002, Red, White, Black, and Blue: A Dual Memoir of Race and Class in Appalachia, 2004; cameraman (film) Evolving Environment, 1972 (Cine Golden Eagle award); editor (film) River of Life, 1975 (U.S. Film Festival award); patentee computerized optical system. Founder, pres. W.Va. Youth Soccer Assn., 1979-84; bd. dirs. Sunrise Mus., Charleston, 1983-86, Renaissance Com., Charleston, 1984-89, Jefferson Co. Hist. Soc., 2002—, Contemporary Am. Theatre Festival, 2002—; mem. Pare Lorentz award panel Internat. Documentary Assn.; trustee U. Charleston, 1985-89; founder W.Va. Assn. Mus., 1990; v.p., sec. W.Va. History Film Project, Inc., 1991-97. Served in USN, 1964-67. Decorated Bronze Star; recipient 2 Cine Eagle awards, cert. Excellence for documentary film work, award Hist. Landmarks Commn. Kanawha County, Tele award, 1997. Mem. Film Arts Guild W.Va. (pres. 1981-87), Orgn. Am. Historians, Am. Hist. Assn., W.V. Hist. Soc., Shepherdstown Rotary, Cress Creek Golf and Country Club. Democrat. Episcopalian. Avocations: tennis, golf, mountain biking, jogging. Office Phone: 304-876-6400, 304-283-5011. Personal E-mail: bill@billdrennen.com.

DRENNER, KARLA, state legislator; b. Sept. 10; 2 children. Environ. cons.; mem. Dist. 86 Ga. House of Reps., 2001—. Adj. prof. Devry U. Author: The True Story of Politics, Prayer and the Power of One; contbr. articles to profl. jours. Democrat. Office: PO Box 348 Avondale Estates GA 30002 also: Ga House of Reps 507 Coverdell Legis Office Bldg Atlanta GA 30334 Office Phone: 404-656-0202. Personal E-mail: dren16999@aol.com.

DRESSLER, ROBERT A., lawyer; b. Ft. Lauderdale, Fla., Aug. 20, 1945; s. R. Philip and Elisabeth Dressler; children: James Philip, Kathryn S. AB cum laude, Dartmouth Coll., 1967; JD cum laude, Harvard U., 1973. Bar: Fla. 1974, D.C. Assoc. Goodwin, Proctor & Hoar, Boston, 1973-75; ptnr. Dressler & Dressler, Ft. Lauderdale, 1975-82; mayor City of Ft. Lauderdale, 1982-86; pvt. practice law Ft. Lauderdale, 1982—2010. Bd. regents State Univ. System, 1987-93; Capt USMC, 1969-72. Named Person of Yr. Fla. Atlantic U., 1993, Disting. Citizen Ft. Lauderdale, 2007. Mem. Greater Ft. Lauderdale C.of C. (bd. govs. 1982-89), Broward County (Pioneer award, 2011), Fla. Bar Assn., Vietnam Vets. Am., Rotary Internat., Tower Forum (bd. govs. 1983-2005), Ft. Lauderdale Forum (moderator 2007-), Phi Beta Kappa. Presbyterian. Avocations: travel, writing. Office: PO Box 2425 Fort Lauderdale FL 33303-2425 Office Phone: 754-223-7392. Business E-Mail: dresslerra@bellsouth.net.

DREW, BENJAMIN ALVIN, JR., astronaut; b. Washington, Nov. 5, 1962; s. Benjamin Drew, Sr. and Muriel Drew. BS in Astronautical Engring., US Air Force Acad., 1984, BS in Physics, 1984; Masters Degree in Aerospace Sci., Embry Riddle U., 1995; Masters Degree in Strategic Studies in Polit. Sci., US Air Force Air U., 2006. 2nd lt. US Air Force Acad., 1984; completed undergraduate pilot tng.-helicopter, earned wings Fort Rucker, Ala., 1985; flew combat missions in ops. Just Cause, Desert Shield/Desert Storm and Provide Comfort Air Force Spl. Ops. Command, 1993; completed USAF Fixed-Wing Qualification, 1993; completed US Naval Test Pilot Sch., 1994; commanded two flight test units and served on Air Combat Command Staff; mission specialist, astronaut NASA, Houston, 2000—; ret. USAF, 2010. Mission specialist STS-118 Mission (Endeavour) to Internat. Space Station, 2007, STS-133-Final Flight of Discovery, 2011; dir. ops. Gagarin Cosmonaut Tng. Ctr., Star City, Russia, 2009. Mem.: Am. Helicopter Soc., Soc. Exptl. Test Pilots. Address: Astronaut Office Lyndon B Johnson Space Center Houston TX 77058

DREW, KATHERINE FISCHER, history professor; b. Houston, Sept. 24, 1923; d. Herbert Herman and Martha (Holloway) Fischer; m. Ronald Farinton Drew, July 27, 1951. BA, Rice Inst., 1944, MA, 1945; PhD, Cornell U., 1950. Asst. history Cornell U., 1948-50; instr. history Rice U., 1946-48, mem. faculty, 1950—, prof. history, 1964—, Harris Masterson, Jr. prof. history, 1983-85, Lynette S. Autrey prof. history, 1985-96, prof. emeritus, 1996—, chmn. dept. history, 1970-80; editor Rice U. (Rice U. Studies), 1967-81, acting dean humanities and social scis., 1973, acting chmn. dept. art and art history, 1996-98. Author: The Burgundian Code, 1949, Studies in Lombard Institutions, 1956, The Lombard Laws, 1973, Law and Society in Early Medieval Europe, 1988, The Laws of the Salian Franks, 1991, Magna Carta, 2004, also articles; editor: Perspectives in Medieval History, 1963, The Barbarian Invasions, 1970; mem. bd. editors Am. Hist. Assn. Guide to Hist. Lit., 1987-94, Am. Hist. Rev. 1982-1985; contbr.: Life and Thought in the Middle Ages, 1967, vol II, 2008. Guggenheim fellow, 1959, Fulbright scholar, 1965, NEH sr. fellow, 1974—75. Fellow Mediaeval Acad. Am. (coun. 1974-77, 2d v.p. to pres. 1985-87, del. to Am. Coun. Learned Socs. 1977-81); mem. Am. Hist. Assn. (coun. 1983-86), Phi Beta Kappa. Home: 9333 Memorial Dr # 306 Houston TX 77024-5739 Office: Rice U Dept History MS 42 PO Box 1892 Houston TX 77251-1892 E-mail: kdrew@rice.edu.

DREW, MARK LIVINGSTON, lawyer; b. Tarboro, NC, Sept. 20, 1961; s. John Edwin and Mildred Jacqueline (Livingston) D.; m. Patricia Alice Faulkner, May 23, 1987; children: Margaret Alice, Mark Livingston Jr., Caroline Addison, David Tillman. BS in Acctg., Wake Forest U., 1983, JD cum laude, 1988. Bar: Ala. 1988, US Dist. Ct. (no. dist.) Ala. 1988. Acct. Arthur Andersen & Co., Charlotte, NC, 1983-85; shareholder Maynard, Cooper & Gale, P.C., Birmingham, Ala., 1988—, mem. exec. com., mng. shareholder. Mem. adv. bd. Office of Advancement of Developing Industries, Birmingham. Mem. Newcomen Soc., Ala., Leadership Ala., Leadership Birmingham, Canterbury United Meth. Ch.; cabinet mem. United Way, 2009; bd. dirs. The Innovation Depot, chmn., 2010—11; bd. visitors Wake Forest U. Sch. Law; mem. chmn. cir. Birmingham Bus. Alliance; mem. exec. leadership team American Heart Assn., chmn., 2010—11; mem. leadership cabinet U. Ala.-Birmingham. Mem. ABA (sect. bus. law exec. coun. 1995—, Young Lawyers Assn. dist. rep. 1991-93, budget dir. 1993-94, dir. 1994-95, cabinet mem. 1993-95, past liason to sect. of bus. law), Birmingham C. of C. (mem. leadership devel. com.), Birmingham Kiwanis Club. Republican. Methodist. Office: Maynard Cooper & Gale PC 2400 Regions Harbert Plz 1901 6th Ave N Birmingham AL 35203-4604 Office Phone: 205-254-1031. Office Fax: 205-254-1999. Business E-Mail: mdrew@maynardcooper.com.

DREW, SCOTT, men's college basketball coach; b. Oct. 23, 1970; s. Homer Drew; m. Kelly Drew; children: Mackenzie, Peyton. BA in Liberal Arts, Butler U., Indpls., 1993; MA, Valparaiso U., Ind., 1994. Team asst., men's basketball Butler U. Bulldogs, 1991—93; asst. coach Valparaiso U. Crusaders, 1993—2001, assoc. head coach, 2001—02, head basketball coach Ind., 2002—03, Baylor U. Bears, Waco, Tex., 2003—. Former 1st v.p., asst. coaches com. Nat. Assn. Basketball Coaches; former com. mem. Nat. Invitation Tournament; asst. coach Athletes in Action, 1995, head coach, 1997. Named Recruiter of Yr., Court Vision, 1999. Office: Baylor Univ Ferrell Ctr One Bear Place #97082 Waco TX 76798 Office Phone: 254-710-3096. Business E-Mail: scott_drew@baylor.edu.

DREWS, JÜRGEN, pharmaceutical researcher; b. Berlin, Aug. 16, 1933; came to U.S., 1991; s. Walter and Charlotte (Schneider) D.; m. Helga Eberlein, July 26, 1963; children: Ulrike, Karoline, Bettina. MD, Free U. Berlin, 1959; Professorship, U. Heidelberg, Fed. Republic of Germany, 1973. Head chemotherapy Sandoz Rsch. Inst., Vienna, 1976-79, head of inst., 1979-82; head internat. pharm. rsch. and devel. Sandoz, Ltd., Basel, Switzerland, 1982-85; dir. pharm. rsch. F. Hoffmann-La Roche Ltd., Basel, 1985-86, chmn. rsch. bd., mem. exec. com., 1986-90; pres. internat. rsch. and devel., mem. exec. com. Hoffmann-La Roche Inc., Basel, 1991-97, pres. global rsch., mem. exec. com. Nutley, NJ, 1996-97; chmn. Internat. Biomedicine Mgmt. Ptnrs., Basel, 1998—2000; mng. ptnr. Bear Stearns Health Innoventures, NYC, 2002—. Prof. medicine U. Heidelberg, 1973—; mem. sci. adv. bd. (jour.) Infection, München, Fed. Republic of Germany, 1973-95, Drug News & Perspectives, Barcelona, Spain, 1988—, Klinische Pharmakologie, München, 1989-2000; bd. dirs. Genentech, Inc., South San Francisco, 1990-97, Protein Design Labs., Mountain View, Calif., MorphoSys GmbH, Munich; bd. dirs., internat. bd. advisors Basel Inst. Immunology, 1986-97; mem. dean's coun. Yale U. Sch. Medicine, 1993-96, chmn. sci. panel inter-company collaboration for AIDS drug devel., 1993-96, chmn. bd. participants inter-company collaboration for AIDS drug devel., 1996-97; mem. adv. com. Mass. Gen. Hosp., Boston, 1994-98; chmn. steering com. Sr. Adv. Group Biotech., 1994-96; chmn. bd. mgmt. EuropaBio, 1997-98; bd. dirs. Human Genome Scis., Rockville, Md. Author: Chemotherapie: Grundlagen und Perspektiven, 1979, Immunpharmakologie, Grundlagen und Perspektiven, 1986, Immunopharmacology, Principles and Perspectives, 1990, In Quest of Tomorrow's Medicines, 1999; editor: (with others) Topics in Infectious Diseases, vol. 1, 1975, vol. 2, 1977; also over 250 articles. Home: 6983 Bridgestone Ct Naples FL 34108-6500 Personal E-mail: info@j-drews.de.

DREYFUSS, LAWRENCE J., energy executive; Joined Plains All American Pipeline, LP, 1981; v.p. Scurlock Permian LLC, 1987—99; sr. mgmt. postions, law dept. Plains All American GP LLC, 1999—2001, assoc. gen. counsel and asst. sec., 2001—06, v.p., 2004—06; assoc. gen. counsel Plains All American Pipeline, LP, 2006, v.p., gen. counsel, comml. and litigation and asst. sec., 2006—13, sr. v.p., gen. counsel, comml. and litigation, 2013. Office: Plains All American Pipeline LP 333 Clay St Ste 1600 Houston TX 77002 Office Phone: 713-646-4100. Office Fax: 713-646-4572.

DREYZEHNER, JOHN JOSEPH, state agency administrator, physician; b. Chgo., July 26, 1963; s. John Edward and Faith Rose D.; m. Jana Kaye Van Fossan, May 6, 1989; children: John Donald, Jason Edward. BS in Psychology magna cum laude, U. Ill., 1985; MD, U. Ill., Chgo., 1989. Cert. in occupl. medicine 1999. Commd. 2nd lt. USAF, 1989, advanced through grades to maj., 1995, chief flight medicine Aeromed. Assessments Hqrs. Air Combat Command Langley AFB, Va., 1994—97; clin. practice in occupl. medicine Va., 1997—2002; dir. Cumberland Plateau Health Dist., Va., 2002—11; acting dir. Lenowisco Health Dist., Va., 2006—08; commr. Tenn. Dept. Health, Nashville, 2011—. Vis. asst. prof. pub. health U. Va.; founding faulty mem. Healthy Appalachia Inst.; adj. prof. East Tenn. State U. Coll. Pub. Health; chmn. adv. com. master pub. health degree program Va. Tech Carilion Sch. Medicine. Fellow American Coll. Occupl. and Environ. Medicine; mem. AMA, American Coll. Preventive Medicine, Assn. Mil. Surgeons US, Aerospace Med. Assn., Nat. Assn. County and City Health Officials; Sigma Chi, Phi Beta Kappa. Avocations: reading, canoeing, hiking. Office: Tennessee Department of Health Cordell Hull Bldg 425 5th Ave N Nashville TN 37243 Office Phone: 615-741-3111.

DREZ, DAVID JACOB, JR., orthopedic surgeon, educator; b. Lake Charles, La., Aug. 21, 1938; s. David Jacob and Hester Adele (Bingham) D.; m. Judith Diane Wolfe, June 5, 1963; children: Susan, Catherine Ann Self, David Jacob III. BS, Tulane U., 1959, MD, 1963. Diplomate Am. Bd. Surgery, Am. Bd. Orthopaedic Surgery. Intern Charity Hosp., New Orleans, 1963-64, resident in gen. surgery, 1964-68, resident in orthopaedic surgery, 1968-71; resident Scottish Rite Hosp., Atlanta, 1969, USPHS Hosp., New Orleans, 1970; pvt. practice Orthopaedic Assocs., Lake Charles, 1971-82; pvt. practice Orthopaedic and Sports Injury Clinic Knee and Sports Medicine Ctr., Lake Charles, 1982-94; pvt. practice Ctr. Orthopaedics, Lake Charles, 1994—2006; pvt. practice, orthop. specialists, 2007—. Staff Lake Charles Meml. Hosp., 1973—, bd. trustees, 1973, 80-82, sec.-treas., 1977, pres., 1981, chief surgery, 1984, 85; med. staff dept. orthopaedics Children's Hosp., New Orleans, 1988; La. state chmn. Orthopaedic Rsch. and Edn. Found., 1987, 90-92; network of orthopedic surgeons U.S. Gymnastics Fedn., 1988—; physician U.S. Soccer Assn., 1988—; examiner Am. Bd. Orthopaedic Surgery, 1989, 91, 92, bd. dirs.; vis. prof. numerous hosps. and univs.; speaker in field. Author: (with R. D'Ambrosia) Prevention and Treatment of Running Injuries, 1982, Prevention and Treatment of Running Injuries, 2d edit., 1989, (with D.W. Jackson) The Anterior Cruciate Deficient Knee-New Concepts in Ligament Repair, 1986, Orthopaedic Sports Medicine: Principles and Practice, 1994 (with Jesse DeLee); author 8 chpts. in books; editor Am. Jour. Sports Medicine, 1988—, Jour. Orthopaedic Techniques, 1993—; co-editor Operative Techniques in Sports Medicine jour., 1993—; mem. editl. bd. Orthopaedics, 1983—, Arthroscopy, 1984-89, Sports Medicine News, 1989—; author 5 video tapes, audio tape; adv. bd. Clin. Update, Sports Medicine, 1983—, Clin. Orthopaedics and Related Rsch., 1987-93; con. rev. bd. Jour. Bone and Joint Surgeons, 1989—; contbr. articles to profl. jours. Team orthopaedist athletic dept. McNeese State U., Lake Charles, 1974—, pres. 100 Club, 1979; co-dir. Runner's Clinic, La. State U. Sch. Medicine, New Orleans, 1978-81; chief physician NAAU Boxing Championship, Lake Charles, 1979; mem. Gov.'s Coun. on Phys. Fitness and Sports, 1981; bd. dirs. Lake Area Runners, 1989-92. Maj. La. N.G., 1963-71. Named to La. Athletic Trainers Assn. Hall of Fame, 1989, McNeese State U. Hall of Honors, 1990. Mem. Acad. Orthopaedic Soc., Am. Acad. Orthopaedic Surgeons, Am. Acad. Sports Physicians, Am. Coll. Sports Medicine, Am. Coll. Surgeons, Am. Orthopaedic Assn., Am. Orthopaedic Foot Soc., Am. Orthopaedic Foot and Ankle Soc., Am. Orthopaedic Soc. Sports Medicine, Arthroscopy Assn. N.Am., Assn. Bone and Joint Surgeons, Assn. Sports Medicine Fellowship Dirs., Mid. Am. Orthopaedic Assn., Assn. Arthritic Hip and Knee Surgery, Australian-Am. Orthopaedic

Soc., Calcasieu Parish Med. Soc., Clin. Orthopaedic Soc., European Soc. Knee Surgery and Arthroscopy, Herodicus Sports Medicine Soc. (past sec., v.p., pres.), Internat. Arthroscopy Assn., Internat. Soc. Knee, La. Orthopaedic Assn. (pres. 1992), La. State Med. Assn., Oscar Creech Surg. Soc., Orthopaedic Rsch. Soc., Soc. Internat. Chirurgie Orthopedique Traumatologie, Soc. Internat. Recherche Orthopedique Tramatologie. Avocations: reading, jogging, travel. Office: 1717 Oak Pk Blvd FL 3 Lake Charles LA 70601-8990 also: Ctr Orthop 1747 Imperial Blvd Lake Charles LA 70607 Office Phone: 337-494-4900, 337-721-7236. Business E-Mail: drezmd@pol.net.

DRIGGERS, TIMOTHY K., corporate financial executive; Contr. EOG Resources, Inc., 1999, v.p., 1999—, v.p., Acctg. and Land Adminstrn., 2000—03, chief acctg. officer, 2003—07, CFO, 2007—. Office: EOG Resources Inc Sky Lobby 2 1111 Bagby Houston TX 77002 Office Phone: 713-651-7000. Office Fax: 713-651-6995. Business E-Mail: tim_driggers@eogresources.com.

DRINKWATER, WILLIAM WAYNE, lawyer; b. Meridian, Miss., Feb. 20, 1949; s. William Wayne and Margaret (Dement) D.; m. Ouida C. Creekmore, June 3, 1972; children: Jennifer Dement, William Woods. BA, U. Miss., 1971, JD, 1974. Bar: Miss. 1974, US Dist. Ct. (no. and so. dists.) Miss. 1974, US Ct. Appeals (5th cir.) 1974, US Supreme Ct. 1982. Law clk. to William C. Keady U.S. Dist. Ct. Miss., Greenville, 1974-76; law clk. to chief justice Warren Burger U.S. Supreme Ct., Washington, 1976-77; assoc. Lake, Tindall, Hunger & Thackston, Greenville, 1977, ptnr, 1977-87, Butler, Snow, O'Mara, Stevens & Cannada, Jackson, Miss., 1987-93, Lake Tindall, LLP, Jackson, Miss., 1993—2001, Bradley, Arant, Boult Cummings LLP, 2001—. Mem. adv. group Civil Justice Reform Act of 1990, 1990-93; mem. model civil jury instrn. com. Miss. Jud. Coll., Jackson, 1989-90; chmn. Gov.'s adv. com. on Yazoo Basin Project, Jackson, 1988-89; Gov.'s com. on Corrections, 1981. 1st lt. US Army, 1971-76. Mem. Am. Law Inst., Am. Acad. Appellate Lawyers, Am. Coll. Trial Lawyers, Miss. Bar Assn. (pres. young lawyers sect. 1982-83), Supreme Ct. Hist. Soc. Office: 188 E Capitol St Ste 450 Jackson MS 39201-2127 Office Phone: 601-948-8000. Business E-Mail: wdrinkwater@bradleyarant.com.

DRISCOLL, CONSTANCE FITZGERALD, education educator, writer, consultant; b. Lawrence, Mass., Mar. 29, 1926; d. John James and Mary Anne (Leecock) Fitzgerald; m. Francis George Driscoll, Aug. 21, 1948; children: Frances Mary, Martha Anne, Sara Helene, Maribeth Lee. AB, Radcliffe Coll., 1946; postgrad., Harvard U., U. Hartford, U. Bridgeport, U. Mass. Secondary sch. tchr., North Andover, Mass., 1946-48; book reviewer N.Y.C. and Boston pubs., 1955-64; asst. conf. edn. dir. U. Hartford, 1964-68; lectr. Pace U., NYC, 1973-74; edn. commentary Radio WVOX, New Rochelle, N.Y., 1974-75; asst. ednl. adv. Nat. Girl Scouts, 1972-74; pres., owner, dir. Open Corridor Schs. Cons., Inc., Bronxville, N.Y., 1972-84; pres., dir. Open Corridor Schs., Inc., Oxford, Mass., 1984—, Worcester, Mass., 2000—, Sarasota, Jacksonville and Bradenton, Fla., 2003—. Dir. assoc. grad. edn. program with U. Hartford, Bronxville, N.Y., 1975-82; dir. grad. edn. program with U. Bridgeport, Greenwich, Conn., 1975-82; creator in svc. edn. programs pub. schs., Norwalk, Conn., 1983-88; assoc. Worcester State Coll., 1984-85, Fitchburg State Coll., 1986-87; dir. assoc. grad. edn. for tchrs. Anna Maria Coll., Paxton, Mass., 1990-94; assoc. grad. tchr. edn. courses Fitchburg State Coll., 1995-99; English instr. grades 9-12, Bais Chana HS for Girls, Worcester, Mass., 2000—, chair English dept., 2000—; provider long distance learning grad. edn. courses, Antigua and Anguilla, 1997—, U. Bridgeport, Conn., 1995—, assoc. agy. for grad. edn. courses for tchrs., 1995—; profl. devel. points provider Mass. State Dept. Edn., 1995—; tutor, cons. Worcester County Sch. Dists., 1989-95; CEU mgr. for Conn. Dept. Edn. O.C.S., Inc., Conn., 1989—; bi-lingual instr. for Indian and Vietnamese students in grades 5-12, 1988-91; dir. grad. edn. courses for tchrs. Mass. Coll. Liberal Arts, North Adams, 1999—; cons. coll./univ. and grad. sch. placement, admissions procedures, 2000—; adviser, cons. Radcliffe Coll. Admissions Coun., 1946-48; summer dir. swim program ARC, North Andover, Mass., 1942-47; cons. Girl Scouts U.S., health guide multicultural program Greater Lawrence, Mass., 1946-48, holiday radio program, Thanksgiving 1774, Antigua and Barbuda; lectr., series for Girl Guides, Antigua, W.I., 1974. Author numerous poems; contbr. articles to profl. jours., local newspapers. Recipient Educator award Nat. Coun. ARC, Washington, 1985, Edn. award Nipmuc Am. Indian Coun., Webster, Mass., 1985. Office: Open Corridor Schs Inc 212 Lakewood Dr Bradenton FL 34210 also: Open Corridor Schs Inc 1015 Atlantic Blvd Ste 273 Atlantic Beach FL 32233 Personal E-mail: opcorridor@aol.com.*

DRISCOLL, DANIEL J., medical geneticist, educator; MD, Albany Med. Coll., 1983; PhD, Indiana U., 1983. Lic. Fla., 1989, diplomate Am. Bd. Pediatrics, 1987, cert. Am. Bd. Clin. Genetics-Med. Genetics, 1990, Am. Bd. Clin. Cytogenetics-Med. Genetics, 1990. Intern Johns Hopkins Hosp., 1984, resident pediat., 1984—86, fellow clin. genetics, 1986—89; prof. pediat. Univ. Fla.; hosp. affiliation include Shands Health Care. Office: University of Florida Shands 1600 SW Archer Rd Gainesville FL 32608 Office Phone: 352-265-0111.

DRISKILL, ROBERT ALLEN, economics professor; b. Lynchburg, Va., Feb. 15, 1949; s. Nelius Kermit and Margaret Martin Driskill; m. Susan Slack, May 22, 1990; children: Michael, Christopher, Christopher Slack. BA, Mich. State U., East Lansing, 1973; PhD, Johns Hopkins U., Balt., 1977. Prof. economics Vanderbilt U., Nashville, 1992—, Ohio State U., Columbus. Contbr. article to profl. jour. Decorated Purple heart (2), Combat Infantryman's Badge US Army. Home: 3186 Parthenon Ave Unit F Nashville TN 37203 Office: Vanderbilt Univ 2301 Vanderbilt Pl Nashville TN 37235 Business E-Mail: robert.driskill@vanderbilt.edu.

DRIVER, JOE LUTHER, insurance agent, consultant; b. Rockwall, Tex., Sept. 29, 1946; s. Marshall Laguin and Alice Elizabeth (Patillo) D.; m. S. DeAnne Browning, Nov. 20, 1993; stepchildren: Eric Browning, Lynsey Browning Peskuski. BBA, U. North Tex., 1971; grad., Garland Citizen's Police Acad., 1993. With Steak & Ale Restaurants, Dallas, 1971—73; instr. Garland (Tex.) Ind. Sch. Dist., 1972; mgr. Marshall Driver Ins., Garland, 1972-73; owner, agt. Joe Driver Ins.-State Farm, Garland, 1973—2014; mem. Dist. 113 Tex. House of Representatives, 1993—2013; mem. LIC Admin. Regs. Comm., 2011—13. Chmn. law enforcement com. Tex. Ho. Reps., 2003—09, mem. environ. regulations com., 2005—09; chmn. Tex. Constl. Revision Coun., 1999—2002, Appropriation Com., Sub Com. Criminal Justice & Pub. Safety, 2009—11; mem. Homeland Security & Pub. Safety Com., 2011—13. Pres. Christian Singles Unltd., Garland, 1979; bd. dirs. First United Meth. Ch., Garland, 1979-81, Garland Econ. and Devel. Authority, 1986, Garland Crimestoppers, 1985-88, 93—, Am. Heart Assn., 1991-93; bd. dirs. New Beginning Family and Violence Prevention Ctr., 1988-91, v.p., 1990-91; chmn. SITE Found. of Garland, Inc., 1991-92; mem. bd. mgmt. Garland YMCA, 1983-85; fundraising chmn. YWCA, 1992; mem. long-range planning com. City of Garland, 1986-88; mem. devel. coun. Baylor Med. Ctr., Garland, 1991-2006; mem. Downtown Citizen Rev. Com., 1991-92; active Tex. Conservative Coalition, 1993—, Rep. Caucus Tex. Ho. of Reps., 1993-2013. Recipient Human Rels. award Dale Carnegie Cos., 1978. Mem. Nat. Assn. Life Underwriters (Nat. Quality award 1978-83, 86-92, 2002), Dallas Assn. Life Underwriters, Garland C. of C. (bd. dirs. 1983-87, chmn. 1986, corp. coun. 1988-90), Rowlett C. of C., Tex. Dist. Exch. Clubs (dist. dir. 1984, Outstanding Dist. Dir. award 1985, Pres.'s award 1986), Noon Exch. Club Garland (bd. dirs. 1982-86, 90-91, pres. 1983, 90, Outstanding Svc. award 1986-87), Leadership Garland Alumni Assn. (bd. dirs. 1990-91), U. North Tex. Alumni Assn. (bd. dirs. 2001-05), Lambda Chi Alpha (pres. 1971). Avocations: fitness training, yoga. Office Phone: 972-276-1116. Personal E-mail: jordriver@tx.rr.com.

DRIVER, WALTER W., JR., lawyer, investment company executive; b. El Paso, Tex., Apr. 10, 1945; s. Walter Williamson and Carolyn Bonds (Mayfield) D.; m. Bettie Townsend Willerson, Dec. 27, 1970; children: Eleanor, Anna, Walter III. AB, Stanford U., 1967; JD, U. Tex., 1970. Bar: Ga. 1970. Chmn., Southeast Goldman Sachs & Co.; assoc. King & Spalding, LLP, 1970—76, ptnr., 1976, chmn. policy com., 1992-94, 98-99, mng. ptnr., chmn., 1999—2005. Bd. dirs. Total Sys. Svcs. Inc., Old Mut. Advisors Funds, Equifax Inc. Mem. exec. com. Children's Mus. Atlanta, 1990-95; bd. dirs. Ctrl. Atlanta Progress, 1993—; chair Celebration of Life Cancer Soc., 1993. Mem. ABA, State Bar Ga., U.S. Golf Assn. (gen. counsel 1997-99, mem. exec. com. 1999—, treas. 2000-01, v.p. 2001—), Ga. State Golf Assn. (gen. coun., exec. com. 1988-97), Atlanta C. of C. (exec. com., bd. dirs.), Piedmont Driving Club, Peachtree Golf Club (bd. dirs.). Office: Goldman Sachs & Co 200 W St New York NY 10282 also: Equifax Inc Bd Directors 1550 Peachtree St NW Atlanta GA 30309 Office Phone: 212-902-1000, 404-885-8000. Office Fax: 212-902-3000, 404-885-8988. Business E-Mail: walter.driver@gs.com.

DROEGEMEIER, KELVIN K., meteorologist, educator; b. Ellsworth, Kans., Aug. 23, 1958; m. Lisa Roevekamp, Sept. 27, 1983. BS in Meteorology with spl. distinction, U. Okla., 1980; MS, U. Ill., 1982, PhD in Atmospheric Sci., 1985. Meteorol. aide Nat. Severe Storms Lab., 1976—78, meteorol. technician, 1978—80; grad. rsch. asst. U. Ill., 1980—85; asst. prof., sch. meteorology U. Okla., 1985—91, co-founder, dep. dir. rsch. Ctr. Analysis and Prediction of Storms, 1989—92, dir. Ctr. Analysis and Predictions of Storms, 1994—2006, dir. emeritus Ctr. Analysis and Predictions of Storms, 2006—, assoc. prof., sch. meteorology, 1991—98, prof., sch. meteorology, 1998—2001, regents' prof., sch. meteorology, 2001—, Roger and Sherry Teigen presdl. prof., 2004—, dir. Sasaki Inst., 2005—, weathernews chair in applied meteorology, 2005—, assoc. vp. rsch., 2005—; founder, dir. Environ. Computing Applications System Rsch. and Ednl. Superconducting Ctr., 1996—2001; co-founder, dep. dir. Engring. Rsch. Ctr. Collaborative Adaptive Sensing Atmosphere, NSF, 2003—. Men. Nat. Sci. Bd., NSF, 2004—, chair Com. on Programs and Plans and Task Force on Cost Sharing; cons. Sperry Comml. Flight Systems Group, Honeywell Corp., 1989—92, Climatol. Cons. Corp., 1997, Am. Airlines, 1997, 1999—, Nat. Transportation Safety Bd., 1997—98; chair SoM Undergraduate Studies Com. U. Okla., 2001—, mem. Williams Chair Search Com., 2001—; mem. bd. advisors Supercomputing Ctr. Edn. and Rsch., 2001—; mem. patent adv. com. U. Okla., 2003—; spkr. in field; fellow NOAA Cooperative Inst. Mesoscale Meteorol. Studies, 1987—. Contbr. articles to profl. jours., chapters to books. Bd. dirs. Norman, Okla. C. of C., 2003—; chmn. Weather and Climate Team, Okla. Econ. Devel. Generating Excellence (EDGE) Gov. Task Force, 2003; deacon Riverside Ch., Norman, 2003—. Recipient Pioneer award, NSF, 2001, Excellence in Aviation award, Fedn. Aviation Adminstrn., 2002. Fellow: Am. Meteorol. Soc. (councilor 2004—), Tau Beta Pi; mem.: Am. Inst. for Aeronautics and Astronautics, Soc. of Indsl. and Applied Math., Am. Assn. of U. Professors, Am. Geophysical Union, Am. Assn. for Advancement of Sci., Sigma Xi Sci. Rsch. Soc., Phi Kappa Phi. Office: U Okla Ctr Analysis and Prediction of Storms Sarkeys Energy Ctr Rm 1110 100 E Boyd Norman OK 73019 Office Phone: 405-325-0453. Business E-Mail: kdroege@tornado.gcn.uoknor.edu, kkd@ou.edu.

DROLLA, JOHN CASPER DODT, JR., lawyer; b. New Orleans, Sept. 29, 1944; s. John Casper Drolla Sr. and Edna Florence (Bauerfeind) Dempsey. AS, Tarleton State U., Stephenvillw, Tex., 1960; BA, U. Tex., Austin, 1963; JD, U. Tex. Sch. Law, 1972. Bar: Tex. 1972, US Dist. Ct. (we. dist.) Tex. 1974, US Ct. Appeals (5th cir.) 1976, US Supreme Ct. 1977, US Ct. Appeals Armed Forces 1988. Briefing clk. to Hon. Leon Douglas Tex. Ct. Criminal Appeals, Austin, 1972-73, rsch. asst., 1973-74, 1976-77; assoc. Philip & Norris, Inc., Austin, 1974-76; founder, sr. atty. Law Offices John C.D. Drolla, Jr., Austin, 1977—. Judge Tex. Ct. Mil. Appeals, 2007—; lectr. in field. Contbr. articles to profl. jours. Chmn. Trial Advocacy Assn., 1971; hon. coun. mem. Habitat for Humanity, 1993—95; bd. dirs. 100 Club Ctrl. Tex., 1990—, Westlake C. of C., 1996—98, Tex. Mil. Forces Found., 1996—2008. Comdr. 25th Trans Co. and Honor Guard US Army, 1965—67, Ft. Sam, Houston, comdr. HHC US Amy Hdqs. Area Command, 1967—68, Vietnam, col. USAR, 1988—93. Fellow: Tex. Bar Found., Coll. State Bar Tex., Travis County Bar Assn.; mem.: Tex. Coll. Real Estate Lawyers, American Law Inst., Fed. Bar Assn., Williamson County Bar Assn., State Bar Tex., Nat. Order Barristers. Avocations: track and field official, stamp collecting/philately, sport cars, outdoor and water related sports. Office: Law Offices of John C D Drolla Jr One Far West Bldg 3410 Far W Blvd Ste 170 Austin TX 78731 Home Phone: 512-327-2001; Office Phone: 512-445-6838. Business E-Mail: drolla@lawdrolla.com.

DRUCKER, RONALD WALTER, rail transportation executive; b. NYC, Dec. 19, 1941; s. Jack and Doris (Blum) D.; m. A. Sibbald Doan, Nov. 24, 1977; children: Julia Alice Ohrt, Jane Sibbald Gregson. BCE, The Cooper Union, 1962; MCE, U. Ill., 1964, PhD, 1966. Chmn. Cooper Union for the Advancement of Sci. and Art; various positions Chessie System R.R.s, Balt., 1966-76, gen. mgr., car utilization, 1979-80, gen. mgr., transp., 1980-81, chief engr. Huntington, W.Va., 1981-85, v.p., transp. Balt., 1985-86; chief engr., sr. v.p. transp., pres. and CEO CSX Rail Transport, Jacksonville, Fla., 1966—92; chmn. CSX Sea-Land Logistics, Alexandria, Va., 1986-91; sr. v.p., CEO CSX Corp., Richmond, Va., 1988-91; chmn. CSX Intermodal, Hunt Valley, Md., 1989-91; chmn., encompass, global logistics CSX Corp., 1989—97; pres., CEO CSX Technologies, Jacksonville, 1991; cons., transp. and tech. CSX Corp., 1992—; chmn., encompass, global logistics AMR, 1989—97. Bd. dirs. Sun Bank North Fla., NA, Jacksonville U., Landstar Logistics Inc., Railworks Corp., 1998., Landstar System Inc., 1994-2009, Landstar System Holdings Inc. (subs. of Landstar System Inc.), 1994-2004 Bd. dirs. Sci. Mus. Va., Richmond, 1989—, Richmond Symphony, 1990—; trustee Jacksonville U., 1988—., New World Symphony Orch., B&O Railroad Mus., LD Pankey Dental Found. Mem. ASCE, Nat. Def. Transp. Assn. (chmn. bd. 1987—), Assn. Am. R.R.s (chmn. info. tech. div. 1991—), Am. R.R. Engring. Assn. Office: CSX Corp 550 Water St Jacksonville FL 32202-5177 Office Phone: 904-359-3200. Office Fax: 904-633-3450. Business E-Mail: rdrucker@csx.com.

DRUMMOND, DORIS WIGGINS, psychologist; b. Ranburne, Ala., Nov. 2, 1938; d. Lee Otis and Lora Lee (Coley) Wiggins; m. J. Ferrell Drummond, Jan. 20, 1961; children: Nancy Lora, Franklin Joseph. AA, Young Harris Coll., Ga., 1959; BS, Jacksonville State U., 1963; MEd, West Ga. Coll., 1973; postgrad., Wesley Coll., Bristol, Eng., 1977-78, Augusta Coll., 1986, Ga. So. Coll., 1987. Tchr. of bus. Carroll County Sch. System, Mt. Zion, Ga., 1964-66; Bowdon, 1973-74; tchr. Carrollton City Schs., Mt. Zion, Bowdon, Ga., 1968-72; tchr. of bus. Jacksonville City Schs., Ala., 1966-67; behavioral psychologist Rome City Schs., Ga., 1981-82, Richmond County Schs., Augusta, Ga., 1982-86, DeKalb County Schs., Atlanta, 1986-90, Carrollton, Ga. Counsellor, Augusta, 1985-86. Ch. sch. tchr. United Meth. Chs., lay minister, Rome, Augusta, Bristol, Eng.; publicity chairperson North Ga. Conf. United Meth. Minister's Wives, Atlanta, 1988-89. Mem. Coun. for Exceptional Children. Home: 85 Azalea Trl Carrollton GA 30116-8960

DRUMMOND, GARRY N., mining company executive; married. BS in Civil Engring., U. Ala., 1961. Chmn., CEO Drummond Co., Inc., 1956—; chmn. bd., dirs. Ala.-By-Products Corp., Birmingham, 1977-80. Mem. Ala. Acad. of Honor, 1989, Ala. Engring. Hall of Fame, 1997, Ala. Bus. Hall of Fame, 2003; bd. dirs. Nat. Mining Assn., Econ. Devel. Partnership, Ala. Coal Assn. Office: Drummond Co Inc 1000 Urban Ctr Dr Ste 300 Birmingham AL 35242 Office Phone: 205-945-6300. Office Fax: 205-945-6440. Business E-Mail: garry.drummond@drummondco.com.

DRUMMOND, JERE A., telecommunications company executive; Pres., CEO BellSouth Comm. Group, Atlanta, BellSouth Telecom., Inc.; with BellSouth Corp, 1962—2001; vice chmn. BellSouth Corp., Atlanta, 2000—01. Bd. dirs. Automotive Component Supplier, 1996—, Centillium Comm., 2000—, AirTran Airways, 2002—, Sci. Applications Internat. Corp., 2003—. Office: AirTran Airways Bd Directors 2702 Love Field Dr Dallas TX 75235-1908 Office Phone: 407-318-5600. Office Fax: 407-318-5900. Business E-Mail: jere.drummond@airtran.com.

DRUMMOND, KIRK G., food service executive; m. Pamela Drummond; 2 children. BS in Bus. Adminstrn., U. Ariz., 1978. With Fisher Drummond Co.; contr. Sysco Corp., Grand Rapids, Mich., 1986—89, CFO, contr. Atlanta, 1989—92, v.p., fin., 1992—97, v.p., contr. Houston, 1997—2000, v.p., 2000—05, CIO, 2000—05, sr. v.p., treas., 2005—. Office: Sysco Corp 1390 Enclave Pkwy Houston TX 77077-2099 Office Phone: 281-584-1390.

DRUMMOND, REE (ANN MARIE DRUMMOND), writer, television personality, photographer, food writer; b. Jan. 6, 1969; d. William Douglas Smith and Gerre Schwert; m. Ladd Drummond, Sept. 21, 1996; children: Alex, Paige, Bryce, Todd. Grad., U. Southern Calif., 1991. Blog writer ThePioneerWoman.com (originally called Confessions of a Pioneer Woman), 2006— (Best Kept Secret Weblog, The Bloggie awards, 2007, Best Food Weblog, The Bloggie awards, 2008, Best Writing of a Weblog, The Bloggie awards, 2008, 2010, Best Designed Weblog, The Bloggie awards, 2009, 2010, Best Photography of a Weblog, The Bloggie awards, 2009, Weblog of the Year, The Bloggie awards, 2009, 2010, 2011, named one of 25 Best Blogs in the World, Time Magazine, 2009, referenced in the Los Angeles Times, New York Times and BusinessWeek), creator (free online community recipe website) TastyKitchen.com, 2009, first major TV debut competiting against Bobby Flay Throwdown! With Bobby Flay, 2010—; author: (cookbook) The Pioneer Women Cooks: Recipes from an Accidental Country Girl, 2009, The Pioneer Woman Cooks: Food from My Frontier, 2012, The Pioneer Woman Cooks: A Year of Holidays: 140 Step-by-Step Recipes for Simple, Scrumptious Celebrations, 2013, (memoir) The Pioneer Woman: Black Heels to Tractor Wheels, 2011 (#2 on the New York Times Best Sellers list for hardcover non-fiction, #2 on the Wall Street Journal Bestseller list); author: (illustrated by Diane deGroat) (children's books) Charlie the Ranch Dog, 2011 (#1 on the New York Times Best Sellers list), Charlie and the Christmas Kitty, 2012, Charlie Goes to School, 2013, (children's books (I Can Read Series) Charlie the Ranch Dog: Charlie's Snow Day, 2013, Charlie the Ranch Dog: Where's the Bacon?, 2013, Charlie the Ranch Dog: Charlie's New Friend, 2014; guest appearances on numerous talk shows including Good Morning America. Today Show, The View, The Chew, The Bonnie Hunt Show & Fox and Friends, featured in Ladies' Home Journal, Woman's Day, People Magazine, More, and Southern Living, host The Pioneer Women, Food Network, 2011—. Named one of Forbes' Top 25 Web Celebrities, 2010. Avocations: gardening, cooking. Office: The Pioneer Woman PO Box 749 Pawhuska OK 74056 Address: The Pioneer Woman 1611 S Utica Ave #343 Tulsa OK 74104-4909 E-mail: ree@thepioneerwoman.com.*

DRUMMOND, WILLA HENDRICKS, neonatologist, educator, information technology developer and executive; b. Harrisburg, Pa., Dec. 5, 1945; d. George Edson and Leah Clementine (Connelly) Hendricks; m. Thomas Weston Drummond, June 1966 (div. 1978). BA cum laude, Brown U., 1966; MD, U. Pa., 1970; MS in Med. Informatics, U. Utah, 1999. Resident in pediat. Children's Hosp. Phila., 1970-72, cardiology fellow, 1972-74; instr. pediat. U. Pa., Phila., 1973-74; rsch. fellow perinatology U. Oreg., Portland, 1974-75; staff pediatrician Kaiser-Permanente Clinics, Portland, 1975-76; instr. neonatology, fellow Cardiovasc. Rsch. Inst.-U. Calif., San Francisco, 1976-78; asst. prof. pediat. U. Fla., Gainesville, 1978-82, asst. prof. pediat. and physiology, 1981-82, assoc. prof. pediat. physiology and vet. med. scis., 1982-88, prof., 1988—, Somanetics Inc., Troy, Mich., 2009—10. Cons. Baxter-Travenol Labs., Deerfield, Ill., 1986-88, co-chair Equine Neonatology Study Group, Gainesville, 1981-91; dir. Neonatology Fellowship Program U. Fla., Gainesville, 1981-85; cons., CIO, chief med. info. officer, ICU Data Sys., Inc., Gainesville, 2001-05, interim CEO, exec. v.p. med. affairs, 2004-06, founder, chief med. info. exec., 2006—08; Cert. Commn. Health Info. Tech. CCHIT Inpatient Experts Panel, 2007-10, patent holder Vital Sync, 2005-, Covidien, Inc. Cons., 2010-. Contbr. numerous rsch. papers and abstracts to profl. jours.; poet: Carousel of Progress, 1979. Emily's List, Named Best Dr. in USA, Best Doctors, Inc., 2005-; named one of America's Top Pediatricians, 2007, 08-11, named to Great Minds of 21st Century, 2010-; rsch. grantee Am. Heart Assn., NIH, Dept. of Def., others, 1976—2006; sr. fellow Med. Informatics, 1997-99, U. Utah. Mem. Am. Physiologic Soc., Soc. Pediat. Rsch., Am. Pediat. Soc., Am. Acad. Pediat.(exec. steering com. Coun. Clin. Info. Tech. 2005-11), Am. Med. Informatics Assn., Sigma Xi, So. Soc. Pediat. Rsch., Internat. Soc. Vet. Perinatology (bd. dirs., pres. 1995-97), Internat. Physicians Prevention of Nuc. War (collective Nobel Peace prize 1985), Union of Concerned Scientists, Nat. Orgn. Women, Nat. Resources Def. Com., Sierra Club, Greenpeace, Friends Earth, Alaska Wilderness League. Democrat. Office: U Fla Coll Medicine PO Box 100296 Gainesville FL 32610-0296 Business E-Mail: willa@drdrummond.net.

DRURY, JOHN R., retail executive; B, Fla. State U. CFO 3three Advt.; co-founder Harris Drury Cohen, Fla., 1980—97; sr. v.p., mktg. AutoNation, Inc., Ft. Lauderdale, Fla., 1997—. Former pres. Advt. Fedn. Greater Ft. Lauderdale, Fla. Office: AutoNation Inc 110 SE 6th St Fort Lauderdale FL 33301 Office Phone: 954-769-6000. Office Fax: 954-769-6537.

DRURY, LEONARD LEROY, retired oil company executive; b. Gillespie, Ill., Nov. 5, 1928; s. Roy August and Regina Loretta (Finnegan) D.; m. Myra Lee Klunk, June 30, 1951; 1 child, Marilyn Jo Drury Chandler. BS in Indsl. Mgmt., St. Louis U., 1950; MBA in Mgmt., U. Houston, 1957. Mgr. systems program info. and computer services Shell Oil Co., NYC, 1966-68, mgr. data processing info. and computer services Menlo Park, Calif., 1968, mgr. acctg. info. and computer services, 1968-69, mgr. MTM bus. systems div. info. and computer services NYC and Houston, 1969-71, mgr. planning Houston, 1971-73, mgr. planning and tech. info. and computer services, 1973-75, asst. treas. fin., 1975-77, gen. mgr. info. and computer services, 1977-80, liaison Shell Ctr. London, 1980-81, gen. mgr. products fin. Houston, 1981-83, v.p. purchasing and adminstrv. services, 1983-86, v.p. info. and computer services, 1986-89, ret., 1989. Bd. dirs. Businessland Inc., 1989—91; bd. mem. 5000 Montrose at Mus., 2010—13, U. St. Thomas Ctr. Faith and Culture, 2010—13; trustee Serra Club NW, Houston, 2012—13. Mem. United Way, Houston, 1982-89; bd. dirs. South Main Ctr. Assn., Houston, 1986-89. Mem.: Houston Bus. Coun. (pres. 1985—86), West Houston Assn. (bd. dirs. 1984—88), The Houstonian Club, Sigma Iota Epsilon. Roman Catholic. Home: 5000 Montrose Blvd Unit 21E Houston TX 77006-6564 E-mail: lldhouston@aol.com.

DRUTZ, JAN EDWIN, pediatrics educator; b. Louisville, Jan. 8, 1942; s. Abe Morris and Lillian (Billig) D.; m. Anne Edwina Sussman, June 7, 1965; children: Jeffrey Benjamin, Lisa Michele, Dana Nicole. BA, U. Louisville, 1964, MD, 1968. Pvt. practice, Houston, 1973-87; intern, then resident Baylor Coll. Medicine, Houston, 1968-71, from clin. asst. prof. to assoc. prof. pediat., 1973—2002, dir. pediat. continuity clinic, 1987—, prof. pediat., 2002—; pres. med. staff Tex. Children's Hosp., 1995, prof. pediats., 2002—. Maj. U.S. Army, 1971-73. Mem. AMA, Harris County Med. Soc., Tex. Pediat. Soc. (adv. com., mem. student preceptorship program 1995-96), Houston Pediat. Soc. (sec. 1984-85, pres. 1988-89), Ambulatory Pediat. Assn. (chmn. continuity clinic spl. interest group 1990-95, edn. com. 1993—). Office: Tex Children Hosp Clin Care Ctr Ste 1540-00 6701 Fannin St Houston TX 77030 Business E-Mail: jdrutz@bcm.edu.

DUBE, VINAY, air transportation executive; b. Feb. 11, 1967; Various positions including v.p. flight scheduling products Sabre Holdings Corp., Southlake, Tex., v.p. airline solutions divsn., Europe, Middle East & Africa, 2002—05, v.p. portfolio mgmt., 2005; v.p. alliance & industry affairs Delta Air Lines, Inc., 2008—10, v.p. Asia Pacific, 2010—. Office: Delta Air Lines Inc PO Box 20706 Atlanta GA 30320-6001 Office Phone: 404-715-2600. Office Fax: 404-715-5042. E-mail: vinay.dube@delta.com.

DUBINA, JOEL FREDRICK, federal judge; b. Elkhart, Ind., Oct. 26, 1947; BS, U. Ala., 1970; JD, Cumberland Sch. Law, 1973. Law clk. to Hon. Robert E. Varner US Dist. Ct. (middle dist.) Ala., Montgomery, 1973—74; pvt. practice law Jones, Murray, Stewart & Yarbrough, 1974—83; magistrate judge US Dist. Ct. (middle dist.) Ala., Montgomery, 1983—86, judge, 1986—90, US Ct. Appeals (11th cir.), 1990—2013, chief judge, 2009—13, sr. judge, 2013—. Mem. Judicial Conf. US; exec. com. mem. Montogomery Judicual Conf. Mem.: FBA (pres. Montgomery chpt. 1982—83), Montgomery County Bar Assn. (chmn. Law Day com. 1975, constrn. and bylaws com. 1977—80, grievance com. 1981—83), 11th Cir. Hist. Soc., Ala. State Bar Assn., Supreme Ct. Hist. Soc., Fed. Judges Assn., Nat. Coun. US Magistrate Judges, Cumberland Sch. Law Alumni Assn., American Inn of Courts (pres. Montgomery chpt. 1993—94), Lions, Phi Delta Phi. Office: US Court Appeals PO Box 867 Montgomery AL 36101-0867 also: US Courthouse Ste C5 1 Church St Montgomery AL 36104 Business E-Mail: jfd@call.uscourts.gov.*

DUBKE, MICHAEL, corporate communications specialist; Grad., Hamilton Coll., Clinton, NY. Co-founder, exec. dir., pres. Americans for Job Security, Alexandria, Va., 1997—2008; founder, ptnr. Crossroads Media, LLC, Alexandria, 2001—; founding ptnr. Black Rock Group, Alexandria, 2009—. Republican. Office: Crossroads Media LLC/Black Rock Group 66 Canal Ctr Plz Ste 555 Alexandria VA 22314 Office Phone: 703-229-1760. Office Fax: 703-299-1761.

DUBOIS, PHILIP LEON, academic administrator, political scientist, educator; b. Oakland, Calif., Oct. 17, 1950; s. Fernand Edmond and Germaine (Goodrich) D.; m. Lisa Lewis, Aug. 28, 1976; 3 children. AB in Polit. Sci. with highest honors, U. Calif., Davis, 1972; MA in Polit. Sci., U. Wis., 1974, PhD in Polit. Sci., 1978. Asst. prof. polit. sci. U. Calif., Davis, 1976—82, faculty asst. to vice chancellors, 1982—83, assoc. prof., 1982—87, assoc. vice chancellor, 1983—90, exec. assoc. dean letters and sci., 1990—91, prof., 1987—91; vice chancellor acad. affairs, provost U. NC, Charlotte, 1991—97, chancellor, 2005—; pres. U. Wyo., 1997—2005. Author (with Floyd Feeney): Lawmaking by Initiative, 1998; author: From Ballot to Bench: Judicial Elections and the Quest for Accountability, 1980; editor: The Analysis of Judicial Reform, 1982, The Politics of Judicial Reform, 1982; contbr. numerous articles, book revs. to law revs. and jours., other profl. publs.; cons. (profl. jours., comml. book pubs.). Scholar, U. Wis., Madison; Ford Found. fellow, Jud. fellow, U.S. Supreme Ct., 1979—80. Mem.: Am. Assn. for Higher Edn., Am. Polit. Sci. Assn. (Edward S. Corwin award 1978), Phi Beta Kappa, Phi Kappa Phi. Democrat. Office: Univ NC Charlotte office Chancellor 9201 Univ City Blvd Charlotte NC 28223 Office Phone: 704-687-5727. Business E-Mail: pdubois@uncc.edu.

DUBOIS, RAYMOND N., medical educator, researcher; BS in Biochemistry, Tex. A&M U.; PhD in Biochemistry, Tex. Southwestern Med. Sch.; MD, U. Tex. Health Sci. Ctr., San Antonio. Osler medicine intern, resident John Hopkins Hosp., Balt.; with Vanderbilt U. Med. Ctr., 1991—, head divsn. gastroenterology, hepatology, and nutrition Nashville, 1998—2003, Mina. C. Wallace prof. medicine and cell biology, 1998—2003, prof. medicine, cancer biology, cell and devel. biology, 2003—; dir. Vanderbilt Digestive Disease Rsch. Ctr., 1999—; Hortnse B. Ingram prof. molecular oncology Vanderbilt-Ingram Cancer Ctr., Vanderbilt U. Med. Ctr., 2004, dir. cancer prevention program, 2005—07; provost, exec. v.p. academic affairs M.D. Anderson Cancer Ctr., Houston, 2007—. Scientific adv. bd. Nat. Colorectal Cancer Rsch. Alliance Found.; bd. scientific advisors Nat. Cancer Inst.; adv. bd. Nat. Inst. Diabetes and Digestive and Kidney Diseases, NIH; chmn. bd. dirs. Keystone Symposia on Molecular and Cellular Biology. Assoc. editor Gasteroenterology and Cancer Rsch.; contbr. articles to profl. jour. Recipient Outstanding Investigator award, AFMR, 2000, Disting. Achievement award, Am. Gastroenterological Assn., 2004. Fellow: AAAS; mem.: Am. Assn. Cancer Rsch. (pres.-elect 2007—, Dorothy P. Landon prize translational cancer rsch. 2004, Richard and Hinda Rosenthal award 2002), Am. Soc. Clin. Investigation, Am. Assn. Physicians, Royal Coll. Physicians. Achievements include first to report the link between cyclooxygenase-2 (COX-2) enzyme and colon cancer. Office: MD Anderson Cancer Ctr 1515 Holcombe Blvd Unit 118 Houston TX 77030 Office Phone: 615-343-0527. Business E-Mail: raymond.dubois@vanderbilt.edu.

DUBOSE, CHARLES WILSON, lawyer; b. Sumter, SC, Mar. 2, 1949; s. Frank Elsivan and Fannie Louise (Wilson) DuB.; m. Patricia Holman Rayle, Dec. 5, 1987; children: Charles Wilson Jr., Margaret Louise Rayle, Frank Elsivan IV. AB magna cum laude, Harvard U., Cambridge, Mass., 1971; JD, U. Va., Charlottesville, 1974. Bar: Ga. 1974, SC 1992, US Dist. Ct. (no. dist.) Ga. 1974, US Ct. Appeals (5th cir.) 1976, US Ct. Appeals (4th cir.) 1978, US Supreme Ct. 1979, US Ct. Appeals (11th cir.) 1981, US Dist. Ct. (mid. dist.) Ga. 1982, US Dist. Ct. SC 2000. Assoc. Kutak, Rock & Huie and predecessor firms, Atlanta, 1974-79; ptnr. Kutak, Rock & Huie, Atlanta, 1979-84; of counsel Griffin, Cochrane & Marshall, PC, Atlanta, 1985-86, ptnr., 1986—92, mng. ptnr., 1989-92; ptnr. Schnader, Harrison, Segal & Lewis, Atlanta, 1992—2000, Atlanta mng. ptnr., 1995-2000; mem. Winkler & DuBose LLC, Atlanta, Madison, 2000—08, DuBose Assoc. LLC, Atlanta, 2009—10, Madison, DuBose Massey Bair & Evans LLC, Madison, Atlanta, 2010—13, DuBose Law Group LLC, Madison, 2013—. Mem. Chief Justice's Commn. on Indigent Def., 2000—02; mem. Ga. Pub. Defender Stds. Coun., 2003-09, chmn., 2007-09; mem. mediation and arbitration panels Am. Arbitration Assn. Elder Peachtree Presbyn. Ch., Atlanta, Madison Presbyn. Ch.; mem. adv. bd. Atlanta's Table, 1991—2006, chmn., 1995; exec. vice chmn. Atlanta Billy Graham Crusade. Fellow Lawyers Found. Ga., Am. Bar Found.; mem. ABA (house of dels. 2000-2006), Am. Law Inst., State Bar Ga. (bd. govs. 1998-2010, chair ind. def. com. 1997—, exec. com. 2006-10, sec. 2009-10), Atlanta Bar Assn. (pres. 1995-96, bd. dir. 1992-97, 00—06, chmn. litig. sect. 1992-93), Lawyers Com. Civil Rights Under Law (Atlanta steering com.), Atlanta Bar Found. (fellow; bd. dir. 1995-96, 00-09), Atlanta Vol. Lawyers Found. (bd. dir. 1995-96), Inst. Continuing Legal Edn. in Ga. (bd. trustees 1995-96, 2009-10), Common Cause Ga., (bd. dir. 2012-), Lawyers Club Atlanta, World Trade Ctr. Atlanta. Avocations: photography, piano, architecture, historic preservation. Home: 1050 East Ave Madison GA 30650-1467 Office: DuBose Massey Bair & Evans LLC 285 N Main St PO Box 192 Madison GA 30650 also: 260 Peachtree St NE Ste 2000 Atlanta GA 30308-3263 Office Phone: 706-342-7900. Business E-Mail: wdubose@duboselawgroup.net.

DUBOSE, KRISTI K., federal judge; b. Brewton, Ala., 1964; BA, Huntington Coll., 1986; JD, Emory U., 1989. Law clk. to Hon. Peter Hill Beer US Dist. Ct. (ea. dist.) La., 1989—90; asst. US atty. US Atty.'s Office (so. dist. Ala.), 1990—93; asst. dist. atty. Covington County Dist. Atty.'s Office, Ala., 1994; dep. atty. gen. Ala. Atty. Gen.'s Office, 1994—96; chief counsel to Sen. Jeff Sessions US Senate, 1997—99; magistrate judge US Dist. Ct. (so. dist.) Ala., 2000—05, judge, 2005—. Office: US Dist Ct So Dist Ala 113 St Joseph St Mobile AL 36602 Office Phone: 251-690-2020.

DUBOW, CRAIG A., former publishing executive; b. Oct. 26, 1954; m. Denise Dubow; 3 children. BS in radio/TV/film, U. Tex., Austin, 1977. Various positions Gannett Co., Inc., 1981—2011, gen. sales mgr. KVUE-TV Austin, Tex., 1987—88, v.p, sta. mgr. KVUE-TV, 1988, v.p., gen. mgr. KVUE-TV, 1988—90, pres., gen. mgr. KVUE-TV, 1990—92, pres., gen. mgr. WXIA-TV Atlanta, 1992—2000; exec. v.p. Gannett TV, 1996—2000; pres., CEO Gannett Broadcasting, 2000—05, Gannett Co., Inc., 2005—06, chmn., pres., CEO, 2006—10, chmn., CEO, 2010—11. Bd. dirs. Nat. Assn. Broadcasters, Assn. Maximum Svc. TV Inc., Broadcast Music Inc. (BMI), Gannett Co., Inc., 2005—11, The Associated Press, Inc., 2008—.

DUBOWSKI, KURT MAX, toxicologist, educator, consultant; b. Berlin, Nov. 21, 1921; came to U.S., 1935; s. Jacques Dubowski and Gertrud (Baron) Steinberg. AB, NYU, 1946; MSc, Ohio State U., 1947, PhD, 1949; LLD (hon.), Capital U., 1984. Diplomate Am. Bd. Clin. Chemistry (pres. emeritus, sec.-treas. emeritus), Am. Bd. of Forensic Toxicology (founding pres., past pres.). Biochemist, asst. dir. labs. Norwalk (Conn.) Hosp., 1950-53; dir. chemistry Iowa Meth. Hosp., Des Moines, 1953-58; state criminalist State of Iowa Divsn. of Criminal Investigation, Des Moines, 1954-58; assoc. prof. clin. chemistry and toxicology U. Fla., Gainesville, 1958-61; George Lynn Cross disting. prof. medicine U. Okla., Oklahoma City, 1961-98, prof. surgery, prof. pathology, dir. toxicology labs., dir. forensic sci. labs. health scis. ctr., mem. clin. staff Univ. Hosps., 1961-2001, emeritus prof., 1998—; prin. rsch. scientist Civil Aerospace Med. Inst. FAA U.S. Dept. Trans., Oklahoma City, 2001—. Cons. clin. chemistry and toxicology Dept. Vets. Affairs Med. Ctr., Oklahoma City, 1962-2001; cons. lab. medicine Okla. Med. Rsch. Found., Oklahoma City, 1967-2001; state dir. tests for alcohol and drug influence, State of Okla., 1967-97, state dir. emeritus, 1997—; chmn. emeritus Bd. Tests for Alcohol and Drug Influence, State of Okla., 2000—; ret. sci. dir. Okla. Dept. Pub. Safety; ret. criminalist Okla. Dept. Pub. Safety/Okla. Hwy. Patrol, Okla. State Bur. Investigation, Oklahoma City Police Dept.; mem. sci. adv. bd. Armed Forces Inst. Pathology, U.S. Dept. Def., 1991-97; mem. Internat. Coun. Alcohol, Drugs and Traffic Safety; mem. exec. bd., co-chair subcom. alcohol pharmacology, toxicology and tech. com. on alcohol and other drugs Nat. Safety Coun.; past advisor subcom. urine drug testing NCCLS; toxicologist advisor DEC program Nat. Hwy. Traffic Safety Adminstrn., U.S. Dept. Transp.; cons. in field; mem. various fed. adv. groups; vis. lectr. and prof. various colls. and univs.; expert witness in forensic sci. matters. Author numerous books; contbr. chpts. to books and articles to profl. jours.; mem. editl. bd. Jour. Forensic Scis., Therapeutic Drug Monitoring, Forensic Sci. Rev.; past mem. editl. bd. Am. Jour. Forensic Medicine and Pathology, Clin. Chemistry, Internat. Microform Jour. Legal Medicine, Jour. Analytical Toxicology. 1st lt. U.S. Army, 1942-55. Recipient Widmark award Internat. Coun. Alcohol, Drugs and Traffic Safety, 1980, CIIT award Chem. Industry Inst. Toxicology, 1983, Cert. of Merit Forensic Scis. Found., 1984, Robert F. Borkenstein award Nat. Safety Coun., 1992, Disting. Svc. to Safety award NSC, 1995, Outstanding Contbn. to Clin. Chemistry award Am. Assn. for Clin. Chemistry, 1996; Kurt M. Dubowski Award established by Internat. Assn. Chem. Testing, 2002; numerous others; named Disting. Alumnus Ohio State U., 1994, hon. Tex. Ranger, 2007; Nat. Rsch. Coun. fellow in phys. scis. Ohio State U., 1948-49. Fellow Am. Acad. Forensic Scis. (founding fellow, disting. fellow, past pres., editor procs., Award of Merit 1980, Rolla N. Harger award 1983), Am. Inst. Chemists (life), Assn. Clin. Scientists (emeritus), Am. Coll. Forensic Examiners (life, Golden Eagle award 1996); mem. AMA, Am. Chem. Soc. (sr., emeritus mem. com. clin. chemistry), Am. Assn. Clin. Chemistry (emeritus, past pres., chmn. com. constn. & bylaws, assn. parliamentarian, Outstanding Clin. Chemist award Tex. sect. 1981, Past Pres.'s award 1986, Presdl. citation 1992, award for outstanding contbn. to clin. chemistry 1996), Indian Acad. Forensic Scis. (hon. life), Southwestern Assn. Forensic Scientists (charter, emeritus), Internat. Assn. Forensic Toxicologists (founding mem.), Internat. Assn. of Chiefs of Police (life), Internat. Assn. Forensic Scis. (charter), Internat. Soc. Clin. Forensic Medicine (founding mem.), Acad. Clin. Lab. Physicians and Scientists (emeritus), Biomed. Engring. Soc. (founding mem./emeritus), Rsch. Soc. Alcoholism (emeritus), Soc. Forensic Toxicologists (charter, emeritus), Soc. Toxicology (emeritus), U. Okla. Univ. Club, Ind. Univ. Club, Phi Lambda Upsilon, Sigma Xi. Avocations: horology, photography, music, travel. Office: PO Box 7245 Oklahoma City OK 73153-1245 Business E-Mail: kurt-dubowski@ouhsc.edu.

DUCA, MICHAEL GERARD, bishop; b. Dallas, June 5, 1952; BA in Psychology with honors, Holy Trinity Sem., U. Dallas; MDiv, Holy Trinity Sem., Univ. Dallas; degre in Canon Law, U. St. Thomas Angelicum, Rome, 1996. Ordained priest Diocese of Dallas, 1978, dir. Office for On-going Formation of Priests, vocations dir., 1985—92; assoc. pastor All Saints, St. Patrick & St. Luke Parishes; campus minister Southern Methodist U., 1985—92; rector Holy Trinity Sem., Dallas, 1996—2008; ordained bishop, 2008; bishop Diocese of Shreveport, La., 2008—. Roman Catholic. Office: Diocese of Shreveport 3500 Fairfield Ave Shreveport LA 71104 Office Phone: 318-222-2006. Office Fax: 318-222-2080.

DUCE, ROBERT ARTHUR, atmospheric chemist, oceanographer, educator; b. Midland, Ont., Can., Apr. 9, 1935; s. Leonard Arthur and Irma Harriet (Gynn) Duce; m. Mary Elizabeth Untz, June 8, 1968; children: Patricia Jean, David Robert. BA cum laude, Baylor U., 1957; postgrad., U. Colo., 1954; PhD in Inorganic and Nuclear Chemistry, MIT, 1964. Teaching asst. dept. chemistry MIT, Cambridge, Mass., 1961-62, rsch. asst. in geochemistry, 1962-63, USPHS predoctoral fellow in air pollution, 1963-64, rsch. assoc. dept. geology and geophysics, 1964-65; from asst. prof. to assoc. prof. chemistry U. Hawaii, Honolulu, 1965-70; assoc. prof. oceanography U. R.I., Kingston, 1970-73, prof. oceanography, 1973-91, dir. Ctr. for Atmospheric Chemistry Studies, 1981-91, dean Grad. Sch. Oceanography, vice provost marine affairs, 1987-91; prof. oceanography and atmospheric scis. Tex. A&M U., College Station, 1991—2004, disting. prof. oceanography and atmospheric scis., 2004—, dean coll. geosciences and maritime studies, 1991-97. Participant disting. lecture series US-USSR Joint Working Group Effects Marine Pollution, 1974; vis. prof. Inst. Marine Scis., U. Tex., Pt. Aransas, 1975, U. East Anglia, Norwich, England, vis. prof. environ. scis., 1997—98; vis. scientist aeronomy lab. NOAA Environ. Rsch. Labs., Boulder, 1977; collaborateur entragner CFR/Nat. Ctr. Sci. Rsch., Gif-sur-Yvette, France, 1976—77; William Evans vis. prof. chemistry U. Otago, Dunedin, New Zealand, 1983; mem. bd. atmospheric scis. and climate NAS/NRC, 1982—86, 1989—93, mem. com. atomospheric chemistry, 1987—90, chmn. com. haze nat. pks. and wilderness areas, 1990—93, chair panel global tropospheric chemistry, 1982—85, mem. ocean studies bd., 2001—07, chair, 2012—, chair com. reviewing US Ocean Sci. Decadal Plan, 2006; sr. vis. fellow Nat. Environ. Rsch. Coun., England, 1984; mem. UN Group Experts Sci. Aspects Marin Environ. Protection, 1986—93, chmn., 2000—03, vice chmn., 2003—06; mem. sci. com. Internat. Geosphere-Biosphere, 2005—11; program bd. govs. Joint Oceanog. Insts., 1987—97, vice chair, 1990—91, Consortium Oceanog. Rsch. and Edn., 1994—97; trustee Univ. Corp. Atmospheric Rsch., 1986—93; mem. exec. com. Ocean Drilling Program, 1987—97, Nat. Assn. State Univs. and Land Grant Colls. Bd. Oceans and Atmospheres, 1993—97; mem. adv. com. geosciences NSF, 1994—97; pres. Internat. Assn. Meterology and Atmosphere Scis., 1995—99; mem. Nat. Sea Grant Rev. Panel, 2000—09; co-chair Com. Evaluate Sci. Ocean Driling, 2009—11; mem. Program Adv. Com. Ocean Observatories Initiative, 2008—12, GEOTRACES Adv. Com., 2010—13, Ocean Rsch. Adv. Panel. Contbr. articles to profl. jours. Capt. USAF, 1957—61. Recipient Rosenstiel award, 1990. Fellow: AAAS (chmn. sect. atmospheric and hydrospheric scis. 1987—88, mem. coun. 1990—93), Oceanography Soc. (pres. 1996—98), Am. Geophys. Union, Am. Meteorol. Soc. (mem. coun. 1988—91); mem.: ICSU (pres. sci. com. oceanic rsch. 2000—04, past. pres. 2004—08), Internat. Coun. Sci., Am. Geol. Inst., Geochem. Soc., Am. Chem. Soc. (chmn.-elect Hawaiian sect. 1969), Sigma Xi, Alpha Chi. Avocation: travel. Office: Tex A&M U Dept Oceanography College Station TX 77843-3146 Home: 145 Pioneer Passage Bastrop TX 78602 Home Phone: 512-549-3626; Office Phone: 979-229-3821. Home Fax: 512-549-3626. Business E-Mail: rduce@ocean.tamu.edu.

DUCEY, MICHAEL E., chemicals executive; b. Columbus, Ohio, Aug. 12, 1948; s. Robert L. and Ruth E. (Elliott) D.; m. Carol J. Starks, June 5, 1971; 1 child, Rebecca Jane. BA, Otterbein Coll., 1970; MBA, U. Dayton, 1980. Sales rep. Dun & Bradstreet Corp., Columbus, Ohio, 1970-73, Borden Agrl. Group, Columbus, 1973-75; fin. analyst Borden Chem., Inc., Columbus, 1975-78, planning supr., 1978-80, mgr., comm. devel., 1980-84, dir., planning, 1984-87; gen. sales mgr. Borden Adhesives & Resins N.Am., Columbus, 1987-92, dir. of mktg., 1992-94, dir., sales & mktg., N.Am., 1994—97; exec. v.p., COO Borden Chem., Inc., 1997—99, pres., CEO, 1999—2002; pres., CEO & bd. dirs. Compass Minerals International, Inc., 2002—06, cons., 2006—; operating ptnr. Apollo Management, 2006—; chmn. TPC Group, Inc., 2009—. Bd. dirs. UAP Holding Corp, 2006—08, Verso Paper Corp., 2007—, Smurfit-Stone Container Corp., 2010—. Dir. Ctrl. Ohio Lung Assn., Columbus, 1988. Mem. Masons, Columbus Athletic Club, Bellevue Athletic Club, Bear Creek C. of C. Republican. Avocations: golf, hunting, reading, physical activities. Office: TPC Group Inc 5151 San Felipe Ste 800 Houston TX 77056-1935 Office Phone: 713-627-7474. Office Fax: 713-626-3650. Business E-Mail: michael.ducey@tpcgrp.com.

DUCKETT, RICK, men's college basketball coach; b. Winston-Salem, NC, Aug. 3, 1957; m. Miller Letitia Duckett; children: Philip, Keigan. BEd, U. NC, Chapel Hill, 1979, MEd, 1980. Grad. asst. coach U. NC Tarheels, 1979—80; asst. coach Harvard U. Crimson, 1980—82, RJ Reynolds HS, Winston-Salem, 1982—83, 1992—93, Jacksonville U. Dolphins, Fla., 1983—84, U. SC Gamecocks, 1984—85, 2001—07, U. Ctrl. Fla. Knights, 1985—86, Wichita State U. Shockers, 1986—92; head coach Fayetteville State U. Broncos, 1993—98, Winston-Salem State U. Rams, 1998—2001, Grambling State U. Tigers, 2008—09; color analyst U. NC Greensboro basketball Sta. WZTK-FM 101.1, 2009—11; asst. coach Tenn. State U. Tigers, 2011—. Former dir. U. SC Offensive Skills Camp. Recipient Coaches award, CIAA Tournament, 1999, 2000; named South Atlantic Coach of Yr., NCAA Divsn. II, 1999. Office: Tennessee State University Basketball Program 3500 John A Merritt Blvd Nashville TN 37209 Office Phone: 615-963-5899. Business E-Mail: rduckett@tnstate.edu.

DUDENHEFER, L. MARK, state legislator; b. Metairie, La., Sept. 25, 1952; m. LaVera Kay Brooks; children: Christian, Rebecca Craven. BS in Economics, La. State U., 1974; MBA, Tulane U., 1987; MCIS, U. Phoenix, 2000. Mem. Stafford County Bd. Supervisors, Va., 2006—11, chmn. Va., 2010—11; mem. Dist. 2 Va. House of Delegates, 2012—, mem. Edn. Com., Transp. Com. & Sci. and Tech. Com. Chmn. Fredericksburg Area Metro Planning Orgn., Quantico Growth Mgmt. Com. Republican. Office: General Assembly Building PO Box 406 Richmond VA 23218 also: PO Box 1570 Stafford VA 22555 Office Phone: 804-698-1002. Office Fax: 804-698-6702. E-mail: DelMDudenhefer@House.virginia.gov.

DUDGEON, MIKE, state legislator; b. Dec. 06; m. Lori; children: Matthew, Daniel, Brandon. B in Elec. Engring., M in Elec. Engring., Ga. Inst. Tech., Atlanta. Tech. profl. Radiant Systems; co-founder Tier One, 2001; co-founder, chief tech. officer Qualia Labs, 2007—; dir. rsch. Hi-Rez Studios; mem. Forsyth County Bd. Edn., 2007—10; mem. Dist. 24 Ga. House Of Representatives, 2011—. Republican. Office: Ga House of Reps 608 Coverdell Legis Office Bldg Atlanta GA 30334 Office Phone: 404-656-0298. Business E-Mail: mike.dudgeon@house.ga.gov.

DUDLEY, GARY EDWARD, psychologist; b. Columbus, Ohio, July 19, 1947; s. Ray Leonard and Mary Virginia (Russi) D.; children: Michelle Denise, Karen Elizabeth. BS, Ohio State U., 1969; MS, U. Miami, 1972, PhD, 1975. Lic. psychologist, Ga., Fla. Tchr. Columbus Pub. Schs., 1969—70; intern in clin. psychology Mt. Zion Hosp. and Med. Ctr., San Francisco, 1972—73; clin. psychologist Met. Dade County Jail, Miami, Fla., 1974—76, Southeast Inst. Criminal Justice, Miami, 1974—76, Ga. So. U., Statesboro, 1976—80; pvt. practice Marietta, Ga., 1980—. Cons. Child Devel. Ctr., Ga. Psycho-Ednl. Network, Atlanta; bd. dirs. svcs. Atlanta Area Psychol. Assocs., PC; pres. Accurate Assessment Svcs. Atlanta. Contbr. articles to profl. jours. NIMH fellow, 1971, 73, VA fellow, 1971. Mem. APA, Nat.

Acad. Neuropsychologists, Am. Bd. Med. Psychotherapists, Southeastern Psychol. Assn., Ga. Psychol. Assn., Nat. Honor Soc. Psychology, Sigma Xi. Office: Doctors Bldg/Windy Hill 2520 Windy Hill Rd Ste 203 Marietta GA 30067-8650 Home Phone: 404-358-1571; Office Phone: 770-953-6401. Personal E-mail: ged69@hotmail.com.

DUDLEY, JULIA CAMPBELL, prosecutor; b. Va., 1960; married; 1 child. BA in Environmental Sci., U. Va., 1982; JD, Mercer U., 1985. Law clerk to Hon. Glen M. Williams US Dist. Ct. (we. dist.) Va., 1985—86, pro se law clk. for judges and magistrates, 1986—88; asst. US atty. (we. dist.) Va. US Dept. Justice, 1988—95, civil atty. Roanoke, 1995—2001, civil chief, 2001—06, 1st asst. US atty. (we. dist.) Va., 2006—, acting US atty. (we. dist.) Va., 2008—09. Office: US Attys Office 310 First St SW Rm 906 Roanoke VA 24011 Office Phone: 540-857-2250. Office Fax: 540-857-2614.

DUDMAN, BRYAN L., energy executive; BBA, Tex. A&M U., Kingsville, 1978. Sr. v.p. World Wide Ops., Smith Tool Divsn., 1993—94, Western Hemisphere Ops. MI Swaco, 1994—2005; joined Smith Internat., 1979; pres., Smith Svcs. Smith International, Inc., 2006—08, exec. v.p.; pres. Drilling and Evaluation, 2008—10, Schlumberger DTR, 2010—. Bd. dirs. Tex. Gulf Coast Chpt. Cystic Fibrosis Found. Mem.: Petroleum Equipment Suppliers Assn. (bd. dirs.), Soc. Petroleum Engrs., Internat. Assn. Drilling Contractors, Am. Assn. Drilling Engrs. Office: Smith International Inc 16740 E Hardy Rd Houston TX 77032 Office Phone: 281-443-3370. Office Fax: 281-233-5199. Business E-Mail: BDudman@smith.com.

DUER, WALTER M., retired corporate financial executive; Degree in Bus. Adminstrn., Wagner Coll., Staten Island, NY; attended, Pace U., Pleasantville, NY. CPA. Nat. mng. ptnr. bus. integration & divestiture practice KPMG LLP, 1968—2004, ret., 2004. Bd. dirs. HCC Ins. Holdings, Inc., 2004—. Mem.: AICPA, Tex. Soc. CPA's. Office: HCC Insurance Holdings Inc 13403 NW Freeway Houston TX 77040 Office Phone: 713-690-7300. Office Fax: 713-462-2401.

DUERR, DAVID, civil engineer; b. Newark, July 4, 1953; s. Warren August and Dorothy (Lanzillo) D.; m. Roberta Kay Apolant, Oct. 12, 1991. B of Engring., Pratt Inst., 1975; MS, U. Houston, 1985. Registered profl. engr. Project engr. Hoffman Internat., Pt. Newark, N.J., 1974-76; chief engr. Williams Crane & Rigging, Richmond, Va., 1976-79; sr. structural engr. Hudson Engring. Corp., Houston, 1980-86; pres. 2DM Assocs., Inc., Houston, 1986—. Frequent lectr. constrn. industry seminars. Contbr. tech. papers to profl. jours. Mem.: ASME (vice chair BTH stds. com. on below-the-hook lifting devices, mem. B30.1 subcom., B30.20 subcom.), ASCE, Specialized Carriers and Rigging Assn., Soc. Automotive Engrs., Am. Coun. Engring. Cos. Achievements include research in the design of pinned connections and development of standards for the design of telescopic hydraulic gantries. Office: 2DM Assocs Inc 9235 Katy Freeway Ste 350 Houston TX 77024-1526

DUFF, WILLIAM GRIERSON, electrical engineer, educator; b. Alexandria, Va., Dec. 16, 1936; s. Johnnie Douglas and Annetta Osceola (Rind) D.; m. Sandra K. Via, June 25, 1983; children: Warren David, Valerie Lynn, Dawn Elizabeth, Deborah Arleen, Kelly Juanita. BEE, George Washington U., 1959, postgrad., 1959-72; MS, Syracuse U., 1969; DSc in Elec. Engring., Clayton U., 1977. Pres. SEMTAS, Fairfax, Va., 1959—. Asst. prof. Capitol Inst. Tech., Greenbelt, Md., 1972—; instr. Interference Control Technologies, Don White Cons., Inc., Gainesville, Va. Author: EMI Handbook, vol. 5, EMI Prediction and Analysis Techniques, 1972, Mobile Communications, 1976, Fundamentals of EMC, 1988, EMC in Telecommunications, 1988; contbr. articles to profl. jours. Counselor Meth. Sr. High Youth Group, 1965-73. Recipient Good Citizenship award DAR, 1955, Math. award George Washington H.S., Alexandria, 1955. Fellow IEEE (pres. EMC Soc., assoc. editor group newsletter 1970—); mem. AIEE (Best Paper award 1961), George Washington U. Engring. Alumni Assn. (pres. 1963-64, Engring. Alumni Svc. award 1980), Springfield Golf and Country Club, Occoquan Water Ski Club (pres. 1976), Sigma Tau, Theta Tau. Home and Office: SEMTAS 7601 S Valley Dr Fairfax Station VA 22039 Office Phone: 703-598-2469. Personal E-mail: wmduff@cox.net.

DUFFEY, WILLIAM SIMON, JR., federal judge; b. Phila., May 9, 1952; s. William Simon and Elinor (Daniluk) D.; m. Betsy Byars, Dec. 17, 1977; children: Charles, Scott. BA with honors in English, Drake U., Des Moines, Iowa, 1973; JD cum laude, U. SC, 1977. Bar: SC 1977, Ga. 1982, US Dist. Ct. (no., mid. and so. dists.) Ga. 1982, US Ct. Appeals (llth cir.) 1983, US Supreme Ct., 1992. Atty. Nexson, Pruet, Jacobs & Pollard, Columbia, SC, 1977-78; assoc. King & Spalding, LLP, Atlanta, 1981—87, ptnr., 1987—94, 1995—2001; dep. ind. counsel Office of the Ind. Counsel, Little Rock, 1994-95; US Atty. (No. dist.) Ga. US Dept. Justice, Atlanta, 2002—04; judge US Dist. Ct. (no. dist.) Ga., Atlanta, 2004—. Adj. prof. U. SC Law Sch., 2000—01; mem. com. on civil justice Ga. Supreme Ct., 2006—. Articles editor SC Lawyer, 1990-94. Pres. Pine Hills Civic Assn., Atlanta, 1984-88; trustee Drake U.; Ga. Rep. Found., Leadership Atlanta; bd. dirs. Ga. Wilderness Inst., 1992-2001, AETV, Atlanta; mem. Peachtree Rd. Race Com., 1993-2002, chmn. Ga. Good Govt. Com., 1995-2001; chmn. bd. advisors Coverdell Leadership Inst., 1995-2002; bd. mem. North Ga. Walk to Emmaus, 1999-2001; founder New Century Forum. Asst. staff judge advocate USAF, 1978—81. Mem. Altanta Bar Assn. (chmn. alt. dispute resolution com. 1984-88), Lawyers Club, Atlanta Track Club (gen. counsel 1993-2001). Methodist. Avocations: running, cooking, woodturning. Office: US Dist Ct No Dist Ga 1721 US Courthouse 75 Spring St SW Atlanta GA 30303-3309

DUFFIN, NEIL W., oil industry executive; b. St. Andrews, Scotland; BS in Mech. Engring., Heriot Watt U. Joined Mobil Oil Co., 1979, producing advisor Europe and Africa Fairfax, Va., 1992—95, ops. and no. North Sea mgr. Aberdeen, Scotland, 1995—98, sr. v.p. Mobil Oil Indonesia, 1998; v.p. ExxonMobil Development Co., exec. v.p., 2006—07, pres., 2007—; v.p. Africa ExxonMobil Prodn. Co., 2004. Office: Exxon Mobil Corp 5959 Las Colinas Blvd Irving TX 75039

DUFFNER, LEE R., ophthalmologist; b. June 3, 1936; m. Alvina Bross, Aug. 31, 1957; children: Fay, Rachel, Tamar. BS Engring., Purdue U., 1957; MS Physiology, Marquette U., Milw., 1961; MD, Med. Coll. Wis., 1962. Diplomate Am. Bd. Ophthalmology. Intern Stanford U., 1962—63; resident U. Miami, Fla., 1966—69; practice medicine specializing in ophthalmology Hollywood, Fla., 1969—; clin. prof. ophthalmology U. Miami Sch. Medicine, 1969—; dir. Am. Bd. Ophthalmology, 1995—2002, chmn., 2002. Pres. town coun. Town of Golden Beach, Fla., 1983—95. Capt. USAF, 1963—66. Fellow: ACS, Am. Acad. Ophthalmology; mem.: Miami Ophthal. Soc. (pres. 1983—84). Avocation: racewalking. Home: 185 Ocean Blvd Golden Beach FL 33160-2208 Office: 2740 Hollywood Blvd Hollywood FL 33020-4826 Office Phone: 954-925-2740.

DUFFY, EARL GAVIN, hotel executive; b. Boston, Oct. 11, 1926; s. William Emmett and Mary Irene (Costello) D.; m. Bernice Rose MacMaster, Feb. 14, 1948; children— Earl Gavin, Joan Irene, Mark Charles, Neil William, Lynn Anne. Student public schs., Boston. In various hotel positions, Boston, 1941-52; sales mgr. Somerset Hotel, Boston, 1952-56; eastern sales mgr. Hotel Corp. Am., Boston, 1956-59, asst. nat. sales mgr., 1959-61, nat. sales mgr., 1961-64; v.p., gen. mgr. Hotel America, Houston, 1964-67, Hartford, Conn., 1967-69, Royal Sonesta Hotel, New Orleans, 1969-71, Soneta Beach Hotel, Key Biscayne, Fla., 1971-76, Boston Park Plaza Hotel, 1977-80; pres. Earl G. Duffy & Assos., 1981—. Guest lectr. Cornell U., 1961, U. Houston, 1965, Wash. State U., 1966, Fla. Internat. U., 1971-76; pres. Greater Hartford Conv. and Visitor's Bur., 1969 Chmn. div. bus. and industry Harris County (Tex.) March of Dimes, 1964-67; pres. New Orleans Jazz Festival, 1970-71. Served with USN, 1943-46. Recipient Golden Host award Wash. State U., 1964 Mem. Skal Club, Am. Hotel and Motel Assn., Hotel Sales Mgmt. Assn. Internat., Greater Boston Hotel and Motor Inn Assn., Mass. Hotel and Motel Assn., New Eng. Innkeepers Assn., Boston Exec. Club. Clubs: Rotary. Roman Catholic. Home and Office: 600 Three Islands Blvd 1503 Hallandale Beach FL 33009

DUFFY, JOHN CHARLES, psychiatrist, educator, consultant; b. Cleve., June 19, 1934; s. John Joseph and Hannah (McIllwee) D.; m. Francoise C. Antonini; children: Charles, Robert, John. Grad., Boston Coll., 1956; MD, N.Y. Med. Coll., 1960. Intern Henry Ford Hosp., Detroit, 1960-61; resident Mayo Clinic, Rochester, Minn., 1963-67; exec. dir. Tucson Child Guidance Ctr., 1971-74; commd. med. officer USPHS, 1974; prof., assoc. chmn. Uniformed Svcs. U. Sch. Medicine, Bethesda, Md., 1974-81; assoc. commr. health affairs FDA, cons. Surgeon Gen., Rockville, Md., 1981-88; asst. surgeon gen. USPHS, 1983-92, chief physician officer, 1983-88; dir. C. Everett Koop Inst. Dartmouth Coll., Hanover, NH, 1992-94; prof. psychiatry Uniformed Svcs. U. Sch. Medicine, Bethesda, 1981-94, clin. prof., 1994—. Nat. and internat. surveyor Joint Commn. on Accreditation of Healthcare Orgns., 1998-2012; founder Integrative Healthcare Solutions; internat. med. cons. Joint Comm. Internat.; prof. U. Ctrl. Fla. Sch. Medicine, 2010-. Author: Psychiatric Morbidity of Physicians, 1964, Psychiatric Issues in the Lives of Physicians, 1966, Child Psychiatry, 1972, 86, Psychiatric Reviews, 1976; founding editor-in-chief Child Psychiatry and Human Devel., 1970-83; editor: Ship's Medical Chest, 1984; mem. editl. bd. MD mag., 1976—. Recipient OutstandingSvc. medal Bd. Regents Uniformed Svcs. U., 1981, Surgeon Gen.'s medallion. Fellow Am. Psychiat. Assn. (life), Aerospace Med. Assn. (assoc.; Longacre medal); mem. Assn. Mil. Surgeons U.S., Sigma Xi. Catholic. Home: 2402 Golf Vista Blvd Viera FL 32955 Office Phone: 638-268-2900. Personal E-mail: jcduffy34@hotmail.com. Business E-Mail: jduffy@medscorp-p.com.

DUFFY, NORMAN VINCENT, chemistry professor; b. Washington, Nov. 1, 1938; s. Norman Vincent and Glenn Mae (Drury) D.; m. Marianne Youdell, Oct. 13, 1962; children: Norman Vincent III, Mary Virginia, Joseph Leslie, Anne-Marie, Maureen Glenn. BS in Chemistry, Georgetown U., 1961, PhD in Chemistry, 1966. NATO postdoctoral fellow chemistry dept. Univ. Coll. London, 1965—66; vis. asst. prof. Kent State U., Ohio, 1966—67, asst. prof. chemistry, 1967—70, assoc. prof., 1970—80, asst. dean arts and scis., 1973—75, assoc. dean, 1975—76, prof. chemistry dept., 1980—96, chmn. dept. chemistry, 1981—86; prof. chemistry Wheeling Jesuit U., 1996—, chmn. dept. biology and chemistry, 1996—2000, chmn. dept. chemistry, 2000—02. Contbr. articles to encys.; prodr. ednl. films in field. Recipient US Prof. of Yr. award, Carnegie Found. for Advancement of Tchg. and Coun. for Advancement and Support of Edn., 2006. Mem. Am. Chem. Soc., The Chem. Soc., Sigma Xi. Roman Catholic. Office: Dept Chemistry Wheeling Jesuit U Wheeling WV 26003 Office Phone: 304-243-4430. E-mail: nduffy@wju.edu.

DUFFY, PATRICK MICHAEL, federal judge; b. Charleston, SC, 1943; BA, The Citadel, 1965; JD, U. S.C., 1968. Bar: S.C., U.S. Dist. Ct. S.C., U.S. Claims Ct., U.S. Ct. Internat. Trade, U.S. Tax Ct., U.S. Ct. Appeals (4th cir.), U.S. Supreme Ct. Asst. county atty. Charleston (S.C.) County, 1973-74; ptnr. Hollings & Hawkins; prin. McNair Law Firm; judge US Dist. Ct. SC, Charleston, 1995—2009, sr. judge, 2009—. With U.S. Army, 1969-71. Mem. ABA, Def. Rsch. Inst., Am. Bd. Trial Advocates (Charleston chpt. pres. 1991, rep. 1988-91), S.C. Bar Assn., S.C. Def. Lawyers Assn., Charleston County Bar Assn. Office: US Dist Ct PO Box 835 Charleston SC 29402-0835 Fax: 843-579-1469.

DUFFY, THOMAS M., transportation services executive, lawyer; b. 1961; BBA, JD, U. Ga. Bar: 1986. Assoc. Peterson Dillard Young Asselin & Powell LLP, 1986—94, ptnr., 1994—97, Troutman Sanders LLP, Atlanta, 1997—98; v.p. Allied Holdings, Inc., Decatur, Ga., 1998—2000, gen. counsel, 1998—, sec., 1998—, sr. v.p., 2000—04, exec. v.p., 2004—. Office: Allied Systems Holdings 2302 Parklake DR NE STE 600 Atlanta GA 30345-2918 Office Phone: 404-373-4285. Office Fax: 404-370-4206.

DUGAS, DAVID ROY, lawyer, former prosecutor; b. New Iberia, La., July 4, 1953; s. Claude Anthony and Gladys Marie (Hippler) D.; m. Dolores Ann Broussard, Mar. 22, 1974; children: Brandy Nicole, Kelly Ann, Mary Katherine. JD, La. State U., 1978. Bar: La. 1978, US Dist. Ct. (mid. dist.) La. 1978, US Dist. Ct. (we. dist.) 1980, US Ct. Appeals (5th cir.) 1981, US Dist. Ct. (ea. dist.) 1984. Assoc. Sanders, Downing, Kean & Cazedessus, Baton Rouge, 1978-80; from assoc. to ptnr. Caffery, Oubre, Dugas & Campbell, New Iberia, 1980—2000; US atty. (mid. dist.) La. US Dept. Justice, 2001—10; of counsel McGlinchey Stafford PLLC, Baton Rouge, 2010—. Dir. Nat. Ctr. for Disaster Fraud US Dept. Justice, 2005—10, exec. dir. Hurricane Katrina Fraud Task Force, 2005—10, co-chmn. Environmental Crimes Policy Com., 2006—10, chair Atty. General's Environmental Issues Advisory Subcommittee, 2006—10. Editor La. State U. Law Rev., 1977. Chmn. Iberia Parish Reps., 1984, Dist. H delegation to Rep. State Convention, 1984. Named US Atty. of the Yr., Fed. Law Enforcement Officers Assn., 2005. Mem. ABA, La. Bar Assn., Iberia Parish Bar Assn., La. Assn. Def. Counsel (bd. dirs. 1985—), Order of Coif, Phi Kappa Phi, Omicron Delta Kappa. Lodges: Kiwanis. Republican. Roman Catholic. Avocations: golf, sailing. Office: McGlinchey Stafford PLLC 301 Main St One American Pl 4th Fl Baton Rouge LA 70825 Office Phone: 225-382-3732. Office Fax: 225-343-3076. E-mail: ddugas@mcglinchey.com.

DUGGAN, CAROL COOK, research and development company executive; b. Dillon, SC, May 25, 1946; d. Pierce Embree and Lillian Watkins (Eller) Cook; m. Kevin Duggan, Dec. 29, 1973. BA, Columbia Coll., 1968; MS, U. Ky., Lexington, 1970. Reference asst. Richland County Pub. Libr., Columbia, SC, 1968—69, asst. to dir., 1970, chief adult svcs., 1971—82; dir. Maris Rsch., Columbia, 1982—. Lectr. Greater Columbia Literacy Coun., SC, 1973—75. Author: A History of the City of Forest Acres, S.C., 1998. Treas. Friends of S.C. Libr., 1995—2003; mem. zoning bd. appeals City of Forest Acres, 1999—; worship com. Washington St. United Meth. Ch., Columbia, SC, 1985—86, 1999—2010, mem. staff-parish rels. com., 1985—91, 2004—07, chmn. staff-parish rels. com., 1993, trustee, 1995—98, mem. adminstr. bd., 1983—86, mem. adminstr. br., 1988—91, mem. adminstr. bd., 1993, mem. ch. coun., 2004—09; exec. bd. United Meth. Women, 1983—2001, treas. unit 7, 1989—91, pres. unit 5, 1992—97, treas., 1998—2010; adminstrv. bd. Washington St. United Meth. Ch., Columbia, SC, 1988—91, 1993; del. SC Ann. Conf. United Meth. Ch., 2004—09. Recipient Sternheimer award, Columbia Coll., 1968. Mem.: PEO (pres. 1983—85, chmn. amendments and recommendations com. 1983—85, historian 1986—87, treas. state conv. 1987—88, historian 1990—92, v.p. 1998—99, del. internat. conv. 1999, historian 2002—), DAR, ALA (chmn. state membership com. 1979—83, councilor 1980—82), SC Pub. Libr. Assn. (pres. 1980—81), SC Libr. Assn. (sec. 1976, exec. bd. 1976, 1978—82), Columbia Coll. Alumnae Assn. (alumnae coun. spl. events com. 1996—, Columbia Coll. Commn. 150 2003, mem. exec. com. 2007—09), Beta Phi Mu. Methodist. Home: 2101 Woodmere Dr Columbia SC 29204-4341 Personal E-mail: icc3612@gmail.com.

DUGGAN, JAMES EDGAR, law librarian, law educator; b. Roanoke, Va., Mar. 24, 1961; s. Daniel David and Margaret Candler (Mallonee) Duggan. BA, Va. Tech., 1983; JD, U. Miss., 1986; MLIS, La. State U., 1987. Bar: Miss. 1987, US Dist. Ct. (southern dist.) Miss., US Ct. Appeals (5th cir.). Ref. libr. So. Ill. U. Sch. Law, Carbondale, 1988—90, from asst. prof. to assoc. prof., 1988—98, computer svcs. libr., 1990—98, dir. info. tech., 1998—2006, prof., 1998—2008, assoc. dir., 2006—08; dir. Law Library, assoc. prof. law Tulane U. Law Sch., New Orleans, 2008—13; asst. editor Law Libr. Jour., 2012—13, editor, 2013—. Del. Synergy The Ill. Libr. Leadership Initiative, 2005, del. Leadership Carbondale class 2006, 2006; pres. bd. trustees Carbondale Pub. Libr., 2001—05, trustee, 1998—2007; trustees Shawnee Libr. Sys., 2001—04, pres. bd. trustees, 2002—03. Scholar West Pub. Co., 1987. Mem.: La. Academic Libr. Info. Network Consort (exec. bd. mem. 2012—13, chair elect 2013—14), Assn. Am. Law Schs. Sect. Law Libr. & Legal Intro. (vice chair 2012—13, chair 2013—14, past chair 2014—), New Orleans Assn. Law Librs. (v.p. 2011—12, pres. 2012—13), La. State U. Sch. Libr. and Info. Sci. (La. State U. Outstanding Alumnus award 2009), Mid-Am. Assn. Law Librs., American Assn. Law Librs. (chair coun. chpt. pres. 1999, exec. bd. 2001—04, v.p., pres.-elect 2007—08, exec. bd. 2007—10, pres. 2008—09, past pres. 2009—10, chair Nominations Com. 2011—12, grant New Orleans chpt. 1987, Call for Papers Competition award 1990, Hall of Fame 2014), Miss. State Bar Assn., Order of the Coif, Beta Phi Mu, Pi Kappa Delta, Phi Alpha Delta. Roman Catholic. Office: Tulane University Law School Law Library Weinmann Hall, Room 320-C 6329 Freret St New Orleans LA 70118 Home: 300 Lake Marina Ave Apt 4BW New Orleans LA 70124-1677 Office Phone: 504-865-5950. Business E-Mail: duggan@tulane.edu.

DUGGAN, KEVIN, information technology professional; b. St. Louis, Feb. 29, 1944; s. Leo Patrick and Jean Claire (McHenry) D.; m. Lillian Carol Cook, Dec. 29, 1973. BA, U. S.C., 1977; MA, Webster U., 1988. Cert. black belt Aikido. With S.C. Nat. Bank, Columbia, 1970—79; mgr. tech. support, 1978—79; dir. info. sci. tech. Midlands Tech. Coll., Columbia, 1979—97; faculty mem. Info. Sys. Tech., 1998—2008. Cons. electronic data processing. Mem. Richland County Friends of Libr., Literacy Coun. S.C.; chmn. fin. com. Washington St. Meth. Ch., 1987-90, chmn. stewardship com., 1982-86, mem. evangelism and membership coms., 1982-86, mem. coun. on ministries, 1982-96, mem. exec. com., 1987-90, mem. adminstrv. bd., 1982-96, 99-2001, lay leader, 1992-96, mem. Missions, 1997-99, mem. ch. coun., 2005-09, mem. fin. com., 2005-; del. to SC United Meth. Ch. ann. conf., 2005-09. Served with USMC, 1963-67. Decorated Bronze Star. Mem. Assn. Sys. Mgr., IBM Users Group, Data Processing Mgmt. Assn., Palmetto Fencing Soc., Amateur Fencing League Am., Rotary. Methodist. Office: PO Box 2408 Columbia SC 29202-2408

DUHE, JOHN MALCOLM, JR., retired federal judge, lawyer; b. Iberia Parish, La., Apr. 7, 1933; s. J. Malcolm and Rita (Arnandez) Duhe; children: Kim Duhe Holleman, Jeanne Duhe Sinitier, Edward M., M. Bofill. Student, Washington and Lee U., 1951—53; BBA, Tulane U., 1955, LLB, 1957. Atty. Helm, Simon, Caffery & Duhe, New Iberia, La., 1957—78; dist. judge State of La., New Iberia, 1979—84; judge US Dist. Ct. We. Dist. La., Lafayette, 1984—88, US Ct. Appeals 5th Cir., 1988—99, sr. judge, 1999—2009. Assoc. editor: Tulane Law Rev., 1956, editor-in-chief:, 1967. Mem.: Omicron Delta Kappa, Order of Coif, Kappa Delta Phi. Home: PO Box 3548 Lafayette LA 70502-3548

DUKE, ELAINE COSTANZO, consulting firm executive, former federal agency administrator; b. Ohio, 1958; d. Frank Costanzo. BS in Bus. Mgmt., NH Coll.; MBA, Chaminade U., Honolulu. Dep. dir. contracting & property mgmt. Smithsonian Instn.; dir. acquisition & grant services Fed. R.R. Adminstrn.; contracting officer USAF; dep. dir. contracting dept. Pub. Works. Ctr. Dept. Navy, US Dept. Def., Pearl Harbor, Hawaii, staff asst. sec. installations and environ., dep. dir. hull, mech. and elec. divsn. in Contracts Directorate Naval Sea Sys. Command, dir. office contract policy; dep. asst. adminstr. Transp. Security Adminstrn., 2002—04; dep. chief procurement officer US Dept. Homeland Security, 2004—06, dep. under sec. for mgmt, 2007—08, under sec. for mgmt., 2008—10; owner, prin. Elaine Duke & Associates, LLC, Woodbridge, 2010—. Bd. dirs. Western Fairfax Christian Ministries, 2010—. Recipient Presdl. Meritorious Rank award, 2007, Silver Medal for Customer Svc., Transp. Security Adminstrn. (TSA), Comdr. Award for Pub. Svc., Dept. Army, Secretary Medal, US Dept. Homeland Security, Disting. Pub. Svc. award, USCG. Office: Elaine Duke & Associates LLC 462 Belmont Bay Dr Woodbridge VA 22191 Office Phone: 703-402-4432. E-mail: elaine@edukeassociates.com.

DUKE, J. RICHARD, lawyer; BSBA, Auburn U.; LLM in Taxation, U. Miami Sch. Law; JD, Samford U. Cumberland Sch. Law. Prin. Duke Law Firm, Birmingham, Ala. Mem. adv. bd. Am. Internat. Depository & Trust, Denver; adj. prof. law Samford U. Cumberland Sch. Law, 1983—99; prof. law Walter H. & Dorothy B. Diamond Grad. Internat. Tax Prog. Thomas Jefferson Sch. Law (formerly St. Thomas U. Sch. Law), Miami, Fla.; prof. law Aristotle U. Coll. Law. Co-author: Offshore Tax Strategies; contbg. editor: Tax Havens of the World; contbr. Named one of Top 100 Attys., Worth mag., 2005—06. Fellow: Royal Soc. Fellows; mem.: Ala. State Bar (tax sect.), Fla. Bar (internat. law sect., tax sect.), ABA (tax sect., real property, probate & trust law sect., internat. law and practice sect.), Inter-Am. Bar Assn., Internat. Bar Assn. (sect. on bus. law, com. on taxes), Soc. of Trust and Estate Practitioners, Internat. Tax Planning Assn. Office: Duke Law Firm Pc 1572 Montgomery Hwy Ste 205 Birmingham AL 35216-4520 Office Phone: 205-823-3900. Office Fax: 205-823-2630. E-mail: richard@assetlaw.com.

DUKE, MIKE (MICHAEL TERRY DUKE), retired retail executive; b. Ga., Dec. 7, 1949; m. Susan Duke; 3 children. BS in Indsl. Engring., Ga. Inst. Tech., 1971. With Federated Dept. Stores, May Dept. Stores, Venture Stores; joined Wal-Mart Stores, Inc., 1979, sr. v.p. logistics Bentonville, Ark., 1995—2000, sr. v.p. distbn., exec. v.p. logistics, 2000, exec. v.p. adminstrn., 2000—03, exec. v.p., 2003—05; pres. Wal-Mart Stores USA, 2003—05; vice chmn. Wal-Mart Stores, Inc., Bentonville, Ark., 2005—09, pres., CEO, 2009—14, chmn. exec. com., adv., 2014—; pres., CEO Wal-Mart International, 2005—09. Bd. dirs. Wal-Mart Stores, Inc., 2009—, US-China Bus. Coun. Mem. advisory bd. U. Ark.; bd. dirs. Arvest-Bank of Bentonville. Named one of The Global Elite, Newsweek mag., 2008, The World's Most Powerful People, Forbes mag., 2009—13, The Bus. People of Yr., Fortune mag., 2010. Mem.: NAE, Internat. Mass Retail Assn. (bd. dirs.). Avocation: golf. Office: Wal-Mart Stores Inc 702 SW Eighth St Bentonville AR 72716*

DUKE, STEPHEN OSCAR, physiologist, research scientist, educator; b. Battle Creek, Mich., Oct. 9, 1944; s. Oscar and Azalee Rosa (Tallant) D.; m. Barbara Alice Rowe, June 2, 1967 (div. Dec. 1993); children: Gregory Ivan, Robin Anne; m. Mary Virginia Duke, Jan. 18, 2009. BS, Henderson State U., 1966; MS, U. Ark., 1969; PhD, Duke U., 1975; PhD (hon.), U. Basque Countray Bilbao, 2008. Plant physiologist So. Weed Sci. Lab., USDA, Stoneville, Miss., 1975-84, rsch. leader, 1984-87, lab. dir., 1987-96, rsch. leader Oxford, Miss., 1996—. Adj. prof. U. Miss., Oxford, 1996—. Co-author: Physiology of Herbicide Action, 1993; editor: Weed Physiology, 2 vols., 1985, Pest Control with Enhanced Environmental Safety, 1993, Porphyric Pesticides, 1994, Herbicide Resistant Crops, 1995, Natural Products for Pest Management, 2006; contbr. articles to profl. jours. Lt. US Army, 1968—70, Vietnam. Decorated Bronze Star; recipient Edminster award USDA, 1986, Disting. Alumnus award Henderson State U., 1989, CIBA-GEIGY/Weed Sci. Soc. Am. award CIBA-GEIGY Corp., 1990, Outstanding Sr. Scientist award USDA, Agr. Rsch. Svc., 2001, Extraordinary Prof. award U. Pretoria RSA, 2002-, Molisch award Internat. Allelopathy Soc.; elected Henderson State U. Acad., 2001. Fellow AAAS, Weed Sci. Soc. Am. (assoc. editor 1978-83, pres. 1996, Outstanding Young Scientist award 1984, Outstanding Article award 1984, Rsch. award 1990); mem. Am. Soc. Plant Physiology (chmn. so. sect. 1985-86), Coun. for Agrl. Sci. and Tech. (bd. dirs. 1993-94), Am. Chem. Soc.(Internat. Rsch. award agrochem. divsn. 2004), So. Weed Soc. (pres. 1995, disting. svc. award 1998), Internat. Weed Sci. Soc. (pres. 2000-04), Internat. Allelopathy Soc. (pres. 2008—). Avocations: gardening, writing. Home: 9 Private Rd 3078 Oxford MS 38655 Mailing: PO Box 3964 University MS 38677 Business E-Mail: sduke@olemiss.edu.

DUKES, DAVID E., lawyer; BA in Fin. Mgmt., Clemson U., SC, 1981; JD cum laude, U. SC, 1984. Bar: SC, US Dist. Ct. SC, US Ct. Appeals (4th, 10th, 11th cirs.), US Supreme Ct. Ptnr. Nelson Mullins Riley Scarborough LLP, Columbia, SC, mng. ptnr., chmn. exec. com. Contbr. articles to profl. jours. Bd. dirs. SC Gov. Sch. for Arts Found., SC Gov. Sch. Sci. and Math.; mem. Clemson U. Pres. Adv. Bd. Named one of The Best Lawyers in America, 2001—11. Fellow: American Bar Found.; mem.: DRI (bd. dirs. 2002—, chmn. drug and device law com. 1999—2001, SC state chmn. 1993—97), SC Def. Trial Atty. Assn., Richland County Bar Assn., Internat. Assn. Def. Counsel (chmn. toxic and hazardous substances litig. com. 1996—98, mem. faculty Trial Acad. 1994), US 4th Cir. Jud. Conf. Office: Nelson Mullins Riley Scarborough LLP Meridian 17th Fl 1320 Main St Columbia SC 29201 Office Phone: 803-255-9451. Office Fax: 803-256-7500. Business E-Mail: david.dukes@nelsonmullins.com.

DUKES, DAWNNA, state legislator; b. Austin, Tex., Sept. 3, 1963; BS in Psychology, Tex. A&M U. Owner, bus. resource planning & mktg. cons. DM Dukes and Associates, Inc.; mem. Dist. 50 Tex. House of Representatives, 1995—2002, mem. Dist. 46, 2003—. Mem.: Alpha Kappa Alpha. Democrat. Roman Catholic. Office: Room EXT E1.504 PO Box 2910 Austin TX 78768 Office Phone: 512-463-0506. Office Fax: 512-481-7864.

DUKES, WINFRED J., state legislator; b. Mitchell County, Ga., Sept. 20; s. Sylvester and Willie Beatrice Dukes. B in History, Mercer U., Macon, Ga.; M in Mgmt., Ga. Coll. and State U., Milledgeville. CEO, contractor & realtor Duke, Edwards and Dukes, Inc., Macon; mem. Dist. 150 Ga. House of Reps., 1997—. Democrat. Office: 920 Highland Ave Albany GA 31701 also: Ga House of Reps 411 Coverdell Legis Office Bldg Atlanta GA 30334 Office Phone: 229-883-8537, 404-656-0127. Business E-Mail: winfred.dukes@house.ga.gov.

DULIN, AMY G., lawyer; BA cum laude, Yale U., New Haven, 1988; JD, NYU Sch. Law, NYC, 1992. Bar: NY 1993, Fla. 1996. Ptnr. Hughes, Hubbard & Reed LLP, Miami, co-chair fin. services group, mem. exec. com. Contbr. articles to profl. jours. Named a Leading Lawyer in Latin America Banking and Internat. Fin., Chambers USA, Chambers Latin America, Chambers Global; named one of The Best Lawyers in America, Derivatives Law and Structured Fin. Law, 2008—11; named to The 45 Under 45, The American Lawyer, 2011. Office: Hughes Hubbard & Reed LLP 201 S Biscayane Blvd Ste 2500 Miami FL 33131-4332 Office Phone: 305-373-5664. Office Fax: 305-371-8759. Business E-Mail: dulin@hugheshubbard.com.

DULLUM, MERCEDES K.C., territorial agency administrator; b. Jamaica; m. Robert L. Lechner. BSc in Applied Biology, Ga. Inst. Tech., Atlanta; MD, Med. Coll. Ga. Cert. Nat. Bd. Med. Examiners, American Coll. Cardiology, American Bd. Thoracic Surgeons, lic. physcian Md., Fla. Internship and residency in surgery U. Miss.; residency in thoracic surgery George Wash. U. Med. Ctr., Washington, clin. prof. surgery, Georgetown U. Hosp., Washington; pvt. practice cardiac surgeon Washington; former staff cardiac surgeon, dir. cardiac surgery and med. dir. internat. patient services Cleve. Clinic Fla.; commr. US VI Dept. Health, St. Thomas, 2012—. Expert panel mem. US Food and Drug Adminstrn.; pres. Women in Thoracic Surgery, 2003—05. Contbr. articles to profl. jours. Recipient Award of Excellence, Jamaica Com., 2007; named Washington's Top Cardiac Surgeon, Washington mag., Physician of Yr., South Fla. Bus. Jour., 2005. Mem.: Soc. Thoracic Surgeons, American Coll. Cardiology, American Heart Assn., Alpha Omega Alpha. Office: US Virgin Islands Department of Health 1303 Hospital Ground Ste 10 St Thomas VI 00802

DUMA, RICHARD JOSEPH, epidemiologist, writer, microbiologist, pathologist, physician, researcher, educator; b. Bethlehem, Pa., Apr. 2, 1933; s. Joseph Anthony and Helen Veronica (Bartek) D.; m. Mary Alyce Fridley, Apr. 18, 1957; 1 child, Scott. BA, Va. Poly. Inst., 1955; MD, U. Va., 1959; PhD, Va. Commonwealth U.-Med. Coll. Va., 1978. Diplomate Am. Bd. Internal Medicine; lic. physician, Fla., Va.; lic. pvt. pilot. Intern, resident then chief, medicine U. Ala. Med. Center, Birmingham, 1959-60, 62-65; research fellow Harvard U. Med. Sch.-Mass. Gen. Hosp., 1965-67; mem. faculty Med. Coll. Va., Richmond, 1967-91, chmn. div. infectious diseases, 1974-92, tenured prof. medicine, infectious diseases and pathology, 1975-92, prof. microbiology, 1977-92. Mem. U. S. Pharmacopeia Adv. Panel on Hosp. Practices, 1971-82, chmn. subcom. rsch., 1976-82, clin. prof. medicine and infectious diseases Med. Coll. Richmond, 1992—; exec. dir. Nat. Found. for Infectious Diseases, 1991-94, v.p. bd. dirs., 1973-75, pres., 1975-91, trustee, 1994-2003, bd. dirs., 2004—09; dir. emeritus, 2010-, chmn. Nat. Coalition for Adult Immunization, 1988-94; didr. infectious diseases and infection control Halifax Med. Ctr., Daytona Beach, Fla., 1995-2012, editl. bd. mem., Infectious Diseases Clin. Practice (editl. bd. mem. 2005-). Mem. bd. visitors Embry-Riddle Aero. U., 1999-; editor, rev. panel Immuno Facts Vaccines and Immunologic Drugs, 2005-; mem., hosp. aquired infection adv. bd. Fla. Dept. Health, 2011-. Served with M.C., USNR, 1960-62. Fellow ACP, Infectious Disease Soc. Am., Royal Soc. Tropical Medicine and Hygiene, Am. Soc. Tropical Medicine and Hygiene, Am. Soc. Rickettsiology, Fla. Infectious Disease Soc. (pres. 1997-99, bd. dirs. 1997-), Fla. Dept. Health Hosp. Acquired Infections (adv. bd. mem.); mem. AAAS, Am. Fedn. Clin. Rsch., Am. Soc. Microbiology, Va. Soc. Microbiology, Am. Soc. Internal Medicine, Va. Soc. Internal Medicine, Richmond Soc. Internal Medicine, So. Soc. Clin. Investigation, Am. Thoracic Soc., Royal Soc. Medicine, Med. Soc. Va., Richmond Acad. Medicine, Acad. of Medicine, Washington, Med. Assn. Fla., Volusia Med. Soc., Daytona Beach Rotary Club, Hammock Dunes Golf & Country Club,, Sigma Xi, Tau Beta Pi. Home and Office: 1 Capri Ct Palm Coast FL 32137 Business E-Mail: rjduma@att.net.

DUMITRU, DANIEL, physiatrist; b. Massillon, Ohio; MD, U. Cin., 1980. Diplomate Am. Bd. Phys. Medicine and Rehab. Resident phys. medicine and rehab. VA Hosp., San Antonio, 1980—83; prof. U. Tex. Health Sci. Ctr., San Antonio, 1983—. Attending physician Audie Murphy Vets. Hosp., San Antonio. Mem.: Am. Assn. Neuromuscular and Electrodiagnostic Medicine, Am. Acad. Phys. Medicine and Rehab. (pres. 2002—03). Office: U Tex Health Sci Ctr Dept RM/PMR 7703 Floyd Curl Dr San Antonio TX 78229-3900

DUNAHOO, EMORY WEST, JR., state legislator; Former ptnr. K & D Transp., Oakwood, Ga.; salesman Robinson Harrison Poultry; mem. Dist. 25 Ga. House of Reps., Atlanta, 2011—. Football coach Johnson HS, Ga.; mem. Blackshear Pl. Bapt. Ch.; bd. dirs. Innsbruck Golf Club and Cmty., Helen, Ga. Republican. Office: 4720 Walnut Ln Gainesville GA 30507 also: Ga House of Reps Coverdell Legis Office Bldg Atlanta GA 30334

DUNBAR, LESLIE WALLACE, writer, consultant; b. Lewisburg, W.Va., Jan. 27, 1921; s. Marion Leslie and Minnie (Crickenberger) Lee; m. Peggy Rawls, July 5, 1942 (dec. Nov. 29, 2009); 1 foster child, Nha Van (dec.) children: Linda Dunbar Knox(dec.), Anthony Paul. MA, Cornell U., 1946, PhD, 1948. Asst. prof. polit. sci. Emory U., Atlanta, 1948-51; chief community affairs Savannah River plant AEC, Aiken, SC, 1951-54; asst. prof. polit. sci. Mt. Holyoke Coll., 1955-58; dir. research So. Regional Council, Atlanta, 1958-61, exec. dir., 1961-65; exec. dir., sec. Field Found., NYC, 1965-80; vis. prof. polit. sci. U. Ariz., 1981. Cons. Fund for Peace, Nat. Urban League, 1981-84; sr. project assoc. social welfare policy, 1985-87, Ford Found.; guardian ad litem State of N.C., 1993-2001. Author: A Republic of Equals, 1966, The Common Interest, 1988, Reclaiming Liberalism, 1990, The Shame of Southern Politics, 2002, Looking For The Future, 2012; co-author: Where We Stand, 2004; American Crisis, Southern Solutions, 2008; editor: Minority Report, 1984; book rev. editor So. Changes, 1989-93. Deacon Watts St. Bapt. Ch., Durham, 1998—2001; bd. dirs. Nation Inst., 1980—86, pres., 1980—84; bd. dirs. Village of Pelham Libr. Bd., 1980—84, pres., 1982—84; bd. dirs. Children's Found., 1980—86, pres., 1982—84, Franklin and Eleanor Roosevelt Inst., 1987—2001, v.p., 1987—92; bd. dirs. Eleanor Roosevelt Inst., 1976—87, Field Found., 1978—80, Minority Rights Group, NYC, 1980—85, Ctr. Nat. Security Studies, 1980—87, Amnesty Internat./U.S.A., 1984—86, Winston Found. for World Peace, 1985—89, Voter Edn. Project, 1987—90, N.C. Coun. Chs., 1991—93, Southeastern Efforts Developing Sustainable Spaces, Inc., 1998—2001, Ruth Mott Fund, 1988—99, chair, 1992—94; bd. dirs., mem. selection com. Windcall Resident Program, 1990—94. Guggenheim fellow, 1954-55; United Negro Coll. Fund scholar-at-large, 1984-85. Fellow So. Regional Coun. (life). Home: 150 Broadway St Apt 420 New Orleans LA 70118-7619 E-mail: lesdunbar@earthlink.net.

DUNBAR, W. ROY, information technology executive; b. Jamaica; Grad. in pharmacy, Manchester U., Eng., 1982; MBA, Manchester U. Mgmt. positions Eli Lilly, 1990—99, v.p., info. tech., chief info. officer, 1999—2003, pres., intercontinental region, 2003—04; pres. global tech. & ops. MasterCard Worldwide (subs. of Mastercard, Inc.), Purchase, NY, 2004—08; CEO Network Solutions, Herndon, Va., 2008—09, acting chmn., advisor, 2009—. Bd. dirs. Humana Inc., EDS Corp. Bd. mem. Exec. Leadership Council Found. Named CIO of the Yr., Information Week mag., 2003. Office: Network Solutions 13861 Sunrise Valley Dr Herndon VA 20171 Office Phone: 703-668-4600. Office Fax: 703-668-5888.

DUNCAN, A. BAKER, investment banker; b. Waco, Tex., Dec. 29, 1927; s. A. Baker and Frances (Higginbotham) Duncan; m. Sally P Witt, Jan. 31, 1953; children: Addison Baker III, Richard Witt, Andrew Prescott. Grad., Woodberry Forest Sch., Va., 1945; BA, Yale U., 1949; MA, U. Tex., 1952. Master Hill Sch., Pottstown, Pa., 1949-51; ptnr. Rotan Mosle & Co. (investment bankers), Houston, 1953—61; headmaster Woodberry Forest Sch., 1962-70; sr. v.p., dir. Rotan Mosle Inc., 1970-78; chmn. Duncan-Smith Co., 1978—. Bd dirs SW Research Inst; devel. com. Episcopal Diocese W. Tex. Mem.: Chi Psi. Democrat. Episcopalian. Home: 610 Garraty Rd San Antonio TX 78209-6149 Office: 711 Navarro Ste 740 San Antonio TX 78205-1786 Office Phone: 210-223-9807. E-mail: mvaaler@duncansmith.com.

DUNCAN, ALLYSON K., federal judge; b. Durham, NC, Sept. 5, 1951; BA, Hampton U., 1972; JD, Duke U., 1975. Bar: NC 1975, DC 1977. Assoc. editor Lawyers Coop. Publ. Co., 1976—77; law clk. to Hon. Julia Cooper Mack DC Ct. Appeals, Washington, 1977—78; appellate atty., asst. to dep. gen. counsel, asst. to chmn. EEOC, 1978—86; assoc. prof. NC Ctrl. U. Sch. Law, 1986—90; assoc. judge NC Ct. Appeals, 1990; commr. NC Utilities Commn., 1991—98; ptnr. Kilpatrick Stockton LLP, Raleigh, NC, 1998—2003; judge US Ct. Appeals (4th cir.), 2003—. Mem.: Wake County Bar Assn. (pres. 2002—03), NC Bar Assn. (pres.-elect 2002).

DUNCAN, CHARLES WILLIAM, JR., investor, former United States Secretary of Energy; b. Houston, Sept. 9, 1926; s. Charles William and Mary Lillian (House) D.; m. Thetis Anne Smith, June 10, 1957; children: Charles William III, Mary Anne. BSChemE, Rice U., 1947; postgrad. mgmt., U. Tex., 1948-49. Roustabout, chem. engr. Humble Oil & Refining Co., 1947; with Duncan Foods Co., Houston, 1948-64, adminstrv. v.p., 1957-58, pres., chmn. adv. bd., 1958-64; pres. Coca-Cola Co. Food Div., Houston, 1964-67; chmn. Coca-Cola Europe, 1967-70; exec. v.p. Coca-Cola Co., Atlanta, 1970-71, pres., 1971-74; chmn. bd., dir. Rotan Mosle Fin. Corp., Houston, 1974-77; dep. sec. US Dept. Def., Washington, 1977-79; sec. US Dept. Energy, Washington, 1979-81. Trustee emeritus, past chmn. Rice U.; lifetime bd. dirs., past treas. The Meth. Hosp. With USAAF, 1944—46. Mem. Coun. Fgn. Rels., Houston Country Club, River Oaks Country Club, Allegro Club, Sigma Alpha Epsilon, Sigma Iota Epsilon. Methodist. Home: 2 Briarwood Ct Houston TX 77019-5801 Office: 600 Travis St Ste 6100 Houston TX 77002-3007

DUNCAN, DONALD WILLIAM, lawyer; b. Baldwin, Md., May 18, 1932; s. William Rush and Mary Alice (MacBlane); children: David (dec.), Lisa (dec. June, 2007); m. Auria Adorno Duncan; 1 child, Roberto Millan. AA, U. Balt., 1956, JD, 1960. Bar: Md. 1960, Fla. 1992. Asso. Haynie & McFerrin, C.P.A., Balt., 1956-61; controller H.C. Weiskettel Co., Balt., 1961-62; v.p., counsel, sec., Balt. Aircoil Co., Inc., 1962-87; pvt. practice Palm Coast, Fla., 1987—. Mem. Md. Bar Assn., Fla. Bar. Republican. Presbyterian. Office Phone: 386-445-0500. Personal E-mail: dwduncan@bellsouth.net.

DUNCAN, JEFF (JEFFREY D. DUNCAN), United States Representative from South Carolina, former state legislator; b. Simpsonville, SC, Jan. 7, 1966; s. John T. and Dianne M. Duncan; m. Melody Ann Hodges, Dec. 3, 1988; children: Graham, John Philip, Parker. BA, Clemson U., 1988; grad., SC Bankers Sch. Cert. Auctioneers Inst. designation, Accredited Auctioneer Real Estate designation. Pres., corp. auctioneer J. Duncan Associates, Clinton, SC; mem. Dist. 15 SC House of Reps., 2002—10; chmn. SC House Agrl., Natural Resources & Environ. Affairs Com., 2007—11; mem. US Congress from 3rd SC Dist., Washington, 2011—, US House Fgn. Affairs Com., Washington, 2011—, US House Homeland Security Com., Washington, 2011—, US House Natural Resources Com., Washington, 2011—. Mem. Clinton Bd. Zoning Appeals, 1995—99. Bd. dirs. Clinton Uptown Devel. Assn., 1993—97, SC Waterfowl Assn., 1997—2002, Piedmont Wilderness Inst., Clinton, 2001—06, Laurens County C. of C., 2002—07. Recipient Palmetto Leadership award from, SC Policy Coun., 2003, Guardian of Small Bus. award, Nat. Fedn. Ind. Bus., 2006; named Legislator of Yr., SC Wildlife Fedn., 2007, SC Recreation & Parks Assn. Republican. Baptist. Office: US House of Representatives 116 Cannon House Office Bldg Washington DC 20515 Office Phone: 202-225-5301.*

DUNCAN, JOHN JAMES, JR., United States Representative from Tennessee; b. Lebanon, Tenn., July 21, 1947; m. Lynn Hawkins; children: Tara, Whitney, John III, Zane. BS in Journalism, U. Tenn., Knoxville, 1969; JD, George Washington U. Nat. Law Ctr., 1973. Bar: Tenn. 1973. Pvt. practice atty., Knoxville, 1973-81; state trial judge Knox County, 1981-88; mem. US Congress from 2nd Tenn. dist., 1988—. Elder Eastminster Presbyn. Ch. Positions capt. US Army Nat. Guard/USAR, 1970—87. Recipient Hartranft award, Airline Operators & Pilots Assn., 1999, Super Hero award, Citizens Against Govt. Waste, Golden Bulldog award, Watchdogs of Treasury; named one of Top 5 Most Fiscally Conservative Members of the House and Senate, Nat. Taxpayers Union. Mem.: Am. Legion, Sertoma Club, Elks, Shriners, Masons. Republican. Office: US House of Representatives 2207 Rayburn House Office Bldg Washington DC 20515 also: 800 Market St Ste 110 Knoxville TN 37902 Office Phone: 202-225-5435.*

DUNCAN, MARIANO, professional baseball coach, retired professional baseball player; b. San Pedro de Macoris, Dominican Republic, Mar. 13, 1963; m. Monique Duncan; children: Mariano Jr., Christopher, Dustin. Infielder LA Dodgers, 1985—89, first base coach, 2006—10; infielder Cin. Reds, 1989-91, Phila. Phillies, 1991-95, NY Yankees, 1996—97, Toronto Blue Jays, 1997, Yomiuri Giants, Japan, 1998; minor league coach Gulf Coast League Dodgers, 2003, Jacksonville Suns, 2004, Las Vegas 51s, 2005, Daytona Cubs, Fla. State League, 2012—. Named to Nat. League All Star Team, Maj. League Baseball, 1994, Dominican Republic Baseball Hall of Fame, 2008. Achievements include leading the National League in: triples (11), 1990; member of World Series championship winning Cincinnati Reds, 1990, New York Yankees, 1996. Office: Daytona Cubs Jackie Robinson Ballpark 110 E Orange Ave Daytona Beach FL 32114-4406

DUNCAN, MEREDITH JOHNSON, law educator; b. 1966; BA in Polit. Sci., Northwestern U., Evanston, Ill., 1988; JD magna cum laude, U. Houston Law Ctr., 1993. Legal asst. Baker & Botts, LLP, 1989—90; intern Tex. Resource Ctr., 1991; law clk. to Hon. Edith H. Jones US Ct. Appeals (5th cir.), Houston, 1993—94, 1996—98; assoc. Vinson & Elkins, LLP, 1994—96, Ahmad & Zavitsanos PC, Houston, 1996; asst. prof. U. Houston Law Ctr., 1998—2004, assoc. prof., 2004—, George Butler rsch. prof. law, 2005—. Contbr. articles to profl. jours. Recipient Faculty of Yr. award, Black Law Students Assn., 2000, Outstanding Prof. of Yr. award, U. Houston Law Ctr. Student Bar Assn., 2002, Enron Tchg. Excellence award, 2005. Mem.: ABA, Tex. Ctr. Legal Ethics & Professionalism, Nat. Assn. Criminal Def. Lawyers, American Law Inst., Nat. Bar Assn., Tex. State Bar, Order of the Coif. Office: Univ Houston Law Center 100 Law Ctr Ste 230 BLB Houston TX 77204 Office Phone: 713-743-2019. E-mail: mduncan@uh.edu.

DUNCAN, MIKE (ROBERT MICHAEL DUNCAN), political organization administrator; b. Oneida, Tenn., Apr. 14, 1951; s. Robert C. and Barbara (Taylor) D.; m. Joanne Kirk, June 3, 1972; children: Robert Michael. BA, Cumberland Coll., 1971; JD, U. Ky., 1974; postgrad., U. Wis., 1977-80; LLD (hon.), Cumberland Coll., 1990; D Pub. Svc. (hon.), Coll. of Ozarks, 2002; D Rb. Svc. (hon.), Morehead State U., 2006. Cert. lener-bus. banking, 1994. V.p. Inez Deposit Bank, 1974—77, exec. v.p., 1977—81, chmn., 1981—, with Louisa, Ky., 1984—; chmn. Cmty. Holding Co., Inez, 1983—; treas. Republican Nat. Com., 2001—02, gen. counsel, 2002—07, chmn., 2007—09; founding chmn. American Crosswords, 2010—; pres., CEO Am. Coalition for Clean Coal Electricity, 2012—. Del. Republican Nat. Conv., 1972, 76, 92, 96, 2000, 04, 08, 2012, chair contest com. 2000, 2012, conv.; nat. committeeman for Ky., 1992-, Rep. Nat. Com., vice chmn. southern region, 1992-2001, exec. com., 1996; chmn. Ky. Rep. Com., 1995; active Govt. Rels. Coun., White House Conf. on Small Bus., 1995; chmn. Govs. Scholars, 1995—98, bd. dirs. 1996—2006; chmn. Bunning for U.S. Senate campaign, 1998; midwest regional chmn. Bush Presdl. campaign, 1999; chmn. Morehead State U., 1985-86; trustee, chmn. Alice Lloyd Coll., Pippa Passes, Ky., 1978—, acting pres., 1993-94; mem. class XX Pres.'s Commn. on Exec. Exch. assigned to White House Office Pub. Liaison as asst. dir.; dir. Christian Appalachian Project, 1995—2009; mem. Pres.'s Commn. on White House Fellows, 2001-06; polit. commentator WYMT-TV, 1999-2007; chmn.transition team Gov.-elect Fletcher, State of Ky., 2003-04; acting sec. revenue; trustee Highlands Regional Med. Ctr., 1977—, sec., 1994 chmn. East Ky. Corp., 1996, vice chmn. Ctr. Econ. Devel. bd. dirs. Cin. Br. of Cleve. Fed. Res. Bank, 1987-90, Tenn. Valley Authority, 2006-2012, chmn., 2009. Named Cumberland Coll. Outstanding Alumnus, 1976, Outstanding Young Man, Ky. Jaycees, 1982; U. Ky. fellow, 1978, White House fellow finalist, 1989; recipient Cmty. Leadership award McConnell Scholars U. Louisville, Cmty. Leadership award, 1999, Vic Hellard award Pub. Svc., 2003; named to U. Ky. Coll. of Law Hall of Fame, 2002. Mem. American Bankers Assn., Ky. Bankers Assn. (pres. 1985-86, dir.), Ky. Bar Assn., Ky. C. of C. (dir.), Kiwanis (lt. gov. 1983-84). Republican. Baptist.

DUNCAN, NEWTON O., otolaryngologist, educator; MD, Baylor Coll. of Medicine, 1978; B in Biol. Sciences, Stanford U., Palo Alto, Calif.; postgrad., Letterman Army Med. Ctr., San Francisco, Calif. Diplomate Am. Bd. Otolaryngology, 1986. Resident surgery Baylor Coll. of Medicine, Houston, 1982—83, resident otolaryngology, 1983—86, asst. clin. prof. depts. of otorhinolaryngology and pediats., chief resident dept. of otorhinolaryngology and communicative sciences; intern gen. surgery Letterman Army Med. Ctr., San Francisco, Calif.; fellow pediatric otolaryngology Univ. of Wash., Seattle, 1990—91, Royal Alexandra Hosp. for Children, Sydney, 1991—92; hosp. affiliations include Texas Children's Hosp., St. Luke's Episcopal Hosp., The Meth. Hosp., Columbia Women's Hosp., Doctors' Surg. Ctr. Decorated Army Commendation medal US Army, Meritorious Svc. medal; named one of the Best Doctors in America, 1996—, the America's Top Doctors, 2000. Fellow: ACS, Am. Acad. of Pediats., Am. Soc. of Pediatric Otolaryngology, Am. Acad. of Otolaryngology - Head and Neck Surgery; mem.: AMA, Am. Cleft Palate-Craniofacial Assn., Harris County Med. Soc., Soc. for Ear, Nose and Throat Advances in Children. Office: Baylor College of Medicine One Baylor Plz Houston TX 77030 Office Phone: 713-798-4951.

DUNCAN, RICHARD RAY, history professor; b. Cin., Aug. 30, 1931; s. Ray Howard and Emma (Swing) D. BA, Ohio U., 1954, MA, 1955; PhD, Ohio State U., 1963. Instr. Kent State U., 1961-64; asst. prof. U. Richmond, Va., 1964-67; prof. Georgetown U., Washington,

1967-2000, prof. emeritus, 2000—. Vis. assoc. prof. Ohio State U., Columbus, summer 1971; chmn. bd. dirs. Duncan Bros. Tire Co., Winchester, Va. Author: Lee's Endangered Left, 1998, Beleaguered Winchester, 2007; editor: Alexander Neil and the Last Valley Campaign, 1996, Maryland Historical Magazine, 1967-74; compiler: Theses and Dissertations on Virginia History, 1986; contbr. articles to profl. jours. Episcopalian. Home: 6101 Edsall Rd Apt 1802 Alexandria VA 22304-6009

DUNCAN, ROBERT D., real estate company executive; m. Marcy Duncan; 6 children. BBA in Bus. Honors Program, U. Tex., Austin, MBA in Fin., LLB. With Trammell Crow Co. (subs. CB Richard Ellis Group, Inc.), Dallas; co-founder, chmn. & mng. prin. Transwestern Investment Co., LLP; founder, chmn. Transwestern Commercial Services, Inc., Houston, 1978—. Founding mem. adv. coun. U. Tex. Real Estate Ctr.; dir. Greater Houston Cmty. Found., Greater Houston YMCA. Mem.: Urban Land Inst., World Pres. Orgn. Office: Transwestern Commercial Services LLC 1900 W Loop S Ste 1300 Houston TX 77027-3218 Office Phone: 713-270-7700. Office Fax: 713-270-6285. Business E-Mail: robert.duncan@transwestern.net.

DUNCAN, ROBERT LLOYD, state legislator, lawyer; b. Vernon, Tex., Aug. 5, 1953; s. Frank Lloyd and Robena Mae (Formby) Duncan; children: Lindsey Elizabeth, Matthew Randall. BS in Agrl. Econs., Tex. Tech. U., Lubbock, 1976; JD, Tex. Tech. U. Sch. Law, 1981. Bar: Tex. 1981, US Ct. Appeals (5th cir.) 1981, US Dist. Ct. (no. dist.) Tex. 1982, US Dist. Ct. (we. dist.) Tex. 1985. Assoc. Crenshaw, Dupree & Milam LLP, Lubbock, 1981-87, ptnr., 1987—; mem. Dist. 84 Tex. House of Representatives, 1993—96; mem. Dist. 28 Tex. State Senate, 1997—. Co-author: Charitable Immunity Liability Tort Reform, 1988, Texas DTPA Reform: Closing the DTPA Loophole in the 1987 Tort Reform Laws and the Ongoing Quest for Fairer DTPA Laws, 1989, A Guide to Texas Workers' Compensation Reform, 1991. Named a Tex. Super Lawyer, Tex. Monthly mag.; named one of Top 10 Legislators, 2001, 2003, 2005. Mem.: ABA, Tex. Assn. Def. Coun., State Bar Tex., Lubbock County Bar Assn. Republican. Baptist. Avocations: reading, golf, hunting. Office: Crenshaw, Dupree & Milam 1500 Broadway 8th Fl Wells Fargo Ctr PO Box 1499 Lubbock TX 79401-3116 also: 1500 Broadway Ste 902 Lubbock TX 79401 also: PO Box 12068 Capitol Station Austin TX 78711 also: Wells Fargo Tower 36 W Beauregard Ave San Angelo TX 76903 also: 119 Avenue B NW Childress TX 79201 Office Phone: 806-762-5281, 806-762-1122, 512-463-0128, 325-481-0028, 940-937-0909.

DUNCAN, TIM (TIMOTHY THEODORE DUNCAN), professional basketball player; b. Apr. 25, 1976; s. William and Ione Duncan; m. Amy Duncan, 2001. BA in Psych., Wake Forest, 1997. Ctr., forward San Antonio Spurs, 1997—. Mem. US Olympic Men's Basketball Team, Athens, 2004. Founder, exec. v.p. Tim Duncan Found. Recipient Naismith Player of Yr. award, 1997, John R. Wooden award, 1997; named NCAA Men's Basketball Player of Yr., AP, 1997, NBA Rookie of Yr., 1998, MVP, NBA Finals, 1999, 2003, 2005, Co-MVP, NBA All-Star Game, 2000, MVP, NBA, 2002, 2003, NBA Player of Yr., The Sporting News, 2002, 2003, Sportsman of Yr., Sports Illus., 2003; named to Western Conf. All-Star Game, NBA, 1998, 2000—11, 2013, All-NBA First Team, 1998—2005, 2007, 2013, NBA All-Defensive First Team, 1999—2003, 2005, 2007—08. Achievements include member of NBA Championship winning San Antonio Spurs, 1999, 2003, 2005. Mailing: San Antonio Spurs 1 AT&T Ctr San Antonio TX 78219*

DUNHILL, ROBERT, advertising executive; b. LA, Sept. 28, 1929; s. Herbert G. and Irma (Meyer); m. Joan Scheer, Dec. 19, 1952; children: Andrew, Candy, Cindy. BS, Adelphi Coll., 1952; MBA, NYU, 1954. Prin. Dunhill Internat. List Co., Inc., NYC, 1952—, pres., chmn., 1975—. With USNR, 1955-57. Mem. Chgo. Assn. of Direct Mktg., Widener U. Alumni Assn., Direct Mktg. Assn., Fla. Direct Mktg. Assn. Republican. Home: 11272 Westland Cir Boynton Beach FL 33437 Office: Dunhill Internat 6400 Congress Ave Ste 1750 Boca Raton FL 33487-2998 Business E-Mail: robert@dunhills.com.

DUNIE, DEBORAH B., military officer; BSEE, Tufts U., 1981; MEE, Stevens Inst. Tech., 1985. Sr. level positions US Dept. of Def., prin. advisor, Under Sec. of Def. for Intelligence; dir., bus. transformation office, US Govt. Nat. GeoSpatial Intelligence Agy., 2002—03; dir., plans and analysis, Under Sec. of Def. for Intelligence US Dept. of Def., 2003—06; exec. v.p., chief tech. officer CACI International, Inc., 2006—. Bd. dirs. Oracle Corp., 1996—2002. Recipient Sec. of Def. Medal, 2006. Office: CACI International Inc 1100 N Glebe Rd Arlington VA 22201 Office Phone: 703-841-7800. Office Fax: 703-841-7882. Business E-Mail: DDunie@caci.com.

DUNKEL, DAVID L., personnel firm executive; b. 1954; Ptnr. Romac, Tampa, 1980; pres., CEO predecessor firm Romac-FMA; CEO, dir. Romac International, 1994—; chmn., pres., CEO kforce-.com, Tampa, Fla., 1994—. Office: Kforce 1001 E Palm Ave Tampa FL 33605

DUNLAP, BENJAMIN BERNARD, academic administrator; b. Columbia, SC; m. Anne Dunlap, 1963; children: Boykin Dunlap Bell, Susannah, Ben. Grad. summa cum laude, U. South, 1959; BA with honors, Oxford U., Eng., 1962, MA, 1966; PhD in English Lang. and Lit., Harvard U., 1967. Mem. faculty Harvard U.; Carolina rsch. prof., prof. English, adj. prof. anthropology U. SC, 1968—93; Chapman Family prof. humanities Wofford Coll., Spartanburg, SC, 1993—2000, pres., 2000—. Moderator Exec. and CEO Seminars Aspen (Colo.) Inst.; lectr. in field. Writer, prodr. (over 200 programs for pub. television). Named Sr. Fulbright lectr., Chulalongkorn U., Bangkok, Chiang Mai U., Thailand; Rhodes scholar, Oxford U., 1959—62, U.S.-Japan Leadership fellow, Japan Soc. N.Y. and Tokyo, 1984—85. Office: Wofford College Office of President 429 N Church St Spartanburg SC 29303 Office Phone: 864-597-4010. Office Fax: 864-597-4018. E-mail: dunlapbb@wofford.edu.*

DUNLAP, WILLIAM, artist, critic, educator; MFA, U. Miss. Prof. Appalachian State U., NC, 1970—79, Memphis State U., 1979—80; art commentator, "Around Town" WETA-TV, Arlington, Va. Spkr. in field; lectr. on art related subjects at colleges, universities, institutions and profl. confs. Represented in permanent collections, Met. Mus. Art, Corcoran Gallery Art, Lauren Rogers Mus., Mobil Corp., Riggs Bank, IBM Corp., Fed. Express, Equitable Collection, Ark. Art Ctr., U.S. State Dept., U.S. Embassies throughout the world, Rogers Ogden Collection, one-man shows include, Corcoran Gallery Art, Nat. Acad. Sci., Aspen Mus. Art, Southeastern Ctr. Contemporary Art, Mus. Western Va., Albany Mus. Art, Cheekwood Fine Arts Ctr., Mint Mus. Art, Miss. Mus. Art, Contemporary Art Ctr., New Orleans, exhibitions include Reconstructed Recollections, Inaugural Exhibition: Story of South, Ogden Mus. Southern Art, New Orleans, 2003—04, What Boys Draw & Other Works, Soren Christensen Gallery, New Orleans, 2004, Panorama Am. Landscape, Gibbes Mus. Art, Charleston, S. C., 2004—05, In Spirit of the Land; co-curator (exhibitions) Winding River: Contemporary Painting from Vietnam, Meridian Internat. Ctr., Washington D.C., 1997—98, Outward Bound: Am. Art Brink of 21st Century, writer Art & Antiques, Washingtonian, Arts Review. Office: WETA TV 2775 South Quincy St Arlington VA 22206 Office Phone: 703-998-2600. Office Fax: 703-998-3401. E-mail: bill@williamdunlap.com.

DUNLEVIE, STEVEN S., lawyer; b. Atlanta, Apr. 24, 1948; BA, UNC, Chapel Hill, 1970; JD, Emory U., 1973. Bar: Ga. 1973, admitted to practice: All Ga. Trial and Appellate Cts., US Dist. Ct. (No. Dist. Ga.). Atty. Office of Judge Advocate, US Navy, Charleston, SC, 1973; assoc. atty. Huie, Ware, Sterne, Brown & Ide (formerly known as Ware & Sterne), Atlanta, 1973—77; ptnr. Ware, Hopkins, Dunlevie & McNairy, Atlanta, 1977—80, Parker, Johnson, Cook & Dunlevie, Atlanta, 1981—96; mem. mgmt. com. Womble Carlyle Sandridge & Rice, PLLC, Atlanta, 1996—, mng. mem. Lt. USNR, 1970—73. Mem.: Ga. State Bar, Internat. Assn. of Attys. and Execs. in Corp. Real Estate, Ga. Bankers Assn. (mem. bank counsel sect.), Am. Judicature Soc., ABA (mem. real property, probate & trust law sect., mem. brokers & brokerage and conveyancing Committees), Atlanta Bar Assn. (mem. corp., banking & real property law sect.). Office: Womble Carlyle Sandridge & Rice PLLC One Atlantic Ctr Ste 3500 271 17th St NW Ste 2400 Atlanta GA 30363-6215 Office Phone: 404-888-7401. Office Fax: 404-870-4828. Business E-Mail: sdunlevie@wcsr.com.

DUNN, BERNARD DANIEL, former naval officer, consultant; b. Providence, Feb. 10, 1934; s. Alexander Gerard and Mary Alice (Fitzpatrick) D.; m. Hilda Hughes Tunney, Jan. 4, 1958; children: Bernard Daniel Jr., Brian Lindsay, Mary Catherine, J. Alexander. BS in Econs., Villanova U., Pa., 1956; MBA in Transp., Mich. State U., East Lansing, 1971. Commd. ensign USN, 1956, advanced through grades to capt.; asst. supply and disbursing officer USS Rushmore, Little Creek, Va., 1957-58; asst. material divsn. officer, stock control divsn. officer Sub Base New London, Groton, Conn., 1958-61; material and fiscal divsn. supt. Ship Repair Facility, Guam, 1961-63; nuclear weapons material divsn. officer Naval Supply Ctr., Oakland, Calif., 1963-64; supply ops. officer Nuc. Weapons Supply Annex, Oakland, Calif., 1964-65; commn. supply officer USS Fox, 1965-68; project officer Naval Supply Sys. Command, Washington, 1968-70; asst. for sea transp. Office Chief Naval Ops., Washington, 1971-73; sr. mem. Mobile Tng. Team to Colombian Navy, Bogota, Colombia, 1973; dir. warehousing, chief transp. office Def. Depot, Tracy, Calif., 1973-76; dep. project mgr., Navy rep. Joint Container Steering Group Office of Sec. of Def., Washington, 1976-77; dir. transp. field ops. divsn. Naval Supply Sys. Command, Washington, 1977-78; head transp. mgmt. and policy br. Office Chief Naval Ops., Washington, 1978-83; comptr./dir. supply Naval Edn. and Tng. Command, Newport, R.I., 1983-85; A-76 program officer Mil. Sealift Command, Washington, 1985; acting dir./chief staff commn. on Merchant Marine and Def., Alexandria, Va., 1985-88; ret., 1988. Bd. dirs., corp. sec. Greenwich Ctr., Inc., East Greenwich, RI, 1988—2002; cons., Alexandria, Va., 1988-91; chief program analyst Resource Cons., Inc., Vienna, Va., 1991-94, sr. supply specialist, 97-98. Life mem. East Greenwich (R.I.) Vol. Fire Dept., 1953—. Decorated Def. Meritorious Svc. medal, Meritorious Svc. medal, Joint Svc. Commendation medal with oak leaf cluster, Navy Meritorious Unit commendation, Air Force Outstanding Unit award, Humanitarian medal, Nat. Def. Svc. medal, Vietnam Svc. medal with one bronze star, Rep. of Vietnam Campaign medal. Mem. U.S. Naval Inst., Nat. Def. Transp. Assn. (pres. San Joaquin chpt. 1974-75), USCG Acad. Found., East Greenwich Vets. firemen Assn., Mil. Officers Assn., Washington Area Navy Supply Corps Assn., Naval Submarine League, USS Rushmore Assn. (founder and charter mem., assoc. treas.1995-2001, 1st v.p. 2003-05), US Navy Meml. Found., USS Fox Assn. Roman Catholic. Avocations: stamp collecting/philately, ice hockey, running, golf. Home: 5817 Shalott Ct Alexandria VA 22310-1427 Personal E-mail: bddunn3@verizon.net.

DUNN, BILL, state legislator; b. Panama Canal Zone, Mar. 3, 1961; m. Stacy Dunn; children: Daniel, Katie, Elizabeth, Rachel, Michael. House rep., Tenn.; state rep. Dist. 16 Tenn., 1995—; rep. caucus parliamentarian; bus mgr. Cortese Tree Specialists. Recipient Agt. of Yr., East Tenn.; named to Person of Yr., C. of C. Mem.: Farm Bur., Tenn. Right Life, Tennes Christian Coalition, Fountain City Rep. Club. Republican. Catholic. Office: 5309 LaVesta Rd Knoxville TN 37918 also: 212 War Memorial Bldg Nashville TN 37243-0116 Office Phone: 615-741-1721, 865-687-4904. Office Fax: 615-253-0276. Business E-Mail: rep.bill.dunn@capitol.tn.gov.

DUNN, CHARLES DEWITT, academic administrator; b. Magnolia, Ark., Dec. 2, 1945; s. Charles Edward and Nora Lucille (Bailey) D.; m. Donna Jane Parsons, Apr. 9, 1966; children: Aimee, James, Joseph, Mary Elizabeth. BA, So. Ark. U., 1967; MA, North Tex. State U., 1970; PhD, So. Ill. U., 1973; cert. inst. ednl. mgmt., Harvard U., 1991. Instr. polit. sci. U. Ark., Monticello, 1969-72, asst. prof., 1972-75; assoc. prof. U. Ctrl. Ark., Conway, 1975-80, prof., 1980—, chmn. dept. polit. sci., 1976-82, dir. govt. rels., 1982-86; pres. Henderson State U., Arkadelphia, Ark., 1986—2008, pres. emeritus, disting. prof., 2008—. Chmn. Commn. Ark.'s Future, 1989-93; chmn. Ark. Higher Edn. Coun., 1992-96; chmn. fin. com. Ark. Cmty. Found. Bd. Dirs., v.p., 2000-02, pres., 2002-03; active Blue Ribbon Commn. Pub. Edn., 2001-02, Ark. Commn. Coordination Edn., 2004-; bd. dirs. Meth. Children's Home, 2003-06. Mem. Am. Assn. State Coll. and Univs., NCAA (pres.'s commn. 1996-97, pres.' coun. 1997-2001, pres. Gulf South conf. 1998-2000, fund selection com. chair, 2009-), Ark. Polit. Sci. Assn. (pres. 1976-77), Conway C. of C. (bd. dirs. 1984-85, v.p. 1985-86), Arkadelphia C. of C. (bd. dirs. 1987-91), Clark County Hist. Assn. (pres. 2010-). Methodist. Office: Henderson State U 1100 Henderson St PO Box 7532 Arkadelphia AR 71999-0001 Home Phone: 870-246-3099; Office Phone: 870-230-5254. Business E-Mail: cddunn@hsu.edu.

DUNN, DELMER DELANO, political science professor; b. Sentinel, Okla., Oct. 31, 1941; s. Robert Patrick and Mildred Marion D.; m. Ann Gregg Swinford, May 15, 1971; children: John Swinford, Kielly McKee BA, Okla. State U., 1963; MS, U. Wis., 1964, PhD, 1967. Asst. prof. polit. sci. U. Ga., Athens, 1967-71, assoc. prof., 1971-77, dir. Inst. Govt., 1973-82, prof., 1977-82, Regents prof., 1982—2006; rsch. assoc. The Brookings Instn., Washington, 1969-70; acting head dept. polit. sci. U. Ga., Athens, 1987-88, assoc. v.p. acad. affairs, 1988-91, dir. Inst. Higher Edn., 2001—02, v.p. instrn., 2002—06; ret; prof. emeritus U. Ga., Athens, 2006—. Vis. fellow dept. polit. sci. faculty of arts Australian Nat. U., Canberra, 1992. Author: Public Officials and the Press, 1969, Financing Presidential Campaigns, 1972, Politics and Adminstration at the Top: Lessons from Down Under, 1997 (Charles Levine Book award 1998); mem. editl. bd. Social Sci. quar., 1988-94; contbr. articles to profl. jours. Trustee Leadership Ga., 1976-82; pres. Clarke/Oconee unit Am. Cancer Soc., 1981-82, chmn., 1982-83; mem. Athens Regional Libr. Endowment Bd., 2008-, Friends of Five Points (Neighborhood Assn.) Mem. Am. Polit. Sci. Assn. (Congl. fellow, 1968-69), Nat. Assn. Schs. of Pub. Affairs and Adminstrn. (pres. 1987-88), Pi Alpha Alpha (nat. pres. 1983-85). Presbyterian. Office: Univ Ga Sch Pub and Internat Affairs Athens GA 30602 Business E-Mail: ddunn@uga.edu.

DUNN, JAMES MILTON, retired religious organization administrator; b. Ft. Worth, June 17, 1932; s. William Thomas and Edith (Campbell) Dunn; m. Marilyn McNeely, Dec. 19, 1958. BA, Tex. Wesleyan Coll., 1953; BD, Southwestern Bapt. Theol. Sem., 1957, ThD, 1966, PhD, 1978; LLD, Alderson-Broaddus Coll., William Jewell Coll.; DHL, Linfield Coll.; DD, Ctrl. Bapt. Theol. Sem., Furman U.; DD (hon.), Franklin Coll., 2004. Ordained to ministry So. Bapt. Conv. and Am. Bapt. Ch. in U.S.A., 1955. Assoc. pastor First Bapt. Ch., Weatherford, Tex., 1955-57; pastor Emmanuel Bapt. Ch., Weatherford, 1957-61; religion instr., campus minister W. Tex. State U., Canyon, 1961-66; dir. christian life commn. Bapt. Gen. Conv. Tex., Dallas, 1967-80; exec. dir. Bapt. Joint Com. on Pub. Affairs, Washington, 1981-99, pres. endowment, 1999—; prof. Christianity and pub. policy Wake Forest U. Div. Sch., 1999—. Sec. bd. Ams. United for Separation of Ch. and State, 1978-88; bd. dirs. Bread for the World, Washington, pres., 1987; chmn. ethics commn. Bapt. World Alliance, McLean, Va., 1975-80; chmn. adv. bd. ProVision Asia, 1985—; bd. dirs. Ch.'s Ctr. for Theology and Pub. Policy, Washington, 1993—02; vis. prof. Wake Forest Div. Sch., 1999—. Editor, co-author: Politics a Guidebook for Christians, 1970, Endangered Species, 1976; co-author: An Approach to Christian Ethics, 1979, Teacher Renewal, 1987; author: (with others) Equal Separation, 1990, The Fundamentalist Phenomenon, 1990, Defining Baptist Convictions, 1996, Proclaiming the Baptist Vision, Religious Liberty, 1997, Why I Am a Baptist, 1999, Baptists in the Balance, 1997, Soul Freedom: Baptist Battle Cry, 2000. Sec. Anti-Crime Coun. Tex., Dallas, 1968-80; founding mem. Dallas Dem. Forum, 1976-80, People for the Am. Way; mem. Fair Campaign Practices Com., Dallas, 1972-76, Gov.'s Juvenile Justice Coun., State of Tex., Austin, 1976-77; pres. Whitsitt Hist. Soc., 2003-04. Recipient Disting. Svc. award Christian Life Commn. of So. Bapt. Conv., 1979, Moore-Bowman Award of Excellence, Tex. Coun. on Family Relations, 1979, Disting. Svc. award Chs. Ctr. for Theology and Pub. Policy, 1993, T.B. Maston Christian Ethics award, 1995, Abner V. McCall Religious Liberty award Baylor U., 1998, Disting. Svc. award Christian Life Commn. Bapt. Gen. Conv. Tex., 1998, Madison-Jefferson award Americans United, 1999, Disting. Svc. medal Colgate Rochester Div. Sch., 2000. Mem. Soc. for the Sci. Study of Religion (Lifetime Svc. award Baptists Today mag., 2009), Hymn Soc. US. and Can. (life), Alumni Assn. London Sch. Econs. and Polit. Sci. (life), Roger Williams Fellowship (life). Baptist. Avocation: music. Office: Baptist Joint Com 200 Maryland Ave NE Ste 302 Washington DC 20002-5797 Office Phone: 336-758-4409. Business E-Mail: dunnj@wfu.edu.

DUNN, MORRIS DOUGLAS, lawyer; b. Ionia, Mich., Nov. 1, 1944; s. Morris Frederick and Lola Adella (Gee) D.; m. Jill Lynn Fasbender, July 22, 1967; children: Brooks, Gillian, Joshua. BSME, U. Mich., 1967; JD, Vanderbilt U., 1970. Bar: NY 1970, US Dist. Ct. (so. dist.) NY 1972, US Ct. Appeals (2d cir.) 1973, US Supreme Ct. 1978. Assoc. Winthrop Stimson, Putnam & Roberts, NYC, 1970-78, ptnr., 1978-84; sr. v.p., mng. dir. Shearson Lehman Bros., Inc., NYC, 1984-85; ptnr. Milbank, Tweed, Hadley & McCloy, NYC, 1985—2009, ret. ptnr., 2009; mng. dir. Dunn Consulting Group, 2009—; mem. bd. dirs. Green Leaf Power LLC, Sacremento, Calif., 2011—; mem. operating exec. bd. Gotham Equity Ptnrs., NY, 2009—11; ptnr. CFSD Group LLC, 2010—; bd. mem. Am. Scottish Found., 2012—. Pres. bd. advisors law sch. Vanderbilt U., 2009—11; bd. trustees Immune Disease Inst., 2006—09; mem. site preservation task force Archaeol. Inst. America, 2009—11; bd. mem. Site Preservation Initiative, Cotsen Inst. Archeology UCLA, 2010—. Contbr. articles to profl. jours. Fellow: Am. Bar Found.; mem.: ABA (fed. regulation of securities com. bus. law sect. 1981—, chair pub. utility, comms. and transp. law sect. 1997—98, bd.govs. 1998—2001), Internat. Bar Assn. (com. chmn. 1990—94), Assn. Bar City NY, Grey Oaks Country Club, Canoe Brook Country Club, Down Town Assn. Home Phone: 239-434-7172; Office Phone: 973-224-3662. Personal E-mail: mddunnjd@comcast.net.

DUNN, PRISCILLA, state legislator; b. Oct. 8, 1943; m. Grover Dunn; 1 child, Karen. BS, Ala. State U., Montgomery; MA, U. Montevallo, Ala. Homeless edn. coord. Bessemer City Schools; mem. Dist. 56 Ala. House of Reps., Montgomery, 1998—2009; mem. Dist. 19 Ala. State Senate, 2009—. Instr. Jefferson County Congress Christian Edn. Bd. mem. Dem. Exec. Com., Ala.; coord. Jefferson County Dem. Conf.; trustee, Sunday sch. tchr. Shady Grove Bapt. Ch.; bd. dirs. Bessemer Civic Ctr.; pres. Concerned Citizens of Bessemer Cut-Off; mem. adv. bd., Jefferson/Shelby counties Am. Cancer Soc. Mem.: Girls, Inc. Ctrl. Ala. (sec.), Humanistic Challengers Federated Club (pres.). Democrat. Baptist. Office: 460 Carriage Hills Dr Bessemer AL 35022 also: Ala State Senate Ala State House 11 S Union St Rm 729 Montgomery AL 36130 Office Phone: 334-242-7793.

DUNN, REBECCA M., telecommunications industry executive; b. Selma, Ala. BS in Math., Auburn U., 1970. Engring. assoc., staff engr., asst. engring. mgr., costs South Ctrl. Bell, asst. engr., 1970, dist. mgr. capital recovery, 1975, ops. mgr. regulatory, asst. v.p., pub. affairs, 1984—87, gen. mgr., bus. mktg. ops., 1987—89; v.p., shared svcs. BellSouth Corp., v.p., corp. affairs, 1989—91, v.p., human resources & corp. svcs., 1991—99, sr. v.p., corp. compliance, corp. sec., 2001; sr. v.p. Bellsouth Corp. Mem. adv. coun. Coll. of Bus., Auburn U.; vol. United Way; bd. dirs. Atlanta History Ctr., Homeward Inc., Ctrl. Atlanta Progress. Office: BellSouth Corp 675 W Peach St Ste 4200 Atlanta GA 30309 Office Phone: 404-249-2000. Office Fax: 404-249-3839.

DUNN, RONNIE GENE, musician; b. Coleman, Tex., June 1, 1953; div.; children: Whitney, Jesse Wayne; m. Janine Dunn. With Brooks & Dunn, 1988—; recording artist Artista, 1991—. Musician: (albums) (with Kix Brooks) Brand New Man, 1991 (Acad. Country Music award Album of Yr., 1992), Hard Workin' Man, 1993 (Grammy award Best Country Vocal Performance by Duo or Group for "Hard Workin' Man", 1993), Waitin' on Sundown, 1994, Borderline, 1996 (Grammy award Best Country Vocal Performance by Duo or Group for "My Maria", 1996), Greatest Hits Collection, 1997, If You See Her, 1998, Tight Rope, 1999, Super Hits, 1999, Steers and Stripes, 2001, It Won't Be Christmas Without You, 2002, Red Dirt Road, 2003, Greatest Hits Collection: Volume II, 2004, Hillbilly Deluxe, 2005 (Single of Yr., Song of Yr. & Music Video of Yr. for Believe, Country Music Assn. Awards, 2006, Song of Yr. for Believe, Acad. Country Music, 2006), Cowboy Town, 2007, (singles) Boot Scootin' Boogie, 1992, We'll Burn That Bridge, 1993, Rock My World (Little Country Girl), 1993, (songs) (8 Seconds soundtrack) Ride 'Em High, Ride 'Em Low, 1994, (with Hank Thompson) Hooked on Honky Tonk, 1997, (with Reba McEntire) If You See Him, If You See Her, 1998, (with Kix Brooks) Indian Summer, 2009 (Duo Video of Yr., CMT Music Awards, 2010); background vocals, chorus: albums T-r-o-u-b-l-e (Travis Tritt), 1992, appears on: albums Common Thread: The Songs of the Eagles, 1994 (Country Music Assn. Album of Yr., 1994). Co-recipient Top New Vocal Duo or Group award, Acad. Country Music, 1991, Entertainer of Yr. award, 1995, 1996, 2001, Top Vocal Duo award, 1991—97, 2000—03, 2005—07, 2008, 2010, Vocal Event of Yr. award, 2007, Home Depot Humanitarian award, 2007, Vocal Duo Yr. award, Country Music Assn., 1992—99, 2001—06, Entertainer of Yr. award, 1994, Favorite Country Group award, Am. Music Awards, 2004, 2005. Office: Brooks and Dunn PO Box 120669 Nashville TN 37212-0669

DUNN, WILLIAM BRUNA, III, journalist; b. Streator, Ill., Jan. 26, 1947; s. William Bruna and Mary Elizabeth (Allgaier) D.; m. Sandra Lee Ann Klein, Aug. 23, 1969; 1 child, William IV. BS in Journalism, U. Fla., 1969. Reporter Orlando (Fla.) Sentinel, 1967-69, mag. editor, 1970-80, dep. mng. editor, 1979-81, mng. editor, 1981-91, assoc. mng. editor, photos, graphics and design, 1991-2001; design editor Orlando (Fla.) Sentinel, 2001—02. Author: Kidding Around, 1973; editor: SHAQ! That Magical Rookie Season, 1993; editor: Martin Andersen: Editor, Publisher, Galley Boy, 1996. Recipient Silver Gavel award ABA, 1974; Gold and Silver medals Soc. News Design, 1984. Mem. Nat. Press Photographers Assn., Soc. Profl. Journalists (past pres. Cen. Fla. chpt.), Soc. of News Design. Roman Catholic. Home: 4 E Vanderbilt St Orlando FL 32804-5925 Home Phone: 407-898-0004. Personal E-mail: willbdunn@aol.com.

DUNNAM, JAMES ROBERT, lawyer, former state legislator; b. Waco, Tex., Dec. 12, 1963; s. Clyde Vance and Vicki (Hohertz) D.; m. Michelle Beth Mansfield, Aug. 15, 1987; children: Lauren Elizabeth, Mason Vance, Rachel Michelle. BBA, Baylor U., 1987, JD, 1987. Bar: Tex. 1988, U.S. Ct. Appeals (5th cir.) 1993, US Supreme Ct., 2006; cert. in civil trial law & family law, Tex. Assoc. Dunnam & Dunnam, LLP, Waco, 1987-93, ptnr., 1994—; mem. Dist. 57 Tex. House of Reps., 1997—2011. Mem. rules adv. com. Tex. Supreme Ct., 1998—2003; chair Tex. Sunset Adv. Commn., 2001—05, House Dem. Caucus, 2003—09, House Dem. Leader, 2009—11, House Select Com. on Fed. Economic Stabilization Funding, 2009—11. Democrat. Methodist. Office: Dunnam and Dunnam LLP 4125 W Waco Dr Waco TX 76710-7110

DUNSHEE, MELANIE J., law librarian, educator; BA, U. Minn.; JD, AMLS, U. Mich. Law firm libr., Detroit; reference libr. Duke U. Sch. Law Libr., Durham, NC, 1994, head reference svcs., 2001—04, dep. dir., sr. lecturing fellow, dir. legal rsch. instruction, asst. dean libr. svcs. Contbr. articles to profl. jours. Mem.: Am. Assn. Law Librs. Office: Duke University Law Library Rm 3046 Box 90361 Durham NC 27708-0361 Office Phone: 919-613-7119. E-mail: Dunshee@law.duke.edu.

DUNSON, WILLIAM ALBERT, biology professor, ecological consultant; b. Cedartown, Ga., Dec. 17, 1941; s. James Blake and Eleanor (Adams) D.; m. Margaret E. Kvashay, Aug. 19, 1963; children: Mary Elizabeth, William Albert, David Brian. BS in Zoology with honors, Yale U., 1962; MS, U. Mich., 1964, PhD, 1965. Teaching fellow U. Mich., Ann Arbor, 1962-63; mem. faculty Pa. State U., University Park, 1965—, prof. biology, 1974-97, prof. emeritus, 1997—; environ. scientist Seminole Tribe Fla., 1997—2002. Adj. prof. biology U. Miami, Old Dominion U., Fla., Atlantic U. (now Atlantic Coll.); chief scientist various internat. oceanographic expdns.; collaborator Everglades Nat. Park. Author: The Biology of Sea Snakes, 1975; contbr. over 140 articles to profl. jours. Queens marine sci. fellow, 1972, hon. Fulbright fellow, 1972; grantee NSF, U.S. Dept. Interior, U.S. Geol. Survey, U.S. EPA. Mem. Soc. for Study Amphibians and Reptiles (jour. edit. bd.). Achievements include study of ecotoxicology, physiological ecology and wetlands ecology. Home: 2535 N Beach Rd Englewood FL 34223 Business E-Mail: wad4@psu.edu.

DUNWODY, EUGENE COX, architect; b. Macon, Ga., July 19, 1933; s. William Elliott and Mary Bennet (Cox) D.; m. Susan Howe Foxworth, June 15, 1957; children: Susan, Eugene Jr., George, Mary Bennet. BS, Ga. Inst. Tech., 1955, BArch, 1956. Registered architect, Ga., Fla. V.p., treas. W. Elliott Dunwody Jr., Macon, 1959-69; pres. Dunwody and Co., Macon, 1969-81, Dunwody, Beeland and Henderson Architects Inc., Macon, 1981-97, Dunwody, Beeland, Azar, Walsh, and Matthews, Architects Inc., Macon, 1997-2000, Dunwody/Beeland, Archs., 2000—, Ga. Tech. Student Coun., 1954—55. Pres. Rotary, Macon, 1974, City Coun., Macon, 1975-87, C. of C., Macon, 1977; dir. Ga. Mcpl. Assn., Atlanta, 1982-83, Nat. League Cities, Washington, 1985-87; chmn. Macon-Bibb County Indsl. Authority, 1992-93, 99, 2000, Macon Econ. Devel. Commn., 1992-2013, chmn., 1992, 93, 99; pres. Macon Symphony Orch., 2000-02, 2010-12; deacon Presbyn. Ch. Named Community leader of Yr. Robins Air Logistics Ctr., Warner Robins, Ga., 1987; recipient Motie Wiggins award for Outstanding elected ofcl. Ga. Mcpl. Assn., Atlanta, 1987, Ga. Tech.'s Dean Griffin Cmty. Svc. award, 2000, Macon Arts Alliance Cultural award, 2002, R. Kirby Godsey Leadership award New Town Macon, 2007. Fellow AIA; mem. Middle Ga. chpt. AIA (pres. 1993), Ga. Assn. AIA (dir. 1992-93). Democrat. Presbyterian. Avocations: golf, piano, choir. Office: Dunwody/Beeland 300 Mulberry St Ste 604 Macon GA 31201-7922 Office Phone: 478-742-5321. Personal E-mail: ecd@dunwodybeeland.com.

DUNWOODY, ANN ELIZABETH, retired military officer; b. Ft. Belvoir, Va., Jan. 14, 1953; d. Harold H. and Elizabeth H. Dunwoody; m. Craig F. Brotchie. BS in Physical Edn., SUNY, Cortland, 1975; MS in Logistics Mgmt., Fla. Inst. Tech., 1988; MS in Nat. Resource Strategy, Industrial Coll. of Armed Forces, 1995. 2d lt. US Army, 1975, advanced through grades to gen., 2008; platoon leader, company exec. officer, battalion adjutant 100th Supply and Transport Battalion, Fort Sill, Okla.; comdr. 226th Light Maintenance Co., Fort Sill, Okla.; cmty. adjutant 8th Infantry Divsn.; comdr. 29th Area Support Group, 5th Quartermaster Detachment, Germany; quartermaster captains assignment officer Military Pers. Ctr., 1984; divsn. property book officer 82d Airborne Divsn., divsn. parachute officer for Desert Shield and Desert Storm, 1990—91; exec. officer 407th Supply and Transp. Battalion; dep. chief staff G4; comdr. 407th Supply and Transp. Battalion, 82d Airborne Divsn., 1992—93, 782d Main Support Battalion, 1993; strategic planner Chief of Staff of US Army; comdr. 10th Mountain Divsn. Support Command, 1996; exec. officer to dir. Defense Logistics Agency, Fort Belvoir, Va.; commdg. gen. 1st Corps. Support Command (Airborne), Fort Bragg, NC, 2000—02; comdr. Surface Deployment & Distbn. Command, 2002—04, US Army Combined Arms Support Command, Fort Lee, Va., 2004—05; dep. chief of staff for logistics (G-4) US Army, Washington, 2005—08; dep. comdr. US Army Materiel Command, Ft. Belvoir, Va., 2008, comdr., 2008—12. Bd. dirs. Logistics Mgmt. Inst., Inc., 2013—, L-3 Communications, 2013—. Decorated Disting. Svc. Medal, Defense Superior Medal, Legion of Merit with one Oak Leaf Cluster, Defense Meritorious Svc. Medal, Meritorious Svc. Medal with Silver Oak Leaf Cluster, Army Commendation Medal, Army Achievement Medal, Nat. Defense Svc. Medal with Bronze Star, SWASM, Kuwait Liberation Medal; named Woman of Yr., USO, 2012. Achievements include being the first woman promoted to the rank of four-star general in the United States Military, November 14, 2008. Avocations: running, sailing, tennis.*

DUPIES, DONALD ALBERT, retired civil engineer; b. Waukegan, Ill., Apr. 17, 1934; s. Renie Bernard and Catherine Marie (Dowe) D.; m. Margaret T. McKibbin, Sept. 29, 1962; children: Mark, Patrick, Peggy, Colleen. BCE, Marquette U., 1957. With Howard, Needles, Tammen & Bergendoff, Milw., 1959—, office engr., 1969-71, engr. in charge, 1971-74, assoc., 1974-79, cons. engr., ptnr., 1980-95. Pres. Great Lakes divsn. HNTB Corp., ret., 1995. Bd. dirs. Centurions of St. Joseph Hosp., Milw., 1971-76; cubmaster Milw. County coun. Boy Scouts Am., 1973-75; mem. Bd. Appeals, Town of Delafield, Wis., 1996-2002. Served with C.E. U.S. Army, 1957-59. Mem. ASCE (nat. dir. 1982-85), Internat. Inst. of Transportation Engrs., Marquette Club of Milwaukee, Marquette U. Engring. Alumni Assn. (dir. Milw. 1976-83pres. 1981-82), Tau Beta Pi, Chi Epsilon. Roman Catholic. Home: 1637 Jardin Ct The Villages FL 32162 Personal E-mail: dadupies@yahoo.com.

DUPLESSIS, ANN, city official, former state legislator; Sr. v.p. Liberty Bank & Trust; mem. Dist. 2 La. State Senate, 2004—10, chair commerce, consumer protection and internat. affairs com., mem. edn. com., judiciary C com., select com. on consumer affairs and tech., select com. on women and children; dep. chief adminstr. officer to Mitch Landrieu Office of Mayor, New Orleans, 2010—. Chmn. La. Serve Commn.; bd. trustees La. State U. Grad. Sch. Banking, La. Utilities Restoration Corp.; mem. adv. bd. State La. Small Bus. Devel. Ctr., The Working Uninsured Task Force, La., Total Cmty. Action, La. Democrat. Office: New Orleans City Hall 1300 Perdido St New Orleans LA 70112

DUPONT, HERBERT LANCASHIRE, medical educator, researcher; b. Toledo, Nov. 12, 1938; s. Robert L. and Martha (Lancashire) DuPont; m. Margaret Wright, June 9, 1963; children: Denise Lorraine, Andrew Wright BA, Ohio Wesleyan U., 1961; MD, Emory U., 1965; doctorate (hon.), U. Zurich, 2004. Diplomate Am. Bd. Internal Medicine. Resident U. Minn. Med. Ctr., Mpls., 1965-67; officer epidemic intelligence svc. CDC Atlanta, infectious disease fellow U. Md. Sch. Medicine, Balt., 1967-69; faculty, prof., dir. Infectious Diseases Program & Clin. Microbiology U. Tex., Houston, 1973—88, dir. Ctr. for Infectious Diseases, Sch. Pub. Health, 2000—, prof. epidemiology, Sch. Pub. Health, 1975—, Mary W. Kelsey chair med. sci., 1988—; chief internal medicine svc. St. Luke's Episcopal Hosp., Houston, 1995—; clin. prof. dept. medicine Baylor Coll. Medicine, Houston, 1995—, vice chmn. dept. medicine, H. Irving Schweppe chair, 1995—; prof. grad. sch. biomed. sci. U. Tex., 2002, Baylor Coll. Medicine, 2004—; adj. prof. infectious diseases, infection control and employee health divsn. internal medicine U. Tex. MD Anderson Cancer Ctr., 2008—; adj. prof. dept. clin. svcs. and adminstrns. U. Houston, Coll. Pharmacy, 2008—. Vaccines and related biologic products adv. com. US FDA, 1989—, cons., 1989—; mid.-east regional infectious disease rsch. program Inst. Medicine, NAS, 1989—94; bd. sci. counselors Nat. Ctr. for Infectious Diseases, CDC, 1992—96; bd. Kelsey Rsch. Found., 2001—, interim pres., 2001, pres., 2008—. Author various med. books; assoc. editor: Am. Jour. Epidemiology, 1978—81, Jour. Infectious Diseases, 1983—88; mem. editl. bd. Clin. Infectious Diseases, 1990—95, Infectious Diseases in Clin. Practice, 1992—, Jour. of Infection, 1997—, Jour. Infectious Diseases, 2006—, mem. editl. adv. bd. Gastroenterology & Hepatology, 2007—, dep. editor Jour. of Travel Medicine, 2003—11; contbr. articles to profl. jours. Lt. comdr. USN, 1967—69. Recipient John P. McGovern Outstanding Tchr., U. Tex.-Houston Med. Sch., 1991, Bronze medal of honor, government of France, 1993, Benjy Brooks award, U. Tex.-Houston, 1997, Disting. Achievement citation, Ohio Wesleyan U., 2006, Maxwell Finland award for Scientific Achievement, Nat. Found. Infectious Diseases, Washington, 2007; Rsch. grant NIH, 1975-, Laureate award, TAIM, ACP, 2008, Pres.'s Scholar award, U. Tex. Health Sci. Ctr., Houston, 2009; Disting. Med. Achievement award Emory U. Sch. Medicine, 2009, TIAA Disting. Med. Educator award. Master ACP; mem. Am. Soc. Clin. Investigation, Infectious Diseases Soc. Am. (counselor 1978-81, sec. 1982-87, pres. 1989-90, Alexander Fleming Lifetime Achievement award 2010), Nat. Found. Infectious Diseases (bd. dirs. 1981-2002, v.p. 1994-97, pres. 1997-99), Am. Clin. and Climatol. Assn. (recorder 2000-05, coun. mem. 2000-, pres.-elect. 2005-06, pres. 2006-07), Am. Epidemiology Soc., Assn. Am. Physicians, U.S. Mex. Found. Sci. and Tech. (com. chair health 1994-99), Tex. Acad. Internal Medicine (bd. dirs. 2003-07), Internat. Soc. Travel Medicine (pres. 1991-93), Am. Coll. Physicians (gov. S. Tex. bd. govs. 2003-07), Alpha Omega Alpha. Republican. Methodist. Office: St Luke's Episcopal Hosp # MC 1-164 6720 Bertner St Houston TX 77030-2697

DUPRE, REGGIE PAUL, former state legislator; b. Jan. 10, 1958; m. Yvonne Edkins; children: Kenny, Melody, Brittney. Dep. sheriff, 1979—85; mem., parish coun., 1988—96; mem. Dist. 53 La. House of Reps., 1996—2002; mem. Dist. 20 La. State Senate, 2003—09; owner Bourg Supermarket Inc.; co-owner Bev's Bouquet Inc. Mem.: KC, C. of C., Vol. Fire Dept. Democrat. Catholic. Fax: 985-873-2016. Business E-Mail: lasen20@legis.state.la.us.

DUPRI, JERMAINE, recording industry executive, music producer; b. Asheville, NC, Sept. 23, 1973; s. Michael and Tina Mauldin; 1 child, Shaniah. Record prodr., 1987—; founder, CEO So So Def Prodns., Atlanta, 1989—; solo artist, 1998—; sr. v.p. Arista Records, 2003—05; pres. Virgin Records Urban Music, 2005—06, Island Records Urban Music divsn., NYC, 2007—09, TAG Records, 2008—. Singer, songwriter (albums) Jermaine Dupri Presents: Life in 1472, 1998, Jermaine Dupri Presents: 12 Soulful Nights, 1998, Instructions, 2001, Green Light, 2004, prodr. for artists including Aaliyah, Destiny's Child, Da Brat, Warren G, Aretha Franklin, Dru Hill, Jay-Z, Alicia Keys, Lil' Kim, Elton John, Kris Kross, Run DMC, Whodini, Usher, Funkmaster Flex, Johnny Gill, Murphy Lee, Ludacris, MC Lyte, Master P., Monica, Chante' Moore, Nelly, New Edition, TLC, Tamia, Tyrese, Lil' Bow Wow, Mariah Carey and others; actor: (films) In Too Deep, 1999, The New Guy, 2002; (TV films) Carmen: A Hip Hopera, 2001, (TV appearances) A Different World, 1992, Moesha, 1996; co-prodr.: (films) Like Mike, 2002; co-author (with Samantha Marshall): Young, Rich and Dangerous: The Making of a Music Mogul, 2007; host (TV series) Cuttin' Up, 2004—. Recipient Prodr. of Yr., Black Entertainment TV (BET) Hip-Hop Awards, 2006; co-recipient Best R&B Song for We Belong Together, Grammy Awards, 2006; named Songwriter of Yr., ASCAP, 1999; named one of The Power 150, Ebony mag., 2008. Achievements include making it to #1 on Top R&B/Hip Hop Chart and #3 on the Billboard 200 for "Jermaine Dupri Presents: Life in 1472" in 1998. Office: So So Def Recordings Inc NW #750 1350 Spring St Atlanta GA 30309-2870

DURACK, DAVID TULLOCH, medical products executive; b. Perth, Australia, Dec. 18, 1944; s. Reginald Wyndham and Grace Enid (Tulloch) D.; m. Carmen Elizabeth Prosser, July 25, 1970; children: Jeremy, Kimberley, Sonya, Justin. BS, U. Western Australia, MB, 1969; DPhil, Oxford U., Eng., 1976. Diplomate Am. Bd. Internal Medicine, Royal Australasian Coll. Physicians, Royal Coll. Physicians U.K. Chief, resident medicine, asst. prof., medicine U. Wash., 1975—77; chief, infectious diseases and internat. health Duke University, Durham, 1977—94, prof., medicine, microbiology & immunology, 1982—94, cons. prof., medicine, 1994; chmn., dept. medicine, chief, divsn. infectious diseases Health Care Internat., Clydebank, Scotland, 1994—95; worldwide med. dir. Becton Dickinson Microbiology Sys., Balt., 1995—99; v.p., corp. med. affairs Becton, Dickinson & Co., 1999, sr. v.p., corp. med. affairs, 2006—. Co-editor: Infections of the Central Nervous System, 1996; contbr. articles to profl. jours. Rhodes scholar, 1969; NIH grantee, 1980, 86-91, grantee R.J. Reynolds Co., 1983-88, Carnegie Corp., 1989-94, grantee Roche Labs., 1991-94. Fellow Royal Coll. Physicians U.K., ACP, Royal Australasian Coll. Physicians, Infectious Diseases Soc. Am., Am. Soc. Clin. Investigation, Am. Fedn. Clin. Research Presbyterian. Avocation: flying. Office: Becton Dickinson and Co 1 Becton Dr Franklin Lakes NJ 07417-1880 Office Fax: 201-847-6475. Business E-Mail: david_durack@bd.com.

DURAND, SYDNIE MAE, state legislator; b. Apr. 30, 1934; m. Alcee John Durand (dec.). Acct., 1970—75; environ. regulation, 1975—92; police juror, 1979—92; house rep. La.; mem. Health & Welfare Com., Ways & Means Com., Retirement Com., House Exec. Com., 1992—; La. state rep. Dist. 46, 1992—. Recipient Outstanding Environmentalist, WOW, Regional Outstanding Citizen, City of St. Martinville, Bishop's medal. Democrat. Roman Catholic. Mailing: PO Box 2840 Parks LA 70582 Office Fax: 318-845-4095.

DURANT, KEVIN WAYNE, professional basketball player; b. Washington, Sept. 29, 1988; s. Wayne and Wanda Pratt. Student, U. Tex., Austin, 2006—07. Forward-guard Seattle SuperSonics, 2007—08, Oklahoma City Thunder, 2008—. Mem. US nat. team FIBA World Championships, Turkey, 2010, Summer Olympic Games, London, 2012. Recipient Oscar Robertson Trophy, US Basketball Writers Assn., 2007, Adolph Rupp Trophy, 2007, Naismith Coll. Player of Yr. award, Atlanta Tipoff Club, 2007, John R. Wooden award, 2007, Gold medal, FIBA World Championship, 2010, Gold medal, men's basketball, Summer Olympic Games, 2012; named McDonald's All-American Game co-MVP, 2006, Jordan All-American Classic Game MVP, 2006, Divsn. 1 Player of Yr., Nat. Assn. Basketball Coaches, 2007, Coll. Basketball Player of Yr., The Sporting News, 2007, 1st Team NCAA All-American, AP, 2007, Nat. Player of Yr., 2007, NBA Rookie of Yr., 2008, 1st Team All-Rookie, NBA, 2008, 1st Team All-NBA, 2010—13, NBA All-Star Game MVP, 2012; named to McDonald's All-American Team, 2006, Western Conf. All-Star Team, NBA, 2010—13. Achievements include being the second overall pick in the NBA Draft, 2007; leading the NBA in: scoring, 2010-12; free-throw percentage, 2013; becoming the youngest scoring champion in NBA history (21 years old), 2010. Office: Oklahoma City Thunder Two Leadership Sq 211 N Robinson Ave Ste 300 Oklahoma City OK 73102*

DURBIN, DEAN D., educational association administrator; BS in Acctg., St. Francis U., Loretto, Pa., 1974. Acctg. supr. McGraw-Hill Companies, Inc., v.p., group contr. constrn. info. group, 1987—94; v.p., CFO, Profl. Pub. Thomson Corp., 1995—97; sr. v.p., chief fin. officer TC Advt. (not Vertis), 1997—2000; CFO Vertis Inc., 2000—04, pres., 2004—06, COO, 2005—06, CEO, 2006, bd. dirs., 2006; exec. v.p., CFO American Media, Inc., 2008—09; CFO Cengage Learning, Inc., 2009—. Bd. dir. Balt. Mus. Industry. Office: Cengage Learning Inc 200 First Stamford Pl Ste 400 Florence KY 41022-6904 Office Phone: 203-965-8600. Business E-Mail: dean.durbin@cengage.com.

DURELL, JACK, psychiatrist; b. NYC, July 5, 1928; s. Sam and Helen (Schwartzman) D.; m. Viviane M. diGioja, May 19, 1955. BA summa cum laude, Harvard U., 1949; MD cum laude, Yale U., 1953. Rsch. biochemist NIMH, Bethesda, Md., 1954-57, chief, sect. of psychiatry, 1963-67; v.p. med. affairs, clin. dir. The Psychiat. Inst., Washington, 1967-72, pres., med. dir., 1972-78; assoc. dir. sci. Nat. Inst. Drug Abuse, Rockville, Md., 1979-86; med. dir. clin. affairs div. Ea. Va. Med. Authority, Norfolk, 1986-87; chmn. dept. psychiatry Mercy Cath. Med. Ctr., Phila., 1987-92; prof. psychiatry U. Pa., Phila., 1987—. Exec. dir. Treatment Rsch. Inst., 1992—; pres. Delta Metrics, 1994—; pres. The Psychiat. Inst. Found., Washington, 1973-78; trustee Phila. Mental Health Care Connection, 1987-89. Editor: The Changing Clinical Picture of Schizophrenia, 1977; asst. editor-in-chief Jour. Psychiat. Rsch., 1966-82, mem. editorial bd., 1982—; contbr. to numerous med. publs. With USPHS, 1953-86. Fellow Am. Psychiat. Assn.; mem. Am. Acad. Psychiatrists in Alcoholism and Addictions (sec.-treas. 1985-93), Am. Psychopathological Assn., Am. Coll. Neuropsychopharmacology. Personal E-mail: jadurell@aol.com, jadurell@gmail.com. Business E-Mail: jdurell@deltametrics.com.

DURHAM, J(OSEPH) PORTER, JR., lawyer, educator; b. Nashville, May 11, 1961; AB in Polit. Sci. and History cum laude, Duke U., 1982, JD, 1985. Bar: Tenn. 1985, Md. 1988, NC 2005. Ptnr. Miller & Martin, Chattanooga, 1990-96, Baker, Donelson, Bearman & Caldwell, Chattanooga, 1997—2003, chmn. corp. dept., 1998—2003; dir. edn. divsn., gen. counsel Duke Endowment, 2003—07; COO, gen. counsel Global Endowment Mgmt. LP, 2007—. Adj. prof. dept. acctg. and fin. U. Tenn., Chattanooga, 1992-98; participant Russian tax code adv. group, 1999; mem. grievance com. NC Bar, 2005-08. Editor Duke Law Mag., 1984-85; contbr. articles to profl. jours. Mem. Balt. Citizens Planning and Housing Assn., 1988-90; career edn. spkr. Explorer Scout program Boy Scouts Am., 1985, 88, 90-92; mem., v.p. bd. dirs., chmn. fin. com. Waxter Ctr. Found., 1989-91; mem., sec. bd. dirs. Assn. for Visual Artists, 1993-96; trustee Good Shepherd Sch., 1992-93, Good Shepherd Endowment, 2003-04; chmn. spl. mgmt. com. Nashville Rehab. Hosp., 1995; trail maintenance vol. U.S. Pk. Svc., 1993-95; mem. adv. com. Chattanooga State Tech. C.C.; bd. dirs. Sr. Neighbors, Inc., 2001-03; mem. investment com. Trinity Episcopal Sch., 2005—09; mem. bd. visitors Davidson Coll., 2006—09, Johnson C. Smith U., 2006-08, trustee, 2008-, Duke Law Sch. 2011-, Trinity Episcopal Sch., 2010-; mem., bd. trustees NC Humanities Coun., 2007-13, Duke Durham Neighborhood Partnership, 2008-12, Blumenthal Performing Arts Ctr., 2012-. Recipient Outstanding Svc. award Waxter Ctr. Found., 1991. Mem. Tenn. Bar Assn., Md. Bar Assn., N.C. Bar Assn., Duke U. Law Sch. Alumni Assn. (bd. dirs. 1994-97), Duke U. Gen. Alumni Assn. (bd. dirs. 1986-92, 2006-09, exec. com. 1989-92). Office: Global Endowment Mgmt LP 550 S Tryon St Ste 3500 Charlotte NC 28202-4012 Office Phone: 704-333-8282. Business E-Mail: pdurham@globalendowment.com.

DURHAM, MICHAEL JONATHAN, investment professional; b. NYC, Jan. 19, 1951; s. Walter Alan and Joyce D. (Packham) D.; m. Marilyn James Marr, May 19, 1984; children: Michael Allen, Elizabeth Marr. BA in Econs., U. Rochester, 1973; MBA in Fin., Cornell U., 1977. Asst. v.p. Bank Julius Bar & Co., NYC, 1978-79; sr. analyst fin. planning American Airlines, Inc., Ft. Worth, 1979-80, mgr. corp. fin., 1980-82, dir. corp. fin., 1982-84, asst. treas. corp. fin., 1984-85, v.p. corp. devel., 1985-87, v.p. fin. and planning, 1987-89, CFO, 1989-95, sr. v.p. fin., CFO, 1989-95; pres., CEO Sabre, Inc., Dallas, 1995-99; pres., CEO and cons. Cognizant Associates Inc., Dallas, 2000—; Non-exec. chmn. Asbury Automotive Group, Inc., 2003—; non-exec. chmn. Hotwire, Inc. Bd. dirs. Acxiom Corp., Culligan Internat., Northwest Airlines, Hertz Global Holdings, SCI Solutions.; bd. dirs. Kinko's Inc., Scheduling.com, GridOne Adv. Corp. and AGL Resources Inc. Trustees coun. U. Rochester, 1992—. Mem. Brookhollow Golf Club. Republican. Episcopalian. Avocations: bridge, golf. Mailing: AGL Resources Inc Bd Directors P O Box 4569 Atlanta GA 30302-4569 Office Phone: 404-584-4000. Personal E-mail: mjdurham@yahoo.com.

DUROCHER, FRANCES A., retired physician, educator; b. Woonsocket, RI, Mar. 11, 1943; d. Armand D. and Teresa (Leverone) DuRocher. BA with honors, Trinity Coll., 1964; MS, Brown U., 1966; postgrad., Woman's Med. Coll., 1970. Med. resident Phila. VA Hosp. and Med. Coll. Pa., 1971-73; assoc. in internal med. Guthrie Clinic Ltd., Sayre, Pa., 1973-79; assoc. in internal medicine Annandale (Va.)

Group Health Assocs., 1979-87; assoc. chair internal medicine Annandale Group Health Assoc., 1986-87; pvt. practice Fairfax, Va., 1987—2004; ret., 2004. Clin. asst. prof. med. and health svcs. George Washington U. Med. Sch., Washington, 1994-2004. Bd. dirs. Fairways of Penderbrook Homeowners Assn., 1993—, sec., 1995-96, pres., 1996-2007. Mem. AMA, ACP-Am. Soc. Internal Medicine, Am. Med. Women's Assn. (exec. bd. br. I, 1985-91, pres. 1987-88), Med. Soc. Va., Med. Soc. No. Va. Avocations: reading, travel.

DURRETT, JAMES FRAZER, JR., retired lawyer; b. Atlanta, Mar. 23, 1931; s. James Frazer and Cora Frazer (Morton) D.; m. Lucretia McPherson, June 9, 1956; children: James Frazer III, William McPherson, Lucretia Heston Miller, Thomas Ratcliffe. AB, Emory U., 1952; postgrad., Princeton U., 1952-53; LLB cum laude, Harvard U., 1956. Bar: Ga. 1955. Ptnr. Alston & Bird (and predecessor firm), Atlanta, 1956-97, retired, 1997. Adj. prof. Emory U. Law Sch., 1961—77. Trustee emeritus Student Aid Found., The Howard Sch. Mem. Am. Law Inst. (life, adv. estate and gift tax project, restatement, second. property, Fed. Income Tax project), Capital City Club, Harvard Club (Atlanta). Presbyterian. Office: Alston & Bird 1 Atlantic Ctr Atlanta GA 30309-3400 Home: 3747 Peachtree Rd Apt 517 Atlanta GA 30319

DUSSEK, STEVEN P., telecommunications industry executive; b. 1956; Grad., Western Ky. U. V.p. ops. McCaw Cellular; pres. McCaw Cellular Comm. Paging Divsn.; sr. v.p., COO PageNet, 1993—95; pres., gen. mgr. AT&T Wireless PCS Markets Northeast, 1995—96; pres. west region Nextel Comm. Inc., 1996—98; pres. Nextel Internat., 1996—98, CEO, COO, 1999; pres., CEO NII Holdings, Inc., 1999, CEO, 1999—2000; exec. v.p., COO Nextel Comm. Inc., Reston, Va., 1999—2001; CEO ScoreBoard Inc., 2002, Am. Cellular Corp.; pres., CEO Dobson Communications Corp., Oklahoma City, 2005—07; CEO NII Holdings, Inc., Reston, Va., 2008—. Bd. dirs. NII Holdings Inc., Am. Cellular Corp., Tatara Systems Inc., Dobson Communications Corp., 2006—07. Bd. dir. Okla. Zoological Soc.; trustee Okla. Health Ctr. Found. Office: NII Holdings Ste 1000 1875 Explorer St Reston VA 20190 Office Phone: 703-390-5100.

DUTKOWSKY, ROBERT M., computer company executive; b. Jan. 2, 1955; BS in Indsl. Engring. & Labor Rels., Cornell U., 1977. Various sr. mgmt. positions, including v.p., distbn., Asia Pacific, worldwide sales & mktg., RS/6000 bus. IBM Corp., 1977—97; exec. v.p., mktg. and channels EMC Corp., 1997—99, pres., data gen., 1999; chmn., pres., CEO GenRad Inc., 2000—02; pres., assembly test divsn. Teradyne Inc., 2001—02; chmn., pres., CEO J.D. Edwards & Co., Inc., 2002—04, Egenera Inc., Marlboro, Mass., 2004—06; CEO, bd. dirs. Tech Data Corp., Clearwater, Fla., 2006—. Bd. dirs. SEPATON Inc., McAfee Inc., 2001—07. Recipient Ellis Island Medal of Honor, 2000. Office: Tech Data Corp 5350 Tech Data Dr Clearwater FL 33760 Office Phone: 727-539-7429. Office Fax: 727-538-7803. Business E-Mail: bob.dutkowsky@techdata.com.

DUTT, KAMLA, retired medical educator; b. Lahore, Punjab, India; came to U.S., 1969; d. Gulzari Lal and Raj Bansi Dutt. BS with honors, Panjab U., Chandigarh, India, 1961, MS in Zoology with honors, 1962, PhD, 1970. Rsch. assoc. Harvard Med. Sch. Sidney Farber Cancer Ctr., Boston, 1972-76; rsch. assoc. Eye Inst. Retinal Fedn., Boston, 1977-80; sr. rsch. assoc. Yale Med. Ctr., New Haven, 1980-81, Emory U., Atlanta, 1981-82; asst. prof. Morehouse Sch. Medicine, Atlanta, 1983-89, assoc. prof., 1989—2001, prof., 2001—11; ret., 2011. Sci. adv. bd. Fernbank Sci. Ctr., Atlanta. Contbr. numerous articles to sci. jours.; author short stories (in Hindi); prodr., actor 3 maj. plays, Atlanta; actor 11 maj. plays, India. Bd. dirs. VSEI (vol. fundraising orgn. for edn. in India), 1973-78; v.p. Indian Am. Cultural Assn., 1985; podium spkr., participant King Week, 1990, 91, 93; spkr. Gandhi Day Celebration, 1984, 85; key participant Intercultural Conf., 1990; main participant joint document Women's Perspective; active human rights issues; stake holder Vision 20/20 Collaborative State of Ga., diversity and edn. coms., 1995. Hindu. Achievements include establishment of human ocular cell lines by gene transfection, used as model for study of eye diseases and tissue engineering. Business E-Mail: kdutt1769@gmail.com.

DUTTON, DELVIS, state legislator; b. Savannah, Ga. m. Danielle Dutton; 2 children. Attended, Ga. So. U., Statesboro. With United Parcel Svc.; founder, well driller Gen. Pump and Well; mem. Dist. 166 Ga. House of Representatives, 2011—. Republican. Christian. Office: PO Box 928 Glennville GA 30427 also: Georgia House of Reps 504 Coverdell Legis Office Bldg Atlanta GA 30334 Office Phone: 912-271-9092, 404-656-0188. Business E-Mail: delvis.dutton@house.ga.gov.

DUTTON, HAROLD V., JR., state legislator; b. Houston, Feb. 17, 1945; s. Harold V. and Mildred Marie (Earle) Dutton; m. Olivia Perdue, 1976; m. Phyllis Faykus, 1987; children: Melonie R., Harold V. III, Peter, Jon Harold. Former pres. Four Star Broadcasting TV; ind. investor & atty.; mem. Dist. 142 Tex. House of Representatives, 1985—. Mem.: NAACP (mem. energy & econ. devel. Com. 1983), Am. Assn. Blacks Energy (regional coord. 1984—), Hope Devel. (bd. chmn. 1983—), St. Elizabeth Hosp. Found. (bd. chmn. 1984—). Democrat. Roman Catholic. Office: 8799 N Loop East Ste 305 Houston TX 77029 also: Room CAP 3N.5 Capitol PO Box 2910 Austin TX 78768 Office Phone: 713-692-9192, 512-463-0510. Office Fax: 713-692-6791.

DUVAL, CYNTHIA, art historian, museum administrator, curator, consultant; b. Port Talbot, South Wales, Oct. 6, 1932; came to U.S., 1972; d. Joseph and Esther (Goldberg) Armstrong; m. Marcel Duval, Aug. 26, 1973; 1 son, Jonathan Armstrong. Degree, Chelsea Sch. Art, London, 1953, U. Arts London. Antiques buyer Harrod's, London, 1972-73; gen. appraiser Sotheby's, N.Y., 1973-77; lectr. Ringling Sch. Art, Sarasota, Fla., 1977-79; adminstr. John and Mable Ringling program Tampa Mus. Art Assocs., Sarasota, 1979-80; sr. curator RMA decorative arts Ringling Mus. Art, Sarasota, 1980-86; advisor State Div. of Culture, 1985-86; grants panelist for visual arts Fla., 1985; asst. dir./curator decorative arts Mus. Fine Arts, St. Petersburg, 1989-93; prof. art history St. Petersburg Jr. Coll., 1994—. Cons. to the dir. Wonders cultural program, City of Memphis; liaison to Gov.'s Mansion, Tallahassee, 1984-85; coord. mus. studies program St. Petersburg Coll.; curator Fla. Internat. Mus., 2003-07; chief curator and curator decorative arts Mus. Arts and Scis., Dayton Beach, 2007-. Author: History of Lighting and Lamps, 1972; Toys of Long Ago, 1972; The Life of a Gentleman, 1972; Love and Marriage, 1972, (catalogs) 500 Years of the Decorative Arts, 1984, Medieval and Renaissance Armor, 1984, Jewelry Through the Ages, 1989, Figures from Life: Porcelain Sculpture from the Metropolitan Museum of Art, 1740-1780, 1992. Recipient Designers Image award Am. Assn. Interior Designers Avocation: study of social history. Home: 28 Cormorant Cir Daytona Beach FL 32119 Office: Mus Arts and Scis Daytona Beach FL 32114 Office Phone: 386-255-0285 316. Business E-Mail: cduval@moas.org.

DUVAL, STANWOOD RICHARDSON, JR., federal judge; b. New Orleans, Feb. 8, 1942; BA, La. State U., 1964, LLB, 1966. Ptnr. Duval, Arceneaux & Lewis, Houma, La., 1966-94, Duval, Funderburk, Sundberry & Lovell, L.L.P., 1966-94; asst. city atty. Terrebonne Parish Consol. Govt., 1970-72, parish atty., 1988-92; judge US Dist. Ct. (ea. dist.) La., New Orleans, 1994—2008, sr. judge, 2008—. Mem. Indigent Def. Bd., 1976-82; elected La. Constnl. Conv., 1973, mem. exec. br. com., Com. to Write Rules of Procedure. Mem. Terrebone Parish; bd. dirs. Covenant House, New Orleans, 2001-. Mem. ABA (adv. com. appellate rules 1997-2003), La. Law Inst. (coun. 1996-2000), Tulane Inns Ct. (pres. 2001-04). Avocations: travel, scuba diving, fishing, performing arts. Office: US Dist Ct Ea Dist 500 Poydras St C368 New Orleans LA 70130

DUVALL, ROBERT, gas industry executive; b. Columbia, SC; BS in Civil Engring., Clemson U., 1984. Registered profl. engr., Ga. Mng. dir., field ops. Atlanta Gas Light Co.; joined AGL Resources, Inc., 1984, various engring. positions, including region mgr., Cumming and North Fulton svc., project mgr., field svc. automation project, mgr., region engring. and ops., v.p., gen. mgr., Va. and Md. ops., 2005—. Former bd. dirs. Atlanta Tech. Coll., Atlanta Union Mission, Greater North Fulton C. of C.; mem. Alpharetta Rotary Club. Office: AGL Resources Inc Ten Peachtree Pl NE Atlanta GA 30309 Office Phone: 404-584-4000. Office Fax: 404-584-3945. Business E-Mail: RDuVall@aglresources.com.

DUVENHAGE, SUSAN B., museum administrator; b. Orchard Pk., NY; BS in Pub. Rels., U. Fla. Profl. accredation in pub. rels. Fla. Pub. Rels. Assn., 1997. Asst. dir., cmty. rels. Shared Healthcare, 1990—98; dir., devel. U. Fla. Found., 1998—2002; various positions including assoc. dir., dept. head exhbns. and pub. programs Fla. Mus. Natural History, Gainesville, 2002—06; pres., CEO Adventure Sci. Ctr., 2007—. Team capt. March of Dimes, United Way of Alachua County; active Gainesville Area C. of C., Pick-An-Angel Program, Alachua County Schs.; bd. dirs. Jr. Achievement North Ctrl. Fla. Mem.: Kiwanis Internat. (past Fla. dist. state chair), Gainesville Kiwanis Club (past pres.). Office: Adventure Sci Ctr 800 Fort Negley Blvd Nashville TN 37203 Office Phone: 615-862-5160. Office Fax: 615-862-5178.

DUXBURY, THOMAS CARL, planetary science professor; b. Fort Wayne, Ind., Jan. 1, 1960; s. John and Justine D.; m. Natalia D.; children. BSEE, Purdue U., 1965, MSEE, 1966. Planetary scientist Jet Propulsion Lab., Pasadena, Calif., 1966—; mem. NASA Mariner mission sci. investigation of Mars, Venus and Mercury, 1969—74; mem. NASA Viking mission sci. team, Mars, Phobos and Deimos investigations, 1974—81; mem. NASA Voyage mission sci. teams, Jupiter and Saturn investigation, 1977—82; project sci. NASA Sci. Internet, 1984—86; mem. US-Russia Joint Working Group for Mars Exploration, 1987—97; mem. Soviet PHOBOS mission, interdisciplinary sci., 1988—89; mem. Clementine mission sci. team for lunar exploration, 1992—94; mem. Russian Mars 96 mission interdisciplinary sci., 1990—96; project mgr. NASA Stardust mission, 1999—2007; NASA Mars Global Surveyor mission sci. team, 1996—2007; mem. European Space Agy. Mars Express mission interdisciplinary sci., 1999—; sci. definition team dep. leader, Clementine II, 1997—98; cartography chair NASA Mars Program, 2002—; scientist Mars Odyssey THEMIS, 2006—; mem. sci. team Mars Reconnaissance Orbiter, 2007—; mem. sci. team Lunar Reconnaissance Orbiter, 2007—09; project mgr. NASA NEXT, 2007—08, NASA EPOXI, 2007—08; prof. GMU Planetary Sci., 2008—, NASA Princ. Inv. Russian Phobos Sample Return Mission, 2008—. Co-author: Television Investigations of Phobos, 1994. Recipient Sci. Achievement medal NASA, Washington, 1972, Burka award Inst. of Navigation, 1973, Achievement awards NASA, 1978-82, Soviet Space Mission Svc. medal, Lavochkin Assn., The Hague, Netherlands, 1991, Innovation award, Popular Mechanics 2006, Program Excellence award, Aviation Week, 2006, Nelson P. Jackson award, Nat. Space Club, 2007, Laureate award, Aviation award, 2007, Stellar award, Rotary Space Achievement, 2007, Nat. Air, Space Mus. Achievement trophy, 2008, medal Russian Spa Agy., 2012, Photos Sample Return Ops. award, 2012. Mem. Am. Geophysical Union, Am. Astronomical Soc., Russian Assn. for Space Sci. & Tech. Achievements include production of first map of another planet's moon; discovery of the Groove Network on Phobos (Mars moon); co-discovery of the Rings of Jupiter, co-discoverer of the Jupiter Lightning; produced the most precise cartographic maps of Mars landing sites for Viking, Pathfinder, Mars Polar Lander, Beagle 2 and MER Spirit and Opportunity; led the world's first planetary mission to return cometary samples to Earth. Home: George Mason University 4400 University Dr 6C3 School of Physics Astron & Comp Sci Fairfax VA 22030 Business E-Mail: tduxbury@gmu.edu.

DUYNE, BETH VAN, mayor, Irving, Texas; children: Katie, Pearce. BA magna cum laude, Cornell U. Pres. BCI Mktg. Group, 2002—; mem. Irving City Coun., Tex., 2004—10; v.p. mktg. Akili, 2008—09; sr. dir. corp. comm. LSG Sky Chefs, 2010—; mayor City of Irving, Tex., 2011—. Voting del. and rep. voting mem. Nat. League of Cities; past chmn. Hackberry Creek Parks Com.; vol. TexasFest; mem. Lyric Stage Guild. Mem.: North Ctrl. Tex. Coun. of Govts., Nat. Assn. of Regional Couns. (rep. voting mem.), Las Colinas PTA (former bd. mem.), Irving Rep. Women's Club (outgoing pres.). Office: City Hall Office of the Mayor 825 W Irving Blvd Irving TX 75060 Office Phone: 972-721-2410. E-mail: bvanduyne@cityofirving.org.*

DWORS, ROBERT F., real estate company executive; BA, Bowling Green State U., Ohio; MBA, Ohio State U., 1967. Sr. v.p., corp. real estate svcs. AutoNation, Inc., Ft. Lauderdale, Fla., 1995—2006; pres., Resort Devel. Cypress Equities, 2006—. Bd. dirs. Bluegreen Corp., 2005—. Office: Cypress Equities 8343 Douglas Ave Ste 300 Dallas TX 75225 Office Phone: 214-561-8800. Business E-Mail: robert.dwors@cypressequities.com.

DWYER, GERALD PAUL, JR., economist, bank executive; b. Pittsfield, Mass., July 9, 1947; s. Gerald Paul and Mary Frances (Weir) Dwyer; m. Katherine Marie Lepiane, Jan. 15, 1966; children: Tamara K., Gerald P. III, Angela M., Michael J. L., Terence F. BBA, U. Wash., 1969; MA in Econs., U. Tenn., 1973; PhD in Econs., U. Chgo., 1979. Economist Fed. Res. Bank, St. Louis, 1972-74, Chgo., 1976-77, asst. v.p. Atlanta, 1997-98, v.p., 1998—2008; dir. Ctr. Fin. Innovation and Stability, 2009—12; asst. prof. Tex. A&M U., College Station, 1977-81, Emory U., Atlanta, 1981-84, sr. rsch. assoc. Law and Econ. Ctr., 1982-84; assoc. prof. U. Houston, 1984-89; prof. Clemson (S.C.) U., 1989-99, acting head dept. econ., 1992-93; vis. prof. scholar Clemson U., 2013—. Vis. scholar Fed. Res. Bank, Atlanta, 1982—84, St. Louis, 1987—89, Atlanta, 1994—97, Mpls., 1995; vis. fin. economist Commodity Futures Trading Commn., Washington, 1990; vis. faculty Ga. State U., 1997, U. Ga., 1999—2000, 2003, U. Rome, 2000—04, U. Carlos III, Madrid, 2005—, Trinity Coll. Dublin, 2009—. Contbr. articles to profl. jours. Recipient Best Article award, Econ. Inquiry, 2006, Disting. Scholar, Assn. Pvt. Enterprise Edn., 2006; fellow, Earhart Found., 1975—77; vis. scholar, Inst. for INternat. Integration Studies, Trinity Coll., 2005, Cambridge Endowment for Rsch. in Fin., Cambridge U., 2006, Ctr. Fin. Analysis and Policy, Cambridge U., 2007; Weaver fellow, Intercollegiate Studies Inst., 1974—75, Rsch. grantee, Earhart Found., NSF. Mem.: Mt. Pelerin Soc., Western Econ. Assn. (bd. dirs. 2005—08), Assn. of Pvt. Enterprise Edn. (exec. com. 2002—06, 2002—06, v.p. 2007—08, pres. 2008—09, exec. com. 2009—10, mem. exec. com. 2012—), Soc. Nonlinear Dynamics and Econometrics (treas. 1997—2003, exec. com. 1997—2006, pres. 2003—05), Am. Fin. Assn., Am. Econ. Assn., Phi Kappa Phi, Beta Gamma Sigma. Avocation: sailing. Office: Dept Economics Clemson University Clemson SC 29634-1309 Business E-Mail: gdwyer@dwyerecon.com.

DWYER, STACEY H., construction executive; BS in Acctg., Southeastern Okla. State U., Durant; MS in Acctg., U. Tex., Arlington. CPA. Auditor Ernst and Young, Ft. Worth, 1989—91; acctg. mgr. D.R. Horton, Inc., Ft. Worth, 1991, with investments divsn., 1996, asst. sec., asst. v.p., 1998—2000, exec. v.p. investor rels., 2000—, treas., 2003—. Office: DR Horton Inc DR Horton Tower 301 Commerce St Ste 500 Fort Worth TX 76102 Office Phone: 817-390-8200.

DYAR, KATHRYN WILKIN, pediatrician; b. Colquitt, Ga., Feb. 20, 1945; d. Patrick McWhorter and Virginia (Wilkin) Dyar; m. James Ansley Patten, Jan. 1, 1985. BS in Biology, Emory U., Decatur, Ga., 1966; MD, Med. Coll. Ga., Augusta, 1970. Resident in pediatrics Eugene Talmadge Meml. Hosp., Augusta, Ga., 1970-72, Georgetown U. Hosp., Washington, 1972-73; pediatrician Children's Clinic, Tifton, Ga., 1973-74, Children and Youth Project, Norfolk, Va., 1974-83, 90-95, dir., 1990-94; pediatrician Hampton (Va.) Health Dept., 1983-90.

DYBALA, KELLY MAYO, lawyer; BA, Okla. State U., 1995; JD, U. Tex., 1998. Bar: Tex. 1998. Ptnr. in the corp. dept. Weil, Gotshal & Manges, LLP, Dallas. Named a Tex. Rising Star, Tex. Super Lawyers/Tex. Monthly, 2009, Leading Lawyer, Banking and Fin. in Tex., Chambers USA, 2010; named to The 45 Under 45, The American Lawyer, 2011. Office: Weil Gotshal & Manges LLP 200 Crescent Ct Ste 300 Dallas TX 75201 Office Phone: 214-746-7898. Office Fax: 214-746-7777. Business E-Mail: kelly.dybala@weil.com.

DYCK, WALTER PETER, gastroenterologist, educator, academic administrator; b. Winkler, Man., Can., 1935; MD, U. Kans., 1961. Diplomate Am. Bd. Internal Medicine, Am. Bd. Gastroenterology. Intern Henry Ford Hosp., Detroit, 1961—62, resident in internal medicine, 1962-63, 65-66; rsch. fellow gastroenterology U. Zurich, Switzerland, 1963—64; fellow enzymology rsch. U. Toronto, Ont., Canada, 1964—65; fellow gastroenterology Mt. Sinai Sch. Medicine, NYC, 1966—68; mem. sr. staff Scott and White Clinic, Temple, Tex., 1968—2006, chmn. dept. rsch., 1969—72, dir. divsn. gastroenterology, 1972—96; prof. medicine, dir. divsn. gastroenterology Tex. A&M Coll. Medicine, 1978—96, sr. assoc. dean, 1996—2003, exec. assoc. dean, 2003—06, prof. emeritus, 2006—; adminstrv. dir. rsch. and edn. divsn., chief acad. officer Scott and White Meml. Hosp., Temple, 1996—2006; sr. advisor Temple Health and Biosci. Econ. Devel. Corp., 2006—11. Mem. gen. medicine study sect. A NIH, 1973-77. Fellow ACP, Am. Coll. Gastroenterology; mem. AMA, Am. Fedn. Clin. Rsch., Am. Gastroenterology Assn., Am. Physiol. Soc., So. Soc. Clin. Investigation, Soc. for Exptl. Biology and Medicine, Am. Pancreatic Assn., N.Y. Acad. Scis. Home: 9424 Hackberry Rd Holland TX 76534 E-mail: wdyck@sw.org.

DYE, THOMAS ROY, political science professor; b. Pitts., Dec. 16, 1935; s. James Clair and Marguerite Ann (Dewan) D.; m. Joan Grace Wohleber, June 29, 1957; children: Roy Thomas, Cheryl Price. BA, Pa. State U., 1957, MA, 1959; PhD, U. Pa., 1961. Asst. prof. polit. sci. U. Wis., Madison, 1962-63; assoc. prof., head dept. polit. sci. U. Ga., Athens, 1963-68; prof., chmn. dept. govt. Fla. State U., Tallahassee, 1968-72, dir. policy scis., 1978-91, McKenzie prof. govt., 1991—98, prof. emeritus polit. sci., 1998—. Vis. prof. polit. studies Bar Ilan U., Israel, 1972, U. Ariz., 1976 Author: Politics, Economics and the Public, 1966, Politics in States and Communities, 1969, 15th edit., 2013, The Irony of Democracy, 1970, 15th edit., 2011, The Politics of Equality, 1971, Understanding Public Policy, 1972, 14th edit., 2012, Power and Society, 1975, 10th edit., 2005, Who's Running America, 1976, Policy Analysis, 1976, Who's Running America-The Carter Years, 1979, Determinants of Public Policy, 1980, Who's Running America-The Reagan Years, 1983, Politics in the Media Age, 1983, Who's Running America-The Conservative Years, 1986, Power Elites and Organizations, 1987, Who's Running America-The Bush Era, 1990, American Federalism: Competition Among Governments, 1990, Politics in America, 1994, 10th edit., 2013, Who's Running America-The Clinton Years, 1994, Politics in Florida, 1998, 2007, Top Down Policymaking, 2000, Who's Running America: The Bush Restoration, 2002, 2013, Who's Running America: The Obama Reign, 2013. 1st lt. USAF, 1961—62. Mem. Am. Polit. Sci. Assn. (sec. 1969-72), So. Polit. Sci. Assn. (v.p. 1974-75, pres. 1976-77), Phi Beta Kappa, Omicron Delta Kappa. Home: 550 Okeechobee Blvd #1710 West Palm Beach FL 33401 Personal E-mail: tomrdye@aol.com.

DYER, CARMEL B., geriatrician; MD, Baylor U., 1984—88. Diplomate Am. Bd. Internal Medicine, Am. Bd. Internal Medicine-geriatrics. Resident Baylor Coll. of Medicine, 1988—91, fellow, 1991—93; hosp. affiliation includes: Meml. Hermann Hosp.-Tex. Med. Ctr. Office: Memorial Hermann-Texas Medical Center 6411 Fannin St Houston TX 77030-1501 Office Phone: 713-704-4000.

DYER, CROMWELL ADAIR, JR., lawyer, legal association administrator; b. St. Louis, Sept. 9, 1932; (parents Am. citizens); s. Adair and Tompie Leora (Giles) Dyer; m. Margaret Copeland Peickert, June 12, 1958 (div. Aug. 1976); children: Gretchen, Jack, Julie, Stephen; m. Susan Aynesworth, Aug. 20, 1977; stepchildren: Carol Godso, Amanda McDonough, Donnella Railsback. BA, U. Tex., 1954; JD, 1961; LLM, Harvard U., 1971. Bar: Tex. 1961, U.S. Dist. Ct. (no. dist.) Tex. 1965, U.S. Ct. Appeals (5th cir.) 1965, U.S. Dist. Ct. (ea. dist.) Tex. 1966, U.S. Ct. Appeals (11th cir.) 1982, U.S. Ct. Appeals (9th cir.) 1999, U.S. Dist. Ct. (we. dist.) Tex. 2003, US Supreme Ct. 2010. Law clk. FTC, Washington, 1960; assoc. Branscomb, Gary, Thomasson & Hall, Corpus Christi, Tex., 1961-62; staff atty. So. Union Gas Co., Dallas, 1962-64; assoc. Dedman & May, Dallas, 1964-65, White, McElroy & White, Dallas, 1965-67; pvt. practice, 1967-73, Tex., 1997—; sec. Hague (The Netherlands) Conf. Pvt. Internat. Law, 1973-78, 1st sec., 1978-93, dep. sec. gen., 1993-97; observer, cons. to intergovtl. orgns., 1976-97. Lectr. Asser Coll. Europe, 1992—96, Sch. Law U. Calif., Davis, Brigitte M. Bodenheimer Meml. Lecture Family, 1996; moderator Common Law Jud. Conf. Internat. Child Custody, Washington, 2000; mem. US dels. Spl. Commn. on Internat. Child Abduction, 2001, 2006; condr. seminars. Honoree of symposium Globalization of Child Law The Role of the Hague Conventions, 1999; co-author: Report on Trusts and Analogous Institutions, 1982; contbr. articles to profl. jours. Mem. adv. com., faculty internat. kidnapping program Nat. Jud. Coll., Reno, 2003; faculty mem. Internat. Parental Abduction Course, Reno, 2004; juror award diploma in internat. law Hague Acad., 1980, 1984—87, 1991, 1994—96, dir. studies, 1985, instr. unfair competition in pvt. internat. law, 1988. Ensign USN, 1954, lt. (j.g.) USNR, 1957. Recipient Leonard J. Theberge award; named hon. mem., Mexican Acad. Pvt. Internat. and Comparative Law. Mem.: ABA (chair com. on internat. family law 2002—03, co-chair 2003—04, law sect. internat. law and practice 2000—, Leonard J. Theberge award for pvt. internat. law), Internat. Law Assn. (Am. br.), Assn. Louis Chatin pour la Def. des Droits de l'Enfant (Paris), Internat. Soc. Family Law, Austin Bar Assn., Acad. Mexicana de Derecho Internacional Privado y Comparado (hon.), Club du jeudi (The Hague) (pres. 1983—85). Office: PO Box 30020 Austin TX 78755-3020 Office Phone: 512-343-7899. Personal E-mail: adairdyer@austin.rr.com.

DYER, DAVID F., apparel company executive; B in Engring., Vanderbilt U. Various Burdines, Miami, 1972-89; from mng. dir. coming home catalog to v. chmn. merchandising Lands' End, Inc., Dodgeville, Wis., 1989-93, v. chmn. merchandising and sales, 1993-94, pres., CEO, 1998—2002; pres., COO Home Shopping Network, 1994-97; catalog/retail cons. Tex. Pacific Group, San Francisco, 1997—98, J. Crew Group, NYC, 1997; CEO Lands' End, 1998—2003; pres., CEO Tommy Hilfiger Corp., 2003—06, Chico's FAS, Inc., 2009—. Dir. ADVO, Inc.; bd. dirs. Lands' End. Office: Chico's FAS Inc 11215 Metro Pkwy Fort Myers FL 33912 Office Phone: 239-277-6200.

DYER, JAMES HAROLD, JR., language educator; b. Christiansburg, Va., Mar. 23, 1946; s. James Harold and Dorothy Louise (Bennett) Dyer. BA in English, Augusta State U., 1970; MEd in English Edn., Ga. State U., 1975, EdS in English Edn., 1978; PhD in Brit. Lit., U. SC, Columbia, 1992. Cert. secondary sch. tchr. S.C. English tchr. Aiken (S.C.) HS, 1975-79; prof. English Ga. Mil. Coll., Ft. Gordon, 1979—2000; prof. grad. English, grad. English MEd program coord. Troy U., Augusta, Ga., 2002—. Grad. tchg. asst. U.S.C., Columbia, 1982—83. Mem.: MLA, Acad. Am. Poets, Children's Lit. Assn., Dickens Fellowship, Lambda Iota Tau (Saul Bellow hon. pres.). Avocations: book collecting, chess, golf. Office: Troy U Dept Grad English 2743 Perimeter Pky Ste 201 Augusta GA 30909 Office Phone: 866-557-8617. Personal E-mail: jimdyer2@netzero.net.

DYER, JANE BALLARD, pilot; b. Easley, SC, Nov. 11, 1957; m. John Dyer, July 13, 1985; 4 children. BSME, Clemson U., 1981. Pilot TWA, 1988; pilot, A300 capt. FedEx, 1989—. Coach, youth basketball, soccer; supporter Habitat for Humanity, Miracle Hill Ministries, Compassion International; leader in ministry for children, youth and young adults; deacon. Pilot USAF. Democrat. Office: PO Box 1000 Easley SC 29641 Office Phone: 864-855-8050. Business E-Mail: jane@janedyerforcongress.com.

DYER, JOHN HUGH, JR., (BUDDY DYER), mayor, Orlando, Florida, lawyer; b. Orlando, Fla., Aug. 7, 1958; m. Karen Caudill, 1979; children: Trey, Andrew Warren. BS in Civil Engring., Brown U., 1980; JD, U. Fla., 1987. Bar: Fla. Lawyer; mem. Fla. State Senate from Dist. 14, Tallahassee, 1992—2002; senate democratic leader; mayor City of Orlando, Fla., 2003—. Vice chmn. Edn. Com.; mem. subcom. B. edn. Ways and Means Com., Rules and Calendar Com., Natural Resources Com., Exec. Bus., Ethics and Elections Com., Tobacco Settlement Implementation Com., Joint Legis Com. on Intergovtl. Rels.; ex-officio mem. Enterprise Fla. Tech. Devel. Bd., 1996; adv. com. Gov.'s Growth Mgmt. Plan, 1993; mem. Classrooms First task force Dept. of Edn., 1993; mem. Fla. Edn. Facilities Study Com., 1994. Editor-in-chief U. Fla. Law Rev., 1987 Henry Toll fellow Coun. on State Govts., 1996; recipient D.I. Rainey Legis. award for outstanding contbns. to quality health care for the citizens of Fla., 1994, Legis. Excellence award Fla. Audubon Soc., 1993, Freshman Friend of Edn. award FTP/NEA, 1993, Outstanding Support award Fla. Assn. Dist. Instructional Materials Adminstrs., 1994, Svc. Appreciation award Athletic Trainers' Assn. Fla., 1995, Legis. Leadership award Fla. Bd. Regents, 1995; named Quality Floridian Fla. League of Cities, 1993, Legislator of Yr., Fla. Assn. Realtors, 1995, Fla. Assn. Social Workers, 1995, Ind. Funeral Dirs., 1996, Internat. Coun. Shopping Ctrs., 1996, Outstanding Legislator Seminole County Pub. Schs., 1995-96, Most Powerful Person in Central Fla., The Orlando Sentinel, 2008. Mem. ABA, Fla. Lawyers Assn. for the Maintenance of Excellence, Fla. Engring. Soc. (James A. Ruth Outstanding Legis. Effectiveness award 1994), Orange County Bar Assn. (bd. dirs. young lawyers sect. 1989-92), Order of the Coif, Golden Key (hon.), Fla. Blue Key. Mayors Against Illegal Guns Coalition. Democrat. Presbyterian. Avocations: fishing, reading, golf. Home: PO Box 1031 Orlando FL 32802-1031 Office: City Hall 400 S Orange Avenue 3rd Fl PO Box 4990 Orlando FL 32805 Office Phone: 407-246-2221. Office Fax: 407-246-2842.*

DYER, JOHN M., corporate financial executive; BBA in Acctg., State U. West Ga.; MBA, Ga. State U. Internal auditor Cox Enterprises, Inc., 1977—80; fin. analyst, mgr., capital asset planning & dir., ops. Cox Comm. (subs. Cox Enterprises, Inc.), 1980—90; regional v.p., v.p., ops. Times Mirror Cable (acquired by Cox Comm.), 1990—95; v.p., fin. planning & analysis Cox Comm. (subs. Cox Enterprises, Inc.), 1995—97; v.p., acctg. & fin. planning Cox Comm. Inc. (subs. Cox Enterprises, Inc.), 1997—98, sr. v.p., mergers & acquisitions, chief acctg. officer, 1998—99, sr. v.p., ops., Western Divsn., 1999—2005, sr. v.p., CFO, 2005—08; exec. v.p., CFO Cox Enterprises, Inc., 2008—. Former bd. dirs. New Eng. Cable TV Assn.; bd. dirs. Cable & Telecom. Assn. for Mktg.; mem., conv. com. Nat. Cable & Telecom. Assn. Office: Cox Enterprises Inc 6205 Peachtree Dunwoody Rd Atlanta GA 30328 Office Phone: 678-645-0000. Office Fax: 678-645-1079. Business E-Mail: John.Dyer@coxinc.com.

DYER, RAYMOND B., diagnostic radiology physician; MD, U. Va., 1977. Diplomate Diagnostic Radiology Am. Bd. Radiology, Ariz., 1981. Intern, internal medicine WFUBMC, 1977—78; resident, diag radiol. U. Va., 1978—81; prof. radiology and urology Wake Forest U. Sch. Medicine, Winston-Salem, NC, 1991—. Contbr. articles to sci. jours. Fellow: Soc. Abdominal Radiology (pres. 2008—09), Am. Coll. Radiology. Office: Wake Forest U Sch Med Medical Center Blvd Winston Salem NC 27157 Office Fax: 336-716-0555. Business E-Mail: rdyer@wakehealth.edu.

DYER, WAYNE WALTER, psychologist, writer, radio and television personality; b. Detroit, May 10, 1940; s. Melvin Lyle and Hazel Irene (Vollick) Dyer; m. Marcelene Louise Dyer (div.); children: Shane, Stephanie, Skye, Sommer, Serena, Sands, Saje; 1 child from previous marriage, Tracy. BS, Wayne State U., Detroit, 1965, MS in Counseling and Ednl. Psychology, 1966, EdD in Counseling and Psychology, 1970. Tchr., counselor Pershing HS, Detroit, 1965-67; dir. guidance/counseling Mercy HS, Farmington, Mich., 1967-71; instr. counselor edn. Wayne State U., 1970—73; staff cons. Herman Kiefer Hosp., Detroit, 1974-75; staff cons., instr. guidance and sch. psychol. pers. Half Hollow Sch. Dist., Huntington, NY, 1973-75; mem. tchg. faculty North Shore U. Hosp., Cornell U. Med. Coll., Manhasset, NY, 1974-75; asst. prof. counselor edn. St. John's U., Jamaica, NY, 1971-74, assoc. prof., 1974-77. Author: Counseling Techniques That Work, 1975, Your Erroneous Zones, 1976, Pulling Your Own Strings, 1978, Group Counseling for Personal Mastery, 1980, The Sky's the Limit, 1980, Gifts from Eykis: A Story of Self-Discovery, 1983, What Do You Really Want for Your Children, 1985, Happy Holidays!, 1986, Real Magic: Creating Miracles in Everyday Life, 1992, Everyday Wisdom, 1993, How to Be a No-Limit Person, 1994, You'll See It When You Believe It: The Way to Your Personal Transformation, 1995, Your Sacred Self: Making the Decision to Be Free, 1995, A Promise Is a Promise: An Almost Unbelievable Story of a Mother's Unconditional Love and What It Can Teach Us, 1996, Manifest Your Destiny: The Nine Spiritual Principles for Getting Everything You Want, 1997, Wisdom of the Ages, 1998, There's a Spiritual Solution to Every Problem, 2001, 10 Secrets For Success And Inner Peace, 2002, It's Never Crowded Along the Extra Mile, 2002, Getting in the Gap: Making Conscious Contact With God Through Meditation, 2002, The Caroline Myss & Wayne Dyer Seminar, 2003, The Power of Intention: Learning to Co-Create Your World Your Way, 2004, Staying on the Path, 2004, Incredible You!, 2005, Inspiration: Your Ultimate Calling, 2006, Being in Balance: 9 Principles for Creating habits to Match Your Desires, 2006, Everyday Wisdom for Success, 2006, Making Your Thoughts Work for You, 2007, Change Your Thoughts - Change Your Life: Living the Wisdom of the Tao, 2007, Living The Wisdom Of The Tao: The Complete Tao Te Ching and Affirmations, 2008, Excuses Begone!, 2009, Wishes Fulfilled, 2012, I Can See Clearly Now, 2014; over 4000 appearances on TV/radio programs including Phil Donohue Show, Tonight Show, Dinah Shore Show, Merv Griffin Show, Mike Douglas Show, Good Morning America, Canada AM, Oprah Winfrey Show, others; contbr. numerous articles to profl. jours.; host (weekly radio show) HayHouseRadio.com, produced several DVD, Compact Discs, videos and cassettes. Served with USN, 1958—62. Recipient Disting. Alumni of Yr., Wayne State U., 1980, Golden Gavel award, Internat. Toastmasters, 1987.

DYESS, BOBBY DALE, lawyer; b. Waxahachie, Tex., Jan. 27, 1935; s. Robert Olin and Rubie Lee (Odom) D.; m. Janet Lee Hassell, Jan. 30, 1960 (dec. 1973); children: Robert Dale, Jonathan David, Julianna Whitfield; m. Sharon Erwin Saylor, June 6, 1974. BA, U. N. Tex., Denton, 1956; JD, So. Meth. U., Dallas, 1959. Bar: Tex. 1959. Ptnr. Elliott, Churchill, Hansen, Dyess & Maxfield, 1965-82, DeHay & Blanchard, 1983-92, Payne & Blanchard, Dallas, 1992—. Chmn. bd. Rainbow Sound, Inc., 1975-85; dir. edn. found. Waxahechie Ind. Sch. Dist., 2004-08, vice chair, 2006-08. Editor: Bests, Life and Health Ins. Edit., 1973-85. Mem. bd. mgmt. East Dallas YMCA, 1970, 1976, campaign chmn., 1976, chmn. bd. mgmt., 1977—79; chief Indian Guides, 1971; chmn. Cub Scout pack com. Boy Scouts Am., 1970; vice chair Baylor Med. Ctr., Waxahachie, Tex., 2004—05, chmn. bd. trustees, 2005—; bd. dirs. Waxahachie Found., 1999—2003, 2009—, chmn., 2011. Mem.: Am. Counsel Assn. (membership chmn. 1976, pres. 1979—80, sec.-treas. 1984—87, membership chmn. 1996—98), Coll. State Bar Tex. (dir. 1996—2010, chmn. 1999—2001), Scribes (bd. dirs. 1976), Am. Soc. Legal Writers, Dallas Bar Found. (charter), Tex. Bar Assn. Presbyterian. Home: 110 Magnolia Dr Waxahachie TX 75165 Office: Payne and Blanchard 500 N Tower Plz of America Dallas TX 75201 Office Phone: 972-938-1181. Personal E-mail: bddyess@att.net.

DYKE, JAMES WEBSTER, JR., lawyer; b. Washington, 1946; BA, Howard U., 1968, JD cum laude, 1971; DHL (hon.), St. Paul's Coll., 1990; LLD (hon.), Va. State Univ., 1991, Univ. Richmond, 1993, Randolph Macon Coll., 2009; Assoc. of Human Letter (hon.), Northern Va. Cmty. Coll., 2008. Bar: DC 1972, Va. 1991, US Supreme Ct. Law clk., Hon. Spottswood W. Robinson III US Ct. Appeals (DC cir.), Washington, 1971—72; domestic policy advisor to Vice Pres. Walter Mondale The White House, Washington, 1977—81; ptnr. Sidley & Austin LLP, 1981—87, Hunton & Williams LLP, 1987—90; sec. edn. Commonwealth of Va., Richmond, 1990—93; ptnr. McGuireWoods, LLP, McLean, Va., 1993—. Adj. prof. Howard U., 1974—76, U. Va., 1976—90; bd. dirs. WGL Holdings, Inc., 2003—, Md. Chamber of Commerce, Washington Gas Holding. Editor (in-chief): Howard Law Jour., 1971. Chmn. Greater Washington Bd. Trade, 2010—; bd. dir. Agnes & Eugene Meyer Found.; mem. adv. bd. George Washington Univ. Va. campus; mem. Comm. to Study Va. State & Local Tax Structure for 21st Century, Va. Joint Commn. on Tech. & Sci., State Coun. on Higher Edn. in Va., 2004—, Arts Coun. of Fairfax, 1999—; bd. dir. American Type Culture Collection, 2004—06; chmn bd. trustees Univ. DC, 2004—09; chmn. Northern Va. Bus. Roundtable, 2001—04, Northern Va. Cmty. Coll. Edn. Found., 2000—02, Fairfax County C. of C., 1999—2000, Metro. Coun. C. of C., 1999—2000; mem. Va. Gov. Commn. on Higher Edn., 1998—2000; chmn. Va. Ctr. for Innovative Tech., 1992—94; mem. Va. State Bd. Edn., 1985—90. Recipient J. Michael Brown award, DuPont Corp.; named one of The 150 Most Powerful People, Washingtonian mag., 2007. Office: McGuire Woods LLP Ste 1800 1750 Tysons Blvd Mc Lean VA 22102-4215 Office Phone: 703-712-5449. Office Fax: 703-712-5221. Business E-Mail: jdyke@mcguirewoods.com.

DYKEMAN, ALICE MARIE, public relations executive; b. Fremont, Nebr., May 18; d. Cecil Victor and Dorothy Lillian (Sillik) Jansen; divorced; children: David Clair, Cinda Cecille Dykeman Nordgren. Pub. relations dir. Meth. Hosp., Dallas, 1961-72; regional pub. info. officer Small Bus. Adminstrn., Dallas, 1972-74; owner Dykeman Assocs. Inc., Dallas, 1974—. Adj. prof. U. Dallas Grad. Sch. Mgmt., Irving, Tex. 1972-78; guest lectr. numerous Univs., and seminars; mem. pub. rels. com. Dallas/Ft. Worth Fed. Exec. Bd., 1973, mem. minority bus. opportunity com., 1974; mem. Gov.'s Coun. on Small Bus., Tex., 1980-81, 500, Inc., 1982-90; chmn. export coun. pub. affairs task force U.S. Dept. Commerce, 1980-83. Contbr. articles to bus., health care and pub. rels. jours. Mem. fgn. visitors com. Dallas Coun. on World Affairs, 1992-98, Dallas Pub. Health Bd., 1972-74, Dallas Urban Rehab. Stds. Bd., 1981-83, Econ. Devel. Adv. Bd., City of Dallas, 1983-86; pres. Concerned Citizens for Cedar Springs, 1982-2006; bd. dirs. Oak Lawn Forum, 1983-92; mem. exec. com. Oak Lawn Com., 1983-95. Recipient Matrix award Women in Comm., Dallas, 1968, 88, Lifetime Achievement award Religion Communicators Coun., 2004. Fellow Pub. Rels. Soc. Am. (accredited, chmn. S.W. dist. 1971-72, bd. dirs. North Tex. chpt. 1966-72, pres. 1969, assembly del. 1970-73, 91, Norm Teich award for contbns. to pub. rels. 2004); mem. North Dallas Fin. Forum (pres. 1991), Nat. Assn. Women Bus. Owners, North Dallas C. of C. (bd. dirs. 1980-82, chmn. networking skills workshop 1990—), co-founder Breakfast Dallas 1994-2008), SMU Mustang Club (bd. dirs. 1996-99, nat. networker 2007-). United Methodist. Office: Dykeman Assocs Inc 4115 Rawlins St Dallas TX 75219-3661 Office Phone: 214-528-2991. Business E-Mail: adykeman@airmail.net.

DYKES, RONALD MITCHELL, hotel executive; BSEE, Auburn U., 1969; MBA, Emory U., 1981; MS in Mgmt., Stanford U., 1986. With Southern Bell, Atlanta, 1971—83; dir. Fin. Mgmt. BellSouth Corp., Atlanta, 1983—85, asst. to the pres., dir., Bus. & Fin. Planning, 1986—88, v.p., Fin., 1989—93, v.p., contr., 1993—95, CFO, 1995—2005. Bd. dirs. Cingular Wireless, 2000—05, Burger King Holdings, Inc., 2007—. Trustee St. Joseph's Health Sys. With Signal Corps. US Army, 1969—71. Sloan fellow Stanford U., 1985-86 Office: Burger King Holdings Inc Bd Directors 5505 Blue Lagoon Dr Miami FL 33126 Office Phone: 305-378-3000. E-mail: ron.dykes@bellsouth.com, rdykes@whopper.com.

DYKEWICZ, MARK STEVEN, physician; b. Flint, Mich., May 21, 1955; s. Richard Alfred and Evelyn Ellen Dykewicz; m. Lenora-Marya Anop. BS, U. Mich., 1977; MD, St. Louis U., 1981. Resident medicine Northwestern U. Med. Sch., Chgo., 1981-84, fellow allergy-immunology, 1984-86, asst. prof. medicine, 1986-90; asst. prof. internal medicine St. Louis U. Med. Sch., 1990—94, assoc. prof., 1994—2002, prof., 2002—09, dir. allergy immunology postgrad. tng. program, 1997—2009, 2013—, chief section allergy and clin. immunology, divsn. immunobiology, prof. internal medicine, 2007—09; dir. Allergy & Immunology Fellowship Program; chief allergy & immunology, sec. pulmonary critical care, allergy & immunologic diseases Wake Forest U. Sch. Medicine, 2009—, St. Louis U. Med. Sch., 2013—, Slavin prof., 2013—; glavin chair; prof. thoraic medicine. Mem. pulmonary allergy drug adv. com. FDA, 1999—2003, chmn., 2001—03; bd. dirs. Am. Bd. Allergy and Immunology, 2004—09. Chief editor Joint Task Force Practice Parameters on Rhinitis, 1998—2008, 2013—. Recipient Disting. Svc. award, Am. Coll. Allergy, Asthma and Immunology, 1999. Fellow ACP, Am. Coll. Chest Physicians, Am. Acad. Allergy-Immunology; mem. Am. Thoracic Soc., Am. Acad. Allergy, Asthma and Immunology (chmn. com. on occupl. lung disease 1998-2000, chmn. com. on adverse reactions to drugs and biols. 2001-03, chmn. com. on rhinitis 2004-05, bd. dirs., 2009-, Spl. Recognition award 1999) Home: 1 Dunleith dr Saint Louis MO 63124 Home Phone: 314-963-9885; Office Phone: 314-977-8828.

DYSART, BENJAMIN CLAY, III, conservationist, engineer, consultant; b. Columbia, Tenn., Feb. 12, 1940; s. Benjamin Clay and Kathryne Virginia (Thompson) D.; m. Betty Blanche Walthall, June 7, 2005. BE, Vanderbilt U., 1961, MS in San. Engring., 1964; PhD in Civil Engring., Ga. Inst. Tech., 1969. Staff engr. Union Carbide Corp., 1961-62, 64-65; from asst. prof. to prof. Clemson U., 1968-90, McQueen Quattlebaum prof. engring., 1982-83, dir. S.C. Water Resources Rsch. Inst., 1968-75, dir. water resources engring. grad. program, 1972-75, adj. prof., 1990-93; facility devel. mgr. Chem. Waste Mgmt., Inc., Marietta, Ga., 1990-91, regional facility devel. mgr. Memphis, 1991; dir. project planning and integration Waste Mgmt., Inc., Washington, 1991-92; pres. Dysart & Assocs., Inc., Nashville, 1992—. Sci. advisor Office Sec. of Army, Washington, 1975-76; mem. EPA Sci. Adv. Bd., 1983-, Reinvention Criteria Com., NACEPT, US EPA, 1998-2000; sr. fellow The Conservation Found., 1985-90; mem. adv. coun. Electric Power Rsch. Inst., 1989-95; mem., chief of engrs. environ. adv. bd. U.S. Army Corps Engrs., 1988-92; mem. Glacier Nat. Park Sci. Coun., Nat. Park Svc., 1988-91; mem. S.C. Gov.'s Wetlands Forum, 1989-90; sec. appointee Outer Continental Shelf Adv. Bd. and OCS Sci. Com. Dept. Interior, 1979-82; mem. S.C. Environ. Quality Control Adv. Com., 1980-90, chmn., 1980-81; mem. Sci. Panel to Rev. Interagy. Rsch. on Impact of Oil Pollution NOAA, Dept. Commerce, 1980; mem. Nuclear Energy Ctr. Environ. Task Force Dept. Energy-So. States Energy Bd., 1978-81; mem. Nonpoint Source Pollutant Task Force EPA, 1979-80; mem. civil works adv. com. Office Sec. Army-Young Pres.'s Orgn., 1975-76; mem. S.C. Heritage Adv. Bd., 1974-76; mem. Pangue Project, ind. review panel, World Bank, 1996-97; chmn. Ga. Erosion & Sedimentation Control Tech. Study Com., 1996-2001; cons. on respect-based stakeholder engagement matters to corp.; sr. assoc. Internat. Council Mining & Metals, London, 2001-02; leader Ind. Review of Compliance Advisor Ombudsman Ofice, World Bank, 2003. Editor: (with Marion Clawson) Managing Public Lands in the Public Interest, 1988, Public Interest in the Use of Private Lands, 1989; contbr. articles on environ. impact, math. modeling in water quality and environ. mgmt. and pub. involvement to profl. jours.; author numerous profl. papers, reports. Trustee Rene Dubos Ctr. for Human Environs., 1985-94, vice chmn., mem. exec. com., 1988-94; trustee Issue Mgmt. Coun., 1997-2003, 2005-; bd. visitors Kanuga Episcopal Conf. Ctr., 1988—. Recipient Tribute of Appreciation for Disting. Svc. EPA, 1981, 86, McQueen Quattlebaum Engring. Faculty Achievement award Clemson U., 1982, Order of Palmetto Gov. S.C., 1984; named Hon. Ky. Col., 1976. Mem. Trout Unltd. (trustee 1990-94), Chattooga River Chpt. Trout Unlimited (bd. dirs. 1988-90), Nat. Wildlife Fedn. (bd. dirs. 1974-90, v.p. 1978-83, pres., chmn. bd. dirs. 1983-85), Assn. Environ. Engring. Profs. (bd. dirs. 1978-83, pres., chmn. bd. dirs. 1981-82), Water Environ. Fedn. (hon., bd. dirs. Rsch. Found. 1989-91), S.C. Wildlife Fedn. (bd. dirs. 1969—, pres., chmn. bd. dirs. 1973-74, S.C. Wildlife Conservationist Yr.), The Ga. Conservancy (bd. trustees 1994-97), Cosmos Club (Washington), Sigma Xi, Tau Beta Pi, Phi Kappa Phi, Chi Epsilon, Omega Rho, Sigma Nu. Episcopalian. Office Phone: 615-828-2902. E-mail: ben@dysartassoc.com.

DYSINGER, PAUL WILLIAM, preventive medicine physician, educator; b. Burns, Tenn., May 24, 1927; s. Paul Clair and Mary Edith (Martin) D.; m. Yvonne Minchin, May 11, 1958; children: Edwin, Wayne, John, Janelle. BA, So. Missionary Coll., 1951; MD, Loma Linda U., 1955; M.P.H., Harvard, 1962. Diplomate Nat. Bd. Med. Examiners, Am. Bd. Preventive Medicine. Intern, Washington, 1955-56; sr. asst. surgeon USPHS; with Blackfeet Indians in Mont., Navajos of Ariz., 1956-58; physician, med. adviser Am. embassy, PhnomPenh, Cambodia, 1958-60; rsch. assoc. dept. preventive medicine Loma Linda U. (formerly Coll. Med. Evangelists), Calif., 1960—62, dir. field sta. Western Tanganyika, 1962—64, adminstrv. asst. div. pub. health, 1964—67, asst. to dean, chmn. dept. tropical health Sch. Pub. Health, 1967—69, asst. dean for acad. affairs and internat. health Sch. Pub. Health, 1969—71, assoc. dean for acad. affairs, 1971—79, assoc. dean emeritus, sch. public health Calif., 2004—, dir. preventive med. residency Sch. of Medicine, 1983-88, clin. prof. emeritus, preventive medicine, 2004; chmn. bd. Devel. Svc. Internat., Williamsport, Tenn., 1992—. Med. cons. dept. Vocat. Rehab., Riverside, Calif., 1964-88; mother and child health cons. Ministry of Health, Tanzania, 1978-80; med. dir. Village Health Program, Punjab, Pakistan, 1980-81, tchr., cons., S.Am. and Caribbean, 1981-83; chief preventive medicine Pettis Meml. VA Hosp., Loma Linda, 1984-88; sr. health advisor Adventist Devel. and Relief Agy., 1988-92; country dir. ADRA, Yemen, 1998-99, local dir.CHIP, 2007- WHO fellow, Somalia, Ethiopia, India, Nepal and Burma, 1969. Fellow Royal Soc. Tropical Medicine and Hygiene, Am. Pub. Health Assn., Am. Coll. Preventive Medicine, Internat. Health Soc. (pres.); mem. AMA, Global Health Coun., Adventist Internat. Med. Soc. (pres. 1983-84), Delta Omega (nat. pres. 1977-78). Adventist. Home and Office: 684 Dry Prong Rd Williamsport TN 38487-2858 Office Phone: 931-583-2792. Personal E-mail: billdysinger@gmail.com.

DYSON, JAMES DAVID, lawyer; BS, La. Tech. U., 1968; JD, Emory U., 1973, LLM, 1980. Bar: Ga. 1974. Asst. atty. gen. State of Ga., 1974—79; sr. atty., asst. sec. Gold Kist, Inc., 1980—98, v.p., gen. counsel & sec., 1998—. Office: Gold Kist Inc 244 Perimeter Ctr Pky NE Atlanta GA 30346-2302 Office Phone: 770-393-5000. Office Fax: 770-393-5262. E-mail: james.dyson@goldkist.com.

DZAU, VICTOR JOSEPH, healthcare executive, cardiologist, director, researcher; b. Shanghai, Oct. 23, 1946; MD, McGill U., 1972. Cert. in internal medicine, subspecialty in cardiovasc. disease. With Harvard Med. Sch. Stanford & Duke U.; intern N.Y. Hosp., 1972-73; resident in medicine Peter Bent Brigham Hosp., Boston, 1974-76, chief resident, 1976-78; fellow in rsch. Mass. Gen. Hosp., Boston, 1976-78, fellow in cardiology, 1979-80; chief divsn. vascular medicine and atherosclerosis Brigham & Women's Hosp., 1984-90; dir. cardiovasc. rsch. ctr. Stanford U. Sch. Medicine, chief divsn. cardiovasc. medicine, 1990-96, assoc. chmn. dept. medicine, 1993-96, chmn. dept. medicine, 1995-96; dir. Am. Heart Assn.-Bugher Found. Ctr. for Molecular Biology, 1991-96; chmn. dept. med., dir. rsch. Brigham & Women's Hosp., 1996—2004; chancellor for health affairs Duke University, 2004—; pres., CEO Duke University Health Systems, 2004—. Asst. prof. medicine, assoc. prof. medicine Harvard Med. Sch., 1980—90, Hersey prof. theory and practice of medicine, 1996—2004; William G. Irvin prof. medicine Stanford U. Sch. Medicine, 1990—96, Arthur L. Bloomfield prof., medicine, 1995—96; bd. dirs. Genzyme, 2000—11, Medtronic, Inc., 2002—,

Duke U. Health System, 2004—; James B. Duke prof. medicine Duke U., 2004—; bd. dirs. PepsiCo, Inc., 2005—, Alnylam Inc., 2007—. Mem.: Inst. Medicine (coun. mem.). Office: Duke U Med Ctr 1 Davison Blvd Box 3701 Durham NC 27710 Office Phone: 919-684-2255. Business E-Mail: victor.dzau@duke.edu.

DZURICKY, DAVID J., gas industry executive; B in Mktg., Syracuse U.; MBA in Fin., U. Pitts. V.p., treas. Consol. Natural Gas Co, 1982—95; sr. v.p., CFO Piedmont Natural Gas Co., Inc., 1995—. Bd. dirs. The United Way Ctrl. Carolinas, Ctrl. Piedmont Cmty. Coll. Found. Mem.: Southeastern Gas Ann. (past bd. dirs.), Am. Gas Assn. (past chmn.fin. com.). Office: Piedmont Natural Gas Co 4720 Piedmont Row Dr Charlotte NC 28210 Office Phone: 704-364-3120. Office Fax: 704-365-3849. Business E-Mail: david.dzuricky@piedmontng.com.

EAGAN, CLAIRE VERONICA, federal judge; b. Bronx, NY, Oct. 9, 1950; d. Joseph Thomas and Margaret (Lynch) E.; m. M. Stephen Barrett, Aug. 25, 1978 (div. 1984); m. Anthony J. Loretti, Jr., Feb. 13, 1988. Student, U. Fribourg, Switzerland, 1970-71; BA, Trinity Coll., Washington, 1972; postgrad., U. Paris, 1972-73; JD, Fordham U., 1976. Bar: N.Y. 1977, Okla. 1977, U.S. Dist. Ct. (no. dist.) Okla. 1977, U.S. Ct. Appeals (10th cir.) 1978, U.S. Supreme Ct. 1980, U.S. Dist. Ct. (we. dist.) Okla. 1981, U.S. Ct. Appeals (5th cir.) 1982, U.S. Dist. Ct. (ea. dist.) Okla. 1988, U.S. Ct. Appeals (Fed. cir.) 1990. Mem. Hall, Estill, Hardwick, Gable, Golden & Nelson, Tulsa, 1978-98, shareholder, 1981-98; magistrate judge US Dist. Ct. (no. dist.) Okla., Tulsa, 1998—2001, judge, 2001—, chief judge, 2005—. Mem. Jud. Conf. Com. on Defender Svcs., 2002—, chair, 2008—. Editor: Fordham Law Rev., 1975—76. Bd. dirs. Okla. Med. Rsch. Found., 2003—, Cath. Charities, Tulsa, 1983-98, Cystic Fibrosis Found., Tulsa, 1982-84; bd. trustees St. Francis Assisi Tuition Assistance Trust, 2006—; mem. Jr. League Tulsa, Inc., 1983—; trustee Gannon U., Erie, Pa., 1995-98; bd. trustee St. Clare Assisi Disadvantaged Schs. Trust, 2008-; bd. dirs. Okla. Sinfonia, Tulsa, 1982-86; adj. settlement judge, Tulsa County, 1990-97. Fellow Am. Bar Found.; mem. Tulsa County Bar Assn., Tulsa Women Lawyers Assn. (pres. 2000-02), 10th Cir. Jud. Conf., Am. Inns of Ct. (master; chpt. pres. 1999-2000, mem. exec. com.). Republican. Roman Catholic. Office: US Dist Ct No Dist Okla 333 W 4th St Ste 411 Tulsa OK 74103-3819 Office Phone: 918-699-4795.

EAGLE, CHRISTOPHER, chef; Grad., Johnson & Wales U., Charleston. Sous chef Brasserie Le Coze, Atlanta, Fusebox; exec. sous chef Ritz-Carlton Aspen; exec. chef JAAN, LA, Cielo, Boca Raton, Fla., 2007—. Named one of Fla.'s Rising Stars, StarChefs.com, 2008. Office: Cielo 501 E Camino Real Boca Raton FL 33432

EAGLEMAN, DAVID M., neuroscientist, educator; b. Albuquerque, Apr. 1971; BA in English, Rice U., Houston, 1993; PhD in Neuroscience, Baylor Coll. Medicine, Houston, 1998. Postdoc. fellow Salk Inst. Biol. Studies, La Jolla, Calif.; faculty U. Tex. Health Sci. Ctr., Houston; asst. prof. dept. neuroscience, asst. prof. dept. psychiatry & behavioral scis. Baylor Coll. Medicine, dir. Lab. Perception & Action. Fellow Inst. Ethics & Emerging Technologies, 2011—. Author: (fiction) Sum: Forty Tales from the Afterlives, 2009, (nonfiction) Why the Net Matters: How the Internet will save Civilization, 2010, Incognito: The Secret Lives of the Brain, 2011; co-author: Wednesday is Indigo Blue: Discovering the Brain of Synesthesia, 2009; mem. edtl. bd. PLoS One, Jour. Vision; contbr. numerous articles to profl. jours. Bd. dirs. Long Now Found., 2010—. Fellow John Simon Guggenheim Meml. Found., 2011. Office: Baylor College Medicine Dept Neuroscience One Baylor Plz Houston TX 77030 Office Fax: 713-798-6699, 713-798-3946. Business E-Mail: eagleman@bcm.tmc.edu.

EAGLES, CATHERINE CALDWELL, federal judge; b. Memphis, Aug. 30, 1958; d. Marvin Bounds and Dorothy Carolyn (Reddell) Caldwell; m. William A. Eagles, Aug. 27, 1983; children: John Ivey, Thad. BA, Southwestern U., Memphis, 1979; JD, George Washington U., 1982. Bar: Mo. 1982, Ark. 1983, N.C. 1984; cert. mediator, N.C. Law clk. to Hon. J. Smith Henley US Ct. Appeals (8th cir.), Harrison, Ark., 1982-84; assoc. Smith Helms Mulliss & Moore, Greensboro, NC, 1984-89, ptnr., 1989-93; judge NC Superior Ct., Greensboro, NC, 1993—2010, US Dist. Ct. (middle dist.) NC, Greensboro, NC, 2010—. Arbitrator American Arbitration Assn., Charlotte, N.C., 1992-93 Assoc. editor ABA Tort & Ind. Practice Sect., 1992—94. Recipient Gwyneth P. Davis Pub. Svc. award, 2000. Mem.: NC Conf. Superior Ct. Judges, NC Assn. Women Attorneys, Joseph Branch Inn Ct., Greensboro Bar Assn., NC Bar Assn. Office: US District Court 324 West Market St Greensboro NC 27401 Office Phone: 336-332-6000.

EAGLES, SIDNEY SMITH, JR., lawyer and retired judge; b. Asheville, NC, Aug. 5, 1939; s. Sidney Smith Sr. and Mildred Truman (Brite) E.; m. Rachel Phillips, May 22, 1965; children: Virginia Brite, Margaret Phillips. BA, Wake Forest U., 1961, JD, 1964. Bar: N.C. 1964. Revisor Gen. Statutes Commn., Raleigh, NC, 1967-70; asst. atty. gen. legis. drafting service Office Atty. Gen. N.C., Raleigh, 1970-74, dep. atty. gen. spl. prosecution divsn., 1974-76; counsel to speaker N.C. State Legislature, Raleigh, 1976-80; ptnr. Eagles Hafer & Hall, Raleigh, 1977-82; judge N.C. Ct. Appeals, Raleigh, 1983—2004, chief judge, 1998—2004; of counsel Smith Moore Leatherwood LLP, 2004—. Adj. prof. Campbell U. Sch. Law, 1977—2010; chmn. N.C. Jud. Stds. Commn., 1994—96; mem. faculty Appellate Judges Sch. Law Sch. NYU, NYC, 1993—99; mem. Uniform Laws Conf., 1968—83, 1992—, life mem., 2000. Co-author: North Carolina Criminal Procedure Forms, 1975, 3d edit., 1989; contbr. articles to profl. jours. V.p. Raleigh Jaycees, 1972-73; mem. Senatorial Dist. Dem. Com., 1979-81; bd. dirs. Wake County (N.C.) Symphony Soc., 1980-81, Women's Aid of Wake County, 1978—82, Carolinas Dist. Kiwanis Found, 2004-2005.; bd. elders, bd. deacons, trustee, tchr. Sunday sch. Hillyer Meml. Christian Ch., 1980—, chmn bd., 1989; bd. visitors Wake Forest U. Sch. Law; vice chair bd. trustees Barton Coll., 1999, chair, 2002-07. Served to capt. USAF, 1964-67; col., ret. 1991. Named Disting. Law Alumnus, Wake Forest U., 1981; N.C. Justice Found. fellow, 1972. Fellow Am. Acad. Appellate Lawyers; mem. ABA (chmn. appellate judges conf. 1993-94, mem. appellate jud. edn. com. 1994-98, ho. of dels. 1992-2009, mem. legal edn. sect. coun. 2002—09), Am. Law Inst. (life), N.C. Bar Assn. (v.p. 1989-90), Wake County Bar Assn. (chmn. exec. com. 1975, pres. 2006—), N.C. State Bar, Execs. Club (pres. 1985), Kiwanis (disting. pres. Raleigh 1986-87, disting. lt. gov. 1995, Kiwanian of Yr. award 1989), Phi Delta Phi, Phi Alpha Delta (James Iredell award 1990), Wake Bar (Chief Justice Joseph Br. Professionalism award 2008). Avocations: politics, reading. Office: Smith Moore Leatherwood LLP PO Box 27525 Raleigh NC 27611 Office Phone: 919-755-8771. Business E-Mail: sid.eagles@smithmoorelaw.com.

EAGLET, ROBERT DANTON, electrical engineer, aerospace scientist, consultant, retired military officer, fighter pilot; b. Cleve., Mar. 2, 1934; s. Albert R. and Dorothy Margaret (Beamer) E.; m. Sally Perry; children: Suzanne Carolyn, Allison Leigh, Kevin Robert. BSEE, U. Ariz., 1962; MSEE, U. So. Calif., 1968, PhD in Elec. Engring. and Physics, 1970. Commd. 2d lt. USAF, 1956, advanced through grades to maj. gen., 1985; forward air contr. in Vietnam CIA & US Army 1st Cav Divsn., 1965-66; chief, classified program, space div. USAF, LA, 1966-68, chief strategic def. div. hdqrs. Washington, 1970-74, mil. asst. to dep. undersec. def., 1974-75; dep. gen. mgr. NATO airborne early warning program Brussels, 1975-79; asst. and dep. chief of staff devel. planning, sys. command USAF, Andrews AFB, Md., 1979-84, dep. comdr. armament divsn. Eglin AFB, Fla., 1984-86, dir. F-16 multinat. fighter program Wright Patterson AFB, Ohio, 1986-89; dep. asst. sec. of Air Force Pentagon, Washington, 1989-91; ret. USAF, 1991; pres. Eaglet Internat. Assocs., McLean, Va., 1991—. Decorated Disting. Svc. medal with oak leaf cluster, Legion of Merit with oak leaf cluster, Silver star, Defense Superior Svc. medal, Disting. Flying Cross with oak leaf cluster, Bronze star with Valor device, Air medal with 25 oak leaf clusters, Purple Heart; named Outstanding Alumnus U. So. Calif. Mem. Air Force Assn. Business E-Mail: eagletrobt@aol.com.

EAKER, CHARLES WILLIAM, chemistry professor; b. St. Louis, May 25, 1949; s. Charles Mayfield and Mildred Catherine (Staples) E.; m. Mary Alice Eisenmann, July 6, 1974; children: Stephanie, Sara Marie. BS, Mich. State U., 1971; PhD, U. Chgo., 1974. Instr. U. Dallas, Irving, Tex., 1976-78, asst. prof., 1978-81, assoc. prof., 1981-89, prof., 1989—; dean Constantin Coll., 2005—. Contbr. articles to profl. jours. Rsch. grantee Robert A. Welch Found., 1984, faculty devel. grantee Arthur Vining Davis, 1980, NSF equipment grantee 1997; recipient Presdl. award U. Dallas, 1987, 91, 95, 96, 98. Mem. Am. Chem. Soc. (rsch. grantee 1978, 88), Sigma Xi. Office: U Dallas 1845 E Northgate Dr Irving TX 75062-4736 Office Phone: 972-721-5384. Business E-Mail: eaker@udallas.edu.

EARLE, BEVERLY M., state legislator; With Bellsouth; former state rep. Dist. 60 NC; state rep. Dist. 101 NC, 2003—; bd. mem. Sos Youth Program, Charlotte Conv. & Visitors Bureau, Mecklenburg County Womens Commn., Summit House, Nevins Ctr., NC Coun. Devel. Disabilities, Exceptional Children's Assistance Ctr., Women's Action New Directions; bd. visitors Johnson C. Smith U. Mem.: Women's Polit. Caucus, Nat. Order Dem. Women, Nat. Conf. State Legislators, Women Govt., League Women Voters. Democrat. Episcopal. Office: North Carolina House of Representatives 300 N Salisbury St Rm 610 Raleigh NC 27603-5925 Office Phone: 919-715-2530. Business E-Mail: Beverly.Earle@ncleg.net.

EARLY, JACK JONES, foundation executive; b. Corbin, Ky., Apr. 12, 1925; s. Joseph M. and Lela (Jones) E.; m. Nancye Bruce Whaley, June 1, 1952; children: Lela Katherine, Judith Ann, Laura Hattie. AB, Union Coll., Barbourville, Ky., 1948; MA, U. Ky., 1953, Ed.D. (So. scholar 1955-56), 1956; B.D., Coll. of Bible, Lexington, Ky., 1956; D.D., Wesley Coll., Grand Forks, ND, 1961; LL.D., Parsons Coll., 1962, Iowa Wesleyan Coll., 1972; Litt.D., Dakota Wesleyan U., 1969; L.H.D., Union Coll., Barbourville, Ky., 1979; D.Adminstrn., Cumberland Coll., 1981. Ordained to ministry Methodist Ch., 1954; pastor Rockhold Circuit, Ky., 1943-44, Craig's Chapel and Laurel Circuit, London, Ky., 1944-47, Trinity Ch., Oak Ridge, summer 1945, Hindman Ch., Ky., 1947-52; dean of men Hindman Settlement Sch., 1948-51; assoc. pastor Park Ch., Lexington, Ky., 1952-54; asst. to pres., dean Athens Coll., Ala., 1954- 55; v.p., dean of coll. Iowa Wesleyan Coll., Mount Pleasant, 1956-58; pres. Dakota Wesleyan U., 1958-69, Pfeiffer Coll., Misenheimer, NC, 1969-71; exec. dir. Am. Bankers Assn., Washington, 1971-73; pres. Limestone Coll., Gaffney, SC, 1973-79; exec. dir. edn. Combined Ins. Co. Am., Chgo., 1979-82, v.p., exec. dir. edn. and communications, 1982-84; pres. Ky. Ind. Coll. Fund, Louisville, 1984-93, pres. emeritus, 1993—; dir. edn., con. Napoleon Hill Found., Northbrook, Ill., 1997—. Pres. W. Clement Stone PMA Communications, Inc., Chgo., 1987—; prof. mgmt., McKendree U., 2002, Three Crusades 1096-1192, 2013, chaplain, General the Hereditary Order the Loyalists and Patriotists Am. Revolution, 2013-. Active Boy Scouts Am.; mem. pres. adv. coun. North Pk. Coll.; mem. Felician adv. bd. Felician Coll.; mem. Ky. Ho. of Reps., 1952-54; bd. dirs. S.D. Found. Pvt. Colls., S.D. Meth. Found., Nat. Coun. on Youth Leadership, Ctr. for Citizenship Edn., YMCA, Motivational Inst., Mid-Am. chpt. ARC, 1980—, W. Clement and Jessie V. Stone Found., Northbrook Symphony Orch., Ky. Mountain Laurel Festival, 1990—, Internat. Coun. on Edn. for Teaching, 1990—; chmn. bd. Religious Heritage Am., 1989-92, Internat. Leadership Network, 1991—; Rep. nominee for Metro Mayor, Louisville, 2002-. Recipient Spoke award Mitchell Jr. C. of C., 1959, Disting. Svc. award, 1960, Disting. Svc. award S.D. Jr. C. of C., 1960, Gaffney Jaycees, 1979, Chief Iron Eyes Cody medal of Peace, 1987, Outstanding Kentuckian award O'Tucks, 1990; named Outstanding Former Kentuckian, 1963; hon. fellow Wroxton Coll., Oxfordshire, Eng.; named to Disting. Alumni Hall of Fame, U. Ky., 1965, Union Coll. Hall of Fame, 2000, U. Ky. Coll. Edn. Hall of Fame, 2006. Mem. Am. Soc. Assn. Execs., Louisville C. of C., Blue Key, Masons (33d degree, chaplain Valley of Louisville chpt. 1990—, Viceroy and Sovereign Red Cross Constantine), Rotary (pres. Louisville 1992-93, dist. 6710 gov. 1996—), First Families Ky. (dep. gov. gen., gov. gen. 2007—), Ky. Soc. SAR (pres. 1998—), Order of Founders and Patriots of Am. (gov. Ky. chpt. 2003-, dep. chaplain st., chaplain gen.), Nat. Guild Soc. Ssh. Margaret Scotland, Soc. War of 1812 in the Commonwealth of Ky. (pres. 1997—), Huguenot Soc. Ky. (pres. 1999—), Huguenot Soc.-Soc. of Manakin (Ky. br. pres. 1999—), Nat. Soc. Sons and Daus. of Pilgrims (gov. Ky. br. 2000—), Gen. for Pub. Rels.-Gen. Soc. of the War of 1812 (v.p. 1998—), Del. State Soc. of Cin., Gen. Soc. Sons of Revolution (gen. chaplain, governor, 2008, gen. chaplain emeritus), Ky. Soc. Colonial Wars (dep. gov. 2008-), Nat. Sojourners Camp #134, Heroes of '76 (E.B. Jones Camp), Jamestowne Soc. (lt. governor, 2008, gov. 2009-), Ky. Co. (chaplain, lt. gov. 2008-, gov. 2009-), First Families of Ga., Baronial Order of Magna Charta (prelate) and Mil. Order of Crusades (Prelate), First Families of Tenn., Kappa Delta Pi, Phi Delta Kappa, Kappa Phi Kappa, Alpha Psi Omega, Theta Phi, Pi Tau Chi, Sigma Beta Delta, Nat. Gavel Soc., Presdl. Families of America (chaplain gen. 2010-), Nat. Soc. Sts. and Sinners, Nat. Soc. Sons Am. Colonists (chaplain gen.), Nat. Order of the Blue and Gray Prelate (chaplain gen.), Order Ams. Armorial Ancestry, Gov. Soc. Colonial Wars in Ky. Republican. Home: 9002 Hurstwood Ct Louisville KY 40222-5716 Home Phone: 502-426-6078.

EARNER, WILLIAM ANTHONY, JR., naval officer; b. Pitts., Nov. 2, 1941; s. William Anthony and Marie Veronica (Ward) E.; m. Jennifer Elizabeth Laurence, Dec. 11, 1971; children: William Andrew, John Laurence. BS, U.S. Naval Acad., 1963; MS, U.S. Naval Postgrad. Sch., 1969; DBA, Harvard U., 1973. Commd. ensign USN, 1963, advanced through grades to vice adm., 1994, 1st lt. USS Blue Yokosuka, Japan, 1963-65, weapons officer USS Black San Diego, 1965-67, ops. officer River Sect. 534 Vietnam, 1967-68, weapons officer USS Dale Mayport, Fla., 1973-75, exec. officer USS Luce, 1975-77, prof. Naval War Coll. Newport, RI, 1977-78, fellow strategic studies group, 1987-88, with Office Chief Naval Ops. Washington, 1978-81, comdg. officer USS Deyo, 1981-83, mil. asst. to dir. NET assesment Office of Sec. Def. Washington, 1983-85, comptr. naval air systems, 1988-90, comdr. Destroyer Squadron Four Charleston, SC, 1985-87, comdr. naval Surface Group Mid-Pacific Pearl Harbor, Hawaii, 1990-92; budget officer Dept. Navy, 1992-94, dep. chief naval ops. (logistics), 1994—96, exec. v.p. Navy Fed. Credit Union Merrifield, Va., 1996—97, sr. exec. v.p. Navy Fed. Credit Union, 1998—2003, COO, Navy Fed. Credit Union, 2003—. Instr. Harvard Grad. Sch. Edn., Cambridge, Mass., 1972-73; adj. prof. Bryant Coll., Smithfield, R.I., 1977-78; COO Navy Fed. Credit Union, 1998—; bd. dirs. Service Source, Inc. Chmn. George Mason dist. Boy Scouts Am., 2000—02; mem. supervisory com. Wescorp Fed. Credit Union, 2004—. Decorated D.S.M., Legion of Merit, Bronze Star with V device. Mem. U.S. Naval Inst., Am. Soc. Mil. Comptrs., Credit Union Exec. Soc., U.S. Naval Acad. Alumni Assn., CUNA Govt. Affairs Com. Avocations: running, gardening. Office: Navy Fed Credit Union PO Box 3000 Merrifield VA 22119-3000 Business E-Mail: william_earner@navyfederal.org.

EARNHARDT, DALE, JR., race car driver; b. Concord, NC, Oct. 10, 1974; s. Dale Earnhardt, Sr. and Brenda Lorraine Gee. Profl. race care driver NASCAR Dale Earnhardt Inc., 1999—2008, Hendrick Motorsports, 2008—; co-owner Chance 2 Motorsports (subs. Dale Earnhardt Inc.), 2002—; owner JR Motorsports, 2002—, Hammerhead Entertainment, Whisky River, Charlotte, 2008—. 1st pl. DirecTV 500 Tex. Motor Speedway, 2000; 1st pl. Pepsi 400 Daytona Internat. Speedway, 2001, 1st pl. Daytona 500, 2004, 2014; 1st pl. MBNA Cal Ripken, Jr. 400 Dover Internat. Speedway, 2001; 1st pl. EA Sports 500 Talladega Speedway, 2001, 2002, 2004, 1st pl. Aarons 499, 2002, 2003; 1st pl. Golden Corral 500 Atlanta Motor Speedway, 2004; 1st pl. Chevy American Revolution 400 Richmond Internat. Raceway, 2004, 1st pl. Crown Royal 400, 2006; 1st pl. Sharpie 500 Bristol Motor Speedway, 2004; 1st pl. Checker Auto Parts 500 Phoenix Internat. Raceway, 2004; 1st pl. USG Sheetrock 400 Chicagoland Speedway, 2005; 1st pl. LifeLock 400 Mich. Internat. Speedway, 2008, 1st pl. Quicken Loans 400, 2012. Guest appearances (TV series) 60 Minutes, 2004, The Tonight Show with Jay Leno, MTV Diary, VH1 Driven, 2003, (film) Talladega Nights: The Ballad of Ricky Bobby, 2006; voice actor: (film) Cars, 2006; author: Driver #8, 2002; exec. prodr., host: (radio show) Dale Jr. Unrestricted, 2006—; (TV series) Back in the Day with Dale Jr., 2006—. Recipient Espy Award for best driver, 2004; named Sprint Cup Series Most Popular Driver, 2003—13; named one of The Most Influential People in the World of Sports, Bus. Week, 2007, 2008, The 100 Most Powerful Celebrities, Forbes.com, 2008. Avocations: water sports, computers. Mailing: c/o Hendrick Motorsports 4400 Papa Joe Hendrick Blvd Charlotte NC 28262*

EARNHARDT, TERESA, race team owner; b. Hickory, NC; d. Hal Houston; m. Dale Earnhardt, 1982 (dec. Feb. 18, 2001); 1 child, Taylor Nicole stepchildren: Kerry, Kelley, Dale Jr. Attended in Comml. Art & Interior Design. Team owner NASCAR; ptnr. Dale Earnhardt, Inc., 1980, CEO, team owner Mooresville, NC, 1982—, pres. Named Outstanding Mother of Yr., Nat. Mother's Day Com., 2002. Achievements include car owner for four Busch Series championships in 1998, 1999, 2004 and 2005; Car owner for two Craftsman Truck Series championships in 1996 and 1997. Office: Dale Earnhardt Inc 1675 Dale Earnhardt Hwy 3 Mooresville NC 28115-8245 Office Fax: 704-663-7945. Business E-Mail: tearnhardt@daleinc.com.

EARP, H. SHELTON, III, endocrinologist, educator; AB in Pre-med., Johns Hopkins U., 1966; MD, U. NC, 1970. Diplomate Am. Bd. Internal Medicine, 1976, Am. Bd. Internal Medicine-endocrinology, diabetes and metabolism, 1977. Resident internal medicine NC Meml. Hosp., Chapel Hill, 1974—75; fellow endocrinology, diabetes and metabolism Univ. NC Hosp., Chapel Hill, 1975—77; asst. prof., medicine; asst. dir. Univ. NC. Lineberger Comprehensive Cancer Ctr., 1977—82, assoc. prof., medicine, assoc. dir., 1982—88, prof., medicine, pharmacology; dep. dir., 1988—97; dir. Univ. NC. Lineberger Comprehensive Cancer Rsch., 1997—; prof. medicine and pharmacology Univ. NC., 1997—. Co-author: (publs.) Angiotensin II Stimulates Protein-Tyrosine Phosphorylation In A Calcium-Dependent Manner, 1990, Signal transduction by integrins: increased protein tyrosine phosphorylation caused by clustering of ß1 integrins, 1991, Cell adhesion or integrin clustering increases phosphorylation of a focal adhesion-associated tyrosine kinase, 1992, The mouse waved-2 phenotype results from a point mutation in the EGF receptor tyrosine kinase, 1994, Cloning and mRNA expression analysis of a novel human protooncogene, c-mer, 1994, and numerous other publs. Rsch. investigator US Army, 1971—74. Mem.: Am. Cancer Soc. (cell and devel. biology study sect. 1989—93, chair 1990—93), Nat. Cancer Inst. (bd. sci. advisors 2002—07), Assn. of Am. Cancer Insts. (bd. dirs. 2001—, pres.-elect 2003—05, pres. 2005—07). Office: University of North Carolina 4009 Genetic Medicine Campus Box 7365 Chapel Hill NC 27599 Office Phone: 919-966-3036. Office Fax: 919-966-3015. E-mail: hse@med.unc.edu.

EARP, NAOMI CHURCHILL, former federal official; b. Newport News, Va., Feb. 15, 1950; d. Robert Henry and Naomi (Johnson) Davis; m. Samuel E. Earp, July 19, 1987. BA, Norfolk State U., 1972; MA, Ind. U., 1977; JD, Cath. U., 1982. Bar: Pa. 1985, Supreme Ct. Social worker City of Norfolk Dept. Welfare, Va., 1972-73, City of Indpls. Employment and Tng., 1973-76; civil rights specialist US Dept. Commerce, Chgo., 1976-79; investigator US Dept. Labor, Washington, 1981-83; pvt. practice as cons. Washington, 1983-85; civil rights specialist Dept. Navy, US Dept. Def., Washington, 1985-86; adminstr. equal opportunity programs USDA, Washington, 1987; atty. US Equal Employment Opportunity Commn. (EEOC), Washington, 1986-87, vice chair, 2003—06, chair, 2006—09. Active Forum Blacks in Agriculture, Washington, 1988, Womens' Action Task Force, Washington, 1988, Nat. Black Rep. Coun. Recipient Am. Jurisprudence award Property Am. Jurisprudence, 1980. Mem. ABA, Supreme Ct. Bar, Pa. Bar Assn., Coun. 100. Republican. Avocations: jogging, biking, dance.

EASLEY, KEVIN A., state legislator; b. Wichita, Kans., May 16, 1960; m. Dea Ann Easley; 3 children. BS in Acctg. and Bus. Mgmt., U. Tulsa. With ind. oil and gas co.; mem. Okla. Ho. of Reps., 10 yrs., Okla. Senate. Mem. Appropriations Com., Deregulation Com., Fin. Com., Gen. Govt. Com., Rules Com., Wildlife Com.; chair Energy, Environ. Resources and Regulatory Affairs Com. Named Legislator or Yr., Okla.Ind. Petroleum Assn., Okla. Mcpl. League, Okla. Rural Water Assn.; Okla. Hwy. Safety Pub. Svc. award, 1987; County Commrs. Bd. Dirs. award, 1991, Okla. Restaurant Assn. award, 1991. Office: State Capitol Bldg 2300 N Lincoln Blvd Oklahoma City OK 73105-4805

EASON, JAMES DAVID, surgeon; b. Memphis, Tenn., Dec. 27, 1960; MD, U. Tenn., 1987. Cert. Am. Bd. Surgery. Resident, surgery Wilford Hall Med. Ctr., Lackland Air Force Base, San Antonio; clin. and rsch. fellow transplant surgery Mass. Gen. Hosp., Boston; clin. fellow surgery Harvard Med. Sch.; prof. transplant surgery U. Tenn. Health Sci. Ctr., Memphis, chief transplantation; program dir. U. Tenn./Meth. U. Hosp. Transplant Inst. Mem. physician adv. com. Patient Access to Transplantation Coalition; mem. Genzyme Liver Transplantation adv. bd. Assoc. editor, editl. bd. American Journal of Transplantation. Maj. USAF. Fellow: American Coll. Surgeons; mem.: Transplantation Soc., Internat. Liver Transplantation Soc., American Soc. Transplant Surgeons, AMA, American Assn. Study of Liver Diseases. Office: Meth U Hospital Transplant Inst 1265 Union Ave S1011 Memphis TN 38104-3499 Office Phone: 901-516-7070. Office Fax: 901-516-9184.

EASON, MARCIA JEAN (MARCY EASON), lawyer; b. Dallas, Aug. 31, 1953; d. John Keller and Sara Marguerite (Prindle) McCarron; m. S. Lee Meredith, Sept. 12, 1981 (div. Oct. 1989); m. David O. Eason, Aug. 21, 1993; stepchildren: Chelsea, Shannon, Valerie. BA magna cum laude, Trinity U., 1975; JD, U. Houston, 1979. Bar: Tex. 1978, U.S. Dist. Ct. (so. dist.) Tex. 1978, U.S. Ct. Appeals (5th cir.) 1979, Tenn. 1985, U.S. Dist. Ct. (ea. dist.) Tenn. 1985, U.S. Supreme Ct. 1985, U.S. Ct. Appeals (6th cir.) 1986, U.S. Ct. Appeals (4th cir.) 1994. Ptnr. Byrnes & Martin, Houston, 1984-85, Miller & Martin PLLC, Chattanooga, 1987—. Pres., bd. dirs. Chattanooga's Kids on the Block, 1987-94; bd. dirs., chair AIM Ctr, Chattanooga, 1993-2005; campaign chair, attys. divsn. United Way, Chattanooga, 1994, leadership, campaign chair, 1998. Fellow: Am. Bar Found., Tenn. Bar Found., Chattanooga Bar Found., Litig. Counsel America; mem. ABA, Tenn. Bar Assn. (pres. 2007-08, v.p. 2005-, bd. govs. 1999-, v.p. 2006-08), Chattanooga Bar Assn. (bd. govs. 2004-05), Nat. Conf. Bar Presidents (exec. coun.), Tenn. Supreme Ct. Commn. (mem. racial and ethnic and gender fairness, mem. enhancing pub. trust in ct. sys.), Tenn. Lawyers Assn. for Women (co-chair com. 1994, treas. 1995-97, pres. 1998). Office: Miller & Martin PLLC 832 Georgia Ave Ste 1000 Chattanooga TN 37402-2289 Office Phone: 423-756-6600. Office Fax: 423-785-8480. Business E-Mail: meason@millermartin.com.

EASON, ROBERT GASTON, psychology professor; b. Bells, Tenn., May 15, 1924; s. William Bryant and Noba (Proctor) E.; m. Dorothy Jean Goodner, Sept. 5, 1952; children— Robert Gregory, Linda Joan. BA, U. Mo., 1950, MA, 1952, PhD, 1956. Postdoctoral fellow physiology UCLA, 1956-57; research psychologist Navy Electronics Lab., San Diego, 1957-67; asst. prof. San Diego State Coll., 1960-63, assoc. prof., 1963-66, prof., 1966-67, U. N.C., Greensboro, 1967-70, excellence prof., 1970-78, Elizabeth Rosenthal Excellence prof., 1978-94, prof. emeritus, 1994—, dept. head, 1967-80. Mem. editorial bd. Internat. Jour. Psychophysiology, 1990-98. Served with USAAF, 1943-46. Fellow APA; mem. Assn. for Psychol. Sci., Eastern Psychol. Assn., Southeastern Psychol. Assn., Soc. Psychophysiol. Rsch., Sigma Xi. Home: 1000 Ridgecrest Dr Greensboro NC 27410-5509 Personal E-mail: bobeason@triad.rr.com.

EASON MCINTYRE, JUDY, state legislator; b. Tulsa, Okla., 1945; d. Del Phillips and Jeanie Hughes P. BS, MS, Univ. Okla. Sr. social svc. supr. Dept. Human Svc., 1967—99, Child Welfare Div.; mem., pres. Tulsa Pub. Sch. Bd.; mem. Dist 73 Okla. House of Representatives, 2002—04; mem. Dist 11 Okla. State Senate, 2005—. Recipient One of 16 Black Women selected for Leadership Tng., NOBL Women & Rutgers U-Eagleton Inst., 2002. Mem.: NAACP. Democrat. Address: 2300 N Lincoln Blvd Rm 429 Oklahoma City OK 73105 Mailing: PO Box 48548 Tulsa OK 74148 Office Phone: 405-521-5598. Business E-Mail: easonmcintyre@oksenate.gov.

EASSON, WILLIAM MCALPINE, psychiatrist, educator; b. Evanston, Ill., July 3, 1931; s. Alexander and Anne Meldrum (Watson) E.; m. Gwendolyn Bowen, May 31, 1958; children: Anne, Jane, David, Michael. M.B., Ch.B., U. Aberdeen, Scotland, 1954, MD, 1967. Fellow in medicine and psychiatry Mayo Clinic, Rochester, Minn., 1956-59; resident in psychiatry U. Sask., 1959-60, instr. psychiatry, 1959-61; fellow in child psychiatry Menninger Clinic, Topeka, 1961-63, staff child psychiatrist, 1963-67; prof. psychiatry, chmn. dept. Med. Coll. Ohio, Toledo, 1967-72; prof., dir. div. child and adolescent psychiatry U. Minn. Med. Sch., Mpls., 1972-74; prof. psychiatry La. State U. Med. Ctr., New Orleans, 1974-96, head dept. psychiatry, 1974-82, prof. emeritus, 1996—. Vis. prof. psychiatry U. Garyounis Med. Sch., Benghazi, Libya, 1979; prof. grad. studies U. Riyadh, Saudi Arabia; U.S.-USSR health scientist, Moscow and Leningrad. Author: The Severely Disturbed Adolescent, 1969, The Dying Child, 2d edit., 1981, Psychiatry Exam. Rev., 5th edit., 1994, Psychiatry Patient Mgmt. Rev., 1977, (with N. Rock) Psychiatry Splty. Bd. Rev., 1991, The Management of the Severely Disturbed Adolescent, 1996; editor: Jour. Clin. Psychiatry, 1977-80. Carnegie fellow, 1956-58; Anderson fellow, 1956-58; WHO fellow, 1976 Fellow Am. Psychiat. Assn. (life). Home: 5218 Saint Charles Ave New Orleans LA 70115-4943

EAST, DON W., state legislator, farmer, retired police officer; b. Surry Co., NC, Dec. 26, 1944; m. Connie East; 1 child, Gina Southern. Attended for Law Enforcement/Criminal Justice, Forsyth Tech. Cmty. Coll., 1964. Farmer, Pilot Mountain, N.C.; commr. Surry Co., 1984—92; mem. NC State Senate, 1994—2000, mem. Dist. 30, 2004—. Mem. agr., environ. and natural resources com., appropriations/base budget com., children and human resources com., ins. com., select com. on tobacco settlement issues, ways and means com., ranking minority mem. appropriations on justice and pub. safety com. Republican. Protestant. Office: NC Senate 300 N Salisbury St 521 Raleigh NC 27603-5925 Office Phone: 919-733-5743. E-mail: Don.East@ncleg.net.

EASTHAM, ALAN WALTER, JR., retired ambassador, lawyer; b. Dumas, Ark., Oct. 16, 1951; s. Alan Walter and Ruth E. (Clayton) E.; m. Carolyn Laux, Aug. 2, 1974; children: Mark A., Michael S.G. BA, Hendrix Coll., Ark., 1973; JD cum laude, Georgetown U., 1982. Bar: D.C. 1982. Mgr. KDDA-AM Radio, Dumas, Ark., 1973-74; vice consul US Embassy, Kathmandu, Nepal, 1975-78; info. officer US Dept. State, Washington, 1978-80, staff mem. office for combating terrorism, 1980-82, desk officer Sri Lanka & the Maldives, 1982-83, polit. officer for India, 1983-84; prin. officer US Consulate, Peshawar, Pakistan, 1984-87; spl. asst. to under sec. polit. affairs US Dept. State, 1987-89; counselor US Embassy, Nairobi, Kenya, 1989-92, Kinshasa, Democratic Republic of Congo, 1992-94, consul gen. Bordeaux, France, 1994-95, counselor New Delhi, 1995-97, dep. chief of mission Islamabad, Pakistan, 1997-99; dep. asst. sec. for South Asian affairs US Dept. State, Washington, 1999—2001, spl. negotiator for conflict diamonds, 2001—02, dir. Ctrl. African affairs, 2002—05, US amb. to Republic of Malawi Lilongwe, 2005—08, US amb. to Republic of Congo Brazzaville, 2008—10; fellow Hendrix Coll., Conway, Ariz., 2010—. Methodist.

EASTLAND, S. STACY, lawyer; b. Houston, Oct. 27, 1948; s. Seaborn and Anne (Stacy) E.; m. Tara Gardner, Mar. 24, 1972; children: Tara Doran, Seaborn Gardner. BS honors, Washington & Lee U, 1971; JD honors, U. Tex., 1974. Assoc. Baker & Botts, Houston, 1974-81, ptnr., 1982—2000; mng. dir. Goldman Sachs & Co., Houston; pvt. practise Houston. Bd. dirs. Houston Estate and Fin. Forum, Camp Mystic, Inc.; mem. Tex. Bd. Legal Specialization in Estate Planning and Probate Law, Estate Planners Nat. Assn. Estate Planners & Coun. Bd. dirs. Oscar Neuhaus Found., St. John Meml. Endowment Fund, Houston chpt. Ortin Soc., DePelchin Children's Ctr., Inst. Child and Family Svcs.; trustee Kelsey-Seabold Found. Recipient Who's Who in Am., Best Lawyers in Am., top trust and estate lawyers. Fellow Am. Coll. Probate Counsel; mem. ABA (coun. 1990—, publs. coord. probate and trust divsn. 1992-93, bylaws and handbook com. 1992—, sec. adv. Revision Uniform Partnership Act 1987—, publs. com. 1992-93, budget and fin. com. 1991-92, chair divsn. coord. ann. meeting programs 1987-89), Am. Coll. Trust and Estate Counsel (bd. regents, chmn. transfer tax study com. 1988-93), Tex. State Bar Assn., Houston Bar Assn., Houston Country Club, Tex. Allegro Club, Internat. Academy of Estate and Trust Law. Episcopalian. Avocations: tennis, golf. Office: 1000 Louisiana Ste 550 Houston TX 77002 Office Phone: 713-654-8484.

EATON, BLAINE (BO), state legislator; b. Taylorsville, Miss. m. Susanne Magee Eaton. Mem. Dist. 79 Miss. House of Reps., 1996—; farmer, logger. Mem.: Nat. Rifle Assn., Forestry Assn., Cattlemen's Assn., Farm Bureau, Lions Club, Mason Lodge. Democrat. Baptist. Mailing: 503 Gambrell St Taylorsville MS 39168-4284 Home Phone: 601-785-4662; Office Phone: 601-260-3278, 601-359-3334. Business E-Mail: beaton@house.ms.gov.

EATON, GORDON PRYOR, geologist, consultant; b. Dayton, Ohio, Mar. 9, 1929; s. Colman and Dorothy (Pryor) E.; m. Virginia Anne Gregory, June 12, 1951; children: Gretchen Maria, Gregory Mathieu. BA, Wesleyan U., 1951, Doctorate (hon.), 1995; MS, Calif. Inst. Tech., 1953, PhD, 1957; Doctorate (hon.), Colo. Sch. Mines, 2001. From instr. geology to asst. prof. Wesleyan U., Middletown, Conn., 1955-59; from asst. prof. to assoc. prof. U. Calif., Riverside, 1959-67, chmn. dept. geol. sci., 1965-67; with U.S. Geol. Survey, 1963-65, 67-81, 94-97; dep. chief Office Geochemistry and Geophysics, Washington, 1972-74; project chief geothermal geophysics Office Geochemistry Geophysics, Denver, 1974-76; scientist-in-charge Hawaiian Volcano Obs., 1976-78; assoc. chief geologist Reston, Va., 1978-81; dean Tex. A&M U. Coll. Geoscis., 1981-83; provost, v.p. acad. affairs Tex. A&M U., 1983-86, prof. emeritus, 2003—; pres. Iowa State U., Ames, 1986-90; dir. Lamont-Doherty Earth Obs. Columbia U., Palisades, NY, 1990-94, U.S. Geol. Survey, Reston, 1994-97. Former mem. Com. on Internat. Edn., Am. Coun. Edn.; bd. earth scis. and resources; ocean studies bd., com. on formation of nat. biol. survey NRC, geophysics study com.; bd. dirs. Midwest Resources, Inc., Bankers Trust; mem., chair adv. com. U.S. Army Command and Gen. Staff Coll.; adv. bd. Sandia Nat. Lab. Geoscis. & Environ. Ctr., Ohio State U. Ctr. Mapping. Mem. editl. bd. Jour. Volcanology and Geothermal Rsch., 1976-78; contbr. articles to profl. jours. Trustee Wesleyan U., 1995-98, Geol. Soc. Am. Found., 1999-2003; pres., bd. dirs. Iowa 4-H Found., 1986-90; mem. adv. bd. Sch. Earth Sci. Stanford (Calif.) U., 1995-2000; mem. U.S. del. sci. and tech. com. Gore-Chernomyrdin Commn., 1996-97; mem. vis. com. Colo. Sch. Mines, 2002-04; mem. water res. adv. com. Island Co., 2001-03. Named Gordon P. Eaton Hall in his honor, Iowa State U., 2003; grantee, NSF, 1955—59; Standard Oil fellow, Calif. Inst. Tech., 1953. Fellow: AAAS, Geol. Soc. Am.; mem.: Am. Geophysical Union. Home: 2505 E Villa Maria Rd Apt 231 Bryan TX 77802-2079 Personal E-mail: vngeaton@suddenlink.net.

EATON, JOEL DOUGLAS, lawyer; b. Miami, Fla., Oct. 31, 1943; s. Joe Oscar and Patricia (MacVicar) E.; m. Mary Benson, June 24, 1967; children: Douglas, Darryl, David. BA, Yale U., 1965; JD, Harvard U., 1975. Bar: Fla. 1975, U.S. Dist. Ct. (so. dist.) Fla. 1976, U.S. Ct. Appeals (5th cir.) 1976, U.S. Supreme Ct. 1978, U.S. Ct. Appeals (11th cir.) 1981, U.S. Ct. Appeals (Fed. cir.) 1996. Ptnr. Podhurst Orseck, P.A. and predecessors, Miami, 1975—. With USN, 1965-71. Decorated Air medal with Bronze Star and numeral 14, Navy Commendation medal with 2 gold stars, Cross of Gallantry (Viet Nam). Mem. ABA, Am. Justice Assn., Am. Law Inst., Fla. Justice Assn., Fla. Bar Assn. (appellate rules com. 1981-2002, chmn. 1989-90, jud. evaluation com. 1995-98, Fla. std. jury instn. com. 1998-2004), Am. Acad. Appellate Lawyers. Democrat. Office: Podhurst Orseck PA 25 W Flagler St Ste 800 Miami FL 33130-1720 Office Phone: 305-358-2800. Business E-Mail: jeaton@podhurst.com.

EATON, ROGER, food products executive; b. South Africa, 1960; arrived in Australia, 1984; Gen. mgr. Kentucky Fried Chicken New Zealand; fin. dir. Kentucky Fried Chicken South Pacific, regional ops. dir.; sr. v.p., mng. dir. South Pacific Yum! Restaurants Internat., Australia, 2000—07; COO, chief devel. officer Yum! Brands, Inc., Louisville, 2008; pres., chief concept officer, KFC Yum! Brands, Inc. (formerly TRICON Global Restaurants, Inc.), Louisville, 2008—. Achievements include 27 consecutive quarters of profitable same store sales growth for Yum! South Pacific. Office: Yum Brands Inc 1441 Gardiner Ln Louisville KY 40213

EAVES, FELMONT FARRELL, III, plastic surgeon; b. June 8, 1962; MD, U. Tenn. Coll. Medicine, Memphis, 1987. Cert. Am. Bd. Plastic Surgery, Am. Bd. Surgery. Intern U. Tex. Southwestern Med. Ctr.; resident gen. surgery Parkland Hosp. U. Texas Southwestern, Dallas; resident plastic surgery Emory U., fellow endoscopic, minimally invasive plastic surgery; practicing minimally invasive, endoscopic surgery, ptnr. Charlotte Plastic Surgery Ctr. Co-author med. textbook; contbr. articles to profl. jours. Mem.: ACS, Southeastern Soc. Plastic & Reconstructive Surgeons, Internat. Soc. Aesthetic Plastic Surgery, Am. Soc. Aesthetic Plastic Surgery (treas., adminstrv. commr., chair patient safety com. 2006—, Sherrill J. Aston award, Lockwood award, Simon Fredricks award), Am. Soc. Plastic Surgeons, Alpha Omega. Office: Charlotte Plastic Surgery Ctr 2215 Randolph Rd Charlotte NC 28207 Office Phone: 704-372-6846, 800-281-2456. Fax: 704-342-0752. Business E-Mail: tvanneste@charlotteplasticsurgery.com.

EBAUGH, HELEN ROSE, sociology educator, researcher; b. San Angelo, Tex., June 21, 1942; d. Arnold and Agnes (Halfman) Fuchs; m. Albert L. Ebaugh, Aug. 3, 1975; children: Sarah, Stephen. BA, Our Lady of Lake U., 1966; MA, U. Tex., 1968; PhD, Columbia U., 1975. Asst. prof., dept. sociology U. Houston, 1973-79, assoc. prof., 1979-89, chmn. dept., 1985-87, prof., 1993—. Author: Out of the Cloister, 1977, Becoming an Ex, 1988, Women in the Vanishing Cloister, 1993, Religion and the New Immigrants, 2000, Religion Acron Border, 2002, The Grulen Movement, 2010. Mem. Am. Sociol. Assn. Home: 2423 Glen Haven Blvd Houston TX 77030-3509

EBBIN, ADAM P., state legislator; b. Huntington, NY, Nov. 10, 1963; BA, American U., Washington, 1985. Mem. Dist. 49 Va. House of Delegates, 2004—12; mem. Dist. 30 Va. State Senate, 2012—, mem. Agr. Com., Conservation and Natural Resources Com., Gen. Laws and Tech. Com. & Local Govt. Com. Mem. edn. com. Nat. Conf. State Legislatures; mem. No. Va. Transp. Commn., Met. Washington Air Quality Commn. Bd. mem. Alexandria Parent Tng. Leadership Inst.; hon. bd. mem. Lincoln at the Crossroads. Fellow, Sorensen Inst. Polit. Leadership. Mem.: NAACP, Met. Washington Coun. Governments, Tenants and Workers United. Democrat. Jewish. Office: Senate of Virginia PO Box 396 Richmond VA 23218 also: PO Box 26415 Alexandria VA 22313 Office Phone: 804-698-7530. Office Fax: 804-698-7651. E-mail: district30@senate.virginia.gov.

EBEL, GREGORY L., energy executive; b. Ontario, Canada, 1964; m. Kimberly Ebel; 2 children. BA, York Univ., Toronto, 1987; grad. advanced mgmt. program, Harvard Bus. Sch. Analyst Decima Rsch., Toronto; chief of staff to Min. of Fin. & Dep. Prime Minister, Govt. of Canada, Ottawa, 1989—93; exec. dir. World Bank Group, Washington, 1993—98; v.p. strategic develop. Westcoast Energy, 1998—2002; mng. dir. mergers & acquisitions Duke Energy, 2002, v.p. investor & shareholder rels., 2002—05; CFO & pres. Union Gas Spectra Energy Corp., Houston, 2005—08, pres., CEO, 2009—. Bd. dir. Spectra Energy Corp., DCP Midstream. Office: Spectra Energy Corp 5400 Westheimer Ct Houston TX 77056-5310

EBERHART, ROBERT CLYDE, biomedical engineering educator, researcher; b. Oakland, Calif., Apr. 17, 1937; s. George Perrin and Roberta Eberhart; m. Carol Eberhart, Aug. 4, 1960; 3 children. AB in Applied Physics, Harvard U., 1958; MS in Mech. Engring., U. Calif., Berkeley, 1960, PhD, 1965. Staff scientist Inst. Med. Scis., San Francisco, 1964—70, sr. scientist, 1970—75; assoc. prof. mech. engring. U. Tex., Austin, Tex., 1975—76; assoc. prof. surgery U. Tex. So. Med. Ctr., Dallas, 1976—86; chmn. biomed. engring. U. Tex. So. Med. Ctr. and U. Tex.-Arlington, 1983—2001; prof. engring. in surgery U. Tex. So. Med. Ctr. and U. Tex., Arlington, 1984—2005; adj. prof. surgery U. Tex. So. Med. Ctr., Dallas, 2006—09, prof. emeritus, 2010—; prof. bioengring. and mech. engring. U. Tex., Arlington, 2006—. Pres. Tex. Stent Tech., 2005—11; bd. sci. advisors Andev, Inc.; cons. in field. Editor: Heat Transfer in Medicine and Biology, 1985; co-editor: Biomaterials-Living Sys. Interactions, 1993—98; contbr. articles to profl. jours., chpts. in books. Recipient C.W. Hall Rsch. award So. Biomed. Engring. Conf., 1987, Career Achievement award Houston Symposium for Biomed. Engring., 1996. Fellow: Biomed. Engring. Soc. (Inaugural fellow 2005), Am. Inst. Med. and Biol. Engring. (founding fellow 1993); mem.: IEEE, ASME (Engr. of Yr. 2007), Biomaterials Soc., Harvard Club. Achievements include patentee nonthrombogenic treatment for med. polymers 1985; patents for expandable biodegradable polymeric stents for combined mechanical support and pharmacological or radiation therapy 2005. Office: U Tex So Med Ctr Dept Surgery 5323 Harry Hines Blvd Dallas TX 75390-9130 Office Phone: 214-648-2052. Business E-Mail: robert.eberhart@utsouthwestern.edu.

EBERLE, CHARLES EDWARD, paper and consumer products executive; b. St. Louis, Mar. 20, 1928; s. Charles Edward and Hazel (Williams) Eberle; m. Nancy Ellen Paddock, Aug. 1, 1953 (div. June 1995); children: Charles Edward, Celia Camille, Julia Lee; m. Denise S. Jackson, Apr. 12, 1997 (dec. Nov. 2002); m. Bonnie M. Shaub, Sept. 28, 2003. BS in Chem. Engring., Washington U., St. Louis, 1949. Prodn. mgr. Procter & Gamble, St. Louis, 1949-55, plant mgr. Lexington, Ky., 1955-57, St. Louis, 1957-60, Sacramento, 1960-64, mgr. mfg. Cin., 1964-79, v.p. mfg., 1979-84, v.p. engring., 1984-85; pres. CEE Enterprises, Cin., 1985-88, Thomas & Eberle Assocs., Inc., Cin., 1986-88; v.p., James River Europe James River Corp., 1988-90, sr. v.p., group exec., 1990, exec. v.p. consumer products bus., 1990-91; pres. CEE Enterprises, Richmond, 1992—2002; chmn. exec. com. Richmond area TEC, Midlothian, Va., 1997-98; v.p. corp. devel. Lloyd Assocs., Inc., Richmond, 1999-2001. Mem. mfg. studies bd. NRC/NAS, 1984-89. Vice pres. bd. trustees Children's Hosp. Med. Ctr., Cin., 1975-78; mem. Cin. Council on World Affairs, 1979-89; v.p. Dan Beard coun. Boy Scouts Am., 1982-85. With U.S. Army, 1951-52. Recipient Engring. Alumni Achievement award Washington U., 1977 Home: 1756 Old Powhatan Est Powhatan VA 23139-7622 E-mail: ceeberle@verizon.net.

EBERLY, CEREE TATE, beverage company executive; b. 1962; BA in Biology, U. Tenn. Joined Coca-Cola Co., 1990, various positions including human resources dir. Latin Ctr. Bus. Unit, v.p. McDonalds divsn., group human resources dir. Europe, chief people officer, 2009—10, sr. v.p., chief people officer, 2010—. Bd. mem. Habitat for Humanity; adv. to bd. Ronald McDonald House Charities. Office: The Coca-Cola Co 1 Coca-Cola Plz Atlanta GA 30313

EBERTS, F. SAMUEL, III, lawyer, medical products executive; BS in Polit. Sci., Loyola U., Chgo., 1977; JD, Boston U., 1982. Assoc. Barnes & Thornburg, 1985—89, Jones Day, 1988—92; chief counsel, Biotech North America divsn. Baxter International, Inc., 1992—96; asst. gen. counsel Allegiance Healthcare Corp., 1996—99, Cardinal Health, Inc., 1999—2001; v.p., gen. counsel, sec. Stepan Co., 2001—04; sr. v.p., gen. counsel Laboratory Corp. of America Holdings, 2004—09, sr. v.p., chief legal officer, 2009—. Office: Laboratory Corp of America Holdings 358 S Main St Burlington NC 27215 Office Phone: 336-229-1127. Business E-Mail: F.Eberts@labcorp.com.

EBONG, ENOH TITILAYO, lawyer; d. Ime James and Rosecleer Sadis Ebong. MA in History, U. Edinburgh, Scotland, 1987; MA in Comm., Annenberg Sch. Communication, U. Pa., Phila., 1989; JD, U. Mich. Law Sch., Ann Arbor, 1997. Assoc. Mintz, Levin, Cohn, Ferris, Glovsky and Popeo, P.C., Boston, 1997—2004; atty. advisor US Trade and Devel. Agy., Arlington, 2004—07, acting regional dir., subsaharan africa, 2007—08, asst. gen. counsel, 2007—10, dep. gen. counsel, 2010—12, gen. counsel, 2012—. Bd. dirs. Wash. Fgn. Law Soc., Washington, 2005—07, Friends Nat. Zoo, Washington, 2011—. Bd. mem. Friends Nat. Zoo, Washington, 2011—12. Democrat. Roman Catholic. Office: US Trade and Development Agency 1000 Wilson Boulevard Ste 1600 Arlington VA 22209 Office Fax: 703-875-4009.

ECHO-HAWK, WALTER R., JR., lawyer; b. Pawnee Reservation, Okla. BA in Polit. Sci., Okla. State U., Stillwater, 1970; JD, U. N.Mex. Sch. Law, Albuquerque, 1973. Bar: Colo. Supreme Ct. 1974, US Dist. Ct. 1974, US Ct. Appeals (8th cir.) 1975, US Supreme Ct. 1977, US Ct. Appeals (10th cir.) 1979, US Ct. Appeals (9th cir.) 1987, Pawnee Nation Supreme Ct. 1994, US Ct. Appeals (DC) 2004, US Ct. Appeals (Fed. cir.) 2007. Assoc. justice Pawnee Nation Supreme Ct., Okla.; sr. staff atty. Native Am. Rights Fund, Boulder, Colo., 1973—2009; gen. counsel Pawnee Nation; of counsel Indian gaming law and gaming practice group Crowe & Dunlevy, Tulsa, Okla. Lectr. in fed. Indian law US Forest Svc. Author: Battlefields and Burial Grounds, 1994; contbr. articles to law jours. Mem. internat. human rights coun. Carter Ctr.; trustee Pawnee Nation Coll.; chmn. bd. dirs. Native Arts and Cultures Found.; mem. Kitkahaki Band Pawnee Nation, Okla. Recipient Civil Liberties award, ACLU Oreg., 1992, Martin Luther King, Jr. Peace award, Met. Coll. Denver, 1998, Spirit Excellence award, ABA Commn. on Opportunities for Minorities in the Profession, 1995, Sarah T. Hughes Civil Rights award, Fed. Bar Assn., 2009; named Martin L. King March Co-Grand Marshal, Martin L. King Ctr., Atlanta, 1993. Mem.: Native Am. Bar Assn. Office: Crowe & Dunlevy 321 S Boston Ave 500 Kennedy Bldg Tulsa OK 74103 Office Phone: 918-592-9874. Office Fax: 918-599-6307. Business E-Mail: walter.echohawk@crowedunlevy.com.

ECHOLS, LELDON E., board member; BS in Acctg., Ark. State U. CPA. Mng. ptnr., audit and bus. adv. practice Arthur Anderson LLP, 1997—2000; exec. v.p., CFO Centex Corp., 2000—06. Bd. dirs. Crosstex Energy, L.P., Holly Corp., Roofing Supply Group Holdings, Inc., Colemont Corp., TXU Corp., 2005—07, Trinity Industries, Inc., 2007—. Mem. AICPA, Tex. Soc. CPAs. Office: Trinity Industries Inc Bd Directors 2525 Stemmons Fwy Dallas TX 75207-2401 Office Phone: 214-631-4420. Office Fax: 214-589-8810. Business E-Mail: leldon.echols@trin.net.

ECK, ROBERT EDWIN, retired physicist; b. Ames, Iowa, Nov. 28, 1938; s. John Clifford and Helen (Behrendt) E.; m. Carolyn Jennie Vodicka, May 11, 1974; children: David Michael, Elizabeth Claire. BA in Physics, Rutgers U., 1960; MS in Physics, U. Pa., 1962, PhD in Physics, 1966; MA in Econs., U. Calif., Santa Barbara, 1973. Sr. rsch. scientist Ford Motor Co., Newport Beach, Calif., 1966-69; project engr. Santa Barbara Rsch. Ctr., Goleta, Calif., 1969-73, asst. mgr. infrared components, 1974-81, mgr. major program, 1982-84, dir. tech., 1985-88, dir./mgr. engring., 1989-95; new bus. devel. mgr.

R.G. Hansen & Assocs., Santa Barbara, Calif., 1995-96; program mgr. Optoelectronics-Textron, Petaluma, 1996-2000; adminstrv. dir. Enhancement Inst., Houston, 2002—03; adj. instr. physics Lone Star Coll., Tex., 2010—11. Bd. dirs. Goleta Edn. Found. Mem. Goleta Noontime Rotary Club (pres. 1989-90). Achievements include patents on superconductors, infrared detector testing and magnetoresistor sensors.

ECK, RONALD WARREN, civil engineer, educator; b. Allentown, Pa., May 11, 1949; s. Warren Edgar and Viola (Ruth) E. BSCE, Clemson U., SC, 1971, PhD, 1975. Registered profl. engr., W.Va. Asst. prof. civil engring. W.Va. U., Morgantown, 1975-80, assoc. prof. civil engring., 1980-84, prof. civil engring., 1984—2008, prof. emeritus, 2008—, dir. rsch. coll. engring., 1994-96; dir. W.Va. Transp. Tech. Transfer Ctr., 1991—2008. Cons. in field. Contbr. articles to profl. jours. Chmn. City Traffic Commn., Morgantown, 1989—2007; mem. Region 3, U.S. DOT, Nat. Def. Exec. Res., 1982-94. Recipient Dow Outstanding Young Faculty award Am. Soc. Engring. Edn., 1980, W.Va. U. Found. Outstanding Tchr. award, 1988, others. Mem. NSPE, Am. Soc. Engring. Edn. (v.p., profl. interest coun., 1987-88), ASCE (pres. W.Va. sect. 1980), Inst. Transp. Engrs. (chmn. expert witness coun. 2003-06), Transp. Rsch. Bd. (chmn. com. on low volume rds. 1990-96), Am. Soc. Safety Engrs. Avocation: backpacking. Home: 609 Valley View St Morgantown WV 26505-2412 Home Phone: 304-599-4022. Business E-Mail: ronald.eck@mail.wvu.edu.

ECKELSON, ROBERT ALAN, orthodontist; b. Cleve., Feb. 2, 1947; s. Sam Robert and Frances (Kaplan) E.; m. Linda Goldstine, July 23, 1984. DDS, Ohio State U., 1971; postgrad., U. Ill., Chgo., 1971-73. Diplomate Am. Bd. Orthodontists. Pvt. practice, Boca Raton, Fla., 1973—. Mem. staff Boca Raton Regional Hosp., 1978—. Bd. dirs. Boca Forum, Boca Raton, 1988-93, pres., 1992-93. Fellow Internat. Coll. Dentists; mem. So. Assn. Orthodontists, Fla. Dental Assn., World Fedn. Orthodontists, Boca Raton Roundtable (pres. 1993-95), Rotary (pres. Boca Raton 1996-97, Paul Harris fellow), South Palm Beach County Dental Assn. (pres. 2000-01), Alpha Omega (pres. Palm Beach/Broward chpt. 1984-86). Avocation: flight instr. Office: 951 NW 13th St Ste 3B Boca Raton FL 33486-2337 Home Phone: 561-495-9198; Office Phone: 561-391-6415. Personal E-mail: dreckelson@yahoo.com.

ECKERT, MICHAEL JOSEPH, television and technology executive, early state private equity capital executive; b. Chgo., Mar. 20, 1947; s. Stephen Michael and Mary Theresa (Kovacs) E.; m. Janis Lynn Kamps, Oct. 28, 1972; children: Eric, Jacob, Morgan. BS in Edn., No. Ill. U., 1969; postgrad., De Paul U., 1969-72. Tchr., coach St. Rita H.S., Chgo., 1969-73; account mgr. Sta. WDHF, Chgo., 1973; sales mgr. Sta. WAIT, Chgo., 1974-76; account exec. John Blair Co., Chgo., 1976-78, sales mgr., 1979-81; gen. sales mgr. Sta. WLAK, Chgo., 1978; v.p. sales The Weather Channel, Chgo. and NY, 1982-85, pres., CEO Atlanta, 1985—99; CEO, The Travel Channel, Atlanta, 1992-93; pres., CEO Pathfire, Inc., Roswell, 2000—07; fellow Ga. Tech. Venture Lab., 2008; chmn. Atlanta Tech., Angel Investors. Cons. Metomedia, Montreal, 1988—92; pres. Prime Time tonight, Atlanta, 1989, Landmark Comm. Broadcast and Video Enterprises Divsn., 1990—; bd. dirs. Pelmorex Inc., Toronto, Der Wetter Kanal, Dusseldorf, Cable TV Advt. Bur., sec, 1993—94, treas., 1995—96, vice chmn., 1997—98; bd. dirs. Multichannel Advt. Bur.; pres. Landmark Comm. Video Networks and Entrprises; chmn. World Cup Com., 1991—95, Golden Cable Ace Award Com., 1992—95, Award Competition Com., 1996; chmn. bd. Vekedeeco, 2011. Active United Way, Atlanta, 1987-88; bd. dirs. Atlanta Symphony Orch., 1996-, Upper Chattahoochee Riverkeeper, 2005, Flux Media, 2008, Tech. Assn. Ga., 2008; chmn. bd. Solo Health, 2008-10, Play On Sports, 2008-12; exec. chmn. Atlanta Tech. Angel Investors; adv. bd. mem. Mother Nature Network, 2008-09; chmn. NOUH Angel Alliance, 2014, Adv. Bd., 2014, Adv. Bd. SNAP, 2014, Adv. Bd. MQUBES, 2014; adv. bd. mem. 4D Nutrition, Idscan, 2014. Recipient Spl. Leadership award ARC, Washington, 1985, 89; named Man of Achievement Phi Kappa Theta, 1994. Mem.: Cable TV Adminstrn. and Mgmt. Soc., Nat. Acad. Cable Programming (bd. dirs. 1985—2000), Nat. Cable TV Assn. (satellite programming com. 1985—2000), Atlanta Alliance Bus. and Edn., Vinngs Club (bd. govs. 1993—96). Avocations: fly fishing, mountain trekking, skiing. Home: 8416 Oak St Apt G New Orleans LA 70118-2058

EDDLEMAN, FLOYD EUGENE, retired language educator; b. Mena, Ark., Dec. 3, 1930; s. Floyd Newton and Ruby Kate (Cannon) E. BSE, U. Cen. Ark., 1951; MA, U. Ark., 1955, PhD, 1961. Teaching asst. English U. Ark., Fayetteville, 1953-55, 56-58; instr. English & Speech U. Colo., Boulder, 1955-56; instr. English Tex. Tech U., Lubbock, 1958-62, asst. prof., 1962-65, assoc. prof., 1965-75, prof., 1975-90, prof. emeritus, 1991—. Author: American Drama Criticism, 1976, 79, 84, 89, 92; co-editor: Almayer's Folly in the Cambridge Edit. of the Works of Joseph Conrad, 1994; contbr. articles to profl. jours. Sgt. US Army, 1951—53. Democrat. Avocation: genealogy. Home: 1309 Cole Ave Mena AR 71953-3722

EDELCUP, NORMAN SCOTT, management and financial consultant; b. Chgo., May 8, 1935; s. Irving L. and Pauline (Bolz) Edelcup. BS in Bus. Adminstrn, Northwestern U., 1957. CPA Fla., Ill. Sr. accountant Arthur Andersen & Co., Chgo., 1957-62; sec.-treas. Acme Printing Ink Co., Chgo., 1962-65; accountant, asst. to chmn. Commonwealth Edison Co., Chgo., 1965-68; sr. v.p., vice-chmn. bd. Keller Industries, Miami, Fla., 1968-76; v.p., treas. Avatar Holdings (formerly GAC Corp.), 1976-80, exec. v.p., treas., chief fin. officer, dir., mem. exec. com., 1980-83; pres., treas., dir. Avatar Properties Inc. (formerly GAC Properties, Inc.), 1976-83, Avatar Properties Credit (formerly GAC Properties Credit, Inc.), 1976-83; vice chmn., chief operating officer Nat. Banking Corp. Fla., Miami, 1983-84; chmn. treas. Scroll Casual Inc., 1983-84; chmn. Fla. Powder Coatings, Inc., Confidata Corp., 1983-87; chmn., treas. First United Leasing Corp., 1983-86; ptnr. E&H Assocs., 1983-91; chmn. Item Processing Am. Inc., Miami, 1987-98. Sr. v.p., dir. Fla. Savs. Bancorp, Pinecrest, Fla., 2001—; bd. dirs. Valhi Inc., Baron Asset Fund. Mayor City of Sunny Isles Beach, Fla., 2003; bd. dirs. Mt. Sinai Med. Ctr. Found., 2003. With AUS, 1958—60. Mem. Am. Inst. CPA's, Fla. Inst. CPA's, Ill. Inst. CPA's, Greater Miami C. of C. (trustee 1979-83). Lodges: Kiwanis. Home: 244 Atlantic Isle Sunny Isles Beach FL 33160 Office: Sunny Isles Beach City Hall 18070 N Collins Ave Sunny Isles Beach FL 33160 Office Phone: 305-947-0606. Personal E-mail: nsedelcup@aol.com.

EDELHAUSER, HENRY F., ophthalmologist, physiologist, educator; b. Dover, NJ, Sept. 9, 1937; married, 1961; 2 children. BA, Patterson State Coll., 1961; MS, Mich. State U., 1964, PhD in Physiology, 1966. Lab. technician Warner Lambert Pharm. Rsch. Inst., 1962-65; from instr. to prof. physiology and ophthalmology Med. Coll. Wis., 1966-89; prof. ophthalmology, dir. rsch. Emory U., Atlanta, 1989—, dir. grants dept. ophthalmology, 1990. Bd. dirs. Am. Fight-for-Sight, Inc., 1975-90; prin. investigator Mt. Desert Island Biol. Lab., 1977; sci. cons. Alcon Labs. Fellow Marquette U., 1966-67; grantee Nat. Eye. Inst., 1969—, Wis. Dept. Nat. Rsch., 1969-71; Olga K. Weiss Rsch. Scholar; named Marjorie and Joseph Heil prof. ophthalmology, 1988, Ferst prof. ophthalmology, 1989. Mem. Assn. Rsch. Vision and Ophthalmology (pres. 1990-91), Am. Physiol. Soc., Am. Acad. Opthalmology (Honor award). Achievements include research in membrane physiology, pathophysiology of eye, fish physiology and eye disease, ocular toxicology, physiological effects of vitrectomy, cellular toxicology and ophthalmic drugs. Office: Emory U Dept Ophthamology Emory Eye Ctr 2600 1365 B Clinton Rd NE Atlanta GA 30322-0001 E-mail: ophthfe@emory.edu.

EDELMAN, THOMAS JEFFREY, energy executive; b. NYC, Jan. 23, 1951; s. Albert I. and Eleanor (Weisman) E.; m. Ingrid M. Ongaro, Sept. 22, 1984; children: Elizabeth G., Eleanor A. BA magna cum laude, Princeton U., 1973; MBA, Harvard U., 1975. With Kuhn Loeb & Co., NYC, 1975—78, Lehman Bros. Kuhn Loeb, NYC, 1975—80; v.p. 1st Boston Corp., NYC, 1980—81; co-founder, pres., bd. dirs. Snyder Oil Corp., Ft. Worth and NYC, 1981—97; chmn. Lomak Petroleum, Inc., Ft. Worth and NYC, 1988; founder, chmn. & CEO Patina Oil & Gas Corp. (merged with Noble Energy, Inc.), 1996—2005; mng. ptnr. White Deer Energy. Bd. dirs. Petroleum Heat & Power Co., Inc., Stamford, Conn., Enterra Corp., Houston, Wolverine Exploration, Houston, Star Gas Corp., Stamford, Command Petroleum Holdings, NL, Sydney, Australia; Noble Energy, Inc., 2005-. Baker scholar Harvard U., 1975. Mem. Univ. Club, Ft. Worth Club, River Club. Republican. Jewish. Home: 770 Park Ave New York NY 10021-4153 Office: White Deer Energy 700 Louisiana St Ste 4770 Houston TX 77002-2722 Office Phone: 713-581-6900. Office Fax: 713-581-6901. Business E-Mail: tedelman@whitedeerenergy.com.

EDELSTEIN, FRANK, retired investment company executive, board member; b. NYC, Dec. 18, 1925; s. Simon and Betty (Joseph) Edelstein; m. Harriet Gold, June 7, 1947; children: Janet, Irving, Robert. BA in Math., NYU, 1948. Sr. v.p. fin. svcs. group Continental Ins. Corp.; corp. v.p. Automatic Data Processing, Inc.; market analyst Paul Devech & Co., NYC, 1949—52; dir. mktg. Manischewitz Co., Newark, 1952—62; exec. v.p. Olivetti Corp. America, NYC, 1963—72; v.p. mktg. Leisure Tech. Co., Lakewood, NJ, 1972—74; pres., chmn. Internat. Ctrl. Bank & Trust Co., El Toro, Calif., 1974—86, CPI Pension Svcs. Co., 1986; v.p. Kelso & Co. Inc., 1986—92, StoneCreek Capital Inc., 1992—2005. Bd. dirs. Ceradyne, Inc, 1984—, DineEquity, Inc., 1987—2010, Ark. Best Corp., 1988—, Kolmar Labs Group, 1996—. Founder, pres. East Brunswick Jewish Ctr., NJ, 1964—65. Served USAAF, 1943—45. Democrat. Jewish. Office: Ark Best Corp Bd Directors 3801 Old Greenwood Rd Fort Smith AR 72903

EDENFIELD, BERRY AVANT, federal judge; b. Bulloch County, Ga., Aug. 2, 1934; s. Perry and Vera E.; m. Vida Melvis Bryant, Aug. 3, 1963. BBA, U. Ga., Athens, 1956, LLB, 1958. Bar: Ga. 1958. Ptnr. Allen, Edenfield, Brown & Wright (and predecessors), Statesboro, Ga., 1958-78; judge US Dist. Ct. (so. dist.) Ga., Savannah, 1978-90, 1997—2006, chief judge, 1990-97, sr. judge, 2006—. Mem. Ga. State Senate, 1965-66. Office: US Dist Ct PO Box 8286 Savannah GA 31412 Office Phone: 912-650-4080.

EDENFIELD, GERALD M., lawyer; b. Guyton, Ga., July 6, 1945; s. Perry and Vera (Berry) E.; m. Sharon Carter; children: Sharri, Kristie, Gerald Malcolm. AB in Polit. Sci. and Philosophy, U. Ga., 1967; JD, Mercer U., 1970. Ptnr. Heyman & Sizemore, Atlanta, 1970-78, Pye, Groover, Edenfield & Dailey, Atlanta, 1978-79, Allen, Brown & Edenfield, Statesboro, Ga., 1979-88, Edenfield, Stone & Cox, Statesboro, Ga., 1988—, Edenfield, Cox, Bruce & Classens, PC, Statesboro, Ga. Active Cancer Soc., United Way, Day for So., Bulloch 2000. Mem. ABA, State Bar Ga. (sec. 2004-06, pres. 2007-08), Atlanta Bar Assn., Am. Trial Lawyers Assn., Ga. Industrial Devel. Assn., Ga. Sch. Bd. Attorneys Assn., Ga. Assn. Trial Lawyers, Ga. Assn. Criminal Defense Lawyers, Atlanta Lawyers Club, Statesboro Bulloch County C. of C. (pres. 1990), Rotary (sgt. arms 1986-87, pres. 1990), Forest Heights Country Club, Chatham Club, Statesboro Rotary Club (pres. 1995); fellow. AAJ, Farmers and Merchants Bank (dir.). Office: Edenfield Cox Bruce & Classens PC 115 Savannah Ave Statesboro GA 30459 also: Edenfield Cox Bruce & Classens PC PO Box 1700 Statesboro GA 30459-1700 Office Phone: 912-764-8600. Office Fax: 912-764-8862. E-mail: gerald@ecbcpc.com.

EDENFIELD, J. MICHAEL, information technology executive; B in Indsl. Mgmt., Ga. Inst. Tech. Regional v.p. American Software, Inc., 1987—91, group v.p., 1991—92, sr. v.p., sales and mktg., N. Am., 1992—94, COO, 1994—97, exec. v.p., 1994—; pres., CEO, bd. dirs. Logility, Inc. (subs. of American Software, Inc.), 1997—; bd. dirs. American Software, Inc., 2001—. Bd. dirs. INSIGHT, Inc. Office: American Software Inc 470 E Paces Ferry Rd Atlanta GA 30305 Office Phone: 404-264-5296. Office Fax: 404-264-5206. Business E-Mail: jedenfield@amsoftware.com.

EDGAR, WALTER BELLINGRATH, retired historian, educator; b. Mobile, Ala., Dec. 10, 1943; s. Ernest, Jr. and Amelia E.; m. Elizabeth Giles, Aug. 6, 1966; children: Eliza, Amelia; m. Cornelia Danforth, Feb. 3, 2007. AB, Davidson Coll., NC, 1965; MA, U. S.C., 1967, PhD, 1969; LLD (hon.), Coker Coll., 1999; HLD (hon.), Coastal Carolina U., 2001; LLD (hon.), Davidson Coll., 2003, Newberry Coll., 2005, The Citadel, 2007. From asst. prof. to prof. history U. SC, Columbia, 1974—2012, dir. Inst. So. Studies, 1980—2012, Neuffer prof. so. studies, 1995—2012, George Washington Disting. prof. history, 1999—2012, Scudder prof. liberal arts, 2001—12, Carolina trustee prof., 2007—12; ret. Author: History of Santee Cooper, 1984, South Carolina in the Modern Age, 1992, South Carolina: A History, 1998, Partisans and Redcoats, 2001; editor: The Letterbook of Robert Pringle, 1972, A Southern Renascence Man: Views of Robert Penn Warren, 1984, The South Carolina Encyclopedia, 2006; host Walter Edgar's Jour., S.C. Pub. Radio. Trustee, Bellingrath Morse Found., Served to capt. U.S. Army, 1969-71; col. Res. Decorated Bronze Star, Legion of Merit; named to Hall of Fame, SC, 2008, SC Higher Edn., 2010. Mem. Soc. Cin., So. Hist. Assn., SC Hist. Assn. (pres. 1982-83), SC Hist. Soc. (pres. 2005-08), South Caroliniana Soc. (pres. 1984-87), Blue Key, Omicron Delta Kappa, Phi Alpha Theta. Business E-Mail: edgar@mailbox.sc.edu.

EDGE, RONALD DOVASTON, physics professor; b. Bolton, Eng., Feb. 3, 1929; arrived in U.S., 1958, naturalized, 1968; s. James and Mildred (Davies) E.; m. Margaret Skulina, Aug. 14, 1956 (div. 1989); children: Christopher James, Michael Dovaston; m. Gertrude Hansen, Dec. 31, 1992. BA, Cambridge U., 1950, MA, 1952, PhD, 1956. Rsch. fellow Australian Nat. U., Canberra, 1954-58; asst. then assoc. prof. physics U. S.C., Columbia, 1958-63, prof., 1964-94, disting. prof. emeritus, 1994—. Rsch. assoc. Yale U., New Haven, 1963-64; vis. prof. Stanford U., Calif. Tech. Inst., U. Munich, U. Sussex, U. Witwatersrand, U. Aarhus, Oak Ridge Nat. Lab., Los Alamos Nat. Lab.; leader 1st Am. team Internat. Physics Olympiad, 1986; judge Internat. Young Physicists Tournament, 1999, 2001. Author: Physics in the Arts, 1973, String and Sticky Tape Experiments, 1978; contbr. articles to profl. jours. Recipient Russell award U. S.C., Guy And Rebecca Forman award tchg. Physics, Vanderbilt U., 1998. Fellow Am. Phys. Soc. (James B. Pegram award 1979), Am. Assn. Physics Tchrs. (apparatus award 1973, v.p. 1995, pres. elect 1996, pres. 1997). Unitarian (past pres. Columbia fellowship) Office: U SC Physics Dept Columbia SC 29208-0001 Home: 619 King St 710 Columbia SC 29205 Personal E-mail: redge@sc.rr.com.

EDGE, TRACY RUSSELL, state legislator; b. Myrtle Beach, SC, Apr. 28, 1967; s. Robert L. and Nettie S. Edge; m. Melissa Renee Pierce, 1994; 1 child, Hannah. BA, U. SC, 1989; MS, W.Va. U., 1991. Former vice chmn. Horry County Rep. Com.; councilman North Myrtle Beach City Coun., 1994—96; mem. Dist. 104 SC House of Reps., 1996—; mng. ptnr. Edge Holdings, LLC; v.p. Burroughs & Chapin Corp. Mem.: North Myrtle Beach Rotary Club. Republican. Baptist. Address: PO Box 2095 Myrtle Beach SC 29577 Mailing: 503B Blatt Bldg Box 11867 Columbia SC 29201 Home Phone: 803-361-2827; Office Phone: 803-734-3013, 803-448-5123. Business E-Mail: te@legis.lpitr.state.sc.us.

EDGELL, LARRY J., state legislator; b. Nov. 16, 1946; m. Cecilia Herrick; children: Eva, Josh. BA, Fairmont State Coll.; MA, Salem Teikyo U. Mem. Dist. 2 W.Va. State Senate, 1998—, majority whip, vice chair Pensions Com., mem. Edn. Com., Fin. Com., Military Com. & Natural Resources Com. Democrat. Mailing: 600 5th St New Martinsville WV 26155 Office: State Capitol Rm 413M Bldg 1 Charleston WV 25305 E-mail: larry.edgell@wvsenate.gov.

EDGERTON, NORMAN B., JR., gastroenterologist; MD, U. of Fla., 1973; attended, U. of South Fla. Lic. Fla., 1976, diplomate American Bd. Internal Medicine, 1976, American Bd. Internal Medicine-gastroenterology, 1981. Intern straight medicine Baylor Coll. of Medicine Affiliated Hosps., 1974, resident internal medicine, 1974—76; fellow gastroenterology Univ. of South Fla. Coll. of Medicine, 1976—78; endoscopy com. St. Joseph's Hosp.; hosp. affiliation includes Tampa Gen. Hosp. Mem. H. Lee Moffitt Cancer Ctr. and Rsch. Inst. Mem. Crohn's & Colitis Found. of America. Mem.: AMA, American Soc. of Gastrointestinal Endoscopy, American Coll. of Gastroenterology, Fla. Med. Assn. (polit. action com.-leader in medicine), Hillsborough County Med. Assn., Liver Club, Gut Club. Office: St Joseph Hospital 3001 W Martin Luther King Blvd Tampa FL 33607-6387 Office Phone: 813-870-4000.*

EDGETT, WILLIAM MALOY, lawyer, arbitrator; b. Balt., Feb. 26, 1927; s. Eugene Albert and Priscilla Ruff (Streett) E.; m. Bronwen Winifred Reese, Nov. 25, 1950. AA, Towson State Coll., 1949; BA, U. Md., 1951, JD, 1959; LL.M., Georgetown U., 1970. Bar: Md. bar 1959. Asst. personnel mgr. Am. Sugar Refining Co., Balt., 1951-55; supr. indsl. relations Westinghouse Electric Co., Balt., 1955-61; sr. labor relations specialist Martin Co., Balt., 1961-64; asst. mgr. indsl. relations Md. Shipbuilding and Drydock Co., Balt., 1964-67; pvt. practice law, 1967—. Asst. prof. Towson State U., 1971-72 Mem. Md. Commn. Nursing, 1974-76; chmn. pub. law bds. Nat. Mediation Bd., 1971—; neutral mem. Nat. R.R. Adjustment Bd., 1971—. Served to staff st. USAAC, 1944-46. Mem. ABA. Nat. Acad. Arbitrators, Am. Arbitration Assn., Am., Roster Arbitrators Fed. Mediation and Conciliation Service. Home and Office: 200 Hampton Cir Bluffton SC 29909-5018

EDMOND, MICHAEL TOOLE, internist; MD, U. Tex., Galveston, 1976. Lic. Tex., 1976, diplomate American Bd. Internal Medicine, 1979, American Bd. Psychiatry and Neurology, 1984. Intern Univ. Tex. Health Sci. Ctr., 1977, resident, 1979, Univ. Health Care, 1980; resident neurology Univ. UT Med. Ctr., 1979—80, Univ. Iowa Hosps. and Clinics, 1980—82; hosp. affiliations include Univ. Med. Ctr., Brackenridge, Seton Med. Ctr., St. David's South Austin Med. Ctr. Office: St David's South Austin Medical Center 901 W Ben White Blvd Austin TX 78704-6903 Office Phone: 512-447-2211.*

EDMONDS, CHRISTOPHER S., investment company executive; BA in Polit. Sci., U. Ala., Birmingham. Lic. series 3 and series 30. Pres., CEO Internat. Derivatives Exch. Group LLC; various positions APB Energy LLC, 1997—2002; various positions through chief devel. officer ICAP Energy LLC, 2002—08; pres. ICE Trust US, LLC, 2010—. Office: IntercontinentalExchange Inc 2100 RiverEdge Pky Ste 500 Atlanta GA 30328 Office Phone: 770-857-4700. Office Fax: 770-857-4755. Business E-Mail: chris.edmonds@theice.com.

EDMONDS, IAN COLIN, electronics executive; m. Mimi Tan. B in Mktg., U. Denver, 1996. Asst. product mgr. Info. Handling Svcs. Inc.; v.p. Zunicom, Inc. (formerly Tech Electro Industries Inc.), 1997—2003; bd. dirs. Zunicom, Inc., 1997—, AlphaNet, Inc. (subs. Zunicom, Inc.), 1999—2006; exec. v.p. through COO, Universal Battery Zunicom, Inc. (formerly Tech Electro Industries Inc.), 2003—06; bd. dirs. Universal Power Group, Inc., 1999—, COO, 2002—09, exec. v.p., 2006—09, interim CFO, 2008—, interim CEO, interim pres., 2009, CEO, pres., 2009—. Bd. dirs. AlphaNet, Inc., 1999—2006, Universal Power Group, Inc., 1999—, Zunicom, Inc. Office: Universal Power Group Inc 488 S Royal Ln Coppell TX 75019-3820 Office Phone: 469-892-1122. Office Fax: 469-892-1123. Business E-Mail: ian@upgi.com.

EDMONDS, SCOTT A., apparel executive; Positions up to pres. Ft. Myers, Fla. divsn. Ferguson Enterprises, Inc., 1980—93; ops. mgr. Chico's FAS, Inc., Ft. Myers, Fla., 1993—94, v.p. ops., 1994—95, sr. v.p. ops., 1996—2000, COO, 2000—01, pres., 2001—03, pres., CEO, 2003—07, chmn., pres., CEO, 2007—. Office: Chicos FAS Inc 11215 Metro Pky Fort Myers FL 33966-1206 Office Phone: 239-277-6200. Office Fax: 239-277-5237.

EDMONDS, TED, state legislator; b. 1943; BS, MA, Eastern Ky. U.; PhD, Union Grad. Sch. Ret. educator; mem. Dist. 91 Ky. House of Reps., 2003—. Mem.: Henson Nursing Home, Breathitt County Fish & Game Club. Democrat. Church Of God. Mailing: 1257 Beattyville Rd Jackson KY 41339 Office: Capitol Annex Rm 466E 702 Capitol Ave Frankfort KY 40601 Home Phone: 606-666-4823; Office Phone: 502-564-8100 ext. 641.

EDMONDSON, JAMES E., state supreme court justice; b. Kansas City, Mo., 1945; m. Suzanne Edmondson; 2 children. BA, Northeastern State U., Tahlequah, Okla., 1967; JD, Georgetown Law Sch., 1973. Asst. dist. atty. Muskogee County, Okla., 1976—78; asst. US atty., 1978—80; acting US atty., 1980—81; prtnr. Edmondson Law Office, 1981—83; judge Okla. Dist. Ct., 1983—2003; justice Okla. Supreme Ct., 2003—, vice chief justice, 2007—08, chief justice, 2009—10. Served in USN, 1967—69. Mem.: Okla. Bar Assn. Office: Okla Supreme Ct Okla Judicial Ctr 2100 N Lincoln Blvd Ste 4 Oklahoma City OK 73105-4907*

EDMONDSON, J.L. (JAMES LARRY EDMONDSON), federal judge; b. Jasper, Ga., July 14, 1947; s. James George and Betty Ruth (Holcomb) Edmondson; m. Eugenia Dettelbach (div. 1992); children: Kelley Eugenia, Alexandra Lisa. BA, Emory U., 1968; JD, U. Ga., 1971; LLM in Jud. Process, U. Va., 1990. Bar: Ga. 1971. Law clk. to Hon. Sidney O. Smith US Dist. Ct. (northern dist.) Ga., Gainesville, Ga., 1971—73; assoc. Webb, Fowler, Tanner & Edmondson, Lawrenceville, Ga., 1973—76, ptnr., 1976—81; mem. Tennant, Davidson & Edmondson, PC, Lawrenceville, 1982—86; judge US Ct. Appeals (11th cir.), Atlanta, 1986—2012, chief judge, 2002—09, sr. judge, 2012—. Instr. U. Ga. Sch. Law, 1975—84. Contbr. articles to profl. jours. Trustee Inst. Continuing Legal Edn., 1980—84. Mem.: Lawyers Club America, ABA, Fellows Ga. Bar Found. (charter), Gwinnett County Bar Assn. (pres. 1980—81), State Bar Ga. (bd. govs.

1982—86), Old War Horse Lawyers Club, Order of Barristers, Pi Sigma Alpha. Episcopalian. Office: US Ct Appeals 11th Circuit 56 Forsyth St NW Rm 416 Atlanta GA 30303-2205*

EDMUNDS, JAMES E., II, state legislator, farmer; b. South Boston, Va., July 21, 1970; m. Jennifer Leigh Wilkerson; children: Paul, Caroline. BS in Bus. Adminstrn., Averett U., 1996. Farmer; mem. Va. Bd. Forestry, Halifax County Bd. Supervisors, 1999—2009; mem. Dist. 60 Va. House of Delegates, Richmond, 2010—. Deacon First Presbyn. Ch. Recipient Farm Pond Mgmt. award, Nat. Remington and Progressive Farmer; named Conservationist of Yr., Izaak Walton League, Halifax County Sportsman's Club. Mem.: NRA, Am. Tree Farm Sys., Nat. Wild Turkey Fedn. (life Conservationist of Yr., Hunting Heritage Landowner Program award 2007). Republican. Office: Va House of Dels Gen Assembly Bldg Rm 805 PO Box 406 Richmond VA 23218 also: PO Box 1115 Halifax VA 24558-1115 Office Phone: 804-698-1060, 434-575-0000. Office Fax: 804-698-6760, 434-575-0077. Business E-Mail: deljedmunds@house.virginia.gov.

EDMUNDS, JEFFREY GARTH, Anglican minister; b. Scottsbluff, Nebr., Sept. 11, 1953; s. Lafe Rees and June LaFawn (Law) E.; m. Rachel Jeanette Hughes, July 17, 1982; children: Jeffrey Garth Jr., Gavin Nathaniel. BA, U. Va., 1975; MLS, Fla. State U., 1976; JD, George Mason U., 1986; LTh, Scott Sch. Theology, 2010. Reference librarian J. Sargeant Reynolds Community Coll., Richmond, Va., 1976-78; spl. instr. U.S. Navy Program for Afloat Coll. Edn., Naples, Italy, 1978-79; devel. rsch. assoc. Georgetown U., Washington, 1979-84; law clk. U.S. Atty.'s Office for Ea. Dist. Va., Alexandria, 1985, U.S. Dept. Labor, Washington, 1985-86; asst. Commonwealth's atty. Pulaski County, Va., 1986-87, City of Petersburg, Va., 1988-89, City of Fredericksburg, Va., 1989-96; atty. pvt. practice, Fredericksburg, 1996—99; reference libr. Ctrl. Rappahannock Regional Libr., Fredericksburg, Va., 1999—. Rector St. Lukes Anglican Cath. Ch., Fredericksburg, Va., 2011—. Founder, Welsh Soc. Fredericksburg, 1991, pres. 1991-93; v.p., dir. Fredericksburg Masonic Mus. Found., 2003—2007; dir. Hist. Fredericksburg Found. Inc., 2008—2010. Anglican. Home: 3524 Waverly Dr Fredericksburg VA 22407-6849 Office: St Luke's Anglican Cath Ch 65 Warrenton Rd Fredericksburg VA 22405 Personal E-mail: rappahannock_rev@yahoo.com.

EDMUNDS, ROBERT HOLT, JR., state supreme court justice; b. Danville, Va., Apr. 17, 1949; s. Robert Holt and Mary (Rucker) Edmunds; m. Linda M. Edmunds; 2 children. Student, Williams Coll., Williamstown, Mass.; BA in English, Vassar Coll., 1971; JD, U. NC, Chapel Hill, 1975; LLM, U. Va., 2004. Bar: NC 1975, Va. 1977. Asst. dist. atty. 18th Judicial Dist., Guilford County, NC, 1978—82; asst. US atty. Mid. Dist. NC US Dept. Justice, Greensboro, 1982—86, US atty. Mid. Dist. NC, 1986—93; ptnr. Stern & Klepfer, 1993—98; assoc. judge NC Ct. Appeals, 1999—2001; assoc. justice Supreme Ct. NC, Raleigh, 2001—. Mem. Atty. Gen. Adv. Subcom. Guideline Sentencing, 1987—93, chair, 1991—93; mem. Atty. Gen. Subcom. Controlled Substances, 1987—93. Contbr. articles to profl. jours. Served in USN, 1975—77. Mem.: Greensboro Criminal Def. Lawyers Assn., Guilford Inn of Ct., Nat. Assn. Former US Attorneys, Greensboro Bar Assn. Office: NC Supreme Ct PO Box 2170 Raleigh NC 27602-2170*

EDSON, EVELYN, history professor, writer; b. Oklahoma City, Nov. 28, 1940; d. Arthur Lewis Edson and Margery Huff Edson-Gould; m. Andrew Austin Wilson, Aug. 15, 1976; children: Meredith Swan Cole, Benjamin Andrew. BA, Swarthmore Coll., Pa., 1962; MA, U. Chgo., 1965, PhD, 1972. Tchr. HS Oakwood Sch., Poughkeepsie, NY, 1962—64; lectr. western civilization U. Chgo., 1966—69; vis. asst. prof. history Roosevelt U., Chgo., 1970—71, assoc. dean continuing edn., 1971—72; prof. Piedmont Va. CC, Charlottesville, 1972—2006, prof. emerita, 2006—. Coll. rep. Chancellor's adv. coun. Va. CC Sys., Richmond, 1983—88; co-chair joint com. transfer students State Coun. Higher Edn. Va., Richmond, 1990—91; mem. adv. bd. western tradition telecourse WGBH, Boston, 1986—88; coun. mem. Nat. Coun. Humanities, Washington, 2000—04; adj. prof. B interdisciplinary studies program U. Va., Charlottesville, 2007—. Author: Mapping Time and Space: How Medieval Mapmakers Viewed Their World, 1997, World Map 1300-1492: The Persistence of Tradition and Transformation, 2007; co-author (with E. Savage-Smith): Medieval Views of the Cosmos, 2004; contbr. articles to profl. jours. Pres. Southside Fellowship, Scottsville, Va., 1990—2004, sec., v.p.; sec. James River Book Club, pres., 1977—2004; bd. dirs. Tandem Sch., Charlottesville, 1990—93, Va. Women's Forum, Charlottesville, 1990—2000, Scottsville Mus., 2004—, Albemarle County Hist. Soc., 2007—08; bd. mem. Scottsville Mus., 2004—, pres., 2011—. Recipient Outstanding Faculty award, State Coun. of Higher Edn., Va., 1990, Eugene Asher Disting. Tchg. award, Am. Hist. Soc. and Soc. for History Edn., 2003; named Disting. Humanities Educator, C.C. Humanities Assn., 1993; fellow summer program India, Fulbright Found., 1980, Nat. Endowment for the Humanities, 1999, Am. Coun. of Learned Societies, 2003—04. Mem.: Fry-Jefferson Map Soc., Va. C.C. Assn., Wash. Map Soc., C.C. Humanities Assn., Medieval Acad., Am. Hist. Assn. (nominating com. 1992—94, program com. 2004). Avocations: reading, gardening, music, hiking.

EDWARDS, CARL, race car driver; b. Columbia, Mo., Aug. 15, 1979; s. Carl Edwards, Sr. Profl. race car driver NASCAR Roush Fenway Racing, 2004—; co-owner Back40 Records, Columbia. 1st pl. Golden Corral 500 Atlanta Motor Speedway, 2005, 1st pl. Bass Pro Shops MBNA 500, 2005, 1st pl. Pep Boys Auto 500, 2008; 1st pl. Pocono 500 Pocono Raceway, 2005, 2008; 1st pl. Dickies 500 Tex. Motor Speedway, 2005, 2008, 1st pl. Samsung 500, 2008; 1st pl. Citizens Bank 400 Mich. Internat. Speedway, 2007; 1st pl. Sharpie 500 Bristol Motor Speedway, 2007; 1st pl. Dodge Dealers 400 Dover Internat. Speedway, 2007; 1st pl. Auto Club 500 Speedway Southern Calif., 2008; 1st pl. UAW-Dodge 400 Las Vegas Motor Speedway, 2008, 1st pl. Kobalt Tools 400, 2011; 1st pl. Ford 400 Homestead-Miami Speedway, Fla., 2008, 2010. Recipient Rookie of Yr., NASCAR, 2003. Office: c/o Roush Fenway Racing 4202 Roush Pl Concord NC 28027

EDWARDS, CHARLENE VERNELL, lawyer; b. Henderson, NC, July 29, 1968; d. Robert Johnson and Edith Vernell (Allred) E. BA cum laude, Campbell U., 1990, JD, 1993. Bar: N.C. 1993, U.S. Dsit. Ct. (ea. dist.) N.C. 1995, U.S. Dist. Ct. (mid. dist.) N.C. 1998, U.S. Dist. Ct. (we. dist.)1999; cert. family fin. mediator, 2003-. Ptnr. Hartley & Edwards, Lillington, NC, 1993-99; pvt. practice Lillington, 1993; owner Charlene Edwards Law Office, 1999—. Child support enforcement atty. Harnett County Clerk Ct., 1994—2006; adj. prof. Campbell U., 1995—2001. Editor: Campbell Law Observer, 1992-93; editor N.C. Supreme Ct. Bd. mem., past pres. Lillington C. of C.; sec.-treas. 11A Jud. Dist., 2013, Lillington Kiwanis Club; lector St. Bernadette Cath. Ch. Recipient Outstanding Alumni award Campbell U., 1996. Mem. ABA, N.C. Assn. Women Attys., N.C. Assn. Trial Lawyers, N.C. Bar Assn., Harnett County Bar Assn. (sec.-treas., 2010-), Federalist Soc. (pres., sec. 1990—, John Madison award 1993), Pi Gamma Mu, Epsilon Pi Eta, Delta Theta Phi. Roman Catholic. Avocation: writing. Home: PO Box 1462 Buies Creek NC 27506-1462 Office: Charlene Edwards Law Office PO Box 2446 130 Pine State St Ste C Lillington NC 27546-2446 Home Phone: 910-893-5554; Office Phone: 910-893-1128. Office Fax: 910-893-1138. Business E-Mail: edwardslaw1@earthlink.net.*

EDWARDS, CHARLES ARCHIBALD, lawyer; b. Lumberton, NC, Sept. 19, 1945; s. Charles Edwin and Elizabeth Gertrude (Gooden) E.; m. Judy Carol Griffin, Aug. 14, 1966; children: Lee McNeill, Caroline Averitt Clark. AB, Davidson Coll., 1967; JD, U. N.C., 1970. Bar: Ga. 1970, U.S. Supreme Ct. 1974, D.C. 1981, N.C. 1987. Assoc. Connerat, Dunn, Hunter, Houlihan, Maclean & Exley, Savannah, Ga., 1970-71, ptnr., 1972-76; ptnr., mem. Constangy, Brooks & Smith, Atlanta, 1976-82; ptnr. Greene, Buckley, Derieux & Jones, Atlanta, 1982-86, Graham & James, Raleigh, NC, 1986-94, Womble Carlyle Sandridge & Rice, PLLC, Raleigh, Winston-Salem, 1994—, labor & employment practice group leader, 1995—2007. Author: Georgia Employment Law, 1983; contbr. articles to profl. publs. Mem. Warrenton Town Coun., 2001—05. Capt. USAR, 1967—74. Mem. ABA, N.C. Bar Assn., State Bar Ga., Atlanta Bar Assn. (chmn. labor law sect. 1983-84). Republican. Episcopalian. Office: Womble Carlyle Sandridge & Rice One W Fourth St Winston Salem NC 27101 Office Phone: 336-721-3795.

EDWARDS, GEORGE CHARLES, III, political science professor, writer; b. Rochester, NY, Jan. 3, 1947; s. George Charles Jr. and Mary Elizabeth (Laing) E.; m. Carmella Rose Pierce, May 22, 1981; 1 child, Jeffrey Allan. BA, Stetson U., 1969; MA, U. Wis., 1970, PhD, 1973. Asst. prof. polit. sci. Tulane U., New Orleans, 1973-78; assoc. prof. polit. sci. Tex. A&M U., College Station, 1978-81, prof., 1981-90, disting. prof., 1990—, Jordan prof. in liberal arts, 1991—, dir. Ctr. for Presdl. Studies, 1991—2001. Vis. asst. prof. U. Wis.-Madison, 1976; vis. prof. U.S. Mil. Acad., West Point, N.Y., 1985-88, Peking U., Beijing, 1993, Hebrew U., Jerusalem, 1997; prof. Oxford U., 2005-06, scis. po-Paris, 2008, Winant prof., 2012-13; John Adams fellow U. London, 2003; pres. Presidency Rsch. Group, 1984-85; lectr. US Dept. State, Europe, 1985, 89, U.S., 1988, 92, 2002-, 2006-08, Brazil, 1988, Australia, 2004; cons. NSF, Washington, 1977—, Internat. Rep. Inst., Moscow, 1994, Ctr. for Strategic and Internat. Studies, Washington, 1990-91, Nat. Acad. Pub. Adminstrn., Washington, 1987-88; bd. dirs. Roper Ctr. Pub. Opinion Rsch.; bd. advisors Stetson U., Transition to Governing Project; bd. acad. advisers Ctr. for Congl. and Presdl. Studies; exec. com. White House Interview Program; mem. Coun. on Fgn. Rels., 2002—. Author: The Public Presidency, 1983, Presidential Leadership, 1985, 90, 94, 97, 99, 2001, 09, 13, Government in America, 1989, 91, 94, 96, 97, 98, 99, 2000, 01, 02, 05, 07, 09, 11, 13, Presidential Influence in Congress, 1980, Implementing Public Policy, 1980, The Policy Predicament, 1978, At the Margins, 1989, On Deaf Ears, 2003, Presidential Approval, 1990, Why The Electoral College Is Bad for America, 2004, Governing by Campaigning, 2006, 07, 11, The Strategic President, 2009, Overreach, 2012; editor: Perspectives on Public Policy-Making, 1975, Studying the Presidency, 1983, Public Policy Implementation, 1984, The Presidency and Public Policy Making, 1985, National Security and the U.S. Constitution, 1988, Researching the Presidency, 1993, New Challenges for the American Presidency, 2004, Presidential Politics, 2005, The Polarized Presidency of George W. Bush, 2007, Oxford Handbook of American Presidency, 2009, Overreach, 2012, Presdl. Studies Quar.; mem. editl. bd. Am. Jour. Polit. Sci., 1985-87, 94—, Jour. Politics, 1997—, Am. Politics Quar., 1981-87, Presdl. Studies Quar., 1978-98, Congress and the Presidency, 1981—, Policy Studies Jour., 1981-83, Am. Rev. Politics, 1994—; contbr. articles to profl. jours. Pres. Greenfield Plaza Condominium Assn., Bryan, Tex., 1980-81; mem. East Tex. 2000 Commn., 1980. Capt. USAR, 1971-79. Decorated for Disting. Civilian Svc. U.S. Army, 1988; Woodrow Wilson fellow, 1969-70, Ford fellow, 1970-73, John Adams fellow U. London, 2003; recipient Career Svc. award. Am. Polit. Sci. Assn. Mem.: Roper Ctr. (bd. dirs. 1997—2008), Coun. on Fgn. Rels., Ctr. Study of Presidency (bd. dirs. 2002—05), Policy Studies Assn., Midwest Polit. Sci. Assn., So. Polit. Sci. Assn. (Pi Sigma Alpha award 2001), Am. Assn. Pub. Opinion Rsch., Am. Polit. Sci. Assn. (sect. pres. 1984—85, Cancer Svc. award 2008), Phi Beta Kappa, Phi Kappa Phi, Phi Alpha Alpha, Phi Alpha Theta, Pi Sigma Alpha. Avocations: collecting art, skiing, tennis, scuba diving, sailing. Home: 2910 Coronado Dr College Station TX 77845-7716 Office: Texas A&M Univ Dept of Polit Sci 4348 TAMU College Station TX 77843 Office Phone: 979-845-9764. Business E-Mail: gedwards@tamu.edu.

EDWARDS, JAMES D., board member; b. Cleve., Tenn., Nov. 4, 1943; s. James D. and Elizabeth (Reynolds) E.; m. Sharon E. Bordelon, May 2, 1968; 1 child, David. BS in Acctg., Bob Jones U., 1964. CPA, Ga. Ptnr., staff acct. Arthur Andersen LLP, Atlanta, 1964—73, mng. ptnr., Atlanta office, 1979—87, mng. ptnr. Americas NYC, 1987—98, mng. ptnr., Global Markets, 1998—2002. Bd. dirs. IMS Health Inc., 2002—, Transcend Svcs, Inc., 2003—, Huron Consulting Group Inc., 2004—, Crawford & Co., 2005—, Cousins Properties Inc., 2007—. Bd. dirs., exec. com. Atlanta C. of C., 1982-85, Woodruff Arts Ctr., Atlanta, 1986-87; chmn. Cen. Atlanta Progress, 1986-87. Mem. Board Room (N.Y.C.),d The Stanwich Club (Greenwich, Ct.) Atlanta Country Club. Office: IMS Health Inc Bd Directors 83 Wooster Hts Fl 5 Danbury CT 06810-7552 Office Phone: 203-845-5200. Office Fax: 203-845-5304. Business E-Mail: jedwards@imshealth.com.

EDWARDS, JOHN, state legislator; Mem. Dist. 38 Ark. House of Reps., 2009—. Democrat. Methodist. Office: State Capitol Rm 350 Little Rock AR 72201 also: 40 Sherrill Rd Little Rock AR 72202 Office Phone: 501-682-6211, 501-682-7771, 501-378-5500. Business E-Mail: jcedwardslaw@aol.com.

EDWARDS, JOHN BEL, state legislator; b. New Orleans, La., Apr. 18, 1979; BS in Engring., US Mil. Acad., 1988; JD, La. State U. Law Sch., 1999. Atty.; mem. Dist. 72 La. House of Reps., 2008—, mem. civil law and procedure com., edn. com., judiciary com., house com. on homeland security, joint com. on homeland security, chair spl. com. on mil. and vets. affairs com. Democrat. Bapt. Office: PO Box 160 Amite LA 70422 also: Capitol Office PO Box 44486 Baton Rouge LA 70804 Office Phone: 985-748-2245, 225-342-6945. Office Fax: 985-748-2247. E-mail: edwardsj@legis.state.la.us.

EDWARDS, JOHN REID, former United States Senator from North Carolina, lawyer; b. Seneca, SC, June 10, 1953; s. Wallace R. and Catherine (Bobbie) Edwards; m. Mary Elizabeth Anania, July 30, 1977 (dec. Dec. 7, 2010); children: Lucius Wade (dec. April 4, 1996), Catharine, Emma Claire, Jack Atticus; 1 child (with Rielle Hunter), Quinn Student Clemson U., 1971; BS with high honors in textile mgmt., NC State U., 1974; JD with honors, U. NC, 1977. Bar: NC 1977, Tenn. 1978, US Dist. Ct. (eastern dist.) NC. Law clk. to Hon. Franklin T. Dupree US Dist. Ct. (eastern dist.) NC, 1977—78; assoc. Dearborn & Ewing, Nashville, 1978-81, Tharrington Smith & Hargrove, Raleigh, NC, 1981-83, ptnr., 1984-92; founder, ptnr. Edwards & Kirby, LLP, Raleigh, NC, 1993-99; US Senator from NC, 1999—2005; dir. Ctr. on Poverty, Work, and Opportunity, U. NC, Chapel Hill, 2005—; sr. adv. Fortress Investment Group LLC, NYC, 2005—. Dem. nominee v.p. US, 2004. Co-author (with John Auchard): Four Trials, 2004; editor: Home: The Blueprints of Our Lives, 2006. Bd. dirs. Urban Ministries, Raleigh, 1996—97; soccer coach Capital Area Soccer League, Raleigh, 1985—97; v.p. Challenge Soccer League, Raleigh; youth basketball coach YMCA Salvation Army, Raleigh; founding trustee Wade Edwards Found., 1996—; mem. adv. bd. Frank Porter Graham Child Devel. Ctr., Chapel Hill, 2000—; visionary com. Edenton St. United Meth. Ch. Recipient Steven J. Sharp Pub. Svc. award Assn. Trial Lawyers America, 1997; named Lawyer of Yr. Lawyers Weekly, 1996. Fellow American Coll. Trial Lawyers; mem. NC Law Review, 1976-77, ABA, ATLA, Inner Circle of Advocates, American Bd. Trial Advocacy, Chief Justice Susie M. Sharp Inns of Ct. (master), NC Acad. Trial Lawyers (v.p., bd. govs.), NC Bar Assn., Tenn. Bar Assn., So. Trial Lawyers Assn., U. NC Law Sch. Alumni Assn. (bd. dirs. 1993-99), Order of Coif, Phi Kappa Phi. Democrat. Meth. Office: U NC 250 E Franklin St Chapel Hill NC 27599*

EDWARDS, JOHN SAUL, state legislator, lawyer; b. Roanoke, Va., Oct. 6, 1943; s. Richard Thomas and Augusta Elizabeth (Saul) E.; m. Catherine Dabney, July 8, 1972; children: John Jr., Dabney, Catherine. AB cum laude, Princeton U., 1966; postgrad., Union Theol. Sem., 1966-67; JD, U. Va., 1970. Bar: Va. 1970, D.C. 1974, U.S. Ct. Mil. Appeals 1971, U.S. Dist. Ct. D.C. 1974, U.S. Ct. Appeals (4th and D.C. cirs.) 1975, U.S. Dist. Ct. (we. dist.) Va. 1976, U.S. Supreme Ct. 1976. Assoc. Sidley & Austin, Washington, 1970, 74-76, Gentry, Locke, Rakes & Moore, Roanoke, 1976-80; U.S. atty. western dist. of Va., Roanoke, 1980-81; ptnr. Martin, Hopkins, Lemon & Carter, P.C., Roanoke, 1981-90, Martin, Hopkins, Lemon & Edwards, P.C., 1990-92; pvt. practice, Roanoke, 1993—; mem. Va. State Senate, 1996—. Mem. Va. Dem. Ctrl. Com., 1978-80, 85-93; chmn. Roanoke City Dem. Com., 1983-85, 6th Dist. Dem. Com., 1987-93; mem. Va. Luth. Homes, Inc., Roanoke, 1978-98, chmn., 1985-98; trustee Roanoke Valley United Way, 1982-88; mem. Roanoke City Civic Ctr. Commn., 1985-93, chmn., 1990-92; mem. Roanoke City Coun., 1993-95, vice mayor, 1994-95. Rockefeller Bros. Theol. fellow, 1966-67. Mem. ABA, Va. Bar Assn. (chmn. criminal law com. 1987-91), Roanoke Bar Assn. (bd. dirs. 1986-88), Am. Trial Lawyers Assn., Va. Trial Lawyers Assn., Nat. Assn. Former U.S. Attys., Omicron Delta Kappa, Raven Soc. Lodges: Kiwanis. Home: 3745 Forest Rd SW Roanoke VA 24015-4509 Office: PO Box 1179 Roanoke VA 24006-1179 Fax: (540) 345-9950. E-mail: jselaw@roacoxmail.com, senator_edwards@roacoxmail.com.

EDWARDS, KATHRYN MARGARET, physician, researcher, educator; b. Williamsburg, Iowa, Aug. 27, 1948; d. Glen Wesley and Betty Jeanne (Heitman) Cranston; m. William John Edwards, June 5, 1970; children: Emily, Kevin, Megan, Gretchen. Student, Grinnell Coll., Iowa; grad., U. Iowa Coll. Pharmacy, 1969; MD, U. Iowa Coll. Medicine, 1973. Diplomate Am. Bd. Pediat., cert. in Pediatric Infectious Disease, lic. Iowa, Ill., Tenn. Resident pediat. Children's Meml. Hosp./Northwestern U. Sch. Medicine, Chgo., 1973—76, fellow infectious diseases, 1976—78; postdoc. fellow, instr. immunology Presbyn. St. Luke's Hosp./Rush Med. Sch., Chgo., 1978—80; asst. prof. pediat., divsn. infectious diseases Vanderbilt U. Sch. Medicine, Nashville, 1980—86, assoc. prof., 1986—91, prof., 1991—, vice-chair clin. rsch., 2001—. Mem. adv. com. immunization practices Ctrs. Disease Control & Prevention, Atlanta, 1991—95; mem. vaccines and related biol. products adv. com. FDA, Washington, 1996—2000. Mem. editl. bd. Infection & Immunity, 2005—07, Pediat., Jour. Infectious Diseases, Pediat. Infectious Disease Jour., Infectious Diseases in Children; contbr. articles to profl jours., chapters to books. Recipient Amos Christie award for Outstanding Tchg., Vanderbilt U. Dept. Pediat., 1983, Stephen R. Preblud award, 2004, Alexander Heard Disting. Prof. award, 2005. Fellow: Am. Acad. Pediat. (mem. exec. com. sect. infectious diseases 1999—2002), Infectious Diseases Soc. America (coun. mem. 2002—05, Mentor award 2006); mem.: Inst. Medicine, Am. Pediatric Soc., Pediatric Infectious Disease Soc. (coun. mem. 1995—99), Soc. Pediatric Rsch., Alpha Omega Alpha. Roman Catholic. Avocations: cooking, reading. Office: Vanderbilt U Sch Medicine Pediat Clin Rsch Office 1116 21st Ave S Nashville TN 37232-0001 Office Phone: 615-322-3078. Office Fax: 615-322-2733. Business E-Mail: kathryn.edwards@vanderbilt.edu.

EDWARDS, MARVIN S., JR., (EDDIE EDWARDS), telecommunications industry executive; Pres. Radio Frequency Sys.; various positions, including pres., N.Am. Cable Sys. Alcatel, 1986—2001; pres., CEO OFS Fitel, LLC, 2001—03, OFS BrightWave, LLC, 2001—03; acting pres. Connectivity Solutions Mfg. Inc., 2004—05, exec. v.p., bus. devel., chmn., 2005; exec. v.p., strategic devel., pres., Wireless Products Group CommScope, Inc., Hickory, NC, 2001—07, exec. v.p., gen. mgr., Wireless Network Solutions Group, 2007—10, pres., COO, 2010—11, pres., CEO, 2011—. Office: CommScope Inc 1100 CommScope Pl SE Hickory NC 28602 Office Phone: 828-324-2200. Office Fax: 828-328-3400. Business E-Mail: marvine@commscope.com.

EDWARDS, OTIS CARL, JR., theology studies educator; b. Bienville, La., June 15, 1928; s. Otis Carl and Margaret Lee (Hutchinson) E.; m. Jane Hanna Trufant, Feb. 19, 1957; children: Carl Lee, Samuel Adams Trufant, Louise Reynes BA, Centenary Coll., 1949; postgrad., Duke U., 1949-51; STB, Gen. Theol. Sem., 1952; postgrad., Westcott House, Cambridge, Eng., 1952-53; STM, So. Meth. U., 1962; MA, U. Chgo., 1963, PhD, 1971; DD, Nashotah House, 1976, U. South, Sewanee, Tenn., 2006. Ordained priest Episcopal Ch., 1954. Curate Episcopal Ch., Baton Rouge, 1953-54, vicar Abbeville, La., 1954-57, Waxahachie, Tex., 1960-61, rector Morgan City, La., 1957-60, priest in charge Chgo., 1961-63; instr. Wabash Coll., 1963-64; asst. prof. Nashotah House, Wis., 1964-69, assoc. prof., 1969-72, prof., 1972-74, sub-dean, 1973-74, acting dean, 1973-74; dean Seabury-Western Theol. Sem., Evanston, Ill., 1974-83, prof., 1983-93, prof. emeritus, 1996; chaplain, scholar in residence Coll. Preachers. Chmn. Coun. for Devel. of Ministry, Episcopal Ch., Coun. Sem. Deans; mem. Bd. for Theol. Edn.; mem. Gen. Bd. Examining Chaplains; vis. prof. Notre Dame, 1986—, Duke U., 1996; rsch. assoc. The Newberry Libr.; interim priest Episcopal Ch., Asheville, NC Author: How It All Began, 1973, The Living and Active Word, 1975, (with Robert Bennett) The Bible for Today's Church, 1979, Luke's Story of Jesus, 1981, (with John Westerhoff) A Faithful Church: Issues in the History of Catechesis, 1981, Elements of Homiletic, 1982, How Holy Writ Was Written, 1989, A History of Preaching, 2004, A Nation with the Soul of a Church, 2013, Runagates in Scarceness, 2013; book rev. editor Anglican Theol. Rev., 1971-76, v.p. of corp., 1975-85; chair editl. bd. Sewanee Theol. Rev., 2002-; contbr. articles and book revs. to various jours. and mags. Chmn. campus affairs com.; trustee Kendall Coll.; sec., co-chair Commn. on Faith and Order Nat. Coun. Chs.; bd. dirs., Native Am. Theol. Assn., U. NC at Asheville Found.; exec. com., Nat. Coun. Chs. in the USA; v.p. bd. dirs. Coll. for Srs./U. NC, Asheville; program com. Kanuga Confs., Inc., Friends of St. Benedict. Recipient Spl. award Mystery Writers Am., 1965, Book of Yr, Acad. Parish Clergy, 2004, Acad. Homiletics Lifetime Achievement award, 2007; grantee The Conant Fund, Pew Foun., St. Paul's Ministry and Mission Found., Indpls., Joseph Cardinal Bernardin award Nat. Coun. Chs., 2008 Mem. Soc. Bibl. Lit., Cath. Bibl. Assn., Am. Acad. Religion, Chgo. Soc. Bibl. Rsch., Acad. Homiletics, (pres.), Societas Homiletica (exec. coun., treas.), Coll. of Preachers (long-range planning com.), Mystery Writers of Am. Democrat. Home: 115 Murphy Hill Rd Weaverville NC 28787-8630 Personal E-mail: ocejunr@gmail.com.

EDWARDS, PAUL BEVERLY, retired science and engineering educator; b. Ridge Spring, SC, Nov. 12, 1915; s. Paul Bee and Chloe Agnes (Watson) E.; m. Sarah Dee Barnes, Apr. 10, 1943 (dec. July 1999); 1 child, Susan Dee Edwards Von Suskil. BS, U. Tampa, 1937; EdM, Harvard U., 1958; EdD, George Washington U., 1972. Owner, operator Edwards' Hobbies, Tampa, Fla., 1938—54; tchr. math. Hillsborough HS, Tampa, 1955—60; head dept. math. King HS, Tampa, 1960—63; coord. Grad. Ctr., supr. edn. and tng. Johns Hopkins U. and Applied Physics Lab., Balt. and Laurel, Md., 1963—75, dir. Grad. Ctr., supr. edn. and tng., 1975—81. Contbr. articles to profl. jours. Mem. Sun City Ctr. Voters League, 1989—, Cmty. Assn., Sun City Ctr., 1987—; mem. Greenbriar Property Owners Assn., Sun City Ctr., 1987—. Lt. comdr. USNR, 1942-46 Named Meritorious Tchr., State Fla., 1962; recipient various fellowships Mem. Ret. Officers Assn., Naval Res. Assn. Avocations: swimming, computers, photography, flying. Home: 6014 Blossom St Houston TX 77007-5002 Personal E-mail: pauldbald@verizon.net.

EDWARDS, S. EUGENE, energy executive; BS in Chem. Engring., Tulane U.; MBA, U. Tex., San Antonio. Process engr. CITGO; cons., refinery econs. Pace Consultants; various managerial pos. in planning and econs., refinery ops., bus. devel., and mktg. Valero Energy Corp., San Antonio, v.p., 1998—2001, sr. v.p. product supply and trading, 2001—05, exec. v.p., chief develop. officer, 2005—. Office: Valero PO Box 696000 San Antonio TX 78269-6000

EDWARDS, STEPHEN ALLEN, lawyer; b. Battle Creek, Mich., July 12, 1953; s. Louis Ward and Elizabeth Yvonne (Stahl) E.; m. Alice Veronica; children: Amelia Hatfield, Nathaniel Gordon. BA with high honors, U. Mich., 1975, JD cum laude, 1978. Bar: Wis. 1978, U.S. Dist. Ct. (ea. and we. dists.) Wis. 1978, Mich. 1980, Pa. 1980, Ga. 1999. Assoc. Godfrey & Kahn S.C., Milw., 1978-80, Pepper, Hamilton & Scheetz, Phila., 1980-82, Morgan, Lewis & Bockius, Phila., 1982-87, ptnr., 1987-98, Kilpatrick Stockton LLP, Atlanta, 1998—. Author: Arbitrage, 1990; exec. editor: The Issuer's Guide to Tax-Exempt Finance, 1994, Municipal Leasing, 2002. Mem. ABA (tax sect.), Ga. Bar Assn., Nat. Assn. Bond Lawyers (chmn. arbitrage seminar 1990, edn. com. 1990-91, bd. dirs. 1991-94, treas. 1994-95), Bond Attys. Workshop (panelist 1984-95, steering com., chmn. arbitrage 1986-87), Pa. Soc. SR (bd. dirs. 1991-94), Phila. Club. Episcopalian. Avocations: bicycling, photography. Home: 360 Cannady Ct Atlanta GA 30350-5622 Office Phone: 404-815-6278. Business E-Mail: sedwards@kilpatrickstockton.com.

EDWARDS, TERESA, professional sports team executive, professional basketball coach, retired professional basketball player; b. Cairo, Ga., July 19, 1964; d. Mildred Edwards and Leroy Copeland. BS in Leisure Studies, U. Ga., Athens, 1990. Guard, Vicenia, Magenta, Italy, 1987-88, Nagoya, Japan, 1989-93, Valencia, Spain, 1994, Tarbes, France, 1994; guard, head coach Atlanta Glory, American Basketball League, 1996—97; guard Minn. Lynx, 2003—04, asst. coach, 2006; dir. player pers. Tulsa Shock, 2010—, interim gen. mgr., head coach, 2011—. Mem. US women's nat. team USA Basketball, 1984—2000, bd. dirs., 2009—. Recipient Gold medal, Women's Basketball, Summer Olympic Games, 1984, 1988, 1996, 2000, Bronze medal, Women's Basketball, 1992, Gold medal, Women's Basketball, Pan American Games, 1987, Bronze medal, Women's Basketball, 1991, Gold medal, FIBA World Championships, 1990, Silver Anniversary award, NCAA, 2010; named Female Athlete of Yr., USA Basketball, 1987, 1990, 1996, 2000; named to Olympic Hall of Fame, Cairo, Ga. Hall of Fame, Nat. HS Hall of Fame, U. Ga. Cir. of Honor, 1996, Ga. Sports Hall of Fame, 2001, Women's Basketball Hall of Fame, 2010, Naismith Meml. Basketball Hall of Fame, 2011. Achievements include the first female athlete to play in five Summer Olympic Games, 1984, 1988, 1992, 1996, 2000. Office: Tulsa Shock One W Third St Ste 100 Tulsa OK 74103

EDWARDS, VICTOR HENRY, chemical engineer; b. Galveston, Tex., Oct. 17, 1940; s. Philip Lacey and Margaret Ruth (Hopkins) E.; m. Mary Margaret Litzmann, June 10, 1963; children: Henry L., Mary E. BA, Rice U., 1962; PhD in Chem. Engring., U. Calif., Berkeley, 1967. Registered profl. engr., Tex. Asst. prof. chem. engring. Cornell U., Ithaca, NY, 1967-73; mgr. adv. tech. U.S. Nat. Sci. Found., Washington, 1971-72; rsch. fellow Merck, Sharp, Dohme Rsch., Rahway, NJ, 1973-76; supr. rsch. engring. United Energy Resources, Houston, 1976-79; vis. prof. environ. engring. Rice U., Houston, 1979-80; sr. process engr. Fluor Engrs. and Constructors, Houston, 1980-82; southwest editor Plant Services mag., Chgo., 1982-85; project engr. Allstates/BE&K, Inc., Houston, 1984-90, lead process engr., 1990-93, process engring. mgr., 1993-94, prin. engr. process and environ., 1994-95; process dir. Aker Kvaerner, Houston, 1995—2007; dir. process safety Aker Solutions, Houston, 2007—11, Kvaerner, 2011—12, IHI Engring. & Constrn. Internat., 2012—13. Tech. adv. com. Mary Kay O'Connor Process Safety Ctr., Tex. A&M U., 1995—, chmn., 2005—11, Centennial Coun. Dept. Chem. & Biomolecular Engring. Rice U., 2009-13. Mem. editl. bd. Chem. Processing mag., 2003-; contbr. articles to profl. jours. Organizing com. Woodlands (Tex.) Harvest Festival, 1979-86; chmn. industry adv. coun. dept. chem. engring. Prairie View A&M U., 1991-94. Named Employee of Yr., 1998; recipient Shield of Irenee award E.I. duPont de Nemours & Co., 1994, 98, 2001, Environ. Excellence award, 1994, Safety, Health, and Environ. Excellence award, 1996, Svc. award Mary Kay O'Connor Process Safety Ctr., 2002, Aker Kvaerner, Design Safety award, 2008. Fellow: AIChE (chmn. Process Plant Safety Symposium 1992, exec. position 1 1993, program co-chmn. 1994, chmn. 1995, South Tex. sect. chmn. 2nd internat. plant ops. and design conf. 1997, chmn. 9th Global Congress Process Safety 2012—13, Disting. Svc. award 1991, Disting. Svc. award Prairie View A&M U. student chpt. 1992, 1994); mem.: Nat. Fire Protection Assn., NSPE, AAAS, Engrs. Coun. Houston (councilor 1987—92), Rice U. Alumni Assn. (class of '62 reunion com. 1982, 1987, 1992, 1997, co-chmn. alumni giving com. 1998, class of '62 reunion com. 2002, 2007—10, co-chmn. alumni giving com. 2007—10, class of '62 reunion com. 2011—12, golden reunion com. mem.), Am. Chem. Soc. (chmn. Ithaca sect. 1969, councilor divsn. biochem. and microbial tech. 1970—77), N.Y. Acad. Scis. (life). Methodist. Avocations: reading, tennis, sailing, golf. E-mail: vhe@alumni.rice.edu.

EFIRD, BRUCE A., retail executive; BSBA, Lenoir-Rhyne Coll.; grad. in Exec. Program, Cornell U. Various positions Food Lion, Inc., 1984—97, Bruno's Supermarkets, Inc., Birmingham, Ala., 1997—2005, sr. v.p., merchandising, 1999—2003, exec. v.p., gen. mgr., 2003—05; exec. v.p., merchandising Meijer, Inc., 2005—07; pres. Fred's, Inc., 2007—, CEO, 2009—. Bd. dirs. Fred's, Inc., 2008—. Office: Freds Inc 4300 New Getwell Rd Memphis TN 38118 Office Phone: 901-365-8880. Office Fax: 901-365-8865. Business E-Mail: befird@fredsinc.com.

EFTEKHARI, NASSER, physiatrist; b. Aug. 15, 1940; MD, U. Tehran, 1965. Diplomate AM. Bd. Phys. Medicine and Rehab. Intern Greater Balt. Med. Ctr., 1967-68; resident in phys. medicine and rehab. Temple U. Sch. Med., Phila., 1968-70, Hahneman Med. U., Phila., 1970-71; rsch. fellow SUNY, Bklyn., 1971-72; chief dept. phys. medicine and rehab. Shafa Rehab. Hosp., Tehran, Iran, 1973-75; dean Coll. of Rehab. Scis., Tehran, 1973-79; phys. med. and rehab. cons. Golestan Clinic, Mehr Hosp., Tehran, 1980-84; staff physician VA Hosp., Miami, Fla., 1985—2005, Mercy Hosp., 1989—, Cedars Med. Ctr., 1989—, Bapt. Health Sys. Hosp. South Fla., Miami, 1996—; chief phys. med. and rehab. svc. VA Hosp., Miami, 1997—2005. Clin. assoc. prof. rehab. medicine U. Miami Sch. Medicine, 2003—. Fellow: Am. Assn. Electrodiagnostic Medicine; mem.: Am. Acad. Phys. Medicine and Rehab., Fla. Soc. Phys. Medicine and Rehab. Office: 8600 SW 92 St Ste 201 Miami FL 33156 Office Phone: 305-206-4726. Business E-Mail: dreftekhari@yahoo.com.

EGAN, MICHAEL JOSEPH, retired lawyer, state legislator; b. Savannah, Ga., Aug. 8, 1926; s. Michael Joseph and Elise (Robider) E.; m. Donna Cole, Apr. 14, 1951; children: Moira Elizabeth, Michael Joseph, Donna, Cole, Roby, John Patrick. BA, Yale U., 1950; LL.B., Harvard U., 1955. Bar: Ga., D.C. Assoc. Sutherland, Asbill & Brennan, Atlanta, 1955-61, ptnr., 1961-77, 79-97, ret. ptnr., 1998; mem. Ga. Ho. of Reps., 1966-77, minority leader, 1971-77; assoc. atty. gen. U.S. Dept. Justice, Washington, 1977-79; mem. Ga. Senate, 1989-2001. Served with U.S. Army, 1945-47, 50-52. Mem. ABA, Atlanta Bar Assn., State Bar Ga., Am. Law Inst. Republican. Roman Catholic. Home: 3145 Argonne Dr NW Atlanta GA 30305-1949 Office: Sutherland Asbill & Brennan 999 Peachtree St NE Atlanta GA 30309-3915 also: 1275 Pennsylvania Ave NW Washington DC 20004-2404 Office Phone: 404-853-8056. E-mail: mjegan@raplaw.com.

EGLE, DAVIS MAX, mechanical engineering educator; b. New Orleans, Jan. 31, 1939; s. Merlin Joseph and Leona (Pujol) E.; m. Judith Johanna Reynolds, June 1, 1963; children: Robert, William. BSME, La. State U., 1960; MS, Tulane U., 1962, PhD, 1965. Registered profl. engr., Okla. Asst. prof., then. assoc. prof. U. Okla., Norman, 1965-73, prof. mech. engring., 1973-99, dir., 1981-90; prof. emeritus U. Okla, Norman, 1999—; DME cons., 1967—. Mech. engr. NASA Langley Rsch. Ctr., Hampton, Va., 1966-67; rsch. engr. Lawrence Livermore (Calif.) Nat. Lab., 1979; biomed. engr. Sports Medicine Specialists, Oklahoma City, 1990-91. Contbr. articles to profl. jours. Fellow Acoustic Emission Working Group (chair 1982-84); mem. ASME, Am. Soc. Nondestructive Testing (chair tech. com. 1979-82, Achievement award 1980). Office: University Okla Sch AME 865 Asp Ave Norman OK 73019-1050 Personal E-mail: dmegle@att.net.

EGLOFF, FRED ROBERT, manufacturers representative, writer, historian; b. Evanston, Ill., Nov. 30, 1934; s. Edward Gottfried and Pearl Elizabeth (Fischrupp) E.; m. Sharon Lee Geyer, June 30, 1962. BS in Commerce, Loyola U., 1956. Asst. adv. mgr. The Englander Co., Chgo., 1956-57; indsl. film svc. Accurate Cinema Svc., Chgo., 1960-62; indsl. sales The EMF Co., Chgo., 1962-69, Avery Internat., Azusa, Calif., 1969-77, The Stanley Works, Hartford, Conn., 1977-78; mfg. rep. ARTCO, Chgo., 1979-99. V.p., bd. dirs. Westerners Internat., Oklahoma City, 1982-2008, pres. 1997-99; cons. ALA, Chgo., 1982-2002; tchr. New Trier Extension, Wilmette, Ill., 1985-2007; adv. bd. Western Outlaw-Lawman History Assn., 1999-2008. Author: El Paso Lawman, 1982, Origin of the Checker Flag, 2006; editor Westerners Brand Book, 1986-96. Bd. dirs. Wilmette Hist. Soc., 1973-77; hist. cons. Wilmette Hist. Mus., 1978; com. mem. Save the Depot Preservation, Wilmette, 1974; sec. Wilmette Sailing Assn., 1974; vis. com. D'Arcy McNickle Ctr. Am. Indian History, Newberry Libr., 1999-02; libr. chmn. Mus. Western Art, Kerrville, Tex., 2009-, bd. dirs., 2011. Recipient Don Russell Meml. award, 1998, Wola Lifetime Achievement award for most outstanding contbns. to western history, 1999, W.I. Living Legend award, 2013; named Remuda Vol. of Yr., 2011, Lifetime Mem. award, Tex. Lions Camp. Mem. Western History Assn., Western Writers Am., Soc. Midland Authors, Chgo. Corral the Westerners (sheriff 1978-80, sidewinder 1984), Windy City BMW Car Club Am. (pres. 1976, Big Wheel 1972, Founders Recognition award 1997), Vintage Sportscar Club (sec. 1972-80, top competitor award 1970, 97), Nat. Cowboy Hall Fame, Soc. Automotive Historians, Wild West History Assn., Tejas Chpt. BMWCCA Southwest Vaqueros Corral San Antonio, Am. Legion, Tex. Lions Camp (life). Republican. Roman Catholic. Avocations: photography, skiing, horseback riding, reading. Personal E-mail: fredegloff@earthlink.net.

EHLE, JOHN MARSDEN, JR., writer; b. Asheville, NC, Dec. 13, 1925; s. John M. and Gladys (Starnes) E.; m. Gail Oliver, Aug. 30, 1952 (div. Apr. 1967); m. Rosemary Harris, Oct. 22, 1967; 1 child, Jennifer Anne. BA, U. NC, 1949; DFA (hon.), NC Sch. Arts, 1981; LHD (hon.), Berea Coll., Ky., 1986, U. NC, Asheville, 1987; DLitt (hon.), U. NC, Chapel Hill, 1990. Faculty U. NC, Chapel Hill, 1951—63; spl. asst. to Gov. Terry Sanford, Raleigh, NC, 1963—64; program officer Ford Found., NYC, 1964—65. Spl. cons. Duke U., 1976-80; co-founder NC Gov.'s Sch., U. NC Sch. Arts, NC Sch. Sci. and Maths. Author: (novels) Move Over, Mountain, 1957, Kingstree Island, 1959, Lion on the Hearth, 1961, The Land Breakers, 1964, The Road, 1967, Time of Drums, 1970, The Journey of August King, 1971, The Changing of the Guard, 1975, The Winter People, 1981, Last One Home, 1983, The Widows Trial, 1989, (biographies) The Free Men, 1965 (Mayflower Soc. cup), The Survivor, 1968, Shepherd of the Streets, 1960, Dr. Frank, Living with Frank Porter Graham, 1993, (non-fiction) The Cheeses and Wines of England and France, with Notes on Irish Whiskey, 1972, Trail of Tears: The Rise and Fall of the Cherokee Nation, 1988; pub. also in several fgn. countries; (screenplay) The Journey of August King, 1996. Apptd. by Pres. Johnson to White House Group for Domestic Affairs, 1964-66, Nat. Coun. Humanities, 1966-70; exec. com. Nat. Book Com., NYC, 1972-75, NC Sch. Arts Found., Winston-Salem, 1970-75; awards commn. State of NC, 1982-93, Mary Reynolds Babcock Found., Winston-Salem, 1985-89; pres. Anne C. Stouffer Found., 1970-80; pres. Awards Com. Edn., 1980-90. With AUS, 1944-46. Recipient Walter Raleigh prize for fiction NC Dept. Cultural Affairs, 1964, 67, 70, 75, 84, State of NC award for lit., 1972, Gov.'s award for Disting. Meritorious Svc., 1978, Lillian Smith prize Southern Regional Coun., 1982, Disting. Alumnus award U. NC, Chapel Hill, 1984, Thomas Wolfe Meml. award Western NC Hist. Assn., 1984, W.D. Weatherford award Berea Coll., 1985, Caldwell award NC Humanities Coun., 1995; named to NC Lit. Hall of Fame, 1997 Mem. PEN, Authors League, Century Club (NYC). Democrat. Methodist. Home: 125 Westview Dr NW Winston Salem NC 27104

EHLERS, KATHRYN HAWES (MRS. JAMES D. GABLER), physician; b. Richmond Hill, NY, Aug. 22, 1931; d. Albert and Edna (Hawes) E.; m. James D. Gabler, Dec. 5, 1959; children— Jennifer K., Emily E. AB, Bryn Mawr Coll., 1953; MD, Cornell U.; MD (Hannah E. Longshore Meml. Med. scholar 1953-57, Elsie Strang L'Esperance scholar 1956-57), 1957. Diplomate: Am. Bd. Pediatrics, Am. Bd. Pediatric Cardiology. Intern N.Y. Hosp., 1957-58, asst. resident pediatrics, 1958-60; fellow in pediatric cardiology Cornell U. Med. Coll., NYC, 1960-64, instr. pediatrics, 1964-66, asst. prof., 1966-70, asso. prof. pediatrics, 1970-75, prof., 1975-96, prof. emeritus, 1996—, vice-chmn. pediat., 1988-96; practice medicine specializing in pediat. cardiology NYC, 1958-96. Contbr. articles to profl. jours. Research trainee N.Y. Heart Assn., 1960-62, Am. Heart Assn., 1962-64. Fellow Am. Coll. Cardiology; mem. N.Y. Heart Assn., Am. Heart Assn., Harvey Soc., Am. Pediatric Soc., Am. Acad. Pediatrics, Alpha Omega Alpha. Personal E-mail: jkgabler@comcast.net.

EHMANN, WILLIAM DONALD, chemistry professor; b. Madison, Wis., Feb. 7, 1931; s. William F. and Victoria V. (Koperski) E.; m. Nancy M. Gallagher, July 16, 1955; children: William J., John M., James T., Kathleen E. BS, U. Wis., 1952, MS, 1954; PhD, Carnegie Inst. Tech., 1957. NRC-NSF rsch. assoc. Argonne Nat. Lab., Ill., 1957-58; mem. faculty U. Ky., Lexington, 1958—, asst. prof., 1958-63, assoc. prof. chemistry, 1963-66, prof., 1966-95, chmn. dept., dir. grad. studies, 1972-76, Coll. Arts and Scis. Disting. prof., 1968-69, univ. rsch. prof., 1977-78, assoc. dean for rsch. Grad. Sch., 1980-84, prof. emeritus, 1995—. Vis. prof. Ariz. State U., Tempe, 1969, Fla. State U., Tallahassee, 1972; cons. Argonne Nat. Lab., 1958-67; rsch. dir. project AEC, 1960-71, Agr. Dept., 1968-70, NASA, 1968-77, NIH, 1977-80, 84-98, DOE, 1983-85, NSF EPSCOR, 1986-91, NIST, 1993-94 Author: Radiochemistry and Nuclear Methods of Analysis, 1991; contbr. articles to profl. jours. Hon. assoc. Sanders-Brown Ctr. on Aging, 1988-95; bd. dirs. U. Ky. Rsch. Found., 1991-93; bd. dirs., exec. com. Alzheimer's Disease Rsch. Ctr., U. Ky., 1990. Recipient William D. Ehmann award Am. Nuclear Soc., 1996, Sturgill award U. Ky., 1987; Fulbright scholar; hon. fellow Australian Nat. U. Inst. Advanced Studies, Canberra, 1964-65, Hall of Fame, U. Ky. Arts & Scis, 2010. Fellow AAAS, Meteoritical Soc.; mem. Am. Chem. Soc. (chmn. Lexington sect. 1963-64, Herty medal for career achievements 1994, nat. award in nuclear chemistry 1996), Ky. Acad. Scis. (bd. dirs. 1964-67, Disting. Ky. Scientist award 1982), Sigma Xi, Phi Lambda Upsilon, Phi Eta Sigma, Phi Theta Kappa. Roman Catholic. Achievements include first analysis (with others) of Apollo Mission lunar samples; research on the chemistry of meteorites, lunar samples and trace elements involvement in neurological diseases; on the etiology of Alzheimer's Disease. Office: U Ky Chem Physics Bldg Lexington KY 40506-0055 Home: 3051 Rio Dosa Dr Apt 228 Lexington KY 40509-1549 Personal E-mail: wdehmann@att.net.

EHRHART, EARL, state legislator; b. Aug. 08; m. Beth Ann; children: Alysse, Quentin, John. BA, U. Ga. Businessman marble & granite industry; mem. 36 Ga. House of Reps., Atlanta, 1989—. Republican. Methodist. Office: 5500 Wright Rd Powder Springs GA 30127-1073 also: Ga House of Reps 245 State Capitol Atlanta GA 30334 Office Phone: 770-943-8568, 404-463-2247. Business E-Mail: earl@ahrhart4emm.com.

EHRLICH, BERNARD HERBERT, lawyer, trade association administrator; b. Washington, Apr. 3, 1927; s. Samuel Zachary and Elsie (Klein) Ehrlich; m. Edna Kraft, June 17, 1951 (div.); children: Vivian Rose, Beverly Denise, Brenda Susan, Lisa Jean. AB, George Washington U., 1946, LLB, 1949, MA, JD, 1950. Pvt. practice, Washington; gen. counsel numerous corps., industries, 1947-89; mgr., gen. counsel Inst. Indsl. Launderers, Washington, 1947-89; counsel KEX Nat. Assn., 1960-94. Counsel Nat. Home Study Coun., 1947—89, Nat. Assn. Cosmetology Schs., 1967—83; gen. counsel KEX Nat. Assn., 1960—95, Accrediting Bur. Health Edn. Schs., 1965—92, Commn. Accredited Truck Driving Schs., 1968—86; mem. adv. panel employee recruitment and job devel. U.S. C. of C., 1967—84; mem. Pres.'s Com. Employing Handicapped, 1975—; pres. Assn. Ret. Attys., Inc., Sarasota. Bd. dirs. Washington B'nai B'rith Hillel Found., 1997—2000; chmn. Darfur: A Genocide We Can Stop, Sarasota, Fla., 2007—; founder Humanity Working End Genocide, 2006—; co-chmn., Holocaust Edn. Program US Holocaust Mus., 2005—11; trustee Temple Emanu-el, Sarasota, 2005—07; programer HWEG, 2006—08. With USN, 1943—45. Recipient Svc. plaque, Am. Inst. Launderers, 1966, Nat. Assn. Trade and Tech. Schs., 1967, Nat. Home Study Coun., 1970, Accrediting Bur. Health Edn. Schs., 1992, Commn. Accredited Truck Driving Schs., 1992, N. F. Cimaglia award, Melody Pub. Co., 2011. Mem.: ABA, Am. Polit. Sci. Assn., Soc. Am. Travel Writers, Am. Soc. Assn. Execs., Am. Hist. Assn., Am. Soc. Internat. Law, Bar Assn. DC, Inst. Indsl. Launderers (hon.), KEX Nat. Assn. (hon.), Nat. Assn. Trade and Tech. Schs. (hon.), Am. Forestry Assn. (life), Phi Beta Kappa, Phi Delta Pi, Nu Beta Epsilon. Jewish. Home and Office: 4907 Lakescene Pl Sarasota FL 34243

EHRMANN, SUSANNA, language educator, photographer, writer; b. Detroit, Oct. 17, 1944; d. Frederick Michael and Stephanie (Fiala) Ehrmann. Student, U. Laval, summer 1965; BA, Antioch Coll., Yellow Springs, Ohio, 1966; MAT, U. Chgo., 1968. Cert. tchr., Ill., Tex., Wis. Tchr. fgn. lang. U. Chgo. Lab. Schs., 1967-74, Maimonides Sch., Brookline, Mass., 1975-76, North Shore Country Day Sch., Winnetka, Ill., 1977-78, Copenhagen Internat. Jr. Sch., 1978-79, Houston C.C., 1979-81, 84, Kinkaid Sch., Houston, 1980-82, Alief Ind. Sch. Dist., Houston, 1982-85, Houston Ind. Sch. Dist., 1990-91, Sch. of the Woods, Houston, 2006—07, T.H. Rogers Mid. Sch., Houston, 2007, Spring Br. Ind. Sch. Dist., Houston, 2008—12, Deutsche Samstagsschule Houston, German Saturday Sch., 2012—; pvt. instr., 1986—; freelance rschr., editor, 1986—; writer, photographer, 1993—; reader Ednl. Testing Svc., 2011—13. Mem. North Ctrl. evaluating teams, Chgo., Rockford, 1971; mem. MAT coordinating com. on Romance langs., U. Chgo., 1971-74, freelance textbook editor in French and German, 1988-96. Creator German Grammar Game, 1982; author, presentor, Bldg. Speaking and Writing Skills, 2007. Reader for the blind, Chgo., 1972-74. NDEA fellow, 1966-68; Goethe Inst. grantee, 1983. Mem. MLA, Am. Assn. Tchrs. of French, Am. Assn. Tchrs. of German. Avocations: reading, needlecrafts, photography, cooking. Home: 1701 Hermann Dr #12F Houston TX 77004-7452 Personal E-mail: susanna17@att.net.

EHSANI, MEHRDAD (MARK), electrical engineering educator, consultant; naturalized, US, 1980; s. Heshmat and Didar (Ahmadi) Ehsani; m. Zohreh Khadem; children: Evan Mancil, Nathaniel William, Sam. MS, U. Tex., 1974; PhD, U. Wis., 1981. Registered profl. engr., Tex. Rsch. engr. Fusion Rsch. Ctr. U. Tex., Austin, 1974-77; rsch. engr. Argonne Nat. Lab., Ill., 1977-81; prof. elec. engring. Tex. A&M U., College Station, 1981, Halliburton prof. elec. engring., 1992, Dresses Industries prof., 1994, dir. Tex. Applied Power Electronics Ctr., 1999, dir. advanced vehicle systems rsch. program, Dow Chem. fellow Coll. Engring., 2001—02, Robert M. Kennedy endowed chair prof. elec. engring., 2004—. Lectr. in field. Author: Converter Circuits for Superconductive Magnetic Energy Storage, 1988, Modern Electrical Drives, 2000; co-author: ANSI/IEEE Standards 936, 1987, Vehicular Power Systems: Land, Sea, Air and Space, 2004, Modern Electric, Hybrid Electric and Fuel Cell Vehicles: Fundamentals, Theory and Design, 2005, 2nd edition, 2009; contbr. articles to profl. jours. Named Outstanding Young Engr., Tex. Soc. Profl. Engrs., 1984, Disting. Lectr., IEEE-Industry Applications Soc., Inds. Elecs. Soc., IEEE Vehicular Tech. Soc., Dow Chem. fellow, Coll. Engring., Tex. A&M U., 2001. Fellow: IEEE (mem. steering com. Vehicle Power and Propulsion Conf., Field award in Undergrad. Tchg. 2003), SAE, Vehicular Tech. Soc. IEEE (bd. govs., bd. dirs., assoc. editor, James R. Evans Avant Garde award 2001), Soc. Automotive Engrs.; mem.: Industry Applications Soc. of IEEE (exec. coun. 1989—93, Disting. lectr.), Power Electronics Soc. IEEE (mem. adminstrv. com. 1990—96, 2005—). Baha'I. Achievements include patents in field. Office: Tex A&M U Dept Elec Engring College Station TX 77843-0001 Office Phone: 979-845-7582. Business E-Mail: ehsani@ece.tamu.edu, ehsani@mail.ece.tamu.edu.

EICHBERG, RODOLFO DAVID, physiatrist, educator; b. Pforzheim, Germany, July 26, 1937; came to the U.S., 1965; s. Julio and Ilse (Schonfarber) E.; m. Yvette Salama, May 21, 1965; children:

William Amadeo, Matias David. Baccalaureate, St. Andrews Scots Sch., Argentina, 1955; MD, U. Buenos Aires, 0963. Diplomate Am. Bd. Phys. Medicine and Rehab., cert. Ind. Med. Rehab. examiner, ringside physician Am. Assn. Profl. Ringside Physicians, diplomate Am. Bd. Disability Analysts, 2008. Intern, resident Grace Hosp. Wayne State U., Detroit, 1965-67; orthopedic surgeon Mar Del Plata, Argentina, 1968-73; resident physical medicine NYU, 1973-75; pvt. practice Rehab. and Electro Diagnosis Assocs., P.C., Tampa, 1975-96, 98—; asst. prof. U. So. Fla., Tampa, 1975-93, clin. assoc. prof., 1994—; chief spinal cord injury rehab. Tampa Gen. Hosp., 1984-96; chief phys. medicine & rehab. VA Med. Ctr., New Orleans, 1997-98; med. dir. Meml. Hosp. Ctr. for Comprehensive Rehab., 1998—2004. Mem. state adv. com. Head Spinal Cord Injuries, Tallahassee, 1976-96; clin. assoc. prof. La. State U. Sch. Medicine, 1997-98; physician advisor State of Fla. Athletic Commn., 1998-99; mem. advisor State of Fla. Agy. for Healthcare Adminstrn., 2001—; cons. MetLife Ins. Co., 2003-, Tech Health, 2010-. Contbr. articles to profl. jours. Bd. trustees Congregation Schaaraizedek, Tampa, 1980-82. Recipient Honors award City of La Paz, Bolivia, 1994, Physician of Yr. award Tampa Bay Latin Am. Med. Soc., 1997. Mem. AMA, Am. Acad. Phys. Medicine and Rehab. (health policy legis. com. 1990-95), Am. Spinal Injury Assn. (internat. rels. rep. S.C. 1990-95), Assn. Med. Latino Americana de Rehab., Colombian Phys. Medicine Rehab. Soc. (corr.), Argentine Soc. Rehab. Medicine (corr.), Fla. Med. Assn., Fla. Soc. Phys. Medicine Rehab. (pres. 1994-96), Hillsborough County Med. Assn. (exec. coun. 2001-03, bulletin editl. bd. 2006-), So. Soc. Phys. Medicine and Rehab. (pres. 1999-2000). Jewish. Avocations: boating, travel, aerobics. Office: Rehab and Electro Diag Assocs PA 2914 N Boulevard Tampa FL 33602-1208 Office Phone: 813-228-7696. Personal E-mail: eichberg@tampabay.rr.com.

EICHENWALD, HEINZ FELIX, physician; b. Switzerland, Mar. 3, 1926; came to U.S., 1936, naturalized, 1945; s. Ernst M. and Stella E.; m. Linda E. Moragné, July 20, 1995; children: Kathryn S., Eric C., Kurt A., Michael M. BA in Biochem. Scis. magna cum laude, Harvard U., 1946; MD, Cornell U., 1950. Intern, sr. asst. resident, sr. resident pediatrician N.Y. Hosp., 1950-51; asst. in pediat. Cornell U. Med. Sch., 1951-53, instr., then asst. prof., 1955-58, assoc. prof., then prof. pediat., 1958-64; USPHS instr. pediat. Emory U. Med. Sch., 1953-55; also vis. physician Grady and Crawford Long hosps., Atlanta; mem. staff N.Y. Hosp., 1958-65, attending pediatrician, 1963-65; vis. asst. prof. Albert Einstein Med. Sch., 1956-58; cons. Hosp. Spl. Surgery, NYC, 1956-64, Patterson (N.J.) Gen. Hosp., 1958-64; prof. pediat., chmn. dept. U. Tex. Southwestern Med. Sch., Dallas, 1964-83; chief-of-staff Children's Med. Ctr., Dallas, 1964—83; chief pediat. Parkland Meml. Hosp., Dallas, 1964—83, prof. emeritus, 2006. Cons. St. Paul, Irving Cmty., Presbyn. Hosps., Dallas; chief hepatitis investigation unit, epidemiology br. USPHS, 1954-55; Richard Bruce Miller lectr. Harvard U. Med. Sch., 1960; lectr. Columbia U. Tchrs. Coll., 1960-64; chmn. Internat. Rsch. Confs. Mental Retardation, 1965-66; chmn. panel anti-infectives NAS-NRC, 1966-69; vis. prof. U. Saigon Med. Sch., 1968-72; Vanuxem lectr. Princeton U., 1970; bd. dirs. Dallas Free Clinic, 1970-74, Children's Devel. Ctr., Dallas, 1974—; mem. bd. maternal and child health NIH, 1974-78; cons. in field, mem. numerous profl. coms. Assoc. editor Pediatric Therapy, 1974; editor Practical Pediatric Therapy, 1985, Current Therapy in Pediatrics, 1989, Pediatric Therapy, 1993; mem. editorial bd. profl. jours.; contbr. numerous articles in profl. publs. Bd. dirs., chmn. exec. com. Lamplighter Sch., Dallas, 1971—1980; bd. dirs. Winston Sch., 1974. Recipient Career Rsch. award NIH, 1963-65, Alexander von Humboldt prize Govt. of Germany (then Fed. Republic Germany), 1979, Weinstein-Goldeson award United Cerebral Palsy Found., 1980; Markle scholar med. sci., 1953. Mem. Harvey Soc., Soc. Pediatric Rsch., Am. Pediatric Soc., Infectious Disease Soc. Am., N.Y. Acad. Scis., Tex. Pediatric Soc., Phi Beta Kappa, Sigma Xi, Alpha Omega Alpha. Personal E-mail: echo18@swbell.net.

EICHLER, CRAIG J., dermatologist; BA in Chemistry, Emory U., Atlanta, 1985; MD, U. Fla., Gainesville, Fla., 1989. Diplomate Am. Bd. Dermatology, 1993. Intern internal medicine Univ. of Fla., Gainesville, Fla.; resident dermatology Univ. of Tex., Galveston, Tex.; staff dermatology dept. Cleve. Clinic Fla Weston, 1993—98, Cleve. Clinic Fla Naples, 1998—2006; staff dermatology divsn. Physicians Regional Med. Group, 2006—, chief dermatology divsn., 2009—; hosp. affiliation include Physicians Regional Med. Ctr. - Pine Ridge. Named one of America's Top Doctors, Castle Connolly Medical Ltd., 1998, 2000, 2002—. Mem.: Fla. Soc. of Dermatology and Dermatologic Surgery (pres. 2004—05), Fla. Med. Assn., Collier County Med. Soc., Am. Acad. of Dermatology. Office: Physicians Regional-Pine Ridge 6101 Pine Ridge Rd Desk 12 Naples FL 34119 Office Phone: 239-348-4400. Office Fax: 239-348-4059.

EICHLER, RODNEY J., energy executive; BS, MS in Geol. Engring., Colo. Sch. Mines. Registered profl. engr., Tex., cert. petroleum geologist. Exploration mgr. Tenneco Oil Co., Denver; v.p. exploration Axem Resources, LLC, Denver; regional exploration/devel. mgr. Rocky Mountain region Apache Corp., Denver, 1993—95, Western region exploration mgr. Houston, 1995—96, Western region v.p., 1996—97, v.p. exploration/prodn. Egypt Cairo, 1997—99, regional v.p., gen. mgr. Egyptian ops., 1999—2003, exec. v.p. Egypt, 2003—09, co-COO, pres.-Internat., 2009—11, pres., COO, 2011—. Pres., dir. Springboard-Educating the Future, Tex. Mem.: Am. Assn. Petroleum Geologists. Office: Apache Corp 2000 Post Oak Blvd Ste 100 Houston TX 77056 Office Phone: 713-296-6000. Business E-Mail: rod@apache.org.

EICKHOFF, MARGARET KATHRYN, consulting firm executive; b. Sedalia, Mo., Apr. 11, 1939; d. Leo Edward and Magdalene (Piatt) E.; m. Alfred James Smith Jr., Mar. 9, 1973. BA, U. Mo., 1960; MA, NYU, 1971. Rsch asst. Van Alstyne Noel & Co., NYC, 1961-62; exec. v.p., treas., sr. economist Townsend-Greenspan & Co. Inc., NYC, 1962-85; assoc. dir. for econ. policy, chief economist Office of Mgmt. & Budget, Exec. Office of the Pres., Washington, 1985-87; pres. Eickhoff Economics, Inc., Naples, 1987—. Former trustee Manhattan Inst., N.Y.C., 1987. Fellow Nat. Assn. of Bus. Economists (pres. 1981); mem. Conf. of Bus. Economists (chmn. 1991), The Econ. Club of N.Y. Office: Eickhoff Economics Inc 1048 Goodlette Frank Rd PO Box 10608 Naples FL 34101

EILAND, CRAIG, state legislator; b. Apr. 4, 1962; m. Melissa Eiland; children: Blake, Tucker, Gray, Delaney. BBA, Baylor U., Waco, Tex., 1984, JD, 1987. Former atty. Ernest H. Cannon, Houston, Mills, Shirley & Bassett, Galveston, Tex.; pvt. practice Houston & Galveston, 1992—; mem. Dist. 24 Tex. House of Reps., 1994—2003, mem. Dist. 23, 2003—. Recipient Pres.'s award, Tex. Pub. Health Assn., Leadership Inst. Class 1977, Nat. Conf. State Legislatures, and several others; named Hospitality Hero, Hotel-Motel Assn. Democrat. Methodist. Office: 9702 E.F. Lowery Expressway Texas City TX 77591 Address: Room CAP GW.05 Capitol PO Box 2910 Austin TX 78768 Office Phone: 800-345-2630, 512-463-0502. Personal E-mail: repeiland@aol.com.

EILAND, GARY WAYNE, lawyer; b. Houston, Apr. 25, 1951; s. William N. and Louise A. (Foltin) E.; m. Sandra K. Streetman, Aug. 4, 1973; children: Trina L. Wuensche, Peter T. BBA, U. Tex., 1973, JD, 1976. Bar: Tex. 1976, U.S. Ct. Claims 1977, U.S. Ct. Appeals (5th cir.) 1978, U.S. Ct. Appeals (11th cir.) 1981, U.S. Supreme Ct. 1989. Assoc. Wood, Lucksinger & Epstein, Houston, 1976-81, ptnr., 1981-91, Vinson & Elkins L.L.P., Houston, 1991—2008, King & Spalding LLP, Houston, 2008—; leader Healthcare Practice Group, Houston, 2008—. Lectr. Aspen Health Care Industry seminars, Aspen Pubs., Inc., Rockville, Md., 1978-89, HLO Health Care seminars, 1990-91; charter mem. health law exam. commn. Tex. State Bd. Legal Specialization, 2002-05. Mem. Tex. Bar Assn. (chmn. health law sect. 1991-92), Am. Acad. Healthcare Attys. (bd. dirs. 1991-97, pres. 1996-97), Am. Health Lawyers Assn. (past pres., exec. com. 1997-98 Greenburg Svc. award 2005), Healthcare Fin. Mgmt. Assn. (pres. Tex. Gulf Coast chpt. 1992-93, Region 9 chpt. liaison rep. 1994-95, compliance officers forum adv. coun. 2000-02, Founders medal of honor 1999), Assn. Am. Med. Colls., Houston Ctr. Club, Bentwater Yacht and Country Club. Office: King & Spalding LLP 1100 Louisiana St Ste 4000 Houston TX 77002-5213 Home: 86 Creekwood Dr Montgomery TX 77356-8469 Office Phone: 713-751-3207. Business E-Mail: geiland@kslaw.com.

EILER, DEREK, marketing executive; m. Sarah Eiler; children: Ryan, Kelsey. BS in Sports Mktg., Bowling Green State U., Ohio, 1993. Intern U. Mich. Athletic Dept., Spl. Olympics, Toledo Mud Hens; univ. services account mgr. Collegiate Licensing Co., 1993—97, v.p., 1997—2000, exec. v.p., 2000—02, COO, 2002—07, sr. v.p., mng. dir., 2007—. Recipient Disting. Alumni award, Bowling Green State Univ., 2002; named one of Forty Under 40, Street & Smith's SportsBus. Jour., 2009. Office: Collegiate Licensing Co 290 Interstate North Circle Ste 200 Atlanta GA 30339 Office Phone: 770-956-0520. Office Fax: 770-955-4491.

EINSPRUCH, BURTON CYRIL, psychiatrist; b. NYC, June 27, 1935; s. Adolph and Mala (Goldblatt) E.; m. Barbara Standen Traeger, Oct. 9, 1960; children: Julia E. Lewis, Alexander Louis, Robert Sands. BA, So. Meth. U., 1956, ScB, 1958; MD, Southwestern Med. Sch., Dallas, 1960. Diplomate Am. Bd. Psychiatry and Neurology (examiner 1974—). Intern Montefiore Hosp., NYC, 1960-61; resident Nat. Hosp. Inst. Neurology, London, 1962; resident, fellow U. Tex., Dallas, 1961—64, adv. devel. bd.; chief resident Parkland Meml. Hosp., Dallas, 1964; instr. psychiatry U. Pa., 1964-66; pvt. practice psychiatry Dallas, 1966—; adv. dir. Am. Nat. Bur. Tex., 2010. Staff Presbyn. and Parkland Hosps.; clin. asst. prof. U. Tex., Health Sci. Center, Dallas, 1966-70, dir. Southwestern Adult Psychiat. Clinic, Dallas, 1966-74; dir. psychiat. service Dallas Geriatric Research Inst., 1974-80; adj. prof. sociology U. North Tex., Denton, 1975-82; cons. staff Baylor U. Hosp., Golden Acres Hosp.; clin. assoc. prof. psychiatry U. Tex. Health Scis. Ctr., Dallas, 1971—; prof. psychiatry U. Tex. Southwestern Med. Ctr., Dallas, 1971—; bd. dirs., founder Dallas Nat. Bank; clin. assoc. prof. psychiatry NYU Med. Ctr., N.Y.C., 1990; adj. prof. Dept. Occupl. and Environ. Med. U. Tex. Med. Ctr., Tyler, Tex., cognitive and neuroscience, U. Tex., Dallas; chmn. bd. dirs. Planned Behavioral Health Care, Inc., Dallas; affiliate Tex. Inst. Rsch. and Edn. on Aging, Health Sci. Ctr. Fort Worth; bd. dirs. Am. Svc. Group; adv. bd. Am. Nat. Bank Tex., 2010. Contbr. articles to profl. jours.; mem. editl. bd.: Tex. Medicine Bd., 1991—2002. Trustee Evans Fedn., NYC, 1986-94, U. Tex., Dallas, 1987—, St. Mark's Sch. Tex., 1987-94, chmn. holocaust studies program bd., 1998—; mem. exec. bd. libr. Southern Meth. U., 1992-97; adv. dir. Leonhardt Fedn., NYC, 1990, Children of Alcoholics Fedn., 1991, 1995; arbitrator, NY and Am. Exchs., NYC, 1984; bd. dirs. Wyndham Internat., 1997-2000; dir. Perot Mus. Nature & Sci., Dallas; bd. trustees, adv. devel., U. Tex., Dallas, 2010, Alumni Bd. Southern Meth. U. Lt. comdr. M.C., USNR, 1964-66. Fellow Am. Psychiat. Assn. (disting. life, Am. Coll. Psychiatrists, Am. Soc. Adolescent Psychiatry, N. Tex. Soc. Adolescent Psychiatry (past pres.); mem. Royal Coll. Psychiatry London, AMA, Tex. Med. Assn. Home: 3505 Lindenwood Ave Dallas TX 75205-3229 Office: 8330 Meadow Rd Ste 117 Dallas TX 75231-3750 Office Phone: 214-369-1636. Personal E-mail: einspruch@charter.net.

EINSPRUCH, NORMAN GERALD, physicist, engineering educator; b. NYC, June 27, 1932; s. Adolph and Mala (Goldblatt) E.; m. Edith Melnick, Dec. 20, 1953; children: Eric, Andrew, Franklin. BA in Physics, Rice U., 1953; MS in Physics, U. Colo., 1955; PhD in Applied Math, Brown U., 1959. Mem. tech. staff, central research labs. Tex. Instruments, Inc., Dallas, 1959-62, mgr. electron transport physics br., central research labs., 1962-68, dir. advanced tech. lab., central research labs., 1968-69, dir. tech., chem. materials div., 1969-72, dir. central research labs., 1972-75, asst. v.p., 1975-77, dir. corp. devel., 1975-76, dir. tech. and planning consumer products, 1976-77; prof. dept. elec. and computer engring. Coll. Engring. U. Miami, Coral Gables, Fla., 1977—2009, dean Coll. Engring., 1977-90, sr. fellow in sci. and tech., 1990—2009, rsch. prof. electrical & computer engring., 2009—, prof., sr. fellow, emeritus dean, rsch. prof., 2009, chmn. dept. indsl. engring., 1994-99. Vis. prof. Rensselaer Poly. Inst., 2001-02, Portland State U., 2009-10; chmn. panel on thin film microstructure sci. and tech. NRC, 1978-79, mem. panel on impact of DoD very high speed integrated circuits program, 1980-81, panel on edn. and utilization of the engr., 1981-82; bd. dirs. ZPower, Inc.; advisor RF Saw, Inc. Author: Electronic Genie: The Tangled History of Silicon, 1998 editor: (series) VLSI Electronics: Microstructure Science, 24 vols., VLSI Handbook, 1985; contbr. articles to profl. jours. Recipient George Washington Honor medal Freedoms Found. Valley Forge. Fellow Am. Phys. Soc., Acoustical Soc. Am., IEEE, AAAS; mem. Golden Key, Iron Arrow, Sigma Xi, Omicron Delta Kappa, Tau Beta Pi, Eta Kappa Nu, Phi Kappa Phi, Alpha Pi Mu, Tau Sigma Delta. Home: 1415 Trillo Ave Miami FL 33146-2312 Office: U Miami Coll Engring PO Box 248581 Coral Gables FL 33124-8581 Home Phone: 305-667-9925; Office Phone: 305-284-3812. Business E-Mail: neinspruch@miami.edu, ngel898@bellsouth.net.

EISELE, GARNETT THOMAS, federal judge; b. Hot Springs, Ark., Nov. 3, 1923; s. Garnett Martin and Mary (Martin) E.; m. Kathryn Freygang, June 24, 1950; children: Wendell A., Garnett Martin II, Kathryn M., Jean E. Student, U. Fla., 1940-42, Ind. U., 1942-43; AB, Washington U., St. Louis, 1947; LLB, Harvard U., 1950, LLM, 1951. Bar: Ark. 1951. Assoc. Wootten, Land and Matthews, 1951—52, Owens, McHaney, Lofton & McHaney, Little Rock, 1956-60; asst. US atty. Little Rock, 1953-55; pvt. practice atty., 1961-69; judge US Dist. Ct. (ea. dist.) Ark., 1970—75, chief judge, 1975—91, sr. judge, 1991—. Legal adviser to gov. Ark., 1966-69. Del. Ark. 7th Constl. Conv., 1969-70; trustee U. Ark., 1969-70. Served with AUS, 1943-46, ETO. Mem. ABA, Ark. Bar Assn., Pulaski County Bar Assn., Am. Judicature Soc., Am. Law Inst. Office: US Dist Ct Ea Dist Ark 500 W Capitol Ave Little Rock AR 72201

EISENBERG, DEBORAH, writer; b. Nov. 20, 1945; BA, New Sch. Coll., NYC, 1969. Prof. creative writing U. Va., 1994—. Author: (story collections) Transactions in a Foreign Currency, 1986, Under the 82nd Airborne, 1992, The Stories (So Far) of Deborah Eisenberg, 1996, All Around Atlantis, 1997, Twilight of the Superheroes, 2007 (First prize in fiction, Libr. of Va.), The Collected Stories of Deborah Eisenberg, 2010 (PEN/Faulkner award for fiction, 2011), (plays) Pastorale, 1982, (stories included in) Best American Stories, 1992, 2004, New Granta Book of the American Short Story, 2007. Recipient O. Henry award, 1986, 1995, 1997, 2001, Whiting Writers' award for fiction, 1987, Friends of American Writers award, 1993, Lit. award, American Acad. Arts & Scis., 1993, REA award for short story, 2000; grantee Ingram-Merrill Found., 1993, Lannan Lit. Found. Fellowship, 2003; fellow John Simon Guggenheim Meml. Found., 1987—88, John T. & Catherine MacArthur Found., 2009. Mem.: AAAL. Office: U Va Dept Creative Writing 219 Bryan Hall PO Box 400121 Charlottesville VA 22904 Office Phone: 434-924-6074. Business E-Mail: de2b@Virginia.EDU, de2b@d1.mail.virginia.edu.

EISENSTADT, G. MICHAEL, diplomat, author, educator, researcher; b. Free City of Danzig (now Gdansk, Poland), Nov. 16, 1928; s. Isidor and Edith (Lange) E.; 1 child, Judith Luzann. BA, Queens Coll., 1951; MS, U. Wis., 1952; postgrad., Russian Inst. Columbia U., 1954—56, Fgn. Svc. Inst., 1982—83. Instr. history Queens Coll., Flushing, NY, 1955-60; jr. officer Am. Embassy, Belgrade, Yugoslavia, 1960-61; cultural officer Am. Consulate Gen., Guayaquil, Ecuador, 1962-63; asst. cultural affairs officer Am. Embassy, Belgrade, Yugoslavia, 1963-67, cultural attaché Warsaw, 1968-71, br. pub. affairs officer Bonn, Fed. Republic of Germany, 1973-76, counselor for pub. affairs Budapest, Hungary, 1977-80, dep. counselor for pub. affairs Bonn, 1983-84, counselor for pub. affairs Belgrade, 1984-88; dep. policy officer Voice of Am., Washington, 1971-73; dir. Office Internat. Visitors USIA, Washington, 1980-82; mem. sr. seminar State Dept., Washington, 1982-83; dir. Office European Affairs USIA, Washington, 1988-89; diplomat-in-residence, adj. prof. fgn. policy NYU, 1989—90; dir. N.Y. Reception Ctr. USIA, 1990-92; sr. rsch. scholar Inst. East Ctrl. Europe Columbia U., 1992-94. Cons. on the Balkans, Ea. and Ctrl. Europe, countries of the former Soviet Union; chmn. coordinating com., chmn. drafting com. Conf. on Peace and Tolerance, Berne, Switzerland, 1992, Istanbul, 1994; chmn. coordinating com. Conflict Resolution Conf., Vienna, 1995; election observer OSCE in Serbia, 1997; coord. Peace and Tolerance Conf. on Kosovo, Vienna, 1999; election observer Appeal of Conscience Found. in Russia, 1999; coord. Peace and Tolerance Conf. II, Istanbul, Turkey, 2005; lectr. in field; moderator Religious Diplomacy Seminar, 2010. Author: Imperfect Memories, 2012; contbr. articles to profl. jours. Sec. Appeal of Conscience Del. to Switzerland, 1997; dir. internat. programs Appeal Conscience Found. With U.S. Army, 1952-54; moderator, Seminar Diplomacy & Religion Dept. State, 2011. Home: 128 Central Park S New York NY 10019 Personal E-mail: gme1@earthlink.net.

EISNAUGLE, ERIC, state legislator; b. Arcadia, Fla., Feb. 6, 1977; m. Carrie Eisnaugle. BS, Fla. Southern Coll., 2000; JD, Vanderbilt U. Law Sch., 2003. Mem. Dist. 40 Fla. House of Reps., 2008—, vice chair econ. devel. policy com., mem. civil justice and courts policy com., criminal and civil justice appropriations com., econ. devel. and cmty. affairs policy coun. Mem. Ninth Jud. Circuit Jud. Nominating Commn. Mem.: Guardian Ad Litem, Down Syndrome Assn. Central Fla. (bd. dirs.). Republican. Office: House Office Bldg 402 S Monroe St Rm 417 Tallahassee FL 32399-1300 also: 2212 Curry Ford Rd Orlando FL 32806-2422 Office Phone: 850-488-9770, 407-893-3141. Business E-Mail: eric.eisnaugle@myfloridahouse.gov.

EISNER, DEAN H., telecommunications industry executive; B in Acctg. & Computer Sci., Purdue U., 1980; MBA, U. Mich. Various exec. mgmt. positions AGB Market Info., London, CBS Corp., General Electric Co., NY, Sony; v.p., bus. devel. Cox Enterprises, Inc.; CEO, Manheim Cox Newspapers Cox Enterprises Inc.; mng. dir., Cox Internat. Cox Enterprises, Inc., 1992—93, treas., 1993; pres., CEO Manheim (subs. of Cox Enterprises, Inc.), 2001—. Bd. dirs. Agora-Gazeta, Alliance Theatre Co., Am. Tower Corp., AutoTrader.com, LLC, 1999—. Bd. dirs. Atlanta C. of C., Atlanta Coll. of Art, Children's Healthcare of Atlanta, Ctr. for Civil and Human Rights, Jerusalem House, Paideia Sch. Endowment, Rotary Club of Atlanta, United Way, Woodruff Arts Ctr.; chmn. EXODUS. Office: Cox Enterprises Inc 6205 Peachtree Dunwoody Rd Atlanta GA 30328 Office Phone: 678-645-0000. Office Fax: 678-645-1079. Business E-Mail: Dean.Eisner@coxinc.com.

EISSENBERG, THOMAS E., psychology professor; b. Oak Ridge, Tenn., Aug. 13, 1965; BA in Psychology and English, Grinnell Coll., Iowa, 1987; PhD in Experimental Psychology, McMaster U., Hamilton, Ontario, Can., 1994. Lectr. McMaster U., 1992—93, Mt. Allison U., Sackville, New Brunswick, Canada, 1993—94; postdoc. fellow behavioral pharmacology rsch. unit Johns Hopkins U. Sch. Medicine, Balt., 1994—96, instr., 1996—97; asst. prof. dept. psychology & Inst. Drug & Alcohol Studies Va. Commonwealth U., Richmond, 1997—. Ad hoc reviewer Clin. Pharmacology & Therapeutics, Drug & Alcohol Dependence, Environ. Health Perspectives, Experimental & Clin. Psychopharmacology, Jour. Pharmacology & Experimental Therapeutics, Jour. Substance Abuse, Pharmacology, Biochemistry & Behavior, Physiology & Behavior, Psychopharmacology; contbr. articles to profl. jours. Recipient Dir.'s Travel award, Nat. Inst. Drug Abuse, 1995, Jr. Investigator Travel award, 1999; scholar Robert Wood Johnson Found., 2000—02. Mem.: Soc. Rsch. Nicotine & Tobacco, Coll. Problems of Drug Dependence, Am. Psychol. Soc., Am. Psychol. Assn. Office: Va Commonwealth U Dept Psychology Box 980205 Richmond VA 23298 Office Phone: 804-225-4617. Business E-Mail: teissenb@vcu.edu.

EISSLER, ROB, state legislator; b. Dec. 6, 1950; m. Linda Eissler; 3 children. BArch, Princeton U., NJ. Pres., exec. recruiter Eissler and Associates; mem. Dist. 15 Tex. House of Representatives, 2002—. Dir. Tex. Edn. Reform Found. Carrier-based attack pilot USN, USS John F. Kennedy. Recipient of several awards and honors. Republican. Office: PO Box 9494 The Woodlands TX 77387 Address: Room E1.408 Capitol Austin TX 78768 also: 431 Nursery Rd B-400 The Woodlands TX 77380 Office Phone: 281-681-9655, 512-463-0797. Office Fax: 281-292-6489.

EITEL, J. TIMOTHY, finance company executive; B in Computer Sci., Metro State Coll., Denver. V.p. Interstate Bank of Denver; joined Raymond James & Assocs. Inc., 1984; sr. v.p. Raymond James Financial, Inc., chief info. officer, 1993—. Office: Raymond James Financial Inc 880 Carillon Pky Saint Petersburg FL 33716 Office Phone: 727-567-1000. Office Fax: 727-567-8915.

EJIMOFOR, CORNELIUS OGU, political scientist, educator; b. Owerri, Nigeria, Oct. 10, 1940; came to U.S., 1963; s. Osuji and Helen Domaonu (Atashia) E.; m. Priscilla Loveth Amaugo, Mar. 10, 1966; children: Cornelia, Caroline, Cornelius Jr., Priscilla, Ebere. AA, Warren Wilson Coll., 1965; BA in Polit. Sci., Wilberforce U., 1966; MPA, U. Dayton, 1967; MA, PhD, U. Okla., 1971. Tchr. Cath. Mission Schs., Emekuku, Nigeria, 1959-63; rsch. asst. U. Dayton, Ohio, 1966-67; instr. polit. sci. Edward Waters Coll., Jacksonville, Fla., 1967-68, prof. polit. sci., 1992—2009, chmn. divsn. arts and scis., 1992-93; grad. asst. U. Okla., Norman, 1968-70; asst. prof. William Paterson Coll., Wayne, NJ, 1970-72; from assoc. prof. to prof. Tuskegee U., Ala., 1972-80, dept. head polit. sci., 1972-77; sr. lectr., reader U. Nigeria, Nsukka, 1980-91, prof. polit. sci., 1991-92. Coord., head, prof. sub-dept. pub. adminstrn. and local govt. U. Nigeria, 1990-92, coord. local govt. tng. programs, 1990-92. Author: British Colonial Objectives and Policies in Nigeria, 1987, Management of Human Resources: A Generic Approach, 1992. Mem. AAUP,

Am. Soc. Pub. Adminstrn., Am. Polit. Sci. Assn., KC (pilot 2010-). Democrat. Roman Catholic. Avocations: swimming, reading, writing. Home: 6450 Sierra Dr Jacksonville FL 32244 Personal E-mail: coejimofor@aol.com.

ELAM, FRED ELDON, retired military officer; b. Seminole, Okla., July 10, 1937; s. Jack Eldon Elam and Maye (Gaskill) E.; m. Judy Teller, Feb. 21, 1959; children: Jacqueline Marie Elam Kabat, Justin Eldon. BS, U. Ark., 1960; MBA, Mich. State U., 1964; grad. strategy mgmt. and naval ops., Naval War Coll., 1977; grad., Harvard Grad. Sch. Bus. Admin., 1998. Commd. 2d lt. U.S. Army, 1960, advanced through grades to maj. gen., 1986, with Div. G-4, 101st Airborne (Air Assault) Fort Campbell, Ky., 1976-77, comdr. Materiel Support Ctr. Waegwan, Republic of Korea, 1977-79, dir. programs and evaluation Army Materiel Command Alexandria, Va., 1979-82; comdg. gen. 19th Support Command, Taegu, Republic of Korea, 1982-84; dir. mgmt. Hdqrs. Dept. Army, Washington, 1984-85; chief U.S. Army Transp., Hdqrs. Transp. Ctr. Fort Eustis, Va., 1985-88; comdr. Joint U.S. Mil. Mission for Aid to Turkey Ankara, 1988-90; asst. dep. chief of staff for logistics, Dept. Army Washington, 1990—2003; v.p. profl. tech. svcs. Advancia Corp., Arlington, Va., 1993—2002; pres. Elam Consulting, 2003—. Mem. lifetime staff and faculty Army Logistics Mgmt. Ctr., Fort Lee, Va., 1971—, Va. Mil. Commn., 1986-88; disting. mem. Transp. Corps Rgt., U.S. Army; counselor Sr. Corps. Ret. Exec., 2005-. Decorated D.S.M., Def. Superior Svc. medal, Legion of Merit, Bronze Star with two oak leaf clusters, Meritorious Svc. medal with two oak leaf clusters, Air medal, Army Commendation medal with three oak leaf clusters, Armed Forces expeditionary medal, Vietnam Svc. medal with four oak leaf clusters, Overseas Svc. ribbon with "4" device, Republic of Vietnam campaign medal, Republic of Korea Svc. medal, Medal of Merit of Turkish Armed Forces, Meritorious Svc. medal; named to US Army Transp. Corps Hall of Fame, 2005. Mem. Assn. US Army, Soc. of 173d Airborne Brigade, Res. Officers Assn. (pres.), Transp. Corps Regimental Assn (nat. pres., hon. col. 2007-11), Beta Gamma Sigma. Avocations: running, reading, military history. Office Phone: 703-644-0753. Personal E-mail: elamjf@msn.com.

ELAM, MERRILL L., architectural firm executive; b. Nashville, June 28, 1943; BArch, Ga. Inst. Tech., 1971; MBA, Ga. State U., 1983; postgrad., Harvard U., 1980. Intern Taylor and Collum Architects, 1967-69; architect, sr. assoc. Heery & Heery Architects & Engrs., Inc., 1969-81, architect, v.p., 1981-84; prin. Scogin, Elam and Bray Architects, Inc., Atlanta, 1984—2000, Mack Scogin Merrill Elam Architects Inc., Atlanta, 2000—. Bd. dirs. Art Papers; vis. critic Miss. State U., 1984, Ga. Inst. Tech., 1985, 89, 90, Auburn U., 1986, Harvard U., 1987, 93, So. Calif. Inst. Architecture, 1990, Clemson U., 1990, Ohio State U., 1991; Harry S. Shure vis. prof. architecture U. Va., 1991; Caudill vis. lectr. architecture Rice U., 1992; Louis Henri Sullivan rsch. prof. architecture U. Ill., 1994; guest lectr. Tulane U., Carnegie-Mellon, Cooper Union, Boston Architecture Ctr., U. Tenn., Miss. State U., Auburn U., U. Fla., Pa. State U., Ariz. State U., U. Va., Princeton U., Va. Polytechnic Inst., Pensselaer Polytechnic Inst., numerous others. Prin. works include Martin Mountain House, Clayton Ga., Heer House, Charlotte, N.C., Roderique Residence, Stone Mountain, Ga., Chmar Residence, Atlanta, Carol Cobb Turner Br. Libr., Morrow, Ga., Gallery for the Bur. Cultural Affairs, Atlanta, Atlanta C. of C. Corp. Hdqrs., High Mus. at Ga.- Pacific Ctr., Atlanta, Tallahassee (Fla.) City Hall, Ga. Power Co. Corp. Hdqrs. Office Bldg., Atlanta, Shelby County Jail, Columbiana, Ala., Crestwood High Sch., Fulton County, Ga., Martin Luther King Jr. Mid. Sch., Atlanta, numerous others. Recipient Ga. Bus. Coun. for the Arts award, 1986, Outstanding Mus. award Gallery and Mus. Assn. Ga., 1986, Urban Design Commn. award of Excellence, High Mus. Ga.- Pacific Ctr., 1987, Buckhead Br. Libr., 1990, Record Houses award House Chmar, 1991, Arnold W. Brunner Meml. Prize in Archit. award, Am. Acad. Arts and Letters., 2011. Mem. AIA (Atlanta chpt., adjudicator, corp., nat. com. design, chair membership com., book ctr. bd. dirs., past chairperson, past exec. com. mem., numerous awards), Ga. State Bd. Architects (past pres.), Architecture Soc. Atlanta (founder, past pres.), Women in Architecture. Office: Mack Scogin Merril Elam Architects 111 John Wesley Dobbs Ave NE Atlanta GA 30303

ELDERS, JOYCELYN (MINNIE JOCELYN ELDERS, MINNIE JOYCELYN LEE), public health service officer, endocrinologist, former Surgeon General of the United States; b. Schaal, Ark., Aug. 13, 1933; d. Curtis and Haller Jones; m. Oliver B. Elders, Feb. 14, 1960; children: Eric D., Kevin M. BA in Biol., Philander Smith Coll., 1952; MD, U. Ark. Med. Sch., 1960; MS in Biochemistry, U. Ark., 1967. Pediatric intern U. Minn. Hosp., Mpls., 1960-61; pediatric resident U. Ark. Med. Ctr., Little Rock, 1961-63, chief pediatric resident, 1963-64, pediatric rsch. fellow, 1964-67, asst. prof. of pediatrics, 1967-71, assoc. prof. of pediatrics, 1971-76, prof. of pediatrics, 1976-87; dir. Ark. Dept. of Health, Little Rock, 1987-93; pres. Assn. of State & Territorial Health Officers, 1992; surgeon gen. US Dept. Health & Human Services, 1993-94; prof. pediatrics Univ. Ark. Med. Ctr., Little Rock, 1994—98, prof. emeritus, pediatric endocrinology, 1998—; medical dir. Apothecus Pharmaceutical Corp., 2006—. Bd. dirs. Nat. Bank of Ark., North Little Rock, 1979-89. Editorial bd. Jour. Pediatrics, 1981—; contbr. articles on pediatrics to profl. jours. Bd. dirs. Northside YMCA, Little Rock, 1973—; vol. vols. in pub. schs., Little Rock, 1973—. 1st lt. U.S. Army, 1953-56. Recipient NIH Career Devel. award, Worthen Bank's Ark. Profl. Woman of Distinction award, 1987; named one of 100 Women of Ark., 1980, Ark. Dem. Woman of Yr. statewide newspaper, 1988, Presdl. award, Ark. Sociological and Anthropological Assn., 1993. Mem. So. Soc. Pediatrics (rsch. pres. 1979-80), Lawson Wilkins Endocrine Soc. (com. chair 1976), Ark. Sci. and Tech. Commn. (sec. 1975-89), Little Rock C. of C. (bd. dirs. 1980—), Endocrine Soc., Acad. Pediatrics, Am. Pediatric Soc. First African Am. US Surgeon General. Office: U Ark Med Ctr 4301 W Markham # 820 Little Rock AR 72205

ELDRIDGE, DAVID CARLTON, art and antique appraiser; b. Lansing, Mich., July 15, 1949; s. Carlton Brady and Blythe (Axford) E.; m. Suzanne Hamrick, Dec. 12, 1970; 1 child, Morgan Worth B.F.A., Ill. Wesleyan U., 1971; postgrad., U. Denver, 1972-73; M.F.A., So. Ill. U., 1974. Accredited sr. appraiser Am. Soc. Appraisers, 1985. Curator exhibits Nature Sci. Park, Winston Salem, NC, 1974; curator exhibits Tenn. State Mus., Nashville, 1974-80; exec. dir. Mus. Arts and Scis., Macon, Ga., 1980-82; dir. Eldridge Appraisals, Naples, Fla., 1982—. Mem. Am. Soc. Appraisers (sr.), Appraisers Assn. America, Royal Instn. Chartered Surveyors. Office: 1839 Imperial Golf Course Blvd Naples FL 34110-8140 Office Phone: 239-598-2225. Personal E-mail: dceldrid@comcast.net.

ELDRIDGE, J. CHARLES, endocrinologist, educator, researcher; b. Chgo., June 7, 1942; s. John Godfrey Eldridge, Carol Boedeker Eldridge; m. Pat Hudler. BA in Biology, North Cen. Coll., Naperville, Ill., 1965; MS in Physiology, No. Ill. U., 1967; PhD in Endocrinology, Med. Coll. Ga., 1971. Instr. biology Orange County C.C., Middletown, NY, 1967—68; rsch. assoc. I.N.S.E.R.M., Bordeaux, France, 1971-72, Med. Coll. Ga., Augusta, 1973; asst. prof. lab. medicine Med. U. S.C., Charleston, 1974-79; asst. prof. physiology and pharmacology Wake Forest U. Sch. Medicine, Winston-Salem, NC, 1979—87, assoc. prof. physiology and pharmacology, 1987—99, prof. physiology and pharmacology, 1999—. Grant reviewer Nat. Inst. Aging, NIH, Bethesda, Md., 1990—93; rsch. cons. EPA, Washington, 1999—, mem. endocrine disruptors methods validation com., 2001—04; ad-hoc mem. Sci. Adv. Panel, 2006—; cons. Internat. Life Scis. Inst., Washington, 1992—94; med. edn. cons. various schs., 1988—; adj. faculty Harvard Macy Inst. Med. Educators, 2001—04; rsch. cons. Nat. Toxicology Program, 2011; mem. Nat. Bd. Med. Examiners Test Com., 2010—13. Mng. editor: Basic Sci. Educator, 1999—2002, mem. editl. bd.: Biology of Reproduction, 2000—05, Jour. Internat. Assn. Med. Sci. Educators, 2002—04; contbr. articles to profl. jours. Coord. United Way, Winston-Salem, 1986—98; elder, deacon, other positions Presby. Ch., 1992—. Recipient Disting. Alumni award, Med. Coll. Ga., 2002, CIBA Toxicology Rsch. award, Novartis Corp., 1995, North Ctrl. Coll., 2011; named to Ottawa Twp HS Hall of Fame, 2013; grantee, NIH, 1976—97, Nat. Inst. Drug Abuse, 1990—98; Macy fellow in edn., Harvard Med. Sch., 2001. Mem.: Soc. for Study of Reproduction, Internat. Assn. for Med. Sci. Educators, Soc. Neurosci., Endocrine Soc., Shriners (bd. dirs. 1988—91). Presbyterian. Avocations: music, travel, cuisine. Office: Wake Forest U Sch Medicine Dept Physiology and Pharmacology Winston Salem NC 27157-1083 Office Phone: 336-716-8570.

ELDRIDGE, JIMMY A., state legislator; b. Jackson, Tenn., Apr. 1, 1948; m. Carolyn Hall; children: Stephen, Michael. Commr., Madison County, Tenn., 1998; entrepreneur Allison-Eldridge Ins. Group, Inc.; state rep. Dist. 73 Tenn., 2003—; Rep. v. chmn.; mem. Children & Family Affairs Com., Health & Human Resources Com.; house rep. Tenn. Mem.: NRA, AARP, State Assn. Profl. Ins. Agts., Jackson-Madison County C. of C., Jackson Symphony Assn., Profl. Ins. Agts. Assn., Fellow Christian Athletes, Pinson Ruritan Club, Jackson Rotary Club. Republican. Office: 29 Emerald Lake Dr Jackson TN 38305 also: 208 War Memorial Bldg Nashville TN 37243-0173 Office Phone: 615-741-7475. Office Fax: 615-253-0373. Business E-Mail: rep.jimmy.eldridge@capitol.tn.gov.

ELDRIDGE, WILLIAM CONNER, JR., federal prosecutor; b. Fayetteville, Ark., 1977; BA, Davidson Coll., NC, 1999; JD, U. Ark. Sch. Law, 2003. Legis. corr. to Senator Blanche Lincoln US Senate, Washington, 1999; legis. asst. to Rep. Marion Berry US House of Representatives, Washington, 1999—2000; law clk. Washington County Prosecutor's Office, Ark., Mitchell, Williams, Selig, Gates & Woodyard PLLC, Little Rock, Bass, Berry & Sims PLC, Memphis, Wright, Lindsey & Jennings LLP, Little Rock; law clk. to Hon. G. Thomas Eisele US Dist. Ct. (eastern dist.) Ark., 2003—04; v.p. credit adminstrn., asst. gen. counsel Summit Bancorp, Inc., Ark., 2004—05, v.p. lending, 2005, regional pres., Summit Bank Arkadelphia, Ark., 2005—06, corp. exec. v.p., sr. counsel, 2006—08, CEO, 2008—10; US atty. (western dist.) Ark. US Dept. Justice, Ft. Smith, Ark., 2010—. Ptnr. Whipple Family Banking Partnership, 2004—09; counsel Whipple Family Ltd. Partnership, 2004—10; bd. dirs., sec.-treas., counsel Horizon Timber Svcs., Ark., 2005—10; bd. dirs. Summit Bancorp, Inc., 2005—10; spl. dep. prosecutor, Clark County, Ark., 2009—10. Bd. dirs. Travel Nurse Across America, North Little Rock, 2004—05. Named Most Likely to Succeed in the Practice of Law, U. Ark. Sch. Law; named one of Top 40 under 40, Ark. Bus. Office: US Courthouse 414 Parker St Fort Smith AR 72901*

ELIN, RONALD JOHN, pathologist, educator; s. John Matthew and Helen Sophia Elin; m. Susan May Krogh, June 14, 1969; children: Derek, Justin. BA, U. Minn., 1960, BS, 1962, MD, 1966, PhD, 1969. Diplomate Am. Bd. Pathology, Am. Bd. Clin. Chemistry. Intern U. Hosp. Calif., San Diego, 1969-70; commd. med. officer USPHS, 1970, advanced through grades to med. dir., 1975; staff assoc. Nat. Inst. Allergy and Infectious Diseases NIH, Bethesda, Md., 1970-73, resident clin. pathology dept., 1973-74, chief clin. pathology dept., 1975-97, chief chemistry svc., 1977-97; vice chmn. pathology U. Louisville, Ky., 1997—2001, chmn. dept. pathology and lab. medicine, 2002. Clin. prof. Uniformed Svcs. U. of Health Scis., Bethesda, 1978-97; initiator, first chmn. Gordon Rsch. Conf. on Magnesium in Biomed. Processes and Medicine, 1978. Contbr. more than 230 articles to profl. jours. Decorated Commendation medal USPHS, 1980, Meritorious Svc. medal USPHS, 1984. Mem. Coll. Am. Pathologists, Am. Soc. Clin. Pathologists; mem. Am. Assn. Pathologists, Am. Assn. Clin. Chemistry (Outstanding Contbns. to Clin. Chemistry in a Selected Area of Rsch. award 1994), Acad. Clin. Lab. Physicians and Scientists (sec.-treas. 1985-87, pres. 1990-91, Gerald T. Evans award 1995). Lutheran. Achievements include research on magnesium metabolism, properties of endotoxin. Office: U Louisville Hosp Dept Pathology and Lab Medicine 627 S Preston St Rm 210 Louisville KY 40202-1675 Home Phone: 502-500-0236; Office Phone: 502-852-4464. Business E-Mail: rjelin01@louisville.edu.

ELKINS, GARY, state legislator; b. Houston, Mar. 15, 1955; m. Julie Ann Elkins; 4 children. BS in Practical Theology, Southwestern Assemblies of God U., Waxahachie, Tex. Real estate agent; pres. Personal Credit Corp.; mem. Dist. 135 Tex. House of Representatives, 1995—. Republican. Pentecostal. Office: 9601 Jones Rd Ste 215 Houston TX 77065 also: Room 4N.03 Capitol PO Box 2910 Austin TX 78768 Office Phone: 932-912-8380, 512-463-0722.

ELKINS, TONI MARCUS, artist, association administrator; b. Tifton, Ga., Feb. 22, 1946; m. Samuel M. Elkins, 1968; children: Stephanie Elkins Sims, Eric Marcus. Student, Boston U., 1965; ABJ, U. Ga., 1968; postgrad., Columbia Coll., SC, 1980-82, postgrad. photography/silk screening. Owner, designer Designs by Elkins, Columbia, 1986—. Supt. fine art SC State Fair Art Exhbn., 1987-96. Auction chair Elegant Egg McKissick Mus., Columbia, 1994; bd. dirs. Trustus Theatre, 1994-96; chmn. SC Playwright's Festival, 1994—. Recipient Best of Show award Internat. Dogwood Festival, 1991, So. Water Color Assn. Pres.'s award, 1992, Purchase award Anderson County Arts Coun., 1992, Meyer Hardware award Rocky Mountain National, 1992, Howard B. Smith award SC Watercolor Ann., 1992, Women of Distinction award Girl Scouts of Congaree Area, Inc., 2000, Tex. Watercolor Soc. Camlin award, So. Watercolor Soc. Cheap Joe's award, Trenholm Artists Guild Pres. award. Mem. Nat. Watercolor Soc. (1st v.p. 2003—), Watercolor U.S.A., S.C. Watercolor Soc., Nat. Watercolor Okla., Penn. Watercolor Soc., Ga. Watercolor Soc., Rocky Mountain Nat. Watercolor Soc., Cultural Coun. of Richland & Lexington Counties (exec. bd. sec. 1990-93), Ctrl. Carolina Cmty. Found. (chmn. devel. 2000—, chmn. nominations 2004-2005), Southeastern Art and Craft Expn. (adv. bd. 1993-94, Elizabeth O'Neill Verner award 1999), Columbia Coll. Com. of 150, Women in Philanthropy (founder 2002). Avocations: reading, swimming, art, rare books. Home: 1511 Adger Rd Columbia SC 29205-1407 Office Phone: 803-206-8492. Personal E-mail: tutata.elkins855@gmail.com.

ELLARD, HENRY AUSTIN, professional football coach, retired professional football player; b. Fresno, Calif., July 21, 1961; m. Lillian Ellard; children: Henry Austin Jr., Christiana, Alexandria, Adriana, Whitney. Attended, Calif. State U., Fresno, 1979—83. Wide receiver LA Rams, 1983—93, Washington Redskins, 1994—98, New England Patriots, 1998; asst. football coach So. Calif. Christian HS, 1999; asst. track and field coach Villa Pk. HS, Calif., 1999—2000; asst. football coach Calif. State U. Fresno Bulldogs, 2000; offensive asst. St. Louis Rams, 2001—02, wide receivers coach, 2003—08, NY Jets, 2009—11, New Orleans Saints, 2012—. Named Player of Yr., Western Athletic Conf., 1983, 1st Team All-Pro, AP, 1984, 1988; named to Nat. Football Conf. Pro Bowl Team, NFL, 1984, 1988, 1989. Achievements include leading the NFL in: yards per punt return, 1983; punt return touchdowns, 1983, 1984; receiving yards, 1988; yards per reception, 1996. Office: New Orleans Saints 5800 Airline Dr Metairie LA 70003

ELLEN, MARTIN M., corporate financial executive; b. Chgo., Dec. 28, 1953; married. BS in Acctg., U. Ill., 1975; M in Mgmt., Northwestern U., 1987. CPA, Ill. Auditor Price Waterhouse, Chgo., 1975-78, sr. auditor, 1978-81, mgr. auditing, 1981-84, sr. mgr. auditor, 1984; controller D&K Fin., Chgo., 1984-86, v.p. fin., 1986—; v.p., CFO Whitman Corp., Cabot Microelectronics Corp., 2001—02; sr. v.p. fin., CFO Snap-on, Inc., 2002—10; exec. v.p., CFO Dr. Pepper Snapple Group Inc. (formerly Cadbury Schweppes Americas Beverages), Plano, Tex., 2010—. Mem. Fin. Exec. Inst., Am. Inst. CPA's, Ill. CPA Soc. Office: Dr Pepper Snapple Group 5301 Legacy Dr Plano TX 75024 Office Phone: 972-673-7000.

ELLER, JEFF, consulting firm executive, former federal official; Attended, Purdue U. Anchor Sta. WAKE Radio, Valparasio, Ind., 1976-77, Sta. WTHI Radio-TV, Terre Haute, Ind., 1977; new dir. Sta. WGOW-Radio, Chattanooga, 1978-80; reporter, anchor Sta. WKRN-TV, Nashville, 1980-85; press sec. to Congressman Bill Boner, Washington, 1985-86, Congressman Bob Carr, Washington, 1986-89, Jill Long for Cong., Ft. Wayne, Ind., 1989; polit. liaison Dem. Congl. Campaign Com., Washington, 1989-91; Fla. state dir. Bill Clinton's Presdl. Campaign, Tallahassee, 1991-92, press sec., polit. communications dir. Little Rock, 1992; dep. asst. to Pres., dir. media affairs The White House, Washington, 1993—94; with Pub. Strategies, Inc., Austin, 1994—2006, pres., CEO, 2006—. Press. sec. Friends of Bob Carr '86, '88, Assn. State Dem. Chairs, Dem. Nat. Conv. '88, Atlanta; press advisor ADO-Civilista, Panama City, 1989, Govt. Panama, 1989-90; comms. dir. Dem. Senatorial Campaign Com., Washington, 1991—. Office: Public Strategies Inc 98 San Jacinto Blvd Ste 1200 Austin TX 78701 Office Phone: 512-474-8848. Office Fax: 512-474-0120.

ELLER, TIMOTHY R., construction and real estate company executive; b. 1948; BS in Constrn. Mgmt., U. Nebr., 1972. With Centex Homes, Ill., 1973, project mgr. Ill., 1975, v.p. Minn., 1977—81, divsn. pres. Minn., 1981—85, pres., CEO, 1991, chmn., 1998—2003; exec. v.p. Centex Real Estate Corp./Centex Homes, Dallas, 1985—90, pres., COO, 1990—96; CEO Centex Real Estate Corp., Dallas, 1991—2002, 2006—, chmn. Dallas, 1998—2003; exec. v.p. Centex Corp., Dallas, 1998—2002, pres., COO, 2002—, bd. dirs., 2002—, chmn., CEO, 2004—09; vice chmn. PulteGroup, Inc., Bloomfield Hills, Mich., 2009—. Bd. chmn. High Prodn. Home Builders Coun. Nat. Assn. Home Builders; life trustee Nat. Housing Endowment. Chmn. policy adv. bd. Harvard U. Joint Ctr. Housing Studies, 2002; bd. trustees Nature Conservancy Tex. Office: Centex Corp 2728 N Hardwood St Dallas TX 75201-1516 also: PulteGroup Inc Ste 300 100 Bloomfield Hills Pkwy Bloomfield Hills MI 48304

ELLERY, JON CHRISTOPHER, literature and language professor; b. Texarkana, Tex., June 30, 1954; s. William Channing and Zenobia Katherine Ellery; m. Celia Elizabeth Norman, Aug. 9, 1976; children: Sarah Katherine, Benjamin Jennings, Elizabeth Claire. BFA, Ark. Tech U., Russellville, 1976; MA, U. Ark., Fayetteville, 1979; PhD, Tex. A&M U., College Station, 1989. Prof. English Angelo State U., Tex., 1990—. Fulbright lectr., rschr. U. Aleppo, Syria, 1999—2000. Co-translator (short stories) Whatever Happened to Antara, 2004; author: Quarry, 2005, All This Light We Live In, 2006. Recipient Tchg. Excellence award, Angelo State U., 2005. Mem.: ACLU, Tex. Inst. Letters, Tex. Assn. Creative Writing Tchrs., Am. Humor Studies Assn., Fulbright Assn., Phi Kappa Phi. Episcopalian. Office: Angelo State Univ 2601 W Ave N San Angelo TX 76909 Business E-Mail: cellery@angelo.edu.

ELLINGTON, CHARLES RONALD, lawyer, educator; b. Cuthbert, Ga., Sept. 3, 1941; s. Charles Bartlett and Annie Claire (Moore) E.; m. Jean Alice Spencer, Apr. 29, 1967; children: Gregory Spencer, Alicia Nicole. AB summa cum laude, Emory U., 1963; LL.B., U. Va., 1966; LL.M., Harvard U., 1978. Bar: Ga. 1967, D.C. 1967. Assoc. firm Sutherland, Asbill and Brennan, Atlanta, 1966-69; mem. law faculty U. Ga. Sch. Law, 1969—2009, prof. law, 1977—, Thomas R.R. Cobb prof. law, 1983-93, dean, 1987-93, J. Alton Hosch prof. law, 1993-99, A. Gus Cleveland prof. legal ethics and professionalism, 1999—2009, Josieh Meigs Disting. tchg. prof., 2007—09; A Gus Cleve. prof. Legal Ethics 2nd Professinalism & Joseph Weiqs Disting. Tchg.; prof. emeritus. On leave as scholar in residence U.S. Dept. Justice, Washington, 1979-80; reporter Standards of the Profession Com., State Bar of Ga., mem. formal adv. opinion bd. Harvard U. fellow in law and humanities, 1973—74. Mem.: Am. Law Inst. Avocation: hiking. Office: Univ Ga Sch Law Herty Dr Athens GA 30602 Business E-Mail: cre@uga.edu.

ELLINGWOOD, BRUCE RUSSELL, structural engineer, educator; b. Evanston, Ill., Oct. 11, 1944; s. Robert W. and Carolyn L. (Ehmen) E.; m. Lois J. Drager, June 7, 1969; 1 son, Geoffrey D. BSCE, U. Ill., 1968, MSCE, 1969, PhD, 1972. Registered profl. engr., D.C. Structural engr. Naval Ship Rsch. and Devel. Ctr., Bethesda, Md., 1972—75; rsch. structural engr., leader structural engring. group Ctr. Bldg. Tech., Nat. Bur. Standards, Washington, 1975—86; prof. civil engring. Johns Hopkins U., Balt., 1986—2000, chmn. dept., 1990—97; chmn. sch. civil and environ. engring. Ga. Inst. Tech., Atlanta, 2000—02, prof. civil engring., 2002—. Lectr., cons. Editor Jour. Structural Safety; mem. editl. bd. Engring. Structures, Probabilistic Engring. Mechanics; contbr. articles to profl. jours. Recipient Dural Research prize U. Ill., 1968, Nat. Capital award for Engring. Achievement D.C. Joint Council Engring. and Archtl. Socs., 1980, Walter L. Huber prize ASCE, 1980, Silver medal U.S. Dept. Commerce, 1980, Markwardt Rsch. prize Forest Products Rsch. Soc., 1988, Lifetime Achievement award Am. Inst. Steel Constrn., 2006; named Engr. of Yr. of U.S. Dept. Commerce, Nat. Soc. Profl. Engrs., 1986. Mem. ASCE (pres. Md. sect. 1998-99, disting. mem. 2010, State of Art in Civil Engring. award 1983, 88, Norman medal 1983, 98, Moisseiff award 1988, Walter P. Moore award 1999, Nathan M. Newmark medal 2006), Am. Concrete Inst., Am. Nat. Stds. Inst., Am. Inst. Steel Constrn. (T.R. Higgins lectureship 1988, Lifetime Achievement award 2006), Nat. Acad. Engring., Sigma Xi, Chi Epsilon, Tau Beta Pi. Presbyterian. Achievements include administered the secretariat of American National Standard Committee A58 on minimum design loads from 1977-84 and was responsible for coordinating and directing revisions to the A58 Standard that culminated in the publication of ANSI A58.1-1982 (now ASCE Standard 7), the first load standard in the U.S. to contain probability-based load combinations for limit states. Such load combinations now are used in Canada, the U.S. and in the Eurocodes now being developed in the common market. Was instrumental in the move by the steel industry toward limit states design. Office: Ga Inst Tech Sch Civil and Environ Engring Dept Civil Engring Atlanta GA 30332-0355 Home Phone: 770-496-5744; Office Phone: 404-894-1635. Business E-Mail: bruce.ellingwood@ce.gatech.edu.

ELLIOT, JARED, financial management consultant; b. Albany, NY, Oct. 15, 1928; s. Henry Melvin and Gladys Dolores (Richter) E.; children: Michael B., Lynn Elliot Sims, Blake R., Jared. B.C.E., Yale

U., 1950; MBA, Stanford U., 1955. Mgr. electronic data processing and mfg. scheduling Lenkurt Electric Co. Inc., San Carlos, Calif., 1955-58; sec., treas. Spectracoat Inc., San Carlos, 1958-61; mng. asso. mgmt. services dept. Arthur Young & Co., San Francisco, 1961-69; v.p. Tex. Gas Resources Corp., Owensboro, Ky., 1969—, treas., 1979-84; v.p. fin. Lightnet, New Haven, 1984-86, ret., 1987; pvt. practice fin. mgmt. cons., 1987—92. Bd. dirs. United Way, Owensboro, 1969-80, pres., 1972; bd. dirs. Community Concert Assn., Owensboro, 1974-77. Served with USN, 1950-53. Democrat.

ELLIOTT, DICK F., state legislator; b. Cassatt, SC, Sept. 26, 1937; m. Martin Oppenheimer; children: Marcy, Evan, Josh, Ali. Owner Elliott Realty Corp., 1959—; major owner Beachwood Golf Club, 1967—; developer, owner Eagle Nest Golf Club, 1970—; mem. Dist 36 SC House of Reps., 1982—92; mem. Dist. 28 SC State Senate, 1993—, mem. Agr. and Natural Resources Com., Fin. Com., Fish, Game and Forestry Com., Invitations Com. & Rules Com. Recipient Woman of Year, Westchester ORT, 1990, Women's Press Club, NY, 1991, Govt award, Westchester Cmty. Opportunity Prog., 1994, honoree, Open Door Med. Ctr., 1995, Careers for the Disabled award, 1996, Svc. award, NY.Jewish War Vet., 1997. Mem.: Mental Health Assn. (bd. mem.), Anti-Defamation League (bd. mem.), America Jewish Com. (vice pres.), Westchester League Women Voters (pres. mamaroneck), Westchester Munic Planning Fedn., Westchester Co. Village Off Assn. (former pres.). Democrat. Presbyterian. Mailing: PO Box 3626 North Myrtle Beach SC 29582 Office: 601 Gressette Bldg Columbia SC 29201 Home Phone: 843-249-1520, 803-771-8711; Office Phone: 843-249-1449, 803-212-6116. E-mail: DE@scsenate.org.

ELLIOTT, EFREM, state legislator; m. Tracie Elliott; 3 children. Grad., Ark. Law Enforcement Acad. Camden; B in Mass Commn., U. Ark., Pine Bluff. Mem. Dollarway Sch. Bd.; with Jefferson-Lincoln County Circuit Ct.; Staff Senator Hank Wilkins, Ark. State Senate; dir., security, 11th jud. Dist.; with, 6th Divsn.; chief of police Altheimer; with, Congressman Mike Ross US House of Representatives; mem. Advocates for Rural Edu.; founder Altheimer Working Together; chmn. Prevention Resource Ctr., Pastor-Parish Rels. Com., Saint James; founder Kops for Kids; pres. Jefferson County Habitat for Humanity; founder Crossroads Resource Ctr.; dir., Pub. Rels. Jefferson County Eco. Opportunity Commn.; dir., security, 6th Divsn. Circuit Ct.; with Pine Bluff; mem. Dist. 11 Ark. House of Representatives, 2011—. Democrat. Office: PO Box 566 Altheimer AR 72004 Office Phone: 870-550-2433. Business E-Mail: efremelliott@aol.com.

ELLIOTT, FRANK WALLACE, lawyer, educator; b. Cotulla, Tex., June 25, 1930; s. Frank Wallace and Eunice Marie (Akin) E.; m. Winona Trent, July 3, 1954 (dec. 1981); 1 child, Harriet Lindsey; m. Kay Elkins, Aug. 15, 1983. Student, N.Mex. Mil. Inst., 1947-49; BA, U. Tex., 1951, LLB, 1957. Bar: Tex. 1957, U.S. Supreme Ct. 1962, U.S. Ct. Mil. Appeals 1974, U.S. Dist. Ct. (no. dist.) Tex. 1987, U.S. Dist. Ct. (so. dist.) Tex. 2003, U.S. Ct. Appeals (5th cir.) 1988. Asst. atty. gen. State of Tex., 1957; briefing atty. Supreme Ct. Tex., 1957-58; prof. U. Tex. Law Sch., 1958-77; dean, prof. law Tex. Tech U. Sch. Law, 1977-80; pres. Southwestern Legal Found., 1980-86; ptnr. Baker, Mills & Glast, Dallas, 1987-88; of counsel Ramirez & Assocs., 1988—; dean Dallas/Ft. Worth Sch. Law, 1989-92; dean Sch. Law Tex. Wesleyan U., 1992-94, prof., dean emeritus, 1994—2013; prof. Sch. Law, TAMU, 2013—. Parliamentarian Tex. Senate, 1969-73; dir. rsch. Tex. Constl. Revision Commn., 1973 Author: Texas Judicial Process, 2d edit., 1977, Texas Trial and Appellate Practice, 2d edit., 1974, Cases on Evidence, 1980, West's Texas Forms, 20 vols., 1977—, West's Texas Practice, vol. 11, 1990, vol. 14, 1996. Served with U.S. Army, 1951-53, 73-74. Decorated Purple Heart. Mem. ABA, Judge Advs. Assn., Am. Judicature Soc., Am. Bar Found., Tex. Bar Found., Dallas Bar Found., Am. Law Inst., N.Mex. Mil. Inst. Alumni Hall of Fame. Home: 1609 Sunset Terr Fort Worth TX 76102 Office: 1515 Commerce St Fort Worth TX 76102-6572 Office Phone: 817-212-3926. Business E-Mail: felliott@law.tamu.edu.

ELLIOTT, JEAN ANN, retired library director; b. Martinsburg, W.Va., Jan. 18, 1933; d. Howard Hoffman and Dorothy Jean (Horn) E. AB in edn., Shepherd U., 1954; MS in libr. sci., Syracuse U., 1957; MS, Shippensburg U., Pa., 1974. Asst. libr. Fairmont U., W.Va., 1957-60; reference asst. U. Pitts., 1960-61; acting libr. Shepherd U., 1961-62, coord. libr. sci., 1962-97. Compiler Jefferson County Hist. mag., 1990. Nat. treas. Palatines of Am., Columbus, Ohio, 1986-88. Mem. ALA, AAUW, DAR (W.Va. treas. 1980-83, 86-89, 95-98, state regent 1998-2001, hon. state regent 2001—), W.Va. Libr. Assn. (election chmn. 1988-90), Jefferson County Hist. Soc., Nat. Soc. Daus. Am. Colonies (nat. libr. 1991-94, hon. state regent 1991—, nat. v.p., blue ridge sect., 2007-09, hon. nat. v.p. blue ridge sect. 2010-), Nat. Soc. Daus. 1812 (nat. libr. 1994-96), W.Va. Soc. Daus. 1812 (state pres. 1991-94, state pres. 2008-, hon. state pres. 1994—), Nat. Soc. Daus. Colonial Wars (state pres. 2001—), Alpha Beta Alpha (nat. exec. sec. 1968-76), Phi Kappa Phi. Presbyterian. Avocations: genealogy, travel, knitting, computers. Home: PO Box 1649 Shepherdstown WV 25443-1649

ELLIOTT, JOYCE, state legislator; b. Willisville, Ark., Mar. 20, 1951; 1 child, Elliott Barnes. BA, So. Ark. Univ., 1973; MA, Ouachita Baptist Univ., 1981. High sch. tchr. various sch. districts in Minn., Fla., Tex. & Ark.; dir. legis outreach SW region The College Bd.; mem. Ark. House of Reps., 2001—06; mem. Dist. 33 Ark. State Senate, 2009—, majority leader, 2009—. Bd. mem. Accelerate Ark., Am. Fedn. Teachers, City Yr. Little Rock, Just Communities Ctrl. Ark., MacArthur Mil. Mus., Nat. Commn. on Writing in America's Sch. & Coll., Women & Children First, Women's Action for New Directions Edn. Fund. Democrat. Mailing: PO Box 4248 Little Rock AR 72214 Office Phone: 501-568-3917. Business E-Mail: elliottj@arkleg.state.ar.us.

ELLIOTT, LARRY PAUL, radiologist, educator; b. Manhattan, Kans., Oct. 16, 1931; s. Leonard Paul and Mary Elizabeth (Myers) E.; m. Betty Lou Hawkins, June 23, 1956; children: Laurie Lou, Mary Elizabeth, Larry Paul. BS, U. Fla., 1954; MD, U. Tenn., 1957. Intern John Gaston Hosp., Memphis, 1957-58; resident in pediat. and pediat. cardiology U. Fla. Hosp., 1958-61; resident in cardiac pathology and cardiovasc. radiology U. Minn. Hosp., 1961-65; assoc. prof. cardiac radiology Washington U. Med. Sch., St. Louis, 1966-67; prof. cardiac radiology U. Fla. Med. Sch., 1967-76; prof. radiology, dir. divsn. cardiac radiology U. Ala. Med. Sch., Birmingham, 1976-81; prof., chmn. dept. radiology Georgetown U. Sch. Medicine, 1981—97, clin. prof., chmn. emeritus, 1996—; clin. prof. radiology Emory U. Med. Ctr., Atlanta, 1997—, Med. U. S.C., 1999—. Chmn. Fac. Practice Group, 1989—; clin. prof. Med. U. S.C., 1999—. Author: Pekannens, 1959, The X-Ray Diagnosis Heart Disease, 1968, 79; editor: Radiology, 1967—, Cardiovascular and Interventional Radiology, 1979—, The Fundamentals of Cardiac Imaging in Infants, Children and Adults, 1990; assoc. editor cardiovasc. sect. Taveras Radiology, 1986; contbr. over 200 articles to med. jours. Vol. Charleston Area Therapeutic Riding Group; camp counselor North Charleston Recreation Inner City Group; tutor Gethsemane's Cmty. Ctr., North Charleston, SC. Recipient Disting. Alumnus award U. Fla., 1981, Outstanding Alumnus award U. Tenn. Med. Sch., 1993; grantee cardiac radiology Nat. Heart Inst., 1968-76, Allied Health Profl. Act, 1970. Fellow N.Am. Soc. Cardiac Radiology (pres. 1977-78), Am. Coll. Cardiology; mem. Radiol. Soc. N.Am., Soc. Cardiac Angiography, Am. Heart Assn., Soc. Thoracic Radiology (founding mem., pres. faculty practice group 1989-93), Feline Freedom Coalition. Home: 2301 Berteau Dr Wake Forest NC 27587

ELLIOTT, LESTER FRANKLYN, plastic surgeon; b. Macon, Ga., Oct. 18, 1950; s. Sewell and Mary Grace E.; m. Elizabeth Wilkinson, May 30, 1981; children: Mary Grace, Elizabeth Ballard. BA, Princeton U., 1972; MD, Vanderbilt Sch. Med., Nashville, 1976. Cert. Am. Bd. Plastic Surgery, Am. Bd. Surgery, lic. Ga., Tenn., La. Resident gen. surgery Vanderbilt U. Hosp., 1976—78, Tulane U. Hosp., New Orleans, 1978—80, chief resident gen. surgery, 1980—81; resident plastic surgery Emory U. Hosp., Atlanta, 1981—83; instr. surgery La. State U., New Orleans, 1983—85, asst. clin. prof. surgery, 1985—87; clin. asst. prof. surgery Emory U., 1987—; cosmetic surgeon Atlanta Plastic Surgery, 1987—, pres. Ga., 1995—2004. Researcher in field. Contbr. articles to profl. jours. Bd. dirs. Atlanta Ballet, 1996—. Clin. orthopaedic fellow Sahlgranska Hosp., Gothenberg, Sweden, 1975. Fellow Am. Coll. Surgeons; mem. Am. Soc. Aesthetic Plastic Surgery, Am. Cleft Palate Assn., Am. Soc. Plastic and Reconstructive Surgeons, Am. Soc. Maxillo-Facial Surgeons, Southeastern Soc. Plastic and Reconstructive Surgeons, La. State Med. Soc., Surg. Assn. La., Ga. Surg. Soc., Ga. Plastic Surgery Soc., New Orleans Surg. Soc., Orleans Parish Med. Soc., Maurice J. Jurkiewicz Soc., Alton Ochsner Surg. Soc., Southern Surgical Assn., Oneiro Travel Club, Cap and Gown Club, Kappa Alpha. Avocations: travel, golf, bicycling, mountain climbing, reading, marathons, hunting. Office: Atlanta Plastic Surgery PC 975 Johnson Ferry Rd NE STE 100 Atlanta GA 30342-1618 Office Phone: 404-256-1311, 888-298-0835. Office Fax: 404-250-3380. Business E-Mail: felliott@atlplastic.com.

ELLIOTT, NORMAN L., gastroenterologist, educator; Grad., USAF Acad.; MD, Yale U., 1979. Diplomate Am. Bd. Internal Medicine, 1982, Am. Bd. Internal Medicine-gastroenterology, 1985. Resident internal medicine Emory Univ. Hosp., 1980—82; fellow gastroenterology Univ. of Ala., 1982—85, instr. digestive disease; team physician Atlanta Braves, 1992—; clin. asst. prof. Emory Univ., Morehouse Med. Sch. Pilot USAF; brig. gen. Ala. Air Nat. Guard. Mem.: ACP, AMA, Atlanta Med. Assn., Med. Assn. of Atlanta, Med. Assn. of Ga., Am. Gastroent. Assn., Am. Coll. of Gastroenterology, Am. Gastroenterology Assn. Office: Atlanta Gastroenterology Associates 550 Peachtree St NE Ste 1600 Atlanta GA 30308 Office Phone: 404-881-1094.

ELLIOTT, SAM, lawyer; BA, U. of South, 1978; JD, U. Tenn., 1981. Bar: Tenn., US Supreme Ct., US Ct. Appeals (6th cir.), US Ct. Appeals (11th cir.), US Dist. Ct. (eastern dist.) Tenn., US Tax Ct. Mem. Gearhiser, Peters, Cavett, Elliott & Cannon, PLLC, Chattanooga. Mem., chair Tenn. Hist. Commn. Fellow: Chattanooga Bar Found., Tenn. Bar Found., American Bar Found.; mem.: ABA, Justices Brock and Cooper American Inns of Ct. (sec. 2005—06), Fed. Bar Assn., Chattanooga Bar Assn. (bd. govs. 1997—2002, pres. 2001), Tenn. Legal Cmty. Found. (bd. mem.), Tenn. Bar Assn. (bd. govs. 2004—, v.p. 2008—09, pres.-elect 2009—10, pres. 2010—11). Office: Gearhiser, Peters, Cavett, Elliott & Cannon, PLLC 320 McCallie Ave Chattanooga TN 37402 Office Phone: 423-756-5171. Office Fax: 423-266-1605. E-mail: selliott@gearhiserpeters.com.

ELLIS, ALFRED WRIGHT (AL ELLIS), lawyer; b. Cleve., Aug. 26, 1943; s. Donald Porter and Louise (Wright) E.; m. Kay Genseke, June 1965 (div. 1976); 1 child, Joshua Kyle; m. Sandra Lee Fahey, Feb. 11, 1989. BA with honors, U. Tex., Arlington, 1965; JD, So. Meth. U., 1971. Bar: Tex., U.S. Dist. Ct. (no., so., ea. and we. dists.) Tex., U.S. Ct. Appeals (5th cir.), U.S. Supreme Ct.; cert. personal injury and civil trial lawyer, Internat. Acad. Trial Lawyers, Litig. Counsel America-Trial Lawyer Hon. Soc. Capt. U.S. Army, 1965—69; atty. Woodruff, Kendall & Smith, Dallas, 1972; ptnr. Woodruff & Ellis, Dallas; pvt. practice Dallas, 1983-96; of counsel Howie & Sweeney, 1996—2003, Sommerman & Quesada, 2003—. Instr. So. Meth. U. Law Sch. Trial Advocacy; past pres. Law Focused Edn., Inc. Past mem. City of Dallas Urban Rehab. Stds. Bd., Dallas Assembly, Salesmanship Club, Dallas; trustee Hist. Preservation League, 1992—94; tournament dir. Dallas Regional Golden Gloves Tournament, 1976—96; pres., bd. dirs. Dallas Coun. on Alcoholism, 1980; pres. Dallas All Sports Assn., 1980; bd. dirs. Dallas Habitat for Humanity, 1998—2002, 2005—08. Recipient award, Dallas Ind. Sch. Dist., 1971—83, Wall Street Jour. award, So. Meth. U. Law Sch., 1972, Hayward McMurray award, Dallas Jaycees, 1975—76, Spl. Recognition award, All Sports Assn., 1977, Cert. of Appreciation for Exceptional & Disting. Vol. Svc., Gov. Mark White, 1983, Cmty. Spirit award, Dallas Bus. Jour., 1993, Disting. Svc. award, Dallas All Sports Assn., 1993, Nancy Garms Meml. award for Outstanding Contbns. to Law Focus Edn., 1996—, Leon Jaworski Tchg. Excellence in Law award, 2002, Jim D. Bowmer Professionalism award, Coll. State Bar Tex., 2010; named Boss of Yr., Dallas Assn. Legal Secs., 1978, Best Lawyer in America, 2002—10; named one of Outstanding Young Men of Am., Jaycees, 1977, Nat.'s Leading Plaintiff Lawyers, Law Dragon, 2007. Fellow: Dallas Bar Found., Tex. Bar Found. (sustaining life, Dan R. Price Meml. award 2003, "D" Mag. Best Personal Injury Lawyers, Dallas 2003, Tex. Monthly Super Lawyers 2003—10), Dallas Assn. Young Lawyers (life); mem.: ATLA, Dallas Minority Bar Assn., William Mac Taylor Inn of Ct. (Judith Sinclair Cmty. Svc. award 2007), Tex. Legal Svcs. Ctr. (bd. dirs. 1999—2002), Tex. Ctr. for Legal Ethics and Professionalism (bd. dirs. 1999—, chmn. 2002—04), Coll. State Bar of Tex. (bd. dirs. 1997—99, Jim Bowmer Profl. award 2009), Am. Coll. Barristers, Tex. Equal Access to Justice Found. (bd. dirs. 1994—96), Tex. Trial Lawyers Assn. (bd. dirs. emeritus), Dallas Trial Lawyers Assn. (pres. 1977, Disting. Cmty. Svc. award 1990), Dallas Bar Assn. (bd. dirs. 1978, v.p. 1987—88, pres. 1990, Presdl. Citation award 2009), State Bar Tex. (bd. dirs. 1991—94, lectr. seminars, Excellence in Diversity award 1994, Outstanding 3d Yr. Dir. award, Judge Sam Williams Local Bar Leadership award), Legal Svcs. of North Tex. (bd. dirs., Outstanding Svc. award 1990), Million Dollar Advocates Forum, Am. Bd. Trial Advocates (sec.-treas. Dallas chpt. 1998, pres. 1999, diplomate, Dayl Found. Excellence award 2004, Dallas Habitat Humanity Family Svcs. award 2009, C. B. Bunkley Cmty. Svc. award 2009, Dallas Lawyers Aux. Justinian award 2010, Justinian award). Avocations: tennis, skiing. Office: 3811 Turtle Creek Blvd #1400 Dallas TX 75219-4461 Office Phone: 214-720-0720. Personal E-mail: al@textrial.com.

ELLIS, ANDREW KINGSLEY (ANDY ELLIS), aerospace defense company executive, former legislative staff member; b. Brookline, Mass., Mar. 16, 1959; s. Gordon Kingsley and Janet (Stewart) E.; m. Susan marie, Dec. 28, 1985; children: Meaghan, Sam, Cameron. BA, U. Vt., 1981; MA, U. So. Calif., 1984, PhD, 1988. Legis. asst. for nat. security affairs to Rep. Duncan Hunter US House of Representatives, Washington, 1985-87; profl. staff US House Armed Services Com., Washington, 1987-90, minority staff dir., 1990—95, staff dir., 1995—2000; v.p. integrated def. systems The Boeing Co., Washington, 2000—08, v.p. strategy Boeing Govt. Ops., 2008—. Bd. advs. ctr. for security policy, Washington, 1989—. Baseball/Soccer coach, Annadale boys and girls club, 1997—. Recipient fellowships, Herman Found., Haynes Found., Olin Found., U. So. Calif., 1982-85. Mem. Phi Beta Kappa. Avocations: golf, running, coaching. Office: Boeing Government Operations 1200 Wilson Blvd Arlington VA 22209

ELLIS, EDWARD R., career officer; BS in Bus. Mgmt., Va. Polytechnic Inst. and State U., 1968; MA in Bus. Stats., U. Ala., 1970; grad., Squadron Officer Sch., 1975, Air Command and Staff Coll., 1984, Air War Coll., 1986, Nat. Security Mgmt. Course, 1988, Nat. War Coll., Fort Lesley J. McNair, Washington, DC, 1991, Harvard Ukranian Nat. Security Program, John F. Kennedy Sch. Govt., Harvard U., 1999. Commd. 2d lt. USAF, 1971, advanced through grades to major gen., 1998; student, undergraduate pilot tng. Craig AFB, Ala., 1971—72; T-37 instr. pilot, 43rd Flying Tng. Squadron, later, flight examiner, 29th Flying Tng. Wing, 1972—77; F-4E pilot, asst. flight comdr. 18th Tactical Fighter Squadron, Elmendorf AFB, Alaska, 1977-80; sect. comdr., ops. officer for dir. student ops. Squadron Officer Sch., Maxwell AFB, Ala., 1980-83, exec. officer to comdt., 1980-83; F-4E pilot, asst. ops. officer then ops. officer 36th Tactical Fighter Squadron, Osan Air Base, Republic of Korea, 1984-86; exec. officer to comdr. 51st Tactical Fighter Wing, Osan Air Base, Republic of Korea, 1984-86; faculty instr., comdr. 3823rd Air Command and Staff Coll. Student Squadron, Maxwell AFB, 1986-88; comdr. 35th Flying Tng. Squadron, Reese AFB, Tex., 1988-90; chief Caribbean Basin br. then chief We. Hemisphere div. Directorate of Strategic Plans and Policy, Joint Staff, Pentagon, Washington, 1991-94; chief flying tng. div. Hdqs. Air Edn. and Tng. Command, Randolph AFB, Tex., 1994-95; comdr. 71st Flying Tng. Wing, Vance AFB, Okla., 1995-97; comdt. Squadron Officer Sch., Maxwell AFB, 1997; comdr. Air Force Accession and Tng. Schs., Maxwell AFB, 1997-99; dep. comdr. 5th Allied Tactical Air Force, Vicenza, Italy, 1999—2000, Combined Air Ops. Ctr. Seven, Larissa, Greece, 2000—01; comdr. Combined Task Force Operation Northern Watch, US European Command, Incirlik AB, Turkey, 2001—02; asst. chief of staff for ops. Hdqs. Allied Air Forces Southern Europe, NATO, Naples, Italy, 2002—04; comdr. 19th Air Force, Air Edn. and Tng. Command, Randolph AFB, Tex., 2004—. Decorated Defense Superior Svc. medal with two oak leaf clusters, Legion of Merit with oak leaf clusters, Meritorious Svc. medal with four oak leaf clusters, Air medal with oak leaf cluster, Aerial Achievement medal with oak leaf cluster, Air Force Commendation medal with oak leaf cluster, NATO medal with Bronze Star (Kosovo). Office: 12FTW/PA Randolph AFB TX 78150

ELLIS, JAMES A., JR., lawyer; b. Lubbock, Tex., Mar. 19, 1943; s. James Alvis and Myrle Alice (Peden) E.; m. Sandra Gay Gillespie, June 18, 1966; children: Claire Ellis Gentry, James Alvis III. BA, Tex. Tech U., 1965; JD, U. Tex., 1968. Bar: Tex. 1968, U.S. Dist. Ct. (no., so., ea. and we. dists.) Tex. 1969, U.S. Ct. Appeals 1970, U.S. Supreme Ct. 1980; cert. in civil trial law Tex. Bd. Legal Specialization. Law clk. to presiding judge U.S. Dist. Ct. (we. dist.) Tex., 1968—69; assoc. Carrington, Coleman Sloman & Blumenthal LLP, Dallas, 1970—74, ptnr., 1975—2008. Pres. Dallas Jr. Bar Assn., 1972. Fellow Tex. Bar Found., Dallas Bar Found.; mem. ABA, State Bar Tex., Dallas Bar Assn. Methodist. Office: 6440 N Central Expy Ste 750 Dallas TX 75206-4136 Office Phone: 214-217-0775. Business E-Mail: jellis@ellistierney.com.

ELLIS, JERRY, state legislator; b. Hugo, Okla., Dec. 11, 1946; s. Willie R.W. and Leona Harline Ellis; m. Cynthia Cox Ellis; 1 child, Tom. B in Animal Sci., Okla. State U., 1969. Laborer, cattle rancher Weyerhaeuser; co-founder, publisher Southeast Times Newspaper; mem. Dist. 1 Okla. House of Representatives, Okla., 2003—08; mem. Dist. 5 Okla. State Senate, 2008—. With armed forces, 1969—72. Recipient Outstanding Svc. award, Friend Working Men & Women award, McCurtain County Dem. Party, 2002. Mem.: Choctaw Electric & Western Farmers (bd. dir.), PACE Local 162, VFW Post 4777, Valliant First United Meth. Ch. (bd. trustees, chmn.), Idabel Rotary Club (pres.), Masonic Lodge 30. Democrat. Mailing: 2300 N Lincoln Blvd Rm 535 Oklahoma City OK 73105-4808 Home: PO Box 317 Valliant OK 74764-0317 Office Phone: 580-286-2628, 580-933-4930, 405-521-5614. Business E-Mail: ellis@oksenate.gov.

ELLIS, JOHN, retired school system administrator, writer; b. Amherst, Ohio, Sept. 15, 1929; s. Edward Pierson and Jean (Scott) E.; m. Carolyn Elizabeth Collier, Dec. 29, 1951; children: Linda Ellis McNeill, Jeanine Ellis Klausing, Jeanette Ellis Hale, John Edward. BS, Bowling Green State U., 1953; MA, Case Western Res. U., Cleve., 1958; EdD, Harvard U., 1964. Tchr. pub. schs., Lorain, Ohio, 1953-54, prin., 1957-61, from asst. supt. to supt. schs. Massillon, Ohio, 1963-66, supt. schs. Lakewood, Ohio, 1966-71, Columbus, Ohio, 1971-77; exec. dep. commr. edn. U.S. Office Edn., Washington, 1977-80; supt. schs. pub. schs., Austin, Tex., 1980-90; commr. NJ Dept. Edn., 1990—92. Adj. prof. ednl. adminstrn. Ohio State U., Columbus, 1971-77. Author: Bonville Search, 2006. With USAF, 1947-49, 54-57. Recipient Massillon Young Man of Yr. award, 1965; named to Saturday Rev. Honor Roll, 1977. Mem. Rotary, Phi Delta Kappa, Pi Kappa Alpha, Phi Alpha Theta, Kappa Delta Pi, Gamma Theta Upsilon. Home: 631Lakeview Blvd AptC407 New Braunfels TX 78130

ELLIS, JOSEPH NEWLIN, retired wholesale distribution executive; b. Tenn., Oct. 19, 1928; s. Richard M. and Pearl A. (Fuqua) E.; m. Barbara Harpster, Sept. 17, 1955; 1 child, Patricia Anne. BS, Northwestern U., 1954. Co-founder LaSalle-Deitch Co., Inc., Elkhart, Ind., 1963, exec. v.p., 1969-72, pres., CEO, 1972—89, chmn. of the bd., CEO, 1989-94; bd. dirs. Decorator Industries Inc., 1993—2011, chmn. audit com.; ret., 1994. With U.S. Army, 1950-52. Home: 1160 Benders Ferry Rd Gallatin TN 37066-5703

ELLIS, LESTER NEAL, JR., lawyer; b. Washington, Aug. 1, 1948; s. Lester Neal and Marie (Brooks) E. BS, U.S. Mil. Acad., 1970; JD, U. Va., 1975. Bar: Va. 1975, U.S. Ct. Appeals (5th cir.) 1977, D.C. 1978, U.S. Ct. Appeals (4th and D.C. cirs.) 1979, U.S. Ct. Appeals (11th cir.) 1982, N.C. 1985, U.S. Supreme Ct. 2000, U.S. Dist. Ct. (ea., mid., we. dists.) N.C., U.S. Dist. Ct. (ea., we. dists.) Va., U.S. Ct. Claims. Trial atty. litig. divsn. Office of JAG, U.S. Dept. Army, Washington, 1975-78; assoc. Hunton & Williams, Richmond, Va., 1978-84, ptnr. Raleigh, NC, 1984—2010, Ellis & Anthony Wake Forest, NC, 2010—. Maj. U.S. Army, 1970-78, col. USAR, 1993-99. Recipient Judge Paul Brosman award U.S. Ct. Mil. Appeals, 1975. Mem.: ABA (chair tort and trial practice steering com., editor-in-chief Tort Source, chair comml. torts commn., chair trial techniques com., tort and ins. practice sect., editor-in-chief Tort and Ins. Law Jour., coun. mem., sect. coun.), NC Bar Assn. (bd. govs., exec. com.), D.C. Bar Assn. (Wake County bd. elections 1986—93, chmn. 1987—93, ct. rules com.), Va. Bar Assn. (spl. issues com. 1982), Phi Kappa Phi. Republican. Presbyterian. Office Phone: 919-562-9925. Business E-Mail: ellis@ellisanthony.com.

ELLIS, MARTHA MCCRACKEN, academic administrator, psychology professor; b. Little Rock, July 29, 1952; d. Mark Maurice and Dorothy Patrina (Carson) McCracken; m. George Elliot Ewing Jr., Apr. 17, 1981 (div. Jan. 1990); m. Steve Erwin Ellis, Oct. 5, 1991; children: Clark Thomas, Cliff Martin. BA, Am. Christian Coll., 1974; MS in Devel. Cognitive Psychology, U. Tex., Dallas, 1979; postgrad., Columbia U., 1984-87; PhD in Higher Edn., U. North Tex. Cert.

eating disorders psychotherapist. Counselor, instr. Eastfield Coll., Mesquite, Tex., 1979-81, adj. prof., 1980-86; counselor Bell and Howell, Irving, Tex., 1984-86; provost, prof. psychology Collin County CC, Plano, Tex., 1986—2000, dir. staff, program and organizational devel., 1991—2000; postdoc SUNY, 1998; pres. Tex. State Tech. Coll., Waco, Tex., 2000—02, Lee Coll., Baytown, Tex., 2002—08; assoc. vice chancellor cmty. coll. partnerships U. Tex. Sys., 2008—; adj. prof. ednl. adminstrn. U. Tex. Austria, 2008—. Author: Laboratory Manual General Psychology, 1989, Life Span Psychology, 1991; (with others) Enhancing Quality of Undergraduate Education in Psychology, 1992; contbr. articles to jours. Advisor Mental Health Adv. Bd., McKinney, Tex., 1987-90; vice chairperson, trustee Collin County Mental Health and Mental Retardation, Plano, 1991-95, chairperson, 1993—95; bd. mem. Baytown C. of C., San Jacinto Meth. Hosp., Rotary Club, Baytown/West Chambers County Econ. Devel. Recipient Outstanding Prof. award Minnie Stevens Piper Found., 1987, Disting. Prof. award Phi Theta Kappa, 1989, Nat. Teaching Excellence U. Tex., 1989, 90. Mem. AACD, APA, Am. Psychol. Soc., N.Y. Acad. Scis., Commn. on Colls. (commr. 2003-09), Assn. Tex. Colls. and Univs. (pres. 2005-08). Avocations: aerobics, gardening, travel. Office: U Tex Sys 601 Colorado St Austin TX 78701-2982 Office Phone: 512-499-2982, 512-579-5087. Business E-Mail: mellis@utsystem.edu.

ELLIS, MICHAEL, law clerk; AB in History, Dartmouth Coll., Hanover, NH, 2006; JD, Yale U., New Haven, 2011. Assoc. dir. strategy Bush-Cheney '04, 2004; assoc. dir. office strategic initiatives The White House, Washington, 2006—07; dep. dir. strategy Romney for Pres., Inc., 2007—08; rschr. Rove & Co., 2008—09; summer assoc. Cooper & Kirk PLLC, 2009; interim assoc. Jones Day, 2010—11; law clk. to the Honorable Amul R. Thapar US Dist. Ct. Ea. Dist. Ky., Covington, 2011—12; law clk. to the Honorable Jeffery S. Sutton US Ct. Appeals for 6th Cir., 2012—. Lt. USNR, 2007—. Named one of 30 Under 30 in Law & Policy, Forbes, 2011. Home: 304 S West St Alexandria VA 22314-5916

ELLIS, MONTA, professional basketball player; b. Jackson, Miss., Oct. 26, 1985; s. Rosa Ellis. Diploma, Lanier HS, Jackson, Miss., 2005. Guard Golden State Warriors, Calif., 2005—12, Milw. Bucks, 2012—13, Dallas Mavericks, 2013—. Named EA Sports Player of Yr., 2005, Mr. Basketball, Miss., 2005, Nat. Co-Player of Yr., Parade Mag., 2005, Most Improved Player, NBA, 2007. Achievements include leading the NBA in: minutes, 2010, 2011. Office: Dallas Mavericks The Pavilion 2909 Taylor St Dallas TX 75226*

ELLIS, RICHARD W., lawyer; b. Raleigh, NC, Apr. 20, 1942; AB, U. N.C., 1964, JD with high honors, 1969. Bar: N.C. 1969. Mem. Ellis & Winters, Raleigh. Assoc. editor N.C. Law Rev., 1968-69. With USNR, 1964-66. Mem. Am. Coll. Trial Lawyers, Interant. Assn. Def. Counsel, Def. Rsch. Inst., N.C. Assn. Def. Attys., Order of Coif. Office: Ellis & Winters LLP PO Box 33550 Raleigh NC 27636 Office Phone: 919-865-7007. Business E-Mail: dick.ellis@elliswinters.com.

ELLIS, RODNEY G., state legislator; b. Houston, Apr. 7, 1954; m. Licia Green-Ellis; 4 children. BA, Tex. So. U.; MPA, Lyndon B. Johnson Sch. Pub. Affairs; JD, U. Tex. Law Sch. Adminstrv. asst. to William Hobby Office of Lt. Gov., Tex., 1976—80; atty. to Chief Justice John Phillips 3rd Ct. Appeals, Austin, 1980—81; legal coun. to commr. Buddy Temple Tex. Railroad Commn., 1981; chief of staff to Rep. Mickey Leland US House of Representatives, 1981—83; former mem. Houston City Coun.; counsel Phillips, King, Smith & Wright Law Firm, 1985—88; mem. Dist 13 Tex. State Senate, Tex., 1990—, pres. pro tempore Tex., 1999—2000; ptnr. Solar & Ellis, 1991—94; atty. of coun. McGlinchey Stafford, 1996—2000; chmn. Apex Securities, Inc.; ptnr. Rice Fin. Products Co.; shareholder The Tagos Group; of counsel Reaud, Morgan & Quinn. Recipient Des. Porres Scholar, 1972—73, EE Worthing Sch., 1975, Lyndon B Johnson Sch. Pub. Affairs Fellow, 1975—77, Earl Warren Legal Trng. Fellow, 1977—94, Houston's Fourth Black City Coun. Mem. Mem.: Houston Intrnet. U. (bd. mem.), Nat. Bar Assn., State Bar of Tex. Democrat. Protestant. Office: 440 Louisiana Ste 575 Houston TX 77002 also: PO Box 12068 Capitol Station Austin TX 78711 also: 2440 Texas Parkway Ste 110 Missouri City TX 77489 also: 10613 Bellaire Blvd Bldg A Ste 126B Houston TX 77072 Office Phone: 713-236-0306, 512-463-0113. Office Fax: 713-236-0604, 512-463-0006.

ELLIS, THOMAS L., neurosurgeon, educator; married; 4 children. MD, U NC Sch. Medicine, 1993. Cert. Am. Bd. Neurological Surgery. Resident U. Fla., 1993—2000; asst. prof., co-dir., Deep Brain Stimulation Program, Residency Program assoc. Dir. Wake Forest U. Sch. Medicine. Mem. Gamma Knife Ctr., 1999—. Contbr. several articles to profl. jours. Office: Wake Forest U Sch Medicine 300 Medical Center Blvd Winston Salem NC 27157 Office Phone: 336-716-6438. Office Fax: 336-716-3065.

ELLIS, THOMAS SELBY, III, federal judge; b. Bogota, Colombia, May 15, 1940; U.S., 1951; 2 children. BSE, Princeton U., 1961; JD magna cum laude (Knox fellow), Harvard U., 1969; diploma in law, Magdalen Coll., Oxford, Eng., 1970. Assoc. Hunton & Williams, Richmond, Va., 1970—76, ptnr., 1976—87; judge US Dist. Ct. (ea. dist.) Va., Alexandria, 1987—2007, sr. judge, 2007—. Temp. mem. sr. common rm. U. Coll., Oxford, 1984; lectr. law Coll. William & Mary, Williamsburg, Va., 1981—83; spkr. in field. Mem. adv. coun. dept. astrophysics Princeton U., 1984—. USN, 1961—66. Office: US Dist Court 401 Courthouse Sq Alexandria VA 22314-5704

ELLIS, TYRONE, state legislator; b. Starkville, Miss., Jan. 31, 1946; m. Arella Rena; children: Stephen, Stephanie. Mem. Dist. 38 Miss. House of Reps., 1980—; mem. Miss. Legis. Black Caucus; ins. exec. & corp. cons.; owner Comml.-Residential Constrn. Co. & Housing Devel. Corp. Pastor Mt. Olivet Mb Ch. Mem.: NAACP, Miss. Arts Handicapped, Moor High Booster Club, Mason. Democrat. Baptist. Mailing: PO Box 892 Starkville MS 39760 Office Phone: 662-324-5433. E-mail: tellis@house.ms.gov.

ELLISON, JAMES OLIVER, federal judge; b. St. Louis, Jan. 11, 1929; s. Jack and Mary (Patton) E.; m. Joan Roberts Ellison, June 7, 1950; 1 son, Scott. Student, U. Mo., Columbia, 1946-48; BA, LL.B., U. Okla., 1951. Bar: Okla. Pvt. practice law, Red Fork, Okla., 1953-55; ptnr. Boone, Ellison & Smith, Davis & Minter, 1955-79; judge U.S. Dist. Ct. (no. dist.) Okla., Tulsa, 1979—, chief justice, now sr. judge. Trustee Hillcrest Med. Center, Institution Programs, Inc.; elder Southminster Presbyterian Ch. Served to capt., inf. AUS, 1951-53. Mem. ABA, Okla. Bar Assn., Tulsa County Bar Assn., Alpha Tau Omega. Office: US Dist Ct The Fed Bldg 224 S Boulder Ave Tulsa OK 74103-3006

ELLISON, KEITH P., federal judge; b. New Orleans, Apr. 29, 1950; BA summa cum laude, Harvard U., 1972; BA 1st class honors, Oxford U., Eng., 1974; JD, Yale U., 1976. Bar: Okla. 1979, Tex. 1985. Law clk. to Hon. Justice Harry A. Blackmun U.S. Supreme Ct., 1977-78; law clk. to Hon. J. Skelly Wright U.S. Ct. Appeals (D.C. cir.), 1976-77; ptnr. Baker & Botts, L.L.P., Houston; pvt. practice Houston, 1978—99; judge US Dist. Ct. (so. dist.) Tex., Houston, 1999—. Editor Yale Law Jour., 1975-76. Rhodes scholar. Mem. ABA, State Bar Tex., Houston Bar Assn. Office: US Dist Ct US Courthouse 515 Rusk Ave Houston TX 77002 Office Phone: 713-250-5806.

ELLISON, LOIS TAYLOR, internist, educator, medical association administrator; b. Ft. Valley, Ga., Oct. 28, 1923; d. Robert James and Annie Maude (Anderson) Taylor; m. Robert Gordon Ellison, Feb. 11, 1945; children: Robert Gordon, Gregory Taylor, Mark Frederick, James Walton, John Charles. BS, U. Ga., 1943; MD, Med. Coll. Ga., 1950. Fellow, Univ. Hosp., Augusta, Ga., 1950-51; mem. faculty Med. Coll. Ga., Augusta, 1951—, prof. medicine and surgery, 1968—2000, assoc. dean, 1974-75, provost, 1975-84, assoc. v.p. planning (hosps. and clins.), 1984—2000, prof. emeritus medicine and surgery, 2000—, med. historian in residence, 2000—, provost emeritus, 2000—. Attending VA Med. Ctr., Augusta; civilian cons. Eisenhower Army Med. Ctr., Fort Gordon, Ga.; mem. coal mine health research adv. council Nat. Inst. Occupational Safety and Health, 1972-75; bd. dirs. East Central Ga. Health Systems Agy., 1976-80, treas., 1978—80; bd. dirs. Oak Ridge Associated Univs., 1979-84; mem. adv. council Univ. Systems Ga., 1975-84; mem. exec. com. Ga. Health Coordinating Council, 1980 Contbr. articles to profl. jours. Bd. dirs. United Way Greater Augusta, 1975-78, chair div. hosp. and health, 1978, chair div. colls. and univs., 1980; mem. adminstrv. bd. Trinity-on-the-Hill United Methodist Ch., Augusta, 1974-77, mem. pastor-parish com., 1978—90, 1998-2001. Recipient: Hall of Fame Alumni award, U. Sys. Ga. Found. Regents, 2009, NIH Rsch. Career award, Lifetime Achievement award Med. Coll. Ga. Sch. Medicine, 1996, Pres. award, Will Ross medal, Am. Lung Assn., 1998, Gov. award Historic Preservation Stewartship, 2004, Sprit of MCG award, 2010, MCG U., 2010, Career award, Lifetime Achievement award, Ga. Health Scis. U., 2011; named Vessel of Life, 2005; included in NIH Nat. Libr. Medicine exhbn., 2003. Fellow Am. Coll. Chest Physicians; mem. Am. Physiol. Soc., Am. Med. Women's Assn., AMA, Assn. Am. Med. Colls., Am. Lung Assn. (bd. dir. 1974—88, sec. 1982-85, pres.-elect 1985-86, pres. 1986-87), Am. Heart Assn. (pres. Ga. affiliate chpt. 1982-83, bd. dir. 1979—87), So. Soc. Clin. Investigation, Am. Lung Assn. of Ga. (pres. 1984-85), Ga. Heart Assn. Home Phone: 706-210-7816; Office Phone: 706-721-4013. Business E-Mail: ellisonl@gru.edu.

ELLISON, LUTHER FREDERICK, oil industry executive; b. Monroe, La., Jan. 2, 1925; s. Luther and Gertrude (Hudson) E.; m. Frances Williams, July 18, 1948 (dec.); children; Constance Elizabeth, Carolyn Williams; m. Patsy Hunter, Nov. 23, 1996. Student, Emory U., 1943-44; BS in Petroleum Engring., Tex. A&M U., 1949, BS in Geol. Engring., 1950. Registered profl. engr., Tex., La. Jr. petroleum engr. Sun Prodn. Co., Kilgore and McAllen, Tex., 1950-52, area petroleum engr. Garcia Field, Tex., 1952-54, Delhi (La.) chief engr., 1954—60, asst. region supt. Dallas, 1960-62, dist. drilling mgr., engr. Corpus Christi, 1962-63, dist. engr. McAllen, 1963-65, supr. engring. Dallas, 1965-66, div. chief petroleum engr., 1966-70, regional mgr. engring., 1970-75, region mgr., 1975-78, dir. devel., 1978-80, v.p. devel., 1980-84; div. v.p., dir. Sun Exploration and Prodn. Co., 1984-86, pres., bd. dirs., 1986—, Dallas C. of C., 1975—88; pres., chief exec. officer Oil & Gas Experts, Inc., Dallas, 1986—, Am. Energy Enterprises Inc., Dallas, 1988—. Pres., dir., mem. exec. com. Nabors-Sun Drilling Co.; dir., mem. exec. com. East Tex. Salt Water Disposal Co.; owner, CEO, pres. Oil & Gas Experts Inc., 1986; spkr. and writer in field. V.p. Northwood Jr. H.S. PTA, Dallas, 1967—68, pres., 1968—69; elder, trustee Preston Hollow Presbyn. Ch. Found.; sr. trustee, 2005—; bd. dirs. Glen Lakes Assn. Lt. j.g. USN, 1943—46. Mem. Tex.-Mid-Continent Oil and Gas Assn. (litig. mem.; Outstanding Achievement award 1964, chmn. area 1964-65, mgr. north region, operating com., Outstanding Performance award 1985—), Am. Petroleum Inst., Soc. Petroleum Engrs., Dallas Engrs. Club, Petroleum Engrs. Club, Dallas Petroleum Club, Park City Club, Northwood Club (Dallas), Lions Club, Premier Club (Dallas), Parents League, Sigma Alpha Epsilon (pres. 1944-45). Office: c/o McKinnon & Assoc Mr Jeff Lyon 10000 N Central Expy Ste 1350 Dallas TX 75231 Office Phone: 214-696-1922.

ELLISON, MARVIN, retail executive; BBA in Mktg., U. Memphis; MBA, Emory U. Various mgmt. and exec. positions including dir., assets protection Target Stores, 1987—2002; joined Home Depot, Inc., 2002, v.p., loss prevention, 2002—04, v.p., global logistics, 2004—05, sr. v.p., global logistics, 2005—06, pres., Northern Divsn., 2006—08, exec. v.p., US Stores, 2008—. Mem. KaBOOM. Office: The Home Depot Inc 2455 Paces Ferry Rd Atlanta GA 30339 Office Phone: 770-433-8211. Office Fax: 770-384-2356. Business E-Mail: marvin_ellison@homedepot.com.

ELLMERS, RENEE JACISIN, United States Representative from North Carolina, nurse; b. Ironwood, Mich., Feb. 9, 1964; m. Brent Ellmers; 1 child, Ben. BS in Nursing, Oakland U., 1990. Surgical intensive care nurse Beaumont Hosp., Mich.; clin. dir. Trinity Wound Care Ctr., Dunn, NC; mem. US Congress from 2nd NC Dist., Washington, 2011—, US House Agrl. Com., Washington, 2011—, US House Fgn. Affairs Com., Washington, 2011—, US House Small Bus. Com., Washington, 2011—. V.p. cmty. devel. C. of C.; bd. mem. Betsy Johnson Hosp. Found., Harnett County Nursing Home Com.; mem. Dunn, NC Planning Bd., 2006—10, chair, 2008—10. Republican. Roman Catholic. Office: US House of Representatives 426 Cannon House Office Bldg Washington DC 20515 Office Phone: 202-225-4531. Office Fax: 202-225-5662.*

ELLSWEIG, PHYLLIS LEAH, retired psychotherapist; b. Irvington, NJ, Apr. 19, 1927; d. Sumar and Jeanette (Geffner) Schwartz; m. Martin Richard Ellsweig, Dec. 25, 1947; children: Bruce, Steven. BS, East Stroudsburg U., Pa., 1947; EdM, Lehigh U., 1966, EdD, 1972. Tchr. Stroud Union High Sch., 1963-66; guidance counselor East Stroudsburg (Pa.) Schs., 1966-68; asst. prof. edn. East Stroudsburg U., 1968; staff psychologist, outpatient supr. Mental Health Center Carbon, Monroe and Pike Counties, Stroudsburg, Pa., 1968-80; pvt. practice in psychotherapy and clin. hypnosis Stroudsburg, 1969-87. Mem. staff Pocono Hosp., 1968—80; pub. spkr. in field; cons. to schs. and pvt. orgns.; tchr. adult edn., Palm Beach County, Fla. Mem. Am. Soc. Clin. Hypnosis, Internat. Soc. Hypnosis, NOW (profl. cons. 1973—). Home: 5500 NW 69th Ave Apt 304 Lauderhill FL 33319-7269

ELLWANGER, THOMAS JOHN, lawyer; b. Summit, NJ, Feb. 26, 1949; s. James Warren and Lorean (Nicholson) E.; m. Sabine S. Ellwanger; children: James Hunter, Margaret Lorean, Stephanie M. Sperando, Jennifer A. Bell. BA, Northwestern U., 1970; JD, U. Fla., 1974. Bar: Fla. 1975, U.S. Dist. Ct. (mid. dist.) Fla. 1976, U.S. Ct. Appeals (11th cir.) 1976, U.S. Dist. Ct. (so. dist.) Fla. 1977, U.S. Tax Ct. Mem. Fowler, White, Gillen, Boggs, Villareal & Banker P.A. (now Fowler, White, Boggs, Banker P.A.), Tampa, Fla., 1975—. Instr. law U. Fla., Gainesville, 1975; adj. prof. Stetson U. Coll. Law, 1997-2000. Editor: Gadsden County Times, 1970-72. Fellow Am. Coll. Trust and Estate Counsel, Fla. Bar (cert. tax lawyer), Hillsborough County Bar Assn. (chmn. com. probate liaison 1985-86, real property probate and trust law sect. 1987-89, 2004-05), Tampa Bay Estate Planning Counsel (pres. 1994-95). Avocations: music, literature, sports. Office: Fowler White Boggs Banker PA 501 E Kennedy Blvd Ste 1700 Tampa FL 33602-5239 Home Phone: 813-250-1606; Office Phone: 813-222-1161. E-mail: tellwang@fowlerwhite.com.

ELLWOOD, SUSIE, publishing executive; b. Ark., 1952; m. Bill Ellwood; 6 children. BSE in Bus., Arkansas State U. Dir., sales, dir., mktg. Nat. Investors Life Ins. Co., Little Rock; v.p., dir., mktg. Arkansas Gazette, Little Rock; various mktg. positions Gannett Co., Inc., Detroit, 1991, v.p., market devel., newspaper divsn., exec. v.p., gen. mgr. USA Today, 2011—12; exec. v.p., gen. mgr. Detroit Media Partnership, 2006—09, CEO, 2009—11; publisher Austin American Statesman & The Statesman Co. Cox Media Group, Austin, 2012—. Bd. dirs. Internat. Newsmedia Mktg. Assn. North America (INMA), 2011—. Mem. CATCH. Recipient Lifetime Achievement award, NAA MD&P Fedn., Disting. Mktg. award, President's Ring award, Gannett Co., Inc.; named Gannett Mgr. of Yr., 2009 Office: Cox Media Group 305 South Congress Ave Austin TX 78704

ELMES, DAVID GORDON, psychologist, educator; b. Newton, Mass., Feb. 15, 1942; s. Leslie and Ruth (Adams) E.; m. Anne Louise Lawrence, June 7, 1963; children: Matthew David, Jennifer Anne. BA, U. Va., Charlottesville, 1964, MA, 1966, PhD, 1967. Mgmt. trainee C & P of Va., 1963; asst. prof. psychology Washington and Lee U., Lexington, Va., 1967-71, assoc. prof., 1971-74, prof., 1975—2007, prof. emeritus, 2007—, head dept. psychology, 1990-2000, co-dir. cognitive sci., 1987-2000. Rsch. assoc. Human Performance Ctr., U. Mich., 1973-74; vis. fellow Univ. Coll., Oxford U., Eng., 1987. Author: Readings in Experimental Psychology, 1978; contbr. articles to profl. jours. Fellow Assn. Psychol. Sci., Va. Acad. Sci.; mem. Psychonomic Soc., Coun. on Undergrad. Rsch. (past pres.), Phi Beta Kappa. Office: Washington and Lee U Dept Psychology Lexington VA 24450-0303 Business E-Mail: elmesd@wlu.edu.

ELMORE, BRUCE ALEXANDER, JR., lawyer; b. Asheville, NC, Nov. 1, 1952; s. Bruce Alexander and Sadie June Elmore; m. Virginia Anne Healy, Nov. 4, 2006; m. Martha Parker, Dec. 28, 1974 (div. Dec. 15, 1990); children: Scott Alexander, Rebecca Anne. BA, U. NC, Chapel Hill, 1974, JD, 1976. Bar: NC 1976. Ptnr. The Elmore Law Firm P.A., Asheville, 1976—2006, 2008—, Cloninger, Elmore, Hensley &Searson PLLC, Asheville, 2006—08. Mem.: WNC ACLU Bd., NC ACLU Bd. (pres. 2006—08), Million Dollar Advocates Forum, Am. Assn. Justice (sustaining mem., NC Super Lawyers award 2012), NC Advocates Justice (benefactor). Liberal. Avocation: motorcycle travel. Home: 169 Windsor Rd Asheville NC 28804 Office: Elmore Law Firm PA 53 N Market St Ste 100 Asheville NC 28801 Office Phone: 828-253-1492. Office Fax: 828-232-2017. Business E-Mail: elmore@theelmorelawfirm.com.

ELROD, BEN MOODY, academic administrator; b. Rison, Ark., Oct. 13, 1930; s. Benjamin Searcy and Frances Othello (Sadler) E.; m. Betty Lou Warren, Aug. 7, 1951; children: Cynthia Lou, William Searcy. BA, Ouachita Baptist U., 1952; ThD, Southwestern Bapt. Theol. Sem., 1962; EdD, Ind. U., 1975. Ordained to ministry Baptist Ch., 1950; pastor First Bapt. Ch., Atkins, Ark., 1951-53, Tioga, Tex., 1955-57, Marlow, Okla., 1957-60, South Side Bapt. Ch., Pine Bluff, Ark., 1960-63; pres. Oakland City (Ind.) Coll., 1968-70, Georgetown (Ky.) Coll., 1978-83, Ind. Colls. of Ark., 1983-88; v.p. devel. Ouachita Bapt. U., Arkadelphia, Ark., 1963-68, 70-78, pres., 1988-97, chancellor, 1998—. Commr. Ark. Econ. Devel. Commn., 2002—09, chmn., 2007; vis. lectr. in field; cons. in higher edn. Contbr. articles to religion jours. Page U.S. Ho. of Reps., 1946-47; trustee Clark County (Ark.) Hosp., 1973-77, chmn., 1975-77; trustee Ark. Bapt. Med. System, 1978, 1989-2001. Recipient Disting. alumnus award, Ouachita Bapt. U., Centinnial achievement award, disting. alumnus award, Southwestern Bapt. Theol. Sem. Mem. Nat. Assn. Ind. Colls. and Univs. (chmn. tax policy commn. 1993), Ark. State C. of C. (bd. dirs. 1990-98), Assn. So. Bapt. Colls. and Schs. (pres. 1996-97), Consortium for Global Edn. (chmn. bd. dirs. 1997-99, mem. exec. com. bd. dirs. 1997-2002). Achievements include having Ben M. Elrod Center for Family and Community at Ouachita Baptist U. named in his honor. Office: Ouachita Bapt Univ Elrod Ctr for Family and Cmty Box 3790 Ouachita Sta Arkadelphia AR 71923-3221 also: 450 Chimney Rock Dr Sherwood AR 72120-5846 Office Phone: 870-245-5320.

ELROD, P. CHRISTOPHER, wholesale distribution executive; BS in Computer Sci., U. SC, Columbia, 1986. Sys. programmer SCE&G, 1987—88; automation engr. Fluor Daniel, 1988—93; global project mgr. MCI, Inc., 1993—2000; v.p. info. sys. ScanSource, Inc., 2000—. Bd. dirs. Brillig Sys. Inc., 1994—. Office: ScanSource Inc 6 Logue Ct Greenville SC 29615 Office Phone: 864-288-2432. Office Fax: 864-288-1165.

EL-SAYED, MOSTAFA AMR, chemistry professor; b. Zifta, Egypt, May 8, 1933; s. Amr and Zakia (Ahmed) El-Sayed; m. Janice Jones, Mar. 15, 1957; children— Lyla, Tarric, James, Dorea Jehan, Ivan Homer BSc, Ein Shams U., Cairo, 1953; PhD, Fla. State U., 1959; Dr honoris causa, Hebrew U., 1993. Research fellow Yale U., 1957; research fellow Harvard U., 1959-60, Calif. Inst. Tech., 1960, 61; asst. prof. chemistry UCLA, 1961-64, assoc. prof. chemistry, 1964-67, prof. chemistry, 1967-94; Julius Brown prof. Ga. Inst. Tech., 1994—, Regent prof., 2000—. Vis. prof. Am. U. Beirut, 1967-68; fgn. prof. U. So. Paris, Orsay, 1976; Sherman Fairchild disting. scholar Calif. Inst. Tech., 1980; cons. Space Tech. Lab, 1962-63, Electro-Optical System, 1963-66, N.Am. Aviation, 1964-65, Navy Electronics Labs., 1969-73, Ford Research Labs., 1970, Northrop Corp., 1979-81; mem. adv. bd. Alexandria Research Ctr., 1979-83; trustee Associated Univs., 1989-92; mem. steering com. Internat. Ctr. Pure and Applied Chemistry, Trieste, Italy, 1988; mem. adv. com. chemistry divsn. NSF, 1990-93; fgn. coun., Inst. Molecular Sci., Okazaki, Japan, 1994; bd. on chem. scis. and technology, NRC 1994-97. Mem. adv. bd. Chem. Physics, Chem. Physics Letters and Accounts of Chem. Research; chief editor Journal Physical Chemistry, 1980-contbr. numerous articles to profl. jours., chpts. to books Mem. chemistry grant selection com. NRC of Can.; mem. chemistry research evaluation panel for directorate of chem. scis. Air Force Office of Sci. Research; mem. rev. com. San Francisco Laser Ctr., radiation lab Notre Dame U., dept. energy and environment Lawrence Berkeley Lab.; mem. NRC com. to survey opportunities in chemistry; mem. vis. com. Brookhaven Nat. Lab., 1986—. Recipient Disting. Teaching award UCLA, 1964, Fresenius nat. award in pure and applied chemistry, 1967; McCoy Research award, chemistry dept. UCLA, 1969, Alexander von Humboldt Sr. U.S. Scientist award Fed. Republic Germany, 1982, King Faisal Internat. Prize in Sci. (Chemistry), 1990, Harris award U. Nebr., 1995, Irving Langmuir award in Chem. Physics, 2002, 2007 Nat. Medal Sci. Fellow Am. Acad. Arts & Scis.; mem. Am. Chem. Soc. (Gold Medal award Calif. sect. 1971, editor in chief Jour. Phys. Chemistry 1980— and editor Internat. Revs. Phys. Chemistry 1984-90, Tolman award 1990, Fla. sect. award 1999), NAS, AAUP, AAAS, Assn. for Harvard Chemists, Western Spectroscopy Assn., N.Y. Acad. Scis., Third World Acad. Scis., Phys. Chemistry Div. Internat. Union Pure and Applied Chemistry (elected, vice chmn. U.S. NRC com. 1987, chmn. 1992). Office: Ga Tech Sch Of Chemistry & Biochemis Atlanta GA 30332-0001

ELSENER, G. DALE, lawyer; b. Frederick, Okla., Mar. 26, 1951; s. Gordon Lee and Anita Lois (Vaughan) Elsener; m. Ann Skidmore; children: Hayley Lynn, Garrett Dale. BS, Okla. State U., 1973; JD, Okla. U., 1976. Bar: Okla. 1976, U.S. Dist. Ct. (ea. and we. dists.) Okla. 1984. Assoc. Richard S. Roberts, Wewoka, Okla., 1976-78; ptnr. Roberts & Elsener, Wewoka, 1979-86; sole practice, 1986. City atty. City of Wewoka, 1986—2007. Mem.: Kingfisher County Bar Assn., Okla. Bar Assn. (real property and mineral law sects.). Office Phone: 405-375-2337. Business E-Mail: gdelsener@pldi.net.

ELSENHANS, LYNN LAVERTY, corporate board member, former oil industry executive; b. May 6, 1956; m. John W. Elsenhans. BA in Applied Math., Rice U., Houston, 1978; MBA, Harvard Bus. Sch., 1980. Numerous positions of increasing responsibility Royal Dutch Shell PLC, 1980—2002, dir. strategic planning, Shell Internat. Ltd. (subs.), 2002—03, CEO Shell Oil Products US, 2003—05, pres. Shell Oil Co., 2003—08, exec. v.p. global mfg. Shell Downstream Inc., 2005—08; pres., CEO Sunoco, Inc., Phila., 2008—09, chair, pres., CEO, 2009—12, exec. chmn., 2012; chair Sunoco Logistics Partners L.P., 2008—10, 2012, chair, CEO, 2010—12. Bd. dirs. Internat. Paper Co., 2007—12, Sunoco, Inc., 2008—12, Sunoco Logistics Partners L.P., 2008—12, Baker Hughes Inc., 2012—, GlaxoSmithKline, 2012—. Mem. council overseers Rice. U. Jones Sch. Bus.; bd.dirs. World Golf Found., Tex. Med. Ctr., Ctrl. Houston, Inc. Named one of The 50 Women to Watch, The Wall St. Jour., 2008, The 100 Most Powerful Women, Forbes mag., 2008—11, The 50 Most Powerful Women in Bus., Fortune mag., 2009—11.

ELSNER, JAMES BRIAN, meteorologist, educator; b. Milw., Oct. 16, 1959; s. Roger Allen and Diane Lucille (Richard) E.; m. Svetoslava Chtilianova Kavlakova, Jan. 7, 1989; children: Ian James, Diana Michelle. BSc, U. Wis., Milw., 1981, MSc, 1984, PhD, 1988. Rsch. scientist U. Wis., Milw., 1989, lectr., 1989-90; asst. prof. dept. meteorology Fla. State U., Tallahassee, 1990-95, assoc. prof., 1995—98, assoc. prof. dept. geography, 1998—2001, prof., 2001—; pres. Climatek Inc., 2001—. Cons. Risk Prediction Initiative, Bermuda, 1995. Co-author: Singular Spectrum Analysis: A New Tool in Time Series Analysis, 1996, Hurricanes of the North Atlantic: Climate and Society, 1999; contbr. articles to profl. jours, chapters to books. Grantee NOAA, 1992, NSF, 1993, 95, 97, 2002, 2004. Mem. Am. Meteorol. Soc., European Geophys. Soc., Am. Assn. Geographers, Xi Epsilon Pi. Office: Dept Geography Fla State U Tallahassee FL 32306-2190 E-mail: jelsner@fsu.edu.

ELSON, EDWARD ELLIOTT, diplomat; b. NYC, Mar. 8, 1934; s. Harry and Esther (Cohn) E.; m. Suzanne Wolf Goodman, Aug. 24, 1957; children: Charles Myer, Louis Goodman, Harry Elson II. Grad., Phillips Acad., 1952; BA in Polit. Sci. with honors, U. Va., 1956; JD, Emory U., 1959; DHL (honoris causa), Talladega Coll., 1995; JD (hon.), Brenau U., 1997. With Atlanta News Agy., Inc., 1959-86, pres., 1967-82, chmn. bd. dir. and pres., 1982—85, chmn. bd. dir., 1985—86; pres. Airport News Corp., Atlanta, 1961-82, chmn. bd. dir., 1982—85; pres. Elson's, Atlanta, 1963-82, chmn. bd. dir., 1982—86; chmn. Gordon County Bank, 1979-83; chmn. bd. dir. W.H. Smith & Son Holdings, PLC, 1985—88; amb. to Denmark U.S. Dept. State, 1993—. Bd. dirs. NationsBank of Ga., Citizens and So. Ga. Corp., Atlantic Am. Corp., Citizens and So. Trust Co., Inc., Genesco Inc., Specialty Coffee Holdings Inc., Mitre Sports Internat. Ltd., RF & P Corp., New & Lingwood Holdings Ltd., Thorkild Kristensen AG, Köllmann AG, Hamton Investment Funds; chmn. W.H. Smith Group PLC, 1986—, Majestic Wine Corp., 1988; hon. pres. Am. Club, Copenhagen, 1993-98; mem. hon. com. European Assn. Jewish Studies' 5th Cong., 1993—; vis. prof. Aalborg (Denmark) U. Mem. publs. com. Commentary Mag., 1967—, chmn., 1975-80. Dir., Am. Coun. Ambs.; bd. dir. So. Regional Coun., 1966—, exec. com., 1986—; bd. govs. Am. Jewish Com., 1966—, trustee, 1977—, chmn. bd. trustees, 1986-89, v.p., 1982-84, treas., 1984-86; v.p. Nat. Found. Jewish Culture, 1990—; mem. Presdl. Commn. on Obscenity and Pornography, 1967-71, Nat. Adv. Commn. Pub. Edn. and Desegregation, 1976-77; mem. funds appeals rev. bd. City of Atlanta, 1971-73, Atlanta-Fulton County Recreation Authority, 1973-80, vice chmn., 1975-80; adv. com. to U.S. Commn. on Civil Rights, State of Ga., 1974—, chmn., 1974-82; chmn. bd. dir. Nat. Pub. Radio, 1977-80, chmn., 1992—; chmn. Nat. Pub. Radio Found.; chmn. so. regional adv. com. to U.S. Commn. on Civil Rights, 1978, U. Va. Bayley Mus., 1986—; pres.'s coun. Brandeis U., 1967—, dir. Reading is Fundamental program, 1975-86, fellow, 1979; trustee Am.-Skandanavian Found., 1998—; bd. visitors U. Va., 1984-92, rector, 1990-92, exec. com. Health Sci. Coun., 1989—, chmn. Real Estate Found., 1990-92; bd. visitors Clark Coll., 1973—, chmn., 1982; trustee Brown U., 1988—, U. Va. Med. Ctr., 1987—, exec. com., 1987—; trustee Am. Briends Brit. Mus., Talladega Coll., 1973—, U. Mid-Am., 1979-82, Am. Fedn. Arts, 1985—, Brenau Coll., 1986—, Hampton Inst., 1986—, Hebrew Union Coll., 1992—, Spellman Coll., 1992—, Jewish Mus., 1992—, Glyndebourne Assn. Am., 1992—; mem. alumni coun. Phillips Acad., Andover, Mass., 1973-76, charter trustee, 1997; pres. coun. Agnes Scott Coll., 1973-82, chmn., 1975-82; mem. coun. White Burkett Miller Ctr. Pub. Affairs, 1990—; dean's adv. bd. Columbia U. Sch. Internat. Affairs and Pub. Affairs; chmn. adv. bd., bd. dir. Southeastern Ctr. Contemporary Art, 1976—; chmn. bd. vis. Emory U. Mus. Art and Archaeology, 1985-92; resource planning com. Nat. Gallery, Washington, 1986—, trustee's coun., 1990—, dir. Coun. Am. Ambs.; chmn. U. Va. Real Estate Found., 1990-92; presdl. del. returning Crown of Stephen to Hungary, 1978; exec. com. U. Va. Health Sci. Coun., 1989—; gov. J.C. Brown Libr., R.I., 1989—; bd. dir. Acad. Corp. Governance, Fordham U.; chmn. bd. trustees Jeffersonian Restoration, 1992—; trustee Nat. Symphony Orch., 1992—; hon. pres. Copenhagen Theatre Cir., 1993-98; exec. com. Assn. Friends Hans Christian Andersen Mus., 1993-98; active Internat. Inst. Strategic Studies, 1995—; assoc. dir. Met. Opera, 2000—; trustee Game Conservancy, exec. coms. mem. Preservation Soc. Palm Beach, 2004—, Soc. of Four Arts, 2004—, vice chmn., 2007; treas. Preservation Found., 2011; vice chair Palm Beach Centennial Com., 2011; gov. Addison Gallery Am. Art; chmn. Inst. Study of Europe Col. U., 2002—; dir. Am. Friends of Nat. Gallery Denmark, trustee, Am. Friends Nat. Mus. Denmark, treas., Preservation Soc. Palm Beach, 2013-, dir., Palm Beach United Way, 2012-, trustee emeritus, Royal Acad. 2012-. Recipient Robert B. Downs award Grad. Sch. Library Sci., U. Ill., 1971, Human Relations award Am. Jewish Com., 1975, Disting. Service award Nat. Pub. Radio, 1979, Inst. Human Relations award, 1982, Merkonom award, 1997, Outstanding Alumnus award Emory U. Law Sch., 2002; Guggenheim fellow, 1994. Mem. Ga. Bar Assn., L.Q.C. Lamar Soc. (v.p. 1973-74, chmn. bd. dirs. 1974-80), Jewish Publ. Soc. (trustee 1974-82, 85—, v.p. 1986-87, pres., 1987-90, chmn. 1990—), Asia Soc. (trustee exec. com. 1999—), Am. Jewish Hist. Soc. (exec. com. 1980—, v.p. 1982-85), Am. Scandinavian Found. (vice chmn. 1998—, St. George's House coun.), Muscular Dystrophy Assn. Am. (v.p. 1972-73, corp. 1973-74), U. Va. Alumni Assn. (bd. mgrs. 1982-84), Soc. for the Four Arts (vice chmn. 2007—), Assn. Governing Bds. Univs. and Colls. (bd. dir.), Nat. Peace Garden Found. (dir., trustee), Royal Acad. U.K. (chair Am. bd.), Inst. Study Europe (co-chair 1999—), European Assn. Jewish Studies (hon. com. 5th congress 1993-98), Coun. Fgn. Rels., Royal Copenhagen Shooting Soc. and Danish Brotherhood, Farmington Country Club, Univ. Club (N.Y.C.), Century Assn., Game Conservancy, USA (trustee), Palm Beach Country Club, Sailfish Club (Palm Beach, Fla.), Whites Club (London), The Beach Club (Palm Beach), Bucks Club (London), Nat. Leadership Coun.-Nat. Mus. Am. Jewish History. Home Fax: 561-833-5044. Personal E-mail: edwardelson@hotmail.com.

ELSON, JAMES MARTIN, retired landmark director; b. NYC, Nov. 25, 1932; s. John James and Elizabeth Jane (Slights) E.; m. Joan Mary Scott Elson, Aug. 21, 1965 (dec. Feb. 15, 1991); children: Elizabeth Joan Elson, Christina Marie Elson, James Scott Elson; m. Karen Sue Porter Elson, Aug. 22, 1992. BA, U. Tenn., 1955; MS, The Juilliard Sch., 1961; Mus. AD, W.Va. U., 1970. 1st lt. US Army, 1955—57; col. USAR, 1957—85, ret.; chmn. vocal dept. Dana Sch. Music, Youngstown (Ohio) State U., 1962-68; grad. asst. Creative Arts Ctr., W.Va. U., Morgantown, 1968-70; chmn., vocal dept. Sch. Music, Winthrop U., Rock Hill, 1970-72; chmn., dept. visual and performing arts Huntingdon Coll., Montgomery, Ala., 1972-76; chmn., dept. fine arts High Point (N.C.) U., 1976—83; exec. dir. Acad. of Music Theatre, Lynchburg, Va., 1984-88; exec. v.p. Patrick Henry Meml. Fdn., Brookneal, Va., 1988-2000, exec. v.p. emeritus, 2000—. Performing arts critic High Point (N.C.) Enterprise, 1977-83. Author: Academy of Music, Lynchburg, Virginia: The Golden Age of Live Performance, 1993, Lynchburg, Virginia: The First Two Hundred Years, 1786-1986, 2004; author, editor: Patrick Henry Essays, 1994, Patrick Henry and Thomas Jefferson, 1997, Patrick Henry in His Speeches and Writings, 2007; editor Lynch's Ferry Mag., 2000-05; contbr. articles to profl. jours. Decorated Meritorious Svc. medal; grantee, Fulbright Commn., 1961—62. Mem.: Coll. Music Soc. (life), Res. Officers Assn. (life), Kappa Sigma Frat., Sphex Club Lynchburg (Va.). Episcopalian. Personal E-mail: jelson@inmind.net.

ELSON, SUZANNE GOODMAN, social services administrator; b. Memphis, Oct. 17, 1937; d. Charles F. and Isabel (Ehrlich) Goodman; m. Edward Elliott Elson, Aug. 24, 1957; children: Charles Myer, Louis Goodman, Harry H. Student, Randolph-Macon Women's Coll., Lynchburg, Va.; BA, Agnes Scott Coll., 1959. Sec. Nat. Coun. Jewish Women, NYC, 1977-79; pres. Nat. Mental Health Assn., 1980-82; trustee emeritus Randolph Macon Women's Coll., 1988-98, 99; hon. trustee Mus. Arts And Design. Chmn. Am. Craft Coun., 1989-92, hon. chmn., 1992-94, hon. trustee, 1994-; Nat. Coun. Medicine Emory U., 1990-95; trustee Va. Mus. of Fine Art., 1992-96, High Mus. Fine Art, 1972-92, Am. Craft Mus., 1999-2007; bd. regents U. System of Ga., 1993-97; adv. bd. Breast Cancer Rsch. Found., 1998-2010; bd. dirs. Friends of Art and Preservation in Embassies, 1999-09; trustee Soc. for the Four Arts, 2003-, Preservation Soc. of Palm Beach, 2004-. Recipient Women of Distinction award, Palm Beach Atlantic U., 2014. Home: 180 Cocoanut Row Palm Beach FL 33480-4121

ELTIFE, KEVIN, state legislator; m. Kelly Eltife; children: Walker, Jack. Grad., U. Tex., Austin. Former mem. Tyler City Coun., Tex.; former mayor City of Tyler; owner Eltife Properties; mem. Dist. 1 Tex. State Senate, 2004—. Steering com. mem. Tyler Civic Arena, Vision 2000; mem. bd. dirs. Tyler Main St., Tyler Cmty. Homes, East Tex. Regional Food Bank; bd. mem. Hospice East Tex. Mem.: Tyler Area C. of C. (bd. dir.). Republican. Roman Catholic. Office: 3304 S Broadway Ste 103 Tyler TX 75701 also: PO Box 12068 Capitol Station Austin TX 78711 also: 101 E Methvin Ste 301 Longview TX 75601 also: 5411 Plaza Dr Ste D Texarkana TX 75503 Office Phone: 903-596-9122, 512-463-0101, 903-753-8137, 903-223-7931. Office Fax: 903-596-9189, 512-475-3751.

ELWES, TIMOTHY, board member; Fin. svcs. cons., 2000—. Bd. dirs. Timothy Elwes & Ptnrs. Ltd., 1978—94, 2000—, Terremark Worldwide Inc., 2000—. Office: Terremark Worldwide Inc Ste 2900 2 S Biscayne Blvd One Biscayne Tower Miami FL 33131 Office Phone: 305-856-3200. Office Fax: 305-856-8190.

ELY, RANDY, federal marshal; Grad., Ft. Worth Police Dept. Tng. Acad., 1972. Traffic cadet Ft. Worth Police Dept., Tex., 1970—73, police officer, 1973—78, detective, 1978—80, sgt., 1980—82, lt., 1982—87, capt., 1987—97, dep. chief, 1997—2002; US marshal, (no. dist.) Tex. US Marshal Svc., US Dept Justice, Dallas, 2002—. Named Ft. Worth's Command Officer of Yr., Officer of Yr., American Legion. Mem.: Tex. Police Assn. (pres. 2001—02), FBI Nat. Associates, Inc. (pres. 2000). Office: US Marshal Federal Bldg 1100 Commerce St Rm 16F47 Dallas TX 75242 Office Phone: 214-767-0836.

ELZINGA, KENNETH GERALD, economics professor; b. Coopersville, Mich., Aug. 11, 1941; s. Clarence Albert and Lettie (Albrecht) E.; m. Barbara Ann Brunson, June 17, 1967 (dec. 1978); m. Terry M. Maguire, Aug. 9, 1981. BA, Kalamazoo Coll., 1963; MA, Mich. State U., 1966, PhD, 1967; LHD, Kalamazoo Coll., 2000. Rsch. economist Senate Antitrust and Monopoly Subcom., 1964; asst. instr. Mich. State U., 1965-66; asst. prof. U. Va., Charlottesville, 1967-71, assoc. prof., 1971-73, prof., 1973—; fellow in law and econs. U. Chgo., 1974; vis. prof. econs. Trinity U., 1984; Thomas Jefferson fellow Cambridge U., 1990, Cavaliers Disting. Tchg. Professorship, 1992-97, Robert C. Taylor prof. econ., 2002—. Spl. econ. advisor to asst. atty. gen., antitrust divsn. Dept. Justice, 1970-71; trustee Hope Coll., 1983-90, Inter-Varsity Christian fellowship, 1992-2000; mem. editl. bd. Antitrust Bull., 1977—; Univ. Disting. vis. prof. Pepperdine U., 2004; Vernon F. Taylor vis. rshc. prof. Trinity U., San Antonio, 2006, Disting. vis. prof. Pepperdine U., 2005. Author: (with others) The Antitrust Penalties, 1976, The Fatal Equilibrium, 1985, Murder at the Margin, 1993, A Deadly Indifference, 1995, The Antitrust Casebook, 3rd edit. 1996. Recipient Thomas Jefferson award U. Va., 1992, Commonwealth of Va. Outstanding Faculty award, 1992, Kenan Enterprise award for tchg. econs., William R. Kenan Jr. Charitable Trust, 1996, Templeton Honor Roll award for Edn. in a Free Soc. John Templeton Found., 1997, Disting. Alumni award Mich. State U., 1999; named Tchr. of the Yr. Phi Eta Sigma, 1992. Mem. ABA, Am. Econs. Assn., Mystery Writers of Am., Am. Law and Econs. Assn., So. Econ. Assn. (pres. 1991), Internat. J.A. Shumpeter Soc., Indsl. Orgn. Soc. (pres. 1979). Presbyterian. Avocations: water-skiing, travel. Office: U VA Dept Econs PO Box 400182 Charlottesville VA 22904-4182 Business E-Mail: elzinga@virginia.edu.

EMBRY, CARLOS BROGDON, state legislator; b. Louisville, Ky., June 29, 1941; s. Carlos Brogdon Embry and Zora Romans E.; m. Wanda Lou Ralph, 1962; children: Laura Ann, Barbara Ann, Carlos Brogdon III. Former co. chmn. local & state programs Young Rep. Nat. Fedn.; former treas. Ky. Rep. Party; mayor Beaver Dam, Ky., 1970—73; judge Ohio County Ky., 1974—77; national committeeman Ky. Young Rep., 1975—77; chmn. 1st Dist. Rep. Com., 1975—78, Ohio County Rep. Com., Ky., 1975—77; judge Ohio county, 1974—77; exec. Ohio county, 1982—89; dir. Ohio county comprehensive employment & training act US Dept. Labor, 1978—81; orgn. chmn. Hopkins Gov. Campaign, 1991; gen. mgr. Embry Newspapers, Inc, 1963—73, 1978—89, Hughes & Coleman, Plc, 1996—2000; tchr. Pleasant Ridge Elem. Sch., 1964—65, Horse Br. Jr High, 1969—70; co owner Embry'S Valley Shopping Ctr., Beaver Dam, 1974—95; Ky. state rep. Dist. 17, 2003—. Contbr. articles; author: (book) How To Add Years To Your Life, 1979. Recipient George Washington Hon. medal, Nat. Freedoms Found., 1970; named Beaver Dam's Outstanding Young Man, Beaver Dam Jaycees, 1969, 1973, Outstanding Young Rep. Ky., Ky. Young Rep. Fedn., 1973—74, Outstanding Young Rep. Nat., Nat. Young Rep., Ohio County Citizen of Yr., Ohio County C. of C., 1982. Mem.: F&AM, Ky. Coun.Crime & Delinquency, Louisville Scottish Rite, Fellow Christian Athletics, Butler/Edmonson Gideons, Ky. Rep. Judge-Exec.'s Assn. (former v. chmn.), Green River Area Devel. Dist. (bd. dir., former chmn.), Ohio County Hist. Soc. (former pres.), Promise Keepers, Kosair Temple Shriners, Hon. Order Ky. Colonels. Republican. Bapt. Mailing: PO Box 1215 Morgantown KY 42261-1215 Office: Capitol Annex Rm 351E Frankfort KY 40601 Office Phone: 502-564-8100 710. Office Fax: 502-782-8820.

EMELY, CHARLES HARRY, trade association executive, consultant; b. Phila., Oct. 30, 1943; s. Charles Walter and Jane Beatty (Stott) E.; m. Susan Elizabeth Lawton, June 18, 1966 (dec. Mar. 1977); 1 child, Charles Walter II; m. Mary Ann Horvath, Sept. 1, 1979; 1 stepchild, Wendy A. Vellrath. Student, Drexel Inst. Tech., 1961-62; BA, Temple U., 1967; MA, Fairfield U., 1974; postgrad., NYU, 1974-76; PhD, Calif. Western U., 1978; postgrad., Ohio U., 1981-82. Adminstrv. asst. City of Phila., 1966-68; nat. rep. ARC, Washington, 1968-70; exec. dir., chief exec. officer Bridgeport, Conn., 1970-77; pres., chief exec. officer Comprehensive Bus. Cons., Ft. Washington, Pa., 1977-86; exec. v.p., chief exec. officer Adhesive & Sealant Council, Washington, 1987-88; pres., CEO Comprehensive Bus. Cons., Inc., Fairfax, Va., 1988—; exec. dir., CEO Internat. Assn. Law Firms, 1988—; exec. dir., COO Am. Soc. Hort. Sci., Alexandria, Va., 1994-97; CEO Am. Railway Engring. and MOW Assn., Landover, Md., 1998—. Chmn. Cmty. Cons. Corps, Ft. Washington, 1980—; sr. cons. Philippine Nutrition Ctr., Manila, 1980; adj. faculty Ohio U., Athens, 1982-83, bd. dirs. ICM Internat., Inc.; comunications officer, U.S.A. Nat. Disaster Med. Sys., 1992—. Mem. bd. mgrs. YMCA, Fairfield, Conn., 1971-75; bd. dirs. Hope Ctr., Inc., Bridgeport, 1972-76, Comprehensive Health Planning Agy., Bridgeport, 1973-74, Found. for Internat. Meetings; mem. Mayor's Energy Adv. Com., Bridgeport, 1973-74, Fayetteville (N.Y.) United Meth. Ch., 1985; trustee, v.p. Mental Health Assn. Conn., 1973-77; mem. adminstrv. bd. Nichols United Meth. Ch., Trumbull, Conn., 1975-77; adv. com. campaign coun. Rep. Nat. Com.; mem. Patriots Soc. Germantown Acad., Ft. Washington, 1978-80; pres. Ambler (Pa.) Symphony Orchestra, 1979-80; mem. Pvt. Industry Council, Ambler, 1979-80, Zanesville, Ohio, 1981-83; mem. parents council Hartwick Coll., Oneonta, N.Y., 1987, bd. trustees, Harford Friends Sch. Mem.: Univ. & Whist Club Wilmington (Del.), Associated Pub. Safety Comm. Officers, Found. for Internat. Meetings, Am. Railway Engring. and Maint. of Way Assn. (CEO 1998—), Nat. Assn. Corp. Dirs. (sec./treas. Washington chpt.), Am. Soc. Assn. Execs. (cert. assn. exec. 1977), Adminstrv. Mgmt. Soc., Am. Mgmt. Assn., Heritage Found., U. Conn. Alumni Assn. (life), Mensa, Officers Club Nat. Naval Med. Ctr. (Bethesda), Rep. Nat. Com. Campaign Coun., Armed Forces Comms. and Electronics Assn., Aircraft Owners and Pilots Assn., Officers Club Marine Corps Base Quantico, Am. Radio Relay League, Renewable Natural Resources Found. (bd. dirs.), Heritage Found. (exec. com.), Rotary, Nat. Assn. Execs. Club, City of Washington Club, Univ. Club, Vesper Club, Phila. Aviation Country Club, Rep. Nat. Com. Pres.'s Club, Elks, Shriners, Masons. Avocations: music, amateur radio, aviation, stamp collecting/philately, travel. Home: 7 Beaver Ridge Rd Stafford VA 22556-6677 Office: Comprehensive Bus Cons Inc PO Box 545 Garrisonville VA 22463-0545 Business E-Mail: chemely@cbc.org.

EMERSON, E. ALLEN, computer science educator; BS in Math., U. Tex., Austin; PhD in Applied Math., Harvard U. Endowed prof. in computer sci. U. Tex., Austin. Mem. of several editl. bds. Co-recipient Kanellakis award, Assn. for Computing Machinery, 1998, Allen Newell award for Excellence in Rsch., Carnegie Mellon Computer Sci. Dept., 1999, A.M. Turning award, Assn. for Computing Machinery, 2007, Test-of-Time award, IEEE Symposium on Logic in Computer Sci., 2006; named Information Sciences Inst. Highly Cited Researcher; named one of Top 1% of the Most Cited Computer Scientists on CiteSeer06. Office: Dept of Computer Sciences Taylor Hall 2.124 The University of Texas at Austin Austin TX 78712 Office Phone: 512-471-9537. Office Fax: 512-471-8885. Business E-Mail: emerson@cs.utexas.edu.

EMERSON, JO ANN H., electric power association executive, former United States Representative from Missouri; b. Washington, Sept. 16, 1950; d. Albert & Sylvia Hermann; m. Bill Emerson, June 22, 1975 (dec. June 22, 1996); children: Victoria, Katharine; m. Ron Gladney, 2000; stepchildren: Elizabeth, Abigail, Alison, Jessica, Stephanie, Sam. BA in Polit. Sci., Ohio Wesleyan U., 1972; DHL (hon.), Westminster Coll., Fulton, Mo. Dep. comm. dir. Nat. Republican Congressional Com. (NRCC), 1984—91; dir. state rels. & grassroots programs Nat. Restaurant Assn., 1991—94; sr. v.p. public affairs American Ins. Assn., 1994—96; mem. US Congress from 8th Mo. Dist., 1996—2013, US House Appropriations Com., 1998—2013; pres., CEO designate Nat. Rural Electric Cooperative Assn. (NRECA), Arlington, Va., 2013—. Mem. PEO Womens's Svc. Grp. (FY chpt.), Cape Girardeau; mem. adv. bd. Arneson Inst. Practical Politics and Pub. Affairs, Ohio Wesleyan U.; co-chair Congl. Hunger Ctr.; bd. dirs. Bread for the World; hon. and life trustee Westminster Coll.; bd. dirs. Presbyn. Children's Home, Farmington, Mo. Recipient Rural Housing Legislator of Yr., Nat. Assn. Home Builders, 2001, Schwarz Pharma Leadership in Pharmacy award, Nat. Assn. Chain Drug Stores, 2002, Ground Water Protector award, Nat. Ground Water Assn., 2005. Mem.: Copper Dome Soc. Republican. Presbyn. Office: National Rural Electric Cooperative Assn (NRECA) 4301 Wilson Blvd Arlington VA 22203 Office Phone: 703-907-5500.

EMERSON, PHILIP G., historic site director; Grad., Randolph-Macon Coll., Ashland, Va., 1981. Exec. dir. Jamestown Settlement, Yorktown Victory Ctr. Jamestown-Yorktown Found., Williamsburg, Va. Former bd. mem. Williamsburg Montessori Sch. Office: Jamestown-Yorktown Found Victory Ctr PO Box 1607 Williamsburg VA 23187-1607

EMERSON, WILLIAM ALLEN, retired investment company executive; b. Columbia, Tenn., July 13, 1921; s. Henry Houston and Mabel N. (Allen) E.; m. Jane Stannard, Oct. 5, 1944; children: Marshal Henry, Shelley, Stacey, Kimberly. AA, St. Petersburg Jr. Coll., 1941; BSBA, U. Fla., 1946. With Merrill Lynch, Pierce, Fenner & Smith, Inc., 1947-87, dir. gen. services div. NYC, 1968-72, Southeast regional dir., corp. dir. Atlanta, 1972-81, sr. v.p., nat. sales dir., 1981-86; dir. Merrill Trust Co. Past vice chmn. bd. trustees St. Joseph-St. Anthony Health Sys. Trustee Oglethorpe U., Atlanta, Mus. Fine Arts, St. Petersburg, Salvadore Dali Mus., St. Petersburg; trustee, past pres. U. Fla. Found. Pilot with USMC, 1942-45. Named Emerson Alumni Hall at U. Fla. in his honor, 2003. Mem.: St. Petersburg Yacht Club, Masons. Republican. Baptist. Home: 3050 82nd Way N Saint Petersburg FL 33710-2220

EMERY, ALAN L., food service executive; b. Mobile, Ala., Mar. 6, 1963; BS in Internat. Affairs, Kennesaw State U., 1991. Dist. mgr. Bennigans, 1992—2007; dist. mgr., internat. cons. Metromedia Restaurant Group, 1992—2007; regional v.p. restaurant ops. Cracker Barrel Old Country Store, Inc., 2007—. Artilleryman USMC, 1982—86. Methodist. Office: Cracker Barrel Old Country Store Inc 305 Hartmann Dr Lebanon TN 37088 Office Phone: 615-444-5533. Office Fax: 615-443-9476.

EMERY, BETH (NANCY BETH EMERY), lawyer; b. Shawnee, Okla., July 9, 1952; d. Paul Dodd Finefrock and Kathryn Jo (Saling) Hutchens; m. Lee Monroe Emery, May 18, 1974. BA with highest honors, U. Okla., 1974; JD, Harvard U., 1977. Bar: D.C. 1981. Atty. advisor USDA, Washington, 1977-79; legal advisor to Commr. Matthew Holden, Jr. Fed. Energy Regulatory Commn. (FERC), Washington, 1979-81; assoc. Pierson, Ball & Dowd and predecessor Sullivan & Beauregard, Washington, 1981-83, Paul Hastings, Janofsky & Walker, Washington, 1983-87, ptnr., 1987-93, Sutherland, Asbill & Brennan, Washington, 1993-97; v.p., gen. counsel, corp. sec. Calif. Ind. Sys. Operator Corp., 1997-99; ptnr. Hopkins & Sutter, Washington, 1999-2001, Ballard, Spahr, Andrews & Ingersoll, LLP, Washington, 2001—03; sr. v.p., gen. counsel, corp. sec. CPS Energy, San Antonio, 2003—06; of counsel Tuggey Rosenthal Pauerstein Sandoloski Agather LLP, 2006—. Nat. adv. bd. USAID Tng. Program, 1994—98; bd. dirs. EnergyConnect Group, Inc., 2010—. Bd. dirs., sec. Park Place Condominium Assn., Inc., Washington, 1982—84; page Continental Congress DAR, 1978—82, chpt. del., 1981, 1984; bd. dirs. New Hope Housing, Inc., Alexandria, Va., 2001—03, chmn. strategic planning com., 2002—03, exec. com., 2003; bd. dirs. Carver Cultural Arts Ctr. Devel. Bd., 2005—. Mem.: ABA (natural resources energy and eviron. law sect. 1990—98, bd. editors Natural Resources & Environment 1990—98, pub. utility law sect., vice chmn. electricity com. 1998—, chmn. program com. 2000—01, chmn. mem. com. 2001—02, chmn. strategic planning com. 2001—02, mem. coun. 2002—, chmn. cmty. involvment 2002—04), Soc. Profl. Journalists, Fed. Energy Bar Assn. (chair tax com. 1986—87, chair FERC ops. and adminstrn. com. 1991—93, chair elec. utility regulation com. 1995—97, chair program com. 1997—98), Mortar Bd., Phi Beta Kappa. Democrat. Office: TRSPA 755 E Mulberry Ste 200 San Antonio TX 78212 Office Phone: 210-225-5000. Office Fax: 210-354-4034. E-mail: bemery@trpsalaw.com.

EMMET, THOMAS ADDIS, JR., college administrator, consultant; b. Detroit, July 26, 1930; s. Thomas Addis and Leona Marguerete (Schneider) E.; m. Anne Marie Baker, Mar. 3, 1972 (dec. Sept. 19, 2001); children: Lynn, Anthony, William Novitsky. PhB, U. Detroit, 1952, MA, 1954; EdS, EdD, U. Mich., 1963; LLD (hon.), St. Norbert Coll., 2001; DHL in Ednl. Leadership (hon.), Quincy U., 2001. Asst. dean U. Detroit, 1953-57, dean men, 1957-64, dean evening coll. arts and scis., 1964-66, asst. prof. higher edn., 1964-67, assoc. v.p. acad. affairs, 1966—67; spl. asst. to pres., prof. edn. Regis U., Denver, 1972-91, pres. higher edn. exec. assocs., 1967-72, 84-86, 89—, sr. adv. to pres., 1991—. Adj. prof. higher edn. Wayne State U., Detroit, 1968-70; chmn. bd. Higher Edn. Group, 1986-89; pres. Thomas A. Emmet & Assos., 1972-84; cons. collective negotiations in higher edn. Edn. Commn. of States, 1971-84; cons. higher edn. Opinion Rsch. Corp., 1984-86; dir. leadership seminars, sr. adviser Am. Council on Edn., 1979-93. Editor: The Acacemic Department and Division Chairman, 1972-94, Collective Bargaining in Postsecondary Institutions: The Impact on the Campus and the State, 1974; assoc. editor Coll. and Univ. Bus., 1969-71; pub. The Department ADvisor, 1985-92. Staff dir. Mich. State Senate Student Unrest Com., 1968-69; exec. sec. Conf. Jesuit Student Personnel Adminstrs., 1956-64; sec. Coun. Student Personnel Assns. in Higher Edn., 1966-69. Recipient Bernard Webster Reed award, 1963, John P. McNichols award U. Detroit, 1986, Alan P. Splete award Coun. Ind. Colls., 2005. Mem. Adult Student Personnel Assn. (v.p. 1961-64), Nat. Assn. Student Personnel Adminstrs. (mem. exec. com. 1961-67, editor Jour. 1962-63), Phi Kappa Phi, Alpha Sigma Nu, Alpha Signa Lambda, Phi Delta Kappa, Phi Eta Sigma. Office: Regis U New Ventures 3333 Regis Blvd Denver CO 80221-1154 Home: 111 Covington PL Thomasville GA 31792-5294 E-mail: heca@aol.com.

EMSLIE, GRAHAM J., child and adolescent psychiatrist, educator; MD, Aberdeen U., 1974. Resident neurosurgery/gen. Aberdeen Royal Infirmary, 1974—75; residenr psychiatry Univ. Rochester & Strong Meml. Hosp., 1978; resident child psychiatry Children's Hosp. Standford Univ., 1980, fellow child psychiatry, 1980—80; prof. psychiatry Univ. Tex. Contbr. articles to profl. publs. Recipient Attention Deficit Disorders Assn.-Southern Region award, 1996, Pamela Blumenthal Meml. Prism award, Mental Health Assn., 2000, Klingenstein Third Generation Found. award for rsch. in Depression or Suicide, 2003. Mem.: Soc. Biological Psychiatry, Tex. Soc. Psychiatric Physicians, Tex. Soc. Child. and Adolescent Psychiatry, Am. Psychiatric Assn., Am. Acad. Child and Adolescent Psychiatry. Office: University of Texas Southwestern Medical Center 6300 Harry Hines Blvd 12th Fl Dallas TX 75235-8589 Office Phone: 214-456-5900. Office Fax: 214-456-4273.

ENDRES, ARTHUR P. (SKIP ENDRES), rail transportation executive; BA, U. Md.; JD, Cath. U. Various positions, house com. including staff dir., full com., House Judiciary Com., exec. dir. & gen. counsel Congl. Commn. on Internat. Migration and Coop. Econ. Devel., 1970—94; majority staff dir., sub com., transp. & hazardous material House Energy and Commerce Com.; spl. coun., sub com. on Commerce and Consumer Protection; asst. v.p., govtl. affairs Burlington Northern Santa Fe, 1994—96, v.p., govtl. affairs, 1996—. Office: Burlington Northern Santa Fe Corp 2650 Lou Menk Dr Fort Worth TX 76131 Office Fax: 817-352-7171.

ENGEL, BERNARD THEODORE, psychologist, educator; b. Chgo., Apr. 18, 1928; s. Marvin I. and Hannah (Hollander) E.; m. Rae Goldberg, Mar. 10, 1951; children: Sandra E., Jeffrey P., Lauren C. BA, UCLA, 1954, PhD, 1956. Jr. rsch. psychologist UCLA, 1956; rsch. psychologist Inst. Psychosomatic and Psychiatric. Research and Tng., Michael Reese Hosp., Chgo., 1957-58; lectr. med. psychology, mem. sr. staff Cardiovasc. rsch. Inst., Sch. Medicine U. Calif., San Francisco, 1959-67; chief behavioral physiology sect., chief Lab. Behavioral Scis. Gerontology Research Center, Nat. Inst. Aging, NIH, Balt., 1967-95; assoc. prof. behavioral biology Johns Hopkins Sch. Medicine, Balt., 1970-82, prof., 1982—. Bd. dirs. Insts. for Behavioral Resources, Inc.; adj. prof. psychiatry and behavioral scis. Duke U. Sch. Medicine, Durham, N.C., 1999—. Contbr. 175 articles to sci. jours.; editorial bds. Applied Psychophysiology and Biofeedback, Jour. of Behavioral Medicine, Psychosmatic Medicine. Served US Army, 1950—52. Recipient award Pavlovian Soc., 1979; cert. of Appreciation, N.C. State Hwy. Patrol, 2003. Fellow AAAS, Gerontol. Sci.; mem. Soc. Psychophysiol. Rsch. (pres. 1970-71), Assn. Applied Psychophysiology and Biofeedback (pres. 1981-82, Disting. Scientist award 2001), Am. Psychosomatic Soc. (sec.-treas. 1981-85, pres. 1985-86, Patricia R. Barchas award in sociophysiology 1999), Gerontol. Soc. Am., Acad. Behavioral Medicine Rsch., Sigma Xi. Personal E-mail: btere@aol.com.

ENGEL, BRYCE, diversified financial services company executive; Grad., U. Nebr., Lincoln, 1991—96. Sr. v.p., leader, call ctr. ops. and Ameritrade clearing TD Ameritrade; exec. v.p. Penson Worldwide, Inc., 2009—. Bd. dirs. Options Clearing Corp., 2006—09. Served ATD Adv. Coun. Named Bus. Progress award, Sarpy County EDC, 2006, top 40 Under 40 program, Midland Bus. Journal, 2007. Office: Penson Worldwide Inc Ste 1400 1700 Pacific Ave Dallas TX 75201 Office Phone: 214-765-1100. Business E-Mail: bengel@penson.com.

ENGEL, JEFFREY P., state agency administrator; B, Johns Hopkins U., Balt., 1977, MD, 1981. Residency, chief residency, fellowship tng. U. Minn., Mpls. Veterans Adminstrn. Med. Ctr., 1981—88; prof. medicine & chief, divsn. infectious diseases East Carolina U. Brody Sch. Medicine, Greenville, 1988—2002; med. dir., hosp. infection control Pitt County Meml. Hosp.; state epidemiologist NC Dept. Health and Human Services, 2002—09, chief, divsn. pub. health epidemiology sect., 2006—09, state health dir. & dir., divsn. pub. health, 2009—12, spl. advisor to the sec. on health policy, 2012—. Office: ND Dept Health and Human Services Adams Building 101 Blair Dr 2001 Mail Service Center Raleigh NC 27699-2001 Office Phone: 919-855-4800.

ENGELAGE, JAMES ROLAND, commercial property manager; b. Springfield, Mo., Dec. 5, 1945; s. Roland C. and Dorothy (Dixter) E.; m. Marcia Cooley, July 5, 1968. BS, Mo. State U., 1965; MS, Troy U., 1968; PhD, St. Louis U., 1977; MA, Ctrl. Mich. U., 1978. Dept. chmn. Montgomery (Ala.) Pub. Schs., 1968-69; asst. prin. Francis Howell Sch. Dist., St. Charles, 1969-74, asst. supt., 1974-75; commd. 2d lt. U.S. Army, 1975—93, advanced through grades to col., 1987; dean Randolph Macon Acad., Front Royal, Va., 1993-94; CEO JAMARC Mgmt. Corp., Winchester, Va., 1994—2003. Evening dir. Temple Schs., Silver Spring, Md., 1982-84; adj. prof. Park Coll., Ft. Myer, Va., 1980-82. Editor: Operation Desert Shield, 1992; contbr. articles to publs. Recipient legion of merit award Dept. Army, Washington, 1993. Mem. Res. Officers Assn. (pres. Chgo. chpt. 1992, Louisville chpt. 1993), Civil Air Patrol (capt. 1973-74), Lions Club (charter 1970-71), Civitans. Republican. Home: 9161 Southern Comfort Ct Weeki Wachee FL 34613-4282

ENGELHARDT, HUGO TRISTRAM, JR., physician, educator; s. Hugo Tristram and Beulah Engelhardt; m. Susan Gay Malloy, Nov. 25, 1965; children: Elisabeth, Christina, Dorothea. BA, U. Tex., Austin, 1963, PhD, 1969; MD with honors, Tulane U., New Orleans, 1972; Dr (hon.), U. Medicine and Pharmacy Gr. T. Popa, Iasi, Romania, 2005, U. Alba Iulia, Romania, 2011. Asst. prof. U. Tex. Med. Br., 1972-75, assoc. prof., 1975-77; mem. Inst. Med. Humanities, 1973-77; Rosemary Kennedy prof. philosophy of medicine Georgetown U., 1977-82; sr. rsch. scholar Kennedy Inst. Ctr. for Bioethics, Washington, 1977-82; prof. depts. internal medicine, cmty. medicine and ob-gyn. Baylor Coll. Medicine, Houston, 1983-2001, prof. emeritus, 2001—; mem. Ctr. for Med. Ethics and Health Policy, Houston, 1983-2001; prof. dept. philosophy Rice U., Houston, 1983—. Chmn. adv. panel on infertility prevention and treatment for office of tech. assessment of the U.S. Congress, 1986-87; vis. scholar Internat. Akad. für Philosophie, Liechtenstein, 1997, Liberty Fund, spring, 1998. Author: Mind Body: A Categorial Relation, 1973, The Foundations of Bioethics, 1986, rev. edit., 1996, Bioethics and Secular Humanism, 1991, The Foundations of Christian Bioethics, 2000; co-author: Bioethics: Readings and Cases, 1987; assoc. editor: Ency. of Bioethics, 1978—83; assoc. editor Jour. Medicine and Philosophy, 1974—84; mem. editl. bd. Poiesis & Praxis, 2001—, Chinese and Internat. Philosophy Medicine, 1998—, sr. editor Jour. Medicine and Philosophy, 1984—, Christian Bioethics, 1995—, (series) Philos. Studies in Contemporary Culture, 1992, Philosophy and Medicine series, 1974—; editor: Clin. Med. Ethics, 1987—2002, Evaluation and Explanation in the Biomedical Sciences, 1975, Philosophical Medical Ethics, 1977, Mental Health, 1978, Clinical Judgment, 1979, Concepts of Health and Disease, 1981, New Knowledge in the Biomedical Sciences, 1982, Scientific Controversies, 1987, The Use of Human Beings in Research, 1988, Sicherheit und Freiheit, 1990, Hegel Reconsidered, 1994, The Philosophy of Medicine, 2000, Allocating Scarce Medical Resources, 2002, Global Bioethics, 2006, The Philosophy Medicine Reborn, 2008, Innovation and the Pharmaceutical Industry, 2008, Bioethics Critically Re Examin: Having Second Thoughts, 2011; author: Viaggi in Italia, 2011. Mem. bioethics com. Nat. Found. March of Dimes, 1975—. Recipient McDonald-Merrill-Ketcham Meml. Excellence award in law and medicine, 2003; Fulbright fellow, 1969-70, Premio Nacional de Bioetica, Assn. Portuguesa de Biotica, Woodrow Wilson vis. fellow, 1988; fellow Inst. for Advanced Studies, Berlin, 1988-89. Mem. Am. Philos. Assn., European Acad. Scis. and Arts. Office: Rice U Dept Philosophy PO Box 1892 Houston TX 77251-1892 Office Phone: 713-348-2491. Business E-Mail: htengelh@rice.edu.

ENGELHARDT, KURT D., federal judge; b. New Orleans, 1960; BA, La. State U., Baton Rouge, 1982, JD, 1985. Law clk. to Hon. Charles Grisbaum La. 5th Cir. Ct. Appeals, 1985—87; pvt. practice atty. La., 1987—2001; judge US Dist. Ct. (ea. dist.) La., New Orleans, 2001—. Office: US Dist Ct 500 Poydras St Rm C367 New Orleans LA 70130 Office Phone: 504-589-7645.

ENGELMAN, KARL, physician; b. NYC, June 23, 1933; s. Samuel and Lillian (Wachs) E.; m. Elaine Kaufman, June 10, 1956; children: Harold Kent, Ross Mitchell, Jeffrey Steven. BS, Rutgers U., 1955; MD, Harvard U., 1959; MA (hon.), U. Pa., 1971. Diplomate Am. Bd. Internal Medicine, Am. Coll. Clinical Phatmacology. Intern, asst. resident, resident in medicine Mass. Gen. Hosp., Boston, 1959-64; clin. asso., sr. investigator, attending physician Nat. Heart Inst., NIH, Bethesda, Md., 1961-70; assoc. prof. medicine and pharmacology Sch. Medicine U. Pa., Phila., 1971-95; chief hypertension sect., dir. clin. research center Sch. Medicine U. Pa. Cons. physician Phila. VA Hosp., 1971-95, Children's Hosp., Phila., 1971-95; clin. prof. medicine Med. U. of S.C., 1996—; cons. Beaufort-Jasper Comprehensive Health Svcs., 1996—, Vols. in Medicine, 2002--. Patentee in field. Med. staff Vols. in Medicine, 2002--. Served with USPHS, 1961-63. Mem. ACP, Am. Coll. Clin. Pharmacology, Internat. Soc. of Hypertention (sci. coun. on hypertension), U.S. Pharmacopeia and Nat. Formullary (adv. coun.), Coun. for High Blood Pressure Rsch. (adv. bd.), Am. Heart Assn., Phila. Doctors Golf Assn., Sea Pines Club. Jewish. Home: 20 Turnberry Ln Hilton Head Island SC 29928-4108

ENGELS, LAWRENCE ARTHUR, retired metal products executive; b. Darlington, Wis., Sept. 26, 1933; s. Henry Morris and Nell Ellen (O'Connor) E.; m. Marilyn Rae Stellick, Sept. 6, 1958; children: Laurie, Michael, Thomas, Stephen BBA, U. Wis., 1959; MBA, Northwestern U., 1970. Dist. credit mgr. U.S. Steel Corp., Chgo., 1959-69; asst. treas. Nat. Can Corp., Chgo., 1969-77; corp. treas. Comml. Metals Co., Dallas, 1977—, chief fin. officer and treas., 1979—, v.p., treas., chief fin. officer Dallas, 1981-99, retired, 1999. Served with USN, 1952-55. Fellow Nat. Inst. Credit; mem. Cash Mgmt. Practitioners Assn. (Chgo. sec. 1975), Chgo. Midwest Credit Mgmt. Assn. (dir. 1973-75), Chgo. Midwest Credit Service Corp. (dir. 1975), Fin. Execs. Inst., Nat. Assn. Corp. Treas.

ENGIBOUS, THOMAS JAMES, retail executive, retired electronics executive; b. St. Louis, Jan. 31, 1953; s. James C. and Emma E. (Buck) E.; m. Wendy; children: Ryan T., Mandie, Christopher Megan. B of Elec. Engring., Purdue U., West Lafayette, Ind., 1975, M of Elec. Engring., 1976, DEng (hon.), 1997. Design engr. SCG, Tex. Instruments, Dallas, 1976-80, dept. mgr., 1980-86, v.p., 1986-91, sr. v.p., 1991-93; exec. v.p., pres. semi-condr. group Tex. Instruments Inc., Dallas, 1993-96, pres., CEO, 1996-98, chmn., pres., CEO, 1998—2004, chmn., 2004—08, J.C. Penney Co., Inc., Plano, Tex., 2012—. Mem. vis. com. Purdue U. Engring., 1995—; bd. dirs. J.C. Penney Co., Inc., Catalyst, US-Japan Bus. Coun., Nat. Ctr. Ednl. Accountability. Dir. Dallas Citizens Coun., 1996—; trustee So. Meth. U.; bd. dir. SW Med. Found. Mem. IEEE, Bus. Roundtable, Bus. Coun., NAE. Roman Catholic. Avocations: boating, water sports, skiing. Office: JC Penney Co Inc 6501 Legacy Dr Plano TX 75024 Office Phone: 972-995-2011. Office Fax: 972-995-4360.

ENGLAND, CHRIS (CHRISTOPHER JOHN ENGLAND), state legislator; b. Aug. 19, 1976; BA in English & Polit. Sci., Howard U., Washington, 1999; JD, U. Ala., 2002. Rep., dist. 70 Ala. House of Reps., Montgomery, 2006—. Mem. Bailey Tabernacle CME, Tuscaloosa, Ala.; bd. dirs. Police Athletic League, PRIDE. Mem.: Alpha Phi Alpha. Democrat. Office: PO Box 2089 Tuscaloosa AL 35403-2089 also: PO Box 20843 Tuscaloosa AL 35402 also: Ala House of Reps Ala State House 11 S Union St Rm 539-B Montgomery AL 36130 Office Phone: 205-535-4859, 205-349-0101, 334-242-7703. Business E-Mail: cengland1@hotmail.com.

ENGLAND, DAN BENJAMIN, accountant; b. Duncan, Okla., Aug. 23, 1955; s. Haskell Thomas and Lillian Lucille (Rouw) E.; m. Mary Elizabeth Metcalf, May 24, 1980; 1 child, Stuart Benjamin. BA, Southeastern Okla. State U., 1977, BS, 1982; MBA, Lincoln U., 2000; MS, Coll. for Fin. Planning, 2003. CPA, Okla. Br. mgr. Curtis Distbg. Co., Durant, Okla., 1978-79; dist. agt. Prudential Ins. Co., Durant, 1980-82; acct. Reedrill Inc., Sherman, Tex., 1982; mgr. Williams and Co. CPAs Inc., Durant, 1983-85; v.p. England Enterprises Inc., Durant, 1985—. Pres. Dan B. England, CPA, Inc., adj. instr. Southeastern Okla. State U., Durant, 1985-86; investment advisor rep., 1993—. Bd. dirs. Red River Arts Coun., Durant, 1986-94. Mem. Nat. Assn. Tax Practitioners, Okla. Soc. CPAs. Republican. Mem. Ch. of Christ. Lodge: Kiwanis (treas. Durant, 1985, sec. 1986, v.p. 1988, pres. 1989). Avocations: golf, tennis, music, art. Office: 206 N 10th Ave Durant OK 74701-4328

ENGLAND, GORDON RICHARD, international business consulting firm executive; b. Balt., Sept. 15, 1937; m. Dorothy England. BSEE, U. Md., 1961; MBA, Tex. Christian U., 1975. Engr. Honeywell Internat., 1961—66; v.p., pres. land sys. General Dynamics Corp., Falls Church, Va., 1986—91, pres. aircraft sys., Ft. Worth divsn., 1991, exec. v.p., 1991—93, exec. v.p. combat sys. group, 1997—2001; pres. Lockheed Ft. Worth Co., 1993—97; sec. Dept. Navy, US Dept. Def., Washington, 2001—03, 2003—06; dep. sec. US Dept. Homeland Security, Washington, 2003, US Dept. Def., Washington, 2006—09; pres. E6 Partners, LLC. Bd. dirs. CACI Internat. Inc, 2009—; mem. Def. Sci. Bd. Vice-chmn. Goodwill Internat.; bd. governors USO; bd. dirs. Ft. Worth Air & Space Mus. Found. Recipient Silver Beaver award, Boy Scouts Am., Silver Knight of Mgmt. award, Nat. Mgmt. Assn., Disting. Pub. Svc. award, US Dept. Def., IEEE Centennial award; named to, Aviation Hall of Fame. Mem.: Beta Gamma Sigma, Omicron Delta Kappa, Eta Kappa Nu. Republican. Office: E6 Partners 8484 Westpark Dr Ste 900 Mc Lean VA 22102 also: E6 Partners 6100 Southwest Blvd Ste 250 Fort Worth TX 76109 Mailing: CACI International Inc Bd Directors 1100 N Glebe Rd Arlington VA 22201 Office Phone: 703-841-7800. Office Fax: 703-841-7882. E-mail: gengland@caci.com.

ENGLAND, JULIE SPICER, former electronics company executive; b. 1957; BS in Chem. Engring., Tex. Tech. U., 1979. First line engr. Tex. Instruments, 1979—89, sr. mem. tech. staff, 1989—94, v.p. quality Semiconductor Group, 1994—98, v.p., 1994—2009, gen. mgr. radio frequency identification bus., 2004—09. Bd. dirs. Intelleflex, 2010—, Checkpoint Systems, Inc., 2010—. Mem. bus. adv. coun. Tex. Tech. Rawl Coll.; founder 3/2 program Tex. Women's U. Recipient Women of Achievement award, Richardson Tex. YWCA, Tex. Tech. U. Disting. Engineer award, Henry Laurence Gantt medal, ASME, 2004, Disting. Info. Sciences award, Assn. Info. Tech. Professionals, 2009; named one of The Top 15 Women Innovators in Bus., PINK mag., 2008; named to Women in Tech. Internat. Hall of Fame, 1998. Mem.: IEEE (sr.), Dallas Women's Found. (Circle of Honor award), Dallas C. of C. (mem. exec. women's roundtable), Soc. Women Engrs. (life). Achievements include patents for related to infrared focal plane array process technology.

ENGLAND, TERRY LAMAR, state legislator; b. Winder, Ga., Aug. 10, 1966; m. Cindy Casper. Owner, operator The Homeport Farm Mart, Winder, 1998—; mem. Dist. 108 Ga House of Reps, Atlanta, 2005—. Republican. Baptist. Office: 1060 Old Hog Mountain Rd Auburn GA 30011 also: Ga House of Reps 245 State Capitol Atlanta GA 30334 Office Phone: 770-867-1601, 404-463-2245. Business E-Mail: englandhomeport2@windstream.net.

ENGLAR, JOHN DAVID, finance educator, textiles executive, lawyer; b. Baldwin, NY, Feb. 19, 1947; s. Jack Donald and Edith (Blackwell) E.; m. Linda Meter, May 10, 1986. BA magna cum laude, Duke U., 1969, JD, 1972. Bar: N.Y. 1973. Assoc. Davis Polk and Wardwell, NYC and Paris, 1972-78; corp. atty. Burlington Industries, Inc., Greensboro, NC, 1978—, v.p., gen. counsel, sec., 1984-93, CFO, 1994-96, sr. v.p. corp. devel. and law, 1995—2003, also bd. dirs., 1990—2003; exec. in residence Fuqua Sch. Bus., Duke U., 2004—07, UNCG Bryan Sch. of Bus., 2005—; disting. practice bus. Elon U. Sch. of Law, 2008—. Bd. dirs. Delphi Corp., 2006—. Chmn. bd. trustees Cen. N.C. chpt. Nat. Multiple Sclerosis Soc., 1984-86, mem. nat. adv. coun., 1988-89; mem. bd. visitors Wake Forest U. Sch. Law, 1984-95, Duke U. Fuqua Sch. Bus., 1995—2005; mem. sch. bd. Our Lady of Grace, 2006—, mem. parish fin. coun., 2006—. Mem. Order of Coif, Phi Beta Kappa. Home: 215 Ridgeway Dr Greensboro NC 27403-1526

ENGLE, CAROLE RUTH, aquaculture economics professor; b. Harrisburg, Pa., July 7, 1952; d. Morris Mumma Engle and Mildred Evelyn (Orris) Wambold; m. Nathan Mayhew Stone, May 30, 1981; children: Reina, Eric, Cody. BA, Friends World Coll., 1975, MS, Auburn U., 1978, PhD, 1981. Vis. prof. U. Centroamericana, Managua, Nicaragua, 1981-83; fisheries economist Inter-Am. Devel. Bank, Santiago, Panama, 1984-85; asst. prof. econs. Auburn U., Montgomery, Ala., 1985-88; assoc. prof. aquaculture econs. U. Ark., Pine Bluff, 1988-94, prof., 1994—; dir., Aguacultural Fisheries Ctr., U. Ark., Pine Bluff, 1989—. Aquaculture coord. U. Ark., Pine Bluff, 1989—; cons. FAO, Rome, 1986, 88. Contbr. articles to profl. jours.; editor conf. proceedings. Mem. World Aquaculture Soc., Am. Fisheries Soc., Am. Assn. Agriculture Econs., So. Agriculture Econs. Assn., Ark. Acad. Scis. Avocations: gardening, reading, swimming. Office: U Ark PO Box 108 1200 University Dr Pine Bluff AR 71601-2799 Business E-Mail: cengle@uaex.edu.

ENGLE, REED LAURENCE, landscape architect; b. Upper Darby, Pa., Jan. 4, 1944; s. Alexander Reed and Alice Lucille (Pickell) E.; m. Dolores Gill Dyson, Dec. 21, 1946; children: Elizabeth Gresham, Louisa Jefferis. BA, Lafayette Coll., Easton, Pa., 1967; MA in Am. History, Lehigh U., Bethlehem, Pa., 1977; M of Landscape Arch., U. Pa., 1986. Archtl. historian John M. Dickey, Media, Pa., 1976-83; hist. architect Nat. Park Svc., Phila., 1983-88, regional hist. landscape architect, 1988-89; chief cultural resources Gettysburg (Pa.) Nat. Mil. Park, 1989-94; cultural resource specialist Shenandoah Nat. Park, Luray, Va., 1994—2007; bd. hist. rev. Savannah, 2008—. Author: Everything Was Wonderful: The C.C.C. in Shenandoah National Park, 1933-1942, 1999, In The Light of the Mountain Moon: An Illustrated

History of Skyland, 1853-2003, 2003; co-author: Story Behind the Scenery, 1998, The Greatest Single Feature, A Sky-line Drive, 2006, (with Darwin Lambert) Herbert Hoover's Hideaway, 2011; author 22 books/hist. structure reports; contbr. numerous articles to profl. jours. Mem. Am. Soc. Landscape Architects (preservation com. 1986—). Achievements include managed restoration of over 20 historic houses and landscapes in Pennsylvania, Delaware and Virginia. Avocations: gardening, reading, travel. Home: 621 E 51st St Savannah GA 31405 Business E-Mail: reedengle@att.net.

ENGLERT, ROY THEODORE, lawyer; b. Nashville, Sept. 11, 1922; s. Roy T. and Ruth Rowe (Tindall) E.; m. Helen Frances Wiggs, Sept. 25, 1948; children: Lee Ann, Roy Jr. BA, Vanderbilt U., 1943; JD, Columbia, 1951; LLM, George Washington U., 1953. Bar: Tenn. 1951, US Dist. Ct. DC 1951, US Supreme Ct. 1955, Internat. Trade 1975. Asst. counsel Office Comptroller of Currency, U.S. Treasury Dept., 1951-58, chief counsel, 1958-62, asst. gen. counsel of dept., 1962-66, dep. gen. counsel, 1966-73; sole practice Washington, 1973-96. Bd. dirs., sec. Walker/Potter Assocs., Inc., Washington, 1973-96; mem. Sr. Seminar in Fgn. Policy, Dept. State, 1963-64, US Assay Commn., 1975; lectr., writer on banking law. Contbr. articles to profl. jours. Judo tech. ofcl. Atlanta Olympics; bd. dirs. Westminster at Lake Ridge, Ingleside at Rock Creek, Ingleside at King Farm. Lt. USNR, 1943—46, participated in D-Day invasion at Normandy. Recipient Exceptional Service award U.S. Treasury, 1972, Gen. Counsel's award, 1973; winner 31 nat. championships in master track events, Gold and Silver medal, World Masters Track Championships. Mem. ABA, Tenn. Bar Assn. Presbyterian. Home: 12183 Cathedral Dr Woodbridge VA 22192-2227 Office: 6720 Bellamy Ave Springfield VA 22152-3023 E-mail: frodo49r@aol.com.

ENGLES, GREGG L., food products executive; b. Durant, Okla., Aug. 16, 1957; AB, Dartmouth Coll., 1979; JD, Yale Univ., 1982. Law clk. Judge Anthony Kennedy, US Ct. Appeals, 1982—83; pres. Engles Capital Corp., 1988—92; chmn., CEO Reddy Ice Co., 1988—95; pres. Engles Mgmt. Corp., 1993—94, Suiza Dairy, San Juan, 1993—95; chmn. Velda Farms, 1994—95; founder, chmn., CEO Suiza Foods, Dallas, 1995—2001; vice-chmn., CEO Dean Foods Co., Dallas, 2001—02, chmn., CEO, 2002—. Bd. dir. Grocery Manufacturers Am. Bd. mem. Southwestern Med. Found., So. Methodist Univ., Dallas Citizens Council, TreeHouse Foods; mem. Dartmouth President's Leadership Council. Mem.: Dallas CEO Roundtable, Young Presidents Org. Office: Dean Foods Co Ste 1200 2515 McKinney Ave Dallas TX 75201-1945

ENGLIN, DAVID L., state legislator; b. Frankfurt, Germany, Aug. 15, 1974; m. Shayna Beth Wolin; 1 child, Caleb. BS in History, USAF Acad., Colo., 1996; MA, Harvard U. Kennedy Sch. Govt., Mass., 1998. V.p. LiveWire Media Rels.; mem. Dist. 45 Va. House of Delegates, 2006—; mem. Privileges & Elections Com., Health, Welfare & Institutions Com., 2006—. Mem. Beth El Hebrew Congregation. Served with USAF, 1992—2004. Decorated Air Force Hist. Found. award, Numerous awards. Mem.: Dem. Svc. Coalition (bd. mem.), Jewish War Vet. USA, Equality Va. NARAL Pro-Choice Va., Del Ray Citizens Assn. (traffic com. chmn.), USAF Acad. Assn. Grad., Air Force Acad. Soc. Washington. Democrat. Jewish. Office: City Hall 301 King St Box 65 Alexandria VA 22314 Office Phone: 703-549-3203. Business E-Mail: DelDEnglin@house.virginia.gov.

ENGLISH, FLOYD LEROY, telecommunications industry executive; b. Nicolaus, Calif., June 10, 1934; s. Elvan L. and Louise (Corliss) E.; children from previous marriage: children: Roxane, Darryl; m. Elaine Ewell, July 3, 1981; 1 child, Christine. AB in Physics, Calif. State U., Chico, 1959; MS in Physics, Ariz. State U., 1962, PhD in Physics, 1965; DSc (hon.), Calif. State U., Chico, 2005. Divsn. supr. Sandia Labs., Albuquerque, 1965-73; gen. mgr. integrated cirs. divsn. Rockwell Internat.-Collins, Newport Beach, Calif., 1973—75; pres. Darcom, Albuquerque, 1975-79; cons in energy mgmt. and acquisitions Albuquerque, 1980-81; v.p. U.S. ops. Andrew Corp., Orland Park, Ill., 1981-82, pres., 1981-82, COO, 1981-82, CEO, 1983-92, also bd. dirs., 1982—, bd. dirs., pres., CEO, 1992—2001, chmn., bd. dirs., CEO, 2001—02, chmn. bd. dirs., 2002—04, chmn. emeritus, 2004. Contbr. articles to profl. jours. 1st lt. U.S. Army, 1954-57; capt. Res., 1957-69 Mem.: IEEE, Internat. Engring. Consortium (bd. dirs. 1984—2002), Exec. Club Chgo. (bd. dirs. 1983—2004). Republican. Presbyterian. Home: 223 Maxan St PMB 301 Port Isabel TX 78578

ENGLISH, JANE, state legislator; b. Lincoln, Nebr., Nov. 9, 1940; m. Don English; children: Steven, Rebecca. BS in Econ. & Fin., Ark. Tech. U., 1981. Sr. project mgr. Ark. Dept. Econ. Devel., 1984—97; exec. dir. Fort Chaffee Pub. Trust, 1997—98, Ark. Workforce Investment Bd. Gov. Cabinet, 2001—04; vol. outreach coord. Support Guard & Res. Dept. Defense, 2001—; mem. Dist. 42 Ark. House of Reps., 2008—. Adv. econ. & workforce policy devel. Rockefeller for Gov. Campaign, 2005. Chmn. Pulaski County Rep. Com., 2004—; mem. Gov. Appointed State Psychology Bd., 2006—, Ark. Veterans Coalition, 2007—, Camp Robinson & Camp Pike Cmty. Coun., 2007—, Little Rock Air Force Base Cmty. Coun., 2007—, Conway C. of C., 2008, Jacksonville C. of C., 2008, North Little Rock C. of C., 2008. Mem.: Ark. Mfrs. Assn. (exec. dir. 1998—2001), Ark. Econ. Developers, Veterans Foreign Wars Aux., Disabled Am. Veterans Aux., North Pulaski Rep. Women, Runyan Acres Vol. Fire Dept. Aux. Republican. Methodist. Office: State Capitol Rm 350 Little Rock AR 72201 Home: 2401 Lakeview Rd Apt L2 North Little Rock AR 72116-9413 Office Phone: 501-682-6211, 501-682-7771, 501-835-7465. Business E-Mail: englishj@arkleg.state.ar.us.

ENGSBERG, MARK DAVID, law librarian, educator; b. St. Louis, Mo., Sept. 25, 1962; s. David Arthur and Evelyn Sue Engsberg; m. Rebecca Baldwin, May 23, 1987; children: Caleb David, Elizabeth Virginia. BA, Drury Coll., 1980—84; JD, Willamette U. Coll. of Law, 1984—87; MA, U. of Ill., 1991—94, PhD, 1994—99, MSLIS, 1999—2000. Bar: Idaho State 1988. Reference libr. Lillian Goldman Law Libr., Yale Law Sch., 2000—01, internat. law libr., 2001, head reference; asst. prof. law, dir. libr. svcs. Hugh F. MacMillan Law Libr. Emory U. Sch. Law. Contbg. author, contbg. editor, bd. mem. Gale Ency. of Everyday Law. Contbr. Law Libr. Jour.; Oxford Ency. of Am. Law. Capt. US Army, 1988—91. Mem.: Internat. Assn. of Law Libraries, Spl. Libraries Assn., Conn. Libr. Assn., Am. Libraries Assn., Am. Assn. of Law Libraries. Office: Emory University School Law Hugh F MacMillan Law Library 1301 Clifton Rd Atlanta GA 30322 Office Phone: 404-727-6983. E-mail: mark.engsberg@yale.edu, mark.engsberg@emory.edu.

ENHOLM, J. ERIC, chemistry professor, department chairman; b. LA, Mar. 27, 1957; s. Don King and Sue Marie Enholm; m. Gann Enholm, May 14, 1994; children: Zoe Orin, Zane Erica. PhD, U. Utah, Salt Lake City, 1985. Prof. chemistry U. Fla., Gainesville, 1998—, assoc. chair, 2003—. Office: Univ Fla Dept Chemistry Gainesville FL 32611

ENNIS, A. LESLIE, gas industry executive; Mgr. sys. maintenance and programming Piedmont Natural Gas Co., Inc., dir. bus. info. solutions, 2001—04, v.p. info. svcs., 2004—. Office: Piedmont Natural Gas Company Inc 4720 Piedmont Row Dr Charlotte NC 28210 Office Phone: 704-364-3120. Office Fax: 704-365-8515.

ENNIS, EDGAR WILLIAM, JR., lawyer; b. Macon, Ga., May 20, 1945; s. Edgar W. and Nelle (Branan) Ennis; m. Judith Anne Godfrey, June 29, 1974; children: William, Branan. BS in Engring. Sci., USAF Acad., Colorado Springs, Colo., 1967; JD, U. Ga., 1971. Bar: Ga. 1971. Commd. 2d lt. USAF, 1967, advanced through ranks to capt., 1970, resigned, 1975; asst. US atty. US Atty.'s Office-Mid. Dist. Ga., Macon, 1975-88; US atty. US Dept. Justice, Macon, 1988-93; of counsel Haynsworth, Baldwin, Johnson & Harper, Macon, 1993-97; ptnr. Haynsworth, Baldwin, Johnson & Greaves LLC, Macon, 1998-99, Constangy, Brooks & Smith LLC, Macon, 1999—2008; superior ct. judge Macon Jud. Cir., 2008—. Office Phone: 478-621-6575.

ENNS, JOHN T., state legislator; b. Enid, Okla. m. Charla Enns. BA, Tabor Coll.; postgraduate studies, Northwestern Okla. State Univ. Rancher, farmer; tchr.; crop loss adjuster USDA; dep. assessor; mem. Dist. 41 Okla. House of Representatives, 2007—. Recipient Okla. Ahead ACCESS award, 2009, Canadian County Caring Kids award, 2007, Legis. of Yr. award, Okla. Dept. Rehab Ctrs., 2006. Mem.: Civil Air Patrol, Nat. Rifle Assn. Republican. Address: 1741 Pawhuska Enid OK 73703 Office: Okla House of Reprs 2300 N Lincoln Blvd Rm 434 Oklahoma City OK 73105 Home Phone: 508-237-0126; Office Phone: 405-557-7321. Personal E-mail: jte67@hotmail.com. Business E-Mail: john.enns@okhouse.gov.

ENOCH, CRAIG TRIVELY, retired judge; b. Wichita, Kans., Apr. 3, 1950; BA, So. Meth. U., 1972, JD, 1975; LLM, U. Va., 1992. Bar: Tex. 1975, U.S. Dist. Ct. (no. & we. dist.) Tex. 1976, U.S. Ct. Appeals (5th cir.) 1979; cert. Civil Trial Law. Assoc. Burford, Ryburn & Ford, Dallas, 1975-77; ptnr. Moseley, Jones, Enoch & Martin, Dallas, 1977-81; judge 101st Dist. Ct., Dallas, 1981-87; chief justice Tex. Ct. Appeals (5th dist.), 1987-92; justice Tex. Supreme Ct., Austin, 1993—2003; chair appellate practice, mem. litigation and govt. rels. sects. Winstead PC, Austin, 2003—11, Enoch Kever PLLC, Austin, 2011—. Pres. Appellate Judges Edn. Inst., 2002—; guest commentator various Nat. TV news programs. Mem. exec. bd. Dedman Sch. Law So. Meth. U., 1990—. Capt. USAFR, 1973-81. Recipient Outstanding Young Lawyer in Dallas, 1985, Disting. Alumni award for judicial svc. So. Meth. U. Dedman Sch. Law, 1999, J. Edward Finch Law Day Speech award, 2001, Disting. Alumni award So. Meth. U., 2006, Outstanding Lead Article award Tex. Tech. Law Rev., 2006-07. Fellow: Dallas Bar Found., Tex. State Bar Found., Am. Bar Found.; mem.: ABA (past chair exec. bd. appellate judges conf. jud. divsn.), Tex. Supreme Ct. (liaison to State Bar of Tex. 1999—2003), Am. Law Inst. Episcopalian. Office Phone: 512-370-2883. Business E-Mail: cenoch@winstead.com.

ENSTROM, TOBIAS, professional hockey player; b. Nordingra, Sweden, Nov. 5, 1984; Defenseman MoDo Hockey (Swedish Elite League), 2002—07, Atlanta Thrashers, 2007—. Mem. Team Sweden, World Jr. Championships, Nova Scotia, 2003, Finland, 2004, Team Sweden, World Championships, Moscow, 2007. Named to NHL YoungStars Game, 2008, All-Rookie Team, NHL, 2008. Office: Atlanta Thrashers Centennial Tower, Ste 1900 101 Marietta St NW Atlanta GA 30303

ENTERLINE, LARRY L., staffing company executive; BSEE with honors, Case Western Res. U.; MBA, Cleve. State U. Mgmt. positions in mktg., sales, engring. and products Reliance Electric Co., 1974—84; v.p. mktg. & sales Bailey Controls Co., 1984—89; sr. mgmt. positions including corp. sr. v.p. worldwide sales & svc. Scientific-Atlanta, Inc., 1989—2000; ptnr. Robinson, Bradshaw and Hinson, P.A., 1990—96; CEO, chmn. bd. dirs. Venturi Ptnrs., Inc. (merged with COMSYS Holding, Inc.), 2000—04; CEO Strategic Management, Inc., 2004—; ptnr. Kennedy Covington Lobdell & Hickman, LLP, 2005—; CEO, bd. dirs. COMSYS IT Partners, Inc., 2006—. Bd. dirs. World Acceptance Corp., 1994—, Pacific Intermedia, Inc., 2004—, Raptor Networks Tech., Inc., 2004—, Concurrent Computer Corp., 2005—. Mem.: IEEE, Am. Staffing Assn., Soc. Cable TV Engrs., Instrument Soc. America, Cable TV Adminstrn. & Mktg. Soc., Tech. Assn. of Pulp and Paper Industry, Women in Cable & Telecomm. Office: COMSYS IT Partners Inc 4400 Post Oak Pky Ste 1800 Houston TX 77027 Office Fax: 713-961-0719.

ENTHOVEN, ADOLF JAN HENRI, accounting educator; b. Nymegan, Utrecht, Netherlands, Apr. 2, 1928; came to U.S., 1953; s. Jaap Philip and Tine Catherina (Croll) E. Postgrad. in Social and Bus. Adminstrn., Netherlands Sch. of Econs., 1946-51; M in Commerce, U. Toronto, 1953; advanced diploma in Econs. Planning and Nat. Acctg., Inst. Social Sci., The Hague, Netherlands, 1957; D of Bus. Econs., Netherlands Sch. Econs., 1960. Dir. Europe Coopers & Lybrand, NYC, 1957-64; sr. investment officer The World Bank, Washington, 1964-66; prof. acctg. U. Ill., Urbana, 1966-68; dir. corp. planning Washington Steele Co., Washington, 1968-70; prof. acctg., dir. ctr. internat. acctg. devel. U. Tex., Dallas, 1976—. Disting. vis. prof. U. NC, 1974—76. Author: Accounting and Economic Development Policy, 1973, Accounting System in Third World Economies, 1977, Accounting Education in Economic Development Management, 1981, Current Value Accounting, 1984. Grantee Ford Found., 1973-74. Mem. Consortium in Internat. Govt. Fin. Mgmt. (bd. dirs.), Govt. Acctg. Assn. (exec. com., internat. com.), Nat. Assn. Accts., (internat. com.), Am. Acctg. Assn. (chmn. internat. com. 1977-80). Clubs: Canyon Creek Country (Richardson). Presbyterian. Avocations: tennis, skiing, reading. Office: U Tex Dallas PO Box 688 Richardson TX 75080 Home: 2413 W Prairie Creek Dr Richardson TX 75080-2654 Home Phone: 972-783-0830; Office Phone: 972-883-2320.

ENZE, CHARLES R., energy executive; b. SD; 2 children. Studied Earthquake & Seismic Resistance, Rice U., Houston; studied Offshore Structures Design, Tulane U., New Orleans; B in civil Engring., SD Sch. Mines & Tech.; grad. Shell's Advanced Mgmt. Program, INSEAD, Fontainebleau, France. Registered profl. engr., Calif., Tex. V.p., engring. & projects Shell Internat. Exploration & Prodn.; mgr. Sandow Power Co. LLC.; chmn., TXU generation constrn. Energy Future Holdings Corp. (formerly TXU corp.), dir., TXU generation constrn., joined, 2006; pres., TXU generation constrn. Energy Future Holdings Corp. (formerly TXU Corp.), 2006—, CEO, TXU generation constrn., 2006—; CEO Luminant Constrn. (subs. of Energy Future Holdings Corp.), 2006—; mgr. Oak Grove Mgmt. Co., 2006—. Bd. dirs. Oak Grove Mining Co. LLC. Office: Energy Future Holdings Corp 1601 Bryan St Energy Plz Dallas TX 75201 Office Phone: 214-812-4600. Business E-Mail: charles.enze@txu.com.

EPPES, THOMAS EVANS, advertising and public relations executive; b. NYC, Aug. 10, 1952; s. Benjamin F. and Eileen (Evans) E.; m. Jennie Spradling, Aug. 2, 1980; children: Benjamin, Jared, Michael. BS, U. So. Miss., 1974. Reporter Jackson (Miss.) Daily News, 1974-75, 76-77, Clearwater (Fla.) Sun, 1975-76; pub. info. coord. Miss. Rsch. and Devel. Ctr., Jackson, 1976-78; press sec. Gov. Bill Waller for U.S. Senate, Jackson, 1978, Maurice Dantin for U.S. Senate, Jackson, 1978; dir. pub. rels. Days Inns Am., Atlanta, 1978-82, Mgmt. Sci. Am., Atlanta, 1982-85; pres., pub. rels. Eric Mower & Assocs. (formerly Price-McNabb), Charlotte, NC, 1985-91, pres., CEO, 1992—94, pres., 1994—, sr. ptnr., bd. dirs. Spkr. nat. confs. on comms. and mktg. Bd. dirs., comms. chmn. United Way of Asheville and Buncombe, 1986-87; campaign dir. Jacksonians for Mayor, Jackson, 1976; bd. advisors U. Colo., Boulder Inc. Sch. Fellow Pub. Rels. Soc. Am. (counselor's acad., exec. bd. counselor's acad. 1998-2000, Coll. of Fellows 2000, Silver Anvil award 1993), Internat. Assn. Bus. Communicators (Gold Quill award 1980, 81), Internat. Comms. Agy. Network (v.p. 2002), Charlotte C. of C. (bd. dirs. 1997), Charlotte Pub. Rels. Soc. Am. (nat. assembly del., bd. dirs. 2005-06, nat. bd. 2006-, Infinity award 2006). Avocation: golf. Office: Eric Mower & Assocs 1001 Morehead Square Dr 5th Flr Charlotte NC 28203-4253

EPPS, ANNA CHERRIE, immunologist, educator, dean interim president; b. New Orleans, July 8, 1930; d. Ernest and Anna L. (Johnson) Cherrie; m. Joseph M. Epps, Sr., Nov. 23, 1968. BS, Howard U., 1951, PhD, 1966; MS, Loyola U., New Orleans, 1959. Technologist clin. lab. dept. Our Lady of Mercy Hosp., Cin., 1953-54; asst. prof., acting chmn. dept. med. tech. Xavier U., New Orleans, 1954-60; technologist dept. medicine La. State U. Sch. Medicine, New Orleans, 1954-60; asst. prof. microbiology Coll. Medicine Howard U., Washington, 1961-69; fellow dept. medicine Sch. Medicine Johns Hopkins U., Balt., 1969; asst. prof., USPHS faculty fellow dept. medicine Tulane U. Sch. Medicine, New Orleans, 1969-71, assoc. prof., 1971-75, prof., 1975—97, assoc. dean student svcs., 1970—97; dir. med. edn. reinforcement and enrichment program Tulane U. Med. Ctr., New Orleans, 1969—97; acting dean, v.p. acad. affairs Meharry Med. Coll., Nashville, 1994—96, dean sch. med., sr. v.p. acad. affairs, 1997—2002, dean emerita, sr. advisor to pres., 2002—. Co-author: Medrep, Tulane U.; co-editor: Medical Education: Responses to a Challenge; mem. editorial bd. Jour. Med. Edn., 1980—; contbr. articles to med. jours. Trustee Children's Hosp., New Orleans, 1977-79; regent Georgetown U., Washington, 1975—; bd. dirs. Diabetes Assn. Greater New Orleans, 1978; mem. La. Bd. Health and Rehab. Svcs., 1978; adv. mem. Kellogg Nat. Fellowship Program, 1981. Recipient award for meritorious rsch. Interstate Postgrad. Med. Assn. N.Am., 1966, Scroll of Merit, Nat. Med. Assn., 1980, Herbert W. Nickens award, AAMC, 2003, dr. harold delancy award, Am. Assn. Blacks Higher Edn., 2008. Mem. Am. Soc. Clin. Pathologists (cert. in med. tech. and blood banking), Am. Soc. Med. Technologists, Am. Assn. Blood Banks (cert. in blood banking), Am. Soc. Tropical Medicine and Hygiene, AAUP, Musser-Burch Soc., Albertus Magnus Guild, Washington Helminthol. Soc., Am. Soc. Bacteriologists, Sigma Xi. Home: 769 Sinclair Cir Brentwood TN 37027-2921 Office: Meharry Med Coll 1005 D B Todd Blvd Nashville TN 37208 Home Phone: 615-371-2404; Office Phone: 615-327-5935. Business E-Mail: acepps@mmc.edu.

EPPS, JAMES A., state legislator; b. Macon, Ga., Sept. 7, 1943; m. Kathryn Epps; children: Pam, Jae, Lesley. AA, Brewton Parker Coll., 1963; BS, Mercer U., 1965, MEd., 1969. Prin. Gorden-Ivey Sch., 1968—77; mem. Twigs County Bd. of Tax Assessors, 1979—82; part-owner Epps & Jones Constrn. Co., 1978—86; commr. Twigs County, 1984—88; chairman Twigs County Bd. of Commrs., 1989—92; mgmt. Epps Bros. Inc., 1986—94, owner, 1994—; mem. Dist. #140 Ga. House of Reps., Ga., 2008—. Democrat. Bapt. Office: Capitol Office 411-E Coverdell Legislative Office Bldg Atlanta GA 30334 also: District Office PO Box 236 Dry Branch GA 31020 Office Phone: 404-656-0126, 478-743-1398. E-mail: bubber.epps@house.ga.gov.

EPSTEIN, DAVID STANLEY, educator, consultant; b. NYC, Apr. 17, 1948; s. Mortimer and Shirley Ruth (Silver) Epstein. BA, Adelphi U., 1970; PhD, St. John's U., Jamaica, NY, 1979. Cert. tchr. NY. Rsch. scientist NY State Inst. Basic Rsch., SI, 1979—80; tchr. NYC Bd. Edn., 1981—99, Richmond Pub. Schs., 1999—2000; lectr. J. Sargeant Reynolds CC, 2002—04, asst. prof. natural sci., 2004—. Cons. in field. Contbr. articles to profl. jours. Mem.: Chemistry Tchr.'s Club NY, Am. Soc. Zoologists, Am. Soc. Microbiologists, Sigma Xi. Democrat. Jewish. Avocation: collecting books. Home: 5018 Sulky Dr Apt 204 Richmond VA 23228 Home Phone: 804-814-6640. Personal E-mail: depstein.6640@verizon.net.

EPSTEIN, JEFFREY S., hair restoration, facial plastic surgeon, otolaryngologist, educator; BA, Swarthmore Coll.; MD, U. of Vt. Coll. of Medicine, 1988. Diplomate Am. Bd. Otolaryngology, Am. Bd. Facial Plastic and Reconstructive Surgery, Am. Bd. Hair Restoration Surgery, 1998. Resident otolaryngology Jackson Meml. Hosp., Miami, Fla., 1989—93; clin. instr. otolaryngology, divsn. of facial plastic surgery Univ. of Miami Sch. of Medicine; solo pvt. practice Miami, 1994—, NY, 2005—; hosp. affiliation includes South Miami Hosp. Found. for Hair Restoration and Plastic Surgery, 2008; past pres. Fla. Soc. of Facial Plastic and Reconstructive Surgery. Fellow: ACS, Am. Acad. Facial and Reconstructive Plastic Surgery. Office: South Miami Hospital 6200 SW 73rd St Miami FL 33143-9990 Office Phone: 786-662-4000.

EPSTEIN, JON DAVID, lawyer, educator; b. Dec. 25, 1942; m. Elizabeth A. Epstein. BS, U. Ill., 1965, JD, 1967. Bar: Ill. 1970, Tex. 1974, DC 1978. Assoc. counsel Blue Cross Assn., Chgo., 1969—74; ptnr. Wood, Lucksinger & Epstein, Houston, 1974—91, Vinson & Elkins LLP, 1991—2007; co-head Health Sect., of counsel Greer, Herz & Adams LLP, Galveston, 2008—. Mem. faculty Aspen Sys. Health Care Seminars, 1974—; adj. prof. U. Houston Coll. Law, 1982—, St. Louis U. Health Sci. Ctr., 1981—91. Contbr. articles to profl. jours. Chmn. bd. dirs. Gulf Coast Chpt. March of Dimes, 1994—95; mem. devel. bd. U. Tex. Med. Br., 2000—; mem. bd. of visitors U. Ill. Coll. Law, 2000—; vol. Epstein program healthlaw U. Ill., 2005—. Officer US Army, 1967. Fellow: Am. Soc. Hosp. Attys. (dir., pres. elect 1985, pres. 1986); mem.: ABA, Hosp. Fin. Mgmt. Assn. (dir. Gulf Coast chpt. 1977—79), DC Bar Assn., Tex. Bar Assn., Houston Bar Assn., Houston Touchdown Club (pres. 1981). Office: 1 Moddy Plz 18th Fl Galveston TX 77550 Office Phone: 409-797-3225. Business E-Mail: jepstein@greerherz.com.

EPSTEIN, ROBERT MARVIN, anesthesiologist, educator; b. NYC, Mar. 10, 1928; s. Nathan B. and Rebecca Epstein; m. Lillian Ray Cohen, Dec. 31, 1950; children: Judith Susan, Neal Myron, Charles Benjamin. BS with distinction, U. Mich., 1947, MD cum laude, 1951. Diplomate Am. Bd. Anesthesiology (dir. 1972-84, pres. 1979-80). Intern U. Mich. Hosp., 1951—52; resident in anesthesiology Presbyn. Hosp., NYC, 1952—53, 1955—56; instr. in anesthesiology and fellow in medicine Columbia U., NYC, 1956—57, assoc., 1957—59, asst. prof., anesthesiology, 1959—65, assoc. prof., 1965—70, prof., 1970—72, U. Va., Charlottesville, 1972—74, Alumni prof., 1974—87, Disting. prof., 1987—92, Harold Carron prof., 1992—2002, dept. chmn., 1972—96, Harold Carron prof. emeritus, 2002—. Mem. anesthesiology tng. com. Nat. Inst. Gen. Med. Scis., NIH, 1966—69; mem. com. on anesthesia NRC, 1970—71; mem. Nat. Bd. Med. Examiners, 1982—90, Am. Bd. Med. Specialities, 1974—95. Editor: Anesthesiology, 1974—79; contbr. numerous articles to profl. jours. Mem. Ednl. Commn. for Fgn. Med. Grads., 1990—95; bd. dirs., sec. U. Va. Health Svcs. Found., 1980—90, pres., 1990—93; trustee Ednl. Commn. for Fgn. Med. Grads., 1991—95, vice chmn., 1994—95; bd. dirs. QualChoice of Va., 1997—2000. With US Army, 1953—55. Fellow Guggenheim fellow, Oxford U., England, 1966—67, NY Heart Assn., 1956—57; scholar in-residence, Inst. Medicine NAS, 1997, sr. scholar, Va. Health Policy Ctr., 1997—2002. Fellow: Royal Coll. Anaesthetists (Eng.); mem.: W.T.G. Morton Soc., Assn. Univ. Anesthesiologists (pres. 1973—74), Anaesthetic Rsch. Soc. (U.K.), Am. Soc. Pharmacology and Exptl. Therapeutics, Soc. Acad. Anesthesia Chmn. (rep. to Coun. Acad. Soc. Assn. Am. Med. Coll. 1984—91, mem. coun.), Am. Soc. Anesthesiologists, Am. Physiol. Soc., Inst. Medicine NAS, AAAS, Alpha Omega Alpha, Sigma Xi, Phi Beta Kappa. Avocations: sailing, photography. Office: Dept Anesthesiology PO Box 800710 Charlottesville VA 22908-0710

ERASMUS, JEREMY JOHN, diagnostic radiologist, educator; MD, U. Witwatersrand, 1982. Diplomate Am. Bd. Radiology-diagnostic radiology, 1993. Clin. intern gen. surgery, internal medicine, and pediatric orthopedics Baragwanath Hosp., 1983—84; clin. resident diagnostic radiology Queen's Univ., Kingston, 1989—93; clin. fellow thoracic imaging Duke Univ. Med. Ctr., Durham, 1994—95; prof. diagnostic radiology dept. The Univ. of Tex. MD Anderson Cancer Ctr. Co-author: (publs.) Comparing the quantification of static, gated, and list mode PET data acquisition of moving objects, 2005, Integrated computed tomography-positron emission tomography in patients with potentially resectable malignant pleural mesothelioma: Staging implications, 2005, Application of the revised lung cancer staging system (IASLC Staging Project) to a cancer center population, 2009, Mycotic pulmonary artery aneurysm due to Aspergillus infection in a patient with leukemia: case report and review of the literature, 2010, Improved long-term outcome with chemoradiotherapy strategies in esophageal cancer, 2010, Computed Tomography Findings Predicting Invasiveness of Thymoma, 2011, and numerous others. Recipient Commendation for Distinguished Med. Svc., South African Med. Corp., 1984—86, Editor's Recognition award, Jour. of Thoracic Imaging, 2009—10, and several others. Office: The University of Texas MD Anderson Cancer Center Radiology Department Unit 1478 1515 Holcombe Blvd Houston TX 77030 Office Phone: 713-792-5878.

ERB, KARL ALBERT, physicist, government official, retired consultant; b. Chgo., June 30, 1942; s. Edgar Gillette and Dorothy (Carsten) E.; children: Janet, Margaret. BA, NYU, 1965; MS, U. Mich., 1966, PhD, 1970. Instr. U. Pitts., 1970-72; instr., asst. prof., assoc. prof. Yale U., New Haven, 1972-80; staff scientist Oak Ridge Nat. Lab., Tenn., 1980-86; program dir. NSF, Washington, 1986-89, dep. dir. physics divsn., 1991; asst. dir. White House Office Sci. and Tech. Policy, Washington, 1989-91; acting assoc. dir. for phys. scis. and engring. White House Office of Sci. and Tech. Policy, Washington, 1991-92, assoc. dir. for phys. scis. engring., 1992-93; sr. sci. advisor NSF, 1993-98; dir. office of polar programs NSF and US Antarctic Program, 1998—2012; chair U. Lapland Arctic Ctr. Sci. Bd., 2009—12; panel expert WmO Exec. Coun., 2009—. Exec. sec. Pres.'s Com. for the Nat. Medal of Sci., 1993-99; exec. com. Fed. Demonstration Partnership, 1996-99; chmn. Coun. Mgrs. Nat. Antarctic Program, 2000-04; U.S. rep. Arctic Sci. Coun. Regional Bd.; vice chair APS Com. on Internat. Sci., 1999-2002, mem. U.S. Nuc. Sci. Adv. Com., Washington, 1983-86; vis. prof. J.W. Goethe U., Frankfurt, 1978; bd. govs. U.S.-Indo. S&T forum, 2001-02. Contbr. articles to physics jours. and encys., chpts. to books. Recipient Pres. Sr. Exec. Svc. Meritorious award, 1998, 2003, Pres.'s Disting. Svc. award, 2006, New Zealand Antarctic medal, 2007, Chevalier, French Legion Merit. Fellow AAAS, Am. Phys. Soc. Office: NSF 4201 Wilson Blvd Arlington VA 22230-0001 Personal E-mail: karlerb7@gmail.com. Business E-Mail: kerb@nsf.gov.

ERDEY, DALE, state legislator; Mem. Dist. 71 La. House of Reps., 2000—07; mem. Dist. 13 La. State Senate, 2008—, vice chair transp., hwys. and pub. works com., select com. on vocat. and tech. edn., mem. health and welfare com., judiciary B com., revenue and fiscal affairs com. Republican. Mailing: Dist Off PO Box 908 Livingston LA 70754 Office Phone: 225-686-2881. Fax: 225-686-7353. E-mail: erdeyd@legis.state.la.us.

ERENSTEIN, ALAN, emergency nurse, legal nurse consultant, staff educator; Grad., Aliquippa Hosp Sch. Radiology, Pa., 1974; student, Aliquippa Hosp. Sch. Radiology, New Wilmington, Pa., 1974; AA in Gen. Studies, LPN, Beaver County C.C., Monaca, Pa., 1977, AS in Nursing, RN, 1979. RN, Fla.; registered radiologic technologist, cert. legal nurse cons. LPN Hamot Med. Ctr., Erie, Pa., 1977-78; team leader Trauma-Neuro ICU and Stepdown Unit Allegheny Gen. Hosp., Pitts., 1979-81, staff nurse Emergency Room, 1981; flight nurse LifeWATCH HCA Wesley Med. Ctr., Wichita, Kans., 1981-91, contigency and float pool, 1991-92, hyperbaric nurse, 1991-92; ER nurse, relief charge nurse, clin. coord., team leader JFK Med. Ctr., Atlantis, Fla., 1992-95; aeromed. specialist Bizjet Air Ambulance, West Palm Beach, Fla., 1994-95; med. edn. cons. Med. Edn. Cons. Am., Tampa, 1994-97; with disaster team Cutler Ridge (Fla.) Field Hosp., 1992; response team Kans. Tornado Wesley Med. Ctr., Wichita, 1991; dept. staff nurse DelRay Med. Ctr., 1995—2013; staff educator emergency dept. Delray Med. Ctr., 2012—13; staff nurse Bethesda Health, Boynton Beach, Fla., 2013—. Paramedic clin. coord. Hutchinson (Kans.) C.C., 1989; skills lab coord. Advanced Trauma Life Support Course, HCA Wesley Med. Ctr., Wichita, 1989-92; lectr.in field; cons. in field, trauma nurse core course-instr.1995-; advanced cardiac life support-instr. 2012 Author: Trauma in Pregnancy, 1990; co-author: LifeWATCH Transport Manual, 1988; contbr. Society Trauma Nurses: Instructor's Resource Manual for Trauma Nursing, The Pregnant Trauma Patient Module, 1998.

ERGAS, JEAN-PIERRE MAURICE, packaging company executive; b. Marseille, France, July 9, 1939; came to U.S., 1989; m. Annie Bourdel, Sept. 4, 1964; children: Nicolas, Yannick, Sebastien and Benjamin (twins). Degree in Economics, Inst. d'Etudes Politiques, Paris, 1962; MBA, Harvard U., 1965. Chmn., CEO Alcan Aluminum Ltd., sr. exec.; mgr. Aluminum Mktg. div. Pechiney, Paris, 1970-73; pres. Cebal Pechiney Packaging, Paris, 1974-82, chmn., CEO and bd. dirs., 1982—; pres. Cegedur Pechiney, Paris, 1982-88, chmn., CEO, 1987-88; also bd. dirs. Pechiney Group, Paris, sr. exec. v.p., 1989—; also bd. dirs. American National Can Co., Chgo., vice chmn., 1989, chmn., CEO, 1989—; chmn. & CEO Bway Corp., Atlanta, 2000—07, non-exec. chmn., 2008—. Bd. dirs. Aplix, Paris., Dover Corp., Compagnie Plastic Omnium SA, 1990-. Chmn. Institut La Boetie, Paris, 1989. 1st lt. French Army, 1965-66. Sachs Found. scholar, 1963. Mem. Harvard Club Paris. Roman Catholic. Avocation: tennis. Office: Bway Corp 8607 Roberts Dr Ste 250 Atlanta GA 30350 Office Phone: 770-645-4800. Office Fax: 770-645-4810. Business E-Mail: jean-Pierre.ergas@bwaycorp.com.

ERICKSON, ROBERT PORTER, psychology professor; b. South Bend, Ind., Feb. 13, 1930; s. Carl Gustav and Elinor (Porter) E.; children: Lars, Nils, David. PhD, Brown U., 1958. Prof. psychology, neurobiology Duke U., Durham, 1961—. Served to lt. (j.g.) USN, 1951-54. Home: 108 Lakeshore Dr Durham NC 27713 Business E-Mail: eric@psych.duke.edu.

ERICKSON, SHANNON, state legislator; b. Raleigh, NC, Apr. 21, 1963; d. William Monroe and Martha Jane (Hattaway) Smith; m. Kendall F. Erickson, Mar. 26, 1983; children: Mariah, Joshua. BA, U. SC, 1997. Tchr/owner/dir. Lowcountry Bldg. Blocks, Inc.; bd. dirs. Beaufort Regional C. of C., 2003—06; pres. SC Child Care Assn., SC, 2005—; residential campaign chair United Way Beaufort County, 2005—06; mem. Dist. 124 SC House of Reps., SC, 2008—. Mem. Gov.'s Adv. Com. Child Care, 2003—. Republican. Cath. Home and Office: Dist/Home Office 129 S Hermitage Rd Beaufort SC 29902 Office: Capitol Office 306A Blatt Bldg Columbia SC 29201 Home Phone: 843-525-1439; Office Phone: 843-986-1090, 803-734-3261. E-mail: shannonerickson@schouse.org.

ERICSON, DAVID FRANK, political scientist, educator; b. Chgo., June 18, 1950; s. Arthur Edward Ericson and Ruth Irene Kessel. BA in Polit. Sci., Wayne State U., 1972; MA in Polit. Sci., U. Mich., 1973, MA in Journalism, 1976; PhD in Polit. Sci., U. Chgo., 1987. Journalist Jackson (Mich.) Citizen-Patriot, 1977, Detroit News, 1978-80; instr. Oberlin (Ohio) Coll., 1986-87; prof. Wichita (Kans.) State U., 1992—, U. Albany SUNY, 2008—09, George Mason U., 2009—. Vis. prof. Washington U., St. Louis, 1987—89, U. Chgo., 1990—91; rsch. fellow Princeton U., James Madison Ctr. Study Am. Ideals and Instns., 2007—08. Author: (book) The Shaping of American Liberalism: The Debates Over Ratification, Nullification, and Slavery, 1993, The Debate Over Slavery: Antislavery and Proslavery Liberalism in Antebellum America, 2001, Slavery in the American Republic: Developing the Federal Government, 1791-1861, 2011; editor: The Liberal Tradition in American Politics: Reassessing the Legacy of Amercian Liberalism, 1999, The Politics of Inclusion and Exclusion: Identity Politics in Twenty-First Century America, 2011; contbr. articles to profl. jours. Grantee Summer Rsch., NEH, 1994, James Madison Ctr. Study of Am. Instns. and Ideals Princeton U., 2007—08; Postdoctoral fellow, John M. Olin Ctr. Study History Polit. Culture, U. Chgo., 1989—90. Mem.: Midwest Polit. Sci. Assn., Am. Polit. Sci. Assn., Phi Beta Kappa, Pi Sigma Alpha. Avocations: tennis, hiking. Office Phone: 703-993-5119. Business E-Mail: dericso2@gmu.edu.

ERIKSON, SHELDON R., oil industry executive; b. Chgo., Sept. 23, 1941; s. Roy A. and Florence Mary (Sheldon) E.; children: Steven, Michael. MBA, Harvard U., 1970. Assoc. Booz, Allen & Hamilton, 1970—75; gen. mgr. General Electric Co., 1975—80; group v.p., plastics and Chemicals Hoover Universal, Ann Arbor, Mich., 1980—82; pres., oilfield services group NL Industries, 1982—86; pres. Joy Petroleum Equipment Co., 1986—87; pres., CEO The Western Co. of N.Am., 1987—95, chmn., 1988—95; pres. Cameron Internat. Corp. (formerly Cooper Cameron Corp.), 1995—2007, CEO, 1995—2008, chmn., 1996—2011. Bd. dir. Cameron International Corp. Bd. dirs. Harvard Bus. Sch. Club, Houston. Office: Cameron International Corp 1333 W Loop S Ste 1700 Houston TX 77027 Office Phone: 713-513-3300. Office Fax: 713-513-3456. Business E-Mail: sheldon.erikson@c-a-m.com.

ERLANDSON, DAVID ALAN, education administration educator; b. Chgo., Jan. 10, 1936; s. Gerald Kenneth and Anna Marie Schlichting E.; m. Gwyneth Ellen Jones, Sept. 21, 1957; children: Paul William, Linda Ann, Daniel Lindsay, Charles David. AB, Wheaton Coll., Ill., 1956; MS, No. Ill. U., 1962; EdD, U. Ill., 1969. Cert. supr. all grades, Ill. Tchr. jr. high sch. Geneva (Ill.) Pub. Schs., 1959-62, Unit 4 Schs., Champaign, Ill., 1962-63, dir. gifted program, 1965-68, asst. prin., 1969-71; tchr. Univ. High Sch., Urbana, Ill., 1963-64; asst. prof. SUNY, Buffalo, 1964-65; dir. Ctr. for Upgrading Ednl. Services, Champaign, 1968-69; asst. prof. Queens Coll. CUNY, Flushing, 1971—77; prof. ednl. adminstrn. Tex. A&M U., College Station, 1977—2006, prof. emeritus, 2006—, head dept. ednl. adminstrn., 1984-92. Dir. Prins.' Ctr., Tex. A&M U., 1983-85, 93-01. Author: Strengthening School Leadership, 1976, Doing Naturalistic Inquiry, 1993, Organizational Oversight, 1996; co-author: School Special Services, 1979, Measurement and Evaluation, 1999, The Emerging Principalship; co-editor School Leadership Library; contbr. 133 articles to books and profl. jours. Served to 1st lt. USMC, 1956-59. Mem. Nat. Assn. Secondary Sch. Prins. (commn. on standards for principalship 1985-88), Am. Ednl. Rsch. Assn., Phi Delta Kappa, Phi Kappa Phi. Democrat. Home: 1107 Glade St College Station TX 77840-4434 Office: Tex A&M U Dept Ednl Adminstrn College Station TX 77843-4226 Business E-Mail: d-erlandson@tamu.edu.

ERLICH, JONATHAN DARIO, professional tennis player; b. Buenos Aires, Apr. 5, 1977; s. Daniel and Susana Erlich. Profl. tennis player ATP, 1996—. Co-founder Jewish Sports Found., 2007—. Achievements include winning 13 career doubles titles, ATP; winning Australian Open to become first Israeli doubles tennis team (with Andy Ram) to win a Grand Slam title, 2008. Avocation: soccer. Office: Renaissance Tennis Mgmt 3111 University Dr Ste 601 Coral Springs FL 33065

ERSHLER, WILLIAM BALDWIN, biogerontologist, educator; b. Syracuse, NY, Jan. 13, 1949; s. Irving Leonard and Eunice (Baldwin) E.; m. Joan Lipstein, Nov. 6, 1971; children: Rachel Eve, Leah Rose. BA, Case Western Res. U., 1970; MD, SUNY Upstate Ctr., Syracuse, 1974. Diplomate Am. Bd. Internal Medicine, Am. Bd. Med. Oncology, Am. Bd. Hematology. Asst. prof. U. Vt., Burlington, 1980-85; assoc. prof. U. Wis., Madison, 1985-89, prof. medicine, 1989-96, dir. U. Wis. Inst. on Aging, 1989-96, head geriatrics, 1989-96; dir. geriatric rsch. Edn. and Clin. Ctr. William Middleton VA Hosp., Madison, 1991-96; prof. medicine, dir. Glennan Ctr. Geriatrics & gerontolog Eastern Va. Medical Sch., Norfolk, 1996-97; dir. Inst. Advanced Studies in Aging and Geriatric Medicine, Washington, 1998—, Nat. Geriatrics Rsch. Consortium, 1998—; rsch. edn. dir. Extended Care Info. Network, 1999—. Dir. Geriatric Oncology Consortium, 2001—; sr. investigator Nat. Inst. Aging, NIH, dep. clin. dir., 2006—10. Editor Jour. Gerontology, 1996-2000; contbr. articles to profl. jours. Recipient Geriatric Leadership award NIH, 1990-96; NIH grantee, 1989—. Fellow Gerontologic Soc. Am.; mem. Am. Geriatrics Soc., Am. Assn. Cancer Rsch., Am. Soc. Clin. Oncology, Am. Soc. Hematology, Assn. Dirs. Acad. Geriatrics (councilor). Jewish. Avocations: running, photography, travel. Office: 6400 Arlingron Blvd Falls Church VA 22042 Business E-Mail: wershler@iasia.org.

ERSKINE, JAMES LORENZO, physics professor; b. Seattle, Oct. 25, 1942; s. Lawrence A. and Elizabeth (Woodbury) E.; m. Julie Ann Grant; children: Michael Grant, John Lawrence. BSEE, U. Wash., 1964, MSEE, 1966, PhD in Physics, 1973. Sr. engr. and cons. Boeing Co., Seattle, 1967-74; rsch. asst. prof. dept. physics U. Ill., Urbana, 1974-77; asst. prof. dept. physics U. Tex., Austin, 1977-82, assoc. prof., 1982-86, prof., 1986—. Trull Centennial prof. Trull Found. U. Tex., 1986. Contbr. numerous articles in fields of solid state physics, magnetism and magnetic materials, surface physics, surface chemistry, and instrumentation. Grantee NSF, R.A. Welch Found., other fed. and pvt. agys. Fellow Am. Phys. Soc.; mem. Am. Vacuum Soc. Office: U Tex Grad Sch Dept Of Physics Austin TX 78712 Office Phone: 512-471-1464. Business E-Mail: erskine@physics.utexas.edu.

ERVIN, GARY W., aerospace transportation executive; B in Math. Sys. Science, U. Calif. V.p., advanced devel. programs Lockheed Martin Corp.; v.p., dep., ACS Northrop Grumman Corp., 2001—02, sector v.p., 2002, v.p., air combat sys. integrated sys. sector, 2002—05, v.p., western region, integrated sys. sector, 2005—07, corp. v.p., pres. integrated sys. sector El Segundo, Calif., corp. v.p., pres., Northrop Grumman aerospace sys., 2008—. Mem.: corp. policy coun. Northrop Grumman Corp. (assoc.). Office: Northrop Grumman Corp 2980 Fairview Park Dr Falls Church VA 22042-4511 Office Phone: 310-553-6262. Office Fax: 310-553-2076. Business E-Mail: Gary.Ervin@ngc.com.

ERVIN, ROBERT MARVIN, lawyer; b. nr. Ocala, Fla., Jan. 19, 1917; s. Richard William and Carrie (Phillips) Ervin; m. Frances Anne Cushing, Dec. 25, 1941; children: Anne Cushing, Robert Marvin Jr. BSBA, U. Fla., 1941, LLB, 1947. Bar: Fla. 1947. Of counsel Ervin, Kitchen & Ervin, Tallahassee, 1947—; part-time US referee in bankruptcy US Dist. Ct. (no. dist.) Fla., 1952-72. Mem. Fla. Constn. Revision Commn., 1966—68; trustee U. Fla. Law Ctr. Assn.; mem. founders com., mem. bd. visitors Fla. State U. Coll. Law. With USMC, 1941—45. Recipient Disting. Svc. award for Legal Edn., John B. Stetson U., 1966, Disting. Svc. award, Armed Forces League, 1966, Medal of Hon. award, Fla. Bar Found., 2003, Lifetime Achievement award, Fla. Supreme Ct. Hist. Soc., 2010; named to Fla. Housing Hall of Fame, 1993. Fellow: Am. Bar Found. (chmn. 1989—90); mem.: ABA (ho. dels. 1966—91, chmn. sect. criminal justice 1975—76, bd. govs. 1979—82, vice chmn. sr. lawyers divsn., chmn. spl. com. on fiscal policy 1984—85, mem. resource devel. coun., mem. audit com.), Nat. Conf. Referees Bankruptcy (pres. 1963—64), Fla. Supreme Ct. Hist. Soc. (pres. 1986—87, chmn. trustees 1987—98), Fla. Bar (pres. 1965—66, Disting. Svc. award 1966), Am. Judicature Soc., Am. Law Inst., Am. Coll. Trial Lawyers (bd. regents 1983—84), Ret. Officers Assn., Am. Bar Retirement Assn. (pres. 1980—82), Fla. Blue Key, Elks, Alpha Kappa Psi, Phi Alpha Delta. Baptist. Home: 530 North Ride Tallahassee FL 32303-5127 Office: PO Box 1170 Tallahassee FL 32302-1170 Office Phone: 850-386-5502. Personal E-mail: ervin090@comcast.net.

ERWIN, FRANK WILLIAM, human resources consultant; b. Elizabeth, NJ, Nov. 22, 1931; s. Frank J. and Jessie (Rugero) E.; m. Bridget E. Taddeo, June 26, 1965. BA cum laude, NYU, 1957. With MBS, 1957-62, asst. to pres., asst. sec. to bd. dirs., 1960-62; dep. dir. div. selection, dir. recruiting ops. Peace Corps, 1962-65; exec. asst. to sec. labor, 1965-68; pres., chmn. Richardson, Bellows, Henry & Co., Inc., 1968-99; advisor FBI, 1995—2007, ePredix, Inc., 1999—, Nat. Skills Stds. Bd., 2001—03, PreVisor, 2011. Chmn. fin. com. Our Lady of Lourdes Ch.; pres. Ridge House Condominium, 2002-05; v.p. Ridge House Condominium, 2001-02. With US Army, 1949—52. Mem. APA, Internat. Assn. for Advancement Pschology, Soc. for Indsl. and Orgnl. Psychology (Disting. Profl. Contbn. award, 2005), Pers. Testing Coun. Met. Washington. Home and Office: 2310 S Rolfe St Arlington VA 22202-1545 E-mail: niwre@ix.netcom.com.

ERWIN, JOSEPH ARNOLD, advertising executive, former political organization administrator; b. Florence, SC, Oct. 23, 1956; s. Henry Brooks Erwin and Isabel (Williams) Kelly; m. Gretchen Elaine Getchell, June 16, 1984; 1 child, Douglas Getchell. BA in Polit. Sci., Clemson U., 1979; postgrad., Sch. of Visual Arts, 1985. Media buyer Leslie Advt., Greenville, S.C., 1980-81, asst. account exec., 1981-82, account exec., 1982, Benton & Bowles, Spartanburg, S.C., 1982-83, Benton & Bowles (merged with DMB&B), NYC, 1983-86; pres., founder Erwin-Penland, Inc., Greenville, 1986—; chmn. S.C. Dem. Party, 2003—07. Cons. Walter Johnson Vol. Com., Greenville, 1986—; cons., vol. communications div. Greenville C. of C., 1987-88; bd. dirs. Freedom Weekend Aloft, Inc. Mem. Palmetto (S.C.) Project, 1989—; mem. staff Palmetto Boys State, Charleston, 1977—; vol. Greenville Little Theatre Bd., 1987—; mem. advt. rev. com. Better Bus. Bur. Mem. Am. Advt. Fedn. (5 Addy's 1984, 7 Addy's 1989, 14 Addy's 1990, 10 Addy's 1991), Am. Assn. Advt. Agys. Democrat. Episcopalian. Avocations: tennis, automobile racing, politics.

ERWIN, MARK A., air transportation executive; Sr. v.p. airport svcs. Continental Airlines, Inc., 1995—2002, dir., pres., CEO Continental Micronesia, Inc., 2002—, sr. v.p. Asia/Pacific & corp. devel., 2004, sr. v.p. corp. develop. & alliances. Dir. Copa Airlines and Copa Holdings, 2004—. Office: Continental Airlines Inc PO Box 4607 Houston TX 77210 Office Phone: 713-324-8601. Office Fax: 713-324-3099. E-mail: mark.erwin@coair.com.

ESAMANN, DOUGLAS F., utilities executive; m. Kimberly Esamann; children: Regan, Kalee, Conley. BS, Ind. U., Bloomington, 1979. Various positions, tax mgr. Pub. Svc. Ind., Inc.(subs. of Cinergy Corp.), Ind., 1979—94, pres. Ind., 2001—04; project mgr., corp. devel. Cinergy Corp., Cin., 1994—96, fin. team, comml. bus. unit, 1996—98, gen. mgr., bus. devel., 1998—99, v.p., CFO, comml. bus. unit, 1999—2001, sr. v.p., Energy Portfolio Strategy & Mgmt., Comml. Bus. Unit, 2004—05, sr. v.p., Energy Portfolio Strategy & Mgmt., 2005—06; sr. v.p., Strategy & Planning Duke Energy Corp., 2006—. Bd. dir. Ctrl. Ind. Corp. Partnership, Ind. Fiscal Policy Inst. Mem.: Ind. Mfrs. Assn. (bd. dir.), Ind. C. of C. (bd. dir.), Indpls. (Ind.) C. of C. (bd. dir.). Office: Duke Energy 526 S Church St Charlotte NC 28202 Office Phone: 704-594-6200. Office Fax: 704-382-4964. Business E-Mail: DEsamann@duke-energy.com.

ESKELAND, PHILIP DOUGLAS, legislative staff member; b. Bklyn., Dec. 19, 1962; s. Per and Elsie Dorothy (Tharaldsen) E.; m. Launa Jean Taylor, Nov. 14, 1992. BA in Polit. Sci., Wheaton Coll., Ill., 1984; MA in Internat. Affairs, Am. U., 1986. Staff asst. to Rep. Dick Armey, Washington, 1985; bus. mgr. Christian Action Coun., Falls Church, Va., 1985-86; writer White House Office of Corr., Washington, 1986-88; legis. asst., legis. dir. to Rep. Ron Marlenee, Washington, 1988—93; legis. dir. to Rep. Dan Manzullo, Washington, 1993-95; staff dir., subcommittee on tax, fin. and exports US House Small Bus. Com., Washington, 1995—2000, dep. chief of staff, policy dir., 2001—. Recipient Bruce Harlow scholarship Bruce Harlow Found., Washington, 1994. Republican. Presbyterian. Office: US House Small Business Com 2361 Rayburn House Office Bldg Washington DC 20515 Office Phone: 202-225-5821. Office Fax: 202-225-3587. Business E-Mail: phil.eskeland@mail.house.gov.

ESLER, ANTHONY JAMES, historian, novelist, educator; b. New London, Conn., Feb. 20, 1934; s. Jamie Arthur and Helen Wilhelmina (Kreamer) E.; m. Carol Eaton Clemeau, June 17, 1961 (div. 1988); children: Kenneth Campbell, David Douglas; m. Helen Campbell Walker, July 24, 1992. BA, U. Ariz., 1956; MA, Duke U., 1958, PhD, 1961. Mem. faculty Coll. William and Mary, 1962-99, prof. history, 1972-99. Vis. prof. Northwestern U., 1968-69. Author: The Aspiring Mind of the Elizabethan Younger Generation, 1966, Bombs, Beards and Barricades: 150 Years of Youth in Revolt, 1971, The Youth Revolution: The Conflict of Generations in Modern History, 1974, Castlemayne, 1974, Hellbane, 1975, Lord Libertine, 1976, Forbidden City, 1977, The Freebooters, 1979, Babylon, 1980, Bastion, 1980, Generations in History: An Introduction to the Concept, 1982, The Generation Gap in Society and History: A Select Bibliography, 1984, The Human Venture, 5th edit., 2004, The Western World: A Narrative History, 2d edit., 1997; co-author: A Survey of Western Civilization, 1987, World History: Connections to Today, 1997, 4th edit., 2007. Fulbright fellow U. London, 1961-62; research fellow Am. Council Learned Socs., 1969-70; Fulbright travel grantee Ivory Coast and

Tanzania, 1983 Mem. World Hist. Assn., Authors Guild. Home: 416 Harriet Tubman Dr Williamsburg VA 23185 Office: Coll William and Mary Dept History Williamsburg VA 23187-8795 Personal E-mail: anthonyesler@aol.com.

ESLER, SUSAN B., human resources specialist; b. Pitts., Pa. Grad., Miami U., Oxford, Ohio, 1983; MBA, Case Western Reserve U., Cleveland, Ohio. V.p., Human Resources and Comm. Ashland Distrbn.; HR specialist Dow Chemicals; compensation cons. Mercer; dir., compensation, benefits and HRIS PepsiCo Food Sys., 1990; mgr., exec. compensation Ashland, Inc., 1999, dir., corp. human resources, 2001—02, v.p., Human Resources, Programs and Svcs., 2002—04, v.p., Human Resources, 2004—06, v.p., Human Resources and Comm., 2006—. Bd. adv. Cin. Children's Mus.; bd. trustees Cin. Mus. Ctr.; mem. One Hundred Wise Women, SOAR. Office: Ashland Inc 50 E RiverCenter Blvd Covington KY 41011 Office Phone: 859-815-3333. Office Fax: 859-815-5053. Business E-Mail: sbesler@ashland.com.

ESPARZA, JAIME, prosecutor; b. El Paso, Tex. m. Noelia Esparza; 4 children. B, Univ. Tex., Austin, 1979; JD, Univ. Tex., 1983. Bar: Tex. 1983, cert.: Tex. Bd. Legal Specialization (in criminal law). Asst. dist. atty. Harris County Dist. Atty. Office, Houston, 1983—87, Office of Dist. Atty. 34th Judicial Dist., El Paso, 1987; asst. pub. defender El Paso County Pub. Defender's Office, 1988—91; asst. county atty. Office of El Paso County Atty., 1992; dist. atty. Office of Dist. Atty. 34th Judicial Dist., 1993—. Office: Office of District Atty El Paso County Courthouse 2d Fl 500 E San Antonio El Paso TX 79901 Office Phone: 915-546-2059. Office Fax: 915-533-5520.

ESPELAND, CURTIS E., chemicals executive; BA in Accounting, Iowa State U.; MBA with honors, U. Chgo. Audit and bus. adv. mgr. Arthur Andersen LLP; joined Eastman Chemical Co., 1996, v.p. fin. Polymers Bus. Group, v.p. fin. Eastman Divsn., v.p., controller, dir. corp. planning and forecasting, dir. fin. Asia Pacific, dir. internal auditing, accounting officer, 2002—08, sr. v.p., CFO, 2008—. Office: Eastman Chem Co 200 S Wilcox Dr Kingsport TN 37660

ESPINOZA, LUIS ALBERTO, medical educator, researcher; arrived in U.S., 1989; m. Lita Rosa Calagua, Mar. 18, 1988; children: Diego, David. MD, Nat. U. Federico Villarreal, Lima, Peru, 1986. Intern internal medicine Hahnemann U., Phila., 1994—95, resident internal medicine, 1995—97; dir. HIV/AIDS Clin. Edn. MCP Hahnemann U., Phila., 1997—; asst. prof. U. Miami Sch. Medicine, Fla., 2001—, dir. HIV/AIDS tng. program, 2005—, assoc. prof. clin. medicine, 2010. Mem. infection surveillance and policy com. Cedars Med. Ctr., Miami, Fla., 2001—02; mem. med. scis. com. A U. Miami Sch. Medicine, 2004. Contr.: 2005 HIV/AIDS Primary Care Guide; contbr. articles to profl. jours. Named Fellow of Yr. in HIV/AIDS, Ortho Biotech, 1993—94. Mem.: Peruvian Am. Med. Soc. (pres. South Fla. chpt. 2004—), Infectious Diseases Soc. Am., Am. Acad. HIV Medicine. Office: U Miami Sch Medicine Ste 858 1400 NW 10th Ave Miami FL 33136 Office Fax: 305-243-4037. Business E-Mail: lespinoza@med.miami.edu.

ESPOSITO, JOHN VINCENT, lawyer; b. Logan, W.Va., Dec. 25, 1946; s. Vito T. and Mary Frances (Lamp) Esposito. BA magna cum laude, W.Va. U., 1968; JD, 1971. Bar: W.Va. 1971, SC 1980, DC 1994. Legis. aide Congressman Ken Hechler, 4th Dist., W.Va., 1971; counsel Hans McCourt; pres. W.Va. State Senate, 1972; instr. So. W.Va. Cmty. Coll., 1972—; founder, sr. ptnr. Esposito & Esposito, Logan, W.Va., Hilton Head Island, SC; formerly sr. ptnr. Washington, 1972—, NYC, 1972—; arbitrator United Mine Workers Am.-Coal Operators Assn.; spl. judge Cir. Ct. Logan County (W.Va.); commr. in chancery Cir. Ct. Logan County; judge Mcpl. Ct. City of Chapmanville, W.Va.; spl. pros. atty. W.Va., Citizen Ambassador to People's Republic of China and Soviet Union for U.S. Legal Del.; founder Citizens Environ. Quality, 1983; of coun. to several Nat. & Internat. law firms; coun. to various Internat., Nat., State, and Local leaders; Citizen's Amb. relative U.S. Legal Sys.; spkr. Nat. & Internat. Forums; fashion model Elite Knot; assisted in formation of Internat. War Crimes Amb., in Democracies establishing their gov., including Solvenia, Bosnia, Romania. Creator, dir. & host TV program, Law USA. Co-author: Laws for Young Mountaineers, 1973—74; author: Law & Sex Come Together in the 90's; co-author (with Dr. John Makay): (coll. textbook) Public Speaking/Theory Into Practice. 2d lt. US Army. Hastings Coll. Law Coll. Advocacy scholarship. Mem.: Acad. Am. Poets, Internat. Platform Assn., US Supreme Ct. Bar, DC State Bar, S.C. Bar, W.Va. State Bar, Am. Judicature Soc., Assn. Trial Lawyers Am., ABA. Office: Ste 303 WatersEdge at Shelter Cove Harbour PO Drawer 5705 Hilton Head Island SC 29938 Office Phone: 843-785-6959.

ESPY, HENRY (CHUCK) WILLIAM, III, state legislator; b. Clarksdale, Miss. m. Lynn Espy; 2 children. V.p. Century Funeral Home; mem. Dist. 26 Miss. House of Reps., 2000—. Mem.: Race Initiative (pastor parish relationship com. mem., nat. coun.), Mason. Democrat. Methodist. Mailing: PO Box 1508 Clarksdale MS 38614 Office Phone: 662-627-4182, 601-359-2421. E-mail: cespy@house.ms.gov.

ESREY, WILLIAM TODD, energy executive, former telecommunications company executive; b. Phila., Pa., Jan. 17, 1940; s. Alexander J. and Dorothy (B.) E.; m. Julie L. Campbell, June 13, 1964; children: William Todd, John Campbell. BA, Denison U., Granville, Ohio, 1961; MBA, Harvard U., 1964. With Am. Tel & Tel. Co., also N.Y. Tel. Co., 1964-69; pres. Empire City Subway Ltd., NYC, 1969-70; mng. dir. Dillon, Read & Co. Inc., NYC, 1970-80; exec. v.p. corp. planning United Telecommunications, Inc. (now Sprint), Westwood, Kans., 1980-81, exec. v.p., CFO, 1981-82, 84-85, CEO, 1985—90; chmn., CEO Sprint Corp., Westwood, Kans., 1990—2003; chmn. Japan Telecom, 2003—04, Spectra Energy Corp., Houston, 2009—. Bd. dirs. Duke Energy Corp., Gen. Mills, Inc. Mem. Birnum Wood, Eagle Springs, Valley Club of Montecito, Phi Beta Kappa. Office: Spectra Energy Bd Directors 5400 Westheimer Ct Houston TX 77056-5310

ESSER, PATRICK J., communications executive; BA in Comm. Media, MA in Comm. Media, U. Northern Iowa. Mem., mgmt. team CableRep (now Cox Media, Inc.), 1981—90, dir., advertising sales, 1990—91, corp. v.p., advertising sales, 1991—99; dir., programming Cox comm., Inc., Hampton Roads, 1976, v.p., ops., Western Divsn., 1999—2000, sr. v.p., ops., 2000—04, exec. v.p., ops., COO Atlanta, 2004—06; pres., CEO Cox Comm., Inc., 2006—. Bd. dirs. Product Info. Network; adv. bd. Compaq; bd. dirs. C-SPAN, CableLabs, Cable in the Classroom. Recipient Heritage Honors Alumni Achievement award, U. No. Iowa, 2003, Cable TV Advertising Bur. President's award. Mem.: Cable TV Pub. Affairs Assn. (bd. advisor), Nat. Cable & Telecommunications Assn. (bd. dir.), Cable & Telecommunications Assn. for Mktg. Ednl. Found. (bd. dir.). Office: Cox Communications Inc 1400 Lake Hearn Dr Atlanta GA 30319 Office Phone: 404-843-5000. Business E-Mail: patrick.esser@cox.com.

ESSLINGER, JOHN THOMAS, lawyer; b. Ephrata, Pa., Aug. 11, 1943; s. Doster Alvin and Lucy Mildred (Ream) E.; 1 child, John David. BA, Yale U., 1965; JD, Georgetown U., 1973. Bar: D.C. 1973, Va., 2009, U.S. Dist. Ct. D.C. 1974, U.S. Supreme Ct. 1974, U.S. Ct. Appeals (D.C. cir.) 1974. Assoc. Morgan, Lewis & Bockius, Washington, 1973-76; ptnr. Schmeltzer, Aptaker & Shepard, P.C., Washington, 1976—2006; gen. counsel Legum & Norman, Inc., Alexandria, Va., 2006—08, Marine Corps. Assn. Quantico, Va., 2008—. Capt. USMC, 1966-70, Vietnam. Decorated with Purple Heart, Bronze Star, With Gold Star. Mem. ABA, Bar Assn. D.C., D.C. Bar Assn., Maritime Adminstrv. Bar Assn. Episcopalian. Avocations: golf, wine, baseball. Business E-Mail: t.esslinger@mca-marines.org.

ESSMYER, MICHAEL MARTIN, lawyer; b. Abilene, Tex., Dec. 6, 1949; s. Lytle Martin Essmyer and Roberta N. Essmyer Nicholson; m. Cynthia Rose Piccolo, Dec. 27, 1970; children: Deanna, Mike, Brent Austin. BS in Geology, Tex. A&M U., 1972; postgrad., Tex. Christian U., 1976; JD summa cum laude, South Tex. Coll. Law, 1980. Bar: Tex. 1980, U.S. Dist. Ct. (no., so., ea. we. dists) Tex. 1982, U.S. Ct. Appeals (5th cir.) 1981, U.S. Ct. Appeals (9th cir.) 1990, U.S. Ct. Appeals (1st cir.) 1993, U.S. Ct. Appeals (7th cir.) 1995, U.S. Ct. Appeals (fed. cir.) 1985, U.S. Ct. Claims, 1981, U.S. Supreme Ct. 1991. Briefing atty. Supreme Ct. Tex., Austin, 1980-81, Haynes & Fullenweider, Houston, 1981-89, Essmyer & Hanby, Houston, 1989-92; atty. Essmyer & Assocs., Houston, 1992-94, Essmyer & Tritico, LLP, Houston, 1994-95, Essmyer, Tritico & Clary, LLP, Houston, 1995-99, Essmyer & Tritico, LLP, Houston, 1999—2007, Essmyer, Tritco & Rainey LLP, Houston, 2007—11, Essmyer & Daniel, P.C., Houston, 2011—. Lead article editor South Tex. Law Jour., 1979. Dem. candidate for state rep., Bryan, Tex., 1972; del. Dem. Party, Houston, 1982, 84; precinct chmn. Harris County Dem. Exec. Com., Houston, 1983-86. Capt. USAF, 1972-78. Nat. Merit Scholar, 1968-72. Mem. ATLA, ABA, Houston Bar Assn. (co-chmn. lawyers in pub. schs. com. 2003-05, co-chair spkrs. com. 2005-06, co-chmn. CLE com. 2011-12), Tex. Trial Lawyers Assn. (dir. 1996—2013), Harris County Trial Lawyers Assn. (dir. 1997—2012), Tex. Criminal Def. Lawyers Assn., Tex. Bar Found., Harris County Criminal Lawyers Assn. (dir. 1986-87), Fed. Bar Assn., Houstonian Club, The Company Onstage (dir. 2001—). Roman Catholic. Home: 1122 Glourie Dr Houston TX 77055-7506 Office: Essmyer & Daniel PC 5111 Center St Houston TX 77007-7328 Office Phone: 713-869-1155. Business E-Mail: messmyer@essmyerdaniel.com.

ESTES, ANDREW HARPER, lawyer; b. Pecos, Tex., Dec. 16, 1956; s. Bobby Frank and Gayle (Harper) E.; m. Deidre Dement, Mar. 19, 1976; children: Andrew Kimble, Jada Catherine. BA, Tex. Tech U., 1977; JD, Baylor Sch. Law, 1979. Bar: Tex. 1980, US Dist. Ct. (no. dist.) Tex. 1980, US Dist. Ct. (we. dist.) Tex. 1981, US Ct. Appeals (5th cir.) 1982, US Supreme Ct. 1983. Ptnr. Lynch, Chappell & Alsup P.C., Midland, Tex., 1980—. Mem. Tex. Tech. U. Coll. Edn. Devel. Coun., Lubbock, 1986-87; vol. Big Bros., Midland, 1983—, bd. dirs., 1985-89; bd. dirs. Hearthstone Temporary Children's Shelter, 1988-92; mem. bd. dirs. Tex. Book Festival, 2001-. Named Big Brother of Yr., Big Bros./Big Sisters of Midland, 1985; recipient Trimble Vol. Svc. award, Leadership Midland Alumni, 1986, Pro Bono Atty. award West Tex. Legal Svcs., 1991. Mem. ABA, Midland County Young Lawyers Assn. (sec., treas. 1987-88, Outstanding Young Lawyer of Midland County 1992), Midland County Bar Assn. (sec., treas. 1987-88, v.p. 1992-93, pres.-elect. 1993-94, pres. 1995-96), State Bar Tex. (Dist. 16 admissions com., dist. 16B grievance com. 1990-93, chmn. 1992-93, bd. dirs. 1999-2002, pres. 2008-09), Tex. Young Lawyers Assn. (bd. dirs. 1987-89), Tex. Bd. Legal Specialization (cert.), State Bar Tex. (pres.2008-09, immediate past pres., 2009-), Phi Delta Phi. Presbyterian. Home: 1505 Princeton Ave Midland TX 79701-5760 Office: Lynch Chappell & Alsup PC The Summit Bldg 300 N Marienfeld St Fl 7 Midland TX 79701-4345 Office Phone: 432-683-3351. Business E-Mail: hestes@lynchchappell.com, hestes@lcalawfirm.com.

ESTES, CRAIG, state legislator; b. Wichita Falls, Aug. 20, 1953; m. Jennifer Estes; children: Abby, Andrew, Mark. BBA, Oral Roberts U., Tulsa, Okla., 1977; grad., Harvard U. Bus. Sch. Owner Pres. Mgr. Program, Mass., 1993. CEO, chmn. Estes, Inc.; mem. Dist. 30 Tex. State Senate, 2001—. Bd. dirs. Tex. Conservative Coalition Rsch. Inst. Mem. Young Life Com. Wichita Falls; elder Presbyn. Ch.; bd. dirs. Wichita Falls Faith Mission, Wichita Falls Boys Club, Young Pres. Orgn., chmn. West Tex. chpt., 1994—96. Mem.: Tex. Agr. Chems. Assn. (pres. 1989), Wichita Falls Rotary Club (bd. dirs.). Republican. Office: State Capitol Room 3E.8 PO Box 12068 Capitol Station Austin TX 78711 also: 2525 Kell Blvd Ste 302 Wichita Falls TX 76308 also: 4401 N I-H 35 #202 Denton TX 76207 also: 1117 Gallagher Dr Ste 340 Sherman TX 75090 Office Phone: 940-689-0191, 512-463-0130, 940-898-0926, 903-868-2347. Office Fax: 940-689-0194.

ESTES, ERNEST L., geologist, educator; b. Evanston, Ill., Mar. 21, 1942; s. Ernest L. and Berit Lillian Estes; m. Mary K. Kolb, Apr. 13, 1967; children: Aaron Judson, Erika Nichol. BS, Lawrence U., Appleton, 1965; MA, Duke U., Durham, NC, 1967; PhD, U. NC, Chapel Hill, 1971. Asst. prof. Lamar U., Beaumont, Tex., 1972—76; prof. Tex. A&M U., Galveston, 1976—; interim head Marine Sci. Dept., 2006—10. Recipient Achievement award, Tex. A&M U., Galveston, 1988, Faculty Disting. Achievement award, Assn. Former Students Tex. A&M U., Galveston, 2001. Avocations: sailing, travel, reading. Office: Tex A&M University Galveston PO Box 1675 Galveston TX 77553 Business E-Mail: estese@tamug.edu.

ESTES, JAMES RUSSELL, botanist; b. Burkburnett, Tex., Aug. 28, 1937; s. Presbyterian Worley and Bessie (Seidlitz) Estes; m. Nancy Elizabeth Arnold, Dec. 21, 1962; children: Jennifer Lynn Estes Varma, Susan Elizabeth Estes Honaker. BS in Biology, Midwestern State U., 1959; PhD in Systematic Botany, Oreg. State U., 1967. Mem. faculty U. Okla., Norman, 1967—, asst. prof., 1967—70, assoc. prof., 1970—82, prof. botany, 1982—96, adj. prof., 2004—, prof. emeritus, 1996—; dir. Okla. Natural Heritage Program, 1981—82, U. Nebr. State Mus., 1996—; curator Bebb Herbarium, 1979—96, curator emeritus, 2004—; prof. biol. scis. U. Nebr. Lincoln, 1996—2002, prof. emeritus, 2002—; assoc. program dir. NSF, 1990—92, program dir., 1993—94, mem. systematic biology adv. panel, 1986—89; interim dir. River Bend Nature Ctr., 2004—05, bd. dirs., 2001—. Mem. ecology adv. panel US Agy. for Internat. Devel., 1991; mem. adv. panel Internat. Biodiversity Conservation Group NIH, 1993, Biotic Surveys and Inventories NSF, 1993, 1996; mem. joint expert group Jordanian-Israeli-Am. Trilateral Coop., 1994—95; cons. World Bank, Global Environ. Trust Fund, Indonesia, 1994—96; cons. in environ. work, 1979—; expert witness in environ. work, 1983—; edtl. bd. mem. Systematic Botany Monographs, 1985—89, Flora N.Am., 1986—92; asst. editor Flora Okla. Project, 1984—96; mem. Flora of Okla. Editl. Com., 2002—; mem. steering com., trustee Flora Okla., Inc., 1985—92. Co-editor: Grasses and Grasslands: Systematics and Ecology, 1981; contbr. articles to profl. jours. Bd. govs United Campus Christian Found., 1976—80; mem. adv. bd. Sutton Urban Wilderness Pk., 1980—; bd. dirs. River Bend Nature Ctr., 2002—, mem. bd. dirs., 2002—04; pres. Lincoln Arts Coun.; bd. dirs., mem. Wichita Falls Symphony Orch. Bd., 2004—. With US Army, 1960—63. Recipient Ortenburger award, Phi Sigma, 1975, Baldwin Study Travel award, Okla. U. Alumni Found., 1976, Outstanding Undergraduate Instr., Mortar Bd., 1990; grantee, NSF, 1963, 1965—70, 1981—87. Mem.: Okla. Acad. Sci. (pres. 1992—93, sec. 1968—69), Southwestern Assn. Naturalists (bd. govs. 1980—83, assoc. editor 1980—82, trustee 1986—93), Bot. Soc. Am., Am. Soc. Plant Taxonomists (past pres. 1987—88, sec. 1980—83, program chmn. 1980—83, pres. elect 1984—85, pres. 1985—86). Democrat. Presbyterian. Achievements include design of. Address: 418 Park St Burkburnett TX 76354-2445 E-mail: jestes@classicnet.net.

ESTEVEZ, ANNE-MARIE, psychologist, lawyer; b. Hiaieah, Fla., Jan. 3, 1968; d. Antonio Jesus and Linda Francis (Murphy) E. BA in Psychology cum laude, U. Miami, 1990; JD, U. Miami Sch. Law, 1993. Bar: Fla., DC. Acct. asst. Project Advisors Corp., Miami, Fla., 1986-87, bookkeeper, 1987-88, asst. to the pres., 1989-90; ptnr. Labor & Employment Morgan Lewis. Author: (ethnographic rsch.) World-War II Vet--Buster Murphy, 1989 (preserved in U. Miami Libr.). Vol. fundraiser and polit. conv. worker for Democrats. Mem. Women in Communications, Inc., Female Execs. of Am., Phi Kappa Phi, Psi Chi, Phi Kappa Alpha. Roman Catholic. Avocations: scuba diving, volunteer work. Office: c/o Morgan Lewis 5300 Wachovia Financial Ctr 200 S Biscayne Blvd Miami FL 33131-2339 Office Phone: 305-415-3330. Office Fax: 305-415-3001. Business E-Mail: aestevez@morganlewis.com.

ESTEVEZ, FELIPE DE JESÚS, bishop; b. Betancourt, Cuba, Feb. 5, 1946; s. Adriano and Estrella Estevez. STL, Univ. Montreal, 1970; MA, Barry Univ., Miami, Fla., 1977; STD, Pontifical Gregorian Univ., Rome, 1980. Ordained priest Diocese of Matanzas, Cuba, 1970; priest Honduras, 1970—75; faculty mem. St. Vincent de Paul Regional Sem., Boynton Beach, Fla., 1975—77; incardinated priest Archdiocese of Miami, 1979; rector St. Vincent de Paul Regional Sem., 1980—86; campus minister Fla. Internat. U., Miami, 1987—2001; dean, spiritual formation St. Vincent de Paul Regional Sem., 2001—03; ordained bishop, 2004; aux. bishop Archdiocese of Miami, 2004—11; bishop Diocese of Saint Augustine, Fla., 2011—. Roman Catholic. Office: Diocese of Saint Augustine 11625 Old St Augustine Rd Jacksonville FL 32258 Office Phone: 904-262-3200. Office Fax: 904-249-3635.

ESTORES, DAVID S., gastroenterologist; MD, U. Philippines, 1985. Diplomate Am. Bd. Internal Medicine, 1989, Am. Bd. Internal Medicine-gastroenterology, 2001. Resident internal medicine St. Lukes Hosp., 1987—89; fellow gastroenterology Univ. Pitts.-Presbyterian Hosp., 1989—92; faculty mem. gastroenterology divsn. Univ. of Miami Leonard Miller Sch. of Medicine, 2000—06; dir. esophegal physiology lab. Univ. of South Fla., 2006; hosp. affiliation include/s Tampa Gen. Hosp. Office: University of South Florida College of Medicine 12901 Bruce B Downs Blvd MDC Box 72 Tampa FL 33612 Office Phone: 813-974-3374. Office Fax: 813-974-7031.

ESTORES, IRENE MISON, physical medicine and rehabilitation physician; b. Quezon City, Philippines, Apr. 14, 1962; MD, Coll. Medicine U. Philippines, 1987. Cert. Phys. Medicine and Rehabilitation, Spinal Cord Injury Medicine. Intern, phys. medicine rehabilitation Sinai Hosp. Balt., Md., 1989—90, resident Md., 1990—93; attending physician U. Miami Hosp., Fla., 2002; staff physician, rehabilitation medicine Miami VA Med. Ctr., 2000—02; project dir. So. Fla. Spinal Cord Injury model system; co-medical dir., spinal cord injury unit Jackson Meml. Hosp. Rehabilitation Ctr.; med. student elective coord., dept. rehabilitation medicine Leonard M. Miller Sch. Medicine, U. Miami, asst. prof., clin. rehabilitation medicine Fla. Office: Jackson Meml Hosp Rehabilitation Ctr Basement Fl 1611 NW 12th Ave Miami FL 33136 Office Phone: 305-585-1320. Office Fax: 305-585-1340.

ESTRELLA MARTINEZ, LOUIS F., territorial supreme court justice; b. San Juan, Nov. 17, 1971; BA, U. PR, 1992, JD magna cum laude, 1996. Legal officer to Hon. Gilberto Gierbolini Ct. Appeals of PR, San Juan; pvt. practice atty. PR, 1999—2011; assoc. justice Supreme Ct. of PR, San Juan, 2011—. Mem. Governor's Adv. Coun. on Youth Affairs, PR, 1993. Office: Supreme Court of Puerto Rico PO Box 9022392 Ponce de Leon Ave Pda 8 San Juan PR 00902-2392*

ESTREN, MARK JAMES, communications executive, television producer, writer, editor; b. NYC, July 12, 1948; s. Solomon and Elaine Estren; m. S. Amber Gordon, July 4, 1986; children: Meredith, Nicholas. BA in Classics and English cum laude, Wesleyan U., 1968; MS in Journalism, Columbia U., 1970; MA in English and Psychology, U. Buffalo, 1973, PhD in English and Psychology, 1978. Producer, reporter, anchor Stas. WBEN & WBEN-TV, Buffalo, 1971-75; exec. producer Stas. WCBS-Radio and TV, NYC, 1975-76, Sta. WCAU-TV, Phila., 1976-79; sr. producer ABC News, NYC and Washington, 1979-80; editor Phila. Inquirer, 1980-81, Miami (Fla.) Herald, 1980-81; exec. producer The Nightly Bus. Report, Miami, Fla., 1981-84; sr. v.p., gen. mgr. Fin. News Network, NYC and L.A., 1984-87; editor-in-chief High Tech. Bus. mag., Boston and NYC, 1987-89; exec. v.p. Infotechnology, Inc., NYC and Washington, 1987-90, UPI, Washington, 1988-90; founder, pres. UPI TV, Fairfax, Va., 1989-90; pres., chief exec. officer TransCentury Comm., Inc., Easton, Conn. and McLean, Va., 1984—. Adj. prof. Columbia U., 1987-89; webmaster www.infodad.com, 1999—; music critic Washington Post, 2005—. Author: A History of Underground Comics, 1974, rev. edit., 1987, 89, 93, Statins. Miraculous or Misguided?, 2013, Prescription Drug Abuse, 2013; co-author: In a Word, 1992, Question Authority to Think for Yourself, 2012, Healing Hormones, 2013, Heal Yourself, 2014; contbg. editor Miami Herald, Bottom Line/Personal, Bottom Line/Tomorrow, Boardroom Reports, Bottom Line/Business, Bottom Line/Health, Bottom Line/Retirement, Bottom Line/Women's Health, Washington Office Mag., Moneysworth, Parent Weekly, Va. Parent News. Trustee Boston Cath. TV Ctr., 1987-89; vice chmn. Arthritis Found., Washington, 1992-94, chmn. commn. com., 1990-92. Pulitzer Found. fellow, 1970. Avocations: classical music, herpetology. Home: 4386 Jib Boom Ct Apt 4F Fort Myers FL 33919-4704 Personal E-mail: infodad@gmail.com.

ESTRIN, HERBERT ALVIN, financial consultant, film company executive; b. Jamaica, NY, May 4, 1925; s. Joseph and Minnie (Haskell) E.; m. Phyllis Glassman, Jan. 28, 1951 (dec. May 22, 2010); children— Myrna Hope, Richard Lawrence. BS in Acctg, N.Y. U., 1949. With Columbia Pictures Industries, Inc., NYC, 1953-73, v.p., 1971-73; v.p., treas., chief fin. officer Prudential Bldg. Maintenance Corp., NYC, 1973-79; v.p., treas. Bolt Corp., South Laguna, Calif., 1979; sr. v.p. fin. and adminstrn. Warner Home Video Inc. subs. Warner Communications, 1981-83; dir. ops. adminstrn. United Satellite Communications Inc., 1983-85; v.p. fin. and adminstrn. Rainbow Home Video div. Rainbow Program Enterprises Co., 1986-88; fin. cons., 1986—. Served with U.S. Army, 1943-46.

ESTRIN, RICHARD WILLIAM, real estate and business broker, retired editor; b. NYC, Apr. 16, 1932; s. Max and Ruth (Lillienthal) E.; m. Alison Kiendl Stewart, Mar. 13, 1971. BA cum laude, CCNY, 1953; grad., Realtor Inst., 2000. Reporter Pk. Row News Svc., NYC, 1953-55; with Newsday, Inc., Long Island, NY, 1955-85, sucessl. Sunday news editor, Part II editor, sr. editor news, until 1983, exec. news editor N.Y.C. Newsday, 1983-85; weekend editor Herald-Tribune, Sarasota, Fla., 1985-86, news editor, 1986-90, asst. mng. editor, 1990-97; v.p. Longview Realty, Longboat Key, Fla., 1999-

2001, pres., 2001—. Recipient First Place Lifestyle Journalism awards J.C. Penney-U. M., 1974, 75 Mem. Phi Beta Kappa. Business E-Mail: longviewrealty@verizon.net.

ESWARAN, SRIDHAR, periodontist, educator; b. Coimbatore, Tamil Nadu, India, Feb. 27, 1979; s. Eswaran Veerakeralam Kuppusamy and Kousalya Eswaran; m. Uphanyasri K. R. Ponussamy, Mar. 7, 2011. BDS, Tamil Nadu Dr MGR Med. U., Chennai, 2001; MS, Stony Brook U., NY, 2006; MS in Dentistry, U. Tex., Houston, 2009. Diplomate Am. Bd. Periodontology, 2010. Rsch. asst. Stony Brook U., NY, 2003—06; asst. prof. U. Tex., Houston Sch. Dentistry, 2009—. Vis. asst. prof. Nathajirao G. Halgekar Inst. Dental Scis. & Rsch. Ctr., Belgaum, India, 2013—. Recipient Bomidalal Trust award, Ragas Dental Coll. and Hosp., India, 2000; Innovation and Ednl. Rsch. grant, U. Tex., Houston Sch. Dentistry, 2011, 2013. Mem.: Am. Dental Edn. Assn. (assoc.), Internat. Congress Oral Implantology (assoc.), Am. Acad. Periodontology (assoc.). Independent. Hindu. Avocations: tennis, camping, running. Office: University Tex Houston Sch Dentistry 7500 Cambridge St Ste # 6422 Houston TX 77054 Office Fax: 713-486-4393. Business E-Mail: sridhar.veerkeralam.esw@uth.tmc.edu.*

ETHELL, JUDY A., former consulting company executive; b. St. Louis, 1958; m. Robert R. Glatz. BS in Acctg., Ea. Ill. U., 1980. CPA. With PricewaterhouseCoopers, LLP, 1982—2001, nat. tour ptnr., 2001—03, ptnr., tax site leader, 2003—05; exec. v.p., chief acctg. officer BearingPoint Inc., McLean, Va., 2005—08, CFO, 2006—08. Recipient Disting. Alumni award, Ea. Ill. U., 2002. Office Phone: 703-747-3000.

ETHERIDGE, ELIZABETH WILLIAMS, history professor; b. McDonough, Ga., May 14, 1928; d. Roy Pierce and Robbie (Williams) Etheridge. AB in Journalism, U. Ga., 1949, PhD in Am. History, 1966; MA in Journalism, U. Iowa, 1962. Asst. dir. News Bur. U. Ga., Athens, 1949-61, 62-63; asst. prof., assoc. prof., prof. history Longwood Coll., Farmville, Va., 1966-92, bd. visitors disting. prof. emeritus history, 1992—. Author: The Butterfly Caste: A Social History of the Pellagra in the South, 1972, Sentinel for Health: A History of the Centers for Disease Control, 1992; (with Sylvia Head) The Neighborhood Mint: Dahlonega in the Age of Jackson, 1986. Mem. AAUP, Orgn. Am. Historians, So. Hist. Assn., Va. Hist. Soc., Phi Beta Kappa, Phi Kappa Phi. Democrat. Presbyterian. Avocations: music, gardening. Home: 706 High St Farmville VA 23901-1818 Personal E-mail: eelibbyeth@gmail.com.

ETHERIDGE, JACK PAUL, arbitrator, mediator, retired judge; b. Atlanta, Mar. 16, 1927; s. Anton Lee and Jessie Shephard (Brown) E.; m. Ursula Schlatter, Feb. 2, 1952; children: Jack Paul, Margaret Ann, Mary Elizabeth. Grad., Darlington Sch., Rome, Ga., 1945; BS, Davidson Coll., 1949; JD, Emory U., 1955. Bar: Ga. 1955. Since practiced in, Atlanta; mem. firm Huie, Etheridge & Harland, 1959-66; mem. Ga. Gen. Assembly from Fulton County, 1963-66; judge Fulton Superior Ct., 1966-76, sr. judge, 1977—, litigation mgr., 1991; faculty Nat. Jud. Coll., Coll. Criminal Justice, Law Sch., U. S.C., 1977-80; assoc. dean Emory U. Law Sch., Atlanta, 1981-88; chief jud. officer Jud. Arbitration and Mediation Svcs., Inc., Atlanta, 1992-98, spl. master nat. class actions, 1999—. Mem. Ga. Crime Commn., 1971-73; bd. dirs. Atlanta Legal Aid Soc., 1960-70. Author: Getting to the Table-A Guide to Preparing for Mediation, 1985. Trustee Davidson Coll., 1966-75; trustee Arts Festival of Atlanta, 1971-74, Atlanta U., 1977-87; chmn. bd. dirs. Atlanta Neighborhood Justice, Inc., Wolfcreek Wilderness Schs., Inc.; Fellow Harvard Law Sch., 1980. Served with USNR, 1945-46; Served with with AUS, 1949-52. Named Young Man of Year in Professions Atlanta Jr. C. of C., 1962 Fellow ABA, Am. Bar Found., Ga. Bar Assn., Internat. Acad. Trial Judges, Ctr. for Pub. Resources; mem. Atlanta Bar Assn. (pres. 1962-63), Nat. Conf. State Trial Judges (chmn. 1978-79), Atlanta Hist. Soc. (trustee 1969-75), Nat. Acad. Pub. Adminstrn., Beta Theta Pi, Omicron Delta Kappa, Phi Alpha Theta. Presbyterian. Home: 4715 Harris Trl NW Atlanta GA 30327-4409 Office Phone: 770-858-1666. Personal E-mail: jetheridge@mindspring.com.

ETTENSOHN, FRANK ROBERT, geologist, educator; b. Cin., Feb. 6, 1947; s. Robert Frank and Aileen Frances (Keman) E.; children: Clare Marie, Marc Francis. BS, U. Cin., 1969, MS, 1970; PhD, U. Ill., 1975. Lic. profl. geologist Ky. Tchr. math. Greenhills-Forest Park City Sch. Dist., Ohio, 1971; from asst. prof. to prof. geology U. Ky., Lexington, 1975—87, prof., 1987—, chmn. dept. geol. sci., 1997—2005; dir. U.K. Honors Program, 2008—12; mem. N.Am. Commn. on Stratigraphic Nomenclature, 2012—; disting. prof. UK Arts & Scis., 2013—14; sr. petroleum geologist US State Dept. Mem. geology adv. com. Coun. for Internat. Exch. Scholars, 1993-96, 2007-10, chmn., 1994-96; bd. dirs., v.p. Ky. Mus. Natural History, 1991-; tech. adv. com. Ea. Oil Shale Symposium, 1992-94; dir. U. Ky. Geology Field Camp, 1977-81, 84-85, 92-93, 95, 97-98, 2001, 09, 11; adv. com. Ky. Water Resources Rsch. Inst., 1998-2001; faculty math. and sci. edn. program U. Ky. Coll. Edn., 1999-; adv. bd. Appalachian Math. Sci. Partnership, 2003-07, U. Ky. AMSTEMM Project, 2005-; Lexington Living Arts & Sci. Ctr., 2013-; vis. prof. China U. Geoscis., Beijing, 2005-06, 08-, Escuela Superior Politecnica del Litoral, Guayaquil, Ecuador, 2005-06.cons., expert witness in field. Editor (tech.): Jour. Paleontology, 1994—97; contbr. articles to profl. jours. Capt. C.E., AUS, 1970. Fenneman fellow, 1969-70, U. Ill. fellow, 1971-74, Jefferson Sci. fellow US State Dept., 2013-2014, grantee US Dept. Energy, 1976-81, NSF, 1987-90, US Bur. Mines, 1990-91, Ky. Coun. on Higher Edn., 1998-2002, NSF/EPSCOR, 2002-05, Geol. Soc. America; recipient Fulbright Lectr. award US Govt., Soviet Union, 1989, Nepal, 2006, ESAAPG Levorsen Best Paper award, 2006-07; named ESAAPG Educator of Yr., 2008, Disting. Prof. U. Ky. Arts & Scis., 2013-2014. Fellow Geol. Soc. Am. (jt. chmn., field trip chmn. ann. mtg. southeastern sect. 2001-02); mem. AAAS, Am. Geol. Inst., Am. Inst. Profl. Geologists (Lifetime Achievement award, Ky. sect.), Am. Assn. Petrol Geologists, Paleontol. Soc., Paleontol. Assn., Paleontol. Rsch. Inst., Internat. Paleontol. Assn., Ky. Acad. Sci., Ky. Soc. Profl. Geologists, Am. Geophys. Union, Nat. Assn. Geosci. Tchr., Nat. Earth Sci. Tchr. Assn., Fulbright Assn., Phi Beta Kappa, Sigma Xi, Phi Kappa Phi, Sigma Gamma Epsilon. Roman Catholic. Avocations: phlately, coin collecting/numismatics, scouting, soccer. Home: 1631 Duntreath Dr Lexington KY 40504-2352 Office: U Ky Earth and Environmental Sciences Lexington KY 40506-0053 Office Phone: 859-257-1401. Business E-Mail: fettens@uky.edu, f.ettensohn@uky.edu.

ETTER, DELORES M., engineering educator, former political appointee; b. 1947; Student, Okla. State U., U. Tex., Arlington; BS in Math., Wright State U., Dayton, Ohio, 1970, MS in Math., 1972; PhD in Elec. Engring., U. New Mex., 1979. Mem. faculty dept. elec. and computer engring. U. N.Mex., 1979-89, assoc. chair dept., 1987-89, assoc. v.p. acad. affairs, 1989; prof. elec. and computer engring. U. Colo., Boulder, 1990-98; dep. under sec. for sci. & tech. US Dept. Def., Washington, 1998—2001, asst. sec. for rsch. devel., & acquisition, Dept. Navy, 2005—08; disting. chair sci. & tech. office naval rsch. US Naval Acad., 2001—05; Tex. Instruments disting. chair engring. edn., dir. Caruth Inst. Engring. Edn. So. Meth. U., Dallas, 2008—. Mem. Naval Rsch. Adv. Com., 1991-97, chmn. 1995-97; vis. prof. info. sys. lab.Stanford U., 1983-84; bd. dirs. Def. Sci. Bd., 1995-98, Nat. Sci. Bd., 2002-2005; prin. U.S. rep. NATO rsch. and tech. bd., tech. cooperation program; mem. bd. vis. Nat. Def. U.; panel mem. numerous studies. Recipient Pub. Svc. award Dept. Navy, 1998, Fed. Women in Sci. and Engring. Lifetime Achievement award. Fellow IEEE (pres., acoustics, speech and signal processing soc. 1988-89, editor in chief Transactions on Signal Processing jour. 1993-95, Disting. lectr. 1996-97, Harriet Rigas award 1998), AAAS, Am. Soc. Engring. Edn.; mem. NAE. Office: So Meth U Caruth Inst Engring Edn PO Box 750278 Dallas TX 75275-0278 Office Phone: 214-768-4262. Fax: 214-768-4007. Business E-Mail: detter@engr.smu.edu.

EUBANK, J. THOMAS, lawyer; b. Port Arthur, Tex., Mar. 17, 1930; s. J.T. and Ada (White) E.; m. Nancy Moore, Feb.10, 1956; children: John, Marshall, Stephen, Laura. BA, Rice U., 1951; JD, U. Tex., 1954. Bar: Tex. 1954, US Supreme Ct. 1960. With Baker Botts L.L.P., Houston, 1954-90, sr. ptnr., 1979-90, sr. counsel, 1999—2008; dir. Sentinel Trust Co., L.B.A., 1997—. Mem. joint editl. bd. Uniform Probate code, 1972-86. Bd. govs. Rice U., 1985-91. Mem. ABA (chmn. sect. real property, probate and trust law 1978-79), Am. Coll. Trust and Estate Counsel (pres. 1984-85, pres. Found. 1986-89, Trachtman lectr. 1986), State Bar Tex. (chmn. sect. real estate, probate and trust law 1972-73, Lifetime Achievement award 2003), Am. Bar Found., Tex. Bar Found. (Outstanding Fifty Yr. Lawyer 2007), Houston Philos. Soc., Rice U. Alumni Assn. (pres. 1979-80, Rice Gold medal 1992), Am. Law Inst., Internat. Acad. Estate and Trust Law, Houston Country, Coronado, Allegro, Thalia, Chevaliers du Tastevin. Home: 26 Liberty Bell Cir Houston TX 77024-6303 Office: 910 Louisiana St Houston TX 77002-4995 Office Phone: 713-229-1688. Business E-Mail: tom.eubank@bakerbotts.com.

EUBANKS, JON S., state legislator; m. Janet Eubanks; 4 children. Degree in Acctg. with honors, Ark. Tech, 1990. CPA. Bd. dirs. Paris Sch. Dist.; pres., bd. dirs. Boys & Girls Club of Paris; pres. North Logan County Farm Bur., bd. dirs.; mem. Dist. 84 Ark. House of Representatives, 2011—. Republican. Office: Arkansas House of Representatives District 84 2543 Greasy Valley Rd Paris AR 72855 Office Phone: 479-963-6217. Business E-Mail: jon@joneubanks.com.

EURE, CASEY, state legislator; b. Jackson, Miss., Mar. 1, 1978; m. Jill Gary; children: Kennedy, Gunner. Attended, U. Southern Miss. Law Enforcement Acad., Miss. Gulf Coast CC. Mem. law enforcement Harrison County Sheriff's Dept., Miss., Miss. Bur. Narcotics; owner Eure Properties, Biloxi, Miss.; mem. Dist. 116 Miss. House of Reps., Jackson, 2011—. Mem.: NRA, Coast Young Professionals, Woolmarket Little League Assn., Harrison County Rep. Club. Republican. Roman Catholic. Office: Miss House of Reps PO Box 1018 Jackson MS 39215 Business E-Mail: ceure@house.ms.gov.

EVANGELISTA, RICHARD T., lawyer; Asst. commr., legal counsel US VI Dept. Labor, Christiansted, head Worker's Compensation, and Appeals and Hearings Divsn. Mem.: VI Bar Assn. (pres. 2010—11). Office: US Virgin Islands Department of Labor 2203 Church St Christiansted VI 00820 also: PO Box 1182 Kingshill VI 00851-1182 Office Phone: 340-773-1994. Office Fax: 340-773-0094. E-mail: rtestx@gmail.com.

EVANS, ANDREW W., energy executive; married. With Nat. Econ. Rsch. Assocs., Cambridge, Mass., Fed. Reserve Bank Boston; v.p., corp. develop., treas. & dir., fin. energy mktg. Mirant Americas; v.p., fin., treas. AGL Resources, 2002—05, sr. v.p., 2005—06, treas., 2005; CFO AGL Resources, Inc., 2005—, exec. v.p., 2006—. Bd. dirs. Heritage Propane, 2002—. Office: AGL Resources PO Box 4569 Atlanta GA 30302-4569 Office Phone: 404-584-4000.

EVANS, BOB, state legislator; b. Hazlehurst, Feb. 3, 1950; m. Jane Allen; children: Jared, Nathan, Benton, Joseph. BA, Miss. State U., 1975; JD, Miss. coll. sch. of law, 1988. Atty., 1988—; mem. Dist. 91 Miss. House of Reps., 2008—. Democrat. Protestant. Home: PO Box 636 Monticello MS 39654 Office: PO Box 1018 Jackson MS 39215 Home Phone: 601-587-9313; Office Phone: 601-587-0615. E-mail: bevans@house.ms.gov.

EVANS, DEBORAH M., food service executive; Grad., Rider U., Lawrenceville, NJ, 1978. Dir. product devel. Kohl's Dept. Stores, 1982—92; v.p. pvt. brand & product devel., home divsn. JC Penney Co., Inc., 2001—06; v.p. product devel., gen. mdse. mgr. Cracker Barrel Old Country Store, Inc., 2007—. Office: Cracker Barrel Old Country Store Inc 305 Hartmann Dr Lebanon TN 37088-0787 Office Phone: 615-444-5533. Office Fax: 615-443-9476.

EVANS, DONALD LOUIS, think-tank executive, former United States Secretary of Commerce; b. Houston, July 27, 1946; m. Susan Marinis; children: Lisa Moon, Jennifer, Donald L. BS in Mech. Engring., U. Tex. Austin, 1969, MBA, 1973; LHD (hon.), U. SC, 2001. Mgr. to chmn. bd. dirs. Tom Brown, Inc., Denver, 1975-2001, CEO, 1985—2001; sec. US Dept. Commerce, Washington, 2001—05; CEO Financial Services Forum, Washington, 2005—. Bd. dirs. TMBR/Sharp Drilling, Inc., Midland, Tex.; non-exec. chmn. Energy Future Holdings Corp., Dallas, 2007—; chmn. Bush/Cheney Presdl. campaign, 2000; mem. Fgn. Intelligence Adv. Bd., Washington, 2006—. Active United Way; campaign chair United Way Midland, 1981, pres., 1989; bd. regents U. Tex., 1995—2001, chmn. bd., 1997—2001; bd. dirs. The Gladney Fund, 1992—96, Scleroderma Rsch. Found., 1992—2000. Recipient Disting. Alumnus award, U Tex., 2002; named to U. Tex. Red McCombs Sch. Bus. Hall of Fame, 2002. Mem.: Independent Petroleum Assn. of America, Permian Basin Petroleum Assn., Rocky Mtn. Oil & Gas Assn., All-Am. Wildcatters, Young Presidents Orgn. Republican. Methodist. Office: Fin Svcs Forum 601 Thirteenth St NW Ste 750 S Washington DC 20005 Business E-Mail: donald.evans@financialservicesforum.org.

EVANS, GERALD WILLIAM, engineering educator, consultant; b. New Albany, Ind., Sept. 29, 1950; s. Robley Warren and Ruth Ann Evans; m. Linda Marie Napierala, May 4, 1974; children: Matthew, Brian. BS in Math., Purdue Univ., West Lafayette, Ind., 1972; MS in Indsl. engring., Purdue Univ., 1974, PhD in Indsl. engring., 1979. Indsl. engr. Rock Island Arsenal, Ill., 1974—75; sr. rsch. engr. Gen. Motors Rsch. Labs, Warren, Mich., 1978—81; asst. prof. U. Louisville, Ky., 1981—87, assoc. prof., 1987—93, prof., 1993—; NSA ASEE faculty fellow Langley Rsch. Ctr., Hampton, Va., 1987; NASA ASEE faculty fellow Kennedy Space Ctr., Cape Canaveral, Fla., 1995. Editor (with others): Applications of Fuzzy Set Methodologies Industrial Enggineering, 1989, Proceedings of the 1993 Winter Simulation Conference, 1993, Proceedings of the 1999 Winter Simulation Conference, 1999. Mem.: Inst. Ops. Rsch. and Mgmt. Scis. (Moving Spirit award 2005), Inst. Insdl. Engrs. (v.p. 1995—97, Divsn. award 1996).

EVANS, HARRY LAUNIUS, pathology educator; b. Mobile, Ala., June 11, 1948; s. Aurelius A. and Anne (Hathaway) E.; m. Cheryl J. Winfrey, June 6, 1970 (div. Dec. 1990); children: Thomas H., Sarah S. BS, Stetson U., 1970; MD, U. Fla., 1974. Diplomate Am. Bd. Pathology. Resident in pathology Vanderbilt U. Med. Ctr., Nashville, 1974-75; fellow in dermatopathology Mayo Clinic, Rochester, Minn., 1977-78; fellow in pathology U.Tex.-M.D. Anderson Cancer Ctr., Houston, 1975-77, asst. prof. pathology, 1978-82, assoc. prof., 1982-90, prof., 1990—. Contbr. articles to med. jours. Mem. U.S.-Can. Acad. Pathology, Arthur Purdy Stout Soc. Surg. Pathologists. Avocations: mountain climbing, music, crossword puzzles. Office: U Tex-MD Anderson Cancer Ctr Dept Pathology 1515 Holcombe Blvd Houston TX 77030-4009 Office Phone: 713-792-3152. E-mail: hevans@mdanderson.org.

EVANS, JAMES (JIM), state legislator; b. Newton, Miss., Oct. 13, 1950; m. Sarah O'Reilly; children: Lilli, Clora. Mem. Dist. 70 Miss. House of Reps., 1992—; minister tchr. Sports Agt & Sports Promoter. Mem.: Mason. Democrat. Mailing: PO Box 1167 Jackson MS 39201 Home Phone: 601-353-7464; Office Phone: 601-948-0517. Business E-Mail: jevans@house.ms.gov.

EVANS, JO BURT, communications executive, rancher; b. Kimble County, Tex., Dec. 18, 1928; d. John Fred and Sadie (Oliver) Burt; m. Charles Wayne Evans II, Apr. 17, 1949; children: Charles Wayne III, John Burt, Elizabeth Wisart. BA, Mary Hardin-Baylor Coll., 1948; MA, Trinity U., 1967. Owner, mgr. Sta. KMBL, Junction, Tex., 1959-61; real estate broker Junction, 1965-74; staff economist, adv. on 21st Congl. Dist., polit. campaign Nelson Wolff, 1974-75; asst. mgr., bookkepper family owned ranches/rental property Junction, 1948—; gen. mgr. TV Translator Corp., Junction, 1968—, sec.-treas., 1980—. Treas., asst. to coord. Citizens for Tex., 1972; historian Kimble Hist. Soc.; mem. Com. of Conservation Soc. to Save the Edwards Aquifer, San Antonio, 1973; homecoming chmn. Sesquicentennial Yr., Junction; treas., asst. coord. New Consitution, San Antonio, 1974; legis. chair Hill Country Women, Kimble County, 1990—; cashier Texan Theatre; campaign chmn. for Challenge U. Mary Hardin, Baylor, 2000; curator Tex. Tech. U. Herbarium, Junction, 2006, Tex. Tech. Junction Campus, 2005-. Named an outstanding Texan, Tex. Senate, 1973. Mem. AAUW (scholarship named in honor 1973), Nat. Translator Assn., Daus. Republic Tex., Tex. Sheriffs Assn., Nat. Cattlewomens Assn., Internat. Platform Assn., Bus. and Profl. Women (pres. 1981-82), Edwards Plateau Tex. Master Naturalists. Republican. Mem. Unity Ch. Home: PO Box 283 Junction TX 76849-0283 Office: 618 Main St Junction TX 76849-4635

EVANS, JOSHUA G., state legislator; b. McComb, Miss., June 27, 1983; m. Brittany Evans. BS in Mass Comm., Middle Tenn State U., 2005. Small bus. owner; UT-MTAS Elected Officials Acad.; intern Tenn. State Senate, 2005; mem. Dist. 66 Tenn. House of Reps., 2008—. Republican. Baptist. Office: 207 War Memorial Bldg Nashville TN 37243 Home: 109 Needham Blvd Rockvale TN 37153-4082 Office Phone: 615-741-2860. Office Fax: 615-253-0283. Business E-Mail: rep.joshua.evans@capitol.tn.gov.

EVANS, LINDA PERRYMAN, foundation administrator; b. Dallas, Apr. 25, 1950; d. Walter Lewis Perryman Jr. and Betty Lou (Slaughter) Williams; married, 1990. BS, U. Tex., 1972; postgrad., East Tex. State U., 1975, So. Meth. U., 1976. Press asst. Pres. Ford Com., Washington, 1976; press asst. Connally for Pres. Com., Washington, 1977-79; adminstrv. asst. Am. Enterprise Inst., Washington, 1980-81; staff asst. The White House, Washington, 1981-83; exec. dir. Dallas Welcoming Com., 1984-85; pres. Linda Perryman & Assocs., Dallas, 1985-87; vice chmn. Stern, Nathan & Perryman, Dallas, 1987-90; v.p., dir., trustee Meadows Found., Dallas, 1987-96, pres., COO, 1996—. Active Charter 100, Dallas; bd. dirs. Tex. Bus. Hall of Fame Found., YWCA Dallas, Equest, Dallas Citizens Coun.; mem. Cattle Baron's Ball com. Jr. League of Dallas, mem. Crystal Charity Ball com.; appointee Coll. Opportunity Act Com. Gov. Bill Clements, 1989; mem. Dallas Assembly. Office: Meadows Foundation Inc Wilson Historic Block 3003 Swiss Ave Dallas TX 75204-6049

EVANS, LISBETH, management consultant, political organization worker, director; b. Clarkton, NC; m. James T. Lambie; 3 stepchildren. BS, MBA, Wake Forest U. Tchr.; with Alex, Brown & Sons Inc., Merrill Lynch, Pierce Fenner & Smith; pres. Health Equity Properties; CEO, bd. dirs. BizNexus; CEO, bd. dirs., sole shareholder West 3d St. Mgmt. Co. Chair N.C. Dem. Party; mem. Dem. Nat. Com.; Dem. chair Women's Campaign Fund. Presbyterian. Office: 8 W 3d Ste 400 Winston Salem NC 27101

EVANS, MARSHA JOHNSON, retired military officer, former non profit and sports association executive; b. Springfield, Ill., Aug. 12, 1947; d. Walter Edward Johnson and Alice Anne Field; m. Gerard Riendeau Evans, June 30, 1979. AB, Occidental Coll., 1968; MA, Fletcher Sch., 1977, MA in Law & Diplomacy, 1977; postgrad., Nat. War Coll., 1988-89. Commd. ensign USN, 1968, advanced through grades to rear admiral, 1993, ret., 1998; mideast policy officer Commander-in-Chief, U.S. Naval Forces, Europe, London, 1977-79; spl. asst. to sec. US Dept. Treasury, Washington, 1979-80; staff analyst Office of Chief Naval Ops., Washington, 1980-81; dep. dir. Pres. Commn. on White House Fellowships, Washington, 1981-82; exec. officer Recruit Tng. Command, San Diego, 1982-84; commanding officer Naval Tech. Tng. Ctr., San Francisco, 1984-86; battalion officer, sr. lectr. polit. sci. U.S. Naval Acad., Annapolis, Md., 1986-88; chief of staff San Francisco Naval Base, 1989-91, US Naval Acad., Annapolis, Md., 1991-92; exec. dir. of the standing com. on mil. and civilian women Dept. Navy, US Dept. Def., 1992-93; comdr. Navy Recruiting Command, Washington, 1993-95; supt. Naval Postgrad. Sch., Monterey, Calif., 1995-97; CEO, nat. exec. dir. Girl Scouts U.S.A., NYC, 1998—2002; pres., CEO Am. Red Cross, Washington, 2002—05; acting commr. LPGA, Daytona Beach, Fla., 2009—10. Mem. bd. visitors U.S. Mil. Acad. at West Point, 2002-06; interim dir. George C. Marshall European Ctr. Security Studies, Garmisch Partenkirchen, Germany, 1996-97; bd. dirs. Weight Watchers Internat., Inc., 2002-, Huntsman Corp., 2005-, Office Depot, Inc., 2006-; mem. advisory coun., LPGA, 2007-08, bd. dirs., 2009-10. Advisory bd. Pew Partnership for Civic Change Pew Charitable Trusts; dir. Naval Acad. Found. White House fellow, 1979; Chief Naval Ops. scholar, 1976; named Exec. of the Yr., Not for Profit Times, 2005 Mem. Mortar Bd., Phi Beta Kappa. Office: c/o Office Depot Inc 2200 Old Germantown Rd Delray Beach FL 33445 Home: 169 Linkside Cir Ponte Vedra Beach FL 32082-2032 Personal E-mail: mevansnps@aol.com.

EVANS, MICHAEL T., state legislator; Grad., Miss. Fire Acad. Firefighter; farmer; mem. Dist. 43 Miss. House of Reps., Jackson, 2012—. Democrat. Office: Miss House of Reps PO Box 1018 Jackson MS 39215 Business E-Mail: mevans@house.ms.gov.

EVANS, ORINDA DALE, federal judge; b. Savannah, Ga., Apr. 23, 1943; d. Thomas and Virginia Elizabeth (Grieco) E.; m. Roberts O. Bennett, Apr. 12, 1975; children: Wells Cooper, Elizabeth Thomas. AB, Duke U., 1965; JD with distinction, Emory U., 1968. Bar: Ga. 1968. Assoc. Fisher & Phillips, Atlanta, 1968-69, Alston, Miller & Gaines, Atlanta, 1969-74, ptnr., 1974-79; judge US Dist Ct. (northern dist.) Ga., Atlanta, 1979—2008, chief judge, 1999—2006, sr. judge, 2008—. Adj. prof. Emory U. Law Sch., 1974-77; counsel Atlanta Crime Commn., 1970-71 Recipient Disting. award BBB, 1972. Mem. Atlanta Bar Assn. (dir. 1979) Democrat. Episcopalian. Office: US Dist Courthouse 1988 US Courthouse 75 Spring St SW Atlanta GA 30303-3309

EVANS, PAT, former mayor, Plano, Texas; b. Abilene, Tex., Feb. 12, 1943; m. Chuck Evans, 1964; 3 children. BA in Govt./History (magna cum laude), U. Tex., Austin, 1964; JD, So. Meth. U. Sch. Law, 1991. Atty. Gay & McCall, Inc., 1991—95; family law instr. Southeastern Paralegal Inst., 1996—97; atty., 1991—; mem., Pl. 2 City Coun. of Plano, 1998—2001, mem., Pl. 3 Tex., 1996; dep. mayor pro-tem Plano, Tex., 2000; mayor City of Plano, Tex., 2002—09. Tchr. Richardson Ind. Sch. Dist., 1964—70; owner landscape design co. Exec. bd. North Tex. Coun. Govts.; exec. com. Dallas Regional Mobility Coun.; mem. Plano Econ. Devel. Exec. Bd.; past. pres. Jr. League, Plano; mem. Metroplex Mayor's Coun., Collin County Mayor's Coun. Recipient Women in Mcpl. Govt. Leadership award, Nat. League of Cities, 2007, Voice of Children award, CASA of Collin County, Hero of Hope award, Collin County's Children Advocacy Ctr.; named Citizen of Yr., City of Plano, 2004, Civic Vol. of Yr. Mem.: State Bar Tex., Metroplex Mayors Assn. (pres.), Voice of Asian-Am. Assn. (hon.), Plano C. of C., Collin County Bar Assn., Arts of Collin County Mayors Assn., Collin County Mayors Assn. Republican.

EVANS, PETER KENNETH, advertising executive; b. Brighton, Eng., Apr. 18, 1935; s. Percy Edward and Doris (McCoy) E.; m. Juana Santana Ramirez, Mar. 31, 1956; children: Luis Miguel, Linda Rosa Del Rocio, Pilar De Los Angeles. Student, Varndean Sch., Brighton, 1946—50; attended, The Open U. Asst. art dir. Grant Advt., Toronto, Ont., Canada, 1958—61; creative group head Goodis, Goldberg, Soren, Toronto, 1961—63; v.p., creative dir. Baker/BBDO, Toronto, 1963—65; creative dir. Kenyon & Eckhardt, Toronto, 1965—67, Mexico City, 1967—68; exec. v.p., creative dir. Vladimir & Evans Inc., Miami, Fla., 1968—71; pres., creative dir. Evans & Ciccarone Inc., Miami, 1971—91; mktg. cons., 1991—; propr. Peter Evans Pipes, 1994—2001, Peter Evans Woodcrafting Solutions, 1998—; cartoonist Islander News, Key Biscayne, Fla., 1996—; owner Peter Evans Photography; pres. Peter Evans Response Marketing & Advertising, 1996—, Peter Evans Creative Services, 1997—. Instr. advt. Fla. Internat. U., Miami, 1974. Author: Jumpstart Marketing for the New Business Owner, 1993, Treasure Your Teeth, 1998; broadcaster radio reading svc. Sta. WLRN-FM (NPR affiliate), Miami, 1990—; playwright: Ruiz, 1982, Unconscious, 1996, Lost, 1997, Bang, 1998; actor: Scrooge, Social Security, 2000; inventor bed elevator, blind dog head protector, perfect wood carvers bench, sander-expander. Leader Jr. Achievement, Miami, 1968; asst. leader Boy Scouts Am., Miami, 1970; bd. dirs. Key Biscayne Music & Drama Club. Armament technician RAF, Fassberg, Germany, 1953-55, ETO. Recipient awards Can. TV Commls. Festival, N.Y. Art Dirs. Show, Clio awards, Andy awards, 100 Best US TV Commls., Printing Industry Am. awards, Top 24 US New Product Introductions, Miami Big Mike awards, Miami Addy awards, Fla. State Addy awards, 1st pl. Fla. Press Assn. awards, 2006, Golden Spike award, Assn. Am. Editl. Cartoonists, 2008, Best Editl. Cartoons of Yr., 2005, 06, 07, 08, 09, 10; named 100 Top US Creative Men Ad Day/USA, Art Dir. of Yr. Greater Miami Ad Fedn, Golden Spike award, Assn. Am. Editl. Cartoonists, 2008. Mem. Nat. Assn. Underwater Instrs., Profl. Assn. Diving Instrs., Dramatists Guild, Nat. Wood Carvers Assn., Am. Birding Assn., Miami Bach Soc., Nat. Audubon Soc., Key Biscayne Beach Club, South Fla. Woodcarvers Club. Anglican. Office: Peter Evans Photography Studio 5 5A Church Street CO6 1TU Colchester England

EVANS, PHILIP G., sports association executive, media consultant; m. Tammy Evans; children: Alex, Logan, Ryan, Henry. B in Hist. and Econs., U. Va., 1984; JD, U. Va. Sch. Law, 1988. Assoc. Latham & Watkins, 1988—93; with Internat. Family Entertainment, Inc., 1995—97; gen. counsel, exec. v.p. bus. and legal affairs, dep. commr. Continental Basketball Assn., 1997—2000; dir. legal and bus. affairs NBA Devel. League, Greenville, SC, 2001—02, pres., 2002—07; founder, pres. Evans Sports and Media Group, Greer, SC, 2007—; pres., gen. counsel SportsQuest, 2009—11; commr. N.Am. Lacrosse League, 2011—. Office: North American Lacrosse League 36 E Main St Somerville NJ 08876 also: Evans Sports and Media Group 3 St Helaine Pl Greer SC 29650-3657 Office Phone: 864-414-5674. Office Fax: 864-848-1445.

EVANS, RICHARD AUSTIN, education educator, consultant; b. Brady, Tex., May 24, 1959; s. Richard Austin Sr. and Dorene Evans; m. Arlene Emma McBee, Aug. 5, 1977; children: Chris, Ray. PhD in Ednl. Psychology, Tex. A&M, 2005. Rschr. assoc., instr., dept. ednl. psychology Tex. A&M U., College Station, 2000—03; asst. prof., coord. undergraduate spl. programs U. Tex. of the Permian Basin, Odessa, 2003—05; asst. prof. James Madison U., Harrisonburg, Va., 2005—08; spl. edn. dept. advisor Angelo State U., San Angelo, Tex. Cons. White Settlement Sch. Dists., Tex., 2005—. Grant advisor Revival Min. Fellowship Internat., Alvarado, Tex., 2004—06. Achievements include research in successful reading programs.

EVANS, RICHARD H., hospital administrator; b. Ogden, Utah, June 13, 1944; s. Hubert H. Evans and Bety Jean (McVean) Roberts; m. Carla Elizabeth Blank, Oct. 18, 1968; children: Eric Richard, Jamie Elizabeth. BS in Bus. Adminstrn., U. Denver, 1966. Chmn. Evans Holdings, LLC., 1999; CEO Madison Sq. Garden Corp., Huizenga Sports, Entertainment Group; COO Gaylord Entertainment Co.; COO, corp. dir. Fla. Panther Holdings; chmn. LifePoint Hospitals, Inc.; With Walt Disney Prodns., Los Angeles and Orlando, 1966-73; dir., Ops. Ringling Bros. & Barnum & Bailey's Circus, Orlando, Fla., 1973-74; asst. mgr., dir., Ops. Marriott's Great America, San Francisco, 1974—75; v.p., prin. XCaliber Corp., Atlanta, 1975—77; pres., CEO & owner Leisure Gen. Corp., Atlanta, 1977—80; chmn., pres. & CEO Radio City Music Hall Prodns., Inc., NYC, 1980. Bd. dirs. Radio City Music Hall TV, N.Y.C. Bd. dirs. N.Y. Conv. and Visitors Bur., N.Y.C., 1982—, Boys Choir of Harlem, N.Y.C., 1984—; co-chmn. arts and entertainment adv. bd. N.Y.C. Partnership, Inc., 1983—; mem. bus. adv. bd. N.Y. State Dept. Commerce, 1984— Mem. Young Pres.' Orgn., Inc. (bd. dirs. Metro N.Y. chpt. 1985—), Assn. for a Better N.Y. Clubs: N.Y. Athletic. Avocations: jogging; swimming; weight-lifting; gardening; family. Office: LifePoint Hospitals Inc 103 Powell Ct Ste 200 Brentwood TN 37027 Office Phone: 614-372-8500. E-mail: richard.evans@lpnt.net.

EVANS, STACEY GODFREY, state legislator; b. Ringgold, Ga., May 05; d. Keith and Kim; m. Andrew Evans, Dec. 2004. B in Economics & Polit. Sci., U. Ga., JD. Atty. Powell Goldstein Frazer & Murphy LLP, Wood, Hernacki & Evans, LLC; mem. Dist. 40 Ga. House of Reps., 2011—. Democrat. Office: PO Box 2523 Smyrna GA 30081 also: Georgia House of Reps 511 Coverdell Legis Office Bldg Atlanta GA 30334 Office Phone: 770-710-4087, 404-656-6372. Business E-Mail: stacey.evans@house.ga.gov.

EVANS, THOMAS R., magazine publisher; Pub., pres. Fast Company; pub. U.S. News & World Report, 1989, pres., editor NYC, 1989—98; pub. Atlantic Monthly Mags.; pres. Atlantic Monthly, 1997—98; CEO, pres. GeoCities, Santa Monica, Calif., 1998—99; chmn., CEO Ofcl. Payments Corp. (formerly U.S. Audiotex), 1999—2002; pres., CEO & bd. dirs. Bankrate, Inc., 2004—. Office: Bankrate Inc 11760 US Hwy 1 Ste 200 North Palm Beach FL 33408-3003 Office Phone: 561-630-2400. Office Fax: 561-625-4540. Business E-Mail: tevans@bankrate.com.

EVANS, TYREKE JAMIR, professional basketball player; b. Chester, Pa., Sept. 19, 1989; s. John and Benita Evans. Attended, U. Memphis, 2008—09. Guard Sacramento Kings, 2009—13, New Orleans Pelicans, 2013—. Actor: (documentaries) Gunnin' For That No. 1 Spot, 2008. Named NBA Rookie of Yr., 2010. Achievements include becoming the fourth player in NBA history to average at least 20 points, five rebounds and five assists per game during his rookie season, 2009-10. Office: New Orleans Pelicans 5800 Airline Dr Metairie LA 70003*

EVANS, WILLIAM EDWARD, hospital administrator, pharmacist, researcher; b. Clarksville, TN, June 27, 1950; s. Buford Joseph and Wanda (Wilson) Evans; m. Diana D. Miller, Sept. 2, 1972; children: Leslie, Kelli McDonald. Pharm.D., U. Tenn., 1974. Asst. prof. Health Sci. Ctr., U. Tenn., Memphis, 1974—75, assoc. prof., 1976—80, prof., 1983—2002; mem., chair St. Jude Children's Rsch. Hosp., Memphis, 1986—2002, dep. dir., exec. v.p., 1999—2002, sci. dir., dep. dir., 2002—04, dir., CEO, 2004—. Editor Pharmacogenetics Journal, London, 2000—00. Editor: (textbook) Applied Pharmacokinetics, 1981 (Volhwiler Award, 1995); author: Pharmacogenomics (Tyler Prize, 2002). Board of Directors Memphis Area Chamber of Commerce, Memphis, 2000—02. Recipient MERIT Award, NIH, 1987, 1995. Fellow: AAAS (Chair, Pharmaceutical Sciences 1998—99), Am. Coll. Clin Pharmacolog (President 1982—83, Therapeutic Frontier Lecture Award 1992); mem.: Am. Soc. Clin. Pharmacology and Therapeutics, Am. Assn. for Cancer Rsch., Am. Soc. Clin. Oncology. Republican. Methodist. Avocation: Golf. Office: St Jude Children's Rsch Hosp 332 N Lauderdale Memphis TN 38105 Home Phone: 901-386-7829; Office Phone: 901-495-3663. Office Fax: 901-525-6869. E-mail: william.evans@stjude.org.

EVATT, PARKER, retired commissioner, state legislator; b. Greenville, SC, Aug. 27, 1935; s. H.D. and Ruby (Parker) E.; m. Jane Mangum, Sept. 2, 1960; children: Katherine, Alan. BS, U. S.C., 1958, M.Criminal Justice, 1978; LLD, Presbyn. Coll., 1977. Exec. dir. Alston Wilkes Soc., Columbia, S.C., 1965-87; mem. S.C. Ho. of Reps., 1975-87; commr. S.C. Dept. Corrections, 1987-95; sr. v.p. Just Care, Inc., 1996—. Mem. adminstrv. bd. Virginia Wingard Meml., United Meth. Ch., del. to gen. conf., 1972, del. to jurisdiction confs., 1972, 76, 80, 84; past lay leader Columbia Meth. Dist. Served with USN, 1958-60, Ret. Cmdr. US Naval Reserve. Recipient numerous awards and citations from civic, religious and profl. orgns. Mem. S.C. Youth Workers Assn. (past pres.), Christian Action Coun. (bd. govs. 1968-71), St. Andrews Jaycees (life), Nat. Assn. Social Workers (named Citizen of Yr. S.C. chpt. 1978), Internat. Halfway Assn. (v.p. 1973-76), Res. Officers Assn. (v.p. Columbia chpt.), Naval Rsch. Assn. (past pres. Carolina chpt.), Rotary, Pi Kappa Alpha. E-mail: PElake156@aol.com.

EVERBACH, OTTO GEORGE, lawyer; b. New Albany, Ind., Aug. 27, 1938; s. Otto G. and Zelda Marie (Hilt) E.; m. Nancy Lee Stern, June 3, 1961; children: Tracy Ellen, Stephen George. BS, U.S. Mil. Acad., 1960; LLB, U. Va., 1966. Bar: Va. 1967, Ind. 1967, Calif. 1975, Mass. 1978. Counsel CIA, Langley, Va., 1966-67; corp. counsel Bristol-Meyers Co., Evansville, Ind., 1967-74, Alza Corp., Palo Alto, Calif., 1974-75; sec., gen. counsel Am. Optical Corp., Southbridge, Mass., 1976-81; assoc. gen. counsel Warner-Lambert Co., Morris Plains, N.J., 1981-83; v.p. Kimberly-Clark Corp., Neenah, Wis., 1984-86, sr. v.p., gen. counsel, 1986—88, sr. v.p. law & govt. affairs, 1988—2003. Served with U.S. Army, 1960-63. Mem. Mass. Bar Assn., Ind. Bar Assn., Calif. Bar Assn.

EVERETT, MALCOLM E., III, medical products executive, retired bank executive; b. Oct. 8, 1946; BA, Ga. U. With First Union Nat. Bank (now Wachovia Corp.), 1978—2001; chmn., pres. North Carolina Bank First Union Nat. Bank, 1995—99, pres. Mid-Atlantic region, 1999—2001, pres. southeast region, 2001; sr. exec. v.p., head corp. and cmty. affairs Wachovia Corp, Charlotte, NC, 2001—04; pres. United Way of Ctrl. Carolinas, 2008—09; vice chmn. Charlotte Mecklenburg Hosp. Authority. Bd. dirs. Piedmont Natural Gas Co., Inc., 2002—. Chmn. Univ. NC, Charlotte; vice chmn., dir., mem. bd. commissioners Carolinas Health Care Sys.; interim pres. & CEO United Way Ctrl. Carolinas, 2008—09. Mailing: Piedmont Natural Gas Bd Directors PO Box 33068 Charlotte NC 28233 Office: Charlotte Mecklenburg Hospital Authority 1000 Blythe Blvd Charlotte NC 28203 Office Phone: 704-355-2000. Office Fax: 704-355-4084. Business E-Mail: malcolm.everett@piedmontng.com.

EVERETT, RALPH BERNARD, think-tank executive; b. Orangeburg, SC, June 23, 1951; s. Francis G.S. and Alethia (Hilton) E.; m. Gwendolyn Harris, June 22, 1974. BA, Morehouse Coll., 1973; JD, Duke U., 1976. Bar: NC 1977, DC 1979. Adminstrv. asst. NC Dept. Labor, 1976—77; legis. asst. Office of Senator Ernest F. Hollings, Washington, 1977—82; minority chief counsel, staff dir. US Senate Com. on Commerce, Sci., Transp., Washington, 1983—87, chief counsel, staff dir., 1987—89; ptnr. Paul, Hastings, Janofsky & Walker, LLP, Washington, 1989—2006; pres., CEO Joint Ctr. for Polit. and Econ. Studies, 2007—. Bd. dirs. Shenandoah Life Ins. Co., Cumulus Media Inc.; mem. adv. bd. Norfolk So. Corp., Washington, 1991; life mem. bd. visitors Duke U. Sch. Law; former mem. Pres.'s Bd. Advs. on Historically Black Colls. and Univs.; head US Del. to World Telecom. Conf., 1998; US amb. to 1998 Internat. Telecom. Union Plenipotentiary Conf.; former bd. trustees Sci. Mus. Va. Former trustee Nat. Urban League, NYC, 1990, former bd. dirs.; senate liaison Clinton/Gore Presdl. Campaign, Washington, 1992; former mem. Congl. Award Found., McLean, Va., 1993—; former mem. Fed. City Coun.; former mem. Pfizer Health Policy Adv. Bd., US, Frederick D. Patterson Rsch. Inst. Adv. Coun., United Negro Coll. Fund, mem. Fed. Comm. Commn. Adv. Com. Diversity Comm. Digital Age, AT&T's Consumer Adv. Panel, Nat. Coalition Black Civic Participation, Black Leadership Forum, Commn. Engage African Ams. Climate Change, with Obama-Biden Trasition Project Agency Review Working Group. Dept. Comm 2008 Named to Power 150, Ebony mag., 2007, 2008. Mem.: Econ. Club Washington, Phi Beta Kappa, Alpha Phi Alpha, Sigma Pi Phi. Democrat. Baptist. Office: Joint Ctr for Polit and Econ Studies 1090 Vermont Ave NW Ste 1100 Washington DC 20005-4928 Office Phone: 202-789-3510. Business E-Mail: ralpheverett@jointcenter.org.

EVERETT, WOODROW WILSON, electrical engineer, educator; b. Newton, Miss., Oct. 11, 1937; s. Woodrow Wilson and Katherine (Thrash) E.; m. Cherry Donna Sarff, Aug. 23, 1958; children: Woodrow W., Leanne Everett Traver. B.E.E., George Washington U., 1959; MS, Cornell U., 1965, PhD, 1968. Project engr. Scott Paper Co., 1959, Ithaca (N.Y.) Rsch. Lab., Atlantic Rsch. Corp., 1962-64; postdoctoral program dir. Rome (N.Y.) Air Devel. Ctr., 1964-75; chmn. bd. N.E. Consortium for Engring. Edn., St. Cloud, Fla., 1975—. Bd. dirs. Device Assos. Corp. N.Y., Masonwood, Inc., Sunoric Corp., ITG, Inc., Thrash Homestead Corp., The Cherwood Corp., SCEEE Svc. Corp. Contbr. articles to profl. jours. Democratic committeeman, Madison County, N.Y., 1976-79; pres. Village of Groton (N.Y.) Appeals Bd., 1966-69; chmn. Groton Planning Bd., 1968-69. Served with USAF, 1959-62. Fellow IEEE (life); mem. Air Force Assn. (life), Res. Officers Assn. (life), Am. Soc. Engring. Edn. Clubs: Rotary. Home: Cherwood Pond King George PO Box 68 Port Royal Sq Port Royal VA 22535-0068

EVERITT, ALICE LUBIN, labor arbitrator; b. Dec. 13, 1936; d. Isador and Alice (Berliner) Lubin. BA, Columbia U., 1968, JD, 1971. Assoc. Amen, Weisman & Butler, NYC, 1971-78; spl. asst. to dir. Fed. Mediation and Conciliation Svc., Washington, 1978-81; pvt. practice labor arbitration Washington, NYC, 1981-87, Petersburg, Va., 1987—. Mem. various nat. mediation and arbitration panels including Fed. Mediation and Conciliation Svc., U.S. Steel and United Steelworkers, Am. Arbitration Assn. Editor: Dept. Labor publ., 1979. Treas., bd. mem. Petersburg Libr. Found., Inc., 2001—; mem. planning commn. City Petersburg, 1992—2000. Mem. Am. Arbitration Assn., Soc. Profls. Dispute Resolution, Indsl. Rels. Rsch. Assn., Civil War Roundtable of Richmond. Office: 541 High St Petersburg VA 23803-3859 Office Phone: 804-733-3200. Personal E-mail: everitt13@verizon.net.

EVERS, GREGORY, state legislator; b. Milton, Fla., June 16, 1955; m. Tami Forehand; children: Stephanie, Jennifer, Rob. Attended, Pensacola Jr. Coll., Fla. Farmer; small businessman; mem. Dist. 1 Fla. House of Reps., Tallahassee, 2001—10, alternating chair joint legis. auditing com., mem. agr. & natural resources policy com., econ. devel. policy com., natural resources appropriations com., pub. safety & domestic security com.; mem. Dist. 2 Fla. State Senate, 2011—. Mem. Yellow River Soil & Water Conservation Dist., 1994-2001, chmn., 1997; pres. Okaloosa County Florida Farm Bur. 1998-2001. Republican. Baptist. Office: 598 N Ferdon Blvd Crestview FL 32536 also: Capital Bldg 308 Senate Office Bldg 404 South Monroe St Tallahassee FL 32399-1100 Office Phone: 850-689-0556, 850-487-5000. Office Fax: 850-689-7932, 850-487-5276. Business E-Mail: evers.greg.web@flsenate.gov.

EVERSON, KEVIN JEROME, artist, filmmaker, educator; b. Mansfield, Ohio; BFA, U. Akron; MFA, U. Ohio. Assoc. prof. art U. Va., Charlottesville, Va. Exhibitions include Centre Pompidou, Paris, Mus. Modern Art, NY, REDCAT, Los Angeles, Calif., Cleveland Mus. Art, Oh., Studio Mus., Harlem, NY, Armand Hammer Mus., Los Angeles, Calif., Whitechapel Gallery, London, Wurttenbergischer Kunstverein, Stuttgart, Hallwalls Contemp. Arts. Ctr., Buffalo, NY, Spaces Gallery, Cleveland, Oh., Am. Acad. in Rome, Rome, Italy, 1K Projectspace, Amsterdam, The Netherlands, Second St. Gallery, Charlottesville, Va., William Busta Gallery, Cleveland, Oh., Whitney Biennial, Whitney Mus. Am. Art, NY, 2012; dir.: (films) Pictures from Dorothy, 2004, Spicebush, 2005, Cinnamon, 2006, Emergency Needs, 2007, The Golden Age of Fish, Telethon, 2009, Erie, 2010, Quality Control, 2011, Rita Larson's Boy, 2011, Early Riser, 2011, Chicken, 2011, Chevelle, 2011. Recipient Am. Acad in Rome prize; fellow, John Simon Guggenheim Mem. Found, Nat. Endowment for the Arts, Ohio Arts Coun., Va Mus. Office: University of Virginia McIntire Dept Art 179 Culbreth Rd, Ruffin Hall Charlottesville VA 22903

EWALD, ROBERT CHARLES, lawyer; b. Phila., Mar. 8, 1940; s. George R. and Dorothy (Edelen) E. BS, Ind. U., 1962; JD, U. Louisville, 1965. Bar: Ky. 1965, U.S. Ct. Mil. Appeals 1966, U.S. Supreme Ct. 1971. Judge adv. USAF, 1965-68; ptnr. Wyatt, Tarrant & Combs LLP, Louisville, 1968—, chmn. Tort & Ins. Practice Group. Bd. dirs. Legal Aid Soc., Louisville, 1970—, chmn. 1991, 92; pres. Jefferson County Pub. Defenders, Louisville, 1970—; mem. Ky. Atty. Adv. Com., Frankfort, 1980—. Mem. Ky. Commn. on Pub. Advocacy, 1990—, chmn. 1993. Mem.: Ky. Bar Assn. (pres. 2006), Louisville Bar Found. (pres. 1986). Avocations: tennis, scuba diving. Office: Wyatt Tarrant & Combs LLP PNC Plaza 500 W Jefferson St Louisville KY 40202 Office Phone: 502-562-7288. Office Fax: 502-589-0309. E-mail: rewald@wyattfirm.com.

EWEN, PAMELA BINNINGS, retired lawyer; b. Mar. 22, 1944; d. Walter James and Barbara (Perkins) Binnings; m. Jerome Francis Ayers, Aug. 22, 1965 (div. July 1974); 1 child, Scott Dylan Ayers; m. John Alexander Ewen, Dec. 13, 1974 (div. Feb. 2003); m. James Craft Lott, Dec. 27, 2003. BA, Tulane U., 1977; JD cum laude, U. Houston, 1979. Bar: Tex. 79, U.S. Dist. Ct. (so. dist.) Tex. 81, U.S. Ct. Appeals (5th cir.) 81. Law clk. Harris, Cook, Browning & Barker, Corpus Christi, Tex., 1977—79; assoc. Kleberg, Dyer, Redford & Weil, Corpus Christi, 1979—80; atty. law dept. Gulf Oil Corp., Houston, 1980—84; assoc. Baker & Botts, L.L.P., Houston, 1980—84, ptnr., 1988—2004; ret. Author: Faith On Trial, 1999, Walk Back the Cat, 2006, The Moon in the Mango Tree, 2008, The Secret of Shroud, 2010, Dancing on Glass, 2011. La. Legis. scholar, New Orleans, 1976—77. Mem.: ABA (forum com. on franchising 1983—85, law practice mgmt. sect., subcom. Women Rainmakers Assn.), Northshore Literary Soc. (founder 2008—), Tenn. Williams Festival (bd. dirs. 2009—), Tex. Assn. Bank Coun., Tex. State Bar (bd. dirs. 1994—97), Am. Petroleum Inst. (com. on product liability 1982—85, spl. subcom. to gen. com. on law), Am. League of Pen Women, New Orleans Pirate's Alley Faulkner Soc. (bd. dirs.), Order of Barons, Jr. Achievement S.E. Tex. (bd. dirs. 1997—2001, bd. dirs. Inprint, Inc. 2002—04, Literary Artist of Yr., St. Tammany Parish, La. 2009).

EWERT, DOUGLAS S., apparel executive; b. Riverside, Calif. married. B in Bus., San Jose State U., Calif. Joined The Men's Wearhouse, Inc., 1995, gen. mdse. mgr., 1996—2000, v.p. merchandising, 1999—2000, sr. v.p. merchandising, 2000—01, gen. mdse. mgr., 2002—05, exec. v.p. merchandising, 2004—05, exec. v.p., COO, 2005—08; pres., COO Men's Wearhouse, Inc., 2008—11, dir., pres., CEO, 2011—. Office: The Mens Wearhouse Inc 6380 Rogerdale Rd Houston TX 77072 Office Phone: 281-776-7200. Business E-Mail: dewert@tmw.com.

EWING, PATRICK ALOYSIUS, professional basketball coach, retired professional basketball player; b. Kingston, Jamaica, Aug. 5, 1962; m. Rita Ewing; children: Patrick Aloysius, Randi. BFA, Georgetown U., 1985. Center NY Knicks, NYC, 1985—2000, Seattle SuperSonics, 2000—01, Orlando Magic, Fla., 2001—02, asst. coach, 2007—12, Washington Wizards, 2002—03, Houston Rockets, 2003—06, Charlotte Bobcats, 2013—. Mem. U.S. Olympic Basketball Teams, 1984, 1992. Recipient Gold medal, men's basketball, Summer Olympic Games, 1984, 1992, Naismith Men's Coll. Player of Yr. award, 1985; named 1st Team All-American, AP, 1983—85, NCAA Final Four Most Outstanding Player, 1984, NCAA Player of Yr., AP, 1985, Rookie of Yr., NBA, 1986, 1st Team All-Rookie, 1986, 1st Team All-NBA, 1990; named to Eastern Conf. All-Star Team, 1986, 1988—97, NBA 50th Anniversary All-Time Team, 1996, Naismith Meml. Basketball Hall of Fame, 2008, Nat. Collegiate Basketball Hall of Fame, 2012. Achievements include member of NCAA Final Four Division I National Championship winning Georgetown University Hoyas, 1984. Office: Charlotte Bobcats 333 E Trade St Charlotte NC 28202*

EWING, R. STEWART, telecommunications company executive; BA in Bus., Northwestern State U., Natchitoches, La. CPA. V.p. fin. Century Tel Inc., Monroe, La., 1983-84, v.p., contr., 1984-89, sr. v.p., CFO, 1989-99, exec. v.p., CFO, 1999—2009; exec. v.p., CFO, asst. sec. CenturyLink, Inc. (formerly CenturyTel, Inc.), Monroe, La., 2009—. Bd. dirs. Progressive Bank. Sr. warden St. Alban's Episcopal Ch.; bd. dirs. N.E. La. Children's Mus.; treas. St. Frederick's H.S.

Athletic Assn., Monroe, La.; bd. dirs., treas. Grace Episcopal Sch., Monroe. Mem. AICPA, Am. Mgmt. Assn., Nat. Assn. Accts., La. Soc. CPAs. Office: CenturyLink Inc PO Box 4065 100 Century Tel Dr Monroe LA 71203

EWING, RAYMOND CHARLES, retired ambassador; b. Cleve., Sept. 7, 1936; s. Thomas Davis and Marion (Andrews) Ewing; m. Jerelyn Patten, Jan. 19, 1962 (dec. May 2006); children: Gregory, Thomas, Joyce, Lillian Patten(dec.); m. Penelope Yung Vut, Jan. 16, 2010. BA, Occidental Coll., 1957; MPA, Harvard U., 1970. Joined Fgn. Svc., Dept. State, 1957; various assignments in Washington, Bern, Switzerland, Rome, Lahore, Pakistan, Vienna, Tokyo, 1957-1977; dir. Office So. European Affairs, Dept. State, Washington, 1977-79; mem. Sr. Seminar, Washington, 1979-80; dep. asst. sec. of state for European affairs, 1980-81; amb. to Cyprus Nicosia, 1981-84; dean Sch. Lang. Studies Fgn. Svc. Inst., Washington, 1985-87; dir. Office Career Devel. and Assignments, Dept. State, 1987-89; amb. to Ghana, 1989-92; chargé d'affaires, a.i. to Tanzania Dar es Salaam, 1992; ret., 1993; mng. editor Mediterranean Quarterly, Washington, 1994—. Mem.: Cyprus Am. Archeol. Rsch. Inst. (bd. dirs. 2000—, pres. 2010), Diplomatic and Consular Officers (bd. govs. 2005—), Am. Fgn. Svc. Assn., Sr. Seminar Alumni Assn. (pres. 2004—07). Episcopalian. Avocations: tennis, golf, travel, reading. Home: 35240 Prestwick Ct Round Hill VA 20141-2504 Office Phone: 202-662-7655. E-mail: medquarterly@aol.com.

EWING, SIDNEY ALTON, veterinary medical educator, parasitologist; b. Emory Univ., Ga., Dec. 1, 1934; s. Aubrey Coleman and Grace Eliza (Prickett) E.; m. Margaret Jane Steffens, Aug. 16, 1963; children— Holly Annette, Ann Krull, Leah Grace. BSA, DVM, U. Ga., 1958; MS, U. Wis., 1960; PhD, Okla. State U., 1964. Instr. U. Wis., 1960; mem. faculty Okla. State U., Stillwater, 1960—65, 1968—72, prof., head dept. vet. parasitology, microbiology and public health, 1968—72, 1979—84, prof., 1984—91, interim assoc. dean for acad. affairs, 1991—92, 2001—03, Wendell H./Nellie G. Krull endowed prof. vet. parasitology, 1992—2003, Wendell H./Nellie G. Krull prof. emeritus, 2004—; assoc. prof. Kans. State U., 1965—67; prof., head dept. Miss. State U., 1967—68; prof., dean Coll. Vet. Medicine, U. Minn., St. Paul, 1972—78. Adv. bd. Morris Animal Found., Denver, 1967-69, cons., 1969-78; animal health com. NRC, 1971-75; adv. panel U.S. Pharmacopeial Conv., 1980-95 Recipient Outstanding Tchr. of Yr. award Okla. State U. Coll. Vet. Medicine, 1970, SmithKline Beecham award for rsch. excellence Okla. State U., 1991, A.M. Mills award for outstanding contbns. to vet. medicine, 1993, Good Neighbor award Radio Sta. WCCO, Mpls.-St. Paul, 1978; commendation Gov. Minn., 1978; named Veterinarian of Yr., State of Okla., 1997; named to Okla. Higher Edn. Hall of Fame, 2000, Paul Harris fellowship, 2009 Mem. AAUP, AVMA, Am. Assn. Vet. Parasitologists (Disting. Vet. Parasitologist 2002), Am. Soc. Parasitologists, Am. Vet. Med. History Soc., Am. Soc. Rickettsiology, World Assn. Advancement Vet. Parasitology, Conf. Rsch. Workers in Animal Diseases (coun. 1980-85, v.p. 1983-84, pres. 1984-85, dedicatee, 89th Ann. Meeting, 2008), Soc. Vector Ecology, Soc. Tropical Vet. Medicine, Minn. Vet. Med. Assn., Okla. Vet. Med. Assn., NY Acad. Sci., Southwestern Assn. of Parasitologists (program officer, pres. elect 2001-02, pres. 2002-2003), Sigma Xi, Phi Kappa Phi, Phi Zeta, Alpha Zeta, Alpha Psi (past nat. pres.), Gamma Sigma Delta, Aghon, Omicron Delta Kappa Office: Okla State U Dept Vet Pathobiology Stillwater OK 74078-2005 Office Phone: 405-744-8177.

EYHARTS, LEOPOLD, astronaut; b. Biarritz, France, Apr. 28, 1957; married; 1 child. Grad. in aero. engring., French Air Force Acad., Salon-de-Provence, 1979; grad. test pilot, Ecole du Personnel Navigant d'Essais et de Réception, France, 1988. Fighter pilot Jaguar squadron French Air Force, Istres AFB, France, 1980—85, wing comdr. Saint-Dizier AFB, France, 1985—88; test pilot Bretigny Flight Test Ctr., Paris, 1988—90; astronaut Hermes spaceplane program Ctr. Nat. d'Etudes Spatiales, Toulouse, France, 1990—94, in charge of parabolic flight testing, 1994—95; back-up cosmonaut for Cassiopeia French-Russian space mission European Space Agy., 1995—96, prime cosmonaut for Pégase mission on Mir Space Sta., 1998; European Space Agy. astronaut, mission specialist candidate Johnson Space Ctr. NASA, Houston, 1998—. Flight engr. Expedition-12 and Expedition-13 Back-up Crews; crew mem. Atlantis STS-122 Mission to deliver the European Space Agency's Columbus Lab. to the Internat. Space Station, 2008. Col. French Air Force. Decorated Légion d'Honneur France, Ordre National du Mérite, Médaille d'Outre Mer; recipient Russian medal of Friendship, Russian medal of Courage. Achievements include logging over 3500 flight hours as a fighter and test pilot in 40 different aircraft types; 21 parachute jumps; logging over 20 days in space. Avocations: reading, computers, sports. Office: NASA Johnson Space Ctr Astronaut Office/CB Houston TX 77058

EYNON, STEVEN SCOTT, pastor; s. John Jerry and Sally Ann Eynon; m. Lori Hunter, June 25, 1983; children: Christopher, Steven. BA summa cum laude, Fla. Christian Coll., Kissimmee, 1984; MMin, Ky. Christian U., 1992. Ordained to ministry Christian Ch., 1984. Min. youth Winter Haven (Fla.) Christian Ch., 1982-84, 1st Christian Ch., Clearwater, Fla., 1985-94; sr. pastor Cmty. Christian Ch., Ft. Lauderdale, Fla., 1994—. Adj. instr. Fla. Christian Coll., 1988, 90, sec. of trustee, 1996-98; v.p. Fla. Christian Youth Conv., Orlando, 1986; bd. dirs. Christianville Mission, Haiti, 1991-96, chmn. bd. dirs., 1993-94; v.p. Fla. Christian Conv., 1998, pres. 1999; active Fla. Ch. Planters Leadership Team, 2003, N.Am. Christian Convention Continuation Com., 2010-, NACC Exec. Com., 2012-. Author: (with others) Ideas, vol. 42, 1987, Good Stuff, vol. 4, 1988, Directions for Your Journey, 2002. Mem. Nat. Right to Life, Washington, 1983-93; vol. Spl. Olympics, Clearwater, 1985-94; scouting coord. Boy Scouts Am., Clearwater, 1986-94; pres. Fla. Christian Coll. Alumni Assn., Kissimmee, 1987-88, v.p., 1985-87; bd. trustees Fla. Christian Coll., 1995-2000; pres. South Fla. Minister's Assn., 1997-98; with mgmt. team LifePoint Christian Ch., 2001-03, New City Christian Ch., 2009-; guest chaplain United States House of Reps., 2011. Named Outstanding Young Min., N.Am. Christian Conv., 1989. Mem. Christ in Youth Planning Coun. (advisor 1986-88), Christian Edn. Conf. (dir. 1988), Nat. Eagle Scout Assn. Avocation: fishing. Home: 9590 NW 31st Pl Sunrise FL 33351-7157 Office: Cmty Christian Ch 10001 W Comml Blvd Fort Lauderdale FL 33351 Office Phone: 954-724-7400. E-mail: seynon@communitycc.com.

EYTCHISON, BRIAN R., food service executive; B, U. Va., 1982. V.p. fin. planning and analysis Cracker Barrel Old Country Store, Inc. Merit badge counselor Boy Scouts America Troop 13, Tenn. Office: Cracker Barrel Old Country Store Inc 305 Hartmann Dr Lebanon TN 37088-0787 Office Phone: 615-444-5533. Office Fax: 615-443-9818.

EZAKI, MARYBETH, hand surgeon, educator; MD, Yale U., 1977. Cert. orthopedic surgery 1985, hand surgery 2000. Resident in orthopedic surgery Univ. Tex. Southwestern Med. Ctr., Dallas, 1978—82; fellow in hand surgery Weyham Pk Hosp., Slough, 1982; assoc. prof. in orthopedic surgery Univ. Tex. Southwestern; hosp. affiliation includes Tex. Scottish Rite Hosp. for Children. Office: Texas Scottish Rite Hospital for Children 2222 Welborn St Dallas TX 75219 Office Phone: 214-559-7842.

FABER, DAVID ALAN, federal judge; b. Charleston, W.Va., Oct. 21, 1942; s. John Smith and Wilda Elaine (Melton) Faber; m. Deborah Ellayne Anderson, Aug. 24, 1968; 1 child, Katherine Peyton. BA, W.Va. U., 1964; JD, Yale Law Sch., New Haven, 1967. Bar: W.Va. 1967, US Ct. Mil. Appeals 1970, US Supreme Ct. 1974. Assoc. Dayton, Campbell & Love, Charleston, 1967-68, Campbell, Love, Woodroe, Charleston, 1972-74; ptnr. Campbell, Love, Woodroe & Kizer, 1974-77, Love, Wise, Robinson & Woodroe, Charleston, 1977-81; US atty. (so. dist.) W.Va. US Dept. Justice, Charleston, 1981—86; ptnr. Spilman, Thomas, Battle & Klostermeyer, Charleston, 1987-91; judge US Dist. Ct. (So. Dist.) W.Va., Bluefield, 1991—2008, chief judge, 2002—07, sr. judge, 2008—. Capt. JAGC USAF, 1968—72, served with USNR, 1973—77, col. W.Va. Air N.G., 1978—92. Mem.: W.Va. Bar Assn., W.Va. State Bar (counsel ethics commn. 1974—76), Phi Beta Kappa. Republican. Episcopalian. Office: 2303 Elizabeth Kee Federal Bldg 601 Federal St PO Box 4278 Bluefield WV 24701 Office Phone: 304-327-8144. Office Fax: 304-347-3171.

FABRE, SHELTON JOSEPH, bishop; b. New Roads, La., Oct. 25, 1963; BA, St. Joseph Sem. Coll., St. Benedict, La., 1985; MA in Religious Studies, Cath. Univ., Louvain, Belgium, 1989. Ordained priest Diocese of Baton Rouge, 1989; pastor St. Joseph, Grosse Tete, La., Immaculate Heart of Mary, Maringouin, La., Sacred Heart of Jesus, Baton Rouge; vicar St. George, Baton Rouge, St. Alphonsus Liguori, Greenwell Springs, La., St. Joseph Cathedral, Baton Rouge, St. Isidore the Farmer, Baker, La.; ordained bishop, 2007; aux. bishop Archdiocese of New Orleans, 2007—. Mem.: Presbyteral Coun., Coll. Consultors. Roman Catholic. Office: Archdiocese of New Orleans 7887 Walmsley Ave New Orleans LA 70125 Office Phone: 504-861-9521. Office Fax: 504-866-2906.

FABRIKANT, CHARLES L., transportation and energy services executive, lawyer; Grad., Columbia U., Harvard U. Bar: New York, DC. Dir., globe wireless GTI Group LLC; chmn., CEO SCF Corp., 2000; pres. Fabrikant Internat. Corp.; chmn., bd. dirs. Chiles Offshore, Inc., 1997—; chmn., pres., CEO Seacor Holdings, Inc., 1989—2010, exec. chmn., 2010—. Bd. adv. GTI Group LLC; bd. dirs. SEACOR Holdings, Inc., 1989, Global Tech. Industries Inc., 2006, Diamond Offshore Drilling, Inc., 2004—. Counselor Ctr. for Strategic and Internat. Studies. Office: SEACOR Holdings Inc 2200 Eller Dr Fort Lauderdale FL 33316 Office Phone: 954-523-2200. Office Fax: 954-524-9185.

FACCINTO, VICTOR PAUL, artist, director; b. Albany, Calif., Oct. 30, 1945; s. Victor A. and Betty Jean (Smith) Pearson; 1 dau., Denise Michelle. BA in Psychology, Calif. State U.-Sacramento, 1969, MA in Art, 1972. Instr. art Calif. State U., 1972-74; asst. to dir. Nancy Hoffman Gallery, NYC, 1974-78; dir. art gallery Wake Forest U., Winston-Salem, NC, 1978—2012. Founding mem. multi-media performance group Three People, 1990; dir., Tree Life, a non-profit Arts Orgn. One-person shows include Mus. Modern Art, NYC, 1975, Collective for Living Cinema, N.Y.C., 1976, Phyllis Kind Gallery, N.Y.C., 1980, 82, 87, 2004, N.C. Mus. Art, 1986, Helander Gallery, N.Y.C., 1991, Millennium Film Workshop, NYC, 1996, 2003, Cleve. Performance Art Festival, 1998, Southeastern Ctr. for Contemporary Art, N.C., 1999, Madison (Wis.) Art Ctr., 2000, Luise Ross Gallery, NYC, 2010; group shows include Luise Ross Gallery, 2007, 09, Whitney Mus. Am. Art, 1972, 73, 74, Mus. Modern Art, NYC, 1978, Barbara Gladstone Gallery, N.Y.C., 1983, Monique Knowlton Gallery, N.Y.C., 1983, Helander Gallery, Palm Beach, Fla., 1988, 90, Am. Visionary Art Mus., Md., 2002; represented in film study collection Mus. Modern Art, N.Y.C., Philip Morris, Inc.; animated film maker: Shameless, 1974. N.Y. CAPS fellow, 1977; N.C. Arts Coun. fellow, 1982, 86, 2000; recipient 1st prize NYU Small Works Competition, 1983. Home: 1950 Cliffside Dr Pfafftown NC 27040-9507 Office: Tree of Life Inc 401 W 4th St Ste 202 Winston Salem NC 27101 Home Phone: 336-924-6086; Office Phone: 336-813-6495. Business E-Mail: faccinto@wfu.edu.

FACE, E. JOSEPH, JR., state banking agency administrator; b. Columbia, SC; married; 2 children. Grad., U. Ala., Ctrl. Mich. U. Joined Va. State Corp. Commn. Bur. Fin. Instns., Richmond, 1979, dep. commr., 1993—99, commr., 1999—. Rep. state regulators Operation Jump-Start Coalition, Am. Fin. Svcs. Assn. and NACCA; mem. com. computerized loan origination working group US Dept. Housing and Urban Devel.; spkr. in field. Contbr. articles to profl. jours. Office: Bureau of Financial Institutions PO Box 640 Richmond VA 23218-0640 Office Phone: 804-371-9657. Office Fax: 804-371-9416. E-mail: joe.face@scc.virginia.gov.

FACEMIRE, DOUGLAS E., state legislator; b. Gassaway, WV, Aug. 22, 1961; s. Eugene and Barbara; m. Tammy Gregory Facemire; children: Corey, Kayla, Jesse. Mem. Dist. 12 W.Va. State Senate, 2008—, vice chair Energy, Industry and Mining Com., mem. Econ. Devel. Com., Enrolled Bills Com., Fin. Com., Mil. Com., Natural Resources Com. & Transp. and Infrastructure Com. Democrat. Baptist. Office: State Capitol Complex Rm 218W, Bldg 1 1900 Kanawha Blvd E Charleston WV 25305 Mailing: PO Box 215 Sutton WV 26601 Office Phone: 304-357-7845, 304-364-9903. E-mail: douglas.facemire@wvsenate.gov.

FACTOR, MALLORY, independent merchant bank and financial relations consulting firm company executive; b. New Haven, Conn., July 16, 1950; s. Martin and Sylvia (Klein) F.; m. Frances Mary Precario, Jan. 2, 1980 (div.); m. Karen Elizabeth Weir, Sept., 2000; 5 children Student, Yale Lang. Inst., 1970; BS, Wesleyan U., 1971; postgrad., Columbia U., 1971-72. Supr. mgmt. cons. services Coopers & Lybrand, NYC, 1972-75; pres., chief exec. officer, chmn. Mallory Factor Inc., NYC, 1976—. Bd. dirs. Internat. Cogeneration Corp., Integrity Fin. Group, Park Lex Med. Mgmt. Ltd.; adv. bd. Continental Nat. Bank Las Vegas; organizer, chmn. Mid-Jersey Nat. Bank; mem. fed. savs. and loan adv. council of Fed. Home Loan Bank, 1987-88; adj. prof. The New Sch. for Social Research's Grad. Sch. for Mgmt. and Urban Professions, 1985-1992, Sch. of Continuing and Professional Studies, NYU, 1992-96; underwriting mem. Lloyds of London, 1987; John C. West Prof. of Internat. Politics and American Govt., The Citadel; bd. governor NY State Banking Dept., 2001-07; chmn. NY Public Asset Fund, 2002-06; vice-chmn., Governor's Island Preservation and Education Corp., 2006-07; co-founder, co-chair The Monday Morning; mem. Coun. on Foreign Relations, vice chair Task Force on Terrorism Financing; chmn. Free Enterprise Fund; sr. fellow House Republican Study Com. 2007-2011; chair Economic Roundtable for the Chairman of the Joints Chiefs of Staff, 2009 Author Shadowbosses, 2012 (#1 on Washington Post Non-Fiction Bestseller and Barnes and Noble Lists, Top 10 Non Fiction Bestseller, New York Times; sr. editor money and politics, TheStreet.com; contbr. articles to profl. publs. including The Wall Street Journal, Christian Monitor, National Review, Forbes Magazine and several others; guest appearances on Fox News, Bloomberg, and CNBC Bd. dirs., mem. exec. com. Bklyn. Acad. Music; vice chmn. bd. Roundabout Theatre, N.Y.C.; adv. bd. mem. American Theater Wing; mem. dean's adv. council New Sch. Social Research Named Man of Yr., Jaycees, Middletown, Conn., 1970 Mem. Pub. Relations Soc. Am. (exec. com.), N.Y. Soc. Assn. Execs., N.Y. C. of C. and Industry, Am. Arbitration Assn., Mktg. Communications Execs. Internat.; Am. Mgmt. Assn. Clubs: Chemist, India House, Army and Navy, N.Y. Athletic. Lodges: Masons. Avocations: piloting; traveling; music. Office: Mallory Factor Inc 211 King St Charleston SC 29401-3128*

FAGALY, WILLIAM ARTHUR, curator; b. Lawrenceburg, Ind., Mar. 1, 1938; s. William James and Dorothy Rae (Wheeler) F. BA, Ind. U., Bloomington, 1962, MA, 1967. Asst. registrar Art Mus., Ind. U., Bloomington, 1965-66; registrar New Orleans Mus. Art, 1966—67, curator collections, 1967-73, chief curator, 1973-80, asst. dir for art, 1980-2001, Francoise Billion Richardson curator African art, 1997—; curator art U. Art Mus. U. La. Lafayette, 2002—03. Guest curator La. Folk Painting exhibit, Mus. Am. Folk Art, 1973, Exhbn. of Contemporary Painting, Corcoran Gallery of Art, Washington, 1989, Preacher Art, Arthur Roger Gallery, New Orleans, 1990, Geography of the Body: The Art of Mignon Faget, Contemporary Arts Ctr., 1995, Preacher Art, Phyllis Kind Gallery, NYC, 1997, Watercolor U.S.A. 1999, Springfield Art Mus., Mo., 1999, Nat. Works on Paper, McNeese State U., Lake Charles, La., It's a Wonderful World, Contemporary Arts Ctr., New Orleans, 2003, Aristides Logothetis, Cue Art Found., NYC, 2003, Tools of Her Ministry: The Art of Sister Gertrude Morgan, Am. Folk Art Mus., 2004, Resonance from the Past: African Sculpture from the New Orleans Mus. of Art, Mus. for African Art, NYC, 2005; adv. panel visual arts and crafts divsn. arts La. Arts Coun., 1978—81, 1992; guest lectr. S.S. Rotterdam, 1983, H.M.S. Queen Elizabeth II, 1986, Sotheby's, NY, 1996; cons. Liberian Pavilion La. World Expn., 1984, Shapes of Power, Belief and Celebration: African Art from New Orleans Collections, 1989, Fritz Bultman: A Retrospective, 1993, Wyo. Art Mus., Laramie, 1995, Oreg. Biennial, Portland Art Mus., 1995, Roots of Am. Jazz: African Mus. Instruments from New Orleans Collections, 1995, He's the Prettiest: A Tribute to Big Chief Allison "Tootie," Montana's 50 Yrs. of Mardi Gras Indian Suiting, Inside the Congo: An Introduction to the Field Rsch. Archives of Frere Joseph Cornet, New Orleans Mus. Art and Monroe Libr., Loyola U., New Orleans, 2006; selection panelist McKnight Found. Fellowship Program, Minn. Coll. Arts and Design, Mpls., 1986, So. Arts Fedn., NEA Arts Regional Artists Fellowships, 1990; selecton panelist 1984 Visual Arts Fellowships, Wyo. Arts Coun., 1993; selection panelist Adolph and Esther Gottlieb Found. Artist Fellowships, NYC, 1995, Western States Art Fedn./NEA, 1996; bd. dirs. Ctr. for African and African-Am. Studies, So. U., New Orleans, Sac-O-Lait-The Keith Sonnier Found., 2002—, Prospect 1 and 2 First Internat. US Biennial, New Orleans, 2007—; bd. advisors Wilkinson County Mus., Woodville, Miss.; adj. curator Univ. Art Mus., U. La., Lafayette, 2002—; founder art activities bus. FUN (Fagaly Unltd.), 2001—; editor Ancestors of Congo Square: African Art New Orleans Mus. Art Scala Publ., 2011. Contbr. articles to profl. jours. NEA fellow, 1985, Visual Arts and Media fellow Miss. Arts Commn., 1994, Visual Arts fellow Wyo. Art Coun., 1994; recipient Mayor's Arts award City of New Orleans, 1997, Gov.'s Arts award La. State Arts Coun., 1997, Charles E. Dunbar Jr. Career Svc. award La. Civil Svc. League, 1999, Isaac Delgado Meml. award Fellows of New Orleans Mus. of Art, 2001, Chevalier de l'Ordre des Arts et des Lettres, République Française, 2006. Mem. Am. Assn. Mus. (mem. vis. com. for Tampa Mus. Art accreditation program 1999). Episcopalian. Office: PO Box 19123 New Orleans LA 70179-0123 Business E-Mail: bfagaly@noma.org.

FAGIEN, STEVEN, ophthalmologist, consultant; b. Neptune, NJ, Mar. 7, 1957; s. Melvin Blumenthal and Sondra Parker; m. Debra L Rattner, Dec. 26, 1981; children: Samantha Michelle, Alyssa Nicole, Kayla Danielle. BS, U. Fla., 1979, MD, 1983. Cert. Am. Bd. Ophthalmology, Am. Soc. Ophthalmic Plastic and Reconstructive Surgery, Am. Acad. Facial Plastic and Reconstructive Surgeons. Internal medicine U. Fla., resident-ophthalmology, 1979—83; fellow-ophthalmic plastic surgery U. Ill., 1987—88; aesthetic eyelid plastic surgery pvt. practice, Boca Raton, Fla., 1988—. Founder Collagenesis, Inc., Beverly, Mass., 1975—2002; educator, instr. Am. Soc. Aesthetic Plastic Surgery, Los Alamitos, Calif.; founder and co-director SEE Internat., Santa Barbara, Calif., 1991—96; cons., med. advisor Allergan, Inc., Irvine, Calif., 1997—, Medicis, Inc, Scottsdale, Ariz., 2002—; founder, pres. Collagen Matrix Technologies, Boca Raton, Fla., 2002—; cons., med. advisor Dermik Aesthetics, Inc, Berwyn, Pa.; chief, dept. surgery Boca Raton Cmty. Hosp., Boca Raton, Fla.; co-dir. Internat. Plastic Surgery Edn. Initiative. Contbr. articles to profl. jours.; mem. editl. adv. bd. New Beauty. Bd. mem. Boca Raton Cmty. Hosp. Recipient Man of Yr., Cystic Fibrosis Found., 2001, Dr. of Yr., Boca Raton Women's Club, 2002; named one of World's Best Plastic Surgeons Specializing in Eyelids, W Mag. Fellow: Am. Soc. Ophthalmic Plastic and Reconstructive Surgery (co-dir.), Am. Acad. Ophthalmolgy; mem.: Allergan's Nat. Edn. Faculty, Am. Soc. Aesthetic Plastic Surgery (assoc.). Achievements include research in new techiques in blepharoplasty; advanced techniques for the use of botulinum toxin type A in facial enhancement; advanced techniques in injectable soft tissue augmentation agents; development of inectable human collagen matrix; research in soft tissue augmentation. Avocations: jazz, music. Office: 660 Glades Road Ste 210 Boca Raton FL 33431 Office Fax: 561-347-0772. E-mail: sfagien@aol.com.

FAHRINGER, CATHERINE HEWSON, retired savings and loan association executive; b. Phila., Aug. 1, 1922; d. George Francis and Catherine Gertrude (Magee) Hewson; m. Edward F. Fahringer, July 8, 1961 (dec.); 1 child, Francis George Beckett (dec.). Grad. diploma, Inst. Fin. Edn., 1965. Notary pub. Fla. With Centrust Bank (formerly Dade Savs. and Loan Assn.), Miami, 1958—85; v.p. Centrust Bank, Miami, 1967—74, sr. v.p., 1974—82, sec., 1975—79, head savs. pers. and mktg. divsn., 1979—83, exec. v.p. office of chmn., 1984, dir., 1984—90, co-chmn. audit com. of bd. dirs., 1990; referral assoc. Referral Network Inc. subs. Coldwell Banker, 1990—. Pub. arbitrator NASD, 1999-2005; sr. citizens bd. City of Coral Gables, 2007-2010. Contbr. articles to profl. jours. Trustee United Way of Dade County (Fla.), 1980-87, chmn. audit com. 1982-84, trustee, Pub. Health Trust, Dade County, 1974-84, sec. 1976, vice chmn., 1977-78, chmn. bd., 1978-81; mem. adv. coun. Women's Bus. Devel. Ctr., Fla. Internat. U., 1993-95; mem. spl. steering com. Breast Cancer Task Force, Jackson Meml. Hosp., 1991; hon. bd. govs. U. Miami, Soc. for Rsch. in Med. Edn.; trustee South Fla. Blood Svc., Miami, 1979-84, vice chmn., 1980, chmn., 1981-84; trustee Dade County Vocat. Found., 1977-81; trustee Fla. Internat. U. Found., 1976-90; trustee emeritus, 1990, v.p. bd., 1978-81, pres. 1982-84; bd. dirs. Sta. WPBT-TV, 1984-2002, founding lifetime dir., 1995, chmn. budget and fin. com., 1986, mem. exec. com. 1985-92, sec. 1987, investment com., 1988-90, vice chmn. 1988-92, mem. fin. com., 1992, chmn. audit and control com., 1994, 2000, 2001, mem., 1997-98; bd. dirs., mem. nominating com. Girl Scout Coun., Tropical Fla., 1985-89, chmn. 1988-89, mem. long range planning com., 1986-88; citizens oversight com. Dade County Pub. Sch. System, 1986-90, chmn. 1988-90; bd. dirs. New World Sch. of Arts, 1987-90, chmn. devel. com., 1987-90, chair New World Sch. of Arts Gala, 1990; mem. Disaster Relief Com., chair Hurricane Disaster Relief Distbn. Ctr., 1992; mem. fin. com., chmn. capital improvement fund com. Coral Gables Congrl. Ch., summer concert series com., chmn. refreshement sub-com.; commd. Stephen min., 1985-1995; mem. grievance com. 11th Jud. Cir. Fla. Bar, 1988-92; bd. trustees United Protestant Appeal, 1994-96; mem. parking adv. bd. City of Coral Gables, 1997-98, bd. of adjustments, 1998-2007, vice chmn., 2001-2003, chmn.2003—2007, sr. citizens adv. bd., 2007-

2011, vice chmn. 2010; mem., 3rd v.p. Bush chpt. Women's Cancer Assn. U. Miami, 1997-99, 2nd v.p., treas. and parliamentarian, 1999-2001, chmn. meml. fund, 1998-2003, 3rd v.p., 2002-03, mem. FIU Bronze Flame Hon. Torcit Soc., 2009. Recipient Trail Blazer award, Women's Coun. of 100, 1977, Cmty. Headliner award, Women in Comm., 1983, Outstanding Citizen of Dade County award, 1984, Honors and Recognition award, Golden Panthers Club of Fla. Internat. U., 1989, Disting. Svc. and Leadership award, Fla. Internat. U., 1991, apprecation, New World Sch. of the Arts, 1990, Meritorious Pub. Svc. award, Fla. Bar, 1991, Outstanding Svc. award, Country Club Coral Gables, 2001, hon. BA, U. Hard Knocks Alderson-Broaddus Coll., 1987, Key to City of Coral Gables for Cmty. Svc., 2000, Dedicated Svc. award, Women's Cancer Assn. of U. Miami, 2001, Outstanding Svc. Award, 2001, Woman's Day Disting. Woman of Svc. Recognition, Coral Gables Congregational Ch., 2006, In The Company of Women Pioneer award, Miami-Dade County, Fla., 2007; named Women of Yr. in fin., Zonta Internat., 1975, amb., Air Def. Arty., 1970, U.S. Army Air Def. Command, 1970, Woman of Yr. in Sports, Links Club, 1986, First Lady of Athletics, Fla. Internat. U., 2003; named one of Notable Women in Miami-Dade County History, Beyond Julia's Daughters 1975-2000, 2007. Mem.: LWV, Women's Union Russia, Fla. Women's Alliance (bd. dirs. 1983—91, pres. 1987—89), Internat. Women's Alliance, Savs. and Loan Pers. Soc. South Fla., Savs. and Loan Mktg. Soc. South Fla. (past pres.), Inst. Fin. Edn. (life; nat. dir., past pres. Local Greater Miami chpt.), Greater Miami Women's Golf Assn. (social dir. 1999—2001), Greenway Women's Golf Assn. (treas. 1988—89), Balt. Women's Golf Assn., Fla. Internat. U. Athletics Club, Golden Panther Club (bd. dirs. 1988—2007, v.p. 1991, pres. 1992—94), Links Fla. Internat. U. Club (v.p. 1992, bd. dirs., sec.), Country Club Coral Gables (treas. women's golf assn 1988—89, sec., bd. dirs., found. trustee 1993, v.p. bd. dirs. 1994, pres. 1995, chmn. bldg. restoration, capital improvement and maintenance com. 1995—99, bd. advisors 1996—2007, liaison City of Coral Gables 1997—99, rear commodore, vice commodore, historian, adv., chair The Fleet 1998, commodore 1999, publicity chmn. woman's bd. 2000—01, pres. women's golf assn. 2001—02, mem. adv. bd. dirs. 2002—, golf adv., directory chair 2003, pres. 2009—10, coord., Ann. Formal Fleet Installation Learning 2011—, Fleet Disting. Svc. award 2010), Dade Bus. and Profl. Women's Club (past pres.). Democrat. Avocations: flower arranging, golf. Personal E-mail: kayaok@aol.com.

FAIELLA, JOANN, mayor, Port St. Lucie, Florida; b. Bklyn. m. Pat Faiella; 3 children. Degree in child devel., Indian River State Coll., Fort Pierce, Fla.; BA in Bus. Adminstrn. Cert. alt. terminal agency coord., comm. tng. officer, crime intelligence analyst Fla. Dept. Law Enforcement. Asst. dir. Colonial Country Day Sch., Port St. Lucie, Fla.; police svc. aide, criminal intelligence analyst Port St. Lucie Police Dept.; mayor City of Port St. Lucie, 2011—. Pub. (handbook) Let Consumers Be Aware. Com. mem. Kids at Hope; mentor for local juveniles. Recipient Child Advocate award, NYC Mayor's Office. Office: City Hall Office of the Mayor 121 SW Port St Lucie Blvd Port Saint Lucie FL 34984-6339 Office Phone: 772-871-5225, 772-873-6339 TDD.*

FAIN, JOHN NICHOLAS, biochemistry educator; b. Jefferson City, Tenn., Aug. 18, 1934; s. Samuel Clark and Virginia Manson (Hunt) F.; m. Ann Duff, June 7, 1958; children: Margaret Ann, John Nicholas Jr., James Clark. BS magna cum laude, Carson-Newman Coll., 1956; PhD in Biochemistry, Emory U., 1960. Rsch. assoc. Emory U., Atlanta, 1960-61; NSF fellow NIH, Bethesda, Md., 1961-62, postdoctoral fellow USPHS, 1962-63; biochemist NIH and Nat. Inst. Arthritis and Metabolic Diseases, Bethesda, 1963-65; asst. prof. Brown U., Providence, 1965-68, assoc. prof., 1968-71, prof., 1971-85, chmn. biochemistry, 1975-85; Van Vleet prof., dept. chmn. U. Tenn., Memphis, 1985-2000, Van Vleet prof. of molecular scis., 2000—. Contbr. numerous articles to sci. jours. Del. gen. assembly United Presbyn. Ch., Providence, 1972. Recipient Disting. Alumnus award Carson-Newman Coll., 1986; fellow Cambridge U., 1977-78; NIH Fogarty fellow, 1984-85; Macy Faculty scholar, 1977-78. Mem. Am. Soc. Biol. Chemists. Democrat. Office: U Tenn Health Scis Ctr Coll Medicine Dept Mol Scis 858 Madison Ste GO1 Memphis TN 38163 Home: 4501 Trezevant Pl 177 N Highland Memphis TN 38111 Office Phone: 901-448-4343. Fax: 901-448-7360. E-mail: jfain@uthsc.edu.

FAIR, MICHAEL L., state legislator, insurance company executive; b. June 16, 1946; s. Paul L. and Hazel C. Fair; m. Judy T. Hodge, July 8, 1969; 1 child, Meredith M. Fair Edmonds. Grad., U. SC. Mem. Dist. 19 SC House of Reps., 1985—95; mem. Dist. 6 SC State Senate, 1995—, chair Corrections and Penology Com. & Subcommittee on Corrections and Pub. Safety. Chmn. corrections and penology com.; mem. edn. com., gen. com., med. affairs com., transp. com., numerous others. Mem. Greenville County Coun., 1976-82. Republican. Office: 211 Gressette Bldg Columbia SC 29202 Mailing: PO Box 14632 Greenville SC 29610-4632 Business E-Mail: FAIRM@scsenate.org.

FAIRBAIRN, URSULA FARRELL, human resources executive; b. Newark, Feb. 5, 1943; d. Henry C. and Clara J. (Ziefle) Otte; m. William Todd Fairbairn III, May 14, 1978; children: W. Todd, Mary, Joyce Sjoberg. BA, Upsala Coll., 1965; MAT in Math., Harvard U., 1966. Instr., numerous mktg. positions IBM Corp., NYC, 1966-78; exec. asst. to sec., White House fellow U.S. Treasury Dept., Washington, 1973-74; exec. asst. to chmn. bd., group dir. IBM Corp., Armonk, N.Y., 1978-79, v.p. mgmt. svcs., then v.p. mktg. ops. west, 1980-84, dir. pers. resources, 1984-87, dir. bus. and mgmt. edn., 1987, dir. edn., 1987-89, dir. edn. and mgmt. devel., 1989-90; sr. v.p. human resources Union Pacific Corp., Bethlehem, Pa., 1990-96; exec. v.p. human resources and quality American Express Co., NYC, 1996—2005; pres, CEO Fairbairn Group, LLC, 2005—. Bd. dirs. VF Corp., Greensboro, N.C., Air Products Corp., Allentown, Pa., Sunoco Corp., Phila., Circuit City Stores, Inc., Richmond, Centex Corp., Dallas. Contbg. author: Managing Human Resources in the Information Age, 1991. Mem. Com. of 200, Catalyst, N.Y.C.; vice-chair Nat. Acad.-HR; chair Pers. Round Table. Mem. Bus. Roundtable, Employee Rels. Com., Labor Policy Assn. Avocations: gardening, art, reading, walking, travel. Office: Centex Corp 2728 N Harwood St Dallas TX 75201-1516 Office Phone: 214-981-5000. Office Fax: 214-981-6859.

FAIRBANK, RICHARD D., diversified financial services company executive; b. 1950; BA in Econs., Stanford U., Calif., 1972, MBA, 1981. Cons. Strategic Planning Assocs., 1981—87; chmn., CEO Capital One Financial Corp., McLean, Va., 1994—2003, chmn., pres., CEO, 2005—; chmn. US region MasterCard, Inc., 2002—04. Bd. dirs. MasterCard US Region, 1995—2004, MasterCard Internat. Global Bd., 2004—. Named Best CEO, Instl. Investor mag., Bus. Leader of Yr., Washingtonian Mag. Office: Capital One Fin Corp 1680 Capital One Dr Mc Lean VA 22102-3491 Office Phone: 703-720-1000.

FAIRCHILD, JOSEPH VIRGIL, JR., finance educator; b. New Orleans, Nov. 26, 1933; s. Joseph Virgil and Georgiana Malone (Bourgeois) F.; m. Judith Champagne, Aug. 12, 1961 (dec. 2005); children: Georgianna, Joseph, Benjamin; m. Marion Peter, Feb. 27, 2009 BS in Geology, La. State U., 1956, MBA, 1961, PhD, 1975. CPA, La. Geologist United Core, Inc., Houston, 1956-57; assoc. acct. Humble Oil & Refining Co., New Orleans, 1963-64; ptnr. L.A. Champagne & Co., Baton Rouge, 1964-69; pvt. practice acctg. Thibodaux, La., 1969-2000; ret., 2000; asst. prof. acctg. Nicholls State U., Thibodaux, 1969-75, assoc. prof., 1975-76, prof., 1976-84, disting. prof. acctg., 1984—2000, asst. dean Coll. Bus., 1985-86, dir. grad. bus. studies, 1982-85, disting. prof. emeritus, 2002—. Vis. prof., acctg. Henderson State U., 2000-04, Am. U. Bulgaria, Blagoevgrad, Republic of Bulgaria, 2004-, Ark. State U., jonesboro, 2005-06, U. Indpls., 2006-09; rsch. reviewer USAF Bus. Rsch. Mgmt. Ctr., Wright-Patterson AFB, Ohio, 1974-84; cons. Def. Sys. Mgmt. Coll., Ft. Belvoir, Va., 1980-81; faculty senate v.p. govt. com., chmn. dean's search com. Author: (with others) The Acquisition and Distribution of Commercial Products, 1980, 1985-86, 1986-87, 1987-88 and 1988-89 Income Tax Guides for State Legislators; contbr. articles to profl. jours.; actor: (TV, movies) The Kingfish-TNT, Orleans-CBS, Deadman Walking; (plays) South Pacific, Arsenic and Old Lace, Brigadoon, Damn Yankees. Mem. St. Genevieve Sch. Bd., Thibodaux, 1979-83, E.D. White Cath. H.S. Bd., 1985-87, chmn. fin. com., 1985-87; lector St. Genevieve Ch., 1975—, choir, 1989—. 1st lt. USAF, 1957-60, lt. col. USAFR ret. Recipient Acad. Excellence award Henderson State U., 2003, 04; Trueblood Prof. Touche-Ross Found., N.Y.C., 1987. Mem. AICPA, Soc. La. CPA's (lectr. seminars, La.'s Outstanding Acctg. Educator 1994), Am. Acctg. Assn., Nat. Assn. Accts., Nicholls State U. Alumni Assn. (Hon. Alumnus award 1991, Case Educator of Yr. 1994). Roman Catholic. Avocations: flying, skiing, photography, fishing. Home: 412 Plater Dr Thibodaux LA 70301-5616 Office: Nicholls State U Dept Acctg Thibodaux LA 70310-0001

FAIRCHILD, KAREN, singer; b. Gary, Ind., Sept. 28, 1969; m. Jimi Westbrook, May 31, 2006; 1 child, Elijah Dylan. Attended, Samford U., Birmingham, Ala. Co-founder Little Big Town, 1999. Singer: (albums) (with Little Big Town) Little Big Town, 2002, The Road to Here, 2005, A Place to Land, 2007, The Reason Why, 2010, Tornado, 2012, (songs) Pontoon, 2012 (Single of Yr., Country Music Assn. Awards, 2012, Best Country Duo/Group Performance, Grammy Awards, 2013), Tornado, 2012 (Video of Yr., Acad. Country Music Awards, 2013). Named Top New Duo/Vocal Group, Acad. Country Music Awards, 2007, Vocal Group of Yr., Country Music Assn. Awards, 2012, 2013, Acad. Country Music Awards, 2013. Office: c/o Sandbox Entertainment 54 Music Square East Suite 200 Nashville TN 37203*

FAIRCLOTH, JOHN, state legislator; b. Greensboro; m. Linda Faircloth; children: Catherine Faircloth, Tammy Faircloth, Laura Faircloth. Grad., U. Louisville; grad. Justice Exec. Program, U. NC, Chapel Hill; AA in Mgmt., BS in Mgmt., Guilford Coll.; M in Pub. Affairs, U. NC, Greensboro. Mem. Covenant Church United Methodist, Boys and Girls Club, High Point ptnrs., High Point Mayor Pro Tem, High Point Housing Authority, High Point Area Arts Coun., Preddy WWII Veterans Found., Rotary Club, Crimestoppers, H.P. Realtors Assoc., Econ. Devel. Commn., City Employee Found., Alliance for Workforce Preparedness, Heart of the Triad Com., Downtown Improvement Com., Core City Steering Com., C. of C., United Way, Human Rels. Commn.; with Greensboro Police Dept., 1961—72, NC Dept. of Justice, 1972—75; chief of police Salisbury, NC, 1975—76, High Point, NC, 1976—92; v.p., owner, broker Coldwell Banker Triad, Realtors, 1994—; mem. High Point City Coun., 2003—08; coun. mem., ward 6 High Point, NC, 2008—10; mem. Dist. 61 NC House of Representatives, 2011—. With USAR, 1957-68. Republican. Methodist. Mailing: 2332 Faircloth Way High Point NC 27265 Office: North Carolina House of Representatives 300 N Salisbury St Room 306A3 Raleigh NC 27603-5925 Office Phone: 336-883-3293, 919-733-5877, 336-841-4137. Office Fax: 336-883-3052. Business E-Mail: John@johnfaircloth61.com, John.Faircloth@ncleg.net.

FAISON, BILL (O. WILLIAM FAISON), state legislator; b. Raleigh, NC, Feb. 7, 1947; m. Lindy Faison; children: Ean, Chasie, Stone, Courtney, Bo; 1 child, Breck. BA, U. NC, Chapel Hill, 1969; JD, U. NC Law Sch., 1972. Assoc. Newsome, Graham, Strayhorn & Hederick, Law Firm, 1972—76, ptnr., 1976—84, Faison & Gillespie Law Firm, 1985—; state rep. Dist. 50 NC, 2005—. Contbr. articles to profl. jours. Recipient Ebby award, NCATL; named Outstanding Young Man of America, Outstanding Lawyers of America. Mem.: ABA, NAACP, Durham County Bar Assn., NC Bar Assn., NC Acad. Trial Lawyers. Democrat. Methodist. Mailing: Dist Off PO Box 51729 Durham NC 27717-1729 Office: North Carolina House of Representatives 300 N Salisbury St Rm 405 Raleigh NC 27603-5925 Office Phone: 919-715-3019, 919-600-6700. E-mail: Bill.Faison@ncleg.net.

FALCO, EDWARD, writer, English educator; b. LA, Nov. 25, 1948; s. Joseph and Edith Falco; m. Jane Braley, June 14, 1980 (div. Sept. 1986); 1 child, Susan; m. Lisa Norris, June 19, 1993; 1 stepchild, Will Stauffer-Norris. BS, SUNY, New Paltz, 1971; MA, Syracuse U., 1979. Part-time instr. Enlish Syracuse U., NY, 1979-84; prof. Va. Tech., Blacksburg, 1984—, dir. MFA program; edits online journal of digital writing The New River. Author: (chapbook of prose poem) Concert in the Park of Culture, 1984, (hypertext poetry collection) Sea Island, 1995; (short stories) Plato at Scratch Daniel's & Othere Stories, 1990, ACID, 1996 (Richard Sullivan prize, 1995, U. of Notre Dame, finalist The Patterson prize), Sabbath Night in the Church of the Piranha: New and Selected Stories, 2005, Wolf Point, 2005, In the Park of Culture, 2005, Burning Man; (novels) Winter in Florida, 1990, (hypertext novel) A Dream with Demons, 1997, Saint John of the Five Boroughs, 2009, The Family Corleone, 2012; stories have been published in journals, including the Atlantic Monthly, Playboy, and TriQuarterly, and collected in the Best American Short Stories, Pushcart prize, and several anthologies, including, Blue Cathedral:Short Fiction for the New Millennium; innovator in the field of digital writing, literary and experimental hypertexts include Self-Portrait as Child w/Father, Circa 1967-1968, 'Charmin' Cleary, and Chemical Landscapes Digital Tales; playwriter Home Delivery (Hampden-Sydney Playwriting award), Radon, Welcome to Castle in the Air, The Center and Possum Dreams Recipient Emily Clark Balch prize The Va. Quar. Rev., 1986, Govs. Screenwriting award Va. Film Office, 1991, Pushcart prize Pushcart Press, 1999, Robert Penn Warren prize in Poetry, The Southern Review, Mishima prize for Innovation Fiction, The Saint Andrews Review, Governor's Award for the Screenplay, Va. Festival of American Film; Individual Artist grantee Va. Commn. Arts, 1992, 95; 2008 NEA Fellowship in Fiction, 2009 Virginia Commission for the Arts Fellowship in Playwriting, Dakin Fellowship, Sewanee Writers' Conf., two individual Artist's Fellowships, Va. Commission for the Arts Unitarian Universalist. Avocation: chess. Office: Va Tech English Dept Blacksburg VA 24061-0112 Address: c/o Neil Olson Donadio and Olson Literary Agency 121 W 27th St Ste 704 New York NY 10001-6207 E-mail: efalco@vt.edu.

FALCO, MARIA JOSEPHINE, political scientist; b. Wildwood, NJ, July 7, 1932; d. John J. and Mafalda M. (Barbieri) F. AB, Immaculata Coll., Pa., 1954; student, U. Florence, Italy, 1954-55; MA, Fordham U., 1958; PhD, Bryn Mawr Coll., Pa., 1963; postdoctoral rsch. fellow, Yale, 1965-66; quantitative data analysis, U. Mich., 1968; mgmt. program, Carnegie-Mellon U., 1983. Instr., then asst. prof. history and polit. sci. Immaculata Coll., Pa., 1957-63; asst. prof. polit. sci. Washington Coll., Chestertown, Md., 1963-64; rsch. asst. Genevieve Blatt; candidate for U.S. Senator from Pa., 1964-65; asst. prof., then assoc. prof. polit. sci. Le Moyne Coll., Syracuse, NY, 1966-73, chmn. polit. sci. dept., 1967-73; prof. polit. sci. Stockton State Coll., Pomona, NJ, 1973-76; chmn. social and behavioral scis. faculty U. Tulsa, 1976-79; dean Coll. Arts and Scis., Loyola U., New Orleans, 1979-85; prof. polit. sci. Loyola U., New Orleans, 1985-86; v.p. acad. affairs DePauw U., Greencastle, Ind., 1986-88, prof. polit. sci., 1988-93, prof. emerita, 1993—. Speaker in field; adj. prof. polit. sci. Tulane U., New Orleans, 1996-97. Author: Truth and Meaning in Political Science: An Introduction to Political Inquiry, 1973, Bigotry: Ethnic, Machine and Sexual Politics in a Senatorial Election, 1980; editor: Through the Looking Glass: Epistemology and the Conduct of Political Inquiry: An Anthology, 1979, Feminism and Epistemology: Approaches to Research in Women and Politics, 1987, Feminist Interpretations of Mary Wollstonecraft, 1996, Feminist Interpretations of Niccolo Machiavelli, 2004, Italy Celebrates the 150th Anniversary of its Unification, 2011; cons. editor Political Parties and the Civic Action Groups; contbr. articles and book revs. to profl. jours. Mem. Mayor's Task Force on Future of New Orleans, 1983-85, Women's Equity Action League, 1979-81, LWV, 1960-63, 82-84; bd. dirs. Inst. for Human Rels., Loyola U., Inst. Human Understanding, New Orleans, 1985-86; pres. Syracuse chpt. New Dem. Coalition, 1970-71; mem. pres.'s coun. Loyola U., New Orleans, 1997-2000, mem. Ars Dean's coun., 2000-06, vol., Arts & Scis., Country Club Estates Cane Assn. Fulbright scholar U. Florence, Italy, 1954-55; faculty fellow in state and local politics Nat. Ctr. for Edn. in Politics, 1964. Mem.: AAUP (v.p. LeMoyne chpt. 1971-72), Womens Caucus Polit. Sci. (pres. 1976, named Mentor of Distinction 1989), Am. Polit. Sci. Assn. (Benjamin Evans Lippincott award com. 1976, chmn. sect. program com. 1975, com. acad. freedom and profl. ethics, chair com. for outstanding conv. paper award women and politics rsch. sect. 1990-91), Midwestern Polit. Sci. Assn. (com. status of women), Northeastern Polit. Sci. Assn., S.W. Polit. Sci. Assn. (outstanding conv. paper com.), Founds. Polit. Theory Group, Common Cause, Great Lakes Coll. Assn. (dean's coun. 1986-88), Assn. Jesuit Colls. and Univs. (dean's coun. 1979-85), Assn. Am. Colls. (coun. for liberal learning 1985-87), Western Polit. Sci. Assn., Ind. Polit. Sci. Assn. (pres., chair 1992-93), Ind. Social Sci. Assn., So. Polit. Sci. Assn., Jefferson Parish LWV (bd. dirs. 1999—, pres. 2001-02), Jefferson Parish Bus. and Profl. Women (1st v.p. 2002-04, pres. 2004-05), East Jefferson Italian-Am. Soc., Am. Instnl. Fedn., Am. Italian Fedn. SE (sec.2013-), Women Better La. (pres., 2012-13), Jefferson Beautification Inc., Women's Opera Guild(connection com. sec. 2013), New Orleans Opera Assn. (mem. adv. com., mktg. com.), Am. Italian Digest New Orleans (hist.), East Jefferson Regional Libr., Eucharistic Min., St. Ann Ch. Roman Catholic. Home: 4709 Tartan Dr Metairie LA 70003 Personal E-mail: msforza2377@yahoo.com.

FALCON, ARMANDO J., JR., consulting firm executive; b. San Antonio, June 4, 1960; married; 2 children. BA, St. Mary's U., 1983; M in Pub. Policy, Harvard U., 1985; JD, U. Tex., 1988. With San Antonio Econ. Devel. Found., 1982; legis. asst. to Com. on Edn. Tex. State Senate, Tex., 1983; law clk. to atty. gen. State of Tex., Austin, 1986—88; pvt. practice; counsel US Ho. of Representatives Com. on Banking & Fin. Services, 1989—91, dep. gen. counsel, 1991—95, gen. counsel, 1995—97; dir. Office Fed. Housing Enterprise Oversight (OFHEO), Washington, 1999—2005; ptnr. The Canonbury Group, Alexandria, 2005—. Office: Canonbury Advisors LLC 1733 King St Third Fl Alexandria VA 22314 Office Phone: 703-838-9552. E-mail: armando@canonburygroup.com.

FALGOUST, DEAN THOMAS, lawyer, accountant; b. Vacherie, La., Oct. 21, 1958; s. Joseph Bienvenue and Rose Mary (Landry) F.; m. Janet Marie Dolese, Aug. 7, 1982; children: Luke Bienvenue, Laura Katherine. BS in Acctg., Nicholls State U., 1978; JD, Loyola U., New Orleans, 1982; LLM in Taxation, NYU, 1983. Bar: La. 1982; CPA, La. Auditor A.A. Harmon & Co., New Orleans, 1978-79; pvt. practice acctg. New Orleans, 1980-81; assoc. Chaffe, McCall, Phillips, Toler & Sarpy, New Orleans, 1982-85; dir. tax, v.p. Freeport-McMoRan Inc., New Orleans, 1985-97; v.p., tax and legal Freeport McMoran Copper & Gold, Inc., New Orleans, 1997—, v.p., gen. counsel, 2003—07, vp, 2007—; v.p., gen. counsel McMoran Exploration Co., 1997—, vp, 1997—; pres. FM Svcs. Co., 2007—. Bd. dirs., chmn. First Am. Bank & Trust, One Am. Corp., Vacherie, legal cons., 1984—. Mem. Loyola Law Rev., 1980-82. Mem. La. Bar Assn., Bus. Coun. New Orleans, New Orleans Police & Justice Found., Fore!Kids Found. Republican. Roman Catholic. Home: 9631 Garden Oak Ln River Ridge LA 70123-2005 Office: Freeport McMoRan Copper & Gold Inc 1615 Poydras St PO Box 61119 New Orleans LA 70161-1119 Business E-Mail: dean_falgoust@fmi.com.

FALK, THOMAS J., health products executive; b. Waterloo, Iowa, 1958; m. Karen Falk; 1 child. B in Acctg., U. Wis., 1980; MS in Mgmt., Stanford U., Calif., 1988. With Alexander Grant & Co.; with internal audit staff Kimberly-Clark Corp., Neenah, Wis., 1983, sr. auditor, 1984, sr. fin. analyst, 1986, dir. corp. strategic analysis, 1987, ops. mgr. infant care, diaper plant Beech Island, SC, 1989, v.p. ops. analysis and control, 1990, sr. v.p. analysis and adminstrn., 1991, group pres. infant and child care, 1993, group pres. N.Am. consumer products, 1995, group pres. global tissue, pulp and paper, 1998—99, pres., 1999—2003, COO, 1999—2002, bd. dirs. Tex., 1999—, CEO Tex., 2002—, chmn. Tex., 2003—. Dallas regional advisory bd. JP Morgan Chase; bd. dirs. Grocery Mfrs. Am., Inc., Centex Corp., 2003—. Bd. govs. Boys and Girls Clubs Am.; bd. dirs. U. Wis. Found. Sloan Fellow, Stanford U. Grad. Sch. Bus., 1988. Office: Kimberly Clark Corp PO Box 619100 Dallas TX 75261-9100 Office Phone: 972-281-1200. Office Fax: 972-281-1435. Business E-Mail: thomas.falk@kimberly-clark.com.

FALLETTA, JOHN MATTHEW, pediatrician, educator; b. Arma, Kans., Sept. 3, 1940; s. Matthew John and Norma (Luke) F.; m. Carolyn Ontjes, June 22, 1963; children: Elizabeth, Matthew. AB, U. Kans., 1962, MD, 1966. Diplomate Am. Bd. Pediat., Am. Bd. Hematology-Oncology. Intern in mixed medicine Kans. U. Med. Ctr., Kansas City, 1966-67; surgeon Epidemic Intelligence Svc., Tex. Children's Hosp. USPHS, Houston, 1967-69; asst. instr. pediat. Baylor Coll. Medicine, Houston, 1967-69, resident, 1969-71, chief resident Tex. Children's Hosp., 1971, postdoctoral fellow hematology-oncology, 1971-73, asst. prof. pediat., 1973-76; assoc. prof. Duke U., Durham, NC, 1976-83, prof., 1984—, chief divsn. hematology-oncology, 1976-94, dir. Clin. Pediat. Lab., 1976-95. Chmn. transfusion com. Duke U. Med. Ctr., 1978—, mem. exec. com. med. staff, 1978—, instl. rev. bd. human rsch., 1979—, chmn., 1994—; mem. instl. rev. bd. human rsch. Baylor Coll. Medicine, 1974-76; mem. acad. coun. Duke U., 1982-86, 87-96, 98-2000, exec. com., 1988, faculty compensation com., 1988—, faculty com. on univ. governance, 1988, trustee-faculty com. to rev. pres., 1989, search com. for pres., 1992; cons. pediat. hematologist-oncologist Charlotte Meml. Hosp., NC, 1978-94, mem. Copernicus Independent Rev. Bd., 2002—, vice-chair, 2004—; mem. med. adv. bd. Children's Cancer Rsch. Fund, 2001—; mem. coun. accreditation Assn. for Accreditation Human Rsch. Protection Programs, Inc., 2005— Contbr. more than 120 articles to Nature, Am. Jour. Ophthalmology, Pediat., New Eng. Jour. Medicine, Clin. Pediat. Oncology, others. Cons. pediat. hematologist-oncologist Project Hope, Pediatric Inst., Krakow, Poland, 1979—; prin. investigator Pediat. Oncology Group, 1981-95, chmn. epidemiology com., mem. prin. investigator's exec. com., new agts. and pharmacology com.; chmn. prophylactic penicillin study I Nat. Heart, Lung and Blood Inst., NIH, 1982-86, chmn. study II, 1987-95; active Cancer Ctr. Support Rev. Com. Nat. Cancer Inst. NIH, 1986-90, NIH Reviewers Res., 1990—, Cancer Clin. Investigation Rev. Com., 1991-96, chmn., 1995-96; trustee Ronald McDonald House Charities, 1986—. Mem. Am. Acad. Pediat., Am. Pediat. Soc., Am. Soc. Clin. Oncology, So. Soc. Pediat. Rsch. (pres. 1981-82), Soc. Pediat. Rsch., NC Pediat. Soc., NC Med. Soc., Phi Beta Kappa, Alpha Omega Alpha. Office: Duke U Med Ctr PO Box 2712 Durham NC 27705-3826

FALLIN, MARY COPELAND, Governor of Oklahoma, former United States Representative from Oklahoma; b. Warrensburg, Mo., Dec. 9, 1954; d. Joseph Newton and Mary (Duggan) Copeland; children: Christina, Price. Attended, Oklahoma Baptist U., 1973—75; BS, Okla. State U., 1977; attended, U. Ctrl. Okla., 1979—81. Bus. mgr. Okla. Dept. Securities, Oklahoma City, 1979-81; state travel coord. Okla. Dept. Tourism, Oklahoma City, 1981-82; sales rep. Associated Petroleum, Oklahoma City, 1982-83; mktg. dir. Brian Head Hotel & Ski Resort, Utah, 1983-84; dir. sales Residence Inn Hotel, Oklahoma City, 1984-87; dist. mgr. Lexington Hotel Suites, Oklahoma City, 1988-90; real estate assoc. Pippin Properties, Inc., Oklahoma City, 1990-94; mem. Okla. House of Reps., Oklahoma City, 1990-94; lt. gov. State of Okla., Oklahoma City, 1995—2007, gov., 2011—; mem. US Congress from 5th Okla. dist., Washington, 2007—11. Chmn. Nat. Conf. Lt. Govs. Mem., del. Okla. Fedn. Rep. Women; mem. Ammerican Legis. Exch. Coun., Nat. Conf. State Legislatures; mem. adv. bd. Trail of Tears; active Crossings Cmty. Ch. Recipient Bi-liner award, 1997, Guardian of Small Bus. award, Small Bus. Adv. award, Nat. Fedn. Ind. Small Bus., Women in the News award, Women in Comm., Clarence E. Page award; named Woman of Yr., Ladies in Comm., 1998, Girl Scouts Am., 1998, Nat. Legislator of Yr., Okla. Ladies in the News, Disting. Former Student, U. Ctrl. Okla.; named to The Okla. Women's Hall of Fame, The Okla. Aviation Hall of Fame, 1998. Mem.: Aerospace States Assn. (chmn. 2003—05). Republican. Office: Office of the Governor Capitol Building 2300 N Lincoln Blvd Room 212 Oklahoma City OK 73105 Office Phone: 405-521-2342. Office Fax: 405-521-4285.*

FALLON, ELDON E., federal judge; b. New Orleans, Feb. 16, 1939; s. Edward and Delia (Koster) F.; m. Cecile Fallon, Sept. 28, 1967. BA, Tulane U., New Orleans, 1959, JD, 1962; LLM, Yale U., 1963. Bar: La. 1962. Assoc. Kierr & Gainsburgh, 1962—68; ptnr. Gainsburgh, Benjamin, Fallon & David, New Orleans, 1968—95; judge US Dist. Ct. (ea. dist.) La., New Orleans, 1995—. Adj. prof. Tulane U. Law Sch., 1975-93, 2000-03. Author: Trial Handbook For Louisiana Lawyers, 1981, 2nd edit., 1992; contbr. articles to profl. jours. Recipient La. Medaille de la Ville de Paris, ABA, 1983, Nat. Pro Bono Publico award, 1987, Pursuit of Justice award, 2005, Herbert Harley award, Am. Judicature Soc., 2005. Fellow Am. Bar Found., Am. Coll. Trial Lawyers, La. Bar Found. (bd. dirs., pres. 1995-96); mem. La. Bar Assn. (sec. treas. 1984, pres. 1985-86, President's award 1980, 88, Lifetime Achievement award 1987, Outstanding Lawyer in La. 1989). Office: US Dist Ct 500 Poydras St C456 New Orleans LA 70130-3313

FALLON, WILLIAM JOSEPH, retired military officer; b. East Orange, NJ, Dec. 30, 1944; m. Mary Elizabeth Trapp; children: Susan, Barbara, William, Christina. BA, Villanova U., 1967; MA in Internat. Studies, Old Dominion, 1982. Advanced through grade to adm. USN, 2005; pilot USS Ranger, 1969; comdr. attack squadron 65 USS Dwight D. Eisenhower, 1984-85; dep. comdr. carrier air wing 8 USS Nimitz; comdr. attack wing 1 Naval Air Sta. Occana, Va., 1989-90, USS Theodore Roosevelt, 1991, comdr. carrier group 8, 1995; comdr. Theodore Roosevelt battle group, comdr. Battle Force 6th Fleet; dep. comdr. in chief, chief staff US Atlantic Fleet, Norfolk, Va., 1996-98, commdr. 2d Fleet, Striking Fleet Atlantic, 1997—2000; vice chief naval ops. USN, Washington, 2000—03; comdr. US Fleet Forces Command & US Atlantic Fleet, Norfolk, Va., 2003—05, US Pacific Command, Honolulu, 2005—07, US Ctrl. Command, MacDill AFB, Fla., 2007—08; ret., 2008.

FAMIGLIETTI, ROBIN, finance company executive; AA in Pre-Professional, Mattatuck Cmty. Coll., 1978; BA in Psychology, Wesleyan U., 1981; MA in Edn., U. South Fla., 1989. Sr. adminstrv. benefits asst. Yale U., 1981—82, internal auditor, 1982—83, sr. staff auditor, 1983—85; tutor Wolcott High Sch., 1985—86; fin. aid counselor Eckerd Coll., 1987—90, assoc. dir., fin. aid, 1993—96; sr. edn. financing specialist Key Bank USA, 1996—97; regional mktg. mgr. Edn. First, 1997—98, dir., bus. devel., 1998—99; sales exec. Fla. USA Funds Svcs., 1999—2001; joined SLM Corp., 2000; v.p. Sallie Mae - SLM Corp., 2007—; nat. sales mgr. USA Funds Services, 2007—. Office: SLM Corp 12061 Bluemont Way Reston VA 20190 Office Phone: 703-810-3000. Office Fax: 703-984-5042. Business E-Mail: robin.famiglietti@salliemae.com.

FANGMAN, KAREN WALKER, school nurse practitioner; b. Lubbock, Tex., Apr. 15, 1951; d. Connie W. and Margaret I. Walker; m. Donnie J. Fangman, Apr. 6, 1973; children: Thomas F. Green, Colby A. BSN, West Tex. A&M U., Canyon, 2005. Cert. sch. nurse, West Tex. AMU WTAMU Nat. Bd., 2005. Cert. nurse aid Kings Manor, Westgate, Hereford, Tex., 1969—72, cert. medication aide, 1970—72, asst. don, 1978—79, staff nurse, 2006—, Hereford Regional Med. Ctr., 2008—; lic. vocat. nurse Amarillo Coll., Tex., 1977—78; RN Deaf Smith Gen. Hosp., Hereford, 1985—, student nurse, 1977—78, NW Tex. Hosp. Sch. Nursing, Amarillo, 1983—84, lvn, 1983—84; dorm parent Cal Farley's Boys Ranch, Tex., 1979—84; grad. nurse Anson Gen. Hosp., Tex., 1984—85, RN; cons. Golden Plains Nursing Home, Hereford, 1986—88; sch. nurse Hereford Ind. Sch. Dist., 1988—, program dir., 2006—; grad. student nurse Tex. Tech. Health Sci. Ctr. Sch. Nursing, Lubbock, 2007—. Composer, singer (cassette tape, CD) The Walkers/Blue Diamonds & Red Roses. Pres. Am. Heart Assn., Hereford, 1985—86; nurse ARC, Hereford, 1989—2008. Recipient Excellence award, DSHS, 1988. Mem.: Gamma Beta Phi, Sigma Theta Tau. Achievements include invention of inflatable bedpan. Home: 312 S Kingwood Hereford TX 79045 Office: Hereford Jr High 704 La Plata Hereford TX 79045 Office Fax: 806-363-7697. Business E-Mail: karenfangman@herefordisd.net.*

FANJUL, ALFIE, JR., (ALFONSO FANJUL), food products executive; b. June 1937; s. Alfonso and Lillian Gomez-Mena Fanjal; m. Tina (div.); children. Grad., Fordham U., NYC. Chmn., CEO Florida Crystals Corp. (Flo-Sun, Inc.), West Palm Beach, Fla., 1960—. Contbr. funds to Dem. Nat. Com. and Dem. Congl. Campaign Com., 1991—; co-chmn. Former President William Clinton's Fla. campaign, 1992; co-sponsored Cuban-Am. fund raiser for Clinton Presdl. Campaign, Miami, 1992. Democrat. Office: Florida Crystals Corp 1 N Clematis St Ste 200 West Palm Beach FL 33401 Office Phone: 561-366-5100. Office Fax: 561-366-5158. Business E-Mail: allie_fanjul@floridacrystals.com.

FANKHAUSER, MARK A., lawyer; b. Wichita, Kans., Dec. 8, 1952; BS, Pitts. State U., 1974; JD cum laude, Harvard U., 1978. Bar: Tex. 1978, bd. cert. (estate planning & probate Law) Tex. Bd. Legal Specialization. Mem. Haynes & Boone, L.L.P., Dallas, 1978-80, Hughes & Luce L.L.P., Dallas, 1980-94; now mem. Little Pedersen Fankhauser, Dallas, 1994—, ptnr. With USAF, 1971—73, air nat. guard, 1973—77, Mo., NH. Fellow Am. Coll. Trust and Estate Counsel, Tex. Bar Found., State Bar Tex., Dallas Bar Assn., mem. IRS TE/GE Coun. Gulf States Area, bd. mem. Am. Heart Assn. Tex., mem. adv. coun. Communities Found. Tex., mem. Dallas Estate Planning Coun. State Bar of Tex. Office: Little Pedersen Fankhauser 901 Main St Ste 4110 Dallas TX 75202-5606 Office Phone: 214-573-2323. Business E-Mail: mfank@lpf-law.com.

FANNIN, JAMES R., state legislator; Mem. Dist. 13 La. House of Reps., 2003—, chair appropriations com., joint legis. com. on the budget, mem. house exec. com., joint legis. com. on capital outlay, legis. budgetary control coun., state bond commn. Democrat. Mailing: Dist Add 320 N 6th St Jonesboro LA 71251 Office Phone: 318-259-6620. Fax: 318-259-6645.

FANNING, BARRY HEDGES, lawyer; b. Olney, Tex., Dec. 5, 1950; s. Robert Allen and Carolyn (Parker) F.; m. Rebecca Sue Cobbs, May 24, 1975 (dec. Mar. 1997); m. Sherri Winn Perry, Mar. 6, 1999 (div. Jan. 25, 2010). BBA, Baylor U., 1972, LL.B., 1973. Bar: Tex. 1973, Fla. 1974, U.S. Dist. Ct. (no., ea. we. and so. dists.) Tex. 1974, U.S. Ct. Appeals (5th and 11th cirs.) 1974. Mem. firm Fanning, Harper Martinson, Brandt & Kutchin, Dallas, 1974—. Social v.p. Dallas Symphony Orch. Guild, 1975-77; mem. Dallas Regional Young Life Bd., 1977—, fund raising chmn., 1982-84, 86-88, 97—; bd. dirs., exec. fin. com. com., Downtown YMCA, 1997—, chmn. cmty. svcs. fund dr., 2003, chmn Advance Gifts Ptnrs. Fund Drive, 2008; mem. Russell Perry Free Enterprise Banquet Com., chmn., 2004; mem. Dallas Bapt. U.; mem. Miss Tex. Pageant Bd., 2003—. Recipient Sam Winstead award, YMCA, 2005. Mem. ABA (vice chmn. young lawyers com. 1980, pub. rels. com. torts sect.), Baylor U. Student Found. (steering com. 1971-72), Baylor Alumni Assn. (bd. dirs. 1978-82, 95), Tryon Coterie (pres. 1971), Highland Park Forensics Found. (pres. 1993-95), Preston Ctr. Legal Assn. (sec. 1993-94, bd. dirs. 1994-95), Dervish Club, Calyx Club, Dallas Baylor Club (bd. dirs. 1976-84, pres. 1981-82), Christian Men's Club, Phi Eta Sigma, Omicron Kappa Delta, Phi Delta Theta. Baptist. Office: Fanning Harper & Martinson 4849 Greenville Ave Ste 1300 Dallas TX 75206 Home: 4627 Westside Dr Dallas TX 75209 Office Phone: 972-860-0327. E-mail: bfanning@fhmbk.com.

FANNING, ELLEN, biology professor, research scientist; BS in Chemistry, U. Wis., Madison; PhD in Virology, U. Cologne, Germany, 1977. Asst. prof. Univ. Konstanz, Germany; prof. and acting chair Inst. for Biochemistry Univ. Munich; now Stevenson Prof. Molecular Biology, Dept. Biological Sciences Vanderbilt Univ., Nashville. Vis. prof. Dept. Genetics Harvard Med. Sch.; mem. editl. bd. Jour. of Virology; assoc. dir. Nat. Inst. Health Tng. Grant of Viruses, Nucleic Acids and Cancer; prof. Howard Hughes Med. Inst. Mem.: German Science Found. Peer Review Bd., Milwaukee Found. Corp. (Shaw Scholar Sci. Adv. Bd.), European Molecular Biology Orgn. Office: Vanderbilt U 2325 Stevenson Ctr 1161 21st Ave S Nashville TN 37235 Office Phone: 615-343-5677. Office Fax: 615-343-6707. E-mail: ellen.h.fanning@Vanderbilt.Edu.

FANNING, JOHN PATTON, state legislator; b. Iaeger, W.Va., Aug. 14, 1934; s. James Patton Fanning and Gertrude Neal F.; m. Kathryn K. Killen; children: Brenda Jean Wells, Deborah Ann Tankersly, John William, Stacy V. Killen. Mgr. Fanning Funeral Home, 1959—; mayor Town of Iaeger, W.Va., 1964—66; mem. Dist 6 W.Va. State Senate, 1968—76, 1984, W.Va., 1996—, chair Natural Resources Com., mem. Banking and Insurance Com., Energy, Industry and Mining Com., Fin. Com. & Rule Com. Mem.: Shriners, Masons, AF&AM, Rotary (pres. 1969—). Democrat. Methodist. Mailing: 52 N PO Box 126 Iaeger WV 24844 Office: State Capitol Complex Rm 214W, Bldg 1 1900 Kanawha Blvd E Charleston WV 25305 Office Phone: 304-938-5331. E-mail: john.fanning@wvsenate.gov.

FANNING, THOMAS ANDREW (TOM FANNING), utilities executive; b. Morristown, NJ, Mar. 12, 1957; s. James E. and Marjorie (Van Morstein) F.; m. Beverly Booher, Mar. 14, 1987; children: Matthew Ryan, Bradley Stephen. BS in Indsl. Mgmt., Ga. Inst. Tech., Atlanta, 1979, MS in Finance, 1980. Financial analyst Southern Co., Atlanta, 1980; with Southern Co. Services, Atlanta, 1983-86, supr., 1988, dir. corporate finance, 1988; treas. Southern Elec. Internat., Atlanta, 1986; sr. v.p. strategy Southern Co., v.p., CFO Miss. Power, exec. v.p., CFO Ga. Power, 1999—2002, pres., CEO Gulf Power, 2002—03, exec. v.p., CFO, treas., 2003—08, exec. v.p., COO, 2008—10, pres., 2010, chmn., pres., CEO, 2010—. Bd. dirs. Southern Co., 2010—. Ga. Fed. Mgmt. scholar, 1979, Nat. Merit scholar adv. bd. Ga. Inst. Tech., 2003-. Mem. Phi Eta Sigma. Office: Southern Company 30 Ivan Allen Jr Blvd NW Bin SC1505 Atlanta GA 30308 Office Phone: 404-505-0590. E-mail: tafannin@southernco.com.

FARBER, ROSANN ALEXANDER, geneticist, educator; b. Charlotte, NC, Nov. 21, 1944; d. J. Wilson Jr. and June Adell (Childs) Alexander; m. Gerald Lee Farber, July 28, 1966 (div. Jan. 1969); m. Thomas Douglas Petes, July 20, 1973; children: Laura Elizabeth Petes, Diana Christine Petes. AB in Biology, Oberlin Coll., 1966; postgrad., U. Pitts., 1967-68, Albert Einstein Coll. Medicine, 1969; PhD in Genetics, U. Wash., 1973. Diplomate in clin. cytogenetics and clin. molecular genetics Am. Bd. Med. Genetics. Postdoctoral fellow Nat. Inst. for Med. Rsch., London, 1973-75; rsch. assoc. Children's Hosp. Med. Ctr., Boston, 1975-77; from asst. prof. to assoc. prof. U. Chgo., 1977-88; assoc. prof. dept. pathology and lab. medicine, program molecular biology and biotechnology, curriculum genetics and molecular biology U. N.C., Chapel Hill, 1988-97, prof., 1997—, prof. dept. genetics, 2001—, assoc. chair dept. genetics, 2007—. Mem. U. N.C. Lineberger Comprehensive Cancer Ctr., 1996—. Contbr. articles to profl. jours. NIH grantee, 1978—. Mem. AAAS, Am. Soc. Human Genetics, Am. Coll. Med. Genetics. Achievements include research in human molecular genetics, somatic cell genetics, cancer genetics. Home: 612 Morgan Creek Rd Chapel Hill NC 27517-4928 Office: U NC CB 7525 Brinkhous-Bullitt Bldg Chapel Hill NC 27599 Office Phone: 919-966-6920. Business E-Mail: rfarber@med.unc.edu.

FARELL, DAN, utilities executive; B in Acctg. & Fin., East Tex. State U.; grad. advanced mgmt. program, Harvard U. CPA Tex. Treas., sec., TU Electric and TU Svcs. subsidiaries Tex. Utilities Co., v.p., TU Electric and TU Svcs. subsidiaries, 1991, chief acctg. officer, 1994, CFO, TU Electric subsidiary, 1994, chmn., Ea. Energy, 1995; mng. dir. TXU Australia, 1995, pres., distbn. divsn. Oncor, 2000; pres. TXU Gas, 2002; CFO, exec. v.p. TXU Corp., Dallas, 2003; sr. v.p., prin. fin. officer TXU Electric Delivery, Dallas, 2004—. Bd. dirs. Victorian Power Exch., Australia, So. Gas Assn., Assn. Tex. Intrastate Natural Gas Pipelines, Energy Reliability Coun. Tex., Leadership Coun. Am. Gas Assn., North Tex. Commn. Dir. North Tex. Commn. United Way; bd. dirs. United Way Met. Dallas; trustee First Bapt. Acad. Mem.: AICPA, Fin. Execs. Inst., Tex. Soc. CPA. Office: TXU Electric Delivery 500 N Akard St Dallas TX 75201-3411 Office Phone: 214-812-4600.

FARENTHOLD, BLAKE (RANDOLPH BLAKE FARENTHOLD), United States Representative from Texas; b. Corpus Christi, Tex., Dec. 12, 1962; BS in Radio, TV and Film, U. Tex., Austin, 1985; JD, St. Mary's U. Sch. Law, San Antonio, 1989. Owner BFP Mobile Entertainment, 1976—84; disc jockey KRYS, Corpus Christi, 1977—78, KZFM, Corpus Christi, 1978—80, KITE, Corpus Christi, 1980, KITY, Llano, 1981, KSJL, San Antonio, 1982; pres. Austin Party Line, 1983—85; atty. Kleberg Law Firm, Corpus Christi, 1989—97; founder, pres. Farenthold Consulting LLC, Corpus Christi, 1997—2010; co-host Lago in the Morning, NewsRadio sta. 1360 KKTX, Corpus Christi, 1999—2010; mem. US Congress from 27th Tex. Dist., Washington, 2011—, US House Oversight & Govt. Reform Com., Washington, 2011—, US House Transp. & Infrastructure Com., Washington, 2011—. Mem. leadership Social Media Club Corpus Christi; bd. dirs. Tex. State Aquarium, Saint James Episcopal Sch., Corpus Christi, 1992—2000. Republican. Episcopalian. Office: US House of Representatives 117 Cannon House Office Bldg Washington DC 20515 Office Phone: 202-225-7742.*

FARENTHOLD, FRANCES TARLTON, lawyer; b. Corpus Christi, Tex., Oct. 2, 1926; d. Benjamin Dudley and Catherine (Bluntzer) Tarlton; children: Dudley Tarlton, George Edward, Emilie, James Doughterty, Vincent Bluntzer (dec.). AB, Vassar Coll., 1946; JD, U. Tex., 1949; LLD, Hood Coll., 1973, Boston U., 1973, Regis Coll., 1976, Lake Erie Coll., 1979, Elmira Coll., 1981, Coll. Santa Fe, 1985. Bar: Tex. 1949. Pvt. practice, 1949-65, 67-76, 80—; mem. Tex. Ho. of Reps., 1968-72; dir. legal aid Nueces County, 1965-67; pres. Wells Coll., Aurora, NY, 1976-80; asst. prof. law Tex. So. U., Houston, Thurgood Marshall disting. vis. prof., 1994-95; exec. dir. Quest Hon. Documentary, 2011. Lawyer; b. Corpus Christi, Tex., Oct. 2, 1926; d. Benjamin Dudley and Catherine (Bluntzer) Tarlton; children: Dudley Tarlton, George Edward, Emilie, James Doughterty, Vincent Bluntzer (dec.). AB, Vassar Coll., 1946; JD, U. Tex., 1949; LLD, Hood Coll., 1973, Boston U., 1973, Regis Coll., 1976, Lake Erie Coll., 1979, Elmira Coll., 1981, Coll. of Santa Fe, 1985. Bar: Tex. 1949. Pvt. practice, 1949-65, 67-76, 80—; mem. Tex. Ho. of Reps., 1968-72; dir. legal aide Nueces County, 1965-67; asst. prof. law Tex. So. U., Houston; pres. Wells Coll., Aurora, N.Y., 1976-80; disting. vis. prof. Thurgood Marshall Tex. So. U., Houston, 1994-95. Mem. Human Relations Com., Corpus Christi, 1963-68, Corpus Christi Citizen's Com. Community Improvement, 1966-68; mem. Tex. adv. com. to U.S. Commn. on Civil Rights, 1968-76; mem. nat. adv. council ACLU; mem. Orgn. for Preservation Unblemished Shoreline, 1964—; Dem. candidate for Gov. of Tex., 1972; del. Dem. Nat. Conv., 1972, 1st woman nominated to be candidate v.p. U.S., 1972; bd. mem. Smothers Bruni Found., Dudley T. Dougherty Found.; nat. co-chmn. Citizens to Elect McGovern-Shriver, 1972; chmn. Nat. Women's Polit. Caucus, 1973-75; mem. Dem. platform com., 1988; trustee Vassar Coll., 1975-83; bd. dirs. Fund for Constl. Govt., Mexican Am. Legal Def. and Ednl. Fund, 1980-83; chmn. Inst. for Policy Studies, 1986-91; mem. bd. dirs. Rothko Chapel, 1997—2007. Mem. Human Rels. Com., Corpus Christi, 1963-68, Corpus Christi Citizens Com. Cmty. Improvement, 1966-68; mem. Tex. adv. com. to U.S. Commn. on Civil Rights, 1968-76; mem. nat. adv. coun. ACLU; mem. Orgn. for Preservation Unblemished Shoreline, 1964—; Dem. candidate for Gov. of Tex., 1972; del. Dem. Nat. Conv., 1972, 1st woman nominated to be candidate v.p. U.S., 1972; nat. co-chair Citizens to elect McGovern-Shriver, 1972; chmn. Nat. Women's Polit. Caucus, 1973-75; mem. Dem. Platform Com., 1988; trustee Vassar Coll., 1975-83; bd. dirs. Fund for Constl. Govt., Ctr. for Devel. Policy, 1983—, Mexican Am. Legal Def. and Ednl. Fund, 198--83; chmn. Inst. for Policy Studies, 1986-91; bd. dirs., bd. mem. (hon.) Rothko Chapel, 1997—, chmn., 2001-07, exec. dir. Quest Honor, 2009 Recipient Lyndon B. Johnson Woman of Yr. award, 1973, Lifetime Svc. award, Dem. Party of Tex., 1998, Molly Ivins Tex. ACLU Lifetime award, 2008. Mem. State Bar Tex. Home: 2929 Buffalo Speedway Apt 1813 Houston TX 77098-1710 Personal E-mail: emailsissy@gmail.com.

FARHO, JAMES HENRY, JR., mechanical engineer, consultant; b. Omaha, June 28, 1924; s. James Henry and Mary (Mena) F.; m. Dummer Ree Mitchem, Nov. 12, 1946; children: Sandra, Joann, Wayne. BSME, U. Nebr., 1965. Enlisted USN, 1942, advanced through grades to sr. aviation chief machinist, 1942-62, ret., 1962; engr. Exxon Rsch. & Engring. Co., Florham Park, N.J., 1965-66, project engr., 1966-68, sr. project engr., 1968-70, engring. group head, 1970-71, engring. sect. head, 1971-78, sr. staff advisor Clinton, N.J., 1978-85; cons. engr. Lighthouse Point, Fla., 1985—. Cons. Exxon Prodn. Rsch., Houston, 1985, Swiki Anderson & Assocs., Bryan, Tex., 1986-87, Glaxo Pharms., Research Triangle, N.C., 1988-91. Mem. VFW, Fleet Res. Assn., Am. Legion, Elks, Sigma Xi. Republican. Roman Catholic. Home and Office: 2401 NE 33rd St Lighthouse Point FL 33064

FARIAS, JOE, state legislator; m. Angie Farias; children: Gabe, Joey, Jaime, Daniel. Novice machinist to supr. tech. tng. sect. City Pub. Svc., San Antonio, 1971—2003, ret., 2003; mem. Dist. 118 Tex. House of Representatives, 2007—. Former mem. Harlandale Ind. Sch. Dist. Bd., St. Leo's Cath. Sch. Bd., San Antonio Zoning Commn. Served with US Army, 1968—71, Vietnam, Germany. Democrat. Office: 660 Southwest Military Dr San Antonio TX 78221 also: Room E1.314 Capitol Extension PO Box 2910 Austin TX 78768 Office Phone: 210-923-0908, 512-463-0714.

FARIELLO, M. ANNA, art educator, project manager, curatorial consultant, museum director; b. Summit, NJ, Feb. 23, 1947; d. Leonard Angelo and Emily (Troianello) F. BA, Rutgers U., 1970; MA, Va. Commonwealth, 1987; MFA, James Madison U., 1993. Art critic Style Weekly, Richmond, Va., 1987; adj. faculty U. Richmond, 1987; designer Sci. Mus., Richmond, 1987; event coord. Va. Mus., Richmond, 1987-88; dir., assoc. prof. Radford U. Museum, Va., 1988-98; assoc. prof. Va. Poly. and State U., 1998—2005; curator Christiansburg Inst., 2000—06; assoc. prof., curator, digital collections Hunter Libr. Western Carolina U., Cullowhee, NC, 2005—. Mem. curators roundtable Va. Mus. Fine Arts, Richmond, 1992—2002; chair Nat. Coll. Art Assn., Boston, 1996; founder Regional Sculpture Competition, 1991—96; chair material culture Smithsonian Folklife Festival, 2001—03. Author: Cherokee Basketry, 2009 From Absurdity to Austerity, 1993 (Addy award 1994), Cherokee Pottery, 2011, Cherokee Carving, 2013, Yellin Metal Workers, 1998, Movers & Makers, 2003, 2005, Blue Ridge Roadways, 2006; co-author: Collaboration, Art and Technology, British Columbia, 1993, Objects and Meaning, 2003, 2005; prodr.: (video series) Profiles of Women Artists, 1992, (photography series) Vernacular Architecture, 2000; editor visual arts Ency. of Appalachia, 2006; presenter/author: Appalachian Craft Revival, Smithsonian Inst., Nat. Women's Mus., Washington, 1993, 99, Twin Myths of Appalachia, Charleston, SC, 1996, Craft Identity, Richmond, Va., 1997, Samuel Yellin, Reynolda Museum, Winston-Salem, NC, 2003, Doris Ulmann, History Mus., Roanoke, Va., 2003. Mem. adv. panel Va. Commn. Arts, Richmond, 1989—92; mem. task force Va. Craft, Richmond, 1989—91; mem. steering com. Yr. of Am. Craft, Richmond, 1991—93; founder, dir. Highland Cultural Coalition, Floyd, Va., 1998—; mem. adv. bd. Blue Ridge Music Ctr., 1999—; bd. dirs. Arts Coun. Blue Ridge, Roanoke, Va., 1994—98; assoc. Tribal Archives, Librs., and Mus., Guardians & Culture Award, 2013. Recipient Univ. Designers Assn. award, 1994, Brown Hudson award, NC Folklore Soc., 2010; Mus. Assessment grantee Inst. Mus. Svcs., Washington, 1993, Spl. Projects grantee, 1988, 89, 95, faculty devel. grantee Radford U., 1991, 92, 94, curator's travel grantee Mid-Atlantic Arts Assn., Balt., 1990, project grantee Va. Comm. Arts,

Richmond, 1989, 2002, project dir., Va. Found. for Humanities, 1999-2000, 2002; rsch. grant Va. Tech. U., 2000; James Renwick sr. rsch. fellow Smithsonian Inst. and Nat. Mus. Am. Art, 1998-2000, Fulbright scholar, 2000, Fulbright museology specialist, 2007-2012; trustee Frontier Culture Mus., 2004-09, grant NC State Libr., 2005-09, Cherokee Preservation Found., 2008- Mem. Am. Assn. Mus. Coll. Art Assn., Southeastern Coll. Art Assn. (nominating com. 1990), NC Folklore Soc. Democrat. Office: PO Box 2212 Cullowhee NC 28723 Office Phone: 828-227-2499. Business E-Mail: fariello@wcu.edu, anna.fariello@icloud.com.

FARIELLO, THERESA M., energy executive; Degree in Polit. Sci., George Washington U.; JD, George Mason U.; LLM in Internat. and Comparative Law, Georgetown U. Congl. aide to Rep. Gerald D. Klecka US House of Representatives, Congl. aide to Rep. John F. Seiberling; mgr. govt. affiars Occidental Petroleum Corp., v.p. internat. rels.; dep. asst. sec. internat. energy policy Office Internat. Affairs, US Dept. Energy; mgr. worldwide pub. policy issues mgmt. dept. ExxonMobil Corp., Irving, Tex., 2001, v.p. Washington, 2009—. Bd. trustees Meridian Internat. Ctr.; bd. dirs. Bus. Coun. for Internat. Understanding. Bd. dirs. Dallas Children's Advocacy Ctr.; mem. Nat. Ocean Industries Assn. Office: Exxon Mobil Corp 5959 Las Colinas Blvd Irving TX 75039-2298 Office Phone: 972-444-1000. Office Fax: 972-444-1348. Personal E-mail: theresa.m.farillo@exxonmobil.com.

FARIS, JACK, association executive; Owner small businesses; pres. Nat. Fedn. Ind. Bus. Mem. nat. bd. dirs. Jr. Achievement; exec. dir. Republican Nat. Fin. Com., 1978-81; campaign dir. Lamar Alexander Gubernatorial Campaign, 1978. Office: Nat Fedn Ind Bus 53 Century Blvd Ste 300 Nashville TN 37214-3693

FARISON, JAMES BLAIR, electrical and biomedical engineer, educator; b. McClure, Ohio, May 26, 1938; s. Blair Albert and Marie Lucille (Ballard) F.; m. Gail Donahue, Mar. 30, 1961; children: Jeffrey James, Mark Donahue. BS summa cum laude in Elec. Engring, U. Toledo, 1960; MS, Stanford U., 1961, PhD, 1964. Registered profl. engr., Tex., Ohio. Asst. prof. elec. engring. U. Toledo, 1964-67, assoc. prof., 1967-74, prof., 1974-95, asst. dean engring., 1969-71, dean engring., 1971-80, prof. elec. engring. and computer sci., 1995-98, prof. bioengring., 1996-98, prof. dean emeritus; prof., chmn. dept. engring. Baylor U., Waco, Tex., 1998—2005, prof., chmn. dept. elec. and computer engring., 2005—07, prof., 2007—08, prof. emeritus, 2008—, part-time faculty mem., coord. BS engring. degree program, 2008—. Adj. prof. Med. Coll. Ohio, 1987-98 Contbr. articles to various profl. jours. Recipient Outstanding Young Man of 1971 award Toledo Jr. C. of C., 1972, Boss of Year award Limestone chpt. Am. Bus. Women's Assn., 1973, Toledo's Engr. Yr. award, 1984, Outstanding Tchr. award U. Toledo, 1986; named Disting. Alumnus U. Toledo, 1983. Fellow Ohio Acad. Sci. (Centennial honoree 1991), Am. Soc. Engring. Edn. (vice chair, program chair, 2002-05, chair 2005-07, past chair 2007-09, multidisciplinary engring. divsn., accreditation activities com. 2005-10, Outstanding Campus Rep. 2003, fellow, 2006); mem. IEEE (sr. mem., Toledo Elec. Engr. of Yr. 1972, 74, 76), NSPE, Ohio Soc. Profl. Engrs. (Young Engr. of Yr. 1973, Citation 1983, Outstanding Engring. Educator 1984), Toledo Soc. Profl. Engrs. (Young Engr. of Yr. 1973), Accreditation Bd. for Engring. and Tech. (program evaluator 1996-2001, 05, engring. accreditation commn. 2006—08, alt. 2008-10), Blue Key, Sigma Xi, Tau Beta Pi, Pi Mu Epsilon, Phi Kappa Phi, Eta Kappa Nu (Outstanding Young Elec. Engr. 1971). Home: 9613 Old Farm Rd Waco TX 76712-6402 Office: Baylor U One Bear Pl # 97356 Waco TX 76798-7356 Business E-Mail: Jim_Farison@baylor.edu.

FARISS, BRUCE LINDSAY, endocrinologist, consultant; b. Allisonia, Va., July 22, 1934; s. Alven Pierce and Hetty Jo (Lindsay) Fariss; m. Cheryl Louise Tomasie, Jan. 18, 1975; children: Bruce Lindsay, Melissa, Margaret, Susan, Henry, Sarah Jane, Caroline, Adam. BS, Roanoke Coll., 1957; MD, U. Va., 1961. Diplomate Am. Bd. Internal Medicine, Am. Bd. Endocrinology. Med. intern U. Va. Hosp., Charlottesville, 1961-62; commd. capt. M.C. U.S. Army, 1962, advanced through grades to col., 1976; gen. med. officer Ft. Monroe, Va., 1962-63; resident in internal medicine Brooke Gen. Hosp., Ft. Sam Houston, Tex., 1963-66; fellow in endocrinology U. Calif., San Francisco, 1966-68; chief endocrine service Madigan Gen. Hosp., Tacoma, 1968-71, chief clin. rsch. svc., 1968-76, asst. chief dept. medicine, 1972-73, dir. endocrine fellowship program, 1971-76, chief dept. clin. investigation, 1979-85, dir. endocrine-metabolism fellowship tng. program, 1979-85; cons. internal medicine MEDCOM Europe, 1976-79; cons. endocrinology to surgeon gen. U.S. Army, 1979-85; with dept. biology Va. Poly. Inst., Blacksburg, 1987-99; sec., treas. Radford Cmty. Hosp., 1998—2000, vice chmn., 2000—02, chmn., 2002—04, chmn. dept. M & D, 2005—06; clin. assoc. prof. Va. Coll. Osteo. Medicine, Blacksburg, 2006—. Contbr. articles to profl. jours. Mem. bd. suprs. Pulaski County, Va., 1988—2004, mem. recreation com. Va., 1989—93, mem. planning commn. Va., 1992—94, vice chmn. Va., 2000—04. Decorated Legion of Merit with oak leaf cluster; recipient Meritorious Svc. award, Office Surgeon Gen. Army, 1977, Roanoke Coll. medal, 1982. Fellow: ACP, Am. Coll. Endocrinology; mem.: Am. Assn. Clin. Endocrinologists, NY Acad. Sci., So. Med. Assn., Am. Diabetes Assn. (trustee 1986—89), Endocrine Soc. (ednl. com. 1980—83), Am. Fedn. Clin. Rsch., S.W. Va. Med. Soc., Alpha Omega Alpha. Office Phone: 540-674-5900.

FARISS, C. MATTHEW, state legislator; b. Lynchburg, Va., May 11, 1968; m. Crystal Dawn Brown; children: Hunter, Bobby, Harrison. Mem. Dist. 59 Va. House of Delegates, 2012—, mem. Agr. Chesapeake and Natural Resources Com. & Militia Police and Pub. Safety Com. Republican. Office: General Assembly Building PO Box 406 Richmond VA 23218 also: 243-C Livestock Rd Rustburg VA 24588 Office Phone: 804-698-1059. Office Fax: 804-698-6759. E-mail: DelMFariss@house.virginia.gov.

FARKAS, DANIEL FREDERICK, food science and technology educator; m. Alice Bridgetta Brady, Jan. 25, 1959; children: Brian Emerson, Douglas Frederick. BS, MIT, 1954, MS, 1955, PhD, 1960. Lic. chem. engr., Calif. Commd. U.S. Army, 1954, advanced through grades to major, 1968, ret., 1974; with Quartermaster Corps, Res., 1958—74; staff scientist Arthur D. Little, Cambridge, Mass., 1960-62; asst. prof. Cornell U. Agrl Expt. Sta., Geneva, NY, 1962-66; rsch. leader We. regional rsch. ctr. USDA, Albany, Calif., 1967-80; prin. Daniel F. Farkas Assocs., 1976—; prof., chair dept. food sci. U. Del., Newark, 1980-87; v.p. process R & D Campbell Soup Co., Camden, NJ, 1987-90; Jacobs-Root prof., head dept. food sci. and tech. Oreg. State U., Corvalis, 1990-2000, prof. emeritus, 2000—. Contbr. more than 50 articles to peer-reviewed sci. and tech. jours. Commd. 2nd lt. US Army, 1954, with, 1955—57, with Res., 1957—74, major, 1974. Recipient Nicholas Appert award, Myron Solberg award. Fellow Inst. Food Technologists; mem. AIChE, Am. Chem. Soc., Am. Inst. Chem. Engrs., Sigma Xi. Achievements include centrifugal fluidized bed food drying system. Initiated basic and applied research leading to the commercial application of ultra-high hydrostatic pressure for food preservation; 5 patents. Avocations: running, sailboat racing.

FARLEY, ALLEN, state legislator; b. Bessemer, Ala. m. Muriel Farley; 3 children. Attended, Jefferson State Jr. Coll., Jacksonville State U.; grad., FBI Nat. Acad. Officer City of Bessemer Police Dept., 1973—77, Jefferson County Sheriff's Office, 1977—2010, asst. sheriff, 2003—10; mem. Dist. 15 Ala. House of Reps., 2011—. Law enforcement liaison officer Jefferson County Sch. Sys., 1990—97. Mem. Grace Life Bapt. Ch., McCalla, Ala.; chmn. auxiliary bd. Jefferson County Salvation Army Adult Rehab. Ctr. Republican. Mailing: Alabama House of Representatives 15th District PO Box 516 Mc Calla AL 35111 Office Phone: 205-477-5617. E-mail: murielfarley@bellsouth.net.

FARLEY, ANDREW DANIEL, lawyer; b. 1964; BA, Washington & Lee U., 1985; JD, George Washington U., 1988. Bar: Tex., Washington, DC. Assoc. Hutchenson & Grundy, Houston; chief counsel Landmark Graphics Corp., 2000—02; asst. gen. counsel, asst. corp. sec., Halliburton KBR, Inc., 2002, chief counsel Internat. Energy Services Group, Halliburton, 2002—03, v.p. Legal of our Energy and Chemicals segment, 2003—06, exec. v.p., gen. counsel, 2006—. Bd. mem. Tex. Gen. Counsel Forum. Office: KBR Inc 601 Jefferson St Houston TX 77002*

FARLEY, CLAIRE SCOBEE, retired petroleum company executive; b. 1959; BS in Geology, Emory U., 1981. Geologist New Orleans exploration and producing divsn. Texaco, 1981, area mgr. for exploration, 1989-92, offshore exploitation mgr., 1992-93; asst. divsn. mgr. ea. region Texaco Exploration and Prodn. Inc., 1993-94, asst. to mgr. office chmn. bd. and CEO, 1994-96; mng. dir., CEO Hydro-Texaco Holdings, Copenhagen, 1996; v.p. Texaco Inc., Lake Charles, La., 1997-99; pres. Texaco N.Am. Prodn., Lake Charles, La., 1997-99; CEO Intelligent Diagnostics Corp., 1999—2001, Trade-Ranger Inc., 2001—02, Jeffries, Randall & Dewey, 2002—05, co-pres., 2005—08, advisory dir., 2008—; mng. ptnr. Castex Energy Partners, 2008—09. Bd. dirs. EnCana, 2008—, FMC Technologies, Inc., 2009—.

FARMAN, ALLAN GEORGE, radiologist, consultant, pathologist, educator; b. Birmingham, Eng., July 26, 1949; came to the U.S., 1980; s. George and Lily (Hewitt) F.; m. Taeko Takemori, May 21, 1996. B Dental Surgery, U. Birmingham, Eng., 1971; PhD, U. Stellenbosch, Cape Town, South Africa, 1977, DSc, 1996; EdS, U. Louisville, 1983, MBA with distinction, 1987. Diplomate Am. Bd. Oral and Maxillofacial Radiology, Japanese Bd. Oral and Maxillofacial Radiology; specialist registration in oral pathology South African Med. and Dental Coun., 2014; lic. specialist Ky. Bd. Dentistry Oral and Maxillofacial Radiology, specialist in dental and maxillofacial radiology, Gen. Dental Coun., UK, 2013. Sr. lectr. oral pathology U. Stellenbosch, Cape Town, 1974-77; head dept. oral biology U. Riyadh, Saudi Arabia, 1978-79; prof., head divsn. radiology and imaging scis. Dental Sch., U. Louisville, 1980—2014; clin. prof. dept. diagnostic radiology Med. Sch., U. Louisville, 1990—2014; rep. to internat. DICOM com. Am. Acad. Oral Maxillofac Radiol., 2010—, rep. to CDT codes maintenance com. ADA, 2012—. Cons. Joint Commn. for Dental Bd. Examination, Chgo., 1984—92, NIH, Bethesda, Md., 1990—; rep. to internat. Digital Imaging & Comm. Medicine Com. Am. Dental Assn., 2001—10; rep. to internat. DICOM com. Am. Acad. Oral Maxillofacial Radiology, 2010—; co-chmn. DICOM Working Group 22, 2003—13; voting mem. US Sub-Tag ISO-TC 106 (Dentistry), 2009—; adj. prof. anatomical sci. and neurobiology U. Louisville, 1990—2014; mem. Integrating Healthcare Enterprise-Radiology Tech. Adv. Com., 2010—; mem. bd. Inter-Societal Accreditation Commn., Conn., 2013—. Author: Oral and Maxillofacial Diagnostic Imaging, 1993, Panoramic Radiology-Seminars on Maxillofacial Imaging and Interpretation, 2007; editor: Advances in Maxillofacial Imaging, 1997, (oral and maxillofacial radiology sect.) Oral Surgery, Oral Medicine, Oral Pathology, Oral Radiology and Endodontics, 1988-95, 2005—09; co-editor CARS Procs., Computer-Assisted Radiology and Surgery, 1998-; dep. editor Internat. Jour. Computer Assisted Radiology and Surgery, 2006—; assoc. editor Radiology Sect. Cranio, Oral Radiology, Acta Stomatologica Croatia, Japan Dental Science Review, Inside Dentistry, eDentico; contbr. more than 400 articles to profl. jours. Recipient DSM, U. Louisville, 2006, MS Student Mentoring award, 2010. Mem. Am. Dental Assn., Japanese Soc. Oral and Maxillofacial Radiology, Internat. Assn. Dento Maxillofacial Radiology (hon.; pres. 1994-97, trust fund chmn. 1997—11), Internat. Congress and Exposition on Computed Maxillofacial Imaging (initiator, founder, organizer 1995—), Am. Acad. Oral and Maxillofacial Radiology (life; editor 1988-95, 2005—09, pres. elect 2007-09, pres., 2009-11), Am. Assn. Dental Schs. (chmn. oral radiology sect. 1988-89), Radiol. Soc. N.Am. (life). Business E-Mail: allan.farman@louisville.edu.

FARMER, HARRY FRANK, JR., public health service officer; b. Daytona Beach, Fla., Nov. 9, 1941; s. Harry Frank and Lottie (Ditson) F.; m. Peggy Hines, Oct. 26, 1973; children: Harry Frank III, Kevin. BA, Stetson U., 1964; MA in History, U. Ga., 1966, PhD in History, 1969; MD, Med. Coll. Ga., 1976. Asst. prof. history Ga. Southwestern Coll., Americus, 1968-69. 71-72; resident in family practice Halifax Hosp., Daytona Beach, Fla., 1976-77; resident in internal medicine Univ. Hosp., Jacksonville, Fla., 1977-80; pvt. practice, New Smyrna Beach, Fla., 1980-90; med. dir. for Medicare, Blue Cross/Blue Shield, Jacksonville, Fla., 1990-92; pvt. practice Ormond Beach, Fla., 1992—; surgeon gen. Fla. Dept. Health, Tallahassee, 2011—. Pres. Endeavors-Physicians Ind. Physicians Assn., Volusia County, Fla., 1993—. Capt. US Army, 1969-71, Vietnam. Decorated Bronze Star, Vietnamese Cross of Gallantry; recipient Disting. Cmty. Svc. award American Coll. Physicians Fla. chapter, 2002 Mem. AMA, American Soc. Internal Medicine, Fla. Soc. Internal Medicine, Fla. Med. Assn. (pres. 2001, editor hist. issue of Jour. 1988-95). Republican. Avocation: reading. Office: Florida Department Health 2585 Merchants Row Blvd Tallahassee FL 32399 Office Phone: 850-245-4321. Office Fax: 850-922-9453.

FARMER, PHILLIP W., board member; b. 1939; BA, Duke U. Various mgmt. and tech. positions General Electric Co., 1962-82; v.p., gen. mgr. govt. support sys. divsn. Harris Corp., Melbourne, Fla., 1982-86, v.p., Palm Bay ops., govt. sys. sector, 1986-88, sr. v.p., sector exec., govt. sys. sector, 1988-89, pres., electronics sys. sector, 1989-91, exec. v.p., 1991, chmn., pres. & CEO, 2000—03. Bd. dirs. Mfrs. Alliance, Vulcan Materials Co., 1999-. Bd. trustees Fla. Inst. Tech.; bd. dirs. Aerospace Industries Assn. Mem. Bus. Roundtable, Electronic Industries Assn. Office: Vulcan Materials Co Bd Directors 1200 Urban Center Dr Birmingham AL 35242 Office Phone: 205-298-3000. Office Fax: 205-298-2960. Business E-Mail: farmerp@vmcmail.com.

FARMER, WILLIAM P., state legislator; b. El Paso, Tex., 1962; m. Janice Farmer; children: William III, Christopher. Engr. Edn. Bullard Co., 1988—91, Ragtheon Co., 1985—88, 1991—99; tax acct. to owner HTI Tax Svc., 1988—; mem. Dist. 88 Ky. House of Reps., Ky., 2003—. Mem.: Refuge, Inc. (bd. dir. 2001—), Kentucky Soc. Enrolled Agts. (pres. 1998—), Good Shepard Episcopal Ch. (treas. 1998—). Republican. Episcopalian. Mailing: 3361 Squire Oak Dr Lexington KY 40515 Office: Capitol Annex Rm 424B 702 Capitol Ave Frankfort KY 40601 Office Phone: 859-272-1425, 502-564-8100 ext. 628. Office Fax: 859-272-1579.

FARMER-BUTTERFIELD, JEAN, state legislator; Health and human svcs. profl.; cons.; state rep. Dist 24 NC, 2002—. Mem. Appropriations com., Ethics com., Commerce, Small Bus. and Entrepreneurship com.; vice chmn. Appropriations Subcom. on Health and Human Svcs.; chmn. Aging com. Democrat. Office: North Carolina House of Representatives 300 N Salisbury St Rm 631D Raleigh NC 27603-5925 Address: PO Box 2962 Wilson NC 27894 Office Phone: 919-733-5898, 252-237-1506. E-mail: Jean.Farmer-Butterfield@ncleg.net.

FARNHAM, CLAYTON HENSON, lawyer; b. New Brunswick, NJ, Aug. 18, 1938; s. Richard Bayles and Naomi Shropshire (Henson) F.; m. Katharine Gross, Sept. 16, 1967; children: Julia Kernan, Richard Bayles II. BA, U. of the South, 1961; LLB, U. Ga., 1967. Bar: Ga. 1968, U.S. Dist. Ct. (no., so. and mid. dists.) Ga. 1968, U.S. Supreme Ct. 1978, U.S. Dist. Ct. (no. dist.) Miss. 1978, U.S. Dist. Ct. (ea. dist.), Tenn. 1997, U.S. Ct. Appeals (5th cir., 11th cir.) 1968, (4th cir.) 1981, U.S. Ct. Appeals (8th cir.) 1992. Law clk. to judge U.S. Dist. Ct., Atlanta, 1967-69; from assoc., to ptnr. Swift, Currie, McGhee & Hiers, Atlanta, 1969-82; ptnr. Drew, Eckl & Farnham, Atlanta, 1983—. Contbr. articles to profl. jours. Lt. (j.g.) USNR, 1961-64. Mem. ABA (coun. TIPS sect. 1989-92), Internat. Assn. Def. Counsel (com. chmn. 1987-89), Ansley Golf Club, Lawyer's Club Atlanta, Old War Horse Lawyer's Club. Home: 30 Inman Cir NE Atlanta GA 30309 Office: Drew Eckl & Farnham 800 W Peachtree St NW PO Box 7600 Atlanta GA 30357 Home Phone: 404-892-2283; Office Phone: 404-885-1400. Business E-Mail: cfarnham@deflaw.com.

FARNSWORTH, WARD, dean, law educator; BA, Wesleyan U., Middletown, Conn., 1989; JD, U. Chgo. Law Sch., 1994. Law clk. to the Hon. Richard A. Posner US Ct. Appeals 7th Cir., 1994—95; law clk. to the Hon. Anthony M. Kennedy US Supreme Ct., Washington, 1995—96; legal advisor Iran-US Claims Tribunal, The Hague, Netherlands, 1996—97; assoc. prof. law Boston U. Sch. Law, 1997—2003, prof. law, 2003—12, Nancy Barton scholar, 2005—12, assoc. dean academic affairs, 2009—12; dean, prof. law U. Tex. Sch. Law, Austin, 2012—. Reporter for Restatement, Third, Torts: Liability for Economic Harm American Law Inst., 2010—. Co-author (with M. Grady): Torts: Cases and Questions, 2004; author: The Legal Analyst, 2007, Classical English Rhetoric, 2010; contbr. articles to profl. jours. Mem.: American Law Inst. Office: University of Texas School of Law Deans Office 727 E Dean Keeton St Austin TX 78705 Office Phone: 512-232-1120.*

FARON, SALLY ROGERS, performing arts association administrator, consultant; b. Augusta, Maine, Oct. 27, 1931; d. Allan Harvard and Edith Robinson Rogers; m. Louis Charles Faron, Dec. 18, 1974. AB, Wellesley Coll., 1953; MA, Boston U., 1957. Tchr., acad. dean Ho. in the Pines, Norton, Mass., 1953—55, 1959—60; tchr. Beverly (Mass.) HS, 1955—57; asst. to headmaster Mac Duffie Sch., Springfield, Mass., 1960—61; adminstr., tchr., prin., acting head Barnard Sch. for Girls, NYC, 1961—74; adminstrv. asst. Bach Aria Festival, Stony Brook, NY, 1981—86; exec. dir. La Musica di Asolo, Sarasota, Fla., 1989—. Editor: (cookbook) Overtures & Artichokes, 1976; contbr. Ency. Indians of the Ams. Pres., bd. dirs. Suffolk Symphony, Smithtown, NY, 1975—80; founder, pres. Suffolk Music Guild, Stony Brook, 1980—86; mem. adv. coun. Bach Aria Festival, Stony Brook, 1980—90; chmn. Young Artists Competition Suffolk County, Stony Brook, 1979—86; mem. cultural exec. com. Sarasota County Arts Coun., 1992—, mem. bd. dirs., 2009—; bd. dirs. Key Chorale, Sarasota, 2004—11, Arts & Cultural Alliance, 2009—; mem. TDC Task Force Sarasota County. Arts Coun., 2009. Recipient Founder's medal, Barnard Sch. for Girls, 1973; grantee, NIMH, 1965—66, 1967. Mem.: Chamber Music Am. Office: La Musica PO Box 5442 Sarasota FL 34277 Office Phone: 941-346-2601. Fax: 941-346-2414. E-mail: salfar544@juno.com.

FARR, BARRY MILLER, physician, epidemiologist; b. Ft. Leonard Wood, Mo., Nov. 15, 1951; s. Alonza Lewis and Alice Louise (Miller) F.; m. Ann Katherine Henry, Oct. 22, 1977; children: Eric Christopher, Ryan Anthony, Jason Alexander. BA in Chemistry, U. Miss., Oxford, 1975; MD, Washington U., St. Louis, 1978; MSc in Epidemiology, London Sch. Hygiene, 1984. Diplomate Am. Bd. Internal Medicine, Am. Bd. Infectious Diseases. Intern U. Va. Hosp., Charlottesville, 1978-79, resident in internal medicine, 1979-81, fellow in infectious diseases, 1981-83; asst. prof. U. Va., 1983-89, assoc. prof., 1989—95, William S. Jordan Jr. prof., 1989, prof. medicine, 1995—2004; prof. emeritus, 2004—. Contbr. articles to profl. jours. Carrier scholar, 1970-74, Culley scholar, 1974-78, Milbank Meml. scholar, 1983-88. Fellow ACP, Infectious Diseases Soc. America, Soc. Healthcare Epidemiology America (pres. 2002). Avocations: photography, writing. Business E-Mail: bmf@virginia.edu.

FARRAR, JESSICA, state legislator; b. Nov. 16, 1966; m. Marco Sanchez. BArch, U. Houston; student, U. Tex. Sch. Law. Arch. Farrar Arch., Houston; mem. Dist. 148 Tex. House of Representatives, Tex., 1995—. Chairwoman Harris County Bi-Partisan Del. State Reps., 1999—2002. Decorated Commendation Texans with Disabilities Assn.; recipient Frankie award, Harris County Dem., 1996, Outstanding Young Alumnus award, U. Houston, 1996. Mem.: LWV, Mexican Am. Legislature Caucus, Hispanic Women Leadership, NOW Legislature, Am. Coun. Young Polit Leaders. Democrat. Office: PO Box 30099 Houston TX 77249 also: Room CAP 4N.07 Capitol Austin TX 78768 Office Phone: 713-691-6912, 512-463-0620. Office Fax: 713-691-3363.

FARRELL, EDMUND JAMES, retired English language educator, writer; b. Butte, Mont., May 17, 1927; s. Bartholomew J. and Lavinia H. (Collins) F.; m. Jo Ann Hayes, Dec. 19, 1964; children: David (dec.), Kevin, Sean. AB, Stanford U., 1950, MA, 1951; PhD, U. Calif., Berkeley, 1969. Chmn. English dept. James Lick HS, San Jose, Calif., 1954-59; supr. secondary English U. Calif., Berkeley, 1959-70; adj. prof. English U. Ill., Urbana, 1973-78; prof. English edn. U. Tex., Austin, 1978—92, prof. emeritus, 1992—; pres. Farrell Ednl. Svcs., Inc., Austin, 1981-97; ret., 1997; asst. chief reader Ednl. Sys. Pearson, 1993—2011. Participant revision lit. objectives Nat. Assessment of Ednl. Progress, Denver, 1972-73, 78; adv. com. Ctr. for the Book, Libr. of Congress, 1980-86; chmn. adv. com. on English, Coll. Bd., NYC, 1974-79, council acad. affairs, 1978-79; guest lectr. local, state and nat. confs. of English tchrs., 1954—; reader compositions for advanced placement program Rider Coll., Princeton, NJ, 1969, 72-77; pres. Calif. Assn. Tchrs. English, 1962-63; sr. editl. cons. EMC Masterpiece Series, 1999-2006. Author (editor): (with others) Exploring Life Through Literature, 1964, Counterpoint in Literature, 1967, Projection in Literature, 1973, Outlooks Through Literature, 1973, Fantasy: Forms of Things Unknown, 1974, Science Fact/Fiction, 1974, Comment, 1976, Myth, Mind and Moment, 1976, I/You, We/They, 1976, Traits and Topics, 1976, Reality in Conflict, 1976, To Be, 1976, Arrangement in Literature, 1979, Purpose in Literature, 1979, Album U.S.A., 1983, Discoveries in Literature, 1985, classic edit., 1989, Patterns in Literature, 1985, classic edit., 1989, Transactions with Literature, 1990, The Perceptive I, 1997; author: Living The English Profession, 2011. With USN, 1945-46. Fellow Nat. Conf. Rsch. on Lang. and Literacy; mem. Nat. Coun. Tchrs. English (field rep. 1970-71, asst. exec. sec. 1971-73, assoc. exec. dir. 1973-78, chmn. commn. lit. 1979-83; trustees rsch. found. 1983-85; fund for tchg. of English 1993-96, Disting. Svc. award 1982, James R. Squire award 1999), Tex. Joint Coun. Tchrs. of English (pres. 1986-87, Disting. English Educator award 1989-90, Disting. Lifetime Svc. award 1999). Unitarian Universalist. Home: 6500 Sumac Dr Austin TX 78731-4117

FARRELL, JOHN MARSHALL, architect; b. Poplar Bluff, Mo., Nov. 2, 1942; s. Marshall Dee and Frieda Mae (Burk) Farrell; m. Susan Martha Garbett, Dec. 7, 1968; children: Kevin, Elizabeth. BArch, Tex. Tech. U., 1965. Registered architect, Tex., N.Mex, Calif., Fla. Designer Skidmore Owings & Merrill, Chgo., 1968—70; project architect Bernard Johnson Inc., Houston, 1970—72, NSHD Inc., 1972—73; prin., corp. dir., project mgr. Goleman & Rolfe Assocs. Inc., 1973—83; former pres. Farrell-Robson Architects Inc.; prin. FKP Architects, Tex., 1998—. Mem. zoning and planning commn. City of West U. Place, Tex., 1980—82. Prin. works include U. Houston at Clear Lake City, 1975, Riverwalk Marriot Hotel, San Antonio, 1978, Oak Ridge HS, Conroe, Tex., 1981, Saida Hilton Condominium, South Padre Island, 1982, Crowne Plaza West Loop Hotel, Houston, 1983. V.p. West U. Little League, 1981—83; mem. adminstrv. bd. St. Luke's United Meth. Ch., Houston, 1982—84. Officer USNR, 1965—68, Vietnam. Mem.: NCARB (cert.), AIA (past. dir. Houston chpt.), Coun. Ednl. Facility Planners, Tex. Soc. Architectx, Briar Club. Office: FKP Architects 8 Greenway Plaza, Ste 300 Houston TX 77046-6501

FARRELL, KEVIN JOSEPH, bishop; b. Dublin, Sept. 2, 1947; BA, U. Salamanca, Spain, 1968, Pontifical Gregorian Univ., Rome, 1971; MA, Pontifical Univ. St. Thomas Aquinas, Rome, 1976, STL, 1977. Ordained priest Congregation of Legionaries of Christ, 1978; incardinated Archdiocese of Washington, 1984; assoc. pastor St. Peter, Olney, 1984, St. Bartholomew, Bethesda, Md., St. Thomas the Apostle, Washington; pastor Annunciation Parish, Northwest Washington, DC, 2000—02; dir., Spanish Cath. Ctr. Archdiocese of Washington, 1986—89, sec. fin., 1989—2001; ordained bishop, 2002; aux. bishop Archdiocese of Washington, 2002—07; bishop Diocese of Dallas, Tex., 2007—. Named a Prelate of Honor, Pope John Paul II, 1995. Roman Catholic. Office: Diocese of Dallas 3725 Blackburn St PO Box 190507 Dallas TX 75219 Office Phone: 214-528-2240. Office Fax: 214-526-1743.

FARRELL, NICHOLAS PATRICK, chemistry professor, researcher; b. Dublin, Apr. 24, 1948; s. Nicholas Patrick and Mary Farrell; m. Erica Farrell; children: Nicole Inaia, Conor Jacob. BSc, U. Coll. Dublin, 1969; PhD, U. Sussex, 1973. Prof. Va. Commonwealth U., Richmond, 1993—. Author: Transition Metal Complexes as Drugs and Chemotherapeutic Agents, 1989; editor: Uses of Inorganic Chemistry in Medicine, 1999, Platinum-Based Drugs in Cancer Therapy, 2000. Recipient Disting. Scholarship award, Va. Commonwealth U., 2003; named Disting. Scholar, 1997. Mem.: Am. Assn. Cancer Rsch., Am. Chem. Soc. Achievements include patents in field; invention of anticancer platinum drugs of clinical relevance. Office: Va Commonwealth Univ 1001 W Main St Richmond VA 23284-2006 Business E-Mail: npfarrell@vcu.edu.

FARRELL, PATRICK, photographer, photojournalist; s. James and Peggie Farrell. BA in TV & Film Prodn., U. Miami, Fla., 1981. Staff photographer Miami Herald, 1987—. Recipient Pulitzer prize for pub. svc., 1993, Sigma Delta Chi award for excellence in photography spot news, Soc. Profl. Journalists, 2008, Pulitzer prize for breaking news photography, 2009, Nat. Headliner award, 2009. Office: Miami Herald One Herald Plaza Miami FL 33132 Office Phone: 305-350-2111.

FARRELL, PETER F., state legislator; b. Alexandria, Va., June 12, 1983; BA in Govt., U. Va., 2006. Mem. Dist. 56 Va. House of Delegates, 2012—, mem. Courts of Justice Com. & Gen. Laws Com. Republican. Office: General Assembly Building PO Box 406 Richmond VA 23218 also: PO Box 87 Richmond VA 23218 Office Phone: 804-698-1056. Office Fax: 804-698-6756. E-mail: DelPFarrell@house.virginia.gov.

FARRELL, THOMAS FRANCIS, II, energy executive; b. Ft. Buckner, Okinawa, Japan, 1954; m. Anne Garland Tullidge; 2 children. BA in Econs., U. Va., 1976, JD, 1979. Ptnr. McGuire, Woods, Beatle & Booth, 1981-95; v.p., gen. counsel Dominion Resources, Inc., Richmond, Va., 1995-97, sr. v.p. corp. affairs, 1997-99, exec. v.p., gen. counsel, corp. sec. Va. Power, exec. v.p., 1999—2003, pres., COO, 2004—06, pres., CEO, 2006—07, chmn., pres., CEO, 2007—; CEO Dominion Energy, 2000—04. Bd. dirs. Dominion Resources, Inc., 2005—, Altria Group, Inc., 2008—. Mem. Va. Bar Assn. (exec. com., chmn. young lawyers sect.), Va. Law Found. (mem. continuing legal edn. com.). Office: Dominion Resources Inc PO Box 26532 Richmond VA 23261-6532 Office Phone: 804-819-2400.

FARRER, MARSHALL B., wine and spirits company executive; 2 children. BA in Polit. Sci., Rollins Coll.; MBA in Internat. Mgmt. & Mktg., Tulane U. Joined Brown-Forman Corp., 1998, dir., Spirits Americas, 2004—06, dir., L. Am. & Caribbean, 2006—10, v.p., 2007—10, mng. dir., Australia, New Zealand & Pacific Islands, 2010—. Office: Brown Forman Corp 850 Dixie Hwy Louisville KY 40210 Office Phone: 502-585-1100. Office Fax: 502-774-7876. Business E-Mail: marshall_farrer@brown-forman.com.

FARRIOR, EDWARD H., otolaryngologist, educator; s. Richard Farrior. BA in Biology, U. of South Fla., Tampa, 1978; MD, U. of Va. Sch. of Medicine, Charlottesville, 1982. Diplomate Nat. Bd. Med. Examiners, 1983, Am. Bd. Otolaryngology, 1989, Am. Bd. Facial Plastic and Reconstructive Surgery, 1991. Intern dept. of gen. surgery St. Joseph's Mercy Hosp., Ann Arbor, Mich., 1982—83; resident dept. of otolaryngology Univ. of Mich. Hosp., Mich., 1983—87; affiliate assoc. prof. voluntary faculty dept. of otolaryngology Univ. of South Fla.; vice chief otolaryngology Tampa Gen. Hosp., 1989—91, 1993—98, chief otolaryngology, 1991—93, vice chief surgery, 1993—95, sec. treas. med. staff, 1996—98. Vis. clin. assoc. dir. dept. of otolaryngology Univ. of Va.; lay rep. Fla. Bar Fee Arbitration Com., 1994—95; presenter, panelist dept of otoralyngology Univ. of Va., Charlottesville, 2004. Actively involved Spring of Tampa Bay, 1993—, bd. dirs., 1998—; volunteer Face to Face Orgn.; bd. dirs. Hillsborough County Assn. for Retarded Citizens, 1990—92. Recipient Physician Humanitarian award, Fla. Med. Bus. Healthcare, 2000, Cmty. Svc. award, Am. Acad. of Facial Plastic and Reconstructive Surgery (AAFPRS), 2002. Fellow: ACS, AAFPRS (credentials Com. 2005—, fellowship dir. 1993—); mem.: AMA, Hillsborough County Med. Assn. (exec. coun. 1996—98, del. 1997—98, v.p. 2001—02, chmn., membership com. 2001—02, del. 2001—05, exec. coun. 2001—05, pres. elect 2002—03, pres. 2003—04, bd. of censors 2004—07, bd. of trustees 2004—08, del. chmn. 2005, Hillsborough Med. Polit. Action Com. Bd. v.p. 2005—08), Fla. Med. Assn., Fla. Soc. of Otolaryngology, Head and Neck Surgery, Fla. Soc. of Facial Plastic and Reconstructive Surgery (sec., treas. 1995, pres. elect 1996, pres. 1997), Am. Acad. Otolaryngology, Head and Neck Surgery, Am. Bd. Facial Plastic and Reconstructive Surgery. Office: Tampa General Hospital 1 Tampa General Cir Tampa FL 33606-3508 Office Phone: 813-844-7000.

FARRIOR, JOSEPH BROWN, otolaryngologist, educator; MD, Emory U. Sch. of Medicine, 1975. Lic. to practice Fla., 1980, diplomate Am. Bd. Otolaryngology, 1981. Resident surgery Johns Hopkins Hosp., Balt., 1976—77, resident otolaryngology, 1977—81, intern, 1976; fellow otolaryngology Farrior Clin., Tampa, Fla., 1979—80, St. Joseph's Hosp., 1979—80, hosp. affiliations include, James A. Haley Veterans' Hosp., Tampa Gen. Hosp., Meml. Hosp. of Tampa; assoc. clin. prof. otolaryngology Univ. South Fla. Coll. of Medicine. Office: St Josephs Hospital 3001 W Martin Luther King Blvd Tampa FL 33607-6387 Office Phone: 813-870-4000.

FARRIS, G. STEVEN, energy executive; Grad. in History and Acctg., Okla. State U. Exec. v.p. Robert W. Berry Inc., 1978—83; v.p. & treas. Terra Resources, 1983—88; v.p. exploration and prodn. Apache Corp., Houston, 1988-91, sr. v.p., 1991-94, pres., COO, 1994—2002, pres., CEO, COO, 2002—09, chmn., pres., CEO, COO, 2009—09, chmn., CEO, 2009—. Mem. Nat. Petroleum Coun. Mem. steering com. Energy Tchrs.; trustee Ucross Found. Office: Apache Corp 2000 Post Oak Blvd Ste 100 Houston TX 77056-4400

FARRIS, ROBERT GENE, transportation company executive; b. Bartlesville, Okla., June 21, 1930; s. Carlton Kittrell and Ruby Lee (Richeson) F.; m. Betty C. Raimond, Dec. 28, 1951; children: Robert Raimond, William Carlton, Jonathan Bradley. BBA, U. Tex., 1952. Safety dir. Valley Transit Co., Inc., Harlingen, Tex., 1955-56, pers. dir., 1956-57, v.p., 1957-62, pres., 1963-99, chmn. bd., also bd. dirs., 1963—. Bd. dirs. Tex. State Bank, Harlingen, Tex. Regional Bancshares, McAllen, Tex., Millennium Fuels Corp., Dallas. Pres. Harlingen Indsl. Found., 1968-69; v.p. Rio Grande coun. Boy Scouts Am., 1971-72; trustee Marine Mil. Acad., Harlingen, 1977—; bd. dirs. Tex. Tourist Coun., Austin, 1980-84; past crusade chmn. Am. Cancer Soc.; past mem. bd. 1st United Meth. Ch., Harlingen. 1st lt. U.S. Army, 1952-54, Korea. Named Friend of Tex. Transit, Tex. Dept. Hwys. and Pub. Transp., 1978. Mem. Nat. Bus Traffic Assn. (bd. dirs. 1980-85), Tex. Motor Transp. Assn. (bd. dirs. 1976-80), Harlingen C. of C. (pres. 1967-68), Rio Grande Valley C. of C. (pres. 1975-76), Algodon Club (past pres.), Phi Gamma Delta. Methodist. Office: Valley Transit Co Inc 219 N A St Harlingen TX 78550-5413 E-mail: bbrfarris@aol.com.

FARSHCHIAN, NASSER, gas industry executive; BS in Civil Engring. and Info. Tech., Cleve. State U. Mgmt positions Bristlecone, SeeCommerce, JB Hunt; dir., supply chain processes Nestle USA; mgmt positions Nestle SA; bd. adv. Aankhen, Inc.; sr. v.p., chief info. officer McJunkin Red Man Corp., 2008—. Office: McJunkin Red Man Corp 835 Hillcrest Dr Charleston WV 25311 Office Phone: 304-348-5211. Office Fax: 304-347-2067. Business E-Mail: nasser.farshchian@mcjunkinredman.com.

FARTHING, WILLIAM P., JR., lawyer; AB, U. NC, Chapel Hill, 1970, JD with honors, 1974. Bar: NC 1974. Ptnr. Parker Poe Adams & Bernstein LLP, Charlotte, chmn. recruiting com., 1984—88, mem. mgmt. com., 1990—2002, vice chmn., 1999—2002, mng. ptnr. of firm, mem. bd. dirs., 2002—. Bd. visitors Johnson C. Smith U., 1985—99, bd. trustees, mem. exec. com., mem. fin. com., 1999—2008, univ. atty.; bd. dirs. Charlotte Repertory Theatre, 1990—99, mem. exec. com., chmn. edn. and outreach com., 1994—98; bd. dirs. Legal Services of So. Piedmont, 2009—10; mem. adv. bd. The Remsen Group's Mng. Ptnr. Forum; bd. advisors Charlotte C. of C. Morehead scholar. Fellow: American Bar Found.; mem.: Nat. Assn. Coll. and Univ. Attorneys, American Employment Law Coun. Office: Parker Poe Adams & Bernstein LLP Three Wells Fargo Ctr 401 S Tryon St Ste 300 Charlotte NC 28202 Office Phone: 704-335-9014. Office Fax: 704-335-9562. Business E-Mail: billfarthing@parkerpoe.com.

FASANO, MICHAEL BENJAMIN, state legislator; b. LI, NY, June 11, 1958; s. Alexander and Joan (Cresswell) Fasano. Attended, St. Petersburg Jr. Coll., Fla., 1987—90. Self-employed Ind. Distbns. Newspapers, 1976—; acctg. exec. Dean Witter Investments, Port Richey, Fla., assoc. v.p.; dir. cmty. and legal affairs Fla. Hosp. Zephyrhills; assoc. v.p. investments Morgan Stanley; mem. Dist. 45 Fla. House of Reps., Tallahassee, 1994—2002; mem. Dist. 11 Fla. State Senate, Tallahassee, 2002—, majority whip, 2006—08, pres. pro tempore, 2008—10, chair transp. and econ. devel. appropriations com., mem. banking and ins. com., comm., energy and pub. utilities com., ethics and elections com., govtl. oversigh and accountability com. Mem., lector St. Thomas Aquinas Cath. Ch. Named Distributor & Salesman of Yr. Times Pub. Co., 1977, Young Rep. of Yr. West Pasco Rep. Club, 1982; named to West Pasco Rep. Club Hall of Fame, 1988. Mem. KC, West Pasco Youth Soccer Assn., Am. Cancer Soc. (bd. mem., chmn. income devel., vol.). Republican. Roman Catholic. Office: 8217 Massachusetts Ave New Port Richey FL 34653-3111 also: 404 Senate Office Bldg 404 S Monroe St Tallahassee FL 32399-1100 Office Phone: 727-848-5885, 850-487-5062. Business E-Mail: fasano.mike.web@flsenate.gov.

FATOVIC, ROBERT DEAN, lawyer; b. Englewood, NJ, Mar. 1965; m. Leeanna D. Black. BS magna cum laude in Fin., Boston Coll., 1987, JD, 1990. Bar: NJ 1991, Fla. 1997. Assoc. Hannoch Weisman, P.C., NJ, 1990—94; asst. divsn. counsel Ryder System, Inc., Miami, 1994—96, assoc. divsn. counsel, 1996, assoc. div. counsel through sr. v.p. & dep. gen. counsel, 1996—2002, sr. v.p. US Supply Chain Operation, High-Tech and Consumer Industries, 2002—04, exec. v.p., chief legal officer, sec., 2004—. Mem.: ABA. Office: Ryder System Inc 11690 NW 105th St Miami FL 33178

FAUGHT, GEORGE E., state legislator; b. Brownfield, Tex., July 14, 1962; m. Becky (Tinnin) F.; children: Tyler, Jamison, Savannah. Grad., Bryan Inst., 1987. Bus. owner Clean Pro; mem. Dist. 14 Okla. House of Representatives, 2007—. Mem.: Muskogee Character Coun., Indian Nations Beekeepers Assn., Nat. Rifle Assn., Muskogee C. of C. Republican. Address: 3220 E Harris Rd Muskogee OK 74403-1669 Office: Oklahoma House of Representatives 2300 N Lincoln Blvd Room 301-A Oklahoma City OK 73105 Office Phone: 405-557-7310. E-mail: george.faught@okhouse.gov.

FAULCONER, ROBERT JAMIESON, retired pathologist, educator; b. Sedlescombe, Sussex, Eng., July 11, 1923; came to U.S., 1925, naturalized, 1932; s. Robert Hoffman and Gladys Alice (Jamieson) F.; m. Virginia Myrl Davis, Aug. 11, 1945; children: Anne Faulconer Hurley, Elizabeth Myrl, Mary Waite, John Edmund. BS, Coll. William and Mary, 1943; MD, Johns Hopkins U., 1947; DSc (hon.), Ea. Va. Med. Sch., 1998. Diplomate Am. Bd. Pathology. Intern Johns Hopkins Hosp., 1948, fellow, 1948-49; resident Presbyn.-U. Pa. Med. Ctr., Phila., 1949-52; pathologist DePaul Hosp., Norfolk, Va., 1954-78, pathologist, dir. labs., 1965-78; clin. prof. pathology Med. Coll. Va., 1972-79; prof. pathology Ea. Va. Med. Sch., 1974-94, chmn., 1978-93, prof. emeritus, 1994—2013. Cons. pathologist U.S. Naval Hosp., Portsmouth, Va., VA Hosp., Hampton, Va., Children;s Hosp., Norfolk, Va. Beach Gen. Hosp.; chmn. Health Svcs. Adv. Bd., Norfolk; mem. adv. com. Va. Cancer Registry. Med. editorial bd. Histology and Histopathology Jour.; contbr. articles on pathology to profl. publs. Pres. Va. div. Am. Cancer Soc., 1963-66, mem. nat. bd. dirs., exec. and sci. rev. coms.; bd. visitors Coll. William and Mary, 1972-76, 79-87, chmn. William and Mary Olde Guarde, 1997-98. With USNR, 1943-46, M.C., U.S. Army, 1952-54. Recipient J. Shelton Horsley award merit, Va. div. Am. Cancer Soc., 1966, Alumni medallion, Coll. William and Mary, 1985. Fellow AAAS; mem. AMA, Internat. Acad. Pathology, Am. Soc. Clin. Pathologists, Coll. Am. Pathologists, Am. Assn. Anatomists, Am. Soc. Clin. Oncology, Am. Assn. Phys. Anthropologists, Va. Soc. Pathology (pres. 1958-59), Norfolk Acad. Medicine (pres. 1964-65), Am. Assn. History of Medicine, Am. Assn. Pathologists, Assn. Pathology Chmn., Cypher Soc. (Coll. William and Mary), Norfolk Yacht and Country Club, Town Point Club (bd. govs.), Commonwealth Club (Richmond), Sigma Xi. Episcopalian. Home: 1507 Buckingham Ave Norfolk VA 23508-1354

FAULK, JOHN, SR., accountant; b. Tex., June 8, 1946; 3 children. BBA in Behavioral Mgmt. Sci., U. Houston, 1971; MBA in Mktg., U. Houston Clear Lake, 1980. Profl. Boy Scout dist. exec. Boy Scouts America Sam Houston Area Coun.; clinic mgr. dept. def. Uniform Svcs. Health Care Clinc Sisters of Charity Health Care Sys.; bus. mgr. Doctor's Hosp., Houston; with Coll. Devel. Office Coll. Natural Sci. & Math. U. Houston; dir. planned giving Episcopal Diocese of Tex.; ret. Mem. Boy Scouts of America, United Meth. Ch., South Belt Ellington C. of C., Greater Heights C. of C.; bd. dirs. U. Houston Clear Lake. With helicopter squadrons USN, 1967—68. Mem.: U. Houston Clear Lake Alumni Assn. Republican. Office: 1701 Hermann Dr # 2206 Houston TX 77004 Office Phone: 832-265-4074. Business E-Mail: john@faulkforcongress.org.

FAULK, MICHAEL ANTHONY, state legislator, lawyer; b. Kingsport, Tenn., Sept. 10, 1953; s. Loy Glade and Rosella E. (Dykes) F.; children: Katherine Lea, Andrew McLain. BS, U. Tenn., 1975; M in Pub. Adminstrn., Memphis State U., 1978, JD, 1979. Bar: U.S. Dist. Ct. (we. dist.) Tenn. 1980, U.S. Dist. Ct. (ea. dist.) Tenn. 1985, U.S. Supreme Ct., 1998; cert. civil trial specialist, Nat. Bd. Trial Advocacy. Dep. clk. to presiding justice Shelby County Chancery Ct., Memphis, 1977-79; assoc. Weintraub & Dehart, Memphis, 1980-82; ptnr. Frazier & Faulk, Church Hill, Tenn., 1982-83; sole practice Church Hill, 1983-93; ptnr. Law Offices of Faulk, May & Coup, Church Hill, Tenn., 1993-96; sole practice Church Hill, 1996—; mem. Dist. 4 Tenn. State Senate, 2009—. Commr. Tenn. Human Rights Commn., Nashville, 1985-92, vice chmn. 1988-92; referee Hawkins County Juvenile Ct., Rogersville, Tenn., 1985-96; bd. commrs. Hawkins County, 1998-2002; bd. dirs. Legal Services Inc., Johnson City, Tenn. Bd. dirs. Upper East Tenn. divsn. Am. Heart Assn., Blountville, 1984-86. Named one of Outstanding Young Men in Am. U.S. Jaycees, 1977, Am. Leading Lawyers, 1993, Super Lawyer of Mid. South, 2007. Mem. ABA, Hawkins County Bar Assn. (pres. 1987-88), Assn. Trial Lawyers Am., Ducks Unltd. (chmn. Holston River chpt. 1984-98). Lodges: Moose. Republican. Baptist. Avocation: outdoors. Office: PO Box 2080 Church Hill TN 37642-2080 Office Phone: 423-357-8088. Business E-Mail: mike@faulklaw.com.

FAULKNER, KRISTINE, communications executive; b. 1968; BS in Comm., Ithaca Coll., 1989; MBA, The Coll. William and Mary, 1998. Bus. devel. mgr. Digital City Hampton Roads, gen. mgr.; dir., internet pub., Daily Press Tribune Interactive, Va., 1998—2000; sr. product mgr., Web Hosting Services Cox Comm. Inc., Atlanta, 2000—04; v.p., product devel. and mgmt. Cox Communications, Inc., Atlanta, 2004—. Named one of 40 Executives Under 40, Multichannel News, 2006. Office: Cox Communications Inc 1400 Lake Hearn Dr Atlanta GA 30319 Office Phone: 404-843-5000. Office Fax: 404-843-5975. Business E-Mail: kfaulkner@cox.com.

FAULKNER, LARRY RAY, foundation administrator, retired academic administrator; b. Shreveport, La., Nov. 26, 1944; s. James Clifford and Doris Louise (Koch) Faulkner; m. Mary Ann Jordan, Aug. 14, 1965; children: Brian Jordan, Susan Louise. BS, So. Meth. U., 1966; PhD, U. Tex., Austin, 1969; DSc (hon.), So. Meth. U., 2000. Asst. prof. chemistry Harvard University, Cambridge, Mass., 1969—73; asst. prof. U. Ill., Urbana-Champaign, 1973—75, assoc. prof., 1975—79, mem. materials rsch. lab., 1978—90, prof., 1979—83, prof. chemistry, dept. head, 1984—89, dean Coll. Liberal Arts and Sci., 1989—94, provost and vice chancellor acad. affairs, 1994—98; prof. chemistry University of Texas, Austin, Tex., 1983—84, pres., 1998—2006, pres. emeritus, 2006—; pres. Houston Endowment, Inc., 2006—. Bd. dirs. Exxon Mobil Corp., 2008—; bd. mem. Temple-Inland Inc., 2004—, Guaranty Fin. Group, 2008—. Author (with A.J. Bard): Electrochemical Methods, 1980, 2d edit., 2001; editor: Jour. Electroanalytical Chemistry, 1980—85; mem. edit. bd.: Jour. Electrochem. Soc., 1975—80. Recipient U.S. Dept. Energy award, 1986. Fellow: Electrochm. Soc., Electrochem. Soc. (v.p. 1988—91, pres. 1991—92, Edward Weston fellow 1969, Young Author's prize 1976, Edward Goodrich Acheson medal 2000), Am. Acad. Arts and Scis. (mem.); mem.: Soc. Electroanalytical Chemistry (Charles N. Reilly award 1998), Am. Chem. Soc. (award in analytical chemistry 1992), Phi Kappa Phi, Phi Beta Kappa (Grad. Rsch. award Tex. Gamma chpt. 1969—70). Office: Houston Endowment Inc 600 Travis, Ste 6400 Houston TX 77002-3000 Office Phone: 713-238-8110. Office Fax: 713-238-8101.

FAULS, THOMAS E. (TED), lawyer; b. Fredericksburg, Va., 1961; AB, Coll. William & Mary, 1983, JD, 1986. Bar: Va. 1986. Assoc. Troutman Sanders LLP, Richmond, Va., 1986—94, ptnr., 1995—, practice group leader, 1998—2007, mng. ptnr. Richmond office, 2006—. Mem.: ABA, Va. Bar Assn. Office: Troutman Sanders LLP Riverside on the James 1001 Haxall Point 14th Fl PO Box 1122 Richmond VA 23219 Office Phone: 804-697-1200. Office Fax: 804-697-1339. Business E-Mail: ted.fauls@troutmansanders.com.

FAUROT, BARBARA S., finance company executive; Attended, Trinity Coll., Hartford. Mktg. assoc. American Express Co.; v.p. mktg. & product mgmt. Citibank; sr. v.p. mktg. General Electric Capital; sr. v.p. mktg. & sales Genworth Financial, Inc., sr. v.p. comm. Office: Genworth Financial Inc 6620 W Broad St Richmond VA 23230 Office Phone: 804-281-6000. Office Fax: 804-662-2414. Business E-Mail: Barbara.Faurot@genworth.com.

FAUST, TEDDY JOE, SR., (JOE FAUST), state legislator; b. Birmingham, Ala., Sept. 13, 1940; m. Sharon Fay Pennington; m. Sharon Faust; children: Teddy Jr., Malory LeBlanc, Andrea Holloway, Christopher. Student in bus., Faulkner CC. Regional sales mgr. & supr. in the retail milk bus.; broker Woodman World Life Ins. Co., 1981—93, Independent Ins.; mem. Baldwin County Commn., Ala., 1996, Ala., 2000, chmn. & vice chmn.; mem. Dist. 94 Ala. House of Reps., 2003—. Bd. mem. Marietta Johnson Sch. Organic Edn.; former bd. mem. Eastern Shore C. of C. Served with Nat. Guard, 1958—66. Mem.: Masons. Republican. Baptist. Office: 20452 Beecher St Fairhope AL 36532 also: Ala House of Reps Ala State House 11 S Union St Rm 524-C Montgomery AL 36130 Office Phone: 251-990-4616, 334-242-7699. Business E-Mail: jfaust@co.baldwin.al.us.

FAVALORA, JOHN CLEMENT, archbishop; b. New Orleans, Dec. 5, 1935; s. Felix J. and Leona M. (Stevens) Favalora. BA in Philosophy and History, Notre Dame Sem., New Orleans, 1958; STL, Pontifical Gregorian U., Rome, 1962; MEd, Tulane U., 1969. Ordained priest Archdiocese of New Orleans, La., 1961, sec. to archbishop, 1963—65, vice chancellor, 1963—65; asst. pastor St. Theresa of the Child Jesus Ch., New Orleans, 1962—70; vice rector St. John Prep., New Orleans, 1964—67, 1968—71; dir. Office of

Permanent Deaconate, New Orleans, 1971—74, Office of Vocations, New Orleans, 1979—81; adminstrv. asst. Notre Dame Sem., New Orleans, 1971—73, rector-pres., 1981—86; pastor St. Angela Merici Ch., Metairie, La., 1973—79; ordained bishop, 1986; bishop Diocese of Alexandria, La., 1986—89, Diocese of St. Petersburg, Fla., 1989—94; archbishop Archdiocese of Miami, 1994—2010, archbishop emeritus, 2010—. Ecclesiastical notary Archdiocese of New Orleans, 1962—64, pro-synodal judge, 1973—79; dean East Jefferson Deanery, New Orleans, 1974—77; vicar Pastoral Planning, New Orleans, 1976—81; chmn. Permanent Diaconate Adv. Com., New Orleans, 1984; consultor Archdiocese of New Orleans, 1984—86. Roman Catholic. Office: Archdiocese of Miami Pastoral Ctr 9401 Biscayne Blvd Miami Shores FL 33138

FAVARO, MARY KAYE ASPERHEIM, pediatrician & family practice, writer; b. Edgerton, Wis., Sept. 30, 1934; d. Harold Wilbur and Genevieve Catherine (Hyland) Asperheim; m. Biagino Philip Favaro, May 31, 1969; children: Justin Peter, Gina Sue. BS, U. Wis., 1956, MD, 1969; MS, St. Louis Coll. Pharmacy, 1965. Instr. pharmacology St. Louis U. and St. Mary's Hosp. Sch. Practical Nurses, 1959-64; staff pharmacist U. Hosps., Madison, Wis., 1964—69; intern Albany Med. Ctr., NY, 1969-70; resident, 1970-71; resident in pediatrics U. SC, Charleston, 1971-72, asst. prof. pediatrics, 1973-75; pvt. practice pediatrics family practice, 1974-99; locumtenens physician, 2000—. Author: The Pharmacologic Basis of Patient Care, 1985, Introduction to Pharmacology, 2012. Mem.: AMA. Roman Catholic. Home: 1407 Southwood Dr Myrtle Beach SC 29575 Office Phone: 843-267-6879. Personal E-mail: maryfav@aol.com.

FAVOLA, BARBARA A., state legislator; b. New London, Conn., June 21, 1955; BS, St. Joseph Coll., 1977; MPA, NYU, 1980. Mem. Dist. 31 Va. State Senate, 2012—, mem. Transp. Com., Local Govt. Com. & Rehab. and Social Services Com. Democrat. Office: Senate of Virginia PO Box 396 Richmond VA 23218 also: 2319 18th St North Arlington VA 22201-3506 Office Phone: 804-698-7651. Office Fax: 804-698-7651. E-mail: district31@senate.virginia.gov.

FAVORS, JOANNE, state legislator; b. Chattanooga, Tenn., Aug. 27, 1942; 4 children. Former cons. health adminstrn.; house rep. Tenn.; mem. Hamilton County Commn., 1998, 2002, Children & Family Affairs Com., Commerce Com., Health & Human Svc. Com., Domestic Rels. Subcom., Small Bus. Subcom., Mental Health Subcom., Profl. Occupation Subcom.; state rep. Dist. 29 Tenn., 2005—. Recipient Mary Walker Hist. Assn. award, award, Tenn. Primary Care Assn., Southside Reunion Disting. Svc. award, Southside & Dodson Ave. Cmty. Health Ctrs. Disting. Svc. award, Tenn. Primary Care Network award; named Nurse of Yr., Dist. 4, Tenn. Nurses Assn. Mem.: Nat. Assn. of State Legislatures, Howard High Sch. Alumni Assn., Hamilton County Dem. Women's Club, Women in Govt., Chattanooga Neighborhood Enterprise, Unity Group, PUSH, Daughters of Elks Temple 364, Ann. Southside Family Reunion Organizer, Elks Springmeade Neighborhood Assn., Tenn. & Am. Nurses Assn., Women's Leadership Coun. Democrat. Baptist. Mailing: PO Box 23286 Chattanooga TN 37422 Office: 25 Legislative Plz Nashville TN 37243-0129 Office Phone: 615-741-2702. Office Fax: 615-253-0351. Business E-Mail: rep.joanne.favors@capitol.tn.gov.

FAVORS, STEVE ALEXANDER, academic administrator; b. Texarkana, Tex., Dec. 30, 1948; s. Clarence L. and Erma (Newton) F.; m. Charlotte A. Edwards, Feb. 12, 1977; children: Steve A., Jonathan A. BS, Tex. A&M U., 1971, MS, 1973, EdD, 1978. Lic. in clin. counseling, Tex. Adminstrv. asst. to dean students Tex. A&M U., Commerce, 1975-77; v.p. student affairs Wiley Coll., Marshall, Tex., 1977-81, Dillard U., New Orleans, 1981-85; vice chancellor for student affairs U. New Orleans, 1985-90; v.p. student affairs Howard U., Washington, 1990-98; pres. Grambling (La.) State U., 1998—, Faculty Senate, 2005—; prof. Honors Coll., 2001—. Mem. Mid-Eastern Athletics Conf. Exec. Coun., 1990—; voting del. NCAA, 1990. Bd. dirs. New Orleans Found., 1985-90, Dollars for Scholars Found., 1983-90; mem. Urban League, New orleans, 1985-90. Recipient Appreciation award U. New Orleans Black Caucus, 1990, Man of the Yr. award Mt. Zion United Meth. Ch., New Orleans, 1988-89, Appreciation award Am. Counseling Assn. (Tex. So. Univ. chpt.), 1987, Svc. award Am. Coll. Pers. Assn., 1986. Mem. Nat. Assn. Student Pers. Adminstrs. (Disting. Svc. award 1988-89), Nat. Assn. for Student Affairs Pers., NAACP, Alpha Phi Omega, Phi Delta Kappa, Omega Psi Phi, Sigma Pi Phi Fraternity. Avocations: basketball, graphic designs, collecting sports cards. Office: Grambling State U Office Pres PO Box 4208 Grambling LA 71245-3091 Office Phone: 318-274-2303. Business E-Mail: favors@gram.edu.

FAW, RICHARD EARL, nuclear engineering educator; b. Ohio, June 22, 1936; s. Robert Harvey and Mary Elizabeth (Baird) F.; m. Beverly A. Giltner, Mar. 25, 1961; children: Jennifer, Andrew; m. Joyce R. Sears, Sept. 8, 2001. BSChemE, U. Cinn., 1959; PhD in Chem. Engring., U. Minn., 1962. Cert. chem. engr., Ohio, nuclear engr., Kans. Prof. nuclear engring. Kans. State U., Manhattan, 1962—2000. Author: Radiological Assessment, 1992; co-author: Principles of Radiation Shielding, 1984, Radiation Shielding, 1996, Fundamentals of Nuclear Science and Engineering, 2002; contbr. articles to profl. jours. Capt. U.S. Army, 1962-64. Fellow Am. Nuclear Soc. (profl. excellence award 1986), mem.; Health Physics Soc. Methodist.

FAWAZ, JED, telecommunications industry executive; V.p., tech., chief info. officer Crown Castle International Corp. Office: Crown Castle International Corp 1220 Augusta Dr Ste 500 Houston TX 77057-2261 Office Phone: 713-570-3000. Office Fax: 713-570-3100. Business E-Mail: jed.fawaz@crowncastle.com.

FAWSETT, PATRICIA COMBS, federal judge; b. Montreal, Can., 1943; BA, U. Fla., 1965, MAT, 1966, JD, 1973. Pvt. practice law Akerman, Senterfitt & Edison, Orlando, Fla., 1973-86; commr. 9th Cir. Jud. Nominating Commn, 1973-75, Greater Orlando Crime Prevention Assn., 1983-86; judge US Dist. Ct. (mid. dist.) Fla., Orlando, 1986—2003, chief judge, 2003—08, sr. judge, 2008—. Trustee Legal Aid Soc., 1977-81, Loch Haven Art Ctr., Inc., Orlando, 1980-84, U. Fla. Law Sch., 2001—; hon. trustee Reago Spiritual Scholarship Found., 1999—; commr. Orlando Housing Authority, 1976-80, Winter Park (Fla.) Sidewalk Festival, 1973-75; bd. dirs. Greater Orlando Area C. of C., 1982-85. Mem. ABA (trial lawyers sect., real estate probate sect.), Am. Judicatures Soc., Assn. Trial Lawyers Am., Fla. Bar Found. (bd. dirs. grants com.), Commn. on Access to Cts., Fla. Coun. Bar Assn. Pres.'s (pres., bd. dirs. 9th cir. grievance com.) Osceola County Bar Assn., Fla. Bar (bd. govs. 1983-86, budget com., disciplinary rev. com., integration rule and bylaws com., com. on access to legal system, bd. of cert., designation and advt., jud. adminstrn., selection and tenure com., jud. nominating procedures com., pub. rels. com., ann. meeting com., appellate rules com., spl. com. on judiciary-trial lawyer rels., chairperson midyr. conv. com., bd. dirs. trial lawyers sect.), Orange County Bar Assn. (exec. coun. 1977-83, pres. 1981-82), Order of Coif, Phi Beta Kappa. Office: US Dist Ct US Courthouse 401 W Central Blvd Rm 3650 Orlando FL 32801 Office Phone: 407-835-4250. E-mail: patricia_fawsett@flmd.uscourts.gov.

FAY, CONNER MARTINDALE, retired marketing executive; b. Chillicothe, Mo., May 9, 1929; s. Vernon Martindale and Corinne (Conner) F.; m. Evelyn Caffey Buford, Dec. 2, 1961; children: Leslie Conner Francesca, Buford Martindale Edoardo, David Curtis Anselmo. BA, Yale U., 1951; MBA cum laude, Harvard U., 1953. Brand mgr. Procter & Gamble Co., Cin., 1956-62; mktg. mgr. Procter & Gamble Co. Italia, Rome, 1962-69; sr. v.p. Clairol Inc., NYC, 1970-89; mgmt. cons., 1989-93; ret., 1993. Mem. bd. fgn. parishes Am. Episcopal Ch., NY, 1977-2005, pres., 1989-2005, emeritus 2006-; bd. dirs. St. Paul's Ch., Rome, 1977-2005, pres., 1989-2001; bd. dirs. St. James Ch., Florence, Italy, 1977-2005, pres., 1989-2005, emeritus 2006-; vice chmn. St. Stephen's Sch., Rome, 1980-94; trustee Samuel and Lois Silberman Fund NY Cmty. Trust, 1993-2012; sr. warden St. Mary the Virgin Episcopal Ch., Chappaqua, NY, 1982-83, 91-93; chmn. coun. of advisors Hunter Sch. Social Work, CUNY, 1985-97, Ashville Symphony Bd., 2011; various offices Yale Alumni Fund, including dir., 1993, chmn., 1996-98, agt., 1996—, 40th, 50th, 55th & 60th reunion spl. gifts co-chair Class of 1951; bd. dirs. Yale Alumni Chorus Found., 2003-2010, v.p., 2004-09; bd. dirs. Katonah Mus. Art, 1995-2008, treas., 2001-03. Recipient Yale medal, 2000. Mem. Am. Indsl. Health Coun. (bd. dirs. 1979-91, chmn. 1988-89), Yale Glee Club Assocs. (pres. 1979-81, treas. 1996-2001, medal 2007). Avocation: music. Business E-Mail: cmfay@charter.net. E-mail: conner.fay@aya.yale.edu.

FAY, KEVIN J., public relations executive; Grad., U. Va.; JD, Am. U. Bar: Va. With Alcalde & Fay, Arlington, Va., 1982—; pres.; bd. visitors U. Va.; bd. mem. LIUNA Lafaren's Charitable Found. Exec. dir. Internat. Climate Change Partnership; counsel Alliance for Responsible Atmosphere Policy. Emeritus chmn. bd. govs. Bishop Denis J. O'Connell HS; bd. dirs. World Children's Choir; mem. Fairfax County Pk. Authority Bd. Recipient Lord Fairfax award, Fairfax County Bd. Supervisors, 2000, Cath. Schools Bus. Partnership award, Cath. Bus. Network No. Va., 1999, 2000, 2010, James L. Eichberg Lifetime Achievement award, 2012, Northern Va. of Yr. award, Leukemia Soc. Ball, Northern Va. Mag., 2012; named Citizen of Yr., McLean Times and Providence Jour., 2012. Office: Alcalde & Fay 2111 Wilson Blvd 8th Fl Arlington VA 22201 Business E-Mail: fay@alcalde-fay.com.

FAY, PETER THORP, federal judge; b. Rochester, NY, Jan. 18, 1929; s. Lester Thorp and Jane (Baumler) Fay; m. Claudia Pat Zimmerman, Oct. 1, 1958; children: Michael Thorp, William, Darcy. BA, Rollins Coll., 1951, LLD, 1971; JD, U. Fla., 1956; LLD, Biscayne Coll., 1975. Bar: Fla. 1956, U.S. Supreme Ct. 1961. Ptnr. firm Nichols, Gaither Green, Frates & Beckham, Miami, Fla., 1956—61, Frates, Fay, Floyd & Pearson (and predecessors), Miami, 1961—70; prof. Fla. Jr. Bar Practical Legal Inst., 1959—65; judge US Dist. Ct. for So. Fla., Miami, 1970—76, US Ct. Appeals (5th cir.), 1976—81, US Ct. Appeals (11th cir.), 1981—94, sr. judge, 1994—; lectr. Fla. Bar Legal Inst., 1959—; faculty Fed. Jud. Center, Washington, 1974—94. Mem. Jud. Conf. Com. for Implementation Criminal Justice Act, 1974—82, Adv. Com. on Codes of Conduct, 1980—87, Ad Hoc Com. on Cameras in the Courtroom, 1983—84, Adv. Com. on Appellate Rules, 1987—90, Eleventh Circuit Standing Edn. Com.; mem. exec. com. Eleventh Circuit Judicial Coun.; co-chmn. Nat. Jud. Coun. for State and Fed. Cts., 1990—. Mem. Orange Bowl Com., 1974—; dist. collector United Fund, 1957—70; mem. adminstrv. bd. St. Thomas U., 1970—; trustee U. Miami, Fla., 1989—; mem., supr. Ind. Counsel, 1994—. Lieutenant USAF, 1951—53. Mem.: ABA, Medico Legal Inst., John Marshall Bar Assn. (past pres.), Dade County Bar Assn., Fla. Bar Assn., Fla. Acad. Trial Attys., Law Sci. Acad., Miami C. of C., U. Fla. Alumni Assn. (dir.), Fla. Coun. of 100, Miami Club, Coral Oaks Club (Miami), Wildcat Cliffs Club (N.C.), Snapper Creek Lakes Club (Miami), Phi Delta Theta (past sec.), Phi Kappa Phi, Pi Gamma Mu (past pres.), Omicron Delta Kappa (past pres.), Phi Delta Phi (past pres.), Order of Coif. Republican. Roman Catholic.

FEASTER, BURNES LYNN, III, critical care specialist; b. Memphis, Tenn. married; 4 children. BA cum laude, U. Fla., 1969—73, MD, 1973—77. Diplomate Am. Bd. Internal Medicine, 1980, Am. Bd. Internal Medicine- pulmonary disease, 1982, Am. Bd. Internal Medicine- critical care medicine, 1998. Instr. Advanced Trauma Life Support; course dir. instr. Advanced Cardiac Life Sipport; intern William Beaumont Army Med. Ctr., El Paso, Tex., 1977—78, resident in internal medicine, 1978—80, staff in pulmonary disease svc., 1982—84, dir. med. intensive care unit, 1982—84; fellow in pulmonary disease Walter Reed Army Med. Ctr., Washington, 1980—82; teaching fellow US Uniformed Health Sci. Med. Sch., Bethesda, Md., 1980—82; chief in pulmonary disease svc. Landstuhi Army Regional Med. Ctr., Germany, 1984—87; cons. in pulmonary disease to 7th med. command Heidelberg, Germany, 1984—87; med. staff St. Petersburg Med. Clinic, Fla., 1987—95; clin. asst. prof. Sch. Medicine Univ. South Fla., 1988—; med. dir. Vocat. tech. Inst. of St. Petersburg, Fla., 1988; nat. faculty mem. Am. Acad. of Allergy and Immunology, 1991—; med. dir. in critical care medicine St. Anthony's Hosp., 1996—; med. dir. Vencor Hosp., 1997—; hosp. affiliation includes Bayfront Med. Ctr. Chmn. spl. care com. Landstuhl Army Regional Med. Ctr., Germany, 1986—87; M.I.C.U. com. St. Anthony's Hosp., St. Petersburg, Fla., 1987—, respitory therapy com., 1987—; chmn. pharmacy and therapeutics com. St. Anthony Hosp., 1989—92, exec. com., 1989—92; chmn. spl. care com. St. Anthony's Hosp., 1996—; intensive care unit com. Edward H. White Meml. Hosp., St. Petersburg, Fla., 1987—90; critical care com. Bayfront Med. Ctr., 1990—, chmn. pharmacy and therapeutic com., 1994—, chmn. cardiac care com., 1997—; SICU com. All Children's Hosp., 1992—; chief of staff Vencor Hosp., 1997—. Office: Bayfront Medical Center 625 6th Ave Ste 475 Saint Petersburg FL 33701-2227 Office Phone: 727-822-6666.

FEATHERMAN, BERNARD, steel company executive; b. May 3, 1929; m. Sandra Green; children: Andrew C., John James. BS, Temple U., Phila., 1951; postgrad., Grad. Bus. Sch., 1951—52, Law Sch., 1952—54, Wharton Sch., U. Pa., 1965—66. Chmn. bd. dirs. Western Metal Bed Co., Phila., 1978-86; with CIATEQ USA, Inc., 1995-98; dir. Pa. Steel and Aluminum Corp. (now Pa. Steel Corp.), Bensalem, 1972—, Wardwell Retirement Complex, Saco, Maine, 1998—2011, Counselling Svcs., Inc., Saco, 1998-2000, Newsletter Pub. Co., Phila., Am. Red Cross So. Maine, 2000—, Am. Red Cross Maine, 2000—10; resident Highland Beach; sec. Villa Costa Condominium Assn.; past CEO C.of C. Maine; past pres. Assn. Steel Distributors; pres. adv. bd. mem. US Small Bus. Adminstrn., 2007—11; regional chair County Phila. Mental Health, Mental Retardation Bd.; mayor Town of Highland Beach, Fla., 2011—; chair Reentry Task Force Sex Offender Sub-Com., Palm Beach Criminal Justice Sys., 2012—. Contbr. articles to profl. jours.; inventor electronics locking locker, columnist Jour. Tribune Maine, 2008-, Host Bus. Today, Channel 3, Biddeford, Maine, 2006-. Mem. exec. bd. Southeast chpt. Nat. Found. March of Dimes, 1969-82, vice-chmn., 1978-80; pres. Phila. Assn. for Retarded Citizens, 1975-77, trustee, 1983-96; trustee Phila. Devel. Disabilities Corp., 1991-96, Equity 591 F8AM, 1990-92; chmn. Mayor's Adv. Com. on Mental Health-Mental Retardation, Phila., 1979-92, bd. dirs. 1993; mem. tax policy and budget rev. com. City of Phila., fiscal adv. com., 1990; bd. dirs. Costar, Inc., 1989-92; co-chmn. Mayor's Small Bus. Adv. Com., Phila., 1979-92, mem., 1979-95; del. White House Conf. on Small Bus., 1980, Pa. del., 1995, vice-chmn., 1986; chmn. small bus. coun. Dem. Nat. Com., 1982-84; fin. chmn. Pa. Dem. Orgn., 1985-86; mem. adv. bd. Coll. Liberal Arts and Scis., Temple U., 1982-91, chmn. incubator program, 1989-91, chmn. Entrepreneurial Inst., 1990; co-dir. Enterpreneurial Inst. U. New Eng., 1996-98; adv. bd. West Chester State U. Bus. Sch., Pa., 1986-87, Frankford Hosp., 1983—85; steering com. entrepreneurial forum Drexel U. Bus. Sch., 1988-91; chmn. 3d Congl. Small Bus. Coun., Phila., 1984-88; bd. dirs. Phila. Citywide Devel. Corp., 1984-96; bd. dirs. Phila. Loan Fund, Inc., 1987-88, ARC, Souther Maine,2004—10, corporator So. Maine Med. Ctr., 2005—09, York County Econ. Devel.Summit Steering Com., 2004; bd. dirs. Coastal Counties Workforce Bd., Topshawn, Maine, 2006-11, Maine Merchants Assn., Augusta, 2006-08; regulatory fairness bd. US Small Bus. Adminstrn., Region 1, 2007—11, chair region 1, 2010-11. Recipient award of appreciation Small Bus. Coun., Dem. Nat. Com., 1983; Gold medal of Honor Adult Trainees Found., Phila., 1976; citation White House Conf. on Small Bus., 1980; named Entrepreneur of Yr. Mid Atlantic Region Supporter of Entrepreneurship, 1990, Ea. Pa. Small Bus. Adv. of Yr. SBA, 1991. Mem. Assn. of Steel Distbrs. (nat. pres. 1975-76, 86-87, named Steel Distbr. of Yr. 1976), Inst. Am. Entrepreneurs (life), Shelving Mfrs. Assn. (nat. chmn. 1977-78), Pa. Soc., Assn. Steel Distbrs. (nat. pres. 1975-76, 86-87, Hunting Park-Germantown Bus. Assn. (pres. 1986-96), Biddeford/Saco C. of C. (bd. dirs. 2002-08, pres., CEO, 2005-08), Rotary, Masons (trustee), B'nai Brith (pres. 1980-82, Nat. Youth Svcs. award Quaker City lodge 1985), Boca Raton Sunset Rotary Club (pres. elect, 2014-). Office: 3614 S Ocean Blvd Highland Beach FL 33487 Office Fax: 561-265-3582. Personal E-mail: bernard@featherman.com.

FEATHERMAN, SANDRA, retired academic administrator, political science professor; b. Phila., Apr. 14, 1934; d. Albert N. and Rebe (Burd) Green; m. Bernard Featherman, Mar. 29, 1958; children: Andrew Charles, John James. BA, U. Pa., 1955, MA, PhD, U. Pa., 1978. Asst. prof. dept. polit. sci. Temple U., Phila., 1978-84, assoc. prof., 1984-91, asst. to pres., 1986-89, pres. faculty senate, 1985-86, dir. Ctr. Pub. Policy, 1986-91; vice chancellor acad. adminstrn., prof. polit. sci. U. Minn., Duluth, 1991-95; pres. U. New Eng., Biddeford, Maine, 1995—2006, pres. emeritus, 2006—; mem. Maine Comm. Jud. Comp, 2005—11; bd. mem. U. Maine Sch. Law Found., 2013—; bd. mem., chair active affairs Fla. Poly U. Mem. New Eng. Assn. Schs. and Coll. Higher Edn. Commn., 2002—06; mem. commn. women in higher edn. Am. Coun. Edn., 2005—08; commr. commn. on accreditation Am. Osteopathic Assn., 2007—; bd. mem. Girl Scout Maine, 2009—. Author: Jews, Black and Ethnics, 1979, Race and Politics at the Millenium, 2000, Higher Education at Risk, 2013; contbr. articles to profl. jours. Nat. bd. Girls Inc., 1971—74; pres. Pa. Fedn. C.C., Girls Inc.; sec. Internat. Women's Forum, Maine, 2002—, pres., 2005—08, mem. Fla., 2011—; bd. Maine Compact Higher Edn., 2003—06, exec. bd., 2003—06; commr. Am. Coun. on Edn. Commn. on Women in Higher Edn., 2005—07; chair Maine Commn. on Jud. Compensation, 2005—; chair ethics commn. State of Maine, 2006—07; chair Gov.'s Blue Ribbon Commn. on Health Care, Maine, 2006—07, Maine, 2006; bd. mem. Girl Scouts Maine, 2009—; adv. bd. Coll. Osteo. Medicine, NY Inst. Tech., 2010—11; bd. mem. Poly. U., 2012—; chair Acad. Affairs Com., 2013—; mem. Palm Beach County Health Care Dist. Audit & Compliance Com., 2013—; gov. Search Com. VGIF NYC, 2011—13; nat. bd. dirs. Women and Founds.-Corp. Philanthropy, 1986—91; bur. osteo. edn. Am. Osteo. Assn., 2004—06; vice chair, commr. Osteo. Coll. Accreditation, 2010—; with Coll Ostea Med., NY Inst Tech., 2010—11, Samuel Fels Found, 1978—, pres., 2007—09; with Maine County Found., 2006—, chair, audit com., 2010—; bd. dirs. Citizens Com. Pub. Edn. Phila., 1977—89, pres., 1979—81; trustee C.C. Phila., 1970—92, chmn. bd. trustees, 1984—86; bd. mem. Samuel Fels Found., 1978—, pres., 2007—; bd. dirs. United Way SE Pa., 1977—89, United Way Pa., 1981—84, U. New Eng., Gulf of Maine Aquarium, Kennebec Girl Scout Coun., Virginia Gildersleeve Internat. Fund., 2003—, chair exec. dir. rsch. com., 2011—; bd. dirs. Vis. Nurse Assn., 2002—03; chair Assembly Pres. Am. Assoc. Coll. Osteopathic Medicine; chmn. Maine Commn. on the State Ceiling on Tax-exempt Bonds, 1999—2000; bd. dirs. Maine Cmty. Found., 2006—, mem. exec. com., 2007—; new dirs. U. Maine Sys. Task Force on New Challenges, 2009—. Recipient Brooks Graves award, Pa. Polit. Sci. Assn., 1982, Cmty. Svc. award, City of Phila., 1984, Women's Achievement award, YWCA, 1989, Adminstr. of Yr. award, Minn. Women in Higher Edn., 1994, Champion of Econ. Growth award, Maine Devel. Found., 2002, Women Who Make a Difference award, Internat. Women's Forum, 2004, Women of Distinction award, 2004, Woman of Distinction award, Kennebec Coun. Girl Scouts USA, 2006, Deborah Morton sward, U. New Eng., Bates award, Maine Osteo. Assn., 2010, Pioneer Of Osteopathic Medicine award, U. New Eng., 2012; named Disting. Daughter Pa., State Pa., 2004. Mem.: AAUW (bd. dirs. Phila. chpt. 1975—78, 1980—91, pres. 1984—86, nat. chair internat. fellowships panel 1987—91, nat bd. dirs. 1993—96, Outstanding Woman award 1986), Maine Media Workshops, Greatness Fund, Am. Coun. Edn. (commn. on advancement racial and ethnic equality 2001—04, commn. women higher edn. 2005—06), Maine Ind. Colls. Assn. (pres. 1998—2000), Greater Portland Alliance Colls. and Univs. (pres. 1997—98), Nat. Assn. Ind. Colls and Univs. (com. policy analysis & pub. rels. 2001—), Am. Polit. Sci. Assn. Office: 3210 S Ocean Blvd Highland Beach FL 33487 Office Phone: 207-602-2306. Business E-Mail: sfeatherman@une.edu.

FEAVER, PETER DOUGLAS, political science educator, consultant, defense analyst; b. Fountain Hill, Pa., Dec. 17, 1961; s. Douglas David and Margaret Ruth F.; m. Karen Michelle Geers, Aug. 11, 1990. BA in Polit. Sci., Lehigh U., 1983; MA in Polit. Sci., Harvard U., 1986, PhD in Polit. Sci., 1990. Tchg. fellow Harvard U., Cambridge, Mass., 1985-90, pre post doctoral fellow, 1985-90; post doctoral rsch. fellow Mershon Ctr., Ohio State U., Columbus, 1990-91; asst. prof. polit. sci. Duke U., Durham, NC, 1991—98, assoc. prof., 1998—2003, prof., 2003—, Alexander F. Hehmeyer prof. polit. sci. and pub. policy, 2009—; dir. def., policy and arms control White House Nat. Security Coun. Staff, Washington, 1993-94, spl. advisor strategic planning and instl. reform, 2005—07. Cons. Inst. Def. Analysis, Alexandria, Va., 1985—98, 2008—; dir. Triangle Inst. Security Studies, Durham, 1999—; co-moderator WashingtonPost-.com Planet War Discussion Group, 2008—09; spkr. in field; co-moderator Shadow Govt. Foreign Policy Com., 2009—. Author: Guarding the Guardians, 1992, Armed Servants, 2003; co-author: Assuring Control of Nuclear Weapons, 1987, Choosing Your Battles, 2004, Getting the Best Out of College: A Professor, 2008, Paying the Human Costs of War, 2009; co-editor: Battlefield Nuclear Weapons, 1988, Soldiers and Civilians, 2001; assoc. editor Armed Forces and Society, mem. editl. bd. Security Studies, Internat. Security; freelance writer: LA Times, Washington Post, Wall St. Jour., NY Times, Weekly Standard, 1990—; contbr. articles to profl. jours., chapters to books. Term mem. Coun. on Fgn. Rels., 1992—97; mem. adv. bd. Duke U. Law Sch. Ctr. on Law, Ethics, and Nat. Security. Lt. comdr. USNR, 1990—99. Recipient Disting. Tchg. award, Trinity Coll., 1994—95, Disting. Undergrad. Tchg. award, Duke U. Alumni Assn., 2001. Mem.: Aspen Strategy Group, Inter Univ. Seminar on Armed Forces and Soc., Internat. Studies Assn., Am. Polit. Sci. Assn., Phi Beta

Kappa. Evangelical. Avocations: golf, basketball, swimming, choral music. Office: Duke Univ Dept Polit Sci 326 Perkins Libr Box 90204 Durham NC 27708 Business E-Mail: pfeaver@duke.edu.*

FECHER, VINCENT JOHN, priest; b. Wilmette, Ill., Feb. 10, 1924; s. Joseph Martin and Emilia Cecilia (Siemer) F. D. Ch. History, Gregoriana, Rome, 1954; MA in Philosophy, Cath. U. Am., 1960; PhD, Angelicum, Rome, 1974; MA in Gerontology, Trinity U., San Antonio, 1981. Ordained priest Roman Cath. Ch., 1950. Sem. prof. Divine Word Sem., Techny, Ill., 1954-59, Manila, Philippines, 1959-64; sec. gen. Soc. of Divine Word, Rome, 1968-74; parish priest San Antonio Archdiocese, 1974—99; pastor Sacred Heart Cath. Ch., Uvalde, Tex., 1980-92, St. John the Evangelist Ch., Hondo, Tex., 1995-99. Author: German National Parishes, 1955, Error, Deception, Incomplete Truth, 1974, Religion and Aging, 1982, The Lord and I, 1990, Man, Woman, and God, 1993, The Voice and The Word, 2005; contbr. articles to profl. pubs. Mem. adv. coun. Tex. Dept. Human Svcs., Austin, 1984-88 Mem. KC, Knights of Holy Sepulcher. Home: 8520 Cross Mountain Trl San Antonio TX 78255-2038 E-mail: countpas@texas.net.

FECHTEL, VINCENT JOHN, legal administrator; b. Leesburg, Fla., Aug. 10, 1936; s. Vincent John and Annie Jo (Hayman) F.; m. Dixie Davenport, Feb. 1992; children: John, Katherine, Elizabeth D., MaryKatherine. BSBA, U. Fla., 1959. Mem. Fla. Ho. of Reps., 1972-78, Fla. Senate, 1978-80; parole commr. U.S. Dept. Justice, Chevy Chase, Md., 1983-96. Served with USNR and Fla. Nat. Guard. Mem. Alpha Tau Omega. Republican. Methodist. Home: 1414 Park Dr Leesburg FL 34748-6736

FEDERLE, MICHAEL, publishing executive; married; 2 children. Student, Tulane U., New Orleans; B, Colby Coll., Waterville, Maine, 1981. Formerly with New Eng. Publs., Camden, Maine, Color Computer mag.; sales devel. mgr. People mag. Time Inc., 1985, assoc. advt. dir. Life mag. NY, 1992, NY advt. dir. Fortune, 1995, assoc. pub. NYC, 1997—99, group pub. Bus. & Fin. Network, 1999—2008; CEO b2b networks Next Jump, Inc., 2008—09; group pub. Mountain divsn. (SKI, Skiing mags., SkiNet.com) Bonnier Corp., 2009—. Office: Bonnier Corp 460 N Orlando Ave Ste 200 Winter Park FL 32789 Office Phone: 212-522-1212.

FEDORA, LARRY, college football coach; B, Austin Coll., Sherman, Tex., 1985. Grad. asst. Austin Coll. Kangaroos, 1986; asst. football coach Garland HS Owls, Tex., 1987—90; tight ends, wide receivers and running backs coach Baylor U. Bears, 1991—96; passing game and wide receivers coach US Air Force Acad. Falcons, 1997—98; offensive coord. Mid Tenn State U. Blue Raiders, 1999—2001; run game coord. U. Fla. Gators, 2002, perimeter game coord., 2003, offensive coord., 2004, Okla. State U. Cowboys, 2005—07; head football coach U. So. Miss. Golden Eagles, 2008—11, U. NC Tar Heels, 2011—. Office: University NC Football c/o UNC Athletic Dept PO Box 2126 Chapel Hill NC 27514 Office Phone: 919-966-2575.

FEEHAN, DANIEL R., finance company executive; BA in Acctg., Tex. A&M U. Audit mgr. Arthur Young & Co.; worked Wedge Group; co-founder, pres. Greer Capital, 1984—88; exec. v.p., fin., adminstrn. Cash America International, Inc., 1988—90, pres., 1990—99, pres., COO, 1999—2000, pres., CEO, 2000—; non-exec. chmn. RadioShack Corp., Forth Worth, Tex., 2011—. Bd. dirs. Cash America Internat., Inc., 1984—, AZZ Inc., 2000—, RadioShack Corp., 2003—. Bd. dirs. Fort Worth Police & Firefighters Meml., Lena Pope Home. Office: Cash America International Inc 1600 W 7th St Fort Worth TX 76102 Office Phone: 817-335-1100. Office Fax: 817-570-1699. Business E-Mail: daniel_feehan@cashamerica.com.

FEEK, JOEY MARTIN, singer; b. 1977; m. Rory Lee Feek; 2 stepchildren. Co-owner Mary Jo's Mealhouse, 2006—. Singer: (albums) (with Joey & Rory) The Life of a Song, 2008, Album #2, 2010, (songs) Cheater, Cheater, 2008, Play the Song, 2009, To Say Goodbye, 2009, That's Important to Me, 2010; performer: (TV series) Can You Duet, 2008—09. Co-recipient Top New Vocal Duo of Yr. award, Acad. Country Music, 2010.

FEEK, RORY LEE, musician, songwriter; b. Atchison, Kans., 1966; m. Joey Martin Feek; 2 children. Co-founder & owner Giantslayer Records, 2004—. Musician: (albums) (Joey & Rory) The Life of a Song, 2008, Album #2, 2010, (songs) Cheater, Cheater, 2008, Play the Song, 2009, To Say Goodbye, 2009, That's Important to Me, 2010; co-author Chain of Love, 2000, The Truth About Men, 2003, Some Beach, 2004, The Upside of Being Down, 2004, How Do You Get That Lonely, 2005, The Best Man, 2005, I Will, 2008, You Can Let Go, 2008, A Little More Country Than That, 2009; performer: (TV series) Can You Duet, 2008—09. With USMC. Co-recipient Top New Vocal Duo of Yr. award, Acad. Country Music, 2010.

FEESE, SUZANNE, lawyer; b. Danville, Ky. BA with honors, Agnes Scott Coll., 1984; JD, Yale Univ., 1987. Bar: Ga. 1988. Law clk. Judge R. Lanier Anderson III, US Ct. Appeals 11th Cir.; ptnr., Tax Practice Group & hiring ptnr., Atlanta King & Spalding, LLP, Atlanta. Trustee Agnes Scott Col.; mem. Chair Council Atlanta Women's Found.; past chairwoman Ga. Ctr. for Children. Mem.: ABA, State Bar Ga. Office: King Spalding Llp 1180 Peachtree St NE Ste 1700 Atlanta GA 30309-7525 Office Phone: 404-572-3566. Office Fax: 404-572-5100. Business E-Mail: sfeese@kslaw.com.

FEI, JAMES ROBERT, engineering executive, consultant; b. Tucson, May 24, 1947; s. Robert Fleming and Barbara Jean (Dukes) F.; m. Patricia Christine Wilson, Aug. 24, 1968; children: Robert Fleming, Christina Kalani. BSME, U. So. Calif., 1969; MS in Ocean Engring., U. Hawaii, 1973. Registered profl. engr., S.C., La., Tex., Ga., Va., N.H., N.C. Design engr. USN, Mare Island, Calif., 1969-70; project mgr. Pearl Harbor (Hawaii) Shipyard, 1970-73; mech. systems engr. Submarine Maintenance Monitoring Systems Office Dept. of the Navy, Washington, 1973-76; chmn., chief exec. officer Life Cycle Engring., Inc., Charleston, SC, 1977—. Bd. dirs., adv. bd. Nat. Bank of S.C., 1985-92; mem. adv. coun. St. Francis Hosp., 1992-95; mem. pres.'s adv. coun. Med. U. S.C., Charleston, 1995-96; mem. Cold War Submarine Meml. Found., exec. com., bd. Mem. SCSPE, NSPE, ASME, Navy League. Republican. Avocations: golf, boating. Office: Life Cycle Engring Inc 4360 Corporate Rd Charleston SC 29405-7445 Home Phone: 843-571-3181; Office Phone: 843-744-7110. Business E-Mail: jfei@lce.com.

FEIDLER, MARK L., investment company executive; BA in Economics, Duke U., 1978; JD, Vanderbilt U., 1981. Assoc., corp. law sec. King & Spalding, 1981—86; with, investment banking dept. Robinson-Humphrey Co., 1986—90; prin. Breckenridge Group, 1990—91; COO Cingular Wireless, 2000—03, bd. dirs., 2005—07; dir., strategic transactions BellSouth Corp. (merged with AT&T), 1991—93, v.p.,corp. devel., 1991—2000, pres., interconnection svc., 1996—98, pres. Bell South Mobility, 1998—2000, chief staff officer, 2004—05, pres., COO, 2005—06. Bd. dirs. MSouth Equity Ptnrs., LLC, NY Life Ins. Co., Equifax Inc., 2007—. Bd. mem. Great Schools Atlanta, Ctr. for Puppetry Arts, Schenck Sch. Office: Equifax Inc Bd Directors 1550 Peachtree St NW Atlanta GA 30309 also: MSouth Equity Partners LLC 2 Buckhead Plz 3050 Peachtree Rd NW Ste 550 Atlanta GA 30305 Office Phone: 404-885-8000, 404-816-3255. Office Fax: 404-885-8988, 404-816-3258. Business E-Mail: mfeidler@msouth.com.

FEIGON, JUDITH TOVA, ophthalmologist, surgeon, educator; b. Galveston, Tex., Dec. 2, 1947; d. Louis and Ethel Feigon; m. Nathan C. Goldman; children: Michael G., Miriam G. AB, Barnard Coll., Columbia U., 1970; postgrad., Rice U., U. Houston, 1970-71; MD, U. Tex., San Antonio, 1976. Diplomate Am. Bd. Ophthalmology. Intern Mt. Auburn Hosp., Cambridge, Mass.; intern, clin. tchg. fellow Harvard U. Med. Sch., 1976-77; resident in ophthalmology Baylor Coll. Medicine, Houston, 1977-80, fellow in retina, 1980-82, clin. faculty, 1982-95; asst. prof. ophthalmology U. Tex. Med. Br., Galveston, 1982-85, clin. asst. prof., 1985-91, clin. assoc. prof., 1992—; pvt. practice medicine specializing ophthalmology, vitreoretinal diseases, surgery, Houston, 1983—. Physician advisor to Houston br. Tex. Soc. to Prevent Blindness, 1987-89, also bd. dirs., mem. staff Meth., St. Lukes, Tex. Children's Hosp. Contbr. articles to profl. publs. Mem. Am. Acad. Ophthalmology, Tex. Med. Assn. Houston Ophthal. Soc., Harris County Med. Soc., U. Tex. San Antonio Alumni Assn., Am. Soc. Retina Specialists, Tex. Ophthalmol. Assn., Houston Ophthal. Soc. (exec. bd. 2000-03). Office: 7515 Main St Ste 650 Houston TX 77030-4599

FEINBERG, HERBERT, wine company executive; b. NYC, June 20, 1926; s. Harry Feinberg and Dorothy (Hurwitz) Goldstein; m. Audrey Frank, Sept. 15, 1948 (div. Mar. 1972); children: Michael (dec.), Mark, Harry; m. Barbara Mays Jones, May 25, 1972 (div. June 1989); 1 child, Candice; m. Sandi Ann Gold, June 1989; 1 child, Tara. BS, U. Ill., 1949. Owner, v.p. Monsieur Henri Wines Ltd., NYC, 1949-72; owner, pres. Hudson Valley Wine Village, Highland, NY, 1972—, Regent Champagne Cellars, Highland, NY, 1988. With USAF, 1944-46. Republican. Jewish. Avocations: tennis, boating. Home: 472 Mariner Dr Jupiter FL 33477

FEINBERG, MIKE, school system administrator; m. Colleen Dippel; 1 child, Gus. BA in Internat. Rels., U. Pa., Phila., 1991. Intern, Senator Paul Simon US Senate, Washington, 1991—92; joined Teach for America Program, 1992; elem. sch. tchr. Houston Ind. Sch. Dist., 1992—94; co-founder (with Dave Levin) Knowledge Is Power Program Found. (KIPP), 1994; founder, sch. dir. KIPP Acad., Houston, 1995—2000; supt. KIPP Houston, 2000—; CEO KIPP Found. Recipient Jefferson Cmty. Svc. award, City of Houston, 1995, Seed of Freedom award, Gulfton Area Neighborhood Orgn., 1997, Salvatori prize for Am. citizenship, Heritage Found., 1999, Crystal award, Presdl. Citizens medal, The White House, 2008; named one of America's Best Leaders, US News & World Report, 2008; Ashoka fellow, 2004. Office: KIPP Houston 10711 KIPP Way Houston TX 77099 Office Phone: 832-328-1051. Office Fax: 832-203-6365. Business E-Mail: mfeinberg@kipp.org.

FEINSTEIN, ROBERT P., dermatologist; b. NYC, July 31, 1941; s. Jerome and May (Wolpin) F.; m. Diane Marla Gutstein, Oct. 25, 1969; children: Steven, Michelle, Suzanne, Gary, Lori. AB in Biology, NYU, 1963, MD, 1967. Diplomate Am. Bd. Dermatology. Intern Kings County Hosp. Ctr., Bklyn., 1967-68; resident in dermatology Columbia U., NYC, 1968-71, assoc. clin. prof. dept. dermatology; chief of dermatology, innoculations and phys. exams. Navy Regional Med. Clinic, Washington, 1971-73; pvt. practice in dermatology Mineola, NY, 1973-99, Smithtown, NY, 1983-2000. Author: (book) Dermatology, 1975, (monograph) Rosacea, 1998, Androgenetic Alopecia, Farre Racouchot Syndrome; contbr. articles to profl. jours. Lt comdr. USNR, 1971-73. Fellow Am. Acad. Dermatology (mem. managed care com., 1995-99, mem. com. physician practice, professionalism study group program for dermatology in 21st cent., vice chmn. adv. bd. 2001-04), Am. Soc. for Dermatologic Surgery, Noah Worcester Dermatology Soc. (mem. bd. trustees 2008-11); mem. AMA, NY State Soc. of Dermatology (pres. 1997-99), L.I. Dermatology Soc. (pres. 1996-98), Suffolk County Dermatology Soc. (pres. 1982-84), Atlantic Dermatology Soc. (bd. dirs. 1995), NY State Med. Soc. (health care delivery sys.). Avocation: golf. Office Fax: 631-824-9393.

FEITO, JOSE, architect; b. Havana, Cuba, Jan. 30, 1929; arrived in U.S., 1961; s. Jose and Herminia (Mayo) F.; m. Bertha A. Abascal, Oct. 7, 1995; children: Patricia Maria, Maria Esther, Jose Alfonso, Sergio P. (dec.). MArch, U. Havana, 1954. Registered arch., Fla. Prin. J. Feito Archs., Havana, 1954-60; assoc. J. DeHaro Archs., Madrid, 1960-61; ptnr. Ferendino et al, Miami, Fla., 1966-79; prin. F&F Archs. and Planners, Miami, 1979-80, F&F Fraga and Feito Archs., Miami, 1980—. Pres. Professio Inc., Miami, 1983-84. Bd. dirs. Dade Co. Shoreline Com., 1986—; chmn. Gov.'s com. for Handicapped, Miami, 1973-75; trustee United Way, Miami, 1979-84. Recipient Meritorious Svcs. citation Gov.'s Com. for Handicapped, 1975. Fellow AIA (pres. Miami South chpt. 1977, Honor award 1985); mem. Fla. Assn. AIA (bd. dirs. 1978, Excellence award 1985), Interam. Businessmen's Assn. (pres. 1978-80), Cuba Soc. Archs. (Gold medal 1957), Cuban Mus. Arts and Culture (founder), Greater Miami C. of C. (mem. bd. govs. 1978-83). Republican. Roman Catholic. Avocations: history, sailing. Office: F&F Fraga & Feito Archs 2151 NW 93rd Ave Miami FL 33172-4804 Home Phone: 305-594-7834. E-mail: ffarchit@bellsouth.net.

FELD, ALAN DAVID, lawyer; b. Dallas, Nov. 13, 1936; s. Henry R. and Rose (Scissors) F.; m. Anne Sanger, June 1, 1957; children: Alan David, Elizabeth S., John L. BA, So. Methodist U., 1957, LL.B., 1960. Bar: Tex. 1960. Since practiced in Dallas; from ptnr. to chmn. bd. Akin, Gump, Hauer, Strauss & Feld, Dallas, 1960-96, sr. exec. ptnr., 1996—. Lectr. Southwestern U. Med. Sch.; chmn. Tex. State Securities Bd. 1985-1991; bd. dirs. Clear Channel Comms., Inc. Contbr. articles to legal jours. Trustee Am. Beacon Funds, So. Meth. U.; bd. dirs. MD Anderson Hosp., Dallas Symphony Orch. Mem.: ABA, Dallas Bar Assn., D.C. Bar Assn., Tex. Bar Assn., Brook Hollow Golf Club, Royal Oaks Country Club (corr.), Salesmanship Club, Dallas Country Club, Phi Delta Phi. Office: Akin Gump Strauss Hauer & Feld 1700 Pacific Ave Ste 4100 Dallas TX 75201-4675 Office Phone: 214-969-2712. Business E-Mail: afeld@akingump.com.

FELD, CHARLES S., information technology executive; BA in Economics, City Coll. NY. Systems engr. IBM Corp., 1970—81; chief info. officer Frito-Lay, Inc., 1981—92; CEO, pres., founder The Feld Group, 1992—2004; chief info. officer Delta Air Lines, Inc., 1997—2000; acting chief info. officer First Data Resources, 2000—02; exec. v.p., portfolio mgmt. EDS, Plano, Tex., 2004—06; sr. exec. v.p., applications svcs. HP Enterprise Services (formerly Electronic Data Systems, LLC), 2006—. Former bd. dirs. Direct Insite Corp., Interliant, Inc. Contbr. articles to profl. jours., articles to Computerworld Executive Suite. Recipient Chief Info. Officer Yr., State of Ga., 1998, Smithsonian award for Tech. Excellence, 2000; named one of 25 IT People to Watch in 1998, Computerworld, 12 Most Influential IT Executives of the Past Decade, CIO mag., 1997, Eight turn-around experts in "Masters of Disaster, Fast Company, 2001. Office: HP Enterprise Services LLC 5400 Legacy Dr Plano TX 75024-3199 Office Phone: 972-604-6000. Office Fax: 972-605-6033.

FELDER-HOEHNE, FELICIA HARRIS, retired librarian; b. Knoxville, Tenn. d. Henry Thomas and Luvilla Tate Harris. BS in English, Knoxville Coll.; MS in Libr. Sci., Atlanta U., 1966; postgrad., U. Tenn., 1972—78. English tchr. McMinn County Schs., J.L. Cook Sch., Athens, Tenn., 1958—60; adminstrv. asst. Knoxville (Tenn.) Coll., 1960—63, adminstrv. asst. to the dir. pub. rels., 1963—65; grad. libr. asst. Trevor Arnett Libr., Atlanta U., 1965—66; head circulation and reserve svcs. Alumni Libr. Knoxville Coll., 1966—69; tchr., libr. summer study skills program United Presbyn. Ch., Bd. Nat. Missions, Knoxville Coll., 1967—68; prof., rsch. libr. John C. Hodges Libr. U. Tenn., Knoxville, 1969—2014; guest lectr. Annual Mary Utopia Rothrock Lecture series East Tenn. Libr. Assn., 2011, U. Tenn. Knoxville. Founder, dir. LARKS: Librs. Linking with At-Risk Students, Knoxville, 1997—; prin. rschr. The George Washington Carver DVD Project, 2003; with Knoxville Police Dept., Harris Burris Meml. Libr., 2009; Knox county mayor Mike Ragslade, 2008; vol. Stars Month Honour Felicia, 2008. Author: A Subject Guide to Basic Reference Books in Black Studies; co-author: (online ency.) Project TAPP: Tennessee Authors Past and Present, 1999—; contbr. Notable Black American Women, Book I, Notable Black American Women, Book II, Behavioral & Social Sciences Librarian;, author poems; contbr. articles to profl. jours. Adv. bd. Mentoring Acad. for Boys, Knoxville, 1997—; sec. to bd. Ctr. for Neighborhood Devel., Knoxville, 2000—02; dir. pub. rels. Concerned Assn. Residents East, Knoxville, 1988—90; active Tenn. Valley Energy Coalition, Knoxville, 1988—90, Town Hall East, Knoxville, 1988—, Save Our Cumberland Mountains, Tenn., 1988—; religious task force World's Fair, Knoxville Internat. Energy Exposition, 1982; pres. Spring Place Neighborhood Assn., Knoxville, 1980—; pk. vol. Knox County Pk. Vol. Corps., 2003—; land devel. com. Knoxville Farmer's Mkt., 2004—05; cmty. action com. Leadership Class 2005; active West End Acad. Outreach, 1989—, Solutions to Issues of Concern to Knoxvillians, 1999—, Tribe One, 2000—, Safety City Outreach of Knoxville PD, 2004—, Cmty. Action Com. Leadership Class, 2005, Teen Challenge, 1985—; bd. dirs. Knoxville-Knox County Libr., 1971—77, sec. to bd., 1972—77; bd. dirs. Knox County Libr. Legacy Found., 2007—; guest Be Pretty Proud program Keep Knoxville Beautiful Bd., 2007, bd. dirs., 2009, Ctr. for Neighborhood Devel., Knoxville, 1998—2002, UT Fed. Credit Union, Knoxville, 1984—89, Knoxville Opera, 1998—2005, 2009—, Knox County Libr. Legacy Found., 2007—; adv. bd. dirs. Knox County Parks and Recreation, 2004—09; adv. bd. dirs. Bd. Probation and Parole State of Tenn., Knoxville, 2003—; mem. YWCA, YMCA. Recipient Cert. of Merit for Contbns. to Edn., Jack and Jill, Inc., 1976, Plaque of Appreciation, Interdenominational Concert Choir, 1976, Religious Svc. award, NCCJ, 1976, Citizen of the Yr. award, Order of the Ea. Star Prince Hall Masons, 1979, Cert. of Appreciation, Knoxville's Internat. Energy Exposition, 1982, Pub. Svc. award, U. Tenn. Nat. Alumni Assn., 1984, Habitat for Humanity award, 1992, Merit award for outstanding achievement, City of Knoxville, Mayor Ashe, 1994, The Humanitarian Libr. Spirit award, 1994, Spl. Svc. commendation, Mayor Victor Ashe, 1994, Spirit award, The Miles 500 Libr., 1994, 1999, 2005, Citation for Svc., Knoxville Police Dept., 1998, Cmty. Cornerstone award, Knoxville News-Sentinel, 1998, Harold B. Love Outstanding Cmty. Involvement award, Tenn. Higher Edn. Commn., 2003, The Vol. Spirit award, U. Tenn., 2003, Plaque of Appreciation, U. Tenn. Fed. Credit Union, 2004, Sincerity Disting. Libr. award, Daily Beacon, 2004, Hardy Liston Symbol of Hope award, U. Tenn., 2006, Vol. Stars award, Knox County, 2008, Adopt A Park Vol. award, Knox County Pks. & Recreation Dept., 2009, award, U. Tenn., 2010, Outstanding Svc. award, Jan Simek, U. Tenn., 2010, award, Ragsdale & Knox County Pks. & Recreation Dept., 2010, plaqe, Mayor Mike Ragsdale & Knox County Pks. & Recreation Dept., 2010, Lifetime Achievement award, Mu Rho chpt., Kappa Alpha Psi Fraternity, U. Tenn., 2011, Diversity Pioneer award, U. Tenn. Librs., 2011, Teamwork award, 2011, Merit Plaque Appreciation award, Knoxville Beautiful Inc., Tenn., 2012, Vol. and Beautification award, Keep Knoxville Beautiful Inc., 2013, Pks. & Recreation Vol. award, Knox County, 2013, 2013, Vol. beautification award, 2013; named Citizen of Yr., Order of Ea. Star, 2004, in her honor Dedicated Svc. Meml. Pk. Bench, Knox County Pks. and Recreation Dept., Mayor Mike Ragsdale, 2006; named one of Outstanding Young Women of Am., 1967; named to U. Tenn. African Am. Hall Fame, 1994. Mem.: LWV, NAACP, ALA, Keep Knoxville Beautiful (bd. dirs. 2009—), Knox County Libr. Legacy (bd. dirs. 2007—), Nat. Mus. Women in the Arts (charter 1981—), East Tenn. Libr. Assn. (guest lectr. 2011), Tenn. Libr. Assn., Knoxville Opera Guild, Dogwood Arts Festival (charter), Citizens Police Acad. Alumni Assn., Beck Cultural Exch. Ctr. (charter mem. 1975—, charter), Met. Opera Guild, Knoxville Opera Co. (re appointed mem. 2009, bd. dirs. 2009—), Character Counts Orgn., Alpha Kappa Alpha (Orchid award Keep Knoxville Beautiful 2006, A Living Legacy award Bronze Pk. Bench 2006). Achievements include the first African American librarian hired at the University of Tennessee campus and faculty in 1969. Avocations: community service, music, poetry, theater. Business E-Mail: ffelder@utk.edu.

FELDMAN, DAVID M., lawyer; b. Lake Charles, La., Aug. 19, 1949; m. Dennie Feldman; children: Cris, Seth, Lera. BA, La. State U., 1970; JD summa cum laude, South Tex. Coll. Law, 1976. Bar: Tex., US Dist. Ct. (so., ea., we., no. dists.) Tex., US Ct. Appeals (5th, 11th cirs.), US Supreme Ct. Employee NASA-Lyndon B. Johnson Space Ctr., 1972—76; ptnr. Vinson & Elkins; mng. ptnr. Feldman, Rogers, Morris and Grover, LLP; city atty. City of Houston, 2010—. Adj. prof. South Tex. Coll. Law. Inf. officer US Army, 1970—72. Named a Tex. Super Lawyer, 2004—09, Tex. Top Notch Lawyer, 2004, 2009; named to Best Lawyers in America, 1987, 2009. Office: City of Houston Legal Dept 900 Bagby 3rd Fl Houston TX 77002 Office Phone: 832-393-6491. Business E-Mail: david.feldman@houstontx.com.

FELDMAN, H. LARRY, lawyer; b. Tyler, Tex., Apr. 18, 1941; s. Henry and Bess (Booken) F.; m. Janice Kay Asner, June 26, 1960; children: Joseph, Katherine. BA, U. Okla., 1963; JD, So. Meth. U., 1966. Bar: Tex. 1966, US Dist. Ct. (no. dist.) Tex. 1969, US Supreme Ct. 1976. Adj. prof. law U. Dallas, 1967-68; mem. dept. tax Peat, Marwick & Mitchell, 1968-69; atty. Marks, Time & Aranson, 1970; ptnr. Feldman, O'Donnell & Neil, Dallas, 1971; sole practice Dallas, 1971—. Mem. ATLA, Tex. Trial Lawyers Assn., Phi Alpha Delta. Jewish. Personal E-mail: janicedallas@hotmail.com.

FELDMAN, JOEL MARTIN, retired judge; b. Atlanta, Jan. 2, 1941; s. Louis Aaron and Rosalie (Bach) F.; m. Debora A. Kirkpatrick; children: Lawrence A., Allison R. AB in Law, Emory U., 1962, JD, 1964. Bar: Ga. 1963, U.S. Dist. Ct. (no. dist.) Ga. 1963, U.S. Ct. Mil. Appeals 1964, U.S. Ct. Appeals (5th cir.) 1963, U.S. Ct. Appeals (11th cir.) 1981, U.S. Supreme Ct. 1967. Asst. legis. counsel Gen. Assembly Ga., Atlanta, 1964-66; asst. atty. gen. State of Ga., Atlanta, 1966-68; asst. dist. atty. Atlanta Jud. Cir., 1968-72, 74; legis. asst., legal counsel Sen. Sam Nunn of Ga., 1973-74; magistrate U.S. Dist. Ct. (no. dist.) Ga., Atlanta, 1974—2006; cert. mil. judge Naval-Marine Corps Trial Judiciary, 1982-92; ret., 2006. Former chmn. North Fulton Citizens Mental Health Adv. Coun.; pres. Temple Sinai Synagogue, Atlanta, 1994-96; chmn. Met. Atlanta 50th Ann. WWII Commemorative Cmty. With USAFR, 1964, capt. USNR, 1964-92. Mem. Fed. Bar Assn., State Bar Ga., Atlanta Bar Assn., Naval League U.S. (pres. Atlanta coun. 1985-86), Naval Res. Assn. (pres. 6th Dist. 1982-83), Fed.

Magistrate Judges Assn. (dir. 11th cir. 1982-83), Atlanta Lawyers Club, Navy League (Atlanta dir., pres.), Naval Order (Atlanta pres., dir.). Home: 9785 LaView Cir Roswell GA 30075 Personal E-mail: feldmanjoel@bellsoath.net.

FELDMAN, MARC DAVID, psychiatrist; b. Kingston, NY, Sept. 9, 1958; AB, Dartmouth Coll., 1980, MD, 1984. Diplomate Am. Bd. Psychiatry and Neurology, Nat. Bd. Med. Examiners. Resident in psychiatry Duke U. Med. Ctr., Durham, NC, 1984-88, asst. prof., 1988-90; chief resident in psychiatry Durham VA Med. Ctr., NC, 1987-88; med. dir. Hill Crest Hosp., Birmingham, Ala., 1990-93; vice chair dept. psychiatry U. Ala., 1993—2002, med. dir. Ctr. for Psychiat. Medicine, 1993—2002, dir. divsn. adult psychiatry, 1994—2002, clinical prof. psychiatry, 2002—. Acting dir. psychosocial support program Duke Comprehensive Cancer Ctr., 1989-90; pvt. practice, 1990-93; med. dir. United Behavioral Sys., 1996—1999. Contbr. articles to profl. jours; author 5 books. Laughlin fellow Am. Coll. Psychiatrists, 1988; Rufus Choate scholar Dartmouth Coll., 1977-79, others. Mem.: Acad. Psychosomatic Medicine, Birmingham Psychiat. Soc., Ala. Psychiat. Assn., Am. Psychiat. Assn., Phi Beta Kappa. Avocations: movies, computers. Office Phone: 205-529-1500.

FELDMAN, MARTIN LEACH-CROSS, federal judge; b. St. Louis, Jan. 28, 1934; s. Joseph and Zelma (Bosse) F.; m. Melanie Pulitzer, Nov. 26, 1958; children: Jennifer Pulitzer, Martin L.C. Jr. BA, Tulane U., 1955, JD, 1957. Bar: La., Mo. 1957. Law clk. to Hon. J.M. Wisdom, U.S. Ct. Appeals, 1958-59; assoc. Bronfin, Heller, Feldman & Steinberg, New Orleans, 1959-60, ptnr., 1960-83; judge US Dist. Ct. (ea. dist.) La., New Orleans, 1983—. Trustee, former chmn. Sta. WYES-TV; spl. counsel to Gov. of La., 1979-83. Contbr. articles to profl. jours. Former nat. sec. Anti-Defamation League; former pres. bd. mgrs. Touro Infirmary; bd. dirs. Public Broadcasting Service, 1978-84, Fed. Jud. Ctr., 1991-95; bd. dirs. Fed. Jud. Ctr., 1991-95. Mem. ABA (chair nat. conf. of fed. trial judges 1996-97), La. Bar Assn. (chmn. law reform com. 1981-82), Mo. Bar Assn., Am. Law Inst., Order of Coif. Republican. Jewish. Office: US Dist Ct 500 Poydras St Rm C555 New Orleans LA 70130

FELDMANN, EDWARD GEORGE, pharmaceutical chemist, pharmacologist, medical scientist; b. Chgo., Oct. 13, 1930; s. Edward Louis and Vera (Arnesen) F.; stepmother Helen E. Whitney; m. Mary J. Evans, Aug. 30, 1952; children: Ann Marie Whittington, Edward William, Robert George, Karen Lynn Zaragoza. BS in Chemistry, Loyola U., Chgo., 1952; MS in Pharmacy (research fellow Am. Found. Pharm. Edn. 1953-55), U. Wis., 1954, PhD in Pharm. Chemistry-Biochemistry, 1955; postgrad. in Med. Scis., Northwestern U., 1956; postgrad., U. Chgo., 1958. Tchg. asst. Loyola U., Chgo., 1951—52; rsch. asst. U. Wis., 1952—53; sr. chemist Am. Dental Assn., 1955—58, dir. divsn. chemistry, 1958—59; assoc. dir. sci. divsn. Am. Pharm. Assn., 1959—60, dir., 1960—85, assoc. editor sci. edit. assn. jour., 1959—60, editor, 1960—97, assoc. exec. dir. sci. affairs, 1970—83, v.p. sci. affairs, 1983—85, project dir. Handbook of Non-Prescription Drugs, 1985—89, mng. editor, 1989—90, project cons. Handbook on Non-Prescription Drugs, 1991—93, mem. adv. panel, 1994—95; exec. sec. Acad. Pharm. Scis., 1983—85; mem. adv. panel Am. Pharm. Assn., 1994—99; pvt. pharm. cons., 1985—; assoc. dir. revision Nat. Formulary, 1959—60; dir. revision Nat. Fomulary, 1960—70. Adv. panel dental drugs Nat. Formulary, 1955-60, Am. Pharm. Assn. Handbook of Non-Prescription Drugs, 1994-95; reviewer Internat. Pharmacopeia, WHO, 1958; spl. lectr., adj. prof. drug standards George Washington U., 1960-64; del. conf. on fellowships Nat. Health Council, 1960; mem. coordinating com. Nat. Conf. Antimicrobial Agts., Soc. Indsl. Microbiology, 1960-63; adv. panel pharm. nomenclature A.M.A.-Am. Pharm. Assn.-U.S. Pharmacopeia, 1961-66, nomenclature com., 1962-66; sec. U.S. Com. Internat. Drug Standards, 1964-65; adv. panel food chems. codex Nat. Acad. Scis.-NRC, 1961-71, liaison rep. to drug research bd., 1968-76; spl. liaison rep. to Commn. of Life Scis., NAS-NRC, 1973-85; lab. com. Am. Pharm. Assn. Found., 1961-75; mem. com. Ebert prize, 1961-75; judge Lunsford-Richardson Pharmacy Awards, 1962-69; cons. Council on Drugs, A.M.A., 1962; vis. scientist Am. Assn. Colls. of Pharmacy, NSF, 1963-66; expert adv. panel on internat. pharmacopeia and pharm. preparation World Health Orgn., 1963-75; mem. US President's Task Force on Hosp. Drug Coverage Under Medicare, 1963-64; drug abuse cons. to Office of US Pres., Lyndon B. Johnson, 1965, drug cons. Office Sec., U.S. Dept. Health, Edn. and Welfare, 1967-70; nomenclature cons. to Commr., U.S. Food and Drug Adminstrn., 1968-71; mem. expert working group Indsl. Devel. Orgn., UN, 1969; organizing com. 31st Internat. Congress Pharm. Scis., 1970-71; mem. NRC, 1971-85; del. U.S. Pharmacopeia, 1970-85, 90-95; mem. Nat. Council on Drugs, 1976-83; scientific adv. bd. Biodecision Labs., Inc., 1987-90; scientific cons. Am. Assn. Pharmaceutical Scientists, 1986-93; pharm. scis. cons. ERGO Sci. Inc., 1992—; steering com. Japan-U.S. Pharmaceutical Scis. Congress, 1987; expert witness congressional drug legis. hearings and civil litigation cases, Drug quality specifications, Fed. legal requirements, Clinical pharmacology and Toxicology, 1965-; lectr. in field. Assoc. editor Drug Standards, 1959-60, editor, 1960; chmn. (1960-70) Nat. Formulary Bd.; editor Jour. Pharm. Scis., 1961-75, cons. editor, 1975-85, 87-89, interim editor, 1991, editor in chief, 1991-94, emeritus editor 1994-95; editor APS Acad. Reporter, 1983-85; author more than 420 articles in field, editor or co-editor 24 ref. books; mem. editorial adv. bd. Index Chemicus, 1968-71; med. contbr. World Book Ency., 1986-88. Mem. membership com. Ravenwood Park Citizens Assn., Falls Church, Va., 1962, adv. mem. medication coverage US Presdl. Commn. Medicare Legis., 1963-64; mem. nominating com., 1971-72; mem. Lake Barcroft Community Assn., 1975-97. Recipient Spl. Recognition award U.S. Pres. Lyndon Johnson, 1965, Man of Yr. award Nat. Assn. Pharm. Mfrs., 1970, Disting. citation U. Wis., 1971, Commr.'s citation FDA, 1975, G.A. Bergy Lectr. award U. W.Va., 1975, Pres. award Am. Assn. Pharm. Scis., 1993. Fellow Acad. Pharm. Scis.; mem. Am. Pharm. Assn. (life, Hon. Mem. award 2005), Am. Chem. Soc. (emeritus), Am. Assn. Pharm. Scis. (charter mem., fellow, fellows selection com. 1989, Pres.'s award 1993), N.Y. Acad. Scis., Nat. Soc. Med. Rsch. (coun. 1961-69), Am. Testing Materials, Coun. Biology Editors, AMA (affiliate), Fedn. Internat. Pharm., US Tennis Assn., Mid-Atlantic Tennis Assn. (chmn. rules com., 1991-96), Fla. Tennis Assn., Sarasota County Sr. Men's Tennis Assn. (team capt. 2003-07), Sleepy Hollow Bath and Racquet Club (Falls Church, Va.), Arlington Tennis and Squash Club, 4-Seasons Tennis Club, Fairfax Golden Racquets Club, Venice (Fla.) Golf and Country Club (bd. mem. tennis assn. 1998-05, pres. 2002-05, mem. sports and health com. 2002-05, mem. Disaster Preparedness Comm. 2006-11), Glenridge on Palmer Ranch, 2010- (hurricane & disaster coord., 2010-, players prodr., 2011-, chmn. Tennis Com., 2011-, Health & Fitness Com., 2011-, Glenridge Adv. Com., 2012-), K.C., Sigma Xi, Rho Chi, Lambda Chi Sigma. Roman Catholic. Personal E-mail: edwardgfeldmann@msn.com.

FELIBERTI CINTRON, ROBERTO, territorial supreme court justice; b. San Juan, Apr. 7, 1963; s. Emilio Feliberti Martinez and Hilda M. Brandes Cintron; m. Lizette Torres Santiago, 1994; 1 child, Hazel Elizabeth. BS in Math., Purdue U., West Lafayette, Ind., 1985; JD with honors, U. PR, 1991. Commd. officer US Navy; legal officer Fed. Ct. for Dist. PR; owner, ptnr. litig. dept. Cancio, Nadal, Rivera & Díaz; judge Ct. of Appeals PR, 2009—11; assoc. justice Supreme Ct. of PR, 2011—. Office: Supreme Court of Puerto Rico PO Box 9022392 Ponce de Leon Ave Pda 8 San Juan PR 00902-2392*

FELICE, STEPHEN J. (STEVE FELICE), computer company executive; b. 1958; BBA, U. Iowa; MBA, U. Houston. Various positions Shell Oil Co.; v.p., planning & devel. Bell Atlantic Customer Services; v.p., gen. mgr., sales and ops. Bell Atlantic Bus. Sys. Svcs. Inc., 1991—95; pres., CEO and bd. dirs. DecisionOne Corp., 1996—99; joined Dell, Inc., 1999, various exec. positions, sales and consulting svcs. orgns., v.p., Corp. Bus. Group, Americas, 2002—05, v.p., Asia Pacific Japan, 2005—07, sr. v.p., pres., Asia Pacific, 2007—09, pres., small & medium bus. Round Rock, Tex., 2009, pres., consumer, small & medium bus., 2009—12, pres., chief commercial officer, 2012—. Bd. dirs. US-China Bus. Coun.; bd. mem. Singapore Econ. Devel. Bd. Office: Dell Inc One Dell Way Round Rock TX 78682 Office Phone: 512-338-4400. Office Fax: 512-283-6161. Business E-Mail: stephen_felice@dell.com.

FELICIANO, LORENZO GONZALEZ, public health service officer; Attending physician Montefiore Med. Ctr., Bronx, NY, 1989—91, Bronx Mcpl. Hosp. Ctr. - Jacobi Hosp., NY, 1989—91, Morrisania Neighborhood Family Care Ctr., Bronx, NY, 1991—93, North Ctrl. Bronx Hosp., NY, 1991—93, Sharon Regional Health System, Pa., 1993—96; clin. instr. Western Pscyhiat. Inst., 1993—96; med. dir. specialized treatment unit II First Hosp. Panamericano, Cidra, PR, 1996—97; med. dir. behavioral health system NW Med. Ctr., Franklin Oil City, PR, 1997—2000; attending physician George Jr. Republic Residential Treatment Ctr., Grove City, Pa., 1997—; chief med. officer Danville State Hosp., Pa., 2001—03; med. dir. Mepsi Ctr., Bayamon, PR, 2003—05; sec. PR Dept. Health, San Juan, 2009—. Consultation liaison svc. chief fellow child and adolescent dept. Columbia Presbyn. Hosp., 1992—93; mem. hospitalization and continuum of care com. Am. Acad. of Child and Adolescent Psychiatry, 1996—2002. Mem.: American Acad. Child & Adolescent Psychiatry (mem. hospitalization and continuum of care com. 1996—2002), Pa. Med. Assn. Office: Puerto Rico Department of Health PO Box 70184 San Juan PR 00936-8184 Office Phone: 787-274-7874. Office Fax: 787-274-5739.

FELIZ, NEFTALI ANTONIO, professional baseball player; b. Azua, Dominican Republic, May 2, 1988; Pitcher Tex. Rangers, 2009—. Named American League Rookie of Yr., Baseball Writers Assn. America, 2010; named to American League All-Star Team, Maj. League Baseball, 2010. Achievements include leading the American League in: games finished (59), 2010; setting Major League Baseball's single-season record for most saves by rookie (40), 2010. Office: Texas Rangers 1000 Ballpark Way Arlington TX 76011

FELKER, G(EORGE) STEPHEN, textile company executive; b. Bronxville, NY, Dec. 15, 1951; s. George W. and Lella (Burnett) Felker; m. Christine Klekner, Nov. 30, 1974; children: George Stephen Jr., Emily Tichenor. BA, U. Va., 1974. Pres., CEO Wacharia Bank; v.p., mktg. Walton Monroe Mills, Inc., Monroe, Ga., 1977—79, exec. v.p., 1979—80, pres., CEO, chmn., 1980—; pres., CEO & bd. dirs. Dacotah Mills, Inc., 1984—89; sales rep. Avondale Mills, Inc. (subs. of Avondale Inc.), 1975—77, supr., mfg. Sylacauga, Ala., 1974; pres., CEO Avondale Inc., 1980—2008, chmn., 1992—. Bd. dirs. Signal Thread Co., Inc., Nat. Cotton Coun., Am. Textile Mfrs. Inst., Textile Edn. Found.; pres., CEO, bd. dirs. Dacotah Mills, Inc., Lexington, NC, 1984—89; bd. dirs. Rock-Tenn Co., 2001—. Pres. Walton County Hist. Soc., Monroe, 1980; bd. dirs. Va. Episcopal Sch. Recipient Innovation award, Textile mag., 2002. Mem.: Ga. Textile Mfrs. Assn. (bd. dirs.), Nat. Assn. Mfrs. (bd. dirs. 1982—85), Walton County C. of C. (bd. dirs. 1980—83), Commerce Club Atlanta, Phi Psi. Office: Avondale Inc 506 S Broad St Monroe GA 30655 Office Phone: 770-267-2226. Office Fax: 770-267-5196. Business E-Mail: gfelker@rocktenn.com.

FELLHAUER, DAVID EUGENE, bishop; b. Kansas City, Mo., Aug. 19, 1939; Attended, Pontifical Coll. Josephinum; JCL, St. Paul U., Ottawa, Can., JCD, 1980; PhD, U. Ottawa, 1979. Ordained priest Diocese of Dallas, Tex., 1965, judicial vicar, 1990; former prof. Holy Trinity Sem., Dallas; ordained bishop, 1990; bishop Diocese of Victoria, Tex., 1990—. Bd. govs. Canon Law Soc. Am. Recipient Role of Law award, Canon Law Soc., 1998. Roman Catholic. Office: Diocese of Victoria 1505 E Mesquite Lane PO Box 4070 Victoria TX 77903-4070 Office Fax: 361-573-0828, 361-573-5725.

FELLOWS, HENRY DAVID, JR., lawyer; b. NYC, Dec. 17, 1954; s. Henry D. Sr. and Mary (Stecko) F.; m. Pam Neal Fellows, May 15, 1982; children: Christopher, Suzanne, Thomas. BSBA, Bucknell U., 1975; JD, Georgetown U., 1978. Bar: Ga. 1978, U.S. Dist. Ct. (no. dist.) Ga. 1978, U.S. Ct. Appeals (11th cir.) 1978, U.S. Supreme Ct. 1997. Law clk. to hon. judge Charles A. Moye Jr. U.S. Dist. Ct. (no. dist.) Ga., Atlanta, 1978—80; assoc. Hurt, Richardson, Garner, Todd & Cadenhead, Atlanta, 1981—87, ptnr., 1987—92, Fellows LaBriola, LLP (and predecessor firm), Atlanta, 1993—. Fellow Am. Coll. Trial Lawyers; mem. ABA, Ga. Bar Assn., Atlanta Bar Assn. (chmn., co-chmn. ct. com. 1992-98, 2004-05, 2007—, bd. dirs. litig. sect. 1999-05, chair, 2005-06, CLE com. bd. dirs. 2001-04, CLE chair 2003-04), Lawyers Club of Atlanta. Avocation: golf. Office: Fellows LaBriola LLP Peachtree Ctr # 2300 South 225 Peachtree St NE Atlanta GA 30303-1701 Business E-Mail: hfellows@fellab.com.

FELLOWS, JOHN, delivery service executive; Grad. in Engring., Dalhousie U. With Can. Nat. Railways; v.p., corp. strategy & devel. Can. Post Corp., Ottawa, Canada; chmn., CEO DHL Holdings Inc., Plantation, Fla., 2001—. Office: DHL Holdings Inc 1200 S Pine Island Rd Ste 600 Plantation FL 33324 Office Phone: 954-888-7000. Office Fax: 954-888-7310.

FELMAN, SHOSHANA, literature and language professor; b. Jan. 29, 1942; PhD, U. Genoble, France, 1970. Faculty Yale Univ., 1970—2004; woodruff prof. comparative lit. and French Emory Univ. Author: (books) La "Folie" dans l'oeuvre romanesque de Stendhal, 1971, La Folie et la chose littéraire, 1978, Le Scandale du corps parlant. Don Juan avec Austin, ou la Séduction en deux langues, 1980, What Does a Woman Want? Reading and Sexual Difference, 1993, The Juridical Unconscious: Trials and Traumas in the Twentieth Century, 2002, numerous books, (articles) Madness and Philosophy or Literature's Reason, 1975, Rereading Femininity, 1981, Postal Survival, or the Question of the Navel, 1985, numerous articles. Office: Emory University North Callaway Center N114 Atlanta GA 30322 Office Phone: 404-727-7875. Business E-Mail: sfelman@emory.edu.

FELTMAN, DOUGLAS S., child and adolescent psychiatrist, educator; MD, U. NC, Chapel Hill, 1985. Diplomate Am. Bd. Psychiatry and Neurology, 1990, Am. Bd. Psychiatry and Neurology-child and adolescent psychiatry, 1991. Resident psychiatry NY Hosp./Cornell Univ./Payne Whitney Psychiatric Clinic, 1985—88, fellow child & adolescent psychiatry, 1988—90; asst. prof. psychiatry Univ. Miami Sch. Medicine; hosp. affiliation includes Univ. Miami,Jackson Meml. Hosp. Office: Jackson Memorial Hospital 1611 NW 12th Ave Miami FL 33136-1096 Office Phone: 305-585-1111.

FENN, ORMON WILLIAM, JR., furniture company executive; b. Tyler, Tex., Mar. 13, 1927; s. Ormon William and Madonna (Muphree) Fenn; m. Lucille Adrianne Kelley (dec.); children: Andrea Lee, Miles Linton, Kelly Sue, Michael Thomas; m. Candace C. Wilkinson, 2005. Student, U. Minn., 1945, Okla. U., 1945, Imperial U., Tokyo, 1946; BS in Applied Econs., Yale U., 1949. Asst. dist. mgr. Armsrong Cork Co., Lancaster, Pa., 1949-59, asst. gen. sales mgr., 1959-70; v.p., gen. sales mgr. Thomasville (N.C.) Furniture Industries, Inc., 1970-74, sr. v.p., gen. sales mgr., 1974-77; exec. v.p. sales and mktg. Stanley Furniture Co. Mead Corp., Stanleytown, Va., 1977-78, pres., vice chmn., 1978-79; pres. CEO Stanley Furniture Co., 1979-82; vice chmn. LADD Furniture Co., High Point, NC, 1982-92, dir., 1982-98. Chmn. emeritus N.C. furnishings export coun. N.C. Dept. Commerce, High Point, 1993—; chmn. N.C. Home Furnishing Coun., 1995-97; past chmn. bd. govs. Western Mdse. Mart, San Francisco; past chmn. market adv. bd. High Point So. Furniture Market Center; past dir. N.C. Furniture Export Office; past chmn. Internat. Home Furnishings Mktg. Assn.; past bd. dirs. Furniture Info. Coun.; past bd. dirs./exec. com. Home Furnishing Coun.; bd. dirs. Am. Furniture Mfrs. Hall of Fame; apptd. by Gov. of N.C. to nat. adv. bd. HandMade in Am.; bd. dirs. Vaughn Bassett Funriture Co., Galax, Va. Past adv. bd. Bryan Sch. Bus. and Econs., U. NC, Greensboro; appt. hon. consul gen. Japan, 1999-2004; bd. dirs. High Point Cmty. Found., bd. trustees. 1st lt. US Army, 1944—52, PTO. Recipient The Order of the Long Leaf Pine award (NC) Gov. Hunt (N.C. highest civilian honor), 1995, Am. Furniture Hall of Fame. Mem. String and Splinter Club (Named to Furn Hall of Fame, 2007), High Point Country Club Episcopalian. Avocations: golf, hunting, physical fitness. Home: 2905 Kippenshire Ln High Point NC 27262-4618 Personal E-mail: billfennoo@hotmail.com.

FENNER, SUZAN ELLEN, lawyer; b. Grand Junction, Colo., Dec. 5, 1947; d. Harry J. and Louise (Bain) Shaw; m. Michael Lee Riddle, Apr. 24, 1969 (div. Feb. 1976); m. Peter R. Fenner, Nov. 24, 1978; children: Laura Elizabeth, Adam Kyle. BA, Tex. Tech U., 1969, JD, 1971. Bar: Tex. 1972, U.S. Dist. Ct. (no. dist.) Tex. 1972. Assoc. Smith & Baker, Lubbock, Tex., 1971-72; law clk. to presiding judge US Dist. Ct., Dallas, 1972-73; assoc. Gardere Wynne Sewell LLP, Dallas, 1973-78, ptnr., 1978—2008. Chair retirement com. Gardere Wynne Sewell LLP, 1973—2006, chair employee benefits practice, 1978—2008, mem. ptnrs. bd., 1991—94, chair tax practice, 2001—06, chair diversity com., 2006—08; bd. dirs. Tex. Lawyers Ins. Exch., 1983—, S.W. Benefits Assn. (formerly S.W. Pension Conf.), 1987—92, pres., 1990—91; bd. dir. Dallas Challenge Inc., 2008—. Bd. dirs. East Dallas Devel. Ctr., 1982—91; Lone Star coun. Camp Fire USA, 1995—2001, v.p. outdoor programs, 1996—98, pres.-elect, 1997, pres., 1998—2000; bd. dir. Episcopal Ch. Women of the Diocese of Dallas, 1992—2002, pres., 1996—2000; del. to triennial nat. conv. Episcopal Diocese of Dallas, 1994, 1997, 2000, asst. chancellor, 1994—2004, exec. coun., 1995—2000, standing com., 2001—04; pres. Episcopal Ch. Women for Episcopal Ch. of Ascension, 1992, bd. dir., 1992—94; pres. Province VII Episcopal Ch. Women, bd. dir., 1999—2002; exec. coun. Province VII of the Episcopal Ch., 1999—2002; mem. vestry Episcopal Ch. of the Ascension, 1996—99, 2005—07, sr. warden, 2007; bd. dir. High Adventure Treks for Dads and Daus., 2005—, vice chair. bd., 2009—, chair. bd. trustees, 2009. Recipient Outstanding Vol. award, Camp Fire USA, Lone Star Coun., 2003. Mem. ABA, Tex. Bar Assn. (chmn. bar. jour. com. 1982-88), Dallas Bar Assn. (treas. employee benefits com. 1998, sec. 1999, v.p. 2000, pres. 2001), Dallas Bus. League (pres. 1986). Avocation: sailing. Home: 600 Goodwin Dr Richardson TX 75081-5603 Office: Gardere Wynne Sewell LLP 1601 Elm St Ste 3000 Dallas TX 75201-4761 Office Phone: 214-999-4576. Business E-Mail: sfenner@gardere.com.

FENNO, EDWARD THORNDIKE, lawyer; b. Detroit, May 25, 1966; s. John Brooks and Judith Fenno; m. Rebecca Patton, Aug. 15, 1992; children: Brant A., Eric P. BA, Princeton U., NJ, 1988; JD, U. So. Calif., 1994. Bar: Calif. 1994, SC 2000. Profl. tennis player Internat. Tennis Fedn., London, 1989—90; assoc. Musick, Peeler & Garrett, LA, 1994—98, Bostwick & Hoffman, Santa Monica, Calif., 1998—99, Moore & Van Allen, Charleston, SC, 2000—06; atty., mng. mem. Fenno Law Firm, LLC, Charleston, SC, 2006—. Vice chmn. ThinkTEC, Charleston, 2004—09. Contbr. articles to profl. jours. Mem. steering com. Charleston Metro Sports Coun., 2001—03. Mem.: ABA (mem. forum on comm. law, IP law sect.), SC. Broadcasters Assn. (assoc.), SC. Press Assn. (assoc.). Avocation: tennis. Office: Fenno Law Firm LLC 171 Church St Ste 160 Charleston SC 29401 Office Fax: 843-577-0460.

FENSTERMACHER, STEPHEN D., corporate financial executive; BA in Govt., U. Notre Dame, Ind.; MBA in Fin. & Acctg., U. Pitts., Pa. CEO, CFO On the Border Cafes, Inc., 1991—95; exec. v.p., CFO The Johnny Rockets Group, Inc., 1995—97; mgmt. cons. Kibel, Green, Issa, Inc., 1998; v.p., acctg., contr. Mannatech, Inc., 1998—99, sr. v.p., CFO, 1999—2008, exec. v.p., global CFO, 2008—09, bd. dirs., chief acctg. officer, co-CEO, CFO, 2009—. Office: Mannatech Inc 600 S Royal Ln Ste 200 Coppell TX 75019 Office Phone: 972-471-7400. Office Fax: 972-471-8135.

FENTON, KEVIN ANDREW, epidemiologist, educator; b. Glasgow, Scotland, Dec. 19, 1966; s. Sydney and Carmen F. MBBS with honors, U. West Indies, Kingston, Jamaica, 1990; MSc in Pub. Health Medicine, London Sch. Hygiene & Tropical Med., 1993; diploma in genitourinary medicine, 1994. Lectr. epidemiology UCL Med. Sch., London, 1995-99; cons. epidemiologist PHLS Communicable Disease Surveillance Ctr., London, 1999; sr. lectr. epidemiology and pub. health Royal Free and Univ. Coll. Med. Sch., London, 1999—2004; dir. HIV & Sexually Transmitted Infections Surveillance Dept. Health Protection Agy., England; chief Nat. Syphilis Elimination Effort Centers for Disease Control, Atlanta, 2005, dir. Nat. Ctr. for HIV/AIDS, Viral Hepatitis, Sexually Transmitted Diseases and Tb Prevention, 2005—. Dir. Big Up, London, 1997-2000; 2d Nat. Survey of Sexual Attitudes and Lifestyles, MRC, 1999, Mayisha Study, AVERT, 1997. Author: Exploring Ethnicity and Sexual Health, 1999. Scholar London Sch. Hygiene and Tropical Medicine, 1992; Carreras post-grad. scholar, 1992; recipient medal in ob-gyn. U. West Indies, 1990, Allenbury prize in internal medicine, 1990. Mem. Faculty of Pub. Health Medicine, Brit. Med. Assn. Office: Nat Ctr for HIV STD TB Prevention Corp Square Bldg 8 Corp Square Blvd Rm 6171 Atlanta GA 30329 Office Phone: 404-639-8000. Office Fax: 404-639-8600. E-mail: kfenton@cdc.gov.

FENVES, GREGORY L., engineering professor, dean; PhD, U. Calif. Berkeley. Prof. civil engring. U. Calif. Berkeley, T.Y. and Margaret Lin Prof. Engring., chair Dept. Civil and Environ. Engring., 2002—07; dean Cockrell Sch. Engring., U. Tex., Austin, 2008—, Jack and Beverly Randall dean's chair for excellence in engring., 2008—. Asst. dir. industry programs Pacific Earthquake Engring. Rsch. Ctr. U. of Calif. Berkeley; mem. Ctr. for Information Technol. Rsch. in the Interest of Society. Recipient Walter L. Huber Civil Engring. Rsch. prize, ASCE, 1995. Office: University of Texas at Austin Dean of Engineering 1 University Station C2100 Austin TX 78712-0284 Office Phone: 512-471-1166. Office Fax: 512-475-7072. E-mail: dean@engr.utexas.edu.

FENWICK, JAMES HENRY, editor, writer, columnist; b. South Shields, Eng., Mar. 17, 1937; came to U.S., 1965; s. James Henry and Ellen (Tinmouth) F.; m. Suzanne Helene Hatch, Jan. 27, 1968. BA, Oxford U., Eng., 1960. Freelance lectr., writer, 1960-65; assoc. editor Playboy mag., Chgo., 1965-71; planning and features editor Radio Times, BBC, London, 1971-77, U.S. rep. NYC, 1978-87; sr. editor Modern Maturity mag., Lakewood, Calif., 1987-90, exec. editor, 1990-91, editor, 1991-98; contbg. editor Get Up and Go!, Age Wave Comm., Lakewood, Calif., 1998-99; editor Next Mag., Palm Springs, Calif., 2000—01, Desert Mag., Palm Springs, 2002—04, food columnist, 2004—, The Desert Sun, Calif., 2004—. Author (with Eric Wadlund): Palm Springs Flavors, 2007. Business E-Mail: fenwickfood@aol.com.

FERDINAND, KEITH C., cardiologist; s. Vallery Ferdinand and Inola Copelin; m. Daphne Pajeaud Ferdinand; children: Aminisha, Jua, Kamau, Rashida. MD, Howard U. Coll. Medicine, Washington, 1976. Cert. Am. Soc. Hypertension, 1999. Clin. prof., cardiology divsn. Emory U., Atlanta, 2006—. Cons. La. Bd. Med. Examiners, New Orleans, 1996—. Contbr. articles to profl. med. jours. V.p. Am. Soc. Hypertension, NYC, 2006—. Recipient Walter M. Booker Cmty. Svc. award, Am. Black Cardiologist Soc., 2002. Mem.: Am. Coll. Cardiology, Assn. Black Cardiologists, Inc. (chief sci. officer 2006—), Am. Heart Assn. (Louis B. Russell, Jr., Meml. award 2002). Office: Assn Black Cardiologists Inc 2400 N St NW Washington DC 20037-1153 Office Fax: 404-201-6601. Business E-Mail: kferdinand@abcardio.org. E-mail: kcferdmd@aol.com.

FERENCE-VALENTA, MARY JEAN, osteopath, health facility administrator; b. Middletown, Pa., Nov. 26, 1969; d. Edward W. and Virginia J. Ference; m. Erik D. Valenta, Sept. 9, 1995; children: Joseph Valenta, Jacob Valenta. BS, St. Vincent Coll., 1992; DO, Chgo. Coll. Osteo. Medicine, 1996. Rsch. intern Pitts. Energy Tech. Ctr., 1991; chemistry analyst Allegheny Power Svc. Corp., Greensburg, Pa., 1992; intern St. Vincent Med. Ctr., Toledo, 1996-97; resident in family practice Toledo Hosp., 1997-99, chief resident, 1998-99; family practitioner Ulrich Profl. Group, 1999; pvt. practice, Kent, Ohio, 1999—2012; med. dir. Child Health Svcs. Portage County, Ravenna, Ohio, 2001—08; family practitioner Viewmont Family Practice, Hickory, NC, 2012—13, Garner, NC, 2013—. Recipient Student Coun. Leadership award, 1996; grantee, Chgo. Coll. Osteo. Medicine Alumni Assn., 1993—95; scholar, Pa. Osteo. Med. Assn., 1995. Mem.: AMA, Catawba County Cancer Task Force (advisor 2013), Robinson Meml. Hosp. (family practice sect. chair 2008—12, performance improvement com.), Am. Acad. Family Physicians, Chgo. Coll. Osteo. Medicine Alumni Assn., Sigma Sigma Phi Alumni Assn. (Am. Osteo. Assn. conv. rep. 1994, sec.-treas. 1994—95). Avocations: jogging, reading, crafts, antiques, interior decorating. Office: 801 Poole Dr Garner NC 27529

FERGUSON, BRADLEY A., corporate financial executive; CPA. Mem., audit practice Arthur Andersen LLP; v.p., treas. MindSpring Enterprises, Inc. (merged with EarthLink, Inc.), 2000—02; v.p., comml. fin. EarthLink, Inc. (merged with EarthLink Network, Inc. and MindSpring Enterprises, Inc.), 2002—05, v.p., contr., 2005—09; prin. acctg. officer EarthLink, Inc., 2008—, CFO, 2009—. Office: EarthLink Inc 1375 Peachtree St Atlanta GA 30309 Office Phone: 404-815-0770. Office Fax: 404-892-7616.

FERGUSON, CHRISTOPHER J., astronaut; b. Phila., Pa., Sept. 1, 1961; s. Norman (Stepfather) and Mary Ann Pietras; m. Sandra A. Cabot; 3 children. BS in Mech. Engrng., Drexel U., 1984; MS in Aeronautical Engrng., Naval Postgraduate Sch., 1991; attended Navy Fighter Weapon Sch. (TOPGUN); grad., Naval Postgraduate/Test Pilot Sch., 1992. Temporary assignment Naval Test Pilot Sch., Naval Air Station, Patuxent River, Md.; flight tng. Fla., Tex.; ordered to F-14 replacement tng. squadron Virginia Beach, Va.; joined Red Rippers of VF-11 deploying to the North Atlantic, Mediterranean and Indian Ocean aboard the USS Forrestal (CV-59); assigned to as the project officer for F-14D weapon separation program Ordinance Branch, Strike Aircraft Test Directorate, NAS Patuxent River, 1992—94; instructor Naval Test Pilot Sch., 1994—95; joined Checkmates of VF-211, 1995; served as F-14 Class Deck officer Comdr. Naval Air Force, Atlantic Fleet; astronaut, pilot NASA Johnson Space Ctr., 1998—. Assigned technical duties in the Astronaut Office Spacecraft Sys. Br. involving the Shuttle Main Engine, External Tank, Solid Rocket Boosters & Software; served as spacecraft communicator (CAPCOM) for STS-118, 120, 128 and 129 missions; pilot Space Shuttle Atlantis (STS-115), 2006; lead CAPCOM STS-118 Mission, 2007; comdr. STS-126 Endeavour mission, 2008, STS-135-Atlantis-The Final Space Shuttle Mission, 2011. Recipient Navy Strike/Flight Air medal, Navy Commendation medal (3), Navy Achievement medal, Def. Meritorious Svc. medal. Mem.: Soc. Exptl. Test Pilots. Avocations: golf, woodworking, running, drums. Office: Astronaut Office CB NASA Lyndon B Johnson Space Ctr Houston TX 77058

FERGUSON, JAMES ELLIOT, II, lawyer; b. Asheville, NC, Oct. 10, 1942; s. James Elliott and Nina (Freeman) Ferguson; m. Barbara Turman, Aug. 17, 1966; children: James Elliot III, Taj, Kali. BA, NC Ctrl. U., 1964; LLB, Columbia U. Sch. Law, NYC, 1967. Bar: NC, US Dist. Ct. (no. dist.) NC, US Ct. Appeals (4th and 8th cirs.), US Supreme Ct. Founding ptnr. Ferguson, Stein, Wallas, Adkins Gresham & Sumter, P.A., Charlotte, NC, 1967—, pres., 1984—. Bd. dirs. Legal Services NC, 1983—89, Nat. Employment Law Project, 1984—88; adj. faculty NC Ctrl. U. Law Sch., 1981, 1988, Harvard U. Law Sch., 1986—92; faculty Nat. Inst. Trial Advocacy. Former gen. counsel & mem. nat. exec. com. ACLU; founder, coord., faculty mem. Black Lawyers South Africa Trial Advocacy Program, Capetown, Durban, Johannesburg; bd. dirs. Southerners for Econ. Justice, 1976—78, pres., 1978—88; bd. dirs. Charlotte-Mecklenburg Urban League, 1984—88. Recipient Lawyer of Yr. award, Nat. Conf. Black Lawyers, 1978, Frank Porter Graham award, NC Civil Liberties Union, 1982. Fellow: American Coll. Trial Lawyers; mem.: AAJ, ABA, Nat. Inst. Trial Advocacy (chair exec. com. 1998—2000), NC Acad. Trial Lawyers (bd. dirs. 1984—92, pres. 2001), NC Assn. Black Lawyers (pres. 1974—76, Outstanding Lawyer of Yr. 1977), Nat. Bar Assn., NC State Bar (mem.Disciplinary Hearing Commn. 1981—90), Inner Circle Advocates, Alpha Kappa Mu. Office: Ferguson Stein Chambers Gresham & Sumter PA 741 Kenilworth Ave Ste 300 Charlotte NC 28204-2873 also: Ferguson Stein Chambers Gresham & Sumter PA 312 W Franklin St Chapel Hill NC 27516 Office Phone: 704-375-8461. E-mail: jamesferguson@fergusonstein.com.

FERGUSON, RICHARD S., investment company executive; BBA in Fin., U. Ga. Fin. advisor Morgan Keegan & Co., Inc., Atlanta, 1987, br. mgr. Athens, Ga., 1994, East regional pres., mem. exec. com., 1999, exec. mng. dir., pres. Pvt. Client Group Memphis, 2010—. Office: Morgan Keegan Morgan Keegan Tower 50 N Front St Memphis TN 38103 Office Phone: 901-524-4100. Office Fax: 901-524-4197.

FERGUSON, THOMAS BRUCE, JR., cardiothoracic surgeon; b. St. Louis, Mo., June 22, 1953; MD, Wash. U., St. Louis, 1979. Cert. Am. Bd. Thoracic Surgery, Am. Bd. Surgery. Resident, gen. & thoracic surgery Duke U. med. Ctr., Durham, NC, 1979—88; hosp. appointment Barnes Hosp., St. Louis; assoc. prof. surgery, divsn. cardiothoracic surgery Wash. U.; staff physician East Carolina Heart Inst.; assoc. dir., cardiothoracic and vascular surgery East Carolina U. Contbr. articles to profl. jours. Office: East Carolina Heart Inst Brody Outpatient Ctr 600 Moye Blvd TA 340 Greenville NC 27834 Office Phone: 252-744-5232. Office Fax: 252-744-5233. E-mail: Fergusont@ecu.edu.

FERNANDES, EDWARD F., lawyer; b. Carver, Mass. BA, Dartmouth Coll., 1980; JD, Columbia U., 1983. Bar: Mass., Tex., US Dist. Ct. (all dists. Tex., Mass. and Ariz.), US Ct. Appeals (1st and 5th cirs.). Ptnr. Weil, Gotshal & Manges, LLP, Houston, Solar & Fernandes, LLP; mng. ptnr. Brobeck, Phleger & Harrison, LLP, Austin, Tex., 2000—03; ptnr. litig. and energy Akin, Gump, Strauss, Hauer & Feld, LLP, Austin, 2003—09; ptnr. litig. and intellectual property Hunton & Williams LLP, Houston, Austin, 2009—. Former dir. Houston Bar Assn.; former pres. Houston Referral Svc.; former adj. prof. U. Houston Sch. Law; mem. steering com. State Bar Tex. Minority Counsel Prog. Mem Econ. Devel. Coun. Greater Austin C. of C. Named a Tex. Super Lawyer, Tex. Lawyers, 2004, 2005, 2006; named one of Top 10 Trial Lawyers in Am., Nat. Law Jour., 2004, Top Comml. Litigators in Austin, Austin Bus. Jour., 2004, 50 Most Influential Minority Lawyers in America, Nat. Law Jour., 2008. Office: Hunton & Williams LLP Bank of America Ctr 700 Louisiana St Ste 4200 Houston TX 77002 also: Hunton & Williams LLP 111 Congress Ave Ste 1800 Austin TX 78701 Office Phone: 713-229-5721, 512-542-5010. Office Fax: 713-229-5750, 512-542-5075. Business E-Mail: efernandes@hunton.com.

FERNANDES, GARY JOE, retail executive; b. San Angelo, Tex., Aug. 10, 1943; s. Arthur and Mattie Lee (Williams) F.; m. Sandra Faye Lyday, June 6, 1964; children: Jennifer Logan, Jeremy Tildon, James Caleb. BA in Economics, Baylor U., 1965. Sys. engr. Electronic Data Sys. Corp., 1969—70, project mgr., 1970—71; sr. v.p. Electronic Data Sys. Corp, Plano, Tex., 1971; account mgr. Electronic Data Sys. Corp., Dallas, 1971—72, br. mgr., 1972—74, mktg. rep., 1974—76; dir., industry mktg. Electronic Data Sys. Fed. Corp., Bethesda, Md., 1976—77, v.p., mktg., 1977—78; pres. Electronic Data Sys. Govt. Svcs., Bethesda, Md., 1978—84, Electronic Data Sys. World, 1984—87; vice chmn. Electronic Data Sys. Corp., 1999; chmn. FLF Investments, 1996; founder, pres. Travel Store Holdings, Inc., 1998; chmn., CEO GroceryWorks.com, 2000—01. Bd. dirs. Wiley Pubs., Westcott Communications, Southland. Bd. dirs. East Tex. State U. Found., Baylor U. Sch. Bus., Boys and Girls Clubs Am. and Greater Dallas. Served to 1st lt. U.S. Army, 1966-69. Mem. Armed Forces Communications and Electronics Assn. (bd. dirs. 1982—). Office: Blockbuster Inc Bd Directors 3000 Redbud Blvd McKinney TX 75069-8228 Office Phone: 214-854-3000. Office Fax: 214-854-3677. Business E-Mail: gary.fernandes@blockbuster.com.

FERNANDES, JANE K., academic administrator, sign language professional; b. Worcester, MA, Aug. 21, 1956; d. Richard Paul and Mary Kathleen (Cosgrove) Kelleher; m. James John Fernandes; children: Sean William, Erin Frances. BA comparative lit., Trinity Coll., Hartford, CT, 1978; MA comparative lit., U of Iowa, Iowa City, IA, 1980, PhD comparative lit., 1986. Acting dir. (ASL prog.) Northeastern U., Boston, 1986—87; chmn. (sign comm.) Gallaudet U., Wash., DC, 1987; coord. (interp. tng.) Kapiolani C.C., Honolulu, 1988—90; dir. Statewide Ctr., Dept. of Ed., Honolulu, 1990—95; v.p. Gallaudet U, Wash., DC, 1995—2000, provost, 2000—06; sr. fellow Johnnetta B. Cole Global Diversity and Inclusion Inst., Atlanta, 2007—; provost, vice chancellor academic affairs U. NC, Asheville, 2008—. Edit. rev. bd. Perspectives in Ed. & Deafness, Wash., DC, 1994—97. Chair State Commn. Persons with Disabilities, Honolulu, 1993—95, mem., 1988—95; mem. (bd. of dir.) Goodwill Indust. of Honolulu, Honolulu, 1992—95; joint com. Am. Annals of the Deaf, 2005—. Recipient Alice Cogswell, Gallaudet U, 1993; Alumni fellow, U. Iowa, 2001. Mem.: Bldg. Bridges Asheville (facilatator), MLK Jr. Assn. Asheville and Buncombe County (bd. dirs. 2010—). Office: U NC CP 01410 1 University Heights Asheville NC 28804-3299 Office Phone: 828-251-6470. Business E-Mail: jfernand@unca.edu.

FERNÁNDEZ, FACUNDO M., science educator; Licenciado en Quimica (MSc) in Chemistry, Buenos Aires U., 1996, Doctor en Ciencias Quimicas (PhD) in Analytical Spectrometry, 1999. Postdoctoral rschr. Zare Group, Stanford U., 2000—01, Wysocki Group, U. Ariz., 2002—03; asst. prof. Ga. Inst. Tech. Sch. Chemistry and Biochemistry, 2004—09, assoc. prof., 2009—. Contbr. several articles to peer-reviewed journals. Recipient Soc. Analytical Chemists of Pittsburgh Starter Grant award, 2004, Am. Soc. for Mass Spectrometry Rsch. award, 2005, NSF Career award, 2007; Doctoral Fellowship, Buenos Aires U., 1996, Summer Rsch. Grad. Student Fellowship, Weizmann Inst. Sci., Israel, 1997, Advanced Doctoral Fellowship for PhD candidates, Buenos Aires U., 1998, Postdoctoral Fellowship World Bank-FOMEC Program, Argentina, 2000, NRC (CONICET) Postdoctoral Fellowship, 2000, Postdoctoral Fellowship Antorchas Found., 2000, Blanchard Fellow, 2006. Office: Sch Chemistry & Biochemistry Ga Inst Technology 901 Atlantic Dr NW L1-244 Atlanta GA 30332-0400 Fax: 404-385-6447; Office Fax: 404-385-4432, 404-894-7452. Business E-Mail: facundo.fernandez@chemistry.gatech.edu.

FERNANDEZ, TONY (OCTAVIO ANTONIO CASTRO FERNANDEZ), professional baseball coach, retired professional baseball player; b. San Pedro de Macoris, Dominican Republic, June 30, 1962; m. Clara Fernandez; children: Joel, Jonathan, Abraham, Andres, Jasmine. Shortstop Toronto Blue Jays, 1983—90, 1993, 1998—99, 2001, San Diego Padres, 1991—92, NY Mets, 1993, Cin. Reds, 1994, NY Yankees, 1995, Cleve. Indians, 1997, Seibu Lions (Japanese Pacific League), 2000, Milw. Brewers, 2001; spl. asst. Tex. Rangers, 2012—. Founder Tony Fernandez Found. Recipient Gold Glove award, 1986—89; named to Am. League All-Star Team, 1986—87, 1989, 1999, Nat. League All-Star Team, 1992, Can. Baseball Hall of Fame, 2008. Achievements include member of World Series championship winning Toronto Blue Jays, 1993. Office: Texas Rangers 1000 Ballpark Way Arlington TX 76011*

FERNANDEZ TORRES, DANIEL, bishop; b. Chgo., Apr. 27, 1964; Ordained priest Diocese of Arecibo, PR, 1995; pastor Our Lady of Mount Carmel Parish, Arecibo; ordained bishop, 2007; aux. bishop Archdiocese of San Juan, 2007—. Roman Catholic. Office: Archdiocese of San Juan Calle San Jorge 201 Santurce Apartado 901967 San Juan PR 00902 Office Phone: 787-727-7373. Office Fax: 787-727-7938.

FERNER, DAVID CHARLES, non-profit management and development consultant; b. Rochester, NY, Mar. 14, 1933; s. John Theodore and Dorothy Flora (Seel) F.; m. Ursula Milda Thieme, Sept. 6, 1958, (dec. Nov. 12, 2002). BA, Amherst Coll., 1955; MEd, U. Rochester, 1957; postgrad., Columbia U., 1961. Dir. student activities U. Rochester, NY, 1956-58; asst. to provost Tchrs. Coll. Columbia U., NYC, 1959-60; asst. dir. devel. St. Lawrence U., Canton, N.Y., 1961-62; dir. devel. Sarah Lawrence Coll., Bronxville, N.Y., 1962-66; cons., v.p. Frantzreb & Pray Assocs., Inc., NYC, 1966-72, v.p., sec. Arlington, Va., 1972-75; pres. Frantzreb, Pray, Ferner & Thompson, Inc., Arlington, 1975-77, David C. Ferner & Assocs., Annandale, Va., 1977—80; v.p., dir. devel. Minn. Orchestral Assn., Mpls., 1980-87; mng. ptnr. Currie, Ferner, Scarpetta & DeVries, Mpls., 1987-99, cons., 2000—. Contbr. articles to profl. publs. Bd. dir. Madeline Island Mus. Camp, 1992-98, Philharm. Soc. NW Fla., 2003-08. Amherst Coll. scholar, 1951-55. Mem. Assn. Fundraising Profls. (bd. dirs. Minn. chpt. 1995-97), Nat. Com. Planned Giving, League Am. Orchs. Home: 192 Orchard Pass Ave Unit 511 Ponte Vedra FL 32081 Personal E-mail: dcferner@hotmail.com.

FERNÓS, MANUEL J., academic administrator; JD, Univ. PR Sch. Law; LLM, NYU; diploma of advanced studies, Complutense Univ. Madrid. Prof. Inter-Am. Univ. PR, Fajardo, 1984—, various positions including chancellor Met. campus, dean of studies and dean Sch. Law, then pres., 1999—. Assoc. mem. bd. pers., jud. br. Supreme Ct. PR, 1985—; bd. dirs. Soc. Educators & Scholars, 1996—; pres. bd. dirs Hispanic Ednl. Telecom. Sys. (HETS), 2003—04, chmn., 2004—06, treas., 2008—; mem. evaluation of jud. nomination com. Govt. PR, 2001—08; mem. adminstrv. bd. Internat. Assn. Universities, 2008—; past pres. Assn. Colleges & Pvt. Universities PR. Office: Inter American U Puerto Rico Call Box 70003 Fajardo PR 00738-7003 Office Phone: 787-863-2390. E-mail: mfernos@inter.edu.

FERRAIOLI, BRIAN K., engineering executive; BS in Accounting, Seton Hall U.; MBA, Columbia U. V.p., CFO Foster Wheeler Power Sys., Inc., 1998—2000, Foster Wheeler USA Corp., 2000—02; v.p., controller Foster Wheeler, Ltd., 2002—07; exec. v.p. fin. The Shaw Group Inc., 2007; exec. v.p., CFO Shaw Group, Inc., 2007—. Mem.: Am. Inst. of CPA. Office: The Shaw Group Inc 4171 Essen Lane Baton Rouge LA 70809

FERRANDO, JONATHAN P., lawyer, automotive executive; b. Kalamazoo, 1966; BA in Econs., U. Mich., 1988; JD, Harvard U., 1991. Atty. Skadden, Arps, Slate, Meagher & Flom, LLP, Chgo., 1991—96; sr. v.p., gen. counsel automotive retail group AutoNation, Inc., Fort Lauderdale, Fla., 1996—2000, sr. v.p., gen. counsel, corp. sec., 2000—04, exec. v.p., gen. counsel, corp. sec., 2005—. Office: AutoNation Inc 200 SW 1st Ave Fort Lauderdale FL 33301*

FERRAZ, FRANCISCO MARCONI, neurological surgeon; b. Floresta, Pernambuco, Brazil, Aug. 14, 1951; arrived in U.S., 1976; Student, Colegio Nobrega, Recife-Brazil, 1967—69; MD, Faculdade de Medicine da Universidade Federal de Pernambuco-Brazil, 1975. Diplomate Am. Bd. Neurol. Surgery. Intern Jamaica Hosp., NYC, 1976—77; resident Georgetown U. Med. Ctr. and Affiliated Hosps., Washington, 1977—82; pvt. practice medicine specializing in neurol. surgery Washington, 1982—; faculty clin. instr. Georgetown U. Sch. Medicine, 1982; faculty clin. assoc. prof. George Washington Sch. Medicine, 1994—; asst. prof. neurosurgery U. La., Ky., 2010—12. Cons. in health care fin., internat. health care. Contbr. articles to profl. jours. Fellow: ACS, Internat. Coll. Surgeons; mem.: AMA, Congress of Neurol. Surgery, Am. Assn. Neurol. Surgeons. Office: 611 S Carlin Springs Rd Ste 105 Arlington VA 22204-1061 Business E-Mail: fferraz@cox.net.

FERREE, CHARLES ELLIOT, internist, educator; MD, U. NC, Chapel Hill, 1980. Diplomate American Bd. Internal Medicine, 1983. Intern Univ. Va. Med. Ctr., 1981, resident internal medicine, 1981—83; asst. prof. medicine Univ. NC; hosp. affiliations includes Carolinas Med. Ctr., Pineville. With NCQH Diabetes Physician Recognition Program, NCQA Heart/Stroke Recognition Program, NCQA Physician Practice Connections-Patient Centered Med. Home. Recipient Top Dr., Charlotte Mag., 2007—08, 2010—11, Best Dr. in America, 2008—10. Office: Mecklenburg Medical Group-Pineville Ste 420 10650 Park Rd Charlotte NC 28210 Office Phone: 704-302-8700. Office Fax: 704-302-8701.*

FERREE, PATRICIA ANN, national learning consultant; b. Middletown, NY, Oct. 5, 1947; d. William Harry and Florence Arlene (Sarr) Krenrich; m. Daniel Milton Ferree, Feb. 13, 1972; children: Patricia Ann, Daniel Milton Jr. AS, Ctrl. Fla. C.C., Ocala, 1969; BS in Nursing, Va. Commonwealth U., 1985. Cert. cardiac nurse therapist; cert. case mgr. 2006-. Critical care nurse Fla. Hosp., Orlando, 1969-76, cardiac nurse therapist, 1976-80, head nurse cardiac rehab., 1980-82; nurse adminstrn., rsch. nurse Va. Heart Inst., Richmond, 1982-86; coord. health care cost containment Cir. City Stores, Inc., Richmond, 1986, mgr. health and safety, 1986-89, corp. mgr. workers' compensation and safety, 1989-94, corp. sr. analyst for managed care in risk mgmt. dept., 1994-97; training quality assurance auditor Concentra Health Svcs., 1997—98, nurse case mgr., 1998—2002, case mgmt. specialist, 2003—04; nat. learning cons. Coventry Worker's Comp Svcs., 2004—12; nat. clin. trainer, 2012—. Choir dir. Courthouse Rd. Seventh-Day Adventist Ch., Richmond, 1983-89, min. music, 1989-94; curriculum com. Richmond Acad. Home and Sch. Leader; chmn. cardiovascular task force Am. Heart Assn., 1984-85; youth leader Tampa 1st Seventh-Day Adventist Ch., 1998-, Tampa First Seventh Day Adventist Ch. Elder, 2010-. Recipient svc. plaque cardiology dept. Fla. Hosp., 1982; Peggy Gibson Meml. nursing scholar, 1967, Fla. Bd. Edn. nursing scholar, 1967-69. Mem. NAFE, Am. Assn. Occupational Health Nurses, Am. Soc. Safety Engrs., Soc. Nursing Profls., Am. Assn. for Cardiovascular and Pulmonary Rehab. (founding), Am. Soc. for Tng. & Devel. (Sun Coast Fla. chpt., nat. chpt.), Richmond Met. Soc. for Cardiac Rehab. (founding), West Coast Regional Case Mgmt. Assn., Phi Kappa Phi, Sigma Zeta, Sigma Theta Tao, Rho Iota. Republican. Avocations: music, computer art, bicycling. Office: Coventry Workers Comp Svcs PO Box 30796 Tampa FL 33630-3796 Office Phone: 813-806-2526. Personal E-mail: patferree@yahoo.com.*

FERRELL, LEE, artist; b. Albany, Ga., Sept. 2, 1951; BA, Valdosta State Coll.; postgraduate studies in art, Univ. No. Dak. Served USAF, 1972—76, served security police USAFR, 1977—84. Mem.: Ga. Artists Guild, Guild Natural Sci. Illustrators, Assn. Med. Illustrators, USAF Security Police Assn., USAF Sergeants Assn., Disabled Am. Veterans, Veterans of Fgn. Wars, Am. Legion. Republican. Christian. Office: PO Box 70834 Albany GA 31721-0834

FERRENDELLI, JAMES ANTHONY, neurologist, educator; b. Trinidad, Colo., Dec. 5, 1936; s. Alex and Edna Ferrendelli; children: Elisabeth, Cynthia, Michael AB cum laude in Chemistry, U. Colo., Boulder, 1958; MD, U. Colo., Denver, 1962. Diplomate Am. Bd. Psychiatry and Neurology. Intern U. Ky. Med. Ctr., 1962-63; resident in neurology Cleve. Met. Gen. Hosp., 1965-68; research fellow in neurochemistry Washington U. Sch. Medicine, St. Louis, 1968-70, asst. prof. neurology and pharmacology, 1970-74, assoc. prof., 1974-77, prof., 1977-95, Seay prof. clin. neuropharmacology in neurology, 1977-95; chmn. dept. neurology U. Tex., Houston, 1995—2006, prof., 1995—, Kraft-Eidmann prof., 1995—. Contbr. numerous articles to profl. jours. Served to capt. M.C., U.S. Army, 1963-65 Recipient rsch. career devel. award USPHS, 1971-76, Founders Day award Washington U., 1981, Disting. Tchr. award, 1993, 94, Disting. Prof. of Yr. award, 1993, NIH grantee, 1971—. Fellow Am. Acad. Neurology; mem. Am. Neurol. Assn., Am. Soc. for Pharmacology and Exptl. Therapeutics (Epilepsy award 1981), Am. Epilepsy Soc. (Lennox lectr. 1991, pres. 1995, William G. Lennox award 2002), Assn. Univ. Prof. Neurology (pres. 2002-04). Avocations: fly fishing, numismatics.

Office: U Tex-Houston Med Sch Dept Neurology 6431 Fannin St Ste 7102 Houston TX 77030-1501 Home Phone: 713-660-9753; Office Phone: 713-500-7080. Business E-Mail: james.a.ferrendelli@uth.edu.

FERRER, DAVID, professional tennis player; b. Javea, Spain, Apr. 2, 1982; s. Jaime and Pilar. Profl. tennis player ATP, 2000—. Achievements include winner (singles) Bucharest, 2002, Stuttgart, 2006, Heineken Open, 2007, Catella Swedish Open, 2007, AIG Japan Open, 2007, Valencia, 2008, Ordina Open, 2008, Acapulco, 2010; winner (doubles) Acapulco, 2005, Vina del Mar, 2005; winner 8 career singles titles, 2 career doubles titles, ATP. Avocations: soccer, basketball, reading. Office: c/o ATP Tour 201 ATP Blvd Ponte Vedra Beach FL 32082

FERRER, MIGUEL ANTONIO, brokerage house executive; b. Ithaca, NY, May 18, 1938; s. Miguel and Conchita (Bolivar) F.; m. Suzan Nudelman, Aug. 1962 (div. 1973); children: Miguel Antonio, Ilena Christine; m. Lizette Gratacos, Sept. 4, 1980 (div. 2000); children: Alejandro Miguel, Augusto Miguel BA, Cornell U., 1959, MBA, 1961. Account exec. Merrill Lynch Pierce Fenner Smith, San Juan, P.R., 1961-65; br. mgr. Eastman Dillon Union Securities, San Juan, 1965-71, pres. CEO ptnr., 1971-73; sr. v.p. Blyth Eastman Dillon & Co., Inc., San Juan, 1973-80, PaineWebber Inc., San Juan, 1980—; chmn. UBS Fin. Svcs., Inc. of P.R., Hato Rey, 1983—2009, PaineWebber Latin Am., 1993-98; CEO, chmn. UBS Trust Co. of P.R., 1997—, UBS Fin. Svcs. PR, 2005—09; chmn. UBS Internat. PR, 2009; dir. Comisión Conmemorativa del Cuadragésimo Aniversario del Fallecimiento del Maestro Pablo Casals, 2014, Fundacion Historica del Tribunal Supremo de Puerto Rico, 2014. Bd. dirs. P.R. Investors Tax Free Fund, Alianza para el Desarrollo de Puerto Rico, Comision Pro Sede ALCA; dir. consultive bd. U. P.R., Rio Piedras, 1989-92; mem. governing bd. P.R. Strategy Project. Bd. dirs. PR Aqueducts and Sewer Authority, San Juan, 1986-88, PR Pub. Broadcasting Corp., 1990-92, Rafael Hernández Colon Found., 1993-2000, U. PR Found., 1995, 2001, PR Mus. Arch. San Juan, Mus. Art PR, San Juan, 2007; pres. fund raising ARC, Rio Piedras, 1990-91; bd. dirs., treas. Casa del Libro, San Juan; founding dir. Found. Friends of PR Acad. of Spanish Lang., 1996—; trustee Cornell U., 2001, 09, Hist. Found. Supreme Ct. PR, 2005. Recipient Top Mgmt. award in fin. Sales and Mktg. Execs. Assn., 1980 Mem. Securities Industry Assn. (founding mem., bd. dirs., past pres.), P.R. Fin. Analysts Assn. (founding mem., past pres.), Alianza el Desarrollo PR (founder, bd. dirs.), Com. Pro Sede ALCA (founder, bd. dirs.), Banker's Club Office: UBS Financial Svcs Inc of PR 250 Munoz Rivers Penthouse Fl #250 Hato Rey PR 00918 Home: Condominio Bristol PH-18 1052 Ashford Ave San Juan PR 00907

FERRER, WIFREDO A., federal prosecutor; b. Miami, Fla., 1966; BA in Economics, U. Miami, Coral Gables; JD cum laude, U. Pa. Law Sch., 1990. Clk. Greenberg Traurig LLP, Miami, 1988, Steel Hector & Davis LLP, Miami, 1989, assoc. litig. dept., 1991—94; law clk. to Hon. Stanley Marcus US Dist. Ct. (southern dist.) Fla., 1990—91; White House fellow, spl. asst. to sec. US Dept. Housing & Urban Devel. (HUD), Washington, 1994—95; counsel, dep. chief of staff to Atty. Gen. US Dept. Justice, Washington, 1995—2000, asst. US atty. (southern dist.) Fla., 2000—06, US atty., 2010—; asst. county atty., chief fed. litig. sect. Miami-Dade County Attorney's Office, 2006—10. Office: US Courthouse 99 NE 4th St Miami FL 33132 also: US Courthouse 500 E Broward Blvd Fort Lauderdale FL 33394*

FERRIER, RICHARD BROOKS, architect, educator; b. Ft. Worth, Mar. 29, 1944; s. Samuel Foster and Opal Birtha (Brooks) F.; m. Lynna Gail Elmore Mindlin; 1 child, Sean Brooks. BA, Tex. Tech U., 1968; MA in Art, U. Dallas, Irving, Tex., 1973. With planning dept. City of Lubbock, Tex., 1962-63; with Atcheson, Atkinson and Cartwright: Architects, Lubbock, 1963-65, Engring. Assocs., Lubbock, 1966-68; mem. faculty U. Tex., Arlington, 1968—, prof. architecture, assoc. dean, 1980-95; prin. Richard B. Ferrier, AIA, architect, Arlington, 1982-91, Firm X Richard B. Ferrier, FAIA, architect, Arlington, 1991—. With Ralph Kelman, architects, Dallas, 1969-70; assoc. William S. Austin, Architect, Arlington, 1976-80; with Comm. Cons., Arlington, 1970-82; mem. architecture adv. bd. Dallas County C.C., 1983-88; architecture critic Ft. Worth Star Telegram, 1989; lectr., juror in field. Contbr. articles and revs. to profl. jours.; prin. works includeNat. Compact House Design Competition, 1990 (First Place), EML House, 1991, Nat. Cowboy Hall of Fame Addition, 1992, DMA Tower, 1993, Nara Toto, 1994, Bar K R Ranch, 1994, Compact House III, 1996, New Lighthouse Ch., 1997; exhibited in numerous group shows, 1968—, including Dallas Mus. Art, 1991-99, Arlington Mus. Art, 1992-2002, Tex. Fine Arts Assn., Austin, 1992-98, Archtl. Gallery, Chgo., 1994. Named Alumni of Yr., Tex. Tech U. Coll. Architecture, 1993; recipient numerous awards Am. Soc. Archtl. Illustrators, 1986—, 12 awards Tex. Architect Graphics Competition, 1988—, amateur animated film award Cannes Internat. Film Festival, 1973, Romieniec award Tex. Soc. Archs., 1997. Mem. AIA (elected to Coll. Fellows 1993, recipient 12 Dallas design awards 1991-2005, 50 Dallas graphic awards 1980—, including 17 honor awards). Democrat. Episcopalian. Home: Firm X 1628 Connally Ter Arlington TX 76010-4516 Office: U Tex Sch Arch PO Box 19108 Arlington TX 76019-0001 Office Phone: 817-469-8605. Fax: 817-469-1856. Personal E-mail: firmx@aol.com.

FERRIOLA, JOHN J., manufacturing executive; Mgr. maintenance and engring. Nucor Steel, Jewett, Tex., 1992—95, gen. mgr. Norfolk, Nebr., 1995—98, Crawfordsville, Ind., 1998—2001, Vulcraft, Grapeland, Tex., 1995; v.p. Nucor Corp., Charlotte, NC, 1996—2001, exec. v.p., 2002—07, COO steelmaking ops., 2007—11, pres., COO, 2011—. Office: Nucor Corp 1915 Rexford Rd Charlotte NC 28211 Office Phone: 704-366-7000. Office Fax: 704-362-4208.

FERRO, MICHAEL T., state legislator; b. Miami, Fla., Apr. 19, 1951; m. Roseann Ferro; children: Brett, Christopher, Adam. BA, West Liberty State Coll.; MA, W.Va U. Mem. Dist. 4 W.Va. House of Delegates, 2008—, mem. Constitutional Revision Com., Judiciary Com., Roads and Transp. Com. & Vet. Affairs and Homeland Security Com. Democrat. Roman Catholic. Office: State Capitol Complex Rm 222E, Bldg 1 1900 Kanawha Blvd E Charleston WV 25305 Mailing: 32 Ninth St Mc Mechen WV 26040 Office Phone: 304-340-3111. E-mail: mtferro@mail.wvnet.edu.

FERRY, DANNY, professional sports team executive, retired professional basketball player; b. Hyattsville, Md., Oct. 17, 1966; s. Bob Ferry; m. Tiffany Ferry; children: Hannah, Grace, Sophia, Lucy, Jackson. Grad., Duke U., 1989. Draft pick LA Clippers, 1989; forward Italian League, 1989—90, Cleve. Cavaliers, 1990—2000, gen. mgr., 2005—10; forward San Antonio Spurs, 2000—03, dir. basketball ops., 2003—05, v.p. basketball ops., 2010—12; pres. basketball ops., gen. mgr. Atlanta Hawks, 2012—. Bd. mem. Hathaway Brown Sch., Shaker Heights, Ohio, Playing for Peace. Named to Duke U. Sports Hall of Fame, 2004. Achievements include member of the NBA Finals championship winning San Antonio Spurs, 2003. Office: Atlanta Hawks 101 Marietta St NW Ste 1900 Atlanta GA 30303

FETTER, TREVOR, healthcare industry executive; b. San Diego, Jan. 16, 1960; married; 2 children. BS in Econs., Stanford U., 1982; MBA, Harvard U., 1986. With investment banking divsn. Merrill Lynch Capital Mkts.; sr. v.p. MGM/UA Comm. Co., 1988; exec. v.p., CFO Metro-Goldwyn-Mayer, Inc.; exec. v.p. Tenet Healthcare Corp., Dallas, 1995—96, exec. v.p., CFO, 1996—2000; chmn., CEO Broad Ln., Inc., San Francisco, 2000—02; pres. Tenet Healthcare Corp., Dallas, 2002—03, pres., acting CEO, 2003, pres., CEO, 2003—. Bd. trustees Healthcare Leadership Coun. Chmn. bd. Santa Catalina Island Conservancy; trustee Santa Barbara Zool. Garden. Office: Tenet Healthcare Corp 13737 Noel Rd Dallas TX 75240

FEUERZEIG, HENRY LOUIS, lawyer; b. Chgo., Dec. 12, 1938; s. Samuel Alexander Feuerzeig and Esther Fleeger; m. Penny Zweigenhaft, Apr. 8, 1967; children: Paul Lawrence, Darcy Elizabeth Coty. BS, U. Wis., 1962; JD, George Washington U., 1970. Bar: D.C., V.I., Fla., Md. Reporter various newspapers, Dubuque, Iowa, Chgo., Madison, Wis., Cin. and Washington, 1962-64, 65-67; assoc. Sachs, Greenebaum, Frohlich & Tayler, Washington, 1970—72; asst. atty. gen. V.I. Dept. Law, St. Thomas, 1972-73, chief civil and adminstrv. law divsn., 1973-74, 1st asst. atty. gen., 1974; ptnr. Feuerzeig & Zebedee, St. Thomas, 1974-76; judge Territorial Ct. V.I., St. Thomas, 1977-87; del., chmn. jud. powers and functions com. 4th V.I. Constl. Conv., 1981; ptnr. Dudley, Topper and Feuerzeig LLP, St. Thomas, 1987—. Mem. supervisory bd. V.I. Law Enforcement Planning Commn., 1978—87, Juvenile Justice and Delinquency Prevention, 1988—2010; mem. V.I. Juvenile Code Revision Task Force, 1978—83, V.I. Criminal Code Revision Task Force, 1978—87, Underwriters, Lloyd's US V.I. Rep., 1989—99; atty. In Fact, 1999—. Mem. Montgomery County (Md.) Dem. State Ctrl. Com., 1970-72; mem. V.I. Indsl. Devel. Commn., 1976; bd. dirs. Environ. Studies Program, St. Thomas, 1977-80, United Way, 1986-92; bd. reps. Hebrew Congregation of St. Thomas, 1983-90, 96-2002, co-chair Bicentennial Campaign com., 1993-97; trustee Antilles Sch., St. Thomas, 1983-91; mem. adv. coun. Youth Multi-Svc. Ctr., 1989-94; dir. Cmty. Found. of V.I., 1990-2003, pres., 1993-94, emeritus dir., 2003-. Sigma Delta Chi scholar, 1962; Congressional fellow Am. Polit. Sci. Assn., 1964-65; named Person of Yr. Hebrew Congregation of St. Thomas, 2003, St. Thomas & St. John Chamber of Commerce Cmty. Svc. award, 2004. Fellow American Bar Found.; mem. ABA (lawyers conf. jud. performance and conduct com. 1984—94), D.C. Bar Assn., Fla. Bar Assn., VI Bar Assn. (pres. 1976), American Law Inst. (life, cons. group for principles of family dissolution, 1992-2000, cons. group for restatement of law governing lawyers, 1992-99), American Judicature Soc., Assn. Trial Lawyers Am., Internat. Soc. Barristers, Order of Coif, Rotary, Harmonic Lodge No. 356, Sigma Delta Chi, Phi Delta Phi. Jewish. Office: Dudley Topper and Feuerzeig LLP 1000 Frederiksberg Gade PO Box 756 Charlotte Amalie VI 00804-0756 Office Phone: 340-715-4443. Personal E-mail: feuerzeig.henry@gmail.com. E-mail: hfeuerzeig@dtflaw.com.

FEULNER, EDWIN JOHN, JR., retired think-tank executive; b. Chgo., Aug. 12, 1941; s. Edwin John and Helen J. (Franzen) F.; m. Linda C. Leventhal, Mar. 8, 1969; children: Edwin John III, Emily V. BS, Regis U., Denver, 1963; MBA, U. Pa., Phila., 1964; PhD, U. Edinburgh, Scotland, 1981; LHD (hon.), Nichols Coll., Dudley, Mass., 1981, Thomas More Coll., Manchester, NH, 2005; degree (hon.), Universidad Francisco Marroquin, Guatemala City, 1982; D in Social Scis. (hon.), Hanyang U., Seoul, Korea, 1982; LLD (hon.), Bellevue Coll., Nebr., 1987, Pepperdine U., Malibu, Calif., 2000, St. Norbert Coll., De Pere, Wis., 2002, Gonzaga U., Spokane, Wash., 1992; DLitt (hon.), Grove City Coll., Pa., 1994; D in Pub. Svc. (hon.), Hillsdale Coll., Mich., 2004. Richard Weaver fellow London Sch. Economics, 1965; fellow Ctr. for Strategic & Internat. Studies (CSIS), 1965—66; pub. affairs fellow Hoover Instn., 1966—68; rsch. analyst US House Republican Conf., 1968-69; confidential asst. to Sec. Melvin Laird US Dept. Def., 1969-70; adminstrv. asst. to Rep. Philip M. Crane US House of Representatives, 1970-74; campaign mgr. Crane for Congress Com., 1972; exec. dir. US House Republican Study Com., 1974-77; pres. The Heritage Found., Washington, 1977—2013, chancellor, chmn. Asian Studies Ctr., 2013; chmn. Inst. European Def. & Strategic Studies, 1977-96; counselor to Vice Presdl. candidate Jack Kemp, 1996; chmn. Asian Studies Ctr. Heritage Found., 2013—; founder Heritage Found., 2013—. US del. IMF/World Bank, 1974—76; mem. exec. com. Presdl. Transition Pres.'s Commn. White House Fellows, 1980—81, mem., 1981—83; pub. del. UN 2nd Spl. Session on Disarmament, 1982; chmn. USIA, 1982—91, U.S. adv. com. pub. diplomacy, 1982—94; mem. Carlucci Comm. Fgn. Assistance, 1983; disting. fellow mobilization concepts Devel. Ctr. Nat. Def. U., 1983—89; White House cons. on domestic policy, 1987; mem. US Com. Improving Effectiveness of UN, 1989—93; mem. adv. com. Am. Polit. Channel, 1994—96; vice-chmn. Nat. Com. Econ. Growth and Tax Reform, 1995—96; mem. Congrl. Policy Adv. Bd., 1997—2001, Internat. Fin. Inst. Adv. Com., 1999—2000; disting. vis. prof. Hanyang U., Seoul, 2001—; mem. Gingrich/Mitchell Task Force on UN Reform, 2005—13; mem. nat. adv. bd. Ctr. Edn. and Rsch. in Free Enterprise, Tex. A&M U., 1995—96; adv. bd. pub. diplomacy collaborative Harvard U.'s Kennedy Sch. Govt., 2009—. Author: Congress and the New International Economic Order, 1976, Looking Back, 1981, Conservatives Stalk the House, 1983, The March of Freedom, 1998, Intellectual Pilgrims, 1999, Leadership for America, 2000, Getting America Right, 2006, The American Spirit, 2012; pub. Policy Rev., 1977-01; contbr. articles to profl. jours., newspapers, chpts. to books. Sec. Korea-U.S. Exch. Coun., 2001—04; chmn. Citizens for Am. Edn. Found., 1985—89; mem. coun. advisors Bryce Harlow Found.; trustee Nat. Chamber Found., 1998—2011; mem. exec. coun. Am.'s Future Found., 1998—; trustee Lehrman Inst., 1981—90, Sarah Scaife Found., 1988—, St. James Sch., 1990—98, Sequoia Nat. Bank, 1987—99, Regis U., 1991—2001, 2005—, Internat. Rep. Inst., 1995—2001, Acton Inst., 1995—2002; vice-chmn. bd. Aequus Inst., 1989—, Intercollegiate Studies Inst., 1979—, chmn., 1989—93, 2003—06; vice-chmn. bd. dirs. Roe Found., 1983—; mem. exec. com. Coun. Nat. Policy, 1993—2001; trustee Am. Coun. Germany, NY, 1982—92, Found. Francisco Marroquin, Inst. Rsch. Econs. Taxation, 1980—87; vice chmn., trustee Manhattan Inst. Policy Studies, 1977—86; mem. bd. visitors George Mason U., 1996—2004; mem. Multimedia Supercorridor Internat. Adv. Coun., Malaysia, 2001—05. Decorated Order of Brilliant Star with Grand Cordon Republic of China, Order of Diplomatic Svc. Merit-Gwanghwa medal Republic of Korea, Presdl. Recognition medal; recipient Washington award, Freedom Found., 1979, 1980, American Eagle award, Invest-in-American Nat. Coun., 1983, Disting. Alumni award, Regis U., 1985, Superior Pub. Svc. award, Dept. of Navy, 1987, Presdl. Citizens medal, 1989, Dir.'s Svc. award, USIA, 1992, Thomas Jefferson Servant Leadership award, Coun. Nat. Policy, 1996, Walter Judd Freedom award, Fund for American Studies, 2004, Truman-Reagan medal of Freedom, 2006, Charles Hoeflich Lifetime Achievement award, Intercollegiate Studies Inst., 2009, Bradley prize, 2012; named Free Enterprise Man of Yr., Tex. A&M U., 1985, Man of Yr., Wharton Sch., 1993; named one of The 50 Most Powerful People in DC, GQ mag., 2007, The Seven Most Powerful Conservatives, Forbes Mag., 2009, Most Influential US Conservatives, The Daily Telegraph, 2010. Mem. American Econs. Assn., Internat. Inst. Strategic Studies, U.S. Strategic Inst., Inst. d'Etudes Politques, Phila. Soc. (treas. 1964-79, pres. 1982-83, 2013-), Mont Pelerin Soc. (treas. 1979-96, 2000-, pres. 1996-98, sr. v.p. 1998-2000), Internat. Com. of the G.K. Chesterton Soc. (chmn. 1989-92), Union League (NYC), Met. Club, Reform Club (London), Bohemian Club (San Francisco), Old. Dominion Boat Club (Alexandria, Va.), Knights of Malta, Knights of the Holy Sepulchre, Alpha Kappa Psi. Republican. Roman Catholic. Office: The Heritage Found 214 Massachusetts Ave NE Washington DC 20002-4958 Office Phone: 202-546-4400. Personal E-mail: ed@feulner.us. E-mail: ed.feulner@heritage.org.*

FEUSTEL, ANDREW J., astronaut; m. Indira Devi Bhatnagar. AS, Oakland Cmty. Coll., Michigan; BS in Solid Earth Sciences, Purdue U., MS in Geophysics; PhD in Geological Sciences, Queen's U., Can., 1995. Auto mechanic Internat. Autoworks, Ltd., Farmington Hills, Mich.; comml. and indsl. glazier Mich.; rsch./tchg. asst. earth and atmospheric sciences dept. Purdue U.; grad. rsch./tchg. asst. Queen's Univ., Canada; geophysicist Engring. Seismology Group, Canada; with Exxon Mobil Exploration Co., Houston; mission specialist, astronaut NASA, 2000—. Crew mem. STS-125-Final Space Shuttle mission to the Hubble Space Telescope, 2009; mission specialist STS-134-Final Flight for Endeavour, 2011. Mem.: Am. Geophysical Union, Soc. of Exploration Geophysicists, U.S.A. Water Skiing Assn., BMW Car Club of America, Sigma Phi Epsilon. Avocations: auto restoration, guitar, water and snow skiing. Office: NASA Astronauts Office Lyndon B Johnson Space Center Houston TX 77058

FIBIGER, JOHN ANDREW, life insurance company executive; b. Copenhagen, Apr. 27, 1932; came to U.S., 1934, naturalized, 1953; s. Borge Rottboll and Ruth Elizabeth (Wadmond) F.; m. Barbara Mae Stuart, June 22, 1956; children: Karen Ruth McCarthy, Katherine Louise. BA, U. Minn., 1953, MA, 1954; postgrad., U. Wis. With Lincoln Nat. Life Ins. Co., Ft. Wayne, Ind., 1956-57; with Bankers Life Ins. Co. Nebr., Lincoln, 1959-73, sr. v.p. group, 1972-73; with New Eng. Mut. Life Ins. Co., Boston, 1973-89, vice chmn., pres., chief operating officer, 1981-89; with Transam Life Cos., 1991-94; exec. v.p., CFO, then pres. Transamerica Occidental Life Ins. Co., LA, 1994-95, chmn., 1995-97. Past vice chmn. Actuarial Bd. for Counseling and Discipline; bd. dirs. Fidelity Life Assn., Genworth Fin. Wealth Mgmt., Contra Fund, Genworth GPS II Fund Life trustee, past chmn. Mus. Sci., Boston, 1989-91; past overseer New Eng. Med. Ctr., Boston Symphony Orch.; past bd. dirs. Menninger Found., past v.p.; mem. fin. com., strategic planning com. L.A. Chamber Orch.; past chmn. Menninger Fund; past bd. dirs. U. So. Calif. Sch. Gerontology; bd. dirs., past mem. exec. com. Austin Symphony Orch.; past trustee Calif. Mus. Sci. and Industry; bd. visitors, Menninger Baylor Meth. Found.; past chmn. Assn. Calif Life Insurance Co.; past founding dir. Boston Classical Orch., mem. fin. acctg. standards bd. adv. comm., 1984-88. With chem. corps US Army, 1957—59. Fellow Soc. Actuaries (past bd. dirs.); mem. Nat. Acad. Social Ins. (founding mem.), Am. Acad. Actuaries (past pres.). Personal E-mail: fibij@aol.com.

FICARRA, ANTHONY MICHAEL, finance company executive; b. Jersey City, Sept. 29, 1942; s. Joseph John Sr. and Doris Veronica (Wattendorf) F.; children: Anthony J., Doris A., Kristen M., Jill E. BS in Mgmt., Fla. Internat. U., 1978. Sys. programmer Thiokol Chem. Co., Denville, 1966; sr. cons. Brandon Applied Sys., NYC, 1966-71; regional mgr. Tymshare, Inc., Norcross, Ga., 1971-83; regional v.p., sr. v.p. & gen. mgr. Automatic Data Processing Co., Cherry Hill, NJ, 1983—88; corp. v.p., info. sys., exec. v.p. & CIO BISys Inc., Cherry Hill, 1988—97; CIO Euronet Worldwide, 1998—2000; tech. cons. United Health Group Americhoice, 2000—02; chief info. officer Aurum Tech. (acquired by Fidelity Nat. Info. Svcs., Inc.); exec. v.p., elec. bus. sys. Fidelity National Information Services, Inc., Jacksonville, Fla., 2002—. Office: Fidelity National Information Services Inc 601 Riverside Ave Jacksonville FL 32204 Office Phone: 904-854-5000. Office Fax: 904-357-1105. Business E-Mail: anthony.ficarra@fisglobal.com.

FICHTNER, JASON J., political science professor, former federal agency administrator; b. 1971; BA, U. Mich., Ann Arbor, 1992; M in Pub. Policy, Georgetown U., Washington, DC, 1995; PhD in Pub. Adminstrn. & Policy, Va. Polytechnic Inst. and State U., 2005. Rsch. asst. Ind. Sector, Washington, 1993—94; economist compliance rsch. divsn. US Dept. Treasury, IRS, Washington, 1995—98; sr. consultant office fed. tax svcs. Arthur Andersen LLP, 1998—99; sr. economist Joint Econ. Com., US Congress, Washington, 1999—2007; assoc. commr. for retirement policy US Social Security Adminstrn., Washington, 2007—09, acting dep. commr., 2008—09, chief economist, 2009—10; sr. rsch. fellow George Mason U., Arlington, Va., 2010—. Adj. prof. Georgetown U. Pub. Policy Inst., Washington, 2006—, Va. Tech. U. Ctr. Pub. Adminstrn. & Policy, Alexandria, Va., 2008—, Johns Hopkins U. Paul H. Nitze Sch. Advanced Internat. Studies, Washington, 2011—. Recipient Colin Campbell award. Mem.: Policy Studies Orgn., American Soc. for Pub. Adminstrn., Assn. for Pub. Policy Analysis and Mgmt., Nat. Tax Assn., American Econ. Assn. Office: Mercatus Center George Mason University 3351 N Fairfax Dr Ste 444 Arlington VA 22201-4433 Office Phone: 703-993-4930. Business E-Mail: jfichtne@gmu.edu.

FICHTNER, MARGARIA, journalist; b. Lakeland, Fla., May 4, 1944; d. August Albert and Margaret Louise (Kelly) Fichtner. BA, Fla. So. Coll., 1966. Feature writer, fashion editor Miami Herald, 1968—92, book editor, 1992—2001, book critic, 2001—03, sr. feature writer, 2003—08, asst. features editor, 2008—10, arts editor, 2010—. Recipient First Pl. Criticism award, Am. Assn. Sunday and Feature Editors, 1996, Fla. Soc. Newspaper Editors, 1997, First Pl. Criticism Green Eyeshade award, Soc. Profl. Journalists, 2000, First Pl. Critical Writing Sunshine State award, 2003. Office: The Miami Herald Pub Co One Herald Plz Miami FL 33132-1693 Home Phone: 305-858-6189; Office Phone: 305-376-3630. Business E-Mail: mfichtner@miamiherald.com.

FICKENSCHER, KEVIN MICHAEL, information technology executive, health services administrator; BS, U. ND, 1973, MD, 1978. Diplomate Am. Bd. Med. Mgmt., Am. Bd. Family Practice. Resident Montefiore Hosp. Med. Ctr., Bronx, N.Y., 1978-80, U. N.D., 1980-82; dir. Ctr. Rural Health, U. N.D., Grand Forks, 1980-89; pres., CEO Kalamazoo (Mich.) Ctr. Med. Studies, Mich. State U., 1989-93; sr. v.p., chief med. officer Aurora Health Care, Milw., 1994-97, Cath. Healthcare West, San Francisco, 1997-99; chmn., sr. v.p. WebMD Corp., 1999—; exec. v.p., chief med. officer, internat. healthcare Perot Systems Corp., 2005—, exec. v.p., strategic initiatives, 2009—; strategy, devel., Dell Healthcare Svcs. Dell, Inc., 2009—. Mem. bd. stewardship trustees Cath. Health Initiatives, Denver; mem. bd. dirs. Dadu Sys. Recipient ND Nat. Leadership award, Emerging Health Care Leader award, 1991; Kellog Nat. fellow, 1985-88., Nat. Rural Health Assn. award, 1989, Third Dist. Med. Soc. award, 1978, Dr. E. L. Grinnell Meml. award, 1978, Sch. of Medicine Recognition award, 1976, Spl. award, 1975 Mem. ACP, Am. Acd. Farm Practice, Nat. Rural Health Assn. (dir. 1989, Pres.'s award 1989). Avocations: gourmet cooking, writing. Office: Perot Systems Corp 2300 W Plano Pky Plano TX 75075 Office Phone: 972-577-0000. Business E-Mail: kevin.fickenscher@ps.net. E-mail: drkevin@pacbell.net.

FIEGEL, JACQUE R., bank executive; d. Harold Leveridge; m. Chris Fiegel; children: Nicholas, Natalie, Nathan. BA in Psychology, Okla. City U., 1976. Cert. So. Methodist U. Grad. Sch. Banking, U. Colo. Boulder Grad. Sch. Bank Investments, Exec. Banking Inst. Teller, controller, CFO, COO, exec. v.p. Coppermark Bank, Oklahoma City, 1976—2009, sr. exec. v.p., COO, 2009—. Bd. dir. Coppermark

Bancshares, Bank & Card Services. Active Am. Heart Assn.; pres. Okla. City U. Nat. Alumni Assn. Bd.; bd. mem. Canterbury Choral Soc.; past chmn. Epworth Villa Retirement Ctr. Named Okla. City Panhellenic Woman of Yr., Alpha Phi; named one of 25 Most Powerful Women in Banking, US Banker, 2008, 25 Women to Watch, 2009, 2010; named to Woman of Yr. Cir. of Excellence, The Jour. Record; finalist Woman of Yr.: 50 Making a Difference. Mem.: EWF Internat., Okla. Econ. Club. Office: Coppermark Bank PO Box 25676 Oklahoma City OK 73125

FIEL, ERIC C., career military officer; BS in Mgmt., SUNY, Buffalo, 1980; M in Mgmt., Troy State U., Ala., 1989; M in Strategic Studies, Air War Coll., Maxwell AFB, Ala., 2001. 2d lt. USAF, 1981—83, navigator tng. and electronic warfare officer tng. 323 Flying Tng. Wing Mather AFB, Calif., 1981—82, MC-130E EWO instr. & exec. officer 8th Spl. Ops. Squadron Hurlburt Field, Fla., 1982—84, 1st lt., 1983—85, standardization and evaluation EWO 1st Spl. Ops. Wing Hurlburt Field, 1984—85, capt., 1985—91, exec. officer 1st Spl. Ops. Wing Hurlburt Field, 1985—86, air staff tng. program with the Office of Asst. Sec. of Air Force Acquisition Washington, 1986—87, chief MC-130 E standardization and evaluation 23d Air Force Hurlburt Field, 1987—88, chief electronic combat divsn. 23d Air Force, 1988—89, exec. officer to the vice comdr. 23d Air Force, 1989—90, aide-de-camp to the comdr. Air Force Spl. Ops. Command, 1990—91, maj., 1991—96, chief North Asia air def. divsn. Joint Intelligence Ctr. Pacific Pearl Harbor, Hawaii, 1994—95, chief crisis mgmt. divsn. Joint Intelligence Ctr. Pacific, 1994—95, dir. ops. 18th Test Flight Squadron Hurlburt Field, 1995—97, lt. col., 1996—2001, asst. dir. ops., dir. ops. and comdr. 4th Spl. Ops. Squadron Hurlburt Field, 1997—99, dep. comdr. 16th Ops. Group, 1999—2000, col., 2001—06, comdr. Aviation Tactics Evaluation Group Ft. Bragg, NC, 2001—03, comdr. 58th Spl. Ops. Wing Kirtland AFB, N.Mex., 2003—05, dir. ops. Air Force Spl. Ops. Command Hurlburt Field, 2005, comdr. Air Force Spl. Ops. Forces, 2005—06, brigadier gen., 2006—09, dep. commdg. gen. Joint Spl. Ops. Command Ft. Bragg, NC, 2006—08, dir. ctr. force structure, requirements, resources and strategic assessments US Spl. Ops. Command Hdqs. MacDill AFB, Fla., 2008—09, maj. gen., 2009—10, chief of staff US Spl. Ops. Command Hdqs. MacDill AFB, 2009—10, vice comdr. US Spl. Ops. Command Hdqs. Washington, 2010—11, lt. gen., 2010—, comdr. Air Force Spl. Ops. Command Hurlburt Field, 2011—. Decorated Def. Superior Svc. medal, oak leaf clusters, Legion of Merit, Disting. Flying Cross, Bronze Star medal, three oak leaf clusters, Def. Meritorious Svc. medal, Air medal, Aerial Achievement medal, Air Force Commendation medal, Joint Svc. Achievement medal, Air Force Achievement medal, oak leaf cluster, Combat Readiness medal, oak leaf cluster, Nat. Def. Svc. medal with bronze star, Armed Forces Expeditionary medal, Kosovo Campaign medal, Afghanistan Campaign medal, Iraq Campaign medal, Global War on Terrorism Expeditionary medal, Global War on Terrorism Svc. medal, Armed Forces Svc. medal, Humanitarian Svc. medal, NATO medal. Office: Air Force Special Operations Command 229 Cody Ave Ste 103 Hurlburt Field FL 32544

FIELD, JAMES BERNARD, internist, educator; b. Fort Wayne, Ind., May 28, 1926; s. Abraham and Clara (Ridner) F.; m. Dorothy Spivey, Sept. 25, 1954; children: Carolyn, Nancy, Douglas, Susan. Student, Harvard Coll., 1944, student, 1946—47; MD cum laude, Harvard Med. Sch., 1951. Diplomate: Am. Bd. Internal Medicine. Intern internal medicine Mass. Gen. Hosp., Boston, 1951-52, asst. resident internal medicine, 1952-53, resident internal medicine, 1953-54; practice medicine specializing in endocrinology Pitts., 1962-78, Houston, 1978-89. Med. officer USPHS, Nat. Inst. Arthritis and Metabolic Diseases, Bethesda, Md., 1954, sr. asst. surgeon, 1954-58, sr. investigator, 1958-60, surgeon, 1958-60, sr. surgeon, 1960-61; asst. in medicine diabetic dept. Kings Coll. Hosp., London, 1957-58; med. officer Nat. Inst. Arthritis & Metabolic Disease, Bethesda, Md., 1961-62; head divsn. endocrinology and metabolism U. Pitts. Sch. Medicine, 1962-78, assoc. prof. medicine, 1962-66, prof. medicine, 1966-78, dir. clin. research unit, 1962-78; Rutherford prof. medicine Baylor Coll. Medicine, Houston, 1978-89, head div. endocrinology and metabolism, 1978-87; vis. prof. dept. exptl. medicine Univ. Coll. Med. Sch., London, 1985-86; dir. Diabetes and Endocrinology Rsch. Ctr., Baylor Coll Medicine, 1980-89; med. adv. bd. Nat. Pituitary Agy., 1967-69; research collaborator Brookhaven Nat. Lab., 1972-85; mem. nat. diabetes adv. bd. HEW, 1977-85, chmn., 1982-85; mem. endocrinology study sect. USPHS, 1965-69, chmn., 1968-69, endocrinology and metabolism tng. grant com., 1970-74, gen. clin. rsch. ctr. rev. com., 1976-79; mem. panel clin. scis. com. study nat. needs biomed. and behavioral rsch. pers. Nat Rsch. Coun., 1976-80; mem. VA merit rev. com. on endocrinology and metabolism, 1982-85; lectr. medicine Harvard Med. Sch., 1992-2002; mem. honors com. Harvard Med. Sch., 1993-2001. Editor (assoc. editor): Metabolism, 1959—69; editor: (editor-in-chief), 1969—2010; editor: (contbg.) Clin.Thyroidology, 1988—2000; contbr. numerous research articles on endocrinology to profl. jours. Bd. dirs. Gen. Clin. Research Centers, 1977-79; physician, vols. Medicine Clin., Hilton Head, 2001—. Served with U.S. Army, 1944-45. Decorated Purple Heart, Bronze Star; recipient Van Meter prize award Am. Goiter Assn., 1961, Prize Boylston Soc., 1951. Mem.: Assn. Am. Physicians, Endocrine Soc. (mem. coun. 1972-75, internat. liaison com. 1972-75, mem. pub. affairs com. 1972-75, mem. awards com. 1972-75, chmn. 1974-75, nominating com. 1982-84, chmn. 1984), Am. Diabetes Assn. (dir. 1968-74, vice chmn. com. on rsch. 1972-73, chmn. com. rsch. 1975-77, mem. established investigator rev. bd. 1975-77, Eli Lilly award 1958), Am. Fedn. Clin. Rsch., Am. Clin. and Climatol. Assn., Am. Physiology Soc., Am. Soc. Clin. Investigation Physician, Mass. Med. Soc. (chmn. com. on ret, physicians 1993-2002, Prize 1951, Vol. of Yr. 2001), Harvard Med. Alumni Assn., (treas. 1997-2000), Sea Pines Country Club (Hilton Head), Alpha Omega Alpha. Home: 4 Hadley Ln Hilton Head Island SC 29926-2912

FIELD, LARRY, anesthesiologist, educator; b. Herrin, Ill., Dec. 11, 1975; s. Larry C. and Linda R. Field. AS, John A. Logan CC, Carterville, Ill., 1995; BA, Southern Ill. U., Carbondale, 1997; MD, University Ill., Peoria, 2001. Diplomate Am. Bd. Anesthesiology, 2006, in critical care medicine 2007. Chief, divsn. anesthesiology critical care, assoc. prof. Med. U. SC, Charleston, 2006—. Office: Medical University SC 25 Courtenay Dr Ste 4200 MC 240 Charleston SC 29425 Business E-Mail: field@musc.edu.*

FIELDER, CHARLES ROBERT, retired oil industry executive; b. Lubbock, Tex., Mar. 9, 1943; s. Clarence Daniel and Ola Marie (Sewell) F.; m. Mary Ruth Wills, May 31, 1964; 1 child, Sara Elizabeth. BBA, Tex. Tech. U., 1965, MS in Acctg., 1972. CPA, Tex. Staff acct. Peat, Marwick, Mitchell & Co., Dallas, 1965-66, Arthur Andersen & Co., Dallas, 1968-69; treasury acct. Halliburton Co., Dallas, 1969-71, treasury supr., 1971-72, asst. treas., 1972-78, treas., 1978-89, v.p., treas., 1990-96; ret., 1997. Mem. AICPA, Fin. Execs. Inst., Tex. Soc. CPAs, Phi Eta Sigma, Beta Alpha Psi, Beta Gamma Sigma, Phi Kappa Phi. Republican. Mem. Ch. of Christ. Office: 11700 Preston Rd Ste 660-392 Dallas TX 75230

FIELDER, PRINCE SEMIEN, professional baseball player; b. Ontario, Calif., May 9, 1984; s. Cecil Fielder; m. Chanel Fielder, 2005; children: Jaden Omari, Haven Cole. First baseman Milw. Brewers, 2005—11, Detroit Tigers, 2012—13, Tex. Rangers, Arlington, 2013—. Recipient Hank Aaron award, Maj. League Baseball, 2007, Nat. League Silver Slugger award, 2007, 2011, American League Silver Slugger award, 2012, Milw. Brewers MVP award, 2007, Josh Gibson Legacy award, Negro Leagues Baseball Mus., 2008; named Brewers Top Newcomer, Baseball Writers Assn., 2006, All-Star Game MVP, Maj. League Baseball, 2011; named to Topps All-Star Rookie Team, 2006, Nat. League All-Star Team, Maj. League Baseball, 2007, 2009, 2011, American League All-Star Team, 2012, 2013. Achievements include leading the National League in: home runs (50), 2007; RBI (141), 2009; walks (114), 2010; winning Major League Baseball's All-Star Home Run Derby, 2009, 2012. Avocation: music. Office: Texas Rangers 1000 Ballpark Way Arlington TX 76011*

FIELDING, DAVID, state legislator; Mem. Dist. 88 House Com. for City, County & Local Affairs; dept. mgr. Kroger, Magnolia; mem. House Pub. Transp. Com.; justice, peace Dist. 8 Columbia County; mem. Dist. 5 Ark. House of Representatives, 2011—. Democrat. Methodist. Office: 909 S Vine Magnolia AR 71753 Office Phone: 870-234-6143. Business E-Mail: david.fielding@arkansashouse.org.

FIELDING, JERRY L., state legislator; b. Richville, Ala., May 9, 1947; m. Libby Fielding; children: Amanda Fielding, Adam Fielding. B, Auburn U., Ala.; JD, Thomas Jones Sch. Law. With Avondale Mills, Inc., 1966—74; ptnr. Bell, Lang, Bell & Fielding, 1974—78; city atty. Childersburg, Ala., Sylacauga, Ala.; presiding cir. judge Talladega, Ala., 1978—2004; mem. Dist. 11 Ala. State Senate, 2011—. Bd. dirs. Frontier Bank, Sylacauga; chmn. Coosa Valley Med. Ctr. Mem. Talladega County Bd. Edn.; bd. dirs. Talladega County Easter Seals Coun., Sylacauga City Sch. Found. Mem.: Talladega County Cattlemen Assn. Democrat. Methodist. Office: Alabama State Senate State House Rm 735 11 S Union St Montgomery AL 36130 Office Phone: 334-242-7898.

FIELDING, RAYMOND EDWIN, writer, communications educator; b. Brockton, Mass., Jan. 3, 1931; s. Walter Howard and Irma Lydia (Nelson) F.; m. Carole Louise Behrens, June 27, 1963. BA, UCLA, 1953, MA, 1956; PhD, U. So. Calif., Los Angeles, 1961. Pres. Ray Fielding Prodns., Los Angeles, 1953-57; asst. to assoc. prof. theater arts UCLA, 1957-65; assoc. prof. radio-TV-film U. Iowa, Iowa City, 1965-69; prof. communication Temple U., Phila., 1969-78; prof., dir. sch. of communication U. Houston, 1978-90; dean Sch. Motion Picture TV and Recording Arts Fla. State U., Tallassee, 1990—2003, dean emeritus, 2003—; v.p., gen. mgr. Zoetrope Images, Inc., Los Angeles, 1980-81; pres. Houston Cons., Inc., 1982—95. Cons. Universal Studios, Los Angeles, 1973-74, Transamerica Corp., San Francisco, 1981—, RKO Pictures, Inc., N.Y.C., 1986—; cons., mem. adv. bd. HIT Films, Inc., Houston, 1985—. Author: The Technique of Special Effects Cinematography, 1965, A Technological History of Motion Pictures and Television, 1967 (Grand prize Venice Film Festival Expn. of Books 1968), The American Newsreel, 1972, rev. edit., 2007, The March of Time, 1935-61, 1978; scriptwriter: (film) The Honorable Mountain, 1955, (TV spls.) Eyewitness to Yesterday, 1978, Yesterday's Witness-A Tribute to the American Newsreel, 1979 (numerous awards including 1st prize Columbus Film Festival, Golden plaque Chgo. Internat. Film Festival), (BBC-TV) Newsreels to Nightly News, 1997; contbr. numerous articles to profl. jours., encys. Recipient Frank Luther Mott Found. Journalism Research award, 1973, Eastman Kodak Gold medal Soc. Motion Picture and TV Engrs., 1991. Fellow Soc. Motion Picture and TV Engrs. (v.p. 1978-79); mem. Univ. Film and Video Assn. (pres. 1967-68), Soc. for Cinema Studies (pres. 1972-74), Industry Film Producers Assn. (pres. 1961-62), Internat. Congress Schs. of Cinema and TV (v.p. 1967-70), Acad. Motion Picture Arts & Scis. Office: Fla State U Sch Motion Pictures TV & Recording Arts Tallahassee FL 32306-2350 Office Phone: 850-644-0453. Personal E-mail: rayrfielding@aol.com.

FIELDS, CLEO, state legislator; b. Baton Rouge, Nov. 22, 1962; m. Debra Horton, 1991; children: Cleo Brandon, Christopher Justin. Former mem. Small Bus. Com., Banking Com., Fin. & Urban Affairs Com.; state rep. Dist. 4 La., 1993—96; state senator Dist. 14, 1989—92; founder Young Adults Positive Action; pres. Cleo Fields & Assocs., CEO, Fields Law Firm. Named Outstanding Young Men in America, 1987. Mem.: Student Govt. Assn. (former pres.). Democrat. Baptist. Mailing: PO Box 94183 Baton Rouge LA 70804 Home Phone: 504-357-3977; Office Phone: 225-342-9793.

FIELDS, CONSTANCE, cardiologist; MD, Northwestern U., 1982. Diplomate American Bd. Internal Medicine, 1988, American Bd. Internal Medicine-cardiovasc. disease, 2001. Intern Rush Presbyn./St. Luke's Med. Ctr., Chgo., resident internal medicine, 1983—85, fellow cardiovasc. disease, 1987—89; fellow Tufts Univ. Sch. of Medicine; hosp. affiliations include West Boca Med. Ctr., Delray Med. Ctr. Office: West Boca Medical Center 21644 State Rd 7 Boca Raton FL 33428-1899 Office Phone: 561-483-8335.*

FIELDS, EDDIE, state legislator; b. Monterey, Calif., Jan. 21, 1967; s. Dennis and Jan; m. Christina Guthrie, May 12, 1990; children: Tailor, Jacie, Tristan. B in Agri-Business, Okla. State U. Lic. vocat. agr. tchr. Cattle rancher & agri-businessman; former dir. Osage Co. Cattleman's Assn., past pres.; former mem. bd. dir. Osage Co. Farm Bur.; former dir. Okla. Cattleman's Assn., life mem., American Quarter Horse Assn., Okla. Quality Beef Network; former mem. bd. dir. Wynona Area C of C; mem. Dist. 36 Okla. House of Representatives, 2008—10; mem. Dist. 10 Okla. State Senate, 2010—. Republican. Baptist. Office: PO Box 366 Wynona OK 74084 also: 2300 N Lincoln Blvd Rm 514B Oklahoma City OK 73105 Office Phone: 405-521-5581. Business E-Mail: efields@oksenate.gov.

FIELDS, JAMES PERRY, dermatologist, dermatopathologist, allergist, pharmacologist, pharmacist; b. Sherman, Tex., July 30, 1932; s. John Galloway and Alma (Goff) F.; m. Linda Hensley, May 30, 1958; children: Timothy Austin, Amy Elizabeth. BS, U. Tex., 1953, MS, 1957; MD, U. Tex., Galveston, 1958. Diplomate Am. Bd. Dermatology, Am. Bd. Allergy and Immunology, spl. competence cert. in dermatopathology. Dir. dept. dermatology USPHS, SI, N.Y., 1964-78; assoc. prof. medicine and pathology Vanderbilt U. Sch. of Medicine, Nashville, 1978-88; pvt. practice, Nashville, 1988—; dir. dermatopathology Lab. of the Mid-South, Nashville, 1988—. From instr. to assoc. clin. prof. dermatology and pathology Columbia U., Coll. Physicians and Surgeons, N.Y.C., 1968-88, assoc. attending dermatologist to dermatologist Presbyn. Hosp., NYC; assoc. clin. prof. medicine Vanderbilt U. Sch. Medicine, Nashville, 1988—. Author (with others): Mycobacterial Diseases, 1991, 2d edit., 2000; contbr. articles to profl. jours. Bd. dirs. Am. Leprosy Missions Internat., Greenville, S.C., 1974—2007, Med. Program cons., 07-, bd. dirs. Am. Registry Pathology, Washington, 80-; vol. med. missionary, United Meth. Vols. in Mission, 1984—2004. Capt. USPHS, 1958-79. Recipient citation for meritorious svcs. President's Com. on Employment of Handicapped, 1970, Meritorious Svc. medal USPHS, 1978, Good Samaritan award Nashville Acad. Medicine, 2002. Fellow ACP (Volunteerism and Cmty. Svc. award in Medicine, Tenn. chpt. 2000), Am. Acad. Allergy and Immunology, Am. Acad. Dermatology, Am. Coll. Allergy and Immunology, Am. Soc. Dermatopathology, Am. Soc. for Dermatologic Surgery, N.Y. Acad. Medicine (sec. 1976-77, chmn. sect. on dermatology 1977-78). Home: 411 Lynwood Blvd Nashville TN 37205-3434 Office: 4301 Hillsboro Rd # 222 Nashville TN 37215-3314 Home Phone: 615-298-1625. Personal E-mail: darmpathlab@earthlink.net.

FIELDS, JAN (JANICE LYNN FIELDS), corporate board member, retired food service executive; b. 1955; m. Doug Wilkins; 2 children. Joined as crew mem. McDonald's Corp., Dayton, Ohio, 1978, various positions, 1978—93, dir. ops., southeast divsn., 1993, v.p Pitts. region, 1994—2000, v.p. Great Lakes divsn., 2000, sr. v.p., chief support officer ctrl. divsn., 2000—03, pres. ctrl. divsn., 2003—06; exec. v.p., COO McDonald's USA, LLC, 2006—10, pres., 2010—12. Bd. dirs. Monsanto Co., 2008—; chair adv. bd. Catalyst, Inc. Bd. dirs. United Cerebral Palsy, Ronald McDonald House Charities, Urban League; mem. Chgo. Network. Recipient WON award, Women's Operator Network, 1988, President's award, McDonald's Corp., 1988, Women Operators Network Recognition award, 2001, Women's Leadership award, 2002, Golden Arch Partners award; named one of The 25 Women to Watch, Crain's Chgo. Bus., 2007, The 50 Most Powerful Women in Bus., Fortune mag., 2007—12, The 100 Most Powerful Women, Forbes mag., 2008, 2009, 2011, 2012.

FIELDS, WILLIAM ALBERT, lawyer; b. Parkersburg, W.Va., Mar. 30, 1939; s. Jack Lyons and Grace (Kelley) F.; m. Prudence Brandt Adams, June 26, 1964. BS magna cum laude, Ohio State U., 1961; postgrad., Harvard Law Sch., 1961-64. Bar: Ohio bar 1964. Since practiced in, Marietta; city prosecutor, 1964-65; acting Judge Marietta Mcpl. Ct.; dir. elections Washington County, 1967-74; profl. bass-baritone soloist. Bd. dirs. Bank One, Marietta, N.A.; lectr. on estate planning and probate matters. Mem. editl. bd. Probate Law Jour. of Ohio. Chmn. Washington County Heart Assn., 1965-67; mem. dist. exec. com. Boy Scouts Am., 1967-74; Treas. County Republican Exec. Com., 1966—; trustee YMCA, Salvation Army; pres. bd. trustees Washington State Community Coll., Marietta; exec. com., trustee Coll. Adminstrv. Scis., Ohio State U.; trustee Appalachian Bible Coll., Bradley, W.Va., 1974-77, Marietta Meml. Hosp., also treas.; bd. dirs. Ohio Valley Port Authority. Recipient Wall St. Jour. award, 1961; named Outstanding Young Man of Marietta, 1968, Outstanding Citizen of Marietta, 1992; named to Ohio Valley Sports Hall of Fame, 2001. Fellow Am. Coll. Trust and Estate Counsel; mem. Ohio Bar Assn. (chmn., bd. govs., probate and trust law sect., mem. splty. bd. Ohio Supreme Ct., splty approval bd. trust, probate, and estate planning), Washington County Bar Assn., Marietta Area C. of C. (v.p., trustee), Am. Mensa, Nat. Soc. of Arts and Letters (bd. trustees), Sigma Chi, Beta Gamma Sigma. Clubs: Rotarian (pres. 1970-71), Homestead Golf & Tennis Club (Hot Springs, Va.). Home: PO Box 87 Warm Springs VA 24484

FIELDS-GOLD, ANITA, retired dean; b. Amarillo, Tex., Oct. 29, 1940; d. Dera and Mamie Maureen (Craig) Bates; m. Maurice Gold; 1 child, William Kyle. Grad. nursing, Jefferson Davis Hosp., 1962; BSN, Tex. Christian U., 1966; MSN, Northwestern State U. La., 1974; PhD, Tex. Women's U., 1980. C.E. coord., asst. prof. Northwestern State U., Shreveport; prof., dean McNeese State U., Lake Charles, La.; ret., 2000. Gov.'s appointee, chmn. S.W. La. Hosp. Dist. Commn., 1989—91; vice chair Region 5 Healthcare Reform Consortium. Mem. allocations com. and loaned exec. United Way, 1991—92, Am. Heart Assn.; vol. Am. Cancer Soc., ARC; bd. pres. Artists Civic Theatre and Studio, 2004—; vice chmn. Region 5 Health Care Reform Consortium, 2005; exec. dir. Region 5 Health Care Authority, 2006—, Region 5 Health Care Redesign Collaborative, 2006—07, DHH liason to La SWIX. Recipient Ben Taub award, 1962, Ann Magnussen award, ARC, 1977, Frances Windham award, ACTA, 2005—06. Mem.: ANA (del.), Lake Charles Dist. Nurses Assn. (bd. dirs., Nurse of Yr. award 1972, 1980), La. Nurses Assn. (past pres. and 1st v.p., Spl. Recognition award 1993, Nightingale Hall of Fame award 2002), Phi Kappa Phi, Delta Kappa Gamma, Sigma Theta Tau (Image of Nursing award 1993). Home: 2339 21st St Lake Charles LA 70601-7946 Personal E-mail: amgold1@suddenlink.net.

FIELEKE, NORMAN SIEGFRIED, economist, educator; b. Kankakee, Ill., Aug. 22, 1932; s. Lessly and Catharine M. (Nicholson) F.; m. Carol A. Curtiss, June 16, 1962 (div. Dec. 1985); children: Andrew, Eric, Michael. BA summa cum laude, Amherst Coll., 1954; AM, Harvard U., 1955, PhD, 1969. Economist, budget examiner Office Mgmt. and Budget, Washington, 1959—64; industry economist Office U.S. Trade Rep., Exec. Office Pres., 1964—65; v.p., economist Fed. Res. Bank of Boston, 1967—97. Dir. econ. rsch. U.S. Internat. Trade Commn., Washington, 1980; cons. IMF, Washington, 1993; adj. prof. Boston U., 1975-76, Brandeis U., 1988-90, Duke U., Durham, NC, 1998-2000; lectr. Osher Lifelong Learning Inst. Duke U., 2001-11. Author: The Welfare Effects of Controls over Capital Exports from the United States, 1971, The International Economy under Stress, 1988; contbr. articles to profl. jours. Lt. USAF, 1955-57. Littauer fellow, 1955, NSF fellow Harvard U., 1967. Home: 213 Carolina Meadows Villa Chapel Hill NC 27517-8503

FIESE, RICHARD KELLY, music educator; b. Beloit, Wis., May 13, 1957; s. Richard and H. Joan Fiese; m. Robin Elizabeth Fiese, July 19. BS, U. Wis.; MusM, PhD, U. Miami, Coral Gables, Fla. Dir. bands, dept. chair Cypress Lake HS, Ft. Myers, Fla., 1980—84; dir. bands West Lab. Sch., Coral Gables, 1984—89; assoc. prof. U. Houston, 1989—95, U. Miami, Coral Gables, 1995—2000; prof. Houston Bapt. U., 2000—. Cons. music edn. Models Assessment Musical Performances Ctr. Arts Adminstrn., Tallahassee, 1996—98. Co-author (with N. DeCarbo): Error Detection for Conductors, 2001, 4th edit., 2006; co-author: (with J.D. Boyle and N. Zavac) A Handbook for Preparing Graduate Papers in Music, 2001, 2d edit., 2004; contbr. chapters to books, articles to profl. jours. Mem.: Tex. Assn. Music Schs. (exec. bd.), Tex. Music Educators, Tex. Music Educators Assn. (columnist Southwestern Musician, exec. bd.), Music Educators Nat. Conf. Republican. Baptist. Office: Houston Bapt Univ 7502 Fondren Rd Houston TX 77074-3298 Office Phone: 281-649-3000 3228.

FIGARI, ERNEST EMIL, JR., lawyer, educator; b. Navasota, Tex., Feb. 18, 1939; s. Ernest Emil and Louise (Campbell) F.; children: Alexandra Caroline, Audrey Elizabeth. BS, Tex. A&M U., 1961; LLB, U. Tex., 1964; LLM, So. Meth. U., Dallas, 1970. Bar: Tex. 1964, US Ct. Appeals (5th cir.) 1965, US Dist. Ct. (no. dist.) Tex. 1964, US Supreme Ct. 1967. Law clk. to judge U.S. Dist. Ct. (no. dist.) Tex., Dallas, 1964-65; assoc. Coke & Coke, Dallas, 1965-70, ptnr., 1970-75, Johnson & Swanson, Dallas, 1975-86, Figari & Davenport, Dallas, 1986—. Adj. prof. law So. Meth. U., Dallas, 1974-79, 81-82, U. Tex., 1980. Contbr. articles to profl. jours. Fellow ABA Found., Tex. Bar Found., Dallas Bar Found.; mem. State Bar Tex. Roman Catholic. Office: Figari & Davenport Bank of Am Plz 901 Main St Ste 3400 Dallas TX 75202-3796 Office Phone: 214-939-2001. Business E-Mail: efigari@figdav.com.

FIGUEREO, JUAN R., corporate financial executive; b. Dominican Rep. BBA in Pub. Acctg., Fla. Internat. U., 1981. CPA. With Arthur Andersen & Co., Miami; v.p., CFO, L.Am. PepsiCo, Inc., 1988—97; v.p., CFO, Europe Frito-Lay (subs. PepsiCo), 1997—99, v.p., bus. integration, Europe, 1999—2000, v.p., mng. dir. Dominican Republic, 2000—03; v.p., mergers & acquisitions Wal-Mart Internat. Co.,

2003—07; exec. v.p., CFO Cott Corp., Inc., 2007—09, Newell Rubbermaid Inc., 2009—. Office: Newell Rubbermaid Inc 3 Glenlake Pky Atlanta GA 30328 Office Phone: 770-418-7000. Office Fax: 770-407-3970. Business E-Mail: juan.figuereo@newellco.com.

FIGURES, VIVIAN DAVIS, state legislator; b. Mobile, Ala., Jan. 24, 1957; m. Michael A. Figures (dec. 1996); children: Akil Michael, Shomari Coleman, Jelani Anthony. BS in Mgmt. Sci., New Haven U., Conn. City councilwoman, Mobile; mem. Mobile City Coun.; mem. Dist. 33 Ala. State Senate, Montgomery, 1997—. Chair edn. com., local legislation No. 3 com. Ala. State Senate. Mem. Ala. Dem. Exec. Com., Ala. New South Coalition; bd. dirs. Big Bros., Big Sister Program Met. Mobile YMCA, Mobile Area C. of C.; mem. exec. com., Homeless Coalition of Mobile, Inc. Democrat. Baptist. Avocations: reading, tennis, travel, physical fitness. Office: 104 S Lawrence St Mobile AL 36602 also: Ala State House 11 S Union St Rm 732 Montgomery AL 36130-2103 Office Phone: 251-208-5480, 334-242-7871. Business E-Mail: vivian.figures@al-legislature.gov.

FIJOLEK, RICHARD M., lawyer; b. Oak Park, Ill., May 31, 1958; AB with honors, Stanford U., 1979; JD, Columbia U., 1982. Bar: Ill. 1982, Tex. 1986. Assoc. Katten, Muchin and Zavis, Chgo., 1982-86, Haynes and Boone LLP, Dallas, 1986-89, ptnr., Bus., 1990—. Author: Complying with FIRPTA, 1989. Named one of best lawyers in Dallas, D Magazine, Tex. Super Lawyers, Tex. Monthly, World's Leading Tax Adv., Euromoney Guide, Leading US Tax Lawyers, best lawyers in Tax Law, Chambers Guide. Fellow: Am. Coll. Tax Counsel; mem.: Tex. Bar Assn., ABA (chmn. Real Estate Tax). Office: Haynes and Boone LLP 2323 Victory Ave Dallas TX 75219-7657 Office Phone: 214-651-5570. Office Fax: 214-200-0442. Business E-Mail: rick.fijolek@haynesboone.com.

FILERMAN, GARY LEWIS, healthcare educator; b. Mpls., Nov. 16, 1936; s. Joseph H. and Bonnie (Kobrin) F.; m. Jane Harding, Sept. 15, 1962; children: Amy Beth, Joseph Harding, Suzanne Louise. BA, U. Minn., 1959, M.Health Adminstrn. (Phillips Found. fellow 1959-60), 1961, MA (W.K. Kellogg fellow 1961-64), 1963, PhD (Milbank travel grantee 1964, Orgn. Am. States fellow 1964), 1970. Adminstrv. resident Johns Hopkins Hosp., 1961-62; acting dir. Minn. Hosp. Assn., 1965; pres. Assn. Univ. Programs in Health Adminstrn., Washington, 1965-93; exec. sec. Accrediting Commn. Edn. Health Services Adminstrn., 1968-80; assoc. dir. PEW Health Professions Commn., Washington, 1993-95; dir. David A. Winston Fellowship, 1986—2007, pres., 1998—2003, Altas Health Found., 2011—. Mem. faculty George Washington U., chmn., prof. dept. health mgmt. and policy, 1998-2000, prof. health svc. adminstrn., chmn., prof. health sys., Georgetown U., 2000—09, sr. v.p., Atlas Rsch. LLC, 2009-; guest scholar Brookings Instn., 1962; sr. health advisor Acae. Ednl. Devel., 1998-2000; cons. in field, advisor Joint Com. Internat., 2006-. Author: A Future of Consequence, 1989; editor Jour. Health Adminstrn. Edn., 1982-93; author articles in field.; mem. editl. bds. profl. jours. Mem. nat. health professions adv. coun. HHS, 1983-87, coun. agy for health care policy and rsch., 1990-92; bd. dirs. Am. Refugee Commn., 1982-2004, Fairfax Audubon, 1989-93, Am. Internat. Health Alliance, Companion Care Assn., 2005-; chmn. Planned Parenthood Metro Washington, 1990-91, bd. dirs. 1989-92; bd. dirs. Ctr. for Transformational Leadership, 2000-02; internat. adv. bd. Vols. of Am., 2003—07, bd. dir. 2008-; trustee Citizens Advocacy Ctr., 2006—, McLean Cmty. Found., 2007-, mem. Inst. Medicine Forum Drug Discovery, Devel. & Translation., 2009- Recipient Silver medal Leuven (Belgium) U., 1972, Disting. Contbn. award Assn. U. Programs Health Adminstrn., 1979, Outstanding Achievement award Regents of U. Minn., 1982, Outstanding Achievement award Ohio State U., 1992, Humanitarian award, Am. Refugee Com., 2005; Salzburg Seminar fellow, 2000. Fellow APHA, Am. Acad. Med. Adminstrn. (hon.), hon. alumni, Univ. Chgo.,1992, diplomate Am. Coll. of Health Care Execs., 1990—; mem. Royal Soc. Health, Assn. Am. Med. Colls., Cosmos Club (Washington), Phi Beta Kappa. Home: 1322 Banquo Ct Mc Lean VA 22102-2707 Office Phone: 202-687-8150.

FILES, DOUGLAS SCOTT, aerospace medicine specialist; b. Ithaca, NY, Mar. 15, 1966; s. Donald Howard and Barbara Distin Files. BA in Linguistics, Mich. State U., East Lansing, 1987; MD, Wayne State U., Detroit, 1994; MPH, U. Utah, Salt Lake City, 2003. Diplomate Am. Bd. Preventive Medicine, cert. aerospace medicine Am. Coll. Preventive Medicine. Rsch. asst. Mich. State U., 1984—87; English tutor Luth. Social Svcs., Lansing, Mich., 1987—90; resident in internal medicine Duke U. Med. Ctr., Durham, NC, 1994—97; internal medicine physician Omni Healthcare, Palm Bay, Fla., 1997—99; brigade surgeon 101st Airborne Divsn., Ft. Campbell, Fla., 1999—2002; resident in aerospace medicine Sch. Aerospace Medicine, Brooks City Base, Tex., 2003—05; chief aerospace medicine 47th Med. Group, Laughlin AFB, Tex., 2005—08; commd. USAF, 2002, advanced through grades to lt. col., 2007. Bd. govs. Hugh O'Brian Youth Leadership, Tex., 2005—08. Decorated Meritorious Svc. medal, Army Commendation medal. Mem.: Aerospace Medicine Assn., Alpha Omega Alpha, Phi Kappa Phi, Phi Beta Kappa. Avocations: travel, running, reading. Office: Flight Medicine 355th Med Group 4171 S Alamo Ave Davis Monthan AFB AZ 85707 also: School of Aerospace Medicine Bldg FEEE 2510 Fifth St Wright Patterson OH 45433

FILLEY, WARREN VERNON, allergist; b. Topeka, Kans., Oct. 27, 1950; MD, U. Kans. Sch. Medicine, 1976. Diplomate Am. Bd. Allergy and Immunology, Am. Bd. Internal Medicine. Intern U. Okla., 1976-77, resident in internal medicine, 1977-79; fellow allergy and immunology Mayo Clin., Rochester, Minn., 1979-81; with Presbyn. Hosp., Oklahoma City; clin. prof. medicine U. Okla. Mem. AMA, Am. Acad. Allergy, Asthma and Immunology, Am. Coll. Allergy, Asthma and Immunology, Okla. Med. Assn. Office: Okla Allergy and Asthma Clin 750 NE 13th St Oklahoma City OK 73104-5051 Home Phone: 405-340-3448; Office Phone: 405-235-0040. Business E-Mail: wfilley@oklahomaallergy.com.

FILLINGANE, JOEY E., state legislator; b. Hattiesburg, Miss., Jan. 10, 1973; Mem. Dist. 101 Miss. House of Reps., 2000—07; mem. Dist. 41 Miss. State Senate, 2007—; atty. Mem.: Lamar County C. of C., Nat Rifle Assn. Republican. Baptist. Home: 8 Westbrook Dr Sumrall MS 39482 Home Phone: 601-271-2070; Office Phone: 601-359-3237. Office Fax: 601-359-2879. E-mail: jfillingane@senate.ms.gov.

FILLMORE, ROBERT M., lawyer; b. Wichita, Kans., 1953; BGS, Univ. Kans., 1975, JD, 1977. Bar: Kans. 1977, Tex. 1986, lic.: US Supreme Ct. 1980. Asst. atty. gen., litig. divsn. State of Kans., 1979—80, spl. asst. atty. gen., 1981—85; ptnr., co-head, regulated industries, govtl. rels. team; head, regulated utilities practice area Hunton & Williams LLP, Dallas, 1985—2009, Justice Tex. Fifth Ct. Appeals, 2009—. Adj. faculty, law Univ. Kans, 1981—82; adj. prof. law Southern Meth. U., Dedman Sch. Law, 2008—09, vis. prof. law, 2009—. Mem.: ABA (chmn., spl. com. on restructuring elec. industry 2003—05), State Bar of Tex. (chmn., vice chmn., sec./treas., mem. coun. pub. utility law section 1997—2001, chmn. appellate judges leis. com., jud. sect. 2010—13), Ctr. Am. and Internat. Law (mem. exec. com, chmn., power energy trading and mktg. com. 2002—04). Office Phone: 214-712-3400.

FILPPULA, VALTTERI, professional hockey player; b. Vantaa, Finland, Mar. 20, 1984; Center Jokerit Helsinki, Finland, Detroit Red Wings, 2005—13, Tampa Bay Lightning, 2013—. Mem. Team Finland, Olympic Games, Vancouver, 2010. Achievements include being a member of Stanley Cup Champion Detroit Red Wings, 2008; being a member of bronze medal winning Finnish Hockey Team, Vancouver Olympics, 2010. Office: Tampa Bay Lightning Hockey Club St Pete Times Forum 401 Channelside Dr Tampa FL 33602*

FILSTON, HOWARD CHURCH, retired pediatric surgeon; b. NYC, Dec. 29, 1935; s. Howard Samuel and Marion (Church) F.; m. Nancy Lee Jameson, June 3, 1961 (dec. Nov. 2002); children: Scott Jameson (dec.), Timothy Howard, Megan Lee Johnson; m. Sandra Kay Stoutt, May 7, 2005. AB, Harvard U., 1958; MD, Case Western Res. U., 1962. Diplomate Am. Bd. Med. Examiners. Intern in gen. surgery Univ. Hosps., Cleve., 1962-63, asst. resident in gen. surgery, 1963-64, 66-68, chief resident, 1968-69; asst. chief resident pediatric surgery Children's Hosp. Phila., 1969-70; instr. pediatric surgery U. Pa. Sch. of Medicine, Phila., 1969-71, chief resident pediatric surgery, 1970-71; asst. prof. pediatric surgery Case Western Res. U. Hosp., Cleve., 1971-76; assoc. prof. pediatric surgery and pediatrics Duke U. Med. Ctr., Durham, NC, 1976-82, chief pediatric surgery, 1976-90, prof. pediatric surgery and pediats., 1982—90, prof. pediatric surgery and pediatrics, U. Tenn. Med. Ctr., Knoxville, 1990-2000, chief pediatric surgery, 1990-2000, vice chmn. dept. surgery, 1992-2000; emeritus prof.of pediat. surgery, 2000—. Specialist site visitor, pediatric surgery, Accreditation Coun. Grad. Med. Edn., 1982-90, 95—2000. Author: Surgical Problems in Children, 1982; author: (with others) The Surgical Neonate, 1978, rev. 1985; assoc. editor, Jour. Pediatric Surgery, 1985-2000; mem. editorial bd. Pediatrics, 1990-97; contbr. articles to profl. jours. Bd. dirs. Pediatric Family Ctr. of N.C. (Ronald McDonald House), Durham, 1980-90, Surgeon Gen.'s Workshop on Drunk Driving, chmn. Citizens Adv. Panel, 1988; mem. exec. bd. Met. Drug Commn., Knoxville, 1993-2000, v.p., 1997-2000, chair DUI task force, 1994-99. Served to capt. U.S. Army, 1964-66. Nat. scholar Harvard U., 1954-58. Fellow ACS (gov. 1992-98), Am. Acad. Pediatrics (surg., exec. com. 1984-91, chmn. 1989-90), Am. Pediatric Surg. Assn. (edn. com. 1984-90, sec., bd. govs. 1994-97), Am. Surg. Assn., So. Surg. Assn.; mem. Alpha Omega Alpha. Republican. Presbyterian (Stephen Minister). Avocations: water sports, sailing. Personal E-mail: hcfilstonmd62@att.net.

FIMIAN, KEITH, property inspection company executive; m. Cathy Fimian; 3 children. BBA in Acctg., Coll. William & Mary, Williamsburg, Va. Cert. pub. accountant; with internat. acctg. KPMG; founder, chmn. U.S. Inspect, Va. Nat. bd. dirs. Legatus. Pres. Youth Leadership Found. Office: US Inspect 3650 Concorde Pky Ste 100 Chantilly VA 20151 Office Phone: 703-293-1400.

FINAN , IRIAL, beverage company executive; b. Castlerea, Ireland, 1956; married; 2 children. B in Commerce, Nat. U. of Ireland, Galway. Acctg. positions Coca-Cola Bottlers Ireland, Ltd., 1981—84, fin. dir., 1984—90; mng. dir. Coca-Cola Bottlers Ulster, Ltd., 1991—93; mng. dir. Romania & Bulgaria Coca-Cola Bottlers, 1994; mng. dir. Molino Beverages, 1995—99; CEO Coca-Cola HBC, Greece, 2001—03; exec. v.p., pres., bottling investments and supply chain Coca-Cola Co., 2004—. Bd. dirs. Coca-Cola HBC, 2001—03, 2005—, Coca-Cola Amatil, 2005—09, Coca-Cola FEMSA, S.A.B. de C.V., 2004—, Coca- Cola Enterprises, 2004—, Alltracel Pharmaceuticals, 2003—07, Eircom Group plc, 2004—; mem. supr. bd. CCE AG, Germany. Non-exec. dir. Co-operation Ireland, NUI Galway Found. Fellow: Inst. Chartered Mgmt. Accountants. Mailing: The Coca-Cola Co P O Box 1734 Atlanta GA 30301 Office Phone: 404-676-2121. Business E-Mail: ifinan@na.ko.com.

FINCH, ROBERT DAVID, mechanical engineer, educator, consultant; b. Westcliff, Essex, England, Aug. 18, 1938; came to U.S., 1963; s. David Nichols and Winifred Laura (Davey) F.; m. Sheila Ann Field, Jan 19, 1963; children: Matthew John, Christine Victoria. BSc, Imperial Coll., London U., 1959; MSc, Chelsea Coll., London U., 1960; PhD, Imperial Coll., London U., 1963. Asst. prof. U. Houston, 1965-67, assoc. prof., 1967-72, prof. mech. engring., 1972—98, prof. emeritus, 1998—. Pres. Am. Acoustics Corp., Sugarland, Tex., 1971—. Author: Introduction to Acoustics, 2005; contbr. papers on acoustics to tech. publs. Fellow Acoustical Soc. Am. (Biennial award 1972); mem. ASME, Am. Phys. Soc. Home: 211 Lombardy Dr Sugar Land TX 77478-3420

FINCH, WARREN LUENBERG, JR., library and museum director, archivist; m. Mary Finch; children: Anne, Kathleen, Joseph. BA, U. South Ala., 1983; MA in History, Auburn U., 1989. Archivist Office Presdl. Librs., Washington, Ronald Reagan Presdl. Libr. Project, Calif., George H. W. Bush Presdl. Libr., College Station, Tex., supervisory archivist, dep. dir., dir., 2004—. Office: Bush Presdl Libr and Mus 1000 George Bush Dr W College Station TX 77845 Office Phone: 979-691-4002. Business E-Mail: warren.finch@nara.gov.

FINCHEM, TIM, PGA Tour commissioner, lawyer; BA, U. Richmond, 1969; JD, U. Va., 1973. Dep. advisor to pres.in the econ. affairs office White House, 1978—79; nat. staff dir. Jimmy Carter-Walter Mondale Presdl. Campaign, 1980; pres. Beckel, Finchem, Toricelli and Assocs., Washington, 1980—84; co-founder Nat. Strategies and Mktg. Group, Washington, 1984—87; v.p., bus. affairs PGA Tour, Inc., Ponte Vedra Beach, Fla., 1987—89, dep. commr., COO, 1989—94, commr. Ponte Vedra Beach, Fla., 1994—. Bd. dirs. KBHome, 2005—. Co-founder World Golf Found., First Tee program; developer World Golf Hall of Fame, World Golf Village. Named one of 50 Most Influential People in Sports Bus., Street & Smith's SportsBus. Jour., 2007—09, The Most Influential People in the World of Sports, Bus. Week, 2007, 2008. Office: PGA Tour Inc 100 PGA Tour Blvd Ponte Vedra Beach FL 32082 Office Phone: 904-285-3700. Office Fax: 904-285-7913. Business E-Mail: tfinchem@pgatourhq.com.

FINCHER, CHAD, state legislator; m. Caresse Hughes; 1 child, Anna Catherine. BS in Forestry Ops., Auburn U., Ala. Lic. real estate agent Ala., Miss., registered forester Ala. Owner, realtor Fincher & Associates Realty Services; mem. Dist. 102 Ala. House of Reps., Montgomery, 2006—. Past chmn. Mobile County Young Republicans; mem. Mobile County Rep. Exec. Com., Mobile County GOP, West Mobile Bapt. Ch.; past. bd. mem. Ct. Apptd. Spl. Advocates, Mobile, Ala.; past pres. Tanner Williams Cmty. Club. Mem.: Ala. Forestry Assn., Ala. Treasure Forest Assn., Ala. Farmers Fedn., Mobile Area Assn. Realtors (mem. govtl. affairs com.), Mobile County Landowners Assn., Citronelle Hist. Soc., Semmes Hist. Soc., Tanner Williams Civic and Hist. Soc. (past v.p.). Republican. Baptist. Office: PO Box 981 Semmes AL 36575 also: Ala House of Reps Ala State House 11 S Union St Rm 528-A Montgomery AL 36130 Office Phone: 251-649-9417, 334-242-7778. Business E-Mail: chad.fincher@alhouse.gov.

FINCHER, RUTH MARIE EDLA, medical educator, dean; b. Hartford, Conn., Dec. 16, 1949; d. Wilber Roe and Hannah Camilla (Andersen) Griswold; m. Michael Edward Fincher, June 26, 1977. BA, Colby Coll., 1972; BMS, Dartmouth U., 1974; MD, Emory U., 1976. Diplomate Am. Bd. Internal Medicine. Intern then resident internal medicine Emory Hosps., Atlanta, 1976-79; practicing internist Pub. Health Svc., Ludowici, Ga., 1979-81; pvt. practice internal medicine Hinesville, Ga., 1981-82; staff physician Am. Lake VA Med. Ctr., Tacoma, Wash., 1982-84; asst. prof. medicine Med. Coll. Ga., Augusta, 1984-89, assoc. prof., 1989-94, prof. medicine, 1994—, vice dean acad. affairs, 1994—. Pres. Clerkship Dirs. in Internal Medicine, Washington, 1992—93; com. chair Nat. Bd. Med. Examiners, Phila., 1995—96, bd. dirs., 2005—; co-chair rsch. in med. edn. com. Assn. Am. Med. Colls., Washington, 1995—96, chair group on ednl. affairs, 1996—97. Co-editor: Clinical Medicine 2nd Edit., 1995; contbr. articles to profl. jours. Bd. dirs. Nat. Bd. Med. Examiners at Large, 2005—07, mem. exec. com., 2007—11. Recipient Edithe J. Levit Disting. Svc. award, Nat. Bd. Med. Examiners at Large, 2011. Master: Am. Coll. Physicians (governor Ga. chpt. 2003—07, bd. dirs. ACP Found. 2003—07, exec. comm. bd. of governors 2004, elected to mastership 2008, J. Willis Hurst Tchg. award 1994, Disting. Tchg. award 1996, Jane F. Des Forges Disting. Tchr. award 2011); mem.: Assn. Am. Med. Colls. (Ednl. Affiars Career scholarship So. Group 2006, Merrel Flair award 2006), Alpha Omega Alpha (bd. dirs. 2003—, Robert J. Glaser Disting. Tchg. award 1996, Daniel S. Tostesen award 2003, Inaugural inductee U. Sys. Ga. Hall of Fame 2004). Avocations: woodworking, gardening, running. Office: Med Coll Ga CB 1843 1457 Laney Walker Blvd Augusta GA 30912

FINCHER, STEPHEN LEE, United States Representative from Tennessee; b. Memphis, Feb. 7, 1973; m. Lynn Fincher; children: John Austin, Noah, Sarah. Mng. ptnr. Fincher Farms, Halls, Tenn.; mem. US Congress from 8th Tenn. Dist., Washington, 2011—, US House Agrl. Com., Washington, 2011—, US House Transp. & Infrastructure Com., Washington, 2011—. Past. pres. Alamo Dixie Youth Baseball, Crockett County Dixie Youth Baseball, United Meth. Men; active Archer's Chapel Meth. Ch., Halls. Republican. United Methodist. Office: US House of Representatives 1118 Longworth House Office Bldg Washington DC 20515 Office Phone: 202-225-4714.*

FINCKE, EDWARD MICHAEL (MIKE), astronaut; b. Pitts., Mar. 14, 1967; s. Edward and Alma Fincke; m. Renita Saikia; 3 children. BSc in Aero. & Astronautics, MIT, 1989, BSc in Earth, Atmospheric & Planetary Sci., 1989; MSc in Aero. & Astronautics, Stanford U., 1990; Msc in Physical Sci. (Planetary Geology), U. Houston, 2001. Commd. 2d lt. USAF, 1989, advanced through grades to lt. col., various assignments, 1990—94, lt. col., mem. 39th flight test squadron, flight test engineer Eglin AFB, Fla., 1994—96; flight test liaison USAF, Gifu Test Ctr., Gifu Air Base, Japan, 1996; astronaut NASA, Houston, 1996—. Technical duties in the Astronaut Office Station Ops. Branch serving as an Internat. Space Station Spacecraft Communicator; back-up crewmember for ISS Expeditions 4 and 6; back-up comdr. for ISS Expeditions 13 and 16; comdr. NASA Extreme Environment Mission Ops. (NEEMO 2); NASA Space Station sci. officer and flight engr. ISS Expedition 9, 2004; ISS comdr. ISS Expedition 18, 2009; mission specialist STS-134 Mission-Final Flight of Endeavour, 2011. Decorated three Commendation medals USAF, two Achievement medals, Meritorious Svc. Medal; recipient DSM, NASA, Spaceflight Medal, ISS Leadership award. Mem.: British Interplanetary Soc., Geological Soc. Am. Achievements include technical duties in the Astronaut Office Station Operations Branch serving as an International Space Station Spacecraft Communicator (ISS CAPCOM); a member and flight engineer of the Crew Test Support Team in Russia; and as the ISS crew procedures team lead and flight engineer; currently back-up comdr. ISS Expedition-13. Avocations: hiking, flying, travel, geology, astronomy, reading, learning new languages. Office: Astronaut Office CB NASA Lyndon B Johnson Space Center Houston TX 77058

FINDLEY, DON AARON, manufacturing executive; b. Gadsden, Ala., June 11, 1926; s. Royal Guy and Hattie Elizabeth (Walden) F.; m. Mary Elizabeth Abernathy, Oct. 22, 1947; children: Elizabeth Jane Findley Dever, David Walden. BS, Auburn U., 1950. Acct. Buckeye Cellulose Corp. Augusta, Ga., 1950-51; acct. Tenn. Eastman Co., Kingsport, 1951-59, gen. supr. standard cost and analysis dept., 1959-64, gen. mgmt. staff, 1964-67, asst. comptroller, 1971-73, comptroller, 1975-79, v.p. fin. and adminstrn., 1979-88; mng. dir. Ectona Fibres Ltd., Cumberland, Eng., 1967-71; asst. comptroller Eastman Chem. Products, Eastman Chem. Internat. Ltd., Kingsport, 1971-73, comptroller, 1975-79, v.p. fin. and adminstrn., 1979-88; asst. comptroller Eastman Chem. Internat. Co., Kingsport, 1971-73, comptroller, 1975-79, Holston Def. Corp.; asst. v.p. Ark. Eastman Co., Carolina Eastman Co., Tex. Eastman Co. Dir. 1st Am. Nat. Bank, Kingsport Bd. dirs. Holston Valley Hosp. and Med. Ctr., Kingsport, 1978-90, treas., 1978-83; dir. United Way of Kingsport, 1994-97. Recipient Achievment award Ala. Soc. C.P.A.s, 1950, Outstanding Acctg. Alumnus award Auburn U., 1981 Fellow Inst. Dirs. (U.K.); mem. Nat. Assn. Accts. (pres. East Tenn. chpt. 1963-64), Tenn. Mfrs. and Taxpayers Assn. (bd. dirs. 1978-86), Delta Sigma Pi, Phi Kappa Phi, Beta Alpha Psi, Greater Kingsport C. of C. (bd. dirs. 1975-77) Clubs: Ridgefields Country (Kingsport) (bd. dirs. 1984-86). Republican. Methodist. Avocations: photography, coin collecting/numismatics, gardening, golf. Home: 100 Nether Ln Apt 224 Kingsport TN 37660

FINE, DAVID JEFFREY, hospital administrator, educator; b. Flushing, NY, Oct. 10, 1950; s. Arnold and Phyllis F.; m. Susan Gory, Dec. 29, 1985; children: Jeffrey Jacob, Christopher Lee. BA, Tufts U., 1972; MHA, U. Minn., 1974; PhD (hon.), U. Southern Miss., 2007. Asst. to dir. U. Calif. Hosp. and Clinics, San Francisco, 1974—76, asst. dir., 1976—78; sr. assoc. dir. U. Nebr. Hosp. and Clinic, Omaha, 1978—83; adminstr. W.Va. Univ. Hosp., Morgantown, 1983—84; pres. W.Va. Univ. Hosps., Inc., Morgantown, 1984—87; pres., COO Health Net, Inc., Charleston, 1985—87; vice provost for health affairs, CEO U. Cin. Health Sys., 1987—90; pres. U. Cin. Med. Assocs., 1988—90; vice chancellor Tulane U. Med. Ctr., New Orleans, 1990—95, emeritus vice chancellor, 1995—; prof., chmn. dept. health sys. mgmt. Sch. Pub. Health and Tropical Medicine Tulane U., New Orleans, 1990—99; pres., CEO New Orleans Region Columbia/HCA Healthcare Corp., 1995—96; pres. Columbia Health Edn. and Rsch. Found., 1996—97, S.E. Med. Alliance, 1998—99; CEO U. Ala. Birmingham Health Sys., 1999—2004; pres., CEO St. Luke's Episcopal Health Sys., Houston, 2004—. Prof. med. econ. and pharmacy U. Cin., 1987-90; vice chair Nat. Ctr. Healthcare Leadership, 2001-07; vis. fellow King Fund Coll.; prof. Dept. Health Svcs. Adminstrn. Sch. Health Related Professions, UAB, 1999-2004, Dept. Health Care Org. and Policy Sch. Pub. Health, 2003-04; Regents prof. Dept. Health Sys. Mgmt., Tulane U. Sch. Pub. Health and Trop. Medicine, 1990-99; prof. mgmt. policy and cmty. health, U. Tex. Sch. Pub. Health, 2004-, prof. medicine Baylor Coll. Med., 2005-; sec.-treas., 2009-10, chair elect, 2010, vice chair Commn. Accreditation Healthcare Mgmt. Edn., Accreditation Coun. Grad. Med. Edn.; cons. in field. Mem. editl. bd. Hospital Formulary, 1982-87, Health Adminstrn. Press, 1991-94, Jour. Health Adminstrn. Edn., 1991-2001; contbr. jour. articles, book chpts. and films. Trustee Monongalia Arts Coun., 1984-86, Cin. Chamber Orch., 1987-91; sec.-treas. Internat. Found. for Pharmacy Edn.,

1990-2001 Recipient James A. Hamilton prize, U. Minn., 1974; Am. Coll. Healthcare Exec. award. Fellow Am. Coll. Healthcare Execs. (Robert S. Hudgens Young Adminstr. of Yr. award 1985, mem. com. on awards and testimonials, Regent, 2009-11), Royal Coll. Medicine; mem. Am. Hosp. Assn. (mem. regional policy bd., mem. ho. of dels., mem. governing coun. sect. on met. hosps.), Am. Assn. Med. Coll. (coun. tchg. hosps. administrv. bd, 2005), Assn. U. Programs in Health Adminstrn. (chmn. 2000-02), Coronado Club, Petroleum Club, Omicron Delta Epsilon, Delta Omega. Episcopalian. Office: St Luke's Episcopal Health Sys 6624 Fannin St Ste 1100 Houston TX 77030 Office Phone: 832-355-7661. Business E-Mail: dfine@sleh.com.

FINE, HOWARD ALAN, management consultant; BS, MBA, NYU. Internat. sales mgr. Pfaff, A.G., Germany; regional sales dir. Brit. Transport Hotels, London; dir. internat. mktg. Sonesta Internat. Hotels, NYC; dir. Pacific mktg. Forte Hotels, LA, dir. Atlantic area and Latin Am. mktg. NYC, v.p. sales and mktg., exec. v.p.; pres. Norwegian Am. Cruise Line, NYC; pres., chief exec. officer Costa Cruise Line, Miami, Fla.; chmn., chief exec. officer Tourism Devel. Internat., Miami; internat. mgmt. cons., advisor to corp. bds. and heads of state worldwide. Bd. dirs. Bahamas Devel. Found., Nassau, Traveling Times, L.A.; spkr., presenter Young Pres.'s Orgn, World Pres.'s Orgn. Contbr. articles to profl. jours. Mem. mayors adv. bd. City of Los Angeles; mem. senatorial commn. Rep. Senatorial Inner Circle, Washington, Presdl. task force to Pres. Bush; bd. dirs. Calif. Dept. Agr. Wine Bd., Ptnrs. for Liveable Places, Washington, NYU Ctr. for Study of Foodservice, Fla. Crime Prevention Commn., Boys Town of Italy, Served to capt. USAR Named Hon. Order Ky. Cols.; named Man of Yr. Am. Jaycees, Man of Yr. Internat. Hotel Industry; recipient Disting. Marker of Yr. Sales and Mktg. Mgmt. Mag., Christopher Columbus award Nat. Columbus Day Com., Spirit of Life Humanitarian award City of Hope; numerous hotel and travel industry awards and citations from fgn. govts. Fellow Inst. Cert. Travel Agts.; mem. Young Pres.'s Orgn. (chmn. World Pres.'s Orgn., Hotelier of World Com. (bd. dirs.), Italian C. of C. (bd. dirs.), Brit. C. of C. (bd. dirs.), Norwegian C. of C. (bd. dirs.), South African C. of C. (bd. dirs.), Greater Ft. Lauderdale C. of C. (bd. govs.), NYU Alumni Fedn., Sigma Alpha Mu, NYU Club (N.Y.C.), 110 Tower Club (bd. dirs.), Harbor Beach Club (bd. dirs.). Avocations: boating, travel, gardening, photography, flying. Office: Tourism Devel Internat PO Box 22323 Fort Lauderdale FL 33335-2323 Office Phone: 954-764-3949. E-mail: hafine@webtv.net.

FINE, J(AMES) ALLEN, insurance company executive; b. May 2, 1934; s. Samuel Lee and Ocie (Loflin) F.; m. Marie Nan Morris, Sept. 1, 1957 (dec. Apr. 1989); children: James A(llen) Jr., W. Morris. Student, Pfeiffer Coll., 1957—58; BS, U. N.C., 1961, MBA, 1965. Sr. acct. Haskins & Sells, CPAs, Charlotte, NC, 1961—62, Watson, Penry & Morgan, Asheboro, NC, 1962—64; instr. U. N.C., Chapel Hill, 1964—65; asst. prof. Pfeiffer Coll., Misenheimer, NC, 1956—66; treas., v.p. adminstrn. Nat. Lab. for Higher Edn. (formerly Regional Edn. Lab. Carolinas and Va.), Durham, NC, 1966—72; organizer, CEO, treas., dir. Investors Title Ins. Co., Inc., Chapel Hill, 1972—, pres.; developer Carolina Forest Subdivsn., Chapel Hill, 1970—78, Springhill Forest Subdivsn., Chapel Hill, 1977—80, Stonycreek Subdivsn., 1978—. Lectr. acctg. U. N.C., Chapel Hill, 1967—70. Area officer ann. alumni giving U. NC, Chapel Hill, 1968—69, 1971—73, 1975—; trustee NC Mus. Art, 2003—07; pres. NC Title Ins. Rating Bur., 2005—; mem. Chapel Hill Downtown Partnership, 2004—06. With USN, 1953—57. Recipient Haskins & Sells Found. award for excellence in accounting, 1961, N.C. Assn. CPAs award for most outstanding accounting student, U. N.C., 1961. Mem.: AICPA, CEDAR Bus. Mgrs. (chmn. nat. exec. com. 1971), U. N.C. Nat. Devel. Com., Nat. Assn. Ins. Commrs. (liaison com. 1987—88, 1994—), Am. Land Title Assn. (rsch. com. 1983—2003, membership com. 1984—85, recruitment, retention subcom. 1985, exec. com. underwriters sect. 1986, 2002—11), Am. Acctg. Assn., N.C. Assn. CPAs, Phi Beta Kappa, Beta Gamma Sigma (treas. 1961). Home: 112 Carolina First Chapel Hill NC 27516-9033 Office: 121 N Columbia St Chapel Hill NC 27514-3502 Office Phone: 919-968-2200. Business E-Mail: jafine@invtitle.com.

FINE, RANA ARNOLD, chemical and physical oceanographer; d. Joseph and Etta (Kreisman) Arnold; m. Shalle Stephen Fine, June 20, 1965 (div. 1979); m. James Stewart Mattson, Jan. 5, 1983. BA, NYU, 1965; MA, U. Miami, 1973, PhD, 1975. Systems analyst Svc. Bur. Corp. Subs. IBM, Miami, 1965-69; rsch. assoc. Rosenstiel Sch. U. Miami, 1976-77, rsch. asst. prof., 1977-80, rsch. assoc. prof., 1980-84, assoc. prof., 1984-90, prof. marine and atmospheric chemistry, 1990—, chair divsn. marine and atmospheric chemistry, 1990-94; assoc. program dir. NSF, Washington, 1981-83. Mem. div. polar programs adv. com. NSF, Washington, 1987-90, geophys. study com. NAS, Washington, 1989-92, ocean studies bd., 1992-98, adv. panel Tropical Ocean/Global Atmosphere Program, 1990-93, chair adv. panel major ocean programs, 1996-98; bd. trustees UCAR 2005—12, chair, 2009-11, Inter-Am. Inst. Global Ch. SSC, 2004-09. Contbr. articles to profl. jours. Vol. guide Vizcaya Mus., Miami, 1967-78, adv. panel mem. methane hydrade rev. 2003-04. Grantee NSF, 1977—, NOAA, 1986—, Office of Naval Rsch., 1983-88, NASA, 1990-97. Fellow: AAAS (chair-elect atm and hydrospheric sci. sect. 2001—04), American Meteorol. Soc. (coun. mem. 2001—04), American Geophys. Union (sec. oceanography sect. 1986—88, pres.-elect oceanography sect. 1994—96, pres. 1996—98, chair honors 2010—12, bd. dirs. 2013—); mem.: Oceanography Soc. Avocations: sailing, scuba diving, fishing, tennis, reading. Office: Rosenstiel School of Marine & Atmospheric Science/MAC University of Miami 4600 Rickenbacker Causeway Miami FL 33149-1031 Office Phone: 305-421-4722. Business E-Mail: rfine@rsmas.miami.edu.

FINK, LESTER HAROLD, retired engineering company executive, educator; b. Phila., May 3, 1925; s. Harold D. and Edna B. (Hopkins) F.; m. R. Naomi Veit, Dec. 10, 1955; children: Lois Hope, Carol Anne. BSEE, U. Pa., 1950, MSEE, 1961. Supr. engr. rsch. divsn. Phila. Electric Co., 1950-74; asst. dir. Electric Energy Systems divsn. Dept. Interior, Washington, 1974-75, ERDA, Washington, 1975-77, Dept. Energy, 1977-79; pres. Systems Engring. for Power, Inc., Vienna, Va., 1979-83; chmn. Carlsen & Fink Assocs., Inc., 1983-89; exec. v.p. ECC, Inc., 1989-96, ret.; pvt. cons. Adj. prof. Drexel U., 1961-74, U. Pa., 1973, U. Md., 1979-80; Attwood assoc. Conf. Internationale de Grande Reseaux Electrique. Patentee underground power transmission and automatic generation control; contbg. author: Large Scale Systems, 1982, Power System Analysis and Planning, 1983; contbr. chpt.: Electronics Engring. Handbook, 1982, 1997; editor, contbg. author: Power Systems Restructuring, 1988, Unlocking the Benefits of Restructuring, 1999. With U.S. Army, 1943-46. Recipient Meritorious Svc. award Dept. Energy, 1979 Fellow IEEE (life), Instrument Soc. Am., Sigma Tau, Eta Kappa Nu, Tau Beta Pi. Presbyterian. Home: 250 Pantops Mountain Rd # WCBR-4 Charlottesville VA 22911-8694 Personal E-mail: lfink@ieee.org.

FINKELMAN, DANIEL P., marketing executive; married; 2 children. Grad. with honors, Grinnell Coll.; grad., Harvard U. Exec. v.p. mktg. Cardinal Health; cons. KcKinsey & Co.; v.p., brand and bus. planning Ltd. Brands, Inc., Columbus, Ohio, 1996—98, sr. v.p., brand and bus. planning, 1999; prin. McKinsey & Co.; mng. dir. Mulberry St. Consulting, LLC; sr. v.p., chief mktg. officer, Retail Svcs. Alliance Data Sys. Inc. Office: Alliance Data Systems Inc 7500 Dallas Pky Ste 700 Plano TX 75024 Office Phone: 214-494-3000. Personal E-mail: dan.finkelman@alliancedata.com.

FINKELSTEIN, DAVID RITZ, physicist, educator, consultant; b. NYC, July 19, 1929; s. Isidore and Esther (Rubinstein) F.; m. Helene Cooper, 1948 (div.); children: Daniel, Beth, Eve; m. Shlomit Ritz, 1981; 1 child, Aria. BS, CCNY, 1949; PhD, MIT, 1953. Asst., then assoc. prof. physics Stevens Inst. Tech., 1954-60; assoc. prof. Yeshiva U., then prof., chmn., dean, 1960-79; prof. physics Ga. Inst. Tech., 1979—2003, prof. emeritus, 2004—. Vis. prof. Tougaloo Coll., 1965, Hebrew U. Jerusalem, 1974; lecturer, Science Monks, 2003 Author: Quantum Relativity, 1996; editor Internat. Jour. Theoretical Physics, 2004; mem. editl. bd. Jour. Math. Physics, 1991-93. Co-chmn. Miss. Project Parents Com., 1965. Ford Found. fellow, 1958; NSF grantee, 1954-96. Fellow Lindisfarne Assn.; mem. AAAS, Am. Phys. Soc., Internat. Quantum Structures Assn. (sec. 1990-93). Jewish. Achievements include research in black holes, high energy physics, space-time quanta, topological physics, gravity, quantum logic and set theory, Clifford algebra. Office: Ga Inst Tech Physics Dept Atlanta GA 30332-0430 E-mail: david.finkelstein@physics.gatech.edu.

FINKENBRINK, RALPH T., corporate financial executive; BS in Acctg., Mount St. Mary's U., Emmitsburg. Staff acct. MBI, Inc., 1984—85; mgr., Inventory Control Dress Barn, Inc., 1985—87; joined Nicholas Financial, Inc., 1988, contr., v.p., fin., 1992—97, sr. v.p., CFO, corp. sec., 1997—. Bd. dirs. Nicholas Fin., Inc., 2002—. Office: Nicholas Financial Inc Bldg C 2454 McMullen Booth Rd Clearwater FL 33759 Office Phone: 727-726-0763. Office Fax: 727-726-2140. Business E-Mail: rfinkenbrink@nicfn.com.

FINKLE, JEFFREY ALAN, professional association executive; b. Newark, Ohio, Apr. 22, 1954; s. Richard James and Margery (Orr) F.; m. Diane Elizabeth Letchford, Aug. 20, 1983 (div. July 1989); m. Vanessa Tracy Brown, Feb. 27, 2010. BSc cum laude, Ohio U., 1976; postgrad., Ohio State U., 1978-80. Legis. dir. Ohio Rep. Party, Columbus, 1976-78; legis. liason Ohio Dept. Mental Health, Columbus, 1978-80; mktg. dir. Systems 80, Bethesda, Md., 1980-81; exec. asst. HUD, Washington, 1981-83, dep. asst. sec., 1983-86; pres., CEO Coun. for Urban Econ. Devel., Washington, 1986—2001; pres, CEO Internat. Econ. Devel. Coun., 2001; CEO Assn. Def. Cmty., 1996—. Mem. adv. com., Ohio U. Inst. for Local Govt. Adminstrn. and Rural Devel., 1986—. Bd. dirs., pres. Bollinger Found., 1989—, Arlington County Va. Econ. Devel. Corp., 1999—2008, Alexandria Econ. Devel. Partnership, 2008-09, D.C. Mktg. Ctr., 1998-2000. Recipient Flax Trust award, Belfast Northern Ireland, 2009, Golden Bear award, Calif. Assn. Local Economic Devel. Sacramento, Calif., 2010, Merit medal, Ohio U. Alumni Assn., 2010. Mem. Housing Rehab. Assn. (bd. dirs. 1986-90), Nat. Assn. Ind. Living Ctrs. (nat. adv. bd. 1987-89), Sr. Living Choices (bd. dirs. 1991-98), Ohio U. Alumni Assn. (past pres. Washington chpt., past bd. dirs. nat. assn.). Republican. Roman Catholic. Avocations: golf, genealogy. Office: Internat Econ Devel Coun 734 15th St NW Ste 900 Washington DC 20005

FINKLER, NEIL J., gynecologic oncologist; Grad., Colgate U., NY; MD, Mt. Sinai Sch. Medicine, NY. Diplomate Am. Bd. Ob-Gyn. Resident ob-gyn. dept. Brigham and Women's Hosp. Harvard Univ., fellow gynecologic oncology Brigham and Women's Hosp., asst. prof. divsn. gynecologic oncology Brigham and Women's Hosp.; dir. gynecologic oncology Boston Univ., Univ. Hosp., Boston City Hosp.; dir. Residency Tng. Program in Ob-Gyn. Mich. State Residents, Orlando Regional Med. Ctr. Residents; founder Gynecologic Oncology program Fla. Hosp. Gynecologic Oncology (former Fla. Hosp. Cancer Inst.), 1992, dir. Gynecologic Oncology Program, dir. Gynecologic Oncology fellowship Tng. Program, prin. investigator clin. trials Gynecologic Oncology Group, co-dir.; tng. Da Vinci Robotic System, 2006; actively involved with Fla. State Univ.; prof. ob-gyn. dept. Univ. Ctrl. Fla., admissions com. mem., mentor Focused Individualized Rsch. Experience; console surgeon Da Vinci Surg. System. Co-author: various publs. Recipient cert. of Off-Tng., da Vinci Surg. System, cert., 2006. Mem.: ACOG, Fla. Soc. of Clin. Oncology, Soc. of Gynecologic Oncology, Am. Assn. of Clin. Oncology. Office: Florida Hospital 601 E Rollins St Orlando FL 32803-1489 Office Phone: 407-200-2422.*

FINLEY, GEORGE ALVIN, III, wholesale and oil industry executive; b. Aurora, Ill., Apr. 25, 1938; s. George Alvin, II, and Sally Ann (Lord) F.; m. Sue Sellors, June 20, 1962 (dec. 1995); m. Phyllis Ann Finley; children: Valerie, George Alvin IV (dec. 2005). BBA, So. Meth. U., 1962; postgrad. Coll. Grad. Program, Ford Motor Co., 1963. Rep. Europe Finco Internat.; trainee Ford Motor Co., Dearborn, Mich., 1962-63, Motor Cars, Inc.; v.p. mktg. Internat. Cars & Motor Ltd., Oakland, Calif., 1963-64, lease mgr. Sequoia Lincoln, 1965; regional mgr. Behlen Mfg. Co., Dallas, 1965-67; pres., CEO CC Distbrs., Inc., Corpus Christi, Tex., 1967—. Guest instr. Sch. Bus., So. Meth. U., pres., 1986-91, Nueces River Authority, 1975-2001; bd. dirs. Contract Svcs. Assn. Am. Sec. Bd. Washington, MD Anderson Hosp. U. Tex., Christus-Spohn Health Sys., exec. com., mem. McDonald Obs., U. Tex., exec. com.; mem. Del Mar Coll. Found. Mem. pres.'s coun. Tex. A&M U., Corpus Christi; bd. dirs. Coastal Bend Alcohol and Drug Rehab. Ctr., 1973—97, 2005—12. Mem. Tex. Wholesale Hardware Assn. (pres. 1991-92), Nat. Assn. Wholesalers, Am. Supply Assn., Wholesale Distbrs. Assn. (bd. dirs. 1994—), Impact Industries Inc. (chmn. bd. Sandwich, Ill. 1986-93), N.Am. Bldg. Material Distbn. Assn., Rotary Internat., State Bar of Tex. (grievance com. 1995-2001), Phi Delta Theta. Democrat. Episcopalian. Achievements include assisted in design, engineering, production, and marketing of the Apollo automobile. Home: 3360 Ocean Dr Corpus Christi TX 78411-1457 Office: CC Distributors Inc 210 Mcbride Ln Corpus Christi TX 78408 Office Phone: 361-289-0200. Office Fax: 361-289-0302. E-mail: gfinley@ccdistributors.com.

FINLEY, GLENNA, writer; b. Puyallup, Wash., June 12, 1925; d. John Ford and Gladys De Ferris (Winters) F.; m. Donald MacLeod Witte, May 19, 1951; 1 child, Duncan MacLeod. BA cum laude, Stanford U., Calif., 1945. Prodr. internat. divsn. NBC, 1945-49; film libr. March of Time, 1949; with news bur. Life Mag., 1950; publicity and radio writer Seattle, 1950-51; freelance writer, 1951-57; contract writer New Am. Libr. Inc., NYC, 1970—. Author numerous books including Master of Love, 1978, Beware My Heart, 1978, The Marriage Merger, 1978, Wildfire of Love, 1979, Timed for Love, 1979, Love's Temptation, 1979, Stateroom for Two, 1980, Affairs of Love, 1980, A Business Affair, 1983, Wanted for Love, 1983, A Weekend for Love, 1984, Love's Waiting Game, 1985, A Touch of Love, 1985, Diamonds for My Love, 1986, Secret of Love, 1987, The Marrying Kind, 1988, Island Rendezvous, 1990, Stowaway for Love, 1992, The Temporary Bride, 1993. Named Matrix Table Woman of Achievement, 1976. Mem.: Women's Univ. Club (Seattle). Republican. Anglican. Home: 9718 Fairway Ridge Rd Charlotte NC 28277

FINLEY, JOHN R., medical insurance company executive; Attended, U. Oxford; BA, Tulsa U.; JD, U. Okla., MA in Pub. Health. Presdl. mgmt. fellow, Pres. US Office of Mgmt. and Budget; spl. asst., Dep. Commr. for Policy, Commr. Office, regulatory counsel, drug evaluation, Office of Compliance US Food and Drug Adminstrn.; assoc. vice chancellor, chief compliance officer U. Kans. Med. Ctr.; co-chmn. Assn. Academic Health Centers; sr. v.p., bus. ethics Amerigroup Corp., chief compliance officer, 2009—. Mem.: Okla. Bar Assn. Office: Amerigroup Corp National Support Ctr 1330 Amerigroup Way Virginia Beach VA 23464 Office Phone: 757-490-6900. Business E-Mail: jfinley@amerigrp.com.

FINLEY, SARA CREWS, medical geneticist, educator; b. Lineville, Ala., Feb. 26, 1930; m. Wayne H. Finley; children: Randall Wayne, Sara Jane. BS in Biology, U. Ala., 1951, MD, 1955. Diplomate Am. Bd. Med. Genetics; cert. clin. geneticist; cert. clin. cytogeneticist. Intern Lloyd Noland Hosp., Fairfield, Ala., 1955-56; NIH fellow in pediatrics U. Ala. Med. Sch., Birmingham, 1956-60; NIH trainee in med. genetics Inst. Med. Genetics, U. Uppsala, Sweden, 1961-62; mem. faculty U. Ala. Med. Sch., 1960-96, co-dir. lab. med. genetics, 1966-96, prof. pediatrics, 1975-96, occupant Wayne H. and Sara Crews Finley chair med. genetics, 1986-96, prof. emerita, 1996—; Disting. Faculty lectr. Med. Ctr., U. Ala. at Birmingham, 1983; mem. staff U. Ala. Hosp., Children's Hosp. Ala. Mem. ad hoc com. genetic counseling Children's Bur., HEW, 1966; mem. ad hoc rev. panel for genetic disease and sickle cell testing and counseling programs, 1980; mem. genetic diseases program objective rev. panel Bur. Maternal and Child Health and Resources Div., HHS, 1989, mem. adv. group on lab. quality assurance, 1989. Birmingham Author papers on clin. cytogenetics, human congenital malformations, human growth and devel. Mem. White House Conf. Health, 1965; mem. rsch. manpower rev. com. Nat. Cancer Inst., 1977-81; mem. Sickle Cell Disease Adv. Com., NIH, 1983-87; chairperson physician's campaign bd. dirs. United Way, 1993-95. Recipient Disting. Alumna award U. Ala. Sch. Med. Alumni Assn., 1989, Med. award Ala. Assn. for Retarded Children, 1969, Turlington award Planned Parenthood of Ala., 1982, Nat. Outstanding Alumnae award Zeta Tau Alpha, 1992, Disting. Alumna award U. Ala. Nat. Alumni Assn., 1994, Brother Bryan Prayer Point award Birmingham Women's Com. of 100, 2001, Gardner award Ala. Acad. Sci., 2002, Local Legend award Am. Med. Women's Assn. Nat. Libr. Medicine, 2004, Lifetime Achievement award Birmingham Bus. Jour., 2003, So. Women of Dist. award So. Women's Ctr., 2005, Martha Myers Role Model award U. Ala. Med, Alumni Assn., 2009, Disting. Svc. award, U. Ala. Med. Alumni Assoc., 2012; co-recipient Will Holmes award Children's Aid Soc. Birmingham, 1999; named Top Ten Women in Birmingham, 1989, Top 31 Most Outstanding Alumnae U. Ala., Tuscaloosa, 1993, Ala. Healthcare Hall of Fame, 2001; Finley-Compass Bank Genetics Conf. Ctr. with portrait opened, 2001. Fellow AMA (founding), Am. Coll. Med. Genetics; mem. Am. Soc. Human Genetics, Med. Assn. Ala. (Samuel Buford Word award 2003, Fifty Year Club 2005), Ala. Acad. Sci., Jefferson County Med. Soc. (pres. 1990), Jefferson County Pediatric Soc., So. Med. Assn., NY Acad. Sci., Caduceus Club, Rotary Club of Birmingham, Phi Beta Kappa, Sigma Xi, Alpha Omega Alpha, Alpha Epsilon Delta, Omicron Delta Kappa, Phi Kappa Phi, Zeta Tau Alpha. Office: U Ala Kaul Bldg 210E Birmingham AL 35294 E-mail: scfinley@webtv.net.

FINLEY, STEPHANIE A., federal prosecutor; b. Pineville, La., 1966; BA in Polit. Sci. magna cum laude, Grambling State U., 1988; JD cum laude, Southern U. Law Ctr., 1991; Grad., Air Command & Staff Coll., 2007. CPA; bar: La. 1991, US Ct. Mil. Appeals 1991. Summer clk. Rapides Parish Sheriff Dept., Alexandria, La., 1988; law clk. La. Dept. Labor, Baton Rouge, 1989—91; summer law clk. Brooke, Morial, Cassibry, Fraiche and Pizza, Baton Rouge, 1990; asst. staff judge advocate USAF, Shaw AFB, SC, England AFB, La., 1991—95, USAFR, Barksdale AFB, La., 1995—; asst. US atty. (western dist.) La. US Dept. Justice, 1995—2010, sr. litig. counsel, 2007—, acting dep. criminal chief, 2008—09, US atty., 2010—. Adj. prof. St. Leo CC, 1993—95; bar examiner Criminal Sect. La. State Bar, 2009—. Contbr. articles to law jours. 1st lt. USAF, 1990—92, capt. USAF, 1992—95, major USAFR, 1999—2007, lt. col. USAFR, 2007—. Decorated Air Force Training Ribbon, Air Force Longevity Ribbon, Air Force Outstanding Unit Award, Air Force Commendation Medal with oak leaf cluster, Armed Forces Reserve Medal, Nat. Def. Svc. Medal, Global War on Terrorism Svc. Medal, Meritorious Svc. Medal. Mem.: ABA, Nat. Black Prosecutors Assn., Louis A. Martinet Soc., Lafayette Parish Bar Found. (bd. dirs. 2004—06), Lafayette Parish Bar Assn. Office: US Attorney's Office Western District of Louisiana 800 Lafayette St, Ste 2200 Lafayette LA 70501 Office Phone: 337-262-6618. Office Fax: 337-262-6783.*

FINLEY, WAYNE HOUSE, medical educator; b. Goodwater, Ala., Apr. 7, 1927; s. Byron Bruce and Lucille (House) F.; m. Sara Will Crews, July 6, 1952; children: Randall Wayne, Sara Jane. BS, Jacksonville State U., 1948; MA, U. Ala., 1950, MS, 1955, PhD, 1958, MD, 1960; postgrad., U. Uppsala, Sweden, 1961-62. Cert. clin. cytogenetics Am. Bd. Med. Genetics, 1983. Sci. tchr. High Sch., Tuscaloosa, Ala., 1949-51; intern U. Ala. Hosps. and Clinics, 1960-61; from asst. prof. to assoc. prof. pediat. U. Ala. Sch. Medicine, 1962-70, prof., 1970-96, asst. prof. biochemistry, 1965-75, prof., 1975-96, asst. prof. physiology and biophysics, 1968-75, assoc. prof., 1975-96, chmn. med. student rsch. day, 1965-75, dir. Lab. Med. Genetics, 1966-96, prof. epidemiology, pub. health and epidmiology, 1975-96, prof. emeritus, 1996—, adj. prof. biology, 1980-96, chmn. faculty coun. Sch. Medicine, 1977-78, 84-87. Dir. med. genetics grad. program U. Ala. at Birmingham, 1983-96, dir. Am. Bd. Med. Genetics approved tng. program, 1978-96, dir. med. genetics residency program, 1995-98; chmn. Carey Phillips Travel Fellowship, 1972—; mem. com. on genetic counseling Children's Bur., Dept. HEW, 1966-67; nat. adv. rsch. resources coun. NIH and HEW, 1977-80; sr. scientist Comprehensive Cancer Ctr., Cystic Fibrosis Rsch. Ctr., Ctr. for Health Risk Assessment and Disease Prevention, 1982-96; bd. dirs. Southeastern Regional Genetics Group, 1982-2000, editor newsletter, 1997-2000; chmn. steering com. Reynolds Hist. Libr. Assocs., 1981-2007, Com. on Future Needs in Med. Genetics, Genetics Svc. Br., USPHS, 1987, Carmichael Fund for Grad. Students, 1989—2009; faculty rep. U. Ala. Sys. Bd. Trustees, 1995-96; senator U. Ala. at Birmingham Faculty Senate, 1995-96; mem. adv. and nominating com. Ala. Healthcare Hall of Fame, 1998—, chmn., 2007-. Author University of Alabama Medical Alumni Association, 1859-2003; contbr. articles on human malformations and clin. cytogenetics to tech. jours. Deacon Dawson Meml. Bapt. Ch., 1960-. With Infantry US Army, 1945—46, Germany, officer Chemical Corps US Army, 1951—53, with USAR, 1946—74, lt. col., ret. Recipient Med. award Ala. Assn. Retarded Children, 1969, Outstanding Educators of Am., 1971, Turlington award, 1982, Disting. Faculty Lectr. award U. Ala. Med. Ctr., 1983, Wayne H. and Sara C. Finley chair in med. genetics U. Ala., Birmingham, 1986, Alumnus of Yr. award Jacksonville State U., 1989, Portrait Reynolds Libr., 1991, Will Gaines Holmes award Childrens Aid Soc., 1999, Brother Bryan Humanitarian award, 2001, Gardner award Ala. Acad. Sci., Samuel Buford Word award Med. Assn. State of Ala., 2003, Lifetime Achievement award Birmingham Bus. Jour., 2003, named to Ala. Healthcare Hall of Fame, 2001; Finley-Compass Bank Genetics Conf. Ctr. established at U. Ala. Birmingham, 2001. Fellow Am. Coll. Med. Genetics (founder, edn. com. 1993-97, program dir. 1996), Royal Soc. Medicine; mem. AMA (Physicians Recognition award 1971, 75, 81, 84, 87, 90, 93, 96), AAAS, N.Y. Acad. Scis., Soc. Exptl. Biology and Medicine, Am. Inst. Chemists, Am. Fedn. Clin. Rsch., Am. Soc. Human Genetics, So. Med. Assn., So. Soc. Pediat. Rsch., Med. Assn. Ala. (counsellor

1990—), Jefferson County Med. Soc. (maternal and child health com. 1975-79, chmn. 1976-77, pres. 1983), Jefferson County Pediat. Soc., Ala. Acad. Sci. (trustee 1991—2001), Caduceus Club (pres. 1984-86), NIH Alumni Assn., U. Ala. Sch. Medicine Alumni Assn. (pres. 1974-75, Disting. Alumni award 1978, Disting. Svc. award 2005, Martha Myers Role Model award 2008), Greater Birmingham Area C. of C. (bd. dirs. 1983-86), Newcomen Soc., Kiwanis (pres. Shades Valley 1973-74), Rotary Club Birmingham, Am. Acad. Pediat. Della Robbia Club (gold mem. 2008), SAR (flag chmn.), ALSSAR, Wayne Finley Breakfast Club, Sigma Xi (pres. U. Ala. Birmingham chpt. 1972-73), Kappa Delta Pi, Phi Delta Kappa, Alpha Omega Alpha, Phi Beta Pi, Omicron Delta Kappa. Baptist. Avocations: reading, golf, genealogy, medical history. Home: 3412 Brookwood Rd Birmingham AL 35223-2023 Office: U Ala Birmingham Dept Genetics Kaul 210 1530 Third Ave S Birmingham AL 35294-0017 Home Phone: 205-969-1942; Office Phone: 205-934-4983. Personal E-mail: wfinley1942@charter.net.

FINNEGAN, PATRICK, academic administrator, military officer, lawyer; b. Fukuoka, Japan; m. Joan Finnegan; children: Katie, Jenna. BS, US Mil. Acad., West Point, 1971; MPA, Kennedy Sch. Govt., Harvard Univ.; JD, U. Va. Bar: Va., U.S. Supreme Ct. Commd. 2d lt. US Army, advanced through grades to brig. gen.; dep. dir. & criminal law instr. JAG Sch., Charlottesville, Va.; staff judge advocate MacDill AFB, Fla.; legal adv. joint spl. ops. command, US European command; staff judge advocate US Mil. Acad., West Point, 1998—99, prof., head dept. law, 1999—2005, dean of academic bd., 2005—10; pres. Longwood U., Farmville, Va., 2010—. Editor: Va. Law Rev.; contbr. articles to profl. legal jours. Decorated Disting. Svc. Medal, Def. Superior Svc. Medal (oak leaf cluster), Legion of Merit, Bronze Star, Meritorious Svc. Medal (two oak leaf clusters), Army Commendation Medal, Army Achievement Medal (two oak leaf clusters), Humanitarian Svc. Medal. Mem.: Phi Kappa Phi, Order of the Coif. Office: Longwood University Office of President 201 High St Farmville VA 23909

FINNERAN, JOHN G., JR., lawyer, diversified financial services company executive; b. Feb. 1950; m. Catherine A. Cotter; 2 children. BA in History, Pa. State U., 1972; JD, Georgetown U. Bar: Va. 1981. Atty. Cleary, Gottlieb, Steen & Hamilton, Washington, 1981—91; assoc. gen. counsel resolutions FDIC, 1991—94, acting dep. gen. counsel, 1994; sr. v.p., gen. counsel, corp. sec. Capital One Financial Corp., McLean, Va., 1994, exec. v.p., gen. counsel, corp. sec. Bd. dirs. Local Initiatives Support Corp., NYC, chmn. local adv. com. Richmond, Va. Recipient Outstanding Liberal Arts Alumni award, Pa. State U. Coll. Liberal Arts, 2003. Office: Capital One Fin Corp 1680 Capital One Dr Mc Lean VA 22102

FINNEY, B. LYNNE, corporate financial executive; Attended, Averett U., 1980. Asst. treas. Alliance One International, Inc. Office: Alliance One International Inc 8001 Aerial Ctr Pkwy Morrisville NC 27560-8417 Office Phone: 919-379-4300. Office Fax: 919-379-4346.

FINNEY, LOWE, state legislator; Sec. Senate Dem. Caucus, treas.; vice chmn. State & Local Govt. Com.; mem. Environment Com., Conservation Com., Tourism Com.; state senator Dist. 27 Tenn., 2007—. Democrat. Office: 312 East Lafayette St Jackson TN 38301 also: 317 War Memorial Bldg Nashville TN 37243-0027 Office Phone: 615-741-1810, 731-424-0461. Office Fax: 731-424-0562, 615-253-0179. Business E-Mail: sen.lowe.finney@capitol.tn.gov.

FINNEY, NIKKY, poet, educator; BA, Talladega Coll. Prof. creative writing and English U. Kentucky, Provost's Disting. Svc. Prof. Mem. Affrilachian Poets Group. Author: (poems) On Wings Made of Gauze, 1985, Rice, 1995 (PEN America Open Book award, 1995), The World Is Round, 2003 (Benjamin Franklin award for Poetry, 2004), Head Off & Split, 2011 (National Book Award-Poetry, National Book Found., 2011), (short stories) Heartwood, 1997; edited The Ringing Ear: Black Poets Lean South. Recipient Kentucky Found. for Women Artists Fellowship award. Office: Univ Kentucky 1349 Patterson Office Tower Lexington KY 40506-0027 Office Phone: 859-257-6997. Business E-Mail: finney@uky.edu.

FINUCANE, ANNE MARIE, bank executive; b. July 18, 1952; m. Mike Barnicle; 4 children. BA with honors, U. NH. Pub. info. officer City of Boston, Boston; dir. creative svcs. Sta. WBZ-TV, Boston; various positions including dir. creative svcs. & broadcast, exec. v.p., dir. corp. devel. and dir. account mgmt. Hill, Holliday, Connors, Cosmopulos, Inc., Boston; prin. Anne Finucane Mktg. & Telecomm., Boston, 1994; sr. v.p., dir. corp. mktg. & comm. FleetBoston Fin. Corp., 1995—99, exec. v.p., chief mktg. officer, 1999—2004; exec. v.p., pres. NE region Bank of America Corp., Boston, 2004—06, global strategy & mktg. officer, 2006—. Bd. dirs. Bank of America Found., Advt. Coun., Inc. Trustee Carnegie Hall, Partners HealthCare Sys., Inc.; bd. dirs. Am. Ireland Fund, Internat. Ctr. Journalists, NY Lit. Partners, John F. Kennedy Libr. Found., Mass. Women's Forum. Named one of 25 Women to Watch, US Banker, 2008, 25 Most Powerful Women in Banking, 2009, 2010, American Banker, 2011, Who's Who in B2B Advt., BtoB Mag., 2009, The 25 Best Marketers, 2009. Office: Bank of America Corp Ctr 100 N Tryon St Charlotte NC 28255 Business E-Mail: anne.finucane@bankofamerica.com.

FIOL MATTA, LIANA, territorial supreme court justice; Grad., Trinity Coll.; M., Columbia U., 1988, JSD, 1996; JD, U. PR. Prof. Inter-Am. U., 1978—88, Pontifical Cath. U.; judge PR Ct. Appeals, 1992—2003; assoc. justice PR Supreme Ct., 2004—. Contbr. articles to profl. jours. Mem.: P.R. Bar Assn. Office: PR Supreme Ct PO Box 9022392 San Juan PR 00902-2392*

FIORCA, JAMES V., gynecologic oncologist, educator; MD, Tufts U., 1982. Diplomate Am. Bd. Ob-Gyn, 2009, Am. Bd. Ob-Gyn-gynecologic oncology, 2009. Resident ob-gyn. dept. Univ. South Fla. Affiliated Hosp., Tampa, 1983—86, fellow gynecologic oncology, 1986—89; fellow breast disease Tufts Univ., Boston, 1990; clin. prof. ob-gyn. dept. Univ. South Fla.; gynecologic oncologist Sarasota Meml. Hosp. Office: Sarasota Memorial Hospital 1888 Hillview St Sarasota FL 34239 Office Phone: 941-917-8383. Office Fax: 941-917-8930.

FIORENZA, JOSEPH ANTHONY, archbishop emeritus; b. Beaumont, Tex., Jan. 25, 1931; s. Anthony and Grace (Galiano) Fiorenza. Grad., St. Anthony HS, Beaumont, Tex., 1947, St. Mary's Sem., LaPorte, Tex. Ordained priest Diocese of Galveston, Tex., 1954; asst. pastor Queen of Peace Ch., Houston, 1954—57; prof. med. ethics Dominican Coll., Houston, 1957—59; adminstr. Sacred Heart Co-Cathedral, Houston, 1959—67; pastor St. Augustine Ch., Houston, 1967—69, St. Benedict Ch., Houston, 1969—72, Assumption Ch., Houston, 1972—73; named Prelate of Honor to his Holiness, 1973; vice chancellor Diocese of Galveston-Houston, Tex., 1972—73, chancellor Tex., 1973—79; ordained bishop, 1979; bishop Diocese of San Angelo, Tex., 1979—85, Diocese of Galveston-Houston, Tex., 1985—2004; archbishop Archdiocese of Galveston-Houston, 2004—06, archbishop emeritus, 2006—. Bd. dirs. U. St. Thomas, Houston, Cath. Near East Welfare Assn., US. Mem.: US Conf. Cath. Bishops (adminstrv. com. 1995—, v.p. 1995—98, pres. 1998—2001). Roman Catholic. Office: Archdiocese of Galveston-Houston 1700 San Jacinto Houston TX 77001

FIORINA, CARLY (CARA CARLETON SNEED FIORINA), not-for-profit executive, former computer company executive; b. Austin, Tex., Sept. 6, 1954; d. Joseph Tyree and Madelon (Juergens) Sneed; m. Todd Bartlem, 1977 (div. 1984); m. Frank J. Fiorina, 1985; 2 stepchildren: Traci, Lori Ann BA in Medieval History & Philosophy, Stanford U., 1976; MBA, Robert H. Smith Sch. Bus. U. Md., College Park, Md., 1980; MSc in Mgmt., MIT, 1989; postgrad., UCLA. Account exec. Long Lines AT&T Corp., 1980, sr. v.p. global mktg., pres., AT&T network systems, North America, 1994—95; exec. v.p. corporate ops. Lucent Technologies, Murray Hill, NJ, 1995—96, pres., consumer products bus., 1996—97, group pres. Global Svc. Provider bus., 1997—99; pres. Hewlett-Packard Co., Palo Alto, 1999—2000, CEO, 1999—2005, chmn., 2000—05; chair, CEO Carly Fiorina Enterprises, 2008—; chair Good360, 2012—. Bd. dirs. Hewlett-Packard Co., 1999-2005, Merck & Co. Inc., 1999-2001, Cisco Systems, Inc., 2001-03, Revolution Healthcare Group, 2005-, Cybertrust, 2005-, Taiwan Semiconductor Mfg. Co., 2006-; mem., US China Bd. Trade., 1999-, US Space Commn., 2004-; contbr. Fox Bus. Channel; chair Republican Victory '08, 2008, The Tech. Policy Inst. 2009-10; vice chair Nat. Republican Senatorial Com. (NRSC), 2011-Author: Tough Choices: A Memoir, 2006. Mem. found. bd. World Econ. Forum; bd. trustees MIT; mem. advisory bd. Found. for Health Coverage Edn.; co-chair US Leadership in Development, Ctr. for Strategic & Internat. Studies (CSIS). Recipient Appeal of Conscience award, 2002, Concern Worldwide Seeds of Hope award, 2003, Leadership award, Private Sector Coun., 2004, Alliance Medal of Honor, Electronics Industries, 2004; named one of The Most Powerful Women in American Bus., Fortune mag., 1998—2005, The 30 Most Powerful Women in America, Ladies Home Jour., 2001, The 100 Most Powerful Women, Forbes mag., 2004, 2010, Top 50 Women To Watch, The Wall St. Jour., 2005, The 25 Most Influential Republicans, Newsmax Mag., 2008; grantee Hon. Fellow, London Bus. Sch., 2001. Republican.

FIORUCCI, MARIANNE, retail executive; BS in Mgmt., Fairleigh Dickinson U., 1983. Buyer Footstar, 1983—95; dir., mdse. planning and allocation Elder Beerman Dept. Stores (Elbee Shoes), 1995—96; mgr., mdse. control Cato, 1996—98; sr. bus. cons. Pricewaterhouse-Coopers, 1998—2000; dir., strategic projects Family Dollar Stores, Inc., 2000—05, divisional v.p., strategy, bus. devel., 2005—07, v.p., planning, allocation, 2007—. Office: Family Dollar Stores Inc 10401 Monroe Rd Charlotte NC 28201-1017 Office Phone: 704-847-6961. Office Fax: 704-847-0189. Business E-Mail: mfiorucci@familydollar.com.

FISCHER, CARL ROBERT, retired health facility administrator; b. Rahway, NJ, Nov. 15, 1939; s. Robert Carlton and Elsie Marie (Wolfarth) F.; m. Lynn Elaine Ekstrand, Mar. 12, 1966; children: Kristen, Leslie, Meredith, Kelly. BSN, Wagner Coll., 1964; MS, SUNY-Buffalo, 1966; MPH, Yale U., 1968. With Yale-New Haven Hosp., 1968-77, assoc. dir., 1975-77; exec. assoc. adminstr. U. Cin. Med. Ctr., 1977-80; exec. dir. clin. programs U. Ark. for Med. Scis., Little Rock, 1980-86; assoc. v.p. health scis., CEO Med. Coll. of Va. Hosps., Richmond, 1986-99; exec. v.p. corp. functions VCU Health Sys., 1999—2002; ret., 2003. Bd. dirs. Univ. Health Systems Consortium, exec. com. 1994-2000, chmn. bd. dirs. 1997-98, chmn. supply and svcs. divsn., 1988-89, 95-96; mem. exec. com. Nat. Assn. Pub. Hosps., 1999-2002. Pres. Ctrl. Va. Health Planning Agy., 1991-93, mem.-at-large, 1997-2002, exec. com., 2000-2002; bd. dirs. Richmond Luth. Home, 2000-01. Mem. Am. Assn. Med. Colls., Am. Hosp. Assn., Va. Hosp. Assn. (bd. dirs. 1986-91, 99-2000, chmn. coun. on adminstrn. and health planning 1988, coun. on assn. devel. 1987-88, physician liaison com. 1989-90, chmn. ctrl. Va. regional planning coun. 1997-99). Personal E-mail: flyfischn@aol.com.

FISCHER, CRAIG LELAND, physician; b. Bklyn., Feb. 17, 1937; s. Emil Carl and Ruth Barbara (Minarcik) F.; m. Sandra Lucile Canfield, Feb. 17, 1962; children: Craig L. Jr., Emil Lewis, Lisa Anne. BS, Kans. State U., 1958; MD, U. Kans., 1962. Diplomate Nat. Bd. Med. Examiners, Am. Bd. Family Practice; cert. anat. and clin. pathology, nuclear medicine. Intern in anatomic pathology Kansas U. Med. Ctr., 1962—63, resident in anatomic pathology, 1963—64, rsch. fellow in pathology (pub. health svc.), nuc. medicine, 1962—64, rsch. fellow pathology, nuc. medicine, 1965—66; resident in clin. pathology, Meth. Hosp. Baylor U. Coll. Medicine, 1967—68; rsch. med. officer Manned Spacecraft Ctr., NASA, Houston, 1965—68, pathologist, chief clin. labs., 1968—71; chief med. ops. Johnson Space, NASA, Houston, 1980—82; assoc. dir. labs. to dir. labs. Eisenhower Med. Ctr., Rancho Mirage, Calif., 1971—72, pathologist, dir. clin. labs., 1972—78, assoc. dir. nuc. med., 1975—78, gen. practice medicine Palm Desert, 1978—80; pathologist, co-dir. Valley Clin. Labs., Palm Desert, 1978—80; gen. practice medicine Indio, Calif., 1982—99; dir. post grad. edn. J.F. Kennedy Hosp., 1982—92; lt. col. USAFR, 1983—97; dir. Fischer and Yao Cons. Pathologists, Indio, 1987—89; pres. Fischer Assocs., Cons. in Pathology, Indio, 1989—95; ptnr. Fischer and Starke Assocs., Indio, 1995—99; sr. aviation med. examiner FAA, 1991—99, 1999—2007; asst. dir. space medicine NASA Johnson Space Ctr., 1999—2001, assoc. dir. clin. lab., 1999—2007, chief, Space Medicine & health Care Sys. Office, 2001—03, asst. dir. internat. space medicine, 2003—07. Clin. prof. dept. preventive medicine and cmty. health U. Tex. Med. Br., Galveston, 2002-07; asst. clin. prof. U. Calif., Irvine, 1986-99; mem. sci. adv. bd. Dept. Air Force, Washington, 1986-90, NAE, NRC; mem. Air Force Studies Bd., Washington, 1987-93; mem. aerospace med. adv. com. Office Space Scis. and Applications, NASA Hdqrs., Washington, 1988-93, chmn. operational medicine discipline working group, Life Scis. Directorate, 1988-92, mem. Shuttle-Mir Joint Sci. Working Group, 1993-94, mem. Adv. Coun. Task Force on the Shuttle-Mir Rendezvous and Docking Missions, 1995; mem. Mir Sci. Program Rev. Panel, 1993-98; mem. Internat. Space Sta. Task Force (Stafford Commn.), 1995-2007; chmn. multinat. med. ops. panel, 2000-04, chmn. Space Medicine Ops. Team, 2000-04, co-chmn. Space Craft Integrated Investigation Team, 2004-07; cons. lab. medicine project tektite U.S. Dept. Interior, 1969-70. Contbr. numerous articles to profl. jours. Capt. USAR, 1964—66, commd., maj, MC USAFR, 1983, commd., lt. col., MC USAFR, 1983, lt. col. USAFR, 1986, with USAFR, 1997, with USAF, Washington. Recipient Group Achievement award NASA Manned Spacecraft Ctr., 1966, 69, 70, Group Achievement award Gemini support team NASA Manned Spacecraft Ctr., Apollo 7 Flight Ops. Team award NASA Manned Spacecraft Ctr., 1969, Sustained Superior Achievement award NASA Manned Spacecraft Ctr., 1969, Superior Achievement award, 1969, Skylab Group Achievement award NASA Johnson Space Ctr., 1974, Presdl. medal of Freedom Apollo 13 Mission Ops. Team, 1970, Group Achievement award NASA Space Shuttle Launch and Ops. Team NASA Manned Spacecraft Ctr., 1982, Meritorious Civilian Svc. award Dept. of Air Force, 1990, Outstanding Contbn. Medicine award, Riverside County Med. Assn., 1996, STS-107 Columbia Contingency Support Team, 2003, Russian Fedn. Space Agy. award for internat. coop. in space exploration, 2005, Exceptional Svc. medal NASA, 2006, Silver Snoopy award Shuttle Comdr. Robert Cabana, 2006, NASA Exceptional Achievement award, 2007, Melbourn W. Boyington award Am. Astronautical Soc., 2007, NASA Outstanding Leadership medal, 2009. Fellow Am. Coll. Preventive Medicine, Am. Coll. Nuc. Physicians, Coll. Am. Pathologists, Am. Soc. Clin. Pathologists (CCE Commr.'s medal 1989), Aerospace Med. Assn. Republican. Presbyterian. Avocations: sailing, tennis, flying. Personal E-mail: clfspacemed@aol.com.

FISCHER, GREG, mayor, Louisville, Kentucky; b. Jan. 14, 1958; s. George and Mary Lee Fischer; m. Alexandra Gerassimides; children: Eleni, george, Nick, Mary. BA in Economics, Vanderbilt U. Founder SerVend Internat., 1980, Iceberg Ventures, 1999; co-founder bCatalyst, 2000; ptnr. and former CEO Dant Clayton Corp.; mayor City of Louisville, Ky., 2011—. Former chmn. Louisville Sci. Ctr. Mem.: Young Presidents Orgn. (chmn.). Democrat. Office: Office of Mayor Metro Hall / 4th Fl 527 W Jefferson St Louisville KY 40202 Office Phone: 502-574-2003.*

FISCHER, JOSEPH MICHAEL, state legislator; b. Covington, Ky., Nov. 14, 1954; s. Thomas A. and Virgilia (Kottman) F.; m. Karen. BA in Econs., Holy Cross Coll., 1976; JD, U. Cin., 1980. Bar: Ohio 1980, Ky. 1981, U.S. Dist. Ct. (so. dist.) Ohio 1981, U.S. Dist. Ct. (ea. dist.) Ky. 1981. Ptnr. Sullivan & Fischer, Cin., 1981-86; from staff atty. to sr. atty. Ohio Nat. Life Ins. Co., Cin.; mem. Dist. 68 Ky. House of Reps., 1999—. City councilman Ft. Thomas, Ky., 1988-89. Mem. ABA, Ky. Bar Assn., Ohio State Bar Assn., Cin. Bar Assn. Republican. Roman Catholic. Avocations: golf, softball, basketball, running. Office: Ky House of Reps 702 State Capitol Annex Rm 429D Frankfort KY 40601 Office Phone: 502-564-8100 ext. 742. Business E-Mail: joe.fischer@lrc.ky.gov.

FISCHER, ROBERT LEE, engineering executive, educator; b. Huntington, W.Va., Feb. 4, 1947; s. Charles Lee and Frances Louise (Pennington) F.; m. Mona Lynn Reeser, Oct. 27, 1966; children: Robert Lee Jr., Amy Lynn, Cory Brandon. Cert. in electronics tech., Huntington East Vocat. Tech., 1965; BA in Physics and Gen. Sci., Marshall U., 1970, MS in Vocat. Tech. Edn., 1976; PhD in Elec. Engring., Kennedy-Western U., 1993. Registered profl. elec. engr., lic. master electrician, cert. plant engr., vibration analyst, Internat. Brotherhood Elec. Workers, Nat. Ctr. Constrn. Edn. and Rsch., Ele. Power Rsch. Inst., instrumentation and controls technician. Electrical engr. J.F. & M. Co., Huntington, 1970-71; electronics prodn. supr. polan ind. div. Wollensak, Inc., Huntington, 1971-72; electrical maintenance supr. ACF Industries, Inc., Huntington, 1972-76, electrical maintenance supt., 1976-78, sr. maintenance engr., 1978-80, plant engr., 1980-84, mgr. plant, prodn. and tooling engring., 1984-85; engr., prin. cons. Fischer Tech. Svcs., Huntington, 1979—; electrical, instrumentation and utilities mgr. Calgon Carbon Corp., Catlettsburg, Ky., 1985-93, maintenance mgr., 1993-94, maintenance svcs. mgr., 1994-2001; instrumentation and controls technician/foreman Pritchard Electric Co., Huntington, 2001—11; physics instr. Mountwest Cmty. & Tech. Coll., Huntington, 2011; solid state electronics instr. ITT Tech. Inst. Huntington, 2012. Robotics instr. Marshall U. Cmty. and Tech. Coll, Huntington, 1986—99; mem. instrumentation and control engring. curriculum adv. com. Shawnee State U., Portsmouth, Ohio, 1995—2000; mem. electronics tech. curriculum advisory com. Mountwest Cmty. and Tech. Coll., Huntington, 2008—; presented an invited paper on industrial power quality problems and their solutions to the plenary session 1997 North Am. Power Quality Symposium. Patentee electronic height control device, robot safety mechanism, Co-Author: Pipeline Electrical & Instrumentation Training Guides, Nat. Ctr. Construction Edn. & Rsch. Elected to West Jr. High Sch. Hall of Fame, Huntington, 1988; recipient Sr.-Under Black Belt-Open 3d Place award United Fighting Arts Fedn. Nat. Karate Tournament, 1984; named W.Va. ambassador of sci. and engring. among all people, 1982. Mem. W.Va. Acad. Sci., The Brucheum Group, Ohio Valley Astron. Soc., Am. Radio Relay League, Six Meter Internat. Radio Club. Democrat. Avocations: amateur radio, martial arts. Home: 4 Willowtree Dr Huntington WV 25704-9154 Office Phone: 304-429-2912. Personal E-mail: fischertek@zoominternet.net.

FISCHER, RUSSELL LEONARD, public relations executive; b. East Orange, NJ, Feb. 4, 1958; s. Harold Martin and Annette Carol Fischer. BA, Boston U., 1980; JD, Antioch U., Washington, 1984. Importer, retailer, owner Fendi of Short Hills, NJ, 1982-92; pub. rels. dir., v.p. IME-Xaminations, Palm Beach, Fla., 1994—. Vol. World Trade Orgn., NYC, battered wives Unity Group, Short Hills, 1995-98; del. reform coun. Am. Jewish Congress, N.Y.C., 1991; adv. bd. Am. Assn. Reform Judaism, Washington, 1995-99; alumni advisor, pres. South Fla. chpt. Boston U. Alumni Assn., 2000-02; active Heritage Soc. Congregation Emanu-El, NYC. Recipient Meritorious and Outstanding Cmty. Svc. award Am. Nat. Red Cross, 1976. Mem.: NJ Importers Assn., Beach Club, Palm Beach, Club Colette, Ocean Point Beach Club, World Trade Ctr. Club, Williams Island Club, Crestmont Country Club. Republican. Avocation: sculpture. Office Phone: 417-383-8095.

FISCHER, STEVEN R., retired diversified financial services company executive; BS in Economics & Acctg., CUNY Queens Coll.; MBA, Baruch Coll., NYC. V.p., regional mgr. Citibank, N.A., 1981—92; sr. v.p., regional mgr. Transamerica Bus. Capital Corp., 1992—97, exec. v.p., divsn. mgr., 1997—2000, pres., 2000—04, North Fork Bus. Capital Corp./Capital One Leverage Fin. Corp., 2004—08. Bd. dirs. ScanSource, Inc., 1995—, chmn. bd. dirs., 2009—; bd. dirs. Falconstor Software Inc., 2001—. Office: ScanSource Inc 6 Logue Ct Greenville SC 29615 Office Phone: 864-288-2432. Office Fax: 864-288-1165.

FISCHLER, ABRAHAM SAUL, retired academic administrator, educator; b. Bklyn., Jan. 21, 1928; s. Morris and Esther P. Fischler; m. Shirley Balter, Apr. 9, 1949; children: Bruce Evan, Michael Alan, Lori Faye. BS in Soc. Sci., CUNY, 1951; MA in Sci. Edn., NYU, 1952; EdD, Columbia U., 1959; DSc (hon.), N.Y. Inst. Tech., 1981; LLD (hon.), Nova U., 1992; BSS (hon.), U. Marnzalis, 2006. Sci. tchr., supr. Ossining (N.Y.) Pub. Schs., 1952-58; instr. Columbia U., NYC, 1958-59; asst. prof. edn. Harvard U. Grad. Sch., Cambridge, Mass., 1959-62; assoc. prof. then prof. edn. U. Calif., Berkeley, 1962-66; dean grad. studies Nova U., Ft. Lauderdale, Fla., 1966-70, James Donn prof., 1966—, exec. v.p., 1969-70, pres., 1970-92; pres. emeritus, univ. prof., 1992—; mem. Broward County Sch. Bd., 1994-98, chair, 1996-97. Vis. prof. nat. and internat. univs., 1963-65; cons. numerous sch. dists., Calif., 1962-67; advisor ednl. pubs.; mem. bus.-edn. adv. com. Alameda-Contra Costa Counties, Calif.; mem. Calif. Elem. Sci. Adv. Com., Sacramento; mem. Overseas Tchrs. Examining Team, Berkeley; bd. dirs. Cardio-Metrics, Inc., Inst. Learning Techs., Inc., Hollywood Med. Ctr., Fla. Med. Ctr., 2000—Author: Modern Science, Grades 7,8,9, 1963; (with others) Science: A Modern Approach, 1966, Modern Science, 1967, Modern Elementary Science: Grades 1 through 8, 1971, Nova U.'s Three National Doctoral Degree Programs: An Analysis and Formative Evaluation, 1977; contbr. numerous articles to profl. jours., author monograph and rsch. reports. Pres. United Way Broward County (Fla.), 1984-85, bd. dirs., 1973-2000, chmn. budget com., 1976-81; chmn. Broward County Overall Econ. Devel. Com., 1980-88, Broward Edn. and Tng. Coun., 1989—; pres. S.E. Fla. Holocaust Meml. Ctr., 1985-87, Temple Beth El, Hollywood, 1988-90; adv. bd. Leadership Broward; mem.

17th Jud. Nominating Commn., Broward County, 1982-86, Ft. Lauderdale Mus. Art, Fla. Philharm., Broward County Crime Commn., Broward Workshop Edn. Task Force, Town of Davie, Fla. Econ. and Indsl. Devel. Bd.; bd. dirs. Hollywood (Fla.) Med. Ctr., 1982—, chmn. bd. dirs., 1985—; pres. Health Care Rsch. and Edn. Found., 1988-89, United Ways Fla., 1990-91; bd. govs. Fla. Bar, 1991-95, Fla. Bar Found., 1996-01; chmn. Hollywood City Master Plan; mem. Broward Ctr. Performing Arts Authority, 1998; co-chair Sun Sentinel Diversity Fund, 2000—; chair Broward Edn. Found., 2002, South Fla. Cmty. Blood Ctrs., 2002, bd. dirs., CEFT Corp. With USN, 1945-47. Recipient Outstanding Mgmt. and Leadership award Sales and Mktg. Execs., Ft. Lauderdale, 1978, Leader of Yr. award Leadership Broward, 1991, Humanitarian of Yr. award E.A.S.E. Found., 1991, Disting. Educator award Assn. Ind. Schs. Fla., 1992, Tree of Life award Jewish Nat. Fund, 1993, Spirit of Broward award, 1994, Lifetime Achievement award Urban League, 1994; named Broward Educator of Yr., Women's Am. ORT, 1997, Disting. Pub. Svc. award ADL, 1998, Sun Sentinel Cmty. Leader of the Yr., 1999, Sun Sentinel Cmty. Svc. award, 2000, Fla. Bar medal of Hon., 2005; DuPont fellow UCLA, 1958, Sci. Manpower fellow Columbia U., 1958-59, Nova Southeastern U. Athletic Hall of Fame, 2007. Fellow AAAS, Phi Delta Kappa; mem. ASCD, NSTA, Assn. for Edn. Tchrs. Sci. (past pres.), Nat. Assn. Research in Sci. Teaching, Soc. Advancement Edn., Soc. Research Adminstrs., Am. Assn. Higher Edn., Nat. Council Univ. Research Adminstrs., Com. of 100, Hollywood, Hundred Club Broward County (pres. 1985-86), Tower Club, Woodmont Country Club, Kappa Delta Pi. Avocations: running, golf, travel. Office: Nova U Office Pres Emeritus 3301 College Ave Fort Lauderdale FL 33314-7796 Office Phone: 954-262-5375. Business E-Mail: fischler@nova.edu.

FISH, A. JOE, federal judge; b. LA, Nov. 12, 1942; s. John Allen and Mary Magdalene (Martin) Fish; m. Betty Fish, Jan. 23, 1971; children: Abigail, Stephen. BA, Yale U., 1965, LL.B., 1968. Bar: Tex. Assoc. firm McKenzie & Baer, Dallas, 1968-80; judge Tex. Dist. Ct., 1980-81; assoc. judge Tex. Appeals Ct., 1981-83; judge US Dist. Ct. (No. Dist.) Tex., Dallas, 1983—2002, chief judge, 2002, sr. judge, 2007—. With USAR, 1968—74. Mem.: Dallas Bar Assn., State Bar Assn. Tex., ABA. Office: US District Court US Courthouse 1100 Commerce St Ste 1528 Dallas TX 75242-1495 Office Phone: 214-753-2310.

FISH, MARDY, professional tennis player; b. Edina, Minn., Dec. 9, 1981; s. Tom and Sally; m. Stacey Gardner, Sept. 2008. Profl. tennis player ATP, 2000—. Recipient Silver medal in tennis, Athens Summer Olympics, 2004; named Comeback Player of Yr., 2006 ATP Awards. Achievements include winning 6 career singles titles, 8 career doubles titles, ATP. Avocations: hockey, baseball. Office: PO Box 648158 Vero Beach FL 32964-8158

FISH, MARY MARTHA, economics professor; b. Albert Lea, Minn., July 17, 1930; d. Charles H. and Olga (Stennes) Thomassen; m. Donald C. Fish, Oct. 1954 (dec.); children: Jill S., Lynn M., Jason M BBA, U. Minn., 1951; MBA Econs, Tex. Tech. Coll., 1957; PhD, U. Okla., 1963. Statis. asst. Iowa Bd. Control, 1951—53; pub. health analyst State of Calif., 1953—54; analytical statistician 46th Med. Gen. Lab., U.S. Army Forces, Tokyo, 1954—57; instr. econs. and bus. Odessa Coll., Tex., 1957—58; asst. prof., then assoc. prof. West Tex. State U., 1961—66; prof. econs. U. Ala., 1966—99, prof. emeritus, 1999—. Prof. econs. Landegg Internat. U., Wienacht, Switzerland, 2000-02; Fulbright lectr. U. Liberia, 1974-75, Gambian Govt., 1978-79, faculty mem. Willamette Inst. "Economics and the Baha'i Faith; cons. in field Co-author: Convicts, Codes and Contraband, 1974; contbr. articles to profl. jours. Founding mem. Nat. Campaign for Tolerance; mem. So. Poverty Tolerance Program, 1995. Grantee U. Ala., 1967-68, 87-89, Dept. Labor, 1978-79; Fulbright rsch. fellow, Taiwan, 1995; Phifer Faculty Scholar, 1998, fellow AAUW, 1960 Mem. Am. Econ. Assn., So. Econ. Assn Mem. Baha'i faith. Home: 18464 Snaffle Ln Culpeper VA 22701 Business E-Mail: mfish@cba.ua.edu.

FISH, STANLEY EUGENE, dean, language educator; b. Providence, Apr. 19, 1938; s. Max and Ida Dorothy (Weinberg) F.; m. Adrienne A. Aaron, Aug. 23, 1959 (div. 1980); 1 dau., Susan.; m. Jane Parry Tompkins, Aug. 7, 1982. BA, U. Pa., 1959; MA, Yale U., 1960, PhD, 1962. Instr. U. Calif., Berkeley, 1962-63, asst. prof., 1963-67, assoc. prof., 1967-69, prof., 1969-74; Kenan prof. English and Humanities Johns Hopkins U., Balt., 1978-85, chmn. dept., 1983-85; Arts and Sci. Disting. prof. English and prof. law Duke U., Durham, NC, 1985-98, chmn. dept., 1986-92; exec. dir. Duke U. Press, Durham, 1994-98; dean U. Ill. Coll. Liberal Arts and Scis., Chgo., 1999—2004; Davidson-Kahn Disting. Univ. Prof. humanities and Law Fla. Internat. U. Coll. Law, Miami, 2005—. Author: John Skelton's Poetry, 1965, Surprised by Sin: The Reader in Paradise Lost, 1967, 97 (Hanford Book award 1998), Seventeenth Century Prose: Modern Essays in Criticism, 1971, Self-Consuming Artifacts, 1972, The Living Temple: George Herbert and Catechizing, 1978, Is There a Text in This Class?, 1980, Doing What Comes Naturally, 1989, There's No Such Thing as Free Speech...And It's a Good Thing Too, 1994 (PEN/Spielvogel-Diamonstein award 1994), Professional Correctness: Literary Studies and Political Change, 1995, The Trouble with Principle, 1999, How Milton Works, 2001; mem. editl. bd. Milton Studies, Milton Quar. Recipient 2d place, Explicator prize, 1968; Am. Council Learned Socs. fellow, 1966; Guggenheim fellow, 1969 Mem. MLA, Am. Acad. Arts and Scis., Milton Soc. (hon. scholar 1991), Spenser Soc. Office: Fla Internat U Coll Law Univ Park Campus Green Library Ste 484 Miami FL 33199 Office Phone: 305-348-7820. Business E-Mail: fishs@fiu.edu.

FISHBACK, DENNIS, information technology executive; Mgmt. Va. Power; with Calif. Ind. Sys. Operator; sr. v.p. & chief info. officer Calpine Corp., San Jose, Calif., 2001—. Named one of the Premier 100 IT Leaders, Computerworld mag., 2004. Office: Calpine Corp 717 Texas Ave Ste 1000 Houston TX 77002 Office Phone: 713-830-2000. Office Fax: 713-830-2001.

FISHEL, PETER LIVINGSTON, finance company executive, accountant; b. Chgo., Apr. 25, 1935; s. Philip W. and Dorothy B. (Livingston) F.; m. Donna Swift, Dec. 17, 1961; children: Pamela Leslie Fishel Saccocio, Patricia Jane Fishel, Françoise Suzanne Fishel. BS, U. Pa., 1959. CPA, Pa., Fla. Agt.-in-charge investigation and civil rights divsn. Commonwealth of Pa. Dept. Justice, 1961-62; contr. Internat. Playtex Corp., 1962-70, BVD Knitwear, 1970-71; corp. contr. BVD Co., Inc., NYC, 1971-73; v.p. fin. BVD Co., Inc. (BVD divsn.), NYC, 1973; chief fin. officer Colebrook Mills, divsn. Bobbie Brooks, Inc., Hialeah, Fla., 1973-77; owner Gen. Bus. Svcs., 1978-86, regional dir. S.E. Fla., 1982-86; pvt. practice acctg., 1987—; mem. adv. com. Oceanmark Fed. Savs. & Loan, 1983-88. Mem. Andover Civic Assn., 1973—2001; mem. citizens adv. com. Met. Dade Police, Miami, Fla., 1981—, treas., 1985—; mem. fin. com. Metro-Dade Pig Bowl, 1985; v.p. Andover Civic Assn., 1986—91; bd. mem. Mosaic Theatre, 2008—10, treas., 2009—10, adv. bd., 2010—13; mem. NMB Pride, 1989—93, bd. dirs., 1991—93, Dade Alumni Club, U. Pa., 1991—; chmn. Bus. Devel. Com. of Aventura Mktg. Coun., 1995—; mem., treas. Coalition Improvement NW Dade, 1996—2013; bd. dirs. Rolling Hills Home Owners Assn., treas., 2003—; season seat holder adv. bd. Florida Panthers, NHL, 2007—10; mem. Aventura Mktg. Coun., 1991—. With M.P. US Army, 1954—56. Mem. AICPA, Pa. Inst. CPAs, Fla. Inst. CPAs, Nat. Assn. Tax Practitioners, Mensa, North Dade C. of C. (bd. dirs. 1978-97, v.p., Businessman of Yr. 1990, Mem. of Month, 1987, 91). Jewish. Home: 8119 S Savannah Cir Davie FL 33328-3033 Office: 2396 NE 172nd St Aventura FL 33160-2923 Home Phone: 305-720-7531; Office Phone: 305-944-0040. Personal E-mail: plfishel@aol.com. Business E-Mail: plfcpa@gmail.com.

FISHEL, ROBERT S., cardiac electrophysiologist, educator; Grad., Cornell U.; MD, NYU, 1987. Diplomate Am. Bd Internal Medicine-cardiovasc. disease, 2005, Am. Bd Internal Medicine-clin. cardiac electrophysiology, 2006. Resident internal medicine Univ. of Mich. Med. Ctr, 1988—90; fellow cardiovasc. disease Emory Univ., 1990—94, fellow cardiac electrophysiology, 1994—95; assoc. clin. prof. medicine Univ. of Miami; founder Fla. Electrophysiology Assocs.; consultative staff Boca Cmty. Hosp., Bethesda Med. Ctr., Delray Hosp., Westside Regional Med. Ctr., Broward Gen. Med. Ctr. Instrument rated pilot. Office: Delray Medical Ctr 5352 Linton Blvd Delray Beach FL 33484-6580 Office Phone: 561-434-0353.*

FISHER, DEREK LAMAR, professional basketball player; b. Aug. 9, 1974; m. Candace Fisher; 4 children. BA in Comm., U. Ark.-Little Rock. Point guard LA Lakers, 1996—2004, 2007—12, Golden State Warriors, 2004—06, Utah Jazz, 2006—07, Oklahoma City Thunder, 2012, 2013—, Dallas Mavericks, 2012. First v.p. NBA Players Assn., 2004—06, pres., 2006—. Active Am. Cancer Soc., Big Brothers and Big Sisters; founder Fisher Fellows Life Skills Program, 2005—. Named Player of Yr., Sun Belt Conf., 1996; named to All-Rookie Team, NBA Western Conf., 1997. Achievements include member of NBA Championship winning Los Angeles Lakers, 2000, 2001, 2002, 2009, 2010. Avocations: fishing, music, travel. Office: Oklahoma City Thunder 100 W Reno Rd Oklahoma City OK 73102

FISHER, DONALD WAYNE, medical association administrator; b. Pitts., Mar. 2, 1946; s. David H.W. and Jean K. F.; children by previous marriage: Kimberly Elizabeth, Jeffrey Wayne. AA, Hinds Jr. Coll., 1966; BS in Biology and Chemistry, Millsaps Coll., 1968; MS in Anatomy, U. Miss., 1970, PhD in Anatomy, 1973; postgrad. in assn. mgmt., U. Md., 1977-79. Cert. assn. exec. Instr. dept. chemistry and biology Hinds Jr. Coll., Raymond, Miss., 1968-74; instr. dept. anatomy U. Miss. Sch. Medicine, Jackson, 1973-74, co-dir. and exec. officer physician asst. program, 1972-74; asst. professorial lectr. George Washington U. Sch. Medicine, 1974—80; exec. dir. Assn. Physician Asst. Programs, Arlington, Va., 1974-80, Am. Acad. Physician Assts., Arlington, 1974-80; pres., CEO Am. Med. Group Assn., Alexandria, Va., 1980—; chmn. Am. Med. Group Corp., Inc., Anceta, 2001—; chmn. bd. Anceta; treas. polit. action com. Am. Med. Group, 1980—. Mem. Nat. Commn. on Allied Health Edn., 1977-80; mem. adv. com. for tng., devel. and utilization of physician extenders Systems Scis., Inc., 1975-80; pres. Am. Acad. Physician Assts. Ednl. and Rsch. Found., 1977-80; sec., treas. Am. Med. Group Found., 1980—; mem. Am. Express Health Care Faculty, 1985-88; mem. bd. dirs. Alliance Bank Va., 2009-. Robert Wood Johnson Found. grantee, 1973-80 Mem. Am. Soc. Assn. Execs. (govt. rels. com. 1980—), Assn. Am. Med. Colls., AAAS, Am. Internat. Health Alliance (bd. dirs. 1992—, treas. 1995-2003, chair 2004-08), Disease Mgmt. Assn. Am. (bd. dirs. 2004-09), Greater Washington Soc. Assn. Execs., Fairfax County Hosp. Assn., Arlington (Va.) C. of C, Am. Internat. Alliance (chair, 2004—08), Alliance Bank of Va. (bd. dirs. 2009-, chmn. 2011-12), Washington First Bank (bd. dirs. 2013-), Maestro Strategies (bd. advisors 2013-). Home: 3814 Ivanhoe Ln Alexandria VA 22310-2170 Office: Am Med Group Assn 1422 Duke St Alexandria VA 22314-3430

FISHER, ERIC A., energy executive, lawyer; b. Columbus, Ind., Apr. 18, 1968; s. Larry S. Fisher and Linda M. Tarry; m. Lauren Maria Dyck, July 27, 1991; 1 child, John Stanton. BS, Tex. A&M U., 1990; JD, U. Tex., 1995. Bar: Tex. 1995. Petroleum acct. Exxon Co., USA, Midland, Tex., 1990-92; assoc. Fulbright & Jaworski LLP, San Antonio, 1995-97; corp. counsel Valero Energy Corp., San Antonio, 1997, v.p. investor rels., corp. v.p. investor and corp. comm., 2007—. Bd. dirs. Human Soc. Bexar County, San Antonio, 1998. Mem. Order of the Coif. Office: Valero Energy Corp 1 Valero Pl San Antonio TX 78249 Office Phone: 210-370-2896. Office Fax: 210-370-2103. E-mail: eric.fisher@valero.com.

FISHER, FENIMORE, business development consultant; b. NYC, 1926; s. Benn and Sadie (Cohan) F.; m. Marcia Obler, Nov. 9, 1952; children: Bennett G., Alan L., Karen Soo. BS in Physics, Columbia U., 1951; MBA, U. Pa., 1952. Staff physicist USN Rsch. Lab., Phila., 1951-52; ops. mgr., chief engr. instrument divsn. Thomas A. Edison Industries, West Orange, NJ, 1952-60; pres. Analogue Controls Inc., Hicksville, NY, 1960-67; corp. v.p. IMC Magnetics Corp., Jericho, NY, 1967-77, pres., CEO, 1977-89, also bd. dirs. Chmn. bd. Hansen Mfg. Co. Inc., Princeton Ind., IMC Ariz. Divsn., Tempe, IMC Fla. Divsn., Miami Lakes, IMC Tenn. Divsn., Camden, IMC Tex. Divsn., Mexia, IMC Western Divsn., Cerritos, Calif., New Eng. Alloys Inc., Lawrence, Mass., Pacific Propeller Inc., Kent Washington, Universal Magnetics Corp., Cerritos, 1989—; exec. v.p. Synergy Gas Corp., 1989-93; bus. devel. cons., 1993-96; v.p. bus. and fin. Dowling Coll., Oakdale, N.Y., 1996-98; exec. dir. Action Long Island, 1999—2001. Contbr. numerous articles on bus. econs., tech. edn., relation with the Far East. Bd. dirs. L.I. Philharm., West Suffolk YM & YWHA, United Way L.I.; chmn. L.I. Forum for Tech., Suffolk Cmty. Planning Coun., Old Westbury Coll. Found.; trustee Dowling Coll. Served to 1st lt. U.S. Army, 1944-46, PTO. Mem.: Eastpoint Golf and Racquet Club (West Palm Beach, Fla.). Home: 6451 Woodthrush Ct Palm Beach FL 33418-1429 Office Phone: 561-801-0100. Personal E-mail: ff1570@aol.com.

FISHER, JACK, medical educator, plastic surgeon; b. Mar. 10, 1947; BCS, U. Ill., 1969; MD, Emory U., Atlanta, 1973. Cert. Am. Bd. Plastic Surgery. Intern George Washington U. Med. Ctr., Washington, 1973-74, resident in gen. surgery, 1974-77, chief resident in gen. surgery, 1977-78; resident in plastic surgery Emory U. Hosp., 1978-80; staff, attending plastic surgeon Mayo Clinic, Rochester, Minn., 1981—86; assoc. clin. prof. dept. plastic surgery Vanderbilt U., Nashville, 1986—. Contbr. articles to profl. jours. Named one of Castle Connolly's America's Top Doctors, 2001—06. Fellow: ACS; mem.: Plastic Surgery Rsch. Coun., Am. Soc. Plastic Surgeons, Am. Soc. Aesthetic Plastic Surgery. Office: 310 23rd Ave N Ste 101 Nashville TN 37203-1525 Office Phone: 615-329-4227. Office Fax: 316-329-8931. Business E-Mail: info@drjackfisher.com.

FISHER, JAMES WILLIAM, pharmacologist, medical educator; b. Tucapau, SC, May 22, 1925; s. Ernest Amaziah and Mamie V. (Turner) F.; m. Carol Barbara Brodarick, June 5, 1947 (dec.), Maryann Hillyer Annis, Sept. 30, 2006; children: Candis Loreen Fisher Rush Smith, Patricia Eileen Fisher Valladares, Richard W., William E., John C., Elaine Marie Fisher Spurr (dec.). BS, U. S.C., 1947; PhD in Pharmacology (USPHS fellow), U. Louisville, 1958. Devel. chemist Armour Pharm. Rsch. Labs., Chgo., 1950-53, Ayerst Pharm. Labs., Rouses Point, NY, 1953—54; pharmacologist Lloyd Bros. Pharm. Co., Cin., 1954—56; instr. pharmacology U. Tenn., 1958-60, asst. prof., 1960-62, assoc. prof., 1962-66, prof., 1966-68; prof., chmn. dept. pharmacology Med. Sch., Tulane U., 1968-96; Regents prof. Tulane U., 1996—99, Regents prof. emeritus, chmn., 1999—. Vis. prof. U. Zambia, Lusaka, 1987, Keio U., Tokyo, 1987, U. Nairobi, 1993; external examiner U. W.I., Trinidad, 1992; vis. scientist Christie Hosp. and Holt Radium Inst., Manchester, Eng., 1963-64; dir. Tulane-Universidad Nacional del Nordeste, Corrientes, Argentina, Pan Am. Health Orgn. Physiol. Scis. Tng. Program, 1972-77; lectr. in field; mem. Nat. Heart, Lung and Blood Inst. (erythropoietin com. 1971-74), mem. NIH hematology tng. grants com., 1977; mem. Cooley's Anemia Nat. Rsch. Com., 1974; pres. So. Blood Club, 1975-77; mem. Wellcome Professorships Com., 1976, 93, 94, 95; mem. pharmacology com. Nat. Bd. Med. Examiners, 1988-92; mem. ad hoc group med. rsch. funding AAMC, 1990-93. Author: Readings on the History of Pharmacology, 1970; editor: Kidney Hormones, Vol. I, 1971, Vol. II, 1977, Vol. III, 1986, Renal Pharmacology, 1971, Handbook of Pharmacology: Blood and Blood Forming Organs, 1992, History of Pharmacology at Tulane, 1834-2004; co-editor: Erythropoiesis, 1975, Erythropoietin and Erythropoiesis, 1981; cons. editor: Erythropoietin, 1968; mem. editl. bd. Proc. Soc. Exptl. Biology and Medicine, 1971-86; contbr. articles to profl. jours. Served to lt. (j.g.) USNR, 1943-46, PTO. Recipient rsch. career devel. award USPHS, 1960-65, Purkinje medal Czechoslovakia Med. Soc., 1975, Golden Sovereign award, 1976, Aspet Exptl. Therapeutics award, 1992, U. Louisville Med. Sch. Alumni award, 1999; named Disting. faculty AOA Honor Med. Soc., 1993; Ann. Tulane Fisher Lectureship established in his honor, 1992. Mem. AAAS, AAUP, Am. Soc. Pharmacology and Exptl. Therapeutics (Sollman awards com. 1981, exptl. therapeutics award com. 1982, 94, alerting network 1986-90, ednl. affairs com. 1986-89, Krayer awards com. 1990, Exptl. Therapeutics award 1992, nominating com. 1997), Soc. Exptl. Biology and Medicine, Am. Soc. Nephrology, Am. Soc. Hematology (sci. affairs com. 1973-74, chmn. erythropoietin subcom. 1973), Assn. Med. Sch. Pharmacology (exec. com. 1979-82, nominating com. 1975, 86, 94, 96, 99, chmn. essential knowledge base in pharmacology com. 1984-95, pres. 1990-92), N.Y. Acad. Scis., Sigma Xi. Home: 67 Grand Canyon Dr New Orleans LA 70131 Business E-Mail: jfisher@tulane.edu.

FISHER, JIMBO (JOHN JAMES FISHER), college football coach; b. Clarksburg, W.Va., Oct. 9, 1965; m. Candi Fisher; children: Trey, Ethan. Attended, Samford U., Birmingham, Ala.; grad., Salem Coll., Winston-Salem, NC, 1989. Quarterback Chgo. Bruisers, Arena Football League, 1988; grad. asst., quarterbacks coach Samford U. Bulldogs, 1988—90, offensive coord., quarterbacks coach, 1991—92; quarterbacks coach Auburn U. Tigers, 1993—98; offensive coord., quarterbacks coach U. Cin. Bearcats, 1999, La. State U. Fighting Tigers, 2000—06, Fla. State U. Seminoles, Tallahassee, 2007—10, head football coach, 2010—. Named Divsn. III Nat. Player of Yr., 1987; finalist Frank Broyles award, 2001. Achievements include being head coach of the BCS National Championship winning Florida State University Seminoles, 2013. Office: Fla State Univ Football c/o Athletics Dept PO Box 2195 Tallahassee FL 32316 Office Phone: 850-644-2545.

FISHER, JOHN MORRIS, association official, business executive, educator; b. Fairhaven, Ohio, Apr. 20, 1922; s. Marion Hays and Bessie (Morris) F.; m. Thelma Ison, Feb. 2, 1947; children: Steven Roger, Linda Lucille. AB, Miami U., Oxford, Ohio, 1947; postgrad., Bklyn. Law Sch., 1950-51, Northwestern U., Evanston, Ill., 1954-55; LLD (hon.), Nasson Coll., 1972. With Belden Mfg. Co., Richmond, Ind., 1941; spl. agt. FBI, 1947—53; exec. staff asst. to v.p. personnel and employee rels. Sears Roebuck & Co., Chgo., 1953—57, chmn. corp. security com., 1957—61; chmn., CEO, oper. dir. Am. Security Coun., 1956—2002, pres., 1957—2002. Pres. Am. Rsch. Found., 1961-90; pres., CEO Am. Security Coun. Found., 1962-87, CEO, 1987-2002, chmn., 1992-2002; pres. Comm. Corp. Am., 1972-80, chmn., 1980—; pres. Am. Coalition Patriotic Socs., 1978-91; adminstrv. chmn. Coalition for Peace Through Strength, 1978-2002; dir. Ctr. for Internat. Security Studies, 1977-83; organizer, pres. Fidelifax, Inc., 1956-57; chmn. merc. divsn. Nat. Safety Coun., 1959-60, 1st vice chmn. trades and svcs. sect., 1961-62. Chmn. Chgo. Retail Safety Conf., 1959-60; spl. adviser Ill. Supt. Pub. Instrn., 1963-64; cons. to Gov. Fla.; cons. to chmn. com. cold war edn. Nat. Gov.'s Conf., 1962-65, Ill. CD Adv. Coun., 1965-68; pres. Am. Coun. World Freedom, 1971-72; mem. exec. com. Nat. Captive Nations Com., 1968-70; bd. visitors Freedoms Found., 1964-65; bd. dirs. Am. Fgn. Policy Inst., 1976-84, Security and Intelligence Fund, 1976-84, James Monroe Libr., 1977-85; pres. Culpeper Meml. Hosp. Found., 1984-86; exec. chmn. U.S. Congl. Adv. Bd., 1982-2002; chmn. Nat. Security Caucus Found., 1997-2002. 1st lt. USAAF, 1943-45. Decorated Air medal with clusters; recipient 10th Anniversary medal and scroll Assembly Captive European Nations, Order Lafayette Freedom award, 1973, Disting. Svc. award Chapel of 4 Chaplains, 1979, Pres. Eagle, Pres. Reagan, 1982, others. Mem. Am. Soc. Indsl. Security (dir. 1959-62), Phi Kappa Tau. Republican. Presbyterian. Office: Comms Corp Am 13195 Freedom Way Boston VA 22713 Home: 13195 Freedom Way Boston VA 22713-4114 Office Phone: 540-547-1700. Personal E-mail: johnmorrisfisher@comcast.net. Business E-Mail: john.fisher@cca.net.

FISHER, JOHN WELTON, II, lawyer, educator, academic administrator; b. Fisher, W.Va., Dec. 11, 1942; s. John Welton and Orrie (Shobe) F.; m. Susan Carol Vass, June 6, 1964; children: John Welton III, Jennifer Lynn. BA, W.Va. U., 1964, JD, 1967. Bar: W.Va. 1967, U.S. Dist. Ct. (no. and so. dists.) W.Va. 1967, U.S. Ct. Appeals (4th cir.) 1969. Law clk. to chief judge U.S. Dist. Ct. (no. dist.) W.Va., 1967-68; assoc. Farmer & Farmer, Morgantown, W.Va., 1968-71; mem. faculty W.Va. U. Coll. Law, 1971—, prof. law, 1977—, acting dean, 1981-82, 92-93, 97-98, dean, 1998—2008, exec. officer univ., 1982-86; magistrate judge U.S. Dist. Ct. No. Dist. W.Va., 1977-98. Reporter Speedy Trial Planning Group, No. Dist. W.Va. Reporter: Local Rules of Practice, Northern District of West Virginia, 1980. Fellow Am.Bar Found., W.Va. Bar Found.; mem. W.Va. State Bar, W.Va. Bar Assn., Fourth Cir. Jud. Conf., Order of Coif. Office: PO Box 6130 Morgantown WV 26506-6130 Office Phone: 304-293-8282. Business E-Mail: John.Fisher@mail.wvu.edu.

FISHER, MIKE, professional hockey player; b. Peterborough, Ont., Canada, June 5, 1980; s. Jim and Karen Fisher; m. Carrie Underwood, July 10, 2010. Center Ottawa Senators, 1999—2011, Nashville Predators, 2011—. Recipient NHL Found. Award, 2012; named to NHL YoungStars Game, 2002. Office: Nashville Predators Bridgestone Arena 501 Broadway Nashville TN 37203

FISHER, RANDALL G., pediatrician, educator; s. Arnold Garth and Geraldine Fisher; m. Melody Ann Cameron, June 29, 1991; children: Garrett Alexander, Grayson Clark. MD, Tulane U. Sch. Medicine, 1988. Cert. in pediatrics Am. Bd. Pediat., 1991. Asst. prof. pediat. Duke U. Sch. Medicine, Durham, NC, 1997—2000, attending faculty, pediatric infectious diseases, 1997—2000; asst. prof. pediat. Ea. Va. Med. Sch., Norfolk, Va., 2000—04, assoc. prof. pediat., 2004—. Attending physician Children's Hosp. King's Daughters, Norfolk, 2000—, dir., infectious diseases clin. divsn., 2001—. Co-author: (textbook) Moffet's Textbook Pediat. Infectious Diseases, 4th edit. Lippincott Williams and Wilkins; co-editor: Pediatric Infections Diseases Macmillan Med. Commn. News reader for blind Triangle

Radio Reading Svc., Durham, 1998—2000; cons. Hampton Rds. Pub. Schs., Va., 2002. Maj. US Army, 1988—94. Decorated Meritorous Svc. medal US Army; recipient Faculty Tchg. award, Ea. Va. Med. Sch. Children's Hosp. King's Daughters, Norfolk, Va., 2005—06, Physician Recognition award, AMA, 1997, 2004, 2007. Fellow: Am. Acad. Pediat.; mem.: AAP, Sect. Infectious Diseases, Va. Chpt., Am. Acad. Pediat., Infectious Diseases Soc. Am., Pediat. Infectious Diseases Soc. Avocation: music. Office: Children's Hosp King's Daughters 601 Children's Ln Norfolk VA 23507 Office Fax: 757-668-8275. Business E-Mail: randall.fisher@chkd.org.*

FISHER, RICHARD WELTON, bank executive; b. LA, Mar. 18, 1949; s. Magnhild and Leslie Welton Fisher; m. Nancy Collins, Sept. 8, 1973; children: Andersen, Alison, James, Texana. Student, US Naval Acad.; BA cum laude, Harvard U., Cambridge, Mass., 1971; student, Oxford U., Eng.; MBA, Stanford U., Calif., 1975. Asst. to Robert Roosa Brown Bros. Harriman & Co., NYC, 1975-77, sr. mgr., 1983-87; exec. asst. to sec. U.S. Dept. Treasury, Washington, 1977-79; mng. ptnr. Fisher Capital Mgmt., Dallas, 1987—97, Fisher Ewing Ptnrs. (Value Ptnrs., Ltd.), Dallas, 1987—97; dep. U.S. Trade Rep. Exec. Office of the Pres., Washington, 1997—2001; vice-chmn. Kissinger McLarty Assocs., Washington, 2001—05; pres., CEO Fed. Res. Bank Dallas, 2005—. Chmn. Stanford U. Sch. Bus. Trust, Palo Alto, 1982—84, Am. Assembly, NY; adj. prof. L.B.J. Sch., U. Tex., 1995—97; mem. Trilateral Commn., 2002. Trustee Brookings Instn., Washington, 2001—05; bd. dirs., mem. exec. com. Dallas Mus. Art, 1985—89; bd. dirs. Dallas Assembly, 1983—97, Boys Club Dallas, 1984, Am. Coun. on Germany, 1985—94, 2004, Russian Am. Enterprise Fund, 1993—98, Goodwill Industries Dallas, 1989—98, treas., 1991—93, chmn., 1993—95. Decorated gran official Order of Bernardo O'Higgins (Chile); recipient Outstanding Achievement award, Stanford U., 1986, Eisenhower Medal for Disting. Pub. Svc., 2006; named Admiral of Tex. Navy, 1987; US-Japan leadership fellow, Japan Soc., 1989, Weatherhead fellow, Harvard U., 2001, hon. fellow, Hertford Coll., Oxford U., 2002. Fellow: Am. Acad. Arts & Scis.; mem.: Philos. Soc. Tex., Met. Club (Washington), Petroleum Club, Harvard Club. Presbyterian. Office: Fed Res Bank Dallas 2200 N Pearl St Dallas TX 75201 Office Phone: 214-922-6000.*

FISHER, ROBERT W., retired food products executive; b. 1937; Pres. Dole Food Co., Inc., 1986—90; COO The Noboa Group, 1991—93; pres. Geest Banana Co., 1993—95; COO The Noboa Group, 1996—98; acting COO Chiquita Brands International, Inc., 2002. Bd. dirs. Geest Banana Co., 1993—95, Chiquita Brands Internat., Inc., 2002—. Office: Chiquita Brands International Inc 550 S Caldwell St Ste 1010 Charlotte NC 28202-2681 Office Phone: 513-784-8000. Office Fax: 513-784-8030. Business E-Mail: rfisher@chiquita.com.

FISHER, SEYMOUR, psychologist, educator; b. NYC, Nov. 4, 1925; s. George and Fannie (Hesselson) F.; m. Carmen Eldridge, June 20, 1959; children: Mark, Andrew. BA, NYU, 1948; PhD, U. N.C., 1952; postgrad., Washington Sch. Psychiatry, 1954-55. Diplomate Am. Bd. Examiners in Psychol. Hypnosis. Clin. psychologist trainee VA Hosp., Roanoke, 1950, psychology trainee, 1952; intern Psychol. Clinic, U. N.C., Chapel Hill, 1950-51; supervising clin. psychologist Walter Reed Army Inst. Rsch., Washington, 1952-58; rsch. psychologist Psychopharmacology Svc. Ctr., NIMH, Bethesda, Md., 1958-60; chief spl. studies unit Psychopharmacology Rsch Br., NIMH, Bethesda, 1960-63; prof. psychiatry (psychology), dir. rsch. tng., dir. psychopharmacology lab., divsn. psychiatry Boston U. Sch. Medicine, 1963-78; prof. dept. psychiatry and behavioral scis., U. Tex. Med. Br., Galveston, 1978—, prof. emeritus, 2000—, assoc. chmn. for rsch., 1978-80, rsch. advisor to chmn. dept., 1980-91, dir. Ctr. for Medication Monitoring, 1987-2000. Vis. prof. Harvard U., Boston U., May to Nov., 1988; cons. NIMH, Chevy Chase, Md., 1964-66, mem. clin. psychopharmacology rsch. rev. com., 1973-77, mem. treatment devel. and assessment rsch. rev. com., 1979-83; cons. Office Naval Rsch., Washington, 1964-66, Mass. Dept. Mental Health, 1969-78, FDA, 1973-77; pres. Boston Mental Health Found., Inc., 1970-72; mem. Commn. on Cmty. Care of Mentally Ill, chmn. tech. com. Hogg Found., 1987-90, planning com. for 50th anniversary rsch. conf., 1988-89 Mem. editl. bd. Psychopharmacology Svc. Ctr. Bull., 1959-63; assoc. editor Psychol. Record, 1960-66; sr. editor vol. on clin. and biobehavioral aspects of cocaine, Oxford U. Press, 1987; mem. adv. bd. Internat. Jour. Methods Psychiatry, 1998-2000; contbr. numerous articles to profl. jours., chpts. in books. Recipient Disting. Alumnus award U. N.C., 1981, Donald E. Francke award for best paper Drug Info. Jour., 1987. Fellow APA (mem. exec. coun. divsn. psychopharmacology 1979-82), Am. Coll. Neuropsychcopharmacology (life, pres. 1984, asst. sec.-treas. 1974-77, chmn. hon. awards com. 1985-87, mem. other coms. 1973-87, emeritus), Soc. Clin. and Exptl. Hypnosis, Internat. Coll. Psychosomatic Medicine, Collegium Internat. Neuro-Psychopharmacologicum (emeritus); mem. Am. Psychopathol. Assn. (exec. coun. 1970-72), Psi Chi, Sigma Xi, Beta Lambda Sigma. Business E-Mail: sfisher@utmb.edu.

FISHER, SUSAN C., state legislator; b. Morganton, NC, Oct. 3, 1955; m. John Fisher; children: Jonathan, Alexandra. Staff US Rep. James McClure Clarke, 1982—84; chmn. Asheville City Bd. Edn., 1993—2001; exec. dir. Kids Voting Buncombe Co., 2001—04; state rep. Dist. 114 NC, 2005—. Mem.: Asheville Burcombe League Women Voters, NC Coun. Women, Asheville Cmty. Theatre. Democrat. Episcopalian. Mailing: 7 Maple Ridge Ln Asheville NC 28806 Office: North Carolina House of Representatives 300 N Salisbury St Rm 504 Raleigh NC 27603-5925 Office Phone: 919-715-2013. E-mail: Susan.Fisher@ncleg.net.

FISHER, WILLIAM LAWRENCE, geologist, educator, dean; b. Marion, Ill., Sept. 16, 1932; s. Henry Adam and Madge Lenora (Moore) F.; m. Marilee Booth, Dec. 18, 1954; children: Leah, Karl, Peter. BS, So. Ill. U., 1954, DSc, 1986; MS, U. Kans., 1958, PhD, 1961; DEng, Colo. Sch. Mines, 2002. Cert. Profl. Geologist Am. Inst. Profl. Geologists, Petroleum Geologist Am. Assn. Petroleum Geologists, Profl. Earth Scientist Soc. Ind. Profl. Earth Scientists. Rsch. scientist Tex. Bur. Econ. Geology, Austin, 1960-68, assoc. dir., 1968-70, dir., 1970-75, 77-94, dir., ad interim, 1999; dir. John A. and Katherine G. Jackson Sch. Geoscis., 2001—05, dean, 2005—06; asst. sec. for energy and minerals Dept. Interior, Washington, 1976—77; prof. dept. geol. scis. U. Tex., Austin, 1969—, dep. asst. sec. energy, 1975—76, Morgan J. Davis prof. petroleum geology, 1984-86, Leonidas T. Barrow chair in mineral resources, 1986—, participating faculty LBJ sch. pub. affairs, 1977—81, chmn. dept. geol. scis., 1984-90, dir. Geology Found., 1984—2006. Vis. prof. dept. geology So. Ill. U., 1967; bd. dirs. Pogo Producing Co.; HRT, SA, geology assoc. bd. U. Kans., 1972-74, 83—; adv. coun. Gas Rsch. Inst., Tex. Energy and Natural Resource; mem. Tex. Sci. Adv. Coun., Gov.'s Energy Coun., White House Sci. Coun., Nat. Petroleum Coun., Pres.' Coun. of Advisors on Sci. and Tech. Panel on Energy R & D and Sec. Energy Adv. Bd.; mem. Tex. 2000 Commn.; bd dirs. Diamond Shamrock, 1987-98, bd. dirs. HRT Trustee, chmn. Southwest Rsch. Inst. With AUS, 1954—56. Shell fellow, 1961; recipient Hedberg medal Inst. for the Study of Earth and Man, 1995, Robert Earll McConnell award Am. Inst. Mining, Metall. and Petroleum Engrs., 2004, Col. Edwin L. Drake Legendary Oilman award, Petroleum History Inst., 2010. Fellow AAAS, Soc. Econ. Geology, Geol. Soc. Am. (councillor); mem. NRC (commn. on geoscis., environ. and resource, chmn. bd. mineral and energy resources, US nat. com. on geology, chmn. bd. on earth scis. and resources, bd. on energy and environ. sys.), Nat. Acad. Engring., Nat. Assoc., Nat. Acads. (nat. assoc. 2003), Am. Inst. Profl. Geologists (pres. Tex. sect. 1979, pres. 1993, Galey Pub. Svc. award, 1985, Parker medal, 1996), Assn. Am. State Geologists (hon. pres. 1981-82), Am. Assn. Petroleum Geologists (hon., pres. 1985-86, trustee, chmn. Found., Sidney Powers Meml. medal award 1994, Heritage award 2006), Am. Geol. Inst. (pres. 1991, trustee, chmn. Found., Campbell medal, 1991, Heroy award, 1997, Milling Legendary Geoscientist medal 2007), Brazilian Assn. Petroluem Geologists (Disting. Acheivement award 2009), Austin Geol. Soc. (hon., pres. 1973-74), Gulf Coast Assn. Geol. Scis. (hon. 1986, pres. 1994, Boyd medal 2002), Tex. Ind. Prodrs. and Royalty Owners (Hats Off award, 2002), Assn. Engring. and Environ. Geologists (Henley award 2009), Tex. Acad. Medicine, Engring. and Sci., Acad. Medicine, Engring. Sci. Tex. (founding mem.), Soc. Sedimentary Geology (Twenhofel medal 2001), Soc. Petroleum Engrs., Soc. Ind. Profl. Earth Scientists, Brazilian Assn. Petroleum Geologists, Engring. & Environ. Geologists(Tex.)(Assoc.) Republican. Achievements include first to introduce the concept of depositional systems linking modern depositional environments to ancient counterparts in 1967; introduced the concept of additional mobile oil recovery and its significance to oil and gas reserves growth. Home: 8705 Ridgehill Dr Austin TX 78759-7342 Office: Univ Tex Dept Geological Scis Austin TX 78712 Office Phone: 512-471-5600. Business E-Mail: wfisher@mail.utexas.edu.

FISHER-HOCH, SUSAN P., epidemiologist, educator; b. Eng., 1940; m. Joseph McCormick, 1992. MB, BS First Class with honors in Pathology, U. London, 1975; MB, BS, LRCP, MRCS, Royal Free Hosp. Sch. Medicine, 1976; MSc in Med. Microbiology, London Sch. Hygiene and Tropical Medicine, U. London, 1978; MRCPath, Royal Coll. Pathologists, Virology, 1981; MD in Epidemiology, U. London, 1981. Lic. Royal Coll. Physicians, 1975. House surgeon St. Luke's Hosp., Guildford, 1975—76; house physician to Dame Sheila Sherlock Med. Unit, Royal Free Hosp., 1975—76; trainee med. microbiologist Oxford Regional Pub. Health Lab., Radcliffe Hosp., 1976—77; sr. registrar, dept. virology St. George's Hosp. Med. Sch., 1979—82, hon. lectr., 1982—; sr. registrar, dept. microbiology Kingston Hosp., 1979—82; Wellcome Trust Fellowship Wellcome Trust Unit, Bangkok and Spl. Pathogens Ref. Lab., Porton Down, 1982—85; cons. med. microbiologist, dir. Viral Zoonoses Lab., Ctrl. Pub. Health Lab., 1985—86; assoc. prof. Emory Sch. Pub. Health, 1991—; dep. br. chief Spl. Pathogens Br., Divsn. Viral and Rickettisial Diseases, Ctrs. for Disease Control and Prevention, Atlanta, 1986—90, acting br. chief, 1988; sr. med. epidemiologist, mycotic diseases br., divsn. baterial and mycotic diseases Ctrs. for Disease Control and Prevention, Atlanta, 1990—93; rsch. prof., dept. pathology Aga Khan U. Med. Sch., Karachi, Pakistan, 1993—97; dir. Laboratoire Jean Mérieux, BSL4, Fondation Marcel Mérieux, Lyon, France, 1993—97; prof. U. Tex. Houston Sch. Pub. Health, Brownsville, 2000—; faculty, grad. sch. biomedical scis. U. Tex. Health Scis. Ctr., Houston, 2001. Invited spkr. in field. Contbr. several articles to profl. jours., chapters to books, scientific papers; writer of invited editls. Lancet, provided expert advice to the lay press and TV, featured in both media and books about hemmorrhagic fever; co-author (with husband): Level 4: Virus Hunters of the CDC. Recipient Chevalier de la Légion d'Honneur, Pres. French Republic, Jacques Chirac, 1999, Medal de la Ville de Lyon, by mayor and former Prime Minister of France, Raymond Barre, 2000, Priz Scientique du Groupe Paris-Lyon, 2000; named one of Women In Technology Internat. Hall of Fame, 2008. Mem.: Royal Coll. Pathologists, Royal Coll. Surgeons. Avocations: skiing, running, backpacking, music, literature, languages, history, art, cooking. Office: U Houston Health Sci Ctr Sch Pub Health U Tex Brownsville 80 Fort Brown Set B Rm 1 334 Brownsville TX 78520 Office Phone: 956-882-5167. Office Fax: 956-882-5152. Business E-Mail: susan.p.fisher-hoch@utb.edu.

FISHMAN, GERALD JAY, astrophysicist; b. St. Louis, Feb. 10, 1943; m. Nancy D.; children: Lisa R., Jodi L. BS in Physics, U. Mo., 1965; MS in Space Sci., Rice U., 1968, PhD in Space Sci., 1970. Rsch. assoc. space sci. Rice U., 1965—69; sr. rsch. scientist Teledyne Brown Engring. Co., 1969-74; prin. investor Gamma Ray Observer, 1978—; sr. staff scientist NASA/Marshall Space Flight Ctr., 1974—98, sr. scientist, 1974—, chief scientist, 1998—. Co-recipient Shaw Found. Prize-Astronomy, Hong Kong, 2011. Mem. AAAS, Am. Astron. Soc., Am. Phys. Soc., Internat. Astron. Union, Sigma Xi. Office: NASA-Marshall Space Flight MSFC Huntsville AL 35812 Office Phone: 256-961-7691. Business E-Mail: jerry.fishman@nasa.gov.

FISHMAN, MARVIN ALLEN, pediatric neurologist, educator; b. Chgo., Feb. 16, 1937; s. Joseph and Mary (Schneider) F.; m. Gloria Brenda Greenberg, Dec. 20, 1959; children: Bradley Steven, Patricia Ann. BS, U. Ill., 1959, MD, 1961. Diplomate Am. Bd. Pediatrics, Am. Psychiatry and Neurology. Intern, then resident in pediat. Michael Reese Hosp. and Med. Center, Chgo., 1961—64; resident in neurology Mass. Gen. Hosp., Boston, 1966—67; fellow in pediat. neurology St. Louis Children's Hosp., 1967—70, dir. Birth Defects Ctr., 1971—79; prof. pediat., neurology and preventive medicine Washington U. Med. Sch., St. Louis, 1970—79, dir. Irene Walter Johnson Inst. Rehab., 1974—79; prof. pediat. and neurology Baylor Coll. Medicine, Houston, 1979—2007, prof. emeritus pediat. and neurology, 2007—, dir. pediat. neurology tng. program, 1979—2004, vice chmn. dept. pediat., 1992—2007; chief neurology svc. Tex. Children's Hosp., Houston, 1979—2004, chief Blue Bird Clinic for Child Neurology, 2003—05. Mem. residency rev. com. for neurology Accreditation Coun. for Grad. Med. Edn., 1991-96, chmn., 1995-96; bd. dirs. Am. Bd. Psychiatry and Neurology, 1991-97, exec. com., 1995-97, v.p., 1996, pres., 1997, cons., 1999-05; cons. Am. Bd. Pediat., 1999-05. Conbr. articles in field, chpts. in books; mem. editl. bd. Jour. Pediat., 1980-87, Jour. Child Neurology, Pediat. Neurology, Annals of Neurology; editor textbook. With USAR, 1964-66. Grantee HEW, Grant Found., Ga. Warm Springs Found., Nat. Found.-March of Dimes. Mem. Am. Soc. Neurochemistry (councilor 1977-79), Child Neurology Soc. (exec. com., councillor 1980-82, sec.-treas. 1984-86, pres.-elect 1986-87, pres. 1987-89, past pres. 1989-90, John B. Hower award 1999), Houston Neurol. Soc. (pres.-elect 1989-90, pres. 1990-91), Am. Acad. Pediat., Am. Acad. Neurology, Am. Neurol. Assn., Am. Pediat. Soc., Soc. Pediat. Rsch., Soc. Neuroscis., Tex. Neurol. Soc. (Lifetime Achievement award 2009). Home: 1523-B Potomac Dr Houston TX 77057-1925 Personal E-mail: mfishman@comcast.net.

FISHMAN, RICHARD G., chemicals executive, lawyer; b. Orange, NJ, June 2, 1952; BA in Economics, Rutgers Coll., 1974; LLM in Tax., NYU School of Law, 1980; JD, Yale Law Sch., 1977. CPA NJ, NY; bar: NJ, NY, La. Dir. internat. and bus. tax planning and assoc. tax counsel Honeywell International, Inc., 1988—2006; dir. of tax and chief tax vounsel Albemarle Corp., 2006—07, v.p., tax and chief tax counsel, 2007—08, v.p., treas., chief tax counsel, 2008—, v.p., interim chief fin. officer, 2010—11. Office: Albemarle Corp Baton Rouge Tower 451 Florida St Baton Rouge LA 70801 Office Phone: 225-388-8011. Office Fax: 225-388-7110. Business E-Mail: richard.fishman@albemarle.com.

FISHMAN, ROBERT, corporate financial executive; HBA, Univ. We. Ontario; MBA, Univ. Pa. CPA, Chartered Acct., Canada, Chartered Fin. Analyst, Assn. for Investment Mgmt. & Rsch. CPA Price Waterhouse, Toronto, England, Germany; fin. mgmt. positions inc. dir. EMEA planning & pricing, dir. mergers & acquisitions, CFO payment solutions NCR Corp., Duluth, Ga., 1993—2005, v.p. corp. planning & asst. contr., 2005—06, v.p., corp. contr., 2007—10, interim CFO, 2007—08, 2009—10, sr. v.p., CFO, chief acctg. officer, 2010—. Office: NCR Corp 3097 Satellite Blvd Duluth GA 30096-5810 Office Phone: 937-445-1936.

FISKE, EDWARD B., editor, journalist; b. Phila., June 4, 1937; s. Edward R., Jr. and Jean B.; m. Dale Alden Woodruff, July 12, 1963 (div. May 1997); children: Julia F. Hogan, Suzanna R. Fiske; m. Helen F. Ladd, June 29, 1997. BA, Wesleyan U., Middletown, Conn., 1959; MA, Princeton Theol. Sem., 1963, Columbia U., 1965; LL.D. (hon.), Occidental Coll., 1991; and others. Religion reporter and editor N.Y. Times, 1964-74, edn. editor, 1974-91. Cons. Pew Forum on Edn. Reform, 1991-92, UNICEF Edn. Mission to Bangladesh, 1993, Internat. Rescue Com. in Cambodia, 1993-94, Acad. Ednl. Devel., 1993—, World Bank, 1995—, UNESCO, 1996—, USAID, 2003-; edn. analyst Asian Devel. Bank, 1994; vis. scholar Victoria U. Wellington, New Zealand, 1998, U. Cape Town, South Africa, 2002, vis. rschr. U. Amsterdam, 2009. Author: Fiske Guide to Colleges, (annual) Smart Schools, Smart Kids, 1990, (with Bruce Hammond) Fiske Guide to Getting into The Right College, 1997, 5th edit., 2014, (with Bruce Hammond) When Schools Compete, 2000, (with Helen Ladd) Fiske What to Do When for College, 2004, (with Hammond) Fiske Nailing the New SAT, 2005, (with Hammond) Elusive Equity: Education Reform in Post-Apartheid South Africa, 2004 (with Ladd); contbr. articles to nat. periodicals. Bd. mem. East Durham Children's Quantitative, Durham, NC Ctr. Internat. Understanding, Central Park Sch. Children, NC Citizen Schs. Wolynsky-Joukowsky fellow Brown U., 1990, Montgomery fellow Dartmouth Coll., 1991. Mem.: Phi Beta Kappa. Home: 1723 Tisdale St Durham NC 27705-5631

FITCH, ROBERT D., orthopedic surgeon; MD, Duke U. Sch. Medicine, NC, 1976. Orthopedic residency Duke U. Sch. Medicine, 1978—82; pediatric orthopedic surgery fellowship Scottish Rite, Tex., 1982—83; chief, pediatric orthopedics Duke U. Med. Ctr. Contbr. articles to profl. publs. Achievements include research in limb lengthening and external fixation; the effects of non steroidal anti-inflammatories on the quality of bone regenerate formed with distraction osteogenesis. Office: Duke U Med Ctr Duke Med Ctr Box 2911 Durham NC 27710 Office Phone: 919-684-3104. Office Fax: 919-681-8703.

FITCHETT, TAYLOR, law librarian; b. 1947; BA, Kans. State U., 1970; MLS, U. Ala., 1979. Acting dir. Law Libr. U. Ala., 1981—83; assoc. libr. Law Libr. Tulane U., 1983—86; dir. Law Libr. U. Cin., 1986—98; assoc. libr. Law Libr. U. Va., 1998—2000, dir. Law Libr. and lectr. gen. faculty, 2000—. Mem.: Va. Assn. Law Libr. (chmn., publications com.), Am. Libr. Assn., Am. Assn. Law Libr. Office: Office of Law Library Director University Virginia 580 Massie Rd Charlottesville VA 22903-1789 Office Phone: 434-924-7725. Business E-Mail: tf2u@virginia.edu.

FITTS, BARRY, healthcare company executive; With HCA, Inc., Columbia, Norton Healthcare; nat. dir., clin.and fin. applications support Catholic Health Initiatives; v.p., fin. application svcs. Community Health Systems, Inc., 2007—. Office: Community Health Systems 4000 Meridian Blvd Franklin TN 37067 Office Phone: 615-465-7000. Business E-Mail: barry_fitts@chs.net.

FITTS, CATHERINE AUSTIN, investment advisor; b. Phila., Dec. 24, 1950; d. William Thomas Jr. and Barbara Kinsey (Willits) Fitts. AA, Bennett Coll., 1970; student, Chinese U., Hong Kong, 1971; BA, U. Pa., 1974, MBA, 1978; postgrad., MIT, 1995. With Dillon, Read & Co., Inc., NYC, 1978-89, sr. v.p., 1984-86, mng. dir., 1986-89, also bd. dirs.; asst. sec. housing, urban devel., fed. housing commr. HUD, Washington, 1989-90; pres., chmn. Hamilton Securities Group, Inc., Washington, 1990-97, Solari, Inc., Tenn., 1998—, Solari Investment Adv. Svcs. LLC, 2006—, Sea Lane Adv. LLC, 2010—; publ. Solari Report. Adv. bd. Fedn. Nat. Mortgage Assn. Fannie Mae, 1992—93; emerging markets adv. com. SEC, 1990—93. Bd. dir. Student Loan Mktg. Assn. Sallie Mae, 1991—94; mem. grad. adv. bd. Wharton Sch., U. Pa., Phila., 1986—95. Home Phone: 731-609-2412; Office Phone: 731-764-2515. Business E-Mail: catherine@solari.com.

FITZ, J. GREGORY, dean, gastroenterologist, educator; BS, U. NC, Chapel Hill, 1975; MD, Duke U., Durham, NC, 1979. Cert. in internal medicine 1982, in gastroenterology 1986. Residency in internal medicine U. Calif., San Francisco, 1979—83, fellowship in gastroenterology, 1983—84; head divsn. gastroenterology and hepatology U. Colo. Health Sciences Ctr.; prof. medicine, dir. gastroenterology fellowship program Duke U. Med. Ctr.; joined U. Tex. SW Med. Ctr., Dallas, 2003, prof., Donald W. Seldin disting. chmn. in internal medicine, Atticus James Gill, MD chair in med. sci., Nadine and Tom Craddick disting. chair in med. sci., dean sch. medicine, exec. v.p. academic affairs, provost, 2009—. Recipient MERIT award, NIH, 2002. Mem.: Assn. American Physicians, American Fedn. Clin. Rsch., American Assn. for Study Liver Rsch., American Gastroenterol. Assn., American Soc. Clin. Investigation (Best Doctors in America 2001—03). Office: University Tex SW Med Ctr at Dallas Office of Dean 5323 Harry Hines Blvd Dallas TX 75390 Office Phone: 214-648-2509. Business E-Mail: greg.fitz@utsouthwestern.edu.

FITZGERALD, EDMUND BACON, electronics executive; b. Milw., Feb. 5, 1926; s. Edmund and Elizabeth (Bacon) F.; m. Elisabeth McKee Christensen, Sept. 6, 1947; children: Karen, Kathleen, Edmund Greer, Rogers Christensen. BSEE, U. Mich., 1946. With Cutler-Hammer, Inc., Milw., 1946-78, v.p. in charge engring., 1959-61, adminstrv. v.p., 1961-63, pres., CEO, 1964-69, chmn., chief exec. officer, 1969-78; vice chmn. Eaton Corp., Cleve., 1978-79; mng. dir. Hampshire Assocs., Milw., 1979-80; pres., dir. No. Telecom, Inc., Nashville, 1980-82; pres. No. Telecom Ltd., 1982-84, chmn. bd. dirs. Mississauga, 1985-90; mng. dir. Woodmont Assocs., Nashville, 1990—. Adj. prof. mgmt. Vanderbilt U., Nashville, 1990—; former chmn., bd. dirs. Milw. Brewers Baseball Club, Inc.; former chmn. Com. for Econ. Devel.; mem. President's Nat. Security Telecom. Adv. Com. Capt. USMCR, 1943-46, 51-52. Named Man of Yr., Milw. Jr. C. of C., 1956 Mem. Nat. Elec. Mfrs. Assn. (pres. 1968). Office: Woodmont Assocs 3434 Woodmont Blvd Nashville TN 37215-1422

FITZGERALD, JOHN THOMAS, JR., religious studies educator; b. Birmingham, Ala., Oct. 2, 1948; s. John Thomas and Annie Myrtle (Walters) Fitzgerald; m. Karol Bonneaux, May 23, 1970; children: Kirstin Leigh, Kimberly Anne. BA, Abilene Christian U., 1970, MA, 1972; MDiv, Yale U., 1975, PhD, 1984. Instr. Yale Coll., New Haven, 1979, Yale Div. Sch., New Haven, 1980—81; from instr. to asst. prof. U. Miami, Coral Gables, Fla., 1981—88, assoc. prof., 1988—2009, prof., 2009—12, dir. honors program, master Hecht Residential Coll., 1987—91, chair religious studies dept., 2010—12; prof. U. Notre Dame, 2012—. Vis. assoc. prof. Brown U., Providence, 1992, Yale Div. Sch., New Haven, 1998—99, New Haven, 2004; vis. rsch. scholar North-West U., Potchefstroom, South Africa, 2006; prof.

extraordinary NW U., Potchefstroom, South Africa, 2008—. Author: Tabula of Cebes, 1983, Cracks in an Earthen Vessel, 1988; editor: Christian Origins sect. Religious Studies Rev., 1994—2002, Friendship, Flattery and Frankness of Speech, 1996, Greco-Roman Perspecitves on Friendship, 1997, Early Christianity and Classical Culture, 2003, Philodemus and the New Testament World, 2004, The Writings of St. Paul, 2007, Passions and Moral Progress in Greco-Roman Thought, 2008, Animosity, the Bible and Us, 2009; contbr. articles to profl. jours. Judge for Silver Knight awards Miami (Fla.) Herald, 1988, 1990. Recipient Max Orvitz Summer Rsch. award, U. Miami, 1985, 1987, 1994, 1995, 1998, 2002, 2009; named Two Bros. fellow, Yale Div. Sch., 1974—75; fellow, Rotary, Tuebingen, Germany, 1975—76. Mem.: Soc. Bibl. Lit. (chmn. com. 1989—96, editor Texts and Translations Series: Greco-Roman Religion 1993—2000, editor Writings from the Greco-Roman World Series 2001—06, chmn. com. 2003—04, sec. 2003—08, coun. 2003—08, chmn. 2008—13, co-chair, early Christianity and the ancient economy sect. 2008—, mem., rsch. & publs. com. 2011—, chmn., rsch. & publs. com. 2012—, rsch. grantee 1997—99), Golden Key Nat. Honor Soc., Iron Arrow Hon. Soc., Omicron Delta Kappa, Phi Kappa Phi (chpt. pres. 1988—89). Home: 15215 SW 78 Ct Palmetto Bay FL 33157-2349 Home Phone: 305-235-4298; Office Phone: 574-631-6607. Business E-Mail: jfitzg10@nd.edu.

FITZGERALD, KEITH, former state legislator, political science professor; b. Springfield, Ohio, Nov. 30, 1956; m. Angela Baker; children: Bridget, Conor. BA, U. Louisville, 1979; PhD, Ind. U., 1987. Assoc. prof. polit. sci. New Coll. Fla., Sarasota, 1994—; mem. Dist. 69 Fla. House of Reps., Tallahassee, 2006—10, dep. policy chair, 2006—08, Dem. caucus policy chair, 2008—10, ranking mem. policy coun., mem. fin. and tax coun., health and family svcs. policy coun., mil. and local affairs policy com., select policy coun. on strategic and econ. planning. Mem. policy coun., fin. and tax coun., health & family services policy coun., mil. & local affairs policy com. Fla. State House of Reps. Author: Face of the Nation: Immigration, the State, and the National Identity; contbr. articles to profl. jours. Adv. coun. Faculty Senates; mem. Sarasota City Charter Rev. Bd.; bd. trustees New Coll. Fla; bd. mem. Suncoast Partnership to End Homelessness. Mem.: Am. Polit. Sci. Assn. Democrat. Roman Catholic. Office: New Coll Fla Divsn Social Scis 5800 Bay Shore Rd Sarasota FL 34243-2197 Office Phone: 941-487-4325. E-mail: fitzgerald@ncf.edu.*

FITZGERALD, KEVIN GERARD, oil industry executive; b. New Orleans, Oct. 31, 1955; s. Patrick Harold Fitzgerald and Rosary Claire (Carallero) Eble; m. Janice Faye Mender, Dec. 20, 1975; children: Kevin Gerard Jr., Shelly Lynn. B magna cum laude in Acctg., U. New Orleans, 1977. CPA, La. Ptnr. Vizzoni & Cooley, CPAs, Kenner, La., 1975-82; asst. treas. Ocean Drilling and Exploration Co., New Orleans, 1982; dir. investor rels. Murphy Oil Corp., 1996—2001, treas., 2001—06, sr. v.p., CFO, 2007—. Mem. AICPA, La. Soc. CPAs (New Orleans chpt.). Clubs: Corp. 25 Investment (Metairie, La.) (treas. 1986), Metaurice Carnival. Roman Catholic. Avocations: fishing, softball. Office: Murphy Oil Corp PO Box 7000 El Dorado AR 71731-7000 Office Phone: 870-862-6411.

FITZGERALD, LISA A., apparel executive; Various merchandising positions Casual Corner; v.p., gen. mdse. mgr. Gymboree; various merchandising positions May Co, The Gymboree Corp., Victoria's Secret; exec. v.p., merchandising, design and creative, interim pres. Lands' End, Inc. (div. of Sears Holdings Corp.), 2008; exec. v.p., brand leader, OshKosh B'gosh Carter's, Inc., 2009—. Office: Carter's Inc 1170 Peachtree St NE Ste 900 Atlanta GA 30309 Office Phone: 404-745-2700. Office Fax: 404-892-0968. Business E-Mail: lisa.fitzgerald@carters.com.

FITZGERALD, PETER GOSSELIN, bank executive, former United States Senator from Illinois; b. Elgin, Ill., Oct. 20, 1960; s. Gerald Francis and Marjorie (Gosselin) F.; m. C. Nina Kerstiens, July 25, 1987; 1 child, Jake Buchanan. AB, Dartmouth Coll., 1982; cert. of attendance, Aristotelian U., Salonica, Greece, 1983; JD, U. Mich., 1986. Bar: Ill. 1986, U.S. Dist. Ct. (no. dist.) Ill. 1986. Assoc. Isham, Lincoln & Beale, Chgo., 1986-88; ptnr. Riordan, Larson, Bruckert & Moore, Chgo., 1988-92; mem. Ill. State Senate, Springfield, Ill., 1993—98, chmn. state govt. ops. com., 1997—98; US Senator from Ill. Washington, 1999—2005; chmn. Chain Bridge Bank, N.A., McLean, Va., 2006—. Counsel Harris Bankmont, Inc., 1992—96; dir. Nat. Coun. Econ. Edn., 2005—07; trustee Nat. Constitution Ctr., 2005—; adv. dir. Transurban Devel., Inc., 2006—08. Rotary Found. internat. grad. scholar, 1982-83. Mem. Econ. Club Chgo. Republican. Roman Catholic. Office: Chain Bridge Bank NA 1445A Laughlin Ave Mc Lean VA 22101 Office Phone: 703-748-2005.

FITZGERALD, TIMOTHY P., public health service officer; Regional managed care officer, gen. mgr., Mid-Atlantic region CIGNA Healthcare; sr. v.p., health care delivery Empire Blue Cross Blue Shield, NY; sr. v.p., healthcare delivery sys. Amerigroup Corp., 2006—. Office: Amerigroup Corp Ste 100 4425 Corporation Ln Virginia Beach VA 23462 Office Phone: 757-490-6900. Office Fax: 757-518-3600. Business E-Mail: tfitzgerald@amerigroupcorp.com.

FITZHUGH, CALVIN CRAIG, state legislator, lawyer; b. Brownsville, Tenn., Mar. 22, 1950; s. James R. and Frances (Craig) F.; m. Pamela Chism, June 8, 1974; children: Elizabeth Marley, Thomas Arthur Craig. BS, U. Tenn., 1972, JD, 1975. Bar: Tenn. 1975, U.S. Dist. Ct. (we. dist.) Tenn. 1975, U.S. Ct. Mil. Appeals 1976. Ptnr. Caldwell & Fitzhugh, Attys., Ripley, Tenn.; v.p., counsel Bank of Ripley, 1988—, bd. dir.; mem. Dist. 82 Tenn. House Reps., 1994—. Scoutmaster troop 63 boy Scouts Am., Ripley, 1988, bd. dirs. West Tenn. dist., Jackson, 1984—; bd. dirs. Tri-County Mental Health Ctr., Covington, Tenn., 1986—. Major USAF, 1976-80. Mem. ABA, Tenn. Bar Assn., Lauderdale County Bar Assn. (pres. 1983—), Ripley C. of C. (pres. 1985-86), Phi Alpha Delta. Democrat. Baptist. Avocation: duck hunting. Office: 33 Legislative Plz Nashville TN 37243-0182 Office Phone: 615-741-2134. Office Fax: 615-741-1446. Business E-Mail: rep.craig.fitzhugh@capitol.tn.gov.

FITZPATRICK, JONATHAN, food service executive; Grad. with honors, Univ. Coll. Dublin, 1992; MA in Banking & Fin., Smurfit Grad. Sch. Bus., Dublin Univ. Various mgmt. positions Diageo plc; pres., COO Tex. Digital Sys. Inc., 2002; v.p. info. tech. Burger King Corp., 2005—07, sr. v.p. devel. & franchising, 2007, sr. v.p. ops. EMEA divsn. (Europe, Middle East, Africa), then exec. v.p. global ops., 2010—11, exec. v.p., chief brand and ops. officer, 2011—. Office: Burger King Corp 5505 Blue Lagoon Dr Miami FL 33126 Office Phone: 305-378-3000. Business E-Mail: JFitzpatrick@whopper.com.

FITZSIMMONS, ELLEN MARIE, lawyer; b. May 1960; BS, Va. Poly. Inst. & State Sch.; JD, Georgetown U. Assoc. Hunton & Williams, Richmond, Va.; sr. counsel CSX Corp., Jacksonville, Fla., 1991—95, asst. gen. counsel, 1995-97, gen. counsel, 1997—2001, sr. v.p., law, 2003, sr. v.p., law & pub. affairs, sec., gen. counsel, 2003—. Bd. dirs. Ameren Corp., 2009—. Office: CSX Corp 500 Water St 15th Fl Jacksonville FL 32202 Office Phone: 904-359-3200. Office Fax: 904-633-3450. Personal E-mail: Ellen_Fitzsimmons@csx.com.*

FITZSIMONS, DENNIS JOSEPH, former broadcast and publishing executive; b. NYC, June 26, 1950; s. Genevieve Theresa (English) F.; m. Ann Christie, Sept. 27, 1980; children: Matthew, Christine. BA, Fordham U., 1972. Account exec. Blair TV, NYC, 1975-77; sales mgr. TeleRep, Inc., Chgo., 1977-78, NYC, 1979-81, dir. spl. projects, 1978-79; dir. advt. sales Viacom Internat., NYC, 1981; dir. sales & mktg. Sta. WVIT-TV, Hartford, Conn., 1981-82; dir. sales Sta. WGN-TV, Chgo., 1982-84, v.p., gen. mgr., 1987—92, Sta. WGNO-TV, New Orleans, 1984-85; v.p. ops. Tribune Broadcasting Co., Chgo., 1985-87; pres. Tribune Television, 1992—94, Tribune Broadcasting Co., 1994—2003; exec. v.p. Tribune Co., 2000—01, COO, 2001—03, pres., 2001—07, CEO, 2003—07, chmn., 2004—07. Bd. dirs. Tribune Co., 2000—07, Media Gen. Inc., 2009—. Vice chmn. United Negro Coll. Fund of Chgo. With U.S. Army, 1970-76. Named Broadcaster of Yr., Broadcasting & Cable, 2003. Mem. Ill. Assn. Broadcasters (bd. dirs.), INTV (bd. dirs.). Roman Catholic. Office: Media General Inc Bd Director 333 E Franklin St Richmond VA 23219 Office Phone: 804-649-6000. Office Fax: 804-649-6898. Business E-Mail: dfitzsimons@mediageneral.com.

FITZWATER, SIDNEY ALLEN, federal judge; b. Olney, Md., Sept. 22, 1953; s. Ivan Welton and Kathleen Elizabeth (Schroeder) F.; m. Nancy Jane Ware, Aug. 6, 1976; children: John Welton, Joseph Leon, James Sidney. BA, Baylor U., 1975, JD, 1976. Bar: Tex. 1977, U.S. Supreme Ct. 1981. Assoc. Vinson & Elkins, Houston, 1976-78, Rain, Harrell, Emery, Young & Doke, Dallas, 1978-82; judge 298th Jud. Dist. Tex., Dallas, 1982-86, US Dist. Ct. (no. dist.) Tex., 1986—2007, chief judge, 2007—. Bd. dirs. Dallas Services for Visually Impaired Children, 1980-85. Mem. exec. com. Dallas County Reps., 1981-82; state del. Tex. Rep. Conv., 1980, 82, 84; mem. exec. com. Tex. Young Reps., 1981-82; bd. dirs. Dallas County Rep. Men's Club, 1984-85. Recipient Baylor U. award of merit, 1983, Ft. Worth Ind. Scho. Dist. Disting. Alumni award 1986; named Outstanding Young Alumnus, Baylor U., 1985; fellow Tex. Bar Found. Mem. State Bar Tex., Dallas Bar Assn., Nat. Order of Barristers, Phi Alpha Delta, Omicron Delta Kappa. Office: US Courthouse 1100 Commerce St Ste 15a3A Dallas TX 75242-1027

FLACH, GLORIA A., aerospace transportation executive; B in Computer Sci., Loyola U., Md., MBA; completed Exec. Mktg. Program, UCLA; completed Gen. Manager's Program, Harvard U. V.p., gen. mgr., targeting sys. divsn., electronic sys. Northrop Grumman Corp., 2004—07, v.p., gen. mgr., Engrng. & logistics, 2007—10, corp. v.p., pres., enterprise shared services, 2010—. Office: Northrop Grumman Corp 2980 Fairview Park Dr Falls Church VA 22042-4511 Office Phone: 310-553-6262. Office Fax: 310-556-4561. Business E-Mail: gloria.flach@ngc.com.

FLACKER, JONATHAN M., geriatrician, educator; BA, Emory U., 1986; MD, U. Chgo., 1990. Diplomate Am. Bd. Internal Medicine, 2003, Am. Bd. Internal Medicine-geriatric medicine, 2008, cert. added qualification in geriatric medicine. Resident internal medicine Univ. Ala. Hosp., 1990—93; fellow in geriatric medicine Hebrew Rehab Ctr. for Aged, 1994—96; hosp. affiliation includes: Emory Univ. Hosp.; asst. prof. dept. medicine, divsn. of geriatric medicine and gerontology Emory Univ.; med. dir. Emma I. Darnell geriat. ctr. Grady Health Sys., med. dir. grady hosp. source program; chief geriatric medicine svc. Grady Meml. Hosp. Office: Grady Health System 80 Jesse Hill Jr Dr SE Atlanta GA 30303 E-mail: jflacke@emory.edu.*

FLAGG, C.A. (CHUCK FLAGG), oil industry executive; B in Chem. Engrng., Villanova U., Pa. Mgmt. positions Texaco Inc.; gen. mgr. Bay/Valley Refining Complex Equilon Enterprises, LLC; gen. mgr. supply optimization Shell Oil Products US; sr. v.p. planning and optimization Tesoro Corp., San Antonio, 2005, sr. v.p. supply and optimization, sr. v.p. strategy, sr. v.p. sys. optimization, 2008—. Office: Tesoro Corp 19100 Ridgewood Pkwy San Antonio TX 78259-1828 Office Phone: 210-283-2000.

FLAGG, JAMES C., educational administrative officer; BS in Economics, Eckerd Coll., 1973; MS in Economics, Tex. A&M U., 1974, MBA, 1976, Ph.D in Acctg., 1988. CPA Tex., 1978. Sr. audit mgr. Coopers & Lybrand, L.L.P.; assoc. prof., acctg. dept., Mays Bus. Sch. Texas A&M University, College Station, Tex., 1988—. Mem. bd. dirs. HCC Ins. Holdings, Inc., 2001—, EGL, Inc., 2003—. Former chmn., minority faculty devel. com. Am. Acctg. Assn.; mem. Tex. State Bd.Pub. Accountancy. Office: Texas A&M University 3577 TAMU College Station TX 77843-3577 Office Phone: 979-458-7643. Office Fax: 979-458-7464.

FLAGG, RAYMOND OSBOURN, retired medical products executive; b. Martinsburg, W.Va., Jan. 31, 1933; s. Dorsey Slemons and Dorothy (Hobbs) F.; m. Ann Quinlan Birmingham, May 19, 1956; children: Richard Matthew, Elizabeth Ann, Catherine Garnett. BA with honors, Shepherd Coll., 1957; PhD in Biology, U. Va., 1961; diploma in advanced mgmt. program, U. N.C., Chapel Hill, 1994. Math tchr. Boonsboro (Md.) High Sch., 1957; rsch. asst. Blandy Exptl. Farm, Boyce, Va., 1957-61; rsch. assoc. U. Va., Charlottesville, 1961-62; dir. botany Carolina Biol. Supply Co., Burlington, NC, 1962-80, v.p., 1980-2000, exec. v.p., 2001—03; v.p. Wolfe Sales Corp., Burlington, 1985-97. Head Cabisco Biotech., Burlington, 1988-91; v.p. Found. for Ednl. Devel., Research Triangle Park, N.C., 1983-85; vice chmn. N.C. Plant Conservation Bd., Raleigh, 1984-88. Contbr. articles to profl. jours. Chmn. Beautification Commn., Burlington, 1976-80, Hist. Dist. Commn., 1981-82; bd. dirs. United Way of Alamance County, Burlington, 1984-88; vice chmn. Tree Adv. Com., Burlington, 1993-2000. Rsch. grant Am. Cancer Soc., 1960, rsch. equipment grant Va. Acad. Sci., 1961; recipient Community Leadership award No. Piedmont Devel. Assn., 1977. Mem. AAAS, Assn. Southeastern Biologists (pres. 1978-79), N.C. Acad. Sci. (pres. 1983-84), Va. Acad. Sci., Rotary (pres. Alamance A.M. 1988-89). Democrat. Presbyterian. Achievements include invention of instant drosophila medium, Carosafe, FlyNap, Sterigel, Planoslo, Vitachrome, Alga-Gro. Office: Carolina Biol Supply 2700 York Rd Burlington NC 27215-3398 E-mail: ray.flagg@carolina.com.

FLAGGS, GEORGE, state legislator; b. Edwards, Miss., Mar. 20, 1953; m. Linda A. Anthony; children: Emmari Genean, Elliott George. Former mem. Planning Cmty., Vicksburg, Miss., Zoning Bd. Appeals, Vicksburg; mem. Dist. 55 Miss. House of Reps., 1988—; counselor Warren County Youth Ct. Mem.: Optimists, Toastmasters, Vicksburg-Warren C. of C., Nat. Rifle Assn., Miss. Chap. Blacks Govt., Nat. Black Caucus State Legislators, Miss. Legislature Black Caucus, Wiseman's Social & Civic Club, Vicksburg Homecoming Benevolence Club. Democrat. Baptist. Mailing: PO Box 1674 Vicksburg MS 39181 Office Phone: 601-359-3755, 601-630-8004. E-mail: gflaggs@house.ms.gov.

FLAITZ, CATHERINE M., former dean, dental educator; BA in Psychology, Creighton U., 1974, DDS, 1978; MS in Pediat. Dentistry, U. Iowa, 1981. Bd. cert. oral and maxillofacial pathology. With Creighton U., U. Iowa, U. Colo.; pvt. practice pediat. dentistry Denver; prof., chair diagnostic sci. Dental Branch, U. Tex., Houston, dir. oral and maxillofacial pathology residency program, 2001—02, interim dean, 2002—04, dean, 2004—09; prof. oral & maxillofacial pathology art pediat. dentistry Dental Branch U. Tex., 1990—. Mem. editl. bd. Pediat. Dentistry, Jour. Dentistry Children, Am. Jour. Dentistry; cons. commn. dental accreditation advanced specialty edn. programs ADA; bd. mem. Friends of the Nat. Inst. of Dental and Craniofacial Rsch., 2005—. Mem. editl. bd.: Archives of Pathology and Laboratory Medicine. Recipient George W. Teuscher Silver Pen award, Jour. Dentistry Children, 2001, William N. Finnegan III Professorship in Dental Scis., U. Tex. Health Sci. Ctr.-Houston, 2005, Pres.'s Scholar award for excellence in tchg., 2004, Jack Harris award, Greater Houston Dental Soc. Alliance, 2009; named Tex. Dentist of Yr., Tex. Acad. Gen. Dentistry, 2005. Fellow: Am. Acad. Pediat. Dentistry (mem. grants and fellowship com., mem. pres. circle); mem.: ADA, Internat. Coll. Dentists, Omicron Kappa Upsilon, Tex. Dental Assn. (Presdl. Svc. award 2010), Internat. Assn. Dental Rsch., Am. Assn. Dental Rsch., Am. Acad. Oral Medicine (mem. clinical investigation and abstract com., Svc. Recognition award 2010), Greater Houston Dental Soc., Am. Acad. Oral and Maxillofacial Pathology (exec. coun.), Am. Dental Edn. Assn., Am. Coll. Dentists. Office: Univ Tex Health Sci Ctr Dental Branch 6516 MD Anderson Blvd Rm 3 0944 Houston TX 77030 Office Phone: 713-500-4420. Office Fax: 713-500-4416. Business E-Mail: catherine.m.flaitz@uth.tmc.edu.

FLANAGAN, CHRISTIE STEPHEN, lawyer; b. Port Arthur, Tex., June 28, 1938; s. Christie John and Rita Catherine (Hancock) F.; m. Gretchen Dowling Neuhoff; children: Mary Eileen, Margaret, Christopher, Michael. BBA, U. Notre Dame, 1960; LLB, U. Tex., Austin, 1962. Bar: Tex. 1962. Assoc. Hutcheson & Grundy, Houston, 1962-68; ptnr. Jenkens & Gilchrist, Dallas, 1968-88, mgr. ptnr., 1982-87, mem., 1988—94, of counsel, 2002—06; exec. v.p., gen. counsel Calif. Fed. Bank, 1994—2002; counsel Hunton & Williams, Dallas, 2007—. Active Dallas Citizens Coun., 1982-92; trustee Hockaday Sch., 1980-86, St. Marks Sch. Tex., 1986-92, Sierra Internat. Found., 1984-88. Mem. ABA, Tex. Bar Assn., Dallas Bar Assn., Salesmanship Club, Fishers Island Club, Brook Hollow Golf Club, Coon Creek Club, Dallas Country Club, Jupiter Island Club. Office: Hunton & Williams 1445 Ross Ave Ste 3700 Dallas TX 75202-2785 Office Phone: 214-468-3323. Office Fax: 214-468-3599. Business E-Mail: cflanagan@hunton.com.

FLANAGAN, CLYDE HARVEY, JR., psychiatrist, psychoanalyst, educator; b. Louellen, Ky., Aug. 21, 1939; s. Clyde H. Sr. and Ruby M. Flanagan; m. Gloria Kay Glymph, June 1, 1961 (div. Feb. 1974); children: Clyde H. III, Christopher Shane; m. Carol Anne Ross, Apr. 13, 1974; children: Patrick Ross, Colleen Helen. BS, Maryville Coll., 1962; MD, U. Tenn. Med. Unit, Memphis, 1966. Cert. Am. Bd. Psychiatry and Neurology in Adult, Child, Adolescent Psychiatry; diplomate Nat. Bd. Med. Examiners. Commd. 2d lt. U.S. Army, 1965, advanced through grades to col. MC, 1980; rotating med. intern U.S. Army Tripler Gen. Hosp., Honolulu, 1966-67; gen. psychiatry resident U.S. Army Walter Reed Gen. Hosp, Washington, 1967-69; child psychiatry resident Walter Reed Hosp., Washington, 1969-71; asst. chief child guidance svc. Walter Reed Army Med. Ctr., Washington, 1971-80; chief Cmty. Mental Health Activity, Ft. Belvoir, Va., 1980-86; asst. head tri-svc. alcohol rehab. dept. Nat. Navy Hosp., Bethesda, Md., 1986-88; dir. gen. psychiat. residency program W.S. Hall Psychiat. Inst., Columbia, SC, 1988-92; mem. clin. faculty, dept. psychiatry, behavioral sci. U. SC Sch. Medicine, Columbia, 1988—, dir. divsn. psychoanalysis dept. psychiat., behavioral sci., 1992—. Candidate in psychoanalysis Washington Psychoanalytic Inst., 1978-88; tng. and supervising analyst, UNC-Duke PSA Inst., 1991-, asst. dir. PSA Inst. Carolinas, Chapel Hill, 1999-2007. Contbr. chapters to books. Recipient Tchr. Yr. award Resident's Gen. Psychiat. Rsch. Program William S. Hall Psychiat. Inst., 1995, Spl. Alumni citation Maryville Coll., 2000. Fellow: Am. Acad. Child and Adolescent Psychiatry (Franklin Robinson award 1975, Disting. fellow), Am. Coll. Psychiatrists (com. pub. edn. 1998—99, Laughlin fellow selection com. 2000—03, membership devel. com. 2003—05), Am. Psychiat. Assn. (disting. life fellow); mem.: Am. Assn. Child Psychoanalysis, Internat. Psychoanalytic Assn., Am. Group Psychotherapy Assn. (founder, cert. group psychotherapist), SC Psychiat. Soc. (chair membership com. 1991—), NC Psychoanalytic Soc., Am. Psychoanalytic Assn. (councilor 1989—2004, cert. in adult, adolescent, and child psychoanalysis 1991). Avocations: fishing, boating. Office: U SC Sch Medicine Dept Neuropsychiatry 3555 Harden St Ext Ste 301 Columbia SC 29203-6894 Business E-Mail: clyde.flanagan@uscmed.sc.edu.

FLANAGAN, GLENDA JANE (GLENDA JANE CHAMBERLAIN), food products executive; b. 1953; BBA in Acctg., U. Tex. Exec. v.p., CFO Whole Foods Market, Inc., 1988—. Bd. dirs. Whole Foods Market Inc., 2004—, Credit Acceptance Corp., 2004—, Golfsmith Internat. Holdings Inc., 2006—. Office: Whole Foods Market Inc 550 Bowie St Austin TX 78703 Office Phone: 512-477-4455. Office Fax: 512-482-7000. Business E-Mail: glenda.chamberlain@wholefoods.com.

FLANAGAN, LOUISE W., federal judge; b. Richmond, Va., June 26, 1962; married; 2 children. Ba magna cum laude, Wake Forest U., 1984; JD, U. Va. Law Sch., 1988. Bar: NC 1988, DC 1989. Law clk. to Hon. Malcolm J. Howard US Dist. Ct. (Ea. Dist.) NC, 1988—89; assoc. Sonnenschein, Nath & Rosenthal, 1989—90, Ward & Smith, 1990—93, ptnr., 1994—99; magistrate judge (part-time) US Dist. Ct. (ea. dist.) NC, 1995—2003, judge, 2003—04, chief judge, 2004—. Mem.: NC Bar Assn. (dispute resolution coun.). Office: US Dist Ct US Post Office & Courthouse 413 Middle St New Bern NC 28560

FLANAGAN, NICHOLAS V., restaurant chain company executive; b. 1966; BSBA, U. Ctrl. Fla., Orlando. From unit mgr. to positions of increasing responsibility including v.p. worldwide franchise ops., sales and devel. S&A Restaurant Corp., Metromedia Restaurant Group, 1991—2004; regional v.p. Cracker Barrel Old Country Store, Inc., 2004—08, v.p. restaurant ops., 2008—10, sr. v.p. restaurant ops., 2010—. Office: Cracker Barrel Old Country Store Inc 305 Hartmann Dr Lebanon TN 37088-0787 Office Phone: 615-444-5533. Office Fax: 615-443-9476.

FLANAGAN, THOMAS JOSEPH, bishop emeritus; b. Rathmore, Ireland, Oct. 23, 1930; M.Div., Oblate Sch. Theology, 1979. Ordained priest Archdiocese of San Antonio, Tex., 1956; ordained bishop, 1998; aux. bishop Archdiocese of San Antonio, Tex., 1998—2005, aux. bishop emeritus, 2005—. Roman Catholic. Office: Archdiocese of San Antonio 2718 W Woodlawn Ave PO Box 28410 San Antonio TX 78228-0410 Office Phone: 210-734-2620. Office Fax: 210-734-0708. E-mail: tflanagan@archdiosa.org.

FLANAGAN, VAN KENT, journalist; b. San Antonio, Sept. 20, 1945; s. Marquiss Monroe and Nina Louise (Fowler) F.; m. Janet Dorothy Robinson, Dec. 16, 1972. BA, Angelo State U., 1968. Reporter, editor San Angelo Standard-Times, Tex., 1966-68; copy editor Fort Lauderdale News, Fla., 1973-74; from news editor to editor Sun. Express-News, San Antonio, 1974-79; from newsman to bur. chief AP, Phila., 1979-80, Columbia, SC, 1980-82, Bismarck, ND, 1982-83, Nashville, 1983—2004; editor, adj. instr. Vanderbilt U., Freedom Forum Diversity Inst., Nashville, 2005—06. Disting. journalist-in-residence, asst. prof. Mid. Tenn. State U., 2005—. Est. Tenn. Intercollegiate Press Assoc., 2008, Est. News Inst. MTSU, 2008, Served with U.S. Army, 1968-72, Vietnam. Decorated Bronze star. Mem.: Investigative Reporters and Editors, Inc., Journalism Edn. Assn., Tenn. Intercoll. Press Assn., Tenn. Coalition for Open Govt. (founding mem., sec. 2004—), Soc. Profl. Journalists (pres. Mid. Tenn. chpt. 1986—87, 2000—03). Presbyterian. Avocations: walking, hiking, reading. Home: 613 Riverview Dr Franklin TN 37064-5514 Office: Ezell Hall Rm 117-B MTSU Murfreesboro TN 37132 Office Phone: 615-898-2495. Personal E-mail: vankent45@comcast.net.

FLANNERY, JAMES WILLIAM, performing arts educator, scholar, theater director and producer, singer; s. James Joseph and Eileen Cotter Flannery; m. Ildiko Elizabeth Pokoly, Sept. 7, 1964; 1 child, Ciaran Pokoly. BA, Trinity Coll., 1958; MFA, Yale Sch. Drama, 1961; PhD, Trinity Coll., Dublin, 1970; DLitt (hon.), Trinity Coll., 1994, U. Ulster, Derry, Ireland, 2001. Dir. Eng. theater U. Ottawa, Canada, 1961—76; chair dept. theater U. R.I., Kingston, 1976—79; chair dept. theatre studies Emory U., Atlanta, 1982—89, Winship prof. arts and humanities, 2001—12, emeritus prof., 2012—. Prodr. Yeats Internat. Theatre Festival, Abbey Theatre, Dublin, 1989—93; founder, dir. W. B. Yeats Found., Atlanta, 1989—; prodr., concerts, symposia, exhbns., films Emory U., Atlanta, 1992—; vis. prof. U. Coll., Dublin, 2013—. Author: (book) W. B. Yeats and the Idea of Theatre; author/singer (book-recording) Dear Harp of My Country: The Irish Melodies of Thomas Moore. Recipient Wild Geese Award for Outstanding Contbn. to Irish Culture, 1994, Gov.'s Award in the Humanities, Ga. Humanities Coun., Atlanta, 2002, Disting. Alumnus Achievement award, Trinity Coll., 2008, SE Emmy award, Atlanta Ctr. Christmas Concert, 2012; named Internat. Assoc., Artist Abbey Theatre, Dublin, 2010; named one of Top 100 Irish Americans, Irish-America Mag., NY, 1990—93, 1998; Disting. Fulbright fellow, Fulbright Commn., UK, 2001. Mem.: Stephens Green Club Burns Atlanta, Global Irish Network, Phi Beta Kappa. Roman Catholic. Business E-Mail: jflanne@emory.edu.

FLANNERY, JOHN PHILIP, lawyer; b. NYC, May 15, 1946; s. John Philip and Agnes Geraldine (Applegate) F.; 1 child by a previous marriage: Diana Elizabeth; m. Holly Lynne Smith, Mar. 1, 2003; 1 stepchild, Alexandra Elizabeth. BS in Physics, Fordham Coll., 1967; BS in Engring., Columbia U., 1969, JD, 1972; student, Art Students League, 1972-73; MS in Info. Sci., George Washington U., 2002. Bar: N.Y. 1973, U.S. Dist. Ct. (so. dist.) N.Y. 1973, U.S. Ct. Appeals (2d cir.) 1973, Va. 1983, U.S. Ct. Appeals (4th cir.) 1985, U.S. Ct. Appeals (D.C. cir.) 1985, U.S. Dist. Ct. (ea. dist.) Va. 1985, U.S. Supreme Ct. 1985. Mem. staff Ford Found. Project to Restructure Columbia U., NYC, 1968; news rep. nat. press rels. IBM, 1970; law clk. Adminstrv. Conf. U.S., 1971, U.S. Ct. Appeals (2d cir.), 1972-74; asst. U.S. atty. Narcotics and Ofcl. Corruption units, So. Dist. N.Y., NYC, 1974-79; sr. assoc. Poletti Freidin Prashker Feldman & Gartner, NYC, 1979-82; spl. counsel U.S. Senate Judiciary Com., 1982, U.S. Senate Labor Com., 1982-83; Dem. candidate U.S. Congress from Va. 10th Dist., 1983-84; pvt. practice in civil and criminal litigation, 1984—; lectr. In Justice America Raw Deal, 2012; contbr. writer Shenandoah Press, 2011—. Spl. counsel Sen. Howard Metzenbaum, 1985-87; asst. dist. atty., Bronx, N.Y., 1986-87; counsel, bd. dir. Washington Internat. Horse Show Assn., 1989-91; legal expert "Crime in D.C.", Fox TV, 1993, "Crime Bill" Wis. Pub. Radio, 1994, "People vs. O.J. Simpson" ABC Network Radio, 1994-95, "Va.'s No Parole" Larry King Live CNN, 1994, "Imprisonment" CBS Morning Show, 1994, Habeas Reform Court TV, 1996, Terrorism, 1996, O'Reilly Factor, Fox News, "Torture", 2004, Fox News "Supreme Court," 2004-05; Fox Maggu Kelly, 2006-, spl. counsel U.S. House Judiciary Com., 1996-97; project dir., spl. counsel U.S. Edn. and Work Force Com., 1997-98; spl. counsel (impeachment proceedings) U.S. Rep. Zoe Lofgren, 1998-99, Washington staff chief, spl. counsel, 1999-2001; vis. exec. George Washington U. Sch. Bus. and Pub. Mgmt., 2002-04; of counsel, Campbell, Miller, Zimmerman, P.C., 2002—; officer, dir. Campbell Miller Zimmerman, PC, 2005—, prin. Campbell Flannery PC, 2010-; lectr. in field. Author: Commercial Information Brokers, 1973, Habeas Corpus Bores Hole in Prisoners' Civil Rights Action, 1975, Pro Se Litigation, 1975, Prison Corruption: A Mockery of Justice, 1980, Conspiracy: A Primer, 1988, Is Innocence Relevant to Execution? If Not, Isn't that Murder?, 1994, Equal Justice For All, 1995, Virginia Governor Allen's No-Parole Plan: A Billion Dollar Wasteland of Prisons, 1995, Pain in America and How our Government Maked it Worse, 2006; tech. columnist, Loudoun Times Mirror, May 2002-04; contbg. columnist Loudoun Times Mirror, 2004—; contbr., writer Purcellville Gazette, 2009-; reporter Brunswick Citizen, 2012-, Opinions, 2012-; editl. mem. Indie Column Left, 2010-12; on-air commentator O'Reilly Factor, Fox News, Chris Matthews' Hardball, MSNBC, 2004—; contbr. columns. in newspapers (Va. Press Assn. award 2011). Mem. legis. commn. Citizen's Union, 1971—72; mem. Arlington Transp. Commn., 1983—85; chmn. bus. coun. Va. Gov.'s War on Drugs Task Force, 1983—84; pres. Franklin Soc., 1979—80; committeeman Dem. Party N.Y. County, 1979—80, Dem. Party Arlington County, 1983—84; coord. N.Y. State Lawyers Com. for Sen. Edward M. Kennedy, 1979—80; dir. Citizens for Sen. M. Kennedy, 1980; del. Dem. Nat. Conf., 1988, Va. Assembly Univ. W.Va., 1990; committeeman Loudoun County Dem. Com., 1995—, sec., 1995—, chmn., 1995—97, mem., 2006—, v.p., 2001; del. 10th Congress and Dist. Com., 1997—; mem. Ctrl. State (Va.) Com., 1997—; del. Dem. Nat. Conv., 2000, 2004, 2008; Va. coord. Kerry for Pres., 2003—04; coord. Clinton Pres., 2008. Recipient U.S. Justice Dept. award for Outstanding Contbns. in Field of Drug Law Enforcement, 1977, U.S. Atty. Gen.'s Spl. Commendation for Outstanding Svc., 1979, FLEOA award, Fed. Law Enforcement Officer's Assn., 1984, NACDL's Marshall Stern award Outstanding Legis. Achievement, 1997, award Va. Press Assn., 2011. Mem. ABA, Assn. Bar City N.Y., N.Y. County Lawyers Assn., Arlington County Bar Assn., Loudon County Bar Assn., Nat. Assn. Criminal Def. Lawyers (chair briefbank com. 1990-91, legis. co-chair 1991-96, dir. 1993-97, President's commendation 1991, 92, 95), Acad. Polit. Sci., Va. Coll. Criminal Def. Attys. (bd. dir. 1993-96), Restoration and Preservation Soc. (bd. dir. 2004-05), Leesburg Rotary (bd. dir. 2004-05). Democrat. Home: Ithaca Manor 38469 Triticum Ln Lovettsville VA 20180 Office: 1602 Village Market Blvd Ste 220 Leesburg VA 20175 Office Phone: 703-771-8344. Personal E-mail: jonflan@aol.com.

FLATO, WILLIAM ROEDER, JR., software development company executive; b. Corpus Christi, Tex., Apr. 20, 1945; s. William Roeder and Juanita Flato; m. Beatrice Pesl, Aug. 22, 1974; children: Amanda Leigh, William Roeder III. BBA, U. Houston, 1967. CPA, Tex. Acct. Hughes Tool Co., Houston, 1966-67, Milchem, Inc., Houston, 1967-72, accounting mgr., asst. contr., corp. contr., 1972-78; v.p. fin., sec., treas. Baker Performance Chems. Inc. (formerly Magna Corp.), Houston, 1978-82, exec. v.p. fin. and planning, sec.-treas., 1982-93; CFO, v.p. fin. CoToCo Techs., Inc., Houston, 1993-97; founder, CFO, v.p. fin. Connective Techs., Inc., Houston, 1996—2010, CEO, pres., 2001—10. Active Country Village Civic Assn.; state chmn. Young Ams. for Freedom, 1964; precinct chmn. Harris County Rep. Exec. Com., 1966-67; chmn. Acctg. Adv. Com., Houston CC Sys., 1996-. With U.S. Army, 1968-69. Decorated Army Commendation medal. Mem. Tex. Soc. CPA, Houston Chpt. TSCPA, Mensa, Tex. Rifle Assn. (life), NRA. Conservative. Presbyterian. Home: 11931 Drexel Hill Dr Houston TX 77077-3009 Personal E-mail: bflato@comcast.net.

FLATT, ADRIAN EDE, surgeon; b. Frinton, Eng., Aug. 26, 1921; came to U.S., 1956, naturalized, 1960; s. Leslie Neeve and Barbara F.; m. Judith Johnson. BA, Cambridge U., 1942, MA, 1945, MBBchir., 1946, MD, 1953, M. chir., 1972. Diplomate: Am. Bd. Orthopedic Surgery. Rotating intern, then resident in gen., plastic and orthopaedic surgery London (Eng.) Hosp., 1946-54, 55-56; mem. faculty U. Iowa Med. Sch., 1956-79; prof. orthopaedic surgery and anatomy, dir. div. hand surgery, chmn. dept. surgery Norwalk (Conn.) Hosp., 1979-82; clin. prof. Yale U. Med. Sch., 1979-82; chief dept. orthopaedics Baylor U. Med. Ctr., Dallas, 1982-92, coord. rsch. Tom Landry Sports Medicine Ctr., 1992-94, dir. edn. dept. orthopaedics, 1995—. Hunterian prof. Royal Coll. Surgeons, 1962; McIlrath guest prof. Royal Prince Alfred Hosp., Sydney, Australia, 1972; Sir R. Watson-Jones lectr. Brit. Orthopaedic Assn., 1986; cons. in hand surgery to surg. gen. U.S. Air Force, 1962— Editor in chief Jour. Hand Surgery, 1981-91; author textbooks, papers in field; patentee artificial wrist and finger joints. Served as officer RAF, 1948-50. Recipient Kappa Delta award Am. Acad. Orthopaedic Surgeons, 1976 Mem. Am. Soc. Surgery Hand(pres.), Brit. Hand Soc.(founder mem.), Brit. Assn. Plastic Surgery (hon.), Group Etude de la Main, Am. Orthopaedic Assn., Am. Acad. Orthopaedic Surgeons, Am. Soc. Plastic and Reconstructive Surgery, British Assn. Orthopaedic Surgeons Office: Baylor U Med Ctr George Truett James Orthopedic Inst 3500 Gaston Ave Dallas TX 75246-2096 Office Phone: 214-820-1989. Business E-Mail: adrianf@baylorhealth.edu.

FLAVIN, PATRICK BRIAN, investment company executive, securities analyst; b. NYC, Mar. 8, 1947; s. Joseph Bernard and Melisande (Barillon) Flavin; m. Deborah Kay Hannon, Jan. 17, 1969; children: Nicole Noelle, Kellie Megan, Casey Eiran. AB, Colgate U., 1968; MBA, U. Utah, 1971. Cert. chartered fin. analyst. Ptnr. Flavin Beardsley & Co., Clearfield, Utah, 1970—72; investment rsch. officer Morgan Guaranty Trust, NYC, 1973—75, asst. v.p. Tokyo, 1975—77, v.p., 1977—82; sr. v.p. Reich & Tang, Inc., NYC, 1982; co-founder, pres., chief investment office Flavin, Blake & Co. Inc., Stamford, Conn., 1992; retired. Bd. dirs. CULP Inc., 1999—. Capt. USAF, 1968—72. Mem.: Inst. Chartered Fin. Analysts. Unitarian. Office: Culp Inc 1823 Eastchester Dr High Point NC 27265 Office Phone: 336-889-5161. Office Fax: 336-889-7246. Business E-Mail: pflavin@culpinc.com.

FLEEGER, DAVID CLARK, colon and rectal surgeon; b. Neubrucke, Germany, July 11, 1959; s. James Elliott and Madge Ellen (Iseminger) F.; m. Jamie Greenstreet, Aug. 16, 1984; 1 child, Lauren Ann. BS, Baylor U., 1981; MD, Tex. A&M U., 1985. Diplomate Am. Bd. Surgery, Am. Bd. Colon and Rectal Surgeons. Resident in gen. surgery Mayo Clinic, Rochester, Minn., 1985-90; fellow in colon and rectal surgery La. State U., Shreveport, 1990-91; ptnr. Ctrl. Tex. Colon and Rectal Surgeons, Austin, 1991—; chief surgery Columbia St. Davids. S. Hosp., 1996-97; chair Cancer Ctr. St. David's Med. Ctr., 1997—2008, co-chair Pain Mgmt. Ctr., 2000—05, chair dept. surgery, 2004—08; exec. bd. Travis County Med. Soc., 2004—. Pres. Travis County Med. Soc., 2007—08; sec., treas., med. staff St. David's Med. Ctr., 2006—08, pres. elect, med. staff, 2008—. Fellow ACS, Am. Soc. Colon and Rectal Surgeons (socioecons. com. 2000-02), Tex. Soc. Colon and Rectal Surgeons (pres-elect 1994, pres. 1994-95); mem. AMA (del.), St. Davids Med. Ctr. (mem. bd. trustees, 2008-09), Am. Soc. Gastrointestinal Endoscopy Surgeons, Soc. Am. Gastrointestinal Endoscopy, Tex. Med. Assn. (chmn. young physician sect., mem. governing coun. 1992-99, chmn. com. on physician distbn. 1999-02, chair coun. practice mgmt. svcs. 2006-08), Ctrl. Texas Blood and Tissue Ctr. (mem. bd. dirs. 2004-08). Avocations: fishing, hunting, photography, kayaking. Office: 4208 Medical Pkwy Austin TX 78756-3310 Office Phone: 512-452-9551.

FLEGLE, JIM L., lawyer; b. Bardwell, Ky., Dec. 3, 1951; s. J.L. and Alice M. (Goodman) F.; m. Ophelia Flegle Camina; children: Lauren Tyler, Brittanie Len, James Brendan, Alexandra Carlisle, James Armand. BA, U. Ky., 1974; JD, U. Va., 1977. Bar: Tex. 1977, US Dist. Ct. (so. dist.) Tex. 1977, US Dist. Ct. (no. dist.) Tex. 1984, US Dist. Ct. (we. dist.) Tex. 1988, US Dist. Ct. (ea. dist.) Tex. 1989, US Dist. Ct. Colo. 2002, US Ct. Appeals (5th and 11th cirs.) 1981, US Ct. Appeals (9th cir.) 1991, US Ct. Appeals (7th cir.) 2004, US Ct. Appeals (fed. cir.) 1994, US Supreme Ct. 1994. Assoc. Bracewell & Patterson, Houston, 1977-83, ptnr., 1983-89, Dallas, 1989—2002, head Dallas office, 1992-98, adv. com., 1996-98; ptnr. Loewinsohn Flegle, LLP, Dallas, 2002—07, Loewinsohn Flegle Deary, LLP, 2007—. Mem. Coll. of the State Bar of Tex., 2003-, criminal justice act vol. atty. panel US Dist. Ct. (no. dist.) Tex.; mem. dean's counsel, U. Va. Law Sch., 1997-; fellow U. Ky., 2006-. Vol. Houston Pro Bono Program, St. Paul's Chamber Music Soc.; mem. corp. campaign com. Dallas Mus. Art, 1994-95, Dallas Hist. Soc., 1991-92. Named Tex. Super Lawyer, Tex. Monthly Mag., 2004, 2005, 2006, 2007—13; named one of Best Lawyers in Am., Woodward/White, Inc., 2007—. Mem. ABA, Tex. Bar Assn. (grievance com. 1996-99, advt. rev. com. 2003-06), Houston Bar Assn., Dallas Bar Assn., Houston Bar Found. (life fellow), Tex. Bar Found., Dallas Bar Found., Am. Bd. Trial Advocates (pres. 2009, treas. 2007), Higginbotham Inn of Ct. (barrister), Raven Soc., Phi Beta Kappa, Omicron Delta Kappa, Sigma Nu. Methodist. Office: 12377 Merit Dr 900 Dallas TX 75251 Office Phone: 214-572-1701. Office Fax: 214-572-1717. Business E-Mail: jimf@lfdlaw.com.

FLEISCHAUER, BARBARA EVANS, state legislator; b. Homestead, Pa., Sept. 1, 1953; d. Fred J. and Eleanor Evans Fleischauer; m. Robert M. Bastress; 1 child, Sarah Eleanor Evans Bastress. BA, Allegheny Coll., 1975; JD, W.Va. U., 1982. Mem. Dist. 44 W.Va. House of Delegates, 1994—2000, Va., 2007—, chair Constl. Revision Com., mem. Health and Human Resources Com., Judiciary Com. & Vet. Affairs and Homeland Security Com. Author: (book) IKEA's Breakthrough in the United States, Sweden Now, 1986, We Can Make It Work-Sweden's Law on the Psycho-social Work Environment, Sweden Now, 1988, Ten Years with the Work Environment Act: High Expectations-Did They Come True?, Working Environ in Sweden, 1988, Employee Family Rights: Maternity Leave, Pregnancy Discrimination and Family Leave. Recipient Award, Nat Energy Law Competition, 1981, Morgantown Bus & Prof Women, 1993. Mem.: NAACP, Bus. & Prof. Women's Clubs America, W.Va. Trial Lawyers Assn., W.Va. State Bar Assn., UNICEF. Democrat. Mailing: 235 High St, Ste 618 Morgantown WV 26505 Office: State Capitol Complex Rm 201E, Bldg 1 1900 Kanawha Blvd Charleston WV 25305 Home Phone: 304-599-7883. E-mail: barbaraf@mail.wvnet.edu.

FLEISCHER, ARTHUR C., medical educator, radiologist; b. Miami, Fla., May 15, 1952; s. Eugene and Lucille Fleischer; m. Leona Fleischer, May 25, 1975; children: Braden, Jared, Amy. BS in Biology, Emory U., 1973; MD, Med. Coll. Ga., 1976. Diplomate Am. Bd. Radiology. Prof. radiology Vanderbilt U. Med. Ctr., Nashville, 1987—, prof. ob-gyn., 1988—, Cornelius Vanderbilt chair, 2011. Author: Principles and Practice of Ultrasonography in Ob/Gyn, 2004, 20 books on diagnostic sonography. Chair Corneluis Vanderbilt, 2011. Named Disting. Alumnus award, Med. Coll. Ga., 2007. Fellow: Am. Inst. Ultrasound in Medicine (bd. govs. 1989—91, William Fry award 1999), Am. Coll. Radiology, Soc. Radiologists in Ultrasound (Cornelius Vanderbilt chair 2011, Larry Mack award 1999, Frank H. Boehm award for continuing med. edn. 2005, C.A.N.D.L.E. award for med. student tchg. 2005, Disting. Alumnus award, Med. Coll. Georgia 2007). Office: Vanderbilt Univ Med Ctr 1161 21st Ave S Nashville TN 37232

FLEISCHMANN, CHUCK (CHARLES J. FLEISCHMANN), United States Representative from Tennessee, lawyer; b. NYC, Oct. 11, 1962; s. Max and Rose Marie Fleischmann; m. Brenda M. Fleischmann; children: Charles, James, Jeffrey. BA in Polit. Sci., magna cum laude, U. Ill., Urbana-Champaign, 1983; JD, U. Tenn. Coll. Law, Knoxville, 1986. Founder, ptnr. Fleischmann & Fleischmann, Chattanooga, 1987—; mem. US Congress from 3rd Tenn. Dist., Washington, 2011—, US House Natural Resources Com., Washington, 2011—, US House Science Space & Technology, Washington, 2011—, US House Small Bus.Com., Washington, 2011—. Past chmn. Chattanooga Lawyers Pro Bono Com. Radio talk show host Chuck Fleischmann Show, Chattanooga. Bd. dirs. Nat. Craniofacial Assn., Cherokee Area Coun. Boy Scouts of America, Chattanooga. Mem.: Chattanooga Bar Assn. (past pres.). Republican. Roman Catholic. Office: US House of Representatives 230 Cannon House Office Bldg Washington DC 20515 Office Phone: 202-225-3271. Office Fax: 202-225-3494.*

FLEMING, ERIK R., former state legislator, paralegal; b. Chgo., Feb. 2, 1965; s. Robert and Joan Fleming; m. Sharon Nacole Yarbrough; 1 child, Sean Christopher stepchildren: Kenneth, James. Grad., Jackson State U., 1987; DD (hon.), U. Life Ch., Modesto, Calif. With Ray Mabus for gov. campaign, 1987; with Mike Park for US Congress campaign, 1988; campaign mgr. for Hon. Henry J. Kirksey Mayor of Jackson, 1993; with Ronnie Musgrove for lt. gov. campaign, 1995; sgt-at-arms Miss. State Senate, 1996; rep. House Reps., Jackson, Miss., 1999—2007; abstinence educator Miss. Cmty. Devel. Corp.; COO New Horizon Ministries, Inc.; paralegal Miss. Immigrants Rights Alliance. Mem. Conservation and Water Resources, Juvenile Justice, Labor and Transp. Coms. Ho. Reps., Jackson, Miss., 1999—2007. Mem. Miss. Families for Kids; national committeeman Young Democrats of America, 1993—95; pres. Young Democrats of Miss., 1991—92; chair exec. com. Hinds County Dem. Orgn., Miss., 1996—99; mem. Miss. Faith-Based Coalition for Cmty. Renewal. Served in Category Area Tng. Program USMC, Operation Desert Storm. Mem.: SCLC, NAACP, Jackson State U. Nat. Alumni Assn., Nat. Sheriff's Assn., Alpha Phi Omega. Democrat. Office: Miss Immigrants RIghts Alliance PO Box 1104 Jackson MS 39215

FLEMING, JOHN CALVIN, JR., United States Representative from Louisiana, physician; b. Meridian, Miss., July 5, 1951; m. Cindy Fleming, 1978; 4 children. B, U. Miss., Oxford, MD, 1976. Cert. Am. Bd. Family Practice. Chief resident family medicine Naval Regional Med. Ctr., USN, Camp Pendleton, Calif., resident drug/alcohol treatment unit Long Beach, Calif., practiced mil. family medicine, dir. drug/alcohol treatment Guam, 1979—81, Charleston, SC, 1981—82; pvt. practice family physician Minden Med. Ctr., La., 1983—2009; mem. US Congress from 4th La. Dist., 2009—. Author: Preventing Addiction: What Parents Must Know to Immunize Their Kids Against Drug and Alcohol Addiction, 2006. Deacon, Sun. sch. tchr., sch. dept. dir. First Baptist Ch., Minden. Mem.: La. Acad. Family Physicians (La. Family Practice Physician of Yr. 2007). Republican. Baptist. Office: US House of Representatives 416 Cannon House Office Bldg Washington DC 20515 also: 6425 Youree Dr Ste 350 Shreveport LA 71105 Office Phone: 202-225-2777, 318-798-2254. Office Fax: 202-225-8039, 318-798-2063.*

FLEMING, JOSEPH Z., lawyer; b. Miami, Fla., Jan. 30, 1941; s. Richard Marion and Lenore C. Fleming; m. Betty Corcoran, Feb. 12, 1947; 1 child, Katherine Anne. BA in English, U. Fla., 1958; postgrad., U. Chgo., 1959, Hague Acad. Internat. Law, 1966; JD, U. Va., 1965; LLM in Labor Law, NYU, 1966. Bar: Fla. 1965, D.C. 1981. Assoc. Paul & Thomson, Miami, 1966-72, ptnr., 1972-74, Fleming & Neuman, 1974-81, Fleming & Huck, Miami, 1981-86, Fleming & Klink, 1987-88, Ford & Harrison, 1996—2001; pvt. practice Miami, 1986—96; with Greenberg Traurig PA, 2001—; mgmt. chair Internat. Labor & Employment Law Com., 2009—. Lectr. in field. Author: Airline and Railroad Labor Law, 1981-; editor, contbg. author Environmental Regulation and Litigation in Florida, 1980, 82, 84-85, 87-88, 90-91, 93-95, 97, 99-2000, 2003-12, Environmental Pollution and Individual Rights, 1978, Reporter's Handbook, 1979—, Historic Preservation Law, 1984-87, 89, 99, 2001, 04-05, 07-, Entertainment, Arts, & Sports Law, 1989-91, 97-99, 2001, 03, 05, 07, 09-12. Trustee Met. Dade County Ctr. for Fine Arts, 1982-86; mem. Biscayne Bay Environ. Task Force Subcom., 1982-83, well field protection adv. com. Dade County Task Force, 1984-87; mem. Noguchi-Bayfront Park Trust, Miami, 1983-89; pres., bd. dirs. Fla. Rural Legal Svcs., 1967-78, Pres.'s Water Policy Implementation Workshops, Dept. of Interior Water Task Force, 1979; bd. dirs. Miami chpt. Am. Jewish Com. Recipient Conservation award Fla. Audubon Soc., 1981, 89, award, Tropical Audubon Soc., 1979, award Dade County Mental Health Assn., 1974, award Miami Design Preservation League, 1982-83, award Progressive Architecture, 1982, Am. Jewish Com. award. Mem. Am. Law Inst., ALI-ABA (continuing profl. edn. com. 1985—2008), Fla. Bar Assn. (chair entertainment arts & sports law sect. 2011-12, past chmn. environ. and land use law sect., labor law and employment discrimination law sect., entertainment, arts and sports law sect., cert. labor and employment law, chair entertainment arts and sports law sect., 2011-), New World Symphony (bd. trustee 2009-11); fellow. Coll. Labor & Employment Lawyers. Home: 34 LaGorce Cir Miami Beach FL 33141-4520 Office: 333 SE 2nd Ave Miami FL 33131 Office Phone: 305-579-0517. E-mail: flemingj@gtlaw.com.

FLEMING, JULIAN DENVER, JR., lawyer; b. Rome, Ga., Jan. 12, 1934; s. Julian D. and Margaret Madison (Mangham) F.; m. Sidney Howell, June 28, 1960; 1 dau., Julie Adrianne. Student, U. Pa., 1951-53; BChemE, Ga. Inst. Tech., 1955, PhD, 1959; JD, Emory U., 1967. Bar: Ga. 1966, D.C. 1967; registered profl. engr., Ga., Calif. Rsch. engr., prof. chem. engring. Ga. Inst. Tech., 1955-67; ptnr. Sutherland, Asbill & Brennan, Atlanta, 1967—. Contbr. articles to profl. jours.; patentee in field. Bd. dirs. Mental Health Assn. Ga., 1970-80; bd. dirs. Mental Health Assn. Met. Atlanta, 1970-80, pres., 1974-75; mem. coun. legal advisors Rep. Nat. Com., 1981-85. Fellow: Am. Bar Found., Am. Coll. Trial Lawyers, Am. Inst. Chemists; mem.: AIChE, AAAS, ABA (coun. sect. sci. and tech. 1980—, vice chmn. 1982—84, chmn. 1985—86, ho. dels. 1990, bd. govs. 1994—95, ho. dels. 1994—96, chmn. spl. citation issues com. 1995—96, coord. commn. legal tech. 1995—97, standing com. tech. and info. sys. 1997—2001), Bleckley Inn of Ct. (master of bench), Nat. Conf. Lawyers and Scientists (chmn. ABA del. 1988—90, standing com. nat. conf. groups 1990, ABA liaison 1990—93, chmn. 1992—93). Achievements include patent for data apparatus. Home: 1248 Oxford Rd NE Atlanta GA 30306-2610 Office: Sutherland Asbill & Brennan 999 Peachtree St NE Ste 2300 Atlanta GA 30309-3996

FLEMING, WILLIAM SLOAN, energy and computer company executive; b. Long Beach, Calif., Aug. 13, 1937; s. William Sloan and Helen Jean Fleming; m. Jacquline M. Carrio, Mar. 9, 1960; children: Katherine A., Kimberly A. BSME, Calif. Maritime Acad., 1958; MBA, Syracuse U., 1970. Commd. ensign USN, 1958, advanced through grades to lt., 1967, attack pilot, 1958—67, disabled in the line of duty, ret., 1967; mech. engr. Carrier Corp., Syracuse, NY, 1967—70; regional sales mgr. Rheem Mfg., Atlanta, 1970—71; market devel. supr. Owens Corning Fiberglas, Toledo, 1971—73; pres. W. S. Fleming & Assocs., Inc., Syracuse, 1975—86, Fleming Group, Syracuse, 1986—87, CEO, chmn. bd., 1987—94; bus. devel. mgr., energy systems group Sci. Applications Internat. Corp. SAIC/Fleming Group, Syracuse, 1994—96; bus. devel. mgr. Sci. Applications Internat. Corp./Energy Sys. Group, 1996—97; exec. v.p. Jacwill Svcs. Inc., Cazenovia, NY, St. Petersburg, Fla., 1997—2007, owner, 2007—. Pres. Enterlog Sys., Inc., Syracuse, 1985—94; chmn. bd. Assn. Intelligent Sys. Tech., Inc., Syracuse, 1986—90. Author: Singer Energy & Economic Building Simulation Computer Program; contbr. articles to profl. jours. Recipient Energy awards, Ctrl. N.Y., 1981. Fellow: ASHRAE (life; chmn. tech. com. 9.6, sys. energy utilization 1981—83, chmn. ad hoc com. 90, energy stds. 1983—84, chmn. tech. com. 6.7, solar energy utilization 1984—86, chmn. nat. program com. 1985—86, mem. edn. coun. 1989—90, rsch. and tech. com. 1991—95, chmn. spl. publs. com. 1998—99, rsch. adminstrn. com. 2000—01, mem. handbook com. 2001—05, chmn. handbook fund subcom. 2004—05, chmn. handbook com. 2005—06, mem. nom. com. 2007—08, honors and awards com. 2007—09, mem. pub. com. 2009—, vice chair pub. com. 2010—11, chair pub.comm 2011—12, Disting. Svc. award 2006, Exceptional Svc. award 2011); mem.: DAV, Assn. Energy Engrs. (charter, mgr., Hall of Fame), Mil. Officers Assn., Am. Legion. Roman Catholic. Avocations: skiing, boating.

FLEMING, WILLIAM WRIGHT, JR., retired pharmacology professor; b. Washington, Jan. 30, 1932; s. William Wright and Esme (Reeder) F.; m. Dolores D. Atchison, Sept. 1, 1952; children: Lisa Marie, Jennifer Amelia, David William. AB cum laude, Harvard U., 1954; PhD (Procter fellow), Princeton U., 1957. Mem. faculty W.Va. U. Med. Ctr., Morgantown, 1960—, prof. pharmacology, 1966—, chmn. dept., 1966-86, Mylan Chmn. of Pharmacology and Toxicology, 1986-99, prof. emeritus, 1999—. Vis. prof. U. Melbourne, Australia, 1969, St. George's Hosp. Med. Sch. U. London, 1978, Flinders U., Adelaide, Australia, 1985, 87, U. Adelaide, 1987; adj. prof. pharmacology U. Pitts. Sch. Medicine, 2005-; cons. Mead Johnson Rsch. Ctr., Evansville, Ind., 1970-77, Spriggs & Hollingsworth Law Firm, Washington, 2004-06; mem. pharmacology-toxicology rsch. program. Nat. Inst. Gen. Med. Scis., NIH, 1973-77, chmn., 1975-77; mem. drug abuse rsch. rev. com. Nat. Inst. Drug Abuse, 1985-89; mem. pharmacology study sect., div. rsch. grants NIH, 1990-94. Mem. editl. bd. Jour. Pharmacology and Exptl. Therapeutics, 1966-85, Life Scis., 1978-90; contbr. articles to profl. jours. USPHS postdoctoral fellow Harvard U., 1957-60; Fogarty sr. internat. fellow, 1978; recipient P.L. MacLachlan award W.Va. U. Med. Sch., 1964, 67, 78, 89, 92, 97, 99; named Outstanding Tchr., W.Va. U. Found., 1978. Mem. AAAS, Am. Soc. Pharmacology and Exptl. Therapeutics (councilor 1975-78, pres. 1981-82, chmn. bd publs. trustees 1984-90, Otto Krayer award 1986, Croker Meml. lectr. 1988, Torald Sollman award 1999), Assn. Med. Sch. Pharmacology (councilor 1977-79, treas. 1977-78, pres. 1986-88), Fedn. Am. Socs. for Exptl. Biology (dir. 1980-83), Internat. Union Pharmacology (del. 1980-83, 91-94, mem. internat. adv. com. for Congress of Pharmacology 1987, exec. com. 1994-98, 2002—06, pres. 1998-2002). Office: WVa U Health Scis Ctr Dept Physiology & Pharmacology Morgantown WV 26506 Home: 1586 Hunter Station Rd Tionesta PA 16353 Personal E-mail: wfle216184@aol.com.

FLEMMING, DAVID PAUL, biologist; b. Kittanning, Pa., Oct. 23, 1953; s. Paul Ross and Jeanne Marie (Seaton) F.; m. Diane Frances MacKenzie, Sept. 17, 1983; children: Daniel Robert, Peter David. BS in Biology, Grove City Coll., 1975; MS in Biology, Bowling Green State U., 1977. Child care worker George Jr. Rep., Grove City, Pa., 1978-79; park naturalist State of Pa.-McConnell's Mill State Park, Portersville, 1979; biologist sect. 7 U.S. Fish & Wildlife Svc., Washington, 1979-80, Atlanta, 1980-83, recovery coord. Denver, 1983-87, biologist endangered species Vero Beach, Fla., 1987-88, chief divsn. endangered species Atlanta, 1988-96, chief ecol. svcs., 1997-98, ecol. svcs. supr., 1998—. Contbg. author: Conservation and Resource Management, 1993. Asst. coach T-ball and soccer YMCA, Lawrenceville, Ga., 1991—92, premier soccer coach Snellville, Ga., 1995—2001; USS Ofcl., 1996—2003. Business E-Mail: dave_flemming@fws.gov.

FLESCHER, HAROLE LEE, retired engineering executive; b. NYC, Oct. 7, 1940; s. Julius Harry and Eileen (Smolen) F.; m. Nancy Tarlin, Aug. 23, 1970 (div. Apr. 1980); m. Judith Rodman, Sept. 2, 1986. BS, NYU, 1961, MS, 1966. Physicist United Nuclear Group, Elmsford, N.Y., 1963-64; engr. Martin Co., Balt., 1964-66; with Raytheon Co., Sudbury, Mass., 1966—2001, prin. engr., dep. mgr. product assurance labs. Cons. Palm Beach Gardens, Fla. Fellow IEEE (Richard M. Emberson award, 2009, served at many levels in IEEE organizations, vol., dir., v.p. technical activities); mem. Am. Soc. Quality Control. Home: 8124 159th Ct N West Palm Beach FL 33418-1877

FLESHER, ROBERT G., oil industry executive; Attended, Tex. A&M U., 1969—73. V.p. ops. ConocoPhillips Can., Calgary, Alberta, sr. v.p. Western Can. conventional devel. and ops., 2006—07; v.p. drilling and prodn. ConocoPhillips, Houston, 2007—; CEO Qatar Gas 3 & 4, Doha. Office: ConocoPhillips 600 N Dairy Ashford PO Box 2197 Houston TX 77252-2197 Office Phone: 281-293-1000.

FLETCHER, ALLEN, state legislator; b. Apr. 9, 1955; m. Penny Fletcher; 3 children. BA in Criminal Justice, M in Criminal Justice, Sam Houston State U. Former mem. pub. integrity rev. group Houston Police Dept., former negotiator, negotiation team, tactical ops. divsn., former supr. office inspector gen., former officer; CEO Resource Protection Mgmt.; mem. Dist. 130 Tex. House of Representatives, 2008—. Republican. Christian. Office: Room E2.906 Capitol Extension PO Box 2910 Austin TX 78768 also: 25222 NW Freeway Bldg 9 Ste 199 Cypress TX 77429 Office Phone: 281-374-0894, 512-463-0661, 281-373-5454.

FLETCHER, GARY, medical insurance company executive; BA in Economics, U. Va., 1975, MBA, 1981; MA in Economics, Va. Commonwealth U., 1984. Corp. projects coord. Anthem, 1986—88, fin. projects coord., 1988—90, dir., managed care support, 1990—98; COO CareSource, 1998—2002; v.p., health plan ops. Amerigroup Corp., 2002—05, pres., CEO, health plan, 2005—. Office: Amerigroup Corp Ste 100 4425 Corporation Ln Virginia Beach VA 23462 Office Phone: 757-490-6900. Office Fax: 757-518-3600. Business E-Mail: gfletcher@amerigroupcorp.com.

FLETCHER, LEROY STEVENSON, mechanical engineer, educator; b. San Antonio, Oct. 10, 1936; s. Robert Holton and Jennie Lee F.; m. Nancy Louise McHenry, Aug. 14, 1966; children: Laura Malee, Daniel Alden. BS, Tex. A&M U., 1958; MS, Stanford U., 1963, Engr., 1964; PhD, Ariz. State U., 1968. Registered profl. engr., Ariz., N.J., Va., Tex., Australia; chartered engr., U.K. Rsch. scientist NASA-Ames Rsch. Ctr., Moffett Field, Calif., 1958-62, dir. aeronautics/aerospace, 1999—2005; instr. Ariz. State U., Tempe, 1964-68; prof. aero., engring. Rutgers U., New Brunswick, 1968-75, assoc. dean, 1974-75; prof., chmn. dept. mech. and aero. engring. U. Va., Charlottesville, 1975-80; dir. Ctr. Energy Analysis, 1979-80; assoc. dean Tex. A&M U., College Station, 1980-88, assoc. dir. Tex. Engring. Expt. Sta., 1985-88, Dietz prof. mech. engring., 1988—2006, Regents prof., 1998—2006, rsch. chair Tex. Engring. Expt. Sta., 2006—. Vis. prof. Tokyo Inst. Tech., 1993; hon. prof. Ruhr U., Bochum, Germany, 1988—; disting. vis. prof. Am. U., Cairo, 1998, Am. U. Sharjah, United Arab Emirates, 2000—; cons. to various industries, govt. labs. and univs.; mem. exec. com. Internat. Ctr. Heat and Mass Transfer, Ankara, Turkey, 1994—, chmn., 1999—2003, fellow, 1998; disting. vis. scholar Hong Kong Poly. U., 2002. Author: Introduction to Engineering Including FORTRAN Programming, 1977, Introduction to Engineering Design with Graphics and Design Projects, 1979; editor: Aerodynamic Heating and Thermal Protection, 1978, Heat Transfer and Thermal Control Systems, 1978. Served to capt. USAF, 1958-61. Recipient Disting. Alumni award Ariz. State U., 1985, Exceptional Achievement medal NASA-Ames, 2002, Outstanding Leadership medal NASA, 2005. Fellow: AIAA (dir. 1981—84, v.p. edn. 1992—95, dir. 1992—98, pres. 1996—97, Lee Atwood award 1982, Enery Sys. award 1984, Thermophysics award 1992, Disting. Svc. award 2002, hon. fellow 2004), AAAS (chair sect. M-engring. 1988—89, Internat. Sci. Coop. award 2003), ASME (bd. govs. 1983—87, pres. 1985—86, Charles Russ Richards award 1982, Heat Transfer Meml. award 1996, hon., medal 2002), Internat. Acad. Astronautics, Pan Am. Acad. Engring., Internat. Astron. Fedn. (Frank J. Malina award 1997), Royal Aero. Soc. U.K., Inst. Engrs. Australia, Accreditation Bd. Engring. and Tech. (dir. 1979—89, 1991—94, 2003—, pres. 2007—08, Linton Grinter award 2002), Am. Astron. Soc. (bd. dirs. 1993—96), Inst. Mech. Engrs. U.K. (James Watt Internat. Gold medal 2005), Am. Soc. Engring. Edn. (dir. 1974—77, v.p. 1978—89, George Westinghouse award 1982, Ralph Coats Roe award 1983, Donald E. Marlowe award 1986, Leighton W. Collins award 1993, Benjamin Garver Lamme award 2001); mem.: Union Panam. Assns. Engrs. (Vector de Oro award 2000), Phi Kappa Phi, Sigma Gamma Tau, Pi Tau Sigma, Tau Beta Pi, Sigma Xi. Office: Tex A&M Univ Dept Mech Engring College Station TX 77843-3123

FLETCHER, LONDON LEVI, professional football player; b. Cleve., May 19, 1975; m. Charne Fletcher; 2 children. Attended, St. Francis Coll., Loretto, Pa.; BA in Sociology, John Carroll U., University Heights, Ohio. Linebacker St. Louis Rams, 1998—2001, Buffalo Bills, 2002—06, Washington Redskins, 2007—. Recipient Carroll Rosenbloom Meml. award, St. Louis Rams, 1998; co-recipient B.J. Blanchard award (with J. Campbell), Washington Redskins, 2007; named Divsion III Linebacker of Yr., 1st Team AP Little All-American, Am. Football Conf. Pro Bowl Alt., NFL, 2002, 2007, Nat. Football Conf. Pro Bowl Alt., 2008, Free Agent of Yr., Dallas Morning Star, 2007; named to Nat. Football Conf. Pro Bowl Team, NFL, 2010, 2011; finalist Gagliardi award. Achievements include tied for the NFL lead in: safeties 1999, 2005; fumble return touchdowns, 2006; member of Super Bowl XXXIV championship winning St. Louis Rams, 2000. Office: Washington Redskins 21300 Redskin Pk Dr Ashburn VA 20147

FLETCHER, SUZANNE WRIGHT, epidemiologist, medical educator, editor; b. Jacksonville, Fla., Nov. 14, 1940; d. Robert Dean and Helen (Selmer) Wright; m. Robert H. Fletcher; children: John Wright, Grant Selmer. BA, Swarthmore Coll., 1962; MD, Harvard Med. Sch., 1966; MSc, Johns Hopkins U., 1973. Diplomate Nat. Bd. Med. Examiners, Am. Bd. Internal Medicine. Intern Stanford (Calif.) U. Med. Ctr., 1966—67, resident, 1967—68; physician 22nd med. detachment U.S. Army, New Ulm, Germany, 1969—70; asst. prof. epidemiology and health Mc Gill U., Montreal, Canada, 1974—77, assoc. prof., 1977—78, asst. prof. medicine, 1973—78; dir. med. clinic dept. medicine NC Meml. Hosp., 1978—82; assoc. prof. medicine U. NC, 1978—83, co-chief divsn. gen. medicine and clin. epidemiology dept. medicine, 1978—86, rsch. assoc. health svcs. rsch. ctr., 1978—90, vice chmn. clin. svcs., 1981—90, prof. medicine, clin. prof. epidemiology, 1983—90, program dir. faculty devel. gen. medicine and gen. pediatrics, 1985—90, co-dir. internat. clin. epidemiology network program Rockefeller Found., 1986—90; prof. ambulatory care and prevention Harvard Med. Sch., 1994, prof. emerita ambulatory care and prevention. Adj. prof. medicine U. Pa., Phila., 1990—93, Jefferson Med. Coll., 1991—93, U. NC, 1994—; physician internal medicine; chmn. NIH Tech. Assessment Conf., 1992, Nat. Cancer Inst. Internat. Workshop, 1993; faculty World Bank Seminar on Preventive Strategies in Med. Edn., Hangzhou, China, 1986; active Ad Hoc NCI Com. on Breast Cancer Detection Rsch., 1986; chair Macy Conf. on Continuing Edn. of Health Profls., 2007. Author: Clinical Epidemiology—The Essentials, 1982, 4t edit., 2005; editor: Annals of Internal Medicine, 1990—93; contbr. chapters to books, articles to profl. jours. Recipient Can. Nat. Health Rsch. Scholar award, Can. Govt., 1975—78; named rsch. grantee, Conseil de la Recherche en Sante du Quebec, 1975—77; grantee, Health and Welfare Can., 1976—78, Robert Wood Johnson Teaching Hosp. Gen. Medicine Group Practice Program, 1980—84, Nat. Ctr. Health Scis. Rsch. and Health Tech., 1985—89, Rockefeller Found. Clin. Epidemiology Resource and Tng. Ctr., 1986—90, NIH, 1987—90, 1997—. Master: ACP (med. knowledge self assessment program 1984—85, clin. practice subcom. 1987, pub. policy subcom. 1988—89); fellow: Coll. Physicians Phila., Am. Coll. Epidemiology (bd. dirs. 1990—93, chmn. pub. com. 1992—94); mem.: APHA, Am. Bd. Internal Medicine (bd. govs. 1981—87), NCI Bd. Sci. Advisors, World Assn. Med. Editors (v.p. 1997—2001), Internat. Clin. Epidemiology Network (bd. dirs.), Inst. Medicine (coun. 1993—96, exec. com. 1993—96), Soc. Gen. Internal Medicine (counsellor 1978—81, pres.-elect 1982—83, pres. 1983—84, co-editor Jour. Gen. Internal Medicine 1984—89, mem. publs. com. 1990—, chmn. Glaser award com. 1991). Unitarian Universalist. Home: 208 Boulder Bluff Trail Chapel Hill NC 27516-9652

FLETCHER, WINONA LEE, retired theater educator; b. Nov. 25, 1926; m. Joseph Grant; 1 child, Betty. BA, Johnson C. Smith U., 1947; MA, U. Iowa, 1951; PhD, Ind. U., 1968. Prof. speech and theatre Ky. State U., Frankfort, 1951-78; prof. theatre and afro-Am. studies Ind. U., Bloomington, 1978-94, prof. emeritus, 1994; assoc. dean COAS, 1981-84. Costumer, dir. summer theatre, U. Mo., Lincoln, 1952-60, 69. Sr. editor: Community Memories: A Glimpse of African American Life in Frankfort, Ky., 2003, editor & ghostwriter: No Way! Memoirs of J. Kenneth Lee, Esq. Recipient Lifetime Achievement award, 1993; Am. Theatre fellow, 1979. Mem. Am. Theatre for Higher Edn., Black Theatre Network, Ky. Hist. Soc., Nat. Assn. Dramatic and Speech Arts, Nat. Theatre Conf., Alpha Kappa Alpha. Home: 317 Cold Harbor Dr Frankfort KY 40601-3011 Personal E-mail: leefle@aol.com.

FLEXON, ROBERT C., energy executive; BS in Accounting, Villanova U. Audit mgr. Coopers & Lybrand; gen. auditor, franchise mgr., controller Atlantic Richfield Co., 1987—2000; v.p. corp. devel. & work process, v.p. bus. analysis, controller Hercules, Inc., 2000—04; exec. v.p., CFO NRG Energy, Inc., Princeton, NJ, 2004—08, exec. v.p., COO, 2008—09, exec. v.p., CFO, 2009; pres., CEO Foster Wheeler USA, Clinton, NJ, 2009—10; CEO Foster Wheeler AG, Clinton, NJ, 2010; CFO UGI Corp., King of Prussia, Pa., 2011; CEO Dynegy, Inc., 2011—. Bd. mem. Foster Wheeler Ltd. Office: Dynegy Inc 601 Travis St Ste 1400 Houston TX 77002-3253 Office Phone: 713-507-6400.

FLICKINGER, CHARLES JOHN, anatomist, educator; b. Bethlehem, Pa., July 13, 1938; s. Wilbur James and Verna (Diehl) F.; m. Agnes Elizabeth Dickel, Feb. 23, 1963; children: Laura Jill, David Paul. AB, Dartmouth Coll., 1960; MD, Harvard U., 1964. Rsch. fellow dept. anatomy U. Colo., Denver, 1964-65, Harvard Med. Sch., Boston, 1965-66; rsch. assoc. Inst. Devel. Biology, U. Colo., Boulder, 1966-67, asst. prof., 1967-70; assoc. prof. dept. anatomy Sch. Medicine, U. Va., Charlottesville, 1971-75, Harvey E. Jordan prof. anatomy, 1982—2002, chmn. dept. cell biology, 1982—2002, prof., 1975—2006; ret.; prof. emeritus Sch. Medicine, U. Va., 2007—. Mem. reproductive biology study sect. NIH, 1979-83; mem. anatomy test com. Nat. Bd. Med. Examiners, 1981-84. Author: (with Brown, Kutchai, Ogilvie) Medical Cell Biology, 1979; contbr. articles to profl. jours.; assoc. editor: Jour. Andrology, 1989-92; adv. editor: Internat. Rev. Cytology, 1974-98; mem. editl. bd. Biology of Reprodn., 1986-89, 2002-04, Jour. Andrology, 1986-89, Anatomical Record, 1972-98. NIH rsch. career devel. award grantee, 1968-70. Mem. Am. Soc. Cell Biology, Am. Assn. Anatomists, Soc. Study Reproduction, Phi Beta Kappa, Alpha Omega Alpha. Home: 2009 Meadowbrook Rd Charlottesville VA 22903-1247 Office: University of Virginia Dept Cell Biology PO Box 800732 Charlottesville VA 22908-0732 Business E-Mail: cjf@virginia.edu.

FLINCHBAUGH, DAVID EDWARD, physicist; b. Poughkeepsie, NY, Oct. 11, 1934; s. Louis David and Lolita Mildred (Hook) F.; m. Heidi Maria Rose, June 15, 1957; children: William David, Laura Jean, Karen Marie, Karl Louis. BS in Physics and Math., Union Coll., 1957; MS in Physics, U. Conn., 1960, PhD in Modern Physics, 1964; cert. computer database mgmt., Harvard U., 1979. Registered profl. engr., Fla., Pa.; cert. tchr., Fla. Rsch. physicist IBM Corp., Poughkeepsie, 1956-57; rsch. assoc. Argonne Nat. Labs., Lemont, Ill., 1958; rsch. scientist United Techs. Rsch. Labs., East Hartford, Conn., 1959-60, 63-65; mgr. R&D Andersen Labs., Bloomfield, Conn., 1965-68; dir. R&D Orlando (Fla.) Rsch. Corp., 1968-69; v.p. R&D Control Laser Corp., Orlando, 1968-71; staff cons. Martin Marietta Aerospace Corp., Orlando, 1971-73, 86-87, Internat. Laser Corp., Orlando, 1975; sr. staff cons. Sperry Microwave Electronics Corp., Clearwater, Fla., 1977-78; program mgr., P.I. Planning Rsch. Corp., Kennedy Space Center, 1978-80; cons. team leader Westinghouse Electric Corp., Pitts., 1980-81; systems engring. mgr. McDonnell Douglas Astronautics Co., Titusville, Fla., 1982-86; v.p., dir. mfg., CEO UroSolutions, Orlando, Fla., 2000—05; sr. v.p. Global Med. Rsch. LLC, Orlando, 2005—. Chief cons., CEO Aerobeam Corp., Orlando, 1971—2002, Dr. David Flinchbaugh & Assoc., P.A., Orlando. Patentee refractive acousto-optic modulators, robotic manipulator system, urinary drainage control valve, others. Vol. instr. ARC, Orlando, 1968-90; lead counselor Boy and Girl Scouts Am., Orlando, 1968—; mem. Nat. Dem. Policy Com., 1984-86. Named Engr. of Yr. Fla. Engring. Soc., Tallahassee, 1984, Fla. Inventor of Yr. Palm Beach Soc. Am. Inventors, 1986—, Nat. Inventor of Yr. Inventor's Soc. South Fla., Ft. Lauderdale, 1988; recipient Environ. Award, Orange Co., Fla., 1998, DaVinci Award, 2002, Albert M. Sargent Progress Award, Soc. Mfg. Engrs., 2003. Fellow IEEE (Engr. of Yr. Orlando sect. 1982, 83, Entrepreneur of Yr. 1998), AIAA (assoc.), Optical Soc. Am., Soc. Mfg. Engrs./Robotics Internat., Laser Inst. Am. (bd. dirs. 1975-79); mem. NSPE, Fla. Coun. Engring. Socs. (exec. com., pres. 1985-86), Inventors Coun. Cen. Fla. (exec. com., pres. 1984—). Presbyterian. Achievements include invention of the UroCycler®; ROSA Westinghouse nuclear service robot. Avocations: music, photography, aviation, swimming, boating. Home: 4855 Big Oaks Ln Orlando FL 32806-7826 Office: Flinchbaugh & Associates 5635 Commerce DR Orlando FL 32839-2977 Office Phone: 407-760-7200. Personal E-mail: drflinchbaugh@aol.com.

FLOCKEN, JEFFERY, healthcare services company executive; BSBA, Calif. State U., Northridge; M in Pub. Health & Hosp. Adminstrn., UCLA, 1978. Interim pres., CEO Cath. Healthcare West, San Bernardino; v.p., Med. Ctrs. Divsn. Unihealth, Northridge; various positions, sr. v.p., COO Northridge Hosp. Med. Ctr. (subs. Unihealth), 1980—89, pres., CEO, 1989—97; sr. v.p., COO St. Joseph Health System, Orange, Calif.; v.p. Tenet Healthcare Corp., Santa Ana, Calif., 2005—07, sr. v.p., ops., 2007—. Former bd. dirs. Hosp. Assn. of Southern Calif.; bd. dirs. Calif. Hosp. Assn., Maternal Outreach Mgmt. Svcs., Calif.; bd. dirs., Orange County Chpt. Am. Red Cross. Office: Tenet Healthcare Corp 1445 Ross Ave Ste 1400 Dallas TX 75202 Office Phone: 469-893-2200. Office Fax: 469-893-8600. Business E-Mail: Jeffrey.Flocken@tenethealth.com.

FLOM, EDWARD LEONARD, retired metal products executive; b. Tampa, Fla., Dec. 10, 1929; s. Samuel Louis and Julia (Mittle) F.; m. Beverly Boyett, Mar. 31, 1956; children— Edward Louis, Mark Robert, Julia Ruth. B.C.E., Cornell U., 1952. With Fla. Steel Corp., Tampa, 1954-93, v.p. sales, 1957-64, pres., dir., 1964-93, ret., 1993. Bd. dirs., mem. exec. com. Com. of 100, Tampa, United Fund Tampa; mem. adv. com. St. Joseph's Hosp., Tampa; bd. dirs. Family Svc. Assn. Tampa, Jewish Welfare Fedn. Tampa; bd. dirs. temple. With C.E., U.S. Army, 1952-54. Mem. Am. Iron and Steel Inst. (bd. dirs.), Fla. Engring. Soc., Young Pres. Orgn., Univ. Club, Palma Ceia Golf and Country Club, Tampa Yacht Club, Gasparilla Krewe, Rotary (bd. dirs. Tampa). Home: 4936 Saint Croix Dr Tampa FL 33629-4831

FLOOD, JOAN MOORE, paralegal; b. Hampton, Va., Oct. 10, 1941; d. Harold W. and Estalena (Fancher) M.; 1 child by former marriage, Angelique. B.Mus., North Tex. State U., 1963; postgrad., So. Meth. U., 1967-68, Tex. Women's U., 1978-79, U. Dallas, 1985-86. Clk. Criminal Dist. Ct. Number 2, Dallas County, Tex., 1972-75; reins. libr. Scor Reins. Co., Dallas, 1975-80; corp. ins. paralegal Assocs. Inc. Group, 1980-83; corp. securities paralegal Akin, Gump, Strauss, Hauer & Feld, 1983-89; asst. sec. Knoll Internat. Holdings Inc., Saddle Brook, N.J., 1989-90, 21 Internat. Holdings, Inc., NYC, 1990-92; dir. compliance Am. Svc. Life Ins. Co., Ft. Worth, 1992-93; v.p., sec. Express Comm., Inc., Dallas, 1993-94; fin. transactions paralegal Thompson & Knight, Dallas, 1994-96; corp. transactions paralegal Jones, Day, Reavis & Pogue, Dallas, 1996-97, Weil, Gotshal & Manges, LLP, 1998—99; corp. paralegal PennCorp. Fin. Group, Inc., Dallas, 1999-2001; debt trade mgr. Patton Boggs LLP, 2001—03, sr. paralegal bus. transactions, 2003; corp. paralegal Carrington, Coleman, Sloman & Blumenthal, LLP, Dallas, 2003—05; freelance paralegal, 2005—13; ret., 2013. Mem. ABA, Tex. Bar Assn. Home and Office: PO Box 190165 Dallas TX 75219-0165 Home Phone: 214-599-0906. Personal E-mail: jmfdallas@msn.com.

FLOOD, KELLY, state legislator; b. Apr. 14, 1959; m. Neil Flood; 1 child, Evan. BA, Fla. State U., 1981. Mem. Dist 75 Ky. House of Reps., 2009—. Democrat. Office: 702 Capitol Ave Rm 357A Frankfort KY 40601 also: 121 Arcadia Park Lexington KY 40503 Office Phone: 502-564-8100 Ext. 675. Office Fax: 859-221-3107.

FLOOD, MARY ANNE, journalist, lawyer, legal media consultant; d. Robert Phillip and Anne Flood. BGS, U. Houston, 1989; JD cum laude, Harvard U., 1993. Bar: Md. 1993, Tex. 1994, D.C. 1994, U.S. Dist. Ct. Md. 1994, U.S. Dist. Ct. Tex. 1994. Reporter The Lansing (Mich.) State Jour., 1976-78; investigative reporter, editor The Houston Post, 1979-90; assoc. Morrison & Foerster, Washington, 1993-94, Rosen & Newey, Houston, 1994-96; staff writer Wall St. Jour., Tex. Journal, 1997—2000; legal journalist Houston Chronicle, 2000—10; legal media cons. Androvett Legal Media & Mktg., Houston, 2010—. Adj. prof. U. Houston, 1997—2001; spkrs. in field. Stringer The N.Y. Times, 1987-90, Reuters News Svcs., 1987-90. Recipient more than 50 awards. Office: Androvett Legal Media & Marketing 1001 McKinney St Ste 470 Houston TX 77002 Office Phone: 713-383-0090. Office Fax: 713-600-3945. Business E-Mail: mary@androvett.com.

FLORA, JOSEPH M(ARTIN), language educator; b. Toledo, Feb. 9, 1934; s. Raymond D. F. and Frances (Ricica) Neumann; m. Glenda Christine Lape, Jan. 30, 1959; children: Ronald James, Stephen Ray, Peter Joseph, David Benjamin. BA, U. Mich., 1956, MA, 1957, PhD, 1962. Instr. U. Mich., Ann Arbor, 1961-62, U. NC, Chapel Hill, 1962-64, asst. prof., 1964-66, assoc. prof., 1966-77, prof. English, 1977—2010, Atlanta prof. so. culture, 2001—06, acting chmn. dept. English, 1980-81, chmn., 1981-91, asst. dean grad. sch., 1967-72, assoc. dean grad. sch., 1977-78; acting dir. Ctr. Study Am. South, 2008—09. Author: Vardis Fisher, 1965, William Ernest Henley, 1970, Frederick Manfred, 1974, Hemingway's Nick Adams, 1982 (Mayflower Cup award 1982), Ernest Hemingway: A Study of the Short Fiction, 1989, Vardis Fisher: Centennial Essays, 2000; editor: The English Short Story, 1880-1945, 1985; co-editor: Southern Writers, 1979, Fifty Southern Writers Before 1990, 1987, Fifty Southern Writers After 1900, 1987, Contemporary Fiction Writers of the South, 1993, Contemporary Poets, Dramatists, Essayists, Novelists of the South, 1994, The Companion to Southern Literature, 2001, Southern Writers: The New Biographical Dictionary, 2006, Reading Hemingway's Men Without Women, 2008; editorial bds. Mem. MLA, South Atlantic MLA (v.p. 1997-98, pres. 1998-99), Western Lit. Assn. (bd. dirs. 1978-81, 83-86, v.p. 1990, pres. 1992), Soc. for Study So. Lit., Thomas Wolfe Soc. (v.p. 1993-95, pres. 1995-97), Phi Beta Kappa, Phi Eta Sigma. Home: 505 Caswell Rd Chapel Hill NC 27514-2705 Office: UNC Dept Of English Chapel Hill NC 27599-3520 Business E-Mail: jflora@email.unc.edu.

FLORES, ANITERE, state legislator; b. Miami, Fla., Sept. 8, 1976; m. Dustin Anderson; 1 child, Maximo Monte Anderson. BA, Fla. Internat. U., 1997; JD, U. Fla., 2001. Bar: Fla. Atty.; dir. cmty. partnerships Fla. Internat. U.; mem. Dist. 114 Fla. House of Reps., Tallahassee, 2004—10, dep. majority leader, 2008—10, chair preK-12 appropriations com., mem. civil justice & courts policy com., edn. policy coun., ins., bus. & fin. affairs policy com., preK-12 policy com.; mem. Dist. 38 Fla. State Senate, 2011—. Mem. cmty. adv. bd. Fla. Internat. U. Honors Coll.; bd. mem. All Children Together, Nat. Assessment Governing Bd., Spectrum Programs, Inc., Nat. Assn. Latino Elected and Apptd. Offcls. Ednl. Fund. Mem.: Cuban-Am. Bar Assn. Republican. Roman Catholic. Office: Ste 309 10691 N Kendall Dr Miami FL 33176 also: Fla State Senate 316 Senate Office Bldg 404 S Monroe St Tallahassee FL 32399-1100 Office Phone: 305-270-6550, 850-487-5130. Business E-Mail: flores.anitere.web@flsenate.gov.

FLORES, BILL (WILLIAM HOSE FLORES), United States Representative from Texas, former oil industry executive; b. Cheyenne, Wyo., Feb. 25, 1954; s. Joe P. and Ruth Ann (Kennedy) Flores; m. Gina Lynn Bass, June 17, 1978; children: William Hose Jr., John Patrick. BBA in Acctg., cum laude, Tex. A&M U., 1976; MBA, Houston Bapt. U., 1985. Staff acct. Peat, Marwick & Mitchell Co., Amarillo, Tex., 1976, sr. acct. Houston, 1976-78; controller ABC, Houston, 1978-80; v.p. fin. Keyes Offshore Cos., Sugar Land, Tex., 1980-90; exec. v.p., dir. marine drilling, CFO Marine Drilling Cos., Inc., Sugar Land, Tex., 1991—97; corp. sr. v.p., CFO Western Atlas Inc., Houston, 1997—98; sr. v.p., CFO TransEnergy, Houston, 1999, Gryphon Exploration Co., Houston, 2001—05; co-founder, pres., CEO Phoenix Exploration Co., Houston, 2006—09; mem. US Congress from 17th Tex. Dist., Washington, 2011—, US House Budget Com., Washington, 2011—, US House Natural Resources Com., Washington, 2011—. Commr. Tex. Real Estate Commn.; bd. trustees Houston Bapt. U.; bd. dirs., past pres. Tex. A&M Assn. Former Students; bd. dirs. Alley Theatre, Houston. Republican. Methodist. Avocations: skiing, flying. Office: US House of Representatives 1030 Longworth House Washington DC 20515 Office Phone: 202-225-6105.*

FLORES, DANIEL ERNEST, bishop; b. Palacios, Tex. s. Fernando Javier and Lydia (Dilley) Flores. Attended, U. Tex., Austin; BA in Philosophy, Holy Trinity Sem., U. Dallas, 1983, MDiv, 1987; DST, Pontifical U. St. Thomas Aquinas, Rome, 2000. Ordained priest Diocese of Corpus Christi, Tex., 1988, sec. to bishop, asst. chancellor; parochial vicar Corpus Christi Cathedral; vice rector St. Mary's Sem., 2002—05; rector St. John Vianney House of Studies; formation faculty St. Mary's Sem., 2001—02; rector Corpus Christi Cathedral, 2005—06; ordained bishop, 2006; aux. bishop Archdiocese of Detroit, 2006—09; bishop Diocese of Brownsville, Tex., 2009—. Roman Catholic. Office: Diocese of Brownsville 1910 University Blvd Brownsville TX 78520 Office Phone: 956-542-2501. Office Fax: 956-542-6751.

FLORES, PATRICK FERNANDEZ, archbishop emeritus; b. Ganado, Tex., July 26, 1929; Grad., St. Mary's Sem., Houston, 1975; D (hon.), St. Mary's Univ., 1995. Ordained priest Diocese of Galveston, Tex., 1956; asst. pastor Diocese of Houston, 1956—63; pastor Guardian Angel parish, Pasadena, Tex., 1963—67, St. Joseph - St. Stephen parish, Houston, 1967—70; ordained bishop, 1970; aux. bishop Archdiocese of San Antonio, Tex., 1970—78; bishop Diocese of El Paso, 1978—79; archbishop Archdiocese of San Antonio, 1979—2004, archbishop emeritus, 2004—. Chmn. Tex. State Adv. Comm. U.S. Commn. on Civil Rights, 1970; nat. chaplain League of United Latin Am. Citizens, 1970. Co-founder Mex. Am. Cultural Ctr., San Antonio, 1972; founder Nat. Hispanic Scholarship Fund, 1976. Recipient Freedom medal, Ellis Island Statue of Liberty 100th Birthday, 1986, Hispanic Heritage award, 1986, Salute to Edn. award, Ford, 1995. Roman Catholic. Mailing: Archdiocese of San Antonio PO Box 28410 San Antonio TX 78228-0410

FLORI, ANNA MARIE DIBLASI, health facility administrator, nurse, anesthesiologist; b. Amsterdam, NY, Oct. 29, 1940; d. Tony Flori and Maria (Macario) DiBlasi Flori; m. Gilberto Flori Flori, May 24, 1986; children: Tammy, Tina, Toni. Degree, Albany Med. Ctr. Sch. Nursing, 1962, Fairfax Hosp. Sch. Nurse Anesthetists, Va., 1972; BS in Anesthesia, George Washington U., 1979; M in Bus. & Pub. Adminstrn., Southeastern U., Washington, 1982; PhD, Columbia Pacific U., 1983. Cert. anesthetist; RN. Staff nurse West Seattle Gen. Hosp., 1962—64; nurse Filmore Buckner, Md., Seattle, 1964—66; staff nurse anesthetist Fairfax Hosp., 1972—73, Potomac Hosp., Woodbridge, Va., 1973; chief nurse anesthetist, 1973—; dir. Potomac Hosp. Sch. for Nurse Anesthetists & Sch. for Nurse Anesthesia; faculty mem. Columbia Pacific U., 1973—90; chief nurse anesthetist No. Va. Anesthesia Assn., 1988—; guest lectr No. Va. CC; guest lectr. Inservice Potomac Hosp., George Washington U. Contbr. articles to profl. jours. Mem.: Nat. Italian Am. Found., Va. Nurse Anesthesia Assn., Am. Assn. Nurse Anesthetists. Home: 12954 Pintail Rd Woodbridge VA 22192-3831 Office Phone: 703-490-5496. Personal E-mail: crnhamf@aol.com.

FLORIN, TODD J., cardiac electrophysiologist, educator; MD, NYU, 1988. Diplomate Am. Bd. Internal Medicine-cardiovasc. disease, 2005, Am. Bd. Internal Medicine-cardiac electrophysiology, 2006. Resident internal medicine Univ. of Mich., 1989—91; fellow cardiovasc. disease Univ. of Md., 1992—95; fellow cardiac electrophysiology; asst. prof. medicine Univ. of Miami; hosp. affiliation includes Mt. Sinai Med. Ctr. Office: Mount Sinai Medical Center 4300 Alton Rd Miami Beach FL 33140-2800 Office Phone: 305-674-2121.

FLORIO, MIKE, sportswriter, lawyer; b. Wheeling, W.Va. m. Jill Florio; 1 child, Alex. B in Engring., Carnegie Mellon U., Pitts.; JD, W.Va. U., 1991. Pvt. practice atty., Pitts., Clarksburg, W.Va.; contbr. NFLTalk.com, 2000; founder, owner, contbr., editor ProFootballTalk-.com, 2001—. Home: 333 E Main St Clarksburg WV 26301-2127

FLOTO, RONALD JOHN, supermarket executive; b. Spangler, Pa., Nov. 12, 1942; s. John Lester and Frances (McCormick) F.; m. Sara Jean Albert, Jan. 6, 1968; children: Lisa, John, Mary, Patricia. BS in Engring., U.S. Mil. Acad., West Point, 1965; MBA, Harvard U., 1971. Special asst. to under sec., transp. U.S. Dept. of Transp., 1971—73; v.p. Masa Feeding Corp., Elk Grove, Ill., 1977—78, Jewel Food Stores, Melrose Park, Ill., 1978—81, Jewel Cos. Inc., Chgo., 1981—83, pres., Jewel's Buttrey Food Stores; pres. Buttrey Food Stores, Great Falls, Mont., 1983—85, Kash n' Karry, Tampa, Fla., 1985—94; CEO, chmn. Kash N' Karry Food Stores; pres., Super K Divsn. Kmart Corp., 1994—97; exec. v.p., pres. Super Kmart Centers, Troy, Mich., 1995—97; CEO Dairy Farm Internat. Holdings Ltd., 1997—2007; founder FLT International, LLC, 2007, pres., 2007—. Bd. dirs. Dairy Farm Internat. Holdings Ltd., Dairy Farm Internat., Food World, Ltd., India and Health & Glow, Ltd., India, Accel Networks, Borders Group, Inc., 2009—. Bd. dirs. Jr. Achievement of Chgo., 1978-81; bd. dirs. Vietnam Vets. Leadership Program, Chgo., 1981-82. Served to capt. U.S. Army, 1965-73. Republican. Roman Catholic. Office: Borders Group Inc 2723 S State St Ste 150 Ann Arbor MI 48104-6188 Office Phone: 734-477-1100. Office Fax: 734-477-1285. Business E-Mail: rfloto@fintech.net.

FLOURNOY, WILLIAM LOUIS, JR., retired landscape architect; b. Raleigh, NC, May 6, 1945; s. William Louis and Flossie (Combs) F. Student, Gardner-Webb Jr. Coll., 1964-66; BS in Recreation and Parks Adminstrn., N.C. State U., 1969, M of Landscape Architecture, 1972. Cons. to City of Raleigh N.C. State U. Sch. Design, 1971—72; community planner Wake County Planning Dept., Raleigh, NC, 1972-80; environ. analysis program mgr. Office Legis. and Intergovtl. N.C. Dept. Environ. and Natural Resources, Raleigh, 1980—2002, sr. conservation specialist Office Conservation and Cmty. Affairs, 2002—05, dir. conservation incentive program nat. resources planning & conservation, 2005—07; mem. leadership coun. NCSU Design Guild, 2010—. Mem. alumni adv. bd. dept. landscape architecture N.C. State U., 1999—2007, chair, 2003—05. Contbr. articles to profl. jours. Bicycle com. NC Dept. Transp., 1974—83, chair, 1974—76, 1978—79; mem. nat. recreational trails adv. com. U.S. Dept. Transp., 1992—94; steering com. Wake County Cmty. Assessment, 1992—94; organizing com. NC Greenways Conf., 1986—95, conf. chair, 1992; active Triangle Open Space Network, 1997—99; bd. dirs. Southeastern U.S. Masters Track and Field, Inc., Raleigh, 1976—82, Triangle Land Conservancy, Rsch. Triangle Pk., NC, pres., 1991—94; bd. dirs. Triangle Greenways Coun., pres., 1989—91, 2008—; bd. dirs. People for Parks, Wake County, NC, pres., 2002—04. Recipient Le Gasse medal, 2010. Fellow Am. Soc. Landscape Architects (treas. N.C. chpt. 1982-86, v.p. 1978-79, awards 1978, 86, 90, 95), N.C. Trails Assn. (bd. dirs. 1977-82, acting pres. 1977), Landscape Architecture Founds., Landscape Architecture Urban Parks Honor Roll, NCSU Coll. Design (Design Smith award, 2009), others. Democrat. Methodist. Avocations: trail construction/maintenance, jogging, canoeing, hiking, bicycling. Home: 520 Polk St Raleigh NC 27604-1960 Personal E-mail: bflournoy@nc.rr.com.

FLOWERS, BETTY SUE, literature and language professor, former library director; b. Waco, Tex., Feb. 2, 1947; d. Paul Davis and Betty Lou (Lewis) Marable; div. John G. Flowers III; 1 child, John Michael. BA with high honors, U. Tex., 1969, MA, 1970; PhD, U. London, 1973. Joined English dept. U. Tex., Austin, 1968, asst. prof. English dept., 1973—79, assoc. prof. English dept., 1979—88, assoc. dean Graduate Studies, 1979-82, 88-90, dir. plan II honors program, 1987-91, prof. English dept., 1989—2001, dir. creative writing, 2000, Kelleher prof. English, 2001—02, adj. prof. English, 2002—09, prof. emerita, 2009—; dir. Lyndon Baines Johnson Libr. and Mus., Austin, Tex., 2002—09. Vis. advisor to sec. USN, 1999; cons. NASA, Exxon, IBM, Shell Internat., London. Author: Browning and The Modern Tradition, 1976, Four Shields of Power, 1987, Extending the Shade, 1990; editor: A World of Ideas, 1988, Joseph Campbell and the Power of Myth: Bill Moyers and Joseph Campbell in Conversation, 1988, (with Lynda E. Boose) Daughters and Fathers, 1988, Moyers: Healing and the Mind, 1992; contbr. chpts. to books, articles to profl. jours. Mem. exec. com. Tex. Com. for Humanities, 1987-90; bd. trustees Tex. Humanities Alliance, 1986-87; mem. envisioning network GM. Recipient Amoco Tchg. Excellence award, 1979, Holloway Tchg. award, 1983, Margaret C. Berry Outstanding Contbn. to Student Life award, 1987, Liz Carpenter Lifetime Achievement award, Women in Comm., 1998, Top Hand award, U. Tex., 1990, Disting. Alumnus award, 2001; named Communicator of Yr., Austin Toastmasters, 1990, Woman Scholar of Yr., Va. Commonwealth Univ., 1996; named a Lone Star Great, Tex. Dept. Commerce, 1992, Piper Prof., Tex., 1997; named an Outstanding Alumna, Waco Ind. Sch. Dist., 1998; grantee, Univ. Rsch. Inst., 1983, 1992; fellow, Ctr. for Internat. Bus. Edn. and Rsch., 1995; Andrew W. Mellow fellowship, Aspen Inst. for Humanistic Studies, 1976, Cranfill Tchg. fellowship, 1986—87. Mem. MLA, Acad. Disting. Tchrs., Nat. Poetry Therapy Assn. (bd. dirs. 1987—), Salado Inst. for Humanities (hon. life mem., bd. trustees, Jungian fellow), Jung Soc. Austin (hon. life. mem.), Phi Beta Kappa, Omicron Delta Kappa. Office: University Tex Dept English Austin TX 78712 Business E-Mail: bflowers@uts.cc.utexas.edu.

FLOWERS, FRANKLIN P., dermatologist, educator; MD, U. Fla., 1971. Diplomate Am. Bd. Dermatology, 1976, Am. Bd. Pathology-dermatopathology, 1981. Intern Univ. Ky. Med. Ctr., 1971—72; resident dermatology Ohio State Univ., Columbus, Ohio, 1972—75; fellow mohs micrographic surgery and cutaneous oncology Univ. Ala., Birmingham, Ala., 1992—93; fellow Am. Coll. of Mohs Micrographic Surgery and Cutaneous Oncology, 1997; dir. dermatol. surg. tng. Univ. of Fla., med. dir. Dermatology and Skin Cancer Ctr., chief dermatology and cutaneous surgery divsn., prof. medicine, hosp. affiliation include Shands. Mailing: University FL Dermatology & Skin Cancer Clinic Park Ave 1014 NW 57th St Gainesville FL 32605 Office: Division of Dermatology & Cutaneous Surgery PO Box 100277 Gainesville FL 32610-0277 Office Phone: 352-265-8001, 352-392-4984. Office Fax: 352-392-5376.

FLOWERS, GARRY W., engineering and construction management company executive; BS, Furman U., Greenville, SC. Joined Fluor Corp., 1978, dir. security, 1987—91, sr. dir. corp. security, 1991—94, v.p., 1994—2004, sr. v.p. indsl. rels., security and health, safety & the environment, 2004—. Mem. Exec. Coun. of US Dept. State, Overseas Security Adv. Coun. Mem.: Internat. Security Mgmt. Assn., Chief Spl. Agts. Assn., Inc. Office: Fluor Corp 6700 Las Colinas Blvd Irving TX 75039 Office Phone: 469-398-7000. Office Fax: 469-398-7255.

FLOWERS, MERLE G., state legislator; b. Camden, Tenn., Oct. 20, 1968; s. Jack and June; m. Stacey Flowers; 3 children. BS in Agrl. Bus. and Econ., Auburn U., 1991; MBA, U. Miss., 1995. Alderman, dir. parks., recreation & beautification City of Section, 1988-92; with Lightfoot, Franklin & White, Birmingham, Ala., Carson-Brooks, Inc., Memphis; dist. mgr. Congressman Roger Wicker, Washington; mem. Dist. 19 Miss. State Senate, 2004—; pres. Flowers Properties LLC. Pres. bd. dirs. Desoto chpt. Habitat for Humanity; bd. dirs. Kudzu Playhouse. Named Top 40 Under 40 Miss. Bus. Jour. Mem. Mason, Shriner (Clown Unit Rookie of the Yr., 1993). Republican. Presbyterian. Avocations: marathon, guitar. Office: PO Box 1018 Jackson MS 39215 Office Phone: 662-349-3983, 601-359-3211. Business E-Mail: mflowers@senate.ms.gov.

FLOWERS, ROBERT SWAIM, medical educator, surgeon; b. Greenville, Ala., Sept. 13, 1934; m. Susan Flowers; children: Swaim, Rob, Christian, Jonathan. BS in Chemistry and Biology, U. Ala., 1955, MD, 1960. Diplomate Am. Bd. Plastic Surgery. Intern U.S. Army Tripler Med. Ctr., 1960-61; battle group surgeon U.S. Army, 1961-63; resident gen. surgery Cleve. Clinic, Ohio, 1963-66, resident plastic surgery Ohio, 1966-68; chmn. plastic surgery sect. Straub Clinic, Honolulu, 1968-72; chmn. dept. plastic surgery Queen's Med. Ctr., Honolulu, 1972-74; asst. clinical prof. plastic surgery U. Hawaii, 1971—; dir., prin. surgeon Plastic Surgery Ctr. of the Pacific Inc., Honolulu, 1975—2009; surgeon, dir. Flowers Clinic, Honolulu, 1993—. Chief, dir. Hawaii Postgrad. Fellowship Prog. Aesthetic & Asian Plastic Surgery; co-founder Gender Identity Clinic, Hawaii U.; vis. prof., lectr. Stanford U., U. Miami, U. Calif., Emory U., U. Zagreb, Yugoslavia, U. Munich, Germany, Columbia Presbyn. U., 1983, Duke U., 1985—86, Cleve. Clinic, 1985, UCLA, 1987, U. Louisville, U. Ala., Saarland U., Germany, 1993, U. Colo., 1994, U. Toronto, U. Manitoba. Contbr. articles to profl. jours., chapters to books. Pres. congregation, choir dir. Calvary By The Sea Luth. Ch., Honolulu, liturgist, lay minister, 1969—2004; bd. dirs. Honolulu Symphony, 2007. Recipient Renaissonce Plastic Surgeon of 20th Century award, Am. Soc. Ophthal. Plastic Surgery; named Top Plastic Surgeon in World, Japanese Soc., Best Aesthetic Surgeon, North America Soc. Aesthetic Surgeons, Japanese Soc. Aesthetic Surgeons, 2001. Fellow: Am. Coll. Surgeons; mem.: AMA, Med. Assn. Ala., Pan-Pacific Surgical Assn., Internat. Soc. Clinical Plastic Surgeons, Internat. Soc. Aesthetic Plastic Surgeons, Honolulu County Med. Soc. (bd. govs. 1990—94), Hawaii Plastic Surgical Socs., Southeastern Soc. Plastic Surgeons (hon.), Australasian Soc. Aesthetics Plastic Surgery (hon.), Northwest Soc. Plastic Surgeons (hon.), Hawaii Med. Assn., Can. Soc. Aesthetic Plastic Surgeons, Calif. Soc. Plastic Surgeons, Oriental Soc. of Aesthetics, Am. Soc. Plastic Surgeons, Am. Assn. Plastic Surgeons, Honolulu Club, Waikiki Yacht Club, Outrigger Canoe Club. Avocations: drawing, painting, writing, sailing, singing, writing, sculpting. Office: Flowers Clinic 4627 Dolly Ridge Rd Birmingham AL 35243-2205 Home: 4627 Dolly Ridge Rd Birmingham AL 35243

FLOWERS, STEPHANIE, state legislator, lawyer; b. Pine Bluff, Ark. d. W. Harold and Margaret (Brown) Flowers; 1 child. BA, Philander Smith Coll., Little Rock; JD, Tex. So. U., Houston, 1979. Bar: Tex. 1982, Ark. 1991. Pvt. practice atty., 1982—; mem. Dist. 17 Ark. House of Reps., 2005—11; mem. Dist. 5 Ark. State Senate, 2011—. Dep. prosecutor Jefferson County Juvenile Ct., 1994. Del. Dem. Nat. Conv., 2008. Mem.: W. Harold Flowers Law Soc., Jefferson County Dem. Women. Democrat. Methodist. Mailing: Dist Address 104 Main St Suite C Pine Bluff AR 71601 Office Phone: 870-535-1032.

FLOWERS, V. ANNE, retired academic administrator; b. Dothan, Ala., Aug. 29, 1928; d. Kyrie Neal and Annie Laurie (Stewart) Flowers. BA, Fla. State U., 1949; MEd, Auburn U., 1958; EdD, Duke U., 1963. Teaching asst. Duke U., Durham, NC, 1963; elem. and secondary sch. tchr., adminstr. Dothan, Dalton, Ga., 1949-61; from assoc. prof. to prof. edn., head dept. Columbia (S.C.) Coll., 1963-68, from assoc. dean to dean, 1969-72; prof. edn. Va. Commonwealth U., 1968-69; tchg. asst. Duke U., 1963, assoc. dean, asst. provost, acting dean, vice provost Trinity Coll. Arts and Scis., 1972-74, prof. edn., chmn. dept., asst. provost ednl. program devel., 1974-80; dean Sch. Edn. Ga. So. Coll., Statesboro, 1980-85; asst. vice chancellor acad. affairs Univ. Sys. Ga., Atlanta, 1985-88, vice chancellor, 1988-90, ret., 1990, vice chancellor emerita, 1990—. Mem. coun. aging and human devel. Duke U., 1974—80; cons. in field. Co-author: Law and Pupil Control, 1964, Readings in Survival in Today's Society, 2 vols., 1978; mem. editl. bd. Ednl. Gerontology, 1979, Jour. Tchr. Edn., 1980—82; contbr. articles to profl. jours. Bd. dirs., mem. exec. com. Learning Inst. N.C., 1976—80; vice chmn. continuing commn. study black colls. related to United Meth. Ch., 1973—76; pres. univ. senate Bd. Higher Edn. and Ministry United Meth. Ch., 1977—80; adv. trustee Queens Coll., Charlotte, NC, 1976—78; mem. bd. visitors Charleston So. U., 1992—93. Delta Kappa Gamma scholar, Duke U., 1963, State of Fla. scholar, Fla. State U., 1949. Mem.: NEA, Nat. Orgn. Legal Problems Edn., Am. Assn. Colls. Tchr. Edn. (bd. dirs., mem. exec. com. 1979—84, pres. 1983—84), Kappa Delta Pi. Home: PO Box 6965 Dothan AL 36302-6965

FLOYD, DAISY HURST, law educator, former dean; BA, MA in Polit. Sci., Emory U., 1977; JD cum laude, U. Ga., 1980. Bar: Ga., TEx. Atty. Alston, Miller & Gaines, Atlanta, 1980—81; instr. Legal Rsch. and Writing Program U. Ga. Sch. Law, 1982—83, dir. Legal Rsch. and Writing Prog., 1983—87; program dir. Paralegal Studies Program Athens Area Tech. Inst., Ga., 1987—89; adj. prof. law Tex. Tech U. Sch. Law, 1990—91, asst. prof., 1991—94, assoc. prof., 1994—96, assoc. dean academic affairs, 1995—2001, prof. law, 1996—2004; dean, prof. law Walter F. George Sch. Law, Mercer U., Macon, Ga., 2004—10, univ. prof. law and ethical found., 2010—. Faculty mem. Nat. Inst. Trial Advocacy (NITA), Nat. Jud. Coll., Tex. Jud. Acad., Tex. Ctr. for Judiciary. Mem. bd. dirs. Lubbock Legal Aid Soc. Recipient New Prof. Excellence in Tchg. award, 1995; named Prof. of Yr., Phi Alpha Delta, 2001; Carnegie scholar, 2001. Fellow: Am. Bar. Found.; mem.: Tex. Bar Found. Office: Walter F George School Law Mercer University 1021 Georgia Ave Macon GA 31207-0001 Office Phone: 478-301-2628. Office Fax: 478-301-2259. E-mail: floyd_dh@law.mercer.edu.

FLOYD, DAVID, state legislator; b. Louisville, Ky., Oct. 2, 1951; m. Cheri Floyd; children: Mindy, Beth. BS, USAF Acad., 1973; MA in Aero. Sci., Embry-Riddle Aero. U., 1987. Entrepreneur Windsor Gardens Retirement Cmtys.; mem. Dist. 50 Ky. House of Reps, 2005—, minority whip; mem. Health & Welfare Com., Local Govt. Com., State Govt. Com. Ret. USAF. Mem.: Nelson County Econ. Devel. Agy., Bardstown Found. for Excellence in Pub. Edn., VFW, Am. Legion, Rotary Club. Republican. Baptist. Office: 702 Capitol

Ave Annex Rm 414 Frankfort KY 40601 Mailing: 102 Maywood Ave Bardstown KY 40004 Home Phone: 502-350-0986; Office Phone: 502-564-8011 698, 502-564-5413, 800-372-7181.

FLOYD, ELMER, state legislator; Mem. Dist. 43 NC House of Reps., 2009—. Mem. Appropriations com., Appropriations Subcom. on Gen. Govt., Commerce, Small Bus and Entrepreneurship com., Edn. com., Edn. Subcom. on Cmty. Colleges, Environ. and Nat. Resources com., Local Govt. II com.; vice chmn. Homeland Security, Military and Veterans Affairs com. With US Army, 1961—63. Democrat. Office: NC House of Reps 16 W Jones St Rm 1311 Raleigh NC 27601-1096 Office Phone: 919-733-5959. Business E-Mail: Elmer.Floyd@ncleg.net.

FLOYD, HENRY FRANKLIN, federal judge; b. Brevard, SC, Nov. 5, 1947; BA, Wofford Coll., 1970; JD, U. SC, 1973. Mem. SC House of Reps., Columbia, 1972—78; pvt. law practice Pickens, SC, 1973—92; cir. judge 13th Jud. Cir. Ct. SC, 1992—2003; judge US Dist. Ct. SC, Spartanburg, 2003—11, US Ct. Appeals (4th Cir.), 2011—. Office: US Court Appeals 1100 E Main St Richmond VA 23219 Office Phone: 864-591-5300.

FLOYD, HUGH, state legislator; b. Parris Island, SC, Jan. 18, 1941; m. Judy Floyd; children: Danna, Evan. Former state rep. Dist. 69, Ga.; mem. Edn. Com., Legislature & Congressional Reapportionment Com.; sec. State Planning & Cmty. Affairs Com.; sales exec. Indusl. Packaging Corp., 1969—2000; state rep. Dist. 99 Ga., 2004—. Democrat. Methodist. Mailing: 744 Omaha Dr Norcross GA 30093 Office: 608 Legis Office Bldg Atlanta GA 30334 Office Phone: 404-656-0298, 770-921-2735. E-mail: hfloyd@legis.state.ga.us.

FLOYD, JOHN ALEX, JR., retired publishing executive; b. Selma, Ala., Feb. 21, 1948; s. John Alex Sr. and Louise (Johnson) Floyd; m. Pamela Lorene Billups, Aug. 14, 1982; children: Ryan Thomas, James Alex. BS, Auburn U., Ala., 1970; MS, Clemson U., SC, 1972, PhD, 1975. Instr. Jefferson State Jr. Coll., Birmingham, Ala., 1975-77; sr. horticulturist Southern Living mag. Southern Progress Corp. (subs. Time, Inc.), Birmingham, 1977-84, editl. dir. Southern Accents, 1985-87, editl. dir. Creative Ideas & Cooking Light mags., 1987-88, dir. mktg. svcs., editor, 1988-91, v.p., editor-in-chief Southern Living, 1991—2008, ret., 2008. Co-author: Southern Living Trees & Shrubs, 1980, Southern Living Garden Guide, 1982, Southern Living Vegetable & Herbs, 1984. Bd. dirs. U NC Bot. Gardens, Chapel Hill, 1988—90, Cmty. Found. Greater Birmingham. Mem.: Garden Writers America, Birmingham Bot. Soc. (pres. 1981, trustee 1984—), Am. Hort. Soc. (bd. dirs. 1991—94), Pi Alpha Xi, Gamma Sigma Delta. Methodist. Office Phone: 205-445-6365. E-mail: john_floyd@timeinc.com.

FLOYD, KAREN KANES, marketing executive, former political organization administrator; b. Houston, Aug. 14, 1962; d. William Henry and Patricia Joan (Smith) Kanes. BA, Goucher Coll., Balt., 1983; JD, U. SC Sch. Law, Columbia, 1986. Bar: SC 1986. Law clk. Swerling & Harpootlian, 1983-86; rsch. asst. U. SC Sch. Law, 1983-86; staff atty. SC State Senate, Columbia, 1986-87; asst. cir. solicitor 7th Jud. Cir., Spartanburg, SC, 1987-88; assoc. King, Hray & Kanes, Spartanburg, 1988—90, ptnr., 1990—92; magistrate Spartanburg Ct., 1992-93, chief magistrate, 1993-94; dir. employee rels. & legal compliance Flagstar Corp., Spartanburg, 1994—96, v.p. employee rels., govtl. affairs, & legal compliance, 1996—98; chmn. Spartanburg County Coun., 1998—2002; CEO The Palladian Group, 1999—; chair SC Rep. Party, 2009—11. Chair State Infrastructure Bank Steering Com., Spartanburg County, 1999—2003, Spartanburg Area Transp. Study, 2000—03; bd. dirs. Spartanburg Area C. of C., 1998—2002, bd. govs., 2005—; founding bd. mem. Susan B. Komen Upstate Race for a Cure, 1998, sec., 1999—2001; bd. dirs. Spartanburg Devel. Coun., 1998—2002, Palmetto Conservation Found., 1998—2002. Elizabeth King Ellicott scholar, Goucher Coll., 1983, Daniel McLeod scholar, U. SC Sch. Law, 1986. Mem.: ABA, American Judiciary Soc., Spartanburg County Bar Assn., SC Bar Assn. Republican. Episcopalian. Avocations: marathon running, scuba diving. Office: Palladian Group 113 W Main St Spartanburg SC 29306 Office Phone: 864-596-7501. Office Fax: 864-596-7502.

FLOYD, NANCY ARTHUR, systems analyst, educator; b. Manchester, NH, June 23, 1938; AB in English, U. NC, Chapel Hill, 1960; PhD in Bus. Info. Sys., Va. Commonwealth U., 1998. Founding instr., data processing for handicapped project Woodrow Wilson Rehab. Ctr. Joint Project VA and IBM, 1972—78; info. sys. tng. dir. & project mgr. Dan River Industries, 1978—81; info. processing instr. Rockingham CC, Guilford Tech. CC, 1981—86; asst. prof., computer info. sys. Eastern Mennonite U., 1986—2000; Planters prof. NC Wesleyan Coll., Jefferson-Pilot prof., assoc. prof. & coord. info. sys. programs, 2000—. Grant, NC ICU, NSF, Title III grant, US Govt. Office: 3400 North Wesleyan Blvd Rocky Mount NC 27804 Business E-Mail: nfloyd@ncwc.edu.*

FLOYD, RAYMOND LORAN, professional golfer; b. Ft. Bragg, NC, Sept. 4, 1942; s. Loren B. and Edith (Brown) F.; m. Maria; children: Raymond Loran, Robert Loran, Christina Loran. Student, U. N.C., 1960. Profl. golfer PGA, 1961-92; profl. golfer Sr. PGA, 1992—. Mem. US team Ryder Cup, 1969, 1975, 1977, 1981, 1983, 1985, 1991, 1993, capt., 1989, asst. captain, 2008. Winner 2000 Ford Sr. Players Championship, Wendy's Champion Tour Sking, 2006, Doral Ryder Open, 1992, GTE North Classic, 1992, Northville Long Island Classic Senior PGA, 1993, Sr. Tour Championship, 1994, Ford Sr. Players Championship, 2000; named Rookie of Year Golf Mag., 1963, 77, Player of Yr., 1976; Runner-up The Boeing Championship, 2006; Three Top Ten Finishes in Nine Starts, 2006; UBS Cup mem. Winning US Team, 2004. Winner PGA tournament, 1969, 82 St. Petersburg Open, 1963, St. Paul Open, 1965, Jacksonville Open, 1969, Am. Golf Classic, 1969, Kemper Open, 1975, Masters, 1976, World Open, 1976, Byron Nelson Golf Classic, 1977, Pleasant Valley Golf Classic, 1977, Brazilian Open, 1978, Greater Greensboro Open, 1979, Canadian PGA, 1981, Vardon Trophy, 1983, Ryder Cup, 1969, 75, 77, 81, 83, 85, Doral Ea. Open, 1980, 81, Tournament Players Championship, 1981, Westchester Classic, 1981, Meml. Tournament, 1982, Memphis Classic, 1982, PGA Championship, 1982, $1Million Sun City Challenge, 1982, Houston Open, 1985, Chrysler Team Championship, 1985, U.S. Open, 1986, Walt Disney/Oldsmobile Classic, 1986, Skins Game, 1988, RMCC Invitational, 1990, Doral-Ryder Open, 1992, GTE North Classic, 1992, Ralph's Sr. Classic, 1992, Sr. Tour Championship, 1992, Thailand Srs., 1992, Northville L.I. Classic, 1993, The Tradition, 1994, Sr. Skins Game, 1994, 95, 96, 97, 98, 06, Las Vegas Srs. Classis, 1994, Sr. Tour Championship, 1994, PGA Srs. Championship, 1995, Burnet Sr. Classic, 1995, Ford Sr. Players Championship, 1996; capt. Ryder Cup, 1989; inducted in PGA/World Golf Hall of Fame, 1989, winner father-son tourn. w/son Raymond Jr., 1995, 96, 97, w/son Robert, 2000, 01, winner Par 3 Shootout, 2000. Office: 505 S Flagler Dr West Palm Beach FL 33401

FLOYD, RICHARD, state legislator; b. Hamilton Co, Tenn., Apr. 17, 1944; 3 children. State rep. Dist. 27, Tenn., 2007—. Fellow: Christian Athletes; mem.: Stuart Heights Bapt. Ch., Nat. Rifle Assn Big Bros.-Big Sisters (Hamilton County), Chattanooga Resource Found., Bethel Bible Village, Pachyderm Club. Republican. Baptist. Office: 306 Altoona Dr Chattanooga TN 37415 also: G-24 War Memorial Bldg Nashville TN 37243-0127 Office Phone: 615-741-2746. Office Fax: 615-253-0304. Business E-Mail: rep.richard.floyd@capitol.tn.gov.

FLOYD, TIM, men's college basketball coach; b. Hattiesburg, Miss., Feb. 25, 1954; s. Lee Floyd; m. Beverly Floyd; 1 child, Shannon. BS in Health & Phys. Edn., La. Tech. U., 1977. Student asst. La. Tech. U. Bulldogs, 1977; asst. coach U. Tex. El Paso Miners, 1978—86, head basketball coach, 2010—, U. Idaho Vandals, 1986-88, U. New Orleans Privateers, 1989—94, Iowa State U. Cyclones, 1994-98; dir. ops Chgo. Bulls, 1998, head basketball coach, 1999—2001, New Orleans Hornets, 2003—04, asst. coach, 2009—10; head basketball coach U. So. Calif. Trojans, 2005—09. Basketball advisor: Glory Road, 2006. Named Coach of Yr., Am. South Conf., 1989, Sun Belt Conf., 1993, Big Eight Conf., 1996. Office: University Tex El Paso Basketball Brumbelow Bldg 500 W University Ave El Paso TX 79968-0579 Office Phone: 915-747-5323.

FLOYD, W. RUSSEL, JR., funeral services company executive; BSBA, U. NC, Chapel Hill, 1972; BA in Psychology, U. NC, Charlotte, 1977. Pres. W. R. Floyd Corp., Spartanburg, 1978—, W. R. Floyd Svcs., Inc., 1978—; v.p., piedmont crematory, pres. Westwood Memorial Gardens, Inc., Spartanburg, 1980—; pres. Business Communications, Inc., 1984—. Bd. adv. Wachovia, Spartanburg, 1994—99; bd. dirs. First Nat. Bank (subs. First Nat. Bancshares, Inc.), Spartanburg, First Nat. Bancshares, Inc., 1999—. Former trustee Spartanburg YMCA; former bd. dirs. First Presbyn. Ch., Spartanburg; pres. Spartanburg Boys Home, 1986—99; mem. Spartanburg Rotary Club. Mem.: SC Perpetual Care Cemetery Bd. Office: W R Floyd Services Inc 2075 E Main St Spartanburg SC 29307-1430 Office Phone: 864-582-5455.

FLUDD, VIRGIL, state legislator; m. Carolyn Fludd; children: Christine, Brendan. Former state rep. Dist. 48, Ga.; state rep. Dist. 66 Ga., 2004—; sec. Banks & Banking Coms.; chmn. Fayette County Del.; mem. Adminstrn. Svcs. Coms., Edn. & Natural Resources & Environ. Coms. Democrat. Mailing: 512 LOB Atlanta GA 30334 Office: PO Box 125 Fayetteville GA 30214 Office Phone: 404-656-7859, 770-460-6383. Fax: 770-460-2216.

FLUR, DORLISA K., retail executive; b. 1965; BS in Computer Sci. & Economics, Duke U., MBA. Various positions, including prin. McKinsey & Co., 1988—2004; sr. v.p., strategy & bus. devel. Family Dollar Stores, Inc., Matthews, NC, 2004—08, exec. v.p., strategy & mktg., 2008—09, exec. v.p., chief merchandising officer, 2009—11, vice chair strategy, chief adminstrv. officer, 2011—. Bd. dirs. Bechtler Mus. Modern Art, NC Blumenthal Performing Arts Ctr., Myers Park United Methodist Church Recipient Phi Beta Kappa, Duke U. Office: Family Dollar Stores Inc 10401 Monroe Rd Matthews NC 28105 Office Phone: 704-847-6961. Office Fax: 704-847-5534. Business E-Mail: dorlisa.flur@familydollar.com.

FLYNN, DAN, state legislator; b. Feb. 21, 1943; m. Susan Flynn. Fin. cons.; mem. Dist. 2 Tex. House of Reps., Tex., 2002—. Mem. State Affairs Sunset Commn. Republican. Office: PO Box 999 Canton TX 75103 also: Room CAP GN.10 Capitol PO Box 2910 Austin TX 78768 Office Phone: 903-567-0921, 512-463-0880.

FLYNN, DONALD F., automotive executive; Grad., Marquette U., 1961. Chmn. LKQ Corp., Inc.; employee David Himmelblau & Co., 1961-65; acct. Arthur Andersen & Co., 1965-72; comptroller, sr. v.p. & CFO Waste Management, Inc., 1972—90; bd. dirs., stockholder Blockbuster Entertainment Corp., 1987—; CEO Discovery Zone, Inc., Fort Lauderdale, Fla., 1992—95, chmn., 1992—96; stockholder Flynn Enterprises, Inc., 1992; vice chmn. Blue Chip Casino, Inc., Michigan City, Ind., 1997—99. Office: LKQ Corp Inc 120 N LaSalle St Ste 3300 Chicago IL 60602 Office Phone: 312-621-1950. Office Fax: 312-621-1969. E-mail: dfflynn@lkqcorp.com.

FLYNN, JAMES S., school system administrator; b. Gallatin, Tenn., Apr. 12, 1964; s. James S. and Lana D. Flynn; m. Natalie S. Wilkins, May 23, 1987; children: James Bracken, John Hunter, Bretton Elizabeth. BS, Western Ky. U., Bowling Green, 1986; MS, Tex. A&M U., Corpus Christi, 1991; EdD, Northern Ky. U., Highland Heights, 2013. Cert. secondary sch. prin. Ky. Edn. Profl. Stds. Bd., 1994, supt. 2001. Dean, sci. tchr. Corpus Christi Acad., 1989—92; tchr., biology, chemistry, physics Greenwood HS, Bowling Green, 1992—94, asst. prin., 1994—97; prin. Shelby County HS, 1997—2003; supt. Simpson County Schs., Franklin, Ky., 2003—. Mem., supt., CEO network, Frankfort, 2006—09; bd. mem. Supts. Adv. Coun. Commr. Edn., Frankfort, 2008—14, Local Supts. Adv. Coun., Frankfort, 2010—14. Bd. mem. Franklin-Simpson C. of C., 2003—14; sports coach Local Youth Soccer and Basketball Leagues, 1994—2013. Recipient Disting. Svc. award, Ky. Dept. Edn., 1995, New Supt. Mentor award, KDE/KASA, 2007, 2012—13, Unbridled Spirit Justice award, Ky. Commn. Human Rights, 2011; named Alumni Hall of Honor, Bowling Green HS, 2014. Mem.: Franklin-Simpson Indsl. Authority (bd. mem. 2003—, Econ. Devel. award 2010), Am. Assn. Sch. Adminstrs., Ky. Assn. Sch. Supts. (Frankfort), Ky. Sch. Bds. Assn., Ky. Assn. Sch. Adminstrs. (bd. mem. 2006—, pres. 2013—), Sigma Chi Fraternity (treas. 1985—86, Best Rusher 1983—85). Democrat. Mem. Christian Ch. (Disciples Of Christ). Avocations: golf, guitar. Home: 207 Cambridge Station Rd Franklin KY 42134 Office: Simpson County Schs 430 S College St Franklin KY 42134 Office Fax: 270-586-2011. Business E-Mail: james.flynn@simpson.kyschools.us.*

FLYNN, MICHAEL S., cardiologist, educator; BA in Chemistry, Miami U., Oxford, Ohio, 1982; MD, St. Louis U., 1986. Lic. Fla., diplomate Nat. Bd. Med. Examiners, 1987, American Bd. Internal Medicine, 1989, American Bd. Internal Medicine-cardiovasc. disease, American Bd. Internal Medicine-interventional cardiology, maintenance of cert. program cardiovasc. disease 2009. Intern internal medicine St Louis Univ. Hosp., 1986—87; resident internal medicine John Cochran Veterans Adminstrn. Hosp., St. Louis, 1987—88, chief resident, 1988—89; resident cardiovasc. disease divsn. of cardiology St Louis Univ., 1989—92, chief resident, 1990—91; fellow interventional cardiology St Louis Univ. Health Sciences Ctr., 1992—94, asst. prof. medicine, 1992—94, assoc. dir. coronary unit, 1992—94; pvt. practice Gulfcoast Cardiology, Naples, Fla., 1994—2007; physician Naples Comty. Hosp., 1994—; clin. asst. prof. Nova Southeastern Univ., Naples, 2008—. Lifetime mem. Mended Hearts Inc.; mem. echo task force Friends of Chgo. Animal Care and Control (FCACC). Recipient Merck, Mosby and Lange Book award, 1986; named Resident of the Year, 1991; named one of Top Interventional Cardiologists, America's Top Doctors (Southwest Fla.), 2004—09. Fellow: Society of Cardiac Angiography and Interventions, American Coll. of Cardiology. Office: Naples Heart Institute 399 Tamiami Trl N Ste 300 Naples FL 34102-5820 Office Fax: 239-261-1714.*

FOARD, DOUGLAS W., historian; b. Balt., Oct. 23, 1939; s. George Winfield and Anna (Herrmann) F.; m. Janet Hess, Aug. 26, 1961; children: Wendy Lynn, Scott Douglas. BA, Randolph-Macon Coll., 1961; MA, U. Va., 1965; PhD, Washington U., 1972; LHD (hon.), Randolph-Macon Coll., 1992, Hampden Sydney Coll., 2001. Asst. to dir. pub. rels. Ferrum (Va.) Coll., asst. prof. history, 1965-70, chair social sci., 1970-79, prof. history, 1972-85, assoc. dean, 1979-81; program officer NEH, Washington, 1985-89; exec. sec. Phi Beta Kappa, Washington, 1989-2001. Adj. prof. history George Mason U., Fairfax, Va. Author: The Revolt of the Aesthetes, 1989, The Imperious Laird 2007; contbr. articles to profl. jours.; guest editor Mag. of History, 1991. Bd. dir. Nat. Humanities Alliance, 1994-2001, mem. exec. com., 1997-2000; bd. dir. Nat. History Day, Washington, 1987-2001; bd. dir. Va. Found. Humanities and Pub. Policy, 1990-96, chmn., 1995-96; trustee Randolph-Macon Coll., 2001—. Recipient Disting. Alumnus award, Randolph-Macon Coll., 2011; grantee Ford Found. 1969-70; James Still fellow U. Ky. 1983, Nat. Defense Act fellow Washington U., 1967-70, Philip DuPont fellow U. Va., 1961-62, Ford Found. fellow Asian Studies, 1967, Nat. Meth. scholar Randolph-Macon Coll., 1960-61; NEH summer seminar Vanderbilt U., 1976. Mem. Soc. Spanish & Portuguese Hist. Studies (newsletter editor 1982-85) Va. Soc. History Tchrs. (pres. 1981-83), Phi Beta Kappa. Address: 38998 Bolington Rd Lovettsville VA 20180

FOEGE, WILLIAM HERBERT, retired public health administrator, educator; b. Decorah, Iowa, Mar. 12, 1936; s. William August and Anne Erika (Ermisch) F.; m. Paula S. Ristad, Dec. 23, 1958; children: David, Michael, Robert. BA, Pacific Luth. U., 1957; MD, U. Wash., 1961; MPH, Harvard U., 1965, DSc (hon.), 1997. Intern USPHS Hosp., SI, NY, 1961-62; epidemic intelligence svc. officer Communicable Disease Ctr., Atlanta, 1962-64; med. officer Immanuel Med. Ctr., Yahe, Nigeria, 1965-66; epidemiologist smallpox eradication/measles control program Nigeria, 1969-70; dir. smallpox eradication program Centers for Disease Control (CDC), US Dept. Health & Human Services (HHS), Atlanta, 1970-73, dir., 1977-83; med. epidemiologist smallpox program Southeast Asia Regional Office WHO, New Delhi, 1973-75; exec. dir. Carter Ctr., Atlanta, 1987-92, health policy fellow, 1986—; Presdl. Disting. prof. internat. health Rollins Sch. Pub. Health Emory U., Atlanta, 1997—2001, emeritus Presdl. Disting. prof. internat. health, 2001—; exec. dir. Task Force for Child Survival and Devel., 1984—99; sr. medical advisor The Bill & Melinda Gates Found., 1999—2001, sr. fellow Global Health Program, 2001—. Cons. WHO, Bangkok, Thailand, 1967, Kinshasha, Zaire, 1968; dep. field coord. Internat. Red Cross Joint Relief Action, Nigeria. Author: House on Fire: The Fight to Eradicate Smallpox, 2011. Bd. regents Pacific Lutheran U., 1997—2006. Recipient Nat. Health Hero award, U. Calif-Berkeley, 1996, Public Welfare medal, Nat. Acad. Sci., 2005, Ivan Allen Jr. Prize for Social Courage, Ga. Inst. of Tech., 2011, Presdl. Medal of Freedom, The White House, 2012; named one of America's Best Leaders, US News & World Report, 2007. E-mail: Bill.Foege@gatesfoundation.org.

FOFT, JOHN WILLIAM, physician, educator; b. LA, May 13, 1928; s. Wilford L. and Mary E. (McMahon) F.; m. Marianne T. Deibler, Mar. 12, 1957; children— John, Christine. BS, U. Nebr., 1951; MD, 1954. Intern Mpls. Gen. Hosp., 1954-55; asst. prof. pathology, dep. dir. clin. chemistry U. Chgo., 1965-67; asso. prof. clin. pathology U. Ala., 1968-70, dir. pediatric-clin. pathology lab., 1968-70, dep. chmn. research clin. pathology, 1969-70, prof., chmn. dept. clin. pathology, 1970-77, clin. prof. dept. pathology, 1977-91; ret., 1991. Chmn. dept. pathology Carraway Meth. Med. Center, 1977-91, Norwood Clinic, 1977-91. Served as capt. AUS, 1955-57,capt. USAF, 1961-64. Nat. Heart Inst. fellow U. Minn. Hosps., 1959-61; Am. Cancer Soc. scholar Argonne Cancer Research Hosp., 1968 Mem. Am. Assn. Pathologists, Ala. Assn. Pathologists, Sigma Xi, Alpha Omega Alpha. Research on clin. lab. systems in developing countries. Home: 235 Inverness Center Dr Apt 354 Birmingham AL 35242-5610

FOGARTY, ANDREW B., rail transportation executive; BA, Hofstra U.; MPA, SUNY; PhD, Fla. State U. Chmn. Nat. Defense Transp. Assn.; sr. v.p., CFO Sea-Land Service Inc.; pres., CEO CSX World Terminals; sec., transp. Commonwealth Va., 1989; sr. v.p., corp. svcs. CSX Corp., 2001—05, spl. asst. to chmn., 2006—; pres. The Greenbrier. Bd. dirs. Danaos Corp., 2006—, The Greenbrier Sporting Club Devel. Co., 2009—, Nat. Defense Transp. Assn. Fellow Nat. Acad. Pub. Adminstrn. Office: CSX Corp 15th Fl 500 Water St Jacksonville FL 32202 Office Phone: 904-359-3200. Office Fax: 804-782-1409. Business E-Mail: andy_fogarty@csx.com.

FOGG, JOSEPH GRAHAM, III, investment company executive; b. Cleve., Oct. 22, 1946; s. Joseph G. Fogg; m. Leslie Kirk Solbert, Jan. 23, 1971; children: Nathaniel, Elizabeth Piper, Whitney Solbert. BA in Economics, Yale U., 1968; MBA, Harvard Bus. Sch., 1970. Co-chmn. Investment Com. Princes Gate, co-founder; founding mem., head Mergers & Acquisitions Dept. and Corp. Fin. Dept. and head worldwide investment banking ops. Morgan Stanley & Co. Inc., sr. mng. dir., adv. dir., 1970—; founder Westbury Capital Ptnrs., LLP, chmn., CEO Westbury, NY, 1991—. Bd. dirs. Maxspeed Corp., Sunnyvale, Calif., 407 ETR Ltd., Toronto, Can., Pardee Resources Inc., Phila., QPass Inc., Seattle, Kennexa Corp., Phila., Aurora Flight Svcs., Manassas, Va., Advanced Interactive Sys, Inc, Seattle, Enesequence, Inc., Authentium, Inc., Crystek, Inc., Sterling, Va, Yale U. Art Gallery, Keewayden Found., Rutland, Vt., Empower America, Washington. Office: Westbury Capital Ptnrs LLP 100 Motor Pky Ste 165 Hauppauge NY 11788 Office Phone: 631-231-4121. Office Fax: 631-231-8121. Business E-Mail: jfogg@westburypartners.com.

FOGLEMAN, RONALD ROBERT, aerospace company executive, retired military officer; b. Juniata County, Pa., Jan. 27, 1942; s. Harry R. and Sara (Landis) F.; m. M. Jane Lauver, June 22, 1963; children: Harry R., William E. BS, USAF Acad., 1963; MA, Duke U., 1971. Commd. 2d lt. USAF, 1963, advanced through grades to gen., 1992, ret., 1997, fighter, mobility and command pilot; chief Tactical Forces Divsn., The Pentagon, Washington, 1979-81; vice comdr. 388th Tactical Fighter Wing, Hill AFB, Utah, 1981-82; dir. fighter ops. Hdqrs. Tactical Air Command, Langley AFB, Va., 1982-83; comdr. 56th Tactical Tng. Wing, MacDill AFB, Fla., 1983-84, 836th Air Divsn., Davis-Monthan AFB, Ariz., 1984-86; dep. dir. Programs and Procedure, Hdqrs. USAF, Washington, 1986-88, dir., 1988-90; comdr. 7th Air Force, 1990-92, US Transp. Command (USTRANSCOM), 1992-94, Air Mobility Command (AMC), 1992-94; chief of staff USAF, Washington, 1994-97; chmn., CEO Durango Aerospace, Inc., 1997—; non-exec. chmn. Alliant Techsystems, Inc., 2009—. Bd. dirs. AAR Corp., 2001—, Alliant Techsystems Inc., 2004—, Alph Security Group Corp. Chmn. Falcon Found., Airlift/Tanker Assn.; bd. dirs. Ft. Lewis Coll. Found., Mitre Corp.; mem. NASA Shuttle Return to Flight Task Group; chmn. Vision 2050: An Integrated Transp. Sys., Nat. Rsch. Council. Mem. Air Force Assn., USAF Acad. Assn. Grads., Daedalians (flight capt. 1983-84, 89-90), Coun. Fgn. Rels. Republican. Methodist. Avocation: rugby. Office: The Durango Group LLC Ste 204 8300 Greensboro Dr Ste 225 Mc Lean VA 22102-3663

FOGLESONG, JAMES STATON (JIM), music educator; b. Lundale, W. Va., July 1922; m. Toni Foglesong; 4 children. B in Music, Eastman Sch. of Music, Rochester, NY. Joined Columbia Records, NYC, 1951; artists & repertoire head Epic Records, NYC, 1951; exec. prodr. RCA Records, NYC, 1963—70; pres. ABC/Dot Records, Nashville, 1970—79, MCA Nashville, Nashville, 1979—84, Capitol Records, Nashville, 1984—89; now cons., independent prodr Nashville, 1984—89; adj. prof., music, Blair Sch. of Music Vanderbilt U, Nashville, 1991—; dir., music bus. program. Trevecca Nazarene U, 1991. Former chmn. of bd. Country Music Found., 1976, 1987, trustee emeritus. Named to Country Music Hall of Fame non-performer category, 2004. Achievements include being credited with furthering careers of Garth Brooks, Reba McEntire, George Strait, Oak Ridge Boys, Tanya Tucker, others. Office: Vanderbilt University 211 Kirkland Hall Nashville TN 37240

FOGLESONG, ROBERT H., mining executive; b. W.Va. m. Mary Thrasher Foglesong; children: David, Mark. BS in Chem. Engring., W. Va. U., 1968, MSc in Chem. Engring., 1969, PhD in Chem. Engring., 1971. Pres. USAF Europe U.; commd. 2d lt. USAF, 1972; instr. pilot 557th Flying Tng. Squadron USAF Acad., Peterson Field, Colo., 1973—76; aide de campe to comdr., 314th Air Divsn. Air Forces Korea, Osau Air Base, Republic of Korea, 1976—77; instr. pilot, comdr. ops. officer, spl. asst to NORAD region USAF, Malmstrom AFB, Mont., 1977—80, pilot, squadron scheduler, 9th tactical fighter squadron Holloman AFB, N.Mex., 1980—82; spl. asst. tactical issues, exec. officer dep. chief of rsch, devel. and acquisition Headqtrs USAF, 1983—85; spl. asst. to comdr., chief combat analysis divsn. Hdqs. Tactical Air Command, Langley AFB, Va., 1985—87; chief of staff, air force, chair, prof. joint and combined warfare Nat. War Coll. Ft. Lesley McNair, 1988—90; pilot F-16, chief of maintenance, 347th Air Tactical Wing USAF, Moody AFB, Ga., 1990—91, comdr., 14 flying tng. wing Columbus AFB, Miss., 1993, comdr., 51st fighter wing Osau Air Base, Republic of Korea, 1994—95; dep. dir., politico-mil. affairs Joint Staff, 1995—97, asst. to chmn., 1997—99; comdr. 12th Air Force and U.S. Southern Command Air Forces USAF, Davis-Monthan AFB, Ariz., 1999—2000, dep. chief of staff Air and Space Ops. Washington, 2000—01, advanced through grades to gen., 2001, vice chief of staff Washington, 2001—03, comdr., Allied Air Component Command, air component comdr. U.S. European Command Ramstein AFB, Germany, 2003—06; pres. Miss. State U., 2006—08; pres., exec. dir. Appalachian Leadership and Education Foundation, 2006—. Bd. dirs. Michael Baker Corp., CDEX, Inc., Massey Energy Co., 2006—. Contbr. articles to mil. and profl. jours. Decorated Defense Superior Svc. medal, Legion of Merit with oak leaf cluster, Meritorious Svc. medal with 3 oak leaf clusters, Aerial Achievement medal with 2 oak leaf clusters, Air Force Commendation medal with 2 oak leaf clusters, Air Force Achievement medal, Korean Nat. Security medal (Samil), Korean Nat. Security medal (Cheon-Su). Office: Massey Energy Co Bd Directors 4 N 4th St Richmond VA 23219 Office Phone: 804-788-1800. Office Fax: 804-788-1870. Business E-Mail: robert.foglesong@masseyenergyco.com.

FOIL, FRANKLIN J., state legislator; b. Baton Rouge, La. m. Tanja Foil; children: Kathleen, Grace, Andy. BA in Polit. Sci., La. State U., 1987; JD, Loyola Sch. Law, 1991. Former judge pro tempore Baton Rouge City Ct.; atty.; mem. Dist. 70 La. House of Reps., 2008—, mem. commerce com., judiciary com., natural resources and environment com., house com. on homeland security, joint com. on homeland security. Comdr. Judge Adv. General's Corp USN. Republican. Presbyn. Office: 320 Somerulos St Baton Rouge LA 70802 also: Capitol Office PO Box 44486 Baton Rouge LA 70804 Office Phone: 225-342-6777, 225-342-6945. Office Fax: 225-342-6785. E-mail: foilf@legis.state.la.us.

FOLCH-SERRANO, KAREN D., psychologist, consultant; b. Mayagüez, PR, Feb. 20, 1969; d. José Folch and Digna J. Serrano. BA in Psychology, U. P.R., Mayaguez, 1991; MS in Clin. Psychology, Carlos Albizu U., San Juan, 1994, PhD in Clin. Psychology, 1998. Cert. forensic psychologist Carlos Albizu U., P.R., 1999, in gerontology U. P.R., San Juan, 2006. Asst. to dir. clin. tng. program Carlos Albizu U., San Juan, 1997—98; dir. Ctr. Clinico Roig, Lucy Lopez Roig and Assocs., San Juan, 1999; clin. psychologist Ramsay Youth Svcs. of P.R., San Juan, 1999—2000, Inst. Psychol. Treatment, San Juan, 2000—02, Clin. Support Group, Inc., San Juan, 2002—08; pvt. practice San Juan, 2002—, Support Therapy Ctr., Inc., Caguas, PR, 2004—05, Caribbean Hosp. Corp., San Juan, 2012—. Cons. in field; lectr. in field; presenter in field. Named Outstanding Student Counselor of Yr., U. PR, 1990, Outstanding Student Gerontology Program, Med. Scis. Campus U. PR, 2006. Mem.: APA. Roman Catholic. Avocations: reading, travel, collecting barbies. Office: 611 Calle Dr Pavia Fernandez Ste 213 San Juan PR 00909-2244 Office Phone: 787-722-3944. Office Fax: 787-722-2170. Personal E-mail: kdfolch@yahoo.com, dr.karendfolch@gmail.com.

FOLDY, SETH LEONARD, public health officer, physician, educator, informatician; s. Leslie and Roma F.; m. Joan Marie Bedinghaus; children: Benjamin, Eva. BA in Human Biology with distinction, Stanford U., 1977; MD, Case Western Res. U., 1982; M in Pub. Health, Medical Coll. Wis., Milw., 2005. Dilomate American Bd. Family Practice, American Bd. Preventive Medicine, Nat. Bd. Med. Examiners. Intern in family practice Cleve. Met. Gen. Hosp., 1982-83, resident in family practice, 1983-85, chief resident in family practice, 1984-85; family physician Great Brook Valley Health Ctr., Worcester, Mass., 1985-87; med. dir. MetroHealth Family Practice, Cleve., 1987-94, dir. cmty. health svcs., 1994-96; med. dir. City of Milw. Health Dept., 1996-98, health commr., 1998—2004; prin. health.e.volution Consulting, 2004—09; med. dir. Healthcare for the Homeless, Milw., 2005—09; adminstr. & state health officer divsn. pub. health Wis. Dept. Health Services, Madison, 2009—10; disting. cons., dir. pub. health informatics & tech. program office Centers for Disease Control & Prevention (CDC), Atlanta, 2010—12; cons. preventive sys. Sethfoldy.Com, 2012—. Asst. prof. family medicine Case Western Res. U., Cleve., 1987-96; assoc. clin. prof. family and cmty. medicine and Population Health, Med. Coll. Wis., Milw., 1996—, clin. prof. health adminstrn. and informatics, U. Wis., Milw., 2001-, adj. prof. dept. population health scis., 2009-10, hon. fellow 2012-, Sch. Medicine & Pub. Health, U. Wis., Madison, 2009-; pub. health systems cons., Ctr. Internat. Health, 2005-09, sr. pub. health cons., e Health Initiative, 2005-08; spl. term appointee Argonne Nat. Lab., Ill., 2004-09 Co-author: Health Information Exchange: From Start-Up to Sustainability, 2007; asst. editor: Urban Family Practice: A Resource Monograph, 1994; editor (newsletter) Urban Health News, 1990-96; assoc. editor Advances in Disease Surveillance, 2006-09. Co-founder, chief med. officer Wis. Health Info. Exch., 2004-09; trustee Friends Sch. in Cleve., 1972-74; nat. com. War Resisters League, NYC, 1970-74; mem. Nat. Health Policy Leadership Coun., Washington, 1991-92, Ohio legis. adv. com. on environ. lead abatement, Columbus, 1994-95, Wis. Turning Point Transformation Team, 1998-2004, Wis. pub. health sys. terrorism & pub. health emergencies legis. coun. com., 2002; mem. info. coun. US CDC, 2000-04, steering com. Rand Inst. Summits on Info. Tech. Infrastructure for Bioterrorism, 2001, Operation Combined Assistance, US Navy Project Hope Tsunami Task Force, 2005; Inst. Medicine, Nat. Rsch. Coun. Com. Biosurveillance Sys., 2008-09, US Health Info. Tech. Policy Com. Info. Exch. Workgroup, 2009-12, Nat. Gov.'s Assn. State Alliance eHealth, 2010; Wis. Homeland Security Coun., 2009-10, White House Nat. Security Staff & Office Sci. & Tech. Policy Biosurveillance Sub-Interagency Policy Com. Sci. & Tech. Workgroup 2011, White House Nat. Sci. & Tech. Coun. Com. Homeland & Nat. Security Biol. Def. Rsch. & Devel. Subcom. Biosurveillance Sci. & Tech. Working Group 2011-12, Fed. Health Arch. Adv. Coun. 2012, US DHHS Health Domain IT Steering Com. 2011-2012, US DHHS Health Reform IT Steering Com. 2010-2011, Lead Team Standards & Interoperability Framework Pub. Health Reporting Initiative, Internat. Joint Commn. Great Lakes Human Health Indicators Workgroup 2013; founder Milw. Pub. Health Found. & Health Champion Award, 2002; bd. dirs. eHealth Initiative & eHealth Inititative Found., 2002-07, Greater Milw. Bus. Group on Health, 2002-, Southeast Wis. Bioterrorism Prepardness Group, Inc., 2003-07, Benedict Ctr., 2007-09, Planning Coun. Health & Human Svcs., 2007-09, Wis. State Lab. Hygiene, 2009-10, Nat. e-Health Collaborative, 2010. Recipient award for Excellence in Info. Tech., Nat. Assn. County & City Health Officers, 1999, Milton & Ruth Roemer Prize for Creative Local Pub. Health, 2002, Pres.'s Vol. Svc. award, 2005, 2007. Fellow Am. Acad. Family Physicians; mem. AMA, APHA (gov. coun. 1992-94, 96-98), Am. Med. Informatics Assn., Health Info. Mgmt. Sys. Soc., Nat. Assn. City & County Health Officers (various coms.), Assn. State & Territorial Health Officials, Pub. Health Leadership Soc., Wis. Med. Soc., Milw. Acad. Medicine (pres. 2009), Milw. County Med. Soc. (chair pub. health com. 1996-, Cmty. Svc. award 1997), Phi Beta Kappa, Delta Omega. Achievements include participated in detecting and elimination of monkeypox virus outbreak from Western Hemisphere. Avocations: fly fishing, hiking, birding. Office Phone: 414-339-3865. Business E-Mail: sfoldy@sbcglobal.net.

FOLEY, ARTHUR JAMES, law firm executive; b. Bklyn., Nov. 14, 1946; s. Arthur James and Grace Mary (Hickey) F.; 1 child, Roger P. Student, Marquette U., 1964-68, St. Joseph's Coll., Phila., 1970. Plant acct. Gen. Box Co., Pa., 1968-70; divsn. controller Farmingdale, N.Y., 1970-73; gen. acctg. mgr. Gen. Instrument Corp., Hicksville, N.Y., 1973-76; comptroller, v.p. mgmt. info. services Nat. Helicopter Corp., Garden City, N.Y., 1976-97; contr. Ventura Air Svcs. divsn. Thomson Ind. Inc., Farmingdale, 1998—2000; contr. Cemetry Gardens Inc., WashingtonMeml. Pk., 2001—06, Law Office Roger P. Foley, 2006—. Office: Law Office Roger Foley PA 524 S Andrews Ave Ste 200N Fort Lauderdale FL 33301 Personal E-mail: art_007@comcast.net.

FOLEY, DAVID EDWARD, bishop emeritus; b. Worcester, Mass., Feb. 3, 1930; Attended, St. Charles Coll.; AB, St. Mary's Sem., 1952, STL, 1956. Ordained priest Archdiocese of Washington, Washington, 1956; ordained bishop, 1986; aux. bishop Diocese of Richmond, Va., 1986—94; bishop Diocese of Birmingham, Ala., 1994—2005, bishop emeritus, 2005—. Roman Catholic. Office Phone: 205-838-8322. Office Fax: 205-836-1910.

FOLEY, GARY J., chemical engineer, computer scientist, federal agency administrator, researcher; b. SI, Mar. 20, 1943; m. Barbara Ickes, 1986; children: William, Karen, Kevin, Ryan, Courtney. BChE, Manhattan Coll., 1964; MS, U. Wis., 1965, PhD in Chem. Engring., 1968. Engr. Am. Oil Co., 1968-73, EPA, 1973—76, 1979—86; dir. Nat. Exposure Rsch. Lab, 1987—93, 1995—2005, acting asst. adminstr. R&D, 1993—2005; dir. Nat. Ctr. for Env. Rsch., 2005—07; dir., exec. Earth Observations Exec., Office Sci. Advisor, 2007—11, Office of R & D, 2011—12; acting dir. RS Kerr Rsch. Ctr., 2012—. Mem. AiChE. Achievements include research in air pollution, acid rain, emissions, transport and fate, human and ecosystem exposure and earth observing systems, total quality management in research organisations, systems analysis for sustainability, ground water studies. Office Phone: 919-541-0711. Business E-Mail: foley.gary@epa.gov.

FOLEY, RITA, consumer products executive; Diploma, U. Geneva, 1974; BA, Smith Coll., 1975; grad. exec. program, Stanford U., 1993. Sales rep. Polaroid Ltd., St. Albans, England, 1975; sales mgmt. positions Harris Lanier, NYC, 1977-82; v.p., sys. ingretion, asst. gen. mgr. Americas Digital Equipment Corp., 1982-97; exec. v.p., worldwide sales, mktg. and global ops. QAD, Inc., 1997-98; ind. cons., 1998-99; sr. v.p., chief info. officer Westvaco Corp. (now MeadWestvaco Corp.), 1999—; pres., consumer products MeadWestvaco Corp., 1999—2006; group pres. AGI Media, 2002—06; bd. dirs., author PetSmart, Inc., 2003—; chmn. Pro Mujer, 2003—, Pro Mujer Int, 2004—07; mem. Internat. Womans Forum, 2005—08, Belizean Grove, 2005—08; advisor Crenshaw Associates, 2007—08, head bd. adv. svcs., 2008—. Bd. adv. Nina McLemore Inc., 2003—; bd. dirs. Dresser-Rand Group Inc., 2007—. Trustee Healthcare Chaplaincy, 2003—. Office: Westvaco Corp 299 Park Ave Fl 13 New York NY 10171-3800 also: Dresser Rand Group Inc Bd Directors 10205 Westheimer Rd Ste 1000 Houston TX 77042 Office Phone: 713-354-6100. Office Fax: 713-354-6110. Business E-Mail: rita.foley@dresser-rand.com.

FOLEY, WILLIAM PATRICK, II, insurance company executive; b. Austin, Tex., Dec. 29, 1944; s. Robert P. Foley; m. Carol J. Johnson, Nov. 15 1969; children: Lindsay, Robert P. II, Countney Diane, William P. III. BS, U.S. Mil. Acad., 1967; MBA, Seattle U., 1970; JD, U. Wash., 1974. Assoc. Streich, Lang, Weeks, Cardon & French P.A., Phoenix, 1974-76; ptnr., pres., dir. Foley, Clark & Nye P.A., Phoenix, 1976-84; pres., CEO Land Resources Corp., Scottsdale, Ariz., 1983-84; chmn., pres., CEO Fidelity National Financial, Inc., Jacksonville, Fla., 1981—2007, chmn., 2007—, Checkers Drive-In Restaurants, Inc., Clearwater, Fla. Chmn. bd., dir., pres., chief exec. officer Fidelity Nat. Fin., Inc., Fidelity Nat. Title Ins. Co. of Calif., Fidelity Nat. Title Ins. Co. of Tenn., Fidelity Nat. Title Ins. Co. of Tex., So. Title Holding Co., Pacific Western Aviation, Inc., Western Am. Exch. Corp., Western Pacific Property & Casualty Agy., Inc., Fidelity Appraisal Group, Inc., Folco Devel. Corp., Western Pacific Acquisitions, Inc., Bristol Investment Corp.; chmn. bd., dir. Western Fin. Trust Co., Rocky Mountain Aviation, Inc.; chmn. bd. dir., chief exec. officer Fidelity Nat. Title Agy., Inc. Fidelity Nat. Title Agy. of Maricopa County, Inc., Fidelity Nat. Title Agy. of Pinal County, Inc., Fidelity Nat. Title Co. of El Paso, Fidelity Nat. Title Co. of Oreg., Ramada Inn Old Town Mgmt., Inc.; numerous other chairmanships and directorships in fin. industry; founder & mng. ptnr. Foley Estates Vineyard & Winery of Calif.; founder & mng. ptnr. LinCourt Vineyards of Calif.; chmn. bd. CKE Restaurants Inc. Mem. Jacksonville C. of C., Fla.; del. Rep. Nat. Conv., 1996; adv. bd. mem. U. Wash. Sch. Law; trustee Found. Bd. U. Calif. Santa Barbara. Capt. USAF. Recipient Semper Fidelis award, Marine Corps Scholarship Found., 1997. Avocations: golf, chess, winemaking. Office: Fidelity Nat Fin Inc 601 Riverside Ave Jacksonville FL 32204-2950

FOLK, THOMAS ROBERT, lawyer; b. Milford, NJ, Jan. 9, 1950; s. Conrad Frank and Isabella Ramsey (Sickels) F.; m. JoAnn Elizabeth Lo Pinto, June 21, 1975; children: Elizabeth Frances, Karina Marie. BS, U.S. Mil. Acad., 1972; JD, U. Va., 1978. Bar: Va. 1978, U.S. Ct. Mil. Appeals 1978, U.S. Ct. Appeals (4th cir.) 1978, U.S. Supreme Ct. 1983, U.S. Ct. Claims 1985, U.S. Ct. Appeals (9th and fed. cirs.) 1985, D.C. 1986., U.S. Dist. Ct. D.C. 1987. Commd. 2d lt. U.S. Army, 1972, advanced to maj., 1983, resigned, 1986, asst. to gen. counsel Washington, 1980-82, atty. litigation, 1983-86; assoc. Hazel & Thomas, P.C., Fairfax, Va., 1986-88, owner, 1989-99; ptnr. Reed Smith LLP, Fairfax, 1999—. Contbr. articles to profl. jours. Mem. Com. Armed Svcs. and Vets. Affairs, 1985-88. Col. USAR, 1995, ret. Mem.: Fairfax Bar Assn. (bd. govs. 1993—97), Va. State Bar (bd. govs. constrn. and pub. contracts 1993—99), West Point Soc. D.C (bd. govs. 1993—99). Home: 4902 Asquith Ct Fairfax VA 22032-2102 Home Phone: 703-503-9475; Office Phone: 703-641-4294. Personal E-mail: tfolk1@cox.net. Business E-Mail: tfolk@reedsmith.com.

FOLKERTS, JEAN, dean, journalism educator; b. Aug. 6, 1945; d. Leonard Folkerts and Betty Manahan; m. Leroy Towns, Aug. 11, 1984; children: Sean, Jenny. BA in Journalism cum laude, Kans. State U., 1967, MS in Journalism and Mass Comm., 1973; MPhil in Am. Studies, U. Kans., 1979, PhD in Am. Studies, 1981. Asst. prof. journalism U. Tex., Austin, 1982-85; assoc. prof., chmn. dept. comm. Mt. Vernon Coll., Washington, 1985-90; assoc. prof. journalism George Washington U., Washington, 1990-94, prof., chmn. dept. journalism, 1994—2006, from acting dir. to prof., dir. Sch. Media and Pub. Affairs, 1995—2001, interim dean Columbian Coll. Arts & Scis., 2001—02, assoc. v.p. special acad. initiatives, 2003—06; dean, disting. alumni prof. Sch. Journalism and Mass Comm., U. NC, Chapel Hill, 2006—. Cons. Food Lion Inc., 1997-98, Newseum, Freedom Forum Found., 1995, Nat. Bank Washington, 1988-89; writer Kans. State U. Counseling Ctr., 1967. Author: Media Voices: An Historical Perspective, 1992, Voices of A Nation: A History of Mass Media in the U.S., 1992, 5th edit., 2009, Media in Your Life: The Role of Mass Media In Society, 1998, 4th edit., 2008; editor Journalism and Mass Comm. Quar., 1992-2002. Grantee AT& T Corp, 1995, Ctr. for Washington Area Studies, 1992. Mem.: Orgn. of Am. Historians, Assn. for Schs. and Depts. of Journalism and Mass comm., Assn. for Edn. and Mass Comm., Phi Kappa Phi. Office: Sch Journalism and Mass Comm U NC at Chapel Hill Campus Box #3365 Chapel Hill NC 27599-1204 Office Phone: 919-962-1204. E-mail: jfolk@email.unc.edu.

FOLLIARD, THOMAS J., automotive executive; s. Thomas J. and Audrey Lee Folliard. BS, Fla. Inst. Tech., 1989. Sr. buyer CarMax Inc., Richmond, Va., 1993, dir. purchasing, 1994—96, v.p. merchandising, 1996—2000, sr. v.p. store operations, 2000—01, exec. v.p. store operations, 2001—06; pres., CEO CarMax, Inc., 2006—. Bd. dirs. Nat. Assn. Basketball Coaches. Office: CarMax Inc 12800 Tuckahoe Creek Pkwy Richmond VA 23238

FOLLIT, EVELYN V., retired retail executive; b. Sept. 10, 1946; Degree in Exec. Planning & Tech., Cornell U., MIT; BA in Math., CUNY, 1970; MBA in Fin. & Info. Sys., Pace U., 1977. Dir., strategic planning Dunn & Bradstreet, 1984—96; v.p., ops. & engring. AC Nielson, 1996—97; sr. v.p., chief info. officer & chief people officer RadioShack Corp., 1997—2005, chief orgnl. enabling svcs., 2003—05; founder, COO Follit Associates, 2005—. Bd. dirs. Catalina Mktg. Corp., 2000—07, Linens N Things, Inc., 2005—06, GetConnected, Inc., 2006—07, Nautilus, Inc., 2007—08; chmn., CIO Coun. Nat. Retail Fedn., 2000—; mem., adv. bd. Ctr. Values Based Leadership, 2002—; bd. dirs. Winn-Dixie Stores Inc., 2006—, Bealls Inc., 2006—. Bd. visitors Tex. Christian U., Fort Worth. Recipient Leadership and Innovation award, Exec. Tech. Mag./Compaq Computer, 2002; named one of Top 10 CIOs in Retailing, Retail Tech. Mag., 1999, Top 10 CIOs Across Am., Info. Week, 1999, 100 Premier IT Leaders in Country, Computerworld, 2001, 25 Most Influential People in Retail, Retail Info Sys. News, 2001, Pioneering Women in Tech., Am. Friends Jerusalem Coll. Tech., 2002. Office: Winn Dixie Stores Inc Bd Directors 5050 Edgewood Ct Jacksonville FL 32254-3699 Office Phone: 904-783-5000. Office Fax: 904-370-7224. Business E-Mail: evelynfollit@winn-dixie.com.

FOLSOM, DAVID, federal judge; b. Murfreesboro, Ark., 1947; Student, So. State Coll., 1965-67; BA, U. Ark., 1969, JD, 1974. Assoc. Young & Patton, 1974-76; ptnr. Young, Patton & Folsom, 1974-90; dep. prosecuting atty. Lafayette County, 1978-81; pvt. practice, 1990-95; judge US Dist. Ct. (ea. dist.) Tex., 1995—2009, chief judge, 2009—. Tchr. Arks. Sr. H.S., 1969-71. Mem. Ark. Bar Assn., Tex. Bar Assn., Ark. Trial Lawyers Assn., Texarkana Bar Asn., Tex. Trial Lawyers Assn., Northeast Tex. Bar Assn., Assn. of Trial Lawyers of Am., Southwest Ark. Bar Assn., Delta Theta Phi. Office: US Dist Ct US Courthouse & Post Office PO Box 2090 Texarkana TX 75504

FOLT, CAROL L., academic administrator, environmental scientist; b. Akron, Ohio; m. David Peart; children: Noah, Tessa. BA in Aquatic Biology, U. Calif., Santa Barbara, MA in Biology; PhD, U. Calif., Davis. Postdoctoral felow W.K. Kellogg Biol. Sta.; faculty mem. Dartmouth Coll., Hanover, NH, 1983—2013, assoc. dir. toxic metals rsch. program, 1998—2000, assoc. dir. ctr. environ. health sciences, 2000—01, assoc. dean of faculty & dean grad. studies, 2001—04, dean of faculty, 2004—09, Dartmouth prof. biol. sciences, 2007—13, provost, 2010—13, interim pres., 2012—13; chancellor U. NC, Chapel Hill, 2013—. Fellow: AAAS. Office: Office of the Chancellor 103 South Bldg Campus Box 9100 Chapel Hill NC 27599-9100 Office Phone: 919-962-1365. Office Fax: 919-962-1647. Business E-Mail: chancellor@unc.edu.*

FOLWELL, DALE ROBBINS, state legislator, investment representative, accountant; b. Raleigh, NC, Dec. 17, 1958; s. Raymond Jackson and Lorraine (Scott) F.; m. Synthia Sexton, Oct. 2, 1988; 1 child, Anna Scott. BS in Acctg., U. N.C., 1984, MS in Acctg., 1986. Former vice pres./ registered investment adv. Deutche Bank Alex Brown; mem. Forsyth County Reps., Winston Salem, 1984; fin. cons. Merrill Lynch, Winston Salem, NC, 1986—90; investment counsel Alex Brown & Sons, West Salem, NC, 1990—97; private investor, 1998—; mem. Dist. 74 NC House of Reps., 2004—. Republican. Avocations: motorcycles, running. Home: 299 S Westview Dr Winston Salem NC 27104 Office: NC House of Representatives 300 N Salisbury St Rm 301A Raleigh NC 27603-5925 Home Phone: 336-748-0046; Office Phone: 919-733-5787. Business E-Mail: Dale.Folwell@ncleg.net.

FONSECA, LIDIA L., health services company executive; BA, U. Calif., Berkeley; MBA, Erasmus U., M in Bus. Informatics. Various positions, including gen. mgr., eBusiness, chief info. officer Philips Med. Sys., 1997—2005, v.p., supply chain mgmt., nuclear medicine divsn., 2003—05; exec. v.p., global ops. & tech. Synarc Inc., 2005—08; sr. v.p., chief info. officer Laboratory Corp. of America Holdings, 2008—. Office: Laboratory Corporation of America Holdings 358 S Main St Burlington NC 27215 Office Phone: 336-229-1127. Office Fax: 336-513-4510. Business E-Mail: lidia.fonseca@labcorp.com.

FONTAINE, R. RICHARD, computer game company executive; Exec. positions Michaels Stores Inc., Ingram Distbn.; pres., CEO Software Etc., 1988—91; exec. v.p. Barnes & Noble, Inc., 1991—93; pres., COO B. Dalton Booksellers, 1991—93; CEO Babbage's Etc., 1996—, GameStop Corp., Grapevine, Tex., 2000—02, chmn., CEO, 2002—08, exec. chmn., 2008—10, chmn. internat., 2010—. Office: GameStop Corp 625 Westport Pky Grapevine TX 76051 Office Phone: 817-424-2000. Office Fax: 817-424-2002.

FONTANALS-CISNEROS, ELLA, art association administrator, information systems specialist; Founder, pres. Together Found., NYC, 1989; founder Together Networks, NYC, 1994; co-founder Cisneros Fontanals Art Found., Miami, 2002—; founder Miami Art Ctrl., 2003—. Bd. dirs. Miami Art Mus., Am. Patrons of Tate, Cintas Found., US Artist, Internat. Women's Forum, Inst. Sustainable Cmtys., US and Pronatura Internat., Fundacion Antonio Cisneros Bermudez; participant UN Conf. Small Island Developing States, Eminent Citizens Group; spl. advisor sec. gen. Habitat II, City Summit, Istanbul, 1996. Named one of Top 200 Collectors, ARTnews Mag.,

2007—12; recipient Spectrum Philanthropy award, Am Red Cross, 2003, Visionary award, Mus. Arts and Design, 2007, Women Together award, UN, 2008. Avocation: collecting contemporary art with strong representations of geometric abstract art from Latin America, video art, and contemporary photography focusing on architecture. Mailing: 5960 SW 57th Ave Miami FL 33143

FONTENOT, HEULETTE (CLO), state legislator; b. July 14, 1961; m. Gail LeBourge. Former house rep., La.; alderman La., 1989—95; state rep. Dist. 71 La., 1996—2001; mem. Environment Com., House & Govt. Affairs Com., Mcpl. Com., Parochial & Cultural Affairs Com., 1996—2001; state senator Dist. 19 La., 2001—02; state senator Dist. 13, 2003—. Mem.: Nat. Youth Sports Coaches Assn., Livingston C. of C., Livingston Leadership, Nat. Rifle Assn. Republican. Baptist. Address: Dist Off PO Box 1238 Livingston LA 70754 Mailing: Capitol Off PO Box 94183 Baton Rouge LA 70804 Office Phone: 504-686-7701. Fax: 225-686-2161. Business E-Mail: fontenoc@legis.state.la.us.

FOODY, JAMES G., retired corporate financial executive; Ptnr. Ernst & Young LLP; pvt. bus. cons. Greenville, SC, 1990—. Bd. dirs. ScanSource, Inc., 1995—, chmn. bd. dirs., 2005—09, chmn. emeritus, 2009—; past bd. dirs. Gates/FA Distbg., Inc. Office: ScanSource Inc 6 Logue Ct Greenville SC 29615 Office Phone: 864-288-2432. Office Fax: 864-288-1165.

FOOSANER, ROBERT STEPHEN, telecommunications industry executive, lawyer; b. Newark, Feb. 1, 1943; s. George and Gertrude (Rood) F.; m. Carol Baber; children: Eve, Matthew, Nellie Ann. BA, Rutgers U., 1965; JD, Washington Coll. Law, 1968. Bar: US Dist. Ct. DC, 1968, US Ct. Appeals DC, 1969. Atty. Broadcast Bur., FCC, Washington, 1968-73, atty. Office Gen. Counsel, 1973-77, supervisory atty., 1977-79, chief policy task force Office of Sci. and Tech., 1979-80, chief policy and mgmt. staff, 1980-81, dep. chief Pvt. Radio Bur., 1981-83; chief Pvt. Radio Bur., 1983-86; ptnr. Jones, Day, Reavis & Pogue, Alexandria, VA., 1986-92; sr. v.p. govt. affairs Nextel Communications, Inc., Washington, 1992—2005; sr. v.p., govt. affairs, chief regulatory officer Sprint Nextel, Reston, Va., 2005—. US del. MF Broadcasting Conf., Buenos Aires, Argentina, 1980, Mobile WARC Conf., Geneva, Switzerland, 1983 Trustee Leukemia Soc. America, Washington, 1976-82. Fellow Radio Club America, 1985. Mem. DC Bar Assn., Bar Assn. DC Office Phone: 703-433-4000.

FOOTE, AVON EDWARD, web developer/producer, communications educator; b. Burnsville, Miss., Sept. 24, 1937; s. Avon Ruble and Lila Frances (Broughton) F.; m. Dorothy Veronica Gargis, Mar. 15, 1960; children: Anthony E., Kevin A., Michele. Cert., NYU, 1961; BS, Florence State U., 1963; MS, U. So. Miss., 1968; PhD, Ohio State U., 1970. Announcer Sta. WJOI, Florence, Ala., 1958-60; prodn. mgr. Sta. WOWL-TV, Florence, 1960-64; advt. coord. Plough Inc., Memphis, 1964-66; faculty adviser Sta. WMSU, U. So. Miss., Hattiesburg, 1966-67; prodr.-dir. telecomm. Ohio State U., Columbus, 1967-69; assoc. prof. broadcasting U. Miss., Oxford, 1971-72; project dir. (part-time) Ohio Valley TV Sys., Columbus, 1972-74, Ohio State, 1972—74; faculty, coord. grad. studies Sch. Journalism/Mass Comm. U. Ga., Athens, 1974-80; prof. broadcasting U. North Ala., Florence, 1980—2008; prof. emeritus, 2008—. Prof., London, 1990-91; awards judge Ohio State Awards, 1968-73; chmn. faculty screening com. Peabody Radio-TV Awards, 1976-79; jury chair NY Festivals Internat. TV awards, 2002-04; founder Worldwide Web pages including Worldserver, 1995, Web cons. chotank.com, flytheshoals.com, fasthealth.com; developer BBC's Web History Computer Collections, Sci. Mus., London, 2006, Gulf War Video Collection, 1992-2001, Libr. Am. Broadcasting, U. Md., College Park, 2002—; faculty Ohio State U., 1972-74; instr. UNA/UCLA, 2004-07; cons. in field. Editor: The Challenges of Educational Communications, 1970, CBS and Congress: The Selling of the Pentagon Papers, 1972, Nat. Assn. Ednl. Broadcasters Broadcasting Rev., 1969-73; author: (with Koenig and others) Broadcasting and Bargaining, 1970, Chotankers, 1982, online author: Burke's Peerage and Gentry, 2003; prodr. ednl. TV programs; editor ref. shelf materials Nat. Pub. Broadcasting Archives, U. Md., College Park, 2002; contbr. and author: www.burkes-peerage.net; contbr. articles to profl. jours. & essays. Bd. dirs. Florence YMCA, 1982-86. Recipient Cmty. Svc. award Florence Civitan Club, 1990, 1st pl. award Corp. Video Profl. Competition Nat. Broadcasting Soc., 1991, regional 1st pl. award, Nat. 3d pl. award Coll. Emmy award Hollywood Acad. TV Arts and Scsi., 1984, Honorable Mention Comedy awards Nat. Broadcasting Soc., 1987; Industry Faculty Seminar fellow Internat. Radio-TV Soc., 1987, NDEA fellow, 1967, NATAS Meml. fellow, 1970. Republican. Anglican. Home: 222 Shirley Dr Florence AL 35633-1434

FOOTE, ELIZABETH ERNY, federal judge; b. Lafayette, La., 1953; BA with honors, La. State U., 1974, JD, 1978; MA, Duke U., Durham, NC, 1975. Law clk. to Hon. William Culpepper 3rd Cir. Ct. Appeals, La., 1978—79; ptnr. Smith Foote Law Firm, LLP (formerly Percy, Smith & Foote), Alexandria, La., 1979—2010; judge US Dist. Ct. (we. dist.) La., Shreveport, 2010—. Bd. trustees La. State U. Law Ctr.; past pres. La. Civil Justice Ctr. Recipient Outstanding Young Career Woman of La. award, La. Bus. & Profl. Women, 1980, Bus. Owner Woman of Excellence award, Ctrl. La. Women Bus. Owners, 1996, Ctrl. La. Woman of Century award, 2000, La. Heroine award, La. Assn. Nonprofit Associations/La. Philanthropy Initiative, 2004, Alexandria Human Rels. Commn. award, 2004. Mem.: La. State Bar Assn. (treas. 1994—96, co-chair disaster relief com. 2005, pres. 2008—09, Pres.'s award 1994), La. Assn. Justice, La. Assn. Def. Counsel. Office: US Dist Ct 300 Fannin St Shreveport LA 71101-3083 Office Phone: 318-934-4780.

FORBES, JAMES RANDY, United States Representative from Virginia; b. Chesapeake, Va., Feb. 17, 1952; m. Shirley Forbes, 1978; 4 children. BA, Randolph-Macon Coll., Ashland, Va., 1974; LLB, U. Va. Sch. Law, Charlottesville, 1977. Atty., ptnr. Kaufman & Canoles PC; mem. Dist. 78 Va. House of Delegates, 1990—98; mem. Dist. 14 Va. State Senate, 1998—2001; mem. US Congress from 4th Va. dist., 2001—. Chmn. Rep. Party Va., 1996—2001. Republican. Baptist. Office: US House of Representatives 2135 Rayburn House Office Bldg Washington DC 20515 also: 505 Independence Pky Ste 104 Chesapeake VA 23320 Office Phone: 202-225-6365.*

FORBES, MORTON GERALD, lawyer; b. Atlanta, July 12, 1938; s. Arthur Mark and Mary Dean (Power) F.; m. Eunice Lee Haynsworth, Jan. 25, 1963; children: John, Ashley, Sarah. AB, Wofford Coll., Spartanburg, SC, 1962; JD, U. Ga., Athens, 1965. Bar: Ga. 1965, US Dist. Ct. (mid. dist.) Ga. 1965, US Dist. Ct. (so. dist.) Ga. 1968, US Dist. Ct. (no. dist.) Ga. 1993, US Ct. Appeals (5th cir.) 1974, US Ct. Appeals (4th cir.) 1972, US Ct. Appeals (11th cir.) 1981. Assoc. Pierce, Ranitz, Lee, Berry & Mahoney, 1967-70; ptnr. Pierce, Ranitz, Berry, Mahoney & Forbes, 1970-76, Pierce, Ranitz, Mahoney, Forbes & Coolidge, 1976-81; ptnr., sec. Ranitz, Mahoney, Forbes & Coolidge, P.C., 1981-91, Forbes & Bowman, Savannah, Ga., 1991—2007, Forbes, Foster & Pool, 2007—. Gen. counsel Ga. Fed. Young Rep. Clubs, 1971-72; guest lectr. dept. dental hygiene Armstrong State Coll., 1970-72. Mem. Savannah Port Authority (now Savannah Econ. Devel. Authority), 1973-2003, chmn., 1979-81; mem. Chatham County Devel. Authority, 1973-80; nat. com. Nat. Fedn. Young Reps., 1973; econ. adv. coun. Coastal Area Planning and Devel. Authority, 1980—; bd. dirs. Savannah Symphony Soc., 1971-75; Ga. del. to Japan/Southeast Trade Mission, Kyoto, Japan, 1983, S.E. Asia USA/Japan Assn. meeting, Birmingham, Ala., 1984. With USN, 1965-67. Recipient Outstanding Service award, Savannah Port Authority, 1981. Mem. ABA, Internat. Assn. Def. Counsel, Fedn. Def. and Corp. Counsel (state rep., admission com.), State Bar Ga., Ala. Def. Lawyer Assn. (hon.), Am. Judicature Soc., Nat. Assn. Bond Counsel, Ga. Def. Lawyers Assn. (v.p. 1987—, mem. exec. com. 1988, bd. dirs., exec. v.p. 1990-91, pres. 1991-92), Savannah Bar Assn. (exec. com. 1989-94, pres. 1992-93), Libel Def. Resource Ctr., Def. Rsch. Inst. (state chmn. 1992-99, bd. dirs. 1999-2002), Savannah Econ. Devel. Action Coun. (founding), Savannah Area Wofford Coll. Alumni Club (past pres.), Soc. of the Cincinnati (Va.), St. Andrews Soc. (v.p., pres.), Soc. Colonial Wars (past gov. dep. gov. gen.), Sons of Revolution (sec. 1988-92), Chatham Club, Savannah Yacht Club, The Landings Club. Republican. Presbyterian. Office: Forbes Foster & Pool PO Box 13929 Savannah GA 31416-0929 Office Phone: 912-352-1190. Business E-Mail: salty@ffp-law.com.

FORBES, THEODORE MCCOY, JR., arbitrator, mediator, retired lawyer; b. Atlanta, Oct. 28, 1929; s. Theodore M. and Mary Beatrice (Christie) F.; m. Margaret Paty, Dec. 12, 1953; children: Theodore McCoy, Margaret Paty. BS in Chemistry, Ga. Inst. Tech., 1950; LLB, U. Va., 1953. Bar: Ga., 1952, D.C. 1973, U.S. Ct. Appeals (5th cir.) 1976, U.S. Ct. Appeals (11th cir.) 1981. Instr. Culver (Ind.) Summer Naval Sch., 1950; from assoc. to ptnr. Smith, Gambrell & Russell, and predecessor firms, Atlanta, 1953—58, ptnr., 1958-91; solo practice, 1992-95. Bd. dirs. Travelers Aid Soc., Atlanta, 1974-90, pres., 1975-76, 86-89; bd. dirs., corp. sec. Shepherd Spinal Ctr., Atlanta, 1975-95; bd. dirs. Ga. Fund for Edn., 1986-89. Lt. (j.g.) USNR, 1950-62. Fellow Ga. Bar Found.; mem. Atlanta Bar Assn., State Bar Ga. (emeritus), Ga. C. of C. (bd. dirs. 1986-95), Capital City Club (life). Avocations: golf, american history, fishing. Home: 2734 Peachtree Rd NW Apt A202 Atlanta GA 30305-2966

FORCE, ROBERT, law educator; b. Phila., Aug. 11, 1934; s. Charles and Dora (Woloshin) F.; m. Ruth Morris, Aug. 18, 1962; children: Joshua Simon, Seth Daniel. BS, Temple U., 1955, LL.B., 1958; postgrad., U. Adelaide, 1958-59; LL.M., NYU, 1960. Bar: Pa. 1961. Law clk. to presiding justice Pa. Ct. Common Pleas., Phila., 1960-61, U.S. Dist. Ct., Phila., 1961-62; instr. Temple U., Phila., 1960-61; assoc. Kleinbard, Bell & Brecker, Phila., 1963-64; asst. prof. Ind. U. Law Sch., Indpls., 1964-67, assoc. prof., 1968; prof. Tulane U., New Orleans, 1969—, Thomas Pickles prof. law, 1979-89, Niels F. Johnsen prof. maritime law, 1989—, acting dean, 1977-78. Dir. emeritus Tulane Maritime Law Ctr. Co-author: Hall's Criminal Law, 1993, Admiralty and Maritime Law: Cases, Notes and Text, vols. 1 and 2, 1997, Marine Pollution: Conventions, Statutes, Cases and Text, 1998, The Law of Seamen, 5th edit., 2003, (with M. Norris) The Law of Maritime Personal Injuries, 2004, (with A.N. Yiawn Poulos and D. M. Davis)Admiralty and Maritime Law, 2005. Fulbright fellow, 1958-59 Mem. ABA, Beta Gamma Sigma, Omicron Delta Kappa Home: 1038 Eleonore St New Orleans LA 70115-4311 Office: 6329 Freret St Ste 255 New Orleans LA 70118-6231 Office Phone: 504-865-5947. Business E-Mail: rforce@law.tulane.edu.

FORD, ANN SUTER, retired family practice nurse practitioner; b. Mineola, NY, Oct. 31, 1943; d. Robert M. and Jennette (Van Derzee) Suter; m. W. Scott Ford, 1964; children: Tracey, Karin, Stuart. RN White Plains Hosp., Sch. Nursing, NY, 1964; BS in Nursing with high distinction, U. Ky., 1967; MS in Health Planning, Fla. State U., 1971, PhD, 1975, MSN, 1992. Nurse U. Ky. Med. Ctr., 1964-65, Tallahassee Meml. Hosp., 1968-69; guest lectr. health planning dept. urban/regional planning Fla. State U., Tallahassee, 1973-76, health planner and research assoc., 1974-76, vis. asst. prof., 1976-77, asst. prof. and dir. health planning splty., 1977-83, assoc. prof., 1982-83, health care analyst and policy cons., 1983-86; med., health program analyst Aging and Adult Svcs. for State of Fla., 1986-90; coordinator Fla. Alzheimer's Disease Initiative, 1986-90; family nurse practitioner Capital Area Physicians' Svcs., 1993-94; assoc. prof. nursing Fla. A&M U., 1994—2002; clin. nurse Tallahassee Meml. Regional Ctr., 1990—2010. Bd. dirs. Regional Fla. Lung Assn., 1986-91; mem. exec. com. human services and social planning tech. dept. Am. Inst. Planners, 1977-83. Author: The Physician's Assistant: A National and Local Analysis, 1975; contbr. articles to profl. jours., chapters to books. USPHS grantee, 1965-67; HEW grantee, 1978; Univ. fellow Fla. State U., 1971-72; recipient Am. Inst. Planners' Student award, 1975. Mem. Am. Planning Assn. (charter mem. human services and social planning tech. dept. 1976-83, chmn. health planning session Oct. 1978, 79, health policy liaison 1979-83, author assn. health policy statement), Am. Health Planning Assn., Fla. Nurses Assn., Phi Kappa Phi, Sigma Theta Tau. Address: 2602 Cline St Tallahassee FL 32308-0810 Personal E-mail: annscott64@comcast.net.

FORD, CRAIG, state legislator; m. Gwen Ford; children: Jon Craig, Wells Elizabeth. BS in Mktg., Auburn U., Ala. Owner Hodges-Ford Ins. Agency; owner, newspaper The Messenger; mem. Dist. 28 Ala. House of Reps., 2000—. Coach Little League Baseball, YMCA, Royal Ambassadors Basketball League; bd. mem. Breakaway Ministries; deacon First Bapt. Ch., Gadsden. Capt. USAR. Recipient Most Outstanding Legislator award, 2006, Friend of Labor award, 2007; named Darden Rehab. Person of Yr., 2003; named to Sr. Citizens Hall of Fame, 2006. Mem.: Ala. Ret. Teachers Assn. (assoc.). Democrat. Baptist. Office: PO Box 8208 Gadsden AL 35902 also: Ala House of Reps Ala State House 11 S Union St Rm 517-F Montgomery AL 36130 Office Phone: 256-413-7611, 334-242-7690.

FORD, DANNY R., state legislator; b. Apr. 25, 1952; m. Sue Hoskins. BS, Eastern Ky. U. Realtor; auctioneer; mem. Dist. 80 Ky. House of Reps., 1982—; minority whip, 1994—95; rep. fl. leader, 1995—2000. Named to Hall of Fame, Ky. Auctioneers Assn. Mem.: Nat. Auctioneers Assn., Nat. Assn. Realtors, Ky. Assn. Realtors, Ky. Auctioneers Assn. (former pres.), Rockcastle Co., C. of C., Cert. Auctioneers Inst. (former bd. govs.), Rockcastle County Rep. Club. Republican. Baptist. Mailing: PO Box 1245 Mount Vernon KY 40456 Office: Capitol Annex Rm 405C Frankfort KY 40601 Office Phone: 606-256-5229, 606-678-0051, 502-564-8100 ext. 693. E-mail: danny.ford@lrc.ky.gov.

FORD, GERALD J. (JERRY), finance company executive; b. Tex., Aug. 1944; BA in Econs., So. Meth. U., 1966, JD, 1969. Bar: Tex. Chmn., CEO First Gibraltar Bank, Tex., 1988-93; chmn. bd. dirs. First Madison Bank; pres., owner Madison Fin., Inc.; founder First United Bank Group, Inc.; chmn., CEO First Nationwide Mortgage Corp., 1994—2002, Calif. Fed. Bank (formerly First Nationwide Bank), 1994—2002, Calif. Fed. Preferred Capital Corp., 1996—2002, Golden State Bancorp (acquired by Citigroup), 1998—2002, CEO, 1996—2002; chmn. First Acceptance Corp. (formerly Liberte Investors, Inc.), 1996—. Bd. dir. Freeport-McMoRan Cooper & Cold, 2000—, AmeriCredit Corp., Fort Worth, Tex., 2003—, McMoRan Exploration Co.; bd. trustees So. Meth. Univ., Dallas, 1992—, chmn. bd. trustees, 2002. Named Among 40 Most Generous, Fortune Mag., 1998; recipient, Disting. Alumni award, SMU, 1995, Mustang award, SMU, 1997. Office: Chairman First Acceptance Corp 3813 Green Hills Village Dr Nashville TN 37215

FORD, JOE THOMAS, retired telephone company executive, former state senator, state legislator; b. Conway, Ark., June 24, 1937; s. Arch W. and Ruby (Watson) F.; m. Jo Ellen Wilbourn, Aug. 9, 1959; children: Alison, Scott. BS, U. Ark., 1959. With Allied Telephone Co., Little Rock, 1959-83, v.p.-treas., 1963-77, pres., 1977-83, Alltel Corp., 1983-87, pres., chief exec. officer, 1987-91, chmn., pres., chief exec. officer, 1991-93, chmn., CEO, 1993—2002, chmn. Little Rock, 2002—07. Mem. Ark. Senate, 1967-82; dir. Comml. Nat. Bank, 1970-85, Little Rock, Security Bank, Conway, Dial Corp., Textron Inc., EnPro Industries Inc. Recipient Disting. Alumni cert. U. Ark., 1987. Baptist. Home: 2500 N Jackson St Little Rock AR 72207-3718

FORD, JOHN, state legislator; m. Mary Ford; children: Jennifer, Jack. BSBA, Univ. Tulsa, 1968. Ret. ConocoPhillips; mem. Dist. 29 Okla. State Senate, 2004—. Mem.: Daybreak Rotary Club (founding mem., pres.), Bartlesville Area Friends of Pks. (founding mem., pres.). Republican. Presbyterian. Office: 2300 N Lincoln Blvd Rm 424A Oklahoma City OK 73105 Home: 748 Brookhollow Ln Bartlesville OK 74006-8216 Home Phone: 918-333-7922; Office Phone: 405-521-5634. Business E-Mail: fordj@oksenate.gov.

FORD, JOHN BASSETT, broadcasting executive; b. Dahlgren, Va., June 8, 1952; s. John Ellsworth and Jean Marie (Arientale) Ford; m. Margaret Ann Smith, Apr. 13, 1985; children: Maureen Griffin, Colin Steven. BA in History, Duke U., Durham, NC, 1974; MPA, U. Tex., Austin, 1980. Devel. officer sta. KERA-TV/FM, Dallas, 1976-78; planning assoc. Nat. Assn. Pub. TV Stations, Washington, 1980-83; v.p. cmty. devel. sta. WHYY, Inc. TV, Phila./Wilmington, Del., 1983-89; v.p. corp. program sponsorships Discovery Channel, Discovery Comm. Inc., Bethesda, Md., 1989-91, sr. v.p. programming, The Learning Channel, 1991-96, sr. v.p., gen. mgr. The Learning Channel, 1996—99, pres. Discovery Health Channel, 1999—2001, pres. new media, Discovery Networks US, 2001—03, pres., gen. mgr. Mil. Channel & Discovery Times Channel, 2007—09; exec. v.p. programming Nat. Geographic Channel, 2003—07; pres. programming ION Media Networks, Inc., 2010—. Adj. prof. U. Del., Newark, 1987—88. Mem.: Nat. Acad. TV Arts & Scis., Nat. Acad. Cable Programming. Avocations: tennis, basketball, skiing, running, golf. Office: ION Media Networks Hdqs 601 Clearwater Park Rd West Palm Beach FL 33401

FORD, KENNETH M., computer scientist, educator; b. Hampton, Va. BS in Mgmt., NH Coll., 1982; MS in Computer Sci., U. West Fla., 1984; PhD in Computer Sci., Tulane U., 1987; PhD (hon.), U. Bordeaux, 2005. Founder, dir., CEO Inst. Human and Machine Cognition U. West Fla., Pensacola, 1990—. Assoc. dir. to dir. Ctr. Excellence and Info. Tech. Ames Rsch. Ctr., NASA, 1997—99; mem. bd. supervisors Fla. Space Authority, 2001—; bd. dirs. itFloriada.com, 2001—; mem. Nat. Sci. Bd., NSF, 2002—08, chmn. Com. on Programs and Plans; mem. adv. bd. Air Force Sci., 2005—; mem. adv. coun. NASA, 2007—; emeritus editor-in-chief AAAI/MIT Press; past pres. Fla. Artificial Intelligence Rsch. Soc.; assoc. Behavioral and Brain Sciences (BBS). Author: over 100 sci. papers, Android Epistemology, 1995, Expertise in Context: Human and Machine, 1997, Knowledge Acquisition as Modeling, 1993; co-author (with Patrick J. Hayes): Advances in Human & Machine Cognition, 1999, On Computational Wings: Rethinking the Goals of Artificial Intelligence, 2003. Recipient Outstanding Leadership Medal, NASA, 1999, U. Rsch. Award, U. West Fla., Golden Apple Award for Teaching, Disting. Teaching Award, Pensacola Area C. of C. Bus. Leader of the Yr. Award, Inst. Human and Machine Cognition U., 2004; named one of 4 most influential citizens working in academia, Fla. Trend Mag., 2004. Fellow: Am. Assn. Artificial Intelligence; mem.: Nat. Assn. of Scholars, IEEE Computer Soc., Assn. for Computing Machinery (ACM), Am. Assn. for the Advancement of Sci. Office: Institute for Human and Machine Cognition 40 S Alcaniz St Pensacola FL 32502 Office Phone: 850-202-4462. Office Fax: 850-202-4440. E-mail: kford@ihmc.us.

FORD, MICHAEL RAYE, lawyer; b. Blackwell, Okla., Sept. 1, 1945; s. Oscar Raye and Lucille Belton (Ray) Ford; m. Rebecca Deal, Nov. 5, 1993; children: Trevor Hawkins, Devin Connor;children from previous marriage: Seth Michael, Jared Raye. Student, Northwestern U., Evanston, Ill., 1963-64; BA, U. Okla., Norman, 1967, JD, 1970; postgrad. (scholar), U. Wis., 1967, Georgetown U., Washington, DC, 1971-72; LLM, George Wash. U., Washington, DC, 1974. Bar: Okla. 1970, US Dist. Ct. (no. dist.) Okla. 1974, US Supreme Ct. 1974, US Ct. Appeals (10th cir.) 1975, US Dist. Ct. (we. dist. north dist.) Okla. 1978, US Ct. Appeals (5th cir.) 1989, US Tax Court 1985, US Court Fed. Claims 1971. Mem. legal dept. Cities Svc. Oil Co., Tulsa, 1970; assoc. Gable, Gotwals, Rubin, Fox, Johnson & Baker, Tulsa, 1974-77; ptnr. Baker, Baker, Wilson, Selph & Ford, Oklahoma City, 1977-79, McKnight, Gasaway, Beck, Seals & Ford, Enid, Okla., 1979-84; pvt. practice, Enid, 1984; ptnr. Ford & Brown, Enid, 1984-86; ptnr., pres., exec. com. mem. Fellers, Snider, Blankenship, Bailey & Tippens, P.C., Oklahoma City, 1987—. Lectr. legal edn. seminars. Articles and book rev. editor: U. Okla. Law Rev., 1969—70; contbr. articles to law jours. Trustee Ctrl. Christian Ch., Enid, 1982—84, deacon, 1981—85, vice chmn. bd., 1984—85, deacon, exec. com., 2008, Westminster Presbyn. Ch., Okla. City, 2009—10. Capt. JAGC US Army, 1971—74. Decorated Meritorious Svc. medal US Army; recipient Leadership Law award, Jour. Record, 2008. Master: The Okla. Acad.; fellow: Okla. Bar Found., Am. Bar Found.; mem.: ABA (mem. com. sect. taxation 1978, vice chair 2001—03, chmn. closely held bus. com. taxation sect. 2003—05, vice chair profl. svcs. com. 2005—08, chair 2008—10), The Okla. Acads., COMMSTAR Program, Okla. City CC Found. (mem. bd. trustees, commstar 2013), Supreme Ct. Hist. Soc., Small Bus. Coun. America, The Group Inc., Enid Estate Planning Coun. (v.p. 1982—83, pres. 1983—84), Am. Law Inst., Okla. Bar Assn. (program chmn. CLE seminar 1982, v.p. taxation sect. 1982—83, chmn. 1983—84), Greater Enid C. of C. (bd. dirs. 1983—85), Kiwanis (1st v.p. 1979—80, com. chmn. Enid 1980—81, bd. dirs. 1982—83, 2d v.p. 1982—83, pres. 1984—85, lt. gov. 1986—87), Order of Coif, Pi Kappa Alpha, Phi Delta Phi. Democrat. Office: Tower 100 N Broadway Ave Ste 1700 Oklahoma City OK 73102 Home Phone: 405-470-0032. Business E-Mail: mford@fellerssnider.com.

FORD, NELSON M., consulting firm executive; b. 1947; married; 3 children. BA in History, Duke U.; M in Edn., U. Del., 1973; attended, U. Pa. Health policy adv. Office Mgmt. & Budget (OMB), Exec. Office of the Pres.; exec. sec. Health Care Financing Adminstrn. US Dept Health & Human Services (HHS); health policy group dir. Coopers & Lybrand; COO Georgetown U. Med. Ctr., 1990—97; pres., CEO Clinipad, 1997—2000; dir. sr. products Humana, 2004—05; dep. asst. sec. for health budgets & fin. policy. Dept. Army, US Dept. Def., 2001—04, prin. dep. for. fin. mgmt. & comptr., 2005—06, asst. sec. for. fin. mgmt. & comptr., 2006—08, acting under sec., 2007—08, under sec., 2008—09; pres., CEO LMI, 2009—. Bd. dirs. Academy-Health. Office: LMI 2000 Corporate Ridge Mc Lean VA 22102 Office Phone: 800-213-4817.

FORD, OPHELIA, state legislator; b. Memphis; State senator Dist. 29, Tenn., 2007—. Mem.: NAACP (life). Democrat. Office: 54 North Arcadian #102 Memphis TN 38103 also: 318 War Memorial Bldg Nashville TN 37243-0029 Office Phone: 901-948-7755, 615-741-1767. Business E-Mail: sen.ophelia.ford@capitol.tn.gov.

FORD, RICHARD, writer; b. Jackson, Miss., Feb. 16, 1944; s. Parker Carrol and Edna (Akin) F.; m. Kristina Hensley, 1968. BA in English, Mich. State U., 1966; MFA, U. Calif., 1970; LHD (hon.), U. Mich., 1998. Adj. prof. Oscar Wilde Ctr. Trinity Coll., Dublin, 2008—11; sr. fiction prof. U. Miss., Oxford, 2011—. Author: (novels) A Piece of My Heart, 1976, The Ultimate Good Luck, 1981, The Sportswriter, 1986 (PEN/Faulkner Citation for Fiction 1986), Wildlife, 1990, Independence Day, 1995, The Lay of the Land, 2006, Canada, 2012 (Andrew Carnegie medal for Excellence in Fiction, American Library Assn., 2013); author: (short stories) Rock Springs: Stories, 1987, Women with Men: Three Stories, 1997 A Multitude of Sins, 2002, Vintage Ford, 2004; author: (plays) American Tropical, 1983; (screenplays) Bright Angel, 1991; editor: (with Shannon Ravenel) The Best American Short Stories, 1990, The Granta Book of the American Short Story, (with Michael Kreyling), Eudora Welty: Complete Novels, 1998, Eudora Welty: Stories, Essays, and Memoir (Eudora Welty), 1998, The Granta Book of the American Long Story, 1999; contbr. articles to popular publs. Recipient Pulitzer prize for Fiction, 1996, PEN/Faulkner prize for fiction, 1996, PEN/Malamud award for excellence in the short story, 2003, Berlin prize American Acad. Berlin, 2003, Cavour prize, 2007, Kenyon prize, 2008; Guggenheim fellow, 1977-98, Endowment for the Arts, 1979-80, 85-86; named a Commandeur L'Ordre Des Arts et Des Lettres, Republic of France, 2004 Mem. U. Mich. Soc. Fellows, American Acad. Arts & Letters; fellow American Acad. Arts & Sciences Office: University of Mississippi W205A Bondurant PO Box 1848 University MS 38677 Office Phone: 662-915-7439.*

FORD, RICHARD EDMOND, lawyer; b. Ronceverte, W.Va., May 3, 1927; s. Grady Williams and Hazel Loraine (Fry) F.; m. Sally Frances Alexander, June 14, 1952; children: Richard Edmond Jr., Sally Anne, Melinda J. Student, U. N.C., 1950; BS in Bus. Adminstrn., W.Va. U., 1951, LL.B., 1954. Bar: W.Va. 1954. Assoc. Holt & Haynes, Lewisburg, W.Va., 1954-55; ptnr. Haynes & Ford, Lewisburg, 1955-74, Haynes, Ford & Rowe, Lewisburg, 1975-96, The Ford Law Firm, Lewisburg, 1997—. Dir. First Nat. Bank Ronceverte, 1986-2009. Bd. dirs. W.Va. U. Found., 1972—2008, Daywood Found., v.p., 1986—; bd. dirs. Faculty Merit Found. W.Va., 1984—2012, W.Va. Legal Svcs. Plan, 1973—79; trustee Greenbrier Coll. for Women, 1960—73; mem. exec. bd. Buckskin Coun. Boy Scouts Am.; mem. adv. bd. Greenbrier C.C. Ctr.; mem. vis. com. Coll. Law W.Va. U., 1972—74; mem. W.Va. Legislature, 1961—64. Served as ensign U.S. Maritime Svc., 1945—47. Recipient Outstanding Alumnus award, W.Va. U., 1988, Law Sch, 80. Fellow ABA (ho. of dels. 1977-80, state chmn., W.Va. 2005-09), Am. Judicature Soc.(state chmn. 2005-09); mem. W.Va. Bar Assn. (v.p. 1965-66, 75-76, pres. 1987-88), Greenbrier County Bar Assn. (pres. 1964-66, 81-82), W.Va. Law Sch. Assn. (pres. 1966-67), Nat. Conf. Commrs. Uniform State Laws, Am. Coll. Real Estate Lawyers, W.Va. U. Alumni Assn. (pres. 1971), W.Va. State Bar (pres. 1978-79), Phi Beta Kappa, Sigma Chi, Phi Delta Phi, Order Vandalia, Masons, KT, Shriners, Lewisburg Elks Club. Democrat. Methodist. Office: The Ford Law Firm 203 W Randolph St Lewisburg WV 24901-1023 Office Phone: 304-645-1858.

FORD, ROBERT, state legislator; b. New Orleans, Dec. 26, 1948; Attended, Grambling State U., Wayne State U. Councilman Charleston City Coun., 1974—92; mem. Dist. 42 SC House of Reps., SC, 1993—, mem. Banking and Ins. Com., Corrections and Penology Com., Gen. Com., Invitations Com., Judiciary Com. & Labor, Commerce and Industry Com. Recipient Triumphant award, 1991; named Legislator of Yr., SC Physical Therapy Assn., 1994; Harvey grant. Democrat. Methodist. Mailing: PO Box 21302 Charleston SC 29413 Office: 506 Gressette Bldg PO Box 142 Columbia SC 29201 E-mail: RIF@scsenate.org.

FORD, ROBERT DALE (DALE FORD), state legislator; b. Jonesborough, Tenn., July 6, 1942; married; 3 children. Mem. Agr. Com., Transp. Com., Pub. Transp. & Hwys. Subcom.; umpire, major league baseball; state rep. Dist. 6 Tenn., 2007—. Spkr. in field. Active St. Jude Children's Hosp., Heart Fund. With U.S. Army. Mem.: East Tenn. Sports Hall of Fame, Kiwanis (bd. dirs.), Puritan Club Bowmantown, Gray Masonic Lodge 575. Republican. Protestant. Avocations: golf, racquetball. Mailing: 678 Brethern Church Rd Jonesborough TN 37659 Office Phone: 615-741-1717. Fax: 615-253-0301. Business E-Mail: rep.dale.ford@legislature.state.tn.us.

FORD, ROLLIN LEE, retail executive; b. 1962; BS in Bus. Adminstrn. and Sys. Analysis, Taylor U. Joined Wal-Mart Stores, Inc., 1983, with distbn. and logistics ops., v.p. splty. distbn./transp., 1996—98, v.p. distbn. ops., 1998—2000, sr. v.p. logistics, 2000—03, exec. v.p. logistics, 2003—06, exec. v.p., chief info. officer, 2006—12, exec. v.p., chief adminstrv. officer, 2012—. Bd. dirs. Thurgood Marshall Scholarship Found. Office: Wal-Mart Stores Inc 702 SW Eighth St Bentonville AR 72716

FORD, SANDRA ELIZABETH, public health service officer, state agency administrator; m. Dominic Conrad Bouchelion. BS in Psychology, Stanford U.; MD, Howard U., MBA in Health Services Adminstrn. Cert. pediatrician. Dep. state health officer, dep. sec. Children's Med. Services Fla. Dept. Health, Tallahassee, 2003—05; dist. health dir. Dekalb County Ga. Dept. Cmty. Health, 2005—; interim dir. Divsn. Pub. Health Ga. Dept. Human Resources, Atlanta, 2008—09. Recipient Robinson/Dickens award; grantee Nat. Med. Fellowship; fellow, Commonwealth Fund. Office: Georgia Department Community Health 455 Winn Way, Room 536 PO Box 987 Decatur GA 30031-1701 Office Phone: 404-294-3789. Office Fax: 404-492-3715.

FORD, TERRENCE JEROD (T.J. FORD), professional basketball coach, retired professional basketball player; b. Houston, Mar. 24, 1983; Attended, U. Tex., 2001—03. Point guard Milw. Bucks, 2003—06, Toronto Raptors, 2006—08, Ind. Pacers, 2008—11, KK Zagreb, Croatia, 2011, San Antonio Spurs, 2011—12; ret. NBA, 2012; vol. coach Austin Toros, NBA Devel. League, Tex., 2012—. Founder T.J. Ford Found., 2004—. Recipient Naismith Trophy, 2003, John R. Wooden Trophy, 2003; named Player of Yr., Sports Illus., ESPN.com and CBSSportsline.com, 2003, Coll. Basketball Player of Yr., The Sporting News, 2003. Office: Austin Toros 12885 N Hwy 183 Ste 207 Austin TX 78750

FORD, THOMAS W., JR., lawyer; b. Austin, Tex., 1955; BA in Acctg., U. Tex., Austin, 1978; JD, U. Houston, 1981. Bar: Tex. 1981. Ptnr., tax dept. Andrews Kurth LLP, Houston. Mem.: Coalition of Publicly Traded Partnerships, ABA, State Bar Tex., Houston Bar Assn., Phi Delta Phi, Beta Alpha Psi, Gamma Delta Sigma, Order of Barons. Office: Andrews Kurth LLP 600 Travis St Ste 4200 Houston TX 77002-3090 Office Phone: 713-220-4498. Office Fax: 713-238-4285. Business E-Mail: tford@andrewskurth.com.

FORD, TRAVIS, men's college basketball coach; b. Madisonville, Ky., Dec. 29, 1969; m. Heather Ford; children: Brook, Kyleigh, Shane. Attended, U. Mo., 1989—90; BS, U. Ky., Lexington, 1994. Head coach Campbellsville U. Fighting Tigers, 1997—2000, Eastern Ky. U. Colonels, 2000—05, U. Mass. Minutemen, 2005—08, Okla. State U. Cowboys, 2008—. Named Southeast Regional MVP, NCAA Men's Basketball Tournament, 1993, Coach of Yr., Mid-South Conf., 1999; named to All-SEC First Team, 1993. Office: Athletics Ctr Okla State U Stillwater OK 74078

FORD, WILLIAM F., banker; b. Huntington, NY, Aug. 14, 1936; s. William Freithaler; m. Diane McDonald, June 11, 1960; children: Eric W., Kristin E. BA in Econs. summa cum laude, U. Tex., 1961; MA, U. Mich., 1962, PhD, 1966; DSc (hon.), Fla. Inst. Tech., 1981; grad. sr. exec. program, Stanford U., 1983. Part-time teaching asst. U. Mich., 1962-63, instr., 1965-66; economist Rand Corp., 1966, cons., 1967-68, 70-71; asst. prof. econs. U. Va., 1967-69; assoc. prof. Tex. Tech. U., Lubbock, 1969-70; prof. econs., dean Transylvania Coll., Lexington, Ky., 1970-71; exec. dir., chief economist rsch. and planning group Am. Bankers Assn., 1971-75; sr. v.p., chief economist Wells Fargo Bank, San Francisco, 1975-80; pres., chief exec. officer Fed. Res. Bank Atlanta, 1980-83; pres., chief operating officer First Nationwide Savs., 1983-85; pres., chief exec. officer Broadview Savs. Bank, Cleve., 1986-89; dean coll. bus. U. Denver, 1990-91; prof. and chair fin. Mid. Tenn. State U., Murfreesboro, 1992—. Mem. faculty Stonier Grad. Sch. Banking, 1976—80; mem. fed. open market com. Fed. Res. Sys., 1982—83; sr. econ. advisor TeleCheck Svcs. Inc., 1992—2001; spkr. in field. Author: Mexico's Foreign Trade and Economic Development, 1968; also over 100 articles, revs., TV script. Bd. vis. Berry Coll., 1984—89. With USN, 1954—57. Woodrow Wilson fellow, 1961; NDEA fellow, 1961-63; Ford Found. fgn. area fellow, Mex., 1964-65; Rotary fellow, Chile, 1970; co-winner Fred M. Taylor Prize U. Mich. Mem. Stanford Grad. Sch. Bus. Adminstrn. Alumni Assn. (bd. dirs. 1985-86), Am. Econ. Assn., U.S. C. of C. (bd. dirs. 1989-91, chmn. econ. policy com. 1990-93), Fellow Nat. Assn. for Bus. Econs. (bd. dirs. 2002-05), Phi Beta Kappa. Methodist. Office: Mid Tenn State U Coll Bus PO Box 27 Murfreesboro TN 37133-0027 Office Fax: 615-898-5962. Business E-Mail: william.ford@mtsu.edu.

FORDHAM, LYNN ANSLEY, pediatric radiologist; b. Corning, NY, Mar. 23, 1963; MD, Tufts U., 1989. Cert. in diagnostic radiology 1993, in pediatric radiology 1998. Pediatric radiology resident U. NC Hosp., 1989—93, sect. chief, pediatric imaging Chapel Hill; fellow Children's Hops. Boston, 1993—94; assoc. prof. radiology U. NC Sch. Medicine. Contbr. articles to profl. publs. Mem.: Soc. for Pediatric Radiology, Radiol. Soc. North America, Am. Roentgen Ray Soc., Am. Inst. of Ultrasound in Medicine, Am. Coll. Radiology, Am. Assn. of Women in Radiology. Office: U NC Dept Radiology Chapel Hill NC 27599 Office Phone: 919-966-3084. Office Fax: 919-966-1994. Business E-Mail: fdh@med.unc.edu.

FORDTRAN, JOHN SATTERFIELD, physician; b. San Antonio, Nov. 15, 1931; s. William M. and Josephine (Bell) F.; m. Jewel Evans, July 25, 1953; children: William, Bess, Josephine, Amy. Student, U. Tex., 1949-52; MD, Tulane U., 1956; DSc (hon.), Med. Coll. Wis., 1988; MD (hon.), Karl Franzens U., Graz, Austria, 1995. Internal medicine intern Parkland Meml. Hosp., Dallas, 1956-57, asst. resident internal medicine, 1957-58; research fellow gastroenterology Mass. Meml. Hosp., Boston, 1960-62; instr. internal medicine U. Tex. Southwestern Med. Sch., Dallas, 1962-63, asst. prof. internal medicine, 1963-67, assoc. prof. internal medicine, 1967-69, prof., 1969-79, chief sect. gastroenterology, 1963-79; chief dept. internal medicine Baylor U. Med. Center, Dallas, 1979-96; pres. Baylor Rsch. Inst., Baylor U. Med. Ctr., Dallas, 1991-2000. Mem. attending staff Parkland Meml. Hosp., Dallas, 1963-79; cons. gastroenterology Dallas VA Hosp., 1963-79. Contbr. articles to profl. jours.; editorial bd. Jour. Clin. Investigation, 1968-73; editor Gastroenterology, 1977-81; co-editor: Gastrointestinal Disease, 5th edit., 1993. Served with USPHS, 1958-60. Recipient King Faisal prize in medicine Saudi Arabia, 1984 Fellow Royal Coll. Physicians Eng.; mem. ACP, Am. Soc. Clin. Investigation (past pres.), Am. Gastroent. Assn. (Disting. Achievement award 1971, Kirsner prize 1990, Disting. Educator award 1991, Friedenwald medal 1993), Am. Gastroenterology Assn. (Lifetime Achievement in Digestive Sci. award, 1999). Office: Baylor U Med Ctr 3500 Gaston Ave Dallas TX 75246-2096 Home: 3408 Hanover St Dallas TX 75225-7643 Office Phone: 214-820-2672. E-mail: johnfo@baylorhealth.edu.

FOREHAND, JOSEPH W., finance company executive; b. Alexander City, Ala. m. Gayle Forehand; 2 children. BS in Indsl. Engring., Auburn U., 1971; MS in Indsl. Adminstrn., Purdue U., 1972. Joined Anderson Consultants, 1972—, various positions with product group, regional dir. products industry, office mng. ptnr. Dallas, head Ams. products group, mng. ptrn. products Dallas and Paris, 1997-98, mng. ptnr. global comms. and high tech market unit; mng. ptnr., CEO Accenture(formerly Anderson), 2001—04; chmn. bd. dirs. Accenture, 2001—06; sr. adv. Kohlberg Kravis Roberts & Co.; chmn. First Data Corp., Atlanta, 2010—. Bd. dir. Aricent Inc., Palo Alto, Calif., 2006—, chmn., 2008—. Recipient Most Influential Cons., Consulting Mag., 2001, Morgan Stanley Leadership award, 2003, Carl S. Sloane award for excellence in mgmt. consulting. Office: First Data Corp 5565 Glenridge Conn NE Atlanta GA 30342-4756 Office Phone: 303-967-8000.

FOREMAN, JEFFREY ERIC, lawyer; b. 1962; BS, Ariz. State U., 1984; JD, John Marshall Law Sch., 1986. Bar: Ill. 1986, Fla. 2000, US Supreme Ct., US Ct. Appeals (11th cir.), US Dist. Ct. (southern and middle dists.) Fla., US Dist. Ct. (northern dist.) Ill. Founding ptnr., prin. Foreman Friedman, PA (formerly Maltzman Foreman), Miami, Fla., Chgo. Named a Top Lawyer, South Fla. Legal Guide, 2011; named one of The Nation's Top Litigators, The Nat. Law Journal, 2009. Avocations: skiing, fishing, boating. Office: Foreman Friedman, PA Suite 2300 2 S Biscayne Blvd Miami FL 33131 Office Phone: 305-358-6555. Office Fax: 305-374-9077. E-mail: jforeman@fflegal.com.

FOREMAN, JOHN WILLIAM, pediatrician, educator; b. Washington, June 23, 1947; s. William Roy and Elizabeth Roberts (McLean) F.; m. Linda Poffenberger, May 27 1973; children: Matthew John, Jennifer Lynne. BS, Duke U., 1969; MD, U. Md., 1973. Diplomate Nat. Bd. Med. Examiners, Pa., Va., N.C., Am. Bd. Pediatrics, subbd. pediatric nephrology. Intern, resident Montreal (Que., Can.) Children's Hosp., 1973-75; asst. chief resident pediatrics Children's Hosp. Phila., 1975-76, fellow pediatric nephrology, 1976-79, staff physician, 1979-86; instr. pediatrics U. Pa. Sch. Medicine, Phila., 1976-79, clin. asst. prof., asst. prof., 1979-85, assoc. prof., 1985-86; assoc. prof. pediatrics Med. Coll. Va., Va. Commonwealth U., Richmond, 1986-90, prof., 1990-93; prof., chief divsn. pediatric nephrology Duke U. Med. Ctr., Durham, NC, 1993—. Cons. WHO, 1984; chmn. med. adv. bd. Nat. Kidney Found. Va., 1989-92, mem. exec. com. pediatric urology and nephrology coun.; mem. pediatric delegation to Chinese Med. Assn. of People's Republic of China, 1982; vis. prof. Fudan U., Shanghai, 2011. Contbr. articles to profl. jours., chpts. to books. Bd. dirs. Transplant Found., Richmond, 1991. Daland fellow Am. Philos. Soc., Phila., 1980-81; grantee Am. Heart Assn., 1984-88, NIH, 1988-91. Fellow: Am. Acad. Pediat.; mem.: Soc. Pediatric Rsch., Am. Pediatric Soc., So. Soc. Pediatric Rsch. (councillor 1989-91), Internat. Pediatric Nephrology Soc. (councillor 1993-98), Am. Soc. Pediatric Nephrology (coun. mem. 2002-06), Am. Soc. Nephrology, chair exec. com. Sect. on Nephrology 2004-10), Am. Acad. Pediat., Am. Bd. Pediat. (bd. mem., pediat. nephrology, 2008-13). Avocation: reading. Home: 9 Streamley Ct Durham NC 27705-5396 Office: Duke U Med Ctr PO Box 3959 Durham NC 27710-0001 Office Phone: 919-684-6627. Business E-Mail: forem001@mc.duke.edu.

FOREMAN, MICHAEL J., astronaut; b. Columbus, Ohio, Mar. 29, 1957; s. James W. and Nancy C. Foreman; m. Lorrie Lee Dancer; 3 children. BSc in Aerospace Engring., U.S. Naval Acad., 1979; MSc in Aeronautical Engring., U.S. Naval Postgraduate Sch., 1986. Commd. lt. USN, 1975, advanced through grades to capt., naval aviator, Patrol Squadron Twenty-Three, Naval Air Systems (NAS) Brunswick, Maine, 1981—89, various assignments, 1990—93, dep. and then Class Desk Officer (chief engr.), Naval Air Systems Command, T-45 Goshawk aircraft program Crystal City, Va., 1993—98; mil. dir. for rsch. and engring. group NAS, Naval Air Warfare Ctr. Aircraft Divsn., Patuxent River; navy liaison to NASA's Advanced Orbitor Cockpit Project Johnson Space Ctr., technical lead, Advanced Orbitor Cockpit Project Team; astronaut NASA, Houston, 1998—. Technical duties Astronaut Office Space Station; liaison, Space Shuttle Branch Johnson Space Ctr. and Kennedy Space Ctr.; dep. Space Shuttle Br.; mission specialist STS-120 mission to Internat. Space Station, 2006; crew mem., mission to deliver the Japanese Logistics Module and the Canadian Spl. Purpose Dexterous Manipulator to the Internat. Space Station (ISS) STS-123 Mission (Endeavour), 2008; mission specialist STS-129 Atlantis Mission, 2009. Decorated Meritorious Svc. medal USN, Navy Commendation medal; recipient Adml. William Adger Moffett Aeronautics award, U.S. Naval Postgraduate Sch., Navy Achievement medal. Mem.: Assn. Naval Aviation, U.S. Naval Acad. Alumni Assn. Avocations: golf, running, skiing, home repair/improvement, time with family. Office: Astronaut Office CB NASA Johnson Space Center Houston TX 77058

FOREST, DANIEL J., Lieutenant Governor of North Carolina; b. Harrisonburg, Va., Oct. 15, 1967; s. Jim and Sue (Wilkins) Forest; m. Alice Forest; children: Jake, Haley, Max, Olivia. BS in Architecture, U. NC, Charlotte, 1993, MA in Architecture. Sr. ptnr., Little Diversified Architectural Consulting, 1988—2009; lt. gov. State of NC, Raleigh, 2013—; pres. NC State Senate, 2013—. Bd. mem. Triangle Leadership Forum, 2003—12. Mem.: Heritage Found. President's Club. Republican. Christian. Office: Office of the Lieutenant Governor 20401 Mail Service Center Raleigh NC 27699-0401 Office Phone: 919-733-7350. Office Fax: 919-733-6595.*

FORESTI, RONALDO M., electronics executive; BEE, U. Sao Paulo, Brazil. Mgr. Digital Equipment Corp., Brazil; bus. group mgr., L.Am., L.Am. Northern Compaq; v.p., gen. mgr., L.Am. Hewlett-Packard Co., Lexmark International, Inc., 2003—08, v.p., Asia Pacific, L.Am., 2008—. Office: Lexmark International Inc 740 W New Cir Rd Lexington KY 40550 Office Phone: 859-232-2000. Business E-Mail: rforesti@lexmark.com.

FORMAN, DONALD T., biochemist, educator; b. NYC, Feb. 27, 1932; s. Jack and Fannie (Jaffee) F.; m. Florence Sporn, Aug. 22, 1953; children: Joan Diane, Steven Lawrence, Debra Helene. BS, Bklyn. Coll., 1953; MS, Wayne State U., 1957, PhD, 1959. Clin. biochemist Mercy Hosp. Med. Center, Chgo., 1959—63; dir. clin. biochemistry, asso. prof. biochemistry and pathology Evanston Hosp./Northwestern U. Med. Sch., Chgo., 1963—78; rsch. prof. U. Stockholm and Royal Postgrad. Med. Sch., London, 1975; prof. pathology and biochemistry U. NC, Chapel Hill, 1978—2002, dir. clin. chemistry, 1978—2002, prof. emeritus pathology and biochemistry, 2002. Cons. clin. chemist, industry and govt., 1965— Editor: Clinical Chemistry, 1976. Served with AUS, 1953-55. Recipient Chgo. Clin. Chemists award, 1974, Sunderman award as clin. scientist for 1986, Spl. Recognition award for clin. chemistry Am. Chem. Soc., 2000; Mich. Heart Assn. fellow, 1957-59 Mem. AAAS, AAUP, Assn. Clin. Scientists (pres. 1973-74), Am. Assn. Clin. Chemistry (dir., award for outstanding contbn. to animal clin. chemistry 1995), Sigma Xi, Phi Lambda Upsilon. Achievements include research on enzymology, inborn errors of metabolism, tumor-associated markers, atherosclerosis, human alcohol metabolism, clinical biochemistry and critical care chemistry. Home: 2559 Owens Ct Chapel Hill NC 27514-1737 Office: U NC Med Sch Dept Pathology Chapel Hill NC 27514 Office Phone: 919-967-9958. E-mail: dforman@nc.rr.com.

FORMANEK, PETER RAEMIN, hotel executive; b. 1943; BA, U. NC, 1966; MBA, Harvard U., 1968. Adminstrv. asst. to pres., asst. prof., bus. adminstrn. LeMoyne-Owen Coll., Tenn.; with Malone & Hyde, Inc., 1968—86, asst. to pres., 1968—73, v.p., Drugs & Rack Svc., 1973—79, group v.p., Retailing, 1979—81, exec. v.p., Splty. Retailing, 1981—86; exec. v.p. Super Drugs, 1969—72, pres., 1972; dir. Autozone Perrigo Co.; dir., Sports Authority, co-founder Auto-Zone, Inc.; pres. Autozone Inc., 1986—94. Bd. dirs. Burger King Holdings, Inc., 2003—. Office: Burger King Holdings Inc Bd Directors 5505 Blue Lagoon Dr Miami FL 33126 Office Phone: 305-378-3000. E-mail: pformanek@whopper.com.

FORMBY, MARK S., state legislator; b. Starkville, Miss., Aug. 16, 1956; s. Lourie N. and Patricia Stuart Formby; m. Rita Elisebeth Gaidamovics. Owner Formby's Flowers, 1979—88; trainer Attitudes Unlimited, 1986—88; co-organizer to congressman Trent Lott, 1988; econ. devel. asst. to US senator Trent Lott, 1989—91; mktg. dir. Delta Data Sys., 1991; mem. Dist. 108 Miss. House of Reps., 1993—; real estate agt. Formby & Assoc. Recipient Eagle Scout award, Boy Scouts, 1973, Citizenship award, Cir. K, Miss. State U., 1979. Mem.: Am. Legislature Exch. Coun., US Jr. C. of C. (v.p. 1986—87, Outstanding State Pres. award 1985), Miss. Jr. C. of C. (pres. 1984—85), Picayune Jr. C. of C. (pres. 1981—82), Ducks Unlimited, Jaycees, Kiwanis Internat., Miss. State U. Alumni. Republican. Southern Baptist. Office: 911 Hwy 43 N Picayune MS 39466 also: Rm 402-B NC PO Box 1018 Jackson MS 39215 Home Phone: 601-798-8917; Office Phone: 601-359-3339, 601-798-3800. Business E-Mail: mformby@house.ms.gov.

FORNAGE, BRUNO DENIS, radiologist, educator; b. Reims, France, July 2, 1949; came to U.S., 1987; s. Louis and Genevieve (Mercier) F.; m. Brigitte Wittmer, Oct. 18, 1991; 1 child, Louis Bruno. MD, Med. Sch. Reims, 1974. Diplomate French Bd. Radiology, French Bd. Oncology. Resident in oncology Inst. Jean-Godinot Regional Cancer Ctr., Reims, 1974-76, resident in radiology, 1976-79, asst. dept. biophysics and nuc. medicine, 1976-82, dir. dept. radiology, 1982-87; assoc. prof. radiology U. Reims, 1986-87; assoc. prof. radiology, chief sect. ultrasound U. Tex. M.D. Anderson Cancer Ctr., Houston, 1987-2000, prof. radiology, 1990—, prof. surg. oncology, 1999—. Author 5 textbooks; editor 2 textbooks; mem. editl. bd. various jours.; editor-in-chief Jour. of Clin. Ultrasound, 1997—; reviewer jours.; contbr. chpts. to books, articles to profl. jours.; patentee in field. Fellow Am. Inst. Ultrasound in Medicine, Soc. Radiologists in Ultrasound, Soc. Breast Imaging; mem. Am. Roentgen Ray Soc., Radiol. Soc. N.Am., Am. Coll. Radiology, Am. Soc. Breast

Disease, Internat. Skeletal Soc., numerous others. Office: U Tex MD Anderson Canc Ctr 1515 Holcombe Blvd Houston TX 77030-4009 Personal E-mail: fornage@swbell.net. Business E-Mail: bfornage@di.mdacc.tmc.edu.

FORNEY, LARRY J., chemical engineer, educator; b. Waterloo, Iowa, Nov. 1, 1944; s. Loren John and Ramona Leary F.; m. Paula Hickey, Aug. 3, 1974; 1 child, Megan Catlin. BS, Case Inst. Tech., Cleve., 1966; MS, MIT, Boston, 1968, ME, 1969; PhD, Harvard U., Cambridge, Mass., 1974. Rsch. engr. Norton Rsch. Corp., Cambridge, Mass., 1968, Walden Rsch. div. Abcor, Inc., Cambridge, Mass., 1972-74; asst. prof. dept. civil engring. U. Ill., Urbana, 1974-79; assoc. prof. chem. engring. Ga. Inst. Tech., Atlanta, 1979—2009, emeritus prof. chem. engring., 2009—. Cons. Comml. Union Ins. Co., 1977, Lockheed Ga. Co., 1982-83, Sverdrup Tech. Inc., 1983-87, Dupont, 1989-91, Leeds & Northrup, 1991, Dow Corning Corp., 1994-96, Chem. Products Corp., 2004, Crystal Clean Technologies, 2006-; phys. scientist USAF Rocket Propulsion Lab., Edward AFB, Calif., 1983. Contbr. articles to profl. jours. Active Clean Air Coun., Ga. Lung Assn., 1980-82. NIH fellow, 1968, SCEEE fellow, 1982, NASA fellow, 1988; recipient: Water award, IChemE, 2008, Food & Drink Processing award, 2010; grantee NSF, 1975-77, EPA, 1976-78, U.S. Dept. Energy, 1977-81, USAF, 1983-84, 1989-95 Ga. FoodPAC, 2002-06. Mem. Am. Inst. Chem. Engrs. (coordinator of sessions 1983, 88, 2000 ann. meetings), Harvard Soc. Engrs. and Scientists, North Am. Mixing Forum, Harvard Club, MIT Club. Achievements include patents for taylor-couette flow: UV disinfection of fluids. Office Phone: 404-713-0923. Business E-Mail: f111144@bellsouth.net.

FORNI, PATRICIA ROSE, nursing educator; b. St. Louis, Feb. 14, 1932; d. Harold and Glenda M. (Keay) Brown. BSN, Washington U., St. Louis, 1955, MS (USPHS trainee), 1957; PhD (USPHS fellow), St. Louis U., 1965; postgrad. (USPHS scholar), U. Minn., summers 1968, 70. Staff nurse McMillan EENT Hosp., St. Louis, summer 1955, Renard Psychiat. Hosp., St. Louis, part-time 1955-57; rsch. asst. Washington U. Sch. Nursing, St. Louis, 1957-59, rsch. assoc., 1959-61, asst. prof., 1964-66, assoc. dean in charge grad. edn., assoc. prof. gen. nursing sci., 1966-68; assoc. prof. pub. health nursing Wayne State U., Detroit, 1968-69; asst. dir. for manpower and edn. Ill. Regional Med. Program, Chgo., 1969-71; project dir. Midwest Continuing Profl. Edn. for Nurses, St. Louis U., 1971-75; dean, prof. nursing So. Ill. U., Edwardsville, 1975-88; dean Coll. Nursing U. Okla., Oklahoma City, 1988—2004, prof. Coll. Nursing, 1988—, dean emeritus, Coll. Nursing, 2008—. Grant proposal reviewer Divsn. Nursing, USPHS, 1972-79, 88, 91, NSF, 1978, U.S. Dept. Edn., 1980; mem. Ill. Implementation Commn. on Nursing, 1975-77, Okla. State Health Plan Adv. Com., 1994—. Mem. peer rev. panel Nursing Outlook, 1987-91; mem. editl. bd. Health Care for Women Internat., 1984—, Jour. Profl. Nursing, 1988-90. Chairwoman articulation of nursing programs task force Okla. State Regents for Higher Edn., 1990-91; bd. dirs. Greater St. Louis Health Sys. Agy., 1976-81, Adult Edn. Coun. Greater St. Louis, 1973-76, Edwardsville unit Am. Cancer Soc., 1981-88. Fellow WHO, Sweden, Finland, 1985. Mem. Nat. League for Nursing (accreditation site visitor 1979—, nominating com. Coun. Baccalaureate and Higher Degree Programs 1979-82, pub. policy and legis. com. 1981-85, bd. dirs. 1991-93, treas. 1991-93, fin. com. 1991-95), Nat. League for Health Care (trustee 1991-93), Nat. League for Nursing Accrediting Commn. (peer review panel, baccalaureate and higher degree programs 1997-2000, 06, commr. 2000-06, chmn. 2001-06), Am. Nurses Assn. (chmn. continuing edn. publs. com. 1975-76), Mo. Nurses Assn. (chmn. edn. com. 1973-77), Greater St. Louis Soc. Health Manpower Edn. and Tng. (chmn. legis. com. 1974-75), Midwest Alliance in Nursing (1st governing bd. 1979-80, 93-96, chmn. nominations com. 1980-81, fin. com. 1993-94, chair fin. com. 1994-96, treas. 1994-96, pres. 1998-2000), Am. Assn. Colls. Nursing (hon., program com. 1978-82, mem.-at-large, bd. dirs. 1990-92, chair rsch. com. 1990-92), Ill. Coun. Deans/Dirs. Baccalaureate and Higher Degree Programs in Nursing (chmn. 1979-81), Am. Acad. Nursing (treas., chair fin. com., gov. coun. 1989-93, editor Newsletter 1982-87), Ill. Nurses Assn. (commn. on adminstrn. 1983-87, commn. on edn. 1987-89), Okla. Nurses Found. (pres. bd. trustees 1990-93), Sigma Theta Tau Internat. (charter mem. Epsilon Eta chpt. 1980). Office: Univ Okla Coll Nursing PO Box 26901 Oklahoma City OK 73216-0901

FORREST, ALLEN WRIGHT, tax consultant; b. Quincy, Mass., Nov. 8, 1941; s. Edwin Wright and Sylvia (Locke) F.; m. Helen Frances Kolb, Nov. 10, 1962; children: Deborah, Teresa, Sandra. BBA, U. N. Fla., 1980, MS in Acctg., 1981. Enrolled agt., IRS. Enlisted USN, 1958, advanced through grades to sr. chief petty officer, 1972, ret., 1977; treas., contr. Fla. Bonded Pools, Inc., Jacksonville, 1977-89; pvt. practice Jacksonville Beach, Fla., 1982-89; pres. Profl. Computer Support Inc., Jacksonville Beach, 1988-90, Forrest & Co., Inc., Jacksonville, Fla., 1989—2003; with USN, 1958—77. Treas. Beaches United Citizens, Jacksonville Beach, 1982. Recipient Carl Burger Meml. Manuscript Nat. Assn. Accts., 1982-83. Mem. Beaches Bus. Assn., Nat. Assn. Tax Profls. Libertarian. Avocation: photography. Office: 1015 Atlantic Blvd 282 Atlantic Beach FL 32233 Office Phone: 904-246-1040. Personal E-mail: mailbox@allenforrest.com.

FORRESTER, J. OWEN, federal judge; b. Columbus, Ga., 1939; BS, Ga. Inst. Tech., 1961; LLB, Emory U., 1966. Bar: Ga. 1966. Assoc. Fisher & Phillips, Atlanta, 1967-69; asst. US atty. US Atty.'s Office (no. dist.) Ga., Atlanta, 1969-76; magistrate US Dist. Ct. (no. dist.) Ga., Atlanta, 1976-81, judge, 1981—2004, sr. judge, 2004—. Office: US Dist Ct 1921 US Courthouse 75 Spring St SW Atlanta GA 30303-3309

FORRESTER, MIKE, state legislator; b. Spartanburg, SC, Feb. 5, 1951; s. Paul Davis Forrester and Peggy Jarrell; m. Connie Carnes, July 13, 1969; children: Brian Michael, Melissa Bishop. BS, State U. NY. V.p. SC ops. Piedmont Natural Gas Co.; mem. Dist. 34 SC House of Reps, 2008—, mem. Agr., Natural Resources and Environ. Affairs Com. Comdr./sgt./maj. USAR. Republican. Office: Dist/Home Office 287 Creekridge Dr Spartanburg SC 29301 also: Capitol Office 402D Blatt Bldg Columbia SC 29201 Home Phone: 864-595-1137; Office Phone: 864-592-6204, 803-212-6792. E-mail: mikeforrester@schouse.org.

FORRY, ROBERT H., lawyer; b. Indpls., 1947; BA magna cum laude, Emory Univ., Atlanta, 1969; JD, Univ. Va., 1972. Bar: Ga. 1972. Assoc. Troutman Sanders LLP, Atlanta, 1972—76, ptnr., energy, govtl. law, 1977—, and sect. chief, pub. law. Named a Super Lawyer, Atlanta Mag., 2004—; named one of America's Leading Lawyers for Bus., Chambers USA, 2004—. Mem.: ABA, Fed. Energy Bar Assn., State Bar Ga. (past chmn., adminstrv. law sect.), Atlanta Bar Assn. Office: Troutman Sanders LLP 600 Peachtree St NE Ste 5200 Atlanta GA 30308-2216 Office Phone: 404-885-3142. Office Fax: 404-962-6559. Business E-Mail: robert.forry@troutmansanders.com.

FORSHEY, MICHAEL S., lawyer; b. Akron, Ohio, May 30, 1956; BA, Univ. So. Fla., 1977; JD magna cum laude, Univ. Houston, 1981. Bar: Tex. 1981, US Dist. Ct. (no., so., ea. & we. dist.) Tex., US Ct. Appeals (5th cir.). Ptnr., Litigation & Dispute Resolution, Bus. Law practices Patton Boggs LLP, Dallas, co-chair wide pro bono com. Contbr. articles to profl. jours. Mem.: Tex. Bar Assn., Dallas Bar Assn. (mem. Bus. Litigation & Sports & Entertainment Law sect., mem. pro bono activities com.), Order of the Barons. Office: Patton Boggs LLP 2000 Mckinney Ave STE 1700 Dallas TX 75201-2085 Office Phone: 214-758-3540. Office Fax: 214-758-1550. Business E-Mail: mforshey@pattonboggs.com.

FORSYTH, BEN RALPH, retired academic administrator, medical educator; b. NYC, Mar. 8, 1934; s. Martin and Eva Forsyth; m. Elizabeth Held, Aug. 19, 1962; children: Jennifer, Beverly, Jonathan. Attended, Cornell U., 1950-53; MD, NYU, 1957; ScD (hon.), UVM, 2009. Diplomate Am. Bd. Internal Medicine. Intern, then resident Yale Hosp., New Haven, 1957-60; postdoctoral fellow Harvard U. Med. Shc., Boston, 1960-61; rsch. assoc. NIH, Bethesda, Md., 1963-66; assoc. prof. med. microbiology and prof. medicine U. Vt., Burlington, 1966—90, prof. emeritus medicine, 1990; sr. exec. asst. to pres. Ariz. State U., Tempe, 1990—2002, pres., 2002—, prof. health adminstrn. and policy, 1992—2002, prof. emeritus health adminstrn. and policy, 2002—. Sr. cons. Univ. Health Ctr., Burlington, 1986-90; sr. adv. Ctr. Future Ariz., Phoenix, Ariz., 2003—. Contbr. articles to profl. jours. V.p., chmn. United Way Planning Com., Burlington, 1974—75, mem. ops. com., 1975—76, bd. dirs., officer, 1977—89; mem. New Eng. Bd. Higher Edn. Com., Burlington, 1985—89; chmn. U. Vt. China Project Adv. Bd., Burlington, 1989—90; trustee U. Vt., Burlington, 1996—2002. Lt. comdr. USN, 1962—63. Sinsheimer Found. faculty fellow, 1966-71. Fellow ACP, Infectious Diseases Soc. Am.; mem. Phi Beta Kappa, Alpha Omega Alpha. Avocations: hiking, photography, travel. E-mail: forsyth@asu.edu.

FORSYTHE, ROBERT ELLIOTT, economics professor; b. Pitts., Oct. 25, 1949; s. Robert Elliott and Dolores Jean (Davis) F.; m. Lynn Maureen Zollweg, June 17, 1970 (div. July 1978); m. Patricia Ann Hays, June 20, 1981; 1 child, Nathaniel Ryan. BS in Quantitative Bus. Analysis, Pa. State U., Univ. Pk., 1970; MS in Statistics, Carnegie-Mellon U., Pitts., 1972, MS in Economics, 1974, PhD in Economics, 1975. Ops. rsch. analyst PPG Industries Inc., Pitts., 1970-72; instr., fin., grad. sch. indsl. adminstrn. Carnegie-Mellon U., Pitts., 1975; asst. prof., bus. economics and mgmt., divsn. humanities and social scis. Calif. Inst. Tech., Pasadena, 1975-81; assoc. prof., economics U. Iowa, Coll. Bus. Adminstrn., Iowa City, 1981-86, prof. econ., 1986-90, chmn. dept. econ., 1990-94; Cedar Rapids prof. bus. Tipple Coll. Bus., U. Iowa, Iowa City, 1992-2000, Leonard A. Hadley Chair in Leadership, 2000—06, prof. emeritus, 2006—, sr. assoc. dean, 1994—2006; dean Coll. Bus. U. South Fla., Tampa, 2006—. Founder Iowa Polit. Stock Market; pres. Iowa Market Systems, Inc., 1993-2000. Assoc. editor Jour. Econ. Behavior and Orgn., 1996-97, Jour. Exptl. Econs., 1997-2004. Dir. Greater Tampa C. of C., 2008—, U. South Fla. Rsch. Found., 2008—, Jr. Achievement West Ctrl. Fla. Recipient State of Iowa Regents award for faculty excellence, 2002; Univ. faculty scholar U. Iowa, 1985-88. Mem. Econometric Soc., Am. Econ. Assn., Econ. Sci. Assn. (sect. head 1989-92, pres.-elect 1992-93, pres. 1993-95). Office: Univ South Fla Coll Bus 4202 Fowler Ave BSN 3403 Tampa FL 33620-5500 Office Phone: 813-974-3229. Business E-Mail: forsythe@usf.edu.

FORT, RANDALL MARTIN, aerospace defense company executive, former federal agency administrator; b. Richmond, Ind., July 4, 1956; Student, U. Cin., 1974-76; BA in Pub. Affairs with distinction, George Washington U., 1978. Various positions with Rep. Willis D. Gradison Jr. US House of Representatives, Cin. and Washington, 1976-80; rsch. asst. Office of Hon. Roo Watanabe M.P., Tokyo, 1980-81; asst. dir., dep. exec. dir. President's Fgn. Intelligence Advisory Bd., Washington, 1982-87; spl. asst. to sec. nat. security, dir. Office Intelligence Support US Dept. Treasury, Washington, 1987-89; dep. asst. sec. for functional analysis and rsch. US Dept. State, Washington, 1989-93; dir. spl. projects TRW, Inc., Washington, 1993-96; chief of staff to pres., COO then co-head global security Goldman, Sachs & Co., NYC, 1996—2006; asst. sec. for intelligence & rsch. US Dept. State, Washington, 2006—09; dir. programs security Raytheon Co., Arlington, 2009—. Luce scholar Henry Luce Found., 1980. Mem. Phi Beta Kappa. Republican. Methodist. Office: Raytheon Co 1100 N Wilson Blvd Arlington VA 22209

FORT, TOMLINSON, chemist, chemical engineering educator; b. Sumter, SC, Apr. 16, 1932; s. Tomlinson and Madeline A. Kean (Scott) F.; m. Martha Kirby, Oct. 13, 1956; children: Tomlinson, III, Frances Clare; m. Nancy H. Blackwelder, Dec. 19, 1998. BS in Chemistry, U. Ga., 1952; MS, U. Tenn., 1957, PhD in Phys. Chemistry, 1957; A.E. and F.A.Q. Stephens postdoctoral fellow, U. Sydney, Australia, 1957-58; cert., Inst. Ednl. Mgmt., Harvard U., 1978. Instr. surface chemistry U. Sydney, 1957—58; rsch. chemist, then sr. rsch. chemist and project leader duPont Co., 1958—65; mem. faculty Case Western Res. U., 1965—73, prof. chem. engring., dir. surfaces research lab., 1971—73; prof. chem. engring. and chemistry, head dept. chem. engring. Carnegie-Mellon U., 1973—80, adj. prof., 1980—83; prof. chemistry and chem. engring., provost U. Mo., Rolla, 1980—82; v.p. acad. affairs Calif. Poly. State U., San Luis Obispo, 1982—83, provost, 1983—86, prof. chemistry and materials sci., 1986—89; Centennial prof. chem. engring., prof. materials sci. Vanderbilt U., Nashville, 1989—2002, Centennial prof. chem. engring. emeritus, 2002—, chair dept. chem. engring., 1989—96. Summer vis. prof. Nat. U. Mex., 1973, U. Copenhagen, 1978, 80; pres. Frances Fort Brown Realty Co., Chattanooga, 1970-94. Author papers on surface and colloid sci. Mem. AAAS, Am. Chem. Soc., Am. Inst. Chem. Engrs., Internat. Assn. of Colloid and Interface Scientists, KP, Sigma Xi, Phi Beta Delta, Gamma Sigma Epsilon, Alpha Chi Sigma, Sigma Chi. Office: Vanderbilt U Dept Chem Engring PO Box 1604 Station B Nashville TN 37235 Home: 217 Lilac Cir Franklin TN 37064-4733 Office Phone: 615-343-6992, 615-591-9215. Personal E-mail: tomlinsonfort@llsouth.net. Business E-Mail: tomlinson.fort@vanderbilt.edu.

FORT, VINCENT D., state legislator; b. New Britain, Conn., May 28, 1956; m. Cheryl Fort; 3 children. BA, Ctrl. Conn. St. Univ., 1978; MA, Atlanta Univ., 1981; post. grad. rsch., Emory Univ. Asst. dir. Martin Luther King Papers Project; prof. Morehouse Coll., 1983—94; sr. asst. Atlanta City Coun., 1994—96; prof. Clark Atlanta Univ., 1996—97; mem. Dist. 39 Ga. State Senate, 1997—. Democrat. Baptist. Office: 305-B Legis Office Bldg Atlanta GA 30334 Home: PO Box 42967 Atlanta GA 30311-9005 Office Phone: 404-656-5091. Office Fax: 404-656-7266. Business E-Mail: vincent.fort@senate.ga.gov.

FORTE, GROVER BERRY, state legislator; With Am. Buildings, Eufaula, Ala.; commr. Dist. 3 Barbour County Commn., Ala.; mem. Dist. 84 Ala. House of Representatives, 2011—. Mem. Southeast Ala. Regional Planning and Devel. Commn., Barbour County Dem. Exec. Com., Tabernacle Bapt. Ch.; bd. mem. Barbour County Hosp. Democrat. Office: Ala House of Reps Rm 540-D 11 S Union St Clayton AL 36030 Office Phone: 334-242-7553. E-mail: berry.forte@alhouse.gov.

FORTE, JUDY, parks director; b. Phoenix City, Ala. m. Michael Forte; children: Michael Brandon, Justin. BS, Tuskegee U., 1980. With Nat. Park Svc., 1978—; park ranger Appomattox Court House Nat. Hist. Park, Va., Tuskegee Inst. Nat. Hist. Site, Ala., Chattahoochee River Nat. Recreation Area, 1980—89; acting supt. Carl Sandburg Home Nat. Hist. Site, NC, 1989—90; supt. Horseshoe Bend Nat. Mil. Park, Ala., 1990; regional chief ranger, acting regional dir. park ops. & edn. Nat. Park Svc. S.E. Regional Office, Atlanta; supt. Martin Luther King, Jr. Nat. Hist. Site, Atlanta, 2006—. Mem.: Internat. Assn. Chiefs of Police, Delta Sigma Theta. Office: Martin Luther King Jr Nat Hist Site 450 Auburn Ave NE Atlanta GA 30312 Office Phone: 404-331-5190. Office Fax: 404-730-3112.

FORTE, LINDA D., finance company executive; Grad. in Leadership Detroit; BS, Bowling Green State U.; MBA in Fin. & Acctg., U. Mich. Joined Comerica, Inc., 1974, various mgmt. positions, Small Business, US Banking, Loan Adminstrn. Groups, human resources and br. adminstrn., sr. v.p., bus. affairs. Bd. dirs. Detroit Symphony Orchestra, Henry Ford Health Sys. Found., New Detroit, Neighborhood Devel. Corp., Detroit, Womens Caring Program, City Year Detroit, Econ. Devel. Corp., Detroit; chmn. Local Devel. Fin. Authority, Michigan Womens Found. Named one of Southeast Michigan's Most Influential Women, Crain's Detroit Bus., 2007; recipient Banker of the Year award, 1990, Nat. Black MBA Assn. H. Naylor Fitzhugh award, 1996, Detroit's 100 Black Bus. Leaders, Crain's Detroit Bus., 1998, Aubrey W. Lee award, Urban Fin. Svcs. Coalition, 2005, John Copeland Cmty. Leadership Legacy award, YMCA, 2005. Office: Comerica Inc Comerica Bank Tower 1717 Main St Dallas TX 75201 Business E-Mail: lforte@comerica.com.

FORTE, STEPHEN MICHAEL, lawyer; b. Bklyn., Feb. 9, 1955; s. Gasper A. and Ellen (Fazio) F.; m. Susan Seavey, Apr. 17, 1982; children: Christina Marie, Stephen Michael Jr. BA, CUNY, Bklyn., 1977; JD, Emory U., 1980. Bar: Ga., NY, Fed. Dist. Cts., US Cir. Cts., US Supreme Ct. Assoc. Macey and Zusmann, Atlanta, 1980-84; ptnr. Smith, Gambrell & Russell, Atlanta, 1984—, mng. ptnr., chmn. of exec. com. Bd. advisors Nat. Paralegal Inst., Atlanta; faculty Nat. Inst. Trial Advocacy, Atlanta; lectr. in field. Contbr. articles to profl. jours. Bd. dirs. Homeowner Assn., Atlanta, 1984-87, Met. Atlanta C. of C., Atlanta Legal Aid Soc., Lawyers Found. Ga., Nat. Diocesan Attorneys Assn.; mem. Civic and Cmty. Assn., Atlanta, 1990-93, Emory U. Bd. Visitors. Named one of The Best Lawyers in America, Comml. Litig.; scholar, NY State Regents, 1973. Mem. State Bar of Ga., Atlanta Bar Assn., Phi Beta Kappa. Roman Catholic. Avocations: sports, classical music, travel. Office: Smith Gambrell & Russell LLP Promenade II Ste 3100 1230 Peachtree St Atlanta GA 30309 Office Phone: 404-815-3556. Office Fax: 404-685-6856. Business E-Mail: sforte@sgrlaw.com.

FORTEZA, ALEJANDRO MARIO, neurologist; b. Cordoba, Argentina, Aug. 25, 1960; married. MD, U. Nat. de Córdoba, Argentina, 1986. Med. dir. Jackson Health Sys., Miami, Fla., 2009—. Assoc. prof. neurology U. Miami Sch. Medicine, Fla., 2001—09. Neurologist Misioneros del Camino, Sumpango, Guatemala, 2007. Recipient America's Top Physicians award, Consumers' Rsch. Coun. America, 2009, Physicians Recognition award, Dade County Med. Assn., 2010, award, Inst. Nat. de Ciencias Neurologicas, 2012. Mem.: World Stroke Orgn., Am. Heart Assn., Am. Acad. Neurology. Office: Jackson Medical Group Specialty Physicians 3801 Biscayne Blvd Ste 230 Miami FL 33137 Office Fax: 305-573-6562; Home Fax: 305-585-1899. Business E-Mail: aforteza@med.miami.edu.*

FORTI, CARL, corporate communications specialist; Grad., George Washington U. Dir. polit. media ops. Wilson Grand Comm., Alexandria, Va.; various positions including dep. comm. dir., issue advocacy dir. and comm. dir. Nat. Rep. Congl. Com., Washington, 1999—2007; dep. campaign mgr., polit. dir. Mitt Romney Presdl. Campaign, 2008; exec. v.p. issue advocacy Freedom's Watch, Washington, 2008—09; co-founder, pres., CEO Black Rock Group, Alexandria, 2009—. Polit. dir. American Crossroads, Washington, 2010—. Republican. Office: Black Rock Group 66 Canal Ctr Plz Ste 555 Alexandria VA 22314 Office Phone: 703-535-3390. Office Fax: 703-535-3391. E-mail: cforti@blackrockgrp.com.

FORTIN, RAYMOND D., lawyer, bank executive; b. 1952; BA, U. Fla., Gainesville, 1974, JD, 1977. Bar: Ga. 1977. Pvt. practice atty., 1977-81; staff counsel The Citizens & So. Corp., 1981-89; mng. atty. SunTrust Banks, Inc., Atlanta, 1989-91, sr. v.p., gen. counsel, 1991—2004, corp. exec. v.p., gen. counsel, corp. sec., 2004—. Office: SunTrust Banks Inc PO Box 4418 Atlanta GA 30302-4418 Office Phone: 404-588-7165. Office Fax: 404-827-6173.*

FORTSON, KAY KIMBELL CARTER, museum and foundation administrator; m. Ben J. Fortson; children: Ben J. III, Lisa Burton, Karen Davis, Kimbell Wynne. BA, Univ. Tex., 1956. Pres. & chmn. bd. trustees Kimbell Art Found. & Museum, Fort Worth, Tex., 1975—. Trustee Tex. Christian Univ.; honorary trustee Modern Art Mus., Fort Worth, Tex. Office: Kimbell Art Foundation Suite 2240 301 Commerce St Ste 2300 Fort Worth TX 76102-4123*

FORTUNA, JULIAN ANTHONY, lawyer, certified public accountant; b. NYC, Feb. 19, 1956; s. Fred and Violet (Ruffini) F.; m. Nancy E. Cohen, May 6, 2006. BA, CUNY, 1977; JD, Rutgers U., Camden, NJ, 1980; LLM, Emory U., 1984. Bar: NY 1981, Ga. 2006; CPA, Ga., Ill. Tax atty. IRS, Atlanta, 1980-84; sr. tax mgr. Deloitte & Touche, 1984—95; v.p., gen. tax counsel InterContinental Hotels Grp., 1995—2007; ptnr. Duane Morris LLP, Atlanta, 2007—08, The Saylor Law Firm LLP, 2008—. Co-author: Changes in Accounting Methods, 1988; contbr. articles to prof. publs. Sect. leader, United Way, Atlanta, 1989. Recipient Am. Jurisprudence award; named one of Best Lawyers in America, 2011. Mem. ABA (tax sect.), Atlanta Bar Assn., NY Bar Assn., Ga. Bar Assn., Internat. Fiscal Assn., Orgn. for Internat. Investment. Roman Catholic. Avocations: photography, golf, tennis, mountain biking, hiking. Home: 1257 Becket DR NE Atlanta GA 30319-1503 Office: The Saylor Law Firm LLP 1175 Peachtree St NE Ste 1450 Atlanta GA 30361-6204 Office Phone: 404-201-2188. Office Fax: 404-892-2400. Business E-Mail: jafortuna@saylorlaw.com.

FOSDICK (BEEBE), CORA PRIFOLD, management consultant; b. San Francisco, Nov. 3, 1937; d. George and Beatrice (Ehni) Prifold; m. Ronald Beebe, Jan., 1959 (div.); m. Donald James Fosdick, Oct. 12, 1997. Student, Hollins Coll., Va., 1955-57, Am. U., DC, 1957-58; BA, U. Mich., Ann Arbor, 1959, MA, 1961; LHD (hon.), Southeastern U., DC, 1993. Adminstrv. asst. Am. Polit. Sci. Assn., 1962-64; rsch. assoc. Inst. Comparative Studies of Polit. Systems, Washington, 1963-65; program planning and evaluation specialist U.S. Office Edn., Washington, 1965-68, planning coord., 1968-73, dir. planning and budget div., 1973-80; prin. dep. asst. sec. for elem. and sec. edn. Dept. Edn., Washington, 1980-81; asst. sec. adminstrn. U.S. Treasury Dept., Washington, 1981-84; dir. office of policy, budget and program mgmt. OSWER, EPA, Washington, 1984-86; dir. office of planning, budget and evaluation Dept. Commerce, Washington, 1986-87; commerce & justice br. chief Office of Mgmt. and Budget, 1987-94, advisor to assoc. dir. gen. govt. and fin., 1994; exec. dir. adminstrn., chief fin. officer Office of Thrift Supervision, Washington, 1994-99; v.p. Jefferson Consulting Group, Washington, 1999—2002; sr. assoc. Kelly, Amdersen & Assocs., Inc., Alexandria, Va., 2002—. Bd. dirs. Treasury Hist. Assn., 2005—. Recipient HEW Superior Svc. award, Presdl. Rank award, 1989; Inst. World Affairs fellow, 1956, Am. Edn. Abroad former fellow, 1960. Fellow: Nat. Acad. Pub. Adminstrn.

(vice chair 2002—03, former bd. mem. adult com.); mem.: Nat. Press Club, Exec. Women in Govt. Home: 4390 King St Apt 1401 Alexandria VA 22302-1551 Office Phone: 571-344-8818, 703-518-8828. Personal E-mail: corabeebe@aol.com.

FOSHEE, DOUGLAS L., gas industry executive; BBA, SW Tex. State U., 1982; MBA, Rice U., 1992; grad., So. Meth. U. Active comml. banking; various positions in fin. and new bus. ventures ARCO Internat. Oil and Gas Co.; COO, CEO Torch Energy Advisors, Inc., 1993—97; chmn., CEO, pres. Nuevo Energy Co.; CFO Halliburton Co., 2001, exec. v.p., COO, 2003; pres., CEO El Paso Corp., Houston, 2003—09, chmn., pres., CEO, 2009—. Pres., bd. mem. Small Steps Nurturing Ctr.; bd. mem. Goodwill Industries, Houston, Tex. Bus. Hall of Fame Found.; mem. coun. of overseers Jones Grad. Sch. Adminstrn., Rice U. Mem.: Houston Prodrs. Forum, Ind. Petroleum Assn. Am. Office: El Paso Corp PO Box 2511 1001 Louisiana St Houston TX 77252-2511

FOSSUM, JERRY GEORGE, electrical engineering educator; b. Phoenix, July 18, 1943; s. George Clayton and Lillian Edith (McNeilis) F.; m. Mary Ellen; children: Kerry Ray, Kelly Lynn. AA, Phoenix Coll., 1963; BSEE, U. Ariz., 1966, MS, 1969, PhD, 1971. Mem. tech. staff Sandia Labs., Albuquerque, 1971-78; assoc. prof. elec. engring. U. Fla., Gainesville, 1978-80, prof., 1980—2006, disting. prof., 2006—, disting. prof. emeritus, 2009—; tech. adv. bd. Astrowatt Inc., 2008—; bd. chmn. Applied Novel Devices Inc., 2007—. Cons. Burr-Brown Rsch. Corp., Tucson, 1970-71, Jet Propulsion Lab., Pasadena, Calif., 1979, Harris Corp., Melbourne, Fla., 1984, Tex. Instruments, Inc., Dallas, 1988-89, 94-96, Ibis Tech. Corp., Danvers, Mass., 1995, Meta-Software, Campbell, Calif., 1995-96, Dynamics Rsch. Corp., San Diego, 1996-02; mem. adv. com. Semiconductor Rsch. Corp., 1991-95; mem. exec. com. IEEE SOI Conf., 1994-97. Author (text book) Fundamentals of Ultra-Thin-Body MOSFETs and FinFETs; contbr. articles to profl. jours.; assoc. editor: Solid-State Electronics, 1979—, IEEE Trans. Computer-Aided Design, 1988-91; patentee in field. Recipient Outstanding Rsch. award, Am. Soc. Engring. Edn., 1979. Fellow: IEEE (life Best Paper award SOI Conf. 1992, J.J. Ebers award Electron Devices Soc. 2004). Office: U Fla Dept Elec and Computer Engr Gainesville FL 32611-6130 Office Phone: 352-392-4921. Business E-Mail: fossum@tec.ufl.edu.

FOSSUM, MICHAEL E., astronaut; b. Sioux Falls, SD, Dec. 19, 1957; s. Merlyn E. and Patricia A. Fossum; m. Melanie J. London; 4 children. BS in Mech. Engring., Tex. A&M U., 1980; MS in Sys. Engring., Air Force Inst. Tech., 1981; disting. grad., USAF Test Pilot Sch., 1985; MS in Phys. (Space) Sci., U. Houston, Clear Lake, Tex., 1997. Commd. USAF, 1980, flight test engr. F-16 test squadron Edwards AFB, Calif., 1985—89, flight test mgr. detachment 3 Air Force Flight Test Ctr., 1989—92; resigned, 1992; sys. engr. NASA, 1993, rep. Flight Crew Ops. Directorate on Internat. Space Sta. redesign, 1993—96, tech. asst. space shuttle, 1996—97, flight test engr. X-38, 1997—98; astronaut, mission specialist candidate NASA, Johnson Space Ctr., Houston, 1998—. Astronaut office lead Space Station flight software development; capsule communicator (CAPCOM) in Mission Control; lead CAPCOM Space Station Expedition-6; crew mem. STS-121 (Discovery), a return-to-flight test mission and assembly flight to the Internat. Space Station, 2006; lead spacewalker, mission specialist STS-124 Mission (Discovery), mission to Internat. Space Station to launch components to complete Japanese Kibo Lab, 2008; crew mem. Internat. Space Station Expedition 28/29 (Soyuz TMA-02M), 2011. Col. USAF Reserves, 1992—. Decorated Meritorious Svc. medal with two oak leaf clusters USAF, Squadron Comdr. Corps of Cadets; named Disting. Mil. Grad., Tex. A&M U. Achievements include logging over 1000 hours in 34 different aircraft. Avocations: jogging, fishing, backpacking, motorcycling. Office: Astronaut Office/CB NASA Lyndon B Johnson Space Ctr 2101 NASA Pkwy Houston TX 77058

FOSTER, ARIAN, professional football player; b. Albuquerque, Aug. 24, 1986; s. Carl Foster and Bernadette Sizemore. B, U. Tenn., Knoxville. Running back Houston Texans, 2009—. Named 1st Team NFL All-Pro, AP, 2010; named to Am. Football Conf. Pro Bowl Team, NFL, 2010—12. Achievements include ledaing the NFL in: rushing yards, rushing touchdowns, 2010; rushing attempts, 2012. Office: Houston Texans Two Reliant Pk Houston TX 77054*

FOSTER, BILL, lawyer, former mayor, St. Petersburg, Florida; s. David and Carol Foster; m. Wendy Holt Foster; children: Christine, Will. BS in Pub. Adminstrn., Samford U., 1985, JD, 1988. Ptnr. Foster and Foster, St. Petersburg, Fla., 1988—; city councilman St. Petersburg City Coun., 1998, 2003, chmn., 2004, 2006; mayor City of St. Petersburg, 2009—14; atty. Graves Injury Law Group, Vero Beach, Fla., 2014—. Mem. Pinellas County Tourist Devel. Coun., Pinellas Planning Coun., Pinellas County Annexation Task Force, Pinellas Assembly, Sunken Gardens Task Force, Neighborhood Svcs. Equities Com., Pub. Art Commn., Internat. Rels. Commn., Code Compliance Com., Cmty. Focus Group on Downtown Devel., Fla. Internat. Mus., Pinellas County Vision 2010 Task Force, St. Petersburg C. of C.; mem. cmty. adv. bd. Jr. League St. Petersburg. Mem.: NAACP, Shore Acres Civic Assn. Office: Graves Injury Law Group 3885 20th St Vero Beach FL 32960*

FOSTER, CHARLES CRAWFORD, lawyer, educator; b. Galveston, Tex., Aug. 1, 1941; s. Louie Brown and Helen (Hall) F.; m. Marta Brito, Sept. 7, 1967 (div. Apr. 1986); children: John, Ruth; m. Lily Chen, Jan. 7, 1989; children: Zachary, Anthony. AA, Del Mar Jr. Coll., 1961; BA, U. Tex., 1963, JD, 1967. Bar: Tex. 1967, N.Y. 1969. Assoc. Reid & Priest, NYC, 1967-69, Butler & Binion, Houston, 1969-73; ptnr. Tindall & Foster, Houston, 1973—2008, Foster Quan LLP, Houston, 2009—. Hon. consul gen. Kingdom of Thailand, 1996—; adj. prof. immigration law U. Houston, 1985-89; bd. dirs. Greater Houston Partnership, 1997-, chmn. econ. devel. adv. bd., chmn., 2000 World Trade Adv. Bd., 1997; chmn. Immigration Task Force, 2006-, Asia Soc.-Tex., bd. trustees, 1990—; bd. dirs. Houston World Affairs Coun., 1990; bd. mem. Inst. Internat. Edn., Houston Ballet Found., Neighborhood Ctr. Interfaith Ministry, Mexican Inst., chmn. Mayoral Adv. Bd. for Internat. Affairs and Devel./Asia, 2012-13; pres. Houston Forum, 2002-04; co-chmn. George Bush Monument Project, 2000-04; pres. The Houston Club, 2000; chmn. Am. Immigration Reform, 2008-, Houston Com. Foreign Rels., 2012-13; co-chmn. James A. Baker Monument Adv. Com., 2009-. Contbr. articles to profl. jours.; portrayed in film, Mao's last Dancer, 2010. Chmn. immigration reform Gov.'s Task Force Tex., 1984—87, chmn., 2008—; mem. Bush-Cheney Transition Adv. Com., 2000—01. Commnd. admiral Texan Navy, 2003. Decorated knight comdr. Order of the Crown (Thailand), Exalted Order of White Elephant (Thailand); Rotary Internat. fellow U. Concepción, Chile, 1964; recipient Houston Internat. Svc. award Houston Jaycees, 1996, Disting. Friend of China award U.S. China Friendship Found., 2000, Human Relations award Am. Jewish Com., 2007; honoree Am. Immigration Law Found., 1998' commd. adm. Tex. Navy, Gov. Rick Perry, 2003, Svc. to Humanity award, Rotary Found., 2006; Wall of Honor Alumni award Del Mar Coll., 2006, Leon Jaworski award Hon. Bar Assn. Aux., 2013. Mem. ABA (chmn. immigration com. internat. law and practice sect. 1982-90, chmn. coordinating com. on immigration and law 1987-89, fgn. rels. com. 2000—), Am. Immigration Lawyers Assn. (pres. 1981-82, Outstanding Svc. award 1985), Tex. Bar Assn. (chmn. com. law on immigration and nationality 1984-86), Tex. Bd. Legal Specialization (chmn. immigration adv. commn. 1979—), Houston Bar Assn., Asia Soc. (trustee 1992—, chmn. Houston Ctr. 1992—). Methodist. Avocations: mountain climbing, photography, travel. Home: 17 Courtlandt Pl Houston TX 77006-4013 Office: Foster Quan LLP 600 Travis St Ste 2000 Houston TX 77006-4013 Office Phone: 713-335-3904. Business E-Mail: cfoster@fosterquan.com.

FOSTER, DALE WARREN, retired political science professor, real estate agent, accountant, management consultant; s. William Henry and Maysie Blanche (Hembree) F. BBA, Tex. A&M U., 1972, MA, 1979, Cert. in Profl. Teaching, 1987; BS, U. Houston, 1981, MEd, 1983; AAS, Houston C.C. Sys., 1982. Cert. in property mgmt. Dept. mgr. J.C. Penney Co., Bryan, 1973-74; shopper advt. mgr. Harte-Hanks Newspapers/Daily Eagle, Bryan, 1975-76; bus. mgr., contr. S.M. Hardee Enterprises, College Station, Tex., 1976-78; ops. mgr. Western Food Svcs., Inc., Pasadena, Tex., 1978-80; internal auditor Hermann Hosp., Houston, 1980-82; high sch. tchr. Cypress-Fairbanks Independent Sch. Dist., Houston, 1983-84; alternative sch. tchr. Alief Independent Sch. Dist., Houston, 1984-88; gov. prof. Houston C.C. System, 1980—2010, chmn. govt. dept. co-op program, 1992—2008; lead instr. Houston C.C. Sys., 1993—2002; supr. student tchr. U. Houston, 1989-90; assoc. chair govt. econ crij divsn., 2003—08; ret., 2010. Adj. instr. North Harris County Coll., Houston, 1983-96; fin. cons. Pro-Trac Econ. Planning Adv. Bd., Denver, 1985-86; Presdl. Scholars lectr. Minority Students Honors Program, Houston, 1986-89; coord. legis. practicum Harris County Congl. Internship Program, 1988—; exch. tchr., The Netherlands, 1992. Co-editor textbook supplement, curriculum guide, departmental political reader; author classroom instructional project. Mem. adv. com. Hermann Affiliated Fed. Credit Union, Houston, 1980-82; mem. fin. coun. Harris County Dem. Com., 1991-93; mem. dean's coun. U. Houston, 1992-96; trustee, treas. Wilmington-Barnard Found., 1992—. Named Tchr. of Yr., Cy.-Fair H.S., 1984, Alief Individualized Study Ctr., 1987, Master Tchr. Nat. Leadership Inst. U. Tex., Austin, 1991, host tchr. Washington Week Intern Program, 1995; recipient Adj. Teaching and Comty. Svc. award North Harris County Coll. Dist., 1990, Teaching Excellence medal Nat. Inst. Staff and Orgn. Devel., 1991, 98, Chancellor's medal Houston CC Sys., 2004; Fulbright scholar, 1992, 98; Robert A. Taft fellow L.B.J. Sch. Pub. Affairs, 1995, Fulbright-Hays fellowship U.S. Dept. Edn., 1998. Fellow Am. Bd. Master Educators; mem. Tex. Jr. Coll. Tchrs. Assn., Tex. Coun. Social Studies, Inst. Mgmt. Accts., Am. Fin. Assn., Fulbright Assn., Houston C.C. Sys. Faculty Assn. (treas. 1997-2000, v.p. 2000-01, pres.-elect 2001-02, pres. 2002-03, Outstanding Tchr. award 1991, Tchr. of Yr. 1997), Phi Theta Kappa, Alpha Phi Omega, Kappa Delta Pi. Baptist. Avocations: travel, reading, bowling, water sports, outdoor activities. Personal E-mail: corps1972@yahoo.com.

FOSTER, JAYNE LYNN ANKRUM, community health nurse; b. Reed City, Mich., Oct. 12, 1944; d. Quinten Wayne and Marshia Agetha (Crum) Ankrum; m. James Anthony Lana, May 4, 1963 (div. Jan. 1975); children: Linda, Michele, Julie; m. Ronald Francis Ayres, Apr. 16, 1977 (div. Sept. 1997); m. Thomas Eugene Foster, Dec. 12, 2004. ADN, Manatee C.C., Bradenton, Fla., 1975. RN Fla., Ga. Staff nurse med.-surg., cardiac, oncology and float team Sarasota (Fla.) Meml. Hosp., 1975—77; nursing supr. Upjohn Healthcare Svcs., Sarasota, 1981—85; staff nurse Devereux Found., Kennesaw, Ga., 1986—89; staff nurse, supr. Vis. Nurse Health Sys., Metro, Atlanta, 1989—97; health clinic nurse Equifax, Atlanta, 1996—97; entertainer JPM Prodn. Co., 1996—97; adv. bd. Waldrop Personal Care, Inc., 1998—2002. Mem. adv. subcom. Waldrop Personal Care, Inc., 1998—2002. Vol. ARC, M.U.S.T., Ministries Health Clinic for Homeless, Marietta, Ga., Summer Olympic Games, Atlanta, 1996; Vol. East Pasco Med. Ctr., Zephyrhills, Fla., 2003; vol. Marietta Mus. History Kennesaw House Marietta, Ga., 2011—. Mem. Am. Legion (hon.), Fla. Nurses Assn. (hon.), Beta Sigma Phi. Achievements include invention of the syringe filling monitor. Home: 4511 Meadow Green Ln NW Acworth GA 30101-4017

FOSTER, JOHN DALE, US marshal; b. 1964; married; 2 children. AA in Polit. Sci., Marshall U., 1986; AA in Fire Sci., CC of the Air Force, 1989; BA, Glenville State Coll., 1991. Trooper W.Va. State Police, Summersville, 1985—90; dep. US marshal US Marshals Svc., US Dept. Justice, Charleston, 1990, judicial security inspector, 2007—10, US marshal (so. dist.) W.Va., 2010—. Served with W.Va. Air Nat. Guard, 1980—2000. Office: US Marshals Service 300 Virginia St E, Ste 3602 Charleston WV 25301 Office Phone: 304-347-5136.

FOSTER, MARTHA TYAHLA, pre-school administrator; b. Coaldale, Pa., Apr. 22, 1955; d. Stephen and Frances (Solomon) Tyahla; m. David Marion Foster, Jan. 3, 1981. BA with distinction, U. Va., 1977, MEd, EdS, U. Va., 1981. Legis. asst. US House of Representatives, Washington, 1977-79; asst. dean summer session U. Va., Charlottesville, 1981; program cons. campus activities U. Houston, 1981; coord. student affairs Capitol Inst. Tech., Kensington, Md., 1982-83, asst. dean students Laurel, Md., 1983-84, assoc. dean students, 1984-86, dean students, 1986-87; dir. Resurrection Luth. Presch., 1997—. Bd. dirs. Curry Sch. Edn. Found. U. Va., 1987-90. Mem. Arlington County Commn. on Status of Women, 1985—88; coun. mem.-at-large Arlington United Way, 1995—98; pres. PTA Arlington Traditional Sch., 1997—98, treas., 1994—95; troop leader Girl Scouts, 1999—2008; chair advancement Boy Scouts Am., Troop 167, 2001—06; bd. dirs. Arlington Arts Coun., 2005—, pres., 2008—; chmn. Christian edn. Christ Meth. Ch., 1994—97. Named Woman of Yr., Bus. and Profl. Women's Club, Vienna, Va., 1986. Mem. Order Eastern Star (worthy matron 1988-89, trustee 1993-96). Methodist.

FOSTER, PAUL L., oil industry executive; BBA, Baylor Univ., 1979. CPA Ariz., 1986. Acctg. supr. So. Union Refining Co.; oil & gas cons. KPMG Peat Marwick; contr. Pride Refining Co.; gen. mgr. mktg. El Paso Refinery; v.p., gen. mgr. Border Refining Co., 1993—97; pres., CEO WRC Refining Co., 1997—2000, Western Refining Co., El Paso, Tex., 2000—09, chmn., CEO, 2009—10; exec. chmn. Western Refining, Inc., El Paso, Tex., 2010—. Bd. dir. Bank of the West. Chmn. El Paso Regional Econ. Develop. Corp., El Paso Am. Red Cross; mem. Tex. Higher Edn. Coord. Bd.; bd. mem. Am. Heart Assn. El Paso, Tex. Econ. Develop. Corp., El Paso Cmty. Found., Sun Bowl Assn.; chmn. Young Presidents Org.; chmn. govt. affairs com. El Paso Bus. Leadership Council; mem. exec. com. El Paso C. of C.; mem. bus. adv. council Univ. Tex., El Paso. Mem.: We. States Petroleum Assn., We. Petroleum Marketers Assn., Nat. Petroleum Refiners' Assn., Am. Inst. CPAs, Ariz. Soc. CPAs, Rep. Senatorial Inner Circle (life), El Paso Downtown Rotary Club. Office: Western Refining Co 6500 Trowbridge Dr El Paso TX 79905

FOSTER, ROBERT WATSON, SR., law educator; b. Charleston, SC, Sept. 24, 1926; s. Thomas Russell and Pamela (Watson) F.; m. Marjorie Ann O'Neil, May 22, 1953; children: Elizabeth, Marjorie, Robert, Mary, Patrick, Pamela. BS, U.S. Mcht. Marine Acad., 1948; LLB, U. SC, 1950; LL.M., Duke U., 1951. Bar: S.C. 1950, U.S. Ct. Mil. Appeals 1952, U.S. Supreme Ct. 1956. From instr. to prof. law U. Louisville, 1951-62; prof. law U. S.C., Columbia, 1962-91, Am. Coll. Trial Lawyers prof., 1979-82, Strom Thurmond prof., chair, 1982-91, disting. prof., dean emeritus, 1991—, dean, 1970-76. Inst. Advanced Legal Studies U. London, 1976-77; fellow Worcester Coll., Oxford U., Eng.; Disting. vis. prof. N.Y. Law Sch., 1977-78; mem. labor panel Fed. Mediation and Conciliation Svc., Am. Arbitration Assn., Nat. Acad. Arbitrators (com. on profl. responsibility and grievances, com. on legislation); mem. com. bankruptcy rules Jud. Conf. U.S., 1978-88; commr. Nat. Conf. Commrs. on Uniform State Laws, Am. Law Inst.; mem. S.C. Jud. Coun., 1970-76. Contbr. articles to profl. jours. With U.S. Mcht. Marine, 1944-48; with USN, 1952-54; capt. Res. ret. Ford Found. fellow Yale Sch. Law, 1959-60; recipient Whitney North Seymour award Am. Arbitration Assn., 1979; Order of the Palmetto, 1991. Mem. ABA, SC Bar (bd. gov. 1974-76), Assn. Am. Law Schs. (com. on accreditation, chmn. SE conf.), AAUP (pres. U. SC chpt. 1966-67), Phi Delta Phi. Clubs: Kosmos, Forest Lake Country, Summit, Carolina Yacht. Home: 1509 Milford Rd Columbia SC 29206-4636 Personal E-mail: foster1509@gmail.com.

FOSTER, SERRIN MARIE, non-profit organization executive; b. Washington, Sept. 17; d. William A. and Donna R. (Hayden) F. BA in Pub. Rels., Old Dominion U., 1977. Freelance pub. rels. specialist, Springfield, Va., 1978-82; program mgr., regional rep. St. Jude Children's Rsch. Hosp., Arlington, Va., 1982-89; dir. devel. Nat. Alliance for Mentally Ill., Washington, 1989-94; exec. dir. Feminists for Life of Am., Washington, 1994-99, pres., 1999—. Mem. adv. bd. Ivy League Coalition for Life, Harvard U., 1997—, Am. Collegians for Life, Washington, 1998—. Author: (books) Pro-Women Answers to Pro-Choice Questions, 2003, Great Speeches in History, 2004—; contbr. Women's Rights, Boston Globe, Cost of Choice; editor-in-chief, contbr. The Am. Feminist mag., 1994—. Susan B. Anthony List, Alexandria, 1997—. Mem. Alpha Phi Women's Found. Avocations: gardening, travel, painting. Office: Feminists Life America PO Box 320667 Alexandria VA 22320

FOSTER, WILLIAM EDWIN (BILL FOSTER), retired men's college basketball coach; b. Ridley Park, Pa., Aug. 19, 1929; s. Howard M. and Viola Jane (Beaston) F.; m. Shirley Ann Junkin, June 17, 1957; children: Vicki R. (dec.), Debra Jo, Julia Ann, Mary K. BS, Elizabethtown Coll., 1954; MEd, Temple U., 1957. Coach, tchr. Chichester (Pa.) High Sch., 1954-57, Abington (Pa.) High Sch., 1957-60; coach, instr. Bloomsburg (Pa.) State Coll., 1960-63; head basketball coach Rutgers U., New Brunswick, NJ, 1963-71, U. Utah, Salt Lake City, 1971-74; head basketball coach, asst. athletic dir. Duke U., Durham, NC, 1974-80, U. S.C., Columbia, 1980-86; head basketball coach, interim athletic dir. Northwestern U., Evanston, Ill., 1986-93, athletic dir., 1993; assoc. commr. S.W. Conf., Dallas, 1993-96; cons. Com. of Big 12 Conf. for basketball, 1996-99; spl. asst. to the commr. Western Athletic Conf., 1999—2005. Chmn. of the bd. Naismith Meml. Basketball Hall of Fame, 1997-98, bd. trustees; pres. Nat. Sports Video Seminars, BF Sports Ltd. Author: (books) Building-Improving Fan Interest in Sports, Filling Seats=Dollars, Earning Dollars For Your Team/Organization/Club By Direct Mail, Upward Mobility In Coaching Basketball. Life trustee Naismith Meml. Basketball Hall of Fame, Springfield, Mass., 2010-. Served with USAF, 1951-52. Named Nat. Coach of Yr., Sporting News Playboy Mag., 1978, S.C. Coach of Yr., 1981, Nat. Invitation Tournament's Man of Yr., Met. Coaches Assn., 2003; named to Sports Hall Fame Elizabethtown Coll., Pa., Rutgers. U., Hall Fame Delaware County (Pa.), Hall Fame Interboro H.S., 2004, Glen-Nor H.S., 2004, NJ Sportwriters Hall of Fame, 2009. Mem. Nat. Assn. Basketball Coaches (past pres., named Co-Coach of Yr. 1978, Sporting News Basketball Coach of Yr., 1978, named to Del. Legends Basketball Hall of Fame, 2010), Met. Intercollegiate Basketball Assn. (elected 2003, Man-of-Yr. Nat. Invitation Tournament, Northwestern U. Legends award 1991). Office: PO Box 635 Galveston TX 77553 Personal E-mail: bfosterbb@aol.com.

FOTTLER, MYRON DAVID, health services educator; b. Boston, Sept. 5, 1939; s. Myron Dustin and Anna Eileen Fottler; m. Carol Ann Fottler, Aug. 11, 1972. BS, Northeastern U., 1962; MBA, Boston U., 1963; PhD, Columbia U., 1970. Asst. prof. SUNY, Buffalo, 1967—75; from assoc. prof. to prof. U. Ala., Tuscaloosa, 1976—83, prof., PhD program dir. Birmingham, 1983—99; prof., program dir. U. Ctrl. Fla., Orlando, 1999—. Cons. numerous legal firms and corps. Author 21 books; contbr. over 40 chpts. to books and over 140 articles to profl. jours. Recipient Hayhew award, Am. Coll. Health Care Execs., 1997, Outstanding Svc. award, Acad. Mgmt.-Healthcare Mgmt. Divsn., 1999, Faculty Pub. of Yr., Am. Acad. Med. Adminstrs., 2001. Episcopalian. Avocation: tennis. Office: Univ Ctrl Fla Coll Health and Pub Affairs 210A HPA2 Orlando FL 32816-0001 Home: 4670 Links Village Dr Unit A 502 Ponce Inlet FL 32127-2008 Home Phone: 386-788-9924; Office Phone: 407-823-5531.

FOULKE, EDWIN GERHART, JR., lawyer, former federal agency administrator; b. Perkasie, Pa., Oct. 30, 1952; s. Edwin G. and Mary Claire (Keller) F. BA, N.C. State U., 1974; JD, Loyola U., New Orleans, 1978; LLM, Georgetown U., 1993. Bar: S.C. 1979, U.S. Dist. Ct. S.C. 1979, U.S. Ct. Appeals (4th cir.) 1979, Ga. 1986, U.S. Ct. Appeals (11th cir.) 1986, D.C. 1989, U.S. Ct. Appeals (D.C. cir.) 1989, U.S. Supreme Ct. 1990, N.C. 1997. Assoc. Thompson, Mann & Hutson, Greenville, SC, 1978-83, Rainey, Britton, Gibbes & Clarkson, Greenville, 1983-85; ptnr. Constangy, Brooks & Smith, Columbia, SC, 1985-90; chmn. Occupational Safety & Health Adminstrn. (OSHA) Rev. Commn., Washington, 1990—94; ptnr. Jackson Lewis LLP, Greenville, SC, 1995—2006; asst. sec. Occupational Safety & Health Adminstrn. (OSHA) US Dept. Labor, Washington, 2006—08; ptnr. Fisher & Phillips LLP, Atlanta, 2008—. Instr. St. Mary's Dominican Coll., New Orleans, 1977-78. Field rep. Reagan/Bush Campaign, Columbia, 1980, S.C. state coord., 1984; sec., treas. Employment Labor Law Sect., Columbia, 1981-82. Named one of The 50 Most Influential EHS Leaders, Occupational Hazards mag., 2008. Mem. ABA, S.C. Bar Assn., Ga. Bar Assn., Greenville County Bar Assn. (chmn. pub. rels. com. 1984-85), SAR, Rotary. Roman Catholic. Avocations: swimming, tennis, skiing, golf. Office: Fisher & Phillips LLP 1075 Peachtree St NE Ste 3500 Atlanta GA 30309 Office Phone: 404-240-4273, 404-231-1400. Office Fax: 404-240-4249. Business E-Mail: efoulke@laborlawyers.com.

FOUNTAIN, JONATHAN EDWIN, family practice physician, educator; MD, U. Fla., 1984. Diplomate American Bd. Family Practice, lic. Fla., 1987. Resident family medicine Duke Watts Family Medicine, Durham, NC, 1984—87; assoc. prof. family medicine Univ. of Fla. Coll. of Medicine; assoc. prof. Fla. State Univ. Sch. of Medicine; hosp. affiliations include Santa Rosa Med. Ctr., Baptist Hosp. Bd. dirs. Pregnancy Resource Ctr. Milton. Office: 6285 Angie Dr Milton FL 32570-5442 Office Phone: 850-626-0400.

FOUNTAIN, LINDA KATHLEEN, health science association executive; b. Fowler, Kans., Apr. 30, 1954; d. Ralph Edward and Ruth Evelyn (Cornelson) Young; m. Andre Fountain. BS in Nursing, Cen. State U., Edmond, Okla., 1976. RN, Okla. Staff nurse med./surg. and coronary care unit Presbyn. Hosp., Oklahoma City, 1976-79; mgr. nursing Hillcrest Osteo. Hosp., Oklahoma City, 1979-80; staff nurse, mgr. Oklahoma U. Teaching Hosp., Oklahoma City, 1981-82; pres. New Life Programs, Oklahoma City, 1981-88, Nursing Entrepreneurs, Ltd., Oklahoma City, 1988—; mgr. Internat. Health Supply, Oklahoma City, 1988—. Coord. lactation cons. program State of Okla.,

1981-98, new life car seat rental program at various hosps., 1983-92, also speaker Success Co., Oklahoma City, 1984—; owner Rainbows Overhead Graphic Media, Oklahoma City, 1984-91; speaker in field. Founder Praxis Coll., Oklahoma City, 1988. Named Mentor of Yr., Okla. Metroplex Childbirth Network, Oklahoma City, 1984; honored for vol. work with families and rescue after Oklahoma City bombing, U.S. Dept. Justice, 1995. Mem. Am. Nurses Assn., Internat. Lactation Cons. Assn., Internat. Platform Assn., Bodyworkers and Wellness Therapies Assn. Avocations: gemology, travel. Office Phone: 405-879-0224. Business E-Mail: Lfountain@praxiscollege.com.

FOUNTAIN, ROBERT ROY, JR., retired engineering company executive, farmer, military officer; b. Norfolk, Va., Jan. 25, 1932; s. Robert Roy and Hilda (Burton) F.; m. Elizabeth Whitmarsh Bean, June 4, 1955; children: Robert, Dorothy, Sally, Edwin. Student, U. Rochester, 1950-51; BS Engring. with distinction, U.S. Naval Acad., 1955. Commd. ensign U.S. Navy, 1955, advanced through grades to rear adm., 1980; nuclear engr. serving in destroyers, cruisers, and nuclear submarines; comdg. officer U.S.S. Sea Devil, 1970-74; comdr. Submarine Devel. Squadron 12, New London, Conn., 1976-78; comdr. U.S. Naval Forces Marianas, comdr. U.S. Naval Base Guam comdr. in chief Pacific rep. Guam and Trust Ter. Pacific Islands, 1979-81; dep. chief Naval Sea Sys. Command, ASW and Undersea Warfare Sys., Navy Dept., Washington, 1981-85; ret., 1985; dir. Offshore Sys. Marine Sys. divsn. Honeywell, Seattle, 1986-88; v.p. Honeywell Advanced Marine Sys. Operation, Mpls., 1988, San Diego, 1989, Arlington, Va., 1990-91; dir. tech. plans & resources Alliant Techsystems Inc., Arlington, Va., 1991-92; mem. Va. Bd. CC, 2011—. Presdl. elector, 1996; mem. Va. Nat. Def. Indsl. Authority, 2005—12, chmn., 2011—12. Decorated Legion of Merit (3), Def. Superior Service medal, Meritorious Service medal (2), Navy Commendation medal. Mem.: SAR, No. Neck Hist. Soc. (pres. 2004—05), Naval Acad. Alumni Assn., Mil. Officers Assn., Naval Submarine League. Home: Stillwater 4750 Zacata Rd Montross VA 22520-3510

FOUST, ROBERT SCHMERTZ, political science professor; b. New Holland, Pa., Jan. 20, 1941; s. Wilson Arbogast and Elizabeth (Schmertz) F. BA in Polit. Sci., Upsala Coll., 1964; MA in Internat. Rels., Lehigh U., Bethlehem, Pa., 1971. Asst. dir. admissions Upsala Coll., East Orange, NJ, 1965-69; legis. asst. Office of Senator Claiborne Pell, Washington, 1970-89; cons. Indochinese Cmty. Ctr., Washington, 1990-91; sr. policy adv. Office of Senator Kent Conrad, Washington, 1991—2005; ret.; assoc. Professorial Lecturer in Legislative Affairs George Washington U., Washington, 2006—. Named Outstanding Young Men of Am., Jaycees, 1973; recipient commendations USCG, U.S. Dept. Vets. Affairs, Disabled Am. Vets., Career Resources Network Assn., Nat. Assn. Federally Impacted Schs., Nat. Head Start Assn. Mem.: Global Cmty. Svc. Found. (bd. advisor). Office: GW 805 21st St NW Washington DC 20052 Personal E-mail: jurongsq@aol.com.

FOUTCH, RANDY A., oil industry executive; b. 1951; BS in Geology, U. Tex.; MS in Petroleum Engring., U. Houston. Mgr. Rocky Mountain Region Anschutz Co.; v.p. exploration Dyco Petroleum; v.p. mid-continent Newfield Exploration Co.; pres. Newfield Mid-Continent; founder, CEO Colt Resources, 1991—96, Lariat Petroleum (merged with Newfield Exploration), 1997—2001, Latigo Petroleum (merged with Pogo Producing Co.), 2002—06; founder, CEO, chmn. Laredo Petroleum, Inc., Tulsa, 2007—. Bd. dirs. Newfield Exploration Co., Bill Barrett Corp., 2006—, Helmerich & Payne, Inc., 2007—. Trustee Cath. Found. of Ea. Okla., U. Tulsa; mem. Boy Scouts of America Indian Nation Coun., America's Nat. Gas Alliance, C.M. Russell Nat. Adv. Bd., Nat. Petroleum Coun.; bd. dirs. Okla. Ind. Petroleum Assn., The Philip Neri Newman Ctr.; chmn. Internat. Soc. of Energy Advocates; pres. Okla. Energy Resources Bd. Recipient Geologists' Pub. Svc. Award; named to Hall of Fame, Tulsa Hist. Soc., 2008. Mem.: Thomas Gilcrease Mus. Assn. Office: Laredo Petroleum Inc 15 W Sixth St, Ste 1800 Tulsa OK 74119 Office Phone: 918-513-4570. Office Fax: 918-513-4571.

FOWLER, BRUCE ANDREW, toxicologist, researcher, public health service official; b. Seattle, Dec. 28, 1945; s. Andrew and Dolores Yvonne F.; children from previous marriage: Glenn Andrew, Randall Bruce. BS in Fisheries, U. Wash., 1968; PhD in Pathology, U. Oreg., 1972. From staff fellow to head metal toxicology Nat. Inst. Environ. Health Scis., Research Triangle Park, NC, 1972—86, head metal toxicology, 1986—87; dir. toxicology program U. Md., 1987—2001; sr. rsch. advisor Agy. for Toxic Substances and Disease Registry, Atlanta, 2002—03, assoc. dir., sci. divsn. toxicology and environ. medicine, 2003—11; scientist environ. health Sr. Biomed. Rsch. Svc. USPHS, 2003—07, disting. cons., 2008—11; Pres.'s rotating prof. U. Alaska, 2006—; adj. prof. Rollins Sch. Pub. Health, Emory U., 2009—; sr. fellow ICF Internat., 2011—14; pvt. practice, 2014—. Prof. pathology U. Md. Med. Sch., 1987—2001, prof. epidemiology and toxicology, 2001—03, dir. lab. of cellular and molecular toxicology dept. of epidemiology and preventive medicine, 2001—03; dir. office collaborative studies on adaptive responses estuarine species U. Md., 1988—2001; Meyer Bodansky lectr. Dept. Pathology, U. Tex. Med. Br., Galveston; adj. assoc. prof. U. NC, NC; temporary adv. WHO; work group mem. Internat. Agy. Rsch. Against Cancer; mem., chmn. Sci. Com. on Toxicology of Metals; mem. Md. Gov.'s Coun. on Toxic Substances, 1988—93, chmn., 1990—93, Dahlem Workshop on Mechanisms of Cell Injury: Implications for Human Health, Berlin, 1985; mem. toxicology info. program com. on toxicology; chmn. com. on measuring lead in critical populations; mem. com. on women in sci. and engring., com. on biologic markers in urologic toxicology NAS/NRC, 1989—93, com. on evaluation on viability of augmenting potable water supplies with reclaimed water, 1996—97, subcom. on arsenic in drinking water, 1997—99; co-chmn. NY Acad. Scis. Conf. on Mechanisms of Chem.-Induced Porphyrinopathies, Rye, NY; fellow Japan Soc. for Promotion Sci., 1990; Swedish Med. Rsch. Coun. vis. prof. Karolinska Inst., 1994—95; Colgate-Palmolive vis. prof. U. Wash., 1998—99; mem. Fulbright scholarship rev. com., Scandinavia, 1999—2001, chair, Scandinavia, 2000—01; mem. nat. metals assessment panel sci. adv. bd. U.S. EPA, 2002—03, mem. nat. metals risk assessment framework review panel sci. advisory bd., 2004—05, mem. all ages lead model review panel sci. adv. bd., 2005—06, mem. clean air sci. adv. lead review panel sci. adv. bd., 2006—08; mem. Particular Matter Rsch. Program Adv. Panel Sci. Adv. Bd., 2008; mem. expert panel Ctr. Evaluation of Risks to Human Reproduction Nat. Toxicology Program, 2003; mem. Nat. Toxicology Program Inter Agy. Comm. Chemical Evaluation & Coord., 2008—, Nat. Toxicology Program Interagency Sci. Review Group, 2008—, US Pharmacopeia Toxicology Expert Com., 2010—, NCEH/ATSDR Liaison to NAS/NRC Com. on Emerging Sci. for Environmental Health Decisions, 2010—11; external peer reviewer EC-WHO REVIHAAP Project, 2012—. Editor: Biological and Environmental Effects of Arsenic, 1983, Mechanisms of Cell Injury: Implications for Human Health, Computational Toxicology: Methods and Applications for Risk Assessments, 2013; co-editor: Mechanisms of Chemical Induced Porphyrinopathies, Handbook on the Toxicology of Metals, 4th edit.; mem. editl. bd. Chemico-Biol. Interacctions, 1980—85, Environ. Health Perspectives, 1981—97, Toxicology and Applied Pharmacology, 1985—96, Internat. Archives of Environ. Health, 1986—, Renal Failure, 1988—, Internat. Jour. Occupl. and Environ. Health, 1994—96, Jour. Biochem. and Molecular Toxicology, 2000—, Open Toxicology Revs., 2006—, Chemistry Ctrl. Jour., 2007—; assoc. editor: Environ. Health Perspectives, 2007—, Open Proteomics Jour, —, Toxicology and Applied Pharmacology, 2011—; contbr. articles to profl. jours., chapters to books. Rsch. fellow Japanese Soc. Promotion of Sci., 1990; Fulbright scholar Karolinska Inst., 1994; finalist Charles C. Shepard award CDC, 2007, 11, Individual Leadership Honor award, NCEH/ATSDR, 2010, CDC-ATSDR, 2011, finalist award PBPK Modelling Group, 2010, Group award Deepwater Horizon Oil Spill Response Team, 2010, Group Honor award, 2011. Fellow Acad. Toxicol. Scis. (bd. dirs. 2006-09); mem. AAAS (recruitment and screening panel ct. apptd. sci. experts project 2000—), Soc. Toxicology (councilor mechanisms of toxicity sect., pres. metals splty. sect. 1996, councilor nat. capitol area regional chpt. 1994-95, v.p. in-vitro splty. sect. 2001-02, pres. in-vitro splty. sect. 2003-04, councilor 2005-07), Am. Coll. Toxicology (councilor 1995-98, councilor, SOT Mixtures Splty. Sect. 2009-10, pres., Mixtures speciality Sect., 2014-. pres. Nat. Capital Area chpt., 2013-14, elect. mem. nominating com., 13-), Soc. Occupl. and Environ. Health (councilor 1988, v.p. 1993), Fulbright Assn. (Ga. Chpt.) (bd. dirs. 2010-11), Internat. Commn. Occupl. Health (chmn. sci. com. toxicology of metals 1996-2002), Profl. Assn. Diving Instrs., Sigma Xi., Nat Cap Area Chapter(pres.), SOT Nominations Com., North Bethsda Rotary Club(bd. dirs., 2013-), Rotary Internat(Paul Harris fellowship, 2014). Office: ICF Internat 9300 Lee Hwy Fairfax VA 22031 Home: 5809 Nicholson Ln Unit 611 North Bethesda MD 20852 Personal E-mail: drtox@earthlink.net.

FOWLER, DAVID, lawyer, state legislator; b. Ft. Ogelthorpe, Ga., June 30, 1958; m. Linda Parker; 1 child, Allison. BS, U. Tenn., Chattanooga, 1980; JD, U. Cin., 1983. Lawyer Spears, Moore, Rebman and Williams; mem. Tenn. Senate 99th-100th Gen. Assemblies, mem. gen. welfare, health and human resources com., mem. judiciary com., mem. select oversight com. on corrections, mem. uniform probate code study commn. Active Signal Mountain Presbyn. Ch., Chattanooga Resource Found., Bethany Christian Svcs. Tenn., Chattanooga Tax Practitioners. Republican. Office: 304 War Memorial Bldg Nashville TN 37243 also: PO Box 1749 Chattanooga TN 37401-1749 E-mail: sen.david.fowler@legislature.state.tn.us.

FOWLER, DAVID WAYNE, architectural engineering educator; b. Sabinal, Tex., Apr. 25, 1937; s. Otis Lindley and Sadie Gertrude (Cox) F.; m. Maxine Yvonne Thomson, Mar. 31, 1961; children: Teresa, Leah. BS in Archtl. Engring., U. Tex., 1960; MS, U. Tex., Austin, 1962; PhD in Civil Engring., U. Colo., 1965. Design engr. W.C. Cotten (Cons. Engr.), Austin, Tex., 1961-62; asst. prof. archtl. engring. U. Tex., Austin, 1964-69, assoc. prof., 1969-75, prof., 1975—, Taylor prof., 1981—, dir. Internat. Ctr. Aggregates Rsch., 1992—, Joe J. King chair, 1998—, chair intercoll. athletics coun. for men. Vis. prof. Nihon U., Japan, 1981, Chulalongkorn U., Thailand, 2001; bd. dirs. Univ. Fed. Credit Union, 1976-84; pres. Internat. Congress on Polymers in Concrete, 1981-87, bd. dirs. Univ. Coop, 2000—. Editor procs. 2d Internat. Congress on Polymers in Concrete, 1978, 2001; contbr. articles to profl. jours. Recipient Teaching award Gen. Dynamics, 1975, Teaching award Amoco Found., 1978, Disting. Engring. Alumnus award U. Colo., 1993, Owen Nutt award ICPIC, 1995, Joe J. King Profl. Achievement award, 2000, Claude Hocott Rsch. award, 2002; named to Acad/ Disting. Tchrs., 2000; cited by Engring.-News Record, 1975, Concrete Repair, 1995; Ford Found. faculty devel. grantee, 1962-64, Disting. Grad. Dept. Civil Archl. and Environ. Engring. U. Tex., 2005. Fellow ASCE (pres. Austin br. 1976-77), Am. Concrete Inst. (Delmar L. Bloem award 1985, bd. dirs. 1993-96, Robert Philleo award 2003), Archtl. Engring. Inst.; mem. NAE, Concrete Rsch. Coun. (chmn. 1996-2002), Concrete Rsch. Found. (chmn. 2000-2001), Am. Soc. Engring. Edn. (chmn. archtl. engring. divsn. 1971-72), Tex. Soc. Profl. Engrs. (bd. dirs. Travis chpt. 1968), Russian Acad. Engring. (hon.), Tau Beta Pi, Chi Epsilon. Mem. Ch. of Christ. Home: 612 Brookhaven Trl Austin TX 78746-5455 Office: Univ Tex ECJ 5208 Archtl Engring Group Austin TX 78712 Office Phone: 512-232-2575. Personal E-mail: dwfowlerpe@austin.rr.com. Business E-Mail: dwf@mail.utexas.edu.

FOWLER, JAMES THOMAS, federal marshal; b. 1960; Grad., Columbia Southern U. Formerly with Knoxville Police Dept., Tenn.; various positions US Marshals Svc., US Dept. Justice, 1989—, including dep. marshal (ea. dist.) Tenn. Knoxville, Tenn., dep. marshal (we. dist.) Tenn. Memphis, US marshal (ea. dist.) Tenn. Knoxvulle, Tenn., 2010—. Office: Fed Bldg 800 Market St Ste 2 3107 Knoxville TN 37902 Office Phone: 865-545-4182.

FOWLER, MICHAEL ROSS, political scientist; b. Washington, Apr. 14, 1960; s. James Randlett and Margaret (Williamson) F.; m. Julie Marie Bunck, May 29, 1989. BA in History, Dartmouth Coll., 1982; MA in Fgn. Affairs, U. Va., 1985; JD, Harvard U., 1986. Bar: Mass. 1986, US Dist. Ct. Mass. 1986, DC 1988, Md. 1990. Scholar-in-residence The White Burkett Miller Ctr. Pub. Affairs, Charlottesville, Va., 1986; assoc. Mintz, Levin, Cohn, Ferris, Glovsky & Popeo, Boston, 1986-90; vis. lectr. Tufts U., Medford, Mass., 1990; rsch. fellow Inst. for Study of World Politics, Washington, 1990-91; vis. lectr. U. Va., Charlottesville, 1991-92; Fulbright scholar U. Ryukyus, Okinawa, Japan, 1992-93; profl. lectr. Georgetown U., 1993-94. Prog. for Int. Studies in Asia lectr. to Vietnam, Inst. for Internat. Rels. in Hanoi, 1995, 02, 08; vis. asst. prof. U. Louisville, 1996-99; vis. scholar U. Ryukyus, Okinawa, Japan, 1999-2000; lectr. to Laos, Inst. of Fgn. Affairs in Vientiane, 2003, 2008; dir. Muhammad Ali Inst. Peacemaking and Conflict Resolution, 2000-05; assoc. prof. U. Louisville, 2000-08, prof. U. Louisville, 2009; vis. lectr. to Mex., U. Colima, 2005; vis. lectr. U. Va., 2011. Author: Winston S. Churchill: Philosopher and Statesman, 1985, Thinking About Human Rights, 1987, Law, Power and the Sovereign State, 1995, With Justice For All?: The Nature of the American Legal System, 1998; Editor: Envisioning Reform: Enhancing UN Accountability in the Twenty-First Century, 2009; Bribes, Bullets, and Intimidation: Drugs and the Law in Central America, 2012. White House intern Carter Adminstrn., Washington, 1979-80. Fulbright scholar, U. Ryukyus, Japan, 2006. Democrat. Office: Univ Louisville Ford Hall Dept Polit Sci Louisville KY 40292 Office Phone: 502-852-4732. Business E-Mail: michael.fowler@louisville.edu.

FOWLER, RICKIE, professional golfer; b. Anaheim, Calif., Dec. 13, 1988; s. Rod and Lynn Fowler. Attended, Okla. State U. Profl. golfer Nationwide Tour, 2008—09, PGA Tour, 2008—. Mem. US nat. team Walker Cup, 2007, 2009, Eisenhower trphy, 2009, The Ryder Cup, 2010. Recipient Ben Hogan award, 2008, Phil Mickelson award, 2008; named PGA Tour Rookie of Yr., 2010. Achievements include winning PGA Tour events: Wells Fargo Championship, 2012. Mailing: 100 PGA TOUR Blvd Ponte Vedra Beach FL 32082

FOWLER, W. RANDALL, energy executive; B in Acctg., La. Tech. U., M in Fin. CPA. Dir., investor rels. Enterprise Products Ptnrs., Houston, 1999; treas., v.p. Enterprise Products GP and EPCO, 2000—05, sr. v.p., 2005; pres., CEO EPCO, Inc., 2007—10, CFO, 2005—, vice chmn., 2010—; sr. v.p. Enterprise GP Holdings, LP, 2005—07, exec. v.p., CFO, 2007—10, Enterprise Products Holdings LLC, 2010—; sr. v.p., treas. & bd. dirs. DEP Holdings LLC, 2006—07, exec. v.p., CFO, 2007—10, pres., CEO, 2010—. Bd. dirs. EPE Holdings, LLC & DEP GP, 2006—10. Office: Enterprise Products Holdings LLC 1100 Louisiana St Houston TX 77002 Office Phone: 713-381-6500. Office Fax: 713-381-8200. Business E-Mail: wfowler@epplp.com.

FOWLKES, JOHN THOMAS, JR., federal judge; b. Washington, 1951; BA, Valparaiso U., 1975; JD, U. Denver Law Sch., 1977. Law clk. Memphis Area Legal Services, Tenn., 1978; asst. public defender Shelby County, Tenn., 1978—79, asst. dist. atty. Tenn., 1979—89, chief adminstrv. officer Tenn., 2002—07; asst. US atty. (western dist.) Tenn. US Dept. Justice, Memphis, 1989—2002, 1st asst. US atty., 1993—97, 2001—02; judge 13th Judicial Dist. Tenn. Criminal Ct., 2007—12; judge US Dist. Ct. (western dist.) Tenn., Memphis, 2012—. Office: US District Court 167 North Main St Rm 242 Memphis TN 38103 Office Phone: 901-495-1200.*

FOX, CHARLES DUNSMORE, IV, lawyer; b. Roanoke, Va., Jan. 12, 1953; s. Charles Dunsmore III and Preston (Wescoat) F.; m. Elizabeth McCabe, Dec. 16, 1989; children: Charles Dunsmore V, Edward Lee McCabe. AB, Princeton U., 1975; MA, Yale U., 1977; JD, U. Va., 1980. Bar: Va. 1980, Ill. 1980. Assoc. Schiff, Hardin & Waite, Chgo., 1980-86, ptnr., 1987—2005, McGuire Woods LLP, Charlottesville, Va., 2005—. Ptnr. chmn. Econs. of Practice of Trusts and Estates Mag., Atlanta, 1995-98; adj. prof. Northwestern U. Sch. Law, 1998-2005; U. Va. Law Sch., 2005-; elected mem. Estate Planning Hall of Fame, 2008. Author: Estate Planning with Life Insurance, 1998, Estate Planning Strategies After Estate Tax Reform, 2001, Estate Planning Manual, 2002, Trust and Fiduciary Law Guide, 2004, Tax Law Guide, 2004, Making Sense of the 2010 Estate Tax Legislation, 2011; mem. editl. bd. Trusts and Estates Mag., 1997-2001, Trust and Investment Mag., 2001—, chair, 2003—. Active U. Va. Law Sch. Found., Charlottesville, 1992-95, vice-chair nat. appeals, 1997-98, chair nat. appeals, 1998-2000; trustee Va. Law Sch. Found., 1998—2013, LaGrange Meml. Found., 1994-96, Episcopal HS, Alexandria, Va., 1995-2001, chair capital campaign, 1998-2001; gen. counsel Cmty. Meml. Found., LaGrange, Ill., 1995—; co-chair planned giving task force Episcopal Diocese of Chgo., 2001-05; bd. dirs. St. Annes-Belfield Found., 2005-08, Arc of Piedmont, 2005-10, Camp Holiday Trails, 2008-. Fellow Am. Coll. Trust and Estate Counsel (co-chair legal edn. com. 2002-05, asst. editor jour. 2004-05, editor 2005-06, regent 2006—12, chair editl. bd. 2008-10, chair comm. com. 2010-11, mem. exec. com., 2011-12), Duke U. Estate Planning Coun. (chair); mem. ABA, Princeton U. Planned Giving Adv. Coun. Democrat. Episcopalian. Avocation: golf. Home: 506 Wellington Pl Charlottesville VA 22903 Office: McGuire Woods LLP Ste 300 Box 1288 310 Fourth St NE Charlottesville VA 22902-1288 Office Phone: 434-977-2500. Personal E-mail: skipfoxiv@embarqmail.com. Business E-Mail: cfox@mcguirewoods.com.

FOX, JAMES CARROLL, federal judge; b. Atchison, Kans., Nov. 6, 1928; s. Jared Copeland and Ethel (Carroll) F.; m. Katharine deRosset Rhett, Dec. 30, 1950; children: James Carroll, Jr., Jane Fox Brown, Ruth Fox Jordan. BSBA, U. N.C., 1950, JD with honors, 1957. Bar: N.C. 1957. Law clk. U.S. Dist. Ct. (ea. dist.) N.C., Wilmington, 1957-58; assoc. Carter & Murchison, Wilmington, NC, 1958-59; ptnr. Murchison, Fox & Newton, Wilmington, NC, 1960-82; judge US Dist. Ct. (ea. dist.) NC, Wilmington, 1982—90, 1997—2001, chief judge, 1990—97, sr. judge, 2001—. Lectr. in field. Contbr. articles to profl. jours. Vestryman, St. James Episcopal Ch., 1973-75, 79-82. Office: US Dist Ct Alton Lennon Fed Bldg PO Box 2143 Wilmington NC 28402-2143

FOX, JOAN PHYLLIS, environmental engineer, company executive; b. Rockledge, Fla., July 16, 1945; d. John A. and Nonie L. (Knutson) Fox. BS in Physics with high honors, U. Fla., 1971; PhD in Civil/Environ. Engring., U. Calif., Bekeley, 1980. Registered profl. engr., Ariz., Fla., Calif., Ga., Wash., Wis., diplomate, Am. Acad. Environ. Engrs., cert. air pollution control, qualified environ. profl., Inst. Profl. Environ. Practice. Engr. Bechtel, Inc., San Francisco, 1964—66, 1971—76; dir. program, prin. investigator Lawrence Berkeley Lab., 1977-81; prin. engr., pres. Environ. Mgmt., Berkeley, Calif., 1981—2006; cons. engr. Fla., 2006—. Guest lectr. dept. conservation and resource studies U. Calif., Berkeley, 1980—84; expert witness in field. Contbr. articles to profl. pubs. Grantee, Dept. Energy, 1976—81, EPA, 1976—81. Mem.: NAS (past mem. com. surface mining and reclamation), Air and Waste Mgmt. Assn., Am. Chem. Soc., Phi Beta Kappa, Sigma Pi Sigma. Achievements include development of methods to analyze air pollutants.

FOX, JOHN WILLIAM, JR., rail transportation executive; b. Radford, Va., May 26, 1947; BSBA, Va. Poly. Inst., 1969. Jr. engr. Norfolk and Western Rlwy. Co., Roanoke, Va., 1969-70, asst. trainmaster Kansas City, Mo., 1970-73, trainmaster St. Louis, 1973, Moberly, Mo., 1973-74, asst. supt. Radford divsn. Roanoke, 1974-76, asst. supt., 1976-80, dir. transp., 1980-83; supt. Shenandoah divsn. Norfolk (Va.) So. Corp., 1983-84, supt. Pocahontas divsn., 1984-90, gen. mgr. no. region, 1990, gen. mgr. ea. region, 1990-93, sales & svc., coal mktg., 1993-95, v.p. coal mktg., 1995-99; sr. v.p. coal mktg. Norfolk Southern Corp., 1999—. Mem. adv. com. continuing edn. Va. Poly. Inst. and State U., Roanoake Valley am. Cancer Soc. Mem. Roanoke C. of C. (bd. dirs.). Office: Norfolk So Corp 3 Commercial Pl Norfolk VA 23510-2108

FOX, MARK, men's college basketball coach; b. Garden City, Kans. m. Cindy Fox; children: Parker, Olivia. Student, Garden City CC, Kans., 1987—89; BS magna cum laude in Phys. Ed., Ea. N.Mex. U., Portales, 1991; MS in Athletic Adminstrn. and Sports Psychology, U. Kans., 1996. Grad. asst. to asst. coach U. Wash. Huskies, 1991—93; asst. coach Kans. State U. Wildcats, 1994—2000; assoc. head coach U. Nev. Wolf Pack, Reno, 2000—04, head basketball coach, 2004—09, U. Ga. Bulldogs, 2009—. Named Don Haskins Western Athletic Conf. Coach of Yr., 2005, 2006. Office: Univ Ga Athletic Dept PO Box 1472 Athens GA 30603 Office Phone: 706-542-1432.

FOX, MATTHEW IGNATIUS, publishing executive; b. NYC, Apr. 10, 1934; s. Matthew I. and Lucille V. (Reilly) F.; children: Cathleen, Matthew, Patricia. AB, Rutgers U., 1956. Field rep. Prentice-Hall, Inc., NYC, 1958-60, editor engring., 1960-67, exec. editor, asst. v.p., 1967-71, exec. editor, 1981-83, editor-in-chief, 1983-85, pub., 1985—; pres. Reston Pub. Co., Va., 1971-81. Cons. in pub., 1987—; bd. dirs. Fairmont Press, Atlanta. Pub. over 1000 books in Enquering & Tech. Dep. mayor, mayor, Riververale (NJ), 1964-67, commr., Bergen County, NJ, 1966-70; del. Fairfax County (Va.) Dem. Com., 1976-81; leader City of Cape May Dem. Party. Mem. Rutgers U. Alumni Assn., Cape May Cottagers and Beach Club, Corinthian Yacht Club. Democrat. Roman Catholic. Home: 1004 Panther Hill Ln Raleigh NC 27603-7864

FOX, MIKE, college baseball coach; m. Cheryl Fox; children: Matthew, Morgan. BA in Phys. Edn., U. NC, Chapel Hill, 1978, MA in Tchg., 1979. Grad. asst. U. NC Tar Heels, Chapel Hill, 1979, head baseball coach, 1998—, Millbrook HS, Raleigh, NC, 1980—81, NC Wesleyan Coll. Battling Bishops, Rocky Mount, 1982—98; athletic dir. NC Wesleyan Coll., 1985—98. Named Divsn. III Nat. Coach of Yr., Am. Baseball Coaches Assn., 1989, Atlantic Region Coach of Yr.,

2006—08, Nat. Coach of Yr., Baseball America, 2008. Achievements include head baseball coach of NCAA Division III national championship winning North Carolina Wesleyan College Battling Bishops, 1989. Office: Univ NC Athletic Dept PO Box 2126 Chapel Hill NC 27515 Office Phone: 919-962-4306.

FOX, RONALD FORREST, physicist, educator; s. Sidney Walter and Raia (Joffe) F.; children: Daniel, Lara. BA, Reed Coll., 1964; PhD, Rockefeller U., 1969. Postdoctoral fellow Miller Inst., U. Calif., Berkeley, 1969-71; asst. prof. Ga. Inst. Tech., Atlanta, 1971-74, assoc. prof., 1974-79, prof., 1979—, Regents prof. physics, 1991—, asst. dir. Sch. Physics, 1982-84, assoc. dir. Sch. Physics, 1986-89, 97-99, acting chair, 1999-2000, chair, 2001—05. A.A. Knowlton lectr. Reed Coll., 1999. Author: Biological Energy Transduction, 1982, Energy and the Evolution of Life, 1988; contbr. over 100 articles to sci. jour., over 20 chpt. to books. Recipient W. Roane Beard Outstanding Tchr. award Ga. Inst. Tech., 1992, Sigma Xi Sustained Rsch. award Ga. Inst. Tech., 1997; fellow Alfred P. Sloan Found., 1974-78, Guggenheim fellow, 1985; grantee NSF, 1973-2003. Fellow Am. Phys. Soc.; mem. NY Acad. Sci. Avocations: racquetball, jazz piano. Office: Ga Inst Tech Dept Physics Atlanta GA 30332-0430 Office Phone: 404-894-5260. Business E-Mail: ron.fox@physics.gatech.edu.

FOX, WILLIAM J., bank executive, former federal official, lawyer; m.; two children. BA in History, Creighton U., Omaha, 1984, JD, 1987. Atty., Bur. Alcohol, Tobacco and Firearms US Dept. Treasury, 1988—93, sr. atty., Bur. Alcohol, Tobacco and Firear, 1993—97, sr. counsel Bur. Alcohol, Tobacco and Firearms, 1997—99, dep. chief counsel Bur. Alcohol, Tobacco and Firearms, 1999—2001, dep. asst. gen. counsel enforcement, 0200—2001, prin. asst., sr. advisor gen. Ccounsel, 2001—02, acting. dep. gen. counsel, 2002, assoc. dep. gen. counsel, 2002—03, dir. fin. crimes enforcement network, 2003—06; sr. v.p., Global AML and Economic Sanctions Exec. Bank of America Corp., 2006—08, 2009—10, sr. v.p. Enterprise Compliance Program Exec., 2008—09, mng. dir., Global AML and Economic Sanctions Exec., 0011—. Recipient Meritorious Rank award, US Dept. Treas. Roman Catholic. Office: Bank of America Corp 100 N Tryon St Charlotte NC 28202 Office Phone: 980-387-2687. Office Fax: 704-683-9303. Business E-Mail: william.fox@bankofamerica.com.

FOXX, VIRGINIA ANN, United States Representative from North Carolina, small business owner; b. NYC, June 29, 1943; m. Thomas A. Foxx; 1 child AB in English, U. NC, Chapel Hill, 1968, MACT, 1972; EdD Curriculum and Tchg./Higher Edn., U. NC, Greensboro, 1985. Sec., rsch. asst. U. NC, Chapel Hill; prof. Caldwell CC, Hudson, NC; prof. sociology Appalachian State U., Boone, NC, asst. dean gen. coll.; dept. sec. mgmt. NC Dept. Adminstrn.; pres., cons. Md. Cmty. Coll., Spruce Pine, NC, 1987—94; owner, operator Grandfather Nursery, Banner Elk, NC; mem. NC State Senate, Raleigh, 1995—2004, US Congress from 5th NC Dist., Washington, 2005—; sec. US House Republican Conf., Washington, 2013—. Mem. Watauga County Bd. Edn., 1976-88. Recipient Outstanding Pub. Official award, NC Christmas Tree Assn., Award for Outstanding Citizenship, Exceptional Pub. Svc., Watauga County League Women Voters, 1988, NC Disting. Women's award, 1990, Order of the Long Leaf Pine, NC Gov. Jim Martin, 1992, Disting. Fundraising award, YMCA, 1993, NC Carpathian award, 1994, Guardian of Small Bus. award, Nat. Fedn. Ind. Bus., 2000, Alan Keith-Lucas Friend of Children award, NC Child Care Assn., 2002, Contbns. to Sociology award, NC Sociol. Assn., 2002, Reagan award, Nat. Republican Congressional Com. (NRCC), 2010. Mem. Nat. Assn. Women Legislators, American Legis. Exch. Conf., NCCBI, NC Ctr. Pub. Policy Rsch., NC Women's Forum. Republican. Office: 6000 Meadowbrook Mall Ste 3 Clemmons NC 27012 also: US House of Representatives 2350 Rayburn House Office Building Washington DC 20515 Office Phone: 202-225-2071, 336-778-0211. Office Fax: 336-778-2290.*

FOYS, ROGER JOSEPH, bishop; b. Chgo., July 27, 1945; AB, Franciscan Univ., Steubenville, Ohio, 1969, STD, 1998. Ordained priest Diocese of Steubenville, Ohio, 1973, vicar gen., 1982—87; instr. canon law St. John Vianney Sem.; ordained bishop, 2002; bishop Diocese of Covington, Ky., 2002—. Named a Prelate of Honor, Pope John Paul II, 1986, Protonotary Apostolic, 2001. Roman Catholic. Office: Diocese of Covington 401 E 20th St 1125 Madison Ave Covington KY 41011-3115

FRAGALE, ALISON R., organizational behavior professor; BA in Math. and Economics magna cum laude, Dartmouth Coll., 1997; PhD in Orgnl. Behavior, Stanford U., 2004. Bus. analyst McKinsey & Co., Inc., Chgo., 1997—99; asst. prof. orgnl. behavior & strategy Kenan-Flagler Bus. Sch., U. NC, Chapel Hill, 2004—, Mary Farley Ames Lee fellow, 2007—. Editl. bd. mem. Orgnl. Behavior and Human Decision Processes, 2007—; contbr. articles to profl. jours. Bd. visitors Nelson A. Rockefeller Ctr. for Pub. Policy and Social Sciences, Dartmouth Coll., 2008—. Mem.: Soc. for Personality and Social Psychology, Acad. of Mgmt. Office: Kenan-Flagler Business School University of NC at Chapel Hill Campus Box 3490, McColl Building Chapel Hill NC 27599-3490 Office Phone: 919-962-3224. Office Fax: 919-962-4425. E-mail: afragale@unc.edu.

FRAGER, ALBERT S., retired food products executive; b. Boston, Dec. 29, 1922; s. Oscar and Anna (Polterak) F.; m. Marion Nathan, June 15, 1950; children: Owen R., Bonnie L. Frager Franks, Laurie J. Burton, Sherri Frager Goodstein. Student, Amos Tuck Sch. Bus., Dartmouth Coll., 1943; BS in Bus. Adminstrn, Northeastern U., 1944. Internal revenue agt. IRS, 1945-56; v.p., controller Stop & Shop, Inc., Boston, 1956-67, treas., 1967-86, fin. v.p., 1969-79, sr. v.p., 1979-86. Past trustee South Palm Beach County Jewish Fedn.; bd. dirs. Donna Klein Jewish Acad.; mem. corp., past bd. overseers Northeastern U.; past pres. Jewish temple. With USNR, 1943-44. Mem. AICPA, Mass. Soc. CPAs. Home: 4740 S Ocean Blvd Apt 911 Highland Beach FL 33487-5354

FRAIM, PAUL D., mayor, Norfolk, Virginia; b. Norfolk, Va., Oct. 26, 1949; m. Elizabeth Peer; children: Annie, Katie, Richard, David. Student, Va. Mil. Inst.; MEd, U. Va.; JD, U. Richmond. Pvt. practice, 1977; ptnr. Heilig, McKenry, Fraim and Lollar, P.C.; mem. city coun. City of Norfolk, 1986—, mayor Va., 1994—; pres. Fraim and Fiorella PC. Chmn. water task force, city coun. City of Norfolk. Mem. Hampton Rds. Planning Dist. Commn.; mem., past chmn. mayor's downtown devel. com. City of Norfolk; past chmn. Hampton Rds. Sports Authority, Hampton Rds. Regional Jail Authority; bd. dirs. Greater Norfolk Corp., Navy League, Forward Hampton Rds.; bd. dirs., treas. Hampton Rds. Partnership; chmn. Hampton Rds. Mayor and Chairs Caucus; past co-capt. football team Va. Mil. Inst.; past coach football U. Va., U. Richmond; bd. dirs. TowneBank; chmn., Norfolk Bd. Recipient Bud Metheny award Old Dominion U., 1995, Tidewater Humanitarian award, National Conference of Christians and Jews, 1998, Port Champion award, Hampton Roads Maritime Assn., 2004; named Man of Yr., Norfolk Sports Club, 1994, Sportsman of Yr., Va. Pilot, 1996, Downtowner of Yr., Downtown Norfolk Coun., 1996. Mem. ABA, Va. State Bar, Va. Bar Assn., Norfolk-Portsmouth Bar Assn., Va. Assn. Def. Attys. Office: City of Norfolk Office of Mayor 1109 City Hall Bldg Norfolk VA 23510*

FRAKER, JACK C., real estate company executive; m. Margaret Fraker; children: Kevin Fraker, Jackie Fraker. BBA, U. Tex., Austin. Exec. v.p. Cushman & Wakefield, Inc.; vice chmn. investment properties Instl. Group CB Richard Ellis Group, Inc., Dallas. Bd. trustees Girls Inc., Dallas, mem., adv. coun., McCombs Real Estate Fin. & Investment Cr, Austin; mem. Urban Land Inst., Soc. of Indsl. and Office Realtors, Nat. Assn. of Investment and Office Properties; bd. govs. North Tex. Comml.Assn. of Realtors. Recipient Deal of the Yr., Dallas Bus. Jour., Top Producer, Cushman & Wakefield, Dallas, 1992-02, No. 1 Investment Sales & Indsl. Broker, Dallas Bus. Jour., 1992, Honorable Mention, SIOR, 2000, Deal of the Yr., 2002, Cooperative Transaction award, 2002, Indsl. Broker of the Yr., North Tex. Chapter, NAIOP, 2002, Stemmons Svc. sward, Dallas, 2003, Gary J. Beban Teamwork award, CB Richard Ellis Group, Inc., 2006, Edward S. Gordon award, 2007. Office: CBRE Suite 700 2100 McKinney Ave Dallas TX 75201 Office Phone: 214-979-6300. Office Fax: 214-979-6518. Business E-Mail: Jack.Fraker@cbre.com.

FRAMKE, GREGORY A., information technology executive; Mktg., sales mgmt. IBM Corp.; prin. equity tech. Morgan Stanley & Co., 1994—99; dir., global equity tech. COO Deutsche Bank Securities, London; exec. v.p., chief info. and ops. officer E*TRADE Financial Corp., NYC, 2000—. Named one of Top 25 Chief Tech. Officers, InfoWorld mag., 2006. Office: E*Trade 671 N Glebe Rd Arlington VA 22203 also: E*Trade Fin Corp 1271 Avenue of the Americas 14th Fl New York NY 10020-1302

FRAMME, LAWRENCE HENRY, III, lawyer; b. Louisville, Oct. 8, 1949; s. Lawrence Henry and Margaret Gertrude (Hayes) Framme; m. Frances Claire Schwacke, Dec. 27, 1969; children: Jessica Marie, Lawrence Henry IV, Benjamin Hayes. BA, Centre Coll., 1971; JD cum laude, Washington and Lee U., 1974. Bar: Va. 1974, US Dist. Ct. Va. 1974, US Ct. Appeals (4th cir.) 1974. Assoc. McGuire, Woods & Battle, Richmond, 1974—81, Lacy & Baliles, 1981—82; mem. firm, dir. Mezzullo, McCandlish & Framme, 1982—90; sec. econ. devel. gov.'s cabinet Commonwealth Va., 1990—92; chmn. Virginians for Progress Found., 1992; v.p. LeClair, Ryan, Joynes, Epps & Framme, 1992—95; prin. Framme Law Firm, 1995—. Co-chmn. gov.'s adv. coun. Workforce 2000, 1990—91. Mem. Va. State Bd. CCs, 1987—90, chmn., 1989—90, Dem Party Va., 1986—90, 2001—03; bd. visitors Va. Commonwealth U., 1992—96; bd. dirs. Downtown YMCA, 1986—95; bd. dirs., sec. Va. Biotech. Rsch. Pk. Authority, 1991—92, 1993—95, 2002—04, Va. Biotech. Rsch. Pk. Corp., 1994—2002, Leadership Metro Richmond, 1991—94; bd. dirs., leagal advisor Richmond Urban League, 1985—86; bd. dirs. Metro Richmond YMCA, 1995—2000; policy bd. mem. Va. Tech Bioinformatics Ctrs., 2001—09. Recipient Legal award, Housing Oppprtunites Made Equal, Richmond, 1983; named Alumni of Yr., Leadership Metro Richmond, 1990. Mem.: VSB, ABA, Richmond Bar Assn., Va. Bar Assn., Omicron Delta Kappa. Roman Catholic. Office: Framme Law Firm PC 2812 Emerywood Pky Ste 220 Richmond VA 23294-3539 Home: 2420 Hanover Ave Richmond VA 23220 Business E-Mail: lframme@frammelaw.com.

FRAMPTON, PAUL HOWARD, physics researcher, educator; b. Kidderminster, Eng., Oct. 31, 1943; came to U.S., 1968; naturalized citizen, 1989; s. Harold Albert and Grace Elizabeth (Howard) Frampton; m. Anne-Marie Frampton, 1993 (div. 2008). BA, U. Oxford, 1965, MA, DPhil, U. Oxford, 1968, DSc, 1984. Rsch. assoc. U. Chgo., 1968—70; fellow CERN, Geneva, 1970—72; vis. prof. Bielefeld U., Germany, 1972, 1999, Syracuse U., 1972—75; vis. assoc. prof. UCLA, 1975—77; vis. scholar Harvard U., Cambridge, Mass., 1978—81; from asst. prof. physics to prof. U. N.C., Chapel Hill, 1981—96; disting. prof. physics Louis D. Rubin Jr., 1996—. Vis. prof. U. Tex., fall 1983, Boston U., 1986-87, U. d'Aix-Marseille, 1993, CERN, 1996, 98, 2000, 2003, Perimeter Inst., 2005, IPMU, Tokyo, 2009-10; chmn. steering com. Workshops on Grand Unification, 1980-89; chmn. organizing com. 1st workshop U. N.H., 1980, 3d workshop, U. N.C., 1982, 10th and last workshop U. N.C., 1989; symposium chair 8th Internat. Symposium on Particles, Strings and Cosmology, U. N.C., 2001 Author: Dual Resonance Models, 1974, 2d edit., 1986, Gauge Field Theories, 1986, 3d edit., 2008, Frampton Festschrift: The Launching of La Belle Epoque of High Energy Physics and Cosmology, 2004, Did Time Begin? Will Time End?, 2009; editor books in field; contbr. 250 articles to profl. jours., also chpts. to books. Gov.'s project dir. for supercollider in N.C., 1987. Fellow AAAS, Am. Phys. Soc., Brit. Inst. Physics. Achievements include research in particle theory, string theory and theoritical cosmology. Office: U NC Dept Physics And Astronomy Chapel Hill NC 27599-3255 Office Phone: 919-962-7207. Personal E-mail: paul.h.frampton@gmail.com. Business E-Mail: frampton@physics.unc.edu.

FRANCESCHETTI, DONALD RALPH, physicist, educator; b. Oceanside, NY, Nov. 21, 1947; s. Nicholas and Lucile Frances (Powell) F.; m. Alice Frizzell, Oct. 2, 1982. BS, Bklyn. Coll., 1969; MA, Princeton U., 1971, PhD, 1974. Rsch. assoc. U. Ill., 1973—75, U. N.C., Chapel Hill, 1975—77, rsch. asst. prof., 1977—79; asst. prof. U. Memphis, 1979—83, assoc. prof., chmn. dept. physics, 1983—86, prof. physics, chmn. dept. physics, 1986—91, interim assoc. v.p. for rsch., 1990—93, interim vice provost for rsch., 1993—96, disting. svc. prof. physics and chemistry, 1996—. Vis. lectr. State U., Utrecht, Netherlands, 1982; Dunavant prof., 2003—, Faundree univ. prof., 2005-; dir. Learning Communities, 2005—. Consulting editor (reference works) Biog. Ency. Mathematicians; contbr. articles to profl. jours. Woodrow Wilson Grad. fellow, 1969-70, NSF Grad. fellow, 1969-72, Postdoctoral Energy-related fellow, 1975-76 Mem.: Am. Phys. Soc., Cognitive Sci. Soc., History of Sci. Soc., Am. Chem. Soc., Sigma Xi, Phi Beta Kappa. Achievements include patent in field. Office: University of Memphis Dept Of Physics Memphis TN 38152-0001 Office Phone: 901-678-5257. Business E-Mail: dfrncsch@memphis.edu.

FRANCESCHINI, NORA, medical researcher; MD, Fed. Univ. Rio Grande do Sul (UFRGS), Brazil, 1986; MPH, U. NC, Chapel Hill, 2004. Diplomate Am. Bd. Internal Medicine, cert. in nephrology. Internal medicine/nephrology residency HCPA (Hospital das Clinicas de Porto Alegre), Brazil, 1987—90; nephrology rsch. fellowship Oreg. Health Sci. U., Portland, 1993—95; internal medicine residency U. Utah Med. Ctr., Salt Lake City, 1995—98; nephrology fellowship Duke U. Med. Ctr., Durham, NC, 1998—2000; instr. medicine, divsn. hephrology & hypertension, Sch. Medicine U. NC, Chapel Hill, 2001—05, posdoc. fellow epidemiology, Sch. Pub. Health, 2005—07, rsch. asst. prof., dept. epidemiology, 2007—. Mem. editl. bd. Clin. Nephrology, 2003—; contbr. articles to profl. jours. Recipient Young Investigator award, Nat. Kidney Found., 2002—03; fellow, Internat. Soc. Nephrology, 1993—95. Mem.: Internat. Genetic Epidemiology Soc., Soc. Epidemiology Rsch., Am. Soc. Nephrology, Internat. Soc. Nephrology. Achievements include research in cardiovascular disease, nephrology and hypertension & genetic epidemiology. Office: Univ NC Dept Epidemiology 137 E Franklin Ste 306 CB #8050 Chapel Hill NC 27514 Office Phone: 919-966-1305. Office Fax: 919-966-9800. E-mail: noraf@unc.edu.

FRANCHITTI, DARIO, race car driver; b. Edinburgh, May 19, 1973; m. Ashley Judd, Dec. 12, 2001 (separated Jan. 2013). Race car driver IndyCar Series Andretti Green, 2003—07; race car driver NASCAR Ganassi Racing, 2008—. 1st pl. Menards A.J. Foyt 225 Milw. Mile, 2004, 2nd pl. ABC Supply Co. A.J. Foyt 225, 2005, 2007; 1st pl. Honda Indy 225 Pikes Peak Internat. Raceway, 2004; 2nd pl. SunTrust Indy Challenge Richmond Internat. Raceway, 2005, 1st pl. SunTrust Indy Challenge, 2007; 1st pl. Firestone Indy 200 Nashville Speedway, 2005, 2nd pl. Firestone Indy 200, 2007; 1st pl. Toyota Indy 400 Calif. Speedway, 2005; 2nd pl. Indy Grand Prix Sonoma Infineon Raceway, 2006; 2nd pl. Kans. Lottery Indy 300 Kans. Speedway, 2007; 1st pl. Indy 500 Indpls. Motor Speedway, 2007, 2010, 2012; 1st pl. Iowa Corn Indy 250 Iowa Speedway, 2007; 2nd pl. Honda 200 Mid-Ohio Sports Car Course, 2007; 1st pl. Peak Antifreeze Indy 300 Chicagoland Speedway, 2007. Recipient Jerry Titus award, Am. Automobile Racing Writers and Broadcasters Assn., 2008; named IndyCar Series Champion, Indy Racing League, 2007. Avocations: reading, video games, skiing. Office: Ganassi Racing 8500 Westmoreland Dr Concord NC 28027

FRANCIS, GREGORY R., Lieutenant Governor of US Virgin Islands; b. St. Croix, VI, Aug. 30, 1951; s. Olric and Hyacinth (Wilson) Francis; m. Cheryl Francis; 4 children. Attended, U. VI. Career mil. svc. US Army/Army Nat. Guard, 1972—99, various responsibilities including command program support specialist, supervisory mil. pers. specialist, recruiting & retention mgr., svc. in Germany, PR, VI, ret. rank of Chief Warrant Officer 4, 1999; VI dir. Office Vets. Affairs, 1999—2001; adminstr. St. Croix, 2001—06; lt. gov. Territory of Virgin Islands, 2007—; commr. Virgin Islands Divsn. Banking & Ins., 2007—. VI del. Nat. Dem. Conv., Boston, 2004; chair St. Croix dist., VI Dem. Party. Mem. Yesterday, Today, Tomorrow Emancipation Com., Crusaders Fraternity, Inc.; founder Friends Helping Friends Fitness Club; vol. Boy Scouts/Girl Scouts of America. Decorated Army Meritorious Svc. medal, Army Commendation medal, Army Achievement medal, Army Good Conduct medal, Army Res. Components Achievement medal, Nat. Def. Svc. medal, Humanitarian Svc. medal, Armed Forces Res. medal, Silver Hourglass, Army Svc. Ribbon, Oversees Svc. Ribbon. Mem.: Vets. Svc. Orgn., Ballet Folkorico Hispanos Unidos, Red Brick Reading Club, King Soloman Grand Lodge (dep. dist. grand master), Caribbean Lodge (pearl), Myron G. Danielson Am. Legion Post 85 (first vice comdr.). Democrat. Office: Office of the Lieutenant Governor 1131 Kings St Ste 101 St Croix VI 00820 Office Phone: 340-773-6449. Office Fax: 340-773-0330. E-mail: Gregory.francis@lgo-vi.gov.*

FRANCIS, JULIE, beverage company executive; d. Butch and Tonie. BBA, Alfred U., 1993. Dir. mktg. Rabun, Hatch & Assoc., Atlanta, 1993—95; key account category mgr. Coca-Cola Enterprises, Atlanta, 1995—96, key account mgr., 1996—97, market devel. mgr. NY divsn. NY, 1998—99, dir. sales NY divsn. NY, 1998—99, sales ctr. mgr. NY divsn. NY, 1999—2001, area v.p. Eastern Great Lakes divsn. Rochester, NY, 2001—02, area v.p. Lakeshore divsn., 2002—04, v.p., gen. mgr. Midwest Bus. Unit, 2005—. Named one of 40 Under 40, Crain's Chgo. Bus., 2005. Office: Coca-Cola Enterprises 2500 Windy Ridge Parkway Atlanta GA 30339

FRANCIS, NORMAN C., academic administrator; b. Lafayette, La., Mar. 20, 1931; s. Joseph Abel and Mabel F.; m. Blanche MacDonald, June 6, 1955; children: Michael, Timothy, David, Kathleen, Patrick, Christine. BA, Xavier U. of La., 1952; JD, Loyola U., New Orleans, 1955; EdD (hon.), Villanova U., 1969; LLD (hon.), Holy Cross Coll., 1969, Seton Hall U., 1969, St. Michael's Coll., 1972, Marquette U., 1977. Dean of men Xavier U. of La., New Orleans, 1957-63, dir. student pers. svcs., 1963-64, asst. to pres. for student affairs, 1964-65, asst. to pres. for devel., 1965-67, exec. v.p., from 1968, pres., 1968—. Trustee Coll. Entrance Exam. Bd., 1972-76, chmn., 1976-78. Commr. New Orleans Civil Svc. Commn., 1969-76; former pres. Urban league New Orleans; former chmn. New Orleans Aviation Bd.; mem. Pontifical Peace & Justice Commn., 1977. Recipient Presdl. Medal of Freedom, 2006; named one of America's Best Leaders, US News & World Report, 2009. Office: Xavier University of La Office of Pres 1 Drexel Ct New Orleans LA 70125-1056

FRANCIS, RON, professional sports team executive, retired professional hockey player; b. Sault Ste Marie, Ont., Can., Mar. 1, 1963; m. Mary Lou Francis; children: Kaitlyn, Michael, Connor. Center Hartford Whalers (now Carolina Hurricanes), 1981—91, Pitts. Penguins, 1991-98, Carolina Hurricanes, 1998—2004, Toronto Maple Leafs, 2004—05; dir player devel. Carolina Hurricanes, 2006—08, asst. gen. mgr., 2007—08, assoc. head coach, dir. player personnel, 2008—. Player NHL All-Star game, 1983, 1985, 1990, 1996. Recipient Frank J. Selke Trophy, 1995, Lady Byng Trophy, 1995, 1998, 2002, King Clancy Meml. Trophy, 2002, NHL Found. Player Award, 2002. Achievements include being a member of Stanley Cup Champion Pittsburgh Penguins, 1991, 1992; having his number, 10, retired by Carolina Hurricanes, 2006; being inducted into the Hockey Hall of Fame, 2007. Office: c/o Carolina Hurricanes RBC Ctr 1400 Edwards Mill Rd Raleigh NC 27607

FRANCO, RICHARD ANTHONY, SR., pharmaceutical company executive, pharmacist; b. NYC, June 9, 1941; s. Vincent and Filomena (DeFeo) F.; m. Dianne Marie Pellecchia, Sept. 6, 1964; children: Richard, Danielle. BS in Pharmacy, St. John's U., NYC, 1963; grad. in Pharm. Mktg. and Mgmt., Long Island U. Registered pharmacist, N.Y., Vt. Community pharmacist Salisbury Pharmacy, Westbury, N.Y., 1963-68; pharm. sales rep. N.Y. area Eli Lilly & Co., Indpls., 1968-70, spl. sales rep., hosp. sales coord., 1970-73, dist. sales mgr., 1975-77, hosp. sales mgr., 1977-79, product mgr., 1979-81, group product mgr., 1981-84; mgr. N.Y. area Dista Products, Indpls., 1973-75; dir. mktg. Glaxo Inc., Research Triangle Park, N.C., 1984-86, v.p. mktg., 1986-88, v.p. comml. devel., 1988-91, v.p., gen. mgr. dermatology divsn., 1991-93, v.p., gen. mgr. Cerenex divsn., 1993-94; pres., CEO, dir. Trimeris, Inc., Research Triangle Park, 1994—97; pres., CEO LipoScience, Inc., co-founder, 1997—2002; pres. DARA Bio-Sciences, Inc., 2005—07, CEO, 2007—, chmn., 2009—. Dir. Entremed Inc., bd. dirs. NeoMatrix, LLC, bd. dirs. Salix Pharmaceuticals, Ltd., bd. dirs. LipoScience, Inc., bd. dirs. DARA BioSciences, Inc., 2005-2008, bd. dirs. DARA BioSciences, Inc., 2009- Mem. N.C. Edn. Forum, Raleigh, 1988, 89; judge N.C. Engrepreneur of Yr., Raleigh, 1990, 95; bd. dirs. United Way, Raleigh, 1990-93. chpt. pres., dir., Rsch. Triangle Chpt., Nat. Assn. of Corp. Dirs. N.Y. State scholar in engring. and nursing, 1959. Mem. Am. Pharm. Assn., Am. Mgr. Assn., Comml. Devel. Assn., Licensing Exec. Soc. Republican. Avocations: golf, reading, gardening, boating. Office: DARA Bio-Sciences Inc Ste 160 8601 Six Forks Rd Raleigh NC 27615 Office Phone: 919-872-5578. Office Fax: 919-861-0239. Business E-Mail: rfranco@trimeris.com.

FRANK, JOE S., lawyer, retired mayor; b. Newport News, Va., Nov. 14, 1942; s. Harry Frank and Dorothy Lilyan (Morewitz); m. Susan Jane Glasser; children: Jason, Melissa, Shelly. BA in Fgn. Affairs with honors, U. Va., 1964; LLB, U. Va. Law Sch., 1967. Bar: Va 1967. Intern Battle, Neal, Harris, Minor and Williams, Charlottesville, Richmond, Washington, 1967; ptnr. David, Kamp & Frank, LLC, Newport News, Va.; vice mayor City of Newport News, 1988-90, 96, mayor, 1996—2010. Mem. Newport News City Coun., 1988—; legal officer Hampton Roads Jaycees. Co-chmn. Hampton Roads Mil. and Fed. Facilities Alliance; mem. exec. com. Va. Peninsula Econ. Devel. Coun.; bd. mem. Hampton Roads Partnership; chmn. Blue Ribbon Commn., Newport News Adv. Com. on Base Realignment and Closure, Mayor's Mil. Affairs Group, Physicians Task Force; mem. Peninsula Alliance For Econ. Devel., Hampton Roads Econ. Devel. Alliance, Governor's Peninsula BRAC Working Group, Governor's Urban Policy Task Force, Hampton Roads Met. Planning Org., Hampton Roads Planning Dist. Commn., Newport News/Williamsburg Internat. Airport Task Force; former pres. bd. dirs. Homebase of Va. Peninsula, Inc.; former bd. dirs. Newport News Alliance for Youth; former chmn. Newport News Advanced Rsch. Ctr. Com., Newport News Dem. Com., Oyster Pt. Devel. Corp.; former vice chmn. Newport News Youth Risk Prevention Com.; former pres. Jewish Fedn. Va. Peninsula, Rodef Sholom Temple; former mem. coord. com. Hampton Roads Crossing; former mem. Hampton Roads Pub. Transp. Alliance, Joint Legis. Task Force on Transit Financing in Hampton Roads. With Army Nat. Guard US Army, 1968—74, hon. mem. Transp. Corps Regiment US Army. Decorated Am. Hero award Hon. Order of St. Christopher; recipient Humanitarian award, Nat. Conf. Christians and Jews, Good Scout award, Colonial Va. Coun. Boy Scouts Am., Disting. Citizen award, Va. Peninsula C. of C.; named Citizen of Yr. Mem.: Newport News Bar Assn., Hampton Roads Mayors and Chairs, Va. Peninsula Mayors and Chairs, Va. Trial Lawyers Assn., Va. State Bar, ABA.

FRANK, LARRY JAMES, library director, writer, consultant; b. Detroit, Oct. 9, 1943; s. George A.; m. Bonnie L. Bonsky; children: Alyssa Ann(dec.), Nathan D. BA magna cum laude, We. Mich. U., 1976, MA with honors, 1977; AMLS, U. Mich., 1979; cert. pub. adm. advanced mgmt. program, Miami U., Oxford, Ohio, 1983; cert. edn., U. Wis., 1996. Exec. dir. Amos Meml. Pub. Libr., Sidney, Ohio, 1981—85, Boyd County Pub. Libr., Ashland, Ky., 1986—95, St. Clair County Libr., Port Huron, Mich., 1995—99, Onondaga County Pub. Libr., Syracuse, NY, 1999—2001, Hinsdale Pub. Libr., Ill., 2001—03, Knox County Librs., Knoxville, Tenn., 2003—10, writer, cons., 2010—. Cons./tchr., missionary The Lang. Inst., Japan Luth. Ch., Tokyo and Niigata, Japan, 1968—71; cons. in libr. design and orgn. Port Huron, 1996—98. Author: (novel) The Arius Scrolls, 2011, Fragments of Faust, 2012, numerous poems; contbr. articles to profl. jours. Bd. dirs. Ky. Coun. on Econ Edn., 1986-95; mem. chronic disease steering com. U. Cin. Children's Hosp., Ashland, 1987-90; mem. bd. visitors U. Tenn. Named Boss of Yr., Jaycees, Ashland, Libr. of Yr., NY Times, 2006, Exec. of Yr., Pub. Rels. Soc. America, 2007; U. Mich. scholar, Ann Arbor, 1978-79. Mem.: PLA, ALA. Avocations: writing, hiking, design, yoga.

FRANK, MICHAEL M., physician; b. Bklyn., Feb. 28, 1937; s. Robert and Helen (Prakin) F.; m. Ruth Sybil Pudolsky, Nov. 5, 1961; children: Robert E., Abigail B., Brice S.H. AB, U. Wis., 1956; MD, Harvard U., 1960. Intern Boston City Hosp., 1960-61; resident in pediatrics Johns Hopkins Hosp., 1961-62, 64-65; vis. scientist Nat. Inst. Med. Research, London, 1965-66; with NIH, 1967-90; chief lab. of clin. investigation, clin. dir. Nat. Inst. Allergy and Infectious Diseases, Bethesda, Md., 1977-90; prof. Duke U. Med. Ctr., Durham, NC, 1990—, chmn.Ddept. Pediatrics, 1990—2004. Mem. ACP, Assn. Am. Physicians, Am. Soc. Clin. Investigation, Soc. Pediatric Rsch., Am. Pediatric Soc., Infectious Diseases Soc., Am. Acad. Allergy, Am. Acad. Pediatrics. Office: Duke U Med Ctr PO Box 3556 Durham NC 27710 Home Phone: 919-489-1964. Business E-Mail: frank007@mc.duke.edu.

FRANKE, J. LANCE, corporate financial executive; BS in Economics, U. Md.; MBA in Fin. & Investments, Washington U. Career sales rep. Xerox Corp.; mgmt. cons. Macro Internat., Inc.; with Sallie Mae, Inc. (Fin. Planning, Analysis, Credit, Leasing, and Pub. Fin. Depts.); v.p., corp. fin. Sallie Mae, Inc., fin. analyst, 1981, sr. v.p., corp. fin., 2004—08; exec. v.p., corp. fin. Sallie Mae - SLM Corp., 2008—. Office: Sallie Mae Inc 12061 Bluemont Way Reston VA 20190 Office Phone: 703-810-3000. Office Fax: 703-984-5042.

FRANKE, WAYNE THOMAS, political and marketing consultant, retired government affairs director, consultant; b. San Angelo, Tex., June 23, 1950; s. Bernard Raymond and Henrietta Elizabeth (Kozelsky) Franke; m. Regina Gale Franke; 1 child, Mauri Jane stepchildren: Colton, Christina. BBA in Gen. Bus., Angelo State U., San Angelo, Tex., 1972. Adminstrv. clk. Gen. Telephone Co. S.W., San Angelo, 1968—72, comm. cons. Irving, Tex., 1972—75, asst. govt. affairs mgr. San Angelo, 1975—78, mgr. govt. affairs Austin, Tex., 1979—86, dir. govt. affairs, 1986—98; owner MJWT Cons., Austin, 1998—; majority owner DOBWEST L.P.; ptnr. Bus. Ptnrs. Ltd., Austin. Mem. legis. affairs com. Tex. Indsl. Devel. Coun., College Station, 1977—84, chmn., Austin, 1981—83, mem. energy and awards coms., 1978—79; mem. US Spkr. Jim Wright's Diplomatic Mission to Moscow, 1987. Fundraiser Boy Scouts Am., Austin, 1987-88, Austin Performing Arts Ctr., 1998-2000; loaned exec. Tarrant County United Way, 1973-74; issues mgmt. adv. coun. North Tex. Commn., Dallas, 1985-87; program chmn. John Ben Shepperd Leadership Forum, Odessa, Tex., 1986, chmn., Austin, 1987, John Ben Shepperd Alumni Forum, 1988; mem. John Ben Shepperd Governing Bd., 1990-91, chmn. fin., 1990-91, fin. com. 1990-92, adv. bd., 1991-93, vice-chmn. John Ben Shepperd Found., 1997-98, chmn., 1998-99, bd. dirs., 1997-; corp. co-chmn. drive United Cerebral Palsy Assn., Austin area, 1990-96; mem. Hays Country Oaks Archtl. Control & Protection Com., 1993-96; steering com., fundraising Travis County Assn. Retarded Citizens; trustee West Tex. Boy's Ranch Found., 1995-2005, treas. exec. com., 1999-2001, chmn. 2001-02; chmn. Tex. Statehood Sesquicentennial Program, 1996; bd. dirs. Angelo State U. Ex-Students Assn., 1999-2005, Hays CISD Edn. Found., 2005-11, Angelo State U. Found., 2006-; vice-chmn 2009-10, chmn 2010-13, pres. cir. mem., 2009-; mem. task force Schs. and Coms. Offering Positive Experiences, Hays ISD, 2003-05; mem. pastoral coun. St. Paul's Cath. Ch., 2007-2009. Recipient External Team Excellence award GTE, 1992-93, Strive for Excellence award, 1992; named Lobbyist of the Year for GTE Corp., 1987, 91, 1989 Disting. Alumnus, Angelo State U.; Wayne Franke Day proclaimed by San Angelo, Tex. City Council Oct. 14, 1989, one of ten Rising Stars of Tex., Tex. Bus. mag., 1988. Mem.: KC (recorder 2003), Lewisville/San Angelo C. of C. (amb. 1974—77, Amb. of Yr. 1975, 1976), Bus. Ins. Consumers Assn. (exec. com. 1990—95), West Tex. C. of C. (state affairs com., legis. adv. coun.), Homeowners Assn., Tex. Self-Ins. Assn. (co-chair legis. com. 1993), Tex. Taxpayers and Rsch. Assn. (state affairs com. 1985—97), Tex. Assn. Bus. and C. of C. (chmn. state affairs com. 1977—79, bd. dirs. Austin chpt. 1985—88, vice chmn. 1987, statewide state affairs com.), Austin Economic Club, St. Paul's Cath. Ch. (vision com. 2001—02, co-chair 2005 St. Paul's parish festival, pastoral coun. 2007—09), Optimists (sec. Irving chpt. 1973—74, v.p. youth work 1974—75, pres. 1975, bd. dirs. San Angelo chpt. 1977, lt. gov. North Tex. dist. 1978—79, Stars of Tex Rodeo-Art Com. 2004—05). Roman Catholic. Avocations: golf, rock work, fishing, tree trimming, camping. Office: MJWT Consulting 1504 San Antonio Austin TX 78701*

FRANKEL, KENNETH M., lawyer; b. NYC, Apr. 22, 1948; BS, U. Pa., 1970; JD with honors, George Washington U., 1973. Bar: Va. 1973, DC 1981, lic.: US Supreme Ct. 1979, US Ct. Appeals (Fed. Cir.) 1982, US Dist. Ct. (Ea. Dist.) Va. 1995. Law clk. to Hon. George Willi US Ct. of Claims, 1973—74; trial atty. US Justice Dept, Antitrust Divsn.; ptnr. Finnegan, Henderson, Farabow, Garrett & Dunner LLP, Reston, Va., leader intellectual property specialties practice group. Bd. dir. DC Computer Law Forum, 1987—92, pres., 1988—89. Mem.: ABA (Litig. Sect., Antitrust Sect., Patent & Trademark & Copy Law Sect.), Va. State Bar, Am. Intellectual Property Law Assn. (chmn. antitrust law com. 2007—09). Office: Finnegan Henderson Farabow Garrett & Dunner LLP Two Freedom Sq 11955 Freedom Dr Reston VA 20190-5675 Office Phone: 571-203-2700. Office Fax: 202-408-4400. Business E-Mail: kenneth.frankel@finnegan.com.

FRANKEL, LOIS JANE, United States Representative from Florida, former state legislator; b. NYC, May 16, 1948; 1 child, Benjamin. BA magna cum laude, Boston U., 1970; JD, Georgetown U. Law Ctr., 1973. Law clk. to Hon. David Norman DC Superior Ct., Washington, 1973—74; asst. public defender West Palm Beach, Fla., 1974—78; ptnr. Searcy Denney, Scarola, Barnhart & Shipley, 1978—94; mem. Dist. 83 Fla. House of Reps., Tallahassee, 1987—93, mem. Dist. 85, 1995—2003, minority leader, 2000—02; mayor City of West Palm Beach, Fla., 2003—11; mem. US Congress from 22nd Fla. Dist., Washington, 2013—, US House Fgn. Affairs Com., 2013—, US House Transp. & Infrastructure Com., 2013—. Chair AIDS Task Force, 1986—90. Recipient Allen Morris Most Promising Freshman award, 1988, Up and Comers Govt. award S. Fla. Bus. Jour.-Price Waterhouse, 1988, Nelson Poynter Civil Liberties award, 1988, Fla. Brotherhood award, 1989, Weizmann Inst. Sci. award, 1989, Brotherhood award Assn. Retarded Citizens/Fla., 1989, Ann. Legis. award Fla. Children's Forum, 1990, First Legis. award Fla. Student Nursing Assn., 1990, Outstanding Legislator award Fla. Fedn. Bus. and Profl. Women, 1990, Commr.'s award for Prevention of Child Abuse and Neglect U.S. Dept. Health and Human Svcs., 1991, Award American Heart Assn., 1992, Polit. Courage award American Lung Assn., 1992; named Freshman Friend Edn. FTP-NEA, 1987, Citizen of Yr. NASW, 1989, Child Adv. of Yr., 1989, Children's Home Soc., 1989, Child Care Connection, 1990. Mem. NOW, LWV, Fla. Bar Assn., Acad. Fla. Trial Lawyers (Freshman award 1987, Outstanding Legislator award 1990), Fla. Assn. Women Lawyers (past pres. Palm Beach County chpt.), Palm Beach County Bar Assn., Jewish Fedn. Palm Beach County, Exec. Women Palm Beaches (Leadership award 1991), Econ. Devel. Coun. Palm Beach County, Gold Coast Bus. and Profl. Women, American Cancer Soc. (bd. dirs. Palm Beach County, Rookie of Yr. award 1994), Jewish Family and Children's Svcs. (dir. Palm Beach County), Domestic Assault Shelter (founder). Democrat. Jewish. Avocations: sports, music. Office: US House of Representatives 1037 Longworth House Office Bldg Washington DC 20515 also: 2500 North Military Trail Ste 490 Boca Raton FL 33431 Office Phone: 202-225-9890, 561-998-9045.*

FRANKLIN, A. DAVID, retired university dean, music educator, journalist; b. River Junction, Fla., Apr. 28, 1940; s. Benjamin Morgan and Roxie Lucille (Conrad) F.; m. Elda Elizabeth Estep, June 4, 1960; 1 child, Elizabeth Anne. BA, Fla. State U., 1962, MA, 1963, PhD, 1968. Asst. prof. music North Ga. Coll., Dahlonega, 1964-66; prof. music Winthrop U., Rock Hill, SC, 1966—2001, prof. emeritus, 2001—, dean Coll. Visual and Performing Arts, 1995—2000, acting assoc. v.p. grad. studies, 2000—01. Editor Jazz Notes, 2001-2002; contbg. writer Cadence Mag., jazz.com; contbr. columns in newspapers, articles and revs. to, critic for profl. jours. Mem. Jazz Journalists Assn. Avocations: reading, travel. Home: 1996 Rosehaven Ln Rock Hill SC 29732-0900 Personal E-mail: davefranklin@comporium.net.

FRANKLIN, ALBERT B., state legislator; Owner A.B. Auto Sales, Action Plus Communications; mem. Dist. 34 La. House of Reps., 2008—, mem. ins. com., judiciary com., transp., hwys. and pub. works com. Democrat. Office: State Capitol PO Box 44486 Baton Rouge LA 70804 Mailing: 2808 E Broad St Lake Charles LA 70615 Office Phone: 225-342-6945, 337-491-2320. Office Fax: 337-491-2020. Business E-Mail: franklina@legis.state.la.us.

FRANKLIN, BENJAMIN, V, English language educator; b. Gallipolis, Ohio, 1939; s. Benjamin IV and Virginia F.; m. Jo Taft, 1962; children: Abigail, Rebecca Jane. BA, BS, Ohio State U., 1965; MA, Ohio U., 1966, PhD, 1969. Asst. prof. U. Mich., Ann Arbor, 1969-76; assoc. prof. U. S.C., Columbia, 1976-81, prof., 1981—2002, disting. prof. emeritus, 2002—. Sr. Fulbright prof. U. Athens, Greece, 1982-84; vis. prof. U. Helsinki, Finland, 1995; Fulbright prof. U. Hannover, Germany, 2002-03. Author: The Other John Adams, 1705-1740, 2003, Jazz & Blues Musicians of South Carolina: Interviews with Jabbo, Dizzy, Drink, and Others, 2008, Research Guide To American Literature: Colonial Literature, 1607-1776, 2010, Commentaries on Jazz Musicians and Jazz Songs: A History of Jazz in Retrospect, 2011; co-author: Anais Nin: An Introduction, 1979; editor: Boston Printers, Publishers, and Booksellers, 1980, On the Left Bank, 1987, Nathaniel Hawthorne: A Documentary Volume, 2003, The Portable Anais Nin, 2011. Bd. mem. Am. Community Schs., Athens, 1983-84. With USAR, 1960-66. Avocations: jazz, baseball. Office: U SC Dept English Columbia SC 29208-0001

FRANKLIN, DANIEL J. (DAN FRANKLIN), otolaryngologist, surgeon; BA in Biomedical Engrng. summa cum laude, Rice U.; MD, Baylor Coll. of Medicine, Houston, 1981. Diplomate Am. Bd. Otolaryngology, 1984, cert. otology, neurotology and skullbase surgery 2004. Resident gen. surgery Baylor Coll. of Medicine, Houston, 1982—84, resident otolaryngology head and neck surgery, 1984—87, fellow otology, neurotology and skullbase surgery, 1987—88, fellow cmty. medicine, former full-time, clin. faculty mem. dept. of otolaryngology head and neck surgery; fellow neurotology Univ. of Zurich, Switzerland, 1988—89; hosp. affiliations include The Meth. Hosp., St. Luke's Episcopal Hosp., Tex. Children's Hosp., Woman's Hosp. of Tex.; physician Rosewood Ear Nose Throat. Pres. Houston Soc. of Otolaryngology. Fellow: ACS, Tex. Soc. of Ophthalmology and Otolaryngology, Am. Acad. of Otolaryngic Allergy; mem.: Tex. Med. Assn., Harris County Med. Soc., Am. Neurotology Soc., Profl. Adv. Bd. of the Ctr. for Hearing and Speech. Office: Rosewood Ear Nose Throat 2500 Tanglewilde Ste 160 Houston TX 77063 Office Phone: 713-781-9660. Office Fax: 713-974-3672.

FRANKLIN, DOUGLAS E., publishing executive; b. 1957; m. Teresa Franklin; 2 children. Grad., U. Dayton, 1979. Newspaper solicitor Dayton Daily News, 1977—83; with Cox Newspapers, Longview, Tex., Springfield, Ohio; bus. mgr. Dayton Daily News, 1986—96; CEO, pres. Cox Ohio Pub., 1986—96; pub. Dayton Daily News, 2004, Palm Beach Post, Atlanta Jour.-Constitution, 2009; exec v.p. Cox Media Group, 2009—. Office: Cox Media Group 6205 Peachtree Dunwoody Rd Atlanta GA 30328

FRANKLIN, H. ALLEN, retired board member; b. 1945; BSEE, U. Ala., MSEE, 1966. Various engrng. positions Southern Co., Birmingham, Ala., 1970-79, exec. v.p., 1991—99, COO, 1999—2001, pres., 1999—2004, chmn., CEO, 2001—04; asst. to exec. v.p. Ala. Power, 1979-81, sr. v.p., 1981-83; pres., CEO Ga. Power, 1994—99. Bd. dirs. Vulcan Materials Co., 2001—. Office: Vulcan Materials Co Bd Directors 1200 Urban Ctr Dr Birmingham AL 35242 Office Phone: 205-298-3000. Business E-Mail: hfranklin@vmcmail.com.

FRANKLIN, JAMES BURKE, lawyer; b. Statesboro, Ga., Mar. 11, 1938; s. Sam J. and Eva Claire (Burke) Franklin; m. Fay Foy Smith, Mar. 20, 1976; children: Julie Foy, Rebecca Claire. BS, Ga. Inst. Tech.; JD, U. Ga. Bar: Ga. 1963, U.S. Dist. Ct. (so., mid., and no. dists.), U.S. Ct. Appeals (11th cir.). Ptnr. Allen, Edenfield, Brown & Franklin (formerly Allen & Edenfield), 1969—74; founding ptnr. Franklin, Taulbee, Rushing, Snipes and Marsh, P.C., and predecessor firms, Statesboro, Ga., 1974—. Magistrate U.S. Dist. Ct. (so. dist.) Ga., 1979—81; chmn. Devel. Authority Bulloch County. Pres. Bulloch County (Ga.) C. of C. Lt. US Army, 1964—66. Recipient Amicus Curiae Award, Ga. Supreme Ct., 2005, Disting. Svc. Scroll, U. Ga. Law Sch., 2005; named Designated Ga. Super Lawyer, 2005, 2006. Mem.: State Bar Ga. (pres. 2001—02), Rotary Club (Statesboro) (pres.). Methodist. Office: 12 Siebald St PO Box 327 Statesboro GA 30458 Home Phone: 912-764-4506; Office Phone: 912-764-9055. Business E-Mail: jfranklin@ftrsm.com.

FRANKLIN, KIRK, singer; b. Fort Worth, Tex., Jan. 26, 1970; m. Tammy Collins, Jan. 20, 1996; 4 children. Choir leader Kirk Franklin & the Family, 1992, Kirk Franklin's Nu Nation, God's Property. Singer: (albums) Kirk Franklin & the Family, 1993, Kirk Franklin & the Family Christmas, 1995, Whatcha Lookin' 4, 1996 (Best Contemporary Soul Gospel Album, Grammy Awards, 1997), God's Property, 1997 (Best Choir Gospel Album, Grammy Awards, 1998), The Nu Nation Project, 1998 (Best Contemporary Soul Gospel Album, Grammy Awards, 1999), The Rebirth of Kirk Franklin, 2002, Hero, 2005 (Best Contemporary R&B Gospel Album, Grammy Awards, 2007), The Fight of My Life, 2007 (Best Contemporary R&B Gospel Album, Grammy Awards, 2009), Hello Fear, 2011 (Best Gospel Album, Best Gospel Song, Grammy Awards, 2012), (songs) Imagine Me, 2005 (Best Gospel Song, Grammy Awards, 2007), Help Me Believe, 2007 (Best Gospel Song, Grammy Awards, 2009). Recipient Best Gospel Artist award, Black Entertainment TV (BET), 2006, Best Male Artist award, Christian30 Video Music Awards, 2006, Favorite Contemporary Inspirational Artist, Am. Music Awards, 2006, Image award for Gospel Artist, NAACP, 2007, 2008, Soul Train award for Best Gospel Album, 2007, Best Gospel Artist award, Black Entertainment TV (BET), 2007; named to Power 150, Ebony mag., 2008. Office: Fo Yo Soul Entertainment Ste 250 17120 Dallas Pkwy Dallas TX 75248 Office Phone: 972-407-9797. Office Fax: 972-407-9688. E-mail: info@FoYoSoulEntertainment.com.

FRANKLIN, LARRY DANIEL, communications company executive; b. Commerce, Tex., July 16, 1942; s. John Asia and Annie Mae (Castle) F.; m. Charlotte Anne Walker, Aug. 18, 1962; children: Kelly Leigh, Kristi Lynn. BBA, East Tex. State U., 1965; MBA, Tex. Tech. U., 1966. Mem. audit staff Arthur Andersen Co., Dallas, 1966-67; controller, treas. Paris Milling Co., Tex., 1967-69; mem. audit staff Price Waterhouse Co., Dallas, 1969-71; asst. copr. dir. acctg. Harte-Hanks Communications, Inc., San Antonio, 1971, corp. dir. fin. services, 1971-72, chief fin. officer, treas., 1972-74, v.p. fin., treas., 1974-75, v.p. fin., sec.-treas., 1975-78, sr. v.p., pres. newspaper ops., 1978-80, pres., chief oper. officer, 1980—, exec. v.p., 1980-84, COO, 1984-91; pres., CEO Harte-Hanks, Inc., San Antonio, 1991—2003, exec. chmn., 2003—05, chmn., 2005—08, chmn., CEO, 2009—. Bd. dirs. Interfirst Bank, San Antonio; bd. dirs. Mailers Coun., 1992—; chmn. audit com. AP; mem. adv. coun. Incarnate Word Coll. Sch. Bus.; past mem. graphic arts adv. com. Rochester Inst. Tech.; mem. mass comm. adv. com. Tex. Tech U., Lubbock; mem. Coll. Comm. Found. adv. coun. U. Tex., Austin, 1989—. Mem. mass comm. adv. com. St. Thomas Episcopal Ch., San Antonio; past mem. program ops. com. United Way, bd. dirs., 1993—; bd. dirs. East Tex. State U. Found., Commerce; bd. dirs. Tex. Rsch. League, 1992—, mem. exec. com., 1994—, mem. chmn.'s leadership coun.; bd. dirs. San Antonio Area Found., 1993—, mem. devel., comm. and mktg. com.; bd. dirs. San Antonio Econ. Devel. Found., 1992—, mem. exec. com., 1993—; trustee S.W. Rsch. Inst., 1993—; mem. devel. bd. U. Tex., San Antonio, 1992—. Recipient Disting. Alumnus award East Tex. State U., 1982, Disting. Acctg. Alumnus award Tex. Tech U., 1984. Mem. AICPA, Fin. Execs. Inst. (founding bd. dirs., past pres. South Tex. chpt.), Am. Newspaper Pubs. Assn. (newsprint com.), So. Newspaper Pubs. Assn. (bd. dirs. 1988—), Newspaper Assn. Am. (bd. dirs. 1991—, chmn. audit com., vice chmn. pub. policy subcom. on state rels.), Am. Press Inst. (bd. dirs.), Tex. Daily Newspaper Assn. (recycling task force), Beta Alpha Psi (Disting. Alumnus award 1984). Office: Harte-Hanks Inc 200 Concord Plaza Dr Ste 800 San Antonio TX 78216-6942

FRANKLIN, ROBERT MCFARLAND, book publisher; b. Memphis, Mar. 13, 1943; s. Robert Dumont and Mary McFarland (Wilson) F.; m. Cheryl Jane Roberts, Jan. 18, 1975; children: Charles McRee, Nicholas Roberts, William Holliday. AB, Yale U., 1965. With Columbia U. Libr., NYC, 1965-66; editor to exec. editor Scarecrow Press, Metuchen, NJ, 1969-79; pres., founder McFarland & Co., Inc., Publishers, Jefferson, NC, 1979—. Pub. Jour. Info. Ethics, 1992—2008, Base Ball: A Jour. of Early Game, 2006—2008, Black Ball: A Negro Leagues Jour., 2008-. Dir., actor Ashe County Little Theatre, Jefferson, 1980—; libr. adv. bd. Appalachian State U., 1995—; pres. Paul and Florence Thomas Meml. Art Sch., Inc., Glendale Springs, NC, 2007-10. With US Army, 1966-68. Recipient Gov.'s Bus. award in arts and humanities, State of NC, 1984, 87, 97, NC State Arts Coun. Outstanding Vol. award 1991, Ashe County Outstanding Vol. award, 2004. Mem. ALA (pub. com. 1984-88, coun. governing body 1988-2000, pay equity com. 1991-93, intellectual freedom com. 1994-96), Am. Soc. for Psychical Rsch. (dir. 1984-88). Avocations: chess, Go, European languages and cultures, acting, canoeing. Home: 338 Cut Laurel Gap Rd Creston NC 28615-9049 Office: McFarland & Co Inc Pubs Box 611 Jefferson NC 28640-0611 Office Phone: 336-246-4460. Business E-Mail: rfranklin@mcfarlandpub.com.

FRANKLIN, ROBERT MICHAEL, JR., academic administrator, theology studies educator; b. Chgo., Feb. 22, 1954; m. Cheryl Goffney; children: Imani, Robert III, Julian DeShazier. Grad., Morehouse Coll., 1975; MDiv, Harvard U., 1978; PhD, U. Chgo., 1985. Protestant chaplain St. Bernard Hosp., 1981—83; dir. field edn. and instruction in religion and psychol. studies U. Chgo. Divinity Sch., 1982—84; asst. dir. ministerial studies Harvard Divinity Sch., Cambridge, Mass., 1984—85, vis. lectr. African Am. Religion, 1986—88, vis. prof., 2002; dean Black Ch. Studies Colgate Rochester Divinity Sch., NY, 1985—89; asst. prof. dir. Black Ch. Studies Candler Sch. of Theology, Emory U., Atlanta, 1989—91, presdl. disting. prof. social ethics, 2003—07; assoc. prof. ethics and society Sch. Law, Emory U., Atlanta, 1994—94, sr. fellow Ctr. for Interdisciplinary Study of Religion, 2001—07; program officer Human Rights and Social Justice Program Ford Found., NYC, 1995—97; pres. Interdenom. Theol. Ctr., Atlanta, 1997—2002, Morehouse Coll., Atlanta, 2007—. Commentator All Things Considered, Nat. Pub. Radio, 2001—; theologian in residence Chatauqua Inst., NY, 2005. Author: Another Day's Journey: Black Churches Confronting the American Crisis, Liberating Visions: Human Fulfillment and Social Justice in African American Thought, Crisis in the Village: Restoring Hope to African American Communities, 2007; cons. Steven Spielberg/DreamWorks prodn. Prince of Egypt. Bd. dirs. Congress of Nat. Black Chs., Ind. Univ. Ctr. on Philanthropy, Ga. Coun. for Humanities, Jessie Ball DuPont Fund, Joseph Lowery Inst. for Justice and Human Rights, Clark Atlanta U.;

mem. adv. bd. Children's Def. Fund's Black Ch. and Cmty. Crusade. Avocations: golf, swimming. Office: Morehouse Coll Office of Pres 830 Westview Dr SW Atlanta GA 30314 Office Phone: 404-215-2645. Office Fax: 404-659-6536. E-mail: rfranklin@morehouse.edu.

FRANKLIN, SHIRLEY CLARKE, community development firm executive, former mayor; b. Phila., May 10, 1945; d. Eugene Haywood Clarke and Ruth (Lyons) White; m. David McCoy Franklin, Feb. 5, 1972 (div. 1986); children: Kai Ayanna, Cabral Holsey, Kali Jamilla. BA, Howard U., 1968, LLD (hon.), 2002; MA, U. Pa., 1969, LLM (hon.), 2007. Contract compliance officer US Dept. Labor, Washington, 1966-68; instr. social scis. Talledega Coll., 1969-71; from dir. to commr. Dept. Cultural Affairs City of Atlanta, 1978-82, chief adminstrv. officer, 1982-90, exec. officer for ops., 1990—2001, mayor, 2002—10; chair, CEO Purpose Built Communities, Inc., Atlanta, 2010—; William & Camille Cosby Endowed Chair Spelman Coll., Atlanta, 2010—. Bd. dirs. Mueller Water Products, Inc., 2010—, Delta Air Lines, Inc., 2011—. Sr. v.p. external rels. Atlanta Com. Olympic Games, 1991—97; mem. Ga. Council for the Arts, Atlanta, 1979—82; trustee Atlanta Symphony Orch., 1977—81, Atlanta Found., 1980—; co-chair Atlanta Regional Commn. on Homelessness; mem. advisory bd. Ga. Women's Polit. Caucus, Atlanta, 1982—84; bd. dirs. Nat. Urban Coalition, Washington, 1980—83, UN Inst. for Tng. & Rsch.; chmn. expansion arts panel Nat. Endowment for the Arts, Washington, 1980—82; majority ptnr. Urban Environ. Solutions, LLC, 1998—; co-chair bd. dirs. Nat. Ctr. for Civil & Human Rights. Recipient Leadership award, NAACP Atlanta chpt., 1987, Disting. Alumni award, Nat. Assn. for Equal Opportunity Higher Edn., 1983, John F. Kennedy Profile in Courage award, John F. Kennedy Libr. Found., 2005; named one of America's Best Leaders, US News & World Report, 2005, The 5 Best Big-City Mayors in America, TIME mag., 2005, The 100 Most Influential Black Americans, Ebony mag., 2006; named to Acad. Women Achievers, YWCA Greater Atlanta, 1986, The Power 150, Ebony mag., 2008. Mem.: Nat. Forum Black Pub. Adminstrs., Chautauqua Circle. Democrat. Avocations: gardening, travel, politics, fine arts. Office: Purpose Built Communities Inc 3445 Peachtree Rd NE Ste 175 Atlanta GA 30326 Office Phone: 404-591-1400.

FRANKLIN, STANLEY PHILLIP, computer scientist, cognitive scientist, retired mathematician; b. Memphis, Aug. 14, 1931; s. Sam and Lily (Rosenblum) F.; m. Jeannie Stonebrook, Apr. 1, 1979; children— Lynn Ann, Michele Suzanne Safa, Phillip Byron, Bruce Eric, Halli Eileen, Elena Simone Berman, Sunny Patrice, Sam Elliot. BS, U. Memphis, 1959; MA, UCLA, 1962, PhD, 1963; NSF post-doctoral fellow, U. Wash., Seattle, 1963-64. Asst. prof. math. U. Fla., 1964-65; assoc. prof., then prof. Carnegie-Mellon U., 1965-72; prof. math., chmn. dept. math. scis. U. Memphis, 1972-84, prof. computer sci., 1984—, co-dir. Inst. for Intelligent Sys., 1987—2004, Dunarant prof. computer sci., 2000—03, W. Harry Feinstone interdisciplinary rsch. prof., 2004—13. Vis. prof. Indian Inst. Tech., Kanpur, Technion, Haifa, Israel; vis. mem. Mathematische Centrum, Amsterdam, Netherlands; condr. workshops, cons. in field. Author research papers and books in field. Served with USMCR, 1951-53. Recipient Bd. Visitors Eminent Faculty award, 1997. Mem. Assn. for Computing Machinery, Am. Assn. for Artificial Intelligence, Cognitive Sci. Soc., Internat. Neural Network Soc., Sigma Xi, Pi Mu Epsilon. Home: 5736 Rich Rd Memphis TN 38120-2086 Office: U Memphis FedEx Institute Technology Memphis TN 38152-0001 Business E-Mail: franklin@memphis.edu.

FRANKS, ALLEN P., retired research institute executive, educator; b. Cleve., Nov. 12, 1936; s. Stanley Arthur and Helen Dorothy (Kulwicki) F.; m. Cary Bajko, Feb. 2, 1963; children: Mathew, Sara. BS, U. Miami, 1959; LLB, Case Western Res. U., 1963, JD, 1968. Cert. chem. engr. Patent atty. B.F. Goodrich Co., Akron, Ohio, 1963-65; chemist, mgr. paint testing lab. PPG Industries, Barberton, Ohio, 1965-66; tech. dir., lab. mgr. Reichhold Chems., Inc., Cuyahoga Falls, Ohio, 1966-76; instr. Inst. Astral Studies, Inc., Akron, 1974-80, pres., 1977-80; mgr. tech. sales Sovereigh Chem. Co., Cuyahoga Falls, 1980-86; pres. I.A.S. Inc., 1986-94; sec.-treas. rsch. divsn. IAA, 1990-95, pres., 1995—2007. Lectr. astrology, biorhythms, tennis Akron U., 1974-79, Kent (Ohio) State U., 1973-77. Contbr. articles to profl. jours. Bd. dirs. Persephone Found., Bath, Ohio, 1974-80, chmn., 1981-86; instr. tennis YWCA, Goodyear Racquet Club. With USCGR, 1954-62. Fellow Am. Inst. Chemists; mem. AAAS, N.Y. Acad. Scis., Ohio Inst. Chemists (treas. 1976-84, pres. 1984-90), Am. Chem. Soc., Akron Rubber Group, N.E. Ohio Rubber Group, Theosophical Soc. South Fla. (treas. 1996-99), Mensa, Intertel, Crystal Lake Country Club, Am. Legion, Fraternal Order Police, Univ. Club, Goodyear Racquet Club, Phi Delta Phi.

FRANKS, CANDACE ANN, state banking agency administrator; b. Memphis, Nov. 18, 1952; d. James William and Barbara Elizabeth Webb; m. Roger Allen Franks, July 23, 1977; 1 child, Ava Elizabeth. BA, Ark. State U., 1974, MA, 1976; JD, U. Ark., 1979. Bar: Ark. 1979. Gen. counsel Ark. State Bank Dept., Little Rock, 1980-95; dep. bank commr. Ark. State Bank Dept., Little Rock, 1995—2007, commr., 2007. Mem. Gov.'s Task Force to Revise Banking Code, Legis. Task Force to Study NAFTA, 1995, Gov.'s Task Force on Interstate Banking, 1997—; mem. legis. com. Conf. State Bank Suprs., Washington, 1997—. Named one of Top 10 Women in Ark., Ark. Bus. Mag., 1996, 97, 98. Mem. Ark. Bar Assn., Pulaski County Bar Assn., Conf. State Bank Suprs. Office: Arkansas State Bank Department Sedgwick Ctr 400 Hardin Rd Ste 100 Little Rock AR 72211-2613 Office Phone: 501-324-9019. E-mail: cfranks@banking.state.ar.us.

FRANKS, HERSCHEL PICKENS, judge; b. Savannah, Tenn., May 28, 1930; s. Herschel R. Franks and Pickens Vada; m. Judy Black; 1 child, Ramona. PA, U. Tenn.; student, U. Md.; JD, U. Tenn., Knoxville; grad., U. Tenn. Bar: Tenn. 1959, US Supreme Ct. 1968. Claims atty. US Fidelity & Guaranty Co., Knoxville, Tenn., 1958; ptnr. Harris, Moon, Meacham & Franks, Chattanooga, 1959—70; chancellor 3d Chancery divsn. Hamilton County, 1970—78; judge Tenn. Ct. Appeals, 1978—, presiding judge, 2004—12. Spl. justice Tenn. Supreme Ct., 1979, 1986—87, 2002—04; presiding judge Hamilton County Trial Cts., 1977—78; spl. judge Tenn. Ct. Criminal Appeals, 1990—92, commn. to study appellate cts., 1990—92. With N.G. USAF, 1949—50, with USAF, 1950—54. Mem.: ABA (Merit award), Inst. Jud. Adminstrn., Chattanooga Bar Assn. (pres. 1968—69, Founds. of Freedom award 1986), Chattanooga Bar Found., Tenn. Bar Found., Tenn. Bar Assn. (Merit award 1968—69, Justice Francis F. Drowota III award 2009), Mountain City Club, City Farmers Club, Optimists (pres. 1965—66, Cmty. Svc. award 1971), Phi Alpha Delta. Mem. United Ch. Of Christ. Office: 333 James Blvd Signal Mountain TN 37377 Home Phone: 423-886-4759.*

FRANKS, JAMIE (JAMES R. FRANKS JR.), lawyer, former political organization administrator; b. Mooreville, Miss., Dec. 26, 1972; BA in Polit. Sci., U. Miss.; JD, Miss. Coll. Law. Mem. Miss. House of Reps. from 19th Dist., 2000—07, chmn. ways & means com., mem. conservation & water resrouces com., pub. health & welfare com.; ptnr. Wheeler & Franks Attys. At Law, Tupelo, Miss.; chmn. Miss. Dem. Party, 2008—12. Mem.: Nat. Shoot to Retrieve Assn., Houston Birdhunters Club. Democrat. Office: 114 S Broadway PO Box 681 Tupelo MS 38802 Office Phone: 662-842-0380, 662-884-5874. Office Fax: 662-690-8947. E-mail: jfranks@wheelerfrankslaw.com.

FRANKS, JOHN JULIAN, anesthesiologist, educator; b. Pueblo, Colo., Apr. 9, 1929; s. Frank Alec and Lila Ethelda (Ownbey) F.; m. Kathryne Jean Sammon, Dec. 27, 1951 (dec. May 1999); children: John Alec, William Thomas, Margaret Lila, Elizabeth Ellen; m. Mary Lou Hawkins Shattuck, Apr. 9, 2004. BA, U. Colo., 1951, MD, 1954. Assoc. dir., dir. clin. rsch. ctr. U. Colo., Denver, 1969-81; assoc. chief of staff rsch. Denver VA Hosp., 1969-82, chief hematology div., 1983; resident in anesthesiology Vanderbilt U. Hosp., Nashville, 1984-86; prof., dir. rsch. div. Vanderbilt U., Nashville, 1987-98, dir. div. organ transplant anesthesia, 1989-98, interim chmn. dept. anesthesiology, 1993-94, prof. emeritus, 1999—. Author chpts. in books; contbr. articles to Jour. Gen. Physiology, Jour. Clin. Investigation, New Eng. Jour. of Medicine, Anesthesiology and N.Y. Acad. Sci.; contbr. numerous articles to profl. jours. Col. USAF, 1955-63, 68-69. NIH grantee U. Colo., 1963-69, 64-82, Vanderbilt U., 1992-96, U.S. VA grantee Denver VA Hosp., 1969-83. Fellow AAAS; mem. Am. Soc. Anesthesiologists, Am. Physiol. Soc., Cen. Soc. Clin. Rsch., Internat. Soc. Thrombosis Haemostosis, Soc. Gen. Physiologists. Business E-Mail: john.frentes@vanderbilt.edu.

FRANKS, RONALD DWYER, dean, psychiatrist, educator; b. Balt., Jan. 15, 1946; s. Wylie and H. Jeanette (Dwyer) F.; m. Vicky Ruth Vicklund; children: Aaron Matthew, Alexis Linda. Student, Albion Coll., 1964-67; MD with distinction, U. Mich., 1971. Intern Virginia Mason Hosp., Seattle, 1971-72; resident in psychiatry U. Colo. Med. Ctr., Denver, 1972-76; instr. psychiatry U. Colo. Sch. Medicine, Denver, 1976-77, asst. prof. psychiatry, 1977-83, assoc. prof., 1983-88, asst. dean student affairs, 1982-84, asst. dean student and curricular affairs, dir. inpatient svcs. dept. psychiatry, 1986-88; dean, prof. psychiatry U. Minn. Sch. Medicine, Duluth, 1988-97; v.p. health affairs East Tenn. State U., Johnson City, 1997—2007, dean James H. Quillen Coll. Medicine, 1997—2006, prof. psychiatry and behavioral scis., 1997—2007; v.p. health scis. U. South Ala., 2007—. Bd. dirs. Bank of Tenn., 2004—07; chmn. State Health Planning and Adv. Bd., Tenn. Contbr. numerous articles to profl. jours. Mem. Med. Assn. State Ala., Am. Psychiat. Assn., Alpha Omega Alpha. Office: VP for Health Sciences Univ of S Alabama 307 N University Blvd CSAB 170 Mobile AL 36688-0002 Office Phone: 251-460-7189. Office Fax: 251-460-6073. Business E-Mail: rfranks@usouthal.edu.

FRANKS, TOMMY RAY, retired military officer; b. Wynnewood, Okla., June 17, 1945; m. Cathryn Carley, Mar. 22, 1969; 1 child, Jacqueline Franks Matlock. BSBA, U. Tex., Arlington, 1971; MS in Pub. Adminstrn., Shippensburg U. Pa., 1985; grad., Armed Forces Staff Coll., U.S. Army War Coll. Commd. 2d lt. U.S. Army, 1967, advanced through grades to gen., 2000; comdr. 2d bn. 78th F.A. 1st Armored Divsn., Germany, 1981-84; dep. asst. chief staff G3 III Corps, Ft. Hood, Tex., 1985-86; comdr. div. arty. 1st Cav. Div., 1987-88, chief staff, 1988-89, asst. divsn. comdr. Operation Desert Shield-Storm, Saudi Arabia, Iraq, 1990-91; asst. comdt. U.S. Army F.A. Sch., Ft. Sill, Okla., 1991-92; dir. La. Maneuvers Task Force, Office Chief of Staff U.S. Army, Ft. Monroe, Va., 1992—94; asst. chief staff C3/J3/G3 UN and combined forces command U.S. Forces Korea, 8th U.S. Army, 1994—95; commdr. second infantry divsn., 1995-97; comdr. 3rd United States Army Ft. McPherson, Ga., 1997-2000; comdr. US Ctrl. Command, MacDill AFB, Fla., 2000—03, Operation Enduring Freedom, Afghanistan, 2001—02, Operation Iraqi Freedom, 2003. Bd. dirs. Bank of America Corp., 2006—09. Co-author (with Malcolm McConnell): (memoir) American Soldier, 2004 (Publishers Weekly Bestseller). Decorated Def. Disting. Svc. Medal, Disting. Svc. Medal with one oak leaf cluster, Legion of Merit with 3 oak leaf clusters, Bronze Star medal with V device and 4 oak leaf clusters, Purple Heart with 2 oak leaf clusters; named Knight Comdr. of the Brit. Empire, 2004, Presdl. Medal of Freedom, 2004. Home: RR 1 Box 86A Roosevelt OK 73564-9764 Office Phone: 813-839-8234. Business E-Mail: admin@tommyfranks.com.

FRANKSON-KENDRICK, SARAH JANE, publisher; b. Bradford, Pa., Sept. 24, 1949; d. Sophronus Ahimus and Elizabeth Jane (Sears) McCutcheon; m. James Michael Kendrick, Jr., May 22, 1982. Customer svc. rep. Laros Printing/Osceola Graphics, Bethlehem, Pa., 1972-73; assoc. editor Babcox Publs., Akron, Ohio, 1973-74, Bill Comms., Akron, Ohio, 1974-75, sr. editor, 1975-77, editor-in-chief, 1977-81; assoc. pub. Chilton Co./ABC Pub., Chgo., 1981-83, pub., 1983-89, group pub. Radnor, Pa., 1989-93; group v.p. Cahners Bus. Info. (formerly Chilton Co.), Radnor, Pa., 1993-98; divsn. v.p. Primedia Intertec, Chgo., 1999—2001. Exec. MBA prof. Northwood U., mem. adv. coun. Mem. oper. com. Primedia Intertec. Recipient Automotive Replacement Edn. award Northwood Inst., 1983, award for young leadership and excellence Automotive Hall of Fame, 1984; bd. dirs. Automotive Hall of Fame. Mem. Automotive Found. for Aftermarket (trustee), Automotive Parts and Accessories Assn. (bd. dirs., exec. com., sec., treas., strategic planning com., edn. com., Disting Svc. award 1993), Automotive Svc. Industry Assn. (bd. dirs. automotive divsn. com.), Automotive Svc. Banyan Golf Club (Wellington, Fla.), Palm Beach Polo and Country Club (Wellington, Fla.), Palm Beach yatch Club(Fla.) Republican.

FRANTZ, ELMAN G., pediatric cardiologist, surgeon; b. Lebanon, Pa., Jan. 17, 1956; MD, Pa. State U., Hershey, 1981. Diplomate Am. Bd. Pediat., Am. Bd. Pediat. Cardiology, lic. NC. Intern pediat. U. NC Meml. Hosp., Chapel Hill, 1981—82, resident pediat., 1982—84, fellowship pediat. cardiology, 1984—85, staff divsn. cardiology; fellowship pediat. cardiology Cardiovasc. Rsch. Inst., San Francisco, 1985—87; assoc. prof. pediat. U. NC Sch. Medicine. Coord. pediat. cardiothoracic transplant team U. NC Meml. Hosp. Contbr. articles to profl. jours. Mem.: Am. Acad. Pediat. Office: U NC Sch Medicine CB 7220 Bldg 311 Burnett Womack Chapel Hill NC 27599 Office Phone: 919-966-4601. Office Fax: 919-966-6894.

FRANTZ, FRANCIS X., telecommunications industry executive, lawyer; married, 1987; 2 children. BA with honors, U. Akron; JD, Ohio State U. Ptnr. Thompson, Hine & Flory; chief legal officer Alltel Corp., Little Rock, sr. v.p., gen. counsel, 1990—2006, corp. sec., 1992—2006, exec. v.p., external affairs, 1998—2006; chmn. Alltel Holding Corp., 2005—06, Swyft Technologies, LLC (formerly XSell, LLC), Jacksonville, Fla., 2010—. Chmn. Windstream Corp., 2006—10, bd. dirs., 2006—. Chmn. USTelecom, 2006—07. Office: Swift Technologies LLC 10151 Deerwood Park Blvd 200-320 Jacksonville FL 32256-0566 Office Phone: 904-854-6700. Business E-Mail: francis.frantz@windstream.com.

FRANZ, FRANK ANDREW, academic administrator, physicist, educator; b. Phila., Sept. 16, 1937; s. Russell Ernest and Edna (Keller) F.; m. Judy Rosenbaum, July 11, 1959; 1 child, Eric Douglas. BS in Physics, Lafayette Coll., 1959; MS in Physics, U. Ill., 1961, PhD in Physics, 1964. Research assoc. U. Ill., Urbana, 1964-65; asst. prof. physics Ind. U., Bloomington, 1967-70, assoc. prof., 1970-74, prof., 1974-85, assoc. dean Coll. Arts and Scis., 1974-77, dean faculties, 1977-82; prof. physics, provost, v.p. academic affairs and research W.Va. U., Morgantown, 1985-91; prof. physics, pres. U. Ala., Huntsville, 1991—2007, prof. emeritus, 2008—, pres. emeritus, 2008—. Guest scientist Swiss Fed. Inst. Tech., Zurich, 1965-67, U. Munich, 1978. Contbr. articles to profl. jours. NSF fellow, 1965-67, Alfred P. Sloan fellow, 1968-70. Fellow AAAS, Am. Phys. Soc.; mem. AAUP (pres. Bloomington, Ind. chpt. 1972-73), Am. Assn. Physics Tchrs., Sigma Xi, Phi Kappa Phi. Avocation: tennis.

FRANZEN, LARRY WILLIAM, aerospace electronics engineer; b. Joliet, Ill., Sept. 6, 1945; s. Elmer William and Evelyn M. (Leonard) F.; m. Pennie Ann Gardner, Aug. 10, 1968 (div. Aug. 1975). A in Applied Tech., DeVry Tech. Inst., 1966; BSEE, Marquette U., 1969. Assoc. engr. McDonnell Douglas Aerospace, St. Louis, 1969-70, engr., 1970-76, sr. engr. Langley AFB, Va., 1977-78, lead engr. Eglin AFB, Fla., 1978-93, sr. project engr., 1994—. Mem. Choctaw Multi-hull Assn., Ft. Walton Yacht Club, Emerald Coast Cyclist. Avocations: sailing, bicycling, skiing. Home: 1421 Bayshore Dr Niceville FL 32578-3401 Office: McDonnell Douglas Aerospace PO Box 1867 Eglin AFB FL 32542-0867

FRASER, RUTH HODGES, city clerk; b. Roanoke, Va., Jan. 15, 1931; d. James Elpherson and Ruth Elizabeth (Morgan) Hodges; m. Leon Menaclus Smith, June 18, 1978 (dec.); children: Dorothy Ruth Smith Swift, Marvis Frances Smith Mills; m. Donald Fraser. Student, Potomac State Coll., 1949-51; cert. mcpl. clk., Old Dominion U., 1982. Cert. mcpl. clk. Va. Legal sec. Commonwealth Atty., Woodstock, Va., 1952-54; adminstrv. asst. Nelson Oil Corp., Mt. Jackson, Va., 1954-56; exec. sec., office mgr. Tidewater Va. Devel. Co., Norfolk, Va., 1956-72; from corp. sec. to purchasing agt. Nepratex Industries, Virginia Beach, Va., 1972-77; realtor, life agt. Real Estate/Ins., 1977—; city clk. City of Virginia Beach, 1978—. Sec.-treas. Hospice Virginia Beach, 1981—86; liaison, coord. Mayor's Sister City Commn., 1993—; mem. IIMC Acad. Advanced Edn., 1984—87, 1987—; founder Z House shelter for battered spouses; Va. state coord. Sister Cities Internat., 2005, parliamentarian bd. dirs., 2006, chair, state coords.; pres. Sister Cities Assn. Vir. Beach, 2010. Recipient Quills award, IIMC Acad. Advanced Edn., 1991, Hon. Recognition Julian F. Hirst award for Disting. Svc., 1994; named Ky. Col., 1993, W.Va. Mountaineer, 1993. Mem.: Va. Mcpl. Clks. Assn. (pres. 1982—84, master mcpl. clk. 2000—, treas. 2002, Clk. of the Yr. 1987), Lifelong Acad. Advanced Edn., Intenrat. Mcpl. Clks. (bd. dirs. 1986—89, chair internat. com. 1989—91, chair year 2000 planning com. 1998—), Pilot Club (officer 1960—72), Shriners, Daus. of Nile (mem. gen. grand chpt. credentials com. 2006—), Order Eastern Star (worthy matron Westminster chpt. #99 1966—67, worthy grand matron grand chpt. Va. 1993—94, worthy matron Westminster chpt. #99 2004—05), Zonta Internat. (bd. dirs. 1983—90). Avocations: crafts, bicycling, ice skating, travel. Home: 1153 Belvoir Ln Virginia Beach VA 23464-6766 Office: City of Virginia Beach Room 281 City Hall Virginia Beach VA 23456 Office Phone: 757-385-8343. E-mail: rhfraser@vbgov.com.

FRASER, TROY L., state legislator; b. Abilene, Tex., Aug. 10, 1949; s. Harold L. and Jo Hudson Fraser; m. Linda Cochran, 1969; children: Chase, Sunny, Andrew. Attended, Angelo State U., U. Tex., Arlington. Founder, former chief devel. officer Palex, Inc. (formerly Fraser Industries); mem. Dist. 69 Tex. House of Representatives, 1987—92; mem. Dist. 24 Tex. State Senate, 1997—. Chmn. Big Spring Ind. Team, 1983—86; dir. Big Spring Ind. Found., 1983—88. Recipient Taxpayers' Advocate award, Texans for Fiscal Responsibility, 2009, Wind Champion Legacy award, The Wind Coalition, 2008, True Agricultural Champion award, Tex. Farm Bureau, 2011, Jack Griesenbeck Leadership in Regionalism award, Capitol Area Coun. of Governments, 2011; named Amb. of Yr., Big Spring C. of C., 1979, Nat. Rep. Legislator of Yr., 1991, Top Legislator in America, Am. Legis. Exch. Coun., 2006, Champion of Free Enterprise, Tex. Assn. of Bus., 2007. Mem.: Big Spring Rotary (pres. 1980—81, dir., dist. cmty. svc. ctr. 1987—99, Rotarian of Yr. 1981). Republican. Methodist. Office: 1920 N Main Ste 101 Belton TX 76513 also: PO Box 12068 Capitol Station Austin TX 78711 also: 500 Chestnut Ste 810 Abilene TX 79602 also: 101 Highway 281 North Ste 203 Marble Falls TX 78654 Office Phone: 254-939-3562, 512-463-0124, 325-676-7404, 830-693-9900.

FRASIER, CURTIS R., lawyer, energy executive; b. Tempe, Ariz. m. Pamela Frasier; 2 children. BA, Ariz. State U., 1977; JD, U. Tulsa, 1982. Joined Shell Oil Co. (subs. of Royal Dutch Shell plc), 1982; COO Tejas Gas Corp. (subs. of Royal Dutch Shell plc); with Shell Internat. Petroleum Co. (subs. of Royal Dutch Shell plc), London, England, 1990; pres., Energy Svcs. Royal Dutch Shell plc, sec., 1992; mgr., Supply Ops. Shell Oil Products Co.(subs. of Royal Dutch Shell plc), 1994—96; pres. Shell Midstream Enterprises (subs. of Royal Dutch Shell plc), 1997—98; various positions, Midstream and Gas & Power businesses Royal Dutch Shell plc, 1998; gen. counsel Royal Dutch Shell Plc, 2002; exec. v.p., Americas Shell Gas & Power Shell Oil Co. (subs. of Royal Dutch Shell plc), 2008—. Office: Shell Oil Co 910 Louisiana St Houston TX 77002 Office Fax: 713-241-4044.*

FRASURE, CARL MAYNARD, political science professor; b. Morgantown, W.Va., Aug. 21, 1938; s. Carl Maynard and Louise (Durham) F.; m. Beverly Brown, Sept. 1, 1962 (div. Aug. 1980); 1 child, Stephanie Frasure Goff. BS, W.Va. U., Morgantown, 1962, MA, 1965, MS, 1966, PhD, 1980; postgrad., Ohio U., Athens, 1985. Cert. secondary tchr., W.Va. Extension prof. W.Va. U., Morgantown, 1966-82; dir. student svcs. Bluefield State U., W.Va., 1982-83; prof. Salem-Teikyo U., W.Va., 1983—2001, chmn. polit. sci. dept. W.Va., 1983—2001, asst. to acad. dean W.Va., 1984-86; prof. Fairmont State Coll., W.Va., 2001—. Cons. W.Va. Dept. Edn., Charleston, 1990; chair social scis. divsn., 1994-2001. Author, editor: W.Va. U. Non-credit Programs Catalog, 1980. Treas. Polit. Action Com. for Better Edn., Clarksburg, 1990; mem. Bridgeport Police Civil Svc. Commn., W.Va., 1993—; mem. Clarksburg Police Civil Svc. Commn, 1994—. Sgt. US Army, 1957-65. US Dept. Edn. grantee, 1966-70, 82-87, Options grantee Brown U., 1991. Mem. Am. Polit. Sci. Assn., W.Va. Polit. Sci. Assn., VFW, Phi Delta Kappa (treas. W.Va. U. chpt. 1984), Lions (treas. Bridgeport chpt. 1987-93, pres. 1993—), Am. Legion, Elks (essay judge Clarksburg chpt. 1983—). Democrat. Episcopalian. Avocations: reading, politics, travel. Home: 1088 Taylor St Clarksburg WV 26301-4227 Office: Fairmont State Coll Locust Ave Fairmont WV 26554 Business E-Mail: cfrasure@fscwv.edu.

FRATELLO, MIKE (MICHAEL ROBERT FRATELLO), sportscaster, former professional basketball coach; b. Hackensack, NJ, Feb. 24, 1947; Student, Montclair State Coll., U. R.I. Asst. coach U. R.I., Kingston, 1971, James Madison U., Harrisburg, Va., 1972-75, Villanova U., Phila., 1976-78, Atlanta Hawks, 1978-82, NY Knicks, 1982-83; head coach Atlanta Hawks, 1983-90, Cleve. Cavaliers, 1993—99, Memphis Grizzlies, 2004—06; NBA color anaylst NBC Sports, 1990-93; NBA analyst Turner Sports, 2000—04, 2007—. Named NBA Coach of Yr., 1986. Office: Turner Sports 1 CNN Ctr 100 International Blvd Atlanta GA 30348

FRATRIK, DEBORAH A., food service executive; B with honors, Temple U., Phila.; MS, East Stroudsburg U., Pa. Various positions including dir. ops. Pizza Hut; dir. ops. TRC; v.p. HR systems & tng. Shoney's Inc.; divsn. pres. Golden Corral; v.p. ops., innovation and tng. Metromedia Restaurant Group, Plano, Tex.; COO Mongolian

Oper. Co. LLC; regional v.p. restaurant ops. Cracker Barrel Old Country Store, Inc. Mem. adv. bd. Kozy Shack Enterprises, Restaurant ABC. Mem.: Women's Foodservice Forum (co-chair mentor com., mem. exec. programs com., bd. dirs.), Mich. Restaurant Assn. (bd. dirs. 2010). Office: Cracker Barrel Old Country Store Inc 305 Hartmann Dr Lebanon TN 37088 Office Phone: 615-444-5533. Office Fax: 615-443-9476.

FRATTO, FRED J., construction executive; BA, Fairmont State U.; MS in Indsl. & Labor Rels., W.Va. U. V.p. human resources Newell Rubbermaid, 1995—99; v.p. human resources & adminstrn. Gulfstream Aerospace, 1999—2002; v.p. human resources Beazer Homes USA, Inc., 2002—04, sr. v.p. human resources, 2004—. Office: Beazer Homes USA Inc 1000 Abernathy Rd NE Ste 260 Atlanta GA 30328-5648 Office Phone: 770-829-3700. Office Fax: 770-481-2808.

FRAZER, JOHN HOWARD, tennis association and retired manufacturing executive; b. Cin., June 3, 1924; s. H. Howard and Amelia (Spieth) F.; m. Joann Elizabeth McEvoy, Nov. 3, 1956; children: John Howard Jr., Victoria S. Frazer. BA, U. Cin., 1948, JD, 1950. Bar: Ohio 1950. V.p. H. Howard Frazer Co., Cin., 1950-62, pres., 1962-76; treas., dir. Cin. Transit Co., 1957-73; dir. Am. Controlled Industries, Cin., 1973-86, pres., 1974-75, exec. v.p., 1975-86; dir. Vulcan Corp., Cin., 1960-91, pres., 1975-88; sec., dir. Valley Industries, 1973-86, Colorpac, Inc., 1973-86. Chmn. U.S. Open Tennis Championships, 1993-94. Chmn. men's com. Cin. Symphony Orch., 1971-73; pres. Cincinnatus Assn., 1969-70; chmn. Western Tennis Championships, Cin., 1970-73; dir. Internat. Tennis Hall of Fame, 1979-2002, hon. life dir., 2002—, exec. com. 1985-2002, chmn. internat. coun. 1996-2007. Served with USAAF, 1942-45. Recipient Highest Effort award, Sigma Alpha Epsilon, 1995, Chmn.'s award, Internat. Tennis Hall of Fame, 2000, Golden Achievement award, 2003; named to, USTA/Midwest Tennis Hall of Fame, 2001, Greater Cin. Tennis Hall Fame, 2004. Mem. USTA (mem. exec. com. 1975—, chmn. sanction and schedule com. 1973-86, bd. dirs. 1986-96, v.p. 1986-88, sec. 1988-90, 1st v.p. 1990-92, pres. 1993-94, chmn. nat. men's ranking com. 1971-73, long-range planning com. 1981-87, internat. com. 1999—, hon. chair 2003—), Internat. Tennis Fedn. (del. 1991-96, mem. com. mgmt. 1993-97, v.p. 1995-97, hon. life counsellor 1997—, mem. vets. com. 1996-99, chmn. vets. com. 1996-97, mem. constl. com. 1997-2003, mem. rewards and recognition com. 2000-, Svc. to Game award 1998), Lawn Tennis Clubs USA, France, Mex., Am. Footwear Industries Assn. (dir.), Rubber Mfrs. Assn. (dir.), Shoe Last Mfrs. Assn. (pres. 1978-79), Univ. Club, Cin. CC, Cin. Tennis Club, Quail Creek CC (Naples), Bay Colony Club (Naples), All-Eng. Lawn Tennis Club (Wimbledon), Royal Poinciana Golf Club (Naples). Home: 148 Mooringe Park Dr Apt L-202 Naples FL 34103 Personal E-mail: bumpy@joandbumpy.com.

FRAZER, VINCENT F., territorial attorney general; b. St. Thomas, VI; m. Anne McLeish; 4 children. BA, Carthage Coll., Kenosha, Wis., 1980; JD, Howard U., Washington, 1984. Paralegal criminal divsn. VI Dept. Law, 1980—81; staff atty. VI Port Authority, 1984—88; pvt. practice, 1988—93; mng. ptnr. Frazer & Williams, 1993—2005; atty. gen. Virgin Islands, Charlotte Amalie, 2007—. Mem. VI Pub. Defenders Adminstrn. Bd., 1999—. Sch. bd. mem. St. Thomas Calvary Christian Acad. Mem.: ABA, VI Com. Bar Examiners, Nat. Assn. Criminal Defense Lawyers, Am. Trial Lawyers Assn., VI Bar Assn. (bd. govs. 1988—89), Alpha Phi Alpha. Democrat. Office: Department of Justice GERS Complex 488-50C Kronprinsdens Gade St Thomas VI 00802 Office Phone: 340-774-5666.*

FRAZIER, GLORIA, state legislator; b. Apr. 19; m. Wayne Frazier. State rep. Dist. 123, Ga., 2007—; mem. Human Relations and Aging Com., 2007—, Banks and Banking Com., 2007—, Pub. Safety and Homeland Security Com., 2007—. Democrat. Home: 2717 Willis Foreman Rd # 1 Hephzibah GA 30815-6936 Home Phone: 706-560-9709; Office Phone: 706-560-0265. E-mail: gloria.frazier@house.ga.gov.

FRAZIER, HILLMAN TEROME, state legislator; b. Jackson, Miss., May 17, 1950; m. Jean Maria Clayton; children: Julian Todd, Gabrielle Patrice, Jordan. Former draftsman; mem. Dist. 67 Miss. House of Reps., 1980—94; mem. Dist. 27 Miss. State Senate, 1995—; atty.; cons. Mem.: NAACP, Career Devel. Ctr., Millsaps Coll. Leadership, Leadership Jackson, Nat. Conf. Black Lawyers, Mason. Democrat. Protestant. Mailing: 2066 Queensroad Ave Jackson MS 39213 Home Phone: 601-982-1871; Office Phone: 601-359-3221, 601-973-3421. Office Fax: 601-359-5957, 601-359-2437. E-mail: hfrazier@senate.ms.gov.

FRAZIER, JOHN R., state legislator; b. Charleston, W.Va., Aug. 2, 1945; s. Charles and Martha; m. Brenda Frazier; 1 child, David S. BS, Concord Coll.; JD, W.Va. U. Circuit judge Mercer County, W.Va., 1981—2006, sr. judge, 2006—07; mem. Dist. 25 W.Va. House of Delegates, 2008—, mem. Banking and Ins. Com., Constitutional Revision Com. & Judiciary Com. Vietnam veteran US Army, 1967—69. Democrat. Presbyterian. Office: State Capitol Complex Rm 221E, Bldg 1 Charleston WV 25305 Home: 893 Platinum Dr Fort Mill SC 29708-8933 Office Phone: 304-340-3396. E-mail: jfrazier@mail.wvnet.edu.

FRAZIER, LESLIE, professional football coach, retired professional football player; b. Columbus, Miss., Apr. 3, 1959; m. Gale Frazier; children: Kieron, Chantel, Corey. BBA, Alcorn State U., Miss., 1981. Defensive back Chgo. Bears, 1981—86; head football coach Trinity Coll. Trojans, Ill., 1988—97; defensive backs coach U. Ill. Fighting Illini, 1998, Phila. Eagles, 1999—2002; defensive coord. Cin. Bengals, 2003—04; defensive backs coach, spl. asst. to the head coach Indpls. Colts, 2005—07; defensive coord. Minn. Vikings, 2007, asst. head coach, defensive coord., 2008—10, interim head coach, 2010, head coach, 2011—13; defensive coord. Tampa Bay Buccaneers, 2014—. Named to The Southwestern Athletic Conf. Hall of Fame, 2007. Achievements include member of Super Bowl XX championship winning Chicago Bears, 1986; assistant coach for Super Bowl XLI championship winning Indianapolis Colts, 2007. Office: Tampa Bay Buccaneers One Buccaneers Pl Tampa FL 33607*

FREDEMAN, BETTY COLEY (BETTY COLEY), retired librarian, editor; b. Corrigan, Tex., Aug. 4, 1933; d. Bennie Boyd and Louise (Long) Gilbert; m. Kenneth Coley, Jan. 27, 1951 (dec. 1991); 1 child, Carol Ann; m. William E. Fredeman, Jan. 16, 1995 (dec. 1999). BS, Sam Houston State U., 1953; MEd, East Texas State U., 1961; MLS, Tex. Women's U., 1980. With registrar's office Tex. A&M U., 1954; tchr. Mesquite (Tex.) Ind. Sch. Dist., 1957-64, elem. librarian, 1964-67, dir. cen. processing ctr., 1964-66; elem. librarian Aldine Ind. Sch. Dist., Houston, 1967-69; law librarian Fulbright and Jaworski, 1969-72; librarian Armstrong Browning Libr., Baylor U., Waco, Tex., 1972-94, ret., 1994. Chair editl. bd. Corr. Dante Gabriel Rossetti, 2002—13; exec. com., sec., curriculum com. SAGE, 2009—12. Editor: My Browning Family Album (Vivienne Browning), 1979, The Correspondence of Dante Gabriel Rossetti, vol. 1-10, 2002-13; contbr. to Studies in Robert Browning and His Circle, 1976, 82, 88, Baylor Browning Interest Series #27, Lot 931: A Reconstruction of Books, Periodicals and Ephemera from the Brownings' Library, 1981, The Browning Collections: A Reconstruction with Other Memorabilia, 1984, Journal of Pre-Raphaelite Studies No. 4, 1995, Pre-Raphaelite and Other Victorian Resources in the Armstrong Browning Library, 1995, others; book rev. editor, bibliographer Studies in Browning and His Circle, Vols. 14, 15, 16; mem. editl. bd. Baylor/Ohio edit. The Complete Works of Robert Browning. Pres. Mesquite Jr. Woman's Study Club, 1966-67; rec. sec. Florence Black Elem. PTA, 1965-67; membership chmn., v.p. Browning Inst. Mem. AAUW (past chpt., sec., pres., state historian, dist. coord., Outstanding Mem. award Waco br. 1980, named gift given to Ednl. Found. 1979), ALA (info. exchange com. Rare Books and Manuscripts Section 1988-90), Browning Inst. (dir. 1984-98), Internat. Browning Soc. (dir. 1976-85), Tex. Libr. Assn. (dist. chmn. 1979-80, publs. com. 1989-91, membership com. 1989-91), Southwestern Libr. Assn., Spl. Librs. Assn., William Morris Soc., Pre Raphaelite Soc., Browning Soc. London, Baylor U. Round Table (rec. sec. 1976, publs. coord. 1977-78, pres. 1983-84), Beta Phi Mu, Delta Kappa Gamma (Zeta scholar 1977, Alpha state scholarship com. 1986-91), Epsilon Chi (treas., pres. 1992-94), SAGE (seminar dir. 2006, exec. com. sec. 2009-10, curriculum com. mem. 2009-12). Baptist. Personal E-mail: bfredeman@austin.rr.com.

FREDERICKS, NANCY, library director; MLIS, U. South Fla., Tampa, 2001. Br. mgr. Pasco County Libr. Cooperative, Land O' Lakes, Fla., 2006—08, e-govt. services mgr. Hudson, Fla., 2008—11, acting libraries dir., 2011, libraries adminstr., chair leadership team, 2011—. Named to Movers & Shakers, Libr. Jour., 2011. Mem.: ALA, Fla. Libr. Assn. Office: Pasco County Library Cooperative Hudson Regional Library 8012 Library Rd Hudson FL 34667 Office Phone: 727-861-3020.

FREDRICK, LAURENCE WILLIAM, astronomer, educator; b. Stroudsburg, Pa., Aug. 27, 1927; s. Ishmeal T. and Grace (Slider) F.; m. Frances I. Schwenk, Feb. 5, 1949; children— Laura Grace, Theodore David, Rebecca Lyn BA, Swarthmore Coll., 1952, MA, 1954; PhD, U. Pa., 1959. Research asst. Sproul Obs., Swarthmore, Pa., 1952-56; research assoc. Flower and Cook Obs., Malvern, Pa., 1957-59; astronomer Lowell Obs., Flagstaff, Ariz., 1959-63; mem. faculty U. Va., Charlottesville, 1963-95, prof. astronomy, 1965-95, rsch. prof., 1995—; prof. U. Vienna, Austria, 1972-73. Cons. in field; Fulbright-Hays exch. lectr., Austria, 1972-73; assoc. astronomer European So. Obs., Munich, Fed. Republic Germany, 1982-83; vis. fellow Australian Nat. U., Canberra, 1991-92. Co-author: Astronomy, 10th edit., 1976, Descriptive Astronomy, 1978, An Introduction to Astronomy, 9th edit., 1980 Served with USN, 1945-48 Named Alumnus of Yr., Milton Hershey Sch., 1961 Mem. Am. Astron. Soc. (sec. 1969-80), Internat. Astron. Union (sec. U.S. nat. com. 1970-80), Am. Inst. Physics (bd. govs. 1969-79), Univs. for Space Research Assn. (trustee), Royal Astron. Soc., Soc. Sci. Exploration (sec. 1981-2005), Sigma Xi Avocations: golf, photography. Home: 2602 Bennington Rd Charlottesville VA 22901-2211 Office Phone: 434-924-4905. Business E-Mail: lwf@virginia.edu.

FREE, VICKY, media executive; Attended, U. of South Carolina, 1988—99; MBA, Northwestern U., 2002—04. Exec. v.p. BET Networks; v.p. entertainment mktg. Turner Broadcasting System, 2005—, v.p. 360 consumer mktg., 2008—. Office: Turner Broadcasting System One CNN Center Atlanta GA 30303 Office Phone: 404-827-1700.

FREEDLAND, STEPHEN JAY, urologist; b. Sacramento, Feb. 15, 1972; s. Richard Allan and Beverly Jane Freedland; m. Inna Shapiro. MD, U. Calif., Davis, 1997. Diplomate Am. Bd. Urology. Resident in urology UCLA Sch. Medicine, 1997—2003; fellow urologic oncology Johns Hopkins Sch. Medicine, Balt., 2003—05; asst. prof. urology and pathology Duke U. Med. Ctr., Durham, 2005—08, assoc. prof., 2008—. Vice chmn. Western Student Med. Rsch. Forum, Reno, 1995—96, chmn., 1996—97, sr. advisor, 1997—98. Contbr. articles to profl. jours. Asst. scout master Boy Scouts America, Davis, 1990—97. Recipient E. E. Osgood award, Western Student Med. Rsch. Forum, 1995, Abe Zarem Rsch. award, UCLA Dept. Urology, 2000, Physician Tng. award, US Dept. Def., 2005, Johns Hopkins Young Investigators award, 2005, Merit award, ASCO Found., 2005, Rising Star in Urology award, Am. Urol. Assn. Found., 2006; Rsch. scholar, US Dept. Def., 2003—10, Am. Found. Urol. Disease/Am. Urol. Assn. Edn. & Rsch., 2004. Mem.: Am. Urol. Assn. (1st prize Miley B. Wesson resident essay competition 2001), Golden Key, Phi Beta Kappa. Jewish. Avocations: travel, basketball. Office: Duke U Dept Surgery / Divsn Urology DUMC 2626 Durham NC 27710 Office Phone: 919-668-8361. Business E-Mail: steve.freedland@duke.edu.

FREEDMAN, RALPH STUART, obstetrician, gynecologist, educator; b. Capetown, South Africa, Feb. 6, 1941; came to U.S., 1975; s. Barry and Hilda (Dick) F.; m. Jennifer M. Goldin, Mar. 7, 1972; children: Paul, Lara. MB, ChirB, Witwatersrand U., Johannesburg, South Africa, 1965, PhD, 1975. Asst. prof. U. Tex. M. D. Anderson Cancer Ctr., Houston, 1977-81, assoc. prof., 1981-87, prof., 1987—. Dir. lab. immunology and molecular biology U. Tex. M. D. Anderson Cancer Ctr., Houston, 1988—. Contbr. articles to profl. jours.; patentee tumor cell surface binding monoclonal antibody, 1995. Mem. Nat. Cancer Adv. Bd. appointed by Pres. Clinton, 2000—06. Eli Lilly fellow, 1976; grantee NCI, 1992, 94, Am. Cancer Soc. Fellow Royal Coll. Ob-gyn.; mem. Felix Rutledge Soc., Am. Assn. Cancer Rsch., Am. Radium Soc., Am. Assn. Immunologists, Am. Coll. Ob-gyn. Avocations: fishing, travel. Home: 215 Electra Dr Houston TX 77079-7336 Office: U Tex MD Anderson Cancer Ctr 1515 Holcombe Blvd # 67 Houston TX 77030-4009 Business E-Mail: rfreedman@mdanderson.org.

FREEDMAN, SANDRA WARSHAW, former mayor; b. Newark, Sept. 21, 1943; m. Michael J. Freedman; 3 children. BA in Govt., U. Miami, 1965. Mem. Tampa (Fla.) City Coun., 1974—, chmn., 1983-86; mayor City of Tampa, 1986-95. Author: Specialties of the House (Recipes for People on the Go!), 2002. Bd. dirs. Jewish Cmty. Ctr., Boys and Girls Clubs Greater Tampa, Hillsborough Coalition for Health, Tampa Cmty. Concert Assn., Hillsborough Edn. Found., Judeo Christian Clinic, NCCJ, Human Rights Task Force; mem. sports adv. bd. Hillsborough Community Coll., 1975-76; sec. Downtown Devel. Authority, 1977-78; bd. dirs., v.p. Fla. Gulf Coast Symphony, 1979-80; vice chmn. Met. Planning Orgn., 1981-82; corp. mem. Neighborhood Housing Service; bd. fellows U. Tampa; mem. steering com. Hillsborough County Council of Govt.'s Constituency for Children; mem. exec. bd. Tampa/Hillsborough Young Adult Forum; chmn. bd. trustees Berkeley Prep. Sch.; trustee Tampa Bay Performing Arts Ctr., Inc., Tampa Mus.; mem. ethics com. Meml. Hosp.; mem. Tampa Preservation, Inc., Tampa/Hillsborough County Youth Council, Davis Islands Civic Assn., Tampa Hist. Soc., Met. Ministries Adv. Bd., Rodeph Sholom Synagogue, Sword of Hope Guild of Am. Cancer Soc., Friends of Arts; chmn. bd. Nat. Civic League, 2008-. Recipient Spessar L. Holland Meml. award Tampa Bay Com. for Good Govt., 1975-76, Human Rights award City of Tampa, 1980, Josephine Howard Stafford award, 2008, award Soroptimist Internat. Tampa, 1981, Status of Women award Zonta of Tampa II, 1986, Woman of Achievement award Bus. & Profl. Women, Jewish Nat. Fund Tree of Life award, Disting. Citizen award U. South Fla., 1995, Nat. Conf. of Christian and Jews Humanitarian award, 1995, Unsung Hero award Tampa Police Dept., 2008, Planned Parenthood Choice award, 2007; named to Fla. Home Builders Hall of Fame. Mem. Hillsborough County Bar Aux., Greater Tampa C. of C., C. of C. Com. of 100 (exec. com.), Fla. League of Cities (bd. dirs.), Tampa Urban League, Nat. Council Jewish Women, U. Miami Alumni Assn., Athena Soc., Hadassah. Office: 3435 Bayshore Blvd Apt 700 Tampa FL 33629-8827

FREEDMAN, SHARON FRIDOVICH, ophthalmologist; b. Durham, NC, May 2, 1959; m. Neil J. Freedman, June 26, 1983. BS, Duke U., 1981; MD, Harvard U., 1985. Diplomate Am. Bd. Opthalmology. Residency in ophthalmology Mass. Eye and Ear, Boston, 1986-89; fellow in pediat. opthalmology Children's Hosp., Boston, 1989-90; fellow in glaucoma Duke Eye Ctr., Durham, 1990-92, asst. prof. to prof. ophthalmology and pediat., 1995—; asst. prof. U. NC, Chapel Hill, 1992-94. Contbr. articles to profl. jours. Office: Duke Med Ctr Box 3802 2351 Erwin Rd Durham NC 27710

FREELAND, ALAN EDWARD, orthopedic surgery educator, physician; b. Youngstown, Ohio, July 30, 1939; s. Harold Edward and Esther Amelia (Hanley) F.; m. Janis Ann Foerschl, Oct. 11, 1969; children: Matthew, Jennifer, Rebecca, Michael. BA, Johns Hopkins U., 1961; MD, George Washington U., 1965. Cert. hand surgery Am. Bd. Orthopaedic Surgery. With Church Home and Hosp., Balt., 1965-66; resident Johns Hopkins Hosp., Balt., 1967-70, Letterman Army Med. Ctr., San Francisco, 1973-75; prof. dept. orthopaedic surgery U. Miss. Med. Ctr., Jackson, 1978—, dir. hand surgery fellowship program, 1991—2004, chief of staff, 1986-87, also bd. dirs. Rowland Med. Libr., 1996-98, prof. emeritus, 2005—. Chief surgery Miss. Meth. Rehab. Ctr., Jackson, 1991-93, pres. elect med. staff, 1994, pres. med. staff, bd. dirs., 1995-97. Author: Stable Internal Fixation of the Hand and Wrist, 1986, The First Twenty-Five Years: History of the American Association for Hand Surgery, 1996, Hand Fractures: Repair, Reconstruction and Rehabilitation, 2000; mem. editl. bd. Orthopedics, Slack, Inc., 1986—2006, Jour. Orthop. Trauma, 1993—2002, Year Book of Hand Surgery, 1997, sect. editor Trauma Update, Orthop., 1989—2006; sect. editor, sr. editor hand surgery: Jour. Orthop. Trauma, 1997—2002; sect. editor Hand Surgery, 1997—2002, bd. editors Microsurgery, 2001—. Mem. Fire Protection Dist., Brandon, Miss., 1990-93; bd. dirs. Miss. Sports Hall of Fame, 2002—. Lt. col. U.S. Army, 1971-78. Fellow: Am Acad. Orthopaedic Surgeons; mem.: S.E. Hand Club (sec.-treas. 1998—2000, v.p. 2001, pres.-elect 2002, pres. 2003), Miss. State Orthopaedic Assn. (pres. Jackson chpt. 1985, pres. 1986), Internat. Fedn. Socs. for Surgery of Hand (chmn. bone and joint com. 1992—2006), Am. Assn. Hand Surgeons (parliamentarian 1994, exec. com., bd. dirs. 1994—2003, historian 1995, treas. 1996—98, historian 1999, v.p. 2000, pres.-elect 2001, pres. 2002, pres. Hand Surgery Endowment 2005—), Am. Soc. Surgery of Hand (governing coun. 1989—92), Am. Orthopaedic Assn. Home: 303 Swallow Dr Brandon MS 39047-6454 Office: 2500 N State St Jackson MS 39216-4500 Office Phone: 601-815-1220. Business E-Mail: afreeland@orthopedics.umsmed.edu.

FREELAND, KEVIN PAUL, automotive executive; b. Cleve., Dec. 3, 1957; s. William Ronald Freeland and Carol Rae (Pankratz) Zelina; m. Lesa Christene Frazer, June 5, 1982 (div. Apr. 1984); 1 child, Lauren Marie; m. Kathleen Kay Wilson, June 20, 1987; children: Bryan Patrick, Brett Wilson, Maggie Louise. BA in Econs., U. Fla., 1981. Area sales mgr. menswear Maas Bros., Naples, Fla., 1981-83, asst. buyer women's coordinates Tampa, Fla., 1983-84; buyer women's sportswear Beall's Dept. Store, Bradenton, Fla., 1984-85, planner women's, jrs., dresses, 1985-87; mgr. distbn. planning & analysis Payless Shoe Source, Topeka, 1987-88, dir. children's distbn., 1988-89, dir. distbn. adminstrn., 1989-90, dir. merchandise planning, 1991-92, v.p. merchandise distbn., 1992-95; v.p. inventory mgmt., sr. v.p. inventory, pres. Musicland divsn. Best Buy Co., Inc., Eden Praire, Minn., 1995—2004; founder, pres. Optimal Advantage, 2004—08; exec. v.p. merchandising, supply chain & info. tech. Advance Auto Parts, Inc., Roanoke, Va., 2008—09, COO, 2009—. Mem. United Way Key Club, Topeka, 1987—, May Dept. Stores Polit. Action Com., St. Louis, 1989—, Friends of Topeka Zoo, 1990—. Mem. U. Fla. 1853 Soc., Profl. Assn. Diving Instrs., Sherwood Lake Club. Republican. Methodist. Avocations: waterskiing, weightlifting, running, skiing, astronomy. Office: Advance Auto Parts 5008 Airport Rd Roanoke VA 24012

FREEMAN, ARTHUR MERRIMON, III, psychiatry professor, dean; b. Birmingham, Ala., Oct. 10, 1942; s. Arthur Merrimon II and Katherine (Lide) F.; m. Linda Poynter; children: Arthur M. IV, Katherin Leigh, Edward Todd. AB in Philosophy, Harvard U., Cambridge, Mass., 1963; MD, Vanderbilt U., Nashville, Tenn., 1967. Diplomate Am. Bd. Psychiatry and Neurology; lic. psychiatrist, Ala., NC, La. Asst. prof. dept. psychiatry and behavioral scis. Stanford U., Calif., 1974—77; prof., vice chmn. dept. psychiatry U. Ala., Birmingham, 1977—90; med. dir. Appalachian Hall Hosp., Asheville, NC, 1990—91; prof., chmn. dept. psychiatry La. State U. Med. Ctr., Shreveport, 1991—2003, dean, 1993—96; prof., chmn. dept. psychiatry Health Sci. Ctr. U. Tenn., Memphis, 2003—05; clin. prof. psychiatry U. Ala., Birmingham, 2006—. Regional med. dir. divsn. mental health La. Dept. Health and Hosps., 1992-94. Author: Psychiatry for the Primary Care Physician, 1979. Bd. dirs. Vols. of Am., Shreveport, 1993-96, Shreveport Symphony, C. of C., 1993-96. Lt. comdr. M.C., USN, 1972-74. Nat. Merit scholar Harvard U., 1959-63; Biochemistry fellow Karolinska Inst., Stockholm, 1965, fellow in hepatic disease Royal Free Hosp., London, 1966, Disting. Paul Harris fellow Rotary Club. Fellow APA (Disting. life fellow, vice-chmn. fin. oversight com.), Am. Coll. Psychiatrists (Laughlin fellow 1971, bd. regents), Acad. Psychosomatic Medicine, So. Psychiat. Assn. (mem. fin. com.); mem. So. Psychiatry Assn., Am. Acad. Psychosomatic Medicine, Royal Coll. Psychiatrists, Collegium Internat. Neuropsychopharmacologia. Home: 3536 Brookwood Rd Birmingham AL 35223 Business E-Mail: amfreeman@utmem.edu.

FREEMAN, BENNY DEAN, engineering educator; b. Hendersonville, NC, Apr. 29, 1961; s. Ruby Jean and Wade Lee Freeman; m. Laurence Veronique Zachar, July 9, 1994; 1 child, Christopher Lee. BS in Chemical Engring., NC State U., 1983; PhD in Chemical Engring., U. Calif., Berkeley, 1988. Profl. Engr., Tex. Bd. Profl. Engrs., 2003. Asst. prof. chemical engring. NC State U., Raleigh, 1989—94, assoc. prof. chemical engring., 1994—97, assoc. dept. head, 1996—2002, prof. chemical engring., 1997—2002, U. of Tex., 2002—, Matthew Van Winkle prof. chem. engring., 2002—05, Kenneth A. Kobe Prof. Chemical Engring., 2005—, Paul D. and betty Robertson Meek & American Petrofina Found. Centennial Prof. Chemical Engring., 2007—. Dir., separations divsn. AIChE, NYC, 2003—. Editor: (book) Polymeric Membranes for Gas and Vapor Separations: Chemistry and Materials Sci., Membrane Formation and Modification, Advanced Materials for Membrane Separations; mem. internat. editl. adv. bd. Membrane Jour. and Korean Membrane Jour., 2003—, mem. editl. bd. Jour. of Applied Membrane Sci. and Tech., 2005—, Jour. of Membrane Sci., 2005—, Open Macromolecules Jour., 2007—, assoc. editor Indsl. and Engring. Chemistry, 2007—. Mem., vice-chair North Am. Membrane Soc., Toledo, Ohio, 2004—; vice chair, exec. com. PMSE Divsn. of the Am. Chem. Soc., Wash., DC, 2000—; mem., internat. adv. bd. Membrane Jour., Seoul, 2003—. Recipient P.V. Danckwerts Sr. Rsch. Prize in Chem. Engring., N.C. State U., 1983, Ea. N.C. Sect. AIChE Award, AIChE, 1983, Spl. Svc. award, N.C. chpt. Tau Beta Pi Engring. Honor Soc., 1983, Berkeley

Outstanding Grad. Instr., U. of Calif., Berkeley, 1986, PMSE Coop. Rsch. Award, Am. Chem. Soc., 2002, Young Investigator award, NSF, 1992—96, ALCOA Found. Rsch. Achievement award, N.C. State U., 1996, Alcoa Found. Disting. Engring. Rsch. award, 2000, Project of the Yr. Award, Strategic Environ. R & D Program, 2001, AIChE Inst. award for Excellence in Idsl. Gases Technology, 2008; Postdoctoral Fellowship, NATO, 1987, E.I. duPont PhD Fellowship, E.I. DuPont de Nemours, Inc., 1982, Berkeley Fellowship, U. of Calif., Berkeley, 1983, Fellowship, Phi Kappa Phi Honor Soc., 1983, Grad. Fellowship, NSF, 1984, Fellowship, Japan Soc. for the Promotion of Sci., 1997, 2001. Mem.: AAAS, Am. Soc. Engring. Educators, Materials Rsch. Soc., North Am. Membrane Soc. (mem., bd. dirs., vice-chair elect 2004—), Am. Chem. Soc. (award for Applied Polymer Sci. 2009), Am. Inst. Chem. Engrs. (dir., separations divsn. 2003—). Achievements include research in Studies of Polymer Science, Mass Transport in Solid Polymers, Membrane Separations, Barrier Materials, and Polymer Spectroscopy. Office: Univ of Texas at Austin Dept Chemical Engring Ctr for Energy & Environmental Resources 10100 Burnet Rd Bldg 133 C0400 Austin TX 78758

FREEMAN, BRENDA, broadcast executive; BS in Chem. Engring., U. Md., MBA in Mktg. and Fin. Mgmt. positions Frito-Lay, Pepsi-Cola; exec. dir. mktg. and spl. events ABC Radio Networks; v.p. consumer mktg. VH1; sr. v.p. integrated mktg. and promotions Nickelodeon and MTVN Kids and Family Group; chief mktg. officer Turner Animation, Young Adults & Kids Media, Atlanta, 2008—. Office: Turner Broadcasting System Inc 1 CNN Ctr 100 Internat Blvd Atlanta GA 30303

FREEMAN, CORINNE, financial analyst, retired mayor; b. NYC, Nov. 9, 1926; d. Bernard J. Hirschfeld and Sidonie (Daxe) Lichtenstein; m. Michael S. Freeman, Mar. 14, 1948; children: Michael L., Stephan J. Student, Adelphi Coll. Sch. Nursing, 1944—47. RN, N.Y., Mass. Nurse numerous hosps. in N.Y. and Mass., 1948-64; mayor St. Petersburg, Fla., 1977-85; mem. Pinellas County Sch. Bd., St. Petersburg, Fla., 1989-98, chmn., 1996-98; bd. trustees Palms of Pasadena Hosp., St. Petersburg, 1998—, dir., 1998—2004. Fin. advisor Prudential Securities, Stephan J. atty wells fargo advisors; bd. dirs. Creativity in Child Care. Chmn. Social Svc. Allocations Com., St. Petersburg, 1972-76, City Budget Rev. Com., 1973-76, Youth Svc. System, Pinellas County, 1975-76, West Coast Regional Water Supply Authority; past mem. community redevel. com. U.S. Conf. of Mayors; past pres. Fla. League Cities; past mem. Pinellas County Mayors Coun.; past mem. Nat. League of Cities Revenue and Fin. Task Force; pres. LWV, St. Petersburg, 1970-72, 75-76; trustee Fire Pension Bd., St. Petersburg, 1989-92, Bayfront Med. Ctr.; dir. Palms of Pasadena Hosp., 1999-2003 Recipient Disting. Alumni award Adelphi U. Mem. Fla. Nursing Assn. Mem.: Treasure Island Yacht and Tennis Club (bd. dirs. 2004—). Republican. Home: 2101 Pelham Rd N Saint Petersburg FL 33710-3659 Office: 700 Ctrl Ave Ste 100 Saint Petersburg FL 33701 Office Phone: 727-551-2303. Business E-Mail: corinne_freeman@wachoviasec.com, corinne_freeman@wfadvisors.com.

FREEMAN, DAVID SCOTT, professional sports team executive, venture capitalist, lawyer; b. Knoxville, Tenn., Dec. 29, 1961; s. Donald W. and Marie A. (Miller) Freeman; 2 children. BS with high honors, U. Tenn., 1984; JD, Vanderbilt U., 1987. Bar: Tex. 1987, Tenn. 1989. Assoc. Locke Purnell Rain Harrell, Dallas, 1987-89, Waller, Lansden, Dortch & Davis, Nashville, 1989-91; founder, chmn., CEO Commodore Med. Svcs., Nashville, 1991—2007; assoc. Farris, Warfield & Kanaday, Nashville, 1995; founder, CEO 36 Venture Capital, 2007—; chmn., gov. Nashville Predators, Predators Holdings LLC, 2007—10. Adj. prof. Vanderbilt U. Sch. Law, 1991—94. Co-author: The Medical Waste Handbook; contbr. articles to law jours. Bd. trustees United Way; mem. Blue Ribbon Com. Country Music Assn. Recipient Cmty. Spirit Award, Nashville Sports Coun., 2008. Mem.: ABA, Beta Gamma Sigma, Nashville Bar Assn., Tenn. Bar Assn., Tex. Bar Assn., Dallas Bar Assn., Phi Kappa Phi.

FREEMAN, DEAN P., corporate financial executive; BS in Fin., U. Conn., 1991; MBA, Rensselaer Poly. Inst., 1999. Held fin. mgmt. positions SPX Corp.; CFO, European ops. Stanley Works Corp.; worked in fin. mgmt. United Technologies Corp.; v.p., fin., Flowserve Pump Divsn. Flowserve Corp., 2006—, v.p., treas., 2009—10, sr. v.p. fin., treas., 2010—. Office: Flowserve Corp Ste 2300 5215 N O'Connor Blvd Irving TX 75039 Office Phone: 972-443-6500. Office Fax: 972-443-6800. Business E-Mail: dfreeman@flowserve.com.

FREEMAN, DONALD WILFORD, real estate developer, horse breeder; b. Brooksville, Fla., Sept. 25, 1929; s. Fred Maxwell and Dovie (Keef) F.; m. Ruby Jane Lewis, Feb. 25, 1956; children: Clifton Lewis, Susan Anne. BS, JD, U. Ala., 1953; LLM, NYU, 1957. CPA Ga., CFP, CLU. Acct. Ernst & Ernst, Atlanta, 1953-55; tax atty. Office Chief Counsel, US Treasury Dept., NYC, 1955-57, West Point Mfg. Co., Ga., 1957-58; treas. Ryder System, Inc., Miami, Fla., 1958-61; v.p., dir. Henderson's Portion Pak, Inc., 1961-63; pres. Biscayne Capital Corp., Miami, 1964-66; dir. Long Range Planning, Kimberly-Clark Corp., Neenah, Wis., 1966—67; sr. assoc. Lazard Freres & Co., NYC, 1967-69; pres. James A. Ryder Corp., Miami, 1969-78; owner Kiyara Arabians, 1978—. With AUS, 1946-48, PTO. 187th parachute inf. regiment, 11th airborne divsn. Mem.: Fla. Inst. CPAs, Beta Gamma Sigma, Phi Kappa Sigma. Anglican. Home: 1314 Parkside Dr Vero Beach FL 32966

FREEMAN, DOUGLAS K., bank executive; BS in Econ., Furman U.; MBA, U. Southern Calif. Exec. v.p., bus. banking Wells Fargo Bank; chief corp. bank exec., chief consumer bank exec. Barnett Banks, Inc.; pres., consumer fin. divsn. Nations Bank, NA; pres., consumer fin. group Bank of Am.; CEO NetBank, Inc., 2002—07, chmn., 2003—07; exec. v.p., chief banking exec. BankAtlantic Bancorp, Inc., 2007—. Mem., Thrift Inst. Advisory Coun.' Fed. Res. Bd.; trustee Furman U. Office: BankAtlantic Bancorp Inc 2100 W Cypress Creek Rd Fort Lauderdale FL 33309 Office Phone: 954-940-5000. Office Fax: 954-940-5250.

FREEMAN, GEORGE C., III, tobacco company executive, lawyer; b. Richmond, Va., May 28, 1963; BA with honors, U. Va., 1985; JD, Yale U., 1989. Bar: Va. 1989, U.S. Ct. of Appeals, 8th Circuit 1990, U.S. Ct. of Appeals, 4th Circuit 1991. Law clerk to Judge Richard S. Arnold U.S. Ct. of Appeals, 8th Circuit, 1989—90; law clerk to Justice Lewis F. Powell U.S. Supreme Ct., 1990—91; assoc. Hunton & Williams, 1991—97; asst. gen. counsel Universal Leaf Tobacco Co., 1997—98, v.p., assoc. gen. counsel, asst. sec., 1998—2001; sec., gen. counsel Universal Corp., Richmond, Va., 2001—06, v.p., 2005—06, pres., 2006—08, pres., CEO, 2008, chmn., pres., CEO, 2008—. Bd. dir. Delta Waterfowl Found., Children's Hosp. & Children's Hosp. Health Svc.; past bd. dir. James River Assn. Mem.: ABA. Office: Universal Corp 1501 N Hamilton St Richmond VA 23230 Mailing: Universal Corp PO Box 25099 Richmond VA 23260 Office Phone: 804-359-9311. Office Fax: 804-254-3582.

FREEMAN, GEORGE CLEMON, JR., lawyer; b. Birmingham, Ala., Jan. 3, 1929; s. George Clemon and Annie Laura (Gill) F.; m. Anne Colston Hobson, Dec. 6, 1958; children: Anne Colston McEvoy, George Clemon III, Joseph Reid Anderson. BA magna cum laude, Vanderbilt U., 1950; LLB, Yale U., 1956. Bar: Ala. 1956, Va. 1958, DC 1974. Law clk. to Justice Hugo L. Black US Supreme Ct., 1956; assoc. Hunton & Williams, Richmond, Va., 1957-63, ptnr., 1963-95, sr. counsel, 1995—. Contbr. articles to profl. jours. Pres. Va. chpt. Nature Conservancy, 1962—63; counsel Va. Outdoors Recreation Study Com. Va. Legis., 1963—65; mem. sect. 301 Superfund Act Study Group Congl. Adv. Com., 1981—82; mem. Falls James Com., 1973—89; chmn. adv. coun. Energy Policy Studies Ctr. U. Va., 1981—85; chmn. legal adv. com. to Va. Commn. on Transp. in the 21st Century, 1986—87; mem. Va. Gov.'s Commn. to Study Historic Preservation, 1987—88, Va. Coun. on the Environment, 1989—91; chmn. Va. Bd. Hist. Resources, 1989—91; mem. The Atlantic Coun., 1986—95; bd. dirs. Nat. Mus. Am. History, 1997—2002; chmn. Richmond City Dem. Com., 1969—71. Lt (j.g.) USN, 1951—54. Fellow Am. Bar Found. (Va. state chmn. 1986-90); mem. ABA (chmn. standing com. on facilities of Law Libr. of Congress 1967-73, coordinating group on regulatory reform 1981-85, nominating com. 1984-87, chmn. civil justice coordinating com. 1990-92, sect. bus. law, sect. coun. 1976-79, chmn. ad hoc com. on Fed. Criminal Code 1979-81, chmn. program com. 1981-82, chmn. ad hoc com. on tort law reform 1986-87, sect. del. to ho. of dels. 1983-87, sec. 1987-88, vice-chmn. and ed. The Business Lawyer 1988-89, chmn.-elect 1989-90, chmn. 1990-91), Richmond Bar Assn., Va. Bar Assn., Am. Law Inst. (coun. 1980—2010, coun. emeritus, 2010-, advisor to coun. on project on compensation and liability for product and process injuries 1986-91, advisor restatement of law, THRD, torts apportionment 1993-97, advisor restatement law THIRD torts gen. prins. injury 1992-96, advisor restatement law THRD torts liability physical & emotional harm, 2001-06), Am. Judicature Soc., Country Club of Va., Knickerbocker Club, Met. Club (DC), Phi Beta Kappa, Phi Delta Phi, Omicron Delta Kappa, Alpha Tau Omega. Democrat. Episcopalian. Avocation: gardening. Office: Hunton & Williams 951 E Byrd St Richmond VA 23219-0005 Home: 4509 Cary St Rd Richmond VA 23221 Home Phone: 804-355-3813; Office Phone: 804-788-8365. Business E-Mail: gfreeman@hunton.com.

FREEMAN, GREGORY L., cardiologist, educator; MD, Loyola U., Chgo., 1976. Diplomate Am. Bd. Internal Medicine, 1979, Am. Bd. Internal Medicine-cardiovasc. disease, 1983. Resident internal medicine Cook County Hosp., Chgo., 1977—79; fellow cardiovasc. disease Loyola Univ. Med. Ctr., Maywood, 1979—81; prof. medicine Univ. of Tex., San Antonio; hosp. affiliation includes Univ. Hosp. Office: Cardiology Clinical Associates Ste 300 4411 Medical Dr San Antonio TX 78229 Office Phone: 210-614-5400.

FREEMAN, JAMES I., retail department store company executive; CPA, mem. mgmt. com. BKD LLP; joined Dillard's, Little Rock, 1988; sr. v.p., CFO Dillard's, Inc., Little Rock. Bd. dir. Dillard's, 1991—. Office: Dillard Dept Stores Inc 1600 Cantrell Rd Little Rock AR 72201

FREEMAN, NEAL BLACKWELL, communications corporation executive; b. NYC, July 5, 1940; s. Malcolm T. and Virginia (Neal) F.; m. Jane Louise Metze, Mar. 19, 1966; children: Malcolm Trowbridge II, James Bragdon, Kathryn R. BA magna cum laude, Yale U., 1962. Asst. to pres. Washington Star Syndicate, 1965-66; assoc. producer TV show Firing Line, 1966-67; exec. editor King Features Syndicate, NYC, 1968-73; v.p., editor King Features div. Hearst Corp., 1973-76; pres. Jefferson Communications, Inc., 1976-86; chmn. bd., chief exec. officer Blackwell Corp., 1982—; dir. Intelsat, Ltd. Exec. prodr. Pub. TV; bd. dirs. Comsat Corp., BTG, Inc., Nat. Rev., Denver Nuggets Profl. Basketball Club, Colo. Avalanche Profl. Hockey Club, GRC Internat., Tutagon Med.; bd. visitors Inst. on Polit. Journ alism, Georgetown U.; chmn. Washington Selection Panel Pres.'s Commn. on White House Fellows, 1998-2002, chmn., Found. Mgmt. Inst., 2000—; chmn. of agts. Yale Alumni Fund; bd. dirs. Corp. for Pub. Broadcasting, 1972-75; bd. dirs., vice-chmn. Ethics and Pub. Policy Ctr. Bd. dirs. Wolf Trap Found., 1984-90. Mem. Colony Found., Yale Club (NYC), York Country Club (Maine), Sigma Delta Chi. Office: The Blackwell Corp 1891 Sycamore Ln Fernandina Beach FL 32034-7857

FREEMAN, ROBERT SCHOFIELD, musicologist, pianist, educator; b. Rochester, NY, Aug. 26, 1935; s. Henry Schofield and Florence Margaret (Knope) F.; m. Carol Jean Morgan, Dec. 10, 1976; children: John Frederick, Elizabeth Poon, Scott Alan Henry. AB summa cum laude, Harvard U., Cambridge, Mass., 1957; MFA, Princeton U., NJ, 1960, PhD, 1967; MusD (hon.), Hamilton Coll., 1988. Instr., asst. prof. Princeton U., 1963-68; asst. prof., assoc. prof. MIT, 1968-73; dir., prof. musicology Eastman Sch. Music, U. Rochester, 1972-96; pres. New England Conservatory, Boston, 1996-99; dean, Effie Marie Cain regents chair in fine arts Coll. Fine Arts U. Tex., Austin, 1999—2006, Susan Menefee raran regents prof. fine arts, 2006—. Chmn. nat. adv. bd. Ctr. for Black Music Research, Chgo., 1985-90; cons. for various Am. U.; vis. assoc. prof. Harvard U., 1972. Author: Opera Without Drama, 1981; contbr. articles to profl. jours. Trustee Conductors' Guild, China. Found. for Edn. and Culture. Harvard Sheldon fellow, 1958, Woodrow Wilson Found. fellow, 1959, Martha Baird Rockefeller Fund fellow, 1963, Fulbright fellow, 1960-62; recipient Civic medal Rochester C. of C., 1982. Mem. Am. Musicol. Soc. (chair New Eng. chpt. 1970-72, coun. mem. 1973-76), Coll. Music Soc. (coun. mem. 1973-76), Neue Bach Gesellschaft (chmn. 1977-82), Nat. Assn. Schs. Music (grad. commn. 1981-85), U. Tex. Club. Avocations: baseball, reading. Office: Coll Fine Arts U Tex at Austin Austin TX 78712 Home Phone: 512-338-4143. Personal E-mail: rf3519@aol.com. Business E-Mail: rsfreeman@mail.utexas.edu.

FREEMAN, THEODORE MONROE, physician; b. Orlando, Fla., Jan. 3, 1955; s. Fred Monroe and Mary Ann (Ridgeway) F.; m. Karen Bonaccorso, Aug. 11, 1978; children: Kathryn Maria, Michelle Terese, Jeannine Nicole, Jason Monroe. BS in Chemistry, Duke U., 1977; MD, U. So. Fla., 1980. Diplomate Am. Bd. Internal Medicine, Am. Bd. Allergy and Immunology. Intern Jacksonville (Fla.) U. Hosp., 1980-81; commd. capt. USAF, 1981, advanced through grades to col., resident internal medicine Keesler AFB Biloxi, Miss., 1981-83, staff physician Dyess AFB Abilene, Tex., 1983-84, fellow allergy and immunology Wilford Hall Med. Ctr., Lackland AFB San Antonio, 1984-86, fellow diagnostic lab. immunology Mass. Gen. Hosp. Boston, 1986-87, staff allergist and immunology Wilford Hall Med. Ctr., 1987-89, chmn. dept. allergy and immunology, program dir., 1989—2001. Med. dir. transplants Wilford Hall Med. Ctr., 1989-2002. Contbr. articles to profl. jours. Fellow ACP, Am. Coll. Allergy and Immunology, Am. Acad. Allergy and Immunology; mem. AMA, Soc. Air Force Physicians. Roman Catholic. Office Phone: 210-614-3923. Personal E-mail: tfree95900@aol.com. Business E-Mail: docfreeman@sanantonioallergydoc.com.

FREEMAN, THOMAS E., bank executive; Bank trainee Citibank, 1975, area mgr., regional credit mgr.; mng. dir. corp. strategy and devel. to consumer lending exec. credit officer to dir. portfolio mgmt. to corp. v.p. comml. real estate Fleet Boston Fin.; prin. KPMG; corp. exec. v.p., mem. mgmt. com. SunTrust Banks, Inc., 2006—, chief credit officer, 2006—07, chief risk officer, 2007—. Office: SunTrust Banks Inc PO Box 4418 Atlanta GA 30302-4418 Office Phone: 404-588-7711. Office Fax: 404-827-6173.

FREER, ROBERT ELLIOTT, JR., lawyer; b. Washington, Jan. 19, 1941; s. Robert E. and Alice (Barry) F.; m. Roberta Stapleton Renchard, Dec. 31, 1972; children: Kimberly Dunlap, R. Elliott III, Ashleigh Hamilton, Daniel Renchard. AB, Princeton U., 1963; JD, U. Va., 1966. Bar: Va. 1966, D.C. 1968, U.S. Supreme Ct. 1973. Trial atty. FTC, 1966-69, atty. advisor to chmn., asst. to gen. counsel, 1969—71; exec. asst. to gen. counsel U.S. Dept. Transp., Washington, 1971-74; Washington counsel Kimberly Clark Corp., 1974-83; staff v.p., 1975-80; corp. v.p., 1980-84; gen. counsel Roswell, Ga., 1983-84; pvt. practice Washington, 1984-2000; founder Free Enterprise Found., 2002—; spl. correspondent Charleston (S.C.) Mercury, 2005—11. Mem. President's Commn. on White House Fellowships, 1985-93; pub. mem. Adminstrv. Conf. U.S., 1981-86; capt. land team President's Pvt. Sector Survey on Cost Control in Fedn. Govt., 1982-83; sec., gen. counsel U.S.-Cuba Bus. Coun., 1994-2000; vis. prof. Citadel Sch. Bus. Adminstrn., 2004-, John S. Grinalds leader in residence, 2005-06; adj. faculty Charleston Sch. Law, 2006-, BB & T vis. prof. ethics free enterprise leadership, 2009-. Author: Citadel Values, 2007, Vol. II, 2010; Contbg. author, editor: Finding Our Roots/Facing Our Future: America in the 21st Century, 1997; contbr. columns to papers; contbr. articles to profl. jours. Founder, chmn. bd. trustees Washington Episc. Sch., 1986-94, chmn. emeritus, 1994—; chmn. bd. visitors Regent U. Sch. Law, 1995-2004, chair emeritus, 2004-; trustee Corcoran Gallery Art, 1986-93, asst. sec., chmn. bylaws com., 1990, sec., 1991; trustee, pres. and CEO Free Enterprise Found., 2002—; chmn. Lawyers for the Republic, 1988-2005; asst. gen. counsel Rep. Nat. Conv., 1984, 88, 92, 96; mem. Parents Coun. Coll. Charleston, 1997, 2002, chmn., 2000-02. Mem. Rep. Nat. Lawyers Assn. (bd. govs. 1985-2000, gen. counsel 1985-89, vice chmn. 1988-89), Washington Met. Area Corp. Counsel Assn. (founder, pres. 1980-81, bd. dirs. 1980-84), Rotary Club Charleston (dir. 2008-10). Office: Free Enterprise Found PO Box 21569 Charleston SC 29413

FREEZE, HUGH, college football coach; b. Senatobia, Miss., Sept. 27, 1969; m. Jill Freeze; children: Ragan, Jordan, Madison. AA, NW Miss. CC, Senatobia, 1990; B in Math., U. So. Miss., Hattiesburg, 1992. Tchr. Briarcrest Christian Sch., Memphis, 1992—2005, assoc. dir. devel., 1998—2000; football offensive coord., defensive backs coach Briarcrest Christian Sch. Saints, 1992—94, head girl's basketball coach, 1994—2005, head football coach, 1995—2004; asst. athletic dir. football external affairs, asst. coach U. Miss. Rebels, 2005, recruiting coord., asst. coach, 2006—07, interim head coach, 2006, head football coach, 2011—, Lambuth U. Eagles, 2008—09; offensive coord., quarterbacks coach Ark. State U. Red Wolves, 2010, head football coach, 2011. Named Region 8-AA Coach of Yr., AP HS Coach of Yr., Dist. 15AA Coach of Yr., 1994, 1995, Coach of Yr., Tenn. Secondary Sch. Athletic Assn., 1998, 2000, 2002, 2004, Dist. 9 Nat. Coach of Yr., Women's Basketball Coaches Assn., 2000, 2001, SE Region Coach of Yr., American Football Coaches Assn., 2009, Mid-South Coach of Yr., 2009. Office: Ole Miss Football 908 All-American Dr PO Box 1848 University MS 38677 Office Phone: 662-915-7547.

FREIDHEIM, CYRUS F., JR., management consultant, board member; b. Chgo., June 14, 1935; s. Cyrus F. and Eleanor Freidheim; m. Marguerite VandenBosch; children: Marguerite Lynn, Stephen Cyrus, Scott. BSChemE, U. Notre Dame, 1957; MBA, Carnegie Mellon U., Pitts., 1963; PhD in Internat. Laws (hon.), Thunderbird American Grad. Sch. Internat. Mgmt., Glendale, Ariz., 1999. Plant mgr. Union Carbide Corp., Whiting, Ind., 1961; cons. Price Waterhouse, Chgo., 1962; fin. analyst Ford Motor Co., Dearborn, Mich., 1963-66; vice chmn. Booz, Allen & Hamilton, Chgo., 1966—2002; chmn., CEO Chiquita Brands International, Inc., Cin., 2002—04; chmn. Old Harbour Partners, 2004—06; pres., CEO Sun-Times Media Group Inc., Chgo., 2006—09. Bd. dirs. HSBC Finance Corp., Inc., 1991—2008, Allegheny Energy, Inc., 2003—, presiding dir., 2010—; bd. dirs. Sitel Corp., 2005—07, Hollinger Internat. Inc., 2005—09. Author: The Trillion Dollar Enterprise, 1998. Trustee Rush U. Med. Ctr., Chgo., 1981—; hon. trustee Brookings Instn., 1998—; life trustee Chg.o Coun. Global Affairs, Chgo. Symphony Orch. Assn. Served with USN, 1957—61. Mem.: Coun. Fgn. Rels., Econ. Club, Chgo. Club. Mailing: Allegheny Energy Inc Bd Directors 800 Cabin Hill Dr Greensburg PA 15601

FREIREICH, EMIL J, hematologist, educator; b. Chgo., Mar. 16, 1927; s. David and Mary (Klein) F.; m. Haroldine Lee Cunningham, Mar. 13, 1953; children: Debra Ann, David Alan, Lindsay Gail, Thomas Jon. BS, U. Ill., 1947, MD with honors, 1949, D.Sc. (hon.), 1982. Diplomate Am. Bd. Internal Medicine. Intern Cook County (Ill.) Hosp., Chgo., 1949-50; resident in internal medicine Presbyn. Hosp., Chgo., 1950-53; rsch. assoc. in hematology Mass. Meml. Hosp., Boston, 1953-55; sr. investigator, head Leukemia Svc. USPHS, Nat. Cancer Inst., Bethesda, Md., 1955-65; prof. medicine U. Tex. System Cancer Ctr., Houston, 1965—, chief rsch. in hematology, 1965-85, head dept. devel. therapeutics, 1972-83, chmn. dept. hematology, 1983-85, dir. Adult Leukemia Rsch. Program, 1985—; prof. medicine U. Tex. Health Sci. Ctr. (Sch. Medicine), 1973—, chief divsn. oncology, 1973-81; mem. faculty Grad. Sch. Med., Health Scis. Ctr., 1965—, dir. Spl. Medical Edn. Programs, 2000—. Mem. rev. com. drug. devel. div. cancer treatment Nat. Carsin Inst., 1975-80; Ruth Harriet Ainsworth chair in devel. therapeutics, 1980—; spl. asst. dir. Nat. Cancer Inst., 1990-91. Assoc. editor Cancer, 1976—, Cancer Research, 1977-86; mem. editorial bd. Oncology News, 1975-90, Cancer Treatment Reports, 1976-80, Leukemia Research, 1976-87, Med. and Pediatric Oncology, 1974—, Leukemia 1987—; contbr. numerous articles on research in hematology and oncology to profl. jours. Recipient Albert Lasker Med. rsch. award, 1972, Charles F. Kettering prize Gen. Motors Cancer Rsch. Found., 1983, Outstanding Investigator award Nat. Cancer Inst., NIH, 1985-92, Alumnus award NIH, 1990; named Alumnus of Yr., U. Ill. Alumni Assn., 1974, Alumni Achievement award, 2000, Pollin prize Columbia U., 2003. Fellow ACP, AAAS; mem. Internat. Soc. Hematology, Am. Soc. Hematology, Am. Fedn. Clin. Research, Am. Soc. Clin. Pharmacology and Therapeutics, Am. Soc. Clin. Oncology (David A. Karnofsky award 1976, pres. 1980-81), Am. Soc. Clin. Investigators, Am. Assn. Cancer Research, Leukemia Soc. Am. (pres. Gulf Coast chpt. 1968-70, trustee 1968-70, Robert Roesler DeVilliers award 1979, grant rev. subcom. 1986-89), Tex. Med. Assn., AMA (editorial bd. jour. 1973-83), Assn. Am. Physicians, Alpha Omega Alpha. Achievements include research in therapy of human acute leukemia and leukocyte physiology. Co-developer of combination chemotherapy and the curative therapy for childhood acute lymphoblastic leukemia. Developed the first successful platelet replacement therapy. Inventor of continuous-flow cell separator. Home: 810 Monte Cello St Houston TX 77024-4515 Home Phone: 713-468-3728; Office Phone: 713-792-2660. Business E-Mail: efreirei@mdanderson.org.

FRELING, RICHARD ALAN, lawyer; b. NYC, June 21, 1932; s. Jack C. and Natalie Freling; children: Richard, Alexandra, Darryl, Robert, Dana. BBA in acctg. with honors, U. Tex., Austin, 1953, JD with honors, 1956. Bar: Tex. 1956, US Dist. Ct. No. Dist. Tex. 1959, US Ct. Appeals 5th Cir. 1961, US Supreme Ct. 1962. Mem. Jenkins & Gilchrist, Dallas; ptnr. Johnson & Wortley, Dallas; sr. ptnr. Hopkins & Sutter, Dallas, 1995—96; of counsel Jones, Day, Reavis & Pogue (now Jones Day), Dallas, 1996—. Mem. exec. adv. committees U. Calif. Securities Regulation Inst., 1973—; adv. bd. BNA/Tax Mgmt.,

1976—. Editor-in-chief Tex. Law Rev., 1955-56; contbr. articles to legal jours. Chmn. Inst. on Oil and Gas Taxation Southwestern Legal Found. (now The Ctr. for Am. and Internat. Law), 1965—68, chmn. taxation divsn., 1968—71, rsch. fellow, 1970—, trustee, 1983—, founder, former chair Symposium on Securities Regulation; trustee St. Mark's Sch. of Tex., 1971—78, mem. exec. com., 1972—75; dir. The Greenhill Sch., 1972—80, mem. exec. com., 1972—75; gov., mem. exec. com. S.W. Outward Bound Sch., 1972—82, vice chmn., 1980—82; trustee Retina Found. of S.W., 1975—90, Pine Manor Coll., Chesnut Hill, Mass., 1982—85, Colo. Outward Bound Sch., 1982—, mem. exec. com., 1986—92; bd. dirs. Friends of Dallas Pub. Libr., 1982—87, Isthmus Inst., Dallas, 1983—89; trustee Aperture Found., 1984—90; bd. dirs. Dallas Symphony Assn., 1984—, v.p. ops., 1988—90, pres., 1990—92, chmn., 1992—94; trustee Dallas Symphony Found.; exec. com., bd. trustee Ctr. for Am. and Internat. Law, 1985—; pres. Sun & Star 1996, Dallas, 1992—96; bd. dirs., mem. ops. com. and spl. projects com. Ctr. for Performing Arts, Dallas, 2006—, trustee, 2007—; mem. Dallas Com. Fgn. Rels. Recipient Faculty Award, U. Tex. Sch. Law, 1981. Fellow Am. Coll. Tax Counsel, Tex. Bar Found.(life); mem. Am. Law Inst. (cons. fed. income tax project 1976—), ABA (chmn. com. corp. stockholder relationships 1979-81, mem. coun. taxation sect. 1982-85), Tex. Bar Assn., Dallas Bar Assn., Tex. Law Rev. Publications Inc., U. Tex. Sch. Law Alumni Assn., Dallas Coun. Fgn. Rels. Office: 5311 Falls Rd Dallas TX 75220 Office Phone: 214-969-4835. Business E-Mail: rfreling@jonesday.com.

FRELS, KELLY, lawyer; b. Lolita, Tex., Dec. 28, 1943; s. Leon A. and Aileen K. Frels; m. Carmela Madden, Sept. 10, 1970; children: Jonathan, Catherine. BS in Edn., Tex. State U., 1966; JD, U. Tex., 1970. Bar: Tex., U.S. Dist. Ct. (so., no., we. and ea. dists.), U.S. Ct. Appeals (5th and 11th cirs.), U.S. Supreme Ct. Sr. ptnr. Bracewell & Giuliani LLP (formerly Bracewell & Patterson), Houston, 1976—, mng. ptnr., 1995—2001, mng. ptnr. Houston office, 2001—03. Contbr. articles to profl. jours. Bd. dirs., mem. exec. com. Greater Houston Partnership, 1998—2003, 2010—12, chair govt. rels. com., 1998—99, chair environ. adv. com., 2000—01, chair clean air task force, 2002—03, chair quality life com., 2002, chair flood task force, 2003, bd. mem. emeritus, 2004—12; chair Tex. Environ. Rsch. Coalition, 2006—12, Ctr. Houston's Future, 2010—12. Mem.: ABA (state bar delegate, house dels. 2004—09), Tex. Ctr. Legal Ethics & Professionalism (chair 2009—10), State Bar Tex. (chmn. sch. law sect. 1977—78, bd. dirs. 1995—98, co-chair legal svcs. for poor task force 1996—97, chair long range planning com. 1997—98, vice chair nominating com. 1997—98, chair lawyer referral com. 1998—2001, chair ann. meeting com. 2002—03, pres.-elect 2003—04, pres. 2004—05, past pres. 2005—06), Houston Bar Assn. (bd. dirs. 1988—96, treas. 1990, 2d v.p. 1991, 1st v.p. 1992, pres. 1994, bd. dirs. 1997—98), Tex. State U. Alumni Assn. (pres. 1973), Houston Club (pres. 1999—2000). Roman Catholic. Home: 5607 Bordley Dr Houston TX 77056-2329 Office: Bracewell & Giuliani 711 Louisiana St Ste 2300 Houston TX 77002-2770 Home Phone: 713-626-7726; Office Phone: 713-221-1203. Business E-Mail: kelly.frels@bgllp.com.

FRENCH, DOUGLAS DEWITT, medical facility administrator; b. Augusta, Ga., Jan. 14, 1954; married. BS, Trevecca Nazarene Coll., 1976; M Health Adminstrn., Xavier U., 1979. Adminstrv. resident St. Thomas Hosp., Nashville, 1978-79, dir. ambulatory svcs. and planning, 1979, dir. mgmt. svcs., 1980, adminstrv. asst., 1980-82, asst. adminstr., 1982-85, v.p., 1985-86; exec. v.p., COO St. Mary's Med. Ctr., Evansville, Ind., 1986-89, pres., CEO, 1979-94; CEO St. Vincent's Hosp., Indpls., 1994; pres., CEO Ctrl. Ind. Health Sys., 1998; exec. v.p., COO Daughters of Charity Nat. Health Sys., 1998—99; COO Ascension Health, 1999—2001, pres., CEO, 2000—04; mng. dir. Sante Health Ventures, 2007—. Bd.dirs. Herman Miller, Inc., 2002—. Fellow: Am. Coll. Health Care Execs. Office: Sante Health Ventures Frost Bank Tower Ste 2950 401 Congress Ave Austin TX 78701 Office Phone: 512-721-1200. Business E-Mail: Douglas_French@hermanmiller.com.

FRENCH, LAYNE BRYAN, lawyer, investor, community volunteer; b. Binghamton, NY, Sept. 29, 1950; s. Lawrence C. and Dorris (Bryan) F.; m. Susan Elaine Penn, July 23, 1983; children: Rebecca Penn, Layne Bryan Jr. BBA in Econs. summa cum laude, U. Houston, 1972; MBA in Fin. summa cum laude, U. So. Calif., 1973, M of Liberal Arts summa cum laude, 1974; JD, Harvard U., 1978. Bar: Tex. 1978. Ptnr. Weil, Gotshal & Manges, Houston, 1986-93; exec. mng. dir. 4F Interests, Houston, 1994—. Founder, former editor Harvard Jour. Law and Pub. Policy. Bd. dirs. St. Luke's United Meth. Ch., Houston Symphony, Emergency Aid Resource Ctr. for Homeless, Christian Community Svc. Ctr.; devel. coun. Tex. Children's Hosp.; vol. lawyer, fin. cons. minority entrepreneurs. Mem. ABA (sects. internat. law and practice, individual rights and responsibilities, bus. law), SAR, Tex. Bar Assn., Houston Bar Assn., Sons Revolution, Sons Colonial Wars, Phi Kappa Phi, Omicron Delta Kappa, Phi Eta Sigma, Beta Gamma Sigma. Home: 11015 S Country Squire St Houston TX 77024-7404 Office: 4F Interests 5650 Kirby Dr Ste 123 Houston TX 77005-2459

FRENCH, MARY B., editor, photographer, poet, retired literature educator; b. Dallas, July 21, 1942; d. Harry Blake and Mary Virginia (Jones) F.; m. Richard Edelin Crouch, Feb. 6, 1965; children: John, Virginia. BA, Coll. William and Mary, 1965; MA, U. Va., 1966. Columnist, reporter Va. Gazette, Williamsburg, 1961-65; mng. editor William and Mary Rev., Williamsburg, 1963-64; asst. editor Microfilm Publ., U. Va., Charlottesville, 1966-67; lectr. Am. lit. and women in lit. U. Va., Falls Church, 1968-99. Instr. English, No. Va. CC, Annandale, 1968-69; instr. English composition George Washington U., Washington, 1970; cons. in lit. humanities project Arlington County Libr., 1976. Author: The State Slate: A Guide to Legislative Procedures and Lawmakers, 1977; compiler: Women in Literature: A Bibliography, 1973; editor (with J.L. Anderson) Microfilm Edition of the Papers of R.M.T. Hunter, 1817-1887, 1966; editor Spokeswoman Mag., 1979-82, Washington Women's Rep. Newsletter, 1979-82; mng. editor Women's News Svc., 1979-82; assoc. editor Career Opportunities News, 1983-96; mng. editor Army Mag., 1984-93, editor, 1993-2002, editor in chief, 2002—; contbr. poetry to several anthologies. Com. on Status of Women, Arlington, Va., 1976, steering com. Coalition on Optimum Growth, 1970-73. Mem. MLA, AAUW (chmn. women's studies, dir. Arlington br. 1974-76, assoc. editor Grad. Women mag. 1982, mng. editor publ. 1983), the Am. News Women's Club, the Acad. of Am. Poets, the Lyon Village Citizens Assoc., Hillsboro Cmty. Assn., English-Speaking Union, Jane Austen Soc., US Congress Periodical Press Corrs.'s Assn., Nat. Trust Hist. Preservation, Preservation Soc. Loudoun County, Old House Group Loudoun County, Loudoun Arts Coun., Soc. Profl. Journalists, Am. Soc. Mag. Editors, Va. Hist. Soc., Land Trust of Va., The Nature Conservancy, Appalachian Trail Conf., Photo Comm. of the Nat. Press Club, (hon.) 101st Airborne Divsn. US Army. Episcopalian. Office Phone: 703-907-2620. E-mail: mfrench@ausa.org.

FRENKEL, EUGENE PHILLIP, physician; b. Detroit, Aug. 27, 1929; s. David Eugene and Eva (Antin) Frenkel; m. Rhoda Beth Smilay, Dec. 21, 1958; children: Lisa Michelle, Peter Alan. BS, Wayne State U., 1949; MD, U. Mich., 1953. Diplomate Am. Bd. Internal Medicine (bd. govs. 1980-87, chmn. subspecialty com. hematology 1980-85), Am. Bd. Hematology, Am. Bd. Med. Oncology. Intern Wayne County Gen. Hosp., Eloise, Mich., 1953-54; resident in internal medicine Boston City Hosp., 1954-55; resident in internal medicine, then instr. U. Mich. Med. Center, 1957-62; mem. faculty U. Tex. Southwestern Med. Ctr., Dallas, 1962—, prof. internal medicine and radiology, 1969—, chief divsn. hematology-oncology, 1962-91, Patsy R. and Raymond D. Nasher Disting. chair in cancer rsch., 1990—, A. Kenneth Pye prof. in cancer rsch., 1994—; chief nuclear medicine, cons. hematology-oncology VA Med. Center, Dallas, 1962-80; Sydney and J.L. Huffines, Jr. disting. chair U. Tex. Southwestern Med. Ctr., 1998—, Elaine Dewey Sammons Disting. chair cancer rsch. in honor of Eugene P. Frenkel, MD, 2003—. Cons. com. evaluation rsch. hematology, nutrtion Nat. Inst. Arthritis and Metabolic Diseases, 1979—82; active Am. Joint Commn. Cancer, 1986—95; interim dir. divsn. hematology-oncology VA Med. Ctr., Dallas, 1995—97; dir. The Boone Pickens Fund for Cancer Rsch. and Treatment Honoring Dr. Eugene P. Frenkel, 2004—. Contbr. rsch. papers in field. Dir. The Boone Pickens Fund, 2004. Officer M.C. USAF, 1955—57. Recipient award, 2008—. Master: ACP (coun. subspecialty secs. 1992—2006), Internat. Soc. Hematology; mem.: Internat. Assn. Study Lung Cancer, Internat. Soc. Hematology (councillor 1992—97), Am. Fedn. Clin. Rsch., Soc. Nuc. Medicine, Am. Urol. Assn., So. Soc. Clin. Investigation, Am. Soc. Clin. Investigation, Am. Soc. Biol. Chemists, Am. Assn. Cancer Edn., Am. Assn. Cancer Rsch., Assn. Am. Physicians, Am. Cancer Soc. (pres. Dallas unit 1970—71, mem. sci. adv. com. clin. investigations II-chemotherapy and hematolog 1978—82, mem. nat. clin. fellowship com. 1978—87, dir. Tex. divsn. 1978—, Emma Freeman prof. 1981—91, mem. internat. rsch. grants com. 1988—90, mem. sci. adv. coun. 1991—97), Am. Soc. Clin. Oncology (chmn. membership com. 1982—85), Am. Soc. Hematology (treas. 1976—84), Alpha Omega Alpha.

FRESEN, ERIK, state legislator; b. Miami, Fla., June 9, 1976; m. Ethel Fresen; children: Adrian, Julian. Legis. aide, 2000—02; mem. Dist. 111 Fla. House of Reps., 2008—, vice chair preK-12 policy com., mem. edn. policy coun., fin. and tax coun., health care regulation policy com., preK-12 appropriations com. Mem. Blue Ribbon Com. on Workforce Housing, Sch. Concurrency Task Force; chmn. Educational Facilities Benefit Dist. Republican. Catholic. Office: House Office Bldg 402 S Monroe St Rm 308 Tallahassee FL 32399-1300 also: 6080 Bird Rd Ste 1 Miami FL 33155-5249 Office Phone: 850-488-4092. Office Fax: 305-663-2011. Business E-Mail: erik.fresen@myfloridahouse.gov.

FRESHWATER, MICHAEL FELIX, hand surgeon, educator; b. NYC, Feb. 4, 1948; s. Jack and Rhonda Freshwater. BS magna cum laude, Bklyn. Coll., 1968; MD, Yale U., 1972. Diplomate Nat. Bd. Med. Examiners, Am. Bd. Plastic Surgery, cert. subspecialist in hand surgery. Asst. resident in surgery Yale New Haven Hosp., 1972-74; fellow in plastic surgery Med. Sch. Johns Hopkins U., Balt., 1974-77; resident, then chief resident in plastic surgery Jackson Meml. Hosp., 1977-78; Kleinert fellow hand and microsurgery Jewish Hosp., Louisville, 1979; pvt. practice medicine specializing in plastic/hand surgery Miami, Fla., 1979—; pres., dir. Miami Inst. Hand and Microsurgery, 1980—; dir. hand and microsurgery Cedars Med. Ctr., 1985—2000, chief surgery, 1988-90. Vol. prof. surgery U. Miami Sch. Medicine, 1979—; vol. faculty mem. Barry U. Sch. Podiatric Medicine and Surgery, 1989—95; vis. prof. Javeriana U., Bogota, 1983—85, Centro Medico de los Andes, 1983—86; cons. Fla. Children's Med. Svc., Tallahassee, 1979—, Fla. Elks Crippled Children Soc., Orlando, 1983—, Fla. Dept. Profl. Regulation, Tallahassee, 1984—95, League Against Cancer, 1983—, Scientists Inst. Pub. Info., 1985—, USCG, Miami Beach, 1992—; editl. bd. Jour. Plastic Reconstructive and Aesthetic Surgery, 2009—; editl. bd. mem. HAND Annals Plastic Surgery Jour. Hand Surgery. Editor: U. Miami Plastic Surgery News, 2004—08; mem. bd. reviewers: Plastic and Reconstructive Surgery, 1976—2004; contbr. chapters to books, articles to profl. jours. Trustee Yale U. Med. Libr., New Haven, 1972—77, 2000—06, D. R. Millard Found., 1987—; bd. dirs. V. and A. Gildred Found., 1980—86, Yale Sch. Medicine Fund, 1991—97, Campaign for Stuyvesant, 2003—; mem. nat. campaign com. Yale Sch. Medicine, 1993—97; mem. Fla. Bar Grievance Com., 1998—2001. Recipient Letter Commendation, Gov. Bob Graham, 1984; fellow Weinberger, NIH, 1974—76; scholar Jonas Salk, CUNY, 1968—72. Fellow: Internat. Coll. Surgeons; mem.: AAUP, AMA (numerous Physicians Recognition awards), Miami Assn. for Surgery of Hand (dir. 1991—), Am. Soc. Peripheral Nerve, Miami Soc. Plastic Surgeons (sec.-treas. 1987—88, v.p. 1988—89, pres. 1989—90, treas. 2007—09), Royal Soc. Medicine, Internat. Soc. Reconstructive Microsurgery, Am. Soc. Reconstructive Microsurgery, Am. Burn Assn., Am. Assn. Hand Surgery, Assn. Yale Alumni in Medicine (bd. dirs. 1998—2000), Grove Isle Club (Miami), Yale Club (Miami, N.Y.), Phi Beta Kappa. Avocation: skiing. Office: 9155 S Dadeland Blvd Ste 1404 Miami FL 33156-2739

FREUDENTHAL, ERNEST GUENTER, technology and business educator; b. Mannheim, Germany, July 22, 1920; came to the U.S., 1937; s. Leopold and Selma (Rosenthal) F.; m. Stephanie Karlsruher, Dec. 26, 1948; children: Pamela Hausman, Joan Fraifeld. BA in Econs., Vanderbilt U., 1948, MA in Econs., 1971. Employee Werthan Industries, Nashville, 1942-44, 46-48, middle mgmt. staff, 1948-69, v.p. mfg., 1969-71, sr. v.p., 1971-90. Adj. assoc. prof. bus., tech., pub. policy, indsl. mktg. Vanderbilt U., Nashville, 1971—. Co-editor: The Holocaust and other Genocide, 2002. Mem. Com. on Employment Projections of the Bus. Rsch. Adv. Coun., Washington, 1997—, Holocaust Edn. Colloquium, 1999—2000; Mem. Bus. Res. Adv. Coun. to the Bur. Labor Statis., Washington, 1981—; chmn. Metro Social Svcs. Commn., Nashville, 1989—2001; commr., treas. Tenn. Holocaust Commn., Inc., 1998—; pres. Jewish Cmty. Ctr., Nashville, 1965—67; trustee Tenn. Hist. Soc., 2000—; bd. dirs. Goodwill Industries of Nashville and Middle Tenn. Staff sgt. US Army, 1944—46, PTO. Recipient Sage award Coun. on Aging, Nashville, 1995. Mem. Jewish Fedn. Nashville (pres. 1974-76), The Temple (pres. 1986-88), Vanderbilt Inst. Pub. Policy Studies, Univ. Club, Phi Beta Kappa. Avocation: hiking. Office: PO Box 1518 Nashville TN 37202-1518 Home: 131 Carnavon Pkwy Nashville TN 37205-3937

FREUND, GERHARD, retired medical educator; b. Frankfurt, Germany, Apr. 21, 1926; came to U.S., 1951; s. Adolf and Martha (Neuhaus) F.; m. Marion Healy, Sept. 24, 1955; children: Anne Freund, Michael S. MD, Goethe U., 1951; MS, McGill U., Montreal, 1957. Mem. Ctr. Neurobiol. Scis. U. Fla., Gainesville, 1967—; assoc. prof. medicine U. Fla. Coll. Medicine, Gainesville, 1970-75, prof. medicine, 1975—, prof. neurosci., 1976—, prof. emeritus, 2000—; chief endocrinology Va. Med. Ctr., Gainesville, 1970—2000. Dir. Alcohol Rsch. Ctr., Gainesville, 1982-87. Fellow Am. Coll. Physicians; mem. Soc. Neurosci., Soc. Biol. Psychiatry, Endocrine Soc., Rsch. Soc. Alcoholism (mem. exec. com. 1981-84). Home: 2515 NW 77 Blvd Apt 407 Gainesville FL 32606-8683 also: 2515 NW 77th Blvd Apt T308 Gainesville FL 32606-8692

FREY, LOUIS, JR., lawyer, federal official; b. Jan. 11, 1934; m. Marcia Turner, 1956; children: Julie, Lynne, Louis III, Lauren, Christine. BA in English cum laude, Colgate U., 1955; JD, U. Mich., 1961; JD (hon.), Rollins Coll., 1977; DSc (hon.), Jones Univ., 1978. Bar: Fla. 1961, U.S. Supreme Ct. 1969, U.S. Ct. of Appeals (5th and 11th cir.), Supreme Ct. Fla., U.S. Dist. Ct. Fla. (mid. dist.). Asst. county solicitor Orange County, Fla., 1961-63; gen. counsel Fla. State Turnpike Authority, 1966-67; congressman US House of Representatives, 1969-79, mem. interstate and fgn. commerce com., sci. and tech. com., select com. on narcotics, sub-com. on communications, sub-com. on energy research; mem. rep. house leadership-rsch. chmn. congress U.S. Ho. of Reps. Rsch. Com., 1993—94; commr. Dept. of Lottery State of Fla., 1987—88; founder Lou Frey Inst. Politics and Govt., U. Ctrl. Fla., 2002—; ptnr. Lowndes, Drosdick, Doster, Kantor & Reed, P.A., Orlando, Fla., 1987—. Del. or alternate del. to most Rep. Conv., 1968—; Rep. State Chmn. Pres. Ford, 1976—; nat. co-chmn., former mem. Congress for Reagan, 1980; nat. fin. com. Bush, 1988—92, pres.-co-chmn., 1996, co-chmn. Dole for pres.; Fla. state fin. com. Pres. Bush, 2000, 2004; counsellor to sec. HUD, 2001, McCain Florida Fin. Com., 2008; alumni bd. trustees Colgate U., 1973—75, 1992—; former mems. Congress, leader dels. to numerous countries including Cuba, Vietnam, China, Slovakia; ofcl. observer Ukraine Election, 2004. Author: Inside The House Former Members Reveal How Congress Really Works, 2001, Political Rules of the Road: Representatives Senators & Presidents Share Their Rules for Success in Congress, Politics & Life, 2009; contbr. weekly column to Fla. newspapers; commentator pub. radio and TV, 1999—; co-author (with George Bush & Bill Brock): Youth of America which became the basis for the 18-year-old vote and the college loan program. Chmn. Fla. Fedn. of Young Reps., 1965-66; treas. Rep. Party Fla., mem. state exec. com., 1966-67; past chmn., mem. exec. com. Fla. Coun. on Econ. Edn., 1991—; chmn. Former Mems. Congress, 1992-94, bd. dirs., 1992—, mem. exec. com., past pres.; candidate Fla. Gov., 1978-86, U.S. Senate, 1980; 1st chmn. Rep. Task Force on Drug Abuse Served with USN, 1955—58, capt. Res. ret., 1978. Recipient Watchdog of Treasury award, 1970, 72, 74, 76, 78, Guardian of Small Bus. award, Disting. Service award Ams. for Constitutional Action, Man of Yr. award Fla. Assn. Broadcasters, 1977, Masada award, 1977, Fla. Coun. on Econ. Edn. Vision award, 2002, Disting. Svc. award, USAFMC, 2009; named Hope for Congress, Life Mag., 1975; named to Sr. Citizens Hall of Fame; named one of 200 Rising Leaders in America, Time Mags., 1974, Best Lawyers in America, 2006-13, Fla. Super Lawyers, 2006. Mem.: Order of the Coif, Phi Gamma Delta, Phi Delta Phi. Lutheran. Home: 139 Genius Dr Winter Park FL 32789-5103 Office: Lowndes Drosdick Doster Kantor & Reed PA 215 N Eola Dr PO Box 2809 Orlando FL 32801-2095 Office Phone: 407-843-4600. Business E-Mail: lou.frey@lowndes-law.com.

FREYTAG, SHARON NELSON, lawyer; b. May 11, 1943; d. John Seldon and Ruth Marie (Herbel) Nelson; children: Kurt David, Hillary Lee. BS with highest distinction, U. Kans., Lawrence, 1965; MA, U. Mich., 1966; JD cum laude, So. Meth. U., 1981. Bar: Tex. 1981, US Dist. Ct. (no. dist.) Tex. 1981, US Dist. Ct. (so. dist.) Tex. 2001, US Ct. Appeals (5th cir.) 1982, US Ct. Appeals (8th cir.) 2001, US Ct. Appeals (fed. cir.) 2002, US Ct. Appeals (9th cir.) 2005, US Ct. Claims 2004, US Supreme Ct. 1993, bd. cert. in civil appellate law: Tex. Bd. Legal Specialization. Tchr. English, Gaithersburg (Md.) H.S., 1966—70; instr. English, Eastfield Coll., 1974-78; law clk. U.S. Dist. Ct. (no. dist.) Tex., 1981-82, U.S. Ct. Appeals (5th cir.), 1982; ptnr. Haynes and Boone, Dallas, 1983—2011, Shoron Freytag Law, 2011—. Vis. prof. law So. Meth. U., 1985-86. Editor-in-chief Southwestern Law Jour., 1980-81; contbr. articles to profl. jours. Dir. devel. bd. U. Tex. at Dallas. Recipient John Marshall Constl. Law award, Baird Cmty. Spirit award, 1995; named Tex. Super Lawyer, 2003, 2004, 2005, 2006, 2007, 2008, 2009, 2010—11, Tex. Lawyer Impact Players award, 2010, Tex. Lawyers Winning Woman award, 2011; named one of 50 Women Tex. Super Lawyers, 2003, 2004, 2005, Best Lawyers in Am., 2005, 2006, 2007, 2008, 2009—10, 2011—13, Best Women Lawyers in Dallas, 2010; Woodrow Wilson fellow. Mem. ABA (past chair, mem. exec. com. and chair long range planning com., coun. appellate lawyers), Fed. Bar Assn. (co-chmn. appellate practice and adv. sect. 1990-91), State Bar Tex. (bd. dir., exec. com. 1997-01, appellate coun. 1995-98), Dallas Bar Assn. (appellate sect.), Dallas Bar Found., Tex. Bar Found., Am. Bar Found., Higginbotham Inn of Ct. (former barrister), Order of Coif, Phi Beta Kappa. Lutheran. Home: 8993 Prairie Knoll Dr Longmont CO 80503

FRIAS, JAIME LUIS, retired pediatrician, clinical geneticist, educator; b. Concepcion, Chile, Mar. 20, 1933; came to U.S., 1970; s. Luis Humberto and Olga Ana (Fernandez) F.; m. Jacqueline May Steel, Apr. 8, 1961; children: Jaime Arturo, Juan Pablo, Patricio Andres, Maria Josefina. MD, U. Chile, 1959. Diplomate Am. Bd. Pediatrics, Am. Bd. Human Genetics. Intern Hospital Regional, Concepcion, 1958-59; resident in pediatrics Calvo Mackenna Hosp., Santiago, Chile, 1960-62; clin. genetics and dysmorphology fellow U. Wis., Madison, 1965-66, U. Wash., Seattle, 1966-67; asst. prof. pediatrics U. Concepcion, 1967-69, U. Fla. Coll. Medicine, Gainesville, 1970-74, assoc. prof., 1974-77, prof., 1977-86, chief divsn. genetics, 1977-86, chmn. med. sch. admissions com., 1983-86; prof., chmn. dept. pediatrics U. Nebr. Med. Ctr., 1986—91; prof. pediatrics U. South Fla. Coll. Medicine, Tampa, 1991—2004, chmn. dept. pediatrics, 1991-99, dir. Birth Defects Ctr., 1999—2004, emeritus prof., 2004—; vis. scientist Nat. Ctr. for Birth Defects and Devel. Disabilities, CDC, Atlanta, 2004—. Chmn. Com. for Protection of Human Subjects, 1975-78; chmn. Fla. Com. on Prevention Devel. Disabilities, 1979-82, chmn. infant hearing screening adv. coun., 1982-86; cons. Spanish Collaborative Project on Congenital Malformation, Madrid, 1983—. Contbr. chpts. to books, articles to profl. jours. Trustee All Children's Hosp., 1991-99, Ronald McDonald Charities Tampa Bay, 1999-2001; exec. com. Assn. Med. Sch. Pediat. Dept. Chmn., 1993-96; steering com. Nat. Folic Acid Coun., 1999-2003. Named Tchr. of Yr., U. Fla. Coll. Medicine, 1978-79, Lewis A. Barness Endowed Chair Pediatrics, 1994-99. Mem. ACP (affiliate; W.K. Kellogg fellow 1965-67), Am. Acad. Pediatrics (com. genetics 1995-2002), Am. Pediatric Soc., Am. Soc. Human Genetics, Assn. Clin. Scientists. Democrat. Roman Catholic. Office: MS E-86 1600 Clifton Rd Atlanta GA 30333 Business E-Mail: jfrias@cdc.gov.

FRIAS, JAMES D., corporate financial executive; BS Acctg., Olivet Nazarene U., 1978. Cost acct. Alberto Culver, 1978—80; contr. Nucor Bldg. Sys., Waterloo, Ind., 1991—94, Nucor Steel, Crawfordsville, Ind., 1994—2001; corp. contr. Nucor Corp., 2001—09, v.p., 2006—09, exec. v.p., CFO, treas., 2010—. Office: Nucor Corp 1915 Rexford Rd Charlotte NC 28211 Office Phone: 704-366-7000. Office Fax: 704-362-4208. Business E-Mail: JFrias@nucor.com.

FRICK, STEPHEN N., astronaut; b. Pitts., Pa., Sept. 30, 1964; m. Jennifer Rhatigan. BSc in Aerospace Engring., U.S. Naval Acad., 1986; MSc in Aero. Engring., U.S. Naval Postgraduate Sch., 1994. Commd. 2d lt. USN, 1986, advanced through grades to comdr.; with strike fighter squadron Naval Air Sta., Cecil Field, Fla., 1988—91; various assignments USN, 1991—94; project officer, test pilot carrier suitability dept. Strike Aircraft Test Squadron, Patuxent River, 1994—96; pilot NASA, Houston, 1996—. Pilot Atlantis STS-110 Mission, 2002; mission comdr. Atlantis STS-122 Mission to deliver the European Space Agency's Columbus Lab. to the Internat. Space Station, 2008. Decorated Air medal with 2 strike flight awards USN, 3 Commendation medals one with combat V, Nat. Defense Svc.

medal. Mem.: Assn. Naval Aviators, Soc. Exptl. Test Pilots, U.S. Naval Acad. Alumni Assn. Avocations: skiing, bicycling, hiking, camping. Office: Astronaut Office CB NASA Johnson Space Center Houston TX 77058

FRIDAY, ELBERT WALTER, JR., federal agency administrator, meteorologist; b. DeQueen, Ark., July 13, 1939; s. Elbert Walter and Mary Elizabeth (Ward) F.; m. Karen Ann Hauschild, Nov. 14, 1959 (dec. Mar. 21, 2007); children: Kristine Ann, Kelly Sue; m. Gay Smith Littleton, Apr. 2, 2008. BS in Engring. Physics, U. Okla., Norman, 1961, MS in Meteorology, 1967, PhD in Meteorology, 1969. Commd. 2d lt. USAF, 1961, advanced through ranks to Col., 1961—81, weather officer, 1961-81, served Vietnam, 1972—73, dir. environ. and life scis., Dept. Def., 1978-81, ret., 1981; dep. dir. Nat. Weather Svc., Silver Spring, Md., 1981-87, dir., 1987-97; asst. adminstr. Office Oceanic and Atmospheric Rsch., Silver Spring, 1997-98; dir. NAS, 1998—2002; Weather News prof. applied meteorology U. Okla., 2002—05, prof. emeritus. Mem. com. on low level wind shear NAS, Washington, 1985-86; U.S. permanent rep. to UN World Meteorol. Orgn., 1988-98, mem. exec. coun., 1988-98; adj. prof. U. Okla., 1998; bd. dirs. Atmospheric Sci. and Climate, NRC, NAS, 1998-2002. Contbr. articles to prof. jours. Elder Calvary Christian Ch., Burke, Va., 1985-89, 2002—, trustee, 1989-93, chmn. bd., 1998-2002. Decorated Bronze Star; recipient Superior Svc. medal Dept. Def., 1981, Presdl. Rank award, 1988, Disting. Achievement award U. Okla., 1992, Fed. Exec. of Yr. award Fed. Exec. Inst. Alumni Assn., 1993. Fellow Am. Meteorol. Soc. (councilor 1988-90, pres. 2003, Cleve. Abbe award 1997); mem. AAAS, Nat. Weather Assn., Sigma Xi. Office Phone: 405-330-8564. Business E-Mail: joefriday@ou.edu.

FRIDMAN, J. ARTURO, colon and rectal surgeon, director; MD, U. Chile, 1967—74. Cert. gen. surgery, diplomate Am. Bd. Surgery, Am. Bd. Colon and Rectal Surgery, 1980. Intern in surgery Sinai Hosp., Balt., 1974—75; resident in surgery Mt. Sinai Hosp., Miami Beach, Fla., 1975—79; fellow in colon and rectal surgery Greater Balt. Med. Ctr., Md., 1979—80; med. staff South Miami Hosp., 1980—2009, chief colon and rectal surgery sect., 1989—98, chief of staff, 1998—2000; med. staff Bapt. Hosp., 1980—2011, asst. chief surgery, 1988—90, chief surgery, 1990—98, chief of staff, 1998—2000, med. dir. dept. med. edn., 2000—. Fellow: Am. Soc. of Colon and Rectal Surgeons, Internat. Coll. Surgeons; mem.: Instituto Nacional de Chile, Gen. José Miguel Carrera, Fla. Surgical Soc. Office: Baptist Hospital Department of Medical Education 8900 N Kendall Dr Miami FL 33176 Office Phone: 786-596-7232. Business E-Mail: Fridmana@bellsouth.net.*

FRIDOVICH, IRWIN, biochemistry professor; b. NYC, Aug. 2, 1929; s. Louis and Sylvia (Appelbaum) F.; m. Mollie Finkel; children: Sharon E., Judith L. BS, CCNY, 1951; postgrad., Cornell U. Med. Coll., 1951-52; PhD, Duke U., 1955; doctorate (hon.), U. Rene Descartes, Paris, 1980. Instr. biochemistry Duke U., Durham, N.C., 1956-58, assoc., 1958—; vis. research assoc. Harvard U., Cambridge, Mass., 1961-62; asst. prof. biochemistry Duke U., 1961-66, assoc. prof., 1966-71, prof., 1971—, James B. Duke prof., 1976—, emeritus, 1996—. Mem. study sect. Am. Cancer Soc., mem. adv. com. biochemistry and chem. carcinogenesis Mem. editorial bd. Jour. Biol. Chemistry, Biochemica Biophysica Acta, Archives of Biochemistry and Biophysics, Biochem. Jour., Bioinorganic Chemistry, Biochemistry, Biochem. Pharmacology, Analytical Biochemistry; contbr. articles to sci. jours. Recipient Founders' award Chem. Industry Inst. Toxicology, 1980, Sr. Passano award Passano Found., 1987, Herty award Ga. sect. Am. Chem. Soc., 1980, Research Career Devel. award NIH, 1959-69, Cressy A. Morrison award N.Y. Acad. Sci., 1984, Townsend Harris medal City U. N.Y., 1990; co-recipient Cresson medal, Franklin Inst., 1997, City of Medicine award, Durham, N.C., 1998, Anlyan Lifetime Achievement award Duke Med. Ctr., 1998. Mem. NAS, Am. Acad. Arts and Scis., Am. Soc. Biol. Chemists (pres. 1982), N.C. Acad. Scis., Oxygen Soc. (pres. 1990), Soc. for Free Radical Rsch. Internat., (pres. 1992), Phi Beta Kappa, Sigma Xi Home: 3517 Courtland Dr Durham NC 27707-5134 Office: Duke U Med Center PO Box 3711 Durham NC 27710-0001 Office Phone: 919-689-5122. E-mail: fridovich@biochem.duke.edu.

FRIEDEL, ROBERT OLIVER, physician; b. Corona, NY, Aug. 4, 1936; s. August W. and Denise G. (D'Aoust) F.; m. Susanne Weber, June 30, 1961; children: Christine, Scott, Karin, Linda. BS, Duke U., 1958, MD, 1964. Diplomate: Am. Bd. Psychiatry and Neurology. Intern Duke U. Med. Ctr., Durham, NC, 1964-65, resident in psychiatry, 1967-70, asst. prof. psychiatry and pharmacology dept. psychiatry, 1970-73, assoc. prof. psychiatry and asst. prof. pharmacology, 1973-74; assoc. prof. psychiatry and pharmacology U. Wash. Sch. Medicine, Seattle, 1974-77, dir. div. psychopharmacology, 1974-77, vice chmn., dir. clin. services dept. psychiatry and behavioral scis., 1975-77; prof., chmn. dept. psychiatry Med. Coll. Va.-Va. Commonwealth U., Richmond, 1977-84; prof., chmn. dept. psychiatry, exec. dir. Mental Health Rsch. Inst. U. Mich., Ann Arbor, 1984-85; v.p. psychiat. medicine and rsch. Charter Med. Corp., Macon, Ga., 1985-90, psychiatrist in chief, 1987-90, sr. v.p. clin. svcs. and rsch., 1990, physician in chief, 1990, also bd. dirs.; prof., chmn. dept. psychiatry U. Ala., Birmingham, 1992-2001; disting. clin. prof., dept. psychiatry Va. Commonwealth U., Richmond, 2001—. Mem. sci. adv. bd. Nat. Edn. Alliance for Borderline Personality Disorder. Author: Borderline Personality Disorder Demystified, 2004, www.bpdemystified.com, 2007, (with others) Behavioral Science: A Selective View, 1972; editor (with L.R. Baxter) Current Psychiatric Diagnosis and Treatment, 1999, (with D. Evans) Current Psychiatry Reports and Current Psychosis and Therapeutic Reports; mem. editl. bd. Jour. Clin. Psychopharmacology, Hosp. and Cmty. Psychiatry, 1986-92; contbr. book chpts. and articles. Bd. dirs. Nat. Mental Health Assn., 1987-92. Served to lt. comdr. USPHS, 1965-67. Fellow Am. Psychiat. Assn. (disting. life); mem. AMA, Am. Coll. Psychiatrists, Soc. Biol. Psychiatry, Med. Soc. Va., Am. Coll. Neuropsychopharmacology (life), Alpha Omega Alpha. Home: 13722 Hickory Nut Point Midlothian VA 23112 Office Phone: 804-744-5261.

FRIEDEN, THOMAS R., federal agency administrator; b. NYC, Dec. 7, 1960; BA, Oberlin Coll., Ohio, 1982; MD, Columbia U. Coll. Physicians & Surgeons, NYC, 1986; MPH, Columbia U. Mailman Sch. Pub. Health, 1986. Med. intern, resident Columbia Presbyn. Hosp., 1986-89; fellow in infectious disease Yale U., New Haven, 1989-90; EIS (epidemiologic intelligence svc.) officer NYC Dept. Health & Mental Hygiene, 1990-92, dir. Bur. Tuberculosis Control, asst. commr., 1992-96, commr., 2002—09; med. officer WHO, New Delhi, 1996—2001; dir. Centers Disease Control & Prevention (CDC), US Dept. Health & Human Services, 2009—, adminstr. Agy. Toxic Substances & Disease Registry (ATSDR), 2009—. Office: CDC 1600 Clifton Rd Atlanta GA 30333 Office Phone: 800-232-4636. Business E-Mail: Tomfrieden@cdc.gov.*

FRIEDENBERG, KAREN ROSEN, real estate executive; b. Savannah, Ga., May 3, 1949; d. Emamuel F. and Thelma Z. (Reed) Rosen; 1 child, Jodi. Student, Harvard U., 1967, U. Ga., 1967-69, U. N.C., 1968; BS in Mass Comm., Emerson Coll., 1971. Exec. trainee Jordan Marsh, Boston, 1974-76; broadcast dir. Rich's, Atlanta, 1976-78; mktg. dir. Northlake Mall, Atlanta, 1978-80, Lenox Square, Atlanta, 1980-82; retail leasing assoc. Trammell Crow Co., Atlanta, 1982-85, Kern & Co., Atlanta, 1985-86, Retail Properties Group, 1986-89; mng. dir. Retail Realty Advisors, 1989, LGB Realty & Devel. Inc., 2000—13. Bd. dirs. Atlanta chpt. Nat. Coun. Jewish Women; patron High Mus. Art. Named Outstanding Woman of Yr., Atlanta Bus. Chronicle, 1990, Best Bacherette in Buckhead award Inside mag., 1990. Mem. Internat. Coun. Shopping Ctrs. Atlanta Bd. Realtors (Top Prodr. award retail divsn. 1990), Comml. Real Estate Women, Midtown Bus. Assn., Buckhead Bus. Assn (grad. Leadership Devel. 1990), Hadassah. Republican. Avocations: aerobics, bicycling, hiking, rafting. Home and Office: PO Box 550622 Atlanta GA 30355

FRIEDHEIM, JERRY WARDEN, museum consultant; b. Joplin, Mo., Oct. 7, 1934; s. Volmer Havens and Billie Alice (Warden) F.; m. Shirley Margarette Beavers, Oct. 17, 1956 (dec. Sept. 15, 2003); children: Daniel Volmer, Cynthia Diane, Thomas Eric; m. Jacqueline Wade Grant, April 24, 2004. BJ, U. Mo., 1956, AM, 1962. Reporter, editor, editorial writer Neosho (Mo.) Daily News, Joplin (Mo.) Globe, Columbia Missourian, 1956-61; instr. journalism U. Mo., Columbia, 1961-62; aide to Congressman Durward Hall from Mo., Washington, 1962-63; legis. asst., pres. sec., exec. asst. to U.S. Senator John Tower from Tex., Washington, 1963-69; dep. asst. Sec. Def. for Pub. Affairs, U.S. Dept. Def., Washington, 1969-72; asst. Sec. Def. for Pub. Affairs, Washington, 1973-74; v.p. pub. and govt. affairs AMTRAK, 1974-75; exec. v.p., gen. mgr. Am. Newspaper Pubs. Assn. and ANPA Found., Washington, 1975-87, pres., 1987-91; pub. Presstime mag., 1980-90; v.p. pub. affairs The Freedom Forum, Arlington, Va., 1991-95; exec. dir. The Freedom Forum Newseum, 1991-93; dep. dir. The Newseum, Arlington, Va., 1995-97, mem. adv. com., 1998—. Bd. dirs. World Press Freedom Com; past chmn. Nat. Press Found. Author: Where are the Voters, 1968. Capt. AUS, 1956-58. Congl. fellow Am. Polit. Sci. Assn.; recipient Disting. Svc. medal Dept. Def., 1972, 74. Home: 46865 Grissom St Sterling VA 20165-3575

FRIEDKIN, THOMAS H., automotive executive; b. 1925; Dir. Pacific Southwest Airlines, San Diego, 1946-87; with Gulf States Toyota, Inc., Houston, 1969—, now chmn. bd. dirs., CEO. Named one of Forbes 400: Richest Americans, 2006—. Office: Gulf States Toyota Inc 1355 Enclave Pkwy Houston TX 77077-2026

FRIEDLAND, MICHAEL LAWRENCE, dean, medical educator; b. Aug. 30, 1942; BS, Bklyn. Coll., 1963; MD, SUNY, Bklyn., 1967. Asst. prof. medicine, dir. hematology/oncology Brown U./Miriam Hosp., Providence, 1973-81; assoc. prof. medicine Med. Coll. Pa., 1981-82; prof. clin. medicine, sr. assoc. dean clin. affairs NY Med. Coll., 1982-87, chmn. dept. medicine, prof. clin. medicine, 1987-92; dean Binghamton Clin. Campus SUNY, Syracuse, 1992-97; v.p.affiliated programs SUNY Health Sci. Ctr., Syracuse, 1993-95; interim exec. v.p. for acad. affairs/dean medicine Tex. A&M U. Sys. Health Sci. Ctr., College Station, Tex., 1997-99; dean of medicine U. Mo. Kansas City, 1999—2001; dean ea. divsn. W.Va. U. Health Scis Ctr., Martinsburg, 2001—04; prof. biomed. sci., v.p. med. programs Fla. Atlantic U., Boca Raton, 2004—, dean Charles E. Schmidt Coll. Biomed. Sci., 2006—. Mem. Medicare Coverage Adv. Com.; v.p. med. programs, founding dean Charles C. Schimet Coll. Medicine, FAU, 2010-. Co-author: (abstract) IME 21st Ann. Session, 1996, (sect. of book) The Chemotherapy Source Book, 1996; contbr. over 50 articles to profl. jours. Bd. dirs. Brazos Valley chpt. Am. Lung Assn., Bryan, Tex., 1998. Mem. AMA (governing coun. sect. on med. schs., chair sect. on med. schs. 2002-04), Mo. State Med. Assn. (coun. on med. edn.). Office: Florida Atlantic Univ Biomed Sci 777 Glades Road PO Box 3091 Boca Raton FL 33431-0991 Home Phone: 561-964-4477; Office Phone: 561-297-2219. Business E-Mail: michael.friedland@fau.edu.

FRIEDLAND, STEVEN I., law educator; b. 1951; BA in Math., SUNY Binghamton, 1978; JD cum laude, Harvard Law Sch., 1981; LLM, Columbia U., NYC, 1994, JSD, 1999. Bar: Mass. 1983, DC 1985, Fla. 1989. Law clk. to judge James L. King US Dist. Ct. (so. dist.) Fla., 1981—82; instr. U. Miami Law Sch., Coral Gables, 1982—83; asst. US atty. for DC US Dept. Justice, Washington, 1983—85; asst., then assoc. prof. Shepard Broad Law Ctr., Nova Southeastern U., Ft. Lauderdale, Fla., 1985—90, prof., 1990—94, 1998—2006; vis. prof. Ga. State U. Coll. Law, Atlanta, 1994—96, U. Ga. Sch. Law, Athens, 1996—97, Elon U. Sch. Law, Greensboro, NC, 2006—07, prof. law, sr. scholar, 2007—, dir. Ctr. Engaged Learning in Law, 2007—. Dollard fellow law, medicine and psychiatry Columbia U. Med. Sch., 1992—93. Co-author (numerous edits.): Techniques For Teaching Law, Teaching the Law School Curriculum; contbr. articles to profl. jours., chapters to books. Mem. services. and programs com. Law Sch. Admissions Coun., 1999—2001, 2009—; bd. advisors Inst. Law Sch. Tchg. Recipient Prof. of Yr. award, NSU Shepard Broad Law Ctr., 2002—03. Mem.: ABA, Assn. American Law Schools, American Law Inst. Office: Elon Univ School of Law 201 N Greene St Greensboro NC 27401 Office Phone: 336-278-9224. E-mail: sfriedland2@elon.edu.

FRIEDLANDER, EDWARD JAY, journalist, educator; b. Portland, Maine, Apr. 24, 1945; s. Otto and Marguerite Evelyn (Smith) Friedlander; m. Roberta Kay Burford, July 12, 1975; 1 child, Erika Anne. BS, U. Wyo., 1967; MA, U. Denver, 1970; EdD, U. No. Colo., 1973. Reporter Denver Post, 1967-68, USIA, Washington, 1968-69; publicist Universal Pictures, NYC, 1969-70; mag. editor Daily Times-Call, Longmont, Colo., 1970-71; media coord. Centaurus HS, Lafayette, Colo., 1972-73; asst. prof. mass communication Ctrl. Mo. State U., Warrensburg, 1973-75; from asst. prof. to assoc. prof. dept. journalism U. Ark., Little Rock, 1975—81, prof., 1981-95, chairperson dept. journalism, 1988-95, emeritus prof., 1996; dir. U. South Fla. Sch. Mass Comm., Tampa, 1995—2010, prof., 1995—2012, emeritus prof., 2013. Cons. Bur. Indian Affairs, Washington, 1972, Ark. Press Assn., Little Rock, 1980—2004; cons., editor FCC, Washington, 1979—81; adminstr. Waldo Proffitt award, 1998—. Author: (book) Excellence in Reporting, 1987, Feature Writing for Newspapers and Magazines, 1988, Feature Writing The Pursuit of Excellence, 7th edit., 2011, Modern Mass Media, 1990, Modern Mass Media, 2d rev. edit., 1994, Medios de Comunicación Social, 1992. German Acad. Exch. Svc. fellow, Bonn, 1982, European Acad. fellow, Berlin, 1984. Mem.: Fla. Press Assocs. (bd. dirs. 2010—11), Soc. Profl. Journalists (officer exec. bd. Ark. profl. chpt. 1986—89, v.p. 1989—91, pres. 1991—92, officer exec. bd. Ark. profl. chpt. 1992—94), Assn. Schs. Journalism and Mass Comm. (exec. com. 1997—2000, 2003—04), Assn. Edn. Journalism and Mass Comm., Kappa Tau Alpha. Office: 4912 Londonderry Dr Tampa FL 33647

FRIEDMAN, ALAN WARREN, humanities educator; b. Bklyn., June 8, 1939; s. Leon and Anne (Markowitz) F.; m. Elizabeth Butler Cullingford, Nov. 22, 1985; children: Eric Lawrence, Scot Bradley, Lorraine Eve, Daniel Butler. Student, U. Edinburgh, Scotland, 1960-61; BA, Queens Coll., 1961; MA, NYU, 1962; PhD, U. Rochester, 1966. Grad. teaching asst. U. Rochester, 1963-64; from instr. English to prof. U. Tex., Austin, 1964—, dir. honors program, 1972-76, chmn. faculty senate, 1987-89, U. Coun., 2011—12; endowed prof. U. Tex., Austin, 2001—. Sr. Fulbright prof. U. Lancaster, Eng., 1977-78, Univ. Coll., Galway, Ireland, 1995; exch. prof. Universite Paul Valery, Montpellier, France, 1985, U. Paris, Sorbonne, 2000. Author: Lawrence Durrell and the Alexandria Quartet, 1970, Multivalence: The Moral Quality of Form in the Modern Novel, 1978, William Faulkner, 1984, Fictional Death and the Modernist Enterprise, 1995, Beckett in Black and Red: The Translations for Nancy Cunard's "Negro", 2000, Party Pieces: Oral Storytelling and Social Performance in Joyce and Beckett, 2007; editor books; contbr. essays and revs. to profl. jours. Chair Dem. Precinct Com.; del. state convs.; founder, 1st pres. Neighborhood Assn., Austin, 1973-74; bd. dirs. Peace Edn. Ctr., Hillel Found., Austin Hospice, Frontline Theatre Co. Recipient Fulbright Rsch. award, 1984—85, 1995, Travel award, France, 1990, Civitatis award, U. Tex.; fellow, NEH, 1970—71. Mem. MLA (del. assembly 1977-79, 82-84, 94-96, exec. com. divsn. on 20th century English lit. 1992-96), AAUP (pres. U. Tex. chpt. 1979-84, nat. coun. 1989-92, nat. exec. com. 1991-92, chair com. governance 1992-95), Tex. Higher Edn. Coord. Bd. (chair faculty adv. com. 1992-95), Tex. Assn. Coll. Tchrs., Nat. Collegiate Honors Coun., Fulbright Alumni Assn. (pres. ctrl. Tex. chpt.), Omicron Delta Kappa. Democrat. Jewish. Office: University Tex Dept English 208 West 21 St Stop B5000 Austin TX 78712-0548 Office Phone: 512-471-4991, 512-471-8376. Business E-Mail: friedman@austin.utexas.edu.

FRIEDMAN, ALLAN HOWARD, neurosurgeon; b. Chgo., Feb. 15, 1949; BS, Purdue U., West Lafayette, Ind., 1970; MD, U. Ill. Coll. Medicine, Chgo., 1974. Cert. in neurol. surgery 1983. Gen. surg. resident Duke U. Med. Ctr., Durham, NC, 1974—75, neurosurg. resident, 1975—78, neurosurg. chief resident, 1978—80, asst. prof., 1981—90, assoc. prof., 1990—93, Guy L. Odom prof. neurol. surgery, 1993—, chief. divsn. neurosurgery, 1996—, co-dir., brain tumor ctr., 1998, co-dir. clin. oncology program, 1998, co-dir. collegiate athlete premed. experience, 2004; vascular fellow U. Western Ontario, London, Canada, 1980—81; chief. divsn. neurosurgery Durham Vets. Adminstrn. Hosp., 1981—89. Co-dir. Rev. and Update in Neurobiology for Neurosurgeons, 1999, Advanced Skull Base Microanatomy and Hands on Dissection Workshop, 2000, 3rd Pan Pacific Neurosurg. Congress, 2000; dir. Rsch. Update in Neurosci. for Neurosurgeons, 2004. Contbr. articles to profl. jours. Recipient David Mortimer Olkon award, U. Ill.; James Scholar of Medicine. Fellow: Am. Coll. Surgeons; mem.: AMA, AMA Stroke Coun., Am. Acad. Neurol. Surgery, Southern Neurosurg. Soc. (chmn. program com. 1985, pres. 1997—98), Am. Assn. Neurol. Surgeons, Neurosurg. Soc. America (chmn. program com. 1985, v.p. 1996—97, chmn., long range planning com. 1999—2000, treas. 2000—03, pres. elect 2005), NC Neurosurg. Soc. (sec. tres. 1995—97, pres. 1997—99), Durham-Orange County Med. Soc., NC Med. Soc., Southern Med. Assn., Congress Neurol. Surgeons (scientific program chmn., upper extremity course 1999), Joint Sect. on Disorders Spine and Peripheral Nerves the Am. Assn. Neurol. Surgeons and the Congress Neurol. Surgeons (course dir. 2000), Joint Sect. on Cerebrovascular Surgery the Am. Assn. Neurol. Surgeons and the Congress Neurol. Surgeons, Omicron Delta Kappa, Sigma Delta Chi, Sigma Pi Sigma. Office: Duke Univ Hosp Box 3807 Durham NC 27710 Office Phone: 919-681-6421. Office Fax: 919-681-7872. Business E-Mail: fried010@mc.duke.edu.

FRIEDMAN, ANDREW, professional sports team executive; b. Houston; s. Kenny Friedman; m. Robin Hochman. BS in Mgmt., Tulane U., New Orleans, 1999. Intern, analyst Bear, Stearns & Co. Inc., 1998—2000; assoc. MidMark Capital, 2000—03; dir. baseball devel. Tampa Bay Rays, 2003—05, exec. v.p. baseball ops., gen. mgr., 2005—. Named Exec. of Yr., The Sporting News, 2008. Office: Tampa Bay Rays One Tropicana Dr Saint Petersburg FL 33705

FRIEDMAN, JAMES WINSTEIN, economist, educator; b. Cleve., Sept. 25, 1936; s. Theodore and Gertrude (Winstein) F.; m. Marcia Sherman, Aug. 11, 1957; children: Nancy Elizabeth, Robert U. Student, MIT, 1954-56; BA, U. Mich., 1959; MA, Yale U., 1960, PhD, 1963; doctorate (hon.), U. Paris, 2004. Instr., then asst. prof. econs. Yale U., 1963-68; assoc. prof. U. Rochester (N.Y.), 1968-72, prof. econs., 1972-83; prof. Va. Poly Inst., Blacksburg, 1983-85; Kenan prof. U. N.C., Chapel Hill, 1985-2001, Kenan prof. emeritus, 2001—. Mem. rsch. staff Cowles Found., 1963-68, asst. dir., 1964-66; vis. prof. U. Bielefeld, Fed. Republic Germany, 1976, 87-88, Hebrew U., Jerusalem, 1979, Cath. U. Louvain, Belgium, 1987, 91, 99, U. Paris, 1991, 93, 2000, U. Alicante, Spain, 1992, U. Kobe, Japan, 1994. Author: Oligopoly and the Theory of Games, 1977, The Theory of Oligopoly, 1983, Game Theory with Applications to Economics, 1986, 2d edit., 1990; co-author: An Experiment in Noncooperative Oligopoly, 1979; editor: Problems of Coordination in Economic Activity, 1994; assoc. editor Japanese Econ. Rev., 1994—2005, Regional Sci. and Urban Econs., 1997-2005, Games and Econ. Behavior, 1998—2005; contbr. articles to profl. jours. Fellow Econometric Soc. (assoc. editor jour. 1975-81), Game Theory Soc. Avocations: cooking, reading.

FRIEDMAN, JEROME B., federal judge; b. Newark, 1943; BS, Old Dominion Coll., 1965; JD, Wake Forest U., 1969. Trust adminstr. First Union Nat. Bank, 1969—70; pvt. law practice, 1970—85; judge Dist. Ct., Juvenile & Domestic Rels., 1985—91, Va. Beach Cir. Ct., 1991—97, chief judge, 1994—97; judge US Dist. Ct. (eastern dist.) Va., 1997—2010, sr. judge, 2010—. Office: Walter E Hoffman US Courthouse 600 Granby St Norfolk VA 23510 Office Phone: 757-222-7004.

FRIEDMAN, KINKY (RICHARD S. FRIEDMAN), writer, musician; b. Chgo., Oct. 31, 1944; s. Tom and Min Friedman. Grad., Univ. Tex., Austin. Vol. Peace Corps, Borneo, 1967; songwriter, 1964—; novelist, 1986—; columnist Tex. Monthly Mag., 2001—; independent candidate, gov. State of Tex., 2005—. Performer (with Texas Jewboys Band): (albums) Sold American, 1973, Kinky Friedman, 1974; performer: (solo) Live from the Lone Star Cafe, 1982, Under the Double Ego, 1983, Old Testaments and New Revelations, 1992, Lasso from El Paso, 1993, From One Good American to Another, 1995, Pearls in the Snow, 1998, Classic Snatches from Europe, 2000; author: Greenwich Killing Time, 1986, A Case of Lone Star, 1987, When the Cat's Away, 1988, Frequent Flyer, 1989, Musical Chairs, 1991, Elvis, Jesus and Coca-Cola, 1993, Armadillos and Old Lace, 1994, Roadkill, 1997, Blast from the Past, 1998, Spanking Watson, 1999, The Mile High Club, 2000, Kinky Friedman's Guide to Texas Etiquette, 2001, Meanwhile, Back at the Ranch, 2002, Kill Two Birds and Get Stoned, 2003, The Great Psychedelic Armadillo Picnic, 2004, Prisoner of Vandam Street, 2004, 'Scuse Me While I Whip This Out: Reflections on Country Singers, Presidents and Other Troublemakers, 2004, Ten Little New Yorkers, 2005, Texas Hold 'Em: How I was Born in a Manger, Died in the Saddle, and Came Back as a Horny Toad, 2005, Cowboy Logic: The Wit and Wisdom of Kinky Friedman (and Some of His Friends), 2006, The Christmas Pig: A Fable, 2006, You Can Lead a Politician to Water, But You Can't Make Him Think: Ten Commandments for Texas Politics, 2007. Founder Utopia Animal Rescue Ranch. Jewish. E-mail: kfcs@kinkyfriedman.com.

FRIEDMAN, LEE S., ophthalmologist; MD, Rosalind Franklin U., 1983. Intern Tampa Gen. Hosp., 1984; resident ophthalmology Univ. of South Fla. Hosp., 1984—87; fellow pediatric otolaryngology Manhattan Eye and Ear Hosp., 1988; hosp. affiliations include Bethesda Meml. Hosp., Boca Raton Regional Hosp., Kimmel Outpatient Surg. Ctr., North County Surgicenter, Outpatient Surgery Ctr., Boca, Palms West Hosp., St. Mary's Hosp., West Boca Med. Ctr. Office: St Mary's Medical Center 901 45th St West Palm Beach FL 33407-2495 Office Phone: 561-844-6300.*

FRIEDMAN, MORTON HAROLD, engineering educator, department chairman; s. Morris Joseph and Florence Rose Friedman; m. Ann Marie Hyde, June 17, 1961; children: David Henry, Catherine Ruth Spencer, Mark Joseph. BChemE, Cornell U., Ithaca, NY, 1957; MS, U. Mich., Ann Arbor, 1958, PhD in Chem. Engring., 1961. Sr. chem. engr. 3M Co., St. Paul, 1960—65; sr. engr., group supr., chief scientist of biomed. programs Johns Hopkins U. Applied Physics Lab., Laurel, Md., 1965—88; prof. chem. and biomed. engring. and pathology, dir. biomed. engring. ctr. Ohio State U., Columbus, 1988—2001; chair dept. biomed. engring., prof. biomed. engring. and medicine Duke U., Durham, NC, 2001—; emeritus prof. biomed. engring., 2009. Recipient Nat. Capital award, DC Coun. Engring. and Archtl. Socs., 1970, Hon. Emeritus Professorship award, Ohio State U., 2005. Fellow: ASME (divsn. chair 1989—90, HR Lissner medal 2000, Richard Skalak award 2007), AAAS, Biomedical Engring. Soc. (pres. 1988—89, Disting. Svc. award 2003, 2005), Am. Inst. Med. and Biol. Engring. (v.p. 1997—99, Disting. Svc. award 1992, 1994), Am. Heart Assn. Office: Duke Univ 136 Hudson Hall Box 90281 Durham NC 27708

FRIEDMAN, NANCY E., pediatric endocrinologist, educator; MD, Va. Commonwealth U., 1975. Diplomate Am. Bd. Pediatrics, 1979, Am. Bd. Pediatrics-pediatric endocrinology, 2003. Resident pediatrics Children's Hosp. Med. Ctr., Univ. of Cin., Ohio, 1975—77, Children's Meml. Hosp., Northwestern Univ., Ill., 1977—78; fellow pediatrics, endocrinology and metabolism Michael Reese Hosp. and Med. Ctr., Ill., 1978—80; physician Duke Univ. Med. Ctr.; asst. clin. prof. pediatrics Duke Univ. Co-author: (publs.) X-linked hypophosphatemic rickets without "rickets", 1991, Methylphenidate in neuropsychological sequelae of radiotherapy and chemotherapy of childhood brain tumors and leukemia, 1992, Effects of calcitriol and phosphorus therapy on the growth of patients with X-linked hypophosphatemia, 1993, A PHEX gene mutation is responsible for adult-onset vitamin D-resistant hypophosphatemic osteomalacia: evidence that the disorder is not a distinct entity from X-linked hypophosphatemic rickets, 1998, Insulin pump therapy in toddlers and preschool children with type 1 diabetes mellitus, 2002. Office: Duke Children's Consultative Services of Raleigh Ste 310 3480 Wake Forest Rd Raleigh NC 27609 Office Phone: 919-862-5363. Office Fax: 919-862-5355.

FRIEDMAN, STUART ANDREW, allergist, immunologist; MD, Universidad de Zaragoza, Spain, 1976. Diplomate Am. Bd. Internal Medicine, 1980, Am. Bd. Allergy and Immunology, 1983, lic. Fla., 1981. Resident internal medicine Winthrop Univ. Hosp., 1978—80; fellow immunology Univ. Cin., 1980—82; hosp. affiliations include Delray Med. Ctr., Boca Raton Cmty. Hosp. Named one of Top Doctors, Gulf Stream Mag., 2009. Office: Boca Raton Community Hospital 800 Meadows Rd Boca Raton FL 33486-2368 Office Phone: 561-955-7100.

FRIEND, EDWARD MALCOLM, III, lawyer, educator; b. Birmingham, Ala., Oct. 12, 1946; s. Edward M. Jr. and Hermione Frances (Curjel) F. BA in History, U. Ala., 1968, JD, 1971. Bar: Ala. 1971. Shareholder Sirote and Permutt, P.C., Birmingham, Ala., 1971—, pres., 1991-93. Chmn. Birmingham Area C. of C., 1990-91; chmn. dist. bd. dirs. Colonial Bank Ala., Birmingham, 1985-2000; chmn. Cmty. Found. of Greater Birmingham, 2008-10; exec. in residence, asst. prof. U. Ala., Birmingham, 1994—2012, chmn. adv. bd. Sch. Bus., 2003-05, chmn. elec., Rotary Club, 2012- Chmn. Birmingham Area chpt. ARC, 1987-88; chmn. bd. NCCJ, 1983, nat. bd., 1981-88; pres. coun. U. Ala., Birmingham, 1980-94, Birmingham Jewish Fedn., 1984-89, United Way Ctrl. Ala., 1984-99, chmn., 1993-94, gen. campaign chmn., 1989; bd. dirs. Childrens Hosp. Ala., 1986-2005; exec. com. Ala. Symphony Assn., 1980-82, bd. dirs., 1982-85, Birmingham Festival Arts, 1978-88, pres., 1984-85, chmn., 1985-86; mem. nat. leadership coun. United Way Am.; pres. Big Bros./Big Sisters Greater Birmingham, 1980, chmn., 1981-83; trustee St. Vincent's Hosp., 1982-86, v.p., 1984-86, Ala. Sch. Fine Arts Found., 1985-91; chmn. Leadership Ala., 1993; bd. dirs. Boy Scouts Am., 1996-2005. Recipient Brotherhood award Nat. Conf. Christians and Jews, 1987; named to Ala. Acad. of Honor; named Lawyer of Yr., Birmingham Legal Secretarial Assn., 1976, Outstanding Alumnus, U. Ala. Sch. Law, 1984, Hon. Outstanding Alumnus, Sch. Bus., U. Ala., 2005, Civic Leader of Yr. award, Nat. Assn. Fundraising Exec. Birmingham, 2010. Mem. Nat. Health Lawyers Assn. (bd. dirs. 1992-95), Farrah Law Soc. (chmn. 1982-84), (hon.) U. Ala. Birmingham Alumnus. Office: Sirote and Permutt PC 2311 Highland Ave South Birmingham AL 35205-4004 Office Phone: 205-930-5116, 205-934-8854. Business E-Mail: efriend@sirote.com.

FRIEND, WILLIAM BENEDICT, bishop emeritus; b. Miami, Oct. 22, 1931; s. William Eugene and Elizabeth Friend. Student, U. Miami, 1949—52; degree, St. Mary's Coll., St. Mary, Ky., 1955, Mt. St. Mary's Sem., Emmittsburg, Md., 1959; MA in Edn., Cath. U. Am., 1965; LLD, St. Leo Coll., 1986. Ordained priest Diocese Mobile-Birmingham, Ala., 1959; parish priest, educator, counselor, adminstr. Diocese of Mobile, 1959—68, vicar for edn., supt. schs. Ala., 1971—76, chancellor adminstrn., vicar for edn., 1976—79; ednl. rsch. adminstr. U. Notre Dame, Ind., 1968—71; ordained bishop, 1979; aux. bishop Diocese of Alexandria-Shreveport, Shreveport, La., 1979—83, bishop, 1983—86, Diocese of Shreveport, Shreveport, La., 1986—2006, bishop emeritus, 2007—. Mem. Nat. Conf. Cath. Bishops, 1979; chmn. Campaign for Human Devel., 1980—93; mem. sci. and human values com. Commn. of Bishops and Scholars, Com. Sci. & Human Values, 1983; chmn. Commn. of Bishops and Scholars, 1986—92, cons., 1993—2006, sec., USCCB, 2000—04; mem. Pontifical Coun. for Culture, 1993—2008. Editor (with Ford and Daues): Evangelizing the Cultures in A.D. 2000, 1990; co-editor (with J. Anderson): The Culture of Bible Belt Catholics, 1995; contbr. articles on Cath. edn., Cath. ch. leadership and mgmt. and theol. reflections to profl. publs. Bd. dirs., v.p. S.E. Regional Hispanic Ctr., Miami, 1986—2008; trustee Notre Dame Sem., 1976—2006, St. Joseph Coll. Sem., New Orleans, 1979—2006; bd. councillors Cmty. Renewal Internat.; chmn. bd. Ctr. for Applied Rsch. in the Apostolate, 1997—2004; mem. adv. bd. The John J. Reilly Ctr. Sci., Tech. and Values U. Notre Dame, 2000—04; bd. dirs. La. Interchurch Conf., La. Catholic Conf., 1979—2006. Decorated Order of Fleur de Lis K.C., knight comdr. with star Knights of Holy Sepulchre of Jerusalem; recipient Presdl. award, Nat. Cath. Ednl. Assn., 1978, O'Neil D'Amour award, Nat. Assn. Bds. Edn., 1982, NCCJ Brotherhood and Humanitarian award, 1987, Human Rels. Coun. award, 2000, Harry Blake award, 2004, Cordinal Cushing medal, Ctr. Applied Rsch. Georgetown U., Wash., 2010. Mem.: World Futures Soc., NY Acad. Scis., Cath. Acad. Sci. USA, KC (former state chaplain La. coun.). Roman Catholic. Avocations: hiking, art, music, reading. E-mail: wfriend@bellsouth.net.

FRIERSON, HERBERT (HERB), state legislator; b. Jackson, Miss., July 19, 1958; Former mem. State Libr. & County Affairs Com.; former tchr. & coach; mem. Dist. 106 Miss. House of Reps., 1992—; real estate broker. Mem.: Nat. Rifle Assn., C. of C., Duck's Unlimited, Mason, Rotary Club. Republican. Baptist. Mailing: 12 Trailwood Lane Poplarville MS 39470 Office Phone: 601-795-6285. Business E-Mail: hfrierson@house.ms.gov.

FRIESECKE, RAYMOND FRANCIS, health company executive, president; b. Mar. 12, 1937; s. Bernhard P. K. and Josephine (De Tomi) F. BS in Chemistry, Boston Coll., 1959; MSCE, MIT, 1961. Product specialist Dewey & Almy Chem. divsn. W. R. Grace & Co., Inc., Cambridge, Mass., 1963-66; market planning specialist USM Corp., Boston, 1966-71; mgmt. cons. Boston, 1971-74; dir. planning and devel. Schweitzer divsn. Kimberly-Clark Corp., Lee, Mass., 1974-78; v.p. corp. planning Butler Automatic, Inc., Canton, Mass., 1978-80; pres. Butler-Europe Inc. Greenwich Conn. & Munich, Germany, 1980; v.p. mktg. and planning Butler Greenwich Inc., 1980-81; pres. Strategic Mgmt. Assocs., San Rafael, Calif., 1981-96; chmn. Beyond Health Corp., 1994—2009, Health-E-America Found., 2000—08; pres. TPED Found., 2008—, Beyond Health Internat., 2009—. Bd. dirs. Better Physiology, Ltd., 2000-05; corp. clk., v.p. Bldg. R&D, Inc., Cambridge, 1966-68. Host, prodr. Beyond Health Show, Sta. KEST, San Francisco, 1994—98, WWNN, 1995—2009, Sta. KBZS, 1998—2001, Stas. WRPT and WSRO, 1999—2001; host, prodr. KYCY, 2001—05; host, prodr. KRLA, KSBN, KFNX, 2003—05, KNTS, 2005—09, KKNT, 2006—09; pub.: Beyond Health News, 1995—2012; author: Management by Relative Product Quality, 1982, The New Way to Manage, 1983, Never Be Sick Again, 2002, Never Be Fat Again, 2007, Never Fear Cancer Again, 2011, Never Feel Old Again, 2013; contbr. articles to profl. jours. State chmn. Citizens for Fair Taxation, 1972-73; state co-chmn. Mass. Young Reps., 1967-69; chmn. Ward 7 Rep. Com., Cambridge, 1968-70; vice-chmn. Cambridge Rep. City Com., 1966-68; bd. dirs. Kentfield Rehab. Hosp. Found., 1986-88, chmn., 1988-91; Rep. candidate Mass. Ho. of Reps., 1964, 66; pres. Marin Rep. Coun., 1986-91; chmn. Calif. Acad., 1986-88; sec. Navy League Marin Coun., 1984-91, v.p., 1994-2000; bd. dirs. The Marin Ballet, 1996-98; bd. dirs. Insts. for Behavioral Physiology, Seattle, 1999-2000; nat. chmn. Project to End Disease, 2005—. 1st lt. U.S. Army, 1961-63. Recipient Green Sch. Green Difference award, 2010; named Businessman of Yr., Bus. Adv. Coun., 2006. Mem. NRA, Nat. Health Fedn., Am. Chem. Soc., Physicians Com. for Responsible Medicine, Marin Philos. Soc. (v.p. 1991-92), Ctr. for Sci. in Pub. Interest, Health Medicine Forum, Assn. of Am. Physicians and Surgeons, Orthomolecular Health Medicine Soc., The World Affairs Coun., Am. Holistic Health Assn., Naval Inst., Milt. Officers Assn. Am., Am. Legion. Office: 6555 Powerline Rd Ste 101 Fort Lauderdale FL 33309 Business E-Mail: mail@beyondhealth.com.

FRIIS-HANSEN, DANA, museum director; b. 1961; BA in Art History, Carleton Coll., 1983. Asst. curator and then curator List Visual Arts Ctr., MIT, Cambridge, Mass., 1985—91; assoc. curator Nanjo and Assocs. pvt. curatorial svc., Tokyo, 1991—95; sr. curator Contemporary Arts Mus., Houston, 1995—99; chief curator Austin (Tex.) Mus. Art, 1999—, interim exec. dir., 2001—02, exec. dir., 2002—. Panelist Pew Fellowships in the Arts, 2002; co-curator TransCulture, Venice Biennale, 1995. Author: Abstract Painting Once Removed, 1998; co-author: Cai Guo-Qiang, 2002, Takashi Murakami, 2000, The History of Japanese Photography, 2003, Terry Allen: Dugout, 2005. Helena Rubenstein fellow, Whitney Mus. Am. Art Ind. Study Program. Office: Austin Mus of Art 823 Congress St Austin TX 78701

FRIOT, STEPHEN P., federal judge; b. Troy, NY, 1947; BA, U. Okla., 1969, JD, 1972. Pvt. practice atty., Okla., 1972—2001; judge US Dist. Ct. (we. dist.) Okla., Oklahoma City, 2001—. Office: US Dist Ct US Courthouse Rm 3102 200 NW 4th St Oklahoma City OK 73102 Office Phone: 405-609-5500. Office Fax: 405-609-5513.

FRIOU, PHILLIP J. (JACK FRIOU), insurance company executive; b. Columbus, Ga., June 26, 1949; s. Phillip John Friou and Janet Ouillette Rosenberg; m. Karen June Knowles, Jan. 10, 1978 (div. Oct. 1980); m. Connie Renee Peters, Dec. 11, 1982; children: Carrie Renee, Catherine Emily. AB in Polit. Sci., U. Ga., 1971; postgraduate student, Columbus Coll., 1977. Mktg. adminstr. Am. Family Life Assurance Co., Columbus, Ga., 1973-75, dept. mgr. policy holder svc., 1975-76, v.p. mktg. comptr., 1976-78, v.p. external affairs, 1978-82, v.p. compliance, 1982-86; sr. v.p. AFLAC, Inc., Columbus, Ga., 1989—; pres. Aflac NY Am. Family Life Assurance Co., 1990—94, sr. v.p. mktg. and agy. devel., 1995—97; sr. v.p. govtl. rels. AFLAC, Inc., 1997—; exec. v.p. adminstrn., bd. dirs. Communicorp, Columbus, Ga., 1986-88, pres., COO, bd. dirs., 1988-89. Bd. mem. Employers Coun. Flexible Compensation. Mem. adv. com. Jed Harris for Ga. House of Reps. campaign, Columbus, 1990. Served in US Army, 1971—73. Mem. Leadership Columbus, Employers Coun. Flexible Compensation, Am. Soc. Health Underwriters, Albany C. of C. Episcopalian. Avocations: golf, skiing, yardwork, reading. Office: Am Family Life Assurance Co 1932 Wynnton Rd Columbus GA 31999 Home: 662 Grey Rock Dr Midland GA 31820-4766 Office Phone: 706-323-3431.

FRISBIE, CURTIS LYNN, JR., lawyer; b. Greenville, Miss., Sept. 13, 1943; s. Curtis Lynn and Edith L. (Brantley) F.; m. Gena F. Johnson, May 30, 1965; children: Curtis L. III, Mark A. BSBA, U. Ala., 1966; JD, St. Mary's U., San Antonio, 1971. Bar: Tex. 1971, US Dist. Ct. (no. dist.), Ga. 1974, US Dist. Ct. (no. dist.), Tex. 1978, US Dist. Ct. (we. dist.), Tex. 1985, US Dist. Ct. (ea. and so. dists.), Tex. 1986, US Dist. Ct. (ea. dist.), Wis. 1986, US Tax Ct. 1986, US Ct. Appeals (5th cir.), 1975, US Ct. Appeals (10th cir.) 1982, US Ct. Appeals (8th cir.) 1987, US Supreme Ct. 1977, US Ct. Appeals (3rd cir.) 2006. Trial atty. Antitrust divsn. U.S. Dept. Justice, Atlanta, 1971-73; assoc. King & Spalding, Atlanta, 1974-77; ptnr. Gardere Wynne Sewell LLP (formerly Gardere & Wynne LLP), Dallas, 1978—. Assoc. editor St. Mary's Law Jour., 1970-71. Bd. dirs. Tex. Hist. Found., 2002—. Capt. USMC, 1966-69, Vietnam. Named Tex. Superlawyers in Antitrust, Tex. Monthly, 2003—11, Outdoorsman of Yr., Beretta Gallery, 2005; named one of Best Lawyers in Dallas, D Mag., 2003—07, Best Lawyers in America, 2006—11; named to Am.'s Leading Bus. Lawyers in Antitrust, Chambers & Ptnrs., 2004—11. Fellow Tex. Bar Found. (life), Dallas Bar Assn. (life); mem. ABA (antitrust and bus. law sect.), Tex. Bar Assn. (antitrust sect., mem. coun. 1995—, vice chair, chair elect 2000-01, chair 2001-02), Dallas Bar Assn. (pres. antitrust and trade regulation sect. 1993), Coll. State Bar Tex., Phi Alpha Delta. Avocations: scuba diving, fishing, hunting. Home: 5605 Palomar Ln Dallas TX 75229-6417 Office: Gardere Wynne Sewell LLP Thanksgiving Tower 1601 Elm St Ste 3000 Dallas TX 75201-4761 Office Phone: 214-999-4757. Business E-Mail: cfrisbie@gardere.com.

FRISHE, JIM, state legislator; b. Potsdam, NY, Apr. 6, 1946; children: William C., Katherine F. Wehland, Erica M. AA, Andrew Coll., Cuthbert, Ga., 1969; BA, U. Fla., 1971. Lic. real estate broker; divsn. leader A.L. Williams; exec. dir. Contemporary Housing Alternatives Fla., Inc.; mem. Fla. House of Reps., Tallahassee, 1984—90, mem. Dist. 54, 2006—, vice chair health care appropriations com., mem. civil justice and courts policy com., govtl. affairs policy com., policy coun. Mem. Bluffs Bus. Assn., Clearwater Hist. Soc., Pinellas County Hist. Soc., St. Petersburg Jaycees, Pinellas Park Boys Club. Republican. Episcopalian. Office: 125 Indian Rocks Rd N Belleair Bluffs FL 33770-1727 also: 322 The Capitol 402 S Monroe St Tallahassee FL 32399-1300 Office Phone: 727-518-3902, 850-488-9960.

FRIST, THOMAS FEARN, JR., hospital management company executive; b. Nashville, Aug. 12, 1938; s. Thomas Fearn and Dorothy (Cate) Frist; m. Patricia Champion, Dec. 22, 1961; children: Trisha, Thomas Fearn III, Bill. BS, Vanderbilt U., 1961; MD, Washington U., 1966. Exec. v.p. Hosp. Corp. Am. (HCA), Nashville, 1968—77, pres., COO, 1977—82, pres., CEO, 1982—85, chmn., 1985—95; vice chmn. Columbia/ Hosp. Corp. Am. Healthcare Corp., Nashville, 1994—97; chmn., CEO Hosp. Corp. Am. Healthcare Corp., Nashville, 1995—2001; chmn. The Frist Found., Nashville. Bd. dirs. Columbia Healthcare. Past v.p. Vanderbilt Bd. Trust; past chair bd. governors United Way of Am. Named Disting. Alumnus, Vanderbilt U., 2002; named one of Forbes 400: Richest Americans, 2006—. Fellow: Am. Coll. Healthcare Execs. (hon.); mem.: Bus. Coun., Bus. Roundtable, Belle Meade Country Club. Presbyterian. Avocations: running, tennis, skiing, flying. Office: Frist Foundation 3100 W End Ave Ste 1200 Nashville TN 37203-1348

FRITCH, HERBERT A., health insurance company executive; BA in Math., Carleton Coll. Actuary Milliman and Robertson; co-founder Sanus Corp. Health Systems, 1982; with Inland Health Plan, 1986—87; regional v.p. Ptnrs. Nat. Healthplans, 1988—91; founder, pres. N.Am. Med. Mgmt., Inc., 1991—99; v.p. managed care PhyCor, Inc., 1995—99; founder NewQuest, LLC (now HealthSpring, Inc.), 2000; chmn., CEO HealthSpring, Inc., 2000—12; pres. HealthSpring, Inc. Cigna Corp., 2012—. Bd. dirs. Predators Holdings LLC. Fellow: Soc. Actuaries; mem.: Acad. Actuaries. Office: HealthSpring Inc Ste 501 9009 Carothers Pky Franklin TN 37067 Office Phone: 615-291-7000. Office Fax: 615-401-4566.

FRITSCH, ERIC G., automotive executive; Regional v.p. Mountain divsn., US automotive parts group Genuine Parts Co., 2008—. Office: Genuine Parts Co 2999 Cir 75 Pky Atlanta GA 30339 Office Phone: 770-953-1700. Office Fax: 770-956-2211. Business E-Mail: Eric_Fritsch@genpt.com.

FRITZ, JIM, professional sports team executive; m. Donna Fritz; children: Zachary, Nicole. grad. in Acctg., M in Acctg., Fla. State U. With Hotel Mgmt. Assocs., PricewaterhouseCoopers; various positions including contr., dir., v.p. fin. & chief of staff Orlando Magic, Ltd., 1994—2004, exec. v.p., bus. ops., 2004—06, CFO, 2006—. Treas. bd. trustees United Arts Ctrl. Fla. Office: Orlando Magic Ltd 8701 Maitland Summit Blvd Orlando FL 32810 Office Phone: 407-916-2400. Office Fax: 407-916-2830.

FRITZ, MARTIN ANDREW, gas industry executive, lawyer; b. Pitts., May 2, 1964; s. George Richard and Margaret Jean Fritz; m. Mary Ellen Bolish, June 3, 1989; children: McKenzie B., Madison K. Degree in Bus. & Economics summa cum laude, U. Pitts., 1986; JD cum laude, Pa. State U., 1992. Bar: Pa. 1993. Assoc. editor, law review Pa. State U.; vice chmn. EQT PAC; sr. staff acct. Ernst & Young LLP, Pitts., 1986-89; atty. Duane, Morris & Hekscher, LLP, Harrisburg, Pa., 1991; various positions, including chief adminstrv. officer, chief info. officer & dep. gen. counsel EQT Corp. (formerly Equitable Resources, Inc.), v.p., pres., midstream, 2008—. NFL agt. NFL Players Assn., Washington, 1997—; CFL agt. CFL Players Assn., Toronto, Can., 1997—; spkr. in field. Editor Dickinson Sch. of Law, Pa. State U., 1990-92. Bd. adv. Johnstown Acctg. U. Pitts., bd. dirs. EQT Found., United Way of Allegheny County, pres. Greater Pitts. Literacy Coun., Mem. atty. adv. com. United Way of Capital Region, Harrisburg, 1996—; membership chmn. Highlands Civic Assn., Mechanicsburg, Pa., 1997; ch. coun. Grace Evang. Luth. Ch., Camp Hill, Pa., 1998—. Presdl. scholar U. Pitts., 1983-86. Mem. AICPA, Am. Assn. of Attys.-CPAs, Ctrl. Pa. Estate Planning Coun., Pa. Bar Assn. (vice-chairperson sports, entertainment, and art law com.), Sports Lawyers Assn. Republican. Lutheran. Avocations: weightlifting, running, golf, travel, music. Home: 101 Green Valley Ln Canonsburg PA 15317-3543 Office Phone: 412-553-5700. Business E-Mail: mfritz@eqt.com.

FRIZZELL, GREGORY KENT, federal judge; b. Wichita, Kans., Dec. 13, 1956; s. D. Kent and Shirley Elaine (Piatt) F.; m. Kelly Susan Nash, Mar. 9, 1991; children: Benjamin Newcomb, Hannah Kirsten, Robert Nash, David Gregory, Elizabeth Piatt, Jubilee Kathryn. BA, U. Tulsa, 1981; JD, U. Mich., 1984. Bar: Okla. 1985, U.S. Dist. Ct. (no., ea. and we. dists.) Okla. 1985, U.S. Ct. Appeals (10th cir.) 1985, U.S. Supreme Ct. 1990. Jud. clk. to judge US Dist. Ct. (No. dist.) Okla., Tulsa, 1984-86; pvt. practice Tulsa, 1986-95; gen. counsel Okla. Tax Commn., 1995-97; dist. judge Tulsa County, 1997—2007, presiding judge, 2006—07; judge US Dist. Ct. (No. dist.) Okla., Tulsa, 2007—12, chief judge, 2012—. Mem. US Jud. Conf. Com. Space and Facilities, Okla. Bar Assn., Rotary, Federalist Soc. Office: US Dist Ct No Okla 333 W 4th St Rm 411 Tulsa OK 74103 Office Phone: 918-699-4780.

FROBERG, BRENT MALCOLM, classics educator; b. Balt., Apr. 8, 1943; s. Lawrence Oscar and Ruth Louise (Lindner) F.; m. M. Gail Galloway, Feb. 27, 1970. BA, Ind. U., 1964, MA, 1965; PhD, Ohio State U., 1972. Instr. U. Tenn., Knoxville, 1968-69; asst. prof. U. S.D., Vermillion, 1970-74, assoc. prof., 1974-96; lectr. Baylor U., Waco, Tex., 2001—08, sr. lectr., 2008—. Cons. Nat. Mythology Exam, Nat. Greek Exam; lectr. in field. Editor: (newsletter) Nuntius, 1978-96; writer Nat. Greek Exam., ATTIC, Level I, 1998-2000. Pres. Friends of the Libr., Vermillion, 1995-97, sec., 1997-99 Mem. Am. Philol. Assn. (award for excellence in tchg. 1994), Am. Classical League, Vergilian Soc. (membership chmn. 1990-94), Classical Assn. Mid. West & South (Ovatio award 1985, chair Manson Stewart scholarship com. 1998), Eta Sigma Phi (exec. sec. 1978-96, hon. life trustee). Avocations: crossword puzzles, travel. Office Phone: 254-710-1399. E-mail: Brent_Froberg@baylor.edu.

FROHLICH, EDWARD DAVID, medical educator; b. NYC, Sept. 10, 1931; s. William and May (Zneimer) F.; m. Sherry Linda Fine, Nov. 1, 1959; children: Marjorie, Bruce, Lara. BA, Washington and Jefferson Coll., 1952; MD, U. Md., 1956; MS, Northwestern U., 1963; DSc (hon.), U. Buenos Aires, 2001. Diplomate Am. Bd. Internal Medicine. Intern, resident D.C. Gen. Hosp., 1956-58; resident Georgetown U. Hosp., Washington, 1958—60; clin. investigator VA Rsch. Hosp., Chgo., 1962-64; assoc. in medicine Northwestern U., 1963-64; staff mem. rsch. divsn. Cleve. Clinic, 1964-69; prof. medicine, physiology and biophysics U. Okla., Oklahoma City, 1969-76, George Lynn Cross rsch. prof., 1975-76; prof. medicine and physiology La. State U., 1976—; clin. prof. medicine, adj. prof. pharmacology Tulane U., 1976—; mem. staff, v.p. edn. and rsch. Alton Ochsner Med. Found., 1976—86, v.p. acad. affairs, 1986—89, disting. scientist, 1986—. Cons. in field. Editor: Pathophysiology-Altered Regulatory Mechanisms in Disease, 1972, 1976, 1984, Rypins' Medical Licensure Examinations, 13th - 18th edits., 1981—2001, Rypins' Intensive Revs., 13 vols., 1996, Take Heart, 1990, Hypertension: Evaluation and Treatment, 1998, Hypertension Atlas, 2009; editor-in-chief: Jour. Lab. and Clin. Medicine, 1973—76, Hypertension, 1994—2002; mem. editl. bd. (jours.) Am. Jour. Cardiology, 1982—91; actor(mem. editl. bd.): (jours.) Am. Jour. Cardiology, 2002—05; consulting editor (jours.) Am. Jour. Cardiology, 2006—, mem. editl. bd. Circulation, 1978—91, Archives of Internal Medicine, 1978—88, Modern Medicine, 1980—2000, Jour. Hypertension, 1994—2003; assoc. editor: Am. Jour. Physiology, Heart Circulation; contbr. chapters to books, articles to profl. jours. Capt. U.S. Army, 1960-62. Recipient Honors Achievement award, Angiology Rsch. Found., 1964, Ann. award, So. Med. Assn., 1971, Janice M. Pfeffer Disting. Lectureship, Internat. Soc. Heart Rsch., 2005, William Harvey award, Am. Soc. Hypertension, 2007; rsch. fellow, Georgetown U. Hosp., 1958—59. Master: ACP (laureate 1996); fellow: AAAS, Coun. High Blood Pressure Rsch. (exec. com. 1972—75, 1981—85, vice chmn. 1986—88, chmn. 1989—91), Am. Coll. Cardiology (gov. La. chpt. 1988—91, bd. trustees La. chpt. 1991—92, 1996—2000, Disting. Scientist award 2005), Royal Coll. Physicians and Surgeons Glasgow (hon.); mem.: Am. Soc. Hypertension (William Harvey award 2007), Polish Acad. Arts Sci. (faculty medicine), Columbian Soc. Cardiology, Peruvian Soc. Cardiology, Assn. Am. Physicians, Am. Soc. Clin. Investigations, So. Soc. Clin. Rsch., Ctrl. Soc. Clin. Rsch., Am. Soc. Nephrology, Am. Physiol. Soc., Am. Soc. Clin. Pharmacology and Therapeutics (past pres.), Am. Soc. Pharmacology and Exptl. Therapeutics, Am. Soc. Clin. Investigation, Soc. Geriat. Cardiology (pres. 2000—01), Inter-Am. Soc. Hypertension (Lifetime Achievement award 1999), Am. Heart Assn. (dir. La. chpt. 1979—83, chmn. Coun. High Blood Pressure Rsch. 1988—91, award of merit 1986, Lifetime Achievement award 1994, Okamoto Internat. award 1994), Internat. Soc. Hypertension (sci. coun. 1974—84, treas. 1980—82, v.p. 1982—84, Astra award 2000), Alpha Kappa Alpha, Phi Sigma, Chi Epsilon Mu. Office: Ochsner Clinic Found 1516 Jefferson Hwy New Orleans LA 70121-2429 Office Phone: 504-842-3700. Business E-Mail: efrohlich@ochsner.org.

FROHOCK, FRED MANUEL, political science professor; b. Perry, Fla., Feb. 7, 1937; s. Fred Clifton and Marie Antonia (Domenech) F.; m. Val Jean Derrick, Sept. 7, 1963; children: Katherine Renee, Christina Marie BA, U. Fla., 1960, MA, 1961; PhD, U. N.C., 1966. Asst. prof. polit. sci. Syracuse U., NY, 1965-68, assoc. prof. NY, 1968-74, prof. NY, 1974—2004, chmn. dept. polit. sci. NY, 1985-89, prof. Florence program Italy, 1969-70, prof., chmn. Madrid program, 1972-74, prof., chmn. London Politics Seminar, 1984—2004; prof., chmn. dept. polit. sci. U. Miami, 2005—, prof., chair London politics seminar, 2008—. Author: Nature of Political Inquiry, 1967, Normative Political Theory, 1974, Public Policy, 1979, Abortion: A Case Study in Law and Morals, 1983, Special Care: Medical Decisions at the Beginning of Life, 1986, Rational Association, 1987, Healing Powers, 1992, Public Reason: Mediated Authority in the Liberal State, 1999, Lives of the Psychics: The Shared Worlds of Science and Mysticism, 2000, Bounded Divinities: Sacred Discourses in Pluralist Democracies, 2006, Beyond: On Life After Death, 2010; contbr. numerous articles to profl. jours. Social Sci. Research Council fellow, 1964-65, 67-68; NEH summer fellow, 1988. Democrat. Roman Catholic. Avocations: golf, watching baseball. Home: 516 Savona Ave Coral Gables FL 33146 Office: U Miami Polit Sci Dept Coral Gables FL 33124 Business E-Mail: f.frohock@miami.edu.

FROMM, GERI-LYNN, gynecologic oncologist, educator; MD, Northwestern U., Ill., 1981; program in med. edn. (hon.). Diplomate Am. Bd. Ob-Gyn, Am. Bd. Ob-Gyn-gynecologic oncology, lic. Tex., 1989. Intern and resident Univ. Pitts.; resident Magee Women's Hosp., 1985; fellow Univ. Tex. MD Anderson Med. Ctr., 1987; assoc. clin. prof. Baylor Coll. of Medicine; physician Tex. Oncology-Houston Med. Ctr.; hosp. affiliations include Pk. Plz. Hosp. and Med. Ctr., Meth. Hosp., Cypress Fairbanks Med. Ctr., Meml. Hermann Hosp. System, Meml. Hermann SW Hosp., Tex. Children's Hosp., Woman's Hosp. of Tex., St. Lukes Episcopal Hosp. Fellow: ACOG; mem.: Soc. of Gynecologic Oncologists, Felix Rutledge Soc., Gynecologic Oncology of Houston (founder and pres.), Soc. of Gynecologic Oncologists. Office: Saint Luke's Episcopal Hospital 6720 Bertner Ave Houston TX 77030 Office Phone: 832-355-1000.

FRONTZ, LESLIE KAY, art educator; b. Cleve., Aug. 23, 1950; d. James W. and Mary K. Robinson; m. Harold O. Frontz, 1972. BA in Psychology, cum laude, Muskingum Coll., New Concord, Ohio, 1972; MA in Edn., Va. Poly. Inst. State U., Blacksburg, 1976; BS in Art, summa cum laude, So. Oreg. State U., Ashland, 1981; MFA in Studio Arts, U. NC, Greensboro, 1986. Studio artist Frontz Studio, Lexington, NC, 1986—; adj. faculty art history Front Range CC, Ft. Collins, Colo., 1989—90; instr. art Wash. State CC, Marietta, Ohio, 1991—92, SW Elem. Sch., Lexington, NC, 1997—2003; adj. faculty art Davidson County CC, Lexington, 2006—08. Adj. faculty, watercolor and art appreciation Rowan-Cabarrus CC, Salisbury, NC, 2011—13; mem., bd. dirs. Ohio Watercolor Soc., Ohio, 1993—94. Exhibitions include Smithsonian Instn., Washington, 1987, Loveland Mus. and Gallery Co., 1990, Davidson County Mus. Art, NC, 1997, Salem Coll. Fine Arts Ctr., 2003, Landfall Found., 2003, So. Watercolor Soc., 2006—08, Soc. Women Artists, London, 2005—10, Am. Watercolor Soc., NYC, 2009—12, Vero Beach Mus. Art, 2011. Vol. asst. exhbns. Loveland Mus. and Gallery, Colo., 1988—90, Davidson County Hist. Mus., Lexington, NC, 2003; mem. exec. bd. Lexington Herb Guild, NC, 1996—2005. Recipient Best of Show, Nat. Art Mart, Colo., 1990, Excellence award, Ohio Watercolor Soc., 1992, Mason award, Batavia Nat. Exhbn., N.Y., 1993, Best of Show, Comer Mus. Art, Ala., 1995, Canson award, Cultural Arts Ctr., Glen Allen, Va., 2006; Holderness fellow, U. N.C., Greensboro, 1985—86. Mem.: Nat. Watercolor Soc. (signature mem.), Am. Watercolor Soc. (signature mem., Ogden and Mary Pleissner Meml. award 2009, High Winds medal 2011, Watercolor Mag. award 2012), Soc. Women Artists (signature mem., HRH Princess Michael of Kent Watercolor award 2007), Southern Watercolor Soc. (signature mem., Canson award 2006, Georg Shook Meml. award 2007), Plein Air Carolina (founding mem.). Presbyterian. Avocations: gardening, travel, writing. Office: Frontz Studio 296 Peace Haven Dr Lexington NC 27292 Office Phone: 336-357-5974. Business E-Mail: hlfrontz@lexcominc.net.*

FROST, PHILLIP, pharmaceutical executive, dermatologist; BA, Univ. Pa., 1957; MD, Albert Einstein Coll., Bronx, NY, 1961. Chmn. dept. of dermatology Mt. Sinai Med. Center, Miami, Fla., 1972—90; chmn. Key Pharms., Miami, Fla., 1972—86; pres. Ivax Corp., Miami, Fla., 1991—95, founder, chmn., CEO, 1987—2006; interim CEO ImClone Systems Inc., NYC, 2005—06, exec. v.p., chief scientific officer, 2006; vice-chmn. Teva Pharmaceuticals Industries, Ltd., 2006—10, chmn., 2010—, Ladenburg Thalmann Fin. Services, Inc., 2006—; chmn., CEO OPKO Health, Inc., 2007—. Bd. dir. Ladenburg Thalmann Fin. Svcs., 2001—02; chmn. IVAX Diagnostics, Inc.; bd. dir. Northrop Grumman Corp., Continucare Corp., Cellular Tech. Svcs.; co-vice-chmn. bd. governors Am. Stock Exchange; chmn. Ladenburg Thalmann Fin. Svcs., 2006—; bd. dirs. Kidville Inc. (formerly Longfoot Comm. Corp.), Prolor Biotech Inc (formerly Modigene Inc.), Ideation Acquisition Corp.; vice chmn. Teva; bd. dir. Castle Brands Inc., 2005—07, bd. dirs., 2008—. Mem. bd. regents Smithsonian Inst.; trustee Scripps Rsch. Inst.; trustee, past chmn. Univ. of Miami. Named one of Forbes 400: Richest Americans, 2006—. Office: OPKO Health Inc 4400 Biscayne Blvd Miami FL 33137 Office Phone: 305-575-6015. Business E-Mail: pfrost@ladenburg.com.

FROST, RICHARD W. (RICK FROST), manufacturing executive; BS in Gen. Studies, La. State U., BS in Indsl. Forest Mgmt.; MBA, Northwestern State U., La. Mgmt. positions Boise Cascade, Scott Paper Co., SAPPI; v.p., ops. mgr. SD Warren Co., 1992—96; v.p., timberlands & procurement Louisiana Pacific Corp., 1996—2002, exec. v.p., procurement & engring., 2002—03, exec. v.p., commodity products, procurement & engring., 2003—04, chmn., CEO, 2004—. Chmn. Forest Resources Assn., 2004—06; vice chmn. Nat. Air. and Stream Coun.; bd. dirs. La. Pacific Corp., 2004—, Tractor Supply Co., 2007—, Forest Products Assn. Can., Am. Forest and Paper Assn., Temperature Forest Found. Office: Louisiana-Pacific Corp 414 Union St Ste 2000 Nashville TN 37219-1711 Office Phone: 615-986-5600. Office Fax: 615-986-5666. Business E-Mail: rick.frost@lpcorp.com.

FROULA, JAMES DEWAYNE, honor society administrator; b. Oak Park, Ill., May 1945; s. James Clarence and Helen Barbara F.; m. Barbara Jean Leftwich, 1968; children: James Matthew, Anna Katherine. BSME, U. Tenn., 1967, MS, 1968. Lic. profl. engr., Tenn. Engr. IBM Corp., Lexington, Ky., 1970-74, engring. mgr. Boulder, Colo., 1974-82; exec. dir., sec.-treas., editor Tau Beta Pi, Knoxville, Tenn., 1982—; pres. Assn. Coll. Honor Socs., 1991-93. Editor: The Bent of Tau Beta Pi, 1982—; patentee magnetic brush roll. 1st lt. U.S. Army, 1968-70, Vietnam. Decorated Bronze Star; fellow NSF, 1967-68. Fellow ASME, NSPE (bd. dirs. Knoxville chpt. 1988-94, Outstanding Engr. 1994), Coun. Engring. and Sci. Soc. Execs., Tenn. Soc. Profl. Engrs. (chair divsn. profl. engrs. in edn. practice 1993-96), Am. Assn. Engring. Socs. (awards com. 1997-2000). Roman Catholic. Avocations: mountain climbing, hiking. Office: Tau Beta Pi PO Box 2697 Knoxville TN 37901-2697

FRY, KELLY DYER, newspaper editor; BA in Journalism, Okla. State U., 1981. Various positions including features editor, gen. mgr. NewsOk.com & dir. multimedia The Oklahoman, Oklahoma City, 1994—2011, editor, 2011—; v.p. news & info. OPUBCO Comm. Group, 2011—. Office: The Oklahoman 9000 N Broadway Oklahoma City OK 73114 Office Phone: 405-475-3247. Business E-Mail: kfry@opubco.com.

FRY, TOM, federal official; b. Richmond, Va., Nov. 13, 1944; s. Tom. Jr. and Louise (Sullivan) F.; 1 child Thomas Hocker. BA, Trinity U., 1966; JD, Southern Meth. U., 1969. Bar: Tex. 1969. V.p. Am. Nat. Resources, Inc.; regional counsel, chief enforcement counsel Economic Regulatory Adminstrn., Dept Energy, dir. field office; ptnr. Cooper, Hayner, Miller, Long & Owen, Dallas; asst. chief anti-trust consumer protection divsn. Tex. Atty. Gen. Office, dir., field office Dallas; now cons. Bd. dirs. Minerals Mgmt. Svc., Pogo Producing Co., 2004—07, Plains Exploration & Prodn. Co., 2007—. Capt. U.S. Army, 1969-1972., pres., Nat. Ocean Industries Assn., 2000-2010, bd. dirs., Interior's Bur. of Land Mgmt. Presbyterian. Avocations: running, golf. Office: Office of Deputy Secretary Dept of the Interior 18 C St Washington DC 20240-0001 also: Plains Exploration & Production Co Bd Directors 700 Milam St Ste 3100 Houston TX 77002 Office Phone: 713-579-6000. Office Fax: 713-579-6611. Business E-Mail: tfry@pxp.com.

FRYE, MARION, state legislator; b. Columbia, SC, Jan. 20, 1945; Mgr. SC Farm Bur. Ins. Office, Saluda; mem. Dist. 39 SC House of Reps., 1999—, mem. Agr., Natural Resources and Environ. Affairs Com. & Invitations and Meml. Resolutions Com. Republican. Office: 323C Blatt Bldg Columbia SC 29201 Mailing: 668 McNeary Ferry Rd Leesville SC 29070 Office Phone: 803-734-3275. E-mail: MBF@schouse.org.

FRYE, PHILLIP D., state legislator; Owner Frye Auto Interiors; state rep. Dist 84 NC, 2003—. Mem. Appropriations com., Appropriations Subcom. on Transp., House Select Com. on Small Bus., Transp. com.; vice chmn. Fed. Rels. and Indian Affairs com. Republican. Mailing: Dist Off PO Box 589 Spruce Pine NC 28777 Office: North Carolina House of Representatives 300 N Salisbury St Rm 639 Raleigh NC 27603-5925 Office Phone: 919-733-5661. E-mail: Phillip.Frye@ncleg.net.

FRYMAN, VIRGIL THOMAS, JR., lawyer; b. Maysville, Ky., Apr. 9, 1940; s. Virgil Thomas and Elizabeth Louis (Marshall) F. AB cum laude, Harvard U., 1962, LLB, 1966. Bar: N.Y. 1967, U.S. Ct. Appeals (2d cir.) 1967, U.S. Dist. Ct. (so. and ea. dists.) N.Y. 1968, U.S. Supreme Ct. 1970, U.S. Ct. Appeals (6th cir.) 1988,U.S. Ct. Appeals (11th cir.) 2002, U.S. Dist. Ct. (ea. and we. dists.) Ky. 1988. Assoc. Cravath, Swaine & Moore, NYC, 1966-73; asst. U.S. atty. U.S. Dist. Ct. (so. dist.) N.Y., NYC, 1973-78; assoc. gen. counsel Price Waterhouse, NYC, 1978-86; staff counsel select com. to investigate covert arms transactions with Iran, U.S. Ho. Reps., 1987; mem. Greenebaum, Doll & McDonald PLLC, Lexington, Ky., 1988—2006. Contbr. to Proving Federal Crimes, 6th edit., 1976. Mem. ABA, Am. Law Inst., Assn. Bar City of N.Y., Ky. Bar Assn., Fayette County Bar Assn., Harvard Club, Idle hour Country Club. Democrat. Episcopalian. Home: Fed Hill Washington KY 41096-0173 Office: Greenebaum Doll & McDonald PLLC 300 W Vine St Ste 1100 Lexington KY 40507-1665 Office Phone: 859-231-8500. E-mail: vtf@gdm.com.

FRYREAR, DONALD WILLIAM, agricultural engineer, researcher; b. Haxtun, Colo., Dec. 8, 1936; s. William Alfred and Majorie (Adams) F.; m. Sherry Janice Watson, Sept. 16, 1956; children: Debra Lou, Kenneth William. BSAE, Colo. State U., 1959; MSAE, Kans. State U., 1962. Registered profl. engr., Tex. Engr. USDA-Agrl. Rsch. Svc., Akron, Colo., 1959-60, Manhattan, Kans., 1960-62, rsch. engr. Temple, Tex., 1962-65, rsch. leader Big Spring, Tex., 1965-97. Erosion cons. UNESCO, Medmine, Tunisia, 1983, Pretoria, South Africa, 1985; project leader for devel. of Revised Wind Erosion Equation. Contbr. articles to profl. jours. Recipient Appreciation award Howard Coll., 1977; Soil Conservation Soc. Am. fellow, 1982. Mem. Am. Soc. Agrl. Engrs. (assoc. editor 1974, SW Dirs. citation 1996), Soil and Water Conservation Soc. (charter pres. 1972), Am. Soc. Agronomy (state pres. 1977), N.Y. Acad. Sci. Baptist. Achievements include development of graded furrow concept for controlling water erosion, techniques for analyzing field erosion data; design and construction of five wind tunnels; design of first field equipment for measuring wind erosion. Office: Custon Products and Cons 7204 S Service Rd Big Spring TX 79720-0546 E-mail: dfryrear@crcom.net.

FRYZEL, MICHAEL E., federal agency administrator, lawyer; b. 1945; m. Gloria Fryzel; children: Scott, Brian, Kimberly. BS in Bus. Adminstrn., Valparaiso U., 1967; MBA, U. Chgo.; JD, Loyola U. Bar: Ill., DC. Dir. adminstrn. and fiscal mgr. Gov.'s Office of Human Resources, Ill.; dir. Ill. Dept. Fin. Institutions, 1982—89; staff asst. to spkr. Ill. House Reps., staff asst. to minority leader; supr. Currency Exchange Divsn. Ill. Dept. Fin. Instns., adminstr. Unclaimed Property Divsn., supr. Consumer Credit Divsn.; commr. Ill. Ct. Claims, 1989—2003; pvt. practice atty. Ill.; DUI prosecutor Ill. Sec. of State; mem. Nat. Credit Union Adminstrn. (NCUA), Alexandria, Va., 2008—, chmn., 2008—09. Mem. Ill. Gov.'s Bd. Credit Union Advisors, 1992—2008, Ill. Gov.'s Task Force on Fin. Svcs., Ill. Gov.'s Fin. Instn. Transition Team; hearing officer Motor Vehicle Review Bd., Ill. Office: Nat Credit Union Adminstrn 1775 Duke St Alexandria VA 22314-3428

FU, CARY T., electronics executive; MS in Acctg., U. Houston. CPA. Contr. Intermedics, 1983—86; treas. Benchmark Electronics, Inc., 1986—96, asst. sec., 1988—90, sec., 1990—96, exec. v.p, Fin. Adminstrn., 1990—92, exec. v.p., 1990—2001, pres., COO, 2001—04, chmn., CEO, 2009—11, chmn., 2011—. Bd. dirs. Benchmark Electronics, Inc., 1986—88, Teradata Corp., 2008—. Office: Benchmark Electronics Inc 3000 Technology Dr Angleton TX 77515 Office Fax: 979-848-5270. Business E-Mail: cary.fu@teradata.com.

FUCHS, MARK, lawyer; BS in Biology, Lewis and Clark Coll., Portland, Oreg.; JD, Willamette U.; MBA, Portland State U. Bar: Oreg. Litig. atty., corp. bds., ins. cos. and product mfr. Bullivant Houser Bailey; corp. atty. Louisiana Pacific Corp., 2001—03, corp. sec., gen. counsel, 2003—, v.p., 2007—. Office: Louisiana Pacific Corp 414 Union St Ste 2000 Nashville TN 37219 Office Phone: 615-986-5600. Office Fax: 615-986-5666. Business E-Mail: mark.fuchs@lpcorp.com.

FUDENBERG, HUGH, neuroimmunologist, educator; b. NYC, Oct. 24, 1928; s. Nathan and Frances (Chackowitz) F.; m. Betty Roof, June 1956 (div.); children: Drew, Brooks, David, Haskell. AB, UCLA, 1949; MD, U. Chgo., 1953; MA, Boston U., 1958. Diplomate Am. Bd. Med. Lab. Immunology. Intern U. Utah Hosp., 1953—54; trainee in hematology New Eng. Ctr. Hosp., Tufts U., Boston, 1954—56; resident Mt. Sinai Hosp., NYC, 1956—57, Peter Bent Brigham Hosp., Harvard U., Boston, 1957—58; rsch. assoc. Rockefeller Inst., NYC, 1958—60; asst. prof. medicine U. Calif. Sch. Medicine, San Francisco, 1960—62, assoc. prof. medicine, 1962—66, prof., 1966—75; assoc. prof. immunology U. Calif., Berkeley, 1965—66, prof. bacteriology and immunology, 1966—75; prof., chmn. dept. basic and clin. immunology and microbiology Med. U. SC, Charleston, 1974—85, prof. medicine, immunology, 1974—88; dir. rsch. NeuroImmuno-Therapeutic Rsch. Found., Spartanburg, SC, 1988—. Adj. prof. pub. health U. Calif., Berkeley, 1966-75; adj. prof. epidemiology U. NC, Chapel Hill, 1977—; vis. prof. univs. and rsch. insts. in US and Europe, including Karolinska Inst., Sweden, Middlesex Hosp., Eng., Harvard U., Yale U., Princeton U., NYU, U. Ala., Wayne State U., U. So. Calif., U. Amsterdam, U. Leiden, U. Paris, U. Glasgow, U. Edinburgh, U. PR, U. Medellin, Colombia, Caracas, Venezuela, U. Innsbruck, Weismann Inst., Israel, Weifang Med. Sch., China, U. Norway, U. Helsinki, also Cancer Rsch. Inst., France, Italy, Russia, and The Netherlands; spkr. in field; mem. nat. adv. coun. Nat. Inst. Allergy and Infectious Diseases, 1981-85; mem. expert adv. panel on immunology WHO, 1962-82; mem. panel biomed. manpower NRC, 1974-78, mem. com. on immunization, 1978-80; mem. nat. task force on multiple myeloma and chronic leukemia NIH, 1966-71; chmn. external evaluation sci. com. U. Merida, Venezuela, 1982-86; mem. sci. adv. bd. UNESCO Internat. Ctr. for Immunology, Lyon, France, 1982-88; chmn. sci. adv. bd. Integra Inst., 1988-92; chmn. bd. sci. direction Inst. Immunology, Weifang Med. Coll., Changdong, China, 1988—; v.p. rsch. Neuro Immunology Therapeutic Rsch. Found., editl. bd. mem., Internat. Jour. Clin. Investigation, 2005, co-editor chief Internat. Jours. Clin. Invest. Author: (with others) Basic Immunogenetics, 1972, 3d edit., 1984, Basic and Clinical Immunology, 1974, 4th edit., 1982 (transl. into 12 lang.), Introduction to Medical Immunology, 1986, 2d edit., 1990; editor: (with others) Phagocytic Mechanisms in Health and Disease, 1972, Biomedical Scientists and Public Policy, 1978; editor: Biomedical Institutions, Biomedical Funding, and Public Policy, 1983; past mem. 35 editl. bds. including African Jour. Clin. and Exptl. Immunology, Annals Allergy, Biomedicine and Pharmacotherapy, Clin. and Exptl. Immunology, Folia Allergologica et Immunologica Clinica, Alzheimer's Longevity and Aging, Hosp. Practice, Jour. Irreproducible Results; co-editor in chief Internat. Jour. Clin. Investigation; contbr. 850 articles to sci. jour.; patentee in field. Mem. nat. adv. coun. Nat. Inst. Allergy and Infectious Diseases, 1981-85; mem. expert adv. panel immunology WHO, 1962-82; mem. panel biomed. manpower Nat. Rsch. Coun., 1974-78, mem. com. on immunization, 1978-80; mem. nat. task force on multiple myeloma and chronic leukemia NIH, 1966-71; chmn. external evaluation sci. com. U. Merida, Venezuela, 1982-86; mem. sci. adv. bd. UNESCO Internat. Ctr. for Immunology, Lyon, France, 1982-88; chmn. sci. adv. bd. Integra Inst., 1988—; chmn. bd. sci. dir. Inst. Immunology, Weifang Med. Coll., Shandong, People's Republic of China, 1988—; v.p. rsch. Neuro Immunology Therapeutic Rsch. Found.; mem. adv. bd. Cambridge Internat. Biog. Centre, 1992; numerous others. Recipient Pasteur medal Inst. Pasteur, 1962, Robert A. Cook medal Am. Acad. Allergy, 1966, Berman medal Am. Acad. Dermatology, 1973, Disting. Svc. award U. Chgo. Med. Alumni, 1973, Petrov Cancer medal Govt. USSR, 1976, Carl Neuberg medal Virchow-Pirquet Med. Soc., 1980, Koch medal German Soc. Microbiology, 1980, von Behringer medal, 1981, Semmelweis medal Hungarian Soc. Immunology, 1981, Metchnikoff Centennial, 1983, Phagocytosis medal Italian Soc. Immunology, 1983, Danish Cancer Soc., 1988, Castelloa di Pietrarossa award, Italy, 1991, Internat. First Prize, Frontiers in Medicine, Italy, 1992, 1st prize Biomed. Rsch. Italian Acad. Arts and Sci., 1992, 20th Century award rsch. sci. med. rsch. and edn., 1993; decorated Order of San Ciriaco, Italy, 1993, Internat. 1st prize in Exptl. Medicine, Italian Govt., 2000; named hon. prof. U. Kuopio, Finland, 1982, U. Claude Bernard, France, 1985, Free Sci. U., Bologna, Italy, 1985, Weifang Med. Coll. Fellow AAAS, Am. Acad. Microbiology; mem. Am. Assn. for Cancer Rsch., Am. Assn. Immunologists (com. for congl. liaison for HEW appropriations, long range planning com.), Am. Rheumatism Assn., Am. Soc. for Clin. Investigation (chmn. com. on pub. info. 1971-74), Am. Soc. Hematology (pres. subdivsn. immunohematology and immunogenetics 1970, subcom. mem., 1974, rsch tchg. methods 1961-65), Am. Soc. Human Genetics (exec. coun. 1969-72), Assn. Am. Med. Sch. Microbiology (chmn., pub. affairs com.), Assn. Am. Physicians, Genetics Soc, Am. Internat. Soc. Blood Transfusion (exec. councillor 1965-71), Internat. Soc. Environment Toxicology and Cancer (bd. councilors), Internat. Soc. Hematology, Internat. Union Immunology Soc. (immunoglobin subcom. mem. 1977), Internat. Platform Assn., Midwinter Conf. Immunologists (founder, past pres.), Royal Soc. Medicine (assoc.), Soc. Clin. Immunology, Am. Soc. Med. Labs., Med. Immunology, Sigma Xi. Business E-Mail: nitrf@charter.net.

FUENTE, DAVID I., retail executive; b. 1946; BS, Purdue U., 1967, MS, 1969. Chmn. SSA & Co., LLC, G100; prof. Case Western Reserve U., 1970—75; dir., mktg. Gould Inc., with Cleve., 1975—79; pres., paint stores group Sherwin-Williams Co., 1979—87; CEO, chmn. Office Depot, Inc., Boca Raton, Fla., 1987—2000; CEO, chmn. & pres. OD Internat., Inc., Delray Beach, Fla., 1987—2000, chmn., 1987—2001. Bd. dirs. Vs Holdings Inc., U. Miami, Boca Raton Cmty. Hosp. Inc., OPEN Sports Network, Inc.; trustee Baron Select Funds; bd. dirs. Ryder Sys. Inc., 1988, Vitamin Shoppe Industries, Inc., 2003—06, Sunrise Sr. Living Inc., 2008—10, Office Depot, Inc., 1987—. Office: Office Depot Inc 6600 N Military Trail Boca Raton FL 33496 Office Phone: 561-438-4800. Office Fax: 561-438-4001.

FUENTE, JUSTIN, college football coach; b. Tulsa, Okla., July 30, 1976; m. Jenny Fuente; children: Cecilia, Caroline. Attended, U. Okla., Norman, 1996—97; B in Fin., Murray State U., Ky., 1999. Quarterback Okla. Wranglers, Arena Football League, 2000—01; quarterbacks coach Ill. State U. Redbirds, 2001—06, offensive coord., 2004—06; running backs coach Tex. Christian U. Horned Frogs, 2007—08, co-offensive coord., quarterbacks coach, 2009—11; head football coach U. Memphis Tigers, 2012—. Named Ohio Valley Conf.

Offensive Player of Yr., 1999; finalist Walter Payton award, The Sports Network, 1999. Office: University of Memphis Football Program 570 Normal AOB Rm #136 Memphis TN 38152 Office Phone: 901-678-5119.

FUGGER, EDWARD F., JR., food products executive; With Price-Waterhouse; various positions, mergers, acquisitions, debt, equity offerings & mng. dir. Bear, Stearns & Co. Inc.; v.p., corp. devel. Dean Foods Co., 2004, sr. v.p., corp. devel. Office: Dean Foods Co 2711 N Haskell Ave Ste 3400 Dallas TX 75204 Office Phone: 214-303-3400. Office Fax: 214-303-3499. Business E-Mail: ed_fugger@deanfoods.com.

FULDA, MICHAEL, political scientist, educator, space policy researcher; b. Liverpool, Eng., Apr. 21, 1939; came to U.S., 1962, naturalized, 1966; s. Boris and Catherine (Von Dehn) F.; m. Rosa Bongiorno, July 19, 1970; children: Robert, George. Student, Polytechnique, Grenoble, France, 1956-57, Tech. U., West Berlin, Germany, 1957-58, Karl Eberhardt U., Tubingen, Germany, 1963-66; MA, Am. U., 1968, PhD in Internat. Studies, 1970. Ballroom dance coor., 2001—; prof. polit. sci. Fairmont State U., W.Va., 1971—2008. Vis. prof. Bauman Moscow State Tech. U., 2002; internat. rels. specialist NASA, Washington, 1979. Author: Oil and International Relations, 1979; (with others) United States Space Policy, 1985; contbr. articles to profl. jours. Bd. dirs. Fairmont Chamber Music Soc., 1983—; W.Va. state com. chmn., dir. space policy Nat. Unity Campaign for John Anderson, 1980; mem. nat. adv. com. John Glenn Presdl. Com., 1984, space policy group Dukakis/Bentsen Com., 1988; dist. advancement com. Boy Scouts Am.; active psychol. ops. Vets. Assn. With U.S. Army, 1962-66. Fellow NASA Marshall Ctr., Huntsville, Ala., 1977, Langley Ctr., Hampton, Va., 1976, Woodrow Wilson Found., 1969-70; grantee Humanities Found. W.Va., 1978-80, NASA W.Va. Space Grant Consortium, 1991-2004; named del. to Aerospace States Assn. by Gov. of W.Va., 2001-08. Fellow AIAA (assoc.), Brit. Interplanetary Soc.; mem. Nat. Space Soc. (dir. 1991-93, 2002-04), German Assn. for Luft and Raumfamrt, Soc. Espacial Mexicana, Nat. Space Club, Assn. Argentina Tech. Space, Inst. for Social Sci. Study of Space (pres. 1988—), Manassas Elks Lodge (edn. com.). Avocations: physical fitness, weightlifting, tango, ballroom dancing. Home: 10911 Wild Ginger Cir # 204 Manassas VA 20109 Office Phone: 304-641-4707. Personal E-mail: mishafulda@gmail.com.

FULGHAM, ALONZO L., not-for-profit organization administrator; b. 1958; m. Celeste L. Fulgham; 3 children. BS, Fisk U., 1980; MA, Nat. Def. U. Pvt. sector adv. US Agy. Internat. Devel. (USAID), Swaziland, 1989, internat. devel. intern, 1992, pvt. sector officer, dir. econ. policy, poverty reduction Jordan, 1993—98, dir. econ. restructuring, energy for Georgia and Azerbaijan, 1998, acting dep. dir. Serbia and Montenegro, 2001, spl. asst. to asst. adminstr., Bur. Asia Near East, 2003, dir. South Asian affairs, Bur. Asia Near East, mission dir., Sr. Fgn. Svc. Afghanistan, 2005—06, COO Washington, DC, 2006—09, acting adminstr., 2009; v.p. Internat. Relief & Devel., Arlington, Va., 2010—. Vol. Peace Corps, Haiti, 1984—86. Named to Power 150, Ebony mag., 2008. Office: Internat Relief & Development 1621 N Kent St 4th Fl Arlington VA 22209 Office Phone: 703-248-0161.

FULGONI, GIAN MARC, Internet research company executive; b. Crickhowell, Brecon, England, Jan. 24, 1948; arrived in US, 1970; BSc in Physics, with honors, Manchester U., 1969; MA in Mktg., Lancaster U., 1970. Exec. v.p. Mgmt. Sci. Assocs., Inc., Pitts., 1970-81; pres. Information Resources, Inc., Chgo., 1981-89, CEO, 1986-98, vice chmn., 1989-90, chmn., 1991-95, bd. dirs.; co-founder, exec. chmn. comScore, Inc., Reston, Va., 1999—. Bd. dirs. US Robotics Inc., 1991—94, Platinum Tech., Inc., 1991—99, Yesmail-.com Inc., 1999—2000, PetMed Express Inc., 2002—, InXpo LLC, 2005—, Advt. Rsch. Found., 2008—; mem. adv. bd. Viewpoints Network, LLC, 2007—. Recipient Wall St. Transcript award, 1992; named Ill. Entrepreneur of Yr., 1991, 2004, Ernst & Young Entrepreneur of Yr., 2008; named to Chgo. Entrepreneurship Hall of Fame, 2008. Mem.: Am. Mktg. Assn., Young Pres. Orgn. Office: ComScore Inc Ste 200 11950 Democracy Dr Reston VA 20190-5624 Office Phone: 703-438-2000. Office Fax: 703-438-2051. E-mail: gfulgoni@comscore.com.

FULKERSON, WILLIAM, hospital administrator, pulmonologist; b. Charlotte, NC, Sept. 8, 1951; Grad., U. N.C., Chapel Hill, 1973; MD, U. N.C., 1977; grad., Duke U. Intern Vanderbilt U. Hosp., Nashville, 1977—78, resident internal medicine, 1978—81, fellow pulmonary disease, 1981—83; asst. prof. medicine Duke U. Sch. Medicine, 1983—90, assoc. prof., 1990—95, prof., 1995—, vice chmn. dept. medicine, 1997—98, chief pulmonary and critical care medicine, 1997—99, exec. med. officer Private Diagnostic Clinic PLLC, 1997—99; chief med. officer Duke U. Hosp., 2000—02, CEO, 2002; sr. v.p. clin. affairs Duke U. Health Sys., exec. v.p. Contbr. articles to profl. jours., chapters to books. Fellow: Soc. Critical Care Medicine, Am. Coll. Chest Physicians; mem.: Am. Thoracic Soc., ACP. Office: Duke Univ 14209 Hosp S Box 3708 Med Ctr Durham NC 27710

FULLENWEIDER, DONN CHARLES, lawyer; b. Milw., Jan. 25, 1935; s. Russell Charles and Anne Mae (Murphy) F.; m. Wendy Lattimer; 1 child, Keith Rabon. BS, U. Houston, 1957, JD, 1958. Bar: Tex. bar 1958; Cert. in family law and civil trials Tex. Bd. Legal Specialization. Assoc. Fred Parks, Houston, 1958-65; partner Haynes & Fullenweider, Houston, 1965-89; pvt. practice, Houston, 1989-93; ptnr. Fullenweider and Wardell L.L.P., 1993-97, The Fullenweider Firm, 1997—2008, Fullenweider Wilhite, 2008—. Adj. assoc. prof. law U. Houston Bates Coll. Law, 1972-74 Mem. 43d Joint Civilian Orientation Conf., 1973; mem. Tex. Bd. Legal Specialization, 1977-98. Recipient Emison award Tex. Acad. Family Specialists, 1993, David Agibson award, 2009; named to State Bar Tex. Hall of Legands, 2004; named one of Best Lawyers in America, 2009, Lawyers of Yr. Family Law, 2009. Fellow Am. Bar Found., Houston Bar Found., Tex. Bar Found. (dir. 1973-76), Am. Acad. Matrimonial Lawyers (pres. Tex. chpt. 1979-81, bd. dirs. 1981-84, treas. 1985-88, pres.-elect 1988-89, pres. 1990-91); mem. ABA, Am. Bd. Trial Advocacy (advocate), Houston Bar Assn. (treas. 1961-62, 2d v.p. 1962-63, dir. 1971, 73, 1st v.p. 1970-73, Outstanding Svc. award 1974), Am. Coll. Family Trial Lawyers (diplomate 1994—), State Bar Tex. (dir. 1973-76, chmn. bd. 1975-76, exec. com. 1976-77, chmn. litigation sect. 1979-81), River Oaks Country Club, Casyine Me Golf & Yacht Club, Sigma Chi, Phi Delta Phi. Office: 4265 San Felipe St Ste 1400 Houston TX 77027-2999 Home: 4265 San Felipe St Ste 1400 Houston TX 77027-2952 Office Phone: 713-624-4100. E-mail: donn012535@aol.com.

FULLER, AARON B., III, information technology executive; BA, Claremont McKenna Coll., Calif.; MA, U. Va. Sr. mgmt. positions Booz-Allen & Hamilton, Gen. Rsch. Corp.; sr. economist Inst. for Def. Analyses, Washington, 1975—80; sr. v.p., operating unit exec. BDM Internat., 1991—98; v.p. Computer Sciences Corp., 1998, v.p., gen. mgr., Navy, Marine Corps and Missile Def., 2004, pres., Def. Mission Engring. and Integration Divsn., 2004—08, pres., enforcement, security and intelligence, N.Am. Pub. Sector, 2008—. Office: Computer Sciences Corp 3170 Fairview Park Dr Falls Church VA 22042 Office Phone: 703-876-1000. Business E-Mail: aaron.fuller@csc.com.

FULLER, MARK EVERETT, federal judge; b. Enterprise, Ala., Dec. 27, 1958; s. Kenneth T. and Rebecca (Phillips) Fuller; m. Mary Elisa Boyd; children: Kailin, Meredith, Everett. BS in Chem. Engring., U. Ala., Tuscaloosa, 1982, JD, 1985. Bar: Ala. 1985, admitted to practice: US Dist. Ct. Ala. 1985, US Ct. Appeals (11th Cir.) 1985. CEO, chmn. bd. Doss Aviation, Inc., Colorado Springs, Colo., 1989—2002; assoc. Cassady, Fuller & Marsh, 1985—86, ptnr., 1986—96; chief asst. dist. atty. 12th Jud. Cir. Ct., Ala., 1996—97, dist. atty., 1997—2002; judge US Dist. Ct. (mid. dist.) Ala., 2002—04, chief judge, 2004—11. Founder Coffee County Teen Court; bd. dir. Coffee County Habitat for Humanity. Chem. Biol. Engring. fellow, 2007, fellow, Ala. Law Found., 2003. Mem.: Ala. Def. Lawyers Assn., Coffee County Bar Assn., Ala. Bar Assn., ABA, Ala. State Rep. Exec. Com., Lions Club, Bench and Bar. Republican. Baptist. Office: US Dist Ct A300 Fed Courthouse Annex One Church St Montgomery AL 36104 Office Phone: 334-954-3640. E-mail: propord_fuller@almd.uscourts.gov.

FULLER, MELVIN STUART, botany educator; b. Livermore Falls, Maine, May 5, 1931; s. George Raymond and Hilda Gordon (Pike) F.; m. Barbara Paul Newman, Apr. 2, 1955; children: Erica Ann, Scott Eliot, Amy Elizabeth. BS, U. Maine, 1953; MS, U. Nebr., 1955; PhD, U. Calif., 1959; Master's ad eundum, Brown U., 1963. Instr. Brown U., 1959, asst. prof., 1960-63, assoc. prof., 1963-64; asst. prof. U. Calif., 1964-65, assoc. prof., 1965-68; prof. botany U. Ga., 1968—, head dept., 1968-73, 86-89, univ. prof., 1990—; vis. agrl. rsch. biologist Sandoz Ltd., Basel, Switzerland, 1983; vis. rsch. prof. U. Uppsala, Sweden, 1985, 86; adj. prof. botany U. Maine, 1992—; emeritus univ. prof. and emeritus prof. botany U. Ga., 1995—. Mem. editorial bd. for publs. in biology McGraw Hill; sec. 2d Internat. Mycol. Congress; organizer Fifth Internat. Fungus Spore Meeting, 1991. Author: The Science of Botany, 1962, Lower Fungi in the Laboratory, 1978, Zoosporic Fungi in Teach. and Research, 1987. Bd. dirs. DaPonte String Quartet, 2002—06. Fellow British Mycological Soc.; mem. Bot. Soc. Am., Mycol. Soc. Am. (counselor 1966-68, 70-72, pres. 1975, Disting. Mycologist Award, 1992), Soc. Study of Growth and Devel., Am. Phythopath. Soc., Gulf of Maine Found. (pres. 1997-99). Achievements include research on growth and development of aquatic fungi, ultrastructure, mechanism of action of fungicides. Home: 1 Kestrel Dr Topsham ME 04086-1725 Personal E-mail: msfuller1@gmail.com.

FULLER, SAMUEL ASHBY, retired lawyer, mining executive; b. Indpls., Sept. 2, 1924; s. John L.H. and Mary (Ashby) F.; m. Betty Winn Hamilton, June 10, 1948; children— Mary Cheryl Fuller Hargrove, Karen E. Fuller Wolfe, Deborah R. BS in Gen. Engring, U. Cin., 1946, JD, 1947; cert. fin. planner, Coll. for Fin. Planning, 1989. Bar: Ohio 1948, Ind. 1951, Fla. 1984. Cleve. claims rep. Mfrs. and Mchts. Indemnity Co., 1947-48; claims supr. Indemnity Ins. Co. N.Am., 1948-50; with firm Stewart, Irwin, Gilliom, Fuller & Meyer (formerly Murray, Mannon, Fairchild & Stewart), Indpls., 1950-85, Lewis Kappes Fuller & Eads (now Lewis & Kappes), Indpls., 1985-89; pres., dir. Irsugo Consol. Mines, Ltd., 1953-80; pres. Freedom Plz. Residents Assn. Coun., 2010—11. Dir. Ind. Pub. Health Found., Inc., 1972-84; staff instr. Purdue U. Life Ins. Mktg. Inst., 1954-61; instr. Am. Coll. Life Underwriters, Indpls., 1964-74; mem. Ind. State Bd. Law Examiners, 1984-96, treas. 1987-88. Bd. dirs. Southwest Social Centre, Inc., 1965-70; mem. Brookshire Homeowner's Assn., pres. 1973; pres., dir. Westminster Village North, Inc., 1981-89. Fellow: Am. Coll. Trust and Estate Counsel, Indpls. Bar Found.; mem.: Freedom Plaza Residents Assn. Coun. (pres. 2010—12), Internat. Assn. Ins. Counsel Rsch. Inst., Fla. Bar, 7th Cir. Bar Assn., Ind. State Bar Assn. (bd. mgrs. 1986—88), English Speaking Union, Ind. Pioneers Soc., Ctr. Ind. Bridge Assn. (pres. 1969), Mil. Order Loyal Legion US (recorder 1970—76, comdr. 1977—80), Masons, Beta Theta Pi. Republican. Roman Catholic. Personal E-mail: samuel105@tampabay.rr.com.

FULLERTON, CAROL, state legislator; m. Gregory L. Fullerton. Mem. Dist. #151 Ga. House of Reps., Ga., 2008—. Democrat. Office: Capitol Office 609 Coverdell Legislative Office Bldg Atlanta GA 30334 also: District Office 639 5th Ave Albany GA 31701 Office Phone: 404-656-0109, 229-883-3881. E-mail: carol.fullerton@house.ga.gov.

FULLINGIM, DWIGHT B., former oil industry executive; b. Memphis, Tex., May 7, 1944; m. Yvonne Butler, 1970; 1 child, Emily. BA in English, Tex. Tech U., 1966; attended, U. Tex. Austin, 1969—70. Publishing rep. Random House Knopf, 1971—72; publishing sales rep. Allyn and Bacon, 1972—73; asst. dir. comm. svcs. Coll. of Mainland, 1973—79; dir. corp. comm. Diamond Drilling Co., 1979—82, Cenergy Corp., 1982—84; pub. rels. cons. Fullingim & Associates, 1984—86; media rels. rep. Lone State Gas Co., 1986—90; sr. pub. affairs staff Saudi Aramco, 1990—2005. Mem. U. North Tex. Friends of the Libr., Adopt-a-Sch. program, St. Christopher's Episc. Ch. of Lubbock, Dallas Mayor's Com. to Hire the Handicapped. Officer, 1st lt. US Army, 1966—68. Mem.: Internat. Pub. Rels. Assn., Sons of Am. Revolution. Democrat. Episc. Office: 1302 Ave Q Lubbock TX 79401 Business E-Mail: dwight@dwight08.com.

FULLWOOD, EMERSON U., board member; B in Econ., NC State U.; MBA, Columbia U.; doctorate (hon.), NC A&T U. Held various sr. mgmt. and mktg. positions, nat. & internat. ops. Xerox Corp., corp. officer, pres., Xerox Worldwide Channels Group, pres., N.Am., exec. chief staff officer, Developing Markets, pres., Worldwide Customer Svcs., retired sr. exec. officer, sales rep., 1972, retired corp. v.p., 1996, retired exec. chief staff, mktg. officer, N.Am., 2004. Former bd. dirs. General Signal Corp.; bd. dirs. SPX Corp., 1998—, Vanguard Group, 2007—, Amerigroup Corp., 2009—. Bd. dirs. Boy Scouts America, Colgate Rochester Crozer Div. Sch., Monroe Cmty. Coll. Found., Rochester Urban League; active leader United Way Greater Rochester; former bd. dirs. Xerox Found. Named one of 75 Most Powerful African-Americans in Corp. America, Black Enterprise Mag., 2007. Office: AMERIGROUP Corp Bd Directors 4425 Corp Ln Ste 100 Virginia Beach VA 23462 Office Phone: 757-490-6900. Office Fax: 757-518-3600.

FULLWOOD, REGINALD, state legislator; b. Jacksonville, Fla., Apr. 4, 1975; BA in Comm., U. North Fla., 1997. Councilman Jacksonville City Coun., 1999—2007; nonprofit exec.; cons.; mem. Dist. 15 Fla. House of Representatives, 2011—. Democrat. Office: 101 E Union St Ste 402 Jacksonville FL 32202-2180 also: Fla House of Reps 1401 The Capitol 402 Monroe St Tallahassee FL 32399-1300 Office Phone: 904-353-2180, 850-488-7417.

FULP, JAMES ALAN, board member, finance company executive, securities firm executive; b. Kernersville, NC, July 11, 1951; s. Charles Lee and Doris (Allen) F.; m. Patricia Jane Withers, May 19, 1973 (div. Apr. 1984); children: Jonathan Charles, Brian Emory; m. Sally Jo Case, Dec. 4, 1984; 1 child, Casey Vance. BA in Economics, NC State U., 1973; MBA, Wake Forest U., 1975. Pres. JJB Hilliard, Louisville, WL Lyons, Inc., Louisville; comml. loan officer First Union Nat. Bank, Charlotte, N.C., 1975-78; v.p. Citizens Fidelity Bank and Trust, Louisville, 1978-81; pres. Hilliard-Lyons Equipment Mgmt., Inc., Louisville, 1981-84, Walnut St. Securities, Inc. (subs. of Life Ins. Co.), St. Louis, 1984-90; pres., fin. instns. divsn. Raymond James Financial Services, Inc. (formerly Investment Management & Research, Inc.), St. Peterburg, 1990—98; exec. v.p., mng. dir., Ind. Contractor Divsn. Raymond James Fin. Svcs. Bd. dirs. Raymond James Fin. Svcs. Mem. Internat. Assn. for Fin. Planning. Republican. Presbyterian. Avocations: tennis, sailing. Office: Raymond James Financial Services 880 Carillon Pky Saint Petersburg FL 33716-1100 Business E-Mail: james.fulp@raymondjames.com.

FULTON, MICHAEL (C. MICHAEL FULTON), lobbyist; m. Teresa Fulton; children: Amanda, Elizabeth. BS, W.Va. U., 1979. Aide to Rep. Robert H. Mollohan US House of Representatives; exec. v.p. GolinHarris, Arlington, Va. Bd. mem. Am. League of Lobbyists, Ctr. for Environmentally Advanced Technologies. Former mem. W.Va. U. Perley Isaac Reed Sch. Journalism Visiting Com. Mem.: Mountain Honorary. Office: GolinHarris 2200 Clarendon Blvd, #1100 Arlington VA 22201 Office Phone: 703-741-7500. Office Fax: 703-741-7501. E-mail: mfulton@golinharris.com.

FULTON, RICHARD T., lawyer; b. Pasadena, Calif., Aug. 30, 1948; BS in Economics, Fla. So. Coll., 1970; JD with high honors, U. Fla., 1977. Bar: Fla. 1977. Ptnr., bus. & real estate law Baker & Hostetler, Orlando, Fla., legal svcs. ptnr., former mem., policy com., former co-chair, nat. real estate practice group, former chair, Fla. real estate practice group, former chair, nat. bus. group. Former bd. mem. Orlando Regional Workforce Develop. Partnership, Inc.; former vice chmn. & bd. mem. Central Fla. Rsch. Park; former chmn. Metro Orlando Economic Develop. Commn. Found. for Edu., Metro Orlando Economic Develop. Commn., 2003—04; former bd. mem. downtown devel. bd. Cmty. Redevelopment Agy. Mem. ABA, Fla. Bar, Orange County Bar Assn. Office: Baker & Hostetler 200 S Orange Ave Ste 2300 Orlando FL 32801-3432 Home Phone: 407-578-2240; Office Phone: 407-649-4005. Office Fax: 407-841-0168. Business E-Mail: rfulton@bakerlaw.com.

FULWILER, ROBERT NEAL, oil industry executive; b. Belton, Tex., Nov. 5, 1937; s. Charles Calvin and Luella (Smith) F.; m. Sylvia Jean Marshall, Dec. 26, 1959; 1 child, Roger Neal. AA, Temple Jr. Coll., 1959; BBA, U. Tex., 1961. Statis. asst. Tex. Eastern Transmission Corp., Houston, 1961-62; adminstrv. asst. subs. LaGloria Oil & Gas, Houston, 1969-76, v.p., 1976; exec. v.p. La Jet, Inc., Houston, 1976-81, pres., 1981-82; chmn. bd. dirs. EnJet Inc., 1982-88; chief exec. officer Trend Energy, Houston, 1989—. Bd. dirs. BFC Assocs., Inc. Author: Competition and Growth in American Energy Markets, 1947-1985, 1968. Mem. Knights of Momus., Aspen Inst. (assoc.), Houston Mus. Fine Arts, Galveston Tex. Country Club. Republican. Mem. Ch. of Christ. Office: Trend Energy 5100 Westheimer Rd Ste 200 Houston TX 77056-5597

FUNDERBURK, LAURIE SLADE, state legislator; b. Camden, SC, Mar. 31, 1975; d. Larry and Betty Horton Slade; m. Harold Williams Funderburk, 1999. BA, U. SC, 1997, JD, 2001. Law clk. SC Senate Judiciary Com., 1990—99; commr. Planning & Zoning Commn., City of Camden, 2001—04; ptnr. Butcher & Funderburk PA, 2003—; mem. Dist. 52 SC House of Reps., 2004—. Mem.: Com. of 100, Kershaw County Bar Assn. (pres. 2004—), Fine Arts Ctr. Kershaw County (sec. 1999—). Democrat. Address: PO Box 188 Camden SC 29021 Office: 422 D Blatt Bldg Columbia SC 29201 Office Phone: 803-734-3044, 803-432-0188. Business E-Mail: funderburkl@scstatehouse.net.

FUNDORA, THOMAS, art director, artist; b. Havana, Cuba, Mar. 7, 1935; came to U.S., 1960; s. Evangelio and Juana Evangelina (Rodriguez) F.; m. Marlene Delgado, Feb. 10, 1954 (div. June 1957). Degree in art journalism, Candler Coll., 1953; degree in modern art and restoration, Escola Arte Bologna, Italy, 1961; student, Escuela San Alejandro, Havana, 1950. Dir. gen., dir. exhbns. Fundora Gallery, Miami, Fla. Pres., bd. dirs. Song Festival, N.Y.C., Internat. Song Festival, Trujillo, Internat. Song Festival, Chiclayo, Festival of Song, Buenos Aires, Internat. Song Festival, Viña del Mar, Miami, others; former sr. v.p. Record World, Internat. Music Rev. mag.; pub., editor USA 23 Millones, Miami. Author: Union Panamericana, Washington, 1959, Galeria Duneen Graham, NYC, 1959, Condon Relley Gallery, NY, 1959, Muestra Arquitectonica Neocolonial Colegio de Arquitectos, Havana, 1959, Emociones, 1963 (award 1964), Lo Mejor de Mi Vida, 1984, Inquietudes, 1988 (award 1990), Tu y Ellos, 1989; exhbns. include Lyceum de La Havana, 1949, Asociacion de Reporters, Havana, 1954, Galeria Gratacielo, Milan, 1961, Galeria del Canale, Venice, Los Grandes de Am., Hotel Woodstock, NY, 1964, Mamma Leones Art Show, NY, 1965 (Internat. Grand prize 1966), Glovier Club, NY, 1965, Hotel Turistas, Trujillo, Peru, 1965, IRT Art Exhibit, Bklyn., 1966 (medalla de plata), Internat. Exhibition Friends of P.R., NYC, 1967, Bienal de Sao Paulo, 1967, Roland de Aenlle Gallery, NY, 1967, Cayre Art Exhibit, 1968, Inst. Arte Latino, Washington, 1968, Inst. P.R., NY, 1969, Internat. Art Gallery, Miami, 1989, Strokes and Motion of Light and Matter, Miami, 1989-90, Martin's Art Gallery, Coral Gables, Fla., 1990, Catalina Art Gallery, Kendall, Fla., 1996, 98, Domingo Padron Art Gallery, Coral Gables, 1997, Frame USA Gallery, Kendall, 1997, Izzo's Artery Gallery, Chgo., 1998, 2001, Ocean Reef Art League, Key Largo, Fla., Estefan Enterprises, Inc., Bongos Cuban Cafe, Miami, 2002, One Ear Soc. Coconut Grove Gallery, 2003, Radisson Mart Plaza Hoter, 2004, Azweart Gallery, Coral Cables, Fla., 2005, Wachovia Bank, Key Largo, Fla., 2006, Strokes and Motion of Light and Matter, VIII, 2008, Gallery at Avalon Island Orlando, Fla, 2008. Named Artist of the Yr. Carteles Mag., 1967. Mem. Assn. Painters N.Y. (pres. 1969-73), Assn. Latin Am. Painters N.Y., Cir. Painters Miami, Monroe Coun. Arts (mem. adv. bd.), Fla. Artists Registry.com Republican. Avocations: fishing, boating, travel. Home: 100 Bahama Rd Key Largo FL 33037-4113 Office Phone: 305-852-1516. Personal E-mail: thomasfund@aol.com.

FUNK, GARY LLOYD, control engineer; b. Fairfax, Okla., Oct. 12, 1944; s. George N. and Maymie Lou Funk. BS, Rose Hulman Inst. Tech., 1966; MS, Purdue U., 1969; PhD, U. Pitts., 1974. Registered profl. engr., Olka., Tex. Rsch. engr. systems control divsn. Gulf Rsch. & Devel. Co., Harmarville, Pa., 1969-72, engr. exploration divsn. on systems and instrumentation, 1972-75; systems and control engr. Applied Automation subs. Phillips Petroleum Co., Bartlesville, Okla., 1975, mem. process tech. divsn., 1975-77, sr. process control engr. computer systems, 1977-83, prin. engr., 1983-87; mgr. process control application and simulation tech. combustion engring. Simcon, Houston, 1987-88; dir. advanced control tech. Brown & Root, USA, Inc., Houston, 1988-91; dir. computer integrated mfg. Cooper and Lybrand Mgmt. Consulting Svcs., Houston, 1991-92; v.p. Computer Integrated Mfg. Process Industry Systemhouse Inc., Houston, 1992—. Chief scientist, 1993-95, prin. cons., 1995—; prin. cons. Foxboro, 1997, prin. mgmt. cons., 1999—, chief cons., 1999-; adj. prof. U. Phoenix, 2000—. Contbr. over 140 articles to profl. jours.; 31 patents in field. Precinct chmn. Dem. Com., 1981. Mem. Okla. Soc. Profl. Engrs. (v.p. 1980-81, 82-83), IEEE, AIChE (treas. mgmt. divsn. 1995, 96, 97, pres. chpt. 1983-84), Nat. Soc. Profl. Engrs., Tex. Soc. Profl. Engrs.,

ISA (nat. dir. automatic control divsn. 1996, 97, 98, nat. dir. robotic and expert sys. divsn., mem. tech. chmn. and pubs. bd. 1999—), Jaycees, Masons, Moose, Elks, Kiwanis. Presbyterian. Office Phone: 918-642-5705. E-mail: g.funk@ieee.org.

FUNK KOBLE, VICKI, librarian; b. Frankfurt am Main, Hesse, Federal Republic of Germany, Apr. 7, 1951; d. George N. and Maymie Lou Funk; m. David Robert Koble, July 11, 1986. BS, Ind. State U., 1971; MLS, Okla. U., 1975; cert. in comparative libraries, Oxford U., Eng., Summer 1978; cert. in Scottish lit., St. Andrews U., Scotland, Summer 1985. Elem. open concept team tchr. Plainfield (Ind.) Pub. Schs., 1971-72; media specialist, tchr. elem. schs. Enid (Okla.) Pub. Schs., 1972-73, librarian, 1973—75; libr. media specialist Bartlesville (Okla.) Sr. H.S., 1975-96. Chmn. library evaluation teams North Cen. Assn., Okla., 1982-86; pres. V.I.E.W. adv. bd. Okla. State Dept. Vocat. Edn., 1980-81; tchr. pub. library continuing adult edn. program, Bartlesville, 1986, social studies methods instr. Okla. Weslyan U., 2005 Storyteller Ednl. TV Bartlesville Cable, 1975-77, Oral Children's Program Pub. Library, 1985-86; book reviewer Okla. State Dept. Libraries "Gushers and Dusters", 1986-87; mem. book rev. selection com. Bartlesville Pub. Library. V.P. Friends of the Pub. Library, Bartlesville, 1986. Recipient Outstanding Svc. award Okla. Dept. Vocat. Edn., 1981; Emiline Libr. scholar Ind. State U., 1970; Innovative Edn. grantee Bartlesville Pub. Edn. Found., 1990, 91. Mem. NEA, AAUW (edn. officer 1980-81), Okla. Edn. Assn., Bartlesville Edn. Assn., Bartlesville Art Assn., Okla. Libr. Assn., Kappa Kappa Iota (v.p. 1990-91, secd. 1996-98). Democrat. Presbyterian. Avocations: bridge, travel, skiing, acting, painting.

FURGESON, WILLIAM ROYAL, JR., federal judge; b. Lubbock, Tex., Dec. 9, 1941; s. W. Royal and Mary Alyene (Hardwick) F.; m. Marion McElroy, Aug. 15, 1964 (div.); m. Juli Ann Bernat, July 29, 1973 (div.); children: Kelly Lynn, Houston, Joshua, Seth, Jill; m. Marcellene Malouf, July 5, 2003. BA in English, Tex. Tech Coll., 1964; JD with honors, U. Tex., 1967. Bar: Tex. 1969, U.S. Dist. Ct. (we. dist.) Tex. 1971, U.S. Ct. Appeals (5th cir.) 1974, U.S. Supreme Ct. 1976. Law clk. to presiding judge U.S. Dist. Ct. for No. Dist. Tex., 1969-70; ptnr. Kemp, Smith, Duncan & Hammond, El Paso, Tex., 1970-94; judge US Dist. Ct. (we. dist.) Tex., Midland/Odessa, 1994—2003, San Antonio, 2003—08, sr. judge, 2008—. Gen. campaign chmn. El Paso United Way, 1979, 1st v.p., 1980, pres., 1981; mem. Jewish Fedn., El Paso, 1980-86; trustee Baylor U. Coll. Dentistry, 1982-86; chmn. YWCA Capital Devel. Campaign, 1986-87. Served to capt. U.S. Army, 1967-69 Decorated Bronze Star; recipient Service award Social Workers of El Paso, 1982, Faculty award U. Tex. Law Sch., 1983, Dean Leon Green award Tex. Law Review, 2001, Jurist of Yr., Tex. Am. Bd. of Trial Advocates, 2004, Outstanding Alumnus, Tex. Tech. U., Lubbock, Tex., 2007. Mem. El Paso Bar Assn. (pres. 1982-83, Outstanding Young Lawyer award 1972), Am. Law Inst., U. Tex. Law Sch. Assn. (pres. 1978), U. Tex. Law Rev. Assn. (pres. 1982-83), El Paso Legal Assistance Soc. (bd. dirs. 1972-78), NCCJ (chmn. El Paso region 1980), ABA, Fed. Bar Assn. (pres. West Tex. chpt. 1987), Am. Law Inst., Tex. Bar Assn. (sec., treas., chair anti-trust and trade regulation sect. 1985-86), Am. Bar Found., Tex. Bar Found. Democrat. Jewish. Office: US Dist Ct 1100 Commerce St Rm 1359 Dallas TX 75242-1001 Office Phone: 210-472-6570, 214-753-2355. Business E-Mail: royal_furgeson@txwd.uscourts.gov.

FURLAUD, RICHARD MORTIMER, pharmaceutical executive; b. NYC, Apr. 15, 1923; s. Maxime Hubert and Eleanor (Mortimer) F.; children: Richard Mortimer, Eleanor Jay, Elizabeth Tamsin; m. Isabel Phelps Furlaud. Student, Institut Sillig, Villars, Switzerland; AB, Princeton U., 1944; LLB, Harvard U., 1947. Bar: NY 1949. Assoc. Root, Ballantine, Harlan, Bushby & Palmer, 1947-51; with legal dept. Olin Mathieson Chem. Corp., 1955-56, asst. to exec. v.p. for finance, 1956-57, asst. pres., 1957-59, v.p., 1959-64, gen. counsel, 1957-60, gen. mgr., v.p. internat. div., 1960-64, exec. v.p., 1964-66, now dir., 1964-94; pres., dir. E. R. Squibb & Sons, Inc., 1966-68; pres., chief exec., dir. Squibb Beech-Nut, Inc. (renamed Squibb Corp. 1971), Princeton, NJ, 1968-74; chmn., chief exec., dir. Squibb Corp. (merged with Bristol-Myers Co.), NYC, 1974-89; pres., bd. dirs. Bristol-Myers Co. (renamed Bristol-Myers Squibb Co.), NYC, 1989-91. Mem. profl. staff Ho. of Reps. Com. Ways and Means, 1954; chmn. emeritus Rockefeller U. 1st lt. JAGC U.S. Army, 1951-53. Mem. Assn. Bar City of N.Y., Coun. on Fgn. Rels., River Club. Home: 745 HiMount Rd Palm Beach FL 33480 Office: 8th Fl West 777 S Flagler Dr West Palm Beach FL 33401 Home Phone: 561-848-2267; Office Phone: 561-515-6016. Personal E-mail: ternaboutx@aol.com.

FURLONG, GEORGE MORGAN, JR., museum program director, retired military officer; b. Muskogee, Okla., Nov. 23, 1931; s. George M. and Anna (Moore) F.; m. Ryland Hagood Blakey, June 5, 1956; children: Morgan, William. BS in Naval Sci., U.S. Naval Acad., 1956; BS in Aero. Engring., U.S. Naval Postgrad. Sch., 1963. Commd. ensign U.S. Navy, 1956, advanced through grades to rear adm. (upper half), 1981; F-14 program mgr. Comdr. Naval Air Forces, U.S. Pacific Fleet, 1973-74; wing comdr. Attack Carrier Air Wing 14, USS Enterprise, 1974-75; comdg. officer USS Ponchatoula, Pearl Harbor, Hawaii, 1975-76, USS Independence, Norfolk, Va., 1977-78; chief of staff U.S. Sixth Fleet, Gaeta, Italy, 1978-80; dir. Air Warfare Systems Analysis Staff, Office Chief of Naval Ops., Washington, 1980-81; comdr. Fighter Airborne Early Warning Wing. U.S. Pacific Fleet, Naval Air Sta., Miramar, San Diego, 1981-83; dep. chief Naval Edn. and Tng., Pensacola, Fla., 1983-85; ret., 1986; exec. v.p. Naval Aviation Mus. Found., Pensacola, 1986-96; dir. devel. Bapt. Health Care Found., Pensacola, 1997—2001; cons. Naval Aviation Mus. Found., 2001—06. Deocorated Legion of Merit with gold star; recipient John Paul Jones award Nat. Navy League Assn., 1971 Home Phone: 850-475-0067; Office Phone: 850-475-0064. Personal E-mail: skipone@aol.com.

FURLOW, MICHAEL H., construction company executive; BA with honors in Acctg., U. West Fla. CPA. CPA Arthur Young & Co.; pres. Ctrl. Fla. Divsn. Pulte Home Corp.; exec. v.p. ops. Beazer Homes USA, Inc., Atlanta, 1997—2009, COO, 1998—2009, divsn. pres. Charleston, Myrtle Beach and Savannah, 2009—. Office: Beazer Homes USA Inc 1000 Abernathy Rd Atlanta GA 30328 E-mail: mh.furlow@beazer.com.

FURMAN, HOWARD, arbitrator, lawyer, mediator; b. Newark, Nov. 30, 1938; s. Emanuel and Lilyan (Feldman) F.; m. Elaine Sheitleman, June 12, 1960 (div. 1982); children: Deborah Toby, Naomi N'chama, David Seth; m. Janice Wheeler, Jan. 14, 1984. BA in Econs., Rutgers U., 1966; JD cum laude, Birmingham Sch. Law, 1985. Bar: Ala. 1985, U.S. Dist. Ct. (no. dist.) Ala. 1986, U.S. Dist. Ct. (so. dist.) Ala. 1996. Designer/draftsman ITT, Nutley, NJ, 1957-61; pers. mgr. Computer Products Inc., Belmar, NJ, 1962-64, Arde Engring. Co., Newark, 1964-66; econs. instr. Rutgers U., New Brunswick, NJ, 1966-74; dir. indsl. rels. Harvard Ind. Frequency Engring. Labs. Divsn., Farmingdale, NJ, 1966-74; commr. Fed. Mediation and Conciliation Svc., Birmingham, Ala., 1974-96; pvt. practice Birmingham, 1985—. Instr. bus. law Jefferson State C.C., 1989-95; instr. human resources mgmt. Nova U., 1993; prof. personal property, adminstrv. law, sales and alternative dispute resolution Birmingham Sch. Law, 1993—2005. Pres. Ocean Twp. (NJ) Police Res., 1968. Recipient ofcl. commendation Fed. Mediation and Conciliation Svc., 1979, 81-82, 88. Mem. ABA, Ala. Bar Assn., Birmingham Bar Assn., Soc. Profls. in Dispute Resolution, Fed. Soc. Labor Rels. Profls., Indsl. Rels. Rsch. Assn., Sigma Delta Kappa. Jewish. Office Phone: 205-969-5598. Personal E-mail: hfesq1@gmail.com.

FURNAD, BOB (VASIL ROBERT FURNAD), retired broadcast executive; b. 1941; BA in Radio/TV, American U., 1967. Film editor, floor dir. Sta. WMAL-TV, Washington, 1961—64, assoc. prodr, dir., 1963—64; radio engineer ABC News, 1964—65, film editor, 1965—68; production mgr. WSWO-TV, Ohio, 1968—69; assignment editor ABC News, 1969—73, field prodr., 1973—76, sr. prodr. GMA News, 1964—83; sr. prodr. World News Tonight Disney ABC Television Group, 1977—80; political dir. CNN, 1983—84; exec. v.p., sr. exec. prodr. CNN USA, 1984—97; pres. CNN Headline News Network, 1997—2001; cons. Intelligent Media Consultants, 2002—06; assoc. prof. broadcast news writing & producing U. Ga., 2009—11. Vis. assoc. prof. U. Ga. Grady Sch. Journalism, 2002—05. Chmn. FaithWorks Christian Fellowship, 2005—10. Recipient George Foster Peabody award, Acad. for cable Excellence Golden-ACE, Emmy award, Overseas Press Club award, Alfred I. duPont award.

FURST, ALEX JULIAN, thoracic and cardiovascular surgeon; b. Augusta, Ga., Aug. 21, 1938; m. George Alex and Ann (Segall) F.; m. Elayne Kobrin, Aug. 11, 1962; children: James Andrew, Jeffrey Michael, Joseph Robert. Student, U. Fla., 1963; MD, U. Miami, 1967. Intern U. Miami Hosp., 1967-68, resident, 1968-72, clin. instr. dept. surgery, 1974-91; chief resident in thoracic and cardiovascular surgery Emory U. Hosp., Atlanta, 1972-73, sr. surg. registrar of thoracic unit, 1972-73, Hosp. for Sick Children, London, 1973-74; practice medicine specializing in thoracic and cardiovascular surgery Miami, Fla.; clin. assoc. prof. surgery and cardiology, chief surg. svc. Miami VA Med. Ctr., 1991—2003, clin. prof., surgery and medicine, chief of surgery; chief surgeon West Palm Beach Med. Ctr., Va., 2000—02; sr. cons. dept. surgery Miami Va Med. Ctr., 2005—. Chief thoracic surgery, pres. med. staff Mercy Hosp.; mem. staff Bapt. Hosp., South Miami Hosp., Doctor's Hosp. (all Miami), North Ridge Gen. Hosp., Ft. Lauderdale; program dir. cardiothoracic surgery U. Miami Sch. of Medicine, 1998-2000. Fellow ACS, Am. Coll. Cardiology, Am. Coll. Chest Physicians; mem. Dade County Med. Assn., Fla. Med. Assn., Heart Assn. Greater Miami, Soc. Thoracic Surgeons, So. Thoracic Surg. Assn. Home: 8802 Arvida Dr Miami FL 33156-2302 Office Phone: 305-575-3157.

FURST, E. KENNETH, financial executive; b. Newark, Oct. 11, 1946; m. Anna Stathis. BS in Econs., U. Pa., 1968, MS in Acctg., 1969. CPA, N.J. V.p. fin. Sea-Land Corp., Edison, NJ, 1971—89; CFO, dir., owner Toledo, Peoria & We. Railway, Ill., 1989—96; CFO, v.p. Golden Eagle Network, Bethel, Conn., 1996—97; owner E. Kenneth Furst, CPA, Short Hills, NJ, 1982—; v.p. RBC Dain Rauscher, Florham Park, 1988—2006; sr. v.p. investments Stifel Nicolaus, 2006—. Chair U. Pa. Secondary Sch. Com., Essex County; past pres., trustee NJ Soc. CPAs-Essex; vice chair Borough Planning Bd., Roseland, NJ. Mem. N.J. Soc. CPA (trustee 1997-2000, pres. Essex chpt. 1995-96), Ct. Apptd. Spl. Adv. (trustee 2000-2005, treas. 2000-03), U. Pa. Club Metro. N.J. (pres. 1995-96, trustee 1971—). Office Phone: 561-982-2652. Business E-Mail: kenneth.furst@stifel.com, ekfurst@alumni.upenn.edu.

FURST, ERIC JONATHAN, physician, surgeon; b. NYC, Dec. 11, 1957; s. Robert Irving and Selmo Barbara Furst; m. Ann Louise Sterling, May 29, 1984; children: Julie, Nicole. BS in Zoology, U. Mass., Amherst, 1980, MS in Pub. Health, 1982; MD, Baylor U., Houston, 1986. Diplomate Am. Bd. Otolaryn. Surgery. Attending physician/surgeon Falls Church Med. Ctr., Va., 1992—95; pvt. practice Springfield, Va., 1995—. Bd. dirs. Congl. Schs. Va., Falls Church, 1993—. Named one of Washington's Top Drs., Washington Mag., 2002, 2005, 2008. Fellow: Va. Soc. Otolaryngology, No. Va. Med. Soc., Am. Acad. Otolaryngology. Avocations: jazz, piano, golf, tennis, scuba diving. Office: 5504 Backlick Rd Springfield VA 22151

FURUBOTN, EIRIK GRUNDTVIG, economics professor; b. NYC, Apr. 18, 1923; s. Konrad Martin and Caroline (Grundtvig) F.; m. Florence Birkby Duckworth; children: Karin Florence, Erik Grundtvig, Kristian George BA, Brown U., 1948; MA, Columbia U., 1950, PhD, 1959. Instr. Wesleyan U., Middletown, Conn., 1953-55; asst. prof. Lafayette Coll., Easton, Pa., 1958-60; assoc. prof. Emory U., Atlanta, 1960-63; prof. SUNY, Binghamton, 1963-67, Tex. A&M U., College Station, 1967-82; James L. West prof. econs. U. Tex., Arlington, 1982-96; rsch. fellow pvt. enterprise rsch. ctr. Tex. A&M U., College Station, 1996—. Com. mem. Tex. A&M Univ. Press, College Station, 1974-82; co-dir. Ctr. for Study of New Instl. Econs., U. Saarland, W.Ger., 1986—; mem. bd. advs. Utrecht Sch. Econs., Utrecht U., Netherlands, 2002. Co-author: (with R. Richter) Neue Institutionen Okonomik, 1996, 4th edit.2010, (with R. Ekeland and P. Gramm) The Evolution of Modern Demand Theory, 1972; co-editor: The Economics of Property Rights, 1974, The New Institutional Economics: An Assessment, 1991, (with R. Richter) Institutions and Economic Theory, 1997, 2nd edit., 2005, also Russian, German and Chinese transls., (with R. Richter) The New Institutional Economics of Markets, 2010; mem. editl. bd. Applied Econs., London, 1971-72; mem. bd. editors So. Econ. Jour., 1979-81, Zeitschrift fur die gesamte Staatswissenschaft, 1984—2011. Trustee Allen Acad., Bryan, Tex., 1974-76; mem. adv. coun. Polit. Economy Rsch. Ctr., Bozeman, Mont., 1984-92; mem. nat. adv. bd. Nat. Ctr. for Privatization, Wichita, Kans., 1985-95. Cpl. U.S. Army, 1942-46, ETO. Francis Wayland scholar Brown U., 1948; named Honorarprofessor für Volkswirtschaftslehre U. Saarland, Fed. Republic of Germany. Mem. Am. Econ. Assn., So. Econ. Assn. (exec. com. 1975-77), Kürschners Deutscher Gelehrten-Kalender, Phi Beta Kappa, Omicron Delta Epsilon, Beta Gamma Sigma, Omega Rho. Republican. Episcopalian. Avocations: antiques, travel. Home: 750 N Rosemary Dr Bryan TX 77802-4307 Office: Tex A&M U Pvt Enterprise Rsch Ctr PO Box 3327 College Station TX 77841-3327 Office Phone: 979-845-7722. Personal E-mail: eirik@furobotn.com. Business E-Mail: perc@tamu.edu.

FURYK, JIM (JAMES MICHAEL FURYK), professional golfer; b. West Chester, Pa., May 12, 1970; m. Tabitha Furyk; children: Caleigh Lynn, Tanner James. Grad. in Gen. Bus., U. Ariz., 1992. Profl. golfer PGA, 1992—. Mem. US team Ryder Cup, 1997, 1999, 2002, 2004, 2006, 2008, 2010, 2012, Presidents Cup, 1998, 2000, 2003, 2005, 2007, 2009, 2011, World Cup, 2003. Winner Nike Miss. Gulf Coast Classic, 1993, Las Vegas Internat., 1995, United Airlines Hawaiian Open, 1996, Argentine Open, 1997, Las Vegas Invitational, 1998, Fred Meyer Challenge, 1998, Doral-Ryder Open, 2000, Mercedes Championship, 2000, Memorial Tournament, 2002, US Open Championship, 2003, Buick Open, 2003, Western Open, 2005, Wachovia Championship, 2006, Canadian Open, 2006, 07, Nedbank Golf Challenge, 2006, Transitions Championship, 2010, Verizon Heritage, 2010, Tour Championship, 2010. Achievements include being a member of the Ryder Cup winning US team, 2008; winning the FedEx Cup, 2010. Avocation: sports. Office: c/o PGA America Box 109601 100 Ave of Champions Palm Beach Gardens FL 33410

FUSCO, ANDREW G., lawyer; b. Punxsutawney, Pa., Jan. 11, 1948; s. Albert G. and Virginia N. (Whitesell) F.; m. Deborah K. Lucas; children: Matthew, Geoffrey, David. BS in Bus. Adminstrn. and Fin., W.Va. U., 1970, JD, 1973. Bar: W.Va. 1973, US Ct. Appeals (4th cir.) 1974, US Supreme Ct. 1977, US Ct. Appeals (fed. cir.) 1985, US Tax Ct. 1995, US Ct. Appeals (9th cir.), 2003. Pvt. practice, Morgantown, W.Va., 1973-85; prin. Fusco & Newbraugh, L.C., Morgantown, 1985-98, The Fusco Legal Group, L.C., Morgantown, 1998-2001; mem. Eckert Seamans Cherin & Mellott, LLC, 2001—08; ptnr. Bowles,Rice, McDavid,Graff & Love LLP, 2008—. Pros. atty. Monongalia County, W.Va., 1977—81; instr. Coll. Bus. and Econs., Law Ctr., W.Va. U., 1975—76, W.Va. U. Sch. Journalism, 1997—2003. Author: Antitrust Law (West Virginia Practice Handbook), 1991; editor, contbg. author: Twenty Feet From Glory (John R. Goodwin), 1970, Business Law (John R. Goodwin), 1972, Beyond Baker Street (Michael Harrison), 1976; gen. editor Baker Street Irregulars Manuscript Series, 2006—. Bd. dirs. W.Va. Career Colls., 1971-76; profl. adv. bd. Childbirth and Parent Edn. Assn., 1975-82, Rape and Domestic Violence Info. Ctr., 1977-81; mem. W.Va. Sec. State's Tribunal on Election Reform, 1977-81; chmn. Monongalia County Drug Edn. Task Force, 1978-80; bd. advisors Nat. Smokers Alliance, 1998-99; vis. com. W.Va. U. Coll. Law, 2000-03. Recipient Am. Jurisprudence award Bancroft-Whitney Publ. Co., 1971; named Outstanding Young Man of Morgantown, 1979. Mem. ABA (bus. torts, civil RICO com., antitrust law sect.), Monongalia County Bar Assn., W.Va. State Bar, Sherlock Holmes Soc. London, Bootmakers of Toronto, Baker St. Irregulars, Sons of Italy, W.Va. Law Sch. Assn., Monongalia Arts Ctr. (pres., treas., vice-chmn., trustee). Democrat. Roman Catholic. Home: 2054 Iron Bridge Cir Morgantown WV 26508 Office: Bowles Rice McDavid Graff & Love LLP 7000 Hampton Ctr Morgantown WV 26505-1720 Home Phone: 304-594-2412; Office Phone: 304-285-2500. Office Fax: 304-285-2575. Business E-Mail: afusco@bowlesrice.com.

FUSELIER, HAROLD ANTHONY, JR., urologist, director, educator; b. Abbeville, La., Dec. 1, 1942; s. Harold Anthony and May Elizabeth (Fowler) F.; m. Ann Valentino, May 17, 1968; children: Harold Anthony III, F. Scott, J. Prentice, Mims Michael. BS, La. State U., Baton Rouge, 1964; MD, La. State U., New Orleans, 1967. Diplomate Am. Bd. Urology. Internship Charity Hosp., New Orleans, 1967-68; residency urology Alton Ochsner Medical Found., 1970-74; mem. dept. urology Ochsner Clinic Found., New Orleans, 1974—2008, chmn. dept. urology, 1989—2002; med. dir. surgery Ochsner Found. Hosp., New Orleans, 1990—2006; clin. prof. urology Tulane U. Med. Ctr., New Orleans, 1988—, La. State U. Med. Ctr., New Orleans, 1990—2008; prof., urology La. State U. Health Sci. Ctr., 2008—. Program dir. La. State U./Ochsner Urology Tng. Program, 1991-2005. Contbr. articles to profl. jours. Capt. USAF, 1968-70. Fellow ACS; mem. Am. Urol. Assn., Soc. Internat. d'Urologie, Soc. for Study of Impotence, Soc. Univ. Urologists. Roman Catholic. Avocations: golf, hunting, fishing. Office: La State Univ Health Sci Ctr 1542 Tulane Ave Rm 547 New Orleans LA 70112 Office Phone: 504-568-2207. Business E-Mail: hfusel@lsuhsc.edu.

FUSTÉ, JOSÉ ANTONIO, federal judge; b. San Juan, Nov. 3, 1943; BBA, U. P.R., San Juan, 1965, LLB cum laude, 1968. Ptnr. Jimenez & Fuste, Hato Rey, P.R., 1968-85; judge US Dist. Ct. PR, San Juan, 1985—, chief judge, 2004—11. Prof. U. P.R., 1975—85, 1996—2002. Office: US Courthouse CH-133 150 Ave Carlos Chardon San Juan PR 00918-1758 Office Phone: 787-772-3120.*

FUTRELL, JOHN WILLIAM, environmental agency executive, lawyer; b. Alexandria, La., July 6, 1935; s. J.W. and Sarah Ruth (Hitesman) F.; m. Iva Macdonald, Aug. 13, 1966; children: Sarah, Daniel. BA, Tulane U., 1957; postgrad., Free U. Berlin, 1958; LLB, Columbia U., 1965. Bar: La. 1966. Atty. Lemle & Kelleher, New Orleans, 1966-71; prof. law U. Ala., 1971-74, U. Ga., 1974-80; pres. Environ. Law Inst., Washington, 1980—2003, Sustainable Devel. Law Assocs., Arlington, Va., 2003—. Lectr. USIA, Japan and India, 1978, Austria, 1979, Sweden, Germany, U.K. and Ireland, 1980, Argentina, 1988, Brazil, 1991, 92, 2004, Mex., 1992, Germany and Chile, 1993, India, 1997, 2000; Woodrow Wilson fellow Smithsonian Instn., Washington, 1978-80. Co-author: Sustainable Environmental Law, 1993. Del. UN Conf. on Water, 1977, White House Conf. Inflation, 1974. Capt. USMC, 1957-62. Recipient Chair's award, Natural Resources Coun. Am., 2005, Career Devel. award, 2008; scholar, Fulbright, 1958. Mem.: ABA (Disting. Achievement award 2004), Am. Law Inst., Sierra Club (nat. bd. dirs. 1971—81, pres. 1977—78, hon. v.p. 2002—), Cosmos Club, Marines' Meml. Club, Phi Beta Kappa, Order of Coif. Office: Sustainable Devel Law Assocs 4600 7th St N Arlington VA 22203 Office Phone: 703-522-0247. E-mail: sdla2003@aol.com.

FYFE, ALISTAIR IAN, cardiologist, scientist, educator; b. Hobart, Tasmania, Australia, Sept. 5, 1960; came to U.S., 1991; s. Ian John and Merrill Millicent (Faragher) F.; children: Alexander Jonathan, Calista Madison, Ethan Alexander. B of Med. Sci., U. Tasmania, 1980, B of Med. Sci. with honors, 1981, MBBS, 1984; PhD in Molecular Biology, UCLA, 1995; MBA, U. Oxford, 2013—. Diplomate Am. Bd. Internal Medicine and Cardiovasc. Disease. Intern Royal Hobart Hosp., 1985-86; resident in internal medicine U. B.C., Vancouver, Can., 1986-89; cardiology fellow U. Toronto, Ont., Can., 1989-91; cardiac rsch. fellow UCLA, 1991-95, asst. prof. medicine and cardiology, 1995-99, dir. Ctr. for Cholesterol and Lipid Mgmt., 1995-98, assoc. mem. Molecular Biology Inst., 1996-98; cardiologist Heart Place, Dallas, 1999—2000, Dallas Heart Group, 2000—04; founder Cardiac Assocs. Dallas, 2004—; dir. primary and secondary cardiac prevention Med. City, Dallas, 2004—. Author: (with others) Progress in Pediatric Cardiology, 1993; contbr. articles to profl. jours. Recipient Fellowship Clinician Scientist award Med. Rsch. Coun., Can., 1992. Fellow Royal Coll. Physicians Can., Am. Coll. Cardiology, Coun. Arterial Sclerosis; mem. Internat. Heart Transplant Soc., Am. Heart Assn. (fellow arteriosclerosis coun., reviewer 1993—, Young Investigator award, 1993, 95), Am. Soc. Clin. Investigation, Am. Diabetes Assn. Achievements include first demonstration of genetic modification of solid organ transplants, cardiac services to Christmas Island Kiribati. Office: Cardiac Assocs Dallas 7777 Forest Ln Ste C 655 Dallas TX 75230-2500 Office Phone: 972-566-8474. Business E-Mail: afyfe@cadmd.com.

GABARRO, JOHN JOSEPH, organizational behavior and business administration educator; b. Worcester, Mass., Aug. 29, 1939; s. Rafael and Joaquina (Canet) Gabarro-Llobel; m. Marilyn Ann Peters, Nov. 18, 1967; children: Jana Pilar, Juan-Carlos. BS, Worcester Poly. Inst., 1961; MBA, Harvard U., 1967, DBA, 1972. Plant process engr. Gen. Foods Corp., Orange, Mass., 1961; devel. engr., project leader Corning Glass Works, Bradford, Pa., 1963-65; research fellow Harvard Business School, Boston, 1970-72, asst. prof., 1972-75, assoc. prof., 1975-79, prof. organizational behavior and bus. adminstrn., 1979-90, chmn. organizational behavior and human resources mgmt., 1987-91, UPS Found. prof. human resource mgmt., 1990—. Cons. govtl. agys., founds., bus. orgns., U.S., Europe; mem. acad. adv. com. Instituto de Estudios Superiores de Empresa, U. Navarra, Spain, 1984—. bd. dirs. Watson Wyatt Worldwide, Inc., 1999- Co-author: Interpersonal Behavior, 1978, Teaching Interpersonal Behavior, 1978, Managing Behavior in Organizations, 1983; author: The Dynamics of

Taking Charge, 1987, Managing People and Organizations, 1992. Trustee Worcester Poly. Inst., 1987—, Am. Inst. Managing Diversity, 1992—. 1st lt. U.S. Army, 1961-63. Foote, Cone and Belding fellow Harvard U., 1967; Harvard Dissertation fellow, 1969; recipient Harvard Bus. Rev. prize McKinsey Found., 1981, Best of Bus. Articles citation Xerox Co., 1981, New Directions in Leadership prize Johnson Smith Knisely Found., 1988. Mem. Acad. Mgmt. (mem. steering com. on careers and socialization 1983-87), Organizational Behavior Teaching Soc. (dir. 1977-80, chmn. Fritz J. Roethlisberger award com. 1984-87), Am. Sociol. Assn. Clubs: Pennhills, Harvard Faculty, Stage Harbor Yacht. Episcopalian. Home: 8 Monadnock Rd Arlington MA 02476-8001 Office: Watson Wyatt Worldwide Inc 901 N Glebe Rd Arlington VA 22203 Office Phone: 703-258-8000. Office Fax: 703-258-8585.

GABBARD, GLEN OWENS, psychiatrist, psychotherapist; b. Charleston, Ill., Aug. 8, 1949; s. Earnest Glendon and Lucina Mildred (Paquet) G.; children: Matthew, Abigail, Amanda, Allison; m. Joyce Eileen Davidson, June 14, 1985. BS, Eastern Ill. U., 1972; MD, Rush Med. Coll., 1975; degree in psychoanalytic tng., Topeka Inst. for Psychoanalysis, 1984. Diplomate Am. Bd. Psychiatry and Neurology. Resident in psychiatry Menninger Sch. Psychiatry, Topeka, 1975-78, mem. faculty, 1978—; staff psychiatrist C.F. Menninger Hosp., Topeka, 1978-83, sect. chief, 1984-89. Med. dir., 1989-94; tng. analyst Topeka Inst. for Psychoanalysis, 1989-2001, dir., 1996-2001; v.p. for adult svcs. Menninger Clinic, 1991-94; clin. prof. psychiatry U. Kans. Med. Sch., 1991-2001; Callaway Disting. prof. Menninger Clinic and Karl Menninger Sch. Psychiatry, 1994-2001; prof. psychiatry Baylor Coll. Medicine, 2001—, Brown Found. chair psychoanalysis, 2003—. Author: With the Eyes of the Mind, 1984, Psychiatry and the Cinema, 1987, 2d edit., 1999, Medical Marriages, 1988, Sexual Exploitation in Professional Relationships, 1989, Psychodynamic Psychiatry in Clinical Practice, 1990, Portuguese transl., 1992, Italian transl., 1992, 2d edit., 1994, Korean transl., 1996, Japanese transl., 1997, 4th edit., 2005, Treatments of Psychiatric Disorders: the DSM-IV Edition, 1995; meml. editl. bd. Am. Jour. Psychiatry, Am. Psychiat. Press; joint editor-in-chief Internat. Jour. Psychoanalysis; contbr. articles to profl. jours. V.p. Topeka Civic Theatre, 1981-82, pres. 1982-83, bd. dirs. 1981-83. Named one of Outstanding Young Men in Am. U.S. Jaycees, 1984. Mem. AAAS, Am. Psychoanalytic Assn. (assoc. editor jour., mem. editl. bd.), Am. Psychiat. Assn. (Falk fellow 1976, Edward A. Strecker award 1994, Disting. Psychiatrist lectr. 1995, C. Charles Burlingame award 1997, Mary S. Sigourney award 2000, Disting. Svc. award 2002, Adolf Meyer award 2004), Sch. Psychotherapy Rsch., Menninger Sch. Psychiatry Alumni Assn. (pres. 1982-83), Alpha Omega Alpha. Avocations: theater, music. Home: 1290 Jimmy Phillips Blvd Angleton TX 77515 Office: Dept Psychiatry Baylor Coll Medicine One Baylor Plz MS 350 Houston TX 77030 Office Phone: 713-798-6397. Business E-Mail: ggabbard@bcm.tmc.edu.

GABEL, GEORGE DESAUSSURE, JR., lawyer; b. Jacksonville, Fla., Feb. 14, 1940; s. George DeSaussure and Juanita (Brittain) G.; m. Judith Kay Adams, July 21, 1962; children: Laura Gabel Hartman, Meredith Gabel Harris. AB, Davidson Coll., 1961; JD, U. Fla., 1964. Bar: Fla. 1964, D.C. 1972. With Toole, Taylor, Moseley, Gabel & Milton, Jacksonville, Fla., 1966—74, Gabel & Hair (formerly Wahl & Gabel), Jacksonville, 1974—98; ptnr., mem. dirs. com. Holland & Knight, Jacksonville, 1998—2001, exec. ptnr., 2002—06, dep. sect. leader litigation sect., 2007—. Mem. Fla. Jud. Nominating Commn., 4th cir., 1982-86.; del. to the Comit-é Maritime Internat. Confs. Sydney, Antwerp, Singapore, Vancouver, Dubrovnik. Pres. Willing Hands, Inc., 1971-72; chmn. N.E. Fla. March of Dimes, 1974-75; mem. budget com. United Way, 1972-74, chmn. rev. com., 1976; bd. dirs. Ctrl. and So. brs. YMCA, 1973-79, Camp Immokalee, 1982-86; elder Riverside Presbyn. Ch., 1970-77, 1980-86, 1990-92, 1997-2003, 2005-12, clk. session, 1975-76, 85-86, trustee, 1988-91; pres. Riverside Presbyn. Day Sch., 1977-79; chmn. Nat. Eagle Scout Assn., 1974-75; pres. Boy Scouts Am., North Fla. Coun. 1993-96, silver Beaver award, 1978; trustee Davidson Coll., 1984-95, Cummer Mus. Art and Gardens, 2012-; Norwegian Consul for N.E. Fla., 1989-; pres. Jacksonville Consular Corps, 1992-93, 1996-2002; mem. nat. adv. bd. Tulane Admiralty Law Inst., 2001—. Capt. U.S. Army, 1964-69. Recipient Holland & Knight's Tillie Fowler Leadership award, 2008; named Internat. Person of Yr., Jacksonville Regional C. of C., 2002, Internat. Bus. Leader of the Decade, 2011. Fellow Am. Coll. Trial Lawyers, Am. Bar Found.; mem. ABA (chmn. admiralty and maritime law com., 1980-81. chmn. media law and defamation torts com. 1988-89. tort and ins. practice sect.), Am. Counsel Assn. (bd. dirs. 1980-82, pres. 1992-93), Maritime Law Assn. U.S. (bd. dirs. 1994-97), Assn. Average Adjusters (U.S.) (overseas subscriber-London), Fla. Bar (chmn. grievance com. 1973-75, chmn. admiralty law com. 1978-89, chmn. media and comms. law com. 1990-91), Southeastern Admiralty law Inst. (bd. govs. 1973-75), Duval County Legal Aid Assn. (bd. dirs. 1971-74, 81-84), Chester Bedell Inn of Ct. (master of bench, sec.-treas. 1990-95), Rotary of Jacksonville (bd. dirs. 1982-84, 88-89, pres. 87-88), World Affairs Coun. of Jacksonville (exec. com. 2001—10), Jacksonville Regional C. of C. (bd. dirs. 2005-12, internat. chair), Jacksonville Econ. Devel. Commn., North Fla. Logistics Adv. Group (chair, 2009), DC Bar, U.S. Dist. Ct. for Middle Dist. Fla. (fed. rules adv. com., 1993-96), Libel Def. Resource Ctr. (mem. def. counsel sect.), First Cast Mfrs. Assn.(bd. dirs. 2010-), Propeller Club Port of Jacksonville (Maritime Person of Yr., 2011), Jacksonville Bar Assn. (Lawyer of Yr.), Jacksonville Internat. Bus. Coalition (vice chair with mayor as chair, 2005-), SW US/Japan Assn., Fla. Del. (chmn., 2011-), Healthcare and Biosci. Coun. Nat. Fla. Democrat. Office: Holland & Knight LLP 50 N Laura St Ste 3900 Jacksonville FL 32202-3622 Office Phone: 904-353-2000, 904-798-7360. Business E-Mail: george.gabel@hklaw.com.

GABERINO, JOHN ANTHONY, JR., lawyer; b. Tulsa, Aug. 6, 1941; s. John A Sr and Elizabeth (McCafferty) Gaberino; m. Marjory Ann Diamond, Aug. 21, 1965; children: Christina M, Megan E, Courtney L, John A III, Kathleen A. AB cum laude, Georgetown U., Washington, DC, 1963, JD, 1966. Bar: Okla 1966, US Dist Ct (no & we dists) Okla, US Ct Appeals (10th cir) 1968, US Tax Ct 1968, US Supreme Ct 1994. Assoc. Huffman, Arrington & Kihle, Tulsa, 1968-75; ptnr. Arrington, Kihle, Gaberino & Dunn, Tulsa, 1975-87, also bd. dirs., 1987-97; sr. v.p., gen. counsel ONEOK, Inc., 1998—2006; shareholder Gable & Gotwals, 2006—. Counsel, bd dirs St Francis Health Sys, Inc, Tulsa, Okla., 1989—97. Chmn. Law Ctr. Alumni Bd. Georgetown U., 1990—92, bd. govs., 1990—2004, chair, 2000—02, bd. dirs., 2000—02; pres. Georgetown U. Club Okla; past chmn. Georgetown U. AAP Okla.; bd. regents Georgetown U., 2002—04; past chmn. Christ the King Bd. Edn.; past pres. bd. trustees Monte Cassino Sch.; bd. dirs. Cascia Hall Sch. Endowment Trust, 2005—11; past chmn. bd. trustees Monte Cassino Sch. Endowment Fund; bd. dirs. W.K. Warren Found, Tulsa Pub. Schs. Found., Tulsa Area United Way, 2000—09, campaign chmn., vice chmn., 2005, chmn. bd. dirs., 2006; bd. dirs. Operation Aware Inc., 1987—95, chmn. bd. dirs., 2006; bd. dirs. The Salvation Army-Tulsa Region, 2002—04, Tulsa CC Found., 2009—12; bd. trustees Okla. Found. Excellence, 2011—. Capt US Army, 1966—68. Recipient John Carroll Medal, Georgetown Univ, 1993. Mem.: NCCJ (bd. dirs. Tulsa chpt. pres. 1993—95, Ann. Dinner honoree 2003), Okla. Fellows of the Am. Bar Found. (chair 2000—01), Tulsa County Bar Found (bd. dirs. 1993—99, pres. 1994), Tulsa Bar Asn (sec. 1988, chmn. constn. and bylaws com., bd. dirs. 1989, 1991—94, pres. 1993), Okla Bar Asn (mem. bd. govs. 1990—92, 1995, v.p. 1995, mem. bd. govs. 1997—99, pres. 1998), Metropolitan Tulsa CofC (bd. dirs. 1996—, chair 2001, CEO 2006), Southern Hills Country Club (mem. bd. govs. 1990—95, 1st v.p. 1991—93, pres. 1994, Tulsa Hall of Fame 2011), Knights Holy Sepulchre (hon. soc. Cath ch.), Phi Beta Kappa. Republican. Roman Catholic. Avocation: golf. Office: Gable & Gotwals 100 W 5th St Ste 1100 Tulsa OK 74103-4217 Office Phone: 918-595-4868. Business E-Mail: jgaberino@gablelaw.com.

GABIG, JEROME S., JR., lawyer; BS in Engring., US Mil. Acad., West Point, NY, 1972; JD, U. Calif., 1977; CSS in Mgmt., Harvard U., 1986. Dir., telecom. law USAF Comm. Command, 1980—83; with USAF Computer Acquisition Ctr., 1983—87; dir., contract law USAF Armament Divsn., 1987—90; dep. SJA USAF Electronic Sys. Ctr., 1990—92; ptnr. Venable, Baetjer, Howard and Civiletti, 1992—99; gen. counsel Time Domain Sys., Inc., Huntsville, Ala., 1999—. Mem. Army Sci. Bd.; mem., procurement process action team NASA, 1997—2000. Named Outstanding Young Mil. Lawyer in Air Force, 1985. Fellow: Nat. Contract Mgmt. Assn. (Delaney award 1993); mem.: ABA (chair info. systems com., pub. contract law sect.). Office: Time Domain Corp 7075 Old Madison Pike ste 250 Huntsville AL 35806 Office Phone: 256-922-9229. Office Fax: 256-922-0387.

GABOS, PAUL G., corporate financial executive; BS in Economics, U. Pa. With Coopers & Lybrand LLP, Dean Witter Reynolds Inc.; joined Lincare Holdings, Inc., 1993, v.p., adminstrn., CFO, 1997—, prin. acctg. officer, sec., 2001—, treas., 2007—. Bd. dirs. MEDNAX, Inc. (known as Pediatrix Med. Group Inc.), 2002—. Bd. dirs. Am. Assn. for Homecare, 2000-. Office: Lincare Holdings Inc 19387 US 19 N Clearwater FL 33764 Office Phone: 727-530-7700. Office Fax: 727-532-9692. Business E-Mail: pgabos@lincare.com.

GABRIEL, EBERHARD JOHN, lawyer, bank executive; b. Bucharest, Romania, Mar. 22, 1942; arrived in US, 1952, naturalized, 1955; s. William and Margaret (Eberhart) Krzyzewski; m. Janice Josephine Jedrzejewski, Aug. 21, 1965; children: John, Stephanie, Christopher. BA in English, St. Joseph's Coll. of Ind., 1963; JD, Georgetown U., 1966. Bar: Md. 1966, U.S. Supreme Ct. 1972, Minn. 1993. Staff atty. Fgn. Claims Settlement Commn., Washington, 1966-68; sr. v.p., gen. counsel Govt. Employees Fin. Corp., Denver, 1968-87; pres., CEO MNC Am. Indsl. Banks, Denver, 1987-89; v.p., asst. gen. counsel and chief compliance officer ITT Consumer Fin. Corp., Mpls., 1989-94; pvt. practice Mpls., 1994-95; coun. Comml. Credit Co., Balt., 1995-99; sr. v.p., gen. counsel Citibank USA, Wilmington, Del., 1995—2002; assoc. gen. counsel CitiFin., Balt., 2002—04; sr. v.p., gen. counsel Citicorp Trust Bank, Irving, Tex., 2004—08; cons., legal and regulatory compliance, 2008—. Fellow St. Joseph's Coll.; sec., treas. Indsl. Bank Savs. Guaranty Corp., Colo., 1973—83, pres., 1983—87; lectr. advanced mgmt. program Am. Fin. Svcs. Assn., 1974—81, 1985, 1987, mem. law com., 1978—89, bd. dirs., 1988—89. Bd. dirs. Jeffco/Lakewood (Colo.) C. of C., 1974—80, 1982—86, chmn., 1984—85; mem. Jefferson County DA Adult Diversion Coun., 1985—89; mem. adv. coun. Colo. Office Regulatory Reform, Colo. Dept. Regulatory Agys., 1984—89; chmn. Lakewood on Parade, 1980; vice chmn. fin. divsn. United Way Metro Denver, 1982; trustee Lakewood Polit. Action com., 1978—89, chmn., 1986—87. Mem.: Am. Counsel Assn. Roman Catholic. Office: 9113 Gardenia Dr Denton TX 76207-8621 Office Phone: 214-662-8893. Business E-Mail: gabelex@aol.com.*

GABRIEL, MICHAEL, psychology professor; b. Phila., May 5, 1940; s. Michael and Josephine (Alesio) G.; m. Linda Prinz, June, 1967 (div.); 1 child, Joseph Michael; m. Sonda S. Walsh, 1984. AB in Psychology, St. Joseph's Coll., 1962; MA, U. Wis., 1965, PhD, 1967. Asst. prof. Pomona Coll., Claremont, Calif., 1967—70; staff psychologist Pacific State Hosp., Pomona, Calif., 1968-70; NIMH sr. postdoctoral fellow U. Calif.-Irvine, 1970-72; asst. prof. U. Tex.-Austin, 1973-77, assoc. prof., 1977-82; prof. psychology U. Ill., Urbana, 1982—2004, appointee Ctr. for Advanced Study, 1990-91, prof. dept. psychology and Beckman Inst., 2004. Area chmn. Biol. Psychology Program, U. Tex., Austin, 1979-82; mem. rev. panel in behavioral and neural scis. NSF, 1988-91, prin. investigator database system for neuronal pattern analysis project NSF, 1992—, ad hoc mem. biopsychology rev. panel, NIMH, 1997-98; faculty Beckman Inst., U. Ill., Urbana, 1989—; chmn. Neuronal Pattern Analysis Group, Beckman Inst., mem. neuroinformatics rev. panel, NIH, 2000-. Co-editor: (with J. Moore) Learning and Computational Neuroscience: Foundations of Adaptive Networks, 1989, (with B. Vogt) Neurobiology of Cingulate Cortex and Limbic Thalamus, 1993; mem. editl. bd. Neural Plasticity, Neurobiology of Learning and Memory. Grantee NIMH, 1978-88, 1998-2002, NIH, 1988-2003, Air Force Office Sci. Rsch., 1988-91, NSF, 1992-2003, NIDA, 1996-2001. Fellow Am. Psychol. Soc., Internat. Behavioral Neurosci. Soc.; mem. Sigma Chi. pioneered methods for simultaneous multi-site recording and analysis of neuron activity during active avoidance learning in behaving animals; performed presently the only neurologic analysis of the neural substrates of active avoidance learning in animals; provided the first documentation of neuron activity in multiple learning-relevant brain areas throughout the course of active avoidance learning; pioneered simultaneous use of de-afferenting lesions and recording of neuron activity in key brain areas to document learning-relevant interactions among involved brain regions; first demonstrated learning-relevant activity (discrimination and reversal of brief-latency neuron activity) in the medial geniculate nucleus (MGm), a region previously believed to be involved in sensory processing but not learning; first demonstration that neurons in the basolateral nucleus of the amygdala play an essential role in the development of discriminative (learning-relevant) neuron activity in the MGm and cingulate cortex; first demonstration in various cytoarchitectural areas of cingulate cortex and anterior thalamus, of early, intermediate and late-developing discriminative neuron activity during learning; first demonstration of training-induced pre-avoidance neuron activity in cingulate cortex; first hypothesized that medial temporal lobe (MTL) and cingulate cortical interactions promote context-based retrieval of learned behavior and memory; first use of dual task strategy to demonstrate context-specific and context-independent neuronal activity in various MTL and cingulate cortical areas; first demonstration that MTL and cingulate cortical interactions are necessary for context-based concurrent learning of two (avoidance and approach) discrimination tasks; first demonstration of latent inhibition (LI) at the neuron level, and dependence of the neural and behavioral LI effect on contextual stimuli; documentation of specific anterior cingulate cortical brain changes resulting from exposure to cocaine in-utero. Office: Beckman Inst Univ Ill Urbana IL 61801-2325 Office Phone: 904-540-9955. Business E-Mail: mgabriel@uiuc.edu, mgabriel@illinois.edu.

GAD, LANCE STEWART, investment advisor, lawyer, private investor; s. Martin Harold and Claire (Entner) G.; m. Helen Alexandra Grevey, Jan. 14, 1972 (div. 1978); m. Janiece Lee Feiden, Feb. 14, 1987. BA cum laude, SUNY, Stony Brook, 1967; JD, Cornell U., 1970, MBA, 1971; LLM in Taxation, NYU, 1975. Assoc. Spear & Hill, NYC, 1971-72, Wien, Malkin & Bettex, NYC, 1972-74; mgr. Wheelabrator-Frye, NYC, 1974-75, Citicorp, NYC, 1975-86, Citibank N.A., NYC, 1975-77, asst. v.p., 1977-79, v.p., 1979-86; v.p., gen. counsel and sec. Citicorp Services, Inc., NYC, 1980-85; v.p. Citicorp Investment Bank, NYC, 1985-86; investment advisor WR Family Assocs., NYC, 1986-90, Am. Securities Corp., NYC, 1986-90; chmn., mng. dir., chief investment officer Greenfield Hill Capital Mgmt., 1991—2009, One Singer Island Capital, 2009—; chmn., pres., treas., dir. The Lance and Janiece Gad Found., Inc., 1987—; special advisor OC Fin. Inc., 2006—09. Deans spl. leadership com. Cornell Law Sch., 2000—10; chmn. 2005 Reunion Campaign Cornell Law Sch. Class of 1970, co-chmn. reunion, 2010; co-pres. family coun. Jewish Home for the Elderly, 2001—04; co chmn. Reunion Cornell Law Sch. Class 1970, 2010. Mem. NY State Bar Assn., Cornell Law Assn., Johnson Sch. Mgmt. Alumni Assn., NYU. Grad. Law Alumni Assn., Cornell Club NY (founding mem.), Temple Judea, Palm Beach Gardens. Mailing: 5310 N Ocean Dr #702 Singer Island FL 33404 Home: 5310 N Ocean Dr #702 Singer Island FL 33404 Office Phone: 561-355-0046. Personal E-mail: gadlance@gmail.com.

GADDIS, PAUL OTTO, university dean; b. Muskogee, Okla., Mar. 20, 1924; s. Paul James and Ida Rose (Oerter) G.; m. Martha Louise Rinker, June 28, 1948; children: Paul James, David Charles, Holly. BS, U.S. Naval Acad., 1946; MS, Rensselaer Poly. Inst., 1949; MBA, MIT, 1961. Mgr. computer systems and finance Westinghouse Electric Corp., Pitts., 1954-68, v.p., corporate devel., 1968-72; cons. corporate devel., prof. mgmt. Wharton Sch.; sr. v.p. U. Pa., Phila., 1972-79; dean Sch. Mgmt. and Adminstrn., U. Tex., Dallas, 1979-86, prof., 1986—2006. Chmn., dir. Globe Ticket Co., Phila., 1975-79; mem. exec. com., dir. Western Savs. Bank, Phila., 1976-79; chmn. exec. com., dir. UNI-COLL Corp., Phila., 1974-79; dir., mem. exec. com. Energy Res. Group, Inc., Wichita, Kans., 1979-86; dir., chmn. audit com. HEI Corp., Houston, Sunbelt Savs. FSB, Dallas; dir. North Park Nat. Corp., Dallas Author: Corporate Accountability, 1964; contbr.: articles to Harvard Bus. Rev.; pub., editor in chief Jour. for Corp. Growth, NYC, 1987—91. Pres. La Napoule Art Found., France, 1979-86. Served with USN, 1946-54., bd. trustees Columbia State Coll. Found., 2009 Mem. Soc. Info. Mgmt., Planning Execs. Inst., Assn. for Corp. Growth. (internat. dir.), Univ. Club (NYC and Dallas), Army and Navy Club (Washington).

GADDIS, RICHARD WILLIAM, management educator; b. Tulsa, May 29, 1941; s. Preston Gilbert and Gladys Leona (Booton) G.; m. Janet Gail Roché, Nov. 23, 1974; 1 child, Jennifer Lee. BA, Northeastern State U., Tahlequah, Okla., 1966, MEd, 1971; EdD, U. Ark., 1988; MS in Mgmt., So. Nazarene U., Bethany, Okla., 1994; grad., Tulsa Citizens Police Acad., Broken Arrow, Okla., 1998, Bartlesville Citizens Police Acad., 2006. Bus. edn. tchr. Vinita (Okla.) High Sch., 1966-74, Oologah (Okla.) High Sch., 1974-77; bus. edn. instr. N.W. Tech. Inst., Springdale, Ark., 1977-86; asst. prof. bus./mktg. edn. SUNY, Oswego, 1988-90; asst. prof. office adminstrn. Lamar U., Beaumont, Tex., 1990-92; MBA/MSM program dir. grad. studies mgmt. So. Nazarene U., Bethany, Okla., 1992—, asst. prof. mgmt., 1992-94, assoc. prof. mgmt., 1994—2001, prof. mgmt., 2002—04, prof. emeritus mgmt., 2004—; prof. bus., dir. adult and grad. studies Okla. Wesleyan U., Bartlesville, Okla., 2004—08; prof. bus. Spartan Coll. Aeronautics & Tech., 2009—, instr., 2011—13. Dir. faculty Okla. Wesleyan U., Bartlesville, Okla., sch. dir. Career Point Coll., Tulsa, Okla., 2008-09, prof. bus. Brown Mackie Coll., Tulsa, 2009-; ind. career programs assessment test adminstr., 2004—; cons., lectr. in field. Contbr. articles to profl. jours. and mags. Mem. Class of XXII, Leadership Tulsa, 1995-96, Spring class Broken Arrow Citizens Police Acad., 2001. Recipient leadership tng. award Mountain-Plains Bus. Edn. Assn., 1974, Dale Carnegie pers. progress award, 1982, Golden Apple award Lamar U. Student Edn. Assn., 1991. Mem. NEA, Am. Vocat. Assn. (new profl. award 1989), Nat. Bus. Edn. Assn., Okla. Edn. Assn. (outstanding educator award 1975, outstanding univ. tchr. of yr. 1997), Okla. Bus. Edn. Assn. (adminstr. of yr. 1994), Northeastern State U. Alumni Assn. (citation of merit 1992), Mountain-Plains Bus. Edn. Assn. (Okla. rep. 1999-2002), Okla. Bus. Edn. Assn. (exec. bd. mem. 1999-2002), Alpha Phi Omega, Delta Mu Delta, Delta Sigma Pi, Kappa Delta Pi, Phi Delta Kappa, Pi Omega Pi, Rho Theta Sigma, Sigma Tau Delta, Delta Pi Epsilon, Alpha Sigma Lambda (nat. councilor). Nazarene. Home: 704 N Kalanchoe Ave Broken Arrow OK 74012 Personal E-mail: rgaddis4@cox.net.

GADDY, JAMES LEOMA, chemical engineer, educator; b. Jacksonville, Fla., Aug. 16, 1932; s. Leoma Ithama and Mary Elizabeth (Edwards) Gaddy; m. Betty Maricella, Sept. 7, 1952; children: James, Teresa. BSChemE, La. Poly. U., 1955; MSChemE, U. Ark., 1968; PhDChemE, U. Tenn., 1972. Registered prof engr, Ark. Process engr. Ethyl Corp., Baton Rouge, 1955-60; project mgr., engring. supr. Ark.-La. Gas, Shreveport, La., 1960-66; assoc. prof. chem engring. U. Mo., Rolla, 1972-79, prof., dir. rsch. ctr., 1979-80; prof., head chem. engring. U. Ark., Fayetteville, 1980-88, disting. prof., 1988-91, emeritus disting. prof., 1991—. Pres Bioethanol Holdings, Fayetteville, 1984—; consult to 15 orgns; teacher numerous short courses in chemical eng for indust; adminr research contracts various cos. and govt. agys. holder numerous US & Foreign Patents; vis. prof. Swiss Fed. Inst. Tech. Zurich, 1978. Mem ed bd: Biomass and Biofuels, Chemical Eng R&D; contbr. to numerous presentations and publs. Mem.: AAAS, AIChE (mem speakers bur), Am Soc Eng Educ, Am Chemical Soc, Omega Chi Epsilon, Alpha Chi Sigma, Tau Beta Pi (Eminent Eng 1976). Baptist. Office: INEOS Bio 1650 Pump Sta Rd Fayetteville AR 72701-7283 Home: 3781 N Sassafras Hill Rd Fayetteville AR 72703 Home Phone: 479-443-4145; Office Phone: 479-571-9926. Personal E-mail: jlgaddy@aol.com.

GADDY, KENNETH C., museum director; BS in Biol., Univ. So. Ala., 1981, BS in Geol., 1983. Curator of Geology Ala. Mus. Nat. History, Tuscaloosa, 1985—87, curator of collections, 1987—91; dir. Paul W. Bryant Mus., Tuscaloosa, 1991—. Lab. tech. Coll. Med., neuroscience dept., Univ. So. Ala., 1979—82; teaching asst. Univ. Ala., 1985, academic tutor, 1987—90, instr. on geology, 2001; instr. Shelton State Cmty. Coll., 1988—92. Past pres. Arcadia Elem. Sch. PTA. Mem.: Southeastern Museums Conf., Ala. Museums Assn. (past pres.), Am. Assn. Museums, Tuscaloosa Area Museums Assn. (v.p., past pres.), Tuscaloosa Convention & Visitors Bureau, Tuscaloosa Hospitality Assn. (past pres.), We. Ala. C. of C. Office: Paul W Bryant Mus Univ Ala 300 Bryant Dr Tuscaloosa AL 35487

GADE, MARVIN FRANCIS, retired paper company executive; b. Clinton, Iowa, Nov. 10, 1924; s. Bernhardt Henry and Anna Mae (Jessen) G.; m. Lorraine F. McDonald, Dec. 2, 1944 (dec.); children: Michael David, Patricia Ann Gade Conn, Steven Dennis, Laura Jean Gade Walls, Mary Kay Gade Brock, Karen Lynn Gade Murphy, Jeffrey Scott; m. Carmell M. Clayton, July 16, 1994. BS in Engring., U. Iowa, Iowa City, 1952; postgrad. exec. program, UCLA, 1960—61. Process instrumentation engr. Standards Brands Co., Clinton, 1946-50; with Kimberly-Clark Corp. (hdqrs.), Neenah, Wis., 1952-88, sr. v.p., group exec., 1974-77, exec. v.p. Coosa Pines, Ala., 1977-88; also dir. Kimberly-Clark Corp.; pres. Kimberly Clark Health Care, Paper and Spltys. Cos., 1981-88, vice chmn. bd., 1983-88. Dir. First Bank of Childersburg, Ala. Bd. dirs. Calif. Water Quality Control Bd., 1964-67, S.C. Tech. Edn. Bd., 1968-70; bd. dirs., sec. Children's Harbor, Alexander City, Ala.; chmn. bd. adv. com. St. Jude's Hosp., Fullerton, Calif., 1962-67; trustee Fulton County Ga. Hosp. Authority, Northside Hosp., Oglethorpe U., Atlanta, Wesley Woods Hosp.,

Atlanta, Woodruff Art Alliance; bd. visitors Emory U., Atlanta. Served as aviator USNR, 1943-46. Home: The Brittany # 705 4021 Gulf Shore Blvd N Naples FL 34103-2232 Personal E-mail: marvgade@embargmail.com.

GAD-EL-HAK, MOHAMED, aerospace and mechanical engineering educator, researcher; b. Tanta, El-Gharbia, Egypt, Feb. 11, 1945; came to U.S., 1968; s. Mohamed Gadelhak and Samira (Hosni) Ibrahim; m. Dilek Karaca, July 19, 1976; children: Kamal, Yasemin. BSc in Mech. Engrng. summa cum laude, Ain Shams U., Cairo, 1966; PhD in Fluid Mechanics, Johns Hopkins U., 1973. Instr. Ain Shams U., Cairo, 1966-68; postdoctoral fellow Johns Hopkins U., Balt., 1973, U. So. Calif., LA, 1973-74; asst. prof. engrng. sci. & systems U. Va., Charlottesville, 1974-76; program mgr. Flow Rsch. Co., Seattle, 1976-86; prof. aerospace & mech. engrng. U. Notre Dame, Ind., 1986—2002; Inez Caudill prof. bioengring., chmn. mech. engrng. Va. Commonwealth U., Richmond, 2002—. Cons. USN, Washington, 1990-91, UN, N.Y.C., 1991, many others; lectr. in field. Author: Flow Control: Passive, Active, and Reactive Flow Management, 2000; assoc. tech. editor AIAA Jour., 1988-91; assoc. editor Applied Mechanics Revs., 1988—; contbg. editor: Springer Verlag's Lecture Notes in Engineering, 1988—; reviewer Jour. Fluid Mechanics, Physics of Fluids, AIAA Jour., Jour. of Aircraft, many others; editor: Advances in Fluid Mechanics Measurements, 1989, Frontiers in Experimental Fluid Mechanics, 1989, Flow Control: Fundamentals and Practices, 1998, The CRC MEMS Handbook, 2002, 2006, Transition and Turbulence Control, 2006, Large-Scale Disasters: Prediction, Control and Mitigation, 2006; contbr. numerous articles to profl. jours. Recipient Alexander von Humboldt prize, 1999; Whitehead fellow Johns Hopkins U., Balt, 1968-73; Freeman scholar, 1998; professeur invité Univ. de Grenoble, France, 1991-92; sr. guest NATO, Paris, 1991, USN Disting. Faculty fellow, 1993; professeur exceptionnel univ. de Poitiers, France, 1994; rsch. grantee USN, 1976-80, USCG, 1976-78, NASA-Ames, 1981, NASA-Langley, 1985-87, 86, ONR, 1981-85, AFOSR, 1982-85, 85, Boeing Co., 1984, NSF, 1986, 95, Flow Industries, Inc., 1986-88, Cortana Corp., 1989-90, ONR, 1991, DARPA, 1991, Bourse de Haut Niveau Ministere de la Recherche et de la Technologie, Paris, 1991-92, NATO, 1991-92, others. Fellow AIAA, Am. Acad. Mechanics, ASME, Am. Phys. Soc. Achievements include patents on method and apparatus for controlling bound vortices in the vicinity of lifting surfaces, for reducing turbulent skin friction, for controlling turbulent boundary layers, for micropumping. Office: Va Commonwealth U PO Box 843015 Richmond VA 23284-3015 Office Phone: 804-828-3576. Business E-Mail: gadelhak@vcu.edu.

GADSBY, ROBIN EDWARD, chemicals executive; b. St. Leonards on Sea, Eng., Mar. 22, 1939; arrived in U.S., 1977, naturalized, 1988; s. John Ernest and Emily Louisa (Burt) G.; m. Olwyn Diane Bowen, Aug. 5, 1961 (div. 1981); children: Tricia Clare, Tracey Carolyn; m. Margaret Alice Fuessel, Dec. 29, 1983 (div. Dec. 15, 2004) MA in Natural Scis., Cambridge U., Eng., 1960, MEng, 1961; MBA, U. Chgo., 1982. CFA. Chem. engr. ICI Billingham (Eng.) div., 1961-62, corp. planner, 1962-65; plant mgr. ICI PLC Agrl. div., Heysham, Eng., 1965-67, chem. engrng. mgr. Billingham, 1967-70, process tech. mgr., 1970-76, research group mgr., 1976-77; pres. Katalco Corp., Oak Brook, Ill., 1978-83; gen. mgr. Rubicon Chems. Inc., Wilmington, Del., 1984-86; pres. polyurethanes group dir. ICI Ams., Inc., Wilmington, 1986—97, pres. chems. and polymers group, 1990-97. Chmn. Cempra Pharma., 2006-09, Cempra Holdings LLC SAB. Mem. AIChE, Am. Chem. Soc., CFA Inst., Inst. Chem. Engrs. (U.K. editl. bd. 1976-77), Internat. Isocynates Inst. (pres. 1990-91), N.Y. Acad. Scis., Fin. Analysts Soc. Phila., Lely Resort and Country Club, (Fla.), Beta Gamma Sigma (U. Chgo. chpt.) Home and Office: PO Box 771150 Vanderbilt Beach FL 34107-1150 Office Phone: 215-796-2053.

GAETZ, DONALD JAY, state legislator; b. Rugby, ND, Jan. 22, 1948; s. Stanley J. and Olive (Knutson) G.; m. Victoria Quertermous; children: Matthew Louis II, Erin Victoria. L.H.D. (hon.), Concordia Coll., 1983. Asst, Senator Milton R. Young US Senate, 1966-67, asst., Senator Everett M. Dirksen, 1968-69; editor Cavalier County Republican, Langdon, ND, 1970-72; exec. dir. Communication Arts, Mpls., 1972-74; gen. sec. Bellin Hosp. Found., Green Bay, Wis., 1974-78; v.p. Methodist Hosp. and Found., Jacksonville, Fla., 1978-81; pres. ABC Home Health Services of Fla., Jacksonville, 1978-81; adminstr. Meth. Hospice, Jacksonville, 1980-81; v.p. Hospice Found., Miami, Fla., 1981-83; exec. v.p. Hospice Care, Inc.-Hospice, Inc., Miami; founder, vice chmn. VITAS Healthcare Corp.; town chmn. City of Seaside, Fla., 1990—91; mem. Okaloosa County Sch. Bd., Fla., 1994—2000, chmn., 1995—96, supt., 2000—06; mem. Dist. 4 Fla. State Senate, Tallahassee, 2006—, chair policy and steering com. on social responsibility, health regulation com., select com. on Fla.'s economy, mem. policy steering com. on energy, environment and land use, policy and steering com. on ways and means, edn. preK-12 com., rules com., mem. health and human svcs. appropriations com. Co-chmn. Nat. Hospice Edn. Project, 1980-82; pres. Nat. Hospice Orgn., 1982-83, chmn. bd., 1983-84. Author: The Flame of Freedom, 1965, Lutheran Social Concern, 1972, Thomas Jefferson Lives, 1976, A Covenant Until Death, 1978, The Case for Hospice, 1981, The High Price of Cutting Kindness, 1983, The Medicare Hospice Benefit at Mid-Passage, 1983; The Impact of Hospice on the DRG Profits-Losses of Acute Care General Hospitals, 1985, others; producer films: That They Might Have Life, 1978 (Gold medal Internat. Film Festival), The Least of These His Brothers and Sisters, 1977 (Silver medal Film Festival of Americas). State campaign chmn. N.D. Republican party, 1968; mem. Pres.'s Commn. on Campus Unrest, 1970; chmn. Fla. Gov.'s Com. on Long Term Health Care, 1980; bd. dirs. Green Bay Area Free Clinic, 1977-78, Wis. Cancer Soc., 1975-78, Family Health Services of Fla., 1981-82. Recipient George Washington Honor medal Nat. Freedoms Found., 1965, Am. Bicentennial Adminstrn. medal, 1976; named Citizen of Yr., NE Assn. to Aid Retarded Children, 1971; Presdl. commendation of merit, 1982, Legis. commendation Mich. Ho. of Reps. and Senate, 1983, Hon. Tarheel award Gov. of N.C., 1983, Founders award Nat. Hospice Orgn., 1985; named Outstanding Adminstr., Wis. Hosp. Assn., 1976, Hon. Commodore of City of Green Bay, 1976, Rosendal award for Disting. Leadership Am. Hospice Movement, 1983. Mem. So. Gerontol. Soc., Am. Soc. Newspaper Editors, Nat. Press Club, Nat. Hospice Orgn. (dir. 1979-84), Fla. State Hospice Orgn. (chmn. 1979-81), Pi Kappa Delta Clubs: Miami Shores Country. Republican. Lutheran. Office: 217 Miracle Strip Pky Fort Walton Beach FL 32548 also: 320 Senate Office Bldg 404 S Monroe St Tallahassee FL 32399-1100 Office Phone: 850-897-5747, 850-487-5009. Business E-Mail: gaetz.don.web@flsenate.gov.

GAETZ, MATT, state legislator; b. Hollywood, Fla., May 7, 1982; s. Don Gaetz. BS, Fla. State U., Tallahassee, 2003; JD, Coll. William and Mary, Williamsburg, Va., 2007. Atty.; mem. Dist. 4 Fla. House of Reps., Tallahassee, 2010—. Mem. Destin C. of C., Ft. Walton Beach C. of C., Navarre C. of C., Niceville Valparaiso C. of C. Bd. mem. AMIkids, Emerald Coast. Mem.: Okaloosa Bar Assn. Republican. Baptist. Office: 1188 Eglin Pky Shalimar FL 32579-1227 also: Fla House of Reps 1003 The Capitol 402 S Monroe St Tallahassee FL 32399-1300 Office Phone: 850-833-9328, 850-488-1170.

GAFFNEY, JAMES J., investment advisor, board member; b. NYC, Sept. 14, 1940; s. Thomas and Mary Agnes (Carroll) Gaffney; m. Eileen McCarthy, Nov. 27, 1964; children: Mary Ellen, Charles. BBA, St. John's U., NYC, 1963; MBA, NYU, 1967. Acct., internal auditor Molycorp, Inc., NYC, 1966-70, corp. contr., 1970-76, v.p., chief acct., 1976-79; v.p., CFO Creusot Loire Steel Corp., Bloomfield, NJ, 1979-81; exec. v.p., fin. Gen. Refractories Co., Bala Cynwyd, Pa., 1981-82, v.p., treas., 1982; pres., CEO Washington Industries, 1985; chmn., CEO Brown Jordan Co., 1986-88, Ayers/Chairmakers Inc., 1988, General Aquatics, Inc., 1995—97; cons. GS Capital Ptnrs. II, L.P., 1997—2003. Bd. dirs. SCP Pool Corp., 1998—, Imperial Sugar Co., 2001—, chmn., 2003—; bd. dirs. Beacon Roofing Inc., 2004—, Armstrong World Industries, 2006—, World Color Press Inc., 2009—10, C&D Technologies, Inc., 2010—. Republican. Roman Catholic. Office: Imperial Sugar Co Bd Directors 1 Imperial Sq 8016 Hwy 90 A Sugar Land TX 77487 Office Phone: 281-491-9181. Office Fax: 281-490-9530. Business E-Mail: james.gaffney@scpoolcorp.com.

GAFFNEY, JOHNNY A., councilman; b. June 26, 1960; s. George and Louise; m. Sonya Gaffney; 1 child, Jocelyn. Grad., U. Fla.; MA in Mgmt., Webster U., MBA; Ed.D, Nova U., 2006. Former branch pres. Barnett Bank of Jacksonville; councilman, Dist. 6 Jacksonville City Coun., Fla., 2007—. Mem. Land Use & Zoning, Transp., Energy & Utilities Coms.; coun. liaison Jacksonville Housing & Cmty. Devel. Commn., Jacksonville Port Authority; mem. Tower Review Com.; alt. Value Adjustment Bd. Mem.: Zoological Soc. (bd. dirs. alt.). Democrat. Office: 117 W Duval St Ste 425 Jacksonville FL 32202 Office Phone: 904-630-1386, 904-630-1384. Business E-Mail: gaffney@coj.net.

GAFFNEY, STEVEN F., information technology executive; BSEE, Lafayette Coll. Various engrng. mgmt. positions Smith Industries, Allied Signal; dir. integrated systems Litton Industries; dir. of programs, avionics divsn. ITT Corp., 1998—2000, pres. & gen. mgr. avionics divsn., 2000—02, v.p. operational excellence, 2002—03, corp. v.p., 2003—05, sr. v.p. global defense bus., 2005—06, sr. v.p. & pres. defense & elec. services, 2006—08; CEO IAP Worldwide, 2008—10; chmn. DynCorp Internat., Falls Church, Va., 2010, chmn., pres., CEO, 2010—. Office: DynCorp Internat 3190 Fairview Park Dr Falls Church VA 22042 Office Phone: 571-722-0210.

GAFFNEY, THOMAS EDWARD, physician; b. East St. Louis, Ill., Nov. 5, 1930; s. John V. and Leola (Heisner) G.; m. Edith Ann Heitholt, June 12, 1954; children— John, David, Michael. AB, U. Mo., 1951, MS, 1953; MD, U. Cin., 1957. Intern Harvard Med. Service of Boston City Hosp., 1957-58; resident medicine Mass. Gen. Hosp., 1958-59; instr. pharmacology, asst. medicine U. Cin., 1959-60; clin. assoc. Nat. Heart Inst., 1960-62; assoc. prof. pharmacology U. Cin., 1962-67, asst. prof. medicine, 1962, dir. div. clin. pharmacology, 1962-72, prof. pharmacology, 1967-72, prof. medicine, 1969-72; prof., chmn. dept. pharmacology, prof. medicine Med. U. S.C., 1972-90, disting. prof., 1986-90; vis. scientist Merck Sharp & Dohme Rsch. Labs., Rahway, NJ, 1989-93; vol. clinician Buncombe County Health Ctr., 1998—2004; prof. medicine U. S.C. Sch. Medicine, Columbia, 2004—; surveillance council Diabetes Initiative SC, 2008—. Cardiovascular panel NAS Drug Efficacy Study, 1967-70; pharmacology and exptl. therapeutics study sect. Nat. Heart Inst., 1967-69; med. adv. bd. Coun. High Blood Pressure Rsch., 1969—; mem. Coun. on Basic Scis. of Am. Heart Assn., 1969—, cardiovascular A study sect., 1972; program rev. com. pharmacology and toxicology Nat. Inst. Gen. Med. Scis., 1971-75, chmn. 1973-75; mem. tech. adv. bd. S.C. Rsch. Authority, 1986-89 Mem. editorial bd. Jour. Pharmacology and Exptl. Therapeutics, 1965-77, Ann. Rev. Pharmacology and Toxicology, 1986-91. Served with USPHS, 1960-62. Recipient Rsch. Career devel. award Nat. Heart Inst., 1962, 67, 72; Myrtle Wreath award for research Hadassah, 1980; Sr. Rsch. fellow NIH, 1989. Mem. Am. Fedn. Clin. Rsch., Am. Soc. Pharmacology and Exptl. Therapeutics, Ctrl. Soc. Clin. Rsch., Am. Soc. Clin. Investigation, Alpha Omega Alpha. Home: 813 Michaelmas Ave Cayce SC 29033-3603 Personal E-mail: tegaff@att.net.

GAFFNEY, THOMAS FRANCIS, principal; b. Rockford, Ill., Aug. 29, 1945; s. Francis William and Catherine Zeta (Haeberle) G.; m. Donna Lee Gottfried, Apr. 17, 1971; 1 child, Cory. BA, Brown U., 1967; MBA, U. Chgo., 1969. CPA Ill. Fin. cons. Duff and Phelps, Inc., Chgo., 1969-70; dir. adminstrn. Masury-Columbia Co. subs. Alberto-Culver Co., Melrose Park, Ill., 1970-75; exec. v.p., dir. Guardian Industries Corp., Northville, Mich., 1975-87; chmn. bd. The Oxford Investment Group, Bloomfield Hills, Mich., 1985-90; prin. Anderson Group, LLC, Bloomfield Hills, Alaska, 1987—; chmn. bd., CEO Automotive Plastic Techs., Inc., Sterling Heights, Mich., 1990-92; chmn. Ashland Products, Inc., Chgo., 1992-95; mng. dir. Raymond James Captial, Inc., St. Petersburg, Fla., 1997—2002. Bd. dirs. Amerus Group, 1982-2005 Decorated chevalier de L'Orde Grand Ducal de le Couronne de Chene (Luxembourg). Mem.: AICPA. Home: 2091 Oceanview Dr Tierra Verde FL 33715-2512 Home Phone: 727-867-3102; Office Phone: 727-866-8729. Business E-Mail: tom@andersongroup.biz.

GAFFORD, RONALD J., construction executive; BS in Bldg. Constrn., Tex. A&M U., 1972; grad. Advanced Mgmt. Program, Harvard U., 1987. Devel. and constrn. ptnr. Trammel Crow Co., 1981—87; project mgr. Henry C. Beck Co., Dallas, 1972—81; pres. Austin Industries, Inc., 1996—, CEO, 2001—, chmn., 2008—. Former chmn., vice chmn. Austin Comml., Inc., Austin Bridge & Road, Inc.; bd. dirs. Trinity Industries, Inc., 1999—, Chaparral Steel Co., 2005—07. Active mem. Dallas Together Forum, Nat. Real Estate Adv. Coun. Trust for Pub. Land; elder Preston Hollow Presbyn. Ch., 1991—; bd. dirs. Dallas Citizens Coun., Dallas Symphony Assn., Trinity Industries, Interfaith Housing Coalition, Lakehill Prep. Sch.; former bd. dirs. Assoc. Gen. Contractors of Am., Dallas chpt. and Tex. Bldg. br., Real Estate Coun., North Tex. Pub. Broadcasting, Vis. Nurses Assn., Greater Dallas C. of C. Office: Austin Industries Inc 3535 Travis St Ste 300 Dallas TX 75204-1466 Business E-Mail: gafford@austin-ind.com.

GAGE, ALEX P., marketing consultant; 2 children. B in Polit. Sci., U. Mich.; grad., Wayne State U., Detroit. With polit. divsn. Market Opinion Rsch., sr. v.p. polit. group, 1989; founder Market Strategies Inc., 1989; co-founder, CEO TargetPoint Consulting Inc, Alexandria, Va., 2003—. Sr. strategist Romney for Pres. campaign, 2008; head Midnight Ride Media. Republican. Office: TargetPoint Consulting Inc 66 Canal St Plz #555 Alexandria VA 22314

GAGLARDI, R. THOMAS, beverage company and hotel executive, professional sports team executive; m. Brittney Gaglardi; 3 children. Degree, U. BC. Pres. Northland Properties Corp.; dir. Leading Brands, Inc., 1998—, sec., 1999—; CEO, pres., bd. chmn. Sandman Hotels, Inns & Suites, Moxie's Restaurants, L.P.; CEO, bd. chmn. Sandman Hotel Group; owner, gov. Dallas Stars, 2011—; part owner Kamloops Blazers (WHL). Founder The Sandman Harvest Found., The Josh Dyck Found.; trustee PA and GM Gaglardi Sr. Citizen's Soc. Avocation: golf. Office: Dallas Stars American Airlines Ctr 2500 Victory Ave Dallas TX 75201 also: 1500 W Georgia St Vancouver BC V6G 2Z6 Canada Office Phone: 604-685-5200.*

GAGNON, STEWART WALTER, lawyer; b. Beaumont, Tex., Jan. 29, 1949; s. Stewart Paul and Helen Anne (Payne) Gagnon; m. Lynn Bass, July 29, 1972; children: Ashley Lynn, Jason Stewart. Student, Trinity U., 1967—69; BA, U. Houston, 1971; JD, South Tex. Coll. Law, 1974. Bar: Tex. 1974, US Dist. Ct. (so. dist.) Tex. 1975, US Ct. Appeals (5th cir.) 1975, US Supreme Ct. 1976. Assoc. Fulbright & Jaworski, Houston, 1974—83, participating assoc., 1983—87, ptnr., 1987—, head family law dept. Mem. Supreme Ct. Commn. on Child Support Guidelines; lectr. Spring Branch Ind. Sch. Dist., 1976—; master/referee Harris County Dist. Cts., Houston, 1977—; mem. Houston Found. Bd. Pub. Trust, 1982—90; mem. exec. com. Tex. State Dem., 1984—90; mem. family and law coun. State Bar Tex., 1990—. Asst. scoutmaster troop 642 Boy Scouts Am., Houston, 1970—, mem. bd. dirs. Sam Houston area coun. Recipient Merit award, Boy Scouts Am., 1982, Silver Beaver award, 1983, Dan R. Price Outstanding Contbns. to Family Law in Tex. award, 1994. Fellow: Am. Acad. Matrimonial Lawyers; mem.: Gulf Coast Legal Found. (bd. dirs., pres. 1991), Tex. Acad. Family Law Lawyers (v.p., pres. 1988), Gulf Coast Family Law Specialists Assn. (dir., pres. 1986—), Tex. Bar Assn., Houston Bar Assn. (mem. dist. 4 admissions com.). Presbyterian. Office: Fulbright & Jaworski LLP 1301 McKinney St Houston TX 77010-3031 Office Phone: 713-651-5151. Office Fax: 716-651-5246. Business E-Mail: sgagnon@fulbright.com.

GAILIUS, GILBERT KEISTUTIS, manufacturing executive; b. Boston, June 21, 1931; s. Joseph B. and Mary K. Gailius; m. Lillian P. Romanskis, Sept. 6, 1954; children: Gregory, Laura, Louise, Gilbert, Linda, Gary. BS in Bus. Adminstrn., Suffolk U., 1958; MBA, Boston Coll., 1962. Plant controller, staff asst. corp. controller Continental Group, NYC, 1954-66; v.p. fin. Foster Grant Co., Inc., Leominster, Mass., 1966-77, Midland Glass Co., Cliffwood, NJ, 1977-78, Am. Biltrite Inc., Wellesley Hills, Mass., 1978—99, v.p. strategic planning, 2001, bd. dirs., 2009. Served with U.S. Army, 1952-54. Mem. Fin. Execs. Inst. Office: Am Biltrite Inc 57 River St Wellesley MA 02481-2013 Home Phone: 239-395-2473.

GAILLARD, JOHN R., wholesale distribution executive; BS in Fin. Mgmt., Clemson U., SC. Mgr. market devel. Duke Energy Corp., 1990—96; regional mgr. sales, mktg., tech. support & logistics functions Gen. Wholesales Distributors; bus. devel. mgr. Catalyst Telecom sales unit ScanSource Inc., 2000—03, v.p. sales & bus. devel. Catalyst Telecom, 2003—04, ScanSource, Inc., 2008—; pres. ScanSource Security Distbn. (subs.) ScanSource Inc., 2004—08. Air def. artillery officer US Army. Office: Catalyst Telecom Inc Ste G 6 Logue Ct Greenville SC 29615-5725 Office Phone: 864-288-2432. Office Fax: 864-288-1165.

GAINER, RONALD WILLIAM, bishop; b. Pottsville, Pa., Aug. 24, 1947; BA, St. Charles Borromeo Sem., Phila., 1969, MDiv, 1973; JCL in Canon Law, Pontifical Gregorian Univ., Rome, 1986. Ordained priest Diocese of Allentown, Pa., 1973; ordained bishop, 2003; bishop Diocese of Lexington, Ky., 2003—. Roman Catholic. Office: Diocese of Lexington 1310 W Main St Lexington KY 40508 Office Phone: 606-253-1993. Office Fax: 606-254-6284.

GAINES, ERNEST JAMES, writer; b. Oscar, La., Jan. 15, 1933; s. Manuel and Adrienne J. (Colar) G., m. Dianne Saulney BA, San Francisco State Coll., 1957; LHD (hon.), Denison U., 1980, Brown U., 1985, Bard Coll., 1985, Whittier Coll., 1986, La. State U., 1987. Prof. English and resident writer U. Southwestern La., Lafayette, 1983—. Writer in residence Denison U., 1971, Stanford U., 1981, Whittier Coll., 1986, U. La. Lafayette, 1983-; vis. prof. Whittier Coll., 1983. Author: Catherine Carmier, 1964, Of Love and Dust, 1967, Bloodline, 1968, The Autobiography of Miss Jane Pittman, 1971, A Long Day in November, 1971, In My Father's House, 1978, A Gathering of Old Men, 1983, A Lesson Before Dying, 1993 (Nat. Book award for fiction 1994), Mozart and Leadbelly: Stories and Essays, 2005; (short stories) The Turtles, 1956, Boy in the Double-Breasted Suit, 1957, Mary Louis, 1960, Just Like a Tree, 1963, The Sky Is Gray, 1963, A Long Day in November, 1964, My Grandpa and the Haint, 1966 Wallace Stenger fellow Stanford U, 1957; Rockefeller grantee, 1970; Guggenheim fellow, 1971, John D. and Catherine T. MacArthur fellow, 1993; recipient Joseph Henry Jackson award San Francisco Found. for "Comeback", 1959, Nat. Endowment for the Arts award, 1967, Black Academy Arts and Letters award, 1972, La. Library Assn. award, 1972; San Francisco Arts Commn. award for excellence of achievement in lit., 1983, Amer. Academy of Arts and Letters lit. award, 1987, Don Passos Prize, 1993, Nat. Humanities Medal, 2000, The Nat. Governors' Arts award, 2000, Acad. of Achievement Golden Plate award, 2001, Sidney Lanier prize for Southern Lit., 2012, Nat. Medal of Arts, Nat. Endowment for the Arts, 2012; named Louisiana Humanist of the Yr., 1993; named to French Order of Arts and Letters, 2000 also: U of Southwestern LA Dept of English PO Box 44691 Lafayette LA 70504-0001 Home: PO Box 81 Oscar LA 70762-0081

GAINES, JAMES EDWIN, JR., retired librarian; b. Dalton, Ga., Feb. 21, 1938; s. James Edwin and Olivia (McCarty) Gaines; m. Sally Martin, Nov. 27, 1965 (div. May 1985); children: Thomas Martin, Robin Jeannette, Steven McCarty; m. Elizabeth Hood, July 28, 1990. BA, Emory U., 1961, MLS, 1964; PhD, Fla. State U., 1977. Tchr. English Marist Coll. H.S., Atlanta, 1961-62; grad. library asst. Emory U., Atlanta, 1962-64; asst. to head of pub. services U. Cin., 1964-65; asst. cataloger Antioch Coll., Yellow Springs, Ohio, 1965-68; dir. library Birmingham-So. Coll., Birmingham, Ala., 1968-74; head librarian Va. Mil. Inst., Lexington, 1976-93; ret., 1994. Contbr. Mem. Com. on Fgn. Rels., Charlottesville, Va., 1982—91; sec. ARC, Rockbridge County, Va., 1993—98, Rockbridge Disability Svcs. Bd., 1993—; v.p. Rockbridge Area Transp. Sys., 2005—08. Mem.: ALA, Va. Libr. Assn. (chmn. coll. and univ. sect. 1979—80), So. Assn. Colls. and Schs. (vis. committeeman 1972—89), Kiwanis (sec. 1985—92, 1999—2001, v.p. 2001—02, pres. 2012—13, sec. 2003—04, 2006—07). Democrat. Presbyterian. Home: 9 Edmondson Ave Lexington VA 24450-1903 E-mail: jegaines@rockbridge.net.

GAINES, RANDAL L., state legislator; B in Sociology, So. U., Baton Rogue, JD. Tax atty. IRS; asst. city atty. City of New Orleans; assoc. prof., dir. criminal justice dept. So. U.; pvt. practice atty.; mem. Dist. 57 La. House of Reps., Baton Rogue, 2012—. Active Winbush / Christwell Scholarship Found.; deacon Bethlehem Missionary Bapt. Ch.; treas. Nat. So. Christian Leadership Conf.; mem. bd. supervisors So. U. Law Sch. Served with US Army, ret. lt. col. La. Nat. Guard. Mem.: VFW, River Region C. of C. Democrat. Office: La House of Reps 900 N 3rd St PO Box 94062 Baton Rouge LA 70804 Business E-Mail: gainesr@legis.la.gov.

GAINES, WEAVER HENDERSON, lawyer; b. Ft. Meade, SD, Aug. 31, 1943; s. Weaver Henderson and Bertha Louise (Harris) G. AB in Philosophy, Dartmouth Coll., 1965; LLB, U. Va., 1968. Bar: N.Y. 1969, Pa. 1979, U.S. Dist. Ct. (so. dist.) N.Y. 1973, U.S. Dist. Ct. (ea. dist.) N.Y. 1975, U.S. Ct. Appeals (2d cir.) 1975. Assoc. Dewey, Ballantine, Bushby, Palmer & Wood, NYC, 1970-79; sr. staff counsel INA Corp., Phila., 1979; asst. gen. counsel, sec. Thyssen-Bornemisza Inc., NYC, 1979-82, v.p. strategic projects, 1982-85; v.p., dep. gen. counsel Mut. of N.Y., NYC, 1985-86, sr. v.p., gen. counsel, 1986-90, exec. v.p., gen. counsel, 1990-92; pres. Unified Mgmt. Corp., 1989-

90; chmn. Ixion Biotechnology, Inc., Alachua, Fla., 1993—2007, CEO, 1993—2002; v.p., mng. dir. Americas Biotech Distributor, LLC, 2005—09; chmn., gen. counsel Nanotherapeutics Inc., 2008—. Bd. dirs. Unified Fin. Svcs., Inc., Nanotherapeutics Inc., Voyetra Turtle Beach, Inc., EccoArray, Inc., Fla. Rsch. Consortium, Inc., Torrey Pines Inst. Molecular Syudies, 2008-, Dance Alive Nat. Ballet; vis. prof. Sch. Law U. Va., 2003—; adv. coun. Keck Grad. Inst. Life Scis. Bd. dirs. N.Y. Lawyers for Nixon, 1972; sr. advisor Bush/Quayle '92. Capt. U.S. Army, 1968-70, Vietnam. Decorated Bronze Star. Mem. ABA, Assn. Bar City N.Y., N.Y. Athletic Club, Haile Plantation Golf and Country Club. Republican. Episcopalian. Office: Nanotherapeutics Inc 13859 Progress Blvd Ste 300 Alachua FL 32615 Office Phone: 386-462-9663 ext. 329. Personal E-mail: weaver.gaines@gmail.com. Business E-Mail: wgaines@nanotherapeutics.com.

GAINETDINOV, RAUL RADIKOVICH, pharmacologist, researcher; b. Mishkino, Bashkiria, Russia, Sept. 1, 1964; s. Radik Akhmetovich Gainetdinov and Lilia Masgutovna Gainetdinova; m. Tatyana Dmitrievna Sotnikova; 1 child, Bulat Raulevich. MD, 2-nd Moscow Med. Inst., Russia, 1988; PhD, Inst. of Pharmacology, Moscow, 1992. Sr. rschr. Inst. of Pharmacology, Moscow, 1994—2004; asst. rsch. prof. Duke U., Durham, NC, 2000—06, assoc. rsch. prof., 2006—. Contbr. chapters to books, articles to profl. jours. Recipient Young Investigator award, Internat. Soc. Neurochemistry, 1993, Investigator award, Tourette Syndrome Inc., 1997, Michael J. Fox Parkinson's Rsch., 2005, 2006. Mem.: NY Acad. Sci., European Behavioral Pharmacology Soc., Soc. for Neurosci. Achievements include development of novel pharmacotherapies for schizophrenia, ADHD; patents pending in field; research in cocaine abuse, Parkinson's disease, schizophrenia. Office: Duke Univ CARL Bldg Rm 487 Research Dr Durham NC 27710 Office Fax: 919-681-8641. Business E-Mail: r.gainetdinov@cellbio.duke.edu.

GAJDOS, LUDOVIT, metal products executive; Pres. CMC Sisak d.o.o., Croatia; pres., gen. dir., bd. mgmt. CMC Zawiercie S.A.; pres. Europe Commercial Metals Co. Bd. supr. CMC Zawiercie S.A. Office: Commercial Metals Co 6565 N MacArthur Blvd Ste 800 Irving TX 75039 Office Phone: 214-689-4300. Office Fax: 214-689-5886. Business E-Mail: ludovit.gajdos@cmc.com.

GALAMBOS, JOHN THOMAS, internist, medical educator; b. Budapest, Hungary, Oct. 29, 1921; came to U.S., 1947; m. Eva G. Cohn; children: Sharon Tobae Galambos McDuff, John Douglas, Michael Robert. BS, U. Ga., 1948; MD, Emory U., 1952. Diplomate Nat. Bd. Med. Examiners, Am. Bd. Internal Medicine, Am. Bd. Gastroenterology. Intern Barnes Hosp., St. Louis, 1952-53; resident U. Chgo. Clinics, 1953-55; dir. gastroenterology teaching program Emory U. Sch. Medicine, Atlanta, 1957-92, dir. gastroenterology labs., 1958-92, dir. div. digestive diseases, 1966-92. Dir. Gastroenterology Clinic Grady Hosp., Atlanta, 1957-92; mem. adv. bd. Nat. Inst. Digestive Diseases, NIH, Washington, 1985-88 Author: Cirrhosis, 1979, Digestive Diseases, 1983; author or co-author 36 book chpts.; contbr. 165 articles to profl. jours. Fellow ACP, Am. Coll. Gastroenterology (pres. 1975), Am. Gastroenterol. Assn., Am. Assn. for Study Liver Diseases, Internat. Assn. for Study Liver Diseases, Alpha Omega Alpha. Republican. Jewish. Avocation: sailing. Office: 95 Collier Rd NW Ste 4075 Atlanta GA 30309-1751 Office Phone: 770-804-0492. Personal E-mail: jgalambos@myway.com.

GALANDIUK, SUSAN, colon and rectal surgeon, educator; b. NYC, Mar. 6, 1957; d. Joseph and Dora (Neu) G.; m. Hiram C. Polk Jr., Dec. 22, 1991. BS cum laude, SUNY, Albany, 1976; MD summa cum laude, Julius Maximilians U., Wuerzburg, Germany, 1982. Diplomate Am. Bd. Surgery, Am. Bd. Colon and Rectal Surgery. Surg. intern Chirurgische Univ. Klinik, Julius Maximilians U., Wuerzburg, Germany, 1982-83, Cleve. Clinic Found., 1983-84, surg. resident, 1984-88; Price fellow in surg. rsch., dept. surgery U. Louisville, 1988-89, colon and rectal surgery fellow dept. surgery, 1989-90, instr. dept. surgery, 1990-91, asst. prof. dept. surgery, 1991-96, assoc. prof., 1996, program dir. sect. colon and rectal surgery, 1999—, prof., 2001—; dir. Price Inst. Surg. Rsch., 2001—; hon. prof. translational surg. rsch. Blizard Inst. Cell & Molecular Sci., 2009—. Presenter in field; editl. bd. mem. Annals Surgery, Brit. Jour. Surgery, Am. Jour. Surgery. Editl. bd. Mayo Clin. Procs.; contbr. chpts. to books, articles to profl. jours. Chmn. fund raising com. ARC, Louisville, 1993, 1995—97, bd. dirs., 1997—2000, chmn. bd., 2001—03; bd. mem. Fund for the Arts, 1996—2009; chair med. adv. com. Ky. chpt. Crohn's and Colitis Found. Am., Louisville, 1993—97, 1999—2003. William E. Lower Fellow Thesis prize, Clinic Found., Cleve., 1986. Fellow ACS, AAUP, Am. Soc. Colon and Rectal Surgeons (mem. chmn. rsch. found. young rschrs. com. 1996—, mem. program com. 1994-96, trustee rsch. found., 2001—, membership com., 2000—); mem. AMA, Am. Med. Women's Assn., Am. Soc. Microbiology, Assn. Acad. Surgery, Assn. Women Surgeons, Collegium Internat. Chirurgiae Digestivae, Jefferson County Med. Soc., Ky. Med. Assn. (mem. cancer com.), Louisville Surg. Soc. (pres. 2005), Hiram C. Polk Jr. Surg. Soc., Ohio Valley Soc. Colon and Rectal Surgeons, Priestly Soc., Soc. Surgery of Alimentary Tract, Soc. Am. Gastrointestinal Endoscopic Surgeons, Soc. Surg. Oncology (mem. corp. rels. and issues, govt. affairs coms.), Southea. Surg. Congress (councillor 1997-99), Surg. Infection Soc., Soc. Univ. Surgeons, Am. Soc. Gastrointestinal Endoscopists, Ctrl. Surg. Assn., Western Surg. Assn., Am. Gastroent. Assn., So. Surg. Assn., Am. Gastroenterol. Assn., Am. Soc. Human Genetics, Am. Soc. Clin. Oncology, Assn. Program Dir. in Colon & Rectal Surgery, Surg. Biol. Club, Soc. Pelvic Surgeons (pres. 2011), Am. Surg. Assn. Greek Catholic. Office: U Louisville Dept Surgery 550 S Jackson St Louisville KY 40202-1622 Office Phone: 502-583-8303.

GALBRAITH, JAMES KENNETH, economics professor; b. Boston, Jan. 29, 1952; s. John Kenneth and Catherine (Atwater) G.; m. Lucy Cam Ferguson, July 28, 1979 (div. Nov. 1991): children: Douglas Aldridge, Margaret Elizabeth; m. Ying Tang, July 1993. AB in Social Studies, Harvard U., 1974; MA in Economics, Yale U., 1977, MPhil in Economics, 1978, PhD in Economics, 1981. Economist banking com. US House of Representatives, Washington, 1975-76, 77-80, exec. dir. joint econ. com., 1981-82, dep. dir., 1983-84; vis. lectr. U. Md., College Park, 1979-80; vis. scholar Brookings Instn., Washington, 1985; vis. assoc. prof. pub. affairs & govt. U. Tex. Lyndon B. Johnson Sch. Pub. Affairs, Austin, 1985-86, assoc. prof. govt., 1986-90, prof. govt., 1990—, dir. PhD program in pub. policy, 1995—97, Lloyd M. Bentsen Jr. chair in govt./bus. rels. Mem. program adv. com. Overseas Devel. Coun., Washington, 1985—; mem. rsch. coun. Econ. Policy Inst., Washington, 1987—, sr. scholar, Levy Economics Inst. Author: Balancing Acts: Technology, Finance and the American Future, 1989, Created Unequal: The Crisis in American Pay, 1998, Inequality and Industrial Change: A Global View, 2001, Unbearable Cost: Bush, Greenspan and the Economics of Empire, 2006, The Predator State: How Conservatives Abandoned the Free Market and Why Liberals Should Too, 2008; co-author: (textbooks) (with Robert L. Heilbroner) The Economic Problem, 1990, (with William Darity, Jr.) Macroeconomics, 1994; co-editor: (with Maureen Berner) Inequality and Industrial Change: A Global View, 2001 Recipient Tex. Excellence in Teaching award U. Tex., 1990; Marshall scholar U. Cambridge, Eng., 1974. Mem. Am. Econ. Assn., Assn. for Pub. Policy Analysis and Mgmt. Democrat. Office: Univ Texas LBJ Sch Pub Affairs SRH 3.237 Austin TX 78713-7450 E-mail: galbraith@mail.utexas.edu.

GALBRAITH, RUTH LEGG, retired dean, home economist; b. Lecompte, La., Nov. 5, 1923; d. Byron S. and Dora Ruth (Lindley) Legg; m. Harry W. Galbraith, June 16, 1950; 1 son, Allan Legg. BS, Purdue U., 1945, PhD, 1950. Chemist E.I. duPont de Nemours, Waynesboro, Va., 1945-46; textile chemist Gen. Electric Co., Bridgeport, Conn., 1946-47; teaching asst. Purdue U., 1947-48, research fellow, 1948-50; prof. textiles and clothing U. Tenn., Knoxville, 1950-55; asso. prof. U. Ill., Urbana, 1956-64, prof., 1964-70, chmn. textiles and clothing div., 1962-70; prof., head consumer affairs dept. Auburn (Ala.) U., 1970-73; dean Sch. Home Econs., head home econs. research, 1973-85. Mem. task force on quality of living Dept. Agr., 1967-68; mem. nat. adv. com. Flammable Fabrics Act, 1971-73; mem. U.S. Dept. Agr. Com. of Nine, 1981-83, chmn., 1983 Mem. editl. bd.: Rsch. Jour. Home Econs., 1973-77, chmn. policy bd., 1978-80; contbr. articles to profl. jours. Recipient Disting. Alumni award Purdue U., 1970 Fellow Am. Inst. Chemists; mem. Am. Home Econs. Assn. (chmn. agy. mem. unit 1975-76, chmn. research sect. 1978-80, Outstanding Home Economist award 1984), Ala. Home Econs. Assn. (pres. 1983-84), Am. Assn. Textile Chemists and Colorists, Am. Chem. Soc., ASTM (3d v.p. com. D-13 textiles 1975-79), Assn. Adminstrs. Home Econs., Nat. Council Adminstrs. Home Econs., AAUW, Sigma Xi, Omicron Nu, Phi Kappa Phi, Delta Kappa Gamma. Home: 368 Singleton St Auburn AL 36830-6317

GALE, FOURNIER JOSEPH, III, lawyer; b. Mobile, Ala., Aug. 3, 1944; s. Fournier J. Jr. and Clara (Beckham) G.; m. Louise Smith, Aug. 7, 1965; children: Carolyn, Jeanette. BA, U. Ala., 1966, JD, 1969; postgrad., Oxford U., summer 1968. Bar: Ala. 1969. From assoc. to ptnr. Cabaniss, Johnston, Gardner, Dumas & O'Neal, Birmingham, Ala., 1969-84; founding ptnr. Maynard, Cooper & Gale, PC, Birmingham, 1984—2011; sr. exec. v.p., gen. counsel Regions Fin. Corp., Birmingham, 2011—. Bd. dirs. McWane, Inc., Birmingham; gen. counsel, bd. dirs. Bus. Coun. Ala., Birmingham, 1977—; bd. dirs., So. Rsch. Inst.; mem. Ala. Permanent Study Commn. on Judiciary, 1977-83; mem. Jefferson County Jud. Nominating Commn., 1993-2000; chmn. Ala. Commn. on Higher Edn., 1998-2003; spl. counsel to Gov. of Ala., 1999-2002. Mem. Leadership Birmingham, 1986-87; pres. U. Ala. Law Sch. Found., 1987-89. Mem. ABA (standing com. on environ. law, standing com. on fed. judiciary), Birmingham Bar Assn. (pres. 1989), Ala. Young Lawyers Assn. (pres. 1976-77), Am. Judicature Soc. (bd. dirs. 1980-85), Jud. Conf. Ala., Am. Bar Found., Ala. State Bar (pres. 2006-07), Kiwanis. Roman Catholic. Office: Regions Fin Corp 1900 5th Ave N Birmingham AL 35203

GALEONE, VICTOR BENITO, bishop; b. Phila., Sept. 13, 1935; s. Angelo and Rita Galeone. BA, Pontifical Gregorian Univ., Rome, 1957, STL, 1961; MEd, Loyola Coll., Balt., 1969. Ordained priest Archdiocese of Balt., 1960; tchr., prin. St. Paul Latin HS, 1962—69; missionary priest Soc. of St. James the Apostle, Peru, 1970—75, 1978—85; pastor St. Thomas More Parish, Balt., 1989—96, St. Agnes Parish, 1996—2001; ordained bishop, 2001; bishop Diocese of Saint Augustine, Fla., 2001—11, bishop emeritus, 2011—. Named a Prelate of Honor, 1995. Roman Catholic. Avocations: fishing, reading. Office: Diocese of St Augustine 11625 Old St Augustine Rd Jacksonville FL 32258 Office Phone: 904-262-3200. Office Fax: 904-262-0698.

GALIL, ZVI, computer scientist, mathematician, dean; b. Tel Aviv, 1947; m. Bella S. Galil; 1 child, Yair. BS in Applied Math., summa cum laude, Tel Aviv U., 1970, MS in Applied Math., summa cum laude, 1971; PhD in Computer Sci., Cornell U., NYC, 1975. Postdoc. rschr. IBM Thomas J. Watson Rsch. Ctr., Yorktown Heights, NY, 1975—76; faculty dept. computer sci. Tel Aviv U., 1976—95, chmn. dept. computer sci., 1979—82, pres., 2007—09; prof. dept. computer sci. Columbia U., 1982—2007, Julian Clarence Levi prof. math. methods & computer cci., 1987—2007, chmn. dept. computer sci., 1989—95, Morris & Alma A. Schapiro prof. engring., 1995—2007, dean Fu Found. Sch. Engring. & Applied Sci., 1995—2007; prof., John P. Imlay Jr. dean computing Ga. Inst. Tech. Coll. Computing, Atlanta, 2010—. Bd. guarantors Italian Acad. Advanced Studies in America, Columbia U., NYC, 1997—2007; bd. dirs. Guglielmo Marconi Internat. Fellowship Found., 1997—. Editor-in-chief Jour. Algorithms, 1988—2004, mng. editor SIAM Jour. on Computing, Soc. for Indsl. and Applied Math., 1991—97; contbr. articles to profl. jours. Fellow: Am. Acad. Arts & Scis., Assn. Computing Machinary; mem.: NAE. Office: Georgia Institute of Technology College of Computing CCB Office 156 266 Ferst Dr Atlanta GA 30332-0765 Office Phone: 404-894-4222. E-mail: galil@cc.gatech.edu.

GALIN, TOMI, healthcare company executive; V.p. Atkinson Pub. Rels.; with HCA, Inc., Renal Care Group, Triad Hosps.; v.p., corp. comm. and mktg. IASIS Healthcare; v.p., corp. comm. Community Health Systems, Inc., 2009—. Office: Community Health Systems Inc 4000 Meridian Blvd Franklin TN 37067 Office Phone: 615-465-7000. Business E-Mail: tomi_galin@chs.net.

GALINSKY, GOTTHARD KARL, classicist, educator; b. Strassburg, Alsace, Feb. 7, 1942; came to U.S., 1961, naturalized, 1971; s. Hans Karl and Edith (Margenburg) G.; children Robert Charles, John Anthony. BA, Bowdoin Coll., 1963; MA, Princeton U., 1965, PhD, 1966. Instr. classics Princeton U., 1965-66; mem. faculty U. Tex., Austin, 1966—, prof. classics, 1972—, chmn. dept., 1974-90, Armstrong Centennial prof., 1985-91, Cailloux Centennial prof., 1991—, Disting. tchg. prof., 1999—, chmn. grad. assembly, 1977-79, chmn. faculty senate, 1981-82. Dir. summer seminars NEH, 1975, 76, 83-85, 97, 02, 05, 07; dir. residential seminar, 1977-78, dir. Collaborative Sch. Project, 1987-89, cons., 1976-78, 80-98; classicist-in-residence Am. Acad. Rome, 1972-73, vis. scholar, 1991; mem. adv. coun. Classical Sch., 1967—, chmn., 1982-85, mem. classical jury, 1970-71; lectr. U.S.-U.K. Edn. Commn., 1973; regional chmn. Mellon Humanities Fellowships, 1982-90; nat. lectr. Phi Beta Kappa, 1989-90; vis. Mellon prof. Tulane U., 1995; vis. prof. U. Nacional de La Plata, 1997; vis. prof. Gutenberg U. Mainz, Germany, 1998, Inst. Advanced Study, Princeton, 2000, U. Tex. Inst. for the Humanities, 2001; rsch. prof. Ruhr-U. Bochum, 2009-2012. Author: Aeneas, Sicily and Rome, 1969, Tibulli Carmina, 1971, The Herakles Theme, 1972, Perspectives of Roman Poetry, 1974, Ovid's Metamorphoses, 1975, The Interpretation of Roman Poetry, 1992, Classical and Modern Interactions, 1992, Augustan Culture, 1996, Cambridge Companion to the Age of Augustus, 2005, Augustus, 2012, Memoria Romana, 2013; mem. editl. bd. Classical World, 1973-76, Vergilius, 1973—, Classical Jour., 1991-98, Auster, 1996—. Mem. Leadership Austin, 1983-84. Fellow Am. Coun. Learned Socs., 1968-69, Fulbright fellow, 1972-73, Guggenheim fellow, 1972-73, NEH fellow, 1993-94; recipient Teaching Excellence award U. Tex., 1970, 76, 99, Robert W. Hamilton Author award U. Tex., 1997; Humboldt Found. sr. rsch. award, 1993, reinvitation award, 1998, Max-Planck Internat. Rsch. award, 2009, hon. doctorate award, Ruhr-U. Bochum, 2011 Mem. Am. Philol. Assn. (Teaching Excellence award 1979, dir. 1980-83), Archaeol. Inst. Am., Classical Assn. Midwest and South (pres. 1980-81), Vergilian Soc. Am. (trustee 1972-76, v.p. 1976-77), Assn. Depts. Fgn. Langs. (exec. com. 1980-83, pres. 1983), Soc. Bibl. Lit., Archeol. Inst. Am., Theodor-Mommsen Gesellschaft. Home: 4508 Edgemont Dr Austin TX 78731-5224 Office: U Tex Dept Classics Austin TX 78712-0308 Office Phone: 512-471-8504. Business E-Mail: galinsky@austin.utexas.edu.

GALL, BERT, lawyer; BA in History and Polit. Sci., Rice U., Houston, 1996; JD, Duke U., Durham, NC, 1999. Law clk. to Judge Karen Williams US Ct. Appeals (4th cir.); atty. Helms Mulliss & Wicker, Charlotte, NC; sr. atty. Inst. Justice, Arlington, Va., 2003—. Named one of Washington's 40 Under 40 Rising Stars, The Nat. Law Jour., 2009. Office: Institute for Justice 901 N Glebe Rd Ste 900 Arlington VA 22203 Office Phone: 703-682-9320. E-mail: bgall@ij.org.

GALL, STANLEY ADOLPH, immunologist, researcher; b. Bismarck, ND, May 31, 1936; s. Adolph and Wilma Thelma (Nickisch) G.; m. Florence Marie Ketterling, Aug. 17, 1958; children: Stanley, Kathryn Louise, Mark Allan, Thomas Andrew. BA, U. Minn., 1958, MD, 1962. Diplomate Am. Bd. Ob-Gyn. Intern U. Oreg. Hosp., Portland, 1962-63; resident in ob-gyn U. Minn. Hosp., Mpls., 1963-66; asst. prof. ob-gyn U. Miami, Fla., 1968-73; assoc. prof. ob-gyn Duke U. Med. Ctr., Durham, NC, 1973-78, prof., 1968—, dir. divsn. perinatal medicine; prof. ob-gyn, assoc. head dept. ob-gyn U. Ill. Coll. Medicine, 1985-89; prof. U. Louisville, 1989—, chmn. dept. ob-gyn., 1989—2000. Contbr. articles to profl. jours. Capt. M.C., U.S. Army, 1966-68. Fellow ACOG (liaison to Adv. Com. for Immunization Practice); mem. Soc. Gynecol. Oncology, Soc. Gynecol. Investigations, Infectious Diseases Soc. Ob-Gyn, Soc. Maternal Fetal Medicine. Episcopalian. Office: U Louisville Dept Ob-Gyn 550 S Jackson St Louisville KY 40202-1622 Office Phone: 502-561-7447. Business E-Mail: sagall@louisville.edu.

GALLAGHER, ANNE PORTER, communications executive; b. Coral Gables, Fla., Mar. 16, 1950; d. William Moring and Anne (Jewett) Porter; m. Matthew Philip Gallagher, Jr., July 31, 1976 (div. July 1998); children: Jacqueline Anne, Kevin Sharkey. BA in Edn., Stetson U., 1972. Tchr. elem. schs., Atlanta, 1972-74; sales rep. Xerox Corp., Atlanta, 1974-76, Rosslyn, Va., 1976-81, No. Telecom Inc., Vienna, Va., 1981-84, account exec., 1984-85, sales dir., 1985-91, mktg. dir., 1995-96; v.p. Fed. Pub. Sector Timeplex Fed. Sys., Inc., Fairfax, Va., 1995-96; bus. devel. dir. Informix Software, Vienna, 1996-97; sr. v.p. Tricor Industries Inc., Alexandria, Va., 1997-98; sr. v.p. fed. sys. Metromedia Fiber Network, McLean, Va., 1999—2002; sr. v.p. bus. devel. Source1 Techs., Arlington, Va., 2002—04; pres. AG Consulting LLC, Alexandria, Va., 2004—. Mem. Pi Beta Phi. Episcopalian. Avocations: running, working out. Home: 4643 Kirkland Pl Alexandria VA 22311-4949 Office Phone: 703-626-9466. Business E-Mail: anne.gallagher@comcast.net.

GALLAGHER, BRIAN, editor; b. 1949; With The Jour. News, Westchester County, NY, 1971—80, Gannett News Svc., Washington, 1980—83, mng. editor, 1983—86; various positions USA Today, McLean, Va., 1986—91, editl. writer, 1991—99, editl. page editor, 1999—2002, exec. editor, 2002—04, editl. page editor, 2004—. Office: USA Today 7950 Jones Branch Dr Mc Lean VA 22108-0605 Office Phone: 703-854-3400. Office Fax: 703-854-2139. Business E-Mail: bgallagher@usatoday.com.

GALLAGHER, BRIAN A., foundation administrator; b. Chgo., 1959; m. Ramona P. Gallagher; children: Katie, Maggie. B in Social Work, Ball State U., Muncie, Ind., 1981, HHD (hon.), 2003; MBA, Emory U., Atlanta, 1992. Joined as a mgmt. trainee United Way, 1981, various positions at US chapters including Winston-Salem, NC, Reading, Pa. and Providence; exec. v.p., COO United Way Met. Atlanta; pres. United Way Ctr. Ohio, Columbus, 1996—2002; pres., CEO United Way America, 2002—, United Way Worldwide, 2009—. Vol. YMCA; bd. trustees Franklin U., Columbus, Columbus Coalition Against Family Violence. Office: United Way America 701 N Fairfax St Alexandria VA 22314

GALLAGHER, CAROL JOY, bishop; b. San Diego, Dec. 24, 1955; d. Donald K. and Elizabeth Anne (WalkingStick) Theobald; m. Mark Paul Gallagher, 1975; children: Emily, Ariel, Phoebe. BA in Writing and Communication, Antioch Coll., Balt.; MDiv, Episcopal Div. Sch., Cambridge, Mass., 1989; ThM, Princeton Theol. Sem., 1998; PhD in Urban Affairs and Pub. Policy, U. Del., 2004. Ordained priest, 1990; asst. Cathedral of the Incarnation, Balt., St. Martin's Ch., Radnor, Pa.; priest-in-charge Trinity Ch., Collingdale, Pa.; rector St. Anne's Ch., Middletown, Del., 1996—2002; consecrated bishop, 2002; bishop suffragen Episcopal Diocese of So. Va., 2002—. Mem. editl. bd. First Peoples Theology Jour. Episcopalian. Office: Episcopal Diocese of So Va 600 Talbot Hall Rd Norfolk VA 23505 Office Phone: 757-423-8287. Office Fax: 757-440-5354.

GALLAGHER, THOMAS C., diversified manufacturing executive; b. 1948; With SP Richards Co., 1983; joined Genuine Parts Co., 1963, exec. v.p., 1989-90, pres., COO, dir., 1990—2004, pres., CEO, dir., 2004—05, chmn., pres., CEO, 2005—12, chmn., CEO, 2012—. Bd. dir. Oxford Industries, STI Classic Funds. Office: Genuine Parts Co 2999 Circle 75 Pkwy NW Atlanta GA 30339-3050

GALLAGHER, THOMAS FRANCIS, physicist; b. Bronxville, NY, Nov. 19, 1944; s. Thomas Francis and Margaret Ann (Sheekey) G.; m. Betty Barbara Cassiman, Sept. 21, 1974; 1 child, Thomas Francis. AB, Williams Coll., Williamstown, Mass., 1966; PhD, Harvard U., 1971. Rsch. assoc. U. Utah, Salt Lake City, 1971-72; postdoctoral physicist SRI Internat., Menlo Park, Calif., 1972-73, physicist, 1973-79, sr. physicist, 1979-83, program mgr., 1983-84; prof. physics U. Va., Charlottesville, 1984-91, Jesse Beams prof. physics, 1991—. Author: (monograph) Rydberg Atoms; assoc. editor Optics Letters, 1985-89; div. assoc. editor Phys. Rev. Letters, 1988-91; mem. bd. editors Physics Reports, 1996—2000; mem. editl. bd. Review of Scientific Instruments, 1999—2003; contbr. more than 200 articles to profl. jours. Named Outstanding Scientist of Va., 1997. Fellow Am. Phys. Soc. (Davisson-Germer Prize in Atomic or Surface Physics 1996), Optical Soc. Am. Roman Catholic. Achievements include patents in field; research on laser spectroscopy of atoms and small molecules, properties of highly excited atoms. Office: Univ of Va Dept Physics Charlottesville VA 22901

GALLAGHER, THOMAS JOSEPH, investment banker; b. Elizabeth, NJ, Jan. 21, 1949; s. T. Stanley and Madeline (Buckley) G.; m. Lindy Allyn Joslow, Nov. 29, 1975; children: James Allyn Buckley, Philip Graham, Charles Bedloe. BA magna cum laude, U. Pa., 1973, MBA, 1975. V.p. PNC Fin. Corp., Phila., 1975-79, Bank of Am. Nat. Trust & Savs. Assocs., San Francisco, 1979-83; v.p. fin., CFO Page Am. Group, Inc., NYC, 1984-85; v.p. investment banking dept. Bankers Trust Co., NYC, 1983-88; sr. v.p., group exec. The Chase Manhattan Bank N.A., NYC, 1988-96; mng. dir., global aerospace CIBC Oppenheimer Corp., NYC, 1996-99; mng. dir. def. and aerospace exec. Wachovia Capital Markets LLC, Charlotte, NC, 1999—2006; mng. dir. Legend Merchant Group Inc., NYC, 2006—07, pres. and COO, 2007—08; mgr. def. advance sys. Boeing Co., 2006; mng. dir. Morgan Joseph, 2009—10; interim CEO, bd. mem. Secondary Sch. Admission Test Bd., Princetown, NJ, 2010—11;

mng. dir., CEO Spectrum Capital Advisors LLC, 2011—13; vice chmn. Spencer Pierce Securities, Princeton, 2013—. Adj. prof. NYU, 1996-99, Georgetown U., 2005-07, adj. prof. and sr. adv., Sch. Foreign Svc. Author: (with Darryl Jenkins) The Handbook of Airline Economics, 1995, (with Gail Butler) Handbook of Airline Marketing, 1998, (with Gail Butler et al) The Handbook of Airline Finance, 1999; advisor Jour. of European Bus. Commr. utilities Town of New Canaan, chmn. 1991-99. Mem. Am. Radio Relay League, The Blue Hill Troupe, The Penn Club (NYC), Stanwich Club, The Wings Club (NYC), The Breakers, Palm Beach, Lawrenceville Club, (South Fla.), Phi Beta Kappa. Republican. Episcopalian. Office: 100 Overlook Ctr Princeton NJ 08540

GALLAHER, ART, JR., university chancellor emeritus, anthropology educator; b. Duncan, Okla., Mar. 22, 1925; s. Art Edward and Mildred Beatrice (Dunaway) G.; m. Dixie Ann Clower, June 6, 1950; children: Erin Brynn, Kell Darren. BA, U. Okla., 1950, MA, 1951; PhD in Social Anthropology; Wenner Gren Predoctoral fellow, U. Ariz., 1956. Asst. prof. to assoc. prof. anthropology and sociology U. Houston, 1956-61; vis. lectr. Rice U., 1961; assoc. prof. anthropology U. Nebr., 1962-63, U. Ky., Lexington, 1963-67, prof., 1967—; acting dir. Ctr. for Devel. Change, 1964-65, dep. dir., 1966-70; chmn. dept. anthropology U. Ky., 1970-72, dean Coll. Arts and Scis., 1972-80, v.p. acad. affairs, 1981-82, chancellor, 1982-89; Weatherhead scholar Sch. Am. Rsch., 1989-90. Author: Plainville Fifteen Years Later, 1961, Perspectives in Developmental Change, 1969, (with H. Padfield) The Dying Community, 1980. Pres., trustee Witter Bynner Found. for Poetry. Served with USCG, 1943-46. Named Disting. Centennial Alumnus U. Ariz., 1989; NSF grantee, 1965-66. Fellow Am. Anthrop. Assn. (exec. bd. 1980-83), Soc. Applied Anthropology (sec.-treas. 1966-76, pres. 1977-78); mem. Am. Ethnol. Soc. (councilor), Alpha Kappa Delta, Omicron Delta Kappa, Pi Alpha Alpha, Acacia Fraternity. Democrat. Unitarian Universalist. Home: 3167 Roxburg Dr Lexington KY 40503-3441

GALLEGO, PETE P., United States Representative from Texas, former state legislator; b. Alpine, Tex., Dec. 2, 1961; m. Maria Elena Ramon; 1 child. BS in Polit. Sci., Sul Ross State U., Alpine, Tex., 1982; JD, U. Tex. Sch. Law, 1985. Asst. atty. gen. State of Tex., Austin, 1986—89; counsel Brown McCarroll, LLP; owner, operator Holland Lofts, Alpine; mem. Dist. 68 Tex. House of Reps., 1991—93, mem. Dist. 74, 1993—2013, chmn. Democratic Caucus, 1991—2001; mem. US Congress from 23rd Tex. Dist., Washington, 2013—, US House Agrl. Com., 2013—, US House Armed Services Com., 2013—. Chmn. Mexican American Legislative Caucus, 2001—09. Named to Sul Ross State U. Hall of Fame; Henry Toll fellow, Nat. Coun. State Governments, 1996—97. Mem.: Nat. Assn. Latino Elected and Apptd. Officials (bd. dirs.), Tex. State Bar. Democrat. Roman Catholic. Office: US House of Representatives 431 Cannon House Office Bldg Washington DC 20515 also: 1915 Veterans Blvd Del Rio TX 78840 Office Phone: 432-837-7383, 512-463-0566, 202-225-4511.*

GALLICK, ROSEMARY, art educator; b. Pitts., Dec. 19, 1949; m. Ross S. Gallick, Jan. 3, 1983; children: May Olivia Silverstein, Joseph Sean Silverstein. BA, SUNY, Stony Brook, 1971; MFA, Pratt Inst., Bklyn., 1974; MPS in Comm., Cornell U., Ithaca, NY, 1976; JD, SUNY, Buffalo, 1981. Prof. art & art history No. Va. Cmty. Coll., Woodbridge, Va., 1990—. Exhibitions include Rock On-Portraits of Rock & Roll Icons (Artistic Achievement award, 2007). Mem.: Popular Culture Assn. Office: No Va Cmty Coll 15200 Neabsco Mills Rd #402 Woodbridge VA 22191 Home Fax: 703-878-5678. Business E-Mail: rgallick@nvcc.edu.

GALLIHER, BLAIN, state legislator; b. Abingdon, Va., Jan. 13, 1949; children: Terry, Charlie. BS in Tech., Jacksonville State U., Ala. Purchasing agt. Gulf State Steel; dir. bus. and industry tng., Calhoun County Gadsden State CC; mem. Dist. 30 Ala. House of Reps., Montgomery, 1994—. Mem. Etowah C. of C., Crosspoint Bapt. Ch.; bd. dirs. Clark Smeltzer Adult Edn. Ctr., Talladega Motor Sports Hall of Fame; mem. adv. bd. C.I.T.Y. Program, Etowah County. Served with US Army, 1968—71. Mem.: Rainbow City Lions Club. Democrat. Baptist. Office: PO Box 4353 Gadsden AL 35904-4353 also: Ala House of Reps Ala State House 11 S Union St Rm 628-C Montgomery AL 36130 Office Phone: 256-832-1201, 334-242-7760. Business E-Mail: blaine2@mindspring.com.

GALLIVAN, MATTHEW S., healthcare services company executive; B, Amherst Coll.; M in Bus., Georgetown U. Rep. Overseas Pvt. Investment Corp., US Export-Import Bank; dir., trade fin. Office of the U.S. Trade Rep.; assoc. v.p., Europe and Americas Health Industry Mfrs. Assn. (now Advamed), 1990—97; pres. Nashville Health Care Coun., 1997—2008; v.p., govt. rels. Community Health Systems, Inc., 2008—. Author: (articles) prospects for health care services and medical technology in global markets. Former bd. dirs. Nashville Tech. Coun., Safety Net Consortium of Mid. Tenn., Tenn. Biotechnology Assn. Office: Community Health Systems Inc 4000 Meridian Blvd Franklin TN 37067 Office Phone: 615-465-7000. Office Fax: 615-371-1068. Business E-Mail: matt_gallivan@chs.net.

GALLMAN, CLARENCE HUNTER, textile executive; b. Rock Hill, SC, Jan. 3, 1922; s. Clarence Calhoun and Hattie (Wood) G.; m. Beatrice Byers; children: Martha Gallman Alewine, Thomas Clarence. BS in Textile Engring., Clemson U., 1943. Various positions with J.P. Stevens, Greenville, S.C. and NYC, 1943-80; sr. v.p. corp. mfg. M. Lowenstein Corp., NYC, 1980-87; group v.p. domestics mfg. Springs Industries, Ft. Mill, S.C., 1987-88, ret., 1988; pres. C. Hunter Gallman Mgmt. Svcs., Greer, S.C., 1988—. Bd. dirs. Textile Hall, Greenville. Mem. J.E. Sirrine Textile Found., Greenville. Served to capt. U.S. Army. Recipient Exec. of Yr. award Assn. Textile Indsl. Engrs., 1982, Chapman award So. Textile Assn., 1985. Mem. S.C. Textile Mfg. Assn. (pres. 1985-86, textile leader of yr. award 1984), Nat. Air Craft Owners & Pilots Assn. Clubs: Greenville Gun, Beechcraft Aero. Lodges: Rotary, Masons, Elks, Shriners. Baptist. Avocations: golf, flying, hunting, skeet shooting.

GALLO, A.C., food products executive; Merchandiser Bread & Circus; v.p. Northeast region Whole Foods Market, Inc., Austin, pres. Northeast region, exec. v.p. ops., COO, 2003—, co-pres., 2004—10, pres., 2010—. Office: Whole Foods Market Inc 550 Bowie St Austin TX 78703-4644 Office Phone: 512-477-4455. Office Fax: 512-482-7000.

GALLO, VINCENT JOHN, financial planner; s. Nicholas and Catherine (Vitiello) G.; m. Blanche Marie Poplin, Apr. 15, 1972; children: Steven, Mark. BA, U. Dayton, 1965; MS in Economics, Miami U., Oxford, 1969. Registered fin. planner; CLU; ChFC; accredited estate planner Nat. Assn. Estate Planning Couns. Mgr. methods engring. Daniel Internat. Corp., Greenville, S.C., 1971-75; exec. v.p. Am. Ind. Elec. Contractors Assn., Arlington, Tex., 1975-77; pres. Vincent J. Gallo & Assocs., Inc., Winston-Salem, N.C., 1977—. Adj. instr. Am. Coll., Bryn Mawr, Pa., 1984-86. Capt. USAF, 1966-71. Served to capt. USAF, 1966-71, bd. mem., Horizons Reidential Care Ctr., 2010, Make a Wish Found., NC Adv. Bd., 2010. Mem. Am. Soc. CLUs and Chartered Fin. Cons. (continuing edn. chmn. 1984, pres. 1988-89), Internat. Assn. Fin. Planners, Nat. Soc. Pub. Accts., NC Planned Giving Coun. (pres. 1997—, accredited estate planner), Winston-Salem Estate Planning Coun. (v.p.), Am. Soc. Pension Actuaries, NC Soc. Accts., Mensa, Million Dollar Round Table, MDRT (life). Avocations: tennis, reading, gourmet cooking, skiing, porsches. Office: 1400 Old mill Cir Ste C Winston Salem NC 27103-2990 Office Phone: 336-765-0122. Business E-Mail: vincegallo@vincegallo.com.

GALLOPOULOS, GREGORY STRATIS, lawyer; b. Detroit, Oct. 8, 1959; s. Nicholas E. and Mary Frances Gallopoulos; m. Christa L. Gallopoulos. AB with highest distinction, U. Mich., 1981, JD magna cum laude, 1984. Bar: Ill. 1984, US Dist. Ct. No. Dist. Ill. 1984, Supreme Ct. Ill. 1984, US Dist. Ct. Ea. Dist. Mich. 1988, US Ct. Appeals 7th Cir. 1990, US Supreme Ct. 1992, US Tax Ct. 1995, US Ct. Fed. Claims 1995, US Ct. Appeals 9th Cir. 1996, US Ct. Appeals Fed. Cir. 2001. Assoc. Jenner & Block LLP, Chgo., 1984-91, ptnr., 1992—2005, firm co-chair tax controversy practice, mng. ptnr., 2005—08; v.p. dep. gen. counsel General Dynamics Corp., Falls Church, Va., 2008—09, sr. v.p., gen. counsel, sec., 2009—. Bd. dir. Chgo. Shakespeare Theater, 2007; trustee Supreme Ct. Hist. Soc., 2009, WETA, 2009. Author: Preserving Error for Appeal in Illinois, 1990, Why Do We Work?, 2006; contr. articles to profl. pubs. Mem. ABA, Order of Coif, Internat. Bar Assn., Phi Beta Kappa. Presbyterian. Office: General Dynamics Corp 2941 Fairview Pk Dr Ste 100 Falls Church VA 22042-4513 Office Phone: 703-876-3000, 703-876-3719. Business E-Mail: ggallopoulos@generaldynamics.com.*

GALLOT, RICHARD, JR., state legislator; Mem. Dist. 11 La. House of Reps., 2000—12; mem. Dist. 29 La. State Senate, 2012—. Mem.: Ruston Jaycees, La. Trial Lawyers Assn., La. State Bar Assn., Kappa Alpha Psi, Phi Alpha Delta Law Fraternity. Democrat. Roman Catholic. Office: PO Box 1117 Ruston LA 71273 Office Phone: 318-251-5019. Business E-Mail: gallotr@legis.la.gov.

GALLOWAY, GALE LEE, oil and gas executive, rancher; b. Pearsall, Tex., Jan. 10, 1930; s. Gerald Glenn and Vida Olga (Tate) G.; m. Connie Bird, July 30, 1965; children: Georgia Gayle, Michael W., Tara Lee. BBA in Econs., Baylor U., 1952; postgrad., Tex A&I U., 1953-54, South Tex. Law Sch., 1960-63. Mgr. gas contracts Tenneco, Houston, 1954-65; sr. v.p. Coastal States Gas, Houston, 1964-73; chmn., pres., CEO Celeron Corp., Lafayette, La., 1973-86; chmn. bd. Entex Inc., Houston, 1987-89, San Antonio, 1994—. Chmn. bd. La. Intrastate Gas, Houston, 1989, GLG Energy, Inc., Austin, Tex., 1989—, Gas Transmission Ltd., London, 1989—; dir. Goodyear Tire & Rubber, Akron, Ohio; bd. dirs. MBank; mem. adv. com. U.S. Senator Commn. Oil and Gas; mem. Interstate Oil Compact Commn. Bd. dirs. Boy Scouts Am., La. Assn. Bus. and Industry, La. State U. Found., Baylor Coll. of Medicine, DeBakey Med. Found.; council trustees Gulf South Research Inst.; chmn. bd. regents Baylor U.; bd. regents Milsaps Coll. Officer USAF, 1952—54. Recipient Carnegie Hero medal Life Saving award, 1982, W.R. White Meritorious Svc. award, 1982, Tex. award for hist. preservation Tex. Hist. Commn., 1994, Disting. Alumni award Baylor U., Silver Beaver award, Boy Scouts Am.; named to Baylor U. Hall of Fame, Baylor Hall of Honor, 1983. Mem. La. Assn. Ind. Producers and Royalty Owners (pres., bd. dirs.), Mid-Continent Oil and Gas Assn. (v.p., exec. com.), Nat. Petroleum Refiners Assn., Am. Petroleum Inst., Calif. Ind. Producers Assn., Ind. Producers Assn. Am., Interstate Natural Gas Assn. Am., Pub. Affairs Research Council, Natural Gas Men Houston, Greater Lafayette C. of C. (bd. dirs.), Natural Gas Men New Orleans, Am. Gas Assn. (bd. dirs.), Austin C. of C. Clubs: City, Petroleum; Austin Country, University (Austin). Home: 4100 Waters Edge Dr Austin TX 78731-5103 Office Phone: 512-917-4294.

GALLOWAY, KENNETH FRANKLIN, engineering professor, dean; b. Columbia, Tenn., Apr. 11, 1941; s. Benjamin F. and Carrie (Dowell) Galloway; m. Dorothy Elise Lamar; children: Kenneth Jr., Carole A. BA, Vanderbilt U., 1962; PhD, U. SC, 1966. Rsch. assoc. Ind. U., Bloomington, 1966—67, asst. prof., 1967—72, assoc. prof., 1972; rsch. physicist Naval Weapons Support Ctr., Crane, Ind., 1972—74; tech. staff Nat. Bur. Standards, Gaithersurg, Md., 1974—77, chief sect., 1977—79, chief divsn., 1980—86; prof. elect. engring. U. Md., 1980—86; prof., dept. head elect. and computer engring. U. Ariz., Tucson, 1986—96; dean, prof. elec. engring. Vanderbilt U. Sch. Engring., Nashville, 1996—. Contbr. articles to profl. jours. Sci. and Tech. fellow, US Dept. Commerce, 1979—80. Fellow: AAAS, IEEE (gen. chmn. Nuc. and Space Radiation Effects Conf. 1985, v.p. Nuc. and Plasma Sci. Soc. 1990, chmn. Radiation Effects Com. 1991—94, chmn. Engring. Rsch. and Devel. Policy Com. 1994, gen. chmn. Internat. Electron Devices Meeting 1997, NPSS Richard F. Shea Disting. mem. award 2007, NPSS Radiation Effects award 2002), Am. Soc. Engring. Edn. (chair Engring. Deans Coun. 2009—11, bd. dirs. 2009—11), Am. Phys. Soc.; mem.: Tau Beta Pi, Eta Kappa Nu, Sigma Xi. Office: Vanderbilt University School of Engineering PMB 351824, 2301 Vanderbilt Pl Nashville TN 37235 Office Phone: 615-322-0720. Office Fax: 615-343-8006. Business E-Mail: kenneth.f.galloway@vanderbilt.edu.

GALT, JOHN WILLIAM, actor, writer; b. Jackson, Miss., Apr. 4, 1940; s. William Neal and Lyndel Janes (Fortenberry) G.; m. Anna Marie Kolenovsky, Dec. 14, 1965 (div. 1973); children: Joseph William, Edward Wayne; m. 2d Diane Renee Wallace, June 6, 1981; children: Christopher Wallace, Geoffrey Warren. Student, U. Md., Munich, 1960-61; BA, Univ. Scis. Am., LA, 1992. Movie trailers voice talent Kim Dawson Agy., 1988—; owner Vox Omnia Prodns., 1999—. Toured as folksinger U.S.A. and Europe, 1960-62; voice talent on numerous radio and TV commls., Dallas, 1965-78, 80—, L.A., 1978-80; 31 film appearances as actor; looped characters in 4 movies; voice of Lyndon B. Johnson in Oliver Stone's JFK, 1992, Forrest Gump, 1994; writer film script Iceman, 1976; contbg. writer For The Love of Benji, 1977; writer screenplay Step Back From Anger, 1986, The Guardians, 1987; v.p. Tex. Ind. Feature Prodns., Inc., 1981-2003, Jackson Galt Creative Enterprise Inc, 1991-99, The Demon King, 2001. Co-author: What Price Paradise, 2001; contbg. writer: The Internal Affair, 1988; assoc. prod.: The Franglys; author, actor, prodr.: Sundown, 2007. With USAF, 1957-62. Recipient Dallas Citizen's Cert. Merit, 1973, Clios (28), Tellys (31), N.Y. Film Festival Silver, Addys (43), CHA Gold Spirit award; several Tops in advt. awards. Mem. NATAS (Heartland chpt.), Actors Equity Assn., SAG, AFTRA, Writers Guild Am., Acad. for Preservation of Talking Pictures. Avocation: martial arts. Personal E-mail: johnwilliamgalt@sbcglobal.net.

GALYA, THOMAS ANDREW, hydrogeologist; b. New Brunswick, NJ, July 11, 1947; s. Andrew Peter and Geraldine Rose Galya; m. Lanora Lucille Bucklew, Jan. 8, 1070. BS, W.Va. U., 1971; MS, U. La., Monroe, 1975; PhD, Miami U., Oxford, Ohio, 1983. Cert. profl. geologist Assn. Profl. Geologists. Geologist Sewell Coal Co.-Pittston Co., Nettle, W.Va., 1972; chief geologist Clinchfield Coal Co.-Pittston Co., Dante, Va., 1978-82; sr. coal geologist, head coal quality group Exxon Coal Resources USA, Inc., Houston, 1982-86; staff geologist Exxon Coal and Minerals Co., Houston, 1986-89; owner, pres. Galya & Assocs., Katy, Tex., 1989; sr. geologist Occidental Petroleum-Island Creek Coal Corp., 1989-91; geologist III W.Va. Divsn. Environ. Protection, Logan, 1991—96, lead geologist statewide Office of Mining and Reclamation, 1996—2002, lead geologist statewide, 1998—2002, Nitro, W.Va.; hydrologist Office of Surface Mining US Dept. Interior, 2002—06, phys. scientist, 2006—. Tchg. asst. U. La., Monroe, 1973-75; tchg. fellow Miami U., Oxford, Ohio, 1975-77, fellow, 1977-78. Mem. Internat. Mine Water Assn., Am. Inst. Profl. Geologists, Am. Assn. Petroleum Geologists, Soc. Sedimentary Geology. Democrat. Roman Catholic. Home: 65 Dogwood Ln Madison WV 25130-1268 Office: Office of Surface Mining 1027 Virginia St E Charleston WV 25301 Office Phone: 304-347-7158 ext. 3047, 304-347-7162 ext. 3047. Personal E-mail: tgalya@yahoo.com. Business E-Mail: tgalya@osmre.gov.

GAMBINO, S(ALVATORE) RAYMOND, lab administrator, educator; b. NYC, Oct. 13, 1926; s. Salvatore Benedict and Rose (Ragona) G.; m. Madeline Russo, Apr. 5, 1953; children: Catherine Rose Garroni, Stephen Raymond. BS, Antioch Coll., 1948; MD, U. Rochester, 1952. Diplomate Am. Bd. Pathology. Dir. labs. Englewood Hosp., NJ, 1961—68; prof. pathology Columbia U., NYC, 1968—82; dir. chemistry labs. Presbyn. Hosp., NYC, 1968—77; dir. labs. St. Luke's-Roosevelt Hosp., 1978—82; chief med. officer, exec. v.p. MetPath, Inc., Teterboro, NJ, 1983—94, exec. v.p., chief med. officer emeritus, 1994—. Adj. prof. pathology Columbia U., N.Y.C., 1983—; mem. Corning (N.Y.) Mgmt. Group, 1984-94; bd. dirs. Ciba-Corning, 1988-94. Co-author: Beyond Normality, 1975; editor: (newsletter) Lab Report for Physicians, 1979-98. Mem. Englewood Cliffs (N.J.) Sch. Bd., 1966-69. Served with USN, 1945-46. Mem. Am. Soc. Clin. Pathologists (editor check sample program 1968-93), Alpha Omega Alpha. Roman Catholic. Avocations: exercise, writing, travel.

GAMBLE, JOHN W., JR., corporate financial executive; B in Elec. Engring., Cornell U.; MBA, Columbia U. Elec. engr. Bethlehem Steel Corp.; treas., GM Can. GM, dir., internat. acquisitions and divestitures; asst. treas., v.p., bus. planning and analysis AlliedSignal Inc., 1996; fin. mgmt. positions through v.p. & CFO indsl. controls Honeywell Internat. (formerly Allied Signal), 1996—2001; prin. acctg. officer Agere Sys. Inc., sr. v.p., treas., 2001—03, sr. v.p., bus. contr., 2003, exec. v.p., CFO, 2003—05, Lexmark International, Inc., 2005—, prin. acctg. officer, 2009—. Office: Lexmark International Inc 740 W New Cir Rd Lexington KY 40550 Office Phone: 859-232-2000. Office Fax: 859-232-2403.

GAMBLE, MARY G(RACE), organizational development professional; b. Evanston, Ill., Feb. 23, 1950; d. John D. and Bertha E. (Flynn) G.; m. John P. Kondrotas. BA with honors, U. Fla., 1971, MBA, 1993, PhD, 2007. Mgr. maj. market Gillette Co., Chgo., 1977-83; asst. regional sales mgr. Atlanta, 1983-85; v.p. sales and mktg. Hemochek Corp., Gainesville, Fla., 1985-89; div. mgr. Environ. Sci. & Engring., Gainesville, Fla., 1989-93; v.p., chief quality officer Hellmuth, Obata & Kassabaum, St. Louis, 1993-99, pres. Competitive Performance Sys., 1999—. Sr. judge Fla. Quality Sterling Award. Bd. mem. Gov.'s Sterling Coun., 1989—; bd. examiners Malcolm Baldridge Nat. Quality Award. Mem. Assn. Jr. Leagues, Hillborough Edn. Found., Athena Soc., Am. Soc. Quality. Republican. Office Phone: 727-224-8878. Personal E-mail: maryggamble@aol.com.

GAMBRELL, DAVID HENRY, lawyer; b. Atlanta, Dec. 20, 1929; s. E. Smythe and Kathleen (Hagood) G.; m. Luck Coleman Flanders, Oct. 16, 1953; children: Luck Coleman, David Henry, Alice Kathleen Hagood, Mary Latimer. BS, Davidson Coll., 1949; JD cum laude, Harvard U., 1952. Bar: Ga. 1951. Pvt. practice, Atlanta, 1952-54, 56—; teaching fellow Harvard Law Sch., 1954-55; ptnr. firm Gambrell & Stolz, LLP, 1963—2007; sr. counsel Baker, Donelson, Bearman, Caldwell & Berkowitz, PC, 2007—. U.S. senator from Ga. to succeed Richard B. Russell Coms. on Banking and Space, 1971-72. Bd. editors: Am. Bar Assn. Jour, 1969-70. Chmn. Ga. Gov.'s Com. on Postsecondary Edn., 1978-79; bd. dirs. Nat. Legal Aid and Defender Assn., 1965-69; chmn. Dem. Party of Ga., 1970-71; trustee Ga. Legal History Found., 1996—, Lawyers Found. of Ga., 1997-2003; bd. dirs., v.p., exec. com. Buckhead Coalition, Inc., 2003—. 1st lt. Inf. Res. US Army, 1949—56. Mem. ABA (ho. of dels. 1975, Outstanding Svc. award 2012), Atlanta Bar Assn. (pres. 1965-66, Leadership award 2007), State Bar Ga. (pres. 1967-68, Disting. Svc. award 2002, 14th Ann. Justice Robert Benham Lifetime Achievement award, 2013), Lawyers Club Atlanta, Ga. C. of C. (bd. dirs. 1989-92), N.C. Soc. Cin., Ga. Hist. Soc. (bd. curators 1999-2001), Met. Club Washington, Piedmont Driving Club, Commerce Club, Capital City Club, Peachtree Golf Club, Sigma Alpha Epsilon, Omicron Delta Kappa. Presbyterian. Home: 3205 Arden Rd NW Atlanta GA 30305-1918 Office: One Buckhead Plaza 3060 Peachtree Rd NW Ste 1890 Atlanta GA 30305 Office Phone: 404-495-5472. Business E-Mail: dgambrell@bakerdonelson.com.

GAMBRELL, LUCK FLANDERS, business executive; b. Jan. 17, 1930; d. William Henry and Mattie Moring (Mitchell) Flanders; m. David Henry Gambrell, Oct. 16, 1953; children: Luck G. Davidson, David Henry, Alice Kathleen, Mary G. Rolinson. Grad., St. Mary's Coll., Raleigh, NC, 1948; AB, Duke U., Durham, NC, 1950; diplome d'etudes françaises, L'Institut de Touraine, Tours, France, 1951. Chmn. bd. dirs. LFG Co., 1960—. Mem. State Bd. Pub. Safety, 1981—90, Chpt. Nat. Cathedral, Washington, 1981—85, World Svc. Coun. YWCA, 1965—, Student Aid Found., Atlanta, 1992—99; life mem. bd. councilors Carter Ctr., Emory U.; mem. bd. advisors Emory U., Atlanta, 2001—04; coun. mem. Presbytery Greater Atlanta, 1988; elder First Presbyn. Ch., Atlanta; bd. dirs. Atlanta Symphony Orch., 1982—85. Recipient East Ga. Coll. Ctr. named in her honor, Swainsboro, Ga., 2002; co-recipient Award, Bronze Statue, "Sightless Among Miracles", Carter Ctr., 2007. Mem.: Atlanta Jr. League, Alpha Delta Pi.

GAMBRELL, MICHAEL W., state legislator; b. Belton, Jan. 10, 1958; s. Aaron and Robbie Gambrell; m. Reene V. Gambrell. BS, Clemson U., 1980. Owner M&R Enterprises, 1983—; mem. Dist. 7 SC House of Reps., 2007—; mem. Edn. Com., Pub. Works Com. Mem.: Anderson County Fire Chiefs Assn. (chmn. 1990—92). Republican. Home: 400 Filter Plant Rd Honea Path SC 29654 Office: 436A Blatt Building Columbia SC 29201 Home Phone: 864-369-0613; Office Phone: 864-844-3614. E-mail: GambrellM@schouse.org.

GAMBRELL, SARAH BELK, retail executive; b. Charlotte, NC, Apr. 12, 1918; d. William Henry and Mary (Irwin) Belk; m. Charles Glenn Gambrell (dec.); 1 child, Sarah Belk. BA, Sweet Briar Coll., 1939; D in Humanities (hon.), Erskine Coll., 1970, U. N.C., Asheville, 1986, Furman U., 1997, Johnson C. Smith U., 2003. Dir. Belk Inc., Charlotte, 1947—2007, hon. dir., 2007—. Trustee Hist. Rural Hill, William Black Home, Montreat, NC; bd. dir. The Andrew Jackson Hist., Mus. Waxhaw; hon. trustee Cancer Rsch. Inst., NYC; hon. trustee emeritus Princeton Theol. Sem., NJ; trustee emeritus Furman U., Charlotte Mus. of History; bd. dirs. Parkinson's Disease Found., NYC, NC Cmty. Found., Raleigh, Hist. Rosedale, Charlotte; bd. dirs., hon. dir. YWCA of Ctrl. Carolinas; hon. bd. dirs. YWCA, NYC. Recipient Algernon Sydney Sullivan award, Queens U., Charlotte, N.C., Univ. award, U. N.C. Chapel Hill, 1993, Woman of Achievement award, YWCA Charlotte, Mary Elizabeth Francis award, Florence Crittenton Svcs., Cmty. Svc. award, Charlotte. Mem.: DAR, Nat. Soc. Daughters Am. Revolution, Women Exec., Fashion Group, Inc. (N.Y.C.), Nat. Soc. Colonial Dames. Home: 300 Cherokee Rd

Charlotte NC 28207-1908 Office: Belk Inc 2801 W Tyvola Rd Charlotte NC 28217-4500 also: 6100 Fairview Rd Ste 640 Charlotte NC 28210 Office Phone: 704-553-8296 ext. 24.

GAN, JIANBANG, agricultural studies educator, economist; s. Darui Gan and Xiujiao Cai; m. Hong Liu; children: Steven, Eric, David. BS, Fujian Agr. and Forestry U., 1982; MS, Iowa State U., 1988, PhD, 1990. Postdoctoral rsch. assoc. Iowa State U., Ames, 1991—92; faculty mem. Tuskegee U., 1992—2001, coord. for internat. project devel., 1992—2001, coord. forest resources program, 1998—2001; assoc. prof. to prof. Tex. A&M U., College Station, 2001—. Adj. prof. Fujian Agr. and Forestry U., Fuzhou, 2005—; mem. exec. adv. bd., cons. AdventGX, College Station, 2004—; mem. nat. grant rev. panels NAS/Ford Found., NSF, USDA; peer reviewer NSF, NRC, USDA, DOE, McGraw Hill, Elsevier, various sci. jours.; co-chmn. conf. rsch. roundtable China-US Rels.: Trade, Diplomacy and Rsch., Beijing, 2005, Development, Energy and Security, Washington, 2007; lectr. in field. Assoc. editor: Can. Jour. Forest Rsch., Southern Jour. Applied Forestry, guest assoc. editor: Forest Sci.; contbr. articles to profl. jours., ency. Recipient Faculty Outstanding Performance award in Tchg., Tuskegee U., 1997; grantee, Biomass R & D Initiative, 2005—, Joint Fire Sci. Program, 2005—, USDA, 1997—, USDA AFRI, 2011—, USDOE, 2012—; vis. scholar Grad. scholar, Fujian Overseas Chinese Scholarship Found. Mem.: Tex. Forestry Assn. (Rsch., Devel. and Innovation award 2010), Internat. Soc. Forest Resource Economics, Soc. Am. Foresters, Xi Sigma Pi, Gamma Sigma Delta (chpt. treas. 1994—96), Sigma Xi. Achievements include research in bioenergy, disturbances and responses, trade and conservation, socially disadvantaged forestland owners; natural resource management, economics and policy in China, Guatemala, India, Senegal, Tanzania, Thailand and The Philippines. Office: Texas A&M U 305 Horticulture/Forest Science Building College Station TX 77843-2138 Business E-Mail: j-gan@tamu.edu.*

GANAWAY, GEORGE KENNETH, psychiatrist, psychoanalyst, educator, researcher; b. Davenport, Iowa, Mar. 22, 1946; s. Kenneth Joseph and Elizabeth Earl Ganaway; m. Elzada Lawson, Dec. 27, 1969; children: Heather, Erin. BS in Clin. Psychology, Duke U., 1968; MD, Emory U., 1973; grad., Emory Psychoanalytic Inst., 2001. Diplomate Am. Bd. Psychiatry and Neurology; lic. physician, Ga. Resident in psychiatry Emory Affiliated Hosps., Atlanta, 1973-76; pvt. practice in gen. adult and adolescent psychiatry Atlanta, 1976—; regional med. advisor Social Security Disability Program, 1997—; pvt. practice psychoanalysis, 2001—; founder, program dir. Ridgeview Ctr. for Dissociative Disorders, Smyrna, Ga., 1987-96; med. cons. dissociative disorders Ridgeview Inst., 1996—2006; asst. prof. psychiatry Emory U. Sch. Medicine, Atlanta, 1976-80, clin. asst. prof. psychiatry, 1981—, Morehouse Sch. Medicine, Atlanta, 1990—; tchg. faculty Emory Psychoanalytic Inst., 1997—, assoc. tchg. analyst, 2002—. Psychiat. cons. Disability Adjudication br. Social Security Adminstrn., Atlanta, part-time, 1980-87, Douglas County Mental Health Clinic, Douglasville, 1977-81, South Cobb Mental Health Ctr., Austell, Ga., 1978-80, Atlanta Depression Clinic of Ctr. Metabolic Studies, 1976-77, others; ann. chmn. S.E. Regional Conf. Dissociative Disorders, 1987-96; med. staff Ridgeview Inst., 1976-98, courtesy staff, 1999-2006. Asst. editor Dissociation: Progress in Dissociative Disorders, 1988-98; assoc. editor Internat. Jour. Clin. and Exptl. Hypnosis, 1995-96; mem. editl. adv. bd. Insight mag.; editl. reviewer Am. Jour. Psychiatry, Child Abuse and Neglect: The Internat. Jour., Jour. Psychology and Theology, Jour. Nervous and Mental Disease, Dissociation: Progress in the Dissociative Disorders; contbr. articles to profl. jours., chpts. to textbooks of psychiatry. Sci. adv. bd. False Memory Syndrome Found., 1992—. Fellow: Internat. Soc. for Study of Dissociation (task force on stds. of practice 1991—96), Am. Psychiat. Assn. (life); mem.: Internat. Psychoanalytical Assn., Atlanta Psychoanalytic Soc. (chair sci. program com. 2001—03, pres.-elect 2003—05, pres. 2005—07), Ga. Psychiat. Physicians Assn., So. Med. Assn., Am. Psychoanalytic Assn. Avocation: collecting maritime antiques. Office: D-201 5064 Roswell Rd NE Ste 201D Atlanta GA 30342-2266 Office Phone: 404-252-4525. Business E-Mail: gkganaway@gmail.com.*

GANDY, GERALD LARMON, rehabilitation counseling educator, psychologist, writer; b. Thomasville, Ga., Feb. 9, 1941; s. Larmon Brinkley and Ruby Wylene (Vickers) G.; m. Patricia Kay Haltiwanger, Jan. 22, 1966. BA, Fla. State U., 1963; MA, U. S.C., 1968, PhD, 1971. Lic. profl. counselor, Va.; lic. clin. psychologist, Va.; nat. cert. rehab. counselor; nat. cert. counselor; cert. profl. qualification in psychology Assn. of State and Provincial Psychology Bds. Profl. counselor U. S.C. Counseling Ctr., Columbia, 1968-70; counseling psychologist VA Regional Office, Columbia, 1970-75, chief counseling psychologist, 1974-75; ind. cons., prof. emeritus Med. Coll. Va., Va. Commonwealth U., Richmond, 1996—, prof., program dir., 1975-95. Chair nat. com. on undergrad. rehab. edn. Nat. Coun. on Rehab. Edn., 1984-89; mem. numerous state and govt. adv. coms., 1970—; cons. in field. Author: Mental Health Rehabilitation, 1995; co-author: Rehabilitation and Disability, 1990; co-author/editor: Rehabilitation Counseling and Services, 1987, Counseling in the Rehabilitation Process, 1999; co-editor: International Rehabilitation, 1980, 89; contbr. numerous articles to profl. jours. Faculty pres. Sch. of Cmty. and Pub. Affairs, VA Commonwealth U., 1989-93. Capt. US Army, 1963-66. Recipient Disting. Svc. award Sch. Cmty. and Pub. Affairs, 1988, School and U. Leadership award, 1993. Fellow Internat. Acad. of Behavioral Medicine, Counseling and Psychotherapy (diplomate); mem. APA, ACA, World Fedn. for Mental Health, Phi Kappa Phi, Sigma Alpha Epsilon. Home: 9030 Stony Point Pkwy Ste 160 Richmond VA 23235-1939 Office Phone: 804-737-6089. Business E-Mail: ggandy@vcu.org.

GANDY, PHILLIP A., state legislator; b. Hickory, Miss., Aug. 28, 1950; m. Peggy McNeil; children: Kimberly Stokley, Gwendolyn King, Joshua. Attended, Southeastern Bapt. Coll., Laurel, Miss. Pastor; mem. Dist. 43 Miss. State Senate, Jackson, 2012—. Republican. Office: Miss State Senate PO Box 1018 Jackson MS 39215 Business E-Mail: pgandy@senate.ms.gov.

GANDY, WINSTON H., JR., cardiologist; MD, Howard U., Washington, DC, 1986. Diplomate Am. Bd. Internal Medicine, 1989, Am. Bd. Internal Medicine-cardiovasc. disease, 2002, cert. echocardiography Nat. Bd. of Echocardiography. Resident internal medicine Emory Univ. Affiliation Hosp., Atlanta, 1986—89; fellow cardiovasc. disease Univ. Ala., Birmingham, 1989—92; gen. cardiologist Piedmont Heart Inst. Fellow: Am. Coll. of Cardiology. Office: Piedmont Heart Institute-Perimeter Ste 385 1140 Hammond Dr Atlanta GA 30328

GANE, STEVE, consumer products company executive; Various positions including pres. Hickory Bus. Furniture Furniture Brands International, Inc., exec. v.p., COO Thomasville Furniture Industries; sr. v.p. Herman Miller, Inc., pres. Geiger Internat., Inc., 2007—, pres. Herman Miller for the Home, 2010—. Office: Geiger International Inc 6095 Fulton Industrial Blvd SW Atlanta GA 30336-0068 Office Phone: 404-344-1100. Office Fax: 404-346-5202.

GANEK, JEFFREY E., telecommunications industry executive; b. 1952; BS in Economics, Carnegie-Mellon U., 1974, MS in Pub. Policy and Mgmt., 1975. Mgmt. positions, corp. devel., mktg. and fin. AT&T Corp., 1976—85; dir., mktg. and corp. devel. MCI Comm. Corp., 1985—91; v.p., mktg. GTE Spacenet, 1991—93; v.p., Asia ops. Global TeleSystems Group, 1993—95; sr. v.p., mng. dir., Comm. Industry Svcs. Lockheed Martin Corp., 1995—99; chmn., CEO NeuStar, Inc., Sterling, Va., 1999—2010, chmn., 2010—. Bd. dirs. comScore, Inc., 2008—. Recipient Entrepreneur Of The Yr., Ernst & Young, 2006. Office: NeuStar Inc 46000 Center Oak Plz Sterling VA 20166 Office Phone: 571-434-5400. Business E-Mail: jeffrey.ganek@neustar.biz.

GANGSTAD, JOHN ERIK, lawyer; b. New Brunswick, NJ, May 16, 1948; s. Edward Otis and Ruth Margaret (Fletcher) G.; m. Cynthia Diane Coffman, July 5, 1974; children: Allison, Erik, Amy. BA, U. Tex., 1970, JD, 1974. Bar: Tex. 1974, U.S. Dist. Ct. (no. dist.) Tex. 1974. Assoc. Turner, Hitchins, McInnery, Webb & Hartnett, Dallas, 1974-76, ptnr., 1977-81, Brown McCarroll & Oaks Hartline, L.L.P., Austin, Tex., 1982-2000, Bickerstaff, Heath et al., Austin, 2000—. Partnership com. State Bar Tex., 1981-98. Bd. dir. Found. for the Homeless, Austin, 1988—. With USNG. Mem. ABA, Tex. Bar Assn., Order of Coif. Presbyterian. Avocations: golf, reading. Home: 7924 Cobblestone Dr Austin TX 78735

GANTZ, CARROLL MELVIN, industrial design consultant, consumer product designer; b. Sellersville, Pa., Sept. 9, 1931; s. Melvin Charles G. and Leona Alberta (Hornberger) Barner; m. Lorraine Sachs, Mar. 5, 1955; children: Erika Christine, Mitchell Allen. B.F.A., Carnegie Mellon U., 1953. Head indsl. design Hoover Co., North Canton, Ohio, 1956-72; mgr. indsl. design Black & Decker, Inc., Towson, Md., 1972-81, dir. indsl. design household products group Shelton, Conn., 1981-86; prof., head dept. design Carnegie Mellon U., Pitts., 1987—92; established Carroll Gantz Design, 1992; designer canal boat St. Helena II, Canal Fulton, Ohio, 1967-70; dir. Am. Canal Soc., York, Pa., 1974-79, 2006—07. Author: Design Chronicles. Significant Mass Produced Products of the 20th Century, 2005, The Industrialization of Design, 2010, Building the St. Helena II, 2012, The Vacuum Cleaner, 2012. Bd. dirs. Stark County Hist. Soc., 1970. Served with Nat. Security Agy. U.S. Army, 1953-56. Recipient Design award Indsl. Designers Inst., 1961, Indsl. Design Excellance award, 1995; Brashear scholar, 1949, IDSA Catalyst award, 2009. Fellow Indsl. Designers Soc. Am. (pres. 1979-80, chmn. bd. 1981-82); mem. SAR, Omicron Delta Kappa, Tau Sigma Delta. Republican. Achievements include patents for original Black & Decker Dustbuster, 1978; 28 others. Personal E-mail: carrgantz@bellsouth.net.

GARAN, RONALD J., JR., astronaut; b. Yonkers, NY, Oct. 30, 1961; s. Ronald Garan, Sr., Linda Lichtblau; m. Carmel Courtney; 3 children. BS in Bus. Economics, SUNY Coll., Oneonta, 1982; M in Aero. Sci., Embry-Riddle Aero. U., 1994; MS in Aerospace Engring., U. Fla., 1996; grad., USAF Fighter Weapons Sch., 1989; attended, US Naval Pilot Sch., Patuxent River Naval Air Station, 1997. Commn. as 2nd lt. USAF, Lackland AFB, Tex., 1984; attended Undergraduate Pilot Tng., earned wings Vance AFB, Okla., 1985; completed F-16 tng. Luke AFB, Ariz.; combat ready F-16 pilot 496th Tactical Fighter Squadron, Hahn Air Base, Germany, 1986—88; reassigned to and served as instr. pilot, evaluator pilot and combat ready F-16 pilot 17th Tactical Fighter Squadron, Shaw AFB, SC, 1988, squadron weapons officer, 1989; flew F-16 combat missions SouthWest Asia, Operation Desert Shield/Desert Storm, 1990—91; weapons sch. instr. pilot, flight comdr., asst. ops. officer USAF Weapons Sch., 1991—94; reassigned to and served as devlop. test pilot, chief F-16 pilot 39th Flight Test Squadron, Eglin AFB, Fla., 1994, dir., Joint Air to Surface Missile Combined Test Force, 1997; ops. officer 40th Flight Test Squadron, 2000; pilot, astronaut NASA, 2000—. Assigned technical duties in the Astronaut Office Station and Shuttle Ops. Branches. NASA, 2002; aquanaut through participation in the joint NASA-NOAA, NEEMO 9 (NASA Extreme Environment Mission Ops.), an exploration research mission held Aquarius., 2006; mission specialist 2 for ascent and entry, perform 3 spacewalks, operate shuttle arm and assist in the activation of Kibo Lab. STS-124 Mission (Discovery), mission to Internat. Space Station to launch components to complete Japanese Kibo Lab., 2008. Founder Manna Energy Found. Decorated Disting. Flying Cross for Combat Valor, Meritorious Svc. Medal, Air Medal, Aerial Achievement Medal, Air Force Outstanding Unit award with Valor, Nat. Def. Svc. Medal, Humanitarian Svc. award, Kuwait Liberation Medal; recipient NASA Superior Accomplishment award, NASA Exceptional Achievement award, Lt. Gen. Claire Lee Chennault award. Mem.: Engineers Without Borders, Internat. Solar Energy Soc., Soc. Exptl. Test Pilots. Avocations: skiing, football, coaching, teaching Sunday School. Office: Astronaut Office/CB NASA Lyndon B Johnson Space Ctr 2101 NASA Pkwy Houston TX 77058

GARAVAGLIA, JAN C., forensic pathologist, chief medical examiner; married; 2 children. AB magna cum laude, St. Louis U. Sch. Medicine, 1978, MD, 1982. Cert. Am. Bd. Pathology in combined anatomic and clin. pathology, Am. Bd. Pathology in forensic pathology. Fellowship, forensic pathology Dade County Med. Examiner's Office, Miami, Fla.; intern, internal medicine St. Louis U. Hosp., 1982, resident, anatomic/clin. pathology dept., 1983—87; assoc. med. examiner Duval County, Jacksonville, Fla., 1988—91, Ga., 1991—93; med. examiner Bexar County Forensic Sci. Ctr., San Antonio, 1993—2003; dep. chief med. officer Med. Examiner's Office, Orlando, Fla., 2003—04; chief med. examiner Orange-Osceola Med. Examiner's Office, Dist. 9, Orlando, Fla., 2004—. Clin. asst. prof., dept. pathology U. Tex. Health Sci. Ctr., San Antonio, 2000, mem. grad. faculty coun., grad. sch. biomedical sci.; given numerous presentations and lectures at various institutions. Published media Jour. of Forensic Sciences, Am. Jour. Forensic Medicine and Pathology, host Dr. G: Chief Medical Examiner (Discovery Channel), 2004—; author: How Not to Die, 2008. Recipient Hidalgo award, Bexar County Commrs. Ct., Tex., 2000. Mem.: Am. Acad. Forensic Scis., Nat. Assn. Med. Examiners. Office: Dist Nine Medical Examiner's Office 2350 E Michigan St Orlando FL 32806-4939

GARBER, DAVID ALEXANDER, dentist, educator; b. Johannesburg; Grad., U. Witwatersrand, South Africa, 1970; postgrad in Periodontics, U. Pa., Phila., 1977, postgrad in Periodontal Prosthesis (Fixed Prosthodontics), 1978, DMD, 1981. Lic. Great Britain, 1970, South Africa, 1970, Nat. Bd. USA, 1976, Pa., 1977, Ga., 1981. Lectr. and clin. instr. Univ. Witwatersrand, South Africa, 1973—74; tchg. fellow form and function of the masticatory system sch. of dental medicine Univ. Pa., 1977—78; editor Fixed Prosthodontics, Clark's Clin. Dentistry, 1985; asst. prof. form and function of the masticatory system sch. of dental medicine Univ. Pa., dir. group clin. practice sch. of medicine, 1978—82, dir. fixed prosthodontics didactic program, 1981—82, dir. fixed prosthodontics (crown and bridge) sch. of medicine, 1981—82, dir. diagnosis and treatment planning seminars, 1978—82, ast. prof. restorative dentistry sch. of dental medicine, 1978—82, asst. clin. prof. periodontics, 1983; spl. letr. esthetic dentistry sch. of medicine Emory Univ., 1984—91; clin. prof. dept. of prosthodontics La. State Univ., 1996—; clin. prof. of periodontics sch. of dental medicine Med. Coll. of Ga., 1987—, clin. prof. of oral rehab. sch. of dental medicine, 1988—; adj. prof. dept. of restorative dentistry Univ. Tex. Health Sci. Ctr., San Antonio, 1999—; dentist Goldstein, Garber and Salama. Editl. bd. Clin. Implant Dentistry and Related Rsch., 2000; sci. cons. Revista Dental Press de Estética, 2006; editor Functional Esthetics and Restorative Dentistry Adv. Bd., 2007—. Co-author: (publ.) Porcelain Laminate Veneers, Bleaching Teeth, orcelain & Composite Inlays and Onlay, Complete Dental Bleaching, (jour.) A Method of Registering Centric Relation, Temp. Stblzn. of Periodontally Involved Teeth, Adjunctive Orthodontics in Oral Rehab., 1977, A Temp. Permanent Splint, 1979, An Alternative to Cast Bridgework in Selected, 1979, various jours. including Loss of Arch Integrity Due to Interproximal Caries, Repair of a Bony Defect Using a Intraoral Exostosis as the Donor Site and Treatment of Posterior Bite Collapse-Occlusal Therapy. Recipient The Sauk Schulger Meml. award for Excellence in Diagnosis and Treatment Planning, Gordon J. Christensen Lectr. Recognition award, The Northeastern Periodontal Soc. Isador Hirschfield award for Clin. Excellence, Prof. of the Year award, Univ. Pa. Fellow: Internat. Coll. of Dentists; mem.: Am. Prosthodontic Soc., Am. Acad. of Periodontics, Am. Acad. of Fized Prosthodontics, Acad. of Osseointegrations, Am. Acad. of Esthetic Dentistry. Office: Goldstein, Garber and Salama LLC Ste 800 600 Galleria Parkway SE Atlanta GA 30339 Office Phone: 404-261-4941. Office Fax: 404-261-4946.

GARBIN, ALBENO PATRICK, sociology educator; b. Girard, Ill., June 20, 1932; s. Cipriano and Angelina (Sommavillia) G.; m. Carol Townsend Nichols, Sept. 3, 1969; children: Angela Marie, Tina Ann, A. Patrick, Carol Anne. AB, Blackburn Coll., 1956; MA, La. State U., 1959, PhD, 1963. Instr., asst. prof. sociology U. Omaha, 1961-64; asst. prof. Fla. State U., Tallahassee, 1964-66; assoc. prof., specialist occupation edn. Ohio State U., Columbus, 1966-68; prof. sociology U. Ga., Athens, 1968-97, prof. emeritus, 1997—. Served in US Army, 1954—56. Recipient rsch. award Am. Personnel and Guidance Assn., 1977, Excellence in Undergrad. Tchg. award U. Ga., 1978, meritorious svc. award Ga. Soc. Assn., 1991. Mem. Am. Sociol. Assn., So. Sociol. Soc., Ga. Sociol. Assn. (v.p. 1984-85, pres. 1986-87). Democrat. Roman Catholic. Avocations: gardening, photography. Home: 85 Timberland Trail Arnoldsville GA 30619-2216 Office: U Ga Dept Sociology Athens GA 30602 Office Phone: 706-542-3218. Business E-Mail: algarbin@uga.edu.

GARCIA, ART A., corporate financial executive; BS in Acctg., Fla. State U. Cert. acct., Fla. Positions in audit services practice including sr. mgr. bus. assurance Coopers and Lybrand LLP, 1984—97; sr. mgr., corp. acctg. Ryder System, Inc., 1997, dir., corp. acctg., 1998—2000, group dir., acctg. svcs., 2000—02, v.p., contr., 2002—05, sr. v.p., contr., 2005—10, exec. v.p., CFO, 2010—; CFO Blue Dot Svcs., Inc., 2000. Office: Ryder System Inc 11690 NW 105th St Miami FL 33178 Office Phone: 305-500-3726. Office Fax: 305-593-4731. Business E-Mail: art_garcia@ryder.com.

GARCÍA, ELBA, dentist, former city councilwoman; b. Mexico City; m. Domingo García; 2 children. Degree in Odontology, U. Autonoma Metropolitana, Mexico City; DDS, Baylor Coll. Dentistry, Coll. Station, Tex. Pvt. practice García-Ibancovichi Dental, Dallas, 1990—; councilwoman, Dist. 1 Dallas City Coun., 2001—09, mayor pro tempore, 2007—09, chair pub. safety com., mem. fin., audit & accountability com., housing com., vice-chair Trinity River Project. Chair City of Dallas Domestic Violence Task Force. Recipient Motherhood Lifetime Achievement award, Dallas Can! Acad., 2006, Advocacy in Film award, Dallas Film Commn., 2006, Aspen Inst.-Rodel Fellowship in Pub. Leadership, 2007, 100 Women of Distinction award, Am. Assn. Univ. Women, 2008, Women of Spirit award, Am. Jewish Congress, 2008, OHTLI award, Inst. of Mexicans Abroad, 2008, Presdl. Citation, Tex. Animal Control Assn., 2008; named Best City Coun. Mem., Dallas Observer, 2002, Citizen of Yr., Oak Cliff Tribune, 2005; named a Most Outstanding Cmty. Leader, Dallas Can! Acad., 2003. Mem.: Oak Cliff C. of C. (Pub. Servant award 2008), Lake Cliff Neighborhood Assn., Greater Hispanic C. of C. (Leadership award 2008). Mailing: Dallas City Hall 1500 Marilla St Rm 5EN Dallas TX 75201-6390 Office Phone: 214-670-4052. Fax: 214-670-3409. E-mail: egarcia@mail.ci.dallas.tx.us.

GARCIA, ELISA DOLORES, lawyer; b. Bklyn., Nov. 8, 1957; d. Vincent Garcia, Jr. and Dolores Elizabeth (Canedo) Marmo; m. John Jay Hasluck, Feb. 28, 1987; children: Brooke Elisabeth, John Neville. BA, MS, SUNY, Stony Brook, 1980; JD, St. John's U., 1985. Bar: N.Y. 1986. Cons. Energy Devel. Internat., Pt. Jefferson, N.Y., 1980-83; assoc. Willkie Farr & Gallagher, NYC, 1985-89; sr. counsel GAF Corp./Internat. Specialty Products, Wayne, N.J., 1989-94; regional counsel for L.Am., Philip Morris Internat., Rye Brook, N.Y., 1994-2000; exec. v.p., gen. counsel Domino's Pizza, LLC, Ann Arbor, Mich., 2000—07; exec. v.p., gen. counsel., corp. sec. Office Depot, Inc., Delray Beach, Fla., 2007—13, exec. v.p., chief legal officer, 2013—. Mem. Glen Rock (N.J.) Planning Bd., 1992-95, chmn., 1994-95. Mem. ABA, N.Y. State Bar Assn., Mich. Bar Assn., Assn. Corp. Counsel Assn. (pres. Mich. chpt.). Roman Catholic. Avocations: gardening, scuba diving. Office: Office Depot Inc 6600 N Military Trl Boca Raton FL 33496-2434*

GARCIA, GERALD, JR., advertising executive; Degree in Petroleum Engring., Tex. A&M U. Sr. editl., exec. mgmt. positions Capital Cities, Gannett; various positions, advt. and newspaper pub. Houston Post, Kansas City Star, Knoxville Journal, LA Daily News; pres., CEO Heartland Capital Corp., McLean, Va., 1995—99; editor San Bernardino County Sun Newspaper, 1999—2000; COO Gregory Welteroth Advt., Montoursville, Pa., 2000—01, pres., 2001—02; joined Aims Worldwide, Inc., 2002; pres. AIMS Worldwide, Inc., chmn., CEO, 2009—. Founder, founding pres. Nat. Assn. of Hispanic Journalists'. Recipient Hall of Fame, Nat. Assn. of Hispanic Journalists, 2005. Office: AIMS Worldwide Inc Ste 450 10400 Eaton Pl Fairfax VA 22030 Office Phone: 703-621-3875. Office Fax: 703-621-3865. Business E-Mail: ggarcia@aimsworldwide.com.

GARCIA, JOE (JOSE ANTONIO GARCIA JR.), United States Representative from Florida, former federal agency administrator; b. Miami, Fla., Oct. 12, 1963; s. Jose Antonio and Carmen Garcia; m. Aileen Maria Ugalde, 1992 (div.); 1 child, Gabriela. AA, Miami Dade Cmty. Coll., 1984; BA in Polit. Sci., U. Miami, 1987; JD, U. Miami Sch. Law, 1991. Dir. refugee resettlement prog. Exodus Project, 1987—91; chmn. Fla. Public Svc. Commn., 1991—2000; exec. dir. Cuban American Nat. Found., 2000—04; v.p. Hispanic strategy Ctr. New Democratic Network (NDN), 2004—08; dir. Office Minority Econ. Impact US Dept. Energy, Washington, 2009—10; mem. US Congress from 26th Fla. Dist., Washington, 2013—, US House Judiciary Com., 2013—, US House Natural Resources Com., 2013—. Democrat. Roman Catholic. Office: US House of Representatives 1440 Longworth House Office Bldg Washington DC 20515 also: 12851 SW 42nd St Ste 131 Miami FL 33175 Office Phone: 202-225-2778, 305-222-0160. Office Fax: 305-222-9397.*

GARCIA, JOXEL, healthcare consultant, former federal agency administrator; b. Arecibo, PR, Feb. 21, 1962; m. Ingrid Grafals; children: Joshua, Kristen. B in pre-med, U. Puerto Rico, 1984; MD, Ponce Sch. Medicine, PR, 1988; MBA, U. Hartford, Conn., 1999; cert. in advanced pelvic endoscopy laser, U. Fla. (Gainesville) Sch. Me., 1991; cert. in advanced hysteroscopic surgery, St. Francis Hosp. Med. Ctr., Hartford, 1993; cert. laparoscopic vaginal hysterectomy, St. Raphael's Hosp., 1993; cert. colposcopic, laparoscopic, and hysteroscopic surgery, The Grad. Sch., Philadelphia, Pena., 1994. Diplomate

Am. Bd. Ob-Gyn. Resident in ob-gyn Mt. Sinai Hosp, Hartford, Conn., 1988-91, chief resident in ob-gyn, 1991-92; asst. dir. St. Francis Hosp. Med. Ctr., Hartford, Conn., 1995-99; resident site dir. in ob-gyn Mt. Sinai Hosp., Hartford, Conn., 1995-96; asst. attending physician St. Francis Hosp. and Med. Ctr., Hartford, Conn., 1995-96; asst. clin. prof. U. Conn. Sch. Med., Farmington, Conn., 1996—; dir. gynecol. endoscopy edn. St. Francis Hosp. Med. Ctr., Hartford, Conn., 1997-99; commr. Conn. Dept. Pub. Health, Hartford, Conn., 1999—2003; dep. dir. Pan Am. Health Org. (PAHO); sr. v.p., sr. medical adv. Maximus Federal Services; asst. sec. for health US Dept. Health & Human Services, Washington, 2008—09; pres., dean Ponce Sch. Medicine and Health Sciences, PR, 2009—12; prin. Internat. Healthcare Solutions Group, LLC, 2009—. Contbr. articles to profl. jours.; inventor laparoscopic trocar port filter. Bd. dirs. Cath. Families Svcs. Capital Region; mem. Cath. Charities. Fellow Am. Coll. Ob-Gyn; mem. AMA, Hartford County Med. Soc., Greater Hartford Ob-Gyn Soc., Am. Soc. Reproductive Med., Internat. Pelvic Pain Soc., Am. Inst. Ultrasound in Med., Soc. Pelvic Reconstructive Surgeons, Am. Assn. Gynecol. Laparoscopists, Soc. Laparoscopic and Endoscopic Surgeons. Avocations: tennis, skiing, music. Office: International Healthcare Solutions Group LLC 204 Guthrie Ave Alexandria VA 22305-1817

GARCIA, JULIET VILLARREAL, academic administrator; b. 1949; m. Oscar E. Garcia; 2 children. BA, U. Houston, 1970, MA in Speech, English, 1972; PhD in Comm. & Linguistics, U. Tex., Austin, 1976; LLD (hon.), U. Notre Dame, 1998; PhD (hon.), Brown U., 2006. Teaching asst. U. Houston, 1970—72; instr. Pan Am. U., Edinburg, 1972; teaching asst. U. Tex., Austin, 1974—76; adj. prof. Pan Am. U., Brownsville, 1977—79; instr. Tex. Southmost Coll., 1972—74, 1976—81, dir. TSC Self-Study, 1979—81, dean arts and scis., 1981—86, pres., 1986—92, U. Tex. at Brownsville, Tex., 1992—. Chmn. bd. dirs. Am. Coun. Edn., 1995; mem. White House Initiative on Ednl. Excellence for Hispanic-Ams.; bd. dirs. Fed. Res. of Dallas/San Antonio; bd. mem. Tex. Commerce Bancshares Inc.; mem. Barack Obama Presdl. Transition Team, 2008—09. Bd. dirs. Carnegie Found. for Advancement of Tchg., Pub. Welfare Found., vice chair adv. com. on fin. aid; bd. trustees Ford Found., 2003—. Recipient Outstanding Tex. Leader Award, John Ben L. Sheppard Leadership Found., 1994, Woman of Distinction, Nat. Conf. of Coll. Women Student Leaders, 1995, John P. McGovern Award, Am. Assn. Colls. of Nursing, 1998, Mujer Regional Award, Nat. Hispana Leadership Inst., 2003, Hispanic Heritage Award for Edn., 2006; named one of The 100 Most Influential Hispanics, Hispanic Bus. Mag., 1993, 1997, 2002, The Most Influential Hispanic Women of Tex., Tex. Hispanic Mag., 1995, The 10 Best Coll. Presidents, TIME mag., 2009. Democrat. Office: U Tex & Tex Southmost Coll Office of Pres 80 Fort Brown St Brownsville TX 78520-4956 Office Phone: 956-544-8200. E-mail: president@utb.edu.

GARCIA, LILLIAN D., human resources specialist; Sr. v.p., human resources Tupperware Brands Corp, 1999—2005; exec. v.p., chief human resources officer Tupperware Brands Corp., 2005—. Office: Tupperware Brands Corp 14901 S Orange Blossom Trail Orlando FL 32837 Office Phone: 407-826-5050. Office Fax: 407-826-8874.

GARCIA, LUIS R., state legislator; b. Marianao, Cuba, Dec. 8, 1945; children: Nicolas Luis, Jorge Luis, Alejandro Luis. AS in EMS Mgmt., Miami-Dade CC, Fla., 1990. Cert. EMT 1974, paramedic 1977, exec. fire officer Nat. Fire Acad., 1997. Ret. chief Miami Beach Fire Dept.; mem. Dist. 107 Fla. House of Reps., Tallahassee, 2006—, ranking mem. pub. safety and domestic security policy com., mem. criminal and civil justice policy coun., joint legis. com. on Everglades oversight, state univs. and pvt. colls. appropriations com. Mem. Miami Beach Sr. High Scholastics Excellence Com.; vice chmn. Fla. Dem. Party; mem. exec. bd. Am. Cancer Soc., Greater Miami Conventions and Visitors Bur., Miami Heart Inst. Mem.: Miami Beach Kiwanis. Democrat. Roman Catholic. Office: 531 SW 12th Ave Miami FL 33130-2413 also: 405 House Office Bldg 402 S Monroe St Tallahassee FL 32399-1300 Office Phone: 305-325-2501, 850-488-9930.

GARCIA, ORLANDO LUIS, federal judge; b. 1952; BA, U. Tex., 1975, JD, 1978. Legis. aide to Hon. Matt Garcia and Ernestine Glossbrenner Tex. Ho. of Reps., 1974-83; atty. Law Offices of Matt Garcia, 1978-85; mem. Tex. Ho. of Reps., 1983-91; atty. Heard, Goggan, Blair & Williams, 1985-90; judge 4th Ct. of Appeals, San Antonio, 1991-94, US Dist. Ct. (we. dist.) Tex., San Antonio, 1994—. Vol. San Antonio State Hosp. Vol. Coun., San Antonio Pro Bono Project. Named One of Ten Best Legislators of 70th Tex. Legislature, State Bar Tex., 1987, Outstanding State Rep. of Yr., Tex. Youth Commn., 1990, Legislator of Yr., Tex. Pub. Employees Assn., 1989, Tex. Alliance for Mentally Ill., 1990, Mem. State Bar Tex., Tex. Bar Found., San Antonio Bar Assn., Tex. Jud. Coun. Office: US Dist Ct US Courthouse 1st Fl 655 E Durango Blvd San Antonio TX 78206-1100

GARCIA, OSCAR NICOLAS, computer science educator; b. Havana, Cuba, Sept. 10, 1936; s. Oscar Vicente and Leonor (Hernandez) G.; m. Diane Ford Journigan, Sept. 9, 1962; children: Flora, Virginia. BSEE, N.C. State U., Raleigh, 1961, MSEE, 1964; PhDEE, U. Md., College Park, 1969. Engr. IBM Corp., Endicott, NY, 1962-63; asst. prof. Old Dominion U., 1963-66, assoc. prof., 1969-70; research asst., instr. U. Md., 1966-69; assoc. prof. U. South Fla., Tampa, 1970-75, prof. computer sci., chmn. dept., 1975-85; prof. dept. elec. engring. and computer sci. George Washington U., Washington, 1985-95; disting. NCR prof. Wright State U., Dayton, Ohio, 1995—2003, chmn. dept. computer sci. and engring., 1995—2003; founding dean Coll. Engring. U. North Tex., Denton, 2003—08, prof. elec. engring., 2008—. Dir. interactive sys. program in info., robotics and intelligent sys. divsn. Computer and Info. Sci. and Engring. Directorate, Intergovtl. Pers. Act, NSF, Washington, 1992-94; cons. and lectr. in field. Author: (with Y.T. Chien) Knowledge-Based Systems: Fundamentals and Tools, 1991. Fellow IEEE (bd. dirs. 1984-85, 2005—, mem. U.S. activities bd. 1984, Profl. Leadership award 1991, Richard M. Emberson award 1994), Computer Soc. of IEEE (pres. 1981-83, awards com. chmn. 2002-03, bd. govs. 2003—, sec. bd. govs. 2003-04, Richard E. Merwin Disting. Svc. award 1988, Meritorious Svc. award 1991), AAAS; mem. Assn. Computing Machinery, Am. Soc. Engring. Edn., Am. Assn. Artificial Intelligence, Sigma Xi, Eta Kappa Nu, Phi Kappa Phi, Tau Beta Pi. Office: U North Tex Coll Engring PO Box 310440 Denton TX 76203-0440 Home: 120 W El Paseo St Denton TX 76205-8590 Office Phone: 940-369-8171.

GARCIA, RENE, state legislator; b. Hialeah, Fla., July 10, 1974; BS in Polit. Sci., Fla. Internat. U., Miami, 1999; MBA in Health Adminstrn and Policy, U. Miami, 2004. Councilman Hialeah City Coun., 1997—99; mem. Dist. 110 Fla. House of Reps., Fla., 2000—08; v.p. cmty. rels. Dade Med. Coll., Fla., sr. v.p. govt. and cmty. rels.; mem. Dist. 40 Fla. State Senate, 2011—. Mem.: Hialeah Flamingo Kiwanis Club (2nd v.p.). Republican. Roman Catholic. Office: Fla State Senate 310 Senate Office Bldg 404 S Monroe St Tallahassee FL 32399-1100 also: 1490 W 68th St Ste 201 Hialeah FL 33014-4590 Office Phone: 305-364-3100, 850-487-5106. Business E-Mail: garcia.rene.web@flsenate.gov.

GARCIA, SERGIO, professional golfer; b. Castellon, Spain, Jan. 9, 1980; s. Victor Garcia. Profl. golfer European Tour, PGA Tour, 1999—; mem. European team Ryder Cup, 1999, 2002, 2004, 2006, 2008, 2012; mem. Spanish team Dunhill Cup, 1999, 2000; mem. Continental European team Seve Trophy, 2000, 2003; mem. Spanish team World Cup, 2001, 2004, 2005, 2009. Recipient Byron Nelson Award, 2008; named Sir Henry Cotton Rookie of Yr., PGA European Tour, 1999. Achievements include winning PGA Tour events including the MasterCard Colonial, 2001 Buick Classic, 2001, 04; Mercedes Championships, 2002; EDS Byron Nelson Championship, 2004; Booz Allen Classic, 2005; The Players Championship, 2008; Wyndham Championship, 2012; winner, international events including the Catalonian Open Championship, 1997; Murphy's Irish Open, Linde German Masters, 1999; Trophee Lancome, 2001; Nedbank Golf Challenge, 2001, 03; Canarias Open de Espana, 2002; Kolon Cup Korean Open, 2002; Mallorca Classic, 2004; Omega European Masters, 2005; HSBC Champions, 2008; Gary Player Invitational; Castello Masters, Andalucia Masters, 2011. Avocations: soccer, computer games. Office: PGA Tour 112 PGA Tour Blvd Ponte Vedra Beach FL 32082

GARCIA, SONIA R., political science professor; d. Minerva M. and Ignacio Garcia; m. Charley A. Garcia, July 8, 1995. BA, St. Mary's U., San Antonio, 1985; MA, U. Ariz., Tucson, 1987; PhD, U. Calif., Santa Barbara, 1994. Co-founder women's studies minora St. Mary's U., San Antonio, coll. prof., 1995—, coord., 2008—. Author: (academic book) Politicas: Latina Public Officials in Texas. Mem.: Western Polit. Sci. Assn. (exec. coun. pres.). Office: St Marys' Univ Polit Sci Dept One Camino Santa Maria San Antonio TX 78228

GARCIA-GRANADOS, SERGIO EDUARDO, portfolio manager, writer, historian; b. June 11, 1942; s. Jorge and Miriam Garcia-Granados; m. Elizabeth Bentley, Apr. 3, 1973; children: Tatiana, Sybil. Law degree with honors, 1960-66, U. San Carlos, Guatemala, 1966; postgrad., U. Paris Inst. Scis. Politique, Paris, 1966-68. Bar: 1968. Rsch. assoc. Hague Acad. Internat. Law, 1969, Internat. Bur. Fiscal Documentation, Amsterdam, 1969-70; ptnr. law firm Saravia y Muñoz, Guatemala City, 1970—81; v.p. sales mgr. Merrill Lynch Capital Markets Internat., NYC, 1982-88; v.p. resident mgr. internat. div. Shearson Lehman Hutton, NYC, 1988—90; portfolio mgr. Lehman Bros., Miami, Fla., 1990—99; sr. portfolio mgr. UBS, Miami, 1999—2009, Morgan Stanley SB, Miami, 2009—. Lectr. tax problems in Central Am. Common Market, U. San Carlos, bus. orgns.,U. Landivar, Globalization of Capital Markets, Guatemalan Mgmt. Assn., 1991; bd. dirs. Miami Soc. Fin. Analysts, 1996—, Miami Symphony Orch., 2004—12. Author: Academia de Geografía e Historia, Revista Anales, 1999, El Siglo de las Luces, Libre Crezca Fecunda (1729-1821), Editorial Magna Terra - Guatemala, 2005; co-author: Cuaderno de Memorias (1900-1922), Artemis-Edinter, 2000, Reminiscencias (1944-51); organizer, 1st editor loose-leaf corp. taxation in Latin Am., Amsterdam, 1970. Bd. dirs. Patronato de Bellas Artes, 1977—84, Guatemala Nat. Theatre Directorate, 1979—82, Cuban Mus. Art, 1994—2000, Miami Symphony Orch., 2004—12, treas., 2006—09. Mem. Colegio de Abogados, Internat. Fiscal Assn. (gen. coun. 1972-80, 2004-12), CFA Inst., Miami Soc. Fin. Analysts (pres. 2005—07), Acad. Geografía e Historia Guatemala, Miami Art Mus. Collectors Coun.*

GARCIA-GREGORY, JAY A., federal judge; b. San Juan, 1944; AB, Assumption Coll., 1966; MA, U. Madrid, 1969; LLB, U. PR, 1972. Law clk. to Hon. Hiram Cancio and Hon. Jose Toledo US Dist. Ct. PR, 1973—74; pvt. practice atty. PR, 1974—2000; judge US Dist. Ct. PR, 2000—. Office: US Dist Ct Clemente Ruiz Nazario US Courthouse 300 Calle Del Recinto S San Juan PR 00901-1907

GARCIA-HOLGUIN, MARY H., child and adolescent psychiatrist; MD, U. Tex., San Antonio, 1991. Diplomate Am. Bd. Psychiatry and Neurology-child and adolescent psychiatry, 1999, Am. Bd. Psychiatry and Neurology, 2007. Resident psychiatry Duke Univ. Med. Ctr., Durham, NC, 1991—94; fellow child & adolescent psychiatry Univ. Tex., San Antonio, 1994—96; hosp. affiliation Nix Med. Ctr. Office: Nix Medical Center 414 Navarro San Antonio TX 78205 Office Phone: 210-271-1800. Office Fax: 210-271-2127.

GARCÍA PADILLA, ALEJANDRO JAVIER, Governor of Puerto Rico; b. Coamo, PR, Aug. 3, 1971; m. Wilma Pastrana, Apr. 7, 2001; children: Ana, Juan, Diego. BA in Polit. Sci. & Economics, U. PR; JD, Interamerican U. of PR. Legal officer Ct. of Appeals of PR; atty. Pedro Ortiz Alvarez, William Elijah Reyes, Jorge R. Jimenez, Fernando Agrait; sec. consumer affairs Commonwealth of PR, PR, 2005—09, gov. San Juan, 2013—; senator at large PR Legislature, 2009—13. Leader Popular Democratic Party, 2011—. Popular Democratic Party. Office: Office of the Governor La Fortaleza PO Box 9020082 San Juan PR 00902-0082 Office Phone: 787-721-7000.*

GARCIA-SILLER, GUSTAVO, archbishop; b. San Luis Potosí, Mexico, Dec. 21, 1956; MA in Psychology, Mexico; MA in Philosophy, Escuela de Verano Para Formadores, Toluca, Mexico; MA in Theology, St. John's Sem., Camarillo, Calif., MDiv. Professed Missionaries of the Holy Spirit, 1975, ordained priest, 1984; rector Missionaries of Holy Spirit House of Studies, Lynwood and Long Beach, Calif., 1990—96, Mount Angel, Oreg., 1996—99; maj. superior Missionaries of Holy Spirit for US, 1999—2003; ordained bishop, 2003; aux. bishop Archdiocese of Chgo., 2003—10; archbishop Archdiocese of San Antonio, Tex., 2010—. Roman Catholic. Office: Archdiocese of San Antonio 2718 W Woodlawn Ave San Antonio TX 78228 Office Phone: 210-734-2620. Office Fax: 210-734-0231.

GARDENIER, JOHN STARK, writer, science/statistical ethicist, open data advocate; b. Portland, Maine, Apr. 10, 1937; s. John Stark and Lucia Esther (Christensen) G.; m. Margaret Elizabeth Mann, Jan. 26, 1962 (dec. 1976); children: Brenda Anne Marshall, Patricia Suzanne Depew, Linda Marie Sievering-Albrecht, Pamela Lee Antoun; m. Turkan Emine Kumbaraci, June 18, 1977; children: George Halil Bonneval, Jason Celal Stark. BA, Yale U., 1959; MS, George Washington U., 1968, DBA, 1973. Tech. staff Computer Scis. Corp., Falls Church, Va., 1968-69; sr. analyst CONSULTEC, Rockville, Md., 1969-71; ops. rsch. analyst USCG, Washington, 1971-90; survey statistician Nat. Ctr. Health Stats., Hyattsville, Md., 1990—2003; ret., 2003. Adj. assoc. prof. George Washington U., 1980-81; prof. lectr. Am. U., Washington, 1982-84; cons. in field. Comdr. USN, ret. Recipient Silver medal US Dept. Transp., 1983, Dir.'s award CDC/Nat. Ctr. for Health Stats., 2000. Mem. AAAS, Am. Statis. Assn. (com. profl. ethics 1994-96, chair com. profl. ethics 1996-99, vice chair com. AAAS reps. 2002-2008), Nat. Assn. Sci. Writers, Naval Res. Assn Avocations: music, golf. Home: 115 St Andrews Dr NE Vienna VA 22180-3660 Office Phone: 703-319-3981. Personal E-mail: drgarden@verizon.net.

GARDENIER, TURKAN KUMBARACI, statistician, researcher; b. Istanbul, Turkey, Nov. 10, 1941; arrived in U.S., 1958; d. Celal and Aysel (Triandafilidu) K.; m. John Stark Gardenier, June 18, 1977; children: Pamela Lee, George HalilBonneval, Jason Celal Stark. AB, Vassar Coll., 1961; MA, Columbia U., 1962, PhD, 1966. Ops. rsch. scientist IIT Rsch. Inst., Chgo., 1966-68; asst. prof., chmn. Middle East Tech. U., Ankara, Turkey, 1968-70; vis. scientist Brookhaven Nat. Labs., Upton, L.I., NY, 1970-71; assoc. dir. Pfizer Pharms., NYC, 1971-73; asst. prof. N.Y. State Maritime Coll., Bronx, NY, 1973-78; health scientist U.S. EPA, Washington, 1978-81; assoc. prof. Am. U., Washington, 1982-84; pres. Pragmatica Corp., Vienna, Va., 1982—. Tech. cons. Analytic Services Corp., Arlington, Va., 1982-90; expert U.S. Energy Info. Adminstrn., Washington, 1982-84; statis. expert EEO, 1990—, statis. cons. Engring. Computer Optecnomics, Annapolis, Md., 1977—; cons. C.R. Cushing Co., Marine Engring., N.Y.C., 1974-77. Organizer, pub. Symposium on Data Efficiency Design; preprocessing pub. Garden-ear Math./Stat. Series for Quanititative Literacy. Corp. mem. Am. Friends of Turkey, McLean, Va., 1983-89; com. mem. World Mut. Service Com., N.Y.C., 1982—; bd. dirs., v.p. Friends of Am. BoardSchs. in Turkey, 1986-88, Am. Turkish Assn., Washington, 1988-90, Washington parents rep. Foxcroft Sch., Middleburg, Va., 1981-84. Grantee, NSF, 1980, CENTO, 1969, NIH/NCI, 1997-2000. Mem. Am. Statis. Assn. (audio-visual graphics com. 1979), Ops. Rsch. Soc. Am. (fin. com. 1980), Soc. Computer Simulation (assoc. editor jour. 1980-84), Soc. Risk Analysis (fin. com. 1980), Soc. Indsl. & Applied Math., Inst. Math. Stats. (life) AAAS (symposium organizer 1979-2011). Avocations: swimming, photography, music composition, multi-media training. Address: Pragmatica Corp 115 St Andrews Dr NE Vienna VA 22180-3660 Home Phone: 703-319-3981; Office Phone: 703-319-9009. Business E-Mail: gardeniert@yahoo.com. E-mail: drgarden@verizon.net.

GARDINER, ANDY, state legislator; b. Orlando, Fla., Jan. 23, 1969; m. Camille Gardiner; children: Andrew Jr., Joanna Lynn. BS in Polit. Sci. & Psychology, Stetson U., DeLand, Fla., 1992. Dir. cmty. and bus. rels. Orlando Health; mem. Dist. 40 Fla. House of Reps., Tallahassee, 2000—08, majority leader, 2004—06; mem. Dist. 9 Fla. State Senate, Tallahassee, 2008—, majority whip, 2008—10, chair transp. com., mem. cmty. affairs com., ethics and elections com., health regulation com., reapportionment com., rules com., joint legis. auditing com. Mem. Orange County Rep. Exec. Com.; bd. dirs. Fla. Hosp. Found. Mem. Rotary, Apopka Foliage Sertoma Club. Republican. Methodist. Office: 1013 E Michigan St Orlando FL 32806-4704 also: 308 Senate Office Bldg 404 S Monroe St Tallahassee FL 32399-1100 Office Phone: 407-428-5800, 850-487-5047. Business E-Mail: gardiner.andy.web@flsenate.gov.

GARDINER, HOBART CLIVE, retired petroleum company executive; b. Boston, Jan. 12, 1929; m. Patricia Williams, Oct. 14, 1950(June 2008), m. Jean Thompson, May 31, 2010. BA, Yale U., 1950; postgrad., U. Central Caracas, Venezuela. Various mgmt. positions Esso Standard Oil Co. S.A., Havana, Cuba, 1954, Panama City, Panama, 1954, San Salvador, El Salvador, 1954-56, Guatemala City, Guatemala, 1956, country mgr. San Jose, Costa Rica, 1956-57, Tegucigalpa, Honduras, Brit. Honduras, 1957-60; asst. employee rels. mgr. Esso Interamerica Inc., Coral Gables, Fla., 1960; pres., gen. mgr. Esso Standard Oil Co., S.A., San Juan, P.R., 1960-62; v.p. Internat. Petroleum Co. Ltd., Bogota, Colombia, 1962-64, ops. mgr. Talara, Peru, 1964-66; pres. Esso Std. Oil (Chile), Santiago, 1966-69; L.Am. area advisor Standard Oil Co. N.J., NYC, 1969-71; v.p. Esso Standard Oil Co. C.Am., Panama, San Salvador, El Salvador, 1971-74; gen. mgr. Esso Chile, Uruguay and Paraguay, Montevideo, Uruguay, 1974-77; pub. affairs program mgr. Exxon Corp., NYC, 1977-79; asst. gen. mgr. Esso Caribbean, Coral Gables, Fla., 1979-81; v.p. fin. and adminstrn. Internat. Exec. Svc. Corps., Stamford, Conn., 1982-84, v.p. L.Am. and Caribbean, 1984-90, exec. v.p., 1990-93, pres., CEO, 1993—2003; ret., 2003. With USMC, 1950—52. Mem.: Piping Rock Club, Gulf Stream Golf Club, Gulf Stream Bath & Tennis Club, Little Club. Episcopalian. Home: 401 E Linton Blvd Apt 477 Delray Beach FL 33483-5028 Personal E-mail: hobartgardiner@gmail.com.

GARDNER, BERNARD, surgeon, educator; b. Bklyn., Oct. 1, 1931; s. Charles and Selma G.; m. Joan E. Mann., Dec. 18, 1954; children: Karen A., Pamela D., Robert A. AB cum laude, NYU, 1952, MD, 1956. Intern Bellevue Hosp. Ctr., NYC, 1956-57; resident Mt. Sinai Hosp., NYC, 1957-58, U. Calif. Med. Ctr., San Francisco, 1961-65; asst. prof. surgery SUNY Downstate Med. Ctr., Bklyn., 1965-68, assoc. prof., 1968-72, prof., 1972; prof. surgery, dir. Bklyn. Cancer Ctr., 1973—; prof., dir. divsn. surg. edn. U. Medicine and Dentistry of N.J., 1983—; dir. dept. surgery Hackensack Med. Ctr., 1983-92. Cons. VA Hosp., Luth. Med. Ctr., Swedish Hosp., Meth. Hosp., Kingsbrook Med. Ctr., all Bklyn., VA Hosp., Newark, N.J. Univ. Hosp., Newark; dir. divsn. surg. oncology Kings County Hosp., 1971; mem. study sect. on cancer edn. Nat. Cancer Inst., 1981-83. Author: (book) Emergency Surgery, 1974, 2d edit., 1986, Basic Surgery: Patient Oriented Text, 1978, 5th edit., 1995, Principles of Cancer Surgery, 1981, 2000, The Value of Corruption in a Democratic Society, prodr.: (plays) Two Mystery Plays, 2008, 5 Plays, 2010. Capt. USAF, 1958-60. Fellow Am. Cancer Soc., 1965-68; Markle fellow, 1968-73; recipient numerous grants, 1962— Fellow Soc. Surg. Oncology (pres. 1994—); mem. Am. Surg. Assn., Soc. Univ. Surgeons, Assn. Acad. Surgery (chmn. com. on issues 1971—), N.Y. Surg. Soc., N.Y. Cancer Soc., Soc. Exptl. Medicine and Biology. Achievements include research on metabolic effects of cancer, mechanism of gall stone dissolution. Personal E-mail: mdbg10012@comcast.net.

GARDNER, DAVID JOHN, communications executive, recording engineer, producer; b. Binghamton, NY, Jan. 8, 1953; s. Daniel Sparrow and Anne Mae (Worthing) G.; m. Nancy Tipton Peacock, 1992; 1 child, Deborah Anne. AA, Broome CC, Binghamton, 1973; BA, Hofstra U., 1975. Prodn. control analyst IBM, Systems Mfg. Div., Endicott, NY, 1971-73; rec. engr. Eye-Full Films, San Francisco, 1972-78; gen. mgr. J.K. Theater Corp., Binghamton, 1975-77; rec. engr. The Image Works, Binghamton, 1977-80; audio/video engr. Sta. WBNG, Binghamton, 1977-78; media technician Nat. Sci. Found., Washington, 1978-79; tech. ops. RCA Americom Svcs., Inc., Princeton, NJ, 1980-84, supr. ops., 1984-86; mgr. network ops. ctr. GE Americom, Inc., Princeton, 1986-90, mgr. Vernon Valley tech. ops., 1990-92, mgr., customer svcs. and ops., 1992-95; dir. media svcs. Orion Atlantic, Rockville, MD, 1995-99; dir. mktg. svcs. Loral Skynet, Bedminster, NJ, 1999—2004, dir. satellite sys. engring., 2004—07; dir., internat. sales engring. Telesat, 2007—10; v.p., engring. US Space LLC, Dulles, Va., 2011—. Owner, pres., rec. engr. Ind. Sound, Binghamton, 1963-; co-founder, COB, bd. dirs. New Orleans Rec. Co., 1980—, Street Rhythm Prodns., Street Rhythm Records, Bklyn., 1980—; instr., lectr., Nat. Def. U. Indsl. Coll. Armed Forces. Mem. Soc. Broadcast Engrs., Soc. Motion Picture and TV Engrs. Lodges: Order of DeMolay. Episcopalian. Achievements include development and implementation of value-added satellite services for multimedia and other customer applications. Avocations: tennis, basketball, audio/video recording. Home: PO Box 205 Springtown PA 18081-0205 Office: US Space LLC 21700 Atlantic Blvd Ste 240 Dulles VA 20166 Business E-Mail: david.gardner@usspacemobile.com.

GARDNER, DONALD F., endocrinologist; MD, U. Ill., 1973. Diplomate Am. Bd. Internal Medicine, 1976, Am. Bd. Internal Medicine-endocrinology, diabetes and metabolism, 1987. Resident internal medicine Vanderbilt Univ. Med. Ctr., Nashville, 1974—76; fellow endocrinology Univ. Fla. Hosp., Gainesville, 1980—83; pvt. practice Meml. City Endocrine Consultants; hosp. affiliations include

Meml. Hermann Meml. City Hosp., Meml. Hermann Katy Hosp. Office: Memorial City Endocrine Consultants Ste 550 1140 Business Center Dr Houston TX 77043 Office Phone: 713-984-8200. Office Fax: 713-984-1113.*

GARDNER, JEFFREY R., telecommunications industry executive; BS in Fin., Purdue U.; MBA, William & Mary U. CPA. Dir., fin. 360 Comm., v.p., gen. mgr. Las Vegas, pres., Mid-Atlantic regional ops., 1994—97, sr. v.p., fin., 1997; joined Alltel Corp. (merged with 360 Comm.), Little Rock, 1998, exec. v.p., CFO, sr. v.p., 2003—05; pres., CEO Alltel Holding Corp., Little Rock, 2005—06, Windstream Corp., 2005—. Bd. dirs. RF Micro Devices Inc. Bd. dirs. Ark. Children's Hosp., Darlington Sch., Ark. Rsch. Alliance; chmn. U. of Ark. for Med. Sciences Ctr. for Distance Health; bd. dirs. Little Rock Regional C. of C., Pulaski Acad. Office: Windstream Corp 4001 Rodney Parham Rd Little Rock AR 72212-2442 Office Phone: 501-748-7000. Business E-Mail: jeffrey.gardner@windstream.com.

GARDNER, JOE C., state legislator; b. Apr. 6, 1944; m. Ella Graham Gardner. Mem. Dist. 11 Miss. House of Reps., 2007—, vice chair agr. com., mem. conservation and water resources com., constn. com., edn. com., judiciary B com., judiciary en banc com., mil. affairs com. Democrat. Baptist. Home: 11084 Curtis Rd Batesville MS 38606 E-mail: jgardner@house.ms.gov.

GARDNER, KERRY ANN, librarian; b. Honolulu, May 19, 1955; d. Byron Patton and Claire Gardner. BA in Polit. Sci. magna cum laude, Temple U., 1976; MA in L.Am. Studies, U. Ariz., 1983, MLS, 1990. Documents libr. FMC Corp., Chgo., 1977-78; rsch. cons., 1983-92; grad. rsch. asst. U. Ariz., Tucson, 1983-86, project mgr., 1990-92; libr. asst. I Phoenix Pub. Libr., 1988-89; mgr. faculty resource libr., English 2d lang. U. Ariz. Ctr., 1989—92; pub. svcs. libr. Bryan Wildenthal Meml. Libr., Sul Ross State U., Alpine, Tex., 1992-95; libr. dir. Am. U., Dubai, United Arab Emirates, 1995-96; literacy libr. Sterling Mcpl. Libr., Baytown, 1996-98; prof., libr. Valle Verde campus, El Paso C.C., 1998—, co-head libr., 2001—02, head libr., 2007—08, 2013—. Indexer Hispanic American Periodicals Index, 1995; maintain GPO Access Web site, 1998—. Contbr. articles to profl. publs. Tchr. English, Literacy Vols. Am., 1991-92, 96-98. Named Libr. of Yr., Border Regional Libr. Assn., 2001; grad. scholar, U. Ariz., 1976—77, 1981—82. Mem.: NEA, ALA, Tex. Libr. Assn. (mem. conf. planning com. 2013—), El Paso Mus. Art Libr. Adv. Bd., Tex. Faculty Assn./El Paso Coun. Higher Edn. (grievance coord. 2009—13, sec. 2011—13, 2013—), Med. Libr. Assn., Friends El Paso Pub. Libr. (sec. 2006—07, bd. dirs. 2007—08, 2013—, sec. 2013—), Tex. State Tchrs. Assn., Border Regional Libr. Assn. (chair publicity com. 1999—2002, chair. Libr. of the Yr. com. 2002—03), Assn. Coll. and Rsch. Librs. (mem. conf. planning com. 2013—), Beta Phi Mu, Reforma. Avocations: travel, birding. Office: El Paso Cmty Coll Valle Verde Campus PO Box 20500 El Paso TX 79998-0500

GARDNER, PAMELA J., sports association executive; b. Green Bay, Wis. children: Coleman Anderson, Meaghan Anderson. Grad., U. Wis., Stout. With Minute Maid Park; dir., comm. Houston Astros Baseball Club, 1989—94, dir., mktg., 1994—96, v.p., mktg., 1996—99, sr. v.p., sales & mktg., 1999—2001, pres., bus. ops., 2001—, COO. Bd. dirs. Ctrl. Houston, Inc., Newfield Exploration Co., 2005—; bd. adv. J.P. Morgan Chase & Co. Bd. dirs. Astros in Action Found., Houston Area Women's Ctr. Named one of 20 Most Influential Women in Sports, Street and Smith's Sports Bus. Jour., 2005; recipient Included in a Spl. Exhibit, Nat. Baseball Hall of Fame and Mus. Cooperstown, Tex. Baseball Hall of Fame, Houston, 2006. Office: Houston Astros Baseball Club Minute Maid Park 501 Crawford Ste 400 Houston TX 77002 Office Phone: 713-259-8000. Office Fax: 713-259-8025.

GARDNER, PAT, state legislator; b. Alpena County, Mich., Mar. 22, 1940; m. Jerry Gardner; children: Anita, Bradley. Former spanish tchr. Cmty. Involvement; former state rep. Dist. 42 Ga.; state rep. Dist. 57 Ga., 2004—; mem. Health & Ecology & Ins. Coms.; vice chmn. Higher Edn. Com. Mem.: Buckhead Bus. Assn., Ga. Conservancy, League Women Voters, America & Ga. Soc. Assn. Execs., Morningside Lenox Pk. Assn. Bd., Midtown Rotary Club. Democrat. Mailing: 609 LOB Atlanta GA 30334 Office: 668 E Pelham Rd Atlanta GA 30324 Office Phone: 404-656-0305, 404-873-9944. Business E-Mail: Pat@patgardner.org.

GARDNER, ROBIN PIERCE, engineering educator; b. Charlotte, NC, Aug. 17, 1934; s. Robin Brem and Margaret (Pierce) G.; m. Linda Jean Gardner, Oct. 21, 1976. B.Ch.E., N.C. State U., 1956, MS, 1958; PhD, Pa. State U., 1961. Scientist Oak Ridge Inst. Nuclear Studies, 1961-63; research engr., asst. dir. measurement and controls lab. Research Triangle Inst., Research Triangle Park, NC, 1963-67; research prof. nuclear engring. and chem. engring., dir. Center Engring. Applications of Radioisotopes, N.C. State U., 1967—. Cons. Oak Ridge Inst. Nuclear Studies, Research Triangle Inst., Oak Ridge Nat. Lab., Internat. Atomic Energy Agy., NASA, AEC, TVA, Alcoa. Author: (with Ralph L. Ely, Jr.), Radioisotope Measurement Applications in Engineering, 1967; regional editor Applied Radiation and Isotopes, Jour. Fine Particle Soc., Nuc. Geophysics; contbr. articles to sci. jours. Served to 1st lt. AUS, 1956. Recipient Alcoa Found. Disting. Rsch. award N.C. State U. Sch. Engring., 1986, Alumni Disting. Grad. Professorship award, 1996, R.J. Reynolds award for excellence in tchg. and rsch., 1998; Centennial fellow Coll. Earth and Mineral Scis., Pa. State U., 1996. Fellow Am. Nuc. Soc. (Radiation Industry award isotopes and radiation divsn. 1984), Am. Nuc. Soc., Am. Soc. Engring. Edn. (Glenn Murphy award for Outstanding Contributions Profession & tchg. Nuc. Engring. 2003, Arthur Holly Compton award Am. Nuc. Soc., 2009), Sigma Xi, Phi Kappa Phi, Phi Lambda Upsilon. Achievements include founding of a successful series of topical meetings entitled Industrial Radiation and Radioisotope Measurement Applications the last four were held in Bologna, Italy, Toronto, Canada, Prague, The Czech Republic, and Kansas City. Home: 3005 Randolph Dr Raleigh NC 27609-6941 Office: NC State U Ctr Engring Applications of Radioisotope Dept Nuclear Engring Raleigh NC 27695-0001 Office Phone: 919-515-3378. Business E-Mail: gardner@ncsu.edu.

GAREN, JOHN EDWARD, economics professor; b. Indpls., Nov. 24, 1953; s. Charles Edward and Luella May Garen; 1 child, Michael John. BA magna cum laude, U. Wash., Seattle, 1976; PhD, Ohio State U., Columbus, 1982. Vis. assoc. prof. Harris Grad. Sch. Pub. Policy Studies, U. Chgo., 1991—92; prof. Dept. Economics, U. Ky., Lexington, 1996—, Gatton endowed prof., 1999—, dept. chair, 2005—; interim co-director Ctr. for Bus. and Economics Rsch., U. Ky., 2004—05. Vis. scholar Nat. Sun Yat-Sen U., Kaohsiung, Taiwan, 2006; adj. scholar Bluegrass Inst. for Pub. Policy Solutions, Bowling Green, Ky., 2008—. Contbr. articles to profl. jours. Grantee Applied Microeconomics Rsch. Program, NSF, 1986-1991, Labor Demand Over Bus. Cycle: Case of Coal, US Dept. Interior, 1987—88, Access of Females to On-the-Job Tng., US Dept. Labor, 1988, Unemployment Ins. Budget and Performance Linkage, 2004-2005, Older Workers in Labor Market, US SBA, 1989-1991, Fiscal Policy and Local Econ. Devel., Nat. Ctr., Real Estate Rsch., 2005, Forces Shaping the Aluminum Industry, Sloan Ctr., Sustainable Aluminum Industry, 2008; fellow Presdl., Ohio State U., 1980-1981. Mem.: Jour. Econs. Fin. (editl. bd. mem. 2003—08), Soc. of Labor Economists, Am. Econ. Assn., Phi Beta Kappa. Office: Dept of Economics Univ of KY 500 South Limestone Lexington KY 40506-0034 Office Fax: 859-323-1920. Business E-Mail: jgaren@uky.edu.

GARFIELD, RANDY ALAN, marketing executive; b. Bronx, NY, Apr. 25, 1952; s. Irving Garfield and Frances Charlotte Patlin Towers; children: Michael Gregory, John Robert. Grad., UCLA, 1974. Cert. travel cons., travel mktg. exec. Quality controller Western region TWA, LA, 1974-75, supr. customer svc. reservation, 1975-78, supr. reservation svcs. Kansas City, Mo., 1978-79, account mgr. passenger sales, 1979-82, mgr. passenger sales Hartford, Conn., 1982-83; v.p. sales S.W. region Royal Viking Line, San Francisco, 1983-86; v.p. sales Universal Studios Hollywood, Universal City, Calif., 1986-89; exec. v.p. mktg. and sales Universal Studios Fla., Orlando, 1989-93; exec. v.p. worldwide sales & travel ops. Disney Destinations Walt Disney Co., Lake Buena Vista, Fla., 1993—; pres. Walt Disney Travel Co., Lake Buena Vista, Fla., 1993—; exec. v.p. sales & travel ops. Walt Disney Parks & Resorts, Lake Buena Vista, Fla., 1993—. Seminar speaker Inst. Cert. Travel Agents, 1983—87; delegate White House Conf. on Tourism. Chmn. bd. Tourism Assn., So. Calif., L.A., 1988-89; bd. dirs. Calif. Tourism Corp., Sacramento, 1988-89, Goodwill Industries Ctrl. Fla., 1990-96, NCCJ, 1990—, Found. for Orange County Pub. Schs., 1990-94; mem. adv. bd. Congl. Travel and Tourism Caucus, 1992-93; trustee Park Coll., Parkville, Mo. Recipient Brass Ring award Internat. Assn. Amusement Parks and Attractions, 1989, 90, Bronze Quill award Internat. Assn. Bus. Communicators. Mem. Travel Industry Assn. Am. (bd. dirs. 1989—, chmn. 1997, award of excellence for tourism promotion 1991, Odyssey award for protecting the environment 1996, Odyssey award for outstanding tourism promotion 1997), Assn. Travel Mktg. Execs. (bd. dirs. 1988—, Atlas award for career achievement in mktg. 1992), Inst. Cert. Travel Agts. (trustee 1995—, vice chmn.). Avocations: fishing, hiking, travel. Office: Walt Disney Parks and Resorts, LLC 1375 E Buena Vista Dr Lake Buena Vista FL 32830-8402 Office Phone: 407-397-6425.

GARFIELD, WINIFRED L., nursing administrator; b. Frederick-sted, St. Croix, VI, July 28, 1941; d. Walter Antonio and Idalia Crystalia (Stephens) L.; m. Victor Conrad Garfield, June 30, 1968; children: Vilma Cecilia, Victor Conrad, Vynette Crystine, Vivicka Celeste. RN, St. Lukes Sch. Nursing, Ponce, PR, 1962; grad. anesthesiology for nurses, Harlem Hosp. Sch., 1966. RN, CRNA, AANA. Staff nurse Knud Hansen Hosp., St. Thomas, VI, 1962-64, nurse anesthetist, 1966-70, nurse anesthetist supr., 1970-89, respiratory therapy instr., 1976-77; campus nurse U. VI, St. Thomas, 1979-82; first aid instr., trainer ARC, St. Thomas, 1973-80; supr. anesthesia and respiratory svc. St. Thomas Hosp., 1980—89; exec. dir. VI Bd. Nurse Licensure, St. Thomas, 1989—. Nurse cons. Educare Sch., Inc., 1970—, asst. dir., 1980—. Recipient Disting. Nurse Cons. award Dept. Health Office Commr., 1982, named Nurse of the Year VI Licensed Practical Nurse Assn., 1986. Mem. VI Nurses Assn. (v.p. 1963-64), Chi Eta Phi (historian, 1963-64), Eta Phi Beta (Alpha Chi chpt). Democrat. Roman Catholic. Avocations: reading, gardening, travel. Home: 394-140 Anna Retreat Charlotte Amalie VI 00803

GARLAND, DAVID ELLSWORTH, dean, theology studies educator; b. Crisfield, Md., Sept. 24, 1947; s. Edward Ellsworth and Ruth (Grey) G.; m. Diana Sue Richmond, Aug. 22, 1970; children: Sarah, John. BA magna cum laude, Okla. Bapt. U., 1970; MDiv., So. Bapt. Theol. Sem., Louisville, 1973; PhD, So. Bapt. Theol. Sem., 1976; postgrad., Eberhard-Karls U., Tubingen, Fed. Republic Germany, 1984-85. Ordained to ministry Bapt. Ch., 1976. Pastor Immanuel Bapt. Ch., Shepherdsville, Ky., 1973-76; asst. prof. So. Bapt. Theol. Sem., Louisville, 1977-83, assoc. prof., 1983-87, prof., 1987—97, Ernest and Mildred Hogan prof. of New Testament, chair Biblical Divsn.; prof. Christian scriptures George W. Truett Theol. Seminary, Baylor U., Waco, Tex., 1997—, assoc. dean academic affairs, 2001, David E. Garland chair preaching, William M. Hinson prof. Christian scriptures, 2005—, dean, 2007—; interim pres. Baylor U., Waco, Tex., 2009—10. Author: Intention of Matthew 23, 1979; contbr. articles to religious publs. With USNR, 1965-71. Mem. Soc. Bibl. Lit., Assn. Bapt. Profs., Inst. Bibl. Rsch. Office: Baylor U Office of Pres One Bear Place #97096 Waco TX 76798-7096 Office Phone: 254-710-3555.

GARLAND, EDWARD T.M., lawyer; b. 1941; BA, U. Ga., 1963; LLB, U. Ga. Sch. Law, Athens, 1965. Bar: Ga. 1964, Ga. Ct. Appeals 1965, Supreme Ct. Ga. 1965, US Dist. Ct. (no. dist.) Ga. 1968, US Ct. Appeals (5th and 11th circs.) 1968, US Supreme Ct. 1972, US Dist. Ct. (so. dist.) Ga. 1987. Ptnr. Garland, Samuel & Loeb, P.C., Atlanta. Named a Ga. Super Lawyer, Law & Politics mag., 2004—11. Mem.: Ga. Trail Lawyers Assn. (v.p. 1968—73), American Assn. Justice, American Bd. Criminal Lawyers, Atlanta Bar Assn. (chmn. 1970, vice chmn. 1977), State Bar Ga., Nat. Assn. Criminal Def. Lawyers (bd. dirs. 1980—86), Ga. Assn. Criminal Def. Lawyers (pres. 1985), Internat. Acad. Trial Lawyers, American Coll. Trial Lawyers. Office: Garland Samuel & Loeb 3151 Maple Dr, NE Atlanta GA 30305-2503 Office Phone: 404-975-0459. Office Fax: 404-365-5041.

GARLAND, GREGORY CYRIL, oil industry executive; b. 1957; BSChemE, Tex. A&M U., 1980. Project engr. Plastics Tech. Ctr., Chevron Phillips Chem. Co., Bartlesville, Okla., 1980—82, sales engr. plastics resins, 1982—86, bus. svc. mgr. advanced materials, 1986—88, bus. devel. dir., 1988—89, mgr. olefins bus. unit, 1989—92, mgr. K-Resin bus. unit, 1992—94, mgr. planning & devel., planning and tech., 1994—95, gen. mgr. natural gas liquids, 1995—97, gen. mgr. Qatar/Middle East, Phillips Petroleum Co., 1997—2000, sr. v.p. planning & strategic transactions, 2000—01, sr. v.p. planning & specialty products, 2001—08, pres., CEO The Woodlands, Tex., 2008—10; sr. v.p. exploration & prodn. Americas, ConocoPhillips, Houston, 2010—12; chmn., CEO Phillips 66, 2012—. Bd. dirs. Phillips 66, 2012—, Amgen, Inc., 2013—. Mem. chem. engring. indsl. adv. bd. Tex. A&M U.; bd. dirs. Jr. Achievement Southeast Tex.; bd. dirs., mem. exec. com. American Chemistry Coun. Mem.: Nat. Petrochemicals & Refining Assn. (bd. dirs., mem. exec. com.). Office: Phillips 66 3010 Briarpark Dr Houston TX 77042 Office Phone: 281-293-6600.*

GARMAN, DAVID KLINE, consulting firm executive, former federal agency administrator; b. Greensboro, NC, May 29, 1957; s. Jack Donald and Jane (Holtzclaw) G. BA in Public Policy, Duke U., 1979; MS in Environ. Sciences, Johns Hopkins U., 1998. Volunteer Peace Corps., Nepal, 1979—80; legis. aide to Senator Richard Stone US Senate, Washington, 1980-81, legis. asst. to Senator Frank Murkowski, 1981-85, chief of adminstrn., exec. asst., 1986-90; profl. staff mem. US Senate Intelligence Com., Washington, 1991-92; spl. projects dir. to Senator Frank Murkowski US Senate, Washington, 1993-94; profl. staff mem. US Senate Energy Subcommittee on R&D, Washington, 1995—2001; asst. sec. for energy efficiency & renewable energy US Dept. Energy, Washington, 2001—05, acting under sec. energy, sci. & the environment, 2004—05, under sec for energy, sci. & the environment, 2005—07; owner, prin. Decker Garman Sullivan & Associates, LLC, Alexandria, Va., 2007—. Recipient E-Visionary award, Electric Drive Transp. Assn., 2003, Secretary's Gold medal, US Dept. Energy, Charles Percy award for Public Svc., Alliance to Save Energy; named to The Energy Efficiency Forum Hall of Fame, 2008. Republican. Episcopalian. Office: Decker Garman Sullivan LLC 500 Montgomery St Ste 400 Alexandria VA 22314 Office Phone: 703-647-6227.*

GARNER, BRYAN ANDREW, law educator, writer, consultant, lexicographer; b. Lubbock, Tex., Nov. 17, 1958; s. Gary Thomas and Mariellen (Griffin) G.; m. Pan Anurugsa, 1984 (div. 2007); children: Caroline Beatrix, Alexandra Bess; m. Karolyne Hu Cheng, Aug. 8, 2010. BA, U. Tex., 1980, JD, 1984; LLD (hon.), Thomas M. Cooley Law Sch., 2000; LLD (hon.), U. LaVerne, 2007, Stetson U. Coll. Law, 2010. Bar: Tex. 1984, U.S. Ct. Appeals (5th cir.) 1985, U.S. Dist. Ct. (no. dist.) Tex. 1986. Law clk. to judge U.S. Ct. Appeals (5th cir.), Austin, Tex., 1984-85; assoc. Carrington, Coleman, Sloman & Blumenthal, Dallas, 1985-88; dir. Tex./Oxford Ctr. for Legal Lexicography U. Tex. Sch. Law, Austin, 1988-90; disting. rsch. prof. law So. Meth. U., Dallas, 1990—. Vis. assoc. prof. law U. Tex., 1988—90; pres. LawProse, Inc., 1990—; vis. scholar U. Salzburg, 1995, 1998, U. Glasgow, 1996, U. Cambridge, England, 1997; chmn. plain-lang. com. State Bar Tex., 1989—95; lectr. in field; cons. in field. Author: A Dictionary of Modern Legal Usage, 1987, 2nd edit., 1995, 3rd edit., 2011, The Elements of Legal Style, 1991, 2nd edit., 2002, Guidelines for Drafting and Editing Court Rules, 1996, Garner's Modern American Usage, 1998, 2nd edit., 2004, 3rd edit., 2009, Securities Disclosure in Plain English, 1999, The Winning Brief, 1999, Legal Writing in Plain English, 2001, The Redbook: A Manual on Legal Style, 2002; co-author (with Justice Antonin Scalia): Making Your Case: The Art of Persuading Judges, 2008; editor: Scribes Jour. Legal Writing, 1989—2000, Texas, as Our Texas, 1984, Black's Law Dictionary, 7th edit., 1999, 8th edit., 9th edit., 2009, Garner on Language and Writing, 2009; mem. editl. bd.: Tex. Law Rev., 1984; contbr. articles to profl. jours. Recipient Henry C. Lind award, Assn. Reporters Judicial Decisions, 1994, Clarity award, State Bar Mich, 1997, Outstanding Young Tex. Ex. award, 1998. Fellow: Tex. Bar Found.; mem.: ABA, Tex. Bar Assn. (chmn. plain lang. com. 1990—), Am. Law Inst. (commn. on bylaws & coun. rules 1993—94), Scribes (exec. bd. 1990—2001, pres. 1997—98), Philos. Soc. Tex., Dictionary Soc. N.Am., Am. Dialect Soc., Grolier Club, Bent Tree Country Club, Friars (abbot 1983—84), Cosmos Club, Phi Beta Kappa. Republican. Avocation: golf. Home: 8133 Inwood Rd Dallas TX 75209 Office Phone: 214-691-8588. Business E-Mail: bgarner@lawprose.org.

GARNER, DOUGLAS RUSSELL, scientific & medical analyst, writer, editor; b. Orange, Tex., Aug. 7, 1953; s. Jim Buck and Ruthie Delores (Seastrunk) G. BA in Biology, U. Tex., 1975; postgrad. in medicine, Creighton U., 1976-77. Pub. health investigator Houston Health Dept., 1979-84; freelance tech. writer, translator Houston, 1984-86; tech. translations editor McElroy Translation Co., Austin, Tex., 1986-96; freelance sci. writer and editor, Austin, 1989—; sci. med. analyst, 2010—. Sci. researcher Calif. Afro-Am. Mus., LA, 1991-92. Author: The Adventures of Teddy Wallace, 1991. Recipient award Charles Palmer Davis Found., 1970. Mem. AAAS. Office: 1105 Larkin San Francisco CA 94109 Mailing: PO Box 7741 Austin TX 78713 Office Phone: 512-460-9284. Business E-Mail: scientific.medical.analyst@gmail.com.

GARNER, ED, state legislator; m. Ginny Garner; children: Jordan, Shelby, Blake. BA, Hendrix Coll. Investment broker T.J. Raney & Sons, 1981—85; with Lasater & Co., 1985—87, Stephens Inc., 1987—94; owner Mama's Manna Bakery, Maumelle, Ark., 1990—; mem. Dist. 41 Ark. House of Reps., 2007—. Republican. Methodist. Address: 4 Pinehurst Way Maumelle AR 72113 Office Phone: 501-663-7880. Business E-Mail: garnere@arkleg.state.ar.us.

GARNER, HAROLD RAY, experimental research physicist, biochemist; b. Feb. 5, 1954; s. Harold R. Sr. and Adelle (Miller) G. BS in Nuclear Engring., U. Mo., Rolla, 1976, PE (hon.), 1994; MS in Nuclear Engring., U. Wis., Madison, 1978, PhD in Plasma Physics, 1982. Registered profl. nuclear engr., Mo. Announcer/technician KMNR-FM Radio, Rolla, 1974-76; nuclear engr. insite program Argonne Nat. Lab., Chgo., 1976; rsch. asst. plasma physics U. Wis., Madison, 1976-82; sr. scientist Gen. Atomics, San Diego, 1982-86, appointed to Inst. for Develop. and Application of Advanced Technology, 1986—93, prin. scientist, 1991—94; prof., biochemistry and assoc. dir., Genome Sci. and Tech. Ctr. U. Tex. Southwestern Med. Ctr., Dallas, 1994—98, Philip O'Bryan Montgomery Disting. Prof. Biochemistry and Internal Medicine, 1997—; program chair, Joint Biomedical Engring. Grad. Program U. Tex. Southwestern Med. Ctr. and U. Tex. at Arlington, 2000—02. Cons. Nanogen, San Diego, 1994—; chmn. Kid Lab, San Diego, 1990-92. Co-author: Karate, 1977; co-author: (chpt.) Biocomputing: Informatics and Genome Projects, 1993, The Polymerase Chain Reaction, 1994; contbr. several articles to profl. jours. Outreach coord. Gen. Atomic, San Diego, 1993. Mem. U. Tex. Southwestern Karate Club (instr.). Achievements include research in micropipette adaptor for spectrophotometers, coaxial microwave absorption diagnostic, spectrophotometer to flurometer convertor, micropipette adaptor for spectrophotometers with temperature control, micropipette adaptor with temperature control for PCR amplification, micropipette adaptor for spectrofluorometers. Office: Univ Tex Southwestern Med Ctr at Dallas 5323 Harry Hines Blvd Dallas TX 75390-9185 Office Fax: 214-648-1445. Business E-Mail: garner@swmed.edu.

GARNER, JAY MONTGOMERY, retired military officer; b. Arcadia, Fla., Apr. 15, 1938; s. James Harley and Consuello Adelaide (Pooser) G.; m. Mary Connie Kreigh, Dec 30, 1958; 1 child, Lori Lee Gibson. BA, Fla. State U., 1962; MA, Shippensburg U., 1983; attended, Air Defense Artillery Sch., Marine Corps. Command and Staff Coll., US Army War Coll., US Army Air Defense Sch., Ft. Bliss, Tex., 1962, Defense Lang. Inst., SW br., Ft. Bliss, 1966-67, Air Defense Artillery Officer Advanced Course, US Army Air Defense Sch., 1969, Vietnam Tng. Ctr. Fgn. Svc. Inst., Dept. State, Washington, 1970-71, Marine Corps. Command and Staff Coll., Quantico, Va., 1974-75, US Army War Coll. Carlisle Barracks, Pa., 1982-83. Commd. 2d lt. US Army, 1962, advanced through grades to lt. gen., 1994, ret., 1997, asst. platoon leader to platoon leader to exec. officer, Battery C, 3d Missile Battalion, 7th Artillery, US Army Europe, 1962-64, inactive Army Nat. Guard, 1964-65, ops. officer 53d Artillery Brigade Maxwell AFB, Ala., 1965-66, asst. subsector advisor, later dep. dist. sr. advisor adv. team 38, mil. assistance command Viet Nam Vietnam, 1967-68, comdr. Battery B, 5th Battalion, 7th Artillery, US Army Air Defense Commd. Franklin Lakes, NJ, 1968, chief, programs br., logistics divsn., office mil. assistance, US Army So. Command Ft. Amador, Panama, 1969-70, dist. sr. advisor, adv. team 36, military assistance commd. Vietnam, 1971-72, S-3, then plans, tng. officer, reserve component study, later S-3, 1st Battalion, 3d Air Defense Artillery, 101st Airborne Divsn. (Airmobile) Ft. Campbell, Ky., 1972-74, staff officer, firepower divsn., requirements directorate, later asst. exec. officer, office dept. chief staff ops. Washington, 1975-78, comdr. 1st Basic Combat Tng. Battalion, tng. and doctrine command, 1978-79, comdr. 2d Battalion, 59th Air Defense Artillery, 1st Armored Division, US Army Europe, 1979-81, comdr. 108th Air Defense Artillery Brigade, 32d Army Air Defense Command, US Army Europe, 1984-86, dir. force requirements (combat support systems) office of dep. chief of staff ops. and plans Washington, 1986-88, dep. commdg. gen. US Army Air Defense

Artillery Ctr., asst. commandant US Army Air Defense Artillery Sch. Ft. Bliss, 1988-90, dep. commdg. gen. V Corps. US Army Europe, 7th Army, 1990-91, commdg. gen. joint task force BRAVO Northern Iraq, 1991, asst. dep. chief staff ops. & plans force devel. Washington, 1992-94, asst. vice chief of staff, 1996-97; commdg. gen. US Army Space and Strategic Def. Command, 1994-96; dir. Office of Reconstruction & Humanitarian Assistance (ORHA), Baghdad, Iraq, 2003. Pres. SY Tech. (now SYColeman Corp.), 1997—2004; bd. dirs. Digital Fusion, Inc., 2005—. Appeared in (documentaries) No End in Sight, 2007. Decorated DSM with oak leaf cluster, Def. Superior Svc. medal with oak leaf cluster, Legion of Merit with 4 oak leaf clusters, Bronze Star, Air medal, Meritorious Svc. Medal, Joint Svc. Commendation Medal, Army Commendation Medal, Combat Infantryman Badge. Democrat. Episcopalian. Avocations: health, exercise.

GARNER, JOSEPH E., management consultant; BA in Social Sciences, St. Mary's Coll., Md.; completed Acquisition Mgmt. Program. Joined Booz Allen Hamilton Holding Corp., 1983, sr. v.p.; pres. ASE Inc. (subs. Booz Allen Hamilton Holding Corp.); exec. v.p. Booz Allen Hamilton Holding Corp., 2001—. Office: Booz Allen Hamilton Holding Corp 8283 Greensboro Dr Mc Lean VA 22102 Office Phone: 703-902-5000. Office Fax: 703-902-3333. Business E-Mail: garner_joseph@bah.com.

GARNER, PAUL TRANTHAM, auditor; b. Cameron, Tex., May 25, 1951; s. W.H. and Dorothy L. (Gohmert) G.; m. Tatyana Tokareva; children: Paul Christopher, Gregory Trantham, Michael Nickolas. BBA, U. Tex., 1973; MS in Bus. Adminstrn., U. No. Colo., 1980. Cert. systems profl. Engr. Tex. Instruments, Inc., Austin, 1980; mgr. performance audit divsn. State of Tex. Auditor's Office, Austin, 1980-95; dir. data svcs. Tex. Workers Compensation Commn., Austin, 1995-98; info. tech. cons. Audit Force, Inc., Dallas, 1998-2000. Asst. city auditor City of Dallas; mem. faculty Austin C.C., 1982; seminar lectr. in field. Mem. Bergstrom-Austin Community Coun. Lt. col. U.S. Army, 1973-99. U.S. Army ednl. scholar, 1969. Mem. Assn. for Systems Mgmt. (pres.), Am. Evaluation Assn., Legis. Prog. Evaluation Soc., Tex. Assn. State Sys. for Computing and Comms. (treas.), Austin Endowment Soc. (bd. dirs.), Austin Bus. Club., Rotary. Avocations: coin collecting/numismatics, scuba diving. Home: 2108 Bishop Dr Flower Mound TX 75028-2142 Office: City Auditor's Office 1500 Marilla 2FN Dallas TX 75201 Home Phone: 972-691-9639; Office Phone: 214-939-2520. E-mail: paultgarner@yahoo.com.

GARNER, ROBERT EDWARD LEE, lawyer; b. Bowling Green, Ky., Sept. 26, 1946; s. Alto Luther and Katie Mae (Sanders) G.; m. Suzanne Marie Searles, Aug. 22, 1981; children: Jessica Marie, Abigail Lee. BA, U. Ala., Tuscaloosa, 1968; JD, Harvard U., 1971. Bar: Ga. 1971, U.S. Dist. Ct. (no. dist.) Ga. 1974, U.S. Ct. Appeals (5th cir.) 1974, U.S. Ct. Appeals (11th cir.) 1981, Ala. 1982, U.S. Ct. Appeals (4th cir.) 1991, S.C. 1992. Assoc. Gambrell, Russell & Forbes, Atlanta, 1972-76, ptnr., 1976-80, Haskell, Slaughter & Young and predecessors, Birmingham, Ala., 1981-88, mng. ptnr., 1986-87, of counsel, 1988-90; gen. counsel, sec. Builders Transport, Inc., 1988-90; ptnr. Nelson, Mullins, Riley & Scarborough, Atlanta and Columbia, SC, 1991-96; mem. Haskell Slaughter Young & Rediker, LLC, Birmingham, 1996—, mng. ptnr., 2000—02. 1st lt. JAGC, USAF, 1971-72. Mem. ABA (com. on fed. regulation of securities, subcom. on disclosure matters and continuous reporting, subcom. on securities registration, ad hoc com. on pub. co. info. practices), State Bar Ga., Ala. State Bar, Birmingham Bar, S.C. Bar, U. Ala. Alumni Assn., Harvard U. Alumni Assn., Am. Soc. Corp. Secs. (mem. tech. com.), Phi Alpha Theta, Pi Sigma Alpha. Republican. Home: 284 Kings Crest Ln Pelham AL 35124-2846 Office: Haskell Slaughter Young & Rediker LLC 2001 Park Pl North Ste 1400 Birmingham AL 35203-2618 Office Phone: 205-254-1417, 205-251-1000. Business E-Mail: relg@hsy.com.

GARNER, TERRI, library and museum director; BA in Polit. Sci., Chatham Coll., Pitts.; MA in History, U. Colo., Denver; PhD in History, U. Maine, Orono. Gen. mgr. bus. svcs. Rocky Mountain and NJ ops. Xerox Corp.; dir., Americas Command Ctr. Sun Microsystems; v.p., svc. and mktg. Intellisource, Denver, 2004—05; exec. dir. Bangor Mus. and Ctr. for History, Maine, 2005—07; dir. Clinton Presdl. Libr. and Mus., Little Rock, 2007—. Office: Clinton Presdl Libr and Mus 1200 President Clinton Ave Little Rock AR 72201 Office Phone: 501-374-4242. Office Fax: 501-244-2883.

GARNETT, STANLEY IREDALE, II, utilities executive, lawyer; b. Petersburg, Va., Aug. 11, 1943; s. Stanley Arthur and Edith (Keirstead) G.; children: Matthew S.A., Andrew F.W. BA, Colby Coll., 1965; MBA, U. Pa., 1967; JD, NYU, 1973. Bar: N.Y. 1974. Sr. fin. analyst Standard Oil Co. of N.J., NYC, 1967-70; assoc. Milbank, Tweed, Hadley & McCloy, NYC, 1973-81; v.p.-legal and regulatory Allegheny Power Sys., Inc., NYC, 1981-90, v.p. fin., 1990-94, sr. v.p. fin., 1994-95; sr. advisor Putnam, Hayes & Bartlett, 1996-97, 98-00; exec. v.p. Fla. Progress Corp., St. Petersburg, 1997-98; ptnr. PA Consulting Group, 2000—04; prin., owner Garnett Consulting Group, Inc., 2004—; operating mgr. CPSD Group LLC. Joseph P. Wharton scholar, 1965-67. Mem. ABA, N.Y. State Bar Assn. Republican. Episcopalian. Home: 2504 Sunset Way Saint Petersburg Beach FL 33706-4127 Business E-Mail: stangarnett@aol.com.

GARNICK, MURRAY R., tobacco company executive; BA in Political Sci., summa cum laude, U. Georgia, JD summa cum laude. Sr. ptnr. Arnold & Porter, Washington; sr. v.p., assoc. gen. counsel, client svcs. Altria Group, Inc. Office: Altria Group Inc 6601 W Broad St Richmond VA 23230 Office Phone: 804-274-2200. Office Fax: 804-484-8231. Business E-Mail: murray.garnick@altria.com.

GAROFALO, RAYMOND E., state legislator; m. Joan Garofalo. BA, JD, Loyola U., New Orleans. Mem. Dist. 103 La. House of Reps., 2012—, mem. Civil Law and Procedure Com., Health and Welfare Com. & Judiciary Com. Owner Interstate Amusements, Proline Productions, Garogalo Investments; ptnr. Park Four Investments. Republican. Office: District Office 204 Etienne Dr Meraux LA 70075 Office Phone: 504-278-6599. Office Fax: 504-278-6597. E-mail: garofalor@legis.la.gov.

GARR, DAVID ROSS, physician, educator; b. Boston, Mass., Sept. 6, 1946; s. Fred Manuel and Ida Shuman Garr; m. Deborah Camille Williamson, Dec. 10, 1976; children: Joshua, Rebecca. BA in Chemistry, Duke U., 1968, MD, 1972. Diplomate Am. Bd. Family Medicine. Resident family practice Highland Hosp., Rochester, NY, 1972—75; med. dir. Family Medicine Group of Tooele, Utah, 1975—81; dir. learning resources family practice residency Mercy Med. Ctr., Denver, 1981—85; clinician, prof., assoc. dean cmty. medicine Med. U. S.C., Charleston, 1985—, exec. dir. SC Area Health Edn. Consortium, 2003—. Office: Med Univ SC MSC 814 19 Hagood Ave Ste 802 Charleston SC 29425

GARRARD, GARDINER W., JR., real estate development and investment company executive; BA, U. NC, Chapel Hill, 1964; LLB, U. Ga. Sch. Law. Law clk to judge Griffin B. Bell US Ct. Appeals (5th cir.); various positions The Jordan Co., Columbus, Ga., 1972—75, pres., 1975—2009; chmn. bd. dirs. Jordan Co., Columbus, Ga., 2009—. Bd. dirs. Synovus Fin. Corp., 1972—, Total Sys. Svcs., Inc., 1982—. Office: The Jordan Co 6001 River Rd Ste 100 Columbus GA 31904 Office Phone: 314-373-7100. Office Fax: 314-373-7339.

GARRARD, V. JANE, consumer products company executive; V.p., investor rels. Tupperware Brands Corp., 2002—07, v.p., internal audit, 2007—. Office: Tupperware Brands Corp 14901 S Orange Blossom Trail Orlando FL 32837 Office Phone: 407-826-5050. Office Fax: 407-826-8874.

GARRETT, ALGIN B., dermatologist, educator; MD, Pa. State U., 1978. Diplomate Am. Bd. Dermatology, 1983. Intern internal medicine Washington VA Med. Ctr. Georgetown Univ. Sch. of Medicine, 1978—79; resident internal medicine Washington VA Med. Ctr., 1979—80; resident dermatology Va. Commonwealth Univ. Med. Ctr., 1980—83, prof., chmn. dermatology dept.; fellow mohs surgery Cleve. Clinic, 1987—88. Office: VA Commonwealth University Department of Dermatology 9000 Stony Point Pky Richmond VA 23235 Office Phone: 804-560-8991.

GARRETT, HENRY, former mayor; Former police officer Corpus Christi Police Dept., former chief of police; fomer mem.-at-large Corpus Christi City Coun.; mayor City of Corpus Christi, Tex., 2005—09. Served with USAFR.

GARRETT, JASON CALVIN, professional football coach, retired professional football player; b. Abington, Pa., Mar. 28, 1966; s. Jim Garrett; m. Brill Garrett. Degree in History, Princeton U., NJ, 1988. Asst. coach Princeton U., 1990; quarterback San Antonio Riders-World League Am. Football, 1991; quarterback Ottawa Rough Riders-CFL, 1992, Dallas Cowboys, Irving, 1993—99, offensive coord., 2007—10, asst. head coach, 2008—10, interim head coach, 2010, head coach, 2011—; quarterback NY Giants, East Rutherford, NJ, 2000—03, Tampa Bay Buccaneers, Tampa Bay, Fla., 2004, Miami Dolphins, Fla., 2004, quaterback's coach, 2005—06. Founder Jason Garrett Starfish Found., 1997—. Named Player of Yr., Ivy League, 1988. Achievements include becoming the highest paid assistant coach in the history of the NFL, 2008. Office: Dallas Cowboys Cowboys Ctr One Cowboys Pky Irving TX 75063 Office Phone: 972-556-9900.

GARRETT, REGINALD HOOKER, biology professor, researcher; b. Roanoke, Va., Sept. 24, 1939; s. William Walker and Lelia Evelyn (Blankenship) G.; m. Linda Joan Harrison, Mar. 15, 1958 (div.); children: Jeffrey David, Randal Harrison, Robert Martin; m. Catherine Leigh Touchton, June 12, 1989 (div.); m. Georgia Cobb Grant, Nov. 27, 2009. BS, Johns Hopkins U., 1964, PhD, 1968. Asst. prof. biology U. Va., 1968-73, assoc. prof., 1973-82, prof., 1982—. Guest prof. U. Paul Sabatier, France, 2003; cons. in field. Author textbooks; contbr. articles to profl. jours. NIH fellow, 1964-68; Fulbright Hays fellow, 1975-76; Thomas Jefferson vis. fellow, 1983; grantee NIH, NSF Mem. Am. Soc. Biochemistry and Molecular Biology, Am. Soc. Microbiology, Am. Soc. Plant Physiology, Soc. Gen. Physiology, Sigma Xi, Phi Lambda Upsilon, Phi Sigma Office: U Va Dept Biology Gilmer Hall Charlottesville VA 22904 Home Phone: 434-293-7277; Office Phone: 434-982-5494. Business E-Mail: rhg@virginia.edu.

GARRETT, RICHARD G., lawyer; b. NYC, Oct. 16, 1948; BA magna cum laude, Emory U., 1970, JD, 1973. Bar: Ga. 1973, Fla 1979; U.S. Dist. Ct. (no. dist.) Ga. 1973, (so. dist.) Fla. 1979, U.S. Dist. Ct. (so. dist. trial bar) Fla. 1979; U.S. Ct. Appeals (5th cir.) 1974; U.S. Ct. Appeals (9th. cir., 11 cir.) 1981; U.S. Supreme Ct. 1981. Program dir., instr. rsch., writing and advocacy Emory U. Sch. Law, 1972-73; chief legal officer and v.p. Greenberg, Traurig, Miami, Fla., prin. shareholder, 1978—. Past chmn. litigation dept., exec. com. bd. dirs. Greenberg, Traurig, Miami. Editor Emory Law Journal, 1972-73. Recipient 1st place and Best Brief award Region V Nat. Moot Ct. Competition, 1972. Mem. ABA, The Fla. Bar Assn., State Bar Ga., Omicron Delta Kappa, Order of the Barristers. Office: Greenberg Traurig LLP 333 SE 2nd Ave Ste 4400 Miami FL 33131-2184 Office Fax: 305-579-0717. Business E-Mail: garrettr@gtlaw.com.*

GARRETT, ROBERTA KAMPSCHULTE, nurse; b. Amityville, NY, Aug. 15, 1947; d. Robert Henry and Gertrude Ann (Schweitzer) Kampschulte; m. Paul R. Garrett Jr., Nov. 26, 1977; children: Samantha Kristine, Kelly Nicole. BS, U. Fla., 1969. RN, Fla.; cert. in oncology nursing. Staff nurse Valley Hosp., Ridgewood, N.J., 1969-70; asst. head nurse Broward Gen. Hosp., Ft. Lauderdale, Fla., 1970-71; CCU nurse Grady Meml. Hosp., Atlanta, 1972-77; nurse to pvt. physician Orlando, Fla., 1977-94; case mgmt. Fla. Healthcare Sys., Orlando, 1996—. Owner 2 Tropical Smoothie stores, Fla., 1999—2002; area developer Tampa/St. Petersburg Tropical Smoothie, 1999—2003; pvt. cons. Med. Record Reviews, 2003—. Republican. Lutheran. Avocation: jogging. Office: Fla Hosp Healthcare Sys 602 Courtland St Orlando FL 32804 E-mail: bobbirn2002@yahoo.com.

GARRETT, SANDY LANGLEY, former school system administrator; b. Muskogee, Okla., Feb. 8, 1943; 1 child, Charles Langley (Chuck). BS in Elem. Edn., Northeastern U., Tahlequah, Okla., 1968, MS in Counseling, 1980; grad. John F. Kennedy Sch. Govt., Harvard U., 1989. Lic. tchr., adminstr., supt. std., Okla. Tchr. Hilldale Schs., Muskogee, Okla., 1968-80; coord. gifted program Hillsdale Schs., Muskogee, Okla., 1980-82; coord. gifted and talented State Dept. Edn., Oklahoma City, 1982-85, dir. rural edn., 1985-87, exec. dir. ednl. svcs., 1987-88, state supt. pub. instrn., 1991-95; sec. edn. Cabinet Gov. of Okla., Oklahoma City, 1988—95; supt. pub. instrn. Okla. Dept. Edn., 1991—2011. Chair State Bd. Edn., Oklahoma City, 1991—, State Vo-Tech. Edn., Oklahoma City, 1991—; bd. dirs. So. Regional Edn. Bd.; regent Okla. Colls., 1991—; mem. Nat. Coll. Bd. Equality Project; chair. Okla. Lit. Initiatives Commn.; mem. So. Regional Ednl. Bd.; treas. Edn. Commn. States, 2004-. Co-author: (curriculum guide) Gifted Galaxy; mem. editorial bd. Rural and Small Schs.; contbr. articles to profl. jours. Co-chair Dem. Party, Muskogee, 1978; del. Dem. Nat. Conv., N.Y.C., 1980, 82; mem. Leadership Okla., 1990. Recipient Cecil Yarbrough award, 1989, Claude Dyer Legis. award, 1989, Silver Beaver award, Boy Scouts Am., 2001; inducted into the Okla. Educators Hall of Fame, 2000, Okla. Women's Hall of Fame, 2001; named one of the Fifty Making a Difference in Okla., The Journal Record; mem, Northeastern State Univ. Alumni Assn. Hall of Fame Mem. Muskogee County Ednl. Assn., Delta Kappa Gamma, Phi Delta Kappa, Delta Kappa Gamma. Democrat. Methodist. Avocations: tennis, swimming, computer programming, travel, politics. Office Phone: 405-521-3301.

GARRETT, T. SCOTT (SCOTT GARRETT), state legislator, surgeon; b. Norfolk, Va., July 22, 1956; m. Whitney Garrett; children: Tyler, Haley Gray. BA in Economics, U. Va., Charlottesville, 1978, MD, 1984. Surgeon, Va., 1989—; healthcare profl. Johnson Health Ctr., Free Clinic Ctrl. Va., Lynchburg Health Dept., Ctrl. Va. Tng. Ctr.; mem. Lynchburg City Coun., Va., 2006—10; mem. Dist. 23 Va. House of Delegates, Richmond, 2010—. Bd. dirs. Integrated Health Care; organizing dir., chmn. nominating and compensation com. Select-Bank. Singer: (choral group) FACination. Eagle scout Boy Scouts America; bd. trustees Peakland United Meth. Ch.; bd. dirs. Greater Lynchburg C. of C., Nat. Civil War Chaplains Mus., Lynchburg Project Lifesaver, James River Coun. for Arts and Humanities; bd. dirs., former pres. Lynchburg Fine Arts Ctr.; mem. adv. com. Va. Legal Aid Soc.; mem. cmty. justice adv. com. Lynchburg Cmty. Ct. Fellow: Am. Coll. Surgeons; mem.: AMA (Physician's Recognition award), Edward R. Woodward Surg. Soc., Am. Cancer Soc. (bd. dirs., former pres.), Lynchburg Acad. Medicine (former pres.), Med. Soc. Va., Va. Surg. Soc., Raven Soc., Lynchburg Optimist Internat. Club, Omicron Delta Kappa. Republican. Office: Va House of Dels Gen Assembly Bldg Rm 718 PO Box 406 Richmond VA 23218 also: 2255 Langhorne Rd Ste 4 Lynchburg VA 24501 Office Phone: 804-698-1023, 434-455-0243. Office Fax: 804-698-6723. Business E-Mail: delsgarrett@house.virginia.gov.

GARRETT, THOMAS A., state legislator; b. Atlanta, Mar. 27, 1972; BA, JD, U. Richmond. Commonwealth atty. Louisa County, Va.; mem. Dist. 22 Va. State Senate, 2012—, mem. Gen. Laws and Tech. Com., Courts of Justice Com., Edn. and Health Com. & Privileges and Elections Com. Republican. Office: Senate of Virginia PO Box 396 Richmond VA 23218 also: PO Box 33 Bumpass VA 23024 Office Phone: 804-698-7522. Office Fax: 704-698-7651. E-mail: district22@senate.virginia.gov.

GARRETT, WILBUR BILL (BILL), magazine editor; b. Kansas City, Mo., Sept. 4, 1930; s. Clay Dean and Cecil Zora (Melton) Garrett; m. Lucille Hall, Dec. 26, 1950; children: Michael Dean, Kenneth Lewis. BJ, U. Mo., 1954; LittD (hon.), U. Miami. With Nat. Geog. Mag., 1954—90, editor, 1980—90; faculty photojournalism workshop U. Mo., 1963—64, 1969—70, 1973—75, 1977—80, 1994; editor Cosmos Jour., 1995—98. Mem. XIX Olympiad Cultural Com.; bd. dirs. Congentrix Energy, Inc., Nat. Geographic Soc., 1980—90, rsch. and exploration com., 1981—90; bd. advisors Corbis Prodns., Inc., Ptnrs. for Livable Cmtys. Designer (photog. exhbn.) U.S. Pavilion, N.Y.'s World Fair, 1965, designer, prodr. (exhibitions) Nat. Geog. Soc. Exhbns. 23d, 24th, 25th Picture of Yr. Competition. Bd. govs. The Nature Conservancy, 1988—98, Am. Land Conservancy; trustee W. Eugene Smith Meml. Fund; founder, pres. La Ruta Maya Conservation Found., 1990; bd. dirs. Heritage U.S.A. With USNR, 1946—52. Decorated Order of the Quetzal Guatemala; recipient Newhouse citation, U. Syracuse, 1963, Nat. Mag. awards for Excellence, 1984, 1989, 1990, 1991, Leadership Medal, UN Environ. Programme, 1990, Chevron Environ. award, 1990, La Pluma Plata, Pres. of Mex., 1990, Rotondi award, Italy, 1998, Linda Schele award, Mesoamerican Arts & Culture, U. Tex., 2006; named to Hall of Fame, Mo. Photojour., 2007. Mem.: Cosmos Club (Washington). Avocation: winemaking. Home and Office: 209 Seneca Rd Great Falls VA 22066-1108 Personal E-mail: billgarret@aol.com.

GARRICK, MIA BUTLER, state legislator; m. Tracy T. Garrick; children: Brian Butler, Cameron M. Butler. BA, U. SC, 1990, JD, 1995. Bd. dirs. Violence Against Women Act; coord., human resources SC C. of C., 1991—92; intern 6th Dist. Congressman Jim Clyburn Steering Com., 1992; bd. dirs. State Office of Victim Assistance, 1999—2001, Cmtys. in Schs. of the Midlands, 2000—03; prin. McLeod Butler Comm., LLC, 2002—; profl. mem. Columbia Lawyers Assn., 2002—04; mem. SC C. of C., 2003; bd. dirs. E. Ctrl. City Consortium, 2003—05; chmn. Rice Creek Sch. Improvement Coun., 2003—04; mem. Pub. Rels. Soc. of America, 2004—, Rice Creek SIC, 2005—07, Leadership SC Alumni Assn., 2006, African Am. Bus. Roundtable, 2006—07; bd. dirs. SC C. of C., 2007—10; mem. Dist. 79 SC House of Representatives, 2011—. Democrat. Office: South Carolina House of Representatives District 79 335D Blatt Bldg Columbia SC 29201 Address: 116 Nautique Circle Columbia SC 29229 Office Phone: 803-212-6794. E-mail: MiaButler@miabutlerforhouse.com.

GARRIDO, AUGIE (AUGUST EDMUN GARRIDO JR.), college baseball coach; b. Vallejo, Calif., Feb. 6, 1939; 1 child, Lisa. B in Phys. Edn., Calif. State U., Fresno, 1961; MEd, Calif. Polytechnic State U., San Luis Obispo, 1966. Minor league baseball player Cleve. Indians Orgn., 1961—66; baseball coach Sierra HS, Tollhouse, Calif., 1966—69; head baseball coach San Francisco State U. Gators, 1969—70, Calif. Polytechnic State U. San Luis Obispo Mustangs, 1970—72, Calif. State U. Fullerton Titans, 1973-87, 1991-96, U. Ill. Fighting Illini, 1987-91, U. Texas Longhorns, Austin, 1996—. Asst. coach US Nat. Team, 1990. Recipient Top Dog award, Fresno State Univ., 2002, Alumnus of Yr. award, athletics, 2002; named Nat. Coach of Yr., 1975, 1979, 1984, 1995, 2002, 2005, Regional Coach of Yr., 1975, 1979, 1984, 1995, 2002, 2004, Coach of Yr., Big West Conf., 1987, 1995, Big 12 Conf., 2002, 2006, 2007; named to Fresno State Hall of Fame, 1993, Tex. Sports Hall of Fame, 2005, Titan Athletics Hall of Fame, Calif. State U. Fullerton, 2005. Achievements include head baseball coach of College World Series NCAA national championship winning California State University-Fullerton Titans, 1979, 1984, 1995; University of Texas Longhorns, 2002, 2005; becoming the all-time winningest head coach in NCAA Division I baseball history, 2003. Office: Univ Tex Austin Dept Intercollegiate Athletics 2400 Inner Campus Dr Austin TX 78712 Office Phone: 512-471-5732.

GARRIOTT, RICHARD ALLEN, game software designer; Co-founder, pres. Origin Systems, Inc. (acquired by Electronic Arts in 1992), 1983—92; several positions, including v.p. bus. develop. and sr. v.p. product develop. Electronic Arts, 1992—95; co-founder Destination Games, Inc. (partnership with South Korean NCsoft Corp., renamed NCsoft N.Am. in Austin, Tex.), 2000—01; exec. prodr., pres. NCsoft N.Am., 2001—. Investor, bd. mem. Space Adventures, Ltd. Creator (games) Akalabeth:World of Doom, Calif. Pacific Computer, 1980, Ultima I, 1980, Ultima II: Revenge of the Enchantress, 1982, Ultima III: Exodus, 1983, Ultima IV: Quest of the Avatar, 1985, Ultima I:The First Age of Darkness, 1987, Ultima V: Warriors of Destiny, 1988, Worlds of Ultima: Savage Empire, 1990, Ultima VI: The False Prophet, 1990, Ultima: Runes of Virtue, 1991, Ultima: Worlds of Adventure 2: Martian Dreams, 1991, Ultima VII: The Forge of Virtue, 1992, Ultima VII: The Black Gate, 1992, Ultima Underworld: The Stygian Abyss, 1992, Ultima VII, Part Two: The Silver Seed, 1993, Ultima VII, Part Two: Serpent Isle, 1993, Ultima VIII: Pagan, 1994, Ultima: Runes of Virtue II, 1994, Ultima Online, 1997, Ultima Collection, 1997, Ultima Online: The Second Age, 1998, Ultima IX: Ascension, 1999, credited games Ring Quest, 1984, Orge, 1986, 2400 A.D., 1987, Times of Lore, 1988, Autoduel, 1988, Omega, 1989, Knights of Legend, 1989, The Need for Speed, 1994, Realms of Arkania Vol. 2: Star Trail, 1994, Crusader: No Remorse, 1995, BioForge, 1995, Exile: Escape from the Pit, 1995, Exile II: Crystal Souls, 1996, Lineage II: The Chaotic Chronicle, 2004, City of Heroes, 2004, City of Villains, 2005, City of Heroes (Deluxe Edit.), 2005, Auto Assault, 2006, Richard Garriott's Tabula Rasa, 2007. Recipient Game Developers Choice award for Lifetime Achievement, 2006. Achievements include being the sixth paying space traveler on the Soyuz TMA-13 spacecraft and the first American to follow a parent into orbit in 2008; known in the industry as Lord British. Office: NCsoft North America Bldg 1 Ste 102 6801 N Capital of Texas Hwy Austin TX 78731-1780

GARRISON, EARL, state legislator; BFA, Tulsa Univ., 1972; PhD in Edn., Univ. Okla., 1976. Rancher, educator; mem. Dist. 9 Okla. State Senate, 2004—. Served USAF. Democrat. Office: 2300 N Lincoln Blvd Rm 533 Oklahoma City OK 73105 Address: 3806 Club View Dr Muskogee OK 74403 Office Phone: 405-521-5533. Business E-Mail: garrisone@oksenate.gov.

GARRISON, J. DANIEL, death care products and services company executive; BS in Adminstrv. Mgmt., Clemson U. Joined Svc. Corp. Internat., 1978, various mgmt. positions, pres., Southeastern region, 1992—98, v.p., internat. ops., 1998—2000, v.p., North Am. cemetery ops., 2000—02, v.p., ops. svcs., 2002—05; sr. v.p., ops. support Service Corp. International, 2005—; cons. Infosys Technologies Ltd. Office: Service Corp International 1929 Allen Pky Houston TX 77019 Office Phone: 713-522-5141. Office Fax: 713-525-5586.

GARRISON, MICHAEL S., lawyer, educator, former academic administrator; b. Fairmont, W.Va., Nov. 6, 1968; m. Heather Malone; children: Julia Grace, Gabriella Malone. BA cum laude, W.Va. U., 1992, JD with honors, 1996. Bar: W.Va. 1996, DC 1999, W.Va. Supreme Ct. Appeals, US Dist. Ct. (no. and so. dists.) W.Va. Adminstrv. asst. instl. advancement W.Va. U., Morgantown, 1993, guest lectr. Coll. Law, 1998—99, adj. prof. Eberly Coll. Arts and Scis., 2002—, pres.-elect, 2007, pres., 2007—08; assoc. Steptoe & Johnson LLP, 1996—2001, Bowles Rice McDavid Graff & Love LLP, 1999; adj. prof. bus. U. Charleston, 1999—2000; cabinet sec. Dept. Tax and Revenue State W.Va., 2001, chief of staff, 2001—03; mng. mem. Spilman Thomas & Battle PLLC, 2003—07, 2008—. Former chmn. W.Va. Higher Edn. Policy Commn. Named one of Ten Outstanding Young Americans, US Jaycees, 2004; scholar St. Anne's Coll., U. Oxford, 1992—93; Henry Toll Fellow, 2003. Mem.: DC Bar Assn., W.Va. Bar Assn. Office: Spilman Thomas & Battle PLLC 150 Clay St, Second Fl PO Box 615 Morgantown WV 26507-0615 Office Phone: 304-291-7926. Office Fax: 304-291-7979. E-mail: mgarrison@spilmanlaw.com.

GARROD, KENNETH J., orthopedist, surgeon; b. Newark, May 11, 1950; s. Roslyn Garrod; m. Beth L. Rosenthal, May 17, 1981; children: Evan, Scott. BS, U. Wis., 1972; MD, U. Medicine and Dentistry NJ, 1977. Cert. in orthopedic surgery and surgery of the hand Am. Bd. Orthopedic Surgery. Attending physician Orthop. Surgery Assocs., Boca Raton, Fla., 1984—95; mem. faculty Miller Sch. Medicine, U. Miami. Physician, pres. South Fla. Hand and Orthop. Ctr., Boca Raton, 2001—. Contbr. articles to profl. jours. Fellow, Tufts U. Med. Sch., Boston, 1983—84. Fellow: ACS, Am. Acad. Orthop. Surgeons; mem.: AMA, Fla. Orthop. Soc., Am. Soc. Surgery of Hand. Avocations: skiing, golf, travel. Office: 1905 Clint Moore Rd Ste 105 Boca Raton FL 33496 Office Fax: 561-998-4246. E-mail: southfloridahand@bellsouth.net.

GARROU, LINDA D., state legislator; b. Atlanta, Jan. 17, 1943; m. John L. W. Garrou. Social studies tchr. Jordan HS, 1964—66; asst. adminstr. Forsyth County Juvenile Justice Coun., 1972—81; dist. adminstr. AOCL, 1987—94, asst. adminstr., 1994—; mem. NC State Legislature, 1996; state senator Dist. 20 NC, 1999—2002; state senator Dist. 32, 2003—. Mem.: Big Brother Big Sister, Winston-Salem Jr. League, Piedmont Triad Leadership, Leadership Winston-Salem. Democrat. Office: NC Senate 300 N Salisbury St Rm 620 Raleigh NC 27603-5925 Address: PO Box 11843 Winston Salem NC 27116 Office Phone: 919-733-5620. E-mail: Linda.Garrou@ncleg.net.

GARSIDE, JOHN W., JR., wholesale distribution executive; Pres., treas. Woodruff Coal Co., 1979—; commr. Mich. Dept. Transp. Mem. bd. dirs. Universal Forest Products, Inc., 1993—, Prab Inc., 1996—. Commr. Mich. Dept. of Transp. Office: Woodruff Coal Co 601 Fairway St Bluefield VA 24605-9428 Office Phone: 276-326-3033.

GARSON, ARTHUR, JR., academic administrator, medical educator; b. NYC; m. Suzan Garson; 2 children. Grad., Princeton U., 1970; MD, Duke U., 1974; MPH, U. Tex., Houston, 1992. V.p. Tex. Children's Hosp.; fellow in pediat. cardiology Baylor Coll. Medicine, 1979, chief pediat. cardiology, 1988, sr. v.p., dean acad. ops., 1995; assoc. vice chancellor health affairs Duke U., 1992; dean, v.p. U. Va. Sch. Medicine, 2002—07, provost, 2007—. Mem. White House Adv. Panel on Health Sys. Improvement; chair quality nat. adv. coun. Agy. Healthcare Rsch. Mem.: Inst. Medicine, Assn. Acad. Health Ctrs., U. Hosps. Consortium, Assn. Am. Med. Colls. (adv. panel on healthcare delivery), Am. Coll. Cardiology (pres. 2000—01, trustee, mem. govt. rels. com., mem. quality of care com.). Office: U Va Health Sys PO Box 800793 Charlottesville VA 22908 Office Phone: 434-924-5118. E-mail: garson@virginia.edu.

GARST, JENNIFER, oncologist; d. John Fredrick and Edna Swindoll Garst; m. Shawn Sendlinger, May 25, 1997; children: Shelby Garst Sendlinger, Jack Garst Sendlinger. MD, Med. Coll. Ga., Augusta, 1990. Diplomate NC State Bd. and ABIM, 2008. Assoc. prof. medicine Duke U. Med. Sys., Durham, NC, 1993—. Founding bd. mem. Nat. Lung Cancer Partnership, Madison, Wis., 2004—05. Recipient Health Care Hero, Triangle Bus., 2008. Achievements include research in Lung Cancer Clincal Research. Office: Regional Cancer Ctr US Oncology 411 Ben Franklin Blvd Durham NC 27704 Office Fax: 919-477-6919. Business E-Mail: garst001@mc.duke.edu.*

GARTMAN, MAX DILLON, language educator; b. Mobile, Ala., May 3, 1938; s. Noah Christopher and Edna Olga (Schwarzauer) G.; m. Marcia Ann Hubbard, Aug. 31, 1962; children: Noel Don, Polly Antoinette, Paul Dillon. AB in French and History, Samford U., Birmingham, Ala., 1960; MA in French, U. Ala., Tuscaloosa, 1962, PhD in Romance Langs., 1974; cert., U. Nice, France, 1985. NDEA fellow U. Ala., Tuscaloosa, 1960-65; prof. Romance langs. Samford U., 1965-82, head dept. fgn. langs., 1975-82; chmn. dept. fgn. langs., prof. romance langs. U. North Ala., Florence, 1982-99, dir. Ctr. for Critical Langs., 1999—2003, prof. emeritus; dir. French program, prof. French and Spanish Bryan Coll., Dayton, Tenn., 2003—05; prof. Spanish and French Chattanooga State CC, 2006—. Pres. Internat. Edn. Travel, Florence, 1982—. Editor SU Faculty Forum Ann., 1967-72; performer rec. The Holy City, 1976. Chmn. Ala. Assn. Fgn. Lang. Tchrs., 1973-74, So. Conf. Lang. Tchg., 1976; bd. dirs. Ala. Humanities Found., 1992-96. Mem. Ala. Assn. Tchrs. of French (chmn. 1995-97), Ala. Consortium for Fgn. Langs. (chmn. 1995-97, 2001-02), Rotary (Paul Harris fellow). Baptist. Avocations: tennis, music, travel. Office: Rm 211 Humanities Bldg Chattanooga State Coll 4501 Amnicola Hwy Chattanooga TN 37406-1097 Personal E-mail: mdgartman@charter.net.

GARTON, DANIEL P., air transportation executive, marketing professional; b. Sheboygan, Wis., May 11, 1957; married; 3 children. BA in Econ., Stanford U., 1979; MBA in Fin., Cornell U., 1982. Assoc. corp. fin. American Airlines, Inc., 1984—86, prin. corp. fin., 1986—87, mng. dir., corp. fin., 1987—88, mng. dir., fin. analysis, 1988—89, v.p., treas., 1989—92, v.p., fin. planning & analysis, 1992—93; sr. v.p., CFO Continental Airlines, 1993—95; pres. AMR Eagle, 1995—98; sr. v.p. AMR Corp. (American Airlines), 1998—2000, exec. v.p., customer services, 2000—02, exec. v.p., mktg., 2002—. Office: AMR Corp 4333 Amon Carter Blvd Fort Worth TX 76155

GARVY, ROBERT ANDREW, investment company executive; MBA in Fin., Ga. State U. Sr. v.p., prin., co-founder cons. divsn. Wilshire Assocs., Inc.; joined INTECH Investment Mgmt. LLC, Janus Capital Group Inc., 1991, pres., CEO, chmn., co-CEO. Mem. Soc. of the Four Arts, Palm Beach; bd. dirs. The Inst. for the Study of Quantitative Fin.; chmn. Town of Palm Beach Gen. Retirement. Mem.: Rosarian Acad. (hon. chmn.). Office: INTECH CityPlace Tower 525 Okeechobee Blvd, Ste 1800 West Palm Beach FL 33401 Office Phone: 561-775-1100. Office Fax: 561-775-1156. Business E-Mail: robertgarvy@intechreports.com.

GARWOOD, JOHN A., state legislator; b. Wilkes, NC, Feb. 8, 1932; s. James Lemuel and Annie Lura Carrigan Garwood; m. Wanda Wadine Bandy Garwood, 1957; children: John B., David A., Susan. Ranking minority mem. NC State Senate; mem. bd. trustees Appalachian State U., 1973—80, chmn., 1978—79, Wilkes County Rep. Exec Com., 1974—79, 5th Congressional Rep. Exec. Com., 1980—81; mem. bd. gov. U. NC, 1985—96; chmn. Wilkes County Bd. Commr., 1991—93; bd. mem. NC State Coll. Life Sci. & Agr., 1995—; state senator Dist. 27 NC, 1997—2002; state senator Dist. 30 NC, 2003—04; state senator Dist. 45 NC, 2005—06; mem. Environ. & Natural Resources Com., Appropriations Edn. Com., Higher Edn. Com., Appropriations Base Budget Com., Edn. Com., Health Care Com., State & Local Govt. Com.; ranking minority mem. Transp. Com. Lay leader & certification lay spkr. United Meth. Ch. Mem.: Wilkes C. of C. (v.p. 1969—70), Elks (exalted ruler 1967—68). Republican. Protestant. Address: 453 Mark Lane N Wilkesboro NC 28659 Fax: 336-838-5378.

GARY, LAWRENCE EDWARD, social work educator; b. Union Spring, Md., May 26, 1939; s. Ed and Henrietta (Mays) G.; m. Robenia Baker, Aug. 8, 1969; children: Lisa Ché, Lawrence Charles André, Jason Edward. BS, Tuskegee Inst., 1963; MPA, U. Mich., 1964, MSW, 1967, PhD, 1970. From lectr. to asst. prof. U. Mich., Ann Arbor, 1968-71; Henry Lucy Moses vis. scholar CUNY-Hunter Coll., 1986-87; Samuel S. Wurtzel prof. Va. Commonwealth U., Richmond, 1990-92; asst. to v.p. acad. affairs Howard U., Washington, 1971-72, assoc. prof. social work, 1971-85, dir. Mental Health Rsch. Ctr., 1974-86, dir. Urban Rsch. Inst., 1972-90, prof. urban studies, 1985-90, prof. social work, 1985—2012, prof. emeritus social work, 2012—. Social welfare com. Nat. Urban League, N.Y., 1986-89; mem. adv. com. D.C. Commn. on Pub. Health, 1984-88; mem. minority rev. com. NIMH, Rockville, Md., 1979-81; youth rsch. com. Lilly Endowment, Indpls., 1987-96; mem. program rsch. commn. Coun. on Social Work Edn., Alexandria, Va., 1999-2002; panel mem. on juvenile crime commn. on law and justice Nat. Rsch. Coun., Washington, 1998-2002; Bush Master tchr. U. Minn., 1996; Karen Honig lectr. U. Ill., Chgo., 1996. Editor: Mental Health: A Challenge to Black Community, 1978, Black Men, 1981; contbr. articles to profl. publs. Mem. vis. com. Sch. Social Work, U. Mich., 1991—96; bd. dirs. Coun. on Social Work Edn., Alexandria, Va., 1992-95; bd. trustees pro tem St. Paul AME Ch., Washington, 1984-99, bd. stewards St. Paul AME Ch., Wash., 2001-2011, charter day dinner alumni com. Howard U., 2010-Recipient Labor of Love award Nat. Head Start Assn., 1984, Disting. Recent Contbns. to Social Work Edn. award Coun. on Social Work Edn., 1996, Alumni Merit award Tuskegee (Ala.) U., 1991, Sons of Thunder award 2d Episcopal Dist. AME Ch., 1997, Svc. Above Self award Fla. Ave. Bapt. Ch., 1999; Eminent scholar Va. State U., 1982; Eminent scholar Norfolk (Va.) State U., 1986, Galt vis. scholar Va. Dept. Mental Health, Richmond, 1994; Disting. scholar Albany (Ga.) State Coll., 1994. Fellow Am. Orthopsychiat. Assn.; mem. NASW (mem. book com. 1997-2002, Disting. Alumni Svc. award U. Mich., 2002), APHA (mem. action bd. 1973-74), Nat. Assn. Black Social Workers (editor jour., Outstanding Leadership and Cmty. Svc. award 1989), Alpha Phi Alpha. Democrat. Avocations: writing, gardening, speaking, swimming, reading. Office: 3504 Tory Cir Ormond Beach FL 32174 Business E-Mail: lgary@howard.edu.*

GARY, RICHARD DAVID, lawyer; b. Richmond, Va., Apr. 25, 1949; s. Morton Nathan and Blanche (Rudy) G.; m. Linda Levene, Aug. 6, 1972; children: Brent Ryan, Lauren Renee. AB in Econs., U. N.C., 1971; JD, U. Va., 1974. Bar: Va. 1974. From assoc. to ptnr.,r egulated industries & govt. rels. Hunton & Williams LLP, Richmond, 1974—, and mem. exec. com. Guest lectr. law Coll. William and Mary, Williamsburg, 1983-90, U. Va. Law Sch., 2004-2005; guest lectr. telecom. Va. Commonwealth U., 2004. Pres. Beth Sholom Home Ctrl. Va., Richmond, 1989-91; chmn. Beth Sholom Home Va., 1991-92, 2005—; v.p. Jewish Cmty. Fedn. Richmond, 2002—. Recipient Disting. Svc. award Beth Sholom Home Ctrl. Va., 1984. Mem. ABA (pub. utilities sect. coun. mem.), Va. State Bar (chmn. adminstrn. law sect. 1982-83), Va. Bar Assn., Fed. Comm Bar Assn., Fed. Energy Bar Assn. Avocation: sports. Office: Hunton & Williams Riverfront Plz East Twr PO Box 1535 Richmond VA 23219-1535 Home: 121 Countryside Ln Richmond VA 23229-7336 Office Phone: 804-788-8330. Office Fax: 804-788-8218. Business E-Mail: rgary@hunton.com.

GARY, STUART HUNTER, lawyer; b. Richmond, Va., Nov. 22, 1946; s. Morton Nathan and Blanche (Rudy) G.; m. Donna (Rothman), Aug. 19, 1967; children: Kenneth Asher, Robin Leigh. BA in Econ., U. Va., 1968; JD, Am. Univ., 1972. Bar: Va., 1972, D.C., 1973, U.S. Dist. Ct. (ea. dist.) Va., 1975, D.C., 1974, U.S. Tax Ct., 1976, U.S. Ct. Appeals (4th cir.), 1975, (D.C. cir.), 1974, U.S. Supreme Ct., 1976. Law clerk D.C. Ct. Appeals, Washington, 1972—73; atty. anti-trust divsn. Fed. Trade Commn., Washington, 1973—74; ptnr. Swift and Gary, Washington, 1974—75, Falcone and Gary, Fairfax, Va., 1975—81; prin. Stuart H. Gary and Assoc., McLean, Va., 1981—85, Stuart H. Gary P.C., McLean, Va., 1992—93, Goodman, Gary, and Lickstein, P.C., 1993—97, Gary and Goodman PLLC, Vienna, Va., 1997—2004, Gary and Regenhardt PLLC, Vienna, 2004—10; mng. shareholder Bailey Gary PC, Washington, Vienna, 2010—11, Gary Regenhardt Goldstein Wade, Tysons Corner, Va., 2011—13, Gary Goldstein Wade PC, 2013—. Bd. cons. Riggs Nat. Bank Va., 1976-88. Editl. bd. Am. U. Law Rev. Washington, 1971-72. Chmn. No. Va. Heart Fund Drive, 1976; bd. dir. No. Va. Jewish Cmty. Ctr., Fairfax, Va.; co-chmn. Am. Assoc. Ben Gurion U. Washington D.C. chpt. Mem. ABA, Va., D.C. Bar Assn., Fairfax County Bar Assn., McLean Bar Assn., Am. Arbitration Assn. (panel of arbitrators). Office Phone: 703-848-2828. Business E-Mail: sgary@garylaw.us.

GARY, WILLIE E., lawyer; b. Eastman, Ga., July 12, 1947; s. Turner and Mary Ella (McNair) G.; m. Gloria R. Gary, Aug. 25, 1978; children: Kenneth, Sekou, Ali, Kobie. BA in Bus. Adminstrn., Shaw U., 1971; JD, N.C. Cen. U., 1974. Bar: Fla., admitted to practice: US Dist. Ct. (So. Dist.) Fla., US Dist. Ct. (Mid. Dist.) Fla. Pvt. practice, Martin County, Fla., 1975-1976; ptnr. Gary, Williams, Parenti, Finney, Lewis, McManus, Watson, & Sperando, P.L. (now Gary, Williams, Finney, Lewis, Watson & Sperando, P.L.), Stuart, Fla., Fla., 1976—. Founder MTBC Network. Founder The Gary Found.; chmn. bldg. fund Evergreen Bapt. Ch. of Indiantown, mem. adult choir; past pres. Young Men's Progressive Assn. of Martin County; chmn. bd. trustees Shaw U.; mem. NAACP, Urban League, Civitan Internat., Fla. Guardsmen, Inc., United Way of Martin County, Martin Mem. Hosp. Found. Coun.; contbr. to various charities. Named Role Model of Yr. Bethune-Cookman Coll., 1989, one of two Coll. Alumni of Yr. United Negro Coll. Fund, 1989; recipient Learned Hand Award, Am. Jewish Com., 1996, Golden Trumpet Award, Turner Broadcasting Co., 1997, Horatio Alger Award, Horatio Alger Soc., 1999; named one of Am.'s Top Black Lawyers Black Enterprise Mag., 2003, 100 Most Influential Black Americans, Ebony mag., 2006; named to Power, 150 Ebony mag., 2008. Mem. ABA, Martin County Bar Assn., St. Lucie Bar Assn., Fla. Bar Assn. (past mem. bd. govs.), Nat. Bar Assn. (past pres. Fla. chpt., Lawyer of Yr.), Fla. Acad. Trial Lawyers, Am. Trial Lawyers Assn., Million Dollar Verdict Club, Phi Alpha Delta. Office: Gary Williams & Parenti Waterside Profl Bldg 221 E Osceola St Ste 300 Stuart FL 34994-2289 also: 320 S Indian River Dr Fort Pierce FL 34950

GARZA, ED, former mayor; b. San Antonio; m. Anna Laura Garza. Student in bus. adminstrn., U. Tex., Austin, 1986—88; B in Landscape Architecture, Tex. A&M U., 1992, MS in Land Devel., 1994. With various planning, devel., real estate fin., landscape architecture, and architecture firms; dir. land planning and devel. Internat. Waterfront Group, San Antonio; elected dist. 7 rep. San Antonio City Coun., 1997—2001; mayor City of San Antonio, 2001—05. Adj. prof. U. Tex., San Antonio, St. Mary's U.; v.p. N.Am. Internat. Trade Corridor Partnership (NAITCP). Mem. San Antonio Trees Bd., CEOs for Cities, Urban Land Inst.; Fannie Mae; Internat. Coun. of Shopping Ctrs.; adv. bd. Nat. League of Cities, 2000—, nominating com., 2003—; bd. advisors Nat. Assn. Latino Elected and Appointed Ofcls. (NALEO); past bd. dirs. Jefferson Neighborhood Assn., Woodlawn Lake Neighborhood Assn.; bd. dirs. Hispanic Elected Local Ofcls., 1998—, pres.; bd. dirs. San Antonio Water Sys., City Pub. Svc., Tex. Municipal League. Named one of 40 Under 40 Rising Stars, San Antonio Bus. Jour., 1996. Democrat.

GARZA, EMILIO MILLER, federal judge; b. San Antonio, Aug. 1, 1947; s. Antonio Peña and Dionisia (Miller) Garza. BA, U. Notre Dame, 1969, MA, 1970; JD, U. Tex., 1976. Assoc. Clemens, Spencer, Welmaker & Finck, San Antonio, 1976—82, ptnr., 1982—87; judge 225th Dist. Ct., Bexar County, San Antonio, 1987—88, US Dist. Ct. (western dist.) Tex., San Antonio, 1988—91, US Ct. Appeals (5th cir.), San Antonio, 1991—2012, sr. judge, 2012—. Adv. coun. U. Tex. San Antonio Coll. Fine Arts and Humanities, 1992—98; adv. bd. Phoenix Inst., 1992—; bd. advisors Hispanic Law Jour. U. Tex. at Austin Sch. Law, 1992—96; adv. com. Notre Dame Law Sch., 1998—; bd. dirs. Symphony Soc. San Antonio, 1987—89; mem. Century Club San Antonio, 1987—88. Capt. USMCR, 1970—79, active duty USMCR, 1970—73. Mem.: San Antonio Bar Assn., State Bar Tex. Office: 8200 I-10 W Ste 501 San Antonio TX 78230*

GASKAMP, ROGER L., management consultant; B in Bus. Mgmt., Tex. A&M U. Various sales mgmt. Willamette Industries; corp. sales mgr. Administaff, Inc., 1993—94, regional sales mgr., 1994—94, v.p., client selection & pricing, 1999—2009, sr. v.p., client selection & pricing, 2009—. Office: Administaff Inc 19001 Crescent Springs Dr Kingwood TX 77339-3802 Office Phone: 281-358-8986. Office Fax: 281-348-3718. Business E-Mail: roger_gaskamp@administaff.com.

GASKIN, FELICIA, biochemist, educator; b. Carlisle, Pa., Jan. 17, 1943; d. Joseph A. and Wanda J. (Rakowski) G.; m. Shu Man Fu, Nov. 29, 1969; children: Kai-Ming, Kai-Mei. AB in Chemistry, Dickinson Coll., 1965; MA in Organic Chemistry, Bryn Mawr Coll., 1967; PhD in Biochemistry, U. Calif., San Francisco, 1969. Postdoctoral fellow Stanford U., Palo Alto, Calif., 1969—71; rsch. assoc. Rockefeller U., NYC, 1971—72, Columbia U., NYC, 1972—74; asst. prof., then assoc. prof. Albert Einstein Coll. Medicine, NYC, 1974—82; prof. Sch. Medicine U. Okla., Oklahoma City, 1982—88, U. Va., Charlottesville, 1988—. Mem. Okla. Med. Rsch. Found., 1982-88. Contbr. articles to profl. jours. Recipient rsch. career devel. award NIH, 1975-80; Nat. Inst. Neurol. Diseases and Stroke spl. fellow, 1972-74. Mem. Am. Soc. Biochemistry and Molecular Biology, Soc. Neurosci. Office: U Va Sch Medicine Box 800203 Charlottesville VA 22908-0001

GASKINS, GARY MICHAEL, US marshal; b. 1955; BS in Criminal Justice, Fairmont State Coll., W.Va., 1994. Trooper Clarksburg detachment W.Va. State Police Dept., 1976—88, promoted through ranks, various assignments in Fairmont, Glenville, Bridgeport, & Morgantown, then capt. Troop 1 Hdqs., 2005—09, ret., 2009; US marshal (northern dist.) W.Va. US Dept. Justice, 2010—. Mem. Project Safe Neighborhood Steering Com., US Dept. Justice, 2005—. Office: US Courthouse Dist Hdqs 500 W Pike St Clarksburg WV 26301 Office Phone: 304-623-0486.

GASKINS, WILLIAM DARRELL, ophthalmologist; b. Columbia, SC, June 7, 1951; s. William and Virginia G. Herron; m. Cynthia Gaile Harper, Sept. 7, 1973; children: William Darrell Jr., Craig E., Trenton F. BS in Pharmacy, U. S.C., 1973; MD, Med. U. S.C., 1977. Diplomate Am. Bd. Ophthalmology. Intern in gen. surgery Med. U. S.C., Charleston, 1977-78; resident in ophthalmology U. Miss. Med. Ctr., Jackson, 1981-84; pvt. practice, Naples, Fla., 1984—. Capt. M.C., USAF, 1978-81. Paul Harris fellow Rotary Internat., 1986. Fellow ACS, Am. Acad. Ophthalmology; mem. AMA, Fla. Soc. Ophthalmology, Collier County Med. Soc. Presbyterian. Avocations: hunting, fishing. Office: 2335 9th St N Ste 304 Naples FL 34103-4457

GASPER, RUTH EILEEN, real estate executive; b. Valparaiso, Ind., July 16, 1934; d. Reuben John and Effie (Wesner) Treons; m. Ralph L. Gasper, May 25, 1957. Student, Purdue U., 1952—56; BA, Govs. State U., 1982. Analyst computer sys. Leo Burnett Advt., Chgo., 1958-69; nat. adminstr. registrars Sports Car Club Am., Denver, 1977-79; pres. Ainslie Inc., Port Orange, Fla., 1982—. Mem. North River Commn. Housing Com., Chgo., 1982-83, fin. com. Mayor's Task Force on Homelessness City of Chgo. Area coord. Concerned Action party, Lansing, Ill., 1977; chief race registrar Ind. N.W. Region Sports Car Club Am., 1969-80; co-founder, Single Rm. Operators Assn., 1987-98; treas. Sand Dollar Home Owners Assn. Inc., 2004-, treas Dolphin Beach Club Condo Assn., 1988-2009 Mem. Fantasy Island II Condo Assn. (sec. 1995-2009, treas., 1995-2009). Avocations: sports car racing, classical music. Personal E-mail: regasper@earthlink.net.

GASTON, CLARENCE EDWIN (CITO GASTON), retired professional baseball coach; b. San Antonio, Mar. 17, 1944; m. Lynda Caesar Gaston; children: Adrian, Carly, Shawn, Rochell. LLD (hon.), U. Toronto, Can., 1994. Outfielder Atlanta Braves, 1967, 75-78, minor league coach, 1981; outfielder San Diego Padres, 1969-74, Pitts. Pirates, 1978; batting coach Toronto Blue Jays, 1982-89, 2000—01, mgr., 1989—97, 2008—10, hitting instr., 2000—02, club amb., spl. asst. to pres. and CEO. Coach Am. League All-Star Team, 1991, mgr., 1993, 1994. Recipient Rube Foster Character award, 1994, Jackie Robinson award, Negro League Hall of Fame, 2008; named Baseball Man of Yr., Toronto-Montreal Baseball Writers Assn. America, 1989, Sportsman of Yr., The Sporting News, 1993; named to Nat. League All-Star Team, Maj. League Baseball, 1970, Blue Jays Level of Excellence, 1999, Can. Baseball Hall of Fame, 2002. Achievements include manager of World Series championship winning Toronto Blue Jays, 1992, 1993; becoming the first African-American to manage a World Series championship winning team, 1992. Home: 1454 Woodstream Dr Oldsmar FL 34677

GASTON, HENRY VICTOR (VICTOR GASTON), state legislator; b. Mobile, Ala., Jan. 15, 1943; s. Emmett Carroll and Jewell (Odom) Gaston; m. Jean Jumonville; children: Hank Victor, George Carroll. BS, U. So. Miss., Hattiesburg; MA, U. So. Ala.; EdD, Auburn U., Ala. Ret. educator, sch. adminstr. Mobile County Pub. Sch. Sys., Ala.; ret. timber farmer Mobile County, Ala.; mem. Dist. 100 Ala. House of Reps., Montgomery, 1982—. Mem. Ala. State Rep. Com., 1970-; vice chmn., Mobile County Rep. Com., Ala., 1974-78; commr., Commn. on Presdl. Scholars, 1981-; del., Rep. Nat. Convention; co-chmn, Am. Legis. Exch. Coun., Ala. Legis. Chpt.; bd. mem. Home of Grace Women, Volunteers America, Penelope House, Mobile Mental Health Ctr., Mobile Assn. Retarded Citizens; deacon Springhill Bapt. Ch. Recipient M.O. Beale Scroll of Merit, Mobile Press Register, 1982, Disting. Alumni award, U. So. Ala., 1982. Mem.: Ala. Forestry Assn., Nat. Assn. Secondary Sch. Principals, Ala. Farm Bur., U. So. Ala. Alumni Assn., Auburn U. Alumni Assn. (life), Scottish Rite, Mason, Phi Delta Kappa. Republican. Southern Baptist. Office: 1136 Hillcrest Crossing W Mobile AL 36695 also: Ala House of Reps Ala State House 11 S Union St Rm 526-C Montgomery AL 36130 Office Phone: 334-242-7675.

GATES, JAMES DAVID, retired professional society administrator; b. East Cleveland, Ohio, July 9, 1927; s. James Adelbert and Margaretta (Voigt) G.; m. Carol Marie Schreiber, June 9, 1956; children: David, Keith, Robert. AB, Hiram Coll., Ohio, 1951; MA, Columbia, 1956; EdD, George Washington U., 1975. Tchr. Maple Heights (Ohio) City Schs., 1951-61; profl. asst. Nat. Council Tchrs. Math., Reston, Va., 1961-63, exec. sec., 1963-76, exec. dir., 1976-95. Mem. faculty U. Va., 1963-66, George Washington U., 1966-75; assoc. dir. Math. Scis. Edn. Bd., Ctr. for Sci., Math., and Engring. Edn., Nat. Rsch. Coun., 1997-99. Mem. Va. Coalition Math. and Sci.; bd. dirs. MathCounts Found.; sec.-treas. Jr. Engring. Tech. Soc. Served with AUS, 1945-46. Fellow AAAS; mem. NEA, ASCD, Nat. Coun. Suprs. Math., Nat. Coun. Tchrs. Math., Math. Assn. Am., Assn. State Suprs. Math., Benjamin Banneker Assn., Assn. Math. Tchr. Educators, Am. Math. Assn. Two-Yr. Colls., Todos: Math. for All, Rotary. Home: 11303 Fieldstone Ln Reston VA 20191-3905

GATES, RICHARD DANIEL, retired manufacturing executive; b. Trenton, Mo., Mar. 27, 1942; s. Daniel G. and Effie Wright (Johnson) G.; m. Jean Gates, Jan. 26, 1966; 1 child, Daniel Wright. BS, U. Mo., 1964; M.C.S., Rollins Coll., Winter Park, Fla., 1968; postgrad., Harvard U., 1976. Mgmt. assoc. Western Electric Co., NYC, 1964-66; bus. mgmt. adminstr. Martin Marietta Aerospace Co., Orlando, Fla., 1966-68, chief indsl. engring., 1968-69; fin. analyst Martin Marietta Co., NYC, 1969-70, sr. acct., 1970-71; controller Dragon Cement Co., divsn. Martin Marietta Co., 1971-72, N.E. divsn. Martin Marietta Aggregates Co., 1972-73; asst. controller, then asst. treas. Rubbermaid, Inc., Wooster, Ohio, 1973-79, treas., 1979-80, v.p., treas., 1980-91, sr. v.p., bus. devel., investor rels. and corp. communications, 1991-98; ret., 1998. Pres. The Rubbermaid Found., Wooster. Mem. Wooster City Fin. Task Force, All Am. City Com.; chmn. Wooster Growth Assn.; active local Cub Scouts.; adviser Art Center, chmn. maj. indsl. capital campaign Boy Scouts Camp; trustee, chmn. Wayne Ctr. Arts; mem. parents' com. St. Paul's Sch., Wesleyan U. Mem. Nat. Assn. Corporate Treas., Main St. Wooster Inc. (bd. trustees), Beta Gamma Sigma, Omicron Delta Kappa. Clubs: Harvard Bus. Sch, Wooster Country (bd. dirs.). Home: 4751 Gulf Shore Blvd N 1606 Naples FL 34103 Mailing: Ste 9-470 88005 Overseas Hwy Islamorada FL 33036

GATES, ROBERT MICHAEL (BOB GATES), academic administrator, former United States Secretary of Defense; b. Wichita, Kans., Sept. 25, 1943; s. Melville A. and Isabel V. (Goss) Gates; m. Rebecca Wilkie Gates, Jan. 7, 1967; children: Eleanor, Bradley. BA in History, Coll. William & Mary, 1965; MA in History, Ind. U., 1966; PhD in Russian & Soviet Hist., Georgetown U., 1974; LHD (hon.), Coll. William & Mary, 1998, U. Okla., 2011. Intelligence analyst CIA, Washington, 1969—72, staff mem. to spl. asst. to dir. for strategic arms limitation, 1972—73, asst. nat. intelligence officer for strategic programs, 1973—74; staff mem. NSC, Washington, 1974—76, staff mem. Ctr. for Policy Support, 1976—77, spl. asst. to the asst. to Pres. for nat. security affairs, 1977—79, dir. Strategic Evaluation Ctr., 1979—80; exec. asst. to dir. CIA, Washington, 1980—81, dir. exec. staff for dir & dep. dir., 1981—82, dep. dir. for intelligence, 1982-86, dep. dir., 1986-89, acting dir., 1986-87, dir., 1991—93; chmn. Nat. Intelligence Coun., Washington, 1983-86; asst. to Pres., dep. asst. to Pres. for nat. security affairs NSC, Washington, 1989-91; pres. Texas A&M U., College Station, Tex., 2002—06, interim dean, George Bush Sch. Govt & Public Service, 1999—2001; sec. US Dept. Def., Washington, 2006—11; chancellor Coll. William & Mary, Williamsburg, Va., 2012—; founding ptnr. RiceHadleyGates, Washington, 2012—. Bd. dirs. Naaco Industries Inc., 1993—2006, Parker Drilling Co., 2001—06, Brinker Internat., Inc., 2003—06, Starbucks Corp., 2012—; mem. Iraq Study Group, 2006; mem. advisory coun. US Global Leadership Coalition, 2012—. Author: From the Shadows: The Ultimate Insider's Story of Five Presidents and How They Won the Cold War, 1996, Duty: Memoirs of a Secretary of War, 2014. Mem. nat. exec. bd. Boy Scouts of America (BSA), 2013—, nat. pres.-elect, 2013, nat. pres., 2014—. Intelligence officer USAF, 1967—69, Whiteman AFB, Mo. Recipient President's Citizens medal, Nat. Intelligence Disting. Svc. medals (3), Disting. Intelligence medals (3), Nat. Security medal, Intelligence medal of merit, Arthur S. Flemming award presented annually to ten most outstanding young men and women in Fed. Svc., Disting. Eagle Scout award, 1993, Henry M. Jackson Disting. Svc. award, 2007, George H.W. Bush award for Excellence in Public Svc., 2007, Presdl. Medal of Freedom, The White House, 2011, Nat. Intelligence Disting. Svc. medal, Office Dir. Nat. Intelligence (ODNI), 2011, Liberty medal, Nat. Constitution Ctr., 2011, Silver Buffalo award, Boy Scouts of America, George Catlett Marshall medal, Assn. US Army, 2013; named Citizen of Yr., Boy Scouts of America, 2007; named one of The 50 Most Powerful People in DC, GQ mag., 2007, 2009, The 100 Most Influential People in the World, TIME mag., 2008, America's Best Leaders, US News & World Report, 2008; named to The Order of the Arrow, Nat. Eagle Scout Assn. Republican. Office: College of William & Mary PO Box 8795 Williamsburg VA 23187*

GATES, STEPHEN FRYE, lawyer, director, former oil industry executive, corporate director; b. Clearwater, Fla., May 20, 1946; s. Orris Allison and Olga Betty (Frye) Gates; m. Laura Daignault, June 10, 1972. BA in Economics, Yale U., New Haven, 1968; JD, MBA, Harvard U., 1972. Bar: Fla. 1972, Mass. 1973, Ill. 1977, Colo. 1986. Assoc. Choate, Hall & Stewart, Boston, 1973-77; atty. Amoco Corp., Chgo., 1977-82, gen. atty., 1982-86, regional atty. Amoco Prodn. Co. (subs.) Denver, 1987-88, asst. treas. Chgo., 1988-91, assoc. gen. counsel, corp. sec., 1991-92, v.p. Amoco Chem. Co., 1993-95, v.p., gen. counsel, 1995-98; exec. v.p., group chief of staff BP Amoco, London, 1999-2000; sr. v.p., gen. counsel, sec. FMC Corp., Chgo., 2000—01; ptnr. Mayer, Brown, Rowe & Maw, Chgo., 2002—03; sr. v.p., gen. counsel ConocoPhillips, Houston, 2003—07; spl. counsel Mayer Brown LLP, Houston, 2008—. Bd. dirs. Nat. Legal Ctr. Pub. Interest, Washington, 1999—2007, Internat. Inst. Conflict Prevention & Resolution, NYC, 2003—, Methode Electronics Inc., Chicago, Ill., 2010—; mem. exec. com. Inst. Energy Law, Dallas, 2003—, chmn., 2010—12. Bd. trustees Newberry Libr., Chgo., 1998—2005, Appleseed Found., 2003—12, co-chair, 2009—11; bd. trustees Charleston Libr. Soc., 2009—, pres., 2011—; mem. Nat. Assn. Corp. Dirs., 2010—, Yale U. Libr. Coun.; mem. adv. bd. Chgo. Vol. Legal Svcs. Found., 1996—98; mem. adv. coun. Chgo. Schweitzer Urban Fellows Program, 1996—2000; bd. dirs. Chgo. Crime Commn., 2000—03; mem. site coun. Drayton Hall, Charleston, 2009—, chair, 2014—; bd. trustees Lowcountry Open Land Trust, 2010—; pres. Drayton Hall, 2014—; bd. dirs. Houston Grand Opera, 2003—08. Knox fellow, 1972—73. Fellow: American Bar Found., Royal Soc. Arts; mem.: ABA, Assn. Gen. Counsel, Yale Club, Chgo. Club, Univ. Club. Office: Mayer Brown LLP 700 Louisiana St Ste 3400 Houston TX 77002 Office Phone: 713-238-2682. Business E-Mail: sgates@mayerbrown.com.

GATES, STEVEN LEON, physician; b. Newton, Kans., Aug. 13, 1954; s. Leon Martin and Mary Lorine (Adams) G.; m. Paula Ellen Banwart, Jan. 1, 1977; children: Stephanie, Scott, Jeffrey. PharmD summa cum laude, SW Okla. State U., 1976; DO, Okla. State U., 1986. Diplomate internal medicine and geriatrics Am. Bd. Internal Medicine. Intern Osteopathic Med. Ctr. Tex., Ft. Worth, 1986-87; resident in internal medicine Dallas/Ft. Worth Med. Ctr., Grand Prairie, Tex., 1987-90; pharmacist M & D Star Drug Store, Okmulgee, Okla., 1976-80; pharmacist, mgr. Wal-Mart Pharmacy Divsn., Okmulgee, Okla., 1980-82; chief med. resident Ready Care Minor Emergency Ctr., Bedford, Tex., 1987-90; jail physician Tarrant County Sheriff's Dept., Ft. Worth, 1989-90; pvt. practice internal medicine Grand Prairie, Tex., 1990-97, Cleburne, Tex., 1997—2006; dir. med. edn. Bay Area Corpus Christi Med. Ctr., Tex., 2007—. Internal medicine physician and minor emergency physician Ready Care Med. Clinic, Bedford, Tex., 1990-91; dir. med. edn. Dallas/Ft. Worth Med. Ctr.-Grand Prairie, 1991-96; clin. asst. prof. dept. medicine U. North Tex., Tex. Coll. Osteopathic Medicine, Ft. Worth, 1990— Fellow Am. Bd. Internal Medicine: mem. Am. Coll. Osteo. Internists (bd. cert. with added qualification in geriatrics), Am. Osteo. Assn., Tex. Osteo. Med. Assn. (trustee 2004—), Assn. Osteo. Dirs. & Med. Educators (nat. bd. trustees), Sigma Sigma Phi. Republican. Avocations: reading, exercise, travel, theater. Office Phone: 361-761-3280. Personal E-mail: sgates5160@gmail.com.

GATEWOOD, WILLARD BADGETT, JR., retired historian, writer; b. Pelham, NC, Feb. 23, 1931; s. Willard Badgett and Bessie Lee (Pryor) G.; m. Mary Lu Brown, Aug. 9, 1958; children: Willard Badgett III, Elizabeth Ellis. BA, Duke U., 1953, MA, 1954, PhD, 1957. Asst. prof. history East Tenn. State U., 1957-58, East Carolina U., 1958-60; assoc. prof. N.C. Wesleyan Coll., 1960-64; prof. U. Ga., 1964-70; Alumni Disting. prof. history U. Ark., 1970-98, ret., 1998, provost and chancellor, 1984-85. Author: Theodore Roosevelt and the Art of Controversy, 1970, Smoked Yankees, 1971, Black Americans and the White Man's Burden, 1975, Slave and Freeman, 1979, Free Men of Color, 1982, Aristocrats of Color, 1990, Arkansas Delta, 1993; mem. bd. editors Ga. Rev., 1968-70, Jour. Negro History, 1972-74, Ark. Hist. Quar., 1992-94. Bd. dirs. Winthrop Rockefeller Found., 1990-96. Recipient Parks Excellence in Teaching award Phi Alpha Theta, 1970, Michael Rsch. award, 1967; Outstanding Teaching award Omicron Delta Kappa, 1979, rsch. award U. Ark. Alumni Assn., 1980, Gingles award Ark. Hist. Assn., 1982, Chancellor's medal, 1994, Ledbetter prize, 1994; Truman Libr. fellow, 1963; Acad. Arts and Scis. grantee, 1962. Mem. So. Hist. Assn. (pres. 1986-87), Ark. Hist. Assn., Orgn. Am. Historians, Phi Beta Kappa. Presbyterian. Personal E-mail: wgatewood@cox.net.

GAU, GEORGE W., finance educator, former dean; BS, U. Ill., Urbana-Champaign, 1969, MS, 1971, PhD in fin., 1975. Asst. prof. fin. U. Okla., 1975—79; asst. to assoc. prof. U. British Columbia, 1979—88; joined faculty McCombs Sch. Bus., U. Tex., Austin, 1988, chair fin. dept., 1992—2002, founding dir. Ctr. Real Estate Fin., 1999—2002, George S. Watson Centennial prof. in real estate, J. Ludwig Mosle Centennial Meml. prof. in investments and money mgmt., Centennial chair is bus. edn. leadership, dean, 2002—08. Co-editor: (book) North American Housing Markets into the Twenty-First Century, 1983; contbr. articles in acad. and profl. jour. Recipient Tchg. Excellence award, Univ. British Columbia, 1984, Adv. Coun. award for tchg. innovation, CBA Found., 1994. Fellow: Homer Hoyt Inst., Urban Land Inst.; mem.: Fin. Mgmt. Assn. (bd. dirs. 1984—86), Am. Real Estate and Urban Econ. Assn. (pres. 1986—87, Rsch. Award 1990). Office: McCombs Sch Business Univ Tex Dept Finance GSB 2-104 Austin TX 78712-1178 Office Phone: 512-471-5921. Office Fax: 512-471-7725. Business E-Mail: ggau@mail.utexas.edu.

GAUDIERI, ALEXANDER V.J., art historian, museum director, educator; b. 1940; married; 1 child. BA, Ohio State U., 1962; diploma, Sorbonne U. Paris, 1962; postgrad., Colgate U., 1963; MBA in Internat. Fin., Am. Grad. Sch. Internat. Commerce, 1965; MA, NYU, 1976. Internat. banking officer Marine Midland Bank, NYC, 1965—71; with Sotheby Parke Bernet, 1972—; dir. Telfair Acad. Arts and Scis., Savannah, Ga., 1977—83; dir. Montreal Mus. Fine Arts, 1983—88; art historian, art cons., 2003—. Adj. prof. mus. studies program Grad. Sch. Arts and Scis., NYU; dir. Samuel F.B. Morse hist. site Locust Grove, Poughkeepsie, N.Y., 1995-96. Mem. bd. sponsors Attingham Park Program, Eng.; bd. dirs. Young Concert Artists, NYC. Barton Kyle Yount scholar. Mem. Assn. Art Mus. Dirs., Am. Assn. Mus. (accreditation commn.), Brit. Nat. Trust, Soc. Archtl. Historians. Home: 926 Village Rd North Palm Beach FL 33408-3336 Office Phone: 561-832-6005. E-mail: gaudieri@bellsouth.net.

GAUT, C. CHRISTOPHER, energy executive; b. 1957; BA in Engring. Sci., Dartmouth Coll.; MBA in Fin., U. Pa. Various fin. mgmt. positions Amoco Corp.; ptnr. Pacific Asset Capital; pres., COO, CFO ENSCO International, Inc., 1988—2003; exec. v.p., CFO Halliburton Co., 2003—07, pres., drilling & evaluation, 2008—09; mng. dir. SCF Ptnrs., Houston; chmn., CEO Forum Energy Technologies. Bd. dirs. KBR, Inc., Ensco plc, 2008—. Mem.: Fin. Execs. Internat., Internat. Assn. Drilling Contractors (mem. exec. com.). Office: Ensco plc Bd Directors 500 North Akard St Ste 4300 Dallas TX 75201-3331 Office Phone: 214-397-3000. Business E-Mail: cgaut@enscous.com.

GAUTHIER, DOREEN ANN, retired librarian; b. Davenport, Iowa, July 18, 1941; d. Clifford H. and Dorothy H. Wildman; m. William E. Gauthier, July 18, 1989. BA, Midland Coll., Fremont. Nebr., 1972; grad. cert., U. Omaha, 1972; MA, U. South Fla., 1996. Children's libr. Keene Meml. Libr., Fremont, Nebr., 1967-77; circulation libr. Pompano Beach (Fla.) Libr., 1978-79; libr. dir. The Doreen Gauthier Lighthouse Point Libr., Fla., 1979—2011. Dir. Fla. Pub. Libr. Assn., Lakeland, 1992—98. Named Librarian of Yr., Fla. Lib. Assn., 2009. Mem. ALA, Fla. Libr. Assn., Broward County Libr. Assn. Episcopalian. Home: 1990 NE 32nd Ct # 44 Lighthouse Point FL 33064-7684 Home Phone: 954-785-0042. Personal E-mail: gauthid22@hotmail.com.

GAUTHIER, ISABEL, cognitive neuroscientist; BA, U. Québec, Montreal, 1993; MS, Yale U., 1995, PhD, 1998. Post doctoral fellowship, psychology, dept. diagnostic radiology Yale U., 1998—99; post doctoral fellowship, psychology, dept. brain and cognitive scis. MIT, 1998—99; head, Object Perception Lab, psychology dept. Vanderbilt U., asst. prof., psychology, 1999—2004, assoc. prof. psychology, 2004—. Panel mem., IGERT prog. NSF, 1999; panel mem., ISBC prog. Nat. Inst. Mental Health, 2002; panel mem., Prog. Project Grant Site Visit NIA, 2003. Contbr. scientific papers articles to profl. jours.; mem. editl. bd. Jour. Exptl. Psychology: General, 2002, Perception and Pyschophysics, 2003. Recipient Young Investigator award, Cognitive Neuroscience Soc., 2002, APA Disting. Scientific award for Early Career Contbn. to Psychology in the area of Behavioral/Cognitive Neuroscience, 2003; co-recipient Troland Rsch. award, NAS, 2008; Grad. Fellowship, Yale U., 1993—97, U. Dissertation Fellowship, 1997—98, NSERC Postdoctoral Fellowship, MIT, 1998—99. Office: Vanderbilt U 301 Wilson Hall/502 Wilson Hall 111 21st Ave S Nashville TN 37203 Office Phone: 615-322-4644, 615-322-1778. Office Fax: 615-322-4706. Business E-Mail: isabel.gauthier@vanderbilt.edu.

GAUTREAUX, NICK, state commissioner, former state legislator; b. Abbeville, La. m. Lynne Mouton Gautreaux; 3 children. Mem. Dist. 26 La. State Senate, Baton Rouge, 2004—10; commr. La. Office Motor Vehicles (OMV), Baton Rouge, 2010—. Mem.: Vermilion Parish Coun. Aging (pres.). Democrat. Office: Louisiana Office Motor Vehicles PO Box 64886 Baton Rouge LA 70896 Office Phone: 225-925-6146.

GAVAGAN, GEORGE R., retired corporate financial executive; b. 1946; Mgr., internal audit Gannett Co., Inc., 1979, asst. contr., dir., acctg. & financial reporting, v.p., corporate acctg. services, 1993—97, v.p., contr., 1997—2011, v.p., chief acctg. officer, 2011—12.

GAVALER, JOAN SUSAN, dance educator, choreographer, performer; d. John Raymond and Judith Stohr Gavaler; m. Robert Lian Foster. BA, Coll. William and Mary, Williamsburg, Va., 1985; MA, Ohio State U., Columbus, 1987. Cert. tchg. mem. Alexander Technique Internat., 1999. Instr. dance Coll. William and Mary, 1994—98, asst. prof. dance, 1998—2001, assoc. prof. dance, 2001—07, prof. dance, 2007—, dept. chair, 2009—14; resident Alexander Technique Tchr. Va. Shakespeare Festival, 2009—14, Beijing Normal U. Dance Dept., 2013. Mem. The Moving Arts Co., Columbus, 1987—90; guest artist Days of Creation, Arts for Kids, Columbus, 1987—94; artistic dir. Gavaler Danceworks, Williamsburg, 1990—96; co-artistic dir. Gravity Optional Dance Co., Williamsburg, 2002—09, Aura Curiatlas Phys. Theatre, 2013—; presenter 8th Internat. Congress F. M. Alexander Technique, Lugano, Switzerland, 2008, 9th Internat. Congress F. M. Alexander Technique, 2011. Choreographer Translations, captured... seeking, Nostalgia (Starry Night Again), Moment, Virus Warning, Even If You Did, Barrier, You Cannot Hear Me, Sextet # 1 With Rests, The Waiting Room, Grace, Dyslexia, Jamestown 2007 Commemoration, Loonatic, Re-Membering, Fiddle Dances, Rapid Eye Movements, Symbol, The Fool and The World, The Abracadabra of Meaning, A Midsummer Night's Dream, Richard III, Newton's Cradle. Recipient Fellowship award for Excellence in Tchg., Alumni Soc., Coll. William and Mary, 2002—03; named Disting. Guest Artist, Southern Dist. AAHPERD Conv., 2005; Nat. Merit scholar, Richard King Mellon, 1981—85, Project grantee, Ohio Joint Program in the Arts and Humanities, 1990, 1991, Greater Columbus Arts Coun., 1991, 1992, 1993. Mem.: Am. Dance Guild (bd. mem. 2003), Alexander Technique Internat., Phi Beta Kappa. Office: Coll William and Mary Dept Theatre Speech Dance PO Box 8795 Williamsburg VA 23187

GAVENDA, JOHN DAVID, physicist; b. Temple, Tex., Mar. 25, 1933; s. Edward and Rose Katherine (Machalek) G.; m. Janie Louise Yeoman, Dec. 22, 1952; children— Victor Joseph, Philip Martin. Student, U. Chgo., 1950-51; BS, U. Tex., Austin, 1954, MA, 1956; PhD, Brown U., 1959. Asst. prof. physics U. Tex., Austin, 1959-62, assoc. prof., 1962-65, assoc. prof. physics and edn., 1965-67, prof., 1967-99, prof. emeritus, 1999—. Contbr. articles on physics of metals and electromagnetic wave propagation to profl. jours. Sr. rsch. fellow Inst. Study of Metals, U. Chgo., 1963, NATO sr. fellow in sci. U. Oslo, 1969. Fellow: Am. Phys. Soc. (Disting Svc. award Tex. Sect. 2009), Tex. Acad. Sci.; mem.: Am. Assn. Physics Tchrs. (Robert N. Little award 1988, Disting. Svc. citation 1997), Phi Beta Kappa, Sigma Xi. Office: Univ Tex Dept Physics 1 University Sta C1600 Austin TX 78712-0264 Office Phone: 512-471-3201. E-mail: gavenda@physics.utexas.edu.

GAVIN, DONALD GLENN, lawyer, educator; b. Newark, Oct. 12, 1942; s. Louis Brooks and Elizabeth (Nievert) Gavin; m. Irene Dunn, Nov. 25, 1965; children: Andrew Scott, Mitchell Bryant. BS in Econs., U. Pa., 1964, JD, 1967; LLM, George Washington U., 1972. Bar: Pa. 1967, D.C. 1972, Va. 1973. Law clk. Ct. Common Pleas, Phila., 1967—68; assoc. to ptnr. Lewis, Mitchell & Moore, Washington and Vienna, Va., 1972—74; founding ptnr. Wickwire, Gavin P.C., Washington, L.A. and Vienna, 1974—2006; shareholder Akerman Senterfitt Wickwire Gavin, 2006—. Lectr. in field. Contbr. articles to profl. jours. Nat. bd. Am. Ceramic Cir. To capt. JAG US Army, 1968—72. Recipient Outstanding Svc. award, US Ct. Federal Claims. Fellow: ABA (past nat. chmn. pub. contract law sect., past chmn. fed. grant legis., policies and remedies com., past chmn. grant coordination com., past chmn. environ. law com., mem. forum on construction industry, mem., former vice-chair tort & insurance practice sect., fidelity and surety com., legal claim divsn., past coun. mem.), Am. Bar Found., Am. Coll. Constrn. Lawyers; mem.: US Coun. Internat. Bus., Internat. Bar Assn. (construction and arbitration com.), Pa. Bar Assn., Va. Bar Assn., US Ct. Fed. Claims Com., Fed. Bar Assn. Home Phone: 703-734-3049; Office Phone: 703-790-8750. Business E-Mail: donald.gavin@akerman.com.

GAVISH, BEZALEL, computer science operations research, information systems educator; b. Dorohoi, Romania, Jan. 23, 1945; came to U.S., 1976; s. Faivish and Tony (Waiseberg) Gropper; m. Dorlen Zukerman, Nov. 6, 1988; children: Ravit, Royi. BSc, Technion, Haifa, Israel, 1966, MSc, 1970, PhD, 1975. Mgr. computer applications IBM Sci. Ctr., Haifa, 1973-76; prof. U. Rochester (N.Y.), 1976-87; Grace Murrey Hopper prof. Naval Postgrad. Sch., Monterey, Calif., 1987-88; prof. computers, info. systems and ops. mgmt. Vanderbilt U., Nashville, 1988—2000; chair, prof. computers, info. tech. and ops. mgmt. So. Methodist U., Dallas, 2000—. Mem. vis. faculty IBM-Watson Rsch. Ctr., Yorktown Heights, N.Y., 1981, AT&T-Bell Labs., Homdel, N.J., 1982; vis. prof. dept. indsl. engring. Technion, 1983-84; cons. GTE Labs., Waltham, Mass., 1986-88, Motorola Satellite Systems. Editor-in-chief Telecommunication Systems--Modeling, Analysis, Design and Management, Electronic Commerce Research; mem. editorial bd. 16 jours.; contbr. more than 100 articles to sci. jours. NSF grantee, 1981-83, Fulbright travel grantee, 1983, 89. Mem. IEEE (sr.), Am. Inst. Indsl. Engrs. (sr.), Ops. Rsch. Soc. Am. (past chmn. spl. interest group on telecomm.), Am. Telecomm. Sys. Mgmt. Assn. (pres.), Assn. Computing Machinery, Inst. Ops. Reserve and Mgmt. Scis. Avocations: tennis, fishing. Office: So Methodist U Cox Sch of Bus Dallas TX 75205 Home: 6441 Norway Rd Dallas TX 75230 Personal E-mail: gavishb2000@yahoo.com.

GAY, HANNAH BERRY, pediatric infectious disease physician, educator; m. Paul E. Gay; children: Stephen Paul, Daniel Evans, Andrew Joseph, Ruth Hannah. BA, U. Miss., 1976, MD, 1980. Diplomate American Bd. Pediat. Pediatric cons. Miss. Dept. Pub. Health, Jackson, 1984; med. missionary Fgn. Mission Bd. So. Bapt. Conv., Addis Ababa, Ethiopia, 1987—93; instr. pediat., adolescent medicine U. Miss. Med. Ctr., Jackson, 1983—84, instr. pediat., pediat. neurology, 1985, asst. dir. pediat. outpatient dept., 1985—86, asst. prof. pediat., pediat. HIV program, 1994—2001, 2001—. SACS rev. self-study - instl. effectiveness com. U. Miss. Med. Ctr., Jackson, 1998—2000; rev. Clin. Pediat., 2001—04; mem. Ryan White Title IV HIVQUAL adv. com., 2002—04. Sec. author (publs.) Jour. Pediat., Jour. Immunology, Jour. Child Neurology. Named one of The 100 Most Influential People in the World, TIME mag., 2013; grantee AIDS Clin. Trial Group Protocol #300, Glaxo Rsch. Inst., 1995-1997, Pediat. and Perinatal Clin. Trials Network, NIH, 1996-2004, Early Intervention Svcs., Ryan White Title III, 1998-2001. Fellow: Am. Acad. Pediat.; mem.: Christian Med./Dental Fellowship. With colleagues responsible for curing a newborn of AIDS by giving the infant who contracted HIV from its mother, anti-HIV drugs within hours of birth in 2013. Office: University of Mississippi Medical Center 2500 N State St Jackson MS 39216 Office Phone: 601-815-2005.*

GAY, ROBERT DERRIL, behavioral health consultant; b. Savannah, Ga., June 23, 1939; s. Roscoe Degomer and Mollie Ann (Jones) G. BA, Oglethorpe U., 1962; MA, Emory U., 1966, PhD, 1984. Dep. dir. Divsn. Mental Health and Mental Retardation Ga. Dept. Human Resources, Atlanta, 1975-77, asst. commr., 1977-78, dir. Divsn. Mental Health and Mental Retardation, 1978-81; dep. dir. DeKalb County Health Dept., Decatur, Ga., 1981-94; dir. DeKalb Community Mental Health, Mental Retardation and Substance Abuse Svc. Bd., Decatur, 1994—2004; ind. cons., 2004—. Vis. instr. Oglethorpe U., 1966, 67, 85-94, Emory U. Sch. Nursing, 1970; mem. Ga. Gov.'s Coun. on Devel. Disabilities, 1978-81, Ga. Gov.'s Coun. on Mental Health and Mental Retardation, 1978-81, DeKalb County Coun. on Devel. Disabilities, 1981-2004 Bd. dirs. St. Joseph's Mercy Care Svcs., 1994-2000. Mem. Am. Sociol. Assn., Nat. Assn. State Mental Health Program Dirs. (bd. dirs. 1978-81), Atlanta Mercy Mobile Health Program (bd. dirs. 1987-94, chair 1991-94), Oglethorpe U. Nat. Almuni Assn. (bd. dirs. 1988-1993, pres. 1990-1991). Home and Office: 308 Oglethorpe Dr NE Atlanta GA 30319-2772

GAYLE, HELENE DORIS, humanitarian organization administrator, pediatrician; b. Buffalo, Aug. 16, 1955; BS in Psychology cum laude, Columbia U. Barnard Coll., 1976; MD, U. Pa., 1981; MPH, John Hopkins U., 1981; LHD (hon.), Jackson State U., 2004; DSc (hon.), Pa. State U., 2004, Smith Coll., 2007, Meharry Medical Coll., 2007, Duke U., 2008; LHD (hon.), Mt. Sinai Sch. Medicine, 2008; DSc (hon.), Morehouse Sch. Medicine, 2008; LHD (hon.), Brandeis U., 2008; DSc (hon.), Agnes Scott Coll., 2009; LLD (hon.), Columbia U., 2009; DSc (hon.), Oberlin Coll., 2011. Diplomate American Bd. Pediatricians. Intern then resident in pediatrics Children's Hosp. Nat. Med. Ctr., Washington, 1981-84; epidemic intelligence svc. officer br. epidemiology divsn. nutrition Ctr. Health Promotion & Edn., 1984-86; preventive medicine resident divsn. evaluation and rsch. office internat. health program Ctrs. Disease Control Ga. State Dept. Health, 1986-87; med. epidemiologist pediatricians and family studies sect., AIDS program Centers for Disease Control (CDC), US Dept. Health & Human Services (HHS), 1987-89, acting spl. asst. minority HIV policy coordination office dep. dir. (HIV), 1988-89, asst. chief sci., 1989-90, chief internat. activity divsn. HIV/AIDS Atlanta, 1990-92, assoc. dir. Washington, 1994-96, dir. Nat. Ctr. HIV, Sexually Transmitted Diseases & Tb Prevention Atlanta, 1995—2001; agy. AIDS coord., chief divsn. HIV-AIDS US Agy. for Internat. Devel. (USAID), Washington, 1992-94; dir. HIV, Tb, reproductive health The Bill & Melinda Gates Found., Seattle, 2001—06; pres., CEO CARE USA (Cooperative for Assistance & Relief Everywhere, Inc.), Atlanta, 2006—. Lectr. Sch. Medicine Morehouse U., 1987—92; lectr. masters in pub. health program Emory U., Atlanta, 1989, 1990, clin. asst. prof. cmty. medicine, 1996—; bd. dirs. Colgate-Palmolive Co., 2010—, Cox Enterprises, 2011—12, The Coca-Cola Co., 2013—; bd. mem. ONE Campaign, 2006—; mem. advisory com. USAID on Voluntary Fgn. Aid (ACVFA), 2007—; trustee Ctr. for Strategic & Internat. Studies (CSIS), 2007—, Rockefeller Found., 2009—. Contbr. articles to profl. jours. Adm. USPHS. Merit scholar, 1981; recipient Henrietta and Jacob Lowenburg prize, 1981, Model Excellence award Colgate-Palmolive Co., 1992, Medal of Excellence Columbia U., 1996, Secretary's Disting. Svc. award US Dept. Health & Human Services (HHS), 1999, Disting. Svc. award Nat. Med. Fellowships, 2003, Disting. Alumnus award, John Hopkins U. Sch. Public Health, Ethics Advocate award Ga. State U., 2009, Katherine Hepburn award Bryn Mawr Coll., 2011; named a Barnard Woman of Achievement Barnard Coll., 2001; named one of The 50 Women to Watch, The Wall St. Jour., 2006, The 100 Most Powerful Women Forbes mag., 2011-13 Mem. AAS, AMA, APHA, American Acad. Pediatrics, American Coll. Epidemiology, Internat. AIDS Soc., Soc. Against AIDS in Africa, Inst. of Med., Coun. on Fgn. Rels. Office: CARE USA 151 Ellis St NE Atlanta GA 30303*

GEALT, MICHAEL A., environmental microbiologist, educator; b. Phila., Nov. 27, 1948; s. Edward Leonard Gealt and Lillian Rose Brenner; m. Maryjanet McNamara, Jan. 2, 1981; 1 child; m. Antonia Malandrucco, May 12, 1967 (div. 1977); 2 children. BA, Temple U., 1970; PhD, Rutgers U., 1974. Rsch. assoc. Med. Sch. Rutgers U., Piscataway, NJ, 1974-76; postdoct. assoc. Inst. Cancer Rsch., Phila., 1976-78; asst. prof. biol. scis. Drexel U., Phila., 1978-84, assoc. prof., 1984-90, prof., 1990-2000, dir. Sch. Environ. Sci., Engring. and Policy, 1994-2000; dean Sch. Engring., Math. and Sci. Purdue U. Calumet, Hammond, Ind., 2000—05, prof. biology, 2000—05, U. Ark., Little Rock, 2006—, dean Coll. Sci. and Math., 2006—. Contbr. articles to profl. jours. Grantee EPA, 1983, 85, 89, NSF, 1981, 94, 97, USAF, 2002. Mem. AAAS, Am. Soc. Microbiology (chair environ. and applied micro divsn. 1995), Am. Soc. Cell Biology, Assn. Environ. Engrs. & Science Profs., Am. Soc. Engring. Educ., Sigma Chi. Avocations: motorcycles, photography. Office: Univ Ark Little Rock 2801 S University Ave Little Rock AR 72204 Office Phone: 501-569-3247. Business E-Mail: magealt@ualr.edu.

GEARHART, G. DAVID, academic administrator, education educator; b. June 1952; s. George A. and Joan (Havens) Gearhart; m. Jane Brockmann; 1 child, Brock; 1 child, Katy Hunt. BA, Westminster Coll., 1974; JD, U. Ark., Fayetteville, 1977, Ed.D in Higher Edn., 1989. Bar: Ark. 1977. Asst. to pres. Westminster Coll., Fulton, Mo., 1976—77, dir. devel. Winston Churchill Meml. and Libr., 1977—78; v.p. devel. Hendrix Coll., Conway, Ark., 1978—82; sr. v.p. devel. and univ. rels. Pa. State U., University Park, Pa., 1985—95, affiliate asst. prof. edn., 1988—95; sr. v.p., mng. dir. Grenzbach Giler & Assocs., Inc., Chgo., 1995—98; vice chancellor univ. advancement, prof. edn. U. Ark., Fayetteville, 1998—, chancellor, 2008—. Author: The Capital Campaign in Higher Education - A Practical Guide for College and University Advancement, 1995, Philanthropy, Fund Raising, and the Capital Campaign: A Practical Guide, 2006. V.p. U. Ark. Fayetteville Campus Found., 2003—; bd. advisors Ark. World Trade Ctr., 2007—; chair bd. dirs. Winthrop Rockefeller Inst., 2007—; mem. adv. bd. Pryor Ctr. for Oral and Visual History, 2006—. Fulbright Fellowship, Merton Coll., Oxford U., 1992. Office: University of Arkansas Office of Chancellor Admin 416 Fayetteville AR 72701 Office Phone: 479-575-6800. E-mail: gdgearh@uark.edu.*

GEARHART, JEFFREY J., retail executive, lawyer; b. 1964; BS, U. Ark., 1986, JD with high honors, 1989. Ptnr. Rose Law Firm, Little Rock, Kutak Rock LLP; v.p., gen. counsel corporate divsn. Wal-Mart Stores, Inc., 2003—07, sr. v.p., dep. gen. counsel, 2007—09, exec. v.p., gen. counsel, 2009—10, 2010—13, corp. sec., 2010—, exec. v.p, global governance, chief legal officer, 2013—. Named to The Ark. Bus. Power List, Ark. Bus., 2011. Mem.: Ark. Alumni Assn. Office: Wal Mart Stores Inc 702 SW 8th St Bentonville AR 72716*

GEARHEART, GARY, sales executive; b. Zeublon, NC; children: Keri, Sara, Leah. BS in Edn., Concord Coll., Athens, W.Va., 1983. Tchr., coach Roanoke County Schools, 1983—84; sales exec., mgr., v.p. sales Acken Signs, 1985—2006; pres. Gearheart's Mens Clothing, 1991—94; sales exec. Tammy Lynn Outdoor, 1995—2006. Former trustee Identity Mgmt. Coun.; former v.p. South Bluefield Merchants Assn.; pres. Sales Exec. Club; dir. Cmty. Found. the Virginias. Mem. exec. com. Mercer County Rep. Party, W.Va. Rep. Party; mem. Bland St. United Meth. Ch.; former bd. mem. Greater Bluefield C. of C. Republican. Mailing: 131 Henderson Dr Bluefield WV 24701

GEARY, RONALD G., race track executive, retired human services company executive; b. Apr. 12, 1947; m. Linda Geary; children: Wendy, Mark. B, U. Ky., Lexington, 1969; JD, U. Louisville, 1974; LLD (hon.), Cin. Bible Coll. and Sem., 1989. Founder, mng. dir. Geary, Balbach and Hardt, 1973—81; ptnr. Barnett and Alagia, 1984—89; pres., cons. Cin. Bible Coll. and Seminary, 1986—89; pres., COO ResCare, Inc., 1990—93, pres., CEO, 1993—2006, chmn., 1998—2010; owner, pres. Ellis Pk. Race Course, Inc., Henderson, Ky., 2006—. Bd. dirs. ResCare, Inc., 1990—2010, Ventas, Inc., 1998—, Alterra Healthcare Corp., 2001—03, First Capital Bank Ky., Apriss, Inc., Pet Suites, Inc., Evansville Icemen, Louisville Exec. Aviation. Sec. of cabinet Jefferson County, Ky., 1984—85; asst. sec. state State of Ky., 1989—90; bd. trustees U. Ky. Office: Ellis Park Race Track 3300 US 41 Henderson KY 42420 Business E-Mail: ron.geary@ellisparkracing.com.

GEBHARD POWELL, JOY LEE (BOK SIN LEE), small business owner; b. Jan. 29, 1936; arrived in U.S., 1956, naturalized, 1962; d. Yong Joon and Chun Jal Lee; m. Jimmy Wayne Powell, Sept. 24, 1960; children: Chun Jal Lee, Miran Victoria, D. Gebhard; m. Karl Ten Eyck Gebhard, Oct. 15, 1995. Grad., Internat. Speech Acad., Pusan, Korea, 1952, Nat. U. Pusan, 1953—55, McMurry Coll., Abilene, Tex., 1956—58; BA, Wayland Bapt. U., Plainview, Tex., 1966; postgrad., Cen. State U., Okla., 1967—68. Cert. antique appraiser and cons. Nurse Rok Med. Sch., Pusan, 1950—53; news anchor Pusan Radio Sta., 1953; sec., ret. choir organizer chaplain's office U.N. Army divsn. 8069, Pusan, 1954—56, Meth. Mission, Pusan, 1955—56, U.S. A.S.C. Office, Ploydada, Tex., 1958, Am. U., Washington, 1958—60; with Washington Post, U.S. Acad. Sci., 1960; with spl. study of prejudice among children grades 1 to 12 Pub. Opinion and Propaganda, 1965—66; tchr. Oklahoma City Sch. Sys., 1968—70; head social studies dept. Dunjee H.S., 1968; tchr. Spanish Carl Albert H.S., 1969; owner Internat. Antiques, Upperville, Va.; founder Healing Inc., 1997. Co-founder Washington Korean Writers Assn., Fairfax, Va., 2008; charter mem. lit. mag. Hiang. Contbr. articles to profl. jours., poetry New Voices in American Poetry, 1978, poems and essays to Korean periodicals. Bd. mem. Buchanan Hall, Upperville, Va., Korean Schs. US, Korean Am. Cult. Com., Washington Assn. for Korean Sch. Mem.: Fauquier County Chamber of Commerce, World Affairs Coun. Washington, Yale Club of Washington, Nat. History Preservation, Smithsonian Assocs., Washington Jeonju Lee Chosun Dynasty Royal Family Assn. (pres.), Sigma Tau Delta (Writers award, McMurry Coll., Abilene, Tex. 1957). Avocations: music, writing, swimming, collecting, travel. Home and Office: PO Box 221 Upperville VA 20185-0221

GEDDY, VERNON MEREDITH, JR., lawyer; b. Norfolk, Va., Apr. 12, 1926; s. Vernon Meredith and Carrie Cole (Lane) G.; m. Marie Lewis Sibley, Dec. 22, 1949; children: Anne Lewis Geddy Cross, Vernon M. Geddy III AB cum laude, Princeton U., 1949; LL.B., U. Va., 1952. Bar: Va. Ptnr. Geddy & Harris (and predecessor firms), Williamsburg, Va., 1952-80; ptnr. McGuire, Woods, Battle & Boothe (and predecessor firms), Williamsburg, Va., 1980-91, Geddy, Harris & Geddy (and predecessor firms), Williamsburg, 1991-99, Geddy, Harris, Franck & Hickman, L.L.P., Williamsburg, 1999—. Former dir. United Va. Bankshares, Nat. Ctr. for State Cts. Mem. Williamsburg City Coun., Va., 1968-80; trustee Colonial Williamsburg Found., 1981-95, Va. Hist. Soc., Richmond, 1981-88, 93-99, Va. Mus. Fine Arts, 1982-91; bd. dirs. Williamsburg Cmty. Hosp., 1969-85, WHRO, Pub. Telecoms. for Hampton Roads, Jamestown-Yorktown Found.; chmn. Williamsburg Cmty. Health Found. Sgt. USAAF, 1944-46, PTO. Named to Raven Soc. Fellow Am. Bar Found. (award 1976); mem. ABA, Va. Bar Assn. (pres. 1972-73), Va. State Bar, Williamsburg Bar Assn. (pres. 1975-93), Omicron Delta Kappa, Commonwealth Club. Episcopalian.

GEDEON, LUCINDA HEYEL, museum director; b. Port Chester, NY, Oct. 13, 1947; d. Philip H. and Isabel (Oldham) Heyel; m. Francis A. Sprout, Feb. 8, 1987. BA, Calif. State U., Long Beach, 1978; MA, UCLA, 1981, PhD, 1990. Asst. curator Grunwald Ctr. UCLA, 1978-81, asst. dir. Grunwald Ctr., 1981-83, acting dir. Grunwald Ctr., 1983-85; chief curator Ariz. State U. Art Mus., Tempe, 1985-91; CEO, dir. Neuberger Mus. SUNY, Purchase, 1991—2004; dir., CEO, Vero Beach Mus. Art, Fla., 2004—. Author: (exhbn. catalogues) Tamarind: Los Angeles to Albuquerque, 1985, Fiber Concepts, 1989 (book) The Art of Leonard Lehrer, 1986; gen. editor: Melvin Edwards Sculpture: A Thirty Year Retrospective, 1993, Shared Beginnings Separate Passages: A Retrospective of the Work of Carol Anthony and Elaine Anthony, 1996, June Wayne; A Retrospective, 1997, Elizabeth Catlett Sculpture: A Fifty-Year Retrospective, 1998, Marisol, 2001, Toshiko Takaezu, 2001, Grace Hartigan, 2001, Masters of Light: Selections of American Impressionism from the Manoogian Collection, 2006, George Rickey Kinetic Sculpture: A Retrospective, 2007, The Reality of Things: Trompe l'oeil in America, 2007, Ships and Shorelines: William Bradford and Nineteenth-Century American Marine Painting, 2010; contbr. articles to profl. jours. Chairperson Tempe Mcpl. Arts Commn., 1989-90; bd. dirs. Balboa Art Conservation Ctr., San Diego, 1986-91, ArtTable, NY, 1995-98, Westchester Arts Coun., 1998-2004; sec., treas., Fla. Art Museums Dirs. Assn., 2012-; mem. Am. Alliance for Arts, Southeastern Art Mus. Conf. Dirs. Assn. Recipient Individual Arts award Westchester Arts Coun., 2002, Chancellor's award Excellence, SUNY, 2002; Edward A. Dickson History of Art fellow UCLA, 1984, Afro-Am. Studies fellow, 1984. Mem.: Am. Alliance of Museums, Assn. Art Mus. Dirs., Southeastern Art Museums Dirs., Indian River County C. of C. (bd. dirs., bd. mem., 2012-). Office: Vero Beach Museum Art 3001 Riverside Pk Dr Vero Beach FL 32963 Office Phone: 772-231-0707 113. Business E-Mail: lgedeon@verobeachmuseum.org.

GEDWED, WILLIAM J., insurance company executive; BS, MBA, U. Houston. Mgmt. positions Health Markets (formerly UICI), No. Richland Hills, Tex., 1997—2001, bd. dirs., 2000—, pres., CEO, 2003—08, chmn., 2005—06; pres., CEO Asparron Capital, LLC. Chmn., pres. & CEO The MEGA Life and Health Insurance Co, Mid-West Nat. Life Insurance Co. of Tenn., Chesapeake Life Ins. Co., Fidelity First Ins. Co. Office: Asparron Capital LLC 1452 Hughes Rd Ste 375 Grapevine TX 76051 Office Phone: 817-865-6570. Office Fax: 817-865-6577.

GEE, ELWOOD GORDON (GORDON GEE), academic administrator, corporate board member; b. Vernal, Utah, Feb. 2, 1944; s. Elwood A. and Vera (Showalter) Gee; m. Elizabeth Dutson, Aug. 26, 1968 (dec. Dec. 1991); 1 child, Rebekah; m. Constance Bumgarner, Nov. 26, 1994. BA, U. Utah, 1968; JD, Columbia U., NYC, 1971, EdD, 1972. Asst. dean U. Utah Coll. Law, Salt Lake City, 1973—74; sr. staff asst., jud. fellow to Chief Justice Warren Burger US Supreme Ct., Washington, 1974—75; prof. law, assoc. dean Brigham Young U. Law Sch., Provo, Utah, 1975—79; prof. law, dean W.Va. U. Coll. Law, Morgantown, 1979—81; pres. W.Va. U., Morgantown, 1981—85, 2014—, interim pres., 2013—14; pres. U. Colo., Boulder, 1985—90, Ohio State U., Columbus, 1990—97, 2007—13, Brown University, Providence, 1998—2000; chancellor Vanderbilt U., Nashville, 2000—07. Bd. dirs. Limited Brands, Inc., 1991—2008, Hasbro Inc., 1999—2010, Massey Energy Corp., 2000—09, Gaylord Entertainment Co., 2002—09, Bob Evans Farms, Inc., 2009—, L Brands, Inc., 2012—. Author: Education Law and Public Schools, 1975, Law and Public Education, 1980, Violence, Values and Justice in American Education, 1982, Fair Employment Practice, 1982. Recipient Good Guy award, Nashville Women's Polit. Caucus, 2004, Elbert P. Tuttle Disting. Achievement award, Pi Kappa Alpha, 2001; named one of The 10 Best Coll. Presidents, TIME mag., 2009; W.K. Kellogg fellowship, 1971—72, Mellon fellow, Aspen Inst. Humanistic Studies, 1977—78. Mem.: ABA, Adminstrv. Conf. US, Phi Kappa Phi, Phi Delta Kappa. Mem. Lds Ch. Office: West Virginia University Office of the Pres PO Box 6301 Morgantown WV 26506 Office Phone: 304-293-5711.*

GEEKER, NICHOLAS PETER, lawyer, judge; b. Pensacola, Fla., Dec. 15, 1944; BA in English, La. Poly. Inst., 1966; JD, Fla. State U., 1969. Bar: Fla. 1969, U.S. Dist. Ct. 1970, US. Supreme Ct., 1980. Assoc. firm Merritt & Jackson, Pensacola, 1969; law clk. U.S. Dist. Judge D.L. Middlebrooks, Tallahassee, 1970-73; asst. state atty. Fla. 1st Jud. Circuit, 1973; asst. U.S. atty. No. Dist. Fla., 1973-76, U.S. atty., 1976-82; sole practice Pensacola, Fla., 1982-85; circuit judge Fla. 1st Jud. Circuit, 1985—. Mem. Fed.-State Joint Com. on Law Enforcement. Mem. Fla. Bar Assn., Fla. Trial Lawyers Assn. (editor Newsletter 1975), Phi Delta Phi. Office: 190 Government St Pensacola FL 32501-5773 Office Phone: 850-595-4439.

GEHRING, DAVID AUSTIN, cardiologist, physician, health facility administrator; b. Bryn Mawr, Pa., Dec. 6, 1930; s. Harry Rittenhouse and Anne Gardiner (Bozarth) G.; m. Joan Helen Lotz, June 7, 1953 (div. Aug. 1982); children: David, Paul, Peter, Sue, Barbara, Eric; m. Victoria Marie Damiano, Sept. 2, 1982 (dec. May 2000); children: Theresa, Judy Lynne, Michael Austin; m. Rose Y. Barron, May 5, 2001. BA magna cum laude, U. Pitts., 1952, MD, 1956; grad., Naples Sch. Real Estate, 2000. Diplomate Am. Bd. Internal Medicine; cert. geriatric medicine. Commd. USN, 1956, advanced through grades to lt. comdr., intern, then resident in internal medicine U.S. Naval Hosp. Phila., 1956—60, mem. staff internal medicine U.S. Naval Hosp., 1960—61, chief internal medicine heart sta. U.S. Naval Hosp. Annapolis, Md., 1961—63, resigned, 1963; cardiologist K.G.E. Med. Group, Woodbury, NJ, 1963—82; cardiologist, pres. Hobbs Cardiology, P.A., N.Mex., 1982—86; med. dir. Polk Ctr., Pa., 1986—91; physician, chief grade VA Med. Ctr., Coatesville, Pa., 1991—97, assoc. chief of staff for ambulatory care, 1993—96, chief med. svc., 1995—96, chief primary care and chief of staff, 1995—96, chief of staff, 1995—96, cardiologist, 1996—97; assoc. med. dir. for correctional med. svcs. South Jersey, 1997—98; med. dir. site South Woodstate Prison, 1997—98; clin. dir. Del. Hosp. Chronically Ill, 1998—99; clin. dir. long term care pub. health divsn. State of Del., 1998—99; physician VA Clinic, Naples, Fla., 2002—10. Clin. dir. Del. Hosp. for Cronically Ill, Smyrna, 1998—99; v.p. Regent Park Villas II Assoc., Inc., Naples, Fla., 1999—2000, pres., 2000—01; realtor VIP Lodge McKee Realtors, 2000—01, VIP Lodge McKee, 2000—01; sect. chief VA Med. Ctr., Salisbury, NC, 2001—02, occupl. health physician, 2002, mem. ethics com., 2001—02, mem. hosp. disaster com., 2002, chair small pox com., 2002; testing cardiologist Anthropometrics United Med. Group, Cherry Hill, NJ, 1974—82; clin. asst. prof. medicine Temple U. Hosp., Phila., 1975—82; adj. asst. prof. medicine Jefferson Meml. Coll., 1981—82; chief cardiac rehab. unit Lea Regional Hosp., Hobbs, 1982—86; chief med. svcs. 829th Sta. Hosp., USAR, Lubbock, Tex., 1984—86; cons. cardiology, Oil City, Pa., 1986—91; staff Franklin (Pa.) Regional Med. Ctr., 1986—90, Oil City Area Health Ctr., 1986—91; teaching staff St. Joseph Hosp., Lancaster, Pa., 1991—97; clin. preceptor U. Pa. Sch. Nursing, 1993—96; cons. Southeastern Vets. Ctr., Spring City, Pa., 1997—98, Providence Med. Ctr., Media, 1997—98; others; assoc. med. dir. Correctional Med. Svcs. South Jersey, 1997—98; mem. adult protective svcs. coun. State of Del., 1998—99; mem. profl. devel. com. Naples Area Bd. Realtors, 2000—01, mem. complaint rev. com., 2000—01; chair pharmacy and therapeutics com. Dept. Health and Social Svcs., State of Del., 1998—99; mem. pharmacy and therapeutics com. for VISN 6 dept. Vet. Affairs, 2001—02, sec.; cons. in field. Author: EKG Workbook, 1972, EKG Workbook I, 1978; contbr. articles to profl. jours. Project dir. 23 Greater Del. Valley Reg. Med. Program, Pa., 1971—75; mem. ACLS Inst. and affiliated faculty Pa. Heart Assn., 1986—98, bd. dirs. N.W. chpt., 1988—90; bd. dirs. Inst. Christianna Hosp., Del., 1998—99; bd. dirs. adv. com., chmn. personnel com. med. health, rehab., drugs and alcohol Venango County, Franklin Parl, Pa., 1986—90, pres., 1988—89; mem. Health Care Adv. Com. to Congressman William F. Clinger, Jr., 23d Dist., 1989—91, Naples Mus. Art, 2000—10; patron Philharmonic Ctr. for Arts, 1998—2010, Carolina Opera, 2001—03; lector St. Joseph Ch., Oil City, 1987—91, eucharistic min., 1990—92, Swedesboro, NJ, 1992—93, Sacred Heart Ch., Mt. Ephraim, 1994—99, lector, 1998—99. Lt. col. USAR, 1983—90, lt. comdr. USN, 1955—63. Recipient Outstanding Svc. award Am. Cancer Soc. NJ, 1967, Benjamin Berkowitz award NJ Heart Assn., 1975, Nat. Def. Svc. medal, 1975, USAR Components Achievement medal, 1988, Letter of Commendation USAR, 1988, 90, Am Def. Commenorative medal, 2014, Pres.'s medal of Merit, Rep. Task Force, 1984, Letter of Commendation Sec. of Vets. Affairs, 1994, Robert Wicarey award, 2009; Cert. of Appreciation, Sec. of State N.Mex., 1982, Venango County Commrs., 1987, 88, 89, 90, Polk Ctr. award of Merit, 1991, Spl. Contbn. award and Mgr. of Yr. award VAMC Coatesville, 1996, Spl. Contbn. award VA Med. Ctr., Salisbury, NC, 2002, Named Am. Top Physician Consumers Rsch. Coun. America, 2008-09, Robert Carey award. Fellow ACP (life, Recognition awards 1967-70), Am. Coll. Cardiology, Am. Coll. Chest Physicians, Coll. Physicians Phila., Am. Coll. Clin. Pharmacology; mem. AMA, Am. Geriat. Soc., St. Jude Soc., Holy Name Soc., Assn. Miraculous Medal (promoter 1987—), Venango County Med. Soc. (pres. 1989-91), Assn. Mil. Surgeons, Mil. Officers Assn. Am. (life), Am. Coll. Physician Execs., Mil. Officers Club Collier County Fla., Am. Legion (chmn. Cable Com., Saturnia Lakes, Naples, Fla.), Mil. Officers Assn. SW Fla., KC.

Republican. Roman Catholic. Avocations: stamp collecting/philately, reading, walking, swimming, opera. Home: 2347 Butterfly Palm Dr Naples FL 34119 Personal E-mail: david34119@yahoo.com.

GEIER, C. DAVID, JR., orthopaedic surgeon; b. May 10, 1973; m. Christian Smith; 1 child, Marshall Conrad. BA in Economics (magna cum laude), Wake Forest U., 1995; MD, Med. U. SC, 1999. Intern, gen. surgery U. Tenn., 1999—2000; resident U. Tenn.,Campbell Clinic, 2000—04; dir. Med. U. SC (MUSC) Sports Medicine; asst. prof., orthop. surgery Med. U. SC (MUSC). Orthop. surgeon James Island Soccer Club; head team physician and orthop. surgeon West Ashley HS; team physician Burke HS, Garrett Acad., North Charleston HS, Academic Magnet HS, Baptist Hill HS, Wash. U., St. Louis, 2004—05, St. Louis Rams, 2004—05, St. Louis Cardinals, 2004—05; provided orthop. coverage Rhodes Coll. Football and Basketball Teams, 2000—04, Memphis Marathon, 2002, Kroger St. Jude Tennis Racquetball Champions, 2003, Cellular South Cup, 2003, US Open Racquetball Championships, 2003; invited presenter in field. Reviewer Am. Jour. Sports Medicine; contbr. chapters to books. Literacy tutot and worked in food shelters in Charleston area MUSC Gives Back, 1996—99. Sports Medicine, Wash. U., St. Louis, 2004—05. Mem.: Omicron Delta Epsilon, Charleston County Med. Soc., Am. Acad. Orthop. Surgeons (cand. mem.), Am. Orthop. Soc. for Sports Medicine (cand. mem.), Phi Beta Kappa, Alpha Omega Alpha. Avocations: weightlifting, reading, politics. Office: Medical University South Carolina 96 Jonathan Lucas St CSB 708 PO Box 250622 Charleston SC 29425 Office Phone: 843-792-4088. Office Fax: 843-792-3843. Business E-Mail: geiercd@musc.edu.

GEIMAN, J. ROBERT, lawyer; b. Evanston, Ill., Mar. 5, 1931; s. Louis H. and Nancy O'Connell-Crowe G.; m. Ann L. Fitzgerald, July 29, 1972; children: J. Robert, William Patrick, Timothy Michael. BS, Northwestern U., 1953; JD, Notre Dame U., 1956. Bar: Ill. 1956, U.S. Ct. Appeals (7th cir.) 1956, U.S. Supreme Ct. 1969. Assoc. Eckert, Peterson & Lowry, Chgo., 1956-64; ptnr. Peterson, Lowry, Rall, Barber & Ross, Chgo., 1964-70, Peterson & Ross, Chgo., 1970-96, of counsel, 1996—. Mem. com. on civil jury instructions Ill. Supreme Ct., 1979-81. Case editor Notre Dame Law Rev., 1956. Bd. advisors Cath. Charities of Archdiocese of Chgo., 1973-96. Fellow Internat. Acad. Trial Lawyers, Am. Coll. Trial Lawyers, Ill. Bar Found.; mem. ABA (aviation com., tort and ins. practice sect. 1980-90), Ill. State Bar Assn. (sec. 1969-70, sec. bd. govs. 1969-71), Chgo. Bar Assn. (aviation law com. 1970-73), Bar Assn. of 7th Fed. Ct. (meetings com. 1968-70, vice chmn. membership com. 1973-75), Soc. Trial Lawyers, Cath. Lawyers Guild of Chgo. (bd. advisors 1973-96), Law Club Chgo., Chgo. Athletic Assn. (pres. 1973). Republican. Home: 4861 River Village Dr Vero Beach FL 32967-7452 Home Phone: 772-794-2254. Personal E-mail: jrobertgeiman@gmail.com.

GEISINGER, HARRY, state legislator; m. Pat Geisinger; 3 children. Attended, Eagletown Inst. of Politics. Former regional commr. US Youth Soccer Assn.; former pres. Riverwalk Condo Assn.; former advisor Nat. Legis. Leaders Conf.; former mem. Nat. Legis. Conf. on Campaign Financing & Ethics; former pres. Ga. Youth Soccer Assn., Ga., Ga. Coaches Assn., Ga.; former pres./chair of bd. Ga. Soccer Assn., Ga.; bd. of dirs. Ashford-Dunwoody Young Men's Christian Assn.; chairman of the bd. Deklab Unit Am. Cancer Soc.; rep. whip Ga. House of Reps., Ga., mem. Dist. #48 Ga., 2005—. Republican. Office: Capitol Office 601-F Coverdell Legislative Office Build Atlanta GA 30334 also: District Office 224 River View Trail Roswell GA 30075 Office Phone: 404-656-0254, 770-594-1510. E-mail: harry.geisinger@house.ga.gov.

GEISLER, JAMES E., manufacturing executive; b. 1966; B in Bus. Adminstrn., U. Ky.; MBA, U. Va., 1993. With United Technologies Corp., 1993—, dir. strategic planning, 1997—99, dir. investor rels., 1999—2001, dir. fin. planning & analysis, 2001—04, v.p. fin., 2004—08, v.p. corp. strategy & planning, 2008; COO, CFO CreoSalus Inc., Louisville. Office: CreoSalus Inc 1044 E Chesnut St Louisville KY 40204 Office Phone: 502-515-1100.

GEITHNER, PAUL HERMAN, JR., retired banker; b. Phila., June 7, 1930; s. Paul Herman and Henriette Antonine (Schuck) G.; m. Irmgard (Hagedorn), Sept. 6, 1956; children: Christina, Amy, Paul. BA cum laude, Amherst Coll., Mass., 1952; MBA with distinction, U. Pa., Phila., 1957. Sec., treas. Ellicott Machine Co., Balt., 1964—68. V.p., sr. v.p., exec. asst. to the chmn. First Va. Banks, Inc., Falls Church, 1968-85, pres., chief adminstrv. officer, 1985-95, bd. dirs., vice chmn., 1986-95; pres. First Va. Life Ins. Co., 1974-96; trustee, mem. investment com. Bridgewater Coll., Va., 1988—. Bd. dirs. Fairfax Symphony Orch., Va., 1988—2004, pres., 1991—92; sec.-treas. Fairfax Symphony Orch. Found., Va., 1999—; bd. dirs. Va. Coll. Fund, 1987—91; trustee Va. Banker Sch. Bank Mgmt., 1988—92. Lt. USNR, 1952—55. Mem. Va. Bankers Assn., (pres. 1992-93).

GELFAND, NEAL, oil industry executive; b. Bronx, NY, Nov. 8, 1944; s. Daniel and Faye (Frank) G.; m. Jane Auerbach, Sept. 11, 1982; children: Alexandra, Laura. BS in Psychology, CCNY, 1965; MS in Indsl. Psychology, Western Mich. U., 1967; PhD in Organizational Psychology, U. Houston, 1972. Ptnr. Hay Assocs., NYC, 1972-80; sr. v.p. human resources Hess Corp., NYC, 1980—2004; pres. Pondfield Group, LLC, Naples, Fla., 2004—. Office: Pondfield Group LLC 295 Grande Way #604 Naples FL 34110 Office Phone: 914-316-7733. Business E-Mail: nealand@mac.com.

GELPI, GUSTAVO ANTONIO, JR., federal judge; b. San Juan, 1965; BA, Brandeis U., 1987; JD, Suffolk U., 1991. Bar: PR 1992. Law clk. to Hon. Juan M. Perez-Gimenez, US Dist. Ct. PR, 1991—93, asst. fed. pub. defender, 1993—97, magistrate judge, 2001—06, judge, 2006—; asst. to atty. gen. PR Dept. Justice, 1997, dep. atty. gen. legal counsel, 1997—99; solicitor gen. Commonwealth of Puerto Rico, 1999—2000; spl. litig. counsel McConnell Valdes, 2001. Adj. faculty Suffolk U., U. PR, Interamerican U. Law Schools. Contbr. of articles to the Federal Lawyer. Mem.: Fed. Bar. Assn. (pres. Puerto Rico Chapter 2000, v.p. first cir. 2002—06, nat. bd. dir. 2006—09, chair audit com. 2008—09, nat. treas. 2012—13, pres.-elect 2013, pres. 2013—, fellow of the found. 2002, life fellow of the found. 2013). Address: Federal Bar Association 1220 North Fillmore St Ste 444 Arlington VA 22201 Office Phone: 787-772-3103.*

GEMIGNANI, MICHAEL CAESAR, clergyman, retired professor and university administrator; b. Balt., Feb. 23, 1938; s. Hugo J. and Dorothy G.; m. Carol A. Federico, June 30, 1962 (dec.); children: Stephen, Susan; m. Nilda B. Keller, May 18, 1985 (dec.) BA, U. Rochester, 1962; MS, U. Notre Dame, 1964, PhD, 1965; JD, Ind. U., 1980. Bar: Ind. 1980, U.S. Dist. Ct. Ind. 1980, Maine 1987, U.S. Dist. Ct. Maine 1987, Tex. 1990; ordained to ministry Episcopal Ch., 1973. Asst. prof. math. SUNY, Buffalo, 1965-68; assoc. prof. Smith Coll., 1968-72; prof., chmn. dept. math. scis. Ind. U.-Purdue U., Indpls., 1972-81; dean Coll. Scis. and Humanities Ball State U., Muncie, Ind., 1981-86; dean Coll. Arts and Scis. U. Maine, Orono, 1986-88; sr. v.p., provost U. Houston-Clear Lake, 1988-91, prof. math. and computer sci., 1991-92; rector St. Paul's Episcopal Ch., Freeport, Tex., 1991—2007; assoc. rector St. Michael's Lc Margues, 2007—10. Vicar St. Francis Episcopal Ch., Zionsville, Ind., 1974-79; pres. Met. Indpls. Campus Ministry, 1975-76, bd. dirs., 1974-81; mem. adv. bd. Ind. Office Campus Ministry, 1973-86, pres., 1983-85; chair divsn. spiritual formation Episcopal Diocese of Tex., 1997-2004; founder, chmn. bd. Brazosport Med. Ctr., 1999-2006. Author: books including Elementary Topology, 1967, 2d rev. edit., 1972, Introductory Real Analysis, 1970, Law and the Computer, 1981, Computer Law, 1985, Legal Guide for EDP Managers, 1989, To Know God: Small Group Exercises in Spiritual Formation, 2001, Spiritual Formation for Pastors Tending the Fire Within, 2002; Making Your Church A House of Healing, 2008; composer; rsch., publs. in math. Mem. Houston Bar Assn., Tex. Bar Assn., ABA, AAAS, Am. Math. Soc. (chmn. N.E. sect. 1970-71, chmn. Ind. sect. 1975-76), Kappa Sigma. Business E-Mail: mgmign@hal-pc.org.

GEMINDER, PHILIP H., II, corporate finance and operations executive; Attended, Mich. State U., 1974; MBA in Ops., Ind. U., South Bend, 1980. CPA Ohio. Various positions, including dir., fin. Honeywell International, Inc., 1978—94; dir., fin. Avery Dennison Corp., 1996—99; v.p., fin. svcs. Graphic Packaging Internat. Corp., 2000—03; v.p., fin. Graphic Packaging Corp., 2003—07, v.p., integration, 2007—08; v.p., chief integration officer Graphic Packaging Holding Co.; v.p. Graphic Business Services, 2009—. Office: Graphic Packaging Holding Co 814 Livingston Ct Marietta GA 30067 Office Phone: 770-644-3000. Office Fax: 770-644-2962. Business E-Mail: geminderp@graphicpkg.com.

GENBERG, IRA, lawyer; b. Newark, July 27, 1947; s. Jack and Ann (Lerman) G.; m. Rosemary Lawlor, Jan. 15, 1981; children: Jack Michael, Anne Rebecca. AB magna cum laude, Rutgers U., 1969; JD, U. Pa., 1972. Bar: Ga. 1972, D.C. 1978. Assoc. Haas, Holland, Levison & Gibert, Atlanta, 1972-75; ptnr. Stokes, Shapiro, Fussell & Genberg, Atlanta, 1975-87; ptnr., head litigation sect. Smith, Gambrell & Russell LLP, Atlanta, 1987—2008; ptnr. Troutman Sanders, 2008. Spkr. Seminar on Constrn. Litigation, Atlanta, 1985, Seminar on Constrn. Law, Atlanta, 1986; co-chmn. Seminar on Trying A Complex Constrn. Case, 1994; chair Associated Owners & Developers Confs., 2004, 06-07. Contbr. articles to Constrn. Bus. Review Mag. Named one of 1000 Great Americans; named to Best Lawyers in Am., Chambers USA, Outstanding Lawyers in Am., Super Lawyers, Top 100 Ga. Super Lawyers, Ga.'s Legal Elite. Mem. Ga. Bar Assn., Atlanta Bar Assn., DC Bar Assn. Office: Troutman Sanders LLP Bank America Tower 600 Peachtree St NE Atlanta GA 30308-2216 Office Phone: 404-885-3740. Business E-Mail: ira.genberg@troutmansanders.com.

GENDRON, TERESA S. (TERI GENDRON), publishing executive; b. 1969; BS in Commerce, U. Va., 1991; MBA, Georgetown U. McDonough Sch. Bus., 2009, Ramon llull U. ESADE Bus. Sch. Sr. mgr. audit KPMG, Washington, 1991—98; joined NII Holdings, Inc., 1999, mng. dir., 2002—05, v.p., financial compliance, 2005—08, v.p., asst. contr., 2008—10, v.p., contr., chief acctg. officer, 2010—11; v.p., contr. Gannett Co., Inc., McLean, Va., 2011—. Office: Gannett Co Inc 7950 Jones Branch Dr Mc Lean VA 22107 Office Phone: 703-854-6000. Office Fax: 703-854-2053.

GENDZWILL, JOYCE ANNETTE, retired health officer; b. Milw., Aug. 8, 1927; d. Felix Vincent and Antoinette Marie (Borske) G.; m. Lauren E. Trombley, June 13, 1952 (div. Jan. 1960); children: Regan Eve Trombley Kovacich, Eugene Vincent, Paul Quentin. BS, U. Mich., 1949, MD, 1952, MPH, 1961. Cert. pub. mgr., Ala. Internship USPHS, Detroit, Cleve., 1952-53; dir. extern edn. Beyer Meml. Hosp., Ypsilanti, Mich., 1953-54; resident in radiology St. Luke's Hosp., Denver, 1954-55; health officer Dickinson-Iron Dist. Health Dept., Stambaugh, Mich., 1959-76; dir. bur. local health svc. Ala. Dept. Pub. Health, Montgomery, Ala., 1976-81, asst. state health officer, 1981-91; ret., 1991. Mem. AMA, So. Med. Assn., Mensa, Phi Beta Kappa, Delta Omega, Phi Kappa Phi.

GENEEN, LAWRENCE I., insurance company executive; Undergraduate, St John's U.; grad. in Advanced Mgmt. Program, Harvard U. Various exec. sales positions and mgmt. positions, ins. brokerage bus. Johnson and Higgins, 1974—92, mng. prin., owner, 1992—97; mng. dir. Marsh & McLennan, Inc., NY, 1997—99. Bd. dirs. Am. Safety Ins. Holdings, Ltd., 2003—, Hartville Group, Inc. Exec. v.p., COO Am. Mgmt. Assn., 1999—2001. Office: American Safety Insurance Holdings Ltd 100 Galleria Pky Ste 700 Atlanta GA 30339 Office Phone: 770-916-1908. Business E-Mail: lgeneen@americansafetyinsurance.com.

GENG, YONG-JIAN, medical educator, researcher; MD, Suzhou Med. Coll., China, 1982; PhD in Clin. Chemistry, Gothenburg U., Sweden, 1994. Instr. Harvard Med. Sch., Boston, 1995—96; asst. prof. Allegheny U. Health Scis., Pitts., 1997—99; assoc. prof. U. Tex., Houston, 2000—04, prof. medicine, 2005—. Cons. Am. Heart; invited spkr. in field. Contbr. scientific papers to profl.publs. Cons. Amercian Heart. Recipient First award, NIH, 1997, ARA award, Park-Davis/Pfizer Found., 2000, Cardiovascular Rsch. award, Fourjay Found., 2001, Edn. award, Wang Kuan Chen Edn. Found., Chinese Acad. Sci., 2005. Fellow: Internat. Union Against Cancer (Internat. Cancer Rsch. Tech. Transfer award 1994); mem.: AAAS, Am. Heart Assn. (mem. sci. coun. on arteriosclerosis, thrombosis, and vascular biology), North Am. Vascular Biology Orgn. Achievements include patents pending in field. Office: Univ Texas 6431 Fannin Street MSB1240 Houston TX 77030

GENTLE, KENNETH WILLIAM, physicist; b. Oak Park, Ill., Oct. 27, 1940; s. William and Cathryn Mary (Spence) G. BS, MIT, 1962, PhD, 1966. Asst. prof. dept. physics U. Tex., Austin, 1966-69, assoc. prof., 1970-75, prof. physics, 1976—, chair dept. physics, 1997-2001. Sloan fellow, 1973-75 Fellow Am. Phys. Soc. Home: 212 Buckeye Trl Austin TX 78746-4420 Office: Univ Tex Dept Physics Austin TX 78712 Home Phone: 512-327-1732; Office Phone: 512-471-7581. Business E-Mail: k.gentle@mail.utexas.edu.

GENTRY, JEFFERY S., tobacco company executive; BS in Zoology, U. NC, Chapel Hill; PhD in Analytical Chemistry, NC State U. Asst. rsch. and tchg. NC State U.; ops. supr. Watkins Motor Lines; R&D chemist R.J. Reynolds Tobacco Co., Winston-Salem, NC, 1986—89, sr. R&D chemist, 1989—93, sr. staff R&D chemist, 1993—96, master scientist, 1996—98, sr. mgr. new product devel., 1998—99, dir. new product devel., 1999—2000, v.p. product devel., 2000—04, exec. v.p. R&D, 2004—08; group exec. v.p. Reynolds American, Inc., 2008—10, exec. v.p. ops., chief scientific officer R.J. Reynolds Tobacco, 2010—. Mem.: Am. Chem. Soc. Office: Reynolds Am Inc 401 N Main St Winston Salem NC 27101

GENTRY, JUDY FENTON, choreographer, educator; d. Mattie Frierson and Joseph Parker Fenton; children: Cristiana Monique, Courtnei Michele. BPE, Vanderbilt U., Nashville, 1975; MPE, Tenn. State U., Nashville, 1983; MEd, Tenn. State U., 1983. Dance instr. Met. Parks & Recreation, Nashville, 1974—79, NW YMCA, Nashville, 1982—88; master dance instructor Malone Dance Studios, Nashville, 1998—2005; founder Tenn. State U., 1980—, choreographer and artistic dir., 1980—. Judge Am. All-Star, United States Dance, Drill Team Championship, Nashville, 1996—98. Choreographer Contemporary Black History Makers, Nashville Minstral Players, coord. Tenn. State Live Arustocrat Bands Sophishcated Ladies; performer: Nat. Assn. Negro Bus. Profl. Women's Clubs. Choreographer/team leader Mt. Gilead Missionary Bapt. Church Prayerful Rhythm Praise Dancers, Nashville, 2005—; mem. Baptist Ch. Recipient Presdl. Disting. Svc. award, Tenn. State U., 2001, Blue and White All Star, 2006, US Hero award, 2009, The Committment Excellence award, 2009; named to Tenn. State U. Coll. Edn. Wall of Fame, 2005. Mem.: Alpha Kappa Alpha. Achievements include founding the Tennessee State Dance Experience Ensemble and Coordinating (and Choreographing) Tennessee State Ni. Aristocrat of Bands. Office: Tenn State Univ 3500 John Merritt Blvd Nashville TN 37209-1561 Office Fax: 615-963-5594. Personal E-mail: jgentry@tnstate.edu. Business E-Mail: jgentry@tnstste.edu.*

GENTRY, ROBERT VANCE, physicist, researcher, writer; b. Chattanooga, July 9, 1933; s. Vance Ault and Sara Frances (Northington) G.; m. Patricia Ann Gentry, Jan. 20, 1953; children: Patricia Lynn, Michael Vance, David Wayne. BS in Physics, U. Fla., 1955, MS, 1956; D.Sc. (hon.), Columbia Union Coll., Takoma Park, Md., 1977. Nuclear engr. Gen. Dynamics Co., Ft. Worth, 1956-58; sr. engr. Martin Co., Orlando, Fla., 1958-59; instr. math. U. Fla., Gainesville, 1959-61, Walla Walla (Wash.) Coll., 1961-62; instr. physics Ga. Inst. Tech., 1962-64; research physicist Archeol. Research Found., Atlanta, 1965-66; mem. faculty Columbia Union Coll., 1966-84, assoc. prof. physics, 1977-84; cons. physicist, 1984-86; research physicist Earth Sci. Assocs., Knoxville, Tenn., 1986—; pres. The Orion Found., 1997—. Guest scientist chemistry div. Oak Ridge Nat. Lab., 1969-82, 89; hon. asst. res. prof. physics U. Tenn.-Knoxville, 1982-83. Author: Creation's Tiny Mystery, 1986, 1986, 1988, 4th edit., 2003; chief rschr.: (video) Fingerprints of Creation (Telly award, 1993); The Young Age of the Earth, 1994; Center of the Universe, 2006; contbr. articles to profl. jours. Grantee NSF, 1962, 1971-77, NASA, 1970-72. Mem. AAAS, Am. Phys. Soc., Am. Geophys. Union, N.Y. Acad. Scis., Sigma Xi Seventh-day Adventist. Adventist. Achievements include discovery of polonium radioactive halos in granites, a new model of the universe to explain the Hubble redshift relation and the 2.7K Cosmic Blackbody Radiation without the use of spacetime expansion-.also that the universe has a nearby Center which is the location of God's Throne-as per Psalm 103:19 (RSV)-and that God's Six-day Genesis creation account is the scientifically correct description of the origin of the universe about 6000 years ago. Home: PO Box 12067 Knoxville TN 37912-0067 Personal E-mail: esa@halos.com.

GEORGE, BOYD L., wholesale distribution executive; BBA, U. Notre Dame; JD, U. Va. Various positions, including chmn., CEO Mchts. Distbrs. Inc. (subs. of Alex Lee inc.), 1969, Instn. Food House, Inc. (subs. of Alex Lee Inc.), 1969, Lowes Food Stores, Inc. (subs. of Alex Lee Inc.), 1969; pres. Alex Lee, Inc., 1992—95, chmn., CEO, 1992—. Bd. dirs. CommScope, Inc. Office: Alex Lee Inc 120 4th St SW Hickory NC 28602 Office Phone: 828-725-4424. Office Fax: 828-725-4435. Business E-Mail: bgeorge@alexlee.com.

GEORGE, DEVERAL D., editor, journalist, advertising consultant; b. Dallas, Nov. 23, 1939; s. Jack Weldon and Lleen Lelia (Hume) G. Student, U. Tex., 1958-61; BA, North Tex. State U., 1964; P.BA, U. Houston, 1974. Copywriter advt. agys., Houston, Dallas, 1964-70; free lance journalist, 1970-73, 75-76; copy and creative dir. Schey Advt., Houston, 1973, Bruce Advt., Houston, 1973-75; editor-in-chief, v.p. Bus. and Energy Internat., Houston, 1976-80; editor Ultra mag., 1980-81; freelance journalist Houston, 1981-83, 84-85; editor Saudi Bus. Mag.; cons. Saudi Research and Mktg. Inc., Houston, Washington, and Jeddah, Saudi Arabia, 1983-84; writer, advt. cons. Dale Carnegie & Assocs., Garden City (NY) and Houston, 1985-90; mng. editor internat. Offshore Mag., Houston, 1991-97; editor Schlumberger Oilfield Rev., 1997-98, Oil and Gas Online, Vertical Net, Horsham, Pa., 1998-2001, Houston, 1998-2001; owner, mng. editor Oil and Gas Internat., Houston, 2001—. Author: Cathedrals of Mexico, and Other Poems, 1963, The Erratic Pilgramage, 1973, The Whole World Cookbook, 1976, The Offshore Atlas, 1995; screenplays: The Monument, 1980, Armageddon, 1981; television series Treasure Hunt, 1984; editor: Worldwide Directory of Petroleum Ministries and National Oil Companies, 1995; mem. editl. bd. Xi'an Petroleum Inst., China. Del., Democratic Conv., 1972; mem. Houston Outdoor Group. Mem. ACLU, Am. Assn. Petroleum Geologists, Soc. Exploration Geophysicists, Geophys. Soc. Houston, Amnesty Internat., World Wildlife Fund, Sierra Club, Human Rights Campaign, Online News Assn., ONE, Am. Soc. Prvention Cruelty to Animals, UNICEF, AARP. Home: 8310 Braesdale Ln Houston TX 77071-1228 Office: PO Box 710046 Houston TX 77071-1030

GEORGE, EDDIE (EDWARD NATHAN GEORGE), entrepreneur, retired professional football player; b. Phila., Sept. 24, 1973; s. Donna George; m. Tamara Johnson-George; children: Eriq, Jaire. BS in Landscape Architecture, Ohio State U., 1996. Running back Tenn. Titans (formerly Tenn. Oilers), 1996—2004, Dallas Cowboys, 2004; ptnr., co-owner The Edge Group; founder, co-owner Eddie's Sports Grill; founder Eddie George Enterprises. Co-founder Visions With Infinite Possibilities Found., 2000—. Recipient Maxwell award, 1995, Heisman trophy, 1995; named NFL Rookie of Yr., 1996, NFL Pro Bowl, 1997—2000; named one of Coll. Football Hall of Fame, 2011. Office: Visions With Infinite Possibilities PO Box 150283 Nashville TN 37215

GEORGE, JAMES NOEL, hematologist, oncologist, educator; b. Columbus, Ohio, Sept. 23, 1938; BA, Ohio State U., MD, 1962. Diplomate Am. Bd. Internal Medicine, cert. in hematology, lic. Okla., Tex., Ohio. Intern, resident dept. medicine Vanderbilt U. Sch. Medicine, Nashville, 1962—63, 1966—67; rsch. hematologist Walter Reed Army Inst. Rsch., Washington, 1963—66; resident in medicine, hematology fellow, chief resident Strong Meml. Hosp., U. Rochester Sch. Medicine, NY, 1967—70; asst. prof., assoc. prof. then prof. dept. med. divsn. hematology U. Tex. Health Sci. Ctr., San Antonio, 1970—90; prof. dept. medicine, chief hematology-oncology sect. U. Okla. Health Sci. Ctr., Oklahoma City, 1990—, George Lynn Cross prof., dept. medicine, 2005—. Mem. transfusion com. Bexar County Hosp., San Antonio, 1970—87; rsch. assoc. Theodor Kocher Inst., Berne, Switzerland, 1975—76; chmn. hematology peer rev. panel Life Scis. Space Flight Experiment prog. NASA, 1978; mem. hematology study sect. 1 NIH, 1986—94; vis. prof. dept. physiol. chemistry U. Wis., Madison, 1987—88; assoc. prof. Hosp. Lariboisiere, U. Paris, 1988—89; mem. adv. bd. Gladstone Found. Labs. Cardiovasc. Rsch., U. Calif., San Francisco, 1991; bd. trustees Gorgas Sci. Found., Inc., Brownsville, Tex., 1992—; staff physician Okla. Blood Inst., Oklahoma City, 1994—; mem. oncology task force Midwest City Regional Hosp., Okla., 1995—. Mem.editl. bd.: Blood Jour., 1985—90; contbr. articles to profl. jours. Capt. M.C. US Army, 1963—66. Fellow: ACP; mem.: So. Soc. Clin. Investigation, Ctrl. Soc. Clin. Rsch., Am. Soc. Hematology (com. on ednl. affairs/tng. 1986—89, sci. subcom. on platelets 1986—89, com. on publs. 1991—, chmn. edn. prog. on platelets 1993—96, ad hoc com. on practice guidelines 1994—, nominating com. 1995, pres. 2005), Am. Soc. Clin. Investigation, Am. Heart Assn. (thrombosis coun., 1st Ann. Lyndon B. Johnson award 1976), Am. Fedn. Clin. Rsch., Alpha Omega Alpha (councilor Tex. Epsilon chpt. 1978—81). Achievements include research in epidemiology, clinical course, and long-term outcomes of platelet disorders.

Office: U Okla Health Scis Ctr 801 NE 13th St Rm 335 PO Box 26901 Oklahoma City OK 73190-0001 Office Phone: 405-271-2330 x48387. Business E-Mail: James_George@ouhsc.edu.

GEORGE, JOYCE JACKSON, lawyer, writer, retired judge, arbitrator, mediator; b. Akron, Ohio, May 4, 1936; d. Ray and Verna (Popadich) Jackson; children: Michael Eliot, Michelle René. BA, U. Akron, 1962, JD, 1966; postgrad., Nat. Jud. Coll., Reno, 1976, NYU, 1983; LLM, U. Va., 1986. Bar: Ohio 1966, U.S. Dist. Ct. (no. dist.) Ohio 1966, U.S. Ct. Appeals (6th cir.) 1968, U.S. Supreme Ct. 1968. Tchr. Akron Bd. Edn., 1962-66; asst. dir. law City of Akron, 1966-69, pub. utilities advisor, 1969-70, asst. dir. law, 1970-73; pvt. practice Akron, 1973-76; referee Akron Mcpl. Ct., 1975, judge, 1976-83, 9th dist. Ct. Appeals, Akron, 1983-89, Peninsula, Ohio, 1989; U.S. atty. No. Dist., Ohio, 1989-93; v.p. adminstrn. Telxon Corp., Akron, 1993-96; pres. Ind. Bus. Info. Svcs., Inc., Akron, 1996—. Tchr., lectr. Ohio Jud. Coll., Nat. Jud. Coll.; cons. in field. Author: Judicial Opinion Writing Handbook, 1981, 3d edit., 1993, 4th edit., 1998, 5th edit., 2007, Referee's Report Writing Handbook, 1992; contbr. articles to profl. publs. Recipient Outstanding Woman of Yr. award Akron Bus. and Profl. Women's Club, 1982; Alumni Honor award U. Akron, 1983, Alumni award U. Akron Sch. Law, 1991; Dept. Treasury award, 1992; named Woman of Yr. in politics and govt. Summit County, Ohio, 1983. Mem.: ABA, Akron Bar Assn., Ohio Bar Assn. Personal E-mail: joycejgeorge@yahoo.com.

GEORGE, PAUL G., mortgage company executive; b. Pasadena, Calif., May 25, 1951; BA in Polit. Sci. & Economics magna cum laude, Occidental Coll., LA; JD, UCLA. With Meserve, Mumper & Hughes, LA; head, human resources Pacific SW Airlines, Inc., San Diego; sr. v.p., human resources United Airlines; mem., interim mgmt. team Waste Management, Inc.; sr. exec. v.p., head, human resources Wachovia Corp., Charlotte, NC, 2001—05; exec. v.p., human resources Freddie Mac - Federal Home Loan Mortgage Corp., 2005—. Active Habitat for Humanity. Mem.: Fin. Svcs. Human Resources Exec. Forum. Office: Federal Home Loan Mortgage Corp 8200 Jones Branch Dr Mc Lean VA 22102-3110 Office Phone: 703-903-2000. Office Fax: 703-903-4045.

GEORGESCU, PETER ANDREW, manufacturing executive; b. Bucharest, Romania, Mar. 9, 1939; came to US, 1954, naturalized, 1954; s. V.C. Rica and Lygia (Bocu) G.; m. Barbara Anne Armstrong, Aug. 21, 1965; 1 son, Peter Andrew. AB cum laude, Princeton U., 1961; MBA, Stanford U., 1963. Joined Young & Rubicam, Inc., NYC, 1963, dir., Mktg., 1977-79, exec. v.p., Ctrl. Region Chgo.; bd. dirs. Young & Rubicam, Inc, Chgo., 1979-82, pres., Internat. NYC, 1982-86, pres., Advt., 1986—94, pres., CEO, 1994—2000, CEO, chmn., to 1999, chmn., Emeritus, 2000—. Bd. dirs. Briggs & Stratton, Inc., Toys "R" Us, Inc., EMI Group Ltd., Levi Strauss & Co., Internat. Flavors & Fragrances Inc., 1999—. Bd dir. Am. Assn. Advt. Agencies, Internat. Advt. Assn., Inc.; adv. bd. mem. Stanford Bus. Sch.; bd dir. A Better Chance, NY Philharm. Named to Adv. Hall of Fame, 2001. Mem. Coun. on Fgn. Rels., Links Club, River Club, Racquet Club, Casino Club, Brooks Club. Office: International Flavors & Fragrances Inc Bd Directors 521 W 57th St New York NY 10019 Office Phone: 212-765-5500. Office Fax: 212-708-7132. E-mail: peter.georgescu@iff.com.

GEPHARDT, DICK (RICHARD ANDREW GEPHARDT), consulting company executive, lawyer; b. St. Louis, Jan. 31, 1941; s. Louis Andrew and Loreen Estelle (Cassell) Gephardt; m. Jane Ann Byrnes, Aug. 13, 1966; children: Matthew, Christine, Katherine. BS, Northwestern U., 1962; JD, U. Mich., 1965. Bar: Mo. 1965. Cons. Goldman Sachs & Co.; sr. advisor FTI Consulting; ptnr. Thompson & Mitchell Law Firm, St. Louis, 1965-76; Dem. committeeman 14th ward, City of St. Louis, St. Louis, 1968—71, alderman 14th ward, 1971-76; mem. Dist. 3 Mo. House of Representatives, 1977—2005; majority leader US Congress from 3d Dist. Mo., 1989—94, minority leader, 1995—2002; founder, pres., CEO Gephardt Group, Washington, 2005—; sr. counsel DLA Piper, LLP, Washington, 2005—. Bd. dirs. US Steel Corp., 2005—, Centene Corp., 2006—, Spirit Aerosystems Holdings, Inc., 2006—, Embarq Corp., 2007—, Ford Motor Co., 2009—, CenturyLink, Inc. (formerly CenturyTel, Inc.), 2009—. Co-author (with Michael Wessel): An Even Better Place: America in the 21st Century, 1999. Pres. Children's Hematology Rsch. Assn., St. Louis Children's Hosp., 1973-76. Served to capt. Air Nat. Guard, 1965—71. Mem.: US Assn. Former Members of Congress, Metro St. Louis Bar Assn., Mo. Bar Assn., Boy Scouts Am., Am. Legion, Mid-Town Club (St. Louis), Kiwanis. Democrat. Baptist. candidate for Dem. presdl. nomination, 1987-88, 2003-04. Office: Gephardt Group 1101 K Street NW Ste 310 Washington DC 20005 Office Phone: 202-403-2150. Office Fax: 202-403-2048. Business E-Mail: richardgephardt@gephardtgroup.com.

GERALD, BARRY, retired radiology educator, neuroscientist; b. Greenville, Miss., Feb. 10, 1934; s. Louis Elmo and Eula (Mitchell) G.; m. Marjorie Brown, Aug. 6, 1955; children: Lucy Gerald Cook, Lee, Paul. Student, U. Miss., Oxford, 1951-54; MD, U. Miss., Jackson, 1958. Diplomate Am. Bd. Radiology. Intern Hermann Hosp., Houston, 1958-59, resident in radiology, 1959-62; fellow in pediatric radiology Children's Hosp. Med. Ctr., Cin., 1962-64; mem. faculty dept. radiology U. Ark., Little Rock, 1964-65, 67-69; dir. radiology dept. Children's Hosp. Med. Ctr., Oakland, Calif., 1965-66; mem. faculty dept. radiology U. Tenn. Coll. Medicine, Memphis, 1969—2009, prof., chmn. dept., 1979-95; fellow in neuroradiology Tufts-New Eng. Med. Ctr., Boston, 1971-72, interim chair dept. radiology, 2004—09, emeritus prof. radiology, 2009. Dir. radiology dept. Le Bonheur Children's Hosp., Memphis, 1983-88, 1991-2002; acting dir. radiology dept. St. Jude Children's Rsch. Hosp., Memphis, 1985-87; trainee Nat. Cancer Inst., 1960-62. Contbr. articles to med. jours., chpts. to books. Fellow Am. Coll. Radiology; mem. Am. Soc. Neuroradiology, Soc. for Pediatric Radiology, Radiol. Soc. N.Am. (councillor 1980-85), Am. Roentgen Ray Soc., Southeastern Neuroradiologic Soc. (founder, pres. 1977-78), So. Radiologic Conf. (pres. 1975-76). Avocations: tennis, history. Home: 177 N Highland St Memphis TN 38111-4747 Personal E-mail: barrygerald@gmail.com.

GERALD, LAURA I., public health service officer; B, Harvard U., Mass., MPH, 2002; MD, Johns Hopkins U., Balt., 1995. Pvt. practice pediatrician; sr. med. cons. NC cmty. care program NC Found. Advanced Health Programs; former sr. advisor to the sec. NC Dept. Health and Human Services, state health dir., dir. divsn. prevention, access and pub. health services, 2012—; exec. dir. NC Health and Wellness Trust Fund Commn., 2010—12. Fellow: American Acad. Pediat.; mem.: NC Pediatric Soc., NC Med. Soc., American Pub. Health Assn. Office: NC Division Public Health 5605 Six Forks Rd 1931 Mail Service Center Raleigh NC 27699-1931 Office Phone: 919-707-5000.

GERBER, DANIEL J., lawyer; b. Greenville, SC, Jan. 14, 1963; BA in Polit. Sci., U. Fla., 1985, JD, 1988. Bar: Fla. 1988, cert.: US Ct. Appeals, 11th Cir. Ptnr. Rumberger, Kirk & Caldwell LLP. Gen. counsel Fla. Pest Mgmt. Assn. Author: Get an Annual Legal Audit, 2002; contbr. articles to profl. jours.; Lectr. in field. Recipient Pres. award, Fla. Pest Mgmt. Assn., 2007; named one of The Nation's Top Litigators, The Nat. Law Jour., 2007. Mem.: Orange County Bar Assn., Def. Rsch. Inst., Fla. Pest Control Assn., Fla. Def. Lawyers Assn., ABA, Fedn. of Def. and Corp. Counsel. Office: Rumberger Kirk & Caldwell PA Lincoln Plz 300 S Orange Ave Ste 1400 Orlando FL 32801 Office Phone: 407-839-4512. Office Fax: 407-835-2012. E-mail: dgerber@rumberger.com.

GERBERDING, JULIE LOUISE, pharmaceutical company executive, former federal agency administrator; b. Estelline, SD, Aug. 26, 1955; m. David Rose; 1 stepchild, Renada. BA in Chemistry & Biology, Case Western Reserve U., Cleve., 1971, MD, 1981; MPH, U. Calif., Berkeley, 1990. Intern and resident, internal medicine U. Calif., San Francisco, chief med. resident, fellow in clin. pharmacology and infectious diseases, assoc. prof. medicine, epidemiology and biostatistics; clin. prof. medicine (infectious disease) Emory U.; founder, dir., Epidemiology Prevention and Interventions Ctr. San Francisco Gen. Hosp., 1987—98; dir., divsn. healthcare quality promotion Centers for Disease Control & Prevention (CDC), US Dept. Health & Human Services, Atlanta, 1998—2001, acting dep. dir. sci., 2001—02, dir., 2002—09; adminstr. Agy. for Toxic Substances and Disease Registry (ATSDR), 2002—09; pres. Merck Vaccines Merck & Co., Inc., Whitehouse Station, NJ, 2010—. Mem. Mayor's AIDS Task Force City of San Francisco, 1985—87; dir., Prevention Epicenter U. Calif., San Francisco; mem., scientific program com. Nat. Conf. on Retroviruses CDC, mem., HIV adv. com., mem., scientific program com., Nat. Ctr. for Infectious Diseases; cons. NIH, AMA, Occupational Safety and Health Adminstrn., Nat. AIDS Commn., U.S. Congress, Congl. Office Tech. Assessment, and WHO.; invited spkr. in field. Edtl. bd. Annals Internal Medicine, assoc. editor Am. Jour. Medicine, peer-reveiwer for numerous types of jours. in the field, contbr. to profl. publs. and textbooks. Recipient Disting. Svc. award, US Dept. Health & Human Services (HHS), 2001, Case Med. Alumni Assn. Disting. Alumnus/a award, Case Western Reserve U., 2003, President's award for Disting. Alumni, 2004; named one of The 100 Most Powerful Women, Forbes mag., 2005—08, The 100 Most Influential People in the World, TIME mag., 2004. Fellow: Infectious Diseases Soc. Am. (chair and co-chair com. profl. devel. and diversity, mem. nominations com., co-chair. annual program com.); mem.: ACP, Nat. Acad. Pub. Adminstrn., Inst. Medicine, Am. Epidemiology Soc., Soc. for Healthcare Epidemiology Am. (mem. AIDS/Tuberculosis com., bd. acad. counselor), Am. Soc. Clin. Investigation, Alpha Omega Alpha, Phi Beta Kappa. Achievements include being the first female director for the CDC. Avocations: scuba diving, reading, gardening. Office: Merck & Co Inc 1 Merck Dr Whitehouse Station NJ 08889

GERDES, LARRY GENE, medical transcription company executive; b. Princeton, Ill., Jan. 15, 1949; s. John and Etta (Muller) G.; m. Ann Adele Zumwalt, Aug. 5, 1972; children: Lindsey, Leslie. BS in Agrl. Sciences with highest honors, U. Ill., 1971; MBA in Fin., Ind. U., 1973. Mem., dean adv. coun., The Kelley Sch. Bus. Ind. U.; pres. Friesland Farms, LLC; CEO Med. Sys. Support of Dallas; gen. ptnr. Sand Hill Fin. Co.; account officer Jefferson Trust & Savs. Bank, Peoria, Ill., 1973-74, asst. v.p., 1975-77; bd. dirs. HBO & Co. (now McKesson), Peoria, contr., 1977-78, v.p., fin., 1979-82, sr. v.p., fin., 1982-85, COO, 1985, exec. v.p., CFO, 1985-87, various positions, 1987—91; gen. ptnr. Gerdes Huff Investments, 1983—; chmn., CEO Transcend Svcs., Inc.; officer Transcend Svcs., Inc, 1993. Bd. dirs. CBOT Holdings, Access Plans, Inc., Delphi Info. Systems Inc., Los Angeles, First Western Health Care, Los Angeles, Med. Sys. Support Inc., Dallas, CME Group Inc., 2007-. Bd. dirs. Tommy Nobis Ctr., J. Kyle Braid Leadership Found., Served with USNG, 1971-77., bd. dirs. Youth Farm Inc., Peoria, 1975-78. Mem.: Atlanta, Buckhead. Republican. Methodist. Avocations: golf, basketball, antique cars, investments. Office: Transcend Services Inc 1 Glenlake Pky Ste 1325 Atlanta GA 30328 also: CME Group Inc Bd Directors 20 S Wacker Dr Chicago IL 60606-7499 Office Phone: 678-808-0600, 312-930-1000. Office Fax: 678-808-0601. Business E-Mail: larry.gerdes@trcr.com.

GERDING, THOMAS GRAHAM, medical products executive; b. Evanston, Ill., Feb. 11, 1930; s. Louis Henry and Helen Frances (Graham) G.; m. Beverly Ann Starnes, June 18, 1955; children: Mark, David, Gail, Genie Ann. Student, U. Notre Dame, 1948-49; BS in Pharmacy, Purdue U., 1952, MS, 1954, PhD, 1960, D (hon.), 2002. From instr. to asst. prof. Purdue U., West Lafayette, Ind., 1956-61; dir. product devel. Pitman-Moore divsn. Dow Chem., Indpls., 1962-64; tech. dir. new products Glenbrook Labs., NYC, 1964-66; dir. product devel. Sterling-Winthrop Rsch. Inst., Rensselaer, NY, 1966-70; v.p. rsch. and devel. Calgon Consumer Products, Rahway, NJ, 1970-77; v.p., dir. rsch. and devel., quality assurance, consumer affairs, engring. Johnson & Johnson Products Inc., New Brunswick, NJ, 1977-88; pres. Thomas G. Gerding, Inc., Georgetown, Tex., 1988-96; dir. Drug Dynamics Inst. U. Tex., Austin, 1988-95; pres. Newform Devel. Labs., Inc., Georgetown, Tex., 1993—. Deans adv. coun. Purdue U. Sch. Pharmacy, 1996—2001, U. Tex. Coll. Pharmacy, 2002—07. Sgt. U.S. Army Med. Svc. Corp, 1954-56. Recipient Disting. Alumni award, Purdue U., 1984, Best Friend award, U. Tex., 2002. Mem.: Am. Assn. Pharm. Scientists, Union League Club (Chgo.). Republican. Achievements include research in pharmaceutics, wound care and unique drug delivery systems; patents in field. Office: Newform Devel Labs Inc 340 Shell Spur Georgetown TX 78628 Home: 30 Wildwood Dr Apt 104 Georgetown TX 78633-5330

GEREIGHTY, ANDREA SAUNDERS, diversified financial services company executive, poet; b. New Orleans, July 20, 1938; d. Andrew Jackson and Jeanne Teresa (Martin) Saunders; m. Dennis Anthony Gereighty Jr., May 19, 1959 (wid.); children: Deni Ann, David Dennis, Peggy T. Cert., Exeter Coll., Oxford, Eng., 1972; BA, U. New Orleans, 1974, MA in English with distinction, 1978. Cotton analyst Anderson-Clayton, Metairie, La., 1956; records retrieval profl. Shell Oil Co., New Orleans, 1956-60; census coord. St. Vincent De Paul Ch., New Orleans, 1960-65; bldg. funds dir. St. Francis Xavier Ch., Metairie, 1965-70; tchr. spl. edn. Deckbar Elem. Sch., Jefferson, La., 1966-70; tchr. English Chalmette (La.) H.S., 1971-73; assoc. prof. English dept. U. New Orleans, 1973-75; tchr. secondary edn. Berlin-Am. H.S., 1980-81; owner, founder, CEO New Orleans Field Svcs. Assocs., 1974—. Guest speaker Delgado Coll., New Orleans, 1989; guest presenter Rabouin Vo-Tech., New Orleans, 1980; lectr., guest presenter poetry at New Sarpy Sch., 1994-95; guest presenter St. Mark's Episcopal Ch., Latter Libr., N.O. Pub. Libr., others. Author: (public opinion polls book) Asking Q's, 1980; (poetry) Illusions and Other Realities, 1974, Restless for Cool Weather, 1990, Season of the Crane, 1994; publ., editor Desire Street, 1997—; author numerous poems. Recipient Coda award Poets and Writers, 1983, Poetry award of honor Nat. League Am. Pen Women, 1973, Deep South Writers, 1984, 88, 90, 92, 94, 95, 96, 97, 98, 99, 2d place award Nuyarikin Poet's Cafe, N.Y.C., Ellipsis Poetry prize, 1983, 85, 87, 90, other poetry awards. Mem. Am. Mktg. Assn., Mktg. Rsch. Assn., Nat. Geneal. Soc., Jefferson Geneal. Soc., Geneaol. Soc. of New Orleans, New Orleans Poetry Forum (dir. 1990—), New Orleans Track Club. Democrat. Roman Catholic. Avocations: poetry, jogging, genealogy, camping. Office: New Orleans Field Svcs 257 Bonnabel Blvd Rear Office Metairie LA 70005-3738 Office Phone: 504-833-0641.

GEREN, CHARLIE, state legislator; b. Oct. 22, 1949; 1 child, Emily. BBA, So. Meth. U., 1971. Deputy US Marshal Svc., 1981—90; founder, former ptnr. Kelly, Green, & Searcy Comml. Real Estate; pres. Railhead Smokehouse Restaurant, LGS Godly Ranch Corp.; mem. Dist. 89 Tex. House of Representatives, mem. Dist. 99 Tex., 2003—. Former bd. mem. Westside State Bank; bd. mem. Worthington Nat. Bank. Recipient of several awards and honors. Mem.: Coca-Cola Bottlers Assn. (former bd. mem., pres.), North Fort Worth Bus. Assn. (former bd. mem.), Greater Fort Worth Assn. of Realtors, Tex. Assn. of Realtors, Fort Worth Restaurant Assn., Tex. Restaurant Assn. Republican. Office: 1011 Roberts Cutoff River Oaks TX 76114 also: Room E2.308 Capitol Extension PO Box 2910 Austin TX 78768 Office Phone: 817-738-8333, 512-463-0610. Office Fax: 817-738-8362.

GERGEL, RICHARD MARK, federal judge; b. Columbia, SC, Aug. 15, 1954; BA, Duke U., 1975, JD, 1979. Bar: SC 1980. Atty. Medlock and Davis, SC, 1980—83; ptnr. to sr. ptnr., prin. Gergel, Nickles and Solomon, PA, Columbia, SC, 1983—2010; judge US Dist. Ct. SC, Charleston, 2010—. Recipient Jonathan Jasper Wright Award, U. SC Black Law Students Assn., 2001. Mem.: SC Supreme Ct. Hist. Soc. (pres. 1998—2000), Jewish Hist. Soc. of SC (past pres.), Columbia Hebrew Benevolent Soc. (past. pres.). Office: US District Court PO Box 835 Charleston SC 29401 Office Phone: 843-579-2610. E-mail: gergel_ecf@scd.uscourts.gov.

GERHARD, H. JOHN, orthopaedic surgeon, retired military officer; b. Portsmouth, Va., Oct. 29, 1955; s. Harry E. and Barbara M. Gerhard; m. Dianne Heath, Aug. 17, 1990; children: Christopher Ansley, Katherine Leigh, J. Stephen, Ian Jonas. BS, US Naval Acad., 1977; MD, Harvard U., Boston, 1981; MS, Indsl. Coll. Armed Forces, 1998. Diplomate Am. Bd. Orthopaedic Surgery, cert. naval flight surgeon Naval Aerospace Med. Inst. Commd. Ens. USN, 1977, advanced through grades to capt.; intern Naval Regional Med. Ctr. San Diego, 1981—82; flight surgeon Carrier Air Wing Two, NAS Miramar, Calif., 1982—84; orthopaedic surgery resident Duke U. Med. Ctr., Durham, NC, 1984—89, fellow hand and upper extremity surgery, 1992—93; staff orthopaedic surgeon Naval Hosp., Camp Lejeune, NC, 1989—92, dir. clin. svcs.; chief orthopaedics, staff orthopaedic surgeon, 1993—96; staff orthopaedic surgeon Brigade Svc. Support Group 4, Ops. Desert Shield/Storm, Iraq, 1990—91, USNS Comfort, Operation Uphold Democracy, Haiti, 1994; physician adviser to pres. Nat. Def. U., Ft McNair, DC, 1996—97; force surgeon USMC Forces, Atlantic, Europe, South, Norfolk, Va., 1998—2001; staff orthopaedic hand surgeon Naval Med. Ctr., Portsmouth, Va., 2001—02; exec. officer/COO Naval Hosp., Beaufort, SC, 2002—05, commdg. officer/CEO Lemoore, Calif., 2005—07. Presenter in field. Decorated various campaign and svc. medals/ribbons Dept. Navy, Ground Combat Action ribbon, Navy And Marine Corps Commendation medal, Meritorious Svc. medal, Legion Of Merit,; recipient USN Surgeon Gen.'s award, Naval Aerospace Med. Inst., Pensacola, Fl, 1980; Trident scholar, US Naval Acad. Fellow: Am. Acad. Orthopaedic Surgeons; mem.: Piedmont Orthopaedic Soc. Office: James A Haley Veterans Hosp Tampa FL 33612 Personal E-mail: d89f04@aol.com. Business E-Mail: h.john.gerhard@va.gov.

GERINGER, STEVEN I., healthcare services company executive; B in Economics, U. Pa., 1968. Sr. mgmt. positions, hosp. mgmt., managed care industry; CEO PCS Health Systems, Inc., pres., 1993, pvt. investor, 1996—; chmn. AmSurg Corp., 2009—, CredenceHealth, Inc.; mem. exec. bd. Cressey & Co. LP; pharmacy benefits mgr., unit Eli Lilly & Co. (acquired by Clinical Pharmaceuticals, Inc.); chmn., oper. ptnr. Qualifacts Sys. Inc. Office: Amsurg Corp Ste 500 20 Burton Hills Blvd Nashville TN 37215 Office Phone: 615-665-1283. Office Fax: 615-665-0755. Business E-Mail: sgeringer@amsurg.com.

GERKENS, HENRY H., trucking executive; m. Marcia Gerkens; 3 children. Degree, Adelphi U. CPA. Acct. Price Waterhouse, 1972; various positions Gen. Host Corp.; v.p. fin. admin. Chiquita Brands Inc.; v.p., CFO Landstar Sys., Inc., Jacksonville, Fla., 1989—94, exec. v.p., CFO, 1994—2001, pres., CFO, 2001, pres., COO, 2001—04, bd. dirs., pres., CEO, 2004—10; chmn., pres., CEO Landstar System, Inc., Jacksonville, Fla., 2010—. Mem.: AICPA, N.Y. State Soc. CPAs. Office: Landstar Sys 13410 Sutton Park Dr S Jacksonville FL 32224

GERMAIN, CLAIRE MADELEINE, law librarian, educator; d. Pierre and Jeanne (Despujols) G.; m. Stuart M. Basefsky, Aug. 16, 1976; 1 child, Nicolas. Licence-es. lettres, U. Paris, 1971, LLB, 1974; M in Comparative Law, La. State U., 1975; M in Law Librarianship, U. Denver, 1977. Reference libr. Duke U. Law Library, Durham, NC, 1977-80, head reference libr., 1982-84, asst. libr., sr. lectr. comparative law, 1984-89, assoc. dir., sr. lectr. comparative law, 1989-93; Edward Cornell law libr., prof. law Cornell U., Ithaca, NY, 1993—2011, prof. law emerita, 2011—; assoc. dean legal info. and Clearance, J Teselle prof. law U. Fla. Frederic G. Levin Coll. of Law, 2011—. Rsch. fellow Max Planck Inst., Hamburg, Federal Republic of Germany, 1980. Author: Germain's Transnational Law Research: A Guide to Attorneys, 1991, (with Szladits) Guide to Foreign Legal Materials, French, 2d edit., 1985; contbr. and editor articles to profl. jours. Recipient French Legion of Honor, 2007, Joseph L. Andrews award, 1992. Mem. ABA, Am. Assn. Law Librs. (pres. 2005-2006), Am. Assn. Law Schs. (chair libr. and tech. com. 1996-98, chair libr. sect. 2004-05). Roman Catholic. Home: 1837 NW 35th Way Gainesville FL 32605 Office: University of Florida Lawton Chiles Legal Information Gainesville FL 32611 Home Phone: 352-519-5200; Office Phone: 352-273-0703. E-mail: germain@law.ufl.edu.

GERNAND, BRADLEY ELTON, archivist, librarian; b. Hugo, Okla., Aug. 29, 1964; s. Charles D. Jr. and Mary Ellen (Akins) G. BA, U. Okla., 1985, MA, 1987, postgrad., 1987—. Archivist Western History Collections, Norman, Okla., 1982-89, Nat. Archives of U.S., Washington, 1989—91, Libr. of Congress, Washington, 1991—2001; libr. mgr. Inst. for Def. Analyses, Alexandria, Va., 2001—. Lachenmeyer Media fellow U. Okla., 1985-87. Independent. Baptist. Avocations: photography, reading, history. Office: Inst for Def Analyses 4850 Mark Center Dr Alexandria VA 22311-1882

GERNON, CLARKE JOSEPH, SR., mechanical and forensic engineering consultant; b. New Orleans, Dec. 27, 1944; s. Edward James and Mary Emma (Harvey) G.; 1 child, Clarke Joseph Jr. BSME, La. State U., 1969, MS in Engring. Mechanics, 1971. Registered profl. engr., La., Tenn., S.C. Mech. engr. Barnard and Burk, Inc., Baton Rouge, 1969-72; project engr. Lurgi-Knost, Inc., Baton Rouge, 1972-73; project mgr. The Rust Engring. Co., Baton Rouge, 1973-78, Imes and Assocs., Inc., Baton Rouge, 1978-86; mech. engr. and owner Futuretech Design, Baton Rouge, 1986—. Patentee in field. Vice chmn. Dixie Elec. Adv. Bd.; founding chmn. Capital Resource Conservation and Devel. Coun., Inc.; major supporter A Child's Wish; mem. Aero-space Task Force of MetroVision Partnership of New Orleans; incorporator and bd. dirs. Plantation Estates Civic Assn., Inc.; past pres. and bd. dirs. La. Miss. Christmas Tree Assn.; bd. dirs. Nat. Christmas Tree Assn., treas.; mem. quarantine adv. com. La. Dept. Agr. for Christmas Trees. Mem. ASME, Am. Welding Soc., So. Bldg. Code Congress Internat., Nat. Fire Protection Assn., Am. Acad. Forensic Scis. Roman Catholic. Avocations: model railroading, tropical fish, ornamental iron work. Office: Futuretech Design PO Box 896 Pearl River LA 70452-0896 Office Phone: 985-863-2909. E-mail: cjg@cgernon.com.

GERRISH, BRIAN ALBERT, theologian, educator, retired minister; b. London, Aug. 14, 1931; s. Albert and Doris G.; children from previous marriage: Carolyn, Paul; m. Dawn Ann De Vries, Aug. 3, 1990; 1 child, Heather. BA, Queens' Coll., Cambridge, Eng., 1952, MA, 1956; cert., Westminister Coll., Cambridge, 1955; S.T.M., Union Theol. Sem., NYC, 1956; PhD, Columbia U., 1958; D.D. (hon.), U. St. Andrews, Scotland, 1984. Ordained to ministry Presbyn. Ch., 1957. Asst. pastor West End Presbyn. Ch., NYC, 1956-58; tutor philosophy of religion Union Theol. Sem., NYC, 1957-58; instr. ch. history McCormick Theol. Sem., Chgo., 1958-59, asst. prof., 1959-63, assoc. prof., 1963-65; assoc. prof. hist. theology U. Chgo., 1965-68, prof., 1968-85, John Nuveen prof., 1985-96, John Nuveen prof. emeritus, 1996—. Disting. Svc. prof. theology Union Theol. Sem., Va., 1996—2002; Cunningham lectr. U. Edinburgh, 1990. Author: Grace and Reason: A Study in the Theology of Luther, 1962, 3d edit., 2005, Japanese transl. 1974, Tradition and the Modern World: Reformed Theology in the Nineteenth Century, 1978, 2d edit. 2007, The Old Protestantism and the New: Essays on the Reformation Heritage, 1982, 2d edit., 2004, A Prince of the Church: Schleiermacher and the Beginnings of Modern Theology, 1984, 2001, Korean transl., 1988, Grace and Gratitude: The Eucharistic Theology of John Calvin, 1993, 2002, Continuing the Reformation: Essays on Modern Religious Thought, 1993, Saving and Secular Faith: An Invitation to Systematic Theology, 1999, The Pilgrim Road: Sermons on Christian Life, 2000, Thinking With The Church: Essays in Historical Theology, 2010; editor: The Faith of Christendom: A Source Book of Creeds and Confessions, 1963, Reformers in Profile, 1967, 2d edit., 2004, Reformatio Perennis: Essays on Calvin and the Reformation in Honor of Ford Lewis Battles, 1981, Reformed Theology for the Third Christian Millennium: The 2001 Sprunt Lectures, 2003; co-editor: Jour. Religion, 1972-85; contbr. articles to profl. jours. Am. Assn. Theol. Schs. faculty fellow, 1961; Guggenheim fellow, 1970; Nat. Endowment Humanities fellow, 1980 Fellow Am. Acad. of Arts and Scis.; mem. Am. Soc. Church History (pres. 1979), Am. Theol. Soc. (Midwest divsn. pres. 1973-74). Home: 9142 Sycamore Hill Pl Mechanicsville VA 23116-5806

GERRY, ROBERT L., III, energy executive; b. NYC, Sept. 20, 1937; m. Sandra Smith; children: Robert L. IV, Lloyd H. Ind. energy industry investor; sr. v.p. Energy Assets Internat. Corp., 1989—90; pres., COO Nuevo, 1990—94, vice chmn., 1994—97; chmn., CEO Vaalco Energy, Inc., 1997—. Bd.dirs. Nuevo, 1990—2004; bd. dirs. Integrity Bank, Plains Exploration & Prodn. Co., 2004—. Trustee Tex. Children's Hosp., 1991—; mem. U. Tex. Adv. Coun. Office: Vaalco Energy Inc 4600 Post Oak Pl Ste 309 Houston TX 77027 Office Phone: 713-623-0801. Office Fax: 713-623-0982.

GERSAPPE, SUNIL, business development director; b. Hyderabad, India, Mar. 30, 1951; arrived in U.K., 1971; s. Raghunandan and Radha Gersappe; m. Kalyani Ganguly, Jan. 24, 1975; children: Avynash, Arjun. B of Commerce, U. Calcutta, India, 1971. Chartered acct., London, fellow, Inst. Chartered Accountants Eng. & Wales, Inst. Dirs. Asst. mgr. Deloitte Haskins & Sells, London, 1975-79; mgr. Produce Brokers, London, 1979-82; v.p. Nascor, Fribourg, Switzerland, 1982-85; pres. Dash Internat., NYC, 1985—86, Indo-Med Commodities, NYC, 1986—97; mktg. dir. Indo-Med Commodities, London, 1995—2010; dir. Business Devel., Franklin Baker Inc, Memphis, Tenn., 2010—. Fellow Inst. Dirs., Internat. Assn. Bus. Leaders (life mem.), Inst. Chartered Accts. Eng. Wales; Mem. Rotary Club Ealing London (treasurer past pres.), Rotary Club Germantown Greater Memphis Tenn. Avocation: travel. Office: Franklin Baker Inc 60 Germantown Ct Ste 210 Cordova TN 38018 Office Phone: 901-881-6681.*

GERSHENHORN, ALAN, delivery service executive; B fin., Univ. Houston. Mgmt. positions UPS, Tex., 1979—93, mgmt. positions internat. mktg., 1993—2002; v.p. mktg. UPS Canada, v.p., ops. dist. mgr., pres., 2002; pres. supply chain solutions glob. transp. & shared services UPS, Atlanta, pres. UPS supply chain solutions ops. Europe, Asia, ME & Africa, 2004—07, pres. UPS Internat., mem. mgmt. com., 2007, chief sales & mktg. officer, 2007—. Office: UPS 55 Glendale Pky NE Atlanta GA 30328

GERSHON, RICHARD (IRA RICHARD GERSHON), dean, law educator; b. Atlanta, July 11, 1957; s. Nathan Isaac and Shifra (Karesh) Gershon; m. Donna Levine; children: Claire, Eve. BA in Polit. Sci., U. Ga., 1979; JD with honors, U. Tenn., 1982; LLM in Taxation, U. Fla., 1983. Bar: Ga. 1982, US Dist. Ct. (northern dist.) Ga. 1982, US Tax Ct. 1983, Fla. 1984. Spl. asst. gen. counsel State Bar Ga., Atlanta, 1983; asst. prof. law Ohio Northern U., Ada, 1983—84, Stetson U. Sch. Law, St. Petersburg, Fla., 1984—86, assoc. prof., 1986—89, prof., 1989—98, academic assoc. dean, 1988—92; dean Tex. Wesleyan U. Sch. Law, Fort Worth, Tex.; founding dean Charleston Sch. Law; dean, prof. law U. Miss. Sch. Law, 2010—. Serves on Miss. Access to Justice Commission, Miss. Bar Professionalism Com., Boys and Girls Clubs Adv. Bd., Diversity Com. of Law Sch. Admission Coun. Author: A Student's Guide to the Internal Revenue Code, 1988, 1995, Life Planning in Florida, 1988, International Tax Guide: United States Income Taxation, 1991; contbr. articles to law jours. Office: University Mississippi School Law PO Box 1848 481 Coliseum Dr Robert C Khayat Law Center University MS 38677 Office Phone: 662-915-6900. E-mail: igershon@olemiss.edu.*

GERSON, IRWIN CONRAD, advertising executive; b. NYC, Mar. 18, 1930; s. Lenore and Charlotte (Steinhause) G.; m. Lenore Greenblatt, Nov. 29, 1953; children: Jill Beth, Matthew Ted. BS, Fordham U., 1953; MBA, NYU, 1959; DHL, Albany Coll. Pharmacy, 1992, L.I. U., 2001. Ter. mgr. Wyeth Labs. divsn. Am. Home Products, 1956-58; account exec., supr. William Douglas McAdams, Inc., NYC, 1958-66, v.p., 1966-68, sr. v.p., 1969-70, exec. v.p., 1971-74, pres., 1974-86, chmn. bd., 1987-96, Lowe McAdams Healthcare, NYC, 1996-98, chmn. emeritus, 1999-2000. Instr. sales mgmt. Columbia Coll. Pharm. Sci., 1967-1997; bd. advisors, v.p. Lifelong Learning Soc., Fla. Atlantic U., 2000-2006, pres., 2006-2011. Mem. editl. adv. bd. US Jour. Drug and Alcohol Dependence, 1977-83. Trustee, bd. dirs. Chemotherapy Found., 1971-86; bd. dir. Nutritional Rsch. Found., 1977-85, Am. Found. for Pharm. Edn., 1996-2003, Conn. Grand Opera, 1983-93, Stamford Chamber Orch., 1985-93; mem. coun. overseers Arnold and Marie Schwartz Coll. Pharmacy and Health Sci., LI U., 1986-90, chmn., 1990-99; bd. trustees Bus. Publs. Audit of Circulation, 1988-95, vice chmn., 1992-93, chmn., 1993-94; bd. trustees LI U., 1989-99; trustee Albany Coll. Pharmacy, Union U., 1993-97. With AUS, 1954-56. Named to Med. Advt. Hall of Fame, 1999. Mem. Am. Assn. Advt. Agys. (bd. govs. NY coun. 1991-95, ea. region 1995-98), Pharm. Advt. Coun. (bd. dirs. 1974-84, treas. 1976-77, v.p. 1979-81), Alpha Zeta Omega. Home: 107 Village Clubhouse Cir Jupiter FL 33458-7826 Office Phone: 561-307-8077.

GERSON, MICHAEL JOHN, columnist; b. NJ, May 15, 1964; s. Michael and Betty Gerson; m. Dawn Soon Gerson; 2 children. BA, Wheaton Coll., Ill., 1986. Aide to Senator Dan Coats US Senate; speechwriter Bob Dole Presdl. Campaign, 1996; journalist US News & World Report; sr. policy adv. The Heritage Found.; chief speechwriter, sr. policy adv. Bush Cheney Presdl. Campaign, 1999—2000; dep. asst. to the Pres., dir. presdl. speechwriting The White House, 2001—02, asst. to the Pres. for speechwriting & policy adv., 2002—05, asst. to the Pres. for policy & strategic planning, 2005—06; Roger Hertog sr. fellow Coun. on Fgn. Rels., 2006—09; op-ed. columnist The Washington Post, 2007—; sr. rsch. fellow Inst. Global Engagement Ctr. on Faith & Internat. Affairs, Arlington, Va., 2009—10; Hastert fellow Wheaton Coll. J. Dennis Hastert Ctr. Economics. Govt. and Pub. Policy, Ill., 2010—; sr. advisor ONE, 2010—; contbr. Ctr. Pub. Justice, Washington, 2010—, vis. fellow, 2012—. Author: Heroic Conservatism: Why Republicans Need to Embrace America's Ideals (And Why They Deserve to Fail If They Don't), 2007; co-author: City of Man: Religion and Politics in a New Era, 2010. Named one of The 25 Most Influential Evangelicals In America, TIME mag., 2005. Republican. Episcopalian. Office: Washington Post 1150 15th St NW Washington DC 20071

GERTLER, JANOS JOHN, electrical engineer, educator; b. Vienna, Sept. 9, 1936; came to U.S., 1981; s. Mor and Marta (Ungar) Gertler; m. Judit Andai, July 29, 1965; 1 child, Nicholas Balazs; m. Eva Anna Vas, Dec. 30, 2000. Diploma in engring., Tech. U., Budapest, Hungary, 1959; candidate in sci., Hungarian Acad. Scis., Budapest, 1967, DSc, 1980. Rsch. assoc. Power Systems Rsch. Inst., Budapest, 1959-65; asst. prof. Tech. U., Budapest, 1965-67; postdoctoral fellow U. Toronto, Ont., Can., 1967-68; sr. rsch. assoc. Automation Rsch. Inst., Budapest, 1968-70, dep. dir., 1971-81; vis. prof., assoc. dean engring. Poly. Inst. N.Y., Bklyn., 1984-85; prof. George Mason U., Fairfax, Va., 1985—. Assoc. vis. prof. Case Western Res. U., Cleve., 1977, vis. prof., 1982-84; cons. Bailey Controls, Cleve., 1983-84, GM, Warren, Mich., 1989-96; plenary spkr. internat. confs., 1974, 86, 91, 92, 93, 94, 95, 2000, 2008. Author: Fault Detection and Diagnosis, 1998; series editor Internat. Fedn. Automatic Control Procs., 1984-96; editor Ann. Revs. in Control, 1996—; contbr. articles to profl. jours. Fellow IEEE, Internat. Fedn. Automatic Control (chmn. publ. bd. 1993-96, 96-99, advisor for life, 1999—); mem. Hungarian Nat. Acad. Scis. (fgn. mem.). Achievements include rsch. in the theory and application of model-based diagnosis in engineering systems; development of generalized parity relation method; isolation-enhanced principal component analysis; application to car engines, macro-model analysis of the effect of offshoring and rehiring on the US economy. Office: George Mason U Elec Engring Dept Fairfax VA 22030 Home Phone: 703-425-3419; Office Phone: 703-993-1604. Business E-Mail: jgertler@gmu.edu.

GERTLER, MEYER H., lawyer; b. New Orleans, Oct. 28, 1945; s. David and Sadie (Redman) Gertler; m. Marcia Raye Goldstein Gertler, Aug. 23, 1967; children: Louis, Danielle, Joshua. BA, Tulane U., 1967, JD, 1969. Bar: La. 1970, US Dist. Ct. (ea. and mid. dists.) 1970, US Ct. Appeals (5th cir.) 1970, US Supreme Ct. 1970. Ptnr. Uddo & Gertler, New Orleans, 1970—76, Gertler & Gertler, New Orleans, 1977—86, Gertler, Gertler & Vincent, New Orleans, 1986—95, Gertler, Gertler, Vincent & Plotkin, 1996—. Mem.: ABA, Am. Assn. Justice, New Orleans Bar Assn., La. State Bar Assn., Asbestos Litig. Group. Democrat. Office: Gertler Law Firm 129 Carondelet St New Orleans LA 70130

GERTZBEIN, STANLEY DAVID, orthopedic surgeon; b. Toronto, Can., Sept. 25, 1941; MD, U. Toronto, Can., 1966. Cert. Am. Bd. Orthop. Surgeons, Am. Bd. Spine Surgery. Fellow, orthop. surgery Royal Coll. Physicians and Surgeons (Can.), 1971; rsch. and clin. fellow Sunnybrook Med. Ctr., Toronto, 1972; spinal tng. London and Hong Kong, 1973; prof. U. Toronto, U. Tex. Med. Sch.; active staff mem. Christus St. Joseph Hosp., Houston; staff mem. Methodist Hosp., Houston; full prof., dept. orthop. surgery Baylor Coll. Medicine, Houston. Vis. prof. and guest lectr. at Colleges, Universities and symposia throughout the world; presenter in field. Adv. editor Spine, Spine Jour.; contbr. article to peer-reviewed jours., chapters to books; guest appearance Miracle Workers (ABC), 2006. Trustee AO Found.; chmn. AO Spine Courses. Mem.: Tex. Orthop. Assn., Tex. Med. Assn., Harris County Med. Soc., Canadian Orthop. Assn., AMA, Am. Acad. Orthop. Surgeons, Internat. Soc. for Study of the Lumbar Spine (exec. bd. dir., Volvo award for the best Basic Sci. Rsch. study 1984), N.Am. Spine Soc. (mem. exec. com.). Office: Baylor Coll Medicine Dept Orthopedic Surgery 6620 Main St 13th Fl Houston TX 77030 Address: Inst for Spinal Disorders 6560 Fannin St Houston TX 77030 also: Christus St Joseph Hosp 1401 St Joseph Pkwy Houston TX 77002 Office Fax: 713-986-5711. E-mail: bkdoctor@aol.com.

GESPASS, DAVID, lawyer; JD, American U. Wash. Coll. Law, 1970. Mem. mil. law office Nat. Lawyers Guild, Okinawa, Japan; pvt. practice atty. Birmingham, Ala., 1978—; ptnr. Gespass and Johnson, Birmingham. Mem. adv. bd. Nat. Police Accountability Project, Boston, 1999—. Editor-in-chief Guild Practitioner, 2004—09. Recipient Golden Jurist award, Birmingham Branch, NAACP. Mem.: Nat. Lawyers Guild (former southern regional v.p., pres., mem. editl. bd.). Office: Gespass & Johnson 825 36th St S Birmingham AL 35222-3505 Office Phone: 205-323-5966. Office Fax: 205-323-5990.*

GETCHELL, E. DUNCAN, lawyer; b. Mobile, Ala., Oct. 12, 1949; B with high honors, Emory U., Ga.; JD with distinction, Duke U., Durham, NC. Assoc. McGuireWoods (formerly McGuire, Woods & Battle); Air Force JAG officer USAF Office of Gen. Counsel; rejoined McGuireWoods (formerly McGuire, Woods & Battle), 1977, ptnr., head appellate litig. practice group, 1981—2009; solicitor gen. Office of Atty. Gen., Va., 2009. Reservist USAFR, 1971—77, capt. USAF, 1975—77. Fellow: Nat. Acad. Appellate Lawyers; mem.: Va. State Bar, Bar Assn. of City Richmond, American Law Inst., Fourth Cir. Jud. Conf. Office: Office of Attorney Gen 900 E Main St Richmond VA 23219 Office Phone: 804-786-2071. Office Fax: 804-786-1991.

GETTE, TIMOTHY J., museum director; b. San Bernardino, Calif. m. Kristi Diane Barton, Oct. 15, 1977; children: Brent Timothy, Rebecca Marie. BA in Journalism, Angelo State U., 1968; M in Mgmt., U. Ark., 1974. Dir., ops. Sixth Fl. Mus., 1997—99; COO Dallas Mus. of Natural History, 1999—2003; exec. dir. Va. Mus. of Natural History, 2004—. Mem.: Kappa Xi. Office: Va Mus of Natural History 21 Starling Ave Martinsville VA 24112 Office Phone: 276-634-4151. Office Fax: 276-634-4199. Business E-Mail: tim.gette@vmnh.virginia.gov, timgette@gette.net.

GETTLEMAN, DAVE, professional sports team executive; m. Joanne Gettleman; children: Aaron, Sam, Ana Jane. BA, Springfield Coll., Mass., 1972; MA in Phys. Edn., Southern Conn. State, 1978; MA in Sports Adminstrn., St. Thomas U., Fla., 1986. Head football coach Spackenkill HS, Poughkeepsie, NY, 1973—78, 1980—81, Kingston HS, NY, 1984—86; scouting intern Buffalo Bills, 1986, scout, 1987, scout rep. for BLESTO, 1988—93; scout Denver Broncos, 1994—98, NY Giants, 1998, pro personnel dir., 1999—2012, sr. pro personnel analyst, 2012; gen. mgr. Carolina Panthers, 2013—. Achievements include being associated with the Super Bowl XXXII winning Denver Broncos, 1997, Super Bowl winning XLII and XLVI NY Giants, 2007, 2011. Office: Carolina Panthers 800 S Mint St Charlotte NC 28202

GEVEDEN, REX D., aerospace and defense manufacturing company executive; B in Engring. Physics, Murray State U., Ky., M in Physics; PhD in Materials Engring., Auburn U., Ala. Pres. Teledyne Brown Engineering, Inc., 2007—; pres., energy and power sys. Teledyne Technologies, Inc., 2008—. Assoc. adminstr. NASA, chief engr., dep. dir., Huntsville, Ala. Mailing: Teledyne Brown Engineering Inc P O Box 070007 Huntsville AL 35807-7007 Office Phone: 256-726-5555. Office Fax: 256-726-5556. Business E-Mail: rex.geveden@tbe.com.

GEWIN, JAMES W., lawyer; b. Tuscaloosa, Ala., Nov. 9, 1940; s. Walter Pettus and Anna (Sledge) Gewin; m. Bradley McLaughlin, July 15, 1972; children: Leslie Stuart, William Hampton. AB, Princeton U., NJ, 1963; LLB, U. Ala. Sch. Law, Tuscaloosa, 1966. Bar: Ala. 1966, US Dist. Ct. (so., no. and mid. dists.) Ala., US Ct. Appeals (5th and 11th cirs.). Law clk. to Hon. Seybourn H. Lynne US Dist. Ct. (no. dist.) Ala., Birmingham, 1966-67; atty., ptnr. Bradley Arant Boult Cummings LLP (formerly Bradley Arant Rose & White), Birmingham, 1967—. Mem. Ala. Bd. Bar Examiners, 1976—78, Ala. State Bd. Bar Commrs., 1991—2000. Bd. trustees Ala. Ballet, 1985—, Girls Inc., Ala. Forest Owners Assn. Fellow: ABA, Ala. Law Found., American Bar Found.; mem.: Ala. Law Inst., Birmingham Bar Assn., American Bd. Trial Advocates, American Coll. Trial Lawyers, Ala. State Bar, American Law Inst., Kiwanis. Office: Bradley Arant Boult Cummings LLP One Federal Pl 1819 Fifth Ave N Birmingham AL 35203 Office Phone: 205-521-8352. Office Fax: 205-488-8352. E-mail: jgewin@babc.com.

GEX, WALTER JOSEPH, III, federal judge; b. Bay St. Louis, Miss., Mar. 20, 1939; BA, U. Miss., 1961, LLB, 1963. With Satterfield, Shell, Williams & Buford, Jackson, Miss., 1963-72, ptnr., 1966-72, Gex, Gex & Phillips, Bay St. Louis, 1972-86; judge US Dist. Ct. (so. dist.) Miss., Gulfport, 1986—2004, sr. judge Miss., 2004—. Mem. FBA, Miss. State Bar Assn. Republican. Roman Catholic. Address: 2012 15th St Ste 592 Gulfport MS 39501-2036

GEYMANN, BRETT F., state legislator; Mem. Dist. 35 La. House of Reps., 2004—, mem. appropriations com., house and govtl. affairs com., retirement com., joint legis. com. on the budget. Republican. Office: Capitol Off 900 N Third St, PO Box 94062 Baton Rouge LA 70804 Address: District Off PO Box 12703 Lake Charles LA 70612-2703 Office Phone: 337-491-2315. Fax: 337-855-8285.

GFELLER, ROBERT J., JR., retail executive; B in Economics, Franklin and Marshall Coll.; MBA in Mktg., NYU. Brand dir., athletic apparel and men's underwear divsns. Champion, Inc.; dir. new products-Planters Snacks, sr. grand mgr., Lifesavers candy, Bubble Yum Nabisco, Inc.; dir., consumer occasions mktg.-retail channels Coca-Cola Co., 1996—99; sr. v.p., gen. merchandising mgr. Lowe's Companies, Inc., 1999—2000, sr. v.p. mktg., advt. and comm., 2000—09, sr. v.p., gen. merchandising mgr. hardlines & bldg. products, 2009—11, exec. v.p., merchandising, 2011—. Office: Lowe's Companies Inc 1000 Lowe's Blvd Mooresville NC 28117 Office Phone: 704-758-1000. Office Fax: 336-658-4766. Business E-Mail: robert.gfeller@lowes.com.

GHAMANDE, SHARAD A., gynecologic oncologist, educator; MD, Bombay U., India, 1990. Diplomate Am. Bd. Ob-Gyn, 2002, Am. Bd. Ob-Gyn-gynecologic oncology, 2003, cert. pediatric gynecology. Resident ob-gyn. dept. Boston Med. Ctr., Mass., 1997; fellow gynecologic oncology Roswell Pk. Cancer Inst., Buffalo, 2000; fellow Meml. Sloan Kettering Cancer Ctr., MD Anderson Cancer Ctr.; asst. prof. Med. Coll. of Ga.; pvt. practice Augusta Oncology Assocs. PC; physician MCG Health. Named one of the Top Doctors in America. Mem.: Alpha Omega Alpha. Avocation: family bonding. Office: MCG Health 1120 15th St Augusta GA 30912-5563 Office Phone: 706-721-6744.*

GHEORGHE, ADRIAN VELICU, safety, engineering management and system engineer, educator; b. Bucharest, Romania, Sept. 12, 1945; naturalized, Austria, 1999; s. Velicu and Frusina Vasile (Cojocaru) Gheorghe; m. Aurora P. Niculescu, July 29, 1972; children: Paul, Alexandra. Degree in engring., Bucharest Poly U., 1968; D in Energy Sys., Bucharest Poly. U., 1971, MS in Engring. and Econs., 1978; degree in engring., Stanford U., 1973; PhD in Sys. Sci., City U., London, 1975; MBA, Acad. Econ. Studies, 1985; PhD in Power Engring., Bucharest Poly. U., Romania, 1971. Asst. prof. Bucharest Poly. U., 1968-75, sr. lectr., 1975-80, prof., 1980—; acting dir. Swiss project risk and safety tech. sys. Swiss Fed. Inst. Tech., Zurich, 1993—2006; project mgr. EC-JRC, Ispra, 2004—05, Regional Vulnerability Assessment, 2004—06; prof. engring. mgmt. and sys. engring., Batten endowed chair sys. engring. Old Dominion U., Norfolk, Va., 2006—; guest prof. Beijing Normal U., 2010—; project mgr. Internat. Sci. Steering Com., Integrated Risk Gov., Beijing, 2011—; chair, dept. energy mgmt. and sys. engring. Old Dominion U, Norfolk, Va.; internat. sci. dir. Ctr. Understanding Change, 2011—; chair dept. engring. mgmt. & sys. engring. Old Dominion U. Norfolk, Va.; chair dept. engring. mgmt. and systems engring, Old Doveivion U., Norfolk, 2013—. Rsch. fellow Stanford (Calif.) U., 1973; sr. rsch. fellow Internat. Inst. Applied Sys. Analysis, Austria, 1976—80, UN Univ., Tokyo, 1978—82, Risø (Denmark) Nat. Labs., 1986, Energy Study Ctr., Netherlands, 1989; civil servant first officer Internat. Atomic Energy Agy., Vienna, 1990—93, sci. sec. Programme DECADES on comparative risk assessment energy sys., 1990—93; project leader Alliance Global Sustainability, MIT, ETH, U. Tokyo; mem. tech. com. Probabilistic Safety Assessment and Mgmt. Internat. Conf., 1996, 1998, 2000, 2002—, 2002; vis. prof. U. Delft, Netherlands, 1997; mem. China Energy Tech. Program, ABB, 1999—2003, Romanian Electricity Tech. Program, Alliance Global Sustainability, 2000—; mem. vulnerability assessment critical infrastructures under sustainability program, 2001—; chmn. Workshop on Risk Mgmt., Ascona, Switzerland, 2001; project mgr. KOVERS-KT, ETH, Zurich, 2001; project mgr. petrochem. industry vulnerability assessment Swiss Re, 2004—05; mem. task force Extended Risk Analysis Switzerland XXI, 2002—; organizer, facilitator Internat. Risk and Governance Coun., Switzerland, 2002; external cons. project U. Tokyo, 2002—; participant, lectr. Crans Montana Forum, Switzerland, 2003; disaster risk mgmt. cons. Swiss Re, 2004—05; expert-at-large on energy security and safety East West Inst., NY and Brussels, 2005—; mem. US intelligent expert grp. on electric power grid interoperability Grid Wise, 2007; spkr. in field, 2007; expert on US Nat. taskforces SAIC Corp., 2007—; keynote spkr. Asian Security Conf., New Delhi, 2010; mem. editl. bd. Annals Romanian Acad. Scientist, 2010; project mgr. Romanian Energy Sys.; mem. DHS Task Force; external reviewer NSF DHS USA Dutch Sci. Found.; guest prof. Beijing Normal U., 2010—; dir. Energy Rsch. Cluster Old Douinion U. Norfolk, Va., 2008; spkr. Strategic Def. Assn., Brussels, 2010; mem. NASA Project Serious Gaming Aviation Risks, 2011; guest editor Spl. Issues with Internat. Critical Infrastuctures & Internat. Jour. Sys. Engring.; mem. Internat. Sci. Steering Com. Integrated Risk Gov. Project; chmn. IEEE Internat. Conf., Va., 2011; dir., Energy Rsch. and Edn. Cluster Old Dominion U., Norfolk, Va., 2008—, chair dept. energy mgmt. & sys. engring., developer, academic cert. energy sys., cyber security and homeland security, 2010—; guest editor Spl. Issues IJ Critical Infrastructure and IJ Sys. of Sys. Engring., 2012; mem. editl. bd. Resilient Energy Sys., Dordrecht, Netherlands, 2012. Author: Applied Systems Engineering, 1982, Decision Processes Dyn. Syst., 1990, Risk Assessment Transportation Dangerous Goods, 1995, Integrated Regional Risk Assessment, 1995, Integrated Fuzzy Logic for Regional Risk Priorization, 1996, Emergency Planning Knowledge, 1996, Risk Engineering,

1999, Electricity and Sustainability: Issues in Debate, 2001, Integrated Risk and Vulnerability Assessment and Management Assisted by DSS, 2005, Critical Infrastructure at Risk, Securing the European Critical Electricity Infrastructures, 2006, Resilient Energy Systems, 2013; author, editor: Cybernetic Systems, 1978; editor: Probability Concept in Risk Analysis, 1996, Integrated Risk and Vulnerability Management, 2005, Internat. Jour. Sys. of Sys. Engring., 2006—, 2007, Springer on the Topic Security, Complex Systems and Governance, 2008—, System of Systems, 2012; mem. editl. bd.: Kluwer Acad. Publ. House, 1995, Internat. Jour. Risk Assessment and Mgmt., 2000, Internat. Jour. Border Security and Immigration Policy, 2007; mem. editl. bd. Springer Acad. Publ. House, Security Complex Systems and Governance, 2008; sr. guest editor: Internat. Jour. Environ. and Pollution, 1994, Risk Analysis, 1980—87, Internat. Jour. Global Energy Issues, 1996, exec. editor: Internat. Jour. Sustainable Devel., 1998, Jour. Critical Infrastructures, 2004, section editor: Energy Security and Homeland Security for the Wiley Handbook for Science and Technology for Homeland Security, 2007; contbr. articles to profl. jours.; coord.: NATO Advance Rsch. Workshop Energy Security at the Black Sea Area, 2008; author: Infranomics: Sustainability Infrastructures & Governnance Springh, Infranomics, 2014. Mem. task force Critical Energy Infrastructures G-8, St. Petersburg, 2006; organiser Internat. Conf., Next Generation Infrastructures, Va. Beach, 2011; keynote spkr. COFES Conf., Phoenix, 2012; hon. pres. Romanian Assn. Protection Critical Infrastructures, 2011—. Lt. maj. Romanian Mil., 1968—69. Ford Found. fellow, 1973, Internat. Rsch. Exch. Bd. fellow, 1980. Fellow: Soc. Risk Analysis-Europe, Soc. Risk Analysis USA (mem. exec. bd. 1990—); mem.: IEEE Conf. (India), IEEE Conf. (Netherlands), Internat. Sci. Dir. Ctr. Understanding Change, Sci. Organising Com. (Rotterdam, Netherlands), EURISC Found. (hon. pres., sr. scientist 1995—), World Security Forum (v.p. 2004—), Internat. Risk Governance Coun. (sci. advisor 2002—05, project mgr. ubiquity of IT and risks on critical infrastructures 2003—04), Japanese NEXUS IDRM, Risk Vulnerability Governance Sustainability First World Risk Congress (organizer mini-symposium Brussels 2003), Romanian Nat. Coll. Def. (lectr. 2002—03, coord., organizer internat. conf. Kyoto, Japan 2003, coord., organizer internat. conf., Beijing 2004), Info. and Knowledge Soc., Romanian Acad. Scis. (mem. think-tank 2000—01), Romanian Acad. Informational Soc. (task force mem.), World Energy Coun. (Living in One World Project 2000), Infosurance, Comm. Mgmt. (hon. pres. 1995), European Inst. Risk, Security, Romanian Soc. Engring. and Mgmt. (pres. 1990), Romanian Mktg. Assn. (sec. 1975—90), N.Y. Acad. Scis., Austrian Soc. Cybernetics (hon.), TRUSTNET, Swiss Soc. Risk and Safety, Swiss Forum Sci. and Energy, Swiss Soc. Info. Tech. Security, World Insts. Disaster Risk Mgmt. Achievements include research in risks national aviation system and the use of UAV. Avocations: jogging, swimming, reading, classical music. Office: Old Dominion U Norfolk VA 23529 Home: 123 Coll Pl Apt 902 Norfolk VA 23510 Business E-Mail: aghcorgh@odu.edu.

GHOVANLOO, MAYSAM, engineer, educator; m. Azadeh N. Shahshahani, Sept. 8, 2001. BS in Elec. Engring., U. Tehran, Iran, 1994; MS in Biomedical Engring., Amirkabir U. Tech., Tehran, Iran, 1997; MS in Elec. Engring., U. Mich., Ann Arbor, 2003, PhD in Elec. Engring., 2004. Sr. rsch. engr. IDEA Co. Ltd. (indsl. Develop. for Electronic Application, Inc., Tehran, Iran, 1994—98; sr. engr. Ctr. for Repair and Reconstruction Med. Devices, Tehran, Iran, 1997—98; founder, CEO Sabz Nagar Rayaneh Co. Ltd., Tehran, Iran, 1998—99; rsch. asst. U. Mich., Ann Arbor, 2000—04; tech. intern Advanced Bionics, Inc., Santa Clarita, Calif., 2002; asst. prof., dept. elec. & computer engring. N.C. State U., Raleigh, 2004—07; asst. prof. Ga. Inst. Tech. Elec. and Computer Engring., Atlanta, 2007—. Cons. Nitinol Devel. Corp., Fremont, Calif., 2004—; tech. reviewer IoP Jour. Contbr. articles to profl. jours., chapters to books. Grantee, N.C. State U., 2005. Mem.: IEEE (tech. reviewer), Sigma Xi, Tau Beta Pi. Achievements include patents pending for Frequency shift keying demodulation methods for wireless biomedical implants; Three dimensional microassembly structures for micromachined planar microelectrode arrays; Shatter-proof microprobes; A compact large voltage compliance high output impedance programmable current source. Home Phone: 404-909-8180; Office Phone: 404-385-7048. Office Fax: 919-515-2285, 404-894-4701. Business E-Mail: mgh@gatech.edu.

GIADROSSI, NICOLETTA, manufacturing company executive; BA in Econ. & Math., Yale U.; MBA, Harvard U. Various positions, including gen. mgr., downstream bus. GE Co., 1995—2005; operating ptnr. LBO France, 2005—06; restructured and managed the divestiture of a family's textile and real estate businessess France, 2006—08; v.p., gen. mgr., European ops. Dresser-Rand Group, Inc., 2009—. Office: Dresser-Rand Group Inc 10205 Westheimer Rd Ste 1000 Houston TX 77042 Office Phone: 713-354-6100. Office Fax: 713-354-6110. Business E-Mail: ngiadrossi@dresser-rand.com.

GIALLOMBARDO, LESLIE, publishing executive; Attended, Salem State Coll., 1975. Adv. dir. The Desert Sun, Palm Springs, Calif., Idaho Statesman, Boise; v.p., adv. The Tennessean, 1995, sr. v.p., mktg., 1999, pres., pub., 2002—05; v.p. advt., newspaper divsn. Gannett Co., Inc., 2006—. Mgmt. positions Reno (NE) Gazette-Jour., Statesman Jour., Salem, Oreg. Named seven time winner Pres.'s Ring. Office: Gannett Co Inc 7950 Jones Branch Dr Mc Lean VA 22107 Office Phone: 703-854-6000. Office Fax: 703-854-2053. Business E-Mail: lgiallombardo@gannett.com.

GIALLORENZI, THOMAS GAETANO, optical engineer; b. NYC, Feb. 28, 1943; s. Amedeo and Eleanor (Spica) G.; m. Margaret Mary Marrin, Sept. 6, 1966; children: Thomas R., Kathy. BS in Engring. Physics, Cornell U., 1965, MS in Engring. Physics, 1966, PhD, 1969. Tech. staff Gen. Tel. & Electronics Lab., Bayside, NY, 1969-70; sect. head, optical techniques br. Naval Rsch. Lab., Washington, 1970-76, head optical techniques br., 1976-79, supt. optical scis. divsn., 1979—. Lectr. in field and at profl. soc. confs. Editor Jour. Lightwave Tech., 1983-88; contbr. over 80 articles to profl. jours.; over 30 patents in field. Mem. adv. bd. U. Va., 1986-92. Recipient Applied Sci. award Rsch. Soc. Am., 1973, Meritorious Civilian Svc. award USN, 1978, Conrad award USN, 1985, Disting. Achievement in Sci. award USN, 2006, Disting. Exec. Rank award Pres. of U.S., 1990, 98, Meritorious Exec. Rank award Pres. of U.S., 1984, 2004, Disting. Civilian Svc. award Dept. Def., 1987. Fellow IEEE (assoc. editor Procs. 1990-95, Lightwave Comms. 1989-92, Harry Diamond award 1986, John Tyndell award 1990), IEEE Laser and ElectroOptics Soc. (pres. 1996), Optical Soc. Am. (editor Jour. Lightwave Tech. 1983-89, assoc. editor Applied Optics 1991-94); mem. Nat. Acad. Engring., U.S. Naval League (Albert Michelson award 1995, USN Rodger Easton award Office of Naval Rsch. 1998). Home: 8704 Side Saddle Rd Springfield VA 22152-2731 Office: Naval Rsch Lab Optical Scis Divsn Washington DC 20375-0001 Office Phone: 202-767-3808. Business E-Mail: giallorenzi@nrl.navy.mil.

GIANNINI, A. JAMES, psychiatrist, educator, researcher, author; b. Youngstown, Ohio, June 11, 1947; s. Matthew and Grace Carla (Nistri) G.; children: Juliette Nicole, Jocelyn Danielle. BS, Youngstown State U., Ohio, 1970; MD, U. Pitts., 1974; postgrad., Yale U., 1974-78, U. London, 1996-97. Diplomate Nat. Bd. Med. Examiners. Intern St. Elizabeth Med. Ctr., Youngstown, 1974, assoc. dir. family medicine, psychiatry, 1978-80; resident in psychiatry Yale U., New Haven, 1975-78, chief resident, 1977-78; assoc. psychiatrist Elmcrest Psychiat. Inst., Portland, Conn., 1976-78; acting ward chief Conn. Mental Health Ctr., New Haven, 1977; assoc. dir. family medicine, psychiatry St. Elizabeth Med. Ctr., Youngstown, 1978-80; from asst. prof. to assoc. prof. dept. psychiatry N.E. Ohio Med. Coll., 1978-84, program dir., 1980-88, prof., 1984-90, vice-chmn., 1985-89; assoc. clin. prof. dept psychiatry Ohio State U., 1983-89, clin. prof., 1989-96; chmn. depts. psychiatry and toxicology Western Res. Care System Hosp., 1985-87, med. dir. toxicology, 1987; acting dir. dual diagnosis unit Youngstown Osteo. Hosp., 1987—2000; pres., corp. med. dir. Chem. Abuse Ctrs., Inc., Ohio and Mich., 1987—2004; med. dir. substance abuse svcs. Cmty. Mental Health Ctr. of Mid. Ga., Dublin, 2004—; lt. col. M.C., U.S. Army, 2004; dir. Opiate Maintenance Clin. Chord Vinson Vet. Med. Ctr., Dublin, 2013. Dir. alumni schs. com. Yale U., New Haven, 1997-2005; vis. prof. Inst. for Scis. Comm. and Sci. Edn., Columbia Coll., Chgo., U. Naples, Italy, 1990, U. Zagreb, Croatia, 1990; examiner in psychology LaTrobe U., Bundoora, Australia, 1988-89; sr. mentor U. Pitts., 2001—05, U. Pitts. Alumni Recruitment Team, 2005-; sr. cons. Fair Oaks Hosp., Summit, N.J., 1979, Regent Hosp., N.Y.C., 1981-96, chmn. Nat. Adv. Council Prevention and Control of Rape, NIMH, Rockville, Md., 1983-86, spl. reviewer mood disorders com., 1995-97; mem. drug abuse clin., behavioral and rsch. rev. com. Nat. Inst. Drug Abuse, Rockville, Md., 1987-88; chief forensic psychiatrist Mahoning County Prosecutor, 1989-97; Am. Participant USIA Drug Abuse program to Cyprus, Italy, Can., Barbados, St. Lucia and Yugoslavia, 1990-94; panelist, moderator Renaissance Weekend, Hilton Head and Charleston, S.C., 1997—; cons. Smith-Kline Labs., McNeil Labs., Excerpta Medica Pubs., Amino Labs., Fund for Am. Renaissance; dir. clin. rsch. Princeton Diagnostic Labs., South Plainfield, N.J., 1987-89; med. dir. med. adv. bd. Neurodata Inc., 1987-89, pres., 1989-2004, med. dir. Chem. Abuse Ctrs. Inc., 1987, corp. med. dir., 1987-97; spl. reviewer initial review group, 1995-97, health, behavior and prevention review com. NIH, Rockville, Md.; ethics com. Mahoning County Mental Retardation Bd., Youngstown, Ohio, 1995-98, treas. 1996-97, vice-chmn., bd. treas., 1997-98; psychiatrist emeritus Stony Lodge Hosp., Briar Cliff Manor, NY; book reviewer Psychiat. Times, 2000—. Author: (with Henry Black) Psychiatric, Psychogenic, Somatopsychic Disorders, 1978; (with Robert Gilliland) Neurologic and Neuropsychiatric Disorders, 1983; (with Andrew Slaby) Overdose and Detoxification Emergencies, 1983; Biological Foundation of Clinical Psychiatry, 1988, (with Andrew Slaby) Drugs of Abuse, 1989, 2d edit., 1996, Comprehensive Laboratory Services in Psychiatry, 1986; (with Philip Jose Farmer) Red Orc's Rage, 1991; (with Andrew Slaby) The Eating Disorders, 1993, 2d edit., 1997, Drugs of Abuse, 2d edit., 1998, Drug Abuse: A Family Guide to Recognition and Treatment, 1999; contbr. numerous articles to profl. jours. Vice chmn. Mahoning County (Ohio) Mental Health Bd., 1982-84, chmn., 1984-86; councilor Nat. Italian Am. Found. Named Ky. Col., 2007; recipient Physician's Recognition award, 1978—, rsch. award Fair Oaks Hosp., 1979, bronze award Brit. Med. Assn., 1983, Outstanding Leadership award Mahoning County Mental Health Bd., 1986, Silver Rose award Assn. Italiano Donati d'Organo, Milan, 1990, Excellence award Yale U. Admissions Com., 2002, Rschr. of Yr. award Western Res. Behavioral Medicine Inst., 2006. Fellow: APA (disting. fellow 2003—11, disting. life fellow 2011—), Royal Soc. Medicine (sub-dean 2005—), Am. Coll. Clin. Pharmacology (sec.-treas. Ohio chpt. 1990—97, nat. govt. affairs com. 1990—2003, steering coun., exec. com. Ohio chpt. 1990—, pres. 1997—2004, nat. edn. com. 2003—04), N.J. Acad. Medicine, Acad. Medicine, Royal Acad. Medicine (Eng.); mem.: Pub. Diplomacy Alumni Assn., Ga. Psychiat. Assn., Acad. Clin. Psychiatry, N.Y. Acad. Scis., Royal Coll. Medicine, European Neurosci., Brit. Brain Soc., Soc. Neurosci., Am. Psychiat. Assn. (fellow 1989—2003, disting. fellow 2003—), Dublin C. of C., Youngstown C. of C. (vice-chmn. health com. 1986—89, chmn. 1989—96), Athletic Club (Atlanta), Atrium Club (Warren, Ohio), Yale Club (Cleve., Pitts., Atlanta), Youngstown Club, Domus (London), Dublin Country Club, Swim and Racquet Club (Poland, Ohio), Morey's (New Haven), Cercola di Corso (Florence, Italy), Sigma Xi. Republican. Roman Catholic. Office: 463 Deer Creek Trail Dublin GA 31021-3248

GIANTURCO, DELIO EMANUELE, management consultant, educator, author; b. Washington, Sept. 28, 1940; s. Elio and Valentine (McGillycuddy) G.; m. Mary Elizabeth Jordan, Jan. 31, 1961; children: Lisa, Grace, Mark. BS in Fgn. Trade, Georgetown U., Washington, DC, 1963; MA, George Wash. U., Washington, DC, 1967. Staff asst. to Robert J. Corbett of Pa. US House of Representatives, Washington, 1960-62, legis. asst. to Robert L.F. Sikes of Fla., 1962-63; sr. v.p. guarantees, ins. and exporter credits, treas., comptroller, exec. v.p., vice chmn., 1st v.p., dir. Export-Import Bank, Washington, 1963-77; pres. First Washington Assocs., 1978—2005. Dir. Fgn. Credit Ins. Assn., N.Y.C., 1971-76; adj. prof. George Mason U., 1995—. Recipient Disting. Faculty award, 2008.

GIARDINO, ANGELO PETER, pediatrician, director; m. Eileen Giardino. MD, U. Pa., Phila., 1987; PhD, U. of Pa. Grad. Sch. of Edn., 1999. Lic. pediatrician Am. Bd. Pediat., 1991, dr. Pa., 1993, Tex., 2005, cert. patient safety officer Quality Colloquium, 2007, physician exec. Certifying Commn. Med. Mgmt., 2007. Assoc. physician, med. dir. cmty. edn. dept., chair quality improvement com. Children's Hosp. Phila., 1993—2002; v.p. clin. affairs St. Christopher's Hosp. Children, Phila., 2002—05; med. dir., chair med. adv. com. Tex. Children's Health Plan, Inc., Houston, 2005—; clin. assoc. physician Baylor Coll. Medicine, Houston, 2005—; attending physician Child Protection Team, Tex. Children's Hosp., Houston, 2005—. Lectr. U. Tex. Sch. Nursing, Houston, 2006—. Author: (book) Helping Children Affected by Abuse: A Parent's and Teacher's Handbook for Increasing Awareness; editor: (books) Child Safety: A Pediatric Guide for Parents, Teachers, Nurses, and Caregivers, Intimate Partner Violence/Domestic Violence, to profl. jours. articles. Bd. mem. US Conf. Cath. Bishops' Nat. Rev. Bd. for Protection of Children, DC, 2004; bd. dirs. Justice for Children, Houston, 2005. Recipient Ronald Reagan award, Nat. Rep. Caucus, 2005, Disting. Child Adv. award, Support Ctr. Child Advocates, 2005, Physician's Recognition award, AMA, 2006—08. Mem.: Am. Coll. Med. Quality, Am. Coll. Physician Execs., Ambulatory Pediatric Assn., Am. Acad. Pediat., Suspected Child Abuse and Neglect, Inst. Safe Families. Office: Tex Children's Health Plan Inc 2450 Holcombe Blvd Ste 34L Houston TX 77021 Home Fax: 832-825-8765. Business E-Mail: apgiardi@texaschildrens.org.

GIBALA, RONALD, metallurgical engineering educator; b. New Castle, Pa., Oct. 3, 1938; s. Steve Anthony and June Rose (Frank) G.; m. Janice Claire Grichor; children: Maryellen, Janice, David, Kristine. BS, Carnegie Inst. Tech., 1960; MS, U. Ill., 1962, PhD, 1964. Engring. technician Crane Co., New Castle, Pa., 1956-59; engr. U.S. Steel Rsch. Labs., Monroeville, Pa., 1960; rsch. asst. U. Ill., Urbana, 1960-64; asst. prof. metallurgy Case Western Res. U., Cleve., 1964-69, assoc. prof., 1969-76, prof. metallurgy and materials sci. and macromolecular sci., 1976-84, co-dir. materials rsch. lab., 1981-84; dir. metallurgy program NSF, 1982-83; prof., chmn. dept. materials sci. and engring. U. Mich., Ann Arbor, 1984-94, L.H. and F.E. Van Vlack prof. materials sci. and engring., 1998—2004, L.H. and F.E. Van Vlack prof. emeritus, 2004—, interim dean Coll. Engring., 2005—06. Dir. electron microbeam analysis lab. U. Mich., Ann Arbor, 2002—04. Contbr. articles to profl. jours.; editor: Hydrogen Embrittlement and Stress Corrosion Cracking, 1984. Pres. Woodhaven Hills Homeowners Assn., 1989—91. Recipient Alfred Noble prize ASCE, 1969, NASA Materials Sci. Divsn. Paper award, 1992; Tech. Achievement award Cleve. Tech. Socs. Council, 1972; vis. research fellow C.E.N.G. Labs., Grenoble, 1973-74; Matthias fellow Los Alamos Nat. Lab., 1991-92, Disting. Merit award U. Ill., 1998; vis. scientist Sandia Nat. Labs., 1998-99. Fellow: TMS (life; bd. dirs. 1981—87), Am. Soc. Metals Internat. (life; chpt. chmn. 1975—76, Outstanding Young Mem. Cleve. chpt. 1971, Albert Sauveur Achievement award 2010); mem.: AAAS, Materials Rsch. Soc. (councillor 1995—97, v.p. 1998, pres. 1999, exec. com. 1995—97, Woody award 2007), Suburban Ski (pres. 1981—82), Alpha Sigma Mu, Tau Beta Pi, Sigma Xi. Democrat. Home: 3450 Lantern Bay Dr Jupiter FL 33477 Office: U Mich Dept Materials Sci Engring Ann Arbor MI 48109-2136 Business E-Mail: rgibala@umich.edu.

GIBBONS, BRENDAN M., apparel executive; Various positions, gen. corp. & securities matters Ropes & Gray LLP; joined Carters, Inc., 2004, v.p., 2008; gen. counsel, sec. Carter's, Inc., 2008—, sr. v.p., corp. affairs, 2009—. Office: Carters Inc 1170 Peachtree St NE Ste 900 Atlanta GA 30309 Office Phone: 404-745-2700. Office Fax: 404-892-0968. Business E-Mail: brendan.gibbons@carters.com.

GIBBONS, JOSEPH A., state legislator; b. NYC, Sept. 23, 1948; m. Ava Parker; children: Avis Williams, Joseph Jr., Stacey Simmons, Charles. BA in Gen. Studies, Calvin Coll., Grand Rapids, Mich.; MPA, John Jay Coll. Criminal Justice, NYC. Pres. Magnetic Imaging Supplies, Inc., Gibbons Consulting Group, Inc.; commr. City of Hallandale Beach, Fla., 2003—06; mem. Dist. 105 Fla. House of Reps., Tallahassee, 2006—, ranking mem. energy and utilities policy com., mem. joint legis. budget commn., select com. on Seminole Indian compact rev., transp. and econ. devel. appropriations com. Mem. Broward County Planning Coun., Fla., 2004—06, Broward County Sch. Bd. WMBE Adv. Coun., Fla.; vice chair, diversity com. Broward League of Cities, Fla. Mem.: Pembroke Pines C. of C., Hollywood C. of C. Democrat. African Methodist Episcopal. Office: Pembroke Pk Town Hall 3150 SW 52nd Ave Ste 203 Hollywood FL 33023-5413 also: 1003 The Capitol 402 S Monroe St Tallahassee FL 32399-1300 Office Phone: 954-893-5006, 850-488-0145.

GIBBONS, JUDITH A., librarian; b. Phila., Nov. 9, 1951; d. John J. and Margaret G. Gibbons; m. Harold M. Staton. BA, Pa. State U., 1972; MS in Libr. Sci., U. Ky., Lexington, 1978; MPA, Ky. State U., Frankfort, 1994. Cert. libr. Ky. Ref. asst. Lexington Pub. Libr., 1977—78, asst. br. mgr., 1978—80, head children's dept., 1980—84; dir. Woodford County Libr., Versailles, Ky., 1984—98; dir. field svcs. divsn. Ky. Dept. Librs. & Archives, Frankfort, 1998—. Adj. faculty U. Ky. Sch. Libr. & Info. Sci., Lexington, 1993—98; mem. State Archives & Records Commn., Frankfort, 1987, State Bd. Cert. of Librs., Frankfort, 1994—98. Contbr. articles to profl. jours. Pres. Woodford County Lit. Coun., Versailles, 1988; grants chair Ky. Book Fair, Frankfort, 2000—; adv. bd. Audio Studio for Reading Impaired, Louisville, 2004—07; bd. dirs. Woodford County Cmty. Edn. Adv. Coun., Versailles, 1989—93, Woodford County C. of C., 1998. Recipient Bus. Equity award, City of Versailles, 1997, Outstanding Pub. Libr. Svc. award, City of Frankfort, 2006; named Woman of Achievement, City of Versailles, 1994. Mem.: ALA (chair pub. awareness com. 2006—), Ky. Pub. Libr. Assn. (chair 1994—95), Ky. Libr. Assn. (sec. 1997—98, James A. Nelson Advocacy award 2008), Southeastern Libr. Assn. (pres. 2004—06). Avocations: reading, hiking, bicycling, gardening. Office: Ky Dept Librs & Archives PO Box 537 300 Coffee Tree Rd Frankfort KY 40602

GIBBONS, JULIA SMITH, federal judge; d. John Floyd and Julia Jackson (Abernathy) Smith; m. William Lockhart Gibbons, Aug. 11, 1973; children: Rebecca Carey, William Lockhart Jr. BA, Vanderbilt U., 1972; JD, U. Va., 1975. Bar: Tenn. 1975. Law clk. to judge US Ct. Appeals, 1975-76; assoc. Farris, Hancock, Gilman, Branan, Lanier & Hellen, Memphis, 1976-79; legal advisor Gov. Lamar Alexander, Nashville, 1979-81; judge 15th Jud. Cir., Memphis, 1981-83, US Dist. Ct. (we. dist.) Tenn., Memphis, 1983—2002, chief judge, 1994-2000; judge US Ct. Appeals (6th cir.), Memphis, 2002—. Recipient Outstanding Judge of Yr. award, Memphis Lawyers, 1985, She Knows Where She's Going award, Girls, Inc., 1992. Master: Leo Bearman, Sr. Am. Inn of Ct.; fellow: Memphis and Shelby County Bar Found., Tenn. Bar Found., Am. Bar Found.; mem.: Ctrl. Gardens Assn., Tenn. Women's Forum, Assn. for Women Attorneys (pres. 1993, Marion Griffin-Frances Loring award 1992), Fed. Judges Assn., Memphis Bar Assn. (Heroine for Women in Law award 2000, Outstanding Judge of Yr. award 2001), Memphis Rotary Club (Treasurer 1991—92, v.p. 1992—93, Paul Harris Fellow, president 1994—95), Phi Beta Kappa, Order of Coif. Presbyterian. Office: US Ct Appeals 970 Federal Bldg 167 N Main St Memphis TN 38103-1816

GIBBONS, LEEZA KIM, television and radio talk show host, writer, journalist; b. Hartsville, SC, Mar. 26, 1957; d. Carlos and Jean Gibbons; m. John Hicks, 1980 (div. 1982); m. Chris Quinten, 1988 (div. 1990); 1 child, Lexi; m. Stephen Meadows, 1991 (dissolved 2005); children: Troy, Nathan; m. Steven Fenton, 2011. Student, U. S.C. Co-host PM Magazine, Beaumont, Tex.; with WFAA-TV Channel 8; co-host Entertainment Tonight, Hollywood, Calif., 1984—2007, John and Leeza, Hollywood, 1993; CEO Leeza Gibbons Enterprises, 1994—; host Leeza, 1994—2000, exec. prodr., 1998—99; host Leeza Live, Blockbuster Top 25 Countdown with Leeza Gibbons, then renamed Hollywood Confidential in 2001, 1995—; co-host, TV new magazine America Now, 2011—; co-host, TV weekly TV news show My Generation, 2011—. Bd. mem. Calif. Stem Cell Research Agy. (CIRM), 2007—; creator Sheer Cover make-up line, HSN: Leeza Gibbons Celebrity Beauty. Host Miss Universe Pageant, The Hollywood Christmas Parade; host, co-prodr. (series) Growing Up Together; film appearances include Maxie, 1985, Robocop, 1987, Robocop 2, 1990, Soapdish, 1991, The Player, 1992, Last Action Hero, 1993, Man of the Year, 2002; performer Dancing with the Stars, 2007; guest host Larry King Live, 2000-05, Who Wants to Be a Millionaire, 2008; guest appearances Murphy Brown, 1990, 1996, Veronica's Closet, 1997, Home Improvement, 1999, The Simpsons, 2000, The Geena Davis Show, 2000, Just Shoot Me!, 2002, Six Feet Under, 2002, The Simple Life, 2004, and several others; co-author Take Your Oxygen First: Protecting Your Health and Happiness While Caring for a Loved One with Memory Loss, 2009, Alzheimer's For Dummies, 2011; author Scrapbooking Traditions, Take 2: Your Guide to Creating Happy Endings and New Beginnings, 2013 Creator Leeza Gibbons Memory Foundation, 2002—, Leeza's Place, 2003—, Leeza's Care Connection, 2003—. Recipient Alfred Mann Found. for Scientific Research Artistic and Philanthropic Visionary award, 2009. Office: Leeza Gibbons Memory Foundation 9000 Sheridan St Ste 162 Pembroke Pines FL 33024

GIBBS, JAMES ALANSON, geologist; b. Wichita Falls, Tex., June 18, 1935; s. James Ford and Clovis (Robinson) Gibbs; m. Judith Walker, June 18, 1966; children: Ford W., John A. BS, U. Okla., 1957, MS, 1962. Lic. geoscientist Tex. Geologist Calif. Co., New Orleans, 1961-63, Lafayette, La., 1963-64; cons. geologist, oil prodr. Dallas, 1964—. Chmn. Five States Energy Co., 1984—. Author: Finding Work as a Petroleum Geologist: Hints to the Jobseeker, 1984,

Becoming an Independent Geologist: Thriving in Good Times and Bad, 1999. Trustee Inst. Study Earth and Man, So. Meth. U. Lt. USNR, 1957—59. Recipient Regents award, U. Okla., 1996, Michel T. Halbouty Outstanding Leadership, 2008. Mem.: AAAS, W. Tex. Geol. Soc., Houston Geol. Soc., Nat. Petroleum Coun., Ind. Petroleum Assn. Am., Am. Inst. Profl. Geologists, Geol. Soc. Am., Am. Geol. Inst. (trustee, William B. Heroy Disting. Svc. award 1994), Soc. Ind. Profl. Earth Scientists (hon.; past chmn. Dallas chpt.), Am. Assn. Petroleum Geologists (hon.; sec. 1983—85, pres. 1990—91, found. trustee 1998—, chmn., Disting. Svc. award 1987), Dallas Geol. Soc. (hon.; pres. 1975—76), Explorers Club, Dallas Petroleum Club, Dallas Country Club, Sigma Xi, Phi Delta Theta, Sigma Gamma Epsilon. Republican. Methodist. Home: 3514 Caruth Blvd Dallas TX 75225-5001 Office: 4925 Greenville Ave Ste 1220 Dallas TX 75206-4015 Office Phone: 214-363-3008. E-mail: jagibbs@fivestates.com.

GIBBS, JOE JACKSON, professional sports team executive, former professional football coach; b. Mocksville, NC, Nov. 25, 1940; m. Pat Gibbs; children: Coy, J.D. Attended, Cerritos Jr. Coll.; BS, San Diego State U., 1964, MS, 1966. Offensive line coach San Diego State U., 1964—66, Fla. State U., 1967-68, U. Southern Calif., 1969-70; running backs coach U. Ark., 1971-72, St. Louis Cardinals, 1973-77; offensive coord. Tampa Bay Buccaneers, 1978, San Diego Chargers, 1979-80; head coach Washington Redskins, 1981—92, head coach, team pres., 2004—07, spl. adv. to owner, 2008—; founder, owner Joe Gibbs Racing, 1991—. Sports commentator NBC, 1993—98. Co-author (with Jerry B. Jenkins): Joe Gibes: Fourth and One, 1992; co-author: (with Ken Abraham) Racing to Win: Establish Your Game Plan For Success, 2003. Named UPI NFL Coach of Yr., 1982, AP NFL Coach of the Yr., 1982, 1983, NFL Coach of the Yr., The Sporting News, 1982, 1983, 1991; named one of The Most Influential People in the World of Sports, Bus. Week, 2007, Redskins' Ring of Fame; named to Pro Football Hall of Fame, 1996. Achievements include being a member of Super Bowl Championship winning Washington Redskins, 1983, 1988, 1992; winning three NASCAR Championships, 2000, 2002, 2005. Office: Joe Gibbs Racing 13415 Reese Blvd W Huntersville NC 28078-7933 Office Phone: 704-944-5000.

GIBBS, RICHARD A., genetics educator, director; BSc with honors, U. Melbourne, 1979, PhD in Genetics and Radiation Biology, 1985. Postdoctoral fellow Baylor Coll. Medicine, 1990, joined, 1991—, Wofford Cain Chair in Molecular and Human Genetics, prof., dept. molecular and human genetics, prof. programs in cell and molecular biology & translationall biology & molecular medicine, dir. Human Genome Sequencing Ctr., 1996—. Contbr. of several articles to profl. publications. Recipient Michael E. DeBakey, MD Excellence in Rsch. award, 2000; Muscular Dystrophy Assn. America Postdoctoral Fellowship, 1986, American Arthritis Found. Postdoctoral Fellowship, 1987, George R. Sampson Disting. Rsch. Fellowship, Muscular Dystrophy Assn., 1988—89. Office: Baylor College Medicine Human Genome Sequencing Ctr One Baylor Plaza MS BCM 226 Houston TX 77030 Office Phone: 713-798-6539. Office Fax: 713-798-5741. Business E-Mail: agibbs@bcm.edu.

GIBBS, ROBERT LANE, consulting firm executive, former White House press secretary; b. Auburn, Ala., Mar. 29, 1971; s. Robert Gibbs and Nancy Gobbs; m. Mary Catherine Gibbs; 1 child. BA in Polit. Sci., NC State U., 1993. Press. sec. to Rep. Bob Ethridge US House of Representatives; spokesman to Senator Fritz Hollings US Senator, 1998; spokesman Senator John Kerry's Presdl. Campaign, 2003, Americans for Jobs, Health Care and Progressive Values, 2003—04; comm. dir. Democratic Senatorial Campaign Com., Barack Obama's Senatorial Campaign, Chgo., 2004; comm. dir. for Senator Barack Obama US Senate, Washington, 2004—08; comm. dir. Senator Barack Obama's Presdl. Campaign, Chgo., 2007—08; asst. to Pres., press sec. The White House, Washington, 2009—11; polit. adv. Barack Obama's 2012 Re-Election Campaign, Washington, 2011—12; contributor NBC News, MSNBC, 2013—; co-founder Incite Agy., Washington, 2013—. Named one of The 50 Most Powerful People in DC, GQ mag., 2007. Democrat.*

GIBNEY, JOHN ADRIAN, JR., federal judge; b. Coatesville, Pa., Oct. 27, 1951; BA in English, Coll. William & Mary, Williamsburg, Va., 1973; JD, U. Va. Sch. Law, 1976. Bar: Va. 1976, US Dist. Ct. (ea. and we. dist.) Va. 1976, US Ct. Appeals (4th cir.) 1980, US Supreme Ct. Law clk. to Justice Harry L. Carrico Supreme Ct. Va., 1976—78; assoc. Bell, Lacy & Baliles, Richmond, Va., 1978—82; asst. atty. gen. Commonwealth of Va., Richmond, 1982—84; assoc. Lacy & Mehfoud PC, Richmond, 1984—87; shareholder, ptnr. Shuford, Rubin & Gibney PC, Richmond, 1987—2003, ThompsonMcMullan PC, Richmond, 2003—10; judge US Dist. Ct. (eastern dist.) Va., Richmond, 2010—. Mem. Chesterfield County Health Care Commn., 2001—; apptd. Va. Mandatory Continuing Legal Edn. Bd. (MCLE), 2009—; bd. dirs. Lawyers Helping Lawyers. Named a Va. Super Lawyer, 2010. Mem.: ABA, Chesterfield Bar Assn., Richmond Bar Assn., Va. Trial Lawyers Assn., Va. Bar Assn., Va. State Bar. Office: Spottswood W Robinson III & Robert R Merhige Jr Fed Courthouse 701 E Broad St Richmond VA 23219 also: Albert V Bryan US Courthouse 401 Courthouse Sq Alexandria VA 22314

GIBSON, AUDREY L., state legislator; b. Jacksonville, Fla., Mar. 15, 1946; 3 children. AA, Fla. CC, Jacksonville, 1976; BS in Criminology, Fla. State U., Tallahassee, 1978. Congl. dist. adminstr. Juvenile Justice Comprehensive Strategy, 1992—98, bd. mem., 1998—99; pub. rels. & legal liaison; mem. Dist. 15 Fla. House of Reps., Tallahassee, 2002—10, Dem. co-floor leader, 2004—06, Dem. floor leader, 2006—08; mem. Dist. 1 Fla. State Senate, 2011—. Bd. dirs. Jax Pride, Northwest Jacksonville Cmty. Devel. Corp.; sec. The Links, Inc., Jacksonville; mem. Jacksonville Cmty. Coun., Dem. Exec. Com., Citizens for Tree Protection, First Coast African Am. C. of C., Manufacturers North Cmty. Adv. Panel. Mem.: Delta Sigma Theta. Democrat. Office: 101 E Union St Ste 104 Jacksonville FL 32202 also: Fla State Senate 226 Senate Office Bldg 404 S Monroe St Tallahassee FL 32399-1100 Office Phone: 904-359-2553, 850-487-5024. Business E-Mail: gibson.audrey.web@flsenate.gov.

GIBSON, CARROLL, state legislator; b. May 26, 1945; BS, Western Ky. U. Mem. State Senate, Ky., Appropriations & Revenue Com., Judiciary Com., State & Local Govt. Com., Vets. Com., Mil. Affairs & Pub. Safety Com.; ret. clk. Grayson County Cir. Ct.; majority whip. Mem.: Grayson County C. of C. Republican. Baptist. Address: PO Box 506 Leitchfield KY 42755 Office: 702 Capitol Ave Annex Rm 242 Frankfort KY 40601 Home Phone: 270-230-5866; Office Phone: 502-564-8100 ext 624, 502-564-2450.

GIBSON, CYNTHIA L., lawyer, multimedia company executive; b. 1964; BA in History with honors, Wake Forest U., 1986; JD, U. Va. Sch. Law, 1989. Cert. sr. profl. human resources, Human Resource Certification Inst., 2006. Ptnr. Katz, Teller, Brant & Hild; sr. v.p., legal Scripps Networks Interactive, Inc., Knoxville, Tenn., 2009, exec. v.p., legal, 2009—12, chief legal officer, corporate sec., 2012—. Mem. Tocqueville Soc. of United Way; gen. counsel., sec., bd. dirs., Knoxville Area Chpt. ARC; fellow Litig. Counsel of America; bd. dirs., vice chmn., Women's Leadership Coun. United Way Worldwide; active United Way of Greater Knoxville; co-chmn. United Way of Greater Cin. Recipient Woman of Distinction award, Great Rivers Girl Scout Coun., 2005. Fellow: Litigation Counsel of America. Avocations: reading, scuba diving. Office: Scripps Networks Interactive Inc 9721 Sherrill Blvd Knoxville TN 37932 Office Phone: 865-694-2700. Office Fax: 865-985-7778. Business E-Mail: cynthia.gibson@scrippsnetworks.com.

GIBSON, EVERETT KAY, JR., space scientist, geochemist; b. Seagraves, Tex., May 13, 1940; s. Everett Kay and Lillie Gertrude (Ivey) G.; m. Mary Morgan Shott, Oct. 13, 1973; 1 son, Bradford Pierce Gibson. BS, Tex. Tech U., Lubbock, 1963, MS, 1965; PhD, Ariz. State U., 1969. Instr. Tex. Tech. U., 1963-65; postdoctoral research assoc. NASA Johnson Space Center, Houston, 1969-70, space scientist, geochemist, 1970-91; sr. scientist NASA-Johnson Space Ctr., 1991—; vis. program mgr. NSF, Washington, 1979; mission sci. advisor Apollo 14; test dir. Lunar Receiving Lab. NASA, 1971, prin. investigator Lunar Sample Analysis Program, 1971-90, mem. Lunar Sample Analysis Planning Team, 1974-77, prin. investigator Planetary Geology Program, 1978-86, prin. investigator Mars Data Analysis Program, 1979-84, prin. investigation Exobiology Program, 1983—. Mem. U.S. Antarctic Meteorite Search Team, 1979-80; adj. prof. geology U. Houston, 1975-90; sr. Leverhulme vis. fellow Open U., Milton Keynes, Eng., 1984-85; cons. The Economist (London), BBC, London; interdiscipline scientist Mars Express/Beagle 2 Mission to Mars, European Space Agy., 2001—. Assoc. editor 5th, 6th, 7th, 8th, 9th and 12th Proc. Lunar and Planetary Sci. Conf., 1974-81; assoc. editor: Chondrules and Their Origins, 1983; contbr. articles to sci. jours. Bd. dirs. Clear Creek Basin Authority, Harris County, Tex., 1974-75; col. Commemorative Air Force, 1983—, life mem., 1987, aircraft sponsor, 1988, exec. officer, 1990-2002; exec. bd. Wings Over Houston Air Show, 1990—. Recipient Laurel Space award Aviation Week and Space Tech., 1972, 97, award for lunar sci. team participation NASA Johnson Space Ctr., 1974, Disting. Achievement award Ariz. State U., 1980, Silver Magnolia award Commemorative Air Force, 1993, 99, Manned Flight Awareness award, 1993, Exceptional Sci. Achievement medal NASA, 1997, Ariz. State U. Hall of Fame award, 1998, Scientist of Yr. award Tex. Acad. of Sci., 2000; Papadopoulos fellow in biology Kinkaid Sch., 2006. Fellow Meteoritical Soc. (sec. 1974-80, councilor 1987-90); mem. Am. Chem. Soc., Internat. Soc. for Study of Origin of Life, AAAS, Am. Geophys. Union, Sigma Xi, Phi Lambda Upsilon. Baptist. Home: 1015 Trowbridge Dr Houston TX 77062-2726 Office: NOW KR Astromaterials Rsch Office NASA Johnson Space Ctr 2101 NASA Rd 1 Houston TX 77058 Personal E-mail: ekgmars@aol.com.

GIBSON, HERMAN, humanities educator, department chairman; b. Natchez, Miss., July 17, 1952; s. Herman Gibson, Jr.; m. Claire Gibson, May 30, 1992; 1 child, Allison Leigh Andrepont. BA in Sociology, La. Tech U., Ruston, 1974; MA in Cultural Anthropology, La. State U., Baton Rouge, 1976; PhD in Sociology, La. State U., 1979. Asst. prof. Drury U., Springfield, Mo., 1979—86; prof., dept. chair Wiley Coll., Marshall, Tex., 1992—95, Henderson State U., Arkadelphia, Ark., 1995—. Contbr. articles to profl. jours. Mem. Oxfam Am. Mem.: Ark. Sociol. and Anthrop. Assn., Midsouth Sociol. Assn. (exec. coun. 2005—07). Methodist. Home: 1050 Caddo St Arkadelphia AR 71923 Office: Henderson State Univ 1100 Henderson St Arkadelphia AR 71999 Business E-Mail: gibsonh@hsu.edu.

GIBSON, JOHN W., gas industry executive; b. Kansas City, Kans. B in engring., Univ. Mo. Refinery engr. Exxon Co. USA; engring. mgmt. positions through exec. v.p. mktg. GPM Gas Corp. Phillips Petroleum Co., 1974—95; exec. v.p. Koch Energy Inc., 1995—2000; pres., COO ONEOK Partners, LP, Tulsa, Okla., 2000—07, pres., CEO, 2007—; CEO ONEOK, Inc., Tulsa, Okla., 2007—09, pres., CEO, 2010—11, vice chmn., 2011, chmn., pres., CEO, 2011—. Bd. mem. Assn. Tex. Intrastate Gas Pipelines, Gas Industry Standards Bd., Interstate Natural Gas Assn. Am. Office: ONEOK Inc 100 W Fifth St Tulsa OK 74103

GIBSON, PRYOR ALLEN, III, former state legislator; b. Forsyth Co., NC, Oct. 12, 1957; s. Pryor and Mary (Pharr) Gibson; m. Barbara Gibson; 1 child. Attended, North Carolina State U.; BS, U. North Carolina, Wilmington, 1978. Precinct chmn., 1980—86; mem., state exec com., 1984—88; treas., Dist. 8, 1985—86; co. party chmn., 1986—88; former vice chmn., commerce com.; former vice chmn. Dist. 33, 1999—2002; mem. NC House of Representatives, 1988—90, mem. Dist. 69, 1990—2011; pres. PEE DEE Co., 1980—; mgr. Myrick Constrn. Inc., 1986—88, exec. dir. Recipient Outstanding Young Man of America, Lions Intetnat., 1987. Mem.: Lions Internat. (dep. dist. gov. 1986, zone chmn. 1985), Rotary Club, Southern Ind. Developers Coun., NC Gen. Contractors. Democrat. Presbyterian. Address: PO Drawer A Troy NC 27371 Home: 1724 Wysong Ct Raleigh NC 27612-6443 Office Phone: 919-715-3007. Business E-Mail: Pryor.Gibson@ncleg.net.

GIBSON, THOMAS JAMES, professional society executive, former naval architect; b. Newark, Apr. 11, 1957; s. Thomas James and Frances Jane (Farley) G.; m. Sheila Buck, May 24, 1980; children: James Farley, Carolyn McCauley. BS in Naval Architecture, US Naval Acad., 1979; M in Marine Affairs, U. RI, 1989. Cmmd. ensign USN, 1979, advanced through grades to lt., 1983, resigned, 1985, sailing instr. Annapolis, Md., 1979-80; missile officer USS Biddle, Norfolk, Va., 1980-82; exec. officer USS Affray, Newport, RI, 1982-84; instr. Surface Warfare Officer Sch., Newport, RI, 1984-85; naval architect Raytheon Co., Portsmouth, RI, 1985-87, mgr. antisubmarine warfare program, 1988—90; Congl. liaison specialist EPA, 1990—92, from assoc. adminstr. office policy econ. and innovation to chief of staff, 2001—04; regulatory and legis. affairs advisor Don Clay Associates, Inc., 1993—95; majority dep. staff dir. and counsel US Senate Com. on environ. and Pub. Works, Washington, 1995—2001; sr. v.p. govt. affairs Portland Cement Assn.; sr. v.p. advocacy Am. Chemistry Coun.; pres. CEO Am. Iron and Steel Inst., 2010—. Active Newport Hist. Soc., 1986, Save the Bay, Providence, 1986, City Planning Bd., Newport, 1986, Aquidneck Island Planning Com., Newport, 1987. Lt. comdr. USNR, 1989—. Mem. USN Inst., Soc. Naval Architects and Marine Engrs., U.S. Naval Acad. Alumni Assn. (v.p. Newport chpt. 1985—). Roman Catholic. Avocations: reading, sailing, bicycling, restoring old homes. Office: Am Iron and Steel Inst 25 Massachusetts Ave NW Ste 800 Washington DC 20001-7406 Office Phone: 202-452-7100.

GIDCOMB, BARRY DOYLE, history professor; b. Nashville, Sept. 27, 1956; s. Byron Doyle Gidcomb and Mary Frances Maxwell; m. Debra Lynn Martin, June 3, 1983; 1 child, Matthew Martin. AS, Columbia State Cmty. Coll., Columbia, Tenn., 1978; BS, Mid. Tenn. State U., Murfreesboro, 1981; MA, Mid. Tenn. State U., 1985; ArtsD in History, Ill. State U., Normal, 2000. Evening coord. Columbia State Cmty. Coll., 1985—92, prof. history, 1992—. Recipient Faculty Appreciation award, Gamma Beta Phi, 1994—95, Disting. Faculty award, Columbia State Cmty. Coll., 2003—04, Pres. medal, 2003—04, Advisor Paragon award, Phi Theta Kappa, 2006. Mem.: Columbia State Faculty Senate (pres. 2008—), Beta Kappa Theta (faculty sponsor 2002—09). D-Liberal. Methodist. Office: Columbia State Cmty Coll 1665 Hampshire Pike Columbia TN 38401 Office Fax: 931-540-2796. Business E-Mail: gidcomb@columbiastate.edu.

GIDDENS, DON PEYTON, engineering educator, researcher; b. Augusta, Ga., Oct. 24, 1940; m. Karin Baldzer; 1 child, Eric. BS in Aerospace Engring., Ga. Inst. Tech., 1963, MS in Aerospace Engring., 1965, PhD in Aerothermodynamics, 1967. Assoc. aircraft engr. Lockheed-Ga. Co., Atlanta, 1963; mem. tech. staff Aerospace Corp., San Bernardino, Calif., 1966-67; asst. prof. Ga. Inst. Tech., Atlanta, 1968-70, assoc. prof., 1970-77, prof., 1977-82, regents prof., 1982-92, chair dept. aerospace engring., 1988-92, dean Coll. Engring., 2002—; eminent scholar Ga. Rsch. Alliance; co-dir. Biomedical Tech. Rsch. Ctr. Ga. Inst. Tech./Emory U., Atlanta, 1987—92, prof., chair Wallace H. Coulter Dept. Biomedical Engring., 1997—2002, now Lawrence L. Gellerstedt Jr. Chair in Bioengineering; dean Whiting Sch. Engring. Johns Hopkins U., Balt., 1992-97. Contbr. articles to profl. jours. Fellow: Am. Heart Assn. Arteriosclerosis, Thrombosis and Vascular Biology Coun., Am. Inst. Med. and Biol. Engineers (founding fellow, pres. 2004—), ASME; mem.: NAE. Avocation: whitewater canoeing. Office: Ga Inst Tech Coll Engring Adminstrn Bldg 225 North Ave NW Atlanta GA 30332-0360

GIDDINGS, HELEN, state legislator; m. Donald Giddings. D (hon.), Paul Quinn Coll., Dallas. Founder, pres. Multiplex, Inc.; mem. Dist. 109 Tex. House of Representatives, 1993—. Recipient of several awards and honors. Democrat. Office: 1510 N Hampton Rd 340 Desoto TX 75115 also: Room CAP 1N.05 PO Box 2910 Austin TX 78768 Office Phone: 942-224-6795, 512-463-0953.

GIDDIS, KEVIN H., investment company executive; Grad., U. So. Miss. Head taxable fixed trading Prin. Fin. Securities, Dallas; head Retail Fixed Income Trading Desk Morgan Keegan & Co., Inc., Memphis, 1998, dead fixed income sales, trading and rsch., 2008—10, pres. Fixed Income Capital Markets Divsn., 2010—, mem. Fixed Income Exec. Com. & Credit Com., mem. Pvt. Client Group's Bus. Leadership Team. Fin. chmn. Collierville United Methodist Ch. Office: Morgan Keegan Morgan Keegan Tower 50 N Front St Memphis TN 38103 Office Phone: 901-524-4100. Office Fax: 901-524-4197.

GIDEL, ROBERT HUGH, real estate investor; b. Ft. Dodge, Iowa, Sept. 19, 1951; s. Wayne D. and Mary A. (Ziegler) G.; m. Linda Carol Lombardo, Oct. 23, 1976; children: Jill, Allison, Robert. BSBA, U. Fla., 1973. Comml. loan officer Century Bank, St. Petersburg, Fla., 1975-77; asst. v.p. N.Y. Life, Washington, 1977-81; exec. v.p. Heller Real Estate Fin. Co., Chgo., 1981-86; pres., mng. dir., bd dirs. Alex Brown Realty Advisors, Balt., 1986-90; mng. dir., bd. dirs. Alex Brown Kleinwort Benson Realty Advisors, Balt., 1990-93; pres., bd. dirs. Brazos Ptnrs. L.P., Dallas, 1993-99; mng. ptnr. Liberty Ptnrs., Orlando, Fla., 1999—2005, also bd. dirs.; chmn. bd. LNR Property Holdings, 2005—07; pres., CEO, bd. dirs. Ginn Co. LLC, 2007—09; chmn., mem., investment adv. coun. State Bd. Adminstrn., Fla., 2009—13; bd. birs. Nationstar Mortgage, 2012—. Pres., COO, bd. dirs. ParagonGroup Inc., 1996-97; CEO, bd. dirs. Meridian Realty Trust VIII, 1997-98; bd. dirs. Fortress Registered Investment Trust, Developers Diversified Realty Corp., Lone Star Opportunity Fund I, II, III, IV, and V, Brazos Fund, 1996-05, Global Signal Inc., U.S. Restaurant Properties, 2001-05, U. Fla. Investment Co., 2010-, Workforce Fla., 2011-, James Madison Inst., 2011-; exec. com. U. Fla. Ctr. Real Estate Studies; mem. bd. dirs. U. Fla. Investment Corp., 2011-. Contbr. articles to profl. publs. Chmn., Bd. trustees Fla. Poly. U., 2012—; bd. dirs. exec. com. Gator Boosters U. Fla. Found., exec. com. bd. dirs., 2009—, pres.; bd. trustees Chayman Fla. Poly. U. Fellow Homer Hoyt Inst. Mem. Nat. Coun. Real Estate Investment Fiduciaries, Pension Real Estate Assn., Assn. Fgn. Investors in Real Estate, Nat. Assn. Real Estate Investment Trusts, Golden Bear Club. Republican. Office: Liberty Capital Advisors 7380 Sand Lake Rd Ste 500 Orlando FL 32819 Home: 9327 Dole Cir Windermere FL 34786-5629 Personal E-mail: RGidel@aol.com. Business E-Mail: rgidel@libertypartnersllc.com.

GIDEON, SHARON LEE, secondary school educator; b. Roswell, N.Mex., Mar. 24, 1955; d. Talmage Dever and Maggie Lee (Payton) Dever Franklin. BA, Baylor U., 1977; MLA, So. Meth. U., 1985. Cert. tchr., Tex. Tchr. Sulphur Springs (Tex.) Ind. Sch. Dist., 1977-80, Klein Ind. Sch. Dist., Spring, Tex., 1980-82, Plano (Tex.) Ind. Sch. Dist., 1982—, So. Meth. U., 2001—02. Author: History and Relationship to it Environment; editor Southwest Who's Who of Professional Wrestling, 2005— Named Notable Woman of Tex., 1984-85, Womwn of Yr., Am. Biographical Inst., 2009, Outstanding Am. Tchr., 2005-6. Mem. NEA, Tex. State Tchrs. Assn. (bd. regions 1991-94), Plano Edn. Assn. (area rep. coord. 1990, 2002-03, chmn. external comm. 1989, pres. 1991-94, 98-99, chair 2002-03), Classical Assn. Mid. and S.Am., Tex. Jr. Classical League, Tex. Fgn. Lang. Assn., Order Ea. Star. Republican. Unity. Home: 1501 Rockshire Dr Plano TX 75074-4007 Office: Plano E Senior HS 3000 Las Rias Blvd Plano TX 75074

GIDLEY, JODI, gas industry executive; b. Wash., Pa. BS in Math., U. Pitts.; MME, Old Dominion U. V.p., Gas Ops. and Capacity Planning AGL Resources, Inc., 2004—07, sr. v.p., MidAtlantic Ops., pres., Elizabethtown Gas, Elkton Gas, & Va. Natural Gas, 2007—; v.p., ops., dir., fin. planning and budgets Virginia Natural Gas, 2004, pres., 2007—, Elkton Gas, Md., 2007—, Elizabethtown Gas, NJ, 2007—. Bd. dirs. Bus. Consortium for Arts Support, Hampton Roads C. of C., Old Dominion U. Ednl. Found., Va. Early Childhood Found. Office: AGL Resources Inc 10 Peachtree Pl NE Atlanta GA 30309 Office Phone: 404-584-4000. Office Fax: 404-584-3714. Business E-Mail: JGidley@aglresources.com.

GIDZENKO, YURI PAVLOVICH, astronaut; b. Elanets, Russia, Mar. 26, 1962; m. Olga Vladimirovna Gidzenko, 1961; children: Sergei, Alexei. Grad., Higher Mil. Pilot Sch., Kharkov, Ukraine, 1983; degree in geodesy and mapping, Moscow State U., 1994. Commd. Russian Air Force, 1983, advanced through grades to col.; test cosmonaut candidate Y.A. Gagarin Cosmonauts Tng. Ctr., Russia, 1987—89, test cosmonaut, 1989—, instr. gen. parachute tng., back-up crew comdr. 17th primary expedition/Euro-Mir-94 program, 1994, mem. crew Mir mission, 1995—96, mem. crew ISS-1, Soyuz transport vehicle comdr., 1996, mem. Soyuz transport transport vehicle/ISS/Space Shuttle, 2000—01, Taxi-3 crew comdr., 2002, dept. chief, 2003—. Named Hero of Russian Fedn. Office: NASA/Johnson Space Ctr co Astronaut Office/CB Houston TX 77058

GIERHART, WANDA MARIE, retail executive; b. 1964; BBA, U. Nebr., Lincoln, 1986. Exec. v.p., chief mktg. officer Ltd. Brands, Inc., 1999—2004; exec. v.p., chief mktg. & merchandising officer Design Within Reach, 2004—06; pres., CEO TravelSmith Outfitters, Inc., 2006—08; mgr., mktg. & circulation Neiman Marcus Direct, 1991—94; sr. v.p., chief mktg. officer Neiman Marcus Group, Inc., 2009—, Neiman Marcus Inc., 2009—. Office: Neiman Marcus Group Inc One Marcus Sq 1618 Main St Dallas TX 75201 Office Phone: 214-743-7600. Business E-Mail: wanda_gierhart@neimanmarcus.com.

GIEVERS, KAREN A., lawyer; b. Culver City, Calif., Apr. 27, 1949; d. Ernest Conrad and Josephine Theresa (Passolt) Prevost; m. Joseph R. Gievers, Nov. 16, 1968 (dec. Feb. 1987); children: Daniel Steven, Donna Ann; m. Frank J. Bach, Nov. 23, 1997. AA, Miami Dade C.C., 1974; BA, Fla. Internat. U., 1975; JD cum laude, U. Miami, 1978.

Bar: Fla. 1978, U.S. Dist. Ct. (so. dist.) Fla. 1978, U.S. Dist. Ct. (mid. and no. dist.) Fla. 1979, U.S. Ct. Appeals (5th cir.) 1979, U.S. Ct. Appeals (11th cir.) 1981, U.S. Ct. Claims 1980, U.S. Supreme Ct. 1982; cert. civil trial atty Fla. Bd. Legal Specialties, 1985, Nat. Bd. Trial Advocacy, 1992. Assoc. Sams, Anderson, Gerstein & Ward, P.A., Miami, 1978, Anderson, Moss, Russo & Gievers, P.A., Miami, 1979-83; ptnr., 1983—87; pvt. practice Karen A. Gievers, P.A., 1987—. Bd. editors: So. Dist. Digest, 1981-85. Lectr. FACT, Miami, 1984; pres. Operation SafeDrive, 1987—; mem. MADD, 1986; bd. trustees We Will Rebuild, 1992-93; candidate treas., ins. commr. State of Fla., 1994, candidate sec. state, 1998. Mem. Fla. Bar Assn. (mem. trial lawyers exec. coun. 1985-88, editor trial lawyers sect. 1984, vice-chmn. evidence com. 1985-88, chmn. 1988-89), Am. Bd. Trial Advocates (pres. elect Fla. 2002), Acad. Fla. Trial Lawyers (chmn. pub. com. 1984-86, bd. dirs. 1985-87, treas. 1988-89, sec. 1987-88, pres. elect 1989-90, pres. 1990-91, recipient Pres.'s award 1986, 90), Assn. Trial Lawyers Am., Dade County Bar Assn. (bd. dirs. 1981-84, 85-87, treas. 1987-88, sec. 1988-89, 2nd v.p. 1989-90, 1st v.p. 1990-91, pres.-elect 1991-92, pres. 1992-93), Dade County Trial Lawyers Assn. (sec. 1984, treas. 1985, pres. 1987), Fed. Bar Assn., Fla. Assn. Women Lawyers, Children's Advocacy Found. (pres., dir. 2000), Zool. Soc. Fla., Fla. Consumer Fedn. (bd. dirs. 1985-87), Lions Internat., Gray Panthers, Banker's, Gov.'s. Democrat. Office: 524 E College Ave Tallahassee FL 32301-2529

GIFFORD, CHARLES K., bank executive; b. Providence, Nov. 8, 1942; s. Clarence H. and Priscilla G.; m. Anne Gifford, Oct. 3, 1964; children: Ramsay, Charles, John, Jessica BA, Princeton U., 1964. Joined First Nat. Bank, 1966—67, loan officer, 1967—70, asst. v.p., 1970—73, v.p., 1973—78, first v.p., 1978, sr. v.p., 1979—81, exec. v.p., 1981—84, group exec., corp. banking group, 1984—87; vice chmn. Bank of Boston Corp. and First Nat. Bank of Boston (sub. of Bank of Boston), 1987—89, pres., 1989—95, chmn., CEO, 1995—99; pres., COO BankBoston and Fleet Fin. Group (merged), 1999—2001, CEO, 2001—02, chmn., 2002—04. Bd. trustees NSTAR Corp., 1999—; bd. dir. CBS Corp., 2005—. Bd. mem. Northeastern U., Boston Symphony Orchestra, WGBH Pub. Broadcasting, Jr. Achievement, Dana Farber Cancer Inst., Dana Farber/Ptnrs. Cancer Care, Greater Boston C. of C.; bd. dirs. Boston Pvt. Ind. Coun., Assn. Res. City Bankers; founding chmn. Success By 6, United Way, 1994-98; chmn. Boston Plan for Excellence in Pub. Schs. Mem. Greater Boston C. of C. (chmn.). Office: Bank of America 100 N Tryon St Charlotte NC 28255 Office Phone: 704-386-5681. Office Fax: 704-386-6699. Business E-Mail: charles.gifford@bankofamerica.com.

GIFTOS, P. MICHAEL, transportation company executive; b. 1947; married. BA, George Washington U., 1969; JD, U. Md., 1974, U. Mo., 1974. Bar: Md. 1974. Also sr. v.p. Atlantic Land and Improvement Co. Inc., Jacksonville, Fla.; sr. atty. Tex. Gas Resources, 1984-85; gen. solicitor CSX Corp., Richmond, Va., 1985-86, gen. counsel, special projects, 1986—88, v.p., law, 1988; v.p. CSX Transp., 1985—89, sr. v.p., gen. counsel rail transport group Jacksonville, Fla., 1990—2000, exec. v.p., chief comml. officer, 2000—04. Bd. dirs. Pacer Internat., Inc., 2004—, Found. Coal, 2005—09, Alpha Natural Resources, Inc., 2009—. Office: Alpha Natural Resources Inc Bd Directors 1 Alpha Place Abingdon VA 24212 Office Phone: 276-619-4410. Personal E-mail: pgiftos@alphanr.com.

GIGLI, IRMA, dermatologist, academic administrator, educator, immunologist; b. Cordoba, Argentina, Dec. 22, 1931; d. Irineo and Esperanza Francisca (Pons de Gigli) Gigli; m. Hans J. Muller-Eberhard. BA, Liceo Nacional Manuel Belgrano, Cordoba, 1950; MD, Universidad Nacional de Cordoba, 1957. Intern Cook County Hosp., Chgo., 1957—58, resident in dermatology, 1958—60; fellow in dermatology NYU, 1960—61; mem. faculty Harvard Med. Sch., 1967—75, asso. prof. dermatology, 1972—75; chief dermatology service Peter Bent Brigham Hosp., Robert B. Brigham Hosp., 1971—75; prof. dermatology and exptl. medicine N.Y. U. Med. Center, NYC, 1976—82, mem. faculty N.Y. Grad. Sch. Med. Scis., dir. Asthma and Allergic Disease Center for Immunodermatology Studies, 1980—91; prof. medicine, chief div. dermatology U. Calif.-San Diego, 1983—95; prof. medicine and dermatology U. Tex. Health Sci. Ctr., Houston, 1995—2003; assoc. dir. Inst. Molecular Medicine for Prevention Human Diseases U. Tex., Houston, 1998—2003, dep. dir., emerita, 2003—09, Walter and Mary Mischer prof. molecular medicine Houston, 1998—2009, Hous J Miller Eber Hard chair; dir. Rsch. Ctr. Immunology and Autoimmune Diseases, 1995—2009; prof. emeritus U. tex. Health Sci. Mem. Nat. Inst. of Allergy and Infectious Diseases Coun., 1978—79, bd. sci. counselors, 1997—; chmn. study sect. Allergy and Immunology Inst., NIH, 1978—83; mem. Guggenheim Found. Western Hemisphere and Phillippines Com. of Selection; adv. bd. NIH Fogarty Internat. Ctr., 1984—97. Bd. dirs. U.S. Civilian R&D Found. Recipient Rsch. award, Am. Cancer Soc., 1970—72, NIH, 1972—76, Disting. Profl. Woman of Yr. award, U. Tex. Health Sci. Ctr. at Houston, 2003, David Martin Carter Mentor award, Am. Skin Assn., 2005; grantee, Guggenheim Found., 1974—75. Mem.: Acad. Medicine, Engring. & Sci. Tex. (bd. dirs.), Am. Acad. Arts and Scis., Henry Kunkel Soc. (councilor 1999—), PEW Latin Am. Fellows Program in Biomed. Scis. (nat. adv. com. 1998—2005), Inst. Medicine/NAS, Am. Dermatol. Assn., Assn. Am. Physicians, Am. Acad. Allergy, Am. Acad. Dermatology, Am. Assn. Immunologists, Am. Soc. Clin. Investigation, Soc. Investigative Dermatology (hon.; pres. 1990—91, Stephen Rothman Meml. award 1996). Home Phone: 858-454-6396. Business E-Mail: irma.gigli@uth.tmc.edu.

GIKAS, CAROL SOMMERFELDT, museum director; b. St. Louis, Oct. 9, 1950; m. Ken Gikas. Student, U. Mo., 1968-70; BA in Studio Art, U. Ark., Little Rock, 1973; MA, U. Tex., 1977; postgrad., U. Calif., summer 1981. Asst. mus. registrar Art. Arts Ctr., Little Rock, 1972-74; assoc. curator Leeds Gallery, U. Tex., Austin, 1977-80; exec. dir. La. Art & Sci. Mus. (formerly La. Arts & Sci. Ctr.), Baton Rouge, 1980—. Mem. grants adv. panel So. Arts Fedn., 1981, Arts and Humanities Coun. Greater Baton Rouge, 1982, 83, divsn. arts La. Arts Council, 1981, 85; mem. adv. bd. USS Kidd/La. Naval Mus., Baton Rouge, 1981, 84, La. Dept. Edn., 1981; state rep. to coun. S.E. Mus. Conf., 1984, 85. Sec. Gov.'s Commn. for Anniversary La. Capitol, 1981, 82; trustee ARC, 1986—; mem. Mayor's Commn. for Bicentennial U.S. Constn. Mem. Am. Assn. Mus., Art Mus. Assn. (regional rep. 1983—), Baton Rouge C. of C. (active Goals Conf. 1984, 85, Leadership Greater Baton Rouge 1985, 86). Office: La Art & Science Mus PO Box 3373 Baton Rouge LA 70821-3373 Office Phone: 225-344-5272. Office Fax: 225-344-9477. E-mail: lasm@lasm.org.

GILBERT, C. TODD, state legislator; b. Newton, Tex., Oct. 19, 1970; Mem. Dist. 15 Va. House of Delegates, 2006—; mem. Courts of Justice Com., Edn. & Milita Police & Pub Safety Com., 2006—. Bd. dir. Shenandoah County Free Clinic; mem. First Baptist Church Woodstock. Mem.: Va. State Bar Assn., Shenandoah County Bar Assn., Page Valley Sportsmen's Club. Republican. Office: PO Box 309 Woodstock VA 22664 Office Phone: 540-459-7550. Office Fax: 540-459-7004. Business E-Mail: DelTGilbert@house.virginia.gov.

GILBERT, FREDERICK E., development planner, Africanist, consultant; b. Mpls., May 28, 1939; s. Eugene Lester and Anne Cecelia (Omlie) G.; m. Jane Arey, June 30, 1962; children: Erik O., Christopher A., Peter A. BA, U. Minn., 1961; MALD, Tufts U., 1963, PhD, 1976. Desk officer for Niger, Upper Volta, Cote d'Ivoire, Dahomey and Togo U.S. AID, Washington, 1974-76, asst. dir. Yaounde, Cameroon, 1976-80, chief Africa econ. policy and analysis Washington, 1980-81, dir. Sahel and West Africa, 1981-83, prin. officer Dar es Salaam, Tanzania, 1983-86, dep. mission dir. Khartoum, Sudan, 1986-88, mission dir., 1988-90, regional dir. Abidjan, Cote d'Ivoire, 1990-93; ind. cons., 1994-97; dir. Famine Early Warning Sys., 1998-2000; ind. cons. Falls Church, Va., 2000—. Bd. dirs. Am. Friends Episcopal Ch. Sudan, 2005—. Mem. ACLU, Am. Fgn. Svc. Assn., Amnesty Internat., World Resources Inst. (policy consultative group on natural resources mgmt. for Africa 1994-97). Episcopalian. Avocations: skiing, tennis, bicycling.

GILBERT, H. STEVEN, engineering and construction management company executive; B in Chem. Engring., Case Western Res. U., Cleve. With Fluor Corp., 1970—, various project mgmt. and gen. mgmt. positions including head telecom. bus. line and head fed. projects. bus. line, office mgr. Irvine, Calif., Houston, Calgary, Alta., Greenville, SC, Chgo., Phila., sr. v.p. bus. and work process integration, sr. v.p. human resources and adminstrn. Office: Fluor Corp 6700 Las Colinas Blvd Irving TX 75039 Office Phone: 469-398-7000. Office Fax: 469-398-7255.

GILBERT, JAMES EASTHAM, academic administrator; b. Bridgeport, Conn., July 1, 1929; s. Carl Ludwig and Anna Maude (Eastham) G.; m. Betty Lee Blankenship, Aug. 26, 1953; 1 child, Gregory Eastham. BS in Psychology, U. N.Mex., Albuquerque, 1954; MA in Psychology, Am. U., Washington, 1962, PhD in Psychology, 1969. Mem. USNR, 1948—60, 1996—2008; interviewer Va. State Employment Service, Alexandria, 1952-53; tng. officer Nat. Security Agy., Washington, 1953-55, rsch. psychologist Ft. Meade, Md., 1957-64, Hdqrs., Sec. to Air Staff, USAF, Washington, 1955-57; assoc. dean adminstrn. Northeastern U., Boston, 1964-71; assoc. vice-chancellor Ind. U.-Purdue U., Ft. Wayne, 1971-78; v.p. acad. affairs Pittsburg (Kans.) State U., 1978-86, interim pres., 1983; pres. East Stroudsburg (Pa.) U., 1986-96, pres. emeritus. Vol. Office Academic Affairs Med. Univ. SC, 1996—2008. Mem. Sigma Xi, Psi Chi, Phi Kappa Phi, Omicron Delta Kappa. Democrat. Home: 1955 Heidelberg Dr Mount Pleasant SC 29464-3966 Personal E-mail: ki4uis@gmail.com.

GILBERT, JILL BARSON, management consultant; b. Syracuse, NY, 1954; d. Zelmar and Thelma Simon Barson; m. Jeffrey S. Gilbert, 1986. MS in Environ. Mgmt., U. San Francisco, 1980; AB in Zoology, Miami U., Oxford, Ohio, 1976; certificate Rice Program for Managers, Rice U., Houston, 2001. Qualified environ. profl. Environ. specialist Diamond Shamrock Corp., Pasadena, Tex., 1977—84; sr. advisor Pilko & Assoc., Inc., Houston, 1984—95; dir. product mgmt. Oracle Corp., 1996—98; dir., corp. strategy and comm. T3, Inc., 1998—2002; pres., CEO Lexicon Systems, LLC, 2002—. Thought leader, environment, health and safety, mgmt. info. sys.; trusted advisor. Author over 150 publs.; columnist IT Insight Column, EM Mag. Troop leader San Jacinto Girl Scouts. Fellow: Air & Waste Mgmt. Assn. (chair gulf coast chpt. 1989—90, chair SW sect. 1994—95, bd. dirs. 1995—98, v.p. 1997—98, charter mem., chair info. solutions com. 2000—04, editl. adv. com. 2002—08, vice chair editl. adv. com. 2007—08, IT Task Force mem.). Avocations: golf, gourmet cooking, yoga. Office: Lexicon Systems LLC PO Box 890433 Houston TX 77289-0433 Office Phone: 281-280-8106. Business E-Mail: jbgilbert@lexicon-systems.com.

GILBERT, LEONARD HAROLD, lawyer; b. Hutchinson, Minn., Apr. 3, 1936; s. Sidney and Clara (Franzblau) Gilbert; m. Jean Buchman, Apr. 21, 1963; children: Jonathan Stuart, Suzanne Elaine. BA, Emory U., 1958; LLB, Harvard U., 1961. Atty. Carlton Fields, Tampa, Fla., 1961—98, Holland & Knight LLP, Tampa, 1999—. Bd. dirs. Gasparilla Sidewalk Art Festival, Tampa, 1970—74, United Way; trustee Tampa Bay Performing Arts Ctr., Lowry Park Zool. Soc., Univ. Cmty. Hosp.; chmn. Art Coun. Tampa, 1973—74; mem. Hillsborough County Bicentennial Commn., Fla., 1973—76, Tampa Charter Revision Com., 1975; pres. Tampa Mus. Art, 1986—87; chmn. bd. fellows U. Tampa, 1986—87, trustee, 1987—2000. With USCGR, 1961—69. Recipient Douglas P. McClurg Professionalism award, Tampa Bay Bankruptcy Bar Assn., 2006, Outstanding Past Local Bar Pres.'s award, Fla. Coun. Bar Assn. Presidents, 1985, Pres.'s award, Fla. Bar, 1985, Young Lawyer Sect. award, 1981, Disting. Svc. award, Am. Coll. Bankruptcy, 2011. Fellow: Fla. Bar Found., Am. Bar Found. (chmn.); mem.: ABA (chmn. sect. gen. practice 1979—80, ho. dels. 1980—90, chmn. creditors' rights com. corps. sect., mem. coun. sect. bus. law 2000—04, standing com. on fed. judiciary 2006—, ho. dels. 2008—, coun. sr. lawyer divsn., bd. dir. ALI-ABA 2009—12), Eleventh Cir. Hist. Soc. (trustee, pres.), Am. Coll. Comml. Fin. Lawyers (pres. 1999—2000), NC Banking Inst. (bd. advisors), Internat. Insolvency Inst. (bd. dirs., sec. 2000—), Internat. Bar Assn. (co-chair insolvency sect.), Am. Coll. Bankruptcy (bd. dirs. 1997—2003, Disting. svc. award 2011), Am. Law Inst., Am. Judicature Soc. (bd. dirs.), Bar Assn. Hillsborough County (pres. 1974—75), Fla. Bar (chmn. sect. corp. banking and bus. law 1970—71, chmn. sect. gen. practice 1972—73, bd. govs. 1975—79, pres. 1980—81), Tampa C. of C. (bd. dirs.), Harvard Law Sch. Assn. Fla. (pres. 1986), Univ. Club, Ye Mystic Krewe Gasparilla, Kiwanis (pres. 1972), Tampa Club (pres. 1986—87). Office: Holland & Knight LLP PO Box 1288 Tampa FL 33601-1288 Office Phone: 813-227-6481. Business E-Mail: leonard.gilbert@hklaw.com.

GILBERT, MARK R., neuro-oncologist, educator; s. Norman and Gloria Gilbert; 1 child, Tess A. MD, Johns Hopkins U., Balt., 1982. Diplomate Johns Hopkins, Md., 1982, cert. Am. Bd. Internal Medicine, 1985, Am. Bd. Neurology and Psychiatry, 1990. Resident/fellow, dept. internal medicine John Hopkins Hops., Balt., 1982—85, resident/fellow, dept. neurology, 1984—88, Keck Found. neuro-oncology fellow, 1986—87; instr. Johns Hopkins Sch. Medicine, Balt., 1988—90; asst. prof. U. Pitts., 1990—96; assoc. prof. Emory U., Atlanta, 1996—2000, M.D. Anderson Cancer Ctr., Houston, 2000—. Contbr. articles to profl. publs. Mem.: Soc. Neuro-Oncology, Am. Soc. Clin. Oncology, Am. Acad. Neurology, Am. Assn. for Cancer Rsch., Alpha Omega Alpha. Office: MD Anderson Cancer Ctr Dept Neuro-Oncology 1515 Holcombe Blvd Box 431 Houston TX 77030

GILBERT, PAUL D., healthcare service executive; BA with honors in Politics, magna cum laude, Wake Forest U., Winston-Salem, NC, 1988; JD, Vanderbilt U. Sch. Law, Nashville, 1991. Ptnr. Waller Lansden Dortch & Davis, LLP, 1999—2006; sr. v.p., gen. counsel, corp. sec. LifePoint Hosps., Inc., 2006—08; chief governance officer LifePoint Hospitals, Inc., 2006—, exec. v.p., chief legal officer, 2008—, chief devel. officer, 2009—. Office: LifePoint Hosps Inc 103 Powell Ct Brentwood TN 37027 Office Phone: 615-372-8500. Business E-Mail: paul.gilbert@lpnt.net.

GILBERT, STEVE, energy executive, lawyer; B in Accounting, Abilene Christian U.; JD, Vanderbilt U. Accountant Bass Family, Fort Worth, Tex., PricewaterhouseCoopers, Fort Worth, Tex.; assoc. atty. Fulbright & Jaworski LLP; joined law dept. Valero Energy Corp., San Antonio, 1993, mng. counsel, v.p. corp. law, asst. sec. and disclosure and compliance officer. Office: Valero Energy Corp PO Box 696000 San Antonio TX 78269-6000 Office Phone: 210-345-2000.

GILBERT-BARNESS, ENID F., pathologist, educator; b. Sydney, May 31, 1927; arrived in U.S., 1952, naturalized, 1975; d. Christian Henry and Mabel (Milne) Fischer; m. James Bryson Gilbert, Aug. 12, 1954; children: Mary M., Elizabeth A., James C. (dec.), Jennifer E., Rebecca D.; m. Lewis Barness, July 5, 1987. MBBS, U. Sydney, 1950, MD, 1983, MD (hon.), 1999; DSc (hon.), U. Wis., 1999, U. Southern Fla.; MD (hon.), U. Sydney, 2004. Diplomate Am. Bd. Pediat., Am. Bd. Clin. Pathology, Am. Bd. Anatomical Pathology, Am. Bd. Pediat. Pathology. Resident Children's Hosp., Boston, Phila., Washington, Brackenridge Hosp., Austin, Tex.; from asst. prof. to assoc. prof. U. W.Va., 1963-70; from assoc. prof. pathology and pediats. to prof. U. Wis., Madison, 1970-93, Disting. Med. Alumni prof., 1986-93, dir. pediat. pathology, 1970-93, prof. emeritus pathology and pediat., 1993—, Disting. Med. Alumni prof. emeritus, 1993—; prof. pathology, pediats. and ob-gyn. U. So. Fla., 1993—. Mem. editl. bds. Pediat. and Devel. Path. Med. jours., 1986—. Author: Introduction to Pathology, 1978, Genetic Aspects Developmental Pathology, 1987, Potters Pathology of the Fetus and Infant, 1997, Atlas Infant and Fetal Pathology, 1998, Metabolic Diseases, 2000, Atlas Embryo Fetal Pathology, 2004, Clinical Use of Pediatric Diagnostic Tests, 2003, Pediatric Autopsy Pathology, 2004; also numerous chpts., articles. Decorated Order of Australia; recipient Disting. Pathologist award, Royal Coll. Pathologists (Australia), 2002; grantee, NIH, 1972—92. Mem. Am. Soc. Clin. Pathology, Soc. Pediat. Pathology (pres. 1986-87), Internat. Acad. Pathology, Internat. Pediat. Pathology Assn. (pres. 1990-92), Teratology Soc., Cardiovasc. Soc. S.Am. (hon.), Am. Pediat. Soc., Am. Acad. Pediat., U.S. Can. Acad. Pathology, Arthur Purdy Stout Soc. Surg. Pathology, N.Y. Acad. Sci., Alpha Omega Alpha. Democrat. Avocation: writing. Home: 3301 Bayshore Blvd #403 Tampa FL 33629 Office: Tampa Gen Hosp Dept Pathology Tampa FL 33601 Office Phone: 813-844-7565. Business E-Mail: egilbert@tgh.org.

GILBERTSON, JOHN S., manufacturing executive; Joined AVX Corp., 1981, sr. v.p., 1990—92, exec. v.p., 1992—97, COO, 1994—2001, pres., 1997—, CEO, 2001—, chmn., 2008—. Bd. dirs. AVX Corp., 1990—2008, Kyocera Corp. ("Kyocera"), 1995—, Kyocera Internat. Inc. ("KII"), 2001—. Mailing: AVX Corp Box 867 Myrtle Beach SC 29578 Office: AVX Corp 801 17th Ave S Myrtle Beach SC 29578 Office Phone: 843-448-9411. Business E-Mail: GilbertsonJ@avxus.com.

GILCHRIST, ERNIE, food products executive; BA in Pub. Adminstrn., Ohio State U. With Seaway Foods, SYSCO, US Foodservice; pres. Vistar Corp., Denver, 2002—06, pres., COO, 2006—08; sr. v.p. strategy and integration Performance Food Group, 2008—. Office: Performance Food Group 12500 W Creek Pky Richmond VA 23238

GILCHRIST, HENRY, lawyer; b. Austin, Tex., Nov. 6, 1924; s. Gibb and Vesta (Weaver) G.; m. Patricia Ann Lynch, Nov. 24, 1951; children: Thomas Gibb, Terri Lynn. BS in Civil Engring., Tex. A&M U., 1948; LLB with honors, U. Tex., 1950. Bar: Tex. 1950, US Supreme Ct. 1971. Assoc. Douglass & McGuire, Pampa, Tex., 1951-52; co-founder Jenkens & Gilchrist, P.C., Dallas, 1952—2007; now of counsel, corp. & securities practice group Hunton & Williams, LLP, Dallas, 2007—. Mem. Rsch. Fellows Southwestern Legal Found., 1976—. Contbr. articles to profl. jours. Bd. dirs. Dallas County Heritage Soc., 1984-87, chmn. bd. trustees, 1978-81, Ctrl. Dallas Assn., exec. com., chmn., 1984-85, Dallas World Salute 1985—, chmn. pres., 1988-90, Theatre Three, 1986-87, Tex. A&M U. Pvt. Enterprise Rsch. Ctr., 1987—, Dallas Bus. Com. for Arts, exec. com. 1988—; adv. coun. Communities Found. Tex., Inc., Dallas Citizens Coun., mem. cultural arts task force; mem. planning and zoning commn. Town of Highland Park, Tex., 1976-84; mem. exec. com. Dallas Mus. Art Trustee and Audit Com., 1988—, chmn. 1988-91, TACA Inc., v.p. 1986-89; mem. devel. coun. Tex. A&M U. Coll. Liberal Arts; mem. Tex. A&M U. Commn. Visual Arts, 1982—, chmn. 1982-88; mem. exec. bd. So. Meth. U. Sch. Theology, 1992—; founder Park Cities Hist. Soc. Served US Army, 1943—46. Mem.: ABA, Ctr. for Am. and Internat. Law, Dallas Bar Assn., Tex. State Bar Assn., Tex. Bar Found. (life), Greater Dallas C. of C. Methodist. Avocations: reading, walking, gardening. Office: Hunton & Williams LLP 1445 Ross Ave Ste 3700 Dallas TX 75202-2799 Office Phone: 214-468-3329. Office Fax: 214-740-7125. Business E-Mail: hgilchrist@hunton.com.

GILCHRIST, JOHN MARK, otolaryngologist; b. Dallas, Dec. 10, 1959; s. Ronald Wallace Jr. and Patricia Gene G.; m. Melissa Paige LaBoon, Jan. 4, 1986; children: Sarah, Claire, Michael. BS, Wheaton Coll., Ill., 1982; MD, U. Okla., Oklahoma City, 1986. Diplomate Am. Bd. Otolaryngology. Intern U. Okla. Med. Ctr., 1986-87, resident otolaryngology, head and neck surgery, 1987-91; mem. staff Mercy Health Ctr., Oklahoma City, 1991—, Bapt. Med. Ctr., Oklahoma City, 1991—2006, Deaconess Hosp., Oklahoma City, 1991—2006; head, otolaryngology sect., dept. of surgery Mercy Health Ctr., Oklahoma City, 1995-2000; pvt. practice Okla. Otolaryngology Assocs., Inc., Oklahoma City, 1991—. Pres. Okla. Acad. of Otolaryngology, 1996-97. Mem. com. Young Life, Oklahoma City, 1987-97. Mem. AMA, Am. Acad. Otolaryngology-Head and Neck Surgery, Okla. Med. Assn., Okla. Acad. Otolaryngology (pres. 1995-). Office: Okla Otolaryngology Assocs 4200 W Memorial Rd Ste 606 Oklahoma City OK 73120-8359 Office Phone: 405-755-1930. Business E-Mail: jmgilchristmd@okoa.org.

GILES, WILLIAM (BILL) T., retail executive; BA in Acct. and Mgmt., Alfred Univ. CPA. With PriceWaterhouse LLP, 1981—90; dir. fin. reporting Melville Corp., 1990—91; asst. contr. Linens 'n Things Inc., Clifton, NJ, 1991—97, CFO, 1997—2000, sr. v.p., CFO, 2000—03, exec. v.p., CFO, 2000—06; exec. v.p. fin., IT & store develop., CFO AutoZone, Inc., 2006—. Office: AutoZone Inc 123 S Front St Memphis TN 38103

GILL, DAVID BRIAN, electrical engineer, educator; b. Columbus, Ohio, Oct. 23, 1957; s. Emery Jr. and Norma Jean Gill; m. Karen Marie Schaar, June 25, 1988. BSEE with highest distinction, Purdue U., 1978, MSEE, 1979, MBA, 1981. Registered profl. engr., Tex. Systems design engr. Owens-Ill., Toledo, 1976-80; engr. Tex. Instruments Def. Group, Dallas, 1981-84, lead engr., 1984-86, mem. group tech. staff, 1986-88, br. mgr., 1988-95, sr. mem. tech. staff, 1995—2001; sr. fellow Raytheon, 2001—. Instr. Purdue U., West Lafayette, Ind., 1978-80, Richland Coll. Engring. Lab., Dallas, 1982-96. Editor lab. manual Control Systems Workbook, 1979. Krannert scholar, 1981. Mem. Purdue Alumni Assn. (life), IEEE, Assn. Old Crows, Phi Eta Sigma, Tau Beta Pi, Eta Kappa Nu, Beta Gamma Sigma, Phi Kappa Phi. Avocations: golf, skeet shooting, hunting. Office: Raytheon 2501 W University Dr Mc Kinney TX 75071-2813

GILL, GERALD LAWSON, librarian; b. Montgomery, Ala., Nov. 13, 1947; s. George Ernest and Marjorie (Hackett) G.; m. Nancy Argroves, Mar. 5, 1977 (div. 1982). AB in History, Philosophy

Religion, U. Ga., Athens, 1971; MA in Libr. Sci., U. Wis., Madison, 1973; postgrad. in Bus. Adminstrn., James Madison U., Harrisonburg, Va., 1978—79. Cert. profl. libr., Va. Cataloger James Madison U., Harrisonburg, Va., 1974-76, reference libr., 1976-87, bus. reference libr., 1987-99, govt. documents libr., 1998—2003, head of reference and govt. documents, 2003—, instr., 1974-80, asst. prof., 1980-90, assoc. prof., 1990—2002, prof., 2002—. Lectr., spkr. nat. and regional groups; cons. in field; mem. faculty senate James Madison U., 1975-79, 96-98, sec. curriculum and instrn. com., 1976-78, chair, 1978-79, univ. coun., 1996-98. Mem. editl. bd. James Madison Jour., 1977-80; reviewer Am. Reference Books Ann.; contbr. articles to profl. jours. Mem. libr. adv. com. State Coun. for Higher Edn. in Va., 1986-87; virtual Va. Coord. Mgmt. Bus. com.; pres. Minor Hill Manorhomes Home Owners Assn., 2004-05, bd. mem., 2006-08. Mem. ALA (chmn. bus. reference svcs. com. 1984-86, sec. law and polit. sci. sect. 1982-85, chmn. bus. reference svcs. discussion group 1986-87, chmn. bus. reference in acad. librs. com. 1988-91, Gale Rsch. award 1991, Bus. Librarianship Excellence award, 1991), AAAS, Am. Soc. for Info. Sci., Va. Libr. Assn. (coun. 1986-87, parliamentarian 1979, 81), Spl. Librs. Assn. (treas. Va. chpt. 1983-85, pres. 1986-87), World Future Soc., Harrisonburg C. of C., Sierra Club. Democrat. Roman Catholic. Avocations: art collecting, writing. Home: 326 Westfield Rd Charlottesville VA 22901-1660 Office: James Madison Univ Carrier Library Mail Stop Code 1704 Harrisonburg VA 22807-0001 Business E-Mail: gillgl@jmu.edu.

GILL, ROSA U., state legislator; m. Jimmie Gill; children: Angie, Natalie. BS in Math., Shaw U. Cert. pub. mgr. Mem. Wake County Bd. Edn., 1999—2009, chairperson, 2007—09; state rep. Dist. 33 NC, 2009—. Mem. Appropriations com., Appropriations Subcom. on Transp., Edn. com., Edn. Subcom. on Presch., Elem. and Secondary Edn., Election Law and Campaign Fin. Reform com., Judiciary II com.; vice chmn. State Govt./State Personnel com. Office: North Carolina House of Representatives 16 W Jones St Rm 1305 Raleigh NC 27601-1096 Office Phone: 919-733-5880. E-mail: Rosa.Gill@ncleg.net.

GILL, TURNER, college football coach; b. Ft. Worth, Tex., Aug. 13, 1962; m. Gayle Gill; children: Jordan, Margaux. Attended, U. Nebr., 1980—83; B in Behavior Analysis, U. North Tex., Denton, 1990. Quarterback Montreal Concordes, Can. Football League, 1984—85; receivers coach Southern Methodist U. Mustangs, 1991; quarterbacks coach U. Nebr. Cornhuskers, 1992—2002, asst. head football coach, 2003, wide receivers coach, 2004; player devel. dir., offensive asst. U. at Buffalo Bulls, 2005, head football coach, 2006—09, U. Kans. Jayhawks, 2009—11, Liberty U. Flames, Lynchburg, Va., 2011—. Minor league player Detroit Tigers, Cleve. Indians. Spokesperson United Way; hon. chmn. Cystic Fibrosis, American Heart Assn., American Diabetes Assn.; bd. mem. Lincoln Children's Mus., Nebr. Recipient Tom Novak award, Herbert Marshall award, MAC Coach of Year, 2007, Coll. Coach of Yr., 2008; named First Team All-Conf., Big Eight Conf., MAC Coach of Year, Sporting News, 2008; named to 1980's All-Decade Team, Big Eight Conf., Nebr. Football Hall of Fame; finalist Heisman Meml. Trophy award, 1983, Paul Bear Bryant award; fellowship, Christians Athletics. Mem.: Black Coaches & Administrators, American Football Coaches Assn. (bd. trustees 2009). Office: Liberty University Football Program 1971 University Blvd Lynchburg VA 24502 Office Phone: 434-582-2040.

GILL, VINCE, country musician, singer; b. Norman, Okla., Apr. 12, 1957; m. Janis Oliver, 1980 (div. 1997); 1 child, Jenny; m. Amy Grant, 2000; 1 child, Corrina. With Pure Praire League, 1980; appeared on Dire Straits album, On Every Street,1991; performed duets with Reba McEntre, Emmylou Harris, Patty Loveless, Ricky Skaggs; solo albums include The Things That Matter, 1985, The Way Back Home, 1987, The Best of Vince Gill, 1989, When I Call Your Name, 1989, Pocket Full of Gold, 1991, I Never Knew Lonely, 1992, I Still Believe in You, 1992, Let There Be Peace on Earth, 1993, When Love Finds You, 1994, Vince Gill and Friends, 1994, Souvenirs, 1995, High Lonesome Sound, 1996, The Key, 1998, Let's Make Sure We Kiss Goodbye, 2000, Next Big Thing, 2003, Christmas, 2003, These Days, 2006, Guitar Slinger, 2011; numerous musical videos. Recipient Grammy award for Best Male Country Performance 1990, 1992, 1994-98, 2003, 2007, for Best Country Song, 1992, 1995, Best Country Collaboration With Vocals, 1991, 1996, Best Country Instrumental Performance, 1998, 2001, 2009, Best Country Gospel Album, 2005, Best Country Album, 2008; 2 Country Music Assn. awards, 1991, Instrumentalist of Yr. award The Nashville Network/Music City News, 1991, 3 Gold albums, 7 Platinum albums, numerous Country Music Assn. awards, including Male Vocalist of Yr., 1991-95, Song of Yr., 1992, 1993, 1996, Entertainer of Yr., 1993, 1994, Album of Yr., 1993, Vocal Event of Yr., 1996, 2007, Country Single of Yr. award Am. Music Awards, 1994, Acad. Country Music awards, 1984, 1992, 1993, Acad. Country Music Home Depot Humanitarian award, 2006, TNN/Music City News awards, 1991-94, 1996, Music City News Songwriters awards, 1990-94, BMI awards, 1987, 1991-93, 1995, 1996, Nashville Music awards, 1994-96, Christian Country Music Assn. awards, 1996, Minnie Pearl award, 1993, Harmony award, 1993, Tennesseean of Yr. award, 1994, Outstanding Nashvillian of Yr. award Kiwanis, 1994, Orville H. Gibson Lifetime Achievement award, 1997; Vince Gill Tenn. PGA Jr. Golf Tournament named in his honor, 1997; named to Country Music Hall of Fame, 2007. Office: c/o Rick Shipp William Morris Agency 1600 Division St Ste 300 Nashville TN 37203 Office Fax: 615-963-3090.

GILLAM, JEREMY, state legislator; b. Aug. 2, 1976; m. Carissa Gillam; 2 children. Grad., Ark. State U., Beebe, 1994; grad. in Psychology Criminology, Ark. State U., Jonesboro, 1999. Mem. US Dept. of Agr. Fruit and Vegetable Adv. Com., Am. Farm Bureau Horticulture Com.; bd. dirs. White County Farm Bureau; mem. Ark. State U. Beebe Devel. Coun.; chmn. Ark. Farm Bureau Horticulture; owner Gillam Farms, 1999—; mem. Dist. 49 Ark. House of Representatives, 2011—. Republican. Baptist. Office: 1825 Missile Base Rd Judsonia AR 72081 Office Phone: 501-729-0042. Business E-Mail: jeremy@growing49.com.

GILLANI, ALEEM, bank executive; B, York Coll., So. Alberta Inst. Tech.; grad. in Advanced Mgmt. Program, Harvard Coll., Cambridge, Mass. Mgmt. accountant (CMA), Soc. of Mgmt. Accountants of Can. With BankBoston, FleetBoston; chief market risk officer PNC Fin. Svcs. Group, SunTrust Banks Inc., corp. treas., 2010, CFO, 2011—; bd. dirs. SunTrust Robinson Humprey Inc. Chmn. market risk coun. Risk Mgmt. Assn., bd. dirs.; serve nat. bd. trustees March of Dimes Found. Office: SunTrust Banks Incorporated 303 Peachtree St NE Atlanta GA 30308 Office Phone: 404-588-7711. Office Fax: 404-332-3875.

GILLENWATER, JEFFREY M., mining company executive, human resources specialist; BBA, Marshall U. Asst. human resources mgr. & human resources mgr. Massey Energy Co.(Rawl Sales & Processing Co.), 1994—96; human resources mgr. Massey Energy Co.(Performance Coal Co.), 1996—99; dir., human resources Massey Energy Co. (subs. of Massey Coal Svcs. Inc.), 1999—2002; dir., external affairs, adminstrn. Massey Energy Co., 2002—09, v.p., human resources, 2009—. Office: Massey Energy Co 4 N 4th St Richmond VA 23219 Office Phone: 804-788-1800. Office Fax: 804-788-1801. Business E-Mail: Jeffrey.Gillenwater@masseyenergyco.com.

GILLESPIE, EDWARD MALCOLM, hospital administrator; b. Mpls., Oct. 19, 1935; s. Harold Livingston and Alice May (Thompson) G.; children: Karin, Timothy, Kenneth. BS, U. Minn., 1957, MPA, 1959, MHA, 1962. Engaged in refugee adminstrn., Linz, Austria, 1958-60; asst. adminstr. Luth. Med. Ctr., Denver, 1962-66; asst. gen. sec. Meth. Bd. Health and Welfare Ministries, Evanston, Ill., 1966-69; adminstr. Meth. Hosp., Rochester, Minn., 1969-74, Univ. Hosp., Augusta, Ga., 1974-91, pres. Health Advance, 1991-92. Bd. dirs. Augusta Area Mental Health, Augusta Speech and Hearing Ctr., St. John's Towers, CSRA Blood Assurance; chmn. hosp. divsn. certification coun. Meth. Health and Welfare. Bd. dirs. local United Way, Boy Scouts Am., Blue Cross Ga., Bankers First; chmn. Augusta Resource Ctr. on Aging, Brandon Wilde. Fellow ACHA; mem. Am. Hosp. Assn., Ga. Hosp. Assn. (chmn.), Rotary Internat. (bd. dirs. Augusta chpt.). Methodist. Home and Office: Health Advance 12 Shadow Brook Cir Augusta GA 30909-3749

GILLESPIE, JOHN DAVID, political science educator; b. Oxford, NC, Sept. 22, 1944; s. Arthur S. and Pauline M. (Pittard) Gillespie; m. Judi K. Flowers, June 11, 1966. BA, Wake Forest U., 1966, MA, 1967; PhD, Kent State U., 1973. Instr., history and polit. sci. Davidson C.C., Lexington, NC, 1967—70; asst. prof. Samford U., Birmingham, Ala., 1973—79; assoc. prof. to prof. to Charles A. Dana prof. polit. sci. Presbyterian Coll., Clinton, SC, 1979—2006, v.p. academic affairs, 1997—2005; pres. SC Ind. Colls. Deans' Coun., 1999—2000; adj. prof. polit. sci. Coll. Charleston, 2007—, The Citadel, 2009—; interviewee ABC-TV, BBC-Radio, CNN-TV, PBS-TV, NPR and others. Author: Politics at the Periphery: Third Parties in Two-Party America, 1993, Challengers to Duopoly: Why Third Parties Matter in American Two-Party Politics, 2012; contbr. articles to profl. jours. Former chmn. Laurens County Dem. Party; mem. SC Dem. Exec. Com.; v.p. Ala. Polit. Sci. Assn., 1978—79; pres. SC Polit. Sci. Assn., 1985—86. Named SC Prof. of Yr., 1993—94, Designated Exemplary Tchr., US Dept. Edn., 1996; fellow, NDEA Title IV, 1970—73, grant, NEH, 1978, Fulbright scholar, China, 1988, Estonia, 1997. Mem.: SC Polit. Sci. Assn., Internat. Soc. Sci. Study Subjectivity, Am. Polit. Sci. Assn. Congregationalist. Home: 6023 Grand Council St Daniel Island SC 29492-8035 E-mail: jdavidgi@gmail.com.

GILLESPIE, MITCH, state legislator; b. Marion, NC, Aug. 19, 1959; m. Barbara Gillespie. State rep. Dist. 49, NC, 1999—2002; state rep. Dist. 85 NC, 2003—; small bus. owner. Republican. Baptist. Office: North Carolina House of Representatives 300 N Salisbury St Room 307B2 Raleigh NC 27603-5925 Address: 185 Cross Creek N Ridge Dr Marion NC 28752 Office Phone: 919-733-5862. Business E-Mail: MitchGillespie@ncleg.net.

GILLET, PAMELA KIPPING, special education educator; EdB in Elem. Edn., Chgo. Tchrs. Coll., 1963; MA in Mental Retardation, Northeastern Ill. U., 1966; PhD in Gen. Spl. Edn./Adminstrn., Walden U., 1976. Cert. elem. edn., early childhood edn., learning disabled, mental retardation, behavior disorders, supt., supr. and dir. spl. edn. 4th grade tchr. Dist. # 83 Mannheim, Franklin Park, Ill., 1963—64; HS spl. edn. tchr. Dist. # 207 Maine Twp., Park Ridge, 1964—67, prevocational coord., 1967—69, dept. chmn. spl. edn. dept., 1969—70; dir. EPDA tchr. tng. program Chgo. Consortium Colls. and Univs., Northwest Ednl. Coop., Palatine, 1970—71; prin. West Suburban Spl. Edn. Ctr., Cicero, 1971—73; supr. West Suburban Assn. Spl. Edn., 1973—75; asst. dir. Northwest Suburban Spl. Edn. Orgn., Palatine, 1975—78, supt. Mt. Prospect, 1978—96; CEC mentoring program dir., 2007—; spl. edn. cons., 1996—. Adj. instr. Northeastern Ill. U., Chgo. State U., Corcordia Coll., Barat Coll., Nat. Coll. Edn., Roosevelt U.; mem. task forces ISBE, 1975—2007, cons. career edn. project, 1977—78, spl. edn. demandate study group, 1983—85; cons. Ednl. Testing Svc.; tchr. edn. coun. Northeastern Ill. U., 1981—97, dean's grant program, 1982—97; workshop leader, 1974—; lectr., cons. in field. Author: Auditory Processes, 1974, rev., 1992, Career Education for Children, 1978, Of Work and Worth: Career Education Programming for Exceptional Children and Youths, 1981, Handbook for board members of volunteer organizations, 2008; contbr. articles to profl. jours., chapters to books. Bd. dirs. Found. Exceptional Children, 1996—2006, pres., 1999—2004. Recipient Cmty. Svc. award, Am. Legion, 1976, 1980, Alumnus of Yr. award, Northeastern Ill. U., 1984, Learning Disabilities of Am. Contributors award, Coun. Understanding Learning Disabilities, 1992, Those Who Excel award of excellence, Ill. State Bd. of Edn., 1994, Outstanding Svc. award, Divsn. Mental Retardation and Devel. Disabilities, 1994, Sleznick award, Coun. of Admin. of Spl. Edn., 1996, Outstanding Contbr. award, Coun. Exceptional Children, 1996, Burton Blatt award, Divsn. on Mental Retardation and Devel. Disabilities, 1997, Spl. Edn. Leadership award, Ill. Adminstrs. of Spl. Edn., 1995, Outstanding Spl. Edn. Adminstr. of Yr. award, 1997, Romaine C Mackie Leadership award, 2010. Mem.: CEC Showcase Session (honoree 2008), Found. for Exceptional Children (pres. 2000—05), Ill. Adminstrs. Spl. Edn. (pres. 1994—95), Coun. Exceptional Children (pres. Ill. chpt. 1975—77, bd. govs. 1977—80, pres. mental retardation divsn. 1983—85, bd. govs. 1986, exec. com. 1989—92, v.p. internat. 1992—93, pres.-elect 1993—94, pres. 1994—95, bd. govs. 1996—2000, bd. dirs. 2000—04, pres.-elect. 2005—06, pres. Pioneers divsn. 2007, Meritorious Svc. award Ill. 1983), Am. Assn. Sch. Adminstrs. Home and Office: 413 Courtlea Oaks Blvd Winter Garden FL 34787

GILLETTE, FRANK C., JR., retired mechanical engineer; m. Jane Gillette; 3 children. BS in Mech. Engring., U. Fla. Mech. designer Pratt & Whitney, 1962-77, chief of structures, 1977-80, engring. mgr. YF119 program, dir. engring. programs F119 engine projects for Govt. Engines and Space Propulsion, 1980-95, dir. advanced mil. programs, 1995-97, dir.-chief engr. F119/JSF engine programs, 1997-98, ret., 1998. Mem. adv. bd. U. Fla. Coll. Engring.; cons. in field. Recipient Disting. Alumnus Disting. Svc. award U. Fla. Coll. Engring., Laurels award Aviation Week, 1991. Fellow ASME, AIAA (assoc.; Nat. Engr. of Yr. award 1991); mem. Soc. Automotive Engrs. (Cliff Garrett Turbomachinery Engring. award 1994). Achievements include design of the RL10 rocket chamber, the turbine section of the J58, father of F119 engine; management of the overall structural engineering effort of the J52, TF30, F100 rockets and preliminary design Nat. Acads., Air Force & Dept. Def. Aerospace Propulsion Commn.; patents in field. Home: 8325 Nashua Dr Palm Beach Gardens FL 33418 Personal E-mail: fcgillette@yahoo.com.

GILLEY, MICKEY LEROY, musician; b. Natchez, Miss., Mar. 9, 1936; s. Arthur Philmore and Irene Frances (Lewis) G.; m. Vivian McDonald, Dec. 27, 1962; 1 son, Gregory Brent. Ptnr. Gilley's Club, Pasadena, Tex., 1971-89; owner Gilley's Theatre, Branson, Mo., 1990—; pres., owner Gilley's Tex. Cafe, 1992—, owner Myrtle Beach, SC, 1995—2000, Gilley's Rest., Pasadena, Tex., 2002—05. Appeared in night clubs in, Houston, New Orleans, Biloxi, Miss., Mobile, Ala., Lake Charles, La., 1957-59; appeared at, Nesadel Club, Houston, 1960-70. Named Most Promising Male Artist, Acad. Country Music 1974, Most Promising Male Artist, Record World 1974, Top New Country Singles Artist, Billboard 1974, Top New Male Vocalist in Album Category, Record World 1975, Most Promising Male Artist, Music City News 1976, Best Male Vocalist, Entertainer of Year, Acad. Country Music 1976; recipient Star in Walk of Fame on Hollywood Blvd., 1984, over 17 #1 records, Grammy award for Orange Blossom Special Nat. Acad. Rec. Arts and Scis., 1981. Mem. Country Music Assn., Acad. Country Music, AFTRA, Musicians Local 65. Clubs: Moose. Office: 3737 Lily St Pasadena TX 77505-2927 Office Phone: 281-998-8480. Business E-Mail: mickey@gilleys.com.

GILLEY, OTIS W., economics professor; b. Ft. Worth, Apr. 10, 1952; s. Wayne Davis and Dorothy Evelyn Gilley; m. Linda Ann Dowling, July 14, 2001; children: Telford James, Telford Joe, Telford Jeremy, Leslie Colwell. BS in Economics, U. Tex., 1974; MS, PhD, Purdue U., West Lafayette, Ind., 1979. Asst. prof. econs. U. Tex., Austin, 1979—84; assoc. prof. econs. U. Alaska, Fairbanks; prof. econs. La. Tech U., Ruston, 1984—, head, econs. and fin., 2004—. V.p. Lions Club, Ruston. Named Clarke Williams CenturyTel Disting. Prof., La. Tech U., 1998—. Mem.: Beta Gamma Sigma. Presbyterian. Avocations: golf, fly fishing, travel. Home: 2805 Foxxwood Dr Ruston LA 71270 Office: Louisiana Tech Univ Dept Economics & Fin Ruston LA 71272 Office Fax: 318-257-4253.

GILLFILLAN, MICHAEL J., investment company executive; BA in History, U. Calif., Berkeley; MBA, UCLA. CEO Wells Fargo Ag Credit Wells Fargo & Co., 1984, head loan portfolio, 1986—99, vice chmn., chief credit officer, mem. sr. mgmt. com., 1999, vice chmn., head Corp. and Comml. Banking Groups, head loan workout group, vice chmn., chief credit officer; ptnr. Neveric LLC, 2000—02, Meriturn Partners, LLC, 2002—. Bd. dirs. UnionBanCal Corp., 2003, Maguire Properties Inc., 2009—. Office: Meriturn Partners LLC 6th Fl 234 Fayetteville St Raleigh NC 27601-1300 Office Phone: 919-882-9966. Office Fax: 919-573-8200. E-mail: mike@meriturn.com.

GILLHAM, NICHOLAS WRIGHT, geneticist, educator; b. NYC, May 14, 1932; s. Robert Marty and Elizabeth (Enright) G.; m. Carol Lenore Collins, June 2, 1956. BA, Harvard, 1954, MA, 1955, PhD (USPHS fellow), 1962. From instr. to asst. prof. Harvard U., 1963-68; assoc. prof. zoology Duke U., 1968-72, prof., 1973-82, James B. Duke prof. biology, 1982—2002, chmn. dept. zoology, 1986—89, profl. emeritus, 2002—. Mem. biochemistry, molecular genetics and cell biology interdisciplinary cluster Pres.'s Biomed. Rsch. Panel, 1975; mem. study sect. in genetics NIH, 1976-80; mem. N.C. Gov.'s Bd. Sci. and Tech., N.C. Gov.'s Task Force on Sci. and Tech., chmn., bd. dirs. Am. Type Culture Collection, 1993-96. Author: (with R. Krueger and J. Coggin) Introduction to Microbiology, 1973, Organelle Heredity, 1978, Organelle Genes and Genomes, 1994, A Life Sir Francis Galton: From African Exploration to the Birth of Eugenics, 2001, Genes, Chromosomes, and Disease, 2011; mem. editl. bd. Genetics, 1975-78, Jour. Cell Biology, 1977-79, Intl. Review of Cytology, 1987-97; sr. editor Plasmid, 1977-86. Served to 1st lt. Med. Service Corps USAF, 1955-58. Postdoctoral fellow USPHS, 1962-63 Spl. fellow, 1967-68; Rsch. Career Devel. grant USPHS, 1972-77; Guggenheim fellow, 1984-85. Mem. Genetics Soc. Am., Sigma Xi. Office: Duke Univ Dept Biology PO Box 90338 Durham NC 27708-1000 Home: 3000 Galleway Ridge A 003 Pittsboro NC 27312 Business E-Mail: gillham@duke.edu.

GILLIAM, JOHN A., lawyer; b. Goldthwaite, Tex., Nov. 3, 1935; s. Ed Burr and Emily Corine (Anderson) Gilliam; m. Sara Ann Swindell, Dec. 26, 1963; children: Joanna, John, Jason. BA, Baylor U., 1958; LLB with honors, U. Tex., 1961. Bar: Tex. 1961, US Dist. Ct. (no., so., ea. and we. dists.) Tex., US Ct. Appeals (5th, 10th and 11th cirs.). Assoc. to ptnr. Thompson & Knight, Dallas, 1961—74; sr. ptnr. to of counsel, comml. litig. practice Jenkins & Gilchrist, 1975—. Trustee, rsch. fellow Ctr. for Am. Law & Justice. Assoc. editor: Tex. Law Rev., 1959. Named one of Best Lawyers in Dallas & Ft. Worth, D mag. Fellow: Dallas Bar Found. (sr., life), Am. Coll. Trial Lawyers, Am. Bar. Found., Tex. Bar Found. (life); mem.: ABA, Patrick E. Higginbotham Am. Inn of Ct. (master emeritus, past pres.), Dallas Bar Assn. (dir. 1981—85), 5th Cir. Bar Assn., Tex. State Bar Assn., Tex. Assn. Def. Counsel (dir.), Am.Bd. Trial Advocates, Phi Gamma Delta, Phi Delta Phi, Alpha Chi, Order of Coif. Baptist. Office: Jenkens & Gilchrist Ste 3200 1445 Ross Ave Dallas TX 75202-2799 Office Phone: 214-855-4306. Office Fax: 214-855-4300. Business E-Mail: jgilliam@jenkens.com.

GILLIARD, WENDELL G., state legislator; b. Charleston, SC, July 1, 1954; s. William and Sinclair Gilliard; children: April Sinclair, Wendell G. Gillard, Keith Demon Gillard. Attended, Devry Sch. Tech, U. Tenn. Former plant operator Albright & Wilson Chem. Plant; former pres. United Steel Workers Local Union; mem. Charleston City Coun., SC, 1997—98; former mayor pro tempore; mem. Dist. 111 SC House of Reps., 2008—. Democrat. Episc. Home and Office: Dist/Home Office PO Box 31641 Charleston SC 29417 Office: 80 Broad St Charleston SC 29401 also: Capitol Office 328A Blatt Bldg Columbia SC 29201 Home Phone: 843-402-9710; Office Phone: 843-209-3123, 843-724-3727, 803-212-6793. Office Fax: 843-720-3959. E-mail: wendellgilliard@schouse.org.

GILLILAND, MARY MARGARETT, healthcare consultant; b. Leland, Miss., Dec. 23, 1942; d. Lindon Edward and Allie Earlene (Saulters) Palmore; m. Carl Ralph Gilliland, Jan. 12, 1963; children: Carl Ralph, Gini Lynn. Diploma in Nursing, Greenwood Leflore, 1963; B of Healthcare Adminstrn., East Tex. State U., 1976; M of Human Rels. and Mgmt., Abilene Christian U., 1978; BS, Tex. Woman's U., 1991, MS, 1993, PhD, 1999. RN, Tex. Staff nurse Sunflower County Health Dept., Indianola, Miss., 1965-66; asst. dir. nursing Presbyn. Hosp. Dallas, 1966-80, assoc. dir. nursing, 1980-87, assoc. exec. dir., 1987-91; healthcare cons. G&S Healthcare Cons., Allen, Tex., 1991—. Contbr. articles to profl. jours. Mem. ANA, Am. Orgn. Nurse Execs., Tex. Orgn. Nurse Execs., Tex. Nurses Assn. (continuing edn. com, Great 100 Nurses 1991), Nurses Alumni Assn. (sec.) Sigma Theta Tau, Phi Kappa Phi. Avocations: walking, reading, tae kwoon do. Home and Office: G&S Healthcare Cons 2101 Rigsbee Dr Plano TX 75074-4913 Office Phone: 214-208-2653. Personal E-Mail: mmpg1@verizon.net.

GILLILAND, MICHAEL S. (SAM GILLILAND), travel company executive; m. Shannon Gilliland; 2 children. BS in Elec. Engring., U. Kans., 1985; MBA, U. Tex., Dallas. Elec. engr. Lockheed Missiles and Space, Austin, Tex.; joined Sabre Holdings Corp., 1988, sr. v.p., gen. mgr., Sabre Bus. Travel Solutions Southlake, Tex., sr. v.p., gen. mgr., product mktg., exec. v.p., chief mktg. officer, 2000—02, group pres., Airlines Solutions bus., 2001—02, pres., CEO, Travelocity, 2002—03, bd. dirs., pres., CEO, 2003—, chmn., 2004—. Office: Sabre Holdings Corp 3150 Sabre Dr Southlake TX 76092 Office Phone: 682-605-1000. Business E-Mail: mgilliland@sabre-holdings.com.

GILLILAND, STANLEY EUGENE, dairy-food microbiology professor; b. Minco, Okla., June 24, 1940; s. Dale W. and Evelyn M. (Barnes) G.; m. Blanche D. King, June 2, 1960 (dec. July 1989); children: Stanley Jr., Stephen, Angela, Amy; m. Jerri Hall, May 26, 1990. BS, Okla. State U., 1962, MS, 1963; PhD, N.C. State U., 1966. Instr. N.C. State U., Raleigh, 1965-67, asst. prof., 1967-72, assoc. prof., 1972-76, Okla. State U., Stillwater, 1976-80, prof., 1980-86, regents prof., 1986-98, regents prof. and Sitlington endowed chair, 1998—. Editor: Bacterial Starter Cultures for Foods, 1985. Recipient Disting. Alumnus award, N.C. State U., 2002. Fellow Am. Acad. Microbiology; mem. Am. Dairy Sci. Assn. (bd. dirs., v.p., pres., Pfizer award 1979, Dairy Rsch. Found. award 1987, Milk Ind. Fedn. Tchr. award 1999, award of honor, 2003), Am. Soc. for Microbiology, Inst. Food Technologists, Coun. for Agrl. Sci. and Tech., Am. Fed. Soc. Food Animal Sci. (v.p., pres.). Baptist. Office: Okla State U Animal Sci Dept & Food and Agri Products Ctr Stillwater OK 74078-0001 Office Phone: 405-744-6071.

GILLINGHAM, ROBERT FENTON, economist, consultant; b. Newark, Nov. 13, 1944; s. Evan Stevenson and Eleanor (Fenton) G.; m. Deborah Lynn Wickham, 1989; children: James Stevenson, Sarah Eleanor. BA, Haverford Coll., 1965; PhD, U. Pa., 1973. Economist Bur. Labor Stats., Washington, 1968-73, chief price rsch. div., 1973-82, dep. assoc. commr., 1982-85; dir. office econ. analysis Dept. Treasury, Washington, 1985-88, dep. asst. sec. for econ. policy, 1988-98; cons. Internat. Monetary Fund, Washington, 1998—. Assoc. editor Jour. Bus. and Econ. Stats., 1982-93; contbr. articles to profl. jours. Mem. Am. Econ. Assn., Am. Statis. Assn., Econometric Soc., Western Econ. Assn. (bd. dirs. 1995-98), Conf. on Income and Wealth, Nat. Acad. Social Ins. Home: 20448 Tappahannock Pl Sterling VA 20165-4786

GILLINGS, DENNIS B., medical products executive; Diploma in Mathematical Statistics, Cambridge U., 1967; PhD in Math., U. Exeter, England, 1972. Prof., biostats. U. NC, Chapel Hill; founder, chmn., CEO Quintiles Transnat. Corp., Durham, NC, 1982—. Named One of 15 Top Biotechnology Execs., Genetic Engring. News, 1994. Office: Quintiles Transnational Corp 4820 Emperor Blvd Durham NC 27703 Office Phone: 919-998-2000. Office Fax: 919-998-2003. Business E-Mail: dennis.gillings@quintiles.com.

GILLIS, JAMES A., gas industry executive; Grad., Lycoming Coll., Williamsport, Pa. Various sales and sales mgmt. positions Union Carbide; founding employee, KMC Telecom Holdings, v.p. southeast region, v.p. market devel., v.p. carrier sales; v.p., sales, mktg. and bus. devel. AGL Networks, L.P., 2004—06, v.p., wholesale markets, 2003—04, pres., 2006—. Mailing: AGL Networks LP P O Box 4569 Location 9300 Atlanta GA 30302 Office Phone: 404-584-3275. Business E-Mail: JGillis@aglresources.com.

GILLIS, JAMES R., publishing executive; Exec. v.p. Globe Comm. Corp.; mng. ptnr. Aders, Wilcox, Gillis; pres., CEO Brand Mfg. Corp.; pres. Source Interlink Companies, Inc., 1998—, COO, 2000—, bd. dirs., 2000—; interim co-CEO Source Interlink Cos., 2006—08. Office: Source Interlink Cos 27500 Riverview Center Blvd Bonita Springs FL 34134 Office Phone: 239-949-4450.

GILLIS, S. MALCOLM, economics professor; AA, Chipola Jr. Coll., Marianna, Fla.; BA, MA, U. Fla.; PhD, U. Ill.; LLD (hon.), Rocky Mountain Coll., Billings, Mont. Asst. prof. economics Duke University, Durham, NC, prof. economics, pub. policy, 1984—93, dean grad. sch., vice provost academic affairs, 1986—91, Z. Smith Reynolds disting. prof. pub. policy, 1990—93, dean, faculty arts & sciences, 1991—93; prof. Harvard University, Cambridge, Mass., 1969—84; pres. Rice University, Houston, 1993—2004, Ervin Kenneth Zingler prof. economics, 2004—. Bd. dirs. HP Enterprise Svcs., AECOM Tech., 1998—, Fed. Res. Bank, Dallas, 1999—2005, Introgen Therapeutics, 2004—, Svc. Corp. Internat., 2004—, Halliburton Co., 2005—, EDS, 2005—; cons. to numerous US govt. agencies and fgn. governments. Author: Public Policies and the Misuse of Forest Resources, 1988, Tax Reform in Developing Countries, 1989, Economics of Development; contbr. articles to profl. jours. Chmn. Econ. Future Commn. for Gov. and Gen. Assembly of State of NC, 1990-91; mem. govt. performance audit com. NC State Legis.; bd. dirs. NC Cargo Authority, 1992-93, US Civilian Rsch. & Devel. Found., Nat. Acad. Sciences Bd. on Sustainable Devel., 1997, Fedn. Am. Scientists, Coun. Higher Edn. Accreditation, 1999-, Bus. and Higher Edn. Forum, 1999-; chmn. vis. com. energy divsn. Oak Ridge Nat. Lab.; bd. mem. Am. Forestry Assn., Nat. Coun. for Sci. and Environment, Houston Advanced Rsch. Ctr., Greater Houston Partnership, Houston Symphony, Tex. Aviation Hall of Fame and Mus., Houston, Tech. Ctr., AMIGOS de Las Americas, St. Lukes Episc. Hosp.; bd. trustees Found. Hosp. Art, Found. Chilean Edn., Ctr. for World Environment and Sustainable Devel.; mem. adv. bd. Tex. Commerce Bank, 1993-98, Arab-Am. Ednl. Found; mem. internat. adv. com. Hainan Province, China. Named Disting. Fulbright Prof., Cath. U. Chile, 1989. Mem.: Assn. Am. Universities (mem. exec. com., chmn. tax com.). Office: Rice University 6400 Fannin Ste 2600 Houston TX 77030 Office Phone: 713-348-2514. Office Fax: 713-348-5479.

GILLISS, CATHERINE LYNCH, academic administrator, dean, nursing educator; b. New Britain, Conn., Apr. 18, 1949; d. James A. and Lorraine Lynch; m. Thomas P. Gilliss, June 6, 1970. BS in Nursing, Duke U., 1971; MS in Nursing, Cath. U. Am., Washington, 1974; D of Nursing Sci., U. Calif., San Francisco, 1983; cert. adult nurse practitioner, U. Rochester, 1979; D (hon.), U. Portland, Oreg., 2007; MA (hon.), Yale; DHL (hon.), Portland. Chmn. dept. family health care U. Calif., San Francisco, 1984-98, prof. emeritus, 1999—; prof. Sch. Nursing, Yale U., New Haven, 1998—2004, dean Sch. Nursing, 1998—2004; dean Sch. Nursing Duke U., 2004—; prof. Helene Fuld Health Trust Duke U. Sch. Nursing, 2004—; vice chancellor nursing affairs, 2004—; gov. appointed mem. NC Inst. Medicine, 2010—. Chair NIH, Nat. Inst. Nursing Rsch. Study Sect., 1997-2000; founding dir. DJNI. Co-author: Toward a Science of Family Nursing, 1989, The Nursing of Families, 1993; Jour. Family Nursing, Jour. Nat. Assn. Hispanic Nurses, Jour. Nat. Black Nurses Assn.; contbr. articles to profl. jours. Bd. dirs. Nat. Coun. Family Relations, 1986-88, Am. Acad. Nursing, 2000-04, Soc. Primary Care Policy Fellows, 1996-99, Nat. Orgn. Nurse Practitioner Faculties, 1994-97. Recipient Disting. Alumna award Duke U. Sch. Nursing, 1991; Pres.'s Fellowship award U. Calif., 1983; Sr. fellow Ctr. for Health Professions, 1996-99, Primary Health Care Policy fellow USPHS, 1993; Regent U. Portland, Oreg., 1994-2000; named to Wall of 100 Disting. Alumni, U. Calif. San Francisco Sch. Nursing, 2007, Lifetime Achievement award in Rsch. Internat. Family Nursing Soc., 2007 Fellow Am. Acad. Nursing (co-chair task force on health disparities 2001-04, co-chair program planning com. 2002, co-chair raise voice campaign 2007-, pres. 2009-, chair strategies planning com. 2009-10); mem. ANA, Nat. Orgn. Nurse Practitioner Faculties (v.p. 1994-95, pres. 1995-96, past pres. 1996-97, mem. adv. bd. nat. coun. state bds. nursing, FNP project, 1995-97), Soc. Primary Care Policy Fellows (bd. dirs., pres. 1996-99), Am. Assn. Colls. Nursing (fin. com., 2006—07.) Office: Duke Univ Sch of Nursing DUMC 3322 Durham NC 27710

GILLMOR, JOHN EDWARD, lawyer; b. Phila., Oct. 26, 1937; s. John Edward and Louise Ann (Porter) G.; m. Allis Dale Brannon, Aug. 17, 1968; children: Sarah, Abigail, Susan, Eleanor, John, Matthew. BA, Swarthmore Coll., 1959; LL.B., U. Pa., 1962. Bar: DC 1962, NY 1963, Tenn. 1972, Pa. 1980. Assoc. Dewey Ballantine Bushby Palmer & Wood, 1962-63, 66-71; v.p., corp. counsel Hosp. Affiliates Internat., Nashville, 1971-78, sr. v.p., gen. counsel, 1978-79; staff v.p., asst. gen. counsel INA Corp., Phila., 1980; sr. v.p., gen. counsel INA Health Care Group, 1981; partner Gillmor, Mills & Gillmor, 1981-83; dir., exec. v.p. Health Am. Corp., 1983-86; ptnr. Gillmor, Anderson & Gillmor, 1986-89, Dearborn & Ewing, 1989-92, Boult, Cummings, Conners & Berry, Nashville, 1992—2008, Bradley Arant Boult Cumings LLP, 2009—. Trustee U. Sch. Nashville, 1990-02; bd. dirs. Nashville Opera Assn., 1996-2007; bd. dirs. Hoosier Care, Inc., 1988-, Am. Eagle Life Care Corp., 2004-10, Edn. Networks Am., 2003-, VTM LLC, 2011-; Nashville Philharmonic Orch. 2006-; with USMC, 1963-66. Mem.: ABA, Nashville Bar Assn., Nashville Bar Found., Tenn. Bar Assn. Republican. Home: 1700 Graybar Ln Nashville TN 37215-2106 Office: Bradley Arant Boult Cummings Conners & Berry 1600 Divsn St Ste 700 Nashville TN 37203 Home Phone: 615-297-3149; Office Phone: 615-252-2305. Business E-Mail: jgillmor@babc.com.

GILMAN, ALFRED GOODMAN, pharmacologist, educator; b. New Haven, July 1, 1941; s. Alfred and Mabel (Schmidt) Gilman; m. Kathryn Hedlund, Sept. 21, 1963; children: Amy, Anne, Edward. BS, Yale U., New Haven, 1962; MD, PhD, Case Western Res. U., Cleve., 1969, DSc (hon.), 1995, U. Chgo., 1991, U. Miami, 1999; DMS (hon.), Yale U., 1997. Pharmacology rsch. assoc. NIH, Bethesda, Md., 1969—71; asst. prof., then assoc. prof. pharmacology U. Va., Charlottesville, 1971—77, prof., 1977—81, dir. med. sci. tng. program, 1979—81; prof. pharmacology, chmn. dept. U. Tex. Southwestern Med. Ctr., Dallas, 1981—2005, Raymond & Ellen Willie disting. chmn. molecular neuropharmacology, 1987—2009, regental prof. pharmacology emeritus, 1994—, interim dean Southwestern Med. Sch., 2004—05, dir. Cecil H. & Ida Green Comprehensive Ctr. Molecular Computational and Sys. Biol., 2004—09, provost, exec. v.p. acad. affairs, dean Southwestern Med. Sch., 2005—09; chief scientific officer Cancer Prevention Inst. Tex., 2009—. Mem. pharmacology study sect. NIH, 1977—81, mem. nat. adv. gen. med. scis. coun., 1992—95; bd. sci. counselors Nat. Heart, Lung Blood & Inst., 1982—86; mem. sci. adv. com. Am. Cancer Soc., NYC, 1982—86; mem. sci. adv. bd. Huntsman Cancer Inst., U. Utah, 1995—2000, Ernest Gallo Clinic & Rsch. Ctr., U. Calif., San Francisco, 1996—2001, Lucille P. Markey Charitable Trust, Miami, 1984—96; mem. sci. rev. bd. Howard Hughes Med. Inst., Bethesda, 1986—93; dir. Regeneron Pharmaceutics, 1989—, Eli Lilly and Co., Inc., 1995—; mem. vis. com. Case Western Res. U. Sch. Medicine, 1995—99; chmn. steering com. Alliance Cellular Signaling, 2000—08. Editor The Pharmacological Basis of Therapeutics; contbr. articles to profl. jours. Recipient Poul Edvard Poulsson award, Norwegian Pharmacology Soc., 1982, Gairdner Found. Internat. award, 1984, Albert Lasker award for basic med. rsch., 1989, Passano Sr. award, Passano Found., 1990, Waterford Biomed. Sci. award, Scripps Clinic & Rsch. Found., 1990, Basic Sci. Rsch. prize, Am. Heart Assn., 1990, City of Medicine award, Durham, NC, 1991, Ciba-Geigy Drew award, 1991, Nobel prize in physiology/medicine, 1994, Disting. Alumnus award, Case Western Res. U., 1995, Am. Acad. Achievement award, 1995, Med. Honor Basic Rsch. award, Am. Cancer Soc., 1995; named to Tex. Hall of Fame, 2001. Mem.: NAS (Richard Lounsbery award 1987), Tex. Acad. Sci. Engring. & Medicine, Am. Acad. Arts & Scis., Inst. Medicine, Am. Soc. Biol. Chemistry, Am. Soc. Pharmacology & Exptl. Therapeutics (John J. Abel award in pharmacology 1975, Louis S. Goodman and Alfred Gilman award 1990, Torald Sollman award 1997). Office: Cancer Prevention & Rsch Inst Tex 5323 Harry Hines Blvd Dallas TX 75390-8520 Office Phone: 214-648-0558. E-mail: agilman@cprit.state.tx.us.

GILMAN, JOHN RICHARD, JR., retired management consultant, sculptor; b. Malden, Mass., July 6, 1925; s. John Richard and Philomene (Gradie) F.; m. Julia Streeter, Feb. 6, 1960; children: Derek, Streeter Gilman Holden. AB, Harvard U., 1946; postgrad., Georgetown U., 1945-46; student, Art Students League, NYC, 1953-55, Sculpture Ctr., 1972-76; MSW, NYU, 1983. Diplomate Am. Bd. Clin. Social Work; lic. clin. social worker, N.Y., R.I. Dir. publicity John H. Breck, Inc., Springfield, Mass., 1949-53, asst. advt. mgr., 1950-53, dir. new products, 1955-56, tech. dir., 1956-63; dir. new products Acco. Labs., Am. Cyanamid Co., Wayne, N.J., 1963; treas., exec. v.p. August Sauter of Am., Inc., NYC, 1964, pres., CEO, 1965-79; pres. John R. Gilman Inc., NYC, 1980-94, ret., 1994. Bd. dir. Slee Internat., Inc., N.Y.C., Finex Mining Co., Reno; assoc. Fisher Cons. Internat. Inc. N.Y.C., 1980-86, C.M. Oppenheim & Co. Inc. N.Y.C., 1981-86; cons. Right Assocs., Inc., Providence, 1986-89. Filmmaker: Water, 1950, Dear Nancy, 1953; sculpture exhbns. include Convergence Internat., Providence, R.I., 1998, Von Liebig Art Ctr., Naples, Fla., 1999 (Sculpture prize), Maine Art Gallery, Wiscasset, Maine, 1999, Winners Circle Art Coun., Fla., 2001, Wynne Hatfield Gallery, Charleston, S.C., 2003; represented in permanent collections: Endicott Coll, Beverly, Mass., Cyanamid, Wayne, N.J., 4Cons Art Ctr. Tiverton, RI, Rock Garden Inn, Sebasco Estates, Maine. Trustee Sculpture Ctr., NYC, 1977-90, exhbn. com., 1980-82, v.p., 1983-86; trustee Augustus Saint-Gaudens Meml., NYC, 1982—, 1st v.p., exec. com., chmn. facilities com., 1988-91, pres., 1991-93, chmn. exhbn. com., 1999-2003, mem., 1994—, fin. com., 1988-2008, chmn. fin. com., 1998-2002, meml. music com., 1997—; bd. dirs. Maine Art Gallery, Wiscasset, 1998-2001, chmn. exhbn. com., 1999-2001. With USNR, 1943-46, trustee emeritus Augustus St. Garden Meml., 2013. Mem. Internat. Sculpture Soc., Art Students League (life), Art Club Washington D.C., Harvard Club (N.Y.C., Boston), Nat. Arts Club (N.Y.C.). Home: 770 Bentwater Cir Apt 101 Naples FL 34108-6776 Personal E-mail: johnrgilman@yahoo.com.

GILMAN, RONALD LEE, federal judge; b. Memphis, Oct. 16, 1942; s. Seymour and Rosalind (Kuzin) Gilman; m. Betsy Dunn, June 11, 1966; children: Laura M., Sherry I. BS, MIT, 1964; JD cum laude, Harvard Law Sch., 1967. Bar: Tenn. 1967, US Supreme Ct. 1971. Ptnr. Farris, Mathews, Gilman, Branan & Hellen, Memphis, 1967—97; judge US Ct. Appeals (6th cir.), 1997—2010, sr. judge, 2010—; chair Appellate Judges Conf. ABA Judicial Divsn., 2007—08. Judge Tenn. Ct. Judiciary, 1979—87; lectr. trial advocacy U. Memphis Law Sch., 1980—97; arbitrator, mediator Am. Arbitration Assoc., 1988—97; arbitrator NASD, 1993—97; referee Pvt. Adjudication Ctr., 1994—97. Contbr. articles to profl. jours. Regional chmn. ednl. coun. MIT, 1968—88; active Chickasaw coun. Boy Scouts Am., 1993—2000; mem. Leadership Memphis; bd. dirs Memphis Jewish Home, 1984—87. Recipient Sam A. Myar Jr. Meml. award for outstanding svc. to legal profession and cmty., 1981. Mem.: ABA (ho. of dels. 1990—97, chair appellate judges conf. jud. divsn. 2007—08), Am. Arbitration Assn. (mem. large, complex case panel 1993—97), Tenn. Bar Assn. (spkr. ho. of dels. 1985—87, pres. 1990—91), Memphis Bar Assn. (pres. 1987), Am. Coll. Trust and Estate Counsel, Am. Judicature Soc., Am. Law Inst., 6th Cir. Jud. Conf. (life). Democrat. Jewish. Office: Fed Bldg 167 N Main St Ste 1176 Memphis TN 38103-1824

GILMAN, SANDER LAWRENCE, liberal arts and sciences professor, historian, writer; b. Buffalo, Feb. 21, 1944; s. William and Rebecca (Helf) G.; m. Marina von Eckardt, Dec. 28, 1969; children: Daniel, Samuel. BA, Tulane U., 1963, PhD, 1968; postgrad., U. Berlin and U. Munich, Ger.; LLD (hon.), U. Toronto, Ont., 1997. Lectr. German St. Mary's Dominican Coll., New Orleans, 1963-64; instr. Dillard U., New Orleans, 1967-68; asst. prof. Case Western Res. U., 1968-69; mem. faculty Cornell U., 1969-94, prof. German, 1976-94, prof. Near Eastern studies, 1984-91, prof. humane studies, 1984-87, Goldwin Smith prof., 1987-94, chmn. dept. German lit., 1974-81, 83-84; fellow dept. psychiatry Cornell U. Med. Coll., 1977-78; prof. history of psychiatry Cornell U., 1978-94; prof. German, history of sci. and psychiatry U. Chgo., 1994-2000, Henry R. Luce disting. svc. prof. Liberal Arts in Human Biology, 1995-2000, disting. svc. prof., 1999-2000; disting. prof. liberal arts & scis. and medicine U. Ill., Chgo., 2000—05; disting. prof. liberal arts & scis. Emory U., 2005—. O'Connor prof. Colgate U., 1982-83; Mellon prof. Tulane U., 1988, Old Dominion prof. English, Princeton U., 1988; Northrup Frye prof. of comparative lit. U. Toronto, Ont., Can., 1989; vis. prof. German lit. Free U. Berlin, 1989; vis. hist. scholar Nat. Libr. Medicine, 1991-92; vis. Rudolph prof. Jewish studies Syracuse (N.Y.) U., 1992; vis. prof. U. Witwatersrand, South Africa, 1994, U. Potsdam, 1996, U. Cape Town, 1996, Ctr. for Advanced Studies in the Behavioral Scis., 1996-97, Getty Inst. for Art and the Humanities, 1998; hon. prof. Free U., Berlin; Berlin prize fellow Am. Acad., Berlin, 2000-01; dir. program in psychoanalysis, Emory U., health sciences humanities initiative. Author, editor.: Bertolt Brecht's Berlin, 1975, Nietzschean Parody, 1976, The Face of Madness, 1976, Klingers Werke, 1978, Begegnungen mit Nietzsche, 1981, On Blackness Without Blacks, 1982, Seeing the Insane, 1982 (reprinted 1996), Difference and Pathology, 1985, Jewish Self-Hatred, 1986, Oscar Wilde's London, 1987, Conversations with Nietzsche, 1987, Diseases and Representation, 1989, Sexuality: An Illustrated History, 1989, Nietzsche on Rhetoric and Language, 1989, The Jew's Body, 1991, Inscribing the Other, 1991, Rasse, Seuche, Sexualitat, 1992, Freud, Race, Gender, 1993, The Case of Sigmund Freud, 1993, Reading Freud Reading, 1993, Reemerging Jewish Culture in Germany, 1994, Jews in Today's German Culture, 1995, Health and Illness, 1995, Franz Kafka: The Jewish Patient, 1996, L'Autre et Le Moi, 1996, Smart Jews, 1996, Yale Companion to Jewish Writing and Thought in German Culture, 1997, Love and Marriage with Death, 1998, Creating Beauty to Cure the Soul, 1998, Making the Body Beautiful, 1999, Jurek Becker: Die Biographie, 2002, (co-editor with Zhou Xun) SMOKE: A Global History of Smoking, 2004, Race and Contemporary Medicine: Biological Facts and Fictions, 2006; mem. editl. bd. Diacritics, 1971-72, Lessing Yearbook, 1974—, German Quar., 1977-86, Confinia Psychiatrica, 1978-80; Oxford Lectures Multiculturalism and the Jews, 2006. Guggenheim fellow, 1972-73, IREX exch. fellow German Democratic Republic, 1976, Soc. for Humanities faculty fellow Cornell U., 1981-82, Nat. Libr. Medicine sr. historian, fellow, 1990-91, Ctr. for the Adv. Study of the Behaviorial Scis. fellow, Stanford, 1996-97, Am. Acad., Berlin, 2000—. Mem. MLA (pres. 1995), Lessing Soc., Am. Assn. Tchrs. German, Soc. Internat. d'Études Littéraires et Psychiatres, Internat. Assn. Germanists. Democrat. Jewish. Office: Emory U Grad Inst Liberal Arts 537 Kilgo Cir S415 Callaway Bldg Atlanta GA 30322 E-mail: sander34@aol.com.

GILMAN, SHELDON GLENN, lawyer; b. Cleve., July 20, 1943; BBA, Ohio U., 1965; JD, Case Western Res. U., 1967. Bar: Ohio 1967, Ky. 1971, Ind. 1982, Fla. 1984, DC 1985, Tenn. 1985, U.S. Supreme Ct. 1987. From assoc. to ptnr. law firms, Louisville, 1972—; ptnr. Lynch, Cox, Gilman & Goodman, P.S.C., Louisville, 1987—. Gen. counsel Louisville Assn. Life Underwriters, 1977, 1978, 1990; adj. prof. law U. Louisville Sch. Law; spkr. in field. Author: Kentucky Estate Planning, 2d edit., 2003; contbr. chapters to books, articles to profl. jours., Estate Planning, UK/CLE-Guides. Bd. dirs., chmn. Louisville Minority Bus. Resource Ctr., 1975—80; bd. dirs., v.p., sec. Louisville Orch., 1982—85; bd. dirs. City of Devondale, Ky., 1976; pres. Congregation Adath Jeshurun, 1986—88; bd. dirs. United Synagogue Cons. Judaism, NY, pres. Ohio Valley region. With JAGC US Army, 1968—71. Named one of Best Lawyers in Am. Employee Benefits Law, Trusts, Estates, 2007. Fellow: Am. Bar Found., Am. Coll. Trust and Estate Counsel; mem.: ACLU (bd. dirs. 1998—2002), Louisville Employee Benefit Coun. (pres. 1980), Ky. Bar Assn. (mem. ethics com. 1982—2011, mem. ethics hotline com. 1990). Office: Lynch Cox Gilman & Goodman 500 W Jefferson St Ste 2100 Louisville KY 40202 Office Phone: 502-589-8591. Business E-Mail: sgilman@lcgandm.com.

GILMER, PENNY JANE, biochemist, educator; b. Hackensack, NJ, Aug. 19, 1943; d. Peter E. and Barbara D. (Joynt) Gilmer; m. Sanford A. Safron, Sept. 9, 1980; children: Helena M., Nathaniel S. BA in Chemistry, Douglass Coll., 1965; MA in Organic Chemistry, Bryn Mawr Coll., 1967; PhD in Biochemistry, U. Calif.-Berkeley, 1972; DSc in Sci. Edn., Curtin U. Tech., 2004. Bank Am.-Giannini postdoctoral fellow Stanford U. (Calif.), 1973—75, USPHS and NIH postdoctoral fellow, 1975—77, acting asst. prof. human biology, 1976—77; asst. prof. chemistry Fla. State U., Tallahassee, 1977—84, assoc. prof., 1984—96, interim assoc. dean coll. arts and scis., 1990—91, assoc. chair chemistry, 1991—93, prof., 1996—; Nancy Marcus prof., chemistry and biochemistry, 2008—. Lectr. in field. Contbr. articles to profl. jour. Recipient Faculty Rsch. award, Fla. State U., 1978, 1984, 1986, 1990, Tchg. Incentive award, 1993—94, Outstanding Cmty. Women award, Am. Assn. U. Women, Tallahassee br., 2006, GK-12 Dissemination award, Nat. Sci. Found., 2006, John Shrum award, Southeastern Assn. Sci. Tchr. Edn., 2007; grantee NIH, 1979—81, Rsch. Corp., 1979—86, 1990—96, Am. Cancer Soc., 1981—83, Jessie Ball duPont Fund, 1987—89, Assn. Women in Sci., 2008; grant, NSF, 1990—2007, 2009—. Fellow: AAAS; mem.: Assn. Sci. Tchr. Edn. (Outstanding Sci. Tchr. Educator 2006), Nat. Assn. Rsch. Sci. Tchg. (bd. 2003—09, pres.-elect 2006—07, pres. 2007—08, past pres. 2008—09), Assn. Women in Sci., Southeastern Immunology Conf. (dir. 1979—84, pres. 1982), Audubon Soc., Am. Chem. Soc., Fedn. Biol. Chemists, Zonta Internat. (pres. Tallahassee Club 1992—93, area 4 dir. dist. 11 2006—08), Sierra Club, Sigma Xi. Democrat. Office: Fla State U Dept Chemistry and Biochemistry Tallahassee FL 32306-4390 Business E-Mail: gilmer@chem.fsu.edu.

GILMORE, ARTIS, academic administrator, retired professional basketball player; b. Chipley, Fla., Sept. 21, 1949; m. Enola Gilmore; 5 children. Attended, Gardner-Webb Jr. Coll., Boiling Springs, NC; grad., Jacksonville U., Fla., 1971. Ctr. Ky. Colonels, American Basketball Assn., Louisville, 1971—76, Chgo. Bulls, 1976—82, 1987, San Antonio Spurs, 1982—87, Boston Celtics, 1988, Fortitudo Bologna, Italy, 1988—89; ret. NBA, 1989; salesman W.W. Gay Mechanical, Jacksonville, Fla., 1999—2007; spl. asst. to the pres. Jacksonville U., 2007—. Named 1st Team NCAA All-American, AP, 1971, Rookie of Yr., Am. Basketball Assn., 1972, MVP, 1972, 1st Team All-ABA, 1972—76, 1st Team All-Rookie, 1972, 1st Team All-Def., American Basketball Assn., 1973—76, All-Star Game MVP, Am. Basketball Assn., 1974, Playoffs MVP, 1975; named to Ea. Conf. All-Star Team, 1972—76, NBA, 1978, 1979, 1981, 1982, We. Conf. All-Star Team, 1983, 1986, Jacksonville U. Athletics Hall of Fame, 1993, Naismith Meml. Basketball Hall of Fame, 2011. Achievements include member of the American Basketball Association championship winning Kentucky Colonels, 1975. Office: Jacksonville University c/o Office of Pres 2800 University Blvd N Jacksonville FL 32211

GILMORE, BRENDA, state legislator; b. Sumner County, Tenn., Dec. 9, 1952; m. Harry Gilmore; 1 child, Erica. Sec. Conservation & Environ. Com.; mem. Commerce Com.; former dir. State Postal Svcs.; with Dept. Gen. Svcs., Tenn., 1979—87; rep. Dist. 1 Nashville Metro Coun., 1999—2006; state rep. Dist. 54, 2007—. Recipient Spirit Leadership award, CABLE, Harriet Foley award, Sr. Citizens Inc.,

Advocacy award, Metro Human Rels. Com., 2004. Mem.: Nat. Hookup Black Women (chair, legis. com.), Tenn. State U. Alumni Assn., Women Nineties, Nashville Women Polit. Caucus, League Women Voters, Nashville CABLE (pres.), NAACP (life), Delta Sigma Theta. Democrat. Baptist. Office: 3009 Vista Valley Ct Nashville TN 37218 also: 22 Legislative Plz Nashville TN 37243-0154 Office Phone: 615-741-1997. Office Fax: 615-253-0361. Business E-Mail: rep.brenda.gilmore@capitol.tn.gov.

GILMORE, VANESSA D., federal judge; b. St. Albans, NY, Oct. 26, 1956; BS, Hampton U., 1977; JD, U. Houston, 1981. Bar: Tex. 1982, U.S. Dist. Ct. (so. dist.) Tex. Fashion buyer Foley's Dept. Store, 1977-79; ptnr. Vickery, Kilbride, Gilmore & Vickery, Houston, 1981-85, 86-94; atty. Sue Schecter & Assocs., Houston, 1985-86; judge US Dist. Ct. (so. dist.) Tex., Houston, 1994—. Spkr. ATLA, San Diego, 1990, ABA, Atlanta, 1991, N.Y.C., 1993, Leadership Tex., Austin, 1992, Hampton U. Alumni Assn., Dallas, 1992, Laredo Bus. and Profl. Women's Assn., 1993, XI Ann. Border Gov.'s Conf., Monterrey, Mex., 1993, Gov.'s Bus. Devel. Coun., Ausitn, 1993, Tex. A&M U., 1993, State Bar of Tex., Austin, 1993, Houston Bus. Coun., 1993, Minority Enterprise Devel. Week, Houston, 1993, Holman St. Bapt. Ch., 1994, Greater Houston Women's Found., 1994, The Kinkaid Sch., 1995, So. Meth. U., Dallas, 1996, South Tex. Coll. of Law, 1996, among others. Contbr. articles to profl. jours. Bd. dirs. Houston Ballet, Tex. So. Univ. Found., Neighborhood Recovery Community Redevel. Corp., 1992-95; chair African Am. Art Adv. Assn., Mus. Fine Arts; mem. scv. acad. nominations bd. Rep. Jack Fields, Tex., 1993, 94; active Texans for NAFTA; mem. Tex. Dept. Commerce, 1991-94, chairperson, 1992-94; mem. adv. bd. St. Joseph's Hosp.; mem. Leadership Tex. Named One of Houston's Black Achievers, Human Enrichment of Life Program, 1989; recipient Citizen of the Month award Houston Defender, 1990, YWCA award, 1991, Austin Met. Resource Bus. Ctr. award, 1991, Houston Bus. and Profl. Men's Club award, 1992, Disting. Svc. award Nat. Black MBA Assn., 1994, Cmty. Svc. award Holman St. Bapt. Ch., 1994. Mem. ABA, NAACP (chair chs. and orgns. com. Freedom Fund banquets 1989-93), ATLA, Am. Leadership Forum, Tex. Trial Lawyers Assn., Tex. Lyceum Assn., Houston Bar Assn., Houston Lawyers Assn., U. Houston Law Alumni (bd. dirs. 1993—), W.J. Durham Legal Soc., Links, Inc. (Mo. chpt., chair LEAD substance abuse and teen pregnancy prevention program 1990-91). Office: US Courthouse 515 Rusk Ave Rm 9513 Houston TX 77002-2605 E-mail: vanessa_gilmore@txs.us.courts.gov.

GILSTRAP, JAMES RODNEY, federal judge, lawyer; b. Pensacola, Fla., May 1, 1957; s. Joseph C. and Wynona Frances (James) G.; m. Sherry Sullivan, June 18, 1977; children: Lauren Gray, Stephen Sullivan. BA magna cum laude, Baylor U., 1978, JD, 1981. Bar: Tex. 1981, US Dist. Ct. (eastern dist.) Tex. 1982, US Ct. Appeals (5th cir.) 1982). Atty., assoc. Abney, Baldwin & Searcy, Marshall, Tex., 1981-84; ptnr. Smith & Gilstrap, Marshall, 1984—2011; county judge Harrison County, Tex., 1989—2002; judge US Dist. Ct. (eastern dist.) Tex., 2011—. Instr. East Tex. Bapt. U., Marshall, 1982-86; bd. dirs. Smith Steel Casting Co., Marshall, 1992—. Pres. Trinity Episcopal Sch., Marshall, 1991-92; trustee The Davidson Found., Marshall, 1992—. Recipient Pres.'s award Harrison County Hist. Soc., 1990. Mem. ABA, Northeast Tex. Bar Assn., Harrison County Bar Assn., Masons, Phi Beta Kappa. Democrat. Baptist. Avocations: water sports, tree farming, reading. Office: US District Court Sam B Hall Federal Bldg 100 East Houston St Rm 125 Marshall TX 75670 Office Phone: 903-935-2912. Office Fax: 903-938-2651.

GIMENEZ, CARLOS ANTONIO, Mayor, Miami-Dade County, Florida; b. Havana, Cuba, Jan. 17, 1954; came to U.S., 1960; s. Carlos Antonio and Mitzi Ann (de Llano) G.; m. Lourdes Maria Portela, June 20, 1975; children: Carlos Julio, Julio Francisco, Lourdes Marie. AA in Gen. Studies, Miami Dade C.C., 1984. Firefighter Miami Fire Rescue, 1975-79, fire lit., 1979-84, fire capt., 1984-87, exec. asst., 1987-88, div. chief, 1988-91, fire chief, 1991—; mem. Miami-Dade Bd. County Commissioners, 2004—11; mayor City of Miami-Dade County, Fla., 2011—. Bd. dirs. Coral Gables Youth Ctr., 1989—. Mem. Dade County Chief Fire Officers Assn. (bd. dirs. 1991—). Republican. Roman Catholic. Avocations: boating, basketball, tennis. Home: 4061 S Le Jeune Rd Miami FL 33146-2854 Office: Office of Mayor 111 NW 1st St Miami FL 33128 Office Phone: 305-375-5071.*

GIMSON, WILLIAM H., III, (BILL GIMSON), health facility administrator; b. 1951; BA, U. Wis., 1973; MBA, Duke U., 2002. Pub. health advisor, Chgo. & NYC Dept. Health Centers for Disease Control & Prevention (CDC), US Dept. Health & Human Services, 1974—81, dir., immunization program, Commonwealth Puerto Rico to acting asst. sect. health Pakistan, 1981—88, dir, fin. mgmt. office, 1996—2003, understudy for the position of dir. financial mgmt. office to assoc. dir. policy coordination, 1988—95, dir., financial mgmt. office, 1995—2003, COO, 2003—09, interim dir., 2009; exec. dir. Cancer Prevention & Rsch. Inst. Tex. (CPRIT), Austin, 2009—. Recipient Presdl. Meritorious Rank award, Presdl. Disting. Rank award, 2005. Fellow: Nat. Acad. Pub. Adminstrn. Office: Cancer Prevention & Rsch Inst Tex (CPRIT) PO Box 12097 Austin TX 78711 Office Phone: 512-463-3190. Office Fax: 512-475-2563. E-mail: cprit@cprit.state.tx.us.

GINEL RODRÍGUEZ, JOSÉ, dean, physician, educator; MD. Joined as asst. prof. pediat. Universidad Ctrl. del Caribe, Bayamon, PR, 1986, dir. clin skills devel., dean medicine, 2004—, pres., 2007—; treas. Ramon Ruiz Arnau U. Hosp., dir. residency program in pediat. Office: Universidad Ctrl del Caribe Office of Dean / Pres Avenida Laurel Santa Juanita Bayamon PR 00960-6032 Office Phone: 787-269-4510. Office Fax: 787-798-4990. Business E-Mail: jose.ginel@uccaribe.edu.

GINEPRI, ROBBY (ROBERT LOUIS GINEPRI), professional tennis player; b. Ft. Lauderdale, FL, Oct. 7, 1982; s. Rene and Nancy Ginepri. Profl. tennis player ATP Tour, 2001—. Achievements include winner, Newport, RI, 2003, Indpls., 2005; mem. US Men's Olympic Team, Beijing, 2008. Office: c/o ATP Tour 201 ATP Boulevard Ponte Vedra Beach FL 32082

GINGRASS, MARY KATHERINE, plastic surgeon; b. Milw., Mar. 31, 1963; m. Christopher Stark. BS cum laude, Boston Coll., 1985; MD, Medical Coll. Wis., Milw., 1989. Diplomate Am. Bd. Plastic Surgery, Nat. Bd. Med. Examiners, Am. Soc. Aesthetic Plastic Surgeons, cert. Advanced Edn. Cosmetic Surgery Am. Soc. Aesthetic Plastic Surgery. Resident gen. surgery So. Ill. U. Sch. Med., 1989—92, resident plastic surgery, burn, 1992—94; fellowship aesthetic surgery, breast reconstruction Nashville Plastic Surgery, 1994—95; plastic, cosmetic surgeon Plastic Surgery Ctr., Nashville, 1995—. Bd. mem. Tenn. Breast Cancer Coalition; chief dept. plastic surgery Baptist Hosp., Nashville; med. staff Baptist Plaza Surgicare Outpatient Surgery Ctr., Nashville, Centennial Med. Ctr., Nashville. Spkr. (in field). Fellow: ACS; mem.: Tenn. Women Med., Tenn. Med. Assn., Am. Med. Assn., Am. Soc. Aesthetic Plastic Surgery, Nashville Acad. Med., Am. Soc. Plastic Surgeons. Office: Plastic Surgery Ctr 1915 State St Nashville TN 37203 Office Phone: 866-433-6066. Office Fax: 615-467-6778.

GINGREY, PHIL (JOHN PHILLIP GINGREY), United States Representative from Georgia; b. Augusta, Ga., July 10, 1942; m. Billie Ayers; children: Billy, Gannon, Phyllis, Laura Neill. BS in Chemistry, Ga. Inst. Tech., 1965; MD, Med. Coll. Ga., 1969. Intern Grady Meml. Hosp., Atlanta; ob-gyn. resident Med. Coll. Ga., Augusta; physician Ga. Ob-Gyn. Affiliates, Marietta, Ga.; mem. Ga. State Senate, Atlanta, 1999—2002, mem. banking and fin. instns. com., edn. com., retirement com., transp. com.; mem. US Congress from 11th Ga. dist., 2003—. Mem. St. Joseph's Cath. Ch., Marietta; mem. Marietta Sch. Bd., 1993-97, also chmn.; bd. dirs. North Cobb divsn. Am. Cancer Soc. Mem.: Ga. Ob-Gyn. Soc., Med. Assn. of Ga., Cobb County Med. Soc., AMA. Republican. Roman Catholic. Office: US House of Representatives 442 Cannon House Office Bldg Washington DC 20515 also: Marietta Dist Office 219 Roswell St Marietta GA 30060 Office Phone: 202-225-2931. Office Fax: 202-225-2944. E-mail: gingrey.ga@mail.house.gov.*

GINN, FRANK, state legislator; b. May 23; m. Robin Tardy Ginn; 1 child, Catherine Ginn. BS in Agrl. Engring., U. Ga., 1985. From mem. services rep. to dir. mem. services Jackson EMC; city mgr., treas. City of Royston, Ga.; city mgr. City of Sugar Hill, Ga.; county mgr. Franklin County, Ga.; mem. Dist. 47 Ga. State Senate, 2011—. Republican. Office: PO Box 1136 Danielsville GA 30633 also: Georgia State Senate 321A Coverdell Legis Office Bldg Atlanta GA 30334 Office Phone: 706-680-4466, 404-656-4700. Business E-Mail: fran.ginn@senate.ga.gov.

GINN, RICHARD VAN NESS, military officer, healthcare executive, author, historian, oral historian; b. Miami, Fla., Mar. 23, 1943; s. Philander Jerome and Alida Loring (Van Ness) G.; m. Angelica Suarez, June 29, 1968; children: Angie Ann, Richard Van Ness. BA, Stetson U., 1965; MHA, Baylor U., 1978; MA, Duke U., 1980; grad. with honors, Army Command/Gen. Staff Coll., 1981, Army War Coll., 1990. Commd. 2d lt. U.S. Army, 1965, advanced through grades to col.; exec. officer, med. co. US Army 173rd Airborne Brigade, Vietnam, 1970—71; aide de camp exec. sec. US Army Med. R & D Adv. Panel Chief Force Devel. USAMRDC, Washington, 1972—76; resident Office Asst. Sec. Def., Health Affairs, Pentagon, Washington, 1977—78; profl. svcs. adminstr. BAMC, Ft. Sam Houston, 1978—80; pers. policy officer Office of Army Surgeon Gen., Washington, 1981-83; spl. asst. to chief Med. Svc. Corps, U.S. Army, Washington, 1983-86; dep. comdr. for adminstrn. SHAPE (Belgium) Med. Ctr., 1986-89; insp. gen. 7th Med. Command, Heidelberg, Germany, 1989-91; chief of staff USAMRDC, Ft. Detrick, Md., 1991-92; chief edn. and tng. Office of Army Surgeon Gen., Va., 1992-93; chief Health Svcs. divsn. Officer Pers. Mgmt., PERSCOM, Alexandria, Va., 1993-95; ret. U.S. Army, 1995; sr. v.p. Capital Health Svcs., Inc., 1996-97, pres., CEO, 1998—2000; historian Office of Army Surgeon Gen., Va., 2001—10, US Navy Bur. Medicine & Surgery, 2010—; oral history editor The Grog: Navy Jour. Med. Culture & History, 2010—. Author: The History of the U.S. Army Medical Service Corps, 1997, In Their Own Words; The 498th in Iraq, 2008; contbr. numerous articles to profl. jours. Bd. dir., sec., v.p. Daventry Cmty. Assn., pres., 2005—. Recipient Sir Henry Wellcome medal and prize, 1977, George Washington Honor medal Freedoms Found., 1978, Pres.'s award Daventry Cmty. Assn., 2005; named Young Fed. Health Care Adminstr., Assn. Mil. Surgeons U.S., 1982, Disting. Honor Grad., U.S. Army-Baylor U. Program in Health Care Adminstrn., 1977, Disting. Mem. U.S. Army Med. Dept. Rgt., 1998. Fellow Am. Coll. Healthcare Execs.; mem. Nat. Capital Healthcare Execs. (prizes scholarly competition 1982, 84), Fed. Health Care Execs. Inst. Alumni Assn., Oral History Assn., Army Hist. Found., Soc. Mil. History, Soc. 173d Airborne Brigade, Order Mil. Med. Merit, U.S. Army War Coll. Alumni Assn., SHAPE Officers Assn., Omicron Delta Kappa (chpt. pres. 1964-65), Sigma Tau Delta, Pi Kappa Phi, Kappa Kappa Psi. Home: 6825 Spring Beauty Ct Springfield VA 22152-3111 Office Phone: 703-912-4326. E-mail: dickginn@aol.com.

GINN, RONN, architect, environmental planner, general contractor; b. Jacksonville, Fla., Apr. 17, 1933; s. Angus Theodore and Joan Adelaide (Bailey) Ginn; children: Sharon Lee, John Norman. AA, U. Fla., Gainesville, 1957, B.Arch., 1960, B.Landscape in Architecture with honors, 1961. Lic. bldg. ofcl. Fla., arch. Fla. Ga., SC, NC, Tenn., Miss., NM, NCARB, gen. contractor Fla., bldg. inspector Fla. and nat. cert. Internat. Codes Coun., registered arch. Nat. Coun. Archtl. Registration Bds. Urban design specialist Model Cities Adminstrn., HUD, Washington, 1967-68; pvt. practice landscape architecture, constrn., environ. planning St. Petersburg, Fla., 1968—; pres. ARG Constrn. Corp., 1975-76, ARG Corp., 1977—, Ginn Corp., 1967-70, Atrium Corp., 1965-72. Urban design lectr. U. N.Mex., 1967; planning cons. State Dept., 1967-68; design cons. Am. Revolution Bicentennial Commn., 1967-69; vis. design critic Rice U., 1974; mem. Pinellas County Bd. Adjustments and Appeals, Fla., 1981-88; mem. Albuquerque Fine Arts Commn., 1965-67, St. Petersburg Design Goals Com., 1971-73; moderator radio program Design in Our Community WPKM, Tampa, Fla., 1971-72; founder, bd. dirs. Pinellas County Red Flag Charrette, 1972-76, Catalyst, St. Petersburg; bd. dirs. Fla. Coun. Clean Air, Fla. Red Flag Charrette; mem. Pinellas County Planning Council, 1972-73 Supervising architect, urban designer: Roswell Ctrl. bus. dist. redesign, N.Mex., 1964, Tucumcari ctrl. bus. dist. redesign, N.Mex., 1967, Treasure Island civic ctr. design, Fla., 1971; architect, urban designer, prin. Atrium One, Albuquerque, 1965-67; contbg. editor Urban Affairs Symposia, 1965-73; guest columnist St. Petersburg Evening Ind., 1974; important works include Albuquerque ctrl. bus. dist. redesign (nat. AIA award 1966), new town Fla. Ctr. (nat. Am. Soc. Landscape Architects award 1970), Brown residence (AIA merit award 1975), Penguin Restaurant, Treasure Island, Fla., 1973, Cross residence, 1974, Sheridan Gallery, 1974, Madeira Beach C. of C., 1975, Greenpepper Restaurant, 1975, Mixon Bldg., Ruskin, Fla., 1976, Congregation Beth Chai Synagogue, Seminole, Fla., 1979, Villa Dos Santos Master Plan, St. Petersburg Beach, Fla., 1979, Congregation Kol Ami Synagogue, Tampa, 1981, Markham residence, St. Petersburg, 1981, The Moorings, Tierra Verde, Fla., 1981, Ginn Residence, St. Petersburg, 1981, Congregation B'nai Israel Synagogue, Clearwater, Fla., 1981, Suncoast Seabird Sanctuary, St. Petersburg, 1982, Lilly Residence, Treasure Island, Fla., 1983, Anchor Bank Office Bldg., St. Petersburg, 1984, 1600 Pasadena Office Bldg., 1984 (nat. design patent), Lighthouse Harbor Marina, 1984, Tugaloo Environ. Edn. Ctr., 1989, Latorre Chiropractic Clinic, 1990, Johnnie Ruth Clarke Health Ctr., 1986. Mayoral candidate City of Treasure Island, Fla., 1973; bldg. dir. City of Seminole, 1975-78; mem. Leadership St. Petersburg, 1978-79; mem. permitting task force City of St. Petersburg, 1999-2001, Mayor's Bldg. Com., 2001-, Agy. Bay Mgmt., 2007-, Stephen Minister, 2007-. Recipient numerous archtl., landscape architecture, urban design awards, Addy awards, 1981, 1982; named Spiffs Person of Courage, 1984. Mem. AIA (nat. com. on regional devel. 1969-76, vice chmn., commr. pub. affairs Fla. chpt.), Am. Inst. Planners, Constrn. Specifications Inst., Am. Inst. Landscape Architects, So. Bldg. Code Congress, Internat. Codes Coun., Fla. Planning and Zoning Assn., Nat. Eagle Scout Assn. (chpt. chmn.), Stephen Min., Deacon, First Presbyn. Ch. Independent. Presbyterian. Avocations: sailing, scuba diving, photography, flying, art. Office: PO Box 11965 Saint Petersburg FL 33733 Office Phone: 727-302-0145. Personal E-mail: ronnginn@aol.com.

GINOBILI, MANU, professional basketball player; b. Argentina, June 28, 1977; m. Marianela Ginobili. Guard Andino, La Rioja, Argentina, 1995—96, Olimpo de Bahía Blanca, Argentina, 1996—97, Basket Viola Reggio Calabria, Italy, 1998—2000, Kinder Bologna, Italy, 2001—02, San Antonio Spurs, 2002—. Mem. Argentine nat. team Summer Olympic Games, Athens, Greece, 2004, Beijing, 2008, London, 2012. Goodwill amb. UNICEF. Recipient Sixth Man of Yr. award, NBA, 2008, Gold medal, men's basketball, Athens Olympic Games, 2004, Bronze medal, men's basketball, Beijing Olympic Games, 2008, Gold medal, Internat. Basketball Fedn. Americas Championship, 2011; named Euroleague Finals MVP, 2001, Italian League MVP, 2000—01, 2001—02; named to Western Conf. All-Star Team, NBA, 2005, 2011. Achievements include being a member of NBA Champion San Antonio Spurs, 2003, 05, 07; being the only player in NBA history to win Olympic Gold medal, NBA Championship, and Euroleague Championship. Office: San Antonio Spurs 1 AT&T Center San Antonio TX 78219

GINSBERG, LEON HERMAN, social work educator; b. San Antonio, Jan. 15, 1936; s. Sam and Lillian (Gindler) G.; m. Elaine Myrna Kaner, July 29, 1956 (div. 1983); children: Robert, Michael, Meryl Sue.; m. Connie Mooney, June 2, 1983; stepchildren: Claire, Kathleen Mooney. BA, Trinity U., 1957; MSW, Tulane U., 1959; PhD, U. Okla., 1966. Dist. dir. B'nai B'rith Youth Orgn., New Orleans, 1958-61; dir. cmty. activities Jewish Cmty. Coun., Tulsa, 1961-63; assoc. prof. Sch. Social Work U. Okla., Norman, 1963-68; prof., dir. Sch. Social Work W.Va. U., Morgantown, 1968-71, prof., dean, 1971-77; commr. human svcs. State of W.Va., Charleston, 1977-84; chancellor W.Va. Bd. Regents for Higher Edn., 1984-86; Carolina disting. prof. Coll. Social Work U. S.C., Columbia, 1986—2006, interim dean, 2002—03, dean, 2003—05; program dir. social work program Appalachian State U., 2006—09; interim chair physics & astronomy, 2009—11. Fulbright prof. U. Pontificia Bolivariana, Medellin, Colombia, fall 1974; cons. tng. programs Peace Corps, Head Start, Cmty. Action, Bur. Indian Affairs, pub. welfare depts. Okla., Pa., W.Va.; sec. S.C. Gov.'s Commn. on Women, 1999—. Author: Social Work Practice in Public Welfare, 1983, The Social Work Almanac, 1992, Understanding Social Problems, Policies and Programs, 1994; co-author, (with Julie Miller-Cribbs): 4th edit., 2005;; author: Conservative Social Policy, 1998, Careers in Social Work, 1998, 2d edit., 2001, Social Work Evaluation, 2001, Thinking About a Social Work Career, 2002, 2d edit., 2005; co-author: Human Services for Older Adults, 1979, 2d edit., 1990, Human Biology for Social Workers, 2004;; editor: Social Work in Rural Communities, 1976, 3d edit., 1998, 5th edit., 2011, Supplement Ency. Social Work, 1990, (book series) Social Issues and Social Problems, 1992—2006; co-editor: Life-Span Development Psychology, 1975, New Management for Social Workers, 1988;: 2d edit., 1995, Understanding Social Problems, Policies, and Programs, 1994, 3d edit., 1999, Information Technologies; editor: Adminstrn. in Social Work, 2002—, Tchg. in Social Work. Mem., sec. Gov.'s Commn. on Women, 2001—05. Capt. AUS, 1957-58. Recipient Disting. Svc. award W.Va. Welfare Conf., 1970, Chauncey Alexander award Nat. Network for Social Work Mgrs., 2005; named W.Va. Social Worker of Yr., 1978, Outstanding Alumnus, Tulane U. Sch. Social Work, 1989, Lifetime Achievement award Coun. Social Work Edn., 2011. Mem. NASW (past nat. sec., comm. com. 1995-98, Rhoda G. Sarnat Internat. award 1998, Carolina Disting. Emeritus Prof. award 2006, Lifetime Achievement award Coun. Social Work Fedn., 2011), Coun. Social Work Edn., Am. Pub. Welfare Assn. (past pres.), Nat. Ctr. for Social Policy and Practice (past chmn. bd.), Internat. Coun. on Social Welfare (past chmn. to U.S. com.), Child Welfare League Am., B'nai B'rith, S.C. Order of the Palmetto. Office Phone: 803-736-1421.

GINSBERG, MYRON DAVID, neurologist; b. Denver, Aug. 26, 1939; s. Morris Seymour and Evelyn (Fishman) G.; children: Deborah Mara, Emily Michelle. BA, Wesleyan U., 1961; MD, Harvard U., 1966. Intern, resident Harvard Med. Svc., Boston City Hosp., 1966-68; neurology resident, fellow Mass. Gen. Hosp., Boston, 1968-70, 72-73; staff assoc. Lab. Perinatal Physiology, NIH, Bethesda, Md., 1970-72; asst. prof., assoc. prof. dept. neurology U. Pa., Phila., 1973-79; assoc. prof. neurology U. Miami Sch. Medicine, 1979—81, prof. neurology, 1981—, dir. cerebral vascular disease rsch. ctr., 1981—2006, dir. neurotrauma clin. rsch. ctr., 1991—95, Peritz Scheinberg endowed chair of neurology, 1992—. Mem. study sect. NIH, Bethesda, 1982-86; nat. rsch. com. Am. Heart Assn., Dallas, 1986-91. Editor: Cerebrovascular Diseases, 16th Princeton Conf., 1989; editor Jour. Blood Flow and Metabolism, 1992-97; contbr. over 300 articles to profl. jours. Lt. comdr. USPHS, 1970-72. Fulbright scholar U.S. Govt., 1961-62; recipient Jacob Javits Neuroscience Investigator award NIH, 1985-92, Willis Lectr. award, Am. Stroke Assn., 2002, Disting. Scientist award Am. Heart Assn., 2003, Disting. Faculty Scholar award U. Miami, 2004. Fellow Am. Acad. Neurology; mem. Am. Neurol. Assn. (membership com. 1990-91), Am. Physiol. Soc., Internat. Soc. Cerebral Blood Flow & Metabolism (dir. 1985-89), Phi Beta Kappa, Alpha Omega Alpha. Office: U Miami Sch Medicine Dept Neurology D4-5 PO Box 016960 Miami FL 33101-6960 Office Phone: 305-243-6103, 305-243-6449. Business E-Mail: mginsberg@med.miami.edu.

GINSBURG, SCOTT K., advertising executive; BA, George Washington U., 1974; JD, Georgetown U, 1978. CEO, bd. dirs. Chancellor Media Corp.; founder Evergreen Media Corp.; co-founder H&G Comm.; CEO Sta. KTRH-AM, Houston, Sta. WNIC, Detroit; co-founder Statewide Broadcasting; chmn. DG FastChannel, Inc., 1998—, CEO, 2003—. Office: DG FastChannel Inc Ste 70 750 W John Carpenter Fwy Irving TX 75039 Office Phone: 972-581-2000. Office Fax: 972-581-2001. Business E-Mail: sginsburg@dgfastchannel.com.

GINTAUTAS, JONAS, physician, scientist, administrator; b. Justinava, Lithuania, Oct. 3, 1938; came to U.S., 1967; s. Jonas and Elena (Zavadzkyte) Sinsinas; m. Kristina Zebrauskaite, June 13, 1970 (div. June 1992); children: Stasys, Pasaka, Vadas; m. Lilija Isodaite, July 13, 2002; 1 child, Justinas. PhD, Northwestern U., 1976; MD, U. Juarez, Mex., 1984; MBA, Century U., 1996. Assoc. prof. Tex. Tech. U., Lubbock, 1975-77; assoc. prof. and dir. rsch. Tex. Tech. U. Health Scis. Ctr., Lubbock, 1979-82; dir. basic and clin. rsch., prof. neurology The Brookdale U. Hosp. Med. Ctr., NYC, 1985—2002; dir. clin. rsch., prof. neurology MediaSys Corp., 2002—. Cons. Amtorg Corp., N.Y.C., 1987-94, Ralex Internat. Co., Boston, 1988-91, Arrow Biomed Inc., Metuchen, N.J., 1988—. Editorial cons. Jour. Aphasia Agnosia Apraxia, 1979—; contbr. articles on pharmacology, anesthesia and surgery to profl. jours. Charter mem. Rep. Presdl. Task Force, Washington, 1982—, Platinum mem., 2002—; mem. Nat. Rep. Senatorial Com., Washington, 1984—, U.S. Senatorial Club, Washington, 1984—; nat. campaign advisor Nat. Rep. Senatorial Com., Washington, 1995-96. Recipient medal of honor Rep. Presdl. Task Force, 1982; rsch. grantee various pvt. and govtl. agys. Fellow Internat. Coll. Physicians and Surgeons (hon.); mem. U.S. Senatorial Club (preferred). Avocations: woodworking, camping, scuba diving, fishing, reading. Home: RR 1 Box 42 Frametown WV 26623-9724 Home Phone: 718-850-0505. E-mail: jgintautas@jhmc.org.

GIPSON, ANDY, state legislator; b. Flowood, Miss., Dec. 21, 1976; m. Leslie Ellen Lehnhoff; children: Joseph, Abigale, Benjamin. BA, Miss. coll.; JD, Miss. coll. sch. of law. Atty. Watkins, Ludlum, Winter & Stennis, 2001—; bus. owner Gipson Land and Cattle, 1995—; mem. Dist. 77 Miss. House of Reps., 2008—. Republican. Baptist. Home: 414 Holly Grove Cir Braxton MS 39044 Office: PO Box 1018 Jackson MS 39215 Home Phone: 601-847-0417; Office Phone: 601-949-4789. E-mail: agipson@house.ms.gov.

GIPSON, JIM, retail executive; Pres. Houchens Industries, Inc., chmn., CEO, 1994—. Office: Houchens Industries Inc 700 Church St Bowling Green KY 42102 Office Phone: 270-843-3252. Office Fax: 270-780-2877. Business E-Mail: jgipson@houchensindustries.com.

GIRARD, JAMES EMERY, chemistry professor; b. Joliet, Ill., July 1, 1945; s. George I. and Mary C. (Jones) G.; children: Krista, Jon, Mark, Steven, Lauren, Alexis. BA, Lewis Coll., Lockport, Ill., 1967; PhD, Pa. State U., University Park, 1971. Research fellow Pa. State U., Univ. Park, 1967-71, postdoctoral fellow, 1971-72; NIH postdoctoral fellow U. Calif., San Diego, 1972-73, vis. prof., summer 1974; asst. prof. Coll. the Holy Cross, Worcester, Mass., 1973-77; staff scientist Gen. Elec. Co. Corp. Research and Devel. Ctr., Schenectady, NY, 1977-79; assoc. prof. The Am. U., Washington, 1979-84, prof., 1984—, chmn. dept. chemistry, 1984—91, 2003—06, 2008—. Franklin fellow US Dept. State, 2009-10, Horace S. & May Davidson Isbell prof. chemistry, 2010, vice chair, Am. U. Faculty Senate, 2010-11, Chair Faculty Senate Am. U., 2011-12, mem. bd. trustees, 2011-12, cons., expert witness in field. Author: (textbooks) Chemistry: An Environmental Perspective, 1994, Chemistry Fundamentals: An Environmental Perspective, 1994, 2d edit., 2003, Principles of Environmental Chemistry, 2005, 2nd edit., 2009, 3rd edit., 2014, Criminalistics: Forensic Science and Crime, 2007, Criminalistics: Forensic Science, Crime & Terrorism, 2010, 3rd edit., 2014; contbr. articles to profl. jours. Recipient Sr. Scholar award The Am. U., 1986-87, Outstanding Svc. award, 2012, Leo Schubert award Washington Acad. Scis., 1995. Mem.: Am. Chem. Soc. Home: 6328 Karmich St Fairfax Station VA 22039-1621 Office: Am U Dept Chemistry 4400 Massachusetts Ave NW Dept Washington DC 20016-8003 Office Phone: 202-885-1791. Business E-Mail: jgirard@american.edu.

GIRGUS, SAM B., English literature educator; b. Dec. 30, 1941; m. Judith Scot-Smith; children: Katya Roberts, Meighan St. John, Jennifer Scot-Smith. BA in American Studies, Syracuse U., NYC, 1962; MA in English, State U. Iowa, Ames, 1963; PhD in American Studies, U. N.Mex., Albuquerque, 1972. Reporter, critic Providence Jour., RI, 1967-69; asst. prof. in Am. studies and English U. Ala., 1972-75, dir., 1973-75; assoc. prof., chmn. dept. Am. studies U. N.Mex., 1975-84, prof. English and Am. studies, 1980-87; prof. English, dir. Am. studies U. Oreg., Eugene, 1987-90; prof. English Vanderbilt U., Nashville, 1990—, dir. Am. studies, 1990-92, chair, dir., film studies, 2003—04. Chmn. disciplinary adv. com. Fulbright Scholars Awards in Am. Culture, 1989-93; cons. USIA visit at Sofia U., Bulgaria, 1985, Los Andes U., Bogota, Columbia, 1992, Hankuk U., Seoul, Korea, 1993, Aarhus U., Odense U., Denmark, 1995; Uppsala chair in Am. studies Uppsala U., Sweden, 1996; acting dir. film studies Vanderbilt U., 2003-04; mem. tchg. com. Soc. for Cinema and Media Studies, 2006, Cinema of Redemption, Levinas and Cinema, King's Coll., London, 2006; lectr. in field. Author: The Law of the Heart: Individualism and the Modern Self in American Literature, 1979, The New Covenant: Jewish Writers and the American Idea, 1984, Desire and the Political Unconscious in American Literature, 1990, The Films of Woody Allen, 1993, 2d edit., 2002, Hollywood Renaissance: The Cinema of Democracy in the Era of Ford, Capra and Kazan, 1998, America on Film: Modernism, Documentary, and a Changing America, 2002, Levinas and the Cinema of Redemption, Time, Ethics and the Feminine, The American Self: Myth, Ideology and Popular Culture, 1981, The New Eden: Consensus and Regeneration in America, 1988, The Outsider: Dissent and Alienation in America, 1988; co-editor: Companion to Woody Allen; guest editor: Am. Literary Realism 1870-1910, 1977; prodr., writer: (film) In Loco Amicis: The New Vanderbilt Story, 2001, Beyond Ontology, 2006, Clint Eastwood's America, Divine comedy in Woody Allen, Capra and Levinas, 1938 in Am. Cinemas, Beyond Being Cinema of Redemption (with Peter Bailey and Sam B. Girgus) The Companion to Woody Allen, 2013, Wood Allen; contbr. articles to profl. jours. With USN, 1963-67. Rockefeller Humanities fellow, 1980-81, Sr. Fulbright lectr. U. Heidelberg, Germany, 1984, Littlejohn Rsch. fellowship; named Prof. of Semester Vanderbilt U., 2006. Fellow Vanderbilt Ctr. Nashville Studies, Ctr for Religion and Cultures, Vanderbilt Ctr. Nashville Studies; mem. MLA, Cinema Studies Assn., Am. Studies Assn., Modernist Studies Assn. Home: 402 Lynwood Blvd Nashville TN 37205-3435 Office: Vanderbilt U Dept English PO Box 1654 Sta B 318 Benson Hall Nashville TN 37235 Office Phone: 615-322-2271. Business E-Mail: sam.b.girgus@vanderbilt.edu.

GIRTH, MARJORIE LOUISA, lawyer, educator; b. Trenton, NJ, Apr. 21, 1939; d. Harold Brookman and Marjorie Mathilda (Simonson) G. AB, Mt. Holyoke Coll., 1959; LLB, Harvard U., 1962. Bar: NJ 1963, US Supreme Ct. 1969, NY 1976. Pvt. practice, Trenton, 1963-65; rsch. assoc. Brookings Instn., 1965-70; assoc. prof. law SUNY Law Sch., Buffalo, 1971-79, prof., 1979-91, assoc. dean, 1986-87; dean Ga. State U. Coll. Law, Atlanta, 1992-96, prof., 1992—2009, prof. emeritus, 2009—. Vis. prof. U. Va. Law Sch., 1979-80, Southeastern Bankruptcy Law Inst., Emory Law Sch., spring 1991, vis. scholar, spring 1996; vis. prof. Warsaw, Poland, 2003, Law Sch. Vytautus Magnus U., Lithuania, 2006; vis. legal educator W.Va. U. Coll. Law Vis. Com., 1994-95; chancellor's search adv. com. Bd. of Regents, 1993-94; mem. com. on standards of the profession State Bar Ga., 1996-2008; mem. commn. on racial and ethnic bias in ct. sys. Ga. Supreme Ct, 1993-95, mem. commn. on equality, 1995-2004, sec., 1998-2000, mem. commn. on access and fairness in the cts., 2004-06; mem. Atlanta Foreclosure Prevention Task Force, Fed. Reserve Bd., 2004-12. Author: Poor People's Lawyers, 1976, Bankruptcy Options for the Consumer Debtor, 1981, (co-author) Bankruptcy: Problem, Process, Reform, 1971. Bd. dirs. Buffalo and Erie County YWCA, 1972-76, Buffalo Unitarian-Universalist Ch., 1981-84, Feminist Women's Health Ctr., 1993-94, ACLU, Ga., 1995-2001, Unitarian-Universalist Congregation of Atlanta, 1999—2003, trustee, Unitarian Universalist Fellowship Chautauqua, 2011-, Meadville Lombard Theol. Sch., 2008-2014, sect., 2009-2014; mem. commn. on peace, justice and human rights Internat. Assn. Religious Freedom, 1976-79; mem Ga. Ct. appeals Centennial Celebration, 2005-06; chmn. Erie County Task Force on Status of Women, 1985-87 Recipient Centennial award for profl. achievement, Alumnae Assn. of Mt. Holyoke Coll., 1972, award for pioneering achievements NY State 8th Jud. Dist. Splty. Bar Assn. and Com. on Women in the Cts., 2000. Fellow Lawyers Found. Ga.; mem. ABA (mem. coun. bus. law sect. 1985-89, chmn. consumer bankruptcy com. 1983-86), Am. Arbitration Assn. (nat. comml. arbitration panel 1997—2011), Assn. Am. Law Schs. (profl. devel. com. 2002-06, nominations com. 1996), Am. Law Inst., NY State Bar Assn. (mem. exec. com. bus. law sect. 1980-91, chmn. bankruptcy law com. 1980-82, chmn. banking corp. bus. law sect. 1986-87, mem. ho. of dels. 1990-91), Am. Law Inst. (elec. mem. 1997-), Law Sch. Admissions Coun. (audit com. 1995-97, 1999—2009, chair, 2007-09, fin. and legal affairs com., 1997-99). Unitarian Universalist. Home: 800 W Fercy St # 6D Buffalo NY 14222 Office: Ga State University Coll Law 800 W Fercy St # 6D Buffalo NY 14222 Business E-Mail: mgirth@gsu.edu.

GISCLAIR, JERRY, state legislator; b. Raceland, La., Feb. 7, 1948; m. Linda Gisclair; children: Gretchen, Andrea, Kristy. Roubstabout Evans Parrafin Svc., 1966; technician/mgr. Latelco & SolaCom, 1971—79; owner E.U.I., 1979—, Coastal Broadcasting, 1993—, Bayou Portuguese Citrus Farms, 2000—; self-employed Donlin Constrn., 2004—; mem. Dist. 54 La. House of Reps., 2008—, mem. agr., forestry, aquaculture and rural devel. com., natural resources and environment com., transp., hwys. and pub. works com., mem. spl. com. on mil. and vets. affairs. Staff sgt. USAF, 1967—71. Democrat. Roman Catholic. Office: PO Drawer 1448 Larose LA 70373 also: Capitol Office PO Box 44486 Baton Rouge LA 70804 also: Business Office Coastal Broadcasting PO Box 135 Larose LA 70373 Home Phone: 985-693-3826; Office Phone: 985-798-7707, 225-342-6945, 985-798-7792. Office Fax: 985-798-7757, 985-798-7793. E-mail: gisclait@legis.state.la.us, jerry@mobiletel.com.

GISH, KATHY OATES, treasurer; b. San Antonio, Tex. 1 children. BBA in Fin., U. Honolulu. Cert. treasury profl. Treasury mgr. CRSS, Inc.; cash mgr. Geosource, Inc.; asst. treas. Sterling Chemicals; treasury mgr. Weatherford International; sr. dir., treasury Sysco Corp., 1998—2000, asst. treas., 2000—, v.p., 2005—. Bd. dirs Houston Treasury Mgmt. Assn., 1996-98, mem.; mem. Nat. Assn. of Corp. Treasurers (NACT), Women's Foodservice Forum (WFF), Houston Treasury Mgmt. Assn. Office: SYSCO Corp 1390 Enclave Pky Houston TX 77077 Office Phone: 281-584-1390. Office Fax: 281-584-2721. Business E-Mail: gish.kathy@corp.sysco.com.

GITNER, GERALD L., air transportation executive, investment banker; b. Boston, Apr. 10, 1945; s. Samuel and Sylvia (Berkovitz) Gitner; m. Deanne Gebell, June 24, 1968; children: Daniel Mark, Seth Michael. BA cum laude, Boston U., 1966. Staff v.p. TransWorld Airlines, NYC, 1972-74; sr. v.p. mktg. and planning Tex. Internat. Airlines, Houston, 1974-80; pres., founder People Express Airlines, Newark, 1980-82; chmn. Pan Am. World Svcs. Inc., NYC, 1982-85, exec. v.p., chief fin. officer, 1983-85; vice chmn. Pan Am. World Airways, NYC, 1982-85, Pan Am Corp., 1984-85; pres. Tex. Air Corp., Houston, 1985-86; CEO, pres. ATASCO USA, Inc., aircraft trading firm, NYC, 1986-89; chmn. D. G. Assocs. Inc., 1986—, Avalon Group, Ltd., NYC, 1990-98; co-chmn. Global Aircraft Leasing Ltd., 1991-98; dir. TWA, Inc., 1993—2002, CEO, 1996-99, chmn., 1997—2002; chmn. bd. Kitty Hawk, Inc., 2002—07; dir. Tricom, S.A., 2004—10, CIFG Holding Inc., 2009—; chmn. eJeT Aviation Holdings, Inc., 2008—. Bd. advisers econs. dept. Boston U.; mem. chancellors coun. U. Mo., St. Louis, 1997—2000. Trustee, mem. exec. com. Boston U., 1984—96, treas. emeritus, 2009—; trustee Rochester (N.Y.) Inst. Tech., 1999—2004. Recipient Disting. Alumni award, Boston U., 1982, 1984. Mem.: Cornell Club N.Y., Phi Alpha Theta.

GITTINS, TIMOTHY LEE, military officer; b. Iowa, 1976; m. Shelley Gittins; children: T.J., Cole. Instructor Captains Career Course, 2007—. Capt. 101st Airborne US Army, Co. C, 1st Sqdn., 61st Cav. Regt. Decorated Purple Heart, Bronze Star, General Douglas MacArthur Leadership Award; named one of The World's Most Influential People, TIME Mag., 2007. Southern Baptist. Office: Captains Career Course Fort Benning GA 31905

GIULIANTI, MARA SELENA, former mayor; b. NYC, June 3, 1944; d. Leon and Bertha (Jablonky) Berman; m. Donald Giulianti, May 29, 1966; children: Stacey Alexander, Michael Alan. BA, Tulane U., 1966. Social worker L.A. County Social Svcs., 1966-68; adminstrv. asst. neurosurg. cons. D. Giulianti, MD, Hollywood, Fla., 1980-83; campaign mgr. City Commr. Suzanne Gunzburger, Hollywood, 1982; mayor City of Hollywood, 1986—90, Fla., 1992—2008. Vice chmn. Broward Employment and Tng. Adminstrn., 1987-89, 92-94, 96-00, 01-02, chmn., 1989-90, 94-96, 00-01, Work Force One chmn., 2002-04, 06-, chmn. pro tem, 2004-05, vice chair 2005-06; exec. bd. Fla. League Cities, Tallahassee, 1986-90, 92—), bd. dirs.; econ. devel. pol. com. Nat. League Cities, Washington, 1987-90, human devel. policy com., 1992-94, fin., adminstrn. and intergovtl. rels. steering com., 1994-02; active Broward County Met. Planning Orgn., 1986-90. Columnist The Digest, Hallandale, Fla., 2001-02, South Fla. Sun-Times, 2002—, Beach Digest, 2002-03; contbr. articles to local newspapers. Pres. Women in Distress, Broward County, 1982-83, bd. dirs., 1983-90, 2006—, trustee, 1994-97, 05-; exec. bd. Nat. Jewish Cmty. Rels. Adv. Coun., 1985-87; v.p. CHARLEE Family Care Homes, Broward County, 1986-88, bd. dirs., 1988-92; mem. Broward County Commn. on Status Women, 1984-86, Fla. Commn. on Drug and Alcohol Concerns, Tallahassee, 1984-85, Broward County Dem. Exec. Com., 1984-88; pres. Hills Dem. Club, 1991-94; trustee Graves Mus. of Archeol. and Nat. History, Dania, Fla., 1993-97; bd. dirs. Hollywood Econ. Growth Corp., 1994-95, 98-99; chmn. Hollywood Cmty. Redevel. Agy., 1992—; v.p. South Broward unit Am. Cancer Soc., 1992-93, bd. dirs., 1993-99. Recipient Hannah G. Solomon award, 1983, Giraffe Stick Your Neck Out award Women's Advocacy--the Majority/Minority, 1986, Leadership award Leadership Hollywood Alumni, 1987, City of Peace award Israel Bonds, Broward County, 1987, Menorah award Histadrut, 1990, Juliette Gordon Low award Girl Scouts Broward County, 1997, Govt. Leadership award, ArtServe, 2002, Gracias award Hispanic Unity, 2000, Cmty. Covenant award, Broward Outreach Ctr., 2001, Breaking the Glass Ceiling award, Ziff Jewish Mus. of Fla., 2002, Spirit of Excellence award Am Bus. Women's Assn., 2003, Woman of Valor award Broward County Jewish Cmty. Ctr., 2003, Founders award Chaminade-Madonna Coll. Prep., 2004; named Broward County Woman of Yr., Am. Jewish Congress, 1988, Woman of Yr. Women in Comms., Inc., 1990, Crystal Vision award Hollywood Art and Culture Ctr., 2000; Honoree Boys & Girls Clubs of Broward, 2001, honoree Holocaust Documentation and Edn. Ctr., 2005; inducted Broward County Women's Hall of Fame, 1996. Mem. Nat. Coun. Jewish Women (nat. bd. dir. 1985-89), Jewish Fedn. So. Broward (chair community rels. com. 1981-82, bd. dir. 1982-90), Broward County Med. Aux. (br. pres. 1977-78), Rotary. Democrat. Avocations: writing, volunteer work, travel. Home Phone: 954-961-5959; Office Phone: 954-921-3321. Business E-Mail: mgiulianti@hollywoodfl.org.

GIVAN, JUANDALYNN DELEATHIA, state legislator, lawyer; d. Leroy and Patricia Givan. B, JD, Miles Coll., Fairfield, Ala. Owner, atty. Givan & Associates; mem. Dist. 60 Ala. House of Representatives, 2011—. Named Profl. Woman of Yr., NAACP, 2010. Democrat. Office: Ala House of Reps Rm 539-A 11 S Union St Montgomery AL 36130 also: PO Box 13803 Birmingham AL 35202 Office Phone: 334-242-7684, 205-326-2466.

GIVEN, KENNA SIDNEY, surgeon, educator; b. Charleston, W.Va., Nov. 22, 1938; s. Virgil and Chessie Given; m. Charlene K. Given; children: Kari, Patrick, Amy. BA, W.Va. U., 1960; MD, Duke U., 1964. Diplomate Am. Bd. Surgery, Am. Bd. Plastic Surgery (chairperson-elect 1996-97, bd. dirs. 1992—). Intern Ind. U. Med. Ctr., Indpls., 1964-65; resident, then chief resident gen. surgery Grady Meml. Hosp./Emory U. Hosp., Atlanta, 1965-69; asst. resident, then chief resident plastic surgery Duke U. Med. Ctr., Durham, NC, 1975-77; clin. instr. surgery Emory U., Atlanta, 1972-74; chief surgery Lanier Meml. Hosp., Langdale, Ala., 1974; prof., chief divsn. plastic surgery Med. Coll. Ga., Augusta, 1977—2001, med. dir. oper. rm., 1989-90. Assoc. dir. burn unit Med. Coll. Ga. Hosp.; cons. Augusta Correctional and Med. Instn.; plastic surgery dir. Children's Med. Svc., 1981—; mem. Residency Rev. Commn. for Plastic Surgery, 1991-2001, chmn., 1994-96; chair Am. Bd. Plastic Surgery, Inc., 1997-99; chmn. residency rev. com. Accreditation Coun. for Grad. Med. Edn., 1994-96; lectr. in field. Contbr. articles to profl. jours. Pres. Med. Rsch. Found. Ga., 1985-88; trustee Plastic Surgery Edn. Found., 1994-97, pres.-elect, 1997; bd. dirs. Augusta Country Day Sch.; bd. dirs. Augusta Prep. Day Sch., 1988, trustee, 1989-90. Fellow ACS; mem. AMA, Am. Assn. Plastic Surgeons (trustee 1994-97), Assn. Acad. Chmn. in Plastic Surgery (pres. 1996-97, bd. dirs. 1985-88, 93—), Southeastern Plastic and Reconstructive Surgery (chmn. continuing med. edn. com. 1987, bd. dirs. 1992-95), Am. Soc. Plastic and Reconstructive Surgery (bd. dirs. 1988), Am. Assn. Hand Surgery, Am. Cleft Palate Assn., Am. Soc. Aesthetic Plastic Surgeons, Internat. Soc. Clin. Plastic Surgeons, Ga. Plastic Surgery Soc. (pres. 1985), Med. Assn. Ga., Richmond County Med. Soc., Southeastern Surg. Congress., So. Med. Assn., Southeastern Soc. Plastic and Reconstructive Surgeons (pres. 1997), So. Surg. Soc. Baptist. Home: 748 Tripps Ct Augusta GA 30909 Office: Med Coll Ga Divsn Plastic Surgery HB-5049 Augusta GA 30912-4080 Office Phone: 706-721-6945. Business E-Mail: kgiven@mcg.edu.

GIVENS, DAVID P., state legislator; b. Dec. 26, 1966; m. Lynne Givens; 3 children. BS in Agr., Western Ky. U., 1989, MA in Comm., 1997. Mng. ptnr. Central Farmers Supply, 1989—; bd. mem. Green River Cattle Co., 2001—; mem. Dist 9 Ky. State Senate, 2009—. Republican. Presbyn. Office: 702 Capitol Ave Rm 215 Frankfort KY 40601 also: PO Box 12 Greensburg KY 42743 Office Phone: 502-564-8100 Ext. 264.

GIVENS, ROY E., state legislator; b. Wellsburg, W.Va, Apr. 27, 1929; s. George D., Anna B. Peters Givens; married; children: Jeff, Susan. Attended, West Liberty State Coll. Ret. sales rep. US Army; bd. dirs. Greater Stubenville C. of C.; past pres. Brooke County Bd. Edn.; mem. Dist 2 W.Va. House of Delegates, 2008—, mem. Govt. Orgn. Com., Pensions and Retirement Com. & Vet. Affairs and Homeland Security Com. Democrat. Office: State Capitol Complex Rm 221E, Bldg 1 Charleston WV 25305 Office Phone: 304-340-3129. E-mail: rgivens@mail.wvnet.edu.

GLADDEN, BRIAN T., computer company executive; b. 1965; BS in Fin., Millersville Univ., 1987. Mgmt. positions General Electric Co., 1989—2007, exec. audit mgr., CFO Healthcares Med. IT, global integration mgr. for acquisition of Marquette Med. Systems; v.p. fin., CFO GE Plastics GE Plastics, v.p., gen. mgr. plastics resins bus., 2005—07, pres., 2007; pres., CEO SABIC Innovative Plastics, 2007—08; sr. v.p., CFO Dell, Inc., Round Rock, Tex., 2008—. Office: Dell Inc 1 Dell Way Round Rock TX 78682

GLADDEN, DEAN ROBERT, arts administrator, educator, consultant; b. Columbus, Ohio, Dec. 27, 1953; s. Cyril Robert and Eileen (Faulkner) G.; m. Jane Frances Tellers, Aug. 27, 1953; children: John Dean, Catherine Eileen. B in Music Edn., Miami U., Oxford, Ohio, 1976; MS in Urban Arts Mgmt., Drexel U., 1978; postgrad., Harvard U., 1998. Exec. dir. Council for Arts of Greater Lima, Ohio, 1977-80, Arts Comm. Greater Toledo, 1980-82; dir. devel. and adminstrn. Great Lakes Theater Festival, Cleve., 1982-86; assoc. mng. dir. The Cleve. Play House, 1986, mng. dir., 1987—2006, Alley Theatre, Houston, 2006—. Cons. Ohio Arts Coun., Cleve., 1977—, chmn. sponsor/touring panel, 1981-83; adj. assoc. prof. U. Akron, Ohio, 1984-87; mem. adv. com. Mandel Sch. of Non-Profit Mgmt., Case Western Res. U., Cleve. Author booklets on the econs. of arts in Ohio, 1981, 83, 85, 87, 89, 91, 93. Mem. League Resident Theatres (exec. com.), Ohio Citizens for Arts (v.p.), Rotary (pres.), Nat. Endownment Arts Theatre Cons. for US Info. Agy. in Budapast(theatre panel) Episcopalian. Avocations: piano, drums. Home: 4022 Lanark Ln Houston TX 77025 Office: Alley Theatre 615 Texas Ave Houston TX 77002 Office Phone: 716-315-3372.

GLADDEN, JOSEPH RHEA, JR., lawyer; b. Atlanta, Oct. 5, 1942; s. Joseph Rhea I and Frances (Baker) G.; m. Sarah Elizabeth (Bynum), Aug. 21, 1965; children: Joseph III, Elizabeth. BA, Emory U., 1964; LLB, U. Va., 1967. Bar: Ga., 1968; U.S. Dist. Ct. (no. dist.) Ga., 1968; U.S. Ct. Appeals (5th cir.), 1968; U.S. Ct. Appeals (11th cir.), 1985. Assoc. King and Spalding, Atlanta, 1967-73, ptnr., 1973-85; v.p., sr. staff counsel The Coca Cola Co., Atlanta, 1985-87, v.p., dep. gen. counsel, 1987-90, v.p., gen. counsel, 1990-91, sr. v.p., gen. counsel, 1991—99, exec. v.p., gen. counsel, 1999—2000; ret. Atlanta, 2001. Bd. dirs. Coca Cola Enterprises, Emory Healthcare; chmn. bd. dir. Wesley Woods Inc., Coca Cola Amatil. Chmn. bd. trustees Agnes Scott Coll.; bd. dir. Atlanta Ballet; trustee Lovett Sch.; Acad. Search Cons. Svc. Mem. ABA (com. corp. law, gen. counsel), Am. Corp. Counsel Assn., Ga. Bar Assn., State Bar Ga., Assn. Gen. Counsel; Atlanta Bar Assn., Health Svcs. Found. (bd. mem.), UVA Miller Ctr. Found. (Chmn. bd.).Commerce Club, Piedmont Driving Club. Home Phone: 540-456-8353. Personal E-mail: sjgladden@mindspring.com.

GLADE, WILLIAM PATTON, JR., economics professor; b. Wichita Falls, Tex., July 29, 1929; s. William Patton and Billie (Hatcher) G.; m. Marlene Louise Joseph, July 10, 1954; children: Anita, Genie, Patton, John. BBA, U. Tex., 1950, MA, 1951, PhD, 1955. Instr., asst. prof. econs. U. Md., 1957-60; asst., assoc. prof. U. Wis., Madison, 1960-65, prof. Sch. Bus. and dept. econs., 1966-71; prof. econs. U. Tex., Austin, 1970—2007, prof. emeritus, 2007—, dir. Inst. L.Am. Studies, 1971-86, dir. Mex. Ctr., 1997-2001; sr. program assoc. Smithsonian Instn. Wilson Ctr., 1987-88, acting sec. L.Am. program, 1989, sr. scholar, 1990-2000; assoc. dir. USIA, 1989-92; mem. rsch. adv. coun. Ctr. for Arts and Culture, 1998—2005. Mem. Mex.-U.S. Commn. Ednl. and Cultural Exch./Fulbright Commn., 2002—07, Am. co-pres., 2002—04; pres. elect Sec. Med. Ctr. Vols., 2009—, pres., 2010—11. Author: Las empresas gubernamentales descentralizadas, 1959, The Political Economy of Mexico, 1963, The Latin American Economies, 1969, Marketing in a Developing Economy - The Case of Peru, 1970; co-editor (with Charles A. Reilly) Inquiry at the Grassroots, 1993; contbr., editor Privatization of Public Enterprises in Latin America, 1991; author, editor: Bigger Economies, Smaller Governments: The Role of Privatization in Latin America, 1996; contbr. articles to profl. jours. Mem. Latin Am. Studies Assn. (v.p. 1978, pres. 1979), S.W. Coun. Latin Am. Studies Assn. (v.p. 1995, pres. 1996), Assn. Cultural Econs., Cosmos Club, Seton Med. Ctr. Austin (vol. pres. elect 2009-10; pres. 2010-11). Office: U Tex Dept Econs Austin TX 78712 Office Phone: 512-471-6811.

GLADSTEIN, MIMI REISEL, theater and literature educator; d. Emil and Regina Rosen Reisel; m. Jay Stephen Gladstein, Aug. 18, 1956; children: Clifford Eric, Denise Robin Halikman-Gladstein, Alfred Martin. BA in Speech and Drama, Tex. Western Coll., 1959; PhD, U. N.Mex, Albuquerque, 1973. Prof. English and Theatre U. Tex., El Paso, Tex., 1968—. Dir. Women's Studies Program U. Tex., 1981—83, chmn. depts. English and Philosophy, 1985—88, exec. dir. Diamond Jubilee, 1988—90, dir. We. Cultural Heritage Program, 1995—97, assoc. dean, 1997—2002, chmn. Dept. Theatre, Dance, and Film, 2002—06. Author: 7 books; contbr. articles to profl. jours., chapters to books. Pres. John Steinbeek Soc. Am., 2006—13; chmn. content com. El Paso Holocaust Mus. and Study Ctr., Tex., 1995—2013. Recipient Burlington No. award, 1988, Angeline Pruis award, 1987, Burkhardt award, 1996, Mentor Appreciation award, Ariz. State U., 2002, Disting. Achievement Svc. to Students award, UTEP, 2006, Sterling Membership award, Rocky Mountain Modern Lang. Assn., 2006, Am Book award, 2009, SW Book award, 2010; named Woman of Yr., El Paso Women's Polit. Caucus, 1975; named to El Paso Commn. for Women Hall of Fame, 2011; grantee, Fulbright Found., 1995, Outstanding Achievement award, Coll. Liberal Arts, 2003; Hall of Fame, El Paso Commn. Woman, 2011, Hall of Hon., El Paso County Hist. Soc., 2011. Home: 5464 Cactus Hill Drive El Paso TX 79912 Office: University of Texas at El Paso El Paso TX 79968 Office Phone: 915-747-6259.

GLANCY, WALTER JOHN, retired lawyer; b. LA, Mar. 8, 1942; s. Walter Perry and Elva Thomasin (Douglass) Glancy; children: Jill Marie(dec.), Gregory Owens. AB, Princeton U., 1964; BA, Oxford U., Eng., 1966; LLB, Yale U., 1969. Bar: Tex. 1971. Law clk. to assoc. justice Byron R. White U.S. Supreme Ct., 1969-70; staff asst. NSC, 1970-71; staff asst. to Peter M. Flanigan, The White House, 1971; assoc. then ptnr. Jackson, Walker, Winstead, Cantwell & Miller, Dallas, 1972-76; ptnr. Hughes & Luce and predecessor, Dallas, 1976-85, Baker & Botts, Dallas, 1985-88, Hughes & Luce, Dallas, 1988-90; pvt. practice Dallas, 1991-95, 97-99; cons. Meyer, Hendricks, Victor, Osborn & Maledon, Phoenix, 1991-95; ptnr. Weil, Gotshal & Manges LLP, Dallas, 1995-96; sr. v.p., gen. counsel, dir Holly Corp., 1999—2008. Adj. lectr. corp. taxation So. Meth. U. Sch. Law, 1988. Note and comment editor Yale Law Jour., 1968-69. Bd. mgmt. Dallas YMCA Urban Svcs., 1975—84; bd. dirs. Dallas Family Guidance Ctr., 1982—96, pres. bd. dirs., 1985—86; bd. dirs. Child & Family Guidance Ctrs., Dallas, 1996—2003, pres. bd. dirs., 2001—02; bd. dirs. Dallas Opera, 1984—88, 1996—97; bd. trustees Hockaday Sch., Dallas, 1989—95; mem. adminstrv. bd. Lovers Ln. United Meth. Ch., Dallas, 1984—86, 1988—89; deacon Park Cities Bapt. Ch., Dallas, 1996—2006. Nat. Merit scholar, 1960-64, Marshall scholar, 1964-66. Mem.: State Bar Tex. (chmn. tax sect. 1985—86, profl. ethics com. 1982—, chmn. profl. ethics com. 1999—2013), Am. Law Inst., Dallas Bar Assn. (chmn. legal ethics com. 1980—81), Order of Coif, Park Cities Rotary Club (pres. 2003—04), Phi Beta Kappa. Republican. Home Phone: 214-361-2732. Personal E-mail: johnglancy@mindspring.com.

GLASER, ARTHUR HENRY, lawyer, mediator; b. Jersey City, May 1, 1947; s. Ned C. and Lorraine I. (Neil) G.; m. Waynelia Potter, Mar. 19, 1994; children: Kimberly N., Kevin M., Daniel J. BS, Hampden-Sydney Coll., 1968; JD, U. Va., 1973. Bar: Ga. 1973, U.S. Dist. Ct. (no. and mid. dists.) Ga., U.S. Ct. Appeals (11th cir.). Assoc. Swift, Currie, McGhee & Hiers, Atlanta, 1973-78, ptnr., 1978-83, Drew, Eckl & Farnham, Atlanta, 1983-98, Self, Glaser & Davis, LLP, Atlanta, 1999—2004, Glaser, Currie, Bullman, Atlanta, 2004—; with Henning Mediation, 1999—. Mem. ABA, Ga. Bar Assn., Am. Coll. Civil Trial Mediators. Presbyterian. Home: 1540 Burnt Hickory Rd NW Marietta GA 30064-1308 Office: Glaser Currie Bullman LLP 1455 Lincoln Pkwy Ste 300 Atlanta GA 30346 Office Phone: 770-563-9305. Business E-Mail: ahg@gcblaw.net.

GLASGOW, AGNES JACKIE, social welfare administrator, therapist; b. El Paso, Tex., July 23, 1941; d. Carl Lecota Pace and Henrietta Ford (Cozart) Robertson; m. Morgan Walton, Sept. 20, 1958 (div. 1979); children: Scotty Gene, Carley Earlene Walton DeVore; m. Phillip Sidney Glasgow, Aug. 9, 1986. Lic., Trinidad State Jr. Coll., Colo., 1968; AAS, Met. State Coll., Denver, 1979, BS, 1980; MPA, U. Colo., Denver, 1987. Cert. substance abuse counselor, Colo., Tenn. Pvt. practice Life Counseling Ctr., Denver, Memphis, 1980—98; coord. masters program for substance abuse Met. State Coll., Denver, 1980—81; exec. dir. Concord Commons Counseling Ctr., Decatur, Ill., 1981—82; child care specialist Adams Cmty. Mental Health Ctr., Commerce City, Colo., 1982—84; adolescent family counselor Parkside Lodge Colo., Thornton, Colo., 1984—86; family therapist Charter Lakeside Hosp., Memphis, 1986—87; counselor, coord. Shelby State Cmty. Coll., Memphis, 1987—88; supr. adolescent and young adult program Meth. Outreach, Memphis, 1988—90; sr. mental health specialist dual diagnosis unit Meth. Hosp. Ctr., 1990—98, relapse prevention specialist, 1994—98; ret., 1998. Cons., part-time instr. Shelby State C.C., Memphis. Contbr. articles to profl. jours. Com. mem. Youth Suicide Task Force, Memphis, 1988—98; pres. Memphis and Shelby County Children and Adolescent Assn., 1990-91. Recipient Vol. of Yr. award United Way, Decatur, Ill., 1982, Cmty. Svc. award scholarship Mental Health Soc., 1983, Outstanding Svc. award, 1989, Disting. Svc. award Sheriff Dept., Memphis, 1988; nominated Diamond award Memphis Mental Health Assn., 1994. Mem. Nat. Orgn. Human Svc. Workers, Nat. Orgn. Substance Abuse Counselors, Am. Assn. Counseling & Devel., Psi Chi (treas. 1979-80). Republican. Lds Ch. Avocations: reading, stained glass, hunting, fishing, sailing.

GLASS, ANDREW JAMES, newspaper editor; b. Warsaw, Nov. 30, 1935; came to U.S., 1941, naturalized, 1948; s. Martin Allan and Wanda (Mosewicka) G.; m. Eleanor Attianese Sorrentino, June 3, 1962; 1 child, Samuel Sorrentino. BA, Yale U., 1957. Fin. reporter N.Y. Herald Tribune, 1959-62, chief congl. corr., 1963-66; mem. nat. staff Washington Post, 1966-68; exec. asst. to Senator Charles Percy, U.S. Senate, Washington, 1968-70; sr. editor Nat. Jour., Washington, 1970-74; Washington corr. Cox Newspapers, 1974-77, chief Washington Bur., 1977-97, sr. corr., 1997—2001; mng. editor The Hill Newspaper, Washington, 2002—04, columnist, 2003—06; contbg. editor Politico, Arlington, Va., 2006—. Syndicated columnist N.Y. Times News Svc., 1980-2001; adj. prof. Philip Merrill Sch. Journalism, U. Md., 2005—09. Chmn. Corr. Com. for Refugee Relief, 1975—78. With US Army, 1958, mem. USAR, 1958—64. Fellow Shorenstein, J.F. Kennedy Sch. Govt., Harvard U., 2001. Mem.: Am. Soc. News Editors, Cosmos Club, Gridiron Club (chmn. Gridiron Found. 2005—), Met. Club Washington. Office: 1100 Wilson Blvd Arlington VA 22209-3921 Office Phone: 703-647-7681. Business E-Mail: aglass@politico.com.

GLASS, DOROTHEA DANIELS, physiatrist, educator; b. NYC; d. Maurice B. and Anna S. (Kleegman) Daniels; m. Robert E. Glass, June 23, 1940; children: Anne Glass Roth, Deborah, Catherine Glass Barrett, Eugene. BA, Cornell U., 1940; MD, Woman's Med. Coll. Pa., 1954; postgrad., U. Pa., 1960—61; DMS (hon.), Med. Coll. Pa., 1987. Diplomate Am. Bd. Phys. Medicine and Rehab. (guest bd. examiner 1978, 89). Intern Albert Einstein Med. Ctr., Phila., 1954-55, clin. asst. dept. medicine, 1956-59, attending phys. medicine and rehab., 1968-70, chmn. dept. phys. medicine and rehab., sr. attending, 1971-85; chief rehab. medicine VA Med. Ctr., Miami, Fla., 1985-95; clin. prof. dept. orthop. and rehab. U. Miami Sch. Medicine, 1985—. Lois Mattox Miller fellow preventive medicine Woman's Med. Coll. Pa., 1955-56, instr. preventive medicine, 1956-59, instr. medicine, 1960-62; resident phys. medicine and rehab. VA Hosp., Phila., 1959-62, chief phys. medicine and rehab., 1966-68, cons., 1968-82; asst. clin. dir. Jefferson Med. Coll. Hosp., Phila., 1963-66, Camden County Stroke Program, Cooper Hosp., Camden, N.J., 1963-66; gen. practice medicine, Phila., 1956-59; asst. med. dir., chief phys. medicine and rehab. Moss Rehab. Hosp., Phila., 1968-70, med. dir., 1971-82, sr. cons., 1982-; mem. active staff Temple U., Phila., 1968-, asso. prof. rehab. medicine, 1968-73, prof., 1973-, dir. residency tng. rehab. medicine, 1968-82; program dir. Rehab. Rsch. and Tng. Ctr., 1977-80, chmn. dept. rehab. medicine, 1977-82; staff physician Hosp. Med. Coll. Pa., Phila., 1955-59, vis. assoc. prof. neurology, 1973-79, clin. prof., 1977-82, vis. prof., 1982-96; mem. cons. staff Frankford Hosp., Phila., 1968-82, Phila. Geriatric Center, 1975-82; mem. active staff Willowcrest-Bamberger Hosp., Phila., 1980-82; asso. phys. medicine and rehab. U. Pa. Sch. Medicine, Phila., 1962-66; asst. prof. clin. phys. medicine and rehab., 1966-68; asst. clin. dir. dept. phys. medicine and rehab. Jefferson Med. Coll., Phila., 1963-66; cons. Vols. in Medicine Clinic, Stuart, Fla., 1996—. Contbr. articles to profl. jours. Mem. profl. adv. com. Easter Seal Soc. Crippled Children and Adults Pa., 1975-82; active Goodwill Industries Phila., 1973-82, Cmty. Home Health Svcs. Phila., 1974-82, Ea. Pa. chpt. Arthritis Found., 1968-82. Recipient Humanitarian Svc. cert. Gov.'s Com. on Employment Handicapped, 1974, Outstanding Alumnae award Commonwealth of Pa. Bd., Hosp. Med. Coll. Pa., 1975, Humanitarian award Pa. Easter Seal Soc., 1981, John Eiselie Davis award Am. Kinesiotherapy Assn., 1988, Carl Haven Young Svc. award, 1994, Disting. Career award Moss Rehab. Hosp., 1997, 2009, award, 2009, Outstanding Svc. and Accomplishments award Fla. Soc. Phys. Medicine and Rehab., 2001, Susan B. Anthony award LWV of Martin County, 2002. Fellow Am. Congress Rehab. Medicine; mem. AMA, Am. Acad. Med. Dirs., Am. Acad. Phys. Medicine and Rehab. (Disting. Clinician award 1995, Krusen award 2000), Am. Assn. Electromyography and Electrodiagnosis (assoc.), Am. Assn. Sex Educators, Counselors and Therapists, Am. Burn Assn., Am. Coll. Angiology, Am. Coll. Utilization Rev., Am. Congress Rehab. Medicine (bd. govs. 1979-85, pres. 1986-87, gold Key award 1989), Am. Heart Assn. (coun. on cerebrovascular disease), Am. Lung Assn. Phila. and Montgomery County (bd. dirs. 1977-79), Am. Med. Women's Assn., Assn. Acad. Physiatrists, Assn. Med. Rehab. Dirs. and Coords., Coll. Physicians Phila., Emergency Care Rsch. Inst., Gerontol. Soc., Internat. Assn. Rehab. Facilities, Internat. Rehab. Medicine Assn., Pan Am. Med. Assn., Fla. Med. Assn., Fla. Soc. Phys. Medicine and Rehab. (pres. 1975-77, Award for Outstanding Svc. in Rehab. Medicine 2001), Pa. Med. Soc. (phys. medicine and rehab. adv. com. 1975-82), Pa. Thoracic Soc., Delaware Valley Hosp. Coun. Forum, Phila. Med. Soc., Phila. PSRO (bd. dirs. 1975-82), Phila. Soc. Phys. Medicine and Rehab. (pres. 1968-69), Laennec Soc. Phila., Royal Soc. Health, Alpha Omega Alpha. E-mail: glassrd@earthlink.net.

GLASS, ROY LEONARD, lawyer; b. Littleton, NH, Jan. 27, 1947; s. Jack Irving and Noreen (Leiuthwait) Kline; children: Shannon Renee, Ashley Leigh; m. Lauren Rachel Adams, Aug. 8, 1998; 1 stepchild, Ariel Adams. AA with honors, St. Petersburg Jr. Coll., Fla., 1971; BA, U. South Fla., 1972; JD, Fla. State U., 1975. Bar: Fla. 1976, U.S. Dist. Ct. (mid. dist.) Fla. 1977, U.S. Dist. Ct. (no. dist.) Fla. 1978, U.S. Supreme Ct. 1979, U.S. Ct. Appeals (11th cir.) 1983; cert. state and fed. mediator, 2005, ct. cert. arbitrator; cert. foreclosure mediator, appellate mediator. Assoc. Meyers, Mooney & Adler, Orlando, Fla., 1976-78, Barrett, Boyd & Bajoczky, Tallahassee, 1978-79; sole practice Tallahassee, 1979-81; ptnr. Deserio & Glass, St. Petersburg, Fla., 1981-82; assoc. Battaglia, Ross, Hastings, Dicus & Andrews, St. Petersburg, 1982-85; sole practice St. Petersburg, 1985—. Lectr. Floridians Against Constl. Tampering, Fla., 1984. Past mem. Roscoe Pound Inst., Capt. U.S. Army, 1966-70, Vietnam. Mem. AAJ (past sustaining mem.), Am. Arbitration Assn., FJA (mem. spkrs. bur.), Fla. Bar Assn. (health law com. 1984-85, chmn. health care profls. subcom. 1984-85, mem. exec. coun. health care sect. 1986-94, mem. spkrs. bur., chair client security fund com. 2003-04, Meritorious Svc. award health law sect. 1994, client security fund com. award for outstanding leadership 2004), St. Petersburg Bar Assn. (legis. com. 1983-85, liaison med. soc., med. rels. com. 1985—, trial lawyers 1987—, mem. spkrs. bur.), Pinellas County Trial Lawyers Assn., St. Petersburg C. of C. (urban solutions task force 1983-84), Phi Delta Phi, Phi Kappa Phi, Beta Gamma Sigma. Clubs: Suncoast Tiger Bay (St. Petersburg, Fang & Claw award 1983), Breakfast Sertoma (Cert. of Appreciation 1984), Westgate High Twelve (Cert. of Appreciation 1987), Am. Coll. Barristers (sr. counsel). Office: 5501 Central Ave Saint Petersburg FL 33710-8050 Office Phone: 727-384-8888.

GLASS, SHERMAN J., JR., oil industry executive; b. Houston, Tex. B in Chem. Engring., Ga. Inst. Tech., Atlanta; M in Chem. Engring., Ga. Inst. Tech. Engr. Baytown refinery, Tex., 1972; tech. and mgmt. positions Exxon Co. USA ExxonMobil Corp., v.p. basic chemicals Americas, Exxon Chem. Co. Houston, 1993—96, v.p. basic chemicals Europe, Exxon Chemical Co. Brussels, 1996, mgr. refining, Exxon Co. Internat., gen. mgr. corp. planning Irving, Tex., 2001—02, pres. ExxonMobil Global Svcs. Co., 2002—05, sr. v.p. basic chemicals, intermediates & synthetics, ExxonMobil Chem. Co., 2005—08, v.p., pres. Refining & Supply Co., 2008—. Mem. bd. trustees Ga. Tech. Found., Inc. Office: Exxon Mobil Corp Hdqs 5959 Las Colinas Blvd Irving TX 75039-2298

GLASSER, WILLIAM ARNOLD, academic administrator; b. Chgo., July 30, 1932; s. Raymond Alfred and Bee (Purdum) G.; m. Laura Jane Parison, Feb. 28, 1957; children: William, Hally. BA in English, SUNY, Binghamton, 1957; MA in English, U. Fla., 1959; PhD in English, U. Iowa, 1965. Instr. English Rollins Coll., Winter Park, Fla., 1959-62, Trinity Coll., Hartford, Conn., 1963-64; asst. prof. Williams Coll., Williamstown, Mass., 1966-70; assoc. prof. Skidmore Coll., Saratoga Springs, N.Y., 1970-77; acad. dean. So. Vt. Coll., Bennington, 1977-83, pres., 1983-97, pres. emeritus, 1997—. Fulbright lectr., Salzburg, Austria, 1972—73. Author: Reclaiming Literature, A Teacher's Dilemma, 1994; New Systems for Managing a College, 2005; The Art of Literary Thieving, 2009; The Autobiography of SATAN, Authorised Edit., 2013, My Other World, Poems for Out-of-the-Ordinary Children, 2013; The Old Man Trilogy; (novel) A Day in the Life Of An Old Man, 2013, What's New, Old Man? 2014, The Old Man in Wonderland, 2014, contbr. articles to profl. jours. Campaign chmn. United Way of Bennington County, 1986; active Bennington County Indsl. Corp., 1986-91; v.p. Assn. Vt. Ind. Colls., 1990-97; mem. Regional Affordable Housing Com., 1989-93. With USAF, 1949—53. Avocation: tennis. Home: 1621 Gulf Blvd Apt 905 Clearwater FL 33767-2930 Personal E-mail: bglasser1@yahoo.com.

GLASSER, WOLFGANG GERHARD, science researcher, educator; b. Oct. 9, 1941; came to U.S., 1969, naturalized, 2001; s. Joachim and Charlotte (Syjatz) G.; m. Heidemarie Reinecke, Mar. 18, 1969; children: Christine Glasser Lamps, Stephan A Degree wood tech., U. Hamburg, 1966, PhD Wood Chemistry, 1969. Rsch. assoc. U. Wash., Seattle, 1969—70, rsch. asst. prof., 1970—71; asst. prof. Va. Poly. Inst. and State U., Blacksburg, 1972—75, assoc. prof., 1975—80, prof. wood chemistry, 1980—2002, assoc. dean rsch. and grad. studies Coll. Natural Resources, 1993—98, prof. emeritus sustainable biomaterials, 2002—; chief sci. officer Cyclewood Solutions Inc., 2013—. Adj. prof. Inst. Paper Sci. and Tech., Atlanta, 1999-2003; dir. Pulp and Paper Rsch. Inst., Sao Paulo, Brazil, 1976, Biobased Materials Ctr., 1988-91; vis. prof. U. Grenoble (France), Centre de Recherche sur Macromolecules Vegetales, Grenoble, 1985, Nat. U. Singapore, 1993, Kyoto (Japan) U., 1998, U. Toulouse, France, 2000, 03, Chalmers U. Tech., Gothenborg, Sweden, 2001-02, U. de Guadalajara, Jalisco, Mex., 2005, U. Henri Poincaré, Nancy, France, 2006, Tech. U. Stockholm, U. Italy, 2008-09, U. Pisa, Italy, 2010, U. Freiburg, Germany, 2012-13; vis. scientist Weyerhaeuser Corp., 2004; chmn. panel NAS, 1974-76; cons. to industry and govt. Mem. editl. adv. group Holzforschung, Braunschweig, Germany, 1985-, Cellulose, 1994-99, editor-in-chief, 2000—12; mem. editl. adv. group Jour. Wood Sci. (Japan), 1998—2009, Jour. Applied Polymer Sci., 1989—2011; patentee in field; contbr. articles to profl. jours.; book editor. Co-recipient George Olmsted award Am. Paper Inst., 1974; recipient Sci. Achievement award Internat. Union Forest Rsch. Orgns., 1986, Anselme Payen award Cellulose, Paper and Textile divsn. Am Chem. Soc., 2000 Fellow Internat. Acad. Wood Sci. Tech.; mem. Am. Chem. Soc. (fellow Cellulose and Renewable Materials divsn., 2003, alt. councilor 1983-85, pub. chmn. 1985-88, chmn. 1990, councilor 1991-2000, program chmn. 1993-96, nominations chair 2002-08), Sigma Xi. Lutheran. Office: Wolfgang and Heidi Glasser 4411 Uppingham Rd Richmond VA 23235 Business E-Mail: wglasser@vt.edu.

GLASSICK, CHARLES ETZWEILER, foundation administrator; b. Wrightsville, Pa., Apr. 6, 1931; s. Gordon J. and Melva G. (Etzweiler) Glassick; m. Mary Williams, Feb. 27, 1952 (dec. 2008); children: Bruce, Judith, Jeffrey, Robert, Jonathan; m. Lois Patterson Bigbee Glassick, 2010. BS with honors, Franklin and Marshall Coll., 1953; MA, PhD, Princeton U., 1957; D.Sc. (hon.), U. Richmond, 1977; L.L.D. (hon.), Dickinson Sch. Law, 1986; LLD, Pepperdine U., 1996, Adrian Coll., 1997; LHD (hon.), Franklin & Marshall Coll., 1997. Rsch. chemist Rohm & Haas Co., Phila., 1957-62; instr. gen. chemistry Temple U., Phila., 1957-62; prof. chemistry Adrian Coll., Mich., 1962-68; v.p. Great Lakes Colls. Assn., Ann Arbor, Mich., 1968-69; assoc. dean acad. affairs Albion Coll., Mich., 1969-71, v.p. acad. affairs, 1971-72; pres. Va. Inst. Scientific Research, Richmond, 1972-77; provost, v.p. acad. affairs U. Richmond, Va., 1972-77; pres. Gettysburg Coll., Pa., 1977-89, Woodruff Arts Ctr., Atlanta, 1990-96; sr. scholar Carnegie Found. Advancement Tchg., Stanford, Calif., 1989-90, acting pres. Menlo Park, Calif., 1995, interim pres., 1996-97, sr. assoc., 1997-2001, sr. assoc. emeritus, 2001—; interim pres. NC Wesleyan Coll., 2000-01, Reinhardt Coll., 2001—02, Thomas U., 2005—06; exec. dir. Thomasville Cultural Ctr. Cons. NSF, 1963—67, NEH, 1971—72, Va. Coun. High Edn., 1972—76; mem. exec. com. Luth. Ednl. Conf. N.Am., 1983—86; mem. Pres.'s Commn. Nat. Collegiate Athletic Assn., 1988—89; interim pres. Converse Coll., 1998—99; interim dir. Scholars Press, 1999—2000; vis. fellow Cambridge U., 2002. Mem. editl. bd. Liberal Education, 1978—82, Educational Record, 1985—97; co-author: Scholarship Assessed-Evaluation of the Professoriate, 1995. Mem. Mental Health and Mental Retardation Task Force Manpower Devel., Richmond, 1975—77, ACE Commn. Minorities; bd. dirs. Hist. Gettysburg/Adams County, 1979—89, Meth. Conf. Homes Aging, 1985—89, Atlanta Cultural Olympiad, 1991—96, Midtown Alliance, 1991—97; bd. dirs, exec. com. Spartanburg Habitat for Humanity, 2002—; bd. dirs. Cmty. Campus Partnership Health, 2003—; trustee, vice-chmn. Eisenhower Soc., 1985—95, Carnegie Found. Advancement in Tchg., 1991—97, Ga. Found. Ind. Colls., 1992—2010, Literacy Action, Inc., 1994—97, Found. Hosp. Art, 1994—; bd. trustees Ga. Found. Ind. Colls., 1996—2010, Thomas U., 2006—12; bd. curators Ga. Hist. Soc., 1997—99; bd. regents Am. Arch. Fedn., 1998—2007; Fulbright sr. scholar specialist, 2002—. Mem.: AAUP, AAAS, Danforth Assocs., NY Acad. Scis., Am. Chem. Soc., Phi Beta Kappa (hon.), Alpha Chi Omega, Omicron Delta Kappa, Beta Gamma Sigma. Methodist. Personal E-mail: CEGlassick@aol.com.

GLASSMAN, ARMAND BARRY, physician, educator, scientist, administrator, pathologist; b. Paterson, NJ, Sept. 9, 1938; s. Paul and Rosa (Ackerman) G.; m. Alberta C. Macri, Aug. 30, 1958; children: Armand P., Steven B., Brian A. BA, Rutgers U., 1960; MD magna cum laude, Georgetown U., DC, 1964. Diplomate in anatomic, clinical pathology & tranfusion medicine Am. Bd. Pathology, Am. Bd. Nuc. Medicine. Intern Georgetown U. Hosp., Washington, 1964-65; resident Yale-New Haven Hosp., West Haven VA Hosp., 1965-69; asst. prof. pathology, Coll. Medicine U. Fla.; chief radioimmunoassary lab. Gainesville VA Hosp., Fla.; practice lab. and nuc. medicine, 1969-71; dir. clin. labs., assoc. prof., prof. pathology, cellular, molecular biology Med. Coll. Ga., Augusta, 1971-76; med. dir. clin. labs. Med. U. SC Hosp., Charleston, 1976-87; attending physician in lab. and nuc. medicine Med. U. SC, 1976-87, assoc. med. dir. Med. U. Hosp. and Clinics, 1982-86, prof., chmn. dept. lab. medicine, 1976-87, med. dir. MT and MLT programs, 1976-87, clin. prof. pathology, lab. medicine, and radiology, 1987—94, acting chmn. dept. immunology and microbiology, 1985-87, assoc. dean Coll. Medicine, 1979-85, asst. and assoc. dean Coll. Allied Health Sci., 1984-87, chmn. hosp. exec. com., 1985-86, acting med. dir. Univ. Hosp. and Clinics, 1985-86; med. dir. clin. labs. Charleston Meml. Hosp., 1976-87; sr. v.p. med. affairs, prof. lab. medicine and nuc. medicine Montefiore Med. Ctr. and Albert Einstein Coll. Medicine, Bronx, NY, 1987-89; v.p., lab. dir. Nat. Reference Lab., Nashville, 1989-92; from clin. prof. to prof. dept. pathology Vanderbilt U., Nashville, 1990-94; dir. Vanderbilt Pathology Lab. Svcs., 1992-94; dir. clin. labs. Vanderbilt U. Med. Ctr., 1993-94, O. Stribling chair, prof., 1994—2006; head and chair divsn./dept. lab. medicine, med. dir. med. tech. and cytogenetic tech. programs U. Tex., M.D. Anderson Cancer Ctr., Houston, 1994—96, med. dir. Med. Tech. & Cytogenetic Tech. programs, 1994—96, 2001—06, dir. sect. cytogenetics, 1994—2005, chair ops. and improvement mgmt. com. dept. hematopathology, 1998—2002; prof. Grad. Sch. Biol. Scis. U. Tex., 1994—2006; prof. emeritus Med. U. SC, 2006—. Adj. prof. Grad. Sch. Biol. Scis. and U. Tex. Health Scis. Med. Sch., 1994-; adv. coun. Trident Tech. Coll., 1976-87; bd. dirs. Fetter Family Health Ctr.; steering com. pathology and lab medicine U. Tex. M.D. Anderson Cancer Ctr., 1998-2000, radiation safety com., 1998-2005, pharmacy and therapeutics com., 2000-06, vice chmn., 2004-06, credentials com., 2002-06, radiation drug rsch. com., 2003-06, chmn. task force on antiemetic drugs, 2003-06, chmn. medication process com., 2004-06, faculty senate rep., 2004-06; founding dir. Sealite, Inc., 1987-99, chmn. bd. dirs., 1995-99; founding dir., bd. dirs. SynthRx, Inc., 2003-07; med. adv. com. Nashville Red Cross Blood Ctr., 1991-94, acting med. dir., 1991-92; v.p., bd. sci. advisors Nat. Health Labs./Nat. Reference Lab., 1992-94; trustee, bd. dirs. Gulf Coast Cmty. Blood Ctr., 1994-2006; cons. in field. Editor, co-editor 4 books; bd. editors Annals of Clin. and Lab. Scis., 1981—, book editor, 2005—; contbr. articles to profl. jours., chpts. to books. Trustee Coll. Prep. Sch., 1979-84, chmn. bd., 1983-84; trustee, bd. dirs., v.p. Mason Prep. Sch., 1984-87; bd. dirs. United Way, 1983-87, Am. Cancer Soc., 1984-87; co-founder, bd. dirs. Glassman Family Fund, 1998-; bd. mem., sec., vice-chmn. Kiawah Island Cmty. Assn., 2007-; mem. comm. com. Town of Kiawah Island, SC, 2006-07; donor M.D. Anderson Cancer Ctr., U. Tex., 1994-, Charleston Breast Cancer, 2006-; founder, chmn. Glassman Family Fund/Fidelity Charitable Gift Fund, 1996-. With USMCR, 1956—64. Johnson and Avalon Found. scholar Georgetown U., 1961-64, State scholar Rutgers U., 1956-60; Recipient Jacobi award in pediatrics, Washington, 1964; named Young Investigator of Yr. Soc. Nuclear Medicine 1971, Outstanding Tchr. Med. Coll. Ga., 1974, Olla Stribling Disting. Chair Cancer Rsch. U. Tex., M.D. Anderson Cancer Ctr., 1994-2006. Fellow ACP, Coll. Am. Pathologists (numerous coms. 1971-2005), Assn. Clin. Scientists (mem. numerous coms. 1969-, pres. 1990-91, exec. com. 1990-95, C.P. Brown lectr, 1995, editor 2006-, Diploma of Honor 1987, Clin. Scientist of Yr. 1993, book editor Annals Clin. and Lab. Scis., 2006-),

Am. Soc. Clin. Pathology (coun. immunohematology and blood banking 1983-89, coun. grad. med. edn. and rsch. 1998—2004, Commr.'s award for Continuing Edn. 1989, nat. contbg. editor to Resident In-Svc. Exam. 2000-04), Coll. Nuc. Medicine, NY Acad. Medicine; mem. Am. Bd. Pathology (transfusion medicine/blood bank test com. 1984-88), Internat. Acad. Pathology, Am. Assn. Pathologists, Soc. Nuc. Medicine (chmn. edn. com. 1973-77, acad. coun. 1979-92), AMA (Physician's Recognition award, instnl. rep. to sect. on med. schs., 1987-94, 2003—), So. Med. Assn., Am. Geriat. Soc. (founding fellow So. divsn.), Am. Soc. Microbiology, Am. Assn. Blood Banks (chmn. cryobiology com. 1974-83, edn. com. 1978-85, sci. program com. 1981-84, autologous transfusion com. 1979-83, bd. dirs. 1984-87, transfusion practices com. 1992-96), Assn. Schs. Allied Health Professions (bd. editors jour. 1979-83), Soc. Cryobiology (treas., bd. dirs. 1978-80), AAAS, NY Acad. Scis., Acad. Clin. Lab. Physicians and Scientists (exec. coun. 1978-85, pres. 1982-83), S.E. Area Blood Bankers (pres. 1979-81, exec. coun. 1980-85), Tenn. Assn. Blood Banks (treas. 1993-94), Am. Coll. Physician Execs., Kiawah Island Cmty. Assn. (bd. sec., mem. various coms. 2007—), Sigma Xi, Alpha Eta, Alpha Omega Alpha. Avocations: tennis, community service. Office: Med Univ SC Dept Microbiology Immunology BSB201 173 Ashley Ave Charleston SC 29425 Personal E-mail: abglassmn@yahoo.com. Business E-Mail: glassma@musc.edu.

GLAZER, BENNETT J., wholesale distribution executive; Attended, Harvard U.; BA in Bus. Adminstrn., U. Tex., Austin. Ter. sales rep. Glazer's Wholesale Drug Co. Inc., Houston, corp. v.p., 1981—96, pres., 1999—2003, chmn., CEO, 2003—. Office: Glazers Wholesale Drug Co Inc 14911 Quorum Dr Ste 400 Dallas TX 75254 Office Phone: 972-392-8200. Office Fax: 972-702-8508. Business E-Mail: bglazer@glazers.com.

GLAZER, MALCOLM, professional sports team owner; b. Rochester, NY, Aug. 25, 1928; m. Linda; children: Avram, Kevin, Bryan, Joel, Ed, Darcie. Pres., CEO First Allied Corp.; chmn. of bd. Zapata Corp., Houston, 1994—2002; owner, pres. Tampa Bay Buccaneers, Fla., 1995—; shareholder Manchester United, 2003—, owner, 2005—. Bd. dirs. Splty. Equipment Cos. Active Am. Cancer Soc., Sloan-Kettering Cancer Ctr., United Jewish Appeal, Jewish Guild for the Blind. Named one of Forbes 400: Richest Americans, 2006—, Most Influential People in the World of Sports, Bus. Week, 2008. Office: Tampa Bay Buccaneers One Buccaneer Pl Tampa FL 33607

GLAZIER, RICK, state legislator; b. Allentown, Pa., June 16, 1955; m. Lise Glazier; children: Philip, Megan. Atty. Hardison and Leone, LLP, 2004—; state rep. Dist. 45 NC, 2002—. Democrat. Jewish. Mailing: Dist Off 2642 Old Colony Pl Fayetteville NC 28303 Office: North Carolina House of Representatives 16 W Jones St Rm 1021 Raleigh NC 27601-1096 Office Phone: 919-733-5601. Business E-Mail: Rick.Glazier@ncleg.net.

GLEASON, SEAN, marketing executive; BA in Comm., U. Va., 1986. Acct. exec. Earle Palmer Brown Advt., Md., 1986—87, Rosenthal Greene & Campbell, Md., 1989—90; copywriter Weitzman/Livingston Advt., Md., 1990; acct. supr. Henry J. Kaufman & Assoc., Washington, 1990—95; v.p. mktg. comm., dir. field mktg. Pizza Hut Yum! Brands, Inc. (formerly PepsiCo, Inc. then Tricon Global Restaurants), 1995—2005; sr. v.p. mktg. & comm. Dr. Pepper Snapple Group, Inc. (formerly Cadbury Schweppes PLC), 2005—09; chief mktg. officer Dave & Buster's, 2009—. Named a Media Maven, Advt. Age, 2008. Mem.: Am. Mktg. Assn. (Dallas-Fort Worth chpt.). Office: Dave & Busters World Hdqs 2481 Manana Dr Dallas TX 75220 Office Phone: 214-357-9558.

GLEIS, LINDA HOOD, physician; b. Louisville, Jan. 28, 1952; d. Edgar Pete Hood and Joan Ray (Brenner) Hulsey; m. Gregory Eric Gleis, Aug. 18, 1973; children: Eric, Matthew, Kevin, Anna. BA cum laude, Bellarmine Coll., 1974; MD, U. Louisville, 1978. Diplomate Am. Bd. Phys. Medicine and Rehab.; lic. physician Ky. Resident Frazier Rehab. Ctr., Louisville, 1978-81, chief resident, 1981, med. staff, 1982—96, dir. residency tng., 1985-95; asst. clin. prof. medicine U. Louisville, Louisville, 1985—; chief phys. medicine and rehab. VA Med. Ctr., Louisville, 1985—2012, med. staff, 1985—, acting chief of staff, 1999-2000; founding ptnr. Rehab. Assoc.-PSC, Louisville, 1985—2003. Spkr. in field. Health care task force Louisville C. of C., 1991—92; dir. JCMS Outreach Program, Inc., 1991-98, 1991—98; mem. cabinet Metro United Way, 1992—94; marriage sponsor Archdiocese of Louisville Holy Spirit Parish Couple to Couple Program, 1991—99; mem. Salute to Cath. Alumni Steering Com., 1991—97, chair, 1993—97; mem. U. Louisville Med. Alumni Bd., 1986—91, v.p., 1989—90, pres., 1990—91; mem. bd. overseers Bellarmine Coll., 1989—95; adv. bd. Jefferson County Office for Women, 1990—94; trustee Spalding U., 1992—2000, vice-chair, 1994—98, chair com. Acad. and Student Affairs, 1995—2000, Spalding U./Presentation Acad. Com., 1995—97, Devel. Com., 1994—95; adv. panel The Physicians Inc., 1993—95; bd. dirs. mem.-at-large U. Louisville Alumni Assn., 1993—2002; bd. dirs. Louisville Cmty. Found., 1992—99, 2001—; med. adv. group Home of the Innocents Pediatric Convalescent Ctr., 1993—95; adv. coun. Louisville Forum, 1995—99; pres. U. Louisville Med. Alumni Bd., 2008—; mem. Leadership Louisville Class of 1992, hon. chair scholarship campaign, 1994; judge exec. Jefferson County Small Bus. Growth Coun., 1992—93, Ky Spinal Cord & Head Injury Rsch. Bd., 2008—. Recipient 1st Ann. Salute to Cath. Schs. Disting. Alumni award Archdiocese Louisville, 1990, Disting. Alumni Svc. award U. Louisville, 1991, Bellarmine Coll. Outstanding Alumnus of Yr., 1991, Assumption H.S. Outstanding Alumna award, Louisville, 1993, Order of Merit U. Louisville Alumni Assn., 1993, Recognition award Ho. of Reps. Commonwealth Ky., 1998; honored with Tribute to Linda Gleis, M.D. Modern Day Heroine Congl. Record, 1992, named to Hall of Fame, Louisville. Ky., 2014. Fellow: Am. Acad. Phys. Medicine and Rehab.; mem.: AMA, Greater Louisville Med. Soc. Found. (chair scholarship com. 2000—), Cath. Edn. Found. (bd. dirs. 2002—), Jefferson County Med. Soc. (treas. 1990—91, physicians Metro United Way campaign chair 1990—94, found. bd. dirs. 1990—96, 1st woman pres. 1991—92, chmn. bd. dirs. 1992—93, bd. dirs. outreach program 1993—99, del. to Ky. Med. Assn. 1993—, 1st v.p. bd. dirs. 1994—96, found. bd. dirs. 1998—), Ky. Acad. Phys. Medicine and Rehab. (sec.-treas. 1988—), Ky. Med. Assn. (com. sch. health, phys. edn. and med. aspects of sports 1988—96, com. on domestic violence 1992—2002, physician orgn. study com. 1993—96, sec.-treas. 1999—), Assn. Acad. Physiatrists (v.p. 1994—95, pres. 1995—96, mem. grad. med. edn. com. 1995—97, sec./program chmn. residency program dirs. coun.), Am. Assn. Electrodiagnostic Medicine. Roman Catholic. Avocations: reading, tennis, golf, sailing. Office: VAMC 117 800 Zorn Ave Louisville KY 40206

GLENDENNING, DON MARK, lawyer; b. Dallas, Dec. 24, 1953; s. Don Thomas and Nancy (Malloy) G.; m. Carol Peterson, Dec. 30, 1979. BA, Rice U., 1976; JD, Stanford U., 1979. Bar: Tex. 1979. Assoc. Rain Harrell Emery Young & Doke, Dallas, 1979-85; ptnr. Rain, Harrell, Emery, Young & Doke, Dallas, 1985-87; shareholder Locke Purnell Rain Harrell, P.C., Dallas, 1987-98; ptnr. Locke Liddell & Sapp LLP, Dallas, 1999—2007, Locke Lord LLP, Dallas, 2007, Dallas mng. ptnr. Past pres. Human Rights Initiative North Tex., Tex., Rice Alumni Assn. DFW; pres. Scenic Dallas, Scenic Tex.; past chair Dallas Zool. Soc., Thanks-Giving Found.; bd. dirs. Arbor Day Found. Parkland Found., Tex. Trees Found.,Dallas Holocaust Mus., KERA, TACA; former dir. Nat. Tree Trust; co-chair New Parkland Campaign. Republican. Presbyterian. Office: Locke Lord LLP 2200 Ross Ave Ste 2200 Dallas TX 75201-6776 Office Phone: 214-740-8623. E-mail: dglendenning@lockelord.com.

GLENN, GERALD MARVIN, marketing, engineering and construction executive; b. Greenville, SC, Aug. 20, 1942; s. Oscar Marvin and Lorene (Ashmore); m. Candice Wilson, Oct. 24, 1986; children: Regina Lynn, Gerald Marvin II, Charles Wilson. BSCE, Clemson U., SC, 1964; Exec. Program Bus. Adminstrn., Columbia U., Harriman, NY, 1980. With Daniel Constrn. Co., Greenville, SC, 1964-77, Fluor Corp., Santa Ana, Calif., 1977-94, sr. v.p. mktg., 1982-85, pres. U.S. ops., 1985-86, exec. v.p., 1986, group pres., dir. Irvine, Calif., 1986-94; owner, prin. The Glenn Group LLC, Ridgeway, Colo., 1994—, Eagle Glen Ranch LLC, Cimarron, Colo., 1994—2006; chmn., pres., CEO, mng. dir. Chgo. Bridge & Iron Co. NV, The Woodlands, Tex., 1996—2006; mng. ptnr. Glenn and Glenn Assets, LLC, The Woodlands, Tex., Magnolia Creek Timber Co., LLC, Trinity County, Tex.; pres. adv. coun. mem. Clemson U. SC. Bd. dir. Woodforest Fin. Group, The Woodlands, Tex., Gas Tech. Inst. Exec. com. mem. Reaching Pines Capital Campaign Montgomery County Women Soc., Tex.; bd. dir. Mont. County Women's Ctr., Tex.; chmn. bd. dirs. Chgo. chpt. Am. Heart Assn., 1999—2001; vice chmn. bd. dir. John Cooper Sch., The Woodlands, Tex.; bd. dir. Jr. Achievement Southeast Tex.; bd. dirs. St. Lukes Episcopal Hosp., Woodlands, Tex.; pres. Adv. Bd. Clemson U. Capt. ARNGUS, Mechanized Infantry. Mem.: ASCE, AIChE, Am. Petroleum Inst., Chgo. Soc., Econ. Club Chgo., Cliffs Vineyard, Beaver Creek Club, Grand Pines Golf Club, Bentwater Yacht and Country Club, 25 Yr. Club Petroleum Industry, Club at Carlton Woods, Woodlands Country Club, Execs. Club Chgo., Fairway Pines Golf Club. Republican. Methodist. Home: 3 Grand Regency Cir The Woodlands TX 77382

GLENN, JAMES H., JR., (JIM GLENN), state legislator, business educator; b. Birmingham, Ala., Feb. 17, 1948; s. James H. and Betty J. G.; m. Cornelia J., July 1, 1972; children: Kimberly, James III. BS, Wis. State U., 1971; MBA, U. Wis., 1974; EdD, U. Ky., 2001. Adj. faculty Concordia Coll., River Forest, Ill., 1985-88; assoc. prof. bus. adminstrn. Owensboro (Ky.) C. C., 1988—; mem. Dist. 13 Ky. House of Reps., 2007—. Adj. faculty Brescia Coll., Owensboro, Ky., 1990-95, Ivy Tech. State Coll., Evansville, Ind., 1991. Contbr. articles to profl. jours. Vol. 4-H, Owensboro, 1990—; elected city commr. City of Owensboro, 2005—06; bd. dirs. Citizen Com. on Edn., Owensboro, Ky., 1989—99, River Park Ctr., Owensboro, Ky., 1992—99, Owensboro Mus., 1993—96. Grad. fellow U. Wis., 1973, Lyman T. Johnson fellow U. Ky., 1998, U. Ky. Extended Campus Coll. Edn. fellow, 1998, 2000. Mem. Ky. Blacks in Higher Edn. (conf. chair 1996), Midwest Bus. Adminstrn. Assn., So. Assn. Colls. and Schs. (mem. vis. team 1995-00). Democrat. Avocations: fishing, cooking, reading about business. Office: Ky House of Reps PO Box 21562 Owensboro KY 42304 Home Phone: 270-686-8760; Office Phone: 270-686-4606, 502-564-8100 ext. 705. Business E-Mail: jim.glenn@kctcs.edu. E-mail: jim.glenn@lrc.ky.gov.

GLENN, JERRY HOSMER, JR., retired language educator; b. Little Rock, Sept. 5, 1938; s. Jerry Hosmer and Anne (Matthews) G.; m. Renate Drexl, July 29, 1978 BA, Yale U., 1960; MA, U. Tex., 1962; postgrad., Free U. Berlin, 1962—63; PhD, U. Tex., 1964. Asst. prof. German U. Wis., Milw., 1964—67; asst. prof. German U. Cin., 1967—69, assoc. prof., 1969—72, prof., 1972—2003, prof. emeritus, 2003—. Dir. honors program U. Cin., 1977—79, head dept., 1980—83. Author: Deutsches Schrifttum der Gegenwart (ab 1945), Francke, 1971, Paul Celan, Twayne, 1973, Paul Celan: Eine Bibliographie, Harrassowitz, 1989, Paul Celan: A Bibliography of English Lang. Secondary Lit. 1955-1996, 1996; (with Jeffrey Todd) Paul Celan: Die zweite Bibliographie, 1998, (with E.P. Harris) Straight White Shield, 2012; mng. editor: Lessing Yearbook, 1969-74; editor: (with Uwe Faulhaber and others) Exile and Enlightenment, 1987; (with Joachim Herrmann and Rebecca Rodgers) Alfred Gong, Early Poems, 1987, Max Kade Occasional Papers, 2001—, (with J. Clausen and others) Iceland's Foggy Nights, 2005; transl. (with Jennifer Kelley) On the Wrong Track, 1993, International Zone, 1999, Too-Late, Too-Early, 2000, (with Clarise Samuels) Landing Attempts, 2000, (with Aine Zimmerman) StadtFluchten/City Escapes, 2004, (with Andrea Engels) Iceland's Foggy Nights, 2005, (with F. Birkmayer) Harvest of Blossoms, 2008, (with Edward P. Harris) White Wings: Preliminary Sketches for a Life of John Hauser, 2008, (with Edward P. Harris)Straight White Shield, 2012. Recipient A.B. Dolly Cohen award disting. excellence in tchg., U. Cin., 1997. Mem. Lessing Soc. (sec-treas. 1968-74), Mideast Honors Assn. (exec. sec. 1977-78, pres. 1979-80), Am. Assn. Tchr. German, Soc. German-Am. Studies (v.p. 1987-89, Outstanding Achievement award, 2004) Republican. Home: 54 Fairway Dr Southgate KY 41071-3025 Personal E-mail: jerry.glenn@uc.edu.

GLENN, LARRY, state legislator; b. July 7, 1947; m. Janet Glenn; children: Scott, Keith, Courtney, Benn. Grad., Northeastern Okla. A&M Coll. With BF Goodrich Plant, Okla., 1970—86; police and fire commr. Miami; fin. commr.; Ottawa County undersheriff; mem. Dist 7 Okla. House of Representatives, 2005—. Democrat. Mailing: Oklahoma House of Representatives 2300 N Lincoln Blvd Rm 502 Oklahoma City OK 73105 Office: 1916 H NW Miami OK 74354 Office Phone: 405-557-7399. E-mail: larryglenn@okhouse.gov.

GLENN, ROBERT KYLE, academic administrator; b. Dallas, Aug. 25, 1953; s.s Rueben Kyle and Elizabeth (Reese) G.; m. Laura Lynn Whitehurst, July 29, 1978; children: Elisabeth Anne, Katherine Whitehurst, Carl Thomas Kyle BS, Birmingham-So. Coll., 1975; MS, U. ALa., 1976; PhD, U. Ala., 1991. Assoc. dir. student affairs Birmingham-So. Coll., Ala., 1976-80, dir. student services, 1980-84; dir. student activities U. North Ala., Florence, 1984—93; dean students S.W. Mo. State U., 1993—99; v.p. student affairs Middle Tenn. State U., Murfreesboro, 1999—2008, vice provost enrollment mgmt., 2002—08, vice provost academic svcs.; pres. Athens State U., 2008—; exec. bd. mem. Southern Assn. Coll. Student Affairs, 2003—08, pres., 2007. Bd. dirs. Muscle Shoals Concert Assn., Florence, 1984—. Chmn. Big Bros./Big Sisters of N. Ala., 1984—, (sec., 1980-84); mem. adminstrn. bd. Edgemont Meth. Ch., Florence, 1984-88; bd. dirs. Neighborhood Housing Auth., Birmingham, 1982. Named one of Outstanding Young Men in Am., 1983. Mem. Internat. Assn. Coll Unions, Nat. Assn. Student Personnel Adminstrs., Omicron Delta Kappa, Kappa Delta Pi., Phi Kappa Phi, Mortar Bd, Delta Mu Delta, Phi Theta Kappa Clubs: Genus Loci (pres. 1979-84). Avocations: golf, bridge, sports, vintage movies. Office: Athens State U Office of Pres 300 N Beaty St Athens AL 35611-1999 Office Phone: 256-233-8201. E-mail: robert.glenn@athens.edu.

GLENN, T. MICHAEL, delivery service executive; b. Memphis; B, U. Miss.; MBA, U. Memphis. With Sales Divsn. Dover Elevator Co.; with dept. corp. sales Fed. Express Corp. (now FedEx Corp.), 1981-83, mgr., 1983-84, mng. dir., dept. mktg., 1984-85, v.p., mktg. N.Am., 1985-92, sr. v.p., Catalog and Remail Svcs. div., 1992-93, sr. v.p., worldwide mktg., customer svc., corp. comm., 1993-98; pres., CEO FedEx Svcs.; exec. v.p., market devel. and corp. comm. FedEx Corp., Memphis, 1998—. Bd. dirs. Renasant Bank, Pentair, Inc., 2007—, Federal Express Corp., 2010—. Bd. dirs. Make-A-Wish Found., United Way of the Mid-South, Autism Speaks Office: Fed Ex Corp 942 S Shady Grove Rd Memphis TN 38120-4117 Office Phone: 901-818-7500. Office Fax: 901-395-2000. Business E-Mail: tglenn@fedex.com.

GLENNON, AMY, publishing executive; Grad., U. Ga., Athens. Copy editor Gwinnett Daily News; joined newsroom Atlanta Journal-Constitution, 1992, various positions in editl., product mgmt. & adminstrn. including gen. mgr. AJC-Gwinnett News edition and sr. dir. product & product mgmt., v.p. circulation, 2010—12, pub., 2012—. Office: Atlanta Journal-Constitution 223 Perimeter Ctr Pky Atlanta GA 30346 Office Phone: 404-526-7237. Business E-Mail: aglennon@ajc.com.

GLEZEN, WILLIAM PAUL, pediatrician, virologist, educator; b. Oblong, Ill., Mar. 15, 1931; s. Ward Anderson and Mary Elizabeth (Brown) Glezen; m. Dorothy Lou Luhman, Aug. 22, 1953; children: Laurie S., Paul L. BS in Biological Scis., Purdue U., Ind., 1953; MD, U. Ill. Coll. Medicine, Chgo., 1956. Diplomate Am. Bd. Pediat. Intern pediat. Wayne County Gen. Hosp., Eloise, Mich., 1956-57; resident pediat. Hurley Hosp., Flint, Mich., 1959-60, NC Meml. Hosp., Chapel Hill, 1960-61, chief resident, 1961-62; chief enteric and respiratory virus unit Kansas City Field Station Ctr. Disease Control, 1962-65; assoc. prof. pediat. U. NC Sch. Medicine, 1965-75; assoc. prof. microbiology and immunology/pediat. Baylor Coll. Medicine, Houston, 1975—77, prof. medicine, microbiology and immunology, 1977—89, prof. dept. molecular virology and microbiology, prof. and head preventive medicine sect., dept. pediat., 1989—. Assoc. attending pediatrician Harris County Hosp. Dist., Houston, 1976—2007; adj. prof., rschr. U. Tex. Ctr. Infectious Diseases, Houston, 1982—; mem. epidemiology and disease control study sect. NIH, 1985—89, mem. adv. com. immunization practices, 1987—90; med. expert Childhood Vaccine Injury Prog., USHHS, 1990—; mem. tnfluenza tech. adv. group Health Care Fin. Adminstrn., 1990—93; mem. task force on adult and maternal immunization Am. Coll. Obstetricians & Gynecologists, 2005—06. Contbr. articles to profl. jours., chapters to books. Comdr. USPHS, 1957—65. Recipient Commr.'s Spl. Citation, FDA, 1997, Disting. Physician award, Pediatric Infectious Disease Soc., 2004, Disting. Sci. Alumni award, Purdue U., 2006. Mem.: Tex. Pediatric Soc., Soc. Pediatric Rsch., Infectious Diseases Soc. America, Am. Pediatric Soc., Am. Acad. Pediat., Am. Epidemiological Soc. Presbyterian. Office: Baylor Coll Medicine Mail Stop BCM280 One Baylor Plz Houston TX 77030 Office Phone: 713-798-5249. Business E-Mail: wglezen@bcm.edu.

GLICK, RICHARD STEPHEN, internist, rheumatologist; b. Pitts., May 18, 1947; s. William and Ruthe (Scher) Glick; m. Joan Marie Skaf, Nov. 2, 1986; children: William Spencer, Michael Andrew. BA cum laude, U. Pa., 1969, MD, 1973. Diplomate Am. Bd. Internal Medicine (also subsplty. bd. rheumatology). Intern U. Mich. Hosp., Ann Arbor, 1973-74, resident, 1974-77; fellow in rheumatology U. Pa., 1977-78, Albany Med. Coll. Hosp., 1978-79; practice medicine specializing in rheumatology and internal medicine Ft. Lauderdale, Fla., 1979—. Contbr. articles to profl. jours. Mem. Am. Coll. Rheumatology, Fla. Soc. Rheumatology. Office: 6405 N Federal Hwy Ste 105 Fort Lauderdale FL 33308-1414 Office Phone: 954-772-3660. Personal E-mail: rglick98@yahoo.com.

GLICK, WILLIAM H., dean, management educator; AB in Psychology, U. Mich., 1975; PhD in Bus. Adminstrn., U. Calif., Berkeley, 1981. Mem. faculty U. Tex., Austin, 1981—95, dir. bus. honors program; mem. faculty Ariz. State U. W.P. Carey Sch. Bus., Tempe, 1995—2005, chair dept. mgmt.; dean, H. Joe Nelson III prof. mgmt. Rice U. Jesse H. Jones Grad. Sch. Mgmt., Houston, 2005—. Vis. prof. INSEAD, 2002. Co-editor (with G.P. Huber): (books) Organizational Change and Redesign: Ideas and Insights for Improving Performance, 1993. Office: Rice U Jesse H Jones Grad Sch Mgmt PO Box 2932 Houston TX 77252-2932 Office Phone: 713-348-5928. E-mail: bill.glick@rice.edu.

GLICKMAN, CARL DAVID, banker; b. Cleve., July 29, 1926; s. Jack I. and Dora R. (Rubinowitz) G.; m. Barbara H. Schulman, Oct. 16, 1960; children: Lindsay Dale, David Craig, Robert Todd. Student, U. Minn., 1944, Inst. Fin. Mgmt., Harvard U., 1970. Pres. Glickman Orgn., Cleve., 1953—; chmn. bd., chief exec. officer Computer Research, Inc., Pitts., 1964-67, Am. Steel & Pump Corp., NYC, 1968-71, Shelter Resources Corp., Cleve., 1971-75; pres. Leader Bldg., Inc., Cleve., 1959—2004, Capital Bancorp., Cleve., 1971-75, Real Property Corp., Cleve., 1975—; spl. ltd. ptnr. Bear Stearns & Co., 1978-85, dir., 1985—, John Carroll U. Chmn. exec. com. Franklin Corp., N.Y.C., 1986-98, Cook United Inc., Cleve., 1986-87, Capital Nat. Bank Cleve., 1970-75; chmn. bd. dirs. Univ. Nat. Bank, Chgo., 1968-70; gen. ptnr. Millbrook Assocs., Chester Union Assocs.; founding gen. ptnr. Park Ctrl. Assocs.; pres. LGT Industries, Durham, N.C., 1987-95; bd. dirs. Royal Petroleum Properties Corp., Jerusalem Econ. Corp., Israel, Custodial Trust Co., Alliance Tyre and Rubber Co., Tel Aviv,Tnuport Ltd., Tel Aviv, Indsl. Structures, Inc., Tel Aviv, Office Max, Inc., InfoTech, Englewood Cliff, NJ, Lexington Corp. Properties, NYC, presiding trustee, chmn. exec. com. Active Mayor's Com. Urban Renewal, 1965-67, Mayors Task Force on Higher Edn., 1967-69; trustee Cleve. Growth Assn., 1972-75; co-chmn. Herzog Loan Fund Cleve. State U., 1970-76; chmn. Med. Arts Hosp., Houston, 1976-86; bd. visitors Case Western Res. Sch. Law; trustee Montefiore Home Aged, Mt. Sinai Hosp., Cath. Diocese Found., Cleve.; grievance com. Cleve. Bar Assn., 1982-85; foreman Cuyahoga County Grand Jury, Cleve., 1984-85; trustee Cleve. State U., 2000—, Cleve. Cath. Diocese Found.; disting. fellow, hon. trustee Cleve. Clinic; nat. chmn. Glickman Urol. Inst. Cleve. Clinic; trustee Cleve. Jewish Fedn., 2006—. With USAAF, 1944-46; trustee John Carron U., Cleve, 2007-. Mem. Am. Bankers Assn., Am. Arbitration Assn. (arbitrator), Beechmont Country Club, Shaker Heights Country Club, Union Club, Standard Club, Harmonie Club, Friars Club, Palm Beach Yacht Club, High Ridge Country Club, Masons, Phi Sigma Delta, Phi Eta Sigma. also: 1 N Breakers Row Palm Beach FL 33480-4021

GLICKMAN, FRANKLIN SHELDON, dermatologist, educator; b. Bklyn., Dec. 14, 1929; s. Arthur Zachary and Hilda (Kurtz) G.; m. Leatrice Sallie Alter, Mar. 29, 1953; children: Todd Scott, Jeff Bret. BA cum laude, Hofstra Coll., 1950; MD, SUNY-Bklyn., 1954; MS in Health Care Mgmt., NYU, 1990. Diplomate: Am. Bd. Dermatology. Intern Flushing (N.Y.) Hosp., 1954-55; resident in dermatology Kings County Hosp., Bklyn., 1957-58, Bronx VA Hosp., 1958-60; practice medicine specializing in dermatology Bklyn., 1960-94; mem. faculty dermatology dept. SUNY-Bklyn., 1960—82, clin. prof., 1982-93, adj. clin. prof., 1993—96; dir. med. edn. Wyckoff Heights Med. Ctr., Bklyn., 1990-96, chmn. dept. grad. med. edn., 1992-96. Author: General Dermatology, 1978, Fundamentals of Dermatology: A Study Guide, 1990; contbr. articles to profl. jours. Served to capt. M.C. USAF, 1955-57. Fellow N.Y. Acad. Medicine, ACP; mem. Am. Acad. Dermatology, Bklyn. Dermatol. Soc. (pres. 1970-72), N.Y. State Med. Soc., Kings County Med. Soc., AMA, N.Y. State Soc. Dermatology (pres. 1983-85), Phi Beta Kappa. Home: 6841 Treves Way Boynton Beach FL 33437-6485 Personal E-mail: fsglickman@comcast.net.

GLIDDEN, ROBERT BURR, academic administrator, music educator, consultant; b. Rippey, Iowa, Nov. 29, 1936; s. Burr Harold and Lora Elsie (Groves) Glidden; m. Rene Colete Siefken, Apr. 26, 1964; children: Melissa, Michele, Briana. BA, U. Iowa, 1958, MA, 1960, PhD, 1966; D of higher edn. adminstrn. (hon.), Bowling Green State U., 2004. Tchr. instrumental music Morrison Community High Sch., Ill., 1958-63, Univ. Schs., Iowa City, 1963-66; asst. prof. music Wright State U., Dayton, Ohio, 1966-67, Ind. U., Bloomington, 1967-69; assoc. prof. music U. Okla., Norman, dir. grad. studies in music, 1969—72; exec. dir. Nat. Assn. Schs. Music, 1972—75, treas., 1977-82, v.p., 1982-85, pres., 1985-88; dean Coll. Musical Arts, Bowling Green State U., Ohio, 1975-79; dean Sch. Music Fla. State U., Tallahassee, 1979-91, provost, v.p. for acad. affairs, 1991-94; pres. Ohio U., Athens, 1994—2004, pres. emeritus, 2004—; interim pres. Cal Poly. San Luis Obispo, 2010—11. Cons., higher edn., condr.; chmn. Coun. Specialized Accrediting Agys., 1976—77; chair Am. Coun. Edn. Commn. Leadership and Instnl. Effectiveness, 1998—2000; chair coun. pres. Mid-Am. Conf., 1997—99. Bd. dirs. Coun. on Postsecondary Accreditation, 1977—84, exec. com., 1979—84, chmn., 1981—83; bd. dirs. Arts, Edn. and Ams., Inc., 1978—81; chmn. advanced placement music com. Coll. Bd., 1977—79; mem. Coun. on Arts Task Force on Edn. Tng. and Devel. Profl. Artists and Art Educators, 1977—78; adv. coun. on accreditation Nat. League for Nursing, 1977—81; edn. adv. com. Nat. Endowment for Arts, 1987, adv. com. for arts in edn., 1989—90; bd. dirs. Coun. for Higher Edn. Accreditation, 1996—2004, chmn., 1996—98. Recipient Disting. Alumni award, U. Iowa, 1997. Mem.: ABA (mem. accreditation comm. 2009—), TIAA-CREF Inst. (cons. 2007—), Ohio Inter-Univ. Coun. (chair 2001—02), Ohio Aerospace Inst. (exec. com. 1995—2004, chair 1998—2000), Ohio Supercomputer Ctr. (governing bd. 1996—2004), Ohio Sci. and Tech. Coun. (biotech. com. 1996—2004), So. Assn. Colls. and Schs. (commn. on coll. 1993—94), Assn. Specialized and Profl. Accreditors (bd. dirs. 1994—96), Coll. Music Soc. (chmn. govt. rels. com. 1976—78, task force on edn. coll. music tchrs. 1987), Mortar Bd., Pi Kappa Lambda (nat. v.p. 1979—81, pres. 1981—85), Omicron Delta Kappa, Phi Kappa Phi, Phi Beta Kappa. Episcopalian. Home: PO Box 88 140 Gibraltar Forge Dr Rockbridge Baths VA 24473 Office Phone: 540-348-6360. Business E-Mail: gliddenr@mac.com.

GLINES, CARROLL VANE, JR., magazine editor; b. Balt., Dec. 2, 1920; s. Carroll Vane and Elizabeth Marion (Cross) G.; m. Mary Ellen Edwards, Oct. 1, 1943; children: Karen Ann, David Edwards, Valerie Jean Student, Drexel Inst. Tech., 1938-40, Canal Zone Jr. Coll., 1946-48, U. Munich, 1948; BBA, U. Okla., 1952, MBA, 1954; MA, Am. U., 1969. Commd. 2d lt. USAF, 1942, advanced through grades to col., 1965; military service, 1941-68; mgr. publs. Nat. Bus. Aircraft Assn., Washington, 1968; assoc. editor Armed Forces Mgmt. mag., Washington, 1969-70; editor Air Cargo mag., Washington, 1970-71, Air Line Pilot mag., Washington, 1971-85, cons. editor, 1985-86, contbg. editor, 1989—2009; sr. editor Aviation Space mag., 1982-85; editor Profl. Pilot Mag., Alexandria, Va., 1986-88, sr. contbg. editor, 1988—, Aviation History mag. (formerly Aviation Heritage mag.), Leesburg, Va., 1990—. Mgr. publs. Air Line Pilots Assn., 1971-85, dir. comms., 1983-85; lectr. U. Dayton, U. Alaska, Am. U Author 36 books; contbr. articles to mags.; gen. editor MacMillan, Air Force Acad. series, 1970-74; editl. cons. Van Nostrand Reinhold, 1980-85; contbg. editor Nation's Bus., 1981-86; mem. adv. bd. Hist. of Aviation Collection, U. Tex., Dallas, 1981-90, 95—, Alaska Aviation Heritage Mus., Anchorage, 1993-99; curator Doolittle Libr., U. Tex., Dallas, 1995— Asst. to v.p. for spl. projects Evergreen Internat. Aviation, 1988-93; active Frontiers of Flight Mus., Dallas Recipient numerous awards from press assns. Freedoms Found., Pres. award Air Force Pub. Affairs Alumni Assn., 2003; inducted into Interboro Hall of Fame, 2003, Glen-Nor Wall of Fame, 2005. Mem. Aviation-Space Writers Assn. (Lauren D. Lyman award), Air Force Assn., Air Force Hist. Found., Soc. Aerospace Communicators, Quiet Birdmen, Soc. Profl. Journalists, Order of Daedalians Home: 1531 San Rafael Dr Dallas TX 75218-4444 Personal E-mail: ceevee1531@sbcglobal.net.

GLITZSBURG, JACQUES, insurance company executive; Ptnr. Stewart Info. Svcs. Corp. Office: Stewart Information Services Corp 1980 Post Oak Blvd Ste 800 Houston TX 77056 Office Phone: 713-627-1310. Office Fax: 713-629-2244. Business E-Mail: jglitzsburg@stewart.com.

GLORIOSO, RICHARD, state legislator; b. Danbury, Conn., Nov. 22, 1943; m. Judy Glorioso; children: Richard, Jeffrey. BA in Math., Northeastern U., Boston, 1967; MA in Mgmt., Ctrl. Mich. U., Mount Pleasant, 1974. Col. USAF, 1967—94; city commr. Plant City, Fla., 1998—2004; mem. Dist. 62 Fla. House of Reps., Tallahassee, 2004—, chair transp. and econ. devel. appropriations com., mem. agr. and natural resources policy com., econ. devel. and cmty. affairs policy coun., select com. on stds. of ofcl. conduct. Decorated Legion of Merit, Meritorious Svc. Medal, Combat Readiness Medal, Vietnam Svc. Medal, Humanitarian Svc. Medal. Mem.: VFW, Airlift Tanker Assn., Am. Legion, Disabled Am. Veterans, Order of Daedalians, Kiwanis. Republican. Baptist. Office: 110 W Reynolds St Ste 204 Plant City FL 33563 also: 222 The Capitol 402 S Monroe St Tallahassee FL 32399 Office Phone: 813-757-9110, 850-488-0807.

GLOVER, CEDRIC BRADFORD, mayor, Shreveport, Louisiana; b. Aug. 9, 1965; s. Elizabeth Bradford Glover, Clarence Ernest Glover. Mem. City Coun., 1990—95, La. House of Reps., La. State Senate from Dist. 4, 1996—2006; mayor City of Shreveport, La., 2006—. Program Coord. Vol. of Am. Lighthouse Program; treas. Shreveport Chpt. of NAACP; pres. Martin Luther King Civic Club; bd. mem. met. YMCA; mem. Goodwill Indsl., Willis-Knighton Neighbor Health Ctr., Gt. Shreveport Econ. Devel. Found., La Exhbn. Mus. Recipient Cmty. Achievement award, La Mcpl. Assn., Polit. Achievement award, Shreveport Black C. of C; named Pub. Ofcl. of Yr., Shreveport Chpt. of Nat. Assn. of Social Workers, Legislator of Month, La Mcpl. Assn. Citizens Against Crime Inc, Legislator of Yr., Rural Caucus. Democrat. Methodist. Achievements include making history as the first African American Mayor of his hometown, Shreveport, LA in 2006. Mailing: Office of the Mayor PO Box 31109 Shreveport LA 71130 Office: Office of the Mayor 505 Travis St Suite 200 Shreveport LA 71101 Office Phone: 318-673-5050.*

GLOVER, DOUGLAS DENNIS, obstetrics, gynecology and pharmacology educator; b. Rowlesburg, W.Va., Feb. 7, 1929; s. Douglas and Iva (Hughes) G.; m. Barbara Anne Brady, Sept. 6, 1958; children: Joseph, William, Donald, Geoffrey, Robert. BS in Pharmacy, W.Va. U., Morgantown, 1951, BS in Medicine, 1959; MD, Emory U., Atlanta, 1961; grad, The Infantry Sch. Ft. Benning Ga., 1951. Diplomate Am. Bd. Ob-gyn. Intern Grady Meml. Hosp., Atlanta, 1961-62, resident, 1962-65; pvt. practice, Marietta, 1965-82; prof. ob/gyn. Marshall U. Sch. Medicine, Huntington, W.Va., 1982-87, W.Va. U. Sch. Med., Morgantown, 1987—2004; prof. Sch. Pharmacy W.Va. U., 1987—. Vis. prof. Zhejiang Med. U., Hangzhou, People's Republic of China, 1993; past operator of 4 rural outreach clinics for disadvantaged pregnant women. Author: From the Everyday to the Extraordinary: West Virginia Pharmacists' Stories, 2009, The Evolution of Pharmacy Education in West Virginia: A History of the School of Pharmacy at West Virginia University 1914-2014, 2012; editor: Current Therapy in Obstetrics, 1988; contbr. articles to profl. jours. Mem. U.S. Pharmacopeial Conv., Inc., 1990—, gen. com. of revision, 1990-2000, chmn. ob-gyn adv. panel, 1990-2000, expert com. on nomenclature and labeling, 1990-2005. Served to 1st lt. AUS, 1952-53, 45th Inf. Divsn., Korea. Decorated Bronze Star, Purple Heart, Expert Inf. Badge, Combat Med. Badge; recipient Outstanding Svc. award W.Va. U., 1972, 87, Outstanding Alumnus award W.Va. U. Sch. Pharmacy, 1982, Disting. Alumnus award, 1999, Dr. James H. Beal award W.Va. Pharmacists Assn., 1989, Sch. Medicine Faculty Recognition award, 1997, 2002, 2005, W.Va.Gov.'s Meritorious Svc. award, 2004, W.Va. U. Most Loyal Mountaineer, 2004, W.Va. U. Sch. Medicine award Excellence Svc. to Sch., 2005. Fellow Am. Coll. Ob-Gyn., Am. Soc. Reproductive Medicine (co-chair sessions mgmt. com. 1990—, chair registrations com. 1992-98), Internat. Infectious Diseases Soc. for Ob-Gyn. (mem. nat. steering com.), Masons (32d deg.), Sigma Xi, Phi Delta Theta (chpt. advisor 1988-2000), Phi Chi, Phi Lambda Sigma. Republican. Presbyterian. Achievements include patents in field; research in placental metabolism and pharmacokinetics of drugs during pregnancy. Avocation: military history. Office: WVa Univ 1136 Health Sci Ctr N Morgantown WV 26506 Home: 1109 Santa Elena Way Johns Island SC 29455-3154 Office Phone: 304-293-4198.

GLOVER, LUCAS HENDLEY, professional golfer; b. Greenville, SC, Nov. 11, 1979; Attended, Clemson Univ. Amateur golfer; winner Sunnehanna Amateur, 2001; profl. golfer, 2001—, Nationwide Tour, 2002—03, PGA Tour, 2004—; winner Okla. Open, 2001, Gila River Classic, 2003, FUNAI Classic, Walt Disney World Resort, 2005, US Open Championship, Bethpage Black, 2009, Grand Slam of Golf, Southampton, Bermuda, 2009, Wells Fargo Championship, 2011. Mem. US team Walker Cup, 2001, Presidents Cup, 2007, 2009. Named 1st Team All-American, 2000—01; named to Clemson Univ. Athletic Hall of Fame, 2005. Office: PGA Tour 100 PGA Tour Blvd Ponte Vedra Beach FL 32082

GLOVER, RENÉE LEWIS, city official; b. 1949; BA, Fisk U., 1970; MA, Yale U.; JD, Boston U., 1975. Ptnr. Seyfarth, Shaw, Fairweather & Ceraldson, NYC, 1983—86; corp. fin. atty. Trotter, Smith & Jacobs, Atlanta, 1986—92; counsel Paul Hastings, Janofsky & Walker, Atlanta, 1992; CEO Atlanta Housing Authority (AHA), 1994—. Recipient Dan Sweat Cmty. Leadership Award, Urban Land Inst., 1998, Masked Award, United Negro Coll. Fund, Inc. and African Heritage Found., 2005, Turner Broadcasting Downtown Cmty. Svc. Award, 2007; named Pub. Official of Yr., Governing Mag., 2002; named one of the Top Ten Am. Women in Govt., Ctr. Am. Women, Ford Found., and Coun. on Excellence in Govt., 2002, Atlanta's Defining Women, Atlanta History Ctr., 2003. Mem.: ABA, Nat. Assn. Securities Profls., Emery Univ. Friends, Mission New Hope, Spelman Coll. Corp. Roundtable, Nat. Bar Assn. Office: Atlanta Housing Authority 230 John Wesley Dobbs Ave Atlanta GA 30303 Office Phone: 404-892-4700.

GLOVER, RUSTY, state legislator; b. Mobile, Ala., Apr. 17, 1966; m. Connie Glover; children: Katie, Kellie. BS in Secondary Edn., MS in Secondary Edn., U. South Ala., Mobile. HS history tchr.; mem. Dist. 102 Ala. House of Reps., Montgomery, 2003—06; mem. Dist. 34 Ala. State Senate, Montgomery, 2007—. Mem. NRA, Christian Educators America, Nat. Right to Life, Ala. Rep. Assembly, U. South Ala. Alumni Assn., Ala. Eagle Forum, Mobile County Rep. Century Club, Gideons. Republican. Baptist. Office: PO Box 2175 Semmes AL 36575 also: Ala State Senate Ala State House 11 S Union St Rm 735-B Montgomery AL 36130 Office Phone: 334-242-7886.

GLOWINSKI, ROLAND, mathematics professor; b. Paris, Mar. 9, 1937; s. Nathan and Anna (Cukiernik) G.; m. Angela Rimok, Nov. 3, 1963; children: Anne, Tania. B, Ecole Polytechnique, Paris, 1960; M, Ecole Nationale Supérieure des Télécommunications, Paris, 1963; PhD, U. Paris, 1970; D (hon.), U. Jyvaskyla, Finland, 2004. Registered profl. engineer; cert. prof. math. Rsch. engr. Office de Radio et Télévision Françaises, Paris, 1963-68, Institut National de Recherches en Informatique et Automatique, Paris, 1968-70; prof. U. Paris VI, 1970—98, chmn. math dept., 1981-85; Disting. prof. U. Houston, 1985—; vis. prof. Inst. Advanced Studies, Hong Kong U. Sci. and Tech., 2008—; hon. prof. Fudan U., Shanghai, 2008. Adj. prof. Rice U., Houston, 1986—, U. Tenn., Knoxville, 2007-, Ben Gurion U., Be'er Sheva, Israel, 2008-; Sherman Fairchild Disting. visitor Calif. Inst. Tech., 1988-89; cons. CNET, Paris, 1968-85, Sci. Rsch. Coun., London, 1978-81; bd. dirs. Electricite de France, Paris, 1990-96, U. Leonardo da Vinci, Paris, 1996-2008; dir. Centre Européen de Recherches et de Formation Avancée en Calcul Scientifique, Toulouse, France, 1992-94; docent prof. U. Jyvaskyla, Finland, 2001—; sci. bd. French Petroleum Inst., 2005- Lt. France Signal Corps, 1958-61. Decorated officer Nat. Merit, knight Order of Acad. Palms, knight Order Legion of Honor, France; recipient Cray prize Selected Jury, Paris, 1988, Marcel Dassault prize French Nat. Acad. Scis., 1996, Zienkiewicz Disting. lectureship, 1999, IMA, 1999, others. Fellow SIAM; mem. Soc. for Indsl. and Applied Math. (Theodore von Kármán Prize, 2004, selected jury), Am. Math. Soc., Academia Europea (London), French Nat. Acad. Tech., French Nat. Acad. Scis., US Assn. for Computational Mechanics (Fluid Dynamics award, selected jury). Office: U Houston Dept Math 651 Philip G Hoffman Hall Houston TX 77204-3008 Office Phone: 713-743-3473. Personal E-mail: angelarim@aol.com. Business E-Mail: roland@math.uh.edu.

GLUCK, MICHELLE H., lawyer; b. Apr. 1959; m. Robert J. Gluck. BA in English, U. Mich., 1980, JD, 1983. Bar: Va. 1983. Assoc. Hunton & Williams, 1983—89; legal cons. Am. Household Inc., 1996—99, Office Depot, 1996—99; v.p., assoc. gen. counsel & asst. sec. The Sports Authority Inc., Ft. Lauderdale, Fla., 1999—2001, Kmart Corp., Troy, Mich., 2001—03; exec. v.p., chief legal officer & corp. sec. LandAmerica Fin. Group Inc., Richmond, Va., 2004—09; sr. v.p., gen. counsel Federal Reserve Bank of Richmond, 2009—. Mem.: Am. Corp. Counsel Assn. (sec., bd. mem. South Fla. Chpt. 2001). Office: Federal Reserve Bank of Richmond 701 E Byrd St Richmond VA 23219 Office Phone: 804-697-8000.

GLUSKI, ANDRÉS R., electric power industry executive; BA, Wake Forest Univ.; MA, Univ. Va., PhD in econ. Exec. v.p. fin. CANTV, Venezuela; exec. v.p. corp. banking Banco de Venezuela; mgmt. positions in Venezuela & Chile AES Corp., Arlington, Va., 1997—2003, sr. v.p. Caribbean & Ctrl. Am., 2003—06, exec. v.p., regional pres. Latin Am., 2006—07, exec. v.p., COO, 2007—11, dir., pres., CEO, 2011—. Mem.: Phi Beta Kappa. Office: AES Corp 4300 Wilson Blvd Arlington VA 22203

GOBILLOT, LORI AURAY, air transportation executive; b. 1961; 3 children. BBA in Finance & Stats., U. Tex., Austin, 1983; JD, U. Tex. Sch. Law, 1993. Mgmt. cons. Arthur Andersen & Co., 1983—86; leasing agent Trammell Crow Co., 1986—89; assoc. Vinson & Elkins LLP, 1993—99; asst. gen. counsel Continental Airlines, Inc., 1999—2008, staff v.p., asst. gen. counsel, asst. sec., 2008—10; v.p. integration mgmt. United Continental Holdings, Inc., Chgo., 2010—. Office: United Continental Holdings Inc 1600 Smith St Dept HQSEO Houston TX 77002 Office Phone: 713-324-2950. Office Fax: 713-324-2687.

GOCKLEY, DAVID (RICHARD DAVID GOCKLEY), opera company director; b. Phila., July 13, 1943; s. Warren and Elizabeth S. Gockley; children: Meredith, Lauren, Adam. Student, New Eng. Conservatory, Boston; BA, Brown U., Providence, 1965, DFA (hon.), 1993; MBA, Columbia U. Bus. Sch., NYC, 1970; DHL (hon.), U. Houston, 1992. Music dir. Newark Acad., 1965-67; drama dir. Buckley Sch., NYC, 1967-69; box office mgr. Santa Fe Opera, 1969-70; bus. mgr. Houston Grand Opera, 1970-71, assoc. dir., 1971-72, gen. dir., 1972—2005, San Francisco Opera, 2006—. Co-founder Houston Opera Studio, 1977; former pres. OPERA America; former chmn. Houston Theater Dist. Prodr. (operas): Nixon in China (Emmy award 1988), Harvey Milk, Florencia en el Amazonas, Porgy and Bess (Tony award, Grammy award 1977), Treemonisha, A Quiet Place, Willie Stark, Resurrection, Carmen, Der Ring des Nibelungen. Bd. dirs. Tex. Inst. Arts in Edn. Recipient Tony award, League NY Theaters & Producers, 1977, Dean's award for Disting. Profl. Achievement, Columbia Bus. Sch., 1982, Music Theater award, Nat. Inst. Music Theater, 1985, William Rogers award, Brown U., 1995. Avocation: tennis. Office: San Francisco Opera 301 Van Ness Ave San Francisco CA 94102 Office Phone: 713-546-0200, 415-551-6271. Business E-Mail: dgockley@sfopera.com.

GODBEY, DAVID CHARLES, federal judge; b. Temple, Tex., Sept. 17, 1957; s. Charles Perry and Bobbye Lee (Wendland) G.; m. Beverly Bell, Nov. 17, 1990; children: John, Ruth. BSEE, BS magna cum laude (hon.), So. Meth. U, 1978; JD magna cum laude (hon.), Harvard U, 1982. Bar: Tex. 1982, US Dist. Ct. Appeals (5th cir.) 1982; bd. cert. civil appellate law. Law clk. to Hon. Irving L. Goldberg 5th cir. U.S. Ct. Appeals, Dallas, 1982-83; assoc. Hughes & Luce LLP, Dallas, 1983-89, ptnr., 1989-94; judge 160th Dist. Ct., Dallas, 1995—2002, US Dist. Ct. (no. dist.) Tex., Dallas, 2002—. Adj. prof. law So. Meth. U., Dallas, 1988-91. Bd. dirs. Suicide & Crisis Ctr., Dallas, 1983-85. Fellow Dallas Bar Found. (chmn. appellate sect. 1996); mem. Mac Taylor Inn of Ct. (barrister), Am. Law Inst. Republican. Methodist. Avocations: Tae Kwon Do, bridge, reading. Office: US Dist Ct (no dist) Tex Rm 1358 1100 Commerce St Dallas TX 75242 Office Phone: 214-753-2700.

GODBOLD, FRANCIS STANLEY, investment banker, security firm executive; b. Charleston, SC, Mar. 4, 1943; s. Francis Stanley and Ula Leigh (Waddey) G.; m. Lelia Elizabeth Harman, Sept. 24, 1966; children: John A., Laura H. Blair. BS in Indsl. Engring. with honors, Ga. Inst. Tech., 1965; MBA, Harvard U., 1969. V.p. Raymond, James & Associates, Inc., St. Petersburg, Fla., 1969-74, sr. v.p., 1974-78, exec. v.p., 1978—; pres. Raymond James Financial, Inc., 1987—2002, vice chmn., 2002—. Regional firms adv. com. NY Stock Exch., 1990-93; bd. dirs. Raymond James Bank, Raymond James Fin. Pres. Baypoint Mid. Sch. Parent Action Com., 1982-83, Bay Vista Parent Action Com., 1979-80; mem. Leadership St. Petersburg, 1974—; mem. Lakewood H.S. Parent Action Com., 1984-90, pres., 1987-88, trustee Ga. Tech. Found., Inc., 2003-; Ga. Tech. Found. Executive Committee (2007 Chmn., Investments Committee(2007-) dir. Ga. Tech. Indsl. and Sys. Engring. Alumni award, 1997, mem. Tampa Bay area regional devel. coun., 1995; bd. dirs. Acad. Prep., 1999-2007, Elk River Properties Owners Assn., chmn. fin. com., 2003-04, pres., 2004-2006; bd. dirs. Banner Elk Heritage Found. Capt. AUS US Army, 1965—67. Mem. Securities Industry Assn. (vice chmn. so. dist. 1980, chmn. 1987, treas. 1986, exec. com. 1988-96, nat. dir. 1995-97, regional firms com. 1995-99, chmn. regional firms com. 1998, tax policy com. 1995-97, nominating com. 1997), Ga. Tech. Alumni Assn. (trustee 2002-05), Harvard Club of West Coast Fla. (sec.-treas 1971-72, v.p. 1972-73, pres. 1973-74), Harvard Bus. Sch. Club (treas. 1984), St. Petersburg Country Club, Elk River Club, Diamond Creek Golf Club, Tau Beta Pi, Phi Kappa Phi, Alpha Pi Mu, Phi Delta Theta. Republican. Office: Raymond James Fin Inc 880 Carillon Pkwy Saint Petersburg FL 33716-1100 Home Phone: 727-867-1962; Office Phone: 727-567-5003.

GODDARD, FRANCES BYRD, clinical social worker; b. Greensboro, NC, Aug. 11, 1939; d. Henry Davis and Blanche Leavell Blake; m. Anthony Edward Goddard, Oct. 10, 1964; 1 child, Caroline Stuart. BA in Sociology with honors, Converse Coll., 1961; MSW, U. N.C., 1963. Lic. social worker; diplomate Am. Bd. Social Work Examiners. Social worker Children's Home Soc., Richmond, Va., 1964-71; supr. of svcs. Coun. of Culpeper, Va., 1971-74; dir. Culpeper Mental Health, 1974-76, Culpeper Family Counseling, 1976—; exec. dir. Am. Assn. State Social Work Bds., Culpeper, 1989-94. Bd. dirs. Va. Mental Health Assn.; founding dir. Soc. Preservation Culpeper History; bd. mem. Va. Soc. Clin. Social Work, 2008—, treas., 2011—12. Author: 6 books in field, studies in field. Recipient Joseph George Lynch award, 2013; grantee, NIMH. Mem. Holloway-Amiss-Leavell Soc. (sec./treas. 1990—), Nat. Clearinghouse on Licensure, Enforcements and Regulations, Nat. Orgn. of Competency Assurance, Va. Commonwealth U. Social Work Adv. Bd. (past chmn.), numerous others. Episcopalian. Avocations: reading, travel, art. Office: Culpeper Family Counseling Ste A 400 South Ridge Pkwy Culpeper VA 22713 Office Phone: 540-825-5337.

GODDESS, LYNN BARBARA, real estate investor; b. NYC, Mar. 3, 1942; d. Eugene Daniel and Hazel Cecile (Kinzler) Goddess. BS, Columbia U., 1963, postgrad., 1964—66. Coord. John M. Burns Assembly Campaign, NYC, 1963; dir. spl. events, projects Kenneth B. Keating Senatorial Campaign, NYC, 1964; dist. dir. fund raising Muscular Dystrophy Assn. Am. Inc., NYC, 1965-66; exec. acct. fund raising, pub. relations Victor Weingarten Co., NYC, 1966-67, Oram Group (formerly Harold L. Oram Inc.), NYC, 1967-70; dir. devel. City Ctr. Music Drama Inc., NYC, 1970; sales person Whitbread-Nolan, NYC, 1971-73; from asst. v.p. to sr. v.p. Cross and Brown Co., NYC, 1973-1985; sr. dir., comml. real estate Cushman & Wakefield, Inc., NYC, 1985—2004; chmn./CEO LYNN LLC, 2004—. Trustee Young Adult Inst.; founder, chmn. The Hazel K. Goddess Fund for Stroke Rsch. in Women., 2000—; mem. external adv. bd. Ga. Brain and Spinal Injury Rsch. Ctr., 2004—. Mem. Nat. Soc. Fund Raisers, Assn. Fund Dirs., Real Estate Bd. NY (named Most Ingenious Broker Yr. 1975), Women's Forum (bd. dirs.). Office: The Hazel K Goddess Fund Stroke Research in Women 1217 South Flagler Dr Suite 302 West Palm Beach FL 33401 Home Phone: 212-288-4287. Personal E-mail: lbg22@earthlink.net.

GODFREY, CULLEN MICHAEL, lawyer, academic administrator; b. Ft. Worth, Apr. 8, 1945; s. Cullen Aubrey and Agnes (Eiland) Godfrey; m. Melinda McDonald, Aug. 29, 1970. BA, U. Tex., 1968, JD, 1970. Bar: Tex. 1969, U.S. Dist. Ct. (we. dist.) Tex. 1971, U.S. Ct. Appeals (5th cir.) 1979, U.S. Supreme Ct. 2004. Ptnr. Sloan, Muller & Godfrey, Austin, Tex., 1969—72; staff atty. Hunt Oil Co., Dallas, 1972—74, Tesoro Petroleum Corp., San Antonio, 1974—75, sr. atty., 1975—78, asst. gen. counsel, 1978—82, FINA, Inc., Dallas, 1982—88, gen. counsel, 1988—90, v.p., sec., gen. counsel, 1990—95, sr. v.p., sec., gen. counsel, 1995—2000; vice chancellor, gen. counsel U. Tex. Sys., Austin, 2000—04; ptnr. Jackson Walker LLP, Austin, 2004—06; gen. counsel Tex. A&M U. Sys., 2006—07; chief legal office Tex. A&M Health Sci. Ctr., 2007—12, attorney, mediator, cons., 2012—. Author: Legal Aspects of the Purchase and Sale of Oil and Gas Properties, 1992; contbr. articles to profl. jours. Trustee Dallas Mus. Art, 1993—95, 1998—2000; gen. campaign chmn. United Way Met. Dallas, Inc., 1999; bd. dirs. Greater Dallas Crime Commn.,

1991—2000, chmn. bd. dirs., 1997—99; bd. dirs. Dallas County Heritage Soc., 1998—2000, United Way Met. Dallas, Inc., 1999—2000, United Way Capital Area, 2005—06; bd. dirs. Cir. 10 Boy Scouts Am., 1999—2000; bd. dirs. Greater Austin Crime Commn., 2003—06, v.p., 2004—06. Recipient Excellence in Corp. Practice award, Am. Corp. Counsel Assn., 1998, Jurisprudence award, Anti-Defamation League, 1999. Fellow: Austin Bar Found. (founder), Dallas Bar Found. (sustaining life fellow), Tex. Bar Found. (sustaining life fellow); mem.: ABA (chmn. subcom. on fgn. investment reporting, internat. law sect. 1984—87), Nat. Conf. Commr. on Uniform State Laws, Am. Law Inst., Ctr. Am. and Internat. Law (rsch. fellow), Tex. Bus. Law Found. (chmn. bd. dirs. 1995—98, bd. dirs.), Tex. Bd. Legal Specialization (bd. cert. oil, gas and mineral law), State Bar Tex. (coll. mem. 1989—, coun. oil, gas and mineral law sect. 1992—95, coun. bus. law sect. 1998—2004, chmn. bus. law sect. 2002—03, Cert. Merit 1999, 2003, Friends of CLE award 2004). Mailing: PO Box 10661 College Station TX 77842 Office Phone: 979-595-8090. Business E-Mail: cmg.991@suddenlink.net.

GODIN, BARB, diversified financial services company executive; B in Finance, U. Western Ont., Can., MBA; Grad., Internat. Sch. Banking. Various positions including dir. consumer underwriting, dir. collections, v.p. credit risk mgmt. and sr. v.p. retail lending and automotive fin. Scotiabank, 1984—98; exec. v.p. consumer risk mgmt., chief consumer risk and credit officer KeyCorp, 1998—2003; exec. v.p. consumer credit Regions Bank, 2003—10, head credit ops. spl. assets and consumer risk, 2009—10; chief credit officer Regions Fin. Corp., 2010—. Named one of The 25 Women to Watch, American Banker, 2011. Office: Regions Financial Corp 1900 Fifth Ave N Birmingham AL 35203

GODIN, MICHAEL S., plastic surgeon; B, Rice U.; grad. with honors, Tulane U. Diplomate Am. Bd. Facial Plastic and Reconstructive Surgery, Am. Bd. Otolaryngology. Intern head and neck surgery Univ. of Calif.; advanced fellow cosmetic and reconstructive surgery Tulane Univ.; fellow dir. facial plastic surgery Am. Acad. of Facial Plastic and Reconstructive Surgery, 2004. Named one of Best Plastic Surgeon, Style Mag., 1999, Best Rhinoplasty Surgeon for Women, Richmond Mag., 2001—09, Top 40 under 40, Inside Bus. Mag. Office: Michael S Godin 410 Libbie Ave Richmond VA 23226 Office Phone: 804-285-8578.

GODSCHALK, DAVID ROBINSON, architect, urban development planner, educator; b. Enid, Okla., May 14, 1931; s. Harold J. and Helen Faye (Robinson) G.; m. Lallie Moore Kain, June 27, 1959; 1 child, David Kennedy. BA, Dartmouth Coll., 1953; B.Arch., U. Fla., 1959; M.Regional Planning, U. N.C., 1964, PhD, 1971. Vice pres. Milo Smith Assos., Tampa, Fla., 1959-61; planning dir. City of Gainesville, Fla., 1964-65; asst. prof. Fla. State U., Tallahassee, 1965-67; editor AIP Jour., Chapel Hill, NC, 1968-71; assoc. prof. U. N.C., Chapel Hill, 1972-77, prof., 1977-94, Stephen Baxter prof. planning, 1994—2004, chmn. dept. city and regional planning, 1978-83. Adj. prof. Kenan Flagler Bus. Sch., U. NC, Chapel Hill, 2005-07; cons. and expert witness in field. Author: (with others) Constitutional Issues of Growth Management, 1979, Land Supply Monitoring, 1986, Planning in America: Learning from Turbulence, 1974, Catastrophic Coastal Storms: Hazard Mitigation and Development Management, 1989, Urban Land Use Planning, 5th edit., 2006, Pulling Together: A Planning and Development Consensus Building Manual, 1994, Cooperating with Nature: Confronting Natural Hazards with Land Use for Planning Sustainable Communities, 1998, 2011, (with others) Hazard Mitigation: Integrating Best Practices into Planning, 2010. Natural Hazard Mitigation: Recasting Disaster Policy and Planning, 1999, Monitoring Land Supply with Geographic Information Systems, 2000; co-author, Sustaining Places: The Role of the Comprehensive Plan, 2012, The Dynamic Decade: Creating the Sustainable Campus for the University of North Carolina at Chapel Hill, 2001-2011, 2012; editor: (with others) Understanding Growth Management, 1989, The Planner as Dispute Resolver, 1989; editor Am. Inst. Planners Jour., 1968-71; mem. editl. bd. Jour. Planning Edn. and Rsch., 1983-89, 93-97, Jour. Am. Planning Assn., 1983-96, 2008-, Jour. Archtl. Planning Rsch., 1991—, Australian Planner, 1997-99, Hazard Mitigation: Integrating Best Practices into Planning, 2010, Eastainable Development projects: Intregrating Design, Development and Regulation, 2013 Mem. Town Coun., Chapel Hill, 1985-89, NC Legis. Rsch. Commn. on Statewide Comprehensive Planning, 1991-93, NC Legis. Commn. on Smart Growth, 1999-2001; bd. dirs. Carol Woods Continuing Care Cmty., 2004—08. With USNR, 1953-56, 61-62; comdr. Res.; ret., 1980. Ret. comdr. USNR. Recipient Disting. Alumnus award Dept. City and Regional Planning, U. N.C., 1996; Disting. Grad. Tchg. awd., U.N.C., 1999. Fellow AICP; mem. Am. Planning Assn. (bd. govs. 1978-79, Profl. Achievement award 1983, Elected Ofcl. award N.C. chpt. 1990), Am. Soc. Planning Ofcls. (bd. dir. 1974-77), Am. Inst. Cert. Planners (Svc. medal 1971), Assn. Collegiate Schs. Planning (Disting. Educator award 2002), NC Botanical Garden Found. (bd. dirs. 2003—11). Office: Univ NC Dept City & Regional Planning Chapel Hill NC 27599-3140 Business E-Mail: dgod@email.unc.edu.

GODWIN, JERRY H., food products executive; Pres. Murphy Farms; pres., COO Murphy-Brown, LLC, 2001—. Office: Murphy-Brown LLC 2822 Hwy 24 W Warsaw NC 28398 Office Phone: 910-293-3434. Office Fax: 910-289-6400. Business E-Mail: jerrygodwin@murphybrownllc.com.

GODWIN, LARRY A., state agency administrator, retired protective services official; m. Nina Elizabeth Barlow; children: Anthony, Lucian, Angelina. BS, Liberty U., Lynchburg, Va. Officer metro narcotics Memphis Police Dept., 1973, patrolman and sgt., instr., homicide investigator, fraud and document investigator, lt. crime response/bomb unit shift supervisor, 1992—98, major, comdr. crime response/bomb unit, 1998—2001, inspector, comdr. spl. svcs., 2001—03, dir. spl. ops., 2003—04, interim dir. police svcs., 2004, dir. police svcs., 2004—11; dep. commr. Tenn. Dept. Safety & Homeland Security, Nashville, 2011—. Pres. Tenn. Pub. Safety Coalition, 2006. Mem.: Memphis Police Found. (founding bd. mem. 2008, pres.), Tenn. Assn. Chiefs of Police (pres. 2006, Director's Choice Award 2007). Office: Tennessee Dept of Safety PO Box 945 Nashville TN 37202

GODWIN, PAMELA JUNE, board member, investment company executive; b. Council Bluffs, Iowa, Mar. 29, 1949; BA in French, Pa. State U., 1970; postgrad., West Chester U., Pa., 1974. Sr. v.p., customer mgmt., credit card divsn. Advanta Corp.; various underwriting/tng. positions Colonial Penn Group, Inc., Phila., 1974-77, mgr., 1977-81, bd. dirs., 1981-84, v.p., 1984-86, 1986-87, sr. v.p., 1987-88; sr. v.p., customer mgmt. Nat. Liberty Corp., Valley Forge, Pa., 1988-93; pres., COO Acad. Ins. Group, Frazer, Pa., 1993-95, Nat. Home Life Assurance Co., Frazer, Pa., 1993-95; acting pres. Womens Way, Phila., 1998-99; pres., COO, personal lines agy. divsn. GMAC Ins. (formerly Integon Corp.), Winston-Salem, NC, 1999—2001; pres. Change Partners, Inc., Havertown, 2001—. Bd. dirs. Unum Group, 2004—. Bd. dirs. Wheels, Inc., J.F. Kennedy Vocat. Tech. Sch., Phila., 1987-88; bd. dirs. Gt. Valley Cmty. Edn. Found., 1991-95, past pres.; mem. Westgate Hills Civic Assn., Havertown, 1974-; mem. Wharton Exec. Edn. adv. bd.; chmn. adv. bd. Pa. State Great Valley, 1996-2000, 2002-; bd. dirs. Winston-Salem C. of C., 1996-2001, Phila. Found., 2003-; mem. Com. of 200, 2000-. Named to Pa. Honor Roll of Women, 1996. Mem. Phila. Forum of Exec. Women (pres. 1998-99), Soc. Property and Casualty Underwriters (past pres. Phila. chpt. 1987-88), Phi Beta Kappa, Phi Sigma Iota. Democrat. Lutheran. Avocations: skiing, walking, reading. Office: Unum Group Bd Directors 1 Fountain Sq Chattanooga TN 37402 Office Phone: 423-294-1011. E-mail: changepartners@comcast.net, pgodwin@unum.com.

GODWIN, RALPH LEE, JR., real estate executive; b. Raleigh, NC, July 20, 1954; s. Ralph Lee Sr. and Hilda Faye (Sellars) G. BS in Commerce, U. Va., 1976; MBA, Dartmouth Coll., 1982. Fgn. exchange trader N.C. Nat. Bank, Charlotte, 1976-78; mgr. N.Y. office 1st Nat. Bank Atlanta, NYC, 1979-80; assoc. corp. fin. Goldman Sachs & Co., NYC, 1982-84; assoc. Eastdil Realty, Inc., NYC, 1984—89; dir. Jones Lang Wootton, U.S.A., NYC, 1989—92; mng. dir., head real estate group Gruntal & Co., Inc., NYC, 1993-98; sr. mng. dir., head equity capital markets Landauer Assocs., Inc., NYC, 1998-99; gen. ptnr. Centurion Realty Ptnrs., L.P., Cochecton, 1999—2004; sr. vice pres. Urdang Capital Mgmt., Charlotte, NC, 2004—06; pres. RCG Longview Realty Svcs., LLC, New Orleans, 2006—10; gen. ptnr. Centurion Realty Services, LLC, Baton Rouge, 2011—. Recipient Devel. cert. DARE Inc., Wilmington, 1984, 88. Mem. NAREIT, Real Estate Bd., N.Y., Urban Land Inst., Nat. Multifamily Housing Coun., N.C. Soc. N.Y., U. Va. Alumni Assn., Dartmouth Coll. Alumni Assn., N.Y. Athletic Club, Omicron Delta Kappa. Republican. Episcopalian. Avocations: fishing, bridge, golf, tennis, sailing. Office: Centurion Realty Svcs LLC 645 Pecan Dr Saint Gabriel LA 70776 Office Phone: 225-319-7015.

GOEPELT, BERNHARD, lawyer, beverage products company executive; b. Germany; Grad., Ruhr-Universitat Bochum. Joined as legal counsel to the German divsn. The Coca-Cola Co., 1992, legal counsel Mid. & Far East group, divsn. counsel Southeast & West Asia Thailand, group counsel Ctrl. Europe, Eurasia & Mid. East and Pacific groups, responsibilities in global mktg., comml. leadership and strategy, Pacific group counsel Atlanta, sr. v.p., gen. counsel and chief legal counsel, 2012—. Office: The Coca-Cola Co PO Box 1734 Atlanta GA 30301*

GOETZ, CHARLES JOHN, law and economics educator; b. NYC, Feb. 20, 1939; m. Judith Condon Goetz; children: Charles III, Daniel, Eric. AB, Providence Coll., 1961; PhD, U. Va., 1965. Asst. prof. U. Ill., 1965-67; assoc. prof. Va. Poly. Inst. & State U., 1967-72, prof. economics, dir. grad. program economics, 1972-75; vis. prof. U. Va. Sch. Law, Charlottesville, 1975-76, prof., 1976-83, Joseph M. Hartfield prof. law, 1983—2006, Hertfield prof. emeritus, 2006—. Co-author: Social Security Hearings and Appeals: A Study of the Social Security Administration Hearing System, 1978, Using Experts: Pre-trial Preparation, Trial Testimony and Settling Cases, 1985, Antitrust Law: Interpretation and Implementation, 1998, 2002, 2006; author, 2009, Cases and Materials on Law and Economics, 1984, Uncommon Common-Sense vs. Conventional Wisdom: The Virginia School of Economics, 1991, What Is Revenue Sharing, 1972; contbr. articles to profl. jours. NATO postdoctoral fellow, 1964-65, Commissioned as Kentucky Col. award, 1980; Patrick Henry award, 2002. Mem. Phi Beta Kappa.

GOFF, GREGORY J., oil industry executive; BS, U. Utah, 1978, MBA, 1981. Joined Conoco Inc., 1981, mng. dir., CEO Conoco JET Nordic, 1998—2000; chmn., mng. dir. Conoco Ltd., England, 2000; pres., Europe and Asia Pacific downstream activities ConocoPhillips, 2002—04, pres., US Lower 48 and Latin America exploration and prodn. bus., 2004—06, pres., strategy, integration and specialty bus., refining, mktg. and transp., 2006—08, sr. v.p., comml., 2008—10; pres., CEO Tesoro Corp., 2010—. Bd. dirs. ChevronPhillips Chem. Co. Mem. downstream com. Am. Petroleum Inst.; nat. adv. bd. U. Utah Bus. Sch. Office: Tesoro Corp 19100 Ridgewood Pky San Antonio TX 78259 Office Phone: 210-626-6000. Office Fax: 210-579-4574. Business E-Mail: gregoryJ.Goff@tsocorp.com.

GOGGANS, GREG, state legislator, orthodontist; m. Jane Goggans; 4 children. Attended, Univ. Ga.; orthrodontic & dental training, Med. Coll. Ga., Univ. Tenn. Orthodontic practice, Douglas, Ga., 1981—; mem. Dist. 7 Ga. State Senate, 2005—. Republican. Baptist. Office: 1300 Hampton Rd Douglas GA 31533 Office Phone: 912-384-1455. Office Fax: 912-383-6428. Business E-Mail: greg.goggans@senate.ga.gov.

GOGUE, JAY (G. JAY GOGUE), academic administrator; b. Waycross, Ga., Sept. 21, 1947; m. Susie Gogue; 3 children. BS, MS, Auburn U.; PhD in Horticulture, Mich. State U. Rsch. scientist Ecological Svc. Div. Nat. Park Svc., 1973—77, chief scientist, 1977—79, chief scientist Div. Interpretation, Park Protection, and Natural Resources Mgmt., 1979—86; prof. Coll. Forest and Recreation Resources Clemson U., 1986—95, assoc. dir. Office Univ. Rsch., 1986—88, v.p. rsch., 1988—95, interim dean Grad. Sch., 1991—92, acting dean Coll. Forest and Recreation Resources, 1994—95, v.p./vice provost agr. and natural resources, 1994—95; provost Utah State U., 1995—2000, prof. Coll. Natural Resources, 1995—2000; pres. N.Mex. State U., 2000—03; chancellor U. Houston Sys., 2003—07; pres. U. Houston, 2003—07, Auburn U., Ala., 2007—. Mem. Tex. Internat. Edn. Consortium; bd. dirs. Greater Houston Partnership, Conference—USA, BioHouston, Inc.; bd. govs. Houston Forum. Mem.: Nat. Assn. State Univs. and Land Grant Colls. (bd. mem. Nat. Resources Ecology Sect.), Sigma Chi, Phi Kappa Phi. Office: Auburn University Office of Pres 107 Samford Hall Auburn University AL 36849 Office Phone: 334-844-4650. E-mail: jgogue@auburn.edu.*

GOHMERT, LOUIE (LOUIS BULLER GOHMERT JR.), United States Representative from Texas, former judge; b. Pittsburg, Tex., Aug. 18, 1953; s. Louis Buller and E. Sue (Brooks) Gohmert; m. Kathryn Ann Bledsoe, June 24, 1978; children: Kathryn Blair, Caroline Sue, Sarah Louise. BA, Tex. A&M U., 1975; JD, Baylor U. Sch. Law, Waco, Tex., 1977; attended, Sch. Internat. Tng., Putney, Vt. Bar: Tex. 1978, US Dist. Ct. (eastern & southern districts) Tex. 1978, US Ct. Appeals (5th cir.) 1986, US Supreme Ct. 1986. Asst. dist. atty. 76th Judicial Dist., Mt. Pleasant, Tex., 1978; assoc. Potter Guinn Law Firm, Tyler, Tex., 1982-86; ptnr. Freeman, Smithson & Gohmert, Tyler, 1986; pvt. practice atty. Tyler, 1986—92; judge Smith County Dist. Ct., Tyler, 1992—2002, 12th Ct. Appeals Tex., 2002—03; mem. US Congress from 1st Tex. Dist., 2005—. Deacon Green Acres Bapt. Ch., Tyler. Capt. JAGC US Army, 1978—82, Ft. Benning, Ga. Mem.: Tex. A&M Alumni Assn. (pres. Smith County chpt. 1988), State Bar Tex., Smith County Bar Assn. (treas. 1989), Rotary. Republican. Baptist. Avocations: sports, creative writing. Office: US House of Representatives 2243 Rayburn House Office Bldg Washington DC 20515 also: 1121 ESE Loop 323 Ste 206 Tyler TX 75701 Office Phone: 202-225-3035.*

GOINGS, EVERETT VERNON (RICK), consumer products company executive; b. Chgo., Oct. 13, 1945; s. Louise Goings; m. Carol Panella; children: Rett, Todd. AB, Guilford Coll., 1969. Dist. sales mgr., regional v.p. Renn Enterprises, 1969-70; pres. Dynamics Inc. (name changed to Dynamark Sec. Ctrs.), 1970-78, Fortcorp, 1979-85; with Avon Products, Inc., 1986—, exec. v.p., N.Am. ops. NYC, 1989, exec. v.p., 1989—; pres. (world-wide) Tupperware (formerly Avon U.S.), NYC, 1989—97; chmn., CEO Tupperware Brands Corp., 1997—. Bd. dirs. R.R. Donnelley & Sons Co., Circuit City Stores, Inc., SunTrust Bank of Ctrl. Fla., N.A., Reynolds Am., Inc. Bd. dirs. Boys & Girls Clubs of Am., N.Y., 1989—. Mem. Direct Selling Assn. (bd. dirs. Washington chpt. 1989—), CTFA, Farmington Country Club. Office: Tupperware Brands Corp 14901 S Orange Blossom Trail Orlando FL 32837 Office Phone: 407-826-5050. Office Fax: 407-826-8268. Business E-Mail: egoings@tupperwarebrands.com.

GOINS, RICHARD ANTHONY, lawyer, educator; b. New Orleans, Mar. 1, 1950; s. James Milton and Vivian (Wiltz) G.; m. Jane Parker, Aug. 18, 1973 (div. Sept. 1987); m. Nannette Smith, Mar. 3, 1990. BA in History cum laude, Yale U., 1968—72; JD, Stanford U., 1972—75. Bar: La. 1975, Calif. 1977. Dep. dir. New Orleans Legal Asst. Corp., 1977-78, exec. dir., 1978-81; law clk. to Hon. A. Duplantier U.S. Fed. Dist. Ct., New Orleans, 1982; asst. prof. Loyola U. Law Sch., New Orleans, 1981-84; ptnr. Adams and Reese, New Orleans, 1987-96, The Goins Law Firm, New Orleans, 1997-99; shareholder Goins Aaron, PLC, 2000—10; spl. counsel Sutterfield & Webb L.L.C., 2011—. Asst. bar examiner torts La. Bar Exam., 1991-96, bar examiner civil procedure, 1996-2004; sec., dir. character and fitness La. Com. on Bar Admissions, 2004-08; chmn. La. Supreme Ct. Com. on Bar Admissions, 2008-10; mem. merit selection panel for selection and appt. of U.S. Magistrate for Ea. Dist. La., 1992-95, 2000; mem. host com. jud. conf. Fed. 5th Cir. Ct. Appeals, 1995; mem. civic justice reform act adv. com. Ea. Dist. La., 2000-06; adj. prof. Loyola U. Law Sch., New Orleans, 1984-92, 2003-05. Co-author: Practical Issues in Class Action Litigation, 1995. Mem. Mayor of New Orleans Overall Econ. Devel. Plan Com., 1991, Orleans Intercmty. Coun., 1992; mem. spl. gifts. com. Yale Alumni Fund, 1991-92; bd. dirs. New Orleans Home Mortgage Authority, 1991-94, City Trust, New Orleans, 1983-94, State Mental Health Advocacy Sys., New Orleans, 1983-84, New Orleans Legal Assistance Corp., 1982-83, Milne Asylum for Destitute Orphan Boys, Inc., 1994-97; Met. Area Com., 1996-2000; Bur. Govtl. Rsch., 2010-. Fellow: La. Bar Found; mem.: ABA (conf. minority ptnrs. 1990—96), Calif. State Bar Assn., 5th Cir. Bar Assn., Fed. Bar Assn. (bd. dir. New Orleans chpt. 1992—99), La. State Bar Assn. (legal aid com. 1978—81, uniform fed. rules com. 1991—92, fed. ct. bench-bar liason com. 1993—99), Master Thomas Moore Inn of Ct. Democrat. Roman Catholic. Avocations: reading, computers. Home: 4412 Mandeville St New Orleans LA 70122-4928 Office Phone: 504-596-2455. Business E-Mail: rgoins@swslaw.com.

GOLD, ALAN STEPHEN, federal judge; b. NYC, 1944; s. Frank and Geraldine (Guenzberg) G.; m. Susan Fine, May 28, 1965; children: Carol, Natalie. BA with high honors, U. Fla., 1966; JD, Duke U., 1969; LLM in Taxation, U. Miami, Fla., 1974. Bar: Fla., 1969, Dade County, Fla. (11th judicial cir.), 1992. Law clk. to Hon. Charles Carrol Fla. 3rd Dist Ct. Appeal, Miami, 1969-71; asst. atty. Met. Dade County Atty's Office, Miami, 1971-75; ptnr. Greenberg, Traurig, Hoffman, Lipoff, Rosen & Quentel, P.A., Miami, 1975-92; judge 11th Cir. Ct., Dade County, Fla., 1992-97, US Dist. Ct. (southern dist.) Fla., Miami, 1997—2011, sr. judge, 2011—. Contbr. articles to profl. jours. Co-gen. counsel Fla. High Speed Rail Transp. Commn., 1985—; city atty. Village of Bal Harbour, Fla., 1976-82; spl. counsel Broward County, Fla., 1984-88; trustee Palmer Sch., Miami, 1987-88; bd. dirs. Actor's Playhouse, Miami, 1989—, South Dade Jewish Community Ctr., Miami, 1985-85; apptd. Fla. Environ. Land Mgmt. Com., 1987. Disting. scholar Fla. State U., 1990; recipient Award for Outstanding Contbn. in Field of Legislative Affairs South Fla. Bldrs. Assn., 1989. Mem. ABA, Fla. Bar. Assn. (com. on environment and land use law 1983-84, Disting. Svc. award 1984), Urban Land Inst. (nat. policy coun. 1988—), Greater Miami Chamber of Commerce (chmn. land use com. 1989-90), American Coll. Real Estate Attorneys Democrat. Jewish. Avocations: trekking, vacationing, raising horses, sail fishing, reading. Office: US District Court Ferguson US Courthouse 400 N Miami Ave Rm 11-1 Miami FL 33128 Office Phone: 305-523-5580.

GOLD, GEORGE MYRON, lawyer, editor, writer, consultant; b. Bklyn., June 28, 1935; s. Harry and Rose Miriam; m. Bunny Winters, Dec. 24, 1960 (dec. Sept 13, 2010); 1 child, Seth Harris; m. Johnette Thompson, Sept. 1, 2012. AB, U. Rochester, 1956; JD, NYU, 1959. Bar: NY 1960. Practice, NYC, 1960-64, 67-78; legal editor Prentice-Hall, Inc., Englewood Cliffs, NJ, 1960-62; assoc. Speiser, Shumate, Geoghan & Law, NYC, 1962-64; assoc. editor Rsch. and Rev. Svc. Am., Inc., Indpls., 1964-67; dir. publs., mng. editor Estate Planners Quar., Farnsworth Pub. Co., Inc., Rockville Centre, NY, 1967-69; editor-in-chief Trusts & Estates Mag., NYC, 1969-76; mng. editor Trust News, NYC, 1976-78; dir. news publs. and info., editor ABA, Chgo., 1978-83; sr. assoc. editor and dir. book divsn. ABA Jour., Chgo., 1984-87; dir. publs. and editor Trial Mag. Assn. Trial Lawyers Am., 1988-89; exec. sr. law editor Lexis/Nexis, Dayton, 1990-93; exec. editor Stevens Pub., Washington, 1993-94, corp. editl. dir., 1994-95, v.p. editl., 1995; sr. acq. editor Harcourt Profl. Pub., Alexandria, Va., 1998—2000; sr. writer, editor Arnold & Porter, 2003—04. Cons., Ashburn, Va., 1995—. Author: The Propriety, Procedure and Evidentiary Effect of a Jury View, 1959, Investments by Trustees, Executors and Administrators, 1961, What You Should Know About Intestacy, 1962, What You Should Know About the Common Disaster, 1962, The Powers of Your Trustee, 1962, What You Should Know About the Antenuptial Agreement, 1963, Who May Be the Beneficiary of Your Will, 1963, What You Should Know About The Spendthrift Trust, 1963, Comprehensive Estate Analysis, 1966, You're Worth More Than You Think, 1966, Medicare Handbook, 1966, The ABCs of Administering Your Estate, 1966, The Will: An Instrument for Service and Sales, 1966, A Tax-Sheltered Pension Plan for the Close-Corporation Stockholder, 1968, Social Security Law in Nutshell, 1968, What You Should Know About Custodial Gifts to Minors, 1968, The Short-Term Trust and Estate Planning, 1976, The Importance of a Will, 1976, The Need for an Experienced Executor, 1976, Tax Tips-99 Ways to Reduce the Bite, 1976, Investment Management: No Job for the Amateur, 1971, Who Manages Your Securities?, 1972, A Woman's Need for Financial Planning, 1972, The Lawyer's Role in the Search for Peace, 1972, True Counselors: Helping Clients Deal with Loss, 1983, Evaluating and Settling Personal Injury Claims, 1991, Cite Checking: A Guide to Validating Legal Research, 1992, The Compliance Pak for HR Managers-Book I (Hiring, Evaluation & Separation), Book II (Severance), 1993, Selling Life Insurance: Overcoming Objections, 1996; editor: Fundamentals of Federal Income Estate and Gift Taxes, 1965-67 (ann.), The R & R Tax Handbook, 1965-67 (ann.),Recovery for Wrongful Death, 1966, Tax-Free Reorganizations, 1968, Guide to Pension and Profit Sharing Plans, 1968, A Life Underwriter's Guide to Equity Investments, 1968, The Tired Tirade, 1968, A Handbook of Personal Insurance Terminology, 1968, The 15th Anniversary Edition of Estate Planners Quar., 1968, You, Your Heirs and Your Estate, 1968, The Farnsworth Letter for Estate Planners, 1968-69, How to Use Life Insurance in Business and Estate Planning, 1969, Human Drama in Death and Taxes, 1970, Don't Bank on It, 1970, The Feldman Method, 1970,Is Trust Marketing Ready for Chiguita Barana, 1973, Directory of Trust Instns., 1969-75 (ann.), English: A Second Language for Lawyers, 1981 LawTalk, 1986-87, The Supreme Court and Its Justices, 1987, Aaron J. Broder on Trial: Reflections of a Master Litigator, 1994, Examining the Science Behind Nutraceuticals, 2001. Mem. Soc. Law Writers (dir.

1972-75), ABA, Am. Law Inst., NY State Bar Assn., Assn. Bar City NY, Estate Planning Council NYC, Nat. Press Club, Soc. Bus. Press Editors, Soc. Scholarly Publ., Soc. Human Resources Mgmt., Am. Soc. Assn. Execs., Newsletter and Electronic Publishers Assn., Washington Independent Writers, Loudon Womens Abuse Ctr. (bd. mem.), Loudoun County Cable TV Commn., Kappa Nu, Pi Alpha Lambda. Clubs: KP. Office Phone: 703-403-0452.

GOLD, JAMES J., retail executive; BA, Tulane U.; MBA, Harvard U. Mem. mdse. tng. program through various mdse., operational positions Neiman Marcus Stores, 1991—97, divsn. mdse. mgr., 2000—02, sr. v.p., gen. mdse. mgr., 2002—04; v.p., last call clearance divsn. The Neiman Marcus Group, Inc., Dallas, 1997—2000; pres. specialty retail Neiman Marcus Group, Inc., Dallas, 2010—; sr. v.p., gen. merchandising Neiman Marcus Direct, 2008—09; pres., CEO Bergdorf Goodman, Inc., 2004—. Office: The Neiman Marcus Group Inc 1618 Main St Dallas TX 75201 also: Bergdorf Goodman Inc 754 5th Ave New York NY 10019 Office Phone: 212-743-7607. Office Fax: 212-872-8677. Business E-Mail: jim@jamesfgoldstein.com.

GOLD, STUART HARRISON, pediatrician; b. Atlanta, June 22, 1955; MD, Vanderbilt U., Nashville, 1981. Cert. in pediat. 1986, in pediatric hematology-oncology 1987. Internship in pediat. U. Colo. Health Sci. Ctr., Denver, 1981—82, residency in pediatric hematol. oncology, 1982—84, chief residency in pediat., 1984—85, fellowship in pediatric hematology oncology, 1985—89; hosp. appointment Meml. Hosp., Chapel Hill, NC; asst. prof. U. NC Sch. Medicine, Chapel Hill, assoc. prof. pediat., clin. rsch. & outpatient clinic dir., Lineberger Comprehensive Cancer Ctr., prof. pediatric hematology oncology divsn., chief pediatric hematology oncology divsn., 2008—. Com. mem. Children's Cancer Group. Contbr. articles to profl. jours. Bd. officer Ronald McDonald House, Chapel Hill. Office: U NC Sch Medicine 407 Macnider Bldg CB 7236 Chapel Hill NC 27599 Office Phone: 919-966-0985. Office Fax: 919-966-7629. Business E-Mail: stuart_gold@med.unc.edu.

GOLDBERG, ALAN JOEL, lawyer; b. Bklyn., Jan. 22, 1943; s. Ralph and Dorothy G.; 1 child, Cary Adam. BA, U. Miami, 1965, JD, 1968. Bar: Fla. 1968, U.S. Supreme Ct., U.S. Ct. Appeals (4th cir.). Ptnr. Goldberg, Young, Goldberg & Borkson, P.A., Ft. Lauderdale, Fla., 1968-82; atty. City of Margate, Fla., 1969-70, City of Tamarac, Fla., 1970-71; pvt. practice Ft. Lauderdale, 1982—. Pres. Diversified Realty Devel., Co., 1996—; bd. dirs. Starmark Internat., 2010—; leadership bd. dirs. Am. Diabetes Assn., 2010—. Mem. Citizen's Task Force on Transp., State of Fla.; mem. Broward County Planning Coun., 1984-92, chmn., 1988, 91; bd. dirs. Boys and Girls Clubs of Broward County, Inc., 1995—, pres., 1999-2000, chmn. bd. dirs., 2000-01 Mem. Fla. Bar Assn. Republican. Office: 6300 NE 1st Ave Ste 100 Fort Lauderdale FL 33334 Office Phone: 954-776-1005.

GOLDBERG, BURTON, pathologist, researcher, educator; b. Milw., Jan. 6, 1927; s. Esrael and Martha Goldberg; m. Geraldine Anne Yencha, Dec. 15, 1984. BS, Northwestern U., 1948, MD, 1950. Internship Cin. Gen. Hosp., 1951-52; residency in pathology Mallory Inst. Boston City Hosp., 1952-55; rsch. fellow in biochemistry MIT, Cambridge, 1955-57; asst. prof. pathology NYU Med. Sch., 1957-59, assoc. prof. pathology, 1959-71, prof. pathology, 1971-84; prof., chmn. dept. pathology U. Wis. Med. Sch., Madison, 1985-93, prof. emeritus, 1993—. Vis. scientist Inst. Pasteur, Paris, 1993-94. Contbr. articles to profl. jours.; contbr. chpt. to Connective Tissue in Histology, 1988. With USN, 1944-45. NIH grantee, 1959—; recipient Career Devel. award USPHS, 1960-70. Mem. Am. Soc. Experimental Pathology, Am. Soc. Biol. Chemistry and Molecular Biology, Am. Soc. Cell Biology. E-mail: bgberg@att.net.

GOLDBERG, DAVID, lawyer; BS in Economics, Tex. Christian U., 1984; JD, St. Mary's U., 1987. Atty. Haynes and Boone, LLP, 1987—95; v.p., gen. counsel & sec. InterTAN, Inc., 1995—99; chief legal counsel RadioShack Corp., Fort Worth, Tex., sr. v.p., gen. counsel & corp. sec., 1999—2007; v.p., gen. counsel & corp. sec. Union Drilling, Inc., 2007—. Office: Union Drilling Inc 4055 International Plz Ste 610 Fort Worth TX 76109-4879 Office Phone: 817-735-8793. Office Fax: 817-735-9226. Business E-Mail: dgoldberg@uniond.com.

GOLDBERG, LARRY M., hospital administrator; BA, U. NC; M in health adminstrn., Duke U. Past position with Deloitte & Touche, NY, Ernst & Young, NY; v.p. hosp. ops. Northwestern Meml. Hosp., Chgo., 1998—2005; CEO, exec. dir. Vanderbilt U. Hosp., Tenn., 2005—. Office: Vanderbilt U Hosp 1161 21st Ave Nashville TN 37232 Office Phone: 615-343-4501. Office Fax: 615-343-7317. E-mail: larry.goldberg@Vanderbilt.Edu.

GOLDBERG, PAUL BERNARD, gastroenterologist, clinical researcher; b. Bklyn., Apr. 11, 1950; s. Samuel and Eva (Turkenitz) G.; m. Harriet Ruth Ferrer, July 8, 1973 (div. 1987); children: Deborah Lynn, Susan Michelle; m. Mary Alice Denaro, June 23, 1990(div. 2007); 1 child, Laura Alicia; m. Sherilyn Marron, Dec. 29, 2011. BA in Chemistry summa cum laude, Cornell U., 1967-71, MD, 1971-75. Diplomate Am. Bd. Internal Medicine, Am. Bd. Gastroenterology. Intern in medicine Hosp. of U. of Pa., Phila., 1975-76, resident in medicine, 1976-78, fellow in gastroenterology, 1978-80, fellow in nutritional support svc., 1979-80; med. coord. and founder nutritional support svc. Lakeland (Fla.) Gen. Hosp., 1980-81; attending physician Halifax Med. Ctr., 1980—, Ormond Meml. Hosp., 1980—, Atlantic Med. Ctr., 1980-2000, Fish Meml. Hosp., New Smyrna Beach, Fla., 1989-99, Peninsula Med. Ctr., 1989-94, Villages Regional Hosp., 2011—, Fla. Hosp. Waterman, 2011—, Leesburg Regional Med. Ctr., 2011—, chmn. dept. medicine, 2012—. Pres. Sunshine Health Care Plan, Inc., 1983-86, v.p., 1986-87; chief staff Humana Hosp., Daytona Beach, 1986-88, trustee, 1986-89, mem. exec. com., 1984-91; mem. rev. bd. Coastal Instnl. Rev., 1990-93, chmn. rev. bd., 1993-96; expert reviewer Fla. Dept. Profl. Regulation, 1990—; pres. med. staff Halifax Hosp., 1996-97; clin. asst. prof. medicine dept. family medicine U. South Fla., 1987-2007. Rschr. and author in field. Physician adv. Daytona chpt. Crohn's and Colitis Found., 1991-95. Recipient Nat. award Ford Future Scientists of Am., 1967, Westinghouse Sci. Talent Search finalist, 1967. Fellow ACP, Am. Coll. Gastroenterology, Am. Gastroent. Soc.; mem. Am. Soc. Gastrointestinal Endoscopy, Am. Soc. for Parenteral and Enteral Nutrition (pres. Fla. chpt. 1991-92), Volusia County Med. Soc. (exec. com. 1991-94, co-chmn. mini internship program 1992-94, 2000-01), Fla. Gastrointestinal Soc., Fla. Med. Assn. (alt. del. to ho. of dels. 1990-95), Fla. Assn. Nutritional Support (1st pres.), Rotary, Phi Beta Kappa, Alpha Omega Alpha. Office: 822 Perkins St Leesburg FL 34748 Office Phone: 352-315-0706. Personal E-mail: pbgoldberg@aol.com.

GOLDBERG, STANLEY IRWIN, real estate company executive; b. Newport News, Va., May 13, 1934; s. David and Sara (Levy) G.; m. Marilyn Levin, Nov. 22, 1963 (dec. Oct. 1970); 1 child, Andrew Garfield. Student, Coll. William and Mary, 1952—54, U. Va., 1954—55. Lic. real estate broker, Va. V.p. Bedding Supply Co., Inc., Newport News, 1956-59, exec. v.p., 1960-61, pres., 1962-70; mng. ptnr. Goldkress Investment Co., Newport News, 1970—, also bd. dirs.; pres. Mut. Realty Corp., Newport News, 1973—. Trustee Temple Sinai, Newport News. Served with USAF, 1957-58. Mem. Nat. Assn. Realtors, Va. Assn. Realtors, Va. Peninsula Assn. Realtors, Elks. Home: 19 Hopemont Dr Newport News VA 23606-2146 Office: 11116 Jefferson Ave Newport News VA 23601-2551 Personal E-mail: asc67@aol.com.

GOLDBERG, WENDY, broadcast executive; B, U. Mich., Ann Harbor; M in Pub. Adminstrn., Harvard U. Sr. adviser Pilot Group; sr. v.p. comm. 6 Flags Entertainment Corp.; spokesperson AOL Time Warner, v.p. comm., America Online; v.p. bus. devel. and strategy Hearst Corp.; exec. v.p. mktg. and comm. clear channel radio divsn. Clear Channel Comm. Inc., Ariz., 2011—. Office: Clear Channel Communications Incorporated Clear Channel Radio 200 E Basse Rd San Antonio TX 78209 Office Phone: 210-822-2828.

GOLDEN, AL, college football coach; b. July 4, 1969; m. Kelly Elizabeth Hanna; children: A.J., Addison, Grace. BA in Pre-Law, Pa. State U., 1991; MS in Sports Psychology, U. Va., 1996. Tight end New Eng. Patriots, 1992; offensive coord. Red Bank Cath. HS Caseys, NJ, 1993; outside linebackers coach Boston Coll. Eagles, 1997—98, linebackers coach, 1999; linebackers coach, recruiting coord. Pa. State U. Nittany Lions, 2000; grad. asst. U. Va. Cavaliers, 1994—96, defensive coord., inside linebackers coach, 2001—04, defensive coord., defensive backs coach, 2005; head football coach Temple U. Owls, 2005—10, spl. teams coord., 2007—09; head football coach U. Miami Hurricanes, 2010—. Recipient Ridge Riley award, Pa. State U., 1991; named Coach of Yr., Mid-America Conf., 2009, Tri-State Coach of Yr., Maxwell Club, 2009. Office: University Miami Football c/o Dept Athletics 5821 San Amaro Dr Coral Gables FL 33146 Office Phone: 305-284-2674.

GOLDEN, DAVID EDWARD, physicist; b. NYC, May 27, 1932; s. Barnet Dade and Rose (Rosenbaum) G.; m. Paula Englander, July 18, 1962; children: Richard, Jeffrey Bertram, Leila Justine. AB, NYU, 1954, PhD in Physics, 1960. Asst. prof. NYU, 1960-61, Adelphi U., Garden City, NY, 1961-62; engring. specialist GTE Lab., Palo Alto, Calif., 1962-63; staff scientist Lockheed Lab., Palo Alto, 1963-68; vis. prof. U. Bari, Italy, 1968-69; sr. scientist Sylvania Electric Products, Danvers, Mass., 1969-70; prof. U. Nebr., Lincoln, 1970-75; George Lynn Gross rsch. prof., chmn. U. Okla., Norman, 1975-85; provost, v.p. acad. affairs, prof. physics U. North Tex., Denton, 1985-89, prof., dir. ctr. for materials characterization, 1989-94, regents prof., 1993—2004; pres. Say It Straight Found., Austin, Tex., 2004—. Cons. autometric divsn. Paramount Pictures, N.Y.C., 1961-62, Tracor, Austin, Tex., 1969-74, Lawrence Radiation Lab., Livermore, Calif., 1975-78, Minn. Mining and Mftg., Mpls., 1984-86, Motorola, 1997-2000, Charles Evans & Assocs., 1998—2000; hon. lectr. Mid-Am. State U. Assn., 1982-83; chmn. Tex. Higher Edn. Coordinating Bd. Com. on Satellite Ednl. Delivery Systems, 1986; lectr. in field. Contbr. articles to profl. jours., chpts. to books. Sr. cons. Say It Straight Found. Grantee various orgns.; fellow Centennial Edn. Program U. Nebr., 1974-75. Fellow Am. Phys. Soc. (com. mem.); mem. AAAS, Materials Rsch. Soc., Sigma Xi. Lodges: Kiwanis. Avocations: jogging, tennis. Home Phone: 512-428-6478; Office Phone: 512-983-4459.

GOLDEN, GERALD SAMUEL, retired national medical board executive; b. Newark, June 8, 1935; s. Clement Harold and Jeannette (Bellat) G.; m. Deborah Ann Berlatsky, March 22, 1959 (dec. 1984); children: Leah Rachel, Ruth Naomi; m. Constance Reisa Abramson, Jan. 26, 1985. AB, Princeton U., 1957; MD, Columbia U., 1961. Diplomate Am. Bd. Pediat., Am. Bd. Psychiatry and Neurology. Asst. prof. of neurology and pediatrics Albert Einstein Coll. of Medicine, Bronx, NY, 1967-73, assoc. prof., 1973-77; prof. pediatrics and neurology U. Tex., Galveston, 1977-84; prof. pediatrics and neurology, dir. ctr. for devel. disabl. U. Tenn., Memphis, 1984-92; v.p. Nat. Bd. Med. Examiners, Phila., 1993—2002, con., 2002—. Adj. prof. neurology U. Pa., 1993—98. Author: Textbook of Pediatric Neurology; assoc. editor: Pediatric Neurology Jour., 1987-92, Jour. of Devel. and Behavioral Pediatrics, 1987-2000, Jour. Epilepsy, 1987-92; contbr. numerous articles to profl. jours. Bd. dirs. Harwood Day Tng. Ctr., Memphis, 1987-92 Memphis-Shelby County Assn. for Retarded Citizens, 1987-92, Memphis Oral Sch. for Deaf, 1987-92, Temple Israel Memphis, 1989-92. Recipient fed. grant Adminstrn. on Devel. Disabilities, 1990, Dept. of Human Svcs., 1990. Fellow Am. Acad. Pediat. (neurology sect. head 1981-83), Am. Assn. Mental Deficiency (v.p. for medicine, 1984-86); mem. Am. Assn. U. Affiliated Programs (bd. dirs. 1987-92, pres. elect 1988-89, pres. 1989-90), Accrediation Coun., United Coun. Neurologic Subspecialties. Democrat. Jewish. Avocations: amateur radio, travel, birdwatching. Personal E-mail: doc.gsg@cox.net.

GOLDEN, LEON, classicist, educator; b. Jersey City, Dec. 25, 1930; s. Nathan and Regina (Okun) G. BA, U. Chgo., 1950, MA, 1953, PhD, 1958. Instr. ancient langs. Coll. William and Mary, 1958-60, asst. prof. ancient langs., 1960-65; assoc. prof. classical langs. Fla. State U., Tallahassee, 1965-68, prof., 1968—, dir. program in humanities, 1976—, chmn. dept. classics, 1986-95. Bd. dirs. Fla. Endowment for Humanities, 1983-87. Author: In Praise of Prometheus: Humanism and Rationalism in Aeschylean Thought, 1966, (with O.B. Hardison Jr.) Aristotle's Poetics, 1968, Aristotle: On Tragic and Comic Mimesis, 1992, Horace for Students of Literature, 1995, Understanding the Iliad, 2004, Achilles and Yossarian. With AUS, 1953-55. Fellow coop. program humanities U.N.C. and Duke, 1964-65; fellow coop. program humanities Soc. for Religion in Higher Edn., 1971-72 Mem. Am. Philol. Assn., Archeol. Inst. Am., Classical Assn. Mid. West and South (pres. So. sect. 1972-74), Phi Beta Kappa. Address: 1526 Parchment Cove Tallahassee FL 32308 E-mail: lgolden352@msn.com.

GOLDEN, PAULA ENGLANDER, psychology, social work, addiction educator, consultant; d. Joseph and Erna (Leser) Englander; m. David E. Golden, July 18, 1962; children: Jeff Bertram, Leila Justine. BS in Physics, Bklyn. Coll., 1956; MS in Physics, NYU, NYC, 1961; MA in Psychology, U. Nebr., Lincoln, 1974, PhD in Psychology, 1977. Cert. therapist and rschr. Level 4 Internat. Bd. Regression Therapy. Sr. scientist Lockheed Missiles and Space Co., Palo Alto, Calif., 1962—67; asst. project dir. U. Okla., Okla., 1975—76, prof., 1976—89; dir. grad. program chem. dependency studies Okla. Alcohol/Drugs Info. Clearinghouse, 1979—89, dir. chem. dependency tng. cert. program, 1979—89, dir., 1980—83, prof. women's studies, 1982—89. Dir. tng., founder Say It Straight Found., Austin, Tex., 1982—; prof. dept. rehab., social work and addictions U. North Tex., Denton, 1989—2004; founder Inst. Studies in Addiction; mem. Substance Abuse & Mental Health Svcs. Adminstrn. Nat. Registry Evidence Based Programs & Practices. Author: Say It Straight: From Compulsions to Choices, 1991; contbr. articles to profl. jours. Mem. Okla. Gov.'s Adv. Commn. on Aging. Grantee Office of Substance Abuse Prevention, HHS, 1989-91; recipient citation Classic Sci. Citation Index, 1981. Mem. APA, Soc. of Psychologists in Addictive Behaviors, Avanta (internat. planning com.), Sigma Xi. Achievements include development of three videotapes for the US Department of Education: Say It Straight: In the Classroom; Say It Straight: Student Support Group; Say It Straight: Family-Community Series. Avocations: yoga, travel, water aerobics. Home and Office: 701 Horseback Hollow Austin TX 78732 Office Phone: 512-428-6478. Business E-Mail: info@sayitstraight.org, paulaeg@sayitstraight.org.

GOLDEN, ROLLAND HARVE, artist; b. New Orlean, Nov. 8, 1931; s. John Ferdinand and Ione (Rolland) Golden; m. Stella Anne Doussan, Aug. 31, 1957; children: Carrie Marie Lambert, Mark Damian, Lucille Marie. Degree, John McCrady Art Sch., 1955—57. Author: Vieux Carrier Courier, Palette Talk, La. Cultural Vistas, Rolland Golden, Journeys of a Southern Artist, 2005, Katrina: Days of Terror, Months of Anguish, 2007, World of Rolland Golden, 1970; one-man shows include New Orleans Mus. Art, Springfield Mus. Art, Mo., Masur Mus. Art, Miss. Hist. Mus., Miss. Mus. Art, 2010, Percy Whiting Art Ctr., one-man shows include USSR, 1976—77, Southern France Touring, 1993—95, La. Old State Capitol Baton Rouge, Celebrating Bicentennial, 2011—12, MS River Exhibition Six Museums, 2010—12, Represented in permanent collections Historic New Orleans Collection, New Orleans Mus. Art, Nat. Arts Club, NY, Pushkin Mus., Moscow, New Orleans Mus. Art, Walter Anderson Mus. Art, Roland Golden Life Love, 2014, OGDEN Mus. Southern Art, 2014, over 100 one-man shows throughout USA. Bd. dirs. Vieux Carre Property Owners, New Orleans, 1970—81, Folsom Rd. Civic Assn., La., 1982—90. Served with USN, 1951—55. Recipient Visual Arts award, Miss. Inst. Arts & Letters, 2011. Mem.: Nat. Arts Club, Watercolor USA, Allied Artists America (hon.; life), La. Watercolor Soc. (life), Nat. Watercolor Soc. Republican. Roman Catholic. Home: 78207 Woods Hole Ln Folsom LA 70437 Personal E-mail: rolandgolden@aol.com.

GOLDEN, TIM ROBERT, state legislator; b. Waycross, Ga., June 3, 1954; son of E Frank Golden & LaVerne Little G; married to Ellen Stewart; children: Seth. BS, Valdosta State Univ., 1977. Staff aide U.S. Senator Sam Nunn, U.S. Congressman Charles Hatcher; pres., owner Golden Printing, Valdosta, Ga.; mem. Dist. 148 Ga. House Reps., 1991—98; mem. Dist. 8 Ga. State Senate, 1999—. Leadership Award, Leadership Georgia Found, 87; Legislator of Year, Georgia Acad Family Physicians, 95; Guardian of Small Bus Award, Nat Fedn Independent Bus, 97 & 98. Kiwanis; Chamber of Commerce; YMCA (president, formerly, board director, 84-); YMCA State Cluster (chairman, formerly); March of Dimes (board director, 90-); Valdosta Methodist Youth Home (board member, currently). Democrat. Methodist. Office: 110 Beacon Hill Valdosta GA 31602 Office Phone: 229-293-0202. Office Fax: 229-241-7732. Business E-Mail: tim.golden@senate.ga.gov.

GOLDENBERG, GEORGE, retired pharmaceutical executive; b. NYC, Mar. 12, 1929; s. Gersh and Rose (Kolpacci) G.; m. Arlene Sondra Yudell, May 22, 1955; children: Steven Alan, Heidi Michele Goldenberg Handelsman, Jeffrey Evan. Student, Bklyn. Coll., 1946-47; BS, Bklyn. Coll. Pharmacy L.I. U., 1951. Pharmacist Dolcorts Pharmacy, NYC, 1951-56; export mgr. Chem. Specialties Co., Inc., NYC, 1956-58; sales mgr. Syntex Chem. Co., Inc., NYC, 1958-60; asst. to pres. Syntex Labs., Inc., NYC, 1960-61; gen. sales mgr. Panray-Parlam Corp., Englewood, NJ, 1961-63; v.p. Ormont Drug & Chem. Co., Inc., Englewood, 1963-64, exec. v.p., dir., 1964-66, pres., dir., 1966-81; sec., dir. Goldleaf Pharmacal Co., Inc., Englewood, 1966-81; pres., dir. Moleculon, Inc., 1982-88; pres., CEO, dir. Argus Pharms. Inc., The Woodlands, Tex., 1988-92. Bd. dirs. Fed. Pharmacal Co., Ft. Lauderdale, Fla., Bedford Acme Surg. Co., Inc., Bklyn., Lawton Labs., Inc., Englewood, Ormont Diagnostics Ltd., London. Trustee L.I. U., Bklyn. Coll. Pharmacy. Mem. Bklyn. Coll. Pharmacy Alumni Assn. (pres.), Fedn. Alumni Assns. L.I. U. (pres.), Am. Pharm. Assn., Englewood Jr. C. of C., Young Pres. Orgn., Am. Mgmt. Assn., Drug and Allied Trades Assn., Delta Sigma Theta. Clubs: B'nai B'rith, The Polo Club of Boca Raton (past pres. bd. govs.), Jewish Fedn. of S. Palm Beach County (mem., bd. dirs.), Delray Med. Ctr. (bd. dirs.). Home: 10672 Fawn River Trail Boynton Beach FL 33437 Personal E-mail: aggpolo@aol.com.

GOLDHAGEN, JEFFREY LEE, city health department administrator; m. Diana Goldhagen; children: Mia, Alanna, Tess, Eva, Julian. MD, U. Pitts.; MPH, U. Minn. Dir., med. programs for surg. aid Children of the World; co-dir., med. anthropology program Case Western Reserve U., Cleve.; med. dir. Cleve. Pub. Health Dept.; assoc. prof., pediat. U. Fla.; dir. Duval Co. Health Dept., Jacksonville, Fla., 1993—. Fellow: Am. Acad. Pediat. Office: Duval County Pub Health 515 W Sixth St MC #24 Jacksonville FL 32206

GOLDMAN, ALAN H., philosophy educator; b. NYC, Aug. 7, 1945; s. Lawrence I. and Florence (Goodman) G.; m. Joan Roslyn Berkowitz, May 29, 1968; children: Michael, David. BA, Yale U., 1967; PhD, Columbia U., 1972. Instr. Columbia U., NYC, 1970-72; asst. prof. Ohio U., Athens, 1972-74, U. Idaho, Moscow, 1974-76; assoc. prof. U. Miami, Coral Gables, Fla., 1977-81, prof., 1981—2002; Kenan prof. Coll. William & Mary, 2002—. Vis. prof. U. Mich., Ann Arbor, 1980; vis. fellow U. Colo., Boulder, 1983, Princeton (N.J.) U., 1976; chmn. philosophy dept. U. Miami, 1988—; editor series in applied ethics Garland Publ., NYC, 1998. Author: Philosophy and the Novel, 2013, Reasons From Within, 2009, Practical Rules, 2002, Aesthetic Value, 1995, Moral Knowledge, 1988, Empirical Knowledge, 1988, Moral Foundations of Professional Ethics, 1980, Justice & Reverse Discrimination, 1979. NEH grantee, 1991; NEH fellow, 1976-77, 2008-09, ACLS fellow, 2007-2008. Mem. Am. Philos. Assn. (program com. 1990-92). Avocations: tennis, golf. Office: Coll William & Mary Dept Philosophy Williamsburg VA 23187 Business E-Mail: ahgold@wm.edu.

GOLDMAN, ARTHUR E., aerospace transportation executive, civil engineer; BS in Civil Engring., Miss. State U., 1977. Registered Profl. Engr.-Civil, 1983. Project mgr. Tenn. Valley Authority, Hartsville, 1976—80; project engr./mgr. Gulf States Utilities, Baton Rouge, 1980—87; engring. mgr. Tenn. Valley Authority, Athens, Ala., 1987—90; with NASA, 1990—, dep. mgr. Space Shuttle Main Engine Project, George C. Marshall Space Flight Ctr. Huntsville, Ala., 1999—2004, mgr. Space Shuttle Main Engine Project, George C. Marshall Space Flight Ctr., 2004—06, dep. dir. John C. Stennis Space Ctr., 2006—08, dir. John C. Stennis Space Ctr., 2010—11, acting dir. Marshall Space Flight Ctr., 2012; exec. dir. Southeast space ops. Aerojet, 2012—. Fed. civil servants' Sr. Exec. Svc., 2004. Recipient NASA Certificate of Appreciation, 1997, NASA Exceptional Achievement medal, 2002, NASA Outstanding Leadership medal, 2007, Presdl. Rank award, 2010; named to Meridian Cmty. Coll. Hall of Fame, Miss., 2010; Sr. Exec. Fellows program, Harvard U., 2002, Congressional Ops. Program, George Washington U., 2003. Office: Aerojet 7047 Old Madison Pike Ste 360 Huntsville AL 35806*

GOLDMAN, BERT ARTHUR, retired professor; b. NYC, Apr. 4, 1929; children: Lisa, Linda. BA, U. Md., 1951; M.Ed., U. N.C., 1956; Ed.D., U. Va., 1960. Mem. faculty U. N.C., Greensboro, 1965—2008, prof., 1971-85, dean acad. advising, 1970-85, prof. higher ednl. adminstrn., 1985—86, acting chair dept. ednl. adminstrn., higher edn. and ednl. rsch., 1987-88, dept. coord. of higher edn., 1991—2005, prof. emeritus, 2006—. Vol. rschr. Greensboro Police Dept., 2010-. Served with U.S. Army, 1951-53. Mem. APA.

GOLDMAN, DANIEL S., cardiac electrophysiology; MD, U. Miss., 1981. Diplomate Am. Bd. Internal Medicine, 1984, Am. Bd. Internal Medicine-cardiovasc. disease, 1987, Am. Bd. Internal Medicine-clin. cardiac electropyhsiology, 2002. Resident internal medicine SUNY Downstate Med. Ctr., 1982—84, fellow cardiovasc. disease,

1984—86; hosp. affiliations include Delray Med. Ctr., Bethesda Meml. Hosp. Office: Delray Medical Center 5352 Linton Blvd Delray Beach FL 33484 Office Phone: 561-498-4440. Office Fax: 561-495-3103.

GOLDMAN, JAY, industrial engineer, educator, dean emeritus; b. Norfolk, Va., Apr. 15, 1930; s. Louis and Rose Goldman; m. Renitta, Dec. 20, 1959 BSME, Duke U., 1950; MSME, Mich. State U., 1951; DSc in Indsl. Engring., Washington U., St. Louis, 1955. Registered profl. engr., Mo. Lectr. indsl. engring. Washington U., 1952-56, asst. prof., 1956-64, acting chmn. human and orgn. factors, 1963-64; dir. dept. indsl. engring. Jewish Hosp., St. Louis, 1960-64; research assoc. dept. hosp. adminstr. U. N.C., Chapel Hill, 1964-68; prof., grad. adminstr. dept. indsl. engring. N.C. State U., Raleigh, 1964-68; prof., chmn. dept. indsl. engring. U. Mo., Columbia, 1968-84, prof. bioengring., 1969-75, prof. bioengring. and advanced automation, 1975-84; dean U. Ala., Birmingham, 1984-96, Disting. Svc. prof. and dean emeritus, 2002—. Cons. to fed., state agys., pvt. industry. Contbr. to textbooks, profl. jours.; producer 6 tech. motion pictures; patentee in field. V.p. Boone County Cmty. Svcs. Coun., 1973-76; bd. dirs. Birmingham Jewish Fedn.; vice-chmn., bd. dirs. Sloss Furnaces Nat. Hist. Landmark; bd. dirs., treas. Jewish Family Svcs. Recipient Editl. award, Hosp. Mgmt. mag., 1969, U. Mo. Faculty Alumni award, 1981, Outstanding Engr. Educator in State award, ASPE, Disting. Svc. award, Engr. Coun. Bhm, 2011; named Ala. Engr. of Yr., ASPE. Fellow Inst. Indsl. Engrs. (trustee, exec. v.p., regional v.p., chpt. pres., v.p. edn. and profl. devel., editl. bd. Trans., Health Svcs. Devel. award 1981, Fred C. Crane award 1999, Medallion award, 2004), Accreditation Bd. Engring. and Tech. (dir., treas., fellow); mem. NSPE; Soc. Health Sys. (bd. dirs., pres.), Nat. Coun. Indsl. Engrs. Acad. Dept. Heads (chmn.), Ala. Soc. Profl. Engrs., American Soc. Engring. Edn., Sigma Xi, Alpha Pi Mu, Tau Beta Pi, Phi Kappa Phi, Omicron Delta Kappa. Home: 6068 Brookhill Cir Birmingham AL 35242 Office: University Ala-Birmingham Sch Engring 1075 13th St S Ste 210 Birmingham AL 35205-3430 Office Phone: 205-934-8400. Business E-Mail: jgoldman@uab.edu.

GOLDMAN, RALPH FREDERICK, research physiologist, educator; b. Boston, Mar. 3, 1928; s. Harry and May (Field) G.; m. Joan R. Krinsky, May 27, 1956; children: Harry, Ellen. BS in Chemistry, U. Denver, 1949; MA in Physiology, Boston U., 1951, PhD in Physiology, 1954; MS in Engring., Northeastern U., Boston, 1962. Lic. bldg. contractor 1990, stock broker 1970, real estate broker 86. Rsch. physiologist Natick Labs. U.S. Army, Mass., 1955—61; dir. div. environ. medicine U.S. Army Rsch. Inst., Natick, 1961—82; prin. cons. Dept. of Army for Environ. Physiology, Natick, 1971—82; chief scientist Multi-Tech Corp., Natick, 1982—88; chief scientist, R&D, clothing and human comfort Comfort Tech., Inc., Plymouth, Mass., 1989—2011; sr. cons. tech. and product devel. Arthur D. Little, Inc., Cambridge, Mass., 1993—97; mgr. Krinsky Realty Co. Inc., 1980—. Adj. prof. Boston U., 1970—2005, N.C. State U., 1989—2005; lectr. MIT, Cambridge, 1974-94; vis. scientist Peoples Rep. of China, 1981—2007; vis. scholar lectr. Springfield (Mass.) Coll., 1977, Ohio State U., 1977, 88; Rohles lectr., Kans. State U., 2008, vis. scholar Otago U., New Zealand, 2013; chmn. rsch. group biomed. effects of clothing, NATO, 1981-86, developed sweating, walking copper man, 1965. Author: 4 books; contbr. 26 chpts. to books, over 500 articles, abstracts and tech. reports to profl. jours. Scoutmaster Boy Scouts Am., Framingham, Mass., 1956-90, exec. bd., 1991-2002; mem. town meeting Town of Framingham, 1983-88, founder, Mil. Ergonomics. Recipient Meritorious Civilian Svc. award U.S. Army R&D Command, 1963, Exceptional Civilian Svc. award Sec. of Army, 1976, Sr. Exec. Svc. award U.S. Civil Svc., 1979, Silver Beaver award Boy Scouts Am., 1981. Fellow: ASHRAE (life; bd. dirs. 1982—85, assoc. editor HVAC&R Rsch. 1995—2001, Disting. Fellow award 1992), Am. Coll. Sports Medicine (editl. bd. 1979—85), Ergonomics Soc. (hon.); mem.: ASTM, IEEE (life; AEMB Coun. 1978—84), Assn. Mil. Surgeons U.S., Am. Physiol. Soc. (editl. bd. 1972—78), Framingham Amateur Radio Assn. (treas. 1970—84), Tarpon Cove Yacht and Racquet Club, Naples, Fla. Jewish. Avocations: piano, gardening, walking. Home: 425 Cove Tower Dr Apt 704 Naples FL 34110-6505

GOLDMANN, JAMES ALLEN, healthcare consultant, author; b. Milw., Feb. 26, 1952; s. Allen Abraham and Ruth Lois (Kolbur) G.; m. Pamela Anne McCole, June 6, 1980; children: Michael, Elissa, Kerry. AB, Harvard Coll., 1974; MHA, Washington U., St. Louis, 1979. V.p. Riverside Meth. Hosp., Columbus, Ohio, 1980—85; COO Children's Med. Ctr., Dallas, 1986—92; cons. APM, Inc., NYC, 1993—96; ptnr. Arthur Andersen, Dallas, 1996—2000, IBM, Dallas, 2001—03, JHD Group, Dallas, 2004—09, Ethos Ptnrs., 2009—, Navigant, 2011—. Contbr. articles to profl. jours. Bd. dirs. Hope Cottage, Dallas, 1989-93; scout leader Boy Scouts Am., Columbus and Grapevine, Tex., 1980-84, 92, 93. Fellow Am. Coll. Healthcare Execs. Avocation: writing.

GOLDSBERRY, RONALD E., board member; b. Wilmington, Del., Sept. 12, 1942; BS, Ctrl. State U., 1964, LHD (hon.), 1988; PhD in Inorganic Chemistry, Mich. State U., 1969. Rsch. chemist, asst. prof. University of California, 1969-72; prodn. mgr. Hewlett Packard Co., 1972-73; mgmt. cons. Boston Cons. Group, 1973-75; dir., Corp. Planning Ops. Gulf Oil Corp., 1975-78; v.p., Bus. Devel. & Planning Occidental Chemical Corp., 1978-81, v.p., gen. mgr., 1981-83; pres., COO Parker Chemical Co., 1983-87; gen. mgr., Plastic & Trim Prodn. Divsn. Ford Motor Co., 1987-90, exec. dir., Sales & Svc. Strategies, 1990-91, gen. sales & mkt. mgr., 1991-94, global v.p., gen. mgr., Global Ford Customer Svc. Ops. Detroit, 1997—99; chmn. OnStation Corp. (formerly Carstation.com), 1999—2006, CEO, 1999—2002. Bd. dirs. Unum Group. Contbr. articles to profl. jours.; patentee in field. Trustee Rockefeller Found. Mem. NAE. Office: Unum Group 1 Fountain Sq Chattanooga TN 37402 Office Phone: 423-294-1011. E-mail: rgoldsberry@unum.com.

GOLDSCHMIDT-CLERMONT, PASCAL J., medical educator, cardiologist, dean; b. Brussels, Apr. 12, 1954; m. Emily Ann Boches. BS, Univ. Libre de Brussels, 1976, MD, 1980. Lic. physician Md., NC, Fla., Belgium. Intern and resident in medicine/cardiology Erasme Acad. Hosp./U. Libre de Brussels, 1980-83; rsch. fellow dept. immunology and microbiology Med. U. SC, Charleston, 1983-86; resident in medicine Union Meml. Hosp., Balt., 1986-88; clin. and rsch. fellow cardiology/cell biology/anatomy Johns Hopkins U., Balt., 1988-91, assoc. prof. dept. medicine/cardiology divsn., 1991-96, dir. Bernard Lab. Vascular Biology, 1991—97; attending CCU Johns Hopkins Hosp., Balt., 1991—97, co-dir. Thrombosis Ctr., 1994-96; co-dir. Henry Ciccarone Ctr. for Prevention Heart Disease, Balt., 1991—97; prof. medicine, dir. Heart and Lung Inst. Ohio State U., Columbus, dir. divsn. cardiology, 1998—2000; joined faculty Duke U., 2000; chief Divsn. Cardiology Duke U. Med. Ctr., chmn. Dept. Medicine; sr. v.p. med. affairs, dean U. Miami Leonard M. Miller Sch. Medicine, 2006—; CEO U. Miami Health Sys., 2007—. Lectr. in field. Contbr. numerous articles and abstracts to profl. jours., chpts. to books; reviewer New Eng. Jour. Medicine, Annals of Internal Medicine, Biochemistry, Blood, Cell, Cell Adhesion and Comm., Circulation Rsch., Jour. Cell Biology, Molecular Biology of the Cell, Am. Heart Assn., NIH. Recipient NATO Sci. award, 1983, 84; grantee Clinician Scientist Award, 1991-93, Syntex Scholars Program, 1992-95, Am. Heart Assn., 1992-94, 95—, NIH, 1992-96, 94-96, 95—; Am. Heart Assn. fellow, 1990, Med. U. S.C., 1984, 85., Jay & Jeasie Schottenstein prize, Ohio State U., 2009 Mem. AAAS, Am. Heart Assn., Am. Soc. Clin. Investigators. Office: Univ Miami Miller Sch Medicine Med Campus R-699 1600 NW 10 Ave Miami FL 33136 Office Phone: 305-243-6545. Office Fax: 305-243-4888. E-mail: pgoldschmidt@med.miami.edu.

GOLDSMITH, BILLY JOE, real estate broker, rancher; b. Blum, Tex., Nov. 6, 1933; s. John T. and Gladys Aileen (Curlee) G.; m. Jean Elizabeth Wendel, Oct. 20, 1962; 1 child, Anne. BS, Tex. A&M U., 1955. Asst., county agrl. agt. Harris County Tex. Extension Svc., Houston, 1957-64; mgr. Rice Coun., Houston, 1964-75, exec. v.p., 1975-95, ret., 1995; owner, broker real estate co. Houston, 1995—; owner Goldsmith Realty, Houston, Bill Goldsmith Agrl. Consulting. Arena dir. Houston Livestock Show and Rodeo, 1966-73; bd. dirs. Tex. Soc. to Prevent Blindness. Ret. US Army, 1955-57. Internat. Rice Festival honoree, 1992, Paul Harris fellow, Rotary. Mem. Tex. Cattle Raisers Assn., Southwestern Cattle Raisers Assn., Nat. Cattlemen's Assn., Houston Livestock Show and Rodeo Rancher, Res. Officer Assn., Harris County Ext. Bd. Advisors. Home: 5826 Cheena Dr Houston TX 77096-5928

GOLDSMITH, JAY PAUL, pediatrician, neonatalogist, educator; s. Jerome and Fannie Goldsmith; m. Terri Lynn Buller, June 28, 1981; children: Lauren Faye, Leighton Elizabeth, Aaron Geoffrey. MD, Albert Einstein Coll. Medicine, Bronx, NY, 1970. Diplomate in neonatal-perinatal medicine Am. Bd. Pediat., 1981. Chmn. dept. pediat. Ochsner Med. Instns., New Orleans, 1978—2000; prof. pediat. Tulane U., New Orleans, 1990—, Elise Schafer chair and sect. head sect. neonatology, 2013—. Cons. So. Gov.'s Task Force on Infant Mortality. Co-editor: (book) Assisted Ventilation of the Neonate, 1981, 1988, 1996, 2003, 2010; contbr. chapters to books. Adv. for children fin. com., sec., treas., pres. Agenda for Children, New Orleans, 1998—. Maj. USAF, 1973—75, George AFB. Recipient Pediatric Educator award, Southern Soc. Pediatric Rsch., 2012. Fellow: Am. Acad. Pediat. (co-chair, neonatal resuscitation program 2000—09); mem.: US Rep. ILCOR, Com. on Med. Liability and Risk Mgmt. Independent. Jewish. Achievements include creator of the Oxygen With Love program to prevent retinopathy of prematurity. Avocations: tennis, skiing, piano. Office Phone: 504-236-3566. Office Fax: 504-895-8023. Personal E-mail: goldsmith.jay@gmail.com.

GOLDSMITH, JEFF CHARLES, management consultant; b. Portland, Oreg., Oct. 31, 1948; BA, Reed Coll., 1970; PhD, U. Chgo., 1973. Dir. health planning, regulatory affairs U. Chgo. Med. Ctr., 1975-82; nat. advisor Ernst & Young, 1982-94; pres. Health Futures, Inc., 1982—; dir. Cerner Corp., 1999—2005, Onfocus Healthcare, 2008—; assoc. prof., pub. health sciences Sch. Medicine U. Va., 2007—. Lectr. U. Chgo. Grad. Sch. Bus., 1979—90, Wharton Sch., U. Pa., 1994—; adv. Burrill Biotech. Capital Fund. Author: Can Hospitals Survive?, 1981, Digital Medicine, 2003, The Long Baby Boom, 2008, The Sorcerer's Apprentice, 2010; mem. editl. bd. Health Affairs, 1990-; contbr. articles to profl. jours. including Harvard Bus. Rev., Jour. AMA, Health Affairs, NEJM. Recipient Woodrow Wilson Nat. Fellowship, 1971. Avocations: skiing, audiophile, native american art, whitewater. Personal E-mail: hfutures@healthfutures.net.

GOLDSMITH, LOWELL ALAN, medical educator; b. Bklyn., Mar. 29, 1938; s. Isidore Alexander and Ida (Kaplan) G.; m. Carol Amreich, June 11, 1960; children: Meredith, Eileen. AB, Columbia Coll., 1959; MD, SUNY, Bklyn., 1963; MPH, U. Rochester Sch. Medicine & Dentistry, 2002. Diplomate Am. Bd. Dermatology. Intern, then resident in medicine UCLA Med. Ctr., 1963-65; resident in dermatology Harvard U. Med. Sch., Boston, 1967-69, asst. prof. dermatology, 1970-73; asst. in dermatology Mass. Gen. Hosp., Boston, 1970-71, asst. dermatologist, 1971-73; assoc. prof. medicine Duke U. Med. Ctr., Durham, NC, 1973-78, prof., 1978-81; James H. Sterner prof. dermatology Sch. Medicine and Dentistry, U. Rochester (NY), 1981-96, chief dermatology unit, 1981-87, acting chmn. dept. medicine, 1985-87, chmn. dept. dermatology, 1987-96; dean Sch. Medicine and Dentistry U. Rochester, 1996-2000, dean emeritus, 2000—; prof. dermatology U. NC, Chapel Hill, 2002—, clin. prof. epidemiology Sch. Pub. Health, 2002—07. Mem. dermatology adv. com. FDA, 1983-87; chmn. Gordon Rsch. Cong. on Epithelial Differentiation and Keratinization, 1987, AAD-CDC Conf. on skin cancer prevention and edn., Washington, 1995; mem. gen. medicine A study sect. USPHS, NIH, 1988-92, chmn., 1990-92; mem. coun. NIAMS, NIH, 1996-99; chmn. med. adv. bd. Nat. Alopecia Areata Found., 1981-87, 90-2002, bd. dirs.; bd. dirs. Monroe Cmty. Hosp., Rochester, Ctr. for Alternatives in Animal Testing, Balt.; chmn. NIH Consensus Conf. on Diagnosis and Treatment of Early Melanoma, Bethesda, Md., 1992. Author, editor: Biochemistry and Physiology of the Skin, 1983, 2d edit., 1991, Physiology, Biochemistry and Molecular Biology of the Skin, 1991, Differential Diagnosis of Skin Disease, 2d edit., 1996; mem. editl. bd. Archives Dermatology, 1981-92, Clinics in Dermatology, 1982-96, Seminars in Dermatology, 1991-96, Jour. Dermatological Sci., 1994-2002; mem. editl. bd. Jour. Investigative Dermatology, 1987-95, editor, 2002-07; editor in chief Journal Watch Dermatology 2006—10, assoc. editor, Rochester Dx: Essential adult Dermatology: Visual Dx: Essential Pediatric Dermatology; Visual Dx: Essential Dermatology in Pigmented Skin; editor in chief, co-founder Logical Images Rochester, NY, 1990-, Fitzpatrick's Dermatology in Gen. Medicine, Mc Hill, NY, 2012; also numerous articles. With USPHS, 1965-67. Recipient Rsch. Career Devel. award USPHS, 1975-80; Macy Found. fellow, 1978-79, Disting. Alumni Achievement award SUNY Downstate, 2013. Mem. Assn. Am. Physicians, Am. Soc. Clin. Investigation, Am. Acad. Dermatology (bd. dirs., Presdl. citation 2003), Soc. Investigative Dermatology (bd. dirs., pres. 1994-95, Rothman Gold medal), Nat. Ichthyosis Found. (chmn. adv. bd. 1981-85), Assn. Profs. Dermatology (bd. dirs. 1984-87, pres. 1992-94), Am. Bd. Dermatology (bd. dirs. 1993-96), NY State Soc. Dermatology (pres. 1985-89), Am. Dermatol. Assn. (bd. dirs. 1996-2001, pres. 2002—03, Buffalo-Rochester Dermatology Soc. (pres. 1987), Rochester Dermatology Soc., Rochester Acad. Medicine, Polish Dermatol. Assn. (hon.), Brit. Dermatology Assn. (hon.), Japanese Dermatology Assn. (hon., DOHI lectr. 2003), Am. Skin Assn. (Martin Carter Mentorship award 2006), Berlin Dermatology Soc. (hon.), Deutsche Dermatologische Gesellschaft (hon.), Alpha Omega Alpha. Office: University NC Dept Dermatology 3100 Thurston-Bowles Bldg CB #7287 Chapel Hill NC 27599 Home Phone: 919-942-9263; Office Phone: 919-929-1572. Business E-Mail: lag1959@gmail.com.

GOLDSTEIN, ADAM M., cruise line executive; m. Cheryl Goldstein; children: David, Julie. Grad. with honors, Princeton U.; JD, Harvard U.; MBA, INSEAD. Sr. v.p. Total Guest Satisfaction, sr. v.p. mktg. Royal Caribbean Internat., Miami, 1988—2002, exec. v.p. brand ops., 2002—05, pres., 2005—07, pres. & CEO, 2007—. Bd. mem. Trust of Our Kids, Inc. Mem.: Travel Industry Assn. Am. (nat. chair 2001). Office: Royal Caribbean Internat 1050 Caribbean Way Miami FL 33132 Office Phone: 305-539-6082. Business E-Mail: agoldstein@rccl.com.

GOLDSTEIN, BARRY DAVID, educational association administrator, pharmacology educator; b. Bklyn., Jan. 7, 1953; m. Gail Goldstein, June 26, 1976; children: Melissa, Beth, Lori. BA in Biology, Adelphi U., 1975; PhD in Pharmacology, U. Medicine and Dentistry NJ, 1979. Rsch. assoc. dept. pharmacology U. Ill., Chgo., 1979-81; asst. prof. dept. pharmacology and toxicology Med. Coll. Ga., Augusta, 1981-86, assoc. prof., 1986-91, interim v.p. acad. affairs, assoc. prof., 1991-92, prof. dept. pharmacology and toxicology, 1991—, v.p. acad. affairs, 1992, provost, 2003—08, sr. v.p. academic affairs, 2008—10; commr. So. Assn. Colleges and Schools, Decatur, Ga., 2009—, v.p. Commn. on Colleges, 2010—. Chairperson State Healthcare Pers. Planning Com., 1996—; mem. top mgmt. adv. com. Internat. Mgmt. Coun., 1994-96; chairperson Gov.'s Health Care Study Com., 1992-93. Contbr. articles to profl. jours. Bd. dirs. Walton Way Temple, 1985-88, 92—; bd. dirs. Augusta Jewish Cmty. Ctr., 1984-93, treas., 1989-90, pres., 1987-89; bd. dirs. Congregation of Children of Israel, 1992—, treas., 1996—; bd. dirs., treas. Augusta Open Door Kindergarten; mem. budget allocation com. United Way, 1992, chair budget panel, 1993, bd. dirs., 1994—; mem. Ga. Environ. Techs. Consortium, 1992—, Augusta Players Bus. and Profl. Alliance, 1993-94, Coll. Bd.-Acad. Assembly, 1992; chmn. Gov.'s Health Care Pers. Study Commn., 1992-93; mem. Ga. Ladders in Nursing Careers planning com. Ga. Hosp. Assn., 1993; judge area sci. fair, 1984. Named to Hicksville Pub. Sch. Hall of Fame, 1987; recipient Disting. Alumnus of the Yr. award U. Medicine and Dentistry of NJ, 1997; NRSA postdoctoral fellow in neurotoxicology, 1979; recipient numerous rsch. grants. Mem. AAAS, Am. Assn. Higher Edn., Am. Soc. Pharmacology and Exptl. Therapeutics, Soc. for Neurosci. (CSRA chpt.), Am. Pain Soc., Internat. Assn. for Study Pain, Soc. Toxicology, Rotary. Home: 1000 Maple Ridge Way Greensboro GA 30642-3933 Office: Southern Association of Colleges and Schools Commission on Colleges 1866 Southern Lane Decatur GA 30033 Office Phone: 404-679-4500. Office Fax: 404-679-4558.

GOLDSTEIN, BURTON BENJAMIN, JR., university professor; b. Atlanta, Mar. 11, 1948; s. Burton B. and Grace Goldstein; m. Kathleen N. Gurley, Aug. 22, 1970; children: Katherine Claire, Alexander Max. AB, U. N.C., 1970; MEd, U. Mass., 1973; JD with honors, U. N.C., 1976. Bar: Ga. 1976. Assoc. dir. urban internship program Yale U., New Haven, 1970-72; assoc. Long, Aldridge & Norman, Atlanta, 1976-80; gen. counsel Solinet, Atlanta, 1980-81; ceo Info. America, Atlanta, 1981-98; gen. ptnr. Networth Ptnrs., Atlanta, 1998—99; venture ptnr. Mellon Ventures, Atlanta, 2000—04; prof. dept. economic & univ. enterpreneur-in-residence UNC, Chapel Hill, 2005—; chmn. Med Fusion Inc., Raleigh, NC, 2009—10; bd. mem. Nourish Internat., 2008—, Medfusion, 2013—; bd. advisor IContact Morrisville, NC, 2008—11. Ex-officio dir. Info. Industry Assn., Washington, 1992-93, adj. prof. Goizueta Sch. of Bus., Emory U., 1997-98. Co-Author: Engines of Innovation (with Holden Thorp) Bd. dirs. SciTrek, Atlanta, 1988-92, High Mus. Art, 1996-2002; chmn. adv. bd. Inst. Arts & Humanities, Chapel Hill, 1991-2001; chmn. Info. Industry Assn. Investment Conf., NYC, 1992-93; pres. Atlanta Chpt. Am. Jewish Com., 2002-04 Named Fast Tech 50, Arthur Andersen, Atlanta, 1988—, Runner-up Entrepreneur of Yr., Ernst & Young & INC Mag., 1991, Entrepreneur of the Yr., Info. Industry, 1991. Mem. Am. Jewish Com., Chancellor's Club U.N.C., Phi Beta Kappa, Order of Golden Fleece, U. Club(NYC) Democrat. Jewish. editl. bd. UNC Law Review, 1976. Office Phone: 919-966-3682. Office Fax: 919-966-4986. Business E-Mail: buck_goldstein@unc.edu.

GOLDSTEIN, BURTON JACK, psychiatrist; b. Balt., Sept. 23, 1930; s. Hyman and Roz (Levin) C.; m. Linda Feuer, June 16, 1989; children: Howard, Herbert, Brian, Esther, Leonard, Mark. BS in Pharmacy, U. Md., 1953, MD, 1960. Diplomate Am. Bd. Psychiatry and Neurology (bd. examiner). Intern Jackson Meml. Hosp., Miami, Fla., 1960-61, NIMH fellow in psychiatry, 1961-63, chief resident, 1963; dir. div. clin. psychopharmacology, dept. psychiatry U. Miami, 1964-92, chief div. research, 1964-71, prof. pharmacology, 1973—, prof. psychiatry, 1973—, acting chmn. dept. psychiatry, 1983-85, prof. epidemiology, pub. health Sch. Medicine, 1999; sr. cons. in psychopharmacology Mt. Sinai Med. Ctr., Miami Beach, 1993—; dir. psychiat. consultation liaison svc. Mt. Sinai Hosp., Miami Beach, 1993—; med. dir. behavioral health U. Miami, Miller Sch. Medicine, 2005—. Mem. bd. advisors Fla. Mental Health Inst., U. South Fla.; cons. in psychiat. rsch. South Fla. State Hosp., West Hollywood; cons. indsl. security program Dept. Def.; cons. VA Psychiatry Svc., Miami; chmn. panel on neuropharmacologic drugs U.S. Pharmacopeial Conv., Inc., 1990-2000, mem. exec. com.; mem. faculty Health Svcs. Ctr., U. Miami, 1996; med. rev. officer dept. athletics U. Miami, 1996—. Mem. editorial bd. Miami Medicine, Clin. Advancement in Treatment of Depression; contbr. chpts. to books, articles to profl. publs. Served to maj. AUS, 1953-62. Fellow Am. Psychiat. Assn. (life), Am. Coll. Psychiatrists, Am. Coll. Clin. Pharmacology, Am. Coll. Neuropsychopharmacology (life); mem. Royal Soc. Health, Am. Assn. Clin. Pharmacology and Chemotherapy, Am. Soc. Addiction Medicine, Collegium Internationale Neuropsychopharmacologium. Personal E-mail: bhls@earthlink.net. Business E-Mail: bgoldste@med.miami.edu.

GOLDSTEIN, DAVID B., geneticist, educator; BS, U. Calif.; PhD in Biol. Sciences, Stanford U., 1994. Wolfson Prof. Genetics, Galton Lab., dept. biology Univ. Coll., London, 1999—2005; dir., Inst. for Genome Sciences & Policy (IGSP) Ctr. for Population Genomics & Pharmacogentics Duke U., NC, 2005—, prof., depts. molecular genetics and microbiology and biology, 2005—. Contbr. several articles to scholarly publications; mem. editl. bds. Current Biology, Annals of Human Genetics, Molecular Biology and Evolution and Human Genomics. Recipient Wolfson Rsch. award for work in human genetics and genomics, Royal Soc. Office: Inst for Genome Sciences & Policy Duke University CIEMAS 101 Science Dr DUMC Box 3382 Durham NC 27708 Address: Inst for Genome Sciences & Policy Ctr for Human Genome Variation Duke Univ LSRC B Wing Rm 330 Box 91009 Durham NC 27708-1009 Office Phone: 919-684-0896. Business E-Mail: d.goldstein@duke.edu.

GOLDSTEIN, JERRY, physicist, educator; BS in Physics, Bklyn. Coll.; PhD in Physics, Dartmouth Coll., Hanover, NH. Prin. scientist space sci. and engring. divsn. S.W. Rsch. Inst., San Antonio, 2003—; adjoint asst. prof. physics and astronomy U. Tex., San Antonio. Contbr. articles to sci. jours. Recipient Macelwane medal, Am. Geophys. Union, 2006; named one of Brilliant 10, Popular Sci. mag., 2006, Forty Under Forty, San Antonio Bus. Jour. Office: Space Sci and Engring Divsn SW Rsch Inst PO Drawer 28510 San Antonio TX 78228-0510

GOLDSTEIN, JOSEPH LEONARD, biochemist, educator, geneticist, educator; b. Sumter, SC, Apr. 18, 1940; s. Isadore E. and Fannie A. Goldstein. BS, Washington & Lee U., Lexington, Va., 1962; MD, U. Tex. Health Sci. Ctr., Dallas, 1966; DSc (hon.), U. Chgo., 1982, Rensselaer Poly. Inst., 1982, U. Paris, 1988, U. Buenos Aires, 1990, So. Meth. U., 1993, U. Miami, 1996, Rockefeller U., 2001. Diplomate Am. Bd. Internal Medicine. Intern, resident in medicine Mass. Gen. Hosp., Boston, 1966—68; clin. assoc. biochemical genetics NIH, 1968—70; fellow med. genetics U. Wash. Sch. Medicine, Seattle, 1970—72; faculty U. Tex. Southwestern Med. Ctr., Dallas, 1972—, Paul J. Thomas chair in medicine, Julie and Louis A. Beecherl disting. chair in biomed. sci., 1977—, regental prof., 1985—. Mem. sci. rev. bd. Howard Hughes Med. Inst., 1978—84, mem. med. adv. bd., 1985—90, chmn. med. adv. bd., 1995—2002; non-resident fellow

Salk Inst., La Jolla, Calif., 1983—94; chmn. awards jury Albert Lasker Med. Rsch. prizes, 1996—. Co-author: The Metabolic Basis of Inherited Disease, 5th edit., 1983; mem. editl. bd. Jour. Clin. Investigation, 1977—82, Ann. Rev. Genetics, 1980—85, Arteriosclerosis, 1981—87, Jour. Biol. Chemistry, 1981—95, Cell, 1983—, Sci., 1985—98; contbr. articles to profl. jours. Bd. trustees Rockefeller U., 1994—, Howard Hughes Med. Inst., 2002—. Recipient Heinrich-Wieland prize, 1974, Pfizer award in enzyme chemistry, Am. Chem. Soc., 1976, Passano award, Johns Hopkins U., 1978, Gairdner Found. award, 1981, NY Acad. Scis.award in biol. and med. scis., 1981, Lita Annenberg Hazen award, 1982, Rsch. Achievement award, Am. Heart Assn., 1984, Louisa Gross Horwitz award, Columbia U., 1984, Albert Lasker award in basic med. rsch., 1985, Nobel Prize in physiology/medicine, 1985, Trustees medal, Mass. Gen. Hosp., 1986, Nat. Medal Sci., 1988, Warren Alpert Found. prize, 2000, Albany Med. Ctr. prize in medicine and biomed. rsch., 2003, Woodrow Wilson award for pub. svc., 2005, Builder of Sci. award, Research!America, 2007. Mem.: ACP (award 1986), NAS (coun. 1991—94, Lounsbery award 1979), Tex. Philos. Soc., Royal Soc. London (fgn. mem.), Inst. Medicine, Am. Philos. Soc., Am. Fedn. Clin. Rsch., Am. Soc. Biol. Chemists, Am. Acad. Arts & Scis., Am. Soc. Human Genetics (William Allan award 1985), Am. Soc. Clin. Investigation (pres. 1985—86), Assn. Am. Physicians, Alpha Omega Alpha, Phi Beta Kappa. Office: U Tex Southwestern Med Ctr 5323 Harry Hines Blvd Dallas TX 75390-9046 E-mail: joe.goldstein@utsouthwestern.edu.

GOLDSTEIN, LARRY BRUCE, neurologist, educator; b. NYC, May 27, 1955; s. Daniel and Sharon Goldstein; children: Sarah, Daniel. AB magna cum laude, Brandeis U., 1977; MD, Mt. Sinai Med. Sch., 1981. Intern Mt. Sinai Hosp., NYC, 1981-82, resident neurology, 1981—85, chief resident, 1985; fellow cereb rsch. Duke U. Med. Ctr., Durham, NC, 1985—87; assoc. Duke U., 1986—88, asst. prof., 1989—95, assoc. prof., 1995—2002, prof., 2002—; dir. Duke Stroke Ctr., NC. Contbr. articles to profl. jours. Recipient Saul Horowitz Jr. award, Mt. Sinai Sch. Medicine, 2004, Chmn.'s award, Am. Heart Assn., 2004; named Nat. Advocate of Yr., 2005. Fellow: Am. Acad. Neurology (G. Milton Shy award 1979); mem.: Am. Neurol. Assn., Am. Stroke Assn. (chair adv. com. 2002—04), Am. Heart Assn. (nat. bd. dirs. 2002—04, chair stroke coun. 2005—07, chair advocacy coord. com. 2008—10, nat. bd. dirs. 2008—11, Meritorious Achievement award 2007, William Feinberg award 2009), Alpha Omega Alpha. Office: Duke Stroke Ctr Duke Univ Medl Ctr PO Box 3651 Durham NC 27710 Office Phone: 919-684-3801. E-mail: golds004@mc.duke.edu.

GOLDSTEIN, MORRIS, international economist; b. NYC, Oct. 13, 1944; s. Lewis and Belle (Hagler) G.; m. Margaret A. Aruck, July 26, 1970; children: Daniel, David, Lewis. AB, Rutgers U., 1966; PhD, NYU, 1971. Economist Internat. Monetary Fund, Washington, 1970-77, sr. economist, 1977-81, advisor, 1981-85, asst. dir., 1985-87, dep. dir., 1987—; Dennis Weatherstone sr. fellow Peterson Inst. Internat. Economics, 1994—. Mem. Coun. Fgn. Rels., Bellagio Group, Pew Task Force Fin. Reaulatorv Reform. Author: Have Flexible Exchange Rates Handicapped Macroeconomic Policy, 1990, Case for International Banking Standard, 1997, The Asian Financial Crisis, 1998, Managed Floating Plus, 2004; co-author: Income and Price Effects in Foreign Trade, 1985, Assessing Financial Vulnerability in Emerging Markets, 2000, Controlling Currency Mismatches in Emerging Markets, 2004, The Future of China's Exchange Rate Policy, 2009; co-editor: International Policv Coordination and Exchange Rate Fluctuations, 1990, Functioning of the International Monetary System, 1996, Debating China's Exchange Rate Policy, 2008; contbr. articles to profl. jours. Mem. Am. Econ. Assn. Avocations: fishing.

GOLEMBIEWSKI, ROBERT THOMAS, management consultant, educator; b. Lawrenceville, NJ, July 2, 1932; s. John and Pauline Pelka Golembiewska; m. Margaret Hughes, Sept. 1, 1956; children: Alice, Hope, Geoffrey. AB, Princeton U., NJ, 1954; MA, Yale U., 1956, PhD, 1958; ScD (hon.), U. Lethbridge, Alb., Can., 1996. Instr. Princeton U., 1958-60; rsch. asst. prof. U. Ill., Champaign, 1960-63; vis. lectr. Yale U., New Haven, 1963-64; assoc. prof. U. Ga., Athens, 1968-71, rsch. prof., 1972—98, disting. rsch. prof., 1998—2002, disting. rsch. prof. emeritus, 2002—. Cons. in field. Author, editor over 85 books; contbr. over 900 articles to profl. publs. Named Ky. col. (hon.) State of Ky. Fellow Acad. of Mgmt., Nat. Acad. of Pub. Adminstrn. Avocations: fly fishing, hunting, coin collecting/numismatics. Home: 145 Highland Dr Athens GA 30606-3211 Office: U Ga Baldwin Hall Athens GA 30602 Office Phone: 706-542-2970. Business E-Mail: rtgolem@uga.edu.

GOLEMON, RONALD KINNAN, lawyer; b. Atlanta, Tex., Nov. 22, 1938; s. William Layton and Avis (Bogle) G.; m. Jacqueline Alice Burst, Sept. 2, 1966; children: Donald Brent, Jennifer Alice. BS in Indsl. Mgmt. Engring., U. Okla., 1961; LLB, U. Tex., 1967. Bar: Tex. 1967, U.S. Ct. Appeals (5th cir.) 1970, U.S. Dist. Ct. (so. dist.) Tex. 1968, U.S. Dist. Ct. (we. dist.) Tex. 1981, U.S. Dist. Ct. (no. dist.) 1986. Engr. asst. Tex. Water Pollution Control Bd., Austin, 1964-67; assoc. Keys, Russell, Watson & Seaman, Corpus Christi, Tex., 1967-71, ptnr., 1971-73, Brown McCarroll, LLP, Austin, 1973—2007; mng. ptnr. Brown McCarroll & Oaks Hartline, 1989-94; pres. KG Strategies LLC, 2008—. Contbg. author The Southwestern Legal Foundation, 40th Annual Institute on Oil and Gas Law and Taxation, 1989, The Southwestern Legal Foundation, 43rd Annual Institute on Oil and Gas Law and Taxation, 1992; contbr articles to profl. jours. Alt. mem. RCRA permit adv. com. U.S. EPA, 1983; mem. Gov.'s Hazardous Waste Task Force, 1984-85; v.p. St. Stephen's Sch. PTA, 1985-86, pres., 1986-87; mem. cmty. adv. bd. Ronald McDonald House, Austin, 1990—. Fellow: Am. Coll. Environ. Lawyers, Am. Bar. Found., U. Tex. Law Alumni Assn. (pres. 1984—85, mem. exec. bd. 1984—86); mem.: ABA (vice chmn. air quality com. 1982—86, chmn. air quality com. 1986—89, mem. coun. 1989—91, vice chmn. sect. natural resources, energy and environ. law 1992—93, chmn.-elect 1993—94, chmn. 1994—95, mem. mkt. rsch. task force 1995—96, mem.standing com. membership and liaison 1997—2000, mem. standing com. constn. & by-laws 2000—03, chmn. 2001—03, chmn. standing com. environ. law 2004—07, bd. govs. 2009—12), UT Law Ctr Global Energy, Arbitration & Environ. Law (adv. bd. 2009—), Travis County Bar Assn., Tex. Mining and Reclamation Assn. (bd. dirs. 1988—2000), State Bar Tex. (chmn. environ. law sect. 1971—72), N.Am. Corriente Assn. (bd. dirs. 2004—10, pres. 2005—10), Tex. Corriente Cattle Assn. (bd. dirs. 2002—05, 2010—12). Avocations: ranching, hunting, skiing, golf. Office: KG Strategies LLC 408 West 14th St Austin TX 78701 Home Phone: 512-327-0721; Office Phone: 512-479-9707. Business E-Mail: kg@kgstrategies.com.

GOLICK, RICH, state legislator; Mem. Ins, Special Judiciary Coms.; house rep. Ga.; state rep. Dist. 30 Ga., 1999—2002; mem. State Inst. & Property Coms., 1999—; state rep. Dist. 34 Ga., 2003—. Republican. Mailing: 2372 Simpson Farm Way Smyrna GA 30080 Office: 601 Legis Office Bldg Atlanta GA 30334 Business E-Mail: rgolick@legis.state.ga.us.

GOLLAHALLI, SUBRAMANYAM RAMAPPA, engineering educator; arrived in US, 1976, naturalized; s. Bagepalli Ramappa and Nagalakshamma Rao Ramappa; m. Rangamani Nadig Gollahalli, Dec. 25, 1967; children: Suma, Anil. BE Mech. Engring., U. Mysore, Karnataka, India, 1963; ME Mech. Engring., Indian Inst. Sci., Bangalore, 1985; MSc Mech. Engring., U. Waterloo, Ont., Can., 1970; PhD Mech. Engring., U. Waterloo, 1973. Registered profl. engr., Okla. Lectr. Indian Inst. Sci., Bangalore, 1965—68; asst. prof. U. Waterloo, 1973—76; from asst. prof. to full prof. U. Okla., Norman, 1976—92, Lesch Centennial prof., 1992—97. Lesch Centennial chair U. Okla., Norman, 1998—, dir. Sch. Aerospace and Mech. Engring., 2001—09; cons. in field Editor: ASME Conf. Proc., 1990, 91, 92; assoc. editor Jour. Energy Resources Tech., 1994-2000, Jour. Engineering Gas Turbines and Power, 1999-2005, editl. bd. mem., jour. combustion, 2009-; contbr. over 250 sci. papers. Advance com. chair Boy Scouts Am., Norman, 1988-90 Recipient Ralph Angus medal Inst. Engrs. Can., 1978, Ralph Teetor award Soc. Automotive Engrs., 1978 Fellow ASME (life; Ralph James award 1993, chair emerging energy tech. com. 1990-93, George Westinghouse gold medal 2005), AIAA (mem. Terrestrial Energy tech. com., Energy Sys.award 2001, Sustained Svc. award 2006), Internat. Soc. Energy, Environment, and Sustainability; mem. Pi Tau Sigma (hon.). Democrat. Hindu. Achievements include research in spray combustion, particularly for delineating the structure of droplet wake flames, turbulent flames in cross-flows, and bio-fuel combustion and emissions. Office: Univ of Oklahoma 865 Asp Ave Norman OK 73019-1050 Office Phone: 405-325-1728. Business E-Mail: gollahal@ou.edu.

GOLLOTT, THOMAS (TOMMY) ARLIN, state legislator; b. Biloxi, Miss., Sept. 29, 1935; m. Zelma Jackson; children: Tanya, Lisa, Jennifer. Mem. Miss. House of Reps., 1968—80; mem. Dist. 50 Miss. State Senate, 1980—; entrepreneur Aaa Transfer & Storage Co. Mem.: C. of C., Nat. Soc. State Legislators (life), Cheshire Home Handicapped (bd. mem., pres.), Fleur de Lis Soc., KofC, Elks, Miss. Arts Fair for Handicapped (former bd. mem.), Boys & Girls Club. Republican. Roman Cath. Mailing: 235 Bayview Ave Biloxi MS 39530 Home Phone: 228-374-1431; Office Phone: 601-359-2220, 228-432-0097. Office Fax: 601-359-2889. Business E-Mail: tgollott@senate.ms.gov.

GOLTRY, THOM, medical products executive; COO, TeamHealth Atlantic Team Health Holdings, Inc. Office: Team Health Holdings Inc 265 Brookview Town Centre Way Ste 400 Knoxville TN 37919 Office Phone: 865-693-1000. Office Fax: 865-539-3073. Business E-Mail: thom_goltry@teamhealth.com.

GOLUB, RICHARD W., colon and rectal surgeon, director, educator; MD, Yeshiva U., NY, 1984. Diplomate Am. Bd. Surgery, Am. Bd. Colon and Rectal Surgery, lic. Fla., NY, Ohio. Intern SUNY, Stony Brook, resident; fellow in colorectal surgery Grant Med. Ctr., Columbus, Ohio; asst. clin. instr. SUNY Downstate Med. Ctr., asst. prof. surgery, assoc. prof. clin. surgery, chief colon and rectal surgery dept., dir. anorectal physiology lab., dir. surgical endoscopy svc.; hosp. affiliations include Doctor's Hosp., Sarasota Meml. Hosp., Fla. Named one of Top 100 Minimally Invasive Surgeons, NY Mag., Best Doctors, America's Top Doctors, Castle Connolly. Fellow: NY Soc. Colon and Rectal Surgeons, Am. Soc. Colon and Rectal Surgeons, ACS; mem.: NY Surgical Soc., Sarasota/LI Chpt. of the Am. Coll. of Surgeons, NY Soc. Gastrointestinal Endoscopy, Soc. for Surgery of the Alimentary Tract, Am. Soc. Gen. Surgeons, Sarasota Surgical Soc., Assn. for Acad. Surgery, Soc. Am. Gastrointestinal Endoscopy, Am. Coll. Gastroenterology. Office: Sarasota Memorial Hospital 3333 Cattlemen Rd Ste 206 Sarasota FL 34232 Office Phone: 941-341-0042.

GOMES, MATTHEW TRAINOR, lawyer; b. Southampton, NY, June 12, 1973; s. Michael Norman and Jane Ellen Gomes; m. Kimberly Marie Arthur, Sept. 1, 2001; children: Dylan Trainor children: Austin Arthur. BA with distinction, U. NC, Chapel Hill, 1991—95; JD cum laude, Wash. & Lee U., Lexington, Va., 1995—98. Bar: Ga. 1998, US Dist. Ct. (no. and mid. dists.), Ga. 1999, US Dist. Ct. (ctrl. dist.), Ill. 2004, US Dist. Ct. (we. dist.), Wis. 2006, US Ct. Appeals (11th cir.) 2002. Law clerk to Honorable Barry J. Stone Ct. Appeals, 4th District, Fla., 1996; internship Office of US Atty. for We. Dist. Va., 1997—98; assoc. Smith, Currie & Hancock LLP, Atlanta, 1998—2003, ptnr., 2003—04; of counsel Nelson, Mullins, Riley & Scarborough, LLP, Atlanta, 2004—06, ptnr., 2007—14, Weinberg, Wheeler, Hudgins, Gunn & Dial, LLC, Atlanta, 2014—. Spkr. Lorman Edn. Svcs., Atlanta, 2000—; young leader coun. mem. Ga. Br. Associated Gen. Contractors, Atlanta, 2003—. Recipient, Phi Beta Kappa, 1995, First Pl. Oralist, Philip C. Jessup Internat. Law Moot Ct. Competition Ea. Regional, 1998, Ga. Super Lawyer Rising Star award, Law & Politics Mag., 2005—06, 2009—, Legal Elite, Ga. Trend Mag., 2012—13. Mem.: ABA, Atlanta Bar Assn. Avocations: travel, history, scuba diving. Office: Weinberg Wheeler Hudgins Gunn & Dial LLC 3344 Peachtree Rd NE Ste 2400 Atlanta GA 30326 Office Fax: 404-875-9433. Business E-Mail: mgomes@wwhgd.com.

GOMEZ, CURTIS V., federal judge; b. St. Croix, VI, Mar. 26, 1962; Transfer, Dickinson Coll., 1981—84; BA, George Washington U., 1983—84; JD, Harvard U. Law Sch., 1986—89. Bar: V.I. 1989, DC 1990. Assoc. Patton, Boggs & Blow, 1989—93; atty. US Dept. Justice, 1997—2001, asst. US atty. (eastern dist.) Va., 2001—02, asst. US atty., Dist. V.I., 2002—05; judge US Dist. Ct. VI, St Thomas, VI, 2005—, chief judge, 2006—. Office: US Dist Judge US Courthouse and Federal Bldg 5500 Veterans Dr Rm 310 St Thomas VI 00802 Office Phone: 340-774-1800. Office Fax: 340-777-8532.

GÓMEZ-JIMÉNEZ, CARLOS, science educator, microbiologist, geneticist; s. Carlos Gómez-Vázquez, Sr. and Emma Jiménez-Gómez BS in Biology with honors, U. PR, Mayagüez, 1986, MS in Microbiology and Genetics, 1992; postgrad., Alliance Theol. Sem. Tchr. asst. U. PR, Mayagüez, 1986-88, 91, biochemistry lab. technician, 1988, full prof. Aguadilla, 1992—; quality assurance analyst Microbiology and Cell Culture Lab. Ortho Biologics, Inc., Manatí, PR, 1989-90; prof. Inter Am. U., Aguadilla, PR, 1991-92, San Germán, 1992—; MCAT, PCAT, and DAT invited prof. Kaplan PR Ctr., 1997—; prof. Pontifica Cath. U. PR, 2000—; chair Dept. Natural Scis. UPR Aguadilla, 2012. Acad. counselor sci. rsch. acad. tchrs. and gifted students Internat. Am. U. PR, San Germán, PR, 1992-, sci. advisor Young Scholars Program-NSF, San Germán, 1992-; cons. drugs, alcohol, violence and HIV/AIDS Prevention programs U. PR, Aguadilla, 1992-; curriculum and course dir., U. PR-Aguadilla, 1992-; mem. over 40 coms. U. PR pres. office & U. PR-Aguadilla, 1992-; dir. honor program, 1996-98, mem. exec. com. Superior Edn. Coun., 1996, 2001; mem. Nat. Collegiate Honors Coun., 1996-; bd. dirs. Assn. Hon. Programs; mentor prof. NSF and U. PR Program, 2001-08; academic senator, mem. adminstrv. bd. U. PR Aguadilla, 2002-08. Editor (newsletters) The Probe-Caribbean Soc. Biotech., Inc., 1994-, Biosfera-U. PR-Aguadilla, 1994-; contbr. articles to profl. jours.; author acad. manuals and modules in Microbiology, Genetics, Human Genetic, and General Biology Co-founder Leguísamo First Baptist Ch., Mayagüez, 1977-; first tenor Mayagüez Municipal Choir, 1994-, ROMANTIEZER Interdenominational Singing Ministry, 1996-; judge,advisor HS and Undergrad. Sci. Competitions, 1987-; liaison U. PR-Aguadilla & Am. Red Cross Assn. Communitarian Svc., 1994-. Mem.: AAAS, PR Soc. Microbiologists (bd. dirs. 1995—97, 2006—, pres. 2008—), Assn. U. Honor Programs (bd. dirs. 1997—), Biostudy 1 (counselor, bd. dirs. 1997—), Assn. Food Sci. Tech. PR, PR Sci. Tchr. Assn., Puertorrican Soc. Mycology (bd. dirs. 2002—08, pres. 2003—04), Caribbean Soc. Biotech. (bd. dirs. 1995—99), Am. Soc. Microbiology, Bapt. Student Union, Beta Beta Beta. Baptist. Avocations: singing, book collecting, French cooking. Office: U PR Aguadilla Dept Nat Scis PO Box 6150 Aguadilla PR 00604-6150 Office Phone: 787-890-2681 ext. 230, 787-890-2681 ext. 226. Office Fax: 787-890-0198. Business E-Mail: cgj_upra@yahoo.com.

GOMORY, RALPH EDWARD, printing company executive; b. NYC, May 7, 1929; s. Andrew L. and Marian (Schellenberg) Gomory; m. Laura Dumper, 1954 (div. 1968); children: Andrew C., Susan S., Stephen H. BA, Williams Coll., 1950; postgrad., Kings Coll., 1950—51, Cambridge U., Eng., 1950—51; PhD in Math., Princeton U., 1954; ScD (hon.), Williams Coll., 1973; LHD (hon.), Pace U., 1986; DSc (hon.), Poly. U., 1987, Syracuse U., 1989, Worcester Poly. U., 1989, Carnegie-Mellon U., 1989. Rsch. assoc. Princeton University, 1951—54, asst. prof., Math., Higgins lectr., 1957—59; with IBM Corp., Yorktown Heights, NY, 1959—86, dir., Math. Sci., Rsch. Divsn., 1965—67, dir., Rsch., 1970—86, v.p., 1973—84, sr. v.p., 1985—89, sr. v.p. for sci. and tech., 1986—89, mem., Corp. Mgmt., 1983—89, dir., Asia Pacific Group, 1982—88. Bd. dirs. Lexmark Internat. Inc., 1991—, Wash. Post Co. Co-author (with William J. Baumol): MIT Press book. Trustee Hampshire Coll., 1977—86, Princeton U., 1985—89, Alfred P. Sloan Found., 1988—, pres., 1989—2007, pres., Emeritus; mem., governing bd. NRC, 1980—83, chmn., com. on mandatory retirement in higher edn., 1989—91. With USN, 1954—57. Recipient Lanchester prize, Ops. Rsch. Soc. Am., 1963, Harry Goode Meml. award, Am. Fedn. Info. Processing Socs., 1984, John Von Neumann Theory prize, Ops. Rschl. Soc. Am. and Inst. Mgmt. Scis., 1984, IRI medal, Indsl. Rsch. Inst., 1985, Engring. Leadership Recognition award, IEEE, 1988, Arthur M. Bueche award, NAE, 1993, Heinz award for Tech., the Economy and Employment, 1998; fellow IBM, 1964; Sheffield Fellowship award, Yale U. Faculty Engring., 2000. Fellow: NAS (coun. 1977—78, 1980—83, 1997—, com. sci. engring. and pub. policy 1985—), Am. Acad. Arts and Scis., Econometric Soc.; mem.: IEEE (hon.), Am. Philos. Soc. (coun. 1986—92), Nat. Acad. Engring. (coun. 1986—92). Home: 260 Douglas Rd Chappaqua NY 10514-3100 Office: Lexmark International Inc Bd Directors 740 W New Cir Rd Lexington KY 40550 Office Phone: 859-232-2000. E-mail: regomory@lexmark.com.

GONÇALVES, C. LOURENÇO, metal products executive; B, Mil. Inst. Engring., Rio de Janeiro; M in Metall. Engring., Fed. U. Minas Gerais. Various positions up to mng. dir. Companhia Siderurgica Nacional, Brazil, 1981—98; pres., CEO Calif. Steel Industries, Inc., 1998—2003; pres., CEO, bd. dirs. Metals USA, Inc., 2003—, chmn., 2006—. Office: Metals USA 2400 E Commercial Blvd Ste 905 Fort Lauderdale FL 33308-4059 Office Phone: 713-965-0990. Office Fax: 713-965-0067.

GONCHAR, SERGEI, professional hockey player; b. Chelyabinsk, Russia, Apr. 13, 1974; Defenseman Washington Capitals, 1994—2004, Boston Bruins, 2004, Pitts. Penguins, 2005—10, Ottawa Senators, 2010—13, Dallas Stars, 2013—. Mem. Team Russia, World Cup, 1996, Team Russia, Olympic Games, Nagano, Japan, 1998, Salt Lake City, 2002, Vancouver, 2010. Named to Second All-Star Team, NHL, 2002, 2003, NHL All-Star Game, 2001, 2002, 2003, 2008. Achievements include being a member of Stanley Cup Champion Pittsburgh Penguins, 2009. Office: Dallas Stars American Airlines Ctr 2500 Victory Ave Dallas TX 75201*

GONG, EDMOND JOSEPH, lawyer; b. Miami, Fla., Oct. 7, 1930; s. Joe Fred and Fayline G.; m. Sophie Vlachos, July 25, 1957 (dec.); children: Frances Fayline, Peter Joseph (dec.), Madeleine, Joseph Fred, II, Edmond Joseph; m. Dana Leigh Clay, Dec. 7, 1988. AB cum laude, Harvard U., 1952, postgrad. in law, 1954-55; JD, U. Miami, 1960. Bar: Fla. 1960. Spl. writer Hong Kong Tiger Standard, 1955-56; staff writer Miami Herald, 1958-59; assoc. firm Helliwell, Melrose and DeWolf, 1960-61; asst. U.S. atty. So. Dist. Fla., 1961-62; mem. Fla. Ho. of Reps., 1963-66, Fla. Senate, 1966-72; trustee Fla. Gulf Realty Trust, 1974-80; pres. Inflahedge Resources Fund, 1969—, Pub. Policy Cons. Inc., 1988—. Sr. pub. policy analyst and legal counsel Everett Clay Assocs., Inc., 1988—; chmn. Fla. Land Sales Advisory Council, 1974-76; vice chmn. Bd. Bus. Regulation, State of Fla., 1976-77; fellow Inst. Politics John Fitzgerald Kennedy Sch. Govt., Harvard U., 1969-70, assoc. dir., 1971-72 Mem. Harvard 350th Commn., 1984-86; mem. com. on univ. resources, bd. overseers and pres. and fellows Harvard Coll., 1984-86; mem. North Key Largo Habitat Conservation Planning Study Com., 1984-88; regional chmn. Selection Com. for Anglo-Am. Conf., Johns Hopkins Sch. Advanced Internat. Studies, 1985; mem. Fairbanks Ctr. Com., Fairbank Ctr. for East Asian Research, Harvard U., 1987-90. Mem. ABA, Fla. Bar, Harvard U. Alumni Assn. (dir.-at-large), Fla. Audubon Soc. (bd. dirs. 1990-93), Coral Reef Yacht Club. Episcopalian. Office: Pub Policy Cons 6161 Blue Lagoon Dr #270 Miami FL 33126

GONSHAK, ISABELLE LEE, nurse, volunteer; b. Newark, Apr. 4, 1932; d. Robert John and Clara Kate (Cooperman) McClelland Barron; m. David M. Gonshak, Aug. 8, 1953; children: Evan J., Brett A., Kathryn Susan. RN, NJ, Fla. Nurse Newark City Hosp., 1953; tchr. Ideal Sch. for Nurse's, Miami, Fla., 1972—74. Vocal soloist numerous TV and social affairs; photographer multiple media, multi-faceted subjects. Bd. dirs. Miami Beach Symphony, 1971—, pres., 1978-79; bd. dirs. South Fla. Symphony; life mem. Opera Guild Soc. Ft. Lauderdale; active Statue of Liberty Refinishing Com; vol. Sarah Westman Davidson Tower at Hadassah Med. Ctr., Israel. Mem. Greater Miami Opera Assn., Hadassah (life) (sr. idol contestant). Jewish. Home: 1700 SW 72d Ave Plantation FL 33317-5037

GONSOULIN, AL A., air transportation executive; Grad. in bus., U. La., Lafayette. Founder, pres., CEO Sea Mar, Inc. (a divsn. of Nabors Industries), 1977—2001; chmn. PHI, Inc., 2001—, CEO, 2004—, former pres. Bd. dirs. Nat. Ocean Industries Assn. Office: PHI Inc 2001 SE Evangeline Thruway Lafayette LA 70508 Office Phone: 337-235-2452. Office Fax: 337-232-6537. Business E-Mail: agonsoulin@phihelico.com.

GONZALES, ALBERTO R., lawyer, law educator, former United States Attorney General; b. San Antonio, Tex., Aug. 4, 1955; s. Pablo and Maria Gonzales; m. Diane Clemons (div. 1985); m. Rebecca Turner; 3 children. Student, USAF Acad., 1975-77; BA in Political Sci., Rice U., 1979; JD, Harvard Law Sch., 1982; LLD, Catholic U. America, 2002; D in Arts & Letters, Miami-Dade Cmty. Coll., 2003; LLD (hon.), U. DC, 2005; D in Assoc. Arts, Houston Cmty. Coll. System, 2005. Bar: Tex. Ptnr. Vinson & Elkins, LLP, Houston, 1982-95; gen. counsel to Gov. George W. Bush State of Tex., Austin, 1995-97, sec. state, 1997—99; justice Supreme Ct. of Tex., Austin, 1999—2000; asst. to Pres. & gen. counsel The White House, Washington, 2001—05; atty. gen. US Dept. Justice, Washington, 2005—07; ind. consulting, mediation & arbitration, 2007—09; founder, prin. Alberto R. Gonzalez, P.C., McLean, Va., 2009—; vis. prof. dept. polit. sci. Tex. Tech. U. Sys., Lubbock, 2009—11; of counsel Waller Lansden Dortch & Davis LLP, Nashville, 2011—;

Doyle Rogers Disting. Chair in Law Belmont U. Coll. Law, Nashville, 2012—. Bd. dirs. Drexel Metals, Inc., 2011—; regular columnist Fox News Latino. Trustee Tex. Bar Found., 1996-99; mem. Tex. Jud. Dists. Bd., 1996-97; bd. dirs. United Way of Tex. Gulf Coast, 1993-94; pres. Leadership Houston, 1993-94; chair Commn. for Dist. Decentralization of Houston Ind. Sch. Dist., 1994; mem. com. on undergrad. admissions Rice U., 1994; chair Republican Nat. Hispanic Assembly of Houston, 1992-94; pres. Houston Hispanic Forum, 1990-92; chair adv. com. Tex. Real Estate Ctr., 1989-90; bd. dirs. Big Brothers & Sisters, Houston, 1985-91, Cath. Charities, Houston, 1989-93 Served in USAF, 1973—75. Recipient: Hispanic Salute award, Houston Metro Ford Dealers, 1989, Commitment to Leadership award, United Way, 1993, Presdntl. Citiation, State Bar of Tex., 1997, Harvard Law Sch. Assn. award, 2002, Outstanding Tex. Leader award John B. Shepperd Public Leadership Forum, 2002, Gary L. McPherson Disting. Alumni award American Coun. Young Political Leaders, 2003, Lifetime Achievement award Travis County Tex. Republican Party, 2003, Good Neighbor award, US-Mex. Chamber of Commerce, 2003, President's award, US Hispanic Chamber of Commerce & League of United Latin American Citizens, 2003, Exemplary Leader award Houston American Leadership Forum, 2004, Hector Barreto Sr. award Latino Coalition, 2005, President's award US Hispanic CHamber of Commerce, 2005, Golden Plate award, Acad. Achievement, 2005, Disting. Leadership award, Leadership Houston, 2006, Honorary Alumnus award Southern Methodist U., 2007, Director's award CIA, 2007, Sec. of Def. medal for Exceptional Public Svc., 2007; named Outstanding Young Lawyer of Tex., Tex. Young Lawyers Assn., 1992, Latino Lawyer of Yr., Hispanic Nat. Bar. Assn., 1999, Disting. Alumnus of Rice U., Assn. of Rice Alumni, 2002, Hispanic American of the Yr. HISPANIC mag., 2005, Lawyer of Yr., ABA Journ., 2007; named one of The Five Outstanding Young Texans, Tex. Jaycess, 1994, The 25 Most Influential Hispanics, TIME mag., 2005; inducted into the Hispanics Scholarship Fund Alumni Hall of Fame, 2003 Mem. Houston Bar Assn., Houston Hispanic Bar Assn. (pres., 1990-91), State Bar Tex. (bd. dirs. 1991-94), Chartered Inst. of Arbitrators, Neutral Internat. Inst. for Conflict Prevention & Resolution, American Law Inst. Republican. Roman Catholic. Office: Waller Lansden Dortch & Davis LLP Nashville City Center 511 Union St Ste 2700 Nashville TN 37219 also: Office Alberto Gonzalez PO Box 1976 Brentwood TN 37024 Office Phone: 615-601-1976, 615-850-8560. E-mail: info@argonzales.com.*

GONZALES, GREG, state banking agency administrator; B cum laude in Hist., Tenn. Technol. U., Cookeville, 1980; law degree, U. Tenn. Rsch. asst. to Sir Patrick Cormack British Parliament, 1980; spl. asst. to Senator Albert Gore Jr. US Senate, 1985—86; positions including gen. counsel, dir. budget, dir. human resources and dir. legis. efforts Tenn. Dept. Fin. Institutions, Nashville, 1986—2005, acting commr., 2005—07, commr., 2007—. Bd. dirs. Money Transmitter Regulators Assn.; mem. bank secrecy act adv. group US Treasury Dept.; sec. Conf. State Bank Supervisors, 2010—. Office: Department of Financial Institutions 414 Union St, Suite 1000 Nashville TN 37219 Office Phone: 615-741-5603. Office Fax: 615-253-6306. E-mail: Greg.Gonzales@state.tn.us.

GONZALES, VERONICA, state legislator; b. June 19, 1964; BA in English and Spanish, Southwest Tex. State U., 1986; JD, U. Tex. Sch. Law, 1991. Ptnr. Kittleman, Thomas & Gonzalez, LLP; mem. Dist. 41 Tex. House of Representatives, Tex., 2004—. Mem.: Hidalgo County Bar Assn. (pres., panel chair), Hidalgo County Young Lawyers Assn. (pres.). Democrat. Office: 4900 N 10th St Mcallen TX 78504 also: Room E2.406 Capitol Extension PO Box 2910 Austin TX 78768 Office Phone: 956-686-5501, 512-463-0578.

GONZÁLEZ, DANIEL E., lawyer; BBA summa cum laude, U. Miami, Fla., 1985; JD summa cum laude, U. Miami Sch. Law, 1988. Bar: Fla., DC, NY, US Dist. Ct. DC, US Dist. Ct. (so. dist.) NY, US Dist. Ct. (so. and mid. dists.) Fla., Supreme Ct. Fla., US Ct. Appeals (11th cir.). Ptnr., dir. internat. litig. & arbitration practice group Hogan Lovells US LLP (formerly Hogan & Hartson LLP), Miami. Contbr. articles to profl. jours. Mam. adv. bd. Inst. Transnational Arbitration, Plano, Tex. Recipient Top Lawyers in South Fla., South Fla. Legal Guide, 2006—09; named one of Legal Elite, Fla. Trend mag., 2007—09. Mem.: ABA, London Ct. Internat. Arbitration, Miami Internat. Arbitration Soc. (bd. dirs.), American Arbitration Assn., Internat. C. of C. (mem. com. to Latin America), Internat. Bar Assn., Dade County Bar Assn. Office: Hogan Lovells US LLP 1111 Brickell Ave Ste 1900 Miami FL 33131 Office Phone: 305-459-6649. Office Fax: 305-459-6550. Business E-Mail: daniel.gonzalez@hoganlovells.com.

GONZALEZ, EDDIE, advertising executive; Attended, NYU. Joined Young & Rubicam Puerto Rico, 1982, mng. dir., 1983; pres., CEO Young & Rubicam Spain, Madrid; chmn., CEO, L.Am. Young & Rubicam Brands, Miami, 2003—, chmn., CEO, Bravo Group, 2006—. Named to 100 Influentials List, Hispanic Bus. Mag., 2006. Office: Young & Rubicam Latin Am Courvoisier Ctr 11 601 Brickell Key Dr Ste 1100 Miami FL 33131 Office Phone: 305-347-1950. Business E-Mail: eddie.gonzalez@yr.com.

GONZALEZ, EDUARDO, state legislator; b. Cardenas, Matanzas, Cuba, Nov. 9, 1969; m. Barbara Gonzalez; children: Evan Mathew, Ethan Angel. Grad. in bus. mgmt. and adminstrn., Miami-Dade CC, 1992. Bus. devel. leader CAC Fla. Med. Ctr.; councilman City of Hialeah, Fla., 1999—2006; mem. Dist. 102 Fla. House of Reps., Tallahassee, 2006—, dep. whip, 2008—09, vice chair govt. ops. appropriations com., mem. civil justice and courts policy com., criminal and civil justice policy coun., edn. policy coun., preK-12 policy com., rules and calendar coun. Bd. mem. City of Hialeah Water and Sewer Dept., 1998. Mem. Fed. Action Strike Team; bd. dirs. Fla. League of Cities, 1999—; mem. exec. com. Mcpl. Loan Coun. Mem.: Miami-Dade County League of Cities (pres.), Kiwanis Club, Flamingo Hialeah. Republican. Roman Catholic. Office: 10001 NW 87th Ave Hialeah FL 33016-1901 also: 209 House Office Bldg 402 S Monroe St Tallahassee FL 32399-1300 Office Phone: 305-364-3066, 850-488-1683.

GONZALEZ, EDWARD, councilman; m. Melissa Gonzalez. Grad., U. Houston; MA in Polit. Sci., U. of St. Thomas. Joined Houston Police Dept., 1991, homicide investigator, sergeant, mem. Hostage Negotiation Team; councilman, Dist. H Houston City Coun., 2009—, mem. Budget and Fiscal Affairs, Devel. and Regulatory Affairs and Transp., Infrastructure and Aviation. Bd. mem. Houston Area Cmty. Svcs., Gulf Coast Cmty. Svcs. Assn.; co-chair Hispanic Outreach Task Force Am. Heart Assn. Mem.: Houston Heights Assn. (chair Crime and Pub. Safety Com.). Office: City Hall Annex 900 Bagby, 1st Fl Houston TX 77002 Office Phone: 832-393-3003. Office Fax: 832-393-3224. E-mail: districth@cityofhouston.net.

GONZALEZ, EMILIO BUSTAMANTE, rheumatologist, educator; b. Asuncion, Paraguay, Jan. 9, 1949; came to U.S., 1974; s. Emilio Gonzalez-Jovellanos and Clara (Bustamante) Gonzalez; m. Elizabeth Ferreira, Jan. 4, 1973; 1 child, Daniel BS Scis. and Humanities, C.A.L. Coll., Asuncion, 1972; MD summa cum laude, Nat. U., Asuncion, 1972. Diplomate Am. Bd. Internal Medicine, Am. Bd. Rheumatology, Am. Bd. Allergy and Immunology. Intern U. Hosp., Asuncion, 1973—74; resident Danbury Hosp., Conn., 1975—78; tchg. fellow allergy and clin. immunology U. Pitts. Sch. Medicine and VA Med. Ctr., 1978—79; mem. staff allergy and clin. immunology Nat. Jewish Hosp. and U. Colo. Affiliated Hosps., Denver, 1979—80; mem. staff clin. immunology and rheumatology U. Tex. Med. Br., Galveston, 1980—81, clin. instr. dept. medicine, 1981—82, asst. prof. medicine, 1982—89, assoc. prof. medicine, 1989—, dir. rheumatology, 2004—, prof. medicine, 2004—; chief rheumatology svc. Grady Meml. Hosp. and Emory U. Sch. Medicine, Atlanta, 1989—; attending physician rheumatology sect. med. svc. VA Med. Svc., Emory U., Decatur, Ga., 1989—; attending physician divsn. rheumatology Emory U. Hosp., Atlanta, 1989—; cons., part-time mem. divsn. rheumatology Emory Clinic and Emory U., Atlanta, 1989—; dir. rheumatology Atlanta Med. Ctr., 1998—2004. Bd. dirs. Arthritis Found., Ga., sci. com.; presenter in field Contbr. articles to profl. jours.; reviewer in field:. Fellow ACP, Am. Coll. Rheumatology; mem. AMA, Am. Acad. Allergy and Immunology, Ga. Rheumatism Soc. (program chmn. 1993-94), Ga. Soc. Rheumatology (pres. 1995-96), Sigma Xi Office: Univ Tex Med Branch Dir Rheumatology 301 University Blvd Galveston TX 77555-0565 Office Phone: 409-772-2863. Office Fax: 409-772-7355. Business E-Mail: ebgonzal@utmb.edu.

GONZALEZ, EUGENE ROBERT, investment banker; s. Eugenio Tomas and Alice Marie (Macdonald) Gonzalez-Mandiola. BA in Internat. Rels., Yale U., 1952; postgrad., Georgetown U., 1954; postgrad. sem. in advanced mgmt., Internat. Mgmt. Devel. Inst., Lausanne, Switzerland, 1967. Econ. officer Dept. Defense, Washington, 1954-57; project fin. officer Devel. Loan Fund (now AID), Washington, 1957-58; fin. mgr. RCA Internat., NYC, 1958-61; fin. instns. specialist Interam. Devel. Bank, Washington, 1961-62, fin. officer, 1962-63, dep. regional rep. for Europe Paris, 1964; exec. v.p. Adela Investment Co., Luxembourg, 1964-74; pres., chief exec. officer Adelatec Mgmt. Cons. Co., 1969-72; mng. dir. Adela Investment Co., 1974-75, pres., chief exec. officer, 1975-76; adviser, regional coordinator Ibero Am. Morgan Stanley Internat., NYC, 1977-89; sr. v.p., head internat. pvt. banking Barclays Bank, NYC, 1989-91; mng. dir. Kidder, Peabody & Co., NYC, 1992-94; pres. Quasar Capital Corp., S.A., 1995—. Author: International Sources of Financing, 1961. Served with US Army, 1952-54. Mem. Nat. Com. on Am. Fgn. Policy, Internat. Assn. Fin. Planners, Am. Soc. Profl. Cons., Presidents Assn., Americas Soc., Spanish Inst., Met. Club (Washington), City Tavern Club (Washington), Brook Club (N.Y.C.), Racquet and Tennis Club (N.Y.C.), Yale Club (N.Y.C.), Pacific Union Club (San Francisco), Zeta Psi Soc. N.Am. Home: Suite 64-A 220 North Zapata Hwy 11 Laredo TX 78043-4464 Office Phone: 212-744-5685. Personal E-mail: egonz88888@aol.com.

GONZÁLEZ, FERNANDO FRANCISCO, professional tennis player; b. Santiago, Chile, July 29, 1980; s. Fernando and Patricia. Profl. tennis player ATP, 1999—. Recipient Chilean Nat. Sports award, 2003. Achievements include winning ARAG ATP World Team Championship title; winning 11 career singles titles, 3 career doubles titles, ATP. Office: ATP 201 ATP Blvd Ponte Vedra Beach FL 32082

GONZALEZ, FREDI JESUS, professional baseball manager; b. Havana, Cuba, Jan. 28, 1964; m. Pamela Gonzalez; children: Gabrielle, Alex Christopher. Mgr. Triple-A Richmond Affiliate Atlanta Braves, 2002; third base coach Atlanta Braves, 2003—06; minor league coach Fla. Marlins, 1992—99, third base coach, 2000—01, mgr., 2006—10, Atlanta Braves, 2010—. Named Nat. League Mgr. of Yr., Sporting News, 2008. Office: Atlanta Braves 755 Hank Aaron dr Atlanta GA 30315

GONZALEZ, HECTOR HUGO, nursing educator; b. Rome, Tex., Mar. 9, 1937; s. Amadeo Lorenzo and Carlotta (Trevino) G. BSN, Incarnate Word Coll., 1963; MSN, Cath. U. Am., 1966; PhD in Edn., U. Tex., 1974. Staff nurse Santa Rosa Med. Ctr., San Antonio, 1962-65; asst. dir. nursing divsn. Incarnate Word Coll., San Antonio, 1968-72; prof., chmn. dept. nursing San Antonio Coll., 1972-92, dir. Ctr. for Assoc. Degree Edn. Rsch. and Svc., 1987-92, prof. and chmn. emeritus, 1993—. Cons. NIMH, 1973, FDA, 1989-93, mem. anesthesiology and respiratory devices panel, mem. dispute resolution panel, 2000—01; numerous ednl. instns. and hosps. in U.S., Mex., P.R., Kuwait; mem. Nat. Adv. Coun. on Alcohol Abuse and Alcoholism, 1976-80; vis. prof. Facultad Enfermería, U. Autónoma Nuevo León, 1980-1990; mem. nat. adv. coun. nurses edn. and practice, 1992-96; mem. panel on nursing practice U.S. Pharmacopeia, 1985-2000. Contbr. articles to profl. jours.; peer reviewer Nursing Outlook, 1983, Advancing Clinical Care. Mem. legis. affairs adv. com. State Senator Glen Kothman, San Antonio, 1983; bd. dirs. Family Svcs. Assn. San Antonio; mem. multidisciplinary academic external com. U. Autonoma de Nuevo Leon, Mex., 1986-88. Capt. nurse corps U.S. Army, 1966-68. Recipient cert. of appreciation Citizens of Bexar County, San Antonio, 1970, Nat. Student Nurses Assn., 1977. Mem. ANA (mem. adv. bd. minority fellowship program 1976-80, Trail Blazer award Minority Fellowship Program 2004), Nat. Assn. Hispanic Nurses (pres. 1982-84, bd. dirs. 1995-97, CEO San Antonio chpt. 1998-2008, project dir. breast cancer tng. grant Am. Cancer Soc. and Nat. Assn. Hispanic Nurses 1992-96, historian 2000—08), Nat. League for Nursing (bd. dirs. 1973-81). Democrat. Roman Catholic. Home: 114 Magnolia Dr San Antonio TX 78212-3115 Office Phone: 210-733-7460. Personal E-mail: hhgzz@sbcglobal.net.

GONZALEZ, JOE MANUEL, lawyer; b. NYC, Aug. 18, 1950; s. Reinaldo Fabregas and Mary Louise (Cermeno) G.; m. Ruia Jane Whiteside, Dec. 30, 1977; children: Matthew Ray, Jane Marie, Jeffrey Joseph, Joseph Manuel. BA, U. South Fla., 1972; JD, Gonzaga U., 1980; LLM in Taxation, Georgetown U., 1981. Bar: Fla. 1981, U.S. Tax Ct. 1983, U.S. Dist. Ct. (mid. dist.) Fla. 1984, U.S. Ct. Appeals (11th cir.) 1984, U.S. Supreme Ct. 1985. Atty. Gonzaga U. Legal Services, Spokane, Wash., 1980; mng. ptnr. Cotterill, Gonzalez, Hayes & Grantham, Fla., 1981-88, Cotterill & Grantham, Pa., 1982-92, Cotterill, Gonzalez & Grantham, Pa., Pa., 1992-93; prin. Joe M. Gonzalez, P.A., 1993—; atty. Hispanic Def. League, Tampa, Fla., 1982-90. Assoc. editor Gonzaga Law Rev. Spl. Report: Pub. Sector Labor Law, 1980. Mem. Sheriff's Hispanic Adv. Coun., Hillsborough County, Fla., 1982-93, City of Tampa Hispanic Adv. Coun., 1983-2006, chmn. 1993-95, U. So. Fla. Hispanic Adv. Bd., 1999-2001; chmn. citizens adv. com. Hillsborough County Planning Commn., 1988-90; pres. Tampa Hispanic Heritage, Inc., 1985-87; co-founder Carnavale En Tampa, Inc., 1986-90; master of ceremonies Gasparilla Sidewalk Art Festival, 1988; mem. police chief's adv. com., 1988-93; sec. Hispanic Bus. Inst. Fla., Inc., 1988-93; dir. Housing and Edn. Alliance, 2001—. Mem.: ABA, Fla. Bar Assn. (jud. nominating prodedures com. 1988-89), Hillsborough County Bar Assn., Assn. Trial Lawyers Am., Nat. Inst. for Trial Advocacy, Complete Census Count Com., Ybor City Rotary Club (Paul Harris fellow 2006), Ybor City Rotary Found. (co-founder, charter mem.), Am. Inns Ct., Phi Delta Phi. Democrat. Presbyterian. Home: 5801 Mariner St Tampa FL 33609-3411 Office: 304 S Willow Ave Tampa FL 33606-2147 Home Phone: 813-639-0680; Office Phone: 813-254-0797. Personal E-mail: joegonzalezpa@aol.com.

GONZALEZ, JORGE JOSE, medical educator; b. Valdivia, Chile, Aug. 13, 1945; came to U.S., 1973; s. Manuel and Emma (Clasing) G.; m. Barbara Hayworth, May 22, 1971; children: Carla Andrea, Maria Cristina. MD, U. Chile, 1971. Resident in internal medicine New Hanover Meml. Hosp., Wilmington, N.C., 1973-76; fellow in endocrinology Med. U. S.C., Charleston, 1976-78; from asst. prof. to assoc. prof. medicine U. N.C. Sch. Medicine, Chapel Hill, 1978-92, prof. medicine, 1992—2007. Program dir. Internal Medicine Tng. Program, Wilmington, 1991-2001. Recipient N.C. Pub. Health Assn. Adult Health Promotion Sect. Spl. commendation, 1989. Fellow Am. Coll. Clin. Endocrinology; mem. Am. Diabetes Assn., Endocrine Soc., Am. Assn. Clin. Endocrinology. Episcopalian. Home: 4921 Nicholas Creek Cir Wilmington NC 28409-3295 Office: Ptnrs Endocrinology & Diabetes 1500 Physicians Dr Wilmington NC 28401-7356 Office Phone: 910-762-9701. Business E-Mail: jgonzalez@partnersed.com.

GONZALEZ, JOSE ALEJANDRO, JR., federal judge; b. Tampa, Fla., Nov. 26, 1931; s. Jose A. and Luisa Secundina (Collia) G.; m. Frances Frierson, Aug. 22, 1956 (dec. Aug. 1981); children— Margaret Ann, Mary Frances; m. Mary Sue Copeland, Sept. 24, 1983 BA, U. Fla., 1952, JD, 1957; LLD, Nova Southeastern U., 1998. Bar: Fla. 1958, U.S. Dist. Ct. (so. dist.) Fla. 1959, U.S. Ct. Appeals 1959, U.S. Supreme Ct. 1963. Practice in, Ft. Lauderdale, 1958-64; claim rep. State Farm Mut., Lakeland, Fla., 1957-58; assoc. firm Watson, Hubert and Sousley, 1958-61, ptnr., 1961-64; asst. state atty. 15th Cir. Fla., 1961-64; cir. judge 17th Cir. Ft. Lauderdale, 1964-78, chief judge, 1969-70; assoc. judge 4th Dist. Ct. Appeals, West Palm Beach; judge US Dist. Ct. (so. dist.) Fla., Ft. Lauderdale, 1978—96, sr. judge, 1996—. Bd. dirs. Arthritis Found., 1962-72; bd. dirs. Henderson Clinic Broward County, 1964-68, v.p., 1967-68. Served to 1st lt. AUS, 1952-54. Recipient Kupferman award Laymen's Nat. Bible Assn., 1991; named Broward County Outstanding Young Man, 1967, one of Fla.'s Five Outstanding Young Men, Fla. Jaycees, 1967, Broward Legal Exec. of Yr., 1978. Mem.: ABA, Broward County Bar, Fla. Bar Assn., Fed. Bar Assn., Am. Judicature Soc., Lenox Club, Kiwanian Club (pres. 1971—72), Fla. Blue Key, Lauderdale Yacht Club, Pittsfield Country Club, Ft. Lauderdale Jaycees (dir. 1960—61), Phi Alpha Delta, Sigma Chi (Significant Sig). Democrat. Office: US Dist Ct 205 US Courthouse 299 E Broward Blvd Fort Lauderdale FL 33301-1944

GONZALEZ, NELSON, computer company executive; Co-founder, CEO Alienware (acquired by Dell. Inc.), Miami, Fla., 1996—. Office: Alienware 14591 SW 120 St Miami FL 33186-8638 Office Phone: 305-251-9797. Office Fax: 305-259-9874. Business E-Mail: nelson@alienware.com.

GONZALEZ, RACHEL A., lawyer; JD, U. Calif. Berkeley, 1994. Atty. Morgan, Lewis & Bockius LLP, 1996—2006; sr. v.p., group counsel mergers & acquisitions Affiliated Computer Services, 2006—08; v.p., dep. gen. counsel Dean Foods Co., 2008—13, exec. v.p., gen. counsel, corporate sec., 2013—. Office: Dean Foods Co 2711 North Haskell Ave Ste 3400 Dallas TX 75204 Office Phone: 214-303-3400.*

GONZALEZ, RAQUEL MARIA, pharmacist; b. Veguitas, Oriente, Cuba, June 1, 1952; d. Ernesto Esteban and Evora Cristina (Ramirez) G. BS in Biology, Ga. Coll., 1974; BS in Pharmacy, Mercer U., 1977. Registered pharmacist, Ga., Fla., Tenn.; registered pharmacist cons., Fla. Staff pharmacist Cobb Gen. Hosp., Austell, Ga., 1978, VA Hosp., Nashville, 1978-79, Decatur, Ga., 1979-81, Lewisburg Cmty. Hosp., Tenn., 1981-89; pharmacist Pharmacy Staffing Svcs. Inc., Brentwood, Tenn., 1989—; chief pharmacist Super D Drug Store # 50, Fayetteville, Tenn., 1989-93; chief of pharmacy Fred's Pharmacy, Lewisburg, Tenn., 1993—. Relief pharmacist Farmer's Market Pharmacy (Kroger), Nashville, 1989—. Mem. Tenn. Pharmacist Assn., Ducks Unltd., Atlanta Ski Club. Republican. Roman Catholic. Avocations: piano, white water rafting, skiing, snorkeling, gardening. Home: RR 1 Box 35 Belfast TN 37019-9801 Office: Fred's Pharmacy #1241 1797 Hwy 100 East Centerville TN 37033

GONZÁLEZ NIEVES, ROBERTO OCTAVIO, archbishop; b. Elizabeth, NJ, June 2, 1950; s. Jesus Hiram and Frances Iris (Nieves) Gonzalez. Grad., St. Joseph Seraphic Sem.; BA, Siena Coll.; MA in Theology, Washington Theol. Union; MA, Fordham Univ., PhD in Sociology; D (hon.), St. Bonaventure Univ., 1980, Siena Coll., 2000, Universidad Central de Bayamon, PR, 2000. Joined Order of Friars Minor, 1970, ordained priest, 1977; cons. Centro Hispano Catolico del Nordeste, NYC, 1977—83; parochial vicar Holy Cross parish, Bronx, NY, 1982—86, pastor, 1986—88; ordained bishop, 1988; aux. bishop Archdiocese of Boston, 1988—95; coadjutor bishop Diocese of Corpus Christi, 1995-97, bishop, 1997—99; archbishop Archdiocese of San Juan, 1999—. Instr. Centro Pastoral del Sur del Bronx, 1979—80; cons., Office of Pastoral Studies Archdiocese of NY, 1979—88; chaplain Lincoln Hosp., Bronx, NY, 1981—82; adj. prof. sociology Fordham U., 1983—85. Contbr. articles to profl. jours. Recipient Presdl. medal, Regis Coll., Weston, Mass., 2000. Roman Catholic. Office: PO Box 9021967 San Juan PR 00902-1967 Office Phone: 787-725-4975.

GONZALEZ-SCARANO, FRANCISCO ANTONIO, neurologist, virologist; b. Ponce, PR, Mar. 23, 1950; s. Francisco and Genoveva (Scarano) Gonzalez-Hernandez; m. Barbara Jean Turner, June 23, 1979; children: Genevieve Carre, Stephanie Katharine, Lisa Frances. BA, Yale U., 1971; MD, Northwestern U., Chgo., 1975; MA (hon.), U. Pa., Phila., 1988. Diplomate Am. Bd. Neurology. Intern Hosp. U. Pa., 1975-76, resident in neurology, 1976-79; fellow U. Pa., Phila., 1979-82, NIMR, London, 1981-82; asst. prof. depts. neurology and microbiology U. Pa., Phila., 1982-88, assoc. prof., 1988-94, prof., 1994—2010, prof. emeritus, 2010—; dean, v.p. med. affairs, John P. Howe Disting. chair U. Tex. Health Sci. Ctr., San Antonio, 2010—. Vice-chair rsch. neurology dept. U. Pa, 1998-99, chair 1999—2010; co-dir. Pa. Ctr. for HIV and AIDS, 1998-2007, Pa. Neurosci. Ctr., 2006—2010; chmn. bd. sci. counselors Nat. Inst. Neurol. Diseases and Stroke, Bethesda, Md., 1993-97, Nat. Adv. Neurol. Diseases and Stroke Coun., 2004—08. Assoc. editor Viral Pathogenesis, 1997; editl. bd. Jour. Neurovirology, 1996-12, Virus Rsch., 1997-2013, AIDS, 1995-2002, GLIA, 1999-12, Jour. Virology, 2000—11, Virology, 2004-2013. Trustee Swarthmore Presbyn. Ch., 1997-2000, session 2004-07. Harry Weaver scholar Multiple Sclerosis Soc., NYC, 1982-87. Fellow: Phila. Coll. Physicians; mem.: Acad. Medicine, Engring., and Sci. Tex., AAMC (coun. dean 2010—), Inst. of Medicine, Am. Soc. Clin. Investigation, Am. Acad. Neurology (mem. sci. issues com. 1985—89, profl. and pub. issues com. 1987—93), Am. Neurol. Assn. (exec. coun. 2001—03, chair sci. prog. com. 2005—07, v.p. 2008—10), Scroll & Key, John Morgan Soc., Penn Club, Alpha Omega Alpha. Presbyterian. Avocation: photography. Office Phone: 210-567-4422. Office Fax: 210-567-3435. Business E-Mail: scarano@uthscsa.edu.

GOOCH, STEVE, state legislator; b. Dahlonega, Ga., Feb. 25, 1967; m. Shannon Gooch; 3 children. MPA, North Ga. Coll. & State U., 1998. Exec. dir. R-Ranch in the Mountains Resort, 1994—2000; chief elected official, sole commr., adminstr. Lumpkin County, Ga., 2000—05, chmn., 2005—09; v.p. comml. group The Norton Agy., 2005—; mem. Dist. 51 Ga. State Senate, 2011—. Bd. dirs. First

Citizens Bank Ga. Chmn. Lumpkin County Bd. Health, Ga. Mountains Regional Devel. Coun., ACCG Gen. Govt. Com.; bd. dirs. Lumpkin County Pub. Bldg. Authority, Holly Theatre, Dahlonega/Lumpkin County C. of C., North Ga. Coll. Sch. Bus. Adv. Coun., Lumpkin County Water & Sewer Authority, Devel. Authority Lumpkin County, Dept. Cmty. Affairs Regional Adv. Coun., Tech. Coll. System Ga.; treas. Dahlonega Rotary Club; exec. coun. Northeast Ga. Boy Scouts; mem. Lumpkin County Leadership Adv. Coun., Lumpkin County Agr. Advisory Coun., Environ. Protection Divsn. Stakeholders Adv. Task Force, Nat. Assn. Counties Environ. Policy Com., ACCG Bd. Mgrs. Republican. Baptist. Office: PO Box Box 600 Dahlonega GA 30533 also: Georgia State Senate 321B Coverdell Legis Office Bldg Atlanta GA 30334 Office Phone: 706-864-5273, 404-656-9221. Business E-Mail: steve.gooch@senate.ga.gov.

GOOD, LYNN JONES, energy executive; b. Apr. 18, 1959; m. Brian Robert Good; 2 children. BS in Systems Analysis & Acctg., Miami U., Oxford, Ohio, 1981. Various positions Arthur Andersen, 1981—2002, ptnr., 1992—2002, Deloitte & Touche LLC, Cin., 2002—03; v.p. finance project strategy Cinergy, 2003, v.p., contr., 2003—05, v.p. finance, contr., 2005, exec. v.p., CFO, 2005—06; sr. v.p., treas. Duke Energy Corp., Charlotte, NC, 2006—07, group exec., pres. comml. business, 2007—09, group exec., CFO, 2009—13, pres., CEO, 2013—, vice chair, 2013—. Bd. dirs. Hubbell Inc., 2009—, Duke Energy Corp., 2013—. Bd. mem. Bechtler Mus. Modern Art, Charlotte, NC. Named one of The 50 Most Powerful Women in Bus., Fortune mag., 2013. Office: Duke Energy Corp 526 S Church St Charlotte NC 28202-1904 Office Phone: 704-594-6200.*

GOOD, MARY LOWE, investment company executive, educator; b. Grapevine, Tex., June 20, 1931; d. John W. and Winnie (Mercer) Lowe; m. Billy Jewel Good, May 17, 1952 (dec. 2005); children: Billy, James. BS, Ark. State Tchrs. Coll., 1950; MS, U. Ark., 1953, PhD, 1955, LLD (hon.), 1979; DSc (hon.), U. Ill., Chgo., 1983, Clarkson U., 1984, Ea. Mich. U., 1986, Duke U., 1987, St. Mary's Coll., 1987, Kenyon Coll., 1988; degree (hon.), Stevens Inst. Tech., 1989, Lehigh U., 1989, Northeastern Ill. U., 1989, U. SC, 1989, NJ Inst. Tech., 1989; degree in law (hon.), Newcomb Coll. Tulane U., 1991; LLD (hon.), Coll. William Mary, 1992; DSc (hon.), Manhattan Coll., 1992, Ind. U., 1992, SUNY, Binghamton, 1994, Rensselaer Polytechnic Inst., 1994, Monmouth U., 1995, La. State U., 1995, Ill. Inst. Tech., 1997, Mich. State U., 1997, U. Mich., 1998; DEng (hon.), Colo. Sch. Mines, 2000; DSc (hon.), U. Ctrl. Ark., Conway, 2007. Instr. Ark. State Tchrs. Coll., Conway, summer 1949; from instr. to asst. prof. La. State U., Baton Rouge, 1954—58, Boyd prof., 1978—80; assoc. prof. to Boyd prof. U. New Orleans, 1958—78; vice pres., dir. Res. R. Uop Inc., 1980—83; pres. Signal Rsch. Ctr. Inc., 1983—85; pres. engineered materials rsch. divsn Allied-Signal Inc., Des Plaines, Ill., 1986—87, sr. v.p.-tech. Morristown, NJ, 1987—93; under sec. of commerce for technology Dept. of Commerce, Washington, 1993-97; mng. mem. Venture Capital Investors LLC, Little Rock, 1997—2005, Fund for Ark., 2005—; emeritus prof. founding dean U. Ark. Little Rock; special advisor chancellor, 2011. Chmn. Pres.'s Com. for Nat. Medal Sci., 1979-82; adv. bd. NSF Chemistry Sect., 1972-76; com. medicinal chemistry NIH, 1972-76, Office of USAF Rsch., 1974-78, chemist divsn. Brookhaven and Oak Ridge Nat. Labs., 1973-83, chem. tech. divsn. Oak Ridge Nat. Lab., catalysis program Lawrence-Berkeley Lab.; bd. dirs. Biogenldec, Inc., 1997-2007, Delta Bank and Trust, Acxiom Inc., 2004-2010, St. Vincent's Health; bd. chem. sci. and tech., Nat. Rsch. Coun., 2003-04, Govt. U., industry roundtable, NRC, 2000-05, Ark. Sci and Tech. Authority, 1998-03, Dialoge Com, Am. Chem. Coun., 2002-05. Contbr. articles to profl. jours. Mem. Nat. Sci. Bd., 1980-91, vice chair, 1984-88, chair, 1988-91; mem. Pres.' Coun. Advisors for Sci. and Tech., 1991-93. Recipient Agnes Faye Morgan rsch. award, 1969, Disting. Alumni citation U. Ark., 1973, Scientist of Yr. award Indsl. R&D mag., 1983, Delmer S. Fahrney medal Franklin Inst., 1988, N.J. Women of Achievement award Douglass Coll., Rutgers U., 1990, Indsl. Rsch. Inst. medal, 1991, Disting. Svc. award NSF, 1992, Roe award ASME, 1993, Gold medal SME, 1995, Earle Barnes award ACS, 1996, Priestley medal, 1997, UCLA Glenn T. Seaborg medal, 1996, Nat. Materials Advancement award Fedn. Materials Socs., 1996, Othmer medal award Chem. Heritage Found., 1998, Henry Michel award, Civil Engring. Rsch. Found., 1998, Heinz award for tech. The Economy and Employment, 2000, Vannevar Bush award NSF, 2004, Gov. Sid McMath Lifetime Achievement award, Lions Found. the Blind, US News and World Report, STEM Leadership award, 2012, 100 Women Leaders in STEM, 2012; AEC tng. grantee, 1967, NSF Internat. travel grantee, 1968, NSF rsch. grantee, 1969-80, Albert Fox Demers award, 1992. Fellow AAAS (Abelson award 1999, pres. 2000, chmn. bd. dirs. 2001), Am. Inst. Chemistry (Gold medal 1983), Chem. Soc. London, Royal Soc. Chemistry (hon.); mem. NAE, Acad. Arts and Scis, Am. Philos. Soc., Swedish Acad. Engring., Am. Chem. Soc. (1st woman dir. 1972-74, regional dir. 1972-80, chmn. bd. 1978, 80, bd. publs., pres. 1987, mem. bd. pub. 2002-, Garvan medal 1973, Herty medal 1975, award Fla. sect. 1979, Charles Lathrop Parsons award 1991, Priestley medal 2001), Internat. Union Pure and Applied Chmistry (pres. inorganic div. 1980-85),Alliance for Sci. and Tech. Rsch. in Am. (chmn. bd. dirs. 2000-), Zonta (past pres. New Orleans club, chmn. dist. status of women com. and nominating com., chmn. internat. Amelia Earhart scholarship com. 1978-88, pres. internat. Found. 1988-93, mem. internat. bd. 1988-90), Rotary Internat., Phi Beta Kappa, Sigma Xi, Iota Sigma Pi (regional dir. 1967-93, hon. mem. 1983), Ark. Women's Forum. Office: U Ark at Little Rock Coll Engring & Information Tech 2801 S University Ave Little Rock AR 72204-1000 Home: 14300 Chenal Pky #7258 Little Rock AR 72211 Office Phone: 501-683-7770. Business E-Mail: mlgood@ualr.edu.

GOOD, MICHAEL LOWELL, anesthesiologist, educator, dean; m. Danette M. Good; 5 children. BS in Computer and Comm. Sci., U. Mich., Ann Arbor, 1980, MD, 1984. Diplomate Am. Bd. Anesthesiology, cert. Nat. Bd. Med. Examiners. Chief resident dept. anesthesiology U. Fla. Coll. Medicine, Gainesville, 1986—87, rsch. fellow dept. anesthesiology, 1987—88, asst. prof. dept. anesthesiology, 1988—93, prof. anesthesiology, 1999—, sr. assoc. dean for VA affiliations, 2004—05, sr. assoc. dean for clin. affairs, 2005—08, interim dean, 2008—09, dean, 2009—; chief anesthesiology svc. Malcom Randall Vet. Affairs Med. Ctr., Gainesville, 1994—96, chief of staff, 1996—99; pres. U. Fla. Health Services Inst., Gainesville, 2007—08; chief of staff Shands HealthCare at the U. Fla. and Alachua Gen. Hosp., 2007—08. Inventor human patient simulator. Mem.: AMA, Fla. Med. Assn., Alachua County Med. Soc., Am. Soc. Echocardiography, Am. Soc. Anesthesiologists. Roman Catholic. Office: U Fla Coll Medicine PO Box 100215 Gainesville FL 32610-0215 Office Phone: 352-273-7500. E-mail: good@anest.ufl.edu.

GOOD, STEPHEN D., lawyer; BS summa cum laude, Wash. and Lee U., Lexington, Va., 1977; JD, Yale U., New Haven, 1980. Ptnr. Gardere Wynne Sewell, LLP, Dallas, mng. ptnr. of firm, 2000—. Atty., pro bono tax advisor to various charities; mem. Dallas Citizens Coun.; former trustee The St. Michael Sch.; bd. dirs. Regional Dallas Chamber; adv. gov. Dallas Symphony Orch. Named to Tex. Super Lawyers, Tax, Tex. Monthly mag., 2003, 2007. Mem.: State Bar Tex., Ark. Bar Assn., NY State Bar Assn., Dallas Bar Assn. Office: Gardere Wynne Sewell LLP 1601 Elm St Ste 3000 Dallas TX 75201 Office Phone: 214-999-4216. Office Fax: 214-797-2829. Business E-Mail: sgood@gardere.com.

GOODALL, JANE, zoologist; b. London, Apr. 3, 1934; d. Mortimer Herbert and Vanne (Joseph) Morris-Goodall; m. Hugo Van Lawick, 1964 (div. 1974); one child, Hugo Eric Louis; m. Derek Bryceson, 1975 (dec. 1980). PhD in Ethology, Cambridge U., 1965; degree (hon.), Wesleyan Coll., Macon, Ga., 2000, U. Minn., 2001, U. Buffalo, NYC, 2001, Ryerson U., Toronto, Ont., Can., 2001, Providence U., Taiwan, 2001, Elon U., NC, 2002, Sweet Briar Coll., Va., 2002, U.Ctrl. Lancashire, UK, 2003, Pecs U., Hungary, 2005, Syracuse U., NYC, 2005, Rutgers State U., NJ, 2005, numerous other univs., 1975—99. Asst., sec. to Dr. Louis S. B. Leakey Coryndon Meml. Mus. Nat. History, Olduvai Gorge, Tanzania; rschr. in animal behavior, sci. dir. Gombe Stream Rsch. Ctr., Tanzania, 1960—2003. Vis. prof. psychiatry, human biology Stanford U., 1971-75; hon. vis. prof. zoology U. Dar Es Salaam, Tanzania, 1973—; lectr. Yale U., 1973; adj. prof. dept., environ. studies Tufts U. Sch. Vet. Medicine, 1987-88; assoc. Cleve. Natural History Mus., 1990; disting. adj. prof. occupl. therapy and anthropology U. So. Calif., 1990; Andrew D. White prof.-at-large Cornell U., 1996-2002; Messenger of Peace UN, 2002—;; spkr. 20/20, Nightline, Good Morning America. Author: My Friends the Wild Chimpanzees, 1967, In the Shadow of Man, 1971, The Chimpanzees of Gombe, 1986 (R.R. Hawkins award for outstanding tech., sci. or med. book, 1986, Award for Outstanding Pub. in Wildlife Ecology and Mgmt., Wildlife Soc. U.S.A., 1986), The Chimpanzee Family Book, 1989, Through a Window, 1990, Visions of Caliban, 1993 (N.Y. Times "Notable Book", 1993, Libr. Jour. "Best Sci-Tech.Book, 1993), Jane Goodall: With Love, 1994, Dr. White, 1999, 40 Years at Gombe, 1999, Brutal Kinship, 1999, The Eagle and the Wren, 2000, Africa in My Blood: An Autobiography in Letters, 2000, Chimpanzees I Love: Saving Their World and Ours, 2001, Beyond Innocence: An Autobiography in Letters, 2001; author: (with Philip Berman) Reason for Hope, 1999; author: (with Marc Bekoff) The Ten Trusts: What We Must Do To Care for the Animals We Love, 2002; author: (with Gary McAvoy and Gail Hudson) Harvest for Hope: A Guide to Mindful Eating, 2005; contbr. Primate Behavior, 1965, Primate Ethology, 1967, Am. Handbook of Psychiatry, 1976, Understanding Chimpanzees, 1990; author (with H. van Lawick): (children's book) Grub: The Bush Baby, 1972; author: My Life With the Chimpanzees, 1988 (Parenting's Reading-Magic award for outstanding book for children, 1989), The Chimpanzee Family Book, 1989, Jane Goodall's Animal World: Chimps, 1989, Animal Family Series, 1989, With Love, 1994, Dr. White, 1999, The Eagle and the Wren, 2000, Chimpanzees I Love: Saving Their World and Ours, 2001; author: (with Alan Marks) Rickie and Henri: A True Story, 2004; author: (films) Miss Goodall and the Wild Chimpanzees, 1963, Among the Wild Chimpanzees, 1984; author: (with Hugo van Lawick) People of the Forest, 1988; author: Chimpanzee Alert, in the Nature Watch Series, 1990, The Life and Legend of Jane Goodall, 1990, The Gombe Chimpanzees, 1990, Jane Goodall: Reason for Hope, 1999, Chimps R Us, 2001, Jane Goodall's Wild Chimpanzees, 2002; contbr. numerous articles to profl. jours. Founder Jane Goodall Inst. for Wildlife Rsch., Edn. and Conservation, 1977—; sci. gov. Chgo. Acad. Scis., 1981—; internat. dir. ChimpanZoo, 1984—; trustee Jane Goodall Inst. U.K., 1988—, Jane Goodall Inst. Can., 1993—; adv. bd. Advocates for Animals, Scotland, 1990—, Albert Schweitzer Inst. for Humanities, 1991—, Trees for Life, 1994—, Dolphin Project Internat. and Dolphin Project Europe, 1995—, Fred Found., Netherlands, 1996—, Lab. Primate Advocacy Group, 2001—, Initiative for Animals and Ethics, Harvard U., 2004—, Friends of Africa Internat., 2005—; mem. internat. adv. bd. Tchrs. Without Borders, 2001—; adv. coun. Cin. Zoo, 2005—. Decorated Dame of Brit. Empire, Legion of Honor (France); recipient Franklin Burr award, Nat. Geographic Soc., 1963, 1964, Centennial award, 1988, Hubbard medal, 1995, Conservation award, Women's Br. N.Y. Zool. Soc., 1974, Albert Schweitzer award, Internat. Women's Inst., 1987, Kyoto prize, Inamori Found., 1990, Tanzanian Kilimanjaro medal for Contbn. to Wildlife Conservation, Pres. Mwinyi, 1996, Mt. Kilimanjaro award, 1996, Pub. Svc. award, Nat. Sci. Bd., 1998, John Hay award, Orion Soc., 1998, Huxley Meml. medal, Royal Anthrop. Inst. Gt. Britain and Ireland, 2001, 2002, Gandhi/King award for Non-Violence, 2001, Benjamin Franklin medal in Life Sci., 2003, Prince of Asturias award, 2003, Gandhi/King award, Nierenberg Prize for Sci. in the Pub. Interest, 2004, European Heroes award, Time Mag., 2004, President's Medal for Exemplary Achievement, Westminster Coll., 2005, Natura award, Pax, 2005, Gold medal award, UNESCO, 2006, 2007 Women of Discovery: Lifetime Achievement award, Wings WorldQuest, Lifetime Achievement award, Jules Verne Adventures, 2006, numerous others; named Internat. Patron, Immortal Chaplains Found., 2006. Fellow: Royal Anthropol. Inst. Gt. Britain and Ireland (hon.); mem.: Academia Scientiarium et Artium Europaea Austria, Deutsche Akademie der Naturforscher Leopoldina (Germany), Soc. Women Geographers, Am. Philos. Soc., Rsch. Ctr. for Human Ethology (fgn.), Am. Acad. Arts and Sci. (hon. fgn.) (hon.), Explorer's Club (N.Y.). Achievements include research in in behavior of free-living chimpanzees in the Gombe National Park, Tanzania; social behavior of the spotted hyena, crocutta crocutta Ngorongoro Conservation Area; on behavior of the olive baboon, Papio anub is, Gombe National Park. Business E-Mail: jginformation@janegoodall.org.

GOODE, DAVID RONALD, retired transportation company executive; b. Vinton, Va., Jan. 13, 1941; s. Otto and Hessie M. (Maxey) G.; m. Susan Skiles, June 22, 1963; children: Christina, Martha. AB, Duke U., 1962; JD, Harvard U., 1965; LHD (hon.), Old Dominion U., 2003; DHL (hon.), Roanoke Coll., 2010. With Norfolk & Western Ry., Roanoke, Va., 1965—82, Norfolk Southern Corp., Va., 1982—92, CEO, 1992—2004, chmn., CEO, 2004—05, chmn., 2005—06. Bd. dirs. Caterpillar, Inc., Delta Air Lines, Russell Reynolds Assocs., Tex. Instruments, Inc. Bd. trustees Gen. Douglas MacArthur Meml. Found., Chrysler Mus., Va. Found. Ind. Colls., Thomas Jefferson Found., Miller Ctr.; mem. Am. Soc. Corp. Execs., The Bus. Coun. Mem. Va. State Bar Assn. Democrat. Presbyterian. Avocation: golf. Home: 7301 Woodway Ln Norfolk VA 23505-3149

GOODEN, CLARENCE W., rail transportation executive; BA in Polit. Sci., U. Ga. COO CSX Corp.; former bd. dirs. CSX Transp. Inc. (subs. CSX Corp.); v.p., system transp. CSX Intermodal (subs. CSX Corp.), 1999—2000, pres., 2001—02; sr. v.p., Mdse. Svc. Group CSX Transp. Inc. (subs. CSX Corp.), 2002—04; exec. v.p. CSX Corp., 2004—08, CSX Transp. Inc. (subs. CSX Corp.), 2004—08; chief comml. officer CSX Transportation, Inc., 2004—, CSX Corp., 2004—, exec. v.p., sales, mktg., 2008—, CSX Transportation, Inc., 2008—. Office: CSX Corp 15th Fl 500 Water St Jacksonville FL 32202 Office Phone: 904-359-3200. Office Fax: 904-633-3450. Business E-Mail: clarence.gooden@csx.com.

GOODENBERGER, DANIEL MARVIN, medical educator; b. McCook, Nebr., Apr. 24, 1948; s. Marvin Eugene and Mary Ellen (Marshall) Goodenberger; children: James Michael, Katherine Elizabeth. BS, U. Nebr., Lincoln, 1970; MD, Duke U., Durham, NC, 1974. Diplomate Am. Bd. Internal Medicine, Am. Bd. Emergency Medicine (examiner 1983-95), Am. Bd. Pulmonary Disease, Am. Bd. Critical Care Medicine. Intern Peter Bent Brigham Hosp., Boston, 1974-75, resident in internal medicine, 1975-76; clin. assoc. Nat. Cancer Inst., Bethesda, Md., 1976-78; fellow pulmonary and critical care medicine Boston U. Med. Ctr., 1985-88; assoc. dir. emergency dept. Arlington Hosp., Va., 1979-82; edn. dir. emergency dept. Georgetown U. Hosp., Washington, 1982-85; dir. emergency svcs. U. Hosp., Boston, 1986-87; dir. pulmonary and critical care fellowship Washington U. Med. Schs., St. Louis, 1989-93; dir. pulmonary cons. svcs. Barnes Hosp., St. Louis, 1990-93, dir. internal medicine residency program, 1992—2006; assoc. prof. medicine Washington U., St. Louis, 1995-99; dir. divsn. med. edn. Washington U. Sch. Medicine, 1998—2006, prof. medicine, 1999—2006; prof., chair dept. medicine U. Nev. Sch. Medicine, Las Vegas, 2006—07; chief med. svc. Dallas VAMC, 2008—13; chief med. svcs. St. Louis VAMC, 2013—; prof., vice-chair, dept. medicine U. Tex., Southwestern Sch. Medicine, 2008—13; prof. medicine Wash. U. Sch. Medicine, 2013—. Chief Wood-Moore Firm, Barnes-Jewish Hosp., 1996-2001. Editor Careers, 1996-98. Lt. comdr. USPHS, 1973-78. Winthrop Breon and Am. Coll. Chest Physicians scholar, 1987. Master ACP; fellow Am. Coll. Chest Physicians; mem. AMA, Am. Thoracic Soc., Am. Clin. and Climatological Assn., St. Louis Met. Med. Soc. (councilor 1997-2000), St. Louis Club, Harbor Point Yacht Club, Phi Beta Kappa, Alpha Omega Alpha. Methodist. Avocations: theater, music, travel, sailing. Office: St Louis VAMC 915 N Grand Blvd Saint Louis MO 63106 Home: 3299 Equestrian Dr Festus MO 63028

GOODENOUGH, JOHN BANNISTER, engineering educator, physicist, researcher; b. Jena, Germany, July 25, 1922; came to US, 1922; parents Am. citizens. s. Erwin Ramsdell and Helen Meriam (Lewis) G.; m. Irene Johnston Wiseman, June 16, 1951. AB, Yale U., New Haven, Conn., 1943; MS, U. Chgo., 1951, PhD, 1952; DHC (hon.), U. Bordeaux, France, 1967; MA (hon.), Oxford U., Eng., 1976; DHC (hon.), U. Santiago de Compostela, 2002. Registered profl. engr. Rsch. engr. Westinghouse Rsch. Corp., 1951-52; rsch. scientist, group leader Lincoln Lab., MIT, 1952-76; prof., head inorganic chem. lab. U. Oxford, England, 1976-86; Virginia H. Cockrell Centennial Chair and prof. engring. U. Tex., Austin, 1986—. Trustee, fellow Neuroscis. Rsch. Program, 1962-76; Centenary lectr. Royal Soc. Chemistry, 1976; vis. Raman prof. Indian Inst. Sci., 1983; hon. prof. Northwestern U., Changchun, China, 1996, Jilin U., Shenyang, China, 1996; cons. in field Author: Magnetism and the Chemical Bond, 1963, Les oxydes des métaux de transition, 1973, Witness to Grace, 2008; assoc. editor Materials Rsch. Bull., 1966—, Jour. Solid State Chemistry, 1968—, Structure and Bonding, 1977—, Solid State Ionics, 1980—, Superconductor Sci. and Tech., 1987, Jour. Materials Chem., 1991—, Chem. of Materials, 1989-92; mem. editl. bd. Jour. Applied Electrochemistry, 1982-89, European Jour. Solid State and Inorganic chemistry, 1992; contbr. articles to profl. jours., chpts. to books. Capt. USAAF, 1942-48. Recipient Solid State Chemistry prize Chem. Soc. UK, 1980, Hon. mem. World Innovation Found., 2002, Fgn. mem., Academia de Ciencias Exactas, Físicas y Naturales, Spain, 2003, Hocott award U. Tex. Austin Coll. Engring., 2001-2002, Enrico Fermi award, 2009, Foreign Member Royal Society (UK), 2010; Inventor of the Yr. award, UT Austin Office of Tech. Commercialization, 2011; UT Mech. Engring. Acad. Disting. Alumni award, 2012; IEEE Medal for Environ. and Safety Technologies, 2012; medal Nat. Acad. Sci., 2012; Nat. medal Sci., 2011; Nat. Alliance for Advanced Tech. Batteries Lifetime Achievement award, 2012. Fellow AAAS, Royal Soc. London (fgn. mem.), Royal Soc. Chemistry, Am. Phys. Soc. (profl.), Indian Acad. Scis. (fgn. assoc.), NAE(co-recipient Charles Stark Draper prize for Engineering, 2014), NAS, Acad. Scis. L'Inst. France (fgn. assoc.), Royal Soc. (London) (fgn. mem.), Materials Rsch. Soc. (hon.), Acad. Sci. Exactas, Fisicas y Naturales (fgn. assoc.); mem. Am. Chem. Soc., Materials Rsch. Soc. (Von Hippel award 1989), Japanese Phys. Soc., Ashmolean Club (Oxford), Skull and Bones, Phi Beta Kappa, Sigma Xi Episcopalian. Achievements include discovery of cathode materials for lithium rechargable batteries. Office: Department of Mechanical Engineering University of Texas at Austin ETC 9.184 204 E Dean Keeton St Stop C2200 Austin TX 78712-1591 Office Phone: 512-471-1646. Business E-Mail: jgoodenough@mail.utexas.edu.

GOODGAME, GORDON CLIFTON, retired minister; b. Jones County, Miss., Oct. 8, 1934; s. J. Clyde and Eloise Hertha (Smith) G.; m. Dianne Fraser, July 29, 1961; children: Gordon Clifton Jr., Gregory Carson, Cathey. BS in Law and Bus., U. Tenn., 1955; MDiv, Emory U., 1958; STM, San Francisco Theol. Sem., 1970, STD, 1974. Sr. min. 1st United Meth. Ch., Pulaski, Va., 1973-74; leader devel. cons. Holston Conf. Coun. Ministries, Johnson City, Tenn., 1974-77; sr. min. 1st United Meth. Ch., Oak Ridge, Tenn., 1977-81, 1st-Centenary United Meth. Ch., Chattanooga, 1981-90; dir. Holston Conf. Coun. Ministries, Johnson City, 1990-93; exec. dir. Southeastern Jurisdictional Adminstrv. Coun., Lake Junaluska, NC, 1994—2000. Del. United Meth. Gen. Conf., 1976, 80, 84, 88, 92, 96, Southeastern Jurisdictional Conf., United Meth. Ch., 1972, 76, 80, 84, 88, 92, 96, 2000; dir. United Meth. Bd. Global Ministries, NYC, 1980-88; mem. World Meth. Coun., 1986-96, United Meth. Gen. Coun. Ministries, 1992-2000. Bd. dirs. Chattanooga United Way, 1983-89, Hospice Chattanooga, 1982-90; trustee Hiwassee Coll., Madisonville, Tenn., 1979-90, pres. bd. trustees, 1989-90; trustee Meth. Med. Ctr. Oak Ridge, 1977-81. Mem. Emory U. Alumni Assn. (bd. govs.), Candler Sch. Theology Alumni Assn. (pres., Svc. award 1992), Rotary (sgt. at arms 1989-90) Givens Estates CCRC Bd., 2006-. Democrat. Home: 2775 S Lakeshore Dr Lake Junaluska NC 28745-8709 Personal E-mail: ggoodgame@charter.net.

GOODING, CHARLES THOMAS, psychologist, educator, retired academic administrator; b. Tampa, Fla., Nov. 18, 1931; s. Charles T. and Gladys (Bingman) G.; m. Shirley Ann Puckett, June 7, 1953; children: Steven Thomas, Carol Ann, David Lee, Mark Charles. BA, U. Fla., 1954, M.Ed., 1962, Ed.D., 1964; postgrad., U. Tampa, 1956-58. Tchr. Meml. Sch., Tampa, 1956-58; asst. prin., then prin. St. Mary's Sch., Tampa, 1958-62; grad. fellow U. Fla., Gainesville, 1962-63, instr., 1963-64; assoc. prof., then prof. SUNY, Oswego, 1964-79, prof. psychology, 1980-98, assoc. dean grad. studies, 1982-89, dean grad. studies and rsch., 1989-95, provost, v.p. for acad. affairs, 1995-98, emeritus, 1998—. Vis. prof. U. Liverpool, Eng., 1979-80; mem. SUNY Chancellor's Task Force on Tchr. Edn., 1984. Author: Learning Theories in Educational Practice, 1971; contbg. author: Florida Studies in the Helping Professions, 1969, Questioning and Discussion: A Multidisciplinary Study, 1988, Research Matters to the Science Teacher, 1992; contbr. articles to profl. jours. Trustee U. of South, 2002-05; bd. dirs. Oswego Coll. Found., 1996-2011, Bishop Gray Inns Found., 2008-. Served to 1st lt. USAR, 1954-56. SUNY Rsch. Found. grantee, 1966, 69-70, NY State Dept. Edn. grantee, 1971-72, 88-94, NSF grantee, 1980-81, 85-88, 90-95. Mem. APA, Ea. Ednl. Rsch. Assn. (v.p. 1979-81, treas., dir. 1983-85, pres.-elect 1987-88, pres. 1989-91, editl. bd. 1991-2000), Am. Ednl. Rsch. Assn. (chair ednl. enterprises SIG, 1994-96). Home: 3730 Cadbury Cir #301 Venice FL 34293 Personal E-mail: tgooding3730@comcast.net.

GOODLATTE, ROBERT WILLIAM (BOB GOODLATTE), United States Representative from Virginia, lawyer; b. Holyoke, Mass., Sept. 22, 1952; m. Maryellen Flaherty, 1974; children: Jennifer, Robert. BA in Govt., Bates Coll., Lewiston, Maine, 1974; JD, Washington & Lee U. Sch. Law, Lexington, Va., 1977. Bar: Mass. 1977, Va. 1978, US Ct. Appeals (4th cir.) 1981. Dist. mgr. to Rep. M.

Caldwell Butler US House of Representatives, 1977—79; pvt. law practice Roanoke, Va., 1979—81; ptnr. Bird, Kinder & Huffman, Roanoke, 1981—93; mem. US Congress from 6th Va. Dist., 1993—; chmn. US House Agrl. Com., 2003—07, ranking mem., 2007—08; vice ranking mem. US House Judiciary Com., 2009—10, chmn., 2013—. Mem. adv. bd. United Way Roanoke Valley, 1988—92; chmn. Roanoke City Rep. Com., 1980—83; chmn. 6th Congressional Dist. Republican Party Va., 1983—88. Republican. Avocations: tennis, swimming, hiking, reading. Office: US House of Representatives 2309 Rayburn House Office Bldg Washington DC 20515 also: 10 Franklin Rd SE Ste 540 Roanoke VA 24011 Office Phone: 202-225-5431.*

GOODMAN, BARRY MICHAEL, lawyer; b. LA, Nov. 22, 1946; s. Ralph Arthur and Natalie Bell (Hamburger) Goodman; m. Susan Lynn Reigrod, June 18, 1969; children: Gregory, Alison. BA in History, Calif. State U., 1967; JD, U. Southern Calif., 1970. Bar: Calif. 1971, DC 1972. Sr. atty. Office of Chief Counsel, Urban Mass Transp. Adminstrn., Washington, 1971—74; dir. Office Pub. Transp., City of Houston, 1974—78; exec. dir. Met. Transit Authority, Houston, 1978—79; pres. Goodman Corp., Houston, 1979—. Mem.: ABA, Transp. Research Bd., Urban Land Inst., DC Bar Assn., Calif. Bar Assn. Jewish. Office: Goodman Corp 3200 TravisSt Ste 200 Houston TX 77006 Office Phone: 713-951-7951.

GOODMAN, BRUCE, insurance company executive; Degree in Elec. Engring., NYU; postgrad., Stanford U. CLU, chartered fin. cons. CEO C2K Tech. Ptnrs., Inc., Livingston, NJ; sr. v.p., chief info. officer MetLife Ins. Co.; pres., corp. svcs. Prudential Ins. Co.; CEO Prudential Svc. Co.; sr. v.p., chief info. officer Humana, Inc., 1999—2002, sr. v.p., chief svc. and info. officer, 2002—. Office: Humana Inc 500 W Main St Louisville KY 40202 Office Phone: 502-580-1000. Office Fax: 502-580-3639. Business E-Mail: bgoodman@humana.com.

GOODMAN, HERBERT IRWIN, petroleum company executive; b. Pitts., Mar. 11, 1923; s. Meyer Irwin and Bessie (Crossof) G.; m. Mary Katherine Schilken, Aug. 12, 1978; children: Michael Christopher, Anne Katheryn, Nancy Hjortshoj, Sara Elizabeth, Mary Elien. BS, U. Pitts., 1943; cert., U. Besancon, 1945; MBA, Harvard U., 1949, AM, 1950. Commd. officer U.S. Fgn. Svc., 1951; served in U.S. Embassy, Copenhagen, 1951-53, Vietnam, 1953-54, U.S. Fgn. Service, Kampuchea, 1954-55; intelligence rsch. officer Dept. State, 1956-57; with Gulf Oil Corp., 1957-84, coord. European sales London, 1957-59; gen. mgr. Pacific Gulf Oil, Tokyo, 1960-64, coord. crude oil dept. Pitts., 1964-66, coord. Far East, 1966-70; pres. Gulf Oil Co. South Asia, Singapore, 1970-72, Gulf Oil Trading Co., Pitts., 1972-80, Gulf Trading and Transp. Co., Houston, 1980-84, GOTCO USA, Inc., Houston, 1984-87, SARMAR LLC, Houston, 1987—; chmn. bd. Applied Trading Sys., Houston, 1988-96, IQ Holdings, Inc., Houston, 1996—2004, pepex.net LLC, 2000—05. Bd. dirs. Houston Livestock Show and Rodeo, Brazil Ethanol, Nanodynamics. Chmn. internat. adv. bd. Tex. A&M U.; bd. dirs. U. St. Thomas Ctr. Faith and Culture. 1st lt. U.S. Army, 1943-46. Decorated Bronze Star; médaille de la Réconnaissance (France). Mem. Am. Petroleum Inst., Coun. on Fgn. Rels., Assn. Internat. Petroleum Negotiators, Harvard Club (N.Y.C.), Racquet Club, Petroleum Club(Houston). Office: SARMAR LLC 510 Bering Dr Ste 300 Houston TX 77057 Business E-Mail: herbg@pepex.net.

GOODMAN, JERRY L(YNN), judge; b. Mangum, Okla., Apr. 17, 1939; s. A.O. and Viola Louise (Bogart) G.; m. Donna K. Rudy, Dec. 16, 1961; children: Courtney L., Polly K., Mallory E., Benjamin R. BA, U. Tulsa, 1961; JD, Georgetown U., 1964. Bar: Okla. 1964. Law clk. antitrust divsn. Dept. Justice, 1962-63; legis. asst. to U.S. Senator J. Howard Edmondson, 1963-64; assoc. David M. Thornton Atty.-at-Law, 1964-65; asst. city atty. City of Tulsa, Okla., 1965-68; ptnr. Owens & Goodman, Tulsa, 1968-70; gen. counsel OTASCO Stores, Tulsa, 1970-74, v.p., gen. counsel, 1974-85, chmn., CEO, 1985-89; spl. counsel Bank of Okla., 1989-90; pres., gen. counsel The Sigma Asset Mgmt. Group, Inc., 1991-92; sec. policy and mgmt., COO Office of Gov., State of Okla., Tulsa, 1992-94; judge Okla. Ct. Civil Appeals, Tulsa, 1994—; chmn. Okla. Bldg. Bds. Commn. Bd. dirs. United Way, 1984—87; chmn., bd. trustees Univ. Ctr. at Tulsa, 1992. Lt. USNR, 1964—70. Mem.: Tulsa County Bar Assn. (v.p. 1971), Okla. Bar Assn., Okla. Jud. Conf. (pres. 2001), Tulsa C. of C. (chmn. 1988). Presbyterian. Office: Okla Ct Civil Appeals 601 State Office Bldg 440 S Houston Ave Tulsa OK 74127-8922 Office Phone: 918-581-2711. Personal E-mail: jlrgoodman1@gmail.com.

GOODMAN, KENNETH LEIGH, state legislator; m. Cindy Shelley Goodman; children: Kenneth L. Goodman, Jr., Kristy McChesney. AA, Wingate U.; BS, Fla. State U. Treas., chmn. Found. of First Health Bd. of Trustees Investment Com.; adv. bd. mem. Centura Bank Local; chmn. First Health Richmond Meml. Hosp. Found.; mem. Found. of First Health Bd. of Trustees, Cole Found. Scholarship Com., Rockingham Parking Authority, Rockingham Rotary Club; chmn. Wingate U. Bus. Affairs Com.; pres. R.W. Goodman, Co., Inc., Rockingham, NC; first pres. Rockingham Downtown Corp.; founder Richmond Transitional Sch.; bd. dirs. First Southern Savings Bank, Richmond County C. of C., Richmond Cmty. Coll. Found.; trustee Richmond Meml. Hosp., Wingate U.; CFO Richmond Yarns Inc., 1990—2009; chmn. Richmond County Bd. of Edn. Accomplishments, 2008; mem. Dist. 66 NC House of Representatives, 2011—. Democrat. Office: 832 Williamsburg Dr Rockingham NC 28379 Address: North Carolina House of Representatives 16 N Jones St Room 1111 Raleigh NC 27601-1096 Office Phone: 919-733-5823, 910-997-2712. Business E-Mail: Ken.Goodman@ncleg.net.

GOODMAN, SEYMOUR EVAN, computer science and international studies educator, researcher, consultant; b. Chgo., June 19, 1943; s. Paul S. and Shirley (Young) G.; m. Diane Margot Samuel, Dec. 18, 1966; children: Richard Michael, Steven Neal. BS, Columbia U., 1965, MS, 1966; PhD, Calif. Inst. Tech., 1970. Asst. prof. applied math. U. Va., Charlottesville, 1970-75, assoc. prof. applied math. and computer sci., 1975-81; prof. mgmt. info. sys. U. Ariz., Tucson, 1981—2000; prof. Sam Nunn Sch. Internat. Affairs Coll. of Computing, Ga. Inst. of Tech., Atlanta, 1999—; co-dir. Ctr. Internat. Strategy Tech. and Policy, 2000—, Ga. Tech. Info. Security Ctr., 2000—. Vis. prof. pub. and internat. affairs, Princeton U., NJ, 1977-79, rsch. fellow, 1978-79; vis. scholar U. Chgo., 1979; mem. Mid. Ea. Ctr., 1992-00; Carnegie Sci. fellow Ctr. Internat. Security and Arms Control, Stanford U., 1994-97; dir. program info. tech. and nat. security, 1996-98, dir. Consortium for Rsch. on Info. Security and Policy, Stanford U., 1998-2000, vis. prof. dept. engring. econ. sys. and ops. rsch., 1998-99; mem. adv. com. Internat. Trade Adminstrn., Dept. Commerce, 1979-82; mem. adv. com. Def. Sci. Bd., Dept. Def., 1981-84, Def. Intelligence Agy., 1983-87, NRC coms., 1985-92, Dept. State, 1987-89; chmn. NRC com. Internat. Devel. in Computer Sci. and Tech., 1987-88; chmn. computer tech.-subpanel NRC panel on Future Design and Implementation of US Nat. Security Export Controls, 2005-07, chmn. NRC Com. on Improving Cybersecurity Rsch. in the US, 2005-07; cons. govtl. agys. Danforth Assoc., 1977-82; Sesquicentennial Assoc. State of Va., 1977; mem. telecom study panel US Dept. Def., 2003-04, chmn. Com. on cybersecurity rsch. in US, NRC. Editor: Technology and Transnational Political Issues, International Information Systems, 1991-93; adv. bd. PRIISM, 1995-97; adv. editor Jour. Global Info. Tech. Mgmt., 1997-2000; mem. editl. bd. Jour. Info. Tech. in Internat. Devel., 2002-; contbr. numerous articles to profl. jours. NSF grantee, 1978-79, 83, 2001-; numerous grant and rsch. contracts Office Tech. Assessment, U.S. Congress, MacArthur Found., 2003-, Los Alamos Nat. Lab., USAF, Battelle Meml. Labs., IBM, Nat. Coun. for Soviet and East European Rsch., Dept. Commerce, Dept. Def., NSF; U.S. participant U.S.-USSR IREX program, 1988-89. Mem. Assn. for Computing Machinery (nat. lectr. 1981-82, com. computing and pub. policy 1981-83, 93—, contbg. editor Internat. Perspectives, Comms. 1991—), Am. Assn. for Advancement of Slavic Studies, Computer Soc. of IEEE (com. on pub. policy 1987-95), Highlands Forum. Office: Sam Nunn Sch Internat Affairs Coll Computing Ga Inst Tech 781 Marietta Ave NW Atlanta GA 30332-0610 Home Phone: 770-455-7554; Office Phone: 404-385-1461. Business E-Mail: goodman@cc.gatech.edu.

GOODMAN, TOBY RAY, lawyer; b. Wichita Falls, Tex., Nov. 2, 1948; s. Johnnie U. and Opal E. (Johnson) G.; m. Lisa C. Schrader, Sept. 14, 1967 (div. 1982); children: Brian Scott, Lauri Ann; m. Gloria Jean Majors, June 14, 1983; 1 child, Christie Louise. BBA, Tex. Christian U., 1971; JD, Baylor U., 1974. Bar: Tex. 1974, U.S. Dist. Ct. (no. dist.) Tex. 1974, U.S. Ct. Appeals (5th cir.) 1977. Asst. city atty. City of Arlington, Tex., 1974-76; ptnr. Remington & Goodman, Arlington, 1976-84, Goodman & Clark, Arlington, 1984—; state rep. State of Tex. Dist. 93, 1990—. Chair Tarrant 2000 Civil Justice, 1989-90; mem. Rep. Caucus Tex. Ho. Reps. Fellow Tex. Bar Found.; mem. Arlington Bar Assn. (dir.), Tarrant County Bar Assn. (dir.); vice chair house comm. Juvenile and Family Issues. Baptist. Office: Goodman & Clark 1600 E Lamar Blvd Ste 250 Arlington TX 76011-4588 Home: 1 Hidden Lake Ct Mansfield TX 76063-5466 Office Phone: 817-460-8171. E-mail: toby@goodmanclark.com.

GOODMAN, TODD, former political organization administrator; Attended, Drew U., Madison, NJ. Formerly with Johnson & Johnson, W. Lorenz Surgical Inc., 2003—05; ops. positions INDN's List, Tulsa, Okla., 2005; field dir. to rep. Andrew Rice Okla. Senate, 2005—06; field dir. Dem. Nat. Com., 2007—08; exec. dir. Okla. Dem. Party, 2008—, comm. dir., 2009, chmn., 2009—11; vice chair Caddo Nation of Okla., 2009—. Democrat. Office: Caddo Nation PO Box 487 Binger OK 73009 Office Phone: 405-427-3366. Office Fax: 405-427-1310.

GOODNIGHT, JAMES H., information technology executive; b. Wilmington, NC, Jan. 6, 1943; m. Ann Goodnight; 3 children. PhD in Statistics, NC State U. Faculty NC State U., 1972-76; co-founder, chmn. SAS Inst. Inc., pres. & CEO Cary, NC, 1976—. Adj. prof. N.C. State U., 1976—. Started SAS inSchool; founder Cary Acad., Cary, NC, 1996. Named one of Forbes 400: Richest Americans, 1999—, World's Richest People, Forbes mag., 2001—, 20th Century's Great Am. Bus. Leaders, Harvard Bus. Sch., 2004, Am.'s 25 Most Fascinating Entrepreneurs, Inc. mag., 2004. Fellow Am. Statis. Assn. Office: SAS Institute Inc 100 SAS Campus Dr Cary NC 27513-2414 Office Fax: 919-677-4444. Business E-Mail: james.goodnight@sas.com.

GOODPASTURE, PHILIP HENRY, lawyer; b. Lisbon, Portugal, Sept. 16, 1960; s. Henry McKennie and Ellen Ingabor (Moller) G.; m. Paige Everett Hargroves, June 25, 1994. BA with high distinction, U. Va., 1982, JD, 1985. Bar: Va. 1985, U.S. Dist. Ct. (ea. dist.) Va. 1985. Assoc. Christian & Barton and predecessor firm, Richmond, Va., 1985-92, ptnr., 1993—2004, vice-chmn. corp. team, 1994-97, mem. exec. com., 1998; ptnr. Williams, Mullen, P.C., 2004—. Dir. Va. League for Planned Parenthood, Richmond, 1989-95, Venture Richmond, 1993-2001, Read to Them, 2006-08, Va. Found. CC Edn., 2008-13, Richmond Fourm, 2010-, Seven Hills Sch., 2011-; mem. Leadership Metro Richmond, 1994, Leadership Devel. Coun. ARC, 1995, World Pediat. Project, 2012-; mem. vestry St. Thomas Episc. Ch., 2007-09. Mem. Va. Bar Assn., Richmond Bar Assn. Office: Williams Mullen 200 S 10th St Ste 1600 Richmond VA 23219 Office Phone: 804-420-6904. Business E-Mail: pgoodpasture@williamsmullen.com.*

GOODRICH, THOMAS MICHAEL, engineering and construction executive, lawyer; b. Milan, Tenn., Apr. 28, 1945; s. Henry Calvin and Billie Grace (Walker) Goodrich; m. Gillian Comer White, Dec. 28, 1968; children: Michael, Braxton, Charles, Grace. BSCE, Tulane U., 1968; JD, U. Ala., 1971. Bar: Ala. 1971. From various mgmt. positions to chmn. & CEO BE & K, Inc., Birmingham, Ala., 1989—95, pres., CEO, 1995—, chmn. bd. dir., 2003—08; pres. Goodrich Mgmt. Co. Bd. dirs. First Comml. Bank, Energen Corp., Birmingham, Synovus Fin. Corp., Columbus, Ga., Altec Inc., Birmingham. With Elsenhowen Exchg. Fellow; exe. bd. Boy Scouts America. Capt. US Army, 1970—72. Office: Goodrich Mgmt Co 3800 Colo Pkwy Ste 430 Birmingham AL 35243

GOODSELL, CHARLES TRUE, public administration educator, researcher; b. July 23, 1932; BA, Kalamazoo Coll., 1954; MPA, Harvard U., 1958, MA, 1959, PhD, 1961. Asst. prof. U. P.R., Rio Piedras, 1961-64; prof. So. Ill. U., Carbondale, 1966-78; prof. pub. adminstrn. Va. Tech., Blacksburg, 1978—2002, prof. emeritus, 2002—. Author: Administration of A Revolution, 1965, American Corporations and Peruvian Politics, 1974, The Public Encounter, 1981, The Social Meaning of Civic Space, 1988, Public Administration Illuminated and Inspired by the Arts, 1995, The American Statehouse, 2001, The Case for Bureaucracy, 4th edit., 2004, Mission Mystique, 2011, The New Case for Bureaucracy, 2014. Recipient Waldo award, Am. Soc. Pub. Adminstrn., 2003; named to Nat. Acad. of Pub. Admin., 1994. Personal E-mail: goodsell@vt.edu.

GOODSON, COURTNEY HUDSON, state supreme court justice; BA magna cum laude, U. Ark., Fayetteville, 1994; JD with high honors, U. Ark., 1997. Law clk. to Judge Frank Arey Ark. Ct. Appeals, 1997—99, law clk. to Judge Terry Crabtree, 1999—2005, judge, 2008—10; assoc. justice Ark. Supreme Ct., Little Rock, 2010—. Liaison to the client security com. and the com. on security and emergency preparedness Ark. Supreme Ct. Mem.: Ark. Assn. Women Lawyers, Ark. Bar Assn., Pulaski County Bar Assn., Washington County Bar Assn., Benton County Bar Assn., Phi Beta Kappa. Office: Arkansas Supreme Court Justice Building 625 Marshall St Little Rock AR 72201 Office Phone: 501-682-6849.*

GOODSON, DOROTHY MOORE, English educator, counselor; b. NC; children: Gina G. Kane, Northington V. BS, Hampton U., 1964, MA, 1970; EdD, Va. Poly. Inst. and State U., 1986. Lic. profl. counselor Va., 75, nat. cert. counselor 1985, realtor. English instr. Hampton City Schs., Va., 1964—69; English and reading instr. Upward Bound Program Hampton U., 1968—76; counselor, guidance dir. Hampton City Schs., 1969—83; supr. Center '70, Coll. Admissions Testing Program, Hampton, 1976—81; English instr. Thomas Nelson CC, Hampton, 1979—82; ins. agent, 1980—82; prof. counselor Norfolk State U., 1983—87, asst. dean student devel., 1987—89, asst. prof., profl. counselor Va., 1983—92, dir. upward bound program, 1989—92; dir. freshman studies, honors, and retention Saint Paul's Coll., Lawrenceville, Va., 1995—97, dir. Ctr. Academic Support Svcs. Spl. Testing, 1997—2001, mem. tchr. Edn. Com. Acad. Comm., chair coun., mem. Strategic Planning Comm., co-chmn., chaiperson freshman studies. Mem. bd. dir. Insight Enterprises Transition Ctr., 1985; mem. First Baptist Ch. East End, Newport News. Recipient Nat. Disting. Svc. Registry award, 1989—90. Mem.: NAACP, NEA (life), Nat. Coun. Negro Women, Va. Edn. Assn., Nat. Assn. for Female Execs., Assn. Measurement and Evaluation in Counseling and Devel., Am. Assn. Counseling and Devel., Delta Sigma Theta Sorority, Kappa Delta Pi Honor Soc. Avocations: reading, music, gardening. Home: PO Box 3349 Hampton VA 23663-0349 Office Phone: 757-719-1641.

GOODSON, TOM, state legislator; b. Marianna, Fla., Feb. 16, 1951; m. Evelyn Watson Goodson; children: Travis, Lindsey. Grad., Brevard CC, Cocoa, Fla.; BS, Fla. State U., Tallahassee, 1975. Road contractor Goodson Paving; mem. Canaveral Port Authority, 2002—10, chmn., 2006—10; mem. Dist 29 Fla. House of Representatives, 2011—. Baptist. Office: 400 South St Ste 1C Titusville FL 32780-5151 also: Fla House of Reps 1101 The Capitol 402 S Monroe St Tallahassee FL 32399-3006 Office Phone: 321-383-5151, 850-488-3006.

GOODSPEED, LINDA A., automotive executive; BS in Mech. Engring., Mich. State U., 1984, MBA, 1989. Engr. Ford Motor Co., 1984—89; various positions General Electric Co., 1996—2001, range product devel. mgr., 1997—99, gen. mgr., Six Sigma divsn., 1999, product gen. mgr., GE Appliances, 1999—2001; pres., COO Partminer, Inc., 2001—02; exec. v.p., chief tech. officer Lennox Internat., Richardson, Tex., 2002—07; with R&D dept. Nissan, 1989—96, v.p., Info. Sys., chief info. officer, Americas, 2008—. Bd. dirs. Am. Electric Power, Columbus McKinnon Corp. Named one of Premier 100 IT Leaders, Computerworld mag., 2007. Office: Nissan 1 Nissan Way Franklin TN 37067 Office Phone: 615-725-1000. Office Fax: 615-725-3343. Business E-Mail: linda.goodspeed@nissan-usa.com.

GOODSTEIN, BARNETT MAURICE, lawyer; b. Dallas, Oct. 1, 1921; s. Arthur Louis and Viola Esther (Levy) G.; m. Mira Brodsky, Jan. 26, 1947; children: Pamela Renee, Heather Ann, Robin Leslie. Student, Rice Inst., 1938—40; BA, MA, U. Tex., 1942; postgrad., U. Wis., 1949—51; JD, So. Meth. U., 1957. Bar: Tex. 1957, U.S. Dist. Ct. (no. dist.) Tex. 1963, U.S. Supreme Ct. Acting dir. case analysis Wage Stblzn. Bd., Dallas, 1951-53; practice of law Dallas, 1957—; pres. Goodstein & Starr, P.C., 1977-91, Goodstein, Starr & Pascoe, P.C., 1991—95; adminstrv. law judge City of Dallas, 1994—95; pvt. practice, 1995—. Lectr. econs. So. Meth. U., Dallas, 1946-48, 51-60; lectr. Massey Realty Coll., Real Estate Inst., Dallas; labor arbitrator, 1953—; former permanent arbitrator City of San Antonio, Police Officers' Assn.; mem. permanent arbitration panel Tinker AFB, Okla., 1984-88, Am. Fedn. Govt. Employees, 1984-90, SW Bell Tel., AT&T, CWA, IBEW, 1988—, FAA, 1993—, Nat. Assn. Air Traffic Specialists, 1994—, Ga. Pacific, 1994—, UPIU, 1994—, U.S. Customs and BP, 2001--, also various VA Med. Facilities, paper and copper industries, others; mem. permanent panel Dallas Area Rapid Transit Sys., 1988-90, 94-96; adminstrv. law judge City of Dallas, 1994-96. Hearing officer work suspensions appeals bd. City of Dallas, 1981-83; trustee Dallas County Sch. Bd., 1980-2005, v.p., 1990-91, 2003-2005; past trustee Temple Emanu-El; mem. legal representation com. Nat. Acad. Arbitrators, 1992-96, chmn. legal affairs com. 1997-99. Served with USAAF, 1942-46, China, 1945-46 Mem.: ABA, Am. Arbitration Assn. (Southwestern adv. coun. 1985—92), Indsl. Rels. Rsch. Assn. (pres. North Tex. chpt. 1985—86, neutral mem. bd. dirs. North Tex. chpt. 1990—92), Nat. Acad. Arbitrators (chmn. S.W. region 1987—88), Tex. Bar Assn. Home: 7750 LBJ Freeway 112 Dallas TX 75251-1288 Personal E-mail: bgoodmb@gmail.com.

GOODWIN, FRANK ERIK, materials engineer; b. Bethlehem, Pa., Jan. 6, 1954; s. Francis Black and Grethe Julie (Andresen) G.; m. Rosalind Ann Volpe, May 30, 1987; children: Adrian Edmond, Marianna Rose. BS, Cornell U., 1975; ScD, MIT, 1979. Plant engr. Chambersburg (Pa.) Engring. Co., 1979-80; devel. dir. Chromalloy Rsch. & Tech., Orangeburg, NY, 1980-82; mgr. devel. Internat. Lead Zinc Rsch. Orgn., Research Triangle Park, NC, 1982-84, mgr. metallurgy, 1984-86, v.p. materials sci., 1986—2004, exec. v.p., 2004—; dir. tech., mktg. devel. Internat. Zinc Assn., Brussels, 2004—. Mem. peer review com. on lead Dept. Energy, Washington, 1987-89. Author: Galfan Galvanizing Alloy & Technology, 1984; editor: Stress Calculations for Zinc Die Castings, 1988, Engineering Properties of Zinc Alloys, 1988; contbr. articles to profl. jours., chpts. to books. Mem. ASM, N.Am. Die Casting Assn. (rsch. com.), N.Y. Acad. Scis. Republican. Episcopalian. Achievements include patents (with other) for new aluminum alloy, new lead alloy for batteries. Office: International Lead Zinc Research Org 1822 E Nc Highway 54 Ste 120 Durham NC 27713-3210

GOODWIN, JEAN MCCLUNG, psychiatrist; b. Pueblo, Colo., Mar. 28, 1946; d. Paul Stanley and Geraldine (Smart) McClung; m. James Simeon Goodwin, Aug. 8, 1970; children: Laura (dec.), Amanda Harding Goodwin, Robert Caleb, Paul Joshua, Elizabeth Cronin Goodwin. BA in Anthropology summa cum laude, Radcliffe Coll., 1967; MD, Harvard U., 1971; MPH, UCLA, 1972. Diplomate Am. Bd. Psychiatry and Neurology, Am. Bd. Forensic Psychiatry, cert. adult psychoanalysis Am. Psychoanalytic Assn., tng. and supervising analyst. Resident in psychiatry Georgetown U. Hosp., Washington, 1972-74, U. N.Mex. Sch. Medicine, 1974-76, asst. dir., dir. psychiat. residents tng., 1979-85; prof. Med. Coll. Wis., 1985-92, U. Tex. Med. Br., Galveston, 1992-98, prof. clin. psychiatry, 1998—; pvt. practice in gen. psychiatry, psychoanalysis. From instr. to assoc. prof. dept. psychiatry U. N.Mex. Sch. Medicine, 1976-85; cons. protective services Dept. Human Services, N.Mex., 1976-84; faculty Ctr. Psychoanalytic Studies, Houston, 1999—, tng. analyst, 2011; founding bd. dirs. Houston-Galveston Trauma Inst.; lectr. in field Author: Effects of High Altitude on Human Birth, 1969, Sexual Abuse: Incest Victims and Their Families, 1982, 2d edit., 1989, Rediscovering Childhood Trauma: Historical Casebook and Clinical Applications, 1993, Mischief and Mercy, 1993; co-author (with Reina Attias) Splintered Reflections: Images of the Body in Trauma, 1999; mem. editl. bd. Jour. Traumatic Stress, 1985-93, Dissociation, 1988-98, Psychotherapy Rev., 1998-2000, Trauma and Dissociation, 2000—; contbr. articles to profl. jours. Chmn. work group on child sexual abuse Surgeon Gen.'s Conf. on Violence and Pub. Health, Leesburg, Va., 1985; mem. adv. bd. Nat. Resource Ctr. on Child Sexual Abuse, 1989-96. Recipient Esther Haar award Am. Acad. Psychoanalysis, 1990, Cornelia Wilbur award Internat. Soc. for Study of Dissociation, 1994; Nat. Cen. Child Abuse and Neglect grantee, 1979-82, Nat. Inst. Aging grantee, 1980-85. Fellow Internat. Soc. Study Dissociation (exec. com. 1991-96), Am. Psychiat. Assn. (dist. br. treas., sec. N.Mex. br. 1980-82, exhibits and programs subcoms. 1985-91; Best Drs. in America, 1994-2013). Democrat. Roman Catholic. Office: 4925 Fort Crockett Blvd Apt 510 Galveston TX 77551-5949 Office Phone: 409-762-1101. Personal E-mail: jmgoodwin@aol.com.

GOODWIN, JOSEPH ROBERT, federal judge; b. Ripley, W.Va., 1942; BS, W.Va. U., 1965; JD, W.Va. U. Coll. Law, 1970. Bar: W.Va. 1970. Ptnr. Goodwin & Goodwin, Charleston, W.Va., 1970-95; city atty. City of Ripley, 1971—72, mcpl. judge, 1972—73; judge US Dist. Ct. (so. dist.) W.Va., 1995—, chief judge, 2007—. Mem. bd. advisors W.Va. U., 1981—86; bd. visitors W.Va. U. Coll. Law, 1995—98.

Served with JAGC US Army, 1965—67. Mem.: ABA, Jackson County Bar Assn., W.Va. State Bar Assn., Order of Coif. Office: 7009 Robert C Byrd US Courthouse 300 Virginia St E Charleston WV 25301 Office Phone: 304-347-3192.

GOODWIN, ROBERT BOOTH, II, federal prosecutor; b. Charleston, W.Va., 1971; BS in Economics cum laude, W.Va. U., 1993; JD, Washington & Lee U., 1996. Bar: W.Va. 1996, Supreme Ct. of Appeals of W.Va. 1996, US Dist. Ct. (southern dist.) W.Va. 1996, US Ct. Appeals (4th cir.) 1997, US Dist. Ct. (northern dist.) W.Va. 2000, US Ct. Appeals (2nd cir.) 2006. Summer law clk. Goodwin & Goodwin, LLP, Charleston, W.Va., 1994, 1995, atty., 1996—2001; asst. US atty. (southern dist.) W.Va. US Dept. Justice, Charleston, W.Va., 2001—10, US atty., 2010—. Bd. mem. Legal Aid Soc. of Charleston (now Legal Aid of W.Va.), 1999—2001. Bd. mem. Friends of Sunrise Mus., Charleston, W.Va., 1999—2001. Mem.: ABA, US Ct. Appeals, Forth Cir. Judicial Conf., Judge John A. Field, Jr. American Inn of Ct., W.Va. Bar Assn., W.Va. U. Alumni Assn. (life). Office: US Attorney's Office PO Box 1713 Charleston WV 25326 Office Phone: 304-345-2200. Office Fax: 304-347-5104.*

GOODWYN, S. BERNARD, state supreme court justice; b. Va., 1961; s. Sam and Dolly Goodwyn; m. Sharon Smith; children: Samuel Jared, Sarah Elizabeth. BA in Econs., Harvard U., Cambridge, Mass.; JD, U. Va. Sch. Law. Ptnr. Willcox & Savage; rsch. assoc. prof. law U. Va. Sch. Law, 1994—95; judge Gen. Dist. Ct., Va., 1995—97, 1st Jud. Cir. Ct., Chesapeake, Va., 1997—2007; assoc. justice Va. Supreme Ct., 2007—. Mem.: Va. Bar Assn. Office: Supreme Ct Va PO Box 1315 100 N Ninth St Richmond VA 23219-1315*

GOOLKASIAN, PAULA A., psychologist, educator; b. Methuen, Mass., Aug. 9, 1948; d. Paul K. and Sadie T. (Touma) G.; m. Francis C. Martin, July 29, 1978; 1 child, Christopher. BA, Emmanuel Coll., 1970; MS, Iowa State U., 1972, PhD, 1974. Asst. prof. U. N.C., Charlotte, 1974-79, assoc. prof., 1979-85, prof. psychology, 1985—, pres. faculty, 1989—. Cons. in field. Exec. editor: Jour. Gen. Psychology. NDEA fellow, 1971-74; grantee NSF, NIH, numerous others. Fellow APA, Assn. Psychol. Scis.; mem. Cognitive Sci. Soc., Psychonomics Soc., Soc. Computers in Psychology (sec.-treas. 1989-91, pres. 1994), Sigma Xi, Phi Kappa Phi. Office: U NC Dept Psychology 9201 University City Blvd Charlotte NC 28223

GOOLRICK, ROBERT MASON, legal consultant; b. Fredericksburg, Va., Mar. 25, 1934; s. John T. and Olive E. (Jones) Goolrick; m. Audrey J. Dippo (div.); children: Stephanie M., Meade A. BA with distinction, U. Va., 1956, JD, 1959. Bar: Va. 1959, DC 1959, US Dist. Ct. DC 1961, US Ct. Appeals (DC cir.) 1961. Assoc. Steptoe & Johnson, Washington, 1959-65, ptnr., 1965-79; pvt. practice Alexandria, Va., 1979-83; cons., Law and Bus., 1983—2008. Instr. U. Va. Law Sch. Author: Public Policy Toward Corporate Growth, 1978, Corporate Mergers and Acquisitions under Federal Securities Laws, 1978. Mem.: ABA (corps. sect.), Raven Soc., Jefferson Soc., Phi Beta Kappa, Order of Coif. Office: PO Box 150672 Alexandria VA 22315-0672 Home: 7408 Spring Village Dr Apt 205 Springfield VA 22150-4490 Office Phone: 703-971-3422. Personal E-mail: rmgoolrick@cox.net.

GOOLSBY, ALLEN CUNNINGHAM, III, lawyer; b. Richmond, Va., Oct. 19, 1939; s. Allen C. Goolsby Jr. and Adelaide Rawles; m. Louanna Godwin. BA, Yale U., 1961; LLB, U. Va., 1968. Bar: Va. 1968, U.S. Dist. Ct. (ea. dist.) Va. Ptnr. Hunton & Williams, Richmond, Va., 1975—. Author: Virginia Corporation Law Practice, 1990, Goolsby on Virginia Corporations, 2002, 2d edit, 2005, 3d edit., 2008 Fellow Am. Bar Found., Va. Bar Found. Office: Hunton & Williams Riverfront Plz East Tower PO Box 1535 Richmond VA 23218-1535 Office Phone: 804-788-8289. Business E-Mail: agoolsby@hunton.com.

GOOLSBY, BRYAN L., lawyer; b. Dallas, Dec. 19, 1950; BBA with honors, Texas Tech U., 1973; JD with honors, U. Tex., 1977. CPA Tex., 1977; bar: Tex. 1977. Mng. ptnr. Locke, Liddell & Sapp, LLP, Dallas, 2001—06, exec. chmn., 2007—, chmn. fin. com. Mem. adv. bd. Dallas region JPMorgan Chase & Co.; assoc. mem. bd. govs. Nat. Assn. Real Estate Investment Trusts, Inc. Mem. Dallas Citizens Coun.; bd. mem. Jr. Achievement of Tex.; dir. Med. Properties Trust; dir. assoc. bd. dirs. So. Meth. U. Edwin L. Cox Sch. Bus.; exec. com. mem. U. Tex. Syst. Law Alumni Assn. Mem.: ABA, Pension Real Estate Assn., Nat. Multi-Family Housing Assn., Greater Dallas C. of C., Royal Oaks Country Club, Beta Gamma Sigma, Phi Delta Phi, Phi Kappa Phi. Office: Locke Liddell & Sapp LLP Ste 2200 2200 Ross Ave Dallas TX 75201 Office Phone: 214-740-8550. Office Fax: 214-740-8800. E-mail: bgoolsby@lockeliddell.com.

GOOLSBY, THOMAS COWART, state legislator, lawyer; b. Dothan, Ala., Sept. 11, 1961; s. Thomas Cowart and Melinda (Merrill) Goolsby; m. Anna Guy, Sept. 21, 1985; 1 child, Fleming. BS, The Citadel, Charleston, SC, 1984; MBA, Golden Gate U., San Francisco, 1987; JD, U. NC, Chapel Hill, 1991. Bar: NC 1992, US Dist. Ct. (ea. dist.) NC 1994, US Ct. Appeals (4th cir.) 1994. Legal counsel NC State Crime Commn./NC Juvenile Law Study Commn., Raleigh, 1991-93; mng. ptnr. Goolsby Law Firm, PLLC, Wilmington, NC, 1993—; mem. Dist. 9 NC State Senate, 2011—. Adj. prof. Campbell Law Sch., Raleigh. Officer USMC, 1984—88. Mem.: Greater Wilmington C. of C., NC Bar Assn. Republican. Avocations: skiing, sailing, scuba diving, rock climbing, mountain biking. Mailing: Goolsby Law Firm PLLC 212 Walnut St Ste 100 Wilmington NC 28401-3991 also: Capitol Office 16 W Jones St Rm 2115 Raleigh NC 27601 Office Phone: 910-763-3339, 919-715-2525. E-mail: Thom.Goolsby@ncleg.net.

GOOLSBY, TONY, state legislator; b. Nov. 9, 1933; m. Toppy Goolsby; children: Cherrie, Brooke, Mellie. Chmn. house adminstrn.; mem. Licensing & Adminstrn. Procedures Com., Pensions & Investments Com., Higher Edn. Com., Sec. Com., Rep. Nat. Conv., Dallas, Steering Com., Tex. Civil Justice League, County Rep. Assembly, Dallas, Greater Dallas Rep. Forum; house rep. Tex.; del. Nat. Legislature Ins. Conf.; Tex. state rep. Dist. 102, 1989—. Recipient Disting. Svc. award, Tex. C. of C., Cert Commendation, Dallas City Coun.; named Outstanding Conservation Legislator, Nat. Ctr. Policy Analysis. Mem.: Southern Meth. U. Mustang Club, Dallas County Rep. Mens Club, America Heart Assn., Prestonwood Homeowners Assn., Richardson C. of C., North Dallas C. of C., Greater Dallas C. of C., Ind. Ins. Agents Dallas, Ind. Ins. Agents Tex. (chmn., regional chmn.), Nat. Fedn. Ind. Bus. Assn. Republican. Methodist. Office: 9696 Skillman Suite 210 Dallas TX 75243 also: Capitol Bldg Rm 1W6 PO Box 2910 Austin TX 78768 also: 6211 W Northwest Hwy Suite G-104 Dallas TX 75225 Office Phone: 512-463-0454, 214-503-1900. Office Fax: 512-463-1121, 214-750-0460.

GORDER, JOSEPH W., energy executive; BBA, U. Mo., St. Louis; MBA, Our Lady of the Lake U. Dir. info. systems Diamond Shamrock, asst. treas., dir. comml./indsl. sales; v.p. bus. devel. Ultramar Diamond Shamrock; sr. v.p. corp. devel. Valero Energy Corp., San Antonio, 2003—05, exec. v.p. mktg. & supply, 2005—, chief comml. officer, 2011—. Office: Valero Energy Corpn PO Box 696000 San Antonio TX 78269-6000

GORDON, BARON JACK, stockbroker; b. 1926; m. Ellin Bachrach, Aug. 20, 1954; children: Jonathan Ross, Rose Patricia, Alison. Midshipman, U.S. Naval Acad., 1946; BS, Lynchburg Coll., 1953; LHD (hon.), Old Dominion U., 2011. Asst. treas. Henry Montor Assocs., Inc., NYC, 1956; v.p., sec. Propp & Co., Inc., NYC, 1957-58; ptnr. Koerner, Gordon & Co., NYC, 1959-62; sr. ptnr. Gordon, Kulman Perry, and predecessor firm, NYC, 1962-71, pres., chmn. bd., 1971—, Palison, Inc., Williamsburg, Va., 1974—; chmn. bd. Rojon Inc., Williamsburg, Va., 1979—, Two Two Inc., 2012—. Mem. N.Y. Stock Exch., White Plains, N.Y., 1974—. Mem. Harrison (N.Y.) Archtl. Rev. Bd., 1970-72, Harrison Planning Bd., 1975-77; bd. dirs. Montefiore Hosp. Assn., YM-YWHA, Lafayette Ednl. Fund, Inc., 1986-92; internat. adv. coun. Mus. of Am. Folk Art, 1990—. Lt. USNR, 1953—55, U.S.S. Midway, naval aide-de-camp to gov. (rank of capt.), 1989—98, Va. Recipient Wisdom award of honor and eminent wisdom; fellow Wisdom Hall of Fame. Mem. Folk Art Soc. (bd. dirs. 1987-95, mem. nat. adv. bd. 1996—), U.S. Naval Acad. Alumni Assn. (life)(pres. cir.), Buttonwood Club. Home: 113 Elizabeth Meriwether Williamsburg VA 23185-5107 Office: Drawer JG Williamsburg VA 23187 Personal E-mail: ebginwmsbg@aol.com.

GORDON, BEN, professional basketball player; b. London, Apr. 4, 1983; Student in Pre-Bus. Adminstrn., U. Conn., Storrs. Guard Chgo. Bulls, 2004—09, Detroit Pistons, 2009—12, Charlotte Bobcats, 2012—. Mem. British Men's Basketball Team, 2008—. Named Big East Tournament Most Outstanding Performer, Sixth Man of Yr., NBA, 2005; named to NCAA Final Four All-Tournament Team, 2004, All-Rookie First Team, NBA, 2005. Avocations: movies, reading. Office: Charlotte Bobcats 333 E Trade St Charlotte NC 28202

GORDON, CYNTHIA T., corporate financial executive; Worked, audit divsn. Ernst & Young LLP; dir., investor rels. and external reporting A Pea in the Pod; dir., corp. planning Zale Corp., 1994, sr. dir., investor rels., 1998—2001, v.p., corp. planning, 2001—03, sr. v.p., contr., 2003—, interim CFO, 2009—. Office: Zale Corp 901 W Walnut Hill Ln Irving TX 75038 Office Phone: 972-580-4000. Office Fax: 972-580-5547. Business E-Mail: cgordon@zales.com.

GORDON, ERIC, professional basketball player; b. Indpls., Dec. 25, 1988; s. Eric and Denise Gordon. Attended, Ind. U., Bloomington, 2007—08. Guard LA Clippers, 2008—11, New Orleans Pelicans (formerly New Orleans Hornets), 2011—. Mem. US nat. team FIBA World Championships, Turkey, 2010. Recipient Gold medal, FIBA World Championship, 2010; named Freshman of Yr., Big-Ten Conf., 2008, 1st Team All-Conf., 2008. Office: New Orleans Pelicans 5800 Airline Dr Metairie LA 70003*

GORDON, FRANK JEFFREY, medical educator; b. Washington, Dec. 5, 1948; married; 2 children. Attended, Case Western Reserve U., 1966-69; BS in Biology, N.Mex. State U., 1972, MA in Psychology, 1974; PhD in Biopsychology, U. Iowa, 1980. Interdisciplinary rsch. fellow U. Iowa, Iowa City, 1978-80, postdoctoral rsch. fellow Dept. Internal Medicine, 1980-81, rsch. scientist, 1981-82; asst. prof. dept. pharmacology Emory U. Sch. Medicine, Atlanta, 1982-88, assoc. prof., 1988—. Spkr. in field. Editl. bd. Am. Jour. Physiology, 1989-93. Mem. com. on risk factors Iowa Heart Assn., 1982. USPHS predoctoral fellow, 1978-80, post-doctoral fellow, 1980-82; rsch. starter grantee Pharm. Mfgs. Assn. Found., 1983-85. Fellow Coun. High Blood Pressure Rsch.; mem. Am. Physiol. Soc., Am. Soc. Pharmacology and Exptl. Therapeutics, Am. Heart Assn. (rsch. investigatorship Ga. affiliate 1987-88, AHA established investigator 1989-94), Soc. Neurosci., Sigma Xi. Achievements include research in brain and spinal cord regulation of peripheral cardiovascular systems in normal and pathological states. Office: Dept Pharmacology Rollins Rsch Ctr Rm 5011 Atlanta GA 30322-0001 Office Phone: 404-727-5893.

GORDON, J. CRAIG, state legislator; b. May 7, 1977; Ceo Statewide Healthcare Inc., 2006—; state rep. Dist. 162 Ga., 2007—; mem. Econ. Devel. and Tourism, 2007—, Retirement and State Planning and Cmty. Affairs Com., 2007—. Recipient Young Entrepreneur of Yr. Spirit of Excellence award, 2005, Black Bus. Profls. Young Exec. of Yr. award, 2006. Mem.: Capitol City Bank & Trust (advisory bd. mem.), Coastal Network Group (charter mem.), 100 Black Men Savannah. Democrat. Office: 714 MLK Suite 100 Savannah GA 31401 Office Phone: 912-231-8958. E-mail: jcraig@statewidehealthcare.com.

GORDON, JEFF, race car driver; b. Vallejo, Calif., Aug. 4, 1971; s. William Grinnell Gordon and Carol Ann Bickford; m. Brooke Sealy, Nov. 26, 1994 (div. June 2003); m. Ingrid Vandebosch, Nov. 7, 2006; 1 child, Ella Sofia. Race car driver NASCAR Hendrick Motorsports, 1993—. 1st pl. Coca-Cola 600 Lowe's Motor Speedway, 1994, 1997, 1998, 1st pl. UAW-GM Quality 500, 1999, 1st pl. Bank of Am. 500, 2007; 1st pl. Brickyard 400 Indpls. Motor Speedway, 1994, 1998, 2001, 2004; 1st pl. Goodwrench 500 NC Speedway, 1995, 1st pl. Goodwrench Svc. 400, 1997, 1st pl. GM Goodwrench Svc. Plus 400, 1998, 1st pl. AC Delco 400, 1998; 1st pl. Purolator 500 Atlanta Motor Speedway, 1995, 1st pl. NAPA 500, 1998, 1st pl. Cracker Barrel 500, 1999, 1st pl. Bass Pro Shops MBNA 500, 2003, 1st pl. Labor Day Classic 500, 2011; 1st pl. Food City 500 Bristol Motor Speedway, 1995, 1996, 1997, 1998, 1st pl. Sharpie 500, 2002; 1st pl. Pepsi 400 Daytona Internat. Speedway, 1995, 1998, 2004, 1st pl. Daytona 500, 1997, 1999, 2005; 1st pl. Slick 50 300 NH Internat. Speedway, 1995, 1st pl. CMT 300, 1997, 1998; 1st pl. Mountain Dew Southern 500 Darlington Raceway, 1995, 1996, 1997, 2002, 1st pl. TranSouth Fin. 400, 1996, 1st pl. Pepsi Southern 500, 1998, 1st pl. Dodge Avenger 500, 2007; 1st pl. MBNA 500 Dover Internat. Speedway, 1995, 1996, 1st pl. Miller 500, 1996, 1st pl. MBNA Platinum 400, 2001; 1st pl. Pontiac Excitement 400 Richmond Internat. Raceway, 1996, 1st pl. Chevrolet Monte Carlo 400, 2000; 1st pl. UAW-GM Teamwork 500 Pocono Raceway, 1996, 1st pl. Pocono 500, 1997, 1st pl. Pa. 500, 1998, 1st pl. Pocono 500, 2007, 2011, 1st pl. Pa. 400, 2012; 1st pl. DieHard 500 Talladega Superspeedway, 1996, 2000, 1st pl. Aaron's 499, 2004, 2005, 2007, 1st pl. UAW-Ford 500, 2007; 1st pl. Hanes 500 Martinsville Speedway, 1996, 1st pl. Goody's Headache Powder 500, 1997, 1st pl. NAPA AutoCare 500, 1999, 1st pl. Va. 500, 2003, 1st pl. Subway 500, 2003, 2005, 1st pl. Advanced Auto Parts 500, 2005; 1st pl. Tyson Holly Farms 400 North Wilkesboro Speedway, 1996; 1st pl. Calif. 500 Calif. Speedway, 1997, 1999, 1st pl. Auto Club 500, 2004; 1st pl. Bud at the Glen Watkins Glen Internat. Raceway, 1997, 1998, 1st pl. Frontier at the Glen, 1999, 1st pl. Global Crossing at the Glen, 2001; 1st pl. Save Mart/Kragen 350 Infineon Raceway, 1998, 1999, 2000, 1st pl. Dodge/Save Mart 350, 2004, 2006; 1st pl. Pepsi 400 Mich. Internat. Speedway, 1998, 1st pl. Kmart 400, 2001; 1st pl. UAW-Daimler Chrysler 400 Las Vegas Motor Speedway, 2001; 1st pl. Protection One 400 Kans. Speedway, 2001, 2002; 1st pl. USG Sheetrock 400 Chicagoland Speedway, 2006; 1st pl. Subway Fresh Fit 500 Phoenix Internat. Raceway, 2007, 2011; 1st pl. Samsung 500 Tex. Motor Speedway, 2009; 1st pl. Ford EcoBoost 400 Homestead-Miami Speedway, 2012. Host: Saturday Night Live, 2003. Founder Jeff Gordon Found., 1999. Named Rookie of Yr., 1993, Winston Cup Series Champion, 1995, 1997, 1998, 2001, NASCAR Driver of Yr., 1995, 1997, 1998, 2001; named one of The Most Influential People in the World of Sports, Bus. Week, 2007, The 100 Most Powerful Celebrities, Forbes.com, 2008; named to McDonald's All-Star Team, 1994, 1995. Achievements include becoming the 2nd youngest Winston Cup Champion ever at age 24. Office: Jeff Gordon Found 4345 Papa Joe Hendrick Blvd Charlotte NC 28262 also: Jeff Gordon Network 7575 Westwinds Blvd NW Ste C Concord NC 28027-3329 Business E-Mail: jgfan@primenet.com.

GORDON, LONNY JOSEPH, artist, educator, dean; s. Lord Gordon and Ruth Rebecca Lee. BFA, U. Tex., 1965; MFA, U. Wis., 1967; DFA, Nishikawa Sch., Tokyo, 1980. Prof. U. Wis., Madison, 1976—91; chmn. dance U. Nev., Las Vegas, 1991—94, dir. devel. Performing Arts Ctr., 1994—98; dean fine arts Ill. State U., Normal, 2004—08, artist in residence, 2008—. Fine arts world outreach prof., 2010-, Am. Kabuki master, choreographer numerous dance works including Radiance, 2011, artist-in-residence; cons. and lectr. in dance and fine arts over 200 profl. dance cos. and ednl. instns.; founder Kinetic Art Theater, Tokyo, 1969, GORDONDANCE, 1968. Contbr. articles to profl. jours. including Japan Modern Dance Quarterly, Okura Lantern, Dance Scope; columnist Capital Times, Asahi Evening News, Korean Times; subject of numerous books and profl. works in dance. Numerous one man world exhbn. watercolor paintings, collage and mixed media works. Pres. U. Nev. Las Vegas Faculty Alliance, 1994—96, 1997. Grantee numerous profl. and ednl. instns., fellow Fulbright-Hays, 1967-69, 83, NEA Choreographers, 1982-83, Japan Found. profl., 1979, Mobile Found., 1971-72, Nev. State Arts Coun., 1992, 93, 94, 95, 96, 97, 98. Mem. Asian Dance Assn. (bd. dirs.), Am. Coll. Dance Festival (bd. dirs. 1987—2004), Fulbright Alumni Assn. Avocations: gardening, body building, writing, painting. Office Phone: 702-203-8761. Personal E-mail: longordon@gmail.com.

GORDON, MARJORIE, lyric-coloratura soprano, opera producer, educator; b. NYC; d. Theodore and Minnie (Glantz) Fishberg; m. Nathan Gordon; children: Maxine, Peter Jon. BA cum laude, Hunter Coll., NYC. Nat. cert. voice tchr. Prof. voice Duquesne U., 1957-59, Wayne State U., 1961-91, Nat. Music Camp, Interlochen, 1963-65, Meadowbrook Sch. Music, 1966-71, U. Mich., 1970, Mich. State U., 1971; soloist, tchr. Am. U.-Wolf Trap Program, Washington, 1973. Spl. edn. cons. Detroit Grand Opera Assn.; adj. prof. Oakland U., Mich.; pres., gen. dir. Piccolo Opera Co., Inc. Solo debut N.Y. Philharm. Symphony, 1950, soprano soloist, NYC Opera, 1955-57, Chautauqua Opera Co., 1949-61, Pitts. Opera, 1956, Interlochen, Mich., Wolf Trap, The Pittsburg Symphony; dir. Detroit Opera Theatre, 1960-72, Piccolo Opera Co., 1961—; soloist with Chgo. Symphony, Phila. Symphony, Pitts. Symphony, other orchs., opera cos., summer stock, on radio and TV; recitals US, Greece, Europe, Can., Israel; editor: Opera Study Guide, 1968—, Three Times One Season with Buffalo Symphony; Pianist accompanist. Mem. music adv. panel Mich. Arts Coun., 1990-; mem. Palm Beach County Cultural Commn., 1992—; opera prodr. Blue Lake Fine Arts Camp, 1993—. Recipient resolution honoring 25th Anniversary Piccolo Opera Co., Mich. Senate; established voice scholarship in perpetuity Nat. Opera Assn. Mem.: AFTRA, Nat. Assn. Tchrs. Singing, Met. Opera Guild, Ctrl. Opera Svc., Nat. Opera Assn., Music Tchrs. Nat. Assn., Am. Guild Mus. Artists, Mich. Music Tchrs. Assn. (voice chmn. 1970—76), Fla. Music Tchrs. Assn., Boca Delray Music Soc., Broward County Music Club, Mu Phi Epsilon. Avocations: handcrafts, swimming, reading, sketching. Office Phone: 800-282-3161. Personal E-mail: leejon51@msn.com.

GORDON, MORRIS AARON, medical mycologist; b. Waterbury, Conn., Apr. 3, 1920; s. Samuel and Anna (Rubinstein) G.; m. Ruth Kathryn McKee, May 22, 1945 (div. 1970); children: Barbara Jean, David Spencer, Sarah Elizabeth. BS, City Coll. N.Y., NYC, 1940; MS, U. Chgo., 1942; PhD, Duke U., 1949. Diplomate Am. Bd. Microbiology; cert. lab. dir., N.Y. Lab. officer Regional Hosp., U.S. Army, Camp Blanding, Fla., 1945-46; mycologist Communicable Disease Ctr., Atlanta, 1949-54; lectr. Emory U., 1952—53; biol. warfare specialist Chem. Corps Training Command, Fort McClellan, Ala., 1954-55; assoc. prof. microbiology Med. Coll. S.C., Charleston, 1955-59; sr. to prin. rsch. scientist, dir. mycology labs. N.Y. State Dept. Health, Albany, 1959-87, dir. clin. microbiology & mycology labs., 1983-87, dir. emeritus clin. microbiology and mycology labs., 1987—96. Study sect. NIH, Washington, 1971-75; adv. com. Brown-Hazen Awards, N.Y.C., 1974-78; cons. VA Hosp., Albany, 1959-96; rsch. prof. Albany Med. Coll., 1975-90. Author: Laboratory Identification of Pathogenic Fungi, 1970; founder/editor Bull. Med. Mycol. Soc. Ams., 1976-94; contbr. over 150 peer reviewed articles to numerous profl. jours. Lt. comdr. USPHS, 1949-54. Recipient various rsch. grants NIH, teaching fellowship Duke U., 1947-49; Fulbright prof., Uruguay, 1978, Inter-Am. fellow La. State U., 1959. Mem. Med. Mycol. Soc. Ams. (pres. 1978-79, Benham award 1988), Internat. Soc. Human and Animal Mycology (v.p. 1982-85, Georg award 1991), Am. Soc. Microbiology (pres. mycology sect.), Phi Beta Kappa, Sigma Xi (pres. Albany chpt. 1972). Achievements include invention of latex test for cryptococcosis; initiation of diagnostic immunofluorescence for human fungal diseases; cultured pathogenic lipophilic yeasts; establishment of first presence in North America and first presence in humans of Dermatophilus infection. Address: 810 Springmoor Dr Apt 193 Raleigh NC 27615

GORDON, SANFORD DANIEL, economics professor; b. Newark, June 23, 1924; s. Harry Louis and Beatrice (Safris) G.; m. Alice Lillian Pressman, May 27, 1948; children— Ellen Ann, Eric Alan. Student, Tulane U., 1942; BS magna cum laude, NYU, 1947, MA, 1948, PhD, 1953. Instr. econ. NYU, 1948-50; mem. faculty State U. Coll., Oneonta, NY, 1950—, prof. econs., 1957—, chmn. dept., 1960—; asst. vice chancellor for policy and planning State U. N.Y. Central Adminstrn., 1972-76, provost for policy analysis, 1976-79; exec. dir. N.Y. State Coun. on Econ. Edn., 1979-89; prof. econs. Russell Sage Coll., 1979-89. Adj. prof. econs. U. So. Fla., 1989-99; lectr. to elder hostels; econ. editor Kennikat Press., Inc., Port Washington, N.Y., 1970—; cons. to govt., industry, banks, pub. schs., 1954—; vis. prof. State U. N.Y., Buffalo, 1965, U. Miami, 1967. Author: (with J. Witchel) An Introduction to the American Economy, 1967, A Visual Analysis of the American Economy, 1968, (with G. Dawson) The American Economy, 1969, Introductory Economics, 1972, 7th edit., 1991; (with Conover and Ramstadder) Business Dynamics, 1982, 2d edit., 1988, The Economy of New York State, 1987, Basic Economic Principles, 1988, Economics U$A: A Resource Guide for Teachers, 1988, (with A. Stafford) Applying Economic Principles, 1994; lectr., writer: pub. TV series The American Economy, Conversations on Economic Issues, 1970—. Mem. Parks Commn., also Charter Revision Commn., Oneonta, 1957—; v.p. Oneonta Brotherhood, 1958; Dem. candidate for 13th Congl. Dist., Fla., for U.S. Ho. of Reps. Served to sgt. USAAF, 1942-44. Recipient Kazajian Found. award, 1967, Bessie B. Moore Service award, 1987, Air medals. Mem. N.Y. Econ. Assn. (past pres.), AAUP (past pres. N.Y. conf.) Home: 3435 Fox Run Rd Unit 235 Sarasota FL 34231-7391 E-mail: budalice@aol.com.

GORE, JOHN CHRISTOPHER, engineering professor; b. King's Lynn, Norfolk, Eng., Apr. 4, 1951; came to U.S., 1982; s. Graham Thomas and Margaret (Elizabeth) G.; m. Joyce Miranda Gnanam, Sept. 13, 1975; children: Simon John, Rachel Elizabeth. BSc in Physics, U. Manchester, Eng., 1972; PhD in Physics, U. London, 1976; BA in Law, Ealing Coll., London, 1983. Physicist Hammersmith Hosp., London, 1975-81; tech. dir. TEM Instruments Ltd.,

Crawley, Eng., 1981-82; hon. rsch. scientist Royal Postgrad. Med. Sch., London, 1981-82; assoc. prof. diagnostic radiology Yale U. Sch. Medicine, New Haven, 1982—87, prof., 1990—2002, chmn. Biomedical Engring. Program, 1997—2001; prof. psychology Yale U., 2001—02; prof. radiology, radiological sciences, biomedical engring., molecular physiology and biophysics and physics Vanderbilt U. Med. Ctr., dir. Ctr. Imaging Sciences, Hertha Ramsey Cress Univ. prof. radiology and radiological sciences. Mem. diagnostic study sect. NIH, Washington, 1989—. Editor in chief: (jours.) Magnetic Resonance Imaging, 1983—, Revs. of Magnetic Resonance in Medicine, 1986—; contbr. 30 chpts. to books and over 100 articles to profl. jours. Recipient Hamer Major scholarship U. Manchester, 1969-72, studentship Sci. Rsch. Coun., London, 1972-75; grantee NIH. Fellow: American Inst. Medical and Biological Enineers, Soc. Magnetic Resonance Medicine, Soc. Magnetic Resonance Imaging, Inst. Physics; mem.: NAE, American Assn. Physicists in Medicine. Office: Vanderbilt University Medical Center AAA 3107 MCN Nashville TN 37232-2675 Office Phone: 615-322-8357. E-mail: john.gore@vanderbilt.edu.

GORE, TIPPER (MARY ELIZABETH GORE), wife of the former Vice President of the United States; b. Washington, Aug. 19, 1948; m. Albert Gore Jr., May 19, 1970 (separated June 1, 2010); children: Karenna, Kristin, Sarah, Albert III. BA in Psychology, Boston U., 1970; MA in Psychology, Vanderbilt U., Nashville, 1975. Freelance photographer; photographer Nashville Tennessean. Author: Raising PG Kids in an X-Rated Society, 1987, Picture This: A Visual Diary, 1996; co-author: The Spirit of Family, 2002, Joined at the Heart: The Transformation of the American Family, 2002. Co-founder Parents Music Resource Ctr., Arlington, Va., 1985; founder Tenn. Voices for Children, 1990; co-chair America Goes Back to Sch. Initiative; chair Congl. Wives Task Force, 1978—79, Pres.'s Coun. on Phys. Fitness & Sports Nat. Youth Fitness Campaign. Recipient Mary Eleanor McGarvah Humanitarian award, Am. Assn. Nurse Attorneys, 1999. Democrat. Office: 3810 Bedford Ave Ste 250 Nashville TN 37215-2563*

GOREN, ISABELLA D. (BELLA GOREN), air transportation executive; b. 1960; BSChemE, U. Tex.; MBA, Southern Meth. U. Chem. engr. DuPont Co., 1983—85; financial analyst through managerial positions, human resources & revenue mgmt. depts. American Airlines, Inc. (subs. AMR Corp.), 1986—92; dir., investor rels. AMR Corp., 1992—94; v.p., finance & adminstrn. AMR Services (subs. AMR Corp.), 1994—96, pres., 1996—98; v.p., customer svc. planning AMR Corp., 1998—2003, v.p., interactive mktg. and reservations, 2003—06, sr. v.p., customer relationship mktg. & reservations, 2006—10, sr. v.p., CFO, 2010—. Bd. dirs. Gap Inc., 2011—. Bd. dirs. Southern Meth. U. Sch. Engring.; mem. Internat. Women's Forum. Office: American Airlines Inc 4333 Amon Carter Blvd Fort Worth TX 76155 Office Phone: 817-963-1234. Office Fax: 817-967-9641. Business E-Mail: bella.goren@aa.com.

GORENSTEIN, DAVID G., chemistry and biochemistry professor; b. Oct. 6, 1945; s. Ben and Shirley (Adelberg) G.; m. Deborah H. Joseph, June 11, 1967; 1 child, Jennifer. BS in Chemistry, M.I.T., 1966; MA in Chemistry, Harvard U., 1967, PhD in Chemistry, 1969. Asst. prof. U. Ill., Chgo., 1969-73, assoc. prof., 1973-76, prof., 1976-85; prof. chemistry Purdue Univ., West Lafayette, Ind., 1985-94; dir. Purdue Biochem. MRI Lab., West Lafayette, Ind., 1985-94, NSF Nat. Biol. Facilities Ctr., West Lafayette, 1987-93, NMR and Structural Biology Cores, West Lafayette, 1988-94; dep. dir. NIH Designated AIDS Rsch. Ctr., West Lafayette, 1993-94; prof. human biol. chemistry and genetics U. Tex. Med. Sch., Galveston, 1994—2008; sr. investigator Sealy Ctr. Molecular Sci. U. Tex. Med. Br., Galveston, 1994—2008; dir. Nuclear Magnetic Resonance Ctr. U. Tex. Med. Br., Galveston, dir. Sealy Ctr. for Structural Biology, 1995—2002, dep. dir. NIEHS Ctr., 1996—2002, Charles Marc Pomerat Disting. Prof. of biology, 1997—2008, vice chmn. human biol. chem. genetics, 1999—2002, assoc. dean rsch., 2006—08; dep. dir. James Willerson Disting. chair Tex. HSC Houston Inst. Molecular Medicine, 2009—; assoc. dean Ut. HSC Houston Inst. Molecular Medicine; founder Am. Biotechnology, 2006—. Dir. Gulf Coast NMR Consortium; founder, chmn. AptaMed, Inc., 2003—; vis. assoc. prof. U. Wis., Madison, 1975; vis. prof. Oxford U., 1977-78, U. Calif., San Francisco, 1986; adj. prof. Biomed. Engring. U. Tex., Austin, 1996—; cons. Baxter Travenol, 1985-95, Merck and Co., 1988, Eli Lilly, 1987-89, Ill. Tool Works, 1973-85, Chronomatic Inc., 1973-85, U.S. Dept. of Labor, 1975, Continental Group, Inc., 1982-84, Abbott Corp., 2001- Abbott Diagnostics, 2002; active numerous univ. coms.; lectr. in field. Editor Bull. of Magnetic Resonance, 1982-99; mem. editorial bd. Magnetic Resonance Revs., 1983-93, Jour. Magnetic Resonance, 1992-99, Biophys. Jour., 1992-98; pub. abstracts; contbr. articles to profl. jours. Grantee: NSF, 1987-93, NIH, 1970—, Eli Lilly, 1988-94 and numerous others; tchg. fellow Harvard U., 1966-69, trainee summer fellow NSF, 1966, predoctoral fellow NIH, 1967-69, Alfred P. Sloan fellow 1975-79, Sr. Rsch. fellow Fulbright, 1977-78, Guggenheim fellow, 1986; recipient Internat. Lectr. award Fulbright, 1978. Fellow AAAS; mem. Am. Soc. for Biochemistry and Molecular Biology, Am. Chem. Soc. (program chmn. divsn. biol. chemistry 1985-87, vice chmn. Purdue sect. 1990-91, chmn. 1991-92), Biophys. Soc., Protein Soc., Sigma Xi, Phi Lambda Upsilon. Achievements include patents in process for Preparing Dithiophosphate Oligonucleotide Analogs via Nucleoside Thiophosphoramidite Intermediates and Beao-Based selection of aptamers; research in proteomics and applications of NMR spectroscopy and other physical techniques to biological systems, theoretical bio-organic chemistry, biomolecular design; cancer and anti-viral drugs development. Business E-Mail: dggorens2@mac.com.

GORES, CHRISTOPHER MERREL, lawyer; b. NYC, Aug. 27, 1943; s. Guido James and Mary (Callaway) G.; children: Ellen, Eugenia. AB magna cum laude, Princeton U., 1965; LLB, Columbia U., 1968. Bar: NY 1968, Tex. 1973, US Dist. Ct (no. dist.) Tex. 1977, US Ct. Appeals Armed Forces. Rsch. asst. to Hon. Jack B. Weinstein US Dist. Ct. (ea. dist.) NY, 1968—69; assoc. Akin, Gump, Strauss, Hauer & Feld, LLP, Dallas, 1973-79, ptnr., 1979—. Bd. dirs. Shakespeare Festival of Dallas, 1982-88. Lt.1972 JAG Corps USNR, 1969—72. Office: Akin Gump Strauss Hauer & Feld LLP 1700 Pacific Ave Ste 4100 Dallas TX 75201-4624 Office Phone: 214-969-2716. Office Fax: 214-969-4343. Business E-Mail: cgores@akingump.com.

GORIE, DOMINIC L. PUDWILL, retired military officer, astronaut; b. Lake Charles, La., May 2, 1957; m. Wendy Lu Williams; children: Kimberly, Andrew. BS in Ocean Engring., US Naval Acad., 1979; MSc in Aviation Systems, U. Tenn., 1990. Designated Naval Aviator, 1981; flew A-7E Corsair with Attack Squadron 46 aboard USS America, 1981—83; transitioned to Strike Fighter Squadron 132, flying the F/A-18 Hornet aboard USS Coral Sea, 1983—86; test pilot Naval Air Test Ctr., 1988—90; assigned to Strike Fighter Squadron 87 flying the F/A-18 aboard the USS Roosevelt, 1990—92; participated in Operation Desert Storm, flying 38 combat missions, 1992; received orders to US Space Command Colo. Springs, 1992—94; reported to Strike Fighter Squadron 106 for F/A-18 refresher tng., 1994; commanded a tour of Strike Fighter Squadron 37; astronaut candidate NASA, 1994, astronaut, 1995—, spacecraft communicator (CAPCOM) in Mission Control for numerous Space Shuttle flights, chief, Astronaut Shuttle Br.; ret. US Navy, 2005. Pilot STS-91 Mission (Discovery), 1998, STS-99 Mission (Endeavour), 2000; crew comdr. STS-108 Mission (Endeavour), 2001; comdr., mission to deliver the Japanese Logistics Module and the Canadian Spl. Purpose Dexterous Manipulator to the Internat. Space Station (ISS) STS-123 Mission (Endeavor), 2008. Decorated Def. Superior Svc. medal, Legion of Merit, Disting. Flying Cross (two) one with Combat "V", Def. Meritorious Svc. medal, Joint Meritorious Svc. medal, Air medal (two), Space Flight medal (three), Navy Commendation medal with Combat "V". Achievements include logged over 5,200 flight hours in over 30 different aircraft; over 600 carrier landings; logged over 32 days in space; pilot STS-91 (1998), STS-99 (2000); crew comdr. STS-108 (2001). Avocations: skiing, bicycling, fishing, hiking. Office: NASA Lyndon B Johnson Space Center Houston TX 77058

GORMAN, MICHAEL STEPHEN, construction executive; b. Tulsa, Aug. 3, 1951; s. Lawrence Matthew and Mary Alice (Veith) G. Student, Colo. State U., 1970-71. Cert. Nat. Assn. Remodeling Industry, 1985, in bldg. energy rating sys. class III Fla. Solar Energy Ctr., Fla. Dept. Cmty. Affairs, 2008. With McGee Constrn. Co., Denver, 1972-74, with sales and estimating dept., 1974-78, gen. mgr., 1978-80, pres., owner, 1980-91; pres. Wisor Group, Boulder, 1990—95; prin. TechKnowledge, 1996—. Cons., author, columnist in remodeling and custom home building; mortgage banker, ins. cons., 1995—; presenter seminars in field. Author: If I Sell You I Have a Job, If I Serve You I Create a Career, 1997; contbg. editor: Remodeling News Mag., 1995—, Profl. Remodeler Mag., 2002—, Home Energy Mag., 2008—. Named one of Industry Leaders, Top 500, Qualified Remodeler Mag., 1980—86; named to Remodeling Mag'.s Big 50 Hall of Fame, 1988. Mem. Nat. Assn. Remodeling Industry (chmn. membership svcs. com. 1987-91, bd. dirs. 1982-91, regional v.p. 1987-89, nat. sec. 1990-91, Man of Yr. 1982, Regional Contractor of Yr. 1988). Avocations: running, sailing, skiing, pilot, diving. Home and Office: 8345 NW 66th St #8371 Miami FL 33166 Home Phone: 303-588-8969; Office Phone: 800-218-5149, 303-588-8969. Personal E-mail: mgbok@aol.com.

GORMAN, STEPHEN E., air transportation executive; b. 1955; BS in Economics, Eureka Coll.; MBA, Bradley U. Former v.p. ops. Aviall Inc., Dallas; former gen. mgr. JT8D engines Pratt & Whitney; v.p. engine maintenance ops. Northwest Airlines Corp., St. Paul, 1996, v.p. engine maintenance ops. and component maintenance, 1997-99, sr. v.p. tech. ops, 1999—2001, exec. v.p. flight & tech. ops., 2001; pres. N.Am. divsn. Krispy Kreme Doughnuts Inc., Winston-Salem, NC, 2001—03; CEO Greyhound Lines, Inc., Dallas, 2003—07; exec. v.p. ops. Delta Airlines, Inc., Atlanta, 2007—08; exec. v.p., COO Delta Air Lines, Inc., Atlanta, 2008—. Chmn. Pinnacle Airlines Inc., 2003—07; bd. dir. Rohn Industries, 2000—03, TIMCO Aviation Services, 2001—04. Office: Delta Airlines Inc PO Box 20706 1030 Delta Blvd Atlanta GA 30320-6001

GORMAN, STEVE M., communications executive; b. 1969; BBA, Rider U., Lawrenceville, NJ, 1991. Product mgr. BellSouth Corp.; dir., small bus. devel. Media One; exec. dir., mktg., High Speed Internet Cox Comm., Inc., product mgr., residential data svcs., 1999; v.p., product mktg. & mgmt., High Speed Internet Cox Communications, Inc., 2003—. Named one of 40 Executives Under 40, Multichannel News, 2006. Office: Cox Communitcations Inc 1400 Lake Hearn Dr Atlanta GA 30319 Office Phone: 404-843-5000. Office Fax: 404-843-5975. Business E-Mail: steve.gorman@cox.com.

GORRIE, M. MILLER, construction executive; b. Birmingham, Ala. m. Frances Gorrie. BS, Auburn U., Ala., 1957. Chmn., CEO Brasfield & Gorrie LLC, Birmingham, Ala., 1995—. Bd. trustees Colonial Properties Trust; bd. dirs. Am. Cast Iron Pipe Co. Bd. dirs. Ala. Symphony Orch., Econ. Devel. Partnership of Ala.; bd. adv. U. Ala. Birmingham Civil Engr.; co-founder Cloister Creek Ednl. Ctr. Recipient Outstanding Corp. Citizen, Nat. Soc. Fund Raising Execs., Tree of Life award, Jewish Nat. Fund, Hope award, Multiple Sclerosis Soc.; named to State of Ala. Engring. Hall of Fame. Office: Brasfield & Gorrie LLC 3021 7th Ave S Birmingham AL 35233-3502 Office Fax: 205-251-1304. Business E-Mail: mgorrie@brasfieldgorrie.com.

GORRY, JAMES A., III, lawyer; b. Wilmington, Del., Mar. 1, 1939; s. James A. Jr. and Carolyn Allmond Gorry; m. Anne Evans, May 7, 1975; children: Scott Baker, Katherine Gorry Brown BA, U. Del., 1961; JD, Washington & Lee U., 1964. Bar: Va. 1964, U.S. Dist. Ct. (ea. dist.) Va. 1968, U.S. Ct. Appeals (4th cir.) 1982, U.S. Supreme Ct. 1982. Atty. U.S. Army-Judge Adv. Gen. Corps, Virginia Beach, Va., 1965-68, Murphy, Bennett & Gorry, Virginia Beach, 1968-72, Broyles, Gorry, Moore & Brydges, Virginia Beach, 1972-82, Taylor & Walker, P.C., Norfolk, Va., 1982-99; ptnr. Williams Muller, P.C, Norfolk, 1999—2006; gen. counsel, corp. sec. Dollar Tree Stores, Inc., Va., 2006—. Commr. in chancery Virginia Beach Cir. Ct., 1985-2006. Capt. U.S. Army, 1964-68. Mem. Va. State Bar (bd. govs. civil litigation sect. 1994-2000), Va. Assn. Def. Attys. (dir. 1993-96), Va. Trial Lawyers' Assn., Va. Bar Assn., Virginia Beach Bar Assn. (pres. 1980), Norfolk-Portsmouth Bar Assn, Internat. Assn. of Def. Coun. Avocations: scuba diving, golf, running. Office: Dollar Tree Stores 500 Volvo Parkway Chesapeake VA 23320 Office Phone: 757-321-5419. Office Fax: 757-321-5111. E-mail: jgorry@dollartree.com.

GORTNEY, WILLIAM EVANS (BILL GORTNEY), career military officer; b. 1955; BA in History & Polit. Sci., Elon Coll., 1977; MA in Internat. Security Afairs, Naval War Coll., 1996. Commd. USNR, 1977; advanced through grades to adm. USN, 2012; assigned to VT-26, Chase Field Naval Air Station, Beeville, Tex., 1978—80, Attack Squadron 82, 1981—84, VFA-125, Naval Air Station Lemoore, Calif., 1984—88, Strike Fighter Squadron 87, 1988—90; aide and flag lt. to Asst. Chief Naval Ops., Washington, 1990—91; exec. officer Strike Fighter Squadron 132, 1991—92, Strike Fighter Squadron 15, 1992—94, comdr., 1994—95, Strike Fighter Squadron 106, East Coast FA-18 Fleet Replacement Squadron, Naval Air Station, Cecil Field, Fla., 1996—97; mem. joint staff J-33 Ops. Dept. US Ctrl. Command (USCENTCOM), 1998—99, chief naval and amphibious liaison element Combined Forces Air Component Comdr.; dep. current ops. Joint Task Force Southwest Asia Operation Southern Watch, 2000—01; dep. comdr. Carrier Air Wing 7, comdr., 2002; chief of staff for comdr. US Naval Forces US Ctrl. Command (USCENTCOM) / US 5th Fleet, 2003—04; dep. chief staff global force mgmt. & joint ops. US Fleet Forces Command (USFLTFORCOM), Norfolk, Va., 2004—06; comdr. Carrier Strike Group 10, 2007—08, US Naval Forces Ctrl. Command (USCENTCOM), US 5th Fleet, Combined Maritime Forces, Bahrain, 2008—10; dir. The Joint Staff, US Dept. Def., Washington, 2010—12; comdr. US Fleet Forces Command (USFLTFORCOM), Norfolk, Va., 2012—. Decorated Def. Superior Svc. Medal, Legion of Merit (four awards), Bronze Star, Def. Meritorious Svc. Medal (two awards), Meritorious Svc. Medal (three awards), Air Medal (three awards), Def. Commendation Medal (three awards), Navy and Marine Corps Commendation Medal, Navy and Marine Corps Achievement Medal, Sea Svc. Ribbon, Overseas Svc. Ribbon. Office: US Fleet Forces Command (USFLTFORCOM) 1562 Mitscher Ave Ste 250 Norfolk VA 23551

GOTCHER, SARA ELIZABETH, theater educator; b. Clarksville, Tenn., Sept. 27, 1958; d. Della Mae and Fredrick Hemmrich; m. James Michael Gotcher. MFA in Acting, Directing, U. Fla., Gainesville, 1983; PhD, La. State U., Baton Rouge, 1990. Prof. theatre Austin Peay State U., Clarksville, Tenn., 1990—. Prodr., actor, dir.: (challenging theatre) Heartbeat to Baghdad, Paradise. Vol. actress, dir. ann. play Clarksville Hist. Soc., 2004—07; dir. ann. play Dinner with the Dead, 2008. Mem.: Southeastern Theatre Assn., Tenn. Theatre Assn. (mid. Tenn. bd. rep. 1992—96), Actors' Equity Assoc. Fla. (assoc.). Democrat. Episcopalian. Office: ASPU 801 Coll St PO 4475 Clarksville TN 37044 Business E-Mail: gotchers@apsu.edu.

GOTLIEB, JAQUELIN SMITH, pediatrician; b. Washington, Oct. 20, 1946; d. Turner Taliaferro and Lois Barbara (Fisk) Smith; m. Edward Marvin Gotlieb, June 25, 1970; children: Sarah Ruth, Aaron Franklin, David Jacob. BS in Zoology, Duke U., 1968; MD, Med. Coll. Va., 1972. Diplomate Am. Bd. Pediat. Rotating intern Med. Coll. Va. Hosps.-Va. Commonwealth U., Richmond, 1972—73, resident in pediat., 1973—74; pvt. practice Richmond, 1974—75, Stone Mountain, Ga., 1976—86, 1987—; resident in pediat. U. Colo., Denver, 1975—76; med. dir., cons. CIGNA Healthplan Ga., Atlanta, 1986—87. Sch. physician Richmond City Schs., 1974-75. Bd. dirs. Ga. Health Found., Atlanta, 1985-95, vice chmn., 1995-99, chmn., 1999-2005; mem. Med. Assn. Ga., Ga. Perinatal Assn., 1987-2002, bd. dirs. 1994-2002, pres. 1999-2000. Recipient Tee Rae Dismukes award, 2003. Fellow Am. Acad. Pediat. (Ga. chpt. bd. dirs. 1996-99, coord. state chpt. Pediat. Rsch. in Office Settings, 1996—, mem. steering com. Pediat. Rsch. in Office Settings, 2005—11), DeKalb Med. Soc. (chmn. com. 1976). Office: Pediatric Center of Stone Mountain LLC 5405 Memorial Dr Ste D Stone Mountain GA 30083-3236 Home Phone: 770-564-2339; Office Phone: 404-296-3800.

GOTTFRIED, MARK FREDRICK, men's college basketball coach; b. Crestline, Ohio, Jan. 20, 1964; s. Joe and Mary Gottfried; m. Elizabeth Kozel; children: Brandon, Mary Layson, Cameron, Aaron, Dillon. Attended, Oral Roberts U., Tulsa, Okla., 1982—83; BA in Comm., U. Ala., Tuscaloosa, 1987; grad. student, UCLA. Asst. coach, recruiter UCLA Bruins, 1987—95; head basketball coach Murray State U. Racers, 1995—98, U. Ala. Crimson Tide, 1998—2009; coll. basketball analyst ESPNU, 2009—11; head basketball coach NC State U. Wolfpack, 2011—. Player Athletes in Action, 1987—88; summer tour coach Poland and Greece, 1989. Named Southeastern Conf. Coach of Yr., 2002. Achievements include assistant coach of the NCAA Final Four national championship winning University of California Los Angeles Bruins, 1995. Office: NC State University Mens Basketball 2500 Warren Carroll Dr Campus Box 8502 Raleigh NC 27695 Office Phone: 919-515-2104.

GOTTUNG, LIZANNE C., health products executive; m. Mark Gottung; 3 children. Employee rels. counselor Kimberly-Clark Corp., 1981, various positions in labor rels., recruiting, tng. and safety, team leader tissue mfg. Lakeview mill Neenah, Wis., ops. mgr. Badger-Globe facility, feminine care plant mgr. New Milford, Conn., 1993, infant care plant mgr., mgr. Nonwovens mill Corinth, Miss., 1997, v.p. human resources Roswell, Ga., 2001—02, sr. v.p. human resources, 2002—. Office: Kimberly Clark 1400 Holcomb Bridge Rd Roswell GA 30076

GOTTWALD, FLOYD DEWEY, JR., chemicals executive, director; b. Richmond, Va., July 29, 1922; s. Floyd Dewey and Anne (Cobb) G.; m. Elisabeth Morris Shelton, Mar. 22, 1947 (dec. Dec. 2003); children: William M., James T., John D.; m. Helga Koch Andrews, July 29, 2005. BS, Va. Mil. Inst., 1943; MS, U. Richmond, 1951. With Albemarle Paper Co., Richmond, 1943-62, sec., 1956-57, v.p., sec., 1957-62, pres., 1962; exec. v.p. Ethyl Corp., Richmond, 1962-64, vice chmn., 1964-68, chmn., 1968-94, CEO, 1970-92, chmn. exec. com., 1970-94, vice chmn., 1994-96. Vice-chmn. Albemarle Corp. Past bd. dirs. Nat. Petroleum Coun.; trustee U. Richmond; mem. River Rd. Bapt. Ch.; past trustee V.M.I. Found., Inc.; mem. bd. visitors Coll. William and Mary, 1993-97; pres. bd. trustees Va. Mus. Fine Arts, 1994-96. Decorated Bronze Star, Purple Heart. Mem. NAM (former bd. dirs.), Am. Petroleum Inst. (bd. dirs.), Am. Chem. Coun. (bd. dirs.), Internat. Game Fish Assn. (trustee 1992—2012), Alfalfa Club, Country Club Va., Commonwealth Club. Office: Albemarle Corp PO Box 2189 Richmond VA 23219

GOTTWALD, THOMAS E., chemicals executive; BS in Chemistry, Va. Mil. Inst.; MBA, Harvard U. Devel. chemist Tredegar Film Products divsn. Tredegar Industries, Inc., 1989—91; devel. chemist, molded products divsn. Ethyl Corp., Sandston and Richmond, Va., 1984—85, product mgr., ethyl petroleum additives divsn. St. Louis, 1985—89, corp. v.p., petroleum additives Richmond, 1991, COO, 1995—2001, pres., CEO, 2001—04; bd. dirs. NewMarket Corp., 1994—, pres., CEO, 2004—. Office: NewMarket Corp 330 South Fourth St Richmond VA 23219 Office Phone: 804-788-5000. Office Fax: 804-788-5688. Business E-Mail: thomas.gottwald@newmarket.com.

GOTTWALD, WILLIAM M., chemicals executive; Corp. sr. v.p. Ethyl Corp.; pres. Whitby, Inc. (subsidiary Ethyl Corp.); v.p., corp. strategy Albemarle Corp., 1996—2001, chmn., 2001—. Bd. dirs. Tredegar Corp., Richmond, Va., 1997—. Office: Albemarle Corp Baton Rouge Tower 451 Florida St Baton Rouge LA 70801 Office Phone: 225-388-8011. Office Fax: 225-388-7686. Business E-Mail: william_gottwald@albemarle.com.

GOUDET, OLIVIER, corporate financial executive; Exec. v.p., CFO Mars, Inc. Office: Mars Inc 6885 Elm St Mc Lean VA 22101 Office Phone: 703-821-4900. Office Fax: 703-448-9678. Business E-Mail: olivier.goudet@mars.com.

GOUGH, GEORGIA BELLE, art educator; b. Oklahoma City, Dec. 21, 1920; d. George John and Lillie Belle (Massongill) Leach; m. Clarence Ray Gough, Feb. 7, 1975. BS, Ctrl. State Coll., 1941; MS, North Tex. State U., 1946; PhD, U. Okla., 1962. Tchr. elementary Dist. 16/Noble County Okla., Lucien, 1941-42; tchr. elementary, art Denison (Tex.) Sch. Dist., 1942-43; tchr. elementary art Oklahoma City Sch. Dist., 1943-47; instr., asst. prof., assoc. prof., prof., prof. emerita U. North Tex., Denton, 1947—. Sec. Nat. Coun. on Edn. Ceramic Arts, 1970-73; craftsman/trustee Am. Crafts Coun., 1976-80; U.S. Del. World Crafts Coun., 1978, 80; sec., pres., hon. mem. Tex. Designer/Craftsmen; Exhibition includes numerous nat. competitional exhbns.; founder Annual Craft Exhbn. Materials Hard and Soft, 1986-. Artist one-woman shows Earth, Water, Fire, Air, 1996, Family Reunion, 2000; contbr. articles to profl. jours.; designer of wall hanging Greater Denton Arts Coun., 1985. Bd. dirs. Greater Denton Arts Coun. Recipient Cmty. Arts Recognition award, 1995; named Ga. and Ray Gough Gallery, 2008. Democrat. Home: 1813 Willowwood St Denton TX 76205-6992

GOULD, ANDREW, oil industry executive; b. UK, Dec. 17, 1946; married; 3 children. B. with honors, U. Wales. With Ersnt & Young, NYC, Schlumberger Ltd., 1975—77, mem. internal audit dept. Paris, 1977—79, contr. Schlumberger Instrument Velizy, 1979—81, contr. FEA Wireline, 1981—82, contr. Forex Neptune, 1982—84, contr.

drilling & prodn. svcs., 1984, v.p. finance Dowell Schlumberger Houston, 1984—85, treas. Atlantic Asia, 1985—86, contr. Wireline & Testing, 1986—90, treas. Schlumberger Ltd. NY, 1990—91, v.p. ops. Sedco Forex, 1991—93, pres. Sedco Forex, 1993—98, pres. Wireline & Testing, 1998—99, pres. Oilfield Svcs. Products, 1999—2002, exec. v.p. Oilfield Svcs. Products, 2002, pres., COO, 2003, chmn., CEO, 2003—11, chmn., 2011—. Non-exec. dir. Rio Tinto. Office: Schlumberger Ltd 5599 San Felipe St Houston TX 77056

GOULD, FRED, entomology and genetics professor; b. NY, USA; BS in Biology, CUNY: Queens Coll., 1971; PhD in Biology, SUNY, 1977. Postdoc. Nat. Sci. Found., 1977—78; rsch. assoc. entomology dept. NC State Univ., 1978—79, asst. prof. entomology dept., 1979—85, assoc. prof., 1985—89, prof. entomology, 1990—93, reynolds prof. dept. entomology, 1993—; adj. prof., 2002—. Recipient George Bugliarello prize, 2007, Alexander Von Humboldt award, 2004; grantee, NSF Nat. Evolutionary Synthesis Ctr., 2004—, Nat. Sci. Found., 2004, and numerous other honors and awards. Mem.: NAS. Achievements include research in Plant-insect interactions; Evolution of moth sexual communication systems; Evolution of resistance in crop pests. Office: North Carolina State University PO Box 7634 840 Method Rd Unit I Raleigh NC 27695-7634 Office Phone: 919-515-1647. Office Fax: 919-515-2824. E-mail: fred_gould@ncsu.edu.

GOULD, HARRY J., III, neurology educator; b. Columbus, Ohio, Mar. 1, 1947; s. Harry J. Jr. and Madeline (Folger) G.; m. Anne Marie Thompson, Jan. 30, 1971 (div. April 21, 2011); children: Trevor Nicholas, Laura Nicole. BS, SUNY, Stony Brook, 1969; PhD, Brown U., 1974; MD, La. State U., 1990. Cert. in neurology and pain mgmt. Asst. prof. Med. Sch. U. Cin., 1974-80; asst. prof. Med. Sch., La. State U., New Orleans, 1980-86, assoc. prof., 1986; assoc. prof. neurology La. State U., New Orleans, 1998—2008, prof. neurology, 2008—; resident in neurology Med. Sch., La. State U., New Orleans, 1990-94; asst. prof. med. sch. La. State U., New Orleans, 1994-98, Tom Benson prof. neurology, dir. Multidisciplinary Pain Ctr.; chief med. officer Oleander Med. Technologies, 2012—. Contbr. articles to profl. jours. With USAR, 1970-76. NSF grantee, 1986-89. Mem. Internat. Assn. for the Study Pain, Soc. for Neurosci., Am. Acad. Neurology, Am. Pain Soc., Am. Acad. Pain Medicine. Republican. Methodist. Avocations: songwriting, banjo, guitar. Home: 1750 St Charles Ave Unit 308 New Orleans LA 70130 Office: La State U Med Ctr Dept of Neurology 533 Bolivar St New Orleans LA 70112-2825 Office Phone: 504-568-4080. Business E-Mail: hgould@lsuhsc.edu.

GOULET, BEVERLY KENYON, air transportation executive; b. 1954; BA, U. Mich., 1976, JD, 1979. Joined American Airlines, Inc., 1993, assoc. gen. counsel, corp. fin., mng. dir., corporate devel., 1999—2002, v.p., corporate devel., treas., chief restructuring officer, 2002—12, sr. v.p., chief integration officer, 2013—. Bd. dirs. YRC Worldwide Inc., 2010—11. Office: American Airlines Inc 4333 Amon Carter Blvd Fort Worth TX 76155 Office Phone: 817-963-1234. Office Fax: 817-967-9641. Business E-Mail: beverly.goulet@aa.com.

GOURLEY, DICK R., dean, pharmacy educator; b. Franklin, Ky., Dec. 26, 1944; m. Greta Ann Kimbrough, Dec. 7, 1968; 1 child, Kristin Marie. BS, U. Tenn. Coll. Pharmacy, 1969, PharmD, 1970. Lic. pharmacist Tenn. Asst. prof. clin. pharmacy Mercer U. Sch. Pharmacy, Atlanta, 1970-72, prof., dean., 1984-89; asst. prof. U. Nebr., Nebr. Med. Ctr., Coll. Pharmacy, Omaha, 1972-73, assoc. prof., 1973-81, prof., 1981-84, chmn. dept. pharmacy practice, 1972—84; prof., dean. Coll. Pharmacy U. Tenn. Health Sci. Ctr., Memphis, 1989—. Cons. Grady Meml. Hosp., Atlanta, 1971—72, Ga. Narcotic Treatment Prog., 1971—72, Shannondale Nursing Home, Knoxville, Tenn., 1971—72, Tri-County Meml. Hosp., Lexington, Nebr., 1975—76, Luth. Med. Ctr., Omaha, 1975—84, Nebr. State Dept. Pub. Instns., 1976—84; bd. dirs. Greater Omaha Pharmacists Assn., 1974—77; vis. prof. U. Sydney, 1978; vis. tutor Ctrl. Inst. Tech., Upper Hutt, New Zealand, 1978; mem. Bd. Pharm Specialists, 1993—, chair, 1995—97. Co-author: Practicing Pharmacist Handbook: Guidlines for the Establishment of High Blood Pressure Control Services by the Practicing Pharmacist, 1977, Handbook for Institutional Pharmacy Practice, 1979, Handbook of Non-Prescription Drugs, 1979, Pharmaceutics and Pharmacy Practice, 1981, Applied Therapeutics for Clinical Pharmacists, 1982, Pharmacy Technicians' Manual, 1988, numerous others; editor: numerous textbooks, ednl. material; contbr. articles to profl. jours., chapters to books. Judge Greater Nebr. Sci. & Engring. Fair, 1973—79; chmn. UNMC Coll. Pharmacy United Way Campaign, 1979—81. Mem.: Fedn. Internat. Pharm., Internat. Found. Pharmacy Edn., Tenn. Pharmacists Assn., Am. Pharm. Assn., Am. Assn. Colleges of Pharmacy, Am. Coun. Pharm. Edn., Am. Soc. Hosp. Pharmacists (bd. dirs. 1981—84), Assn. Pub. Health Observatories, APHA (bd. trustees 2008—10), Rho Chi, Phi Delta Chi. Office: U Tenn Coll Pharmacy 847 Monroe Ave Memphis TN 38103-4901 Office Phone: 901-448-6036. Business E-Mail: dgourley@uthsc.edu. E-mail: dgourley@bellsouth.net.

GOUSE, S. WILLIAM, JR., mechanical engineering executive, researcher; b. Utica, NY, Dec. 1931; s. S. William and Charlotte G.; m. Jacqueline Ann McLaughlin, Aug. 6, 1955; children: Linda Ellen, S. William III. S.B., S.M., Mass. Inst. Tech., 1954, Sc.D., 1958. Instr. mech. engring. MIT, 1956-57, asst. prof., 1957-61, 62-65, assoc. prof., 1965-67, lectr., 1967-68; prof. mech. engring., prin. rsch. engr. Transp. Rsch. Inst., Carnegie-Mellon U., 1967-69; staff mem. Office Sci. and Tech. of Exec. Office of the Pres., Washington, 1969-70; assoc. dean Carnegie Inst. Tech. and Sch. Urban and Pub. Affairs Carnegie-Mellon U., 1971-73, dir. Environ. Studies Inst., 1971-73, adj. prof. engring. and pub. policy, 1980-90; dir. Office R&D, sci. advisor to sec. U.S. Dept. Interior, 1973-75; acting dir. Office Coal Rsch., 1974-75; dep. asst. adminstr. fossil energy ERDA, 1975-77; chief scientist MITRE Corp., 1977-79, v.p., 1979-80, v.p., gen. mgr. Ctr. for Civil Systems, 1980-84, sr. v.p., gen. mgr. Ctr. for Civil Systems, 1984-90, 1990-92, sr. v.p., 1992-94; mng. dir. Energy Sys. and Tech., 1994—. Cons. and mem. panels various industry and govt. agys. including U.S. Dept. Commerce, U.S. Office Sci. and Tech., NSF; mem. rsch. adv. com. Electric Power Rsch. Inst., 1973-76; chmn. rev. adv. bd. on coal liquefaction Internat. Energy Agy., Paris, 1981-82; mem. energy engring. bd. NRC, 1985-88; U.S. rep. to comm. energy conservation in indsl. processes World Energy Conf., 1984-89; mem. com. on environ. and energy aspects of waste handling World Energy Coun., vice chmn. com. on efficient use of energy utilization using high tech.; mem. adv. bd. Aspen Inst. Humanistic Studies Com. Pub. Policy Issues Energy and Resources, 1982-95; internat. adv. bd. World Energy Coun.; dir. Colshire Group, 1997; tech. advisor AB Volvo, 1996-2000; tech. adv. bd. Earth First Techs., 2002-03; assoc. dir. Aspen Inst., 1996. Editorial bd. Internat. Jour. Environ. Studies, 1971-81; editor-in-chief Energy Systems and Policy, 1973-93; assoc. editor Energy Sources, 1994-2001; contbr. to books, profl. jours., and congl. testimony. Mem. vis. com. mech. engring. dept. MIT, 1978-85. Served with ordnance AUS, 1961-62. Visking Corp. fellow, 1954-55; GE W. Rice Jr. fellow, 1955-56; recipient Ralph Teetor award Soc. Automotive Engrs., 1966; Sir A.L. Mudslior lectr in tech. Al Alagappa Chettiar Coll. Tech., U. Madras, 1969; Disting lectr. mech. engring. Pa. State U., 1980; recipient Outstanding Svc. award No. Area Environ. Coun., Allegheny County, Pa., 1973, Meritorious Svc. award ERDA, 1976, 60th Lord Melchett Medal Lectr. Inst. Energy London, 1994. Fellow ASME, AIAA (assoc.); mem. SAE, U.S. Energy Assn. (bd. dirs. 1987-88, 91-92, audit com. 1992—), Cosmos Club, Explorers Club Washington group (bd. dirs. steering com., 2001-2004, sec., 2004-07. Office Phone: 540-399-9825. Personal E-mail: swgjmg@alum.mit.edu. Business E-Mail: swg11@hughes.net.

GOVAERTS, FRANK, beverage company executive, lawyer; BA in Law, Cath. U. Leuven, Netherlands, 1981; MA in Law, Cath. U. Leuven, 1984; M in European Law, U. Liege, 1986; BA in Economics, U. Hasselt, 1987. Teaching asst., econ. law Cath. U. Leuven, 1984—85; legal counsel Janssen Pharmaceutica, 1987—93; region counsel, benelux and denmark Coca-Cola Co., 1993—96; v.p., legal benelux Coca-Cola Enterprises, Inc., 1996—2001, corp. counsel, EU group, 2001—02, gen. counsel, EU group, 2002—, v.p., gen. counsel, 2009—. Office: Coca Cola Enterprises Inc 2500 Windy Ridge Pkwy Atlanta GA 30339 Office Fax: 770-989-3788. Business E-Mail: FGovaerts@na.cokecce.com.

GOVAN, JERRY N., JR., state legislator; b. Orangeburg, SC, Mar. 17, 1958; s. Jerry N. and Roberta W. Govan; m. Wanda Elaine Gibson, 1984; children: Shawantra, Jeri, Nicole, LaWanda. BA, SC State U., 1982. Pers. specialist US Dept. Navy, 1979—80; recruiting officer SC Dept. Health & Environ. Control, 1984; asst. dir. pers. SC State U., 1984—85, dir. Small Bus. Develop. Ctr., 1985—86; coord. 1st jud. cir. SC Cir. Ct., 1989—90; mem. Dist. 95 SC House of Reps., 1993—. Mem. Orangeburg County Dem. Party, 1980—86; chmn. SC Dem. Party, 1984—86, Young Dems. America, 1985—87. Mem.: Orangeburg Kiwanis (bd. dir. 1992), Primary Prevent Profls. SC. Democrat. Methodist. Address: PO Box 77 Orangeburg SC 29116 Mailing: 530C Blatt Bldg Columbia SC 29201 Office Phone: 803-533-6402, 803-734-3012. E-mail: jng@legis.lpitr.state.sc.us.

GOVE, SUE E., sporting goods company executive; b. 1958; BBA in Acctg., U. Tex., Austin. Acct. Zale Corp., 1980, with, 1980—89, v.p., 1989, sr. v.p., corporate planning, 1996—97, exec. v.p., CFO, 1998—2002, COO, 2002—06; cons. Alvarez & Marsal Bus. Consulting, L.L.C, 2006—07, Prentice Capital Mgmt., LP, 2007—08; exec. v.p., COO Golfsmith Internat. Holdings, Inc., Austin, 2008—09, exec. v.p., CFO, COO, 2008—12, pres., COO, CFO, 2012, pres., CEO, 2012—. Bd. dirs. Zale Corp., 2004—06, AutoZone, Inc., 2005—, Golfsmith Internat. Holdings, Inc., 2012—. Office: Golfsmith International Holdings Inc 11000 N ih35 Austin TX 78753 also: AutoZone Inc 123 S Front St Memphis TN 38103 Office Phone: 512-837-8810. Business E-Mail: sue.gove@golfsmith.com.

GOVIL, NARENDRA KUMAR, mathematics professor; b. Aligarh, India, Jan. 5, 1940; arrived in U.S., 1983, naturalized; s. Panna Lal and Kamla Devi (Agrawal) G.; m. Urmila Agrawal, Feb. 1, 1964; children: Sanjay, Sandeep. BSc, Agra U., India, 1957; MSc in Math., Aligarh Muslim U., India, 1959; PhD in Math., U. Montreal, Can., 1967. Lectr. Concordia U., Montreal, 1967-68, asst. prof., 1968-70, Indian Inst. Tech., New Delhi, 1970-78, assoc. prof., 1978-80, prof., 1980-85; assoc. prof. Auburn (Ala.) U., 1985-86, prof., 1986—2011, alumni prof., 2011—12, alumni prof., assoc. chair math. and stats. dept., 2012—. Vis. scientist Dalhousie U., Halifax, Canada, 1980; vis. prof. U. Alta., Edmonton, Canada, 1981, Auburn U., 1983—85; mem. exec. com. Forum Interdisciplinary Math, Delhi, 1989—91, 2007—09; reviewer Math. Reviews. Co-author: Great Mathematician Shrinivas Ramanujan (in Hindi), 2005; co-editor: Fourier Analysis, Approximation Theory and Applications, 1997, Approximation Theory, 1998, Frontiers in Interpolation and Approximation, 2007; contbr. articles to profl. jours.; editor: Australian Journal of Mathematical Analysis and Applications; assoc. editor Jour. Inequalities and Applications, European Journal of Pure and Applied Mathematics, mem. editl. Bd. Internat. Jour. Math. and Math. Scis., Jour. Inequalities and Spl. Functions, Pure Math. Scis., Jour. Complex Analysis, Asia Pacific Journal of Mathematics, Journal of Complex Analysis and Applications. Pres. India Cultural Assn. East Ala., 1991; mem. exec. India Cultural Assn. East Ala., Auburn, 1986, 96-97. Recipient Outstanding Advisor award, Auburn U. Coll. Scis. & Math., 2010, Alumni Professorship award, Auburn U., 2011. Fellow: Nat. Acad. Scis. India (life); mem.: Indian Math Soc. (life). Avocations: music, reading. Home: 523 Owens Rd Auburn AL 36830-2513 Office: Auburn Univ Dept Math Auburn AL 36849 Office Phone: 334-844-6558. Business E-Mail: govilnk@auburn.edu.

GOWDY, MARJORIE E., museum director; M in Liberal Scis., U. NC, Greensboro, 2008. Exec. dir. Ohr-O'Keefe Mus. Art, Biloxi, Miss., 1992—. Spkr. in field. Mem.: Rotary Club. Office: Ohr-O'Keefe Mus Art 1596 Glenn Swetman St Biloxi MS 39530 Office Phone: 228-374-5547. Business E-Mail: marjie@georgeohr.org.

GOWDY, TREY (HAROLD W. GOWDY III), United States Representative from South Carolina; b. Greenville, SC, Aug. 22, 1964; s. Hal and Novalene Gowdy; m. Terri Dillard; children: Watson, Abigail. BA in History, Baylor U., Waco, Tex., 1986; JD, U. SC Sch. Law, 1989. Law clk. to Hon. John P. Gardner SC Ct. Appeals; law clk. to Hon. G. Ross Anderson, Jr. US Dist. Ct. (Dist. SC), Anderson; atty. Nelson Mullins Riley & Scarborough LLP, Greenville; fed. prosecutor Office US Atty. US Dept. Justice, Greenville, 1994—2000; solicitor Seventh Jud. Cir. Ct., Spartanburg, SC, 2000—; mem. US Congress from 4th SC Dist., Washington, 2011—, US House Judiciary Com., Washington, 2011—, US House Edn. & the Workforce Com., Washington, 2011—, US House Oversight & Govt. Reform Com., Washington, 2011—, US House Ethics Com., 2013—. Republican. Baptist. Office: US House of Representatives 1404 Longworth House Office Bldg Washington DC 20515 Office Phone: 202-225-6030. Office Fax: 202-226-1177.*

GOYER, ROBERT ANDREW, pathology educator; b. Hartford, Conn., June 2, 1927; s. Andrew R. and Cecelia P. (Castonguay) G.; m. Mary Ellen Wilke, Feb. 4, 1955; children: Barbara, John, Peter, Ellen. BS, Holy Cross Coll., 1950; MD, St. Louis U., 1955. Diplomate: Am. Bd. Pathology. Intern St. Francis Hosp., Hartford, 1955-56; resident in pathology St. Louis U. Hosps., 1956-60; practice medicine specializing in pathology St. Louis, 1956-65; instr. pathology St. Louis U., 1960-62, asst. prof., 1962-65, Sch. Medicine, U. NC, Chapel Hill, 1965-68, assoc. prof., 1968-71, prof. pathology, 1971-74, adj. prof. pathology, 1979-87; clin. pathologist Cardinal Glennon Meml. Hosp. for Children, St. Louis, 1961-62, dir. labs., 1962-64; staff pathologist NC Meml. Hosp., Chapel Hill, 1965-74; chief pathology U. Hosp., London, Ont., Canada, 1974-79; prof. pathology Health Scis. Centre, U. Western Ont., Canada, 1974-79, 87-92, prof. emeritus, 1992—; dept. dir. Nat. Inst. Environ. Health Scis., Research Triangle Park, NC, 1979-87; pvt. cons. health effects, toxic metals Chapel Hill, 1992—. Nat. assoc. Nat. Acads.; mem. com. WHO/IPCS, NAS, NRC. Contbr. articles to profl. jours.; mem. editl. bd. Yearbook Pathology, 1979-88, AMA Archives of Pathology, 1973-82. Served with USN, 1945-47. Recipient Merit award, Soc. Toxicology, 2004; Nat. Found. fellow, 1959—60. Mem. Coll. Am. Pathology, Am. Assn. Pathologists, Internat. Acad. Pathology, Soc. Exptl. Biology and Medicine, Soc. Toxicology (Merit award 2004). Roman Catholic. Achievements include research in experimental pathology and metal toxicology. Office: 6405 Huntingridge Rd Chapel Hill NC 27517 Office Phone: 919-419-1804. Personal E-mail: robert_goyer@msn.com.

GOYNE, RODERICK A., lawyer; b. Denver, Aug. 13, 1949; BA with highest honors, hist., U. Tex., Arlington, 1971; JD cum laude, Harvard U., 1974. Bar: Tex. 1974. Ptnr. Baker & Botts LLP, Dallas. Recipient Am.'s Leading Bus. Lawyers, Chambers USA Guide, 2003—, Tex. Super Lawyer, Tex. Monthly and Law & Politics, 2003—08, Internat. Who's Who of Capital Markets Lawyers, 2005—, Best Lawyers in Dallas, D Mag., 2005, Best Lawyers in Am., 2006—. Mem. ABA, State Bar Tex. (chmn. legal opinions com. bus. law sect. 1992), Am. Coll. Investment Counsel (trustee, former pres.), Tex. Assn. Bank Counsel, Dallas Bar Assn., TriBar Opinion Com. Office: Baker & Botts LLP 2001 Ross Ave Ste 900 Dallas TX 75201-2917 Office Phone: 214-953-6527. Office Fax: 214-661-4527. Business E-Mail: rick.goyne@bakerbotts.com, sharon.phillips@bakerbotts.com.

GRABOWSKI, BETH, artist, educator; d. John Stanley and Marion Frances Wormald Grabowski; m. James R. Symon, Aug. 2, 1986; 2 children. BA in Studio Art, U. Va., Charlottesville, 1978; MFA, U. Wis., Madison, 1985. Asst. prof U. NC, Chapel Hill, 1985—91, assoc. prof., 1991—95, prof., dept. art, 1995—, Zachary Taylor Smith disting. term prof., art, 2012—. Pres. SGC Internat., 2012—. Author: (book) Printmaking: A Complete Guide to Materials and Processes; exhibitions include Contemporary Printmaking, China Gallery, Beijing, A Tribute to Kathe Kollwitz. Recipient Johnston award, U. NC Chapel Hill, 1993, Undergrad. Tchg. award, 1994—97, Provost's award, UNC-CH Provost's office, 2005—06, 2009—10; fellow fellowship, Inst. Arts & Humanities, 1989; Bowman & Gordon Gray Professorship, 1994—97, fellowship, Inst. Arts & Humanities, 1994, 2004, Academic Leadership fellow, Inst. Arts & Humanities, UNC-Chapel Hill, 2008, Artist's Project grant, NC Arts Coun., 1988, Artist's fellowship, 1991—93, 1998—2000. Mem.: Southern Graphics Coun. Internat. (v.p. 1993—95). Office: University NC Chapel Hill CB# 3405 Hanes Art Ctr Chapel Hill NC 27599 Office Fax: 919-962-0722. Business E-Mail: beth.grabowski@unc.edu.*

GRACA, THOMAS JOHN, education educator, lawyer; b. Chgo., Feb. 7, 1975; s. Mark S. and Linda Mae Graca; m. Clare Elizabeth Bedell, Mar. 30, 1997. BS in Speech Commn., Tex. Christian U., Ft. Worth, 1995, M in Theol. Studies, 2000; MEd, U. Tex., Arlington, 1998; EdD, Tex. A&M U., Commerce, 2004; JD, Southern Meth. U., Dallas, 2004. Bar: Tex. 2004; cert. tchr. Tex., 1998. Asst. prof. U. Tex., Arlington. Contbr. articles to profl. jours. Mem.: ABA, Assn. Study of Higher Edn., Dallas Bar Assn., Edn. Law Assn., Am. Ednl. Rsch. Assn. Office: U Tex UTA Box 19575 Arlington TX 76019-0227 Office Fax: 817-272-2530. Business E-Mail: tgraca@uta.edu.

GRACE, MARCELLUS, pharmacy educator, retired dean; b. Selma, Ala., Oct. 17, 1947; s. Capp and Mary (Davis) G.; m. Laura Dunn, Sept. 8, 1973; children: K'Chebe M., Syreeta L., Marcellus Jr. BS in Pharmacy, Xavier U. La., 1971; MS in Hosp. Pharmacy, U. Minn., 1975, PhD in Pharmacy Adminstrn., 1976. Registered pharmacist, La., Ohio, Calif., Minn., D.C. Hosp. pharmacy resident USPHS Hosp., Balt., 1971-72, staff pharmacist Boston, 1972-73, Thrifty Drug Stores, LA, 1973; asst. dir. pharmacy Bethesda Hosps., Cin., 1975; dir. pharmacy svcs. Tulane U. Med. Ctr., New Orleans, 1976-77; assoc. prof., asst. dean Howard U., Washington, 1979-82; asst. prof. clin. pharmacy Xavier U. La., New Orleans, 1976-78, dean, 1983-99, prof. pharmacy adminstrn., 1999—2004; assoc. dean Howard U. Sch. Pharmacy, 2004—06; ret. Mem. adv. coun. Nat. Heart Lung and Blood Inst., NIH, Bethesda, 1990-93; mem. Walgreens Pharmacy adv. coun., 1993-97; chair pharmacy panel Peer Health Professionscommn., 1991-92; bd. dirs. New Orleans Regional Med. Complex, 1993-98, Ernest N. Morial Asthma and Respiratory Disease Ctr., 1995—, La. Cancer and Lung Trust Fund, 1995-98, Alton Ochsner Med. Found., 1996—. Contbr. articles and abstracts to profl. jours. Recipient Bowl of Hygeia award, 1998, Wendell T. Hill award Assn. Black Hosp. Pharmacists, 2000. Mem. Am. Assn. Colls. Pharmacy (bd. dirs. 1992-94), N.Y. Acad. Scis., Assn., Rho Chi. Democrat. Baptist. Avocations: automobile restoration, flying. Address: 1735 N Broad St New Orleans LA 70119 Personal E-mail: lgrace4@cox.net.

GRACE, NANCY ANN, news correspondent, former prosecutor; b. Macon, Ga., Oct. 23, 1958; d. Mac and Elizabeth Grace; m. David Linch, Apr. 21, 2007; children: Lucy Elizabeth, John David. BA, Mercer U., Macon, 1981; JD, Walter F. George Sch. Law, Macon, 1984; LLM, NYU. Bar: 1984. Law clk. to fed. ct. judge; practiced antitrust/consumer protection law with FTC; spl. prosecutor Ga. Dist. Atty.'s Office, Atlanta-Fulton County, 1987—96; anchor, host Court TV's Closing Arguments, 1996—2007; sub. host Larry King Live, CNN, 2003—05; radio show host Rapid Fire with Nancy A. Grace, Clear Channel's KNEW-AM, 2004—; host Nancy Grace, HLN (formerly CNN Headline News), 2005—, Swift Justice with Nancy Grace, 2010—11. Litig. instr. Ga. State U. Coll. Law; bus. law instr. Ga. State U. Sch. Bus.; appears as legal commentator for numerous cable and network programs including ABC's The View, The Oprah Winfrey Show, CNN's Larry King Live, Dr. Phil. Author (nonfiction): Objection!: How High-Priced Defense Attorneys, Celebrity Defendants, and a 24/7 Media Have Hijacked Our Criminal Justice System, 2005 (NY Times bestseller); author: (novels) The Eleventh Victim, 2009 (NY Times bestseller), Death on the D-List, 2010; contbr. articles to various law jours.; contestant Dancing With the Stars, 2011, exec. prodr., writer, actress (TV films) The Eleventh Victim, 2012, TV series appearances Drop Dead Diva, 2010—13, Raising Hope, 2012. Former staff mem. Atlanta Battered Women's Ctr. Hotline. Recipient Gracie award for individual achievement as best prog. host, Am. Women in Radio & TV; named one of The 100 Most Powerful Women in Entertainment, Hollywood Reporter, 2011. Mem.: State Bar Ga. Achievements include compiling a perfect record of nearly 100 felony convictions at trial and no losses while at Atlanta-Fulton County Dist. Atty.'s Office. Office: CNN NY Bureau One Time Warner Ctr New York NY 10019 also: CNN Headquarters 1 CNN Ctr Atlanta GA 30303*

GRACE, RICHARD EDWARD, engineering educator; b. Chgo., June 26, 1930; s. Richard Edward and Louise (Koko) Grace; m. Consuela Cummings Fotos, Jan. 29, 1955; children: Virginia Louise, Richard Cummings(dec.). BS in Metall. Engring., Purdue U., West Lafayette, Ind., 1951; PhD, Carnegie Inst. Tech., Pitts., 1954. Asst. prof. Purdue U., West Lafayette, Ind., 1954—58, assoc. prof., 1958—62, prof., 1962—2000, head sch. materials sci. and metall. engring., 1965—72, head divsn. interdisciplinary engring. studies, 1970—82, head freshman engring. dept., asst. dean engring., 1981—87, v.p. student svcs., 1987—95, dir. undergrad. studies program, 1995—2000, prof. emeritus, v.p. emeritus, 2000—. Apptd. Ind. Commn. on Aging by Gov. of Ind., 2005—; cons. to Midwest industries. Contbr. articles to profl. jours.; author: When Every Day Is Saturday, 2002, 2nd edit., 2010. Named Sagamore of Wabash, Gov. of Ind., 1995. Fellow Am. Soc. Metals (tchr. award 1962), Am. Soc. Engring. Edn. (Centennial medallion 1993), Accreditation Bd. Engring. and Tech. (past dir. and officer engring. edn. and accreditation com., related engring. com., Grinter award 1989); mem. Minerals, Metals and Materials Soc. (bd. dirs. 1987-90), Lafayette Symphony Found. Bd. (pres. 1993-1995), Wabash Valley Trust Hist. Preservation (Johanna Downie Preservation award, 2009), Lafayette Country Club, Rotary, Elks, Tau Beta Pi, Omicron Delta Kappa, Phi Gamma Delta. Achievements include conference room in Neil Amstrong Hall is named after him given by Purdue School of Materials Engineering. Home: 2175 Tecumseh Park Ln West Lafayette IN 47906-2118 Office: Purdue Univ Neil Armstrong Hall Sch Materials Engring 701 W Stadium Ave West Lafayette IN 47907-2045 Home (Winter): 3155 Gulf of Mexico Dr Longboat Key FL 34228 Business E-Mail: regrace@purdue.edu.

GRACEY, JAMES STEELE, retired coast guard officer, management consultant, director; b. Newton, Mass., Aug. 24, 1927; s. Ernest James and Edna Alicia (Steele) G.; m. Dorcas Randall Neal, June 15, 1949; children: Kevin, Cheryl, Pamela BS, U.S. Coast Guard Acad., 1949; MBA, Harvard U., 1956. Commd. ensign USCG, 1949, advanced through grades to adm.; comptr. 2d Coast Guard Dist., St. Louis, 1962—65; dep. Governors' Island project and Coast Guard Base, NY, 1965—69; chief programs divsn. Chief of Staff's Office, Washington, 1969—74; chief of staff 5th Coast Guard Dist., Portsmouth, Va., 1974; comdr. 9th Coast Guard Dist., Cleve., 1974—77; chief of staff Coast Guard Hdqrs., Washington, 1977—78; comdr. Coast Guard Pacific Area and 12th Coast Guard Dist., San Francisco, 1978—81, Coast Guard Atlantic Area and 3d Coast Guard Dist., NYC, 1981—82; commandant USCG, Washington, 1982—86; sr. fellow Inst. for Higher Def. Studies, Capstone, 1986—2001. Chmn. Fed. Exec. Bd. Cleve., 1976-77; coord. regional emegency transp. Fed. Region IX, 1978-81; bd. dirs. Marine Spill Response Corp., chmn. audit com., 1991-2003; bd. dirs. Maguire Group, Inc., 1998-2009, Maguire Group Conn., Inc., chmn., 1993-98; advisor New Sulzer Diesel Group, 1991-95; cons. Mitre Corp., 1987-92; vis. lectr. Nat. Def. U., Navy, Air and Army War Colls., Fgn. Svc. Inst., Presdl. Classroom, Sloane Fellows, MIT, Kennedy Sch. Govt., Harvard U., 1982-86; bd. mgrs. Am. Bur. Shipping, 1982-86; leader U.S. del. to Internat. Maritime Orgn., UN Assembly, 1983, 85; bd. visitors Mich. Maritime Acad Mem. world bd. govs. USO, 1982-91; trustee, chmn. Calvary United Meth. Ch., 1988-2001, chmn. ch. coun., 2001-09, fin. commn., ch. coun. Decorated Legion of Merit with gold star, D.S.M. with gold star; named Bay Stater of Yr., Maritime Man of Yr., San Diego NL Man of Yr.; recipient Michelob Schooner award, San Francisco Honor medal Mem. Ret. Officers Assn./Mil. Officers Assn. Am. (bd. dirs. 1986-92), Coast Guard Found. (bd. dirs.), Navy League, Nat. Mil. Family Assn. (advisor 1986-2002), Assn. for Rescue at Sea (bd. dirs., vice chmn. 1988-97, chmn. 1997-2003), Army-Navy Country Club Home: 1411 21st St S Arlington VA 22202-1507

GRACIDA, RENE HENRY, bishop emeritus; b. New Orleans, June 9, 1923; s. Enrique J. and Mathilde (Derbes) Gracida. BA in Architecture, U. Houston, 1950; MDiv, St. Vincent Coll., Latrobe, Pa.; JD, St. Leo Coll. Mem. faculty Sch. Architecture, U. Houston, 1948-51; architect Donald Barthelme & Assocs., Houston, 1949-51; ordained priest Archdiocese of Miami, 1959; asst. pastor Holy Family Parish, North Miami, Fla., 1961-62, St. Coleman Parish, Pompano Beach, Fla., 1962-63, St. Matthew Parish, Hallandale, Fla., 1963-64; adminstr. St. Ambrose Parish, Deerfield Beach, Fla., 1964; asst. pastor Visitation Parish, North Dade, Fla., 1964-65; adminstr. St. Ann Parish, Naples, Fla., 1965-67; pastor Nativity Parish, Hollywood, Fla., 1967-69; rector St. Mary Cathedral, Miami, Fla., 1969-71; aux. bishop Archdiocese of Miami, 1971; ordained bishop, 1972; pastor St. Patrick Parish, Miami Beach, Fla., 1971-72, St. Kiernan Parish, Miami, 1973-75; bishop Diocese of Pensacola-Tallahassee, 1975-83, Diocese of Corpus Christi, Tex., 1987—97, bishop emeritus, 1997—. Mem. Liturgical Conf., 1959-72; mem. Archdiocesan Bldg. Commn., Archdiocese of Miami, 1964-73, sec., 1962-65, chmn., 1967-73, West Coast Deanery, Human Rels. Bd., 1965-67; senator Priests Senate, 1967-69, archdiocesan consultor, 1967-75; chmn. Broward Deanery, Human Rels. Bd., 1969-72, vicar gen., 1969-75; mem. steering com. Biennial Congress Worship, 1966-68; mem. Dade County Community Rels. Bd., 1972-75; aux. bishop Archdiocese Miami, 1971-75, supt. edn., 1973-75; chmn. com. on migration and tourism Nat. Conf. Cath. Bishops, 1975-80; nat. episcopal promoter of Apostleship of the Sea in U.S., 1975-89; mem. Episc. adv. bd. P.A.D.R.E.S. (Orgn. Mex.-Am. Priests), 1975—; Episc. adv. bd. Word of God Inst., 1975—; Episc. liaison for edn. Tex. Cath. Conf., 1986—. Archtl. works include: remodeling St. Vincent Archabbey Basilica, Latrobe, Ch. of the Nativity, Hollywood, St. Ambrose Ch, Deerfield Beach. Pres. Community Action Fund; bd. dirs. Community Act Fund, 1966-72; mem. bishop's com. liturgy Nat. Conf. Cath. Bishops, 1972-77, chmn., 1977-78, mem. policy and rev. com., 1973-77; chmn. ad. hoc. com. on migration and tourism Nat. Conf. Cath. Bishops, 1975-80; cons. Pontifical Commn. for Pastoral Care of Migrants and Tourists, 1978-83; v.p. Am. Immigration and Citizenship Conf., 1977-82; bd. dirs. Cath. Relief Services, 1981-88; trustee Nat. Shrine Immaculate Conception, Washington, 1984—; mem. adv. council South Tex. Eye Found., 1984—; honorary bd. dirs. Stop Child Abuse and Neglect, Inc., 1985—; bd. dirs. Cath. Telecommunications Network of Am., 1985-88; mem. South Tex. Regional Studies Ctr., Kingsville, 1985; mem. com. on social devel. and world peace Nat. Conf. Cath. Bishops, 1985-88; mem. Gov.'s Task Force on Border Econ. Devel., 1985-86; mem. statewide adv. com. Tex. State Aquarium, 1986—; mem. exec. com. Gulf Coast Coun. Boy Scouts Am., 1987—; bd. dirs. Inst. Religion and Democracy, 1986, Sta. KEDT-TV, KKED-FM, 1986—, Cath. Communications Found., 1988—; trustee Cath. Mut. Relief Soc., 1989—, Tex. A&I U. Found., Inc., 1989—; mem. St. Gregory Found. Latin Liturgy Episcopal Adv. Bd., 1989—, NCCB Pro-Life Activities com., 1989-92, cons. Hispanic Affairs com., 1992—, bd. dirs. Catholic Campaign for Am., 1991—, mem. Nat. Adv. Bd. Youth Evangelization Project U. Steubenville. 1991—. Served with USAAF, 1943-45. Decorated Air medal with 2 oak leaf clusters; named Grand Prior So. Lieutenancy Equestrian Order Knights of the Holy Sepulchre Jerusalem, 1986. Mem. Guild for Religious Architecture, Phi Kappa Phi. Roman Catholic. Office: Diocese of Corpus Christi PO Box 2620 620 Lipan St Corpus Christi TX 78403-2620 Office Phone: 361-855-8540. Office Fax: 361-852-3308.

GRACIN, HANK, lawyer; b. Massapequa Pk., NY, Jan. 27, 1957; s. Bernard Tobias and Ada (Rosenberg) G. BA with honors, SUNY, Binghamton, 1978; JD cum laude, NYU, 1981. Bar: N.Y. 1982, U.S. Dist. Ct. (so. dist.) N.Y. 1982. Assoc. Sullivan & Cromwell, NYC, 1981-83, Schulte Roth & Zabel, NYC, 1983-86, Fulbright Jaworski & Reavis McGrath, NYC, 1986-90; corp. counsel Computer Assocs. Internat., Inc., 1990-94; ptnr. Lehman & Eilen, 1994—2009; founding ptnr. Gracin & Marlow LLP, 2010—. Advisor OTCQX market. Editor: Private Placements and Restricted Securities, 1981. Recipient NY Super Lawyers, 2009—10, 2012—13; named to Top Attys. NY, 2012. Mem. South Palm Beach County Bar Assn., Palm Beach Bar Assn., Order of Coif (NYU chpt.). Avocations: bicycling, reading, piano. Office: Gracin & Marlow LLP Mission Bay Office Plz 1825 NW Corporate Blvd # 110 Boca Raton FL 33431-8559 Home Phone: 561-243-1363; Office Phone: 561-237-0804. Business E-Mail: HGracin@gracinmarlow.com.

GRADDICK, CHARLES ALLEN, judge; b. Mobile, Ala., Dec. 10, 1944; s. Julian and Elvera (Smith) G.; m. Corinne Whiting, Aug. 19, 1966; children: Charles Allen, Herndon Whiting, Corinne. BS, U. Ala.; JD, Cumberland Sch. Law, 1970. Bar: Ala. 1970. Clk. Ala. Supreme Ct., 1970; asst. dist. atty. County of Mobile, Ala., 1971-75, dist. atty. Ala., 1975-79; atty. gen. State of Ala., Montgomery, 1979-87; ptnr. Thorton, Farish and Gaunt, Montgomery, 1987-89, Anderson, Graddick and Nabors, P.C., Montgomery, 1989-90; dist. atty. Montgomery County, Montgomery County, Ala., 1991-93; ptnr. Graddick & Belser, P.C., Montgomery and Mobile, 1992-99, Sims, Graddick & Dodson, Mobile, 2000—04; presiding cir. judge Mobile County, 2004—. Served with USNG, 1969-96. Named Outstanding Young Man of Mobile, Mobile Jaycees, 1976, State Conservationist of Yr., Ala. Wildlife Fedn.; recipient cert. appreciation Ala. Peace Officers, 1978, Appreciation award Optimists, 1978. Mem. Ala. Bar Assn., Mobile Bar Assn., Nat. Assn. Attys. Gen., Ala. Cir. Judges Assn. Office: Paul W Brock Inn of Court Govt Plaza 205 Government St Ct Rm 8600 Mobile AL 36644 Office Phone: 251-574-5639. E-mail: charlie.graddick@alacourt.gov.

GRADY, LEE TIMOTHY, pharmaceutical chemist; b. Chgo., Mar. 21, 1937; s. Thomas Aloysius and Lentella Kathryn (Eibel) G.; m. Ann Marie Gill, Aug. 8, 1964; children: Patricia Ann, Meghan Elizabeth. BS in Pharmacy with high honors, U. Ill., 1959, PhD in Chemistry, 1963. Registered pharmacist, Ill., Va., Md. Analyst CIA, Langley, Va., 1963—65; sr. rsch. pharmacologist Merck Inst. Therapeutic Rsch., West Point, Pa., 1965-68; dir. drug standards lab. Am. Pharm. Assn. Found., Washington, 1968-74; dir. drug rsch. and testing lab. U.S. Pharmacopeia, Rockville, Md., 1975-78, v.p., dir. stds. devel., dir. drug stds., 1979-99, v.p., dir. emeritus, 2000—. Expert com. WHO, Geneva, 1980-87; temp. advisor Pan Am. Health Orgn., Washington, 1984; observer Internat. Conf. Harmonization, 1990-2000; mem. Pharmacopeial Discussion group, U.S., Japan, Europe, 1989-2000; cons. in field. Contbr. articles to sci. jours.; sci. editor U.S. Pharmacopeia National Formulary, 1980-2000, 3rd edit., 2010. Docent Nat. Mus. Am. History, 2000—12, Nat. Mus. Natural History, 2010-; vol. Nat. Park Svc, Fairfax County Med. Res. Corp., 2004—12. Recipient rsch. award Am. Soc. Hosp. Pharmacists, 1982. Fellow AAAS, Am. Assn. Pharm. Scientists; mem. Am. Pharm. Assn. (J.L. Powers rsch. achievement award 1990), Cath. Acad. Scis. U.S. (sec.), Order of Holy Sepulchre, Rho Chi, Phi Kappa Phi, Sigma Chi. Roman Catholic. Avocations: swimming, hiking. Personal E-mail: ltgrady@verizon.net.

GRAF, ALAN B., JR., delivery service executive; b. Evansville, Ind., 1953; BS, MBA, Ind. U. With FedEx Corp., Memphis, 1980—, exec. v.p., CFO, 1996—. Bd. dir. Nike Inc., Kimball Internat., Mid-Am. Apartment Communities, Methodist Healthcare. Mem. Dean's adv. council Kelley Sch. Bus.; trustee Univ. Memphis Herff trust; mem. adv. bd. Univ. Memphis Tiger clubs. Office: FedEx Corp 842 S Shady Grove Rd Memphis TN 38120

GRAF, HANS, conductor, music director; b. Marchtrenk, Austria, Feb. 15, 1949; m. Margarita Graf; 1 child, Anna. Studied conducting with Franco Ferrera, Arvid Jansons, Sergiu Celibidache; diplomas in piano and conducting, Music Conservatory, Graz, Austria. Music dir. Iraqi Nat. Symphony Orch., Baghdad, 1975—76; music coach Vienna State Opera, 1977—84; music dir. Mozarteum Orch., Salzburg, Austria, 1984-94, Calgary Philharm. Orch., 1995—2003, Orchestre National Bordeaux Aquitaine, France, 1998—2004, Houston Symphony, 2001—. Artist-in-residence Shepard Sch. Music, Rice U.; guest condr. Vienna Symphony, Vienna Philharm., Leningrad Philharm., Pitts. Symphony, Boston Symphony. Decorated Chevalier l'Ordre de la Legion d'Honneur France, 2002; recipient First prize, Karl Bohm Competition, 1979. Avocation: fine wine. Office: Houston Symphony 615 Louisiana St Suite 102 Houston TX 77002

GRAGG, KARL LAWRENCE, lawyer; b. Watertown, NY, Sept. 25, 1946; s. Karl Lawrence and Pauline (Sykes) G.; m. Maureen Gilluly, Dec. 13, 1975; children: Meaghan Christina, Erika Lawrence, Jenny Camille. BS, Fla. State U., 1968; JD, U. Fla., 1974, LLM in Taxation, 1975. Bar: Fla. 1975, U.S Dist. Ct. (so. dist.) Fla., U.S. Tax Ct., U.S. Ct. Appeals (5th cir.). Assoc. Mershon, Sawyer, Johnson, Dunwoody & Cole, Miami, Fla., 1975-80, ptnr., 1980-82, Gunster, Yoakley, Criser & Stewart, Palm Beach, Fla., 1982-84, Walker Ellis Gragg & Deaktor, Miami, 1984-86, White & Case, LLP, Miami, 1987—. Adj. prof. law U. Miami, 1978-89; mem. tax com. Fla. Ho. of Reps., Tallahassee, 1983. Contbr. articles to U. Fla. Law Rev. Vol. Miami United Way, 1977-80; bd. dirs. New Word Sch. of the Arts Found., 1998—, Bapt. Health Sys. Found., 2004—; trustee U. Fla. Law Sch. Found., 2004—. Mem. ABA (taxation sect.), Nat. Assn. State Bar (chmn. 1986), Am. Coll. Tax Counsel, Fla. Bar Assn. (tax sect., chmn. tax sect. 1991, chmn. coun. of sect.), Nat. Assn. Indsl. and Office Parks (bd. dirs. 1989-91), Ctr. for Health Techs., Inc. (bd. dirs. 1992-98), Japan Soc. South Fla. (bd. dirs. 1990-98), Miami City Club (bd. dirs. 2004—). Office: White & Case LLP 200 S Biscayne Blvd Ste 4900 Miami FL 33131-2352 Office Phone: 305-371-2700. E-mail: LGragg@whitecase.com.

GRAGLIA, LINO ANTHONY, lawyer, educator; b. Bklyn., Jan. 22, 1930; s. Pasquale and Antoinette (Romeo) G.; m. F. Carolyn Pennington, July 17, 1954; children: Donna, Carol, Laura. BA, CCNY, 1952; LLB, Columbia U., 1954. Bar: N.Y. 1954, D.C. 1957, Tex. 1980, U.S. Supreme Ct. Atty. U.S. Dept. Justice, Washington, 1954-57; pvt. practice law Washington and NYC, 1957-66; prof. law U. Tex., Austin, 1966—. Author: Disaster by Decree: The Supreme Court Decisions on Race and the Schools, 1976. Recipient George Washington medal Freedoms Foundation at Valley Forge, 1989. Republican. Avocations: tennis, biking, hiking, billiards. Office: U Tex Sch Law 727 E 26th St Austin TX 78705-3224 Office Phone: 512-232-1363.

GRAHAM, BILLY (WILLIAM FRANKLIN GRAHAM), evangelist; b. Charlotte, NC, Nov. 7, 1918; s. William Franklin and Morrow (Coffey) G.; m. Ruth McCue Bell, Aug. 13, 1943 (dec. June 14, 2007); children: Virginia Leftwich, Anne Morrow, Ruth Bell, William Franklin, Nelson Edman. BA, Wheaton Coll., Ill., 1943; ThB, Fla. Bible Inst., Tampa, 1940; ThB numerous hon. degrees, including, Houghton Coll., NY, Baylor U., The Citadel, William Jewell Coll. Ordained to ministry So. Baptist Conv., 1939; pastor First Bapt. Ch., Western Springs, Ill., 1943-45; charter v.p. Youth for Christ Internat., Chgo., 1945-50; pres. Northwestern Coll., Mpls., 1947-52; worldwide evangelist, 1949—; founder, chmn. Billy Graham Evangelistic Assn., 1950—; host weekly radio program Hour of Decision, 1950—; founder World Wide Pictures, Inc., Burbank, Calif., 1951—; evangelist Crusade Telecasts. Author: Peace with God, 1953, World Aflame, 1965, The Jesus Generation, 1971, Angels: God's Secret Agents, 1975, How To Be Born Again, 1977, The Holy Spirit, 1978, Till Armageddon, 1981, A Biblical Standard for Evangelists, 1984, Approaching Hoofbeats, 1983, Unto the Hills, 1986, Facing Death and The Life After, 1987, Answers to Life's Problems, 1988, Hope for the Troubled Heart, 1991, Storm Warning, 1992, Angels: God's Secret Agents, 1995, Just As I Am: The Autobiography of Bill Graham, 1997, Hope for Each Day: Words of Wisdom and Faith, 2002, Living in God's Love: The New York Crusade, 2005, The Journey: How to Live by Faith in an Uncertain World, 2006, Wisdom for Each Day, 2008, Storm Warning, 2010, Nearing Home, 2011, The Reason for My Hope: Salvation, 2013; also writer of daily newspaper column. Hon. chmn. Lausanne Congress World Evangelization, 1974. Recipient Bernard Baruch award, 1955, Humane Order of African Redemption, 1960, Gold award George Washington Carver Meml. Inst., 1964, Horatio Alger award, 1965, Internat. Brotherhood award NCCJ, 1971, Sylvanus Thayer award Assn. Grads. U.S. Mil. Acad., 1972, Franciscan Internat. award, 1972, Man of South award, 1975, Liberty Bell award, 1975, Templeton prize for Progress in Religion, 1982, Presdl. Medal of Freedom, The White House, 1983, William Booth award Salvation Army, 1989, Congl. Gold Medal, 1996; Freedom award Ronald Reagan Presdl. Found., 2000, Hon. Knight Comdr. Order British Empire, 2001; named to The Gospel Music Hall of Fame, Gospel Music Assn., 1999. Baptist. Address: Billy Graham Evangelistic Assn 1 Billy Graham Pkwy Charlotte NC 28201 Office: Billy Graham Evangelistic Assn Media and Public Relations Department PO Box 1270 Charlotte NC 28201-1270

GRAHAM, CHARLES VINSON, state legislator; m. Kelly Graham; 6 children. BS, Pembroke State U., 1973; MEd, Appalachian State U., 1983; EdD, Lehigh U., 1991. Ret. educator; business owner; mem. Dist. 47 NC House of Representatives, 2011—. Democrat. Office: 479 Bee Gee Rd Lumberton NC 28358 Address: North Carolina House of Representatives 16 W Jones St Room 1315 Raleigh NC 27601-1096 Office Phone: 910-739-3969, 919-715-0875. Personal E-mail: charles.graham10@gmail.com. Business E-Mail: Charles.Graham@ncleg.net.

GRAHAM, DAVID BOLDEN, food products executive; b. Miami Beach, Fla., Feb. 10, 1927; s. Robert Cabel and Bertha Eugenia (Hack) G.; m. Stuart Hill Smith, Sept. 1, 1956; children: Bird, Ellen, Darnall, Lamar, Lyle, Gerard, Barbara, David Bolden. Student, Colegio de san Bartolome, Bogota, Colombia, 1946; BS, Georgetown U., 1949; postgrad., Harvard Bus. Sch., 1950. Chmn. Graham Farms, Inc., Washington, Ind., 1950-99, Graham Cheese Corp., Washington, 1950-99; sec. Bal Harbour Shops, Fla., 1956—57, Graham Bros., Inc., Washington, 1950-72. Author: Taco Tales 2012, The Hockey Duck, 2013, Showdown at the Grotto, 2013, The Secret Spy, Mission Moscow; contbr. articles on agr., transp. and early fur traders to various publs. Past pres. Washington Planning Commn., Regional Planning Commn.; past bd. dirs. Hist. Landmarks Found., Ind.; mem. revolving fund com., mem. rural preservation com.; past mem. Ind. Agrl. Adv. Coun.; past mem. adv. coun. Bur. Water and Mineral Resources; past mem. Natural Resources Commn.; mem. various Meth. awareness coms.; dir. Ind. Regional Hwy. Coalition; v.p. I-69 Mid-Continent Hwy. Coalition; past pres. Nat. Turkey Fedn.; mem. Olympic Yachting Staff, 1996; active Coast Guard Aux., Lic. Master Great Lakes or Inland Waters, FCC Marine Radio Lic. Lt. col. USAF Res., 1949-77. Mem. Columbia Club (Indpls.), Rotary (hon., past pres., Paul Harris fellow), Atlantic Cruising Club, Inland Yacht Club, Elks, Soc. of Children's Book Writers, N.Am. Fishing Club (life), Fla. Writers Assn., Villages Polo. Republican. Roman Catholic. Home and Office: Sumter Place 1550 Killingsworth Way #301 The Villages FL 32162

GRAHAM, DAVID BROWNING, lawyer; b. Wildwood, NJ, Dec. 20, 1942; s. William Browning and Mary Graham; m. Linda Lea Beasley, Feb. 20, 1971; children: Owen, Mary. BS, La. State U., 1966, JD, 1969. Bar: La. 1969, D.C. 1972, Va. 2003, U.S. Ct. Appeals (D.C. cir.) 1974, Ill. 1980, Ohio 1999, Va. 2004. Atty. U.S. EPA, Washington, 1972-73; corp. counsel Nat. Rural Elec. Coop. Assn., Washington, 1973-77; dir. office hearing and appeals U.S. Dept. Interior, Arlington, Va., 1977-79; dep. gen. counsel Velsicol Chem. Corp., Chgo., 1979-84; ptnr. Freedman, Levy, Kroll & Simonds, Washington, 1984-89, Kaye, Scholer, Fierman, Hays & Handler, Washington, 1989-92, Howrey & Simon, Washington, 1992-98, Baker & Hostetler, Cleve., 1998—2003, Kaufman & Canoles, Williamsburg, Va., 2003—. Mem. bd. advisors Toxics Law Reporter, Washington, 1987—, Chem. Waste Litigation Reporter, Washington, 1986—. Co-author: New Approaches to Environmental Law and Agency Regulation: The Daubert Litigation Approach, 2000, Emergency Response Planning--A Critical Investment, 2006; contbr. articles to profl. jours. Mem. ABA (former officer sect. environ., energy and environ. law), Va. Bar Assn. (environ. law bd. govs.). Presbyterian. Avocations: running, skiing. Home: 221 William Claiborne Williamsburg VA 23185

GRAHAM, DERRICK W., state legislator; b. 1958; BA, Ky. State U.; MA, Ohio State U. Educator Frankfort Ind. Schs.; mem. Dist. 57 Ky. House of Reps., 2003—; mem. Edn. Com., Local Govt. Com., 2003—04. Mem.: Franklin County Coun. Family Abuse, Inc. (former bd. dir.), Frankfort Salvation Army, MCA Youth Assn. (Ky.). Democrat. Ame. Mailing: 157 Bellemeade Dr Frankfort KY 40601 Office: Capitol Annex Rm 329F Frankfort KY 40601 Office Phone: 502-564-8100 ext. 639.

GRAHAM, DONALD LYNN, federal judge; b. Salisbury, NC, Dec. 15, 1948; s. Ernest Jethro and Mildred (Donald) G.; m. Brenda Joyce Savage, Sept. 27, 1969; 1 child, Sherrian Lynne. BA magna cum laude, W.Va. State Coll., 1971; JD, Ohio State U., 1974. Bar: Ohio 1974, U.S. Ct. Mil. Appeals, 1974, Fla. 1980, U.S. Dist. Ct. (so. dist.) Fla. 1980, Supreme Ct. 1980, U.S. Ct. Appeals (5th and 11th cirs.) 1981. Asst. US atty. US Dist. Ct. (so. dist.) Fla., Miami, 1979-84; ptnr. Raskin & Graham, Miami, 1984-91; judge US Dist. Ct. (so. dist.) Fla., Miami, 1991—. Instr. U. Md., Hanau, Fed. Republic Germany, 1977-78, Embry Riddle U., Homestead, Fla., 1978-79. Maj., asst. staff judge adv. U.S. Army, 1974-79. Recipient Arthur S. Fleming award Washington Jaycees, 1982, Superior Performance award U.S. Dept. Justice; named one of Outstanding Young Men of Am., 1984. Mem. Assn. Trial Lawyers Am., Nat. Bar Assn., Fed. Bar Assn. (so. Fla. pres. 1984-85, treas. 1982-83), Fla. Bar Assn., N.Y. Bar Assn., Ohio Bar Assn., Wilkie D. Ferguson Jr. Bar Assn., NAACP, Alpha Phi Alpha. Democrat. Baptist. Avocations: fishing, reading. Office: US Dist Ct Ferguson US Courthouse 400 N Miami Ave Rm 13-4 Miami FL 33128 Office Phone: 305-523-5130.

GRAHAM, FRANKLIN (WILLIAM FRANKLIN GRAHAM III), evangelist, missionary; b. Asheville, NC, July 14, 1952; s. Billy and Ruth Bell Graham; m. Jane Austin Cunningham, 1974; children: William Franklin IV, Roy, Edward, Jane Austin. BA, Appalachian State U., Boone, NC, 1978; doctorate (hon.), Whitworth Coll., Toccoa Falls Coll., LeTourneau U., Lees McRae Coll., Nat. U., Liberty U. Bd. mem. Samaritan's Purse, 1978—, pres., CEO, 1979—; evangelist Billy Graham Evangelistic Assn. (BGEA), 1989—, first vice chmn., 1995—, CEO, 2000—, pres., 2001—. Bd. dirs. Harvest Christian Fellowship. Author: Bob Pierce: This One Thing I Do, 1983, Rebel with a Cause, 1995, Miracle in a Shoebox, 1995, Living Beyond the Limits, 1998, The Name, 2002, It's Who You Know: The One Relationship that Makes All the Difference, 2002, Kids Praying for Kids, 2003, A Wing and a Prayer, 2005; co-author (with R. Rhoads): All For Jesus: A Devotional, 2003. Recipient William Booth award, Salvation Army; named Tar Heel of Yr., The News & Observer, Charlotte, NC, 1992, Daniel of Yr., World mag., 2002. Office: BGEA 1 Billy Graham Pky Charlotte NC 28201 also: Samaritan's Purse PO Box 3000 Boone NC 28607 Office Phone: 704-401-2432, 828-262-1980. Office Fax: 828-266-1053.

GRAHAM, LAWRENCE SHERMAN, political science educator, management consultant; b. Daytona Beach, Fla., July 12, 1936; s. Marion Webster and Mary Virginia (Sherman) G.; m. Jane Sharp Merrell, June 8, 1961; children: Merrell Anne Shearer, Virginia Carroll, Lauren Richards, Katherine Lugar. BA, Duke U., 1958; MA, U. Wisc., 1961; PhD, U. Fla., 1965. Prof. govt. U. Tex., Austin, 1965—, assoc. v.p. internat. programs, 2000—04, mem. chancellors coun., 2006—, adj. faculty, LBJ sch. pub. affairs, 2009—10, co-dir., Telluride Assn. Summer Seminar HS Srs., 2010; vis. fulbright fellow Sch. Policy Studies, U. Ulster, Jordanstown, Northern Ireland, 2008—09. Exch. scholar NRC-NAS, Romanian Acad., 1977-78, Yugoslav Acad., 1981, internat. project dir. Nat. Assn. Schs. Pub. Affairs, Washington, 1987-89; cons. mgmt. devel. program UN Devel. Program, NYC, 1989-93, dir. Brazil Ctr., U. Tex., 1995-2000; adv. pub. adminstrn. Inst. Pub. Adminstrn., Lima, Peru, 1967-68. Author: Romania: A Developing Socialist State, 1982, The State and Policy Outcomes in Latin America, 1990, The Portuguese Military and the State, 1993, Politics and Government: A Brief Introduction, 1994, The Politics of Governing: A Comparative Introduction, 2006; editor: Contemporary Portugal: The Revolution and its Antecedents, 1979, In Search of Modern Portugal: The Revolution and Its Consequences, 1982, The Polish Dilemma: Views from Within, 1987, The Political Economy of Brazil, 1990. Mem. NATO Fellowship Rev. Com., 1994, chair, 1995—96. Recipient Rsch. award Calouste Gulbenkian Found., Portugal, 1971, 79-80, Angola and Mozambique, 1972, Hoover Inst., Stanford, 1988; collaborative projects grantee Internat. Rsch. and Exchs. Bd., Poland, 1984, Ford Found., 1986, 96-2001, Rockefeller Found., 1993, 96; rsch. fellow NATO, 1993. Mem. Am. Soc. Pub. Adminstrn. (pub. adminstrn. review bd. 1973-77, chair internat. and comparative adminstrn. 1981-82, 89-90), Internat. Polit. Sci. Assn., Internat. Acad. of Portugese Culture (corrs. mem.), Portuguese-Am. Leadership Coun., Am. Polit. Sci. Assn. Episcopalian. Home: 3404 Mt Barker Dr Austin TX 78731-5725 Office: Univ Tex Dept Of Govt Austin TX 78712 Business E-Mail: l.graham@mail.utexas.edu.

GRAHAM, LINDSEY OLIN, United States Senator from South Carolina; b. Seneca, SC, July 9, 1955; s. Florence James and Millie Graham. BS in Psychology, U. SC, 1977, MPA, 1978, JD, 1981, LLD (hon.), Southern Wesleyan U., Central, SC, SC State U., Orangeburg, Erskine Coll., Due West, SC, Coker Coll., Hartsville, SC; LHD (hon.), Winthrop U., Rock Hill, SC, Coll. Charleston, SC, Allen U., Columbia, SC; HD (hon.), Francis Marion U., Florence, SC; D in Public Svc. (hon.), Presbyn. Coll., Clinton, SC; D in Public Adminstrn. (hon.), The Citadel, Charleston. Area def. counsel Shaw AFB, 1982-84; cir. trial counsel USAF Europe, 1984-88; asst. county atty. County of Oconee, SC, 1988-92; pvt. practice, 1988-94; city atty. Central, SC, 1990-94; mem. SC House of Reps., 1992—95, US Congress from 3d SC Dist., 1995—2001, US House Edn. & Workforce Com., 1995—2002, US House Internat. Rels. Com., 1995—98, US House Judiciary Com., 1997—2002, US House Armed Services Com., 1999—2002; US Senator from SC, 2002—; mem. US Senate Judiciary Com., 2002—, US Senate Armed Services Com., 2002—, US Senate Health, Labor, Edn. & Pensions Com., 2002—04, US Senate Budget Com., 2004—, US Senate Veterans Affairs Com., 2007—, US Senate Agrl., Nutrition & Forestry Com., 2007—09, US Senate Select Com. on Aging, 2007—, US Senate Select Com. on Intelligence, 2007—09, US Senate Homeland Security & Govtl. Affairs Com., 2009—. Bd. dirs. Rosa Clark Free Med. Clinic, Seneca, SC; mem. Anderson Chamber of Commerce, Corinth Bapt. Ch. Served as Major with SC Air N.G., 1989—95, Desert Shield/Desert Storm, served with USAF Res., 1995—2004, col. USAF Res., 2004—. Decorated Meritorious Svc. medal; recipient Minuteman of Yr. award, Res. Officers Assn., 2004. Mem.: Retired Officers Assn., American Cancer Soc. (Oconee County Chpt. fundraising chmn.), Seneca Sertoma, American Legion Post 120, Walhalla Rotary. Republican. Baptist. Office: US Senate 290 Russell Senate Office Building Washington DC 20510 Office Phone: 202-224-5972, 864-888-3330. Office Fax: 202-224-4003, 864-888-3335.*

GRAHAM, MALCOLM, state legislator; m. Kim Graham; children: Cortney Janaye, Nicole Ranaye. Bachelor's degree, Johnson C. Smith U., 1985. Exec. dir. Carolinas Minority Supplier Devel. Councils, Inc., 1987—96; nat. client rels. mgr., v.p. minority bus. devel. Bank of Am.; sr. exec. Bovis Lend Lease; commr. Charlotte, 1999—2004; bus. cons.; state senator Dist. 40 NC, 2005—. Democrat. Office: NC Senate 300 N Salisbury St Rm 622 Raleigh NC 27603-5925 Office Phone: 919-733-5650. Business E-Mail: Malcolm.Graham@ncleg.net.

GRAHAM, MICHAEL PAUL, lawyer; b. Leavenworth, Kans., May 15, 1948; s. K.L. and Norma D. (Whiteside) Graham; m. Pamela Jeanne Haymes, Feb. 21, 1976; children: Sarah Kathryn, Patrick Edward. AB, Dartmouth Coll., 1970; JD, Harvard, 1973. Bar: Tex. 1973. Assoc. Baker & Botts, Houston, 1973—80; ptnr., 1981—; bd. govs. Texans for Lawsuit Reform. Mem.: Houston Bar Found., Houston Bar Assn. Office: Baker & Botts 910 Louisiana St Ste 3000 Houston TX 77002-4991

GRAHAM, ROBERT ALBERT, physicist, researcher; b. Dallas, Feb. 11, 1931; s. John Mark and Eleanor Ball (Evans) Graham; m. Lettie Barbara Umphres, Sept. 1, 1951 (dec.); children: Stephanie Ann Graham Farrow, Mark Lee, Stuart Russell; m. Nell Heard Griffin, Apr. 6, 1996. AA, Allen Jr. Coll., 1951; BSCE, U. Tex., 1954, MS in Engring. Mechanics, 1958; DSc in Materials Sci. and Engring., Tokyo Inst. Tech., 1990. Rsch. engr. S.W. Rsch. Inst., San Antonio, 1956-57; staff mem. Sandia Nat. Labs., Albuquerque, 1958-83, disting. mem. tech. staff, 1983-96; dir. rsch. Tome Group, 1996—. Adviser NAS, Washington, 1982—, Ctr. Explosives Tech. Rsch., Socorro, N.Mex., 1983—88, U. N.Mex, Albuquerque, 1988—; lectr. in field. Editor: Proc. 1981 Shock Conference, Proc. 1983 Shock Conference, N.Mex. Genealogist, 1974—75, High Pressure Exptl. Processing of Ceramic Trans. Tech., 1987; co-editor: Shock Waves in Condensed Matter, 1982, 1983, 1984, High Pressure Explosive Processing of Ceramics, 1987; editor-in-chief Springer-Verlag book series on Shock Compression of Condensed Matter, 1988—96; mng. editor: Shock Waves Internat. Jour., 1991—96, The Heard Family of Uvalde County, Texas, 2005, Effie Rheiner Garner-Blanco Creek Orphan- Within A Heartbeat of the White House, 2010; author: Solids Under High Pressure Shock Compression: Mechanics, Physics and Chemistry, 1993; translator, 1995; author: 3 Families in the Westward Expansion, 2004, in Chinese; contbr. articles to profl. jours. V.p. Amigos de las Ams., Albuquerque, 1968—70; host family Am. Field Svc., Albuquerque, 1969; active Uvalde County Tex. Hist. Commn. 1st lt. US Army, 1954—56. Recipient Excellence award, Dept. Energy, 1983, G. B. Sawyer Meml. award, Sawyer Rsch. Products, 1984, George E. Duvall award, Am. Phys. Soc., 1993. Fellow: AAAS, Internat. Shock Wave Inst., Am. Phys. Soc. (organizing com. 1979, 1983, topical conf. 1993); mem.: IEEE (sr.; local arrangements chmn. 1975), Am. Chem. Soc., Materials Rsch. Soc., Phi Theta Kappa, Chi Epsilon, Tau Beta Pi. Achievements include patents in field. Home and Office: 608 Cenizo Blvd Uvalde TX 78801-4009

GRAHAM, WILLIAM THOMAS, lawyer; b. Waynesboro, Va., Oct. 24, 1933; s. James Monroe and Margaret Virginia (Goodwin) G.; m. Kent Hill, Feb. 1, 1958; children: Ashton Cannon, William Thomas Jr. AB in Econs., Duke U., 1956; JD, U. Va., 1962. Bar: NC 1962, Va. 1962, DC 1970, US Supreme Ct. 1970. Assoc. Craige, Brawley and predecessor firms, Winston-Salem, NC, 1962-64; ptnr. Craige, Brawley, Horton & Graham, Winston-Salem, 1965-69; asst. gen. counsel HUD, Washington, 1969-70; ptnr. Billings & Graham, Winston-Salem, 1971-75; judge N.C. Superior Ct., 1975-79; pvt. practice Winston-Salem, 1981-87; commr. of banks State of N.C., Raleigh, 1987-95; counsel Patton Boggs, LLP, Raleigh, 1995-98; pvt. practice William T. Graham Law Office, Raleigh and WinstonSalem, 1999—. Chmn. N.C. Inst. for Constl. Law, 2003—, mng. dir., 2007—08. Chmn. Forsyth County Reps., Winston-Salem, 1966-69, 73-75, George Bush for Pres., NC, 1988. With US Army, 1957-58. Mem. Old Town Club. Republican. Methodist. Avocation: travel. Home: 465 Sheffield Dr Winston Salem NC 27104 Office Phone: 336-725-3884. E-mail: wtggtw@aol.com.

GRAHAM-MOORE, BRIAN EDWARD, retired educator, consultant; b. Evansville, Ind., Oct. 30, 1935; s. Joseph G. and Ruth (Shaughnessy) Moore; m. Audrey Evans, Jan. 7, 1959 (div. Apr. 1982); children:Susan K., Michael J.; m. Robin Graham, May 6, 1982. BA, Northwestern U., 1961; MA, Washington U., St. Louis, 1967, PhD, 1970. Employer rep. Ill. State Employment Office, Chgo., 1961-64; human resources staff Helene Curtis Industries, Chgo., 1964—66; asst. prof. Grad. Sch. Bus. U. Chgo., 1968—72; from assoc. to full prof. McCombs Bus. Sch. U. Tex., Austin, 1972—99, emeritus prof., 1999—. Author: (monograph) Sharing Gains of Productivity, 1978, (with others) Scanlon Way to Improved Productivity, 1983, Productivity Gainsharing, 1983, Gainsharing and Employee Involvement, 1991, rev. edit., 1995. With US Army, 1957—58, Hon. Discharge. Avocations: flying, fishing, bicycling. Office Phone: 512-585-5180. Business E-Mail: gmoore@utexas.edu.

GRAHMANN, CHARLES VICTOR, bishop emeritus; b. Halletsville, Tex., July 15, 1931; Student, Assumption-St. John's Sem., Tex.; MS, Our Lade of the Lake, 1966. Ordained priest Archdiocese of San Antonio, Tex., 1956, aux bishop Tex., 1981—82; ordained bishop, 1981; bishop Diocese of Victoria, Tex., 1982; coadjutor bishop Diocese of Dallas, 1989—90, bishop, 1990—2007, bishop emeritus, 2007—. Roman Catholic. Home: 8520 Cross Mountain Trl Apt San Antonio TX 78255-2039 Office Phone: 214-528-2240. Office Fax: 214-528-0287.

GRAINGER, MICHAEL J., board member; BS in Acctg., U. Montevallo, Ala. CPA, Calif. CFO Coble Systems, Inc., Nashville, 1980-86, Book Group, Sullivan Graphics, Inc., 1986-90; v.p., contr. Ingram Industries, Inc., 1990-96, CFO, 1996; exec. v.p., worldwide CFO Ingram Micro, Inc., Santa Ana, Calif., 1996—2001, pres., COO, 2001—04. Bd. dirs. ScanSource, Inc., 2004—. Office: ScanSource Inc Bd Directors 6 Logue Ct Greenville SC 29615 Office Phone: 864-288-2432. Office Fax: 864-288-1165. Business E-Mail: michael.grainger@scansource.com.

GRALLA, EUGENE, natural gas company executive; b. NYC, May 3, 1924; s. Jacob and Anna Ruth (Kleiman) G.; m. Beverly Dorman, Apr. 7, 1946; children: Rhona Gralla Spilka, Steven Stuart. BS, U.S. Naval Acad., 1945; MBA, Harvard U., 1947. Commd. ensign USN, 1945, advanced through grades to comdr., 1961; served sea duty, 1947-49, 54-56; control officer (Naval Supply Depot, Guantanamo Bay), Cuba, 1959-61; with (Office Asst. Sec. Def. for Installations and Logistics), 1961-64; ret., 1966; dir. data systems planning Trans World Airlines, NYC, 1966-68; corp. dir. mgmt. info. systems Internat. Paper Co., NYC, 1968; v.p. electronic data processing Columbia Gas System Service Corp., Wilmington, Del., 1969-73; sr. v.p. Columbia Gas Distbn. Cos., Columbus, Ohio, 1973-86, pres., 1986-89, ret., 1989. Mem. Harvard Bus. Sch. Club, Palm Beach Club, Mil. Officers Assn. Am., Masons. Home: 7641 La Corniche Cir Boca Raton FL 33433-6007 Personal E-mail: bevandgene@aol.com.

GRALLA, MILTON, retired publisher; b. Bklyn., Jan. 28, 1928; s. Meyer and Julia (Barnett) G.; m. Shirley Edelson, Aug. 31, 1950; children— Edward, Karen, Dennis. BA in Journalism, CCNY, 1948; LHD (hon.), Yeshiva U., 1991. News reporter, 1948-51; co-founder nat. bus. news agy. NYC, 1951-55; co-founder, exec. v.p. Gralla Pubs., NYC, 1955-93; ret., 1993. Adj. prof. journalism NYU, Ramapo Coll., Yeshiva U., 1989—; del. leader Reawakening 1990-91, Moscow, 1990. Author: How Good Guys Grow Rich, 1995. Candidate for Congress, N.J., 1974; chmn. Israel Salute parade, 1993-94. Recipient major awards (trade) Govt. of Israel, (community service) Brandeis U., United Jewish Appeal, Orgn. Rehab. Through Tng., NCCJ, medal of honor Ellis Island. Mem. Friars Club, 24 Karat Club. Republican. Jewish.

GRAMMIG, ROBERT JAMES (BOB GRAMMIG), lawyer; b. Oceanside, Calif., June 15, 1956; s. Richard Adolf and Mary Elizabeth (Spisak) G.; m. Laurel Jean Lenfestey, Aug. 10, 1996; children: Clare Marie, James Richard, Grace Caroline, Julia Laurel. BA summa cum laude, U. Pa., 1978, MA, 1978; JD, Harvard U., 1981. Bar: Fla. 1982, DC 1986, US Dist. Ct. (mid. dist.) Fla. 1982, US Ct. Appeals (11th and 5th cirs.) 1982, US Supreme Ct. 1985. Law clk. to Hon. Thomas A. Clark US Ct. Appeals (5th and 11th cirs.), Atlanta, 1981-82; assoc. Holland & Knight LLP, Tampa, Fla., 1982-88, ptnr., 1989—, mem. dir. com., 1993—99, 2004—, nationwide practice group leader, securities law and pub. companies, 2005—. Bd. dirs. Fla. Chamber of Comm., 2011—. Contbr. articles to profl. jours. Bd. dirs. Child Abuse Coun., Tampa, 1993-97, Fla. C. of C., 2011-; bd. govs. Crisis Ctr. Tampa Bay, 2006-; mem. Leadership Tampa, 1994-95; sec. Tampa Bay Internat. Trade Coun., 1994, vice chmn., 1995, mem., Golden Triangle Tampa Bay. Mem. Hillsborough County Bar Assn., Tampa Bay Coun. on Fgn. Rels. Fla. Chptr., German Am. C. of C., US-Austrian C. of C.(sec. 2012-), Phi Beta Kappa. Republican. Roman Catholic. Office: Holland & Knight LLP 100 N Tampa St Ste 4100 Tampa FL 33602-4322 Office Phone: 813-227-8500. Business E-Mail: rgrammig@hklaw.com.

GRAMS, DANA A., gas industry executive; 4 children. Attended, USAF Acad., Colo. Springs, 1976; BS in Petroleum Geology, Tex. A&M U., Coll. Sta., 1980. Reservoir geologist Natural Gas Pipeline Co. America, 1980—83, adminstrv. asst. to v.p., gas supply, 1983; mgr., gas supply MidCon Svcs., 1983—87; v.p. Venture Resources - Midcon JV, 1987—89; mgr., natural gas trading Phibro Energy USA, 1989—95; v.p., trading Shell, Coral Energy, 1995—2000; v.p., asset mgmt. Sequent Energy Mgmt., AGL Resources, 2001—04; sr v.p., bus. devel. AGL Resources, 2004—07; pres. Pivotal Energy Development (divsn. of AGL Resources), 2007—. Republican. Roman Catholic. Office: Pivotal Energy Development Two Allen Ctr 1200 Smith St Houston TX 77002 Office Phone: 832-397-1700. Office Fax: 832-397-3713. Business E-Mail: DGrams@aglresources.com.

GRANADE, CALLIE VIRGINIA SMITH, federal judge; b. Lexington, Va., Mar. 7, 1950; d. Milton Hannibal and Callie Dougherty (Rives) Smith; m. Fred King Granade, Oct. 9, 1976; children: Taylor Rives, Milton Smith, Joseph Kee. BA, Hollins Coll., 1972; JD, U. Tex., 1975. Bar: Tex. 1975, Ala. 1976, U.S. Ct. Appeals (5th cir.) 1976, U.S. Dist. Ct. (so. dist.) Ala. 1977, U.S. Supreme Ct. 1980, U.S. Ct. Appeals (11th cir.) 1981. Law clk. to chief judge John Godbold US Ct. Appeals (5th cir.), Montgomery, Ala., 1975-76; asst. US atty. US Atty.'s Office (So. Dist. Ala.), Mobile, 1977—2001; sr. litigation counsel US Dept. Justice, Mobile, Ala., 1987-90; chief criminal sect. US Atty.'s Office, Mobile, 1990-97; 1st asst. US Atty. Southern Dist. of Ala., 1997—2001, interim US Atty., 2001—02; judge US Dist. Ct. (so. dist.) Ala., 2002—03, 2010—, chief judge, 2003—10. Mem. ABA, Fed. Bar Assn., Ala. State Bar Assn., Tex. State Bar Assn., Mobile Bar Assn., Am. Coll. Trial Lawyers. Presbyterian. Office: US Dist Ct So Dist Ala 113 St Joseph St Mobile AL 36602

GRANGER, BRENDA ANN, museum director; b. Midwest City, Okla., Sept. 4, 1966; d. Esten Elzo Peck and Neoma Nadine Passmore; m. Edward William Granger, Nov. 28, 2000. BS, Okla. State U., Stillwater, 1988; MA, U. Ctrl. Okla., Edmond, 1991. Cert. tchr. Okla., Mo. Intern Guggenheim Mus., 1990; architectural historian Meacham and Assoc., U. Okla., Norman, 1991-92; vol. coord., promotions mgr. Harn Homestead Mus., Oklahoma City, 1992-94; exec. dir. Edmond Hist. Soc. and Mus., Okla., 1994—2005, Okla. Mus. Assn., 2005—. Adminstr., coord. Historic Edmond: An Illustrated History, 2000. Mem. Okla. Visual Arts Coalition, 1999-2005, Edmond Millennium Com., 2000; bd. dirs. Holocaust Resource Ctr. of Okla., 1997-2002; former mem. Edmond Visual Arts Commn.; former mem. Edmond Culture Dist, bd. dirs. Assn. of Fundraising Prof., 2003—09; mem. com. Day of Philantropy, 2000—, task force Gov., Signage, 2005— Recipient Citation Mil. Order of the Purple Heart, 2000, Award for Continuous Svc. in the Arts Edmond Arts and Humanities Coun., 2001. Mem. Am. Assn. of Mus., Okla. Mus. Assn. (bd. dirs. 1998-2005, Cert. Recognition 1997), Okla. Hist. Soc., Nat. Alliance State Mus. Assn. Avocations: art, travel, volunteering, bicycling. Office: Okla Mus Assn 2100 NE 52d St Oklahoma City OK 73111 Business E-Mail: bgranger@okmuseums.org.

GRANGER, KAY, United States Representative from Texas; b. Greenville, Tex., Jan. 18, 1943; BS magna cum laude, Tex. Wesleyan U., 1965, DHL (hon.); D in Pub. Svc. (hon.), Tenn. Wesleyan Coll. Prin., owner G&R Ins. Agy., Ft. Worth, Kay Granger & Assocs.; mem. zoning com. City of Ft. Worth, 1981—89, mem. pvt. industry coun., 1988-89, city councilwoman, 1989-91, mayor, 1991-95; mem. US Congress from 12th Tex. dist., 1997—, vice chair House Rep. Conf., 2007—09. Author: What's Right About America?, 2006. Bd. visitors USAF Acad.; bd. trustees Southwestern U., Georgetown, Tex. Recipient Cmty. Health Defender award, Nat. Assn. Cmty. Health Centers, 2006, Nat. Assn. Manufacturers award, 2006, Brotherhood/Sisterhood citation, Nat. Conf. Cmty. & Justice Ft. Worth/Tarrant County Region, 2006; named to Tex. Women's Hall of Fame, 1999, Ft. Worth Bus. Hall of Fame. Mem.: Meadowbrook Bus. & Profl. Womens Assn., East Ft. Worth Bus. & Profl. Assn. (bd. dirs.), Internat. Sister Cities Assn., Am. Planning Assn., East Ft. Worth C. of C. Republican. Methodist. Office: US House of Representatives 1026 Longworth House Office Bldg Washington DC 20515 also: 1701 River Run Rd Ste 407 Fort Worth TX 76107 Office Phone: 202-225-5071.*

GRANGER, ROBERT ALAN, mechanical and aerospace engineering educator; b. Evanston, Ill., Aug. 7, 1928; s. Robert Alan and Kathleen (Buehr) G.; m. Ruth Nickerson, Oct. 7, 1951; children: Erin Alyson. BA, Pomona Coll., 1955; MS, Drexel Inst. Tech., 1959; PhD, U. Md., 1970. Sr. rsch. scientist Martin Co., Balt., 1955-60; prin. engr. Boeing Co., Renton, Wash., 1975; prof. mech. and aerospace engring. U.S. Naval Acad., Annapolis, Md., 1960-98, discipline dir., 1972-75; ret., 1998. Prof. emeritus U.S. Naval Acad., Annapolis, 2001; adj. prof. LSC Coll., 1999, lectr., U. Cambridge (Eng.), 2000—; fellow (hon.) Cambridge (England) U., 1991; pub., CEO Sci. Archives, Inc., 1997; sci. contbr. editor Daily Sun newspaper, 1988-99; cons. NASA, Boeing Co.; vis. prof. U. Petroleum and Minerals, Saudi Arabia, 1977-79, U. Zurich, Switzerland, 1978, Yale U., 1989; dir. Vortex Dynamics Symposium von Karman Inst., Brussels, Belgium; dir., prin. lectr. Introduction to Wing Flutter Symposium, 1991. Author: Fluid Mechanics, 1985, Unified Method of Aeroelasticity, 1986, Experiments in Fluid Mechanics, 1986, Design of Spacecraft, 1988, Introduction to the Flutter of Winged Aircraft, 1992, Experiments in Heat Transfer and Thermodynamics, 1994, Fluid Mechanics, 1994, Life on Mars, 1997, One is Infinity, 2007; contbr. over 800 articles to profl. publs. Served with U.S. Army, 1950-52, Korea. Ford Found. fellow, 1965; recipient USN Meritorious Civilian award, 1996, Euler Math. prize, 1999. Hon. mem. Inst. Modern Physics (Athens, Greece); mem. AIAA, Kappa Mu Epsilon, Alpha Gamma Sigma. Republican. Avocations: composing, mountain climbing, writing, tennis, swimming. Home: 31 Hickory Head Hammock Lady Lake FL 32159-8868 Personal E-mail: ragranger@embarqmail.com.

GRANOF, MICHAEL H., finance educator, department chairman; b. NYC, June 16, 1942; s. David H. and Diana (Simon) G.; m. Dena Gloria Hirsch, Aug. 27, 1972; children: Leah, Joshua AB, Hamilton Coll., 1963; MBA, Columbia U., 1965; PhD, U. Mich., 1972. CPA, Tex. Sr. acct. Coopers & Lybrand, NYC, 1966-68; asst. prof. to prof. acctg. U. Tex., Austin, 1972-84, chmn., acctg. dept., 1984—88, Ernst & Young disting. centennial prof., chmn. acctg. dept., 1984—, and prof., LBJ sch. pub. affairs, 1999—. Mem. Nat. Coun. on Govtl. Acctg., 1982-84, Govtl. Acctg. Stds. Adv. Coun., Norwalk, Conn., 1984-90, Assn. Govt. Accts. Fin. Mgmt. Standard Bd., 2007-10, Fed. Acctg. Standards Adv. Bd., 2009-; Fulbright prof. Coun. for Internat. Exch. Scholars, Hebrew U., Jerusalem, 1978-79; edn. adv. com. U.S. Comptr. Gen., 2001—, adv. coun. on govtl. auditing stds., 2005—; vis. prof. U. Tel Aviv, 1981; bd. trustees Assn. Govt. Accts. Acad. for Govtl. Accountability, 2005—. Author: How To Cost Your Labor Contract, 1973, Financial Accounting: Principles and Issues, 1977, 4th edit., 1990, Accounting for Managers and Investors, 1983, 2d edit., 1993, Government and Not-for-Profit Accounting, 1998, 4th edit., 2007, Core Concepts in Government and Not-for -Profit Accounting, 2003; co-editor: Government Accounting and Auditing Update, 1989-97. Co-pres. Congregation Agudas Achim; treas. Austin Area Urban League. With USCG, 1965-66, standard bd. Govt. Acctg., 2010-Erskine fellow U. Canterbury, Christchurch, N.Z., 1983 Mem. AICPAs (com. on govt. acctg. and auditing), Am. Acctg. Assn. (chmn. pub. sector sect. 1981-82), Tex. Soc. CPAs (chmn. govt. acctg. standards com.), Govt. Fin. Officers Assn., Assn. Govt. Accts. Jewish. Home: 7310 Valburn Dr Austin TX 78731-1146 Office: U Tex Dept Acctg CBA 4M 202 Austin TX 78712 Business E-Mail: michael.granof@mccombs.utexas.edu.

GRANOLLERS, MARCEL, professional tennis player; b. Barcelona, Apr. 12, 1986; s. Javier and Montse Granollers. Profl. tennis player ATP, 2003—. Achievements include winning 1 career title final, 5 career doubles title, ATP; winning (singles) Houston, 2008, (doubles) Moscow, 2009, Buenos Aires, 2009, Costa Do Sauipe, 2009, 2010, Chennai, 2010. Office: c/o ATP Tour Inc 201 Atp Tour Blvd Ponte Vedra Beach FL 32082-3211

GRANT, ANTHONY, men's college basketball coach; b. Apr. 15, 1966; m. Christina Harrell; children: Anthony, Preston, Jayda Danielle, Makai. Grad., U. Dayton, Ohio, 1987. Player Miami Tropics, USBL, 1987; asst. coach Miami Sr. HS, 1987—92; head coach Miami Ctrl. HS, 1992—93; asst. coach Stetson U. Hatters, 1993—94, Marshall U. Thundering Herd, 1994—96, U. Fla. Gators, 1996—2001, assoc. head coach, 2002—06; head coach Va. Commonwealth U. Rams, 2006—09, U. Ala. Crimson Tide, 2009—. Recipient Sharpenter Meml. Rebounding award, 1987; named Coach of Yr., Colonial Athletic Assn., 2007; named one of Top Future Coaching Prospects, Sports Illustrated, The Sporting News. Office: Dept Intercollegiate Athletics Univ Ala Box 870393 Tuscaloosa AL 35487 Office Phone: 205-348-4551.

GRANT, DANIEL ROSS, retired academic administrator; b. Little Rock, Aug. 18, 1923; s. James Richard and Gracie (Sowers) Grant; m. Betty Jo Oliver, June 17, 1947; children: Carolyn, Shirley, Ross. BA, Ouachita Bapt. U., 1945; MA, U. Ala., 1946; PhD, Northwestern U.,

1948. Asst. prof. polit. sci. Vanderbilt U., 1948-54, assoc. prof., 1954-63, prof., 1963-70, dir. Urban and Regional Devel. Ctr., 1968-70; pres. Ouachita Bapt. U., Akadelphia, Ark., 1970-88, pres. emeritus, 1988—. Assoc. dir. Harris County Home Rule Commn., Houston, 1957; vis. prof. mcpl. govt. and planning Thammasat U., Bangkok, 1958—59; cons. U.S. Adv. Commn. Intergovernmental Rels., 1962—67; mem. adv. com. federalism and met. govt. Nat. Com. Econ. Devel., 1969—73. Author (with others): (book) Plan of Metropolitan Government for Nashville and Davidson County, 1956, Metropolitan Surveys: A Digest, 1958, The States and Metropolis, 1968, Government and Politics: An Introduction to Political Science, rev. edit., 1971; author: The Christian and Politics, 1968; author: (with Lloyd Omdahl) State and Local Government in America, 6th edit., 1993. Chmn. Coop. Svcs. Internat. Edn. Consortium (name now Consortium Global Edn.), 1987—88, cons., 1988—90, pres., 1990—98; active So. Bapt. Found., 1959—60, Ark. Bapt. Found., 1991—97, vice chmn., 1995—96, chmn., 1996—97; mem. regional rev. panel Harry S Truman Scholarship Found., 1982—96, chmn., 1984—96; active Ark. Postsecondary Edn. Planning Commn., 1980—89; mem. Ark. Higher Edn. Coordinating Bd., 1997—2010, vice chmn., 2002—04; mem. commn. religious liberty and human rights Bapt. World Alliance, 1971—95, vice chmn., 1985—90; mem. edn. commn. So. Bapt. Conv., 1973—80, chmn., 1978—80; 1st v.p. Ark. Bapt. State Conv., 1989—91; pres. Assn. So. Bapt. Colls. and Schs., 1984—85. Mem.: Am. Soc. Pub. Adminstrn., Ark. Polit. Sci. Assn., Am. Polit. Sci. Assn., Arkadelphia C. of C. (bd. dirs. 2000—02), Rotary (pres. 1986—87). Home: 4 Glendale Pl Arkadelphia AR 71923-3529 Office: Ouachita Bapt Univ PO Box 3636 Arkadelphia AR 71998-3636 E-mail: dangrant@suddenlink.net.

GRANT, J. KIRKLAND, lawyer, educator; b. Monroe, Mich., Feb. 14, 1943; s. Stanley Gordon and Neva Alene (Piper) G.; 1 child, Alexandra. BBA, U. Mich., 1965, JD cum laude, 1967. Bar: Mich. 1968, NY 1970, SC 1975, US Supreme Ct. 1979. Acct. Peat Marwick Mitchell, Detroit, 1964-65; asst. prof. Ga. State U., 1967-70, U. Toledo, 1970-71; assoc. counsel Sullivan & Cromwell, NYC, 1970-72; prof. U. SC, 1972-80; dean, prof. Del. Law Sch., Wilmington, 1980-83; assoc. counsel Bingham, Dana & Gould, Boston, 1983-84; prof. law Touro Law Sch., Huntington, NY, 1984—2006, emeritus prof., 2006—; academic dean Touro Law Ctr., Huntington, NY, 1984-85; pvt. practice Charleston, SC, 1987—, Huntington, NY, 1984—2006; disting. vis. prof. Charleston Sch. Law, SC, 2005—. Vis. scholar Columbia U., 1980, Harvard U., 1982-83; chair com. on legal edn. NY State Bar Assn, 1992-95; cons. in the field; comml. and securities arbitrator; arbitrator, mediator U.S. Dist. Ct. Author: Securities Arbitration, 1994; reporter Revision of SC Bus. Corp. Law, 1981; editor: Lexis Nexis NY Corp. Law Handbook, 1986-2010; contbr. articles to profl. jours. Mem. ABA, Am. Law Inst. (life), Scribes, Alexander Hamilton Inn of Ct. (pres. 1998-2000, 2002—06), Petigrue Inn, Harvard Club (NY), Sand Dollar Club (Folly Beach), Hist. Ansonbourough Neighborhood Assn. (pres.), Folly Beach SC Planning Commn. (commr.). Office: Charleston Sch Law 83 Mary St Charleston SC 29402 Home: 24 Wentworth St Charleston SC 29401 Office Phone: 843-377-2416. Business E-Mail: grantlaw@usa.com.

GRANT, JAMES W., state legislator; b. Tampa, Fla., Sept. 20, 1982; BS in Mktg. & Polit. Sci., Auburn U., 2006; JD, Stetson U., 2009. Atty. The Grant Law Group; mem. Dist. 47 Fla. House of Representatives, 2011—. Republican. Office: 12956 N Dale Mabry Hwy Tampa FL 33618-2806 also: Florida House of Reps 1003 The Capitol 402 S Monroe St Tallahassee FL 32399-1300 Office Phone: 813-265-6280, 850-488-0275.

GRANT, JOHNNY, state legislator; b. Milledgeville, Ga. m. Carol Thornton; children: Rebecca, Michael, Daniel. Grad., Ga. Inst. Tech.; MPA, Ga. State Univ. Mem. Dist. 25 Ga. State Senate, 2004—. Republican. Episcopalian. Office: 321 A Legis Off Bldg Atlanta GA 30334 Mailing: PO Box 1458 Milledgeville GA 31059 Office Phone: 404-656-0082. Office Fax: 404-657-3248. Business E-Mail: johnny.grant@senate.ga.gov.

GRANT, JOSEPH MOORMAN, finance company executive; b. San Antonio, Oct. 30, 1938; s. George William and Mary Christian (Moorman) G.; m. Sheila Ann Peterson, Aug. 26, 1961; children: Mary Elizabeth, Steven Clay. BBA, So. Meth. U., 1960; MBA, U. Tex., 1961, PhD, 1970. Banking officer Citibank, NYC, 1961-65; sr. v.p., economist Tex. Commerce Bank (N.A.) also Tex. Commerce Bancshares, Houston, 1970-73; pres., dir. Tex. Commerce Bank, Austin, 1974-75; chmn., CEO Tex. Am. Bankshares/Ft. Worth, 1986-89; pres. Tex. Am. Bank/Ft. Worth, 1976-89, chmn., CEO, 1983-89; exec. v.p., CFO Electronic Data Systems, Dallas, 1990-98; chmn., CEO Tex. Capital Bancshares, 1998—. Bd. dirs. Vignette Corp., Chaparral Steel. Author: (with Lawrence L. Crum) The Development of State-Chartered Banking in Texas, 1978, The Great Texas Banking Crash, 1996. Trustee Tex. Christian U., 1989-94, So. Meth. U., 1980-89; chmn. adv. coun. Coll. Bus. Adminstrn. Found., U. Tex., Austin; trustee Dallas County C.C.; bd. dirs. North Tex. Commn., 1976-86, chmn., 1981-82; trustee Paul Quinn Coll., 1995-98; bd. dirs. Communities Found. Tex., KERA; chmn. Woodall Rodgers Park Found. Recipient Man of Yr. award Anti-Defamation League B'nai B'rith, 1988, Banker of the Year award Am. Banker, 2001; named to Disting. Alumni, U. Tex. at Austin, Coll. Bus. Adminstrn., 1982, Hall of Fame U. Tex. Coll. Bus. Adminstrn., Austin, 1999, Am. Banker, 2001, Ernst & Young's Entrepeneur of Yr. fin. svs., 2002, Dallas Citizen's Coun., 2002. Mem. Ft. Worth C. of C. (past chmn.), Dallas C. of C., Young Pres. Orgn. (bd. dirs. 1980-89, internat. pres. 1987-88, exec. com.), Blue Key, World Presidents Orgn., Exch. Club, Sigma Alpha Epsilon. Episcopalian. Home: 4305 Overhill Dallas TX 75205 Office Phone: 214-932-6610.

GRANT, WALTER MATTHEWS, retired lawyer and corporate executive; b. Winchester, Ky., Mar. 30, 1945; s. Raymond Russell and Mary Mitchell (Rees) G.; m. Ann Carol Straus, Aug. 5, 1967; children: Walter Matthews II, Jean Ann, Raymond Russell II. ABJ, U. Ky., Lexington, 1967; JD, Vanderbilt U., 1971. Bar: Ga. 1971, Tenn. 1992. Assoc. Alston & Bird, Atlanta, 1971-76, ptnr., 1976-83; v.p., gen. counsel, sec. Contel Corp., Atlanta, 1983-91; sr. v.p., gen. counsel Smith & Nephew Inc., Memphis, 1991-93; sr. v.p., gen. counsel, sec. The Actava Group Inc., Atlanta, 1993-96, Bruno's Supermarkets, Inc., Birmingham, Ala., 1996—2002. Editor in chief Vanderbilt Law Rev., 1970-71, Ga. State Bar Jour., 1979-82. Baptist.

GRANTHAM, MARK E., lawyer; BA in History, U. Va., 1973; JD, Georgian Ct. U., 1977. Bar: Georgia 1977, Florida 1982. Mng. ptnr. DLA Piper. Named Georgia Super Lawyer, Law and Polit Mag.; named one of America's Leading Lawyers for Bus., Chambers USA, Georgia's Legal Elite, Georgia Trend Mag., 2004, The Best Lawyers in America. Fellow: Am. Bar Found.; mem.: FBA, ABA, Internat. Bar Assn. Office: DLA Piper 1201 West Peachtree St Ste 2800 Atlanta GA 30309-3450 Office Phone: 404-736-7801. E-mail: mark.grantham@dlapiper.com.

GRAPHIA, GARY P., lawyer, construction executive; b. Baton Rouge, Sept. 4, 1962; m. Rene Graphia. Degree in Fin., La. State U., JD, 1991. Various positions, including asst. v.p. Texas Commerce Bank; assoc. Phelps Dunbar LLP, Kean, Miller, Hawthorne, D'Armond, McCowan & Jarman LLP, 1995—99, ptnr., 1999; gen. counsel The Shaw Group Inc., 1999—2006, corp. sec., 1999—2007, chief legal officer, 2006—07, exec. v.p., corp. devel. & strategy, 2007—08; exec. v.p., COO Shaw Group, Inc., 2008—. Bd. trustees La. Arts & Sci. Mus., 2002—, La. State U. Paul M. Hebert Law Ctr., 2003—. Named one of "40 under 40", Baton Rouge Bus. Report, 2001. Office: The Shaw Group Inc 4171 Essen Ln Baton Rouge LA 70809 Office Phone: 225-932-2500. Office Fax: 225-987-3328. Business E-Mail: gary.graphia@shawgrp.com.

GRASS, FRANK JOSEPH, career military officer; b. Arnold, Mo., May 19, 1951; AA in Environmental Technology, St. Louis Cmty. Coll, 1975; BS in Liberal Arts, Metropolitan State U., 1985; MS in Nat. Security Strategy, Nat. War Coll., 2000; Grad., Nat. Def. U., 2006. Joined US Army Nat. Guard, Mo., 1969, advanced through ranks to gen., 2012; platoon leader Detachment 1, 220th Engineer Co., Festus, Mo., 1981; project officer US Army Corps of Engineers, St. Paul, 1982—84; platoon leader Company D, 15th Engineer Battalion, 9th Infantry Divsn., Ft. Lewis, Wash., 1984, exec. officer, 1984—85, battalion motor officer, 1985—86; S4 880th Engineer Battalion, Jefferson Barracks, Mo., 1986; comdr. 220th Engineer Co., Festus, Mo., 1986—88; civil engineer 35th Engineer Brigade, Jefferson Barracks, Mo., 1988; asst. prof. mil. sci. Mo. State U., Springfield, Mo., 1988—91; engineer exercise project officer US Army South, Ft. Clayton, Panama, 1992—94; chief exercise section, exercise branch US Army Nat. Guard Readiness Ctr., Arlington, Va., 1994—97, chief ops. divsn., 2000—03, G-3, 2003—04; comdr. 203rd Engineer Battalion, Joplin, Mo., 1997—99; dep. dir. US Army Nat. Guard, 2004—06; dir. mobilization & reserve component affairs US European Command (EUCOM), 2006—08; dir. ops. US Northern Command (USNORTHCOM), Peterson AFB, 2008—10, dep. comdr., 2010—12; chief Nat. Guard Bur., Arlington, Va., 2012—. Decorated Def. Disting. Svc. medal, Def. Superior Svc. medal, Legion of Merit, Meritorious Svc. medal, Army Commendation medal, Army Achievement medal, Army Reserve Component Achievement medal, Nat. Def. Svc. medal, Global War on Terrorism Svc. medal, Armed Forces Svc. medal, Humanitarian Svc. medal, Armed Forces Reserve medal; recipient Bronze Order of the De Fleury medal, Army Engineer Assn., Mo. Conspicuous Svc. medal, Mo. Nat. Guard, Honorable Order of St. Barbara, US Field Artillery Assn., Disting. Svc. medal, Nat. Guard Assn. US, Washington Army Nat. Guard Legion of Merit, State of Washington. Office: The National Guard Bureau 111 South George Mason Dr Arlington VA 22204*

GRASSO, ALFRED, engineering company executive, systems engineer; b. Worcester, Mass., Sept. 19, 1958; s. Ciriaco and Tommasina (Pirracci) Grasso; m. Michele Therese Casciaro, Aug. 22, 1987. BSEE, U. Mass., Amherst, 1980; MS in Computer Sci., Worcester Poly. Inst., 1993. Engr. Westinghouse Electric Corp., Balt., 1980-84; sr. engr. ARINC Research Corp., Annapolis, Md., 1984-86; with MITRE Corp., Bedford, Mass., 1986—, tech. dir. Battlefield Sys. Divsn. Ft. Monmouth, NJ, v.p., chief info. officer McLean, Va., 1999—2001, sr. v.p., gen. mgr. Washington Command, Control and Comms. (WC3) Ctr., 2001—04, dir. Command, Control, Comms., and Intelligence (C3I) Federally Funded Rsch. and Devel. Ctr. (FFRDC), 2004—07, pres., CEO, 2006—, mem. bd. trustees. Adj. prof. Anne Arundel CC, Arnold, Md., 1984—85; advisor Picker Engring. Program, Smith Coll., Dept. Sys. and Info. Engring., U. Va.; mem. US Army Sci. Bd.; bd. dirs., exec. com. mem. Armed Forces Comm. and Electronics Assn.; cons. STRATCOM Strategic Adv. Group; mem. Def. Sci. Bd., 2010—. Contbr. articles to profl. jours. Mem.: AVSA, AFCEA, IEEE, Order of Engrs. Roman Catholic. Avocations: astronomy, racquetball, tennis, computers. Home: 12165 Brecknock St Oakton VA 22124-2348 Office: MITRE Corp 7515 Colshire Dr Mc Lean VA 22102-7539

GRATZ, JAY M., metal products executive; b. NYC; m. Pam Gratz; 1 child, Kimberly. B in Econ. and Chemistry, SUNY, Buffalo, 1973; M of Mgmt. in Fin. and Acctg., Northwestern U., 1975. CPA, Ill. Various positions Inland Steel Industries, Inc., Chgo., 1975-81, asst. mgr., 1981-84, asst. mgr. cash and investments, 1984-86, mgr. fin. planning and analysis, 1986, v.p. fin., v.p. fin. Ryerson Tull, Inc., 1994-96; v.p., CFO Inland Steel Industries, 1994—98, Ryerson, Inc., Chgo., 1996—98, exec. v.p., CFO, 1999—2007, pres., Ryerson Coil Processing Divsn., 2001—07. Bd. dirs. Trex Co., Inc., 2007—. Office: Trex Co Inc 160 Exeter Dr Winchester VA 22603 Office Phone: 540-542-6300. Office Fax: 540-678-1820. Business E-Mail: jgratz@trex.com.

GRAUER, PHYLLIS A., pharmacist; BS in Pharmacy, Ohio State U.; PharmD, Kans. U. Cert. palliative care cert. Program, Ohio Northern U. Pres. Palliative Care Consulting Group, 1999—2006; v.p., Clin. Svcs. HospiScript Svcs. LLC, 2007—; clin. pharmacist cons., 2009—; asst. clin. prof. The Ohio State U. Coll. Pharmacy, 2009—. Pharmacist section leader Nat. Coun. Hospice and Palliative Profls.; mem. Nat. Hospice and Palliative Care Orgn. (NHPCO). Mem.: Oxford Internat. Ctr. (hon. bd. dirs.). Office: HospiScript Services LLC 4525 Executive Park Dr Ste 100 Montgomery AL 36116-1648 Office Phone: 334-240-1494. Business E-Mail: grauer.1@osu.edu.

GRAVELLE, MICHAEL L., lawyer; BBA, JD, Southern Meth. U. Atty. Baker & McKenzie; joined Alltel Info. Svcs., Inc. (acquired by Fidelity Nat. Info. Svcs., Inc.), 1993, v.p., 1996—2000, gen. counsel, sec., 1996—2006, sr. v.p., 2000—06; sr. v.p., gen. counsel, sec. Fidelity Nat. Info. Services, Inc., 2006, exec. v.p. legal, 2006—10, corp. exec. v.p., chief legal officer, corp. sec., 2010—. Office: Fidelity National Information Services Inc 601 Riverside Ave Jacksonville FL 32204 Office Phone: 904-854-5000. Office Fax: 904-357-1105. Business E-Mail: michael.gravelle@fnf.com.

GRAVES, JAMES EARL, federal judge, former state supreme court justice; b. 1953; m. Bettye Ramsey; 3 children. BA in Sociology, Millsaps Coll., 1975; JD, Syracuse U., 1980; MPA, Syracuse U. Maxwell Sch. Citizenship & Public Affairs, 1981; LLD (hon.), Millsaps Coll. Clerk Dept. of Community Devel., Syracuse, NY, 1978—79; staff atty. Central Miss. Legal Services, Jackson, Miss., 1980—83; ptnr. Murrain & Graves, 1983—84; assoc. atty. Walker & Walker, 1984—86; legal counsel Health Law Div., Miss. Atty. Gen. Office, 1986—89, Human Services Div., Miss. Atty. Gen. Office, 1989—90; special asst. atty. gen. State of Miss., 1986—90, dir. child support enforcement div. Dept. Human Services, 1990—91; cir. ct. judge 7th Cir. Dist., 1991—2001; justice Miss. Supreme Ct., 2001—11, presiding justice, 2009—11; judge US Ct. Appeals (5th Cir.), Jackson, 2011—. Adj. prof. media and civil rights law Jackson State U., 1980—97; instr. trial advocacy Harvard Law Sch., 1998—2000. Active pub. sch. activities; coach student mock trial teams. Recipient Judge of Yr. award, Nat. Conf. Black Lawyers, 1992, Thurgood Marshall award, Jackson's Martin Luther King Celebration, 1994, 2002, Commissioner's award, US Dept. Health & Human Services, 2001, Special Achievement award, Jackson Federal Exec. Assn., 2002, Humanized Ed. award, Miss. Assn. of Educators, 2002; named Parent of Yr., 2000—01. Mem.: Miss. Bar Found. (Law-Related Public Ed. award 2002), Magnolia Bar Assn. (Govt. Service award 1993, R. Jess Brown award 1994, Govt. Service award 1998), Hinds County Bar Assn. (Innovation award 2000), Nat. Bar Assn. (Disting. Jurist award 1996). Office: US Court Appeals 5th Cir 245 E Capitol St Ste 200 Jackson MS 39201

GRAVES, JOHN WILLIAM, historian; b. Little Rock, June 25, 1942; s. William A. and Mabel (Morehart) G. BA in History, U. Ark., 1964, MA, 1967; PhD in History, U. Va., 1978. Grad. tchg. asst. U. Ark., 1965-66; instr. history U. S.W. La., LaFayette, 1966-68; rsch. asst. U. Va., Charlottesville, 1971-72; instr. history S.W. Tex. State U., San Marcos, 1972-77; coll. assistance migrant program, freshman studies coord., basic skills specialist, lectr. St. Edward's U., Austin, Tex., 1979—85; assoc. prof. then prof. history Henderson State U., Arkadelphia, Ark., 1985—, chmn. dept. social scis., 2002—. Rep. Sch. Liberal Arts Faculty Senate, 1987-88; Rep., Dept. Social Sci. Faculty Senate, 2002-03. Author: Town and Country: Race Relations in an Urban-Rural Context, Arkansas, 1865-1905, 1990 (Arkansiana award Ark. Libr. Assn. 1991, Commendation award Am. Assn. for Study of State and Local History 1993); contbr. articles to profl. jours. Bd. dirs. Soc. for Preservation of Mosaic Templars of Am. Bldg., Hillcrest Residents Assn., Little Rock, Black History Adv. Com. State of Ark.; adv. bd. dept. Ark. heritage Mosaic Templars Am. Ctr.; rep. Coalition of LIttle Rock Neighborhoods. Recipient Disting. Svc. award Henderson State U., 1999-2000, Disting. Rsch. award Henderson State U., 2001-2002; Stonewall Jackson Meml. fellow Ark. History Commn., 1965, Philip Francis DuPont fellow U. Va., 1969-71. Mem. AAUP (pres. chpt. 1999-2001), So. Hist. Assn., Ark. Hist. Assn. (v.p. 1987-92, pres. 1992-96), Ark. History Coun. (Ark. sec. of state), Audubon Soc. (pres. Bastrop County Tex. 1985), Defenders of Wildlife, Environ. Def. Fund, Ark. Nature Conservancy, Nat. Trust for Hist. Preservation, Hist. Preservation Alliance Ark., Quapaw Qtr. Assn., Student Sen. U. Ark. (grad. sch. rep. 1965-66), Tau Kappa Epsilon (pres. 1964), Phi Alpha Theta. Home: 5218 G St Little Rock AR 72205-3517 Office: Henderson State U Dept History Arkadelphia AR 71999-0001 Fax: (870) 230-5144. E-mail: johnwgrav@aol.com, gravesj@hsu.edu.

GRAVES, LORRAINE ELIZABETH, dancer, educator, coach; b. Norfolk, Va., Oct. 5, 1957; d. Thomas Edward and Mildred Fayette (Odom) G. BS, Ind. U., 1978. Dancer, Regisseuse Dance Theatre of Harlem, NYC, 1978—, ballet mistress, 1980—, prin. dancer, 1980, artistic asst., 1998—. Tchr./coach Dance Theatre of Harlem, 1998-99, 2001, guest ballet mistress, 2001—; guest tchr. N.C. Sch. of Arts, Winston-Salem, 1987, 93, Gov.'s Sch. for Arts, U. Richmond, 1990—, Carlton Johnson Acad. of Dance, 1991-95, Okla. Summer Arts Inst., 1993-94, The Flint Sch. Performing Arts, Flint Youth Ballet, 2001—, Dance Theatre of Harlem, Kennedy Ctr. Residency Program, 1993-95, 98—, Worcester Sch. Performing Arts, 1997, Greenville Ballet, 2001; resident guest tchr. Gov.'s Sch. for Arts, Norfolk, 1988-91, mem. faculty, 1996—; guest tchr. Worcester Sch. Performing Arts, 1997; resident guest tchr. S.C. Gov.'s Sch. for Arts, 1995-97; guest tchr. Va. Ballet Theatre, 1996—, artistic advisor, 1998—; guest tchr. Va. Sch. for the Arts, 1997—, resident guest tchr., 2003—; educator, judge Dance Olympus, 1997—; judge Internat. Dance Challenge, 1998—; guest faculty Mid-States Regional Dance Festival, 1999; mem. faculty SERBA Festival, Roanoke, Va., 2003, masters & mentors program Dance Theater of Harlem, 2006-; mem. Links, Inc., 2006-, Mayor's Task Force, 2008-; bd. mem. Todd Rasenlieb Dance Co., guest tchr. Battle Va. Internat., 2009-. Dancer Dance Theatre of Harlem as Princess of Unreal Beauty in live TV prodn. of Firebird, 1982, as Myrta, Queen of the Willis in NBC prodn. of Creole Giselle, 1987, performed at White House, 1981, also at the closing ceremonies of the 1984 Olympics, toured with Dance Theatre of Harlem, USSR, 1988, South Africa, 1992, guest artist Young People's Concert series, N.Y. Philharm., 1988, Detroit Symphony, 1989, River City Ballet, Memphis, 1991, 1992, N.W. Fla. Ballet, 1994, prin. dancer Va. Ballet Theatre, Norfolk, 1996—, Dance Theatre of Harlem, 1999, guest ballet mistress, 1999—, regisseuse Dance Theatre of Harlem, 1989—96. Mem. artistic com. Young Audiences of Va.; chmn. Norfolk Commn. on the Arts and Humanities, 2006—; mem. program com. Young Audiences Va.; sec., treas. Graves Funeral Home, Inc. Fellow Am. Guild Mus. Artists. Episcopalian. Avocation: teaching younger dancers.

GRAVES, TOM (JOHN THOMAS GRAVES JR.), United States Representative from Georgia, former state legislator; b. St. Petersburg, Fla., Feb. 3, 1970; m. Julie Howard, 1996; children: JoAnn, John, Janey. BBA in Finance, U. Ga.; Grad., Coverdale Leadership Inst. Mem. Dist. 10 Ga. House of Reps., 2003—05, mem. Dist. 12, 2005—10; mem. US Congress from 9th Ga. Dist., Washington, 2010—13, US Congress from 14th Ga. Dist., 2013—. Recipient Guardian of Small Bus. award, Nat. Fedn. of Ind. Bus., Legislative Entrepreneur of the Yr. award, Freedom Works Found.; named Legislator of the Yr., American Legislative Exch. Coun., 2009, 9th Dist. Republican Party, 2009, Ga. Retail Assn. Mem.: American Legislative Exchange Coun. Republican. Baptist. Office: US House of Representatives 432 Cannon House Office Bldg Washington DC 20515*

GRAVES, WILLIAM H., minister; b. Brownsville, Tenn., June 19, 1936; s. Johnnie and Leatha Graves; m. Donna Bentley; children: Jacquelyn Graves Thomas, Ameera, William II. BA, Lane Coll., Jackson, Tenn.; D in Ministry, Claremont Sch. Theology. Asst. pastor St. John's Christian Meth. Episcopal Ch., Detroit; pastor Phillips Temple Christian Meth. Episcopal Ch., LA; sr. bishop, CEO Christian Meth. Episcopal Ch., Memphis, 2006—, chair dept. fin. Pres. Nat. Youth Conf.; rep. Christian Meth. Episcopal Ch. World Coun. Chs., India, World Meth. Conf., London, Dublin, Honolulu; chair com. on Episcopacy Christian Meth. Episcopal Ch. Nat. bd. mem. Tenn. Valley Authority. Named to Power 150, Ebony mag., 2008. Mem.: Nat. Congress Black Chs. (immediate past pres. bd. dirs.), NAACP (nat. bd. mem.). Office: Christian Meth Episcopal Ch 4466 Elvis Presley Blvd Memphis TN 38116 Business E-Mail: WHGraves@aol.com.

GRAY, ANN MAYNARD, broadcasting company executive; b. Boston, Aug. 22, 1945; d. Paul Maynard and Pauline Elizabeth MacFadyen; children: Richard R. Gray III, Dana Maynard Gray. BA, U. Mich., 1967; MBA, NYU, 1971. With Chase Manhattan Bank, NYC, 1967-68, Chem. Bank, NYC, 1968-73, asst. sec., 1971-73; asst. to treas., then asst. treas. ABC, Inc., 1974-76, treas., 1976-81, v.p. planning, 1979-86; v.p. Capital Cities/ABC, Inc., 1986—; sr. v.p. fin. ABC TV Network Group, 1988-91; pres. Diversified Pub. Group Capital Cities/ABC, Inc., 1991—97. Bd. dirs. Duke Energy Corp., Phoenix Companies Trustee Martha Graham Ctr. of Contemporary Dance, N.Y.C., 1989-92, Cancer Care, Inc., 1991—. Mailing: Duke Energy Corp Bd Directors 526 S Church St Charlotte NC 28202-1803

GRAY, DONALD MELVIN, molecular and cell biology educator; b. Milton, Pa., Apr. 4, 1938; s. Harry Seal and Edith Sophia (Larrison) G.; m. Carla Christine Winlund, Sept. 10, 1970. BA, Susquehanna U., 1960; MS, Yale U., 1963, PhD, 1967. Postdoctoral fellow U. Calif., Berkeley, 1967—70; asst. prof. molecular and cell biology U. Tex. at Dallas, Richardson, 1970—76, assoc. prof., 1976—83, prof., 1983—2012, program head, 1989—95, 2004—07, emeritus prof., 2012—. Contbr. articles to profl. jours. Fogarty Sr. Internat. fellow European Molecular Biology Lab., Heidelberg, Fed. Republic of Germany, 1977-78; NIH grantee U. Tex. at Dallas, 1972-93, NSF grantee, 1994-98, Welch Found. grantee, 1972—2010. Fellow AAAS; mem. Am. Chem. Soc., Biophys. Soc. Office: Univ Tex at Dallas Molecular and Cell Biology 800 W Campbell Rd Richardson TX 75080

GRAY, FESTUS GAIL, electrical engineer, educator, researcher; b. Moundsville, W.Va., Aug. 16, 1943; s. Festus P. and Elsie V. (Rine) G.; m. Caryl Evelyn Anderson, Aug. 24, 1968; children: David, Andrew, Daniel. BSEE, W.Va. U., 1965, MSEE, 1967; PhD, U. Mich., 1971. Instr. W.Va. U., Morgantown, 1966-67; asst. prof. Va. Poly. Inst. and State U., Blacksburg, 1971-77, assoc. prof., 1977-82, prof., 1983—2003, prof. emeritus, 2003—. Vis. scientist Rsch. Triangle Inst., N.C., 1984-85; faculty fellow NASA, 1975; cons. Inland Motors, Radford, Va., 1980, Rsch. Triangle Inst., 1987—; researcher Rome Air Devel. Ctr., N.Y., 1980-81, Naval Surface Weapons Ctr., Dahlgren, Va., 1982-83, Army Rsch. Office, 1983-86, NSF, 1991-93, 98-2001, ARPA, 1993-96, Wright-Patterson AFB, 1995-99; publs. chmn. Internat. Symposium on Fault Tolerant Computing, Ann Arbor, Mich., 1985. Co-author: Structured Logic Design with VHDL, 1993, VHDL Representation and Synthesis, 2d edit., 2000; contbr. articles to sci. jours. Assoc. treas. Northside Presbyn. Ch., Blacksburg, 1986—, bd. deacons, 1980-83; coach S.W. Va. Soccer Assn., Blacksburg, 1980-86; asst. scoutmaster Boy Scouts Am., 1990—. Grantee NSF, Office Naval Rsch., NASA, Adv. Rsch. Projects Agy; Teaching fellow U. Mich., 1967-70. Mem. IEEE (chpt. chmn. 1979-80), Computer Soc. IEEE, Sigma Xi. Democrat. Achievements include research on fault tolerance, diagnosis, testing and reliability issues for VLSI, distributed and multiprocessor computer architectures, modeling and synthesis with VHOL, modeling and design with hardware description languages. Home: 304 Fincastle Dr Blacksburg VA 24060-5036 Office: Va Poly Inst and State U Blacksburg VA 24061-0111

GRAY, FRED DAVID, lawyer; b. Montgomery, Ala., Dec. 14, 1930; s. Abraham and Nancy G.; m. Bernice Hill, June 17, 1956; children: Deborah R., Vanessa, Fred D., Stanley F. BS, Ala. State U., 1951; JD, Case Western Res. U., 1954. Bar: Ala. 1954, Ohio 1954, U.S. Dist. Ct. (mid. dist.) Ala. 1955, U.S. Supreme Ct. 1956, U.S. Ct. Appeals (5th cir.) 1958, U.S. Dist. Ct. (no. dist.) Ala. 1963, U.S. Tax Ct. 1968, U.S. Ct. Appeals (11th cir.) 1982. Sr. ptnr. Gray, Langford, Sapp, McGowan, Gray & Nathanson, Montgomery and Tuskegee, Ala., 1983—. Vis. prof., Charles Hamilton Houston Chair N.C. Central Univ. Sch. of Law, Durham, NC. Author: (book) Bus Ride to Justice, 1995, The Tuskegee Syphilis Study, 1998. City atty. City of Tuskegee, 1965—; cooperating atty. NAACP Legal Def. Fund, Inc.; local gen. counsel Tuskegee U.; spl. asst. to atty. gen. State of Ala., 1975; past mem. Ala. Adv. Com. U.S. Commn. on Civil Rights; mem. Tuskegee Civic Assn. (life, award 1981); elder Tuskegee Ch. of Christ; chmn., trustee Southwestern Christian Coll., Terrell, Tex. Recipient Constl. Law award Ala. Civil Liberties Union, 1968, Disting. Alumni award Ala. State U., 1974, Social Engr.'s citation, 1975, Martin Luther King, Jr. Meml. Drum Major award Southern Christian Leadership Conf., 1980, Black Achievers award, Ala. chpt. SCLC 1981, Fletcher Reed Andrews Grad. Yr. award Case Western Res. U., 1985, Man Yr. award Southwestern Christian Coll., 1986, Charles Hamilton Medallion of Merit Washington Bar Assn., 1986; honored by Miller Brewing Co. Gallery of Greats: Black Attys. Counsels for the Cause, 1989; named to The Trial Lawyer Hall of Fame, 2011 Mem. ABA, Assn. Trial Lawyers Am., Ala. Trial Lawyers Assn., Ala. State Bar Assn. (pres.-elect 2001-02, pres. 2002-03), Nat. Bar Assn. (pres. 1985-86, 1st Ann. Equal Justice award 1977), Macon County Bar Assn. (past pres.), Nat. Bar Inst., NAACP (life), Soc. Benchers, Omega Psi Phi, Sigma Pi Phi. Represented Rosa Parks when she was arrested for not giving up her seat on a Montgomery bus, 1955. Office: Gray Langford et al PO Box 830239 Tuskegee AL 36083-0239 also: 400 S Union St Ste 205 Montgomery AL 36104-4316

GRAY, HUGH M., metal products executive; BSc in Math. & Physics, Glasgow U., Scotland, MBA. Pres. tech. divsn. of a Bethlehem Steel subs.; pres. and CEO of a computer software and mgmt. consulting co.; dir. info. tech. and CIO of computer software and metal roofing companies; dir. info. tech. Metals USA Holdings Corp., 2000—03, v.p., chief info. officer, 2003—. Mem. bd. dirs. Nashville C. of C. Internat. Bus. Coun. Office: Metals USA Holdings Corp 2400 E Commercial Blvd Ste 905 Fort Lauderdale FL 33308-4059 Office Phone: 713-965-0990. Office Fax: 713-965-0067.

GRAY, J. CHARLES, lawyer, former cattle rancher; b. Leesburg, Fla., Mar. 26, 1932; s. G. Wayne and Mary Evelyn (Albright) G.; m. Saundra Hagood, Aug. 18, 1955; children: Terese Ren. John Charles Jr., Lee Jerome. BA, U. Fla., 1955, LLB, 1958, JD, 1962. Bar: Fla. Supreme Ct., State and Fed. Cts. County atty. Orange County, Fla., 1977—85; founder, chmn. Gray Robinson, P.A., Attys. Chmn. Fla. Turnpike Authority, 1965-67; city solicitor City of Orlando (Fla.), 1960-61; pres. Santa Gertrudis Breeders Internat., 1981-83; dir. Nat. Cattleman's Assn., 1981-83. Trustee U. Ctrl. Fla. Found.; bd. dirs. Fla. TaxWatch, Fla. Earth Found., Orlando Remembered. Recipient J. Thomas Guerney Lifetime Svc. award, 1998, James B. Green award for Econ. Devel., 1998, Legacy award Greater Orlando Leadership Found., 2005, John Young History Maker award, 2008, Le Roy Collins Lifetime Achievement award Leadership Fla., 2009; inducted into U. Fla. Hall of Fame, Fla. Blue Key, Roast & Toast Fla. Pub. Rels. Assn.,2003, J.A. Lauriet Hall of Fame, 2003, Fla. Most Outstanding Bus. Legacy award Orlando Bus. Jour. Ctr., 2009, Named 50 Most Powerful People, Orlando Mag., 2008 Mem. ABA, Fla. Bar Assn., Orange County Bar Assn., Martindale Hubble Rating AV, Citrus Club of Orlando (past dir.), Univ. Club of Orlando (past dir.), Seven Seas Cruising Assn. (commodore, World Circumnavigator award, bd. dirs. O'Force, adv. bd. "Seeds of Peace"). Republican. Episcopalian. Office: Ste 1400 301 E Pine St Orlando FL 32801-2725 Office Phone: 407-843-8880. Personal E-mail: charlie.gray@gray-robinson.com. Business E-Mail: cgray@gray-robinson.com.

GRAY, JIM, mayor, Lexington, Kentucky; b. 1953; s. James Norris Gray and Lois Howard. Grad., Vanderbilt U. Pres. and CEO Gray Constrn.; vice mayor City of Lexington, Ky., 2007—10, mayor Ky., 2010—. With Gay & Lesbian Victory Fund; trustee Berea Coll. Loeb Fellow, Harvard U., 1996. Democrat. Office: Office of the Mayor 200 E Main St Lexington KY 40507 Office Phone: 859-258-3100. Office Fax: 859-258-3194. E-mail: mayor@lexingtonky.gov.*

GRAY, MYRON A., delivery service executive; Degree in Bus. Adminstrn.; completed Advanced Mgmt. Program, INSEAD, Fontainebleau, France, Yale Sch. of Bus. Part-time package handler United Parcel Service of America, Inc. (UPS), Tenn., 1978, ops. supr., 1984, with Rocky Mountain Dist., pres., Americas region, v.p., COO, Southeast Tex. Dist., 1995, v.p., Southwest region, 2002—04, v.p., North Ctrl. region, 2004—08, v.p., Americas region, 2008—09, pres., U.S. ops., 2009—. Bd. govs. The Atlanta Police Found., Nat. Urban League, Boys & Girls Clubs of America. Office: United Parcel Service Inc 55 Glenlake Pky NE Atlanta GA 30328 Office Phone: 404-828-6000. Office Fax: 404-828-7666. Business E-Mail: MGray@ups.com.

GRAY, NANCY ANN OLIVER, academic administrator; b. Dallas, Apr. 23, 1951; d. Howard Ross and Joan (Dawkins) Oliver; m. David Nelson Maxson, Oct. 5, 1985; children by previous marriage: Paul, Jeff, Scott. BA, Vanderbilt U., 1973; MEd, North Tex. State U., 1975; attended, Vanderbilt U., 1976-79; PhD (hon.), Presbyterian Coll., 2002. Cert. fund raising exec. Tchr. Highland Park High Sch., Dallas, 1973-75; chmn. drama dept. Harpeth Hall Sch., Nashville, 1975-77; assoc. dir. devel. Vanderbilt U., Nashville, 1977-78, assist. dean students, 1978-80; dir. spl. gifts U. Louisville, 1982-86; dir. major gifts Oberlin Coll., Ohio, 1986-90; dir. capital programs The Lawrenceville Sch., NJ, 1990-91; v.p. devel. and univ. rels. Rider U., Lawrenceville, NJ, 1991-98; v.p. sem. rels. Princeton Theol. Sem., NJ, 1998-99; pres. Converse Coll., Spartanburg, SC, 1999—2004, Hollins U., Roanoke, Va., 2005—. Trustee Princeton Theol. Sem., 2000—; bd. dirs. Tuition Plan Consortium, 2008-, Spartanburg Day Sch., 2000-2002, Vanderbilt U., Nashville, 1973-77, Found. Ind. Higher Edn., 2006-09, vice chair resource devel., Coun. Ind. Colls., 2010-14, United Way of Roanoke Valley, 2006-12; bd. dirs. Brevard Music Ctr., 1999—2005, Wye Faculty Seminar, 2000-04, treas. Women's Coll. Coalition, 2009-13; chair Coun. Independent Colls. Va., 2008-09, mem. bd. dirs., 2010-13, South Assn. Sch. & Univ., 2013-, bd. dirs., 2013. Home: Hollins U PO Box 9630 Roanoke VA 24020 Office: Hollins U PO Box 9625 Roanoke VA 24020 Office Phone: 540-362-6321. Business E-Mail: ngray@hollins.edu.

GRAY, ROBERT F., JR., lawyer; BBA, U. Mich., 1972, MBA, 1974; JD, U. San Diego, 1977; LLM, NYU, 1978. Bar: Calif. 1977, Tex. 1978, DC 1979. With Fulbright & Jaworski LLP, Houston, 1978—2005; ptnr. and head global energy practice group Mayer, Brown, Rowe & Maw LLP, Houston, 2005—. Bd. dir. Jr. Achievement of Houston/Gulf Coast, 1996—2001; adv. bd. dir. Houston Tech. Ctr., 2000—; bd. dir. Houston Entrepreneur's Found., 2000—; bd. mgrs. Cougar Investment Fund, 2001—; dean's adv. bd. Univ. Houston C.T. Bauer Coll. Bus., 2002—. Named a Tex. Super Lawyer, Tex. Monthly Mag., 2003. Fellow: Tex. Bus. Law Found.; mem.: ABA (Tex. State Liaison, com. on corp. laws 1990—98), State Bar Tex. (chmn. bus. law sect. 1995—96), State Bar of Calif., Houston Bar Assn., DC Bar. Office: Mayer Brown Rowe & Maw LLP 700 Louisiana St Ste 3400 Houston TX 77002-2790 Office Phone: 713-238-2600. Business E-Mail: rgray@mayerbrown.com.

GRAY, ROBERT STEELE, publishing executive, editor, writer; b. Beaumont, Tex., Oct. 6, 1923; s. Fred and Ruth Louise (Lewelling) G.; m. Nellie Frances McGuinness, July 3, 1945; children: Robert Steele, Laura, Ruth Ellen (Mrs. Sommy L. Ham). BS, U. Houston, 1954. Newcaster Sta. KPRC-AM, Houston, 1947; news dir. Sta. KNUZ, Houston, 1948-49; reporter Citizens Papers, Houston, 1950; newsfilm dir. Sta. KPRC-TV, 1951-56; writer Houston Post, 1956-60; founder, pub. editor Cordovan Corp., Houston, 1960—, chmn. bd., 1982—; pub. Cordovan Bus. Jours., Houston, 1971; co-founder Golfer Mags., Inc., 1984—2001. Author: Survivor, 1998. 2nd lt. USMCR, 1942-46, to 1st lt. 1951-52, Korea. Mem.: Soc. Profl. Journalists. Home and Office: 607 Houghton Rd Katy TX 77450

GRAY, VIRGINIA HICKMAN, political science professor; b. Camden, Ark., June 10, 1945; d. George Leonard and Ethel Massengale (Bell) Hickman; 1 child, Brian Charles. BA with honors, Hendrix Coll., 1967; MA, Washington U., St. Louis, 1969, PhD, 1972. Asst. prof. polit. sci. U. Ky., Lexington, 1971-73; from asst. prof. to assoc. prof. U. Minn., Mpls., 1973-83, prof., 1983-2000, chairperson dept. polit. sci., 1985-88; Winston Disting. prof. polit. sci. U. N.C., Chapel Hill, 2001—. Guest scholar Brookings Inst., Washington, 1977-78; vis. prof. U. Oslo, 1985, Nankai U., 1988, U. B.C., 1992, U. N.C., 1993-94; NSF vis. prof. for women, 1993-94. Co-author: The Organizational Politics of Criminal Justice, 1980, Feminism and the New Right, 1983, Politics in the American States, 9th edit., 2008, 10th edit., 2013 American States and Cities, 1991, 2d edit., 1997, The Population Ecology of Interest Representation, 1996, Minnesota Politics and Government, 1999; Interest Groups and Health Care Reform across the United States, 2013. Bd. dirs. Health Ptnrs. Inc., 1992-2001, chair, 1999-2001. Fellow Woodrow Wilson Found., 1970, NDEA, 1969-70; grantee Swedish Bicentennial Found., 1985; recipient rsch. assistantship NSF, 1968-69, rsch. grant NSF, 1997-2001; scholar in residence Rockefeller Ctr., Bellagio, Italy; Investigator award Robert Wood Johnson Found., 2003-06; named Disting. Alumnus Hendrix Coll., Career Achievement award, State Politics & Policy Sec., Am. Polit. Sci. Assn., 2005, Virginia Gray Book award, Am. Polit. Sci. Assn., 2013. Mem. Am. Polit. Sci. Assn. (coun. 1990-92), Midwest Polit. Sci. Assn. (coun. 1984-86, v.p. 1997-99, pres. 2003-2004), Policy Studies Orgn. (coun. 1977-79), So. Polit. Sci. Assn., Western Polit. Sci. Assn. Democrat. Office: U NC Dept Polit Sci CB 3265 Hamilton Hall Chapel Hill NC 27599-3265 Office Phone: 919-843-5602. E-mail: vagray@email.unc.edu.

GRAYBEAL, JACK DANIEL, chemist, educator; b. Detroit, May 16, 1930; s. Paul Herman and Polly Dale (McClintic) G.; m. Evelyn Alice Nicolai, June 13, 1954; children: Daniel Lee, David Eugene, Dale Kevin. BS in Chemistry, W.Va. U., 1951; MS in Chemistry, U. Wis., 1953, PhD in Chemistry, 1955. Mem. tech. staff Bell Tel. Labs., Holmdel, NJ, 1955-57; asst. prof. chemistry W.Va. U., Morgantown, 1957-63, assoc. prof., 1963-68; assoc. prof. chemistry Va. Poly. Inst. and State U., Blacksburg, 1968-69, prof., 1969-97, assoc. head dept., 1975-95, prof. emeritus, 1997—. Author: Molecular Spectroscopy, 1988; contbr. articles to profl. jours. Mem. Am. Chem. Soc., Phi Lambda Upsilon (nat. editor 1981-87, nat. sec. 1987-96, nat. pres. 1996-2002, nat. historian 2002—10), Sigma Xi. Avocations: stamp collecting/philately, photography. Home: 312 Apperson Dr Blacksburg VA 24060-3641 Office Phone: 540-552-4073. Personal E-mail: graybealjd@verizon.net.

GRAYDON, FRANK DRAKE, retired accounting educator, administrator; b. Ovalo, Tex., Feb. 11, 1921; s. Alonzo Otis and Jennie Lewis (Drake) G.; m. Mary Elizabeth Galt, June 16, 1943; children: Geoffrey Galt, David Drake. BBA, Tex. Tech. Coll., 1941; MBA, Northwestern U., 1943. CPA Tex. Pub. acct. David Himmelblau & Co., Chgo., 1942-44; lectr. in acctg. Northwestern U., Chgo., 1942-44; instr. acctg. Tex. Tech. Coll., 1944-45; chief acct. U. Houston, 1945-46; asst. prof. acctg. U. Tex., 1946-50; with fin. statement sect. Ctrl. Contrs. Office Ford Motor Co., Dearborn, Mich., 1950-51; budget examiner Agys. of Higher Edn., Legis. Budget Bd., Austin, Tex., 1951-55; fin. planning staff Temp. Commn. on Higher Edn., Austin, 1954-55; budget dir. and prof. acctg. U. Tex. Sys., Austin, 1955-90, spl. counsel budget and fin., Office of the Chancellor, 1990-93, budget dir. emeritus, 1993—; prof. acctg. emeritus U. Tex., Austin, 1993—. Mem. AICPA. Home: 8158 Ceberry Dr Austin TX 78759-8743 Home Phone: 512-345-9180.

GRAY-LITTLE, BERNADETTE, academic administrator, psychology professor; b. Washington, NC, Oct. 21, 1944; d. James and Rosalie (Lanier) Gray; m. Shade Keys Little, Nov. 21, 1971; children: Maura, Mark. BA, Marywood Coll.; MS, St. Louis U., PhD in Psychology. Asst. prof. psychology U. NC, Chapel Hill, 1971-76, assoc. prof., 1976-82, prof. psychology, 1982—2009, chair Dept. Psychology, 1993—98, sr. assoc. dean undergraduate edn., 1999—2001, dean Coll. Arts and Scis., 2004—06, exec. vice chancellor, provost, 2006—09; chancellor U. Kans., 2009—. NIMH fellow, 1967-68, Fulbright fellow, 1970-71, NRC fellow, 1982-83. Fellow Am. Psychol. Assn.; mem. Phi Beta Kappa. Office: University of Kansas Office of Chancellor 230 Strong Hall Lawrence KS 66045 Office Phone: 785-864-3131. Office Fax: 785-864-4120. E-mail: chancellor@ku.edu.*

GRAYSON, ALAN MARK, United States Representative from Florida; b. NYC, Mar. 13, 1958; s. Daniel Franklin and Dorothy Ann (Sabin) Grayson; m. Lolita Botado, Apr. 27, 1990 (separated 2014); children: Skye, Star, Sage, Storm, Stone. BA in Urban Studies magna cum laude, Harvard U., Cambridge, Mass., 1978, MA in Public Policy, 1983, JD cum laude, 1983. Bar: Colo. 1984, DC 1985, US Dist. Ct. DC, US Dist. Ct. (eastern dist.) Va., US Ct. Fed. Claims, US Ct. Appeals (4th & Fed. Circuits). Law clk. Colo. Supreme Ct., Denver, 1983-84, US Ct. Appeals DC, Washington, 1984-85; assoc. Fried, Frank, Harris, Shriver & Jacobson, Wash., 1985—90; founder, pres. IDT Corp., 1990—91; prin. Grayson & Kubli PC, Orlando, Fla., 1991—2008; mem. US Congress from 8th Fla. Dist, Washington, 2009—11, US Congress from 9th Fla. Dist, 2013—, US House Financial Services Com., 2009—11, US House Space, Sci. & Technology Com., 2009—11, 2013—, US House Fgn. Affairs Com., 2013—. Lectr. George Wash. U. Founder, officer Alliance for Aging Rsch. Named Lawyer of Yr., Taxpayers Against Fraud, 2006, Humanitarian of Yr., Fla. Civil Rights Assn., 2007; named one of The 50 Politicos to Watch, Politico, 2010; finalist Trial Lawyer of Yr., Trial Lawyers Assn., 2006. Democrat. Jewish. Office: US House of Representatives 430 Cannon House Office Bldg Washington DC 20515-0908 also: 5842 S Semoran Blvd Orlando FL 32822 Office Phone: 202-225-9889, 407-615-8889. Office Fax: 202-225-9742, 407-615-8890.*

GRAYSON, JOANN HESS, psychology professor; m. Phillip Grayson; 2 children. PhD, Washington U., St. Louis. Asst. prof. to prof. psychology James Madison U., Harrisonburg, Va., 1976—. Past chair Gov.'s Adv. Bd. on Child Abuse and Neglect, Va. Contbr. articles to profl. jours.; editor, pub.: Va. Child Protection Newsletter, 1981—. Recipient TIAA-CREF Va. Outstanding Faculty award, State Coun. Higher Edn. Va., 2004, Commr.'s award for Va., Adminstrn. Children, Youth and Families, US HHS Adminstrn. Children and Families, 2005, Champion for Children award, Prevent Child Abuse Va., 2006, US Prof. of Yr. award, Carnegie Found. for Advancement of Tchg. and Coun. for Advancement and Support of Edn., 2006; named Va. Women in History, Va. Libr. Assn., 2009. Office: Dept Psychology James Madison U MSC 7704 Harrisonburg VA 22807 Office Phone: 540-568-6482. E-mail: graysojh@jmu.edu.

GRDEN, NANCY L., medical insurance company executive; Grad., U. Del.; BS in Economics, Bucknell U.; MS in Urban & Regional Planning, U. SC, MBA. Chief mktg. officer FHC Health Sys.; exec. v.p., mktg. svcs. NationsBank; founder, pres. Avenir, LLC; staff dir. Nat. Conf. State Legislatures, 1975—78; exec. asst. HUD, 1978—80; rsch. analyst U. SC, 1980—82; exec. v.p. BofA, 1983—92, ValueOptions, 1992—2001; CEO Lifescape, LLC, 1999—2000; joined Amerigroup Corp., 2001, exec. v.p., 2008—. Office: Amerigroup Corp 4425 Corporation Ln Virginia Beach VA 23462 Office Phone: 757-490-6900. Office Fax: 757-222-2330. Business E-Mail: nancy.grden@valueoptions.com.

GREASON, MURRAY CROSSLEY, JR., lawyer; b. Wake Forest, NC, Dec. 12, 1936; s. Murray Crossley and Evelyn Elizabeth (Hackney) G.; m. Joan Millicent Wilder. BS magna cum laude, Wake Forest U., 1959, JD magna cum laude, 1962. Bar: N.C. 1962. Assoc. firm Womble Carlyle Sandridge & Rice, PLLC, Winston-Salem, NC, 1965-70; mem. firm Womble Carlyle Sandridge & Rice, Winston-Salem, NC, 1970—; mng. ptnr. firm Womble Carlyle Sandridge & Rice, PLLC, Winston-Salem, 1988-96. Vis. lectr. Wake Forest U., 1972-74. Pres. Winston-Salem Estate Planning Coun., 1973; trustee Denmark Loan Fund, scholarships to Wake Forest U.; bd. visitors Wake Forest Law Sch., 1983-07, 2009-; chmn. 1994-2000; trustee Wake Forest U., 1990, vice chmn., 1997-2002, chmn., 2003-05, vice chmn., 2005-06; life trustee, 2008-; chmn. N.W. N.C. chpt. ARC, 1996; chmn. bd. United Way Forsyth County, 1995; mem. Commn. on Ministry Episcopalian Diocese N.C., 1983-93; bd. dirs. Winston-Salem Alliance, 2000-05, Idealliance, 1998—2007, Wake Forest U. Health Scis., 2000—10, Wake Forest U. Baptist Med. Ctr., 2006-10, Wake Forest Innovation Quarters, 1999-, Cmty. Care Ctr., 2004—, The NC Railroad Co., 2004—11; adv. bd. The Wachovia Corp., 1999—2006, chmn 2003-06; adv. bd. Amarr Co., 2000—12. Capt. JAG, AUS, 1962-65. Fellow Am. Coll. Tax Coun.; mem. ABA, N.C. Bar Assn. (I. Beverly Lake Pub. Svc. award 2005), Order of Long Leaf Pine, Forsyth County Bar Assn. (pres. 1986-87), Winston-Salem C. of C. (bd. dirs., vice chmn. 2001, chmn. 2002), Wake Forest U. Alumni Assn. (pres. 1973), Forsyth Country Club, Phi Beta Kappa, Omicron Delta Kappa. Episcopalian. Home: 745 Arbor Rd Winston Salem NC 27104-2209 Office: Womble Carlyle Sandridge PLLC One W 4th St Winston Salem NC 27101 Office Phone: 336-721-3616. Business E-Mail: mgreason@wcsr.com.

GREASON, THOMAS A., state legislator; b. Ft. Leavenworth, Kans., Sept. 16, 1970; m. Mary Beth Greason; children: Matthew, Jenna, Grace. BS in Systems Engring., US Mil. Acad., West Point, NY, 1993; MBA in Fin., George Mason U., Fairfax, Va., 2000. Leadership positions Qwest, Exodus, UUNet Technologies; financial analyst, mgr. capital markets Charles E. Smith Reality, Inc; v.p. global services, east Savvis Comm., Inc.; exec. v.p. Current Analysis, Inc.; house del. Dist. 32 Va. House of Dels., Richmond, 2010—. Active Loudoun County C. of C.; mem. Econ. Devel. Commn.; vice-chmn. membership, Goose Creek dist. Boy Scout America; mem. exec. coun. Loudoun Sch. Bus. Partnership; mem. selection com. Wash. Post Agnes Myer Tchr. of Yr. 2d lt. Corps of Engineers US Army, 1993—2000, served with Va. Nat. Guard, 2000—03. Republican. Office: Va House of Dels Gen Assembly Bldg Rm 513 PO Box 406 Richmond VA 23218 also: PO Box 651293 Potomac Falls VA 20165 Office Phone: 804-698-1032, 703-203-3203. Office Fax: 804-698-6732. Business E-Mail: deltgreason@house.virginia.gov.

GREAVER, JOANNE HUTCHINS, mathematics educator, writer; b. Louisville, Aug. 9, 1939; d. Alphonso Victor and Mary Louise (Sage) Hutchins; 1 child, Mary Elizabeth Turner. BS in Chemistry, U. Louisville, 1961, MEd, 1971; MAT in Math., Purdue U., 1973. Cert. tchr. Pres. Math Mentors Inc., 1962—. Part-time faculty Bellarmine U., Louisville, 1982-2002, U. Louisville, 1985-2001, Spalding U. 2009-, Pathways Prog. U. Louisville, 2010-; project reviewer NSF, 1983—; advisor Council on Higher Edn., Frankfort, Ky., 1983-86; active regional and nat. summit on assessment in math., 1991, state task force on math., assessment adv. com., Nat. Assessment Ednl. Progress standards com.; charter mem. Commonwealth Tchrs. Inst., 1984—; mem. Nat. Forum for Excellence in Edn., Indpls., 1983; metric edn. leader Fed. Metric Project, Louisville, 1979-82; mem. Ky. Ednl. Reform Task Force, Assessment Com., Nat. Framework, Nat. Assessment Ednl. Progress Rev. Com.; lectr. in field. Author: (workbook) Down Algebra Alley, 1984; co-author curriculum guides. Recipient Presdl. award for excellence in math. tchg., 1983; named Outstanding Citizen, SAR, 1984; named to Hon. Order Ky. Cols.; grantee, NSF, 1983, Louisville Cmty. Found., 1984—86. Mem. Greater Louisville Coun. Tchrs. of Math. (pres. 1977-78, 94-95, Outstanding Educator award 1987), Nat. Coun. Tchrs. of Math.

(reviewer 1981—), Ky. Coun. Tchrs. of Math. (pres. 1990-91, Jefferson County Tchr. of Yr. award 1985), Math. Assn. Am., Phi Delta Kappa Internat., Kappa Delta Pi, Delta Kappa Gamma, Zeta Tau Alpha. Democrat. Presbyterian. Avocations: tropical fish, gardening, handicrafts, travel. Home: 11513 Tazwell Dr Louisville KY 40241 E-mail: jogreaver@aol.com.

GREBE, MICHAEL J., wholesale distribution executive; Grad., U. Mich. With AB Bonnierforetagen; pres. IPCO Safety, Inc. (acquired by Airgas, Inc.), 1991—96; group v.p. Airgas, Inc., 1997—98; COO Interline Brands, Inc., 1998—2004, pres., 1999—, CEO, 2002—; pres., CEO Interline Opco (subs. of Interline Brands, Inc.), 2004—, chmn., 2007—, Interline Brands, Inc., 2007—. Bd. dirs. Restaurant Technologies, Inc. Bd. dirs. Leadership Jacksonville. Officer, Naval Nuclear Propulsion Program USN. Office: Interline Brands Inc 701 San Marco Blvd Jacksonville FL 32207 Office Phone: 904-421-1400. Office Fax: 904-358-2486. Business E-Mail: mgrebe@interlinebrands.com.

GREEHEY, WILLIAM EUGENE (BILL GREEHEY), energy executive; b. Ft. Dodge, Iowa, 1936; married. BBA, St. Mary's U., San Antonio, 1960. Auditor Price Waterhouse & Co., 1960-61; sr. auditor Humble Oil & Refining Co., 1961-63; sr. v.p. finance Coastal Corp., 1963-74; with Valero Energy Corp., San Antonio, 1974—2007, chmn., CEO, 1979—2005, pres., 1998—2003, chmn., 2006—07, Valero L.P., 2006—07, Valero GP Holdings LLC, 2006—07, NuStar Energy LP, San Antonio, 2007—. Founder Greehey Family Found., 2004—. Served with USAF. Office: NuStar Energy LP 19003 W Interstate 10 San Antonio TX 78257-9518

GREEN, AL, soul and gospel singer; b. Forest City, Ark., Apr. 13, 1946; s. Robert and Cora G. Founder, ordained minister Full Gospel Tabernacle, Memphis, 1976—; pres. Green Enterprises, Inc., Al Green Music. Formerly rec. artist with Bell, then with Hi-Records (earning 4 gold albums, 7 gold singles, 2 platinum albums); songs recorded include: Rhymes, 1975, Let's Stay Together, Tired of Being Alone, How Do You Mend a Broken Heart, Back up Train, Love and Happiness, Sailin' on the Sea of Your Love, 1980 (Grammy award for Best Male Soul Gospel Performance, 1983, Going Away (Grammy award for Best Male Soul Gospel Performance, 1986), Everything's Gonna Be Alright, 1987 (Grammy award for Best Male Soul Gospel Performance, 1987), As Long as We're Together, 1987 (Grammy award for Best Male Soul Gospel Performance, 1989), Funny How Time Slips Away (Grammy award for Best Pop Collaboration with Vocals, 1994), (with John Legend) Stay with Me (By the Sea), 2008 (Grammy award for Best R&B Performance by Duo with Vocals, 2009), (with Anthony Hamilton) You've Got the Love I Need, 2008 (Grammy award for Best Traditional R&B Vocal Performance, 2009; albums: The Lord Will Make a Way, 1980 (Grammy award for Best Traditional Soul Gospel Album, 1981), Higher Plane, 1981 (Grammy award for Best Contemporary Soul Gospel Album, 1982), Precious Lord, 1982 (Grammy award for Best Traditional Soul Gospel Album, 1982), I'll Rise Again, 1983 (Grammy award for Best Male Soul Gospel Performance, 1983, He is the Light, 1986, I Get Joy, 1989, Love Ritual, 1990, One in a Million, 1991, Love is Reality, 1992, Al Green Gets Next to You, 1993, Your Heart's in Good Hands, 1995, Feels Like Christmas, 2001, I Can't Stop, 2003, Everything's OK, 2005, Lay It Down, 2008; appeared in Broadway prodn.: Your Arms Too Short to Box with God, 1982. Recipient Grammy award for Lifetime Achievement, 2002; inducted into the Rock & Roll Hall of Fame, 1995, Gospel Music Hall of Fame, Gospel Music Assn., 2004. Office: Full Gospel Tabernacle 787 Hale Rd Memphis TN 38116

GREEN, ASA NORMAN, academic administrator; b. Mars Hill, Maine, July 22, 1929; s. Clayton John and Annie Glenna (Shaw) G.; m. Elizabeth Jean Zirkelbach Ross, May 27, 1965; 1 son, Stephen Richard Ross. AB cum laude, Bates Coll., Lewiston, Maine, 1951; MA, U. Ala., 1955; LL.D., Jacksonville U., Ala., 1975. Rsch. dir. Ala. League Municipalities, Montgomery, 1955-57; city mgr. Mountain Brook, Ala., 1957-65; exec. sec. Ala. Assn. Ins. Agts., 1965-66; dir. devel. Birmingham-So. Coll., 1966-71; dir. devel. and communications Dickinson Coll., Carlisle, Pa., 1971-73; pres. Livingston (Ala.) U., 1973-93; pres. emeritus Livingston U., 1993—; pres. U. So. Ala. Found., 2004—. Cons. NCAA Pres.'s Commn., 1993—99; instr. polit. sci. U. Ala. Ext. Ctr., Montgomery and Birmingham, 1955—57, 1958—60. Author: Revenue for Alabama Cities, 1956. Mem. adminstrv. bd. Livingston United Methodist Ch., 2005—; bd. dirs. U. South Ala. Found., 1997—, pres. Ala., 2004—. With CIC US Army, 1952—54. Grad. fellow So. Regional Tng. Program in Pub. Adminstrn., 1951 Mem.: Phi Beta Kappa. Independent. Methodist. Office: PO Box 1466 Livingston AL 35470-1620 Home Phone: 205-652-7999.

GREEN, DANIEL MICHAEL, pediatric oncologist; b. Seattle, May 30, 1946; s. Daniel Marie and Margaret Ann (Johnson) Green; m. Lydia Ann Betz, Jan. 7, 1984; children: Amy Lynn, Sarah Ann, Daniel Joseph. BS, MIT, 1969; MD cum laude, St. Louis U., 1973. Diplomate Am. Bd. Pediatrics, in pediatric hematology-oncology Am. Bd. Pediatrics. Intern in pediat. Boston City Hosp., 1973-74, resident in pediat. hematology-oncology, 1974-75; fellow in pediatric oncology Sidney Farber Cancer Inst., Boston, 1975-78; fellow in hematology/oncology Children's Hosp. Med. Ctr., Boston, 1975-78; rsch. fellow in pediat. Med. Sch. Harvard U., Boston, 1975-78; cancer rsch. pediatrician II Roswell Park Meml. Inst., Buffalo, 1978-90; attending physician Roswell Pk. Cancer Inst., Buffalo, 1990—2008; spl. cons. in hematology-oncology Children's Hosp. Buffalo, 1978-85, from asst. attending to assoc. attending physician, 1985-89, attending physician, 1989—2008; rsch. asst. prof. Sch. of Medicine and Biomed. Scis. SUNY, Buffalo, 1978-82, from asst. prof. to assoc. prof., 1982-90, prof., 1990—2008. Author: Diagnosis and Management of Malignant Solid Tissues in Infants and Children, 1985, Long Term Complications of Treatment for Cancer During Childhood and Adolescence, 1989; mem. editl. bd. Pediatric Blood and Cancer, ad hoc reviewer Am. Jour. Pediatric Hematology/Oncology, Jour. Clin. Oncology, Cancer, Pediat., Med. and Pediatric Oncology; contbr. articles to profl. jours. Recipient, Buffalo Bills Found., 1988—90, Nat. Cancer Inst., 1991—; grantee, ACS Instnl., 1980—81, Dorothea Haus Ross, 1984—85, AROCC, 1985—90. Mem.: St. Jude Children's Rsch. Hosp. (mem. dept. epidemiology & cancer control 2008—), Soc. Pediat. Rsch., N.Y. Acad. Scis., Am. Soc. Hematology, Am. Pediat. Soc., Am. Soc. Pediat. Hematology-Oncology, Am. Acad. Pediat. (exec. com. 1992—94, oncology-hematology sect.), Internat. Soc. Pediat. Oncology (sci. com. 1989—95, sec. gen. 1999—2005), Am. Fedn. Clin. Rsch., Am. Assn. Cancer Rsch., Am. Soc. Clin. Oncology. Office: Dept Epidemiology and Cancer Control St Jude Children's Rsch Hosp 262 Danny Thomas Pl Mail Stop 735 Memphis TN 38105-2794 Office Phone: 901-595-5915. Office Fax: 901-595-5845. Business E-Mail: daniel.green@stjude.org.

GREEN, DARRELL, retired professional football player; b. Houston, Feb. 15, 1960; m. Jewell Green; children: Jerrell, Jared, Joi. Student, Tex. A&I; BS, St. Paul's Coll., Lawrenceville, Va., 1998, LHD (hon.), 2002, Marymount U., Arlington, Va., 1999, Washington U., 2002. Cornerback Washington Redskins, 1983—2002; founder Darrell Green Enterprises. Founder Darrell Green Youth Life Found., 1988—, Darrell Green Bus. Coun.; bd. mem. Balt.-Washington 2012 Olympic Bid Com., NFL/NFLPA Sept. 11th Relief Fund, Loudoun Edn. Found.; chair Pres. Bush's Coun. on Svc. and Civic Participation, 2003. Named to NFL Pro Bowl 1984, 86, 87, 90, 91, 96, 97, NFL All-Pro Team, 1986, 87, 90, 91, NFL 1990's All Decade Team, NCAA Divsn. II Hall of Fame, Tex. Sports Hall of Fame, Lone Star Conf. Hall of Honor, Javelina Hall of Fame, Pro Football Hall of Fame, 2008; recipient Walter Payton NFL Man of Yr. award, 1996, Bart Starr award, 1997. Achievements include being a member of Super Bowl Championship winning Washington Redskins, 1988, 1992. Office: Darrell Green Enterprises 21515 Ridgetop Cir Ste 290 Sterling VA 20166 Office Phone: 703-719-9174. Business E-Mail: infor@darrellgreen.com.

GREEN, DAVID, retail executive; Founder Greco Products, 1970—72; founder & CEO Hobby Lobby Stores Inc., 1972—. Named one of Forbes 400: Richest Americans, 2009. Office: 7707 SW 44th St Oklahoma City OK 73179

GREEN, GENE (RAYMOND EUGENE GREEN), United States Representative from Texas; b. Houston, Oct. 17, 1947; s. Garland B. and Evelyn (Clark) Green; m. Helen Lois Albers, 1970; children: Angela, Christopher. BBA, U. Houston, 1971; JD, U. Houston Bates Coll. Law, 1977. Bar: Tex. 1977. Mem. Dist. 95 Tex House of Reps., 1973—81, mem. Dist. 140, 1981—85; mem. Dist. 6 Tex. State Senate, 1987—93; mem. US Congress from 29th Tex. dist., 1993—; chair US House Standards of Official Conduct Com., 2008—09. Recipient Legis. Open Door award, Nat. Assn. Credit Mgmt., 2003, Medal of Honor for directing funding for cancer rsch., US Oncology, Inc., 2003, Disting. Cmty. Health award, Nat. Assn. Health Centers, 2003, 2008, Alfred K. Whitehead Legis. award, Internat. Assn. Fire Fighters, 2004, Safety Net Champion award, Nat. Assn. Hospitals, 2007, Champion of Women's Health award, Susan G. Komen for the Cure Advocacy Alliance, 2008, Honor award, Houston Bur. Tuberculosis Control, 2008; named Legislator of Yr., Nat. Coun. Cmty. Behavioral Healthcare, 2008. Mem.: Coastal Conservation Assn., Tex. Hist. Soc., League United Latin Am. Citizens (hon.). Democrat. Methodist. Office: US House of Representatives 2470 Rayburn House Office Bldg Washington DC 20515 also: 11811 I 10 East Ste 430 Houston TX 77029 Office Phone: 202-225-1688.*

GREEN, GRANT S., JR., consulting firm executive, former federal agency administrator; b. Seattle, June 16, 1938; s. Grant S. and Eveleth (Solberg) G.; m. Virginia Dondy; children: Kelley, Shelley, Tana. BA in Polit. Sci., U. Ark., 1960; MS in Mgmt., George Washington U., 1978. Commd. 2d lt. U.S. Army, 1961, advanced through grades to col., ret., 1983; various mgmt. positions Sears World Trade, Washington, 1983-86; exec. sec., spl. asst. to pres. US nat. security affairs NSC, Washington, 1986-87; asst. sec. def. US Dept. Def., Washington, 1987-88; v.p. IPAC, Washington, 1989—96; chmn., pres. Global Marketing & Development Solutions Inc. (GMDS), Alexandria, 1996—2000, chmn., 2005—; under sec. for mgmt. US Dept. State, Washington, 2001—05; pres. American Support You Fund, 2007—10. Mem. bd. USO, 1987—96; mem. advisory bd., Budget of the Future for the US Dept. State, 2007-, commr., US Commn. Wartime Contracting in Iraq & Afghanistan (CWC), 2009- Recipient Disting. Pub. Svc. award US Dept. Def., Disting. Svc. award, US Dept. State Mem. Assn. U.S. Army, Ret. Officers Assn., Am. Legion. Republican. Avocations: boating, golf, skiing. Office: GMDS Solutions Inc 2121 Eisenhower Ave Alexandria VA 22314 Office Fax: 703-299-9213.

GREEN, HOLCOMBE TUCKER, JR., investment company executive; b. Atlanta, Sept. 29, 1939; s. Holcombe Tucker and Mary Katharine (Woltz) Green; m. Nancy Reade Hall, June 18, 1966. AB, Yale U., 1961; LLB, U. Va., 1967; DBA (hon.), Piedmont Coll., 1995; MA (hon.), Yale U., 1998. Bar: Ga. 1967. Assoc. firm Hansell & Post, Atlanta, 1967-70, mem. firm, 1970-87, mgmt. com., 1980-87; CEO Green Capital Investors L.P., Atlanta, 1987—2004; chmn., CEO WestPoint Stevens, Inc., 1992—2003; prin. Birch Comm. Inc. Bd. dirs. Vytech Industries, Inc., 1987—2007, Birch Comm. Inc., 1995—, Cumulus Media Inc., 2000—09; bd. dirs., chmn. Rhodes, Inc., 1988—96; chmn. HBO & Co., 1990—98. Bd. dirs. Child Svc. and Family Counseling Ctr., 1972—85, pres., 1982—84; active Leadership Atlanta, 1974—75; trustee Atlanta Bot. Garden, 1976—92, pres., 1982—84; bd. dirs. High Mus. Art, 1982—96, Yale U. Art Gallery, 1992—, Atlanta Ballet, 1987—89, Ga. Conservancy, 1987—92, Atlanta Hist. Soc., 1993—96; trustee Taft Sch., 1987—2000; trustee, vice chmn. investments Woodruff Arts Ctr., 1990—98; chmn. Yale Devel. Bd., 1998—2005; fellow Yale Corp., 1999—2005; hon. Swedish consul State of Ga., 1988—96. Served to lt. (j.g.) USN, 1961—64. Mem.: Headwaters, Raven Soc. Va., Ocean Forest Golf Club, Doubles Club, Homosassa Fishing Club, Nine O'Clocks Club, Piedmont Driving Club, Capital City Club, Wade Hampton Golf Club, Chatooga Club, Royal Order Polar Star, Order Coif. Democrat. Presbyterian. Home: 2774 Andrews Dr #9 Atlanta GA 30305

GREEN, HOWARD A., dermatologist; Grad., George Wash. U.; MD, Boston U., 1985. Diplomate Am. Bd. Internal Medicine, 1988, Am. Bd. Dermatology, 2004. Resident internal medicine Thomas Jefferson Univ. Hosp., Phila., 1986—88; fellow mohs surgery Boston Univ. Med. Ctr., Boston, 1992—93; resident dermatology Harvard Med. Sch. Boston Mass. Gen. Hosp., Boston, Beth Israel Hosp., Children's Hosp., Lahey Clinic, New Eng. Deaconess Hosp., Brigham and Women's Hosp., Harvard Cmty. Health Plan., 1988—92; staff Dermatology Assocs., P.A. of the Palm Beaches; hosp. affiliation include St. Mary's Med. Ctr. Author publs. dozens of sci. papers on mutagenesis, skin cancer, lasers and wound healing, and has several med. patents. Named one of America's Top Doctors, Castle Connolly Med., LTD. Office: Dermatology Associates PA of the Palm Beaches 120 A Butler St West Palm Beach FL 33407 Office Phone: 561-659-1510.

GREEN, HUBERT GORDON, university professor, pediatrician; b. Dallas, Tex., Oct. 31, 1938; s. Hubert Gordon and Mary Belle G.; m. Jean A. Green, June 7, 1969; children: Nancy Elaine, David Gordon, Whitney Anne, Emily Erin. BA, Rice U., 1962; MD, U. Texas Southwestern, Dallas, 1968; MPH, U. California, Berkeley, 1972. Diplomate Am. Bd. Pediatrics. Intern Children's Med. Ctr., Dallas, 1968-69; resident U. Washington, Seattle, 1969-71; assoc. prof., pediatrics and biometry U. Arkansas Med. Sch., Little Rock, 1972-77; deputy dir., Divsn. Health Svcs. Delivery region VI USPHS, Dallas, 1977-83; dir. Dallas County Health Dept., 1983-90; dean U. Tex. Southwestern Sch. Health Professions, Dallas, 1991—2006; prof. family and cmty. medicine U. Tex. Southwestern Med. Sch., 2006—. Arkansas Children and Youth Project, (assoc. med. dir., 1972-73), Little Rock; Arkansas Children's Hosp., (med. dir., 1973-77), Little Rock; Handicapped Children's Ctr. and Child Devel. Clinic, Arkansas Dept. Health (dir., 1975-77), Little Rock; bd. dirs. Tex.-Mex. Border Health Task Force, Tex. Contbr. articles to med. jours. Lt. USNR, 1962-64. Recipient HRSA Administrator's award, Darryl Mace Presdl. award, Max Cole award. Fellow Am. Acad. Pediat., Tex. Pub. Health Assn., Royal Soc. Medicine; mem. APHA, Assn. Schs. Allied Health Professions, Tex. Assn. Pub. Health Physicians, Tex. Pediat. Soc., Tex. Med. Assn., Tex. Soc. Allied Health Professions, Dallas County Med. Soc., Alpha Omega Alpha. Avocations: travel, art. Office: U Tex Southwestern Med Ctr 5323 Harry Hines Blvd Dallas TX 75390-9082 Office Phone: 214-648-6579. Business E-Mail: gordon.green@utsouthwestern.edu.

GREEN, LARRY, councilman; BA, U. Houston, 1987; JD, Tex. Southern U., 1992. Dist. dir. to Rep. Sheila Jackson Lee US House of Representatives; v.p. devel. and govt. affairs Thurgood Marshall Coll. Fund, 2007—08; CEO HoustonWorks USA, 2008—; councilman Dist. K Houston City Coun., 2012—. Office: City Hall Annex 900 Bagby, First Floor Houston TX 77002 Office Phone: 832-393-3016. E-mail: districtk@houstontx.gov.

GREEN, LISA CANNON, editor; b. Marshall, Ky., May 7, 1962; d. Walter L. and Phyllis (Jones) Cannon; m. Bob Dale Green, May 31, 1980; children: Emily, Ethan. BA in Journalism and English, Murray State U., 1983. With The Post-Intelligencer, Paris, Tenn., 1983-84, The Jackson (Tenn.) Sun, 1984-90; data desk editor The Tennessean, Nashville, 1990—. Office: The Tennessean 1100 Broadway Nashville TN 37203-3134 Office Phone: 615-259-8275. Business E-Mail: lgreen@tennessean.com.

GREEN, LOUIS HARRY, retired surgeon; b. Houston, Jan. 21, 1923; MD, U. Tex. Med. Br., 1947. Diplomate Am. Bd. Surgery. Intern D.C. Gen. Hosp., Washington, 1947—48; resident surgery Meml. Hosp., Houston, 1948—49, Houston VA Hosp., 1951—54, Baylor Affiliated Hosps., Houston; emeritus clin. assoc. prof. Baylor Coll. Medicine, Houston; emeritus staff Meth., St. Luke's Episcopal, Tex. Children's, Hermann Hosps.; lectr., dept. biology U. Houston NSM, 2012—13; lectr. ICA NSM, 2012—13, Coll. NMS, 2013—. Commencement keynote spkr., natural scis. and math. U. Houston, 2005, 2005, commencement spkr., selector NSM, 2007, scholar, 2007, lectr., dept. biology, 2013. Named Disting. Alumnus U. Houston, 1989, Great Texan Chron's and Colitis Found. Am., 1975. Fellow: ACS; mem.: AMA, Houston Surg. Soc. (pres. 1991—92, pres. elect. 1990—91). Personal E-mail: barbara.louis@gmail.com.

GREEN, MARK FREDRICK, federal prosecutor; b. Ft. Smith, Ark., Nov. 6, 1953; BBA, U. Okla., 1978; JD, U. Okla. Coll. Law, 1978. Bar: Okla. 1978, US Dist. Ct. (eastern dist.) Okla. 1978, US Ct. Appeals (10th cir.) 1979, US Dist. Ct. (northern dist. Okla.) 1980. Asst. US atty. (eastern dist.) Okla. US Dept. Justice, Muskogee, 1978—83, US atty., 2010—; ptnr. Green & Green, 1983—91; pvt. law practice Muskogee, 1993—2010. Mcpl. ct. judge City of Muskogee; tribal prosecutor Bur. Indian Affairs, US Dept. Interior; past mem. Muskogee City Coun., Cherokee Nation Environ. Protection Commn., Okla. Scenic Reviers Commn.; bd. dirs. City of Muskogee Housing Authority. Mem.: Okla. Bar Assn., Muskogee County Bar Assn. Office: US Attorneys Office 520 Denison St Muskogee OK 74401-6007*

GREEN, MARY T., ophthalmologist; MD, Baylor U., 1982. Diplomate American Bd. Ophthalmology, 1988. Intern Baylor Coll., 1982; resident ophthalmology Baylor Coll. Med. Affil. Hosps., 1983—86; fellow cornea and refractive surgery La. State Univ. eye Ctr., 1986—87; hosp. affiliation includes St. Luke's Episcopal Hosp. Office: St Luke's Epsicopal Hospital 6720 Bertner Ave Houston TX 77030-2697 Office Phone: 832-355-1000.*

GREEN, MAURICE RICHARD, retired neuropsychiatrist; b. Chgo., Oct. 28, 1922; divorced; children: Melissa, Suzanne, Constance. BS, Northwestern U., 1942; BM, Northwestern U. Med. Sch., 1945, MD, 1946; cert. in Psychoanalytic Tng., William Alanson White Inst., NYC, 1954. Diplomate Am. Bd. Psychiatry and Neurology. Intern Passavant Hosp., Chgo., 1945-46; resident in psychiatry Bronx (N.Y.) VA Hosp., 1948-51; cons. psychiatrist Brookwood Hall, East Islip, L.I., N.Y., 1955-58; staff psychiatrist Psychiatric Clinic Ct. Spl. Sessions, 1956-60; cons. psychiatrist Bleuler Psychotherapy Ctr., Queens, N.Y., 1956-68; rsch. psychiatrist, mem. psychiat. epidemiology sect. William Alanson White Inst., NYC, 1968-72; attending geriat. psychiatrist Albert Einstein Med. Sch., 1974-76; attending child and adolescent psychiatrist Harlem Hosp. of Columbia Presbyn. Med. Ctr., NYC, 1974-75; med. dir. geriat. and family psychiatry Lincoln Hosp., 1974-76; chief psychiatrist Family Ct. Svcs. divsn. South Beach Psychiat. Ctr., SI, N.Y., 1976-80; sr. attending psychiatrist Columbia-Presbyn. at St. Luke's-Roosevelt Hosp., NYC, 1978—; cons. psychiatrist Liaison-Consultation Svc. NYU Med. Ctr., NYC, 1985-86; psychiatrist spl. evaluation and treatment unit Rockland Psychiat. Ctr., 1985-87; ret., 2010. Mem. faculty William Alanson White Inst., N.Y.C., 1957—09; cons. Goddard Coll., 1961-68; assoc. attending psychiatrist Bellevue Hosp., 1962-85; clin. prof. psychiatry NYU Med. Sch., 1964—2003; mem. med. bd. Roosevelt Hosp., 1965-76; prin. investigator Diamox-Thiamine Research Unit Nathan S. Kline Research Inst., 1987; project dir. Brain Chemistry of Schizophrenia at Nathan Kline Inst., 1988-93; med. dir. Neurologic Sys., Inc., 1987; presidium Inst. for Brain Function Rsch., Inc., 1987; mem. Treatment Innovations Task Force-Soc. for Traumatic Stress Studies, 1987. Author: Interpersonal Psychoanalysis: Selected Papers of Clara Thompson, 1971, Psicoanalisi interpersonale, 1972, L'Esperienzce Prelogica, 1972, Violence and the Family, 1980; (with Edward S. Tauber) Prelogical Experience, 1959; assoc. editor Contemporary Psychoanalysis jour., 1968-80; contbr. articles to profl. jours. Project dir. Nathan Kline Rsch. Inst., 1988—. Fellow: N.Y. Acad. Medicine, Am. Acad. Child and Adolescent Psychiatry (com. on hospitalization of children, nat. legis. network 1982—86), Am. Psychiat. Assn. (com. on aging N.Y. Dist. br.), Am. Orthopsychiat. Assn. (publs. com. Anniversary Vol. 1968—71); mem.: Am. Acad. Psychoanalysis, Am. Assn. Geriat. Psychiatry, Internat. Soc. Psychoneuroendocrinology, Am. Assn. Psychosocial Rehab., Soc. Biol. Psychiatry, Nat. Assn. Patients Rights and Advocacy, Physicians for Social Responsibility, N.Y. Soc. Clin. Psychiatry, N.Y. Coun. Child Psychiatry. Home: 7480 Beechnut St Apt 319 Houston TX 77074-4507 Office Phone: 212-595-9774. Personal E-mail: mauriegreen@msn.com.

GREEN, MIKE, professional hockey player; b. Calgary, Alta., Canada, Oct. 12, 1985; Defenseman Washington Capitals, 2005—. Player NHL YoungStars Game, 2007. Named to All-Rookie Team, American Hockey League, 2006, All-NHL team, Sporting News, 2009, First All-Star Team, NHL, 2009, 2010, NHL All-Star Game, 2011. Achievements include setting NHL record for consecutive games with a goal by a defenseman, 2009. Avocation: golf. Office: c/o Washington Capitals Verizon Center 601 F St NW Washington DC 20004 also: 627 N Glebe Rd, Ste 850 Arlington VA 22203

GREEN, PAUL WARREN, state supreme court justice; b. San Antonio, Mar. 6, 1952; s. Hubert William and Leah (Tritt) G.; m. Judith Ellen Keppler, Aug. 4, 1973; children: W. Paul, John K. BBA, U. Tex., 1974; JD, St. Mary's U., San Antonio, 1977. Bar: Tex. 1977, U.S. Dist. Ct. (we. dist.) Tex. 1982, U.S. Ct. Appeals (5th cir.) 1985, U.S. Dist. Ct. (so. dist.) Tex. 1990. Ptnr. Green, McReynolds & Reed, San Antonio, 1977—95; judge San Antonio Ct. of Appeals, 1995—2004; justice Tex. Supreme Ct., 2005—. Bd. dirs. Halfway House of San Antonio, 1978-90, pres., 1985. Fellow Tex. Bar Found., San Antonio Bar Found.; mem. ABA (mem. house of delegates

1991-93), State Bar Tex. (dir. 1993-94), San Antonio Bar Assn. (pres. 1991-92). Avocations: golf, sailing, hunting. Office: Tex State Supreme Court PO Box 12248 Austin TX 78711*

GREENBERG, DAVID I., tobacco company executive; Grad., Williams Coll.; JD, MBA, U. Chgo., 1981. Legis. rep. Staff of Ralph Nader, 1975—77; legis. dir., gen. counsel Consumer Fedn. Am., 1981—84; ptnr. Arnold & Porter, 1984—88; staff v.p. Washington rels. Philip Morris Mgmt. Corp., 1988—90, v.p. corp. affairs strategy and devel. NYC, 1998—99; v.p. govt. affairs Philip Morris Cos., 1990—92; v.p. corp. affairs Europe Philip Morris Internat., Brussels, 1992—98, sr. v.p. corp. affairs, 1999—2001; sr. v.p., chief compliance officer Altria Group., Inc., NYC, 2001—. Mem.: Phi Beta Kappa. Office: Altria Corporate Services Inc 615 Maury St Richmond VA 23224-4121 Office Phone: 917-663-3620. Business E-Mail: david.greenberg@altria.com.

GREENBERG, HARVEY, gynecologic oncologist; MD, SUNY, Buffalo, 1971. Diplomate Am. Bd. Ob-Gyn, Am. Bd. Ob-Gyn-gynecologic oncology, lic. Tex., 1987. Intern Flower-Fifth Ave. Hosp., 1972, resident, 1976; fellow NY Med. Coll., Valhalla, 1978; hosp. affiliations include Del Sol Med. Ctr., LAs Palmas Med. Ctr., Univ. Med. Ctr. of El Paso, R E Thomason Gen. Hosp., Providence Meml. Hosp. Named Recognized Dr., HealthGrades. Office: Providence Memorial Hospital 2001 N Oregon St El Paso TX 79902 Office Phone: 915-577-6011.*

GREENBERG, HOWARD, publishing executive; b. Miami, Fla. married. BBA in Fin., U. Miami, 1971. Various circulation positions Miami Herald, 1971—81; v.p., circulation dir. Denver Post, 1981—84; various positions including circulation sales & mktg. mgr., v.p., dir. devel. & v.p., circulation dir. Sun-Sentinel Co., Ft. Lauderdale, Fla., 1984—2002, v.p. circulation & ops., 2002—04, sr. v.p., mng. dir., 2004—05, sr. v.p., gen. mgr., 2005—07, pres., CEO, 2007—, pub. South Fla. Sun-Sentinel, 2007—, pub. Orlando Sentinel, 2008—, gen. mgr. WSFL-TV Miami, 2008—. Chmn. Broward Alliance, Ft. Lauderdale, 2004—05. Office: Sun-Sentinel 500 E Broward Blvd Ste 900 Fort Lauderdale FL 33394-3019 Office Phone: 954-356-4229. E-mail: hgreenberg@sun-sentinel.com, hgreenberg@tribune.com.

GREENBERG, PAUL, editor; b. Shreveport, La., Jan. 21, 1937; s. Ben and Sarah (Ackerman) G.; m. Carolyn Levy, Dec. 6, 1964; children: Daniel, Ruth Elizabeth. BA Journalism, U. Mo., Columbia, 1958, MA in History, 1959; student, Columbia Grad. Sch., NYC, 1960—62; LittD, Rhodes Coll., Memphis, 1995; DHL, Lyon Coll., Batesville, Ark., 2007. Lectr. Am. history Hunter Coll., 1962; editorial page editor Pine Bluff (Ark.) Comml., 1962-66, 67-92; syndicated columnist, 1970—; editorial page editor Ark. Dem. Gazette, Little Rock, 1992—. Editl. writer Chgo. Daily News, 1966-67; adj. faculty history U. Ark., Pine Bluff, 1978-82, vis. Fulbright fellow, 1985, mem. faculty in journalism, 1991; commentator BBC, 2004; media fellow Hoover Inst., 2005. Author: Resonant Lives, 1991, Entirely Personal, 1992, No Surprises, 1996, To Life, 1999. Served to capt. U.S. Army, 1969. Recipient Grenville Clark award for best editl., 1964, Pulitzer prize editl. writing, 1969, award Nat. Newspaper Assn., 1968, U. Mo. Sch. Journalism award, 1983, Walker Stone award for editl. writing, 1985, 86, Pulitzer Prize finalist for editl. writing, 1986, H.L. Mencken Writing award, 1987, William Allen White Journalism award U. Kans., 1988, Green Eyeshade award, 1997, 2005, Carmage Walls award, 2003. Jewish. Office: Arkansas Democrat Gazette Capitol at Scott Little Rock AR 72202

GREENBERG, RAYMOND SETH, academic and health facility administrator, educator; b. Chapel Hill, NC, Aug. 10, 1955; s. Bernard George and Ruth Esther (Marck) G.; m. Leah Daniella Dacus, Oct. 23, 1988. BA in Chemistry, U. N.C., 1976, PhD in Epidemiology, 1983; MD, Duke U., 1979; MPH, Harvard U., 1980; DMS (hon.), The Citadel, 2001; DS (hon.), Simpson Coll., 2002. Asst. prof. sch. medicine Emory U., Atlanta, 1983-86, assoc. prof., 1986-90, dep. dir. Winship Cancer Ctr., 1985-90, chair epidemiology/ biostat., 1988-90, prof., dean sch. pub. health, 1990-95; v.p. for acad. affairs, provost Med. U. SC, Charleston, 1995-99, pres., 2000—. Chair preventive medicine Nat. Bd. Med. Examiners, Phila., 1991-93; chair epidemiology study sect. NIH, Bethesda, Md., 1992-94; bd. sci. counselors Nat. Inst. for Dental and Craniofacial Rsch., Bethesda, 1994-99, mem. blue ribbon panel on rsch. tng. and career devel., 1999; chair adv. coun. Prudential Ctr. for Health Care Rsch., Atlanta, 1994-96; chair Harvard Adv. Com. on Electromagnetic Fields and Human Health, Boston, 1994-98; adv. com. on rsch. and med. grants, Am. Cancer Soc., Atlanta, 1994-96; breast and cervical cancer early detection and control adv. com., Ctrs. for Disease Control and Prevention, Atlanta, 1996-2000; adv. com. on agrl. health risks, Harvard Ctr. for Risk Analysis, Boston, 1996-99; clin. adv. bd. Deloitte and Touche Health-care Consulting Group, 1997-99; chair sci. adv. panel 3M Corp., 1998-2002; chair bd. trustees S.C. Gov.'s Sch. Sci. and Math., 2004-08; bd. sci. counselors Nat. Ctr. Health Stat., 2004-08; mem. adv. bd. McKesson Corp., 2005—, Soc. Fellows and Scholars, Nat. Ctr. Minority Health; mem. S.C. Commn. on Healthcare Access, 2004-05. Author: Medical Epidemiology, 1993, 4th edit., 2005, Epidemiologia Medica, 1995, 3d edit., 2004; contbr. articles to profl. jours. Bd. dirs. Ga. divsn. Am. Cancer Soc., 1987-93, Carolina Art Assn., 1996-98, Trident United Way, 1999-2002, Trident Urban League, 2006—; mem. Gov.'s Task Force on Higher Edn., 2006., chair bd. mem. Sea Grant, 2008-, bd. SC Rsch. Authority, 2000-Recipient SC Order of Palmetto, 2005; named hon. alumnus, Med. U. S.C. Coll. Medicine Alumni Assn., 2006. Fellow Am. Coll. Epidemiology (pres. 1990-91); mem. APHA, Am. Epidemiology Soc. Democrat. Jewish. Office: Med U SC Colcock Hall 179 Ashley Ave Charleston SC 29425 Office Phone: 843-792-9005. Business E-Mail: greenber@musc.edu.

GREENBERG, STEPHEN BARUCH, dean, medical educator; b. May 24, 1944; BA, Johns Hopkins U., 1966; MD, U. Md., 1970. Herman Brown tchg. prof. Baylor Coll. Medicine, Houston, 1990—, vice chmn. dept. medicine, 1990-1999, sr. v.p., dean of med. edn., 2006—; chief medicine svc. Ben Taub Gen. Hosp., Houston, 1990, assoc. chief staff, 1990, assoc. chmn. Dept. Medicine, 2000, chair, 2004—06. Office: Baylor Coll Medicine One Baylor Plaza Houston TX 77030 E-mail: stepheng@bcm.edu.

GREENE, DAVID, surgeon, researcher; BA magna cum laude, Harvard U., 1989; MD, Yale U., 1993. Diplomate Am. Bd. Med. Examiners, Am. Bd. Otolaryngology, Am. Bd. Facial Plastic Surgery. Rsch. fellow NIH, Bethesda, Md., 1990—90; resident otolaryngology head and neck surgery U. Calif., San Francisco, 1993—98, chief resident head and neck surgery, 1997—98; fellow facial plastic surgery Stanford U., Calif., 1998—99; clin. instr. facial plastic surgery Stanford U. Med. Ctr., 1998—99; staff surgeon Palo Alto Vets. Health Sys., 1998—99; staff otolaryngologist, head and neck surgeon Physicians Regional Med. Ctr. (formerly Cleveland Clinic), Naples, Fla., 1999—2011, chmn., 2001—. Contbr. articles to profl. jours. Recipient Spl. Thanks and Recognition award, VA, 1999, Physician Recognition award, AMA, 2001, Am. Top Doctors, Consumer Rsch. Coun. America; named Am. Top Physician, Consumer Rsch. Coun. America; named one of Best Physicians Am., Castle-Connolly's Top Drs.; John Harvard scholar, Harvard U., 1986, Harvard Coll. scholar, 1986, Harvard Detur scholar, 1985. Fellow: Am. Rhinologic Soc., Am. Acad. Otolaryngology (Achievement award 2001); mem.: ACS, Am. Acad. Facial Plastic Surgery (Best Clin. Rsch. Paper award 1999), Phi Beta Kappa. Office: 1112 Goodlette Rd N Ste 203 Naples FL 34102 Office Phone: 239-263-8444. Office Fax: 239-263-6120.

GREENE, DON HOWARD, product designer; b. Norcross, Ga., July 9, 1958; m. s. Paul Howard and Patricia Anne (Knox) G.; Cheryl Jeanne Garner, June 9, 1984; children: April Elizabeth, Adam Garner, Anna Rebecca. B of Indsl. Engring., Ga. Inst. Tech., 1980; MBA, Ga. State U., 1988. Registered profl. engr., Ga. Mfg. engr. Sci.-Atlanta, Inc., Atlanta, 1981-82; indsl. engr. Sci.-Atlantic, Inc., Atlanta, 1982-84; staff indstrl. engr. Inst. Indsl. Engrs., Atlanta, 1984-88, tech. ops. mgr., 1988-91, product devel. mgr., 1991—94, total quality mgmt. facilitator, 1991—94, exec. dir., 2005—; dir. mem. services and ops. Polaris Internat., 1994—2000; mng. dir., International Gas Turbine Institute Am. Soc. Mech. Engineers, 2000—05. Mem. NSPE, Inst. Indsl. Engrs., Tau Beta Pi, Alpha Pi Mu, Beta Sigma Gamma. Methodist. Office: Inst Indsl Engrs Ste 200 3577 Pkwy Ln Norcross GA 30092

GREENE, EDWARD A., food service executive; b. 1955; BA in Internat. Rels., Bradley U., Peoria, Ill.; M in Internat. Mgmt., Thunderbird The Am. Grad. Sch. Internat. Mgmt. Started career with The Pillsbury Co.; sr. positions Metromedia Restaurant Group, Metromedia Steakhouses, Inc., Burger King Corp.; v.p. food and packaging purchasing Restaurant Services, Inc.; sr. v.p. strategic initiatives CBRL Group, Inc., 2005—. Office: Cracker Barrel Old Country Store Inc 305 Hartmann Dr Lebanon TN 37088 Office Phone: 615-444-5533. Office Fax: 615-443-9818.

GREENE, GERALD E., state legislator; b. Jan. 20, 1948; AA, Andrew Coll.; BA, Ga. So. Coll.; MEd, Ga. Southwestern Coll. Tchr.; cattleman; mem. dist. 134 Ga. Ho. of Reps., Atlanta, 1983, mem. dist. 149, 2004—; chmn. interstate coop. com.; mem. appropriations, agr. and consumer affairs coms.; also state inst. and property com. Sec., Randolph Dem. Party. Mem. Hist. Soc. Democrat. Baptist. Home: RR 3 Box 316 Cuthbert GA 31740-9619 Office: State Capitol Rm 401 Atlanta GA 30334

GREENE, GREGORY F., leasing company executive; BA in Economics, U. Pitts.; MBA, Barry U. Various positions NationsBank; sr. v.p., global talent mgmt. Ryder System, Inc., sr. v.p., field human resources, mgr., exec., internat. compensation, 1993, dir., human resources, internat. divsn., 1996, sr. v.p., strategic planning and devel., 2003, exec. v.p., chief human resources officer, 2006—. Bd. trustees Barry U.; bd. dirs. Fla. C. of C. Office: Ryder System Inc 11690 NW 105th St Miami FL 33178 Office Phone: 305-500-3726. Office Fax: 305-593-4731. Business E-Mail: Gregory_Greene@Ryder.com.

GREENE, HUNTER V., state legislator; b. July 1, 1966; Mem. Dist. 66 La. House of Reps., 2005—, chair ways and means com., joint legis. com. on capital outlay, mem. house exec. com., joint legis. com. on the budget, state bond commn. Republican. Office: State Capitol 900 N Third St, PO Box 94062 Baton Rouge LA 70804 also: Law Off 8708 Jefferson Hwy, Ste B Baton Rouge LA 70809-2233 Office Phone: 225-342-7259. E-mail: larep066@legis.state.la.us.

GREENE, JOHN JOSEPH, lawyer; b. Marshall, Tex., Jan. 19, 1946; s. William Henry and Camille Anne Greene. BA, U. Houston, 1969, MA, 1974; JD, South Tex. Coll., 1978. Bar: Tex. 1978, US Supreme Ct. 1982. Asst. atty. City of Amarillo, Tex., 1978-79, Harris County, Tex., 1979-83; pvt. practice, 1983—; city atty. City of Conroe, Tex., 1983-89; sr. asst. city atty. City of Austin, Tex., 1990—2006; pvt. practice, 2006—. Served to capt. USAR, 1969—76. Decorated Bronze Star, Air medal. Roman Catholic.

GREENE, JULE BLOUNTE, lawyer; b. Dublin, Ga., Aug. 15, 1922; s. Jule B. and Bette (O'Neal) G.; m. George Williams, Aug. 22, 1952; children: James Herschel, Bradley O'Neal. AB, Mercer U., 1949, LL.B., 1950. Bar: Ga. 1950, U.S. Supreme Ct. 1960. Atty. SEC, Atlanta, 1950-53, Washington, 1956-58, atty.-in-charge Miami, Fla., 1958-69, regional adminstr. Atlanta, 1969-82; regional counsel Nat. Assn. Securities Dealers, Atlanta, 1982-90; pvt. practice law Macon and Waycross, Ga., 1953-56, Dublin, Ga., 1990—. Former mem. Atlanta Fed. Exec. Bd., Interagy. Bd. U.S. Civil Service Examiners; former v.p., dir. Peachtree Fed. Credit Union.; former treas., dir. Mental Health Assn. Met. Atlanta. Served with A.C. AUS, 1942-46. Recipient award for exemplary achievement in pub. adminstrn. William A. Jump Meml. Found., 1958

GREENE, KIMBERLY SCHEIBE, utilities executive; b. 1966; m. Ted Greene; 2 children. BS in Engring. Sci. & Mechanics, U. Tenn., Knoxville, 1988; MS in Biomedical Engring., U. Ala., Birmingham, 1990; MBA, Samford U., Birmingham, 1996; postgrad., Harvard U., 2011. Various positions of engring., strategy, and leadership Southern Co., 1991—94, structuring, asset mgmt. Southern Energy Inc. (now GenOn), 1994—2002; dir. portfolio mgmt. Southern Co. Generation & Energy Mktg., 2002—03, sr. v.p. finance, treas., 2003—07; pres., CEO Southern Co. Services, 2013—; exec. v.p. financial services, CFO Tenn. Valley Authority, 2007—10, group pres. strategy & external relations, 2010—12, exec. v.p., chief generation officer, 2012—13. Mem. advisory bd. U. Tenn. Coll. Engring.; bd. mem. master engring. program U. Ala., Birmingham; bd. mem. Electric Power Rsch. Inst. Mem.: Exec. Women in Energy, Tenn. Women's Forum, Covenant Health (bd. dirs.), Knoxville Chamber (bd. dirs.), Knoxville Symphony Orchestra (bd. dirs.). Office: Southern Company Services Inc 30 Ivan Allen Jr Blvd NW Atlanta GA 30308

GREENE, MARGARET H., telecommunications industry executive; b. Nebr. JD, U. Nebr., 1972; LLD (hon.), Georgetown Coll., 1975. Assoc. solicitor Dept. Energy, Washington; atty. pvt. practice; with legal dept. South Ctrl. Bell, 1983; cabinet sec. Gov. Commonwealth Ky., 1996; v.p., gen. counsel Bellsouth Telecomm., 1996—98; pres. Bellsouth Corp., Ky., 1991—95, pres. regulatory and external affairs, 1998—, pres. Mem. adv. com. rsch., devel. and tech. So. Govs. Assn.; bd. dors. High Mus. Art, Atlanta; mem. nat. bd. vis. U. Louisville Bus. Sch. Mem.: ABA, Nebr. Bar Assn., Ky. Bar Assn., D.C. Bar Assn., Ala. Bar Assn., U.S. Telecom Assn. (chair). Office: BellSouth Corp 675 W Peach St Ste 4200 Atlanta GA 30309 Office Phone: 404-249-2000. Office Fax: 404-249-3839.

GREENE, MARK W., plastic surgeon; Med. degree, U. Tex. Health Sci. Ctr., San Antonio; dental degree, U. Tenn. Ctr., Memphis. Diplomate Am. Bd. Plastic Surgery, Am. Bd. Oral and Maxillofacial Surgery. Intern in anesthesia Univ. Tex. Health Sci. Ctr., San Antonio, resident in oral and maxillofacial surgery; resident in surgery Methodist Med. Ctr., Ohio; resident in plastic and reconstructive surgery Northeast Ohio Univ. Coll. Medicine, Akron. Named to, New Beauty Mag., 2010. Mem.: Bexar County Med. Soc., Tex. Soc. Plastic Surgeons, Am. Soc. Aesthetic Plastic Surgery, Am. Soc. Plastic Surgeons. Office: Mark W Greene M D Remington Oaks Office Bldg Ste 110 525 Oak Centre Dr San Antonio TX 78258 Office Phone: 210-653-4993. Office Fax: 210-599-4626.

GREENE, THOMAS L., hand surgeon; MD, Ohio State U., 1975. Cert. orthopedic surgery 1983, hand surgery 2000. Resident in surgery Univ. Mich. Med. Ctr., Ann Arbor, 1975—77, resident in orthopedic surgery, 1977—80; fellow in hand surgery St. Vincent's Hosp., Indpls., 1980—81; hosp. affiliations include St. Joseph's Hosp., Tampa Gen. Hosp. Office: Tampa General Hospital 1 Tampa General Circle Tampa FL 33606-3508 Office Phone: 813-844-3508.

GREENE, WALTER BLAIR, pediatric orthopedist; b. Fayetteville, NC, July 21, 1946; BS, Davidson Coll.; MD, Univ. NC Med. Sch., 1972. Cert. Am. Bd. Orthopaedic Surgery. Intern in orthopaedic surgery Parkland Meml. Hosp., Dallas, 1972—73; resident in pediatric orthopaedics Univ. NC Sch. Med., Chapel Hill, 1973—77; fellow in pediatric orthopaedic surgery Newington Children's Hosp., Conn., 1977—78; assoc. prof. pediatrics & orthopaedic surgery Univ. NC Sch. Med., Chapel Hill, 1983—89, prof. pediatrics & orthopaedic surgery, 1989—95; J. Vernon Luck prof. orthopaedic surgery Univ. Mo. Sch. Med., Columbia, 1996—2003, chmn. Dept. Orthopaedic Surgery, 1996—2002; pediatric orthopaedic surgeon OrthoCarolina, Charlotte, NC, 2003—06, Cape Fear Orthopaedic Clinic, Fayetteville, NC, 2007—. Editor: Netter's Orthopaedics; author: Essentials of Musculoskeletal Care; co-author: Clinical Measurement of Joint Motion; contbr. articles to profl. jours.; mem. editl. bd. Jour. of Pediatric Orthopaedics. Mem.: Am. Acad. Orthopaedic Surgeons, Pediatric Orthopaedic Soc., Am. Med. Soc. Office: Cape Fear Orthopaedic Clinic Ste 801 4140 Ferncreek Dr Fayetteville NC 28314 also: Ste 108 6000 Ramsey St Fayetteville NC 28311 Office Phone: 910-484-2171, 919-484-3222.

GREENFIELD, GEORGE B., radiologist; b. NYC, May 4, 1928; s. Jacob and Rose (Wolf) G.; m. Barbara Anne O'Driscoll, Mar. 3, 1956; children: Edward James, Sheelagh Anne. BA, NYU, 1949; MD, State U. Utrecht, Netherlands, 1956. Diplomate: Am. Bd. Radiology, Am. Bd. Nuclear Medicine. Intern Bridgeport (Conn.) Hosp., 1956-57; resident radiology Presbyn.-St. Lukes Hosp., Chgo., 1957-60; practice medicine, specializing in radiology Chgo., 1960—; radiologist Cook County Hosp., 1961-66, asst. dir. diagnostic radiology, 1966-69; assoc. prof. radiology U. Ill., 1966-69; prof., chmn. dept. radiology Chgo. Med. Sch., 1969-74, Mt. Sinai Hosp. Med. Center, 1969-89; prof. diagnostic radiology Rush Med. Coll., 1975-87; pres. med. staff Mt. Sinai Hosp. Med. Center, 1983-85; prof. radiology Cook County Grad. Sch. Medicine., Chgo. Med. Sch., 1987-89, vice chmn. dept. radiology, 1988-89; prof. radiology U. South Fla., Tampa, 1989—2003, prof. emeritus, 2004—. Attending radiologist H. Lee Moffitt Cancer Ctr. & Rsch. Inst., Tampa, 1989—2006. Author: Radiology of Bone Diseases, 5th edit., 1990; sr. author: A Manual of Radiographic Positioning, 1973, Computers in Radiology, 1985, Imaging of Bone Tumors, 1995 Imaging of Arthritis, 2001; contbr. articles to profl. jours. Trustee Mt. Sinai Hosp., 1986-89. Served with U.S. Army, 1951. Fellow Am. Coll. Radiology; mem. AMA, Chgo. Med. Soc., Chgo. Roentgen Soc., Am. Roentgen Ray Soc., Radiol. Soc. N.Am., Inst. Medicine Chgo., Internat. Skeletal Soc., Soc. Skeletal Radiology, Sigma Xi.

GREENFIELD, JOSEPH CHOLMONDELEY, JR., physician, educator; b. Atlanta, July 20, 1931; s. Joseph Cholmondeley and Agnes (Game) Greenfield; m. Mary Ruth Fordham, Aug. 13, 1955; children: Mary Agnes, Ruth Ann, Susan Lee. AB in History, Emory U., 1954, MD, 1956. Intern, resident in medicine Duke Med. Ctr., Durham, NC, 1956—59, mem. staff, 1962—2001, asst. prof. medicine, 1962—65, assoc. prof. medicine, 1965—70, prof. medicine, 1970—, dir. heart sta., 1972—2001, James B. Duke disting. prof., 1981—, chief cardiovasc. divsn., 1981—89, chmn. dept. medicine, 1983—95; staff., dir. heart sta. VA Med. Ctr., Durham, 1962—; clin. assoc. NIH, USPHS, 1959—62, mem. cardiovasc. and pulmonary study sect., 1974—78, chmn., 1975—78. Author: A Quail Hunter's Odyssey, 2004, 2009, Duke Cardiology Fellows Training Program, Origin to the Present, 2004, Bawna Babu, 2005, Duke Chief Medical Residents, 2005; contbr. 200 articles to profl. jours. Fellow: ACP, Am. Coll. Cardiology (disting. sci. award 1985); mem.: NRA (life), Inst. Medicine, Assn. Am. Physicians, Am. Physiol. Soc., Am. Soc. Clin. Investigation, SCV, Safari Club Internat., Kappa Alpha, Alpha Omega Alpha, Phi Beta Kappa. Methodist. Home: 1212 Virginia Ave Durham NC 27705-3264 Office: Duke U Med Ctr PO Box 3246 Durham NC 27715-3246 Office Phone: 919-286-6951. Business E-Mail: green045@mc.duke.edu.

GREENLAW, MARILYN JEAN, retired adult education educator; b. St. Petersburg, Fla., Apr. 1, 1941; d. Hinckley and Dorothy Rebecca (Ball) G. BA, Stetson U., 1962, MA, 1965; PhD, Mich. State U., 1970. Elem. tchr. Broward County schs., Ft. Lauderdale, Fla., 1962-64; ele. cons. Harper and Row Publs., Evanston, Ill., 1965-69; from asst. to assoc. prof. U. Ga., Athens, 1970-78; from assoc. to full prof. U. North Tex., Denton, 1978-87, regents prof., 1987—2005, ret., 2005. Cons. Scholastic Publs., N.Y.C., 1978-87, Houghton Mifflin Co., Boston, 1984-94, Tex. Instruments, Dallas, 1981-85, Coordinating Bd., Austin, Tex., 1987-91. Author: Ranch Dressing: The Story of Western Wear, 1993, Welcome to the Stock Show, 1997; co-author: Storybook Classrooms, 1985, Educating the Gifted, 1988; editor book rev. column Jour. Reading, 1981-84, The New Adv., 1987-94. Mem. Friends of the Denton Pub.Libr., 1984—, pres., 1995-97, 2001-, Keep Denton Beautiful, pres., 2003; bd. dirs. Denton Libr., 1992-97, chair, 1995-96. Recipient Arbuthnot award, 1992, Disting. Svc. award Tex. State Reading Assn., 1996, Pres.'s Coun. Disting. Svc. award U. North Tex., 1996, Disting. Alumni award Stetson U., 1999, Literacy Leadership awrad U. North Tex., 2005. Mem.: ALA (com. chairperson 1984—85), Greater Denton Arts Coun. Bd., Internat. Reading Assn. (com. chairperson 1980—90, Arbuthnot award 1992), Nat. Coun. Tchrs. of English (com. chairperson 1980—, Outstanding Leadership in Edn. award 1976), Kiwanis (pres. 2002—), Phi Kappa Phi (v.p. 1986—87), Phi Delta Kappa (pres. 1982—83, Outstanding Young Educator award 1981). Republican. Avocations: reading, gardening, photography. Home: 2600 Sheraton Rd Denton TX 76209-8620

GREENSPUN, PETER D., lawyer; b. Phila. BS, LaSalle Coll., Phila., 1975; JD, George Mason U. Sch. Law, Fairfax, Va., 1978. Bar: Va. 1978, US Dist. Ct. (ea. dist.) Va. 1978, US Ct. Appeals (4th cir.) 1986, DC 1996, US Ct. Appeals (9th cir.) 2005, US Dist. Ct. (we. dist.) Va., US Supreme Ct. Atty. Greenspun Shapiro Davis & Leary PC, Fairfax, 1978—. Named one of The Legal Elite, Va. Bus. mag., 2000—05, Washington's 75 Best Lawyers, Washingtonian mag., 2002, Washington's Big Guns-Top 30 Lawyers, 2004, Washington DC Area's Best Lawyers, Washington Post Mag., 2006, Top 100 Trial Lawyers from Va., American Trial Lawyers Assn., 2007, Top Criminal Lawyers, Northern Va. Mag., 2010. Mem.: FBA, AAJ, ABA (house of delegates 1993—94, 2004—08), Va. Trial Lawyers Assn. (chmn. criminal law sect. 1999), Va. State Bar (mem. com. fed. judgeships 1998—, coun. mem. 2009—), Va. Assn. Criminal Def. Lawyers (bd. dirs. 1993—2008, pres. 1995, 2007—08), Nat. Assn. Criminal Def. Lawyers. Office: Greenspun Shapiro Davis & Leary PC 3955 Chain Bridge Rd 2nd Fl Fairfax VA 22030 Office Phone: 703-352-0100. E-mail: pdg@greenspunlaw.com.

GREENSTEIN, JOEL SANDOR, industrial engineering educator; b. Chgo., May 7, 1952; s. Benjamin and Muriel Greenstein; m. Katherine Marie, Sept. 1, 1982 (dec., 2011); children: Claire Elizabeth, Seth Michael, Paul David BS, U. Ill., 1973, PhD, 1979; MS, Stanford U., 1974. Cert. profl. ergonomist. Asst. prof. indsl. engring. and ops. rsch. Va. Poly. Inst. & State U., Blacksburg, 1979-85; assoc. prof. indsl. engring. Clemson U., SC, 1985—. Contbr. articles in field to profl. jours. Mem. Am. Soc. Engring. Edn., Assn. for Computing Machinery, Human Factors and Ergonomics Soc., Inst. Indsl. Engr., Usability Profl. Assn. Office: Clemson U Dept Indsl Engring Clemson SC 29634-0920 Office Phone: 864-656-5649. Business E-Mail: iejsg@clemson.edu.

GREENWOOD, ROBERT SAMUEL, pediatric neurologist; b. Frederick, Okla., June 12, 1943; s. Gorman and Ruth (Dittmar) G.; m. Dana Sue Reno, Aug. 20, 1966; children: Holly, Brian. BS, U. Tex., 1965, MD, 1968. Cert. Am. Bd. Pediatrics, 1974, in child neurology Am. Bd. Neurology, 1979. Intern Children's Hosp., St. Louis, 1968—69, resident in pediatrics, 1969—70, resident in pediatric neurology, 1970—71, 1973—75; chief mil. pediatrician Andrew Rader Clinic, Washington, 1971-73; fellow pediatrics, asst. neurologist Washington U., St. Louis, 1975-77, rsch. instr., neurosurgery, 1977; asst. prof. neurology Univ. NC, Chapel Hill, 1977-83, assoc. prof. to prof. neurology, 1983—. Med. dir. Epilepsy and Anticonvulsant Drug Rsch. Lab., 1980-87. Author: Pediatric Neurology, 3rd. edit., 1983; contbr. articles to med. jours. Recipient Nat. Rsch. Svc. award Nat. Inst. Neurologic and Communicative Disorders and Stroke, 1975-77, co-investigator rsch. grantee, 1984-91; prin. investigator rsch. grantee NIDR, 1989—. Mem. AAAS, Am. Acad. Pediatrics (exec. com. computer and other techs. 1990—), N.C. Neurol. Soc. (v.p. 1990—), N.C. Epilepsy Assn. (profl. adv. bd. 1977—), N.Y. Acad. Scis., Child Neurology Soc., Soc. for Neurosciences. Office: Univ NC Dept Neurology Ste 751 101 Manning Dr Chapel Hill NC 27599 Office Phone: 919-966-8160. Office Fax: 919-966-2922.

GREER, J. RONNIE, federal judge; b. Mountain City, Tenn., 1952; BS, East Tenn. State U., 1974; JD, U. Tenn., 1980. Spl. asst. to Gov. Lamar Alexander, Nashville, 1980—81; pvt. practice atty. Tenn., 1981, Greeneville, Tenn., 1983—2003; campaign mgr. Robert Beard US Senate Campaign, 1981—82; county atty. Greene County, Tenn., 1985—86; state senator Tenn. Gen. Assembly, 1986—94; judge US Dist. Ct. (ea. dist.) Tenn., Greeneville, 2003—. Office: US Dist Ct 220 W Depot St Ste 405 Greeneville TN 37743 Office Phone: 423-639-0063.

GREER, JEFF, state legislator; b. Mar. 8, 1964; Owner Greer Ins. Agy.; mem. Meade Co. Sch. Bd., 1993—2006; mem. Dist. 27 Ky. House of Reps., 2007—. Mem.: Meade County Area C. of C. Democrat. Methodist. Mailing: 2125 Highway 79 Brandenburg KY 40108 Home Phone: 270-422-3764; Office Phone: 502-564-8100 ext. 603. Fax: 270-422-5010. Business E-Mail: jeff.greer@lrc.ky.gov.

GREER, K. GORDON, banker; b. Tulsa, Oct. 28, 1936; s. H.K. and Afton (Goodman) G.; m. Nancy Lang, Nov. 22, 1958; children—Keith G., Scott A. BS in Banking and Fin., Okla. State U., 1958. Pres. Liberty Nat. Bank, Oklahoma City, 1958-84; CEO The First Nat. Bank and Trust Co., Tulsa, 1984—89; pres. Bank IV, Wichita, Kans., 1989—96; vice chmn. BancFirst Corp., Tulsa, 1996—. With Air Force N.G., 1958-64 Named to Hall of Fame, Bus. Adminstrn. Sch. Okla. State U., 1984 Mem. Am. Bankers Assn., Okla. Bankers Assn. (pres. 1983-84), So. Hills Country. Republican. Methodist. Avocation: golf.

GREER, LYNN, state legislator; b. Rogersville, Ala. m. Becky Greer; 4 children. Attended, U. Ala., Huntsville; BSEE, Auburn U., Ala. Elec. engr. NASA Space Programs, Huntsville, Cape Kennedy; rep. Ala. House of Representatives, 1974—81, 2002—06, mem. Dist. 2, 2011—; pub. svc. commr., 1981—90; divsn. dir. Ala. Dept. Econ. and Cmty. Affairs, 1993—95; owner, mgr. marine dealership; gen. contr., developer. Former bd. dirs. Elk River Devel. Agy., Shoals Econ. Devel. Authority; fund adminstr. Ala. Rsch. Inst. Mem. First Bapt. Ch., Rogersville, Ala.; former mem. Southern States Energy Bd.; mem. SE Low-Level Radioactive Waste Compact, 1993—95; adminstr. Ala. Aerospace Commn. Republican. Office: Ala House of Reps 11 S Union St Montgomery AL 36130 also: 115 East Mobile St Florence AL 35634 Office Phone: 334-242-7576, 256-767-5707.

GREER, MARK FRANCIS, information technology executive; b. Washington, Apr. 28, 1954; s. Richard Edwin and Marion Cecilia Greer; m. Donna Therese Weber, June 22, 1985; children: Matthew C., Alexander F., Kathleen M., Andrew W. BS, Duke U., Durham, NC, 1976; MS, Naval Postgrad. Sch., 1991. Liaison officer USN/Def. Intelligence Agy., Ottawa, Ont., Canada, 1984—87; asst. intelligence officer USN/Carrier Group 7, San Diego, 1987—89; project mgr. USN/Atlantic Fleet Hdqs., Norfolk, Va., 1991—93; commanding officer USN/Fleet Intelligence Ctr., Rota, Spain, 1993—96; asst. chief of staff for intelligence USN/Carrier Group 8, Norfolk, 1996—98; dir. info. tech., program mgr. USN/Office of Naval Intelligence, Washington, 1998—2003; dep. chief info. officer Def. Intelligence Agy., Washington, 2003—07; v.p. McNeil Tech., Inc., 2007—. Leader Boy Scouts Am., 1994—. Capt. USN, 1978—2003. Mem.: Naval Intelligence Profls., Armed Forces Comm. Elec. Assn. (v.p. govt. affairs 2001—, Meritorious Svc. in Intelligence award 2003). Office: McNeil Tech 6564 Loisdale Ct Ste 500 Springfield VA 22150 Office Fax: 703-921-1610. Business E-Mail: mgreer@mcneiltech.com.

GREESON, TODD, state legislator; b. Mar. 7, 1971; A, Northeast State Jr. Coll.; BS in Polit. Sci., Athens State Coll., BBA in Mgmt.; MPA, Troy State U., Ala. Farmer; ins. agent; mem. Dist. 24 Ala. House of Reps., Montgomery, 1998—; employee Northeast Ala. CC. Mem. Ft. Payne & Rainesville C. of C.; past chmn. DeKalb County Young Republicans; mem. Mountain View Bapt. Ch. Mem.: Ala. Cattleman's Assn., Ft. Payne Kiwanis. Republican. Baptist. Office: Ala House of Reps Ala State House 11 S Union St Rm 528-A Montgomery AL 36130 Office Phone: 256-638-4418 ext. 375, 256-632-3963, 334-242-7743.

GREGANTI, MAC ANDREW, physician, educator; b. Cleveland, Miss., Apr. 13, 1947; s. Mack Americo and Grace Margaret (Barbati) G.; m. Susan Taylor, Aug. 8, 1971; children: Paul Andrew, Mack Taylor, Mary Catherine. BS summa cum laude, Millsaps Coll., 1969; MD summa cum laude, U. Miss., 1972. Diplomate Am. Bd. Internal Medicine, Am. Bd. Geriat. medicine. Intern U. Rochester, NY, 1972-73, resident NY, 1973-75; instr. dept. medicine U. Miss. Sch. Medicine, Jackson, 1975-76, asst. prof., 1976-77, U. N.C. Sch. Medicine, Chapel Hill, 1977-83, assoc. prof., 1983-90, prof., 1990—, chief div. gen. medicine, 1986-91, assoc. chair for clin. affairs, 1991-99, acting chmn., 1999-2000, vice-chmn., 2000—. Dir. med./pediatric residency U. N.C. Dept. Medicine, Chapel Hill, 1980-86, dir. medicine residency, 1981-86. Contbr. articles on med. edn. and patient care to profl. jours. Fellow: ACP; mem.: Am. Geriatrics Soc., Alpha Omega Alpha. Roman Catholic. Avocations: tennis, golf, photography, computers. Office: Univ NC Chapel Hill Dept Medicine 125 Macnider Hall Cb 7005 Chapel Hill NC 27599-7005 Office Phone: 919-966-3063.

GREGORY, ANN YOUNG, editor; b. Apr. 28, 1935; d. David Marion and Pauline (Adams) Young; m. Allen Gregory, Jan. 29, 1957; children: David Young, Mary Peyton BA high distinction with departmental honors, U. Ky., 1956. Sec. Ky. Edit. TV Guide, Louisville, 1956; traffic mgr. Sta. WVLK, Lexington, 1956—61; part-time tchr. adult basic edn. Wise County Sch. Bd., St. Paul, Va., 1966—72; adminstrv. asst. Appalachian Field Svcs., Children's TV Workshop, St. Paul, 1971—74; editor, co-pub. Clinch Valley Times, 1974—. Pres. Clinch Valley Pub. Co., Inc., St. Paul, 1974—; mem. mktg. com. Mountain Empire TechPrep Consortium, 1993— Editor, text writer: The Flood of '77 in the St. Paul Area, 1977; weekly newspaper columnist: Of Shoes...and Ships...and Sealing Wax, 1974— V.p. St. Paul PTA, 1970-73; trustee Lonesome Pine Regional Libr. Bd., 1972-80, chmn., 1978-80; chmn. com. to establish br. libr. in St. Paul, opened 1975; mem. adv. bd. Pro-Art, Wise County chpt. Va. Mus. Fine Arts, 1979-86; co-leader Brownie troop Girl Scouts U.S.A., 1971-76, bd. dirs. Appalachian coun., 1983-95, 1st v.p., 1985-91; mem. adv. bd. Wise County YMCA, 1977-80; mem. Wise County Bd. Edn., 1975-2005, vice-chmn., 1981-95, 99, chmn., 2000-01; pres. So. Region Sch. Bds. Assn., 1987-88; mem. Va. Edn. Block Grants Adv. Com., 1981-86, Region I State Literacy Coun., 1989-91; mem. Local Vocat. Adv. Coun., 1980—, chmn., 1981—; mem. statewide planning coun. Va. Dept. Edn.; mem. Va. Coun. on Vocat. Edn., 1987-95, chmn., 1989-91; mem. exec. com. Va. H.S. League, 1984-88 (Lifetime Achievement award, 2001); past pres. Wise County Humane Soc., Inc.; bd. dirs. Va. Sch. Bds. Assn., 1979-89, pres., 1985-86; bd. dirs. Va. Literacy Found., 1987-89, Appalachian Ednl. Lab., 1995-2001, bd. chmn., 2000, amb., 2005—, Quarter Century Club, Va. Sch. Bd. Assn., 2002; sec., treas. S.W. Va. Pub. Edn. Found. Bd., 1993—; edn. chair Wise County C. of C.; mem. Mountain Empire C.C. Found. Bd., 1994—2010; mem. adv. com. Va. State Supt. Pub. Instrn., 1993-96; mem. devel. and cmty. rels. com., mem. music adv. com. Clinch Valley Coll.; mem. adv. bd. Wise Appalachian Regional Hosp., 1995-98; mem. Wise County Info. Tech. Task Force, 1998—; bd. dirs., sec. St. Paul Tomorrow Steering Com., 1998-2000; mem. adv. com. WISE-FM, U. Va. Coll., Wise; bd. dirs. St. Paul Tomorrow, Inc., sec., 2001—; High Knob design com., 2007-12; bd. trustees High Knob Enhancement Corp., 2008-12. Named Outstanding Clubwoman of Yr., St. Paul Jr. Women's Club, 1964, 66, Outstanding Citizen, S.W. Va. dist. Va. Fedn. Women's Clubs, 1968, Woman of Yr. Wise County/Norton Dem. Women's Club, 1986, Citizen of Yr., Wise County C. of C., 1990; recipient Rufus Beamer award Va. Poly. Inst., 1989, William P. Kanto Meml. award for contbns. to edn. Clinch Valley Coll., Mountain Empire C.C. and Wise County and Norton Pub. Schs., 1990, Literacy award S.W. Reading Coun., 1994, Lifetime Achievement award Va. H.S. League, 2001; Ky. Broadcasters Assn. scholar, 1956 Mem. Va. Press Assn. (1st pl. award for editl. writing 1976), Nat. Press Women, Va. Press Women, Nat. Newspaper Assn., Women in Comm., Nat. Sch. Bds. Assn. (pub. rels. com., nominating com. 1987, Quarter Century Club award Va. chpt., 2002), Mortar Bd., Delta Kappa Gamma (hon., Alpha Psi chpt.), Phi Beta Kappa, Alpha Delta Pi, Chi Delta Phi, Alpha Epsilon Rho, Alpha Lambda Delta, Theta Sigma Phi Democrat. Methodist. Home: PO Box 303 Saint Paul VA 24283-0303 Office: PO Box 817 Saint Paul VA 24283-0817 Business E-Mail: cvtimes@verizon.net.

GREGORY, BECKY (REBECCA ANN GREGORY), lawyer, former prosecutor; BA, U. Dallas, 1972; JD, St. Mary's U., 1978. Bar: Tex. 1979, US Dist. Ct. (no., ea. and so. dist.) Tex., US Ct. Appeals (5th cir.). Asst. US atty. (no. dist.) Tex. US Dept. Justice, first asst. US atty. (ea. dist.) Tex., 2002—05, with Office Intelligence Policy & Review Washington, 2004; judge 283rd Judicial Dist. Ct., State of Tex., Dallas, 2005—07; ptnr. Curran, Tomko, & Tarski LLP, Dallas, 2007—08; US atty. (ea. dist.) Tex. US Dept. Justice, 2008—09; sr. counsel to atty. gen. State of Tex., 2009—. Exec. bd. North Tex. High Intensity Drug Trafficking Area Assn. (HIDTA); steering com. mem. North Tex. Electronic Crimes Task Force; vis. assoc. prof. Dedman Sch. Law, So. Meth. U.; instr. Nat. Advocacy Ctr. Recipient Spl. Agent award, US Dept. State. Mem.: Dallas Bar Assn., State Bar of Tex., FBI InfraGard Assn., Exec. Women of Dallas. Office: Office of Atty Gen Capitol Sta PO Box 12548 Austin TX 78711-2548 Office Phone: 409-839-2538.

GREGORY, BRIAN, men's college basketball coach; b. Mt. Prospect, Ill. m. Yvette Gregory; children: Isabella, Elyse. Attended, US Naval Acad., 1985—86; BA in Secondary Edn., Oakland U., Rochester, Mich., 1990; M in Athletic Adminstrn., Mich. State U., East Lansing, 1992. Asst. coach Mich. State U. Spartans, 1990—96, 1999—2001, assoc. head coach, 2001—03; asst. coach U. Toledo Rockets, 1996—97, Northwestern U. Widcats, 1997—99; head basketball coach U. Dayton Flyers, 2003—11, Ga. Inst. Tech. Yellow Jackets, 2011—. Hon. chmn., pledge campaign United Way, 2007; participant Operation Hardwood, Persian Gulf, 2008; spokesperson Real Men Wear Pink; active Secret Smiles. Named Atlantic 10 Conf. Coach of Yr., CBS Sportsline.com, collegeinsider.com, 2005. Achievements include head coach of the National Invitational Tournament championship winning University of Dayton Flyers, 2010. Office: Ga Inst Tech Mens Basketball c/o Ga Tech Athletic Assn 150 Bobby Dodd Way NW Atlanta GA 30332-0455 Office Phone: 404-894-5425.

GREGORY, CHAUNCEY KLUGH, state legislator; b. Mar. 18, 1963; s. D. C. and Eleanor Eleanor (Tillman) Gregory; m. Sherri Cauthen, 1986; children: Marshall, Ellen Gray. State senator Dist. 16, SC, 1993—; mem. Corrections & Penology Com., Fish, Game & Forestry Com., Gen. Judiciary & Rules Com., State Senate, SC; pres. Builders Supply Co. Republican. Baptist. Address: PO Box 1381 Lancaster SC 29721 Mailing: 606 Gressette Bldg Columbia SC 29202 Office Phone: 803-283-8481. Business E-Mail: 513@legis.l-pitr.state.sc.us.

GREGORY, LORI-DON M., lawyer, healthcare company executive; BA in Govt. & History, Coll. William and Mary, 1985; JD, Widener U. Sch. Law, 1990. Atty. Shapiro & Burson, 1994—97; sr. counsel Amerigroup Corp., 2003—05, assoc. gen. counsel, 2005—06, dep. chief compliance officer, counsel, 2008—. Office: Amerigroup Corp 4425 Corporation Ln Virginia Beach VA 23462 Office Phone: 757-490-6900. Office Fax: 757-518-3600. Business E-Mail: lgregory@amerigroupcorp.com.

GREGORY, LOUIS P., lawyer, gas industry executive; b. 1955; BA, Stephen F. Austin State U.; JD, Tex. Tech U., 1981. Bar: Tex. 1981. Assoc. Jenkens & Gilchrist, Dallas; prtnr. Gregory, Self & Beuttenmuller, Dallas; from assoc. counsel to sr. v.p., gen. counsel Lomas Financial Corp., Dallas, 1988—96; cons. Siena Holdings, Inc. (formerly Lomas Financial Corp.), 1996—98, Nomas Corp. (formerly Lomas Mortgage), 1996—98; atty. short-term lending & real estate devel. McManemin & Smith, Dallas, 1999—2000; sr. v.p., gen. counsel Atmos Energy Corp., Dallas, 2000—. Mem.: ABA. Office: Atmos Energy PO Box 650205 Dallas TX 75265-0205

GREGORY, MICHAEL J., mining company executive, human resources specialist; b. Petoskey, Mich., June 25, 1947; Watson Louis and Winifred Rosine (Martin) G.; m. Karen Jane Busch, Aug. 12, 1972; children: Sarah, Patrick. BS Metall. Engring., Mineral Processing, Mich. Tech., 1969; MBA, Ohio State U., 1979. Registered profl. engr., Tex.; lic. Tex. Assn. Realtors. Sales engr. Am. Cynamid Co., Wayne, NJ, 1969-74; pres. North Am. Consultants, Inc., Dallas, 1988; mgr. preparation North Am. Coal Corp. (NACoal, subs. NACCO Industries, Inc.), Dallas, 1974, corp. preparation engr., mgr. adminstrv. svcs., mgr. tech. svcs., mgr. sales and mktg., 1989, v.p. southern ops., human resources, 2006—08; v.p. engring., human resources, internat. ops. North American Coal Corp., 2008—; gen. mgr. San Miguel, 2004—06. Instr. Richland Community Coll., Dallas, 1988—. Commr. Dallas North Soccer Assn., 1983—. With U.S. Army, 1970-71. Named Boss of Yr., Am. Bus. Women's Assn., 1982. Mem. AIME (awards com. 1986-90), Tex. Assn. Realtors. Roman Catholic. Avocations: jogging, biking, racquetball. Office: North American Coal Co 5340 Legacy Dr Ste 300 Plano TX 75024-3141 Business E-Mail: michael.gregory@nacoal.com.

GREGORY, ROGER LEE, federal judge; b. Phila., July 17, 1953; s. George Lee and Fannie Mae (Washington) G.; m. Carla Eugenia Lewis, Sept. 6, 1980; children: Adriene Leigh, Rachel Leigh. BA, Va. State U., 1975; JD, U. Mich., 1978. Bar: Mich. 1978, Va. 1980, US Ct. Appeals (6th cir.) 1978, US Ct. Appeals (4th cir.) 1980. Assoc. atty. Butzel, Long, Gust, Klein & Van Zile, Detroit, 1978-80, Hunton & Williams, Richmond, Va., 1980-82; mng. ptnr., chmn. litigation sec. Wilder & Gregory, Richmond, 1982—2001; judge US Ct. Appeals (4th cir.), Richmond, 2001—. Bd. visitors Va. Commonwealth U., Richmond, 1985-;adj. prof. Va. State U., 1981-1985. Bd. dirs. Indsl. Devel. Authority, Richmond, 1984—, Richmond chpt. YMCA, 1989—. Me. Cen. Va. Legal Aid Soc. (exec. com.), Old Dominion Bar Assn. (pres.), Richmond Bar Assn. (bd. dirs.), Metro C. of C. (bd. dirs. 1989—), Alpha Kappa Mu, Alpha Mu Gamma. Baptist. Office: US Ct Appeals 4th Cir 1000 E Main St Rm 212 Richmond VA 23219

GREGORY, SARA BETH, state legislator; b. Sept. 5, 1982; BA in Polit. Sci., U. Ky., 2003, JD, 2007. Legis. asst. to the Rep. caucus Ky. State Legislature, Frankfort, 2004; law clerk to Hon. Eugene E. Siler, Jr. US Ct. of Appeals; atty. Carroll & Turner, PSC, Monticello, Ky.; mem. Dist. 52 Ky. House of Reps., Frankfort, 2011—. Mem.: Ky. Bar Assn., Order of Coif. Republican. Baptist. Office: Kentucky House of Reps Annex Rm 429B 702 Capitol Ave Frankfort KY 40601 Office Phone: 502-564-8100 ext. 673. Business E-Mail: sara.gregory@lrc.ky.gov.

GREGORY, WILTON DANIEL, archbishop; b. Chgo., Dec. 7, 1947; s. Wilton and Ethel Duncan Gregory. Attended, Niles Coll., Loyola U., Chgo., St. Mary of Lake Sem., Mundelein, Ill.; PhD in Sacred Liturgy, Pontifical Liturgical Inst., Sant'Anselmo, Rome, 1980; HHD (hon.), Lewis Univ., Ill., St. Louis U.; LHD (hon.), Xavier Univ., Cincinnati, McKendree Coll., Ill. Ordained priest Archdiocese of Chgo., 1973; assoc. pastor Our Lady of Perpetual Help Parish, Glenview, Ill.; mem. faculty St. Mary of the Lake Sem.; master of ceremonies to Cardinals Cody and Bernardin; ordained bishop, 1983; aux. bishop Archdiocese of Chgo., 1983—94; bishop Diocese of Belleville, 1994—2005; archbishop Archdiocese of Atlanta, 2005—. Recipient Sword of Loyola, St. Louis U., 2004, Cardinal Bernadin award, Cath. Common Ground Initiative, 2006; named to Martin Luther King Bd. of Preachers, Morehouse Coll., 2006, Power 150, Ebony mag., 2008. Roman Catholic. Avocations: travel, music, racquetball, golf. Office: Archdiocese of Atlanta 2401 Lake Park Dr SE Ste 100 Smyrna GA 30080-8859 Office Phone: 404-888-7802.

GREIG, BRIAN STROTHER, lawyer; b. Austin, Tex., Apr. 10, 1950; s. Ben Wayne Greig and Virginia Ann (Strother) Higgins; m. Jane Ann Sentilles, June 17, 1972; children: Travis Darden, Grace Hanna. BA, Washington and Lee U., 1972; JD, U. Tex., 1975. Bar: Tex. 1975, US Dist. Ct. (ea. dist.) Tex. 1976, US Ct. Appeals (5th cir.) 1976, US Dist. Ct. (so. dist.) Tex. 1977, US Dist. Ct. (we. dist.) Tex. 1980, US Supreme Ct. 1980, US Dist. Ct. (no. dist.) Tex. 1984, US Ct. Appeals (11th cir.) 1984. Law clk. to chief judge US Dist. Ct., Beaumont, Tex., 1975-76; sr. ptnr. Norton Rose Fulbright, Austin, 1976—, mem. policy com., 2004—09; chair Global Labor & Employment Dept., 2008—. Mem. Austin Tomorrow On-Going Goals Assembly Com., 1981; pres. Austin Mgmt. Lawyers Forum, 1987, 1993. Editor-in-chief Tex. Assn. Bus. Employment Law Handbook; mem. editl. bd. Tex. Labor Letter, 1994-2001. Pres. Austin Lawyers and Accts. for Arts, 1981; trustee Laguna Gloria Art Mus., Austin, 1983-91, pres., 1989-90, chmn., 1990-91; bd. dirs. Zachary Scott Theater Ctr., Austin, 1981; devel. bd. Inst. Texan Cultures, 1991-98; trustee Westminster Manor Health Facilities Corp. of Travis County, Tex., 1991-96, sec., 1995-96; trustee St. Stephen's Episcopal Sch., 1995-2001. Headliners Found., 2006; pres. Austin Mus. Art, 1991-92, trustee, 1991-93; bd. dirs. Capital of Tex. Pub. Telecomms. Coun., chair KLRU-TV, 2009-10. Fellow Tex. Bar Found. (life), Am. Coll. Labor and Employment Lawyers; mem. ABA, FBA, Am. Arbitration Assn. (employment adv. coun. 1995—2000), Tex. Bar Assn., Travis County Bar Assn., Tex. Commn. on Human Rights (chmn.'s task force), Tex. Assn. Bus. (bd. dirs. 2000-), Austin Area Rsch. Orgn., 2009-, Tarry House Club, Headliners Club (trustee 1998-, pres. 2008, chmn. 2013-), Austin Assembly, Chattooga Club. Roman Catholic. Avocations: hunting, fishing. Office: Norton Rose Fulbright 98 San Jacinto Blvd Ste 1100 Austin TX 78701-4255 Office Phone: 512-536-4510. Business E-Mail: brian.greig@nortonrosefulbright.com.

GREINER, KENNETH DONALD, JR., retired management consultant, health facility administrator; b. Cushing, Okla., Aug. 19, 1938; s. Kenneth Donald Greiner and Billie Alene (Williams) Greiner; m. Leitner Louise Jarrell, Sept. 2, 1961; children: Katherine Louise Pierce, Kenneth Donald III, Jennifer Lee Burrell, Cheryl Sue Gumerson. BS in Econs., Okla. State U., 1960; MBA, Harvard U., 1962; BS in Health Care Adminstrn., Okla. Bapt. U., 1977. Adminstrv. asst. Doric Corp., Oklahoma City, 1962-64; asst. to treas. Skelly Oil Co., Tulsa, 1964-66; loan officer AID, Lahore, Karachi, Pakistan, 1966-69; ptnr. Resource Analysis and Mgmt. Group, Oklahoma City, 1969-74; v.p., dir. Texas Internat. Co., Oklahoma City, 1974-76; chmn. Grace Living Ctrs. (formerly Amity Care Corp.), Oklahoma City, 1976—2002; pres. Grouper Mgmt. Co., (Formerly Nursing Home Properties), 2002—; ptnr. Ams. Mgmt. Svcs. LLC, 2003—06. Asst. bankruptcy trustee Four Seasons Nursing Ctrs. Am., 1972—73; bd. dirs. Cmty. bnk Warr Acres, 1972—82, Will Rogers Bank, 1983—94; br. adv. dir. Oklahoma City Nations Bank, 1994—97; bankruptcy trustee Gulf South Corp., 1974, Cleanerator Corp., 1974, Preferred Commodity Options Corp., 1974—75; bd. dirs. Secret Harbour Beach Resort, 2004—07. Treas., bd. dirs. Neighborhood Svcs. Orgn., Oklahoma City Met. Area, 1978—83; chmn. bd. New World Sch., Oklahoma City, 1973—74; mem. Putnam City Sch. Bd., 1988—93, pres., 1992—93; dir. Cowboy Golf, Inc., 1992—2003; trustee Hillcrest Hosp., Oklahoma City, 1989—93; dir. Emergency Med. Svcs. Authority, Oklahoma City, Tulsa, 1998—2001; mem. bd. govs. Okla. State U. Found., 1994—, trustee, 1998—2009, vice chmn., 2004—05, chmn. bd., 2005—07, Papal Found. Investment Com., 2007—11, Opportunity Internat. Bd. Govs., 2008—, Cath. Social Ministries, Archdiocese of Oklahoma City, 1977—86. Mem.: Nat. Assn. Bds. Examiners Nursing Home Adminstrs. (pres. 1994—96), Okla. State Bd. Nursing Homes (bd. dirs. 1988—92), Nursing Home Assn. Okla. (exec. bd. 1988—2003, v.p. 1990—92), Okla. State U. CBA Assocs. (pres. 1993—94), Equestrian Order Holy Seplechre, Ski Island Lake Inc. (pres. 1984—87), Quail Creek Golf and Country Club (v.p., dir. 1998—2001), Bus. Boosters Club (pres. 1985), Harvard Bus. Sch. Alumni Club (pres. Oklahoma City 1970—71), Phi Delta Theta Alumni (pres. Oklahoma City 1969—71). Republican. Roman Catholic. Office: 4350 Will Rogers Pkwy Ste 350 Oklahoma City OK 73108

GREKOS, ZANNOS G., cardiologist; b. Jersey City, Apr. 27, 1965; BS in Chemistry and Biology, Fla. Atlantic U., Boca Raton, 1986; MD, U. South Fla. Coll. Medicne, 1990. Diplomate Am. Bd. Internal Medicine, cert. in cardiovasc. diseases. Intern, resident internal medicine Tampa Gen. Hosp./U. South Fla. H. Lee Moffitt Cancer & Rsch. Inst., 1990—94, fellow cardiovasc. diseases, 1993—96; assoc. clin. prof. cardiology Nova Southeastern U., Ft. Lauderdale, Fla.; dir. Regenocyte Therapeutic Stem Cell Clin. Ctr., Naples, Fla. Mem. sci. adv. bd. US Repair Stem Cell Inst. Fellow: Am. Acad. Pediat., Am. Acad. Cardiology; mem.: Internat. Soc. Stem Cell Rsch. Achievements include development of many protocols used for adult stem cell therapy throughout the world; using adult stem cell therapy to treat congestive heart failure, cardiomyopathy, peripheral artery disease, coronary artery disease, kidney disease, ischemic heart disease, pulmonary disease and early senile dementia. Office: Regenocyte Therapeutic 9500 Bonita Beach Rd Ste 210 Bonita Springs FL 34135 Office Phone: 239-333-1239. Office Fax: 239-333-2891.

GREMP, JOHN T., energy executive; b. 1951; B in Bus., Lewis & Clark Coll.; MBA, U. Calif., Berkeley. Mgr., western region, mgr., ops., Wellhead Equipment Divsn. FMC Technologies, Inc., Houston, various positions through regional mgr., asst. divsn. contr., fin. analyst Chgo., 1975, materials mgr., Automotive Svc. Divsn., 1977, asst. purchasing mgr., Def. Divsn., 1980, materials divsn., Ordnance Divsn., 1981, with, Wellhead Equipment Divsn., 1983, gen. mgr., Asia Pacific and Middle East region, 1990, gen. mgr., fluid control divsn., 1995, gen. mgr., energy prodn. sys., 2002, v.p., energy prodn. sys., 2004, exec. v.p., energy sys., 2007—10, pres., COO, 2010—11, pres., CEO, 2011, chmn., pres., CEO, 2011—. Bd. dirs. Joy Global, Inc., 2011—, FMC Technologies, Inc., 2011—. Bd. dirs. Offshore Energy Ctr., Petroleum Equipment Suppliers Assn.; bd. adv., Employer Support of the Guard & Res. U.S. Sec. Def. Office: FMC Technologies Inc 1803 Gears Rd Houston TX 77067 Office Phone: 281-591-4000. Office Fax: 281-591-4102. Business E-Mail: john.gremp@fmcti.com.

GRENDLER, PAUL FREDERICK, historian, educator; b. Armstrong, Iowa, May 24, 1936; s. August Paul and Josephine Lucy (Girres) G.; m. Marcella T. McCann, June 16, 1962; children: Peter, Jean. BA, Oberlin Coll., 1959; MA, U. Wis., 1961, PhD, 1964. Lectr. history U. Pitts., 1963-64, U. Toronto, Ont., Canada, 1964—65, asst. prof., 1965—69, assoc. prof., 1969—73, prof., 1973—98; prof. emeritus, 1998. Postdoctoral fellow Inst. Rsch. in Humanities U. Wis., Madison, 1967—68. Author: Critics of the Italian World, 1530-1560, 1969, The Roman Inquisition and the Venetian Press, 1540-1605, 1977 (Marraro prize 1978), rev. Italian transl., 1983, Culture and Censorship in Late Renaissance Italy and France, 1981, Schooling in Renaissance Italy, 1989 (Marraro prize 1989), paperback, 1991, 1995, Italian transl., 1991, Books and Schools in the Italian Renaissance, 1995, The Universities of the Italian Renaissance, 2002 (Marraro prize 2002), paperback edit., 2004, The European Rennissance in Am. Life, 2006, Renaissance Education Between Religion and Politics, 2006, The University of Mantua, the Gonzaga, and the Jesuits, 1584-1630, 2009; editor: An Italian Renaissance Reader, 1987, 2d edit., 1992, Roman and German Humanism 1450-1550, 1993, Renaissance Quarterly, 2000-03; editor-in-chief: Ency. of Renaissance, 6 vols., 1999, 2d printing, 2000 (Dartmouth medal 2000, Roland H. Bainton prize 2000), Renaissance. An Encyclopedia for Students, 4 vols., 2004; assoc. editor Europe 1450-1789, 6 vols., 2004; mem. editl. bd., exec. com.: Collected Works of Erasmus, from 1976; contbr. articles to profl. jours. Fulbright fellow Italy, 1962-63; Can. Council fellow, 1970-71; Am. Council Learned Socs. fellow, 1971-72; I Tatti fellow Harvard U. Ctr. for Italian Renassance Studies, Florence, Italy, 1970-72; sr. fellow Soc. for Humanities Cornell U., 1973-74; Guggenheim Meml. fellow, 1978-79; Social Scis. and Humanities Research Council Can. fellow, 1979-80, 85-86; Woodrow Wilson Internat. Ctr. for Scholars fellow, 1982-83; Nat. Humanities Ctr. fellow, 1988-90; grantee NEH, 1989-92; Connaught fellowship, 1998. Mem.: Renaissance Soc. Am. (v.p. 1991-92, pres. 1992-94), Am. Cath. Hist. Assn. (pres. 1984), Am. Philos. Soc., Soc. Italian Hist. Studies (sr. scholar citation 1998; v.p. 2001-03, pres. 2003-05). Address: 110 Fern Ln Chapel Hill NC 27514-4206 Personal E-mail: paulgrendler@gmail.com.

GRENIER, BEAU, lawyer; m. Joy Grenier; children: John, Dede, Evans, Carolyn. BA, U. Va., Charlottesville; JD, Vandebilt U. Law Sch. Bar: Ala., US Dist. Ct. (no. dirst) Ala. Atty. Bradley Arant Boult Cummings LLP, Birmingham, Ala., 1983—, ptnr., chmn of bd. Bd. dirs. Ala. Symphony Orch., Boy Scouts America Greater Ala. Coun.; past pres. & trustee Highlands Sch. Named one of The Best Lawyers in America, Corp., Mergers & Acquisitions and Securities Law, 2009; named to Ala. Super Lawyers, 2009. Mem.: Phi Beta Kappa, Rotary Club Birmingham. Office: Bradley Arant Boult Cummings LLP One Federal Pl 1819 Fifth Ave N Birmingham AL 35203 Office Phone: 205-521-8355. Office Fax: 205-488-6355. Business E-Mail: bgrenier@babc.com.

GRESHAM, DOLORES R., state legislator; b. July 16, 1942; married. Mem. Dist. 94; house rep. Tenn., 2003—08; mem. Dist. 26 State Senate, Tenn., 2009—. Recipient CP Boyd award, WestStar, 2000; named Citizen of Yr. Fayette County, 2000. Mem.: Hardeman County Right to Life, Fayette County & Tipton County Livestock Assns., Local Workforce Investment Bd. (former dir.), Nat. Cattlewomens Assn. (former dir.), Fayette Cares (former pres.), Tenn. Cattlewomens Assn. (former pres.), Fayette County C. of C. (former pres.), Fayette County Foster Care Rev. Bd., Fayette County Forestry Assn., SW Tenn. Cmty. Coll. Found., Fayette Haywood Enterprise Cmty., NRA & Nat. Skeet Shooting Assn. (life), Tenn. Farm Bur. Republican. Roman Catholic. Office: 3515 Country Club Rd Somerville TN 38068 also: 308 War Memorial Bldg Nashville TN 37243 Office Phone: 615-741-2368. Office Fax: 901-465-6330. Business E-Mail: sen.dolores.gresham@capitol.tn.gov.

GRESHAM, REGINA GINA HARWOOD, psychology professor, researcher; b. Gadsden, Ala., July 12, 1963; PhD, U. Ala., Tuscaloosa, 1998. Cert. in edn. psychogy Ala., 1998. Prof. U. West Ga., Carrolton, 2001—03, U. Ctrl. Fla., Orlando, 2003—. Educator Gadsden City Schs., Ala., 1988—99. Recipient Excellence in Undergrad. Tchg. award, U. Ctrl. Fla., 2007. Office: Univ Ctrl Florida PO Box 161250 Orlando FL 32816-1250 Business E-Mail: drginag@yahoo.com.

GREY, ROBERT J., JR., lawyer; b. Richmond, Va., Aug. 5, 1950; BS, Va. Commonwealth U., 1973; JD, Washington & Lee U., 1976. Bar: Va. 1978. Ptnr. Grey & Wesley, 1978—82; asst. prof. Va Commonwealth U., Sch. Bus., 1979—82; ptnr. Mays & Valentine, 1985—95, LeClair Ryan, Richmond, Va., 1996—2002, Hunton & Williams LLP, 2002—. Bd. dirs. Margaretten Corp., 1994, Va. Biotechnology Rsch. Park Corp., 2000—, Legal Services Corp., Washington, 2010—; bd. dirs. & mem. ea. regional adv. bd. Jefferson Nat. Bank, 1995—97; mem. Va. state bd. advisors Wachovia Bank, 1999—2000; interim exec. dir. Leadership Coun. on Legal Diversity, 2009—. Chmn., Va. State Alcoholic Beverage Control Bd., 1982-85; pres., Richmond Crusade for Votes, 1988-90; chmn., Youth Matters, 1995-98; co-chmn., MAPS steering com., 1997-2000; chmn., Greater Richmond Partnership, 1999-2000. Recipient Alumni Star award, Va. Commonwealth U. Sch. Bus., 1995, Disting. Leader award, Nat. Assn. Cmty. Leadership, 1997; Flame Bearer award, UNCF, The Coll. Fund, 1998; Hon. mem., Wash. and Lee U. Sch. Law, 1993. Mem. ABA (chair ho. dels. 1998-2000 bd. govs., exec. com. 1998-2000, pres-elect 2003-04, pres. 2004-05), Grtr. Richmond C. of C. (chair 1996-97); mem. Va. State Bar (pres., Young Lawyers Conf. 1982-83, chair., Commn. on Women & Minorities in the Profession 1985-86, chair, Legal Ethics Com. 1986-87); Am. Law Inst.; Nat. Bar Assn. (Wiley A. Branton award 1998, Gertrude E. Rush award 2003); Old Dominion Bar; Richmond Bar Assn.; DC Bar; Va. Bar Assn. Office: Hunton & Williams LLP Riverfront Plz E Tower 951 E Byrd St Richmond VA 23219-4074 E-mail: rgrey@hunton.com.

GREYSON, SANDY, councilwoman; Councilwoman Dist. 12 Dallas City Coun., 1997—2005, 2011—, mem. Pub. Safety Com., 1997—2005, chair City of Dallas Domestic Violence Task Force, 1998—2004, chair Legis. Affairs Com., 1999—2001, chair Transp. and Telecommunications Com., 2001—05, vice chair Trinity River Com., 2002—05, vice chair Quality of Life, 2011—. Columnist The Advocate Mag., 2008—11; bd. mem. Save Open Space, 2009—; vice chair Domestic Violence Legal Help Ctr., 2010—; vice chair Sixth Floor Mus. Dallas County Hist. Found., 2009—11; pres. League of Women Voters of Dallas, 2009—11. Office: Dallas City Hall Room 5FS 1500 Marilla St Dallas TX 75201 Office Phone: 214-670-4067. Office Fax: 214-670-5117.

GRICHNIK, JAMES MICHAEL, dermatologist; b. Memphis, May 10, 1961; BA summa cum laude, Washington U., 1982; PhD, Baylor Coll. Medicine, Houston, 1988; MD, Harvard Med. Sch., Boston, 1990. Intern Beth Israel Hosp., Boston, 1990—91; resident Duke U. Med. Ctr., Durham, NC, 1991—94, asst. prof. divsn. dermatology dept. medicine, 1994—2000, assoc. prof. divsn. dermatology dept. medicine, 2000—08; prof. dept. dermatology U. Miami, 2008—. Contbr. articles to profl. jours. NIH-MSTP predoctoral fellow, 1982-86, Dept. Cell Biology predoctoral fellow, 1986-87, Postdoc. fellow, 1987-88. Mem.: Pan Am. Soc. Pigment Cell Rsch., Am. Assn. Cancer Rsch., Am. Acad. Dermatology, Soc. Investigative Dermatology. Office: University Miami Miller Sch Medicine Rm 912 BRB 1501 NW 10th Ave Miami FL 33136 Office Phone: 305-243-6045.*

GRIER, TERRY B., school system administrator; s. O. F. and Alfreda Grier; m. Nancy Kay Miller, Jan. 24, 1998; children: Danielle Peckham, Anna Peckham, Jason Brooks children: Cynthia Leigh. BS, East Carolina U., Greenville, NC, 1972, MA, 1974, MA, 1977; EdD, Vanderbilt U., Nashville, 1983. Cert. sch. adminstrn. NC Dept. Pub. Instrn. Supt. McDowell County Schs., Marion, NC, 1984—87, Amarillo Ind. Sch. Dist., Tex., 1987—88, Darlington County Schs., SC, 1988—91, Akron Pub. Schs., Ohio, 1991—94, Sacramento City Schs., 1994—95, Williamson County Schs., Franklin, Tenn., 1996—2000, Guilford County Schs., Greensboro, NC, 2000—08, San Diego Unified Sch. Dist., 2008—09, Houston Independent Sch. Dist. (HISD), 2009—. Cons. New Brunswick Sch. Supts., Canada. Contbr. articles to profl. jours. Mem. Commn. on Gang Prevention and Intervention, San Diego; bd. dirs. Nat. Sch. Pub. Rels. Assn., Rockville, Md., 2002—04; bd. dirs., past pres. Horace Mann League of USA, Wash., 1985—2005; mem. membership com. Coll. Bd., NYC, 2004—05; bd. dirs. Nat. Dropout Prevention Network, Forward Greensboro III, 2004—05; bd. govs. 2 Those Who Care, NC, 2000—05; bd. dirs. YMCA of San Diego County. Recipient Silver Ladle award, Leukemia Found., State Svc. award, NC United Way, Outstanding Alumni award, East Carolina U., Gold Award of Excellence, SC Sch. Pub. Rels. Assn., Disting. Alumnus award, Vanderbilt U. Peabody Coll., 2008; named Lion of Yr., St. Pauls Lions Club, 1982, Regional Supt. of Yr., Piedmont Triad Edn. Consortium, NC Supt. of Yr., NC Assn. Sch. Adminstrs. and NC Sch. Bd. Assn., 2008; named to Exec. Educator 100, Exec. Educator Mag. Mem.: NC Assn. Supervision and Curriculum Devel. (pres. 2004—05, Disting. Educator award). Avocation: travel. Office: Houston Independent Sch Dist (HISD) 4400 W 18th St Houston TX 77092 Office Phone: 713-556-6300. Office Fax: 713-556-6323. E-mail: HISDSuperintendent@houstonisd.org.*

GRIERSON, KEVIN WILLIAM, lawyer; b. Ridgewood, NJ, July 27, 1965; s. John William and Sandra Grace Grierson; m. Lynda Giselle Paccone, Oct. 16, 2010; children: Kyle Broaddus, Kendall Noble Minor, Kirk William Troy. BA in Biology, U. Va., Charlottesville, 1987, JD, 1992; MA in Biology, Coll. William and Mary, Williamsburg, Va., 1989. Registered: US Patent and Trademark Office (patent atty.) 1998, bar: U.S. Ct. Appeals (fed. cir.) 2002, U.S. Ct. Appeals (4th cir.) 1994, Va. 1993, U.S. Dist. Ct. (ea. dist.) Va., U.S. Dist. Ct. (we. dist.) Va., U.S. Bankruptcy Ct. (ea. dist.) Va. Law clk. to Justice Henry H. Whiting Supreme Ct. of Va., Winchester, 1992—93; atty. Jones, Blechman, Woltz & Kelly, P.C., Newport News, Va., 1993—99; of counsel Willcox & Savage, P.C., Norfolk, Va., 1999—2009; ptnr. FisherBroyles LLP, Williamsburg, 2009—. Mem. bd. regents Leadership Inst. of the Va. Peninsula, Hampton, 2005—08, participant, 2004—05; mem. Ft. Monroe Redevel. Planning Steering Com., Hampton, 2006—07; chmn., parish fin. coun. Our Lady Mt. Carmel Roman Cath. Ch., Newport News, 2005—12; pres. Our Lady of Mt. Carmel Home and Sch. Assn., Newport News, 2001—03; bd. dirs. Thomas Nelson C.C. Ednl. Found., Hampton, 2005—08. Echols scholar, U. Va., 1983—87. Mem.: Williamsburg Bar Assn., Nat. Assn. Patent Practitioners (bd. dirs. 2004—12), ABA, Internat. Trademark Assn. (mem. bull. com. 2006—09). Roman Catholic. Achievements include development of Excellence in Innovations Award for Tech Nite. Home and Office: FisherBroyles LLP 2736 Holly Ridge Ln Williamsburg VA 23185 Office Phone: 757-726-7799. Office Fax: 866-521-5663. Business E-Mail: kgrierson@fisherbroyles.com.

GRIEVE, WILLIAM ROY, psychologist, educator, educational administrator, researcher; b. NYC, Mar. 15, 1917; s. Walter Stuart and Grace G.; m. Harriet Bush, Mar. 30, 1978; children: Leslie Lynne Grieve Bainbridge, Davelyn Anne Grieve Sandhowe. Student, SUNY, Oswego, 1934—35; BS, NYU, 1937, MA, 1938; EdD, Rutgers U., 1954. Tchr. secondary edn., NYC, 1938—48; rsch. fellow Ohio State U., Columbus, 1942; ind. arts editor High Point Mag. N.Y.C. Bd. Edn., 1984—85, textbook and instrnl. materials com., 1954—65, curriculum specialist Bur. Curriculum Rsch., 1948—50, supr., adminstr. secondary edn., 1950—65; prof. NYU, NYC, 1965—72, ombudsman Sch. Edn., 1969—71, rsch. predictive testing specialist in vocat./tech. edn.; prof. grad. program NYU/U. PR, NYC, 1966—79; ESSA, ESAA, and ESEA evaluation studies in reading, math., ESL and indsl. edn. NY, NJ, Conn., Mass., Md., 1970—83; assoc. dir. evaluation studies divsn. Psychol. Corp., 1972—75; dir. Ednl. Planning and Rsch. Inc., Boston, 1975—83, pres. Glencove, NY, 1983—, Stuart, Fla., 1983—. Asst. examiner ind. edn., supervision, guidance lics., NYC Bd. Edn., 1950-72; chmn. ind. edn. standing com. Bd. Supts., NYC, 1960-65; adj. prof. psychology L.I. U., Bklyn., 1965-70; adj. prof. edn. NY Inst. Tech., Westbury, 1981-86, SUNY, Westbury, 1986-89; cons. NY C.C. orthotics and prosthetics, 1966, NC State U., 1968, Pub. Edn. Assn./Nat. Alliance Businessmen, NY, 1968-72, Citibank, PR, 1970, Met. Mus. Art (The Art of Black Africa), NYC, 1970, Sta. UFT-TV, NY, 1970; Young and Raubicam, NY, 1974; cons. Cautaulds Internat., Mobile, Ala., 1975, Rheem Mfg., Chgo., 1975, Bankers Trust, NYC, 1975, Republic Steel, Akron and Canton, Ohio, 1977, Rheem Mfg, Chgo, 1979, S.W. Regional Lab., Calif., 1980, N.Y. State Dept. Edn., 1985—, job and task analysis, equal opportunity test devel., alt. edn. programs, coop. edn., work study, career edn., tng. and devel., 1990—; prof., U. PR, Rio Piedras, 1966-67, rsch. predictive testing specialist, 1970-83; cons., industry and commerce in pers. analysis, job and tittle description, hiring and promotion, 1999-2010. Contbr. articles to profl. jours. Bd. mgrs. Prospect Park YMCA, Bklyn., 1960-65; adviser desegregation measures Boston Pub. Schs., 1976-81. With U.S. Army, 1944-45. Mem.: Am. Psychol. and Guidance Assn., Am. Assn. Tchr. Educators, Am. Vocat. Assn., Am. Vocat. Ednl. Rsch. Assn. (charter), N.Y. Schoolmasters Club, Kappa Delta Pi, Kappa Phi Kappa, Epsilon Pi Tau, Phi Delta Kappa. Home: 5485 SE Running Oak Cir Stuart FL 34997-1651 Office Phone: 772-220-6010. Personal E-mail: haribil@aol.com.

GRIEVES, ROBERT BELANGER, engineering and language educator; b. Evanston, Ill., Oct. 15, 1935; s. Roy and Marie (Belanger) Grieves; m. Sandra Lee Artman, Dec. 10, 1966; children: Christopher Robert, Jaime Robert. BA in Russian with highest distinction, Northwestern U., 1956, MS in Chem. Engring, 1959, PhD in Chem. Engring, 1961. Asst. prof. civil engring. Northwestern U., Evanston, Ill., 1961—64; from asst. prof. to assoc. prof. civil and environ. engring. Ill. Inst. Tech., Chgo., 1964—67; prof., chmn. Dept. Chem. Engring. U. Ky., Lexington, Ky., 1967—79, dir. Ky. Water Resources Rsch. Inst., 1973—82, assoc. dean adminstrn., grad. programs and rsch. Coll. Engring., 1976—82; prof. civil engring. U. Tex., El Paso, Tex., 1982—94, dean Coll. Engring., 1982—89, dir. Slavic Lang. Program, 1989—94. Cons. to industry in air and water pollution control; spl. employee, mem. effluent stds. and water quality info. adv. com. U.S. EPA, Washington, 1975—79; mem. commn. on environ. health U.S. Armed Forces Epidemiol. Bd. Office Surgeons Gen., Washington, 1962—79. Contbr. over 150 articles to profl. jours. Mem.: Tau Beta Phi, Phi Beta Kappa. Achievements include research in phys.-chem. separations, indsl. waste treatment. Home: 705 Cresta Mira Dr El Paso TX 79912-2622

GRIFFIN, ELEANOR, publishing executive; BA in Journalism and Political Sci., U. Ind. Merchandising mgr. Southern Living mag. Southern Progress Corp. (subs. Time Inc.), 1977—87, promotions mgr. Southern Living & Southern Accents mags., 1987—91, creative svcs. dir. Southern Living, Southern Accents, Travel South, 1991—92, editl. coord. Southern Living, 1992—93, exec. editor, 1993—2001, editl. dir. custom pub. divsn., 2001—02, v.p., editor-in-chief Cottage Living, 2004—08, v.p., editor-in-chief Southern Living, 2009—10, v.p. brand devel., 2010—. Office: Southern Progress Corp 2100 Lakeshore Dr Birmingham AL 35209-6721

GRIFFIN, J. TIMOTHY, air transportation executive; Grad., Fla. Atlantic U.; M, U. Wash. With Am. Airlines; sr. v.p. schedules and pricing Continental Airlines; sr. v.p. market planning and systems NW Airlines Corp., Minn., 1993—99, exec. v.p. mktg. & distbn., 1999—2010. Office Phone: 612-726-2111.

GRIFFIN, MICHAEL DOUGLAS, aerospace scientist, former federal agency administrator; b. Aberdeen, Md., Nov. 1, 1949; BS in Physics, Johns Hopkins U., 1971, MS in Applied Physics, 1983; MS in Aerospace Sci., Cath. U., 1974; PhD in Aerospace Engring., U. Md., 1977; MS in Elec. Engring., U. So. Calif., 1979; MS in Civil Engring., George Washington U., 1998; MBA, Loyola Coll. Registered engr., Md., Calif. With Computer Scis, Corp., Jet Propulsion Lab.; dep. for tech. Strategic Defense Initiative Orgn., 1986—91; chief engr., assoc adminstr. for exploration NASA, Washington, DC, 1991—94; sr. v.p. program devel. Space Industries Internat., gen. mgr. Houston; exec. v.p., chief tech. officer Orbital Scis. Corp., Dulles, Va., 1995—2002; pres., COO In-Q-Tel, Arlington, Va., 2002—04; head Space Dept. Applied Physics Lab., Johns Hopkins U., Laurel, Md., 2004—05; adminstr. NASA, 2005—09. Adj. prof. U. Md., Johns Hopkins U., George Washington U. Author: (textbook) Space Vehicle Design. Recipient Exceptional Achievement Medal, NASA, Disting. Pub. Svc. Medal, US Dept. Def.; named Hon. Chancellor, Fla. So. Coll., 2008; named one of The 100 Most Influential People in the World, TIME mag., 2008. Fellow: Am. Astronautical Soc., AIAA (Space Sys. Medal); mem.: NAE, IEEE, Internat. Acad. Astronautics. Avocations: golf, flying, skiing, scuba diving, amateur radio.

GRIFFIN, ROBERT LEE, III, professional football player; b. Camp Lester, Okinawa, Japan, Feb. 12, 1990; s. Robert Lee and Jacqueline Griffin; m. Rebecca Liddicoat, July 6, 2013. B in Polit. Sci., Baylor U., Waco, Tex., 2010. Quarterback Washington Redskins, 2012—. Recipient Davey O'Brien Nat. Quarterback award, Davey O'Brien Found., 2011, Heisman Meml. Trophy, Heisman Trophy Trust, 2011; named Coll. Football Player of Yr., AP, 2011, NFL Offensive Rookie of Yr., 2012; named to The Nat. Football Conf. Pro Bowl Team, NFL, 2012. Office: Washington Redskins 21300 Redskin Park Dr Ashburn VA 20147

GRIFFIN, STEPHEN M., law educator, former dean; BS, U. Kans., 1979, JD, 1983; LLM, NYU, NYC, 1986. Rsch. instr. NYU; Bigelow fellow U. Chgo.; faculty mem., Rutledge C. Clement, Jr. prof. in constl. law Tulane U. Law Sch., New Orleans, 1989—, vice dean academic affairs, 2001—04, 2006—09, interim dean, 2009—10. Author: American Constitutionalism: From Theory to Politics, 1996; contbr. articles to profl. jours., chapters to books. Recipient Sumter Marks award, 2000, Felix Frankfurter Disting. Tchg. award, 2002. Mem.: Am. Polit. Sci. Assn. Office: Tulane University Law School Weinmann Hall Rm 230 F 6329 Freret St New Orleans LA 70118 Office Phone: 504-865-5910. Business E-Mail: sgriffin@tulane.edu.

GRIFFIN, TIM (JOHN TIMOTHY GRIFFIN), United States Representative from Arkansas, former federal prosecutor, lawyer; b. Charlotte, NC, Aug. 21, 1968; m. Elizabeth Griffin. BA in Economics, Hendrix Coll., Conway, Ark., 1990; JD, Tulane Law Sch., New Orleans, 1994; attended, Oxford U. Bar: Ark., La. Assoc. Jones Walker Waechter Pointevent Carrere & Denegre, New Orleans, 1994—95; assoc. ind. counsel investigating Henry Cisneros US Dept. Justice, 1995—96; sr. counsel US House Govt. Reform Com.; dep. rsch. dir. Bush-Cheney Campaign, Rep. Nat. Com., 2000, rsch. dir., 2004; dep. comm. dir. Republican Nat. Com., 2004; spl. asst. to US atty. (eastern dist) Ark. US Dept. Justice, Little Rock, 2001, spl. asst. to asst. atty. gen. Washington, 2001—02; spl. asst. to Pres., dep. dir. Office Polit. Affairs The White House, Washington, 2005; interim US atty. (eastern dist) Ark. US Dept. Justice, Little Rock, 2006—07; founder, prin. Griffin Law Firm PLLC, Griffin Pub. Affairs LLC, 2007—10; mem. US Congress from 2nd Ark. Dist., Washington, 2011—, US House Armed Services Com., 2011—, US House Fgn. Affairs Com., 2011—, US House Judiciary Com., 2011—. Maj. JAG USAR, Army JAG, 172d Stryker Brigade Combat Team, Brigade Operational Law Team 101st Airborne Divsn. US Army, 2006, Mosul, Iraq. Decorated Combat Action Badge, Army Commendation Medal. Fellow: Ark. Bar Found. Republican. Office: US House of Representatives 1232 Longworth House Office Bldg Washington DC 20515 Office Phone: 202-225-2506. Office Fax: 202-225-5903.*

GRIFFITH, DANIEL ALVA, geography educator; b. Pitts., Nov. 15, 1948; s. Donald Sanford and Mary Jane (McClain) G.; m. Diane Elaine Swartz, Jan. 3, 1970; children: Darren Lee, Michele Renee. BS, Indiana U. of Pa., 1970, MA, 1972; MS, Pa. State U., University Park, 1985; PhD, U. Toronto, Ont., Can., 1978; DSc with honors, Indiana U.

of Pa., 2006. Instr. Ryerson Polytech. U., Toronto, 1975-78; from asst. prof. to full prof. SUNY, Buffalo, 1978-88; prof. geography Syracuse U., NY, 1988—2003, dir. stats. program, 1991—95, chair, 1995—97; prof. geography U. Miami, Fla., 2003—05; prof. geospatial info. scis. U. Tex., Dallas, 2005—. Adj. prof. Coll. Environ. Sci. and Forestry, 1992-2003; vis. EPA/EMAP rsch. affiliate stats. dept. Oreg. State U., Corvallis, 1990-93; vis. rsch. prof. Erasmus U., Rotterdam, 1992, U. Rome, 1995; dep. dir. NY State program in geographic info. and analysis Syracuse U., 1989-90; ASI dir. NATO Sci. Affairs, Brussels, 1979-82, 85, cons. Peru Minister Edn., 2000-01; Leverhulme vis. prof. Cambridge U., 2004; vis. rschr. Max Planck Inst. Demographic Rsch., Rostock, Germany, 2005, invited lectr. Polish Acad. Scis, Acad. Sinica Taiwan, 2007. Author: Spatial Autocorrelation, 1987, Advanced Spatial Statistics, 1988, Statistical Analysis for Geographers, 1991, Spatial Regression Analysis on the PC, 1993, Multivariate Statistical Analysis for Geographers, 1997, A Casebook for Spatial Statistical Data Analysis, 1999, Spatial Autocorrelation and Spatial Filtering, 2003, Nonstandard Spatial Statistics and Spatial Econometrics, 2011, Spatial Statistics and Geostatistics, 2013; contbr. articles to profl. jours. Recipient Award Pa. Geog. Soc., 1999; NSF grantee, 1981, 83-85, 88-90, 92-93, 95-97, 99, 2002, 2004-14; Fulbright fellow, 1992-93, rsch. fellow ASA/USDA-NASS, 1999, Guggenheim fellow, 2001-02; named to Ashbel Smith Endowed chair U. Tex., Dallas, 2005; fellow U. Miami; sr. specialist Fulbright Found., 2006. Fellow AAAS, Regional Sci. Assn. Internat. (pres. 1996-97), NY Acad. Scis., Spatial Econometrics Assn. (founding fellow 2007), Internat. Collaborative Ctr. Geocomputation Studies, Wuhan U. (adv. com. mem.); mem. Am. Statis. Assn., Assn. Am. Geographers (chair 1987-88, Nystrom Dissertation award 1980, Pub. Domain Computer Software award 1994, 97, Disting. scholarship honor 2010, Outstanding Svc. award, 2013), Internat. Geog. Union (mem. commn. on modelling geog. sys. steering com. 2008-), Sigma Xi (Syracuse chpt. pres. 1999-2000). Democrat. Methodist. Avocation: travel. Home: 5804 Bracknell Dr Allen TX 75002-5473 Office: Sch Econ Polit and Policy Scis Univ Texas Richardson TX 75083 Office Phone: 972-883-4950. Business E-Mail: dagriffith@utdallas.edu.

GRIFFITH, G. SANDERS, III, lawyer; b. June 27, 1953; B, LaGrange Coll., 1974; JD, U. Ga., 1977. Atty. Davidson & Calhoun, 1978—88; v.p. Synovus Fin. Corp., 1988—92, gen. counsel, 1988—2007, exec. v.p., sec., 1992—95, sr. exec. v.p., 1995; sr. v.p. Total System Services, Inc., various positions, 1988, sr. exec. v.p., gen. counsel & sec., 2007—. Mem., bank counsel sect. Ga. Bankers Assn., Fin. Svcs. Roundtable; bd. dirs. Columbus Regional Health Care System; bd. trustee LaGrange Coll.; mem. Govs. Jud. Nominating Commn., Columbus Met. Airport Commn., Assn. of Corp. Counsel. Mem.: ABA, Am. Soc. of Corp. Secretaries, Am. Corp. Counsel Assn., Am. Bankers Council, Ga. Bar Assn., Columbus Bar Assn. Office: Total System Services Inc 1 TSYS Way Columbus GA 31902-2567 Office Phone: 706-649-2310. Office Fax: 706-649-4266. Business E-Mail: sandersgriffith@tsys.com.

GRIFFITH, HOWARD MORGAN (MORGAN GRIFFITH), United States Representative from Virginia, former state legislator, lawyer; b. Phila., Mar. 15, 1958; s. A. Hundley and Charlotte Virginia (Burford) Griffith; m. Hilary Davis; children: Davis, Starke 1 stepchild, Abby. BA with honors, Emory & Henry Coll., Va., 1980; JD, Washington Lee U., Lexington, Va., 1983. Bar: Va. 1983, US Dist. Ct. (dist. Va.) 1985. Assoc. Lutins & Shapiro, Roanoke, Va., 1983—84; pvt. practice Salem, Va., 1984—87, 1989—2007; ptnr. Griffith & Varney, Salem, 1987—89; mem. Dist. 8 Va. House of Delegates, 1994—2010, majority leader, 2000—10; ptnr., head Roanoke/Salem office Albo & Oblon LLP, 2007—; mem. US Congress from 9th Va. Dist., Washington, 2011—, US House Energy & Commerce Com., Washington, 2011—. Advisor, sponsor Legal Explorers Post Boy Scouts of America, Salem, 1988—89, dist. chmn., 1988—91, mem. Blue Ridge Mountains Coun., chmn. Catawba dist., 1984—86; bd. visitors Emory & Henry Coll.; mem. state ctrl. com. Rep. Party Va.; chmn. Salem Rep. Party, 1986—88, 1991—94; mem. St. Paul's Episc. Ch., Salem; bd. dirs. Legal Aid Soc. Roanoke Valley, 1991—92, Stonegate Swim Club, Salem, 1991—; former mem. bd. dirs. Easter Seals Va.; bd. trustees Jamestown-Yorktown Found. Recipient Silver Beaver award, Boy Scouts of America, 1994. Mem.: Salem/Roanoke County Bar Assn. (pres. 1995—96), Va. Bar Assn., Lions (bd. dirs. 1988—90). Republican. Episcopalian. Avocations: swimming, ornithology, ichthyology. Office: US House of Representatives 1108 Longworth House Office Bldg Washington DC 20515 Office Phone: 202-225-3861.*

GRIFFITH, MARTHA, retired small business owner, controller; b. Brockton, Mass., Sept. 9, 1945; d. Ishmael Hayes and Jettie L. (Dudley) Davis; m. Jack C. Griffith, May 29, 1965 (dec. June 1984); children: Michael S., David M.; m. Dan H. Fries, Nov. 5, 1994. Student, U. Ark., 1962—64; BA, Ball State U., 1967. Prin. Griffith Acctg. Co., Indpls., 1968-70; probate adminstr. Johnson & Weaver, Indpls., 1970-74; pers. adminstr. Hercules Inc., Houston, 1974-76; adminstr. Lapin Totz & Mayer, Houston, 1976-80; bus. mgr. Pasadena (Tex.) Citizen, 1980-84; contr. Houston Cmty. Newspapers, 1984-88, DCI Pub., Alexandria, Va., 1989-90, Telescan Inc., Houston, 1990-93, Advolink, Inc., 1993-99, Suncoast Post-Tension, Inc., Houston, 1999—2005; prin., owner Kitty's Korner, 2005—14. Commr. Houston coun. Boy Scouts Am., 1983-99, vol. tax preparer AARP, Local Hosp., 2005-13, Mchood Hosp., 2005; mem. Silver Hair Legislature, 2013- Recipient Dist. Merit awards Boy Scouts Am., Houston, 1983. Mem. NAFE, Internat. Newspaper Fin. Execs. (com. mem. 1986-89), Collier Jackson Users Group (moderator 1986-89). Democrat. Baptist. Avocations: dance, boating, travel. Home: 2210 W Jody Rd Apt D4 Florence SC 29501-2059 Personal E-mail: mgriffith542@yahoo.com.

GRIFFITH, W.E.B. (WILLIAM EDMUND BUTTERWORTH III), writer; b. Newark, Nov. 10, 1929; s. William Edmund and Gladys Schnable Butterworth. PhD in Mil. Fiction (hon.), Norwich U. Author: (Brotherhood of War series) The Lieutenants, 1982 (Ala. Author's award Ala. Libr. Assn., 1982), The Captains, 1982, The Majors, 1983, The Colonels, 1983, The Berets, 1984, The Generals, 1986, The New Breed, 1987, The Aviators, 1988, Special Ops, 2002, (The Corps series) Semper Fi, 1986, Call to Arms, 1987, Counterattack, 1990, Battleground, 1991, Line of Fire, 1992, Close Combat, 1993, Behind the Lines, 1996, In Danger's Path, 1999, Under Fire, 2002, Retreat, Hell!, 2004, (Badge of Honor series) Men in Blue, 1991, Special Operations, 1991, The Victim, 1991, The Witness, 1992, The Assassin, 1993, The Murderers, 1995, The Investigators, 1998, Final Justice, 2003, The Traffickers, 2009, The Vigilantes, 2010, (Honor Bound series) Honor Bound, 1994, Blood and Honor, 1997, Secret Honor, 2000, The Honor Of Spies, 2009, Death and Honor, 2008, (Men At War series) The Last Heroes, 1997, The Secret Warriors, 1998, The Soldier Spies, 1999, The Fighting Agents, 2001, The Saboteurs, 2007, The Double Agents, 2008, (Presidential Agent series) By Order of the President, 2005, The Hostage, 2006, The Hunters, 2007, The Shooters, 2008, Black Ops, 2009, The Outlaws, 2010; numerous other titles under pseudonyms W. E. Butterworth, Eden Hughes, Webb Beech, Walker E. Blake, Edmund O. Scholefield, Edmund O. Scholefield, Patrick J. Williams. Served with US Army, Germany 1946-1947, Korea 1951-1953. Mem.: Spl. Ops. Assn. (hon.), Marine Raider Assn. (life), Marine Combat Correspondants (life).

GRIFFITHS, JEFFREY W., electronics executive; BA, Albright Coll.; MBA, Temple U. Merchandising mgr. Electronics Boutique Inc., 1984—84, v.p., merchandising, 1987—96, sr. v.p., merchandising & distribution, 1996—98, Electronics Boutique Holding Corp., 1998—2001, pres., CEO, 2001—05, Lumber Liquidators, 2006—. Bd. dirs. Philadelphia Academies Inc., Electronics Boutique Holdings Corp., 2001—05, THQ Inc., 2005—, Lumber Liquidators, 2006—. Bd. trustees Albright Coll. Office: Lumber Liquidators Inc 3000 John Deere Rd Toano VA 23168 Office Phone: 757-259-4280. Business E-Mail: jgriffiths@lumberliquidators.com.

GRIFFITHS, KAREN, mobile data services company executive; Ind. cons.; fin. dir. Europe/Africa concentrate ops. Coca-Cola Co.; CFO Europe Ingram Micro Inc., sr. v.p.; CFO Acision, Ga., 2011—. Office: Acision 6404 International Pkwy Ste 2048 Plano TX 75093-8246 Office Phone: 404-812-8070.

GRIFFY, THOMAS ALAN, physics professor; b. Oklahoma City, Dec. 16, 1936; s. Judson H. and Dicie (Johnston) G.; m. Peggy Lynn Walker, June 6, 1958; children— David, Alan, Marjorie BA, Rice U., 1959, MA, 1960, PhD, 1961. Asst. prof. physics Duke U., Durham, NC, 1961—62; research assoc. High Energy Physics Lab., Stanford U., Calif., 1962-65; assoc. prof. physics U. Tex., Austin, 1965—68, prof., 1968—2004, chmn. dept., 1974—84, assoc. dean grad. sch., 1970—73, 1996—2000, prof. emeritus, 2004—. Contbr. articles to profl. jours. Fellow: Am. Phys. Soc. Methodist. Office: U Tex Dept Physics Austin TX 78712 Home: 6806 Pioneer Pl Austin TX 78757 Home Phone: 512-453-6328. Personal E-mail: tom@tgriffy.com.

GRIGGS, SCOTT, councilman, lawyer; m. Mariana Griggs, 2002. BS in Chemistry, Tex. A&M U.; JD, U. Tex. Ptnr. Griggs Bergen LLP, 2004—; councilman Dist. 3 Dallas City Coun., 2011—, vice chair Housing Com. Pres. Fort Worth Ave. Devel. Group, 2007—10. Office: Dallas City Hall Room 5FS 1500 Marilla St Dallas TX 75201 Office Phone: 214-670-0776. Office Fax: 214-670-5117.

GRIJALVA MOSQUERA, VICTOR ELIAS, energy executive; b. Guayaquil, Ecuador, July 13, 1938; s. Hector Elias and Eugenia (Mosquera) G.; m. Eva Maria, Jan. 5, 1963; children: Victor, Tania, Christina. BSEE, Carnegie Mellon U., 1962; MSEE, U. Pa., 1963. V.p., gen. mgr., far east EHS, Singapore, 1977—79, v.p., gen. mgr., Eastern Hemisphere, S.Am., 1979—82; gen. mgr., component test sys. Fairchild Automatic Test Equipment, San Jose, Calif., 1982—84; vice chmn. Schlumberger Ltd.; with tech and field mgmt., Schlumberger Surenco Schlumberger Surenco (subs. of Schlumberger Ltd.), Venezuela, 1966—76; tech. mgr., Tech. Svcs. Schlumberger Ltd., Paris, 1976—77, v.p., personnel NYC, 1984—85, exec. v.p., 1989, pres., Wireline N.Am., Well Svcs. Houston, 1985—86, pres., wireline testing N.Am., Well Svcs., 1986—89. Bd. dirs. Transocean, Inc., 2002—, Dynegy Inc., 2006—. Contbr. articles to profl. jours. Mem. AIEE, Soc. Petroleum Engrs., Am. Petroleum Inst. Patentee in field. Office: Dynegy Inc Bd Directors 601 Travis St Ste 1400 Houston TX 77002-3253 Office Phone: 713-507-6400. Office Fax: 713-507-6808. Business E-Mail: victor.grijalvamosquera@dynegy.com.

GRIMALDI, JAMES THOMAS, private investor; b. Elizabeth, NJ, Dec. 8, 1928; s. Anthony and Helen (Bernatt) G.; m. Norma Miriello, June 17, 1951; children: Patricia Ann, Pamela Gay, Donna Lynne. BS in Econs., U. Pa., 1951; MBA, Columbia U., 1955. CLU, 1964. Br. acct. Watson-Flagg Engrng. Co., Paterson, N.J., 1953-56; from agt. to sr. asst. dist. mgr. Met. Life Ins. Co., Paterson, Ridgewood, N.J., 1956-61; reg. agy. dir., asst. v.p. Am. Amicable Life Ins. Co., Ft. Lauderdale, Fla., 1961-66; v.p. mktg. Inland Life Ins. Co., Chgo., 1966-69; exec. v.p. Peoples Home Life Ins. Co. Ind., 1969-71, Fed. Life & Casualty Co., Battle Creek, 1970-71; pres., chief exec. officer, also dir. Peoples Home Life Ins. Co. of Ind., 1971-74; pres., CEO, bd. dirs. Fed. Life & Casualty Co., 1971-74, Keystone Co., Boston, 1974-76, Cornerstone Fin. Svcs., Inc., Boston, 1974-76; exec. v.p. sales Keystone Custodian Funds, Inc., Boston, 1974-76; engaged in pvt. investments, 1976—. Mem. faculty De Paul U., Chgo., 1969. 1st lt. USAF, 1951-53; bd. dirs., Mich. C. of C., 1972-74; trustee, Cmty. Hosp. Assn., Battlecreek, Mich. 1971-74. Recipient Spl. Tribute as Outstanding Citizen, State of Mich., 1974 Mem. Sales Mktg. Execs. Internat., Am. Soc. CLU, Nat. Assn. Life Underwriters, Am. Mktg. Assn., Assn. Individual Investors, Life Assn. Mich. (pres. 1973, exec. com.), Nat. Assn. Security Dealers, Acad. Polit. Sci., U. Pa. Alumni Assn., Columbia U. Alumni Assn. Home: 4300 Sharon Rd Apt 528 Charlotte NC 28211

GRIMES, DALE MILLS, physics and electrical engineering educator; b. Marshall County, Iowa, Sept. 7, 1926; s. LeRoy and Helen (Mills) G.; m. Janet LaVonne Moore, Mar. 22, 1947(dec. 9 Feb. 2013); children: Prudence Rae, Craig Alan. BS in Physics, Math. and Chemistry, Iowa State U., Ames, 1950, MS in Physics and Math, 1951; PhD in Elec. Engring, U. Mich., Ann Arbor, 1956. From rsch. assoc. to assoc. prof. elec. engring. U. Mich., 1951-61, prof. elec. engring., 1961-76; chief scientist Conductron Corp., Ann Arbor, 1960-63; prof. elec. engring., chmn. dept. U. Tex., El Paso, 1976-79, pres. grad. faculty, 1978—79; prof. elec. and computer engring. Pa. State U., 1979-91, chmn. dept., 1979-86, prof. emeritus, 1992—. Adj. prof. physics U. Ky., 1996—2000; cons. Environ. Rsch. Inst. Mich., US Dept. Transp., GM Corp., 1968—91; vis. prof. elec. and computer engring. U. Tex.-Austin, 1985—86; chief scientist Crale, Inc., 1985—95. Author: Electromagnetism and Quantum Theory, 1969, Automotive Electronics, 1974, Advanced Electromagnetics: Foundations, Theory, Applications, 1995, Electromagnetic Origin of Quantum Theory and Light, 2002, 2d edit., 2005, Riding Asteroid 869, 2007, Photon Creation Annihilation Continuum Electromagnetic Theory, 2012. With USNR, 1943—46. Fellow AAAS; Am. Phys. Soc. Achievements include patents in field; research in automotive radar, biconical antennas, quantum theory, electromagnetic radiation. Home: 5505 Overdale Ln Raleigh NC 27603 Personal E-mail: dale.grimes@gmail.com.

GRIMES, RUSSELL NEWELL, inorganic chemist, educator; b. Meridian, Miss., Dec. 10, 1935; s. Newell Cleveland and Marion Esther (Zehner) G.; m. Nancy Farrow Hall, Sept. 21, 1962; children— Susan, David BS in Chemistry, Lafayette Coll., 1957; PhD in Chemistry, U. Minn., 1962; postdoctoral, Harvard U., 1962, U. Calif., Riverside, 1962-63. Asst. prof. chemistry U. Va., Charlottesville, 1963-68, assoc. prof. chemistry, 1968-73, prof. chemistry, 1973—2003, chmn. dept. chemistry, 1981-84, prof. emeritus, 2003—. Guest prof. U. Canterbury, N.Z., 1974-75, U. Heidelberg, Fed. Republic of Germany, 1986, 1997-98. Author: Carboranes, 1970, 2nd edit., 2011; editor: Metal Interactions with Boron Clusters, 1982, Inorganic Syntheses Vol. 29, 1992; contbr. over 240 articles to profl. jours. Grantee Office Naval Rsch., 1965-83, Army Rsch. Office, 1983—, NSF, 1976—; Fulbright sr. rsch. scholar, New Zealand, 1974-75; recipient Alexander von Humboldt Sr. Rsch. prize, 1996. Fellow AAAS; mem. Am. Chem. Soc. (sec.-treas. inorganic divsn. 1981-84, grantee 1965—), Corp. Inorganic Syntheses (pres. 1997-2000), Sigma Xi (President's and Visitors' rsch. prize 1981, 85, 96). Office: U Va Dept Chemistry Mccormick Rd Charlottesville VA 22904-0001 E-mail: rng@virginia.edu.

GRIMES, STEPHEN HENRY, retired state supreme court justice; b. Peoria, Ill., Nov. 17, 1927; s. Henry Holbrook and June (Kellar) G.; m. Mary Fay Fulghum, Dec. 29, 1951; children: Gay Diane, Mary June, Sue Anne, Sheri Lynn. Student, Fla. So. Coll., 1946—47; BS in Bus. Adminstrn. with honors, U. Fla., 1951, LLB with honors, 1954; LLD (hon.), Stetson U., 1980. Bar: Fla. 1954, U.S. Dist. Ct. (no. and so. dists.) 1954, U.S. Ct. Appeals (5th cir.) 1965, U.S. Supreme Ct. 1972. Since practiced in, Bartow, Fla.; ptnr. Holland and Knight and predecessor firm, Tallahassee, 1954-73, 98—; judge Ct. Appeals 2d Dist. Fla., Lakeland, 1973-87, chief judge, 1978-80; chmn. Conf. Fla. Dist. Cts. Appeals, 1978-80; justice Fla. Supreme Ct., Tallahassee, 1987-97, chief justice, 1994-96; chair Article V Task Force, 1994-96, Supreme Ct. Workload Study Commn., 2000—01. Mem. Fla. Jud. Qualification Commn., 1982-86, vice chmn., 1985-86; chmn. Fla. Jud. Coun., 1989-94. Contbr. articles U. Fla. Law Rev., 1951, 54. Bd. dirs. Bartow Meml. Hosp., 1958-61, Bartow Libr., 1968-78; trustee Polk C.C., Winter Haven, Fla., 1967-70, chmn., 1969-70; bd. govs. Polk Pub. Mus., 1976-82; bd. dirs., chmn. Elder Care. Lt. (j.g.) USN, 1951-53. Fellow Am. Coll. Trial Lawyers; mem. ABA, Fla. Bar Assn. (bd. govs. jr. bar 1956-58, bd. dirs. trial lawyers sect. 1967-69, sec. 1969, vice chmn. appellate rules com. 1976-77, vice chmn. tort litig. rev. commn. 1985-86), 10th Cir. Bar Assn. (pres. 1966), Bartow C. of C. (pres. 1964), Rotary (dist. gov. 1960-61). Episcopalian (sr. warden 1964-65, 77). Office: Holland & Knight LLP 315 S Calhoun St Ste 600 Tallahassee FL 32301-1856 Home Phone: 850-668-2098; Office Phone: 830-425-5661. Business E-Mail: steve.grimes@hklaw.com.

GRIMM, BEN EMMET, library director, consultant; b. Jersey City, Sept. 27, 1924; s. Benjamin Harrison and Eunice Blanche (Whitenack) G.; m. Jean Kay Bohrer, Aug. 19, 1950 (div. 1982); children: Jeffrey, Kevin, Mark, Wendy; m. Lucy Ann Taylor, Jan. 21, 1989. BA, Washington and Lee U., 1949; MS, Columbia U., 1950. Librarian youth services Detroit Pub. Libr., 1950-52; sr. librarian Fair Lawn (N.J.) Pub. Libr., 1952-54; reference and reading librarian Montclair (N.J.) Pub. Libr., 1955-56; asst. dir. Montclair (N.J.) Pub. Libr., 1956-61; dir. Belleville (N.J.) Pub. Libr., 1961-72, Jersey City Pub. Libr., 1973-85; prin. Grimm/McPherson Assocs., Montclair, N.J., 1988-92; ind. libr. cons., 1992-93. Chmn. Hudson County Audio-Visual Aids Commn., 1975-85; cons. libr. bldgs., svcs. and adminstrn., 1966-93; cons., mem. state aid constrn. adv. bd. N.J. State Libr., 1985-88, chmn. adv. coun. Libr. Svcs. and Constrn. Act, 1979-83. Mng. editor Libr. Trustee Newsletter, 1978-80. Bd. dirs. Orange County (Va.) Hist. Soc., 1994-96, pres., 1995; bd. dirs. Orange County Libr. Found., 1995-98, v.p., 1997-98; bd. dirs. Rapidan Found., 1999—2010, treas., 2003-2010; bd. dirs. The Arts Ctr. in Orange, 2002-03. With USAAF, 1942-45. Decorated D.F.C., Air medal with oak leaf clusters. Mem. N.J. Libr. Assn. (pres. 1968-69). Home and Office: PO Box 145 Rapidan VA 22733-0145 Personal E-mail: bgrimm92@yahoo.com. Business E-Mail: b.e.grimm@hotmail.com.

GRIMM, JAMES R. (RONALD), management consultant; b. Monroe, Mich., Nov. 5, 1935; s. Carl S. and Annie B. (Platt) G.; m. Carol Ann Forman, Aug. 24, 1957; children: James R., Phillip H. BS in Bus. Adminstrn, Ariz. State U., 1958. Dir. internal audit Motorola, Inc., Phoenix, 1961-68; bus. and fin. mgr. Europe Motorola Semicondr. Co., Geneva, 1968-70; dir. internat. fin. Fairchild Camera & Instrument Co., Mountain View, Calif., 1970-71; v.p. internat. fin. Computer Scis. Corp., Los Angeles, 1971-74; sr. v.p., chief fin. exec. Pertec Computer Corp., Los Angeles, 1974-80; exec. v.p. fin. and adminstrn. MAPCO, Inc., Tulsa, 1980-84; v.p., chief fin. officer Greyhound Corp., Phoenix, 1984-88; pres. Internat. Bus. Cons., Phoenix, 1988—; sr. v.p., CFO Gulf States Steel Ala., Gadsden, Ala., 1998—2000; pres. JCP Properties, LLC, Gadsden. Bd. dirs. Petro Star Inc., Fairbanks, Alaska, Infinite Tech. Corp., Dallas. Contbr. articles to Inst. Internal Auditors publs., 1964-68. Inducted into Ariz. State U. Hall of Fame, 1982 Mem. Inst. Internal Auditors (founder and 1st pres. Phoenix chpt. 1963), Fin. Exec. Inst., Gadsden Country Club. Home: 527 Mistletoe Holw Gadsden AL 35901-5739 Personal E-mail: gjim4al@aol.com.

GRIMM, JOHN LLOYD, marketing professional; b. NYC, Oct. 21, 1945; s. Judson and Nanette Grimm; m. Stephanie L. Cassagne, Dec. 23, 1969; children: Samantha, Jonathan. BBA, Tulane U., 1967, MBA, 1969. Asst. prof. Dillard U., New Orleans, 1969-82; pres. Multi-Quest Internat. Inc., New Orleans, 1966—, Analytical Studies Inc., New Orleans, 1966—, Sybersurveys Inc., New Orleans, 1966—. Author: Interviewer's Handbook & Training Manual, 1970. Chmn. rsch. com. United Way, New Orleans, 1988-89, 94—, mem. mktg. com., 1986-88; mem. mktg. com. YMCA, New Orleans, 1985-98; mem. pub. rels. com. Goodwill Industries, New Orleans, 1986-89. Named Prof. of the Yr., Dillard U., 1981. Mem. Am. Mktg. Assn. (pres. New Orleans chpt. 1985-87, 94-95, treas. 1984-85, sec. 1983-84), Market Rsch. Assn. (tangipahoa master guidance v.p.), New Orleans Camellia Soc., Baton Rouge Camellia Soc., Mobile Camellia Soc., Gainesville Camellia Soc., Ft. Walton Beach Camellia Soc., So. Calif. Camellia Soc. South Ala. Camellia Club. Avocation: growing and showing camellias. Office: Multi-Quest Internat Inc 708 Rosa Ave Metairie LA 70005-2145 Office Phone: 504-835-3507. Business E-Mail: research@multi-questintl.com.

GRIMSHAW, JAMES ALBERT, JR., retired language educator; s. James A. and John Maurine Grimshaw; m. Glenda Darlene Hargett, June 10, 1961; children: Courtney Anne, James A. IV. BA in English, Tex. Tech. U., 1962, MA in English, 1968; PhD in English, La. State U., 1972. Commd. 2d lt. USAF, 1962, advanced through grades to lt. col., ret., 1983; instr. in English USAF Acad., Colorado Springs, 1968-70, asst. prof., 1970-74, assoc. prof., 1974-80, prof., 1980-83; prof. and dept. head Tex. A&M U. (formerly East Tex. State U.), Commerce, 1983-90, prof., 1990—2005; regent's prof. Tex. A&M U. Sys., 1995—; prof. emeritus Tex. A&M U. (formerly East Tex. State U.), 2007. Pres. Northeast Tex. Orgn. of Lang. Educators, Commerce, 1984-85, S. Cen. Assn. Depts. English, 1984-85, Tex. Assn. Depts. English, Commerce, 1988-89; chmn. Robert Penn Warren Adv. Group, Bowling Green, Ky., 1990-98; pres. Robert Penn Warren Circle, Durham, N.C., 1991-93. Author: The Flannery O'Connor Companion, 1981, Understanding Robert Penn Warren, 2001; compiler: Robert Penn Warren: A Descriptive Bibliography, 1981; editor: Cleanth Brooks at the United States Air Force Academy, 1980, Robert Penn Warren's A Brother to Dragons: A Discussion, 1983, Time's Glory: Original Essays on Robert Penn Warren, 1986, The Paul Wells Barrus Lectures, 1983-89, 1990, Friends of Their Youth: Cleanth Brooks and Robert Penn Warren, 1993, Cleanth Brooks and Robert Penn Warren: A Literary Correspondence, 1998, (with James A. Perkins) Robert Penn Warren's All the King's Men: Three Stage Versions, 2000, (with William Bedford Clark) RWP: An Annual of Robert Penn Warren Studies, 2001-05, Dictionary of Literary Biography: Robert Penn Warren Documentary Volume, 2006; gen. editor Sam Rayburn Series on Rural Life, 1997-2005. Mem. vestry Epiphany Episcopal Ch., Commerce, Tex., 1989-91, sr. warden, 95-96; chair, Army Residence Cmty. Book Club 2007-2013; treas., ARC Protestant Chapel Coun., 2008-09; supporter Courtney Anne Grimshaw Fowler Equine Therapeutic Program, Tex. A&M U., 2012. Decorated Bronze Star medal, 1966, Hon. Ky. Col., 2005; recipient Disting. Faculty award, Faculty Senate East Tex. State U., Commerce, 1988, 95, East Tex. State U. Honors Prof. of Yr. award, 1993, Tex. Assn. of Coll. Tchrs. Disting. Faculty Tchg. award, 1992-93; named to the Flannery

O'Connor Vis. Professorship, Ga. Coll., Milledgeville, 1977, vis. fellow in bibliography, Beinecke Rare Book & Manuscript Libr., Yale U., New Haven, Conn., 1979-80, Regents Prof. award, East Texas State U., 1995-97; Regents Prof. award, Texas A&M U. Sys., 1997-; Professor Emeritus, Tex. A&M U. Commerce, 2007. Mem. Robert Penn Warren Cir. Episcopalian. Avocations: swimming, gardening, chess, 5-string banjo, reading. Home: 7400 Crestway Dr Apt 1115 San Antonio TX 78239-3096 Personal E-mail: jagrimshaw@satx.rr.com.

GRIMSLEY, DENISE, state legislator; b. Lakeland, Fla., Sept. 21, 1959; 1 child, Nicole Pace. AS, Polk CC, Winter Haven, Fla.; BA, Warner So. Coll., Lake Wales, Fla.; MBA, U. Miami, Fla. V.p. Grimsley Oil Co., Inc.; registered nurse; citrus grower; mem. Dist. 77 Fla. House of Reps., Tallahassee, 2004—, chair health care appropriations com., vice chair select policy coun. on strategic and econ. planning, mem. gen. govt. policy coun., health and family svcs. policy coun., joint legis. budget commn. Mem.: Highlands County Citrus Growers Assn., Fla. Cattlemen's Assn., Lake Placid Morning Rotary Club. Republican. Baptist. Office: 205 S Commerce Ave Ste B Sebring FL 33870 also: 222 The Capitol 402 S Monroe St Tallahassee FL 32399 Office Phone: 863-385-5251, 850-488-3457.

GRIMSLEY, DEXTER, state legislator; b. Abbeville, Ala. BS in Psychology, Northwestern State U., Natchitoches, La., 1993. Chief juvenile probation officer Henry County, Ala., 1995—; mem. Dist. 85 Ala. House of Representatives, 2011—. Democrat. Office: Ala House of Reps Rm 537-F 11 S Union St Montgomery AL 36130 Office Phone: 334-242-7740.

GRINNEY, JAY, health facility company executive; b. Racine, Wis., Mar. 20, 1951; s. Leo Richard and June Louise (Christensen) G.; children: Naomi Hope, Rachel June, Matthew Jay; m. Ellen Heath, May 4, 1988. BA in Psychology, St. Olaf Coll., 1973; MHA, Washington U., Saint Louis, Mo., 1981, MBA, 1981. Adminstrv. resident The Meth. Hosp. System, Houston, 1982-83, asst. v.p., 1982-84, sr. v.p., 1985; CEO, Rosewood Med. Ctr. HCA Healthcare Co., Houston, 1990—92, COO, Houston region, 1992—93, pres., Houston region, 1993—96, pres., Eastern group Nashville, 1996—2004; pres., CEO HealthSouth Corp., Birmingham, 1999—, bd. dirs., 2004—. Treas., bd. dirs. The People's Community Clinic, St. Louis, 1979-81; adj. instr. Washington U., Houston, 1988—. Mem. allocations com. Houston United Way, 1988. Mem. Am. Coll. Healthcare Execs. (mem. regent's adv. coun. 1986—), Am. Hosp. Assn., Tex. Hosp. Assn., Greater Houston Hosp. Coun. (fin. com. 1985). Avocations: weightlifting, running, skiing, horseback riding. Office: HealthSouth Corp One HealthSouth Pkwy Birmingham AL 35243 Office Phone: 205-967-7116. Office Fax: 205-969-3543. Business E-Mail: jay.grinney@healthsouth.com.

GRINOLS, EARL LEROY, III, economist, educator; s. Earl Leroy and Betty A. G.; m. Anne Dudley Bradstreet, Feb. 2, 1978; children: Kimberly Anne, Lindsay Elizabeth, Daniel Stephen. BS in Economics, U. Minn., 1973, BA in Math. summa cum laude, 1973; PhD in Econs., MIT, 1977. Asst. prof. econs. Cornell U., Ithaca, N.Y., 1977-84; assoc. prof. U. Ill., Champaign, 1984-87, prof., 1988—2005; sr. economist Coun. of Econ. Advisers, Washington, 1987-88; disting. prof. Baylor U., 2004—. Cons. Dept. Labor, Washington, 1985-86; vis. prof. U. Chgo., 1991. Author: Uncertainty and the Theory of International Trade, 1987, Microeconomics, 1994, Gambling In America: Costs and Benefits, 2004, Health Care for Us All: Getting More For Our Investment, 2009. Grad. fellow NSF, 1973-76. Mem. Am. Econ. Assn., Econometric Soc., Assn. Christian Economists, Royal Econ. Soc., Phi Beta Kappa. Home: 104 Cantor Ct Woodway TX 76712-8818 Office: 357 Hankamer Sch Bus Baylor U One Bear Pl #98003 Waco TX 76798-8003 Business E-Mail: earl_grinols@baylor.edu.

GRISCHKOWSKY, DANIEL RICHARD, research scientist, educator; b. St. Helens, Oreg., Apr. 17, 1940; s. Oscar Edward and Christine Hazel (Olsen) G.; m. Frieda Rosa Bachmann; children: Timothy and Stephanie (twins), Daniela BS, Oreg. State U., 1962; AM in Physics, Columbia U., 1965, PhD in Physics, 1968. Postdoctoral studies Columbia U., NYC, 1968-69; mem. rsch. staff IBM Watson Rsch. Ctr., Yorktown Heights, NY, 1969-77; sci. advisor to dir. rsch. div. IBM, Yorktown Heights, 1978; mgr. atomic physics with lasers group IBM Watson Rsch. Ctr., Yorktown Heights, 1979-83, mgr. ultra-fast sci. with lasers group, 1983-93; Regents prof., Bellmon chair optoelectronics Sch. Elec. and Computer Engring. Okla. State U., Stillwater, 1993—. Chmn. Internat. Coun. on Quantum Electronics, 1989-93, Am. Phys. Soc./Optical Soc. Am./IEEE Joint Coun. on Quantum Electronics, 1989-93. Contbr. articles to profl. jours.; patentee in field. Recipient Boris Pregel award N.Y. Acad. of Sci., 1985, Kenneth J. Button prize Internat. Soc. IR, mm and THz Waves. Fellow IEEE, Am. Phys. Soc. (chmn. laser sci. topical group 1993-94), Optical Soc. Am. (R.W. Wood prize 1989, William F. Meggers award 2003). Office: Okla State U Sch Elec Computer Engring Stillwater OK 74078-0001 Business E-Mail: daniel.grischkowskyg@okstate.edu.

GRISHAM, JOHN RAY, JR., writer; b. Jonesboro, Ark., Feb. 8, 1955; m. Renee Jones, May 8, 1981; children: Ty, Shea. BS in Acctg., Miss. State U., 1977; JD, U. Miss. Sch. Law, 1981. Bar: Miss. 1981. Pvt. law practice, Southaven, Miss., 1981-91; mem. Dist. 7 Miss. House of Reps., Jackson, 1984-90. Author: (novels) A Time to Kill, 1989, The Firm, 1991, The Pelican Brief, 1992, The Client, 1993, The Chamber, 1994, The Rainmaker, 1995, The Runaway Jury, 1996, The Partner, 1997, The Street Lawyer, 1998, The Testament, 1999, The Brethren, 2000, A Painted House, 2001, Skipping Christmas, 2002, The Summons, 2002, The King of Torts, 2003, Bleachers, 2003, The Last Juror, 2004, The Broker, 2005, Playing for Pizza, 2007, The Appeal, 2008 (#1 Publishers Weekly bestseller), The Associate, 2009 (#1 Publishers Weekly bestseller), Ford County, 2009 (#1 Publishers Weekly bestseller), The Confession, 2010 (#1 Publishers Weekly, NY Times bestsellers, Harper Lee prize for Legal Fiction, 2011), The Litigators, 2011, Calico Joe, 2012, The Racketeer, 2012, Sycamore Row, 2013, (nonfiction) The Innocent Man: Murder and Injustice in a Small Town, 2006, (children's books) Theodore Boone: Kid Lawyer, 2010, Theodore Boone: The Abduction, 2011, Theodore Boone: The Accused, 2012, Theodore Boone: The Activist, 2013, (screenplays) The Gingerbread Man, 1998; prodr. (films) A Time to Kill, 1996; exec. prodr.: (TV films) The Street Lawyer, 2003; actor, dir., prodr. (films) Mickey, 2006. Democrat. Baptist. Office: Doubleday Pub 1540 Broadway New York NY 10036-4039 Address: c/o Agent David Gernert 18th Fl 136 E 57th St New York NY 10022*

GRISWOLD, NANCY J., federal judge; b. 1960; BA, La. State U., 1980; JD, Baylor U. Law Sch., 1983. Pvt. law practice, Dallas, Shreveport, La.; chief judge La. Workers Compensation Ct., 1990—93; adminstrv. law judge Office Hearings & Appeals Social Security Adminstrn. (SSA), Shreveport, La., 1995—2002, chief adminstrv. law judge, 2002—04, regional chief adminstrv. law judge Boston, 2004—06, dep. chief adminstrv. law judge Office Disability Adjudication & Review Washington, 2006—10; chief adminstrv. law judge Office Medicare Hearings & Appeals US Dept. Health & Human Services, Washington, 2010—. Mem.: Colo. Bar Assn., La. Bar Assn., Tex. Bar Assn. Office: Office Medicare Hearings & Appeals US Dept Health & Human Services (HHS) 1700 N Moore St Ste 1800 Arlington VA 22209 Office Phone: 703-235-0635. Office Fax: 703-235-0700. E-mail: nancy.griswold@hhs.gov.*

GRIVNER, CARL J., telecommunications industry executive; BA, Lycoming Coll. Mgmt. positions IBM, Ameritech; pres., CEO Advanced Fibre Comm.; CEO we. hemisphere Cable & Wireless, 1998—99; chmn., CEO Worldport Comm., 1999—2000; exec. v.p., global ops. Global Crossing, Inc., Rochester, NY, 2000—02, COO, 2000—03; bus. mgr. XO Communications, LLC, Rochester, Va., CEO Reston, Va., 2003—. Vice-chmn. CompTel. Served USMC, 1975—78. Office: Xo Communications Llc 13865 Sunrise Valley Dr Herndon VA 20171-6187 Office Phone: 703-547-2000. Business E-Mail: carl.grivner@xo.com.

GROAT, CHARLES GEORGE, geologist, former federal agency administrator; b. Westfield, NY, Mar. 25, 1940; married, 1963; 2 children. AB, U. Rochester, 1962; MS, U. Mass., 1967; PhD in Geology, U. Tex., 1970. Rsch. geologist Bur. Econ. Geology, U. Tex., Austin, 1968-71, assoc. dir., 1971-75, assoc. prof. dept. geol. sci., 1971-76, acting dir. Bur. Econ. Geology, 1975-76; assoc. prof. geol. sci., chmn. University of Texas, El Paso, 1976-78; dir. La. Geol. Survey, 1978-90; exec. dir. Am. Geol. Inst., 1990-92; dir. La. State U. Ctr. Coastal Energy & Environ. Rsch. Lab., Baton Rouge, 1992-95, U. Tex. Ctr. for Environ. Resource Mgmt., El Paso, 1995-98; assoc. v.p. rsch. University of Texas, El Paso, 1998; dir. U.S. Geol. Survey US Dept. Interior, Reston, Va., 1998—2005; dir. Ctr. for Internat. Energy & Environ. Policy University of Texas, Austin, 2005—, chair energy & mineral resources, Dept. Geological Sciences, 2005—. Bd. dirs. Plains Exploration & Production Co., 2007—. Mem. Geol. Soc. Am., Am. Assn. Petrol Geologists, Am. Geophys. Union, Am. Assn. for Higher Edn. Achievements include research in geology of energy resources, environmental aspects of resource extraction, geomorphology of coastal and arid areas, water resources, science education. Office: U Tex Austin Charles Groat Dept Geological Sciences 1 University Station C1100 Austin TX 78712

GROB, GEORGE FREDERICK, independent program evaluator; M in Math., Georgetown U., 1969. Comptr. Office of Asst. Sec. Def.; ops. rsch. analyst Office of Asst. Sec. Navy for Fin. Mgmt.; dir. planning and policy coordination Office of Asst. Sec. Planning and Evaluation, USHHS, 1976-88; chair evaluation and inspection round table PCIE, Washington, 1994—2002; dep. insp. gen. for evaluation and inspections USHHS, Washington, 1988—2002, asst. insp. gen. for evaluation and inspections, 2004—05, dep. insp. gen. mgmt. and policy, 2002—05; exec. dir. Citizens Health Care Working Group, 2005—06; pres. Ctr. for Pub. Program Evaluation, 2006—. Mem. Am. Evaluation Assn. Office: Center for Public Program Evaluation 200 E Main St Purcellville VA 20132 Office Phone: 540-454-2888. Business E-Mail: georgefgrob@evaluationcenter.net.

GROENDYKE, JOHN D., transportation executive; Chmn. GTI Ins. Co., Inc., James, Inc.; chmn., pres. Bell Transport, Inc. (subs. Groendyke Transport, Inc.), Oringderrf Tank Line, Inc. (subs. Groendyke Transport, Inc.), Transport Co., Inc. (subs. Groendyke Transport, Inc.), Triple "A" Transport (subs. Groendyke Transport, Inc.); with Groendyke Transport, Inc., 1965, chmn., CEO Enid, Okla., 1984—. Bd. dirs. Ctrl. Svc. Corp., Ctrl. Nat. Bank, OG&E, 2003—, OGE Energy Corp., 2003—. Office: Groendyke Transport Inc 2510 Rock Island Blvd Enid OK 73701-1342 Office Phone: 580-234-4663. Business E-Mail: jgroendyke@groendyke.com.

GROETZINGER, JON, JR., lawyer, pharmaceutical, aerospace executive, educator; b. NYC, Feb. 12, 1949; s. Jon M. and Elinor Groetzinger; m. Carol Marie O'Connor, Jan. 24, 1981; 3 children. AB magna cum laude, Middlebury Coll., 1971; JD in Internat. Legal Affairs, Cornell U., 1974. Bar: N.H. 1974, N.Y. 1980, Mass. 1980, Fla. 1982, Md. 1985, Ohio 1991, U.S. Supreme Ct. 1980. Assoc. McLane, Graf, Greene, Raulerson and Middleton, P.A., Manchester, NH, 1974-76; atty. John A. Gray Law Offices, Boston, 1978—81; pvt. practice NH, Boston, 1977-81; chief internat. counsel Martin Marietta Corp., Bethesda, Md., 1981-88; pres., exec. v.p. Martin Marietta Overseas Corp., Bethesda, 1984-88; sr. v.p., gen. counsel, corp. sec. Am. Greetings Corp., Cleve., 1988—2003; CEO, pres. LifePill, Cleve., 2004—05; vis. prof. law Case Western Reserve Sch. Law, Cleve., 2007—; vis. prof. bus. U. Akron Coll. Bus. Administrn., 2007. Chmn. internat. adv. bd. Case Western Res. U. Law Sch., 1995-; bd. mem. Can.-US Law Inst., 1995-; dir. Case Abroad At Home, 2007-; US Nat. dir., 2008-10, exec. cmty. dir. 2008-10; China Legal Programs dir., 2010-13, Sino-Am. Law Commerce Inst., 2012-. Contbr. articles to profl. pubs. Trustee Middlebury (Vt.) Coll., 1974—76, bd. overseers, 1977—; bd. dirs. Cleve. Coun. on World Affairs, 1992—98, 2000—, vice chmn., 2002—06, chmn. strategic planning com., 2000—02, exec. com., 2000—05, trustee, 1992—96, 1998—2005, The Conf. Bds. Coun. Chief Legal Officers, 1996—2003, membership chmn., 1997—98, program chair, 1999—2000, coun. chmn., 2000—02; chmn., pres. Greater Cleve. Gen. Counsel Assn., 2001—04; bd. dirs. Lake Erie Coll., 2002—07, vice chmn., 2005—06, chmn. bd., 2006—07. Mem. ABA, ASIL, NH Bar Assn., Fla. Bar Assn., Ohio Bar Assn., Cleve. Bar Assn., Md. Bar Assn., Am. Soc. Corp. Secs. (sec. Ohio chpt. 1995-2006, v.p. 1996-97, pres. 1997-98, adv. com. 1998-2006), Soc. Benchers, Phi Beta Kappa. Office Phone: 216-870-0622. Personal E-mail: jongretz@gmail.com.

GROH, GINA MARIE, federal judge; b. Hagerstown, Md., 1964; BS, Shepherd U., 1986; JD, W.Va. U. Coll. Law, 1989. Atty. Steptoe & Johnson LLP, Martinsburg, W.Va., 1989—91, Mell, Brownell & Baker LLP, Washington, 1991—95, Semmes, Bowen & Semmes, Balt. & Hagerstown, Md., 1995—98; asst. prosecutor Berkeley County, W.Va., 1998—2002, Jefferson County, W.Va., 2002—06; judge 23 Judicial Cir. W.Va. Circuit Ct., 2006—12; judge US Dist. Ct. (northern dist.) W.Va., 2012—. Recipient McMurran Scholar award, Shepherd U. Roman Catholic. Office: US District Court PO Box 471 1125 Chapline St Ste 1000 Wheeling WV 26003 Office Phone: 304-232-0011.

GRONBACH, TYLER D., communications executive; BA, Marist Coll. Worked LCI Internat.; sr. dir. pub. rels. Qwest Communications International, Inc., 1998—2000, v.p., corp. comm., 2000—05, R.H. Donnelley Corp., 2005—07, v.p., corp. comm. and adminstrn., 2007, sr. v.p., corp. comm. and adminstrn., 2007—. Office: R H Donnelley Corp 1001 Winstead Dr Cary NC 27513 Office Phone: 919-297-1600. Office Fax: 919-297-1285.

GRONEFELD, RALPH G., JR., healthcare services executive; B, Bellarmine U. CPA. Exec. v.p., ops., Youth Svcs., v.p. Youthtrack, Inc. (subs. Res-Care, Inc.), Alternative Youth Svcs., Inc. (subs. Res-Care, Inc.); dir., internal audit ResCare, Inc., 1995, interim sr. adminstr., west region, 1995—96, CFO, 1998—2001, exec. v.p., Cmty. Svcs. Group, 2001—02, pres., Cmty. Svcs. Group, 2002—07, pres., CEO and bd. dirs., 2006—; mem. North Peak Capital LLC. Bd. dirs. Health Enterprises Network. Exec. bd. adv., Rubel Sch. of Bus. Bellarmine U.; mem., adv. com. on Job Corps US Dept. of Labor. Office: Res Care Inc 9901 Linn Station Rd Louisville KY 40223-3808 Office Phone: 502-394-2100. Office Fax: 502-394-2206. Business E-Mail: rgronefeld@rescare.com.

GROOMS, LAWRENCE K. (LARRY GROOMS), state legislator; b. Berkeley County, SC, Mar. 20, 1964; m. Carol Grooms. BS, Clemson U., 1987. Pres., CEO GTI Corp., 1989—; mem. Dist. 37 SC State Senate, 1998—; mem. Agr. Com., Natural Resources Com., Corrections & Penology Com., Med. Affairs Com., Fish, Game & Forestry Com., 1999—. Republican. Baptist. Mailing: 131 Indian Field Dr Bonneau SC 29431 Office: 203 Gressette Bldg Columbia SC 29201 Office Phone: 803-212-6400. Office Fax: 843-825-3948. E-mail: STR@scsenate.org.

GROSCH, LAURA DUDLEY, artist, educator; b. Worcester, Mass., Apr. 1, 1945; d. Daniel Swartwood and Edith Dudley (Taft) G. BA in Art History, Wellesley Coll., 1967; BFA in Painting, U. Pa., 1968. Solo exhbns. include Mint Mus. Art, Charlotte, N.C., 1974, Jerald Melberg Gallery, Charlotte, 1984, 87, Greenville (N.C.) Mus. Art, 1987, Greenville County Mus. Art, 1987, Christa Faut Gallery, Davidson, N.C., 1990, 93, 96, Rock Sch. Arts Found., Valdese, N.C., 2000, Millennium exhbn., Valdese, 2000, others; group exhbns. include Impressions Gallery, Boston, 1973, Rose Mus. Glenbow-Alberta Gallery, Can., 1974, New Orleans Mus. Art, 1975, Bklyn. Mus., 1976, Visual Arts Ctr. Alaska, 1978, Print Club, Phila., 1980, Palazzo Venezia, Rome, 1984, Syracuse U., N.Y., 1987, Wellesley (Mass.) Coll., 1997, Mint Mus. Art, Charlotte, N.C., 2002, Christa Faut Gallery, Cornelius, N.C., 2003, 04, 05, 06, 07, 08, 09, 10, Charlotte Wine and Food, 2004, 250 Years of Art, Winston-Salem, N.C., 2004, Sommerhill Gallery, Chapel Hill, NC, 2006, 07; represented in pub. collections Boston Pub. Libr., Bowdoin Coll., Brunswick, Maine, Brit. Mus., London, Bklyn. Mus., Fla. State U., Manhattan Coll., Mus. Fine Arts, Boston, N.Y. Pub. Libr., Ringling Mus., Sarasota, Fla., Smithsonian Inst., Washington, UCLA, Newark Pub. Libr., Minn. Inst. Arts, Honolulu Acad. Arts, Dayton (Ohio) Art Inst., Carnegie Mellon U., Pitts., Free Libr. Phila., Victoria and Albert Mus., London, many others. Office: PO Box 10 Davidson NC 28036-8006 Home Phone: 704-892-1723; Office Phone: 704-892-1723.

GROSS, BRUCE E., construction executive; Sr. v.p., treas., contr. Pacific Greystone; v.p., CFO Lennar Corp., Miami, Fla., 1997—. Office: Lennar Corp 700 NW 107th Ave Ste 400 Miami FL 33172-3154 Office Phone: 305-559-4000. Office Fax: 305-226-4158.

GROSS, GARY NEIL, allergist, physician; b. Fort Lewis, Wash., July 25, 1944; s. Norman Harold and Dorothy Naomi (Bercie) G.; m. Elaina Wee, Mar. 23, 1974; children: Risa, Lara. BA, U. Tex., 1967; MD, Southwestern Med. Sch., Dallas, 1969; MBA, Southern Methodist U., Dallas, 1987. Diplomate Am. Bd. Internal Medicine, Am. Bd. Allergy and Clin. Immunology. Intern U. Utah Med. Ctr. Hosp., Salt Lake City, 1969-70, resident, 1970-71; fellow Nat. Jewish Hosp., Denver, 1971-74; founding physician Dallas Allergy and Asthma Ctr., Tex., 1979—; med. dir. Pharm. Rsch. and Cons., Dallas, 1992—; clin. prof. internal medicine Southwestern Med. Sch., Dallas, 1994—. Contbr. articles to profl. jours. Bd. dirs. Am. Jewish Com., Dallas, 1990-94, Am. Lung Assn., 1978-88, Temple Emanuel Brotherhood, 1978-80. Fellow Am. Coll. Physicians, Am. Acad. Allergy Asthma and Immunology (chmn. seminars com., 1987-88, chmn. pub. edn. com., 1989-90, Outstanding Vol. Clin. Faculty award 2004, Disting. Svc. award 2003); mem. Fedn. Regional State Local Allergy Socs. (gov. reg. 5, 1992-, chmn. 1993-94), Joint Coun. Allergy Clin. Immunology (sec. bd. dirs. 1992-96, exec. v.p. 1998-). Jewish. Avocations: bicycling, skiing, photography. Office: 5499 Glen Lakes Dr Ste 100 Dallas TX 75231-4383 Office Phone: 214-691-1330. Personal E-mail: gary.gross@daac-prc.com.

GROSS, HARRIET P. MARCUS, religious studies and writing educator; b. Pitts., July 15, 1934; d. Joseph William and Rose (Roth) Pincus; children: Sol Benjamin, Devra Lynn AB magna cum laude, U. Pitts., 1954; cert. religious tchg., Spertus Coll. Judaica, Chgo., 1962; MA, U. Tex., Dallas, 1990, postgrad., 1998. Assoc. editor Jewish Criterion Pitts., 1955—58; publs. writer B'nai B'rith Vocat. Svc., 1956—57; group leader Jewish Cmty. Ctrs. Met. Chgo., 1958—63; columnist Star Publs., Chicago Heights, Ill., 1964—80; pub. info. specialist Operation ABLE, Chgo., 1980—81; dir. religious sch. Temple Emanu-El, Dallas, 1983—86; freelance writer, 1986—; columnist Dallas Jewish Life Monthly, 1992—96, Dallas Jewish Week, 2000—04, Tex. Jewish Post, Dallas, 2004—. Lectr. U. Tex., Dallas, 1994-98; tchr. writing Homewood-Flossmoor (Ill.) Park Dist., Brookhaven Jr. Coll., Dallas; advisor journalism program Prairie State Coll., Chicago Heights, 1978-80; mem. adv. bd. The Creative Woman Quar. Publ., Gov.'s State U., Governors Park, Ill., The Mercury U. Tex., Dallas Bd. dirs., sec. Family Svc. and Mental Health Ctr. South Cook County, Ill., 1965-71; active Park Forest (Ill.) Commn. on Human Rels., 1969-80, chmn., 1974-76; bd. dirs. Ill. Theatre Ctr., 1977-80, Jewish Family Svc. Dallas, 1982-95, Dallas Jewish Hist. Soc., 1995—; mem. Dallas Jewish Edn. Com., 1992-95; adv. bd., Tycher Libr., 2007-. Recipient Humanitarian Achievement award Fellowship for Action, 1974, Honor award Anti-Defamation League B'nai B'rith, 1978, Cmty. Svc. award Dr. Charles E. Gavin Found., 1978, 1st Ann. Leadership award Jewish Family Svc., 1990, Katie award Dallas Press Club, 1995; inducted into Park Forest Hall of Fame, 2000, Tex. Press Women State Writing award, 2003, 2009, Communicator Achievement award, 2010, Lifetime Svc. award, 2012. Mem. Nat. Fedn. Press Women, Press Women Tex., Ill. Woman's Press Assn. (named Woman of Yr. 1978), Intertel (pres. Gateway Forum Dallas 1984-85), Nat. Assn. Temple Educators, Mensa, Soc. Profl. Journalists, Dallas Press Club, Nat. Soc. Newspaper Columnists, Am. Jewish Press Assn. (Simon Rockower Personal Commentary award 2006, 2010), Phi Sigma Sigma Jewish. Achievements include development of 1st community newspaper action line column. Office: 8560 Park Ln # 23 Dallas TX 75231-6312 Office Phone: 214-691-8840. E-mail: harrietgross@sbcglobal.net.

GROSS, MARILYN AGNES, artist, audiologist, small business owner; b. Rolla, Mo., Jan. 23, 1937; d. John Andrew and Florence Margaret (White) Robertson; m. James Dehnert Gross, Jan. 9, 1960; children: Kathleen Ann, Terrence Michael, Brian Andrew, Kevin Matthew. Student, U. Mo., 1955; BS, St. Louis U., 1958; Cert., Washington Sch. Art, 1978. Audiologist Bur. Maternal and Child Health U.S. Dept. Pub. Health, Washington, 1959; pvt. practice speech therapist Millington, Tenn., 1959—60; owner, dir. Marilyn's Studio, Creative Systems for Creative People, Streator, Ill., 1983—93, Osprey, Fla., 1993—; bus. mgr. Pathology Services, Streator, 1984—93; art represented by Toby Falk NYC, 1988—90. Exhbn. coord. Arts Week Community Project, Streator, 1982; visual arts rep. Ill. Pub. Sch. System on Improvement of Fine Arts Curriculum, 1986; speaker numerous civic orgns. and clubs; participant numerous art seminars and confs. Exhbns. include Ill. Valley Art League (award) 1975, 76, Town and Country, Ottawa, Ill. (award), 1975, 76, 77, (award) 78, (2 awards) 79, (award) 81, Streator Centennial, 1976, North Light mag. Competition, Westport, Conn., 1977, Internat. Soc. Artists Competition, N.Y.C., 1978, Ann. Town and Country State Art Show, Peru, Ill., (3 awards) 1979, (4 awards) 80, (award) 81, 82, Urbana, Ill., 1979, 80 (State award), Pekin, 1980, Ill. Valley Art League Silver Ann. Show, 1980, Ducks Unlimited Contest, 1980, Link Gallery, Oglesby, Ill., 1981, Streator Arts Happening, 1982, Ill. Watercolor Exhbn., Glenview (traveling exhbn. award), 1983, Springfield, 1985, Ill. Art League Lakeview Mus., 1984, Springfield (Ill.) Art

Assn., 1985, Gallery 100 Premier Exhbn., Chgo., 1985, Limelight Club, Chgo., 1986, Galesburg Civic Art Ctr., 1987, North Coast Coll. Soc., 1988 (2 awards), Hiram (Ohio) Coll., 1988, Adirondack Nat. Exhbn. of Am. Watercolors, Old Forge, N.Y., 1988, Riverlands '88 Exhbn., Hopkinsville, Ky., 1988, Ft. Wayne (Ind.) Mus. Art, 1988, 89, Alice and Arthur Baer Competitive Exhbn., Chgo., 1988 (award), 48th Nat. Competition, Fine Arts Mus. of South, Watercolor Soc. Ala., Mobile, 1989, Soc. Exptl. Artists Nat. Juried Exhibit, U. North TX, 1994, Western Colo. Watercolor Exhbn., Nat. Juried Exhbn., Grand Junction (Juror's Award), 1997, Watercolor USA, Nat. Juried Exhbn., Springfield (Mo.) Mus. Art, 1998, Am. Watercolor Soc. Exhbn., Salmagundi Club, N.Y.C., 1998, Internat. Soc. Exptl. Artists, Internat. Juried Exhibit, U. North Tex., Ft. Worth, 1998 (award), Ariz. Aqueous, 1999, Nat. Juried Exhbn., Tubac (Ariz.) Ctr. for the Arts, 1999, 8th Annual Internat. Soc. Exptl. Artists Exhbn., Huntsville Mus. of Art, 1999, 19th Ann. Faber Birren Natl. Color Exhbn., U. Conn., Stamford, 1999, Intuitive Art, Rosemary Ct. Galleries, Sarasota, 2000, No. Trust Exhbn., Longboat Key, Fla., 2000, Internat. Soc. Exptl. Artists Exhbn., Dennos Mus., Traverse City, Mich., 2001, 6th Ann. Nat. USA Acrylic Painters' Assn. Exhbn., Segretto Contemporary Art Gallery, Santa Fe, 2002, Watermedia, 2003, Houston, 2003, Challenge of the Champions, 2003, SLMM Exhbn. "Illuminations", Ft. Meyers, Fla., 2008, Canvas Project, Atlanta, 2009, Creator's Collectors Galleria, Sarasota, Fla., 2010; one-woman shows include: Engle Ln. Gallery, Streator, 1980, 81, 82, 84, 85, Illini Union Gallery, Urbana, 1982, Dai-Ichi Kangyo, Ltd., Chgo., 1983, Atrium Gallery We. Ill. U., Macomb, 1983, John G. Blank Ctr. for Arts, Michigan City, Ind., 1984, 1st Nat. Bank of Morton (Ill.) Gallery, 1985, Birchwood Farms Estate, Harbor Springs, Mich., 1988, L'Attitude Gallery, Sarasota, Fla., 2003, Womens Resources Ctr., Sarasota, Fla., 2011-12; gallery shows include Copley Soc., Boston, 1983-86, Lakeview Mus. Gallery, Peoria, Ill., 1983-88, Springfield Art Assn. Gallery, 1983—, The Prism Gallery, Evanston, Ill, 1987-88, Ft. Wayne Mus. Art Gallery, 1988, Artisan's Gallery, Petoskey, Mich., 1988-90, Hodgell Gallery, Sarasota, Fla., 1995-2002, L'Attitude Gallery, Sarasota, 2002-03, Boston, 2002—03; represented in numerous corp. and pvt. collections; painting selected for books: Best of Watercolor, 1995, Creative Watercolor, 1996, Abstracts in Watercolor, 1996, Creative Inspiration, 1997, Painting Color, Best of Watercolor Series, 1997, Painting Composition, Best of Watercolor Series, 1997, Watercolor Mag., Spring 2001, The Collected Best of Watercolor, 2002, Splash 7: A Celebration of Light, 2002; Watercolor Magic Mag., Spring, 2002 The Art of Layering: Making Connections, 2004, Collage In All Dimensions, 2005, The Artist's Muse: Unlock The Door To Your Creativity, 2006, A Walk Into Abstracts: How did They Do That?, 2011; author: Gift of Love, 1975 (Peter Herring Poetry award), The President's Book, 1971, Studio Log: Making it Happen-Creative Systems for Creative People, 1988. Mem. St. Anthony's Parents Club, 1966-82; rep. White House conf. on library and info. services, 1978. Recipient photography award CICCA Interclub Comp., 1981, 82, (3 awards) 83, 2 photography awards Pictorialists Comp., 1982, painting award Binney & Smith Corp., 1982, photography award Fuji Photo Comp., 1983, profl. award Ill. Art League, 1984; named Artist of Month Springfield (Ill.) Art Assn. Gallery, 1983; represented in numerous biographies and revs. in newspapers and books. Mem. Am. Med. Soc. Aux., Assn. Clin. Scientists Aux., Am. Soc. Clin. Pathologists Aux., Coll. Am. Pathologists Aux., LaSalle County Med. Soc. Aux., Am. Speech and Hearing Assn. (cert.), Internat. Soc. Artists (charter), Associated Photographers Internat., Am. Watercolor Soc. (assoc.), Nat. Watercolor Soc. (assoc.), Midwest Watercolor (assoc.), Nat. Collage Soc. (signature mem.), Fla. Watercolor Soc. (assoc.), Ill. Art League, Ky. Watercolor Soc., Ala. Watercolor Soc., Nat. Acrylic Painters Assn. (signature mem.), Internat. Soc. Exptl. Artists (signature mem.), Soc. of Layerists. in Multimedia (signature mem.) Knickerbocker Artists N.Y., Soc. Painters in Casein and Acrylics, Chgo. Artists Coalition, Pictoralists Club, Delta Sigma Epsilon, Sigma Alpha Eta, Delta Zeta (State Day award 1958). Republican. Roman Catholic. Home: 374 MacEwen Dr Osprey FL 34229-9233 Office Phone: 941-966-4219. Personal E-mail: marigro@comcast.net.

GROSS, PAUL ALLAN, health products executive; b. Va., Oct. 1, 1937; s. Albert and Cynthia (Saxe) G.; m. Gail Byrd, Nov. 19, 1966; children: Lorri, Garry, Randy. Degree, U. Richmond, 1959; BA, U. Ga., 1961; MHA, Va. Commonwealth U., 1964; cert. in hosp. adminstrn., U. Miami, Jackson Meml. Hosp. Adminstrv. resident in hosp. administrn. Tampa Gen. Hosp., Fla., 1964; adminstrv. asst. Dallas County Hosp. Dist., 1964-66, asst. adminstr., 1966-69, sr. asst. adminstr., 1969-70, assoc. adminstr., 1971-72; clin. assoc. prof. hosp. med. care U. Tex. Southwestern Med. Sch., 1964-72, Sch. Allied Health Scis., Dallas, 1964-72; exec. dir. Humana Inc. Suburban Hosp., Louisville, 1972-76; v.p. Fla. region Humana Inc., Miami, 1976-81; sr. v.p. Pacific Region Humana Inc., Newport Beach, Calif., 1981-84, exec. v.p., pres. hosp. div., 1984-92; ret. Humana Inc., 1992; prof., health administr. Va. Commonwealth U./Med. Coll. Va., 1992-95, prof. emeritus, 1996—. Nat. cons. emeritus Surgeon Gen. USAF, 1987—; vice chmn. bd. trustees MedEcon, Inc., Louisville, 1993-96, also bd. dirs.; bd. dirs. St. Anthony Pub. Co., Washington, 1993-96; advisor KBL Healthcare Inc., Comprehensive Med. Mgmt., Inc., N.Y.C. 1993-96. Contbr. articles to profl. jours. Mem., chmn. U.S. Selective Svc. System Local Bd. 154, Newport Beach, 1983, Bd. 13, Louisville, 1982-2002; bd. assocs. U. Richmond, Va., 1990-96; bd. dirs. St. Francis High Sch., Louisville, 1989-92; bd. dirs. Louisville Zool. Found., 1989-96, chmn. investment com., 1992; mem. adv. bd. Sch. Nursing, 1992-96, Spalding U., 1997; chmn. devel. bd. Jefferson County C.C., Kentuckiana Edn. and Work Force Com.; bd. dirs U.S. Selective Svc. Bd., 1981-2002, emeritus 2002—; preceptor Fellowship Program-Edn. with Industry, USAF, 1986-92; bd. dirs. Spaulding U., 1996-97, Lake/Sumter County United Way, 2005-07, LifeStream Behavioral Ctr., 2004-; bd. mem., treas. chair fin. com. Comprehensive Med. Mgmt. Inc, 1993-96; bd. dirs. Med. Coll. Va. Found., chmn. audit and applications com., 1993-2000; pres. bd. dirs. Pelican Cove Two Condo Assn.; bd. dirs. Hospice of Lake and Sumter County, Fla, 2005-; CRA adv. bd., mem, chmn. City of Tauares Fla., 2005-08. With USNR, 1955—63. Recipient Humana Club award, Ctrl. Region, Louisville, 1974—76, Presdl. medallion, Va. Commonwealth U., 1995; named Outstanding Adminstr., Ctrl Region Humana, 1975, 1976. Fellow Am. Coll. Health Care Execs. (ethics com., chmn. inv. droped sect. 1993—); mem. Tex. Hosp. Assn., Hosp. Coun. So. Calif. (chmn. multi-instnl. corp. liaison com. 1983—), United Hosp. Assn. Calif., Fedn. Am. Healthcare Sys. & Am. Hosp. Assn. (hon. life). Home: PO Box 311 Terra Ceia FL 34250-0311 E-mail: pagross144@comcast.net.

GROSSMAN, HERBERT BARTON, urologist, researcher; b. Tampa, Fla., June 25, 1945; s. Benjamin and Pauline (Mattis) G.; m. Amy C. Becker, Aug. 24, 1969; children: Beth, Sara, Rebecca. BA, La Salle Coll., Phila., 1966; MD, Temple U., 1970. Diplomate Am. Bd. Urology. Surg. intern U. Mich. Med. Ctr., Ann Arbor, 1970-71; surg. resident St. Joseph Mercy Hosp., Ann Arbor, 1973-74; urology resident U. Mich. Med. Ctr., Ann Arbor, 1974-77; instr. U. Mich. Med. Sch., Ann Arbor, 1977-78; rsch. and clin. fellow Meml. Sloan-Kettering Cancer Ctr., NYC, 1978-80; asst. prof. U. Mich. Med. Sch., Ann Arbor, 1980-85, assoc. prof., 1985-90, prof., 1990-94; dir., urologic oncology U. Mich. Cancer Ctr., Ann Arbor, 1986-94; prof. U. Tex. M.D. Anderson Cancer Ctr., Houston, 1994—2010; dep. chair Dept. Urology U. Tex. MD Anderson Cancer Ctr., 1998—2008, clin. prof., 2011—, Singapore Nat. Med. Rsch. Coun., 2003, 2008, 2012. Cons. Taubman Med. Libr., 1985—94, The Med. Letter, 1991, Jour. Vascular Surgery, 1991; reviewer VA Merit Rev. Bd. for Surgery, 1986, NIH Pathology B Ad Hoc (SI) Study Sect., 1988, NIDDK Ad Hoc Rev. Groups 12 and 13, 1992, Med. Rsch. Coun., UK, 1999, Dutch Cancer Soc., 1999, 2001, cons., 2010—; reviewer NCI Spl. Emphasis Panel, 1999, 2000—11, 2003—04, 2010—11; spl. reviewer NIH Exptl. Therapeutics Study Sect., 1986, reviewer spl. study sect., 1995, reviewer cancer ctr. support grant, 1996; reviewer NCI Rev. Group/subcom. 4, 1997; external reviewer Alta. Cancer Bd., 1998; mem. surg. quality control and edn. com SW Oncology Group, 1980—90, GU com., 1980—, organ site chmn. for local bladder cancer, 1991—2000; surg. oncology adv. com. dept. surgery U. Mich. Med. Ctr., Ann Arbor, 1981—82, dept. surgery computer sys. adv. com., 1983—88, cancer ctr. clin. rsch. com., 1987—94, laser safety com., 1987—94, med. sch. admissions com., 1988—94, patient care com., 1989—90, hosps. quality mgmt. com., 1990—94, rsch. coord. sect. urology, 1991, fin. adv. com., adv. promotion com. for primary rsch. staff dept. surgery, 1993—94; med. practice subcom. U. Tex. M.D. Anderson Cancer Ctr., Houston, 1994—2010, grad. med. edn. com., 1994—2004, surveillance com., 1994—95, dir. clin. rsch., 1994—2004, dep. chmn. dept. urology, 1998—2008, clin. study sect. rev. grants program, 2002—10, vice chmn., 2002—03, chmn., 2003—04; prostate cancer adv. com. Mich. Dept. Pub. Health, 1993—94, clin. rsch. com. mem., 1994—2000, chmn., 1997—2000, dir. bladder cancer multidisciplinary rsch. program, 1999—2004; mem. sci. adv. bd. Anthra Pharms., Inc., 1994—2004, Fujirebio Diagnostics Inc., 2003—07; cons. NCI early detection rsch. network, 2002, PhotoCure, 2003—12, Viventia Biotech., 2006—12, Ferring Pharms., 2007—10, Oncomethylome, 2009—10, Nucleix, 2013—; ad hoc reviewer NCI subcom. E, 2003—04, US Army Med. Rsch. and Materiel Command, 1999; mem. NCI program for assessment of clin. cancer tests strategy group, 2003—, co-chair, 2006—; mem. NCI PACCT strategy group, 2004—; molecular biology rev. panel FAMRI, 2001—06, chair therapeutic intervention; chmn. Tengion Data Safety Monitoring Bd., 2010—. Mem. editl. bd. Oncology Reports, 1998—, Jour. Urology, 1999—2007, sect. editor Urologic Oncology, 2000—10, Molecular Oncology, 2007—; contbr. articles to profl. jours., chapters to books. Capt. USAF, 1971—73. Recipient 2d prize Ferdinand C. Valentine Urology Essay Contest, 1980, also numerous rsch. grants; named to W.A. "Tex" and Deborah Moncrief, Jr. Disting. Chair in Urology, 1994, Vis. Professorship award in urology, Pfizer/AUA, 2004; Ferdinand C. Valentine fellow N.Y. Acad. Medicine, 1979-80, clin. fellow Am. Cancer Soc., 1979-80. Office: U T MD Anderson Cancer Ctr 1515 Holcombe Blvd # 1373 Houston TX 77030-4009 Office Phone: 713-792-3250.

GROSSMAN, MARC ISAIAH, consulting firm executive, former diplomat; b. L.A., Sept. 23, 1951; s. Melvin and Estelle Grossman; m. Mildred Patterson, May 29, 1982; 1 child, Anne. BA, U. Calif., Santa Barbara, 1973; MSc in Internat. Rels., London Sch. Econs./Polit. Sci., 1974. Polit. officer US Embassy, Islamabad, Pakistan, 1977-79; staff asst. Bur. Near Eastern and South Asian Affairs US Dept. State, 1979-80; dep. spl. adviser to Pres. Jimmy Carter The White House, Washington, 1980; chief profl. staff US Dept. State Transition Team, 1980; country officer for Jordan US Dept. State, 1981-83; polit. officer US Mission to NATO, 1983; dep. dir. pvt. office of sec. gen. NATO, 1984-86; exec. asst. to dep. sec. US Dept. State, 1986-89; dep. chief US Embassy, Ankara, 1989-92; exec. sec., spl. asst. to sec. US Dept. State, Washington, 1993-94, US amb. to Turkey Ankara, 1995-97, asst. sec. for Europe & Canadian affairs Washington, 1997-98, asst. sec. for European affairs, 1998-2000, dir. gen. Fgn. Svc., 2000-01, under sec. for polit. affairs, 2001—05, spl. envoy to Afghanistan & Pakistan, 2011—13; profl. lectr. Georgetown U. Edmund A. Walsh Sch. Fgn. Svc., 2006—10; vice chmn. The Cohen Group, Washington, 2005—; Kissinger Sr. Fellow Yale U., New Haven, 2013—. Chair bd. trustees Masters Program Edmund A Walsh Sch. Fgn. Svc., Georgetown U. Recipient Disting. Svc. award, US Dept. State, 2005; named a Career Amb., 2004. Mem. American Friends of the London Sch. of Economics, Army & Navy Club (Washington). Avocations: reading, travel, sports. Office: The Cohen Group 500 8th St NW Ste 200 Washington DC 20004

GROSSMAN, MINDY FAYE, broadcast executive; b. 1957; married; 1 child. Attended, Manhattanville Coll., George Washington U. Various sr. positions Oxford Industries; v.p., Sales & Merchandising Tommy Hilfiger; pres., Chaps Ralph Lauren Divsn., sr. v.p., Menswear Warnaco, Inc., 1991—94; v.p., New Bus. Devel. Polo Ralph Lauren Corp. (formerly Polo Fashions, Inc.), 1994—95; pres., CEO Polo Jeans Co., 1995—2000; global v.p., head, Apparel Nike, Inc. (formerly Blue Ribbon Sports, Inc.), 2000—06; CEO IAC Retailing, 2006—08, HSN, Inc., 2008—. Bd. dirs. Scotts Miracle-Gro Co., 2006, HSN, Inc., 2008—, Bloomin' Brands Inc., 2012—. Bd. dirs. East Harlem Sch. at Exodus House, NYC, Nat. Retail Fedn., Cosmetic Exec. Women.; chmn. Fashion Inst. Tech.; bd. advisor J. Baker Sch. Retail, Wharton Sch. Bus. Recipient Innovator of the Yr. award, Ernst & Young, 2012; named one of The 100 Most Powerful Women, Forbes mag., 2009, 2011—13, The Top 50 Women in World Bus., Financial Times, 2010. Jewish. Office: HSN Inc 1 Hsn Dr Saint Petersburg FL 33729-0001 Office Phone: 727-872-7069. E-mail: mindy.grossman@hsn.net.*

GROSSMAN, REX, professional football player; b. Bloomington, Ind., Aug. 23, 1980; s. Daniel and Maureen Grossman; m. Alison Miska, 2005. Student, U. Fla, 1999—2003. Quarterback Chgo. Bears, 2003—08, Houston Texans, 2009, Washington Redskins, 2010—. Recipient Ed Block Courage award, 2006; named MVP, Southeast Conf. Championship Game, 2000. Office: Washington Redskins 21300 Redskin Park Dr Ashburn VA 20147

GROSSMAN, ROBERT GEORGE, neurosurgeon, department chairman; b. NYC, Jan. 24, 1933; s. Ferenc and Vivian (Isenberg) Grossman; m. Ellin Friedman, June 26, 1955; children: Amy, Kate, Ruth. BA, Swarthmore Coll., 1953; MD, Columbia U., 1957. Diplomate Am. Bd. Neurosurgery. Intern Strong Meml. Hosp., Rochester, NY, 1957-58; resident Presbyn. Hosp., Columbia U., NYC, 1960-63; acad. practice medicine, specializing in neurol. surgery Houston, 1973—; from instr. to assoc. prof. neurol. surgery U. Tex. S.W. Med. Sch., 1963-68; from assoc. prof. to prof. neurol. surgery Albert Einstein Coll. Medicine, 1969-73; prof., chmn. div. neurol. surgery U. Tex. Med. Br., Galveston, 1973-80; prof., chmn. dept. neurol. surgery Baylor Coll. Medicine, 1980—2005; assoc. dean clin. affairs Baylor Coll. Medicne, 2002—05; dir. Neurol. Inst., chmn. dept. neurosurgery Meth. Hosp., Houston, 2005—13. Chmn. neurology B study sect. USPHS, NIH, 1972—74; mem. bd. sci. counsellors Nat. Inst. Neurol. Diseases and Strok, NIH, 1993—96. Author (with W. D. Willis): Medical Neurobiology, 3d edit., 1981; chmn. editl. bd.: Jour. Neurosurgery, 1987. With US Army, 1958—60. Mem.: ACS, Soc. Neurol. Surgeons (pres. 1995), Am. Acad. Neurol. Surgery (v.p.), Am. Bd. Neurol. Surgery (chmn. bd. dirs. 1989—90), Soc. Univ. Surgeons, Am. Assn. Neurol. Surgeons. Home: 2002 Sunset Blvd Houston TX 77005-1651 Office: Tex Med Ctr Scurlock Tower 6560 Fannin St Ste 944 Houston TX 77030-2706 Office Phone: 713-441-3800. Business E-Mail: rgrossman@tmhs.org.

GROSSMAN, ROBERT LOUIS, lawyer; b. Cleve., Dec. 20, 1954; s. Sidney and Lillian Belle (Davis) G.; m. Rochelle Carol Shear, Nov. 7, 1987; children: Zachary, Jonathan, David, Andrew. BA with honors, Ohio State U., 1975, JD with Honors, 1978, MA with honors, 1979. Bar: Ohio 1978, Fla. 1982, U.S. Ct. Appeals (5th cir.) 1979. Law clk. U.S. Dist. Ct. (so. dist.) Ohio, Columbus, 1977-78; sr. atty. U.S. Govt. EEOC, Houston, 1979-82; shareholder Greenberg, Traurig, P.A., Miami, 1982—; co-chmn. Isreal Practise, 2001—. Editor: Florida Corporate Practice, 2d edit., 1991. Chmn. South Dade Jewish Leadership Coun., 1997-99; bd. dirs. Greater Miami Jewish Fedn. South Dade, 1987—, campaign chmn., 1995-97, chmn., 1997-99; bd. dirs. Greater Miami Jewish Fedn., 1995—2008, mem. exec. com., 1997-99; bd. dirs. Alper Jewish Cmty. Ctr., 1997-00, exec. com., 1998-00; bd. dirs. Children's Bereavement Ctr., 2000-08, Orgn. Leadership Advancement Miami, 2001-03; chmn. Exec. Inst. OLAM, 2001-03; bd. dirs. Beacon Coun., 2000-02, 2008-09; chmn. Exec. Inst. for Orgn. for Leadership Advancement in Miami, 2001-03; chmn. Fedn. Agy., Day Sch. and Synagogue Campaign, 2003-08; bd. dirs. Temple Beth Am., 2003-05, Project Interchange, 2005-, Jewish Nat. Fund, 2005-, United Jewish Cmtys. Israel Advocacy Com., 2005-09; chair econ. devel. Greater Miami Jewish Fedn., Yerucharn, Israel, 2008-. Donald Becker Meml. scholar Ohio State U., 1975, 76, fellow, 1978; Robert Russell fellow Greater Miami Jewish Fedn., 1998; recipient Stanley C. Myers Young Leadership award Greater Miami Jewish Fedn., 1999, Put Something Back Cmty. award, 2003. Mem. ABA (corp. securities sect.), The Fla. Bar, Dade County Bar Assn., Order of Coif. Avocations: sports, reading, travel. Office: Greenberg Traurig 333 SE 2nd Ave Ste 4400 Miami FL 33131-2184 Home Phone: 305-661-5370; Office Phone: 305-579-0756. Business E-Mail: grossmanb@gtlaw.com.

GROTE, GORDON, publishing executive; Pres. response mktg. svcs. Dex One. Office: Dex One Corp 1001 Winstead Dr Cary NC 27513 Office Phone: 919-297-1600. Office Fax: 919-297-1285. Business E-Mail: gordon.grote@dexone.com.

GROTON, JAMES PURNELL, lawyer, arbitrator; b. Newport News, Va., Oct. 29, 1927; s. Lafayette Watson and Mary (Skidmore) Groton; m. Lora Frances Webster, June 13, 1953 (dec. Mar. 1999); m. Eve Oxford, May 6, 2006 (dec. Sept. 13, 2011); children: James Purnell, Hunter W., Molly Groton Urban, Lora Groton Rust. AB cum laude, Princeton U., 1949; LLB, U. Va., 1954. Bar: D.C. 1954, Ga. 1955, U.S. Supreme Ct. 1964. Assoc. Sutherland, Asbill & Brennan, Atlanta, 1954—61, ptnr., 1961—2001. Lectr. to profl. socs. on prevention dispute and constrn. Editor: (articles) Va. Law Rev., 1953—54; contbr. articles to profl. jours. Chmn. Constrn. Industry Dispute Avoidance and Resolution Task Force, 1991—94; bd. dirs. Atlanta Coun. for Internat. Visitors, 1968—75; bd. dirs., treas. N.W. Ga. coun., Girl Scouts U.S., 1973—79; trustee South Kent Sch., Conn., 1973—77, Nat. Assn. Women in Constrn. Edn. Found., 1993—98. Sgt. USMC, 1946—48, capt. USMC, 1950—52. Recipient medal excellence, Engring. News-Record, 1993. Fellow: Chartered Inst. Arbitrators, Coll. of Comml. Arbitrators, Am. Coll. Constrn. Lawyers (pres. 2000—01); mem.: AIA (hon. Bronze medal 1984), Ga. Arbitrator's Forum (pres. 2011), Princeton Alumni Assn. Ga. (v.p. 1964—77), Internat. Inst. Conflict Prevention and Resolution (Alternative Dispute Resolution awards 1988, 1994), Ga. Coun. Sch. Bd. Attys. (exec. com. 1971—78), Nat. Assn. Coll. and Univ. Attys., Nat. Sch. Bds. Assn. Coun. of Sch. Attys., Am. Arbitration Assn. (nat. panel constrn. arbitrators 1970—, bd. dirs. 1990—2002, nat. constrn. dispute resolution com. 1992—, internat. panel arbitrators 2001—, Whitney North Seymour medal 1983), Atlanta Bar Assn. (chmn. constrn. sect. 1992—93), State Bar Ga., Nat. Acad. of Constrn., Old War Horse Lawyers Club, Piedmont Driving Club, Peachtree Club, Phi Delta Phi. Democrat. Episcopalian. Office: Ste 2300 999 Peachtree St NE Atlanta GA 30309-3996 Office Phone: 404-853-8071. Business E-Mail: jim.groton@sutherland.com.

GROUT, ROBERT W., lawyer; b. Memphis, Nov. 2, 1944; s. M. Wayne and Evelyn (McClure) G.; m. Marsha Karkula, Aug. 12, 1967; children: Brad, Taylor. BA in Econs., Vanderbilt U., 1966; LLB, U. Va., 1969. Bar: Ga. 1969, Ga. Supreme Ct. 1970, Ga. Ct. of Appeals 1970, U.S. Dist. Ct. (no. dist.) Ga. 1975, U.S. Supreme Ct. 1975. Assoc. Troutman, Sanders, Lockerman & Ashmore, Atlanta, 1969-73; ptnr. Troutman Sanders LLP, Atlanta, 1974-85, sr. ptnr., sect. chief, corp. dept., 1986—2006, mem., opinion com. Seminar speaker Atlanta Bar Assn., 1986-99. Bd. dirs. Ashford-Dunwoody YMCA, 1984-93, Met. Atlanta YMCA, 1998-2004, Boy Scouts of Am. Troop, 1986-92; pres. Neighborhood Civic Assn., 1984—2004; mem. fin. com. Cherokee Town & Country Club, 1991—2003, pres. 2003-04. Named a Super Lawyer, Atlanta Mag., 2006—09; named one of America's Leading Bus. Lawyers, Chambers USA, 2003—08, Legal Elite, Ga. Trend Mag., 2003—08. Mem. ABA, State Bar Ga., Atlanta Bar Assn., Dunwoody Rotary Club (dir. 1984-91), Ravinia Club. Avocations: hunting, fishing, computers, photography. Office: Troutman Sanders LLP 600 Peachtree St NE Ste 5200 Atlanta GA 30308-2216 Office Phone: 404-885-3152. Office Fax: 404-962-6789. Business E-Mail: bob.grout@troutmansanders.com.

GROVE, JEFFREY SCOTT, family practice physician; b. Paxton, Ill., Sept. 21, 1964; s. Ronald Edwin and Delores Ann (Martensen) G.; m. Karen Beth Hanlon, June 17, 1989; children: Garrett Jeffrey, Victoria May. BS in Biology, Fla. So. Coll., 1986; DO, Southeastern Coll. Osteo Med., North Miami Beach, Fla., 1990. Diplomate Am. Bd. Quality Assurance and Utilization Rev. Physicians; bd. cert. family practice and in geriatrics. Intern Suncoast Hosp., Largo, Fla., 1990-91, resident in family practice, 1991-93; pvt. practice SunCoast Family Med. Assocs., Largo, 1993—. Med. dir. Barrington Properties, Largo, 1994-97, Oak Manor Nursing Ctr., Largo, 1993-2000, Drew Village Nursing Ctr., Clearwater, Fla., 1996-99, Highland Pines Nursing Ctr., 1999-2000; rep.-at-large exec. com. Suncoast Hosp., 1995-2000, chief adminstrv. resident, 1992-93, family practice tchg. staff, geriatrics program dir., 1993-96, faculty devel. com., 1994—2006, legal compliance comm., 1998—2006; mem. quality assurance/utilization rev. com., 1993—2006, med. dir. of quality assurance/utilization rev. dept., 1995—06; bd. dirs. Suncoast Cmty. Care PHO, Largo, 1994-98, med. dir., 1998; clin. asst. prof. family medicine Nova Southeastern U. Coll. Osteo. Medicine, North Miami Beach, 1994-2000, clin. assoc. prof., 2000—; clin. instr. Kirksville Coll. Osteo. Medicine, 1993—; trustee SunCoast Hosp. Found., 1996-2002, SunCoast Hosp., 1998—06; regional med. dir. Tampa Bay for Elder Health. Vice-chmn. bd. trustees SCH Found., 1997-98, chmn., 1998-99; trustee St. Paul's Sch., 2003—09, chmn. devel. com., 2005—07; bd. trustees health professions divsn. Nova Southeastern U., 2009-. Named to Outstanding Young Men of Am.; recipient Disting. Trustee award SCH Found., 2000. Mem.: Am. Coll. Osteopathic Family Practitioners (nat. bd. govs. 2004—, v.p. 2011—12, pres.-elect 2012—, pres. 2013—, Fellows award 2002, Disting. fellow 2013), Pinellas County Osteo. Med. Soc. (bd. govs. 1995—, treas. 1996—99, pres. 2000—03, Physician of Yr. 2002—03, Distinguished Svc. award 2007), Fla. Soc. Am. Coll. Osteo. Family Physicians (chmn. membership com. Fla. chpt. 1997—99, trustee 1997—2010, treas. 1999—2000, v.p. 2000—01, pres. 2001—02, Physician of Yr. 2003—04, Distinguished Svc. award 2009), Fla. Osteo. Med. Assn. (trustee 2001—, exec. com. 2005—, 1st v.p. 2009—10, pres. 2011—), Am. Osteo. Assn. (mem. coun. continuing med. edn. 2006—09, vice-chmn. coun. on continuing med. edn. 2006—, chmn. coun. continuing med. edn. 2009—, mem. Bur. of State Govt. Affairs), Nova Southeastern U. Coll. Osteo. Medicine Alumni Assn. (v.p. 2000—01, pres. 2002—03, Disting. Alumni award 2001, Disting. Alumni Achievement award 2003), Scouting Res., Nat. Eagle Scout Assn. (life). Republican. Methodist. Avocations: golf, stamp collecting/philately, travel, skiing. Office: SunCoast Family Med Assocs 12020 Seminole Blvd Largo FL 33778 also: 120 Medical Blvd Ste 103 Spring Hill FL 34609 Office Phone: 727-588-9572.

GROVER, ROSALIND REDFERN, oil and gas company executive; b. Midland, Tex., Sept. 5, 1941; d. John Joseph and Rosalind (Kapps) Redfern;m. Arden Roy Grover, Apr. 10, 1982; 1 child, Rosson. BA in Edn. magna cum laude, U. Ariz., 1966, MA in History, 1982; postgrad. in law, So. Meth. U. Libr. Gahr H.S., Cerritos, Calif., 1969; pres. The Redfern Found., Midland, 1982—89; ptnr. Redfern & Grover, Midland, 1986—; pres. Redfern Enterprises Inc., Midland, 1989—. Chmn. bd. dirs. Flag-Redfern Oil Co., Midland. Sec. park and recreation commn. City of Midland, 1969-71, del. Objectives for Convocation, 1980; mem., past pres. women's aux. Midland Cmty. Theatre, 1970; chmn. challenge grant bldg. fund, 1980, chmn. Tex. Yucca Hist. Landmark Renovation Project, 1983, trustee, 1983-88; chmn. publicity com. Midland Jr. League, Midland, Inc., 1972, chmn. edn. com., 1976, corr. sec., 1978; 1st v.p. Midland Symphony Assn., 1975; chmn. Midland Charity Horse Show, 1975-76; mem. Midland Am. Revolution Bicentennial Commn., 1976; trustee Mus. S.W., 1977-80, pres. bd. dirs., 1979-80; co-chmn. Gov. Clements Fin. Com., Midland, 1978; mem. dist. com. State Bd. Law Examiners; mem. bd. visitors Hockaday, 2001-03; trustee Midland Meml. Hosp., 1978-80, bd. gov., 2006-, Permian Basin Petroleum Mus., Libr. and Hall of Fame, 1989-98, Midland Cmty. Theatre, 2005—. Recipient HamHock award Midland Cmty. Theatre, 1978. Mem. Ind. Petroleum Assn. Am., Tex. Ind. Producers and Royalty Owners Assn., Petroleum Club, Racquet Club (Midland), Horseshoe Bay (Tex.) Country Club, Phi Kappa Phi, Pi Lambda Theta. Republican. Office: 303 W Wall Ste 2102 PO Box 2127 Midland TX 79702-2127 Office Phone: 432-683-9137. E-mail: rozgrover@aol.com.

GROWCOCK, TERRY D., manufacturing executive; b. 1945; BS in Bus. Mgmt., U. St. Francis. Exec. King-Seeley Corp., United Technologies, Universal Nolin, Paragon Electric; v.p., gen. mgr Robertshaw Automotive; exec. v.p., gen. mgr. Manitowoc Ice, 1994—95; pres. Manitowoc Foodservice Group, 1995—98, The Manitowoc Co., Inc., 1998—2002, CEO, 1998—2007, chmn., 2002—08. Bd. dirs. Harris Corp., 2005—, Harsco Corp., 2008—, Carlisle Companies Inc., 2008—. Chmn. Wis. Mfrs. & Commerce. Office: Carlisle Companies Inc Bd Directors 13925 Ballantyne Corporate Pl Ste 400 Charlotte NC 28277 Office Phone: 704-501-1100. Office Fax: 704-501-1190. Business E-Mail: tgrowcock@carlisle.com.

GRUBB, EDGAR HAROLD, automotive executive; b. Harrisburg, Pa., May 8, 1939; s. Harold E. and Ruth (Longenecker) G.; m. Patricia A. Kerwin, Dec. 14, 1963; children: Dennis, Lisa, Mary, Jennifer. BS, Pa. State U., 1961; MBA, Calif. State U., Fullerton, 1967. CPA, Calif. Cons. mgr., auditor Coopers & Lybrand, San Francisco and L.A., 1967—72; group contr. Crown Zellerbach Corp., San Francisco, 1972—75, gen. mgr., packaging papers, 1976—77, dir., Planning, 1978—80, v.p., Consumer, 1981—82, v.p., Contr., 1983—84, sr. v.p., CFO, 1984—86, Lucky Stores, Inc., Dublin, Calif., 1986—89; sr. v.p. Transamerica Corp., 1989—93, exec. v.p., CFO, 1993—99, joined, 1989. Bd. dirs. Goodwill Industries of Alameda/Contra Costa/Solano Counties, CarMax, Inc., 2007—. Trustee Mills Coll., Oakland, Calif. Capt. USMC, 1961-65, bd. dirs., AAA of Northern Calif., Nev. & Utah, NCNU Ins. Bur., AAA Club Affiliates Mem. AICPA, Calif. Soc. CPA's, Fin. Execs. Inst. Roman Catholic. Office: CarMax Inc Bd Directors 12800 Tuckahoe Creek Pky Richmond VA 23238 Home: 41 Comistas Ct Walnut Creek CA 94598-4523 Office: Transamerica Corp 600 Montgomery St Ste 2300 San Francisco CA 94111-2770 Office Phone: 800-519-1511. E-mail: edgar_grubb@carmax.com.

GRUBB, WILLIAM FRANCIS XAVIER, consumer products company executive, marketing professional; b. NYC, Aug. 11, 1944; s. William Martin and Eileen F. (Donnelly) G.; m. Eileen B. O'Leary, Apr. 4, 1964; children: Catherine E., William M., Kerri A., Christopher M. BA in Econs., Fordham U., 1966; MBA in Mktg. and Fin., Seton Hall U., 1972. bd. dirs. several privately-held cos. Mktg. and sales exec. Black & Decker, Towson, Md., 1968-79; v.p. mktg. Atari, Sunnyvale, Calif., 1979-81; chmn., pres. New West Mktg., Mountain View, Calif., 1981; pres., chief exec. officer, chmn. Imagic, Los Gatos, Calif., 1981-84; exec. v.p. Dataspeed, 1984-85; pres. Axlon Inc., 1985-86; exec. v.p., gen. mgr. Worlds of Wonder, Inc., Freemont, Calif., 1986-87; pres., chief exec. The Complete PC, San Jose, Calif., 1987-93; CEO, ICTV Inc., Los Gatos, Calif., 1994-96; CEO Millenia Software Inc., Saratoga, Calif., 1996—; pres. Toolz Ltd., Palo Alto, Calif., 1998-99; CEO Grubb Enterprises LLC, Pawleys Island, SC, 1999—. Guest editor The Dual Office of The Future. Bd. regents Holy Names Coll. Nominee BillBoard Mag. Video Game Hall of Fame, 1984. Avocation: photography. Office: Grubb Enterprises LLC 45 Rookery Trl Pawleys Island SC 29585-5266 Home: 109 Black Duck Rd Pawleys Island SC 29585-5266 Personal E-mail: wfxgrubb@aol.com.

GRUBBS, WILLIAM J., corporate financial executive; B in Computer Sci., U. NH. Pres., CEO TRS Staffing Solutions; CEO Spring Group plc., 2000—01, Spring Tech. Staffing Svcs. Ltd., 2001—02; COO Spring Group plc., 2002—05; sr. v.p., chief mktg. & corp. devel. officer Spherion Corp., 2005—07, exec. v.p., COO, 2007—. Office: Spherion Corp 2050 Spectrum Blvd Fort Lauderdale FL 33309 Office Phone: 954-308-7600. Office Fax: 954-308-7666.

GRUBER, IRA DEMPSEY, historian, educator; b. Phila., Jan. 6, 1934; married; 3 children. AB, Duke U., 1955, AM, 1959, PhD, 1961. Instr. history Duke U., 1961-62; fellow Inst. Early Am. History and Culture, 1962-65; asst. prof. Occidental Coll., 1965-66; from asst. prof. to assoc. prof., 1966-74; prof. Rice U., Houston, from 1974, now Harris Masterson emeritus history prof., chmn. dept. history, 1983-87. Master Hanszen Coll., Rice U., 1968-73; John F. Morrison prof. U.S. Army Command and Gen. Staff Coll., 1979-80; vis. prof. mil. history U.S. Mil. Acad., 1984-85, 92-93; mem. hist. adv. com. USAF, 1987-91, Dept. Army, 1992-95; trustee Soc. for Mil. History, 1987-95. Author: Lord Howe and Lord George Germain, 1965, The American Revolution as a Conspiracy: The British View, 1969, The Howe Brothers and the American Revolution, 1972, The Education of Sir Henry Clinton, 1990, Books and the British Army in the Age of the American Revolution, 2010; co-author: Classical Traditions in Early America, 1976, Reconsiderations on the Revolutionary War, 1978, Limits of Loyalty, 1980, Arms and Independence, 1984, Against All Enemies, 1986, America's First Battles, 1986, Warfare in the Western World, 1996, Between War and Peace, 2011; editor: John Peebles American War, 1998; mem. editl. bd. Jour. of Mil. History, 1995—99, chair editl. bd., 1999—2009. Recipient Samuel Eliot Morison prize, Soc. Mil. History, 2013. Home Phone: 713-668-4062; Office Phone: 713-348-4947. Business E-Mail: gruber@rice.edu.

GRUBER, J. RICHARD, museum director; b. Louisville, Mar. 30, 1948; s. James Richard Sr. and Mary Jane G.; children: Shen, Kalen. BA in English, Xavier U., 1971; MA in History of Art cum laude, U. Colo., 1980; M in Philosophy History of Art, U. Kans., 1982, PhD, 1987. Asst. dir. Jefferson County Archives & Records Service, Louisville, 1971-72, hist. preservation, 1972-74; art critic Colo. Daily, Boulder, 1977-78; lectr. history of art U. Colo., Colorado Springs, 1979-81; research fellow Nat. Mus. Am. Art, Washington, 1982-83; curator collections Memphis Brooks Mus. Art, 1983-85, acting dir., 1984-85, dir., 1985-89, Wichita Art Mus., Kans., 1989-91; gallery dir. Peter Joseph Gallery, NYC, 1991—93; dep. dir. Morris Mus. Art, 1993—99; dir. Ogden Mus. Southern Art, U. New Orleans, 1999—. Dir. design, installation and edn. Rameses the Great Exhbn., Memphis, 1985-87; faculty U. New Orleans. Author (exhbn. catalogue) Memphis in Memphis, 1984, Memphis: 1948-50, 1986, In Plain View-Irwin Kremen, 1987, We Like Ike (Wichita Art Mus.), 1990, The Dot Man: George Andrews of Georgia (exh. cat), 1994, Robert Rauschemberg: Major Printed Works (exh. cat), 1995, Nelhe Mac Rave (exh. cat), 1996, William Christenberry: The Early Years, 1954-1968, Robert Rauschemberg: Through the LPAS, 1996, From Madison to Manhatton: The Art of Benny Andrews 1977-1997, 1997, Thomas Hart Benton and The American South, 1998, Wolf Kahn: Painting the South, 1999, Robert Stackhouse,1999, William Christenberg: Art of Family,2000, Richard Julley: Sculpting Glass, 2007, The Art of the South 1890-2003, 2004, Missing New Orleans, 2005, Dunlap: Million Dunlap, 2006 Mem. policy com. Memphis Ctr. City Commn., 1985—; mem. adv. bd. Jr. League Memphis, 1984—; bd. dirs. Life Blood, Memphis, 1987, Wichita Airport Authority Art Com., Wichita Pub. Art Task Force, Downtown Action Corp. Adv. Com. Pre-doctoral fellow Nat. Mus. Am. Art-Smithsonian Instn., 1982-83; travel grantee Kress Found., 1983, fellow, 1982-83; grantee U. Colo., 1977;recipient Francis Gassner award Mempher Chapter AIA, 1988, Author of Yr., Ga., 1998, Book of Yr., Missing New Orleans, 2006, Humanities of Yr. Louisiania Endowment Humanities, 2007 Mem. Am. Mgmt. Assn. (pres.'s assn.), Am. Assn. Mus. Office: Ogden Mus Southern Art 925 Camp St New Orleans LA 70130

GRUBER, JOHN BALSBAUGH, physics professor; b. Hershey, Pa., Feb. 10, 1935; s. Irvin John and Erla R. (Balsbaugh) G.; m. Judith Anne Higer, June 20, 1961; children: David Powell, Karen Leigh, Mark Balsbaugh. BS, Haverford Coll., Pa., 1957; PhD, U. Calif., Berkeley, 1961. NATO postdoctoral fellow Inst. Tech. Physics, Tech. U. Darmstadt, Germany, 1961-62, gastdozent, 1961-62; asst. prof. physics UCLA, 1962-66; asso. prof. physics Wash. State U., Pullman, 1966-71, prof. chem. physics, 1971-75; asst. dean Wash. State U. (Grad. Sch.), 1968-70, assoc. dean, 1970-72; prof. physics, dean Coll. Sci. and Math., N.D. State U., Fargo, 1975-80; prof. physics and chemistry, v.p. for acad. affairs Portland (Oreg.) State U., 1980-84; prof. physics San Jose State U., 1984—2005, acad. v.p., 1984-86, v.p. devel., 1986, dir. Inst. for Modern Optics, 1992—2005, chmn. dept. physics, 2001—05; prof. rsch. physics and astronomy U. Tex., San Antonio, 2005—13. Vis. prof. Joint Ctr. Grad. Study, Richland, Wash., 1964-66, Ames Lab., Dept. of Energy, Iowa State U., 1976-80; Disting. vis. prof. U.S. Navy Naval Weapons Ctr., China Lake, Calif., 1984-93, Stanford U., 1993-2000; invited lectr., U.S., Can., Europe, 1966—; cons. in laser physics and spectroscopy Aerospace Corp., El Segundo, Calif., 1962-65, Douglas Aircraft and McDonnell Douglas Astronautics Co., Santa Monica, Calif., 1963-69, N.Am. Aviation, Space and Info. Systems, Downey, Calif., 1964-66, Battelle-Northwest, Richland, Wash., 1964-69, Los Alamos (N.Mex.) Sci. Lab., 1969-71, 73-74; mem. task force lunar exploration sci. Apollo, NASA, 1964-69, 71-73; cons. Army Rsch. Lab., Adelphi Ctr., U.S. Army, 1991—2012, IBM, 1985-90, GTE, 1986-89, Lasergenics, 1986-2005, Night Vision Lab. U.S. Army, Ft. Belvoir, 1993—2005, Deltron, 1990-91, Rey Tech Corp., 1998-2002, Laser Sci. and Tech., 1999—, Bicron Corp., 2000-03, Spectragen Corp., 2000, SAIC, 2002-06, Battelle, 1994-03, 05-12, Aculight Corp., 2003-06, Newtec Corp., 2003-04, CACI Techs., 2004; pres. The Gruber Group, 2005-; mem. Rare Earth Rsch. Conf. Com., 1976-83, exec. com., 1977-83, sec. bd. dirs., 1979-84; gen. conf. chmn. XIV Internat. Rare Earth Rsch. Conf., 1979, Novel Laser Sources and Materials, 1992; exec. sec. Internat. Frank H. Spedding Award, 1979, 83, Willig award, 1986, Internat. Spencer prize for outstanding contbrn. to sci., 1987, Pres.'s Scholar, 1994-95, Outstanding Achievement awards U.S. Dept. Def., 1995-96, 98, 01-05, Nom. U.S. Asst. Sec. Def. (Spl. Ops.), 1986-87; chmn. U.S. Navy/ASEE Postdoctoral Selection Bd., 1988-2002, U.S. Nat. Inst. Sci. and Tech. Postdoctoral Selection Bd., 1989-91; mem. rev. panel U.S. Navy/ASEE Grad. Fellowship Program, 1990-02; chmn., mem. NASA/ASEE program rev. bd., 1994-98; chmn. Internat. Conf. on Novel Laser Sources and Applications, San Jose, Calif., 1993, chmn. Battelle U.S. Dept. Def. Scholarship Program, 1994-01; mem. Battelle Sci. Bd. Selection Grad. Scholarship Fellows, 1998-99; PhD examiner physics U. Tex., San Antonio, 2009-. Co-author (with U.V. Valiev & G. W. Burdick) Magnetooptical Spectrocopy of Rare Earth Compounds, 2012, Contbr. articles to profl. jours., chpts. to books; holder numerous patents in laser sci. and tech. Trustee Symphony Bd. Fargo-Moorhead Symphony Orch., 1978-80; mem. N.D. State Bd. PTA; chmn. Univ., Coll. and Pub. Sch. Rels. Bd., 1979-80; active Boy Scouts Am.; trustee Pullman Pub. Libr., 1973-75, N.D. Symphony Orchs. Assn., 1978-80; mem. planning commn. City of Pullman, 1972-75; bd. dirs. Westminster Found., 1982-84. Recipient Outstanding Merit and Performance award San Jose State U., 1990, San Jose State Pres.'s Scholar, 1994-95, Dist. Tchr./scholar award, 1996, 97, 99, award in the field of lasers and electro-optics U. Chgo., 1995, Citation for Svc. and Achievement Dept. of Def., 1996, Award for Rsch. into night vision devices U.S. Army, 1997, 2001, 05, Outstanding World Leadership in Sci. award Acad. Scis., Poland, 1998, Outstanding Rsch. award San Jose State U., 2005; grantee AEC-ERDA, 1963-75, NSF, 1966-72, 76-78, 92—2008, U.S. Army Rsch. Office, Durham, 1979-80, Am. Chem. Soc. Petroleum Rsch. Funds, 1979-80, Dept. Energy, 1979-84, Dept. Def., 1984—2012, Office Naval Rsch., 1987—2002, Office Naval Tech., 1988-93, Dept. Def., DARPA, 1998-2006; fellow NASA Ames Lab., 1993-95; vis. scholar Stanford U., 1993-2000. Fellow Am. Soc. Engring. Edn. (disting.), Am. Phys. Soc. (chmn. nat. mtg. sessions), Am. Acad. Spectral Scis.; mem. AAAS, IEEE (sec. lasers and electro-optics 1995-96), NSF (reviewer and panel mem. divsn. material sci. 1994—), N.Y. Acad. Scis., N.D. Acad. Sci., Oreg. Acad. Sci., Acad. Scis. of Ukraine, Nat. Acad. Scis. (com. on lasers and electro-optics), Coun. Colls. Arts and Scis., Optical Soc. No. Calif. (v.p. 1992, pres. 1993), Lasers and Electro-optics Soc. (mem. program com. nat. meeting 1995), Internat. Soc. Optical Engring. (bd. dirs. 1993), Phi Beta Kappa, Sigma Xi, Phi Kappa Phi, Sigma Pi Sigma, Phi Sigma Iota. Office: Univ Tex at San Antonio Dept Physics and Astronomy San Antonio TX 78249-0697 Office Phone: 210-458-5748. Office Fax: 210-458-4919. Personal E-mail: johnbgruber@yahoo.com. Business E-Mail: john.gruber@utsa.edu.

GRUBERG, CY, educational administrator; b. Kingston, NY, Aug. 23, 1928; s. Joseph and Sara J. (Jacobson) G. BS, Rider U.; MA, Syracuse U., 1949; postgrad. guidance and counseling, Columbia U.; postgrad., NYU, Hofstra U., Harvard U., Adelphi U., U. Maine, U. Vt.; PhD, Columbia Pacific U., 1980. Tchr., guidance counselor Wellington C. Mepham HS, Bellmore, NY, 1949-60; guidance counselor, dean and dir. guidance Lynbrook HS, LI, 1960-66; asst. prof. SUNY at New Paltz, 1966-67; dir. pupil pers. svcs. and guidance Hastings-on-Hudson HS, NY, 1967—85; dir. coll. counseling Univ. Sch. Nova Southeastern U., Ft. Lauderdale, Fla., 1985-2000, pvt. ind. cons., 2000—. Group leader summer resident camps, 1950—55; mem. faculty Inst. Beau Soliel, Villars, Switzerland, 1955; tour dir. summer tours, US, Europe, Russia, Israel, Mexico, Can., 1961—71; instr. adult edn. Mepham High Sch., 1950-55; mem. faculty Roosevelt Sch., summers 1949-50; admissions interviewer Columbia U., 1985; faculty of Focus at Tufts U., Medford, Mass., summer 1990-91. Cons. N.C.C.J.; Active local drives Nat. Cerebral Palsy Assn., Am. Cancer Soc., Muscular Dystrophy Found., Cystic Fibrosis Found. (bd. dirs. Mid-Hudson Valley Region, NY), Leukemia Soc. Am., also, Community Scholarship drives; exec. bd. Nassau County Boys and Girls Week Com.; adv. com. Hastings Youth Employment Svc.; adv. coun. Graham Home; chmn. Hastings Student Project Com.; Mem. Hastings Safety Commn.; bd. dirs. Echo Hills Mental Hill Clinic, Dobbs Ferry, NY; vol. Cleve. Clinic Hosp., Weston, Fla. Technician 3rd grade, World War II, with Army Med. Corps, 1946, 1st lt. USAR, 1959. With Army Med. Corps. Recipient Nat. citation Parents' mag., 1960-65; scholar workshop human rels. U. Maine, 1958; recipient William O. Hamilton award Key club NY State, 1964, 72; June 3, 1981 proclaimed Cy Gruberg Day, Westchester County, NY Execs.; named to Sr. Hall of Fame, Broward County, Fla, 2000; named Vol. of Yr. Cleve. Clinic Hosp., Fla., 2004. Mem. VFW, NY State Tchrs. Assn., NY State Pers. and Guidance Assn., Am. Guidance and Pers. Assn., Am. Indian Edn. Found. (hon. scholarship com. mem.), Westchester-Putnam-Rockland Pers. and Guidance Assn., NEA, So. Assn. Coll. Admissions Counselling, Am. Ednl. Rsch. Assn., Nat. Assn. for Coll. Admissions Counseling, Am. Legion, Jewish War Vets., Broward County, Fla. Pub. Libr. Found., Phi Delta Kappa, Zeta Beta Tau. Clubs: B'nai B'rith, Kiwanis. Personal E-mail: doccy24@aol.com.

GRUCHACZ, ROBERT S., real estate company officer; b. Bloomfield, NJ, May 15, 1929; s. Stanley A. and Mae (Zalenski) G.; m. LaVerne T. Stein, Mar. 2, 1957; children— Robert S., Thomas A., Christopher J. BS, Seton Hall U., 1950; MBA, NYU, 1971; student, Advanced Mgmt. Program, Harvard U., 1973. C.P.A., N.J. With Arthur Young & Co., C.P.A.'s, 1955-58, Sterling Drug Inc., NYC, 1958-65; controller Nabisco Inc., 1965-72, asst. to pres., 1973-74, 76—, v.p., 1979-84; broker Dunes Mktg. Group and Sea Pines Realty, 1985-2001; exec. v.p. Aurora Products, 1974-76. Served as 1st lt. USAF, 1952-54. Mem. AICPA. Home: 11 Timber Marsh Ln Hilton Head Island SC 29926-2790 Personal E-mail: bobgruchacz@aol.com.

GRUCZA, DAN, manufacturing executive; BSChemE, Auburn U., Ala.; M in Indsl. Engring., Auburn U.; degree in law, Faulkner U., Montgomery, Ala. Mgr. environ., health and safety Gen. Elec.; dir. safety and environ. compliance Walter Industries, Inc.; v.p. environ., health and safety Mueller Water Products, Inc., 2006—. Office: Mueller Water Products Inc Ste 1200 1200 Abernathy Rd NE Atlanta GA 30328 Office Phone: 770-206-4200. Office Fax: 770-206-4235. Business E-Mail: dgrucza@muellerwp.com.

GRUDEN, JAY, professional football coach; b. Tampa, May 4, 1967; s. James and Kathy Gruden; m. Sherry Gruden; children: JJ, Joey, Jack. BS, U. Louisville, 1989. Grad. asst. U. Louisville Cardinals, 1990—91; quarterback Barcelona Dragons, World Football League, 1991, Tampa Bay Storm, Arena Football League, 1991—96; offensive coord. Nashville Kats, Arena Football League, 1997; head coach, gen. mgr. Orlando Predators, Arena Football League, 1998—2001, 2004—08, quarterback, 2002—03; offensive asst. Tampa Bay Buccaneers, 2002—08; head coach, gen. mgr. Fla. Tuskers, United Football League, 2010; offensive coord. Cin. Bengals, 2011—13; head coach Washington Redskins, 2014—. Named Arena League MVP, 1992. Achievements include member of Arena Football League championship winning Tampa Bay Storm, 1991, 1993, 1995, 1996; head coach of Arena Football League championship winning Orlando Predators, 1998, 2000. Office: Washington Redskins 21300 Redskin Pk Dr Ashburn VA 20147*

GRUM, CLIFFORD J., retired manufacturing executive, board member; b. Davenport, Iowa, Dec. 12, 1934; s. Allen F. and Nathalie (Cate) Grum; m. Janelle Lewis, May 1, 1965; 1 child, Christopher J. BA, Austin Coll., Sherman, Tenn., 1956; MBA, Wharton Sch., U. Pa., 1958. Formerly with Republic Nat. Bank, Dallas; v.p. fin. Temple Industries, Diboll, Tex.; treas. Time, Inc., NYC, 1973-75, pub. Fortune mag., 1975-79, v.p., 1975-80, exec. v.p., 1980-83; CEO Temple-Inland, Inc., Diboll, 1983-2000, chmn., 1991-2000, ret., 2000. Bd. dirs. Cooper Industries plc, 1982—2005, vice chmn., 2004—05; bd. dirs. Premark Internat., 1986—99, Trinity Industries Inc., 1995—2007, Tupperware Brands Corp., 1996—. Mailing: Tupperware Brands Corp Bd Directors 14901 S Orange Blossom Trail Orlando FL 32837

GRUNDER, FRED IRWIN, retired industrial hygienist, consultant; b. Detroit, Aug. 17, 1940; s. Fritz and Mary Kathrine (Irwin) G.; m. Barbara Ann Ward, May 7, 1966; children: John Frederick, Robert William. BS in Engr. Physics, U. Mich., 1963, MS in Physics, 1967. Diplomte Am. Bd. Indsl. Hygiene; cert. indsl. hygienist. Rsch. assoc. U. Mich., Ann Arbor, 1960-69; chemist G.D. Clayton & Assocs., Southfield, Mich., 1969-72; lab. dir. Bethlehem Steel Corp., Pa., 1972-85; dir. indsl. hygiene Am. Med. Labs., Fairfax, Va., 1985-92; mgr. lab. accreditation programs Am. Indsl. Hygiene Assn., Fairfax, 1992—2002; indsl. hygiene cons. Fishersville, Va., 2002—; v.p. SAW Habitat for Humanity. Sect. editor: Methods for Biological Monitoring, 1988. Scoutmaster Boy Scouts Am., Bethlehem, 1972-84; pres. U. Mich. Club, Lehigh Valley, 1980-84; mem. toxic planning and oversight panel Chesapeake Rsch. Consortium, Solomons Island, Md., 1990-91, lab. assessor AIHA Lab. Accreditation Avg. LLC, 1992, 2004—; bd. dirs. Nat. Coop. Lab. Accreditation, 1997-98, pres., 1998-2000, past pres., 2000-01, evaluation coord., 2004-07. Fellow Am. Indsl. Hygiene Assn.; mem. Am. Chem. Soc., Am. Acad. Indsl. Hygiene. Democrat. Methodist. Avocations: reading, stamp and coin collecting, gardening. Personal E-mail: fgrunder@ntelos.net.

GRUNEWALD, MARK HOWARD, law educator; BA, Emory U., 1969; JD with highest honors, George Washington U., 1972. Bar: DC 1973, Va. 1979. Assoc. Arent, Fox, Kintner, Plotkin & Kahn, Washington, 1972—73; atty. advisor Office of Legal Counsel US Dept. Justice, 1973—76; from asst. prof. to assoc. prof. law Washington and Lee U. Sch. Law, Lexington, Va., 1976—86, prof. law, 1986—2002, assoc. dean, 1992—96, interim dean, 1999—2000, 2010—12, James P. Morefield prof. law, 2002—. Editor-in-chief George Washington Law Review. Mem.: Order of Coif. Office: Washington and Lee University School of Law 457 Sydney Lewis Hall 1 Denny Circle Lexington VA 24450 Office Phone: 540-458-8526. Office Fax: 540-458-8488. E-mail: grunewaldm@wlu.edu.

GRUNSFELD, JOHN M., astronaut, astronomer; b. Chgo. s. Ernest A. Grunsfeld III; m. Carol E. Schiff; 2 children. BS in Physics, MIT, 1980; MS in Physics, U. Chgo., 1984, PhD in Physics, 1988. Vis. scientist U. Tokyo, Inst. Space and Astronautical Sci., 1980—81; grad. rsch. asst. U. Chgo., 1981—85, NASA grad. student fellow, 1985—87, W.D. Grainger Postdoctoral fellow in Exptl. Physics, 1988—89; sr. rsch. fellow Calif. Inst. Tech., 1989—92; astronaut NASA Johnson Space Ctr., Houston, 1992—; chief scientist NASA, 2003—04. Recipient 3 Space Flight medals, NASA, 2 Exceptional

Svc. medals, DSM, 2003, Disting. Alumni award, U. Chgo. Achievements include 5 space flights, 3 to Hubble Space Telescope, 8 space walks, more than 50 days in space. Avocations: bicycling, flying, music, sailing. Office: Astronaut Office/CB NASA Johnson Space Ctr Houston TX 77058

GRUSKIN, JAMES, marketing services company executive; Media investment banker Morgan Stanley, Lehman Bros.; v.p. bus. devel., corp. contr. Jour. Register Co., 2002—04; asst. v.p. fin. R.H. Donnelley Corp., 2004—, (merged with Dex One Corp., 2010). Office: Dex One Corp 1001 Winstead Dr Cary NC 27513 Office Phone: 919-297-1600. Office Fax: 919-297-1285. Business E-Mail: james.gruskin@rhd.com.

GUADERRAMA, DAVID CAMPOS, federal judge; b. Las Cruces, N.Mex., 1954; BA, N.Mex. State U., 1975; JD, U. Notre Dame Law Sch., 1979. Ptnr. Guaderrama & Guaderrama, 1980—86; chief public defender El Paso County, 1987—94; dist. judge 243rd Dist. Ct. Tex., El Paso, 1995—2010; magistrate judge US Dist. Ct. (western dist.) Tex., El Paso, 2010—12, judge, 2012—. Office: US District Court 525 Magoffin Ave El Paso TX 79901 Office Phone: 915-534-6005. Office Fax: 915-534-6724.*

GUARINO, ANTHONY MICHAEL, pharmacologist, educator, consultant, counselor; b. Framingham, Mass., Dec. 11, 1934; s. Alfred V. and Nellie L. (Beatrice) G.; m. Aida Iris Gerena, Nov. 9, 1957; children: Theresa, Elizabeth, Barbara, Cathie, Tom, Gregory, Paula, Phil, Richard, Paul. BS in Chemistry, Boston Coll., 1956; MS in Chemistry, U. R.I., 1963, PhD in Pharmacology and Toxicology, 1966; MA in Counseling, Liberty U., Lynchburg, Va., 1993. Lic. profl. counselor. Lt. comdr. USPHS, 1966, advanced through grades to capt., 1979; staff fellow pharmacology-toxicology rsch. assoc. program Nat. Heart Inst., NIH, Bethesda, Md., 1966-68; rsch. pharmacologist NCI Nat. Cancer Inst., NIH, Bethesda, Md., 1968-73, chief lab. toxicology, 1973-80; regulatory pharmacologist Ctr. for Drugs and Biologics-FDA, Md., 1980-84; lab. dir. fishery rsch. br. FDA, Dauphin Island, Ala., 1984-93; marriage and family counselor Cath. Social Svcs., Mobile, Ala., 1993—2006, The Carpenter's House, Mobile, 2007—. Adj. prof. U. South Ala. Coll. Medicine, Mobile, 1996-; vice chmn. com. on animals as monitors in environ. hazards NAS. Contbg. author: Handbook of Experimental Pharmacology—Concepts in Biochemical Pharmacology, 1971, Handbook of Experimental Pharmacology, Antineoplastic and Immunosuppressive Agents, 1974, Methods in Cancer Research, 1979, Pesticides and Xenobiotics Metabolism in Aquatic Organisms, 1979, Pesticides and Xenobiotics Metabolism in Aquatic Organisms, 1979, Cisplatin—Current Status and New Developments, 1980, Modern Pharmacology, 1982; contbr. 106 articles to profl. jours. Mem. Am. Soc. Pharmacology and Exptl. Therapeutics, Soc. Toxicology, Am. Chem. Soc., Am. Assn. Christian Counselors. Roman Catholic. Office: Carpenter's House PC 601 Bel Air Blvd Ste 409 Mobile AL 36606 Office Phone: 251-476-9994. Business E-Mail: amguarino@earthlink.net.

GUASTAFERRO, ANGELO, space science administrator, consultant; b. Hoboken, NJ, June 4, 1932; s. Carlo and Rafaela Nancy (Gioffi) G.; m. Eleanor Lago, Sept. 12, 1954; children: Carl, Mark, John Brian. BS in Mech. Engring, N.J. Inst. Tech., 1954; MBA, Fla. State U., 1963; A.M.P., Harvard U., 1984. With NASA, 1963-85, dep. mgr. Viking project, 1974-76; dir. planetary programs NASA Hdqs., Washington, 1979-81; dep. dir. Ames Research Center, Moffett Field, Calif., 1981-85; v.p., program dir. Lockheed Missiles & Space Co., 1985-96, exec. dir., 1994-96; CEO, chmn. bd. n View Corp., Newport News, Va., 1996; pres., CEO View Corp., Newport News, Va., 1996—98; exec. cons. AG Cons., Williamsburg, Va., 1998—; exec. ptnr., lectr. NASA and Fla. Inst. Tech., 1998—. Bd. trustees Internat. Space U., 1993-96; chmn. bd. dirs. View Corp., 1995-2002; sci. adv. com. NJIT. Chair bd. dirs. Hampton Rds. Tech. Coun. Served with USAF, 1955-58. Recipient Langley Spl. Achievement award NASA, 1974, 77, 78, Outstanding Leadership medal, 1977, Superior Performance award, 1980, Exceptional Service medal, 1981, Presdl. Meritorious rank, 1982; Disting. Alumnus NJIT, 1997. Fellow AIAA (Space Systems medal 1982), Am. Astronautics Soc.; mem. Mars First Landing Soc. (pres. 1978-79), Internat. Astronautics Fedn. (bd. dirs.), Tau Beta Pi (eminent engr. 1989). Roman Catholic. Office: AG Cons 124 Peter Lyall Williamsburg VA 23185-8902 Office Phone: 757-258-3039. Personal E-mail: gusg@cox.net.

GUBBINS, KEITH EDMUND, chemical engineering educator; b. Southampton, Eng., Jan. 27, 1937; came to U.S., 1962; m. Pauline Margaret Payne, June 28, 1960; children: Nick, Vanessa. B.Sc. in Chemistry, Queen Mary Coll., U. London, 1958; Diploma in Chem. Engring., King's Coll., U. London, 1959, PhD in Chem. Engring., 1962. Vis. lectr. U. London, Eng., 1960-62; postdoctoral fellow U. Fla., Gainesville, 1962-64, asst. prof., 1964-68, assoc. prof., 1968-72, prof., 1972-76; T.R. Briggs prof. engring. Cornell U., Ithaca, NY, 1976-98, T.R. Briggs prof. engring. emeritus, 1998—; dir. Cornell U., Sch. Chem. Engring., Ithaca, NY, 1983-90; W.H. Clark disting. univ. prof. N.C. State U., Raleigh, 1998—; co-dir. N.C. State U., Ctr. for High Performance Simulation, Raleigh, 2004—; dir. Inst. Computational Sci. & Engring., 2008—12. Vis. cons. theoretical physics divsn., U.K. Atomic Energy Authority, Harwell, U.K., 1971; vis. prof. dept. physics U. Guelph, 1971-73, 76, U. Kent, Canterbury, Eng., 1975, dept. chemistry U. Oxford, 1979-80, 86-87, Kyoto U., Japan, 1987, Chiba U., Japan, 1999, dept. chem. engring. U. Calif., Berkeley, 1982, Australian Nat. U., Canberra, 1993, Imperial Coll., London, 1970-71, 94, 2002, 2011, U. Paris-Sud, 2001-02, dept. chem. engring. U. Wis., 1993, U. Hong Kong, 2007, U. Manchester, 2009; vis. fellow Fulbright Sr. scholar Australian Nat. U., 1993-94; mem. NAS com. to study formation of Nat. Resource Ctr. for Computing in Chemistry, 1976-77, NRC Assessment Bd. to rev. NIST programs, 1988-91; cons., lectr. in field. Mem. editl. bd. Molecular Physics, 1978-87, 95—2012, Jour. Chem. Physics, 1995-98, Molecular Simulation, 1986-, assoc. editor, 1990-2006; assoc. editor AIChE Jour., 1988-91; editor: Topics in Chem. Engring., Oxford U. Press, 1991—2008; del. Oxford U. Press, 1991-2008. Recipient best paper ann. award Can. Soc. Chem. Engring., 1973; named Eppley Found. fellow Imperial Coll. London, 1970-71, Guggenheim fellow, 1986-87, sr. vis. fellow (SERC award) U. Oxford, 1986-87, vis. fellow (SERC award) Imperial Coll., London, 1994, medal Found. Molecular Modeling and Simulation, 2012, Rossini Lecture award, Internat. Assn. Chem. Thermodynamics, 2012, Lennard Jones Lecture award., Royal Soc. Chemistry, 2013; Royal Soc. vis. professorship, Hong Kong, 2007; Disting. Vis. fellow Royal Acad. Engring., 2009. Mem. NAE, AAAS, AIChE (program com. 1974-81, Alpha Chi Sigma award 1986, William H. Walker award 2000, fellow 2003), Am. Chem. Soc. (Joel Henry Hildebrand award in Theoretical and Exptl. Chemistry of Liquids, 2007), Am. Inst. Physics, Chem. Soc. (London). Home Phone: 919-841-5671. Personal E-mail: kgubbins@aol.com. Business E-Mail: keg@ncsu.edu.

GUELLI, PETE, professional sports team executive; b. Rochester, NY; m. Patty Guelli; children: Gunner, Grayson. Grad., SUNY, Brockport. Sales and mktg. profl.; sr. v.p. bus. ventures Buffalo Bills, 1998—2009; exec. v.p., chief sales and mktg. officer Charlotte Bobcats, 2009—. Office: Charlotte Bobcats 333 E Trade St Charlotte NC 28202

GUERIN, DEAN PATRICK, metal products executive; b. St. Paul, Feb. 21, 1922; s. Joseph Henry and Della (Booth) G.; m. Jo Alice Maryman, Sept. 3, 1959; children: Dean William, Stephen Patrick, Mark Joseph. BSBA, Boston U., 1949. With Sperry Gyroscope Co., NYC, 1940-42; registered rep. Chas. A. Day & Son, Boston, 1946-49, Dallas Rupe & Son, 1949-51; from exec. v.p. to chmn. bd. dirs., pres. & CEO Eppler, Guerin & Turner, Inc., Dallas, 1951—88; CEO, chmn. bd. dirs. Gen. Aluminum Corp., 1995; ind. dir. cos., 1994—. Chmn. Archaea Solutions, Inc.; bd. dirs. Components Corp., Tex. Internat., Houston, 1964-66, Cir. K Corp., 1967-93, Dallas Airmotive Inc., Am. Fed. Bank, Dallas, 1989-93, and numerous others; guest lectr. North Tex. U., Tex. Christian U. Past trustee Marine Mil. Acad.; mem. Bus. Adv. Coun. North Tex. U., Naval War Coll. Found.; mem. planning & policy devel. com. Selwyn Sch.; with Investment Com. Dallas Mus. Art & Arbitrator NY Stock Exch. With USMCR, 1942-46, PTO. Mem. Dallas Country Club, Chandler's Landing Yacht Club (former commodore & gov.), Dallas Petroleum Club. Republican. Episcopalian. Avocations: sailing, skiing, scuba diving. Home: 1401 Vino Blanc Ct Southlake TX 76092-8862 Office Phone: 214-520-0197. Personal E-mail: deanguerin1@att.net.

GUERRA, DONNA T., bank executive; Sr. acct. Deloitte & Touche, 1988—89; v.p., fin., investment, purchasing Jefferson Guaranty Bank, Metairie, La., 1989—97; fin. cons. Oil Mop, LLC, Belle Chasse, La., 2003—05; sr. v.p., CFO, asst. sec. Hibernia Homestead Bank, 2005—; CFO, asst. sec. Hibernia Homestead Bancorp, Inc., 2008—. Sr. internal cons., fin. divsn. Ochsner Found. Hosp., 1998—2001. Office: Hibernia Homestead Bancorp Inc 325 Carondelet St New Orleans LA 70130 Office Phone: 504-522-3203.

GUERRA, FERNANDO A., pediatrician, health facility administrator; b. San Antonio, 1939; m. Beverly Guerra; 6 children. BA, Univ. Tex.; MD, Univ. Tex. Med. Br., Galveston, 1964; MPH, Harvard Univ. Diplomate Am. Bd. Pediatrics. Intern San Francisco Gen. Hosp., 1964—65; resident U. Tex. Hosps., Galveston, 1967—69, U. Tex. Bexar County Tchg. Hosps., San Antonio, 1969—71; staff pediatrician Santa Rosa Children's Hosp., San Antonio, 1970—; fellow in pub. health Harvard U., Boston, 1982—83; founder, med. dir. Barrio Family Health Clinic, San Antonio; dir. health MetroHealth, San Antonio, 1987—. Clin. prof. pediatrics Univ. Tex. Health Sci. Ctr., San Antonio; bd. trustees Urban Inst., Inst. Medicine Bd. on Children and Families, CDC Adv. Com. on Immunization Practices; founding scholar Pub. Health Leadership Inst.; adj. prof. Univ. Tex. Sch. Pub. Health, USAF Sch. Aerospace Med., Brooks AFB. Contbr. numerous articles to profl. jours. Fellow: Am. Acad. Pediats. (spokesman for Internat. Yr. of the Child 1979); mem.: APHA, Tex. Med. Assn., Inst. of Medicine of NAS. Office: MetroHealth 332 W Commerce San Antonio TX 78205-2489 Office Phone: 210-207-8731.

GUERRA, JUAN LUIS, musician; b. Santo Domingo, Dominican Republic, June 7, 1957; s. Gilberto Guerra and Olga Seijas; m. Nora Vega; children: Jean-Gabriel, Paulina. Grad., Nat. Conservatory Music, Santo Domingo, Berklee Coll. Music, Boston. Founding band mem. 440, 1984. Musician: (albums) Mientras Mas Lo Peinso, 1987, Bachata Rosa, 1990 (Grammy award, Best Tropical Latin Album, 1992), Burbujas de Amor, 1990, El Original 4.40, 1990, Bilirrubina, 1991, Tu, 1991, Mudanza y Acarreo, 1991, Areito, 1992, Fogaraté, 1994, Romance Rosa, 1995, Ojalá que Llueva Café, 1995, Ni Es Lo Mismo Ni Es Igual, 1998, Para Ti, 2004, La Llave de Mi Corazón, 2007 (Record of Yr., Album of Yr., Song of Yr., Best Tropical Song, Best Engineered Album, Latin Grammy Awards, 2007, Grammy award, Best Tropical Latin Album, 2008, Group Tropical Album of Yr., Billboard Latin Music Awards, 2008), Archivo Digital 4.4, 2007. Recipient Latino Spl. award, Music Acad. Spain, 2005, Hon. Lifetime Achievement award, Premio Lo Neustro Awards, 2007, Spirit of Hope award, Billboard, 2005, Music Icon award, BMI Singer/Songwriter Assn., 2006, Person of Yr. award, Latin Grammy Awards, 2007, Hot Latin Songs Artist of Yr., Prodr. of Yr., Billboard Latin Music Awards, 2008. Office: c/o Integrity Music 1000 Cody Rd Mobile AL 36695

GUESS, JAMES DAVID, lawyer; b. Lampasas, Tex., Jan. 21, 1941; s. David Ira and Lila Blanch (Reagan) G.; m. Susan Lawyer, Dec. 19, 1981; children: Corey, Stephanie, Casey, Chris. BS in Edn., Southwestern U., 1963; JD, St. Mary's U., 1968. Bar: Tex. 1968, U.S. Dist. Ct. (we. dist.) Tex. 1974, U.S. Ct. Appeals (5th cir.) 1974, U.S. Dist. Ct. (so. dist.) Tex. 1978, U.S. Dist. Ct. (no. dist.) Tex. 1982. Assoc. Groce Locke & Hebdon, San Antonio, 1968-74, ptnr., 1975-86; shareholder Groce Locke & Hebdon P.C., San Antonio, 1986-96, Jenkens & Gilchrist, San Antonio, 1996-99, Law Offices of James D. Guess, San Antonio, 1999—. Sustaining mem. Products Liability Adv. Coun.; mem. Am. Bd. Trial Advs. With USN, 1961—67, Vietnam. Mem.: Internat. Assn. Def. Counsel, Def. Rsch. Inst. (bd. dirs. 1998—2001), Tex. Assn. Def. Counsel (past pres.). Avocations: sports, golf, hunting. Home Phone: 210-494-4582; Office Phone: 210-340-1403. E-mail: jamesdguess@sbcglobal.net.

GUEST, FLOYD EMORY, JR., lawyer; b. Oglethorpe, Ga., May 5, 1929; s. Floyd Emory and Eula Belle (Jones) G.; m. Mary E. Vick, Oct. 12, 1955 (div. 1959); 1 child, Victoria Elizabeth; m. Martha J. Roy, Oct. 12, 1963 (dec. 2008); children: Alyson Jane, Emory Roy; m. Nola W. Ash, Dec. 26, 2011. AB in Bus. Adminstrn., Duke U., 1952; JD, U. Tex., 1962; MS in Fin. Svcs., Am. Coll., 1980. Bar: Tex. 1962. V.p., controller Cosmopolitan Life, Houston, 1952-59; trust officer Bank of Southwest, 1962-67, Capital Nat. Bank, 1967-69; chmn. Profl. Businessmen Assn. Retirement Plans Co., Houston, 1969—2004. Pres. Southgate Civic Assn., Houston, 1967, 68. Served with USMC, 1946—50, served to captain USAFR, 1950—67. Mem. SAR, Tex. Bar Assn., Houston Bar Assn., Houston Estate Planning Coun. Delta Theta Phi Law Frat. (pres. Houston alumni 1964). Lodges: Downtown Optimist (pres. 1982-83), Masons, K.T. Republican. Home: 19 Poplar Hill Pl The Woodlands TX 77381 Home Phone: 713-952-9479; Office Phone: 281-693-2222. Personal E-mail: floydguest@hotmail.com.

GUGLIELMINO, LUCY MARGARET MADSEN, education educator, researcher, consultant; b. Charleston, SC, Feb. 20, 1944; d. Robert Allen and Margaret Webb (Rodgers) Madsen; m. Paul Joseph Guglielmino, July 31, 1965; children: Joseph Allen, Margaret Rose. BA in English magna cum laude, Furman U., 1965; MEd in English and Edn., Savannah Grad. Ctr., 1973; EdD in Adult Edn., U. Ga., 1977. Tchr. English various pub. schs., Mass., NJ, SC, Ga., 1965-72; vis. asst. prof. adult and cmty. edn. Fla. Atlantic U., Boca Raton, 1978-87, asst. prof., 1987-88, assoc. prof., 1988-90, prof., 1991—2011, chmn. dept. ednl. leadership, 1991-94, dir. Melby Cmty. Edn. Ctr., 1994—2000, prof. emeritus, 2012; extraordinary prof. North West U. Potchefstroom, South Africa, 2012—. Cons. AT&T, Motorola, Westvaco, S.E. banks, U. Coimbra, Portugal, Northwest U., South Africa, U. Paris; bd. dirs. South Fla. Ctr. for Ednl. Leaders. Author: Adult ESL Instruction: A Sourcebook, 1991, Community Education and Florida's Future: Proceedings of the Commissioner's Summit, 1997; co-author: Administering Programs for Adults, 1997; author: (adult form) Self-Directed Leaning Readiness Scale, 1978, 3 other forms and translations into 20 other langs., 1979—2011, Learning Preference Assessment, 1991; editor: Florida GED Teachers' Handbook, 1999, 2001, Florida GED Teachers' Lesson Bank, 2001, Internat. Jour. Self-Directed Learning, 2003—; contbr. over 100 articles to profl. jours., chapters to books. Recipient Tchr. of Yr. award Coll. Edn., Fla. Atlantic U., 1990, Outstanding Achievement award 1991, Presdl. Merit award, 1993, Profl. Excellence award, 1998, Malcolm Knowles Meml. award for outstanding lifelong contbn. to rsch. in self directed learning, 2002, Commn. of Profs. of Adult Edn. Career Achievement award, 2010, Fla. Atlantic U. Alumni Assn. Talon-Faculty Leadership award, 2010; named to Fla. Adult and Cmty. Edn. Hall of Fame, Fla. Adminstrs. Adult and Cmty. Edn., 1992; Internat. Adit & Continuing Edn. Hall of Fame, 2012. Mem. AAUW, Nat. Cmty. Edn. Assn., Am. Assn. for Adult and Continuing Edn., Commn. Profs. Adult Edn. (chmn. self-directed learning task force 1987-88, 90-91), Fla. Adult Edn. Assn. (bd. dirs. 1989-90), Internat. Soc. for Self-Directed Learning (co-chair, bd. dirs. 2006-10, chair 2011-), Phi Kappa Phi, Phi Delta Kappa. Episcopalian. Avocations: reading, swimming, bicycling, flower arranging, gardening, boating. Home: 7339 Reserve Creek Dr Port Saint Lucie FL 34986 E-mail: lguglie@fau.edu.

GUGLIELMONE, ROBERT ERIC, bishop; b. NYC, Dec. 30, 1945; BA in Edn., St. John's Univ.; MDiv, Immaculate Conception Sem., Huntington, NY, 1978. Tchr. Patchogue-Medford High Sch., NY, 1968—73; ordained priest Diocese of Rockville Ctr., NY, 1978; parochial vicar St. Martin of Tours parish, Amityville, NY, 1978—86; dir. pastoral info. & dean of seminarians Immaculate Conception Sem., Huntington, NY, 1986—93; pastor St. Frances de Chantal, Wantagh, NY, 1993—2004; dir. priest personnel Diocese of Rockville Ctr., 2004—07; rector St. Agnes Cathedral, Rockville Ctr., NY, 2007—09; ordained bishop, 2009; bishop Diocese of Charleston, SC, 2009—. Diocesan chaplain Boy Scouts, 1983—90; assoc. nat. chaplain Nat. Catholic Com. on Scouting, 1986—89; chaplain Internat. Conf. on Scouting, 2000—08. Roman Catholic. Office: Diocese of Charleston 119 Broad St PO Box 818 Charleston SC 29402 Office Phone: 843-853-2130. Office Fax: 843-724-6387.

GUI, JAMES EDMUND, architect; b. Wooster, Ohio, Aug. 13, 1928; s. Harry Ludwig and Mabel Josephine (Olson) Gui; m. Anne Louise Outram, Oct. 15, 1955; children: Linda Anne, Jeffrey Allen. BArch, Ohio State U., 1954. Assoc. firm Charles F. McKirahan & Assocs., Archs., Ft. Lauderdale, Fla., 1958—63; chief specifications Archs. Collaborative, Cambridge, Mass., 1963—67; propr. James E. Gui, Archtl. and Specifications Cons., Belmont, Mass., 1967—2005, ret., 2005. Prin. works include Archs. Collaborative, Benjamin Thompson & Assocs., Cambridge Seven Assocs., Archtl. Resources Cambridge, Inc., Harvard, MIT, Juilliard Sch. Music, Lincoln Ctr., NYC, U.S. Pavillion Expo 67, Montreal, New Eng. Aquarium, Children's Hosp. Med. Ctr., Harvard U. Law Sch. Complex, Harvard Gutman Libr., Harvard Obs., Kirkland Coll., Berkshire CC, Tufts U. Dental Health Ctr., Independence Nat. Hist. Pk. Visitors Ctr., Navy Pier, Chgo., Wilmington Jewish Cmty. Ctr., Faneuil Hall Marketplace, Boston, Harborplace, Balt., Seaport Market, NYC, Pier 17, Bayside Marketplace, Miami, Century City Market, LA, Harvard Kennedy Sch. Govt., Cambridge, Ordway Music Theater, Mpls., Union Sta. Restoration, Washington, Va. Performing Arts Ctr., Richmond, Va. Recipient Disting Alumnus award, Ohio State U., 2003. Mem.: Constrn. Specifications Inst. Home Phone: 843-785-7641; Office Phone: 843-785-7645. Personal E-mail: jandagui1@aol.com.

GUICE, JEFFREY S., state legislator; b. El Paso, Tex., Dec. 22, 1959; m. Belinda Gryder. Attended, U. Southern Miss. Real estate broker; mem. Dist. 114 Miss. House of Reps., 2008—. Republican. Presbyterian. Office: PO Box 1018 Jackson MS 39215 Home: PO Box 549 Ocean Springs MS 39566-0549 Home Phone: 228-872-2994; Office Phone: 228-875-1131. E-mail: jguice@house.ms.gov.

GUICE, W. DAVID, state legislator; b. Asheville, NC, July 4, 1955; m. Kerry Lynne Guice; children: Lindsey, Colby. AS, Montreat Anderson Coll., 1977; BS in Social Work, Mars Hill Coll., 1979. Former instr. NC Justice Acad.; former parole ops. mgr. NC Dept. Correction, former ERT leader; chief probation & parole officer Transylvania & Henderson Counties; co-owner Old Hickory House, 1987—2007; commr. Transylvania County, 2000—08; mem. Dist. 113 NC House of Reps., 2009—12. Republican. Home: 297 Cardinal Dr Brevard NC 28712 Office Phone: 919-715-4466. Business E-Mail: David.Guice@ncleg.net.

GUIDRY, GREG G., state supreme court justice; JD, La. State Univ., 1985; postgraduate study, Univ. Witwatersrand, Johannesburg, So. Africa. Bar: La. 1985. Atty. Liskow & Lewis, New Orleans; asst. us atty. US Dept. Justice Ea. Dist. La., 1990—2000; judge La. Dist. Ct. 24th Dist., 2000—06, La. 5th Cir. Ct. Appeal, 2006—08; assoc. justice La. Supreme Ct., 2009—. Mem.: La. Bar Found., La. 5th Cir. Judges Assn. (pres.), Judge John C. Boutall Inn of Ct. (pres.), Order of the Coif. Office: La Supreme Ct 400 Royal St New Orleans LA 70130 Office Phone: 504-310-2300.*

GUILLEN, RYAN, state legislator; b. Oct. 27, 1977; m. Dalinda Guillen; 1 child, Cinco Demi. BS, Tex. A&M U., College Station. Rancher, educator; small business owner; mem. Dist. 31 Tex. House of Representatives, Tex., 2002—. Democrat. Office: 100 N FM 3167 Ste 212 Rio Grande City TX 78582 also: Room EXT E1.320 Capitol Extension PO Box 2910 Austin TX 78768 Address: PO Box 689 131 W Main St Benavides TX 78341 also: 4735 Loma Vista Dr Laredo TX 78046 Office Phone: 956-716-4838, 512-463-0416, 361-256-3970, 956-794-1767.

GUILLORY, CURTIS JOHN, bishop; b. Mallet, La., Sept. 1, 1943; MDiv, Cath. Theol. Union, 1973; M of Christian Spirituality, Creighton U., 1986. Ordained priest Society of the Divine Word, Rome, 1972; aux. bishop Archdiocese of Galveston-Houston, Tex., 1987—2000; ordained bishop, 1988; bishop Diocese of Beaumont, 2000—. Roman Catholic. Office: Diocese of Beaumont PO Box 3948 Beaumont TX 77704-3948 Office Phone: 409-838-0451. Office Fax: 409-838-5411. E-mail: bishop@dioceseofbmt.org.

GUILLORY, ELBERT LEE, lawyer, state legislator; b. Opelousas, La., June 24, 1944; s. Macie and Lucille (Green) G.; m. Mary Marks, Dec. 21, 1965 (div. 1981); 1 child, Elbert Lee II; m. Yvonne Guillory, Aug. 8, 1987; 1 child, Imani Malique. Student, Southern U., 1961-64; BA, Norfolk State Coll., Va., 1968; JD, Rutgers U., 1971; postgrad., N.Y. Theol. Sem., 1971-72. Bar: N.J. 1972, La. 1986. Exec. dir. Paterson (N.J.) Action Civic Team, 1970-71; instr. Rutgers Law Sch., Newark, 1971-72; div. dir. Pa. Human Rights Dept., Harrisburg, 1972-73; exec. dir. Md. Commn. on Human Rights, Balt., 1973-77; affirmative action mgr. Balt. Region Rapid Transit System, 1977-79; exec. dir. Seattle Human Rights Dept., 1980-81; pvt. practice Opelousas, La., 1981-85, 87—; mng. atty. Acadiona Legal Svc. Corp., Opelousas, 1985-87; mem. Dist. 40 La. House of Reps., 2004—09; mem. Dist. 24 La. State Senate, 2009—. Bd. dirs. Acadiona Legal Svcs. Corp, Lafayette, La., 1987—. Columnist: Metropolitan Mag., African Am. News and World Report; contbr. to Balt., Seattle and Afro-Am. newspapers. With U.S. Navy, 1964-68. Recipient scholarships to Southern U., 1961, Rutger U., 1968, N.Y. Theol. Sem., 1971, Superior Pub. Svc. award, Afro-Am. Newspapers, Harriet Tubman Community Svc. award, Assn. of Black Media Workers, Bishop Spotswood Leadership award, Md. State Conf. NAACP branches, Disting. Svc. Citation, Frontiers Internat., Humnitarian award, Md.

Assn. Human Rights Agys., Disting. Health and Community Svc. award, Community Health Coun. Md., others. Mem. ABA, ATLA, N.J. Bar Assn., Fed. Bar Assn., Am. Acad. Polit. Sci., Am. Soc. Pub. Adminstrs., La. Bar Assn., Lt. Landry Parish Bar Assn., S.E. La. Lawyers Bar Assn., La. Trial Lawyers Assn., Opelousas-St. Landry C. of C. (v.p. for govtl. affairs), La. Fedn. Families for Children's Mental Health (pres. bd. dirs.). Democrat. St. Landry. Avocations: mountain climbing, skiing, swimming, photography, dance. Office: 660 E Landry St Opelousas LA 70570-7320 also: 633 E Landry St Opelousas LA 70570 also: State Capitol P O Box 44486 Baton Rouge LA 70804 Office Phone: 337-943-2457, 225-342-6945. Fax: 337-943-2459.

GUILLORY, MICKEY JAMES, state legislator; b. Mamou, La., Feb. 2, 1941; m. Helen Aucoin; children: Vicky, John. State police officer; mem. Dist. 41 La. House of Reps., 2004—, mem. adminstrn. of criminal justice com., agr., forestry, aquaculture and rural devel. com., appropriations com., joint legis. com. on the budget, mem. house com. on homeland security, joint com. on homeland security. Named one of Best Elected Official; named to Citizen of Yr., Citizen Action, King, Basil Swine Festival, 2006. Democrat. Pentecostal. Address: PO Box 986 Eunice LA 70535 Office: Capitol Off 900 N Third St, PO Box 94062 Baton Rouge LA 70804 Home: 516 Rozas Rd Eunice LA 70535 Fax: 337-457-5649. E-mail: larep041@legis.state.la.us.

GUILTINAN, RICHARD J., corporate financial executive; BBA in Acctg., U. Notre Dame, 1976; attended in Tuck Exec. Program, Dartmouth Coll., 1993. CPA. Served, acctg., fin. mgmt., oper. positions Caltex Corp., 1985—2001, CFO, 2000—01; cons. Chevron, 2002—03; v.p., chief acctg. officer Flowserve Corp., 2004—10, sr. v.p., chief acctg. officer, 2010—. Bd. dirs. North Am. Technologies Group, Inc. Office: Flowserve Corp Ste 2300 5215 N O'Connor Blvd Irving TX 75039 Office Phone: 972-443-6500. Office Fax: 972-443-6800. Business E-Mail: rguiltinan@flowserve.com.

GUIMARAES, TOR, IT researcher, professor; s. Nestor and Elsa Guimaraes; m. Valerie Guimaraes; children: Erik, Sarah, Melissa. AA in Bus. Adminstrn., Pasadena City Coll., Calif., 1969; BS, Calif. State U., 1973, MBA, 1974; PhD in Mgmt. IS, U. Minn., Mpls., 1981. Instr. St. Cloud State U., Minn., 1974—77, asst. prof., 1979—81, full prof., 1986—87, 1987—91; dir., MIS post grad. cert. program Weatherhead Sch. Mgmt., Cleve., 1981—86; vis. expert mgmt. IT Fudan U., Shanghai, 1988, 1990; endowed chair prof. Tenn. Tech U., Cookeville, 1991—. Cons. and mem. bd. dirs. PMR, Inc, Knoxville, Tenn., SERPLAN, Inc., San Palo, Brazil, SIRA Internat., Campinas, Brazil. Contbr. articles to profl. jours. Recipient Caplenor Faculty Rsch. award, Tenn. Tech U., 1999, Highly Commended award, Emerald Literati Network, 2006, Citation of Excellence award, ANBAR Electronic Intelligence; named one of Top Rschrs. in World, Decision Scis. Inst., 1999. Office: Tennessee Tech Univ 1105 N Peachtree JH 412 Cookeville TN 38505

GUIN, JUNIUS FOY, JR., federal judge; b. Russellville, Ala., Feb. 2, 1924; s. Junius Foy and Ruby (Pace) G.; m. Dorace Jean Caldwell, July 18, 1945; children: Janet Elizabeth Smith, Judith Ann Mullican, Junius Foy III, David Jonathan. Student, Ga. Inst. Tech., 1940-41; AB magna cum laude, U. Ala., JD with honors, 1947; LLD, Magic Valley Christian Coll., 1963. Bar: Ala. 1948. Sr. ptnr. Guin, Guin, Bouldin & Porch, Russellville, 1948—73; commr. Ala. Bar, 1965-73, 2d v.p., 1969-70; judge US Dist. Ct. (no. dist. Ala.), Birmingham, 1973—89, sr. judge, 1989—. Pres. Abstract Trust Co., Inc., 1958-73; sec. Iuka TV Cable Co., Inc., Haleyville TV Cable Co., Inc., 1963-73; former dir., gen. counsel First Nat. Bank of Russellville, Franklin Fed. Savs. & Loan Assn. of Russellville.; Lectr. Cumberland-Samford Sch. Law, 1974, U. Ala. Sch. Law, 1977 Chmn. Russellville City Planning Com., 1954-57; 1st chmn. Jud. Commn. Ala., 1972-73; mem. Ala. Supreme Ct. Adv. Com. (rules civil procedure), 1971-73; mem. adv. com. on standards of conduct U.S. Jud. Conf., 1980-87, mem. com. on Fed.-State Jurisdiction, 1982-88, mem. ad hoc com. on cameras in the courtroom, 1982-83; Rep. county chmn., 1954-58, 71-72, Rep. state fin. chmn., 1972-73; candidate for U.S. Senator from, Ala., 1954; Ala. Lawyers' Finance chmn. Com. to Re-elect Pres., 1972; former trustee Ala. Christian Coll., Faulkner U., Magic Valley Christian Coll., Childhaven Children's Home; elder Ch. of Christ. Served to 1st lt., inf. AUS, 1943-46. Named Russellville Citizen of Year, 1973; recipient Dean's award U. Ala. Law Sch., 1977 Mem. ABA (mem. spl. com. on resdl. real estate transactions 917-73), Am. Radio Relay League, Ala. Bar Assn. (com. chmn. 1965-73, Award of Merit 1973), Jefferson County Bar Assn., Fed. Bar Assn., Am. Law Inst., Ala. Law Inst. (dir. 1969-73, 76—), Am. Judicature Soc., Farrah Law Soc., Farrah Order Jurisprudence (now Order of Coif), Phi Beta Kappa, Omicron Delta Kappa, Delta Chi. Office: US Dist Ct No Dist Ala Hugo Black Courthouse 1729 5th Ave N Birmingham AL 35203-2000

GUINN, JOHN E., state legislator; Attended, Mo. Auction Sch., 1984. Sales & mktg.; mem. Dist. 37 La. House of Reps., 2008—, mem. agr., forestry, aquaculture and rural devel. com., natural resources and environment com., transp., hwys. and pub. works com. Republican. Office: State Capitol PO Box 44486 Baton Rouge LA 70804 Mailing: PO Box 287 Jennings LA 70546 Office Phone: 225-342-6945, 337-824-0376. Office Fax: 337-824-4780. Business E-Mail: guinnj@legis.state.la.us.

GUION, KATHLEEN R., retail executive; BA, Loyola U. Various oper. positions, including v.p., Chesapeake divsn. The Southland Corp., 1979—97; dist. mgr., zone mgr., ops. mgr. and divsn. mgr., Midwest divsn. 7-Eleven, Inc., v.p., gen. mgr. Chesapeake, 1987—97; pres., COO E-Z Serve Corp., 1997—98; oper. ptnr. Devon Ptnrs., 1999—2000; pres., CEO Duke & Long Distbg. Co., 2000—03; exec. v.p., store ops. Dollar General Corp., 2003—05, exec. v.p., store ops. and store devel., 2005, exec. v.p., divsn. pres., store ops. and store devel., 2005—. Office: Dollar General Corp 100 Mission Ridge Goodlettsville TN 37072 Office Phone: 615-855-4000. Office Fax: 615-855-5252. Business E-Mail: kguion@dollargeneral.com.

GUIROLA, LOUIS, JR., federal judge; b. Baltimore, Sept. 5, 1951; BA, William Carrey Coll., 1973; JD, U. Miss., 1979. Assoc. Boyce Holleman & Assocs., P.A., 1979-80; asst. dist. atty. Miss. Dist. Atty.'s Office, Miss., 1980-84; county bd. atty. Jackson County Port Authority, 1984-86; ptnr. Guirola & Jackson, 1986-90; dep. chief criminal divsn., lead Crime and Drug Envorcement Task Force, 1990-93; magistrate judge US Dist. Ct. (wc. dist.) Tex., 1993-96, US Dist. Ct. (we. dist.) Miss., 1996—2004, judge, 2004—10, chief judge, 2010—. Adj. prof. William Carey Coll., 1979-81, U. So. Miss., 1981-85. Office: 2012 15th St Ste 814 Gulfport MS 39501

GULARI, ESIN, chemical engineering educator, dean; b. Istanbul, Turkey, July 12, 1946; d. Fahri and Selma (Ozdamar) Cetegen; m. Erdogan Gulari, June 28, 1969; 1 child, Bora. BS, Robert Coll., Istanbul, Turkey, 1969; MS, Calif. Inst. Tech., 1970, PhD, 1973. Postdoctoral fellow SUNY, Stony Brook; asst. prof. Coll. Engring. Wayne State U., Detroit, 1979—83, assoc. prof., 1983—87, prof., 1987, chair Chem. Engring. and Materials Sci. (CHEMS) Dept., 1993—2000; chief tech. officer nanoSEC; dir. Chem. and Transport Sys. Divsn., Engring. Directorate NSF, Washington, 2000—04, acing asst. dir. Engring. Directorate, 2001—03; dean Coll. Engring. and Sci. Clemson U., 2006—. Mem. Nat. Sci. Bd., NSF, 2008—, vice chmn., 2010—. Contbr. articles to profl. jours. Fellow: Am. Inst. Chem. Engrs.; mem.: Com. of the Advancement of Women Chemists and Chem. Engrs. (mem. exec. bd.), Coun. on Chem. Rsch. (chair 2003), Am. Phys. Soc., Am. Chem. Soc. Office: Clemson University School Materials Science and Engineering 109 Riggs Hall Clemson SC 29634 Office Phone: 864-656-3202. E-mail: egulari@clemson.edu.

GULBRANDSEN, PATRICIA HUGHES, physician; b. May 9, 1940; d. Patrick Boland and Anne Hughes; m. Jon Alf Gulbrandsen, Mar. 6, 1972 (dec. Oct. 1984). BA, Cornell U., 1962; MD, U. Pa., 1967; MPH, Johns Hopkins U., 1980. Cert. Am. Bd. Disability Analysts; diplomate Am. Bd. Phys. Medicine and Rehab., Am. Bd. Occupl. Medicine. Rotating intern Chgo. Wesley Meml. Hosp., 1967-68; resident in neurology Pa. Hosp., Phila., 1968-69, Georgetown U. Hosp., Washington, 1972-74; fellow in gynecologic endocrinology Chelsea Hosp. for Women, London, 1969-71; resident in phys. medicine and rehab. Good Samaritan Hosp., Phoenix, 1974-76; commd. maj. U.S. Army, 1979, advanced through grades to lt. col., 1982; with Walter Reed Army Med. Ctr., Washington, 1979-81; occup. medicine officer U.S. Army/Army Environ. Hygiene Agy., Aberdeen Proving Ground, Md., 1981-83; resigned U.S. Army, 1983; med. dir. USN/Naval Surface Warfare Ctr., White Oak, Md., 1984-89, NASA Hdqs., Washington, 1990-93; acting chief med. officer Hdqs. FBI, Washington, 1995; med. officer Orgn. Am. States, Washington, 1999—2001; occupl. health phys., cons. Def. Intelligence Agy., Bolling AFB, Washington, 2001—03; NIOSH occupl. medicine physician Dept. Energy Worker Advocacy Program, 2004; pvt. practice Gulbrandsen Energy Medicine, LLC, 2006—. Occupl. medicine Profl. Occupl. Health Svcs., 1997-98; staff physiatrist, head consultation svc. New Eng. Med. Ctr. Hosps., Boston, 1977-78; instr. neurology and phys. medicine and rehab. Tufts U. Sch. Medicine, Boston, 1977-78; med. cons. Fairfax County (Va.) Health Dept., 1990, Hummer and Assocs., Cleve., 1990-93, Allied Med. Cons., Inc., Washington, 1994-95, AspenMed Svcs., Inc., 1995-96, 01-03, The Westwood Group, 2004, Gulbrandsen Energy Medicine, LLC, 2006—, Occu Save, Inc., Lanham, Md., 1996, staff privileges Drs. Cmty. Hosp., 1996-98, Hummer Whole Health Mgmt., 1998-99. Personal E-mail: mddocg@yahoo.com.

GULESERIAN, KRISTINE JANE, surgeon, thoracic surgeon, educator; AB in Classics-Greek, Harvard Coll., 1990; MD, Boston U. Sch. Medicine, 1994. Cert. Am. Bd. Thoracic Surgery, Am. Bd. Surgery. Resident, gen. surgery Brown U. Sch. Medicine, 1994—99; resident, thoracic surgery Washington U. Sch. Medicine, 2001—03; fellow, cardiovascular tissue engring. Children's Hosp. Boston, 1999—2001, fellow, pediat. cardiovascular surgery, 2003—04; asst. prof., cardiothoracic surgery Southwestern Med. Sch. Contbr. several articles to profl. jours. Recipient Outstanding Chief Resident award, Brown U. Dept. Surgery, 1999, Kaplan Cardiovascular Rsch. award, Children's Hosp. Boston, 2000, Corgentech Clin. Rsch. Scholarship, Soc. Thoracic Sugery, 2004, Hudson Found. Clin. Rsch. award, Children's Med. Ctr. Dallas, 2006. Mem.: Am. Heart Assn., Soc. Heart Valve Disease, So. Thoracic Surgical Association, Internat. Soc. Heart & Lung Transplantation, Soc. Thoracic Surgeons. Achievements include led team of doctors responsible for the heart and liver transplant of 3 year old girl at Children's Medical Center at Dallas in 2005, 7 year old in 2009. Address: U Tex Southwestern Med Ctr Dallas 5323 Harry Hines Blvd Dallas TX 75390-8835 Office: Childrens Med Ctr Dallas 1935 Medical District Dr Dallas TX 75235 Office Phone: 214-456-5000. Office Fax: 214-456-5015.

GULLACE, MARLENE FRANCES, systems engineer; b. Ft. Belvoir, Va., Jan. 12, 1952; d. Amerigo Francis and Martha Arlene Guy; m. Gerald Lynn Tolley, June 26, 1970 (div. Nov. 1974); 1 child, Gerald Lynn Tolley Jr.; m. Salvatore Gullace, Nov. 19, 1976 (div. Apr. 1991). AA in Pre-Law, Cochise Coll., 1979; BA in Polit. Sci., U. Ariz., 1982; AA in Computer Sci. and Bus., Chaparral Coll., 1985; MS in Sys. Engring., George Washington U., 2008. Realtor, entrepreneur, inventor, Sierra Vista, Ariz., 1977-84; ADP instr. Chaparral Coll., Tucson, 1985; model Barbizon, Tucson, 1986-87; clk. HUD/FHA, Tucson, 1987-88; computer programmer DOD Inspector Gen., Arlington, 1988-89; programmer analyst US Army Corps of Engrs., USAF, Washington, 1989-91, Calibre Sys. Inc., Falls Church, Va., 1991; cons., sys. analyst/programmer EDP, Vienna, Va., 1991-93; info. engr. Ogden/Anteon Corp., Vienna, 1993-96, Orkand Corp., 1996, SRA Internat., Inc., 1997-00, SRA Internat., 2000—01, SAIC, 2002—04, Lockheed Martin, 2004—10, The SI Org., 2011—. Patented toy, registered trademark. Realtor assoc. Cochise County Bd. Realtors, 1977-84. Mem. IEEE, Fed. Women's Program at SBA (sec. 1976). Baptist. Avocations: art, design, crafts, sewing. Home: 7829 Piccadilly Dr Warrenton VA 20186-8623

GULLEDGE, SANDRA SMITH, publicist; b. Great Lakes, Ill., July 6, 1949; d. Dennis and Olga Smith. BS, Northwestern U., 1971; MA, Annenberg Sch Comm., U. So. Calif., 1986. Columnist Camarillo Daily News, Calif., 1971-76; editor Fillmore Herald, Calif., 1976-78; pub. info. officer Oxnard Union High Sch. Dist., Calif., 1980-82, Ventura County Cmty. Coll. Dist., 1982-83; pub. rels. dir. Murphy Orgn., Oxnard, Calif., 1983-84, sr. adminstr., customer comms.; editor Forum and Solutions GTE, Irving, Tex., 1984—93; mktg. spec. USAA Alliance Svc., San Antonio, 1995-99; pres. Crimson Horse Entertainment & Publ.Co., LLC, 2000—. With Abandoned Bataan: One Man's Story of Survival, by Oliver Red Allen, as told to Mildred Allen, 2002. Pres. Northwestern U. Alumni Club Greater San Antonio. Recipient Hon. Mention award, Assn. Women Comms. San Antonio Profl. Chpt., 2004, Katie awards, Press Club Dallas, 1991—92, Bronze Quills award, Internat. Assn. Bus. Communicators Dallas, 1991—93, Bronze Quill Merit award, 1991—92, Silver Quill Merit award, 1992, TOPS finalist, Dallas Advertising League, 1991, Best of Tex. award, Pub. Rels. Soc. Tex., 1992, John Swett award, Calif. Tchr. Assn., 1974, Women Helping Women award, LA, 1979. Business E-Mail: crimsonhorse@usa.net.

GULLICK, CARL L., former state legislator; b. Greenville, Mar. 20, 1953; s. Leo and Cleo Gullick; m. Lynn Preston; children: Helen, Mitchell. Former adj. prof. Wingate U.; mem. Edn. & Pub. Works Com., Met. Transit Commn., 1998—2001; chmn. York County Coun., 1993—2001; mem. Dist. 48 SC House of Reps., 2007—09; cons. Gullick & Assoc. Host WB TV Series, ETV TV Series. Recipient Eddie Black award, Keepers of Culture award; Paul Harris fellow. Mem.: Luray C. of C. (former v.p.), Lake Wylie C. of C., York County Regional C. of C. (chmn. 2005), Allocations Commn. (former chmn.), Trident Area United Way, Keystone (bd. dir. 2005), Charlotte Regional Partnership (bd. dir. 1994—2001), Charleston Personnel Assn. (former v.p.), RFATS (former chmn.), Rock Hill Rotary Club. Republican. Home: 1425 Timber Ln McAlester OK 74501-7287 Home Phone: 803-517-9368; Office Phone: 803-656-5000, 803-734-3011. Business E-Mail: GullickC@schouse.org.

GULLIFORD, BILL, councilman; m. Harriet Gulliford; children: Tripp, Thad, Katherine, Elizabeth. Grad., U. Fla. With Pilot Equipment Co.; ptnr. Major Machinery & Equipment LLC; commn. mem. City of Atlantic Beach, Fla., mayor Fla., 1988—93; councilman Dist. 13 Jacksonville City Coun., 2011—. Office: Jacksonville City Council 117 W Duval St Jacksonville FL 32202 Office Phone: 904-630-1397. E-mail: Gulliford@coj.net.

GULLING, MARK V., consumer products company executive; BS in Math. and Economics, Ashland U., 1974; grad. exec. edn. program, Duke U., 1991. Sys. analyst, corp. info. sys. divsn. Eastman Kodak Co., 1974, various positions, 1974—85, info. sys. dir., Eastman Savs. and Loan, 1986—89, with, 1989, reengineering project mgr., 1991—92, info. sys. dir., bus. imaging sys. and office imaging bus., 1993—96, program mgr., corp. enterprise resource planning initiative, 1996—98, asst. CIO, 1998—2000, acting CIO, 2000—01, CIO, v.p. Rochester, NY, 2001—03, dir., global shared svcs., v.p., 2003—06; pres., global bus. svcs. MeadWestvaco Corp., Glen Allen, Va., 2006—. Recipient CEO Diversity award, 2002. Office: MeadWestvaco Corp 501 S 5th St Richmond VA 23219-0501 Office Phone: 804-444-1000. Business E-Mail: Mark.Gulling@meadwestvaco.com.

GULYA, AINA JULIANNA, otologist, neurotologist, skull base surgeon; b. Syracuse, NY, Feb. 3, 1953; d. Aladar and Sylvia E. Gulya; m. William R. Wilson, May 21, 1983. AB cum laude, Yale Coll., 1974; MD with distinction in rsch., U. Rochester, 1978. Diplomate Am. Bd. Otolaryngology. Intern, jr. resident in gen. surgery Beth Israel Hosp., Boston, 1978-80; resident in otolaryngology Mass. Eye and Ear Infirmary, Boston, 1980-83; fellow in otology/neurotology Bapt. Hosp. Ear Found., Nashville, 1983-84; asst. prof. surgery George Washington U., Washington, 1984-87, assoc. prof. surgery, 1987-90, clin. prof. surgery, otolaryngology, head and neck surgery, 1998—2005; assoc. prof. otolaryngology and head and neck surgery Georgetown U., Washington, 1990-94, prof., 1994-96; chief clin. trials br. Nat. Inst. on Deafness and other Comm. Disorders, Bethesda, Md., 1996-2000, chief clin. trials epidemiology biostats. sect., 2000—; ret., 2005; clin. trials project officer NIH. Assoc. examiner Am. Bd. Otolaryngology, 1993-97, bd. dirs., 1997-2002, oral exam. leader for otology, 2000-02, chair neurotology sub-specialty cert. com., 2000-02, cons. Nat. Inst. on Deafness and Other Comm. Disorders. Co-author: Anatomy of the Temporal Bone With Surgical Implications, 1986, 95, author, 2007; contbr. articles, to profl. jours., 2007; assoc. editor Am. Jour. Otology, 1989-99; co-editor Surgery of the Ear, 5th edit., 2002, 6th edit., 2009, sr. editor, 2010. Bd. dirs. Deafness Rsch. Found., 1994—2001. Recipient Libr. award, Rochester Acad. Medicine, 1975, presdl. citation, Am. Otol., Rhinol. and Laryngol. Soc., 1999. Mem.: Am. Acad. Otolaryngology, Head and Neck Surgery (bd. dirs. 1995—97, Honor award 1991, Disting. Svc. award 2001), Am. Neurotology Soc. (coord. for continuing med. edn. 1990—95), Am. Otological Soc. (coun. 1993—, editor-libr. 1995—2000, trustee rsch. fund 1993—2001, pres.-elect 1999—2000, pres. 2000—01). Avocation: water-skiing.

GUNDERSON, CLARK ALAN, orthopedic surgeon; b. Watertown, SD, Aug. 27, 1948; s. Harvey Alfred and Eugenie (Tulson) G.; m. Robbie Gunderson; children: Ashley, Camille Student, U. Minn., 1966-69; BS, U. S.D., 1971; MD, Baylor Coll. of Medicine, 1973. Diplomate Am. Bd. of Orthopaedic Surgery, 1979. Intern in gen. surgery Charity Hosp., New Orleans, 1973-74, resident in orthopedic surgery, 1974-78; chief of surgery Lake Charles (La.) Meml. Hosp., 1980-83, 90-91, sec., treas. med. staff, 1983-87, pres. med. staff, 1992-93, also trustee, 90-94, chief of surgery, 1998-99; clin. assoc. prof. La. State U. Sch. of Medicine, New Orleans, 1987-90. Bd. dirs. Arthritic Found. La., 1987. Mem. AMA, ACS, Am. Acad. Orthopaedic Surgeons (bd. councilors 2002, com. on state com. 2002), La. Orthopaedic Assn. (pres. 1995-96), Calcasieu Parish Med. Soc., La. State Med. Soc., N.Am. Spine Assn., Mid Am. Orthopaedic Assn., La. Orthopaedic ASsn. (exec. com. 1993—), Lake Charles Country Club (pres. 1987-89), Clin. Orthopedic Rsch. Soc., Sigma Chi. Avocation: golf. Office: 2615 Enterprise Blvd Lake Charles LA 70601-7675

GUNDLACH, HEINZ LUDWIG, investment banker; b. Dusseldorf, Germany, July 6, 1937; came to U.S., 1969, naturalized, 1980; s. Heinrich Otto and Ilse (Schuster) G.; m. Cornelia T. Gundlach; children: Andrew, Annabelle, Julia Olivia. LLD, U. Heidelberg, 1962; JD, U. Law Sch., Wuerzburg. V.p. Thyssen A.G. Dusseldorf, 1964-68; v.p., partner Loeb, Rhoades & Co., NYC, 1969-75; vice-chmn., CEO Fed-Mart Corp., San Diego, 1975-81; vice chmn., chief exec. officer successor cos. Sunbelt Investment Holdings, Inc., 1981-88; chmn. successor cos. Trucolor Foto Inc., 1981-88, Clearfoto, Inc., 1981-88; mng. dir. Dean Witter Reynolds, Inc., NYC and London, 1988-91; prin., chmn. Cardinal Capital Corp., Palm Beach, Fla., 1991—. Served with W. Ger. Army, 1958-59. Mem. Farmington Country Club, Keswick Golf Club. Republican. Office Phone: 561-317-6699.

GUNDY, MIKE, college football coach; b. Midwest City, Okla., Aug. 12, 1967; s. Ray and Judy Gundy; m. Kristen Gundy; children: Gavin, Gunnar, Gage. B in Secondary Edn., Okla. State U., Stillwater, 1990. Receivers coach Okla. State U. Cowboys, 1990, quarterbacks coach, 1991—93, 1995, offensive coord., 1994, offensive coord., assoc. head coach, 2001—04, head coach, 2005—; quarterbacks coach, passing coord. Baylor U. Bears, 1996; receivers coach U. Md. Terrapins, 1997—98, quarterbacks coach, 1999—2000. Recipient Eddie Robinson Coach of Yr. award, Football Writers Assn. America, 2011, Paul "Bear" Bryant Coll. Coach of Yr. award, Nat. Sportscasters & Sportswriters Assn., 2011; named Outstanding Freshman Quarterback, The Sporting News, 1986, Big 12 Conf. Coach of Yr., AP, 2010, Coach of Yr., Big 12 Conf. Coaches, 2010. Office: Okla State Univ Athletics Okla State Univ Athletics Ctr Stillwater OK 74078

GUNELIUS, SUSAN, advertising executive, writer; Mktg. and branding expert; with AT and T Corp., Hong Kong and Shanghai Banking Corp.; owner Women on Bus.; featured columnist entrepreneur.com; featured blogger Progress forbes.com; featured blogger Cox Communications kudzu.com; featured blogger Guide for Blogging about.com; pres. and CEO KeySplash Creative Inc. Author: (books) Kick-ass Copywriting in 10 Easy Steps, HArry Potter: The Story of a Global Business Phenomenon, 2008, Blogging All-in-One For Dummies, 2009, Building Brand Value The Playboy Way, 2009, Google Blogger Dummies, 2009, 30-Minute Social Media Marketing: Step-by-step Techniques to Spread the Word about Business, 2010, The Complete Idiot's Guide to WordPress, 2011, Content Marketing For Dummies, 2011; cinematographer:. Mem.: Network Solutions Social Media (adv. bd. mem.). Home: 10845 Lemay Dr Clermont FL 34711-8033 Office Phone: 652-243-4339.

GUNN, ALBERT EDWARD, JR., internist, health facility administrator, lawyer, educator; b. Port Washington, NY, Oct. 31, 1933; s. Albert Edward and Esther Frances (Williams) G.; m. Joan Marie Jacoby, May 18, 1968; children: Albert Edward III, Emily Williams Gunn, Andrew Robert, Clare Margaret Gunn Berchelmann, Catherine Ann, Philip David. BS, Fordham Coll., 1955, LLB, 1958; MB BCh BAO, Nat. U. Ireland, Galway, 1967. Bar: NY 1958, US Ct. Mil. Appeals 1959, DC 1972, US Supreme Ct. 1972, US Ct. Appeals (DC cir.) 1972; diplomate Am. Bd Internal Medicine, lic. physician Pa., NY, Va., Tex., Eng., Wales. Owner, agt. Albert E. Gunn Ins. Agy., Port Washington, 1953-65; 2nd lt. USAF, 1955, active to 1st lt., 1958—61, SAC served in res., 1961—75, capt., 1962; intern Montefiore Hosp., NYC, 1967-68; resident internal medicine Roosevelt Hosp., NYC,

1968—70; USPHS trainee and fellow neurology U. Rochester, NY, 1970—72; asst. dir. govtl. rels. AMA, Washington, 1972-74; med. dir. Geriat. Svcs. Suffolk County, Hauppauge, NY, 1974-75, Rehab. Ctr., U. Tex./M.D. Anderson Cancer Ctr., 1975-88, chief rehab. sect., 1988-93, chief geriat. sect., 1993-2000, dep. chmn. dept. internal med. spltys., 1998-2000; prof. mgmt. and policy scis. U. Tex. Houston Sch. Pub. Health, 2001—. Asst. prof. medicine U. Tex. Med. Sch., Houston, 1976-80, assoc. prof., 1980-2000, prof., 2000-08, assoc. dean for admissions, 1979-2006, spl. adv. to the President, 2006-08; med. dir. Region IV, Tex. Med. Found., 1986-93; del.-at-large White House conf. on Handicapped Individuals, 1977; pres. Mus. Med. Sci., 1990; cons. CDC, Legal Svcs. Corp., Nat. Libr. Medicine. Co-author: Rehabilitation of the Cancer Patient, 1976, AIDS in Africa, 1988; editor, contbg. author: Cancer Rehabilitation, 1984; mem. editl. bd. Cancer Bull., 1977-90, Gerontology and Geriatrics Edn., 1984-2003, Linacre Quar.; contbr. articles to profl. jours Pres. Cath. Evidence Guild, Fordham, NY, 1953-54; mem. nat. adv. health coun. HEW, 1974-75; mem. adv. com. Nat. Inst. Law Enforcement and Criminal Justice, Law Enforcement Assistance Adminstrn., U.S. Dept. Justice, 1974-76; mem. bd. regents Nat. Libr. Medicine, NIH, 1983-87, chmn., 1986-87, chmn. lit. selection tech. adv. com., 1988-91; bd. dirs. Right to Life Advs., 1977-78, Tex. Med. Ctr. Libr., 1990. Recipient Gold Key award, Highest Ranking Cadet Officer La Salle Military Acad., 1951, Gold medal Constitutional Law, Fordham Law Sch., 1958. Mem. Tex. Med. Assn. (hon. mem. 2010-, trustee ins. trust, chmn. bd. trustees 1997-2000), Harris County Med. Soc. (hon. mem. 2010-, exec. bd. 1986-90, v.p. 1998), Royal Coll. Physicians London (licentiate), Royal Coll. Surgeons Eng., Houston Acad. Medicine (bd. dirs. 1986-90, pres. 1990), Houston Bar Assn. (50 Yr. Svc. award 2008), DC Bar, Cath. Med. Assn. (regional bd. dirs. 1992—2011, Thomas Linacre award 1997), NRA (life), Res. Officers Assn. (life), Am. Legion (life), KC, Army and Navy Club, Cosmos Club, Petroleum Club Houston, Fellowship Cath. Scholars. Home and Office: 3514 Glen Haven Blvd Houston TX 77025-1306

GUNN, CLARE ALWARD, travel consultant, writer, retired educator; b. Grandville, Mich., Oct. 28, 1916; s. Fred Melvin and Lila Barton (Alward) G.; married; children: Thomas, Bruce, Richard, William. BS in Landscape Architecture, Mich. State U., 1940, MS in Land and Water Conservation, 1952; PhD in Landscape Architecture, U. Mich., 1965. Prof. dept. tourism-recreation devel. Mich. State U., East Lansing, 1945-66; vis. prof. tourism Sch. Travel Industry Mgmt. U. Hawaii, 1966-67; prof. tourism-recreation devel. Tex. A&M U., College Station, 1967-74, prof. dept. recreation, park and tourism scis., 1975-85, prof. emeritus, 1985—. Prof. resources recreation Oreg. State U., summer 1974; prof. Sch. Landscape Arthitecture, U. Guelph, Ont., Can., 1974-75; vis. prof. Clemson U., 1989; cons. state tourism plans N.Y., 1986, Okla., 1987, Wash., 1988, Del., 1990, Ill., 1993; cons. analysis tourism potential Whiteman Park, Perth, Australia, 1989; cons. South African Tourism Bd., 1988, natural resource potential for Tourism in Del., 1991; mem. task force Moorea & Tourism, French Polynesia, 1990, tourism potential Finger Lakes Region, N.Y., 1989-91, resort devel. plan Chun-Cheon Lake Area, Korea, 1991; tourism plan Newfoundland, Labrador, Can., 1994; prepared Agenda Item 13 World Tourism Conf., The Pilippines, 1980, major destination zone study for Can., 1982. Author: A Concept for the Design of a Tourism-Recreation Region, 1965, An Annotated Bibliography of Resource Use of the Texas Gulf Coast, 1969, Vacationscape: Designing Tourist Regions, 3d edit., 1997, Chinese edit., 1998, Tourism Planning, 3d edit., 1994, 4th edit., 2002, Western Tourism: Can Paradise Be Reclaimed, 2004, Motel Planning and Business Management, 1964, others; contbr. articles to profl. jours. Mem. George Bush Libr. Com., College Station, 1994; chair adv. com. CVB of Bryan, College Station, 1992-93; mem. sch. bd. Okemos (Mich.) Dist., 1958-64. Recipient Tex. Gov. award, 1984, Disting. Alumni award Landscape Architecture Program, Mich. State U., 1999; named mem. emeritus Internat. Acad. for Study of Tourism, 2001. Fellow Am. Soc. Landscape Architects (Spl. award 1973); mem. Travel and Tourism Rsch. Assn. (bd. dirs., Lifetime Achievement award 2001), Rotary Internat. (hon.; chmn. dist. group study exch. com. 1992-93, chair dist. exch. com. 1992-94, Role of Fame award 1990), Gamma Sigma Delta, Epsilon Sigma Phi, Beta Gamma Sigma, Phi Kappa Phi, Sigma Lambda Alpha (Disting. Mem. award 1991). Methodist. Avocations: photography, travel, sketching. Home: 2345 Manor Dr Apt 37 Bryan TX 77802-1910

GUNN, LEE DELTON, IV, lawyer; b. Dearborn, Mich., Sept. 20, 1959; s. Lee Delton Gunn III and Madeline Evelyn (Lorenz) Currier; m. Tracy Raffles, May 12, 1995. BS in Bus. Adminstrn., U. Fla., 1980, JD, 1982. Bar: Fla. 1983, U.S. Dist. Ct. (mid. dist.) Fla. 1983, U.S. Ct. Appeals (11th cir.) 1983; bd. cert. in civil trial Fla. Bar 1990., Nat. Bd. Trial Advocacy 1993. Assoc. Shackleford, Farrior, Stallings & Evans, P.A., Tampa, Fla., 1983-88, shareholder, 1988-90; founding shareholder Gunn, Ogden & Sullivan, P.A., Tampa, Fla., 1990—99, Gunn Merlin, P.A., Tampa, 2000—04, Gunn Law Group, P.A., Tampa, 2005—. Mem. pres.'s coun. U. Fla. Contbr. articles to profl. jours. Mem. Am. Justice Assn., Fla. Justice Assn. (Eagle founder), Am. Bd. Trial Advocacy. Office: Gunn Law Grp PA 400 N Ashley Dr Ste 2050 Tampa FL 33602-4344 Office Phone: 813-228-7070. Office Fax: 813-228-9400. Business E-Mail: lgunn@gunnlawgroup.com.

GUNN, PHILIP, state legislator; b. Hattiesburg, Jan. 27, 1963; m. Lisa Watkins Gunn. Mem. Dist. 56 Miss. House of Reps., 2004—, mem. conservation and water resources com., judiciary A com., judiciary en banc com., juvenile justice com., pub. utilities com., mem. wildlife, fisheries and pks. com. Republican. Baptist. Address: 101 Pinehaven Cove Clinton MS 39056 Office Phone: 601-355-8321. Business E-Mail: pgunn@house.ms.gov.

GUNN, RICHARD WALLACE, JR., state legislator; m. Gayle Gunn; children: Scott Gunn, Daniel Gunn. BSBA, U. NC, Chapel Hill. Mem. Home Builders Assn., U. NC Ednl. Found; chmn., Budget Review United Way of Alamance County; v.p. Equity Securities Corp., 1982—85, Synco, Inc., 1982—85; pres., bd. dirs. Alamance Bus. Club, 1988—95; bd. adv. Alamance Cmty. Coll. Real Estate, 1989—91; pres., bd. dirs. Burlington-Alamance Association of Realtors, 1987—89, 1995—96; state dir. NC Assn. of Realtors, 1995—96; pres., bd. dirs. Burlington Downtown Corp., 1995—2001; pres. Alamance Multiple Listing Svcs., Inc., 1990—91, Gunn and Assocs., LLC, 1985—; owner ERA Gunn Realty, 1988—; vice chmn. Alamance County C. of C., 1998; bd. dirs. Salvation Army Boys & Girls Club, 1999—2002; mem. Govt. Affairs Com., 2002—; pres., bd. dirs. Alamance Country Club, 2003—06; mem. Dist. 24 NC State Senate, 2011—. Republican. Presbyterian. Office: PO Box 308 Burlington NC 27216 also: NC Senate 300 N Salisbury St Room 312 Raleigh NC 27603-5925 Business E-Mail: Rick.Gunn@ncleg.net.

GUNSON, DOUGLAS ROBERT, lawyer; b. L.A., 1962; m. Blythe Gunson; children: Jessica, Jonathan, Rebecca, Christina, William, Nathanael, Eliza. BA in Economics, Brigham Young U., 1985; JD, Brigham Young U. J. Reuben Clark Law Sch., 1989. Assoc. Moore & Van Allen, PLLC, NC, 1989—90, Parker, Poe, Adams & Bernstein LLP, NC, 1990—94; chief legal officer SGL Carbon Corp., NC, 1994—2000; gen. mgr. corp. legal affairs Nucor Corp., Charlotte, NC, 2005—. Avocations: basketball, jogging, golf, reading. Office: Nucor Corp 2100 Rexford Rd Charlotte NC 28211 Office Phone: 704-972-1832. Office Fax: 704-362-4208. E-mail: dgunson@nucor.com.

GUNTER, BRADLEY HUNT, capital management executive; b. Norfolk, Va., Dec. 8, 1940; s. J.A. and Virginia (Whalen) G.; m. Susan Mason Hart, Dec. 27, 1962 (div. 1977); m. Anne Macon, Nov. 7, 1985 (dec. 1994); m. Meredith Laura Strohm, Dec. 16, 1994;children: Bradley Hunt, Valerie Mason, Bradford Macon. BA, U. Richmond, 1962; MA, U. Va., 1963, PhD, 1969. Instr. Washington and Lee U., Lexington, Va., 1967-69; asst. prof. Boston Coll., 1969-71; editor Econ. Rev. Fed. Res. Bank, Richmond, Va., 1971—80, corp. sec., 1973—80; pres. Bartleby's Inc., Richmond, 1980-85; dir. found. rels. U. Va., Charlottesville, 1985-86; investment broker Scott and Stringfellow, Richmond, 1987-89; mng. dir. Scott & Stringfellow Capital Mgmt., Richmond, 1989-97, pres., CEO, 1997—2000; pres. Investment Mgmt. of Va., LLC, Richmond and Charlottesville, 2000—. Cons. NEH, Washington, 1975—80. Author: Studies in The Waste Land, 1971, Guide to T.S. Eliot, 1970, Checklist of T.S. Eliot, 1969; contbr. articles to profl. jours. Chmn. fund drive United Way, Richmond, 1980; mem. arts and scis. alumni coun. U. Va., mem. Emeritus Soc., Coll. Found.; pres., bd. dirs. New Va. Rev.; pres. Arts Coun. Richmond; chmn. Hist. Richmond Found.; bd. dirs. Poe Found., Va. Ctr. for the Book; bd. dirs., chmn. U. Va. Cancer Ctr., U. Va. Health Scis. Coun., mem.; mem. regional bd. Sorensen Inst. for Polit. Leadership; chmn. U. Va. Ann. Giving Adv. Bd.; trustee United Way Greater Richmond; cons. mem. U. Va. Bd. Visitors; vestryman St. Paul's Ch., Richmond, 1975—78; trustee St. Paul's Endowment Fund, Inc., 1975—97; bd. dirs. St. Christopher's Sch. Found., Richmond, 1981—85, Richmond Ballet, Big Bros. Richmond Inc., Va. Found. for Humanities and Pub. Policy, Scott and Stringfelow Ednl. Found., Elk Hill Farm, Tuesday Evening Concert Series. Mem. Va. Coun. on Econ. Edn. (bd. dirs.), U. Va. Alumni Assn. (chpt. pres. Richmond 1981), U. Va. Coun. Chairs, U. Va. Coun. Founds., Va. Soc. Mayflower Descs. (bd. dirs.), Country Club Va., Colonnade Club, Focus Club, Univ. Club NY, Farmington Country Club, Phi Beta Kappa, Omicron Delta Kappa. Episcopalian. Avocation: walking. Office: Investment Mgmt of Va 310 4th St NE Charlottesville VA 22902-5266 Home Phone: 434-923-3870; Office Phone: 434-220-0356. Business E-Mail: bgunter@imva.net.

GUNTER, JACK PERSHING, plastic surgeon, otolaryngologist; b. Ft. Smith, Ark., Oct. 7, 1937; s. Jack and Charlene Gunter; m. Deborah Dawson, Mar. 21, 1992; children: Ashley, Page, Courtney. BA, Westminster Coll., Fulton, Mo., 1959; MD, U. Okla., Oklahoma City, 1963; postgrad. in Facial Plastic and Reconstructive Surgery, Mercy Hosp., Pitts., 1968-69. Diplomate Am. Bd. Otolaryngology, Am. Bd. Plastic Surgery. Intern U. Ark. Med. Ctr., 1963-64, resident in gen. surgery, 1964-65; resident in otolaryngology Tulane U. Eye, Ear, Nose & Throat Hosp., New Orleans, 1965-68; NIH fellow in facial, plastic and reconstructive surgery Mercy Hosp., Pitts., 1968-69; assoc. prof. otolaryngology U. Tex. Health Sci. Ctr., Dallas, 1969-76, chmn. divsn. otolaryngology, 1971-74, clin. assoc. prof. otolaryngology, 1976-91; resident in plastic surgery U. Mich. Hosp., Ann Arbor, 1978-80; clin. prof. otolaryngology U. Tex. Health Sci. Ctr., Dallas, 1991—; clin. asst. prof. plastic surgery U. Tex. Southwestern Med. Sch., Dallas, 1980-86, clin. assoc. prof., 1986-91, clin. prof., 1991—; pvt. practice Dallas, 1981—. Guest lectr. in field; founder, chmn. Dallas Rhinoplasty Symposium. Co-editor, pub. Dallas Rhinoplasty: Surgery by the Masters, 2nd edit. Recipient Westminster Coll. Alumni Achievement award, 1990; named to Best Doctors in America, 1993—. Fellow ACS; mem. Am. Soc. Plastic and Reconstructive Surgery (Aesthetic award for video tape of Primary Rhinoplasty via the Open Approach, 1993), Am. Soc. Plastic Surgeons (President's award, 2004), Am. Assn. Plastic Surgeons, Am. Soc. for Aesthetic Plastic Surgery (Tiffany award for best paper, 1989), Am. Acad. Facial Plastic and Reconstructive Surgery, Am. Acad. Facial Plastic and Reconstructive Surgery, Am. Acad. Otolaryngology, AMA, Dallas County Med. Soc., Tex. Med. Assn., Tex. Soc. Plastic Surgeons, Rhinoplasty Soc., Inc. (founding mem. 1996). Avocation: golf. Office: 8144 Walnut Hill Ln Ste 170 Dallas TX 75231 Office Phone: 214-369-8123. Office Fax: 214-369-2984. Business E-Mail: drgunter@gunter-center.com, info@gunter-center.com.

GUNTER, JOSEPH CLIFFORD, III, lawyer; b. Ft. Worth, Apr. 26, 1943; s. Joseph Cliford Jr. and Helen (Wright) G.; children: Joseph Clifford IV, Grant Norwood. BA, U. Tex., 1965, JD, 1967. Bar: Tex. 1967. Assoc. McDonald Sanders Ginsberg New Kirk Gibson & Webb, Ft. Worth, 1967-68; ptnr. Bracewell & Patterson, Houston, 1968—2005, Bracewell & Guiliani, Houston, 2005—. Adv. Am. Bd. Trial Advocates. Lt. USNR, 1967-73. Fellow Am. Coll. Trial Lawyers, Tex. Bar Found., Houston Bar Found.; mem. ABA, State Bar Tex., State Bar Colo., Internat. Acad. Trial Lawyers. Episcopalian. Avocations: golf, tennis, skiing, sailing. Office: Bracewell & Giuliani 711 Louisiana St Ste 2300 Houston TX 77002-2781 Home Phone: 713-526-3766; Office Phone: 713-221-1213. Business E-Mail: clifford.gunter@bgllp.com.

GUNTER, MICHAEL DONWELL, lawyer; b. Gastonia, NC, Mar. 26, 1947; s. Daniel Cornelius and DeNorma Joyce (Smith) Gunter; m. Barbara Jo Benson, June 19, 1970; children: Kimberly Elizabeth, Daniel Cornelius III. BA in History with honors, Wake Forest U., 1969; JD with honors, U. NC, 1972; MBA with honors, U. Pa., 1973. Bar: NC 1972, US Dist. Ct. (mid. dist.) NC 1974, US Tax Ct. 1975, US Supreme Ct. 1979, US Claims Ct. 1982, US Ct. Appeals (DC cir.) 1985, US Ct. Appeals (4th cir.) 1992. Mem. Womble Carlyle Sandridge & Rice PLLC, Winston-Salem, NC, 1974—, chmn. employee benefits practice group, employee benefits counsel. Bd. dirs. Indsl. Belting, Inc. Contbr. articles to benefit jours. Mem. NCAA cert. com. Wake Forest U., former mem. athletic dept. long-range planning com., former pres. Deacon Club, former mem. athletic coun., former mem. alumni coun., mem. bd. visitors Hall of Fame com.; coach youth basketball Winston-Salem YMCA, 1981—90; mem. Hall of Fame Selection Com.; advisor Winston-Salem United Way Christmas Cheer Toy Shop, 1975; bd. dir. Centenary Meth. Ch., 1980, Goodwill Industries, 1987—; forum chmn. bd., sec. chmn. fin. com., chair CEO search com., mem. cmty. problem solving com. United Way, 1988—99; mem. Leadership Winston-Salem. Named one of Best Employee Benefits Lawyers in Am., Nat. Law Jour., Best Lawyers in Am.; William E. Newcombe scholar, U. Pa., 1972—73. Fellow: Am. Coll. Employee Benefits Counsel (charter); mem.: ABA, Assn. Pvt. Pension and Welfare, ESOP Assn., Profit Sharing Coun. Am., Winston-Salem Estate Planning Coun. (past bd. dirs.), Forsyth County Bar Assn., N.C. Bar Assn. (former chmn. tax sect., mem. continuing legal edn. com., mem. sports and entertainment law com.), So. Pension Conf., Forsyth Country Club (former pres., bd. dirs.), Rotary (former bd. dirs. Reynolda Club), Order of Coif. Democrat. Methodist. Avocations: golf, fishing. Home: 128 Ballyhoo Dr Lewisville NC 27023-9633 Office: Womble Carlyle Sandridge and Rice PLLC One W Fourth St Winston Salem NC 27101 Office Phone: 336-721-3607. Office Fax: 336-733-8392. Business E-Mail: mgunter@wcsr.com.

GUNTER, RUSSELL ALLEN, lawyer; b. Amarillo, Tex., Feb. 21, 1950; s. J.B. and Shirley Ann (Russell) G.; children: Kim, Sarah, Laura, Rachel. BS in Polit. Sci., So. Ark U., 1972; JD, Tex. Tech U., 1975. Bar: Ark., 1975, Tex, 1975, U.S. Dist. Ct. (ea. and we dists.) Ark. 1975, U.S. Dist. Ct. (no. dist.) Tex. 1976, U.S. Ct. Appeals (8th cir.), 1980, U.S. Supreme Ct. 1986. Assoc. Gaines N. Houston, Little Rock, 1975-79, Wallace, Dover & Dixon, P.A., Little Rock, 1979-90, McGlinchey Stafford Lang P.L.L.C., Little Rock, 1990-97; Cross, Gunter, Witherspoon & Galchus P.C., Little Rock, 1997—. Mem. ABA (com. on practice and procedure before NLRB labor sect.), Soc. for Human Resource Mgmt. (cert. sr. profl. in human resources), Ark. Bar Assn., Tex. Bar Assn., Ark. State C. of C. (bd. dirs.). Office: 500 Clinton Ave Ste 200 Little Rock AR 72201-1747 Home Phone: 501-771-0399; Office Phone: 501-371-9999. Business E-Mail: rgunter@cgwg.com.

GUNTER, WILLIAM DAWSON, JR., (BILL GUNTER), insurance company executive, consultant; b. Jacksonville, Fla., July 16, 1934; s. William Dawson Gunter and Tillie S. Gunter; children—Bart, Joel, Rachel, Rebecca. BSA. with high honors, U. Fla., 1956. Tchr. pub. schs., Live Oak and Orlando, Fla., 1956, 1958; ins. agt., agy. mgr. Ctrl. Fla., 1959—72; mem. Fla. State Senate, 1966—72, U.S. Congress from 5th Fla. dist., 1973—74; treas., ins. commr. State of Fla., Tallahassee, 1976—88; CEO Bill Gunter & Assocs. (govt. cons.), Tallahassee, 1989—; chmn. Rogers, Gunter, Vaughn Ins., Inc., Tallahassee, 1997—; sr. v.p., pres. Rogers-Atkins Ins., Rogers, Atkins Gunter & Assocs. Ins., Inc., 1989—96. Sr. v.p. Southland Equity Corp., Orlando, Fla.; pres. Southland Capital Investors, Inc., Orlando, 1975-76; chmn. Fla. Assn. Ins. Agts., 2009-10. Bd. dirs. Central Fla. Fair Assn. Served with U.S. Army, 1956-58. Recipient good govt. award Fla. State Jaycees, 1972; named Floridian Fla. Dept. State, 2013. Mem. U. Fla. Nat. Alumni Assn. (pres. 1985-86), Orlando Area C. of C. (past dir.). Clubs: Jaycees, Kiwanis, Rotary, Masons, Tiger Bay, Economic Club Fla.(pres. 2012) Democrat. Office: 1117 Thomasville Rd Tallahassee FL 32303-6223 Home: 1117 Savannah Trace Tallahassee FL 32312 Office Phone: 850-386-1111. Business E-Mail: wgunter@rgvi.com.

GUNTHER, WILLIAM DAVID, retired academic administrator, economics professor; b. Balt., Oct. 11, 1940; s. William E. and Geneva (Gee) Gunther; m. Irene Leveja Reineks, Jan. 8, 1966; children: William B., Kristine A., Jennifer R. BS, Kent State U., 1962, MA, 1965; PhD, U. Ky., 1969. Asst. prof. econs. U. Ala., Tuscaloosa, 1968-72, assoc. prof. econs., 1972-76, prof. econs., 1976—98, assoc. dean for rsch., 1988-98; dean sch. bus. U. So. Miss., Hattiesburg, 1998—2003, prof. econs., 1998—; dir. Bur. Bus. and Econ. Rsch., 2005—10. Contbr. articles to profl. jours. Bd. dirs. Spl. Olympics Ala. Fulbright scholar Fulbright Commn., 1972, Faculty fellow USAF, 1979. Mem.: Soc. Paper Money Collectors, Internat. Banknote Soc. Avocations: boating, coin collecting/numismatics, paper money collecting. Business E-Mail: wdg@mypchouse.com.

GUNZBURGER, SUZANNE NATHAN, municipal official, social worker; b. Buffalo, July 12, 1939; d. Lawrence Emil and Ruth Lucille (Wohl) Nathan; m. Gerard Josef Gunzburger, Apr. 10, 1960; children: Ronald Marc, Cynthia Anne, Judith Lynn. BS in Edn., Wayne State U., 1959; MSW, Barry U., 1974. Tchr. pub. schs., Detroit, 1959-63, Trumbull, Conn., 1963-66, North Miami Beach, Fla., 1967-68, Broward County, Fla., 1968-72; pvt. practice clin. social work Hollywood, Fla., 1975—; vice mayor City of Hollywood, 1983-84, 85-87, city commr., 1982-92; commr. Broward County, 1992—, vice chair, 1993—94, 1998—99, chair, 1994-95, 99-2000. Chmn. Met. Planning Orgn., Broward County, 1984—87, 1989, Statewide Human Rights Adv. Com., 1988—89; pres. Broward County Mental Health Bd., 1984; active Broward County Commn. Status Women, 1978—82, White House Conf. Families, Balt., 1980; del. Broward County League Cities, 1988—92; mem. adv. bd. Broward Homebound, 1991—; mem. Broward Children's Svc. Bd., 1989—92, Broward County Water Adv., 1992—94, 1997—98, 2005—06, 2008, Broward County Cmty. Redevel. Agy., 1992—, South Fla. Regional Planning Coun., 1992—94, 1998—99, treas., 1999; mem. Broward County Planning Coun., 1995—2001, vice-chmn., 1996—98, chair planning coun., 2000—01, Broward County Cultural Affairs Coun., 1996—2006, 2008, Broward County Cultural Coun. Planning Com.; Broward chair Concert Assn. of Fla., Inc., 1996—; mem. Broward Children's Svc. Bd., 1998—; bd. dirs. Environ. Coalition Broward County, 1982—89, 1997—2000, Fla. Assn. of Counties, 1992—, Broward Alliance, 1992—2000, Broward Children's Svcs., 1997, Children's Svcs. Coun., 2001—, chair, 2007—09; champion for children Broward Youth Summit, 2007; Outstanding Mother Health Mothers, Health Babies, 2007; adv. bd. Homeless Initiative Partnership, 2007—. Named Broward County Woman of Yr., 1990, Humanitarian of Yr., David Posnack, Jewish Cmty. Ctr., 1994, Environmentalist of Yr., Broward County Environ. Coalition, 1994, Polit. Leader of Yr., The Vanguard Chronicle, 1999, Dem. of Yr., Broward Dem. Exec. Com., 2000, Woman of Valor, David Posnack JCC, 2003, First Lady Broward, Broward County Fair, 2004; recipient Woamn of Yr. in Govt. award Women in Comms., 1983, Disting. Achievement award Am. Jewish Congress, 1990, Fla. Philharm. Woman of Style and Substance, 1995, Woman of Distinction award March of Dimes, 1996, Heart award Children's Consortium, 1996, Disting. Alumni award Barry U., 1996, Jesse Portis Helms Dem. of Yr. award Dolphin Dem. Club, 1996, Gracias award Hispanic Unity, 1999, Polit. Alliance of Yr. award Dolphin Dem. Club, 1999, Cmty. Covenant award Broward Outreach Ctr., 2005, Com Leadership award Hispanic Unity, Women of Style and Substance, Social Activist award; inductee Broward County Women's Hall of Fame, 1995, Woman of Distinction award City of Hollywood, 1997, Women's Polit. Caucus, 1997, Encore award Art Serve, 2004; Jewish Mus. Fla., Queen Esther Court Honoree, 2004. Mem. Nat. Assn. Social Workers (diplomate clin. social work), Internat. Acad. Behavioral Med., Counseling and Psychotherapy (diplomate profl. psychotherapy), Am. Acad. Behavioral Med. (clin. mem.), Nat. Coun. Jewish Women (pres. 1980-82, Hannah G. Solomon award 1989), Met. Planning Orgn., Israel Bond Coun., Hollywood C. of C. (leadership devel. 1990—), Kiwanis (South Fla. Regional Planning Coun. 2007-). Democrat. Avocations: reading, swimming, travel. Office: Office Bd County Commrs Govtl Ctr Rm 412 115 S Andrews Ave Fort Lauderdale FL 33301-1818

GUPTA, SANJAY, neurosurgeon, medical correspondent, journalist; b. Novi, Mich., Oct. 23, 1969; s. Subhash and Damyanti Gupta; m. Rebecca Olson, May 15, 2004; children: Sage Ayla, Sky, Neal. BS in Biomedical Scis., U. Mich., Ann Arbor; MD, U. Mich. Med. Ctr., 1993. Diplomate American Bd. Neurol. Surgery, cert. med. investigator. Neurosurgical fellowship Semmes-Murphy Clinic, Memphis, U. Mich. Med. Ctr.; White House fellow, spl. advisor to First Lady, 1997—98; gen. neurosurgeon, asst. prof. dept. neurol. surgery Emory U. Sch. Medicine, Atlanta, 2001—; health and med. news reporter Cable News Network (CNN), Atlanta, 2001—, chief med. corr. Founder, dir. CNN's Fit Nation Initiative, 2006—; assoc. chief neurosurgery svc. Grady Meml. Hosp., Atlanta; neurosurgeon Emory U. Hosp. Author: Chasing Life: New Discoveries in the Search for Immortality to Help You Age Less Today, 2007 (NY Times bestseller), Cheating Death: The Doctors and Medical Miracles that Are Saving Lives Against All Odds, 2009 (NY Times bestseller), Monday Mornings, 2012; host (TV series) House Call with Dr. Sanjay Gupta, CNN, 2005—, Fit Nation, 2008—, (podcast) Paging Dr. Gupta, CNN.com, guest host CBS News Sunday Morning, 2007, Larry King Live, 2009, spl. corr. CBS News, columnist TIME mag., reg. contbr. health & med. news reports Anderson Cooper 360°, American

Morning, 60 Minutes; exec. prodr.: (TV series) Monday Mornings, 2013. Bd. dirs. Lance Armstrong LiveStrong Found. Recipient Humanitarian award, Nat. Press Photographers Assn., 2003, News & Documentary Emmy award, 2006, Health Comm. Achievement award, AMA Med. Comm. Conf., 2009, Mickey Leland Humanitarian award, Nat. Assn. Multi-Ethnicity in Comm., 2009; named Journalist of Yr., Atlanta Press Club, 2004; named a Pop Culture Icon, USA Today, 2003; named one of Sexiest Men Alive, People Mag., 2003, Ten Most Influential Celebrities, Forbes mag., 2011. Mem.: Coun. Fgn. Rels., Congress Neurol. Surgeons, American Assn. Neurol. Surgeons. Achievements include in 2004, covering the tsunami disaster in Sri Lanka that took more than 155,000 lives in Southeast Asia, contributing to the 2005 Alfred I. DuPont-Columbia award for CNN; in 2006, contributing to CNN's Peabody award-winning coverage of Hurricane Katrina, revealing that official reports that Charity Hospital in New Orleans had been evacuated were incorrect; consideration for the position of Surgeon General of the US by President Barack Obama in 2009. Office: Grady Memorial Hospital 80 Jesse Hill Dr SE Atlanta GA 30303 also: Cable News Network PO Box 105366 One CNN Ctr Atlanta GA 30348 Office Phone: 404-778-1398.*

GURA, ALAN, lawyer; b. Tel Aviv, Jan. 2, 1971; BA in Govt., Cornell U., Ithaca, NY, 1992; JD, Georgetown U. Law Ctr., 1995. Bar: Calif. 1995, US Dist. Ct. DC, US Dist. Ct. (no., ea., so. and ctrl. dists.) Calif., US Dist. Ct. (ea. dist.) Va., US Ct. Appeals (2nd, 4th, 5th, 6th, 9th, 11th, fed. and DC cirs.), US Supreme Ct. Law clk. to Hon. Terrence W. Boyle US Dist. Ct. (ea. dist.) NC, 1995—96; dep. atty. gen. Calif. Dept. Justice, 1996—98; assoc. Sidley & Austin, Washington, 1998—2000; counsel US Senate Judiciary Com., 2000—01; founding ptnr. Gura & Possessky, PLLC, Alexandria, Va., 2001—. Named one of Washington's 40 Under 40 Rising Stars, The Nat. Law Jour., 2009. Mem.: State Bar. Calif., Va. State Bar, DC Bar, Federalist Soc. Office: Gura & Possessky PLLC 105 Oronoco St # 305 Alexandria VA 22314-2015 Office Phone: 703-835-9085.

GURA, PHILIP FRANCIS, English and American literature educator; b. Ware, Mass., June 14, 1950; s. Oswald Eugene and Stephanie (Koziara) G.; m. Leslie Ann Cohig, Aug. 4, 1979; children: David Austin, Katherine Blair, Daniel Alden. BA, Harvard Coll., 1972; PhD, Harvard U., 1977. Instr. Am. Lit. Middlebury (Vt.) Coll., 1974-76; asst. prof. U. Colo., Boulder, 1976-80, assoc. prof., 1980-85, prof., 1985-87, U. N.C., Chapel Hill, 1987—98, prof., English, adj. prof. religious studies, 1998—2000, William S. Newman disting. prof. Am. lit. and culture, 2000—. Lectr. in field. Author: The Wisdom of Words, 1981, Critical Essays on American Transcendentalism, 1982, A Glimpse of Sion's Glory, 1984, The Memoirs of Stephen Burroughs, 1988, The Crossroads of American History and Literature, 1996, (with James Bollman) America's Instrument: The Banjo in the Ninteenth Century, 1999, Buried from the World: Inside the Massachusetts State Prison, 1829-1831, 2001, C.F. Martin and His Guitars, 1796-1873, 2003, Jonathan Edwards: America's Evangelical, 2005, American Transcendentalism: A History, 2007, The American Antiquarian Society: A Bicentennial History, 2012, Jonathan Edwards: Writings from the Great Awakening, 2013, Truth's Ragged Edge: The Rise of the American Novel, 2013; editor Early Am. Lit., 1989-99. Recipient Post-Baccalaureate Disting. Tchg. award, U. NC, 2004, Disting. award Divsn. Early Am. Lit., 2008; Sr. fellow NEH, 1985-86, Charles Warren Ctr. fellow Harvard U., 1980-81. Mem.: MLA (Disting. Scholar award, 2008), Colonial Soc. Mass., Am. Antiquarian Soc. (James Russell Wiggins lectr. 2004, Mellon Dist. scholar 2006, Peterson fellow, 1989, 1998, 2003, Disting. award, 2006-07), Inst. Early Am. History and Culture (Nat. coun. 1991-94), Nat. Book Critics Cir. (Finalist Non-Fiction, 2008), Soc. Am. Historians. Office: Wm Newman Disting Prof CB3520 University NC Dept English Chapel Hill NC 27599-3520

GURA, PHILIP PAUL, lawyer; BA, Emory Univ., 1981; JD, Georgetown Univ., 1984. Ptnr. Nelson Mullins, 2000—02, Sutherland, Asbill & Brennan LLP, 2002—05; v.p. legal, gen. counsel Racetrac Petroleum, Inc., Atlanta, 2005—. Office: Racetrac Petroleum Inc Ste 100 3225 Cumberland Blvd Atlanta GA 30339 Office Phone: 770-431-7600. Office Fax: 770-319-7944.

GURIAN, MAL, telecommunications executive; b. NYC, Nov. 17, 1926; s. George Joseph and Rose (Graff) G.; m. Gloria Dickler; children: Randy Harlan, Nancy Ellen Newman. Ptnr. Mal Gurian Assocs., NYC, 1946-77; v.p. Radio Telephone Corp., NYC, 1960-83; sr. v.p. Aerotron, Inc., Raleigh, NC, 1965-81; v.p. Oki Advanced Comm., Hackensack, NJ, 1981-84; pres. Oki Telecom, Fairlawn, NJ, 1984-88, Cartell, Inc., Romulus, Mich., 1988, Cellcom Cellular Corp., Fairfield, NJ, 1989-91; CEO Universal Cellular, Inc., Anaheim, Calif., 1992; chmn., CEO Global Link Comm., Inc., Irvine, Calif., 1993—; pres., CEO Authentix Network, Inc., Tucson, 1995-98, 99—, chmn., 1998-2001; pres., CEO SimplySay, LLC, Tucson, 2001—02, Mal Gurian Assocs., Bradenton, Fla., 2002—. Adv. I-Control, Campbell, Calif., 2002-03; bd. adv. pres. Ea. Profl. Photographers Assn., NYC, 1951-53; exec. advisor TRW Wireless Commn., Sunnyvale, Calif., 1994; advisor Sims Comms., Inc., Delray Beach, Fla., 1994-98; arbitrator Am. Arbitration Assn., 1994-2002; bd. electronic comm. Rangestar Internat., San Jose, Calif., 1996-98; bd. advisor Genesis Campus, LP, 2003-09; bd. dirs. Airbee Wireless; bd. advisor Mobility Ventures, 2005-09; advisor Valmarc Corp., 2009-, Blip.Fm, 2009-. Active Old Tappan (NJ) First Aid Corp., 1966—. Cpl. USMC, 1943-46. Decorated Air medal; recipient Alexander S. Popov Hon. medal, St. Petersburg Electrotech. U., Russia, 1995. Fellow Radio Club Am. (life mem., v.p. 1976-92, exec. v.p. 1993, pres. 1994, pres. emeritus 1995—, Spl. Svcs. award 1986, Sarnoff citation 1988, Fred Link award 1989, inducted into Wireless Hall of Fame, 2003); mem. Am. Assn. Pub. Safety Comm. Officers, Nat. Assn. Bus. and Ednl. Radio (bd. dirs. 1977-84, Chmn.'s award 1986. Office Phone: 941-752-1133. Personal E-mail: mgurian@tampabay.rr.com. Business E-Mail: mgurian@malgurianassoc.com, mgurian@tampabay.com.

GURICH, NOMA DIANE, state supreme court justice; b. South Bend, Ind., Sept. 26, 1952; d. John and Ramona Gurich; m. John E. Miley. BA in Polit. Sci. magna cum laude, Ind. State U., 1975; JD, U. Okla., 1978. Bar: Okla. 1978, US Dist. Ct. (western dist.) Okla., US Dist. Ct. (northern dist.) Okla., US Ct. Appeals (10th cir.), US Supreme Ct. Assoc. Cheek, Cheek and Cheek, Oklahoma City, 1978, Abowitz & Welch, Oklahoma City, 1982, ptnr.; presiding judge Okla. Workers Compensation Ct., 1988—98, judge, 1989—92; dist. judge 7th Judicial Dist., Okla. County, 1998—2011, presiding judge, 2003—04; justice Okla. Supreme Ct., 2011—. Faculty mem. Okla. U. Law Sch. Grad. Sch. of Successful Trial Advocacy. Mem. Application Screening Com. Okla. Sch. Sci. and Math. Recipient Profl. Responsibility Award. Master: William J. Holloway, Jr. American Inn of Ct. (pres. 2007—08); mem.: Okla. Judicial Conf., Okla. County Bar Assn., Okla. Bar Assn. (Mona Salyer Lambird Spotlight Award 2003), Kiwanis Club of Oklahoma City (pres. 2006—07). Office: Supreme Court Oklahoma Jud Ctr 2100 N Lincoln Blvd Ste 1 Oklahoma City OK 73105 Office Phone: 405-521-3839.*

GURNEY, ROBERT M., architectural firm executive; m. Thérèse Baron Gurney; 2 children. Fellow, Am. Inst. Architects, 2002. Founder, prin. architect Robert M. Gurney Architect, FAIA, Alexandria, Va. Bd. dirs. Am. Inst. Architects Northern Va. Chpt., mem. design com., mem. schools connection com.; mem. state design com. Va. Soc. AIA, mem. honors com. Contbr. articles to numerous nat. and internat. jours. Recipient more than 100 local, regional and national design awards including, Nat. Honor award, Am. Inst. Architects, Four Nat. Housing awards, Wood Design award. Office: 113 S Patrick St Alexandria VA 22314 Office Phone: 703-739-3843. Office Fax: 703-739-0033. Business E-Mail: rmg@robertgurneyarchitect.com.

GUSKEY, THOMAS ROBERT, education educator; b. Johnstown, Pa., Feb. 15, 1950; s. Robert C. and Evelyn M. (Yarnick) G. BA, Thiel Coll., 1972; MEd, Boston Coll., 1975; PhD, U. Chgo., 1979. Tchr. St. Andrew's Sch., Erie, Pa., 1972-74; rsch. asst. Boston Coll., Chestnut Hill, Mass., 1974-75; teaching asst. U. Chgo., 1975-78; rsch. cons. Chgo. Bd. Edn., 1975-76, dir. R&D, 1976-78; dir. rsch. Ctr. for Improvement of Teaching, Chgo., 1980-82; asst. prof. edn. U. Ky., Lexington, 1978—81, assoc. prof., 1981—85, prof., 1985—2007; disting. svc. prof. Georgetown Coll., 2008—09; prof. edn. psychology U. Ky., 2009—. Chmn. dept. edn. policy studies and evaluation U. Ky., Lexington, 1995-96; spl. asst. to chancellor U. Kentucky, 1996-98; co-dir. Ctr. Advanced Study of Assessment, Georgetown Coll., 2008-09; vis. prof. various colls. and univs.; cons. edn. systems. Author: Implementing Mastery Learning, 1985, 2d edit., 1997, Improving Student Learning, 1988, High Stakes Performance Assessment, 1994, (with J. Block and S. Everson) School Improvement Programs, 1995, (with M. Huberman) Professional Development in Education, 1995, Communicating Student Learning, 1996, (with J. Block and S. Everson) Comprehensive School Reform: A Program Perspective, 1999, Evaluating Professional Development, 2000, (with J. Bailey) Implementing Student-Led Conferences, 2001, (with Bailey) Developing Grading and Reporting Systems for Student Learning, 2001, How's My Kid Doing? A Parents' Guide to Grades, Marks, and Report Cards, 2002, Benjamin S. Bloom: Portraits of an Educator, 2006, 2nd edit., 2012, The Teacher as Assessment Leader, 2009, The Principal as Assessment Leader, 2009, Practical Solutions to Serious Problems in Standards-Based Grading, 2009, (with J. Bailey) Developing Standards Based Report Cards, 2010, (with L. Jung) Grading Exceptional and Struggling Learners, 2012, (with L. Jung) Answers to Essential Questions About Standards, Assessments, Grading and Reporting, 2013, On Your Mark: Challenging the Conventions of Grading and Reporting, 2014; editor Elem. Sch. Jour., 1990—, Focus on Learning, 1996—, Ednl. Measurement: Issues and Practice, 1997—, NASSP Bull., 2005—, Profl. Devel. Edn., 2011-. Named to Outstanding Young Men of Am., 1981; Ky. Col., 1994; recipient U. Ky. Wethington award, 2004, 05, Disting. Alumnus award Thiel Coll., 2005, Athletic Hall of Fame, 2010, Millman award Consortium Rsch. Ednl. Accountability Tchr. Evaluation, 2010. Mem. APA, ASCD, Am. Ednl. Rsch. Assn. (Outstanding Contbns. Relating Rsch. to Practice award 2006, named fellow, 2009), Am. Evaluation Assn., Am. Ednl. Pubs. (Disting. Achievement award, 2010), Assn. Ednl. Pubs. (Disting. Achievement award 2010), Nat. Soc. for Study of Edn., Nat. Staff Devel. Coun. (Article of Yr. award 1996, 99, 2002, Book of Yr. award 1996, 2002, Best Non-Disseration Rsch. Award, 2003, Best Staff Devel. Evaluation, 2008, Field award, 2009), Nat. Coun. on Measurement in Edn., Phi Delta Kappa. Home: 2108 Shelton Rd Lexington KY 40515-1170 Office: U Ky Coll Edn 307 Dickey Hall Lexington KY 40506-0001 Office Phone: 859-257-5748. Business E-Mail: guskey@uky.edu.

GUSKIEWICZ, KEVIN M., sports medicine researcher, educator; m. Amy Guskiewicz; children: Jacob, Nathan, Adam, Tessa. BS in Athletic Training, West Chester U., 1989; MS in Exercise Physiology/Athletic Training, 1992; PhD in Sports Medicine, U. Va., 1995. Asst. prof. Dept. Exercise and Sport Sci. U. NC, Chapel Hill, 1995—2001, dir. Undergraduate Athletic Training Edn. Program, 1995—2002, dir. Sports Medicine Rsch. Lab., 1996—2008, dir. Grad. Studies & Grad. Admissions, 1998—2005, assoc. prof., 2001—04, prof., 2004—, dept. chair, 2005—, academic leadership fellow Inst. For Arts & Humanities, 2008—, Mary Lily Kenan Flagler Bingham disting. prof., 2009—, co-dir. Matthew Gfeller Sport-Related Traumatic Brain Injury Rsch. Ctr.; asst. prof. Dept. Orthopaedic Surgery Sch. Medicine, U. NC, Chapel Hill, 1998—2001, assoc. prof., 2001—04, prof., 2004—. Recipient Kenneth Knight Outstanding Rsch. Manuscript, Jour. Athletic Training, 1997, NATA-REF New Investigator Award for Athletic Training Rsch., 1999, Medal for Disting. Athletic Training Rsch., 2006; named a MacArthur Fellow, John D. & Catherine T. MacArthur Found., 2011; fellow American Coll. Sports Medicine, 2003. Fellow: American Acad. Kinesiology and Physical Edn. Office: University of North Carolina Department of Exercise and Sports Scienc 204 Fetzer Hall CB# 8700 Chapel Hill NC 27599 Office Phone: 919-962-5175. Office Fax: 919-962-0489. E-mail: gus@email.unc.edu.

GUSTAFSON, JIM, broadcast executive; Gen. mgr. Sta. WCCO-AM-FM, Mpls., 1995-98, Renda Broadcasting, Ft. Myers, 1998—. Office: Renda Broadcasting Corporation 10915 K Nine Dr Bonita Springs FL 34135-6802

GUTH, CARYL JOY, retired anesthesiologist; b. Peoria, Ill., 1935; m. John Falstad, 1968 (dec. 2001). AA, Mars Hill Coll., 1955; BS, Wake Forest U., 1957, MD, 1962. Diplomate Am. Bd. Anesthesiology. Intern U. Kans. Med. Ctr., Kansas City, 1962-63; resident in anesthesiology U. Pa. Hosp., Phila., 1963-65; instr. dept. anesthesiology Wake Forest U. Bapt. Hosp., Winston-Salem, NC, 1965; fellow in anesthesiology Queen Victoria Hosp., Sussex, Eng., 1966; instr. U. Nijmegan, Netherlands, 1966; bd. dirs. Mills Hosp., San Mateo, Calif., 1994—96, Mills-Peninsula Health Sys., Burlingame, 1994—2002; former chmn. dept anesthesiology Mills-Peninsula Hosps., San Mateo, Calif., ret. Mem. bd. sci. and policy advisors Am. Coun. Sci. and Health, 1995—; ind. Nikken wellness cons., 1996-; holistic and integrative medicine physician San Mateo, 1998-2003, Advance, NC, 2003-. Bd. visitors Wake Forest U. Bapt. Med. Ctr., Winston-Salem, NC, 2004—. Recipient Crisp-Casey award for best female athlete, Wake Forest U., 1957, Mars Hill Coll. Disting. Alummna of Yr. award, 2012, NC Baptist Heritage award, Wake Forest Baptist Med. Ctr., 2013. Mem. AMA, Am. Soc. Anesthesiology (del. 1976-2000, chair com. on comms. 1987-90, chair com. profl. diversity 1995-97, ann. meeting program organizer 1983-84, 87-88, 94, 97), Calif. Med. Assn. (chair com. splty. socs. 1983-84), Calif. Soc. Anesthesiology (past pres., editor bull. 1976-79, asst. treas. 1979-81, pres.-elect 1981-82, pres. 1982-83, Disting. Svc. award 2006), San Mateo County Med. Assn. (bd. dir. 1984-86, chair med. staff affairs com. 1985-86), Coy C. Carpenter Philanthropic Soc., Wake Forest U. Soc., Pres.'s Club Wake Forest U. (endowed WFU womens golf scholarship 2007—), Wake Forest U. Deacon Club (bd. dirs. 2008-, lead challenge campaign Dianne Daily GOlf Learning Ctr., 2010, exec. com. 2013-, named Deacon Club Mem. of Yr. award 2010), Wake Forest U. Med. Alumni Assn. (bd. dir. 1999—, sec. 2003-04, pres.-elect 2004-05, pres. 2005-06, dean's leadership coun. 2006—; Disting. SVc. award 2010, Half Century Class Rep. Lead Physicians Oath Class, 2012), Wake Forest U. Med. Alumni Reunion Class 1962 Campaign (chair 2011-12). Achievements include establishing and endowed chair in complementary and integrative medicine Wake Forest U. Bapt. Med. Ctr., 2002. Home: 105 Willowbrook Pl Advance NC 27006-9480 Office Phone: 336-998-6112. Personal E-mail: cguth@triad.rr.com. Business E-Mail: drguth@yahoo.com.

GUTHRIE, BRETT (STEVEN BRETT GUTHRIE), United States Representative from Kentucky, former state senator; b. Florence, Ala., May 18, 1964; s. Lowell M. and Carolyn P. (Holt) Guthrie. BS in Mathematical Economics, US Mil. Acad., 1987; MA in Public & Pvt. Mgmt., Yale U., 1997. Dir. ops. Trace Die Casting; mem. Dist. 32 Ky. State Senate, Frankfort, 1998—2009; mem. US Congress from 2nd Ky. Dist., Washington, 2009—. Vol. Potter Children's Home; bd. dirs. United Way; mem. Warren County Rep. Exec. Com. Mem.: American Soc. Quality, Nat. Assn. Mfg. Republican. Christian. Office: US House of Representatives 308 Cannon House Office Bldg Washington DC 20515 also: 1001 Center St Ste 300 Bowling Green KY 42101 Office Phone: 202-225-3501, 270-842-9896. Office Fax: 202-226-2019.*

GUTHRIE, CHRIS, dean, law educator; BA in Polit. Sci. with distinction & honors, Stanford U., 1989; EdM, Harvard U., 1991; JD, Stanford U., 1994. Program evaluator Gen. Acctg. Office, Kansas City Regional Office, 1989—90; counselor Higher Edn. Info. Ctr., Boston, 1990—91; assoc. labor & employment group Fenwick & West LLP, Palo Alto, Calif., 1994—96, cons. atty., 1996—98; assoc. prof. U. Mo. Sch. Law, 1996—2002, assoc. dean, 2000—01, 2002; prof. Vanderbilt U. Law Sch., 2002—, assoc. dean academic affairs, 2004—08, dean, John Wade-Kent Syverud prof. law, 2009—. Vis. prof. Wash. U. Sch. Law, 2000, Northwestern U. Law Sch., 2004; spkr. in field. Contbr. articles to law jours. Office: Vanderbilt U Law Sch Dean's Suite Room 108 131 21st Ave S Nashville TN 37203-1181 Office Phone: 615-322-9800. E-mail: chris.guthrie@vanderbilt.edu.*

GUTHRIE, JUDITH K., federal judge; b. Chgo., July 13, 1948; d. David Curtis and Kathleen McAfee G.; m. John H. Hannah, Jr., May 9, 1992 (dec. 2003); m. Matthew Watson, May 28, 2006. Student, Ariz. State U., 1966—68; BA, St. Mary's U., 1971; JD cum laude, U. Houston, 1980. Bar: Tex. 1981, U.S. Dist. Ct. (ea. dist.) Tex. 1982, U.S. Ct. Appeals (5th cir.) 1982, U.S. Dist. Ct. (no. dist.) Tex. 1983, U.S. Dist. Ct. (we. dist.) Tex. 1984, US Supreme Ct., 2002. Editor Am. Coun. Edn., Washington, 1972-73; exec. asst. Tex. Ho. Reps., Austin, 1973-75; lobbyist Bracewell & Patterson, Austin, 1975-80, assoc. Houston, 1980-81; briefing atty. Tex. Ct. Appeals, Tyler, 1981-82; ptnr. Hannah & Guthrie, Tyler, 1982-86; magistrate judge U.S. Dist. Ct. (ea. dist.) Tex., Tyler, 1986—. Instr. legal asst. program, Tyler Jr. Coll., 1986-87; apptd. Tex. Jud. Coun., 1991-97, gender bias task force, 1991-92; lectr. in field. Contbr. articles to profl. jours. Adv. bd. Main St. Project; legal asst. adv. bd. Tyler Jr. Coll., 1986—2007, chmn. adv. bd., 1996—2007; mem. Citizens Commn. Tex. Jud. Sys., 1992—93; bd. dirs. Habitat for Humanity, 2003—08; former Dem. chmn. Smith County; bd. dirs. Found. Women's Resources, Leadership Am., Leadership Tex. Mem.: ABA (Fed. trial judges legis. com. 1991—93), Smith County Bar Assn. (chmn. law libr. com. 1985—2001), State Bar Tex. (dist. 2A grievance com. 1990—, chmn. 1995—96, second term mem. 2002—08), 5th Cir. Bar Assn., Fed. Magistrate Judges Assn., Am. Judges Assn. Office: US Dist Ct 300 Fed Bldg & US Ct House 211 W Ferguson St Tyler TX 75702-7212 Office Phone: 903-590-1077.

GUTHRIE, M. PHILIP, corporate financial executive; b. Vicksburg, Miss., Mar. 26, 1945; s. Marion P. Jr. and Aileen (Perry) G.; m. Beverly Alice Blackmon, June 2, 1966; children: Philip Todd, Edward Tait, Stuart Trent. BS, La. Tech U., 1967; MBA, U. Mich., 1968. CPA, La., Tex. Sr. cons. Price Waterhouse & Co., Houston, 1968-72; v.p. fin. and mfg. Vicra div. Baxter Labs., Dallas, 1972-78; v.p. fin., CFO, treas. S.W. Airlines Co., Dallas, 1978-81; exec. v.p., CFO, Braniff Internat., Dallas, 1981-84; pres. Diamond Mgmt. Group, Dallas, 1984-89; mng. dir. Mason Best Co., Dallas, 1989—98; chmn., CEO, Am. Eagle Group, Inc., Dallas, 1992—96; CEO Aircraft Interior Resources Group Inc., 1998—2003, Intech Aerospace Group, LLC, 2004—05, Denham Ptnrs., LLC, 2004—. Bd. dirs. Ariel Holdings, Inc., Bermuda, Mainstream Data, Inc., Salt Lake City, Safeguard Bus. Sys., Ft. Washington, Pa., Internat. Autotech, Dallas, Westmark Sys., Inc., Austin, Tex., Sunrise Pubs., Inc., Bloomington, Ind., Bristol Group (Buenos Aires), Alpargatas (Buenos Aires), Neuro Resource Group, Inc., Dallas, Rsch. Frontiers Inc.; CEO Neuro Holdings Internat. LLC, 2004-. Assoc. bd. dirs. So. Meth. U. Grad. Sch. Bus., Dallas, 1985—. Mem. AICPA, Fin. Execs. Inst., Nat. Assn. Casualty and Surety Execs., Soc. Internat. Bus. Fellows, Tex. Soc. CPA's, Coun. of Ins. Co. Execs.,Nat. Assn. Copr. Dirs., Phi Kappa Phi, Omicron Delta Kappa, Beta Gamma Sigma, Delta Sigma Pi, Beta Alpha Psi. Office: Three Lincoln Ctr 5430 LBJ Fwy Ste 1200 Dallas TX 75240 E-mail: mphilipguthrie@sbcglobal.net.

GUTHRIE, NANCY PEOPLES, state legislator; b. Havre de Grace, Md., June 15, 1952; m. George Guthrie. BA, Pa. State U., 1975. TV reporter, 1979—83; state liaison Office of Senator Robert Byrd, US Senate, 1985—92; asst. dir. info. mgmt. US Forest Svc., 1992—93; v.p. state govt. rels. The Arnold Agency, 1993—96; pres., owner Capitol City Comm., 1996—; mem. Dist. 30 W.Va. House of Delegates, 2007—, chair Fed. Stimulus Utilization Com., vice chair Interstate Cooperation Com. Democrat. Lutheran. Mailing: 5300 Kanawha Ave Charleston WV 25304 Office: State Capitol Complex Rm 227E, Bldg 1 1900 Kanawha Blvd E Charleston WV 25305 Office Phone: 304-925-8681. E-mail: nguthrie@mail.wvnet.edu.

GUTHRIE, WALLACE NESSLER, JR., naval officer; b. NYC, Feb. 22, 1939; s. Wallace Nessler and Rena Otis (Robertson) G.; m. Virginia Dale Sargeant, June 7, 1961; children: Wallace Edward, Gail Elizabeth, Virginia Lynn. BS, U.S. Naval Acad., Annapolis, Md., 1961; MS, Rollins Coll., 1972, EdS, 1981. Commd. ensign USN, 1961, advanced through ranks to rear adm., 1987; edn. specialist Naval Tng. Systems Ctr., Orlando, Fla., 1967-89; dep. dir. Navy Res., Washington, 1989-92; dir. tng., supt. schs. Am. Forces Info. Svc., 1993-97. Past head Naval Acad. Candidate Selection Com., 9th Congl. Dist., Fla. Sr. officer adv. panel Joint Mil. Intelligence Coll.; bd. dirs., trustee Navy Mut. Aid Assn., Cornerstone Bible Ch. Mem. Naval Res. Assn. (life), Res. Officers Assn. (life), Surface Navy Assn. (life), Naval Submarine League, Clan Guthrie (bd. dirs.), St. Petersburg Hist. Soc. (bd. trustees, bd. dirs.), Friends of Weedon Island (bd. dirs.). Republican. Avocations: camping, boating, fishing, hiking. Office Phone: 727-522-7978. E-mail: wgguthrie@tampabay.rr.com.

GUTIERREZ, JUAN RESTREPO, corporate financial executive; B in Geology, MS in Geology, U. South Fla., Tampa. Gen. mgr. Mineral and Geol. Consulting Co., 2006; pres., bd. dirs. Chancery Resources, Inc., CEO, 2008—09, COO, CFO, treas., sec., 2008—. Lectr. Universidad Pontificia Bolivariana, Colegiatura Colombiana de Diseno; lectr., optical mineralogy, igneous and metamorphic petrology Universidad Nacional de Colombia. Office: Chancery Resources Inc 4553 Jimmy Doolittle Dr Ste 5 Addison TX 75001-5456 Office Phone: 214-288-9897. Office Fax: 972-930-7202.

GUTIERREZ, ROLAND, state legislator; m. Sarah Sanchez; children: Izabella, Victoria. BA in Polit. Sci., U. Tex., San Antonio; JD, St. Mary's U. Sch. Law. Pvt. atty., San Antonio; mem. Dist. 3 San Antonio City Coun., 2005—08; mem. Dist. 119 Tex. House of Representatives, 2008—. Democrat. Office: 3319 Sidney Brooks San Antonio TX 78235 also: Room E1.316 Capitol Extension PO Box 2910 Austin TX 78768 Office Phone: 210-532-2758, 512-463-0452.

GUTMANN, KATE (KATHLEEN M. GUTMANN), delivery service executive; b. Troy, NY, 1968; BS in Mktg., Siena Coll., Loudonville, NY. Sales and mktg. mgr. United Parcel Svc., mktg. intern, 1989, dir. strategic sales southeast region, 1996—99, dir. sales mktg. South Calif. Dist., 1999—2002, dir. mktg. pacific region, 2002—03, v.p. sales southeast region, 2003—06, v.p. mktg. Europe region, Africa & Middle East, 2006—08, pres. enterprise sales, 2008—11, pres. worldwide sales, 2011—. Office: United Parcel Service 55 Glenlake Parkway NE Atlanta GA 30328 Office Phone: 800-742-5877.

GUYETTE, JAMES M., manufacturing executive; b. 1945; married; 5 children. BS Bus. Adminstrn. & Econs., St. Mary's Coll., Moraga, Calif., 1967. Exec. v.p., mktg. & planning United Air Lines Inc., with, 1967, various mgmt. positions, 1967-79, v.p., personnel, sr. v.p., 1979-85, exec. v.p., ops., 1985, v.p. mktg. planning., 1992; bd. dirs. Rolls-Royce plc; chmn., pres. & CEO Rolls-Royce North America, Inc. (subs. of Rolls-Royce, plc), 1997—. Bd. dirs. Internat. Aero Engines, PrivateBancorp Inc., Priceline.com Inc., 2003—. Bd. Regents St. Mary's Coll., U. Ill. Bus. Adv. coun.; devel. coun. Alexian Bros. Med. Ctr., Elk Grove Village, Ill.; various leadership positions United Way Crusade Mercy; bd. dirs. United Way, PrivateBancorp., bd. dirs. Wings Club, Smithsonian Mus. — Air & Space Mus., US C. of C., Flight Safety Found., bd. regents St. Mary's Coll. — Moraga CA, bd. govs. Aerospace Industries Assn. Office: Rolls-Royce North America Inc 1875 Explorer St Ste 200 Reston VA 20190 Office Phone: 703-834-1700. Office Fax: 703-709-6086. Business E-Mail: james.guyette@priceline.com.

GUYNN, JACK (GEORGE C. GUYNN), retired bank executive; b. Staunton, Va., 1942; BS in Indsl. Engring., Va. Polytech. Inst. and State U., 1964; MS in Indsl. Mgmt., Ga. Inst. Tech., 1969; Grad., Harvard Bus. Sch.for Mgmt. Devel., 1974. Joined Fed. Res. Bank Atlanta, 1964, first v.p., COO, 1984—96, pres., CEO, 1996—2006; ret., 2006. Bd. advisor ING Americas; bd. dirs. Genuine Parts Co., 2006—, Oxford Industries, Inc., 2007—, Acuity Brands, Inc., 2008—. Advisory bd. Va. Tech.; bd. councilors Carter Ctr.; bd. trustees Furman U., Oglethorpe U.; bd. dirs. Midtown Alliance, Atlanta, Cmty. Found.; bd. trustees Ga. Tech. Found.; mem. exec. bd. Atlanta Area Coun. Boy Scouts Am. Mem.: Atlanta Rotary Club. Office: c/o Acuity Brands Inc Ste 2400 1170 Peachtree St NE Atlanta GA 30309

GUYNN, ROBERT WILLIAM, psychiatrist, educator; b. Streator, Ill., Oct. 27, 1942; s. William Digby and Helen Louise (Dancey) G. BA, Mich. State U., 1963; MD, Johns Hopkins U., 1967. Diplomate Am. Bd. Psychiatry and Neurology. Clin. fellow Nat. Inst. of Mental Health, Washington, 1970-73; asst. prof. Dept. of Psychiatry and Behaviorial Scis. U. Tex., Houston, 1973-76, assoc. prof., 1976-83, vice-chmn., prof. psychiatry, 1983—2010, interim chmn., 1987-89, chmn., 1989—2007, prof. emeritus, 2010—. Dir. U. Tex. Mental Scis. Inst., 1987—2007; exec. dir. Harris County Psychiat. Ctr., 1988—2007; sr. oral examiner Am. Bd. Psychiatry and Neurology, 1994—2003, mem. written exam com., 1998—2007, chair, 2008—; dir. Acad. Psychiatry, 2008—, editl. bd., 2006—08. Contbr. articles to profl. jours. and book chpts.; mem. editl. bd. Internat. Rev. Psychiatry, 1988-93, editor-in-chief, 1989-93. Bd. dirs. Vols. of Am., Houston, 1982—88; with Passages, 1991—94; mem. adv. bd. The Gathering Place, The Club House, 2004—07. Surgeon USPHS, 1970—73. Recipient Psychiat. Excellence award, Tex. Soc. Psychiat. Physicians, 2000. Fellow Am. Psychiat. Assn. (disting.), Am. Coll. Psychiatrists; mem. Am. Soc. Biol. Chemistry, Tex. Rsch. Soc. on Alcoholism (pres. 1985-87), Tex. Soc. of Am. Assn. Psychiat. Adminstrs. (treas. 1990-91, pres. 1992-93), Biochem. Soc., Rsch. Soc. on Alcoholism, Houston Psychiat. Soc. (v.p. 1989-90, pres. 1991-92), Harris County Med. Soc. (bd. ethics 1989-92), Tex. Dept. Mental Health and Mental Retardation (med. adv. com. 1997—2003), Mental Health and Mental Retardation Auth. (adv. bd. 1992—). Avocations: printmaking, painting. Office: 1941 East Rd Houston TX 77054 Office Phone: 713-486-2554. Business E-Mail: robert.w.guynn@uth.tmc.edu.

GUYTON, ROBERT A., cardiothoracic surgeon, medical educator; BS in Physics with great distinction, U. Miss., 1967; MD magna cum laude, Harvard Med. Sch., 1971. Bd. cert. Am. Bd. Surgery, Am. Bd. Thoracic Surgery, lic. Ga. Asst. resident, surgery Mass. Gen. Hosp., Boston, 1971—73, 1975—77, sr. resident, surgery, 1977—78, clin. fellow, surgery, 1977—78, chief resident, cardiothoracic surgery, 1979; clin. assoc. surgery Branch Nat. Heart & Lung Inst., Bethesda, Md., 1973—75; chief resident, cardiothoracic surgery Children's Hosp. Med. Ctr., Boston, 1978—79; asst. prof. surgery Emory U. Sch. Medicine, Atlanta, 1980—84, assoc. prof. surgery, 1984—90, Disting. Charles Ross Hatcher, Jr. prof. surgery, 1990—, dir., cardiothoracic residency training program, 1990—, chief, Divsn. Cardiothoracic Surgery, Dept. Surgery, 1990—; dir., Cardiothoracic Rsch. Lab. Carlyle Fraser Heart Ctr., Crawford Long Hosp., Atlanta, 1980—85, chief, cardiac surgery, 1987—95; co-dir. Emory-Georgia Tech. Biomedical Tech. Rsch. Ctr., Atlanta, 1986—92; chief, cardiothoracic surgery Emory U. Hosp., Atlanta, 2006—. Mem., transfusion com. Crawford Long Hosp., 1980—91, mem., infection control com., 1980—91, chmn., surgical intensive care unit com., 1980—91, critical pathway com. for cardiac surgery, 1993—95; co-dir. Emory-Ga. Tech. Biomedical Tech. Rsch. Ctr., Atlanta, 1986—90; chmn., new program develop., long range planning com. Emory U. Sch. Medicine, 1986—88, mem., univ. priorities com., 1988—91, mem. faculty com. on appointments and promotions, Office of the Dean, 1995—98; bd. dirs. exec. com. Emory Clinic, 1990—98, 1991—93; critical pathway task force for cardiac surgery Emory U. Hosp., 1994—; mem. Emory U. Sys. Healthcare Internet Com., 1995—97; chmn. Am. Coll. Cardiology/Am. Heart Assn. com. on guidelines for coronary artery bypass, 1997—2006; mem. Emory Healthcare Info. Tech. Com., 1999—2001, Emory Healthcare Managed Care Contract Com., 1999—; mem. valve adv. bd. Medtronic, Inc., 1999—; bd. dirs. Thoracic Surgery Found. for Rsch. and Edn., 2006—; invited lectr. in field. Co-editor: Cardiopulmonary Bypass Principles and Techniques of Extracorporeal Circulation; mem. editl. bd. Clin. Cardiology, 1989—, guest editor The Annals of Thoracic Surgery, 1988—98, Seminars in Thoracic and Cardiovascular Surgery, 1995, manuscript reviewer Jour. Am. Coll. Cardiology, Circulation, Am. Jour. Thoracic and Cardiovascular Surgery; contbr. articles to med. jours. Lt. comdr. US Pub. Health Svc., 1973—75. Recipient Award for Outstanding Rsch., Harvard Med. Sch., Mass. Med. Soc., 1971. Fellow: ACS; mem.: So. Surgical Assn., Am. Soc. for Artificial Internal Organs, Soc. for Thoracic Surgery End., Andrew G. Morrow Soc., Am. Heart Assn., AMA, Ga. Med. Assn., Atlanta Med. Assn., Thoracic Surgery Found. for Rsch. and Edn. (bd. dirs.), Thoracic Surgery Dirs. Assn., So. Thoracic Surgical Assn., Soc. Thoracic Surgeons (mem. program com. 1988—91, com. on edn. and resources 1989—91, chmn., com. on scientific program for 1990 interim meeting 1990, chmn., program com. 1990—91, treas.-elect 1996—97, internet liaison com. 1997—2000, treas. 1997—2002, mem. exec. com. 1997—2004, first-v.p. 2002—03, mem. Coun. on Health Policy & Relationships, chair, workforce on comm. 2005—, chair Workforce on Comm.), Am. Surgical Assn., Am. Coll. Cardiology, Am. Assn. Thoracic Surgeons (Evarts A. Graham Meml. Traveling Fellowship Com. 1990—94, mem. governing coun. 1992—95, Evarts A. Graham Meml. Traveling Fellowship Com. 1993—94, co-chmn., com. on continuing med. edn. 1995—96), Alpha Omega Alpha, Omicron Delta Kappa, Phi Kappa Phi. Achievements include patents pending in field. Office: The Emory Clinic Inc Bldg A Rm 2223 1365 Clifton Rd NE Atlanta GA 30322 Office Phone: 404-778-3836. Office Fax: 404-778-5039.

GUZICK, DAVID S., academic administrator, hospital administrator; b. 1952; MD, NYU, 1979, PhD. Resident in ob-gyn. John Hopkins Hosp., 1979—83; fellow in reproductive endocrinology U. Tex. Southwestern Med. Sch., 1983—85; dir. divsn. reproductive endocrinology Magee Women's Hosp., U. Pitts.; assoc. prof. U. Pitts., 1986—94, prof., 1994—95; chief svc. ob-gyn. Strong Meml. Hosp., Rochester, NY; Henry A. Thiede prof. and chair ob-gyn. U. Rochester Sch. Medicine and Dentistry, 1995—2002, dean and prof. ob-gyn., 2002—09; sr. v.p. health affairs U. Fla., 2009—; pres. UF & Shands Health Sys., 2009—; bd. chmn. UF Shands and Shands Jacksonville, 2009—. Named one of America's Best 400 Doctors for Women, Good Housekeeping mag. Mem.: Inst. Medicine, Soc. Assisted Reproductive Tech., Soc. Reproductive Endocrinologists, Am. Soc. Reproductive Medicine, The Endocrine Soc., Am. Bd. Obstetrics and Gynecology, Coun. Chairs of Obstetrics and Gynecology, Soc. Gynecologic Investigation, Am. Gynecologic and Obstetric Soc., Soc. Scholars. Office: UF & Shands The University Fla Academic Health Sys 1600 SW Archer Rd Gainesville FL 32608

GUZMAN, EVA MARTINEZ, state supreme court justice; b. Chgo., 1961; m. Tony Guzman; 1 child, Melanie Alexis. BBA, U. Houston; law degree, South Tex. Coll. Law. Pvt. practice atty.; judge 309th Dist. Ct. Harris County, 1999—2001; assoc. justice Tex. 14th Ct. Appeals, Houston, 2001—09, Tex. Supreme Ct., Austin, 2009—. Adj. faculty mem. U. Houston Law Ctr.; sr. fellow Am. Leadership Forum. Mem. adv. coun. The Salvation Army Boys and Girls Clubs of Met. Houston; bd. mem. Tex. Ct. Appointed Spl. Advs., The Escape Ctr., Wesley Cmty. Ctr., The Chinquapin Sch.; bd. mem. Greater Houston Area chpt. ARC. Recipient Woman on the Move Award, Tex. Exec. Women, 2006, Pres.'s Award for Outstanding Com. Svc., Houston Bar Assn., Judge of Yr. Award, Mex. Am. Bar Assn. Tex. Found., 2009; named Appellate Judge of Yr., P.O.L.I.C.E. Inc., Houston Police Officers Union, Latina Judge of Yr., Hispanic Nat. Bar Assn., 2009. Mem.: Am. Law Inst. Republican. Office: Tex Supreme Ct 201 W 14th St Rm 104 Austin TX 78701 Office Phone: 512-463-1312.*

GUZZO, DANA F., construction executive; Grad., Old Dominion U. Dir. internal audit W. R. Grace and Co., 2001—04; v.p. Martin Marietta Materials, Inc., 2004—, contr., 2005—, chief acctg. officer, 2006—. Office: Martin Marietta Materials Inc 2710 Wycliff Rd Raleigh NC 27607 Office Phone: 919-781-4540. Office Fax: 919-783-4535.

GWATHMEY, JOE NEIL, JR., retired broadcast executive; b. Brownwood, Tex., Jan. 4, 1941; s. Joe Neil and Grace Christine (Henry) G.; m. Linda Sue Sams, Aug. 22, 1965; children: Sara Lynn, David Alan. BA, Howard Payne Coll., 1963; postgrad., U. Denver, 1963-64, George Washington U., 1964-65. Sta. mgr. Sta. KUT-FM, Austin, 1965-71; mem. founding bd. dirs. Nat. Pub. Radio, Washington, 1970, various mgmt. positions, 1971-83, v.p., 1983-88; pres. Tex. Pub. Radio, San Antonio, 1988—2006; ret., 2006. Review panel chair United Way Bexar County, San Antonio, 1994-97; mem. adv. coun. Coll. Fine Arts U. Tex., Austin, 1990-93; trustee Tex. Student Publs., Austin, 1995-98; mem. bd. advisors N.Y. Festivals, 1986—2006, Riverwalk Jazz, 2005-; mem. bd. dirs. World Affairs Coun., San Antonio, 1999—2008, Low Vision Resource Ctr., 2004-11. Recipient Edward R. Murrow award Corp. Pub. Broadcasting, 1988. Protestant. Avocation: reading. Home: 2926 Meadow Cir San Antonio TX 78231-1720

GWIN, DOROTHY JEAN BIRD, retired psychology professor, dean; b. Smith County, Tex., June 26, 1934; d. Joseph William and Elva Gracie (Elledge) Bird; m. Clinton Dale Gwin, Nov. 21, 1964; 1 child, Clinton Bird. BBA, East Tex. State U., 1954, MS, 1955; EdD, U. Kans., 1958. Lic. psychologist, La. Tchr. Thomas Jefferson High Sch., Port Arthur, Tex., 1954—55; resident dir. U. Kans., Lawrence, 1955-57; sch. psychologist Caddo Parish Schs., Shreveport, La., 1958-67, con. psychologist, 1967-70; prof. psychol., edn. Centenary Coll., Shreveport, La., 1967-79, 1996—, dean, 1979-92, dean enrollment mgmt., 1993—96, prof. edn., psychol. and dir. alumni rels., 1992-93, prof., 1996—97; exec. dir. Cmty. Found. Shreveport-Bossier, Shreveport, La., 1997—2004; bd. dirs. Christus Schumpert Med. Ctr., 2001—04; ret., 2004. Bd. dirs. Vol. of Am., Shreveport, 1967-70; pres. bd. dirs. Southfield Sch., Shreveport, 1984-86, bd. dirs. 1974-87. Fulbright U.S. Ednl. Adminstrs. grantee to Germany, 1990, Japan, 1997. Mem. Am. Pers. Guidance Assn. (life). Home: 429 Prestwick Ct Nashville TN 37205-5016 Personal E-mail: dbgwin@bellsouth.net.

GWIN, ROBERT G., oil industry executive; BS, U. So. Calif., LA; MBA, Duke U. Fuqua Sch. Bus., Durham, NC. CFA, Chartered Fin. Analyst Inst. Merchant banker Prudential Capital Group, mng. dir.; chmn., pres., CEO Prosoft Learning Corp.; CEO Cmty. Broadband Ventures, LP; v.p. fin., treas. Anadarko Petroleum Corp., 2006—08, pres., CEO, dir. Western Gas Holdings, LLC, 2007—, sr. v.p., 2008—09, sr. v.p. fin., CFO, 2009—. Bd. dirs. Storm Ventures Internat., Theatre Under the Stars. Office: Anadarko Petroleum Corp 1201 Lake Robbins Dr The Woodlands TX 77380 Office Phone: 832-636-1000.

HAAS, EDWARD LEE, management consultant; b. Camden, NJ, Nov. 9, 1935; s. Edward David and Mildred Haas; m. Maryann Lind, Dec. 27, 1958; children: John Eric, Gretchen Haas Theodore. BA, LaSalle U., Phila., 1958. Cryptanalyst Nat. Security Agy., Ft. Meade, Md., 1958—59; mgr. sys. devel. RCA Corp., Cherry Hill, NJ, 1966—71; mgr. computer tech. svcs. Gen. Tire & Rubber Co., Akron, Ohio, 1971—74; sr. mgr. computer applications R & D Ernst & Young LLP, Cleve., 1974—75, nat. dir. software products, 1976—77, chief info. officer, nat. dir. software products, 1977—80, nat. ptnr., 1978—82, cons. sr. ptnr. Phila., NYC, L.A., 1983—95; ind. mgmt. cons. L.A., 1996—98; v.p. info. tech. Sunbeam Corp., Boca Raton, Fla., 1998—99; ind. mgmt. cons. NYC, 2000—. 1st lt. arty. US Army, 1958—59. Mem.: Tournament Players Club (Sawgrass), Plantation Country Club. Republican. Roman Catholic. Office Phone: 904-285-5735.

HAAS, JOANNA E., museum director; With Ohio Ctr. Sci. & Industry; Spirit of Ford dir. Ford Motor Co., Dearborn, Mich., 1999—2001; dir. Henry Ford Mus., Dearborn, Mich., 2001—03; Henry Buhl, Jr. dir. Carnegie Sci. Ctr., Pitts., 2003—08; dir. Louisville Sci. Ctr., 2008—. Office: Louisville Sci Ctr 727 West Main St Louisville KY 40202 Office Phone: 502-561-6100.

HAAS, JOSEPH MARSHALL, retired petroleum consultant; b. Alexandria, La., June 21, 1927; s. Samuel and Lulu Susan (Haupt) H.; m. Mary Louise Nance, June 4, 1949 (dec. Jan. 1950); 1 child, Samuel Douglas; m. Marion Barker, Apr. 9, 1954; children: Joseph Marshall, Suzanne M., Thomas B., Katherine L. B of Mech. Engring., Ga. Inst. Tech., 1949. With Gen. Am. Oil Co., Dallas, 1949-78, asst. v.p. prodn. and engring., 1957—60, v.p. engring., 1960—78, bd. dirs., 1978—83. Pres., bd. dirs. Conejo Investments Inc., 1994—; mgr. Tiger Bend Gen. Ptnr. LLC, 2005-. With USNR, 1945-46. Mem. Am. Inst. Mining and Metall. Engrs., Masons (32 degree, Shriner), Dallas Petroleum Club, Tau Beta Pi, Sigma Chi, Pi Tau Sigma. Methodist. Home: 1119 Challenger St Austin TX 78734-3801 Office: 1123 Challenger St Austin TX 78734-3801

HAASS, CHRISTOPHER (CHIP), city councilman; b. July 29; City councilman Dist. 10, San Antonio. Mailing: PO Box 839966 San Antonio TX 78283-3966 Office: 1802 NE Loop 410, Ste 102 San Antonio TX 78217 Office Phone: 210-824-7355, 210-207-7063. Office Fax: 210-207-7027, 210-824-7506.

HABENICHT, PETER A., advertising and marketing professional; BA in Mktg. with honors, U. Notre Dame, 1978; MS in Journalism, Va. Commonwealth U., 1984. V.p. strategic planning and client leadership Rightminds, 2001—05; v.p. corp. comm. LandAmerica Fin. Group, Inc., 2005—08; smart network liaison Studio Squared, 2010—. Office: Studio Squared c/o The Martin Agency One Shockoe Plz Richmond VA 23219-4132 Office Phone: 804-698-8000. Office Fax: 804-698-8001.

HABICHT, FRANK HENRY, retired manufacturing executive; b. Chgo., Sept. 4, 1920; s. Geroge Jr. and Gertrude A. (Tronc) H.; m. Jeanne Ellen Patrick, Mar. 9, 1943; children: Pamela, Patricia, Frank Henry II. BSME, Purdue U., 1942; postgrad., Cornell U., Ithaca, NY, 1942, Am. U., Washington, DC, 1944. From sales engr. to pres. Marshall & Huschart Machinery Co., Chgo., 1946-70; vice chmn. Cone-Blanchard Machine Co., Windsor, Vt. and Aldridge, England, 1971-74; chmn. bd., pres. United Tech. Corp., Chgo., 1970-81; pres. Steego Tech. Corp., West Palm Beach, 1981-86; chmn., pres. Corp. Assocs., Inc., 1986-97, ret., 1997. Tech. cons. US Dept. Def., Washington, 1963-64; pres. UNISIG Corp., 1980-86, King & Gavaris Cons. Engrs. Inc., 1980-84; US projects mgr. Boehringer GmbH, Germany, 1989-95; 1997; lectr. in field; bd. dirs. Am. SIP Corp., Botemp Corp., Switzerland. Author: Modern Machine Tools, 1964; contbr. articles to profl. jours. Mem. def. indsl. plant equipment com. Dept. Def. Lt. comdr.USN, 1942-45. Mem. ASME, Am. Machine Tool Distbrs. Assn. (dir., past pres.), Fabricating Mfrs. Assn. (dir., past pres.), Assn. of RAF Warbirds, Conf. Bd. (exec. coun.), Order Knights St. John of Jerusalem, Oakbrook Polo Club, Palm Beach Club, Palm Beach Yacht Club, Governor's Club, Soc 4 Arts (Palm Beach), Navy League (bd. dirs.), Masons. Episcopalian. Avocations: hunting, fishing, tennis.

HABORAK, GEORGE EDWARD, retired academic administrator, educator; b. Bridgeport, Conn., Oct. 8, 1936; s. Gerorge Albert and Helen Genivieve (Olsen) H.; m. Cecilia Yvonne Eggleston, Aug. 28, 1965; children: Chris, Kevin, Dana. AB in Classical Lang., Boston Coll., 1960, MA in Philosophy, 1961; MA in Math., Wayne State U., 1964; PhD in Math., Cath. U. Am., 1971. Asst. prof. math. US Naval Acad., Annapolis, Md., 1964-71; with Coll. Charleston, SC, 1971—2005, prof. math. SC, 1976—2005, sr. v.p. student affairs SC, 1979—2001. Author: (with others) Calculus with Analytic Geometry, 1971, revised, 1982. Pres. Nativity Sch. Bd., Charleston, 1977-81; bd. dirs. Low Country chpt. ARC, treas., 1993-94, chmn., 1994-95; pres. Carolina Hearing Aid Bank, 2002-05. Leads grantee U.S. Dept. Transp. and S.C., 1986-89, U.S. Dept. Edn. grantee, 1989-92. Mem. Am. Coll. Pers. Assocs., Nat. Assn. Student Pers. Adminstrs. (state coord. legal issues 1986-92), Math. Assn. Am., So. Assn. Coll. Student Adminstrs., Rotary (treas. 1983-84, sec. 1984-85, pres. 1985-86, Paul Harris fellow 1991), Order of Omega, Omicron Delta Kappa, Alpha Phi Omega, Sigma Phi Epsilon (dist. gov. S.C. 1992—). Personal E-mail: ghaborak@hotmail.com.

HACKENSON, ELIZABETH, electric power industry executive; b. 1960; BS, NY State U. IT mgmt. positions EDS, Computech, TRW, Grumman and Sperry; with UUNET, Concert Communication, MCI Inc., Ashburn, Va., 1997—2006, exec. v.p., chief info. officer, 2004—06; chief info. officer Lucent Technolgies, Murray Hill, NJ, 2006; head, info. systems & info. tech. Alcatel Lucent, New Providence, NJ, 2006—08; sr. v.p., chief info. officer AES Corp., Arlington, Va., 2008—. Bd. dirs. Serena Software, Inc., San Mateo, Calif., 2006—; bd. dirs LGS, 2007—. Named one of Top 200 Female Executives, The Washington Post, 2004, Premier 100 IT Leaders, Computerworld, 2006. Office: AES Corp 4300 Wilson Blvd 11th Fl Arlington VA 22203 Fax: 601-460-8269.

HACKNEY, JAMES ACRA, III, industrial engineer, consultant, retired manufacturing executive; b. Washington, NC, Sept. 27, 1939; s. James Acra Jr. and Margaret Dunston (Hodges) H.; m. Constance Garrenton, June 5, 1961; children: Kenneth Ross, Jane H. Kemsley. BSME, N.C. State U., Raleigh, 1961, BS in Indsl. Engring, 1962. Licensed profl. engr., NC, Licensed master 100T US Coast Guard. With Hackney Industries, Inc., Washington, NC, 1961—95, chief engr., 1961—63, asst. gen. mgr., 1963—65, exec. v.p., gen. mgr., 1965—70, pres., CEO, 1970—90, chmn. bd. dirs., 1990—95; pres., CEO Hackney Group, Inc., Washington, 1995—; bd. dirs., sec. Freeway Holdings, Inc., Washington, NC, 2004—; bd. dirs. PENC Ednl. Found., Inc., 2008—14. Bd. dirs. Sprint Mid-Atlantic Telecom, Wake Forest, N.C., 1987-97, Bank of Am., client adv. bd, 1995-. Chmn. Blackbeard dist. Boy Scouts Am., 1970-74, pres. East Carolina Cncl., 1976-77, mem. nat. exec. bd., 1987-, pres. S.E. Region, 1987-89; chmn. bd. trustees Beaufort County Hosp., 1975-77; trustee N.C. State U., Raleigh, 1979-87, chmn. bd. trustees, 1985-87; mem. Interam. Scout Com., World Orgn. Scout Movement, 1984-88; lay Eucharistic min. Zion Episcopal Ch., Washington, N.C., 2002-, Vestryman 2012-; gen. campaign chmn. Beaufort County United Way, 1998-2000; mem. adv. cncl. Sch. Engring., East Carolina U., 2004-; bd. dirs. Shepard Cancer Ctr. Foundn., Washington, 2011-; mem. adv. cncl. Sch. Mech. and Aerospace Engring., N.C. State U., 2002-09; bd. dirs. NC Engring. Found., Inc., 1977-1979, 2008-. Officer US Army, 1962—69. Recipient Disting. Service award Washington Jaycees, 1970; Silver Beaver award Boy Scouts Am., 1975, Silver Antelope award, 1982, Disting. Eagle Scout award, 1980, Silver Buffalo award, 1992; Youth of the Ams. award World Orgn. Scout Movement, 1990, John Southam Journalism award Sail Am., 1997; named N.C. Small Businessman of Yr., SBA, 1971, Young Engr. of Yr., NSPE, 1971; St. George Epicopal award, 2007, Cliff Dochterman award Internat. Fellowship Scouting Rotarians, 2005. Fellow NSPE; mem. Inst. Indsl. Engrs. (chpt. pres. 1967-68), Profl. Engrs. N.C. (pres. Ea. Carolina chpt. 1971-72, state sec. 2000-01, state treas. 2001-02, pres.-elect 2002-03, pres. 2003-04, Outstanding Young Engr. 1970-71), NC Chamber(bd. dirs. 1979-86), Washington C. of C. (pres. 1972-74, Outstanding Cmty. Svc. award 2000), N.C. State U. Alumni Assn. (bd. dirs. 1976-80, Outstanding Young Alumnus 1975, Disting. Engring. Alumnus 1984, Watauga Medal 1997), Rotary (pres. 1978-79), Pamlico Plantation Yacht Club (commodore 1993). Episcopalian. Avocations: sailing, trumpet, amateur radio.

HACKNEY, JOE, state legislator; b. Chatham County, NC, Sept. 23, 1945; s. Herbert and Ida; m. Betsy Hackney; 2 children. Attended, NC State U.; AB, UNC, Chapel Hill, 1967; JD, UNC Law Sch., Chapel Hill, 1970. Rsch. asst. & law clk. Assoc. Justice Frank Huskins, 1970—71; asst. dist. atty. Orange & Chatham Counties, 1971—74; ptnr. Epting & Hackney, 1974—; mem. Dist. 24 NC House of Reps, 1981—2002, spkr. pro tem., 1999—2002, mem. Dist. 54, 2003—, dem. leader, 2003—04, majority leader, 2005—06, spkr. of the house,

2006—. Legislator of Year Award, NC Wildlife Fedn, 1985. Orange Co Bar Association (president, 1974-75); District 15-B Bar Association (president, 1980-81). Democrat. Baptist. Office: North Carolina House of Representatives 300 N Salisbury St Room 612 Raleigh NC 27603-5925 Office Phone: 919-733-3451, 919-733-5860, 919-728-0449. Business E-Mail: Joe.Hackney@ncleg.net.

HACKNEY, VIRGINIA HOWITZ, lawyer; b. Phila., Jan. 11, 1945; d. Charles Rawlings and Edith Wrenn (Pope) Howitz; m. Barry Albert Hackney, Feb. 15, 1969; children: Ashby Rawlings, Roby Howison, Trevor Pope. BA in Econs., Hollins Coll., 1967; JD, U. Richmond, 1970. Bar: Va. 1970. Assoc. Hunton & Williams, Richmond, Va., 1970-77, ptnr., capital fin., real estate, 1977—, also dep. gen. counsel. Pres. Am. Acad. Hosp. Attys. Chgo., 1992-93. Mem. agy. evaluation com. United Way of Greater Richmond, 1981-86; sustainer Jr. League of Richmond; mem. and fellow Am. Health Lawyers Assn. (pres. 1992-93, bd. dirs. 1988-94). Recipient Women of Achievement award, Met. Richmond Women's Bar Assn., 1998, Distinction award Va. Women Attys. Assn., 2006; named Outstanding Woman in Field of Law, YWCA, Richmond, 1981. Fellow Am. Health Lawyers Assn. (past pres.); mem. ABA (forum com. health law 1982—), Va. State Bar (long range planning com. 1985-90, chmn. standing com. lawyer discipline 1986-90, exec. com. 1988-90, Bar Coun. mem. 1984-90), Va. Bar Assn. Avocations: book tapes, reading, boating, jogging/walking. Office: Hunton & Williams Riverfront Plz East Tower 951 E Byrd St Richmond VA 23219-4074 Office Phone: 804-788-8263. Office Fax: 804-788-8218. Business E-Mail: vhackney@hunton.com.

HADDAD, EMILE, construction executive; Civil engr. Lic. engr., Calif.; contracting Calif. Pres., Western Region Lennar Corp., chief investment officer, 2009—. Bd. dirs. Home Aid of Orange County; mem. Urban Land Inst. Active, Mare Island, Hunters Point, Treasure Island & Villages Tustin Marine Air Station, active, Heritage Fields El Toro Marine Base. Office: Lennar Corp 700 NW 107th Ave Miami FL 33172 Office Phone: 305-559-4000. Office Fax: 305-226-4158. Business E-Mail: emile.haddad@lennar.com.

HADDOCK, RAYMOND EARL, retired career officer, major general; b. Oklahoma City, Sept. 26, 1936; s.Clyde William and Ida Belle (Lemmon) H.; m. Brunhilde Ernestine Becker, Oct. 21, 1960; children: Ralph William, Ronald Raymond, Karen Elizabeth Haddock Fralen. BS in Chemistry, W. Tex. State U., Canyon, 1958; MS in Pub. Adminstrn., Shippensburg Coll., Pa., 1977; grad., US Army War Coll., Carlisle Barracks, Pa., 1977. Commd. 2d lt. US Army, advanced through grades to maj. Gen., capt. and maj. advisor to Vietnam forces, 1966—67, bn. comdr. Pershing Missile Bn., 56th FA., 1973-75, pers. staff officer (G-1) 8th Inf. Div. Germany, 1975-76, dir. internat. programs Tng. and Doctrine Command Fort Monroe, Va., 1977-80, comdr. 9th Div. Arty. Fort Lewis, Wash., 1980-83, chief of staff Tng. Ctr. Fort Dix, NJ, 1983-84, comdg. gen. Pershing Missile Command 56th FA. Germany, 1984-87; comdr., dir. US mil. forces US Command, Berlin, 1988-90; comdg. gen. US Army Security Assistance Command, Alexandria, Va., 1990-92; v.p. ITT Def. Internat., McLean, Va., 1993—2003, ret., 2003. Participant fall of Berlin wall, reunification of Germany and US-Soviet nuclear forces treaty, 1987. Ret. maj. gen. US Army. Decorated D.S.M. with two oak leaf clusters; Fed. Order of Merit, Berlin; Order of Merit (Fed. Republic Germany); Gold Nat. Def. medal (France). Avocations: sailing, fishing, jogging, hunting, genealogy. Personal E-mail: raybrunih@yahoo.com.

HADDOCK, RONALD WAYNE, board member; b. St. Elmo, Ill., July 29, 1940; s. Clarence and Marie (Price) H.; m. Sandra Sue Thomas, Sept. 1957; children: Roni Sue Haddock Campey, Mark Tayler, Rick Wayne. B in Mech. Engring., Purdue U., 1963. Chmn. AEI Svcs., LLC, Rubicon Offshore Internat., Safety-Kleen Sys., Inc.; with Exxon Corp., 1963—86; staff, mgmt. positions Baton Rouge Refinery, 1963—71; specialties econs. coord., adminstrv. mgr., planning mgr. Refining Dept. Houston hdqrs., 1971—75, corp. planning mgr., v.p. for refining, 1978—81; ops. mgr., refinery mgr. Baytown Refinery, 1975—78; exec. asst. to chmn., Exxon Corp. Hdqrs. NYC, 1981—82; v.p., dir., Esso Eastern Houston hdqrs., 1982—85; exec. v.p., COO FINA, Inc., Dallas, 1986—88; pres., CEO Fina, Inc., Dallas, 1998—2000; exec. chmn., CEO & bd. dirs. Prisma Energy Internat. Ltd., 2003. Bd. dirs. Alon USA Energy, Inc., Adea Solutions, Inc., SWS Group, Inc., 2002—05, Trinity Industries, Inc., 2005—. Mem. Dallas Morning News Energy Adv. Bd.; hon. consul of Belgium in Dallas; mem. Dallas Together Forum; chmn.'s adv. bd. Dallas Arboretum; mem. Gov.'s Bus. Coun.; mem. bd., Zale Lipshy Hosp., Sci. Pl. Named Man of Yr. Belgian-Am. Chamber, Disting. Engring. Alumnus Purdue U, Humanitarian of Yr. Anti-Defamation League; recipient award Multiple Sclerosis Dinner of Champions, Chmns. award D/FW Minority Bus. Devel. Coun., Entrepreneurs award African Am. Women, Advocate of Yr. award Golden Triangle Minority Bus. Coun. Mem. Am. Petroleum Inst. (bd., com. hon. dirs., mgmt. com., Ind. Reputation Strategic Issues Grp.), Nat. Petroleum Coun. (bd., coordinating com.), Chems. Mfrs. Assn. (bd., Responsible Care Com., Fin. Com.), Ind. Petroleum Assn. Am. (regional adv. bd.), Tex. MidContinenta Oil and Gas Assn. (exec. com.), Petrochem. Industry Founders Club, 25 Yr. Club Petroleum Industry, Dallas Petroleum Club (adv. com. chmn., past pres.), Dallas Wildcatters (past pres.), Brook Hollow Golf Club, Bd. Dallas Citizens Counc., co-chair, Dallas Together Forum, bd., The Science Place. Methodist. Avocations: jogging, music. Office: Trinity Industries Inc Bd Directors 2525 Stemmons Fwy Dallas TX 75207-2401 Office Phone: 214-631-4420. Office Fax: 214-589-8810. Business E-Mail: ronald.haddock@trin.net.

HADLER, NORTIN MARVIN, rheumatologist, clinical investigator, educator; b. NYC, Nov. 13, 1942; s. Morris H. and Lucille C. (Hochberg) H.; m. Carol S. Spiegel, June 20, 1965; children: Jeffrey A., Elana B. AB, Yale U., 1964; MD, Harvard U., 1968. Diplomate Am. Bd. Internal Medicine, Am. Bd. Rheumatology, Am. Bd. Allergy and Immunology, Am. Bd. Geriatrics. Intern, resident then fellow Mass. Gen. Hosp., Boston, 1968-70; clin. assoc. ARB-NIAMDD, NIH, Bethesda, Md., 1970-72; asst. prof. medicine and microbiology U. N.C., Chapel Hill, 1973-78, assoc. prof., 1978-85, prof., 1985—. Author: Medical Management of the Regional Musculoskeletal Diseases: Backache, Neck Pain, Disorders of the Upper and Lower Extremities, 1984, Last Well Person: How to Stay Well Despite the Health-care System, 2004, Occupational Musculoskeletal Disorders, 2004, Worried Sick: A Prescription for Health in an Overtreated America, 2008, Stabbed in the Back: Confronting Back Pain in an Overtreated Society, 2009; co-author: Arthritis and Society: The Impact of Musculoskeletal Disease, 1985; co-editor: The Yearbook of Rheumatology, Arthritis, and Musculoskeletal Disease, 1999; contbr. articles to profl. publs. Surgeon USPHS, 1970-72. Avocation: bicycling. Office: U NC Dept Med 3300 Thurston Bldg Chapel Hill NC 27599-7280 Office Phone: 919-966-4191.

HAEFELE, CHAD M., library and information scientist; BS in Computer Info. Sci., Grove City Coll., Pa., 2004; MLIS, U. Pitts., 2005. Page Fairport Pub. Libr., NY, 1998—2001, clk., 2001—04; intern Rochester Pub. Libr., NY, 2003; entertainment editor, computer scientist The Collegian, Grove City, Pa., 2002—04; tech. support, lab attendant U. Pitts. Barco Law Libr., 2004—05; reference & instruction libr., lectr. U. Ala., Huntsville, 2005—07, interim dept. head distance learning, 2007; emerging technologies libr., computer sci. subject specialist U. NC, Chapel Hill, 2007—. Named to Movers & Shakers, Libr. Jour., 2011. Office: University NC at Chapel Hill Davis Library CB# 3922 208 Raleigh St Chapel Hill NC 27514-8890 Office Phone: 919-962-1151. Business E-Mail: chaefele@email.unc.edu.

HAEFFNER, ROBERT, corporate financial executive; B in Economics & Mgmt., Trinity Coll., Deerfield, Ill.; MBA, U. Miami. CPA. Sr. mgr. Deloitte; asst. v.p., bus. process devel. JM Family Enterprises, Inc.; bd. dirs. JM&A Group (subs. JM Family Enterprises, Inc.), acctg. mgr., v.p., CFO. Office: JM&A Group 500 Jim Moran Blvd Deerfield Beach FL 33442 Office Phone: 954-429-2295. Office Fax: 954-596-7448. Business E-Mail: robert.haeffner@jmfamily.com.

HAEMMERICH, DIETER, biomedical engineer; PhD, U. Wis., 2001. Scientist U. Wis., Madison, 2001—04; asst. prof. dept. pediatric cardiology Med. U. SC, Charleston, 2004—08, assoc. prof. dept. pediatric cardiology, 2008—; pres. Med. Engring. Innovations LLC, Madison, 2005—. Cons. Bard Electrophysiology, Lowell, Mass., 2000—01, Richmar, Inc., Inola, Okla., 2002—03, Biosense-Webster, Diamond Bar, Calif., 2003—04; adj. prof. bioengring. Clemson U., 2004—. Contbr. chapters to books. Mem.: IEEE (assoc.). Achievements include invention of multiple probe radiofrequency ablation; radiofrequency assisted resection device. Office: MUSC 165 Ashley Ave PO Box 250915 Charleston SC 29425 Personal E-mail: haemmeri@hotmail.com.

HAFTER, JEROME CHARLES, lawyer; b. Orlando, Fla., May 16, 1945; s. Jerome Sidney and Mary Margaret (Fugler) H.; m. Jo Cille Dawkins, July 18, 1976; 1 child, Jerome Bryan. BA summa cum laude, Rice U., 1967; BA with first class honours, Oxford U., 1969, MA, 1976; JD, Yale U., 1972. Bar: Miss. 1974, U.S. Ct. Appeals (5th cir.) 1974, U.S. Dist. Ct. (no. and so. dists.) Miss. 1974. Law clk. to presiding judge U.S. Ct. Appeals (5th cir.), Jackson, Miss., 1972—73; assoc. Lake, Tindall, Hunger & Thackston (now Lake Tindall LLP), Greenville, Miss., 1973—76, ptnr., 1976—2001, Phelps Dunbar LLP, Jackson, 2001—. Chmn. Miss. Bd. Bar Admissions, Jackson, 1979-2002; sec., treas. Hafter Realty Inc., Greenville, 1969-92, pres., 1992—; mem. gov.'s constn. commn., Jackson, 1985-87; sec., gen. counsel Delta and Pine Land Co., Scott, Miss., 1993—2007. Author: Family History of Peter Quin, 1964, 2d. rev. edit., 1970. Pres. Downtown Improvement Assn. Greenville, 1980—2001, Common Cause/Miss., 1976—78; mem. Greenville City Election Commn., 1978—, Greenville Mcpl. Sch. Bd., 1988—2013, pres., 1995—96, 1999—2000, 2002—03, 2006—07, 2011—12; chmn. com. on tax Miss. Econ. Coun., Jackson, 1985, 1987, 1996—98; pres. Greenville Area C. of C., 1992; v.p. I-69 Mid-Continent Hwy. Coalition, 1992—. Marshall scholar, 1967-69; Leadership Miss. Program fellow, 1976-77; Best Lawyers in Am., 2001-. Fellow: Miss. Bar Found.; mem.: ABA (young lawyer divsn. 1980—82, law sch. accreditation com. 1998—2002, coun. sect. legal edn. and admissions to bar 2000—06, chmn. bar admissions com. sect. on legal edn. and admission to bar 2006—07, coun. sect. legal edn. and admissions to bar 2007—11, vice chmn. com. on issues affecting legal profession, chmn. 2009—10), Miss. Bankruptcy Conf. (chmn. com. on bankruptcy rules 1988), Am. Law Inst., Am. Judicature Soc., Nat. Conf. Bar Examiners (MBE com. 1986—88, trustee 1989—2000, chmn. 1998—99, chmn. tech. com. 2000—), Fed. Bar Assn. (v.p. no. Miss. 1977—78, 1981—82), Miss. Bar Assn. (bd. dirs. young lawyers divsn. 1976—79, chmn. sect. corp. fin. bus. law 1989—90, pres. fellows young lawyers divsn. 2000—01), Washington County Hist. Soc. (pres. 1981), Greenville C. of C. (bd. dirs. 1976—79, pres. 1992—93), Kiwanis (Greenville pres. 1978—79, lt. gov. 1982—83), Oxford & Cambridge Golfing Soc. (Rye, Eng.), Annandale Golf Club (Madison, Miss.), Huntercombe Golf Club (Nuffield, Eng.), Greenville Golf and Country Club (v.p. 1977—79), Vincents Club (Oxford, Eng.), Phi Beta Kappa. Episcopalian. Home: 315 Wetherbee St Greenville MS 38701 Office: Phelps Dunbar LLP PO Box 23066 PO Box 16114 Jackson MS 39236-6114 Office Phone: 601-360-9347. Personal E-mail: hafter@tecinfo.net. Business E-Mail: hafterj@phelps.com.*

HAGAN, KAY RUTHVEN, United States Senator from North Carolina; b. Shelby, NC, Mar. 26, 1953; d. Joseph P. Ruthven and Jeanette (Chiles) Rithven; m. Chip Hagan; 3 children. BA in American Studies, Fla. State U., 1975; JD, Wake Forest U., 1978. Bar: NC. Pvt. law practice, Shelby, NC; mem. Dist. 32 NC State Senate, Raleigh, 1999—2003, mem. Dist. 27, 2003—09; US Senator from NC, 2009—; mem. US House Health, Edn. Labor & Pensions Com., 2009—, US House Armed Services Com., 2009—, US House Small Bus & Entrepreurship Com., 2009—, US Senate Banking Com., 2011—. Named one of North Carolina's 10 Most Effective Senators, NC Ctr. for Public Policy Rsch. Democrat. Presbyterian. Office: US Senate 521 Dirksen Senate Office Building Washington DC 20510 also: 310 New Bern Ave Raleigh NC 27601 Office Phone: 202-224-6342, 919-856-4630.*

HAGE, LILLIAN C., organization administrator, director, dean; d. McKinley H. and Doris Trent; Masters, Marshall U., Huntington, W.Va., 1978; Doctorate, Truth and Liberty Bible Coll., Hurricane, W.Va., 2005. Teen dir. Hurricane Bible Coll., 1977—2011; prin. Truth and Liberty Ch. Sch., Hurricane, 1979—2011; dir. program activities Camp Grace, Milton, W.Va., 1994—2010; academic dean Truth and Liberty Bible Coll., Hurricane, 1996—2011; asst. to CEO Faith Mission, Hurricane, 2001—11; tchr. risk young adults, 2012—. Avocations: water color, flower arranging, interior decorating. Personal E-mail: lilie1954@yahoo.com.

HAGEE, MICHAEL W., foundation administrator, retired military officer; b. Va., Dec. 1, 1944; BS in Engring. with distinction, U.S. Naval Acad., 1968; MSEE, U.S. Naval Postgrad. Sch., 1969; MA in Nat. Security/Strategic Studies, Naval War Coll., 1987; Grad., Command and Staff Coll., 1982, U.S. Naval War Coll., 1987. Commd. 2d lt. USMC, 1968, advanced through grades to gen., 2003, ret., 2006; command positions include 1st Btn., 8th Marines, 1988-90; dir. humanities & social sci. divsn. US Naval Acad., 1990—92; commanding officer 11th Marine Expeditionary Unit, 1992-93; various to exec. asst. to asst. commandant USMC, 1993-94; dir. character devel. divsn. US Naval Acad., 1994-95; sr. mil. asst. to dep. sec. US Dept. Def., Washington, 1995-96; exec. asst. to dir. CIA, Washington, 1995-96; dep. dir. ops. US European Command, Stuttgart, Germany, 1996-98; dir. strategic planning and policy US Pacific Command, 1999—2000; commd. gen. I Marine Expeditionary Force, 2000—02; comdt. USMC, Washington, 2003—06; pres., CEO Adm. Nimitz Found., Fredericksburg, Tex., 2009—. Decorated Def. Disting. Svc. medal, Legion of Merit with two gold stars, Bronze Star with Combat "V", Def. Meritorious Svc. medal, Def. Superior Svc. medal, Meritorious Svc. medal with one gold star, Navy Achievement medal with one gold star, Joint Meritorious Unit award, Combat Action Ribbon, Southwest Asia Svc. medal, Nat. Def. Svc. medal, Armed Forces Expeditionary medal, Nat. Intelligence Disting. Svc. medal, Vietnam Svc. medal, Vietnam Campaign medal, Kuwait Liberation medal Office: Admiral Nimitz Foundation 328 E Main St Fredericksburg TX 78624

HAGEN, MICHAEL DALE, family physician educator; b. St. Louis, Nov. 11, 1949; s. Hubert Dale and Gwendel (Carden) Hagen; m. Barbara Carroll Keifer, Aug. 21, 1971; children: Laura Carrol, Sandra Ann. BS in Biology, Denison U., 1971; MD cum laude, U. Mo., Columbia, 1975. Cert. family practice bd. Pvt. practice Family Medicine Assocs., Aurora, Mo., 1978—81; asst. prof. dept. family practice U. Ky., Lexington, 1981—87, assoc. prof. dept. family practice, 1987—92, prof. dept. family practice, 1993—, interim chmn. dept. family practice, 1992—93, assoc. chmn. dept. family practice, 1993—97, project dir., computer-based assessment, 1996—; assoc. dir. assessment methods Am. Bd. Family Practice, 2003—05; v.p. assessment methods devel. Am. Bd. Family Medicine, 2005—07, sr. v.p., 2008—. Fellow clin. decision making New Eng. Med. Ctr., Boston, 1987—89; at-large dir. Am. Bd. Family Practice, Lexington, 1991—96, pres., 1995—96; residency rev. com. family practice Accreditation Coun. for Grad. Med. Edn., Chgo., 1994—97. Author: Saunders Review Family Practice, 1992, 1997, 2002; contbr. articles to profl. jours. Mem.: AMA, Omicron Delta Kappa, Soc. for Med. Decision Making, Am. Acad. Family Physicians (clin. policies task force 1994—95), Phi Kappa Phi, Alpha Omega Alpha. Presbyterian. Avocations: amateur radio, gardening. Home: 2012 Blairmore Rd Lexington KY 40502-2435 Office: Am Bd Family Medicine 1648 McGrathiana Pky 5th Fl Lexington KY 40511 Office Phone: 888-995-5700. Business E-Mail: hagen@theabfm.org. E-mail: hagenmd@prodigy.net.

HAGEN, RICHARD J., JR., brokerage house executive; BA in Bus. and Mktg., Southampton Coll. Pres. SureTrade; v.p. retail brokerage divsn. FOLIOfn; head online brokerage strategy H&R Block; co-founder, pres., COO TradeKing, Charlotte, NC, 2006—. Office: TradeKing PO Box 49050 Charlotte NC 28277-3432 E-mail: rhagen@tradeking.com.

HAGEN, VERONICA M., textile manufacturing company executive; b. 1947; BS in Internat. Rels., U. So. Calif., LA; attended exec. edn. program in fin., U. Pa. Wharton Sch., Phila.; attended exec. leadership program, Harvard U., Mass. Entrepreneur in the metals industry; pres. Metal Sales Assocs.; exec. v.p. distbn. and indsl. products Alumax, Inc., Cressona, Pa., 1996—98; joined Alcoa, Inc., 1998, v.p. Alcoa North Am. Extrusions, 2000—03, exec. v.p. engineered products bus., pres. engineered products, 2001—03, v.p., chief customer officer, 2003—04; pres., CEO Sappi Fine Paper N.Am., 2004—07; CEO, bd. dirs. Polymer Group, Inc., 2007—. Former bd. dirs. Covanta Energy Corp., Jacuzzi Brands; bd. dirs. Newmont Mining Corp. of Canada Ltd., 2005—, Southern Co., 2008—. Mem.: The Econ. Club Chgo., Chgo. Network, Women Corp. Dirs., The Com. of 200 (dir. at large). Office: Polymer Group Inc 9335 Harris Corners Pky Ste 300 Charlotte NC 28269 Office Phone: 704-697-5100. Office Fax: 704-697-5116. Business E-Mail: veronica.hagen@polymergroupinc.com.

HAGER, BILL, state legislator; b. Pipestone, Minn., Feb. 6, 1947; BA in Math., U. No. Iowa, Cedar Falls, 1969; MEd, U. Hawaii, Honolulu, 1972; JD, U. Ill., Urbana-Champaign, 1974. Adminstrv. asst. US House of Representatives, Washington; mid. sch. math. tchr.; mem. West Des Moines Sch. Bd.; asst. atty. gen. Office of Atty. Gen., Iowa; from first dep. commr. ins. to commr. ins. State of Iowa; atty., reinsurance arbitrator; mem. Boca Raton City Coun., Fla., 2002—09; dep. mayor City of Boca Raton; mem. Dist. 87 Fla. House of Representatives, 2011—. Republican. Office: 301 Yamato Rd Boca Raton FL 33431-6607 also: Fla House of Reps 1101 The Capitol 402 S Monroe St Tallahassee FL 32399-1300 Office Phone: 561-470-6607, 850-488-2234.

HAGER, JOHN HENRY, former lieutenant governor and homeland security director, former federal agency administrator; b. Durham, NC, Aug. 28, 1936; m. Margaret Dickinson Chase, Feb. 27, 1971; children: John Virgil, Henry Chase. BSME, Purdue U., 1958; MBA, Harvard U., 1960; degree (hon.), Averett Coll., 1999, Mary Washington Coll., 1999, U. No. Va., 1999. Various positions Am. Tobacco Co., 1961—84; lt. gov. Commonwealth of Va., Richmond, 1998—2002; asst. to the Gov. for Commonwealth Preparedness State of Va., Richmond, 2002—04; asst. sec. for spl. edn. & rehabilitation svc. US Dept. Edn., Washington, 2004—07; chmn. Va. Rep. Party, Richmond, 2007—08. Past chmn. Disability Commn., Faith Based Cmty. Svcs. Task Force; past co-chmn. Com. on Ednl. Infrastructure; past vice-chmn. Gov.'s Commn. on Transp. Policy; bd. dir., past vice-chair Aerospace State Assn.; dir. Jamestown Yorktown Found. Inc.; hon. chmn. Greater Richmond Conv. Ctr.; dir., chmn. Sorensen Inst. Polit. Leadership; dir. Ctr. for Politics, past dir. Jamestown 2007, Jamestown Yorktown Fdn., Va. Free, Thomas Jefferson Inst. Pub. Policy; dir. Lead Va., Va. 21, Va.; chmn., sr. navigator; chmn. Stratford Hall Nat. Coun.; former mem. US Access Bd.; past dir. Partnership for Urban Va., Greater Richmond Chamber., Va. State C of C; trustee, exec. com., fin. com. Va. Mus. Fine Arts; 1st v.p., dir. Va. Pub. Safety Found., Inc.; past pres., trustee, exec. com. Children's Hosp.; Met. Richmond Conv. and Vis. Bur. (past chmn., dir., founding dir.); Va. Health Care Found. (past chmn., dir., exec. com.); 7th Dist. Rep. Party (past vice chmn. 3rd district, exec. com. mem. past precinct, ward and campaign chmn.); Rep. Party of Va. and del./alt. to 9 natl. convs. (past treas. chmn., past exec. com. mem., state ctrl. com. mem.); ruling elder 1st Presbyn. Ch., Richmond; mem. drug task force Va. State Crime Commn. 2nd lt. U.S. Army, 1960-61, capt. USAR., dir. Richmond Convention & Visitor Bureau. 2nd lt. US Army. Named one of The Outstanding Young Men of America, 1976, Man of Yr., Tobacco Internat. Mag., 1990; named a Disting. Engring. Alumnus, Purdue Sch. Engring., 2007; recipient Alumni Citizenship award Purdue U., 1987, Svc. award Richmond Rep. Com., 1992, Disting. Alumni award Durham Acad., 1992, Good Govt. award Richmond First Club, 1996, Tourism Leadership award Met. Richmond Convention and Visitors Bur., 1997, Lettie Pate Whitehead Evans award Westminster-Canterbury, 1997, Citizenship award Va. Coun. Indians, 1998, Heritage award, Radford U., 2000, Vol. Fundraiser of Yr. award ARC, 2004, Humanitarian award Nat. Conf. Cmty. & Justice, 2002, Volunteer Fundraiser of the Yr. award, Am. Red Cross, 2004, Father of Yr. award, 2006, Richmond Bus. Hall Of Fame, 2012, Outstanding Virginian award, 2012. Mem. Am. Legion, Va. C. of C. (dir.), Nat. Assn. Lt. Govs. (mem. exec. com., So. sector chmn.), So. Growth Policies Bd., Adv. Bd. Tobacco History Corp., Jamestown-Yorktown Found., Richmond Rep. Party Com., Richmond German, Richmond Hundred (past pres., dir.), City of Richmond Electoral Bd. (past chmn.) Pub. Affairs Group (past chmn.), Forum Club (past pres.), Commonwealth Club (past dir.), Custis Fishing and Hunting Club (dir.), Country Club Va. (past pres. and CEO, past dir.), West Chop Club(dir.), Maymont Found. (past pres., dir.). Republican. E-mail: johnhager1@comcast.net.

HAGER, MIKE, state legislator; Mem. Dist. 112 NC House of Representatives, 2004, 2011—. Republican. Office: 342 Walking Horse Trail Rutherfordton NC 28139 Address: North Carolina House of Representatives 300 N Salisbury St 306C Raleigh NC 27603-5925 Office Phone: 828-748-2378, 919-733-5749. Business E-Mail: Mike.Hager@ncleg.net.

HAGERMAN, JOHN DAVID, lawyer, investment advisor; b. Houston, Aug. 1, 1941; s. David Angle and Noima L. (Clay) H.; m. Linda J. Lambright, June 25, 1975; children: Clayton Robert, Holly Elizabeth. BBA, So. Meth. U., 1963; JD, U. Tex., Austin, 1966. Bar: Tex. 1966, U.S. Ct. Appeals (5th cir.) 1967, U.S. Supreme Ct. 1969; cert. civil trial law, 1980-95; real estate broker Tex. Pres., owner Hagerman & Sereau, Inc., The Woodlands, Tex., 1966—. Condr. bank creditor rights seminars; mem. adv. bd. Amegy Bank. Contbr. articles to profl. jours. Res. dep. sheriff Montgomery County, Tex.; former bd. dirs. 100 club of Montgomery County Fair Assn., 1978—, Montgomery County Hosp. Dist. Found., Seven Coves Homeowners Assn. Mem.: ABA, Houston Philosophy Soc., Comml. Real Estate Assn. Montgomery County, Tex. Assn. Bank Counsel, Tex. Assn. Civil Trial Specialists, Houston Outdoor Advt. Assn., Houston Bar Assn., Tex. Bar Assn., River Oaks Country Club, Briar Club, Woodlands Country Club, Petroleum Club (Houston), Woodlands Rotary Club, Beta Theta Pi. Republican. Avocations: golf, tennis, jogging, shooting. Office: Hagerman & Seureau Inc 24800 I-45 Ste 100 The Woodlands TX 77386-1987 Office Phone: 281-367-8800.

HAGGARD, MERLE RONALD, musician; b. Bakersfield, Calif., Apr. 6, 1937; s. James Frances and Flossie Mae (Harp) H.; m. Leona Hobbs, 1957 (div. 1964); children: Dana, Marty, Kelli, Noel; m. Bonnie Owens, Jan. 28, 1968 (div. 1978); m. Leona Williams, Oct. 7, 1978 (div. 1983); m. Debbie Parret, June 1, 1985 (div. 1991); m. Theresa Lane, Sept. 11, 1993; children: Jenessa, Benion. Grad. high sch. Rec. artist Capitol Records, 1963-76, Tally Records, 1977—, MCA Records, 1977-81, CBS Records, 1981-89, Curb Records, 1990—; pres. Shade Tree Music Pub. Co., 1970—, Hag Prodns. Inc., 1973—. Singer: (solo albums) Strangers, 1965, Swinging Doors and the Bottle Let Me Down, 1966, I'm a Lonesome Fugitive, 1967, Branded Man/I Threw Away the Rose, 1967, Sing Me Back Home, 1968, The Legend of Bonnie and Clyde, 1968, The Best of Merle Haggard, 1968, Mama Tried, 1968, Pride in What I Am, 1969, Okie from Muskogee, 1969, Merle Haggard Close Up, 1969, Same Train, a Different Time, 1969, A Portrait of Merle Haggard, 1969, A Tribute to the Best Damn Fiddle Player in the World (Or, My Salute to Bob Wills), 1970, The Fightin' Side of Me, 1970, Hag, 1971, Someday We'll Look Back, 1971, The Land of Many Churches, 1971, Let Me Tell You About a Song, 1972, It's Not Love (But It's Not Bad), 1972, The Best of the Best, 1972, I Love Dixie Blues, 1973, A Chrismas Present (Something Old, Something New), 1973, If We Make It Through December, 1974, Merle Haggard Presents His 30th Album, 1974, Keep Movin' On, 1975, It's All in the Moves, 1976, My Love Affair with Trains, 1976, The Roots of My Raising, 1976, Ramblin' Fever, 1977, A Working Man Can't Get Nowhere Today, 1977, Songs I'll Always Sing, 1977, My Farewell to Elvis, 1977, Eleven Winners, 1978, I'm Always on a Mountain When I Fall, 1978, The Way it Was in '51, 1978, Serving 190 Proof, 1979, The Way I Am, 1980, Back to the Barrooms, 1980, Big City, 1981, Rainbow Stew-Live at Anaheim Stadium, 1981, Songs for the Mama That Tried, 1981, Greatest Hits, 1982, Going Where the Lonely Go, 1982, Going Home for Christmas, 1982, That's the Way Love Goes, 1983, It's All in the Game, 1984, His Epic Hits, The First Eleven...To Be Continued, 1984, Kern River, 1985, Amber Waves of Grain, 1985, Merle Haggard: His Best, 1985, A Friend in California, 1986, Out Among the Stars, 1986, A Friend in California, 1986, Chill Factor, 1988, Merle Haggard's Greatest Hits, 1988, 5:01 Blues, 1989, Blue Jungle, 1990, Super Hits, 1993, Merle Haggard 1994, 1994, Super Hits, Vol. 2, 1994, Merle Haggard 1996, 1996, 16 Biggest Hits, 1998, Live at Billy Bob's Texas, 1999, Ford the Record, 43 Legenday Hits, 1998, 40 #1's, 2004, Ultimate Collection, 2000, If I Could Only Fly, 2000, A Cabin in the Hills, 2001, The Peer Sessions, 2002, Haggard Like Never Before, 2003, I Wish I Was Santa Claus, 2004, Unforgettable, 2004, Chicago Wind, 2005, Tough Country Heroes, 2006, Hag, The Best of Merle Haggard, 2006, The Bluegrass Sessions, 2007, Hag's Christmas, 2007, Live from Austin, Texas '78, 2008, I Am What I Am, 2010, Working in Tennessee, 2011; (albums with Bonnie Ownes) Just Between the Two of Us, 1966; (albums with The Strangers) Instrumental Sounds of Merle Haggard's Strangers, 1969, Introducing My Friends the Strangers, 1970, Getting to Know the Strangers, 1970, Honky Tonkin', 1971, Totally Instrumental...With One Exception, 1973; (albums with Willie Nelson) Pancho and Lefty, 1981, Seashores of Old Mexico, 1987; (albums with George Jones) A Taste of Yesterday's Wine, 1982, Kicking Out the Footlights...Again, 2001; (albums with Leona Williams) Heart to Heart, 1983; (with Willie Nelson and George Jones) Walking the Line, 1987; (albums with Albert E. Brumley), Two Old Friends, 2001; (albums with Willie Nelson & Ray Price), Last of the Breed, 2007; actor: (TV appearances) Doc Elliot, 1974, The Waltons, 1976, Centennial, 1979; (TV movies) Huckleberry Finn, 1975, All American Cowboy, 1985; author: Sing Me Back Home, 1981, Down Every Road, 1996, My House of Memories, 1999 Inducted into Nashville Songwriters Hall of Fame, 1977, Country Music Hall of Fame, 1994, Okla. Music Hall of Fame, 1997; recipient 18 awards Acad. Country and Western Music, 56 Achievement awards Broadcast Music Inc., 7 awards Shade Tree Music Pub., 7 gold album awards, 1 platinum album award, 4 awards Music City News, Kennedy Ctr. Honors, John F. Kennedy Ctr. for Performing Arts, 2010; named Songwriter of Yr., Nashville Songwriters Assn. 1970, 81, also 5 outstanding writer achievement awards; Grammy award for Best Male Country Vocal Performance, 1984, Country Collaboration with Vocals, 1998, Poets award, Acad. Country Music, 2009. Mem. Country Music Assn. (6 awards), Am. Fedn. TV and Rec. Artists, Screen Actors Guild, Am. Fedn. Musicians. Office: c/o Bobby Roberts Co Inc PO Box 1547 Goodlettsville TN 37070-1547

HAGHIGHI, ALIAKBAR MONTAZER, mathematics probability and statistics, queueing theory educator; arrived in USA, 1985, naturalized, 1992; s. Mohammed Ali and Roghayeh (Jaafari) M.; m. Shanin Hamidi, Feb. 20, 1971; children: Mahyar, Mahroo. BA in Math., San Francisco State U., Calif., 1966; MA in Applied Maths., San Francisco State U., 1971; PhD in Probability and Statis. Queueing Theory, Case Western Res. U., Cleve., 1976. Cert. in tchg. CC. Asst. prof. Inst. Statistics, Tehran, 1968-81; assoc. prof. Nat. U. Iran, Tehran, 1981-85; vis. scientist McMaster U., Hamilton, Ont., Can., 1984; lectr. Mt. San Antonio Coll., Walnut, Calif., 1985; vis. prof. Calif. State U., Fullerton, 1985; assoc. prof. math. Benedict Coll., Columbia, S.C., 1985-88, prof. math., 1988—2002; prof. head dept. maths. Prairie View A&M U., 2002—. Chmn. dept. math. Benedicft Coll., 1988—; lectr. in field; cons. in field. Contbr. articles to profl. jours. Mem. Am. Math. Soc., Soc. Indsl. & Applied Maths., Math. Assn. Am., Iranian Math. Soc., S.C. Acad. Scis. Muslim. Avocations: reading, music. Office: Prairie View A&M University LW Minor St WR Banks Building Prairie View TX 77446 Business E-Mail: amhaghighi@pvamu.edu.

HAGY, DAVID LEE, conductor; b. Indpls., Apr. 16, 1953; s. Lloyd Rollen and Mary Ora (Breeze) H. MusB, Ind. U., 1977; MusM, Yale U., 1984, M Mus. Arts, 1986, D Mus. Arts, 1991. Asst. condr. Ft. Wayne (Ind.) Philharm., 1974-78; music dir. Omaha Area Youth Orchs., 1978-82; asst. condr. Norwalk (Conn.) Symphony, 1987-93; music dir. Salisbury (N.C.) Symphony, 1988—, Greensboro (N.C.) Symphony Youth Orch., 1993-97, Winston-Salem Youth Symphony, 2002—08; asst. condr. Greensboro Symphony, 1993-97; dir. of orch. Wake Forest U. Orch., Winston-Salem, N.C., 1995—. Office: Salisbury Symphony Orch PO Box 4264 Salisbury NC 28145-4264 Business E-Mail: dhagy@wfu.edu.

HAHM, THOMAS X., plastic surgeon; Grad., MD, Emory U., Atlanta; tng. in Gen. Surgery and Plastic Surgery, U. Louisville; surg. tng. in Craniofacial and Cosmetic Surgery, Johns Hopkins U., Balt. Staff plastic surgeon Roper/St. Francis Hosp. System, Trident Health System, East Cooper Hospital; plastic surgeon Carolina Aesthetic Plastic Surgery Inst. Mem.: Am. Soc. of Aesthetic Plastic Surgery (candidate mem.), Am. Soc. of Plastic Surgery (candidate mem.), AMA, SC Med. Assn., Alpha Omega Alpha. Office: Carolina Aesthetic Plastic Surgery Institute 9213-C University Rd Charleston SC 29406 also: Carolina Aesthetic Plastic Surgery Institute 180 Wingo Way Ste 205 Mount Pleasant SC 29464-1811 Office Phone: 843-884-1400.

HAHN, GEORGE THOMAS, materials engineering educator, researcher; b. Vienna, July 28, 1930; came to U.S., 1938; s. Rudolph and Stella (Honig) H.; m. Frances Cutler, May 24, 2009; children: Claudia Abbott, Elizabeth. BSME, NYU, 1952; MS in Metall. Engring., Columbia U., 1956; ScD in Metall. Engring., MIT, 1959. Rsch. engr. Westinghouse Rsch. Labs., Pitts., 1952; cons. Mfg. Labs., Cambridge, Mass., 1956-60; rsch. assoc. metal sci. sect. Battelle Meml. Inst., Columbus, Ohio, 1960-66, mgr. metal sci. sect., 1966-79; prof. materials sci. and engring. Vanderbilt U., Nashville, 1979-98, prof. materials sci. and engring. emeritus, 1998—, chmn. dept. materials sci. and engring., 1988-93; co-dir. Ctr. Materials Tribology, Nashville, 1987-96; pres. Mechanics & Materials Techs. Inc., Nashville, 1988—. Co-editor: Fracture, 1959, Fast Fracture and Crack Arrest, 1977, Crack Arrest Methods, 1980; co-author: Structural Shear Joints, 2005; contbr. numerous articles to profl. jours. Capt. USAF, 1953—57. Fellow Am. Soc. Metals (Campbell Meml. Lectr. 1981), Metall. Soc. Avocation: painting. Office: Vanderbilt U Dept Mech Engring Box 1592 Sta B Nashville TN 37235 Personal E-mail: georgethahn@comcast.net.

HAHN, JOHN WILLIAM, retired insurance company executive; b. NYC, July 12, 1940; s. Ferdinand J. and Evelyn H. H. (Hauser) Hahn; m. L. Dale Mazza, 1963; children: Nancy, John. BA, Queen's Coll., 1962; postgrad., Harvard U., Cambridge, Mass., 1973-74. With Atlantic Mut. Cos., NYC, 1963—2002, v.p., adminstrv. svcs., 1963—2002, sr. v.p., adminstrv. svcs. Roanoke, Va., 1978-85, exec. v.p., adminstrn. Madison, NJ, 1985—2002; exec. cons., 2002—. Mem. exec. com., bd. dirs. Ins. Value Added Network Svc., Conn., 1985—92; mem. std. com. Agy. Co. Orgn. R & D; spl. advisor Artbase, NYC, 2003—; bd. dirs. Luxury Market Coun. With USMC, 1959—66. Mem.: Alliance Productive Tech. (chmn. bd. dirs. 1997—98), Mil. Family Support Ctr., Inc. (exec. v.p. 2005—10), AGENA Corp. (chmn. bd. dirs. 1993—95), Waters Edge Country Club, Hidden Valley Country Club (Va.), Harvard Club (NYC). Home: 85 Loving Cir Penhook VA 24137-5225 Office Phone: 540-798-5420. Personal E-mail: pmd261@aol.com.

HAIDET, JEFFREY K., lawyer; BA, Miami U., Ohio, 1982; JD magna cum laude, U. Toledo, Ohio, 1985. Bar: Ga. Ptnr. McKenna Long & Aldridge LLP, Atlanta, chmn. Contbr. articles to profl. jours. Youth basketball and soccer coach; mem. dean's adv. coun. U. Toledo Coll Law; bd. dirs. Nat. Commerce Club, St. Joseph's Mercy Found., Ga. C. of C.; bd. dirs., gen. counsel Points of Light/Hands on Network; gen. counsel 2004 G-8 Organizing Com. Mem.: ABA, Ga. Bar Assn., Atlanta Bar Assn. Office: McKenna Long & Aldridge LLP 303 Peachtree St NE Ste 5300 Atlanta GA 30308-3265 Office Phone: 404-527-4012. Office Fax: 404-527-4198. Business E-Mail: jhaidet@mckennalong.com.

HAIK, RICHARD T., SR., federal judge; b. Lafayette, La., 1950; BS, U. SW La., 1971; JD, Loyola U., New Orleans, 1975. Assoc. Haik & Broussard, 1975-79; ptnr. Haik, Broussard & Haik, 1979-81, Haik, Haik & Minvielle, 1981-84; judge La. State Dist., New Iberia, 1984-91, US Dist. Ct. (we. Dist.) La., Lafayette, 1991—2002, 2009—, chief judge, 2002—09. With USAR, 1978-81; USNG, 1971-78. Mem.: La. Dist. Judge's Assn. (exec. com. 1988—91), Nat. Coun. Juvenile and Family Ct. Judges (steering com. alcohol and substance abuse), Iberia Parish Bar Assn., La. Bar Assn., ABA. Office: US Dist Ct 800 Lafayette St Ste 4200 Lafayette LA 70501-6879

HAIKALA, MADELINE HUGHES, federal judge; b. New Orleans, 1964; BA, Williams Coll., 1986; JD, Tulane U. Law Sch., 1989. Atty. Lightfoot, Franklin & White LLC, Birmingham, Ala., 1989—2011; magistrate judge US Dist. Ct. (northern dist.) Ala., 2012—13, judge, 2013—. Adj. prof. appellate law Cumberland Sch. Law, 1998—2005. Office: US District Court Hugo Black Courthouse 1729 5th Ave N Birmingham AL 35203 Office Phone: 205-731-1712.*

HAIL, KAREN LEE, bank executive; b. 1954; 4 adopted children. Founding exec. officer MidSouth Bancorp, 1984—, bd. dirs., 1988—, sr. exec. v.p., COO; CFO, dir. MidSouth Bank (subsidiary of MidSouth Bancorp). Mem. technology com. Independent Community Bankers of Am. Active Big Brothers/Big Sisters. Named one of 25 Women to Watch, US Banker, 2005, 2006, 2008, 25 Most Powerful Women in Banking, 2007. Office: Midsouth Bancorp 102 Versailles Blvd Lafayette LA 70501

HAIL, MICHAEL WAYNE, political science professor; b. 1966; AB in Internat. Economics, Ctr. Coll. Ky., 1989; MA in Govt., Eastern Ky. U., 1992; PhD in Polit. Sci., U. Del., 2003. Adj. instr. polit. sci. U. Del., Newark, Del., 1992—95; dir. rural telecom. policy inst. U. Ky., Lexington, Ky., 1995—98, dir. planning, policy, & rsch. Ctr. Rural Develop., 1995—98, assoc. dir. Inst. Federalism & Intergovernmental Relations, 2004—; adj. instr. govt. Eastern Ky. U., Richmond, Ky., 1996—98; adj. asst. prof. polit. sci. U. NC, Greensboro, NC, 1998—99, rsch. assoc. Bryan Sch. Bus. & Econ., 1998—99, assoc. dir. Ctr. Study of Social Issues, 1998—99; dir. rsch., asst. to dean of IRAPP Morehead State U., Morehead, Ky., 2000—06, adj. asst. prof. govt., 2000—01, asst. prof. govt., 2001—06, spl. asst. to pres. for fed. govt. rels., 2004—08, dir. MPA program, IRAPP, 2007—, asst. dean IRAPP, 2007—, assoc. prof. govt., 2007—. Bd. trustees Harry S. Truman Scholarship Found., 2013—. Named Faculty Mem. of Yr., Morehead State U., 2007. Mem.: Ky. Polit. Sci. Assn. (pres. 2007, assoc. exec. sec. 2008—13), Midwestern Polit. Sci. Assn., Southern Polit. Sci. Assn. (program com. conf. 2005, 2009), Am. Polit. Sci. Assn. (mem. governing coun. 2007—10, Teaching Excellence award 2008), Pi Sigma Alpha (Hon. award 1992, Teaching Excellence award 2008). Office: Morehead State University Inst Regional Analysis & Public Policy UPO Box 699 Morehead KY 40351 Office Phone: 606-783-5407. Personal E-mail: mc_hail@yahoo.com. Business E-Mail: m.hail@morehead-st.edu.*

HAILE, LAWRENCE BARCLAY, lawyer; b. Atlanta, Feb. 19, 1938; children: Gretchen Vanderhoof, Eric McKenzie (dec.), Scott McAllister. BA in Econs, U. Tex., 1958, LLB, 1961. Bar: Tex. 1961, Calif. 1962. Law clk. to U.S. Judge Joseph M. Ingraham, Houston, 1961-62; pvt. practice San Francisco, 1962-67, LA, 1967—. Instr. UCLA Civil Trial Clinics, 1974, 76; lectr. law Calif. Continuing Edn. of Bar, 1973-74, 80-89; nat. panel arbitrators Am. Arbitration Assn., 1965—. Mem. editl. bd. Tex. Law Rev, 1960-61; contbr. articles profl. jours. Mem. State Bar Calif., Tex., U.S. Supreme Ct. Bar Assn., Internat. Assn. Property Ins. Counsel (founding mem., pres. 1980), Vintage Motorsports Coun. (past pres.), Phi Delta Phi, Delta Sigma Rho. Office: 2503 Canyon Creek Dr Richardson TX 75080 Office Phone: 310-415-8516. Personal E-mail: hailelaw@aol.com.*

HAILEY, JAMES R., health insurance company executive, pharmacist; MBA, St. Joseph's U.; PharmD, U. Miss. With SmithKlineBeecham Pharm. Co.; various positions including v.p. specialty markets, chief pharmacy officer, sr. v.p. pharmacy svcs., exec. v.p. prescription mgmt. svcs. Coventry Health Care, Inc., 1994—2009; sr. v.p., pres. pharm. ops. HealthSpring, Inc., 2009—. Mem. Am. Pharmacists Assn., Joint Commn. of Pharmacy Practitioners, Acad. of Managed Care Pharmacy; pres. The Found. of Managed Care Pharmacy. Fellow: Acad. Managed Care Pharmacy (mem. membership com., chmn. pharm. industry rels. com., dir.); mem.: Am. Pharmacist Assn. Office: HealthSpring Inc Ste 501 9009 Carothers Pky Franklin TN 37067 Office Phone: 615-291-7000. Office Fax: 615-401-4566.

HAIMAN, ROBERT JAMES, editor, journalist, educator, media consultant, expert witness, critic; b. Norwich, Conn., May 6, 1936; s. Albert and Letta (Cone) H.; m. Elizabeth Royce Greenlaw, Sept. 26, 1964 (div. Aug. 1996); 1 child, Robert Greenlaw. Student, U. Conn., 1953-55; BS, U. Fla., 1957. Reporter St. Petersburg (Fla.) Times, 1958-60, copy editor, 1962-63, nat. editor, 1964-66, mng. editor, 1966-76, exec. editor, 1976-83; pres., mng. dir. Poynter Inst. Media Studies, 1983-96, pres. emeritus and disting. editor in residence, 1997—. Bd. dir. Times Pub. Co., St. Petersburg; trustee Fla. InterAm. Scholarship Found.; mem. minority mgmt. task force Inst. Journalism Edn. Mem. pres. round table Eckerd Coll.; trustee Poynter Inst. Media Studies, St. Petersburg; mem. Pulitzer Prize jury, 1977, 90, 91, 96, 97; internat. adv. bd. Inst. Advancement Journalism, Johannesburg, South Africa; mem. nat. adv. bd. Inst. for Journalists and Pub. Policy Gordon Pub. Policy Ctr. Brandeis U.; expert witness. Mem. bd. advisors U. Fla. Coll. Journalism and Comms.; elder Presbyn. Ch.; trustee Bayfront City Found.; sr. fellow Freedom Forum, Washington, 1998—; mem. Pres.'s coun. U. Fla., U. South Fla., chmn. campus adv. bd., 1989—91; mem. adv. bd. U. Fla. Internat. Ctr.; mem. journalism adv. bd. Knight Found., Inst. Current World Affairs, Hanover, NH, Tampa Bay Com. Coun. on Fgn. Rels. With USMC, 1961. Named Disting. Alumnus, U. Fla., 1988. Mem. AP Mng. Editors Assn. (pres. 1982), Am. Soc. Newspaper Editors (dir. 1992-98), Internat. Press Inst. (Vienna), World Editors Forum (Paris), Interam. Press Assn. Miami, St. Petersburg Yacht Club, Dragon Club, Quarterback Club, Golden Triangle Club, Soc. Profl. Journalists. Independent. Home: 5155 Isla Key Blvd S Apt 103 Saint Petersburg FL 33715-1687 Office: 801 3rd St S Saint Petersburg FL 33701-4920

HAIN, J. TRAVIS, bank executive; BSBA, Washington U.; MBA, Duke U. Joined Bank of America Corp., 1985; founding ptnr. Banc of America Capital Investors, 1993; joined Bank of America Merrill Lynch Capital Partners, 2002, mng. dir., global head, 2009—. Former bd. dirs. Clean Earth, Inc., Titan Towers, LP, WorldStrides, LLC; bd. dirs. Eurofresh Farms Inc., FlexSol Holding Corp., Bargo Energy Co., 1999—, Muzak Holdings Fin. Corp., 2006—, Muzak Holdings LLC, 2006—, Hertz Corp., 2009—, Hertz Global Holdings, Inc., 2009—. Office: Bank of America 100 N Tryon St Charlotte NC 28255 Office Phone: 980-386-4710. Office Fax: 980-386-6432. Business E-Mail: jh@muzak.com.

HAINES, DAVID W., social sciences educator; b. Middletown, NY, Apr. 15, 1947; s. Howard B. and Grace S. Haines; m. Karen E. Rosenblum, Jan. 31, 1986. PhD, Am. U., Wash., 1976. Adminstrv. mgr. VA Workers' Compensation Commn., Richmond, Va., 1990—97; prof. George Mason U., Fairfax, Va., 1997—2008. Pres. Soc. Urban, Nat. and Transnational, Global Anthropology, Arlington, Va., 2006—08. Author: (monograph) The Limits of Kinship: South Vietnamese Households, (textbook) Cultural Anthropology: Adaptations, Structures, Meanings; editor: Refugees in America in the 1990s. Recipient Thcg. Excellence award, George Mason U. Office: George Mason Univ Soan 3g5 Fairfax VA 22030 Business E-Mail: dhaines1@gmu.edu.

HAINES, KENNETH H., sports television broadcasting and marketing executive; b. Spokane, Sept. 5, 1942; s. Kenneth A. and Helen Elizabeth (Evans) H.; m. Stephanie Marie Phelps, Nov. 23, 1981; 1 child, Avery Jordan. BA, Dakota Wesleyan U., 1964; MA, U. Wyo.; MS, Troy State U., 1970; CAGS, Va. Tech., 1976. News dir. KORN TV, Mitchell, SD, 1962-64; sta. mgr. KUWR Radio, Laramie, Wyo., 1965-67; gen. mgr. KLME Radio, Laramie, 1967-68; instr. flight ops. U.S. Army, Ft. Rucker, Ala., 1968-70; from dir. radio, tv, film to dir. pub. affairs, univ. rels. Va. Tech., Blacksburg, 1970-81; from exec. v.p., COO to pres., CEO, Raycom Sports, Charlotte, NC, 1981—2002, pres., CEO, 2002—. Exec. prodr. Elvis Graceland, 1987-97; bd. dirs. Charlotte Sports Commn., ACC Properties; trustee Dakota Wesleyan U.; exec. dir. Continental Tire Bowl, 2002—; mem. Tar Heel of the Week; 2005; bd. dirs. Charlotte Coll. Football, 2010-. Bd. dirs. Sunshine Football Classic, 1989—2000, Charlotte Basketball Challenge, 1987—90, Diet Pepsi Tournament Champions, 1988-2001, Blockbuster Bowl, 1990-93; tournament dir. LPGA Golf, 1997—; exec. dir. Continental Tire Bowl, Meineke Car Care Bowl, 2002-09 Named Reporter of Yr., UPI, 1967, Opperman Disting. Lectr., Dakota Wesleyan U., 1998, Outstanding TV Sports Exec., All-Am. Football Found., 1999, Outstanding Bowl Dir., Football Found., 2004, Alumnus of Yr., Dakota Wesleyan U., 2005; recipient golden award Coun. Support Higher Edn., 1978, 4th Most Powerful award Atlantic Coast Conf., Orlando, Sentinel, 2009., Pres. award Atlantic Coast Conf., 2011-12 Mem. Am. Assn. Agr. Writers, Am. Coll. Pub. Rels. Assn. (exceptional achievement award 1974), Va. Press Assn., Coun. for Advancement and Support of Edn. (pres. univ. faculty club 1980-82), Nat. Acad. TV Arts and Scis. (judge), Charlotte C. of C. (bd. dirs.), Phi Kappa Delta, Pi Delta Epsilon, Omicron Delta Kappa. Avocations: sports, photography, television, travel, reading. Office: Raycom Sports 1900 W Morehead St Charlotte NC 28208-5228 Home: 1909 Bent Branch Rd Charlotte NC 28226-5500 E-mail: khaines@raycomsports.com, ken9542@aol.com.

HAIR, WILLIAM BATES, III, librarian, dean; b. Gastonia, NC, Mar. 16, 1952; s. William Bates and Lou (Holland) Hair; m. Mary Elizabeth Timanus, Dec. 9, 1972; children: Melissa Bain, Laura Elizabeth, Megan Holland. BS, U. Tenn, 1976; MDiv, Mid-Am. Bapt. Theol. Sem., 1980; MLS, Vanderbilt U., 1982. Sales rep. Groves Thread Co., Gastonia, NC, 1972—73; youth min. Lexa Bapt. Ch., Ark., 1977—78; libr. asst. Mid-Am. Bapt. Theol. Sem., Memphis, 1978—80, cataloger and tech. svcs. head, 1980—82, dir. libr., 1982—88, Golden Gate Bapt. Theol. Seminary, Mill Valley, Calif., 1988—94; faculty mem. Baylor U., Waco, Tex., 1994—, assoc. prof., assoc. dean, dir. Univ. Librs., interim dean librs. Trustee Memphis and Shelby County Pub. Libr. and Info. Ctr., 1983, v.p., 1985, pres., 1986—87. Mem.: ALA, Calif. Library Assn., Southeastern Library Assn., Tenn. Library Assn., Tenn. Theol. Library Assn. (v.p. 1985), Am. Theol. Library Assn., Kappa Sigma, Beta Phi Mu. Republican. Home: 316 Tree Grove Cir Waco TX 76712-6474 Office: Baylor U One Bear Pl #97143 Waco TX 76798 Office Phone: 254-710-3591. Office Fax: 254-741-9855. Business E-Mail: bill_hair@baylor.edu.

HAIRE, ROBERT PHILLIP, state legislator; b. Caretta, Va., May 1, 1936; s. Herman E. and Pauline (Jackson) Haire; m. Constance Mullinnix Haire, May 28, 1983; children from previous marriage: Phillip, Scott, Anne, Tate. BA, U. NC, 1958, JD, 1961. Bar: NC 1961, US Ct. Mil. Appeals 1964, US Supreme Ct. 1965, US Ct. Appeals (4th cir.) 1978. Town atty., Sylva, NC, 1969—; mem. NC House of Representatives, 1999—2002, mem. Dist. 119, 2002—; trustee Western Carolina U., 1993—; mem. Western N.C. Regional Econ. Devel. Commn., 1994—96; asst. majority counsel US Senate Select Com. Presdl. Affairs, Washington, 1973; dir. First Union Nat. Bank, Sylva, WNC Legal Svcs., Sylva. Del. Dem. Nat. Conv., 1972; past lay leader First United Meth. Ch., Sylva; bd. govs. U. NC, Chapel Hill, 1981—93. With JAGC USAF, 1962—65. Mem.: NC Dist. Bar Pres.'s (chair 1993—94). Office: Haire & Bridgers PA 21 Colonial Sq Sylva NC 28779-5147 also: PO Box 727 Sylva NC 28779 also: 300 N Salisbury St Rm 609 Raleigh NC 27603-5925 Office Phone: 919-715-3005, 828-586-1771. E-mail: Phillip.Haire@ncleg.net.

HAIRSTON, WILLIAM, author, poet, playwright, former actor; b. Goldsboro, NC; s. William Russell and Malissa (Carter) H.; m. Enid Carey, June 2, 1957; 1 dau., Ann Marie. BA, U. Northern Colo., Greeley; degree, Columbia & NYU. Mng. editor D.C. Pipeline, 1973-78; pub. adminstr. city govt. Washington; rschr. NY Pub. Libr. Theatre mgr., adminstr. N.Y. Shakespeare Festival, 1963—65, Greenwich Mews Theatre, 1963, Arena Stage, Washington, 1965—66. Prodr.: (plays) Walk in Darkness, Swan Song of the 11th Dawn, Double Dare, Black Antigone; author Ira Aldridge-The London Conflict (Group Theatre's Best Playwright award, 1988), (novels) The World of Carlos, 1968, Sex and Conflict, 1993, Spaced Out!, 1998, Showdown at Sundown, 1999, The History of the National Capital Area Council/BSA, 1998, Passion and Politics, 2001, Swan Song, 2003, It's Human Nature, 2004, Spaced Out! A Space Adventure, 2008, Suburban Ghetto, 2010, (poetry and prose) Passion and Compassion, 2002; author: (prodr., dir.) (plays) Curtain Call Mr. Aldridge, Sir; dir.: (plays) Jerico-Jim Crow; actor: (feature role films) Take the High Ground, 1953; (TV series) Harlem Detective; author: (films) US Informasion Agency: Apollo-11 Man On The Moon, and other stories; actor: (smaller roles in movies and TV shows), (summer stock) The Hasty Heart, Louisana Purchase, Respectful Prostitute, No Time for Sergeants, The Petrified Forest. Former chmn. D.C. Police and Firefighters Retirement and Relief Bd.; active Nat. Capital Area coun. Boy Scouts Am., mem., Schomburg Ctr. Rsch. Black Culture Divsn. NY Pub. Libr. Ford Found. theater grantee Arena Stage, 1965; Nat. Endowment for the Arts lit. grantee, 1967; recipient Silver Beaver award NCAC/BSA, 1988, Meritorious Pub. Svc. award D.C., 1990, Honored Alumni award U. Northern Colo., Appreciation award, Merit award, Outstanding Performance Rating award, Sustained Superior Performance award, Faithful & Dedicated Svc. award, Wash., Meritorius Pub. Svc. award, 1990, Apple Oscar award, Silver Beaver award, Nat. Capital Area Coun., Boy Scouts America, 1988, winner, Group Theatre Playwriting award, Seattle, 1987-88. Mem.: Dramatists Guild.

HAJDIK, LLOYD A., corporate financial executive; BBA cum laude, Tex. State U. CPA. Various positions, audit practice Ernst & Young LLP, 1989—95; contr., Energing. Svcs. Cliffs Drilling Co., 1995—97; various acctg. & fin. positions Shell Oil Co., 1997; contr., Baroid Drilling Fluids and Zonal Isolation Product Svc. Lines Halliburton Co., 1997—2000; sr. mgr., SEC Reporting and Acctg. Svcs. Compaq Computer Corp. (now Hewlett Packard), 2000—02; asst. corp. contr. NL Industries, Inc., 2002—03; v.p., corp. contr. Helix Energy Solutions Group Inc., 2003—08; chief acctg. officer Helix Energy Solutions Group, Inc., 2004—, sr. v.p., fin., 2008—. Mem.: AICPA, Tex. Soc. CPAs. Office: Helix Energy Solutions Group Inc 400 N Sam Houston Pky E Ste 400 Houston TX 77060 Office Phone: 281-618-0400. Office Fax: 281-618-0505. Business E-Mail: lhajdik@helixesg.com.

HAJEK, JOSEF, consumer products company executive; BA in Acctg., DePaul U. Sr. tax mgr. Price Waterhouse, 1987—96; v.p., Tax Tupperware Brands Corp., 2001—06, sr. v.p., Tax and Govt. Affairs, 2006—. Office: Tupperware Brands Corp 14901 S Orange Blossom Trail Orlando FL 32837 Office Phone: 407-826-5050.

HAJEK, OTOMAR, mathematician, educator; b. Beograd, Serbia, Dec. 22, 1930; arrived in U.S., 1966, naturalized, 1974; s. Frantisek Josef and Ruzena (Houdekova) Hajek; m. Olga Barbara Nemcova, Feb. 12, 1955; 1 child, Michael. Diploma in math., Caroline U., Prague, Czech. Rep., 1953, candidate sci., 1963; RNDr, Caroline U., Prague, Czech Rep., 1966. Asst. prof. Czech Inst. Tech., Prague, 1953-56, sr. asst. prof., 1956-60; sci. officer Research Inst. Computing Machinery, Prague, 1960-65; sr. sci. officer Caroline U., Prague, 1965-66; assoc. prof. Case Western Res. U., Cleve., 1966-69, prof. math., 1969—, prof. sys. engring., 1988-96, prof. emeritus, 1996—. Author: (book) Dynamical Systems in the Plane, 1968, Pursuit Games, 1975, 2nd edit., 2008, Control Systems in the Plane, 1991, 2nd edit., 2009; co-author: (book) Local Semi-Dynamical Systems, 1969; co-editor: Global Differentiable Dynamics, 1970. Recipient von Humboldt prize, 1975; Deutsche Forschungsgemeinschaft fellow, Bonn, 1979, 1990, Fulbright fellow, 1990. Mem.: Union Czech Math. and Physicists, Fulbright Assn., von Humboldt Assn., Czechoslovak Soc. Arts and Scis., Am. Math. Soc. Lutheran. Home: 11330 Savannah Dr Fredericksburg VA 22407-9109 Personal E-mail: ohajek1@verizon.net.

HAKE, RALPH F., manufacturing executive; b. Cin., Jan. 25, 1949; m. Robin Hake; 1 child, Mark. BBA, U. Cin., 1971; MBA, U. Chgo., 1975. Joined Mead Corp., 1975, v.p. adminstrn. Escababa, Mich., 1980-84, dir. corp. devel. Dayton, Ohio, 1984-87; various positions including v.p. fin. planning & analysis, v.p. planning & devel., contr., sr. exec. v.p. ops., pres. N.Am. appliance group and CFO Whirlpool Corp., Benton Harbor, Mich., 1987—99; exec. v.p., CFO Fluor Corp., Aliso Viejo, Calif., 1999—2001; chmn., CEO Maytag Corp., 2001—06; chmn. Smurfit-Stone Container Corp., Chgo., 2010—11, ITT Exelis, 2011—. Bd. dirs. Maytag Corp., 2001—06; bd. dir. ITT Corp., 2002—11, Owens-Corning Inc., 2006—; bd. dirs. Smurfit-Stone Container Corp., 2010—11, RockTenn Co., 2011—, ITT Exelis, 2011—. Served in U.S. Army, 1971-73. Mem. NAM (bd. dirs.). Avocations: woodworking, reading. Office: ITT Exelis 1650 Tysons Blvd Ste 1700 Mc Lean VA 22102

HAKES, JAY EDWARD, library director, former federal agency administrator; b. Gallipolis, Ohio; m. Anita Zervigon. Grad., Wheaton Coll., 1966; M, Duke U., 1968, PhD, 1970. Tchr. polit. sci. U. New Orleans, 1970-77; with AID, Dept. of Interior, Exec. Office of Pres., 1977-80; state energy dir. Fla. Gov. and U.S. Senator Bob Graham, 1980-93; adminstr. Energy Info. Adminstrn., U.S. Dept. Energy, Washington, 1993-2000; dir. Jimmy Carter Presdl. Libr. and Mus., Atlanta, 2000—. Office: Jimmy Carter Presdl Libr and Mus 441 Freedom Pky NE Atlanta GA 30307-1498 Office Phone: 404-865-7100. Business E-Mail: jay.hakes@nara.gov.

HALABE, UDAYA BHATTA, civil engineering educator, researcher; arrived in US, 1985, naturalized; s. Gangadhar Bhatta and Shailaja Bhatta H.; m. Anjali Marathe; children: Esha Bhatta H., Shivali Bhatta H. BE in Civil Engring., U. Roorkee, India, 1984; M in Tech. (Civil Engring.), Indian Inst. Tech., Kanpur, India, 1985; MS in Civil Engring., MIT, 1988, MS in Mgmt., 1990, PhD in Civil Engring., 1990. Registered profl. engr., W. Va. Asst. prof. W.Va. U., Morgantown, 1990-96, assoc. prof., 1996-2001, prof., 2001—. Contbr. numerous articles to profl. jours. and conf. proceedings, over 100 sci. papers, over 40 rsch. reports. Recipient Nat. James M. Robbins Excellence Tchg. award, 2012. Fellow: ASCE, Structural Engring. Inst., Am. Soc. Nondestructive Testing; mem. Am. Concrete Inst., Chi Epsilon, Tau Beta Pi. Hindu. Avocations: walking, reading, tennis, swimming. Home: 1504 Foxtrot Dr Morgantown WV 26508-9175 Office: W Va U PO Box 6103 Engring Sci Bldg Rm #613 Morgantown WV 26506-6103 Office Phone: 304-293-9934. Business E-Mail: uhalabe@alum.mit.edu.

HALBERT, JON S., insurance company executive; B in Acctg., Abilene Christian U. Co-founder, COO Advance PCS, Inc., vice chmn. Irving, Tex., 2000—. Bd. dir. Phytel, 2005—. Office: Advance PCS Inc 750 W John Carpenter Fwy Ste 1200 Irving TX 75039 Office Phone: 469-524-4700. Office Fax: 469-524-4702.

HALBOUTY, THOMAS C., oil and gas company executive; BBA in Acctg., U. Houston. CPA; cert. mgmt. acct. With Am. Exploration, Quintana, Gulf Oil; mem. America's Energy Practice Andersen Consulting; v.p., chief info. officer Pioneer Natural Resources Co., 1997—. Bd. dirs. Energistics, former vice chair. Advisor Coun. on Competitiveness. Office: Pioneer Natural Resources Co Ste 200 5205 N O'Connor Blvd Irving TX 75039 Office Phone: 972-444-9001. Office Fax: 972-402-7023.

HALDEMAN, JOE WILLIAM, writer; b. Okla. City, June 9, 1943; s. Jack Carroll and Lorena (Spivey) H.; m. Mary Gay Potter, Aug. 21, 1965. BS in Physics and Astronomy, U. Md., 1967; MFA in Writing, U. Iowa, 1975. Assoc. prof. writing program MIT, 1983—. Author: War Year, 1972, The Forever War, 1975, Mindbridge, 1976, Planet of Judgment, 1977, All My Sins Remembered, 1977, Infinite Dreams, 1978, World Without End, 1979, Worlds, 1971, (with Jack C. Haldeman II) There Is No Darkness, 1983, Worlds Apart, 1993, Dealing in Futures, 1985, Tool of the Trade, 1987, Buying Time, 1989, The Hemingway Hoax, 1990, Worlds Enough and Time, 1993, 1968, 1995, None So Blind, 1996, Saul's Death and Other Poems, 1997, Forever Peace, 1997, Forever Free, 1999, The Coming, 2000, Guardian, 2002, Camouflage, 2004, Old Twentieth, 2005, War Stories, 2005, A Separate War, 2006, The Accidental Time Machine, 2007, Future Weapons of War, 2007, Marsbound, 2008, Starbound, 2010; editor: (with Martin H. Greenburg and Charles Waugh) Body Armor: 2000, 1986, Supertanks, 11987, Spacefighters, 1988; editor: Cosmic Laughter, 1974, Study War No More, 1977, Nebula Awards 17, 1983. Served with U.S. Army, 1967-69. Decorated Purple Heart; recipient Hugo award World Sci. Fiction Soc., 1976, 77, 91, 95, 98, Nebula award Sci. Fictions Writers Am., 1975, 91, 93, 98, 2001, Rhysling award Sci. Fiction Poetry Assn., 1984, 91, 2001, World Fantasy award, 1993, John W. Campbell award Sci. Fiction Rsch. Assn., 1998, James Tiptree award, 2004, SFWA Grandmaster award, 2010. Mem. Sci. Fiction Writers Am. (treas. 1970-73, chmn. grievance com. 1977-79, pres. 1992-94), Authors Guild, Writers Guild, Poets and Writers, Inc., Nat. Space Inst. E-mail: haldeman@mit.edu.

HALE, DAVID JASON, federal prosecutor; b. Ft. Campbell, Ky., June 30, 1967; s. H. David and Brenda T. Hale; m. Ann F. Hale, Aug. 26, 1989; children: Caroline, John David. BA, Vanderbilt U., 1989; JD, U. Ky., 1992. Bar: Ky. 1992, US Dist. Ct. (eastern & western districts) Ky. 1992, US Ct. Appeals (6th cir.) 1992. Assoc. Brown Todd & Heyburn, PLLC, Louisville, 1992-94; asst. US atty. (western dist.) Ky. US Dept. Justice, Louisville, 1995-99, US atty., 2010—; counsel Reed Weitkamp Schell & Vice, PLLC, Louisville, 1999—2002, ptnr., 2002—10. Project coord. (video) What is a Living Will?, 1999. Nat. pres. Coll. Democrats America, Washington, 1988-89; mem., bd. dirs. State YMCA Ky. Youth Assn., Frankfort, 1996—. Mem. ABA, FBA, Ky. Bar Assn., Louisville Bar Assn., Louisville Urban League (bd. dirs. 2000), Ky. Ednl. TV. Democrat. Office: US Attorneys Office Bank of Louisville Bldg 510 W Broadway Louisville KY 40202 Office Phone: 502-582-5911. Office Fax: 502-582-5097.*

HALE, EARL F., JR., mediator, arbitrator; b. Ranger, Tex., Aug. 17, 1945; AB cum laude, Stanford U., 1967; JD cum laude, Columbia U., 1970. Bar: Tex. 1970, NY 1980. Former ptnr. Carrington, Coleman, Sloman & Blumenthal, LLP, Dallas; atty. sole practice, Dallas. Recipient Disting. Faculty award, Tex. Ctr. Legal Ethics and Professionalism; named Super Lawyers, Tex. Lawyers; named one of Best Lawyers in Dallas, D Mag. Fellow: Dallas Bar Found., Tex. Bar Found. (life); mem.: Am. Health Lawyers Assn., Assn. Conflict Resolution, Assn. Atty.-Mediators, Dallas Bar Assn., ABA. Office: 4144 North Central Expy Ste 225 Dallas TX 75204 Office Phone: 214-515-0199. Office Fax: 214-515-0192. Business E-Mail: efhale@earlhale.com.

HALE, JEAN R., bank executive; Joined Community Trust Bancorp, Inc., 1969, compliance & CRA officer, exec. v.p., sr. lendor, sr. v.p., comml. lending, v.p., comml. lending; chmn. Cmty. Trust and Investment Co. (subs. of Cmty. Trust Bancorp, Inc.), Cmty. Trust Bank, Inc. (subs. of Cmty. Trust Bancorp, Inc.); pres. Community Trust Bancorp, Inc., 1999—, CEO, 2001—, chmn., 2004—. Bd. dirs. Commonwealth Seed Capital, LLC. Bd. dirs. KCTCS Found. Office: Community Trust Bancorp Inc 346 N Mayo Trail Pikeville KY 41501 Office Phone: 606-432-1414. Office Fax: 606-437-3345. Business E-Mail: haleje@ctbi.com.

HALE, MARIE STONER, performing company executive; b. Greenwood, Miss. Student in Piano, U. Miss., Hattiesburg; studied with Richard Ellis, Christine du Boulay, Jo-Anna Kneeland, David Howard. Tchr. Ellis/du Boulay Sch., Chgo., Jo-Anna Kneeland Imperial Studios, Palm Beach County, Fla.; co-founder Ballet Arts Found., West Palm Beach, Fla., 1973-86; founder, artistic dir. Ballet Fla., West Palm Beach, 1986—2009; founder Dance Florida Acad., 2009—. Office: Dance Fla Acad PO Box 8036 West Palm Beach FL 33407-0036 Office Phone: 561-832-8941.

HALE, STEVE, state legislator; b. Memphis, Mar. 28, 1954; m. Cindy Rials; children: Jennifer Hale Brunetti, Jay. Attended, NW Miss. CC, Senatobia; BS in Bus. Adminstrn., Miss. State U. With Hale Lumber Co.; alderman City of Senatobia, 1989—93, mayor, 1993—2001; chief of staff Miss. Devel Authority, 2002—03, exec. dir.; sr. policy advisor econ. devel. to Ronnie Musgrove Office of Gov., Miss.; dir. bus. devel. Miss. Dept. Employment Security; planning dir. Tate County, Miss.; mem. Dist. 10 Miss. State Senate, Jackson, 2012—. Democrat. Baptist. Office: Miss State Senate PO Box 1018 Jackson MS 39215 Business E-Mail: shale@senate.ms.gov.

HALEY, NIKKI RANDHAWA, Governor of South Carolina, former state legislator; b. Bamberg, SC, Jan. 20, 1972; m. Michael Haley, Sept. 6, 1996; children: Rena, Nalin. BS in Accounting, Clemson U., 1994. Acctg. supervisor FCR, Inc., 1994—96; CFO Exotica Internat., 1996—2004; mem. Dist. 87 SC House of Reps., Columbia, 2004—10, majority whip, 2006—10; gov. State of SC, Columbia, SC, 2011—. Bd. dirs. Lexington Medical Found., 2004, Lexington Sheriff's Found., 2004—06. Author: (memoir) Can't Is Not An Option: My American Story, 2012. Bd. mem. Mt. Horeb United Methodist Church. Named one of The 50 Politicos to Watch, Politico, 2010, The Politics 40 Under 40, TIME Mag., 2010. Mem.: NRA, West Metro Rep. Women, Lexington Rotary Club. Republican. Methodist. Office: Office of the Governor 1205 Pendleton St Columbia SC 29201 Office Phone: 803-734-5167. Office Fax: 803-734-2100.*

HALFACRE, ROBERT GORDON, ombudsman, landscape architect, horticulturist, educator; b. Newberry, SC, June 22, 1941; s. Edwin Harvey and Lela (Ruff) H.; m. Carolyn F. Halfacre, Jan. 24, 1963 (div. Jan., 1980); children: Angela, Robert. BS, Clemson U., 1963, MS, 1965; PhD in Horticulture, Va. Poly. Inst., 1968; MLA, N.C. State U., 1973. Registered landscape architect, S.C. Asst. prof. N.C. State U., Raleigh, 1968-71, assoc. prof., 1971-74; assoc. prof. horticulture Clemson (S.C.) U., 1974-79, prof., 1979-90, Alumni disting. prof., 1990—2006, univ. ombudsman, 1998—. Landscape architect Landscape Archtl. Svcs., Clemson, 1977—; mem. Planning Commn. City of Clemson, 1990-93; pres. faculty senate, Clemson U., 1989-90, bd. visitors, 1992-94, chmn. grievance bd., 1996-98. Author: Carolina Landscape Plants, 1971, Keep 'em Growing, 1972, Fundamentals of Horticulture, 1975, Horticulture, 1979, Plant Science, 1987, Landscape Plants of the Southeast, 5th edit., 1989. Dir. Horticulture Gardens, Clemson U., 1974-77; pres. bd. dirs. Daniel H.S. P.T.A., Clemson, 1985-86; chmn. United Way Campaign, Clemson U., 1996-97. Recipient Silver Seal award Nat. Coun. State Garden Clubs, 1984, Helen S. Hull award, 1979, Sigma Xi Rsch. award, 1968, Outstanding Tchr. award N.C. State U., 1970, Outstanding Faculty award AAUP, 1997. award for Faculty Excellence, Clemson U. Bd. Trustees, 1997. Mem.: Internat. Ombudsman Assn. (bd. dirs. 2005—07), Univ. and Coll. Ombuds Assn. (bd. dirs. 2004—05), Am. Soc. Hort. Sci. (Julian C. Miller rsch. award 1968, L.M. Ware Outstanding Tchr. award So. region 1982), Am. Soc. Landscape Archs., Nat. Ombudsman Assn. Republican. Lutheran. Avocations: water-skiing, writing, tennis, travel. Office: Clemson U 101 Clemson House 410 N Palmetto Blvd Clemson SC 29631-5107 Home Phone: 864-985-1123; Office Phone: 864-656-4353. Office Fax: 864-656-4373. Business E-Mail: ombudsman@clemson.edu.

HALFORD, CURTIS, state legislator; m. Charlotte Halford; children: Lori, Bradley. Ret. Dyer Fiberglass; former commr. Gibson Co.; mem. bd. dir. Casey Counseling Ctr. Peer Support Group; mem. Gibson Co. Rep. Party, Dyer Sta. Planning Com.; mem. Dist. 79 Tenn House of Reps., 2008—. Vet. USAF. Republican. Presbyterian. Mailing: 127 Old Dyer Trenton Rd Dyer TN 38330 Office: 106 War Memorial Bldg Nashville TN 37243 Office Phone: 615-741-7478. Business E-Mail: rep.curtis.halford@capitol.tn.gov.

HALL, ADAM STUART, lawyer; b. Atlanta, June 19, 1971; s. Andrew Clifford Hall and Patricia Ann Bursten. BA with honors, U. Fla., 1993, JD with honors, 1996. Bar: Fla. 1997, U.S. Dist. Ct. (so. dist.) Fla. 1997, U.S. Dist. Ct. (mid. dist.) Fla. 1998. Intern Supreme Ct. Fla., Tallahassee, 1995; assoc. Andrew Hall & Assocs., P.A., Miami, Fla., 1997-98, Hall, David and Joseph, P.A., Miami, 1998—2005; ptnr. Hall, Lamb and Hall, P.A., Miami, 2005—. Chmn. unsecured creditor's com. Inre Telephone Co. Ctrl. Fla., Inc., Orlando, 1998-99. Mem. U. Fla. Coll. Law Alumni Coun., Gainesville, 1997—; mem. young leadership coun. United Way of Dade County, Miami, 1997—. Mem. ABA, ATLA, Acad. Fla. Trial Lawyers, Dade County Bar Assn. Avocations: scuba diving, skiing, football. Office: Offices at Grand Bay Plza 2665 S Bayshore Dr Penthouse 1 Miami FL 33133*

HALL, ANDREW CLIFFORD, lawyer; b. Warsaw, Sept. 16, 1944; arrived in U.S., 1949, naturalized, 1954; s. Edmund and Maria (Hahn) Hall; m. Gail Meyers, 1993. BA, U. Fla., 1965; JD with high honors, U. Fla. Coll. Law, 1968. Bar: Fla. 1968, U.S. Dist. Ct. (so. dist.) Fla. 1968, U.S. Dist. Ct. (no. dist.) a. 1971, U.S. Ct. Appeals (5th cir.) 1971, Ga. 1973, U.S. Supreme Ct. 1974, U.S. Ct. Appeals (D.C. cir.) 1974, U.S. Ct. Appeals (11th cir.) 1981. Law clk. to judge U.S. Dist. Ct.; assoc. Haas, Holland, Levison, Gilbert, Atlanta, 1970—72, Frates, Floyd, Pearson, Stewart, Miami, 1972—75; ptnr. Storace, Hall & Hauser, Miami, 1975—79, Hall & Hauser, Miami, 1979—82; founder, mng. ptnr. Hall, Lamb and Hall, P.A., Miami, 1982—; Kleh vis. prof. Internat. Law Boston U. Coll. Law, 2013. Trustee emeritus, Coll. Law Found. U. Fla., past mem., Law Ctr. Coun., Holland Law Ctr.; bd. editors Sch.'s Law Rev.; Kleh vis. prof. internat. law Boston U. Coll. Law, 2013. Nat. bd. mem. Am. Jewish Com.; chmn. Holocaust Meml. Miami Beach, 2012—. Recipient Learned Hand award, AJC, 2009; named one of Best Lawyers in America. Mem.: AAJ, ABA, South Fla. Transplant Found. (pres.), Greater Miami Jewish Fedn. (bd. dirs.), Fla. Justice Assn., Acad. Fla. Trial Lawyers (diplomate), Am. Judicature Soc., Fla. State Bar Assn., Hebrew Immigrant Aid Assn. (nat. bd. dirs., bd. mem.), Order of Coif, Phi Alpha Delta, Phi Kappa Phi. Democrat. Home: 3515 Bayshore Villas Dr Miami FL 33133 Office: Hall Lamb and Hall PA 2665 S Bayshore Dr Penthouse 1 Miami FL 33133

HALL, CARL WILLIAM, agricultural and mechanical engineer; b. Tiffin, Ohio, Nov. 16, 1924; s. Lester and Irene H.; m. Mildred Evelyn Wagner, Sept. 5, 1949; 1 dau., Claudia Elizabeth. BS, B. in Agrl. Engring. summa cum laude, Ohio State U., 1948; M.M.E., U. Del., 1950; PhD, Mich. State U., 1952. Registered profl. engr., Mich., Ohio. Instr. U. Del., 1948-50, asst. prof., 1950-51, Mich. State U., 1951-53, assoc. prof., 1953-55, prof., 1955-70, chmn. dept. agrl. engring., 1964-70; dean, dir. research (Coll. Engring.); prof. mech. engring. Wash. State U., Pullman, 1970-82, pres. WSU Rsch. Found., 1973-82; dep. asst. dir. Directorate for Engring. NSF, 1982-90; ret., 1990. With ESCOE, Inc., Washington, 1979; dist. vis. prof. Ohio State U., 1991; del. to USSR, 1958, 1987; mem. Wash. State mission to Libya, 1977; mem. engring. edn. del. to People's Republic of China, 1978, Indonesia, 1978, 1993, 1994; co-chmn. NRC-India Nat. Sci. Acad. Workshop, New Delhi, 1979; with ACA, Inc., 1956—70, pres., 1962—70; chmn. Nat. Dairy and Food Engring. Conf., 1953—66; mem. postgrad. edn. select com. USN, Monterey, Calif., 1975; rsch. fellow Japan Soc. Promotion Sci., 1991; cons. in field. Author: (over 30 books) The Age of Synthesis, 1995, Laws and Models, 1999, Biographical Dictionary of People in Engineering Literature, 2008; founding editor, emeritus: Drying Technology: Taylor & Francis, Inc.; contbr. articles to profl. jours., chpts. to books. Staff sgt. infantry US Army, 1943—46, ETO. Decorated Bronze Star and CIB; recipient Disting. Faculty award, Mich. State U., 1963, Centennial Achievement award, Ohio State U., 1970, Massey-Ferguson Edn. medal, 1976, Max Eyth medal, Germany, 1979, Medal du Merite, France, 1979, Silver medal, Paris, 1980, Cyrus Hall McCormick medal, 1984, Disting. Svc. award and medal, NSF, 1988, Excellence in Drying award, IDS, 1990, Food Engring. award and medal, 1993, Disting. Alumni award, Ohio State U., 1983, 2003, Mich. State U., 2004, Internat. Peace prize, United Collateral Conv., 2005, Mech. Engring. Disting. Career award, U. Del., 2006, Lifetime Achievement award, Internat. Drying Symposium, 2008, Global R & D Drying; named Engr. of Yr., DC Coun. Engrs. and Archs., 1999. Fellow: Am. Soc. Agr. and Biol. Engrs. (life; pres. 1974—75), ASME (life; v.p. rsch. 1993—95), AAAS (life), Internat. Commn. Agrl. Engrs. (v.p. 1965—74), Accreditation Bd. Engring. and Tech., Am. Inst. Med. and Biol. Engring.; mem.: VFW, NAE, Inst. Biol. Engring. (Verma Lifetime Visionary award), Inst. Food Tech., Am. Soc. Engring. Edn. (life), Engrs. Coun. for Profl. Devel. (exec. com., bd. dirs., sec.

1973—74, chmn. EAC-ABET engring. accreditation commn. 1979—80), Va. Soc. Profl. Engrs. (pres. No. Va. chpt. 1987—88), Wash. Soc. Profl. Engrs. (nat. dir. 1975—79), Am. Inst. Biol. Scis., Nat. Inf. Assn., Combat Infantrymens Assn. (life), Philos. Soc. Washington (life), 99th Inf. Divsn. Assn., Univ. Club Wash., Phi Lambda Tau, Gamma Sigma Delta, Phi Kappa Phi, Sigma Xi, Tau Beta Pi (life). Achievements include rsch. in energy, drying, food engring., properties of materials and biomass. Office: Engring Info Svcs 2454 N Rockingham St Arlington VA 22207-1033 Office Phone: 703-534-8321.

HALL, CAROL K., chemical engineering educator, researcher; b. Bklyn., Apr. 23, 1946; d. Harris J. and Celia Klein; children: Katherine, Adam, Norah. BA, Cornell U., 1967; MA, SUNY, Stony Brook, 1969, PhD, 1972. Postdoctoral rsch. assoc. Cornell U., Ithaca, NY, 1973-76; mem. tech. staff Bell Labs., Murray Hill, NJ, 1976-77; asst. prof. Princeton U., NJ, 1977-85; assoc. prof. N.C. State U., Raleigh, 1985-87, prof., 1987-98, Alcoa prof., 1998—; prof. Camille Dreyfus Disting. U., 2007—. Contbr. more than 200 articles to profl. jours. Recipient Outstanding Rsch. award N.C. State U. Alumni Assn., 1992, Disting. Grad. Prof. award, 1998, Disting. Engring. Rsch. award N.C. U. Alcoa Found., 1994. Mem. NAE, AIChE, Am. Chem. Soc., Biophys. Soc., Assn. for Women in Sci. (pres. local chpt. 1993-94). Achievements include research in application of statistical thermodynamics and computer simulation to problems in chemical engineering and chemistry. Office: NC State U PO Box 7905 Raleigh NC 27695-0001 Home: 434 Yarmouth Rd Raleigh NC 27608-1030

HALL, CHARLES WASHINGTON, lawyer; b. Dallas, June 30, 1930; s. Albert Brown and Eleanor Pauline (Hopkins) H.; m. Mary Louise Watkins, Aug. 3, 1957; children: Kathryn Louise, Allison Ash (dec.), Charles Washington III. BA, U. of South, 1951; JD, So. Meth. U., 1954, LLM in Taxation, 1959. Bar: Tex. 1954. Ptnr. Storey, Armstrong & Steger, Dallas, 1954-57; sr. ptnr. Fulbright & Jaworski, Houston, 1957—. Mem. adv. com. on tax litigation Dept. Justice, 1979-80; dir. Friedman Ind., Inc., Tex. Med. Ctr., Inc. Houston; mem. Commr. Internal Revenue Adv. Group, 1990-91; mem. adv. coun. U.S. Claims Ct., 1988-2006. Pres., trustee Sarah Campbell Blaffer Found., Houston; dir. Goodwill Industry, Houston, 1977-84; trustee Inst. Religion, Houston, 1990-2000, Killson Found., Houston, pres. & trustee, M.D. Anderson Found., Houston, Allbritton Found., Houston, Allbritton Art Inst., Waco, Houston Child Guidance Ctr., 1984-86, The Howell Family Found., Houston; pres. John S. Dunn Found., 2008-11; trustee, treas. Ctr Am. Internat. Law, 1973-2005 (formerly Southwestern Legal Found.), Dallas, 1973-2006; S.W. Rsch. Inst., San Antonio, 1974-2005; gov. Houston Forum, 1992-95, trustee Camp Allen Conf. Ctr., Navasota, Tex., 2001-10, Trustee Episcopal Found., Houston, 2008-11, Episcopal Ch. Corp. Recipient Disting. Alumni award, So. Meth. U., 1989. Fellow Am. Bar Found.; mem. ABA (chmn. sect. taxation 1987-88, ho. dels. 1991-95, nat. conf. lawyers and CPAs chmn. 1988-1990), Houston Bar Assn., Dallas Bar Assn., State Bar Tex. (chmn. sect. taxation 1970-71, Lifetime Achievement in Taxation award 2006, Recognized Tax Legend award 2012), Internat. Bar Assn., Am. Coll. Tax Counsel (regent 1982-91), Am. Law Inst., River Oaks Country Club, Coronado Club(Houston),(pres. 1992), Met. Club (Washington), Old Baldy Club (Saratoga, Wyo.), Adrienne Helis Malvin Med. Rsch. Found., Diana Helis Henry Med. Esch. Found. Episcopalian. Office: Fulbright & Jaworski LLP 1301 Mckinney St Ste 5100 Houston TX 77010-3031 Office Phone: 713-651-5268.

HALL, CLARK, state legislator; Farmer; mayor Marvell, Ark.; mem. Dist. 13 Ark. House of Reps., 2007—. Democrat. United Methodist. Address: 302 Elm St Marvell AR 72366 Office Phone: 870-829-3382. Business E-Mail: hallc@arkleg.state.ar.us.

HALL, DANIEL J., state legislator; b. Beckley, W.Va., July 26, 1974; s. Garry, Peggy. BA, Marshall U., 1997. Tchr. Raleigh County Bd. Edn., 1997—99; claims handler State Farm Ins., 1999—2005, Nationwide Ins., 2005—; mem. Dist. 22 W.Va. House of Delegates, 2008—. Democrat. Office: State Capitol Complex 1900 Kanawha Blvd E Rm 230E, Bldg 1 Charleston WV 25305 also: PO Box 339 Oceana WV 24870 Office Phone: 304-340-3119, 877-565-3447. E-mail: djhall@mail.wvnet.edu.

HALL, DEANGELO, professional football player; b. Chesapeake, Va., Nov. 19, 1983; married; 2 children. Student in sec. edn., Va. Polytechnic Inst. and State U., Blacksburg, 2004. Cornerback Atlanta Falcons, 2004—07, Oakland Raiders, 2008, Washington Redskins, 2008—. Vol. Atlanta Coaches Acad., 2004. Named Pro Bowl MVP, NFL, 2011; named to The All-American Team, NCAA, 2002, The Nat. Football Conf. Pro Bowl Team, NFL, 2005, 2006, 2010; finalist Jim Thorpe award, 2003. Achievements include leading the NFL in: fumble return yards, 2005. Office: Washington Redskins 21300 Redskin Pk Dr Ashburn VA 20147*

HALL, FRANK JERRY, mathematics professor; BA, St. Marys U., San Antonio, Tex., 1965; MS, U. Houston, 1967; PhD in Math., NC State U., Raleigh, 1973. Prof. Ga. State U., Atlanta, 1978—. Contbr. articles to profl. jours. Office Phone: 404-413-6432. Business E-Mail: matfjh@langate.gsu.edu.

HALL, FRANK W., oil and gas company executive; BBA in Acctg. & Bus. Mgmt., U. Tex., San Antonio; MBA in Corp. Fin. with honors, U. Dallas. Mem. audit staff Touche Ross & Co., 1977—80; contr. Riddle Oil Co., 1980—83; ptnr. Hall, Brock & Co., 1983—89; sr. fin. analyst Oryx Energy Co., 1989—98; mgr. fin. reporting Pioneer Natural Resources Co., 1998—2005, asst. contr., 2005—07, corp. contr., 2007—08, v.p., chief acctg. officer, 2008—, Pioneer Natural Resources GP, LLC, 2008—. Office: Pioneer Natural Resources Co Ste 200 5205 N O'Connor Blvd Irving TX 75039 Office Phone: 972-444-9001. Office Fax: 972-402-7023.

HALL, FRANKLIN PERKINS, lawyer, former state legislator; b. Amelia, Va., Dec. 12, 1938; s. Perkins Lee and Lois E. Hall; m. Phoebe Ann Poulterer, July 26, 1969; children: Kimberly Ann, Franklin P. Jr. BS, Lynchburg Coll., 1961; MBA, Am. U., 1964, JD, 1966. Bar: Va. 1966. Aide US Senate, Washington, 1964; asst. sec. Dept. HUD, Washington, 1968-69; sr. ptnr. Hall & Hall, Richmond, 1969—; mem. Dist. 69 Va. House of Delegates, 1976—2010. Chmn. bd. Cardinal Savs. and Loan Assn., Richmond, Va., 1979-84; chmn. bd. Commonwealth Bank, Richmond, 1984—; spl. counsel Va. Gen. Assembly, Richmond, 1970-75. Chmn. bd. Cen. Richmond Assn., 1974-75; pres. Richmond Jaycees, 1972-73; dem. minority leader Va. Ho. Dels., 2001 Recipient Disting. Svc. award Richmond Jaycees, 1972, Award Va. Jaycees, 1974, Disting. Citizen award Nat. Mcpl. League, 1976; named Outstanding Young Man of Va. award, 1973. Mem. Va. Trial Lawyers Assn. (bd. govs. 1982-84), Richmond Bar Assn. (exec. com. 1973-76), Soc. Advancement Mgmt., Newcomen Soc. Democrat. Presbyterian. Office: Hall & Hall 1401 Huguenot Rd Ste 100 Midlothian VA 23113-2662

HALL, HARRY H., agricultural economics educator; b. Cassville, Mo., Aug. 14, 1934; s. Bert L. and Cynthia Jane (Smith) H.; m. Betty Sue Dowler, June 4, 1961; children: Brian E., Janet Anne. BS, U. Mo., 1956; MS, Okla. State U., 1964; PhD, Iowa State U., 1969. Asst. county agt. U. Mo., Columbia, 1956-57, assoc. county agt., 1959-61; rsch. asst. Okla. State U., Stillwater, 1961-63, Iowa State U., Ames, 1963-65, rsch. assoc., 1965-69; prof. agrl. econs. U. Ky., Lexington, 1969—99; ret., 1999. Contbr. articles to profl. jours. With U.S. Army, 1957-59. Mem. Am. Agrl. Econs. Assn., So. Agrl. Econs. Assn., Phi Eta Sigma, Alpha Zeta, Gamma Sigma Delta, Phi Kappa Phi. Office: U Ky Dept Agrl Econs Lexington KY 40546-0276 Office Phone: 859-257-7272 ext 250. Business E-Mail: hhall@uky.edu.

HALL, JACQUELYN DOWD, historian, educator; Founder, dir. So. Oral History Program. Recipient Nat. Humanities medal Pres. Clinton and First Lady Hilary Rodham Clinton, 1999.

HALL, JAMES H(ERRICK), JR., philosophy educator, writer; b. Houston, Oct. 20, 1933; s. James Herrick and Loula Ben (Vining) H.; m. Bonlyn Goodwin, 1957 (div. 1977); children: Christopher Vining, Jonathan Goodwin; m. Myfanwy Seaver Monroe, 1977; 1 child, Charles Trevor. AB, Johns Hopkins U., 1955; BD, Southeastern Sem., Wake Forest, NC, 1958, ThM, 1960; PhD, U. N.C., Chapel Hill, 1964. Instr. philosophy U. N.C., Chapel Hill, 1960-62; asst. prof. Furman U., Greenville, SC, 1963-65; assoc. prof. U. Richmond, Va., 1965-74, chmn. dept. philosophy, 1965—89, 1999—2004, prof., 1974—2005, The Thomas chair, 1982—2005, Thomas prof. emeritus, 2005—, guest dir., 1999—2001. Author: Knowledge Belief and Transcendence, 1975, Logic Problems, 1991; (with others) Biblical and Secular Ethics, 1988, Philosophy of Religion, 2003, Practically Profound, 2005, Tools of Thinking, 2005. Mem. vestry St. Paul's Episcopal Ch., Richmond, 1988-91, 2004-08, sr. warden, 2007-08; profl. ch. musician, Chapel Hill, Raleigh, Balt., Washington, Richmond. Rsch. grantee Duke Found., Durham, 1964, Mednick Trust, 1973-74; named Disting. Educator, U. Richmond, 2001, Outstanding Prof., 2005; Coun. for Philosophic Studies fellow, Grand Rapids, 1973, U. Warwick fellow, Coventry, U.K., 1989-90, Kenan fellow U. NC, 1960-61. Mem. AAUP (chpt. pres. 1991-92), ACLU, Am. Philos. Assn., Soc. for Philosophy of Religion, So. Soc. for Philosophy and Psychology, Omicron Delta Kappa. Democrat. Episcopalian. Avocations: choral music, travel, computers. Home: 209 Wood Rd Richmond VA 23229-7538 Office: U Richmond Dept Philosophy North Ct Richmond VA 23173 Business E-Mail: jhall@richmond.edu.

HALL, JAMES RANDAL, federal judge; b. Augusta, Ga., Nov. 9, 1958; s. James Marcus and Gary Patricia (Ross) H.; m. Mary Suzanne Crowder, Dec. 19, 1981; children: Mary Catherine, Elizabeth Hinson. BA, Augusta Coll., 1979; JD, U. Ga., 1982. Bar: Ga. 1982, U.S. Dist. Ct. (no. dist.) Ga. 1982, U.S. Tax Ct. 1983, U.S. Dist. Ct. (so. dist.) Ga. 1984. Assoc. Sanders, Mottola, Haugen & Goodson, Newnan, Ga., 1982-84; ptnr. Avrett & Hall, P.C., Augusta, 1984-85; gen. counsel, v.p., sec. Bankers First Corp., Augusta, 1985—96; ptnr. J. Randal Hall, P.C./Hall U Mullins, P.C., 1996—99, Hunter, Maclean, Exley & Dunn, P.C., 1999—2003, Warlick, Tritt, Stebbins & Hall, LLP, 2004—08; judge US Dist. Ct. (so. dist.) Ga., 2008—. Lectr. Inst. Fin. Edn., Augusta, 1989—; treas. Bankers First Com. for Quality Govt., Augusta, 1988—. Bd. dirs., ex-officio Augusta Port Authority, 1987-88; chmn. Augusta So. Nats. Inc., 1987-88, Evang. com. Trinity Meth. Ch., Augusta, 1989-91; bd. dirs. Richmond County Consumer Adv. Bd., Augusta, 1988-89; bd. dirs. Augusta Coalition for Children and Youth, 1991-93, pres. 1993-94. Mem. ABA (savings instn. subcom.), Augusta Bar Assn., Am. Corp. Counsel Assn., State Bar Ga. (corp. counsel com., legal econs. com., arrangements for meetings com.), Assn. Fin. Svcs. Holding Cos. (holding cos. law com. 1987—), Leadership Augusta (bd. dirs. 1991-93), Lions (pres. Augusta chpt.), Phi Delta Phi. Avocations: golf, running, reading, gardening. Office: US Dist Ct PO Box 1130 Augusta GA 30903

HALL, JOHN WESLEY, JR., lawyer; b. Watertown, NY, Jan. 28, 1948; s. John Wesley and Mary Louise Hall; m. Alison Hall; children: Justin William, Mark Daniel, Juliana Gebb. BA, Hendrix Coll., 1970; JD, U. Ark., 1973. Bar: Ark. 1973, US Dist. Ct. (ea. and we. dists. Ark.) 1973, US Ct. Appeals (8th cir.) 1973, DC 1975, US Ct. Appeals (5th cir.) 1976, US Supreme Ct. 1976, US Ct. Fed. Claims, 1984, Tenn. 1988, US Ct. Appeals (fed. cir.) 1988, US Ct. Appeals (6th cir.) 1991, Nev. 1993, US Ct. Appeals (9th cir.) 1995, NY 1996, US Dist. Ct. (so. dist. NY), 1999, US Ct. Appeals (2nd cir.) 1999, US Dist. Ct. (dist. Nev.) 2000, US Dist. Ct. (ea. dist.) Tex. 2004, US Dist. Ct. (mid. dist.) Tenn. 2005. Law clk. Ark. Supreme Ct., Little Rock, 1974; dep. pros. atty. Office Pros. Atty., Little Rock, 1973-79, head career criminal divsn., 1978-79; pvt. practice atty., 1974—. Instr. trial advocacy Ark. Pros. Attys. Assn., 1977-79; adj. prof. Sch. Law, Grad. Sch. Criminal Justice, U. Ark., Little Rock, 1985-88, 91; mem. Ark. adv. com. US Commn. Civil Rights, 2003-04; war crimes trial Spl. Ct. Sierra Leone, 2004-06; speaker to lawyer and police groups. Author: Search and Seizure, 3rd edit., 2000, Professional Responsibility in Criminal Defense Practice, 3rd edit. 2005, Trial Handbook for Arkansas Lawyers, 5th edit., 2007; editor, author: Arkansas Prosecutor's Trial Manual, 1976-77, Arkansas Extradition Manual, 1978; editor: (with B. Scheck and P. Neufield) DNA: Understanding, Controlling, and Depleting the New Evidence of the 90's, 1990; contbr. articles to law jours. Recipient Robert C. Heeney Meml. award, 2002. Fellow Am. Bd. Criminal Lawyers; mem. NACDL (life, bd. dirs. 1989-95, 97-2003, officer 2003-, mem. ethics adv. com. 1990-2005, lawyer's assistance strike force 1994-97, exec. com. 2000-01, 03-, Robert C. Heeney Meml. award 2002), Ark. Bar Assn. (ho. dels. 1976-79), Ark. Assn. Criminal Def. Lawyers (pres. 1987-89, Champion of Justice award 2003), NY State Assn. Criminal Def. Lawyers, First Amendment Lawyers Assn., Internat. Criminal Bar, Internat. Criminal Def. Attys. Assn. Episcopalian. Office: John Wesley Hall Jr PC 1311 Broadway Little Rock AR 72202-4843 Office Phone: 501-371-9131.

HALL, KATHY, continuing education director; b. Covington, Ky., Feb. 15, 1953; d. Joseph B. and Mary Louise (Weindel) Dusing; m. Harold G. Hall, Oct. 6, 1973; children: Becky, Amy, Sarah. AA, Eastern Ky. U., 1973, BS in Nursing, 1978; MS in Nursing, Bellarmine U., 1999. Med.-surg. staff nurse Good Samaritan Hosp., Lexington, Ky., 1973; infection control nurse Pattie A. Clay Hosp., Richmond, Ky., 1975-93, orientation instr., 1978-82, quality assurance dir., 1982-93; nurse epidemiologist U. Ky. Chandler Med. Ctr., Lexington, 1993—99; edn. dir. Shriners Hosp. for Children, Lexington, 1999—2002; dir. continuing edn. and devel. Coll. Health Sci. Ea. Ky. U. Mem.: NNSDO, KNA, ANA, Ctrl. KY Staff Devel. Group, Sigma Theta Tau. Office: CHS Continuing Edn and Devel 202 Perkins Bldg Ea Ky U 521 Lancaster Ave Richmond KY 40475-3102 Office Phone: 859-622-2143. Business E-Mail: Kathy.Hall@eku.edu.

HALL, KENNETH RICHARD, chemical engineering professor, consultant; b. Tulsa, Okla., Nov. 5, 1939; s. Snipes Webster and Selina Rose (Scarpin) H.; m. Janet Beulah Blood, June, 1964 (div. 1975); children: Tara Marie, Deirdre Rene; m. Frieda Maria Karner, Mar. 12, 1976; children: Kent Max, Keith Anton, Krysta Maria. BS ChemE, U. Tulsa, 1962; MS, U. Calif., Berkeley, 1964; PhD, U. Okla., 1967. Registered engr., Tex. Asst. prof. U. Va., Charlottesville, 1967-70, 71-74; asst. to pres. ChemShare Corp., Norman, Okla., 1970; sr. rsch. engr. AMOCO, Tulsa, 1970-71; vis. prof. U. Louvain, Belgium, 1971-72; assoc. prof. Tex. A&M U., College Station, 1974-78, prof., 1978—, dir. Thermodynamics Rsch. Ctr., 1979-85, 97-2000, asst. dir. Tex. Engring. Experiment Sta., 1985-88, assoc. dean engring., 1987—94, 2002—03, from assoc. dir. to dep. dir., 1988—94, 2002—03, 2007—, assoc. dep. chancellor for engring., 1990—94, 2002—03, 2007—, interim head petroleum engring., 1991, interim head chem. engring., 1994; dir. CTS divsn. NSF, Va., 1994-96; GPSA prof. Tex. A&M U., College Station, 1997-2000, Jack E. and Frances Brown chair, 2001—, head dept. chem. engring., 2002—06; assoc. dir. Tex. Engring. Experiment Station, 2007—09; dep. dir. Tax Engring. Experiment Sta., 2009—11; assoc. dir. Tex. Engring. Exptl. Station, 2011—, assoc. vice chancellor engring., 2011—; assoc. dean R&GS Tex. A&M U. Qatar, 2011—. Cons. OPC Engring., Houston, 1980-85, Quantum Tech., Houston, 1981-85; cons. Precision Measurement Inc., Duncanville, Tex., 1981-90; bd. dirs. Lorax Corp., Syn Fuels. Contbr. articles to profl. jours. Recipient numerous grants for research. Mem.: Am. Inst. Chem. Engrs. (chmn. ctrl. Va. chpt. 1969, chmn. cyrogenics 1977—79, exec. position II South Tex. sect. 1991—92, bd. dirs. fuels and petrochems. divsn. 1992—94), Am. Chem. Soc. Avocations: sports, reading. Home: 1401 Millcreek Ct College Station TX 77845-8352 Office: Tex A&M U Dept Chem Engring College Station TX 77843 Home Phone: 979-696-3579; Office Phone: 979-845-3357.

HALL, KEVIN D., apparel company executive; b. 1959; BS in Biology, Wabash Coll., 1981; MBA in Mktg., Ind. U., 1985. Various mgmt. positions including gen. mgr., Vidal Sassoon bus. worldwide Procter & Gamble Co., 1985—2001; sr. v.p., mktg. Fidelity Investments Tax-Exempt Retirement Svcs. Co., 2001—05; adv. bd. & cons. Affinova Inc., 2005—06; chief mktg. officer Hanesbrands, Inc., 2006—08, exec. v.p., 2006—, gen. mgr., Outerwear Strategic Bus. Unit, 2008—. Past pres. Kelley Sch. Bus. Office: Hanesbrands Inc 1000 E Hanes Mill Rd Winston Salem NC 27105 Office Phone: 336-519-4400.

HALL, LARRY D., state legislator; Atty.; state rep. Dist. 29 NC, 2007—. Mem. Edn. com., Edn. Subcom. on Universities, Fin. com., Judiciary I com., Sci. and Tech. com.; vice chmn. Fin. Instns. com.; chmn. Homeland Security, Military and Veterans Affairs com. Democrat. Mailing: PO Box 25308 Durham NC 27702 Office: North Carolina House of Representative 300 N Salisbury St Rm 510 Raleigh NC 27603-5925 Office Phone: 919-682-8823, 919-733-5872. Business E-Mail: Larry.Hall@ncleg.net.

HALL, LAURA, state legislator; b. Sandy Springs, SC, Jan. 25, 1943; m. John Hall; 1 child, Janeka. BS, Morris Coll., Sumter, SC; MA, Ohio State U. Adminstr. Calhoun CC; mem. Dist. 19 Ala. House of Reps., Montgomery, 1993—. Mem. Madison County Dem. Women, Madison County Women's Polit. Caucus; past mem. bd. dirs. Constitution Hall Village; mem. adv. bd. dirs. AID Action Coalition, Ctrl., North Ala. Health Ctr. Democrat. Roman Catholic. Office: 100 St Clair Huntsville AL 35810 also: Ala House of Reps Ala State House 11 S Union St Rm 518 Montgomery AL 36130 Office Phone: 256-539-5441, 256-539-5444, 334-242-7688, 256-859-2234. Business E-Mail: laura.hall2@att.net.

HALL, LAWRENCE, secondary school educator; s. Leroy and Ocie Hall; children: Reginald Dwight, Lawrence Jr., Trevis Devaughn, Drayton Davion. AAS in Adminstrv. Mgmt., CC Air Force, Maxwell AFB, Ala., 1987, AAS in Instrnl. Tech., 1993; BS in Mgmt. Studies, U. Md., College Pk., 1997; BSBA, Columbia Coll., Mo., 2000. Cert. in tchr. tng. track Coll. Bibl. Studies Tex., Houston, 2007; lic. master instr. US Air Force Tex., Lackland Air Force Base, 1987, cert. aerospace sci. instr. US Air Force Ala., Maxwell AFB Ala., 2000, advanced aerospace sci. instr. 2008. Sr. master sgt. (e8) USAF, 1972—98; adminstrv. CLK and NCOIC adminstrv. sect. 357th Tactical Fighter Squadron, Davis-Monthan Air Force Base, Ariz., 1972—77; NCOIC wing self-inspections and squadron adminstrn. 67th Tactical Reconnaissance Wing and 12th Tactical Reconnaissance Squadron, Bergstron Air Force Base, Tex., 1977—79, NCOIC maintenance adminstrn., wing adminstrn., and unit adminstrn., 1980—82; NCOIC mission rels. US Mil. Tng. Mission To Saudi Arabia, Dhahran, 1979—80; chief adminstrn. 7580th Ops. Squadron, Rhein-Main Air Base, Germany, 1982—84; mil. tng. instr. Basic Mil. Tng. Sch., Lackland Air Force Base, Tex., 1984—88; chief info. mgmt. 6906 Electronic Security Squadron, Brooks Air Force Base, Tex., 1988—89, Electronic Security Command, Kelly Air Force Base, Tex., 1989—92; chief, ops. info. mgmt. 6903rd Electronic Security Group, Osan Air Base, Republic of Korea, 1992—93; chief, base info. mgmt. 768th Air Base Squadron, Neubruecke Army Installation, Germany, 1993—94; sta. supt. Dallas Mil. Entrance Processing Sta., 1994—98; aerospace sci. instr. Cedar Hill HS, Tex., 2000—02, Klein HS, Houston, 2002—03, Lamar Consol. HS, Rosenberg, Tex., 2003—10, B.F. Terry HS, Rosenberg, 2010—. Decorated Def. Meritorious Svc. medal, Air Force Meritorious Svc. medal with 4 oak leaf clusters, Joint Svc. Commendation medal, Air Force Commendation medal with 2 oak leaf clusters, Air Force Achievement medal, Air Force Good Conduct medal with 7 oak leaf clusters, Nat. Def. Svc. medal with bronze star. Conservative. Baptist. Avocations: travel, music, reading. Office Fax: 832-223-3401; Home Fax: 281-239-2298.

HALL, NEVA L., retail executive; Attended, Lab. Inst. Merchandising, NYC. V.p., divisional mdse. mgr. fine apparel Neiman Marcus Stores, Dallas, 1991—96, v.p. pub. rels., 1996—97, sr. v.p. gen. mdse. mgr., 1997—2002, exec. v.p., 2002—. Office: Neiman Marcus Stores One Marcus Sq 1618 Main St Dallas TX 75201

HALL, O.B. GRAYSON, JR., (GRAYSON HALL), bank executive; b. 1957; Grad., Stonier Sch. Banking; BS in Economics, U. South, Sewanee, 1979; MBA, U. Ala., Tuscaloosa, 1980. Sr. exec. v.p., head, lines bus., ops. and tech. group AmSouth Bank, AmSouth Bancorporation; sr. exec. v.p., gen. bank group Regions Bank, Regions Financial Corp., participant, mgmt. trainee program, 1980, head, ops. tech. group, 1993—2004, mgr., consumer banking, comml. banking, and wealth mgmt., 2005—06, head, gen. bank group, 2006—08, vice chmn., 2008—, pres., COO, 2009—10, pres., CEO, 2010—. Bd. dirs. Regions Financial Corp., 2008—, Zep Inc., 2009—. Bd. dirs. RR Park Found., Birmingham; past leadership volunteer United Way of Ctrl. Ala., Birmingham C. of C.; mem. Leadership Birmingham, 2001—. Mem.: Ala. Better Bus. Bureau (bd. dirs.), Young Bus. Leaders Birmingham (bd. dirs.). Office: Regions Financial Corp 1900 Fifth Ave N Birmingham AL 35203 Office Phone: 205-944-1300. Office Fax: 901-580-3915. Business E-Mail: bgrayson.hall@regions.com.

HALL, RALPH MOODY, United States Representative from Texas; b. Fate, Tex., May 3, 1923; s. Hugh and Maude Hall; m. Mary Ellen Murphy, Nov. 14, 1944 (dec. Aug. 27, 2008); children: Hampton, Brett, Blakeley. Attended, Tex. Christian U., Ft. Worth, U. Tex., Austin; LLB, Southern Meth. U., Dallas, 1951. Bar: Tex. 1951. County judge Rockwall County, Tex., 1950-62; mem. from Dist. 9 Tex. State Senate, 1962-72, pres. pro tempore, 1968—69; pres., CEO Tex. Aluminum Corp., 1967—68; gen. counsel Tex. Extrusion Co., Inc.; counsel Howmet Corp., 1970—74; founding mem., chmn. Lakeside Nat. Bank, Rockwall, Tex.; mem. US Congress from 4th Tex. Dist., 1981—; ranking mem. US House Sci., Space & Technology Com., 2007—11, chmn., 2011—13, chmn. emeritus, 2013—. Pres. State Judges & Commissioners Assn. Tex., 1958—59. Sr. grade lt., aircraft carrier pilot USN, 1942—45. Mem.: VFW, American

Legion, Rotary. Republican. Methodist. Office: US House of Representatives 2405 Rayburn House Office Bldg Washington DC 20515 also: 104 N San Jacinto St Rockwall TX 75087 Office Phone: 202-225-6673.*

HALL, ROBERT JOSEPH, internist, educator; b. Buffalo, June 4, 1926; s. Joseph M. and Florence C. (Kirst) H.; m. Dorothy Nowak, Aug. 28, 1948; children: Thomas R., Kathleen A. Hall Noble, Mary J. Hall Stuart, Michael F., Steven E. Student, Canisius Coll., Buffalo, 1943-45; MD, U. Buffalo, 1948. Diplomate Am. Bd. Internal Medicine, Sub Bd. Cardiovascular Disease (mem. cardiovascular disease sect. 1969-75). Intern Mercy Hosp., Buffalo, 1948-49; commd. 1st lt. M.C. U.S. Army, 1948, advanced through grades to col., 1966; resident in internal medicine Walter Reed Gen. Hosp., Washington, 1949-52, resident in cardiovascular diseases, 1956-57; asst. cardiovascular research Walter Reed Army Inst. Research, 1957-58; service in Korea and Japan, 1952-55; chief cardiology service Brooke Gen. Hosp., Ft. Sam Houston, Tex., 1961-66, Walter Reed Gen. Hosp., 1966-69; ret., 1969; clin. assoc. prof. medicine Georgetown U. Med. Sch., 1967-69; clin. prof. medicine Baylor U. Coll. Medicine, Houston, 1969—, prof. emeritus, 2004—; clin. prof. medicine U. Tex. Med. Sch., Houston, 1977—; med. dir. Tex. Heart Inst., Houston, 1969-93, chmn. exec. com. profl. staff, 1969-93; dir. div. cardiology St. Luke's Episcopal Hosp., Houston, 1969-95, assoc. chief med. service, 1970-83; dir. edn., cardiology Tex. Heart Inst. Tex. Heart Inst. and St. Luke's Episcopal Hosp., 1992—2002, dir. emeritus, 2002—. Cons. Tex. Children's, VA, Brooke Gen. hosps., M.D. Anderson Hosp. and Tumor Inst.; mem. cardiovascular study sect. NIH, 1958-61; mem. phys. evaluation team Gemini project NASA, 1958-61; mem. nat. adv. heart counseil Dept. Def., 1966-69; adv. council Mended Hearts, 1970-78 Contbr. numerous articles med. jours. Mem. President's Adv. Panel Heart Disease. Decorated Legion of Merit; recipient Disting. Alumnus award Canisius Coll., 1995. Fellow A.C.P., Am. Coll. Cardiology (gov. 1968-71-74, chmn. bd. govs. and trustee 1973-74); mem. Am. Heart Assn. (fellow council clin. cardiology; pres. Houston chpt. 1974-75, advisor corp. cabinet 1980-86), Assn. Mil. Surgeons U.S., Assn. Advancement Med. Instrumentation, Pan Am. Med. Assn. (chmn. sect. cardiovascular diseases 1978-81), Assn. Univ. Cardiologists, Tex. Med. Assn., Tex. Cardiology Club, Harris County Med. Soc., Houston Cardiology Soc. (chmn. 1976-77), Houston Soc. Internal Medicine, Alpha Omega Alpha, 1948—. Home: 5504 Sturbridge Dr Houston TX 77056-1623 Office: 6624 Fannin St Ste 2480 Houston TX 77030-2309 Business E-Mail: rjhall@wt.net.

HALL, STEPHEN CHARLES, lawyer; b. Carmel, Calif., Sept. 14, 1948; s. Melvin Wiley and Dorothy Louise (Hoyt) H.; m. Kristi Lee Roberts, Feb. 23, 1983; children: Spencer Stephen Rodrigo, Rachel Genevieve Cristina, Trevor Charles. AB, Dickinson Coll., 1971; JD, Vt. Law Sch., 1977. Bar: Pa. 1978, Va. 1979, U.S. Dist. Ct. (ea. dist.) Va. 1982, U.S. Dist. Ct. (we. dist.) Va. 1990, U.S. Ct. Appeals (4th cir.) 1982. Title atty. Chgo. Title Inst. Co., Richmond, Va., 1978-79; assoc. Edward E. Willey Jr., P.C., Richmond, 1979-82; ptnr. Willey & Hall, P.C., Richmond, 1983-88; assoc. Hazel & Thomas, P.C., Richmond, 1988-90, ptnr., 1990-94, Keith & Hall, Richmond, 1994—2003, Hairfield Morton PLC, Richmond, 2004—. Contbr. articles to profl. jours. Past chmn. bd. trustees St. Michael's Episcopal Sch. Mem. Richmond Bar Assn. (past chmn. publs. com.), Chesterfield County Bar Assn. (past pres. 2003—), Bon Air Bus. and Profl. Assn. (fellow, past pres.), Salisbury Country Club, Litigation Counsel America. Episcopalian. Avocations: golf, photography. Office: Hairfield Morton PLC 2800 Buford Rd Ste 201 Richmond VA 23235 Office Phone: 804-320-6600. Business E-Mail: shall@hmalaw.com.

HALL, W. KEITH, state legislator; b. July 3, 1959; Founder, pres., CEO Benetech Mining Materials Inc.; mem. Dist. 93 Ky. House of Reps., 2001—. Democrat. Office: PO Box 466 Phelps KY 41553 also: Capitol Annex Rm 466C 702 Capitol Ave Frankfort KY 40601 Office Phone: 606-456-3432 ext. 25, 502-564-8100 ext. 635.

HALLADAY, LAURIE ANN, public relations consultant, food products executive; b. Monroe, Mich., Aug. 18, 1945; d. Alvin John and Florence (Lowrey) Kohler; m. Edward L. Howell, Aug. 27, 1966; m. 2d Fredric R. Halladay, May 24, 1980. BJ, U. Mo., 1967. Reporter, staff writer Copley Newspapers, LA, 1967-69; account exec. Furman Assocs., LA, 1969-71, v.p., 1971-74; account supr. Bob Thomas & Assocs., LA, 1974-76, v.p., 1976-78; v.p., sr. ptnr. Fleishman-Hillard, Inc., St. Louis, 1980-84; owner, operator McDonald's, Portland, Oreg., 1984-87, McDonald's McStop of Mid.-Mo., Kingdom City, 1988-92. Chmn. press ops. for Budweiser/G.I. Joe's Portland 200 Indy Car Race, 1984-87; mem. advt., promotions com. Hollywood Boosters, 1986. Bd. dirs. Waterman Place Assn., St. Louis, 1983; mem. pub. rels. com. Winston Churchill Meml., Fulton, 1988-92. Recipient Merit award Calif. Press Women, 1969, Lulu award Los Angeles Women's Ad Club, 1976, McDonald's Outstanding Store award, 1985, 86, 89, 90, 91. Mem. PRSA (Prism award 1977), Soc. Am. travel Writers (assoc. 1981-84), Women in Comm. (dir. St. Louis 1980-82), Nat. Tour Assn., Mo. Travel Coun., Delta Delta Delta (alumna adviser 1989, 90, v.p. Delta Xi House Corp. 1991, collegiate dist. officer 1991, 94, regional program chmn. 1994, program resource team pub. rels. specialist 1995-96, nat. chmn. pub. rels. 1996, cons. pub. rels. chpt. 1998-2000), Delta Delta Delta (trident coorespondent Sarasota Alumnae chpt. 2009-10). Home: 2313 Jessie Harbor Dr Osprey FL 34229 Personal E-mail: halladayl@yahoo.com.

HALLAM, HOWARD, food service executive; JD, U. Tex.; MBA, Southern Meth. U. Chmn., CEO Ben E. Keith Co., pres., COO, 1979—. Office: Ben E Keith Co 601 E 7th St Fort Worth TX 76102-5501 Office Phone: 817-877-5700. Office Fax: 817-338-1701. Business E-Mail: howardhallam@benekeith.com.

HALLAM, ROBERT G., wholesale distribution executive; b. Dallas, Sept. 16, 1941; BBA, U. Tex., Austin, 1964, JD, 1966. Various positions Ben E. Keith Co., 1969—79, chmn., CEO Ft. Worth, 1979—. Office: Ben E Keith Co 601 E 7th St Fort Worth TX 76102-5501 Office Phone: 817-877-5700. Office Fax: 817-338-1701. Business E-Mail: rghallam@benekeith.com.

HALLEN, BARRY, philosopher, educator; b. Chgo., Apr. 5, 1941; s. George and Betty Hallen; m. Carla De Benedetti, Apr. 30, 1986. BA in Philosophy, Carleton Coll., 1963; MA in Philosophy, Boston U., 1968, PhD in Philosophy, 1970. Lectr. in philosophy U. Lagos, Lagos, Nigeria, 1970—75; from lectr. to reader in philosophy U. Ife, Ile-Ife, Nigeria, 1975—83, reader in philosophy, 1983—88; project dir. UNESCO, Milan, 1989—98; vis. prof. philosophy Morehouse Coll., Atlanta, 1997—2000, prof. philosophy, 2000—, chmn. dept. philosophy and religion, 2001—08. Assoc. W.E.B. DuBois Inst. Harvard U., Cambridge, Mass., 1995—. Co-author: Knowledge, Belief & Witchcraft, 1997; author: The Good, The Bad & the Beautiful, 2000, African Philosophy: The Analytic Approach, 2006, A Short History of African Philosophy, 2009. Borden Parker Bowne Fellow, Boston U., 1968—69, Fulbright rsch. grantee, 2003. Mem.: Internat. Soc. African Philosophy and Studies (pres. 2004—06), Soc. African Philosophy in N.Am. (gen. sec. 1998—2006). Avocations: sailing, bicycling, writing detective stories. Office Phone: 404-215-2607. Business E-Mail: bhallen@morehouse.edu.

HALLER, THOMAS, facilities services company executive; Attended, Pa. State U., 1975—77. Nat. mktg. dir. Sanitors, 1991—2001; regional dir. ABM Industries, Inc., 2001—; regional sales mgr. ABM Industries Inc., 2002—08; regional dir. sales ABM Industries, Inc., 2006—. Mem.: Houston Bldg. Owners and Mgrs. Assn. (SW conf. com. co-chmn. 2009, Allied Mem. of Yr. award 1995, 1999). Office: ABM Janitorial Services 2131 Gulf Central Dr Houston TX 77023 Office Phone: 713-928-5344. Office Fax: 713-928-2143. Business E-Mail: thaller@abm.com.

HALLGREN, WENDY, engineering company executive; BA in Govt. & Economics magna cum laude, Georgetown U., 1989; JD cum laude, U. Mich., 1994. Bar. Washington, D.C., Tex., Calif. Assoc. Hogan and Hartson LLP, Washington, 1994—97, Gibson, Dunn & Crutcher LLP, Orange, Calif., 1997—2002; mem., legal dept. Fluor Corp., 2002—04, v.p., corp. compliance, 2004—. Contbg. editor U. Mich.jour. Law Reform. Office: Fluor Corp 6700 Las Colinas Blvd Irving TX 75039 Office Phone: 469-398-7000. Office Fax: 469-398-7255. Business E-Mail: Wendy.Hallgren@fluor.com.

HALLIDAY, WILLIAM ROSS, retired physician, speleologist, writer; b. Atlanta, May 9, 1926; s. William Ross and Jane (Wakefield) H.; m. Eleanore Hartvedt, July 2, 1951 (dec. 1983); children: Marcia Lynn, Patricia Anne, William Ross III; m. Louise Baird Kinnard, May 7, 1988. BA, Swarthmore Coll., 1946; MD, George Washington U., 1948. Diplomate Am. Bd. Vocat. Experts. Intern Huntington Meml. Hosp., Pasadena, Calif., 1948-49; resident King County Hosp., Seattle, Denver Children's Hosp., L.D.S. Hosp., Salt Lake City, 1950-57; pvt. practice Seattle, 1957-65; with Wash. State Dept. Labor and Industries, Olympia, 1965-76, med. dir., 1970—76, Wash. State Div. Vocat. Rehab., 1976-82; staff physican N.W. Occupational Health Ctr., Seattle, 1983-84; med. dir. N.W. Vocat. Rehab. Group, Seattle, 1984, Comprehensive Med. Rehab. Ctr., Brentwood, Tenn., 1984-87. Dep. coroner King County, Wash., 1964—66. Author: Adventure Is Underground, 1959, Depths of the Earth, 1966, 2d edit., 1976, American Caves and Caving, 1974, 82, Floyd Collins of Sand Cave, 1998; co-author: (with Robert Nymeyer) Carlsbad Cavern: The Early Years, 1991; editor Jour. Spelean History, 1968-73, Hawaiian Volcanoes, 2005; contbr. articles to profl. jours. Cons. Egyptian Environ. Affairs Agency; v.p. North Cascades Conservation Coun., 1962—63; pres. Internat. Speleological Found., 1981—87, Internat. Union Speleol. Com. on Volcanic Caves, 1992—98, hon. pres., 1998—; asst. dir. Internat. Glaciospeleological Survey, 1972—76; mem. Gov.'s North Cascades Study Com., 1967—76; chmn. Hawaii Speleol. Survey, 1989—97; dir. We. Speleol. Survey, 1957—83, dir. rsch., 1983—96. Served to lt. USNR, 1949—50, served to lt. comdr USNR, 1955—57. Recipient medal Geol. Soc. China; named Alumnus of Yr., George Sch., 1992. Fellow Am. Coll. Chest Physicians, Nat. Speleological Soc. (hon., bd. govs. 1950-2001), Explorers Club; mem. Nat. Trust (Scotland), Geol. Soc. Am., Mars Soc., Ukrainian Speleological Assn. (hon.), Seattle Tennis Club, Internat. Union Conservation Nature World Com. on Protected Areas.

HALLIGAN, JAMES EDMUND, state legislator, retired academic administrator, retired chemical engineer; b. Moorland, Iowa, June 23, 1936; s. Raymond Anthony and Margaret Ann Halligan; m. Ann Elizabeth Sorenson, June 29, 1957; children: Michael, Patrick, Christopher. BS in Chem. Engring., Iowa State U., MS in Chem. Engring, 1962, MS, 1965, PhD in Chem. Engring., 1968. Registered profl. engr., Okla. Process engr. Humble Oil Co., 1962-64; mem. faculty Tex. Tech U., 1968-77; dean engring. U. Mo., Rolla, 1977-79, U. Ark., Fayetteville, 1979-82, vice chancellor for acad. affairs, 1982-83, interim chancellor, 1983-84; pres. N.Mex. State U., Las Cruces, 1984-94, Okla. State U., Stillwater, 1994—2003, pres. emeritus, 2003—07; mem. Dist. 21 Okla. State Senate, 2008—. Mem. Gov. Tex. Energy Adv. Council, 1972-74; prof. achievement citation engr. Iowa State U. Coll. Engring., 1984. Served with USAF, 1954-58. Recipient Disting. Teaching award Tex. Tech U., 1972, Disting. Research award, 1975, 76; Disting. Teaching award U. Mo., Rolla, 1978, Disting. Achievement citation Iowa State U. Alumni Assn., 1996. Mem. AIChE, Rotary, Tau Beta Pi, Phi Kappa Phi, Pi Mu Epsilon. Republican. Roman Catholic. Home: 6321 West Coventry Stillwater OK 74074 Office: 2300 North Lincoln Blvd Room 416 Oklahoma City OK 73105 Office Phone: 405-521-5572. Personal E-mail: halligan3@suddenlink.net. Business E-Mail: halligan@oksenate.gov.

HALLINAN, PATRICK K., civilian military employee; b. 1956; m. Doreen Hallinan; children: Matthew, Rachel. AA in Liberal Arts, Suffolk Cmty. Coll., Long Island, BA in Social Sci. magna cum laude. Joined as laborer LI Nat. Cemetery, NY, 1977, advanced through positions including work supr., asst. cemetery dir., dir.; assoc. dir., Office of Field Programs Nat. Cemetery Adminstrn., Dept. Vet. Affairs, Arlington, Va., 2003—08, dir., Office of Field Programs, 2008—10; supt. Arlington Nat. Cemetery, 2010—13; exec. dir. Army Nat. Military Cemeteries, Arlington, 2013—. Dir. Calverton Nat. Cemetery, NY, 1994. Infantry squad leader USMC. Recipient 1995 Leadership VA award, VA Dep. Sec. Hershel Gober; co-recipient VA Secretary's award, Sec. Anthony Principi, 1994. Mem.: DAV (life). Office: Arlington National Cemetery Arlington VA 22211*

HALLOCK-MULLER, PAMELA, oceanographer, educator, geobiologist, consultant; d. Graydon B. and Marjorie L. Hallock (dec.); m. Robert Glenn Muller, Aug. 22, 1969. BA in Zoology, U. Mont., 1969; MSc in Oceanography, U. Hawaii, 1972, PhD in Oceanography, 1977. Asst. prof. earth scis. U. Tex. of Permian Basin, Odessa, 1978-83; assoc. prof. marine sci. U. South Fla., St. Petersburg, 1983-88, prof., 1988—. Participant Nat. Undersea Rsch. Ctr. Fla. Keys, Saturation Mission, 1994; mem. Sci. Party Ocean Drilling Program Leg 194, 2001; assoc. editor Jour. Foraminiferal Rsch., Washington, 1985—; mem., editl. bd. Marine Micropaleontology Jour., 1990-2012, Geology, 1996-98. More than 130 articles to profl. publs. Vol. speaker Pinellas County (Fla.) Schs. Speaker Bur., 1984-98; judge local, regional, and state sci. fairs, Fla., 1989—; vol. Pinellas Coastal Cleanup, St. Petersburg, 1988-; expert sci. judge Spoonbill Regional of Nat. Ocean Scis. Bowl, 2006-, ARCS Tampa Bay, 2011-. ARCS fellow U. Hawai'i Manoa, 1976, German Acad. Exch. Svc. rsch. fellow, Kiel, Germany, 1978; summer faculty fellow NASA Goddard Space Flight Ctr., 1987, Elected fellow Paleontological Soc., 2012; recipient Outstanding Educator award Assn. Women Geoscientists, 1999; named Minority Program's Mentor of Yr., Alfred P. Sloan Found., 2012. Fellow: Cushman Found. for Foraminiferal Rsch. (bd. dirs. 1989—, v.p. 1992, 2010, pres. 1995-96, 2011), Geol. Soc. America (W. Storrs Cole Rsch. award 1994), Paleontol. Soc.; mem.: Assn. Women Geoscientists (Outstanding Educator award 1999, disting. spkr.), Soc. Sedimentary Geology (v.p. Permian Basin sect. 1982-83, paleontology councilor 1997-98), N.Am. Micropaleontol. Soc., Am. Acad. Underwater Scis., Assn. Women in Sci. Progressive. Avocations: scuba diving, canoeing, natural history. Office: University S Fla Coll Marine Sci 140 7th Ave S Saint Petersburg FL 33701-5016

HALLORAN, WILLIAM FRANK, English educator; b. Spearfish, SD, Sept. 12, 1934; s. William Patrick and Frances Marie (Perrin) H.; m. Mary Helen Griffin, July 29, 1961; children— Julia Frances, William David. BA magna cum laude, Princeton, 1956; MA, Duke, 1959; PhD, Duke U., 1965; Dr. Phil. h.c., Justis Liebig Universität, Giessen, Fed. Republic Germany, 1989. Instr. English U. N.C., 1963-64; instr. English NYU, 1964-66; asst. prof. English U. Wis.-Milw., 1966-68, asso. prof., 1968-72, prof., 1972-98; prof. emeritus, 1998—; asso. dean Coll. Letters and Sci., 1969-72, dean, 1972-95; dep. project leader Zayed U., United Arab Emirates, 1998. Cons. North Ctrl. Assn., 1973-2000, commr.-at-large, 1988-92. Served with U.S. Army, 1957. Recipient Uhrig Teaching award U. Wis.-Milw., 1968 Mem. MLA, AAUP, Midwest Modern Lang. Assn. (exec. com. 1971-74), Coun. of Colls. of Arts and Sci. (bd. dirs. 1984-90, pres.-elect 1987-88, pres. 1988-89), Am. Inst. Fgn. Study (bd. advisors 1980-89), Nat. Assn. State Univs. and Land Grant Colls. (commn. on arts and scis. 1986-91, chmn. 1987), Phi Kappa Phi, Crown Colony (Ft. Myers). Episcopalian. Home: 8893 Crown Colony Blvd Fort Myers FL 33908-5611 Personal E-mail: wfh30@hotmail.com.

HALLUM, HUDSON, state legislator; Grad. in the paramedic program, Ark. State U.; completed fire standards program, So. Ark. U. Paramedic, firefighter West Memphis Fire Dept., Ark.; mem. Dist. 54 Ark. House of Reps., 2011—. Mem.: Ark. Ambulance Assn., Ark. State Firefighters Assn., West Memphis C. of C., Marion C. of C., Marion Rotary Club, Crittenden County Leadership. Democrat. Baptist. Office: 611 N River Wind Dr Marion AR 72364 Office Phone: 901-301-5650. Office Fax: 870-733-1168. Business E-Mail: hudson.hallum@arkansashouse.org.

HALLUMS, BRUCE A., food service executive; V.p. internal audit and loss prevention Cracker Barrel Old Country Store, Inc. Bd. dirs. Lebanon/Wilson County C. of C. Office: Cracker Barrel Old Country Store Inc 305 Hartmann Dr Lebanon TN 37087 Office Phone: 615-444-5533. Office Fax: 615-443-9476.

HALLWORTH, RICHARD, health services executive; BS in Acctg., Bentley Coll., Mass. CPA Coopers & Lybrand; ptnr. Ernst & Young, LLP; CFO Tufts Health Plan, 1994—98, sr. v.p. adminstrn., 1998—2002, COO, 2002—05, American Service Group, Inc., Brentwood, Tenn., 2006, pres., 2007—, CEO, bd. dir., 2009—; pres., CEO, dir. Prison Health Services, Inc. (subs. American Service Group, Inc.), Brentwood, Tenn., 2006—. Office: Am Svc Group Inc 105 Westpark Dr Ste 200 Brentwood TN 37027 Office Phone: 615-373-3100. Office Fax: 615-376-1350.

HALPERN, PAUL G., retired history professor; b. NYC, Jan. 27, 1937; s. Harry and Teresa (Ritter) H. BA with honors, U. Va., 1958; MA, Harvard U., 1961, PhD, 1966. Instr. Fla. State U., Tallahassee, 1965-66, asst. prof., 1966-70, assoc. prof., 1970-74, prof. dept. history, 1974—2005; emeritus prof., 2005—. Vis. prof. strategy dept. Naval War Coll., Newport, R.I., 1986-87. Author: The Mediterranean Naval Situation, 1908-14, 1971, The Naval War in the Mediterranean, 1914-18 1987, A Naval History of World War I, 1994, Anton Haus: Österreich-Ungarns Grossadmiral, 1998, The Battle of the Otranto Straits, 2004; editor: The Keyes Papers, 3 vols., 1972-81, The Royal Navy in the Mediterranean, 1915-1918, 1987, The Mediterranean Fleet, 1919-1929, 2011. Mem. Naval Aviation Mus. Found., Pensacola, Fla., Naval War Coll. Found., Newport, R.I. 1st lt. U.S. Army, 1958-60. Fellow Woodrow Wilson Nat. Fellowship Found., 1958. Fellow Royal Hist. Soc.; mem. Am. Hist. Assn., The Navy Records Soc. (coun. 1968-72, 82-86, 2010-), Naval Rev., U.S. Naval Inst., Friends of Imperial War Mus., Naval Hist. Found., Soc. for Mil. History, Phi Beta Kappa, Phi Eta Sigma. Avocations: model ship collecting, book collecting, model soldier collection. Home: 3103 Brandemere Dr Tallahassee FL 32312 Personal E-mail: phalpern@fsu.edu.

HALPIN, DANIEL WILLIAM, engineering educator, consultant, writer; b. Covington, Ky., Sept. 29, 1938; s. Jordan W. and Gladys E. (Moore) H.; m. Maria Kirchner, Feb. 8, 1963; 1 child, Rainer. BS, U.S. Mil. Acad., 1961; MSCE, U. Ill., 1969, PhD, 1973. Research analyst Constrn. Engring. Research Lab., Champaign, Ill., 1970-72; faculty U. Ill., Urbana, 1972-73; mem. faculty Ga. Inst. Tech., Atlanta, 1973-85, prof., 1981; A.J. Clark prof., dir. Constrn. Engring. and Mgmt. U. Md., 1985-87; dir. divsn. Constrn. Engring. and Mgmt. Purdue U., West Lafayette, Ind., 1987—2006, interim head Sch. Civil Engring., 2000—01, Bowen engring. head of constrn. engring. and mgmt., 2006—06, prof. emeritus, 2006—. Cons. constrn. mgmt.; vis. assoc. prof. U. Sydney, Australia, 1981; vis. prof. Swiss Fed. Inst. Tech., 1985, U. Karlsruhe, Germany, 1998; vis. scholar Tech. U., Munich, 1979; vis. lectr. Ctr. Cybernetics in Constrn., Bucharest, Romania, 1973; cons. office tech. assessment U.S. Congress, 1986-87; mem. JTEC Team to evaluate constrn. tech., Japan, 1990; juror emeritus Constrn. Innovation Forum, 1994. Author: Design of Construction and Process Operations, 1976, Construction Management, 1980, 4d edit., 2011, Internat. Student Version, 2011, Planung und Kontrolle von Bauproduktionsprozessen, 1979, Constructo - A Heuristic Game for Construction Management, 1973, Financial and Cost Control Concepts for Construction Management, 1985, Planning and Analysis of Construction Operations, 1992, Financial Management and Accounting Fundamentals for Construction, 2009. Served with C.E., U.S. Army, 1961-67, commissioned 2nd lt. US Army, advanced through grades to capt., co. commander, Vietnam, 1966-67 Decorated Bronze Star; recipient Lifetime Achievement award INFORMS Constrn. sect., Coll. Simulation, 2004; named Disting. Civil and Environ. Engring. Alumnus, U. Ill., 2008; grantee NSF, Dept. Energy, NIOSH. Mem. ASCE (hon.; past sect. pres. 1981-82, chmn. constrn. rsch. coun. 1985-86, Walter L. Huber prize 1979, Peurifoy Constrn. Rsch. award 1992, named disting. mem., 2006, Halpin award Est. 2011), Am. Soc. Engring. Edn., Nat. Acad. Constrn. (elected 2003), Constrn. Industry Inst. (rsch. com. 1996-2012, Carroll H. Dunn award, 2006), Sigma Xi. Methodist. Office Phone: 859-331-1185. Business E-Mail: halpin@purdue.edu.

HALTER, HANK, air transportation executive; b. 1965; BS in Acctg. summa cum laude, Villanova U., 1987; MBA, Duke U. Fuqua Sch. Bus., 1993. CPA. Sr. acct. Ernst & Young LLP, Phila., 1987—91; analyst, sr. mgr. Am. Airlines, 1993—98; v.p. finance & ops. Delta Air Lines Inc., 2000—01, v.p., asst. controller, 2002—05, v.p., controller, 2005, sr. v.p. finance, controller, 2005—08, sr. v.p., CFO, 2008—. Bd. dirs. Metro Atlanta Boys & Girls Club, Delta Cmty. Credit Union; bd. trustees Delta Heritage Mus.; adv. bd. CFO Roundtable Atlanta Chpt. Office: Delta Air Lines Inc PO Box 20706 Atlanta GA 30320-6001 Office Phone: 404-773-3146, 404-538-3304. E-mail: Hank.Halter@delta.com.

HALTER, HENRY JAMES, JR., (DIAMOND JIM HALTER), retail executive; b. Fernandina, Fla., Feb. 28, 1947; s. Henry James and Grace (Bealey) H.; m. Wanda O'Quinn, Mar. 15, 1970; children: Jennifer, John, Elizabeth, Amelia. BS in Mgmt., Valdosta State Coll., 1970. Residential mem. Am. Inst. Real Estate Appraisers, 1974, sr. real property appraiser Soc. Real Estate Appraisers, 1974, diamond cert. Gemological Inst. Am. Sales mgr. Southwestern Co., Nashville, 1969; collection mgr. Fla. Title & Mortgage Co., Jacksonville, 1970-72; appraiser Richard Hamilton & Assocs., Jacksonville Beach, 1972-74; exec. v.p. Developers Investors Svc. Corp., Jacksonville, 1975-78; pres. A-Coin and Stamp Gallery, Inc., Jacksonville, 1978-81; ptnr. Jacksonville Precious Metals, 1981, Sidetrack Video Arcade Chain, Ga., 1982-84; pres. Diamond House Corp., Valdosta, Ga., 1985—88, J-Mart Jewelry Outlets, Inc., Tifton, Ga., 1988-91, chmn.

bd., 1990-91; pres. K&H Ltd., Valdosta, 1992-94; exec. dir. Soc. for Legalization of Drugs, Valdosta, 1994-97. Sr. appraiser Collectors Road Show, 2006—10; bus. cons., 1996—. Author: May I Help You, 1988, LIZ, Inc., 1998, Meister Poker, 2012; co-author Olympic Awareness award for 1996 Olympic Games, 1994—95, voice of Ernie Beaver for nationally syndicated TV cartoon Coots and Critter, 1996. Mem. exec. bd. Alapaha coun. Boy Scouts Am., 1982—2013, South Ga. Coun., 2013—; youth spkr. Atlanta Com. Olympic Games, selected local hero torch bearer Olympic Games, Atlanta, 1996; mem. Ga. Small Bus. Task Force; pres. Valdosta H.S. Band Boosters Inc., 2002—03; co-founder Boy Scouts Am. Olympic Expo, 2000—05; with ALAPAHA coun. Eagle Scout Class Boy Scouts America; bd. dir. Park Ave. United Meth. Ch., Valdosta, 1986—88; mem. exec. com. Lowndes County Rep. Party, 1995—, chmn. edn. com., 2009—; charter dir. Redirecting Attitudes of Persons; mem. Alumni Bd. Valdosta State U., LIR instr., 2012—. Recipient Addy award, 1980, 83, God and Svc. nat. award Meth. Ch. and BSA, Cmty. Hero Torch Bearer, Coca Cola Olympic Torch Relay, 1996, Evangelism award King Solomon Missionary Bapt. Ch., 2000; named Adm. in Ga. Navy, 1983, Outstanding Ga. Citizen, 1990. Master. Mason, Knights Templar; mem. Nat. Speakers Assn., Toastmasters, Sertoma, Vigil Honor, Order of the Arrow, Rotary, Am. Numismatic Assn. (life), Hasan Shrine Temple & Valdosta Shrine Club, Fla. United Numismatists (life), Alpha Phi Omega, Sigma Iota (charter. pres.;life). Home and Office: 208 Breckenridge Dr Valdosta GA 31605-6402 Personal E-mail: jim_halter@hotmail.com.

HALTER, JON CHARLES, retired magazine editor, writer; b. Hamilton, Ohio, Nov. 24, 1941; s. Sam Lesher and Helen Louise (Olds) H.; m. Corina Garcia, Feb. 14, 1968; children: Jon Julian, Helen Margaret. BA, Syracuse U., 1964, MA, 1966. Vol. U.S. Peace Corps, Venezuela, 1966-68; asst. editor Nat. Petroleum News mag. McGraw-Hill Inc., NYC, 1968-72; editor, writer Boys' Life mag. Boy Scouts Am., North Brunswick, NJ, 1972-79, Irving, Tex., 1979-90, exec. editor Scouting Mag., 1990-94; editor Scouting Mag., Irving, Tex., 1994—2007, Exploring Mag., Irving, Tex., 1994—98. Author: Bill Bradley: One to Remember, 1974, Reggie Jackson: All-Star in Right, 1975, Top Secret Projects of World War II, 1978, Their Backs to the Wall: Famous Last Stands, 1980, Letters from the Sixties: College, Peace Corps, Marriage, 2013; contbr. articles to profl. jours. Mem. Soc. Profl. Journalists, Authors Guild. Democrat. Presbyterian. Avocations: reading, model building, walking. Home: 2502 Vernell Way Round Rock TX 78664 Personal E-mail: jchalter@yahoo.com.

HALVERSEN, DAVID T., plastics company executive; Sr. v.p., bus. devel. and comm. Tupperware Brands Corp., 1996—2002, sr. v.p., bus. devel. and planning, 2002—03, group pres., L.Am. and BeautiControl, 2003—05, group pres., Asia Pacific and BeautiControl Mexico, 2005—06, group pres., Asia Pacific and N.Am., 2006—09, group pres., N.Am. and beauty, 2009—. Office: Tupperware Brands Corp 14901 S Orange Blossom Trail Orlando FL 32837 Office Phone: 407-826-5050.

HALVERSON, PAUL KENNETH, state agency administrator, public health service officer; b. Downey, Calif., Mar. 21, 1959; s. Kenneth Gunnar and Doris M. (Laury) H.; m. Andrea Edwina Stenken, June 14, 1980; children: Melissa Nathalie, Kara Elizabeth. AA, Glendale Coll., 1980; BS, Ariz. State U., 1982, M of Health Svcs. Adminstrn., 1984; D Health Policy and Adminstrn., U. N.C., 1994. Various clin. positions John C. Lincoln Hosp., Phoenix, 1975-79; adminstr. Lincoln Inst. Surgery & Truama, Phoenix, 1979-84; adminstrv. resident Health Cen. System, Mpls., 1984; v.p. Mercy Med. Ctr., Coon Rapids, Minn., 1984-86; pres., chief exec. officer Cen. Mich. Community Hosp., Mt. Pleasant, Mich., 1986-92; asst. prof. dept. health policy and adminstrn. U. N.C., Chapel Hill, 1993—97, sr. fellow Ctr. for Pub. Health Practice, 1994—97, exec. liaison Office of Dean Sch. Pub. Health, 1995—97; pres., CEO Health Faculty Cons., Inc., Chapel Hill, 1993—97; dir. div. public health systems & mem. sr. sci. staff Ctr. for Disease Control, Atlanta, 1997—2004; prof. & chmn. health policy & mgmt. dept. Boozman Coll. Public Health, Univ. Ark., 2004—05; dir. div. health Arkansas Dept. of Health and Human Svc., Little Rock, 2005—. Sr. hosp. mgmt. specialist Rsch. Triangle Inst., Research Triangle Park, N.C., 1995-97; adj. prof. Ctrl. Mich. U., Mt. Pleasant, 1986-92; pres., CEO Meridian Home Care, Inc., Mt. Pleasant, 1988-92. Chmn. bd dirs. Ctrl. Mich. Health Policy Coun., 1987-92; bd. dirs. United Way of Isabella County, Mt. Pleasant, 1987-92, Am. Heart Assn., Mt. Pleasant, 1988-92. Mem. Am. Hosp. Assn., Am. Mgmt. Assn., Med. Group Mgmt. Assn., Am. Coll. Healthcare Execs. (mem. regent's adv. coun. 1989—), Pres.'s Assn., Mich. Hosp. Assn. Republican. Avocations: photography, microcomputers, travel. Office: Health Div 4815 W Markham St Little Rock AR 72205-3867 Home Phone: 501-954-9990. Business E-Mail: phalverson@healthyarkansas.com.*

HALVERSON, STEVEN THOMAS, construction executive, lawyer; b. Enid, Okla., Aug. 29, 1954; s. Robert James Halverson and Ramona Mae (Ludke) Selenski; m. Diane Mary Schueller, Aug. 21, 1976; children: John Thomas, Anne Kirsten. BA cum laude, St. John's U., 1976; JD, Am. U., Washington, DC, 1979. Bar: Va. 1979. Asst. project dir. ABA, Washington, 1977-79; with Briggs & Morgan, St Paul., Minn., 1980-83; sr. v.p. M.A. Mortenson Co., 1984-99; pres., CEO Haskell Co., Jacksonville, Fla., 1999—. Chmn. Jacksonville Symphony; bd. dir. CSX Corp., ACIG Ins. Co., U. North Fla., PSS World Med., Inc., 2008-. Co-author: Federal Grant Law, 1982, The Future of Construction, 1997; contbr. articles to profl. jour. Mem. ABA, Wash., DC, Fla. Con. 100 (vice chmn. 2008-), Constrn. Industry Roundtable (dir. 2006-), CSX Corp. (2006-). Republican. Roman Catholic. Office: The Haskell Co 111 Riverside Ave Jacksonville FL 32202-4921 Office Phone: 904-791-4500. Office Fax: 904-475-7681. E-mail: sthalver@thehaskellco.com.

HALVERSTADT, DONALD BRUCE, urologist, educator; b. Cleve., July 6, 1934; s. Lauren Oscar and Lillian Frances (Jones) H.; m. Margaret Ann (Marcy), Aug. 4, 1956; children: Donna, Jeffrey, and Amy. BA magna cum laude (hon.), Princeton U., 1956; MD cum laude (hon.), Harvard U., 1960. diplomate Am. Bd. Urology. Intern, then resident in surgery Mass. Gen. Hosp., Boston, 1960—62, resident in urology, 1964—67; pvt. practice medicine specializing in urology Okla City, 1967; chief pediatric urology svc. Okla. Children's Meml. Hosp., Okla. City, 1967; clin. prof. urology and pediat. U. Okla. Med. Sch., 1970; chief staff Okla. Children's Meml. Hosp., Okla. City, 1974—79; interim provost U. Okla. for Health Sci., Okla. City, 1979—80; CEO State of Okla. Tchg. Hosp., 1980—83; spl. asst. to pres. for Hosp. affairs Okla. U., 1980—84; vice chair dept. urology U. Okla. Med. Sch., 1982; bd. dir. State of Okla. Tchg. Hosp.; CEO State Regents for Higher Edn., 1988—93. Mem. U. Okla. Bd. Regents, 1993-2000, (chmn. 1999); founder, vice chmn., dir. Lincoln Nat. Bank, Oklahoma City, 1984-2003; bd. dir. BancFirst of Okla., 2004-, Compensation Comm., 2010, vice chair bd. gov. Okla. Med. Ctr. Hosp. Sys., 1998—; bd. dir. Triad Hosp., Inc., chair compliance com., 2000—2007, nominating com. dir. Legacy Hosp. Partners Inc., Chair, Compliances com., 2008-. Contbr. articles to med. journals. Vice chair bd. gov. Univ. Health Ptnrs.; pres., chmn. bd. Okla. Ind. Phys. Svc. Corp., 1986-96; trustee Columbia Presbyn. Hosp., 1990-96, chmn., 1995-96; bd. dir. Nat. Assn. Basketball Coaches FDTN; athletic dir. adv. coun. U. Okla., 2003. Fellow ACS; mem. AMA (Physicians Recognition Award 1969, 72, 79, 82, 85, 91, 94, 96, 99, 2002), Am. Urol. Assn., Am. Acad. Pediat., Soc. Pediat. Urology, Am. Soc. Nephrology, Soc. Univ. Urologists, So. Med. Assn., Okla. Med. Assn., Okla. County Med. Soc., Okla. State Regents for Higher Edn., Am. Coll. Physician Exec., Assn. Governing Bd. Coll. and Univ. (bd. dir., sec. 1996-97, treas. 1997-98). Presbyterian. Business E-Mail: donald-halverstadt@ouhsc.edu.

HALWIG, J. MICHAEL, allergist; b. Denver, Apr. 15, 1954; s. John Philip and Hilda (Fuggis) H.; m. Nancy Diane Graupman, June 14, 1975; children: Courtney Elizabeth, J. Christopher. BA, Johns Hopkins U., 1975; MD, Northwestern U., Chgo., 1980. Diplomate Am. Bd. Allergy and Immunology, Am. Bd. Internal Medicine. Intern in internal medicine Northwestern U. Meml. Hosps., Chgo., 1980-81, resident in internal medicine, 1981-83; allergy fellowship Northwestern U. Med. Sch., Chgo., 1983-85; practice medicine specializing in allergy, asthma, immunology Atlanta, 1985—. Instr. Northwestern U. Med. Sch., Chgo., 1984-85, admissions amb., 1989—75; clin. asst. prof. Emory U. Sch. Medicine, 1989—95. Bd. dirs. Am. Lung Assn. Ga., 1996—2001. Fellow Am. Coll. Allergy, Asthma and Immunology (allergy practice and practice guidelines com. 1992—95), Am. Acad. Allergy, Asthma and Immunology (Managed Care Key Contact Network 1996—2000); mem. AMA, Asthma and Allergy Found. of Am. (nat. chpt. bd. dirs., chpt. rels. and devel. com. 1997-99, mktg. and fundraising com. 1997-99, Ga. chpt. founder, bd. dirs., med. dir. 1995-99, chmn. med. adv. com. 1995-99), Joint Coun. on Allergy and Immunology, Med. Assn. Ga. (rep. Coun. on Legis. 1989-95), Allergy, Asthma and Immunology Soc. Ga. (pres. 1993-95, v.p. 1991-93, program chmn. 1991-93, co-chmn. third party payors com. 1992—95, rep. Ga. medicare carrier adv. com. 1993—), So. Med. Assn., Cobb County Med. Assn., Cobb Area Pediat. Soc., Wellstar Health Care Sys. (pediat. asthma task force 1996-2001, asthma/COPD task force 1998-2001), Ga. Partnership for Caring, Phoenix Soc. (bd. dirs., 2007-08). Presbyterian. Avocations: running, jazz, exercise, reading. Office: 1620 Mulkey Rd Ste 100 Austell GA 30106-8116 Home: 2132 W Village Crossing Smyrna GA 30080 Home Phone: 404-351-7418. Business E-Mail: mhalwig@atlantaallergy.com.

HAM, KENNETH T., astronaut, military officer; b. Plainfield, NJ, Dec. 12, 1964; s. Ed and Marion Ham; m. Linda J. Hautzinger (div.); children: Ryan, Randy; m. Michelle Lucas. BS in Aerospace Engring., USN Acad., Annapolis, Md., 1987; MS in Aeronautical Engring., Naval Postgrad. Sch., Monterey, Calif., 1996. Commd. ensign USN, Annapolis, 1987; advanced through grades to lt. commdr.; crew mem. NASA Zero -g rsch. aircraft, Ellington Field, Houston, 1987; student pilot USN, 1988—89; trainee and mem., airwing strike leader on missions Privateers VFA-132 and Gunslingers VFA-105 included combat missions Bosnia and N. Iraq, 1989—91; student aeronautical engring. USN, Monterey, Calif., 1991—93, test pilot trainee NAS Patuxent River, Md., 1993—94, lead carrier suitability test pilot F/A-18E/F, 1997—98; team mem. USN F/A-18E/F Super Hornet Integrated Test Team, 1994—96; astronaut NASA Johnson Space Ctr., Houston, 1998—. Pilot STS-124 Mission (Discovery), mission to Internat. Space Station to launch components to complete Japanese Kibo Lab., 2008; commander STS-132 Mission (Atlantis)-Last Flight for Atlantis, 2010. Mem.: Soc. Exptl. Test Pilots, USN Acad. Alumni Assn. Achievements include 3,700 flight hours in more than 40 different aircraft; over 300 carrier landings and 300 land based arrested landings. Avocations: aviation, skydiving, skiing, running, weightlifting, snow and water skiing, scuba diving. Office: Astronaut Office/CB NASA Lyndon B Johnson Space Ctr 2101 NASA Pkwy Houston TX 77058

HAMBY, ROGAN, library and information scientist, director; BA in English Lit., Coker Coll., Hartsville, SC, 1997; MLIS, U. SC Davis Coll., Columbia, 1999. Tchg. asst. U. SC Davis Coll., 1998—99; reference librarian, automation support coord, mgr. virtual village Pub. Libr. Charlotte Mecklenburg County, Charlotte, NC, 1999—2007; tech. cons., 2007—08; sys. adminstr., librarian Florence County Libr. Sys., SC, 2008—11; dir. info. technologies and innovation SC State Libr., Columbia, 2011—. Contbr. articles to profl. jours. Mem. info. tech. solutions com. State Agencies for SC. Named one of New Leaders for SC Libraries, 2011; named to Movers & Shakers, Libr. Jour., 2011. Mem.: ALA, SC Libr. Assn. Office: SC State Library 1500 Senate St Columbia SC 29201 Office Phone: 803-734-8651. Business E-Mail: rhamby@statelibrary.sc.gov.

HAMDY, RONALD CHARLES, geriatrician; b. Alexandria, Egypt, July 31, 1946; came to U.S., 1985; s. Charles and Mary Hamdy; m. Eleanor Gertrude Hamdy, Aug. 19, 1977; children: Conrad, Gerard, Ronan. MB, ChB with honours, U. Alexandria, 1968, DM, 1971. Rotating intern U. Alexandria, 1968-69; resident in internal medicine Al-Gomhouriya Gen. Hosp., Alexandria, 1969-70; resident registrar internal medicine U. Alexandria Main Tchg. Hosp., 1970-72; sr. ho. officer geriatric and internal medicine Farnborough (Eng.) Hosp., Kent, 1972-73; registrar in geriatric medicine Bromley (Eng.) Group of Hosps., Kent, 1974; sr. registrar in geriatric medicine King's Coll. Group Hosps., London, 1975-77; consulting physician St. John's Hosp. Richmond (Eng.), Twickenham & Roehampton Health Authority, 1977-85, chmn. dept. clin. gerontology, ethics rsch. com., 1981-85; prof. internal medicine, Cecile Cox Quillen prof. geriatric medicine, head divsn. gerontology East Tenn. State U., Mountain Home, 1985—, Cecile Cox Quillen prof. geriatric medicine, head divsn. gerontology, 1990—, dir. osteoporosis ctr., 1997—; chief geriat. VA Med. Ctr., Mountain Home, 1985-88, assoc. chief of staff geriatric and extended care, 1988—2004. Hon. sr. lectr. geriatric medicine St. George's Hosp. Med. Sch., U. London, 1981-85; planning team for elderly Wandsworth Health Care, 1982-85; med. dist. initiated peer rev. orgn. VA Hosps., Dist. 8, 1986-89; vis. prof. Health Care for Elderly, U. London, 1991-93; Burroughs Wellcome vis. prof. geriatric medicine Royal Soc. Medicine, 1994-95; co-chmn. pharmacy and therapeutics com. VA Med. Ctr., Johnson City, Tenn., chmn. adverse drug reaction com.; chmn. program com. Coll. Medicine Continuing Med. Edn., East Tenn. State U.; mem. Gov.'s task force on Alzheimer's Disease, Tenn., task force on edn., prevention and detection of osteoporosis; mem. advisor to pub. guardian 1st Tenn. Devel. Dist.; adv. bd. Colonial Hill Health Care Ctr., Johnson City, Golden J-55, Johnson City Med. Ctr. Hosp., Inc.; sr. health adv. com. 1st Tenn. Regional Health Office; adj. clin. prof. divsn. clin. nutrition and psychiatry East Tenn. State U., editor in chief, Jours. Clin. Densitometry, 2010-. Author: Diuretic Therapy in the Older Patient, 1978, Paget's Disease in Bone, Assessment and Management, 1981, Geriatric Medicine: A Problem Oriented Approach, 1984; editor: (with J. Turnbull, M. Lancaster, L. Norman) Alzheimer's Disease: A Handbook for Caregivers, 1990, 3d edit., 1998; mem. editl. adv. bd. Revs. Clin. Gerontology, South Med. Jour., Geriatria; reviewer for med. jours.; contbr. chpts. to books, articles to profl. jours. Fellow ACP (com. geriat. 1987-90, chmn. com. geriat. MKSAP IX 1991-94), Royal Coll. Physicians, Royal Soc. Medicine; mem. Internat. Soc. Clin. Densitometry, Am. Geriat. Soc. (membership com., reviewer jour., ann. meeting planning com. 1993), Gerontol. Soc. Am., Royal Coll. Surgeons, So. Med. Assn. (vice-chmn. coun. 1995-96, chmn. coun. 1996-97, v.p. 1997-98, pres.-elect 1998-99, pres. 1999-2000, editor geriatric medicine sect. Dial-Access program, from assoc. councilor to councilor state Tenn., chmn. adv. com. sci. activities, reviewer jour., assoc. editor So. Med. Jour. 1995-2000, editor 2000-2010, editor in chief, Jour. Clin. Deusitometry), So. Assn. Geriatric Medicine (pres. 1990-92), So. Assn. for Primary Care (editor clin. revs.), Tenn. Med. Assn. (reviewer jour.), Tenn. Geriat. Soc. (founding), Brit. Med. Assn., Brit. Geriat. Soc., Bone and Mineral Soc., Alzheimer's Assn. (pres. bd. dirs. N.E. Tenn. chpt. 1990-91). Office: Ea Tenn State U Coll Medicine PO Box 70429 Johnson City TN 37614-1704 Office Phone: 423-439-8830. Business E-Mail: hamdy@etsu.edu.

HAMED, KEVIN, biology professor; m. Misty Hamed. BS in Biology, Tenn. Technol. U.; MS in Biology, East Tenn. State U., Johnson City; doctoral student, U. Tenn. Nature ctr. mgr. Steele Creek Pk., Bristol, Tenn., 1995—2003; faculty mem. Va. Highlands CC, Abingdon, 2003—, asst. prof. biology. Named Va. Prof. of Yr., Carnegie Found. for Advancement of Tchg. and Coun. for Advancement and Support of Edn., 2009; grantee Va. CC Chancellor's Faculty Fellowship, 2009. Mem.: Soc. for Study Amphibians and Reptiles, Am. Soc. Ichthyologists and Herpetologists. Office: Va Highland CC OTC 1208 100 VHCC Dr Abingdon VA 24210 Office Phone: 276-739-2431. Office Fax: 276-739-2595. Business E-Mail: khamed@vhcc.edu.

HAMEL, DANA BERTRAND, retired academic administrator; b. Rumford, Maine, Aug. 9, 1923; s. Donat H. and Louise (Kenison) H.; m. Shirley Elmeree Smith Knavel, Dec. 19, 1945; children: Dana Randolph, Michelle, April. AB, Ashland Coll., Ohio, 1951; MA, Ohio State U., 1952; EdD, U Cin., 1962; AA in Humanities (hon.), Southside Va. C.C., 2004; AA in Humane Letters (hon.), Va. Western C.C., 2005. Master watchmaker Thomas J. Apryle & Sons, Johnstown, Pa., 1946; owner Hamels, Jewelers, Conemaugh, Pa., 1946-48; mem. mgmt. dept. Gen. Motors Inst., Flint, Mich., 1955-57; dean adminstrv. affairs Ohio Coll. Applied Sci. and Ohio Mechanics Inst., Cin., 1957-63, acting pres., 1961-62, exec. v.p., dean of faculties, 1962-63; dir. Roanoke Tech. Inst., 1963-64; exec. dir. Va. Dept. Tech. Edn., Richmond, 1964-66; founding chancellor Va. Community Coll. System, Richmond, 1966-79, cons., 1979-80; cons. to pres., dir. spl. acad. programs Va. State U., Petersburg, 1980-961980—; exec. dir. Va. Ctr. Pub./Pvt. Initiatives; pres. Hamel & Assocs., Richmond, 1996—. Coord. for offices of Va. Sec. of Edn. and Dept. of Edn. for WorkForce 2000, V-Quest Programs, 1992-96; co-chair Metro Richmond 2000; acting dir. Adminstrv. Affairs, CEBAFA. Founder, Gov.'s liaison SURA/Continuous Electron Beam Accelerator Facility, 1983—; trustee, v.p. 1983-99, Southeastern Univs. Rsch. Assn., Inc., 1981—; mem. Va. Adv. Coun. Vocat. Edn.; bd. dirs. Richmond Eye and Ear Hosp. Authority, 1989—, Ctr. Excellence, Inc., Richmond Cmty. HS, 1981—; chmn. bd. Va. Edn. Rsch. 1981-85, Network for Supercomputers, 1986—; sr. cons. 1986-93, So. Growth Policies Bd. Tech. Coun., 1987-95; Va. coord. Vamanuf Networking, 1990—; exec. dir. Mfg. Networking and Indsl. Modernization Project, 1992—; interim exec. dir. Va. Alliance Mfg. Competitiveness, 1993—; interim dir. Sch. to Work Program, 1994-95. With USAAF, 1942-45. Scribes acad. scholar, Ashland Coll. Mem. So. Assn. Schs. and Colls. (former pres.), Am. Assn. Jr. Colls. (commn. on legis.), Nat. Coun. State Dirs. (former chmn.), Am. Soc. Engring. Edn., Am. Psychology and Guidance Assn., Nat. Assn. for Gifted Children, Am. Coll. Pers. Assn., Cin. Guidance and Pers. Assn., Va. League Nursing (pres. 1987), Forum Club, Masons, Kiwanians, Phi Delta Kappa, Psi Chi, Iota Lambda Sigma.

HAMEL, DOUGLAS E., lawyer; b. Anchorage, Feb. 21, 1951; BA, U. Va., 1972, JD, 1976. Bar: Tex. 1976. Ptnr., co-head Employment Litig. and Labor Sect. Vinson & Elkins LLP, Houston. Chmn. Civil Svc. Commn. City of Houston, 1984-87. Office: Vinson & Elkins First City Tower 1001 Fannin St Ste 2300 Houston TX 77002-6760 Office Phone: 713-758-2036. E-mail: dhamel@velaw.com.

HAMEL, MATTHEW EDWARD, consumer products company executive, lawyer; b. NYC, Jan. 15, 1960; s. Rodolphe and Marilyn Vivian (Johnsen) H.; m. Lena Birgitta Nilsson, Aug. 9, 1986; 1 child, Emilie Lisa. BA in Economics and Polit. Sci., Yale U., 1982; JD, U. Chgo., 1986. Bar: N.Y. 1987. Assoc. White & Case, NYC and Stockholm, 1986; divsn. gen. counsel, Internat. Bus. Devel. Colgate-Palmolive Co.; v.p., gen. counsel & sec. Dow Jones Reuters Bus. Interactive LLC; assoc. gen. counsel, v.p., law, Enterprise Media Group. Dow Jones & Co; exec. v.p., gen. counsel & sec. Brown-Forman Corp., 2007—. Fulbright scholar, Sweden, 1982-83. Mem. ABA, Assn. Bar City N.Y. Office: Brown Forman Corp 850 Dixie Hwy Louisville KY 40210 Office Phone: 502-585-1100. Office Fax: 502-774-7876. E-mail: matt_hamel@b-f.com.

HAMENT, ANDREW STANTON, lawyer; b. Salina, Kans., Jan. 4, 1955; s. Carrol and Barbara June Hament; m. Priscila Morgan Fenton, May 5, 1990; children: Blake Fenton, Caroline Adams. BA in Humanistic Studies, John Hopkins U., Balt., 1977; JD, U. Balt., 1981. Bar: Fla. 1981. Assoc. Muller & Mintz, PA, Miami, Fla., 1981—87; sr. counsel labor law Harris Corp., Melbourne, 1987—90, European counsel Brussels, Belgium, 1990—93, sr. counsel aerospace Palm Bay, Fla., 1993—95; ptnr. Holland & Knight, LLP, Melbourne, 1995—2003, Gray Robinson, PA, 2003—06, Ford & Harrison, LLP, 2006—. Contbr. articles to profl. jours. Mem. human resource mgmt. South Brevard Soc., Melbourne, 1995; past bd. mem. Bridges, Inc., Melbourne, 2000—08; mem. US Mid. Dist. Advisory Com., 2002—; past bd. mem. United Way Brevard, Melbourne, 2005; past trustee Holy Trinity Acad., Melbourne, 2005; mem. Space Coast March Dimos Leadership Team, 2012. Recipient Atty. of Yr. award, Harris Corp., 1990. Mem.: Inns Ct. (barrister), Acad. Fla. Mgmt. Attys. (charter mem.). Republican. Achievements include successfully argued Bruer vs. Jim's Concrete of Brevard actions under Fair Labor Standards Act before the US Supreme Court, 2003. Office: Ford & Harrison LLP 1901 S Harbor City Blvd Melbourne FL 32901 Office Phone: 321-724-5633. Business E-Mail: ahament@fordharrison.com.

HAMERMESH, DANIEL SELIM, economics professor; b. Cambridge, Mass., Oct. 20, 1943; s. Morton and Madeline (Goldberg) H.; m. Frances Witty, Dec. 18, 1966; children: David J., Matthew A. AB, U. Chgo., 1965; PhD, Yale U., 1969. Asst. prof. Princeton (N.J.) U., 1969-73; assoc. prof. Mich. State U., East Lansing, 1973-76, prof., 1976-93, chmn. dept., 1984-88; Edward Everett Hale centennial prof. economics U. Tex., Austin, 1993—2008, Sue Killam prof. economics, 2008—; prof. labor economics Maastricht U., 2009—. Rsch. dir. ASPER-U.S. Dept. Labor, Washington, 1974-75, rsch. assoc. Nat. Bur. Econ. Rsch., 1979-; vis. prof. Harvard U., Cambridge, Mass., 1981, Latrobe U., Melbourne, Australia, 1987, Gadjah Mada U., Indonesia, 1990, Australian Nat. U., 1991, Rijksuniversiteit Limburg, The Netherlands, 1992, New Econ. Sch., Moscow, 1993, Hebrew U., Jerusalem, 1995, Erasmus U., The Netherlands, 1997, U. Bristol, Eng., 2000, U. Aberdeen, Scotland, 2002, McMaster U., 2003, U. Mich., 2004; mem. econ. adv. panel NSF, 1995-97; program dir. Inst. for Study of Labor, Bonn, Germany; chmn. sci. adv. bd. German Inst. Econ. Rsch., 2003-09. Mem. bd. editors Am. Econ. Rev., 1990-94; co-editor Econ. Letters, 1994-98, Labour Econs., 1996-00, Jour. Population Econs., 2001-03, Ind. and Labor Rels. Rev., 2004—. Pres. Congregation Kehillat Israel, Lansing, 1988-90. Recipient Best Article award Western Econ. Assn., 1987, Parents' Assn. Centennial Teaching fellow U. Tex., 1995-96, Pres.'s Assocs. Tchg. Excellence award U. Tex., 2008; NSF rsch. grantee, 1980-82, 84-86, 86-91,

95—2003. Fellow Econometric Soc., Soc. Labor Economists (pres. 2000-01); mem. Am. Econ. Assn., Midwest Econ. Assn. (pres. 1988-89). Jewish. Avocations: running, classical music. Office: U Tex Dept Econs Austin TX 78712 Home Phone: 512-206-0908; Office Phone: 512-475-8526. Business E-Mail: hamermes@eco.utexas.edu.

HAMERMESH, RICHARD G., management professor; b. Altadena, Calif., Feb. 10, 1948; s. Bernard and Sylvia (Molberger) Hamermesh; m. Lorie Ann Shapiro, June 21, 1970; children: Joshua, Molli. BA, U. Calif., Berkeley, 1969; MBA, Harvard U., 1971, D in Bus. Adminstrn., 1976. Prof. mgmt. practice Harvard Business School, Boston, asst. prof., 1976—81, assoc. prof., 1982—87, MBA Class of 1961 prof. mgmt. practice, 2002—, faculty chair Healthcare Initiative; co-founder, mng. ptnr. Ctr. for Exec. Devel., Cambridge, Mass., 1987—2001. Bd. dirs. BE Aerospace Inc., 1987—. Author: Making Strategy Work, 1986, Fad-Free Management: The Six Principles That Drive Successful Companies and Their Leaders, 1996; co-author: New Business Ventures And The Entrepreneur, 2006; editl. bd. Harvard Bus. Review; contbr. articles to profl. jours. Founding pres. New Schs. Found., Mass., 1986—87. Jewish. Avocations: swimming, tennis. Home: 33 Woodland Rd Newton MA 02166 Office: Harvard Business School Rock Center, Rm 109 60 North Harvard St Boston MA 02163 also: BE Aerospace Inc Bd Directors 1400 Corporate Ctr Way Wellington FL 33414 Office Phone: 561-791-5000, 617-495-4179. Office Fax: 561-791-7900. Business E-Mail: richard_hamermesh@beaerospace.com, rhamermesh@hbs.edu.

HAMES, MICHAEL J., electronics executive; BSEE, U. Notre Dame, Ind. Joined Texas Instruments, Inc., 1980, v.p. worldwide DSP bus., 1982, DSP mktg. mgr., US DSP product mgr., sr. v.p., mgr. application specific products Dallas. Mem.: IEEE. Office: Tex Instruments Inc PO Box 660199 Dallas TX 75266-0199 Office Phone: 972-995-2011. Office Fax: 972-995-4360.

HAMILTON, ANTHONY, singer; b. Charlotte, NC, Jan. 28, 1971; m. Tarsha McMillian; children: Aaron Michael, Nolan Anthony, Anthony, Romero, Tristen. Barber; signed to Uptown Records, NYC, 1993—95, various music labels, 1996—2003, So So Def Records, 2003—. Singer: (albums) XTC, 1996, Comin' from Where I'm From, 2003, Soulife, 2005, Ain't Nobody Worryin', 2005, The Point of It All, 2008, Back to Love, 2011, (songs) (with Al Green) You've Got the Love I Need, 2008 (Grammy award for Best Traditional R&B Vocal Performance, 2009); background vocals (songs) Po' Folks, 2002 (nominated for Grammy award for Best Rap/Sung Collaboration, 2003). Recipient J Cool Like That award, Black Entertainment TV (BET), 2006. Office: Zomba Label Group 3923 7th St S Arlington VA 22204 Office Phone: 703-979-5483.

HAMILTON, BUFFY J., school librarian; EdS in Instrnl. Tech. & Sch. Libr. Media, U. Ga., Athens, 2005. HS English tchr., tech. integration specialist Cherokee County Sch. Dist., Ga.; librarian Creekview HS, Canton, Ga. Adj. instr. Lyrasis; mem. adv. bd. Sch. Libr. Monthly, Libr. Media Connection; mem. inter-divisional com. on info. literacy American Assn. Sch. Libraries / Assn. Coll. and Rsch. Libraries, 2010—12. Named to Movers & Shakers, Libr. Jour., 2011. Mem.: ALA, Profl. Assn. Ga. Educators, Assn. Coll. and Rsch. Librarians, American Assn. Sch. Librarians (social media chair, mem. nat. conf. com. 2011), Ga. Libr. Media Assn. (comm. chair 2010, 2011). Office: Creekview HS Library 1550 Owens Store Rd Canton GA 30115 Office Phone: 770-720-7600 ext. 253. Business E-Mail: buffy.hamilton@cherokee.k12.ga.us.

HAMILTON, CARL HULET, retired academic administrator; b. Morris, Okla., Sept. 30, 1934; s. Alva H. and Olah E. (Pryor) H.; m. Gloria Joyce Gore, Sept. 3, 1954; children: Ray, Carla Jo, Deanna Jean. ThB, Southwestern Coll., 1956; BA, Oklahoma City U., 1957; MA, U. Tulsa, 1962; PhD, U. Ark., 1968. English tchr. Southwestern Coll., Oklahoma City, 1957-60; editor Oral Roberts Evangelistic Assn., Tulsa, 1960-62; English tchr., editor Oral Roberts U., Tulsa, 1966-68; acad. dean, 1968-75; provost Oral Roberts U., Tulsa, 1975-84; adminstr. World Evangelism, San Diego, 1984-86; chief of staff Feed the Children, Oklahoma City, 1986-88; provost, chief acad. officer Oral Roberts U., 1989-98; ret., 2001. Min. adminstrn. First United Meth. Ch., 1999-2001, pastor Ketchum United Meth. Ch., 2006-07. Republican. Methodist. Avocations: fishing, water sports, motorcycling. Home: PO Box 488 Disney OK 74340-0488 Home Phone: 918-435-4788. E-mail: piscatore@brightok.net.

HAMILTON, CARLOS ROBERT, JR., endocrinologist, academic administrator, consultant; b. Houston, June 12, 1939; s. Carlos Robert and Berta (Denman) H.; m. Carolyn Burton, Aug. 12, 1961; children: Carlos R. III, Patricia Frances. BA, U. Tex., 1961; MS, MD with honors, Baylor Coll. Medicine, 1966. Diplomate Am. Bd. Internal Medicine, Am. Bd. Endocrinology and Metabolic Diseases. Intern in internal medicine Johns Hopkins Hosp., Balt., 1966-67, asst. resident in internal medicine, 1967-69, chief resident in medicine, 1970-71; clin. and rsch. fellow Harvard Med. Sch./Mass. Gen. Hosp., Boston, 1969-70; asst. prof. medicine Johns Hopkins U. and Hosp., Balt., 1971-72; staff endocrinologist Wilford Hall USAF Med. Ctr., San Antonio, 1972-74; clin. prof. medicine Baylor Coll. Medicine, Houston, 1974—; clin. prof. medicine Med. Sch. U. Tex., Houston, 1999-2000, prof. internal medicine, 2000—, spl. asst. to pres., 2000—. Cons. endocrinology and internal medicine Med. Clinic of Houston, L.L.P., 1974—2000; med. advisor employee benefit com. Southwestern Bell Tel. Co., 1975—93; attending physician in endocrinology Ben Taub Gen. Hosp./Baylor Coll. Medicine, 1980—; attending physician, mem. active staff The Meth. Hosp./Meml.-Hermann Hosp., Houston, 1974—; mem. active staff St. Luke's Episcopal Hosp., 2000—, Meml. Hermann Hosp., 2000—; practicing physicians adv. coun. U.S. Dept. HHS, 2003—07; mem. health, sci. and rsch. com. World Anti-Doping Agy., Montreal, 2003—07. Contbr. articles to profl. jours. Dist. and coun. chair, area pres., regional bd. dirs., v.p. Boy Scouts Am., Houston, Atlanta, Irving, Tex., 1980—; bd. regents Tex. Woman's U., 1999-2001; chair, bd.dirs. Mus. Health and Med. Sci., Houston, 2006-08. Recipient Dist. award of merit, Silver Beaver award, Silver Antelope award, Disting. Eagle Scout award, Silver Buffalo award Boy Scouts Am., 1982-99. Fellow ACP (bd. dirs. Tex. chpt., Mead-Johnson Residency scholar 1970, bd. dirs. Tex. Acad. Internal Medicine and ACP-ASIM health and pub. policy com., Tex. Laureate award 2003, Named Advocate of Yr., 2006), Am. Coll. Endocrinology (trustee 1999-2000, sec.-treas. 2001-02, chancellor 2005-06, pres. 2007-08); mem. SAR (bd. dirs. Paul Carrington chpt. 1992—, pres. 1993), Am. Soc. Internal Medicine (bd. dirs. polit. action com. 1995-98, Key Congl. Contact of Yr. 1996), Am. Assn. Clin. Endocrinologists (bd. dirs. 1995—, chair legis. and regulatory com. 1998-2000, sec. exec. com. 2000-01, treas. 2001-02, v.p. 2002-2003, pres.-elect 2003-04, pres. 2004-05, Disting. Svc. award, 2010), Tex. Med. Assn. (exec. com. polit. action com. 1989-01, chair 1995, 96), Harris County Med. Soc. (bd. dirs. 1992-99, pres.-elect 1998, pres. 1999), Kiwanis (bd. dirs. Houston chpt. 1986-95, pres. 1995), Alpha Omega Alpha, Sigma Xi; Master ACE. Office: U Tex Health Sci Ctr 7000 Fannin Rm 1732 Houston TX 77030 Office Phone: 713-500-3825. Business E-Mail: carlos.r.hamilton@uth.tmc.edu.

HAMILTON, CLYDE HENRY, federal judge; b. Edgefield, SC, Feb. 8, 1934; s. Clyde H. and Edwina (Odom) Hamilton; children: John C., James W. BS, Wofford Coll., 1956; JD with honors, George Washington U., 1961. Bar: SC 1961. Reference asst. US Senate Libr., Washington, 1958—61; assoc. J.R. Folk, Edgefield, 1961—63; assoc., gen. ptnr. Butler, Means, Evins & Browne, Spartanburg, SC, 1963—81; judge US Dist. Ct. SC, Columbia, 1981—91, US Ct. Appeals (4th cir.), Richmond, Va., 1991—99, sr. judge, 1999—. Gen. counsel Synalloy Corp., Spartanburg, 1969—80. Mem. editl. staff: Cumulative Index of Congl. Com. Hearings, 1935—58, bd. editors: George Washington Law Rev., 1959—60. Pres. Spartanburg County Arts Coun., 1971—73, Spartanburg Day Sch., 1972—74, sustaining trustee, 1975—81; past mem. steering com. undergrad. merit fellowship program and estate planning coun. Converse Coll., Spartanburg; trustee Spartanburg Meth. Coll., 1979—84; bd. commrs. on grievances and discipline SC Supreme Ct., 1980—81; del. Spartanburg County, 4th Congl. Dist. and SC Rep. Convs., 1976, 1980; active, past chmn. fin. com. and adminstrv. bd. Trinity United Meth. Ch., Spartanburg, trustee, 1980—83. Capt. USAR, 1956—62. Recipient Alumni Disting. Svc. award, Wofford Coll., 1991, The Order of The Palmetto, Gov. Beasley, SC, 1999. Mem.: SC Bar Assn., Piedmont Club (bd. govs. 1979—81). Office: US Ct Appeals 4th Cir 1901 Main St Columbia SC 29201-2443 Office Phone: 803-765-5461.

HAMILTON, DAGMAR STRANDBERG, lawyer, retired educator; b. Phila., Jan. 10, 1932; d. Eric Wilhelm and Anna Elizabeth (Sjöström) Strandberg; m. Robert W. Hamilton, June 26, 1953; children: Eric Clark, Robert Andrew Hale, Meredith Hope. AB, Swarthmore Coll., 1953; JD, U. Chgo. Law Sch., 1953—55, Am. U., 1961. Bar: Tex. 1972. Atty. civil rights divsn. U.S. Dept Justice, Washington, 1965-66; asst. instr. govt. U. Tex., Austin, 1966-71; lectr. Law Sch. U. Ariz., Tucson, 1971-72; editor, rschr. Assoc. William O. Douglas U.S. Supreme Ct., Washington, 1962-73, 75-76; editor, rschr. Douglas autobiography Random House Co., 1972-73; staff counsel Judiciary Com. US House of Representatives, 1973-74; asst. prof. L.B. Johnson Sch. Pub. Affairs U. Tex., Austin, 1974-77, assoc. prof., 1977—83, assoc. dean, 1983—87, prof., 1983—2006, prof. emeritus, 2007—. Interdisciplinary prof. U. Tex. Law Sch., 1983—2006; vis. prof. Washington U. Law Sch., St. Louis, 1982, U. Maine, Portland, 1992; Godfrey Disting. vis. prof. U. Maine Law Sch., 2002; vis. fellow U. London, QMW Sch. Law, 1987—88; vis. prof. U. Maine, Portland, 2002; vis. fellow U. Oxford Inst. European & Comparative Law, 1998. Contbr. to various publs. Mem. Tex. State Bar Assn., Am. Law Inst., Assn. Pub. Policy Analysis and Mgmt., Swarthmore Coll. Alumni Coun. (rep.), Kappa Beta Phi (hon.), Phi Kappa Phi (hon.). Democrat. Mem. Soc. Of Friends.

HAMILTON, DANIEL P., state legislator; b. Miami, Fla., Aug. 17, 1976; s. Glenn Hamilton; m. Kelly Hamilton; children: Caroline, Rivers, Greyson. BS in Orgnl. Comm., Bob Jones U., 1998. Congl. aide to Rep. Jim DeMint US House of Representatives, 1999—2001; mng. ptnr. Keller Williams Realty, 2005—; pres., CEO Hamilton Mgmt. Group; mem. Dist. 20 SC House of Reps., 2009—. Republican. Christian. Office: 312A Blatt Bldg Columbia SC 29201 Home: PO Box 6088 Greenville SC 29606-6088 Home Phone: 864-244-0663; Office Phone: 864-527-7685, 803-212-6795. Business E-Mail: DanHamilton@schouse.org.

HAMILTON, EUGENE FORREST, state legislator; b. Olive Branch, Miss., Oct. 4, 1941; m. Patricia Bennett Hamilton. Mem. Dist. 6 Miss. House of Reps., 2004—, vice chair exec. contingent fund, mem. county affairs com., Medicaid com., municipalities com., pub. health and human svcs. com. Mem.: NARD, NPIB, Miss. Pharmacists Assn. Republican. Baptist. Address: 7410 Hamilton Cir N Olive Branch MS 38654 Office Phone: 662-893-7400. Business E-Mail: efhamilton@house.ms.gov.

HAMILTON, JOHN MAXWELL, professor, author; b. Evanston, Ill., Mar. 28, 1947; s. Maxwell Millings and Elizabeth Curran (Carlson) H.; m. Regina Frances Nalewajek, Aug. 19, 1975; 1 child, Maxwell Janek. BA in Journalism, Marquette U., Milw., 1969; postgrad., U. N.H., 1971-73; MS in Journalism, Boston U., 1974; PhD in Am. Civilization, George Washington U., 1983. Reporter Milw. Jour., 1967-69; free-lance journalist Washington, 1973-75; fgn. corres. L.Am., 1976-78; spl. asst., asst. adminstr. Agy. for Internat. Devel., Washington, 1978-81; staff assoc. House Fgn. Affairs Subcom. Internat. Econ. Policy/Trade, Washington, 1981-82; chief U.S. fgn. policy corres. Internat. Reporting Info. Sys., Washington, 1982-83; dir. Main St. Am. and the Third World, Washington, 1985-87; sr. counselor World Bank, Washington, 1983-85, 87-92; dean and prof. Manship Sch. Mass. Comm. La. State U., Baton Rouge, 1992—2010, exec. vice chancellor, provost, 2010—12, Hopkins Breazeale found. prof. Baton Rouge, 1998; commentator MarketPlace Pub. Radio Internat., 1991—2004; sr. scholar Woodrow Wilson Internat. Ctr. Scholars, 2012—. Bd. dirs., treas. Internat. Ctr. for Journalists, Lamar Advt. Corp.; lectr. Brazil, Republic of Ga., UK, Hongkong, others; Pulitzer prize juror, 1999—2000; chair adv. com. Knight Internat. Press Fellowships; judge Scripps Howard Nat. Journalism award, 2001, 2004, 2006, 2010; fellow Shorenstein Ctr. Press, Politics and Pub. Affairs, Kennedy Sch., Harvard U., 2002. Author: Main Street America and the Third World, 1986, 2d edit., 1989, Edgar Snow: A Biography, 1988, revised, 2003 (Critics Choice, L.A. Times, Frank Luther Mott-Kappa Tau Alpha Rsch. award 1988), Entangling Alliances: How the Third World Shapes Our Lives, 1990; co-author: (with George Krimsky) Hold the Press: The Inside Story on Newspapers, 1996, Casanova Was A Book Lover: And Other Naked Facts and Provocative Curiosities About Reading, Writing and Publishing, 2000, Journalism's Roving Eye: A History Am. Foreign Reporting, 2009; editor:(book series) From Our Special Correspondent, 2007—; author chpts. in books; contbr. numerous articles to profl. jours. including Balt. Sun, Bull. of Atomic Scientists, Boston Globe, Chgo. Tribune, Christian Sci. Monitor, Columbia Journalism Rev., Fgn. Affairs, Journalism Studies, Journalism and Mass Comm. Quar., LA Times, NY Times, The Nation, others. Officer USMC, 1969—73. Recipient By-Line award, Marquette Coll. Journalism, 1993, Goldsmith prize, 2010, Tankard Book award, 2010; named Journalism Adminstr. of the Yr., Freedom Forum, 2003; grantee, Ford Found., Carnegie Inst., Knight Found., Scripps-Howard Found., others, 1985—. Mem.: Assn. Schs. Journalism and Mass Comm., Soc. Profl. Journalists, Coun. Fgn. Rels., Met. Club (Washington). Democrat. Office: La State Univ Manship Sch Mass Cmn Baton Rouge LA 70803-0001 Home: 1077 30th St NW Apt 606 Washington DC 20007 Office Phone: 225-578-2002. Business E-Mail: jhamilt@lsu.edu.

HAMILTON, JOSEPH HANTS, JR., physicist, researcher; b. Ferriday, La., Aug. 14, 1932; s. Joseph Hants and Letha (Gibson) H.; m. Jannelle Jauree Landrum, Aug. 5, 1960; children: Melissa Claire, Christopher Landrum. BS, Miss. Coll., Clinton, 1954; MS, Ind. U., Bloomington, 1956, PhD, 1958; DSc (hon.), Miss. Coll., Clinton, 1982; PhD (hon.), Nat. U. Frankfurt, Germany, 1992, U. Bucharest, Romania, 1999, U. St. Petersburg, Russia, 2001, Joint Inst. for Nuc. Rsch., 2004, Ravi Shankar Shukla U., India, 2006, Berea Coll., Ky., 2007, Eastern Ky. U., 2012. Mem. faculty Vanderbilt U., Nashville, 1958—, prof. physics, 1966—, Landon C. Garland prof. physics, 1981-92, Landon C. Garland disting. prof. physics, 1992—, chmn. dept., 1979-85; adj. prof. Tsinghua U., China, 1986—; vis. disting. lab. fellow Our Ridge Nat. Lab., 2000—. Hon. adv. prof. Fudan U., People's Republic of China, 1988—; NSF postdoctoral fellow U. Uppsala, Sweden, 1958-59; rsch. fellow Inst. Nuclear Studies, Amsterdam, 1962; vis. prof. U. Frankfurt, 1979-80, 90, 98, U. Louis Pasteur, Strasbourg, France, 1991; mem. adv. panel Nat. Heavy Ion Labs., 1971-73; mem. nat. policy bd. Holifield Heavy Ion Facility, 1974-84; organizer, chmn. exec. com., prin. investigator Univ. Isotope Separator, Oak Ridge, 1970-95; organizer Univ. Radioactive Ion Beam Consortium, 1996; cons. Oak Ridge Nat. Lab., 1972—; mem. coun. Oak Ridge Assoc. Univs., 1974-80, bd. dirs., 1995-97; organizer, dir. Joint Inst. for Heavy Ion Rsch., Oak Ridge, 1980—; mem. Oak Ridge Health Agreement Steering Panel for State of Tenn., 1993-00; sci. and tech. advisor coun. for State of Tenn., 1994-01; chmn. Internat. Conf. Internal Conversion Processes, 1965, Internat. Conf. Radioactivity in Nuclear Spectroscopy, 1969, Internat. Conf. Future Directions in Studies Nuclei far from Stability, 1979, Internat. Conf. Dirs. Nuclear Structure Rsch., 1984; co-chmn. Internat. Workshop Physics with a Recoil Mass Spectrometer, 1986; chmn. Internat. Symposium on Reflections and Directions in Low Energy Heavy Ion Physics, 1991, Internat. Conf. on Fission and Properties of Neutron Rich Nuclei, 1997, Internat. Symposium Perspectives in Nuclear Physics, 1998; co-chair Second Internat. Conf. on Fission and Properties of Neutron Rich Nuclei, 1999; chair third Internat. Conf., on fission and properties neutron rich nuclei, 2002; co-chair fourth Internat. Conf. on Fission and Properties of Neutron Rich Nuclei, 2007; dir. Vanderbilt Summer Sci. Collaborative for High Sch. Students and Tchrs., 1991-2004; chair Fifth Internat. Conf. Fission and properties of Neutron Rich Nuclei, 2012. Co-author: Science: Faith and Learning, 1972, ORAU from the Beginning, 1980, Graphical Representation of K-shell and Total Internal Conversion Coefficients from Z=30-104, 1984, Modern Atomic and Nuclear Physics, 1996, rev. 2010; co-author, editor: Internal Conversion Processes, 1966, Radioactivity in Nuclear Spectroscopy, 1972, Reactions Between Complex Nuclei, 1974, Future Directions in Studies of Nuclear Far from Stability, 1980, Microscopic Models in Nuclear Structure Physics, 1989, Reflections and Directions in Low Energy Heavy Ion Physics, 1993, Structure of the Vacuum and Elementary Matter, 1997, Fission and Properties of Neutron Rich Nuclei, 1998, Perspectives in Nuclear Physics, 1999, Fission and Properties of Neutron Rich Nuclei, 2000; Third Internat. Conf. Fission and properties of Neutron Rich Nuclei, 2003, Fourth Internat. Conf. Fission and properties of Neutron Rich Nuclei, 2008, Fifth Internat. Conf. Fission and properties of Neutron Rich Nuclei, 2013; assoc. editor Jour. Physics G: Nuc. Physics, 1984-87; internat. advisor nuc. physics World Sci. Pub. Corp., 1986-91, Jour. Modern Physics Letters A, 1986-91; mem. editl. bd. Progress in Particle and Nuc. Physics, 1993-98, editl. bd. mem. McGraw-Hill Yearbook in Sci. and Tech., 2009-, McGraw-Hill Encyclopedia Sci. and Tech., 2010-; assoc. editor Internat. Jour. Modern Physics, 2010-; contbr. articles to profl. jours., chpts. in books. Mem. Mayor Nashville Citizens Adv. Com. Housing, 1970-74; bd. dirs. Vineyard Conf. Center, Louisville, 1972-77, Danforth assoc., 1965-86, So. Bapt. Conv. Hist. Commn., 1983-91. Recipient Harvie Branscomb Disting. Prof. award Vanderbilt U., 1983-84, Humbolt prize W. Germany, 1979, Order Golden Arrow Outstanding Alumni award Miss. Coll., 1985, Sutherland prize for rsch., 1988, Guy and Rebecca Forman award for outstanding physics tchg., 1990, Thomas Jefferson award for svc. in univ. couns., 1995, Jeffrey Nordhaus award for excellence in undergrad. tchg., 1996, Outstanding Sci. Tchr. award, Tenn., 1998, First Outstanding Svc. award Oak Ridge Associated U., 2000, D. Ilkovic Gold medal Slovak Acad. Sci., 2002; Internat. Sci. and Tech. Cooperation award, Peoples Republic China 2002, GN. Flerov Prize Russia 2003; named State of Tenn. Outstanding Prof. of Yr. Coun. Advancement and Support Edn., 1991; grantee NSF, 1959-76, ERDA-Dept. Energy, 1975—. Fellow AAAS (Internat. Cooperation award 1996), Am. Phys. Soc. (vice chmn. Southeastern sect. 1972-73, chmn. 1973-74, mem. coun. 1994-2004, Jesse Beams Gold medal for rsch. 1975, George Peagram Gold medal tchg. 1988, Francis Slack gold medal for Svc. 2000); mem. Academia Europaea, Am. Assn. Physics Tchrs., Am. Inst. Physics (governing bd. 2004-07), Sigma Xi (chpt. pres. 1970). Home: 305 Mountainside Dr Nashville TN 37215-4324 Office Phone: 615-322-2456. Business E-Mail: j.h.hamilton@vanderbilt.edu.

HAMILTON, LEONARD, men's college basketball coach; Attended, Gaston CC, NC; B in Phys. Edn., U. Tenn., Martin, 1971; M in Phys. & Health Edn., Austin Peay State U., Clarksville, Tenn., 1973. Grad. asst. Austin Peay State U. Governors, 1971—73, asst. coach, 1973—74, U. Ky. Wildcats, 1974—80, assoc. head coach, 1980—86; asst. coach Okla. State U. Cowboys, 1986—90; head basketball coach U. Miami Hurricanes, Fla., 1991—2000, Washington Wizards, 2001, Fla. State U. Seminoles, 2002—. Named Nat. Coach of Yr., UPI, 1995, Big East Conf. Coach of Yr., 1995, 1999, Ea. Basketball Coach of Yr., 1999, Coach of Yr., Black Coaches Assn., 2000, Atlantic Coast Conf. Coach of Yr., 2009, 2012; named to U. Tenn. Martin Athletic Hall of Fame, U. Miami Athletic Hall of Fame, Austin Peay State U. Athletic Hall of Fame, Gaston County Hall of Fame, 2007; finalist Coach Wooden Keys to Life award, 2000. Office: Fla State Univ Athletics Dept 403 Stadium Dr W Rm D0107 PO Box 2195 Tallahassee FL 32316 Office Phone: 850-644-5229.

HAMILTON, MARK, state legislator; b. Apr. 21; life ptnr. Claudia Hamilton; 2 children. State rep. Dist. 82, Ga., 2007—; mem. Judiciary Non Civil com., Sci. and Tech. com., Agr., and Information and Audits Com., 2007—; house rep. Ga.; vice pres. Legal Mktg., Hill Mfg. Inc. Mem.: coaches cmty. youth sports teams, Tucker Civic Assn. and the Anti-Defamation League, Tucker Bus. Assn., Northlake Cmty.Alliance. Republican. Baptist. Office: 108 Colony Dr Ste 400 Cumming GA 30040 Office Phone: 770-844-6768. Fax: 770-844-6232. E-mail: mark.hamilton@house.ga.gov.

HAMILTON, MIKE (TUFFY), state legislator; b. Sept. 30, 1961; m. Terry Hamilton. Restaurant owner; mem. Dist. 19 Tex. House of Representatives, 2002—. Republican. Office: PO Box 119 Mauriceville TX 77626 also: Room E2.318 Capitol Extension Austin TX 78768 Office Phone: 409-745-3644. Office Fax: 512-463-0412.

HAMILTON, REBECCA, state legislator; b. Okla. City, Okla., Jan. 8, 1948; d. George and Betty Hamilton; m. Rodney Hargrave; 2 children. Mem. Okla. House Reps., 1980—86; mem. Dist. 89 Okla. House of Representatives, 2003—. Democrat. Mailing: 2433 SW 26th Oklahoma City OK 73108 Home: 919 SW Grand Blvd Oklahoma City OK 73109 Office: 2300 N Lincoln Blvd Rm 510 Oklahoma City OK 73105 Office Phone: 405-635-1689, 405-557-7397, 405-635-1687. Business E-Mail: rebeccahamilton@okhouse.gov.

HAMILTON, ROBERT WOODRUFF, retired legal association administrator, educator; b. Syracuse, NY, Mar. 4, 1931; s. Walton Hale and Irene (Till) H.; m. Dagmar S. Strandberg, June 2, 1953; children: Eric Clark, Robert Andrew, Meredith Hope. BA, Swarthmore Coll., 1952; JD, U. Chgo., 1955. Bar: D.C. 1956, U.S. Ct. Appeals (D.C. cir.) 1960, U.S. Supreme Ct. 1965. Law clk. to justice Tom Clark US Supreme Ct., Washington, 1955-56; assoc. Gardner, Morrison & Rogers, Washington, 1956-64; assoc. prof. law U. Tex., Austin, 1964-67, prof., 1967—2004, prof. emeritus, 2004—, Minerva House Drysdale Regents chair in law. Rsch. dir. U.S. Admin. Conf., Washington, 1972-73; vis. prof. U. Pa., U. Minn., Washington U., St.

Louis, others; Godfrey Disting. prof. law U. Maine Law Sch., 1992, 2003; mem. rev. panel on new drugs HEW, Washington, 1974-77. Author: Texas Practice, vols. 19 and 20, 1973, Cases on Corporations, 1975; author: (with Jonathan Macey) 9th rev. edit., 2005; author: Cases on Contracts, 1984, 2d rev. edit., 1992, Nutshell on Corporations, 1980, 5th rev. edit., 2000, Cases on Corporate Finance, 1984, 2d rev. edit., 1989, Fundamentals of Modern Business, 1990, Money Management for Lawyers and Clients, 1993, Business Organizations: Unincorporated Businesses and Closely Held Corporations, 1996, Business Basics for Law Students, 2d edit., 1998; author: (with Richard Booth) 3d edit., 2002. Chmn. bd. dirs. U. Tex. Coop., 1989-01, U. Coop. Soc., Austin, 1989-02; elected mem. Westlake Hills (Tex.) City Coun., 1969-72; chmn. zoning commn. Westlake Hills, 1983-87. Rsch. grantee U. Tex., 1970, 84, 92, 97. Mem. ABA (reporter), Am. Law Inst., Tex. Bar Assn. (partnership com., corp. laws com.), Tex. Bus. Law Found., Order of Coif. Democrat.

HAMILTON, RYAN, marketing professor; BS in Applied Physics, Brigham Young U., 1999; PhD in Mktg., Northwestern U., 2008. Asst. prof. mktg. Goizueta Bus. Sch., Emory U., 2008—. Contbr. articles to profl. jours. Mem.: Soc. for Judgement and Decision Making, Soc. for Consumer Psychology, Assn. for Consumer Rsch. Office: Emory University Goizueta Business School 1300 Clifton Rd NE Atlanta GA 30322 Office Phone: 404-727-9892. Office Fax: 404-181-6313. E-mail: ryan_hamilton@bus.emory.edu.

HAMILTON, STEVEN M., plastic surgeon; b. Houston, Aug. 25, 1954; MD, Baylor U., 1983. Cert. Plastic Surgery, 1992. Resident U. Tex. Health Sci. Ctr.; pvt. practice Houston; staff mem. St. Luke's Episcopal Hosp. Avocation: fishing. Office: 6624 Fannin St Ste 1650 Houston TX 77030 also: 22999 Highway 59, N, Ste 250 Kingwood TX 77339 Office Phone: 713-797-1007, 713-348-3344. Office Fax: 713-797-0633.

HAMILTON, SUSI, state legislator; m. Steve Hamilton; 1 child, Parker Elizabeth. BA in History, U. NC, Chapel Hill, 1994; MPA, U. NC, Wilmington, 2004. With Hist. Preservation and Downtown Devel., 1997—98; assoc. planner Hist. Preservation Planner, Wilmington, NC, 1998—2000; sr. planner Long Range Planning, Wilmington, NC, 2000—01; bd. dirs., pres. Hist. Wilmington Found., 2001—11; exec. dir. Wilmington Downtown, Inc., 2001—07; bd. dirs. Junior League of Wilmington, 2003—05; Del. A State Pub. Affairs Assoc. Wilmington Chpt., 2003—05; pres. Carousel Ctr. for Abused Children, bd. dirs., 2003—, Wilmington Rotary Club, 2004—07, Brooklyn Arts Ctr. as St. Andrews, 2005—, Girls, Inc., 2005—08, Wilmington Childrens Mus., 2007—10; regional v.p. NC Downtown Devel. Assoc., 2004—07; chmn. Cucalorus Film Festival, 2007—; with, mktg. Govtl. Rels. & Bus. Devel. Cons., 2007—; founder, CEO Hamilton Planning, 2007—; mem. Greater Wilmington C. of C. Fundraising Com., 2007—09; mem. District 18 NC House of Representatives, 2011—. Democrat. Office: 206 Nun St Wilmington NC 28401 Address: North Carolina House of Representatives 16 W Jones St Rm 1319 Raleigh NC 27601-1096 Office Phone: 919-733-5754. Business E-Mail: susi@susihamilton.com, Susi.Hamilton@ncleg.net.

HAMILTON, THOMAS ALLEN, financial planner insurance agent, securities representative; b. Oklahoma City, July 7, 1947; s. Vernon (Carlton) and Hazel (Margie) H.; m. Deborah; children: Travis Matthew, Heather Lynne. BBA Mktg. and Mgmt., Okla. U., 1969. Registered securities rep. Mass. Fin. Group, 1984, Sunesco, 1994, LifeMark Securities, Okla. City, 1995, Leonard Securities, Inc., 2003. Dept. mgr. J.C. Penney, Oklahoma City, 1969-71; spl. agt. CNA Ins., Oklahoma City, 1971-74; group cons. Mass. Mut. Ins. Co., Oklahoma City, 1974-79, qualified plan cons.; bus./estate/ins. cons. Mass Mut. Ins. Co., Oklahoma City, 1979-93; ins./investment cons. Sun Fin. Group, Oklahoma City, 1993-95; owner Hamilton Fin./Ins. Svs.-licensed in securities, property/casualty, life/health, disability, employee benefit plans, retirement and investment planning, 1979—; registered rep. Leonard Securities, Inc., Oklahoma City, 2003—. Past chmn. troop 177 Boy Scouts Am., Oklahoma City, 1987-88; mem. Crossings Cmty. Ch. Mem. Nat. Assn. Ins. and Fin. Advisors, Nat. Assn. Health Underwriters, Oklahoma City C. of C. Republican. Protestant. Home: 6100 W Gun Hill Way Oklahoma City OK 73132 Office: 5830 NW Express Way # 359 Oklahoma City OK 73132 Office Phone: 405-608-0295.

HAMILTON, VIRGINIA VAN DER VEER, historian, educator; b. Kans. City, Mo., Sept. 7, 1921; d. McClellan and Dorothy (Rainold) Van der Veer; m. Lowell S. Hamilton, Aug. 4, 1946; children: Carol (dec.), David. AB, Birmingham Coll., Ala., 1941, MA (Ford Found. Fund Adult Edn. fellow), 1961; PhD, U. Ala., 1968, LittD, 1992. Staff writer AP, Washington, 1942—46, Birmingham News, 1948—50; asst. prof. history U. Montevallo, Ala., 1951—55; asst. prof., asst. to pres. pub. rels. Birmingham-So. Coll., 1955—65; lectr. in history U. Ala., Birmingham, 1965—68, asst. prof., 1968—71, assoc. prof., 1971—75, prof., 1975—87, prof. emerita, 1987—. Author: Hugo Black: The Alabama Years, 1972, Alabama: A History, 1977, The Story of Alabama, 1980, Your Alabama, 1980, Seeing Historic Alabama, 1982, rev. edit., 1996, Lister Hill: Statesman from the South, 1987, Looking For Clark Gable and Other 20th Century Pursuits, 1996, Teddy's Child: Growing Up in The Anxious Southern Gentry Between the Great Wars, 2009; editor: Hugo Black and the Bill of Rights, 1978. Faculty Rsch. grantee U. Ala. at Tuscaloosa, 1969, U. Ala. at Birmingham, 1973-74, 74-75. Mem. So., Am. Hist. Orgn., Am. Historians, Soc. Am. Historians, Ala. Assn. Historians, Ala. Hist. Soc. Office Phone: 205-821-7652.

HAMILTON-KEMP, THOMAS ROGERS, organic chemist, educator; b. Lebanon, Ky., May 13, 1942; s. Thomas Rogers and Catherine Rose (Hamilton) K.; m. Lois Ann Groce, Sept. 13, 1980. AA, St. Catharine Coll., 1962; BA, U. Ky., 1964, PhD in Chemistry, 1970. Asst. prof. natural products chemistry U. Ky., Lexington, 1970-75, assoc. prof., 1975-85, prof., 1985—2005, prof. emeritus, 2005—. Contbr. articles to profl. jours. Mem. SAR, Am. Chem. Soc., Am. Soc. Hort. Sci., Sigma Xi, Gamma Sigma Delta Democrat. Roman Catholic. Home: 2025 Williamsburg Rd Lexington KY 40504-3015 Home Phone: 859-276-4728.

HAMLEN, KEVIN WILLIAM, computer scientist, educator; b. Buffalo, June 2, 1976; s. William Arthur and Susan Margaret Hamlen; m. Rebecca Anne Geiger, July 1, 2006. BS, Carnegie Mellon U., Pitts., 1998; MS, Cornell U., Ithaca, NY, 2002, PhD, 2006. Rschr. Cornell U., Computer Sci. Dept., 1998—2006; asst. prof. computer sci. U. Tex., Dallas, 2006—. Tech. cons. Microsoft Rsch., Redmond, Wash., 2001—01. Leader Bible study, pianist Cornell Grad. Christian Fellowship, Ithaca, 1998—2006. Fellow, Lockheed Martin, 1998—99; scholar, Carnegie Mellon U., 1994—98. Mem.: Phi Beta Kappa, Phi Kappa Phi. Evangelical. Achievements include invention of certified program-rewriting as a means of enforcing computer security.

HAMLIN, DENNY, race car driver; b. Nov. 18, 1980; Profl. race car driver NASCAR Sprint Cup Series, 2005—; NASCAR driver Joe Gibbs Racing, 2006—. 1st pl. Pocono 500 Pocono Motor Speedway, 2006, 1st pl. Pa. 500, 2006, 2009, 1st pl. Gillette Fusion ProGlide 500, 2010; 1st pl. Lenox Indsl. Tools 300 NH Internat. Speedway, 2007, 1st pl. Sylvania 300, 2012; 1st pl. Goody's Cool Orange 500 Martinsville Motor Speedway, 2008, 1st pl. TUMS Fast Relief 500, 2009, 2010, 1st pl. Goody's Fast Pain Relief 500, 2010; 1st pl. Chevy Rock & Roll 400 Richmond Motor Speedway, 2009, 1st pl. Air Guard 400, 2010; 1st pl. Samsung Mobile 500 Tex. Motor Speedway, 2010, 1st pl. AAA Tex. 500, 2010; 1st pl. Southern 500 Darlington Raceway, 2010; 1st pl. Heluva Good! Sour Cream Dips 400 Mich. Internat. Speedway, 2010, 2011; 1st pl. Subway Fresh Fit 500 Phoenix Internat. Speedway, 2012; 1st pl. STP 400 Kans. Speedway, 2012; 1st pl. IRWIN Tools Night Race Bristol Motor Speedway, 2012; 1st pl. AdvoCare 500 Atlanta Motor Speedway, 2012. Named Raybestos Rookie of Yr., NASCAR Sprint Cup Series, 2006. Office: Joe Gibbs Racing 13415 Reese Blvd W Huntersville NC 28078

HAMM, HAROLD GLENN, oil industry executive; b. Lexington, Okla., Dec. 11, 1945; s. Leland Albert and Jane Elizabeth Hamm; m. Sue Ann Hamm, 1987 (separated 2012); 5 children. LHD (hon.), U. Okla., 2009. Chmn., pres., CEO Continental Resources, Inc. (formerly Shelly Dean Oil Co.), Oklahoma City, 1967—2005; chmn., ptnr. Hiland Holdings GP, LP, 2004—. Bd. dirs. Continental Resources, Inc., 1967—, Hiland Holdings, LLC, 2004—, Complete Production Services, Inc., 2005—. Recipient Energy Advocate of the Yr. award, 2009; named one of The Forbes 400: Richest Americans, 2007—, The 100 Most Influential People in the World, TIME mag., 2012; named to The Enid Public Sch. Found. Hall of Fame, 2008, The Okla. Ind. Petroleum Assn. Wildcatters Hall of Fame, 2011. Mem.: Nat. Stripper Well Assn., Okla. Independent Petroleum Assn. (chmn. 2005—07). Office: Continental Resources Inc PO Box 269000 Oklahoma City OK 73126 Office Phone: 580-233-8955, 405-234-9000.

HAMMAD, ALAM E., international business consultant, author, educator; 1 child, Adam. BA in Commerce, Cairo Poly. Inst., Egypt, 1965; MS in Mktg., La. State U., Baton Rouge, 1971; D in Bus. Adminstrn., George Washington U., 1977. Advisor Min. State & Gov. of Dhofar, Oman, 1977-79; advisor Min. Petroleum and Minerals, Oman, 1979; advisor to min., head planning Min. Agr. and Fisheries, Oman, 1979-83; chmn. MicroAge Computers Corp., Va., 1984-86; prof., lectr. George Washington U., Washington, 1984-88; internat. cons., 1984—; pres., founder Pizza Club, Inc., Va., 1987-97; vis. prof. George Washington U., 1988—90; trustee George Mason U., 1994—98; vice rector, 1996—98. Mem. found. com. Sultan Qaboos U., 1981-86; pres. Info. Security Found., 1991-93; chmn. found. com. Oman Nat. Fisheries Co., 1980-81, chmn. Founding Com., Oman Bank Agr. and Fisheries, 1981-82; bd. dirs. Oman Sun Farms Co., 1979; bd. dirs. Oman Devel. Bank, 1979-83; class A contractor, 1987-; founder Am. Global Pub., 1992—; pub. policy expert Heritage Found., 1996—; writer Okaz Saudi Newspaper, 1996-97, Gulf News, 1992-93; sr. assoc. Ctr. Strategic and Internat. Studies, 1997-2001; Va. Gov. conf. asst., 1998-2001; advisor GLG Policy and Econ. Coun., 2005. Author: Development of Agriculture and Fisheries in Oman, 1981, Agriculture, Animal Wealth, Water Resources and Fisheries of Oman, 1987, Islamic Banking: Theory and Practice, 1989, Encyclopedia of Computer Terms, English-Arabic, 1994, Dictionary of Computer Terms, English-Arabic, 1994; editor Newsweek in Arabic, 2000, Encyclopedia of Computer and Internet Terms, English-Arabic, 2008; contbr. articles to profl. jours., radio, TV shows. Chmn. pub. affairs, exec. vice chmn., 1st vice chmn. Alexandria Rep. City Com.; pres. Nat. Arab-Am. Rep. Coun., 1994; mem. George Washington Dist. Com., Boy Scouts Am.; vice rector, 1996-98; commr. Alexandria Indsl. Devel. Authority, 1996-98; mem. Nat. Policy Coun., No. Va. Rep. Bus. Forum, Com. for a Safe Va., Campaign for Honest Change, Empower Am., Bachelor 95 & Master Commr. Sci. 97 U. Scouting; chmn. advancement Rep. Party Va., 1994-96; mem. Rep. Presdl. Task Force; nat. advisor New Majority Coun., 1997; mem. Alexandria Citizen Police Acad., 1997, cmty Polit. leadership Inst., 1998, Cmty. Emergency Response Team, 2012, Alexandria Citizens Acad, 2012, pres. Alexandria Citizen's Police Acad. Assn., 1998, Comm. VA Coun., 2000; maj. gen. mil. Aide-de-Camp to Va. Gov., 2001; vol. Bush-Cheney Presdl.Transition. Com., 2001, Presdl. Inaugural Com., 2001; grad. FBI Citizens Acad., 2002; mem. Rep. Nat. Com., Nat. Rep. Senatorial Com., 2002; sec., bd. dirs. Alexandria Police Found., 2002-, Hon. Police Captain, 2010, Alex Cir Court Commr. Jury, 2010 Decorated Order of Sultan Qaboos (Oman); recipient Outstanding Cmty. Svc. award Am. Indian Exch., 1994, Recognition honor Immigrant Ams.-Orgn. Chinese Am., 1996, Scroll of Achievements George Mason U., 1998, Outstanding Svc. award VA Prof. Occupl. Reg. Bd., 1999, Alexandria Chief of Police award, 2000, Appreciation cert. VA DPOR, 2001, Patrick Henry award VA Gov., 2001 Mem. Am. Coun. Trustees and Alumni, Beta Gamma Sigma. Home: 819 S Fairfax St Alexandria VA 22314-4311 Home Phone: 703-548-4840. Personal E-mail: alamehammad@aol.com.

HAMMER, KIM D., state legislator; m. Karen Hammer; 3 children. B in Bibl. Counseling, Trinity Coll., Newburgh, Ind. Mem. First Bapt. Ch., Benton; case mgr., regional dir. Harmony Grove Public Sch., Benton; interim mgr. West Dept. Store, 1977; pastor Oakdale Bapt. Ch., Judsonia, Ark., 1980—84; trustee Budd Creek Bapt. Camp, 1983—85; pastor Lakeside Bapt. Ch., Des Arc, Ark., 1984—89; mem. Prairie County Home Health Svcs., 1986—88, Des Arc Vol. Ambulance Svcs., 1988—90; vol., chaplain svcs. Birch Tree Mental Health Unit, 1991—92; assoc. pastor, adminstr. Holland Chapel Bapt. Ch., Benton, Ark., 1992—2006; vol., chaplain svcs. Saline Meml. Generations Unit, 1993—95; mem. Saline Meml. Hosp. Home Health, 1992—96; chmn. Saline Meml. Hospice, 1994—95, vol., chaplain svcs., 1995—97, Ctrl. Ark. Hospice, 1996—97; mem. Ark. Hospice Found., 1999—99, Cmty. Christian Care Clinic, 2000—04, Benton Pub. Sch. Restructuring Com., 2001—03, Organized Patriotic Svc., 2002; bd. dirs. City Reach, 2002—05; candidate, Dist. 28 Ark. House of Representatives, 2006; chaplain Saline Meml. Hospice, 2008—; mem. Dist. 28 Ark. House of Representatives, 2011—. Republican. Office: 1411 Edgehill Dr Benton AR 72015 Office Phone: 501-840-3841. Personal E-mail: kimdhammer@yahoo.com.

HAMMERSCHMIDT, JOHN PAUL, former United States Representative, Arkansas, lumber company executive; b. Harrison, Ark., May 4, 1922; s. Arthur Paul and Junie (Taylor) H.; m. Virginia Sharp, deceased; 1 child, John Arthur. Student, The Citadel, U. Ark., Okla. State U.; BS in Bus. Mgmt., Canbourne U., London, MA in Philosophy magna cum laude; PhD in Internat. Studies, Wallingham U., London; LLD (hon.), U. Ark., 2011. Ordained elder, deacon in Presbyn. Ch. Chmn. bd. Hammerschmidt Lumber Co., Harrison, 1946-84; mem. 90th-102d Congresses from 3d Ark. Dist., 1967-93. Mem. Pub. Works and Transp. Com., 1967-93, ranking mem., 1987-93; mem. V.A. Com., 1967-93, ranking mem., 1973-86; bd. dirs. 1st Fed. Bank of Ark.; sr. chmn. bd. 1st Fed. Bankshares of Ark.; chmn. emeritus N.W. Ark. Coun.; nat. committeeman Ark. Citizen of Yr. Com.; mem. Presdl. Commn. on Aviation Security and Terrorism; mem. Pres.'s task force on Vets. Health Care; mem. Claude and Mildred Pepper Found., 1989-90 (PVA Speedy award), bd. Met. Washington Airports Authority; past chmn. bd., trustee Ark. State U., U. of the Ozarks; committeeman Nat. Rep. Party, 2002; bd. mem. Arks. Western Found., 2006-2010. Chmn. Ark. Republican Com., 1964-66; mem. Rep. Nat. Finance Com., 1960-64, nat. Rep. committeeman from, Ark., 1976-80; mem. Harrison City Coun., 1948, 60, 62. Served as pilot USAAF, World War II, CBI. Decorated Air medal with 4 oak leaf clusters, D.F.C. with 3 oak leaf clusters, 3 Battle Stars, The China War Meml. medal, Meritorious Svc. award VFW Congl. award, Silver Helmet award, Nat. Order Trenchrats Legis. Svc. award, Award for Life Svc. to Vets., Boy Scouts Golden Eagle award, 2012; named. Ark. Citizen of Yr., 1991, Ark. Aerospace Found. Hall of Fame, 1991. Mem. Ark. Lumber Dealers Assn. (past pres.), Midwest Lumbermens Assn. (past pres.), Harrison C. of C. (named Man of Yr. 1965), Am. Legion, Masons (33 degree-Grand Cross), Scottish Rite, Shriners, Jesters, Elks, Rotary (past pres. Harrison). Republican. Presbyterian. Office Phone: 870-391-3325, 870 741 9250. Personal E-mail: jph@northark.edu, jphzz@cox.net.

HAMMES, GORDON G., chemistry professor; b. Fond du Lac, Wis., Aug. 10, 1934; s. Jacob and Betty (Sadoff) H.; m. Judith Ellen Frank, June 14, 1959; children: Laura Anne, Stephen R., Sharon Lyn. AB, Princeton, 1956; PhD, U. Wis., 1959. NSF postdoctoral fellow Max Planck Inst. fur physikalische Chemie, Göttingen, Germany, 1959-60; from instr. to assoc. prof. Mass. Inst. Tech., Cambridge, 1960-65; prof. Cornell U., Ithaca, NY, 1965-88, chmn. dept. chemistry, 1970-75, Horace White prof. chemistry and biochemistry, 1975-88, dir. biotech. program, 1983-88; prof. U. Calif., Santa Barbara, 1988-91, vice chancellor, 1988-91; prof. Duke U., Durham, NC, 1991—2007; vice chancellor Duke U. Med. Ctr., Durham, NC, 1991-98; univ. disting. svc. prof. biochemistry Duke U., Durham, NC, 1996—2007, emeritus, 2008—. Mem. physiol. chemistry sect., phys. biochemistry study sect., Tng. grant com. NIH; bd. counselors Nat. Cancer Inst., 1976-80; mem. adv. coun. chemistry dept., Princeton, 1970-75, Poly. Inst. NY, 1977-78, Boston U., 1977-92; mem. NRC, US nat. com. for biochemistry, 1989-95. Author: Principles of Chemical Kinetics, 1978, Enzyme Catalysis and Regulation, 1982; author: (with I. Amdur) Chemical Kinetics: Principles and Selected Topics, 1966, Thermodynamics and Kinetics for the Biological Sciences, 2000, Spectroscopy for the Biological Sciences, 2005; author: Physical Chemsitry for the Biological Sciences, 2007; editor: Biochemistry, 1992—2003; contbr. articles to profl. jours. NSF sr. postdoctoral fellow, 1968-69; NIH Fogarty scholar, 1975-76 Mem. NAS, Am. Acad. Arts and Scis., Am. Chem. Soc. (award biol. chemistry 1967, editl. bd. jours., exec. com. div. phys. chemistry 1976-79, exec. com. div. biol. chemistry 1977-88, com. profl. tng. 1985-92, task force on biotech. 1989-90), Am. Soc. Biochemistry and Molecular Biology (coun., editl. bd. jour. pres., William C. Rose award 2002), Phi Beta Kappa, Sigma Xi, Phi Lambda Upsilon. Home: 7515 Pelican Bay Blvd 7A Naples FL 34108 Business E-Mail: gordon.hammes@duke.edu.

HAMMETT, SUZANNE, bank executive; Grad., Wellesley Coll.; completed Mgmt. Tng. Program, Harvard U. With Chem. Bank, Chase Manhattan; joined JP Morgan Chase & Co., 1977, mng. dir.; exec. v.p., chief credit policy officer JPMorgan Chase & Co., head credit risk policy, 2004; exec. v.p., chief risk officer Radian Group, Inc., 2005, Capital One Financial Corp., 2007—. Bd. dirs. Lydall, Inc., 2000—. Trustee JP Morgan Chase Trust Found. Named one of 25 Women to Watch, US Banker, 2010, American Banker, 2011. Office: Capital One Financial Corp 1680 Capital One Dr Mc Lean VA 22102 Office Phone: 703-720-1000. Office Fax: 703-720-2306. Business E-Mail: suzanne.hammett@capitalone.com.

HAMMICK, PATRICIA A., retired energy executive; b. 1946; BS in Chem. Physics & Math., Rice U., 1968; MSc in Physics, U. Calif., Riverside, 1970; PhD in Math. Statistics, George Washington U., 1989. With Gulf Oil, 1979—83; COO Natural Gas Supply Assn., 1983—96; v.p., strategic planning Columbia Energy Group, Reston, Va., 1997—98, sr. v.p., strategy & corporate comm., 1998—2000; chmn. Dynegy Inc., Houston, 2011. Bd. dirs. Consol Energy, Inc., 2001—, Dynegy Inc., 2003—11, SNC-Lavalin Group Inc., 2007—; adj. prof. George Washington U., 2001—03.

HAMMON, JOHN WILLIAM, JR., medical educator, thoracic surgeon; b. Springfield, Mo., Mar. 9, 1942; m. Mary Lisa Hammon; children: Ian, Dudley, Daniel. BA, Drury Coll., 1964; MD, Tulane U., 1968. Diplomate Am. Bd. Surgery, 1978, Am. Bd. Thoracic Surgery, 2008. Intern Duke U. Med. Ctr., Durham, NC, 1968—69, resident, 1969—70, resident, gen./thoracic surgery, 1972—77, tchg. scholar cardiac surgery, 1977—78; asst. prof. surgery Vanderbilt U., Nashville, 1978—83, assoc. prof. surgery, 1983—89, prof. dept. cardiac and thoracic surgery, 1989—91; chief cardiac and thoracic surgery VA Hosp., Nashville, 1987—91; Howard Holt Bradshaw prof., chmn. Bowman Gray Sch. Medicine, Winston-Salem, NC, 1991—95; prof. surgery Sch. Medicine Wake Forest U., Winston-Salem, NC, 1995—2009; prof. surgery emeritus Walce Forest U. Sch. Med. Winstonsalem, NC, 2009—. Prin. investigator NIH Grants, 1979—2008; fed. drug. admstr. Cardiac Devices Panel, 2009—. Mem. editl. bd. Jour. Surg. Rsch., 1986—91, Cardiac Chronicle, 1986—91, Annals of Thoracic Surgery, 1991—2002, Jour. Cardiac Surgery, 1993—2012, Jour. Thoracic and Cardiovascular Surgery, 2006—. Lt. comdr US Naval Hosp., 1970—77. Recipient Disting. Alumni award, Drury Coll., 1989, 2001; scholar, NIH, 1974. Mem.: ACS (gov. 2002, membership com. 2002—04), Soc. Thoracic Surgeons (standard and ethics com. 2008—), N.C. Surg. Assn. (pres. 2006—07), Winston-Salem Surg. Assn. (pres. 1999—2000, historian 2013—), So. Thoracic Surg. Assn. (v.p. 1999—2000, pres. 2007—08, pres.'s award for best sci. paper 1985), Am. Assn. Thoracic Surgery (residents com. 1999—2003, membership com. 2002—05, sci. and govt. affairs com. 2007—, sci. affairs and govt. relation com. 2007—), Omicron Delta Kappa. Avocations: golf, fishing. Office: Dept Cardiothoracic Surgery Medical Ctr Blvd Winston Salem NC 27157-1096 Office Fax: 336-716-3348. Business E-Mail: jhammon@wfubmc.edu.

HAMMON, MICKY, state legislator; m. Pam Hammon; children: Jake, Colter, Davis-Anne. Degree, Calhoun County CC, Ala. Ind. elec. contractor; mem. Dist. 4 Ala. House of Reps., Montgomery, 2002—. Mem. Tenn. Valley Tng. Ctr. Mem. Nat. Fedn. Ind. Bus., Associated Builders & Contractors, Bus. Coun. Ala., Morgan County Econ. Devel. Assn., US C. of C., Decatur C. of C. Republican. Office: 1344 E Upper River Rd Decatur AL 35603 also: Ala House of Reps Ala State House 11 S Union St Rm 523-C Montgomery AL 36130 Office Phone: 334-242-7709.

HAMMOND, CHARLES BESSELLIEU, obstetrician, gynecologist, educator; b. Ft. Leavenworth, Kans., July 24, 1936; s. Claude G. and Alice (Sims) H.; m. Peggy A. Hammond, June 21, 1958; children: Sharon L., Charles B. BS, The Citadel, 1958; MD, Duke U., 1961. Diplomate Am. Bd. Ob-Gyn. Intern in surgery Duke U., 1961-62, resident in ob-gyn, 1962-63, 66-69, fellow in reproductive endocrinology, 1963-64, asst. prof. dept. ob-gyn, 1969-73, asso. prof., 1973-78, prof., 1978-81, E.C. Hamblen prof. emeritus, 1981—2010, chmn., 1980—2002. Contbr. in field. Served with USPHS, 1964-66. Fellow Royal Coll. Ob-gyn. (ad eundeum), Soc. Ob-gyn. Can. (hon.); mem. AMA, Am. Fertility Soc. (pres. 1985), ACOG (chmn. dist. IV 1997-2000, pres. 2002), Am. Assn. Ob-Gyn. Found. (pres. 1996-2002), Assn. Profs. Obstetrics and Gynecology, Am. Gynecol. and Obstet. Soc. (pres. 1993-94), Soc. Gynecol. Investigation, Am. Gynecol. Soc., Am. Assn. Obstet. and Gynecology, N.C. Med. Soc., N.C. Soc. Obstetricians and Gynecologists (pres. 1985), Am. Gynecol.

Club (pres. 1994), Inst. of Medicine. Presbyterian. Home: 2827 McDowell Rd Durham NC 27705-5604 Office: Duke U Med Ctr PO Box 3853 Durham NC 27710 Business E-Mail: hammo005@mc.duke.edu.

HAMMOND, DAVID ALAN, stage director, educator; b. NYC, June 3, 1948; s. Jack and Elizabeth Alida (Furno) H. BA magna cum laude, Harvard U., 1970; MFA, Carnegie-Mellon U., 1972. Mem. faculty Juilliard Theatre Ctr., NYC, 1972-74; asst. conservatory dir. Am. Conservatory Theatre, San Francisco, 1974-81, assoc. stage dir., 1974-78; dir. Summer Tng. Congress, 1976-80, resident stage dir., 1979-81. Adj. assoc. prof. acting and directing Yale Sch. Drama, New Haven, 1981—85; adj. prof. dept. dramatic art U. NC, Chapel Hill, 1985—88, prof., 1988—2006, emeritus prof., 2007—; prof. theatre studies Guilford Coll., Greensboro, NC, 2007—, arts divsn. chair, 2009—; artistic dir. PlayMakers Repertory Co., Chapel Hill, 1985—92, 1999—2006, artistic dir. emeritus, 2006—, assoc. producing dir., 1992—99, theatre studies chair, 2013—; guest artist Pacific Conservatory Performing Arts, 1976, U. Wash., 1977, 2007, SUNY, Purchase, 1979, Am. Repertory Theatre, Moscow Art Theatre Sch., Inst. for Advanced Theatre Tng. at Harvard U., 2006—, Tisch Sch. Arts/NYU, NYC, 1999—2010; guest dir. Aspen (Colo.) Music Festival, 1974—75, San Francisco Opera, 1978, Carmel (Calif.) Bach Festival, 1979—80, Sherwood Shakespeare Festival, Oxnard, Calif., 1981, Roundabout Theatre, NYC, 1983, Valley Shakespeare Festival, Saratoga, Calif., 1984, 1986, 1988, Shakespeare Festival of Dallas, 1990, Teatro Alianza, Montevideo, 1992, 1994, 1997, Inst. Teatral El Galpon, Montevideo, 1995, Opera Co. NC, 1998, 1999; resident dir. Yale Repertory Theatre, New Haven, 1981—85; Arts Am. cultural specialist U.S. Info. Svc., 1992, 1994; guest prof. Escuela Mcpl. de Arte Dramatico, 2003, Escuela de Expression Teatral Anglo-o.m.b.u., 2003, El Univ. del Plata, Montevideo, 2003; Escuela Del actor, Montevideo, 2013. Recipient Drama-Logue Critics award, LA, 1980, 81, Florencio award, Montevideo, 1992, Playmaker award, 2005, Thangle Theatre Review award, 2005, named Triangle Theatre Person of Yr., 2005. Mem. Soc. Stage Dirs. and Choreographers, Actors' Equity, Am. Guild Mus. Artists, Dramatists' Guild, Nat. Theater Conf., Assn. for Theatre in Higher Edn. Office: Guilford Coll Dept Theatre Studies Founders 086 5800 W Friendly Ave Greensboro NC 27410 Office Phone: 336-316-2477. Business E-Mail: hammondda@guilford.edu.

HAMMOND, FRANK JEFFERSON, III, lawyer; b. Moss Point, Miss., Sept. 18, 1953; s. Frank Jefferson Jr. and Jane (Laird) H.; m. Gale Ray, May 30, 1975; children: Katharine Blakeney, Benjamin Laird. BBA, U. Mis., 1974, JD, 1976; LLM, U. Fla., 1978. Bar: Miss. 1977, U.S. Dist. Ct. (no. dist.) Miss. 1977, U.S. Dist. Ct. (so. dist.) Miss. 1977, U.S. Ct. Appeals (5th cir.) 1977, U.S. Tax Ct. 1978, U.S. Ct. Appeals (11th cir.) 1980, U.S. Supreme Ct. 1989. Mem. Corlew, Krebs & Hammond, P.A., Pascagoula, Miss., 1978-84, Watkins & Eager, PLLC, Jackson, Miss., 1984—. Adj. prof. U. Ala. Sch. Law, Mobile, 1983; adj. faculty U. So. Miss., Gautier, 1983-84; bd. dirs. Merchants and Marine Bank, Pascagoula, Miss. Bd. trustees Dantzler Meml. Meth. Ch., Moss Point, 1981-84. U. Fla. Grad. Council fellow, 1977; Richard B. Stephens scholar, 1978. Mem. Miss. State Bar (chmn. sect. estates and trusts 1988-89), Phi Kappa Phi, Beta Alpha Psi, Beta Gamma Sigma, Omicron Delta Kappa. Home: PO Box 650 Jackson MS 39205-0650 Office: Watkins & Eager PLLC 400 E Capitol St Ste 300 Jackson MS 39201-2610

HAMMOND, HERBERT J., lawyer, arbitrator, mediator; b. Santa Fe, May 19, 1951; m. Myra Hammond; children: Ariel, Jay. BS magna cum laude, U. N.Mex., 1973; JD, NYU, 1976. Bar: Tex. 1977, U.S. Patent and Trademark Office 1977. Sr. ptnr. Thompson & Knight, Dallas, 1994—. Author: Tex. Intellectual Property Handbook 20th ed., 2011; contbr. articles to profl. jours. Mem. Am. Law Inst., State Bar Tex. (sec., intellectual property section 2013-2014, chair computer sect. 1994-95) Am. Intellectual Property Law Assn., Dallas Bar Assn. (chmn. intellectual property sect. 1998), Phi Beta Kappa. Office: Thompson & Knight 1722 Routh St Ste 1500 Dallas TX 75201 Office Phone: 214-969-1607. Business E-Mail: herbert.hammond@tklaw.com.

HAMMOND, MARK, state official; b. Lancaster, SC, Nov. 29, 1963; m. Ginny Hammond; children: Matthew, Ross, Grace. BA in Polit. Sci., Newberry Coll., SC, 1986; MEd, Clemson U., SC, 1988. Juvenile probation officer SC Dept. Youth Services; criminal investigator 7th Cir. Solicitor's Office, Spartanburg County, SC, 1990—96; clk. of cts. Spartanburg County, 1996—2002; sec. of state State of SC, Columbia, 2002—. Mem. St. Paul United Meth. Ch., Spartanburg. Henry Toll fellow, Coun. State Governments, 2007. Republican. Office: Office of the Secretary of State 1205 Pendleton St Suite 525 Columbia SC 29201 Office Phone: 803-734-2170. Office Fax: 803-734-1661. Business E-Mail: rdaggerhart@sos.sc.gov.*

HAMMOND, ROY JOSEPH, reinsurance company executive; b. St. Louis, Jan. 9, 1929; s. Edward Herman and Alvera Ann (Herzog) H.; m. Donna LaSalle Perkins, Apr. 12, 1951 (div. July 2001); children— Douglas Edward, Donald Erwin, Laura Ann Hammond Budniakiewicz; m. Gloria June Kirkpatrick, Dec. 19, 2001. BS, Northwestern U., Evanston, Ill., 1954; JD, DePaul U., Chgo., 1959. Bar: Ill. bar 1959. With Am. Mut. Reins. Co., Chgo., 1963-91, v.p., then sr. v.p., gen. counsel and sec., 1967-76, pres., chief exec. officer, bd. dirs., 1976-91; pres., chief exec. officer Whitehall Cons., Ltd., Camden, NC, 1991—; pres. Wheeling Mcpl. Park Dist., Ill., 1963-65. Past mem. Reins. Assn. Am., bd. dirs., 1976—86. Served with U.S. Army, 1946-48, treas. Good Shepherd Luth. Ch. Mem. ABA, Ill. State Bar Assn., Internat. Assn. Def. Counsel, Fedn. Ins. and Corp. Counsel, Chgo. Casualty Adjusters Assn. (pres. 1972-73), Chgo. Yacht Club. Republican. Lutheran. Home and Office: Whitehall Shores 201 Azalea Dr Camden NC 27921-6991 Business E-Mail: ehh@mchsi.com.

HAMMOND, THOMAS J., securities exchange company executive; BSBA, Lewis U., Romeoville, Ill. Commodities acct. Rosenthal and Co., 1980—82; mgr., delivery and compliance Goodman, Manaster and Co., 1982—84; mgr., clearing house MidAmerica Commodity Exch., 1984—86; mem. svcs. rep. The Clearing Corp. (formerly Bd. of Trade Clearing Corp.), 1986, sr. mem. svcs. rep., 1986—89, mktg. mgr., 1989—90, mgr., Mem. Svcs. Group, 1990—92, mem. svcs. dir., 1992—94, v.p., clearing ops., 1994—2000, exec. v.p., COO, 2000—03; joined Chgo. Bd. of Trade (now CME Group), 2003, mng. dir., trading ops.; pres., COO ICE Clear US (subs. Intercontinental-Exchange, Inc.), 2007—. Participates, Working Group on Fin. Markets Chgo. Fed. Res. Bank; bd. dirs., Fin. Svcs. Divsn. and Chgo. Ops. Divsn. Futures Industry Assn. Office: IntercontinentalExchange Inc 2100 RiverEdge Pky Ste 500 Atlanta GA 30328 Office Phone: 770-857-4700. Office Fax: 770-857-4755. Business E-Mail: thomas.hammond@theice.com.*

HAMNER, REGINALD TURNER, lawyer; b. Tuscaloosa, Ala., June 4, 1939; s. Raiford Samuel and Ellie Wells (Turner) Hamner; m. Anne Ellen Young, Nov. 8, 1969; children: Patrick Turner, William Christian. BS, U. Ala., 1961, JD, 1965. Bar: Ala. 1965, US Dist. Ct. (mid. dist.) Ala. 1966, US Ct. Appeals (5th cir.) 1966, US Ct. Mil. Appeals 1968, US Supreme Ct. 1968, US Ct. Appeals (11th cir.) 1981. Law clk. Supreme Ct. Ala., Montgomery, 1965; dir. legal-legis. affairs Med. Assn., State of Ala., 1968-69; sec., exec. dir. Ala. State Bar, Montgomery, 1969-94; ct. project coord. U.S. Dist. Ct. (Mid. Dist.) Ala., Montgomery, 1995—2006. Bd. dirs. S.E. br. YMCA, Montgomery, 1978—81; former legal counsel govtl. adv. panels investigating Ala. Prison Sys.; vice chmn. State Child Welfare Com.; bd. dirs. Attys. Ins. Mut. Ala., Inc., 1989—2008; sec., treas. Ala. Law Found., 1987—93; chmn. Ala. Rhodes Scholarship Com., 1989—94; bd.dirs. Ala. Humanities Found., 2004—. With JAG USAF, 1965—68, col. USAFR. Named Disting. alumnus, U Ala., 2004. Fellow: Am. Bar Found. (life; state chmn. 1994—95); mem.: ABA (mem. ho. dels. 1972—76, 1985—89, 1993, 1965—), Jud. Conf. U.S. Ct. Appeals (11th cir. 1981—96), Ala. Law Inst. (coun.), Ala. Coun. Assn. Execs. (pres. 1984), Am. Soc. Assn. Execs. (commr. certification com. 1978—79), Nat. Assn. Bar Execs. (pres. 1978—79), Am. Judicature Soc., U. Ala. Nat. Alumni Assn. (pres. 1989—90), Montgomery Country Club, Delta Tau Delta, Phi Alpha Delta, Alpha Epsilon Delta, Omicron Delta Kappa. Episcopalian. Home: 7518 Wynford Cir Montgomery AL 36117-7498 Office: US Courthouse One Church St Ste Rm 400 FMJ Montgomery AL 36104 Office Phone: 334-324-4372.

HAMPLE, JUDY G., academic administrator; BA in Speech Comm. and Secondary Edn./French, David Lipscomb U.; MA, PhD in Comm., Ohio State U. Univ. fellow, asst. dir. intercollegiate debate Ohio State U.; faculty dept. speech comm. U. Ill., Champaign-Urbana; divsn. dir. dept. comm. arts and scis. Western Ill. U., assoc. dean for budget and pers. Coll. Arts and Scis.; dean Coll. Liberal Arts and Scis. Emporia State U., 1983—86; dean Coll. Arts and Scis. Ind. State U., 1986—93; sr. v.p. acad. affairs U. Toledo, 1993; vice chancellor planning, budget and policy analysis, vice chancellor and chancellor bd. regents State Univ. Sys. Fla., 1998—2001; chancellor Pa. State Sys. of Higher Edn., Harrisburg, 2001—08; pres. U. Mary Washington, 2008—. Cons.-evaluator North Cen. Accreditation Assn.; pub. cons.-evaluator ABA. Co-editor: Teaching in the Middle Ages, 3 vols.; editor: Studies in Medieval and Renaissance Teaching; contbr. articles to profl. jours. Office: U Mary Washington George Washington Hall, Rm 103 1301 College Ave Fredericksburg VA 22401 Office Phone: 540-654-1301. Office Fax: 540-654-1076.

HAMPTON, BENJAMIN BERTRAM, brokerage house executive; b. NYC, Aug. 3, 1925; s. max and Pauline (Weinberger) H.; m. Elizabeth Golub-Cohen, Oct. 16, 1975; 1 child by previous marriage, Roger Neil; stepchildren: Laurence, James, Lisa. B Aero. Engring., NYU, 1947; cert. in mech. engring., Pa. State Coll., 1945; MBA, Harvard U., Cambridge, Mass., 1949. Sales mgr. Carew Products, Inc., NYC, 1949-51; project mgr. Emerson Radio & TV Corp., 1951-52; div. mgr. Paragon Oil Co., Mineola, NY, 1952-55; mgmt. cons. E.N. Kagan & co., NYC, 1955-60; exec. asst. to pres. mktg. sect. Fed. Pacific Electric co., Newark, 1960-62; asst. to pres. Seagrave Corp., NYC, 1962-63; v.p. Swingline Inc., Long Island City, N.Y., 1963-68, exec. v.p., 1968-71, bd. dirs., 1970-71; exec. v.p., bd. dirs. Poloron Products Inc., New Rochelle, N.Y., 1971-73, pres., CEO, bd. dirs., 1973-74; exec. v.p., bd. dirs. West Chem. Products, Inc., Long Island City, 1975-78; prin. Hampton Assocs., 1979-82; v.p. Merrill Lynch Pierce Fenner & Smith, Great Neck, NY, 1982—2007; ret., 2007. Co-chmn. N.Y. State fin. com. J.F. Kennedy presdl. campaign, 1960. With AUS, 1944-46. Mem. Harvard Club, Pi Lambda Phi. Home: Apt B 6224 Island Bend Boca Raton FL 33496 Personal E-mail: bhampton08@comcast.net.

HAMPTON, CATHY, lawyer; b. Magnolia, Miss. B, Spelman Coll., Atlanta; JD, Harvard U. Law Sch., Mass. Bar: Ga., NY, DC. Assoc., atty. in corp. securities and internat. fin. law Shearman & Sterling, NYC; atty. in mktg., advt. and gen. corp. law NBA, NYC; v.p., asst. gen. counsel EarthLink, Inc.; gen. counsel, sec. EarthLink PeoplePC; v.p., gen. counsel, sec. RARE Hospitality Internat., Inc.; city atty. City of Atlanta, 2010—. Mem. Class of 2003 Leadership Atlanta; mem. Cascade United Meth. Ch.; bd. mem. VOX Youth Comm., Women's Resource Ctr.; chair Atlanta Women's Found. Econ. Justice Program. Named one of 30 Nat. Leaders Under 30, Ebony mag. Mem.: ABA, Nat. Bar Assn., Assn. Corp. Counsel, Ga. Assn. Black Women Attorney's, Gen. Counsel Roundtable, Delta Sigma Theta. Office: City of Atlanta Dept Law 68 Mitchell St Ste 4100 Atlanta GA 30303 Office Phone: 404-330-6400. Office Fax: 404-546-9379. Business E-Mail: lawdepartment@atlantaga.gov.

HAMPTON, JAMES WILBURN, hematologist, oncologist; b. Durant, Okla., Sept. 15, 1931; s. Hollis Eugene and Ouida (Mackey) Hampton; m. Carol McDonald, Feb. 22, 1958; children: Jaime, Clay, Diana, Neal. BA, U. Oklahoma, 1952, MD, 1956. Int. U. Okla. Hosps., 1956-57, res.; instr. to prof. U. Okla., Oklahoma City, 1959-77; clin. prof. med., 1977—. Mem. admissions bd., 1965—; bd. dirs., 1995—2006; head hematology/oncology, 1972—77; head hematology, mem. Okla. Med. Rsch. Found., Oklahoma City, 1972—77; dir. cancer prog. and med. oncology Bapt. Med. Ctr., 1977—85; med. dir. Cancer Ctr. S.W., 1985—94, Troy and dollie Smith Cancer Ctr., 1994—; mem. Internat. Com. Thrombosis and Hemostasis; cons. NIH, Biomed. and Nat. Cancer Inst., Karolinska Inst., Stockhom; vis. scientist Career Devel. Award, 1966—67; vis. prof. U. NC, Chapel Hill, 1966; founder Stewart Wolf Soc., 1967, pres., 1990—92; founder Robert Montgomery Bird Soc., 1973, pres., 1996—98. Contbr. articles to profl. jours. Chmn. Network Cancer Prevention and Control Rsch. Am. Indians/Alaska Natives Nat. Cancer Inst.; mem. Intercultural Cancer Coun., 1996—, chair-elect, 2000—01, chair, 2001—02; initiator Hospice Oklahoma County, 1990—99; bd. dirs. Am. Cancer Soc., mem. at large, nat. bd. dirs., 1990—96; mem. com. task force Cancer Socio-Economically Disadvantaged, 1990—2002; chmn. Okla. divsn. svc. and rehab. com., collaborating ptnr. Pres. Bush Dialogue on Cancer, 1999—; chmn. Okla. Pain Initiative, 1996; mem. adv. com. Office Minority Health NIH, 1996—99; co-chmn. Save St. Paul's Episcopal Cathedral Com., 1983; chmn. bishop's Okla. com. Indian ministry, mem. province VII Indian com., alt. del. Diocesan Conv. Okla., 1991—95, chmn. bishop's Okla. com. Indian work, mem. province VII Indian com., alt. del., 2000—05; mem. coun. combating racism Epis. Ch. Am., 1995—97, del. to elect bishop to Okla., 2007, del. to Diocesan Conv., 2007. Recipient Humanitarian award, ACS, 1999, honor by Lakota Tribe at Mayo Clinic, 1999, Leap of Faith award, Intercultural Cancer Coun., 2006; named Physician of the Yr., U. Okla. Alumni Assocs., 1998; Career Devel. grantee, NIH, 1966—76. Fellow: ACP; mem.: AMA (mem. minority affairs consortium, mem. steering com. 1997—2000), Intercultural Cancer Coun. (chairperson 2003), Am. Psychosomatic Soc., So. Soc. Clin. Investigation, Am. Soc. Clin. Oncology, Am. Soc. Hematology, Assn. Am. Pathologists, Am. Phyhsiol. Soc., Assn. Am. Indian Physicians (pres. 1978—79, 1988—89, Indian Physician of the Yr. award 1987), Internat. Soc. Thrombosis and Hemostasis, Oklahoma County Med. Soc. (editor bull. 1981—, bd. dirs. 1982—85, 1989—91), Ctrl. Soc. Clin. Rsch. (assoc. editor Jour. Lab. and Clin. Med. 1975—76), Am. Fedn. Clin. Rsch. (pres. midwest sect. 1970—71), English Speaking Union, Blue Cord Club, Oklahoma City Golf and Country Club, Chaine des Rotisseurs. Home: 1414 N Hudson Ave Oklahoma City OK 73103-3721 Office: Mercy Cancer Ctr 4205 Mcauley Blvd Ste 375 Oklahoma City OK 73120 Office Phone: 405-751-7343. Business E-Mail: james.hampton@mercy.net.

HAMPTON, MARK GARRISON, architect; b. Tampa, Fla., July 17, 1923; s. Ham Stonewall and Laura (Bingenheimer) H. BS, B.Arch., Ga. Inst. Tech., 1949. Owner Mark Hampton, Architect, Tampa, 1952-65, Miami, Fla., 1974—; partner Herbert H. Johnson Assocs., Miami, 1966-73. Prin. works include Chemistry and Life Sci. bldgs, U. So. Fla., Tampa, 1961, First Fed. Office Bldg, Sarasota, 1973, Mark Hampton Exhibition U. Miami, 2010. Bd. dirs. Lannan Found., Palm Beach, Fla., 1972-88; pres. Tampa Art Inst., 1958, 64. Served with inf. AUS, 1943-46. Decorated Bronze Star, Purple Heart; recipient award Homes for Better Living competition, 1957, 62; Nat. Design award Horizon Home program, 1963 Fellow AIA (juror Nat. Honor awards 1963, 64, medal of honor for design Fla. Central chpt. 1974, award of honor for design 1987, test of time award 1987). Episcopalian. Office: Mark Hampton Architect FAIA 3900 Loquat Ave Miami FL 33133-5622 Office Phone: 305-443-6946.

HAMPTON, ROBERT WESLEY, corporate financial executive; b. Phila., Aug. 20, 1951; s. Robert W. Hampton and Edna M. (Walsh) Corby; m. Jenifer H. Bryan, May 4, 1974; children: John, Rebecca. BS, Pa. State U., 1973. CPA, Tex. V.p., CFO HWC Energy Svcs.; sr. mgr. Price Waterhouse, Houston and Phila., 1973-86; v.p., acctg. American Exploration Co., 1986-89; area mgr., North Sea Ops. Tidewater Inc., Aberdeen; v.p., treas. & CFO Hornbeck Offshore Svc., Inc. (acquired by Tidewater Inc.), Galveston, Tex., 1990; joined Oil States International, Inc., 2001, v.p., fin. & acctg., sr. v.p., acctg., corp. sec. Mem. AICPA, Fin. Execs. Inst., Tex. Soc. CPAs, Kappa Sigma. Republican. Roman Catholic. Avocation: golf. Home: 1440 Canal St New Orleans LA 70112-2703 Office: Oil States International Inc Three Allen Ctr 333 Clay St Ste 4620 Houston TX 77002 Office Phone: 713-652-0582. Office Fax: 713-652-0499. Business E-Mail: robert.hampton@oilstatesintl.com.

HAMRA, SAMEER T., plastic surgeon, educator; b. Ponca City, Okla., July 16, 1937; MD, U. Okla., 1963. Diplomate Am. Bd. Surgery, 1970, Am. Bd. Plastic Surgery, 1977. Intern gen. surgery U. Okla., 1963—64, resident plastic surgery, 1964—68, NYU Med. Ctr., NYC, 1970—73; fellowship surgery U. Lausanne, Switzerland, 1965—66; staff mem. Mary Shiels Hosp., Dallas; assoc. clin. prof. plastic surgery U. Tex. Southwestern Med. Ctr., Dallas. Mem.: Am. Soc. Plastic Surgeons, Am. Assn. Plastic Surgeons, Am. Soc. Aesthetic Plastic Surgery. Office: 9301 North Central Expressway #551 Dallas TX 75231-9080 Home: 9301 N Central Expy Ste 551 Dallas TX 75231-0819 Office Phone: 866-773-9181. Office Fax: 214-754-9080. E-mail: drhamra@drhamra.com.

HAMRICK, HARVEY J., pediatrician; b. Rutherfordton, NC, July 8, 1940; MD, U. NC Sch. Medicine, 1967. Intern, pediat. NC Meml. Hosp., Chapel Hill, 1967—68, resident, pediat., 1968—70, chief resident, pediat., 1970—71, fellow, pediat., 1972; hosp. appointment U NC Hosps., Chapel Hill, dir., pediat. residency tng. program; prof., pediat. U NC Sch. Medicine. Contbr. articles to profl. jours. Office: U NC Pediat Edn Office 30137 NC Womens Hosp 101 Manning Dr CB# 7593 UNC Sch Medicine Chapel Hill NC 27599-7593 Fax: 919-966-8419.

HAMRICK, WILLIAM (BILL), III, state legislator; b. Carrolton, Ga., 1906; BBA, Auburn Univ.; JD, Ga. State Univ., 1992. Lawyer, Carrolton, Ga.; mem. Dist. 30 Ga. State Senate, 2000—. Republican. Methodist. Mailing: PO Box 368 Carrollton GA 30112 Office: 121-H State Capitol Atlanta GA 30334 Office Phone: 770-214-8210. Business E-Mail: bill.hamrick@senate.ga.gov.

HAN, CHIEN-PAI, statistics educator; b. Hunan, China, Dec. 17, 1936; came to U.S., 1960; s. Chung-Shih and Pei-Wen Han; M. Maria Han, Aug. 28, 1965; children: Richard, Julie. BA, Nat. Taiwan U., Taipei, 1958; MA, U. Minn., 1962; PhD, Harvard U., 1967. Asst. prof. stats. Iowa State U., Ames, 1967-69, assoc. prof., 1970-75, prof., 1975-82; prof. math. U. Tex.-Arlington, 1982—. Statis. cons. Mus. N.Mex., Santa Fe, 1965; vis. asst. prof. Harvard U., Cambridge, Mass., 1970 Author: (with T.A. Bancroft) Statistical Theory and Inference in Research, 1981; mem. editl. bd. Comms. in Stats. Theory and Methods, 1975-92, Jour. Statis. Rsch., 1994; assoc. editor Comms. in Stats., 1993—; co-editor Jour. Probability and Statis. Sci., 2004—, Jour. Applied Probability and Stats., 2006—. Fellow Am. Statis. Assn. (pres. Iowa chpt. 1971-72); mem. Internat. Statis Inst. (elected), Inst. Math. Stats., Internat. Assn. Engrs., Internat. Assn. Survey Statisticians, Internat. Chinese Statis. Assn. (bd. dirs. 1987-92, pres. 2000), Sigma Xi, Mu Sigma Rho. Office: U Tex Dept Math PO Box 19408 Arlington TX 76019-0408

HAN, NONG, artist, sculptor, painter; b. Seoul, Oct. 10, 1930; arrived in U.S.A., 1952, naturalized, 1958. Commr. Asian Art Commn. Asian Art Mus. San Francisco, The Avery Brundage Collection, city and county of San Francisco, 1981—84. One-man exhbns. paintings and or sculpture include Ft. Lauderdale, Fla. Mus. Arts, Santa Barbara-,Calif. Mus. Art, Crocker Art Mus., Sacramento, 1965, Ga. Mus. Art, Athens, 1967, El Paso, Tex. Mus. Art, 1967, Nat. Mus. History, Taiwan, 1971, Nihonbashi Gallery, Tokyo, Japan, 1971, Shinsegye Gallery, Seoul, Korea, 1975, Nat. Mus. Modern Art, Seoul, 1975, San Francisco Zool. Garden, 1975, Tongin Art Gallery, Seoul, 1978, Consulate Gen. Republic of Korea, L.A., 1982, Choon Chu Gallery, Seoul, 1982, Mee Gallery, Seoul, 1984, 86, Leema Art Mus., Seoul, 1985, Tong A Dept. Store, Taegu, Korea, 1986, Tongso Gallery, Masan, Korea, 1986, Han Kwang Art Mus., Pusan, Korea, 1986, Union de Arte, Barcelona, Spain, 1987, Acad. de Belles Arts, Sabadell, Spain, 1987, Nong Hyup Art Mus., Ft. Lee, N.J., 1995, The Info. Ctr. Korean Embassy, Washington, 1997; Gallery Art Exchange, N.Y.C., 1998, Korean Cultural Ctr., Annandale, Va., 1999, Paeksang Meml. Hall The Korea Times, Seoul, 2000, The Korea Central Daily, Vienna, Va., 2001, YTN, 24 hour news channel Seoul, Korea, 2004, KM Art Ctr., Sandy Spring, Md., 2005, Visitor's Ctr. Mormon Ch., Kensington, Md., 2005, Seoul Gallery, Korea, 2006; numerous group exhibits including most recently Taipei Gallery Taiwanese Cultural Ctr., N.Y.C., 1998, Fisher Gallery U. So. Calif., L.A., 1998, Japanese Am. Nat. Mus., L.A., 1998, Bedford Gallery, Dean Lesker Regl. Ctr. for the Arts, Walnut Creek, 1998, The Kaohsing Museum of Fine Art, 1998, Taipei Mus. of Fine Arts, 1998, Marugame Genichiro Inokuma Mus. of Contemporary Art, Japan, 1999, Fukuoka Asian Art Mus., Fukuoka City, 1999, Akita Senshu Mus. Art, Akita City, 1999, San Francisco De Young Art Mus., 2008, The Isamu Noguchi Found. & Garden Mus., Long Island, NY, 2009; represented in numerous permanent collections including, Santa Barbara Mus. Art, Anchorage Alaska Hist. and Fine Art Mus., Museo de Arte, Lima, Peru, Govt. Peru, Nat. Mus. History, Govt. of Republic of China, Oakland, Calif. Art Mus., Ga. Mus. Art, Athens, Korean Embassy, Lima, Peru, Nat. Mus. of Modern Art, Nat. Mus. Korea, Govt. of Republic of Korea, Seoul, Nat. Gallery of Modern Art, New Delhi, India, Asian Art Mus. San Francisco, Govt. of People's Republic China, Beijing and Shanghai, Palacio de la Zarzuela, Madrid, Palacio de la Moncloa, Madrid, The Korean Embassy, Madrid, Mus. Art de Sabadell, Spain, Mus. Nat. des Beaux-Arts, Monte Carlo, Monaco, The Philatelic Mus. Palais des Nations, Geneva, Korean Embassy, Wash., Nat. Mus., Manila, Philippines, Daesung Group, Seoul, YTN, Seoul, Asian-Am. Modern Art Shifting Currents, 1900-1970 Fine Arts Mus. San Francisco, others; author: Nong Questions, 1982. Chmn. San Francisco, Seoul Sister City Com., city and county San Francisco, 1981-84.

Served in U.S. Army, 1956-59; USAF, 1959-60. Recipient numerous awards including citations from Republic of Korea; Cert. Disting. Achievement, State of Calif., 1982, Proclamation City and County of San Francisco, 1982; Nong Stamp issued in his honor UNISEF, 1996. Office Phone: 703-901-8246, 703-944-1984.

HANBURY, GEORGE LAFAYETTE, II, university president and professor; s. Emmette Cecil and Ada Christine (Nelligar) H.; m. Jana Hanbury; 1 stepchild, Jia; children from previous marriage: George Lafayette III, Melissa Lee. BS in Bus. Adminstrn., Va. Tech., Blacksburg, 1966; MPA in Pub. Adminstrn., Old Dominion U., Norfolk, Va., 1977; postgrad. in Leadership, U. Va., Charlottesville, 1983; PhD in Pub. Adminstrn., Fla. Atlantic U., Boca Raton, 2001. Asst. to city mgr., Norfolk, 1967-70; asst. city mgr. Va. Beach, 1970-74; city mgr., 1974-82, Portsmouth, Va., 1982-90, Ft. Lauderdale, Fla., 1990-98; exec. v.p. and chief oper. officer Nova Southeastern U., Ft. Lauderdale, 1998—2010, pres., 2010—. Bd. dirs. United Way Broward County, Broward Libr. Found.; bd. govs. Mus. Art; bd. advisors. Bus. Devel. Bd. Palm Bach County; exec. com. Broward Workshop. Recipient Eagle Scout award, Boy Scouts, 2010, SEFLIN award, 2006, Valor award, Am. Diabetes Assn., 2005, Leadership award, Broward City County Mgrs. Assn., 2000; named Downtowner of Year, Ft. Lauderdale C. of C., 2013, Eae Found. Humananitarian of Year, 2011, Leader of Year, Leadership Broward Found., 2007, Man of Year, Rotar Club Davie, 2006. Mem. Internat. City Mgmt. Assn., Am. Soc. Pub. Adminstrs., Pi Alpha Alpha. Methodist. Avocations: boating, scuba diving, swimming. Home: The Four Seasons 333 Sunset Dr Apt 807 Fort Lauderdale FL 33301-2655 Office: Nova Southeastern Univ 3301 College Ave Fort Lauderdale FL 33314-7796 Office Phone: 954-262-7575. Business E-Mail: hanbury@nova.edu.

HANCE, JAMES HENRY, JR., (JIM HANCE), private equity firm executive, retired bank executive; b. St. Joseph, Mo., Sept. 16, 1944; s. James Henry Sr. and Kathryn (Lichty) H.; m. Beverly Vaughan Smith, May 20, 1960; children: Samantha, Lindsay, Meredith, Blair. BA in Econs., Westminster Coll., 1966; MBA in Fin., Washington U., 1968. CPA. Ptnr. Price Waterhouse, Phila. and Charlotte, NC, 1968-85; chmn. bd. Consolidated Coin Caterers Corp., Charlotte, 1985-86; exec. v.p., chief acctg. officer NCNB Corp., Charlotte, 1987-88; CFO Bank of America Corp. (formerly NationalBank), Charlotte, 1988—2004, co-vice chmn., 1988—2004; sr. adv. Carlyle Group, NYC, 2005—; chmn. Sprint Nextel Corp., 2007—. Bd. dirs. Rayonier Corp., 2004-, Cousin Proprties Inc., 2005-, Duke Energy Corp., 2005-, Sprint Nextel Corp., 2005-, Morgan Stanley, 2009-, Ford Motor Co., 2010-. Bd. dirs. Microelectronis Ctr., NC, Rsch. Triangle Pk., 1988; trustee Presbyn. Hosp. and Presbyn. Hosp. Health Svcs. Corp., Charlotte, 1989, Charlotte Country Day Sch., 1990; mem. acctg. and fin. commn. Bank Adminstrn. Inst., Rolling Meadows, Ill., 1989. Fellow Soc. Internat. Bus. Fellows. Republican. Presbyterian. Office: The Carlyle Group 520 Madison Ave New York NY 10022*

HANCOCK, JAMES HUGHES, federal judge; b. Montgomery, Ala., 1931; BS, U. Ala., Tuscaloosa, 1953; LLB, U. Ala., 1957. Bar: Ala. Law clk. to Hon. John L. Goodwyn Ala. Supreme Ct.; ptnr. Balch and Bingham, Birmingham, Ala., 1957-73; judge U.S. Dist. Ct. (no. dist. Ala.), Birmingham, 1973—96, sr. judge, 1996—. Lt. US Army, 1953—55. Mem.: Ala. Bar Assn. Office: US Dist Ct No Dist Ala Hugo Black Courthouse 1729 5th Ave N Birmingham AL 35203

HANCOCK, JOHN C., pharmacologist; b. Lockwood, Mo., Aug. 20, 1938; s. Daniel L. and Cordelia O. (Chandler) H. BS, U. Mo., Kansas City; MS, U. Tex., Galveston, 1965, PhD, 1968. Instr. U. Conn., Storrs, 1968-69, asst. prof. Farmington, 1969-71, La. State U., New Orleans, 1971-73, assoc. prof., 1973-77; prof. East Tenn. State U. Coll. Medicine, Johnson City, 1977—, dep. chair, 1985—, prof. emeritus, 2006—, interim chair, 1996—98, 2003—05. Peer rev. panel Am. Heart Assn., Tenn., 1991—; presenter in field. Author (software) Autonomic Pharmacology; contbr. articles to profl. jours. Grantee NIH, Named Tchr. of Yr. East Tenn State U., 2001 Mem. Am. Soc. Pharmacol. Exptl. Therapeutics, Neurosci./Am. Heart Assn. (coun. on hypertension), Soc. Neurosci. (Applachian chpt.), Sigma Xi. Achievements include research on the role of sensory peptides in the regulation of blood pressure, physiopathology of ganglion transmission in hypertension; characteristics of ganglion transmission in the rat. Business E-Mail: hancock@etsu.edu.

HANCOCK, KELLY, state legislator; m. Robin Harrison; children: Chloe, Skylar, Harrison. Degree in bus., Baylor U., Waco, Tex. Former farmer, rancher; with family-founded chem. distbn. co. Chem. Logistics; former bd. mem. Birdville Ind. Sch Dist.; mem. Dist. 91 Tex. House of Representative, 2006—. Recipient Emerging Bus. award, Fort Worth C. of C.; named one of 40 Under 40, Tarrant Bus. Press. Republican. Office: 7101 Burns St Fort Worth TX 76118-2343 also: PO Box 185096 Fort Worth TX 76181 also: Room E2.910 Capitol Extension PO Box 2910 Austin TX 78768 Office Phone: 817-590-9280, 512-463-0599.

HANCOCK, WILLIAM FRANK, JR., professor; b. Richmond, Va., Jan. 4, 1942; s. William Frank and Gladys Elizabeth (George) H.; m. Donna G. Hosmer, May 18, 1968 (div.), Joy T. Shelley, Dec. 14, 2010; children: Peter James, Jeffrey William, Jennifer Beth. BBA, U. Iowa, 1964; MBA, U. Pa., 1966; postgrad., Capella U. CPA, CLU, CPCU, CMA, CDP. Exec. asst. to exec. v.p. John Hancock Mut. Life Ins. Co., 1966-69; mgmt. cons. Keane Assocs., 1969-74, regional mgr., 1974-75; v.p., gen. mgr. comml. sys. SofTech, Inc., Waltham, Mass., 1975-79; dir. internat. sales and field ops. Nixdorf Computer Co., Burlington, Mass., 1979-80; mgr. mktg. Digital Equipment Corp., 1980-84, electronic commerce mgr., 1984-97; mgmt. cons. electronic commerce Grant Thornton LLP, 1997—98; mgmt. cons., nat. electronic commerce practice Ernst & Young, LLP, 1998—2000; prin. IBM Corp., 2000—02; mng. dir. 3 Rivers Assocs., Mills River, NC, 2002—. Adj. prof. acctg. and fin. Grad. Sch. Bus., Northeastern U., Boston, 1966—, sr. instr. acctg. Grad. Sch. Bus. Babson Coll., Wellesley, Mass, 1985—; assoc. dean and prof. Sch. Mgmt., Cambridge Coll., 2002—2008; prof. Jinan U., China, 2007, assoc. dean, acctg. and fin. prof. Hult Internat. Bus. Sch., 2008-, Cambridge, Mass.; bd. dirs. Ctrl. Cambridge Bus. Assn. Treas. Pilgrim Ch.; trustee Sherborn Libr.; chmn. Sherborn coun. Boy Scouts Am. With U.S. Army, 1967-72. Recipient Outstanding Teacher of Yr. Awd., Northeastern Univ., 1989, Prof. of Yr., Hult Internat. Bus. Sch., 2011. Mem. AICPA, Data Processing Mgmt., Nat. Assn. Accts., Assn. Computing Machinery, Boston C. of C., Exec. Club Boston, Wharton Alumni Club, U. Iowa Alumni Assn., Cambridge Bus. Assn. (bd. dirs. 2008-). Presbyterian. Home and Office: 3 Rivers Assocs 52 N Mission Hills Ct Mills River NC 28759 Office Phone: 828-707-6147. Personal E-mail: william.hancock@morrisbb.net.

HANDEL, MORTON EMANUEL, retired film company executive, management consultant; b. NYC, Apr. 12, 1935; s. Benjamin and Mollie (Heller) H.; m. Irma Ruby, Aug. 5, 1956; children: Mark, Gary, Karen. BA, U. Pa., 1956; postgrad., NYU, 1957-59; DHum (hon.), U. Hartford, 2002. V.p. Dale Plastic Playing Card Corp., NYC, 1955-57; gen. mgr. Handel Nets & Fabrics Corp., NYC, 1957-62; pres. A.M. Industries, Inc., Farmingdale, NY, 1962-68, Allan Marine, Inc., Deer Park, NY, 1969-71; chmn. bd. Marlow Yacht Corp., Deer Park, 1969-71; v.p. fin., sec.-treas. Aurora Products Corp. (subs. Nabisco Inc.), 1971-73, sr. v.p., CFO, 1973—74; v.p. fin., CFO Coleco Industries Inc., 1974—78, sr. v.p., CFO, 1978—82, exec. v.p. fin. and adminstrn., 1982-83, exec. v.p. corp. com., 1983-85, exec. v.p. corp. devel., 1985-88, chmn., dir., CEO, 1988—90; pres., dir. Morton Handel Co., Inc., Boca Raton, Fla., 1990—. Pres. and dir. Ranger Industries, Inc., Bloomfield, Conn., 1997-2001; chmn. bd. dirs. Marvel Entertainment, Inc., NYC, 1997—2009; bd. dirs. Linens 'N Things, Clifton, NJ, 2000-06, Trump Entertainment Resorts, 2005-08, dir., Concurrent Computer Corp., 1991-2002, dir. Comp USA, 2002-05. Pres. Rochdale Village Civic Assn., 1964-65; pres. bd. dirs. Hartford Symphony Orch., 1976—; bd. dirs. Jewish Children's Svc. Corp., 1976-78; corporator St. Francis Hosp., 1982—; bd. dirs. One Thousand Corp., 1983-95, Greater Hartford Arts Coun., Inc., 1987-89, Hebrew Home for the Aged, 1989—2004; regent U. Hartford, 1990—; vice chmn. bd. regents U. Hartford, 1992-2000; trustee, vice chmn. Hartt Sch. Music, 1991—; bd. dirs. Jewish Fedn. of Greater Hartford, 1996-2000, Hartford Dispensary Inc., 1996-2002; bd. overseers Bushnell Ctr. for Performing Arts, 2002—; trustee Jewish Cmty. Found., 2005-08. Mem. Am. Mgmt. Assn., Fin. Execs. Inst., Alpha Epsilon Pi. Office: Morton Handel Co Inc 3475 Windsor Pl Boca Raton FL 33496 Home: 41 Ranger Ln West Hartford CT 06117-3040 Office Phone: 561-995-8586.

HANDEL, RICHARD CRAIG, lawyer; b. Hamilton, Ohio, Aug. 11, 1945; s. Alexander F. and Marguerite (Wilks) H.; m. Katharine Jean Carter, Jan. 10, 1970. AB, U. Mich., 1967; MA, Mich. State U., 1968; JD summa cum laude, Ohio State U., 1974; LLM in Taxation, NYU, 1978. Bar: Ohio 1974, S.C. 1983, U.S. Dist. Ct. (so. dist.) Ohio 1975, U.S. Dist. Ct. S.C. 1979, U.S. Tax Ct. 1977, U.S. Ct. Appeals (4th cir.) 1979, U.S. Supreme Ct. 1979; cert. tax specialist. Assoc. Smith & Schnacke, Dayton, Ohio, 1974—77; asst. prof. U. S.C. Sch. Law, Columbia, 1978—83; ptnr. Nexsen, Pruet, Jacobs & Pollard, Columbia, 1983—87, Moore & Van Allen, Columbia, 1987—88, Nexsen Pruet Jacobs & Pollard, Columbia, 1988—89; chief tax policy and appeals S.C. Tax Commn., Columbia, 1989—95; chief coun. Policy S.C. Dept. Revenue, Columbia, 1995—2003, sr. adminstr., gen. counsel, 2003—06, sr. adminstr., gen. counsel policy, 2006—12. Adj. prof. U. S.C. Sch. Law, 1990—2001, 2003, 2011—. Contbr. articles to legal jours. Bd. dirs. Friends of Richland County Pub. Libr., 1993-99. With U.S. Army, 1969-70, Vietnam. Recipient Outstanding Law Prof. award, 1980—81; Gerald L. Wallace scholar, 1977—78. Mem.: ABA (vice-chmn. com. tax procedures 1993—94, chmn. membership state and local taxes com. 1997—2007, sec. 2003—05, vice chair state and local taxes com. 2005—08, com. stds. tax practice), Order of Coif., S.C. Bar Assn. Office: SC Dept Revenue PO Box 12265 301 Gervais St Columbia SC 29211 Home Phone: 803-254-0439; Office Phone: 803-777-3611. Personal E-mail: handel.rick@gmail.com. Business E-Mail: handelr@law.sc.edu.*

HANDLER, JEROME SIDNEY, anthropology educator; b. NYC, Sept. 3, 1933; children: Joshua Martin, Lisa Frances. BA, UCLA, 1956, MA, 1959; PhD, Brandeis U., 1965. From asst. prof. to prof. anthropology So. Ill. U., Carbondale, 1964-93, prof. Black Am. studies, 1993-95, prof. emeritus, 1995—. Olive B. O'Connor vis. prof. Am. instns. Colgate U., Hamilton, N.Y., 1971-72; hon. rsch. asst. Univ. Coll., London, 1966-67; staff archaeologist New World Archaeol. Found., Chiapas, Mex., 1957; cons. AID, fall, 1964, Peace Corps, summer 1969; cons. Libr. of Congress, 1998, 99, 2000, 01, panelist NEH, 1977-79, 82, NSF, 2004; mem. adv. com. African Burial Ground, N.Y.C., GSA, 1991-93. Author: A Guide to Source Materials for the Study of Barbados History, 1627-1834, 1971, The Unappropriated People: Freedmen in the Slave Society of Barbados, 1974, Supplement to A Guide to Source Materials for the Study of Barbados History, 1991; co-author: Plantation Slavery in Barbados: An Archaeological and Historical Investigation, 1978, Searching for a Slave Cemetery in Barbados: A Bioarcheological and Ethnohistorical Investigation, 1989, co-author: Enacting Power: The Criminalisation of Obeah in the Anglophone Caribean, 2012 Vis. rsch. fellow U. W.I., Jamaica, 1969-70, Barbados, 1983; rsch. assoc. Rsch. Inst. for Study of Man, N.Y.C., 1978-79; vis. scholar Ctr. for Afro-Am. Studies, UCLA, 1980, dept. Afro-Am. Studies, Harvard U., summer 1992; Rsch. grantee NSF, 1966-67, 71-73, Wenner-Gren Found. Anthrop. Rsch., 1971-72, 87, Rsch. Inst. Study Man, 1962, 70, NIH, 1965, Am. Philos. Soc., 1968, Nat. Geographic Soc., 1987, NEH Inst. for Coll. Tchrs., 1997-98; NEH fellow, 1969-70, 75-76, 79; Travel grant Am. Coun. Learned Socs., 1977, grantee Social Sci. Rsch. Coun. and Am. Coun. Learned Socs. Joint Com. on Latin Am. Studies, 1983; Nat. Humanities Ctr. fellow, 1982-83, John Carter Brown Libr. fellow, 1985, 88, 2002, 06, 07, DuBois Inst. Afro-Am. Rsch. fellow Harvard, 1989-90; fellow Va. Found. Humanities, 1995-99, sr. fellow, 2002; Va. Found. sr. fellow, 2002—; fellow Libr. Co. Phila., 2002; Sch. Am. Rsch. fellow, Santa Fe, summer 2004. Fellow Am. Anthrop. Assn. (rep. to Am. Coun. Learned Socs. 1985-90); mem. Caribbean Studies Assn. (past mem. exec. council) Office: Va Found Humanities 145 Ednam Dr Charlottesville VA 22903-4629 Office Phone: 434-924-3296.

HANDLER, RICHARD, educational association administrator, anthropologist; b. Indiana, Pa., May 17, 1950; s. Earl and Phoebe Handler; m. Wendy Zomparelli, Mar. 3, 2007; children: Molly Rose, Louis Cole Hanlder. BA, Columbia U., NYC, 1972; PhD, U. Chgo., Ill., 1979. Asst. prof. Lake Forest Coll., Ill., 1980—86; prof. U. Va., Charlottesville, 1986—, assoc. dean. Author: (book) Nationalism and the Politics of Culture in Quebec. Exec. bd. mem. Am. Anthrop. Assn., Washington, 2000—03. Humanities fellowship, NEH, 1991. Home: 325 7 1/2 St SW Charlottesville VA 22903 Office: Univ Virginia PO Box 400133 Charlottesville VA 22904-4133 Business E-Mail: rh3y@virginia.edu.

HANDLEY, LEON HUNTER, lawyer; b. Lakeland, Fla., Sept. 9, 1927; s. Driskle Hubert and Mamie (Denmark) H.; m. Mary Virginia Wolfe, May 2, 1953; children: Leon Hunter, Mary Ellen, Laura Catherine, Leann Virginia. BSBA with honors, U. Fla., Gainesville, 1949, JD, 1951. Bar: Fla. 1951, US Dist. Ct. (so. dist.) Fla. 1952, US Dist. Ct. (mid. dist.) Fla. 1962, US Supreme Ct. 1956, US Ct. Appeals (5th cir.) 1960, US Ct. Appeals (11th cir.) 1981. Pres. Gurney & Handley, Orlando, Fla., 1951—2005; ptnr. Rumberger, Kirk & Caldwell, P.A., Orlando, 2005—. Bd. dirs. Orlando/Tampa Cracker Groves, Inc., Orlando, 1964—; v.p., bd. dirs. So. Indsl. Savs. Bank, Orlando, Claude H. Wolfe, Inc., Orlando, 1969—, chmn., bd. dir. Beneficial Savings Bank, Tampa; pres., chmn. bd. dirs. Mine & Mill Supply Co., Lakeland, 1966—; gen. counsel, life dir., past pres. Cen. Fla. Fair; chmn. bd. trustees Sta. WMFE-TV. Pres. Chesley Magruder Charitable Trust; elder Presbyn. Ch.; trustee Lake Highland Prep. Sch., Orlando. Warrant officer US Maritime Svc., 1945-46, ETO; sgt. US Army, 1946-48, Korea; capt. USAFR, 1949-59. Named one of Best Lawyers in Am.; named to U. Fla. Hall of Fame. Fellow Am. Coll. Trial Lawyers; mem. ABA, Am. Bd. Trial Advocates (Fla. Trial Lawyer of Yr. 1966, advocate), Orange County Bar Assn. (past pres.; Wm Trickle Professionalism award, 2010), Fla. Bar Assn. (past pres. sta. jr. bar sect., bd. govs. 1959-60), Fedn. Ins. and Corp. Counsel, Internat. Assn. Def. Counsel, Assn. Def. Trial Attys., Trial Attys. Am., Am. Judicature Soc., Pres.'s Coun. (founder U. Fla. chpt.), Citrus Club, Orlando Country Club, Univ. Club, Masons (grand orator Fla. 1982, 86), K.T., Shriners, Scottish Rite (33d degree, insp. gen. hon. 1979), Rotary (pres. Orlando chpt. 1984, Paul Harris fellow), Travelers' Century Club, Fla. Blue Key (pres. 1951), Phi Delta Phi, Alpha Tau Omega (pres. U. Fla. chpt. 1951), Phi Kappa Phi, Alpha Kappa Psi, Beta Gamma Sigma. Republican. Avocations: jogging, handball. Office: Rumberger Kirk & Caldwell PA PO Box 1873 Orlando FL 32801 Home: 70 W Lucerne Cir Apt 1715 Orlando FL 32801 Office Phone: 407-872-7300 ext. 2159. Office Fax: 407-841-2133. Business E-Mail: lhandley@rumberger.com.

HANDY, F. PHILIP, investment company executive, educational association administrator; BA in Economics cum laude, Princeton U.; MBA, Harvard U. CEO ComBanks Corp.; securities analyst Fidelity Mgmt. and Rsch., Boston, 1968—70; v.p., investment banking Donaldson, Lufkin & Jenrette, Inc., NYC, 1970—76; CEO Multiple Bank Holding Co., Orlando, Fla., 1976; founder, owner Winter Park Capital Co., 1980—97, ptnr., 1980—97; mng. dir. EGI Corp. Investments, 1996—99; chmn. Strategic Industries, LLC, CEO, 2001—. Bd. dirs. Anixter Internat., Inc., Wink Comm., Inc., WCI Cmtys., Inc., Owens Corning, 2006—, iDine Rewards Network, Inc., 2008—. Chmn. Fla. State Bd. Edn., 2001—; active Edn. Governance Reorganization Task Force, 2000—; trustee, treas., mem. exec. com. Northfield Mount Hermon Sch.; mem. bd. overseers Rollins Coll. Crummer Grad. Sch. Bus.; mem., pres. bd. trustees Orlando Mus. Art; active Govs. Commn. on the Future of Fla. Environment, 1989—90; bd. dirs. PRIDE (Prison Rehabilitative Industries and Diversified Enterprises, Inc.) of Fla., 1989, chmn. bd.; bd. dirs. Govs. Fla. Coun. of 1000. With USAR, 1966—73. Mem.: Chief Execs. Orgn. Avocations: long distance running, mountain biking. Office: Strategic Industries LLC 11660 Alpharetta Hwy Ste 350 Roswell GA 30076-3878 Office Phone: 770-619-2898. Office Fax: 850-245-9667. Business E-Mail: fhandy@strategicind.com.

HANDY, JOHN W., shipping company executive, retired military officer; b. Raleigh, NC, Apr. 29, 1944; BS in History, Meth. Coll., 1966; Diploma, Squadron Officer Sch., 1972, Air Command and Staff Coll., 1979; MS in Systems Mgmt., U. So. Calif., 1979; Diploma, Air War Coll., 1982, Nat. War Coll., 1984; postgrad., Harvard U., 1993. Commd. 2d lt. USAF, 1967, advanced through ranks to gen., 2000; various assignments to dir. of programs and evaluations Hdqtrs. USAF, Washington, 1995-97; comdr. 21st Air Force, McGuire AFB, N.J., 1997-98; dep. chief of staff for installations and logistics Hdqtrs. USAF/The Pentagon, Washington, 1998-2000; vice chief of staff USAF/The Pentagon, Washington, 2000—01; comdr. U.S. Transp. Command, Scott AFB, Ill., 2001—05; exec. v.p. Horizon Lines, LLC, Charlotte, NC, 2005—. Bd. dir. Alien Tech., 2006—, American Roll-On Roll-off Carrier, Am. Auto Logistics; bd. trustee Methodist Coll., Fayetteville, NC, St. Louis Sci. Ctr. Decorated Def. Disting. Svc. medal, Disting. Svc. medal, Legion of Merit with oak leaf cluster, Meritorious Svc. medal with three oak leaf clusters, Air medal with oak leaf cluster, Antarctica Svc. medal, Vietnam Svc. medal with three svc. stars, Republic of Vietnam Gallery Cross with Palm, Order of Sword, 2005, others. Office: Horizon Lines Inc 4064 Colony Rd Ste 200 Charlotte NC 28211

HANEMAN, VINCENT SIERING, JR., consulting engineer, educator, dean; b. Orange, NJ, Feb. 19, 1924; s. Vincent Siering and Helen (Harris) H.; m. Adelaide Russell, Oct. 3, 1961 (dec.); children: Charles Frederick; m. Barbara Gilliam, June 1, 2002. S.B., MIT, 1947; MS in Aero. Engring, U. Mich., 1950, PhD, 1956. Registered profl. engr., Ohio, Okla., Tex., Ala., Alaska. Asst. head flight research Project Meteor, Mass. Inst. Tech., 1947-49; project head automatic wind tunnel data reduction U. Mich., 1949-51; project officer analogue computer research Wright Air Devel. Center, Ohio, 1951-52; assoc. prof., asst. dept. head aero. engring. Air Force Inst. Tech., Wright Patterson AFB, Ohio, 1955-59; chief spl. projects div. guidance and control directorate Air Force Ballistic Missile Div., 1959-60; pres., sr. asso. Haneman Assos., Richardson, Tex., 1960-66, Stillwater, Okla., 1967-72, Auburn, Ala., 1972-73; chmn. bd. Haneman Assos., Inc., Richardson, Stillwater and Auburn, 1961-73, exec. v.p. Stillwater, 1966-67; prof. mech. engring., dir. engring. research, asso. dean Coll. Engring., Okla. State U., 1966-72; prof. aeros. engring., dean Sch. Engring., Auburn U., 1972-80; prof. mech. engring., dean sch. engring. U. Alaska, Fairbanks, 1980-91, prof. emeritus, dean emeritus sch. engring., 1991—. Cons. flight simulator project U. Mich., 1952-55, Gen. Electric Co., Gen. Dynamics, Space Tech. Labs., Chance Vought Corp., Ling Temco-Vought, Nat. Acad. Scis., Union Carbide, Auburn U., State of Ark., U. Tex. Pan-Am., Brownsville, others. Contbr. articles on instrumentation, control and guidance, aircraft performance, engring. edn. to tech. jours. Mem. Army Sci. Adv. Panel, 1967-77; chmn. night low level com. Project Master, Point of Contact Airmobile. Served to 1st lt. USAAF, 1943-45, MTO; to maj. USAF, 1951-60; to maj. gen. Res., moblzn. asst. to dep. chief staff for research and devel. Decorated D.S.M., Legion of Merit with oak leaf cluster, D.F.C. with oak leaf cluster, Air medal with 7 oak leaf clusters, Air Force Commendation medal. Assoc. fellow Am. Inst. Aeros. and Astronautics; fellow Am. Soc. Engring. Edn. (past sec. mech. and aero. divs., past nat. chmn. aero. div., past mem. gen. council, past mem. exec. com., past chmn. engring. research council, past 1st v.p., chmn. dean's inst. 1978, chmn. planning factors com. Engring. Coll. Council 1976-80, pres. 1980-81), Am. Astronautical Soc. (sr.), Am. Helicopter Soc., IEEE, Nat. Soc. Profl. Engrs. (ethics com. 1974-75, nat. chmn. Engring. Week 1977, 78, chmn. cost of engring. edn. com., nat. dir. 1979-80), Ala. Soc. Profl. Engrs. (state chmn. Engring. Week 1973-76), Alaska Soc. Profl. Engrs. (pres. 1985-86, pres. Fairbanks chpt. 1982-83, gov. 1974—, exec. com. Sustaining U. Program com.), Nat. Conf. Advancement Research (ad hoc mem. exec. com. 1977-79), Sigma Xi, Tau Beta Pi, Sigma Tau, Phi Kappa Phi, Pi Epsilon Gamma, Sigma Nu. Address: 1906 Leonard St #4 Columbus GA 31906

HANEN, ANDREW SCOTT, federal judge; b. Elgin, Ill., Dec. 10, 1953; s. Eugene Edward Hanen and Phyllis Jean (VanderWorker) Fee; m. Diane Dillard, Jan. 5, 1980. BA, Denison U., 1975; JD, Baylor U., 1978. Bar: Tex. 1978, U.S. Dist. Ct. (no., so., ea., and we. dists.) Tex. 1978, U.S. Ct. Appeals (5th and 11th cirs.) 1978, U.S. Supreme Ct. 1978. Briefing atty. Supreme Ct. Tex., Austin, 1978-79; ptnr. Andrews & Kurth, Houston, 1979; judge US Dist. Ct. (so. dist.) Tex., Brownsville, 2002—. Gen. counsel Sunshine Kids, Houston, 1983—; mem. Harris County Jud. Qualifications Com., Houston, 1984—. Fellow Tex. BarFound., Houston Bar Found.; mem. ABA, Houston Bar Assn. (chmn. com. 1984—, Pres. award 1985), Houston Young Lawyers Assn. (treas. 1986, Outstanding Service award 1982, 83, 85). Clubs: Tex. (Houston). Office: US Dist Ct US Courthouse 600 E Harrison St Brownsville TX 78520 Office Phone: 956-548-2591.

HANES, RALPH PHILIP, JR., network technician; b. Winston-Salem, NC, Feb. 25, 1926; s. Ralph Phillip and Dewitt H (Chathan); m. Joan Audrey Humpstone, Jan. 14, 1950 (dec. Jan. 1983); m. Mary Charlotte Metz, Dec. 23, 1984. Grad., Woodberry Forest Sch., Orange, Va., 1944; student, U. NC, Chapel Hill, 1944-46; BA, Yale U., New Haven, Conn., 1949; LHD (hon.), St. Andrews Coll., Laurinburg, NC, 1981; DFA (hon.), NC Sch. of Arts, Winston-Salem, 1987; HHD (hon.), Wake Forest U., Winston-Salem, 1990. With Hanes Cos., Inc. (formerly Hanes Dye and Finishing Co.), Winston-Salem, NC, 1950-93; pres. Hanes Dye and Finishing Co., 1965-68, chmn. bd., 1968-88, chmn. emeritus, 1988-93; chmn. bd. Ampersand, Inc., 1976-85. Mem. coun. of sr. fellows Salzburg Seminars in Am.

Studies. Author: How to Get Anyone to Do Anything, 2006; cons. editor: Performing Arts Rev., 1981—85, Jour. Arts Mgmt. and Law, 1981—86, mem. editl. adv. bd.: Art Economist, 1982—86. Mem. (appt. by Pres. L. B. Johnson) Nat. Coun. Arts, 1965—70; mem. Moravian Music Found., 1963—65; founder/mem. bd. visitors NC Sch. Arts, 1985—, trustee exec. com., 1966—78; bd. visitors Barter Theatre State Theatre of Va., 1967—75; assoc. fellow Jonathan Edward Coll., Yale U., 1971—74; mem. Spoleto Festival, 1979—86, Nat. Mus. Am. Art, Renwick Gallery, 1976—89, Alliance for Arts Edn., 1976—79; mem. exec. com. Nat. Coun. for Arts and Edn., 1976—79; mem. adv. coun. for arts Fed Res. Bank of Richmond, 1977—78; mem. Bus. Com. for Ars Arena Stage, Washington, 1980—86; mem. Gov.'s Coun. Bus., Arts and Humanities, 1977—85; mem. fine arts com. Fed. Res. Bank of Washington, 1979—81; mem. adv. bd. Pauline Koner Dance Consort, 1977—80; mem. Arts Resources Corp., 1981—83; chmn. Am. Art Forum, 1986—87, bd. dirs., 1986—90, Arena Stage, 1990—92; com. mem. State of NC award, 1993; mem. Yr. of Mountains Commn., NC, 1995—96; corp. mem. Woods Hole Oceanog. Inst., 1994—98; mem. coun. advisors Blue Ridge Pky., 1998—; exec. com. Ambs. for the Arts, NEA, 1999—; mem. Art Based Elem. Schs., 2000; founder/commr. Winston-Salem Commn. Cultural Affairs, 2001—; co-chair Artsignite Fest., 2002; initiator New River Blue Way, N.C., Va., W.Va., 2002; mem. adv. bd. Blue Ridge Rural Land Trust, 2003—; craft adv. com. Mint Mus., Charlotte, 2004—; mem. Winston-Salem Commr. Cultural Affairs, 2001—; mem. coun. of advisors Blue Ridge Pkwy, 2002—; initiator New River VA Blueway, 2002, H. John Heinz III Ctr. for Sci., Econs. and the Environment, 2004—; arts cons. Govt. of Austria, 1978; bd. dirs. Nat. Coun. Friends of Kennedy Ctr., 1975—80; mem. founding com. Agri-Rsch. Extension Network of N. Am., 1995—97; chmn. cabinet Spl. Olympics World Games, 1999; bd. dirs. (appt. by Pres. J.F. Kennedy) Nat. Cultural Ctr. for Performing Arts, 1962—65; bd. dirs. Am. Symphony Orch. League, 1958—61; trustee Salem Coll., 1961—64; bd. dirs. Jargon Soc. Inc., 1966—69, pres., 1968—75; founder NC State Arts Coun., chmn., 1964—66; founder/bd. dirs. Ams. for the Arts (formerly Am Coun. Arts), 1960—69; pres. Ams. for the Arts, 1964—66, vice chmn., 1967—69; mem. nat. adv. com. Brevard Sch. Music, 1969—74, Am. Crafts Coun., 1970—72, Appalachian Trail Conf., 1973—76; chmn. com. on music Yale U. Coun., 1970—73; bd. dirs. Nat. Audubon Soc., 1972—78, John. W. and Anna H. Hanes Found., 1974—, So. Appalachian Highlands Conservancy, 1974—78, Old Salem Inc., 1974—77, Isaak Walton League Am., 1974—78, Nature Conservancy, 1975—79; bd. dirs. (apptd. by Pres. Gerald Ford) Kennedy Ctr. for the Performing Arts, 1975—80; bd. dirs. Salzburg Seminar of Am. Studies, 1978—82, Am. Land Trust, 1976—93, Arts Internat., 1981—85; adv. com. Am. Farmland Trust, 1983—97; mem. internat. coun. NYC Ballet, 1984—86; trustee emeritus Kennedy Ctr. for the Arts, Washington, 1999—; bd. govs. Nat. Com. for the New River, N.C. Va., W. Va., 1999—2001; commissioner of cultural affairs Nat. Com. for the New River, N.C., Va., W. Va., 2001—; mem. internat. coun. Mus. Modern Art, 1978—83. Recipient Chmn.'s award, NEA, 1966, 2005, Gov.'s award for preservation of natural area, 1969, pub. svc. award, State of NC, 1976, Morrison award for the Arts, 1977, Swan award, Tenn., 1970, award, NC Soc. of NYC, 1979, Cmty. Svc. award, Winston-Salem Urban League, 1979, Conservation award, Isaac Walton League Am., 1982, award for disting. svc. to arts, Nat. Gov.'s Assn., 1982, NC Gov.'s award in fine arts, 1982, awards, Winston-Salem chpt. NAACP, 1983, Nat. Medal of Arts Amb. for the Arts presented by Pres. George Bush, 1991, award, Piedmont Opera Theatre, 1992, tribute, Nat. Arts Club, NYC, 1995, Southeastern Ctr. for Contemporary Arts Leadership award, 1998, Young Leadership award, Winston-Salem Arts Coun., 2000, Charlotte & Philip Hanes Art Gallery award, Wake Forest U., 2001, Excellence award, Downtown Winston-Salem, 2003, award, Phil and Charlotte Hanes Student Commons Bldg., NCSA, 2003, Winston-Salem Found., 2003, Founder award, Nat. Assn. of State Arts Agencies, 2005, Disting. Svc. to the Arts award, NEA, 2005, Entrepreneurial Am. Leadership award, Ptnrs. for Livable Places, 2007, Innovation award, Trenthot Ctr. (USMS), 2008; named Young Man of Yr., Winston-Salem Jaycees, 1958, NC Jaycees, 1958, Hon. Comdr., USS NC, 1998. Mem.: Assn. Fundraising Profls., Am. Assn. Fund Raising Profls. (Lifetime Achievement award 2005, 2002), Nat. Assn. of State Arts Agencies (Nat. Endorsement for the Arts Chmns. award 2005, Founder award 2005), Piedmont Triad Entrepeneurs Network, Piedmont Triad Partnership Bd., Century Assn. (NYC), Walpole Soc., Wilderness Soc., Royal Soc. Arts, Ut Prosim Soc., Pa. Acad. Fine Arts, N.Am. Mycological Assn., Nat. Wildlife Fedn., East African Wildlife Soc., Appalachian Consortium, World Bus. Coun., Trout Unltd., S.E. Coun. on Founds., Peale for Visual Arts (Phila.), Appalachian Trail Conf., Am. League Anglers, Potomac Appalachian Mountain Club, Isaac Walton League, Curri-tuck, Bohemian Club, Cane River Club, Twin City Club, Piedmont Club, Met. Club (Washington), Lotos Club (NYC), Yale Club (NYC). Home and Office: PO Box 1704 Winston Salem NC 27102-1704 Office Phone: 336-761-0570. E-mail: rph@rphanes.com.

HANEY, GREG, state legislator; m. Rhonda Barrett. Attended, Miss. Gulf Coast CC, U. So. Miss., Hattiesburg. Real estate broker; mem. Dist. 118 Miss. House of Reps., Jackson, 2012—. Mem.: Nat. Assn. Realtors, Miss. Assn. Realtors, Miss. Gulf Coast Realtors, Harrison County Rep. Club. Republican. Baptist. Office: Miss House of Reps PO Box 1018 Jackson MS 39215 Business E-Mail: ghaney@house.ms.gov.

HANGER, EMMETT WILSON, state legislator; b. Staunton, Va., Aug. 2, 1948; m. Sharon Michael; children: Shelley R., E. Michael, Scott T., Heidi Y., Chad N. Comml. real estate commr.; pres., CEO Dominion Bus. Sch.; pres. Dominion Bus. Svc.; chief adminstrn. Va. Coll.; commr. revenue Augusta County, 1979—82; state del. Dist. 26 Va., 1983—91; former mem. Fin. Com., Conservation & Natural Resources Com., Claims Com.; state senator Dist. 24, 1995—; mem. Agr. Com., Conservation & Natural Resources Com., Local Govt. Com., Privileges Com., Elec., Rehab. & Soc. Svc. Com. Mem.: Parent-Tchr. Assn., Ruritan. Republican. Church Of Brethren. Mailing: PO Box 2 Mount Solon VA 22843-0002 Fax: 540-885-6157. E-mail: district24@sov.state.va.us.

HANKENSON, E(DWARD) CRAIG, JR., performing arts executive; b. Mankato, Minn., Apr. 12, 1935; s. Edward Craig and Ethel Irene (Favre) H.; m. Francis Joyce Hall, Mar. 23, 1957 (div. 1978); 1 child, Meridith Joyce.; m. Catherine Ann Donaldson, 1981; 1 child, Jennifer Leigh. MusB, Eastman Sch. Music, 1957, MusM, 1959. Head voice and opera dept. Auburn U., Ala., 1959-62; bus. mgr. Chautauqua Opera Assn., NY, 1958-61, stage mgr., 1957-59, stage dir., 1962; mgmt. intern San Francisco Opera Co., 1962-65; assoc. dir. Brevard Mus. Center, NC, 1965-68; gen. mgr. Saratoga Performing Arts Ctr., NY, 1968-75, dir., 1975—78; exec. dir. Wolf Trap Found. Performing Arts, Vienna, Va., 1978-81; pres. Producers, Inc., 1980; dir., chmn. dept. arts mgmt. and events U. South Fla., Tampa, 1983-86; pres. KiddyCart Inc., 1987—, Producers, Inc., 1981—; chmn. bd. PI-CASTAR, 1985—. Dir. Rochester Comty. Opera, N.Y., 1957-59; mem. Title III adv. coun. N.Y. Dept. Edn., 1969-75, N.Y. Gov.'s Commn. on Arts in Edn., 1978; cons. N.Y. Coun. on Arts; coun. bd. Rensselaer Poly. Inst.; cons. theater constrn. and mgmt. Concord Pavillion, Calif., Blossom Music Ctr., Cleve., Art Park, Buffalo, Mud Island, Memphis, Tampa Bay Performing Arts Ctr., Tampa, Robin Hood Dell, Phila.; ops. cons. Worcester Ctr. Performing Arts, 2005—. Prodr.: (TV spls.) Snow White, PBS, 1973, Al Hirt and Pete Fountain Together, PBS, 1979, Great Jazz Pianists, PBS, 1979-81, Brigadoon, Majestic Theatre, N.Y.C., 1980-81, Lionel Hampton's Return to the Paradise, PBS, 1988, Thames Live Cinema, Radio City Music Hall, 1988; nat. tour of Show Boat, 1980, Kiss Me Kate and Taming of the Shrew, Washington Internat. Jazz Festival, 1980, nat. tour Pete Fountain, Jerry Mulligan and Al Hirt, 1982, 83, Tom Paxton, Dab O' Dixie, 1987, translator: Haydn's Lo Speziale, 1958, Smetana's Bartered Bride, 1964; creator Ticket Reservation Systems, 1968, prodr. of Glenn Miller, Artie Shaw, Woodie Herman, Helen O'Connell, Warren Covington, Don Cornell, Pied Pipers BigBand Nat. Tour Show, 1993; prodr.: (tours) Midnight in the Garden of Good and Evil, 1999, Last Swing of the Century, 1999, Irish Christmas, 1999. Bd. dirs. Capitol Area Resident Opera Co., 1969-71; mem. alumni adv. bd. Eastman Sch. Music, 1974-78; mem. com. performing arts Leukemia Soc. Am., Inc.; mem. spl. adv. com. on spl. projects and presenting orgns. Nat. Endowment for the Arts, 1979-80; elder, mem. ruling session Temple Ter. Presbyn. Ch., 1990—, chmn. rsch. and planning, 1992—; bd. dirs., sec. Ter. Landings Assn.; youth group leader H.S., 1996—, Terrace Presbyn. Ch., 1996—; small group leader, Montreat, NC, Youth Conf., 2000, 01, leader 12-step program, 2001; pres. Univ. Cmty. Civic Assn., 1997—; mem. adv. bd. Tampa Habitat for Humanity, 2000—, mem. com., 2001; bd. dirs. Parents Coun. Hollins U., 2001-, vice chmn., 2003—; co-chair Hollins U. Parents Coun., 2003-04, chair, 2004—. Recipient citation Ctrl. Theaters, Moscow, 1973. Mem. Internat. Assn. Concert and Festival Mgrs. (dir.), Performing Arts Assn. N.Y. (pres. 1972-78), Orgn. Summer Festival Mgrs. (moderator 1971-79, dir), N.Y. Fedn. Music Clubs (dir.), Saratoga Springs C. of C. (dir. 1969-72, chmn. promotion com. 1970-72), Council of Pres.'s, Albany League Arts, Saratoga Springs PTA (pres. 1972-73), Temple Terrace C. of C. (spl. events com., bd. dirs., bd. dirs. Farmer's Market), Univ. Cmty. Civic Assn. (pres.), Pleasant Terr. Civic Assn. (pres. 2004—), Rotary (chair programming com., bd. dirs. 2003—, bd. dirs. Temple Terr. chpt. 2003—), Hollins U. Parents' Coun. Bd., Temple Terrace Police (adv. coun., 2000—) Republican. Presbyterian. Achievements include conceiving process of computerized event tickets, motivation for creation of company Tickeron and consulted for creation of the Ticketron ticket system. Home: 5109 Oakhaven Ln Tampa FL 33617-1032 Office: Producers Inc 11806 N 56th St Tampa FL 33617-1652 Office Phone: 813-988-8333. Office Fax: 813-985-3293. Personal E-mail: craighank@verizon.net. Business E-Mail: craigh@producersinc.com.

HANKINS, RANDAL L., retail executive; Pres. Dillard Nat. Bank, 2004—06; v.p. Dillard's, Inc., 2006—. Office: Dillard's Inc 1600 Cantrell Rd Little Rock AR 72201 Office Phone: 501-376-5200. Office Fax: 501-399-7831. E-mail: randy.hankins@dillards.com.

HANLEY, THOMAS RICHARD, engineering educator; s. Thomas Jesse and Dorothy Louise (Hay) H.; m. Norma Kathryn Decker, Dec. 27, 1979; children: Thomas Jeffrey, Alan Michael, Andrew Richard, Caitlin Marisa. BSChemE, Va. Poly. Inst., 1967; MSChemE, Va. Poly. Inst. & State U., 1971, PhDChemE, 1972; MBA in Mgmt., Wright State U., 1975. Registered profl. engr., Ky. Devel. engr. AF Materials Lab., Wright Patterson AFB, Ohio, 1972-75; asst. prof. Tulane U., New Orleans, 1975-79; assoc. prof. Rose-Hulman Inst. Tech., 1979-83; prof., dept. head La. Tech. U., Ruston, 1983-85; prof., chmn. dept. Fla. State U., Fla. A&M U., Tallahassee, 1985-91; dean Speed Sci. Sch. U. Louisville, 1991—2003; provost Auburn (Ala.) U., 2003—05, v.p., 2005—06, prof., 2006—. Divsn. advisor NSF, Washington, 1987-93; presenter at numerous nat. and internat. profl. confs. Contbr. articles to profl. jours. Bd. dirs. Plasticolors, Ashtabula, Ohio, 1997-2013, AAES, Washington, 2007-10. Capt. USAF, 1972—75. Recipient award Soc. Am. Mil. Engrs., 1966, 67, Acad. award Am. Legion, 1967, Ralph R. Teetor Ednl. award SAE, 1989, Outstanding Engr. in Edn. award Ky. Soc. Profl. Engrs., 1994; grantee NSF, Nat. Renewable Energy Lab., GE, Colgate-Palmolive, United Catalysts, IKA Works, Swan Biomass, Toro, Olin, Stone and Webster. Fellow AIChE (profl. devel. recognition cert. 1980, student chpt. advisor award 1979, bd. dirs., NYC 2006-08); mem. Am. Soc. Engring. Edn., Nat. Assn. Basketball Coaches, Sigma Xi, Phi Kappa Phi, Tau Beta Pi, Phi Lambda Upsilon, Omega Chi Epsilon. Office: Auburn U Dept Chem Engring Auburn AL 36849 Home Phone: 502-228-0161; Office Phone: 334-844-7773. Business E-Mail: hanley@auburn.edu.

HANMER, STEPHEN READ, JR., retired federal official; b. Denver, Aug. 15, 1933; s. Stephen Read and Mary Virginia (Marchant) H.; m. Lois Eileen Boteler, June 25, 1955; children: Susan Eileen Hanmer Alexander, Stephen Read III, Sara Lynn Black. BS in Phys., Va. Mil. Inst., Lexington, 1955; MS in Aerospace Engring., MSME, U. So. Calif., 1964. Commd. 2d lt. U.S. Army, 1956, major, 1965, lt. col., 1968, comdg. 6th bn., 32d Artillery Vietnam, 1968, col., 1975, retired, 1977; assoc. prof. dept. mechanics U.S. Mil. Acad., 1964-67; def. plans div. staff mem. U.S. Mission to NATO, Brussels, 1978-81; dir. theater nuclear force policy Office of Sec., Dept. Def., Washington, 1981-84; prin. dep. asst. sec. Internat. Security Policy Dept. Def., Washington, 1984-85; amb., dep. head U.S. del. Strategic Arms Reduction Talks, 1985-87, amb., chief U.S. del., 1988-89; dep. dir. ACDA, 1989-93; asst. to pres. Kaman Scis. Corp., Alexandria, Va., 1993-98; ret., 1998. Mary Moody Northen chair dept. internat. studies Va. Mil. Inst., 2002. Bd. advisors. Va. Military Inst. Found., 2011. Decorated Legion of Merit, Bronze Star; recipient Meritorious Civilian Svc. medal U.S. Dept. Def., 1981, Sec. of Def. medal, 1987, Sr. Exec. Svc. Disting. Exec. award, 1988, Sec. State Superior Honor award, 1993, Disting. Honor award ACDA, 1993. Mem. St. Andrews Soc. Washington (sec. 1995-96, v.p. 1997, 2004, pres. 2006), Am. Legion Post#18 (comdr. 2010), Sertoma Club (bd. dirs. 1977), Am. Def. Preparedness Assn., VMI Found. (bd. advisor, 2011). Republican. Episcopalian. Business E-Mail: readandlois@cox.net.

HANN, ROY WILLIAM, JR., civil engineer, educator; b. Okla. City, Mar. 21, 1934; s. Roy W. and Irene (Billups) H.; m. Ann Mullman, Dec. 27, 1960 (div. Apr. 1983); children: Kimberly Anne, Sharon Irene, Roy Lee, Karen Bea; m. Martha D'Anne Metting, June 23, 1984; children: Tyson Orion, Heather Eileen. BS, U. Okla., 1956, MCE, 1957, PhD, 1963. Registered profl. engr., Okla., Tex., bd. cert. gen. environ. engr.; lic. real estate broker, Tex. Engr. C.H. Guernsey and Assos., Oklahoma City, 1959-60; asst. prof. civil engring U. S.C., Columbia, 1962-64; asst. prof. civil engring. dept. environ. engring. div. Tex. A&M U., Coll. Sta., 1965—67, assoc. prof., 1967—71, prof., rsch. engr., 1971—2010, prof. emeritus, 2010—, head environ. engring. div., 1970—75, 1981—86, dir. sea grant program, 1976—77; dir. Inst. for Oil Spill Tech. Tex. Engring. Experiment Sta., 1991—2010. Pres. Civil Engring. Systems, Inc., Internat. Spill Tech. Corp., Hann Investments; owner, operator Spring Valley Ranches; cons. in field. Author: Fundamental Aspects of Water Quality Management, 1972; contbr. articles to profl. jours. With USPHS, 1957—59; mem. Bryan-College Station Apt. Assn., 1973—2005, pres., 1975—76, dir., 1977—84. Recipient Palladium medal Nat. Audubon Soc. and Am. Assn. Engring. Socs., 1983. Fellow: ASCE (life Paper award 1970—72), Am. Water Works Assn. (Outstanding Paper award 1969), Tex. Soc. Profl. Engrs. (Named Outstanding Young Engr. Brazos chpt. 1969), Am. Acad. Environ. Engring., U. Okla. Alumni Assn. (life), Tau Beta Pi (life), Omicron Delta Kappa (life), Chi Epsilon (life), Sigma Chi (life), Sigma Xi (life). Achievements include research in computer methods, oil pollution control and water supply, water pollution. Home: 1300 Walton Dr College Station TX 77840-2529 Business E-Mail: rwhannpe@yahoo.com.

HANNA, GEORGE VERNER, III, lawyer; b. Shelby, NC, Mar. 2, 1943; s. George and Mildred Mae (McSwain) H.; m. Linda Faye Tyndall, May 4, 1982 (div.); children: George Verner IV, Mark W., Elizabeth P.; m. Deborah Henson Hannon, Apr. 14, 1984. AB, U. N.C., 1965, JD, 1968. Bar: N.C. 1968, U.S. Dist. Ct. (we. dist.) N.C. 1969, U.S. Dist. Ct. (ea. dist.) N.C. 1972, U.S. Dist. Ct. (mid. dist.) 1974, U.S. Ct. Appeals (4th cir.) 1976, U.S. Supreme Ct. 1976; cert. mediator N.C. Dispute Resolution Commn. Law clk. N.C. Supreme Ct., Raleigh, 1968-69; assoc. Moore & Van Allen, PLLC, Charlotte, NC, 1969-73, ptnr., 1974—. Arbitrator Am. Arbitration Assn. Past vice-chair bd. mgrs. Harris YMCA, Charlotte; past chmn. bd. mgrs. McCrorey YMCA, Charlotte; past pres., bd. dirs. Legal Svcs. So. Piedmont, Charlotte; past bd. chair Coun. Children's Rights (formerly Children's Law Ctr.), Charlotte; past chair YMCA Cmty. Devel. Bd.; former mem. UNC Law Sch. Alumni Bd. Recipient Dr. I Beverly Lake Public Service award NC Bar Assn, 2010, Diversity in Business award Diversity Coun. Carolinas, 2006, Willie J. Stratford, Sr. Diversity award Greater Charlotte YMCA, 2008, Julius L. Chambers Diversity Champion award Mecklenburg County Bar, 2009, Inaugural Disting. Pro Bono Svc. award Coun. Children's Rights, Legal Aid of NC and Legal Svcs Southern Piedmont Fellow: Am. Bar Found.; mem.: ABA, NC Chief Justice's Commn. Equal Access to Justice, Mecklenburg Bar Found. (past pres.), Mecklenburg County Bar (past pres.), N.C. Bar Assn. (past bd. govs.), Quail Hollow Club. Home: 244 Hempstead Pl Charlotte NC 28207-1922 Office: Moore & Van Allen PLLC Bank of Am Corp Ctr 100 N Tryon St Ste 4700 Charlotte NC 28202-4003 Home Phone: 704-377-0618; Office Phone: 704-331-1030. Office Fax: 704-378-2030. Business E-Mail: georgehanna@mvalaw.com.

HANNA, WILLIAM JOHNSON, electrical engineering educator; b. Longmont, Colo., Feb. 7, 1922; s. William Grant and Anna Christina (Johnson) H.; m. Katherine Fagan, Apr. 25, 1944 (dec. 1993); children: Daniel August, Paul William; m. Helen Yeager McCarty, Sept. 19, 1996. BSEE, U. Colo., 1943, MS, 1948, D in Elec. Engring., 1951. Registered profl. engr., Colo. Mem. faculty U. Colo., 1946-91, prof. elec. engring., 1962-91, prof. emeritus, 1991—; ret., 1991. Cons. in field; mem. Colo. Bd. Engring. Examiners, 1973-85; with Ponderosa Assocs., Lafayette, Colo. Author articles, reports. Served to 1st lt. AUS, 1943-46. Recipient Faculty Recognition award Students Assn. U. Colo., 1956, 61, Alfred J. Ryan award, 1978, Archimedes award Calif. Soc. Profl. Engrs., 1978, Outstanding Engring. Alumnus award U. Colo., 1983, Faculty Service award, 1983; named Colo. Engr. of Yr. Profl. Engrs. Colo., 1968; named to Hon. Order of Ky. Cols. Mem. IEEE, Am. Soc. Engring. Edn., Nat. Soc. Profl. Engrs. (pres. Colo. 1967-68), Nat. Coun. Examiners Engring. & Surveying (pres. 1977-78, Disting. Svc. award with spl. commendation 1990), AIEE (chmn. Denver 1961-62) Clubs: Masons. Republican. Presbyterian. Home: 888 Richardson Rd Fortson GA 31808-6010 Office Phone: 307-666-8112.

HANNAH, JAMES, state supreme court chief justice; b. Dec. 26, 1944; BSBA in Acctg., U. Ark., JD. Pvt. practice Lightle, Tedder, Hannah & Beebe; city atty. City of Searcy, Ark., 1969—78; juvenile judge White County, 1976—78; chancery,probate judge 17th Jud. Dist., 1979—2000; assoc. justice Ark. Supreme Ct., 2001—04, chief justice, 2005—. Faculty adv. Nat. Jud. Coll. Former chmn. of bd. of adv. Wilbur Mills Alcoholism Treatment Ctr. Mem.: Ark. Bar Assn., Ark. Jud. Coun. (pres. 1995—96, bd.), Ark. Bd. of Pardons and Paroles (sec. 1972—79), White County Bar Assn. (former pres., treas., sec.), Am. Judges Assn. Office: Ark Supreme Ct Justice Bldg Rm 230 625 Marshall St Little Rock AR 72201 Business E-Mail: jim.hannah@arkansas.gov.*

HANNAH, JOHN ROBERT, SR., accountant; b. Monroe, La., Aug. 11, 1939; s. Robert Ruskin Hannah and Berta (Gilliland) Nelson; m. Elizabeth Girdner, Dec. 26, 1965; children: Allison, John Robert Jr. BS, La. State U., 1960. CPA, Tex. Acct. Arthur Young & Co., Houston, 1960-70, Peters & Smith, Midland, Tex., 1970-71; ptnr. Hannah & Trott, Midland, 1971-72; contr. Western States Producing Co., San Antonio, 1972-73; v.p. fin. Sommers Drug Stores Co., San Antonio, 1973-77; pvt. practice acctg. San Antonio, 1987—; ptnr. Peters, Anders & Hannah, San Antonio, 1978-86. Seminar speaker Bexar County Med. Soc., San Antonio, 1981. Fin. chmn. YMCA, San Antonio, 1975-82, chmn., 1982-83; adminstr. Bible Study Fellowship, San Antonio, 1977-83; bd. dirs. Morningside Ministries, 1991, Christian Ministry Assistance, 1992—, treas.; chmn. bd. trustees Alamo Heights United Meth. Ch., 1998. Lt. USN, 1961-65. Mem. Am. Inst. CPA's, Tex. Soc. CPa's, Fin. Execs. Internat., Execs. Internat. Club (San Antonio, pres. 1975-76). Methodist. Home: 102 Castleoaks Dr San Antonio TX 78213-2303 Office: 800 Navarro St Ste 210 San Antonio TX 78205-1725

HANNEMAN, RODNEY ELTON, metallurgical engineer; b. Spokane, Wash., Mar. 14, 1936; s. Christie Luther and Viva Helen (Sugrue) H.; married; 3 children. BS in Phys. Metallurgy, Wash. State U., Pullman, 1959; MS in Metallurgy, MIT, Cambridge, 1961, PhD, 1964; grad., GE Mgmt. Devel. Inst., 1979. With GE Co., Schenectady, 1963-81, mgr. materials characterization lab., 1977-80, mgr. materials programs, 1980-81; v.p. research, devel. and energy resources Reynolds Metals Co., Richmond, Va., 1981-85, v.p. quality assurance and tech. op., 1985-98; dir. Face Internat., 1988—2002; chmn. Aluminum Assn. Tech. Comm., 1989—97; pres. Mgmt. and Tech. Consultants, Richmond, Va., 1998—2002. Mem. vis. com. dept. materials sci. and engring. MIT, 1975—80, mem. adv. bd. Materials Processing Ctr, 1980—97; mem. adv. bd. U. Va., 1982—87, chmn. indsl. adv. bd. grad. engring. program, 1983—86; chmn. rsch. coordinating coun. Gas Rsch. Inst., 1985—87, adv. coun., 1988—2001; bd. dirs. Materials Properties Coun., 1982—90; mem. adv. com. Va. Ctr. for Innovative Tech., 1999—2002; adv. bd. Commonwealth Grad. Engring., Richmond, 1996—2006. Exec. v.p. found. bd. Sci. Mus. Va., 1989—09; v.p. Civic Assn., 1990-92. Recipient Alumni Achievement award Wash. State U., 1978; Joint Engring. Coun. award, 1984 Mem. AIME, MAPI, SAE, Am. Soc. Metals (Geisler award 1971, Engring. Materials Achievement award 1973), Am. Chem. Soc. (Chem. Innovator award 1970, Edison medallion 1979), Indsl. Rsch. Inst., Sigma Xi. Achievements include patents in field. Personal E-mail: rhannem@aol.com.

HANNER, BOB, state legislator; b. Apr. 19, 1945; m. Linda AnnMatthews Hanner; children: Rob, Jeff, Jeff. Former state rep. Dist. 133, Ga.; state rep. Dist. 131, 1974—92; state rep. Dist. 159, 1993—2002; state rep. Dist. 148, 2004—; chmn. natural resources & environ. com.; mem. appropriations com.; mem. game com.; mem. fish com.; mem. pks. com.; mem. Ga. House Rep.; mem. ins. & securities; mem. estate & bus. analysis; farmer. Mem.: Terrell County C. of C., US Jaycees (past dir.), Lions, Mason. Democrat. Baptist. Mailing: 9610 Plains Hwy Parrott GA 31777-9505

HANNER, Z. FRANK, museum director; b. Winston-Salem, NC; m. Patsy Doolittle; children: Tricia, Christy. BS in History, Appalachian State U., Boone, NC; EdM in History, Armstrong State Coll.,

Savannah, Ga. Inf. soldier US Army; served with 2d Inf. Divsn., Korea, 101st Airborne Air Assault, Ft. Campbell, Ky.; mem. staff 24th Inf. Divsn. Mus., Ft. Stewart, Ga., Nat. Inf. Mus., Ft. Benning, Ga., 1981—, dir., 1995—. Office: Nat Infantry Mus Bldg 396 Baltzell Ave Fort Benning GA 31905-5593 Office Phone: 706-545-2958. Office Fax: 706-545-5158. E-mail: zachary.f.hanner@us.army.mil.

HANNES, WILLIAM F., oil and gas company executive; BS in Petroleum Engring., Texas A&M U., 1981. With Mobil and Superior Oil; dir. bus. devel. Parker & Parsley, 1997—2001, v.p. engring. and devel., 2001—05; exec. v.p. worldwide bus. devel. Pioneer Natural Resources Co., 2005—07; exec. v.p. bus. devel. Pioneer Southwest Energy Partners, LP, 2007—10, Pioneer Natural Resources Co., 2007—10, exec. v.p. South Tex. ops., 2010—. Office: Pioneer Natural Resources Co Ste 200 5205 N O Connor Blvd Irving TX 75039 Office Phone: 972-444-9001. Office Fax: 972-969-3576.

HANRAHAN, LAWRENCE MARTIN, healthcare consultant; b. Cin., Mar. 9, 1961; adopted s. Robert Donald and Mary Francis (Doran) Hanrahan, s. Barry Wright and Kathryn Regina Kinkaid; m. Madeleine Carol Routon. AB in Chemistry, Miami U., 1983; MD, U. Cin. Coll. Medicine, 1988; MBA, U. Tex. Grad. Sch. Bus., 1992. Founder, owner Landscaping group, Cin., 1975—85; chief ultrasound tech., instr., rsch. assoc. Good Samaritan Hosp. Peripheral Vascular Lab., Cin., 1983—84; instr., technologist Clin. Vascular Lab. Christ Hosp., Cin., 1986; tech. cons., instr. Biosound, Inc., Indpls., 1983—89; surg. rsch. fellow divsn. surgery Boston U. Sch. Medicine; instr. peripheral vascular technologist Seton Med. Ctr., Austin, 1991; summer assoc. health care ops. Deloitte & Touche, Houston, 1991, cons. health care ops., 1991—92, sr. cons., 1992—94, mgr. health care ops., 1994—; sr. assoc. healthcare provider cons. William M. Mercer, Inc., Houston, 1995—97; co-founder Hanrahan Williams LLC, Houston, 1997—2000; dir. Genesis Healthcare Internat., Inc., Houston, 2000—01; co-founder, chmn. Interna Quality Healthcare, Profl. Connection, L.P., Houston, 2001—04; sr. mgr. Capgemini US LLC, 2004—05, Accenture, 2005—, global head health facility devel., 2005—10; prin. PWC, 2010—. Founder, chmn., pres. MLH Industries, Inc. (formerly CORE Med. Techs., Inc.), Houston, 1992—; sr. mgr., treas. Miami Med. Edn. and Devel., Miami U., 1975-79; com. mem. Disting. Lecture Series, U. Tex. Sch. Bus., Austin, 1990-91; founding pres. Tex. Bus. Hall of Fame Found. Scholarship Alumni Assn., 1992-93; bd. dirs., exec. com., 1992-93; mem. adv. bd. Healthcorp MBA, Owen Sch., Vanderbilt U., 2005-06; lectr. health-care adminstrn. program U. Houston, 2002—. Contbr. articles to profl. jours. Finalist ACS resident competition, 1990, San Diego State U. Entrepreneurship competition; winner New Eng. Surg. Soc. resident competition, 1990; Tex. Bus. Hall of Fame Found. scholar, 1991, Abell-Hanger Endowed presdl. scholar, 1991, Accenture HLS Innovation award, 2006. Mem. AMA, Soc. for Vascular Tech., Mass. Med. Soc., Harris County Med. Soc., Med. Student Surg. Soc., Tex. Med. Assn. (chair com. on physician access 1999-2006, alt. del. 2003-06, del. 2006-, cons. coun. on med. edn. 2006—), Harris County Med. Soc., Greater Houston Partnership, Engring. Health Issue Com., Beta Theta Pi. Achievements include patents in field. Avocation: jazz music. Office Phone: 713-356-4206. Business E-Mail: lawrence.m.hanrahan@us.pwc.com.

HANRAHAN, ROBERT JOSEPH, chemist, educator; b. Chgo., Jan. 7, 1932; s. James Richard and Lucille Florence (Granger) H.; m. Mary Ellen Hogan, Oct. 28, 1957; children: Ann Marie, Sheila Frances, Robert Joseph, Margaret Evyleen. BS, Loyola U., Chgo., 1953; PhD, U. Wis., Madison, 1957. Research chemist Pure Oil Co., Crystal Lake, Ill., 1953; teaching asst., research asst. Monsanto research fellow U. Wis., Madison, 1953-57; NSF postdoctoral fellow Leeds (Eng.) U., 1957-58; asst. prof. phys. chemistry U. Fla., 1958-64, assoc. prof., 1964-71, prof., 1971—2004, chmn. phys. chemistry div., 1977-86, prof. emeritus, 2004—. Vis. sci. Hahn-Meitner Inst. Nuclear Research, Berlin, 1976; cons. in field. Patentee in field; contbr. articles to profl. jours. AEC rsch. grantee, 1963-74; ERDA grantee, 1975-77; Dept. Energy grantee, 1977-88, 2001-06; Dreyfus Found. grantee, 1983. Mem. Am. Chem. Soc., Am. Phys. Soc., Radiation Research Soc., AAAS, Am. Soc. Mass Spectrometry, Inter-Am. Photochem. Soc. Democrat. Roman Catholic. Achievements include rsch. in chem. effects of nuclear radiation and on solar energy systems. Home: 3730 NW 16th Pl Gainesville FL 32605-4848 Office: U Fla Dept Chemistry Gainesville FL 32611 Office Phone: 352-392-1442. Business E-Mail: hanrahan@chem.ufl.edu.

HANSBARGER, L. CLARK, dean; b. Welch, W.Va. m. Christine Hansbarger. Grad., Duke U. Sch. Economics and Bus. Adminstrn., Durham, NC, Med. Coll. of Va. Sch. Medicine. Dir. W.Va. Dept. Health, 1981—85; divsn. dir. gen. pediat. U. N.Mex., med. dir. of pediat. ambulatory services, dean grad. med. edn.; assoc. v.p. health sciences, dean sch. medicine, dir. med. edn. W.Va. U., Charleston, 2002—. Office: WVa University Sch Medicine Robert C Byrd Health Sciences Ctr 3110 MacCorkle Ave SE Charleston WV 25304-3110 Office Phone: 304-347-1206. Office Fax: 304-347-1298. Business E-Mail: chansbarger@hsc.wvu.edu.

HANSELMAN, RICHARD WILSON, entrepreneur; b. Cin., Oct. 8, 1927; s. Wendell Forest and Helen E. (Beiderwelle) H.; m. Beverly Baker White, Oct. 16, 1954; children: Charles Fielding, II, Jane White. BA in Econs, Dartmouth Coll., 1949. V.p. merchandising RCA Sales Corp., Indpls., 1964-66, v.p. product planning, 1966-69, v.p. product mgmt., 1969-70; pres. luggage divsn. Samsonite Corp., Denver, 1970-73, pres. luggage group, 1973-74, exec. v.p. ops., 1974-75, pres., 1975-77; sr. v.p. Beatrice Foods Co., Chgo., 1976-77, exec. v.p., 1977-80; pres., COO, dir. Genesco Inc., Nashville, 1980-86, CEO, 1981-86, pvt. investor, corp. dir., 1986—. Dir. Forward Air. Hon. trustee Com. for Econ. Devel. Served with U.S. Army, 1950-52. Mem. Belle Meade Country Club, Union League, Phi Kappa Psi. Office: 104 Westhampton Pl Nashville TN 37205

HANSEN, KEN, telecommunications industry executive, electronics executive; BSEE, MSEE, U. Ill., Urbana-Champaign. With BiCMOS Technologies, CMOS; various sr. tech. and mgmt. positions Motorola, Freescale Semiconductor, Inc., v.p., chief devel. officer, 2007—09, sr. fellow, 2007—, v.p., chief tech. officer, 2009—. Sr. mem. IEEE. Achievements include patents for 12. Office: Freescale Semiconductor Inc 6501 W William Cannon Dr Austin TX 78735 Office Phone: 512-895-2000. Business E-Mail: ken.hansen@freescale.com.

HANSEN, KENNETH D., lawyer, ophthalmologist; b. Seattle, 1947; s. George R. and Elaine D. H.; m. Barbara Caleen, Oct. 8, 1976; 1 son, David Scott. BS in Psychology, U. Wash., 1969, JD, 1972, MD with honors, 1976. Bar: Wash. 1972, Mich. 1977, Ill. 1984, D.C. 1986, U.S. Supreme Ct. 1981; diplomate Am. Bd. Ophthalmology. Legal counsel Assn. Wash. Bus., Olympia, 1972-73; asst. atty. gen. State of Wash., Seattle, 1973-74; v.p., gen. counsel NW Med. Rsch. Found., Seattle, 1976-86; pres. Internat. Health Found., 1986—; intern medicine U. Mich. Hosp., Ann Arbor, 1977, resident in ophthalmology, 1978-80; sr. med. staff Henry Ford Hosp., Detroit, 1981-82; dir. ophthalmology Carbondale (Ill.) Clinic, 1983-86, chmn. dept. surgery, gen. counsel, 1984-86; clin. asst. prof. ophthalmology and med. humanities So. Ill. U., Carbondale, 1983-86; clin. asst. prof. ophthalmology U. Md., Balt., 1986—92; pres., gen. counsel Internat. Inst. for Biomed. Rsch., 2002—11. Med.-legal adv. com. U. Mich. Hosp. System; cons. Nat. Def. Med. Coll., China; charter coun. mem. practicing physicians adv. coun. to Sec. of U.S. Dept. Health and Human Svcs., 1992-97; lectr. in field. Assoc. editor Trauma, 1995-97, Wash. Law Rev., 1971-72; contbr. articles to profl. jours. Recipient U. Wash. Med. Thesis Award, Gold Medal Egyptian Med. Syndicate, 1986; William Wallice Wilshire Meml. scholar; Anna C. Dunlap Meml. scholar; Grad. Rsch. fellow, 1975-76; recipient Rod Rose award Soc. Rsch. Adminstrs., 1989. Fellow Am. Coll. Legal Medicine (jud. coun., model statutes com., Pres.'s award 1989), Internat. Coll. Surgeons; mem. ABA, AMA, Wash. State Bar Assn., Mich. Bar Assn., Ill. Med. Soc. (med.-legal coun.), Ill. Bar Assn., Mich. Med. Schs. Coun. Deans (med.-legal adv. com.), Mich. Ophthalmology Soc. (Rsch. award 1981), Am. Acad. Ophthalmology, D.C. Bar Assn., Phi Delta Pi, Phi Eta Sigma, Pi Sigma Epsilon. Baptist. Home: 5917 Bayview Cir Gulfport FL 33707 Personal E-mail: eyeus1@yahoo.com. E-mail: kdhmd@hotmail.com.

HANSEN, THOMAS C., footwear manufacturing company executive; Pres. Square One; creative dir. Leo Burnett, Tracy-Locke, Y&R; worked American Airlines, Inc., Frito Lay, Hallmark, McDonald's, Miller Brewing Co., Sears, Tabasco; pres., CEO, founding ptnr. Gigasphere Group of Companies, 2002—04; chief mktg. officer TM Advt., 2004—05, pres., 2005—09; CEO Heelys, Inc., 2009—. Office: Heelys Inc Ste 100 3200 Belmeade Dr Carrollton TX 75006 Office Phone: 214-390-1831. Business E-Mail: thomash@heelys.com.

HANSHAW, JOHN, health products executive; Pres., CEO St. Marks Hospital, pres., Mountain Divsn., 2006—, HCA, Inc., 2006—. Office: HCA Inc 1 Park Plz Nashville TN 37203-1548 Office Phone: 615-344-9551. Business E-Mail: john.hanshaw@hcahealthcare.com.

HANSON, LAURA C., geriatrician, educator; MD, Harvard U., 1986. Diplomate Am. Bd. Internal Medicine, 1989, Am. Bd. Internal Medicine-geriatric medicine, 2002, Am. Bd. Internal Medicine-hospice & palliative medicine, 2009. Resident internal medicine Brigham & Women's Hosp., 1986—88, Univ. NC Hosp., 1988—89, fellow geriatric medicine, 1989—91; assoc. prof. geriatric medicine Univ. NC Sch. of Medicine, co-dir. palliative care program. Office: University of North Carolina Hospitals 101 Manning Dr Chapel Hill NC 27514-4220 Office Phone: 919-966-4131. E-mail: lhanson@med.unc.edu.

HANSON, VICTOR ARTHUR, gerontologist, retired surgeon; b. Syracuse, NY, May 5, 1933; s. Victor Arthur Sr. and Dorothy (Burns) H.; m. Mary Diane Nadijcka, Sept. 13, 1985. AB, Princeton U., 1955; MD, U. Pa., 1959. Diplomate Am. Bd. Surgery. Intern then resident, instr. surgery U. Pa. Hosp., Phila., 1964-69, chief resident, 1968-69; instr. surgery SUNY, Syracuse, N.Y., 1969-71, asst. prof. surgery, 1971-78, clin. asst. prof. surgery, 1978-80; asst. prof. surgery Thomas Jefferson U., Phila., 1980-88; pvt. practice Syracuse, 1969-80; dir. rsch. VA Med. Ctr., Wilmington, Del., 1983-87; pvt. practice Wilmington, Del., 1987-90; staff surgeon HMO, Atlanta, 1990-96; pvt. practice in geriatrics Atlanta, 1996—; ret. surgeon. Contbr. articles to profl. jours. Lt., naval flight surgeon, USN, 1961-64, Vietnam. Grantee Am. Heart Assn., 1975, FDA, 1988, Merit Rev. X Z Vets. Adminstn. Hosp. System. Fellow ACS; mem. AMA, Med. Assn. Ga., Med. Assn. Atlanta, Soc. Surgery of the Alimentary Tract, So. Med. Assn. Avocations: tennis, model railroading. Home: 3875 W Nancy Creek Ct NE Atlanta GA 30319-4803 Office Phone: 404-255-6894. Personal E-mail: vahanson@bellsouth.net.

HANSON, VICTOR HENRY, II, newspaper publisher; b. Augusta, Ga., Aug. 17, 1930; s. Clarence Bloodworth, Jr. and Elizabeth (Fletcher) H.; m. Elizabeth Stallworth, Dec. 29, 1953; children: Clarence Bloodworth III, Victor Henry III, Elizabeth Mickel, Mary Fletcher, Robert Stallworth. Grad., Choate Sch., 1949; student, U. Va., 1949-51; BA, U. Ala., 1954. With Birmingham (Ala.) News & Post Herald, 1946-54, 57—, gen. mgr., 1963-83; with advt. and prodn. dept. WAPI-TV, Birmingham, 1954-55; v.p. Birmingham News Co., 1960-79, pres., 1979-2000, pub., 1983-2000. Bd. dirs. Art Fund, Inc.; elder Presbyn. Ch. Served to capt. USAF, 1955-57. Recipient Tree of Life award, Nat. Jewish Fund, 1991. Mem. SAR, Soc. of Cincinnati, N.C. Soc. of Cincinnati, Mountain Brook Club, The Club, Kappa Alpha. Office: 402 Office Park Dr Ste 201 Birmingham AL 35223 Home: 400 University Park Dr Apt 281 Birmingham AL 35209-8825 Home Phone: 205-967-5970; Office Phone: 205-879-8562. Business E-Mail: vhiil@me.com.

HARAGAN, DONALD ROBERT, academic administrator, geologist, educator; b. Houston, Apr. 15, 1936; s. Donald William and Mary (Thompson) H.; m. Willie Mae O'Berry, July 2, 1966; children—Shannon Lea, Shelley Jo. BS, U. Tex., 1959, PhD, 1969; MS, Tex. A & M U., 1960. Registered profl. engr., Tex. Research asst. Tex. A & M U., College Station, 1959-60; research scientist U. Tex., Austin, 1960-66, instr., 1966-69; asst. prof. Tex. Tech. U., Lubbock, 1969—72; assoc. prof. Tex. Tech U., 1972—78, prof. geosci., 1978—, dept. chmn., 1972—77, 1980—83, interim dean, 1985, interim v.p., 1985—86, v.p. for acad. affairs and research, 1986—88, exec. v.p., provost, 1988—; interim pres. Tex. Tech. U., 1996, pres., 1996—2000, pres. emeritus, 2000—, interim chancellor, 2006. Contbr. articles in field to profl. jours. Mem. Am. Soc. Civil Engrs., AAAS, Am. Meteorol. Soc., Am. Water Resources Assn., Tex. Acad. Sci. Home: 6914 Nashville Dr Lubbock TX 79413-6002 Office: Tex Tech U Honors Coll Lubbock TX 79409 Office Phone: 806-742-0031.

HARATI, YADOLLAH, neurologist, educator; MD, Iran, 1970. Diplomate American Bd. Psychiatry and Neurology-neurology, 1978. Resident in neurology Univ. Nebr. Affiliated Hosp., Omaha, 1971—74, Baylor Coll. of Medicine Affiliated Hosp., Houston, 1974—75, fellow in neuromuscular disease, 1975—76; prof. in neurology Baylor Coll.; hosp. affiliation includes St. Luke's Episcopal Hosp. Office: St Luke's Episcopal Hospital 6720 Bertner Ave Houston TX 77030-2697 Office Phone: 832-355-1000.*

HARBACH, ED (FRANK EDWIN HARBACH), management and technology consulting executive; b. 1954; married. BS in Sys. Analysis, Miami U., Ohio, 1976. With Accenture Ltd., 1998—2000, CIO, mng. ptnr. Japan, 2000—03, mng., ptnr., head, client satisfaction and quality, 2003—04; COO BearingPoint, Inc., 2006—07, pres., CEO, 2007—09. Bd. dirs. BearingPoint, Inc., 2007—. Office: Bearingpoint LLC Bd Directors 1676 Intl Dr Ste 900 Mc Lean VA 22102 Office Phone: 703-747-3000, 703-915-9468. Business E-Mail: f.harbach@bearingpoint.com.

HARBAUGH, JOSEPH DELBERT, law educator, former dean; b. June 15, 1939; s. Kenton E. and Giovanna D. (Fusco) H.; m. Leona R. Noon, June 17, 1961; children: Regina, Denise, Laurie, Wendolyn; m. Barbara J. Britzke, July 23, 1982; children: Elizabeth, Andrew, Nicholas. BS in Polit. Sci., St. Joseph's Coll., 1961; LLB, U. Pitts., 1964; LLM, Georgetown U., 1967. Bar: D.C. 1965, Conn. 1965, U.S. Ct. Appeals (2d cir.) 1967, U.S. Supreme Ct. 1968, Pa. 1979. Chief pub. defender Conn. Cir. Ct., 1965-68; assoc. prof. Sch. Law U. Conn., 1968-72; with Sch. Law Duke U., 1972-74; prof. Sch. Law Temple U., Phila., 1974-82; vis. prof. Law Ctr. Georgetown U., 1982-84; prof. law Am. U., 1984-87; dean T.C. Williams Sch. Law U. Richmond, Va., 1987-95; prof. law Shepard Broad Law Ctr., Nova Southeastern U., Davie, Fla., 1995—, dean, 1995—2008. Majority chief counsel Pa. Senate Judiciary Com., 1978-80, minority chief counsel, 1980-85; cons. to continuing legal edn. orgns. Author: (with McDonald) Task Analysis of the Criminal Justice Attorney, 1977; editor: Comparative Analysis of ABA Standards for Criminal Justice with Connecticut Law, Rules and Practice, 1973, Lawyer Negotiation Training Materials, 1988, (with Bastress) Interviewing, Counseling and Negotiating: Skills for Effective Representation, 1990; videotapes include: (with Britzke) Basics of Interviewing, 1982, Basics of Negotiating, 1984, (with Guernsey and Zwier) The Negotiator, 1995; contbr. articles to profl. jours. Mem. ABA (ho. of dels., pres.'s task force on profl. competency 1981-83, 92—, mem. accreditation com. 1982-88, chmn. legis. com. criminal justice sect. 1982-83), Pa. Bar Assn., Assn. Am. Law Schs. (del. to ABA Ho. of Dels. 1983-86, 92—, mem. exec. com. 1980-82). Democrat. Office: Nova Southeastern U Shepard Broad Law Ctr Leo Goodwin Sr Hall 3305 College Ave Fort Lauderdale FL 33314 E-mail: harbaughj@nsu.law.nova.edu.

HARBIN, BEN L., state legislator; m. Hope Harbin; children: Caitlin, Benjamin Hampton. Former state rep. Dist. 80, Ga.; state rep. Dist. 113, 1994—2002; state rep. Dist. 118, 2004—; mem. Appropriations Com., Ins. Com., Legislature & Congl. Reapportionment Com.; bus. owner; bd. mem. Crossroads Acad. Collaboration. Mem.: Columbia County Found. Children, Optimist, Kiwanis. Republican. Address: 4468 Columbia Rd Martinez GA 30917-1959 Mailing: State Capitol 612 Legis Off Bldg Atlanta GA 30334 Office: Po Box 211959 Augusta GA 30917 Office Phone: 706-855-6700. Fax: 706-863-8959. Personal E-mail: bharbin@juno.com. Business E-Mail: bharbin@legis.state.ga.us.

HARBISON, ED, state legislator, broadcast journalist, motivational speaker; b. Prattville, Ala., Aug. 25, 1941; m. Cecilia Harbison; children: Edward, Ladena. Grad., Career Acad. Sch. Broadcasting, 1969, Troy State U., Ala. Broadcast journalist, pub. rels. cons., Columbus, Ga., 1994—; mem. Dist. 15 Ga. State Senate, Atlanta, 1993—. Second v.p. Muscogee County Sch. Bd., Columbus, 1985—; former mem. Columbus Charter Rev. Commn., Mayor's Com. for Drug-Free Columbus, Community Task Force on Gangs, Columbus Cable TV Study Commn.; grad. Leadership Columbus, 1990; bd. dirs. A.J. McClung YMCA; chmn. Ga. Legis. Black Caucus, 2003—. Sgt. USMC, 1963-67. Recipient numerous awards for profl. accomplishments and community svc., including Dr. John W. Townsend award, ann. award for best regularly scheduled TV newscast AP, PUSH Excellence award, award of support Bambino League, honored by Alpha Kappa Alpha, citation NAACP, 1989, award for outstanding contbns. to African-Ams., Columbus Times, Outstanding Man of Yr. award Men's Progressive Club, 1994; named One of 50 Most Influential African-Ams. in Columbus, Phenix City, Ft. Benning, Ga., Among 50 Most Influential African Am. in Ga., Ga. Forum Newspaper, 2004. Mem. Ga. Assn. Newscasters (former officer). Mailing: PO Box 1292 Columbus GA 31902-1292 Office Phone: 706-687-3899. Business E-Mail: ed.harbison@senate.ga.gov.

HARCROW, EDWARD EARL, lawyer; b. Carrizozo, N.Mex., Mar. 4, 1954; s. James Earl and Nettie (McInnes) H.; m. Julie A., Apr. 16, 1987; children: Ashley Nicole, James Earl. BS, Tex. Tech. U., 1976, JD, 1979. Bar: Tex. 1979, U.S. Dist. Ct. (no. dist.) Tex., U.S. Ct. Appeals (5th cir.) 1979. Asst. dist. atty. Lubbock (Tex.) Dist. Atty. Office, 1979-80, Tarrant Dist. Atty. Office, Ft. Worth, 1980-83; ptnr. Shannon, Gracey, Ratliff & Miller, Ft. Worth, 1985-99, mng. ptnr., 1995-96, ptnr. in charge of tech., 1996-99; ptnr. Haynes & Boone, Ft. Worth, 1999—2009; gen. counsel Dallas Ft. Worth Med. Ctr., 1990—2009. Bd. dirs. Planned Parenthood North Tex., 1987-92; fellow Tex. Bar Found., 1991—. Office: 1304 W Abram St STE 100 Arlington TX 76013-1752

HARDAWAY, G. A., state legislator; b. June 18, 1954; 3 children. BS in Finance, DePaul U. Real estate investor; Tenn. State Repr., Dist. 92 Tenn. Ho. Reprs., 2007—. Mem.: Rose Parks Academy, NAACP. Democrat. Baptist. Office: 109 War Memorial Bldg Nashville TN 37243-0192 also: 1243 Worthington St Memphis TN 38114 Office Phone: 615-741-5625. Office Fax: 615-741-1005. Business E-Mail: rep.ga.hardaway@capitol.tn.gov.

HARDBERGER, PHILLIP DUANE, former Mayor, San Antonio, judge, lawyer, journalist; b. Morton, Tex., July 27, 1934; s. Homer Reeves and Bess (Scott) H.; m. Linda Morgan, May 1968; children: Amy, Kimberlea Moser. BA, Baylor U., 1955; MS, Columbia U., 1960; LL.B., Georgetown U., 1965. Reporter Waco (Tex.) News Tribune, 1952-54; press rep. Tex. Baptist Conv., 1958-59; assoc. editor Mil. Pub. Inst., NYC, 1961; exec. sec. Peace Corps, 1962-66; spl. asst. to dir. OEO, 1967-68; trial lawyer, 1968-94; chief justice Fourth Ct. of Appeals, State of Tex., San Antonio, 1994—2003; mayor City of San Antonio, San Antonio, 2005—09. Author: Texas Courtroom Evidence, Texas Workers' Compensation Trial Manual; contbr. articles to profl. jours. Served to capt. USAF, 1955-58. Home: 319 W Hollywood Ave San Antonio TX 78212-2211 Office: Cox Smith Matthews Inc 112 East Pecan Ste 1800 San Antonio TX 78205 Office Phone: 210-554-5500. Business E-Mail: phardberger@coxsmith.com.

HARDCASTLE, RICK L., state legislator; b. Sherman, Tex., Apr. 6, 1956; m. Nancy Hardcastle. Rancher, owner in the chemical and fertilizer businesses; operator Rolling H Cattle Co.; mem. Dist. 68 Tex. House of Representatives, 1998—. Republican. Office: 1930 Fannin Vernon TX 76384 also: Room 4N.04 Capitol PO Box 2910 Austin TX 78768 Office Phone: 940-553-3825, 512-463-0526.

HARDEN, BUDDY, state legislator; m. Linda Harden; 2 children. Former supr. US. Dept. of Agr.; former CEO Ga. Pharmacy Assn., Ga.; pres./chief exec. officer Harden Pharmacy Consultants; dist. pres. Ga. Mcpl. Assn., Ga., 2009; mayor City of Sylvester, Ga.; mem. Dist. #147 Ga. House of Reps., Ga., 2008—. Republican. Office: Capitol Office 404-C Coverdell Legislative Office Bldg Atlanta GA 30334 also: District Office 458 Lakeshore Way Cordele GA 31015 Office Phone: 404-656-0109, 229-535-6050. E-mail: buddy.harden@house.ga.gov.

HARDEN, JAMES E., JR., professional basketball player; b. LA, Aug. 26, 1989; s. James Harden and Monja Willis. Attended, Ariz. State U., Tempe, 2007—09. Guard Oklahoma City Thunder, 2009—12, Houston Rockets, 2012—. Mem. US nat. team Summer Olympic Games, London, 2012. Named 1st Team All-American, AP, Nat. Assn. Basketball Coaches, US Basketball Writers Assn., The Sporting News, Basketball Times, 2009, 1st Team All-Pacific 10 Conf., 2009, Pacific 10 Conf. Player of Yr., 2009, NBA Sixth Man of Yr., 2012; named to Western Conf. All-Star Team, NBA, 2013. Office: Houston Rockets 1510 Polk St Houston TX 77002*

HARDEN, MICHAEL, state legislator; b. Aug. 16; m. Janelle Harden. Attended, Emmanuel Coll., Toronto Airport Christian Fellowship Sch. of Ministry. Former surveillance officer Dept. Juvenile Justice; correctional officer Alto Prison, 1999; campaign coord. Charlie Norwood for Congress, 2002; mem. Dist. #28 Ga. House of Reps., Ga., 2008—. Republican. Office: Capitol Address 411-C

Coverdell Legislative Office Bldg Atlanta GA 30334 also: District Office PO Box 1189 Toccoa GA 30577 Office Phone: 404-656-0126. E-mail: micheal.harden@house.ga.gov.

HARDEN, ROGER ARTHUR, allergist, immunologist; BS in Chemistry, U. Notre Dame; MD, Johns Hopkins U., 1978. Diplomate Am. Bd. Internal Medicine, 1981, Am. Bd. Allergy and Immunology, 1983, lic. Tex., 1982. Intern Baylor Health Care System, 1978—79, resident internal medicine, 1979—81; fellow allergy and immunology Univ. Mich. Med. Ctr., 1981—83; hosp. affiliations include St. David's South Austin Hosp., Seton Med. Ctr.; pvt. practice allergy and immunology Austin, Tex. Office: Roger A Harden MD 11623 Angus Rd Ste 11 Austin TX 78759 Office Phone: 512-338-1366.*

HARDESTY, DAVID CARTER, JR., lawyer, educator; b. Sept. 20, 1945; m. Susan B. Hardesty, 1968; children: Ashley, D(avid) Carter III. AB, W.Va. U., 1967; MA, Oxford U., Eng., 1969; JD, Harvard U., 1973. Bar: W.Va. 1973. Tax commr., sec. Econ. Devel. Authority, State of W.Va., Charleston, 1977-80; chmn. Mcpl. Bond Commn., 1977-80; assoc. Bowles Rice McDavid Graff & Love, Charleston, 1973-77, ptnr., 1981-95, of counsel, 2008—; pres. W.Va. U., Morgantown, W.Va., 1995—2007, emeritus prof., law, 1995—. Chmn. W.Va. Tax Study Commn., 1982-84; mem. W.Va. Asian Trade Missions, 1978-79, 95; chmn. W.Va. Roundtable, Inc., 1994-95; mem. adv. bd. Nat. Security Higher Edn., 2005-07; frequent spkr. at govt., edn. and bus. group meetings. Chancellor United Meth. Ch., W.Va., 1986-95; trustee Univ. Sys., 1989-95, 1st chmn., 1989-91; trustee W.Va. Wesleyan Coll., 1986-94, Nat. 4-H Coun., 2000—, chair bd. trustees, 2004—; mem. Gov.'s Energy Task Force, 2001-; mem. Nat. Assn. State Univs. and Land Grant Colls., 1995-2007, W.Va. Rhodes Scholar Selection Com., 1980-2000, sec., 1991-98; bd. advisors W.Va. U., 1980-89, chmn. bd. advisors, 1987-89; bd. dirs. United Meth. Charities W.Va., 1978-94; bd. dirs. Greater Kanawha Valley Found., 1980-89; chmn. W.Va. Tax Study Commn., 1982-84; mem. W.Va. Asian Trade Missions, 1978-79, 95; chmn. W.Va. Roundtable, Inc., 1994-95; mem. adv. bd. Nat. Security Higher Edn., 2005-07; frequent spkr. at govt., edn. and bus. group meetings. Rhodes scholar, 1969. Mem.: ABA, 4th Cir. Jud. Conf., W.Va. Bar Assn., W.Va. U. (hon.; pres.). Mailing: West Virginia University PO Box 6130 Morgantown WV 26506 Business E-Mail: dhardesty@wvu.edu.

HARDGRAVE, J. JEFFREY, energy executive; married; 4 children. BBA, Dallas Baptist U. Lic. pilot FAA. Various profl. and leadership positions TXU Gas, 1979; region mgr. TXU Pipeline Svcs. Dir. Operations, 1979; joined Atmos Energy Corp., 2004, v.p., Non-Metro Ops., Mid-Tex Divsn., v.p., Customer Svc., 2007—10; with Acquisition TXU Gas Assets, 2004; v.p. Atmos Energy Pipeline Tex. Mem. Habitat for Humanity, Spl. Olympics, United Way of Metropolitan Dallas, The Senior Source. Recipient TXU Leadership award, 2000, TXU Diversity award, 2001. Baptist. Office: Atmos Energy Corp 2 Lincoln Ctr 5420 LBJ Fwy Ste 1528 Dallas TX 75240 Office Phone: 972-934-9227. Office Fax: 972-855-3040. Business E-Mail: jeff.hardgrave@atmosenergy.com.

HARDIMAN, JOSEPH RAYMOND, investment firm executive; b. Salisbury, Md., May 27, 1937; s. Leonard Roy and Virginia Mildred (Darden) H.; m. Katherine McCampbell, Mar. 23, 1963; children: Katherine Hughes, Elizabeth Gore. BA, U. Md., Coll. Pk., 1959; LLB, U. Md., Balt., 1962. Bar: Md. 1962. Law clk. to Hon. Hall Hammond Md. Ct. of Appeals, 1962-63; assoc. Miles & Stockbridge, Balt., 1963-68; exec. v.p., sec., dir. Robert Garrett & Sons, Inc., Balt., 1968-75; gen. ptnr. Alex. Brown & Sons, 1975-87, mng. dir., COO, 1984-87; pres., CEO, dir. Nat. Assn. Securities Dealers, Inc., 1987-97, Nasdaq Stock Market, Inc., 1987-97. Bd. dirs. Franklin Resources, Inc., Brown Adv. Mutual Funds, Ch. Bd. dirs. Arthritis Found., Md., 1975-79, pres., 1976-78; bd. dirs. Balt. Urban Coalition, 1975-78, U. Md. Med. Sys., 1980-86, Fund for Ednl. Excellence, 1984-91, Ctr. for the Study of the Presidency, 1992-97, U. Md. Found., 1992-2000, U. Md. Balt. Found., 2000—; steering com. Baltimore County Charter Rev. Commn., 1977-78; trustee St. Paul's Sch. for Girls, 1978-86, Balt. Sch. for the Arts, 2002-06, Balt. Chesapeake Bay Outward Bound, 2005-, Securities Industry Found. Econ. Edn., 1988-96; adv. bd. U. Calif. Securities Regulation Inst., 1988-97; bd. visitors U. Md. Sch. Law, 1990—, Am. Bus. Conf., Con. on Competitiveness, 1994-97, Fla. Coalition Preservation, 2007-. Mem. Md. Club, Elkridge Club (Balt.), Gulfstream Club (Fla.), Order of Coif, Phi Delta Theta, Omicron Delta Kappa. Home: 540 Old School Rd Delray Beach FL 33483

HARDIN, DALE WAYNE, political science professor; b. Peoria, Ill., Sept. 9, 1922; s. James P. and Lucille Maureen (Elgin) H.; m. Sandra L. Gorzen, July 3, 1939; children: Bradley J., Stacy Alexander, Rebecca Kuplas, J. Scott Keaton. AB in Polit. Sci., George Washington U., 1949, JD, 1951. Bar: Va. 1951, D.C. 1951, U.S. Dist. D.C. 1951, U.S. Ct. Appeals (D.C. cir.) 1951. Assoc. Mills & Partridge, Washington, 1951; spl. agent FBI, Washington, 1951-54; fin. counsel ICC, Washington, 1954-55, legis. counsel, 1955-64, presdl. appointee as commr., 1967-77, vice chmn., acting chmn. agy., 1971-73, chmn. rates divsn., 1975-77; Presdl. appointee, mem. Adminstrv. Conf. U.S., 1969-72; dir. dept. transp. and comm. U.S. C. of C., Washington, 1964-66; v.p. govt. affairs Overmeyer Co., Washington, 1966-67; spl. counsel Am. Trucking Assn., Washington, 1967; assoc. prof. polit sci. S.W. Tex. State U. (now Tex. State U.), San Marcos, Tex., 1977—, assoc. prof. emeritus, 1989—2006, acting dean sch. liberal arts., 1986-87, chmn. dept. home econs., 1990-92; ret. law educator, 2000. Gen. counsel Transp. Assn. Am., Washington, 1959; exec. v.p. GC Wheaton Van Lines, Indpls., 1981-82; moderator 14th Ann. Seminar, State Bar Tex., 1982, moderator profl. devel. program gen. paralegal skills, 1988, standing com. on legal assts., 1988-00; chmn. Tex. forum IV Conf. Legal Asst. Educators, 1985, chair forum VII, 1988; presenter papers in field. Bus. sec. George Washington U. Sch. Law Rev., 1951. Bd. dirs. U. Christian Ch., 2006—. With USMC, 1942—46, PTO. Mem. Soc. Former Spl. Agents FBI. Fed. Bar Assn., Va. State Bar., D.C. Bar, Phi Delta Phi. Avocation: golf. Home: 54 Rainey St #406 Austin TX 78701-4311 E-mail: docnsand@austin.rr.com.

HARDIN, EUGENE BROOKS, JR., bank executive; b. Wilmington, NC, Oct. 18, 1930; s. Eugene Brooks Hardin and Roberta Gilmour (Sterling) Demme; m. Olivia Lynch, Aug. 16, 1958; children: John Haywood II, Olivia Cary. BS, U. N.C., 1952. With Wachovia Bank & Trust Co., Wilmington, 1956—, asst. v.p., 1957-60, v.p., 1962-68, sr. v.p., 1969-72, sr. v.p., regional exec. Raleigh, 1972-79, regional v.p., 1979-95; cashier Burlington, NC, 1961-62; ret., 1995. Bd. dirs. Wachovia Bank, Raleigh, N.C. Pres., bd. dirs. Babies Hosp., Wilmington, 1968-72; pres. United Fund, 1970; treas., trustee Episcopalian Diocese East Carolina, 1965-72; chmn. Raleigh Civic Center Authority, 1978-81; chmn. Raleigh-Durham Airport Authority, 1981-82; chmn. bd. trustees St. Mary's Coll., 1979-85; bd. dirs. Children's Home Soc. N.C. Served with USNR, 1948-49; to 1st lt. USAF, 1952-56. Mem. Robert Morris Assos. Clubs: Civitan (pres. Wilmington 1971-72); Carolina Yacht (Wrightsville Beach); Carolina Country (Raleigh); Cape Fear Country (Wilmington); Land Fall (Wilmington). Home: 404 Drummond Dr Raleigh NC 27609-7006 Office Phone: 919-782-4875.

HARDIN, HAL D., lawyer, former judge, US attorney; BA, Middle Tenn. State U.; JD, Vanderbilt U., 1968. Bar: Tenn., Wash. D.C., Tex., Ky., U.S. Ct. Claims, U.S. Tax. Ct., U.S. Ct. Mil. Appeals, U.S. Supreme Ct. Dir. St. Louis Job Corps Ctr.; vol. Peace Corps. Assn., emeritus bd. mem.; asst. dist. atty.; pvt. practice; presiding judge Nashville Trial Cts., 1976-77; spl. judge Ct. of Appeals; U.S. atty. Middle Dist. Tenn., 1977-81; practice law Nashville, 1981—. Adj. prof. Aquinas Coll., 1975—76; faculty emeritus Nashville Sch. Law; vice-chair Nashville Charter Revision Com. Bd. dirs. Nat. Assn. Former U.S. Atty., 1993—96, 2012—, Leadership Nashville, 1983, Capital Case Resource Ctr., 1988—95, Leadership Alumni Assn., 1985. Fellow: Tenn. Bar Found.; mem.: Washington Bar Assn., Ky. Bar, Am. Bd. Trial Advs. (nat. bd. dirs. 1988—89, pres. Tenn. Chpt. 1990), Tenn. & Nat. Crime Def. Attys. Assn., 6th Cir. Jud. Coun. (life), Tex. Bar Assn., Tenn. Bar Assn. (gen. counsel 1982—90), Nashville Bar Assn. (bd. dirs. 1983—85, v.p. 1985, Criminal Law Excellence award 2006). Office: 211 Union St Ste 200 Nashville TN 37201 Office Phone: 615-369-3377. Business E-Mail: hal@hardinlawoffice.com.

HARDIN, JAMES NEAL, language educator, publisher; b. Nashville, Feb. 17, 1939; s. James N. and Ina M. (Anderson) H.; m. Anne Farr. AB summa cum laude, Washington and Lee U., 1960; postgrad., U. Berlin, 1960-61; PhD, U. NC, 1967. Prof. German lit. U. S.C., Columbia, 1969—98. Pres. Hardin Pub. Inc.; cons. in field. Author: Co-founder, Camden House, imprint published by Boydell & Brewer Ltd., Johann Beer, 1983, Johann Beer Bibliographie, 1984, Christian Gryphius Bibliographie, 1985, J.C. Ettner Bibliographie, 1988; editor: Der Verliebte Oesterreicher, 1977; editor/co-editor: Dictionary of Lit. Biography, Vols. 59, 66, 69, 81, 85, 90, 94, 97, 118, 124, 129, 133, 138, 148, 194 and 168, Goethe's Wilhelm Meister's Travels, 1991; founder, co-editor: Studies in German Language, Literature and Linguistics, Works of Christian Gryphius, 2 vols., 1985; contbr. articles to profl. jours. and mags. Capt. U.S. Army, 1967-69. Decorated Army Commendation medal; recipient Alexander von Humbolt award, 1974-75, Russell award for scholarship, 1979, German-Am. Friendship award, 2004; Fulbright scholar, 1960-61 Mem. MLA, South Atlantic MLA, Gothe Soc. Personal E-mail: jnh@reagan.com.

HARDIN, JAMES W., botanist, educator, herbarium curator; b. Mar. 31, 1929; BS, Fla. So. Coll., 1950; MS, U. Tenn., 1951; PhD, U. Mich., 1957. Instr. U. Mich., 1956-57; from asst. prof. to prof. NC State U., Raleigh, 1957-68, prof., 1968-96, emeritus prof., 1996—, curator herbarium, 1957—96. Vis. prof. Mountain Lake Biological Sta. U.Va., summers 1962, 64, 83, U. Okla. Biological Sta., summers 1967, 70; mem. exec. com. Flora Southeastern US, 1966-97; endangered species com. NC Dept. Natural & Econ. Resources, 1973-74, natural areas adv. com., 1973-79; mem. plant conservation sci. com. NC Dept. Agriculture, 1980-97, chmn. 1987-97; mem. endangered species com. NC Wildlife Resources Commn., 1976-78, NC State Mus. Natural Hist., 1975-78; pres. Highlands Biological Station, Inc., 1963-69, trustee, 1958-69, sec., 1960-63; invited symposium speaker. Author: Human Poisoning, 1974, Textbook of Dendrology, 2001; mem. editl. com. Am. Jour. Botany, 1964-66; mem. editorial bd. Brittonia, 1964-67, Brimleyana, 1975-97; reviewer jours. in field. Trustee Highlands Biol. Found., 1976—. Recipient Outstanding Tchr. award, NC State U., 1966—67, 1969—70. Mem. Am. Soc. Plant Taxonomists (pub. policy com. 1976-78, editorial bd. 1964-67, editor-in-chief Systematic Botany 1985-91, pres. elect 1991-92, pres. 1992-93, past pres. 1993-94, Cooley award 1958), Southern Appalachian Botanical Club (v.p. 1959-60, pres. 1964-65, Bartholomew award 1994), Botanical Soc. Am. (editorial com. 1964-66, chair southeastern sect. 1968-69), Assn. Southeastern Biologists (Meritorious Teaching award 1991, chmn. local arrangements 1966, 77, v.p. 1968-69, pres. 1979-80, editor ASB Bull 1980-86), Soc. Economic Botany (chmn. local arrangements 1979), Phi Kappa Phi, Sigma Xi (exec. com. N.C. chpt. 1962-63, sec. 1965-66, treas. 1966-67, v.p. 1967-68, program chmn. 1968-69, pres. 1969-70). Home: 204 Furches St Raleigh NC 27607-4056 E-mail: jwhardin@nc.rr.com.

HARDIN, P. RUSSELL, foundation administrator; BA with high distinction, U. Va., Charlottesville, 1979; JD with honors, Duke U., NC, 1982. Lawyer King & Spalding, Atlanta, 1982—88; joined The Woodruff & Whitehead Foundations, Atlanta, 1988, pres. Robert W. Woodruff, Joseph Whitehead, Lettie Pate Evans & Lettie Pate Whitehead Foundations, 2006—. Bd. trustees Northwestern Mutual, Milw., 2011—. Office: The Robert W Woodruff Foundation 191 Peachtree St NE Ste 3540 Atlanta GA 30303*

HARDIN, PAUL, III, law educator; b. Charlotte, NC, June 11, 1931; s. Paul and Dorothy (Reel) Hardin; m. Barbara Russell, June 8, 1954; children: Paul Russell, Sandra Mikush, Dorothy Holmes. AB, Duke U., 1952, JD, 1954; LHD (hon.), Clemson U., 1970, Coker Coll., 1972; LittD (hon.), Nebr. Wesleyan U., 1978; LLD (hon.), Adrian Coll., 1987, Monmouth Coll., 1988; HHD (hon.), Wofford Coll., 1989; LLD (hon.), Rider Coll., 1990; LHD (hon.), Duke U., 1994. Bar: Ala. 1954. Practiced in, Birmingham, 1954, 1956—58; asst. prof. Duke Law Sch., 1958—61, assoc. prof., 1961—63, prof., 1963—68, univ. trustee, 1969—74, 1995—2001; pres. Wofford Coll., Spartanburg, SC, 1968—72, So. Methodist U., Dallas, 1972—74, Drew U., Madison, NJ, 1975—88; chancellor U. NC, Chapel Hill, NC, 1988—95, chancellor emeritus, 1995—; interim pres. U. Ala., Birmingham, Ala., 1997. Vis. prof. U. Tex., 1960, U. Pa., 1962—63, U. Va., 1974; dir. Smith Barney mut. funds. Author (with Sullivan, others): The Administration of Criminal Justice, 1966; author: (with Sullivan) Evidence, Cases and Materials, 1968; contbr. articles to profl. jours., law revs. Chmn. Human Rels. Com., Durham, NC, 1961—62; pres. Nat. Assn. Schs. and Coll. of United Meth. Ch., 1984; mem. gen. conf. United Meth. Ch., 1968, 1976, 1980, 1984; chmn. Nat. Commn. on United Meth. Higher Edn., 1975—77. Served with CIC US Army, 1954—56. Mem.: Order of Coif, Carnegie Found. for Advancement Tchg. (bd. dirs. 1990—98), Phi Beta Kappa. Home: 379 Carolina Meadows Vil Chapel Hill NC 27517-7521

HARDIN, RUSTY (RUSSELL HARDIN JR.), lawyer; b. Durham, NC, Oct. 6, 1941; m. Tissy Hardin; children: Russell, Thomas. BA, Wesleyan U., Middletown, Conn., 1965; JD, So. Meth. U. Dedman Sch. Law, Dallas, 1975. Bar: Tex. 1975, US Ct. Dist. Ct (no. and so. dists.) Tex., US Ct. Appeals (5th cir.), US Supreme Ct. Asst. dist. atty. Harris County, Tex., 1975—90, felony divsn. chief Tex., 1983—90; founding ptnr. Hardin, Beers, Hagstette & Davidson, 1991—96; founder, pres. Rusty Hardin & Associates, P.C., Houston, 1996—. Faculty Tex. Dist. & County Attorneys Prosecutor Sch., 1983—98, Nat. Coll. Dist. Attorneys, 1986—92, U. Houston Law Found. Continuing Legal Edn., 1992—99; Whitewater chief trial counsel US Office Ind. Counsel, 1994; spl. counsel State Bar Tex. Disciplinary Counsel, 1996—97, Nat. Inst. Trial Advocacy, 1998; spl. trial counsel Jud. Conduct Commn., 2001. Founder Tex. People Against Crime, 1990. Named a Go-to-Lawyer for Civil Def. Litig., Tex. Lawyer mag., 2002, Go-to-Lawyer for Comml. Litig., 2007, Tex. Super Lawyer, Tex. Monthly, 2003—07; named one of Houston's Top Lawyers, H Mag., 2006, The 25 Greatest Tex. Lawyers of the Past Quarter-Century, Tex. Lawyer mag., 2010. Fellow: Tex. Bar Found.; mem.: ABA (administr. rules of evidence com.), State Bar Tex. (Prosecutor of Yr. 1989), Houston Bar Assn., American Bd. Trial Advocates. Office: Rusty Hardin & Assocs PC 5 Houston Ctr 1401 McKinney Ste 2250 Houston TX 77010 Office Phone: 713-652-9000. Office Fax: 713-652-9800. Business E-Mail: rhardin@rustyhardin.com.

HARDING, HARRY, dean, political scientist, educator, consultant; b. Boston, Dec. 21, 1946; s. Harry and Vernette (Vickers) H.; m. Roca Lau, July 5, 1971; 1 child, James V. L. AB in Pub. and Internat. Affairs summa cum laude, Princeton U., NJ, 1967; MA in Polit. Sci., Stanford U., Calif., 1969, PhD in Polit. Sci., 1974. Polit. sci. instr. Swarthmore Coll., Pa., 1970-71; acting asst. prof. polit. sci. Stanford U., 1971-73, asst. prof., 1973-79, assoc. prof., 1979-83; sr. fellow The Brookings Instn., Washington, 1983—94; dean, Elliott sch. internat. affairs, prof. internat. affairs and polit sci. George Wash. U., Washington, 1995—2005, univ. prof., 2007—09; dir. rsch. and analysis Eurasia Group, NYC, 2005—07; dean, prof. pub. policy and politics Frank Batten Sr. Sch. Leadership and Pub. Policy U. Va., Charlottesville, 2009—. Vis. asst. prof. U. Calif.-Berkeley, 1977, vis. prof. U. Washington, Seattle, 1988; coord. East Asia program Woodrow Wilson Internat. Ctr. Scholars, Washington, 1979-80; adj. prof. Georgetown U.; vis. fellow, ctr. China rels. The Asia Found.; counselor, chair China task force Eurasia Group; bd. govs. Nanyang Technol. Univ. S. Rajaratnam Sch. Internat. Studies, Singapore. Author: Organizing China: The Problem of Bureaucracy, 1949-76, 1981, China's Second Revolution: Reform After Mao, 1987, China and Northeast Asia: The Political Diemnsion, 1988, A Fragile Relationship: The US and China Since 1972, 1992; editor: China's Foreign Relations in the 1980s, 1984, Sino-American Relations, 1945-1955, 1989; co-editor (with F. Frankel): The India-China Relationship: What the United States Needs to Know, 2004; contbr. chpts. in books, articles to profl. publs. Mem. US-PRC Joint Commn. on Sci. and Technol. Cooperation, Washington, 1981—83, Def. Policy Bd., Washington, 1998—2001; pres. Assn. Profl. Schs. Internat. Affairs, Washington, 1996—97; dir. Atlantic Coun. the US, Washington, 1996, Nat. Com. on US-China Rels., Washington, 2001; mem. sr. adv. panel on the long term strategic framework Asian Devel. Bank, Manila, Philippines, 2000—01; trustee World Affairs Coun., No. Calif., San Francisco, 1978—83, The Asia Found., San Francisco, 1992, Taipei, 1996; chmn. China coun. The Asia Soc., NYC, 1983—91. Hoover Inst. on War, Revolution and Peace Nat. fellow, 1977-78; recipient Walter J. Gores award for teaching Stanford U., 1975, Ohira Meml. prize, 1986. Mem. Am. Polit. Sci. Assn., Assn. Asian Studies, Internat. Inst. Strategic Studies, Coun. Fgn. Rels., Phi Beta Kappa. Clubs: Cosmos (Washington); Princeton (NY). Office: Frank Batten Sch Leadership and Pub Policy Garrett Hall 200A 235 McCormick Rd PO Box 400893 Charlottesville VA 22904-4893 Office Phone: 434-924-0812. Business E-Mail: hhyb@virginia.edu.*

HARDING, ROBERT A., security firm executive, retired military officer; b. NYC, May 13, 1948; BA in Bus. Adminstrn., Bowie State U.; MBA, Salve Regina U.; M in Nat. Security and Strategy, US Naval War Coll. Commd. 2d. lt. US Army, 1969, advanced through grades to maj. gen.; comdr. Aerial Exploitation Hdqs. Co., Fort Bragg, NC, HUMINT and Counterintelligence Battalion, Republic of Korea, Counterintelligence Group, the 902d, Fort Meade, Md.; staff assignment US Forces Command, US Forces Korea, US Army Europe, US Army PERSCOM, US Army Intelligence and Security Command; J2 intelligence directorate US So. Command, Panama; dir. intelligence coordination Joint Interagency Task Force-East; dir. ops. Def. Intelligence Agency (DIA), 1997—2000; sr. human intelligence officer US Dept. Def., dir. Def. Human Intelligence Svc., dir. Def. Attache Sys., dir. Ctrl. MASINT Office, functional mgr. intelligence collection mgmt.; dep. chief staff, G-2 US Army, 2001; exec. v.p. ops. Innovation Logistics Techniques, McLean, Va.; pres., CEO Harding Security Assocs., LLC, 2003—10. Decorated Def. Disting. Svc. Medal, Army Disting. Svc. Medal, Def. Superior Medal, Legion of Merit with three oak leaf clusters, Def. Meritorious Svc. Medal, Meritorious Svc. Medal with two oak leaf clusters. Office: Harding Security Associates Ste 525 1430 Spring Hill Rd Mc Lean VA 22102

HARDMAN, LAURA JONES, volunteer, board member; d. Boisfeuillet Jones; m. John Barnett Hardman; 3 children. Grad. with honors, Emory Coll., Atlanta, 1967. Faculty Harvard U. Inst. Politics, Cambridge, Mass.; with Great Am. Mortgage Investors, 1969—74; exec. v.p. Wakefield Co., 1975—76; bd. dirs. Kaiser Foundation Health Plan Georgia, Inc, 1985—. Bd. visitors Emory U., 1981—83, bd. trustees, 1983—. Former trustee Woodruff Arts Ctr., Atlanta Coll. Art., Atlanta Ballet Co., Ctr. Puppetry Arts; ops. mgr. Carter-Mondale Transition Planning Group, Atlanta, 1976; bd. dirs. Alliance Theatre Co., Atlanta, chmn. bd. dirs., 1981—85. Recipient Emory medal, Assn. Emory Alumni, 1998. Mem.: Phi Beta Kappa. Office: Kaiser Permanente Nine Piedmont Ctr 3495 Piedmont Rd NE Atlanta GA 30305 Office Phone: 404-364-7000. Office Fax: 404-364-4998. Business E-Mail: laura.hardman@emory.edu.

HARDWAY, WENDELL GARY, retired academic administrator; b. Bolair, W.Va., Mar. 5, 1927; s. Ressie Bruce and Elsie Clennen (Miller) H.; m. Hannah Lou Garrett, July 12, 1950. BS, W.Va. U., 1949, MS, 1953; PhD, Ohio State U., 1959. Tchr. Troy (W.Va.) High Sch., 1949-54; asst. prof. sci. Glenville (W.Va.) State Coll., 1954-57, assoc. prof. edn., 1959-61, prof., chmn. div. edn., dir. student teaching, 1961-66; pres. Bluefield (W.Va.) State Coll., 1966-73, Fairmont (W.Va.) State Coll., 1973-88, ret., 1988. Pres. United Way, Fairmont, 1976; mem. Glenville City Council, 1958-64; pres. W.Va. Intercollegiate Athletic Conf., 1977-78. Served with AUS, 1945-46. Named Man of Yr., Bluefield Jaycees, 1969, Disting. Pioneer, Glenville State Coll., 1985, Outstanding Alumnus, W.Va. U. Coll. Agr., 1987. Hardway Libr. at Bluefield State Coll. and Hardway Hall (adminstrn. bldg.) at Fairmont State Coll. named in his honor. Mem. Phi Delta Theta (pres., alumni assoc. 1900-92), Gamma Sigma Delta, Phi Delta Kappa, Kappa Delta Pi. Methodist. Home: 2206 Heritage Pointe Morgantown WV 26505-3065 Personal E-mail: hlg@aol100.com.

HARDWICK, NELSON L., state legislator; b. Conway, SC, Sept. 19, 1951; m. Marty Hardwick; children: Nada, Ira, Melissa. BSChemE, Clemson U., SC, 1973, MS in Environ. Engring., 1977. Mem. Dist. 106 SC House of Reps., SC, 2004—. Republican. Mailing: 411 Blatt Bldg Columbia SC 29201 Home: 714 Cedar Dr N Surfside Beach SC 29575 Office Phone: 803-734-2967. Business E-Mail: HardwickN@scstatehouse.net.

HARDY, ASHTON RICHARD, retired attorney; b. Gulfport, Miss., Aug. 31, 1935; s. Ashton Maurice and Alice (Baumbach) H.; m. Katherine Ketelsen, Sept. 4, 1959; children: Karin H. Wood, Katherine H. Foster. BBA, Tulane U., 1958; JD, Tulane U. Law Sch., New Orleans, 1962. Bar: La. 1962, FCC, 1976, US Supreme Ct., 1975. Lt. USNR, 1958—66; ptnr. Jones, Walker, Waechter, Poitevent, Carrere & Denegre, New Orleans, 1962-74, 76-82; gen. counsel FCC, Washington, 1974-76; ptnr. Fawer, Brian, Hardy, Zatzkis, New Orleans, 1982-86, Hardy & Popham, 1986-88, Walker, Bordelon, Hamlin, Theriot & Hardy, New Orleans, 1988-92, Hardy, Carey, Chautin & Balkin, New Orleans, 1992—2000. Gen. counsel La. Assn. Broadcasters, 1976-86, Greater New Orleans Assn. Broadcasters, 1976—88, La. Assn. Advt. Agys., 1982-86; lectr. in field; advance rep. to Pres. U.S., 1971-74. Bd. dirs. New Orleans Mission, 1989-, Met. Crime Commn. New Orleans, 1993-, v.p., 2006-, vice chmn., 1997-2002, United Christian Charities, 1993-99, Prison Fellowship/La.,

1976—; bd. dirs. Nat. Religious Broadcasters Assn., 2004—. Lt. USN, 1958—60. Named to Hall of Fame, Greater New Orleans Broadcasters Assn., 2001. Mem. La. Bar Assn. (del. house of dels. 1987-92), FCC Bar Assn., Nat. Religious Broadcasters (nat. bd. dirs. 2003-), Metairie Country Club (pres. 1986). Republican. Evangelical. Avocations: golf, scuba diving. Personal E-mail: arhardy@bellsouth.net.

HARDY, DORCAS RUTH, business and government relations executive; b. Newark, July 18, 1946; d. C. Colburn and Ruth (Hart) H.; m. Samuel V. Spagnolo. BA, Conn. Coll., 1964-68; MBA, Pepperdine U., 1976. cert. sr. advisor. Legis. rsch. asst. U.S. Senator Clifford P. Case, Washington, 1970; spl. asst. White House Conf. Children and Youth, Washington, 1970-71; exec. dir. Health Svcs. Industry Commn., Cost of Living Coun., Washington, 1971-73; asst. sec. Calif. Dept. Health, Sacramento, 1973-74; assoc. dir. U. So. Calif. Ctr. Health Svcs. Rsch., 1974-81; asst. sec. human devel. svcs. HHS, Washington, 1981-86; US commr. Social Security Washington, 1986-89; pres. DR. Hardy & Assocs., 1989—, A Pub. Policy Firm, Wash., DC; exec. v.p. Pub. Issue Mgmt., Washington, 2001—03. Chmn. bd., CEO Work Recovery, Inc., Tucson, 1996-98; bd. dirs. Options Clearing Corp., 2000-06, First Coast Svc. Options, Inc., 1998-2009; chmn. Ind. Trustees Wright Investors Svc. Managed Funds; Social Security Advisory Bd., 2002-; chmn. vocat. rehab. and employment task force VA, 2003-04; chmn. policy com. 2005 White House Conf. on Aging, 2004-06. Author: Social Insecurity: The Crisis in America's Social Security System and How to Plan Now for Your Own Financial Survival, 1992. Mem. Girl Scouts USA, Friends of Our chalet com., 2006-, Girl Scout Commonwealth Coun., Va.; Va. Bd. Rehab. Svcs., 1998-2002, bd. visitors, U. Mary Wash., 2000-04, bd. dirs. Com. on Developing Am. Capitalism; former chmn. Pres.'s Task Force on Legal Equity for Women. Mem.: Soc. Cert. Sr. Advisors. Office: Washington Metro Office 11407 Stonewall Jackson Dr Spotsylvania VA 22551-4608 Office Phone: 540-972-1552.

HARDY, EVA TEIG, retired energy executive; B in Polit. Sci., Hood Coll., Frederick, Md.; M in Govt. and Pub. Adminstrn., Am. U. Urban planner City of Portsmouth, Va.; sec. health and human resources for Gov. Gerald L. Baliles State of Va., 1986—90; with Dominion Resources, Richmond, Va., 1990—, sr. v.p. Va. Power, 1997, sr. v.p. external affairs & corp. comm., 1999—2006, exec. v.p. external affairs & corp. comm., 2007—08, exec. v.p., sr. adv. to chmn., 2008—09; sr. policy advisor & cons. McGuireWoods, 2009; interim state dir State of Va, 2009. Mem. State Coun. Higher Edn. Va., 2005—; bd. mem. Va Advanced Study Strategies. Recipient Lifetime Achievement award, Urban League of Greater Richmond, Flame Bearer of Edn. award, United Negro Coll. Fund, Wilder Sch. Pub. Svc. award, Va. Commonwealth U., 2005; named one of Outstanding Women of Greater Richmond in Govt. and Politics, YMCA. Mailing: c/o Va Advanced Study Strategies 820 Bruce St South Boston VA 24592

HARDY, JOHN CHRISTOPHER, physicist, researcher, educator; b. Montreal, Que., Can., July 10, 1941; s. Noel Woodburn and Ethel May (Collins) H.; m. Lynn Helen Frederick, June 3, 1964 (div.); children: Ericka, Kirsten, Bruce, Alana; m. June Dennie, July 5, 1997; stepchildren: Benjamin, Samantha. BSc, McGill U., Montreal, 1961, MSc, 1963, PhD, 1965. NRC Can. postdoctoral fellow Oxford Nuc. Physics Lab., 1965—67; Miller rsch. fellow Lawrence Radiation Lab., Berkeley, Calif., 1967—69, staff physicist, 1969—70; assoc. rsch. officer Atomic Energy Can. Ltd., Chalk River, Ont., 1970—74, sr. rsch. officer, 1975—83, head nuc. physics br., 1983—86, asst. v.p., 1986—89, dir. tandem accelerator superconducting cyclotron divsn., 1989—97; prof. physics Tex. A&M U., College Station, 1997—2006, disting. prof., 2006—. Sci. assoc. CERN, Geneva, 1976-77; program adv. coms. Oak Ridge Nat. Lab., UNISOR, 1979-85, HHIRL, 1991-92, HRIBF, 1999-2006, chmn., 2000-06; program adv. coms. Lawrence Berkeley Lab., Super HILAC, 1983-86, Cyclotron, 1994-99, chmn., 1995-99; program adv. com. Nat. Superconducting Cyclotron Lab., 1990-93; mem. adv. bd. TRIUMF, 1992-98, U. Chgo. rev. com. physics divsn. Argonne Nat. Lab., 1999, program adv. com ATLAS, 2007-; mem. sci. policy com. HRIBF, Oak Ridge Nat. Lab., 2002—; mem., JSA program com. SURA, 2008-. Contbr. articles to profl. jours. and books; editor North Renfrew Times, 1972-97; mem. editl. bd. Nuc. Physics News Internat., 1995-97, Phys. Rev. C. Jour., 1980-82, 95-97; divisional assoc. editor, Phys. Rev. Letters, 2009-. Chmn. bd. dirs., co-founder Deep River Sci. Acad., 1986-97, trustee 1997—2003. Recipient D.W. Ambridge prize, McGill U., 1965, Disting. Achievement award for rsch., Assn. Former Students, Tex. A&M U., 2006. Fellow: Am. Phys. Soc. (DNP program com. 1999—2001, exec. com. DNP 2002—04, chair DNP publs. com. 2003—04, Tom W. Bonner prize 2006), Royal Soc. Can. (v.p. acad. III 1992—95, chmn. fundraising com. 1994—97, Rutherford medal in physics 1981); mem.: Can. Assn. Physicists (Herzberg medal 1976). Office: Tex A&M U Cyclotron Inst College Station TX 77843-3366 Office Phone: 979-845-1411. Business E-Mail: hardy@comp.tamu.edu.

HARDY, R. DEAN, construction executive; BS in Engring., NC State U. Joined Martin Marietta Materials, Inc., 1972, v.p., gen. mgr. Greensboro Dist., pres. Carolina Divsn., 2006—. Office: 2710 Wycliff Rd Raleigh NC 27607-3033 also: Martin Marietta Materials Inc 413 S Chimney Rock Rd Greensboro NC 27409-9260 Office Phone: 336-668-3253. Office Fax: 336-668-1092.

HARDY, RICHARD EARL, rehabilitation counseling educator; b. Victoria, Va., Oct. 11, 1938; s. Clifford E. and Louise (Hamilton) H.; 1 son, Jason Elliott. BS, Va. Poly. Inst. and State U., 1960, MS, 1962, EdD, 1966. Rehab. counselor State of Va., Richmond, 1961-63; rehab. advisor HHS, Washington, 1964-66; chief psychologist S.C. Dept. Rehab., Columbia, 1966-68; prof. chmn. dept. rehab. counseling Med. Coll. Va., Richmond, 1968-96, prof. and chair emeritus, 1996—. Former bd. mem. S.C. State Bd. Psychology, former ABPP candidate examiner; internat. cons. to numerous countries including Turkey, Iraq, Peru, Uruguay, South Africa, Brazil, Thailand Author, editor: International Rehabilitation: Approaches and Programs, Hemingway: A Psychological Portrait, 1988, Gestalt Psychotherapy, 1991, Hispaniola Episode: A Mental Health Allegory, 1992, (with J.G. Cull) The Brass Chalice: Drug Prevention Stories and Information for Children and Youth, 1994, Counseling in the Rehabilitation Process, 1999, Woodpeckers Don't Get Headaches: The Psychology of Stress, Relationships, and Addiction, 2001, numerous others. Recipient Nat. award Nat. Rehab. Assn., 1976; recipient Nat. award Am. Assn. Workers for Blind, 1976, Outstanding Grad. award Med. Coll. Va./Va. Commonwealth U., Dept. Rehab. Counseling, 1997, Richard E. Hardy endowed scholarship Med. Coll. Va., 1998, Outstanding Scholar award U. Md. Sch. Edn., 2006. Fellow Am. Psychol. Soc., Assn. Allied & Preventive Psychology; mem. Am. Assn. Vol. Action Scholars, Phi Kappa Phi. Office: Va Commonwealth U 6962 Forest Hill Ave Richmond VA 23225

HARDYMON, JAMES FRANKLIN, board member; b. Maysville, Ky., Nov. 11, 1934; s. Kenneth Thomas and Pauline (Strode) Hardymon; m. Rebecca Gay Garred, June 25, 1960; children: Jennifer, Frank. BSCE, U. Ky., 1956, MSCE, 1958. V.p. planning and devel. Browning divsn. Emerson Electric Co., Maysville, 1970—73, exec. v.p. Browning div., 1973—76, pres. spl. products divsn. St. Louis, Ky., 1976—79, v.p. corp. group and pres. Skil divsn. Chgo., 1979—83, from vice chmn. to pres., COO St. Louis, 1986—89; COO Textron, Inc., Providence, 1989—90, CEO, 1991—98, chmn., 1993—99. Bd. adv. Investcorp International, Inc.; bd. dirs. Lexmark Internat. Inc., 1998—, Circuit City Stores, 1998—; chmn. WABCO Holdings Inc., 2007—09, bd. dirs., 2009—. With US Army, 1958—59, with US Army, 1961—62. Recipient Corp. Devel. award, ASME, 1976. Republican. Mem. Christian Ch. Mailing: Lexmark International Inc Bd Directors 740 W New Circle Rd Lexington KY 40550 Office Phone: 859-232-2000. Office Fax: 859-232-2403. Business E-Mail: jhardymon@lexmark.com.

HARE, JOSHUA MICHAEL, cardiologist, educator; b. South Africa, Apr. 4, 1962; s. Philip and Isadora Hare; m. Lee Susan Cohen, Oct. 17, 1999. BA in Biochemistry with honors, U. Pa., Phila., 1984; MD, Johns Hopkins U., Balt., 1988. Cert. FLEX, diplomate Am. Bd. Internal Medicine, 1991, Am. Bd. Cardiovasc. Disease, 1995. Intern in medicine Johns Hopkins Hosp., 1989; fellow in internal medicine Johns Hopkins U., Boston, 1991; resident in medicine Johns Hopkins Hosp., Boston, 1991; fellow in cardiovasc. disease Brigham and Women's Hosp., Boston, 1994; rsch. fellow in medicine Harvard U., 1994; asst. prof. medicine Johns Hopkins U. Sch. Medicine, Balt., assoc. dir. cardiac transplant program, prof. medicine and biomedical engring.; Louis Lemberg prof. medicine Miller Sch. Medicine, U. Miami, 2006—, chief divsn. cardiology, 2006—, dir. interdisciplinary stem cell inst., 2006—. Recipient Young Investigator award, Am. Coll. Cardiology, Clin. Investigator Devel. award, Nat. Heart Lung and Blood Inst., SmithKline Beecham Jr. Faculty award. Fellow: Am. Heart Assn.; mem.: Am. Soc. Clin. Investigation, Assn. U. Cardiologists. Achievements include being one of the main pioneers in cardiovasc. stem cell therapy. Office: Clin Rsch Bldg Miller Sch Medicine U Miami 1120 NW 14th St11th Fl Miami FL 33136 Office Phone: 305-243-1998. Office Fax: 305-243-1894.

HARGETT, TRE, state official; b. Ripley, Tenn., Feb. 7, 1969; m. Dawn Hargett; 1 child. BBA in Acctg., Memphis State U., 1991, MBA in Mktg., 1992. Financial planner Nationwide Ins., 1993—95; mktg. dir. Tri-State Case Mgmt., Inc., 1995—97; mem. Tenn. House of Reps., 1996—2006, treas. Republican caucus, 1999—2000, Republican leader, 2002—05; mortgage banker Bartlett Mortgage, 1997—98; dir. cmty. rels. Rural/Metro Corp., 1998—2005, v.p., 2005—09; sec. of state State of Tenn., Nashville, 2009—. Mem. Housing Corp. Recipient Bob James Outstanding Svc. award, 1999, J. Wayne Johnson Meml. award; named Legislator of Yr., Tenn. PTA, 1999; named one of The Republican Rising Stars in Tenn. Politics, The Tennesseean, 1999. Mem.: Mid. South Workers Compensation Assn. Republican. Southern Baptist. Office: Office of the Secretary of State 1st Fl State Capitol Nashville TN 37243 Office Phone: 615-741-2819. Office Fax: 615-741-5962. Business E-Mail: tre.hargett@state.tn.us.*

HARGIS, V. BURNS (BURNS HARGIS), academic administrator, lawyer; b. Victoria, Tex., Oct. 29, 1945; s. A.V. and Rosalie (Burns) H.; m. Ann Whiting, June 8, 1969; children: Matthew Burns, Kathryn Ann. BS in Acctg., Okla. State U., 1967; JD, U. Okla., 1970. Bar: Okla. 1970. Pres. Okla. County Bar Assn.; commd. 2nd lt., mil. intelligence US Army, 1967; capt. USAR, Fin Corp., 1970—77; pres., bd. dirs. Neighborhood Homes, Inc., 1973; ptnr. Reynolds, Ridings & Hargis, 1975-89; dir. Hartzog, Conger, Cason & Hargis, 1989-94; with McAfee & Taft, 1994-97; chmn., Okla. Agrl. & Mech. Colleges Oklahoma State University, pres., 2008—. Bd. dirs. Bank of Okla., Tulsa, Okla.; vice chmn. Bank of Okla. Fin. Corp., 1997—2008; bd. dirs. Chesapeake Energy Corp., 2008—. Vice chmn. Okla. Constl. Revision Commn., Okla. State Election Bd., 1975-80; legal counsel Okla. State Rep. Com., 1971-73; bd. dirs. Neighborhood Services Orgn.; pres., bd. dirs. Oklahoma City Cmty. Food Bank, 1978-87; exec. com. Last Frontier Council, 1988—; chmn. Mayor's Econ. Devel. Com., Oklahoma City, 1986; chmn. Okla. Commn. Human Svcs., 1987, Downtown Okla. City, Inc., 2007—; sr. warden All Souls Episcopal Ch., 1974-78; bd. regents, chmn. Okla. State U., 2005; vice-chmn. Okla. City Meml., 2005., mem. Commn. of the North Ctrl. Assn. of Colleges & Schs. Fellow Am. Bar Found., Okla. Bar Found. (trustee, pres. 1987); mem. Okla. Bar Assn. (Outstanding Cmty. Svc. award 1986), Okla. County Bar Assn. (pres. 1982, Leadership award 1986), Okla. City Golf and Country Club, Rotary (pres., bd. dirs. Oklahoma City 1986), Greater Okla. City C. of C. (chmn. 2003-04), United Way Ctrl. Okla (chmn., 2005-06). Republican. Avocations: golf, tennis, squash. Office: Oklahoma State University 219 Student Union Stillwater OK 74078-1012 Office Phone: 405-744-5000. Office Fax: 405-744-5285. Business E-Mail: vbhargis@okstate.edu.*

HARGROVE, DONNA L., lawyer; BS, U. Tenn.; JD, U. SC. Atty. mergers & acquisitions and gen. corp. matters Womble Carlyle Sandridge & Rice, PLLC; lead corp. in-house counsel BB&T Insurance Svc., Inc.; gen. mgr. AmWINS Group, Inc., 2008—. Mem.: NC Bar Assn. Office: AmWINS Group, Inc 4725 Piedmont Row Dr, Ste 600 Charlotte NC 28210

HARGROVE, ERWIN CHARLES, JR., political science professor; b. St. Joseph, Mo., Oct. 11, 1930; s. Erwin Charles and Gladys Lenore (France) H.; m. Lynne Douglas, Apr. 10, 1961 (div. Jan., 1991); children: John, Amy, Sarah; m. Julia Hamilton, Sept. 21, 1991. BA, Yale U., 1953, PhD, 1963. From asst. prof. to prof. polit. sci. Brown U., Providence, 1960—76, prof., dept. chair polit. sci., 1971—73; sr. fellow Urban Inst., Washington, 1973—76; prof. polit. sci., dir. Inst. for Pub. Policy Studies Vanderbilt U., Nashville, 1976-85, chmn. dept. polit. sci., 1992-96, prof. polit. sci. emeritus, 2000—, lectr. dept. history, 2004—; vis. prof. dept. politics Leeds U., Leed, England, 1996—97. Author: Presidential Leadership, Personality and Political Style, 1966, Professional Roles in Society and Government: The English Case, 1972, The Power of the Modern Presidency, 1974, The Missing Link: The Study of Implementation of Social Policy, 1975, Jimmy Carter as President, Leadership and the Politics of the Public Good, 1988 (Richard E. Neustadt award, 1988), Prisoners of Myth: Leadership of the Tennessee Valley Authority, 1933-1990, 1994, The President as Leader: Appealing to the Better Angels of Our Nature, 1998, The Effective Presidency: Lessons on Leadership From John F. Kennedy to George W. Bush, 2007; co-author (with Michael Nelson): Presidents, Politics and Policy, 1984; editor: The Future of the Democratic Left in Industrial Democracies, 2003; co-editor (with Paul Conkin): TVA, Fifty Years of Grass Roots Bureaucracy, 1983; co-editor: (with Samuel Morley) The President and the Council of Economic Advisers: Interviews with CEA Chairmen, 1984; co-editor: (with Jameson Doig) Leadership and Innovation: A Biographical Perspective on Entrepreneurs in Government, 1987; co-editor: (with John Glidewell) Impossible Jobs in Public Management, 1990; co-editor: (with John E. Owens) Leadership in Context, 2003. With U.S. Army, 1954-56. Democrat. Episcopalian. Home: 662 Timber Ln Nashville TN 37215-1120 E-mail: Erwin.C.Hargrove@Vanderbilt.edu.

HARIDOPOLOS, MIKE, state legislator; b. Huntington, NY, Mar. 15, 1970; m. Stephanie Bressan; children: Alexis, Hayden, Reagan. BA, Stetson U., 1992; MA, U. Ark., 1993. Coll. prof., author; mem. Dist. 30 Fla. House of Reps., Tallahassee, 2000—03; mem. Dist. 26 Fla. State Senate, Tallahassee, 2003—, majority whip, 2006—08, pres., 2010—. Faculty mem. Bob Graham Ctr. for Pub. Svc., U. Fla. Republican. Baptist. Office: 420 Senate Office Bldg 404 S Monroe St Tallahassee FL 32399-1100 also: 8167 Andover Way Melbourne FL 32940-2400 Office Phone: 321-752-3131, 850-487-5056. Business E-Mail: haridopolos.mike.web@flsenate.gov.

HARIG, ROBERT J., food service executive, human resources specialist; b. 1950; BA in Polit. Sci., The Citadel, Charleston, SC. Formerly with Metro Media Restaurant Group, v.p. human resources Ponderosa Inc. Dayton, Ohio, 1989; v.p. field human resources Cracker Barrel Old Country Stores Inc., 2000—04; sr. v.p. human resources Cracker Barrel Old Country Store, Inc., 2004—. Office: Cracker Barrel Old Country Store Inc 305 Hartmann Dr Lebanon TN 37088-0787 Office Phone: 615-444-5533. Office Fax: 615-443-9818.

HARING, ROBERT WESTING, newspaper editor; b. Salem, Mo., Nov. 13, 1932; s. Arthur S. and Martha I. (Westing) H.; m. Jo M. Houser, June 1, 1957 (dec. Nov. 1991); children: Robert A., Joel B., Jon G.; m. Carolyn Scudder, May 20, 1995. AA, Kans. City CC, Mo., 1951; BJ, BA in History, U. Mo., 1954. Reporter So. Illinoisan, Carbondale, Ill., 1954-55, city editor, 1957-59; writer AP, Little Rock, 1959-61, corr. Tulsa, 1961-64, asst. bur. chief Columbus, Ohio, 1964-67, bur. chief Newark, 1967-71, exec. NYC, 1971-75; Sunday editor Tulsa World, 1975-81, exec. editor, 1981-95; ret., 1998. Chmn. Goodwill Industries, Tulsa, 1990-94; bd. dirs. River Parks Authority, Tulsa, 1985-93; pres. Tulsa Zoofriends, 1994-96; chmn. Tulsa Mentoring Coun., Tulsa Lit. Coalition, 1996-98; initiated price earnings ratio in newspaper stock tables, 1973, project re-directory nationnide telephone book recycling, 1986. With U.S. Army, 1955-57. Avocations: running, walking, bicycling. Home: 1620 S Detroit Ave Tulsa OK 74120-6214 Home Phone: 918-599-7413; Office Phone: 918-520-4432. Personal E-mail: harings2@sbcglobal.net.

HARKER, VICTORIA DUX, publishing executive; b. NYC, Oct. 24, 1964; d. Paul A. and Mary Ellen (Duva) Dux; m. Drew Alan Harker, June 24, 1989; children: Zachary Paul, Ethan, Benjamin. BA in English & Economics, U. Va., 1986; MBA, Am. U., 1990. Financial analyst Arnold & Porter LLP, Washington, 1986-89; from financial mgr. to sr. mgr. bus. analysis & devel. MCI, 1990, dir. mass markets bus. analysis & planning, v.p. financial mass markets, 1996—98; CFO MCI Group WorldCom Inc., 1998—2000; acting CFO, treas. MCI, 2002—06; exec. v.p., CFO AES Corp., 2006—12; CFO Gannett Co., Inc, McLean, Va., 2012—. Bd. dirs. Darden Restaurants, Inc., 2009-, Xylem, Inc., 2011-, AES Gener S.A., 2011-, Huntington Ingalls Industries, 2012- Mem. Mt. Vernon Coll. Inst. on Women in Work, Washington, 1992-94; adv. American U. MBA Alumni Coun., Washington, 1993-94; bd. visitors U. Va., 2012- Mem. American Mgmt. Assn., Women's Golf Assn., Jr. League Assn. Northern Va. (chair placement com. 1991-93). Avocations: golf, reading, travel. Office: Gannett Co Inc 7950 Jones Branch Dr Mc Lean VA 22107-0150

HARKEY, JOHN NORMAN, retired judge; b. Russellville, Ark., Feb. 25, 1933; s. Olga John and Margaret (Fleming) H.; m. Willa Moreau Charlton, May 24, 1959; children— John Adam, Sarah Leigh. AS, Marion Inst., Ala., 1952; LLB, BS, BSL, U. Ark., 1959, JD, 1969. Bar: Ark. 1959. Since practiced in, Batesville; pros. atty. 3d Jud. Dist. Ark., 1961-65; ins. commr. Ark., 1967-68; chmn. Ark. Commerce Commn., 1968-69; spl. justice Ark. Supreme Ct., 1988; judge juvenile divsn. Ark. 16th Dist., 1989-90; sr. ptnr. Harkey, Walmsley and related firms, Batesville, 1970-92; chancery and probate judge 16th Jud. Dist., Batesville, Ark., 1993-98, circuit and chancery judge, 1999—2002, circuit judge, 2002—08, ret., 2009. 1st lt. USMCR, Korea. Named Outstanding Trial Judge, Ark. Trial Lawyers Assn., 2005. Mem. Ark. Bar Assn., Am. Bar Register, U.S. Marine Corps Heritage Found. Home: 490 Harkey Rd Batesville AR 72501-9294 Home Phone: 870-793-5849.

HARKEY, ROBERT SHELTON, retired lawyer; b. Charlotte, NC, Dec. 22, 1940; s. Charles Nathan and Josephine Lenora (McKenzie) H.; m. Barbara Carole Payne, Apr. 2, 1983; 1 child, Elizabeth McKenzie. BA, Emory U., 1963, LLB, 1965. Bar: Ga. 1964, U.S. Dist. Ct. (no. dist.) Ga. 1964, U.S. Ct. Appeals (1st, 5th, 7th, 9th and 11th cirs.) 1964-86, U.S. Supreme Ct. 1964. Assoc. Swift, Currie, McGhee & Hiers, Atlanta, 1965—68; atty. Delta Air Lines, 1968—74, gen. atty., 1974—79, asst. v.p. law, 1979—85, assoc. gen. counsel, v.p., 1985—88, gen counsel, v.p., 1988—90, gen. counsel, sr. v.p., 1990—94, gen. counsel, sr. v.p., sec., 1994—2003; ret., 2004. Coun. mem. Emory U. Law Sch., 1997—2003; bd. adv. Emory U. Med. Sch., 2004—. Unit chmn. United Way, Atlanta, 1985; trustee Woodruff Arts Ctr., 1995-2001; bd. vis. Emory U., 1999-2000; bd. dirs. Chris Kids, Inc., chmn., 2004. Lt. jg. USNR, 1968-79 Mem. ABA (com. gen. counsels), Air Transport Assn. (chmn. law coun. 1996-98), State Bar Ga. (chmn. corp. counsel sect. 1992-93), Atlanta Bar Assn., Corp. Counsel Assn. Greater Atlanta (bd. dirs. 1990), Cherokee Town and Country Club. Avocations: tennis, reading. Personal E-mail: robertharkey@att.net.

HARKINS, JOSH, state legislator; b. Jackson, Miss., Apr. 5, 1974; m. Andrea Scales; 1 child. Attended, Miss. State U. Real estate broker; mem. Dist. 20 Miss. State Senate, Jackson, 2012—. Mem.: ACI Real Estate and Home Builders Assn., Flowood C. of C. Republican. Baptist. Office: Miss State Senate PO Box 1018 Jackson MS 39215 Business E-Mail: jharkins@senate.ms.gov.

HARLAN, JIM, energy executive; m. Mary Ellen Harlan; children: Arief, Ryan. BS in Engring., Wash. U.; MPP in Pub. Policy, Harvard U. Sch. Govt., 1977; PhD in Pub. Policy, Harvard U. With US Synthetic Fuels Corps. Policy and Planning Office, White House Office of Energy Policy and Planning; co-founder Natural Gas Storage and Acquisition Co., 1992; dir. iCAD Inc., 2008. Coach Mandeville's Pelican Park and Soccer Club; vol. Boy Scouts America, St. Paul's HS Marching Wolves Band Booster Club. Democrat. Office: 59002 Pine Bay Ln Lacombe LA 70445 Office Phone: 985-809-9847. Business E-Mail: info@harlanforcongress.org.

HARLAN, STEPHEN DONALD, personal care industry executive; b. St. Louis, Oct. 24, 1933; s. Stephen Donald and Mary Edith (Baker) Harlan; m. Mary Joan Heath, 1958; children: Ann, Donald. BS in Acctg., U. Mo., 1959. Mem., staff PMM & Co., 1959—67, ptnr., 1967—70, ptnr. in charge, audit Long Range Planning and Rsch. Group, 1970—75, mng. ptnr., 1975—87; with KPMG Peat Marwick, 1959—92, mng. ptnr., 1987, vice chmn., 1987—92; pres. H.G. Smithy Co., 1992, chmn., 1993—2001; ptnr Harlan Enterprises, LLC, 2001—. Bd. dirs. ING Direct Bank, Friedman, Billings, Ramsey Group, Inc., 2003—08, Sunrise Sr. Living Inc., 2007—. Vice chmn. DC Fin. Responsibility and Mgmt. Assistance Authority, 1995. With US Army, 1953—56. Recipient Merit award, U. Mo., 1976. Mem.: AICPA, Met. Washington Bd. Trade, Columbia Country Club, Georgetown Club, Met. Club. Home: 9621 Beman Woods Way Potomac MD 20854-5466 Office: Sunrise Senior Living Inc Bd Directors 7900 Westpark Dr Ste T900 Mc Lean VA 22102-4217 Office Phone: 703-273-7500. Office Fax: 703-744-1601. Business E-Mail: stephen.harlan@sunrise-al.com.

HARLE, THOMAS STANLEY, radiologist; b. Detroit, Aug. 17, 1932; s. Edward John and Daisy Odell (Bacon) H.; m. Barbara Janette Chrestman, Oct. 15, 1960; children: Blair Thomas, Timothy John.

Student, Mich. State U., 1950-53; BS, Northwestern U., 1954; MD, Northwestern U., Chgo., 1957. Diplomate Am. Bd. Radiology (trustee 1987-99). Intern Passavant Meml. Hosp., Chgo., 1957-58; radiology resident Brooke Army Med. Ctr., San Antonio, 1958-61, asst. chief radiology, 1964-65; radiologist Ft. Detrick, Frederick, Md., 1961-62, Kelsey Seybold Clinic, Houston, 1965-66; chief of radiology Irwin Army Hosp., Ft. Riley, Kans., 1962-64; asst. prof., then assoc. prof. Baylor Coll. Medicine, Houston, 1966-69; assoc. prof. Duke U. Med. Ctr., Durham, NC, 1969-71; prof. U. Tex. Med. Sch., Houston, 1975-78, 80-82, chmn. dept. radiology, 1975-78; prof. Mich. State U., East Lansing, 1978-80, U. Tex. M.D. Anderson Cancer Ctr., Houston, 1982-1997, asst. v.p. acad. affairs, 1982-90, assoc. v.p. acad. affairs, 1990-94; prof. dept. radiology Wake Forest U., Winston Salem, NC, 1997—, Isadore Meschan disting. prof. radiology, 2001—. Contbr. articles to profl. jours., chpts. to books. Maj. U.S. Army, 1958-65. Fellow Am. Coll. Radiology; mem. Assn. Univ. Radiologists (pres. 1983-84), Radiol. Soc. N.Am. (pres. 1993), European Assn. Radiologists (hon.), Faculty of Radiologists, Royal Coll. Surgeons in Ireland (hon.), Brit. Inst. Radiology (hon.). Republican. Baptist. Avocation: architecture. Office: Wake Forest U Medical Center Blvd Winston Salem NC 27157-0001 Office Phone: 336-716-4316. Business E-Mail: tharle@wfuhmc.edu.

HARLESS, PATRICIA FINCHER, state legislator; b. Houston; m. Sam Harless; 1 child, Samuel Justin. BS in Bus. Mgmt., LeTourneau U., Longview, Tex. Owner, CFO Fred Fincher Motors, Houston, 1984—; mem. Dist. 126 Tex. House of Representatives, 2006—. Mem. Tex. Motor Vehicle Bd., 1998—2005. Mem.: Heights C. of C., CyFair C. of C., NW C. of C., Houston Livestock Show & Rodeo, Tex. Fedn. Rep. Women, Cyfair Rep. Women, Tex. Tea Rep., Northwest Forest Rep. Women, Am. Heart Assn., NW Harris County Divsn. (former pres.), 100 Club of Houston, Cherry Tree Rep. Club. Republican. Baptist. Office: 6605 Cypresswood Dr 240 Spring TX 77379 also: Room E2.410 Capitol Extension PO Box 2910 Austin TX 78768 Office Phone: 281-376-4114, 512-463-0496.

HARLEY, DAVID H., facial plastic surgeon; Grad. cum laude, Dartmouth Coll.; MD, Vanderbilt U. Diplomate Am. Bd. Otolaryngology, Am. Bd. of Facial Plastic and Reconstructive Surgery. Residency Vanderbilt Univ. Med. Ctr.; residency plastic and reconstractive surgery Methodist Hosp., Houston; plastic surgery residency St. Joseph Med. Ctr.; trained cancer reconstructive surgery MD Anderson Med. Ctr.; tng. plastic surgery, head and neck surgery ACGME; staff physician Charles George VA Med. Ctr., Asheville, 2008—. Recipient Hospital award of Excellence, Dean's award of Distinction. Mem.: Alpha Omega Alpha (Vanderbilt chpt.). Office: Biltmore Plastic Surgery 1249 Hendersonville Rd Asheville NC 28803 Mailing: Biltmore Plastic Surgery 902 N Church St Greenville SC 29601 Office Phone: 828-274-1009, 864-232-2332. Office Fax: 828-274-4418, 828-274-4418.

HARLIN, RAY M., corporate financial executive; b. 1951; BSBA, U. Tenn., Knoxville. Ptnr. Arthur Andersen LLP, 1972—97; exec. v.p. fin. US Xpress Enterprises, Inc., 1997—, CFO, bd. dirs., 2000—. Office: US Xpress Enterprises Inc 4080 Jenkins Rd Chattanooga TN 37421 Office Phone: 423-510-3000. Office Fax: 423-510-3318. Business E-Mail: RHarlin@usxpress.com.

HARLOW, LARRY (BRYCE LARIMORE HARLOW), lobbyist, former federal official; b. Oklahoma City, Jan. 21, 1949; married; 2 children. BA, George Washington U., 1971. Legis. specialist EPA, Denver, 1972-76, spl. asst. to adminstr., dir. Office Legislation Washington, 1981; dir. govtl. rels. Grocery Manufacturers of America, Inc., 1976-81; dir. Office Congressional Rels. FTC, 1981-85; spl. asst. to Pres. for legis. affairs The White House, Washington, 1985-89; assoc. dir. for legis. affairs Office Mgmt. & Budget, Exec. Office of the Pres., Washington, 1985-86; dep. under sec. for legis. affairs US Dept. Treasury, Washington, 1989—91; v.p. Timmons & Co., Inc., Washington, 1991—2000, pres., CEO, 2000—10; vice chmn. Prime Policy Group, Washington, 2010—11; founder Harlow Govt. Relations, Washington, 2011—. Script mgr. Republican Nat. Convention, 1992, 1996, asst. dir. official proceedings, 2000, dir. official proceedings, 2004. Named one of The 50 Top Lobbyists, Washingtonian mag., 2007, The Top Lobbyists in Washington, The Hill, 2010. Republican.

HARMAN, JOHN R., construction executive; V.p., gen. mgr. Martin Marietta Magnesia Specialties, LLC, Martin Marietta Materials, Inc., pres. Office: Martin Marietta Magnesia Specialties 8140 Corporate Dr, Ste 220 Nottingham MD 21236 also: 2710 Wycliff Rd Raleigh NC 27607 Office Phone: 410-780-5500.

HARMEL, MEREL HILBER, anesthesiologist, educator; b. Cleve., May 19, 1917; s. Louis and Hermine (Greenbaum) H.; m. Armide Chilcoat, July 2, 1944 (dec. 1988); children: Nancy Armide, Ruth Courtney, Priscilla Gover, Mary Louise; m. Ernestine Friedl Levy, Dec. 27, 1990. BA, Johns Hopkins U., 1938, MD, 1943; PhD in Sci. (hon.), Downstate Med. Ctr., SUNY, 2010; DSc (hon.), SUNY, Downstate, 2010. Diplomate Am. Bd. Anesthesiology. Fellow in anesthesiology NRC; anesthesiologist-in-chief Albany Med. Ctr., 1948-52, Kings County Med. Ctr., Bklyn., 1952-68, pres. med. bd., 1958-62, chmn. exec. com., 1964-65; cons. L.I. Jewish, St. Albans Naval, Maimonides, St. John's Episcopal, VA hosps., N.C. Eye and Ear Hosp., Durham; assoc. prof. anesthesiology (surgery) Albany Med. Coll., 1948-52; prof., chmn. dept. anesthesiology SUNY Downstate Med. Ctr., 1952-68, Pritzker Sch. Medicine, U. Chgo., 1968-71; prof. anesthesiology Duke Med. Ctr., Durham, NC, 1971—, chmn. dept. anesthesiology ctr., 1971-83, prof. anesthesiology, 1983-87, Merel H. Harmel prof. anesthesiology, 2002, prof. emeritus, 1987—; prof. anesthesiology Duke U. Med. Ctr., Durham, 2002—; lectr. Duke U., 2010; Roderick Calverly lectr., 2009. Vis. prof. dept. anesthesiology Sch. Medicine, Johns Hopkins U., 1985-; endowed Merel H. Harmel chair, anesthesiology Duke U. Sch. Medicine, 2008. Contbr. articles to profl. jours. Named Disting. Alumnus Johns Hopkins Sch. Medicine, 2003; Commonwealth fellow Oxford U., 1961-62, hon. mem. Sr. Common Rm., Pembroke Coll., 1961; named Merel Harmel vis. lectureship in his honor Duke U. Med. Ctr., 1983, Merel H. Harmel chair dept. anesthesiology in his honor, 2003, Tribute honor, SUNY Downstate Med. Ctr., 2008. Fellow Am. Coll. Anesthesiology (bd. govs.), Royal Coll. Anaesthesia Faculty; mem. AMA, Am. Soc. Anesthesiologists (Living History Series), Assn. Univ. Anesthetists, Duke U. Med. Ctr. Founders Soc., Johns Hopkins U. Soc. Scholars, Japan Soc. Anesthesiologists (hon.), Assn. Anesthesiologists Français (hon.), Oxford Soc. Carolinas (hon. sec. 1990—, W.G. Anlyan Lifetime Achievement award 1999). Business E-Mail: harme001@mc.duke.edu.

HARMER, DON STUTLER, physicist, educator, nuclear engineer; m. Carolyn Wood, 1952 (div. 1964); children: Diana H. Brown, Katherina H. Lucey, Nancy H. Wiggers; m. Lee DeLoache, Dec. 22, 1965; children: David Stutler, Muffin Louise Blakeney, Jonathan Aubrey. Student, USN Electronics Schs., Great Lakes, Ill. and Washington, 1946-47; BS in Chemistry cum laude, George Washington U., 1952; PhD in Nuclear Chemistry, UCLA, 1956; postgrad., N.C. State U., 1960. Postdoctoral fellow Brookhaven Nat. Labs., Upton, N.Y., 1956-59; prof. physics and nuclear engring. Ga. Inst. Tech., Atlanta, 1959—. Cons. on solar neutrino experimental physics rsch. Brookhaven Nat. Labs., 1959-67; cons. computer systems design Digital Equipment Corp., Maynard, Mass., 1967-76; cons. hardware and software design, systems tng. CompuCom Inc., Atlanta, 1986-89; performed experimental rsch. on blood coagulation and in vitro tagging Ferst Rsch. Ctr., Atlanta, 1960-67; designed and implemented numerous on-line computer data acquistion and control systems. Contbg. author (textbook) Introduction to Computer Technology and Interfacing, 1970; contbr. more than 80 articles on physics and computer systems to profl. jours.; patentee in field. With USN, 1946-48, USNR, 1948-53. Recipient Outstanding Mentor award, 1992; named Faculty Mem. of Yr., 1992-93. Fellow Am. Inst. Chemists, Am. Inst. Physics, Am. Nuclear Soc., Southeastern MGT Register (past pres.), Peachtree MG Registry, MG Car Club, Sigma Nu. Episcopalian. Home: 3926 Harts Mill Ln NE Atlanta GA 30319-1854 Business E-Mail: don.harmer@physics.gatech.edu. E-mail: mgnut@mindspring.com.

HARMON, BILL W., state legislator; State rep. Dist. 37, Tenn., 2003—; mem. Transportation Com., Commerce Com., Pub. Transportation & Hwys. Subcom., Joint TennCare Oversight Com.; exec. Sequatchie County; dir. Bus. Devel., North Valley Med. Plz. Democrat. Office: 107 Harmon Rd N Dunlap TN 37327 also: 24 Legislative Plz Nashville TN 37243-0137 Office Phone: 615-253-0264, 615-741-6849, 423-949-5100. Business E-Mail: rep.bill.harmon@capitol.tn.gov.

HARMON, MELINDA FURCHE, federal judge; b. Port Arthur, Tex., Nov. 1, 1946; d. Frank Cantrell and Wilma (Parish) Furche; m. Frank G. Harmon III, Oct. 16, 1976; children: Mary Elizabeth, Phelps, Francis. AB, Harvard U., 1969; JD, U. Tex., 1972. Bar: Tex. 1973, U.S. Dist. Ct. (so. dist.) Tex. 1974, U.S. Dist. Ct. (no. dist.) Tex. 1975, U.S. Dist. Ct. (ea. dist.) Tex. 1978, U.S. Ct. Appeals (5th and 11th cirs.) 1981, U.S. Supreme Ct. 1982, U.S. Ct. Claims 1987. Law clk. to presiding judge U.S. Dist. Ct. (so. dist.) Tex., Houston, 1973-75; atty. Exxon Co., Houston, 1975-88; judge 280th Jud. Dist. Ct. Tex. State Trial Ct., ctrl. jurisdiction, 1988-89; judge US Dist. Ct. (so. dist.) Tex., Houston, 1989—. Mem. Tex. Bar Assn., Am. Inns of Ct., Houston Bar Assn., Harvard Radcliffe Club. Roman Catholic. Office: US Dist Ct 515 Rusk St Ste 9114 Houston TX 77002-2605

HARMON, MIKE, state legislator; b. Harrodsburg, Ky., 1966; m. Lynn Harmon Harmon; children: Tori, Elizabeth. State rep. Dist. 54, Ky., 2003—; mem. Elections Com., Constnl. Amendments & Intergovt Affairs Com., Health & Welfare Com., Tourism Devel. & Energy Com., 2003—04. Republican. Mailing: PO Box 458 Junction City KY 40440 Office: Capitol Annex Rm 429J Frankfort KY 40601 Home Phone: 859-854-6328; Office Phone: 859-238-9717, 502-564-8100 ext. 677. Fax: 859-239-9494.

HARMON, ROBERT GERALD, physician executive; b. Barnsdall, Okla., Mar. 20, 1944; s. Thomas Frederick and Eleandor Virginia (Colley) H.; children: Rex, Susan. BA in Zoology, Washington U., 1966, MD, 1970; MPH, Johns Hopkins U., 1977. Diplomate Am. Bd. Preventive Medicine. Intern, then resident U. Colo. Med. Ctr., Denver, 1970-73; asst. prof. health svcs. and internal medicine U. Wash., Seattle, 1977-80; chmn. dept. community medicine Maricopa Med. Ctr., Phoenix, 1980-85; dep. dir. Maricopa County Divsn. Pub. Health, Phoenix, 1980-82, dir., 1983-85; dir. Dept. Health State of Mo., Jefferson City, 1986-90; clin. prof. U. Mo. Sch. Medicine, Columbia, 1986-90; adminstr. Health Resources Svcs. Adminstrn. USPHS/HHS, Rockville, Md., 1990-93; sr. v.p. MetraHealth Ctr. for Corp. Health Inc., Oakton, Va., 1994-95; v.p., nat. med. dir. Optum divsn. United-Health Group, McLean, Va., 1996—2004; dir., chief med. officer Ctr. for Health Care Policy and Evaluation Ingenix/United Health Group, Eden Prairie, Minn., 2004—05; dir. Duval County Health Dept., Jacksonville, 2006—12; physician exec. Cerner Corp, 2013—. Clin. prof. Sch. Medicine, U. Fla., 2007-. & Col. Health, U North Fla, Jacksonville, 2009-. Contbr. over 70 articles to profl. jours. Bd. dirs. Partnership for Prevention, DC, 1996-2005, Nat. Bd. Pub. Health Examiners, DC, 2005-2010; with commd. corps USPHS, 1974-75, 90-93. Decorated Meritorious Svc. medal USPHS. Fellow Am. Coll. Preventive Medicine (pres. 2003-05); mem. Nat. Assn. County Health Ofcls. (pres. 1983-85), Assn. State and Territorial Health Ofcls. (exec. com. 1987-90), Ariz. County Health Ofcls. Assn. (founder, pres. 1984-85), Omicron Delta Kappa, Delta Omega. Unitarian Universalist. Avocation: sports. Office Phone: 816-260-3273. Business E-Mail: bob.harmon@cerner.com.*

HARMS, JOHN KEVIN, lawyer; b. Bitburg Air Base, Germany, Oct. 19, 1960; s. William Robert and Catherine Dorothy (Heslin) H.; m. Pamela Tinkham, 1988; children: William Cameron Harms, Wade Devlin Harms. Student Wash. Seminar in Econ. Policy, Am. U., 1981; BPA magna cum laude, Loyola U., New Orleans, 1982; JD, Northwestern U., 1985; MBA, Western New Eng. Coll., 1989; postgrad., US Army Command and Gen. Staff Coll., 1997, USAF Air War Coll., 1997, US Navy Coll. Continuing Edn.; M in Strategic Studies, US Army War Coll., 2006; degree in Strategy & Policy, Naval War Coll., 1999, degree in Nat. Security Decision Making, 2002. Bar: Ill. 1985, U.S. Army Ct. Mil. Review 1986, U.S. Ct. Mil. Appeals 1991, Mass. 1994. Commd. 2d lt. USAR, 1982, advance through grades to col., 1982—2005, comdr. 151st Legal Support Orgn. Alexandria, Va., 2005—, commdr., 2005—09; aide-de-camp to commdg. gen. 33d Inf. Brigade, Army Nat. Guard, Ill., 1983—85; rsch. asst. Am. Bar Found., Chgo., 1985; mem. North Western Law Review, 1985; legal assistance atty. Office Staff Judge Adv., Ft. Devens, Mass., 1986, atty.-adv., environ. law specialist, 1992—95; trial def. counsel US Army Trial Def. Svc., Ft. Devens, 1986—87, sr. def. counsel, 1987—90; mem. 1st del. of Am. criminal lawyers People to People Internat., 1987; deputy staff judge adv. Mil. Traffic Mgmt. Command Ea. Area, Bayonne, NJ, 1990—92; internat. ops. atty. Third Mil. Law Ctr., USAR, Boston, 1992—95; chief counsel Devens Res. Forces Tng. Area, Mass., 1995—96; atty., adv. govt. contracts, chief environ. law Electronic Sys. Ctr., Hanscom AFB, Mass., 1996—2003; adminstrv. and contract law atty. 94th Regional Support Command, USAR, Ft. Devens, 1996—2000, dep. staff judge adv., 2000—04; assoc. gen. counsel environment, basic realignment and closure Defense Logistics Agy., Fort Belvoir, Va., 2003—05, joint ops. law atty. USAR Joint Reserve Forces, 2004—05, assoc. gen. counsel environment, installations and enterprise support, 2005—. Aide-de-camp to commdg. gen. 33d Inf. Brigade, Army Nat. Guard, Ill., 1983—85; rsch. asst. Am. Bar Found., Chgo., 1985; mem. North Western Law Review, 1985; legal assistance atty. Office Staff Judge Adv., Ft. Devens, Mass., 1986, atty.-adv., environ. law specialist, 1992—95; trial def. counsel US Army Trial Def. Svc., Ft. Devens, 1986—87, sr. def. counsel, 1987—90; mem. 1st del. of Am. criminal lawyers People to People Internat., 1987; deputy staff judge adv. Mil. Traffic Mgmt. Command Ea. Area, Bayonne, NJ, 1990—92; internat. ops. atty. Third Mil. Law Ctr., USAR, Boston, 1992—95; chief counsel Devens Res. Forces Tng. Area, Mass., 1995—96; atty., adv. govt. contracts, chief environ. law Electronic Sys. Ctr., Hanscom AFB, Mass., 1996—2003; adminstrv. and contract law atty. 94th Regional Support Command, USAR, Ft. Devens, 1996—2000, dep. staff judge adv., 2000—04; assoc. gen. counsel environment, basic realignment and closure and property Defense Logistics Agy., Fort Belvoir, Va., 2003—05, joint ops. law atty. Joint Reserve Forces, 2004—05, assoc. gen. counsel environment, installations and enterprise support, 2005—; counsel sys. acquisition R & D Def. Fed. Acquistion Regulation Supplement Com., 2009-; dep. counsel streamlined IT, 2008-. Cubmaster Cub Scout Pack 50, Boy Scouts Am., 1999—2001; leader den Weblos/Boy Scouts Am., 2001—03; mem. sixth ring U.S. Olympic Com., 2003; silver level U. S. Olympic Com., 2006; trustee N. Ctrl. Charter Essential Sch., Fitchburg, Mass., 2002—04, sec., 2003—04; treas. Fed. Bar Assn., Environment, Energy, and Natural Resources Sect., 2008—. Named Outstanding Young Man Am., 1988. Mem. ABA, Fed. Bar Assn., Assn. U.S. Army, Navy League U.S., Boston Bar Assn. (mem. environ. law sect.), Bluekey Nat. Honor Fraternity, Alpha Sigma Nu, Delta Sigma Pi, Beta Gamma Sigma. Avocations: walking, writing, Karate. Office: Office Gen Counsel Defense Logistics Agency 8725 John J Kingman Rd Ste 1644 Fort Belvoir VA 22060 Office Phone: 703-767-6066. Business E-Mail: john.harms@us.army.mil.

HARMS, RUSSELL K., corporate financial executive; m. Elvia Harms. B in Acctg., U. Wis., Whitewater; MBA in Fin., Loyola U., Chgo., 1997. CPA. Contr. Spring Br. Med. Ctr. (subs. of HCA, Inc.), 1983—86; CFO Scott Gen. Hosp. (subs. of HCA, Inc.), Georgetown, Ky., 1986; CFO, MidAmerica Divsn. HCA, Inc., 2001—05, CFO, Ctrl Group Nashville. Bd. dirs. Am. Red Cross., United Cerebral Palsy Mid Tenn. Office: HCA Inc One Park Plz Nashville TN 37203 Office Phone: 615-344-9551. Business E-Mail: russell.harms@hcahealthcare.com.

HARNER, JAMES LOWELL, language educator; b. Washington, Ind., Mar. 24, 1946; s. Thomas Lloyd and Ruth Ellen (Clark) H.; m. Darinda Jane Wilson, Aug. 26, 1967; 1 child, Lenée Francais. BS magna cum laude, Ind. State U., 1968; MA, U. Ill., 1970, PhD, 1972. Prof. English Bowling Green (Ohio) State U., 1971-88, Tex. A&M U., College Station, 1988—. Author: Literary research Guide, 1989 (Choice Mag. Outstanding Acad. Book 1990), 5th edit., 2008 (Choice Mag. Outstanding Acad. Title 2008), 6th electronic ed., 2014 (Prose award, 2009), English Renaissance Prose Fiction, 1978, 3d edit., 1992, On Compiling an Annotated Bibliography, 1983-2000, Samuel Daniel and Michael Drayton, 1980, Directory of Scholarly Presses, 1991, (online database) World Shakespeare Bibliography Online, 1996—, (Besterman medal 1997, Besterman/McColvin medal, 2001, hon. mention MLA Disting. Bibliography prize, 2006); editor World Shakespeare Bibliography, 1988—, Essential Bibliographies Series, 1985-96;chair, Southwest Region Marshall Scholarship Selection Comm., 2009-11; mem. editl. bd. Seventeenth-Century News, 1973-92, Lit. Rsch., 1984-99, Shakespeare Yearbook, 1992—, Shakespeare Quar., 1993—2009, Literature Online, 2006-13. Recipient Prose award, Am. Assn. Pub., 2009. Mem. MLA, The Bibliog. Soc., Shakespeare Assn. of Am., Internat. Shakespeare Assn., Bibliog. Soc. Am. Democrat. Presbyterian. Avocations: book collecting, travel, manuscript collecting. Home: 4736 Stonebriar Cir College Station TX 77845 Office: World Shakespeare Bibliog Tex A&m U Dept English College Station TX 77843-4227 Home Phone: 979-690-9353; Office Phone: 979-845-3400. Business E-Mail: j-harner@tamu.edu.

HARNESS, WILLIAM WALTER, lawyer; b. Apr. 14, 1945; s. Walter W. and Mary E. (Bukowski) Harness; m. Carolyn Margaret Barnes, Jan. 4, 2969; children: Matthew William, Michael Andrew. BA, U. Iowa, 1967; JD, Cleve. State U., 1974. Bar: Ohio 1975, U.S. Dist. Ct. (no. dist.) Ohio 1975, D.C. 1976, U.S. Dist. Ct., D.C. 1976, U.S. Ct. Appeals (D.C. dist.) 1976, U. S. Dist. Ct. N.C. (we. dist.) 1979, U.S. Ct. Appeals (1st cir.) 1980, U.S. Ct. Appeals (4th cir.) 1981, U.S. Ct. Appeals (5th cir.) 1981, U.S. Ct. Appeals (11th cir.) 1981. Mem. labor rels. staff Monogram Industries, Cleve., 1970—75; asst. counsel Nat. Treasury Employees Union, Washington, 1975—77, nat. counsel Atlanta, 1977—. Lectr. Emory U., Atlanta, 1978—; participant various seminars Ga. State U.; pres. Spring Mill-Kingsborough Ct. Corp., Atlanta; arbitrator Fin. Industry Regulatory Authority; mem. Dept. Homeland Security Design Team, 2003. 1st lt. US Army, 1967—70. Mem.: ABA (com. on fed. labor mgmt. 1981—84), Indsl. Rels. Rsch. Assn., Soc. Fed. Labor Rels. Profls. (Lifetime Achievement award 2004). Home: 1285 Mile Post Dr Atlanta GA 30338-4756 Office: National Treasury Employees Union 3475 Lenox Rd NE Ste 690 Atlanta GA 30326-3220

HARNETT, JOSEPH DURHAM, oil industry executive; b. Paterson, NJ, Aug. 23, 1917; s. James Harold and EMily (Steele) H.; m. Wilhelmina Nordstrom, June 21, 1941 (dec. July 1958); children: Gordon D., Linda C., Ralph H., David S.; m. Nancy Beam. BS, Purdue U., 1939. With Consol. Edison Co., NYC, 1939, Worthington Pump & Machinery Corp., 1940, Standard Oil Co., Cleve., 1941-80, v.p., 1957-68, sr. v.p., 1968-70, exec. v.p., 1970-77, pres., 1977-80; chmn. Com. Representing Co. Design Construction Trans Alaska Crude Oil Pipeline, 1975—77. Mem. Am. Petroleum Inst. (bd. dirs.), Country Club Cleve., Pepper Pike Club, Everglades Club, Lost Tree Club. Presbyterian. Home: 11090 Turtle Beach Rd # 204 North Palm Beach FL 33408-3423 Office: Moore and Ellrich 4400 P G A Blvd Ste 400 Palm Beach Gardens FL 33410-6557

HARNITCHEK, MARK D., federal agency administrator; BA, Pa. State U., 1977; M in Mgmt., Naval Postgrad. Sch., Monterey, Calif., 1987. Dep. comdr. US Transp. Command, Scott AFB, Ill.; dir. Def. Logistics Agy., Fort Belvoir, Va., 2011—. Vice adm. USN. Office: Defense Logistics Ageny Andrew T McNamara Bldg 8725 John J Kingman Rd Fort Belvoir VA 22060-6221 Office Phone: 703-767-5200.

HARPER, ALAN, state legislator; m. Jean Harper; children: Brant, Sam. Grad., U. Ala., 1986. With Tuscaloosa County Indsl. Devel. Authority; mem. Dist. 61 Ala. House of Reps., Montgomery, 2006—. Mem. DCH Regional Med. Ctr. Instl. Rev. Commn., Tenn-Tom Waterway Devel. Coun. Named Alumnus of Yr. Univ. Ala. Sch. Comm., 2001. Mem. Econ. Devel. Assn. Ala., Aliceville Area C. of C., Gordo Area C. of C., Reform C. of C., Pickens County Cattlemen's Assn., Aliceville Rotary Club. Democrat. Office: 419 Memorial Pky E Aliceville AL 35442 also: Ala House of Reps Ala State House 11 S Union St Rm 538-C Montgomery AL 36130 Office Phone: 205-373-6611, 334-242-7732. Business E-Mail: aharper@nctv.com.

HARPER, A(LFRED) J(OHN), II, lawyer; b. El Paso, Tex., Aug. 11, 1942; s. Mosely Lloyd and Marion M. (McClintock) H.; m. Cynthia Newkam; children: A. John, Leslie J. BA, North Tex. State U., 1964; LLB cum laude, So. Meth. U., 1967. Bar: Tex. 1967, US Dist. Ct. (so. dist.) Tex. 1967, US Dist. Ct. (no. dist.) Tex. 1975, US Dist. Ct. (we. dist.) Tex. 1976, US Dist. Ct. (ea. dist.) Tex. 1995, US Ct. Appeals (5th cir.) 1968, US Ct. Appeals (9th cir.) 1976, US Ct. Appeals (10th cir.) 1984, US Ct. Appeals (6th cir.) 1990, US Ct. Appeals (1st cir.) 1991, US Ct. Appeals (2d cir.) 1995, US Ct. Appeals (8th cir.) 2002, US Supreme Ct. 1971. Assoc. Fulbright & Jaworski, LLP, Houston, 1967-74, ptnr., 1975—2007, and former head, labor and employment law dept. Sr. counsel cert. labor and employment law specialist State Bar Tex. bd. legal specialization, 1990-2008, Morgan Lewis Bockius LLP, 2008-. Editor Jour. Air Law and Commerce, 1966-67; contbr. articles to profl. jours. With USMCR, 1960-66. Named a Tex. Super Lawyer, Tex. Monthly Mag., 2003—09; named to The Best Lawyers in Am., 2002—09, Chambers USA, 2005—09. Fellow Coll. Labor and Employment Lawyers; mem. ABA (past coun., labor and employment law sect., past mgmt. co-chmn. com. on devel. law under Nat. Labor Rels. Act, past mgmt. co-chmn. meetings and insts. com., labor law sect.), Tex. Bar Assn., Order of Coif, Houston Country Club. Republican. Methodist. Office: Morgan Lewis Bockius LLP Ste 4200 1000 LA Houston TX 77002 Office Fax: 713-890-5001. Business E-Mail: aharper@morganlewis.com.

HARPER, DIANE, lobbyist; Profl. staff asst. US House of Representatives, Washington, 1979—88; v.p. legis. affairs Northrop Grumman, Washington, 1989—. Named one of Washington's Top Lobbyists, The Hill, 2010. Office: Northrop Grumman Corp Govt Rels 2980 Fairview Park Dr Falls Church VA 22042-4511 Office Phone: 703-875-8400.

HARPER, EDWIN LELAND, corporate financial executive, manufacturing executive; b. Belleville, Ill., Nov. 13, 1941; s. Horace Edwin and Evelyn Ruth (Wright) H.; m. Lucy Davis, Aug. 21, 1965; children: Elizabeth Allen, Peter Edwin. BA with honors, Principia Coll., 1963; PhD, U. Va., 1968. Guest scholar Brookings Instn., Washington, 1965-66; lectr. Rutgers U., 1966-68; staff Bur. of Budget, Washington, 1968-69; sr. cons. Arthur D. Little, Inc., Washington, 1969; spl. asst. to pres. of U.S., 1969-72; asst. dir. Domestic Coun., Washington, 1970-72; v.p. INA Corp. (now CIGNA), Phila., 1973-74; pres., chief exec. officer Air Balance, Inc., Chgo., 1975; sr. v.p. strategic planning, chief adminstrv. officer Certain Teed Corp., Phila., 1976-78; v.p. Emerson Electric Co., St. Louis, 1978-81; dep. dir. Office of Mgmt. and Budget; asst. to pres. of U.S. Ronald Reagan, Washington, 1981—83; chmn. Pres.'s Coun. on Integrity and Efficiency in Govt., 1982-83, Fed. Property Rev. Bd., 1982-83; dir., exec. v.p. Dallas Corp. (formerly Overhead Door Corp.), Dallas, 1983-86; sr. v.p., CFO Campbell Soup Co., Camden, NJ, 1986—92, acting co-CEO, 1991—92; CEO Assurant Inc., 1998—2000, COO, 1998—2000; pres., CEO Assn. Am. Railroads, Washington, 1992—97, chmn. CEO Commondore Applied Techs., 1997, exec. v.p. CFO Am. Security Group Fortis, 1997—2000, sr. v.p. govt. rels. Washington, 2000—10. Dep. exec. dir. platform com. Rep. Conv., 1976; mem. Pres.'s Commn. on Pers. Interchange, Washington, 1976-79, 81-83, Pres.'s Commn. on Indsl. Competitiveness, 1983-86, Pres.' Commn. Exec., Legis. and Judicial Salaries, 1987; chmn. White House Fellows Selection Com., Phila., 1990, 91; bd. dirs. Phila. Suburban Corp., 1988-92, Allied Capital, 2005-10. Contbr. articles to profl. jours. Recipient Louis Brownlow award, 1969, Exec. Govt. award Opportunities Industrialization Corp. Am., 1982, Person of Yr. award Washington chpt. Inst. Internal Auditors, 1982, Spl. Commendation Assn. Fed. Investigators, 1983; Ford Found. grantee, 1965. Mem. Nat. Acad. Pub. Adminstrn., Fin. Execs. Inst., U.S. C. of C. (econ. policy pub. affairs com.), Met. Club Washington, Raven Soc., Omicron Delta Kappa. Republican.

HARPER, GREGG, United States Representative from Mississippi, lawyer; b. Jackson, Miss., June 1, 1956; s. C. Douglas and Lois (Livingston) H.; m. Sidney Hancock, Aug. 11, 1979. BS in Chemistry, Miss. Coll., 1978; JD, U. Miss., 1981. Bar: Miss. 1981, U.S. Dist. Ct. (no. and so. dists.) Miss. 1981, U.S. Ct. Appeals (5th cir.) 1981. Atty. Sanford and Harper, 1995—2009; city prosecutor City of Brandon, Miss., 2003—09, City of Richland, Miss., 2006—09; mem. US Congress from 3rd Miss. Dist., 2009—, US House Ethics Com. (formerly House Standards of Official Conduct Com.), 2009—. Legal vol. 2000 Presdl. Recount, Fla., 2000, Ohio, 2004; legal vol. for Senator Jim Talent, 2006. Bd. atty. Miss. Baptist Children's Village, 2004—; del. Rep. Nat. Convention, Phila., 2000, NY, 2004; chair Rankin County Rep. Exec. Com., 2000—08. Named one of The 50 Politicos to Watch, Politico, 2010. Mem. Assn. Trial Lawyers Am., Miss. Bar Assn., Miss. Trial Lawyers Assn. (bd. govs. 1986—). Republican. Southern Baptist. Office: US House of Representatives 307 Cannon House Office Bldg Washington DC 20515 also: 1 Research Blvd Ste 206 Starkville MS 39759 Office Phone: 202-225-5031, 662-324-0007. Office Fax: 202-225-5797, 601-823-5512.*

HARPER, HENRY H., retired military officer; b. Ft. Benning, Ga., Aug. 24, 1934; s. H.M. and Frances Louise (Hearn) Harper; m. Helen Harpe, Apr. 2, 1960; children: Cynthia Jane, Linda Leigh BS, U. Md., 1964; MA, George Washington U., 1965; Disting. grad., Indsl. Coll. Armed Forces, 1973. Commd. officer U.S. Army, 1954, advanced through grades to maj. gen., 1980, dep. comdg. gen. Armaments Command Rock Island, Ill., 1977-79, dir. logistics U.S. European Command Stuttgart, Fed. Republic Germany, 1979-82, comdg. gen. Depot System Command Chambersburg, Pa., 1982-86, ret., 1986; corp. sr. v.p. Synovus Fin. Corp., Columbus, Ga., 1986-95; ret., 1995. Dir. Ga. State Golf Assn., 1999—. Chmn. bd. dirs. Easter Seals West Ga., Inc.; chmn., bd. dirs. Goodwill Industries, Springer Opera House; bd. dirs. Universal Bank. Decorated Disting Svc. medal, Def. Superior Svc. medal Legion of Merit w/OLC, Bronze Star medal, Army Commendation medal, Senior Parachutist Badge, Aviator Badge. Mem. Assn. U.S. Army (bd. govs., dir. Chambers Fort chpt. 1982-85), Columbus C. of C. (bd. dirs.). Episcopalian. Avocations: golf, jogging. Home Phone: 706-323-9019. Personal E-mail: g2mmhm@knology.net.

HARPER, JAMES EDWARD, JR., academic administrator; b. Newnan, Ga., Apr. 6, 1964; s. James Edward and Lois Mae Harper; m. Jacqueline Sharon Layne, Aug. 4, 1984; children: James Edward III, Jessica Sharon. BA, Lee Coll., Cleve., Tenn., 1986; MDiv, Ch. of God Theol. Sem., Cleve., Tenn., 1990; D of Ministry, Fuller Theol. Sem., Pasadena, Calif., 2002. Ordained Minister Ch. of God, Cleve., Tenn., 1984. Min. of youth Princeton Ch. of God, NC, 1990—91, Farmington Heights Ch. of God, Wilson, NC, 1991—94, Coastal Cathedral Ch. of God, Savannah, Ga., 1994—97; sr. pastor Eastwood Ch. of God, Swainsboro, Ga., 1997—98; assoc. pastor Live Oak Ch. of God, Hinesville, Ga., 1998—2000; instr. in youth and family ministry Lee U., Cleve., Tenn., 2000—01, campus pastor and dir. of campus ministries, 2001—. Author: (text book) Launching A Forever Faith, 2004 (AIM/CTC Book of Yr., 2005). Min. Lee U., Cleve., 2000. Mem.: Nat. Youth Leaders Assn. (assoc.), Assn. Of Christians in Student Devel. (assoc.), Assn. of Youth Ministry Educators (assoc.), Alpha Gamma Chi (life). Conservative. Church Of God. Avocation: sports. Office: Lee Univ 1120 North Ocoee St Cleveland TN 37320-3450 Business E-Mail: jharper@leeuniversity.edu.

HARPER, MARY SADLER, wealth advisor and relationship manager; b. Farmville, Va., June 15, 1941; d. Edward Henry and Vivien Morris (Garrett) Sadler; m. Joseph Taylor Harper, Dec. 21, 1968; children by previous marriage: James E. Hatch III, Mary Ann Hatch Czajka (dec.). Cert., Fla. Trust Sch., U. Fla., 1976. Registered securities rep., Fla., gen. securities prin., fin. and ops. prin., options prin., mcpl. securities prin., investment mgmt. advisor, wealth adv. specialist. Dep. clk. Polk County Cts., Bartow, Fla., 1964-67; rep. Allen & Co., Lakeland, Fla., 1967-71; with First Nat. Bank, Palm Beach, Fla., 1971-89, sr. v.p., 1984-86, S.E. Bank N.A., Palm Beach, 1986-89, 1st United Bank, 1997-98; pres., CEO Palm Beach Capital Svcs., Inc., 1986-88; mng. dir. Investment Svcs., Palm Beach Capital Svcs. Divsn., 1988; v.p. investments, trustee J.M. Rubin Found, Palm Beach, 1983—; v.p. sec., sr. v.p. investment divsn. Island Nat. Bank & Trust Co., 1989-97; chair, dir., pres., CEO Island Investment Svcs., Inc. (A Wachovia Co.), Palm Beach, 1989-98; also bd. dirs., mng. exec., sr. v.p. Wachovia Investments, Palm Beach, 1998-2000; sr. v.p. Wachovia Bank N.A., 1999-2000; sr. v.p., investment mgmt. advisor Wachovia Securities, Inc., 1999—2000; sr. v.p. investments, wealth adv. specialist Legg Mason, Wood, Walker, Inc., 2000—05; dir. pvt. banking Credit Suisse Securities, LLC, 2005—13; pres. J.M. Rubin Found., 2013—. Adv. coun. Nuveen, 1987-99, pres.'s coun., Legg Mason, 2001, chmn.'s coun., 2002-05. Adv. panel Palm Beach County YWCA, 1985, mem. endowment com., 1990—93; mem. pres.'s club Jupiter Med. Ctr. Found., 1989—; life mem. Juno Beach Civic Assn.; profl. endowment com. Rehab. Ctr. for Children and Adults, 1998—2002; chmn. Palm Beach adv. bd. Palm Beach Nat. Bank & Trust Co., 2000—01; dir., v.p. Friends of Abused Children, 2001—03; mem. Fla. History Mus.; dir. Ctr. for Family Svcs., 2003—; bd. dirs. Biomotion Found., 2002—05, pres., 2004—05; mem. Palm Beach Hist. Soc., 2004—. Mem. Inst. CFPs (assoc.), Nat. Assn. Securities Dealers (dist. com. 1995-98), Fin. Planners Assn., Fin. Women Internat., Fla. Securities Dealers Assn., Exec. Women of Palm Beaches (fin. com. 1985-92), Internat. Soc. Palm Beach (treas., trustee 1986—), Jupiter Med. Ctr. Found. (pres.'s club 1989—), Loxahatchee Hist. Soc. (bd. dirs. 1991-93, chair devel. com. 1992-93), Sebring, Fla. Hist. Soc. (life), Jupiter/Tequesta C. of C. (assoc.), United Daus. of Confederacy, Gov.'s Club, Pub. Securities Assn. (exec. rep.), Jonathans Golf Club, Flagler Mus. (Palm Beach, Fla.), Rotary (Palm Beach Found. com. 1990-2009, bd. dirs. 1992-94, 2001-, co-chair, 1997, chair Rotary Internat. Found., Palm Beach 1998-2006, Paul Harris fellow 1992), Lighthouse Ctr. for the Arts (life), Norton Art Mus. (patron), Palm Beach Yacht Club, Ritz Carlton Club (Jupiter, Fla.), Palm Beach County Hist. Soc., Palm Beach Preservation Found. Democrat. Baptist. Avocations: reading, history. Home: 800 Ocean Dr PH 4 Juno Beach FL 33408-1730 Office: Flagler Ctr Tower 777 S Flagler Dr Ste 1320 West Palm Beach FL 33401 Business E-Mail: msharper@jnrf.org.

HARPER, MICHAEL JOHN KENNEDY, obstetrics and gynecology educator; b. London, Feb. 25, 1935; arrived in U.S., 1964, naturalized, 1969; s. John Kennedy and Helen Malvina (Koeller) Harper; m. Marian Wedd, July 23, 1960 (div. Feb. 1982); children: Charlotte G. K., Tristram J. K., Felicity W. K.; m. Ann Carlene Vandeventer, Feb. 16, 1985; 1 child, Helen H. K. BA in Agr., U. Cambridge, Eng., 1957, MA, 1961, PhD in Reproductive Physiology, 1962, ScD, 1979; diploma, U. Reading, Eng., 1958; MBA, U. Tex., San Antonio, 1984. Tech. officer pharm. divsn. Imperial Chem. Industries Ltd., Cheshire, Eng., 1960-64, 65-66; vis. scientist Worcester Found. for Exptl. Biology, Shrewsbury, Mass., 1964-65, staff scientist, 1966-68, sr. scientist, 1968-72; med. officer Human Reproduction Sect. WHO, Geneva, 1972-75; assoc. prof. U. Tex. Health Sci. Ctr., San Antonio, 1975-81, prof. ob-gyn. and physiology, 1981-93; prof. ob-gyn. and cell biology Baylor Coll. Medicine, Houston, 1993-95; prof. ob-gyn Eastern Va. Med. Sch., Arlington, 1995—2010, dir. Consortium for Indsl. Collaboration in Contraceptive Rsch./CONRAD Program, 1995—2010, prof. emeritus, 2010—. Lectr. Clark U., 1971; cons. NIH, Bethesda, Md., 1970—, WHO, Geneva, 1974—87, USAID, Arlington, Va., 1988—95, Andrew W. Mellon Found., NYC, 1991—2005; mem. IOM com. Contraceptive Rsch. and Devel.: Looking to the Future, 1996, New Frontiers in Contraceptive Rsch., 2004. Author: (book) Birth Control Technologies, 1983, Birth Control Technologies, paperback edit., 1985; contbr. articles to profl. jours. Recipient Woodman prize, U. Cambridge, 1956, Agr. Food Products prize, U. Reading, Eng., 1958, Rsch. Career Devel. award, NIH, 1968—72. Fellow: Soc. Biology (Eng.); mem.: Am. Physiol. Soc., Soc. Study of Reproduction, Endocrine Soc., Soc. Study of Fertility (Eng.), Soc. Endocrinology (Eng.). Achievements include invention of alkene/alkanol derivatives, Tamoxifen, alkene derivatives. Avocations: classical music, reading, hunting, automobiles, genealogy. Personal E-mail: mjkharper@msn.com, mjkharper@gmail.com.

HARPER, RAY, men's college basketball coach; b. Greenville, Ky., Oct. 11, 1961; m. Shannon Harper. Attended, U. Tex., 1981—82; BS, Ky. Wesleyan Coll., Owensboro, 1985; M, Western Ky. U., Bowling Green, 1995. Grad. asst. Va. Commonwealth U. Rams, 1985—86; asst. coach Ky. Wesleyan U. Panthers, 1987—90, assoc. head coach, 1991—96, head basketball coach, 1996—2005, Oklahoma City U. Stars, 2005—08; asst. coach Western Ky. U. Hilltoppers, 2009—12, head basketball coach, 2012—. Named Great Lakes Valley Conf. Coach of Yr., 1998—2000, 2002, 2003, NCAA Divsn. II Nat. Coach of Yr., 1999—2002, Sooner Athletic Conf. Coach of Yr., 2006, 2007, NAIA Divsn. I Nat. Coach of Yr., 2008. Achievements include head coach of NCAA Division II National Championship winning Kentucky Wesleyan University Panthers, 1999, 2001; head coach of NAIA Division 1 National Championship winning Oklahoma City University Stars, 2007, 2008. Office: Western Ky University Basketball Program EA Diddle Arena 1605 Avenue of Champions Bowling Green KY 42101-6412

HARPER, ROBERT WALTER, III, museum director; b. Tallahassee, Apr. 8, 1945; s. Robert Walter Harper, Jr. and Dorothy Peters Harper; m. Alicia Anne Von Hoefling, Oct. 29, 1972; children: Robert Walter IV, Wiley Martel. BA in Art History, Fla. Atlantic U., Boca Raton, 1972. Curator Hist. St. Augustine Preservation Bd., Fla., 1973—80; exec. dir. Lightner Mus., St. Augustine, 1980—. Contbr. articles to profl. jours. Mem.: Fla. Trust Hist. Preservation (bd. mem. 1989—92), Hist. Archtl. Rev. Bd. (licentiate; chmn. 1992—98), St. Augustine Art Assn. (assoc.; bd. mem. 1979—82), Nat. Trust Hist. Preservation (assoc.), Am. Assn. Museums (assoc.). Democrat-Npl. Episc. Avocations: sailing, gardening, reading, travel, art, historic preservation. Home: 232 Saint George Saint Augustine FL 32084 Business E-Mail: lightner@aug.com.

HARPER, SANDRA STECHER, academic administrator; b. Dallas, Sept. 21, 1952; d. Lee Roy and Carmen (Crespo) Stecher; m. Dave Harper, July 6, 1974; children: Justin, Jonathan. BS in Edn., Tex. Tech. U., 1974; MS, U. N. Tex., 1979, PhD, 1985; grad. mgmt. devel. program, Harvard U., 1992. Speech/reading tchr. Nazareth H.S., Tex., 1974-75; speech/English tchr. Collinsville H.S., Tex., 1975-77, Pottsboro H.S., Tex., 1977-79; instr. comm. Austin Coll., Sherman, Tex., 1980-82; rsch. asst. U. N. Tex., Denton, 1982-84; from asst. prof. to assoc. prof. comm. McMurry Coll., Abilene, Tex., 1985-95; dean Coll. Arts and Scis. McMurry U., Abilene, 1990-95, asst. dir. NEH univ. core curriculum project; v.p. for acad. affairs Oklahoma City U., 1995-98; provost, v.p. for acad. affairs Tex. A&M U., Corpus Christi, 1998—2006, prof. comm., 1998—2006; pres. Our Lady of the Lake Coll., Baton Rouge, 2006—13; healthy sys. exec., edn. Franciscan Missionaries of Our Lady Health Sys., 2008—12; chair La. Assn. Independent Colls. & U., 2010—12; chair, exec. com. La. Campus Compact, 2010—12; bd. dirs. Assn. Fransiscan Colls. & U., 2011—13; pres. McMurry U., Abilene, Tex., 2013—. Vis. instr. comm. Austin Coll., Sherman, 1985; CIES mentor for Russian adminstr. from Moscow State U., Ulyanovsk, 1995-96; mem. adv. bd. Coll. Am. Indian Devel., 1995-98; critic judge Univ. Interscholastic League, Austin, 1980-93; mem. adv. bd. Univ. Rsch. Consortium, Abilene, 1990-95; mem. formula adv. com., mem. instrn. and operation formula study com. Tex. Higher Edn. Coordinating Bd., 1999-2004, mem. adv. com. AA in Tchg., 2003-04; mem. working group Am. Assn. State Colls. and Univs. Am. Democracy Project, 2002-06; mem. student fin. assistance commn. and tuition trust authority, La., 2006—13, master plan postsecondary edn. workforce devel. workgroup, 2007-09. Contbr. articles to profl. jours.; author: To Serve the Present Age, 1990; co-author U.S. Dept. Edn. Title III Grant; mem. editl. bd. Soc. for the Advancement of Mgmt. Jour., 1999—. Planner TEAM Abilene, 1991; del. Tex. Commn. for Libr. and Info. Svcs., Austin, 1991; chair Abilene Children Today: Life and Cmty. Skills Task Force, 1994-95; del. Oklahoma City Ednl. TV Consortium, 1997-98; bd. dirs. South Tex. Pub. Broadcasting, 1998-2004, Leadership Corpus Christi, Southern Assn. Colls. and Schs. Commn. on Colls., 2013-, Assn. Cath. Colls. and Univs., 2013; bd. trustees St. Joseph's Sem. Coll., Covington, La., 2012-; mem. gov.'s exec. devel. program Class XVIII, LBJ Sch. Pub. Affairs, U. Tex., Austin, 1999, S. Tex. Regional Leaders Forum, 2001-02. Media Rsch. scholar Ctr. for Population Options, 1989; recipient Corpus Christi YWCA Women in Careers Secondary Edn. award, 2000. Mem. Nat. Comm. Assn., Tex. Pub. Univ. Chief Acad. Officers Assn. (v.p. 2003-04, pres. 2004-05), Soc. for Advancement of Mgmt. (Mgmt. Excellence award 2005, Named Disting. Alumni Tex. Tech. U. Coll. Edn., 2011), Am. Coun. Edn. (mem. commn. lifelong learning 2008-11). Democrat. Roman Catholic.

HARPER, THELMA MARIE, state legislator; b. Williamson County, Tenn., Dec. 2, 1940; d. William and Clora Thomas Claybrooks; m. Paul Wilson Harper; children: Dylan Wayne, Linda Gail. Former county commr. Davidson, Tenn.; foreman 5th Circuit Ct. Grand Jury, Tenn., 1977—79; del. Dem. Nat. Conv., 1980; mem. Davidson County Dem. Exec. Com., Tenn., 1980—82, 2nd Coun. Dist. Dem. Exec. Com., 1980—, Tenn. Voters Coun.; city councilwoman Nashville; state senator, Dist. 19 Tenn., 1989—; state senator Dist. 19 Majority Whip; entrepreneur Paul Harper's Convenience Markets, 1972—; fin. analyst Ins. Co., 1978—. Mem.: YMCA (bd. dir., co-chmn. 1971—), Nashville Women's Polit. Caucus (state sec. 1980—81), Nat. Hook-up Black Women (first v.p. 1980—), Cable, Inc., Davidson County Dem. Women's Club. Democrat. Church Of Christ. Mailing: PO Box 281047 Nashville TN 37228 Office: 303 War Memorial Bldg Nashville TN 37243-0219 Office Phone: 615-741-2453, 615-228-6466. Business E-Mail: sen.thelma.harper@capitol.tn.gov.

HARPER, TRUDY A., electric power industry executive; BSEE, MSEE, Tenn. Technological U.; MBA, Southern Meth. U. Exec. dir. Tenaska Mktg. Ventures (subs. Tenaska Inc.); pres. Tenaska Ga. Partners LP (subs. Tenaska Inc.), Tenaska Power Svcs. Co. (subs. Tenaska Energy, Inc.). Office: Tenaska Power Services Co 1701 E Lamar Blvd Ste 100 Arlington TX 76006-7320 Office Phone: 817-303-1850. Business E-Mail: t_harper@tenaska.com.

HARPER ANGEL, DENISE (DENISE HARPER ANGEL), state legislator; b. Nov. 24, 1953; children: Erica, Ashley. Chief of staff Property Valuation Adminstr. Office, 1973—90; property valuation adminstr. Jefferson County, 1990—; state senator Dist. 35 Ky., 2005—; mem. State senate, Ky., Appropriations & Revenue Com., Health & Welfare Com., Econ. Develop Com., Tourism & Labor Com. Named one of Adminstr. of Yr., Outstanding Dep. Property Valuation, 1989, 1996. Mem.: Women's Network., Nat. Coun. Jewish Women, Louisville Forum, Met. Louisville Women's Polit. Caucus, River City Bus. & Profl. Women. Democrat. Roman Catholic. Address: 2521 Ransdell Ave Louisville KY 40204 Office: 214 Capitol Annex Frankfort KY 40601 Office Phone: 502-452-9130, 502-564-8100 ext. 633.

HARPER-BROWN, LINDA, state legislator; b. 1948; m. Bill Harper-Brown; children: Timothy, Terry, Craig. CPA. Mem. Dist. 105 Tex. House of Representatives, 2002—. Republican. Office: 100 Decker Ct Ste 110 Irving TX 75062 also: Room E2.212 Capitol Extension PO Box 2910 Austin TX 78768 Office Phone: 972-717-2871, 512-463-0641.

HARPOLE, PAUL, mayor, Amarillo, Texas; m. Jenny Harpole; children: Amy Martin, Daniel. BBA in Mktg., U. N.Mex., Albuquerque, 1976. V.p., gen. mgr. John Chandler Ford, 1982—2009; pres. Paul Harpole Motors, LLC, 2009—; mayor City of Amarillo, Tex., 2011—. TIRZ rep. Downtown Amarillo, Inc., 2009—11. Active United Way, Second Chance Found.; pres. so. region Boy Scouts America, com. chmn. & asst. scoutmaster St. Thomas Troop 87; mem. men's club St. Thomas the Apostle Ch., pres.; mem. Salvation Army Bd. Crew chief US Army. Decorated Army Commendation medal US Army, Air medal, Air medal with a V for Valor. Mem.: Lions Club, Kappa Alpha. Office: City Hall Office of the Mayor 509 S E Seventh Ave Amarillo TX 79105-1971 Office Phone: 806-378-3000, 806-378-4229 TDD. Office Fax: 806-378-9394.*

HARPOOTLIAN, RICHARD ARA (DICK HARPOOTLIAN), lawyer, former political organization administrator; b. Bklyn., Jan. 23, 1949; s. Harold C. and Joan (Williams) Harpootlian; m. Pamela McCreery, Jan. 1, 1972. BS, Clemson U., 1971; JD, U. S.C., 1974. Bar: SC 1974. Asst. solicitor Solicitor's Office (5th cir.), Columbia, SC, 1975-77, dep. solicitor, 1977-83; solicitor Solicator's Office (5th cir.), Cola, SC, 1991-95; ptnr. Swerling & Harpootlian, Columbia, SC, 1983-90; pvt. practice atty. Richard A. Harpootlian P.A., Columbia, SC, 1995—; chmn. SC Dem. Party, 1998—2003, 2011—13. Democrat. Methodist. Office: Richard A Harpootlian PA PO Box 1090 Columbia SC 29202 E-mail: ratt@harpootlianlaw.com.

HARRELL, BRETT ALEXANDER, state legislator; b. Decatur, Ga., July 1, 1961; s. Bobby Alexander and Vivian Claire (Horton) Harrell; m. Diane Kokinos, Apr. 11, 1987; 1 child, Briggs. AA in Bus. Adminstrn., DeKalb Coll., Decatur, 1982; BBA in Mktg. and Fin., U. Ga., 1983. Sales rep., account mgr. Lever Bros. Co., Atlanta, 1983-84, dist. sales asst. Southeast, 1985, area sales mgr. Washington, 1986; ptnr. Kokinos Kreations, Snellville, Ga., 1987-89; owner American Speedy Printing, Snellville, 1986—2005; exec. dir. Evermore Hwy. Cmty. Improvement Dist., Stone Mountain, Ga., 2003—09; sales assoc. Advanced Disposal Services, 2009—; mem. Dist. 106 Ga. House of Reps., 2011—. Mayor City of Snellville, 2000—03. Mem.: Snellville Commerce Club, Gwinnett County C. of C., Rotary Club Snellville (sec. 1995—96). Republican. Roman Catholic. Office: PO Box 1135 Snellville GA 30078 also: Ga House of Reps 512 Coverdell Legis Office Bldg Atlanta GA 30334 Office Phone: 404-656-7859. Business E-Mail: brett.harrell@house.ga.gov.

HARRELL, CARLTON (BENJAMIN CARLTON HARRELL), retired editor, writer; b. Mamie, NC, Oct. 1, 1929; s. Taylor Smith Jr and Nellie Augusta (Gallop) Harrell; m. Audrey Jeanine Tarkenton, Apr. 26, 1952; children: Melissa Ann, Sheila Lynn. Student, U. N.C., 1947-49. Reporter Daily Advance, Elizabeth City, N.C., 1950-52, 53-56, Goldsboro (N.C.) News-Argus, 1956-57, Durham (N.C.) Sun, 1957-64, state editor, 1964-65, asst. city editor, 1965-69, city editor, 1969-72, mng. editor, 1972-90; assoc. editor Herald-Sun, Durham, 1991-96, editor emeritus, columnist, 1996—. 2d lt US Army, 1952—53. Mem.: Hist Preservation Soc Durham, Res Officers Asn, Am Soc Newspaper Eds. Home and Office: 410 Argonne Dr Durham NC 27704-1428

HARRELL, GAYLE B., state legislator; b. Nashville, Tenn., Oct. 21, 1943; m. James E. Harrell; children: Stephanie, Jennifer, James Jr., Melinda. Mem. Dist. 81 Fla. House of Reps., Fla., 2000—08, 2011—; pres. Rep. Club Martin Co., 1999, bd. dir.; mem. Martin County Rep. Exec. Com., Port St.Lucie Rep. Club; adjunct faculty mem. Indian

River Cmty. Coll.; bd. dir. & pres. Tri-Co TEC, 1985; mem. funding bd. Hibiscus Children's Ctr., 1985—, pres., 1998, bd. dir.; founding mem. & pres. Hibiscus Children's Cent Guild, 1985, v.p., 1997—98; bd. dir. Barn Theatre, 1985, pres., 1985; state chmn. FMA Alliance Legislature Comm. Network, 1998. Former elder & deacon First Presbyn. Ch., former lay reader. Recipient Outstanding Volunteer in Social Svcs. award, United Way Martin Co., 1992. Republican. Presbyterian. Office: Capitol Office 417 House Office Bldg 402 S Monroe St Tallahassee FL 32399-1300 also: 751 SE Port St Lucie Blvd Port Saint Lucie FL 34984-5211 Office Phone: 772-398-2786, 850-488-8749.

HARRELL, JAMES A., III, manufacturing executive; MBA. Joined Sonoco Products Co., 1985, divsn. v.p. indsl. products/paper, Europe, 2002—07, staff v.p. global operating excellence, indsl. products divsn., 2007—08, divsn. v.p., gen. mgr. paper N.Am., 2008—09, v.p., gen. mgr. indsl. converted products, 2009—10, v.p., North American Indsl. Carriers Divsn., 2010—. Office: Sonoco Products Co mail code W53 1 N Second St Hartsville SC 29550-3305 Office Phone: 843-339-6678. Office Fax: 843-339-6078. Business E-Mail: james.harrell@sonoco.com.

HARRELL, ROBERT W., JR., state legislator; b. Orangeburg, SC, Mar. 7, 1956; s. Robert W. Harrell Sr. and Charlotte (Davis) Harrell; m. Catherine Smith, July 21, 1979; children: Trey, Charlotte. BS in Fin. & Ins., U. SC, 1978. Ins. agent, 1980—; owner Palmetto State Pharmaceuticals; mem. Dist. 114 SC House of Reps., 1993—, majority leader, 1997—99, spkr. of the house, 2005—. Republican. Presbyterian. Office: 506 Blatt Bldg Columbia SC 29211 Address: 2000 Sam Rittenberg Blvd Ste 124 Charleston SC 29407 Office Phone: 803-572-1500, 803-734-3125. Business E-Mail: HSP@schouse.org.

HARRELSON, NANCY, construction and real estate development company executive; b. Mullins, SC, Jan. 18, 1954; d. Harvey and Ruth Pulley; m. Larry Harrelson; children: Joseph, Amy Lucking. Grad., Okla. Bapt. Inst., 1978. With sales dept. ERA Bob Linn and Assocs., 1983—88, Caldwell Banker Real Estate, 1989—94; mem. mgmt. Angle Constrn. Co., 1988—2001, Creative Home Concepts, 2001—08. Republican. Baptist. Office Phone: 843-229-1999. Business E-Mail: lharrelson@roadrunner.com.

HARRELSON, STEVE, state legislator, lawyer; b. Texarkana, Tex., Mar. 3, 1974; m. Lori Harrelson; 1 child. BA in Polit. Sci., U. Ark., Fayetteville, 1996; JD, U. Ark., Little Rock, 2000. Bar: Ark. 2000, US Dist. Ct. (ea. and we. dist.) Ark. 2000, Tex. 2002, US Dist. Ct. (ea. dist.) Tex. 2002, La. 2003, US Dist. Ct. (we. dist.) La. 2003, US Supreme Ct. 2008. Ptnr. Harrelson Law Firm, Texarkana, Ark.; mem. Dist. 1 Ark. House of Reps., 2005—10, majority leader, 2009—11; mem. Dist. 21 Ark. State Senate, 2011—. Bd. dirs. Ct. Appointed Spl. Advocates Assn., 2005—, pres., 2007; bd. dirs. Opportunities Inc., 2005—, Ark. Lit. Coun., Ark. Prostate Cancer Found. Recipient Citizenship award, Texarkana Police Dept., Ark., 2005, Leadership award, Martin Luther King, Jr. Commn. Texarkana, 2007, Legis. award, Ark. Dist. Judges Coun., 2007, Outstanding Legislator award, Ark. Cir. Clerks Assn., 2007, First Branch award, Ark. Jud. Coun., 2008; named Atty. of Yr., Tex. Young Lawyers Assn., 2007. Mem.: ABA, Ark. State Bar Assn., Assn. Trial Lawyers America, Ark. Trial Lawyers Assn., La. State Bar Assn., La. Trial Lawyers Assn., Texarkana Bar Assn., Tex. State Bar Assn., Tex. Trial Lawyers Assn. Democrat. Christian. Office: Capitol Address 3911 Jack Cullen Dr Texarkana AR 71854 also: 300 N State Line Ave Texarkana AR 71854 Office Fax: 870-772-0302. Business E-Mail: steve@steveharrelson.com.

HARRIGAN, THOMAS MICHAEL, federal agency administrator; b. Bklyn., 1959; married; 4 children. BS, CUNY John Jay Coll., 1982; Grad., Diplomatic Language Svc. Inst., 1993; MA in Edn., Seton Hall U., 1999. Spl. agent NY Field Divsn. Drug Enforcement Adminstrn. (DEA), 1987—94, spl. agent Bangkok Country Office, 1994—96, group supervisor Newark Field Divsn., 1996—99, staff coord. Office Congressional & Public Affairs, 1999—2000, sect. chief Dangerous Drugs and Chemicals Sect., 2000—01, dep. chief Office of Domestic Ops., 2001—03, sr. advisor to chief domestic ops., asst. spl. agent in charge Washington Field Divsn. & High Intensity Drug Trafficking Area Task Force W.Va., 2003—04, chief enforcement ops, 2004, chief ops, asst. adminstr., 2008—12, dep. adminstr., 2012—. Recipient Administrator's award, Drug Enforcement Adminstrn. (DEA), 1992, 1999, Outstanding Svc. award, Monmouth County, NJ, 1999, Spl. award of Honor for Outstanding Svc. & Dedication to Law Enforcement, Internat. Narcotic Enforcement Officers Assn., 2001, US Customs & Border Protection award for Exceptional Svc., 2007, Asst. Atty. General's award, US Dept. Justice, 2008, Presdl. Rank award for Disting. Svc., 2009; named Outstanding Investigator of the Yr., NYC Dept. Investigation, 1984. Mem.: Fed. Law Enforcement Officers Assn. Office: Drug Enforcement Adminstrn (DEA) Mailstop AXS 8701 Morrissette Dr Springfield VA 22152*

HARRINGTON, KATHY, state legislator; married; 2 children. Real estate broker Prudential Carolina Realty; state senator Dist. 43 NC, 2010—. Republican. Office: NC Senate 16 W Jones St 2113 Raleigh NC 27601-2808 Address: 3324 Lincoln Lane Gastonia NC 28056 Office Phone: 919-733-5734. Business E-Mail: Kathy.Harrington@ncleg.net.

HARRINGTON, RICK, psychology professor; s. Keith S. and Grace L. Harrington; m. Cynthia A. Thompson, June 17, 1985. BA, U. Tex., Austin, 1975; PhD, U. Tex., Arlington, 1981. Lic. psychologist Tex. State Bd. Examiners Psychologists, 2013. Pvt. practice, Houston, 1984—87; prof. psychology U. Houston, Victoria, 1987—, chair social & behavioral sci. divsn., 2009—. Contbr. articles to profl. jours.; author: (book) Stress, Health & Well-Being: Thriving in the 21st Century. Recipient Tchg. Excellence award, U. Houston, Victoria, 1990—91; fellow, U. Houston, 1981—84. Mem.: APA, Victoria Area Psychol. Assn. (pres. 1990—91), Psi Chi, Phi Beta Kappa. Avocation: running. Office: University Houston-Victoria 3007 N Ben Wilson Victoria TX 77901-5731 Business E-Mail: harringtonr@uhv.edu.

HARRIS, AARON, management consultant; b. Birmingham, Ala., Oct. 27, 1930; s. Moses and Fannie (Williams) H.; m. Edna Mabel Turner, May 13, 1954; children: Kevin Brian, Edwin Maurice. BA, Talladega Coll., 1952; MS, Columbia U., 1959; postgrad., Princeton U., 1961. Trainee Bklyn. Pub. Library, 1956-59; asst. librarian Burroughs Wellcome Co., Tuckahoe, NY, 1959-64; assoc. librarian IBM Corp., East Fishkill, NY, 1964-66; library mgr. IBM Research Lab., San Jose, Calif., 1966-73; personnel exec. IBM Corp., San Jose, 1973-77; v.p. Discovery Sys., Inc., 1974—2005; data processing mgr. IBM, 1977-80, mgr. tng. and devel., 1980-84, mgr. human resources info. systems, 1985-88; program mgr. mgmt. devel. Rolm Systems, Santa Clara, Calif., 1988-91. Adv. instr. IBM Mgmt. Inst., 1992; cons.; pres. Amistad Assocs. Gen. chmn. Citizens Com. on Schs., San Jose, 1969-71; mem. San Jose CSC, 1974-78; foreman pro tem Santa Clara County Grand Jury, 1979-80; candidate San Jose Sch. Bd., 1969, 73; past bd. dirs. Santa Clara chpt. ARC, Mus. Art, San Jose; bd. dirs. Opera San Jose, 1986-92, Santa Clara County Urban League, 1984-87; San Jose Planning Commr., 1989-92; bd. dirs. Am. Civil Liberties Union Ala., 1996-99; conf. pres. laymen's coun. AME Zion Ch., trustee. With AUS, 1952-55. Recipient Citizen of Year award Omega Psi Phi, 1970, Outstanding Contbn. award Omega Psi Phi, 1991, Disting. Laity award, Lay Coun., Ame Zion Ch., 2010. Mem. Talladega Coll. Alumni Assn. (pres. Birmingham chpt. 1995-2000, Outstanding Contbn. award 2000, Outstanding Alumnus award Talladega Coll. 2005). Mem. AME Zion Ch. Home and Office: 341 Turnberry Rd Birmingham AL 35244-3291 E-mail: AaronAt75@yahoo.com.

HARRIS, ALAN N., energy executive; b. 1953; m. Karen Harris; 5 children. B in Acctg., Northeastern Okla. State U.; MBA, U. Tulsa. CPA. Group v.p. Duke Energy Gas Trransmission, CFO; dir. gas acctg. Panhandle Eastern Pipe Line and Trunkline Gas, 1982; contr. of trunkline Texas Eastern Transmission, 1995, Algonquin Gas Transmission, 1997, v.p. controllers and strategic planning, 1999, treas., 2000; sr. v.p. of strategic devel. and planning Westcoast Energy Inc.; exec. v.p. Duke Energy Gas Transmission, 2002, group v.p., CFO; chmn. Interstate Natural Gas Assn. of America; COO Spectra Energy Corp., 2008—, chief devel. officer, 2008—. Mem.: AICPA, Fin. Execs. Inst. Office: Spectra Energy Corporation 5400 Westheimer Court Houston TX 77056-5310 Office Phone: 713-627-5400.

HARRIS, BEN M., education educator; b. Chgo., Feb. 8, 1923; s. Eva Mae (Barber) Sands; m. Mary Lee Christian, Sept. 28, 1948 (dec. June 06, 2006); children: Kim Christian, Tamara Lee. AA, Glendale Coll., 1943; BA, UCLA, 1948, MEd, 1951; EdD, U. Calif., Berkeley, 1958. Cert. elem. tchr., secondary tchr., prin., sch. adminstr., Calif. Chemist Desert Chem. Co., Twenty Nine Palms, Calif., 1943-44; tchr. Burbank Jr. HS, Calif., 1948-51; curriculum coordinator Inyo County Schs., Independence, Calif., 1951-54; tchr. Lafayette Elem. Sch., Calif., 1954-55; dir. curriculum Lafayette Sch. Dist., 1955-56, dir. pers., 1956-57; acad. asst. dept. edn. U. Calif., Berkeley, 1957-58; asst., then assoc. prof. U. Tex., Austin, 1958-68, prof. edn. adminstrn., 1968-87, M.K. Hage Centennial prof. edn., 1987, prof. emeritus, 1988—. Cons. Ministry Edn., Venezuela, 1973, Bahrain, 1985, Effective Border Schs. R&D Initiative, 1995-96, U. Sch. Collaborative project, Austin Pub. Schs., 1995-97; vis. prof. U. Wash., Seattle, 1976, U. Tex., San Antonio, 1989, U. Tex. Pan Am., Edinburg, 1992, 1997-2002; planning cons. Ministry of Edn., Egypt, 1987, Venezuela, 1973, 75, Malaysia, 1989, 91; UNESCO advisor U. Cordoba, Spain, 1971, U. Petroleum and Minerals, Dharan, 1979; advisor Lagoven, S.A. Venezuela Petroleum, 1991-92, Am. 2000 New Generation Schs. Project, Austin, 1991-92; vis. lectr. Taiwan Tchrs. Coll., Taichung/Kaochsfungand, 1994; dir. evaluation effective schs. border project, Edinburgh, 1995-97; co-dir. Visioning the Future Project Austin (Tex.) Ind. Sch. Dist., 2004. Author: Supervisory Behavior in Education, 1963, 3d edit., 1985, Developmental Teacher Evaluation, 1986, Inservice Education for Staff Development, 1980, 2d edit., 1989; (with others) Inservice Education: A Guide to Better Practice, 1969, Personnel Administration in Education, 1980, 3d edit., 1992, Invention*Developmental Teacher Evaluation Kit; co-developer Diagnostic Executive Competency Assessment System, 1988, Performance Criteria for School Executives, 1991, Summary Report on Formative Evaluation of Partner School Progress, 1997; mem. editl. bd. Handbook of Rsch. on School Supervision, 1998; co-author: Visioning the Future for Austin Senior High Schools, 2004, Cooperative Superintendency Project, 2004; contbr. chpts. to books and articles to profl. jours. Served with USNR, 1944-46. Fulbright scholar U. Teheran, Iran, 1962-63, Bahrain, 1985. Mem. ASCD (nat. bd. dirs. 1973-75, 80-82), Am. Edn. Rsch. Assn., Coun. Profs. of Instrnl. Supervision (pres. 1976-77), Sam Bass Theatre Assn., Trad. Jazz Club, Fulbright Alumni Assn., Phi Delta Kappa. Avocations: country and western dancing, singing, gardening. Office: U Tex Austin Dept Ednl Adminstrn D5400 George Sanchez Bldg 310 Austin TX 78712 Home: 1525 East Palm Valley Blvd Apt 1406 Round Rock TX 78664 Home Phone: 512-248-9284. Office Fax: 512-471-5975.

HARRIS, BENJAMIN HARTE, JR., lawyer; b. Sept. 12, 1937; s. Ben H. and Mary Cade (Aldridge) Harris; m. Martha Elliott Lambeth, Aug. 26, 1961; children: Benjamin Harte, Wayt. AB, Davidson Coll., NC, 1959; JD, U. Ala., 1962. Bar: Ala. 1964, US Dist. Ct. (so. dist.) Ala. 1965, US Ct. Appeals (5th cir.) 1981, US Supreme Ct. 1971, US Ct. Appeals (11th cir.) 1981, US Tax Ct. 2000. Assoc. Johnstone, Adams, Bailey, Gordon & Harris (formerly Johnstone, Adams, May, Howard & Hill, LLC), Mobile, Ala., 1964-70; mem. Johnstone, Adams, Bailey, Gordon & Harris, Mobile, 1971. Past chmn. Atty's Ins. Mut. Ala., past bd. dirs. Past bd. dirs., past pres. Boys' Club, 1989-95; past chmn., past trustee UMS Prep Sch.; past v.p., bd. dirs. Gordon Smith Ctr.; past mem. stds. com. United Way; past sr. warden, All Saints Episc., mem. vestry, 2005-07, treas., 2008-09. Fellow: Ala. Law Found. (life; past. pres., past trustee, past pres.), Am. Bar Found. (life); mem.: Nat. Conf. Bar Pres. (past exec. coun.), 11th Cir. Ct. Appeals Hist. Soc. (pres. 2009—13, trustee), Ala. Jud. Commn., Am. Arbitration Assn., Am. Judicature Soc., Ala. Def. Lawyers Assn., Ala. Law Sch. Found. (past pres., trustee, Pipes Disting. Alumnus award 2003), Ala. Law Inst., Ala. State Bar (bd. commrs. 1978—87, mem. exec. com., trustee bar found., past chmn. disciplinary commn., past pres., State bar award 2010), Mobile County Bar Assn. (exec. com. 1980—87), ABA (past ho. of dels., past bd. govs.), Athelstan Club, Murray House (pres. 2003—04, past dir. 2006—08), Mobile Rotary Club (Paul Harris fellow), Brock Inn of Ct. (pres. 1996—98). Episcopalian. Office: PO Box 1988 Mobile AL 36633-1988 Office Phone: 251-441-9205, 251-432-7682. Business E-Mail: bhh@johnstoneadams.com.

HARRIS, CHARLES EDISON, banker, lawyer; b. Ft. Lauderdale, Fla., Sept. 16, 1946; s. Thomas Edison and Margaret (Bailey) H.; m. Jeanne Dammas, June 17, 1969; children: David Edison, Ginger Suzanne, Brian Charles. BA, U. Fla., 1969; JD, Harvard U., 1972. Bar: Fla. 1972, D.C., 1987, U.S. Dist. Ct. (mid. dist.) Fla. 1978, U.S. Supreme Ct. 1978. Assoc. Maguire, Voorhis & Wells PA, Orlando, Fla., 1972-73; gen. counsel, sec. Sun Banks, Inc., Orlando, 1973-75, sr. v.p. adminstrn., sr. v.p. legal affairs and sec., 1976-81; asst. prof. law U. Fla., Gainesville, 1975-76; pvt. practice Orlando, 1981-84; ptnr. Arky, Freed, Stearns, Watson, Greer, Weaver & Harris, P.A., Orlando, 1984-85, Smith, Mackinnon, Mathews, Harris & Christiansen, P.A., Orlando, 1985-89; chmn. bd. Mid-State Federal Savings Bank, Ocala, Fla., 1987; vice chmn., cfo Starwood Vacation Ownership Inc.; CEO Mid-State Federal Savings Bank, Ocala, 1988, acting pres., 1988-89; CEO Allen C. Ewing & Co; chmn., pres. Synagen Capital Ptnrs., Inc., Orlando, 1989; investor & dir. Intellon, Ocala, Fla., 1994, chmn. & pres., 2001; CEO Intellon (sold to Atheros Communications, Inc.), Ocala, Fla., 2002—09. Bd. dirs. Atheros Communications, Inc., 2010—. Author: Business Negotiating Power: Optimizing Your Side of the Deal, 1983; co-author: Computer Contract Negotiations, 1981, Major Equipment Procurement, 1983. Served to capt. U.S. Army Res., 1969-77. Mem. ABA, Fla. Bar Assn., D.C. Bar Assn. Office Phone: 352-237-7416. Office Fax: 352-237-7616.

HARRIS, CHRISTOPHER J., state legislator, lawyer; b. Pasadena, Calif., Feb. 22, 1948; m. Tammy Harris, Feb. 22, 1948. Student, Tex. Christian U.; JD, Baylor U., 1974. Pvt. practice law, Arlington, Tex.; mem. Dist. 93 Tex. House of Representatives, 1985—90; mem. Dist. 10 Tex. State Senate, 1991—2002, mem. Dist. 9, 2003—. Vice chmn. Tex. Sunset Commn., 2001. Honored by Nat. Child Support Enforcement Assn., Tex. Civil Justice League, Tex. State Bar family law sect., Tarrant County Family Bar Assn., Fort Worth and Dallas C. of C., Ret. Tchrs. Assn., Humane Soc. North Tex., Future Farmers Am., Tex. Mpcl. Officers League, Am. Subcontractors Assn., Tex. Assn. Alcoholism and Drug Abuse Counselors, Tex. State Troopers Assn. Mem.: Tex. State Bar Assn., Arlington Bar Assn., Tarrant County Family Law Bar Assn., Tarrant County Bar Assn. Republican. Episcopalian. Office: 2001 E Lamar Blvd Ste 150 Arlington TX 76006 also: PO Box 12068 Capitol Station Austin TX 78711 Office Phone: 817-461-9109, 512-463-0109.

HARRIS, CHRISTY FRANKLIN, lawyer; b. Greensboro, NC, Dec. 8, 1945; s. Luther Franklin and Rebecca Ann (Bluster) H.; children: Stacey Lynn, Aubrey Leigh. AA, Oxford Coll., Emory U.; BA, U. Fla., Gainesville, 1967; JD with honors, U. Fla., 1970. Bar: Fla. 1970, U.S. Dist. Ct. (mid. dist.) Fla. 1970, U.S. Ct. Mil. Appeals 1971, U.S. Ct. Appeals (11th cir.) 1984. Assoc. Holland & Knight, Lakeland, Fla., 1970, 1973—74; pres. Canan & Harris P.A., Lakeland, 1974—76; pres., sr. atty. Harris, Midyette & Clements P.A., Lakeland, 1976—89, Harris & Midyette, P.A., Lakeland, 1989—91, Harris, Midyette, Geary, Darby & Morrell, P.A., Lakeland, 1991—98, Harris, Midyette & Darby, P.A., Lakeland, 1998—2000; shareholder Peterson & Myers, P.A., Lakeland, 2000—03; of counsel Kinsey, Vincent, Pyle, P.L., Daytona Beach, Fla., 2003—. Mem. 10th cir. Grievance Com., Lakeland, 1976—79, 1983—86, vice chmn., 1979, chmn., 1986; mem. Unauthorized Practice of Law Com., 1983—86; bd. dirs. Internat. Speedway Corp., 1984—. Bd. dirs. Program to Aid Drug Abusers, Lakeland, 1975-76, Campfire, 1979-85. Served to capt. USMCR, 1968-77, mil. judge, 1972-73, bd. dirs. Automobile Competition Com. US(ACCUS), judge FIA Internat. Tribunal. Named to Hon. Order of Ky. Cols., 1974 Mem. Volusia County Bar Assn., Attys. Title Fund Svcs. LLC, Grand Am. Rd. Racing Assn., LLC (founding mem.), Order of Coif, Art League Daytona Beach, Phi Beta Kappa, Phi Kappa Phi, AMA Pro Racing (mng. bd. mem. 2010-13). Republican. Home: 6022 S Williamson Blvd Port Orange FL 32128 Office: Kinsey Vincent Pyle PL 150 S Palmetto Ave Ste 300 Daytona Beach FL 32114 Business E-Mail: cfh@kvplaw.com.

HARRIS, CLIFFORD JOSEPH, JR., (T.I., TIP HARRIS), rap artist; b. Atlanta, Sept. 25, 1980; s. Clifford Harris Sr. and Violeta Morgan; m. Tameka Cottle, July 31, 2010, children: Clifford King III, Major Philant; children: (from a previous relationship) Messiah YaMajesty, Domani Uriah, Dehjah Imani. Launched film prodn. co. Grand Hustle Films, 2005—; founder, co-CEO Grand Hustle Records, 2005—; owner Club Crucial, Atlanta. Singer: (albums) I'm Serious, 2001, Trap Muzik, 2003, Urban Legend, 2004, King, 2006 (Billboard Music award for Best Album of Yr., 2006, BET Hip Hop CD of Yr., 2006), In Da Streets, 2007, T.I. vs T.I.P., 2007 (Favorite Rap Album, Am. Music Awards, 2007), Paper Trail, 2008, No Mercy, 2010, Trouble Man: Heavy is the Head, 2012, (songs) What You Know, 2006 (BET Hip Hop Video of Yr., 2006, Grammy award for Best Rap Solo Performance, 2007), (with Justin Timberlake) My Love, 2006 (Grammy award for Best Rap/Sung Collaboration, 2007), (with Jay-Z) Swagga Like Us, 2008 (Grammy award for Best Group Rap Performance, 2009); co-exec. prodr. (film soundtracks) Hustle & Flow, 2005; actor: (films) ATL, 2006 (BET award for Best Hip Hop Movie, 2006), American Gangster, 2007, Takers, 2010, Identity Thief, 2013; (TV series) Boss, 2012; reality TV personality, exec. prodr. T.I.'s Road to Redemption, 2009; author: Power & Beauty: A Love Story of Life on the Streets, 2011, Trouble & Triumph: A Novel of Power & Beauty, 2012. Recipient Lisa Lopez award for Comty. Svc., 2005, Most Stylish Male award, Black Entertainment TV (BET) Awards, 2005, Best Male Hip Hop Artist award, 2006—07, Hip Hop MVP of Yr., BET Hip Hop Awards, 2006, Rap Artist of Yr., Rap Album Artist of Yr., Rap Songs Artist of Yr., & Videoclips Artist of Yr., Billboard Music Awards, 2006, Favorite Male Rap Artist, Am. Music Awards, 2007, Best Male Video for Live Your Life, MTV Video Music Awards, 2009. Office: Grand Hustle PMB 161 541 10th St Atlanta GA 30318

HARRIS, DAVID FORD, management consultant, retired federal official; b. Hillsboro, Mo., Feb. 14, 1931; s. Walter Dunklin and Nelle (Landrigan) H.; m. Erna Beckmann, Mar. 5, 1964; children: Christopher Beckmann, Stefanie Ford. BS, U.S. Mil. Acad., West Point, 1954; MBA, Stanford U., 1961. Budget officer Post Office Dept., Washington, 1964-68, spl. asst. postmaster gen., 1968-70; chief adminstrv. officer, sec. Postal Rate Commn., Washington, 1970-83; sec. to bd. govs. U.S. Postal Svc., Washington, 1983-95; ret., 1995; mgmt. cons. representing N.Am. for CB Group, Santiago, Chile, 1996—. Capt. U.S. Army, 1954-64. Mem. West Point Alumni Assn., Stanford Alumni Assn. Roman Catholic. Home and Office: 3643 Trinity Dr Alexandria VA 22304-1840 Office Phone: 703-751-6945.

HARRIS, DEL WILLIAM, professional sports team executive, professional basketball coach; b. Plainfield, Ind., June 18, 1937; m. Ann Harris; 1 child, Nik; children: Larry, Alex, Stan. BA, Milligan Coll., Tenn., 1959; MA, Ind. U., 1965. Ordained minister, Christian Ch., 1958. HS coach, 1959-64; head coach Earlham Coll. Quakers, Richmond, Ind., 1965-74; asst. coach Utah Stars, Am. Basketball Assn., 1974-75, U. Utah Utes, 1975-76, Houston Rockets, 1976-79, basketball coach, 1979-83; scout Milw. Bucks, 1983-86, asst. coach, 1986-87, v.p. ops., 1987, head coach, 1987-91, LA Lakers, 1994-99; asst. coach Dallas Mavericks, 1999—2008, Chgo. Bulls, 2008—09, NJ Nets, 2009—10; gen. mgr., head coach Tex. Legends, NBA Devel. League, 2010—12, gen. mgr., 2012—. Head coach PR Superior League, 1969—75, Chinese Olympic Men's Basketball Team, Athens, Greece, 2004; motivational spkr. Intercontinental Tng. Systems Inc., 1982—84; advisor Can. Nat. Team, 1993—94, Team USA, World Games, Toronto, Canada, 1994, asst. coach, Athens, 1998. Author: Multiple Defenses, 1971, Zone Offense, 1975, Winning Defense, 1995; juvenile novel Playing the Game, 1982; appeared in (movie) Space Jam, 1996, (TV) Diagnosis Murder, 1996, In the House, 1997 (TV), Over The Top, 1997 (TV); commentator: ESPN Spanish Radio, 1996. Bd. dirs. Wis. Leukemia Soc., 1989, Milw. Athletes Against Childhood Cancer Fund; hon. chairperson Easter Seals Milw. High Sch. Classic, Vince Lombardi Golf Classic, Leukemia 6 Hours for Life Telethon; spokesperson St. Francis Children's Ctr., Milw., Spl. Olympics; founder Del and Ann Harris Found. Recipient Disting. Houstonian award, 1981; named NBA Coach of Yr., 1995; named to Nat. Assn. Intercollegiate Athletics Hall of Fame, Ind. Basketball Hall of Fame, Earlham Coll. Hall of Fame, Milligan Coll. Hall of Fame; Eli Lilly fellow, 1965. Mem.: SAG. Office: Texas Legends 2601 Avenue of the Stars Ste 300 Frisco TX 75034

HARRIS, DEVIN LAMAR, professional basketball player; b. Milw., Feb. 27, 1983; s. Terry and Julie Harris. Attended, U. Wis., 2001—04. Guard Dallas Mavericks, 2004—07, 2013—, NJ Nets, 2007—11, Utah Jazz, 2011—12, Atlanta Hawks, 2012—13. Named Player of Yr., Big Ten Conf., 2004; named to Ea. Conf. All-Star Team, NBA, 2009. Office: Dallas Mavericks The Pavilion 2909 Taylor St Dallas TX 75226*

HARRIS, DIANA KOFFMAN, sociologist, educator; b. Memphis, Aug. 11, 1929; d. David Nathan and Helen Ethel (Rotter) Koffman; m. Lawrence A. Harris, June 24, 1951; children: Marla, Jennifer. Student, U. Miami, 1947-48; BS, U. Wis., 1951; postgrad., U. Oxford, Eng., 1968-69. Advt. and sales promotion mgr. Wallace Johnston Distbg. Co., Memphis, 1952-54; welfare worker Tenn. Dept. Pub. Welfare, Knoxville, Tenn., 1954-56; instr. sociology Maryville (Tenn.) Coll., 1972-75, Fort Sanders Sch. Nursing, Knoxville, 1971-78, U. Tenn., Knoxville, 1967—; series editor Garland Pub., Inc., 1989—. Author: Readings in Social Gerontology, 1975; author: (with Cole) The Elderly in America, 1977; author: The Sociology of Aging, 1980, 3d edit., 2007; co-author: Sociology, 1984, Annotated Bibliography and Sourcebook: Sociology of Aging, 1985, Dictionary of Gerontology, 1988, Teaching Sociology of Aging, 1991, 5th edit., 2000, Maltreatment of Patients in Nursing Homes: There Is No Safe Place, 2006; co-editor: Encyclopedia of Ageism, 2005; aging series editor Garland Pub., Inc., 1989—; contbr. articles to profl. jours. Chmn. U. Tenn. Coun. on Aging, 1979—; organizer Knoxville chpt. Gray Panthers, 1978; mem. Govnr.'s Task Force on Preretirement Programs for State Employers, 1973, White Ho. Conf. on Aging, 1981; bd. mem. Knoxville-Knox County Coun. on Aging, 1976, Sr. Citizens Info. and Referral, 1979, Sr. Citizens Home-Aide Svc., 1977; del. E. Tenn. Coun. on Aging, 1977. Recipient Meritorious award Nat. U. Continuing Edn. Assn., 1982, Pub. Svc. award Nat. Alumni Assn., 1992, Appreciation award Assn. Gerontology in Higher Edn., 1994, Appreciation award for excellent scholarly contbn. to ednl. gerontology lit. Ednl. Gerontology jour., 1996; grantee Retirement Rsch. Found., 1997—. Mem. Am. Sociol. Assn., AAAS, Gerontol. Soc. Am., Popular Culture Assn., So. Sociol. Soc., So. Gerontol. Soc. (pres.'s award 1984), N. Central Sociol. Assn., London Competitor's Club, Nat. Contest Assn., Knoxville Kontestars. Home and Office: U Tenn Dept Sociology PO Box 50546 Knoxville TN 37950-0546 Business E-Mail: dharris@utk.edu.

HARRIS, EMMYLOU, singer; b. Birmingham, Ala., Apr. 2, 1947; d. Walter and Eugenia; m. Tom Slocum, 1969 (div.); children: Hallie, Meghann. Attended, U. NC, Greensboro; PhD (hon.), Berklee Coll. Music, 2009. Singer, 1967; toured with Fallen Angels Band, performed across Europe and US; appeared in rock documentary The Last Waltz, 1978; albums: The Gliding Bird, 1969, Pieces of the Sky, 1975, Elite Hotel, 1975 (Grammy award for Best Female County Vocal Performance, 1976), Luxury Liner, 1977, Quarter Moon In A Ten Cent Town, 1978, Profile: Best of Emmylou Harris, 1978, Blue Kentucky Girl, 1979 (Grammy award for Best Female Country Vocal Performance, 1979), Light of the Stable, 1979, Roadie, 1980 (Grammy award for Best Country Performance, 1981), Evangeline, 1981, Last Date, 1982, White Shoes, 1983 (Grammy award for Best Female Country Vocal Performance, 1984), The Ballad of Sally Rose, 1985, Thirteen, 1986, Trio (with Dolly Parton and Linda Ronstadt), 1987 (Acad. Country Music award for Album of Yr., 1987, Grammy award for Best Country Performance, 1988), Angel Band, 1987, Bluebird, 1988, Duets, 1990, At the Ryman, 1992 (Grammy award for Best Country Performance, 1993), Cowgirl's Prayer, 1993, Songs of the West, 1994, Wrecking Ball, 1995 (Grammy award for Best Contemporary Folk Album, 1996), Spyboy, 1998, A Tribute to Tradition, 1998 (Grammy award for Best Country Collaboration with Vocals, 1999), The Horse Whisperer, 1998, Red Dirt Girl, 2000 (Grammy award for Best Contemporary Folk Album, 2001), O Brother, Where Art Thou?, 2001 (Grammy award for Album of Yr.), Nobody's Darling But Mine, 2002, Stumble Into Grace, 2003, The Very Best of Emmylou Harris: Heartaches & Highways, 2005 (Grammy award for Best Female Country Vocal Performance, 2006), All I Intended to Be, 2008, Hard Bargain, 2011, Old Yellow Moon (with Rodney Crowell), 2013 (Grammy award for Best Americana Album, 2014); co-writer, co-prodr.: (with Paul Kennerley) The Ballad of Sally Rose, 1985. Pres. Country Music Found., 1983. Recipient Orville H. Gibson Lifetime Achievement award, 1996, Patrick J. Leahy Humanitarian award-Americana Music awards Lifetime Achievement Performer, 2002; named Female Vocalist of Yr., Country Music Assn., 1980, Golden Plate award, Acad. Achievement, 2004; named to Ala. Music Hall of Fame, 2003, Country Music Hall of Fame, 2008. Fellow: Am. Acad. Arts and Sciences. Office: Vector Management 1607 17th Ave S Nashville TN 37212-2875*

HARRIS, ERNEST LEO, state legislator; b. Louisville, Ky., Dec. 23, 1947; s. Ernest Leo and Dorothy Eggenspiller Harris; m. Janet Lynn Coleman, 1977; children: Jonathan, David, Anne. State senator Dist. 26, Ky., 1995—; mem. Agr. & Natural Resources Com., Banking & Ins. Com., Local Govt. Com., State Govt. Com.; comml. airline pilot; dairy & tobacco farmer. Mem.: Farm Bur., C. of C., VFW. Republican. Baptist. Address: 4306 S Hwy 1694 Prospect KY 40059 Mailing: PO Box 1073 Crestwood KY 40014 Home Phone: 502-241-8307; Office Phone: 502-564-8100 605. Fax: 502-241-8307.

HARRIS, FRANCES FLINTROY, university administrator, civic worker; b. Monroe, La., Feb. 17, 1937; d. Mose Flintroy and Annie (Henry) Collins; m. Charles Blunt, July 11, 1955 (div. July 1967); children: Lorenzo, Alonzo, Sylvia Ann, Robert Earl;. BA, Tulane U., 1985; M in Social Work, Southern U., New Orleans, 1990. Cert. YWCA, 1997. Sec. Grambling U., La., 1963—68, State Farm Ins., Monroe, La., 1968—75; rehab. dir. City of Monroe, La., 1975—81; asst. administr. tchr. edn. Tulane U., 1982—87; u. adminstrv. asst. Covenant House, New Orleans, 1987—89, VOA super case mgmt., 1990—92; ret., 2005. Social worker nurse midwifery ctr. Lakeland Med. Ctr., 1992—93. Pres. Sickle Cell Anemia Found., Monroe, 1977—81. Mem.: New Orleans Women's Bowling Assn., Nat. Bowling Assn., Am. Legion Aux., Nat. Assn. Negro Bus. and Profl. Women, Nat. Assn. Female Execs. Democrat. Baptist. Avocations: bowling, swimming, sports, piano. Mailing: 1765 Coliseum St Apt 306 New Orleans LA 70130

HARRIS, HUGH R., mortgage company executive; BS, Auburn U. Mortgage banker South Trust Mortgage, Birmingham, Ala., 1974—83; sr. v.p., mgr. residential production and secondary mktg. Mortgage Corp. of South, Birmingham, Ala., 1983-86, pres., 1986-88; vice chmn. BancBoston Mortgage Corp., 1988-93, pres., COO, 1993—96, Homeside Lending Inc. (formerly BancBoston Mortgage Corp.), 1996—2000, pres., CEO, 2000—01; pres. fin. services tech. divsn. Fidelity Nat. Financial and Fidelity Nat. Info. Services, 2003—06; dir., pres., CEO Lender Processing Services, Inc., Jacksonville, Fla., 2011—. Bd. govs., legis. com. Mortgage Bankers Assn. Am. (co-chmn Fannie Mae Liason com., mem. edn. com., past chmn. Single Family com.), mem. Mortgage Bankers Assn. Ala. (past v.p.), mem. Fannie Mae Regional adv. bd. and Fannie Mae Nat. Adv. Coun., adv. bd. Lender Svcs. Inc., Residential Mortgage Ins. Corp., bd. dirs. Freedom Securities Corp. Office: Lender Processing Services Inc 601 Riverside Ave Jacksonville FL 32204

HARRIS, J(ACOB) GEORGE, health products executive; b. Kings Mountain, NC, Sept. 5, 1938; s. James A. and Carolyn (Hord) H.; m. Sondra Gilbert, Mar. 29, 1959; children: Cynthia, Susan, David. BA in Math., Duke U., 1960. With Am. Hosp. Supply Corp., 1960-84, region mgr. South San Francisco, 1964-67, pres. Port Credit, Ont., Canada, 1967-70, v.p. ops. Evanston, Ill., 1970-71, pres. dietary products div. McGaw Park, Ill., 1971-74, corp. v.p. Evanston, 1974-78, exec. v.p., 1978-84; chmn., chief exec. officer Health Group Inc., Nashville, 1984-85; founder, pres., CEO Pinnacle Care Corp. (merged Mariner Health Group), 1985-94; pres., COO Mariner Health Group, 1994; ret., 1994; formerly bd. dirs. Mariner Health Group. Bd. dirs. Union Spl. Corp., Chgo., Monoclonal Antibodies, Inc., Mountain View, Calif., Electro Neucleonics Inc., Health Group, Electro-Biology Inc., Dialogic Comm. Corp. Bd. dirs. Highland Park (Ill.) Hosp., 1981-84; trustee McCormick Sem., Chgo. Mem. Scientific Apparatus Mfrs. Assn. (bd. dirs.), Richland Country Club. Home: 1204 Beddington Park Nashville TN 37215-5810 Office Phone: 615-414-7553. Personal E-mail: bocaj1938@aol.com.

HARRIS, JAMES B., geology professor; BS in Geology, Ea. Ky. U., 1982; BS in Geophysics, U. Houston, 1985; MS, U. Ky., 1989, PhD Geology/Geophysics, 1992. Prof. geology Milsaps Coll. Contbr. articles to profl. jours. Named Miss. Prof. of Yr., Carnegie Found. for Advancement of Tchg. and Coun. for Advancement and Support of Edn., 2009. Office: Millsaps College Dept Geology 1701 N State St Jackson MS 39210 Office Phone: 601-974-1343. Office Fax: 601-974-1345. E-mail: harrijb@millsaps.edu.

HARRIS, JOHN F., editor-in-chief; b. 1963; m. Ann O'Hanlon; children: Liza, Griffin, Nikki. BA in American History, Carleton Coll., Northfield, Minn., 1985. Intern The Washington Post, 1985, reporter, Va. and Washington region stories, 1985—90, reporter, Va. state govt. and politics Richmond, 1990—94, reporter, Washington and nat. staff Washington, 1994—95, reporter, Clinton White House, 1995—2001, polit. editor, nat. polit. editor, 2005—06; co-founder, editor-in-chief The Politico, Arlington, Va., 2006—; editor-in-chief Politico.com, Arlington, Va., 2007—. Author: The Survivor: Bill Clinton in the White House, 2005; co-author (with Mark Halperin): The Way to Win: Clinton, Bush, Rove and How to Take the White House in 2008, 2006; guest panelist Washington Week and other radio shows, guest appearances Face the Nation. Recipient Aldo Beckman award, White House Corr. Assn., 1999, Prize for Disting. Reporting on the Presidency, Gerald R. Ford Libr., 2001; named one of The 50 Most Powerful People in DC, GQ mag., 2009; Guest Scholar, Brookings Institution, 2003. Office: Politico 1000 Wilson Blvd Ste 601 Arlington VA 22209 Office Phone: 703-647-7998.*

HARRIS, JOHN W., real estate company executive; BA, U. N.C.; postgrad., Am. U. Lic. real estate broker N.C., S.C., Tenn., Ga., Va. Bldg. mgr. The Bissell Cos., Inc., v.p., pres., Lincoln Harris, LLC (formerly The Harris Group), Charlotte, NC, 1992—. Dir. emeritus USAir, Inc.; bd. dirs. Dominion Resource, Inc., Richmond, Va., Piedmont Natural Gas. Mayoral appointee Airport Adv. Com.; past chmn. bd. trustees U. N.C., Chapel Hill; past chmn. Charlotte organizing com. NCAA Final Four; active Charlotte Regional Partnership; dir. Charlotte-Mecklenburg Hosp. Authority. Recipient Man of Yr. award, Charlotte News, 1984, Cornerstone award, Charlotte Region Comml. Bd. Realtors, 1994. Mem.: Charlotte C. of C. (chmn. 1990), Urban Land Inst., Charlotte Regional Comml. Bd. Realtors, Nat. Collegiate Athletic Found. Office: Lincoln Harris 100 N Tryon St Charlotte NC 28202

HARRIS, JUDITH ANN WHITE, occupational health nurse, educator; b. Springfield, Ohio, Mar. 6, 1939; d. Willis and Tennessee Belle (Poole) Martin; m. Allen G. Harris, Mar. 21, 1986; 1 child by previous marriage, Denise Marian Womble. Student, U. South Fla., 1978-85, BS/MS in Psychology, 2000. RN, Fla.; cert. tchr., Fla. Nurse Dr. Robert Tapogna, Springfield, Ohio, 1960-62, Springfield City Hosp., 1962-65, Dr. Robert Beam, Springfield, 1965-75; ednl. coord., instr. med. assisting Sarasota Vocat. Ctr., Fla., 1977-82, instr. med. assisting program, chmn. dept., 1982-84, 89-91, instr. health svc. oocupations, placement coord. health occu, 1985-88; dept. chmn. Allied Health, 1989-95; v.p. Jara Villas Commous Assn., 2008—; pres. Jora III Villas, 2008—. Bd. dirs. Fla. Bd. Inc.; pres. J.W. Harris Pub. Co.; cruise ship lectr. for Princess, Royal Caribbean and Celebrity Cruise Lines; v.p., sec. Al Harris Pest Control, Inc. 1996-; dir. adv. & mktg., 2000-. Author: J.W. Harris Medical Assisting Review Manual, 1995, Templin, 2002; contbr. articles to profl. jours. Vol. Children's Breath Clinic, Sarasota, 1977-79, Kidney Found., Sarasota, 1982, ARC, Sarasota, 1976-88; dir. Spl. Care Unit, 1984-88; v.p. Sons of Norway, 1993-95; choir soloist Beneva Christian Ch., 1989—, deaconess, 1993-96, elder 1997—, chmn. Health Care Svcs. Dept., 1996—, vice chmn. bd. dirs., 2001-02, chmn. bd., 2002—; asst. state dir. Fla. Good Sons, 1993-94; bd. dirs. Fla. Bd. Camping Assn., Inc., sec., 1999--, newsletter editor, 1996—; chmn. FVA Leadership Forum, 1992—; parish nurse and chmn. health svcs. dept. Beneva Christian Ch., 1995—; pres. FVA Post Pres.'s Club, 1999—; 1st v.p. Sarasota Bay Republican Women's Club Federated, 1998-2001; mem. Sarasota Tiger Bay Club, 1999—, Sarasota Homebuilders Assn., 1999—; sec. Acorn Glass Bowling League, 2000—. Named Outstanding Vocat. Tchr. Sarasota County Sch. Bd., 1985, Woman of Impact for Edn., Sarasota County Commn. on the Status of Women, 1995. Mem. Am. Vocat. Assn. (Outstanding Vocat. Tchr. region II 1985, Vocat. Tchr. Yr. 1987), Health Occupations Educators (vice chmn. policy com. 1985-86), Nat. Assn. Health Occupations Tchrs. (v.p. region II 1984-86, pres. elect 1988, pres. 1989-91), Fla. Vocat. Assn. (bd. dirs. 1983-85, pres. 1987-88, Pres. award 1984, Outstanding Vocat. Educator region 23 award 1982, Sarasota Mayors award 1984, Gov.'s Proclamation for Outstanding Tchg. 1987, chmn. leadership forum 1993—), Health Occupations Educators Assn. Fla. (pres. 1983-84, chmn. legis. com. 1985-93, Outstanding Tchr. 1983), Sarasota County Vocat. and Adult Edn. Assn. (pres. 1978-80, editor newsletter 1978-83), Am. Assn. Med. Assts., Good Sams Inc. Fla. (asst. state dir. dist. 12 1993-95), Fraternal Order of Eagles Aux. (dist. 3 auditor 1995-96, eagle nurse 1995-97, chair health care dept. 1995—, condr. 1996—), Sarasota Bay Republican Women's Club (life; v.p. 1998—), Women's Coun. Realtors (ways and means chair 2002-, corr. sec. 2003, rec. sec. 2004), Sarasota Assn. Realtors, Ladies of Oriental Shrine N.Am., Sunrise Rotary Club (Paul Harris fellow, 2002-, Rotary Internat. Sustaining Mem. 2002-), Tara Country Club (soc. com. mem., co-chair commn. com. 2011-) Tiger Bay Club, Delta Kappa Gamma, Phi Kappa Phi. Avocations: swimming, camping, knitting, sewing, biking. Home: 6417 Liberty Ave Bradenton FL 34203

HARRIS, JUSTIN T., state legislator; b. Muskogee, Okla., Aug. 25, 1975; s. Michael and Linda Harris; m. Marsha Frederick; children: Ethan Harris, Caelan Harris, Isaiah Harris. B in Human Environ. Sci., U. Ark. Mem. West Fork City Coun.; vice chmn. Planning Commn.; bd. adv. Children & Families, Little Rock; mem. Budget & Personnel Com.; owner Growing God's Kingdom Inc., Ark., Growing God's Kingdom Preschool, West Fork, Ark., 2003—09; mem. Dist. 87 Ark. House of Representatives, 2011—. Republican. Office: PO Box 880 West Fork AR 72774 Office Phone: 479-871-8542. Personal E-mail: justin.harris@arkansashouse.org.

HARRIS, LANCE, state legislator; Attended, Northwestern State U., Natchitoches, La., La. Coll., Pineville. Business exec.; mem. Dist. 25 La. House of Reps., Baton Rogue, 2012—. Republican. Office: PO Box 13555 Alexandria LA 71315-3555 also: La House of Reps 900 N 3rd St Baton Rouge LA 70804 Office Phone: 318-767-6095. Business E-Mail: harrisl@legis.la.gov.

HARRIS, NANCY L., information technology executive; BS in Journalism, Northwestern U., MS in Mktg. Worked Andersen Consulting; dir., field mktg., dir., product mktg., devel. mgr. BMC Software; dir., mktg. and product mgmt. ClearCommerce, 2000—01; sr. v.p., ops. Forgent Networks, Inc., v.p., mktg., 2001, gen. mgr., NetSimplicity, 2003, COO, 2008—, pres., CEO, 2009—. Bd. dirs. Forgent Networks Inc., 2009—. Office: Forgent Networks Inc 108 Wild Basin Rd Austin TX 78746 Office Phone: 512-437-2700. Office Fax: 512-437-2365. Business E-Mail: nancy_harris@forgent.com.

HARRIS, PATRICE A., III, physician, public health service officer; b. Bluefield, W.Va. B in Psychology, W.Va. U., M in Counseling, MD. Resident in psychiatry Emory U., Ga., fellow in child psychiatry; sr. policy fellow Emory U. Sch. Law; pvt. practice physician Ga.; med. dir. Fulton County Dept. Behavioral Health and Devel. Disabilities, Ga.; dir. health services Fulton County Govt., Ga. Founding pres. Ga. Psychiatry PAC. Mem.: AMA (mem. governing coun. on legis. 2003—, chair governing coun. on legis. 2010—11, bd. trustees 2011—, mem. governing coun. Women Physicians Congress), American Psychiatric Assn. (bd. mem., del. to the AMA), Med. Assn. Ga. (mem. coun. on legis., mem. com. on constn. and by-laws), Ga. Psychiatric Physicians Assn. (bd. mem., pres.), Alpha Kappa Alpha. Office: Fulton County Health and Human Services 141 Pryor St Atlanta GA 30303

HARRIS, RAYMOND CLEMENT, nephrologist, educator; b. Nashville, Tenn., Mar. 26, 1952; s. Raymond Clement and Elizabeth Lay Harris; m. Paula Jean Messenheimer, Sept. 26, 1982; children: Matthew Clement, William Alexander. BS, Yale U., 1974; MD, Emory U., 1978. Intern U. Calif., San Francisco, 1978—79, med. resident, 1979—81; renal fellow Brigham & Women's Hosp., Boston, 1982—86; asst. prof. Vanderbilt U. Hosp., Nashville, 1986—91, assoc. prof., 1991—98, prof., 1998—, dir. divsn. nephrology & hyptertension; dir. Vanderbilt O'Brien Ctr. for Study of Kidney Disease, Nashville. Office: Vanderbilt U Med Ctr Medicine Dept D-3100 Med Ctr N Nashville TN 37232-0001 Home Phone: 615-385-4575; Office Phone: 615-322-2150.

HARRIS, RICHARD JOHN, social sciences educator; b. Belgrade, Minn., Apr. 5, 1948; s. Johnny Lee and Marjorie (Meyers) H.; m. Carolyn Besser (div. 1993); children: Karl, Mark; m. Juanita M. Gillette Firestone, Apr. 18, 1994. BA, Macalester Coll., 1971; MA, Cornell U., 1974, PhD, 1976. From asst. to full prof. U. Tex., San Antonio, 1976—, rsch. prof. Ctr. for Policy Studies, 2006—07. Project dir. Alamo Area Cmty. Info. Sys., 2000—04; vis. prof. Univ. Klagenfurt, Austria, 2002; sr. faculty rschr. Defense Equal Opportunity Mgmt. Inst., Patrick AFB, Fla., 2007—09, 2011; disting. vis. prof. US Air Force Acad., Colo., 2009—10. Contbr. articles to profl. jours.; editor: The Politics of San Antonio: Community Progress and Power, 1983. Active Odyssey of the Mind, San Antonio Sch. Sys., 1994-95; mem. faculty adv. com. U. Tex. Sys., Austin, 1994-96; sec. gen. faculty U. Tex., 1991-96. Staff sgt. USAFR, 1969-74. Recipient cert. of achievement Black Legis. Caucus, U.S. Congress, 1996; postdoctoral fellow U. So. Calif., 1980-82. Mem. Am. Sociol. Assn., Population Assn. of Am., Am. Acad. Polit. and Social Scis., Southwestern Social Sci. Assn., Tex. Econ. and Demographic Assn. (bd. dirs.), Alpha Kappa Delta. Office: Univ Tex San Antonio Dept Social Work San Antonio TX 78249

HARRIS, RICHARD LEE, engineering executive, retired military officer; b. Bellevue, Pa., Dec. 26, 1928; s. Everette Lee and Marjorie Anna (Messer) H.; m. Patricia Ann Walton, Dec. 12, 1953; children: Sandra Jo, Carole Jill, William Walton, Robert Lee. BS, U.S. Mil. Acad., West Point, NY, 1951; student, Army Engr. Sch., 1951-59; MS, MIT, 1956; grad., Oak Ridge Sch. Reactor Tech., 1957, Command and Gen. Staff Coll., 1963, Nat. War Coll., 1967. Designated sr. parachutist, nuclear reactor comdr. registered profl. engr., Pa., Tex. Commd. 2d lt. U.S. Army, 1951, advanced through grades to maj. gen., 1973; with (32d Engrs. Combat Bn.), 1951; co-comdr. (13th Engrs. Combat Bn., 7th Inf. Divsn.), Korea, 1952-53; res. engr. (Phila. Engrs. Dist.), 1953-54; engrs. supply officer Columbus Depot, 1954-55; tech. ops. officer AEC, NYC, 1957-59; officer in charge (SM-1A Nuclear Power Plant), Alaska, 1960-62; with (U.S. STRIKE Command), 1963-65; bn. comdr. (20th Engrs. Combat Bn.), Vietnam, 1965-66; with Office Chief of Staff, U.S. Army, 1967-68, Hdqrs. U.S. Army Pacific, 1968-70; comdr. divsn. support command (1st Cav. Divsn.), Vietnam, 1970-71; asst. comdt. Army Engrs. Sch., 1971-73; dir. mgmt. info. sys. Office Chief Staff Army, Hdqrs. Dept. Army, 1973-76; comdr. U.S. Army Tng. Ctr.-Engr. and Ft. Leonard Wood, Mo., 1976-78; divsn. engr. North Ctrl. Engr. Divsn., 1978-80; ret., 1980; v.p. Radian Corp., Austin, 1980-93; ret., 1993. Decorated D.S.M., Legion of Merit with 4 oak leaf clusters, Bronze Star with 2 oak leaf clusters, Air medal with 4 numerals, Joint Services Commendation medal, Purple Heart. Fellow: Soc. Am. Mil. Engrs.; mem.: Mil. Officers Assn., Assn. U. S. Army, Phi Kappa Phi. Home: 8817 Balcones Club Dr Austin TX 78750-3042 Personal E-mail: richardlharris@msn.com.

HARRIS, ROBERT SHIELDS, finance educator; b. Eden, NC, Nov. 6, 1949; married; 2 children. BA in economics summa cum laude, Davidson Coll., 1971; PhD in economics, Princeton U., 1977. Faculty Wharton Sch. Bus., U. Pa., 1975-78, Kenan-Flagler Bus. Sch., U. NC, Chapel Hill, 1978—88, U. Va. Darden Sch. Bus., Charlottesville, 1988—, assoc. dean faculty, 1990—93, Charles C. Abbott prof. bus. adminstrn., dean, 2001—05, C. Stewart Sheppard prof. bus. adminstrn., 2005—; v.p., chief learning officer United Tech. Corp., 1998—2001. Vis. prof. London Grad. Sch. Bus.; vis. scholar Oxford U.; cons. and expert witness in field. Assoc. editor: Fin. Mgmt., Jour. Fin. Rsch., Fin. Review, Jour. Applied Fin., author: books, articles, cases and tutorials. Mem.: Williamsburg Investment Trust (bd. chair), Fin. Mgmt. Assn. (past v.p. fin. edn., trustee). Office: University Va Darden Sch Bus PO Box 6550 Charlottesville VA 22906-6550 Office Phone: 434-924-4823. Business E-Mail: HarrisR@darden.virginia.edu.

HARRIS, RUTH HORTENSE COLES, retired accounting educator; b. Charlottesville, Va., Sept. 26, 1928; d. Bernard Albert and Ruth Hortense (Wyatt) Coles; m. John Benjamin Harris, Sept. 2, 1950; children: John Benjamin Jr., Vita Michelle. BS, Va. State U., 1948; MBA, NYU, 1949; EdD, Coll. William and Mary, 1977; LHD, Va. Union U., 1998. CPA, Va. Instr. commerce dept. Va. Union U., Richmond, 1949—53, asst prof., 1953—64; head dept., 1956—69; assoc. prof., head dept. Va. Union U., Richmond, 1964—69, prof., dir. divsn. commerce, 1969—73, dir. Sydney Lewis Sch. Bus. Adminstrn., 1973—81, prof. acctg., 1981—85, 1987—97, chmn. dept., 1987—97, mem. mgmt. team Sch. Bus., 1985—87, disting. prof. emeritus, 1997—. Bd. dirs. Am. Assembly Collegiate Schs. Bus., St. Louis, 1976-79; mem. adv. bd. Intercollegiate Case Clearing House, 1976-79; mem. state adv. coun. Cmty. Svc. and Continuing Edn. (Title I) Agy., Charlottesville, 1977-81. Chmn. Interdeptl. Com. on Rate-Setting for Children's Facilities, Richmond, 1983-85; bd. dirs. Richmond Urban League; mem. agy. evaluation comn. United Way Greater Richmond; mem. fin. sec. Va. Commonwealth chpt. Nat. Coalition 100 Black Women; participant Va. Heroes, Inc., Richmond, 1991-94, 96. Recipient tchg. excellence award Sears Roebuck Found., 1990, Outstanding Faculty award Va. Coun. for Higher Edn., 1992, Eboné Image award No. Va. chpt. Nat. Coalition of 100 Black Women, 1993,

Serwa award Va. Commonwealth chpt., Nat. Coalition 100 Black Women, 1989, Tenneco Excellence in Tchg. award United Negro Coll. Fund, 1995; named Belle Ringer of Richmond, 1992, Richmond Br. Nat. Assn. U. Women; Hon. award Dominion Power's Strong Men and Women, 1998. Mem. AICPA (Outstanding Va. Educator award), AARP (Cmty. Svc. award 2005), Va. Soc. CPA (com., Outstanding Va. Educator award, Disting. Career in Acctg. Edn. award). Baptist. Achievements include first African-American female CPA in Commonwealth of Virginia. Avocations: ringing handbells, reading, playing piano. Home: 2816 Edgewood Ave Richmond VA 23222-3518 Personal E-mail: hortense2@aol.com.

HARRIS, SCOTT BLAKE, lawyer; b. NYC, June 18, 1951; s. Stanley Robert and Adele Jean (Ganger) Harris; m. Barbara Straughn, Aug. 5, 1978. AB magna cum laude, Brown U., 1973; JD magna cum laude, Harvard U., 1976. Bar: DC 1977, US Ct. Appeals (DC cir.) 1978, US Supreme Ct. 1983. Law clk. to Hon. Gerhard A. Gissell US Dist. Ct. DC, Washington, 1976-77; assoc. Williams & Connolly LLP, Washington, 1977-84, ptnr., 1984-93; chief counsel Bur. Export Adminstrn., US Dept. Commerce, Washington, 1993-94; chief internat. bur. FCC, Washington, 1994-96; ptnr. Gibson, Dunn & Crutcher LLP, Washington, 1996-98; mng. ptnr. Harris, Wiltshire & Grannis LLP, Washington, 1998—2009; gen. counsel US Dept. Energy, Washington, 2009—11; exec. v.p. legal & external affairs NeuStar, Inc., Sterling, Va., 2011—. Mem. adv. bd. Ctr. Wireless Tech., Va. Tech. U., 1996—2003; adj. prof. Georgetown U. Law Ctr., 1996, 2001—02. Columnist: Aviation Week, 2000—01, Space News, 2001—05. Trustee Fed. Comm. Bar Assn. Found., 1997—2000. Recipient Marconi-Bell award, Nat. Assn. Radio & TV Engineers, 2004. Mem.: ABA (co-chair telecom. com., sect. internat. law 1999—2002), US ITU Assn. (bd. dirs. 1999—2003), Fed. Comm. Bar Assn. (co-chair online comm. com. 2000—02, co-chair legislation com. 2004—05, co-chair annual seminar 2006—08), Phi Beta Kappa. Office: NeuStar Inc 21575 RidgeTop Cir Sterling VA 20166 Office Phone: 571-434-5400.

HARRISON, C. LASH, lawyer; BBA, Emory U., Ga., 1962, LLB, 1965. Bar: Ga. Mng. ptnr. Ford & Harrison LLP, Atlanta, 1978—, chmn. of exec. com. Mem. bd. visitors Emory U., 1999—2002, mem. exec. com.; mem. Emory U. Law Sch. Coun.; bd. trustees Trinity Sch., chmn. of bd. Named one of The Best Lawyers in America, Labor and Employment Law; named to Ga. Super Lawyers, Law & Politics mag. Mem.: ABA, Ga. Bar. Assn., Atlanta Bar Assn. Office: Ford & Harrison LLP 271 17th St NW Ste 1900 Atlanta GA 30363 Office Phone: 404-888-3801. Office Fax: 404-888-3863. Business E-Mail: lharrison@fordharrison.com.

HARRISON, CLIFFORD, chef, small business owner; Grad., Calif. Culinary Inst., San Francisco, 1987; postgrad, U. Hawaii. Chef, co-owner Bacchanalia, Atlanta, Floataway Cafe, Ga., Quinines; chef with Judy Rogers Zuni Cafe, San Francisco; chef with Bob Kinkead 21 Federal, Nantucket Island, Mass.; chef Bimini Twist, NY, La Petite Ferme, NY, Grolier Club, NY. Elected mem. James Beard Found. Named one of America's Best New Chefs, Food & Wine mag., 1995. Office: Bacchanalia 1198 Howell Mill Rd Atlanta GA 30318

HARRISON, DAVID GLENN, medical educator, cardiologist; BS, Okla. State U., Stillwater, 1970; MD, U. Okla., Okla. City, 1974. Cert. internal medicine Nat. Bd. Examiners, 1976, cardiovasc. diseases 1979. Intern Duke Hosp., Durham, NC, 1974—75, resident, 1975—77; fellow Duke U., 1977—79; clinical instr. U. NC, Charlotte, 1979—80; clinical cardiologist Nalle Clinic, Charlotte, 1979—80, U. Iowa, Iowa City, 1980—90, fellow, 1980—82, assoc. in cardiovasc. Coll. Medicine, 1980—82, asst. prof. medicine, 1982—87, dir. sect. cardiology, 1984—89, assoc. prof. medicine, 1987—90; prof. medicine Emory U. Sch. Medicine, Atlanta, 1990—, interim dir., 1999—2000, dir. cardiology, 2000—; dir. sect. cardiology Atlanta VA Hosp., 1991—94, 1998—2000. Mem. Iowa affiliate study sect. Am. Heart Assn., 1982—85, mem. Great Plains regional review com. study sect., 1983—88, mem. com. regional and nat. rsch., 1987—88, chmn. Great Plains regional review study sect., 1987—88, mem. nat. review com. study sect., 1987—90, chmn. credentials com., 1992—94, mem. vascular biology study sect., 1991—94, mem. nat. study sect. vascular biology, 1992—95, chmn. marcus selection com., 1993—95, mem. exec. com. coun. on circulation, 1993—95, chmn. sci. conf. planning com., 1993—95, vice chmn. exec. com. coun. on circulation, 1995—98, chmn. exec. com. coun. on circulation, 1998—99, mem. program com. coun. basic cardiovasc. sciences, 1999—2000, mem. rsch. planning and evaluation com., 2000—01, fellow coun. basic cardiovasc. sciences, 2001—, mem. rsch. com., 2002—04; mem. med. student adv. com. U. Iowa, 1983—84, mem. house staff adv. com., 1983—90, mem. U. aminal care com., 1983—90, mem. house staff evaluation com., 1986—90, mem. promotions com., 1988—90; chmn. merit review study sect. VA, 1990—94; mem. NIH experimental cardiovasc. sciences study sect., 1992—97, 1993—95; mem. sci. adv. com. Atherogenics, Inc., 1995—; mem. rsch. planning Emory U. Health Svcs. Ctr., 1997; mem. rsch. strategic planning, dept. medicine Emory U., 2000; mem. sci. adv. bd. VasoPharm, Inc., 2000—; mem. adv. bd. Novartis Angiotensin/ARB, 2000—; mem. heart ctr. steering com. Emory Heart Ctr., 2002—; mem. governing bd. Carlyle Frazier Heart Ctr. Crawford Long Hosp., 2003—; mem. Proteomics, Chemical and Structural Biology Strategic Planning com., 2003—. Mem. editl. bd. Circulation, 1990—94, Journal of Cardiovascular Pharmacology, 1991—, Trends in Cardiovascular Medicine, 1992—93, Endothelium, 1992—96, Journal of Vascular Medicine and Biology, 1993—98, Circulation Research, 1995—, Journal of Clinical Investigation, 1997—, Arteriosclerosis, Thrombosis and Vascular Biology, 1999—, Hypertension, 2000—. Recipient Individual Nat. Rsch. Svc. award, NIH, 1980, Clinical Investigator award, 1981, Clinician Scientist award, Am. Heart Assn., 1981, Established Investigator award, 1987, Novartis award for Hypertension Rsch., 2004, Disting. Achievement award, 2003, J. Willis Hurst Internal Medicine Residency Program Mentorship award, Emory U., 2004. Mem.: Oxygen Soc., Am. Assn. U. Cardiologists, Soc. Vascular Medicine and Biology, Am. Soc. Clinical Investigation, Am. Physiol. Soc. (fellow cardiovasc. sect. 1988—), Ctrl. Soc. Clinical Rsch., Am. Fedn. Clinical Rsch. Midwest Sect., Assn. Am. Physicians. Office: Woodruff Meml Bldg Rm 319 Emory U 1639 Pierce Dr Atlanta GA 30322 Office Phone: 404-727-8386. Office Fax: 404-727-3585. Business E-Mail: dhar02@emory.edu.

HARRISON, EMMETT BRUCE, JR., corporate communications counselor; b. Lanett, Ala., Apr. 3, 1932; s. Emmett Bruce and JeNelle (Williams) H.; m. Patricia DeStacy, Aug. 26, 1973; children by previous marriage: Susan, Emmett, Joe. AB, U. Ala., 1954; postgrad., Cath. U. Am., 1966-67. Mng. editor Talladega (Ala.) News, 1955; polit. reporter Columbus (Ga.) Ledger, 1956; adminstrv. asst. to U.S. Rep. K.A. Roberts Washington, 1957-61; pub. rels. dir. Mfg. Chemists' Assn., Washington, 1961-69; v.p. Freeport Minerals Co., NYC, 1969-73; pres. Harrison Assocs., Washington, 1973-77; pres., chmn. E. Bruce Harrison Co., Inc., Washington, 1978—97; chmn., CEO EnviroComm Internat., 1992—. Instr. bus. studies Georgetown U. Washington DC; bd. dirs. PR News. Author: Going Green: How to Communicate Your Company's Environmental Commitment, 1993, Corporate Greening 2.O: Create and Communicate Your Company's Climate Change and Sustainability Strategies, 2008, Leadership Comms, 2012, How Leaders Communicate in the Modern American Corporation, 2014; prodr. plays at Dramarena, NYC, Washington Theatre Club and Arena Stage, Washington, 1966-69. Asst. press mgr. J.F. Kennedy campaign Ala., 1960; mem. U.S. Coun. Internat. Bus.; del. UN Conf. on Environ., Rio de Janiero, 1992, People to People Amb. to China, 2005. Named Outstanding Journalism Grad., U. Ala., 1954; named to 100 Most Influential Pub. Rels. People in the 20th Century PR Week mag., 2000, Washington Pub. Rels. Hall of Fame, 2000; recipient AP Radio award, 1956, Nat. Endowment of Arts Play award, 1969, Betsy Plank award, U. Ala. Comm. Dept., 2003. Fellow Pub. Rels. Soc. Am. (named Top 100 People 20th Century award 2000, Washington PR Hall Fame 2000), Counselors Acad. (chair 1990—), Arthur W. Page Soc. (bd. 1989-96, sec. 1994-96, exec. dir. 1997-98; Disting. Svc. award 2009), Pa. State U. Oral History, Nat. Press Club, Senate Press Secs. Club, Chemists Club N.Y., Soc. Profl. Journalists (bd. 2003-06), Guest Svcs. Inc. (bd. 1998-2001), Washington Golf and Country Club, Sigma Delta Chi (bd. com. 1991-93), Omicron Delta Kappa, Pi Kappa Phi. Methodist. Home: 3201 N Vermont St Arlington VA 22207-4480 Office Phone: 202-204-3077. Business E-Mail: bruceharrison@envirocomm.com.

HARRISON, ESTHER M., state legislator; b. Columbus, Miss. Mem. Dist. 41 Miss. House of Reps., 2000—, chair state libr. com., mem. edn. com., interstate cooperation com., Medicaid com., ports, harbors and airports com., univs. and colls. com. Mem.: SCLC, NAACP, League Voters, NANBPW, Eastern Star, Zeta Phi Beta. Democrat. African Methodist Episcopal. Mailing: 924 S 7th St Columbus MS 39701 Office Phone: 601-359-9390. E-mail: eharrison@house.ms.gov.

HARRISON, FAYE VENETIA, anthropologist, educator, writer; b. Norfolk, Va., Nov. 25, 1951; d. James and Odelia Blount (Harper) Harrison; m. William Louis Conwill, May 17, 1980; children: Giles Harrison-Conwill, L. Mondlane Harrison-Conwill, Justin Harrison-Conwill. AB, Brown U., 1974; MA, Stanford U., 1977, PhD, 1982. Asst. prof. anthropology U. Louisville, 1983-89; assoc. prof. U. Tenn., Knoxville, 1989-97, prof., 1999—2004, Lindsay Young prof. in humanities, 2002—04; prof., grad. dir. women's studies U. S.C., Columbia, 1997-99; prof. anthropology and African Am. studies U. Fla., Gainesville, 2004—, dir. African-Am. studies, 2007—10. Adj. assoc. prof. U.Binghamton, SUNY, 1996—98; adj. prof. Union Inst. and U., 2002—05; internat. assoc. Ctr. Culture, Identity, and Edn., U. British Columbia, 2007—; vis. prof. U. Suriname, 2011. Author: Outsider Within: Reworking Anthropology in the Global Age, 2008; editor, contbg. author: Black Folks in Cities Here and There, 1988, Decolonizing Anthropology, 1991, 2d edit., 1997; editor, contbg. author 3rd edit., 2010; editor, contbg. author: W.E.B. DuBois and Anthropology, 1992, American Anthropologist Contemporary Forum: Race and Racism, 1998, African-American Pioneers in Anthropology, 1999, Resisting Racism and Xenophobia, 2005, assoc. editor: Urban Anthropology, 1992—2010, cons. editor: Women and Aging, 1990—96, Identities: Global Studies of Culture and Power, 1992—2010; mem. editl. com. Critique of Anthropology, 1995—99, Annual Rev. Anthropology, 1995—2000, Am. Anthropologist, 2000—05, mem. editl. bd. U. Tenn. Press, 1996—97, mem. adv. com. Womanist Theory and Rsch., 1990—2004, Transforming Anthropology, 1990—; author, performer: (one woman show) The Other Side of Paradise; Three Women; One Struggle; contbr. articles to profl. jours. & chapters in anthologies. Mem. Nat. Alliance Against Racist and Polit. Repression, 1973—89, Black Women Organized for Power, Lousiville, 1984—86, Alliance Against Women's Oppression, Lousiville, 1988—89, E. Tenn. Coalition Against State Killing, 1995—97, 1999—2004, So. Human Rights Organizers Network, 2000—; organizer Ky. Rainbow Coalition, Lousiville, 1987—89; mem. Sister Song Reproductive Health & Rights Collective, 2002—; mem. adv. bd. Knoxville Roman Cath. Diocese's Justice, Peace, Integrity of Creation, 1996—97, St. Francis House (for homeless), 2010—; mem. Ky. Alliance Against Recist & Polit. Repression, 1988—. Recipient Cert. of Merit, U. Louisville Pres. Office, 1989, Phi Beta Kappa U. Tenn. chpt., 1993, Hardy Liston, Jr. Symbol of Hope award for Promotion Cultural Diversity, U. Tenn. Commn. Blacks, 2003, Disting. Contbn. to Study of N.Am. award, Soc. Anthropology N.Am., 2004, Zora Neale Hurston award, Southern Anthrop. Soc., 2007, President's Award, Amer. Anthrop. Assoc., 2007, Legacy Scholar Award, Assoc. Black Anthropologists, 2010; Ford Found. fellow, 1987—88, Andrew W. Mellon Visiting fellowship, U. Cape Town, Spring, 2011. Mem.: Internat. Union Anthrop. and Ethnol. Scis. (co-chair commn. anthropology women 1993—98, chair commn. anthropology women 1998—2009, mem.-at-large, exec. com. 2003—13, pres. 2013—), Assn. Black Anthropologists (pres. 1989—91, Legacy Scholar award 2010), Am. Anthrop. Assn. (exec. bd. dirs. 1990—91, 1999—2001, ann. meeting exec. program chair 2007, mem. comm. World Anthropologies 2007, chair sub com. tchg. rsch. 2010—11, mem. standing com. World Anthropology). Avocations: art, theater, dance. Office: Univ Fla Turlington Hall Gainesville FL 32611 Personal E-mail: fevenetia@yahoo.com.

HARRISON, GAIL L., retired insurance company executive; b. Danbury, Conn., Aug. 18, 1947; d. Richard Frank and Lucille R. Harrison; m. Larry T. Suiters, Aug. 2, 1987; 1 child, Michael Leighton Suiters. BA in Govt., Cornell U., 1969. Rsch. and legis. asst. Senator Walter F. Mondale, Washington, 1969—76; issues dir., speechwriter Mondale Vice Presdl. Campaign, Washington, 1976; asst. to v.p., issues devel V.P. Walter F. Mondale, 1977—80; founder, ptnr., founding prin. Wexler Group, 1981; exec. v.p., prin. Powell Tate (divsn. of Weber Shandwick Worldwide), 2000—07. Bd. dirs. Allmerica Fin. Corp., Worcester, Mass.; trustee, prin. Coun. for Excellence in Govt., Washington, 1994—; trustee Bryce Harlow Found., Washington, 1998—. Mem. parenting group St. Peter's Ch., 1993—. N.Y. State Regent's schoalr, 1965-69. Mem. Forum on Religion and Diplomacy, Mortar Board, Phi Beta Kappa. Episcopalian. Avocations: golf, reading.

HARRISON, GEORGE BROOKS, engineer, researcher, retired military officer; b. Greenville, SC, July 30, 1940; s. William Henry and Mary Carter (Ogburn) Harrison; m. Pennie Maria Jenkins, Nov. 29, 1963; children: Taylor Leigh, Todd Henry, Tracy Elizabeth. BS in Engring. and Pub. Policy, USAF Acad., 1962; MBA, U. Pa., 1970. Cert. flight instr. single and multi-engine instrument glider, lic. airline transport pilot. Commd. 2d lt. USAF, 1962, advanced through grades to maj. gen., 1989; fighter pilot, forward air contr. and instr. 557th and 436th Tactical Fighter Squadron, Fla., Vietnam, 1963—69; joint exercise planner U.S. Readiness Command, MacDill AFB, Fla., 1971-74; grad. Armed Forces Staff Coll., Norfolk, Va., 1974; ops. officer 13th and 25th Tactical Fighter Squadron, Udorn, Thailand, 1974-75; comdr. 4485th Test Squadron, Eglin AFB, Fla., 1975-78; grad. Air War Coll., Montgomery, Ala., 1979; wing comdr. 479th Tactical Tng. Wing, Holloman AFB, N.Mex., 1982-86; chief joint ops. divsn. Orgn. of Joint Chiefs of Staff, Washington, 1984-86; dept. chief staff plans USAF Europe, Ramstein AFB, Germany, 1986-89, dep. chief staff ops., 1991-92; asst. chief staff studies and analyses Hdqrs. USAF, Washington, 1989-91; comdr. Air Warfare Ctr., Eglin AFB, Fla., 1992-93; comdr. combined/joint task force USAF, S.W. Asia, 1993; comdr. Air Force Operational Test and Evaluation Ctr., Kirtland AFB, N.Mex., 1994-97; prin. rsch. engr., assoc. dir. Ga. Tech Rsch. Inst., 1997—; mil. affairs cons. CNN, 1997—. Mem. sci. adv. bd. USAF, Washington, 1998—; sponsor Mil. Ops. Rsch. Soc., 1989—91; U.S. del. NATO Adv. Group Aerospace R & D, Paris, 1989—91; lectr. to mil., tech. and civic groups, 1982—. Contbr. articles to mil. jours. Mem., lt. col. CAP, SC, N.Mex., Ga., 1978—; dist. commr. Boy Scouts Am., Germany, 1986—89, coun. commr., 1991—92, exec. coun. N.Mex., 1995—97; exec. v.p., bd. dirs. Air Warrior Courage Found., 1998—; bd. dirs. Nat. Mus. Aviation, 1998—, Ga. Aviation Hall of Fame, 2005; mem. Atlanta Regional Airport Authority. Decorated DSM with oak leaf cluster, DFC, Air medal with eleven oak leaf clusters, Legion of Merit with one oak leaf cluster, Def. Superior Svc. medal; recipient Lt. Gen. Glen Kent Leadership award, USAF, 2005. Fellow: Beta Gamma Sigma; mem.: Air Force Assn., Quiet Birdmen, Order of Daedalians (flight capt. 1987—89, 2003—05). Baptist. Avocation: aviation. Home: 109 Middleton Dr Peachtree City GA 30269 Office: Ga Tech Rsch Inst 250 14th St NW # 548 Atlanta GA 30318-5712 Home Phone: 404-358-8120; Office Phone: 404-407-7136. Business E-Mail: george.harrison@gtri.gatech.edu.

HARRISON, GORDON RAY, retired engineering executive, consultant, research scientist; b. Wister, Okla., Dec. 14, 1931; s. Trannie Gordon and Isah Lee (Ray) H.; m. Barbara Ann Herndon, June 22, 1957; children: William Andrew, Melissa Leigh, Lori Jeanne, Amanda Ray. BS in Physics, U. Central Ark., 1952; MS, Vanderbilt U., 1954, PhD, 1958. Sr. staff engr. and engring. mgr. Sperry Microwave, Clearwater, Fla., 1957-71; prin. research scientist to lab. dir. Engring. Expt. Sta., Ga. Inst. Tech., Atlanta, 1971-83; v.p. Electromagnetic Scis., Inc., Atlanta, 1983-91; ind. cons. tech., bus., 1991—2010. Contbr. chpt. to book, numerous articles to profl. jours.; patentee microwave ferrimagnetic garnets. Fellow IEEE; mem. Soc. Microwave Theory and Techniques, Magnetics Soc., Mustang Club Am., Sigma Xi. Democrat. Methodist. Personal E-mail: bahgrh@bellsouth.net.

HARRISON, GUY (O.L. HARRISON IV), consulting firm executive; b. Dallas, Oct. 22, 1971; s. Orrin Lea and Paula Diane Harrison; m. Tandy Claycombe, Nov. 18, 1995; 1 child. BA in Govt., Dartmouth Coll., Hanover, NH, 1994. Assoc. US House Rules Comm., 1998—99; legis. dir. to Rep. Pete Sessions, US House of Reps., 1999—2000, chief of staff, 2000—08, dep. legis. dir., 1997—98; exec. dir. Nat. Republican Congressional Com. (NRCC), Washington, 2008—12; ptnr. OnMessage Inc., Alexandria, Va., 2013—. Named one of The Fabulous 50, Roll Call, 2009. Mem.: Univ. Club, Washington DC, Theta Delta Chi. Republican. Episcopalian. Office: OnMessage Inc 815 Slaters Ln 1st Fl Alexandria VA 22314 Office Phone: 703-683-3806.*

HARRISON, J. KEVIN, cardiologist, educator; MD, NYU, 1984. Diplomate Am. Bd. Internal Medicine, 1988, Am. Bd. Internal Medicine-cardiovasc. disease, 2001, Am. Bd. Internal Medicine-interventional cardiology, 2003. Resident internal medicine Johns Hopkins Hosp., Balt., 1984—87; fellow cardiovasc. disease Duke Univ. Med. Ctr., Durham, NC, 1988—90, hosp. affiliation includes; prof. medicine Duke Univ., Durham, NC. Office: Duke University Medical Center PO BOX 3331 Durham NC 27710 Office Phone: 919-681-3763. Office Fax: 919-681-9774.

HARRISON, JAIME R., political organization administrator, communications executive; BA, Yale U.; JD, Georgetown U. COO, dir. program devel. Coll. Summit Inc.; dir. floor ops., counsel for House Majority Whip James Clyburn US House of Representatives; exec. dir. House Dem. Caucus; prin. Podesta Group, Washington; first vice chair SC Dem. Party, Columbia, chair, 2013—. Named one of Fabulous Fifty Moves and Shakers Behind the Scenes on Capitol Hill, Roll Call, 35 Stellar Staffers Under 35, The Hill, 100 Emerging and Established African-American Leaders Who Are Making Extraordinary Contributions, The Root mag., 2010, Top 40 Lawyers Under 40, Nat. Bar Assn. and Impact DC. Democrat. Office: SC Democratic Party PO Box 5965 Columbia SC 29250 also: Podesta Group Ste 1000 W 1001 G St NW Washington DC 20001 Office Phone: 202-879-9301. E-mail: jaime@scdp.org, jharrison@podestagroup.com.

HARRISON, JAMES HODGES, state legislator; b. Greenwood, SC, Apr. 11, 1951; s. William H. and Mary H. Harrison; m. Pamela Ann Salley, 1977; children: Catherine Salley, Molly Tarrant. BA, The Citadel, 1973; JD, U. SC, 1976. Pvt. practice, 1976—78, 1990—; gen. counsel SC Alcoholic Beverage Control Commn., 1978—89; mem. Dist. 75 SC House of Reps., 1989—, chair Judiciary Com., mem. Subcommittee on Constl. Laws. Col. USAR, 1976—2003. Mem.: SC & Richland County Bar Assn., East Columbia Rotary. Republican. Presbyterian. Office: 512 Blatt Bldg Columbia SC 29201 Home: 1639 Williams St Apt 200 Columbia SC 29201-2267 Home Phone: 803-783-0777; Office Phone: 803-734-3120, 803-256-0049. E-mail: hju@legis.lpitr.state.sc.us.

HARRISON, JOE, state legislator; BBA, Nicholls State U. Fin. planner; mem. Dist. 51 La. House of Reps., 2008—, mem. appropriations com., judiciary com., natural resources and environment com., joint legis. com. on the budget. Republican. Office: Capitol Office State Capitol PO Box 44486 Baton Rouge LA 70804 Home: PO Box 1809 Gray LA 70359-1809 Office Phone: 800-935-2081, 225-342-6945. Office Fax: 985-655-9011. E-mail: harrisoj@legis.state.la.us.

HARRISON, JOHN D., state banking agency administrator; m. Barbara Harrison; 5 children. B in Bus. Adminstrn. and Mktg., Troy U., 1967; grad., La. State U. Grad. Sch. Banking, 1988. Ptnr., v.p. C&H Trucking Co., Inc., 1976—97; owner, pres. Crenshaw Land and Timber Co., 1981—; CEO First Citizens Bank of Luverne, 1983—2003; mayor Luverne, Ala., 1988—2003; dir. Ala. Dept. Cmty. and Econ. Affairs, 2003—05; supt. Ala. State Banking Dept., 2005—. Bd. trustees Ala. Forestry Assn. Forest Fund. Bd. trustees Troy U. Named Alumnus of Yr., Troy U., 1992. Office: Alabama State Banking Department PO Box 4600 Montgomery AL 36103-4600 Office Phone: 334-242-3585. Office Fax: 334-242-3500. E-mail: john.harrison@banking.alabama.gov.

HARRISON, JOHN RAYMOND, foundation administrator, retired publishing executive; b. Des Moines, June 8, 1933; s. Raymond Harrison and Dorothy (Stout) Harrison Cohen; m. Lois Cowles, June 24, 1955 (div. Apr. 1981); children: Gardner Mark, Kent Alfred (dec.), John Patrick, Lois Eleanor; m. Mary Gee MacQueen, Sept. 5, 1981 (div. 2000); m. Bonnie Lynne Anderson, Aug. 26, 2000; stepchildren: Jennifer Alicia Stuart, Michael Christopher Anderson. Grad., Phillips Exeter Acad., 1951; AB, Harvard U., 1955, postgrad. Sch. Bus., 1955-56; DHL (hon.), Fla. So. Coll. With various papers throughout the U.S.; vice pres. N.Y. Times Co., ret.; chmn. Harrison Charitable Found., Sarasota, Fla. Dir. Internat. Herald-Tribune, Paris, 1974-91. Bd. dirs. Ft. Pierce (Fla.)-St. Lucie County Indsl. Devel. Coun., 1959-62, Ft. Pierce Meml. Hosp., 1959-62, Lincoln Pk. Child Care Ctr., Ft. Pierce, 1959-62, Gainesville United Fund, 1965, Boys Club Gainesville, 1965, U. Fla. Found., 1967, YMCA Greater Lakeland, 1967-69, Human Rels. Coun. Lakeland, 1967-69, Boys Club Lakeland, ARC, 1967-69; trustee Robert H. Anderson Found., Ridge Sch., Bartow, Fla., High Mus., 1988-94; mem. Pres.'s Resources Coun. Wellesley (Mass.) Coll.; mem. bd. counsellors Fla. So. Coll., 1974; mem. bd. visitors Emory U., 1984, pres., 1986; trustee Westminster

Schs., 1989-92, Kennesaw State Coll. Found.; mem. bd. councillors Carter Presdl. Ctr.; mem. bd. overseers Harvard U., 1995-2001; bd. trustees Ringing Sch. Art and Design, 2003. Recipient Pulitzer Prize for editl. writing, 1965, Nat Headliners award for pub. svc. editl. writing, Nat. Headliners Club, 1972, Walker Stone award for editl. writing Scripps-Howard Found., 1974, 76, Silver Gavel award for pub. svc. editls. ABA, 1977, Sigma Delta Chi Bronze medal, 1970, 73. Mem. Greater Lakeland C. of C. (dir. 1966-67), Associated Harvard Alumni (dir. 1979-82), Spee Club, Hasty Pudding Inst. 1770 (grad. dir.), Harvard Club (N.Y.C., Boston, Ga. bd. dirs.), Oaks Club-Sarasota, Fla.

HARRISON, KEVIN CHARLES, US marshal; b. 1953; BA, Nicholls State U., Thibodaux, La., 1976. Trooper La. State Police, 1979—86, chief dep. Assumption Parish Sheriff's Office Napoleonville, La., 1984; various positions of increasing responsibility DEA, 1986—2005, asst. spl. agent in charge New Orleans, 2005—10; US marshal (mid. dist.) La. US Dept. Justice, Baton Rouge, 2010—. Office: US Courthouse 777 Florida St Room G 48 Baton Rouge LA 70801 Office Phone: 225-389-0364.

HARRISON, LYNN HENRY, JR., cardiovascular surgeon, educator; b. Oklahoma City, Jan. 8, 1944; s. Lynn Henry and Vera Alice (Pritchett) H.; m. Lura Ann Wright, June 21, 1969; children: Parker, Tyler. BA, Yale U., 1966; MD, U. Okla., 1970. Diplomate Am. Bd. Surgery, Am. Bd. Thoracic Surgery. Clin. assoc. surgery Nat. Heart and Lung Inst., Bethesda, Md., 1972-74; resident surgery Duke University, Durham, NC, 1970-72, 74-78, teaching scholar surgery, 1978-79; asst. prof. surgery U. Okla. Sch. Medicine, Oklahoma City, 1979-84; clin. asst. prof. La. State U. Sch. Medicine, New Orleans, 1986-89, clin. assoc. prof., 1989, assoc. prof. surgery, chief sect. cardiovascular surgery, 1993-98, prof. surgery, 1998—, Craighead chair surgery, 2002; ptnr. The O'Neill Surg. Group, New Orleans, 1984-91; pres. Crescent Surg. Assocs., Marrero, La., 1991-93; prof., chief cardiac surgery U. Mass., Worcester, 2006—09; clin. dir. cardiac surgery Baptist Health Cardiac & Thoracic Surgical Group, Miami, 2009—. Pres. Southern Soc. Clin. Surgeons, Washington, 2005—06. Contbr. articles to numerous profl. publs. Bd. dirs. Ballet Okla., Oklahoma City, 1983-85. With, 1972—74, Bethesda, Md. Recipient Alan J. Stanley prize, U. Okla. Sch. Medicine, 1967. Fellow ACS (counselor La. chpt. 1988—, pres. 1995, gov. 1998-2004); mem. Assn. Acad. Surgery, Soc. Thoracic Surgeons, Am. Assn. Thoracic Surgery, So. Surg. Assn., Surg. Assn. of La. (pres. 1996), Andrew G. Morrow Soc., David C. Sabiston Jr. Surg. Soc., Timberlane Country Club (bd. dirs.). Avocations: golf, hunting. Office: Baptist Health 8900 N Kendall Dr Miami FL 33176 Office Phone: 786-596-5991.

HARRISON, MICHAEL, state legislator; b. Sept. 9, 1958; married; 2 children. State rep. Dist. 9, Tenn., 2003—; former Hancock county exec. sessions judge. Mem.: Rural Health Assoc. Tenn., NE Cmty. Svcs. Sneedville, NE Regional Health Coun., Hancock Cmty. Partners. Republican. Baptist. Office: 115 Green Acres Dr Rogersville TN 37857-5183 also: 206-A War Memorial Bldg Nashville TN 37243-0109 Office Phone: 615-741-7480. Office Fax: 615-253-0210. Business E-Mail: rep.mike.harrison@capitol.tn.gov.

HARRISON, PHILIP, architect; BA in Visual Arts and Philosophy, Harvard U., Mass., 1986, MArch, 1993. Arch. Nix, Mann. and Associates; joined as an arch. Perkins + Will, 1993, mng. dir., pres., CEO. Bd. dirs. Perkins + Will. Mem. Atlanta Urban Design Commn.; bd. dirs. Mus. Design Atlanta, Liguria Study Ctr. for Arts and Humanities; bd. trustees Nat. Bldg. Mus. Fellow: AIA (mem. large firm roundtable exec. com.); mem.: Leadership Atlanta. Office: Perkins Will 1315 Peachtree St NE Atlanta GA 30309-7515 Office Phone: 404-443-7663. Business E-Mail: phil.harrison@perkinswill.com.

HARRISON, PRICEY, state legislator; Ret. comm. atty.; mem. Dist. 57 NC House of Reps., 2004—. Mem. Judiciary I com., Marine Resources and Aquaculture com., Pub. Utilities com, Election Law and Campaign Fin. Reform com.; vice chmn. Appropriations com., Energy and Energy Efficiency com., Environ. and Natural Resources com.; chmn. Appropriations Subcom. on Natural and Econ. Resources. Democrat. Office: 16 W Jones St Rm 1218 Raleigh NC 27601-1096 Office Phone: 919-733-5771. Business E-Mail: Pricey.Harrison@ncleg.net.

HARRISON, RICHARD WAYNE, lawyer; b. Marfa, Tex., June 23, 1944; AA, Schreiner U., 1964; BBA, U. Tex., Austin, 1966, JD, 1968. Ptnr. Florence & Harrison, Hughes Springs, Tex., 1968-69; pvt. practice Hughes Springs, Tex., 1969-73; asst. atty. gen. Atty. Gen.'s Office of Tex., Austin, 1973-74, chief tax divsn., 1974-76, spl. asst. atty. gen., 1976-78; ptnr. McGinnis, Lochridge & Kilgore, Austin, 1978-87, Jones, Day, Reavis & Pogue, Austin, 1987-94; mng. ptnr. Harrison & Rial LLP, Austin, 1994—2000; owner Rick Harrison & Assocs., Austin, 2000—02; ptnr. Fritz, Byrne, Head & Harrison RLLC, Austin, 2002—. Pres. Hughes Springs Indsl. Found., 1970; Cass County chmn. Salvation Army, 1970—72; chmn. Hughes Springs United Fund Drive, 1972; mem. Austin Convocation Cursillo Steering Com., 1983—86, chmn., 1985—86; precinct chmn. Cass County Dem. Com., 1969—73; area coord. Lloyd Bentsen for Senate Com., 1970; trustee, treas. St. Andrew's Episcopal Sch., Austin; sr. warden St. Luke's-on-the-Lake Episcopal Ch., 1984. Named Best Lawyers in America, 2007—13; named a Tex. Super Lawyer Comml. Litig., 2007—13, Best Lawyer, 2007—14; named one of 500 Leading Plaintiffs Lawyers in America, Lawdragon Mag., 2007, Intellectual Property Lawyer, 2012. Fellow: Tex. Bar Found. (life); mem.: Schreiner U. Former Student Assn. (bd. dirs. 1984—88), Cass County Bar Assn. (past pres.), Travis County Bar Assn., State Bar of Tex. (fed. jud. com. 1980—83, bar jour. com. 1980—83), Barton Creek Country Club, Masons. Democrat. Office: Fritz Byrne Head & Harrison LLP 98 San Jacinto Blvd Ste 2000 Austin TX 78701 Home: 2301 S 5th St Apt 26 Austin TX 78704 Office Phone: 512-476-2020.

HARRISON, SHAWN, state legislator; b. Anderson, Ind., Mar. 20, 1965; m. Susan Gall; children: Ethan, Sarahcate. BA in Polit. Sci., U. South Fla., 1987; JD, U. Fla., 1990. Atty. Wetherington, Hamilton, Harrison & Fair, P.A., Tampa; councilman Tampa City Coun., chmn. pro-tem, 2004—07; small bus. owner, founder Med. Collection Group, LLC, 2002—; mem. Dist. 60 Fla. House Reps., 2010—. Republican. Methodist. Avocations: biking, outdoor activities, skiing, golf. Office: Fla House of Reps 1301 The Capitol 402 S Monroe St Tallahassee FL 32399-1300 Office Phone: 813-983-3300, 850-488-3087. Business E-Mail: shawn.harrison@myfloridahouse.gov.

HARRISON, TERRY, former state legislator; b. McAlester, Okla., Oct. 9, 1972; m. Amy Mitchell Harrison; 3 children. BS, Okla. State Univ., 1995; JD, Okla. Univ., 1999. Mem. Dist. 18 Okla. House of Representatives, 2003—11. Mem.: Grand Ave. Meth. Ch. Democrat. Methodist. Address: 316 E Choctaw Hartshorne OK 74547 Mailing: 500 E Creek Ave Mcalester OK 74501 Office Phone: 405-557-7376, 918-302-1302. E-mail: harrisonte@lsb.state.ok.us.

HARROZ, JOSEPH, JR., dean, law educator; BA in Economics with distinction, U. Okla., 1989; JD, Georgetown U., 1992. Legis. dir., legal counsel to Senator David L. Boren US Senate, Washington; atty. Crowe and Dunlevy, Okla.; v.p. exec. affairs U. Okla., 1994—96, gen. counsel, chief legal counsel to pres., 1996—2008, v.p., 2010—; adj. prof. U. Okla. Coll. Law, 1997—2010, dean, dir. Law Ctr., 2010—, prof. law, Fenelon Boesche chair law, 2010—; pres. Graymark Healthcare, Inc., 2008—10. Founding dir. Okla. Appleseed Ctr. for Law and Justice; mem. bd. and exec. com. Okla. Found for Excellence; chmn., trustee Ivy Mutual Funds Waddell & Reed, trustee Advisor Mutual Funds; cons. MTV Assocs., 2004—05. Mem.: Phi Beta Kappa. Office: University of Oklahoma College Law 300 Timberdell Rd Norman OK 73019 Office Phone: 405-325-4699. E-mail: jharroz@ou.edu.*

HART, C(HARLES) W(ILLARD), JR., zoologist, curator; b. Farmville, Va., Jan. 30, 1928; s. Charles Willard and Etta Catharine (Sawyer) H.; m. Margaret Waddell Gordon, Sept. 17, 1957 (div. Jan. 1958); m. Nancy Dabney Gardner, June 9, 1962. BA, Hampden-Sydney Coll., Va., 1949, BS, 1950; postgrad., Fla. State U., 1950-52, 53-54; MA, U. Va., 1951. Instr. biology Washington Coll., Chestertown, Md., 1954-55, Randolph Macon Woman's Coll., Lynchburg, Va., 1955-56; med. editor Smith, Kline & French Labs., Phila., 1956-58; editor sci. publs. Acad. Natural Scis., Phila., 1958-70, dir. water pollution studies, 1968-74; asst. to dir. Natural History Mus., Smithsonian Instn., Washington, 1974-79, curator dept. invertebrate zoology, 1979-92, chmn. dept., 1988-91, rsch. scientist, curator, 1992-96, rsch. scientist emeritus, 1996—. Author: A Dictionary of the Non-Scientific Names of Freshwater Crayfishes, 1994; (with Janice Clark) An Interdisciplinary Bibliography of Freshwater Crayfishes from Aristotle Through 1987, 1989; editor: (with P. Holt and R. Hoffmann) The Distributional History of the Biota of the Southern Appalachians, Part I: Invertebrates, 1969, (with S.L.H. Fuller) Pollution Ecology of Freshwater Invertebrates, 1974, Pollution Ecology of Estuarine Invertebrates, 1979, (with Dabney G. Hart) The Ostracod Family Entocytheridae, 1974; contbr. numerous articles to profl. jours. Mem. Phila. Rep. City Com., 1966-68; bd. dirs. Archbold Ctr. for Tropical Rsch., Dominica, 1987-96. Fellow AAAS; mem. Am. Soc. Zoologists (com. on rsch. in systematic biology 1974-78), Crustacean Soc. (treas. 1981-85), Biol. Soc. Washington (editor Procs. Biol. Soc. Washington 1978-80, sec. 1986-88), Assn. Southeastern Biologists (editor ASB Bull. 1961-72, pres. 1970-71), Coun. Biology Editors (treas. 1968-71), Explorers Club, Cosmos Club Washington (mem., chair, program com. 1996-98), Cosmos Club Found. (trustee 1998-2005, advisor 2005-), Phi Beta Kappa, Sigma Xi. Episcopalian. Avocations: web page design and maintenance, flying, sailing, jewelry design and fabrication, cartography of Bermuda. Home: 6449 Walters Woods Dr Falls Church VA 22044-1424 Personal E-mail: henry5cat@verizon.net. E-mail: winston@patriot.net.

HART, CHRISTOPHER R., state legislator; b. Columbia, SC, Sept. 22, 1972; s. Glennah and Maxsena Thomas Days Hart; m. Tara Robertson. BA, Howard U., 1997; JD, U. SC, 2000. Mem. Dist. 73 SC House of Reps., 2007—, mem. Med., Mil., Pub. and Mcpl. Affairs Com. & Subcommittee on Health and Environ. Affairs Com.; adj. prof. Benedict Coll. Mem.: SC Bar Assn., Nat. Bar Assn., SC Trial Lawyers Assn., Omega Psi Phi. Democrat. Home: 5219 Burke Ave Columbia SC 29203 Office: 432B Blatt Building Columbia SC 29211 Home Phone: 803-740-1953; Office Phone: 803-734-3061. Business E-Mail: HartC@schouse.org.

HART, DUDLEY, professional golfer; b. Rochester, NY, Aug. 4, 1968; m. Suzanne Hart; children: Rachel, Abigail, Ryan. Grad., U. Fla. Profl. golfer, 1990—. Achievements include winning Bell Canadian Open, 1996, Honda Classic, 2000. Office: PGA Tour 100 PGA Tour Blvd Ponte Vedra FL 32082

HART, ERIC MULLINS, consumer products company executive; b. Clanton, Ala., May 6, 1925; s. Eric and Myrtle (Mullins) H.; m. Joy Porter, May 16, 1953; children: Anne Porter, Eric Mullins. BS, U. Ala., 1946; grad., Harvard Advanced Mgmt. Program, 1970. With Internat. Paper Co., 1946-69, asst. to v.p.-treas., 1962-64, comptroller, 1964-69; treas. Red River Paper Mill, Inc., 1964-69; fin. v.p. Lever Bros. Co., 1969-83, dir., 1969-83, Unilever U.S. Inc., 1981-83, Macmillan, Inc., 1975-88; exec. in residence Columbia U. Bus. Sch., 1983-88. Trustee King Sch., Stamford, Conn., 1970-76. Mem. Union League Club (N.Y.C.), Lakewood Golf Club, Fairhope Yacht Club, Sigma Alpha Epsilon. Home: 1257 Government St Apt 219 Mobile AL 36604-2451

HART, JAMES WARREN, retired athletic administrator, professional football player; b. Evanston, Ill., Apr. 29, 1944; s. George Ezrie and Marjorie Helen (Karsten) H.; m. Mary Elizabeth Mueller, June 17, 1967; children: Bradley James and Suzanne Elizabeth (twins), Kathryn Anne BS, So. Ill. U., 1967. Quarterback St. Louis Cardinals Profl. Football Team, 1966—83, Washington Redskins Profl. Football Team, 1984; radio sports personality Sta. KMOX, 1975—84, Sta. KXOK, 1985—86; sports analyst Sta. WGN Radio, Chgo., 1985—89; athletics dir. So. Ill. U., Carbondale, 1988—99, assoc. chancellor for external affairs, 1999—2000, spl. asst. to vice chancellor for instnl. devel., 1999—2002; head coach So. Ill. Spl. Olympics, 1973—90, Mo. Spl. Olympics, 1976—78; co-owner Dierdorf & Hart's Steak House, St. Louis. Co-author: The Jim Hart Story, 1977. Gen. campaign chmn. St. Louis Heart Assn., 1974-88; hon. chmn. St. Louis Sr. Olympics, 1986-88 Recipient Brian Piccolo Nat. YMCA award for most civic minded profl. athlete, 1980; named Most Valuable Player in Nat. Football Conf., 1974, Most Valuable Player with St. Louis Cardinals, 1973, 1975, 1978, Man of Yr., St. Louis Dodge Dealers, 1975—76, Miller High Life, 1980, St. Louis Sports Hall of Fame; named to So. Ill. U. Sports Hall of Fame, 1978, Mo. Sports Hall of Fame, 1998, Mo. Valley Conf. Hall of Fame, 2001, Chicagoland Sports Hall of Fame, 2003. Mem.: AFTRA, NFL Players Assn. (Byron Whizzer White award 1976), Fellowship Christian Athletes. Republican.

HART, JAMES WHITFIELD, JR., retired public relations executive, lawyer; b. Greenwood, Fla., Dec. 20, 1935; s. James Whitfield Sr. and Lela (Cox) H.; m. Patricia Ann Landrum, Mar. 11, 1961; children: William Gordon, Melanie Ann. AA, Chipola Coll., 1956; JD, U. Ala., 1973; MBA, MIT, 1982. Bar: Ala. 1974, Colo. 1976; cert. flight instr. News dir., anchorman Sta. WTVY-TV, Dothan, Ala., 1958-60, Sta. WSFA-TV, Montgomery, Ala., 1960-62; exec. dir. Am. Petroleum Inst., Montgomery, 1962-75; mgr. pub. affairs Gulf Oil Corp., Atlanta, 1975-76, dir. pub. affairs Denver, 1976-81, sr. dir. pub. affairs Pitts., 1981-85; sr. v.p. Blue Cross/Blue Shield, Jacksonville, Fla., 1985-86; sr. v.p., gen. mgr. Hill & Knowlton, Denver, 1986-88; v.p. pub. affairs PanEnergy Corp., Houston, 1988-97; v.p. Duke Energy Corp., 1997-99; ret. Res. dir. pub. affairs Office Sec. Air Force, 1988-95; bd. dirs. Vita-Living, Inc.; chmn. interstate natural gas Am. Pub. Affairs Com., 1994. Adv. bd. City of Sugar Land Airport; former pres. Ala. N.G. Assn.; bd. dirs. Opportunity Fla., Boy Scouts Am.; pres. Chipola Jr. Coll. Found. Brig. gen. USAFR, 1990-95. Decorated Disting. Svc. medal, Legion of Merit, Meritorious Svc. medal, Air Force Commendation medal; recipient Meritorious Svc. award and Disting. Svc. award State of Ala., Outstanding Young Man of Am. award U.S. Jaycees, 1965, Outstanding Pub. Rels. Practitioner award, 1991, Pub. Rels. Practitioner of Yr., 1996; named Alumnus of Yr., Chipola Coll., 2007. Mem. ABA, Pub. Rels. Soc. Am., Tex. Pub. Rels. Assn. (bd. dirs., chmn. pub. affairs coun. 1996, pres. 1996, Gold Spur award 1999), Coun. Assn. Execs. (former pres.), Am. Petroleum Inst., Am. Gas Assn., Pub. Affairs Coun. (past chmn.), Res. Officers Assn. (life), Air Force Assn. (life), Tex. Coun. Econ. Edn. (bd. dirs.), Tex. Rsch. League (bd. dirs.), Forum Club Houston, Houston Club, Univ. Club Houston, Fed. Aviation Agy.(Wright Brothers Master Pilot award 2009-), Rotary, Marianna Rotary Club (pres.), Sigma Delta Kappa (former chancellor). Baptist. Home: 7371 Cox Rd Bascom FL 32423-9411 E-mail: jimwhart@digitalexp.com.

HART, JOHN CLIFTON, lawyer; b. Chgo., Apr. 29, 1945; s. Clifton Edwin and Eleanor (Zielinski) H.; m. Dianne Lynn Wenzel, Jan. 18, 1969; children: David Clifton, Steven Philip, Kristin Dianne. BS, Loyola U., Chgo., 1967; postgrad., Northwestern U. Sch. Law, Chgo., 1967—69; JD, U. ND, Grand Forks, 1972. Bar: Minn. 1973, US Dist. Ct. Minn. 1973, Tex. 1979, US Dist. Ct. (no. dist.) Tex. 1979, US Dist. Ct. (we dist.) Tex. 1981, US Dist. Ct. (ea. dist.) Okla. 1981, US Dist. Ct. (ea. dist.) Tex. 1984, US Dist. Ct. (no. dist.) Okla. 1999, US Ct. Appeals (5th and 8th cirs.) 1980, US Supreme Ct., 1997. Ptnr. Robins, Zelle, Larson & Kaplan, Mpls., 1973-81; v.p. Gollaher & Hart, Dallas, 1981-84; pres. Hart & Engen, Dallas, 1984-87, Hart & Assocs., Dallas, 1987-88; mng. ptnr. SW regional office Robins, Kaplan, Miller & Ciresi, 1988-93; ptnr. Cantey & Hanger LLP, 1993-98, Brown, Dean, Wiseman, Proctor, Hart & Howell LLP, Fort Worth, 1998—. Contbr. articles to profl. jours. Maj. USAF, 1969-79. Mem.: ABA, Am. Bar Found., Tex. Bar Found., Loss Exec. Assn., Fedn. Def. and Corp. Counsel, Tarrant County Bar Assn., State Bar Tex. Republican. Lutheran. Office: Brown Dean Wiseman Proctor Hart & Howell LLP Ste 200 306 W 7th St Fort Worth TX 76102-4905 Office Phone: 817-820-1112. Business E-Mail: jhart@browndean.com.

HART, JOSEPHINE L., state supreme court justice; BA, Ark. Tech U.; JD, U. Ark. Law clk. to Justice Frank Holt Ark. Supreme Ct., Little Rock, spl. chief justice, spl. justice, assoc. justice position 4, 2012—; asst. Judge Advocate Gen.; atty. Gregg, Hart, and Farris, Batesville, Ark.; legal advisor 306 Civil Affairs Group; asst. Staff Judge Advocate; comdr. 32nd JAG. Bd. dirs. Mountain View Gen. Hosp. Asst. adj. gen. US Army. Mem.: Independence County Bar Assn., Ark. Bar Assn., ABA. Office: Arkansas Supreme Ct 625 Marshall St Little Rock AR 72201

HART, KEVIN JOHN, poet, educator; b. London, July 5, 1954; arrived in Australia, 1966; s. James Henry and Rosina (Wootton) H. BA with honors, Australian Nat. U., 1976; PhD, U. Melbourne, 1986. Tchr. Geelong (Australia) Coll., 1979-83; lectr. dept. philosophy U. Melbourne, Australia, 1984-85, lectr. dept. English, 1986-87; lectr. lit. studies Deakin U., Geelong, 1987-90, sr. lectr., 1991; assoc. prof. dept. English Monash U., Melbourne, Australia, 1991-95, prof. dept. English, 1995—2002; visiting prof. Georgetown U. Dept. English, 1996-97; Notre Dame prof. philosophy and lit. U. Notre Dame, 2007—07; Edwin B. Kyle prof. christian studies, courtesy prof. English, French U. Va., 2007—. Vis. prof. dept. philosophy Villanova U., 2001. Author: The Departure, 1978, The Lines of the Hand, 1981, Your Shadow, 1984, The Trespass of the Sign, 1989, expanded edit., 2000, Peniel, 1991, A.D. Hope, 1992, New and Selected Poems, 1995, Dark Angel, 1996, Nineteen Songs, 1999, Wicked Heat, 1999, Samuel Johnson and the Culture of Property, 1999, Madonna, 1999, How to Read a Page of Boswell, 2000, Flame Tree: Selected Poems, 2001, (with K. Headlam) Night Music, 2002, Postmodernism: A Beginner's Guide, 2004, The Dark Gaze: Maurice Blanchot and the Sacred, 2004, Young Rain, 2008, Morning Knowledge 2011, Kingdom of God, 2014; editor: The Oxford Book of Australian Religious Verse, 1994, The Fifth Question and After: Poems for Tomaz Salamun, 2001; Nowhere without No: In Memory of Maurice Blanchot, 2003, The Power of Contestation: Perspectives on Maurice Blanchot, 2004, Derrida and Religion, 2004, The Experience of God: A Postmodern Responce, 2005, Counter-Experiences: Reading Jean-Lnc Marion, 2007, ed. The Exorbitant: Emmanuel Levinas between Jews and Christian, 2010, Clanteshine Encounters: Philosophy in the Narratings of Maruice Blanchst, 2010, Jean-Luc Marion: The Essential Writings, 2012; translator: The Buried Harbour: Selected Poems of Giuseppi Ungaretti, 1990. Recipient Tillyard Prize, 1976, John Shaw Neilson award, 1977, Fellowship Australian Writers, 1977, Harri Jones Award, 1983, Wesley Michel Wright Award, 1984, NSW Premier's award, 1985, Victorian Premier's award, 1985, Grace Leven award U. Sydney, 1991 and 1995, Christian Brennan award, 1999, Graybeal-Gowan prize, 2008; elected fellow, Australian Acad. of Humanities, 1994, Fel., Xavier Tilliette Inst., Rome, 2008, Acad. Catholic Theology, 2010. Roman Catholic. Avocations: cooking, walking. Office: Dept Religious Studies University Va Charlottesville VA 22904 Office Fax: 434-924-1467. Business E-Mail: kevinhart@virginia.edu.*

HART, RONALD WILSON, radiobiologist, educator, toxicologist, business adviser; b. Syracuse, NY, Mar. 23, 1942; s. Wilson and Annabell Hart. BS, Syracuse U., 1967; MS, U. Ill., 1970, PhD, 1971; postgrad. (Nat. Cancer Inst. trainee), Oak Ridge Nat. Lab., 1973. USPHS trainee, 1970-71; asst. prof. dept. radiology Ohio State U., Columbus, 1971-75, dir. radiation biology rsch. divsn., 1971-82, assoc. prof. depts. biology, biophysics, preventive medicine, 1976-78, assoc. prof. pharmacology, medicinal chemistry dept. preventive medicine, 1977-78, dir. chem., biomed. environ. rsch. group dept. preventive medicine, 1977-82, prof. depts. radiology, preventive medicine, pharmacology, medicinal chemistry, vet. pathobiology, 1978-82; dir. Nat. Ctr. for Toxicological Rsch., Jefferson, Ark., 1980-92, Disting. scientist in residence, 1992-2000; rsch. prof. Strang Cancer Prevention Rsch. Ctr. Rockefeller U., 2000—04, dir., hart mgmt., 2008—; venture ptnr. Sail Venture Capital, 2008—12; ptnr. LA Sustainability Fd, 2010—12; gen. ptnr. Global Tech Deployment Fd, 2012—; chair Adv. Bd. Greener Cap, 2011—13. Disting. prof. U. Poona, India, 1978—2004, Cairo U., 1989—2010; disting. prof. carcinogenesis Guang Zhou Med. Coll., China, 1988—; adj. prof. U. Ark. Med. Sci., 1980—2010, U. Tenn. Health Scis., 1983—2012; adj. prof. pharmacology Coll. Pharmacy U. Ark., 1997—2010; cons. Oak Ridge Nat. Lab., 1971—75, Brookhaven Nat. Lab., 1975—78, Argonne Nat. Lab., 1975—78, EPA, 1976, 1978, Am. Indsl. Health Coun., 1978, PPG Industries, 1978, Informatics, 1978—80, FDA, 1980; mem. NAS/NRC Bd. Toxicology and Environ. Health Hazards, 1976—82; mem. insteragy. staff group Office Sci. and Tech. Policy Exec. Office of Pres., 1982—85, chmn., 1983—85; chmn. bd. dirs. Ark. Sci. and Tech. Authority, 1983—84, mem., 1985—88; bd. dirs. Miltos Pharms., 2006—08, Water Chef, Inc., 2007—08, Immunovative, Inc., 2007—08, SNTech., 2007—, WNKO Battery, 2007—, Geo Vidio, LLC, 2007—09, ZUMA, 2008—09, SpectRX, 2006—, vice chair, 2011—; mem. adv. bd. Miss. State U., 1987—96, St. Renatus, 2009—, bd. dirs., Aerofarms, mem. adv. bd., 2009—; adv. bd. Petrotech, 1991—92, VoiceNet, 1998—99, Waterchef, Inc., 2001—03, Micromed Labs., 2002—06, Biomed, 2002—08, Applied DNA Sci., Inc., 2003—05, Fla. A&M U. Rsch. Ctr., 1985—2004, Omega Foods, 2004—05, Met. Area Networks, 2004, Ship OK, LLC, 2004—06, Biophora, Inc., 2005, Neogenix Ind., 2006—10, Ice Energy, 2007—10, Flex Energy, 2009—11, Therapy's Solutions, 2009—11, Motor Excellence, 2009—10, vice chair, 2010—11, Biz NGO, 2011—; bd. visitors Memphis State U., 1984—90; chair task force risk assessment/risk mgmt. HHS, 1985, chmn. com. coordinate environ., health and related programs, 1985—88; chmn. sci. panel Agt. Orange working group, 1986—88; mem. USAF toxicology rev. panel, 1987; chmn. intergovtl. Task Force Tech. Transer, 1987—88,

DHHS Task Force Tech. Transfer, 1987—88; mem. Inter Govt. Commn. Competitiveness, 1987—94; apptd. del. US-USSR Emerging Leaders Summit; chmn. Sci. and Tech. Commn., 1988; disting. adj. prof. Moscow State U., 1989—2011, Guanzou Med. U., China, 1988—, U. Udina, Italy, 1999—2002; chmn. Ark. Sch. Math. and Sci. Found., 1997—2003; adv. bd. St. Regeneris, 2009—; bd. dirs. G Therm Inc., 2011—12. Editor-in-chief: Toxicology Indsl. Health, 2000—12; contbr. chapters to books, articles to profl. jours. Recipient Hopkins award for grad. rsch., 1971, Japanese Med. Assn. award, 1978, Karl-August-Forester award, West Germany, 1980, award of merit, FDA, 1982, 1985, 1986, Sr. Exec. Svc. award, 1982, 1984, 1985, Commr.'s Spl. citation, 1987, Superior Svc. award, USPHS, 1983, Gov.'s award Outstanding Svc., State of Ark., 1985, Letter of Commendation, Pres. of US, 1985, Pres. Rank award Outstanding Accomplishment, Guangzhou Med. Coll., 1988, Bose medal, Bose Inst., 1994, Ednl. medal, U. Ark., 2005; named Outstanding Alumnus, Syracuse U., 1976. Fellow: AAAS, Am. Assn. Clin. Chemistry, Risk Analysis Soc., Gerontol. Soc., Am. Coll. Toxicology (past pres.); mem.: Sr. Execs. Assn., Photochem. and Photobiol. Soc., Biophys. Soc., Radiation Rsch. Soc., Sigma Xi. Office: 4821 Crestwood Little Rock AR 72207 Personal E-mail: rhart99@comcast.net.

HARTE, CHRISTOPHER M., investor, former publishing executive; BA, Stanford U.; MBA, U. Tex. Pub. Centre Daily Times, State Coll., Pa., 1986—89, Akron Beacon Jour., Ohio, 1989—92; pres. Portland Press Herald/Maine Sunday Telegram, 1992—94; chmn., pub. Star Tribune, Mpls., 2007—09. Mem. exec. adv. bd. Avista Capital Partners; bd. dirs. Harte-Hanks, Inc., 1993—, Geokinetics, 1997—, Crown Resources Corp., 2002—06. Mem. adv. coun. Univ. Tex. Coll. Natural Sciences Found., 2009—10. Mem.: Tex. Audubon Soc. (adv. bd.), Nat. Audubon Soc. (bd. dirs., asst. sec. & chair Governance Com.). Office: Geokinetics Inc Corp Hdqs Bd Directors 1500 CityWest Blvd Ste 800 Houston TX 77042

HARTKE, ANITA, real estate broker; d. Vance and Martha Hartke; children: Ryan, Hanna, Wyatt. BA in Psychology, Salem Coll., W.Va. Lic. real estate broker. Broker Nat. Realty, Amissville, Va. Mem. Culpeper County C. of C., Fauquier County C. of C. Democrat. Lutheran. Office: Nat Realty LLC 3192 Rancelee Way Amissville VA 20106 Office Phone: 703-987-4410. Business E-Mail: anita@nationalrealty.biz.

HARTLE, ROBERT WYMAN, retired literature and language professor; b. Kongmoon, China, Sept. 1, 1921; s. Jacob Everett and Margaret (Wyman) H.; m. Ann Dorothy Mordhorst, Jan. 5, 1980; 1 son, Robert Wyman, Jr.; children by previous marriage: Shirley Ann (Mrs. Jan McDaniel), John Wyman. BA, MA, U. Tex., 1947; AM, Princeton U., 1949, PhD, 1951. Instr. French Princeton U., 1950-53, asst. prof., 1953-60; assoc. prof. modern langs. U. Oreg., 1961-63; asst. prof. Romance langs. Queens Coll. (now CUNY-Queens Coll.), NYC, 1960-61, prof., chmn. dept. Romance and Slavic langs., 1963-65, assoc. dean faculty, 1964-65, dean faculty, 1965-70, prof., 1972-87, prof. emeritus, 1987—, chmn. ad hoc legal affairs com., mem. univ. acad. senate, 1979-81, dir. PhD program in France, 1970-72, mem. senate. Founder, dir. programs of study abroad, 1963-70; vis. prof. Inst. Liberal Arts, Emory U., 1985-93. Author: Index du vocabulaire du théâtre classique: Racine, 8 vols, 1956-64; transl. Tartuffe (Molière), 1963; contbr. articles on the iconography of Alexander the Great, 17th century French art and architecture, Hellenistic Art, 1955—; French translator Papers of Robert Morris, 1973-84, Papers of Thomas Jefferson, Princeton U. Press, 1986-2010. Bd. dirs. Am. Ctr. for Students and Artists, Paris, 1970-78; eucharistic minister Atlanta VA Med. Ctr., 2007-. Decorated officer Ordre des Palmes Académiques (France), knight Order of Merit (Italy), officer's cross Order of Merit (Germany). Mem. MLA, AAUP (pres. chpt. 1975-80) Home: 1803 Westminster Way NE Atlanta GA 30307-1134 E-mail: rwhartle@comcast.net.

HARTLEY, CYNTHIA A., human resources specialist; b. 1949; BA in English, Roosevelt U., Chgo.; MA in Orgn. Behavior, George Williams Coll., Ill.; MBA, U. Chgo. V.p., human resources Dames & Moore, Inc., National Gypsum Co., Sonoco Products Co., 1995—2002, sr. v.p., human resources, 2002—. Bd. dirs. SCBT Financial Corp., 2011—. Office: Sonoco Products Co 1 N Second St Hartsville SC 29550 Office Phone: 843-383-7000. Business E-Mail: cynthia.hartley@sonoco.com.

HARTLEY, MICHAEL J., travel company executive; CEO Cheap Tickets, Inc., Honolulu, 1986—. Recipient Hawaii Ernst & Young Entrepreneur of Yr. award, 2000. Office: Cendant Travel PO Box 41005 Nashville TN 37204-1005

HARTMAN, FREDERICK COOPER, retired biochemist; b. Memphis, Aug. 17, 1939; s. Fred Francis and Raymie Constance (Cooper) H.; m. Patricia Jean Ballard, Sept. 7, 1961; children: Patricia Suzanne, Sheila Katherine. BS in Chemistry, Memphis State U., 1960; MS in Biochemistry, U. Tenn., 1962, PhD in Biochemistry, 1964; postgrad., U. Ill., 1964-66. Sr. rsch. biochemist Oak Ridge (Tenn.) Nat. Lab., 1966—99; group leader protein chemistry Oak Ridge Nat. Lab., 1972-99, sect. head molecular and cellular scis., 1975-88, dir. biology divsn., 1988-97; prof. dept. biochemistry U. Tenn., Knoxville, 1999—2004; ret., 2004. Mem. editl. bd. Jour. Biol. Chemistry, BioSci., Jour. Protein Chemistry; contbr. numerous articles to profl. jours. Grantee Dept. Agr., 1978-2003, NSF, 1980-87; fellow USPHS, 1962-64, NIH, 1963, 65. Fellow AAAS; mem. Am. Chem. Soc. (Pfizer award 1979, nominating com. 1982), Am. Soc. Biol. Chemists (nominating com. 1979, 81), Am. Soc. Plant Physiologists, Protein Soc., Sigma Xi. Home: 9172 Sugarland Dr Jacksonville FL 32256 Personal E-mail: fredchartman@aol.com.

HARTMANN, BRUCE, publishing executive; m. Tami Hartmann; children: Melissa, Jacquelyn, Brian. BA in Journalism, W. Va. U., 1979. Adv. positions Nashua Telegraph; advt. positions Balt. (Md.) Sun, 1981—87; mgr. Lowell (Mass.) Sun, 1987—90; advt. dir. Knoxville News-Sentinel (subs. of E.W. Scripps Co.), 1990—93, asst. gen. mgr., 1993, gen. mgr., v.p., 1993—98, pub. Knoxville, Tenn., 1998—2009, corp. v.p., sales, 2009—. Pres. Hist. Tenn. Theatre Found.; bd. dirs. Knoxville Area Chamber Partnership, Knoxville (Tenn.) Area Chamber Partnership, Knoxville (Tenn.) Zoo, Knoxville (Tenn.) Sports Cup, United Way, Knoxville, St. Mary's Found., Knoxville. Office: Knoxville News Sentinel Co 2332 News Sentinel Dr Knoxville TN 37921-5766

HARTMANN, FREDERICK WILLIAM, newspaper editor; b. Wilmington, Del., Feb. 3, 1928; s. William and Louise (Askani) H.; m. Mary Lucille Nelson, Oct. 16, 1954; children: Michele Mary, Randi Lucille, Frederick Andrew, Eric William, Adam Nelson BA, U. Del., 1951; postgrad., Am. U., 1952; MS, Columbia U. Grad. Sch. Journalism, 1953. Reporter AP, NYC, 1954; dir. news and sports WDEL Radio, Wilmington, 1954-56; reporter Morning News, News-Jour. Co., Wilmington, 1956-60, asst. city editor, 1961-62, city editor, 1962-64, Morning and Evening Jour., 1964-67, met. editor, 1967-72, asst. to pres., 1972-74, dir. corp. mktg., 1974-75, exec. editor, 1975-80, v.p., 1977-80; mng. editor Fla. Times-Union, Jacksonville, 1980-83; exec. editor Times-Union/Jacksonville Jour., Jacksonville, 1983-88, Times-Union, Jacksonville, 1988-98, ret., 1998. Lectr. U. Del., 1971, 72; Pulitzer prize juror, 1981, 82 Mem. budget com. United Way of Del., 1973, 74; v.p. Brandywine Little League, 1973; bd. dirs. United Cerebral Palsy Assn. of Del., 1970-72. Served with AUS, 1946-48 Mem.: Theta Chi. Home: 3852 Mcgirts Blvd Jacksonville FL 32210-4337 Home Phone: 904-387-4025. Personal E-mail: freditor39@bellsouth.net, hartmann39@att.net.

HARTMAYER, GREGORY JOHN, bishop; b. Buffalo, Nov. 21, 1951; Attended, St. Joseph Cupertino Friary, Ellicott City, Md.; M in theology, St. Anthony on Hudson; M in pastoral counseling, Emmanuel Coll., Boston; M in Edn., Boston Coll. Professed Order of Friars Minor Conventual (Franciscan), 1970, solemn professed, 1973, ordained priest, 1979; guidance counselor Archbishop Curley High Sch., Balt., 1979—85, prin., 1985—88, Cardinal O'Hara High Sch., Tonawanda, NY, 1988—89, St. Francis High Sch., Athol Springs, NY, 1989—94; tchr. John Carroll High Sch., Fort Pierce, Fla., 1995; pastor St. Philip Benizi parish, Jonesboro, Ga., 1995—2010, St. John Vianney parish, Lithia Springs, Ga., 2010—11; appointed bishop, 2011; bishop Diocese of Savannah, Ga., 2011—. Roman Catholic. Office: Diocese of Savannah Pastoral Ctr 601 E Liberty St Savannah GA 31401 Office Phone: 912-201-4100. Office Fax: 912-236-0848.

HARTNETT, WILL FORD, lawyer; b. Austin, Tex., June 3, 1956; s. James Joseph and Emily (High) Hartnett; m. Tammy Lynn Cotton, Dec. 7, 1996; children: Will, Winston, Warner. BA, Harvard U., 1978; JD, U. Tex., 1981. Bar: Tex. 1981, U.S. Ct. Appeals (5th cir.) 1985, U.S. Supreme Ct. 1985; cert. in Estate Planning and Probate Law Tex. Bd. Legal Specialization. Assoc. Turner & Hitchins, Dallas, 1981-82; ptnr. The Hartnett Law Firm, Dallas, 1982—; mem. Dist. 114 Tex. House of Representatives, 1990—2013. Bd. dirs. Tex. Guaranteed Student Loan Corp., Austin, 1987-90; chmn. Judiciary Com., Tex. House of Representatives, 2001-2007. Co-author: Annual Survey of Wills and Trusts, 1986. Recipient of several awards and honors. Fellow: Tex. Bar Found., Am. Coll. Trust and Estate Coun.; mem.: SAR, Dallas Bar Assn., Order of Malta, Mensa, St. Nicholas Soc., Harvard Club Dallas (bd. dirs., treas. 1983—95, 2006—09, 2013—). Republican. Roman Catholic. Office: 2920 N Pearl St Dallas TX 75201 Office Phone: 214-742-4655. Business E-Mail: will@hartnettlawfirm.com.

HARTON, HERBERT LYNN, banker; b. Asheboro, NC, July 15, 1961; s. Herbert Clarence and Linda Lou (York) H.; m. Debra Ann Fretwell, July 12, 1981; children: Sara Elizabeth, Katherine Leigh. BS, Wake Forest U., 1983; postgraduate, NC State U., 1986-87, E. Carolina U., 1987-88. Chief credit officer Regions Fin., Union Planters; with, corp. bus. banking mgr., regional loan adminstrn., and comml. banking mgr. Br. Banking and Trust Co., mgmt. trainee Wilson, N.C., 1983-84, fin. analyst, 1984, mgr., comml. lending tng., 1984-85, bus. svcs. mgr. Graham, N.C., 1985-86, regional loan adminstr. Wilson, 1988; exec. v.p., chief risk officer and chief credit officer South Financial Group, Inc. (acquired by TD Bank Financial Group), 2007, chief comml. banking officer, 2008, pres., CEO and dir., 2009—. Mem. Robert Morris Assocs. Treas. Habitat for Humanity, Wilson, 1990—. Republican. Baptist. Office: BB&T 223 Nash St W Wilson NC 27893-3801 also: South Financial Group Inc 1701 Rte 70 E Cherry Hill NJ 08034 Office Phone: 856-751-2739. Business E-Mail: hharton@thesouthgroup.com.

HARTSELL, FLETCHER LEE, JR., state legislator; b. Concord, NC, Feb. 15, 1947; s. Fletcher Lee and Doris Wright Hartsell; m. Tana Renee Honeycutt, 1972; children: Fletcher Lee III, Whitney Paige, Alice Tyson. Former atty. Cabarrus County, atty., 1985—, Hartsell, Hartsell & White Pa, Concord, NC, 1972—, Cabarrus County Schs., 1979—; state senator Dist. 22 NC, 1991—2002; state senator Dist. 36, 2003—. Mem.: Rotary, 9A Jud. Dist. Bar Assn., Cabarrus County Bar Assn., NC Bar Assn., Am. Bar Assn. Republican. Baptist. Address: PO Box 368 Concord NC 28026-0368 Office: NC Senate 300 N Salisbury St Rm 300 C Raleigh NC 27603-5925 Office Phone: 919-733-7223. E-mail: Fletcher.Hartsell@ncleg.net.

HARTSELL, HORACE ED, college president; m. Joyce Powell; 6 children. BS, U. Fla.; MS, Fla. Atlantic U.; D in Adminstrn. of Higher Edn., Auburn U. Founder East Ark. C.C.; with Broward C.C., Fla. Atlantic U.; pres. Pensacola Jr. Coll., 1990-98, pres. emeritus, 1999—; interim pres. Daytona Beach C.C., 1998-99. Vice-chair, chair Fla. Coun. of Pres.; mem. coun. Pres.'s Legis. com. Founder, mem. Leadership Fla. Named Bus. and Profl. Leader of Yr. Pensacola News Jour., 1983; recipient Disting. Life Svc. award Fla. Assn. of C.C., 1997, Adminstrn. Commn. award, 1997. Mem. Pensacola Area C. of C. (chmn.). Office: Daytona Beach Cmty Coll PO Box 2811 Daytona Beach FL 32120-2811 Home: 317 S 3RD ST Pulaski TN 38478-3803

HARTSFIELD, JAMES KENNEDY, JR., orthodontist, geneticist; b. Decatur, Ala., Feb. 12, 1955; s. James Kennedy and Shirley Joann (Bridwell) H.; m. Karen Lee Whitaker, May 8, 1977; 1 child, Kennedy Whitaker. BS in Biology cum laude, U. SC, Columbia, 1977; DMD in Dental Medicine, Med. U. SC, Charleston, 1981; MS in Med. Genetics, Ind. U., Indpls., 1983; MMSc in Oral Biology, Harvard U., Boston, 1987; PhD in Med. Scis., U. South Fla., Tampa, 1993. Diplomate Am. Bd. Med. Genetics., Am. Bd. Orthodontics. Intern Hillsborough Dental Rsch. Clinic, Tampa, Fla., 1981-82; clin. fellow Ind. U., Indpls., 1982-83; rsch. fellow Harvard U., Boston, 1983-86, Mass. Gen. Hosp., Boston, 1984-86; clin. fellow U. South Fla., Tampa, 1986-87, asst. prof., 1987-93; assoc. prof. Sch. Dentistry and Sch. Medicine, Ind. U., Indpls., 1993—99, prof. Sch. Dentistry and Sch. Medicine, 1999—2008, adj. clin. prof. Sch. Dentistry and Sch. Medicine, 2008—; prof., E. Preston Hicks Endowed Chair in Orthodontics and Oral Rsch., Coll. Dentistry U. Ky., 2008—, prof., Coll. Medicine, 2010—. Adj. prof. U. Ill. at Chgo. Coll. Dentistry; dir. Teratogen Info. Svc., U. South Fla., 1987-93; dir. oral facial genetics divsn. Sch. Dentistry Ind. U., 1993-, acting chmn. oral facial devel., 1998-99, chmn., 1999-2002, interim chmn. orthodontics and oral facial genetics, 2007—; pres. Meridian Orthodontics, PC, 2003-08; dir. hereditary genomics lab. U. Ky. Coll. Dentistry, 2008—, dir. grad. orthodontic program residency, 2011; editl. rev. bd. mem. Am. Jour. Orthodontics and Dentofacial Orthops., 2008-, Angle Orthodontist, 2011-. Mem. editl. bd. Jour. Dental Rsch., 2007-09; rev. bd. mem. Internat. Jour. Oral Maxillofacial Implants; editl. bd. mem., Internat. Jour. Dentistry, contbr. articles to profl. jours. Med. adv. coun. Osteogenesis Imperfecta Found., 2007—. Recipient Physician-Scientist award NIH, 1989, 1st Ind. Rsch. Support and Transition award, 1996, B.F. Dewell Meml. Biomed. Rsch. award Am. Assn. Orthodontists Found., 2001, Disting. Faculty award Ind. U. Sch. Dentistry Alumni Assn., 2003; named Outstanding Faculty of Yr., Ind. Dental Assn., 2004. Fellow Am. Coll. Med. Genetics (founding), Am. Coll. Dentists, Coll. of Diplomates of Am. Bd. Orthodontics; mem. ADA, Am. Soc. Human Genetics, Am. Assn. for Dental Rsch., Edward H. Angle Soc. Orthodontists (Midwest Component), Internat. Assn. Dental Rsch. (v.p. craniofacial biology group 2003-04, pres. 2005-06), Internat. Coll. Dentists, Soc. Craniofacial Genetics (pres. 1989-90), Am. Dental Edn. Assn., Am. Cleft Palate Assn., Am. Assn. Orthodontists, Harvard Soc. for Advancement of Orthodontics (v.p. 2006-07, pres. 2007-09), Confs. on Orthodontic Advances in Sci. and Tech. (bd. dirs. 2006—). Presbyterian. Avocations: music, boating. Office: U Ky Coll Dentistry Rm D-406 800 Rose St Lexington KY 40536-0297 Office Phone: 859-323-5371. Office Fax: 859-257-8878. Personal E-mail: drHartsfield@post.harvard.edu. Business E-Mail: James.Hartsfield@uky.edu.

HARTWELL, STEPHEN, investment company executive; b. Phila., Apr. 10, 1915; s. Stephen Warren and Elizabeth (Thompson) Hartwell; m. Elizabeth van Laer Speer, Feb. 21, 1946 (div. Jan. 1973); children: Stephen Warren II, Robert van Laer; m. Norma Bostick, Dec. 9, 1978. BS in Adminstrv. Engring., Lafayette Coll., 1936. Investment analyst Pa. Co. Banking & Trusts, 1936-41; procurement officer electronic equipment CAA, 1947-48; indsl. specialist AEC, 1948-49, chief progress and stats. sect., prodn. div., 1949-51, chief constr. engring. reports br., 1951-54; exec. v.p. Atomic Devel. Securities Co. (and successor cos.), 1954-68; v.p. Washington Mut. Investors Fund, Inc., 1968-81, pres., 1981-85, chmn., 1985—2001, chmn. emeritus, 2001—. Pres. Washington Investment Advisers Inc., 1992—2002; chmn. Tax Exempt Bond Fund Md., Tax Exempt Bond Fund Va., 1986—97, chmn. emeritus, 1997—; pres. Colchester Corp., Woodbridge, Va., 1971—, bd. dirs.; chmn. WMIF Mgmt. Corp., Washington, 1986—, Hartick LLC, 1997—; bd. dirs. Wentz Corp., Wilmington, Del., Johnston Lemon Group Inc.; trustee Ameribanc Investors Group, 1985—95. Mem. Fairfax County Planning Commn., 1961—67, chmn., 1964—66; mem. No. Va. Regional Planning and Econ. Devel. Commn., 1963—64; bd. govs. Gunston Hall Sch.; active Mt. Vernon Life Guards, 1992—, chmn., 1998—2005; trustee Am. U., 1983—88, trustee emeritus, 1988—; trustee Woodlawn Found., 1983—89; trustee, treas. Found. for Mid. East Peace, 1993—, Fairfax Hosp. Assn., 1986—93, Inova Health Sys., 1987—96, chmn. investment and pension com., 1997—2005; chmn. Jefferson Hosp., Alexandria, Va., 1986—92, Va. Coll. Bldg. Authority, Richmond, 1994—2001; mem. Commonwealth Coun., Richmond, 1998—, Fairfax County Rep. Com., 1955—61, 1966—70, 1979—81. Maj. US Army, 1941—45. Mem.: NASD (Dist. 10 com. 1968—71), SAR, Nat. Economists Club, Washington Soc. Investment Analysts, Met. Club, Mt. Vernon Country Club, Phi Alpha (pres.), Zeta Psi (trustee Ednl. Found. 1997—2005, pres. 1999—2000). Home: PO Box 1907 Clayton GA 30525-0048 Home Phone: 703-780-8867; Office Phone: 202-842-5670. Personal E-mail: stephcom@verizon.net.

HARTZ, STEVEN EDWARD MARSHALL, lawyer, educator; b. Cambridge, Mass., July 11, 1948; s. Louis and Stella (Feinberg) H.; m. Janice Lindsay, June 12, 1976. AB magna cum laude, Harvard Coll., 1970; JD, U. Chgo., 1974. Bar: N.Y. 1975, U.S. Dist. Ct. (so. and ea. dists.) N.Y. 1975, U.S. Ct. Appeals (2d cir.) 1975, Fla. 1979, U.S. Dist. Ct. (so. dist.) Fla. 1979, U.S. Tax Ct. 1979, U.S. Ct. Appeals (5th cir.) 1979, U.S. Supreme Ct. 1979, U.S. Ct. Appeals (11th cir.) 1981, U.S. Dist. Ct. (mid. dist.) Fla. 1984. Assoc. Cleary, Gottlieb, Steen & Hamilton, NYC, 1974-79; asst. U.S. atty. U.S. Dept. Justice, Miami, Fla., 1979-82, dep. chief criminal divsn., chief fraud and pub. corruption sect., 1981-82; sole practice Miami, Fla., 1982-90; of counsel Akerman, Senterfitt & Eidson, P.A., Miami, 1980, ptnr., shareholder, 1991—. Lectr. dept. English, U. English, U. Miami, 1984, adj. assoc. prof., 1985-86. Co-author: Housing, A Community Handbook, 1973; author: The Practical Guide for New Lawyers, 2010. Vol. atty. Mobilization for Youth Legal Svcs., N.Y.C., 1978. Recipient Dirs.' award U.S. Dept. Justice, 1981; Fulbright Hays scholar, 1970. Mem. ABA, FBA, Fla. Bar Assn., N.Y. State Bar Assn., N.Y.C. Bar Assn., Dade County Bar Assn., Phi Beta Kappa. Office: One Southeast 3rd Ave 28th Fl Miami FL 33131-4943 Business E-Mail: steven.hartz@akerman.com.

HARVARD, BEVERLY JOYCE BAILEY, federal marshal; b. Macon, Ga., Dec. 22, 1950; d. Arcelious and Irene (Perkins) Bailey; m. Jimmy C. Harvard, 1972 1 child, Christa BA, Morris Brown Coll., 1972; MS, Ga. State U., 1980. Cert. FBI Nat. Acad. Police officer Atlanta Police Dept., 1973—79, dep. chief of police, 1982—94, acting chief of police, 1994, chief of police, 1994—2002; affirmative action specialist Atlanta Dept. Pub. Safety, 1979—80, dir. pub. affairs, 1980—82; dir. Transp. Security Coordination Centers Transp. Security Adminstrn. (TSA), dep. fed. security dir.; US marshal (no. dist.) Ga US Marshals Svc., US Dept. Justice, 2010—. Commr. Commn. Accreditation for Law Enforcement Agys., 1991; bd. dirs. Coun. on Battered Women, 1991; trustee Leadership Atlanta, 1991;adv. bd. dir. Big Bros./Big Sisters, 1986—, Atlanta Victim/Witness Assistance Program, 1985—. Named Outstanding Atlantan, 1983, Alumna Yr., Morris Brown Coll., 1985, Bronze Woman Yr., Iota Phi Lambda, 1986, Woman Achiever Atlanta YWCA, YWCA Woman of Yr., 1996. City Govt. Woman of Yr., 1995, 100 Most Influential Georgians; recipient Trailblazer award for Law Enforcement City of Atlanta, TBS Trumpet award, 1999. Mem. Internat. Assn. Chiefs Police (tng. com. Ga. chpt.), Nat. Orgn. Black Law Enforcement (chmn. program), Bus. System Planning Team, Ga. State U. Alumni Assn. (bd. dirs. Atlanta chpt.), Delta Sigma Theta (parliamentarian). Office: US Marshals Service 75 Spring St SW Atlanta GA 30303 Office Phone: 404-331-6833.

HARVEY, ALBERT C., lawyer; b. Knoxville, Tenn., June 30, 1939; m. Nancy Rutherford; children: Anne, Elizabeth. BS, U. Tenn., 1961, JD, 1967. Law clk. Tenn. Supreme Ct.; asst. to pub. defender Shelby County, 1969-71; ptnr. Thomason, Hendrix, Harvey, Johnson & Mitchell, Memphis; adj. faculty U. Memphis Sch. Law, 2010—. Instr. med. and dental jurisprudence U. Tenn., Memphis. Bd. editors Tenn. Law Rev. Pres. Goodwill Boys Club, 1983-85; active YMCA, Arthritis Found., Citizens Assn. Memphis and Shelby County, Shelby County War Memls.; sr. warden of vestry Calvary Episcopal Ch. Maj. gen. USMCR, comdg. gen. 4th Marine divsn. Recipient Sam A. Myar, Jr. award Tenn. Bd. Law Examiners, 1978. Fellow: Am. Coll. Trial Lawyers, Tenn. Bar Found. (pres. 1993—94), Am. Bar Found. (life); mem.: Memphis Area C. of C. (pres. mil. affairs coun.), Am. Inns. of Ct., Memphis Bar Assn. (v.p. 1989, pres. elect 1990, pres. 1991, pres. young lawyers divsn., Lawyer award 2009), Tenn. Bar Assn. (pres. 2002—03), Am. Bd. Trial Advocates (adv.), Am. Judicature Soc. (nat. bd. dirs.), ABA (bd. govs., ho. dels. charter mem. and coun. sect. litigation, young lawyers sect., fellow young lawyers divsn., com. on ethics and profl. responsibility, chair standing com. on law and nat. security, ethics 2000 spl. com.), Navy League, U. Tenn. Nat. Alumni Assn. (pres. Memphis chpt., nat. bd. govs.), Ctrl. Garden Area Assn. (pres.), Memphis Rotary Club (officer, bd. dirs.), Univ. Club Memphis (pres.), Kiwanis, Phoenix Club (1st v.p.). Office: Thomason Hendrix Harvey Johnson & Mitchell 29th Fl 1 Commerce Sq Memphis TN 38103 Office Phone: 901-525-8721. Business E-Mail: Harveya@ThomasonLaw.com.

HARVEY, JOHN ARTHUR, nuclear physicist; b. Saskatoon, Sask., Can., Dec. 14, 1921; naturalized U.S. citizen; married; 2 children. BSc, Queen's U., Ont., Can., 1945; PhD in Physics, MIT, 1950. Physicist Atomic Energy Can., Ltd., 1945-46; rsch. asst. MIT, 1946-50; assoc. physicist Brookhaven Nat. Lab., 1951-55; physicist Oak Ridge Nat. Lab., 1955-93, dir. linear accelerator, 1965-93, retired, 1993, cons., 1993—. Rsch. prof. U. Tenn., 1995—. Home: 108 Ogontz Ln Oak Ridge TN 37830-3905 Office: Oak Ridge Nat Lab PO Box 2008 Oak Ridge TN 37831-6354 E-mail: harveyjm@icx.net.

HARVEY, KERRY B., federal prosecutor; b. Madisonville, Ky., 1957; BS, Murray State U., Ky., 1978; JD, U. Ky. Coll. Law, 1982. Claims svc. rep. Progressive Casualty Ins. Co., Mayfield Village, Ohio, 1978—79; law clk. to state prosecutor Commonwealth Atty.'s Office, Murray, Ky., 1980; law clk. Shaw, Spangler & Roth, Denver, 1981; assoc. Brown, Todd & Heyburn, Louisville, 1982—84; Marshall County atty. Benton, Ky., 1986—94; ptnr. Owen, Harvey & Carter, Benton, 1991—2008; gen. counsel, acting inspector gen. Commonwealth of Ky. Cabinet Health & Family Services, Frankfort, 2008—10; US atty. (eastern dist.) Ky. US Dept. Justice, 2010—. Adj. instr. U. Louisville Sch. Law, 1983, U. Ky. Coll. Law, 1983, Murray State U., 1984; bd. dirs. BMC Bancorp, Inc./Bank of Marshall County, Benton, 1989—94, United Commonwealth Bank, F.S.B., Murray, 1992—98, CBT Corp., Paducah, Ky., 1994—98, Hopfed Bankcorp, Inc./Heritage Bank, Inc., Hopkinsville, Ky., 2001—08. Bd. dirs. Marshall County Chamber of Commerce, 1985—88. Office: US Attorneys Office 260 W Vine St Ste 300 Lexington KY 40507 Office Phone: 859-233-2661. Office Fax: 859-233-2666.*

HARVEY, MARK N., cardiac electrophysiology; MD, U. Okla., 1988. Diplomate Am. Bd. Internal Medicine-clin. cardiac electrophysiology, 2001, Am. Bd. Internal Medicine-cardiovasc. disease. Intern gen. surgery Mt. Sinai Hosp., 1988; resident cardiovasc. disease Univ. of Mich., 1988—89, fellow cardiac electrophysiology and pacing, 1989—92; hosp. affiliation includes Okla. Heart Hosp., joined, 1998. With Cystic Fibrosis Found. Mem.: ACP, Heart Rhythm Soc., Am. Coll. of Cardiology. Office: Oklahoma Heart Hospital Physicians 4050 W Memorial Rd Fl 3 Oklahoma City OK 73120 Office Phone: 405-608-3800.

HARVEY, PATRICIA KIKO, air transportation executive; BS, U. So. Calif., MS in Acctg. CPA. Sr. autid mgr. PricewaterhouseCoopers; dir. franchise revenue & planning Taco Bell Corp.; v.p. internal audit Starbucks Coffee Co., Seattle; v.p. corp. audit Delta Air Lines, Inc., 2009—. Office: Delta Air Lines Inc PO Box 20706 Atlanta GA 30320-6001 Office Phone: 404-715-2600. Office Fax: 404-715-5042. E-mail: kiko.harvey@delta.com.

HARVEY, ROBERT W., investment company executive; BS in Mech. Engring., Tex. A&M U, 1978; MBA, Harvard U., 1982. Vice chmn., exec. v.p. Reliant Energy Inc. (formerly Reliant Resources, Inc.), 1999—2005, group pres., wholesale, 2003; pres. RWH Ventures, LLC, 2005—. Bd. dirs. McKinsey & Co., Inc., 1982—99, TRC Companies, Inc., 2007—. Chmn. bd. trustees Tex. A&M Found.; mem. Vision 2020 adv. coun. Tex. A&M, mem. univ. sys. chancellor's century coun.; mem. Corps of Cadets Devel. Coun.; vice chmn. Ctrl. Houston, Inc., Ctrl. Houston Civic Improvement, Inc.; bd. dirs. Houston Zoo, Inc., United Way Tex. Gulf Coast, Alexis de Tocqueville Soc. Cabinet, The Post Oak Sch. Office: RWH Ventures LLC 1558 Kirby Dr Houston TX 77019-3302 Office Phone: 713-520-7905. Business E-Mail: rharvey@trcsolutions.com.

HARVEY, WILLIAM BRANTLEY, JR., lawyer, retired lieutenant governor; b. Walterboro, SC, Aug. 14, 1930; s. William Brantley and Thelma (Lightsey) H.; m. Helen Coggeshall, Dec. 30, 1952; children: Eileen L., William Brantley, III, Helen C., Margaret D., Warren C. AB in Polit. Sci., The Citadel, Charleston, SC, 1951, LLD (hon.), 1978; JD magna cum laude, U. S.C., Columbia, 1955. Bar: SC 1955. Since practiced in, Beaufort, SC; sr. ptnr. Harvey & Battey; mem. S.C. Ho. of Reps. from Beaufort County, 1958-74, chmn. rules com., mem. constl. revision com.; lt. gov. State of S.C., 1974-78. Bd. dirs., past chmn. Carolina Motor Club (AAA); mem. exec. com. Assoc. Marine Inst., past chmn.; bd. dirs., sec. AMI Kids Beaufort; past chmn. Beaufort County Transp. Com.; pres. SC Bar, 1986—87; mem. SC State Bd. Tech. and Comprehensive Edn., AMI Found. Former commr. S.C. Dept. Hwys. and Pub. transp.; former commr., vice chmn. S.C. Parks, Recreation and Tourism Commn.; mem. Coastal Caroline coun. Boy Scouts Am.; Lowcountry Habitat for Humanity, Mustard Seed Found.; bd. dirs., vice chmn. Historic Beaufort Found.; bd. dirs. Beaufort Symphony Orch. Lt. artillery US Army, 1952—54. Decorated Order of Palmetto Gov. James B. Edwards, SC. Mem. ABA, S.C. Bar Assn., Beaufort County Bar Assn., Rotary, Phi Beta Kappa, Kappa Alpha, Phi Delta Phi, Omicron Delta Kappa. Presbyterian (elder). Avocations: sailing, hunting, fishing, reading. Home: 501 Pinckney St Beaufort SC 29902-4739 Office: Harvey & Battey Attys PO Box 1107 1001 Craven St Beaufort SC 29902-5577 Home Phone: 843-524-2935; Office Phone: 843-524-3109. Office Fax: 843-524-6973. Business E-Mail: wbharvey@harveyandbattey.com.

HARVICK, KEVIN, race car driver; b. Bakersfield, Calif., Dec. 8, 1975; m. DeLana Linville, Feb. 28, 2001. Student, Bakersfield Jr. Coll., 1997. Racecar driver Richard Childress Racing, Welcome, NC, 2000—. 1st pl. Cracker Barrel Old Country 500 Atlanta Motor Speedway, 2001; 1st pl. Tropicana 400 Chicagoland Speedway, 2001, 2002; 1st pl. Brickyard 400 Indpls. Motor Speedway, 2003; 1st pl. Ford City 500 Bristol Motor Speedway, 2005; 1st pl. Subway Fresh 500 Phoenix Internat. Speedway, 2006, 1st pl. Checker Auto Parts 500, 2006, 1st pl. AdvoCare 500, 2012; 1st pl. AMD at The Glen Watkins Glen Internat., 2006; 1st pl. Chevy Rock and Roll 400 Richmond Internat. Raceway, 2006, 1st pl. One Last Race to Make the Chase 400, 2011; 1st pl. Sylvania 300 NH Internat. Speedway, 2006; 1st pl. Daytona 500 Daytona Motor Speedway, 2007, 1st pl. Coke Zero 400, 2010; 1st pl. Aaron's 499 Talladega Superspeedway, 2010; 1st pl. CARFAX 400 Mich. Internat. Speedway, 2010; 1st pl. Auto Club 400 Auto Club Speedway, Fontana, Calif., 2011; 1st pl. Goody's Fast Relief 500 Martinsville Speedway, Va., 2011; 1st pl. Coca-Cola 600 Charlotte Motor Speedway, 2011. Named Rookie of the Yr., Busch Series, 2000, Winston Cup Raybestos, 2001, champion, NASCAR Winston West, 1998, Busch Series, 2001, 2006, Brickyard 400, 2003, Daytona 500, 2007. Achievements include becoming the first driver in NASCAR history to run full-time on both the Busch and Winston Cup series, a total of 70 races, in one season (2001); first to be named Winston Cup rookie of the year the same season that he earned the Busch Series Championship (2001). Avocations: riding ATV's and go karts, video games, remote control cars, skeet shooting. Office: c/o Richard Childress Racing PO Box 1189 Welcome NC 27374-1189

HARWELL, AUBREY BIGGS, lawyer; b. Nashville, June 9, 1942; s. Aubrey B. and Grace Cleveland (Follin) H.; m. Carlana Christine H.; children: Aubrey B. III, Christopher F. BA, Vanderbilt U., 1964, JD, 1967. Bar: Tenn. 1967, U.S. Dist. Ct. Appeals (6th cir.) 1971, U.S. Supreme Ct. 1971. Assoc. Cornelius, Collins, Neal & Higgins, Nashville, 1967-71; ptnr. Neal & Harwell, Nashville, 1971—. Lectr. law Vanderbilt U., Nashville, 1979; ind. counsel to chmn. Fed. Home Loan Bank Bd., Washington, 1986; bd. dir Piedmont Natural Gas Co., 2002-; bd. dir. NID Corp.; holder Chair of Excellence, Middlei Tenn., Univ. Coll. Bus. Bd. mem. Meharry Med. Coll., Vanderbilt Med. Ctr., Cmty. Found. Mid. Tenn., Tenn. Performing Arts Ctr., Boy Scouts Am., nat. treas. Recipient Silver Buffalo award Boy Scouts Am. Mem. ABA, Am. Bd. Trial Advocates (bd. dirs.), Nat. Assn. Criminal Def. Lawyers, Tenn. Bar Assn., Nashville Bar Assn. (pres. 1994), Nashville City Club, Richland Country Club. Democrat. Baptist. Avocations: fishing, scuba diving, hunting, tennis. Office: Neal & Harwell 2000 One Nashville Pl Nashville TN 37219

HARWELL, BETH HALTEMAN, state legislator; b. Norristown, Pa., Sept. 24, 1957; married; m. Sam Harwell; 3 children; 2 children. BA, David Lipscomb U., 1978; MS, George Peabody Coll., 1979; PhD, Vanderbilt U., 1982. Bd. trustees Centennial Med. Ctr.; adv. bd. mem. Cohn Adult Learning Ctr. & Womens Network; mem. bus. adv. coun. David Lipscomb U.; bd. dir. Knowles Sr. Citizens Ctr.; assoc. prof. Belmont U., 1986—90; state rep. Dist. 56 Tenn., 1988—; chmn. Tenn. State Rep. Party, 2001—04. Mem.: AMI (Nashville) (advisor bd. mem.), Leadership Nashville, Families First (advisor coun., statewide advisor coun.), Am. Heart Assn. (Tenn. chap. bd. dir.), Nashville Vanderbilt Club (bd. dir.). Republican. Church Of Christ. Office: 42 Wyn Oak Nashville TN 37205 also: 107 War Memorial Bldg Nashville TN 37243-0156 Office Phone: 615-385-0357, 615-741-0709. Office Fax: 615-741-4917. Business E-Mail: rep.beth.harwell@capitol.tn.gov.

HARWELL, DAVID WALKER, retired judge; b. Florence, SC, Jan. 8, 1932; s. Baxter Hicks and Lacy (Rankin) H.; married; children: Robert Bryan, William Baxter. LL.B., JD, U. S.C., 1958; HHD (hon.), Frances Marion U., 1987; D in Pub. Svc. (hon.), Coastal Carolina U., 2006. Bar: S.C. 1958, U.S. Dist. Ct. S.C. 1958, U.S. Ct. Appeals 1964, U.S. Supreme Ct. 1961. Circuit judge 12th Jud. Ct. S.C., 1973-80; justice S.C. Supreme Ct., 1980-91, chief justice, 1991-94; ret., 1994; spl. counsel Nelson, Mullins, Riley and Scarborough. Mem. S.C. Ho. of Reps., 1962-73. Served with USNR, 1952-54. Mem. Am. Bar Assn., Am. Trial Lawyers Assn., S.C. Bar Assn., S.C. Trial Lawyers Assn. (Portrait and Scholarship award 1986). Presbyterian. Office Phone: 843-448-3500, 843-446-5673. Business E-Mail: david.harwell@nelsonmullins.com.

HARWELL, ROBERT BRYAN, federal judge; b. Florence, SC, 1959; BA, Clemson U., 1980; JD, U. SC, 1982. Law clk. to Hon. G. Rodney Peeples State of SC Jud. Dept., 1983; law clk. to Hon. Ross Anderson Jr. US Dist. Ct. SC, 1983—84; pvt. practice atty. Florence, 1984—2004; judge US Dist. Ct. SC, Florence, 2004—. Mem. SC Army Nat. Guard, 1987—92. Office: US Dist Ct 401 W Evans St Florence SC 29501 Office Phone: 843-676-3800.

HASENYAGER, RICHARD L., JR., library director; BS in Elem. Edn., Ohio State U., Columbus, 1994; MLS, Sam Houston State U., Huntsville, Tex., 2000; doctoral student in info. sci., U. North Tex., Denton, 2005—. 5th grade tchr. Alief Ind. Sch. Dist., Houston, 1996—98, libr. media specialist, 1998—2001; part-time GED & ESL instr. Harris County Dept. Edn., Houston, 1998—2001; libr. media specialist Katy Ind. Sch. Dist., Katy, Tex., 2001—07, jr. high libr. media specialist, 2006—07; dir. libr. services North East Ind. Sch. Dist., San Antonio, 2007—. Adj. reference librarian Cy-Fair Coll., Cypress, Tex., 2003—07; adj. instr. U. North Tex., 2007—. Named to Movers & Shakers, Libr. Jour., 2011. Mem.: ALA, Tex. Libr. Assn., Tex. State Teachers Assn., American Soc. Info. Sci. & Tech., Assn. Libr. and Info. Sci. Educators, Tex. Assn. Sch. Libr. Administrators. Office: North East Ind School District 8961 Tesoro Dr San Antonio TX 78217 Office Phone: 210-407-0001. Business E-Mail: rhasen@neisd.net.

HASHMI, SAJJAD AHMAD, finance educator, dean; b. India, Dec. 20, 1933; m. Monica Ruggiero; children: Serena, Jason, Shawn, Michelle. BA, U. Karachi, 1953, MA, 1956; PhD in Ins., U. Pa., 1962. Lectr. Ohio State U., Columbus, 1962-64; asst. prof. Roosevelt U., Chgo., 1964-66; prof. Ball State U., Muncie, Ind., 1966-83, chmn. dept. fin., 1973-83; Jones disting. prof., dean emeritus Sch. Bus. Emporia (Kans.) State U., 1983—2003. Tech. advisor Ind. Arts Commn.; vice chmn. bd. trustees Kans. Ins. Edn. Found.; appeared on TV and radio programs, testified before NY, Kans. and Ind. legis. coms.; cons., spkr. in field. Author: Insurance is a Funny Business, 1972, Automobile Insurance, 1973, Contemporary Personal Finance, 1985, Make Every Second Count, 1989, Strategies for The Future, 1990; contbr. articles to profl. jours. Named Prof. of Yr., Ball State U. Students, 1971, Outstanding Tchr. of Yr., Ball State U., 1970. Mem. Am. Risk and Ins. Assn., Midwest Fin. Assn., Fin. Mgmt. Assn., Emporia C. of C., Emporia Country Club, Rotary, Beta Gamma Sigma, Sigma Iota Epsilon, Alpha Kappa Psi, Gamma Iota Epsilon, Phi Kappa Phi. Home: 13804 Siena Loop Bradenton FL 34202-2442 Personal E-mail: shashmi58@gmail.com.

HASKELL, DAVID G., biology professor; married. BA in Zoology, U. Oxford, England; PhD in Ecology and Evolutionary Biology, Cornell U., Ithaca, NY. Prof. biology Sewanee: U. of South, Tenn. Owner Cudzoo Farm, Sewanee. Contbr. articles to profl. jours. Named Tchr. of Yr., Soc. Sewanee Scholars, 2007, Tenn. Prof. of Yr., Carnegie Found. for Advancement of Tchg. and Coun. for Advancement and Support of Edn., 2009. Office: Sewanee: University of South Spencer Hall 159 735 University Ave Sewanee TN 37383 Office Phone: 931-598-1918. Business E-Mail: dhaskell@sewanee.edu.

HASKINS, V. LYLE, retired academic administrator; b. Bellingham, Wash., Dec. 6, 1938; s. Victor and Doris Haskins; m. Annette McFarland, Aug. 22, 1959; children: Cheryl Jeanice Rodriquez, Laura Terese Mendenhall. PhD in History, U. Okla., Norman, 1968. Dean, coll. social sciences Northeastern State U., Tahlequah, Okla., 1975—93, dean, coll. social & behavioral sci., 1993—2004, interim assoc. v.p., academic affairs, 2005—06, history prof., cons., academic affairs, 2006; emeritus prof., history and dean Coll. Social and Behavioral Scis., 2006—. Office: Northeastern State Univ 600 N Grand Ave Tahlequah OK 74464 Business E-Mail: haskins@nsuok.edu.*

HASLAM, BILL (WILLIAM EDWARD HASLAM), Governor of Tennessee, former mayor; b. Knoxville, Tenn., Aug. 23, 1958; s. Jim and Natalie L. Haslam; m. Crissy Haslam, 1981; children: Will, Annie, Leigh. BA in History, Emory U. Mgr. Pilot Travel Centers, 1983—85; pres. Pilot Corp., 1985—2003; owner Tenn. Smokies; mayor City of Knoxville, 2003—11; gov. State of Tenn., 2011—. Bd. mem. Adv. Coun. on Hist. Preservation, 2008—, Tenn. Tech. Devel. Corp., 2008—. Chmn. East Tenn. Ctr. for Non-Profit Mgmt.; chmn. & pres. Project GRAD; exec. com. chmn. Young Life of Knoxville; campaign chmn. Foothills Land Conservancy; vice chmn. Knoxville Mus. Art; former bd. mem. Cornerstone Found. and World Vision, Emerald Ave. Youth Found., Diversity Task Force of Nine Counties, One Vision; elder Cedar Springs Presbyn. Ch. Mem.: Salvation Army (chmn.), United Way of Greater Knoxville (chmn.). Republican. Presbyterian. Avocations: bicycling, running. Office: Office of the Governor 1st Floor State Capitol Nashville TN 37243 Office Phone: 615-741-2001. E-mail: bill.haslam@tn.gov.*

HASLAM, JAMES A., III, retail executive, professional sports team executive; b. Mar. 9, 1954; m. Susan Bagwell; children: Jim, Whitney, Cynthia. BA in Mktg., U. Tenn., Knoxville. Joined Pilot Corp., Knoxville, Tenn., 1976, v.p. sales devel. and ops., 1980, pres., CEO, 1996—, Pilot Travel Centers, LLC (also known as Pilot Flying J), 2001—; part owner Pitts. Steelers, 2008—12; owner Cleve. Browns, 2012—. Bd. dirs. Ruby Tuesday, Inc., First Horizon Nat. Corp., Anderson Media Corp., Innovation Valley, Inc.; mem. Fed. Res. Bd. Energy Adv. Coun. Bd. dirs. Clayton Family Found., U. Tenn. Athletics, United Way of Greater Knoxville and Lakeshore Pk. Mem.: Nat. Assn. Truckstop Operators (bd. dirs.), Nat. Assn. Convenience Store Operators (mem. leadership coun.). Office: Pilot Corp PO Box 10146 Knoxville TN 37939-0146 Office Phone: 865-588-7488.

HASLETT, JIM (JAMES DONALD HASLETT), professional football coach; b. Pitts., Dec. 9, 1955; m. Beth Haslett; children: Kelsey, Chase, Libby. BA in Elem. Edn., Ind. U., Pa., 1978. Linebacker Buffalo Bills, 1979—85, NY Jets, 1987; asst. football coach U. Buffalo Bulls, 1988-89; asst. coach LA Raiders, 1993-94, Pitts. Steelers, 1996-99; head coach New Orleans Saints, 2000—05; defensive coord. St. Louis Rams, 2006—08, interim head coach, 2008; head coach Fla. Tuskers, United Football League, Orlando, 2009; defensive coord. Washington Redskins, 2010—. Named NFL Defensive Rookie of Yr., AP, 1979, Coach of Yr., NFL, 2000; named to Coll. Football Hall of Fame, 2002. Office: Washington Redskins 21300 Redskin Pk Dr Ashburn VA 20147

HASS, JOSEPH MONROE, automotive executive; b. Syracuse, NY, July 28, 1955; s. Joseph Monroe and Susan Faith (Betts) H.; m. Lisa Michelle Palmer, Aug. 14, 1982. BS in Secondary Edn., Tenn. Temple U., 1977. Diesel mechanic Cummins Engines Tenn., Chattanooga, 1978-81, mgr. tng. Nashville, 1981-85; svc. fl. foreman Cummins Cumberland, Nashville, 1985-86, CompuChek technician, 1986-87, fleet systems support engr., 1987-89, tech. advisor, instr., 1989-90, dir. devel., 1990—2013; dir. electrical safety Cumminus Crosspoint, 2013—. Diesel mechanic Cummins Engines Tenn., Chattanooga, 1978—81, tng. mgr., Nashville, 1981—85; svc. fl. foreman Cummins Cumberland, 1985—86, compu-chek technician, 1986—87, fleet sys. support engr., 1987—89, tech. advisor, instr., 1989—90, devel. dir., 1990—2013; dir., elec. safety Cummins Crosspoint, 2013—. Mem. ASTD, Am. Assn. Individual Investors, Citizens Against Govt. Waste, Exptl. Aircraft Assn., Heritage Found., AOPA Avocations: music, sailing, carpentry, bicycling, reading, flying. Office: Cummins Crosspoint LLC 706 Spence Ln Nashville TN 37217-1190 Home Phone: 615-865-7250. Business E-Mail: joseph.m.hass@cummins.com.

HASSEL, RUDOLPH CHRISTOPHER, language educator; b. Richmond, Va., Nov. 16, 1939; s. Rudolph Christopher and Helen Elizabeth (Poehler) H.; m. Sedley Louise Hotchkiss, June 16, 1962; children: Bryan Christopher, Paul Sedley. BA, U. Richmond, 1961; MA, U. N.C., 1962; PhD, Emory U., 1968. English instr. Mercer U., Macon, Ga., 1962-65; asst. prof. Vanderbilt U., Nashville, 1968-73, assoc. prof., 1973-85, prof., 1985—2003, prof. emeritus, 2003. Dir. grad. studies English dept. Vanderbilt U., 1974-81, dir. undergrad. studies, 1991, 99-00; mem. exec. com. Folger Inst., Washington, 1986-95; cons. State of Tenn., Nashville, 1987-93; cons. for various univ. presses and profl. jours. Author: Renaissance Drama and the English Church Year, 1979, Faith and Folly in Shakespeare's Romantic Comedies, 1980, Songs of Death, 1987, Shakespeare's Religious Language: A Dictionary, 2005; contbr. articles to Shakespeare Quar., Shakespeare Jahrbuch, Comparative Drama, Studies in Philology, others, poems to Vanderbilt Rev., Arts and Letters. Mem. choir Christ Episcopal Ch., Nashville, 1974-95, outreach vol., 1974—, vestryman, 1980-83; vol. United Way, Vanderbilt U., 1980—, Habitat for Humanity. Woodrow Wilson Found. fellow, 1962; Emory U. fellow, 1965; Folger Libr. fellow, 1976; Am. Philol. Soc. fellow, 1986. Mem. MLA, Internat. Shakespeare Assn., Shakespeare Assn. Am., Malone Soc., Omicron Delta Kappa, ACLS, Phi Beta Kappa. Avocations: biking, hiking, tennis, gardening, woodcrafting. Home: 107 Pembroke Ave Nashville TN 37205-3728 Office: PO Box 129B Nashville TN 37202-0129 Business E-Mail: r.chris.hassel@vanderbilt.edu.

HASSELBACH, KARLHEINZ, retired literature educator; b. Giessen, Germany; arrived in US, 1965; s. Adolf and Elisabeth Hasselbach; m. Ingrid Tiesler, June 10, 1972. PhD, Philipps U., Marburg, Germany, 1971. Asst. prof. Fla. State U., Tallahassee, 1965—72; assoc. prof. Tulane U., New Orleans, 1974—86, prof., 1986—2005, chmn. dept. Germanic and Slavic languages, 1978—82, dept. chair Germanic and Slavic languages, 1989—95, emeritus, 2005. Author: The Dialects of the Region of the Central Vogelsberg in Germany (vol. 76 of Deutsche Dialekt- Geographie), 1971, Thomas Mann: Doktor Faustus, 1978, 1986, Thomas Mann: Doktor Faustus, vol. 24 of Oldenbourg-Interpretationen, 1988, 1996, Georg Büchner: Lenz, 1986, Georg Büchner: Lenz, vol. 5 of Oldenbourg-Interpretationen, 1988, Bertolt Brecht: Kalendergeschichten, vol. 32 of Odlenbourg-Interpretationen, 1990, 1997, Georg Büchner, Reclam, 1997, 2d rev. edit., 1999; contbr. articles to profl. jours. on Thomas Mann, Ernst Jünger, romanticism, and socio-linguistics. Mem.: AAUP, ACTA, Nat. Assoc. Scholars.

HASSELL, STEPHEN C., information technology executive; BS in Computer Sci., US Naval Acad., Annapolis, 1988; MBA, Northwestern U., Chgo., 1995. Officer US Navy, 1988—95; mgr., strategic planning Newport News Shipbuilding, 1995—96, dir., process innovation, 1996—98, v.p., chief info. officer, 1998—2002; pres., CEO Naptheon Inc. (subs. Newport News Shipbuilding), 2001—02; chief info. officer Invensys, 2002—04; v.p. & chief info. officer Emerson Electric Co., 2004—10; pres. Avocent Corp. (acquired by Emerson Network Power), 2010—. Decorated Navy Commendation medal; recipient CIO 100 award, CIO Mag. Office: Avocent Corp 4991 Corporate Dr Huntsville AL 35805 Office Phone: 256-430-4000. Office Fax: 256-430-4030. Business E-Mail: stephen.hassell@avocent.com.

HASSELMAN, RICHARD B., retired rail transportation executive; b. Jersey City, Nov. 28, 1926; s. Benjamin R. and Clara A. (Borchert) H.; m. Mildred E. Schaber, May 29, 1954; children: Richard Dwight, James Christopher. BME, Yale U., 1947; MBA, NYU, 1949. Student engr. N.Y. Ctrl. R.R., 1947-49, trainee, 1949—52, brakeman, 1952-53, signalman, freight agt., 1953; transp. insp. Ea. region Syracuse, NY, 1953-55; trainmaster Mohawk divsn. Albany, NY, 1955-57; divsn. trainmaster Syracuse divsn., 1957; divsn. supt. Boston & Albany divsn. Springfield, Mass., 1957-59; dist. transp. supt. Western region Cleve., 1959-60; gen. supt. yards and terminals N.Y. Ctrl. Sys., NYC, 1960-63; gen. mgr. Ind. Harbor Belt and Chicago River & Ind. R.R., Hammond, Ind., 1963; gen. mgr. No. Region N.Y. Ctrl. R.R., Detroit, 1964, gen. mgr. So. Region Indpls., 1964-66, gen. mgr. Western Region Cleve., 1967; asst. v.p. transp. N.Y. Ctrl. Sys., NYC, 1967-68; v.p. transp. Penn. Ctrl., Phila., 1968-76; pres. Ind. Harbor Belt R.R., 1968-87; sr. v.p. ops. Consol. Rail Corp., Phila., 1976-89; transp. cons., 1989—. Home: 5289 Ladyfinger Lake Rd Sanibel FL 33957-2436

HASSEMAN, DEAN MICHAEL, lawyer; b. Abington, Pa., Mar. 15, 1946; s. Charles L. and Doreen C. (Herzog) H.; m. Mary Kay Powers, Aug. 14, 1971; children: K. Mariah, C. Abigail. BA in Polit. Sci., Northeastern U., 1968; JD, U. Va. Sch. Law, 1971. Bar: Pa. 1971, Okla. 1983, US Dist. Ct. (eastern dist.) Pa. 1975, US Dist. Ct. (northern dist.) Okla. 1990, US Ct. Appeals (DC cir.) 1990, Temporary Emergency Ct. Appeals, US Supreme Ct. 1977; cert. treas., 2006, Va. Darden Grad. Sch. Bus. Asst. defender Defender Assn. Phila., 1971-72; sr. atty. Sun Refining & Mktg. Co., Phila., 1972-82, Sun Pipe Line Co., Tulsa, 1982-87; gen. counsel Williams Pipe Line Co., Tulsa, 1987-91; sr. counsel Citgo Petroleum Corp., Tulsa, 1991—98, sr. corporate counsel, 1998—2002, acting gen. counsel, 2003—06, gen. counsel, chief compliance officer, 2006—. Legal advisor gen. com.

transp. American Petroleum Inst., 1987-90; bd. dirs. Williams Employees Credit Union, 1990-93; mem. legal adv. com. Marine Preservation Assn., state affairs com. Assn. Oil Pipe Line Cos., legal com. Colonial Pipe Line Co., Explorer Pipe Line Co. Recipient HBJ/ACC Champion of Diversity award, 2009, Huminity Corp. Counsel Assn. Employer of Choice award in South & SE Region; named one of Best Assn. Corp. Counsel, Houston Bus. Jour., 2009. Mem. ABA, Okla. Bar Assn., Tulsa County Bar Assn. Democrat. Unitarian Universalist. Avocations: horseback riding, tennis. Office: Citgo Petroleum Corp PO Box 4689 Houston TX 77210 Office Phone: 832-486-1700. Office Fax: 832-486-1817. E-mail: dhassem@citgo.com.

HASSETT, BRENDAN, mathematics professor; b. Apr. 1, 1971; BA in Math., Yale Coll., 1992; MA, Harvard U., 1994, PhD, 1996. Dickson instr. math. U. Chgo., 1996—2000; vis. instr. Inst. Mittag-Leffler, Stockholm, 1997; vis. scholar inst. math. sciences Chinese U. Hong Kong, 2000—01; asst. prof. math. Rice U., 2000—03, assoc. prof. math., 2003—06, prof. math., 2006—, chair dept. math., 2009—. Author: (books) Introduction to algebraic geometry, 2007, Arithmetic Geometry, 2009. Recipient Charles W. Duncan Jr. Achievement award for Outstanding Faculty, Rice U., 2009. Office: Dept Math Rice U MS 136 6100 S Main St Houston TX 77005 Office Phone: 713-348-5261. Business E-Mail: hassett@rice.edu.

HASSON, JAMES KEITH, JR., lawyer, educator; b. Knoxville, Tenn., Mar. 3, 1946; s. James Keith and Elaine (Biggers) Hasson; m. Jayne Young, July 27, 1968; 1 child, Keith Samuel. BA, Duke U., 1967; JD, 1970. Bar: Ga. 1971, DC 1971. Assoc. Sutherland, Asbill & Brennan, Atlanta, 1970—76; ptnr., 1976; prof. law Emory U., Atlanta, 1976—94; chmn. bd. dir. House-Hasson Hardware Co., Knoxville, 2000—. Dir. Gary and Mary West Wireless Health Inst., 2010—. Editor: Jour. Taxation; contbr. articles profl. jour. Mem. Atlanta Civilian Rev. Bd.; trustee Met. Atlanta Crime Commn., chmn., 1986—87; trustee Foxfire Fund, 1988—2001, A.D. Henderson Found., 2005—; chmn. bd. dirs. Foxfire Fund; chmn. bd. trustees Reinhardt Coll., 2001—06; elder 1st Presbyn. Ch., Atwater, 2008—. Recipient Pres. Disting. Svc. award, 1980. Mem.: ABA (com. chmn. 1983—85), Atlanta Bar Assn. (counsel 1977—80), Leadership Atlanta, Peachtree Club. Presbyterian. Home: 3185 Chatham Rd NW Atlanta GA 30305-1101 Office: Sutherland Asbill & Brennan 999 Peachtree St NE Ste 2300 Atlanta GA 30309-3996 Office Phone: 404-853-8083. Business E-Mail: jim.hasson@sutherland.com.

HASSON, JANET, publishing executive; BA in Bus. Adminstrn., Ea. Wash. U. With The Spokesman-Rev., assoc. pub. jour. of bus.; circulation and mktg. exec. the Cin. enquirer Gannett Co. Inc., 1997, circulation dir. the Idaho statesman Boise, Idaho, 1999, pres. the jour. news Westchester County, NY, 2011—; v.p. circulation Rochester (NY) Dem. and Chronicle, 2004; joined Detroit Media Partnership, 2005, sr. v.p., v.p. circulation, pub. Detroit free press, pub. the Detroit news. Served newspaper assn. of America's liaison com. Audit Bur. of Circulations; served adv. bd. SW Detroit Salvation Army. Recipient Gannett Pres.' Ring award. Office: Gannett Company Incorporated 7950 Jones Branch Dr Mc Lean VA 22107-0150 Office Phone: 703-854-6000.

HASTINGS, ALCEE LAMAR, United States Representative from Florida, former federal judge; b. Altomonte Springs, Fla., Sept. 5, 1936; s. Julius C. and Mildred L. Hastings; children: Chelsea, Alcee Jr., Leigh. BS in Zoology & Botany, Fisk U., Nashville, 1958; student, Howard U. Sch. Law; JD, Fla. A&M U., 1963. Bar: Fla. 1963. Assoc. Allen & Hastings, Ft. Lauderdale, 1963-66; pvt. practice atty. Ft. Lauderdale, 1966-77, 1989—92; judge Cir. Ct. Broward County, Fla., 1977-79, US Dist. Ct. (southern dist.) Fla., 1979-89; mem. US Congress from 23d Fla Dist., Washington, 1993—2013, US Congress from 20th Fla Dist., 2013—. Lectr., cons. Peace Corps Vols., Avon Park, Fla., 1966. Host (TV series) Pride, Sta. WPLG, columnist West Side Gazette. Trustee Broward Cmty. Coll., Bethune Cookman Coll.; bd. dirs. Urban League Broward County, Child Advocacy, Inc., Broward County Sickle Cell Anemia Found., Fla. Voters League, Broward County Coun. Human Rels. Recipient Humanitarian award, Broward County Young Democrats, 1978, Sam Delevoe Human Rights award, Cmty. Relations Bd. Broward County, 1978, Glades Festival of Afro Arts award, Zeta Phi Beta, 1981, Chairman's award, Nat. Bar Assn., 1981; named Citizen of Yr., Zeta Phi Beta, 1978, Man of Yr., Com. Italian American Affairs, 1979; named one of The 100 Most Influential Black Americans, Ebony mag., 2006; named to The Power 150, 2008. Mem.: NOW, NAACP, Miami-Dade C. of C., Am. Civil Liberties Union, Family Christian Assn. Democrat. Office: US House of Representatives 2353 Rayburn House Office Bldg Washington DC 20515-0923 also: 2701 W Oakland Park Blvd Ste 200 Fort Lauderdale FL 33311 Office Phone: 202-225-1313, 954-733-2800. Office Fax: 202-225-1171, 954-735-9444. E-mail: alcee.pubhastings@mail.house.gov.*

HASTINGS, KELLY, state legislator; m. Anika Howell Hastings; 1 child. Grad., U. NC; BS in Commn., Mktg. & Mgmt., Appalachian State U. Bd. dirs. Pregnancy Resource Ctr., Boy's and Girl's Club; mem. Nat. Rifle Assoc.; with Rotary, Jaycees; mem. NC Farm Bureau, NC Assoc. of Realtors; mem. Dist. 110 NC House of Representatives, 2008—. Mil. USMC. Republican. Office: 405 Jane St Cherryville NC 28021 also: North Carolina House of Representatives 16 W Jones St Room 2123 Raleigh NC 27601-1096 Office Phone: 704-473-3468, 919-715-2002. Business E-Mail: Kelly.Hastings@ncleg.net.

HASWELL, CARLETON RADLEY, banker; b. Milw., May 18, 1939; s. Clayton Lyman and Jane (Radley) H.; m. Almut Haberkamp, Dec. 10, 1966; children—Angela, Robin. BS, Northwestern U., 1961; MBA, NYU, 1967. Chief internat. credit officer Chem. Bank, NYC, 1963-87; dir. Chem. Internat. Inc., NYC, 1981-86, Chem. Internat. Fin., NYC, 1981-84; pres. Carleton Haswell Assocs., 1987—. Treas. P.G. Islanders; counselor S.C.O.R.E. With US Army, 1961—63. Republican. Home and Office: Villa 514 2645 W Marion Ave Punta Gorda FL 33950-5979

HATCH, HELEN DAVIS, architect; m. Edward M. Hatch, Apr. 6, 1994; children: Charles M., Katelyn Jane. BA, Agnes Scott Coll., Decatur, Ga.; MArch, Harvard Grad. Sch. Design. Arch. Thompson, Ventulett, Stainback & Assocs., Atlanta, 1973, positions up to mem. prins. adv. group, v.p. client rels., 1994—; prin., dir. hospitality design Cooper Carry, Atlanta, 1985—94. Adj. faculty mem. U. Hawaii Sch. Architecture, Manoa. Past chair Atlanta Dist. Coun. Urban Land Inst., trustee, dist. coun. counselor, mem. policy and practice com.; chair Mayor's Walkable Atlanta Task Force; bd. mem. Beltline Partnership; mem. alumni coun. Harvard Grad. Sch. Design; mem. adv. coun. Savannah Coll. Art and Design; mem. steering com. Metro Atlanta C. of C.; mem. environ. com. Leadership Atlanta. Named Outstanding Alumna, Agnes Scott Coll.; named to Women of Excellence, Bus. to Bus. Mag. Fellow: AIA. Office: TVS Internat 2700 Promenade Two 1230 Peachtree St NE Atlanta GA 30309-3591 Office Phone: 404-888-6600. Office Fax: 404-888-6700. E-mail: hhatch@tvsa.com.

HATCH, JOHN D., lawyer; b. Atlanta, Aug. 26, 1942; s. Ernest Healey and Charlotte Blanchard (Chazal) H.; m. Pamela Faye Carr, June 13, 1964; children: Wendy H. Duncan, A. Candice Hatch, Teresa H. Caraker. AA, Ctrl. Fla. Jr. Coll., Ocala, 1962; BS, Fla. State U., 1964; JD, Georgetown U., 1971. Bar: Fla. 1971, Conn. 1972, Tex. 1992, U.S. Dist. Ct. Conn. 1973, U.S. Dist. Ct. (no. dist.) Tex. 1992, U.S. Tax Ct. 1979, U.S. Supreme Ct. 1979; gen. securities lic., gen. prin. lic. Lt. USNR, 1964-71; atty. AEtna Life & Casualty, Hartford, Conn., 1971-74, counsel, 1974-83; v.p. and gen. counsel Continental Corp., NYC, 1983-85; v.p. spl. ops. Comml. Life Ins. Co., Piscataway, N.J., 1985-87; v.p. and gen. counsel Associated Madison Cos., Inc., NYC, 1987-88; sr. v.p. Resource Deployment, Inc., NYC and Ft. Worth, 1988-91; pres. Ins. Horizons, Inc., Ocala, Fla., 1992—, John D. Hatch, P.C., Ocala, 1992—. Gen. counsel Am. Health & Life Ins. Co., Ft. Worth, 1995—; bd. dirs. Pub. Svc. Mut. Ins. Co., N.Y.C., London and Midland Gen. Ins. Co., London, Ont. Mem. ABA (chmn. TIPS employee benefits com. 1983-84, TIPS fin. svcs. com. 1992-93), Assn. Life Ins. Counsel, Fed. Bar Assn., Internat. Assn. Ins. Law. Republican. Roman Catholic. Avocations: reading, boating, tennis. Office: John D Hatch Pc 1267 Berkshire Ln Tarpon Springs FL 34688-7631

HATCH, NATHAN ORR, academic administrator; b. May 17, 1946; m. Julia Gregg; 3 children. AB summa cum laude, Wheaton Coll., 1968; AM, Washington U., 1972, PhD, 1974. Postdoctoral fellow Johns Hopkins U., 1974-75; from asst. prof. to prof. history U. Notre Dame, South Bend, Ind., 1975-88, dir. grad. studies dept. history, 1980-83, assoc. dean Coll. Arts and Letters, dir. Inst. for Scholarship in the Liberal Arts, 1983-89, acting dean Coll. Arts and Letters, 1988-89, v.p. for grad. studies and rsch., 1989-96, prof., 1989, provost, 1996—2005, Andrew V. Tackes prof. history, 1999—2005; pres. Wake Forest U., Winston-Salem, NC, 2005—. Author: The Sacred Cause of Liberty: Republican Thought and the Millennium in Revolutionary New England, 1977, The Democratization of American Christianity, 1989 (Albert C. Outler prize Am. Soc. Ch. History 1989, 1989 Book prize Soc. for Historians of Early Am. Republic, co-winner John Hope Franklin Publ. prize Yale U. Press 1990); also articles; editor: The Professions in American History, 1988; co-editor: The Bible in America: Essays in Cultural History, 1982, Jonathan Edwards and the American Experience, 1988. Bd. dirs. United Way St. Joseph County, Ind., 1987-92; trustee St. Joseph's Med. Ctr., 1994, chair bd. trustees, 1997-99; mem. nat. adv. bd. Salvation Army, 1997-99; trustee Fuller Theol. Sem., 1998—; mem. Nat. Coun. Humanities, 2000—. Recipient Paul Fenlon Teaching award U. Notre Dame, 1981; Am. Coun. Learned Socs. fellow, 1976, Fred Harris Daniels fellow Am. Antiquarian Soc., 1977, Charles Warren fellow Harvard U., 1977-78; grantee Lilly Endowment, 1979, Ind. Com. for the Humanities, 1981-82, NEH, 1981-85. Mem. Johns Hopkins Soc. Scholars, Am. Soc. Ch. Hist. (pres. 1993), Phi Beta Kappa. Office: Wake Forest University 211 Reynolds Hall Box 7226 1834 Wake Forest Rd Winston Salem NC 27109 Office Phone: 336-758-5112. E-mail: hatch@wfu.edu.*

HATCH, ROSS RIEPERT, weapon system engineering executive; b. NYC, Sept. 6, 1934; s. Aylmer Roscoe and Ebba (Riepert) H.; m. Phyllis Anne Hess, July 21, 1961; children: Robert Ross, Michael Aylmer. BS in Engring., U.S. Naval Acad., Annapolis, Md., 1956; MS in Engring. Electronics, U.S. Naval Postgrad. Sch., Monterey, Calif., 1964; MS in Fin. Mgmt., George Washington U., 1972. Commd. ensign USN, 1956, advanced through grades to capt., 1977, ret., 1985, dept. head destroyers, cruisers, ice-breakers, 1956-71; commanding officer guided missile destroyer USS Semmes (DDG-18), Charleston, S.C., 1971-72; commanding officer guided missile cruiser USS Belknap (CG-26), Norfolk, Va., 1979-82; head missile br. Office of Chief Naval Ops., Washington, 1972-76; program mgr. Naval Sea Sys. Command, Washington, 1976-79, dir. combat sys., 1982-85; strike/cruise missile program mgr. Applied Physics Lab.-Johns Hopkins U., Laurel, Md., 1985-96, asst. dept. head power projection dept., 1996—99; apptd. prin. profl. staff Johns Hopkins U., 1989; ret., 1999. Cons. in field. Editor procs. Precision Strike Tech. Symposium, 1990-98. Scoutmaster Boy Scouts Am., 1972-75. Recipient Legion of Merit, Sec. of Navy, Arlington, Va., 1985; Hatch Outcrop Antarctica named in his honor U.S. Bd. of Geographic Names, Washington, 1962. Fellow Explorers Club, mem. IEEE (life), Precision Strike Assn. (bd. dirs. 1988—2012), U.S. Naval Inst., Glacier Soc. (advisor, historian 1999—2010), Belknap Assn. (historian 2002—). Episcopalian. Avocations: photography, studio art glass, travel, history, computers. Home: 16 Salisbury Dr Apt 7215 Asheville NC 28803-3518

HATCHELL, DENNIS G., retail executive; B, U. Colo., 1971. Various positions including v.p., gen. mgr. western grocers SuperValu, Denver, 1972—80; pres. Merchant Distributors, Inc., 1980—86; group v.p. merchandising and store ops. H.E. Butt Grocery Co., San Antonio, 1986—89; pres. Lowes Food Stores, Inc., 1989—95; pres., COO Alex Lee, Inc., Hickory, NC, 1995—2011, vice chmn., 2011—12; pres., CEO The Pantry, Inc., Cary, NC, 2012—. Mem.: Nat. Assn. Wholesale Distributors (bd. dirs.). Office: The Pantry Inc 305 Gregson Dr Cary NC 27511

HATCHELL, SYLVIA R., women's college basketball coach; b. Gastonia, NC, Feb. 28, 1952; m. Sammy Hatchell; 1 child, Van. BS cum laude in Phys. Edn. and Health, Carson-Newman Coll., 1974; MS, U. Tenn., 1975. Coach jr. varsity women's team U. Tenn.; head coach Francis Marion Coll., 1976, U. NC, Chapel Hill, 1986—. Asst. coach US World U. Games team, 1983, 85, coach, 1995; ct. coach US Olympic basketball try-outs, 1984, 92; basketball event staff Olympic Games, LA, 1984; asst. coach US team 1988 Olympic Games, Goodwill Games and World Championships. Named Nat. Coach of Yr., USA Today, 1994, Coll. Sports Mag., 1994, Converse Nat. Assn. Intercollegiate Athletics Regional Coach of Yr., 1986, AMF-Voit Championship Coach, 1986, Coll. Basketball Coach of Yr., Athletes Internat. Ministries, 1995, Carson-Newman Disting. Alumnus of the Yr., 1994; named to Francis Marion U. Athletic Hall of Fame, 1993, Women's Basketball Hall of Fame, 2004; recipient Naismith award, 2006. Mem. Women's Basketball Coaches Assn. (pres. 1996-97, past bd. dirs.), Amateur Basketball Assn. US (women's games com.). Office: U NC Dept Athletics PO Box 2126 Chapel Hill NC 27514-2126 Office Phone: 919-962-5187. E-mail: shatchel@email.unc.edu.

HATCHER, BARBARA A., lawyer; BA, U. NH, 1977; JD, Wake Forest U., 1980. Atty. Squire, Sanders & Dempsey, Washington; asst. gen. counsel Burlington Industries; v.p., gen. counsel GNB Technologies Inc.; group counsel, transp. bus. group Exide Technologies, Alpharetta, Ga., 2000—04, dep. gen. counsel, asst. sec., 2004—06, exec. v.p., gen. counsel, 2006—. Office: Exide Technologies 13000 Deerfield Pkwy Bldg 200 Alpharetta GA 30004 Office Phone: 678-566-9000. Office Fax: 678-566-9188.

HATCHER, CHARLES ROSS, JR., surgeon, health facility administrator; b. Bainbridge, Ga., June 28, 1930; s. Charles Ross and Vivian Elizabeth (Miller) Hatcher; m. Phyllis Gregory Slappey, July 9, 1988; children from previous marriage: Marian Barnett Thorpe, Charles Hatcher III. BS magna cum laude, U. Ga., 1950; MD cum laude, Med. Coll. Ga., 1954. Intern Johns Hopkins Hosp., Balt., 1954-55; resident surgery Peter Bent Brigham Hosp., Boston, 1955-56, Johns Hopkins Hosp., 1958-62; prof. surgery, chief cardiothoracic surgery Emory U. Sch. Medicine, Atlanta, 1971-90; dir., CEO Emory Clinic, Atlanta, 1976-84; v.p. health affairs, dir. Woodruff Health Scis. Ctr., Emory U., 1984-96, dir. emeritus; chmn., CEO Emory HealthCare, 1995-96. Bd. dirs. Life of the South Corp., Japan Am. Soc. Contbr. Capt. US Army, 1956—58. Mem.: ACS, So. Thoracic Surg. Assn. (pres. 1984), So. Surg. Assn., Am. Cancer Soc., Soc. Thoracic Surgeons (pres. 1986—87), Am. Assn. Thoracic Surgery, Am. Surg. Assn., Am. Coll. Chest Physicians (bd. regents 1977—81, bd. govs. 1974—77), Am. Coll. Cardiology (bd. govs. 1976—80), Johns Hopkins Soc. Scholars, Gov.'s Club Tallahassee, Fla., Bainbridge Country Club, Piedmont Driving Club, Rotary Club (bd. dirs. Atlanta chpt. 1976—80), Capital City Club, Alpha Omega Alpha, Sigma Xi, Phi Beta Kappa. Methodist. Home: 1105 Lullwater Rd NE Atlanta GA 30307-1245 Office: Emory U Woodruff Health Scis Ctr 1440 Clifton Rd NE Ste 318 B Atlanta GA 30322-1013 also: 1440 Clifton Rd NE Ste 318B Atlanta GA 30322 Office Phone: 404-778-5860. Business E-Mail: charles.hatcher@emoryhealthcare.org.

HATCHER, JAMES A., lawyer, communications executive; b. Macon, Ga., Feb. 20, 1952; BA, Furman U., 1974; JD, U. SC, 1977. Assoc. Sell & Melton, Macon, Ga., 1977—79; corp. legal counsel, sec. Cox Comm., Inc. (subs. Cox Enterprise, Inc.), Altanta, 1979—92; sec., gen. counsel Cox Enterprise, Inc., 1987—93; v.p., gen. counsel Cox Comm., Inc. (subs. Cox Enterprise, Inc.), 1992, v.p., legal & regulatory affairs, 1995—99; sr. v.p., legal & regulatory affairs Cox Communications, Inc., 1999—. Recipient Diversity Champion award, Walter Kaitz Found., 2005. Mem.: Ga. Bar Assn., SC Bar Assn., Bd. Dir. Diversity Com. State Bar Assn. Ga. Office: Cox Communications Inc 1400 Lake Hearn Dr Atlanta GA 30319 Office Phone: 404-843-5000. E-mail: jim.hatcher@cox.com.

HATCHER, JOE BRANCH, management consultant; b. Ft. Worth, July 28, 1936; s. W. Joe and Jessie Mae Hatcher; m. Irma Gail Collins, Apr. 18, 1957; children: Gregory Layne, Geoffrey Alan, Gailyn. BA, U. Wichita, 1960; MA, U. Kans., 1967, PhD, 1968. Mem. English lit. faculty Baker U., Baldwin City, Kans., 1966-74; asst. to pres. Park Coll., Kansas City, Mo., 1974-75; v.p. Albion (Mich.) Coll., 1976-81; pres. Hendrix Coll., Conway, Ark., 1981-91; vice chmn. 1st Comml. Bank, Little Rock, 1992-95, also bd. dirs., 1992-95; cons. Hatcher & Assocs., Conway, 1995—. Mem.: Conway C. of C. Methodist. Avocation: tennis. Office: 916 Heather Cir Conway AR 72034-9395 Office Phone: 501-269-3185. Personal E-mail: jhatcher@cyberback.com.

HATCHER, ROBERT DEAN, JR., geologist, educator, research scientist; b. Madison, Tenn., Oct. 22, 1940; married; 2 children. BA in Geology and Chemistry, Vanderbilt U., 1961, MS in Geology, 1962; PhD in Structural Geology, U. Tenn., Knoxville, 1965. Registered profl. geologist Ga., Tenn., SC. Tchg. asst. Vanderbilt U., Nashville, 1960-62, U. Tenn., Knoxville, 1962-65; mem. staff Humble Oil and Refining Co., New Orleans, 1965—66; asst. prof. geology Clemson U., SC, 1966-70, assoc. prof. geology, 1970-76, prof. geology, 1976-78, Fla. State U., Tallahassee, 1978-80, U. SC, Columbia, 1980-86; staff mem. Oak Ridge Nat. Lab., Tenn., 1986—2000; mem. faculty, disting. scientist, prof. tectonics and structural geology U. Tenn., Knoxville, 1986—. Part-time geologic mapping Tenn. Divsn. Geology, 1961-64, SC Divsn. Geology, 1966-82, Ga. Geol. Survey, summer, 1970, NC Divsn. Mineral Resources, 1974-80; mem. rev. panel NSF, 1982, 85, 95, US Geol. Survey Adv. Com. Nat. Coop. Geologic Mapping Program, 1995-2006; mem. NAS Bd. Radioactive Waste Mgmt., 1990-96; mem. nuc. reactor safety com. NRC, 1993-95; mem. Nat. Coop. Geologic Mapping Prog. Adv. Com., 1996-. Author: Structural Geology: Principles, Concepts and Problems, 1990, 1995; co-author: Phys. Geology: Principles, Processes and Problems, 1976, Lab. Manual for Structural Geology, 1990, US Appalachian and Ouachita Orogens, 1990; co-editor: Contbns. to the Tectonics and Geophysics of Mountain Chains, 1983, Variscan-Appalachian Dynamics: The Building of the Late Paleozoic Basement, 2002, Four-D Framework of Continental Crust, 2007; editor: Geol. Soc. Am. Bull., 1981—88; contbr. scientific papers, articles to profl. jours. Grantee NSF, 1968-70, 70-72, 76-78, 78-79, 79-87, 89-92, 2004, Duke Power Co., 1974-75, Westinghouse Elec. Corpn., 1974-75, Nuc. Regulatory Commn., 1978-79, 2009-10, 11-, Dept. Energy, 1993-2005, Conoco-DuPont Found., 1997, 98, Tenn. Valley Authority, 1998, US Geol. Survey, 1997-2009, 2011, recipient Appreciation award, 2007; named hon. citizen of W.Va., 1998. Fellow: Geol. Assn. Can., Geol. Soc. Am. (chmn. exec. com. 1991—92, pres. 1993, exec. com. 1999—2007, chair Geol. Soc. Am. Found. bd. trustees, exec. com. 2005—07, found. bd. trustees, Disting. Svc. award 1988, Penrose medal 2006), AAAS; mem.: Ga. Geol. Soc., East. Tenn. Geol. Soc., Carolina Geol. Soc., Am. Geophys. Union, Am. Assn. Petroleum Geologists (I.C. White Meml. award (eastern sect.) 1997, John T. Galey award from Eastern Sect. 2001, Outstanding Educator award Eastern sect. 2011), Am. Geol. Inst. (pres. 1996, Ian Campbell medal 2006), Sigma Xi. Office: U Tenn Dept Earth and Planetary Scis 1412 Circle Dr 306 Earth and Planetary Scis Bldg Knoxville TN 37996-1410 Office Phone: 865-974-6565. Business E-Mail: bobmap@utk.edu.

HATCHER, SAMUEL F., lawyer, diversified financial services company executive; BA, Davidson Coll., 1968; JD, Yale U., 1971. Ptnr. Alston & Bird, Atlanta, 1976; gen. counsel Equitable Real Estate, 1989—2001; pvt. practice Atlanta, Columbus, Ga.; exec. v.p., gen. counsel, corp. sec. Synovus Financial Corp., Columbus, Ga., 2008—. Office: Synovus Fin Corp 1111 Bay Ave, Ste 500 PO Box 120 Columbus GA 31902 Office Phone: 706-649-2311. Office Fax: 706-641-6555.

HATCHETT, MATT, state legislator; b. Laurens, Apr. 12; m. Kim Hatchett; children: Emily, Camille. BS in Applied Math., Presbyn. Coll., Clinton, SC. Methods analyst Delta Air Lines, Inc., mem. stockholder rels and corp. contributions dept.; owner Hangers Cleaners, Nathans Famous Hotdogs, Brusters Real Ice Cream; councilman Dublin City Coun., 1999—2009, mayor pro-tem, 2006—07; mem. Dist. 143 Ga. House of Representatives, 2011—. Republican. Office: 100 Canterbury Rd Dublin GA 31021 also: Georgia House of Representatives 601 Coverdell Legis Office Bldg Atlanta GA 30334 Office Phone: 404-656-0254. Business E-Mail: matt.hatchett@house.ga.gov.

HATFIELD, BENNETT K., mining executive; BS in Mining Engring., Va. Poly. Inst. & U. Exec. v.p. El Paso Energy Coastal Coal Co., 2001—03; exec. v.p., COO Massey Energy Co., 1998—2001; pres., Eastern ops. Arch Coal, inc., 2003—05; pres., CEO & bd. dirs. International Coal Group, Inc., Ashland, Ky., 2005—. Office: International Coal Group Inc 300 Corporate Ctr Dr Scott Depot WV 25560 Office Phone: 255-760-2400. Business E-Mail: bhatfield@intlcoal.com.

HATFIELD, GREGORY M., drilling company executive; CPA. Corp. acct. Rowan Companies, Inc., Houston, prin. acctg. officer, contr., 2005—10, v.p., contr., 2010—. Office: Rowan Companies Inc 2800 Post Oak Blvd Ste 5450 Houston TX 77056 Office Phone: 713-621-7800. Office Fax: 713-960-7560.

HATFIELD, JOHN MARK, state legislator; b. Waycross, Ga., Sept. 29, 1969; State rep. Dist. 117, Ga., 2005—. Republican. Mailing: 411 Legis Off Bldg Atlanta GA 30334 Business E-Mail: mhatfield@wayxcable.com.

HATGIL, PAUL PETER, artist, sculptor, educator; b. Manchester, NH, Feb. 18, 1921; s. Peter H. BS, Mass. Coll. of Art, 1950; MFA, Columbia U., 1951. Cert. Friends Smithsonian, Washington, Admiral Nimitz Found., Nat. Mus. Pacific War Fredericksburg, Tex. Instr. art U. Tex., Austin, 1951-54, asst. prof., 1954-56, assoc. prof., 1956-67, prof., 1967-85, prof. emeritus, 1985—, design curator Archer M. Huntington Gallery Mus., 1965-68. Vis. instr. Columbia U. (summer) 1958; designed and installed Tex. Pavilion Exhbn., N.Y. World's Fair; coord. for Gov. John Connolly's Exhbn. of Art and Conf. on the Arts; aux. edn. officer Dist. 8 U.S. Coast Guard, 1965-74; bd. dirs. AHEPA Nat. Ednl. Found., Washington, 2003—. Author: Establishing Residency in Greece. 1988, (autobiography) Apostolos, The Immigrant's Son, 1990; (book) Contemporary Encaustic Painting, 1994; contbr. numerous articles and papers to profl. jours. One man shows include Baylor U. Gallery, Bass Concert Hall, U. Tex.; exhbns. include: 42 annual faculty exhbns. U. Tex., Austin, 2d, 3d, 4th Internat. Invitational Exhbn. of Ceramic Art Smithsonian Mus., Washington, 2d, 3d and 7th Nat. Decorative Arts Exhbns., Wichita, Kans., Internat. Invitational Exhbn. of Ceramic Art Iowa State U., Ceder Rapids, Flatbed Print Gallery, 1985-2003, St. Stephen's Emeriti Exhbn., Tex., Austin Mus. Fine Arts, Austin Mus. Art, La Guna Gloria Mus. Art, 2003-2004, Biennale Internat. dell'arte Contemporanea, Firenze, Italy, 2002, U. Mus. Fine Arts, Waco, Tex., 2002, Flatbed Press, Austin, Tex., SPAZIO Gallery, Austin, 2003-07, Hatgil Art Exhbn., Tex. Mid-Century Modernists Exhbn., Dallas, Austin Gallaries, Fine Arts Assocs., The Charles Umlauf Mus., Austin; pvt. collections including St. Paul's Luth. Ch., U. Tex. Bus. Administrn. Bldg., Huston Tillotson Coll., Seguin Luth. Coll., U. Tex. Faculty Club, U. Tex. Coll. Fine Arts, Woodlands Corp., Houston, Zapata Corp., Houston, Warren Cravens Corp., Houston, U.S. Mil. Ins. Corp., Harry Litwin Industries, Wichita, Kans., Coopers & Lybrand Corp., Houston, Cesar Design Inc., Cleve., Abilne (Tex.) 1st Nat. Bank, Tchr. Retirement Sys., Austin, FAA, Panama C.Z., Austin (Tex.) Mus. Art, Fox Collection, Austin, Tex., Voutsinas Collection, Elgin, Tex., Iatrou Collection, Austin, Tex., Martin Mus. Art, Baylor U., Waco, Tex., 2010, 2011, 2012, Blanton Mus. Fine Arts, U. Tex., Austin, 2013, Wichita Art Mus., Kans., Carl R. McQueary Collection, Austin; videos collections include Ceramic History 1951-1976, Baylor U. Archives, Art in Texas - 1951-2000, Baylor U.; work featured in Encaustic Painting, 2000. With USAF, 1943—45, PTO. Recipient Estelle Grey Meml. prize in art, Margaret Flowers prize in art, White Mus., San Antonio, Wolff and Marx prize in art, Dallas Mus. of Fine Arts; purchase prizes Dallas Mus. of Art, Laguan Gloria Mus. Austin, Citation AHEPA Nat. Ednl. Found., 2008; grantee U. Tex. Mem. Am. Hellenic Ednl. and Progressive Assn. (pres. Stephen F. Austin chpt. 312, dist. gov., 1999-2002, mem. bd. dirs. nat. ednl. found. bd. 2003-07, Citation 2007). Home: 2203 Onion Creek Pky Unit 7 Austin TX 78747-1648 Business E-Mail: propph@mail.utexas.edu.

HATHAWAY, MELISSA E., consulting company executive, former federal official; b. 1968; BA, American U.; Grad., US Armed Forces Staff Coll. Rschr. Evidence Based Rsch.; prin. Booz Allen Hamilton; sr. advisor to dir. of nat. intelligence, cyber coordination exec. Office Nat. Intelligence (ODNI), 2007—09; sr. dir. for cyberspace NSC, Washington, 2009; pres. Hathaway Global Strategies, LLC, 2009—; sr. adv. Belfast Ctr. for Sci. & Internat. Affairs John F. Kennedy Sch. Govt., Harvard U., 2009—. Chair Nat. Cyber Study Group (NCSG); dir. Joint Interagency Cyber Task Force (JIACTF), 2008; bd. dirs. Terremark Worldwide, Inc., 2010—.

HATHCOCK, BONITA CATHERINE (BONNIE HATHCOCK), managed health care company executive; b. Chambersburg, Pa., Oct. 30, 1948; d. John McGillis Gentry and Lola Vaneda (Showaker) Wood; m. Lindsay Levoy Hathcock, Apr. 14, 1984. BS in Bus., Shippensburg State U., 1971; MBA, Nova Southwestern U., 1989; grad. Exec. Human Resource Program, Stanford U. Instr. bus. Cen. Pa. Bus. Sch., Summerdale, 1972-75; with Xerox Corp., various locations, 1975-84, product planning mgr. Dallas, 1982-84; dir. mktg. edn. Datapoint Corp., San Antonio, 1984-85, sr. dir. corp. edn., 1985, sr. dir. worldwide edn., 1985-87; various positions including dir. corp. tng. and v.p. human resources Siemens-Rolm, Boca Raton, Fla.; v.p. human resources U.S. Airways; sr. v.p., chief human resources officer Humana Inc., Louisville, 1999—. Prin. bcG Enterprises (profl. awareness tng. co.) Dallas, 1982-84. Avocations: cooking, swimming, reading, walking, writing. Office: Humana Inc The Humana Bldg 500 W Main St Louisville KY 40202

HAUENSTEIN, GEORGE CAREY, life insurance executive; b. Hattiesburg, Miss., May 8, 1936; s. George Jacob Jr. and Earline (Allsup) J.; m. Marjorie Rutland, Aug. 27, 1960; children: Ruth Hauenstein Austin, George Jacob III. Student, Miss. State U., Starkville, 1954-56; BS, U. So. Miss., 1961. CLU Am. Coll. Prin. Hauenstein & Assocs., LLC, Laurel, Miss., 1962—. Contbr. articles to numerous profl. publs.; spkr. profl. convs. and symposia. Mem. Jones County Econ. Devel. Authority, Laurel; bd. dirs. Miss. Easter Seal Found., 1966, Laurel Community Concert Assn., 1990—; chmn. dist. xi Am. Heart Assn. 1964-65; ruling elder Evang. Presbyn. Ch.; bd trustees French Camp Acad., Chamberlain-Hunt Acad., U. So. Miss. Found., mem. estate planning coun. Served to Sgt. U.S. Marine Corps, 1956-58. Otho Smith fellow U. Miss., 1989; named to Hall of Fame The New England, 1982. Mem. Nat. Assn. Ins. and Fin. Advisors, Soc. Fin. Svc. Profls., Internat. Ins. Soc., Assn. for Advanced Life Underwriting, Miss. Estate Planning Coun., Miss. Assn. Ins. Fin. Advisors, Miss. Soc. Fin. Svc. Profls., Million Dollar Round Table (exec. com. 1986-90, pres. 1989, Top of the Table). Avocations: scuba, hunting, fishing. Office Phone: 601-428-4393. E-mail: gchclu@lycos.com.

HAUENSTEIN, GLEN W., air transportation executive; BBA in Fin., Stetson U., DeLand, Fla., 1982. Internat. contr. Continental Airlines, Inc., 1987, v.p., scheduling, 1998—2001, sr. v.p., scheduling, 2001—03, sr. v.p., network, 2003; vice gen. dir., chief comml. officer, COO Alitalia, 2003—05; exec. v.p., chief network and revenue mgmt. Delta Air Lines, Inc., Atlanta, 2005—06, exec. v.p., network planning and revenue mgmt., 2006—. Office: Delta Air Lines Inc 1030 Delta Blvd Atlanta GA 30320-6001 Office Phone: 404-715-2600. Office Fax: 404-715-5042.

HAUGHT, JAMES ALBERT, JR., journalist, editor; b. Reader, W.Va., Feb. 20, 1932; s. James Albert and Beulah (Fish) H.; m. Nancy Carolyn Brady, Apr. 22, 1958; children: Joel, Jacob, Jeb, Cassie Student, Morris Harvey Coll., 1950—52; part-time, W.Va. State Coll., 1960—63. Apprentice printer Charleston Daily Mail, 1951—53; reporter Charleston Gazette, 1953—, varied positions as night and weekend city editor, music and film critic, govt., schs., suburban, religion and investigative reporter, 1970—82, assoc. editor, 1983—92, editor, 1992—. Author: Holy Horrors, 1990, Science in a Nanosecond, 1990, The Art of Lovemaking, 1992, Holy Hatred, 1994, 2000 Years of Disbelief, 1996, Honest Doubt, 2007, Amazon Moon, 2007, Fascinating W.Va., 2008, Fading Faith, 2010; sr. editor: Free Inquiry mag., 1996—, contbr. to 84 mags. and essays, chapter to books Recipient award Headliners Club, 1971, 1st Ann. Consumer Writing prize Nat. Press Club, 1973, Nat. Hwy. Safety Writing award Uniroyal Tire Co., 1975, First Amendment award Sigma Delta Chi, 1977, People for Am. Way, 1986, Merit award ABA, 1977, Consumer Writing prize Nat. Press Club, 1979, 83, Spl. award Religion Newswriters Assn., 1980, Health Journalism award Am. Chiropractic Assn., 1981, 83, Nat. award for edn. reporting Edn. Writers Assn., 1989, Hugh M. Hefner First Amendment award Playboy Found., 1989, Benjamin Fine award for edn. reporting Nat. Assn. Secondary Sch. Prins., 1990, Clarion award Women in Comm., 2000, 02-03, Nat. Headliners award, 2001, Green Eyeshade award, 2003, Edn. Writers Assn. award, 2009, Gov.'s Civil Rights award, 2010. Democrat. Unitarian Universalist. Home: 15 Killen Hollow Dr Cross Lanes WV 25313-3516 Office: Charleston Gazette 1001 Virginia St E Charleston WV 25301-2895 Office Phone: 304-348-5199. Business E-Mail: haught@wvgazette.com.

HAUGHT, WILLIAM DIXON, lawyer, writer; b. Kansas City, Kans., June 12, 1939; s. Walter Dixon and Florence Louise (Rhoads) H.; m. Julia Jane Headstream, July 22, 1967; 1 dau., Stephanie Jane. BS, U. Kans., 1961; LL.B., U Kans., 1964; LL.M., Georgetown U., 1968. Bar: Kans. 1964, Ark. 1971. Assoc. Stanley, Schroeder, Weeks, Thomas & Lysaught, Kansas City, Kans., 1968-70; ptnr. Wright, Lindsey & Jennings, Little Rock, 1970-91; pvt. practice Little Rock, 1991-95; ptnr. Haught & Wade, 1996—. Author: Arkansas Probate System, 1977, 7th ed. 2005, (with others) Probate and Estate Administration: The Law in Arkansas, 1983. Served to capt. USAR, 1964-68, Korea, Washington. Mem. ABA (coun. chmn. coms.), Am. Coll. Trust and Estate Counsel (regent, editor studies program, chmn. editl. bd., state chair), Internat. Acad. Estate and Trust Law, Am. Law Inst., Am. Counsel Assn., Ark. Bar Assn. (chmn. probate law sect., chmn. econs. of law practice com., chmn. agrl. law com., chmn. juris law reform com.), Ctrl. Ark. Estate Coun., Pulaski County Bar Assn., Ark. Bar Found., Country Club of Little Rock. Presbyterian. Office: Haught & Wade 111 Center St Ste 1320 Little Rock AR 72201-4405 Office Phone: 501-375-5257. Business E-Mail: wdh@haughtwade.com.

HAULMAN, CLYDE AUSTIN, economics professor; b. Riverdale, Md., June 29, 1943; s. Clyde Austin and Dorothy Evans Haulman; m. Fredrika J. Teute, May 18, 1985; 1 child, Catherine Anna. BA, Fla. State U., Tallahassee, 1965, MS, 1967, PhD, 1969. Prof. economics Coll. William and Mary, Williamsburg, Va., 1969—, dean. undergraduate studies, 1989—93, chair. dept. music, 1996—97, asst. to pres., 1997—99, chair dept. economics, 2003—. Vis. assoc. prof. U. Ctrl. Fla., Orlando, 1977—79; fulbright sr. lectr. Wuhan U., China, 1985—86; scholar residence Commonwealth Ctr., Study Am. Culture, Williamsburg, 1993—94; fulbright disting. lectr. Chinese U., Hong Kong, 1994—95; resident fellow Va. Humanities Ctr., Charlottesville, 1995. Author: (book) Virginia and the Panic of 1819; editor: US Employment and Training Programs. Bd. mem. Williamsburg Social Svcs. Adv. Bd., 1996—98, Big Brothers-Big Sisters, Williamsburg, 1998—2008, Williamsburg-James City County Sch., 1999—2000, Williamsburg Area C. of C., 2002—04; commr. Williamsburg Redevelopment and Housing Authority, 2000—08; bd. mem., fin. chair Leadership Hist. Triangle, Williamsburg, 2003—08; city coun., vice mayor City of Williamsburg, 2000—08. Recipient Outstanding Academic Book, Choice, 1983, Thomas Jefferson award, Coll. William and Mary, 2002, President's award, 2002, Faculty Initiate, Phi Beta Kappa, 2004. Avocations: book collecting, model railroad. Office: Coll of William and Mary Williamsburg VA 23187 Office Fax: 575-221-1175. Business E-Mail: cahaul@wm.edu.

HAUMSCHILD, MARK JAMES, pharmacist; b. West Bend, Wis., Apr. 6, 1951; s. James Harlow and Helen Marie (Bohn) H.; m. Mary Jo Snider, Oct. 15, 1976; 1 child, Ryan James. BA in Chemistry, Fla. Atlantic U., 1973; BS in Pharmacy, U. Fla., 1976; MS in Mgmt., U. South Fla., 1982; PharmD, Mercer U., 1984. Cert. nuc. pharmacist; cert. nutritional support pharmacist; cert. geriatric pharmacist. Continuing edn. instr. St. Petersburg (Fla.) Jr. Coll., 1977-81; staff pharmacist Morton F. Plant Hosp., Clearwater, Fla., 1976-78, nuclear pharmacy coordinator, 1978-83, clin. pharmacist, 1984-86, resident, 1984-85; ctr. mgr. Foster Infusioncare, St. Petersburg, 1986-88; gen. mgr. Healthinfusion Inc., St. Petersburg, 1988-95; pres. Pharm D. Cons., Largo, Fla., 1984—; regional dir. ops.-Fla. UPC Health Network, Clearwater, Fla., 1995-98; scientific mgr. Aventis, Inc., Largo, 1998—2004; dir. Sanofi-Aventis, Inc., 2005—12, Nat. Outcomes Liaison, 2013—. Adj. instr. Coll. Pharmacy, U. Fla., Gainesville, 1980-86, 2003-. Fellow Am. Soc. Cons. Pharmacists; mem. Am. Soc. Hosp. Pharmacists, S.W. Soc. Hosp. Pharmacists, Am. Pharm. Assn. (cert. in nuclear pharmacy), Soc. Nuclear Pharmacy, Am. Coll. Hosp. Adminstrs., S.W. Fla. Soc. Hosp. Pharmacists (cert. nuclear pharmacist), Beta Gamma Sigma, Phi Kappa Phi, PQA. Republican. Avocations: golf, walking, reading, snowboarding, surfing. Home and Office: Sanofi 12494 104th Ter Seminole FL 33778-3407

HAUSER, DAVID L., communications executive; b. 1951; m. Nancy Hauser; 3 children. BA in Bus. Adminstrn., Furman U., SC; MBA, U. NC, Charlotte; grad. in Exec. Prog. of Profl. Mgmt. Edn., U. NC, Chapel Hill. CPA; cert. purchasing mgr. With Duke Energy, 1973—2009, various acctg. positions including contr., v.p. procurement svcs. and materials, sr. v.p. global asset devel., 1997—98, sr. v.p., treas., 1998—2003, acting CFO, 2003—04, group v.p., 2004—06, CFO, 2004—06, group exec., CFO, 2006—09; chmn., CEO FairPoint Communications, Inc., 2009—. Bd. dirs. FairPoint Communications Inc., 2009—, Enpro Industries. Trustee NC Blumenthal Performing Arts Ctr.; mem. bus. adv. coun. U. NC, Charlotte. Mem.: AICPA, NC Assn. CPA. Address: FairPoint Communications Inc Suite 250 Box F 521 E Morehead St Charlotte NC 28202 Office Phone: 704-594-6200.

HAUSERMAN, JACQUITA KNIGHT, management consultant; b. Donalsonville, Ga., Apr. 23, 1942; d. Lendon Bernard and Ressie Mae (Robinson) Knight; m. Mark Kenny Hauserman, July 8, 1978 (div. Mar. 1998). BS in Math., U. Montevallo, Ala., 1964; MA in Tchg. Math., Emory U., 1973; MBA in Fin., Ga. State U., 1978. Fin. analyst Cleve. Electric Illuminating Co., 1982-83, gen. supr. employment svc., 1983-85, sr. corp. planning advisor, 1985-86, dir. customer svc., 1986-88, v.p. adminstrn., 1988-90; v.p. customer svc. & cmty. affairs Centerior Energy Corp., Independence, Ohio, 1990-93, v.p. customer support, 1993-95, v.p. bus. svcs., 1995-97; v.p., chief devel. officer Summa Health Sys., Akron, Ohio, 1999-2000; prin. Arcadia Consulting, Pepper Pike, Ohio, 2000—. Home and Office: 2901 Greenflower Ct Bonita Springs FL 34134-4387 E-mail: jhauserman@johnrwood.com.

HAVARD, KENNETH E., state legislator; Grad. in indsl. instrumentation & design, La. State U. Oil & gas bus. developer; mem. Dist. 62 La. House of Reps., Baton Rouge, 2012—. Republican. Office: PO Box 217 Jackson LA 70748 also: La House of Reps 900 N 3rd St Baton Rouge LA 70804 Office Phone: 225-634-7470. Business E-Mail: havardk@legis.la.gov.

HAVENS, HARRY STEWART, retired federal official, management consultant; b. Little Rock, Dec. 18, 1935; s. Ralph Murray and Catherine Clara (Clark) H.; m. Frances Jones, June 12, 1960 (dec. 2010) BA in Econs. magna cum laude, Duke U., 1957; BA in Philosophy, Politics, Econs., Oxford U., England, 1959, MA, 1963. Economist U.S. Budget Bur., Washington, 1964-66, budget examiner, 1966-70, chief housing br., 1970-72; chief income maintenance br. U.S. Office Mgmt. and Budget, Washington, 1972-74, dep. dir. human resources divsn., 1972—74; dir. program analysis divsn. U.S. GAO, Washington, 1974-80, asst. comptroller gen., 1980-93; pvt. practice cons. Washington, 1993—2007. Cons. Orgn. Econ. Coop. & Devel., Paris, 1993-2007, U.S. GAO, 1993-96, Supreme Soviet of Russian Fedn., 1992-93, State Duma of Russian Fedn., 1994. Contbr. articles to profl. jours.; contbr. book chpts. Rhodes scholar, 1957. Home and Office: 4515 Neptune Dr Alexandria VA 22309-3129 Personal E-mail: havensh@aol.com.

HAVENS, MURRAY CLARK, political scientist, educator; b. Council Grove, Kans., Aug. 21, 1932; s. Ralph Murray and Catherine Clara (Clark) H.; m. Agnes Marie Scharpf, July 5, 1958 (dec. 1969); children: Colin Scott, Theresa Agnes; m. Carolyn Trost, May 5, 1997. BA, U. Ala., 1953; MA, Johns Hopkins U., 1954, PhD, 1958. Postdoctoral fellow Brookings Instn., Washington, 1958-59; asst. prof. polit. sci. Duke U., 1959-61; from asst. prof. to prof. U. Tex., Austin, 1961-73; vis. lectr. U. Sydney (Australia), 1966; prof. polit. sci. Tex. Tech U., Lubbock, 1973-98, chmn. dept., 1975-83, prof. emeritus, 1999—. Author: City Versus Farm?, 1957, The Challenges to Democracy, 1965, The Politics of Assassination, 1970, Assassination and Terrorism, 1975, Texas Politics Today, 1995; book rev. editor Jour. Politics, 1971-83; contbr. numerous articles to profl. jours. With AUS, 1954—56. Mem.: AAUP, Am. Polit. Sci. Assn., So. Polit. Sci. Assn., Southwestern Polit. Sci. Assn. (pres. 1983—84), Phi Beta Kappa. Home: 804 Deer Foot Ct Nashville TN 37221

HAVIGHURST, CLARK CANFIELD, law educator; b. Evanston, Ill., May 25, 1933; s. Harold Canfield and Marion Clay (Perryman) H.; m. Karen Waldron, Aug. 28, 1965; children: Craig Perryman, Marjorie Clark. BA, Princeton U., 1955; JD, Northwestern U., 1958. Bar: Ill. 1958, N.Y. 1961. Assoc. Debevoise Plimpton Lyons & Gates, NYC, 1958, 61-64; assoc. prof. law Duke U., Durham, NC, 1964-68, prof., 1968-86, William Neal Reynolds prof., 1986—2002, emeritus, 2005—; interim dean Duke U. Sch. Law, 1999. Dir. Program on Legal Issues in Health Care Duke U., 1969-88; adj. scholar Am Enterprise Inst. Pub. Policy Rsch., 1976-2005; resident cons. FTC, Washington, 1978, Epstein, Becker & Green, Washington, 1989-90; scholar in residence Inst. Medicine of NAS, Washington, 1972-73, RAND Corp., Santa Monica, 1999. Author: Deferred Compensation for Key Employees, 1964, Regulating Health Facilities Construction, 1974, Deregulating the Health Care Industry, 1982, Health Care Law and Policy, 1988, 2d edit., 1998, Health Care Choices: Private Contracts as Instruments of Health Reform, 1995; editor Law and Contemporary Problems jour., 1965-70. With U.S. Army, 1958-60. Mem. Inst. Medicine of Nat. Acad. Sci., Order of Coif Home: 1109 Fearrington Post Pittsboro NC 27312 Office: Duke U Sch Law PO Box 90360 Durham NC 27708-0360 Office Phone: 919-613-7061. Business E-Mail: hav@law.duke.edu.

HAVNER, KERRY SHUFORD, civil engineering and solid mechanics educator, scientist; b. Huntington, W.Va., Feb. 20, 1934; s. Alfred Sidney and Jessie May (Fowler) H.; m. Roberta Lee Rider, Aug. 28, 1954; children: Karen Elese Smith, Clark Alan, Kris Sidney. BSCE, Okla. State U., Stillwater, 1955, MS, 1956, PhD, 1959. Registered prof. engr., Okla. Stress analyst Douglas Aircraft Co., Tulsa, 1956; from instr. to asst. prof. civil engring. Okla. State U., Stillwater, 1957-62; sr. stress and vibration engr. Garrett Corp., Phoenix, 1962-63; sect. chief solid mechs. rsch. missile/space systems divsn. McDonnell-Douglas Corp., Santa Monica, Calif., 1963-68; lectr. civil engring. U. So. Calif., LA, 1965-68; assoc. prof. civil engring. N.C. State U., Raleigh, 1968—75, prof. civil engring., 1975—82, prof. civil engring. and materials sci., 1982-99, prof. emeritus, 1999—. Sr. vis. prof. dept. applied math. and theoretical physics U. Cambridge, 1981, 89; vis. fellow Clare Hall, Cambridge, 1981; tchr. link fellow NC Sci., Math. and Tech. Edn Ctr., 2003—. Author: Finite Plastic Deformation of Crystalline Solids, 1992, re issue, 2008; contbg. author: Mechanics of Solids, The Rodney Hill 60th Anniversary Volume, 1982; contbr. articles to profl. jours. including Jour. Applied Math. and Physics, Jour. Mechs. and Physics of Solids, Acta Mechanica, Procs. and Phil. Trans. Royal Soc., Philos. Mag., others; bd. editor hon. sci. adv. bd. Mechs. of Materials, 1981-2006; editl. adv. bd. Internat. Jour. Plasticity, 1986-2010. 2d lt. US Army, 1961, 1st lt. USAR, 1962. Rsch. grantee NSF, 1971, 74, 76, 78, 81, 83, 87, 91, 94; recipient Melvin R. Lohmann medal Okla. State U., 1994. Fellow ASCE (sec. engring. mechs. divsn. 1983-85, chmn. 1987-88, chmn. engring. mechs. adv. bd. 1990-91, chmn. ASCE-CERF awards com. 1991-94; assoc. editor Jour. Engring. Mechs. 1981-83), Am. Acad. Mechanics (assoc. editor Mechanics, 1991-97); mem. ASME, Soc. Engring. Sci., Soc. Indsl. and Applied Math., Sigma Xi (edn. com. 2004—08, Leroy Record Fund Com., 2008-10). Democrat. Methodist. Achievements include theories and analyses of anisotropic hardening and finite deformation in crystalline materials, particularly metals. Home: 3331 Thomas Rd Raleigh NC 27607-6743 Office: NC State U PO Box 7908 Raleigh NC 27695-7908 Office Phone: 919-515-7632. Business E-Mail: havner@ncsu.edu.

HAWARI, AYMAN I., engineering educator, director; BS in Nuc. Engring., U. Mo., Rolla; MS in Nuc. Engring., U. Mich., Ann Arbor; PhD in Nuc. Engring., U. Mich. Prin. nuc. engr. ABB Combustion Engring. Nuc. Power, Windsor, Conn., 1998—2000; asst. prof. nuc. engring. U. Cin., 2000—02; dir. nuc. reactor program NC State U., Raleigh, 2002—. Contbr. scientific papers in field. Recipient Alcoa Found. Engring. Rsch. Achievement award, NC State U., 2007; grantee Nuc. Energy Rsch. Initiative grants, Dept. Energy, 2000—, Maj. Rsch. Instrumentation grant, NSF, 2005—08. Mem.: IEEE, Am. Nuc. Soc., Sigma Xi, Phi Eta Sigma, Alpha Nu Sigma. Achievements include research in neutron thermalization, very high temperature reactors, nuclear fuel, and research reactor utilization. Office: NC State Univ Dept Nuclear Engring PO Box 7909 2500 Stinson Dr Raleigh NC 27695-7909 Office Fax: 919-513-1276. Business E-Mail: ayman.hawari@ncsu.edu.

HAWES, CLAY ERIK, lawyer; b. Murfreesboro, Tenn., Dec. 10, 1969; s. Clayton E. Hawes and Kathleen Joan Nelson; m. Melissa Kaye Giles, May 18, 2004; 1 child, Hayden Carter. BS in Econs., U. Minn., 1992, JD, 1995. Bar: Minn. 1995, Nev. 2001, Tex. 2003. Ptnr. Fulbright & Jaworski, LLP, Houston, 2006—08, Morgan, Lewis & Bockius LLP, Houston, 2008—. Mem.: ABA, Am. Intellectual Property Law Assn., Fed. Cir. Bar Assn. Avocations: running, travel, scuba diving, skiing, Tae Kwon Do. Office: Morgan Lewis & Bockius LLP 1000 Louisiana Ste 4200 Houston TX 77002 Office Phone: 713-890-5000. Business E-Mail: chawes@morganlewis.com.

HAWES, WILLIAM KENNETH, communication educator, author; b. Grand Rapids, Mich., Mar. 6, 1931; s. William Kenneth and Cora Elizabeth (Tibble) H.; m. Ella Margaret Plant, Aug. 13, 1961 (dec. 1998); children: William III, Robert Ernest. AB, Eastern Mich. U., 1955; AM, U. Mich., 1956, PhD, 1960. Tchg. asst. U. Mich., Ann Arbor, 1956-57; instr. English and speech Eastern Mich. U., Ypsilanti, 1956-60; asst. prof., mgr. KTCU Tex. Christian U., Ft. Worth, 1960-64; vis. assoc. prof., mgr. WUNC U. NC, Chapel Hill, 1964-65; assoc. prof., mgr. KUHF U. Houston, 1965—70, prof., 1976—. Admissions bd. Biomed. Program, Sch. Allied Health Scis., U. Tex. Health Sci. Ctr., Houston, 1974-95; prof. U. Houston program, London, 1984, 94; J. William Fulbright lectr. Nat. Chenghi U., Taipei, Taiwan, 2001; resident Rockefeller Found., Bellagio, Italy, 2003. Author: The Performer in Mass Media, 1978, 2010, American

Television Drama, 1986, Television Performing, 1991, Ante La Cámara, 1993, Chinese edit., 1999, Public Television: America's First Station, 1996, Live Television Drama, 1946-1951, 2001, Filmed Television Drama, 1952-1958, 2002, Caligula and The Fight for Artistic Freedom, 2009, Pub. Televiosion: Creators(KUMT), 2013; contbg. author: Understanding Radio, 1967, 85, La Radio: Une Carrière, 1970, Understanding Television, 1978, Television Station Management and Operations, 1989; editor: Pornography Cinema Community Standards, 1975, 4th edit., 2006; prodr., creator TV series including Video Workshop, 1967—2006; film guest Fed. Republic of Germany, 1981, Arts Tour India, 2010. Active Houston Pub. TV, Fulbright Found.; established William Hawes Family scholarship U. Mich., Sch. Music, Theatre & Dance, 2006, U. Houston, Valenti Sch. Comm., 2007. Jack LeRoy Bush Meml. scholar U. Mich., 2007; recipient Avery Hopwood award U. Mich., 1957, Rockwell award, 1996, Gulf Coast Film and Video award, 2004; grantee U. Houston and/or NEH, 1981, 83, 86-87, 91, 2003. Mem.: ACLU, Acad. TV Arts and Scis., Mus. of Fine Arts Houston, Am. Film Inst. Home: Parc V-902 3600 Montrose Blvd Houston TX 77006-4658 Office: University of Houston Jack J Valenti Sch of Communication Houston TX 77204-4072 Office Phone: 713-743-2863. Office Fax: 713-743-2604. Business E-Mail: whawes@uh.edu.

HAWK, DAVID B., state legislator; b. Greeneville, Tenn., June 21, 1968; m. Julia R. Hawk; 2 children. State rep. Dist. 5, Tenn., 2003—; chmn. Greene County United Way Small Bus. Div., 1995—98; mem. Greene County Rep. Party; youth baseball coach Greeneville County Pks. & Recreation. Haberdasher. Mem.: Little Theatre Greeneville, Inc., Kiwanis Club Greene Co. Republican. Lutheran. Office: 407 Crockett Ave Greeneville TN 37745 also: 219 War Memorial Bldg Nashville TN 37243 Office Phone: 615-741-7482. Business E-Mail: rep.david.hawk@capitol.tn.gov.

HAWK, PHILLIP MICHAEL, retired service corporation executive; b. Oklahoma City, June 14, 1939; s H. M. and Rosetta (Cross) H.; m. Nancy Batton, Aug. 13, 1966; children— Tabatha Lynn, Phillip Michael BBA, U. Okla., 1961. Pub. rels. exec. Coca Cola Co., Dallas, 1961-63; salesman svc. Reynolds Metals Co., Dallas, 1963-65; corp. dir. mktg. Cole Pubs. Co., Dallas, 1965-71; sr. v.p. Club Corp. of Am., Dallas, 1972-90; pres. Interclub Corp., Blackwell, Tex., 1990-93, CEO club acquisiton and devel., 1993—2001; CEO Clubnet, Kingwood, Tex., 1996—2001. Bd. dirs. Club Corp. Mex. Exec. v.p. United Golf Group, N.Y.C., 1998-2000; v.p. Acquisitions Renaissance Golf Group, LLC, 2001-11; ptnr. Caminata Mgmt. LLC, 2008-12. Independent. Avocation: golf. Office: 5362 Keswick Dr Frisco TX 75034 Personal E-mail: phil.hawk@att.net.

HAWKINS, ELINOR DIXON (MRS. CARROLL WOODARD HAWKINS), retired librarian; b. Masontown, W.Va., Sept. 25, 1927; d. Thomas Fitchie and Susan (Reed) Dixon; m. Carroll Woodard Hawkins, June 24, 1951; 1 child, John Carroll. AB, Fairmont State Coll., 1949; BS in Libr. Sci., U. N.C., 1950. Children's libr. Enoch Pratt Free Libr., Balt., 1950-51; head circulation dept. Greensboro (N.C.) Pub. Libr., 1951-56; libr. Craven-Pamlico Libr. Svc., New Bern, N.C., 1958-62; dir. Craven-Pamlico-Carteret Regional Libr., New Bern, N.C., 1962-92. Storyteller children's TV program Tele-Story Time, 1952-58, 63—; bd. dirs. Triangle Bank of New Bern. Mem. New Bern Hist. Soc., 1973—, Tryon Palace Commn., 1974—; mem. adv. bd. Salvation Army. Recipient Order of Long Leaf Pine award, Gov. Bev. Perdue, 2012. Mem. N.C. Assn. Retarded Children, Pilot Club (pres. 1957-58, v.p. 1962-63). Baptist. Home: PO Box 57 Cove City NC 28523-0057

HAWKINS, FRANK NELSON, JR., investor relations and public relations/communications consultant, writer; b. Macon, Ga., Sept. 2, 1940; s. Frank N. and Lottie (Norton) H.; m. Inge Lehmitz, Apr. 22, 1967; children: Liv Marion Taylor, Daphne Virginia Moss. BA, Cornell U., 1962; grad, Def. Lang. Inst., 1964. Corr. AP, New Delhi, 1969-70, Jakarta, Indonesia, 1970-71, chief bur. Manila, 1971-73, chief Middle East svcs. Beirut, 1973-75; bus. mgr., adminstrv. dir. AP-Dow Jones, London, 1975-80; dir. corp. rels. Knight-Ridder, Inc., Miami, Fla., 1980-83, v.p. corp. rels. and planning, 1983-94; pres. Access Asia Group, Hong Kong, 1994-95; founder, CEO Hawk Assocs., Inc., 1995—; founder, prin. Hibiscus Mktg. Author: Ritter's Gold, 1980. Capt. Intelligence Corps, U.S. Army, 1963-67. Mem. Assn. Former Intelligence Officers, Zool. Soc. Fla. (pres. 1992-93), Fla. Keys Electric Corp. (bd. dirs.), Upper Keys Rotary Club (pres. 2002-03), Audobon Soc., Secure Outcomes(bd. dirs.), PHI Group(bd. dirs.), Fla. Keys History and Discovery Found.(bd. dirs.) Office: Hawk Assocs Inc 227 Atlantic Dr Key Largo FL 33037 Home: 102 Pelican Rd Tavernier FL 33070 Office Phone: 305-451-1888.

HAWKINS, HAL KENNETH, pathologist; b. Bartlesville, Okla., Aug. 11, 1945; s. Guy Rodgers and Sarabeth (Barbour) H.; m. Barbara Patterson Reed, Sept. 6, 1969 (div. Apr. 1992); children: David, Heidi, Brian, Russell. PhD, Duke U., 1971, MD, 1972. Asst. prof. Duke U. Med. Sch., Durham, N.C., 1973-79, Emory U. Sch. Medicine, Atlanta, 1979-83, Baylor Coll. Medicine, Houston, 1983-93; assoc. prof. U. Tex. Med. Br., Galveston, 1993—2002, prof., 2002—. Pathologist Shriners Burns Hosp., Galveston, 1996-. Mem. U.S. Canadian Acad. of Pathology. Office: 300 University Blvd Rt 0747 Galveston TX 77550 Office Phone: 409-770-6635. Business E-Mail: hhawkins@utmb.edu.

HAWKINS, JOHN DAVID, state legislator; b. Spartanburg, SC, Mar. 2, 1968; s. David O. and Doretha Ann (O'Shields) Hawkins; m. Andrea Allison Moore, 1991. Former mem. Judiciary Com.; law clerk to hon. EC Burnett III Supreme Ct. Justice SC, 1994—96; state rep. Dist. 34 SC, 1997—2001; atty. Hawkins & Lister, Spartanburg, 1996—; state senator Dist. 12 SC, 2001—. Recipient award, Phi Beta Kappa, 1991. Republican. Baptist. Address: 2992 Reidville Rd Spartanburg SC 29301 Office: SC State Legislature 602 Gressette Bldg Columbia SC 29202 Home Phone: 864-576-9932; Office Phone: 864-574-8801, 803-212-6008. Business E-Mail: DH@scsenate.org.

HAWKS, BARRETT KINGSBURY, lawyer; b. Barnesville, Ga., July 13, 1938; s. Paul K. and Nettie Glenn (Barrett) H.; m. S. Kathleen Pafford, Apr. 3, 1965 BBA, Emory U., 1960, LL.B., 1963; LL.M., Harvard U., 1964. Bar: Ga. Clk. Supreme Ct. Ga., 1963; Assoc. Gambrell, Russell, Moye & Richardson (now Smith, Gambrell & Russell), Atlanta, 1961-65; assoc. Sutherland, Asbill & Brennan, Atlanta, 1965-70, ptnr., 1970-82, 93—, Paul, Hastings, Janofsky & Walker, 1982-93. Served to lt. comdr. USNR. Mem. ABA (mem. coun. group pub. utility, transp. and comms. law sect.), State Bar Ga. (bd. govs. 1981-88), Atlanta Bar Assn., D.C. Bar Assn., Emory Law Sch. Alumni Assn. (pres. 1996-97), Emory Law Sch. Coun. (chmn., 1997-98), Capital City Club, Highlands Country Club. Presbyterian. Office: Sutherland Asbill & Brennan 999 Peachtree St NE Ste 2300 Atlanta GA 30309-3996 Office Phone: 404-853-8164. Business E-Mail: barrett.hawks@sutherland.com.

HAWTHORNE, BRUCE N., lawyer; b. Dearborn, Mich., Sept. 21, 1949; BBA with distinction, U. Mich., 1971; MBA, U. Detroit, 1972; JD, Vanderbilt U., 1975. Bar: Ga. 1975. Ptnr. King & Spalding LLP, Atlanta; lead outside counsel Sprint Corp., Overland, Kans., exec. v.p., chief staff officer, 2003—04; exec. v.p., gen. counsel, sec. Electronic Data Systems Corp., Plano, Tex., 2004—05; co-founder, mng. dir. Consigliere Group LLC, 2008—10; ptnr., devel. chmn. Arnell Golden Gregory LLP (AGG), Atlanta, 2010—11; corp. v.p., gen. counsel, sec Huntington Ingalls Industries, Inc. (HII), 2011—. Mng. editor Vanderbilt Law Rev., 1974-75. Mem. ABA (fed. regulation of securities com., corp., banking and bus. law sect. 1983—), State Bar Ga., Atlanta Bar Assn., Order of the Coif, Beta Gamma Sigma. Office: Huntington Ingalls Industries Inc 4101 Washington Ave Newport News VA 23607 Office Phone: 757-380-2000. Office Fax: 757-380-4713.

HAY, FRED J., education educator, librarian, editor; b. Toccoa, Ga., Oct. 3, 1953; s. Samuel Hutson and Dorothy Churchill Hay; m. Valentina Maiewskij, Feb. 4, 1983; 1 child, Nikolai Mikhail. BA, Rhodes Coll., Memphis, Tenn., 1975; MA, U. Va., Charlottesville, Va., 1981; PhD, U. Fla., Gainesville, Fla., 1985; MLIS, Fla. State U., Tallahassee, Fla., 1987. Asst. prof. St. Cloud State U., Minn., 1985—86; libr. Fla. Hospitality Edn. Program (FSU), Tallahassee, 1987; ast. prof., social sciences libr. Kans. State U., Manhattan, 1988—89; reference libr. Harvard U., Cambridge, Mass., 1989—94; prof., libr. Appalachian State U., Boone, NC, 1994—; Anne Belk Disting. prof., 2007—; prof. appalachian studies. Editl. bd. mem. Appalachian Jour., Boone, NC, 2000—, Coll. & Rsch. Librs., Chgo., 1993—2008, book rev. editor, 1996—2008; grant reviewer Nat. Endowment for the Humanities, Washington, 2000—03, Editl. Bd. Choice, 2008—; bd. dirs. NC Preservation Consortium; exec. com. mem. Social Scis. Librs. Sect. Internat. Fedn. Libr. Assns. Author: (scholarly book) Goin' Back To Sweet Memphis: Conversations With The Blues, African-American Community Studies in North America; editor: When Night Falls, Kric Krac: Haitian Folktales, Documenting Cultural Diversity in the Resurgent American South; guest editor: Black Music Rsch. Jour., 3 issues. Mem. Bd. of Adjustments, Boone, NC, 1999—2013, Town Coun., Boone, 2013—; commr. Internat. Congress Anthrop. and Ethnological Scis., 1991—98; exec. com. mem. Social Scis. Librs. Section, Internat. Fedn. Libr. Assn.; cons. Appalachian Coll. Assn., 2011, Nat. Mus. African-Am. Music, 2012—; bd. dirs. NC Preservation Consortium, 2009—. Recipient Brenda McCallum Meml. Award, Am. Folklore Soc., 1997; Douglas W. Bryant Fellowship, Harvard U., 1992-93, LSTA Digitization grant, 2001, Blue Ridge Nat. Heritage Area grant, 2005, Preservation grant, NC Preservation Consortium, 2005. Mem.: Progressive Librarian's Guild, NC Folklore Soc., Am. Anthrop. Assn., Internat. Fedn. Libr. Assn., Ctr. Black Music Rsch., Assn. of Coll. and Rsch. Libraries, ALA, Appalachian Studies Assn. Avocations: gardening, contemplation, music, social and environmental activism. Home: 261 East View Dr Boone NC 28607 Office: Appalachian State Univ WL Eury Appalachian Collection Boone NC 28608 Business E-Mail: hayfj@appstate.edu.*

HAY, JESS THOMAS, retired finance company executive; b. Forney, Tex., Jan. 22, 1931; s. George and Myrtle Hay; m. Betty Jo Peacock, 1951 (dec. 2005); children: Deborah Hay Spradley, Patricia Hay. BBA, So. Meth. U., 1953, JD magna cum laude, 1955. Bar: Tex. Assoc. Locke, Purnell, Boren, Laney & Neely, 1955-61, partner, 1961-65; pres., chief exec. officer Lomas Fin. Corp., Dallas, 1965-69, chmn. bd., chief exec. officer, 1969-94; chmn. bd., chief exec. officer, trustee Lomas & Nettleton Mortgage Investors, 1969-92; chmn., CEO Capstead Mortgage Corp. (formerly Lomas Mortgage Corp.), 1985-91. Chmn. HCB Enterprises Inc, 1996-2007; bd. dirs. Hilltop Holding, Inc., Viad Corp.; former bd. dirs. Exxon Mobil Corp., AT&T (SBC Comm.) Trinity Industries Inc., M Corp., Republic Fin. Svcs., Allied Fin. Co., Money Gram Internat., bd. mem., Friends Nat. World War Meml., mem. adv. bds., Briscoe Ctr. Am. History Studies, U. Tex. Austin, U. Tex. Press, John Glenn Sch. Pub. Policy Ohio State U. Former mem., nat. fin. chmn. Dem. Nat. Com., bd. trustees, governing body Southern Meth. U., former chmn. bd. regents U. Tex. Sys.; former mem. Dallas Citizens Coun., Dallas Assembly; mem. Greater Dallas Planning Coun.; mem. WWII Meml. Adv. Bd.; bd. dirs. Tex. Rsch. League, North Tex. Food Bank, Child Care Partnership Dallas, Dallas County Hist. Found.; chmn. bd. Tex. Found. for Higher Edn.; trustee Southwestern Med. Found. Recipient Disting. Svc. award, Assn. Governing Bds. Univs. and Colls., 1987, Disting. Alumnus award, Southern Meth. U., 1977, Santa Rita award, U. Tex. Sys., 1991. Mem. ABA, Dallas Bar Assn., Tex. Bar Assn., Am. Judicature Soc., Newcomen Soc. N.Am., U.S. C. of C. Methodist. Home: 7236 Lupton Cir Dallas TX 75225-1737 Home Phone: 214-368-4059; Office Phone: 214-368-0531.

HAY, LEWIS, III, utilities executive; b. 1955; BSEE, Lehigh U., Bethlehem, Pa., 1977; M in Indsl. Adminstrn., Carnegie-Mellon U., Pitts., 1982. Gen. foreman US Steel Corp., Pitts., 1977-80; v.p., mng. ptnr. strategy practice Strategic Planning Assocs., Washington, 1982-91; exec. v.p., CFO US Foodservice Inc., Columbia, Md., 1991-99; CFO FPL Group, Inc., Juno Beach, Fla., 1999—2000, CEO, 2001—02, chmn., CEO, 2002—08, NextEra Energy, Inc. (formerly FPL Group, Inc.), Juno Beach, Fla., 2008—. Bd. dirs. Capital One Fin. Corp., Harris Corp.; mem. exec. com. Nuc. Energy Inst. Office: NextEra Energy Inc 700 Universe Blvd Juno Beach FL 33408-0420

HAY, PETER HEINRICH, law educator; b. Berlin, Sept. 17, 1935; s. Edward and Margot (Tull) H.; 1 child, Cedric. BA, JD, U. Mich., 1958; D (hon.), U. Pecs, Hungary, 2012. Prof. law U. Ill., Champaign, 1963-91, dean Coll. Law, 1979—89; L.Q.C., Lamar prof. law Emory U., Atlanta, 1991—2012, prof. emeritus, 2012—, interim dean, chief exec. and acad. officer, 2001—02. Hon. prof. U. Freiburg, Germany, 1976—; prof. U. Dresden, Germany, 1994-2000; dean, 1997-2000; vis. prof. Stanford 1966, Ctrl. European U., Budapest, Hungary, 1995-, Bucerius Law Sch., Hamburg, Germany, 2005-. Author: Law of the United States, 2002, 3rd edit., 2010, Internationales Privatrecht, 4th edit., 2010; co-author: Conflict of Laws, 5th edit., 2010; contbr. over 80 articles to profl. jours. Recipient Rsch. prize von Humboldt Found., Germany, 1990; Fulbright rsch. prof., 1992; Jean-Monnet prof., Bonn, Germany, 1994. Mem. Am. Law Inst., Internat. Acad. Comparative Law, Am. Soc. Comparative Law, Soc. Legis. Compare (France), Gesellschaft fuer Voelkerrecht (Germany), Wissenschaftliche Vereinigung fuer Zivilprozessrecht (Germany), Dresdner Juristische Gesellschat (Germany). Office: Emory U Sch Law G523 Gambrell Hall 1301 Clifton Rd Atlanta GA 30322-2770 Office Phone: 404-727-6896. Business E-Mail: phay@law.emory.edu.

HAYDEN, LINDA C., librarian, educator; b. Hazard, Ky. d. Walter H. and Nancy Catherine (Gott) Combs. BA, Coll. of William and Mary, 1966; MA in Teaching, Spalding U., 1976, postgrad., 1987; MSLS, U. Ky., 2002. Cert. elem. and early childhood edn. tchr., Ky., cert. public mgr., Governmental Svc. Ctr., Ky. Tchr. York County Pub. Schs., Poquoson, Va., 1966-67; asst. coord. children's svcs. Louisville Free Pub. Libr., 1969-74; tchr. Ursuline Spl. Edn. Ctr., Louisville, 1975-79; tchr., owner Multi-Handicapped Tutoring, Louisville, 1979-80; tchr. J-Town Presch., Inc., Jeffersontown, Ky., 1983-84; therapist Pine Tree Villa Nursing Home, Louisville, 1982-84; asst. prin., tchr. Brown's Lane Acad., Louisville, 1984-86; tchr. Jefferson County Pub. Schs., Louisville, 1986-94; access svcs. libr., reference and interlibr. loan libr., acad. libr., assoc. prof. Ky. State U., 1994—2010, faculty senate, 2005—07, 2008—10; pvt. practice, 2010—. Part-time pub. rels. and outreach asst. Ky. Commn. on Cmty. Volunteerism and Svc., 1998-99; mem. faculty senate Ky. State U., 2005-2010. Vol. tutor ESL with refugees, 1990—91. Mem.: ALA, ACRL, Ky. Libr. Assn., Leadership Edn. Alumni Assn., Internat. Soc. for Tech. in Edn., Delta Delta Delta Sonority (Alpha Mu chpt., Coll. William & Mary), Pi Lambda Theta. Democrat. Avocations: music, sports, outdoors, cooking, computers.

HAYDEN, TIM, marketing executive; BA in Polit. Sci., S.W. Tex. U., 1995. Co-founder & pres. GamePlan Mktg. & Events, LLC, Austin, Tex., 2003—. Mem. communication coun. Greater Austin C. of C., 2000—, chair media relations task force, 2004—06, vice-chair comm., 2006—; amb. Capital City African-Am. C. of C., 2003—05; bd. dirs. & exec. com. Meals on Wheels & More, 2003—; chair Ballet Austin Mktg. Coun., 2006—. Recipient Communication Vol. of Yr. award, Greater Austin C. of C., 2005, Austin Under 40 award for Bus./Entrepreneurship, 2006. Mem.: Sigma Phi Epsilon. Office: GamePlan Mktg & Events LLC Ste 207 1634 E Cesar Chavez St Austin TX 78702-4456 Office Phone: 512-275-1336. Office Fax: 512-275-1339.

HAYES, ANN CARSON, retired computer company executive; b. Hamlin, Tex., Apr. 25, 1941; d. Fred Elbert and Nona Faye (Riddle) Carson; m. James Russell Brown, May 7, 1959 (div. July 1973); children: James Allen Brown, Daniel Russell Brown, Robert Anthony Brown, Debra Faye Brown; m. Robert Lee Hayes, Nov. 15, 1975. AAS, Howard Coll., Tex., 1972; student, Regents Coll., NYC, 1986. Lic. ins. agt. Nat. Assn. Self-Employed. Freelance artist, Big Spring, Tex., 1956-76; real estate agt. Century 21, Littleton, Colo., 1976-78, Huntsville, Ala., 1978-79; art dir. Hayes and Co., Splendora, Tex., 1979—; CEO Hayes Enterprises, New Caney, Tex., 2000—11. Executor Hayes Tax Svc., New Caney. Democrat. Episcopalian. Avocations: sculpting, glass etching. Home: 1308 Stanford Ave Big Spring TX 79720-5142 Personal E-mail: achayes1@yahoo.com.

HAYES, JACKIE E., state legislator; b. Marion, SC, Oct. 12, 1961; m. Mandy Hayes; 3 children. BA, Catawba Coll., 1984. Athletic dir., head football coach; mem. Dist. 55 SC House of Reps., SC, 1999—. Mem.: Athletic Adminstrn. Assn. SC (pres.). Democrat. Presbyterian. Mailing: 333D Blatt Bldg Columbia SC 29211-1867 Address: 240 Bermuda Rd Dillon SC 29536 E-mail: jh@legis.lpitr.state.sc.us.

HAYES, LARRY B., retired lawyer; b. Atlanta, Oct. 4, 1939; s. Luther F. and Ruby (Thomas) H.; m. Rebecca Thomason, Feb. 7, 1959; children: Laura Alison, Lawrence Bruce. BS in Pharmacy, U. Fla., 1962; JD, St. Mary's U., 1977. Bar: Tex. 1978, U.S. Dist. Ct. (we. dist.) Tex. 1979, U.S. Ct. Appeals (5th cir.) 1979; cert. personal injury trial law, Tex. Trial counsel Windle Turley PC, Dallas, 1978-82; ptnr. Ware & Hayes, Dallas, 1982-83; sr. trial atty. Green, Hayes & Ryan, Dallas, 1983-86; ptnr. Cantey & Hanger, Ft. Worth, 1986—2006; ret., 2006. Mem. Tex. Bar Assn., Tex. Assn. Def. Counsel, Def. Rsch. Inst., Tarrant County Bar Assn., Tarrant County Civil Trial Lawyers Assn., Phi Delta Phi. Home: 1155 Oceanshore Blvd Unit 305 Ormond Beach FL 32176 Office Phone: 817-929-4625.

HAYES, MICHAEL JOSEPH, retail executive, investment banker; b. Altoona, Pa., June 8, 1941; s. Francis C. and Mary E. (Curren) H.; m. Christina L. Casselbury, Apr. 21, 1966; children— Barbara, Michelle, Michael Joseph BA in Econs., Lycoming Coll., 1963; postgrad., Gen. Motors Inst. Mgmt., 1965; cert., N.Y. Inst. Fin., 1969. Prin. Hayes Fin. Corp., NYC; dir. Petro Corp., Houston; dir., fin. services dept. Oppenheimer and Co., gen. ptnr. NYC, 1977-82, exec. v.p., mng. dir., corp. fin. and fin. svcs., 1982-85, co-mng. corp. fin. dept., 1983-85; mortgage banker Advance Mortgage Co., Southfield, Mich., 1979-84; CEO Fred's, Inc., 1989—2009, mng. dir., 1989—, chmn., 2004—. Bd. dirs. Fred's, Inc., 1987. Mem. fin. com. N.J. Republican Party, 1982. Served with USAR, 1963-68 Mem.: Ridgewood Country (N.J.). Roman Catholic. Avocations: golf; squash; bridge. Office: Fred's Inc 4300 New Getwell Rd Memphis TN 38118 Office Phone: 901-365-8880. Office Fax: 901-328-0354. Business E-Mail: mhayes@fredsinc.com.

HAYES, ROBERT BRUCE, former college president, educator; b. Clarksburg, W.Va., Nov. 15, 1925; s. Bruce and Ruby (Hitt) H.; m. Ruth Harrison, July 19, 1947 (dec.); children: Steven, Ruthann, Mark; m. Kathleen Peters. Student, Fairmont State Coll., W.Va.; BA, Asbury Coll., Wilmore, Ky., 1950; MEd, U. Kans., 1956, EdD, 1960. Tchr., prin. elem. and secondary schs., Kans., 1951-57; chmn. dept. edn. and psychology Asbury Coll., Wilmore, Ky., 1957-59; dir. tchr. edn. Taylor U., Upland, Ind., 1959-65; dean Coll. Edn. Marshall U., Huntington, W.Va., 1965-74, pres., 1974-83; prof. ednl. adminstrn. Coll. Edn., Marshall U., 1983-90; exec. v.p. Warner So. Coll., Lake Wales, Fla., 1991-92; interim dean coll. bus. Marshall U., Huntington, W.Va., 1992-93, coord. accreditation, 1993-95, pres. emeritus, 1992—, provost, 1996-97, 99; interim v.p. Cmty. & Tech. Coll., 1995-97; interim pres. Marshall Cmty. and Tech. Coll., 2006—07; curriculum cons. Robert C. Byed Institute. Mem. W.Va. Adv. Com. Tchr. Edn., 1965-74; dir. Twentieth St. Bank Editor, contbr.: 1966 Yearbook of Assn. Student Teaching. Bd. dirs. Cabell-Wayne United Way, 1981; chmn. bd. Green Acres, 1983; commr. Cabell County (W.Va.), 1983-88. Served with USMCR, 1944-46. Recipient Green Acres award for contbn. to mentally retarded, 1972, Golden Knight award Nat. Mgmt. Assn., 1981 Mem. Huntington Area C. of C. (dir. 1974-83), Phi Delta Kappa, Kiwanis. Methodist. Home: 347 Bradley Foster Dr Huntington WV 25701-9451 Office: Marshall Cmty and Tech Coll Huntington WV 25755-0001 Office Phone: 304-696-3064, 304-781-1668.

HAYES, ROBERT WESLEY, JR., state legislator, lawyer; b. Rock Hill, SC, Dec. 19, 1952; s. Robert Wesley and Wilbur (Kirkland) H.; m. Sarah Mellon Shurley, Jan. 8, 1977; children: Robert Wesley III, James Creighton, Margaret Mellon. BS, US Mil. Acad., 1975; JD, U. SC, 1983. Bar: S.C. Commd. 2d lt. U.S. Army, 1975; with 82d Airborne Divsn., 1975-80; resigned, 1980; practiced in Rock Hill, S.C.; mem. SC House of Reps., 1985-91; mem. Dist. 15 SC State Senate, 1991—, chair Ethics Com. Mem. banking and ins. com., corrections and penology com., edn. com., fin. com., med. affairs com.; bd. dirs. Guardian Fidelity Mortgage Corp., Nat. Bank York County. Mem. U. S.C. Law Rev., 1981-83. Bd. dirs. Westminster Ctr., Inc., Rock Hill Sch. Dist. Found.; chmn. York dist. Boy Scouts Am., 1985-91; campaign chmn. Rock Hill United Way, 1992. Lt. col. S.C. Army N.G., 1980—. Recipient Outstanding Young Am. award S.C. Jaycees, 1990. Mem. S.C. State Bar (exec. coun. young lawyers divsn. 1984-87), S.C. N.G. Assn. (exec. com. 1990-92), Order of Coif. Republican. Presbyterian. Mailing: 1486 Cureton Dr Rock Hill SC 29732-7754 Office: 205 Gressette Bldg Columbia SC 29202 Office Phone: 803-212-6410, 803-324-2400. E-mail: set@scsenate.org.

HAYES, SANDRA K., food service executive; Grad., Okla. State U., 1977. Dist. mgr. Paul Harris Stores, Inc., 1985—91; regional dir. Disney Store, 1992—99; v.p. merchandise a& ops. Universal Studios Hollywood Theme Park, LA, 1999—2002; regional v.p. retail ops. Cracker Barrel Old Country Store, Inc., 2003—. Office: Cracker Barrel Old Country Store Inc 305 Hartmann Dr Lebanon TN 37088-0787 Office Phone: 615-444-5533. Office Fax: 615-443-9476.

HAYES, SYLVIA RICHMOND, music educator; b. Lawrenceburg, Tenn., 1936; d. Edward David and Blanche Audrey (Sells) Richmond; m. Gene Edwin Hayes. BS, George Peabody Coll. Tchrs., MusM, 1968; postgrad., Tenn. State U.; postgrad. in data processing, Columbia State CC. Band dir. & tchr. English HS, Loretto, Tenn.; dir. band & tchr. music Coffman Sch., Lawrenceburg, 1972—89, Leoma Sch., Tenn., 1989—94; tech. coord. Lawrence County Sch. Sys., 1994—. Choir, music dir. & sec. Baptist Ch. Mem.: NEA, Music Educators Nat. Conf., Mid. Band and Orch. Assn., Tenn. Edn. Assn., Mid. Edn. Assn. (Tenn.), Lawrence County Edn. Assn. (treas. bd. dirs., sec. 1988—98, pres. 1998—99), Bus. and Profl. Women's Club (Career Woman of Yr. 1972), Lioness Club (pres. 1977—78). Democrat. Office: Lawrence County Bd Edn 700 Mahr Ave Lawrenceburg TN 38464

HAYES, WILLIAM B., corporate financial executive; BS in Acctg., U. N.C., Greensboro. CPA 1990. With audit dept. KPMG LLP; exec. v.p., treas., CFO Monogram Biosciences, Inc.; sr. v.p., fin. Laboratory Corp. of America Holdings, 2000, sr. v.p., fin. investor rels., corp. comm., 2004—06, exec. v.p., CFO, treas., 2005—. Bd. dirs. Monogram Biosciences, Inc., 2009—. Bd. dirs. Alamance Regional Med. Ctr., 2009-. Office: Laboratory Corporation of America Holdings 358 S Main St Burlington NC 27215 Office Phone: 336-229-1127. Office Fax: 336-436-1205. Business E-Mail: william_hayes@labcorp.com.

HAYES, WILLIAM MEREDITH, pilot, retired military officer; b. San Antonio, Mar. 28, 1947; s. Oscar Junior and Mary Kathryn (Leuthart) Hayes; m. Beverly Jeanne Lowe, May 20, 1972; children: Loren Elaine, Colin Meredith. BA, Western Ky. U., 1971. Cert. naval aviator, airline transport pilot FAA. Commd. ensign USCG, 1973, advanced through grades to capt., 1994; asst. ops. officer USCG Base, Honolulu, 1973-74; pub. affairs officer USCG Air Sta., Mobile, Ala., 1975-78; tng. officer USCG Group/Air Sta., Corpus Christi, Tex., 1978-81; head Falcon jet tng. USCG Aviation Tng. Ctr., Mobile, 1981-87; air ops. officer USCG Air Sta., Miami, Fla., 1987-92, exec. officer Elizabeth City, NC, 1992-94; commdg. officer USCG Activities, San Diego, 1994-97; chief office of ops. 8th C.G. Dist., New Orleans, 1997; pilot Humana, Inc., Louisville, 1997—. Bd. dir. USO, San Diego, Armed Svcs. YMCA, San Diego; mem. mil. adv. coun. C. of C. San Diego, 1994—. Contbr. articles to profl. jours. Recipient Humanitarian Svc. medal USCG, Corpus Christi, 1978, Commendation medal USCG, Miami, 1992, Achievement medal USCG, Elizabeth City, 1994, Meritorious Svc. medal, 1997. Mem. SCV, Amateur Radio Relay League, Sons of the Am. Revolution, Delta Tau Delta (life, chpt. v.p. 1969-70). Avocations: fishing, amateur radio, golf. Home: 2420 Napoleon Blvd Louisville KY 40205-2011 Office: Humana 1180 Standiford Ct Louisville KY 40213-2019 Office Phone: 502-580-0452. Business E-Mail: wmhayes@insightbb.com.

HAYFORD, MICHAEL D., corporate financial executive; b. 1960; B in Acctg., U. Wis., La Crosse, B in Computer Sci.; MBA, Northwestern U. CPA. Consulting positions Andersen Consulting LLP (now Accenture); joined Metavante Corp., 1992, head, ops., 1992—93, chief info. officer through gen. mgr., fin. products group & exec. officer of subs. groups, 1993—2001, CFO, treas., 2001—07, sr. exec. v.p., 2004—07, COO, 2006—07; sr. v.p. Marshall & Ilsley Corp., 2006; sr. exec. v.p. Metavante Technologies, Inc., 2007—08, COO, 2007—09, pres., 2008—09; corp. exec. v.p., CFO Fidelity National Information Services, Inc., 2009—. Former bd. dirs. NYCE Payments Network, LLC; bd. dirs. Metavante Corp., 2004—07, West Bend Mutual Ins., Metavante Technologies Found., Inc. Bd. dirs., La Crosse Found. U. Wis. Office: Fidelity National Information Services Inc 601 Riverside Ave Jacksonville FL 32204 Office Phone: 904-854-5000. Office Fax: 904-854-4124. Business E-Mail: michael.hayford@fisglobal.com.

HAYNES, CATHARINA D., federal judge, lawyer; b. Melbourne, Fla., Nov. 9, 1963; m. Craig Alan Haynes, Aug. 20, 1988. BS in Psychology, Fla. Inst. Tech., 1983; JD, Emory U., 1986. Bar: Tex. 1986, cert.: consumer and comml. law 1997, US Supreme Ct., bar: US Ct. Appeals (5th & 10th Cir.), US Dist. Ct. (no., so., ea., we. dist.) Tex. Assoc. Thompson & Knight LLP, Dallas, 1986—88, Baker & Botts LLP, Dallas, 1988—94, ptnr., 1995—98, 2007—08; judge 191st Dist. Ct. Tex., Dallas, 1999—2006; presiding judge Dallas Civil Dist. Ct., Dallas, 2005; judge US Ct. Appeals (5th Cir.), Dallas, 2008—. Founding fellow Dallas Assn. Young Lawyers Found., 2002—; volunteer judge Pro Bono Clinic Lega Aid Northwest Tex., 2003—06; chair Tex. Ct. Reporters Cert. Bd., Austin, 2003—06. Mem. Dallas Inn Ct., 1990—91, Attorneys Serving the Cmty., 2006—; bd. mem. Vickery Meadow Learning Ctr., 2005—, volunteer instr., 2003—. Recipient Jo Anna Moreland Outstanding Com. Chair award, Dallas Bar Assn., 1996, 2002, Outstanding Bd. Mem. award, Dallas Women Lawyers Assn., 2003, Louise B. Raggio award, 2004, Award of Excellence, Dallas Assn. Young Lawyers Found., 2005, Presdl. Commendation, State Bar Tex., 2006, Outstanding Achievement award, Fla. Tech. Alumni Assn., 2006; named a Tex. Super Lawyer, Tex. Monthly & Law & Politics, 2007; fellow, Coll. State Bar Tex., 2001—, Dallas Bar Found., 2002—. Mem.: Dallas Assn. Women Lawyers (mem. advisory bd. 2003—07), Coll. State Bar Tex. (mem. 1991—), State Bar Tex. (Supreme Ct. Tex. Jury Task Force 1996—97, mem. ins. law section coun. 2002—, profl. ethics com. 2006—07), Dallas Bar Assn. (co-chair, judiciary com. 1996, at-large dir. 2001, ADR section coun. 2001—03, co-chair, bench/bar conf. com. 2002, co-chair courthouse com. 2005). Office: US Ct Appeals 1100 Commerce St Rm 1452 Dallas TX 75242 Office Phone: 214-653-6609.

HAYNES, DAVID S., otolaryngologist, educator; b. Sept. 27, 1960; BA in Biology, Spanish Lit. with honors, U. of Tenn., Knoxville, 1979—83; MD with honors, U. of Tenn., Memphis, 1983—87. Lic. Tenn., 1996, Ala., 1995, diplomate Am. Bd. Otolaryngology, 1994, Am. Bd. Otolaryngology (Neurotology), 2004. Intern gen. surgery Vanderbilt Univ. Med. Ctr., Nashville, 1987—88, resident gen. surgery, 1987—89, resident otolaryngology head and neck surgery, 1989—93, mem. contract com., 1996—2000, dir. adult and pediatric cochlear implant program, med. dir. Vanderbilt hearing and balance ctr., dir. divsn. of otology neurotology, 1996—, coord. med. student preceptorship, 1998—, dir. the otology group of Vanderbilt, 2004—, dir. neurotology fellowship program, 2006—, fellow otology neurotology Vanderbilt academic leadership course Nashville, 2006; clin. instr. dept. of otolaryngology Vanderbilt Univ. Sch. of Medicine, 1994—95, asst. prof. dept. of hearing and speech sciences, 1996—2001, asst. prof. dept. of otolaryngology, 1996—2001, interviewer, admissions com., 1999—2001, med. student advisor, 2000—, assoc. prof. dept. of hearing and speech sciences, 2001—, assoc. prof. dept. of otolaryngology, 2001—; full time faculty Vanderbilt Univ. Medicine Ctr., 1995—, Monroe Carell Jr. Children's Hosp., 1996—; fellow otology neurotology The Otology Group The Ear Found., Nashville, 1994—95; active staff St. Thomas Hosp., 1996—, Bapt. Hosp., 1997—, Veterans' Adminstrn. Med. Ctr., 1998—2000, St. Thomas Surgicare, 2002—, Nashville Surgery Ctr., 2006—; courtesy staff Centennial Med. Ctr., 1999—. Preceptor dept. of biomedical engring., 1998—2000; vis. prof. Tulane Univ. Med. Ctr., New Orleans, 2000, W.Va. Univ. Sch. of Medicine, 2000, Va. Mason Med. Ctr., Seattle, 2003, Univ. of Tenn. Health Sci. Ctr. Coll. of Medicine, 2004, Univ. of Tex. Southwestern, Dallas, 2005, Med. Univ. of SC, Charleston, SC, 2005, Mayo Clinic Med. Ctr., Rochester, Minn., 2005, Cornell Univ. Weill Coll. of Medicine, NY, 2006, Univ. of Mich., Ann Arbor, Mich., 2006, Case Western Reserve Univ., Cleve., 2006, Oreg. Health Sciences Univ., Potland, Oreg., 2006, Univ. of Ark., 2006, Pan Am. Otology and Neurotology Symposium, Bogota, Columbia, 2007, Univ. of Miss. Med. Ctr., Jackson, Miss., 2009, Univ. of Ind. Med. Ctr., Indpls., 2009, Madigan Army Med. Ctr., Tacoma, 2009. Co-author: (publs.) Cochlear Implants in Children: Surgeon's Role in Educational Management, Evaluation and Treatment of the Patient with Vertigo, 1999, 2001, Neurophysiologic Intraoperative Monitoring, 2005. Bd. dirs., chmn. menieres com., chmn. continuing med. edn. com. The Ear Found., 1994; sec., treas. Deafness Rsch. Found., 2004—08, pres., 2008. Recipient Honor award, Am. Acad. of Otolaryngology Head and Neck Surgery, 2004, Vanderbilt Univ. Med. Ctr. Academic Leadership Course, 2007; named to Top Physicians, Guide to America, 2005, Best Doctors, 2007—08, 2008—09; finalist First Pl. Resident Rsch. Competition, Vanderbilt Univ. Med. Ctr., 1991, First Pl. Poster Competition, Triological Soc. Southern Sect., 2002. Mem.: ACS, AMA, Am. Otol. Soc., The Triological Soc. (sci. program chmn. 1997, program com. 2007, nominating com. 2007), William House Cochlear Implant Study Group, Surgeon's Adv. Bd. Cochlear Corp., Southern Med. Assn., Am. Acad. of Facial Plastic and Reconstructive Surgery, Med. Soc. of Mobile County, Med. Assn. of the State of Ala., Nashville Acad. of Otolaryngology (pres. 2003), Prosper Menière Soc. (bd. dirs. 2000—), Am. Acad. of Otolaryngology Head and Neck Surgery, Am. Neurotology Soc. (assoc.; neurotology fellowship com. 2007—), The Kappa Sigma Frat. Lambda Chpt. Office: St Thomas Office The Otology Group of Vanderbilt 4230 Harding Rd Ste 503 W Nashville TN 37205 Office Phone: 615-222-6099. Office Fax: 615-222-2384. E-mail: david.haynes@vanderbilt.edu.

HAYNES, JOE M., state legislator; b. Sumner County, Tenn., Oct. 8, 1936; m. Barbara Haynes; children: Jeff, Scott, Mandy Young. Commr., Goodlettsville, Tenn., 1976—88; vice mayor, 1986—88; state senator Dist. 20 Tenn., 1985—; chmn. Dem. Caucus; mem. Judiciary Com., Fin. Com., Ways & Means Com., State & Local Govt. Com.; state senate atty. Tenn. Recipient Pres' award, Dem. Women's Club Davidson County, Appreciation award, Assn. Retarded Citizens Tenn., 1987, 1988, Greater Nashville Regional Coun., Nashville Firefighters Assn., Tenn. Housing Industry Conf., Tenn. Emergency Number Assn., 1995, Senator Joe M. Haynes award, 1992, Tenn. Citizen Action Legislature Leadership award, 1996; named Outstanding Legislator of Yr., Consulting Engrs. Tenn., Legislator of Yr., Tenn. Devel. Dist. Assn., 1996, State Legislator of Yr., Nat. Assn. Rehab. Profl. Pvt. Sector. Fellow: Nashville Bar Assn. (pres. & dir.); mem.: Donelson-Hermitage C. of C. (dir.), Old Hickory C. of C., Madison C. of C., Tenn. & America Trial Lawyers Assns., Tenn. & America Bar Assns., Goodlettsville & C. of C., Kiwanis Club, Mason, Shriner, Elks. Democrat. Presbyterian. Office: 219 Moss Trail Goodlettsville TN 37072 also: G19 War Memorial Bldg Nashville TN 37243-0220 Office Phone: 615-859-3529, 615-741-6679. Business E-Mail: sen.joe.haynes@capitol.tn.gov.

HAYNES, JOHN MABIN, retired utilities executive; b. Albany, NY, Apr. 22, 1928; s. John Mabin and Gladys Elizabeth (Phillips) H.; m. Marion Enola Hamilton, Apr. 7, 1956; children: John David, Douglas Hamilton, Robert Paul. BS, Utica Coll., Syracuse U., 1952. Accountant Price Waterhouse & Co., NYC, Syracuse, NY, 1953-61; successively auditor, adminstrv. asst., asst. treas., treas., treas. and v.p., sr. v.p. Niagara Mohawk Power Corp., Syracuse, 1961-88; past pres., chmn., dir. N.Y. Bus. Devel. Corp., Albany. Past dir., pres. N M Uranium, Inc.; past dir., treas. Canadian Niagara Power Co. Ltd.; past treas. Moreau Mfg. Co., St. Lawrence Power Co.; past treas. Empire State Power Resources, Inc.; past dir. and treas. Beebee Island Corp.; past bd. dirs. treas. Opinac Investments Ltd., Opinac Energy Ltd., Opinac Holdings Ltd.; past mng. dir. Niagara Mohawk Fin. N.V. Mem. Westhill Cen. Sch. Bd. Edn., 1968-73, pres., 1969-71; treas. Henderson County Humane Soc., 1989-90. With AUS, 1945-47. Mem. Nat. Assn. Accountants (past dir.), Am. Gas Assn. (fin. com.), Fin. Execs. Inst. Clubs: Bond of Syracuse (past dir.), Masons. Home: Apt 352 400 Wesley Dr Asheville NC 28803 Personal E-mail: jack_hay352@msn.com.

HAYNES, JOHNSON, internist, educator, pulmonologist; BS, Tuskegee U., Ala., 1975; MD, U. South Ala., Mobile, 1980. Faculty U. South Ala., 1988—2007, prof. medicine, 1995—. Dir. USA Sickle Cell Ctr. U. South Ala., 2001—07. Vestry mem. Good Shepherd Episcopal Ch., Mobile, Ala., 2005—. Named to America's Top Doctors, Castle Connolly Med. Ltd., 2001—07. Fellow: ACP (life), Am. Coll. of Chest Physicians (life); mem.: Alpha Omega Alpha Honor Soc. Anglican. Achievements include research in acute lung injury in sickle cell disease. Office: Univ South Ala Med Ctr 2451 Fillingim St Mobile AL 36617

HAYNES, RICHARD (RACEHORSE HAYNES), lawyer; b. Houston, Apr. 3, 1927; BBA, U. Houston, 1951, JD, 1956. Bar: Tex. 1956. Pvt. practice, 1956—. Adj. prof. law U. Houston, 1972—73; mem. permanent tchg. faculty Nat. Coll. for Criminal Def. Charter mem. Coll. Edn., Challenge Club, U. Houston; chmn. bd. regents Nat. Coll. for Criminal Def., 1980—81; mem. Nat. Neurofibromatosis Found.-Tex. Chpt.; bd. mem. Coll. Edn. Found. Bd., U. Houston. Paratrooper officer. Recipient Tex. Lifetime Achievement award, Mexican Am. Bar Assn., 2004, Outstanding Alumni award, U. Houston, Law Alumni award, Golden Plate award, Am. Acad. Achievement; named one of Top Criminal Def. Lawyers, The Best Lawyers in Am., 5th edit. (book), 10 Best Trial Lawyers, The Trial Lawyers (book). Fellow: Internat. Acad. Trial Lawyers, Tex. Bar Found.; mem.: ABA, Houston Law Found. (bd. dirs.), Houston Bar Assn. (bd. dirs.), Harris County Criminal Lawyers Assn. (bd. dirs., named Lawyer of Yr. 1999), Tex. Trial Lawyers Assn., Tex. Criminal Def. Lawyers Assn. (bd. dirs.), Tex. Bar Assn. (bd. dirs.), Nat. Assn. Criminal Def. Lawyers, Am. Judicature Soc., Am. Bd. Trial Advs., Internat. Soc. Barristers, Phi Alpha Delta (alumni advisor 1979—80). Office: Richard Haynes & Assocs PC 314 N Post Oak LN # 2Fl Houston TX 77024-5904 Office Phone: 713-868-1111.

HAYNES, ROBERT VAUGHN, retired academic administrator, historian; b. Nashville, Nov. 28, 1929; m. Martha Farr, Dec. 25, 1952; children: Catherine Anne, Carolyn Alice, Charles Allen. BA, Millsaps Coll., 1952; MA, Peabody Coll., 1953; PhD, Rice U., 1959. Mem. faculty U. Houston, 1956-84, prof. history, 1967-84, acting dir. Afro-Am. studies, 1969-71, interim dir. libraries, 1976-78; dir. libraries U. Houston central campus, 1978-80, assoc. provost, 1980-81, dep. provost, 1981-84; v.p. acad. affairs Western Ky. U., Bowling Green, 1984-96, prof., 1996—2009, prof. emeritus, 2010. Vis. prof., Black studies cons. U. Ala., 1970; dir. Inst. Cultural Understanding, 1971; mem. adv. planning com. Tex. Conf. on Library and Info. Services, 1978-79 Author: A Night of Violence: The Houston Riot of 1917, 1976, The Natchez District and the American Revolution, 1976, The Mississippi Territory and the Southwest Frontier, 2010, Bellewood: A Preshy Teriew Haven For Homeless Children, 2012; editor: The Houston Rev., 1981-84; Contbr. articles to profl. jours. Mem. Houston United Campus Christian Life com., 1973-81; chmn. ch. and soc. com. Synod of Tex., Presbyn. Ch. U.S.A., 1970-73; treas. Houston Com. on the Humanities, 1978-79. Served with USAF, 1950-51. Recipient McLemore prize, 2010,; Danforth assoc., 1969, Carnegie fellow, 1952—53, Nat. Endowment Humanities fellow, 1973. Mem. Am. Hist. Assn., Orgn. Am. Historians, So. Hist. Assn., Miss. Hist. Soc., Inst. Early Am. History and Culture, Tex. Assn. Coll. Tchrs. (past chpt. pres.), Phi Kappa Phi (past pres.). Democrat. Office: Dept History Western Ky U Bowling Green KY 42101

HAYNES, RYAN A., state legislator; b. May 8, 1985; BA, U. Tenn., Knoxville. Banker; mem. Dist. 14 Tenn. House of Reps., 2008—. Republican. Baptist. Mailing: PO Box 22091 Knoxville TN 37933 Office: 203 War Memorial Bldg Nashville TN 37243 Office Phone: 615-741-2264. Business E-Mail: rep.ryan.haynes@capitol.tn.gov.

HAYNES, ULRIC ST. CLAIR, JR., retired dean; b. Bklyn., June 8, 1931; s. Ulric St. Clair and Ellaline (Gay) H.; m. Yolande Toussaint, Sept. 20, 1969; children: Alexandra, Gregory. BA, Amherst Coll., 1952; JD, Yale U., 1956; LLB (hon.), Ind. U., 1981, John Jay Coll., 1981, Fisk U., 1982, Ala. State Coll., 1982; JD, Butler U., 1988; LLB (hon.), Mercy Coll., 1994, Amherst Coll., 2012. Exec. asst. N.Y. State Dept. Commerce, Albany, 1956-57; adminstrv. officer UN European Office, Geneva, 1959-60; asst. to rep. Ford Found., Lagos, Nigeria, Tunis, Tunisia, 1960-63; asst. officer in charge Moroccan affairs Dept. State, Washington, 1963, officer in charge Southwest Africa and High Commn. Ters. Affairs, 1963-64; mem. NSC staff White House, 1965-66; pres. Mgmt. Formation Inc., NYC, 1966-70; sr. v.p., ptnr. Spencer Stuart and Assocs. Mgmt. Consultants, NYC, 1970-72; v.p. for mgmt. devel. Cummins Engine Co., Columbus, Ind., 1972-74, v.p. for Mid-East and Africa, 1974-77, v.p. internat. bus. planning, 1981-83; ambassador to Algeria Am. Embassy, Algiers, Algeria, 1977-81; acting pres. SUNY/Coll. at Old Westbury, 1985-86; pres. AFS Intercultural Programs, NYC, 1986-88; cons. NYC, 1989-91; exec. dean Hofstra U. Sch. Bus., Hempstead, NY, 1991-96; exec. dean internat. rels. Hofstra U., Hempstead, NY, 1996—2003; adj. prof. internat. rels Rollins Coll. and U. Ctrl. Fla., 2004—05; disting. vis. scholar University of Central Florida, 2008—, Fla. Southern Coll., 2008—10. Bd. dirs. Pall Corp., 1994-2010 Contbr. articles to profl. publs. Selection com. Henry Luce Found. Asian Scholars Program; trustee Deep Springs Coll., 1999-04. Root-Tilden scholar; John Hay Whitney scholar; Leopold Schepp Found. scholar. Mem. Coun. Fgn. Rels., Yale Club of N.Y.C., Am. Acad. Diplomacy, Atlantic Coun. US., Coun. Am. Ambs. Democrat. Episcopalian. Home: 2403 Timothy Ln Kissimmee FL 34743 Personal E-mail: uhaynesjr@yahoo.com.

HAYNES, WILLIAM JOSEPH, JR., federal judge; b. Memphis, 1949; BA, Coll. St. Thomas, 1970; JD, Vanderbilt U., Nashville, 1973. Asst. state atty. gen. Tenn. Atty. Gen.'s Office, 1973—77, sr. state asst. gen., 1977—78, dep. state atty. gen., 1978—84; pvt. practice atty. Nashville, 1984; magistrate judge US Dist. Ct. (mid. dist.) Tenn., Nashville, 1984—99, judge, 1999—. Adj. prof. Southeastern Paralegal Inst., 1986—90, Vanderbilt U. Sch. Law, 1987—94, 1997—98. Office: US Dist Ct Rm A845 801 Broadway Nashville TN 37203 Office Phone: 615-736-7217.

HAYNIE, THOMAS POWELL, III, physician; b. Hearne, Tex., Aug. 9, 1932; s. Thomas Powell Jr and Sue Cummings Haynie; m. Bette Flossel, Mar. 10, 1956 (dec. Apr. 2002); children: David Powell, Amy Cummings, Sue Cummings, Garner Powell; m. Charlotte Peters, Dec. 18, 2004. Student, U. South, Sewanee, Tenn., 1949-51, U. Tex., Austin, 1951-52; MD, Baylor U., 1956. Diplomate Am Bd Internal Med, Am Bd Med Oncology, Am Bd Nuclear Med. Intern, then resident in internal medicine U. Mich. Med. Center, Ann Arbor, 1956-60, instr., 1960-62; asst. prof. medicine, dir. nuclear med. service U. Tex. Med. Br., Galveston, 1962-65; assoc. prof. medicine U. Tex.-M.D. Anderson Cancer Ctr., Houston, 1965-75; prof. U. Tex.-M.D. Anderson Hosp. and Tumor Inst., Houston, 1975-95, James E. Anderson prof. nuclear medicine, 1988-95, prof. emeritus of nuclear medicine, 1995—, chief sect. nuclear medicine, 1967-84, chmn. dept. nuclear medicine, 1984-93, head dept. internal medicine, 1977-84. Adj prof radiology Baylor Col Med, Houston, 1996—; pres Am Col Nuclear Med, 1993—94; consult in field. Contbr. articles in field, chapters to books; editor: Jour Nuclear Med, 1985—89. Mem.: AMA, ACP, AAAS, Am. Coll. Radiology, Tex. Assn. Physicians Nuclear Medicine, Tex. Med. Assn., Soc. Nuclear Medicine, Assn. Univ. Radiologists, Am. Thyroid Assn., Radiol. Soc. N.Am., Am. Coll. Nuclear Medicine, Am. Coll. Nuclear Physicians, Order St. Lazarus of Jerusalem, Sigma Xi, Phi Gamma Delta. Episcopalian. Office: U Tex-MD Anderson Cancer Ctr 1515 Holcombe Blvd Houston TX 77030-4009 Home: 771 Lakewood Ct Lewisville TX 75077-8686 Personal E-mail: thaynie@swbell.net. Business E-Mail: thaynie@mdanderson.org.

HAYNSWORTH, HARRY JAY, IV, law educator; b. Greensboro, NC, Apr. 9, 1938; s. Harry J. Jr. and Ruth (Eberhardt) H. AB, Duke U., 1961, JD, 1964; postgrad., U. Denver Law Center, 1972; MAR, Luth. Theol. So. Sem., 1989; LLD (hon.), William Mitchell Coll. Law, 2004. Bar: SC 1965, Minn. 2005, U.S. Supreme Ct. 2005. Assoc. Haynsworth, Perry, Bryant, Marion & Johnstone, Greenville, SC, 1964-69, ptnr., 69-71; assoc. prof. law U. SC, 1971-74, prof., 1974-90, assoc. dean, 1975-76, 85-86, acting dean, 1976-77; of counsel Nexson, Pruet, Jacobs & Pollard, Columbia, SC, 1986-90, Briggs & Morgan, Mpls., 2005—11; dean, prof. law So. Ill. U., Carbondale, 1990-95; dean, pres. William Mitchell Coll. Law, St. Paul, 1995—2004; dean emeritus William Mitchell Coll. Law, 2004—. Vis. prof. U. Leeds, Eng., 1978-79; commr. Nat. Conf. Commrs. on Uniform State Laws, 1992—; mem. S.C. Legis. Consumer Law Com., 1975-80. Author: Comments, S.C. Consumer Protection Code, 1983, 2d edit. 1990, Organizing a Small Business Entity, 1986, Marketing and Legal Ethics: The Rules and Risks, 1990, others; contbr. articles to profl. jours.; mem. editorial bd.: Am. Bar Assn. Jour, 1977-83, chmn. editorial bd., 1982-83. Chmn. bd. S.C. Commn. for Blind, 1973-75; bd. dirs. Greenville County Housing Commn., S.C., 1970-71; v.p., dir. United Speech and Hearing Ctr., Greenville, 1970-71; trustee Heathwood Hall, 1976-86, Randolph-Macon Women's Coll., Lynchburg, Va., 1970-75, Minn. Zoo, 1999—2011; chair, 2006—08; trustee Episc. Diocese Minn., 2006—. Mem. ABA (small bus. com., spl. cons. corp. laws com. 1978-82, coun. sect. bus. law 1988-92), S.C. Bar Assn. (vice chmn. consumer and comml. law com. 1975-78, sec., exec. com. 1972-75, exec. dir. 1971-72), Va. Bar Assn., Am. Law Inst., 4th Cir. Jud. Conf., S.C. Bar Assn. Home and Office: 108 Addingtons Williamsburg VA 23188 Personal E-mail: hhaynsworth@gmail.com.

HAYS, RICHARD R., lawyer; b. Tulsa, Okla., Mar. 25, 1960; AB, Harvard U., Cambridge, Mass., 1982; MSc, U. Edinburgh, Scotland, 1984; JD, Vanderbilt U., Nashville, 1986. Bar: Ga. 1986. Ptnr. Alston & Bird LLP, Atlanta, chmn. litig & trial practice group, mem. mgmt. com., mng. ptnr., 2008—. Editor: Vanderbilt Law Rev. Bd. mem. Ga. Shakespeare, Harvard of Ga., Vanderbilt Law Sch., United Way, Alexis de Tocqueville Soc., Alumni Coun. Leadership, Atlanta; bd. dirs. Commerce Club, Midtown Alliance. Rotary scholar. Mem.: Midtown Alliance (bd. dir.), Atlanta CC (exec. com. mem.), Commerce Club (bd. dir.). Office: Alston & Bird LLP One Atlantic Ctr 1201 W Peachtree St NW Atlanta GA 30309-3424 Office Phone: 404-881-7360. Office Fax: 404-253-8654. Business E-Mail: richard.hays@alston.com.

HAYS, ROBERT D., JR., lawyer; b. Cleveland, Tenn. BA summa cum laude, U. NC, Chapel Hill, 1980; JD, Vanderbilt U., 1983. Bar: Ga. 1983. Assoc. King & Spalding LLP, Atlanta, 1983—91, ptnr., 1991—, chmn., 2006—, chair tort litig. practice group. Morehead scholar, U. NC, Patrick Wilson scholar, Vanderbilt U. Mem.: ABA (litig. sect., product liability sect.), Ga. Product Liability Com. (founding mem.), Ga. Def. Lawyers Assn., Def. Rsch. Inst. (trial tactics & techniques com.), Product Liability Adv. Coun. Office: King Spalding LLP 1180 Peachtree St NE Ste 1700 Atlanta GA 30309-7525 Office Phone: 404-572-4674. Office Fax: 404-572-5100. E-mail: rhays@kslaw.com.

HAYS, STEPHEN ROBERT, pediatrician, anesthesiologist; b. Syracuse, NY, Dec. 17, 1964; MS, Yale U., 1987; MD, John Hopkins U., 1991. Cert. Pediatrics, Pediatric Critical Care Medicine, Anesthesiology. Intern, pediatrics John Hopkins U., Balt., 1991—92, resident, pediatrics, 1992—94, resident, anesthesia, 1994—97, fellow, pediatric anesthesia, 1996—99, fellow, pediatric critical care medicine, 1996—99; dir., pediatric pain services Vanderbilt Children's Hosp., 2003—; asst. prof. anesthesiology and pediatrics Vanderbilt U. Med. Ctr., Nashville, 1999—2006, assoc. prof. anesthesiology and pediatrics, 2006—. Office: Vanderbilt Children Hosp 2200 Childrens's Way RM 3115 Nashville TN 37232 Office Phone: 615-936-0023. Office Fax: 615-936-4294. Business E-Mail: stephen.hays@vanderbilt.edu.

HAYSBERT, JOANN WRIGHT, academic administrator; b. Kingstree, SC, 1948; d. Norwood and Lillie Mae (Scott) Wright; m. Barral Stanley Hershel Haysbert; children: Andre, Nineveh, Nazareth, Jordan, Samaria. BA, Johnson C. Smith U., Charlotte, NC, 1969; MEd, Auburn U., 1974, EdD, 1978. Coordinator rsch. and program planning Macon County Pub. Sch. System, Tuskegee, Ala., 1971-76; title IX coordinator Auburn U., Ala., 1976—78; instr. psychology Alexander City State Jr. Coll., Va., 1977—78; asst. prof. edn. Va. State U., Petersburg, 1978-80, dir. lab. sch., 1978—80; dir. women and minorities program Hampton U., Va., 1981-82, asst. v.p. acad. affairs, dir. summer session, asst. provost acad. affairs, provost, COO, 1998—2005, acting pres., 2003—04; pres. Langston U., Langston, Okla., 2005—. Cons. in field. Author ednl. materials. Mem. Va. Nat. Identification Program for Advancement of Women in Higher Edn. Adminstrn.; bd. dirs. State Chamber, Coll. Bd., Leadership Okla., Nat. Campus Compact. Ford Found. fellow, 1973. Mem. AAUW, Nat. Assn. Women Deans, Adminstrs. and Counselors, Nat. Assn. Summer Sessions (chmn. com. 1986-88), Assn. Univ. Summer Sessions, Commn. on Women in Higher Edn., Am. Coun. Edn., Phi Delta Kappa. Avocations: reading, music. Office: Langston Univ PO Box 907 Langston OK 73050 Office Phone: 405-466-3388. Office Fax: 405-466-3461. Business E-Mail: jwhaysbert@lunet.edu.

HAYTAIAN, PETER D., lawyer, healthcare company executive; BA in Mktg. & Comm., Clarkson U., Potsdam, NY; JD, St. John's U. Sch. Law. Pres., CEO Amerigroup NJ Inc.; CEO, Northeastern Region Amerigroup Corp. Office: Amerigroup Corp 4425 Corporation Ln Virginia Beach VA 23462 Office Phone: 757-490-6900. Office Fax: 757-518-3600. Business E-Mail: phaytaian@amerigroupcorp.com.

HAYWOOD, DAVE, musician; b. Augusta, Ga., July 5, 1982; s. Van and Angie Haywood; m. Kelli Cashiola, Apr. 14, 2012. Grad., U. Ga. Founding band mem. Lady Antebellum, 2006—. Musician: (albums) Lady Antebellum, 2008, A Merry Little Christmas, 2010, Need You Now, 2010 (Best Country Album, Record of Yr., Grammy Awards, 2011), Own the Night, 2011 (Best Country Album, Grammy Awards, 2012), On This Winter's Night, 2012, Golden, 2013, (songs) I Run to You, 2009 (Single of Yr., Country Music Assn. Awards, 2009, Best Country Performance by Duo or Group with Vocals, Grammy Awards, 2010), Need You Now, 2009 (Single Record of Yr., Song of Yr., Acad. Country Music Awards, 2010, Group Video of Yr., CMT Music Awards, 2010, Single of Yr., Country Music Assn., 2010, Best Country Performance by Duo or Group with Vocals, Song of Yr., Grammy Awards, 2010, Top Country Song, Billboard Music Awards, 2011), Hello World, 2010 (Group Video of Yr., CMT Music Awards, 2011), We Owned the Night, 2011 (Group Video of Yr., CMT Music Awards, 2012, 2013), Downtown, 2013. Named Top New Duo or Group, Acad. Country Music, 2008, Top Vocal Group of Yr., 2010, 2011, 2012, New Artist of Yr., Country Music Assn., 2008, Vocal Group of Yr., 2010, 2011, Favorite Country Band, Duo or Group, American Music Awards, 2010, 2011, 2012, 2013, Top Country Artist, Billboard Music Awards, 2012. Office: Capitol Records Nashville 3322 W End Ave #11 Nashville TN 37203*

HAYWOOD, H(ERBERT) CARL(TON), psychologist, educator; b. Taylor County, Ga., July 2, 1931; s. Howard Chapman and Rosebud (Smith) H.; m. Nancy Patricia Roberts, Oct. 5, 1951 (div. Mar. 1971); children: Carlton, Terence, Elizabeth, Kristin; m. Dona June Wooldridge Tapp, Sept. 6, 1993 (div. Mar. 2000). AB, San Diego State Coll., 1956, MA, 1957; PhD, U. Ill., 1961. Lic. clin. psychologist Tenn. Mem. faculty George Peabody Coll. (merged with Vanderbilt U. 1979), Nashville, 1962—94, Alexander Heard disting. svc. prof., 1993-94, prof. psychology, 1969-93, prof. spl. edn., 1975-79, prof. emeritus, 1994—, dir. mental retardation rsch. tng. program, 1968-70; dir. Inst. Mental Retardation and Intellectual Devel., 1970-73, Office Rsch. Adminstrn., 1974-76, John F. Kennedy Ctr. Rsch. Edn. and Human Devel., 1971-83; prof. neurology Vanderbilt U. Sch. Medicine, 1971-93; prof. psychology and edn., dean grad. sch. edn. & psychology Touro Coll., NYC, 1993-2000. Vis. prof. U. Toronto, 1965-66; sr. fellow Vanderbilt Inst. Pub. Policy Studies, 1983-88; chmn. Nat Mental Retardation Research Center Dirs., 1979-82; adv. bd. Ill. Inst. Developmental Disabilities, Chgo., 1970-78, Eunice Kennedy Shriver Center Mental Retardation, Waltham, Mass., 1973-80, Tenn. Dept. Mental Health, 1964-92; mem. nat. child health and human devel. council NIH, 1983-88; cons. President's Com. on Mental Retardation, 1968-73; mem. sci. rev. com., health research facilities br., div. edn. and research facilities NIH, 1967-71 Author (with Brooks and Burns): Bright Start: Cognitive Curriculum for Young Children, 1992; editor: Brain Damage in School Age Children, 1968; author (with Lidz): Dynamic Assessment in Practice, 2007; editor: Social Cultural Aspects of Mental Retardation, 1970; editor: (with Begab and Garber) Prevention of Retarded Development in Psychosocially Disadvantaged Children; editor: (with J.R. Newbrough) Living Environments for Developmentally Retarded Persons, 1981; editor: (with D. Tzuriel) Interactive Assessment, 1992; editor: (with S. Friedman) Developmental Follow-Up: Domains, Concepts, and Methods, 1994; editor: Am. Jour. Mental Deficiency, 1969—79, Jour. Cognitive Edn. and Psychology, 1999—2006; mem. editl. bd.: Jour. Abnormal Child Psychology, 1973—89, Contemporary Psychology, 1982—85, Acta Paedologica, 1983—87, Jour. Mental Deficiency Rsch., 1984—2001, Internat. Rev. Rsch. in Mental Retardation, 1982—97; contbr. articles on child devel., motivation, cognitive edn., psycho assessment and mental retardation to profl. jours. Trustee Am. U. Rome, 2000—04. With USN, 1950-54. Recipient Myrtle Wreath Citation of Honor, So. Region Hadassah, 1979. Fellow Am. Assn. Mental Retardation (v.p. psychology 1975-77, 1st v.p. 1978-79, pres. 1980-81, Leadership award, 1985, Rsch. award, 1989), APA (pres. Div. 33 1978-79, mem. Coun. of Reps. 1980-82, Edgar A. Doll award, 1988), Assn. for Psychol. Sci.; mem. Internat. Assn. Cognitive Edn. (pres. 1988-92, Disting. Svc. award, 1995), Soc. Rsch. in Child Devel., Inst. Medicine. Democrat. Episcopalian. Avocations: piano, organ, choral conducting. Business E-Mail: carl.haywood@vanderbilt.edu.

HAYWOOD, THEODORE JOSEPH, physician, educator; b. Monroe, NC, Feb. 13, 1929; s. Jesse Beman and Mary (McDonald) H.; m. Nancy Hume Ferguson, Dec. 21, 1959; children: Elizabeth Linscott, Keene McDonald, Mark Shepard. BS, The Citadel, 1948; MD, Vanderbilt U., 1952. Diplomate: Am. Bd. Pediatrics, Am. Bd. Allergy and Immunology. Pvt. practice allergy, Houston, 1958—; mem. staff Tex. Children's Hosp., 1958—, mem. active staff Pediatrics, 1963—; mem. faculty Baylor U. Coll. Medicine, 1958—, clin. assoc. prof. pediatrics and allergy, 1977—. Assoc. mem. U. Tex. McDonald Obs., 2000—, bd. visitors dept. astronomy, 2007—. Served with M.C. AUS, 1955-57. Fellow Am. Coll. Allergists, Am. Acad. Allergy and Immunology, Am. Acad. Pediatrics; mem. Sigma Xi. Clubs: River Oaks Country (Houston). Republican. Episcopalian. Home: 2923 Ferndale Pl Houston TX 77098-1117 Office: McGovern Allergy & Asthma Clinic 4710 Bellaire Blvd Ste 200 Bellaire TX 77401-4505 Home Phone: 713-522-5600; Office Phone: 713-661-1444. Business E-Mail: mac@mcgovernallergy.com.

HAZEL, LOWELL C., state legislator; BA in Polit. Sci., U. New Orleans, 1990; attended, Fed. Law Enforcement Tng. Ctr. U.S. Border Patrol Acad., Artesia, N. Mex., 1992; JD, Thomas M. Cooley Law Sch., Lansing, Mich., 2000. Atty.; mem. Dist. 27 La. House of Reps., 2008—, mem. adminstrn. of criminal justice com., agr., forestry, aquaculture and rural devel. com., appropriations com., joint legis. com. on the budget, mem. house com. on homeland security, joint com. on homeland security. Republican. Office: State Capitol PO Box 44486 Baton Rouge LA 70804 Mailing: 1013 Main St Pineville LA 71360 Office Phone: 225-342-6945, 318-767-6082. Office Fax: 318-767-6084. Business E-Mail: hazelc@legis.state.la.us.

HAZELRIGG, GEORGE ARTHUR, JR., systems engineer, educator; b. Summit, NJ, Oct. 28, 1939; s. George Arthur Hazelrigg and Dorothy Hetty (Howell) Orr; m. Lauretta Blanche Powell, Aug. 31, 1968; children: George A. III, Geoffrey A. BS, N.J. Inst. Tech., 1961, MS, 1963; MA, Princeton U., 1966, MSE, 1968, PhD, 1969. Cert. glider flight instr. Engr. Curtiss-Wright, Wood Ridge, NJ, 1961-63, Jet Propulsion Lab, Pasadena, Calif., 1966-67; staff sci. Gen. Dynamics, San Diego, 1968-71; rsch. staff Princeton U., 1971-75; dir., systems engr. Econ, Inc., Princeton, 1976-82; dep. divsn. dir. NSF, Arlington, Va., 1982—; prof. of systems engring. (sabbatical) Inst. for Advanced Engring., Seoul, 1993. Dir. ECON, Inc., Princeton, 1974-84; cons. Princeton Synergetics, Inc., 1986-2000. Author: Systems Engineering: An Approach to Information-Based Design, 1996, Fundamentals of Decision Making for Engineering Design and Systems Engineering, 2012; editor: Opportunities for Academic Research in a Low Gravity Environment, 1986; assoc. editor Jour. Spacecraft and Rockets, 1977-82. Named Disting. Alumnus, N.J. Inst. Tech., Newark, 1989. Fellow ASME; mem. AIAA, Am. Soc. for Engring. Edn., Tau Beta Pi. Avocations: aviation, hang-gliding. Home: 8427 Idylwood Rd Vienna VA 22182-5309 Office: NSF 4201 Wilson Blvd Arlington VA 22230-0001 E-mail: ghazelri@nsf.gov.

HAZELTINE, RICHARD DEIMEL, physics professor; b. Jersey City, June 12, 1942; s. L. Alan and Elizabeth (Barrett) H.; m. Cheryl Pickett, June 27, 1964; children: Richard Eliot, Susannah Elizabeth. AB, Harvard Coll., 1964; MS, U. Mich., 1966, PhD, 1968. Lectr. physics U. Mich., 1968; rsch. scientist US Naval Rsch. Lab, 1969; with Inst. Advanced Study, Princeton, 1969-71; rsch. scientist assoc. U. Tex. Austin, 1971-75, rsch. scientist Fusion Rsch. Ctr., 1975-83, asst. dir. Inst. Fusion Studies, 1982-86, prof. physics, 1986—, chmn. Dept. Physics; chair Fusion Energy Sci. Adv. Com. US Dept. Energy, 2000—. Vis. scientist Aspen Ctr. Physics, 1970; acting dir. Inst. Fusion Studies U. Tex. Austin, 1987-88, 91, dir., 1991—; mem. Nat. Rsch. Coun.; chmn. and mem. numerous profl. coms. and boards; cons. in field. Author: Plasma Confinement, 1992, The Framework of Plasma Physics, 1998; assoc. editor Revs. Modern Physics; mem. editorial bd. Phys. Rev. A, 1978-79, The Physics of Fluids, 1978-80; contbr. over 100 articles to profl. jours. Scholar Harvard Coll., Horace H. Rackman predoctoral fellow. Fellow Am. Phys. Soc. (chmn. divsn. of plasma physics); mem. Sigma Xi, Phi Kappa Phi. Office: University of Texas at Austin Department of Physics 1 University Station C1600 Austin TX 78712-0264 Office Phone: 512-471-1152. Office Fax: 512-471-9637. E-mail: rdh@physics.utexas.edu, chair@physics.utexas.edu.

HAZEN, SAMUEL N, hospital administrator; b. July 30, 1960; m. Glenna Hazen; 2 children. B in fin., U. Ky., 1982; MBA, U. Nev., 1988. Various positions, including fin. mgmt. tng. program Humana, 1983; various positions HCA, Inc., 1983—, CFO, North Tex. Divsn., 1994, CFO, Western Group, 1995—2001, pres., Western group Tenn., 2001—. Office: HCA Inc 1 Park Pl Nashville TN 37203 Office Phone: 615-344-9551. Business E-Mail: samuel.hazen@hcahealthcare.com.

HEACOCK, DAVID, electronics executive; BS in Interdisciplinary Engring. and Mgmt., Clarkson U., Potsdam, NY, 1983; MBA, U. North Tex., Denton, 1988. With Benchmarq Microelectronics, 1990—98, Unitrode Corp., 1998, dir. portable power products; Joined Texas Instruments, Inc., Dallas, 1999, mgr. battery mgmt. product line, v.p. portable power mgmt. bus. unit, 2003, sr. v.p., mgr. high-volume analog and logic, 2007—. Achievements include patents in field. Office: Tex Instruments Inc PO Box 660199 Dallas TX 75266-0199 Office Phone: 972-995-2011. Office Fax: 972-995-4360.

HEAD, CHRISTOPHER T., state legislator; b. Commerce, Ga., Jan. 13, 1963; m. Elizabeth Ann Frost; children: Victoria, Abigail, Michael. BMUS, U. Ga., 1985. Mem. Dist. 17 Va. House of Delegates, 2012—, mem. Fin. Com. & Militia Police and Pub. Safety Com. Recipient Roanoke Regional Small Bus. of Yr., 2009. Mem.: Va. Assn. Home Care and Hospice, Roanoke Regional C. of C., Downtown Roanoke Kiwanis. Republican. Office: General Assembly Building PO Box 406 Richmond VA 23218 also: PO Box 19130 Roanoke VA 24019 Office Phone: 804-698-1017. Office Fax: 804-698-6717. E-mail: DelCHead@house.virginia.gov.

HEAD, ELIZABETH, lawyer, arbitrator, mediator; b. Rochester, Minn., Dec. 17, 1930; d. Walter Elias and Ruth Winnogene (Evesmith) Bonner; m. C. J. Head, Dec. 30, 1950; 1 child, Alison Elizabeth. BA, U. Chgo., 1949, JD, 1952. Bar: Ill. 1952, Calif. 1955, N.Y. 1958, U.S. Supreme Ct. 1963, DC 1978. Atty. Nat. Labor Rels. Bd., Washington, 1953-54; assoc. Johnston & Johnston, San Francisco, 1954-56; atty. Aminoil Inc., San Francisco, 1956-57; tchg. assoc. Law Sch. Columbia U., NYC, 1957-58, gen. counsel, 1989-97; assoc. Skadden Arps, NYC, 1958-60; atty. Coca-Cola Corp., NYC, 1961-65; assoc. Kaye Scholer, NYC, 1965-72, ptnr., 1973-82; mem. Hall & Estill, Tulsa, 1983-87; vis. fellow antitrust analysis Fed. Energy Regulatory Commn., Washington, 1987-89; arbitrator, mediator N.Y. Stock Exch., Nat. Assn. Securities Dealers, 1998—; mediator fed. cts. Trustee Mary Baldwin Coll., Staunton, Va., 1983—87. Mem.: ABA (mem. standing com. dispute resolution 1983—90), Assn. Bar City of N.Y. (mem. non-profit orgns. com. 1989—90, chair 1992—95, mem. health law com. 1997—2000), Century Assn., Phi Beta Kappa, Order of Coif. Avocations: travel, music, art, theater. Home: 38595 Purple Martin Ln Hamilton VA 20158-9439 Personal E-mail: elizabethhead@nyc.rr.com.

HEAD, HAYDEN WILSON, JR., federal judge; Student, Washington and Lee U., 1962-64; BA, U. Tex., 1967, LLB, 1968. Bar: Tex. 1968, US Dist. Ct. So. Dist. Tex. 1968. Assoc. Head & Kendrick, Corpus Christi, Tex., 1968—69, 1972—76, ptnr. Corpus Christi, Tex., 1976-81; judge US Dist. Ct. (so. dist.) Tex., Corpus Christi, 1981—2003, chief judge, 2003—09, sr. judge, 2009—. Chmn. 5th Cir. Com. on Criminal Pattern Jury Instr., 1986—; mem. Jud. Conf. U.S. Com. on Security and Facilities, 2002—06; mem. U.S. Jud. Conf., 1998—2006. Contbr. to profl. publs. Lt. Judge Adv. Gen. Corps. USN, 1969—72. Fellow: Tex. Bar Found.; mem.: Hon. Reynolds G. Garzan Am. Inn Ct. (pres. 2000), Jud. Conf. US (com. automation & tech. mem. 1991—92, 5th circuit dist. judges rep. 1998—2001, 5th circuit dist. judges rep. com. security & facilities 2002—06), Dist. Judges Assn. (5th circuit pres. 1996—98, pres. elect. 1994—96, v.p. 1992—94, sec.-treas. 1990—92), Fed. Judges Assn., State Bar Tex. Office: US Dist Ct 1133 N Shoreline Blvd Corpus Christi TX 78401 Office Phone: 361-888-3148.

HEAD, JONATHAN FREDERICK, cell biologist; b. Syracuse, NY, Nov. 23, 1949; s. Arthur Everard and Lillian Myrtle (Hendra) H.; m. Priscilla Catherine Tambone, July 28, 1984; 1 child, Catherine Elizabeth. BS in Zoology, Syracuse U., 1971; MA in Biology, Bklyn. Coll., 1977; PhD in Biology, Fordham U., 1985. Rsch. asst. Naylor Dana Inst. Disease Prevention/Am. Health Found., Valhalla, NY, 1974-78, Cornell U. Med. Coll., NYC, 1978, Mt. Sinai Sch. Medicine, NYC, 1978-84, rsch. assoc., 1984-86, rsch. asst. prof., 1986-87; dir. tumor cell biology Ctr. Clin. Scis./Internat. Clin. Labs., Nashville, 1986-89; pres. Mastology Rsch. Inst., Baton Rouge, 1989—, Oncbiomune, LLC, Baton Rouge, 2005—. High Complexity Clin. Lab. dir. Am. Bd. Bioanalysis, 1988—; med. lab. dir. Clin. Chemistry, State of Tenn., 1988—; clin. lab. scientist/specialist, State of La., 1995—; adj. assoc. prof. Tulane U. Sch. Medicine, New Orleans, 1989—, La. State U. Vet. Sch., Baton Rouge, 2005-; adj. prof. Delta State U., Cleve., Miss., 1992—; dir. R&D Med. Thermal Diagnostics, Baton Rouge, 1995-2001, Innovative Dug Techs., Edmond, Okla., 1999-2005; rschr. and lectr. in field of cancer. Contbr. articles, abstracts and chpts. to sci. publs. Mem. State of La. Adoption Cmty. Adv. Bd., 1992-95. Mem. AAAS, Am. Assn. Cancer Rsch., Am. Soc. Clin. Oncology, Am. Acad. Thermology, Soc. Immunotherapy of Cancer, Am. Soc. Breast Disease, European Soc. Med. Oncology, NY Acad. Scis. Methodist. Home: 6144 Hagerstown Dr Baton Rouge LA 70817-3917 Office: Mastology Rsch Inst 17050 Med Ctr Dr 4th Fl Baton Rouge LA 70816 Home Phone: 225-753-4939; Office Phone: 225-755-3070. Business E-Mail: jhead@eehbreastca.com.

HEADINGTON, TIMOTHY, oil industry executive; BS, Univ. Okla. Dir. Headington Inst.; founder & pres. Headington Oil., 1977—. Named one of Forbes 400: Richest Americans, 2009. Office: 2711 N Haskell Ave Ste 2800 Dallas TX 75204-2940

HEALD, MARK AIKEN, physicist, educator; b. Princeton, NJ, Jan. 27, 1929; s. Mark Mortimer and June (Kilts) H.; m. Jane Dewey, June 9, 1952; children: Kathryn, John S., Charles K. BA, Oberlin Coll., 1950; MS, Yale U., 1951, PhD, 1954. Mem. rsch. staff Project Matterhorn Princeton U., NJ, 1954—59; mem. faculty Swarthmore Coll., Pa., 1959—, prof. physics, 1970—92, prof. emeritus, 1992—. U.S. tech. del. UN Conf. Peaceful Uses of Atomic Energy, 1958; NSF sci. faculty fellow Culham Lab., U.K. AEA, 1963-64, Plasma Physics Lab., Princeton, 1969-70, vis. staff, 1974-75; vis. scientist Plasma Fusion Ctr., MIT, 1978-79. Author: (with C.B. Wharton) Plasma Diagnostics with Microwaves, 1965, (with W.C. Elmore) Physics of Waves, 1969, (with J.B. Marion) Classical Electromagnetic Radiation, 1980, 95, 2013. Mem. Phi Beta Kappa, Sigma Xi. Home: PO Box 284 Pleasant Hill TN 38578-0284 E-mail: mheald@frontiernet.net.

HEALEY, DAVID LEE, investment company executive; b. Pomona, Calif., Dec. 13, 1950; s. Robert Lincoln Sr. and Bernice (Mayes) H.; children: Paul Marcus, Elaina Rose. BS, U. Tulsa, 1978, postgrad. in law, 1979-80; cert., N.Y. Inst. Fin., 1980. Sales mgr. Magnavox, Tulsa, 1978-80; dir. tng. First State Fin., Tulsa, 1980-81; asst. v.p. Prudential-Bache Securities, Tulsa, 1981-86, E.F. Hutton, Tulsa, 1986-91, UBS PaineWebber, Inc., Tulsa, 1991—. Sales cons., Tulsa, 1981—. Judge Miss Teen USA pageant, 1984; chair endowment fund adv. com. Tulsa YWCA. Sgt. USAF, 1974-78. Mem. Internat. Assn. Fin. Planners (bd. dirs. 1984), Toastmasters Internat. (speakers bur.). Republican. Baptist. Avocations: computers, auto restoration, public speaking. Home: RR 1 Box 120 Cleveland OK 74020-9729 Office: UBS 2431 E 61st St 8th Fl Tulsa OK 74136-1211

HEALY, JOSEPH FRANCIS, JR., lawyer, retired air transportation executive; b. NYC, Aug. 11, 1930; s. Joseph Francis and Agnes (Kett) H.; m. Patricia A. Casey, Apr. 23, 1955; children: James C., Timothy, Kevin, Cathleen M., Mary, Terence. BS, Fordham U., 1952; JD, Georgetown U., 1959. Bar: D.C. 1959. With gen. traffic dept. Eastman-Kodak Co., Rochester, NY, 1954-55; air transp. examiner CAB, Washington, 1955-59; practiced in Washington, 1959-70, 80-81; asst. gen. counsel Air Transport Assn. Am., 1966-70; v.p. legal Eastern Air Lines, Inc., NYC and Miami, Fla., 1970-80; ptnr. Ford, Farquhar, Kornblut & O'Neill, Washington, 1980-81; v.p. legal affairs Piedmont Aviation, Inc., Winston Salem, NC, 1981-84, sr. v.p., gen counsel, 1984-89, ret., 1989; sr. v.p., gen. counsel Trans World Airlines Inc., Mt. Kisco, NY, 1993-94. Mem. bd. visitors Sch. Law Wake Forest U., 1988-96. 1st lt. USAF, 1952-54. Mem.: Nat. Aero. Assn., Phi Delta Phi, Beta Gamma Sigma. Home: 104 Overlink Ct Lynchburg VA 24503-3200

HEAPHY, TIMOTHY JOHN, federal prosecutor; b. New Haven, Conn., 1964; BA, U. Va., 1986, JD, 1991. Bar: Calif. 1992, DC 1995, Va. 2004. Law clk. for Hon. John A. Terry US Ct. Appeals (DC Cir), 1991—92; litig. assoc. Morrison & Foerster, San Francisco, 1992—94; asst. US atty. DC US Dept. Justice, 1994—2003, asst. US atty. (western dist.) Va., 2003—05, US atty., 2009—; ptnr. McGuireWoods LLP, 2005—09. Adj. prof. law, fed. criminal practice and trial advocacy U. Va. Sch. Law; lectr. Nat. Advocacy Ctr., US Dept. Justice, Columbia, SC; mem. cmty. resource adv. group Office of Chief Officer for Equity and Diversity, U. Va., Charlottesville, 2006—; bd. dirs. First Amendment Monument, Thomas Jefferson Ctr. for Free Expression, 2006—, Charlottesville Police Found., 2006—, Va. Fair Trial Project. Contbr. articles to profl. jours. Bd. dirs. Pres.'s Commn. on Equity and Diversity, U. Va., 2003—04, Charlottesville/Albemarle Commn. on Children and Families, 2003—06, Sorensen Inst. for Polit. Leaders Program, 2005. Named one of Top 40 Lawyers Under 40, Nat. Law Jour., 2003. Office: Office of US Attorney PO Box 1709 Roanoke VA 24008-1709 Office Phone: 540-857-2250. Office Fax: 540-857-2614.*

HEARD, KEITH G., state legislator; b. Sept. 19, 1956; Former state rep. Dist. 75, Ga.; mem. Athens Clarke County Airport Authority; sec. Ins. Com.; mem. Appropriations Com., Intra Govt. Coord. Com., Ways & Means Com., House Rep., Ga.; state rep. Dist. 89, Ga., 1992—2002, Dist. 114, 2004—; agt. Allstate Ins. Co.; bd. mem.

Gabeo Corp. Roundtable & Athens Tutorial Program; chmn. Pvt. Industry Coun. Mem.: Athens C. of C., Nat. Ga. & Athens Assn. Life Underwriters (past bd. mem.). Democrat. Baptist. Address: 3100 Atlanta Hwy Athens GA 30606-3331 Mailing: 509 Legis Off Bldg Atlanta GA 30334 Office: 370 Woodridge Circle Athens GA 30601 Office Phone: 404-656-0220. Fax: 706-548-7952. Business E-Mail: kheard@legis.state.ga.us.

HEARD, LARRY, real estate company executive; b. Houston; BBA in Fin., Baylor U. With Joe A. McDermott, Inc. (devel. and leasing divsn.), Houston, 1981—84; joined Transwestern Commercial Services, Inc., Houston, 1984, pres., S.W. region, 1996—2002, exec. v.p., Houston divsn., 1996—2002, pres., CEO, bd. dirs., 2002—. Bd. dirs. SEARCH. Adv. bd. Hankamer Sch. Bus. Baylor U.; bd. dirs. SEARCH. Mem.: Urban Land Inst. (mem. exec. com. Houston), Baylor Bear Found. (past pres. Houston chpt.), Young Pres. Orgn. (exec. com. Houston chpt.). Office: Transwestern Commercial Services Inc 1900 W Loop S Ste 1300 Houston TX 77027 Office Phone: 713-270-7700. Office Fax: 713-270-6285. Business E-Mail: larry.heard@transwestern.net.

HEARINGTON, JOSEPH W., JR., tobacco company executive; b. 1961; Grad., Old Dominion U., 1983. Corp. dir., internal auditing Universal Corp. Office: Universal Corp 1501 N Hamilton St Richmond VA 23230 Office Phone: 804-359-9311. Office Fax: 804-254-3582. Business E-Mail: hearingtonj@universalleaf.com.

HEARL, PETER R., former food service executive; b. Sydney, 1951; m. Helen I. Hearl; 3 children. BCom, U. New South Wales, Australia, 1973. Mgmt. positions Exxon, 1973—91; dir KFC ops. PepsiCo, Sydney, 1991—93, KFC mgmt. positions London, 1993—96; regional v.p. KFC & Pizza Hut, Sydney, 1996—97, Yum! Restaurants Internat., Hong Kong, 1997—98, exec. v.p. Dallas, 1998—2002; pres., chief concept officer Pizza Hut, Dallas, 2002—06; exec. v.p., chief people officer Yum! Brands, Inc., Louisville, 2002, COO, chief develop. officer, 2006—08.

HEARN, GEORGE M., state legislator; b. Charlotte, NC, Nov. 28, 1951; s. George M. Hearn Sr. and Martha Hearn; m. Kaye Gorenflo, Feb. 14, 1980; 1 child, Kathleen Wrenn. BA, Duke U., Durham, NC, 1974; JD, U. SC, 1977. Mem. SC Bd. Bar Examiners, 1986—2008; mem. Dist. 105 SC House of Reps., 2008—. Bd. dirs. Horry County Red Cross, 1990—92, Horry County Shelter Home, 1995—2000, Conway Hosp. Found., 1998—2004. Republican. Episc. Office: 1100 Oak St Conway SC 29526 also: Capitol Office 320C Blatt Bldg Columbia SC 29201 Office Phone: 803-212-6796, 803-212-6796. E-mail: georgehearn@schouse.org.

HEARN, KAYE GORENFLO, state supreme court justice; b. Delaware, Ohio, Jan. 30, 1950; d. James F. and Kathleen (Haines) Gorenflo; m. George M. Hearn, Feb. 16, 1980; 1 child, Kathleen Wrenn. BA cum laude, Bethany Coll., 1972; JD cum laude, U. SC, 1977; LLM, U. Va., 1998. Law clk. to Hon. Julius B. Ness SC Supreme Ct., 1977—79; trial lawyer Stevens, Stevens, Thomas, Hearn, and Hearn, 1979—86; family ct. judge 15th Judicial Dist., SC, 1986—95, chief adminstrv. judge SC, 1987—95; judge SC Ct. Appeals, 1995—99, chief judge, 1999—2009; justice SC Supreme Ct., 2009—. Mem. SC Bd. of Bar Examiners, 1984—86, Nelson Mullins Riley & Scarborough Professionalism Com., Chief Justice's Commn. on the Profession, Alternative Dispute Resolution Commn., 2005—; pres. S.C. Conf. Family Ct. Judges, 1992—93, Coun. of Chief Judges of Courts of Appeal, 2005—06; adj. prof. Charleston Law Sch., 2006—. Named portrait honoree, SC Trial Lawyers, 2004. Office: SC Supreme Ct PO Box 11330 Columbia SC 29211 Office Phone: 803-734-1890, 803-734-1080.*

HEARTFIELD, THAD, federal judge; b. Port Arthur, Tex., 1940; Student, Notre Dame U., 1959-60, Southwest Tex. Jr. Coll., 1960; BA, St. Mary's U., 1962, JD, 1965. Asst. dist. atty. Jefferson County, 1965-66; assoc. Weller, Wheelus & Green, 1966-69; city atty. Beaumont, 1969-73; ptnr. O'Brian, Richards & Heartfield, 1973-77, Crutchfield, DeCordova, Brocato & Heartfield, 1981-85; dir. Lower Neches Valley Authority, 1983-94; judge US Dist. Ct. (eastern dist.)Tex., 1995—2003, chief judge, 2003—09, sr. judge, 2010—. Adv. dir. St. Elizabeth Hosp., 1992—94. Office: US Dist Ct Fed Bldg and US Courthouse 300 Willow St Ste 212 Beaumont TX 77701

HEATH, BILL, state legislator; b. Columbus, Ga., Oct. 20, 1959; m. Susan Heath; children: William, Sandy. BS in Elec. Engring. Tech., Southern Tech. Inst., Ga. Mem. Dist. 18 Ga. House Reps., 2002—04; mem. Dist. 31 Ga. State Senate, 2005—, apptd. adminstrn. fl. leader, 2006—. Mem. West Ga. Regional Airport Authority, 1992—2002; gov. apptd. mem. Met. Atlanta Rapid Transit Authority Overview Com., 2007—. Deacon Abeline Bapt. Ch. Republican. Southern Baptist. Mailing: 2225 Cashtown Rd Bremen GA 30110 Office Phone: 770-537-5234. Office Fax: 770-537-6383. Business E-Mail: bill.heath@senate.ga.gov.

HEATH, FRED MILTON, library director, educator; b. Dothan, Ala., Aug. 26, 1944; s. Fred Milton and Mary Glenn Marsh Heath; m. Carol Jean Benton, Aug. 6, 1966; children: Laura Elizabeth Heath Case, Joseph Benton. BA in History, Tulane U., 1966; MA in History, U. Va., 1968; MLS, Fla. State U., 1973; EdD in Edn. Adminstrn., Va. Tech., 1980. Commd. 2d lt. USAF, 1968, rose through ranks to capt., 1972; assoc. reference libr. U. Richmond, Va., 1973—74; asst. dir. pub. services Radford U. Libr., 1974—80; dean libr. services U. North Ala., Florence, 1980—87; dir. libraries Tex. Christian U., Ft. Worth, 1987—93; dean Tex. A&M U. Libraries, College Station, 1993—2003; vice provost, dir. U. Tex. Libraries, Austin, 2003—. Interim dir. Network Ala. Acad. Librs., Montgomery, 1984—85; chair coun. libr. dirs. Assn. Higher Edn. North Tex., 1990—93; pres. Va. Libr. Assn., 1978—79; editor Libr. Adminstrn. and Mgmt. Assn. Jour. ALA, 1992—93; founding adv. bd. SPARC, 1999—2001. Co-editor: Libraries Act on Their Libqual and Findings, 2004; mem. editl. bd. Tex. A&M U. Press., 1993—2003, mem. editl. adv. bd. Libr. Quar., 2003—. Grantee Fund for Improvement of Postsecondary Edn., 2000, NSF, 2001, Telecomm. and Informatics Task Force, Tex., 2002. Mem.: Tex. Coun. State Univ. Librs. (pres. 1998—2000), Greater Midwest Libr. Consortium (pres. 1998—99), Assn. Rsch. Librs. (pres. 2002—03). Avocations: golf, kayaking, running, photography. Home: 5909 Tom Wooten Dr Austin TX 78731 Office: U Tex at Austin Mail Stop 5400 Austin TX 78713 Office Phone: 512-495-4350. E-mail: fheath@austin.utexas.edu.

HEATH, RICHARD EDDY, lawyer; b. NJ, Nov. 15, 1930; s. W. Eddy and Dorothy (Brown) H.; m. Beth M., June 17, 1955; children: Ellen Louise, David Montgomery, Karen Elizabeth, Deborah Anne. BA cum laude, Swarthmore Coll., Pa., 1952; LLB cum laude, Harvard U., Cambridge, Mass., 1955. Bar: NY, Fla. Tchg. fellow Harvard Law Sch., Cambridge, Mass., 1955—56; assoc. Hodgson and Russ, Buffalo, 1956—61, ptnr., 1961—. Trustee Children's Hosp., Buffalo, 1975-98; trustee U. at Buffalo Found., 1966-89, sec., 1976—. Recipient Walter P. Cooke award U. Buffalo, 1978. Office: 140 Pearl St Ste 100 Buffalo NY 14202-4040 Office Phone: 716-856-4000.

HEATH, STAN, men's college basketball coach; b. Detroit, Dec. 17, 1964; m. Ramona Webb; children: Jordan, Joshua. B in Social Sci., Ea. Mich. U., Ypsilanti, 1988; M in Sports Adminstrn., Wayne State U., Detroit, 1993. Asst. basketball coach Lincoln HS, Ypsilanti, 1987—88, Hillsdale Coll. Chargers, 1988—89; asst. basketball coach, head jr. varsity coach Albion Coll. Britons, 1989—91; asst. basketball coach, assoc. head coach Wayne State U. Warriors, 1991—94; asst. basketball coach Bowling Green State U. Falcons, 1994—96, Mich. State U. Spartans, 1996—2001; head basketball coach Kent State U. Golden Flashes, 2001—02, U. Ark. Razorbacks, 2002—07, U. So. Fla. Bulls, 2007—. Named Mid-American Conf. Coach of Yr., 2002, Big East Conf. Coach of Yr., 2012. Office: Univ So Fla Mens Basketball ATH 100 4202 E Fowler Ave Tampa FL 33620 Office Phone: 813-974-3252.

HEATHCOTT, FORREST, automotive executive; m. Chris Heathcott; 2 children. BS in Mktg., Harding U., 1975. V.p., nat. sales and remarketing World Omni Fin. Corp. (subs. of JM Family Enterprises, Inc.); various regional and nat. positions, including nat. mgr. Nissan Motor Corp., 1979—93; dir., remarketing Southeast Toyota Distbrs., LLC (subs. of JM Family Enterprises, Inc.), 1993, group v.p., distbr. ops., group v.p., asst. gen. mgr., 1999—2004, asst. gen. mgr., 1999—2007, sr. v.p., 2004—07; pres. JM&A Group (subs. of JM Family Enterprises, Inc.), 2007—; exec. v.p. JM Family Enterprises, Inc., 2007—. Chmn. Boca Raton C. of C. Office: JM Family Enterprises Inc 100 Jim Moran Blvd Deerfield Beach FL 33442 Office Phone: 954-429-2000. Office Fax: 954-429-2300. Business E-Mail: forrest.heathcott@jmfamily.com.

HEATON, JOE L., district judge; b. Alva, Okla., 1951; s. Joe D. and Doris E. H.; m. Dee Anne Barbour, 1980; children: Andrew, Adam. BA, Northwestern Okla. State U., 1973; JD, U. Okla., 1976. Bar: Okla., 1976, U.S. Dist. Ct. (we. dist.) Okla. 1978, U.S. Ct. Appeals (10th cir.) 1985. Legis. asst. U.S. Senator Dewey Bartlett, Washington, 1976-77; atty. Fuller, Tubb & Pomeroy, P.C., Oklahoma City, 1977-92, 93-96; U.S. atty. U.S. Dept. Justice We. Dist. Okla., Oklahoma City, 1992-93, first asst. U.S. Atty., 1996—2001; judge US. Dist. Ct. (we. dist.) Okla., 2001—. State rep. Okla. Ho. of Reps., Oklahoma City, 1984-92, minority leader, 1988-91. Editor U. Okla. Law Rev., 1976. City councilman City of Alva, 1972-73. Office: US Courthouse Ste 3108 200 NW 4th St Oklahoma City OK 73102-5628 Office Phone: 405-609-5600.

HEATON, STUART ALAN, lawyer; b. Orange, Calif., Mar. 28, 1956; m. Carolyn T. Heaton. BA in Biology, Calif. State U., Fullerton, 1979; JD, UCLA, 1982; MBA, Vanderbilt U., 1991. Bar: Fla. 1982, Tenn. 1989. Atty. Preddy, Kutner, Rubinoff, Brown & Thompson, Dixon, Dixon, Hurst & Nicklaus, Miami; v.p., gen. counsel Thomas Nelson Inc., 1989—96; asst. gen. counsel Lockheed Martin Corp., 1997—2002; v.p., gen. counsel, corp. sec. CarMax Inc., Glen Allen, Va., 2002—05; sr. v.p., gobal bus. devel. WorldSpace, 2005—09; prin. Stuart A. Heaton & Assocs., 2009—10; ptnr. Vasallo Sloane, PL, 2010—. Mem.: Assn. of Corp. Counsel, Richmond Bar Assn., Va. Bar Assn., Tenn. Bar Assn., Fla. Bar Assn., ABA. Office: Vasallo Sloane PL 301 E Pine St Ste 250 Orlando FL 32801-2744 Office Phone: 407-622-6751.

HEBALD, MILTON ELTING, sculptor; b. NYC, May 24, 1917; s. Nathan and Eva (Elting) H.; m. Cecile Rosner, June 10, 1938 (dec. Feb. 1998); 1 child, Margo; m. Kathleen Arc, Feb. 12, 2000. Student, Art Students League, 1927-28, Nat. Acad. Design, 1931-32, Beaux Arts Inst. Design, 1932-35. Tchr. Am. Artist Sch., 1940-41, Cooper Union, 1945-53, Bklyn. Mus. Art Sch., 1946-52, Skowhegan Art Sch., summers 1950-52, U. Minn., 1949, Long Beach (Calif.) State, summer 1968. Recipient 2d prize Social Security Competition, U.S. Govt. relief in Post Office, Toms River, N.J. 1940, 2d prize Wings for Victory 1942, 1st prize Bklyn. Mus. 1950, 2d prize Pa. Acad. 1951, 1st prize N.Y.C. Dept. Pub. Works for East Bronx Tb Hosp. 1953, Prix de Rome in Sculpture 1955-58); Commns. include facade Equador Pavilion, N.Y. World's Fair, 1939; trophy, Rep. Aviation Co., 1942, Turtle Tent; play sculpture, Phila., 1954, Isla Verdi Aeroport, San Juan, P.R., 1954, 16 foot bronze group, East Bronx (N.Y.), Tb Hosp, 1954; portrait bust of Archibald MacLeish, Am. Acad. Arts and Letters, 1957; bronze relief Zodiac, Pan Am. Terminal, Kennedy Airport, 1957-58, Ackland Meml, U. N.C., 1961, James Joyce Monument, Zurich, Switzerland, 1966, Marshall Field Meml, Sun-Times Bldg., Chgo., 1966, Shakespeare Group, Central Park, N.Y.C., 1973; heroic head C.V. Starr, Tokyo, 1974; Shakespeare relief, Oslo, Norway, 1975, Joyce Portrait, Tower Mus., Dublin, 1975, Starr Portrait, Tokyo and Hong Kong, 1975, Dancing Family group, Delora Art Ctr., St. Charles, Ill., 1979, Richard Tucker Monument, N.Y.C., 1980, Romeo and Juliet bronze, Wilshire Blvd, Los Angeles, 1981, Olympics L.A. 1984 monument, 2 bronzes, Los Angeles YMCA sculpture garden, 1986, Dancing Family group, The Great Escape Park, Lake George, N.Y., 1988, others, one-man exhbns. include, ACA Gallery, N.Y.C., 1937, 40, Grand Central Moderns, N.Y.C., 1950, 54, Schneider Gallery, Rome, Italy, 1957, Nordness Gallery, N.Y.C., 1959-71, Cheekwood Center, Nashville, 1968, 78, Mickelson Gallery, Washington, 1972, 78, Aschehoug Gallery, Oslo, 1975, Sestiere Gallery, Rome, 1975, Yares Gallery, Scottsdale, Ariz., 1975, 78, Heritage Gallery, Los Angeles, 1978, Gilman Gallery, Chgo., 1978, Harmon Gallery, Naples, Fla., 1978, 81, 84, Randall Gallery, N.Y.C., 1978, Foster Harmon Gallery Am. Art, Sarasota, Fla., 1981, Bronze Plaque 100 Anni, Scuola Artiglieriadi Bracciano, 1988, Life Size Group, Ft. Wayne, Ind., 1988; group shows include, Arte Figurativo, Rome, Italy, 1964, 67, Carnegie Inst., Pitts., 1967, Va. Mus. Fine Arts; represented permanent collections, N.Y. Acad. Arts and Letters, Notre Dame U., N.J., Phila. Mus., Whitney Mus. Am. Art, Yale, U. Ariz., U. N.C., Brandeis U., Columbia (S.C.) Mus. Art, Ackland Meml., Tel Aviv Mus., Israel, Nat. Portrait Gallery, Smithsonian Instn., Washington, Joyce Mus., Dublin, Oslo U., Bergan, Norway, Privatbank, others. Fellow Am. Acad. in Rome; mem. Ahnual Am. Group. Subject of monograph by Frank Getlein, Milton Hebald: A Studio Book, 1971, also revs. and articles. Office: Harmon Meek Gallery 599 Tamiami Trl N Ste 309 Naples FL 34102-5631 Mailing: Milton Hebald Rev Trust 223 N Guadelupe St #528 Santa Fe NM 87501

HEBERT, BOBBY JOSEPH, JR., radio personality, retired professional football player; b. Galliano, La., Aug. 19, 1960; m. Teresa Hebert; children: Ryan, Cammy, T-Bob, Bo. Attended, Northwestern State U., Natchitoches, La. Quarterback Mich. Panthers, USFL, 1983-84, Oakland Invaders, USFL, 1985, New Orleans Saints, 1985-92, Atlanta Falcons, 1993—96; ret. NFL, 1996; sports radio show co-host Sta. WWL 870 AM / FM 105.3, New Orleans, 2005—. Named to Nat. Football Conf. Pro Bowl Team, NFL, 1993, New Orleans Saints Hall of Fame, 1999, La. Sports Hall of Fame, 2000. Office: WWL 870 AM / FM 105.3 400 Poydras St Ste 800 New Orleans LA 70130 Business E-Mail: cannon@wwl.com.

HEBERT, JAMES R., epidemiologist, educator; b. Hartford, Conn., Oct. 3, 1949; s. Roger Adrian and Aldea Naomi (St. Amand) H.; m. Hazel Jane Teas, Feb. 27, 1982; 1 child, Christine Joyce. BS in Biology, Boston U. Coll. Liberal Arts, 1971; MSPH in Environ. Health and Epidemiology, U. Wash. Sch. Pub. Health & Cmty. Medicine, Seattle, 1980; ScD in Nutritional Epidemiology, Harvard U. Sch. Pub. Health, Cambridge, Mass., 1984. Epidemiologist, sr. scientist Am. Health Found., NYC, 1985—89, head, nutritional epidemiology, chief, biostats., 1985—89, assoc. chief, epidemiology, 1988—89; prof., epidemiology U. Mass. Sch. Pub. Health, Amherst, 1989—99, Med. U. SC, Charleston, 2004—; assoc. prof., medicine & epidemiology U. Mass. Med. Sch., Worcester, 1989—95, prof., medicine & epidemiology, 1995—99, assoc. dir., preventive & behavioral medicene, 1995—99, dep. dir., cancer prevention & control, 1998—99; prof., epidemiology & biostats. U. SC Arnold Sch. Pub. Health, Columbia, 1999—, dir., nutrition ctr., 1999—2002, chair, epidemiology & biostats, 1999—2002; dir., SC statewide cancer prevention & control program U. SC, 2003—, disting. prof., health scis., 2006—. Project dir., P.I. Madras U., Chennai, India, 1978—80; data analyst & computer programer Harvard U. Demography & Population Scis., Boston, 1982—83; cons., nutrition & epidemiology UNICEF, Kampala, Uganda, 1983, nutrition advisor, 1984; assoc. dir. Hollings Cancer Ctr. MUSC, Charleston, 2003—06; review com. U. Alabama, Birmingham, 2006—. Contbr. articles to profl. jours. Grant reviewer, Bd. Agy. Breast Cancer Rsch. US Army, 1996. Recipient Dean's award, Grad. Sch. U. Wash., 1979, Rsch. award, Oxfam-UK, 1979, Promotion award, Zurich, Switzerland, 1983, Pub. Health award, Harvard U. Sch., 1983; named Eminent Scientist of Yr., World Sci. Forum, 2004, Leading Scientist of World, Internat. Biog. Ctr., Cambridge, 2005; Fulbright Sr. Rsch. fellow, US Info. Agy., 1997—98. Mem. Am. Pub. Health Assn., Am. Inst. Nutrition, Am. Soc. Clin. Nutrition, Soc. Epidemiolog Rsch., Internat. Epidemiolog. Assn., Am. Soc. Clin. Pathologists (cert. hematologist), AAAS, N.Y. Acad. Sci., Mass. Pub. Health Assn. Democrat. Achievements include discovery of a link between dietary fat and suppression of immune function; discovery of a relationship between obesity and breast cancer recurrence; proposition of a link between menthol cigarette smoking and esophageal cancer; development of methods to measure dietary intake, studies to investigate the role of diet and psychosocial factors in cancer. Home: 6049 Robinwood Rd Columbia SC 29206 Office: Univ SC Dept Epideniology & Biostats Statewide Cancer Prevention & Control Program Columbia SC 29208 Office Fax: 803-734-5259. Business E-Mail: jhebert@sc.edu.

HEBERT, TROY, state commissioner, former state legislator; b. La., Apr. 19, 1966; s. Elton Charles Hebert; children: Hailey, Chad. Sugarcane farmer, 1983—88; mem. Iberia Parish Coun., 1991—95; mem. Dist. 48 La. House of Reps., Baton Rouge, 1996—2007; mem. Dist. 22 La. State Senate, Baton Rouge, 2008—10; commr. La. Office Alcohol & Tobacco Control (ATC), Baton Rouge, 2010—. Mem.: Jeanerette C. of C. Independent. Catholic. Office: Louisiana Office Alcohol & Tobacco Control PO Box 66404 Baton Rouge LA 70896 Office Phone: 225-925-4041.

HEBRA, ANDRE, surgeon; b. Sao Paulo, Brazil, Mar. 26, 1959; s. Alexius Von and Gerda Von Hebra; m. Jennifer Duncan Duncan, Aug. 18, 1990. MD, Med. U. SC, Charleston, 1987. Diplomate in gen. surgery Am. Bd. Surgery, 1992, in pediat. surgery 1996. Chief, surgeon divsn. pediat. surgery Children's Hosp. Med. U. SC, 2007—. Decorated Meritorious Civilian Svc. medal USN. Mem.: Alpha Omega Alpha. Office: Medical University SC 96 Jonathan Lucas St 417 CSB MSC 613 Charleston SC 29425 Office Phone: 843-792-3853. Office Fax: 843-792-3858. Business E-Mail: hebra@musc.edu.*

HECHT, NATHAN LINCOLN, state supreme court chief justice; b. Clovis, N.Mex., Aug. 15, 1949; s. Harold Lee and Mary Loretta (Byerly) H. BA, Yale U., 1971; JD cum laude, So. Meth. U., 1974. Bar: Tex. 1974, D.C. 1975, U.S. Dist. Ct. D.C. 1975, U.S. Dist. Ct. (no. and we. dists.) Tex. 1976, U.S. Ct. Appeals (D.C. cir.) 1975, U.S. Ct. Appeals (5th cir.) 1976, U.S. Supreme Ct. 1979. Law clk. to judge U.S. Ct. Appeals (D.C. cir.), 1974-75; assoc. Locke, Purnell, Boren, Laney & Neely, Dallas, 1976-80, ptnr., 1981; dist. judge 95th Dist. Ct., Dallas, 1981-86; judge Tex. Ct. Appeals (5th Dist.), 1986-89; justice Tex. Supreme Ct., Austin, 1989—, chief justice, 2013—. Contbr. articles to profl. jours. Bd. visitors So. Meth. U., Dallas, 1984-87; trustee Children's Med. Found., Dallas, 1983-89; bd. dirs. Children's Med. Ctr. North, Dallas, 1985-89; elder Valley View Christian Ch., Dallas, 1981—. Lt. USNR, 1971—79. Named Outstanding Young Lawyer of Dallas, Dallas Assn. of Young Lawyers, 1984. Fellow Tex. Bar Found., Am. Bar Found.; mem. ABA, Dallas Bar Assn., D.C. Bar Assn., Am. Law Inst. Republican. Avocations: piano, organ, jogging, bicycling. Office: Tex Supreme Ct PO Box 12248 201 West 14th Room 104 Austin TX 78711*

HECHT, WILLIAM DAVID, retired accountant; b. NYC, Nov. 7, 1941; s. Adolph J. and Lillian (Shore) H.; m. Francine Rosen, Aug. 22, 1964; children: Peter, Dana, Allison. BS in Acctg., Queens Coll., 1962; JD, Bklyn. Law Sch., 1971; LLM in Taxation, NYU, 1974. Bar: N.Y. 1972. Ptnr., mem. mgmt. com. Weiser LLP, NYC, 1964—2008. Mem. faculty Found. Acctg. Edn., N.Y.C.; lectr. in field. Contbr. articles to CPA Jour. Mem. ABA, AICPA, N.Y. State Soc. CPAs, N.J. State Soc. CPAs, N.Y. State Bar Assn. Republican. Jewish. Avocations: skiing, basketball. Home: 10233 Spyglass Way Boca Raton FL 33498 Office Phone: 212-375-6584. Business E-Mail: whecht@mrweiser.com.

HECK, JAMES BAKER, retired education educator; b. Columbus, Ohio, Aug. 26, 1930; s. Arch O. and Frances (Agnew) H.; m. Jo Ann Gatton, Nov. 18, 1950; children: Janice M., Judith L., J. Jeffrey. BS in Edn., Ohio State U., 1953, MA, 1961, PhD, 1967. Comml. sales engr. Ohio Bell Tel. Co., Dayton, 1955-57; tchr. Ohio Pub. Schs., Dayton, 1957-59, sch. counselor, 1959-60; from instr. to asst. dean faculties Ohio State U., 1960—67, assoc. dean faculties Office Acad. Affairs, 1967-68, asst. prof. edn., 1967—68, prof., dean, dir. Mansfield campus, 1971-78; prof., dean Coll. Edn. U. Del., Newark, 1968-71; prof., dean regional campus affairs U. South Fla., 1978-81, prof., assoc. v.p. acad. affairs, 1981-84, prof., assoc. v.p. acad. affairs, dir. office of tech., 1984-86, prof., dean Sch. Extended Studies & Learning Techs., gen. mgr. pub. broadcasting Sta. WUSF-TV/FM, WSFP-TV/FM, spl. asst. to provost, dir. office tech., 1986-90; prof., gen. mgr. Sta. WSFP-TV/FM, 1990-96, Sta. WUSF-TV/FM, 1990—2002; exec. dir. WUSF advancement Sta. WUSF TV/FM, 2002—03; ret., 2003. Mem. bd. adminstrv. reps. U. South Fla. Pub. Broadcasting, 1999-2002; asst. state supr. for guidance svc. Ohio Dept. Edn., 1962-63; Am. Coun. on Edn. fellow in acad. adminstrn. U. Ill., 1965-66; evaluator Nat. Coun. for Accreditation Tchr. Edn., 1972-78; mem. planning com. Nat. Conf. Br. and Regional Campus Adminstrs., 1973-82, chmn., 1972, 80; chmn. planning com. Am. Coun. Edn. Acad. Fellows Working Reunion, 1972, 79, 85; vice chmn. Am. Coun. Edn. Coun. Fellows, 1980-81, chmn., 1981-82, exec. com., 1980-83, chmn. S.E. Region Conf., 1988, mem. alumni rels. com.; mem. U. South Fla. Interdisciplinary Ctr. on Digital and Computational Video, 1999-2002; co-chair Internat. Workshop on Digital and Computational Video, 1999, 2000; cons., lectr. in field. Co-author: Counseling; Selected Readings, 1962, Educational Administration: Selected Readings, 1965, 2d edit., 1971, Analysis of Educational Change in Ohio Public Schools, 1968; contbr. articles to profl. jours. Gen. chmn. Mansfield Area United Way campaign, 1975, bd. dir., 1976-78, v.p., 1977, 78; bd. dir. Mansfield Symphony Orch., 1972-78, pres., 1978; bd. dir. Rsch. for Better Schs., Inc., 1968-71, pres., 1970-71; mem. Kiwanis Club Mansfield, 1971-78, bd. dir., 1974-78; mem. citizens adv. com. Richland County Regional Planning Commn., 1973-74, bd. dir., 1975-78, v.p.; mem. Manpower Adv. Coun. Richland and Morrow Counties, 1977-78; trustee Hillsbrough County Hosp. Authority, Tampa, Fla., 1980-84, Tampa Heart Ctr., 1982-84; sec.-treas., 1983-84; mem. Leadership Tampa, 1982-83, Leadership Tampa Alumni, 1983-2003, 2006-07, Leadership Tampa Bay, 1992-2003; mem. Tampa-Hillsborough Cable adv. com., 1984-92, vice chmn., 1987-88, chmn., 1988-92; instl. rep. PBS and Nat. Pub. Radio, Am. Pub. TV Stas. 1986-2002, Legis. adv., APTS, 1995-2001; market fund adv. com. CPB, 1996; steering com. Higher Edn. Telecomm. Consortium, 1995-2001; steering com., pub. broadcasting joint licensee Consortium, 1996-2001; bd. dir. Fla. Pub. Broadcasting Svc. Inc., 1986-2002, chair Long Range Planning Com., 1988-93, treas., 1991-93, vice chair, 1993-95, chair, 1995-97, chair programs and ops. com., 1993-95, exec. com. 1991-99; bd. dir. Program Resources Group, 1993-2001, exec. com., 1995-2001, vice-chair, sec., 1995-2001; mem. Palma Ceia United Meth. Ch., 1980-2009, choir 1980-2009, chair coun. on ministries, 1985-86, chair pipe organ com., 1985-91, chair adminstrv. bd., coun., 1987-89, 93-98; mem. pastor parish com., 1990-92, 96-98, chair, 1992; mem. choir Palma Ceia Presbyn. Ch. and Choir, 2013-; mem. Master Chorale of Tampa Bay, 1983—, mem. bd. trustees, vol. devel. officer; bd. dir. Chorale Masterworks Festival, Inc., 1987—, v.p., 1991-93, chair and pres., 1993-95, 97-99, 2000-01, exec. com., 2002—, exec. advisor, 2004-, co-chair longrange planning com., 2005-06, chair Devel. Com., 2006-08, trustee of the Season, 2007-08, v.p., 2011-, mem. Tampa Oratorio Singers, 2013-; bd. mem., USF Clarion Soc., 2008-, chair, Membership Com., 2011-12; bd. dir. Southern Ednl. Comms. Assn., 1986-97, mem. budget and fin. com., 1989-91. bd. dir. Nat. Edn. Telecom. Assn., 1997-2002, long range planning coun. 1997-98; mem. Tampa Bay Area Com. Fgn. Rels., 2002—; mem. classical music festival, Eisenstadt, Austria, 2002, 06, 08. With USAF, 1953-55; USAFR, ret. 1973. Recipient Best Comprehensive Grassroots Program award, Am. Pub. TV Stas., 1999; Nat. Def. Edn. Act fellow, Ohio State U., 1961. Mem. Assn. Higher Edn. (life), Ohio State U. Assn. (life), Nat. Univ. Continuing Edn. Assn. (instnl. rep., bd. dirs. region III, honors and awards com. 1986-90), Greater Tampa C. of C. (chmn. emergency preparedness task force 1991-94), Civitan (club founding pres. 1980-82), Tampa Rotary (chair music com. 2003-2004, 2006-2013, Paul Harris fellow), Columbus North H.S. ALumni Club (life), Phi Delta Kappa (life), Kappa Delta Pi, Phi Kappa Phi. Democrat. Presbyterian. Personal E-mail: jim@jbheck.com.

HECK, PATRICK GEORGE, legislative staff member, lawyer; b. Cin., Feb. 27, 1957; s. James L. and Helen Jean (Thaman) H.; m. Debbie Ann Knott, Feb. 29, 1992; children; Patrick Thaman, Josephine Jorgeanne. Student, U. London, 1978; BS in Polit. Sci. and Econs., American U., 1979; JD, U. Toledo Coll., 1982; LLM in Taxation, Georgetown U., 1998. Bar: Ohio 1982. Congl. asst. US House of Representatives, Washington, 1978-81; advance person Office of V.P., Washington, 1980; clk. courtroom Lucas County Common Pleas Ct., Toledo, 1981-82; tax law specialist, employee plan and exempt organization divsn. IRS, Washington, 1983-85, trial atty., Office of Chief Coun., 1985—88; asst. counsel US House Ways and Means Com., Washington, 1988—95; sr. mgr., Nat. Tax Dept. Ernst & Young, LLP, Washington, 1995—2000; tax counsel, chief investigative counsel US Senate Fin. Com., 2000—03, chief tax counsel, chief investigative counsel, 2003—. Mem. ABA. Office: Ernst & Young LLP 1225 Connecticut Ave NW Washington DC 20036-2604 Address: US Senate Finance Com 219 Dirksen Senate Office Washington DC 20510 Office Phone: 202-224-4515.

HECKEL, JOHN LOUIS (JACK HECKEL), aerospace management executive; b. Columbus, Ohio, July 12, 1931; s. Russel Criblez and Ruth Selma (Heid) H.; m. Jacqueline Ann Alexander, Nov. 21, 1959 (div. 1993); children: Heidi, Holly, John; m. Linda Holleran, Aug. 1, 1994. BS, U. Ill., 1954; PhD with honors, Nat. U. San Diego, 1984. Divsn. mgr. Aerojet Divsn., Azusa, Calif., 1956-70, Seattle and Washington, 1956-70; pres. Aerojet-Space Gen. Co., El Monte, Calif., 1970-72, Aerojet Liquid Rocket Co., Sacramento, 1972-77; group v.p. Aerojet Sacramento Cos., 1977-81; pres. Aerojet Gen., La Jolla, Calif., 1981-85, chmn., CEO, 1985-87; pres., COO GenCorp., Akron, 1987-94, bd. dirs., Teraphysics Corp. Bd. dirs. WD-40 Corp., Petritech, Corp. Bd. dirs. San Diego Econ. Devel. Corp., 1983-86, Akron Regional Devel. Bd., Akron Gen. Hosp., Summit County United Way; pres. Summit Edn. Partnership Found., Akron. Recipient Disting. Alumni award U. Ill. Ann. Alumni Conv., 1979 Fellow AIAA (assoc.); mem. Aerospace Industries Assn. Am. (gov. 1981), Navy League U.S., Am. Def. Preparedness Assn., San Diego C. of C. (bd. dirs.), Teraphysics Corp. (bd. dir.). Office Phone: 239-948-0306. Personal E-mail: jheckel4@comcast.net.

HECKSTALL, JOE, state legislator; m. Andrea Heckstall. Former state rep. Dist. 48, Ga.; former state rep. Dist. 55 Ga.; former TV talk show host; sec. State Planning & Cmty. Affairs Com.; mem. Defense & Vet. Affairs & Special Judiciary Coms.; house rep. Ga.; state rep. Dist. 62 Ga., 2004—; motivational spkr.; sales trainer. Democrat. Address: 2713 Briarwood Blvd East Point GA 30344-5316 Mailing: State Capitol 509 Legis Off Bldg Atlanta GA 30334

HEDDEN, KENNETH FORSYTHE, chemical engineer; b. Glendale, Calif., Aug. 13, 1941; s. Marion William and Pauline (Forsythe) H.; m. Ann Ellen Young, Jan. 26, 1963 (div. 1990); children: Randolph, Stephen, William; m. Suzanne A. Whitlock, Feb. 10, 1990. BS, U. Calif., Berkeley, 1963; PhD, U. Calif., Davis, 1968; M in Pub. Adminstrn., U. Ga., 1980. Registered profl. engr., sanitarian, specialist microbiologist. Research fellow Tufts U. Med. Sch., Boston, 1968-70; research assoc. Purdue U., Lafayette, Ind., 1970-72; lab. supr. Anheuser-Busch, Inc., Lafayette, 1972-75; sanitary engr. U.S. Army Environ. Hygiene Agy., Aberdeen (Md.) Proving Ground, 1975-78, EPA, Athens, Ga., 1978-83, chem. engr. Environ. Monitoring Systems Lab. Las Vegas, Nev., 1983-88; environ. engr. Warner Robins Air Logistics Ctr., Robins AFB, Ga., 1988-94, environ. chemist, 1994—2006. Contbr. articles to profl. jours. Col. ret. USAR. Mem. Conf. Fed. Environ. Engrs., Sigma Xi, Alpha Chi Sigma. Republican. Baptist. Avocations: gardening, bowling, stamp collecting/philately, woodworking, black powderguns. Home: 1736 Hwy 49 Fort Valley GA 31030-6802 Home Phone: 478-825-7213. Personal E-mail: eaglestationinc@hotmail.com.

HEDGEBETH, REGINALD D., lawyer; BS, Pa. State U.; JD, Harvard U., 1996. Bar: Ga. 1996. Fin. analyst GE Capital Corp., Atlanta; assoc. King & Spalding, LLP; v.p. legal Home Depot Inc., Atlanta; sr. v.p., gen. counsel, sec. Circuit City Stores Inc., Richmond, Va., 2005—09; gen. counsel Spectra Energy Corp., Houston, 2009—. Mem.: State Bar Ga. Office: Spectra Energy Corp 5400 Westheimer Ct Houston TX 77056-5310 Office Phone: 713-627-5400.

HEDMAN, VICTOR (VICTOR ERIK OLOF HEDMAN), professional hockey player; b. Örnsköldsvik, Sweden, Dec. 18, 1990; Defenseman Modo Hockey (Swedish Elite League), Örnsköldsvik, Sweden, 2007—09, Tampa Bay Lightning, 2009—. Mem. Team Sweden, World Jr. Championships, Czech Republic, 2008, Ottawa, Ont., Canada, 2009. Achievements include being the second overall draft pick in NHL entry draft, 2009. Office: Tampa Bay Lightning Hockey Club St Pete Times Forum 401 Channelside Dr Tampa FL 33602

HEDRICK, KIRBY L., energy executive; BS in Mech. Engring., U. Evansville, Ind., 1975. Pres., CEO Phillips Gas Co., Houston, 1986-94; sr. v.p., refining, mktg. and transp. Phillips Petroleum Co., Bartlesville, Okla., 1994-97; exec. v.p. Upstream Phillips Petroleum Co., 1997—2000. Bd. dirs. Noble Energy, Inc., 2002—. Office: Noble Energy Inc Bd Directors 100 Glenborough Dr Ste 100 Houston TX 77067 Office Phone: 281-872-3100. Office Fax: 281-872-3111. Business E-Mail: khedrick@nobleenergyinc.com.

HEEBE, FREDERICK JACOB REAGAN, federal judge; b. Gretna, La., Aug. 25, 1922; s. Bernhardt and Marguerite (Reagan) H.; m. Doris Stewart, Oct. 6, 1984; children by previous marriage: Frederick Riley, Adrea Dee. BA, Tulane U., 1943, LLB, 1949. Bar: La. 1949. Practice in, Gretna, 1949-60; judge divsn. B 24th Jud. Dist. Ct., Jefferson Parish, La., 1961—66; judge US Dist. Ct. (ea. dist.) La., New Orleans, 1966—72, chief judge, 1972—92, sr. judge, 1992—. Mem. Community Welfare Council Jefferson Parish, from 1957; chmn. Jefferson Parish Bd. Pub. Welfare, 1953-55; Mem. Jefferson Parish Council, 1958-60, vice chmn., 1958-60; Bd. dirs. Social Welfare Planning Council New Orleans, New Orleans Regional Mental Center and Clinic, W. Bank Assn. for Retarded. Served to capt., inf. AUS, World War II. Decorated Purple Heart, Bronze Star. Mem. Am., La., New Orleans, Fed. bar assns., Am. Judicature Soc., Phi Beta Kappa. Office: US Dist Ct 500 Poydras St Rm C107 New Orleans LA 70130

HEEBNER, DAVID K., manufacturing executive, retired military officer; b. Feb. 15, 1945; BS in Mech. Engring., Worcester Polytechnic Inst., 1967; MS in ops. rsch., Naval Postgrad. Sch., 1976; MA in nat. security & strategic studies, Naval War Coll., 1986. Advanced through grades to lt. gen. U.S. Army, 1967—99, served overseas in Korea, Vietnam, Germany & Israel, comdr. 10th Air Defense Artillery Brigade, dir. theater missile defense, Ballistic Missile Defense Org., asst. divsn. comdr. 2d Armored Divsn., dir. program analysis & evaluation, 1994—97, asst. vice chief of staff, 1997—99; v.p. strategic planning General Dynamics Corp., Falls Church, Va., 2000—02, sr. v.p. planning & develop., 2002—05, sr. v.p., pres. land systems, 2005—08, exec. v.p. marine systems, 2009—10, exec. v.p. combat systems, 2010—. Office: Gen Dynamics Corp 2941 Fairview Park Dr Falls Church VA 22042-4513

HEEG, PEGGY A., lawyer, former gas industry executive; b. Louisville, June 25, 1959; BA in Polit. Sci. with honors, U. Louisville, 1983, JD, 1986. Bar: Ky. 1986, DC 1987, Tex. 1987. With Tenneco Energy, El Paso Corp., 1996—97, v.p., assoc. gen. counsel, regulated pipelines, 1997—2001, sr. v.p., dep. gen. counsel, 2001, exec. v.p., gen. counsel, 2002—04; ptnr. Fulbright & Jaworski, LLP, 2004—. Legal advisor to commr. Charles Stalon Fed. Energy Regulatory Commn., 1988; bd. dirs. El Paso Tenn. Pipeline Co. Mem.: ABA, Interstate Natural Gas Assn. Am., DC Bar, State Bar Tex., Ky. Bar Assn., Energy Bar Assn. Office: Fulbright & Jaworski LLP 1301 McKinney Ste 5100 Houston TX 77010-3095 Office Phone: 713-651-5151. Office Fax: 713-651-5246. E-mail: pheeg@fulbright.com.

HEESACKER, MARTIN, psychologist, educator; b. Warwick, Va., Apr. 25, 1956; s. Bernard Andrew and Mary (NeCasek) H. BS with highest honors, U. So. Miss., 1977; MS in Psychology Counseling, U. Mo., 1981, PhD in Psychology Counseling, 1983. Lic. psychologist, Ohio, Fla. Counselor, intern U. Mo., Columbia, 1981-83; asst. prof. psychology So. Ill. U., Carbondale, 1983-86, Ohio State U., Columbus, 1986-89; assoc. prof. psychology U. Fla., Gainesville, 1989—95, prof. psychology, 1995—, chmn., dept. psychology, 2000—07. Cons. Covington Industries, Opp, Ala., 1983-84, North Fla. Evaluation and Treatment Ctr., Gainesville, 1996—, SOAR Am., Inc., Melbourne, Fla., 1990—; lectr. in field. Editorial bd. Jour. Counseling Psychology, 1987-95, Contemporary Psychology, 1995—; editor Profiles of Adjustment, 1994; contbr. articles to profl. jours., chpts. to books. Recipient Grad. Rsch. award Mo. Psychol. Assn., 1982, Davis Productivity award Fla. Tax Watch, 1994; Fulbright scholar USIA, 1987; Lilly fellow Eli Lilly Endowment, 1988. Fellow APA (counseling psychology divsn., co-chair Gt. Lakes regional conf. 1987-88, new profls. com. 1986-87, Early Career award 1989); mem. Midwestern Psychol. Assn., Soc. Advancement Social Psychology, Soc. Exptl. Social Psychology, Sigma Xi. Avocations: sailing, jogging, swimming. Office: Dept Psychology U Fla 027 Psychology Bldg PO Box 112250 Gainesville FL 32611-2250 Office Phone: 352-273-2136. Business E-Mail: heesack@ufl.edu.

HEESTAND SKINNER, DIANE ELISSA, retired health professions educator; b. Boston, Oct. 9, 1945; d. Glenn Wilson and Elizabeth (Martin) Heestand. BA, Allegheny Coll., 1967; MA, U. Wyo., 1968; edn. specialist, Ind. U., 1971, EdD, 1979; MPH, U. Ark. Med. Sci., 2007. Asst. prof. communication Clarion (Pa.) State Coll., 1971; asst. prof. learning resources Indiana U. of Pa., 1971-72; asst. prof. communication U. Nebr. Med. Ctr., Omaha, 1972-74; assoc. prof. learning resources Tidewater Community Coll., Virginia Beach, Va., 1975-78; ednl. cons. U. Ala. Sch. Medicine, Birmingham, 1978-81; dir. learning resources, assoc. prof. med. edn. Mercer U. Sch. Medicine, Macon, Ga., 1981-88; asst. dean ednl. devel. and resources Ohio U. Coll. Osteopathic Medicine, 1989-90; assoc. prof. clin. med. edn., dir. biomed. communications U. So. Calif. Sch. Medicine, LA, 1990-95, acting chair dept. med. edn., 1992-95; prof., dir. office ednl. devel. U. Ark. for Med. Scis., Little Rock, 1995—2007, prof., assoc. dean. Coll. Health Related Prof., 2008—12, prof., dir. interprofessional edn., 2012—13; assoc. dean emerita, 2012. Cons. Lincoln (Pa.) U., summer, 1975; vis. fellow Project Hope/China, Millwood, Va., summer, 1986; vis. scholar, U. Nigeria, Jos U., 2005-2006 Author (teleplay) Yes, 1968 (award World Law Fund 1968); producer, dir. (slide tape) Finding a Way, 1980 (1st Pl. award HESCA 1981, Susan Eastman award 1981). Vol. Habitat for Humanity; UAMS vol. Grantee, Porter Found., 1984, Ark. Dept. Higher Edn., 1996—97, UAMS Spl. Devel., 1997—99; Family and Preventive Medicine fellow, Health Resources and Svcs. Adminstrn., 2003—04. Mem. Health Scis. Comm. Assn. (bd. dirs. 1982-86, pres.-elect 1987-88, pres. 1988-89, Spl. Svc. award 1990), Assn. Ednl. Comm. and Tech. (pres. media design and prodn. div. 1985-86), Assn. Biomed. Comm. Dirs. (bd. dirs. 1993-95), Soc. of Dirs. of Rsch. in Med. Edn. (steering com. 2000—, chair-elect 2002, chair 2003), Generalists in Med. Edn. (steering com. 1998-2001, chmn. 1999-2000). Democrat. Presbyterian. Avocations: tennis, gardening, golf. Personal E-mail: deskinner009@gmail.com.

HEFFERNAN, EDWARD J., financial services company executive; B, Wesleyan U.; MBA, Columbia Bus. Sch. Corp. fin. Credit Suisse First Boston, 1986—90; v.p., mergers, acquisitions Citicorp., 1990—94, First Data Corp., 1994—98; mergers, acquisitions & IPO mgmt. positions Alliance Data Sys. Corp., 1998—2000, exec. v.p., CFO, Alliance Data, 2000—09, pres., CEO. Bd. dirs. Alliance Data Sys. Corp., 2009—, VALOR Comm. Group, Inc., 2005—06. Office: Alliance Data Systems Inc 7500 Dallas Pkwy Ste 700 Plano TX 75024-4006 Office Phone: 972-348-5100. Business E-Mail: Edward.Heffernan@alliancedata.com.

HEFFERNAN, THOMAS CARROLL, English literature and American studies educator; b. Hyannis, Mass., Aug. 19, 1939; arrived in Japan, 1984; s. Thomas (Hugh) Carroll and Mary Elizabeth (Sullivan) H.; m. Nancy Elizabeth Iler, 1972 (div. 1977). BA in English, Boston Coll., 1961; MA in English Lit., Victoria U. Manchester, Eng., 1963; PhD in English Lit., Sophia U., 1990. Asst. lectr. English U. Manchester, 1964-65, U. Bristol, Eng., 1965-66; instr. English U. Hartford, West Hartford, Conn., 1967-70, N.C. State U., Raleigh, 1971-73; poet in the schs. N.C. Dept. Pub. Instrn. and Arts Coun., Raleigh, 1973-77; lectr. English and humanities Program for Afloat Coll. Edn., USN, Norfolk (Va.) & San Diego, Calif., 1982-84; lectr. in English, history and philosophy U. Md., Asian Divsn., Tokyo, 1984-92; vis. prof. English U. Kagoshima, Japan, 1992-94; prof. English and Am. studies Kagoshima Prefectural Coll., Japan, 1994—2005; vis. prof. English, theater and fgn. langs. St. Andrews Presbyn. Coll., 2005—10; lectr. English and Theater Dept., U. NC, Pembroke, 2012—. Editor, pub., dir. Yorick Books, Boston and Hartford, 1967-71; dir., poetry instr. Martha's Vineyard Writers Workshop, Vineyard Haven, Mass., 1973-77; vis. artist in poetry N.C. Arts Coun., N.C. Dept. C.Cs., Raleigh, 1977-81; vis. artist in poetry S.C. Arts Commn., Columbia, 1981-82; editor, pub. Plover/Chidori, Okinawa, Japan, 1987-92; editor, CAIRN: The New St Andrews Review, Laurinburg, NC, 2005-2009; lectr. in field. Author: The Liam Poems, 1981 (Roanoke-Chowan 1982), Art and Emblem: Early 17th Century English Poetry of Devotion, 1991, Gathering In Ireland, 1996, Christmas Gifts in South Japan, 2002, White Edge, Curling Wave, 2003; editor (Celtic issue) Internat. Poetry Rev., 1979, CAIRN: The St. Andrews Rev., 2005—09; contbr. chpts. to books and articles to profl. jours. Recipient Mainichi Internat. Haiku award in English, Mainichi Daily News, Japan, 1985, 87-93, 97, 2d pl. in English, 1999-2000, 06, Portfolio Poetry award Poetry Ctr.-Guilford Coll., Greensboro, N.C., 1983, Mainichi Culture Seminar Haiku award Mainichi Daily News/Japan Air Lines, Tokyo, 1986, Internat. Haiku award Itoen Co., Tokyo, 1990, 1995, Kusamakura Internat. Haiku Grand prize, 2006. Mem. Associated Writers and Writing Programs, Coll. English Assn., Internat. Ezra Pound Conf., Haiku Soc. Am., NC Haiku Soc. Avocations: singing, walking, travel. Personal E-mail: thomasheffernan@yahoo.com. Business E-Mail: thomas.heffernan@uncp.edu.

HEFLIN, MARTIN GANIER, diplomat, political scientist; b. Oklahoma City, July 5, 1932; s. Martin Henry and Eugenia Marie (Gabel) H.; m. Sydney Daffin Lewis, Nov. 24, 1954; children— Martin Hays, Stephanie Anne Heflin Pace BA, U. Okla., 1954, MA, 1957; post-grad., U. Redlands, 1955, U. Tex., 1958-59. Vice consul U.S. Consulate, Ponta Delgada, Portugal, 1960-62, U.S. Consulate Gen., São Paulo, Brazil, 1962-64; 2d sec. U.S. Embassy, Tokyo, Japan, 1964-68; prin. officer U.S. Consulate, Sapporo, Japan, 1968-71; fgn. affairs officer U.S. Dept State, Washington, 1971-74; consul, econ. and commerce U.S. Consulate Gen., São Paulo, 1974-76; dir. U.S. Trade Ctr. U.S. Dept. Commerce, São Paulo, 1976-78; counselor econ. and comml. affairs U.S. Embassy, New Delhi, India, 1979-83; minister-counselor, sr. Fgn. Service; prin. officer U.S. Consultate Gen., Monterrey, Mexico, 1983-87; sr. fellow Ctr. for Study of Fgn. Affairs, Fgn. Service Inst., Dept. State, 1987-89; mng. dir. The Naiad Corp., 1990—. Served to 1st lt. USAF, 1954-56. Mem. Am. Fgn. Service Assn., Am. Legion, Phi Delta Theta Roman Catholic. Avocations: golf, photography. Home: 4411 NW 12th Pl Gainesville FL 32605-5500 Personal E-mail: nikkihef@gmail.com.

HEFNER, DAVID STUART, health facility administrator, academic administrator; b. Boston, Tex., July 20, 1954; s. John Hardin and E. Patricia (Schwartz) H.; div. 1984; children: Tonia Marie, Brandi Lynn. BBA, U. Tex., 1976; M in Personnel Adminstrn., Brigham Young U., 1982. Founder, CEO Cons. Concepts, Inc., Salt Lake City, 1978, mng. ptnr., 1978—94; hosp. adminstr. Crook County Hosp., Sundance, Wyo., 1978-80, Tooele Valley Hosp., Utah, 1980-82; program mgr. BSL Tech., Salt Lake City, 1982-85; acting exec. dir., COO Penn State Milton S. Hershey Med. Ctr., Hershey, 2003, exec. dir., COO, 2003—06; sr. ptnr. CSC Global Health Solutions, 2006; pres. U. Chgo. Med. Ctr., 2006—09; sr. adv. Assn. American Med. Colleges (AAMC), Washington, 2009—; exec. v.p. clinical affairs Ga. Health Sciences U., Augusta, Ga., 2011—; CEO MCG Health Inc., Augusta, Ga.; CEO, chief strategy & transformation officer Physicians Practice Group, Augusta, Ga., 2011—. Mem.: Am. Arbitration Assn. (panel arbitrator). Office: Georgia Health Sciences University 1120 15th St Augusta GA 30912

HEFT, MARC W., medical educator, researcher; s. Harold Heft; m. Ann Gary; children: Adrienne, Sara, Jordan. BS, U. Pa., Phila., 1970; DMD, 1974, MA; PhD, Am. U., Washington DC, 1982. Clin. assoc. N.I.D.R., NIH, Bethesda, Md., 1975—79, postdoc. fellow, 1979—82; sr. staff fellow N.I.A., NIH, Balt., 1982—84; asst. prof. U. Fla., Gainesville, 1984—, assoc. prof., prof. Mem., cmty. investment adv. com. United Way, Alachua County, Fla., 2006—07; mem., cmty. adv. bd. Wuft Fm, Gainesville, 1992—97. Comdr. USPHS, 1975—79, Besthesda. Recipient Sigma Xi, 2003; Harald Löe Scholar, Am. Assoc for Dental Schs. NIDCR, 1999. Fellow: AAAS (chair, sec. 2001—07), Sigma Xi (Elected mem. 2003), Gerontol. Soc. Am. (Fellow); mem.: ADA, Internat. Assn. for Study of Pain (mem., task force on pain in the elderly 1993—95), Am. Dental Edn. Assn. (chair, behavioral sciences sect. 1999—2001), Am. Assn. Dental Rsch. (pres. 2007—08). Achievements include research in Aging, Oral Health In Aging And Pain. Office: Univ Florida 1600 SW Archer Rd D8-6 Gainesville FL 32610-0416

HEGAR, GLENN, state legislator; b. Nov. 25, 1970; m. Dara Hegar. BA, Tex. A&M U., 1993; MA, JD, St. Mary's U., 1997; LLM, U. Ark., 1998. Farmer; mem. Dist. 28 Tex. House of Representatives, 2003—07; mem. Dist. 18 Tex. State Senate, 2007—. Recipient of several awards and honors. Republican. Lutheran. Office: PO Box 1008 Katy TX 77492 also: PO Box 12068 Capitol Station Austin TX 78711 Office Phone: 281-391-8883, 512-463-0118.

HEGDE, ASHOK, research scientist, educator; s. Narayan and Susheela Hegde; m. Lalita Hegde, June 18, 1990; 1 child, Monica. MS, U. Agrl. Scs., Bangalore, India, 1983; PhD, Ctr. for Cellular and Molecular Biology, Hyderabdad, India, 1990. Rsch. scientist iv Columbia U., NY, 1997—2000; assoc. prof. Wake Forest U. Health Scis., Winston Salem, NC, 2001—. Cons. NIH, Bethesda, Md., 2001—. Grantee Grant for Rsch. on Proteolysis and Long-Term Memory, NIH, 2000—. Mem.: Soc. for Neuroscience. Achievements include discovery of proteolysis as mechanism underlying long-term memory. Office: Wake Forest U Health Scis Med Ctr Blvd Winston Salem NC 27157

HEGGEN, ARTHUR WILLIAM, insurance company executive; b. Eureka, Calif., Aug. 9, 1945; s. Arlo Murray and Edna Marie (Nelson) H.; m. Betty Louise Roddy, Nov. 21, 1970; children: Cherilyn, Christopher. BS in Indsl. Adminstrn., Acctg., Iowa State U., 1967. CPA, Iowa, Fla.; CPCU, FLMI, AIAF. Audit staff mgr. Ernst & Whinney, Des Moines, 1971-84; sr. v.p., treas. Am. Bankers Ins.

Group, Inc., Miami, Fla., 1984-96; exec. v.p. Am. Bankers Ins. Co., Miami, 1996-99, Assurant Solutions (formerly Assurant Group), Miami, 1999—. Bd. dirs. YMCA of Greater Miami; pres. Iowa Ptnrs. of the Yucatan, Des Moines, 1984; pres., treas. Des Moines Hearing Speech Ctr., 1976-82. Capt. USMC, 1967-70, Vietnam. Fellow Life Mgmt. Inst.; mem. AICPA, Soc. CPCU, Fla. Inst. CPAs, Ins. Acct. & Sys. Assn. Office: Assurant Solutions 11222 Quail Roost Dr Miami FL 33157-6543 also: Assurant Solutions 260 Interstate North Cir NW Atlanta GA 30339-2210 Office Phone: 305-253-2244, 305-252-6916.

HEGGERS, JOHN PAUL, retired surgery, immunology and microbiology educator; b. Bklyn., Feb. 8, 1933; s. John and May (Hass) H.; m. Rosemarie Niklas, July 30, 1977; children: Arn M., Ronald R., Laurel M., Gary R., Renee L., Annette M. BA in Bacteriology, Mont. State U. now U. Mont., 1958; MS in Microbiology, U. Md., 1965; PhD in Bacteriology and Pub. Health, Wash. State U., 1972. Diplomate Am. Bd. Bioanalysis; cert. wound specialist Am. Acad. Wound Mgmt.; cert. Advanced Burn Life Support provider. Med. technologist U.S. Naval Hosp., St. Albans, N.Y., 1951-53; bacteriologist Hahnemann Hosp., Worcester, Mass., 1958-59; commd. 2d lt. U.S. Army, 1959, advanced through grades to lt. col., 1975; mem. staff dept. bacteriology 1st U.S. Army Med. Lab., NYC, 1959-60; chief clin. lab., food svc. divsn. & diet kitchen U.S. Army Hosp., Verdun, France, 1960-63; chief virology and rickettsiology div. dept. microbiology 3d U.S. Army Med. Lab., Ft. McPherson, Ga., 1965-66; instr. bacteriology Basic Lab. Sch., Ft. McPherson, 1965-66; chief diagnostic bacteriology 9th Med. Lab., Saigon, Vietnam, 1966-67; chief microbiology div. dept. pathology Brooke Gen. Hosp., Ft. Sam Houston, Tex., 1967-69; chmn. dept. microbiology U.S. Army Sch. Med. Tech., Ft. Sam Houston, 1967-69; instr. bacteriology evening div. San Antonio Jr. Coll., 1969; lab. scis. officer Office Surgeon Gen., Washington, 1972-74; microbiologist spl. mycobacterial disease br. div. geog. pathology Armed Forces Inst. Pathology, Washington, 1973, spl. asst. to dir., 1973-74; chief clin. rsch. lab. clin. rsch. svc. Madigan Army Med. Ctr., Tacoma, 1974-76, asst. chief clin. investigation svc., 1976-77; instr. immunology, parasitology and mycology Clover Park Vocat. Tech. Inst., 1976-77; ret., 1977; assoc. prof. dept. surgery U. Chgo., 1977-80, prof., 1980-83; prof. surgery Wayne State U., Detroit, 1983-88; prof. surgery, microbiology and immunology U. Tex. Med. Br., 1988—2005; ret., 2005. Dir. clin. microbiology Shriners Burn Hosp., Galveston, Tex., 1988-2005. Author: Current Problems in Surgery, 1973, Quantitative Bacteriology, 1991; contbr. articles to profl. jours.; contbg. editor: Jour. Am. Med. Tech., 1972-2000. Pres. Aloe Rsch. Found., 1989-92, vice-chmn. 1992-95; Svc. award dedicator. Decorated Bronze Star; Legion of Merit; recipient cert. of appreciation A.C.S., 1969, cert. appreciation Armed Forces Inst. Pathology, 1974, Valley Forge Honor cert. Freedoms Found., 1974 Fisher award in med. tech., Fisher Scientific, Am. Med. Techs., 1968, 82, Gerard B. Lambert award, 1973, Ednl. Found. Rsch. award Am. Soc. Plastic and Reconstructive Surgery, 1978, Alumni Achievement award Wash. State U., 1993, Disting. Alumni award U. Mont., 1994, cert. appreciation for volunteering for operations Noble Eagle and Enduring Freedom, U.S. Army Reserve Command Personnel, 2002. Fellow NY Acad. Sci., Am. Acad. Microbiology, Royal Soc. Tropical Medicine and Hygiene, Am. Geriat. Soc.; VFW (life), mem. Nat. Registry Microbiologists (chmn. exec. coun. 1976-79), Am. Soc. Microbiology (chmn. com. tellers 1974-75), Wash. Soc. Am. Med. Technologists (pres. 1975-77), Wash. Soc. Med. Tech. (chmn. sect. microbiology sci. assembly, dir. 1975-77), Assn. Mil. Surgeons U.S. (life), Am. Soc. Clin. Pathologists (assoc.), Am. Med. Technologists (Disting. Svc. award 1975, Exceptional Merit award 1976, nat. dir. 1979-80, nat. sec. 1980-82, nat. v.p. 1982-84, Technologist of Yr. 1983), Am. Burn Assn. (chmn. rsch. com., 2d v.p. bd. trustees 2002, plaque of appreciation for dedicated svc., 2004, Pres.'s continuing edn. award 1981, At Large award 1986, Robert B. Lindberg award 1991, 92, 2004, Curtis P. Artz Disting. Svc. award 1996), Plastic Surgery Rsch. Coun., Surg. Infection Soc. (charter), Am. Assn. Bioanalysts (William N. Reich Outstanding Achievement award 2007), Ill. State Soc. Med. Technologists (v.p. 1979), Internat. Soc. Burn Injuries, Vietnam Vets. Assn. (life), Masons (32d degree, knight comdr. Ct. Honor), Shriners (ritualistic potentate), Sigma Xi

HEGI, FREDERICK B., JR., investment company executive; b. 1943; Grad., So. Meth. U., 1966; MBA, Harvard U., 1968; PhD, U. Tex., 1970. With First Chgo. Co., 1970-73; v.p. Cooper Industries, Dallas, 1973-82; pres. Valley View Capital, Dallas, 1982-87; founding ptnr., prin., mem. adv. bd. Wingate Partners, Dallas, 1987—; chmn., pres., CEO Kevco Inc., 1999—2002; chmn., interim pres. & CEO United Stationers, Inc., 1996—97, chmn., 1997—2011. Bd. dir. Lone Star Tech Inc., Drew Industries Inc., Tex. Capital Bancshares Inc., United Stationers, Inc., 1995—2012. Office: Wingate Partners 750 N Siant Paul St Ste 1200 Dallas TX 75201

HEGSTROM, WILLIAM JEAN, retired mathematics professor; b. Macomb, Ill., Oct. 21, 1923; s. Carl William and Thelma (Canavit) Hegstrom; m. Grace Ann Paladino, May 3, 1944 (dec. Nov. 29, 2005); children: Elizabeth Louise, William Jean II, Jean Kilbourne. Studied, Western Ill. U., 1941—42; BSc, Rutgers U., 1949, EdM, 1952; postgrad., U. Fla., 1961; MA in Tchg., Purdue U., 1964; postgrad., Fla. Atlantic U., 1965—68; EdD, U. Miami, 1971. Tchr. S. Plainfield Jr. H.S., NJ, 1949—52, Bernardsville H.S., NJ, 1952—54, Oak St. Sch., Bernardsville, NJ, 1954—55, Summit H.S., NJ, 1955—58, Delray Beach Jr. H.S., Fla., 1958—65; chmn., math. dept. John I. Leonard H.S., Lake Worth, Fla., 1965—68; dir. Palm Beach County Rsch. Project, 1966—68; adj. prof. Fla. Atlantic U., 1965—69, assoc. prof., 1969—70; counselor coord. John Leonard Adult Ctr., Lake Worth, Fla., 1965—68; supr. rsch. and evaluation Palm Beach County Sch. Bd., West Palm Beach, Fla., 1970—74; adj. prof. Palm Beach Jr. Coll., 1981—88, Palm Beach Atlantic Coll., 1984—86, asst. prof., 1986—87; cons. math. prof. Palm Beach County Sch. Bd., 1985—87; ret., 1987. Contbr. articles to profl. jours. With USAAF, 1942—46. Mem.: NEA, Am. Assn. Individual Investors. Home: 225 NE 22nd St Delray Beach FL 33444-4221

HEICHEL, GARY HAROLD, agronomist, educator; b. Park Falls, Wis., Nov. 9, 1940; s. Harold H. and Bernice I. (Comp) Heichel; m. Iris Fehl Martin, Apr. 24, 1988. BS, Iowa State U., 1962; MS, Cornell U., 1964, PhD, 1968; D in Natural Scis. (hon.), Swiss Fed. Inst. Tech., Zurich, 1998. Asst. plant physiologist Conn. Agrl. Expt. Stats., New Haven, 1968-73, assoc. plant physiologist, 1973-76, plant physiologist, 1976, USDA Agrl. Rsch. Svc., St. Paul, 1976-90, acting rsch. leader, 1988-90; head agronomy dept. U. Ill., Urbana, 1990-95, interim head plant pathology dept., 1994-95, head crop scis. dept., 1995—2004, prof. emeritus, 2004—. Adj. prof. agronomy U. Minn., 1976—90; program mgr. USDA Competitive Rsch. Grants Office, 1981; bd. dirs. Coun. Agrl. Sci. and Tech., 2005—09; pres. Whiting's Neck Farm Estates, Inc., 2005—07. Contbr. chapters to books, articles to profl. jours. Pres., mem. adminstrv. bd. Cheshire (Conn.) United Meth. Ch., 1973—76, v.p. Cheshire Land Trust, 1975—76. Named Civil Servant of the Yr., Twin Cities Fed. Exec. Bd., St. Paul, 1984; Paul Harris fellow, Rotary Internat., 2002. Fellow: AAAS (chair sect. 0 1997—98); mem.: Potomac Headwaters Resources Conservation & Devel. Coun. (bd. dirs. 2008—, chair 2010—), Coun. Agrl. Sci. & Tech. (bd. dirs. 2004—08), Am. Soc. Plant Physiologists (trustee 1988—90), Am. Soc. Agronomy (pres. North Ctrl. sect. 1991—93, pres. 1997—98, Svc. award 2001), Crop Sci. Soc. Am. (pres. 1991—92, Monsanto Crop Sci. Disting. Career award 2006), Shepherdstown Rotary Club (bd. dirs. 2008—), Urbana Rotary (bd. dirs. 1997—99). Avocations: classical music, reading, hiking, gardening. Office: U Ill Dept Crop Scis 1102 S Goodwin Ave AW-101 Urbana IL 61801-4730 Business E-Mail: gheichel@uiuc.edu.

HEIDEN, CHARLES KENNETH, metal products executive, consultant, retired military officer; b. Detroit, July 7, 1925; s. Carl William and Elsie Mae (Langley) H.; m. Nancy Earle Gray, June 7, 1949; 1 son, Charles Gray. BS, U.S. Mil. Acad., 1949; MS in Mech. Engring, U. Mich., 1957; grad. mgmt. execs. program, U. Pitts., 1971. Registered profl. engr., Ky. Enlisted U.S. Army, 1943, commd. 2d lt., 1949, advanced through grades to maj. gen., 1977; services in Panama, France, Korea and Vietnam; dep. dir. ops. Nat. Mil. Command Center, Joint Chiefs of Staff, 1973-74; dir. enlisted personnel U.S. Mil. Personnel Center, Washington, 1974-76; comdr. U.S. Army Mil. Personnel Center, 1977-80; comdg. gen. U.S. Army Tng. Ctr., Ft. Dix, N.J., 1980-81; pres., dir. Montel Metals Inc., 1981-83, Cedar Lake Lodge Inc., La Grange, Ky., 1982—98, chmn. bd. dirs., 1982—98, dir. emeritus, 1998—; cons. Computer Simulation, 1987-98; dir. Cedar Lake Inc., Louisville, 1993—98, 2012—, chmn. bd. dirs., 1993—98; dir. Seven Counties Svcs., 2000—07, treas., 2004—05. Bd. dirs. Park Glen Heights Assn., Annandale, Va., 1974-76; bd. dirs. Seven Counties Svcs., 2000-07, treas., 2004-05; pres. Our Saviour Luth. Ch., Arlington, Va., 1974-76; mem. code enforcement bd. City Jeffersontown, Ky., 1998-2000. Decorated D.S.M., D.F.C., Legion of Merit with 3 oak leaf clusters, Air medal with 10 oak leaf clusters, Joint Services Commendation medal, Army Commendation medal with 2 oak leaf clusters, Meritorious Service medal with oak leaf cluster; Cross of Gallantry with silver star Vietnam; recipient Pace award Office Sec. Army, 1963 Mem. Armed Forces Relief and Benefit Assn. (dir. 1977-81), West Point Alumni Assn., Forest Garden Assn. (chmn. and pres. 2001—04), Am. Legion, U.S. Army War Coll. Alumni Assn. Lutheran. Home: 10500 Forest Garden Ln Louisville KY 40223-6166 Personal E-mail: heidenck@bellsouth.net.

HEIDT, LARRY P., energy executive; Pres., CEO Peter Bawden Drilling (acquired by Noble Drilling Corp); exec. v.p. Noble Drilling Corp.; pres., North Sea ops. Nabors Industries Ltd., pres., US Lower 48 land drilling ops., Nabors Drilling USA, LP, 1997—2004, spl. asst. to chmn., 2004, chmn., CEO, Nabors Well Svcs., 2009—. Office: Nabors Well Services Ste 1000 515 W Greens Rd Houston TX 77067 Office Phone: 281-874-0406. Office Fax: 281-775-8462. Business E-Mail: lheidt@nabors.com.

HEIL, GENE D., retail executive; b. Elmont, NY, 1955; BS in Mgmt., Jones Coll., Fla., 1977. Divisional mdse. mgr. May Department Stores Co., 1974—85; owner, pres. Lectron Svcs. Inc., 1985—91; regional v.p. stores Dillard's, Inc., 1991—. Office: Dillard's Inc 1600 Cantrell Rd Little Rock AR 72201 Office Phone: 501-376-5200. Office Fax: 501-399-7831. E-mail: gene.heil@dillards.com.

HEIM, MICHAEL A., energy executive; Officer of exploration & prodn., mktg. and midstream subsidiaries The Coastal Corp., exec. v.p., COO Coastal Field Services, 1997—2001, pres. Coastal States Gas Transmission Co., 1997—2001; energy industry cons., 2001—03; exec. v.p., COO Targa Resources Corp., 2004—11, pres., COO, 2012—. Office: Targa Resources Inc 1000 Louisiana Ste 4300 Houston TX 77002 Office Phone: 713-584-1000. Office Fax: 713-584-1100.

HEIMBERG, MURRAY, pharmacologist, biochemist, physician; b. Bklyn., Jan. 5, 1925; s. Gustav and Fannie (Geller) H.; children by previous marriage: Richard G., Steven A.; m. Anna Frances Langlois Knox, July 12, 1964; stepchildren: Larry M. Knox, David S. Knox. BS, Cornell U., Ithaca, NY, 1948, MNS, 1949; PhD in Biochemistry (NIH fellow), Duke, 1952; MD, Vanderbilt U., 1959. NIH Postdoctoral fellow in biochemistry Med. Sch. Washington U., St. Louis, 1952-54; research asso. physiology Med. Sch. Vanderbilt U., 1954-59, asst. prof. to prof. pharmacology, and asst. prof. medicine, 1959-74; prof., chmn. dept. pharmacology, prof. medicine U. Mo., 1974-81; prof. and chmn. dept. pharmacology, prof. medicine, endocrinology and metabolism U. Tenn., Health Sci. Ctr., Memphis, 1981-96; Van Vleet prof. pharmacology U. Tenn., Memphis, 1986-96, Disting. prof. pharmacology and medicine, 1996-99, disting. prof. pharmacology and medicine emeritus, 2000—. Cons. NSF, NIH; cons., established investigator Am. Heart Assn.; attending physician U. Tenn. Hosps. and Memphis VA Hosp.; dir. emeritus lipid metabolism clinic U. Tenn. Med. Group. Contbr. articles to profl. jours. Served with inf. AUS, 1943—45, ETO. Decorated Purple Heart, Bronze Star; recipient Lederle Med. Faculty award; research grantee. Fellow AAAS, Am. Coll. Clin. Pharmacology, Am. Heart Assn.; mem. Am. Soc. Biol. Chemistry and Molecular Biology, Am. Soc. Pharmacology and Exptl. Therapeutics, Endocrine Soc., Am. Diabetes Assn., So. Soc. Clin. Investigation, Nat. Lipid Assn. Home: 105 Devon Way Memphis TN 38111-7711 Office Phone: 901-448-4748. Personal E-mail: murrayhmd@gmail.com. Business E-Mail: mheimberg@uthsc.edu.

HEIMBINDER, ISAAC, lawyer; b. Bklyn., May 15, 1943; s. David and Evelyn (Brown) H.; m. Sheila Marie Mooney, Aug. 3, 1970; children: Susan, Daniel, Erin, Michael. BS in Bus., Am. U., 1965; JD, NYU, 1968. Atty. Debevoise and Plimpton, NYC, 1969-72; corp. counsel U.S. Home Corp., Clearwater, Fla., 1973-77, v.p. legal affairs Houston, 1977-79, CFO, 1979-86, pres. COO, 1986-95, co-CEO, pres. COO, 1995-99; chmn., CEO HomeWrite Inc., Houston, 2000—01; vice chmn., pres., COO Kimball Hill Homes, 2001—06; chmn. Buildtopia, 2007—. Named one of 100 Most Influential People in Homebuilding Industry in 20th Century, Builder Mag., 1999; recipient Homebuilder of Yr. award Profl. Builder, 1994 Mem. NY Bar Assn., Fla. Bar Assn., Tex. Bar Assn., Nat. Assn. Home Builders (former mem. high prodn. home builders coun.), Order of Coif, Omicron Delta Kappa.

HEIN, JAY FOREST, religious studies educator, former federal official; b. Shawano, Wis., 1965; BA in Social Sci., Eureka Coll., Ill.; M in Polit. Studies, U. Ill. Springfield. With Dept. Pub. Aid, Ill., Office Sec. of State, Ill. State Libr.; welfare reform policy adv. to Gov. Tommy Thompson, 1994—97; exec. dir. civil soc. programs Hudson Inst., 1997—2004; founding pres. Sagamore Inst. Policy Rsch., Indpls., 2004—06; dep. asst. to Pres., dir. office Faith-Based and Cmty. Initiatives The White House, 2006—08; Disting. sr. fellow, dir. program for faith & svc. Baylor U. Inst. for Studies of Religion, Waco, 2008—. CEO Found. Am. Renewal, 2002—06. Co-author, editor: book The New Wisconsin Idea: Replacing Entitlement Welfare with Personal Empowerment, The Welfare of Britain. Office: Institute for Studies of Religion One Bear Pl #97236 Waco TX 76798 Office Phone: 254-710-7555. Office Fax: 254-710-1428. E-mail: jay_hein@baylor.edu.

HEINDL, PHARES MATTHEWS, lawyer; b. Meridian, Miss., Dec. 14, 1949; s. Paul A. and Leila (Matthews) H.; children: Lori Elizabeth, Jesse Phares, Jared Matthews. BSChemE, Miss. State U., 1972; JD, U. Fla., Gainesville, 1981. Bar: Fla. 1981, Calif. 1982, US Dist. Ct. (cen. dist.) Calif. 1983, US Dist. Ct. (mid. dist.) Fla. 1983; registered patent atty., USPTO, 2009; cert. civil trial lawyer Fla. Bar. Assoc. Lafollette, Johnson et al, LA, 1982-83, Sam E. Murrell & Sons, Orlando, Fla., 1983-84; pvt. practice Orlando, Fla., 1984-93, Altamonte Springs, Fla., 1993—. Program com. Volie Williams Jr. Inns of Ct., 2003. Precinct coord. Freedom Coun., Orlando, 1986; pres. Friends of the Wekiva River, 1999—2001. Mem. Fla. Bar Assn., Calif. Bar Assn., Seminole County Bar Assn. (pres. civil trial sect. 1998), ATLA, Christian Legal Soc. (past pres. Ctrl. Fla.), Lit. Counsel America-Lawyers Honor Soc., Fla. Acad. Trial Lawyers, Workers Compensation Rules Com. Republican. Avocation: kayak racing. Office: PO Box 1009 Marco Island FL 34146 Business E-Mail: phares@heindllaw.com.

HEINEMEIER, DAN C., science association director; b. 1957; m. Meredith Heinemeier; 2 children. BS in Fgn. Svc., Georgetown U., Washington. Cert. assn. mgmt. Am. Soc. Assn. Execs./U. Md., assn. exec. Am. Soc. Assn. Execs., 1999. With Electronic Industries Assn. (now Alliance), 1980—98, exec. dir. govt. rels., 1984—90, v.p. govt. divsn.; pres. Govt. Electronics & Info. Tech. Assn., Arlington, Va., 1998—2008; COO TechAmerica, 2008—. Past chmn. oper. com. Coun. Def. and Space Industry Assns., mem. policy com. Office: TechAmerica 601 Pennsylvania Ave NW N Bldg Ste 600 Washington DC 20004 Office Phone: 202-682-9110.

HEININGER, S(AMUEL) ALLEN, retired chemical company executive; b. New Britain, Conn., June 13, 1925; s. Alfred D. and Erma Geraldine (Kline) H.; m. Barbara Ashenfelter Griffith, June 16, 1948 (dec. Oct. 6 1994); children: Janet, Kathryn, Kenneth, Keith; m. Margot Moran Danis, Nov. 27, 1998. AB, Oberlin Coll., 1948; MS, Carnegie Inst. Tech., 1951; D.Sc., 1952. Research chemist Monsanto Chem. Co., Dayton, Ohio, 1952-56, group leader, 1956-58, project mgr. devel. dept. Organic Chems. div. St. Louis, 1958-59, mgr. fine chems. intermediates and market exploration sect., 1959-65, dir. comml. devel., 1965-67, dir. food and fine chems., 1967-71, dir. corp. plans and devel., 1971-74; gen. mgr. plasticizers div. Monsanto Indsl. Chems. Co., St. Louis, 1974-76; dir. corp. research lab. Monsanto Chem. Co., St. Louis, 1977, v.p. research and devel., 1977-79, v.p. corp. plans and bus. devel., 1980-86, v.p. resource planning, 1986-90; retired, 1990. Contbr. articles to profl. jours.; U.S., fgn. patentee in field. Alderman City of Warson Woods, Mo., 1961—65, police commr., 1967—71; trustee St. Louis Sci. Ctr., 1997—2003, Repertory Theatre, 1998—2000; bd. dirs. Episcopal City Mission, 1998—2001, Gen. Protestant Children's Home, 1999—2004, Chem. Heritage Found., 2003—06. Served to lt. USNR, 1943—46. Fellow Am. Assn. Adv. Sci.; mem. Am. Chem. Soc. (pres.-elect 1990, pres. 1991, chmn. pension and investment com., Charles Lathrop Parsons award, 2007), Indsl. Rsch. Inst. (pres. 1987-88), Soc. Chem. Industry, N.Y. Acad. Scis., U.S./Mex. Found. (bd. dirs.), Old Warson Country Club, St. Andrews Club (Delray Beach), St. Louis Club. Republican. Episcopalian. Personal E-mail: alheininger@aol.com.

HEINLE, RICHARD ALAN, lawyer; b. New Kensington, Pa., May 13, 1959; s. Robert Alan and Barbara Jane (Klimeck) H.; m. Sharon Eileen Farrell, Oct. 20, 1990; children: Kelly, Kyra, Casey. AB with highest honors, U. Chgo., 1981; JD cum laude, Georgetown U., 1984. Bar: Ill. 1984, Fla. 1994. Assoc. Arnstein & Lehr, Chgo., 1984-89, Foley & Lardner, Chgo., 1989-93, ptnr. Orlando, Fla., 1994—2003, Pohl & Short, P.A., Winter Park, Fla., 2003—. Counsel BBB Ctrl. Fla., Orlando, 1996-03. Bd. dirs. Better Bus. Bur. Ctrl. Fla., 2003—09. Mem.: Fla. C. of C. (bd. dirs. 1999—2000), Mfrs. Assn. Ctrl. Fla. (bd. dirs. 1995—2005), Phi Beta Kappa. Roman Catholic. Avocations: golf, running. Home: 8100 Vineland Oaks Blvd Orlando FL 32835-8215 Office: Pohl & Short PA 280 W Canton Ste 410 Winter Park FL 32789 Office Phone: 407-647-7645. Business E-Mail: rheinle@alumni.uchicago.edu.

HEINRICH, CAROLYN J., political science professor; BA summa cum laude, Beloit Coll., 1989; MA, U. Chgo., 1991, PhD, 1995. Rsch. assoc. U. Chgo. Ctr. for Social Program Evaluation, 1993—97, assoc. dir., 1997—2000; rsch. assoc. Am. Bar Found., 1995—97, U. Chgo., 1997—2000; rsch. dir. U. Chgo.-Pew Charitable Trusts Study on Pub. Mgmt. and Govt. Performance, 1997—2000; asst. prof. pub. policy U. NC, Chapel Hill, 2000—03; assoc. prof. La Follette Sch. Pub. Affairs, U. Wis.-Madison, 2003—06, prof., 2006—11, dir., 2008—11; assoc. dir. rsch. and training Inst. for Rsch. on Poverty U. Wis.-Madison, 2004—11, affiliated prof. econs., Regina Loughlin Scholar, 2007—11; Sid Richardson prof. pub. affairs U. Tex. LBJ Sch. Pub. Affairs, Austin, 2011—, dir. Ctr. Health and Social Policy, 2011—; affiliated prof. economics U. Tex., Austin, 2011—. Spkr. in field. Contbr. articles to profl. jours. Recipient Lewis E. Severson Award for Excellence in Econs., Ruth Coleman Peterson Prize in Govt. and Internat. Rels. Mem.: Internat. Soc. Policy Monitoring Network, Am. Polit. Sci. Assn., Soc. Labor Econ., Midwest Econ. Assn. (first v.p. 2007—08), Am. Econ. Assn., Am. Soc. Pub. Adminstrn. Office: University Tex Lyndon B Johnson Sch Public Affairs PO Box Y Austin TX 78713-8925 Office Phone: 512-471-3200. Business E-Mail: cheinrich@austin.utexas.edu.

HEINS, JOHN D., human resources specialist; B in Bus. Adminstrn. & Ops. Rsch. Mgmt., U. Fla., 1977. Mgr. human resources planning and comml. ops. Fla. Power & Light; v.p. human resources and adminstrv. svcs. JM Family Enterprises, dir. corp. planning and human resources svcs.; sr. v.p. chief human resources officer Spherion Corp., 2006—. Office: Spherion Corp 2050 Spectrum Blvd Fort Lauderdale FL 33309 Office Phone: 954-308-7600. Office Fax: 954-308-7666.

HEIRD, WILLIAM CARROLL, pediatrician, educator; b. Decatur, Tenn., Jan. 27, 1936; s. C.T. and Mary Edna (Ward) H.; m. Jane Ray, Aug. 21, 1960. BS, Maryville Coll., Tenn., 1958; MS, Vanderbilt U., Nashville, 1963, MD, 1964. Intern Vanderbilt U. Med. Ctr., Nashville, 1964-65; resident Babies Hosp. Columbia-Presbyn. Med. Ctr., NYC, 1965-67; asst. prof. pediatrics Coll. Physicians and Surgeons Columbia U., NYC, 1971-77, assoc. prof. pediatrics Coll. Physicians and Surgeons, 1977-89; prof. pediatrics Baylor Coll. Medicine, Houston, 1990—; pediatrician Children's Nutrition Rsch. Ctr., Houston. Co-editor: Protein and Energy Needs During Infancy, 1987; editor: Nutritional Needs of the 6-to-12 Month Old, 1991; contbr. numerous articles to profl. publs., chpts. to books. Capt. USAF, 1967-69. Mem. Am. Pediatric Soc., Soc. for Pediatric Rsch., Am. Soc. Nutrition, Am. Acad. Pediatrics. Office: Children's Nutrition Rsch Ctr 1100 Bates St Houston TX 77030-2600 Office Phone: 713-798-7177. Business E-Mail: wheird@bcm.edu.

HEISER, ARNOLD MELVIN, astronomer; b. Bklyn., Feb. 9, 1933; s. Hyman Samuel and Sadie (Kretchmer) H.; m. Vivian Carol Jacobs, June 6, 1964; children: Naomi Elizabeth, David Alan. AB, Ind. U., 1954, MA, 1956; PhD, U. Chgo., 1961. Rsch. asst. Ind. U., 1954-56; rsch. fellow U. Chgo., 1956-61; asst. prof. physics and astronomy Vanderbilt U., Nashville, 1961-66, assoc. prof., 1966-99, prof. emeritus, 1999—. Dir. A.J. Dyer Obs., 1972-86; H. Shapley vis. prof. Am. Astron. Soc., 1969—. Subscriptions editor Comms. of the Internat. Amateur-Profl. Photoelectric Photometry, 1993-99; contbr. articles to profl. jours. Mem. Am. Astron. Soc., Internat. Astron. Union, Tenn. Acad. Sci., Sigma Xi. Office: Vanderbilt Univ Dyer Observatory 1000

Oman Dr Brentwood TN 37027-4143 Home: 753 Glendevon Dr West Haven CT 06516-7921 Office Phone: 615-373-4897, 615-438-4290. Business E-Mail: a.heiser@vanderbilt.edu.

HEISS, HARRY GLEN, archivist; b. Fort Smith, Ark., Jan. 3, 1953; s. Fred William and Mary Kathryn (Hall) H. BA, U. Ark., 1975, MA, 1984; archives cert., Western Wash. U., 1979. Archives intern Oreg. State Archives, Salem, 1979; asst. archivist Smithsonian Instn. Archives, Washington, 1980-85; archivist Nat. Air and Space Mus., Washington, 1985-87, Jefferson Nat. Expansion Meml., Nat. Pk. Svc., St. Louis, 1988-91, Libr. Congress, Washington, 1991-2000, Shenandoah Nat. Park, Nat. Pk. Svc., Luray, Va., 2000—02, Bur. Pub. Debt, U.S. Dept. Treasury, Washington, 2002—. Democrat. Avocations: bicycle touring, camping. Home: 23333 Mountain Valley Rd Millboro VA 24460 Office: 257 Bosley Industrial Park Dr Parkersburg WV 26101 Home Phone: 540-322-1778; Office Phone: 304-480-5335. Office Fax: 304-480-5334. Business E-Mail: Harry.Heiss@bpd.treas.gov.

HEITER, MATTHEW STEPHEN, lawyer; b. Ft. Campbell, Ky., Oct. 1, 1960; m. Judy Anthony, Dec. 10, 1958; children: Emma Celeste, Charles Anthony. BA, U. of Miss., Oxford, 1982; JD, Vanderbilt U., Nashville, 1985. Bar: Tenn. 1985. Exec. v.p., gen. counsel IPIX Corp., Reston, Va., 1999—2002; chair securities practice group Baker, Donelson, Bearman, Caldwell & Berkowitz, Memphis, 2002—10. Contbr. chapters to books. Named one of Top 40 Under 40, Memphis Bus. Jour., 1999; named to Best Lawyers in Am., Woodward/White, Inc., 2005—10, Chambers Leading Bus. Lawyers, 2010. Mem.: ABA, Memphis Bar Assn. (chair bus. law sect.), Tenn. Bar Assn. Home: 1376 Carr Ave Memphis TN 38104 Office: Baker Donelson Bearman Caldwell & Ber 165 Madison Ave Memphis TN 38103 Business E-Mail: mheiter@bakerdonelson.com.

HEITMEIER, DAVID R., state senator; m. Cathy Chifici, 1985; children: Leah, Meghan. BS, U. Southwestern La., 1984; OD, U. Houston, 1987. Founder Heitmeier & Armani - Med. & Surgical Eyecare, managing ptnr.; mem. Dist. 7 La. State Senate, 2008—, vice chair judiciary B com., interim mem. senate and govtl. affairs com., mem. health and welfare com., revenue and fiscal affairs com., transp., hwys. and pub. works com. Democrat. Roman Catholic. Office: PO Box 94183 Baton Rouge LA 70804 Mailing: 3501 Holiday Dr Ste 225 New Orleans LA 70114 Office Phone: 225-342-2040, 504-361-6356. Office Fax: 504-361-6358. Business E-Mail: heitmeid@legis.state.la.us.

HEITMEIER, FRANCIS C., state legislator; b. New Orleans, Aug. 2, 1950; s. Dewey J. and Barbara Cargol H. Heitmeier; m. Rai Lynn Umbach, 1972; children: Cody, Cory. Dep. assessor, New Orleans, 1972—73; mem. Dem. Exec. Com., 1978—; bd. dir. Greater New Orleans Tourist Com.; state rep. Dist. 102 La., 1984—92; state senator Dist. 7, 1992—; asst. mgr. Tel. Co.; mem. Headmasters Coun. Holy Cross Sch. Mem.: Little Sisters Poor (exec. bd.), Kiwanis, Greater New Orleans Football Offcls., Jaycees. Democrat. Catholic. Address: 2601 General Collins Ave New Orleans LA 70114 Mailing: 3709 General De Gaulle Dr New Orleans LA 70114 Fax: 504-361-9794.

HEITZENRATER, JAMES F., hospital administrator; BA, Marshall U., W. Va.; MA in healthcare adminstrn., Ctrl. Mich. U. Asst. adminstr. Colin Anderson Ctr., W.Va.; adminstr. Marcum & Wallace Meml. Hosp., Irvine, Ky., Methodist Sugar Land Hosp.; pres. St. Mary's Medical Ctr. Campbell County, 2010—. Mem. Program Planning Com. DePelchin Children's Ctr.; bd. mem. Fort Bend Econ. Devel. Coun., Fort Bend C. of C. Fellow: Am. Coll. Healthcare Exec. (diplomat). Office: St Marys Med Ctr Campbell County 923 E Ctrl Ave La Follette TN 37766

HELANDER, ROBERT CHARLES, lawyer, arbitrator, contributing editor; b. Chgo., Oct. 30, 1932; s. William Eugene and Grace Pauline H.; m. Betty Jane Vinson, Apr. 8, 1961; children: Diana Chaffin, Alexander Christian, Nicholas Charles. BA, Amherst Coll., 1953; JD, Harvard U., 1956, PMD, 1971. Bar: D.C. 1956, Ill. 1956, N.Y. 1979, U.S. Supreme Ct. 1960. Practice law, Chgo., 1956-62; Amherst fellow in Mid. East, 1960-61; mem. firm Helander, Farmanfarmaian & Ghany, Tehran, Iran, 1962-65; assoc. gen. counsel Internat. Basic Economy Corp., Lima, Peru, 1965-68, v.p., 1968-71, v.p. devel. and adminstrn., gen. counsel NYC, 1971-73; group v.p. and pres. Internat. Basic Economy Corp. Housing Internat., NYC, 1973-76; ptnr. firm Jones, Day, Reavis & Pogue (Surrey & Morse), NYC, 1976-93; ptnr. Kaye, Scholer LLP, NYC, 1993—2001. Panelist Am. Arbitration Assn., 1986—, Internat. Ctr. for Settlement of Investment Disputes of World Bank, 2005—; contbg. editor Met. Corporate Counsel. Pres. Accion Internat., 1978-88; chmn. Pan Am. Soc., 1979-88, Am. Fund for Ind. Univs., 1987—, Fund for Multinat. Mgmt. Edn., 1981-91; bd. dirs. Internat. Law Inst., 1975, Ams. Soc., 1982—, Univ. Andes Found., 1983—, Overlook Hosp. Found., 2006-09, Near East Found., 1977-2008, Bolivarian Soc., 1980—, IESA Found., 1991—, St. Timothys Sch., 2007-10, chmn. Internat. Coun. Escuela Superior Adminstrn. de Negocios, 1999—; dir. The Americas Endowment (Orgn. Am. States), 2003-; mem. bd. disting. advisors Am. Coms. on Fgn. Rels., 2006-10. Named Comendador, Orden del Sol (Peru). Fellow Am. Bar Found. (life); mem. ABA (chmn. inter-Am. law com. sect. internat. law and practice 1978-83, editor-in-chief Inter-Am. Legal Materials 1983-91, del. to Inter-Am. Bar Assn.), Assn. Bar City N.Y. (inter-Am. affairs com.), Inter-Am. Bar Assn., Am. Fgn. Law Assn. (pres. 2001-04), Coun. Fgn. Rels., Carnegie Coun., Century Assn. Republican. Episcopalian. Home and Office: 86 Macfarlane Dr Apt 6F Delray Beach FL 33483 Office Phone: 917-345-8250. Personal E-mail: rhelander@hotmail.com.

HELCK, CHESTER B., investment company executive; m. Abby Helck. B, W.Va. U. Inst. Tech., 1974; grad., U. Pa. Product mktg., territory mgr. Deere & Co.; investment rep. Edward D. Jones & Co.; sr. v.p. Raymond James Financial Services, Inc. (formerly Investment Management & Research, Inc.), 1997—99, exec. v.p., 1999—2002, Raymond James Financial, Inc., v.p., bus. devel., 1989, pres., COO, 2002—; chmn. Raymond James Tech. Adv. Group. Bd. dirs. Raymond James Fin., Inc., Securities Industry and Fin. Markets Assn., Raymond James Ltd, Raymond James & Assocs., Inc. Office: Raymond James Financial Inc 880 Carillon Pky Saint Petersburg FL 33716 Office Phone: 727-567-1000.

HELEEN, MARK L., lawyer, finance company executive; BA, Bucknell Univ.; JD, Univ. Pitts. Atty. PNC Bank, Tucker Arensburg PC, Pitts. & Phila.; atty. positions through v.p., dep. gen. counsel SLM Corp. (Sallie Mae), Reston, Va., 1998—2008, sr. v.p., gen. counsel, 2008—09, exec. v.p., gen. counsel, 2009—. Office: SLM Corp 12061 Bluemont Way Reston VA 20190

HELFRICK, ALBERT DARLINGTON, electronics engineering educator, consultant, department chairman; b. Camden, NJ, June 10, 1945; s. Eugene G. and Irma (Darlington) H.; m. Toni Venezia, May 6, 1989; children: A. Karl, Rachel. BS, Upsala Coll., East Orange, NJ, 1969; MS, N.J. Inst. Tech., 1973; PhD, Clayton U., Mo., 1988. Registered profl. engr., N.J. Sr. rsch. engr. Singer-Kearfott Div., Little Falls, NJ, 1969-72; sr. engr. Kay Elemetrics, Pine Brook, NJ, 1972-77; sr. project engr. Cessna Aircraft, Boonton, NJ, 1977-84; prin. engr. RFL Industries, Boonton, 1984-89; cons. engr. Boonton, 1989-92; prof. electronics engring. Embry-Riddle Aero. U., Daytona Beach, 1992—2003, chair engring. sci. dept., 2003—05, chair elec. and sys. dept. and mech., civil and engring. sci. dept., 2005—10, prof. elec. engring., 2010—. Mem. com. Radio Tech. Commn. for Aeros., Washington, 1980-85, 93—; mem. adj. faculty Upsala Coll., 1972-73, Kean Coll., NJ, 1979-81, Fairleigh Dickinson U., 1986-87; instr. aerospace U. Kans., 2006-. Author: Practical Repair and Maintenance of Communications Equipment, 1983, Modern Aviation Electronics, 1984, 2d edit., 1994, Electronic Instrumentation and Measurement Techniques, 1985, Modern Electronic Instrumentation and Measurement Techniques, 1990, Electrical Spectrum and Network Analyzers, 1991, Practical Aircraft Electronic Systems, 1994, Avionics Test Equipment Handbook, 1997, Principles of Avionics, 1999, 01, 04, 07, 10, 13, Electronics in the Evolution of Flight, 2004; assoc. editor Jour. Aerospace Computing, Info. and Communication; tech. editor IEEE Transactions on Aerospace and Electronic Systems; also contbr. 70 articles. Bd. dirs. Aircraft Electronics Assn. Edn. Found. Sgt. U.S. Army, 1969-71, Vietnam. Recipient award RF Design mag., 1988, Excellence in Rsch. award Embry-Riddle U., 2001, Outstanding Faculty award 2006. Fellow AIAA (assoc.) (Digital Avionics award 2013), Radio Club Am. (bd. dirs. 1989-90, 92-94, sec. 1990-91); mem. IEEE (life) (sr., chmn. Daytona Beach sect., editor IEEE Transactions and Aerospace Electronics Sys., named Outstanding Faculty Educator, Fla. Coun. 2006). Achievements include patents in magnetic recording tape erasure, a method of frequency synthesis, antenna coupling device, method of coupling GPS to VHF navigation equipment, passive radar. Home: 2925 Betty Dr Deland FL 32720-1945 Office: Embry-Riddle Aero U 600 S Clyde Morris Blvd Daytona Beach FL 32114-3900

HELLAND, GEORGE ARCHIBALD, JR., manufacturing executive, federal official; b. San Antonio, Nov. 28, 1937; s. George Archibald and Ruth (Gorman) H.; m. Josephine Howell, June 9, 1962 (div. 1989); children: Jane Elizabeth, Thomas Gorman; m. Antonia Scott Day, Nov. 24, 1990. BS in Mech. Engring., U. Tex., 1959; MBA with distinction, Harvard U., 1961. Registered profl. engr., Tex. With Cameron Iron Works, Inc., Houston, 1961-77, asst. sales mgr., 1963, dist. sales mgr., 1964, dist. sales mgr., U.K., Africa, 1965, product mgr., 1966, plant mgr., Leeds, Eng., 1967, mgr. oil tool products, 1968, v.p., 1969-75, exec. v.p., 1975-77; with Weatherford Internat., Inc., Houston, 1977-79, v.p., 1977, pres., CEO, dir., 1978-79; pres., CEO McEvoy Oilfield Equipment Co. (name changed to Sii McEvoy div. Smith Internat., Inc. 1980), Houston, 1979-85; pres., bd. dirs. McCall Industries, Inc., Houston, 1986-87; gen. mgmt. cons., 1987-90; dep. asst. sec. of energy for export assistance U.S. Dept. Energy, Washington, 1990-93; v.p. Dresser Industries, Inc., Houston, 1993—97. Sr. assoc. Cambridge Energy Rsch. Assocs., 1997—; pres. Lockwood Corp., Gering, Nebr., 1986—91; chmn. bd. dirs. SIE Internat., Inc., Ft. Worth, 1986—87, Gas Turbine Efficiency Holdings Corp., 2002—04; prin. Innova Ptnrs., 1988—90; bd. dirs. NSGroup, Newport, Ky., 2000—06, Hunting PLC, London, 2001—11, Skip's Clothing, Ephrata, Pa., 2006—07; chmn. bd. dirs. Tokheim Corp., Ft. Wayne, Ind., 2001—03; adv. dir. Athens Group, Austin, Tex., 2012—. Bd. dirs. Jr. Achievement Worldwide, Colorado Springs, 1993-2008; trustee S.W. Rsch. Inst., Eurasia Found., Washington; mem. exec. com. Jr. Achievement of S.E. Tex., 1975-2008; mem. engring. adv. coun. U. Tex., 2000-. Recipient Five Outstanding Young Texans award Tex. Jr. C. of C., 1972; named Outstanding Young Houstonian Houston Jr. C. of C., 1972; Disting. Grad. Sch. Engring. U. Tex., 1977. Mem. ASME, Am. Inst. Mining, Metall. and Petroleum Engrs., Am. Petroleum Inst. (bd. dirs.), Inst. Gas Engrs. (U.K.), Tex. Soc. Profl. Engrs., Am. Wellhead Equipment Assn. (pres. 1967), Petroleum Equipment Suppliers Assn. (pres. 1976-77), Houston C. of C., Tau Beta Pi, Phi Eta Sigma, Pi Tau Sigma, Sigma Nu, Friars Soc. Presbyterian. Home and Office: 3635 Overbrook Ln Houston TX 77027-4127 Office Phone: 713-961-4475. Personal E-mail: ghelland@mba1961.hbs.edu.

HELLER, ADAM, chemist, researcher; b. Cluj, Romania, June 25, 1933; came to U.S., 1962; s. Ephraim and Blanche (Nissel) H.; m. Ilana Grossbard, July 26, 1956; children: Ephraim, Jonathan. MSc, Hebrew U., 1957, PhD, 1961; D honoris causa, Upsalla U., Sweden, 1991; degree honoris causa, CUNY, 2008. Postdoctoral rsch. assoc. U. Calif., Berkeley, 1962-63; mem. tech. staff Bell Labs., Murray Hill, NJ, 1963-64, 75-77, GTE Labs., Bayside, NY, 1964-70, mgr. exploratory rsch. Waltham, Mass., 1970-75; head electronic materials rsch. dept. AT&T Bell Labs., Murray Hill, 1977-88; prof. chem. engring. U. Tex., Austin, 1988—. Co-founder, chief sci. advisor TheraSense Inc., 1996—2003; guest prof. Coll. de France, 1982-, The Berkeley Lectures (Chem. Engring.) 1991. Editor: Semiconductor Liquid Junction Solar Cells, 1977, Inorganic Resists, 1982; contbr. articles to profl. jours.; patentee in field. Recipient Chemistry of Materials award, Am. Chem. Soc., 1994, Faraday medal Royal Chem. Soc., London, 1996, Spiers medal, 2000, Charles N. Reilley award, Electroanalytical Soc., 2004, Fresenius Gold medal, Soc. German Chemists, 2005, Chem. Engring. Practice award, Am. Inst. Chem. Engrs., 2005, 2007 Nat. Medal Technology and Innovation, Creative Invention award, Am. Chemical Soc., 2008. Fellow AAS, Electrochem. Soc.; mem. NAE, Am. Acad. Arts & Scis. Jewish. Achievements include co-inventor of first substantiantially painless blood glucose monitoring system for diabetes management; subcutaneously implanted continuous glucose sensors for diabetes management; invention of lithium batteries, liquid lasers, electrochemical solar cells, photocatalytically self-cleaning windows and coatings. Business E-Mail: heller@che.utexas.edu.

HELLER, JAMES STEPHEN, law librarian, educator; b. Detroit, Apr. 11, 1950; s. Benjamin Heller and Vera Frances (Broder) Schumer; m. Janet Louise Crowther, Oct. 27, 1985; children: Benjamin William, Seth Joseph. BA, U. Mich., 1971; JD cum laude, U. San Diego, 1976; MLS, U. Calif., Berkeley, 1977. Bar: Calif. 1976, D.C. 1978. Assoc. law librarian Nat. Law Ctr., George Washington U., Washington, 1977-80; dir. Civil Library, U.S. Dept. Justice, Washington, 1980-83; dir., asso. prof. law Law Library, U. Idaho, Moscow, 1983-88; dir. Law Libr., prof. law Marshall-Wythe Sch. Law, Coll. of William and Mary, Williamsburg, Va., 1988—. Co-author: Copyright Handbook, 1984; contbr. articles to legal jours; author: The Librarian's Copyright Companion, 2004. Mem. Am. Assn. Law Librs. (chmn. copywrite com. 1982-83, 93-94, chmn. awards com. 1991-92, chair edn. com. 1994-95, pres., 1998-99), Northwest Consortium Law Librs. (chmn. 1987-88), Va. Assn. Law Librs. (pres. 1994-95), Southeastern Assn. Law Librs., ACLU (v.p. Moscow-Latah com. 1987-88). Jewish. Office: William & Mary School Law PO Box 8795 Williamsburg VA 23187-8795 Office Phone: 804-221-3252. E-mail: heller@wm.edu.

HELLERSTEIN, WALTER, lawyer; b. NYC, June 21, 1946; s. Jerome Robert and Pauline Alice H.; m. Nina Laurie Salant, Aug. 31, 1970; children: Michael, Margaret. AB, Harvard U., 1967; JD, U. Chgo., 1970. Bar: D.C. 1970, Ill. 1976, N.Y. 1989. Law clk. U.S. Ct. Appeals (2d cir.), NYC, 1967-71; atty. Air Force Gen. Counsel's Office, Washington, 1971-73; assoc. Covington & Burling, Washington, 1973-75; asst. prof. law U. Chgo., 1976—78; assoc. prof. law U. Ga., Athens, 1978-84, prof. law, 1984-98, Francis Shackelford prof. taxation, 1999—, disting. rsch. prof., 2011—; of counsel Morrison & Foerster, NYC, 1986-96; ptnr. Sutherland, Asbill & Brennan, Atlanta, 1996-98, of counsel Washington, 2004—08, KPMG, 1999—2004. Cons. Orgn. Econ. Coop. and Devel., 1999—, UN, 2000; trustee Am. Tax Policy Inst., 2006—2011. Co-author: State and Local Taxation of Natural Resources, 1986, State Taxation, vols. 1 & 2, 3d edit., rev. edit., 2014, Streamlined Sales and Use Tax, 2008-09, edit., State and Local Taxation, 9th edit., 2009, Taxing Global Digital Commerce, 2013; mem. editl. bd. Nat. Tax Jour., 1983-2004, Multistate Tax Analyst, 1986—; chmn. editl. adv. bd. State Tax Notes, 1991—, Jour. Taxation, 1993—; contbr. articles to profl. jours. Recipient Multistate Tax Commn. 25th Ann. award for outstanding contbn. 1992, BNA Tax Mgmt. Latcham award, 2007. Fellow Am. Coll. Tax Counsel; mem. ABA, Nat. Tax Assn. (dir. 1981-83 Holland Medal, 2008), Ill. State Bar Assn., D.C. Bar Assn., Am. Law Inst., Order of Coif, Phi Beta Kappa. Home: 239 Westview Dr Athens GA 30606-4731 Office: U Ga Law Sch Athens GA 30602-6012 Home Phone: 706-353-0865; Office Phone: 706-542-5175. Business E-Mail: wallyh@uga.edu.

HELLMUTH, GEORGE WILLIAM, architect; b. Detroit, Nov. 21, 1942; s. George Francis and Mildred Lee (Henning) H.; m. Camille Byrns Carmody, Feb. 20, 1965 (div. 2003); children: George, Holly, Julie, Emily. BA in Architecture, Yale U., 1964; MBA, Eastern N.Mex. U., 1969; BArch, CCNY, 1979. Sr. prin. Hellmuth, Obata & Kassabaum, Washington, 1971—2006, cons., 2007—08; dir. Mid-Atlantic Region FXFOWLE, 2009—10; prin. Perkins & Will, 2010—11, EVP Page Southerland Page, 2011. Capt. USAF, 1965—69. Mem.: AIA. Roman Catholic. Home: 2721 N Ohio St Arlington VA 22207 E-mail: george.hellmuth@perkinswill.com.

HELLYAR, MARY JANE, film equipment company executive; b. May 27, 1953; BA in Chemistry & Math., Coll. St. Catherine, St. Paul; MSChemE, MIT, Cambridge, PhD in Chem. Engring., MBA in Mgmt. of Tech. Rsch. scientist Kodak Rsch. Labs. Eastman Kodak Co., Rochester, NY, 1982, various positions in R & D, film mfg. and chem. process devel., with consumer imaging in strategic planning function, 1994, dir. Color Product Platform, 1995, gen. mgr. Consumer Film Bus., Consumer Imaging, v.p., 1999, pres. Display and Components Group, 2004, sr. v.p., 2005—07, pres. Film & Photofinishing Systems Group, 2005—07, pres. Film Products Group, 2007—09, exec. v.p., 2007—09; CEO Technocorp OLED, Rochester, NY, 2009—12; corporate v.p. Tredegar Corp., Richmond, Va., 2012—; pres. Tredegar Film Products Corp., Richmond, Va., 2012—. Office: Tredegar Corp 100 Boulders Parkway Richmond VA 23225 Office Phone: 804-330-1000.*

HELM, BOB (ROBERT WILBUR HELM), manufacturing executive, former federal official; b. LaCrosse, Wis., Aug. 19, 1951; s. Wilbur and Avis (Smale) H.; m. Sandra K. Howard, May 31, 1975 BA, U. Wis., LaCrosse, 1973; MA, Fletcher Sch. Diplomacy, Tufts U., 1975. Profl. staff mem. Los Alamos Lab., 1975-79, Senate Budget Com., Washington, 1979-82, Nat. Security Coun., Washington, 1982-84; asst. sec. def., comptr. US Dept. Def., Washington, 1984-88; v.p., bus. devel. Honeywell Inc., 1989; corp. v.p., legis. affairs Northrop Grumman Corp., 1989—93, v.p., govt. rels., 1993—2010; sr. v.p., planning and devel. General Dynamics Corp., 2010—. Named one of Washington's Top Lobbyists, The Hill, 2010. Office: General Dynamics Corp Govt Relations 2941 Fairview Pk Dr Ste 100 Falls Church VA 22042-4513 Office Phone: 703-876-3000. Office Fax: 703-876-3125. Business E-Mail: rhelm@generaldynamics.com.

HELM, DEWITT FREDERICK, JR., professional society administrator, consultant; b. Charlotte, NC, Apr. 24, 1933; s. DeWitt Frederick Sr. and Blanche Buchanan (DeBusk) H.; divorced; children: DeWitt Frederick III, Mary McNair Helm Bishop; m. Anne M. Valle, Mar. 1, 2002. BS in History, Davidson Coll., NC, 1956. Mgr. advt. Vick Chem. Co., NYC, 1956-63; mgr. consumer products Pfizer, Inc., NYC, 1963-66; mgr. consumer product acquisition and devel. A.H. Robins Co., Richmond, Va., 1966-69; exec. v.p. Miller Morton Co., Richmond, 1969-72, pres., 1972-81, Miller Morton of Can. Ltd., 1969-81; sr. v.p. Jack Morton Prodns. Inc., Washington, 1981-84; exec. v.p. Assn. Nat. Advertisers, Inc., NYC, 1984, pres. & CEO, 1984-93, also bd. dirs.; mng. ptnr. DH Assocs., Palm City, Fla., 1994-97, The Advt. Partnership LLC, Bearfort, SC, 1996—. Deacon, elder Presbyn. Ch., United Meth. Ch., 1990-2003; trustee Christ Ch., NYC, 2000-03; bd. dirs. Nat. Tobacco Festival, Richmond, 1977-81, Traffic Audit Bur., NYC, 1984-93. With U.S. Army, 1956-58. Mem. Consumer Healthcare Products Assn. (bd. dirs., exec. com. 1972-80, chmn. 1973-75), Coun. Better Bus. Burs. (bd. dirs. 1989-93), Am. Advt. Mus. (founding dir., nat. bd. 1987—), Smithsonian Instn.'s Ctr. for Advt. History (adv. bd. 1989—), Advt. Coun. (bd. dirs., treas. 1984-93, life bd. dirs. 2002—), Advt. Rsch. Found. (bd. dirs. 1984-93), World Fedn. Advertisers (bd. dirs., mgmt. com. 1984-93), Media-Advt. Partnership for Drug-Free Am. (mgmt. bd.), Wintergreen (Va.) Club, Sky Club, Met. Club (N.Y.C.), Harbour Ridge Club (Fla.). Presbyterian. Office Phone: 843-441-0566. Personal E-mail: taphelm@gmail.com.

HELM, GORDON K., controller; Grad., Oral Roberts U., 1975, MBA, 1978. CPA. Internal auditor Helmerich & Payne, Inc., 1991, contr., 1993—, chief acctg. officer, 2003—08, v.p., 2008—. Office: Helmerich & Payne Inc 1437 S Boulder Ave Ste 1400 Tulsa OK 74119 Office Phone: 918-742-5531. Office Fax: 918-742-0237.

HELM, T. KENNEDY, III, lawyer; b. Louisville, July 2, 1946; s. T. Kennedy Helm Jr. and Nell Hoge Helm; m. Elizabeth Jennifer Schmick, May 30, 1970; children: T. Kennedy IV, Mary Emily Mitchell, Helm Ryan. BA, Yale U., 1968; MA, Ind. U., 1970; JD, U. Va., 1974. Former 5th & 6th grade geography tchr.; assoc. Stites & Harbison, Louisville, 1974—79, ptnr., 1979—, chmn., 1997—. Former mem. bd. dirs. Nat. City Bank Ky.; former bd. mem. Whayne Supply Co., Griffin & Co. Contbr. articles to profl. jours. Mem. Louisville and Jefferson County Urban Renewal Commn., 1975—76; bd. dirs. Louisville Mus. Natural History and Sci., 1979—82, Louisville Zoo Found., 1993—97, Greater Louisville, Inc., Louisville Urban League, 2005—, vice chmn. devel., 2006; bd. trustees Ky. Country Day Sch., 1988—94, 1995—98, Simmons Coll., Ky.; mem. adv. bd. Summerbridge of Ky., 1992—96; mem. bd. advisors Presentation Acad., 1995—97; bd. overseers U. Louisville, 2000—. Mem.: ABA, Ky. Bar Assn., Louisville Bar Assn., Mng. Ptnr. Forum (mem. midwestern adv. bd.), Japan Am. Soc. Ky. (bd. dirs.), Tri-State Golf Assn. (bd. dirs. 1996—, pres. 1998). Office: Stites & Harbison PLLC 400 W Market St Ste 1800 Louisville KY 40202-3352 Office Phone: 502-681-0449. Office Fax: 502-587-6391. Business E-Mail: khelmiii@stites.com.

HELMAN, STEPHEN JODY, lawyer; b. Houston, Dec. 14, 1949; m. Gail Stevenson, 1974; children: Kimberley Brooke, Courtney Elizabeth, Caitlin Rebecca. BA in Spanish and Religion, So. Meth. U., Dallas, 1971; postgrad., Perkins Sch. Theology, 1971—73; JD with honors, U. Tex., 1978. Bar: Tex., 1978; cert. estate planning and probate law, 1987. Assoc. Graves, Dougherty, Hearon & Moody, Austin, Tex., 1978-85, ptnr., shareholder, 1985-93; ptnr. Osborne, Lowe, Helman & Smith, LLP, Austin, 1993-2000, Osborne & Helman, LLP, Austin, 2001—05, Osborne, Helman, Knebel & Deleery, LLP, 2006—. Exam commr. in estate planning and probate law, Tex. Bd. Legal Specialization, 1990-94. Contbr. articles to profl. jours.

Fellow Am. Coll. Trust and Estate Counsel (mem. profl. standards com. 1990-93); mem. ABA (mem. real property, probate, and trust law sects.), Coll. of the State Bar of Tex., State Bar Tex. (mem. real property, probate and trust law sects.), Travis County Bar Assn. (mem. probate and estate planning sect., pres. 1991-92, dir. 1989-92, ex-officio dir. 1992-93), Order of Coif. Avocations: nature photography, hiking. Office: Osborne, Helman, Knebel & Deleery LLP 301 Congress Ave Ste 1910 Austin TX 78701-4041 Office Phone: 512-542-2000. Business E-Mail: sjhelman@ohkdlaw.com.

HELMERICH, HANS CHRISTIAN, oil industry executive; b. Tulsa, Okla., Sept. 4, 1958; s. Walter Hugo III and Peggy Josephine (Varnadow) H.; m. Lea Calhoon, Aug. 23, 1980; children: Isaac Breaker, Shelby Kate, Maxim Rainer, Sunday Lane, Hailey Beth. BA in Govt., Dartmouth Coll., 1981. Cert. program mgmt. devel. Harvard U., 1985. Asst. to pres. Helmerich & Payne, Inc., Tulsa, 1981-85, v.p., 1985-87, exec. v.p., 1987, COO, 1987—89, pres., bd. dirs., 1987—, CEO, 1989—. Bd. dirs. Atwood Oceanics, Inc., Fed. Res. Bank of Kansas City, 1996—, Cimarex Energy Co., 2002-. Commr. Tulsa Devel. Authority, 1986-87; bd. dirs. Hillcrest Med. Ctr. Assocs., Tulsa, 1982—, Gilcrease Mus. Assn., Tulsa, 1983—, Tulsa Area Unit Way, 1984—, Young Pres.'s Orgn., Inc., 1988—, Tulsa Boys' Home, 1990—; trustee Okla. Futures, Oklahoma City, 1987—, Fuller Theol. Sem., 1989—; dir. Indian Nations Coun., Tulsa, 1994, Okla. Heritage Assn., 1995—. Home: 2955 S Rockford Rd Tulsa OK 74114-5324 Office: Helmerich & Payne Inc 1437 S Boulder Ave Tulsa OK 74119 also: Cimarex Energy Co Bd Directors 1700 Lincoln St Ste Denver CO 80203 Office Phone: 918-742-5531, 303-295-3995. Office Fax: 918-742-0237, 303-295-3494. Business E-Mail: hans.helmerich@hpinc.com.

HELMICK, FRANK G., career military officer; b. 1953; BS, US Mil. Acad., 1976; MS in Mgmt., US Naval Postgraduate Sch.; grad., Armed Forces Staff Coll., 1989, US Army War Coll., 1998. Commd. 2d. lt. US Army, 1976, advanced through grades to lt. gen., 2008; platoon leader 1st Battalion, 5th Cavalry, 1st Cavalry Divsn., Fort Hood, Tex., 1976; exec. officer and co. comdr. 7th Cavalry Divsn., Fort Hood, Tex.; comdr. 3rd Battalion, 504th Parachute Infantry Regiment, 82nd Airborne Divsn., Fort Bragg, NC, Ranger Training Brigade, Fort Benning, Ga.; asst. divsn. comdr. maneuver 24th Infantry Divsn., Fort Riley, Kans., 2002—03; asst. divsn. comdr. (ops.) 101st Airborne Divsn., Operation Iraqi Freedom, 2003; sr. mil. advisor to dep. sec. of defense US Dept. Defense, Washington, 2004—06; commdg. gen. US Army So. European Task Force, Vincenza, Italy, 2006—08, Multi-Nat. Security NATO Transition Command-Iraq, NATO Training Mission-Iraq, Operation Iraqi Freedom, 2008—09, XVIII Airborne Corps. & Ft. Bragg, Ft. Bragg, NC, 2009—. Chief ops. and intelligence divsn. J-34, The Joint Staff, Washington; chief ops. anti-terrorism J-3, The Joint Staff, Washington. Decorated Defense Disting. Svc. Medal, Disting. Svc. Medal, Defense Superior Svc. Medal, Legion of Merit (with 2 Oak Leaf Clusters), Bronze Star Medal, Meritorious Svc. Medal (with 3 Oak Leaf Clusters), Joint Svc. Commendation Medal, Army Commendation Medal (with 5 Oak Leaf Clusters), Army Achievement Medal (with Oak Leaf Cluster), Ranger Tab, Expert Infantryman Badge, Master Parachutist Badge, Air Assault Badge, Office of Sec. of Def. Identification Badge, Joint Chiefs of Staff Identification Badge. Office: XVIII Airborne Corps & Ft Bragg 2175 Reilly Rd Stop A Fort Bragg NC 28310

HELMICK, WALTER DOLPH, state legislator; b. Bergoo, W.Va., Apr. 25, 1944; s. Dolph Walter and Cleo Blevins Helmick; m. Rita Faye Hedrick; children: Sam, Tim, Brian, Shelley. BA, W.Va. Inst. Tech., 1993. Mem. Pocahontas County Bd. Edn., 1976—78; pres., mem. Pocahontas County Commn., 1978—89; mem. W.Va. House of Delegates, 1988—89; mem. Dist. 15 W.Va. State Senate, 1990—, chair Fin. Com., mem. Agr. Com., Banking and Insurance Com., Econ. Devel. Com., Energy, Industry and Mining Com., Natural Resources Com. & Rules Com. Pres. H and S Welding Supply, 1973—87, Allegheny Med. Equipment Co., 1983—86; v.p. Quaill Hollow Mining Co., 1987—88; exec. dir. Pocahontas County Devel. Authority, 1996—97. Recipient Outstanding Pub. Svc. award, Hillsboro, W. Va., 1986. Mem.: North Ctrl. Cmty. Action, Region IV Coun., Huntersville AF&AM, Scottish Rite, Masons (master 1978), York Rite, Marlington Little League Football & Basketball (former pres.), Kiwanis. Democrat. Presbyterian. Mailing: HC 82 Box 130 Marlinton WV 24954 Office: State Capitol Complex Rm 465M, Bldg 1 11900 Kanawha Blvd E Charleston WV 25305 E-mail: walt.helmick@wvsenate.gov.

HELMKAMP, KATRINA L., manufacturing executive; b. 1965; BS in Indsl. Engring. and Mgmt. Scis., Northwestern U., 1987; MBA, Northwestern U. Kellogg Grad. Sch. Mgmt., 1992. Various positions including v.p. and dir. Chgo. office Boston Consulting Group, Inc.; pres. The Terminix Internat. Co. L.P., 2005—07; group pres. Servicemaster Co., Servicemaster Global Holdings, 2006—07; v.p. refrigeration Whirlpool Corp., 2007—10, sr. v.p. product bus. teams, 2010; CEO SVP Worldwide, 2010—. Office: SVP Worldwide 1224 Heil Quaker Blvd La Vergne TN 37086

HELMREICH, JONATHAN ERNST, history professor; b. Brunswick, Maine, Dec. 21, 1936; s. Ernst Christian and Louise Bertha (Roberts) H.; m. Martha Anne Schaff, Aug. 22, 1959 (div. 1978); children— Anne Linden, Dana Louise, Douglas Ernst Folger; m. Nancy L. Ross, Feb. 21, 1979. BA magna cum laude, Amherst Coll., 1958; MA, Princeton, 1959, PhD, 1961; postgrad. (Fulbright grantee), Free U. of Brussels, 1961-62. Teaching asst. Princeton, 1961; asst. prof. Allegheny Coll., Meadville, Pa., 1962-66, asso. prof., 1966-72, dean of instrn., 1966-81, prof., 1972-98, prof. emeritus, coll. historian, 1998—. Author: Belgium and Europe: A Study in Small Power Diplomacy, 1976, Gathering Rare Ores: The Diplomacy of Uranium Acquisition, 1943-54, 86, U.S. Relations with Belgium and the Congo, 1940-60, 98, Eternal Hope: The Life of Timothy Alden, Jr., 2001, (with others) Rebirth: A History of Europe since World War II, 1st ed. 1992, 2nd ed. 2000 Through All The Years: A History of Allegheny College, 2005; editor: To Petersburg with the Army of the Potomac: The Civil War Letters of Levi Bird Duff, 105th Pennsylvania Volunteers, 2009; editor: Student as Soldier: The Civil War Letters of James D. Chadwick, 2011, That Fearful Month at Fair Oaks: The Civil War Journal of James F. Rusling, 2011; contbr. articles to profl. publs. Mem. Pa. Trial Judge Nominating Commn. for Crawford County, 1973-75; Pres., bd. dirs. United Housing Corp. of Meadville, Fairview Housing Corp. of Meadville; bd. mem. French Creek Valley Conservancy, 1994-2006, United Way at Western Crawford County, 1996-99; bd. govs. Erie Philharmonic, 2007-11; bd. mgrs. Greendale Cemetery, Meadville, 1990-2011. Mem. Am. Hist. Assn., Crawford County Hist. Soc., Phi Beta Kappa, Pi Gamma Mu, Phi Alpha Theta. Clubs: Rotarian. Democrat. Methodist. Mailing: 1031 Sand Castle Rd Sanibel FL 33957 Business E-Mail: jhelmrei@allegheny.edu.

HELMS-VANSTONE, MARY WALLACE, anthropology educator; b. Allentown, Pa., Apr. 15, 1938; d. Samuel Leidich and Mary (Wallace) Helms; divorced. BA, Pa. State U., State College, 1960; MA, U. Mich., 1962, PhD, 1967. Instr. Wayne State U., Detroit, 1965-67; asst. prof. Syracuse (N.Y.) U., 1967-68; lectr. Northwestern U., Evanston and Chgo., Ill., 1969-79; prof. U. N.C., Greensboro, 1979—2004, prof. emerita, 2004—, head dept. anthropology Greensboro, 1979-85. Author: Asang: A Miskito Community, 1971, Middle America, 1975, Ancient Panama, 1979, Ulysses' Sail, 1988, Craft and the Kingly Ideal, 1993, Creations of the Rainbow Serpent, 1995, Access to Origins, 1998, The Curassow's Crest, 2000; contbr. articles to profl. jours. Fellow: Am. Anthrop. Assn.; mem.: Medieval Acad. Am., So. Anthrop. Soc. (pres. 1980—81, procs. editor 1982—94), Am. Ethnological Soc., Am. Soc. Ethnohistory (pres. 1976). Avocations: travel, painting, musical activities, crafts. Office: Univ NC Dept Anthropology PO Box 26170 Greensboro NC 27402-6170

HELSEL, GORDON C., JR., state legislator; b. Hampton, Va., Jan. 9, 1947; m. Joyce Rasnick; children: Scott, Brian. Degree in occpl. safety and health, Thomas Nelson CC, Hampton. Mem. piping dept. Newport News Shipbuilding, Va.; ret. owner York Box and Barrel Mfg. Co., Inc., Va.; councilman City of Poquoson, Va., 1982—94, vice mayor, 1990—94, mayor, 1996—2011; del., Dist. 91 Va. House of Delegates, Richmond, 2011—. Mem., former chief Poquoson Vol. Fire Co., Va.; mem. Liberty Bapt. Ch., Va., C. of C., BB&T Adv. Bd., Met. Planning Dist. Inf. C Co.-2nd Bn. 35th Inf., 4th Inf. Divsn. US Army, 1966—71, Vietnam. Decorated Two Purple Hearts, Bronze Star for Valor. Mem.: VFW, Mil. Order Purple Heart of USA, Peninsula Mil. Alliance. Republican. Office: PO Box 2571 Poquoson VA 23662 also: Va House of Delegates Gen Assembly Bldg PO Box 406 Richmond VA 23218 Office Phone: 757-969-9036, 804-698-1091. Business E-Mail: delghelsel@house.virginia.gov.

HELTMAN, ROBERT FAIRCHILD, distribution executive; b. Lakewood, Ohio, May 11, 1934; s. Fairchild Long and Sarah Agnes (Fleck) H.; m. Melody Elaine Valentine, Feb. 14, 1992; children: Ken, Kathy, Daniel, Kim, Karen, David, Kerri, Summer. BS, Oberlin Coll., 1956. Mktg. & exec. staffing mgr. GE Co., 1960-88; pres. Leading Edge Products & Svcs., Inc., Hendersonville, NC, 1987—. Contbr. articles to mags.; author: Reflections of A long Term Part Time Woodturner. Treas., pres. Homeowner's Assn., Palatine, Ill.; chmn. bd. dir. Erie (Pa.) City and County Librs.; pres. Adv. Coun. on Vocat. Edn. Pa.; chmn., bd. dirs. Hendersonville County Food Co-op; past pres., past bd. dirs, mem. Something Spl. Enterprises & Career Opportunites, Inc.; bd. dir. Carolina Mountain Woodturners; editor Mountain Woodturner, 2004-07; chmn. Blue Ribbon Com. Illegal Innigration Henderson County, NC, 2007, chmn., Henderson County Bd. Elections, 2013. Mem. Masons, Shriners. Republican. Achievements include invention of Ultimate Hiking Staff; BBOBB; Heltman Hollowing Tool; Heirloom Genealogical Baby Cradle, PocketPics-Stylus. Avocations: writing, reading, gardening, photography, woodturning. Office: Leading Edge Products & Svcs Inc PO Box 545 Hendersonville NC 28793-0545 Office Phone: 828-692-9333. Business E-Mail: bobh@leadingedgepands.com.

HELTON, MIKE (MICHAEL GREGORY HELTON), sports association executive; b. Bristol, Va., 1953; With radio stations, Bristol, Tenn.; pub. rels. dir. Atlanta Motor Speedway, 1980—85, gen. mgr., 1985—86; from dir. mktg. to gen. mgr. Daytona Internat. Speedway, 1986—87; gen. mgr. Talladega Superspeedway, 1987—89, pres., 1989—94; v.p. Internat. Speedway Corp, 1989; v.p. competition NASCAR, Daytona Beach, Fla., 1994—98, sr. v.p., 1998—99, sr. v.p., COO, 1999—2000, pres., 2000—. Bd. dirs. NASCAR. Named one of The Most Influential People in the World of Sports, Bus. Week, 2008. Office: NASCAR 1801 W International Speedway Blvd Daytona Beach FL 32115

HEMBREE, WILLIAM A., state legislator; b. Mar. 8, 1966; m. Beth Hembree; 1 child, William Jr. Former Dist. 67, 2004—; former mem. Govt. Affairs Coms., Motor Vehicles Coms., Community Affairs Coms., State Planning Coms., Defense & Vet Affairs, Health & Ecology & U. Sys. Ga. Coms.; nat. pres. Distributive Education Clubs America, 1985; house candidate, 1990; state rep. Dist. 98 Ga., 1992—97; pub. svc. commn. candidate, 1996; citizen mem. Atlanta Ga. Regional Commn., 1997; state rep. Dist. 98 Ga., 1999—2002; house rep. Ga.; state rep. Dist. 46 Ga.; real estate asset mgr. Irt. Mem.: Muscular Dystrophy Assn. (nat. youth chmn.), C. of C. Republican. Methodist. Office: 609 Legis Office Bldg Atlanta GA 30334 Mailing: 4159 Pool Rd Winston GA 30187-2024 Home Phone: 770-942-1656; Office Phone: 770-955-4406. Business E-Mail: bhembree@legis.state.ga.us.

HEMINGWAY, RICHARD WILLIAM, law educator; b. Detroit, Nov. 24, 1927; s. William Oswald and Iva Catherine (Wildfang) H.; m. Vera Cecilia Eck, Sept. 12, 1947; children: Margaret Catherine, Carol Elizabeth, Richard Albert. BS in Bus, U. Colo., 1950; JD magna cum laude (J. Woodall Rogers Sr. Gold medal 1955), So. Meth. U., 1955; LL.M. (William S. Cook fellow 1968), U. Mich., 1969. Bar: Tex. 1955, Okla. 1981. Assoc. Fulbright, Crooker, Freeman, Bates & Jaworski, Houston, 1955-60; lectr. Bates Sch. Law, U. Houston, 1960; assoc. prof. law Baylor U. Law Sch., Waco, Tex., 1960-65; vis. assoc. prof. So. Meth. U. Law Sch., 1965-68; prof. law Tex. Tech U. Law Sch., Lubbock, 1968-71, Paul W. Horn prof., 1972-81, acting dean, 1974-75, dean ad interim, 1980-81; prof. law U. Okla., Norman, 1981-83, Eugene Kuntz prof. oil, gas and natural resources law, 1983-92, Eugne Kuntz prof. emeritus oil, gas & natural resources law, 1992—. Author: The Law of Oil and Gas, 1971, 2d edit., 1983, lawyer's edit., 1983, 3d edit., 1991, West's Texas Forms (Mines and Minerals), 1977, 2d edit., 1991; contbg. editor various law reports, cases and materials. Served with USAAF, 1945-47. Mem. Tex. Bar Assn., Scribes, Order of Coif (faculty), Beta Gamma Sigma. Lutheran. Avocation: amateur radio. Home Phone: 469-330-8775. Personal E-mail: rheming1@sbcglobal.net.

HEMMADY, GOKUL V., corporate financial executive; BS in Commerce, U. Bombay; MBA, Yale U., 1990. Chartered acct. Various sr. level internat. fin. positions Citibank, US West, Inc.; dir., internat. fin. US West Internat.; asst. treas. ADC Telecomm., 1997, CFO, 1997—2007, treas., 1998—2003, v.p., 1998—2007, contr., 2002—03; exec. v.p., CFO NII Holdings, Inc., 2007—. Mem.: Inst. Chartered Accountants India. Office: NII Holdings Inc Ste 1000 1875 Explorer St Reston VA 20190 Office Phone: 703-390-5100. Office Fax: 703-547-5269. Business E-Mail: ghemmady@nii.com.

HEMPFLING, LINDA LEE, retired nurse; b. Indpls., July 28, 1947; d. Paul Roy and Myrtle Pearl (Ward) H. Diploma, Meth. Hosp. Ind. Sch. Nursing, 1968; postgrad., St. Joseph's Coll., Joliet Jr. Coll. Cert. in profl. healthcare mgmt. 2009; med. audit specialist, 2000. Charge nurse Meth. Hosp., Indpls., 1968; staff nurse operating rm. Silver Cross Hosp., Joliet, Ill., 1969; charge nurse oper. rm. Huntington Hosp., 1969-73; night supr. oper. rm., post anesthesia care unit Hermann Hosp., Houston, 1973-76, unit mgr., purchasing coord. oper. rms., 1976-83; RN med. auditor, quality improvement, tng. coord. Nat. Healthcare Rev., Inc., Houston, 1984—98; RN med. auditor RelayHealth, 1999—2011. Future Nurses Am. scholar, 1965, Nat. Merit scholar, 1965. Mem.: Am. Assn. Med. Audit Specialists, Tex. Med. Auditors Assn., Assn. PeriOperative Registered Nurses. Home Phone: 713-729-7303.

HEMUS, SIMON C., consumer products company executive; Attended, London Bus. Sch., 1966. Sr. v.p., mktg. Avon Products, Inc., 1988—93; group pres., CEO, direct selling divsn. Sara Lee Corp., 1993—2005; group pres., internat. beauty Tupperware Brands Corp., 2005—07, pres., COO, 2007—. Office: Tupperware Brands Corp 14901 S Orange Blossom Trail Orlando FL 32837 Office Phone: 407-826-5050. Office Fax: 407-826-8874.

HENDERSON, ARNOLD GLENN, architect, educator; b. Shawnee, Okla., Nov. 10, 1934; s. Henry Glenn and Pearlalee H.; m. Beatriz Eugenia Chavez Escandon (dec. Oct. 2011); children: Eric Neal, Alex Jon. B.Arch., U. Okla., 1961; BS in Architecture; BS in Engring., U. Okla., 1961; MS in Architecture, Columbia U., 1964. Asst. prof. architecture U. Ill., Urbana, 1964-68; assoc. prof. U. Okla., 1968-73, prof., 1973—2002, prof. emeritus, 2002—, disting. lectr. Norman, 1984, 88; pvt. practice architecture Norman, Okla., 1975—. Author: Document for an Anonymous Indian, 1974, The Surgeon General's Collection, 1976, Architecture in Oklahoma, 1978, (with others) The Point Riders Great Plains Poetry Anthology, 1982; co-editor: (with others) Point Riders Press, 1974-; painting exhbns. in Ind., Ill., Okla., La., Wyo., Ark., Kans., Ala., Colo., Tex. and London; author of poetry. Chmn. Norman Housing Authority, 1972-77; mem. Hist. Preservation and Landmark Commn., Guthrie, Okla., 1979-81; chmn. Okla. Hist. Preservation Rev. Com., 2004-10. Served with U.S. Army, 1953-55. Grantee NSF, Nat. Endowment Arts, AIA, Okla. Arts Coun., Okla. Humanities Com., Graham Found. for Advanced Studies in the Fine Arts. Fellow AIA (award of excellence 1976); mem. Okla. Hist. Soc. (Shirk Meml. award 1991, Okla. Humanities award, 2013), Soc. Archl. Historians, Sigma Tau. Democrat. Roman Catholic. Home: 1208 Barkley Ave Norman OK 73071-4812 Office: U Okla Coll Arch Norman OK 73019-0001 Home Phone: 405-364-6770. E-mail: ahenderson@ou.edu.

HENDERSON, BARRY L., bank executive; Grad., Va. Tech. Loan exec. United Way, 1980, campaign chmn., 2005, bd. chmn., 2008; exec. v.p., head, western va. region comml. bus. SunTrust Banks, Inc., 2000, pres., CEO, western Virginia region, 2007—. Vice chmn. The United Way, Roanoke Valley; bd. dirs. YMCA, Roanoke Valley, Va. Western Cmty. Coll. Recipient F. Wiley Hubbell award. Office: SunTrust Banks Inc 303 Peachtree St NE Atlanta GA 30308 Office Phone: 404-588-7711. Office Fax: 404-332-3875. Business E-Mail: barry.henderson@suntrust.com.

HENDERSON, DWIGHT FRANKLIN, dean, educator; b. Austin, Tex., Aug. 14, 1937; s. Ottis Franklin and Leona (Bady) H.; m. Connie Chorlton, Dec. 24, 1966; 1 dau., Patricia Ross. BA, U. Tex., 1959, MA, 1961, PhD, 1966. Assoc. prof. Ind. U., Ft. Wayne, 1966-68, chmn. dept. history, 1968-71, assoc. prof. history, 1971-80, chmn. arts and scis., 1971-76, dean arts and letters, 1976-80, acting chancellor, 1978-79; prof. history, dean Coll. Social and Behavioral Scis. U. Tex., San Antonio, 1980-2000, acting v.p. acad. affairs, 1986-87, interim dean Coll. Engring., 2000-2001; Fulbright lectr. East China Normal U., Shanghai, 2002; dir. Freshman Initiative, 2003—05. Author: Private Journals of Georgiana Gholson Walker, 1963, Courts for a New Nation, 1971, Congress, Courts, and Criminals, 1985; Co-Author (with Ruth Lofgen)Mitchell Lake Wildlife Refuge: An Illustrated History, 2008. Bd. dirs. Ft. Wayne Philharm. Orch., 1973-74, Pub. Transp. Corp., Ft. Wayne, 1975-77, Vis. Nurse Assn., San Antonio, 1989-94, 95-96, Vis. Nurse Assn. Hospice South Tex., 1996-2002, Employment Network, 1990-96,; pres. Mitchell Lake Wetlands Soc., 2004-09, 12-, mem. vol. svcs. Coun. San Antonio State Living Links, 2012-; docent Mitchell Lake Audubon Ctr., 2004-, mem. stewardship bd., 2006-10; mem. Tex. Master Naturalists, 2010-. With AUS, 1962-64. Tex. Soc. Colonial Dames fellow, 1964-65, 65-66; Ind. U. fellow, 1968, 70, 72, Fulbright U.S.-German Internat. Edn. Adminstrs. Program, 1993. Mem.: Tex. Assn. Deans of Liberal Arts and Scis. (bd. dirs. 1992—98, v.p. 1994, pres. 1995—97), Phi Alpha Theta, Delta Sigma Rho. Home: 18222 Redriver Sky San Antonio TX 78259 Office: U Tex Dept History 6900 N Loop 1604 W San Antonio TX 78249

HENDERSON, GEORGE, educational sociologist, educator; b. Hurtsboro, Ala., June 18, 1932; s. Kidd Large and Lula Mae (Crawford) H.; m. Barbara Ann Beard, Aug. 9, 1952; children: George, Michele, Faith, Lea, Joy, Lisa, Dawn. Student, Mich. State U., 1950-52; BA, Wayne State U., 1957, MA, 1959, PhD in Ednl. Sociology, 1965. Caseworker Ch. Youth Service, Detroit, 1957-59; social economist Detroit Housing Commn., 1960-61; dir. cmty. svcs. Detroit Urban League, 1961-63; program dir. Mayor's Com. for Detroit Youth, 1963-64; asst. dir. delinquency control tng. center Wayne State U., 1964-65; asst. dir. intercultural rels. Detroit Pub. Schs., 1965-66, asst. to supt., 1966-67; assoc. prof. sociology and edn. U. Okla., 1967-69, Sylvan N. Goldman prof. human rels., 1969—2006, prof. edn., assoc. prof. sociology, 1969—2006, David Ross Boyd prof. human rels., 1985—2006, Regents' prof. human rels., 1989—2006, Kerr-McGee Presdl. prof., 2001—05; dean U. Okla. Coll. Liberal Studies, 1996-2000; dir. human rels. U. Okla., 2000—06. Chmn. dept. human rels. U. Okla., 1969-95; vis. prof. sociology Langston U., 1969-70; disting. vis. prof. U.S. Air Force Acad., 1980-81; cons. in field. Author: Foundations of American Education, 1970, Teachers Should Care, 1970, America's Other Children, 1971, To Live in Freedom, 1972, Education for Peace, 1973, Human Relations, 1974, Human Relations in the Military, 1975, A Religious Foundation of Human Relations, 1977, Introduction to American Education, 1978, Understanding and Counseling Ethnic Minorities, 1979, Police Human Relations, 1981, Transcultural Health Care, 1981, Physician-Patient Communication, 1981, The Human Rights of Professional Helpers, 1983, The State of Black Oklahoma, 1984, Psychosocial Aspects of Disability, 1984, 2004, 2011, Mending Broken Children, 1984, College Survival for Student Athletes, 1985, International Business and Cultures, 1987, Understanding Indigeneous and Foreign Cultures, 1989, 2006, Values in Health Care, 1991, Social Work Interventions, 1994, Cultural Diversity in the Workplace, 1994, Migrants, Immigrants and Slaves, 1995, Human Relations Issues in Management, 1996, Our Souls to Keep, 1999, Rethinking Ethnicity and Health Care, 1999, Ethnicity and Substance Abuse, 2002, Excellence in College Teaching and Learning, 2007, Race and the University, 2010, A Human Relations Approach to Multiculturalism in K-12 Schools. Recipient Outstanding Achievement award Human Rels. Assn., 1975, Human Rels. award Met. Human Rels. Commn. Nashville, 1979, Okla. Dept. of Mental Health award, 1996, Okla. Found. for Excellence medal for outstanding coll./univ. tchr., 2000; named to Okla. Higher Edn. Hall Fame, 2003, Okla. Hall Fame, 2003. Mem. AAUP, ACD, Am. Sociol. Assn., Nat. Assn. Human Rights Works, Assn. Black Sociologists, Inter-Univ. Seminar on Armed Forces and Soc., Internat. Soc. Law Enforcement and Criminal Justice Instrs., Am. Assn. High Edn. (Black Caucus award for Ednl. Svc. 1993), Golden Key, Omicron Delta Kappa, Delta Tau Kappa, Phi Kappa Phi, Kappa Alpha Psi. Democrat. Home: 2616 Osborne Dr Norman OK 73069-5031 Office: 601 Elm Ave Norman OK 73019-3100 Business E-Mail: clsdean@ou.edu.

HENDERSON, GEORGE ERVIN, lawyer; b. Pampa, Tex., June 7, 1947; s. Ervin L. and Elizabeth (Yoe) Henderson; m. Linda L. Dalrymple, Aug. 22, 1970; children: Andrew, Elizabeth. BA, Tex. Christian U., 1969; JD, Yale U., 1972. Bar: Tex. 1972, U.S. Dist. Ct. (so. dist.) Tex. 1974, U.S. Dist. Ct. (we. dist.) Tex. 1978. Assoc. Fulbright & Jaworski, Houston, Austin, Tex., 1972-79, ptnr. Austin, 1983—2007, of counsel, 2008—; ptnr. Sneed & Vine, Austin, 1979-

82. Adj. instr. law U. Tex., Austin, 1983—85. Contbr. articles to profl. jours. Mem. rules com. S. Tex. Youth Soccer Assn., 1993—; mem. Greater Austin Soccer Coalition, Austin, 1995—98; elder Univ. Presbyn. Ch., Austin, 2001—04, 2007—. Capt. USAR, 1972—78. Mem.: ABA, Am. Bankruptcy Inst., Tex. Bar Found., Travis County Bar Assn. (chmn. 1988—89, vice-chmn. 1997—98, mem. bankruptcy law sect.), Tex. Assn. Bank Counsel (pres. 1985—86), State Bar Tex. (mem. articles 2 and 2A revision subcom. 2005—, chmn. corp. banking and bus. law sect. 1983, mem. coun. corp. banking and bus. law sect. 1985—88), Capital Soccer Club (pres. 1993—95), Austin Yacht Club. Office: Fulbright and Jaworski 98 San Jacinto Blvd Ste 1100 Austin TX 78701-4255 Office Phone: 512-536-4524.

HENDERSON, GLORIA MASON, retired literature and language professor; d. William Lester and Alice (Carter) Mason; m. Harold Henderson, Sept. 1, 1957; children: Harold Mason, Daniel Scott. BA, Hendrix Coll., 1958; MA, Vanderbilt U., 1967; PhD, Ga. State U., 1974. Tchr. Alice Bell Elem. Sch., Knoxville, Tenn., 1958-60, Glynn Acad., Brunswick, Ga., 1960-65, Wills High Sch., Smyrna, Ga., 1965-66; grad. asst. Ga. State U., Atlanta, 1971-73; tchr. DeKalb Coll. (presently Georgia Perimeter Coll.), Clarkston, Ga., 1974-85; prof. English Gordon State Coll., Barnesville, Ga., 1985—2005; chmn. lit. and lang., 1985-94. Editor: Literature and Ourselves: A Thematic Introduction for Readers and Writers, 1994, 97, 2001, 03, 06, 09. Named Dist. STAR Tchr., Ga., 1965. Mem. AAUW, Soc. for Study of So. Lit., South Atlantic MLA, Iris Murdoch Soc., Am. Conf. for Irish Studies, Assn. for Interdisciplinary Study of Arts. Democrat. Methodist. Avocations: reading, swimming, travel. Home: 2442 Chapel Hill Rd Griffin GA 30224 Personal E-mail: gmhenderson@mindspring.com.

HENDERSON, HORACE EDWARD, World War II historian, peace advocate; b. Henderson, NC, July 30, 1917; s. T. Brantley and Maude (Duke) H.; m. Vera S. Schubert; children by previous marriage: Terri Kelley, Elizabeth Smith. Student, Coll. William and Mary, 1934—37, Yale U., 1941—42. Owner Henderson Real Estate & Ins., Williamsburg, Va., 1947—52; coord. Nat. Automobile Dealers Assn., Washington, 1954—56; dir. gen. World Peace Through Law Center, Geneva, 1964—69; chmn. bd. Henderson Real Estate, McLean, Va., 1964—66; exec. dir. World Assn. Judges, 1968—69; pres. Cmty. Methods, Inc., 1969—76; chmn. Congress Reform Com., Washington, 1976; exec. v.p. Am. Lawmakers Assn., Washington, 1977; pres. Williamsburg Vacations, Inc., 1969—84. Chmn., pres. Nat. Assn. for Free Trade, San Francisco, 1986-87; mem. adv. bd. Mut. Security Agy., 1952-53; mem. Pres.'s Conf. on Indsl. Safety, 1952-53; exec. com. U.S. Com. for UN, 1954; dir. Nat. Citizens Com. for Hoover Report, 1954; indsl. adv. com. Fed. Civil Def. Adminstrn., 1952-53; cons. to dir. ICA, 1956; dir. spl. liaison, spl. asst. to dep. under sec. state, Washington, 1958, dep. asst. sec. state internat. orgn. affairs, Washington, 1959-60; dir. Exile Orgns. Free Europe Com., 1962; U.S. del. to ILO, UNESCO, FAO, WHO, ECOSOC, UN. Author: The Greatest Blunders of World War II, 2002, The Scots of Virginia--America's Greatest Patriots, 2001, The Final Word on War and Peace, 2004. Local, state and Nat. pres. US Jaycees, 1947-53; chmn. Va. Rep. party, 1962-64, Americans for Asian Security and Freedom, 1961; campaign dir. Am. Nationalities for Nixon-Lodge, 1960, Rep. candidate for Congress, 1956, for lt. gov. Va., 1957; permanent chmn. Va. Rep. Conv., 1957; asst. nat. dir. Rockefeller for Pres. campaign, 1964, Scranton for Pres. Campaign, 1964; ind. Candidate for U.S. Senator, 1972; mem. Williamsburg (Va.) City Coun., 1948-50; chmn. Com. Against Recognition Red Hungary, 1963; World vice chmn. Operation Brotherhood, 1954-55; owner Powhatan Hist. Corp., Williamsburg, Va., 1957; chmn. World Campaign Conv. for Peaceful Settlement Internat. Disputes, 1975-95, Assn. for Devel. Edn., Washington, 1978-80, World Peace Treaty Campaign, 1997-05; chmn. Coalition World Union Fedn., 2006; pres. Internat. Domestic Devel. Corp., 1975; trustee Valley Forge Found., 1952-55, Jr. C. of C. War Meml. Hdqrs.; elder, deacon Presbyn. Ch. Pvt. Capt., C.E. AUS, 1942-46. Recipient spl. citizenship award Am. Heritage Found., 1953; named Outstanding Jaycee of World, 1954; Nominee Nobel Peace prize, 2007. Mem. US C. of C. (dir. 1954), Yale Club, St. Andrew's Soc., Sigma Alpha Epsilon. Visited 47 countries organizing young men's civic groups, 1953-54. Home: Apt 822 1925 Burnt Bridge Rd Lynchburg VA 24503-2246

HENDERSON, J. NEIL, medical anthropologist; b. Sulphur, Okla. m. Carson Henderson; children: Matt, Kara, Gabriela. BA in Sociology and Anthropology, U. Ctrl. Fla., 1973; MS in Psychol. Anthropolgy, Fla. State U., 1975; PhD in Medical Anthropology, U. Fla., 1979. Prof. U. Okla. Health Scis. Ctr., Oklahoma City. Faculty advisor Native Am. Pub. Health Student Assn., 2001—; external adv. bd. ctr. health equality, ctr. excellence in partnership for cmty. outreach U. Ariz., Tucson, 2006; cons. ethnogeriatrics nat. com. US Bur. Health Professions; grant reviewer NIH; project coord. U. South Fla. Geriatric Edn. Ctr.; dir. Am. indian Dibetes Prevention Ctr. Contbr. articles to profl. jours., chapters to books; co-author: The Culture of Long-Term Care: Nursing Home Ethnography, 1995, Social and Behavioral Foundations of Public Health, 2001. Pres. Assn. Anthropology and Gerontology, 1996; oversight com. diversity Nat. Alzheimer's Assn., 2004—; com. mem. Kellogg/ASPH disparities task force Am. Schs. Pub. Health, 2005—; com. mem. prevention rsch. workgroup Ctrs. Disease Control Nat. Pub. Health Action Plan to Promote and Protect Brain Health, 2006—. Recipient Outstanding Employee award, U. South Fla. Suncoast Gerontology Ctr., Achievement award in Native Am. health, U. Okla. Coll. Pub. Health, 2006, Leadership in Prevention award Native. Am. Health, Loma Linda U. Sch. Pub. Health, 2006; Okla. Ctr. Am. Indian Diabetes Health Disparities grant, NIH, 2007—. Mem.: Choctaw Nat. Okla. Achievements include research in health and disease in Native American/Alaska Native populations, Hispanics and African Americans; the cultural construction of health and disease; intercultural health communication; impact of organizational culture on health care dynamics; institutional and informal long term care strategies in rural and urban communities; development of a needs assessment project on cardiovascular health and service needs for large Native American tribes; developed and conducted cultural competence workshops for Native American tribes; developed and operated multicultural support groups for caregivers to victims of dementing diseases such as Alzheimer's. Office: 801 NE 13th St # 253 Oklahoma City OK 73104-5005 Office Phone: 405-271-7500. Business E-Mail: neil-henderson@ouhsc.edu, twohawkinstitute@cox.net.

HENDERSON, JAMES RONALD, industrial real estate developer; b. Columbus, Nebr., Dec. 2, 1947; s. Bill and Roeburta (Hamrick) H.; m. Jamey Lee Blevins, June 30, 1972 (div. Mar. 1993); children: Benjamin James, Katrin Lee, Joseph Marion. BSBA, Okla. State U., 1970. Commd. 2d lt. USAR, 1970, advanced through grades to maj., 1987, ret., 1992; appraiser Dorchester Cos., Tulsa, 1970-72; devel. mgr. Wolf Point Properties, Tulsa, 1972-82; v.p. Mager Mortgage Co., Tulsa, 1972-78; mktg. dir. Tulsa Port of Catoosa, Okla., 1987-89; pres. J. Ronald Henderson Real Estate, Tulsa, 1978—, Henderson Exploration Co., Tulsa, 1982—. Mng. dir. Wolf Point Indsl. Pky. Owners Assn., Tulsa, 1984—. Organizer, incorporator Tulsa Charity Fight Night, Inc., 1993; organizer N.E. Okla. Econ. Devel. Assn., 1988. Maj. USAR ret. Mem. Nat. Assn. Indsl. and Office Pks. (pres. Tulsa chpt. 1990), Propeller Club Port of Catoosa (pres. 1987). Southern Baptist. Avocations: backpacking, history, geology. Office: Henderson Cos 1643 E 15th St Tulsa OK 74120-6044

HENDERSON, JOHNNY, mathematician, educator; b. Santa Monica, Calif., Mar. 26, 1951; s. Ernest Elijah and Madora Allene Henderson; m. Darlene Baxter; 1 child, Kathryn Strunk. BS, U. Ark., 1973, MS, 1975; PhD, U. Nebr., 1981. Asst. prof. math. U. Mo., Rolla, 1981—84; alumni prof. math. Auburn U., Auburn, 1984—2000, Scharnagel prof. math., 2000—02; disting. prof. math. Baylor U., Waco, Tex., 2002—; bd. chmn. Abilene Christian U., Tex., 2007—08, adv. bd., math. dept., 2004—09; com. mem. Am. Math. Soc., 2009—. Author: Boundary Value Problems for Functional Differential Equations, 1995, Implusive Differential Equalizations and Inclusions, 2007, Impulsive Differential Inclusions: Fixed Point Approach, 2013; contbr. articles to profl. jours.; mem. editl. bd. Jour. Math. Analysis and Applications, Comms. on Applied Nonlinear Analysis, Journ. Difference Equations and Applications, Differential Equations and Applications, Involve: A Jour. Math., others. Vol. Wesley Terr. Retirement Ctr., Auburn, 1984—2002, Meadowlands Terr. Retirement Ctr., Waco, 2002—10. Recipient Tchg. Excellence award, 1982, Outstanding Tchg. award, U. Mo., 1984, Outstanding Achievement award, Ark. Coll., 1993, Trio Achievement award, Ark. Assn. Student Assistance Programs, 1994, Alumni Achievement award, U. Nebr., 1995, Outstanding Tchg. award, Lamdba Sigma Soc., 2002, Mortar Bd. Tchg. award, Laurel chpt. Baylor U., 2006, Elsevier award, 2005—10, Recognition award, Phi Kappa Chi Baylor U., 2011; fellow, Tamkang U, Taiwan, 1999, 2001, U. NSW, 2003; Raybould fellow, U. Queensland, Australia, 1997. Fellow: Am. Math. Soc. (com. coms. mem. 2009—11, Simons grant com. mem. 2011); mem.: Internat. Soc. Difference Equations (adv. bd. 2001—03), Internat. Fedn. Nonlinear Analysts, Math. Assn. Am. (Disting Tchg. award 2001), Sigma Xi. Office: Baylor University Dept Math One Bear Pl #97328 Waco TX 76798 Business E-Mail: johnny_henderson@baylor.edu.

HENDERSON, MILTON ARNOLD, professional society administrator; b. Chattanooga, June 22, 1922; s. Milton Arnold and Margaret (Rawlings) H.; m. Joyce Crowder (dec. Nov. 13, 1977); children: George, Linda (dec.), Philip.; m. Betty Ann Harnage, Aug. 20, 1982. BS, Northwestern U., 1948. Asst. sales mgr. Coca-Cola Bottling Co., Savannah and Macon, Ga., 1948—54; with Gideons Internat., Chgo., 1954-63, field rep., 1954-55, promotion mgr., 1955-56, with Nashville, 1964—, exec. dir., 1956-87, exec. dir. emeritus, 1987—. Editor The Gideon Mag., Gideon Info. Bull., Gideon News Brief, 1956-87; author: Sowers of the Word, a 95-Year History of The Gideons International, 1899-1994, 1995; attended Gideon convs. and meetings in 74 countries, 1956—. 1st lt. USAAF, 1942-46; capt. USAF, 1951-52. Recipient Community Leader of Am. award, 1969, Personalities of the South award, 1975, Disting. Alumnus award Howe Mil. Sch., Ind., 1985. Mem. Am. Mgmt. Assn., Nashville City Club. Republican. Presbyterian. Home: 2524 Stones River Ct Nashville TN 37214-1425

HENDERSON, PHYLLIS, state legislator; b. Cin., Ohio, Nov. 14, 1959; d. Edward and Bessie (Cross) Bertaux; m. Richard Henderson; 3 children. BA, U. Cin., 1982; MPA, Ind. U., 1984. Field ops. supr. US Census Bureau; v.p., govtl. affairs Greater Greenville C. of C.; bd. dirs. Greenville Area Devel. Corp., Greenville County Planning Commn.; campaign mgr. to congressman Jim DeMint, 1988; mem. Greenville County Coun., 2000—04, chmn., 2003—04; pres. Eastside High Sch. PTA, 2010—; mem. Dist. 21 SC House of Representatives, 2010—. Republican. Office: South Carolina House of Representatives District 21 522D Blatt Bldg Columbia SC 29201 Address: 110 Silver Creek Ct Greer SC 29650 Office Phone: 803-212-6883.

HENDERSON, RICHARD D., state legislator; b. Mar. 15, 1971; Co-owner C&H Block & Concrete; mem. Dist 74 Ky. House of Reps., Ky., 2007—. Recipient C. of C. Leadership award, 2003. Democrat. Christian. Office: Ky Legislature Annex Rm 466D 702 Capitol Ave Frankfort KY 40601 Home: 120 Dove Trace Dr Mount Sterling KY 40353-8313 Office Phone: 502-564-8100 ext. 642. Business E-Mail: richard.henderson@lrc.ky.gov.

HENDERSON, STANLEY DALE, lawyer, educator, arbitrator; b. Monona, Iowa, June 17, 1935; s. Leon Gilbert and Iva Elizabeth H.; m. DeArliss Garretson, June 15, 1957; children: Lesli Kara, Heidi Elizabeth, Holly Ann. AB, Coe Coll., 1957; postgrad. (Woodrow Wilson fellow), Cornell U., 1957-58; postgrad., U. Chgo. Law Sch., 1958-59; JD, U. Colo., 1961. Bar: Colo. 1961, Va. 1973. Law clk. U.S. Dist. Ct., Denver, 1961-62; mem. firm Williams and Zook, Boulder, Colo., 1962-64; mem. faculty U. Wyo. Coll. Law, 1964-69; prof. law U. Va. Law Sch., Charlottesville, 1970—2004, F.D.G. Ribble prof. law, 1976—2004, prof. emeritus, 2004. Vis. prof. law Ind. U., 1974, Harvard Law Sch., 1978-79, Pepperdine U., 1992-93; arbitrator AAA and FMCS, 1970—. Author: Labor Law; author: (with Dawson, Harvey and Baird) Contracts; author: (with Meltzer) Labor Law; contbr. articles to profl. jours. Mem. Va. State Bar, Am. Law Inst., Am. Arbitration Assn., FMCS, Order of Coif, Phi Beta Kappa, Phi Kappa Phi. Democrat. Presbyterian. Home: 1615 King Mountain Rd Charlottesville VA 22901-3003 Office: U Va Sch Law Charlottesville VA 22901 Office Phone: 434-924-3522. Business E-Mail: sdh6k@virginia.edu.

HENDERSON, THOMAS HENRY, JR., lawyer, former legal association executive; b. Birmingham, Ala., Feb. 4, 1939; s. Thomas Henry and Edna (Green) H.; m. Elaine Dauphin (div. 1983); children: Ashley, Michelle; m. Paulette Machara, June 1988. BSBA, Auburn U., 1961; JD, U. Ala., 1966; LLM, Nat. Law Ctr., George Washington U., 1987. Bar: D.C. 1970, Ala. 1966. Trial atty. organized crime and racketeering sect. U.S. Dept. Justice, Washington, 1966-70, dep. sect. chief mgmt. labor sect., 1970-73; dep. chief counsel, subcom. on adminstrn. practice and procedure U.S. Senate, Washington, 1973-74; dep. sect. chief mgmt. and labor sect. Dept. Justice, Washington, 1974-76, chief pub. integrity sect., 1976-80, sr. counsel criminal divsn., 1980-83; bar counsel D.C. Ct. Appeals, Washington, 1983-87; CEO ATLA- NSW Am. Assn. Justice, Washington, 1988—2005, ret., 2005—09. Columnist Bar Counsels Page, Washington Lawyer mag., bi-monthly, 1983-87. Pres. Christmas in April, Washington, 1986-87. Recipient Justic Howell Heflin award, ATLA, 2004; named Disting. Practitioner of Law, U. Ala. Law Sch., 2004. Mem. Am. Soc. Assn. Execs. (bd. dirs. 1994-97, vice chair 1997-98, Key award 2003), Omicron Delta Kappa. Avocations: golf, skiing, exercise, outdoor adventure.

HENDLEY, DAN LUNSFORD, retired bank executive; b. Nashville, Apr. 26, 1938; s. Frank E. and Mattie (Lunsford) H.; m. Patricia Fariss, June 18, 1960; children: Dan Lunsford, Laura Kathleen. BA, Vanderbilt U., 1960; grad., Rutgers U., 1969; postgrad., Program Mgmt. Devel., Harvard, 1972. With Fed. Res. Bank Atlanta, 1962-73, v.p., officer in charge Birmingham br., 1969-73; v.p., exec. v.p. AmSouth Bancorp, 1973-77; exec. v.p. First Nat. Bank Birmingham, 1976-77, pres., 1977-79, chmn. bd., chief exec. officer, 1979-83; pres., chief operating officer, bd. dirs. Am South Bank, N.A., 1983-90; v.p. bus. affairs Samford U., Birmingham, Ala., 1991-94; ret., 1994. Trustee Children's Hosp., Samford U. With Tenn. Air N.G., 1961-67. Mem. Kiwanis, Mountain Brook Club, The Club. Baptist. Home: 3258 Dell Rd Birmingham AL 35223-1318 Personal E-mail: danandpat@charter.net.

HENDREN, JIMM LARRY, federal judge; b. Gravette, Ark., 1940; BA, U. Ark., 1964, LLB, 1965. Atty. Little & Enfield, 1968-69; pvt. law practice Bentonville, Ark., 1970-77, 79-92; chancellor, probate judge Ark. 16th Chancery Dist., 1977-78; judge US Dist. Ct. (western dist.) Ark., 1992—2012, chief judge, 1997—2012, sr. judge, 2012—. Served to lt. comdr. JAGC, USN, 1965-70, USNR, 1970-83. Mem. ABA, Ark. Bar Assn. Office: Hammerschmidt Fed Bldg Rm 559 35 E Mountain Fayetteville AR 72701 Office Phone: 479-444-7876.*

HENDREN, KIM D., state legislator; b. Gravette, Ark., Feb. 6, 1938; m. Marylea Hutchinson, 1958; children: Mark, Jim, Gayla, Hope. BS, Univ. Ark., 1960. Engr., owner Hendren Plastics; mem. City Coun., Sch. Bd., Gravette, Ark., Ark. House of Reps., 2001—02; mem. Dist. 6 Ark. State Senate, 1979—83, mem. Dist. 1, 2001—03, mem. Dist. 9, 2003—, minority leader, 2009—11. Mem.: Ark. Bd. Profl. Engineers, Ark. Real Estate Coun. Republican. Mailing: 1501 Hwy 72 SE Gravette AR 72736 Office Phone: 501-787-6500. Office Fax: 501-787-6116. Business E-Mail: hendrenk@arkleg.state.ar.us.

HENDRICK, JOSEPH RIDDICK, III, (RICK HENDRICK), race team owner; b. Warrenton, NC, July 12, 1949; s. Joe and Mary Hendrick; m. Linda Hendrick. Co-founder Hendrick Automotive Group, NC; founder Hendrick Motorsports (formerly All-Star Racing), NC, 1984, now chmn., CEO NC. Technical advisor Days of Thunder, 1990. Founder Hendrick Found. for Children; founder, bd. mem. Hendrick Marrow Program, 1997—. Decorated Order of the Long Leaf Pine; recipient Horatio Alger Award, 2006; co-recipient Leadership for Life Award, Marrow Found., 1999; named one of 50 Most Influential People in Sports Bus., Street & Smith's SportsBus. Jour., 2009. Mem.: NC Motorsports Assn. (vice chmn.). Achievements include being the car owner for six NEXTEL Cup championships, one Busch Series championship and three Craftsman Truck Series championships. Office: Hendrick Motor Sports Ltd 4440 Papa Joe Hendrick Blvd Charlotte NC 28262

HENDRICKS, LAURA J., residential and commercial cleaning company executive; BA in Liberal Arts, Xavier U., Cin. Cert. total quality mgmt., Six Sigma Green Belt. Mng. dir., ops. FedEx in, Cin.; v.p., distrbn. and Production Planning Cintas, regional business dir., 2000—05, v.p., supply chain, 2005—07; pres., COO, Merry Maids Servicemaster Co., Servicemaster Global Holdings, 2007—. Recipient Five Star award, FedEx, 1996, 1999. Office: The ServiceMaster Co 860 Ridge Lake Blvd Memphis TN 38120 Office Phone: 901-597-1400. Office Fax: 630-663-2001. Business E-Mail: Laura.Hendricks@servicemaster.com.

HENDRIKSEN, ROGER S., mining executive; BA in Economics and Polit. Sci., U. Utah, 1986; MS in Internat. Mgmt., Garvin Sch. of Internat. Mgmt. Dir., investor rels., corp. comm. Cooper Tire & Rubber Co.; dir., investor rels. Massey Energy Co., 2007—. Mem. Alliance Investor Rels. Coun., Nat. Investor Rels. Inst. Office: Massey Energy Co PO Box 16429 Bristol VA 24209-6429 Office Phone: 804-788-1800. Office Fax: 804-788-1801. Business E-Mail: investor@masseyenergyco.com.

HENDRIX, DANIEL T., textile manufacturing company executive; m. Betsy Hendrix; children: Lauren, John. BS in Acctg. with honors, Fla. State U., 1977. Fin. mgr. Interface, Inc., Atlanta, 1983, sec., treas., 1984—85, CFO, v.p. fin., 1985—95, sr. v.p., 1995—2000, exec. v.p., 2000—01, pres., CEO, 2001—. Bd. dirs. Global Imaging Sys., Inc., 2003—07, Am. Woodmark Corp., 2005—. Office: Interface Inc 2859 Paces Ferry Rd SE Ste 2000 Atlanta GA 30339-6216 Office Fax: 706-882-0500. Business E-Mail: dhendrix@interfaceglobal.com.

HENDRIX, DENNIS RALPH, energy executive; b. Selmer, Tenn., Jan. 8, 1940; s. Forrest Ralph and Mary Lee (Tull) Hendrix; m. Jennie L. Moore, Dec. 28, 1960; children: Alisa Lee, Natalie Moore, Amy Louise. BS, U. Tenn., 1962; MBA, Ga. State U., 1967. CPA Ga. Staff acct., cons. Arthur Andersen & Co., Atlanta, 1962—65; faculty Ga. Inst. Tech., 1965—67; sr. cons. Touche, Ross & Co., Memphis, 1967—68; pres. United Foods, Inc., Memphis, 1968—73; asst. to pres. Tex. Gas Transmission Corp., Owensboro, Ky., 1973—75, pres., 1976—83, chief exec. officer, 1978—83; vice chmn. CSX Corp., 1983—84; exec. v.p., dir. Halliburton Co., Dallas, 1984—85; COO Tex. Eastern Corp., Houston, 1985—86, CEO, pres. & bd. dirs., 1986—89; CEO PanEnergy Corp., 1990—95, chmn., 1995—97. Bd. dirs. Allied Waste Industries, Duke Energy Corp., Grant Prideco, Inc., M.D. Anderson Cancer Ctr. Outreach Corp., Newfield Exploration Co., Pool Energy Svcs. Co., Tex. Commerce Bancshares, Tex. Med. Ctr., Spectra Energy Corp., 2006—. Bd. dirs. Nat. Jr. Achievement, U. Tenn. Devel. Coun., Greater Houston Partnership Bd.; chmn. The Robert A. Welch Found., 1995, Harris County Children's Protective Svcs. Fund, Baylor Coll. Med.; campaign chmn. United Way of Tex., Gulf Coast, 1993; mem. Mus. Fine Arts, Houston, Ctr. for Strategic and Internat. Studies. Mem.: Nat. Petroleum Coun. (vice chmn. 1995), Interstate Natural Gas Assn. Am. (bd. dirs., chmn. 1994), Am. Petroleum Inst. (bd. dirs.), Castle Pines Club, Eldorado Country Club, Forum Club (bd. dirs.), River Oaks Country Club, Houston Ctr. Club, Ramada Club, Burning Tree Club. Presbyterian. Office: Spectra Energy Corp Bd directors 5400 Westheimer Court Houston TX 77056 Office Phone: 713-627-5400. Office Fax: 713-627-4691. Business E-Mail: dhendrix@spectraenergy.com.

HENDRIX, LAURA HROMYAK, lawyer; d. George Frank Jr. and Cecelia (Brown) Hromyak; m. Stewart Douglas Hendrix, Oct. 16, 1993. BA in History, Washington U., St. Louis, 1989; JD, U. Ky., 1992; student, U. Louisville, 1994. Bar: Ky. 1993. Law clk. McBrayer, McGinnis, Leslie & Kirkland, Frankfort, Ky., 1989-90; jud. clk. Hon. William Graham, Frankfort, 1991-93; staff atty. Ky. Higher Edn. Assistance Authority, Frankfort, 1994-95; gen. counsel Exec. Br. Ethics Commn., Frankfort, 1995-96, Legis. Rsch. Commn., Frankfort, 2004—, health policy analyst, mem. com. health and welfare, 1996—99, com. staff adminstr. elections and constitutional amendments, 1999—2004, gen. counsel, 2004—. Editor: Citizen's Guide to the Kentucky Constitution. Mem. Bluegrass Theatre Guild, Frankfort, 1984—, Frankfort Younger Woman's Club, 1999—2003, Hearn Elem. PTA, 2001—, Immanuel Baptist Ch., 1999—. Mem.: Ky. Bar Assn., Ky. Historical Soc., Kappa Alpha Theta. Avocations: singing, reading, dance, cooking, playing piano. Office: Legis Rsch Commn Rm 300 State Capitol Bldg Frankfort KY 40601 Business E-Mail: laura.hendrix@lrc.ky.gov.

HENDRIX, MARK D., finance company executive; BA with honors, Rice U., MBA in Fin. Assoc. ptnr. Andersen Consulting; exec. v.p., e-business, chief info. officer Coral Energy; sr. v.p., chief info. officer Reliant Resources, Inc., 2000; officer Sirius Solutions LLC. Adj. prof. Rice U. Office: Sirius Solutions LLC 1233 W Loop S Ste 1800 Houston TX 77027 Office Phone: 713-888-0488. Office Fax: 713-888-0235. Business E-Mail: mhendrix@sirsol.com.

HENDRY, ROBERT RYON, lawyer; b. Jacksonville, Fla., Apr. 23, 1936; s. Warren Candler and Evalyn Marguerite (Ryon) H.; children by previous marriage: Lorraine Evalyn, Lynette Comstock, Krista Ryon. BA in Polit. Sci., U. Fla., 1958, JD, 1963. Bar: Fla. 1963; bd. cert. in internat. law. Assoc. Harrell, Caro, Middlebrooks & Whiltshire, Pensacola, Fla., 1963-66, Hewlliwell, Melrose & DeWolf, Orlando, Fla., 1966-67, ptnr., 1967-69; ptnr., pres. Hoffman, Hendry, Parker & Smith and predecessor Hoffman, Hendry & Parker, Orlando, Fla., 1969-77, Hoffman, Hendry & Stoner and predecessor, Orlando, Fla., 1977-82, Hendry, Stoner, Sims & Sawicki, Orlando, Fla., 1982-88, Hendry, Stoner, Townsend Sawicki & Brown, Orlando, Fla., 1988-92, Hendry, Stoner, Sawicki & Brown, Orlando, Fla., 1992—2002, Hendry, Stoner, DeLancett & Brown, Orlando, Fla., 2002—05, Hendry, Stoner & Brown, Orlando, Fla., 2005, Hendry, Stoner, Calandrino & Brown, PA, Orlando, Fla., 2005—09, Hendry, Stoner & Brown P.A., Orlando, Fla., 2009—. Author: U.S. Real Estate and the Foreign Investor, 1983; contbr. articles to profl. jours. Mem. Dist. Export Coun., 1977-91, vice chmn., 1981, chair, 1995-2006, chair emeritus, 2007—, mem. nat. steering com., 1997-06, trade issues com., 2007—; bd. dirs. World Trade Ctr. and predecessor, Orlando, 1979-89, pres., 1980-82, 84; chmn. Fla. Gov.'s Conf. on World Trade, 1983; chmn. Fla. coun. on internat. edn., 1993-96; mem. internat. fin. and mktg. adv. bd. U. Miami Sch. Bus., Fla., 1979-90, bd. trustees, Orlando Mus. Art, 1982-, sec v.p., 2003-06, sec., 2007-,chmn. Commn. on Internat. Edn., 1986-88; bd. dirs. Econ. Devel. Commn. of Mid-Fla., 2001-03, Metro Orlando Econ. Devel. Commn., 2000—, bd. dirs., Caribbean Cmty. Found., Inc., 2003—; mem. Metro Orlando Internat. Bus. Coun., 1994-96, Metro Orlando Internat. Affairs Commn., 1995—, Fla. Econ. Summit, 1996-00; mem. internat. trade and econ. devel. bd. and audit com. Enterprise, Fla., 1997-00; chmn. Fla. Trade Grant Review Panel, 1998-01; mem. adv. com. Enterprise Fla. Internat. Bus. Devel., 2000—; bd. dirs. Gulf of Mexico States Partnership, Inc., 2001—, Enterprise Fla. Stakeholders Coun., 2005—08, Golden Rule Found., bd. dirs, 2000—; co-chair Gulf of Mex. Accord Com. on Legal Infrastructure, 2002—; bd. advisors Fla. Free Trade Area of the Ams., 2001-03; mem. steering com. Orlando Area Com. on Fgn. Rels., 2002—; mem. internat. programs adv. com. U. Fla. Levin Coll. of Law, 2000—. Lt. U.S. Army, 1958-60, capt. Army N.G., 1960-70. Mem. Fla. Coun. Internat. Devel. (bd. dirs. 1972-85, chmn. 1977-79, adv. bd. 1985-95, chmn. emeritus, 1991—, vice chair 1995-96, chair 1996-98), Fla. Bar (bd. cert. internat. lawyer 1999—, vice chmn. internat. law com. 1974-75, chmn. com. 1976-77, mem. exec. coun. internat. law sect. 1982—, original internat. law certification com. 1998—2000, chmn. 2001, Internat. Law Cert. Com., 2010, Fla. Assn. Voluntary Agys. for Caribbean Action (bd. dirs. 1987—, pres. 1989-91, past pres. 1991-92), Caribbean Cmty. Found. (v.p., bd. dir. 2003-12), Orange County Bar Assn. (treas. 1971-74, mem., 1975-2008), Scottish Exec. (founding mem. 2002-), Soc. Internat. Bus. Fellows, Brit.-Am. C. of C. (bd. dirs. 2000-04, sec. 1984-85), Swiss Am. C. of C. (sec. Fla. chpt. 1996—89), German Am. Bus. Chamber of Fla.(dir. 2005-08). Office Phone: 407-843-5880. Business E-Mail: rhendry@lawforflorida.com.

HENEGAN, JOHN C(LARK), lawyer; b. Mobile, Ala., Oct. 14, 1950; s. Virgil Baker and Marie (Fife) Gunter; m. Morella Lloyd Kuykendall, Aug. 5, 1972; children: Clark, Jim. BA in English and Philosophy, U. Miss., 1972, JD with honors, 1976. Bar: Miss. 1976, US Dist. Ct. (no. dist.) Miss. 1976, NY 1978, US Dist. Ct. (so. dist.) NY 1979, US Ct. Appeals (5th and 11th cirs.) 1982, US Ct. Appeals (2nd cir.) 1984, US Dist. Ct. (so. dist.) Miss. 1984, US Ct. Appeals (fed. cir.) 1995, US Supreme Ct. 1995, US Ct. Appeals (6th cir.), 2011, US Ct. Appeals (4th cir.), 2013. Law clk. to judge U.S. Ct. Appeals (5th cir.), 1976-77; atty. Dewey, Ballantine, Bushby, Palmer & Wood, NYC and Washington, 1977-81; exec. asst., chief of staff to Gov. William Winter Jackson, Miss., 1981-84; mem. Butler, Snow LLP, Ridgeland, Miss., 1984—. Lectr. U. Miss. Ctr. for Continuing Legal Edn., 1985, 87, Miss. Jud. Coll., Oxford, 1982, Miss. Press. Assn. Ann. Conv., 2005, 08; mem. lawyers adv. com. U.S. Ct. Appeals for 5th Cir. Jud. Conf., 1991-93. Editor-in-chief Miss. Law Jour., 1976; editor Miss. Lawyer, 1985; contbr. articles to legal jours. Bd. dirs. Mississippians for Ednl. Broadcasting, Jackson, 1983-90, North Jackson Youth Baseball, Inc., 1991-97, Ctr. and Ctrl. S.W. Miss. Legal Svcs., 1997-04, Wells United Meth. Ch.; mem. Miss. Ethics Commn., Jackson, 1984-87, chair adv. bd. William Winter Inst. Racial Reconciliation, 2010—13. Fellow Am. Acad. Appellate Lawyers, Miss. Bar Found.; mem. ABA, FBA, Miss. Bar Assn. (chmn. Law Day USA 1983, chmn. appellate practice sect., 2012-13), Miss. Def. Lawyers Assn., 5th Cir. Bar Assn., Fed. Circuit Bar Assn., Hinds County Bar Assn. (bd. dir. 2002-08, sec., treas. 2004-05, v.p. 2005-06, pres. 2006-07), Jackson C. of C., Am. Inns of Ct. (bencher Charles Clark chpt.), Phi Kappa Phi, Phi Delta Phi, Omicron Delta Kappa, Sigma Chi. Avocation: reading. Home: 2441 Eastover Dr Jackson MS 39211-6727 Office: 1020 Highland Colony Pky Ste 1400 Ridgeland MS 39158-6010 Office Phone: 601-985-4530. E-mail: john.henegan@butlersnow.com.

HENINGTON, DAVID MEAD, retired library director; b. El Dorado, Ark., Aug. 16, 1929; s. Bud Henry and Lucile Check (Scranton) H.; m. Barbara Jean Gibson, June 2, 1956; children— Mark David, Gibson Mead, Paul Billins. BA, U. Houston, 1951; MS in L.S., Columbia U., 1956. Young adult libr. Bklyn. Pub. Libr., 1956-58; head lit. and history dept. Dallas Pub. Libr., 1958, asst. dir., 1962-67; dir. Waco (Tex.) Pub. Libr., 1958-62, Houston Pub. Libr., 1967-95; ret., 1995. Served with USAF, 1951-55. Council on Library Resources fellow, 1970-71; recipient Liberty Bell award Houston Bar Assn., 1976 Mem. ALA, AIA (hon. mem. Tex. chpt.), Am. Mgmt. Assn., Tex. Libr. Assn. (Libr. of Yr. 1976, Disting. Svc. award 1993), Philos. Soc. Methodist. Home: 6225 San Felipe St Houston TX 77057-2809 Personal E-mail: dmhenington@comcast.net.

HENKE, MICHAEL JOHN, lawyer, educator; b. Evansville, Ind., Aug. 3, 1940; s. Emerson Overbeck and Beatrice (Arney) H.; children: Blake, Paige, Britt; m. Judith Sanders Campbell, 2008. BA summa cum laude, Baylor U., 1962, LLB, 1965; LLM, NYU, 1966. Bar: Tex. 1965, D.C. 1967, Va. 2010. Assoc. Covington & Burling, Washington, 1966-73, Vinson & Elkins, Washington, 1974—75, ptnr., 1976—2004; sec., gen. counsel Space Adventures, Ltd., 2005—. Adj. prof. U. Va. Law Sch., 1988-94, 96—; chmn. pro bono adv. com. Legal Aid Soc., D.C., 1990-96, trustee, 1992-06, chmn. ways & means com., 1997-2000, v.p., 2000—02, pres., 2002-04; Washington adv. coun. Baylor Washington Program, 1989-92; sesquicentennial coun. of 150 Baylor U., 1993-95. Author: (with others) Petroleum Regulation Handbook, 1980, Natural Gas Yearbook, 1995; mem. editl. bd. Nat. Gas Mag., 1992-97, Best Lawyers in America, 1989—2005, Best Lawyers in Washington, 1997, Worlds Leading Competition and Antitrust Lawyers, 1997—2005, World's Leading Litigation Lawyers, 1997—2005; contbr. articles to profl. jours. Founder, chmn. Old Presbyn. Meeting House Day Care Ctr., Alexandria, Va., 1970-74; trustee Alexandria Country Day Sch., 2000-03. Recipient Gladys award La. State U. Sch. Law, 2003; Kenneson fellow. Mem. ABA (chmn. energy antitrust subcom. litigation sect. 1987-88, vice chmn. energy litigation com. 1988-89, chmn. 1989-92, chmn. ann. fall meeting 1993, divsn. dir. 1993-95, co-chmn. audiotaping and videotaping com. 1995-96, co-chmn. ins. coverage litigation com. 1996-98, coun. 1998-2001, co-chair task force on judiciary 2001-03, Pres.'s Commn. on 21st Century Judiciary 2002-03), D.C. Bar Assn., Tex. Bar Assn., Va. State Bar, Baylor U. Alumni Assn. (bd. dirs. 1994-98, mem. sesquicentennial coun. 2006-08), The Breakfast Club (Charlottesville), Met. Club (Washington), Farmington Country Club (Charlottesville). Democrat. Avocations: skiing, fly fishing, tennis, golf. Home: 1832 Wayside Pl Charlottesville VA 22903 Business E-Mail: mhenke@velaw.com.

HENKE, ROBERT J., federal commissioner, former federal agency administrator; b. Chgo., 1966; BA in Govt. & Internat. Rels., Notre Dame U., 1988; MPA, Syracuse U.; Grad., GE Fin. Mgmt. Program, 1993—96. Presdl. mgmt. intern to asst. sec. (fin. mgmt. & comptr.) Dept. Navy, US Dept Def., 1997—99; profl. staff mem. Subcommittee on Def. US Senate Appropriations Com., 1999—2004; prin. dep. under sec., comptr. US Dept. Def., 2004—05; asst. sec. for mgmt. US Dept. Veterans Affairs, 2005—09. Commr. Commn. on Wartime Contracting in Iraq & Afghanistan (CWC), 2009—. Office: Commission on Wartime Contracting in Iraq & Afghanistan 1401 Wilson Blvd Ste 300 Arlington VA 22209 Office Phone: 703-696-9362. Office Fax: 703-696-9393.

HENKEL, HERBERT LUDWIG, diversified industrial products company executive; b. Reid, Austria, Apr. 22, 1948; m. Gloria Henkel; 2 children. BS in Aerospace Engring., Poly. U., 1970, MS in Mech. Engring., 1972; MBA, Pace U., 1979. Mem. tech. staff Bell Labs.; design engr. Grumman Aerospace; v.p. sales and mktg. Chgo. Pneumatic Tool Co., Hilti, Inc.; pres., COO Southern Fastening Sys. and Unifast Industries, Inc.; pres. Greenlee Textron, Rockford, Ill., 1987-93; pres. indsl. products segments Textron, Inc., 1993-98, exec. v.p., 1998-99, COO, 1998-2000, pres., 1999-2000; chmn., pres., CEO Ingersoll-Rand Co. Ltd., 2000—. Bd. dirs. Pitney Bowes, 1999—2005, Ingersoll-Rand Co. Ltd., 2000—, C.R. Bard Corp., 2002—, 3M Corp., 2007—. Avocations: woodworking, golf, tennis. Office: Ingersoll-Rand Co Ltd 800 E Beaty St Davidson NC 28036 Office Phone: 704-655-5822.

HENLEY, ERNEST JUSTUS, retired chemical engineering professor; b. Sept. 30, 1926; BS, U. Del., 1950; D Engring. Sci., Columbia U., 1953. Asst. prof. nuc. and chem. engring. Columbia U., NYC, 1953-59; prof. chemistry and chem. engring. Stevens Inst. Tech., Hoboken, NJ, 1959-64; chief of party AID Mission, Rio de Janeiro, 1964-66; prof. chem. engring. U. Houston, 1964—. Founder, bd. dirs. Maxxim Med., St. Petersburg, Fla.; bd. dirs. Circon Corp., St. Petersburg, Fla., Procedyne Corp., New Brunswick, NJ; tech. cons.; founding dir. RAI Rsch., 1953-82, Henley Healthcare, 1984-2000. Pres. The Henley Found. Office: U Houston Dept Chemical Engineering Houston TX 77204-0001 Personal E-mail: henleyej@aol.com.

HENLEY, MELVIN B., state legislator; b. Aug. 25, 1935; BS, MBA, Murray State U.; PhD, U. Miss. Bus. owner; mem. Dist. 5 Ky. House of Reps., 2004—. Enlisted USAAF, 1954—58. US Chem. Soc. Republican. Baptist. Address: 1305 S 16th St Murray KY 42071 Office: 329J Capitol Annex Frankfort KY 40601 also: Annex Rm 432C 702 Capitol Ave Frankfort KY 40601 Office Phone: 502-564-8100 ext 611, 502-564-8100 611.

HENNE, PRESTON A., engineering executive; m. Connie Henne; children: Matthew, Lauren, Alexis. BS in Aero. and Astronautical Engring. with honors, U. Ill., 1969; MS in Engring., Calif. State U., Long Beach, 1974, postgrad. in Bus. Adminstrn. Project aerodynamicist McDonnell Douglas Corp., 1969-94, sect. chief aerodynamics tech. programs, br. chief aerodynamics configuaration design and devel., mgr. advanced program aerodynamics and acoustics, chief design engr. MD-80 program, v.p., gen. mgr. MD-90 program; sr. v.p. GV program Gulfstream Aerospace Corp. (subs. of General Dynamics), Savannah, Ga., 1994—. Spkr. in field. Editor Applied Computational Aerodynamics, 1990; contbr. articles to profl. jours. Recipient Outstanding Recent Alumnus award U. Ill., 1982, Mgmt. award NASA, 1984, Outstanding Alumnus award U. Ill., 1989. Fellow AIAA (applied aerodynamics tech. com., Engr. of Yr. 1996); mem. NAE, Sigma Gamma Tau, Phi Kappa Phi, Sigma Tau, Tau Beta Pi. Avocations: skiing, golf, mountain biking. Office: Gulfstream Aerospace Corp PO Box 2206 Savannah GA 31402-2206 Home: 5 Ravenwood Rd Hilton Head SC 29928-3380

HENNEKE, DAN, metal products executive; BBA in Acctg., U. Houston, 1971. CPA. With Arthur Andersen & Co.; v.p. fin. Bldg. Products Group Metals USA, Inc., 2003—05, v.p., corp. contr., 2005—. Office: Metals USA, Inc 2400 E Commercial Blvd Ste 905 Fort Lauderdale FL 33308-4059 Office Phone: 713-965-0990. Office Fax: 713-965-0067.

HENNESSEY, AUDREY KATHLEEN, computer researcher, educator; b. Fairbanks, Apr. 4, 1936; d. Lawrence Christopher and Olga Virginia (Strandberg) Doheny; m. Gerard Hennessey, Mar. 10, 1963; children: Brian, Kate. BA, Stanford U., 1957; HSA, U. Toronto, Ont., Can., 1968; PhD, U. Lancaster, Eng., 1982. Asst. dir. European sales U. Soc., Heidelberg, Germany, 1959—61; landman's asst. Union Oil Co. Calif., Anchorage, 1962; sys. analyst No. Telephones, New Liskeard, Canada, 1962—63; adminstr. group pension Mfgs. Life Ins., Toronto, 1963—65; instr. office sys. Adult Edn. Ctr., Toronto, 1965—68; lectr. office sys. Salford Coll. Tech., Lancashire, England, 1968—70; sr. lectr. data processing Manchester Met. U., England, 1970—79; lectr. computation U. Manchester Inst. Sci. and Tech., 1979—82; assoc. prof. computer sci. Tex. Tech. U., Lubbock, 1982—86, assoc. prof. info. sys., 1987—94, prof. info. sys., 1994—2001; pres., CEO ISOA Inc., 1994—2002; dir. Internat. Ctr. Informatics Rsch., 1996—2000; v.p., gen. mgr. YMG/Rudolph Tech. Inc., 2002—03; pres., CEO Internat. Ctr. Informatics Rsch. Inc., Colleyville, Tex., 2002—09; mng. dir. Konsult Europe Ltd./ICIR, 2002—09; pres. Hennessey Mgmt. LLC, 2002—. Dir. Inst. for Studies of Orgn. Automation/Tex. Tech. U., Lubbock, 1987-95; vis. instr. Fed. Law Enforcement Tng. Ctr., Glynco, Ga., 1984-88; adj. prof. West Tex. A&M U., Canyon, 1994-95, U. Alaska, Anchorage, 1995, U. Tex., Dallas, 1995-98; mem. NATO panel of experts on visualization of massive data sets, 1996-98; election judge Tarrant County, Tex., 2010. Author: Computer Applications Project, 1982; contbg. author: Semiconductor International, 1998, 2002; editor (procs.) Office Document Architecture Internat. Symposium, English version, 1991; contbr. articles to profl. jours. Organizer Explorer Scouts Computer Applications, Lubbock, 1983-85; treas. Tivoli Wines LLC, 2006—. Recipient various awards, Tex. Instruments, 1982—86, 1994, Xerox Corp., 1985, Halliburton, 1986, Sys. Exploration, 1987, State of Tex., 1988—93, 1996—99, Knowledge-based Image Analysis award, USN Tencap, 1991—96, Immunization Tracking Sys. award, Robert Wood Johnson Found., 1993, Sematech S77 award, 1994, award, Leica GmbH, 1994—2001. Mem.: IEEE (contbg. author Systems Man Cybernetics 1984), Assn. Info. Tech. Profls. (chpt. pres. 1989, Disting. Info Sci. award 1992), Assn. Computing Machinery, Soc. Mfg. Engrs., Spl. Interest Group for Artificial Intelligence (JEDEC working group ISO semiconductor defect data stds. 1999—2002), Sigma Xi Rsch. Soc. (chpt. pres. 1996—97). Achievements include 18 patents in field. Office: 1205 Hall Johnson Rd #9 Colleyville TX 76034 Office Phone: 817-479-0565. Personal E-mail: akhennessey@aol.com.

HENNESSY, DANIEL KRAFT, lawyer; b. Summit, NJ, Jan. 4, 1941; s. Robert Emmett and Agnes Lyons (Lindle) H.; m. Susan Elizabeth (Bettina) Ware, June 17, 1972; children— Mary Elise, Daniel Joseph, Michael Ware, Catherine Anne. BS with highest honors, U.S. Naval Acad., 1963; JD cum laude, Harvard U., 1970. Bar: Tex. 1970. Ptnr. Hughes & Luce (formerly Hughes & Hill), Dallas, 1973—2006, Garfield Traub Devel. LLC, 2007—, gen. counsel prin., 2007—. Bd. regents Ave Maria U., 2005—06. Editor: Harvard Law Rev, 1969-70. Mem. bd. advisers Jesuit Coll. Prep. Sch., Dallas, 1975-88; bd. dirs. Dallas-North Tex. region NCCJ, 1976-83, Catholics United for Faith, Inc., 1982-99, Greater Dallas Right to Life Ednl. Found., 1974-86, The Highlands Sch., 1986—, Cath. Pro-life Com. of North Tex., 2001—, Legatus Internat., Dallas chpt., 2003-12; chmn. bd. visitors Coll. St. John Fisher & Thomas More, 2006-12; mem. bd. dirs. Birth Choice Dallas, 2011-. Lt. USN, 1963—67, Vietnam. Decorated knight grand cross Equestrian Order of Holy Sepulchre of Jerusalem, Knight of Malta, Knight Constantinian Order of St. George. Mem. Dallas Bar Assn., State Bar of Tex., KC. Roman Catholic. Home: 4405 Beverly Dr Dallas TX 75205-3001 Office Phone: 972-716-3848. Personal E-mail: hennesdk@yahoo.com.

HENNESY, GERALD CRAFT, artist; b. Washington, June 11, 1921; s. Gerald Craft and Frances Lee (Moore) H.; m. Elizabeth Ann Lovering, Mar. 4, 1950; children: Kathleen, Paul, Brian, Shawn, Hugh, Craig. Student, Corcoran Sch. Art, 1939, George Washington U., 1940; BS, U. Md., 1948. Enlisted U.S. Navy, 1942, advanced through grades to comdr., 1956; mgmt. analyst U.S. Air Force Hdqrs., Pentagon, Washington, 1948-52, 53-56; asst dir. for orgn. and mgmt. AEC, 1956-72; artist, dir. Studio of Hennesy, Clifton, Va., 1972—. One man shows include PLA Gallery, McLean, Va., 1967, Tolley Galleries, Washington, 1983, Venable Neslage Galleries, Washington, 1993, Marin-Price Galleries, Chevy Chase Md., 1995-96, 98, 2000, 02, 04, 07, 09, 10, 11, 12, 13, Prince Royal Gallery, Alexandria, Va., 1999, 2003, 05, Byrne Gallery, Middleburg, Va., 2009, 10, 11, 12, 13; exhibited works at Corcoran Gallery Art, Washington, 1957, 59, 67, Smithsonian Inst., Washington, 1962, 64, Allied Artists of Am., N.Y.C., 1974, 75; represented in permanent collections at U.S. Ho. of Reps., Washington, Md. State Exec. Mansion, Annapolis, Nat. Hdqrs. Am. Legion, Washington, Nat. Hdqrs. DAR, Washington, Hdqrs. FDIC, Washington, others. Decorated Air medal with one star. Republican. Home and Office: 6811 White Rock Rd Clifton VA 20124-1434

HENNIGAN, ROB, professional sports team executive; b. Worcester, Mass. s. Bob and Lynn Hennigan; married. B in Broadcast Journalism, Emerson Coll., Boston, 2004. Intern San Antonio Spurs, 2004—05, basketball ops. asst., 2005—07, dir. basketball ops., 2007—08; dir. coll. & internat. player devel. Oklahoma City Thunder, 2008—10, asst. gen. mgr. player pers., 2010—12; gen. mgr. Orlando Magic, 2012—. Office: Orlando Magic 400 W Church St # 250 Orlando FL 32801-2515

HENNIGHAUSEN, NED, consumer products company executive; BS in Biology, High Point U. Sr. v.p., ops. & supply chain ConAgra Foods, 1997—2002; exec. v.p., production ops. Lorillard Tobacco Co. Office: Lorillard Tobacco Co 714 Green Valley Rd Greensboro NC 27408 Office Phone: 336-335-7000. Office Fax: 336-335-7414. Business E-Mail: nhennighausen@lortobco.com.

HENRICH, SARAH E., museum director; BA in Art History, Muhlenberg Coll., Allentown, Pa.; MFA in Museology, Syracuse U., NY, 1982. Acting dir. Rockwood Mus., Wilmington, Del., 1979—80; collections/edn. curator Hist. Speedwell, Morristown, NJ, 1982—84, dir., 1986—96; collections curator Fort Dix Mus., NJ, 1984—86; exec. dir. Hist. Soc. of Rockland County, New City, NY, 1996—2001, Mus. of Am. Quilter's Soc., Paducah, Ky., 2001—03, Headley-Whitney Mus. of Decorative Art, Lexington, Ky., 2005—; dir. Murray State U. Galleries, Ky., 2004—05. Mus. cert. insp. Ctr. for Mil. History, US Dept. Def., 1984—; cons. HH Cultural Resources & Consortium, 2003—; asst. prof. art Murray State U., 2004—05. Trustee Hist. Morris Visitors Ctr., 1990—95, pres., 1994—95. Mem.: NJ Assn. Mus. (trustee 1987—90), Northern NJ Mus. Roundtable (co-founder 1986), NJ Hist. Commn. (pub. programs advisor 1993—96, grant reviewer 1994—99), Ky. Hist. Consortium (trustee 2002—), Paducah Rotary, Lexington Rotary Club. Office: Headley-Whitney Mus 4435 Old Frankfort Pike Lexington KY 40510 Office Phone: 859-255-6653. Office Fax: 859-255-8375. Business E-Mail: seh@headley-whitney.org.

HENRIQUES, GEORGE L., medical products executive, information technology executive; Chief info. officer Webster Vet. Supply, Inc., 2000—06; pres., Webster Vet. Supply Patterson Companies, Inc., 2006—. Bd. dirs. Am. Vet. Distbrs. Assn. Mem.: Am. Vet. distbrs. Assn. (assoc.). Office: Webster Veterinary Supply Inc 3867 Pine Ln Bessemer AL 35022 also: Patterson Companies Inc 1031 Mendota Heights Rd Saint Paul MN 55120 Office Phone: 651-686-1600. Office Fax: 651-686-9331. Business E-Mail: george.henriques@pattersoncompanies.com.

HENRY, CAMERON, state legislator; BS in Polit. Sci., La. State U.; MBA in Fin., Tulane U. Former legis. aide State Rep. Steve Scalise; former bd. mem. Jefferson Parish Sch.; adjunct prof. Delgado's Coll. of Bus. and Tech.; bus. analyst Bearing Point Inc.; mem. Dist. 82 La. House of Reps., 2008—, mem. house & govtl. affairs com., labor & indsl. rels. com., ways & means com., joint legis. com. on capital outlay, spl. com. on mil. & vets. affairs. Republican. Office: 201 Evans Rd Ste 101 New Orleans LA 70123 also: Capitol Office PO Box 44486 Baton Rouge LA 70804 Office Phone: 504-736-7135, 225-342-6945. Office Fax: 504-736-7137. E-mail: henryc@legis.state.la.us.

HENRY, CHARLES L., manufacturing executive; b. Chattanooga, 1941; m. Kay Henry; 4 children. BS in Engring. Physics, U. Tenn., 1963. Process engr. E. I. du Pont de Nemours and Co., 1963, various positions, 1963—84, v.p. Wilmington, Del., 1984—86, group v.p., 1986—93, exec. v.p., CFO, 1993—96; chmn., pres., CEO Johns Manville Corp., Denver, 1996—2004. Bd. dirs. Lennox Internat. Inc., 2000—, Ga. Gulf Corp., 2003—09. Office: Lennox International Inc Bd Directors 2140 Lake Park Blvd Richardson TX 75080 Office Phone: 972-497-5000. Office Fax: 972-497-5292. Business E-Mail: henry.charles@lennoxintl.com.

HENRY, FRANCIS J., JR., management consultant; BS in Quantitative Methods, U. Va.; MBA in Fin. & Investments, George Washington U. Joined Booz Allen Hamilton Holding Corp., 1977; v.p. ASE Inc. (subs. Booz Allen Hamilton Holding Corp.); former bd. dirs. Booz Allen Hamilton Holding Corp., chmn., Employee Capital Accumulation Plan, exec. v.p., 2009—. Former bd. dirs. Panthea Strategic Leadership Advisors. Mem., Nat. Coun. of Smithsonian Nat. Mus. of the Am. Indian. Office: Booz Allen Hamilton Holding Corp 8283 Greensboro Dr Mc Lean VA 22102 Office Phone: 703-902-5000. Office Fax: 703-902-3333. Business E-Mail: francis_henry@bah.com.

HENRY, G. WILLIAM, pediatrician; b. 1951; MD, Ind. Univ., 1977. Cert. Am. Bd. Pediatrics, 1982, in pediatric cardiology Am. Bd. Pediatrics, 1985. Intern in pediatrics Ind. Univ., Indpls., 1977—78, resident in pediatrics, 1978—79; fellowship in pediatric cardiology

Univ. NC, Chapel Hill, 1979—82, prod. of pediatrics, chief of pediatric cardiology div., dir. Children's Heart Ctr. Office: UNC Sch Med 5160Q Bioinformatics Bldg 130 Mason Farm Rd Chapel Hill NC 27599-7220 Office Phone: 919-966-4601. Office Fax: 919-966-6894.

HENRY, JANICE K., corporate board member, retired construction materials company executive; b. 1951; BS, Columbia Union Coll.; MBA, George Washington U. Various financial mgmt. positions Martin Marietta Corp., 1974-94; v.p., CFO Martin Marietta Materials, Inc., 1994—96, v.p., treas., CFO, 1996—98, sr. v.p., treas., CFO, 1998—2000, sr. v.p., CFO, 2000—05, sr. v.p., 2005—06. Bd. dirs. Inco Ltd., 2004—06, North American Galvanizing & Coatings, Inc., 2008—, Cliffs Natural Resources Inc., 2009—, W.R. Grace & Co., 2012—. Trustee Peace Coll., Raleigh.

HENRY, KATHLEEN MARIE, international marketing consultant; b. Stillwater, Okla., Sept. 24, 1950; d. Irl Wayne and Hulda Mary Henry. BS, U. Ctrl. Okla., Edmond, 1972. Community relations dir./account exec. Lowe Runkle Advt., Oklahoma City, 1972-74, account coordinator, 1975; sales promotion cons. McDonald's Corp., Houston, 1974, regional advt. supr. Southfield, Mich., 1975, regional advt. mgr., 1976-78, nat. local store mktg. mgr. Oak Brook, Ill., 1978-80, staff dir., nat. store mktg./sales promotion, 1980-82, home office dir. nat. store mktg./sales promotion, 1982-83, dir. nat. sales promotion, 1983-84, internat. mktg. dir., 1984-85; mktg. dir. McDonald's System France, 1985-86, McDonald's System Europe, 1985-88, v.p. mktg., 1988-97; pres. Henry Jamieson Assocs., Tulsa, Okla., 1997—; pres., COO Zepper Entertainment, Tulsa, 2004—07. Publicity chmn. Keep Okla. Beautiful, 1973-74; publicity chmn. Muscular Dystrophy Assn. Am., Okla. chpt., 1973-74; bd. dirs. Southfield Arts Coun., Mich., 1976-78; commr. Lake Keystone Planning and Zoning Commn., 1999—2007; bd. dirs. Perry H.S. Alumni Assn., 1999—; bd. dirs. sec. Keystone Peninsula Property Owners Assn., 1998—2010; commr. State of Okla. Film and Music Commn., 2005—11; bd. dir. Tulsa Symphony Orch., 2007—; branding com. chmn., strategic planning com. chmn. exec. com. Recipient Chgo. YWCA Leadership award, 1978, Disting. Former Student award U. Ctrl. Okla., 1979, Bronco award U. Ctrl. Okla. Centennial, 1991; named Outstanding Sr. Woman U. Ctrl. Okla., 1972, Outstanding Greek Woman, 1972. Mem. U. Ctrl. Okla. Alumni Assn. (dir. 1974, 1998-2002, found. bd. dirs. 1999—), U. Ctrl. Okla. Centennial Commn., Sigma Kappa. Office: 754 S Norfolk Ave Tulsa OK 74120

HENRY, LAURIN LUTHER, public affairs educator; b. Kankakee, Ill., May 23, 1921; s. Laurimer Luther and Jeanette Belle (Wagner) H.; m. Kathleen Jane Stephan, May 18, 1946; children— Stephanie Jane, Robin Leigh. BA, DePauw U., 1942; MA, U. Chgo., 1948, PhD, 1960. Staff asst. Public Adminstrn. Clearing House, Chgo. and Washington, 1950-55; research asso., sr. staff mem. Brookings Instn., Washington, 1955-64; prof. govt. and fgn. affairs U. Va., 1964-78; dean Sch. Community and Public Affairs, Va. Commonwealth U., Richmond, 1978-86, prof., 1986-87, prof. emeritus, 1987—. Guest scholar U. Va., 1988-95; vis. prof. Johns Hopkins U.; cons. to govt. Author: Presidential Transitions, 1960, The NASA-University Memorandum of Understanding, 1967; co-author: Presidential Election and Transition of 1960-61, 1961; contbr. articles profl. publns. Served with USNR, 1942-46. Recipient L.D. White prize Am. Polit. Sci. Assn., 1961. Fellow Nat. Acad. Pub. Adminstrn. (sr.), Nat. Assn. Schs. Public Affairs and Adminstrn. (pres. 1971-72), Am. Soc. Pub. Adminstrn., Phi Beta Kappa, Phi Kappa Phi. Home: 500 Crestwood Dr Apt 1204 Charlottesville VA 22903-4853

HENRY, MICHAEL, retail executive; Attended, Georgetown U., 1976; MBA in Mktg., Columbia U., 1982. Exec. dir., YSL mktg. YSL Beauty, 1995—99, Sanofi Beauty, 1996—99; v.p., promotional mktg. Lancome, 1999—2002; sr. v.p., beauty merchandising HSN, Inc., 2002—. Office: Home Shopping Network Inc 1 HSN Dr Saint Petersburg FL 33729 Office Phone: 727-872-1000. Office Fax: 727-872-6615. Business E-Mail: michael.henry@hsn.net.

HENRY, MITCH, health products executive; B in Computer Sci., Ctrl. Mo. State U.; MBA, U. Mo. With Kans. U. Med. Ctr., Deloitte & Touche Consulting, Trans World Airlines, Panhandle Ea. Pipeline, Kansas City, Mo.; sr. dir., info. tech. Hoechst Marion Pharm., Switzerland; info. officer Eli Lilly & Co., London; CIO PCS Health Sys., Phoenix, 1997—2000; sr. v.p., CIO AdvancePCS (formerly PCS Health Sys. and Advance Paradigm), 2000—. Office: AdvancePCS Inc 750 W John Carpenter Fwy Ste 1200 Irving TX 75039 Office Phone: 469-524-4700. Office Fax: 469-524-4702.

HENRY, NICHOLAS LLEWELLYN, retired public administration educator; b. Seattle, May 22, 1943; s. Samuel Houston and Ann (Connor) H.; m. Muriel Bunney; children: Adrienne Richardson, Miles Houston. BA, Centre Coll. Ky., 1965; MA, Pa. State U., 1967; MPA, Ind. U., 1970, PhD, 1971. Asst. to dean Coll. Arts and Scis.; instr. Ind. State U., 1967-69; vis. asst. prof. U. N.Mex., 1971-72; asst. prof. polit. sci. U. Ga., 1972-75, assoc. prof., 1975-78, prof., 1978-87, dir. Ctr. Pub. Affairs, 1975-80, dean Coll. Pub. Programs, 1980-87; prof., pres. Ga. So. U., Statesboro, 1987-98, prof. polit. sci., 1998—2009. Author or editor 12 books; contbr. numerous articles to profl. jours. Recipient Author of Yr. award Assn. Sci. Jours., Laverne Burchfield award ASPA, 2002; named One of 100 Most Influential People in Ga., Ga. Trend, 1994. Fellow Nat. Acad. Pub. Adminstrn.; mem. Cosmos Club (Washington). Office: Ga So U PO Box 8009 Statesboro GA 30460-1000 Business E-Mail: nic_henry@georgiasouthern.edu.

HENRY, RONALD JAMES WHYTE, academic administrator, physicist, educator; b. Belfast, No. Ireland, Feb. 5, 1940; came to U.S., 1965; s. William James Louis and Mary Ann (Whyte) H.; children: Norah Lynn, Andrea Marie. BSc, Queen's U., Belfast, 1961, PhD, 1964. Asst. lectr. Queen's U., 1964-65; rsch. assoc. Goddard Space Flight Ctr., Greenbelt, Md., 1965-66; asst. physicist Kitt Peak Nat. Obs., Tucson, 1966-69; assoc. prof. La. State U., Baton Rouge, 1969-73, prof., 1973-89, chmn. dept. physics and astronomy, 1976-82, dean basic scis., 1982-89; sr. v.p. acad. affairs Auburn (Ala.) U., 1989-91; provost, exec. v.p. for acad. affairs Miami U., Oxford, Ohio, 1991-94; provost, v.p. acad. affairs Ga. State U., Atlanta, 1994—. Com. on undergrad. sci. edn. Nat. Rsch. Coun., 1998-2004; bd. trustees CAEL, 2005-. Fellow Am. Physics Soc. Republican. Avocation: golf. Office: Ga State U Atlanta GA 30302-3999 Office Phone: 404-413-2574. E-mail: rhenry@gsu.edu.

HENRY, SHIRLEY ANN, legislative audit manager; d. Woodrow Wilson and Maymie Katherine Smith; m. Herman Gregg Henry, Jan. 19, 1980. BS summa cum laude, Western Ky. U., 1976; grad., Tenn. Govt. Exec. Inst., 1996. CPA Tenn., 1981, CGFM, 1995. Jr. legis. auditor Divsn. State Audit, Nashville, 1977, sr. legis. auditor, 1977-80, legis. audit mgr., 1980—. Active United Meth. Women, asst. leader, comm. coord., v.p., treas., 1992-2003; treas. Old Hickory (Tenn.) United Meth. Ch., 1995-2003; tutor Dupont Hadley Mid Sch., Old Hickory, 1993-95, Vol. Literacy, Nashville, 1996-99; vol. auditor Christian Cmty. Outreach Ctr., Old Hickory, 1992-95, vol., 2001-2003; bd. dirs. Nashville Adult Literacy Coun., 1999-2001. Mem. AICPA, Assn. Govt. Accts. (awards com., newsletter chair, membership com, sec., pres.-elect), Nashville Chpt. Assn. Govt. Accountants (sec., 2009-10, pres.-elect, 2010-). Avocations: reading, antiques, cross stitch. Office: Comptroller Treasury Divsn State Audit James K Polk Bldg Ste 1500 Nashville TN 37243-1402 Home Phone: 615-338-4043; Office Phone: 615-401-7897. Business E-Mail: shirley.henry@tn.gov.

HENRY, VIC HOUSTON, lawyer; b. Big Spring, Tex., 1958; s. Don Vernor and Patricia Jean H.; m. Candace Lee McComb, Dec. 27, 1980; children: Taylor McComb, Lee Houston. BA with highest honors, U. Tex., Austin, 1980; JD cum laude, Georgetown U., Washington, 1983. Bar: Tex. 1983, U.S. Ct. Appeals (5th, 8th, 10th and D.C. cirs.) 1985, U.S. Ct. Appeals (fed. cir.) 1987, U.S. Dist. Ct. (no. dist.) Tex. 1983, U.S. Dist. Ct. (ea. and we. dists.) Tex. 1985, U.S. Dist. Ct. (ea. and we. dists.) Okla. 1985, U.S. Dist. Ct. (ea. and we. dists.) Ark. 1985, U.S. Dist. Ct. (no. dist.) Ala. 1985, U.S. Claims Ct. 1986, U.S. Supreme Ct. 1985, Okla. 2008. Law clk. to presiding justice U.S. Dist. Ct., Dallas, 1983—84; assoc. Storey Armstrong Steger & Martin, Dallas, 1984—88, ptnr., 1989—97, Henry Oddo Austin & Fletcher, P.C., Dallas, 1997—. Mem. adv. group Civil Justice Reform, U.S. Dist. Ct. (no. dist.) Tex., 1990; speaker seminars including Am. Corp. Counsel Assn., 1987, Notre Dame U. Sch. of Law, 2000-02, Georgetown U. Law Ctr., 2001. Adminstrv. asst. Tex. Senate, Austin, 1976-78, Tex. Ho. of Reps., Austin, 1979-80, U.S. Ho. of Reps., Washington, 1980-82; chmn. deacons Gaston Ave. Baptist Ch., Dallas, 1988, 2002-04; bd. dirs. United Cerebral Palsy of Dallas, 2004-. Mem. ABA, Tex. State Bar, Conf. Freight Counsel, Transp. Lawyers Assn., Dallas Inn Ct. (barrister 1988-91). Avocations: travel, fly fishing, golf, kayaking. Office: Henry Oddo Austin & Fletcher PC 1700 Pacific Ave Ste 2700 Dallas TX 75201-7353 Office Phone: 214-658-1900.

HENRY, WILLIAM ED, state legislator; b. Hartselle, Ala., July 30, 1970; m. Wendi Henry; 2 children. BS in Radiol. Sciences, Mid-Western State U., Tex., 2006. Med. sales rep GE Med. Divsn., 1997—2002; dir. radiology Woodland Med. Ctr., 2000—02; CT technologist Decatur Gen. Hosp., 2002—07; cardiac CT specialist The Heart Ctr., 2007—; mem. Dist. 9 Ala. House of Representatives, 2011—. Radiol. technologist USAF, 1993—97. Republican. Office: 2128 6th Ave SE Ste 504 Decatur AL 35601 also: Ala House of Reps Rm 524-A 11 S Union St Montgomery AL 36130 Office Phone: 256-260-2146, 334-242-7736.

HENSARLING, JEB, United States Representative from Texas; b. Stephenville, Tex., May 29, 1957; m. Melissa Fore; children: Claire, Travis. BA in Economics, magna cum laude, Tex. A&M U., 1979; JD, U. Tex., Austin, 1982. State dir. to Rep. Phil Gramm US House of Representatives, 1985—89; atty. Oppenheimer, Harrison, Blend & Tate, San Antonio; owner, prin. F-H & Assocs., Dallas; v.p. Maverick Capital, Dallas, 1993—96; owner San Jacinto Ventures, 1996—99; v.p. Green Mountain Energy, Austin, 1999—2001; CEO Family Support Assurance Corp., Dallas, 2001—02; mem. US Congress from 5th Tex. Dist., Washington, 2003—; chmn. US House Republican Conf., Washington, 2011—13, US House Financial Services Com., Washington, 2013—; co-chair Joint Select Com. on Deficit Reduction, Washington, 2011. Exec. dir. Nat. Republican Senatorial Com. (NRSC), 1991—93; chmn. Republican Study Com., 2007—09. Mem. adv. bd. Children's Edn. Fund; bd. dirs. American Cancer Soc.-Dallas Metro Area, Tex. Pub. Policy Found. Recipient True Blue award, Family Rsch. Coun., Spirit of Enterprise award, Small Bus. Adv. award, Hero of the Taxpayer award, Fighter for Free Enterprise award. Republican. Episcopalian. Office: US House of Representatives 2228 Rayburn House Office Bldg Washington DC 20515 Office Phone: 202-225-3484.*

HENSCHEL, DONALD FRANCIS, JR., theater educator, artist, designer; b. Princeton, Minn., July 31, 1945; s. Donald Francis and Mary Elizabeth Henschel; children: Donald Francis III, Erin Rosemary. BA, Dickinson State U., ND, 1968; MA, Colo. State U., Ft. Collins, 1970. Cert. Illuminating Engring. Soc. N.Am., 1986. Prof. theatre design Midwestern State U., Wichita Falls, Tex., 1970—, chmn. speech & theatre, 1981—83. Theatre, dramas, comedies, operas, musicals, (Faculty Mem. of Yr., 2008). Dir. Greater Wichita Falls Alliance Performong Arts, 1998—2001. Recipient Hardin Scholar, Hardin Found. MSU, 1983, Scenic Design award, AMOCO. Fellow: US Inst. Theatre Tech.- SW (pres., sec., treas. 1990—2004, Founder's award 2000). Liberal. Avocations: travel, camping, sailing, flying. Home: 4801 Augusta Ln Wichita Falls TX 76302 Office: Midwestern State Univ 3410 Taft Wichita Falls TX 76308 Office Fax: 940-397-4909. Business E-Mail: don.henschel@mwsu.edu.

HENSGENS, BOB, state legislator; BBA, U. Southwestern La. Nursing home adminstrn.; mayor Twp. of Gueydan, La., 2007—11; mem. Dist. 47 La. House of Reps., Baton Rogue, 2012—. Republican. Roman Catholic. Office: 407 Charity St Abbeville LA 70510 also: La House of Reps 900 N 3rd St Baton Rouge LA 70804 Office Phone: 337-893-5035. Business E-Mail: hensgensb@legis.la.gov.

HENSHAW, JOHN LESTER, consulting firm executive, former federal agency administrator; b. Aug. 27, 1949; m. Jane Henshaw; 4 children. BS in Biology, Appalachian State U., 1971; student, U. Del., 1971—72; MPH in Environ. Health Adminstrn. & Industrial Health, U. Mich., 1974. Landscape engr., 1971—72; with Dept. Health & Social Svc. State of Del., 1972—73; indsl. hygienist Monsanto Co., St. Louis, 1975—77, indsl. hygiene specialist, 1977—81, mgr., corp. indsl. hygiene, 1981—85, corp. dir., quality & compliance assurance, environment, safety & health, 1991—97, corp. dir. quality and compliance assurance, corp. stewardship environ. safety & health, 1995—97, corp. indsl. hygiene dir., safety & environ. health, 1985—91; dir. environ., safety & health Solutia, Inc., St. Louis, 1997—2000, Astaris, LLC, St. Louis, 2000—01; sr. adv. to sec. US Dept. Labor, Washington, 2001, asst. sec. Occupational Safety & Health Adminstrn. (OSHA), 2001—04; pres. Henshaw & Associates, Inc., Sanibel, Fla., 2005—. Served in Air Nat. Guard, 1984—2000. Recipient Kusnetz award, Am. Indsl. Hygiene Assn., 1988, Disting. svc. award, 1999, Disting. Alumnus award, U. Mich., 2002, Pres. award, Am. Soc. Safety Engineers, 2004, Disting. Alumni Svc. award, U. Mich., 2004. Home: Henshaw & Associates Inc 461 Lighthouse Way Sanibel FL 33957 Personal E-mail: john.henshaw@comcast.net.

HENSINGER, MARGARET ELIZABETH, real estate broker, associate, horticultural and agricultural advertising and marketing executive; b. Jackson, Mich., Aug. 31, 1950; d. John Kenneth and Inez Estelle (McVay) H.; m. William C. Pixley, Apr. 26, 1985; children: William Christopher, Patrick Edward. BS, Eastern Mich. U., 1973. Lic. realtor-broker, Fla. Salesperson Hunter Pub. Co., Winston-Salem, N.C., 1974-76, Josten's-Am., Topeka, 1976-77; editorial asst. Mich. Dept. Agriculture, Lansing, 1977-80, U. Fla., Apopka, 1981-82; pres. Country Carousel, Inc., Mt. Dora, Fla., 1983—2010; editor, pres. Green Pages Ltd., Mt. Dora, 1984-88; owner, pres. Sunbelt Mktg. Services, Inc., Mt. Dora, 1982-99; pub. Fax-It-Green The Hort Fax Directory, 1987-98; pres., treas. Duragreen Mktg. USA, Inc., Mt. Dora, 1990-99; broker owner Coldwell Banker All Stars Realty, Mt. Dora, Daytona Beach Shores, Ponce Inlet, 2003—10; broker assoc. ERA Tom Grizzard Inc. Mt. Dora, Fla., 2010—; co-owner Bithlo & Waldo Motocross Tracks, 2003—, Orlando, Fla., Waldo. Comptr. Adventure Yacht Harbor, Inc., Daytona Beach, Fla., 1999-2005; mem. 5th dist. com. for unlicensed practice of law Fla. Supreme Ct., 2001-2004, mem. Fifth Cir. Judicial Grievance Com., 2010-13. Mem. Leadership Am., Fairfax, Va., 1990; pres. Our Turning Point Ranch, Inc., 2009-. Mem. Nat. Assn. Women in Horticulture (v.p., past pres., organizer), Am. Soc. of Advt. Promotion, Mt. Dora C. of C. (exec. bd., bd. dirs., sec. 1988-89, v.p. 1989-95, pres. 1996), Golden Triangle Federated Rep. Women's Network (pres. 1995-96, 2003-2004, 2013, bd. dirs.), Ice House Theatre (Mt. Dora, Fla.). Republican. Avocations: reading, travel, gardening, motorcross. Office: ERA Tom Grizzard Inc 600 N Donnelly St Mount Dora FL 32757 Office Phone: 352-735-4433.

HENSLEY, JOSEPH (JOEY HENSLEY), state legislator; b. July 28; married. State rep. Dist. 70, Tenn., 2003—; Republican caucus treas.; house rep. Tenn.; mem. Health & Human Resources Com., State & Local Govt. Com.; former chmn. Lewis County Sch. Bd.; commr. Lewis County, med. examiner; vice chmn. Lewis County Health Coun.; res. St Francis Hosp., Memphis, 1983—86; Staff Lewis Comm Hosp. Fellow: Am. Acad. Family Physicians; mem.: AMA, Tenn. Acad. Family Physicians, Lewis County Youth Coun., Lewis County Edn. Found., Lewis County C Of C. Republican. Presbyterian. Office: 106 War Memorial Bldg Nashville TN 37243-0170 also: 855 Summertown Hwy Hohenwald TN 38462 Office Phone: 615-741-7476. Business E-Mail: rep.joey.hensley@capitol.tn.gov.

HENSON, ANNA MIRIAM, retired otolaryngologist, retired medical educator; b. Springfield, Mo., Nov. 7, 1935; d. Bert Emerson and Esther Miriam (Crank) Morgan; m. O'Dell Williams Henson, Aug. 1, 1964; children: Phillip, William. BA, Park Coll., Parkville, Mo., 1957; MA, Smith Coll., 1959; PhD, Yale U., 1967. Instr. Smith Coll., Northampton, Mass., 1960-61; rsch. assoc. Yale U., New Haven, 1967-74; instr. U. N.C., Chapel Hill, 1975-78, rsch. asst. prof., 1978-83, rsch. assoc. prof., 1983-86, prof. Sch. Medicine dept. otolaryngology, 1986—2001; ret., 2001. Mem. study sect. on hearing rsch. NIH, Bethesda, Md., 1990-93. Contbr. articles to profl. jours. Fulbright scholar, Australia, 1959-60; NIH grantee, 1975—2003. Mem. Assn. for Rsch. in Otolaryngology, Sigma Xi. E-mail: mmhenson@med.unc.edu.

HENSON, CHRISTOPHER L., bank executive; b. Boone, NC, June 17, 1961; BS, High Point U., NC. Mgmt. devel. prog. BB&T Corp. (Branch Banking and Trust Co.), 1985, city exec. Wilson and Greensboro, NC, pres. Hampton Roads region, pres. Atlanta region, pres. Ga. state, sr. exec. v.p., 2004—, CFO, 2005—. Bd. mem. Ga. C. of C., Atlanta C. of C., Hampton Roads C. of C., Atlanta Buckhead Coalition. Bd. mem. Hampton Roads YMCA, United Way South Hampton Roads, Old Dominion U. Intercollegiate Found., Va., Va. Marine Sci. Mus. Office: BB&T Corp Hdqs 200 W 2nd St Winston Salem NC 27101 Office Phone: 336-733-2000. Office Fax: 336-733-2470.

HENSON, MICHELE, state legislator; b. Boston, Mass., Aug. 29, 1946; m. Doug Henson. Former state rep. Dist. 55, Ga.; former state rep. Dist. 87 Ga., 2004—; state rep. Dist. 57 Ga., 1990—92; state rep. Dist. 65 Ga., 1993—2003; former sec. ins. com.; vice chmn.; mem. Health & Ecol., Intra-Govt. Coord. & Appropriations Com.; house rep. Ga.; adminstr. Metro Dental Svcs., 1985—. Democrat. Jewish. Mailing: 4140 Creek Stone Court Stone Mountain GA 30083-4202 Office: 401 CAP Atlanta GA 30334 Office Phone: 404-292-6165, 404-656-0254. Fax: 404-296-8685. E-mail: mhenson@legis.state.ga.us.

HENSON, O'DELL WILLIAMS, JR., retired anatomy educator; b. Kansas City, Mo., Jan. 11, 1934; s. O'Dell Williams and Natalie (Smith) H.; m. Miriam Morgan, Aug. 1, 1964; 1 child, Phillip William. BA, U. Kans., 1957, MA, 1960; PhD, Yale U., 1964. From instr. to assoc. prof. dept anatomy Yale U., New Haven, 1964-74; prof. dept cell biology and anatomy U. N.C., Chapel Hill, NC, 1974—2004, ret., 2004. Chmn. Commn. Anatomy, N.C., 1982-2003. Recipient Phi Sigma award 1960, Alexander Von Humbolt award 1982, Cen. Carolina Bank Excellence in Tchg. award 1982, NIH-Nat. Inst. Deafness and Other Communicative Disorders Claude Pepper award, 1989. Fellow AAAS. Home: 317 Reade Rd Chapel Hill NC 27516-1509 E-mail: owh@med.unc.edu.

HENSON, STEVE, state legislator; b. Indpls., Ind., Mar. 30, 1959; AB, Univ. Ga., 1981. Vocational tchr. & adminstr. Henson Training Inst.; mem. Dist. 55 Ga. State Senate, 1991—99, mem. Dist. 41, 2003—. Democrat. Episcopal. Office: 2643 Sterling Acres Dr Tucker GA 30084 Office Phone: 404-243-5127. Office Fax: 678-937-1672. Business E-Mail: steve.henson@senate.ga.gov.

HENTGES, DAVID JOHN, microbiology educator; b. LeMars, Iowa, Sept. 18, 1928; s. Romaine Francis and Geneva Mae (Kruger) Hentges; m. Kathleen Edwina Mullan, Dec. 28, 1957; children: Stephen Edward, Kathleen Marie, Margaret Ann. BS, U. Notre Dame, 1953; MS, Loyola U., Chgo., 1958, PhD, 1961. Asst. prof. Creighton U. Sch. Medicine, Omaha, 1964-67, assoc. prof., 1967-68, U. of Mo. Sch. of Medicine, Columbia, 1968-72, prof., 1972-81, interim chmn., 1976-79; prof., chmn. Tex. Tech. U. Sch. Medicine, Lubbock, 1981-96, vice provost for rsch., dean grad. sch. biomed. scis., 1996-98, assoc. dean basic scis., 1996-98, dean emeritus, 1998—. Editor: Human Intestinal Microflora, 1983, Medical Microbiology, 1986, Microbiology and Immunology, 2d edit., 1995; regional editor Microbial Ecology in Health and Disease, 1987-96; mem. editl. bd. Infection and Immunity, 1983-92, Anaerobe, 1998-2004; contbr. chpts. to books and articles to profl. jours. Lay gen. chmn. Diocesan Cath. Appeal, Lubbock, 1989, 1997; co-exec. dir. Cath. Found. Diocese of Lubbock, 1998—2002, treas. bd. dirs., 2008—. Decorated knight grand cross Order of the Holy Sepulchre, knight of merit with star Constantinian Order of St. George. Fellow Am. Acad. Microbiology (emeritus); mem. Cath. Acad. Scis., Soc. for Microbial Ecology and Disease (pres. 1987-89), Rotary Club, Sigma Xi. Roman Catholic. Avocations: gardening, fly fishing. Home: 4601 88th St Lubbock TX 79424-4107 Home Phone: 806-794-5529. Personal E-mail: djh18micro@hotmail.com.

HEPP, WALTER R., cardiac electrophysiologist; MD, Tufts U., 1984. Diplomate Am. Bd. Internal Medicine, 1987, Am. Bd. Internal Medicine-cardiovasc. disease, 1989, Am. Bd. Internal Medicine-clin. cardiac electrophysiology, 2004. Resident internal medicine New Eng. Deaconess Hosp., 1985—87; fellow cardiovasc. disease Univ. of Pa. Med. Ctr.- Presbyn., 1987—90; hosp. affiliation includes Sarasota Meml. Hosp. Office: Sarasota Memorial Hospital 1950 Arlington St Ste 400 Sarasota FL 34239 Office Phone: 941-917-4250.

HEPPNER, DONALD GRAY, JR., medical consultant; b. Lynchburg, Va., 1956; s. Donald Gray Sr. and Nathalie (Ward) H.; m. Mary Virginia Leach, June 12, 1983; children: Charlotte Nathalie, Virginia Dearing, William Lynch. BA in Biochemistry/German Lit., U. Va., 1978, MD, 1983. Diplomate Am. Bd. Internal Medicine, 1986, Am. Bd. Infectious Diseases, 1990, 2003, 13, Gen. Staff Coll, Ft. Leavenworth, Tex., 1993. Commd. capt. U.S. Army, 1987, advanced through grades to col., 2002; intern in internal medicine U. Minn. Hosps. and Clinics, Mpls., 1983-84, resident in internal medicine, 1984-86; rsch. assoc. Dight Lab., U. Minn., Mpls., 1987; with emergency medicine dept. Abbot North Western Hosp., Mpls., 1986-88; fellow infectious diseases U. Md., Balt., 1988-90; infectious disease officer Dept. Immunology, Walter Reed Army Inst. of Rsch., Washington, 1990-93; asst. chief dept. immunology Armed Forces Rsch. Inst. Med. Scis., Bangkok, 1993-94, chief dept. immunology and medicine, 1994-97; overseas malaria vaccine trial coord. dept. immunology Walter Reed Army Inst. Rsch., Forest Glen, Md., 1997-99, chief dept. immunology, 2001—06; dir. U.S. Army Malaria Vaccine Program, 2001—07, acting dir. divsn. communicable diseases and immunology, 2006, dir. divsn. of malaria vaccine devel., 2006—08; dep. comdr. Walter Reed Army Inst. Rsch., 2008—11; v.p. clin. devel. Crucell Biologics, Johnson & Johnson Co., Rockville, Md., 2011—12; sr. scientist TASC Inc., Lorton, Va., 2012—. Attending physician Walter Reed Army Med. Ctr., Washington, 1991-93, 2003-06; advisor NRC, 1995-97. Contbr. more than 102 articles to profl. jours. Mem. Com. on Fgn. Rels., Charlottesville, Va., 1983—. Decorated Order Mil. Med. Merit; recipient Legion of Merit, Kiwanis Internat. World Svc. medal, 2009, Vanguard award, TASC Inc., 2013, Johnson & Johnson Leadership award, 2011; named Alumnus of Yr., Va. Episcopal Sch., 2011; finalist Berry prize, Fed. Medicine, 2008. Fellow: ACP, Royal Asiatic Soc., Royal Geog. Soc., Am. Soc. Tropical Medicine and Hygiene; mem.: VFW (life), Coun. Fgn. Rels.(Wash.), Sons Revolution Va. Soc., Armed Forces Infectious Disease Soc. (life), Order of St. John (hospitaller 2009—13, officer 2010—, bd. gov. 2010—12, priory chpt. mem. 2012—, vice chancellor 2013—), Sons Am. Revolution Va. Soc., Soc. Colonial Wars State of Va., Aztec Club 1847, Soc. War 1812, U. Va. Alumni Assn. (life), Am. Legion, Mil. Order Fgn. Wars. Achievements include development and testing of malaria vaccines for military and public health benefit. Office: Heppner Associates LLC 9441 Brenner Ct Vienna VA 22180 E-mail: grayheppner@gmail.com.

HERBEL, VERN D., insurance company executive; Exec. v.p. United American Insurance Co., 2002—04, pres., 2004—07, exec. v.p., Globe and American Income, 2002—, CEO, 2004—; exec. v.p., chief adminstrv. officer Torchmark Corp., 2006—. Office: Torchmark Corp 3700 S Stonebridge Dr Mc Kinney TX 75070-8080 Office Phone: 972-569-4000. Office Fax: 972-569-3282. Business E-Mail: vherbel@torchmarkcorp.com.

HERBERT, JAMES ARTHUR, retired art educator, artist, filmmaker; b. Boston, Feb. 13, 1938; s. James Arthur and Bernice Frances (Burns) H. AB magna cum laude, Dartmouth Coll., 1960; M.F.A., U. Colo., 1962. Instr. U. Colo., 1962; artist-in-residence Yale Summer Sch. Art and Music, 1965; mem. faculty dept. art U. Ga., Athens, 1962—; fellow Guggenheim Found., 1971—72, 1989—90; prof. U. Ga., 1973—, rsch. prof., 1992—, disting. rsch. prof. art, 1999—2006, disting. rsch. prof. emeritus, 2006—. One-man shows include Babcock Galleries, NYC, 1967, U. Colo., Boulder, 1972, Poindexter Gallery, NYC, 1972, 1973, 1974, 1976, Mus. Modern Art, 1970, 1972, 1974, 1977, 1981, 1988, 1994, 1998, 1999, 2005, Walker Art Ctr., Mpls., 1973, 1982, Harvard U., 1973, High Mus. Art, Atlanta, 1979, Kennedy Ctr., Washington, 1981, Libr. of Congress, 1983—, Museu Tropical, Lisbon, Lisbon, Portugal, 1993, Art Gallery Toronto Can., 1994, Oberhausen Internat. Film Festival, Germany, 1999, Brit. Coun., Cologne, Germany, 1999, Film Mus. Munich, 1999, Atl. Contemporary Art Ctr., 2000, Mus. Modern Art, NYC, 2005, exhibited in group shows at Krannert Art Mus., Urbana, Ill., 1974, New Orleans Mus. Art, 1975, 1980, 1989, Whitney Mus. Am. Art, 1969, 1973, 1974, 1983, Westdeutsche Kurzfilmtage, Oberhausen, W. Ger., 1970, 1972, 1989, 1992, 2001, La Cinémathèque Royale de Belgique, Knokke-Heist, Belgium, 1974—75, Mus. Modern Art, NYC, 1979, P.S. 1, 1979, Stedelijk Mus., Amsterdam, 1982, Kennedy Ctr., Washington, 1983, Monique Knowlton Gallery, NYC, 1983, IRCAM, Pompidou Ctr., Beaubourg, France, 1984, Cinémateque Française, Beaubourg, 1985, Bibliotheque Nat., Avignon, France, 1985, Mus. Modern Art, NYC, 1986, 1991, LA County Mus. Art, 1988, Carnegie-Mellon U. Art Gallery, Pitts., 1988, Va. Mus. Fine Art, Richmond, Va., 1988, Southeastern Ctr. for Contemporary Art, Winston-Salem, N.C., 1988, Corcoran Gallery of Art, Washington, 1989, Kuznetsky Most Exhbn. Hall, Moscow, 1989, Art Gallery of Ont., 1989, Long Beach Mus. Art, Calif., 1989, 1991, Norton Galley Art, Palm Beach, 1989, Sheridan Opera House, Telluride, Colo., 1989, 1991, 1993, Mus. Fine Arts, Boston, 1990, Art Inst., Chgo., 1990, Pacific Film Archive, Berkeley, Calif., 1991, Walker Art Ctr., Mpls., 1991, Sundance Theatre, Park City, Utah, 1992, Melbourne Internat. Film Theatre, Australia, 1992, European Media Art Theatre, Osnabrück, Germany, 1992, Toronto Film Festival Theatre, Can., 1992, NY Film Festival at Lincoln Ctr., 1992, Inst. de Estadios Norteamericanos, Barcelona, Spain, 1992, Melbourne Internat. Film Mus., Australia, 1992, Eldorado Theatre, Royal Palace, Antwerp, Belgium, 1993, Odense Internat. Film Theater, Denmark, 1993, Fifth Media Festival Theatre, Hertogenbosch, The Netherlands, 1993, Vienna Shortfilm Mus., Antwerp (Belgium) Sinema festival Theatre, 1993, Rio Internat. Festival Hall, Rio de Janiero, Brazil, 1993, Sydney Internat. Film Mus., Australia, 1994, Vherskě Hradiště, Czech Republic, 1994, Kunstencentrum, Leuveen, Netherlands, Gaumont Marignan Theater, Paris, 1995, Toronto Internat. Film Festival, 1997, 1999, Sundance Film Festival Theater, Park City, Utah, 1998, 1999, Rotterdam Internat. Film Festival, The Netherlands, 1998, 1999, 2000, Edinburgh Internat. Film Festival, Scotland, 1999, Rio Internat. Film Festival, Brazil, 1999, Sao Paulo Internat. Film Festival, 1999, Film Theatre Brit. Coun., Cologne, Germany, 1999, Staatliche Galerie Moritzburg, Halle, Germany, 1999, Mus. Nat. Ctr. de Arte Reina Sofia, Madrid, Spain, Regensburger Kurzfilmwoche, Germany, 2003, Metropolis Kino Hamburg, 2003, Oberhausen Internat. Film Festival, 2004, London Film Festival, 2005, No. Ireland Internat. Film Festival, Belfast, 2006, Buenos Aires Internat. Festival of Ind. Cinema, 2006, The Era of New Horizons Internat. Film Festival, Wroctaw, Poland, 2006, Rotterdam Internat. Film Festival, 2007, O.K. Harris Gallery, NY, 2007, Represented in permanent collections NYU, Am. Fedn. Arts, Royal Film Archives Belgium, Centre Beaubourg, Paris, Mus. Modern Art, NYC, Whitney Mus. Am. Art, Cornell U., Am. Film Inst., Chase Manhattan Bank, Coca Cola USA, Herbert F. Johnson Mus. Art at Cornell U., Walker Art Ctr., Mpls., Anthology Film Archives, NYC; author: Stills: Photographs by James Herbert, 1992. Recipient Awards in the Visual Arts, Rockefeller Found., 1987; Woodrow Wilson fellow, 1960-62; grantee Am. Film Inst., 1969, Nat. Endowment Arts, 1975, 78, 81, 82, Louis Comfort Tiffany Found., 1980, Rockefeller Found., 1993; commn. Libr. of Congress, 1983, Adolph and Esther Gottlieb Found., 1991. Office: U Ga Sch Art Athens GA 30602

HERBKERSMAN, WILLIAM G. (BILL), state legislator; b. Bedford, Ohio, June 30, 1958; s. Donald and Kate Herbkersman; m. Mary Margaret Kinzer, Nov. 29, 1986; children: Shelby, Cole. Mem. Dist. 118 SC House of Reps., 2003—. Mem. Gov.'s Coun. Global Warming. Mem.: Bluffton YMCA (founding mem.). Republican. Mailing: 151 Gascoigne Bluff Bluffton SC 29910 Office: 308B Blatt Bldg Columbia SC 29201 Address: 896 May River Rd Bluffton SC 29910-5833 Home Phone: 843-757-5424; Office Phone: 803-734-3063, 843-757-7900. E-mail: Herbkersman@scstatehouse.net.

HERBST, ROBERT LEROY, organization executive; b. Mpls., Oct. 5, 1935; s. Walter Peter and Bernice Mickey (Mikkelson) H.; m. Evelyn Clarice Elford, Sept. 22, 1956; children— Eric Elford, Peter Robert, Amy Jo. BS in Forest Mgmt, U. Minn., St. Paul, 1957. Dep. commnr. Minn. Conservation Dept., 1966-69; nat. exec. dir. Izaak Walton League Am., 1969-70; commr. natural resources State of Minn., 1971-77; asst. sec. fish, wildlife and parks Dept. Interior, Washington, 1977-81, sec., Jan. 20-26, 1981; exec. dir. Trout Unltd., 1981-90; pres. Lake Superior Ctr., Washington, 1990-92, A-S5 Energy Co., Reno, Nev., 1997-98; Washington rep. TVA, Washington, 1992-96; CEO, chmn. bd. dirs. Global Environment & Tech. Found., Annandale, Va., 1996—. Instr. U. Minn., 1954; mem. adv. faculty N. Am. Sch. Conservation, 1969-77; chmn. Gt. Lakes Fisheries Commn., 1978-80, steering com. Nat. Fishing Week, 1991; mem. U.S. Commn. UNESCO, 1978-79, Pres. Carter's Interagency Coun., 1978-80; co-chmn. Nat. Adv. Coun. Environ. Edn., 1989, chmn., 1990-92; mem. U.S. bd. Environ. Ctr. for Ctrl. and Ea. Europe, 1997—, chmn. bd. dirs.; chmn. bd. dirs. Nat. Wildlife Refuge Assocs., 1998-2001. Author: Careers in Environment, 1973; contbr. articles to profl. jours. Mem. nat. bd. Boy Scouts Am., 1969—77; exec. bd. Viking Coun., 1975—76; bd. govs. African Inst. Econs. Edn. and Devel., 1980; pres. Nat. Watershed Protection Ctr., 1994; U.S. rep. Regional Environ. Ctr. for Ctrl. and Ea. Europe, chair bd. dirs.; chmn. bd. Nat. Reach Coun.; mem. Annandale United Meth. Ch., 1969—77. Recipient Nat. Svc. award Izaak Walton League Am., 1971; Silver Beaver award Boy Scouts Am., 1977; Disting. Svc. award U. Minn., 1969, 2003, Washington Acad. Sci. award, 2001, Outstanding Achievement award U. Minn., 2003; named Pub. Adminstr. of Yr. in Minn. Am. Soc. Pub. Adminstrn., 1976; named to Nat. Fresh Water Fishing Hall Fame, 2003, Wall-Outstanding Alumni, U. Minn., 2005. Mem. Natural Resource Coun. Am. (chmn. 1989-91, Honor award 1994), Land Between Lakes Assn.(chmn. 1982-91, trustee 1981-91). Democrat. Office: Global Environment Technol 2900 S Quincy St Ste 375 Arlington VA 22206-2279 Office Phone: 703-379-2713. Business E-Mail: bherbst@getf.org, bherbs@getf.org.

HERCULES, DAVID MICHAEL, chemistry professor, consultant; b. Somerset, Pa., Aug. 10, 1932; s. Michael George and Kathryn (Saylor) H.; m. Nancy Catherine Miller, Sept. 23, 1957 (div. 1968); 1 dau., Kimberly Ann; m. Shirley Ann Hoover, Dec. 14, 1970; children: Sherri Kathryn, Kevin Michael. BS, Juniata Coll., 1954; PhD, MIT, 1957. Asst. prof. Lehigh U., 1957-60; assoc. prof. Juniata Coll., Huntington, Pa., 1960-63; asst. prof. MIT, 1963-68, assoc. prof., 1968-69, U. Ga., Athens, 1969-74, prof., 1974-76; prof. dept. chemistry U. Pitts., 1976-94, chmn., 1980-89, Miles prof., 1990-94; chmn. dept. Vanderbilt U., Nashville, 1995—2003, Centennial prof., 1995—2007, Centennial prof. emeritus, 2007—. Mem. vis. com. for chemistry Lehigh U., 1980-84; vis. prof. Mich. State U., 1972; chmn. Gordon Research Conf. on Electron Spectroscopy, 1974, Gordon Research Conf. on Analytical Chemistry, 1966; co-chmn. Internat. Conf. Chemiluminescence, 1972; univ. rep. Council on Chem. Research, 1980-88; mem. program com. Pitts. Conf. on Analytical Chemistry and Applied Spectroscopy, 1977-94; mem. vis. scientist program NSF, 1964-76 Mem. editorial bds.: Applied Spectroscopy, 1963-65, Analytical Chemistry, 1964-67, Jour. Electron Spectroscopy, 1971-77, Environ. Analytical Chemistry, 1973—, Spectrochimica Acta, 1973-83, Talanta, 1974-80, Spectroscopy Letters, 1975—, The Scis., 1979-84, Trends in Analytical Chemistry, 1980-88, Jour. Trace and Microprobe Techniques, 1980-93, Fresenius Zeitschrift für Analytische Chemie, 1987-; patentee (in field). Recipient Benedetti-Pichler award Am. Microchem. Soc., 1987, Achievement in Analytical Chemistry award Ea. Analytical Symposium, 1988, prize Alexander von Humboldt Found., 1984, Disting. Alumnus award Juniata Coll., 1989, Pres.'s Disting. Rsch. award U. Pitts., 1990; John Simon Guggenheim Meml. fellow, 1973. Mem. Am. Chem. Soc. (Petroleum Research Fund adv. bd. 1978-80, chmn. div. analytical chemistry 1977-78, analytical chemistry award 1986, Arthur W. Adamson award disting. svc. in advancement of surface chemistry 1993, Pitts. sect. award 1997), Soc. Applied Spectroscopy (Lester W. Strock medal New Eng. sect. 1981, Pitts. Spectroscopy award 1996), Am. Vacuum Soc., Photoelectric Spectrometry Group, Pa. Acad. Scis., Spectroscopy Soc. Pitts. (award 1996), Soc. Analytical Chemists Pitts., Sigma Xi Home: 200 Olive Branch Rd Nashville TN 37205-3220 Office: Vanderbilt U Dept Chemistry Box 1822, Sta B Nashville TN 37235 Office Phone: 615-343-5230. Business E-Mail: david.m.hercules@vanderbilt.edu.

HERGENROEDER, ALBERT C., pediatrician, educator; BS, U. Pitts., 1976, MD, 1980. Diplomate Am. Bd. Pediatrics, 1993, Am. Bd. Pediatrics-sports medicine, 2004, Am. Bd. Pediatrics-adolescent medicine, 2009. Resident pediat. Duke Univ. Med. Ctr., Durham, 1981—83; fellow adolescent medicine Univ. Washington, Seattle, 1984—85; head of sports medicine sects. Baylor Coll. Med., head of adolescent medicine, prof. pediat.; chief young women's clinic Tex. Children's Hosp., chief sports medicine clinic, chief adolescent medicine svc. Fellow: Soc. for Adolescent Medicine, Am. Acad. of Pediat., Am. Coll. of Sports Medicine; mem.: Soc. for Pediatric Rsch., Am. Bd. of Pediat. Office: Texas Children's Hospital Clinical Care Center 11th Fl 6701 Fannin St CC 1710.00 Houston TX 77030 Office Phone: 832-822-4887.

HERLIHY, JAMES P., critical care specialist, educator; MD, Georgetown U., 1984. Diplomate Am. Bd. Internal Medicine, 1987, Am. Bd. Internal Medicine- pulmonary disease, 2004, Am. Bd. Internal Medicine- critical care medicine, 2005. Resident in internal medicine Letterman AMC, San Francisco, 1985—87; fellow in cardiovascullar disease Mass. Gen. Hosp., Boston, 1991—95; assoc. clin. prof. Baylor Coll. of Medicine; hosp. affiliation includes St. Luke's Episcopal Hospital. Office: Saint Luke's Episcopal Hospital 6624 Fannin Ste 1700 Houston TX 77030 Office Fax: 713-790-9408. E-mail: phka@aol.com.

HERLONG, HENRY MICHAEL, JR., federal judge; b. Washington, June 1, 1944; s. Henry Michael Sr. and Josie Payne (Blocker) H.; m. Frances Elizabeth Thompson, Dec. 30, 1983; children: Faris Elizabeth, Henry Michael III. BA, Clemson U., 1967; JD, U. S.C., 1970. Bar: S.C. 1970, U.S. Ct. Appeals (4th cir.) 1972, U.S. Dist. Ct. S.C. 1972. Legis. asst. to Senator Strom Thurmond US Senate, Washington, 1970-72; asst. US atty. US Dept. Justice, Greenville, SC, 1972-76, Columbia, SC, 1983-86; magistrate judge US Dist. Ct. SC, Columbia, SC, 1986-91, judge Greenville, SC, 1991—2009, sr. judge, 2009—; prin. Coleman & Herlong, Edgefield, S.C., 1976-83. Dir. Edgefield (S.C.) Devel. Bd., 1978-83, S.C. Assn. of Counties, 1980-83; active S.C. Rural Devel. Bd., 1980-83, Edgefield County Coun., 1979-83. Capt. USAR, 1970-75. Mem. S.C. Bar, Edgefield County Bar, Lions Club, Sertoma Club. Republican. United Methodist. Avocations: hunting, fishing, gardening.

HERMAN, DAVID CHRISTOPHER, ophthalmologist; b. Mpls., Oct. 25, 1957; s. Wallace Martin and Katherine Ann Herman; m. Karen Herman; children: Nicole Marie, Daniel Christopher. BS, U. Ill., Urbana, 1979; MD, Mayo Med. Sch., Rochester, Minn., 1983; MS in Med. Mgmt., U. Texas, Dallas, 2000. Cert. Am. Bd. Ophthalmology, 1988. Sr. staff fellow NIH, Bethesda, Md., 1987—88; cons. in ophthalmology Mayo Clinic, Rochester, 1988—2011; dir. Mayo Clinic Employee & Cmty. Health, 2007—11, Mayo Clin. Affiliated Network, 2010—11; pres., COO Vident Health, Greenville, NC, 2011—12, pres. CEO, 2012—. Bd. mem. Minn. Bd. Med. Practice, Mpls., 1990—99; bd. trustees Minn. Med. Assn., Mpls., 1994—96; med. dir. Mayo Clinic Rochester, 2003—07, exec. bd., 2007—10; bd. dirs. Immanuel-St. Joseph's Health Sys., Mankato, 2005—11, Inst. Clin. Sys. Improvement, Bloomington, Minn., 2006—11, St. Mary's Hosp., Rochester, 2007—10, Rochester Meth. Hosp., 2007—11, Mayo Health Sys., 2009—11. Bd. dirs. Am. Bd. Opthalmology, 2014—, NC Chamber, 2014—; bd. trustees Ronald McDonald House, Rochester, 2004—11, Ronald McDonald House Charities, 2011—. Fellow: Am. Acad. Ophthalmology; mem.: NC Hosp. Assn. (mem. policy devel. com. 2012—). Avocation: aviation. Office: Vidant Health 2100 Stantonsburg Rd PO Box 6028 Greenville NC 27835-6028 Home: 3007 Westview Dr Greenville NC 27834*

HERMAN, ROBERT A. (BOB HERMAN), oil industry executive; b. Seattle, 1959; BSMechE, Wash. State U., Pullman, 1982. Rotating equipment engr. Sohio Alaska Petroleum Co., Prudhoe Bay, 1982—87; various positions in refining ops., maintenance, turnaround, project mgmt., tech. support and refining mgmt. BP, Tosco, Premcor, ConocoPhillips, 1987—2002; mgr. Bayway refinery ConocoPhillips, 2002—05, gen. mgr. refining bus. improvement, 2005—08, pres. refining, mktg., & transp. Europe, 2008—10, v.p. health safety & environ., 2010—12; sr. v.p. health, safety & environment, projects & procurement Phillips 66, Houston, 2012—. Past bd. mem. NW Constrn. Consumers Coun., Europia, CONCAWE. Office: Phillips 66 3010 Briarpark Dr Houston TX 77042*

HERMAN, RUSSELL LELAND, mathematics, physics professor; b. Manchester, NH, Apr. 23, 1951; m. Ann Diggs, Dec. 14, 2004; children: EliJacob Weinstock-Herman, Arianna Zimmerman, Nathan Moshe Weinstock-Herman, Shoshana Joele Weinstock-Herman, Avi Micah Weinstock-Herman. BS in Math., Empire State Coll., SUNY, 1981; MA in Physics, Temple U., 1982; PhD in Physics, Clarkson U., Potsdam, NY, 1988, MS in Math., 1986. Math. and physics prof. U. NC, Wilmington, 1990—, chair physics & physical oceanography, 2009—; editor in chief Jour. Effective Tchg., 2006—. Vis. asst. prof. St. Lawrence U., Canton, 1988—90. Recipient Disting. Tchg. professorship, U. NC Wilmington, 2005, Chancellor's Tchg. Excellence award, 2005, Bd. Gov.'s award for Tchg. Excellence, U. NC, 2006; numerous grants in ednl. rsch., NSF and U. N.C. Wilmington, 1991—2005. Mem.: Am. Assn. Physics Tchrs., Soc. for Indsl. and Applied Math., Am. Math. Soc., Math. Assn. of Am., Am. Phys. Soc. Office: U NC Wilmington 601 S College Rd Wilmington NC 28403 Business E-Mail: hermanr@uncw.edu.

HERMES, CLINTON DANIEL, lawyer; s. Terry and Lisa Hermes; m. Susan Fieselman, Aug. 11, 2001. BA, Yale U., New Haven, Conn., 1994—98; JD, Harvard Law Sch., Cambridge, Mass., 1998—2001. Atty. Ropes & Gray LLP, Boston, 2001—07; sr. v.p., gen. counsel St. Jude Children's Research Hosp., Memphis, 2007—. Panelist, spkr. in field., 2001—. Co-author: (book) HIPAA and Human Subjects Research, 2003; editor: (journal) Harvard Journal of Law and Technology, 2000—01; contbr. articles to profl. jours. Dir., pres. Tutoring in Elem. Schools, New Haven, 1995—97; dir. Battered Women's Advocacy Project Legal Rsch. Bur., Cambridge, Mass., 1999—2001; vice chmn., instl. rev. bd. Judge Baker Children's Ctr., Boston, 2003—04; pro-bono counsel Psychoanalytic Couple and Family Inst. of New Eng., Boston, 2004—; mem. adv. bd. Am. Law Found. Recipient Deb Levi Pro Bono award, 2005; named New Haven Youth of the Yr., Mayor of the City of New Haven, 1997; named one of the 15 Outstanding Young Healthcare Lawyers (under 40) nationally, Nightingale's Healthcare News, 2004; scholar, Ala. Law Found., 2000; Nat. Merit Scholar, 1994. Mem.: ABA, Am. Health Lawyers Assn., Mass. Bar Assn., Boston Bar Assn., Nat. Polit. Sci. Honor Soc. Avocations: hiking, travel. Office: St Jude Children's Research Hospital 262 Danny Thomas Pl Memphis TN 38105

HERNANDEZ, CARLOS, mayor, Hialeah, Florida; b. Camaguey, Cuba, Mar. 8, 1961; m. Nancy Hernandez; children: Kayla, Hunter. B in Orgnl. Leadership, St. Thomas U., Miami, Fla. Ret. comdr. Hialeah Police Dept., Fla.; councilman Hialeah City Coun., 2005—11, coun. v.p., 2007—09, coun. pres., 2009—11; mayor City of Hialeah, 2011—. Office: Office of the Mayor City of Hialeah 501 Palm Ave Hialeah FL 33010 Office Phone: 305-883-5800. Business E-Mail: mayorchernandez@hialeahfl.gov.*

HERNANDEZ, CARLOS MANUEL, lawyer; b. Sancti Spiritus, Las Villas, Cuba, July 30, 1954; came to U.S., 1962; s. Pedro M. and Maria Teresa (Leon) H.; m. Deborah Lee Pautsch, Aug. 16, 1980; children: Alicia Maria, Monica Lynn, Cecilia Elena. BSCE, Purdue U., 1976; JD, U. Miami, 1979. Bar: Fla. 1979, Mo. 1981, U.S. Dist. Ct. (so. dist.) Fla. 1980, U.S. Dist. Ct. (we. dist.) Mo. 1981, U.S. Ct. Appeals (5th and 11th cirs.) 1981, Ohio 1985. Assoc. Kavanaugh & Leiby, Miami, Fla., 1979-81; assoc. counsel Burns & McDonnell Engr., Co., Inc., Kansas City, Mo., 1981-84; asst. counsel Armco, Inc., Middletowm, Ohio, 1984-86, Parsippany, N.J., 1986-88, assoc. counsel, 1988—2001; gen. counsel, sec. Fleming Co. Inc., 2001—04, Internat. Steel Group Inc., 2004—05, Mittal Steel USA Inc., 2005—06; gen. counsel Arcelor Mittal Am., 2006—07; exec. v.p., chief legal officer, corp. sec. Fluor Corp., Irving, Tex., 2007—. Republican. Roman Catholic. Office: Fluor Corp 6700 Las Colinas Blvd Irving TX 75039*

HERNANDEZ, KENNETH J., dean; MBA, Pace U., 1973. Dean, workforce devel. Houston Cmty. Coll. Northeast, 1997—. Master chief USN, 1984—2008, Houston. Business E-Mail: kenneth.hernandez@hccs.edu.

HERNÁNDEZ DENTON, FEDERICO, supreme court chief justice; b. Santurce, PR, Apr. 12, 1944; s. Federico and Teresa (Denton) Hernandez-Morales; m. Isabel Pico, 1966. BA, Harvard U., 1966, JD, 1969. Bar: PR 1971. Dir. Consumer Rsch. Ctr. and Bus. Adminstrn. Rsch. Ctr. U. PR, 1970-72; dir. PR Consumer Svc. Adminstrn., 1973; sec. PR Dept. Consumer Affairs, 1973-76; asst. prof. Law Sch. Interam. U., PR, 1977-84, dean PR, 1984-85; justice Supreme Ct. PR, San Juan, 1985—2004; pres. PR Bd. of Bar Examiners, 1987—2004; chief justice PR Supreme Ct., San Juan, 2004—; pres. Jud Evaluations Comm., 2007—. Pres. PR Bd. Bar Examiners, 1987—; chairperson Jud. Code Comm., 2003—05; mem. bd. dir. Conf. of Chief Justices, 2007—. Mem. ABA, Am. Law Inst., PR Bar Assn. Office: Supreme Ct of PR PO Box 9022392 San Juan PR 00902-2392 Office Phone: 787-724-3535. Business E-Mail: federico.hernandez@ramajudicial.pr.*

HERNANDEZ LUNA, ANA E., state legislator; b. Reynosa, Mexico; m. Greg Luna. BS in Polit. Sci. and Psychology, U. Houston; JD, U. Tex. Sch. Law, 2004; attended, U. New South Wales, Sydney. Former staff mem. and chief of staff to Representative Jessica Farrar Tex. House of Representatives, 1998—2002, former staff mem. to Representative Joe Moreno, 2002—04, mem. Dist. 143, 2005—; property, tax, real estate & right of way atty. ConocoPhilips; former atty. Mostyn Law Firm; atty. Carrigan, McCloskey & Roberson, LLP. Fellow: Tex. Bar Found.; mem.: Hispanic Bar Assn. Houston (bd. dirs.), State Bar Tex., Latinas on the Rise (co-founder 1998, former exec. dir., fundraiser), Am. Heart Assn. (mem. policy coun.). Democrat. Office: 1233 Mercury Dr Houston TX 77029 also: Room E1.212 Capitol Extension PO Box 2910 Austin TX 78768 Office Phone: 713-675-8596, 512-463-0614.

HEROS, ROBERTO COSME C., neurosurgeon; b. Havana, Cuba, Sept. 27, 1942; m. Deborah O.; children: Elsa, Rob, Carlos. MD, U. Tenn., Memphis, 1968. Diplomate Am. Bd. Neurol. Surgery. Intern in surgery Mass. Gen. Hosp., Boston, 1968-69; asst. resident gen. surgery, 1969-70; resident in neurosurgery, 1972-77; asst. in neurosurgery, 1976-77; attending neurosurgeon Presbyn. U. Hosp., Pitts., 1977-79; assoc. chief neurosurgery, 1979-80; asst. prof. neurosurgery U. Pitts., 1977-80, dir. neurosurgery residents ednl. program, 1979-80; asst. prof. surgery Harvard Med. Sch., Boston, 1980-83; assoc. prof. surgery, 1983-89; prof. surgery, 1989-90; Lyle A. French prof., chmn. dept. neurosurgery U. Minn., 1990-95; prof., chair dept. neurol. surgery U. Miami, 1995—. Dir. U. Miami Internat. Health Ctr. Chmn. editl. bd. Neurosurgery, 1988; contbr. articles to profl. jours. Chmn. Brain Attack Nat. Coalition, neurovasc. com. World Fedn. Neurosurg. Soc. Maj. USAF, 1970—72. Recipient Medal of Surgery U. Tenn., 1968, Dean's medal, 1968. Fellow: ACS; mem.: World Congress Neurol. Surgeons (v.p. 1986—87, pres. 2005—09), Neurosurg. Soc. Am., Am. Acad. Neurol. Surgeons (pres. 2001), Am. Assn. Neurol. Surgeons (pres. 2002), Alpha Omega. Office: U Miami Med Sch 1095 NW 14th Terr Miami FL 33136-1407 Office Phone: 305-243-4572. E-mail: rheros@med.miami.edu.

HERRAN, MANUEL A., supermarket chain executive; b. Santander, Spain, 1937; arrived in Cuba, 1951, arrived in US, 1966; m. Nyria Herran. Salesman, Miami, 1967—71; joined Sedano's Mgmt., Inc., 1971, chmn., pres., CEO; co-founder, dir. US Century Bank, 2002—. Office: Sedano's Management Inc 3140 W 76th St Hialeah FL 33018 Office Phone: 305-824-1034. Office Fax: 305-556-6981. Business E-Mail: manuel.herrn@sedanos.com.

HERRERA, GUILLERMO ANTONIO, pathologist, educator, researcher; b. Havana, Cuba, Mar. 16, 1952; came to U.S., 1967; s. Guillermo S. and Olga (Del Castillo) H.; m. Elba A. Turbat, Dec. 23, 1972; 1 child, Marlene F. Student, U. Miami, 1970; MD cum laude, U. P.R., 1975. Diplomate Am. Bd. Pathology, Am. Bd. Anat. and Clin. Pathology; cytopathology added qualification bd.; lic. physician Fla., N.Mex., Ala., Miss., La., Mo. Intern categorical pathology Brooke Army Med. Ctr., Ft. Sam Houston, Tex., 1975-76, resident pathology, anatomic and clin., 1975-79, chief resident, 1978-79; asst. prof. dept. pathology Sch. Medicine and Dentistry U. Ala., Birmingham, 1982-87, scientist II Nephrology Rsch. and Tchr. Ctr. Sch. Medicine, 1982-88, dir. nephropathology Schs. Medicine and Dentistry, 1987-88, assoc. prof. dept. pathology, 1987-88, prof. pathology, head surg. pathology, 1991-95, sr. scientist Comprehensive Cancer Ctr., 1991-95, acting med. dir. Sch. Cytotech., 1991-93, faculty mem. Grad. Sch., 1991-95; assoc. prof., head surg. pathology U. Miss. Med. Ctr., 1989-91; head surg. pathology, attending pathologist VA Hosp., Birmingham, 1991-95; sr. scientist, co-dir. EM Core Facility Comprehensive Cancer Ctr. Ala., 1991-95; prof. pathology, medicine, cell biology La. State U., Shreveport, 1996—2006, chmn. dept. pathology, 1996—2006; prof. St. Louis (Mo.) U., 2006—, chmn. dept. pathology, 2006—. Assoc. pathologist Palm Beach Pathology, Good Samaritan Hosp., West Palm Beach, Fla., 1988-89; faculty Grad. Sch. U. Miss., 1989-91; cons. pathologist VA Hosp., Jackson, 1990-91; attending pathologist, head surg. pathology VA Hosp., Birmingham, 1991-95; acting med. dir. Sch. Cytotech., U. Ala., Birmingham, 1991-93, acting head cytopathology, 1991-93, faculty mem. Grad Sch., 1991-95; sr. scientist Comprehensive Cancer Ctr. Ala., co-dir. EM Core facility, 1991-95; cons. Overton Brooks VA Hosp., Shreveport, La. Mem. editl. bd.: Ultrastructural Pathology and Pathology Case Revs., 1995—, Human Pathology and Applied Immunohistochemistry and Molecular Morphology, 2001—, manuscript reviewer: Applied Pathology, Diagnostic Cytopathology, Am. Jour Medicine, Am. Jour. Kidney Diseases, Archives of Pathology and Laboratory Medicine, 2005, Ultrastructural Pathology, Stain Tech. and Histochemistry, Am. Jour. Clin. Pathology, Pathobiology, Human Pathology, Cancer, Kidney Internat., Pathology Rsch., Practice and Annals of Saudi Medicine, Am. Jour. Pathology, mem.: NIH rev. panel, assoc. editor: Ultrastructural Pathology Jour., 2004—; contbr. articles to profl. jours., chpts. to books. Maj. M.C., U.S. Army, 1974-82, col. USAR, 1988-96, ret. Grantee U. P.R., 1972-75, Brooke Army Med. Ctr., Ft. Sam Houston, 1978-79, U. Ala., Birmingham, 1983-86, 87-88, Universita Degli Studi di Milano, 1984, VA, 1986—, Nat. Cancer Inst., 1991—, NIH, 1992—, Ala. Kidney Found., 1992-93, Leukemia Soc. Am., 1997-99. Mem.: N.Y. Acad. Scis., Birmingham Soc. Pathologists (v.p. 1987—88), Tex. Electron Microscopy Soc., Internat. Acad. Pathology, Arthur Purdy Stout Soc. Surg. Pathologists, Am. Soc. Nephrology, Rsch. Soc., Soc. Advancement Sci., Renal Pathology Soc. (chmn. tng. com. 1996—98, sec.-treas. 1999—2005), Soc. Ultrastructural Pathology (sec.-treas. 1988—91, treas. 1991—99), Electron Microscopy Soc. Am., Armed Forces Soc. Lab. Scientists, Am. Soc. Clin. Pathology, Alpha Omega Alpha. Roman Catholic. Home: 3583 Conroy Rd Apt 1117 Orlando FL 32839 Office Phone: 314-577-8475. Business E-Mail: gherrer1@slu.edu.

HERRICK, JOHN DENNIS, financial planner, consultant, retired food products executive; b. St. Paul, Oct. 8, 1932; s. Willard R. and Gertrude (O'Connor) H. BA, U. St. Thomas, 1954; MBA (hon.), U. Laval, 1969. Field auditor Gen. Mills, Inc., Mpls., 1954-59, acctg. supr. Kankakee, Ill., 1959-61, adminstrv. mgr. Chgo., 1961-62, mgr. auditing Mpls., 1962-65, mgr. new bus. devel., 1965-66, dir. adminstrn. and controller Smiths Food Group (subs.) London, 1966-68; pres. Gen. Mills Cereals Ltd., Toronto, Ont., Canada, 1969-71; chmn. bd., pres., chief exec. officer Gen. Mills Canada, Inc., Toronto, Ont., Canada, 1971-86; chief operating officer Borden & Elliot, Toronto, 1986-89; cons. West Beach, Fla., 1989—; pres. J.D. Herrick Found. Past chmn. Grocery Products Mfrs. of Can., Toronto; dir. CP Express & Transport, Toronto; adv. bd. American Coll. Louvain, Belgium. Past pres. Jr. Achievement Can., Toronto, 1970-71, Am. Club; past chmn. Toronto Area Inds. Devel. Bd., Emmanuel Convalescent Found., Toronto, Toronto Harbour Commn.; past pres., mem. coun. Bd. Trade Met. Toronto; past vice-chmn. Nat. Theater Sch. Can., Montreal; bd. dirs., past pres. Cath. Charities Palm Beach; mem. pres.'s coun. U. St. Thomas; chmn.'s adv. bd. Rep. Nat. Com., Roundtable NRSC; mem. PNST, treas. Rep Exec. Com., Palm Beach County; bd. past pres. DePorres P.L.A.C.E.; bd. dirs. Liberty Ednl. Forum; bd. govs. U. St. Thomas Law Sch.; rector's coun. St. Vincent de Paul Seminary, bd. treas. Palm Beach Symphony. Capt. USAF, 1954-57; dir. Cath. MED Missionary Bd., NYC. Decorated knight grand cross Knights of Holy Sepulchre, Order of St. John, knight comdr. Order of Polonia Restituta; recipient Queen's Silver Jubilee medal, 1978, Queen's Golden Jubilee medal, 2003, Bishop Cretin award, 2004; named Disting. Alumnus, U. St. Thomas, 1984. Mem.: Can. C. of C. (past chmn., gov.), Club Colette, PB, Palm Beach Yacht Club, Capital Hill Club (Washington), KC, NY Athletic Club, Royal Can. Yacht Club, Empire Club, Beefeater Club. Roman Catholic. Home: 701 South olive Ave #1416 West Palm Beach FL 33401

HERRING, CHARNIELE L., state legislator, political organization administrator; b. Santo Domingo, Dominican Republic, Sept. 25, 1969; BA in Economics, George Mason U., 1993; JD, Catholic U., 1997. Atty.; mem. Dist. 46 Va. House of Delegates, 2009—, House minority whip, 2012—; chair Dem. Party of Va., 2012—. Trustee Hopkins House. Mem.: Rotary. Democrat. Office: PO Box 11779 Alexandria VA 22312 also: General Assembly Bldg PO Box 406 Richmond VA 23218 Office Phone: 804-698-1046. Office Fax: 804-698-6746. E-mail: DelCHerring@house.virginia.gov.*

HERRING, JERONE CARSON, retired lawyer, bank executive; b. Kinston, NC, Sept. 27, 1938; s. James and Isabel (Knight) H.; m. Patricia Ann Hardy, Aug. 6, 1961; children: Bradley Jerone, Ansley Carole. AB, Davidson Coll., 1960; LL.B., Duke U., 1963. Bar: N.C. 1963. Assoc. McElwee & Hall, North Wilkesboro, N.C., 1965-69; ptnr. McElwee, Hall & Herring, North Wilkesboro, 1969-71; exec. v.p., sec., gen. counsel Br. Banking & Trust Co., Winston-Salem, NC, 1971—2003, BB&T Corp., Winston-Salem, 1995—2003. Mem. bd. adv. U. N.C. Ctr. Banking and Fin.; mem. bd. visitors Davidson Coll.; mem. bd. trustees Mountain Retreat Assn. Bd. dirs. Montreat Conf. Ctr. Devel. Found., Black Mountain Swannanoa Valley Found.; mem. Town of Montreat Planning and Zoning Commn., 2004-10; Served to capt. U.S. Army, 1963-65. Mem. NC Bar Assn. Presbyterian. Personal E-mail: jherring123@charter.net.

HERRING, MARK RANKIN, state attorney general, former state legislator; b. Johnson City, Tenn., Sept. 25, 1961; m. Laura Herring; children: Peyton, Tim. BA in Fgn. Affairs & Economics, U. Va., 1983, MA in Fgn. Affairs, 1986; JD, U. Richmond Sch. Law, 1990. Atty. Turner Parks & Herring P.L.C., Leesburg, Va., 1990—99; town atty. Town of Lovettsville, 1992—99; bd. supervisors Loudoun County, 2000—03; prin. The Herring Law Firm, P.C., Leesburg, Va., 2000—10, Herring & Turner, P.C., Leesburg, Va., 2011—14; mem. Dist. 33 Va. State Senate, Richmond, Va., 2006—14; atty. gen. Commonwealth of Va., Richmond, Va., 2014—. Mem.: Olive Branch Lodge #114 and Alexandria Scottish Rite, NAACP Loudoun Chpts., Loudoun County Bar Assoc., Leesburg Kiwanis Club, Loudoun County ChofC. Democrat. Presbyterian. Office: Attorney General's Office 900 East Main St Richmond VA 23219 Office Phone: 804-786-2071.*

HERROD, HENRY GRADY, III, pediatrics professor, allergist, immunologist; b. Oakland, Calif., Apr. 30, 1945; MD, U. Ala., 1972. Cert. allergy and immunology; cert. pediats. Intern U. Wash., Seattle, 1972-73, resident in pediats., 1973-74; resident rsch. assoc. in allergy and immunology NIH, Bethesda, Md., 1974-76; fellow in allergy and immunology Duke U., Durham, 1976-78; physician Le Bonheur Childrens Med. Ctr., Memphis; prof. U. Tenn., Memphis, dean, 1998—2005; fellow Urban Child Inst., Memphis, 2005—. Mem. AAAI, AAI, AAP, APS. Office: Urban Child Inst 600 Jefferson # 221 Memphis TN 38105 Home Phone: 901-685-6016; Office Phone: 901-576-1355. Business E-Mail: hherrod@utmem.edu.

HERRON, EDWIN HUNTER, JR., energy consultant; b. Shreveport, La., June 7, 1938; s. Edwin Hunter and Helen Virginia (Russell) H.; m. Frances Irvine Hunter, June 27, 1959; children: Edwin, David, Ashley. BS in Chem. Engring., Tulane U., 1959, MS, 1963, PhD (NSF fellow 1963-64), 1964. Rsch. engr. Exxon Rsch. & Engring. Co., Linden, N.J., 1959-61; sr. rsch. egnr. Exxon Prodn. Rsch. Co., Houston, 1964-66; corp. planning advisor Esso Europe, London, Eng., 1966-74; fin. analyst Exxon Corp., NYC, 1974-78; v.p. Gruy Petroleum Tech., Inc., McLean, Va., 1978-84; pres. Petro-Analysis, Inc. (named changed to Hunter Trading Co. Inc.), 1984—, Petroleum Equities, Inc., 1987—; dir. petroleum projects CORE Internat., Inc., 1989—; pres. Petroleum Holdings, Inc., 1993—; dir. World Energy Sys. Inc., 1999—2005. Contbr. articles to profl. publs. Recipient Levey award Tulane U., 1970. Mem. Soc. Petroleum Engrs. (sr.), Am. Inst. Chem. Engrs., Sci. Rsch. Soc., Soc. Tulane Engrs., Tau Beta Pi. Office: Petroleum Equities Inc 8000 Towers Crescent Dr Ste 1350 Vienna VA 22182-6207 Office Phone: 703-743-9877. Business E-Mail: hunter.herron@petroleumequities.com.

HERRON, ROY BRASFIELD, political organization administrator, former state legislator; b. Martin, Tenn., Sept. 30, 1953; m. Nancy Carol Miller; children: Benjamin, John, Rick. Grad. with highest honors, U. Tenn. at Martin; grad. in Divinity and Law, Vanderbilt U. Staff mem. senator, Gore, 1984; pres., 1987—88; cooper senator, 1993; state rep. Dist. 76 Tenn., 1987—96; state senator Dist. 24 Tenn., 1994—2013; atty & businessman; adj. faculty Vanderbilt Law Sch.; chmn. Tenn. Dem. Party, Nashville, 2013—. Contbr. articles to profl. jours. Mem.: Muscular Dystrophy Assn., Crime Stoppers, Farm Bur., C. of C., Weakly County & Tenn. Bar Assn., Quail Unlimited, Ducks Unlimited, Habitat for Humanity, Rotary Club. Democrat. Methodist. Office: Tennessee Democratic Party 1900 Church St Ste 203 Nashville TN 37203*

HERSHBERGER, RAY E., cardiologist, educator; b. Lincoln, Nebr., Sept. 22, 1953; BA, Goshen Coll., 1975; MD, U. Nebr., 1978. Cert. Internal Medicine, 1981, Cardiovascular Disease, 1989. Resident internal medicine Washington Hosp. Ctr., DC, 1978—79, U. Kans. Sch. Medicine, Wichita, 1979—81; fellowship cardiology U. Utah Hosp., Salt Lake City, 1985—90; fellowship cardiac transplant Utah Cardiac Transplant Program, Salt Lake City; dir. cardiac transplantation, prof. medicine in cardiology Oreg. Health & Sci. U., Portland; prof. medicine, assoc. chief cardiology, dir. Advanced Heart Failure Therapies Program, dir. Translational Cardiovascular Genetic Medicine Miller Sch. Medicine, U. Miami, 2007—. Founder, prin. investigator Familial Dilated Cardiomyopathy Rsch. Project. Office: U Miami PO Box 019132 Miami FL 33101 Office Phone: 305-243-7067. Office Fax: 305-243-7069. E-mail: rhershberger@med.miami.edu.

HERSHNER, ROBERT FRANKLIN, JR., judge; b. Sumter, SC, Jan. 21, 1944; s. Robert Franklin and Druie (Goodman) H.; m. Sally Sinclair, May 19, 1990; children: Bryan, Andrew. AB, Mercer U., 1966, JD, 1969. Bar: Ga. 1971, U.S. Dist. Ct. (mid. dist.) Ga. 1971, U.S. Dist. Ct. (so. dist.) Ga. 1979, U.S. Ct. Appeals (11th cir.) 1981, U.S. Supreme Ct. 1978. Atty. Ga. Legal Svcs. Corp., Macon, 1972; assoc. Adams, O'Neal, Hemingway & Kaplan, Macon, 1972-76; ptnr. Kaplan & Hershner, P.A., Macon, 1976-80; judge U.S. Bankruptcy Ct. for Mid. Dist. Ga., Macon, 1980—, chief bankruptcy judge, 1986—. Active Fed. Jud. Ctr. Com. on Bankruptcy Edn., 1990—99, chmn., 1994—99; elected mem. bd. Fed. Jud. Ctr., 2001—. Contbr. Georgia Lawyers Basic Practice Handbook, 2d edit., Post-Judgment Procedures, 1979; cons. Norton Bankruptcy Law and Practice. V.p. Macon Heritage Found., 1977-78. Capt. U.S. Army, 1970-75. Mem. Ga. Bar Assn., Macon Bar Assn., Nat. Conf. Bankruptcy Judges (gov., v.p. 1996-97, pres. 1997-98), Blue Key, Phi Eta Sigma. Methodist. Office: US Bankruptcy Ct PO Box 86 Macon GA 31202-0086 Office Phone: 478-749-6861.

HERSON, ARLENE, television host producer, journalist, television personality, radio commentator; b. NYC; d. Sam and Mollie (Friedman) Hornreich; m. Milton Herson, June 16, 1963; children: Michael, Karen. Student, Queens Coll., 1957, New Sch. for Social Rsch., NYC, 1960. Exec. sec. Tex McCrary, Inc., NYC, 1958—60; asst. to William L. Safire, Safire Pub. Rels., NYC, 1960—62; columnist Advisor, Inc., Middletown, NJ, 1974—78; prodr., host The Arlene Herson Show, NYC, 1978—, Manhattan Cable TV, 1980—; owner eBay Store, 2010—; talent coord. Showtime, 2013—. Syndicated on Tempo TV, 1988, Channel Am., 1989-93, Boca Raton Ednl. TV, 2006-2010; spokesperson Storer Cable TV, Monmouth County, 1989-91, Nutri/Sys., Monmouth and Ocean Counties, 1989-90; news anchor Nostalgia Cable TV Network at Rep. Nat. Conv., 1993; cons., talent coord. Super Annuities, 1993-94; moderator debate on capital punishment, 1998; moderator panel on assisted suicide, 1999; panelist radio program Fla. Forum NPR, 2004—2010; panelist, interviewer The Am. Sr. Side-WXEL-Nat. Pub. Radio, 1999-04; co-host radio sta. WJNA, Lunch Bunch; entertainment chmn. Polo Club, 2001—2010; master of ceremonies Calvacade of Stars, 2004—10, Wings of Memory Soc., 2005-; mem. grievance com. Fla. Bar, 2003-06; presdl. appointee US Holocaust Meml. Coun., 2004-2009, mem. com. on conscience, 2006-; mem. Fla. Film and Entertainment Adv. Coun., 2005—2010, vice chmn. membership, 2006-, keynote spkr. Fla. Atlantic U. 2009, Palm Isles Country Club, 2010; lectr., spkr. in field. Contbg. writer The Washington/Hampton Connection Dan's Papers, 1993-98, The Hill Newspaper, 1994-98; exec. prodr. The Magic Flute, conductor Victor Borge, DAR Constitution Hall, Washington, 1995, 1776, 1997; exec. prodr., casting dir. (musical) 1776, DAR Constitution Hall, Washington, 1996, encore prodn., 1998; prodr. 1776 (featuring current mems. of Congress), 1998; interviewer Steven Spielberg's Shoah Found., 1997-99; host WXEL-TV Pledge Drive, 2000, patron, Boca Raton Mus. Art, 2011, Theatre Arts Guild, 2011, Impact 100, 2011, Polo Club Grievance Com., 2011, elect. mem., Tennis Com., 2011, cmty. Rels. Com., 2011, South Fla. Legacy Light Chmn., 2011; featured in documentary "The Embrace of Aging", 2013-. 92d St. Y benefit com. Variety-The Children's Charity; active Women's Project and Prodns., 1992; com. mem. Children's Psychiat. Ctr., 1971-90, Monmouth Park Charity Fund, 1980-90; corp. exec. bd. Family and Childrens Svcs., 1985—90; life mem. N.Y. chpt. Brandeis U. Libr. Fund; dir.'s resource coun. Nat. Women's Econ. Alliance; social com. Westbridge Condominium; fin. chmn. Mike Herson for Congress, 1994, fin.com. March of Dimes, 1995; profl. women's coun. Nat. Mus. of Women in the Arts, 1994; com. mem. Vicent T. Lombardi Cancer Rsch. Ctr., 1994-98, Parkinson's Action Network, 1996; publicity chmn.exhbn. for Israel Tennis Ctrs. Excalibur Soc. of Lyn U., 1996—2008; adv. coun. mem. Jewish Edn. Ctr., 2009—; adv. coun. to co-chmn. Rep. Nat. Com., 1997—2000; active Power of Women Effecting Renewal, 1997; 2d decade coun. Am. Film Inst., 1998; bd. dirs. A Healing Among Nations, 1999; active Soc. of 100, Fla. Philharm. Orch., 1999; benefit com. Caldwell Theatre, 1999; bd. dirs. Miami City Ballet; founder Israel Children's Ctrs., 2000; bd. dirs. Fla. Film and Entertainment Adv. Coun., 2001—08; mem. com. Shaare Zedek Med. Ctr., 2001; honors bd. dirs. Miami City Ballet, 2000—05; com. mem. Ctr. for the Arts, 2001—03, Palm Beach Cultural Coun., 2001—03; corp. exec. com. Ctrl. Park Conservancy, Women of Washington; corp. exec. com. mentor program Women's Econ. Devel. Coun.; bd. dirs. Miami City Ballet Sch., 2001—03; exec. com. Cmty. Rels. Coun., 2001—03; leadership coun., exec. com. Rep. Jewish Coalition, 2002—; mem. Garnet Soc. PBS, Nat. Pub. Radio, 2004—; life mem. Boca Raton cancer unit Papanicolau Corps for Cancer Rsch., 2002—; mem. Boca Raton Mus. Art, 2002—, coun. trustees, 2001—03; apptd. by Gov. Jeb Bush Fla. Film Entertainment Coun., 2004—08; founder Lippy Leadership Soc., 2005; mem. com. on conscience U.S. Holocaust Mus., 2006; vice chmn. membership Fla. Film and Entertainment Adv. Coun., 2006—08; nat. chair Legacy Light Soc.-US Holocaust Meml. Mus., 2009—; life mem. Hadassah, 2010; adv. bd. mem. Next Generations, 2011—; exec. com. mem. Jewish Edn. Ctr., 2010; entertainment chmn. Hadassah luncheon, 2011, Cmty. Relations Com., 2011, Grievance Com. Polo Club, 2011; elect. mem. Tennis Com., Polo Club, 2011; bd. mem. Boca Raton Hist. Soc., 2012—; patron Boca Raton Mus. Art, 2012—; master ceremonies Showtime Series, 2011—; sponsor Talent Coord. Showtime, 2013; bd. mem. Festival Arts, 2013; mem. Oral History Project Boca Raton Hist. Soc., 2013; founder Women Against Alzheimers, 2013—; adv. coun., presdl. appointment Take Pride in Am., 1993; bd. dirs. women's activities campaign Sen. Jacob J. Javits, NYC, 1968, Monmouth Mus., 1982—86, Will Rogers Inst., 1992—, Washington Symphony Orch., 1994—98, v.p., 1994; bd. dirs. Boca Raton Ednl. TV, 2001—08, Palm Beach Internat. Film Festival, 2005—, Together Against Gangs, 2006; membership chmn. Palm Beach Internat. Film Festival, 2008; mem. Legacy Light Soc., 2007—, Keepers Gate, 1993—, Leadership Soc. Lynn U., 2013—; spkr. Symposium Genocide, 2012—; sponsor Live at Lynn Series, 2013—; bd. mem. Festival of Arts, 2013. Recipient CAPE award for best talk show on Cable TV Network, 1984-93, Best Single Program with Suzanne Sommers, 1988, Woman of Achievement in Comm. award Adv. Commn. on Status of Women, 1986, Pub. and Leased Access (PAL) award for best talk show Paragon Cable TV, N.Y.C., 1988, spl. resolution N.J. Assembly, 1988, Willie award for outstanding svc. Will Rogers Inst., 1992, Leadership award Wings Memory Soc., 2009, Honor medal, Jewish Ednl, Ctr. South Fla., 2009, Lifetime Achievement award, Chabad of Boca, 2013; named Disting. Alumni mem. Waldorf Astoria, 1998; nominated Cable Ace award Best Talk Show nationwide The Arlene Herson Show, 1987, 89, 2009, Spl. Appreciation award, Palm Beach Internat. Film Festival, 2011, Leadership award US Holocust Meml. Mus. Legacy Light Soc, 2011-, Lifetime Achievement award, Chabad East Bera, 2013-, Master Ceremonies A Time to Celebrate award, 2013-. Mem. NAFE, NATAS, Nat. Acad. Cable Programming, Nat. Assn. Profl. Women, Women in Comm., Women in Cable, Women in Film and Video, Am. Women in Radio and TV, Power Women Effecting Renewal, Internat. Radio and TV Soc., Internat. Newswoman's Assn., Rep. Gov's. Assn., Nat. Press Club, Friends for Life, Friars Club (house com. 1993, admissions com. 1994—), Bethesda Country Club, Lotos Club, East River Tennis Club, Excalibur Soc. of Lynn U., Seagate Beach Club, Boca Raton Rep. Club, Polo Club (cmty. rels. com. 1998-99, social com. 2000-, entertainment chmn. 2001-05), Palm Beach Rep. Club, Profl. Bus. Forum, Boca Raton Roundtable (bd. dirs. 2009), Hadassah (life), NXT Generation (life), Leadership Soc. Lynn U. Avocations: tennis, swimming, reading. Fax: 561-998-4776. E-mail: aherson123@aol.com.

HERTOG, JOHN HERMAN, transportation executive; b. Mpls., July 26, 1927; s. Herman and Adriana Jacomina (Zegers) Hertog; m. Violet Ellen Ackerman, July 22, 1950; children: John, Judith Ann, Linda, Susan, Pamela, Nancy. BCE, U. Minn., 1950. With No. Pacific R.R., St. Paul, 1946—70, asst. div. supt., 1964—66, asst. to gen. mgr., 1966—67, div. supt., 1967—70; with Burlington No. Inc., St. Paul, 1970—, sr. vp. ops., 1976—80, sr. v.p. coal and taconite, 1981—. Dir. Trailer Train Co. With US Army, 1945—46. Mem.: St. Paul C. of C., Masons, St. Paul Athletic, Elks. Republican. Office: 1 Continental Plz Fort Worth TX 76102

HERTZ, ARTHUR HERMAN, communications executive; b. Bklyn., Sept. 10, 1933; s. Edwin Carl and Blanche H.; Stephen R., Andrew P. BBA, U. Miami, Fla., 1955, postgrad., 1955-56. Acct. Aetna Mortgage Co., Miami, Fla., 1955, Wometco Enterprises, Inc., Miami, 1955-60, contr., v.p., 1960-64, sr. v.p., 1964-71, exec. v.p., treas., CFO, 1971-81, COO, 1981-84, chmn., CEO, 1985—; exec. v.p., COO WEI Enterprises Corp., Miami, 1984-85; exec. v.p. Wometco Broadcasting Co., Inc., Miami, 1984-85. Past pres. Orange Bowl Com.; past chair City of Miami Off St. Parking Authority; past chair Pub. Health Trust, Miami Dade County; past chmn. audit com. bd. trustees U. Miami. Mem. AICPA, Fla. Inst. CPAs, Greater Miami C. of C. (gov. 1975-78), Iron Arrow, Phi Kappa Phi, Omicron Delta Kappa, Phi Eta Sigma. Home: 610 Fluvia Ave Coral Gables FL 33134-7016 Office: Wometco Enterp PO Box 149019 Coral Gables FL 33114-9019 Office Phone: 305-529-1403. Business E-Mail: Arth@wometcoent.com.

HERTZ, KENNETH THEODORE, healthcare executive; b. Jackson Heights, NY, Aug. 19, 1951; s. Irwin R. and Dorothy S. H.; m. Debra Pitre, July 12, 1997. BA in Spl. Studies, SUNY, Fredonia, 1974; cert. med. and dental practice mgmt., Loyola U., 1992. Cert. med. practice exec.; fellow Am. Coll. Med. Practice Execs., 2010. Gen. mgr. Cape Cod Symphony, West Barnstable, Mass., 1974-75; mng. dir. Tulsa Philharm., 1975-78; pres., gen. mgr. Atlanta Ballet, 1979-89; instr. continuing edn. Oglethorpe U.; dir. Atlanta Great Artists Series, 1989-90, Atlanta Arts Devel. Svcs., 1989-90; exec. dir. New Orleans Symphony, 1990-91; adminstr. M.D. Care, Inc., New Orleans, 1991-95; dir. acquisitions and network devel. Tenet Healthcare, New Orleans, 1995-96, area mgr. practice ops., 1996-97; adminstr. MacArthur Surg. Clinic, Alexandria, La., 1977—2002, KTH Cons. LLC, 2003—05; sr. cons. MGMA Health Care Cons. Group, 2005—08, prin., 2008—; med. assoc. MGMA Med. Group. Mem. dance panel City of Atlanta, 1983-89, Ga. Coun. for Arts, 1984-88, NEA, 1985-87; dir. Dance/USA, 1985-89; mem. adv. bd. cert. program in med./dental practice mgmt. Loyola U., 1993—; mem. Pres.'s Adv. Coun., De La Salle H.S., 1993-2000. Chmn. Atlanta C. of C. Cultural Programming Task Force, 1987—89, Atlanta C. of C. "Arts Alive", art celebration, 1986, Ga. Profl. Arts Caucus, 1983—85; bd. dirs. Big Bros./Big Sisters, 1988—89, Arts Festival Atlanta, BVA, 1986—90, Bus. Vols. for Arts, New Orleans Ballet Assn., 1996—98, Rapides Symphony Orch., 1998—2000, Ballet Alexandria, 2000—, Am. Jewish Com., Atlanta, 1967. Mem. Midtown Bus. Assn. (dir. 1984-89), Ga. Citizens for Arts, Am. Symphony Orch. League, La. Med. Group Mgmt. Assn. (bd. dirs. 2001—, sec. 2003—, v.p., 2004-05), Ctrl. La. Med. Group Mgmt. Assn. (v.p. 2001-02, pres. 2002—), Alpha Phi Omega E-mail: khertz@mgma.com.

HERZ, NATHAN (BEN), occupational therapy professor; BS in Occupational Therapy, Eastern Ky. U., 1990; MBA, Averett U., Danville, Va., 1999; D of Occupational Therapy, Creighton U., Omaha, 2004. Chair rehabilitation svcs. Jefferson Coll. Health Scis., Roanoke, Va., 2000—04; asst. prof., program dir. dept. occupational therapy Med. Coll. Ga., 2004—. Bd. dirs. Columbia Parkinson's Support Group, SC. Recipient Disting. Svc. award, Med. Coll. Ga., 2008. Mem.: Ga. Occupational Therapy Assn., Am. Occupational Therapy Assn. Achievements include research in Parkinson's disease and the use of interaction video gaming systems, such as Wii and Wii Fit game systems, and how it relates to rehabilitation. Office: Med Coll Ga Dept Occupational Therapy 1120 15th St Augusta GA 30912 E-mail: nherz@mcg.edu.

HERZ, WERNER, retired chemistry professor; b. Stuttgart, Germany, Feb. 12, 1921; came to U.S., 1937, naturalized, 1944; s. Alfred and Hedwig (Loewenstein) H.; m. Marcia Lucile King, Feb. 22, 1945; children— Michael John, Patrick Werner, Monica Lucile, Andrea Lauren. BA, U. Colo., 1943, MA, 1945, PhD, 1947. Instr. math. U. Colo., 1946—47; Am. Cyanamid fellow U. Ill., 1947—49; with Fla. State U., Tallahassee, 1948—. Prof. chemistry Fla. State U., Tallahassee, 1959—, Robert G. Lawton disting. prof., 1987—96; mem. chemistry panel Cancer Chemotherapy Nat. Svc. Ctr., 1959—62, NSF, 1961—64; cons. Nat. Cancer Inst., 1962—65; mem. cancer chemotherapy study sect. NIH, 1962—66, mem. medicinal chemistry study sect., 1970—74. Author: The Shape of Molecules, 1963; mem. editl. bd.: Jour. Organic Chemistry, 1962-63, sr. editor, 1963-89; editor: Fortschritte der Chemie Organischer Naturstoffe, 1969-2006; bd. editors: Planta Medica, 1978—, Phytochemistry, 1981— Mem. Am. Chem. Soc. (councilor Fla. sect. 1960-79, adv. bd. Petroleum Rsch. Fund 1970-72), Chem. Soc. London, Phi Beta Kappa, Sigma Xi, Sigma Pi Sigma, Alpha Chi Sigma, Pi Mu Epsilon, Phi Lambda Upsilon Research and numerous publs. on isolation and structure determination of plant products with emphasis on possible applications to chemotaxonomy and cancer chemotherapy, structure synthesis and transformations of terpenoid substances; studies of molecular rearrangements in chemistry. Home: 314 Saratoga Dr Tallahassee FL 32312-2041 Office: Fla State U Dept Chemistry Tallahassee FL 32306-4390 Office Phone: 850-644-2774. Business E-Mail: herz@chem.fsu.edu.

HERZOG, LAURA LEFLER, state official, former legislative staff member; b. Tenn., 1980; d. Jack H. and Mary C. (White) Lefler; m. John Thomas Herzog; 1 child. BA, U. Tenn., Knoxville, 2001. Intern Dateline NBC, NYC, NBC News Bur., London; constituent rels. dir. to Senator Lamar Alexander US Senate, Washington, 2003—04, dep. press sec., 2004—06, press sec., 2006, to Senator Bob Corker, US Senate, Washington, 2007—09, comm. dir., 2010—14; dep. dir. for comm. Gov. Bill Haslam State of Tenn., Nashville, 2014—. Republican. Office: Office of Governor 1st Fl State Capitol Nashville TN 37243*

HERZOG, RONALD PAUL, bishop; b. Akron, Ohio, Apr. 22, 1942; Ordained priest Diocese of Natchez-Jackson, Miss., 1968; ordained bishop, 2005; bishop Diocese of Alexandria, La., 2005—. Roman Catholic. Office: Diocese of Alexandria PO Box 7417 Alexandria LA 71306 Office Phone: 318-445-2401 203. Office Fax: 318-767-1230. Business E-Mail: rherzog@dioceseglex.org.

HESS, DENNIS WILLIAM, chemical engineering educator; s. John William and Dorothy E. (Miller) H.; m. Patricia Ruth Weidner, June 1, 1968; children: Amy R., Sarah E. BS in Chemistry, Albright Coll., 1968; MS in Phys. Chemistry, Lehigh U., 1970, PhD in Phys. Chemistry, 1973. Staff researcher Fairchild Semiconductor, Palo Alto, Calif., 1973-77; from asst. prof. to prof. chem. engring. U. Calif., Berkeley, 1977-91; prin. investigator Materials and Molecular Research div. Lawrence Berkeley Lab., 1978-84, Ctr. for Adv. Materials, Lawrence Berkeley Lab., 1983-85; asst. dean Coll. Chemistry U. Calif., Berkeley, 1982-87; vice chmn. dept. chem. engring U. Calif., Berkeley, 1988-91; chmn. dept. chem. engring. Lehigh U., Bethlehem, Pa., 1991-96; William W. LaRoche jr. prof. chem. and biomolecular engring. Ga. Inst. Tech., Atlanta, 1996—2008; Thomas C. Deloach jr. prof. Chem. and Biomolecular Engring. GA Inst. Tech., Atlanta, 2008—; dir. NSF Materials Rsch. Sci. & Engring. Ctr. Ga. Inst. Tech. Editor Electrochem. and Solid State Letters, 2004-2012, ECS Jour. Solid State Sci. and Tech., 2012-; contbr. articles to profl. jours. Fellow AAAS, AIChE (Charles M.A. Stine award 1999), The Electrochem. Soc. (pres. 1996-97, Thomas D. Callinan award 1993, Solid State Sci. and Tech. award 2005); mem. Am. Chem. Soc., Am. Inst. Physics, Materials Rsch. Soc., Sigma Xi, Tau Beta Pi. Office: Ga Tech Sch Chem and Biomolecular Engring 311 Ferst Dr Atlanta GA 30332-0100 Office Phone: 404-894-5922. E-mail: dennis.hess@chbe.gatech.edu.

HESSELS, JAN-MICHIEL, stock exchange executive; b. The Hague, Netherlands, Dec. 21, 1942; came to US, 1982; s. Johan H. and Emmy H.P. (Boots) H.; s. Liesbeth W.M. Hillen, Nov. 12, 1970; children: Maartje, Laurien, Pieter. LLM, Ryks U., Leiden, Holland, 1966; postgrad., London Sch. Econs., 1966—67; MA in Finance and Bus. Adminstrn., U. Pa., 1969. Trainee S.G. Warburg & Co., London, 1967; asst. to gen mgr. Overseas Devel. Bank, Geneva, 1969-70; assoc. McKinsey & Co., NYC, 1968, engagement mgr. Amsterdam, 1971-73; corp. treas. Akzo N.V., Arnhem, Netherlands, 1973; pres. Akzo Ltda., Sao Paulo, Brazil, 1977—82; exec. v.p. Akzona Corp., Asheville, 1982—85; CEO NV Deli Universal, Rotterdam, 1985—90, Vendex Internat. NV / Royal Vendex KBB NV, 1990—2000; chmn. Euronext NV, 2000—07, NYSE Euronext, NYC, 2007—. Dir. Robrasco A.A., Rio de Janeiro, 1980-82; pres. Fontanus Argentina S.A., Buenos Aires, 1977-82; mem. supervisory bd. Schiphol Group N.V., 1993-2006, Royal Vopak N.V., Netherlands, 1999-2005, Laurus N.V., Netherlands, 1998-2004, B&N.com Inc., 1999-2003; mem. supervisory bd. Royal Philips Electronics N.V., Netherlands, also chmn. bd. dirs., Heineken N.V., Netherlands, 2001-12, Fortis N.V., Netherlands, Belgium, 2001-07, dep. chmn. 2007-09; chmn. supervisory bd. Schiphol Area Devel. Co., Netherlands, 1993-2006, SC Johnson Europlant B.V., Netherlands, Stichting Particuliere Historische Buitenplaatsen (Dutch Assn. Pvt. Hist. Estates), Dutch National Com. Rembrandt 400; serves on the internat. adv. bd. Blackstone Group, SC Johnson Corp. Pres. Escolha Rainha Juliana, Sao Paulo, 1981-82. Office: NYSE Euronext Inc 11 Wall St New York NY 10005

HESTAND, JOEL DWIGHT, minister, evangelist; b. Henrietta, Tex., May 23, 1939; s. Dee Lathell and Jack Fern (Gamble) H.; m. Carolyn Somers, June 12, 1959; children: Paul Daniel, Joe Randall. Student, Odessa Coll., Tex., 1963-66; diploma, Brown Trail Sch. Preaching, Ft. Worth, Tex., 1968-70, Sunset Sch. Missions, Lubbock, 1973; BA, Theological U. Biblical Studies, 1990, MA, 1995, DM, 2007. Evangelist Ch. of Christ, various locations, 1968—; missionary Tanzania, E. Africa, 1973-75, Chimala Mission and Hosp., Mbeya, Tanzania, 1994-95. Police chaplain Naperville (Ill.) Police Dept., 1977-83; ednl. dir. Rockford (Ill.) Christian Camp, 1977-82, bd. dirs., 1977-82; instr. Fishers of Men Evangelism, Frankfort, Ky., 1984-2007. With USAF, 1957-66. Republican. Home: 515 Winters St River Oaks TX 76114 Office Phone: 502-227-0092.

HESTER, HORTENSE, retired physical education educator; b. Montgomery, Ala., Oct. 16, 1931; d. Roland Arthur and Josie Lee (Almon) Hester. AB, Judson Coll., 1954; MA, U. Ala., 1959; D in Phys. Edn., Ind. U., 1972. Cert. secondary tchr. Ala. Phys. edn. tchr. Andalusia HS, Ala., 1954—56; math. tchr. Capitol Heights Jr. HS, Montgomery, 1957—58; grad. asst. U. Ala., Tuscaloosa, 1958—59, Ind. U., Bloomington, 1964—66. Phys. edn. instr. James Madison U., Harrisonburg, Va., 1959—64; prof., chmn. dept. phys. edn. U. West Ala., 1966—86; ret. Sec. Presbyn. Women of Ch., Livingston, 1967—68; area coord. Ala. Spl. Olympics, 1972—86; chmn. City Recreation Bd., 1972—82. Mem.: AAHPERD, Phys. Edn. & Recreation (co-adviser student sect. 1972—73), Ala. State Assn. Health, Judson Coll. Alumnae Assn. (bd. dirs. 1981—87), Nat. Assn. Phys. Edn. in Higher Edn. (charter mem.), Ind. U. Alumni Found., Delta Kappa Gamma. Home: 3321 Oxmoor Ln Montgomery AL 36111-3316

HESTER, PHILLIP D., engineering company executive; BSEE, MSEE, U. Tex. Various leadership & exec. tech. positions IBM Corp.; co-founder Newisys (now Sanmina-SCI Co.), CEO, 2000—05; v.p. Advanced Micro Devices, Inc., 2005—06, chief tech. officer, 2005—08, sr. v.p., 2006—08; tech. cons., 2008—; sr. v.p. rsch. and devel. National Instruments Corp., 2009—. Bd. dirs. AMI Semiconductor Inc., 2006—, ON Semiconductor Corp., 2006—. Chmn. AMD Techn. Coun.; mem. IBM Corporate Tech. Coun. Mem.: RS/6000. Office: Nat Instruments Corp 11500 N Mopac Expwy Austin TX 78759-3504

HESTER, ROSS WYATT, retired manufacturing executive, small business owner; b. Amarillo, Tex., Aug. 23, 1924; s. Wyatt Langford and Nettie Estelle (Horne) H.; m. Elizabeth Ruth Hobbs, May 28, 1948 (div. Aug. 1984); children: Sherry Gail, Randal Ross, Debra Renee, Stephen Keith, Jeffry Wyatt. BA, Austin Coll., Sherman, Tex., 1947. Vice pres. Hester's Office Supply, Inc., Lubbock, Tex., 1947-60; pres. Caprock Bus. Forms, Inc., Lubbock, 1960-90, chmn. bd., 1990-96; ret., 1996; owner Off Broadway Used Books, Lubbock, 2007—14. Trustee Austin Coll., 1987-99. With USAAF, 1943-46, CBI. Recipient Disting. Alumnus award Austin Coll., 1984. Mem. Printing Industry Assn. Tex. (pres. 1988-89). Republican. Presbyterian. Avocations: tennis, reading, travel.

HESTER, THOMAS RODERICK, JR., plastic surgeon, educator; b. Cairo, Ga., Mar. 24, 1942; Grad., Emory U., Atlanta, 1963, MD, 1967. Cert. Am. Bd. Surgery, 1973, Am. Bd. Plastic Surgery, 1980. Intern surgery Grady Meml. Hosp., Atlanta, 1967—68; resident plastic reconstructive surgery Emory Affiliated Hosps., 1968—72; chief surgery Colquitt County Meml. Hosp., Moultrie, Ga., 1972—76; chief resident plastic surgery Emory U., 1976—78; assoc. prof. plastic and reconstructive surgery Emory U. Sch. Medicine, 1980—93, program dir. divsn. plastic surgery, 2001; asst. prof. plastic and reconstructive surgery Emory U., 2001—, chief divsn. plastic surgery, 2001—, William G. Hamm chair plastic surgery, 2005—; founder Paces Plastic Surgery, 1993—. Contbr. articles to med. jours., chapters to books. Maj. USAR, 1973—76. Recipient Best Jour. Article, Aesthetic Soc. Ednl. Rsch. Found., 1997. Fellow: Am. Coll. Surgeons; mem.: AMA, Southeastern Surg. Soc., So. Med. Assn., Med. Assn. Atlanta, Jurkiewicz Soc., James C. Thoroughman Surg. Soc., Ga. Med. Assn., Ga. Soc. Plastic Surgeons, Southeastern Soc. Plastic and Reconstructive Surgeons, Am. Assn. Plastic Surgeons, Am. Soc. Aesthetic Plastic Surgery (Simon Fredericks award 1992), Internat. Soc. Aesthetic Plastic Surgeons, Am. Soc. Plastic Surgeons, Alpha Omega Alpha Honor Med. Soc. Office: Paces Plastic Surgery 3200 Downwood Cir Ste 640A Atlanta GA 30327 also: Emory Divsn of Plastic and Reconstructive Surgery Emory Crawford Long Hosp 550 Peachtree St, SE, 8th Fl, Ste 4300 Atlanta GA 30308 Office Phone: 404-351-0051, 678-420-7045. Office Fax: 404-351-0632.

HESTERBERG, EARL J., automotive executive; BA, Davidson Coll.; MBA, Xavier Univ. With Nissan Motor Corp., 1982—98, v.p., gen. mgr. Nissan div., 1991—95, v.p. sales Nissan Europe, 1996—98; pres., CEO Gulf States Toyota, 1998—99; v.p., mktg.,sales & svc. Europe Ford Motor Corp., 1999—2004, v.p. No. Am. mktg., 2004—05; pres., CEO Group 1 Automotive, Inc., Miami, Fla., 2005—. Office: Group 1 Automotive Ste 500 800 Gessner Houston TX 77024 Office Phone: 713-647-5700.

HESTON, JERRY D., child and adolescent psychiatrist, educator; MD, U. South Fla., Tampa, 1981. Diplomate Am. Bd. Psychiatry and Neurology, 1988, Am. Bd. Psychiatry and Neurology- child and adolescent psychiatry, 1989, Am. Bd. Pediatrics, 2004. Intern LeBonheur Children's Hosp., 1982, resident pediat. Memphis, 1982—84; resident psychiatry Univ. Tenn. Affiliated Hosp., Memphis, 1984—86, fellow child & adolescent psychiatry, 1986—88; clin. prof. psychiatry Univ.Tenn. Coll. Medicine. Office: The University of Tennessee Health Science Center 920 Madison Ave Memphis TN 38163 Office Phone: 901-448-3420. Business E-Mail: jheston@uthsc.edu.

HETHERINGTON, EILEEN MAVIS, psychologist, educator; b. Nov. 27, 1926; BA, U. B.C., 1947, MA, 1948; PhD in Psychology, U. Calif.-Berkeley, 1958. Clin. psychologist B.C. Child Guidance Clinic, 1948-51, sr. psychologist, 1951-52; clin. internship Langley Porter Clinic, 1956-57; instr. psychology San Jose State Coll., 1957-58; asst. prof. Rutgers U., 1958-60; from asst. prof. to prof. U. Wis., 1960-70; prof. psychology U. Va., Charlottesville, 1970-99, James Page prof. psychology, 1976-99, prof. emeritus, 1999—, dept. chmn., 1980-84. Editor Child Devel., 1971-77; rschr. in personality devel. and childhood psychopathology, the role of family process and parent characteristics on normal and deviant behavior in children, the effects of divorce and remarriage on families, parents and children. Bd. dirs. Found. for Child Devel. Recipient Disting. Scientist award Am. Assn. for Marriage and Family Therapy, 1988, Am. Family Therapy Assn., 1992, Burgess award Nat. Coun. on Family Rels., 2000. Mem. APA (pres. divsn. 7, 1978-79, Stanley Hall Disting. Scientist award 1987, Disting. Scientist award 1993), Soc. Rsch. in Child Devel. (pres. 1985-87, Disting. Scientist award 1995), Soc. Rsch. in Adolescents (pres. 1986-88, Disting. Scientist award 1988, William James Disting. Scientist award 1994), Am. Psychol. Soc. (Disting. Scientist award 2004).

HETHERINGTON, MARC J., political science professor; BA in Polit. Sci. summa cum laude, U. Pitts., 1990; PhD in Govt., U. Tex., Austin, 1997. Lectr., dept. govt. U. Va., Charlottesville, 1997—98; asst. prof., dept. govt. Bowdoin Coll., Brunswick, Maine, 1998—2004; assoc. prof. dept. polit. sci. Vanderbilt U., Nashville, 2004—09, prof. dept. polit. sci., 2009—. Chair, Am. politics search com. Vanderbilt U., 2004—05, dir. grad. studies, 2005—. Co-author (with W. Keefe): Parties, Politics, and Public Policy in America, 2003; author: Why Trust Matters: Declining Political Trust and the Demise of American Liberalism, 2005; mem. editl. bd.: Polit. Behavior, 2005—09; contbr. articles to profl. jours., chapters to books. Recipient Emerging Scholar award, Am. Polit. Sci. Assn., 2004; fellow Ctr. the Study Democratic Politics, Princeton U., 2001—02. Mem.: Midwest Polit. Sci. Assn. (sect. chair, polit. psychology and pub. opinion 2002, polit. participation 2005). Office: Vanderbilt Univ Dept Polit Sci VU Station B #351817 Nashville TN 37235-1817 Office Phone: 615-322-6240. Business E-Mail: marc.j.hetherington@vanderibilt.edu.*

HETTRICK, GEORGE HARRISON, lawyer; b. Piney River, Va., Aug. 15, 1940; s. Ames Bartlett and Frances Caryl (O'Brian) H.; m. Lee Ann Hettrick; children: Heather White Hettrick Brugh, Edward Lord. BA, Cornell U., 1962; JD, Harvard U., 1965. Bar: Va. 1965. Assoc. Hunton & Williams LLP, Richmond, Va., 1965-73; spl. counsel Gov. of Va., 1970—71; ptnr., bus. practice group Hunton & Williams LLP, Richmond, Va., 1973—, and chmn., cmty. svc. com. Managing ptnr. Hunton & Williams Church Hill Neighborhood Pro Bono Law Office, Richmond, Virginia, 1990-, Hunton & Williams U. Va. Law Sch. Pro Bono Partnership Office, Charlottesville, Virginia, 2003-; chmn. Community Svc. com. Contbr. articles to profl. jours. Pres. bd. trustees Va. Episcopal Sch., Lynchburg, 1978—81; spl. counsel Gov. of Va., Richmond, 1971—72; vice-chmn. bd. dirs. Va. Port Authority, Norfolk, 1970—75, former commr., vice-chmn.; Va. State adv. com. Neighborhood Assistance Program; past dir., chmn. Peter Paul Devel. Ctr., Inc.; bd. dirs. Lawyers Helping Lawyers, 1992—, St. Mary's Hosp., 1996—2005, St. Francis Hosp., Regional Meml. Med. Ctr, Greater Richmond Bar Found., 1999—, pres., 2003—05; mem. Henrico County Cmty. Svcs. Bd., Va., 1997—2005, chmn., 2002—03; bd. dirs. Chesterfield/Colonial Heights Drug Ct. Found., 2002—; bd. dirs., vice chair Va. Network Nonprofit Orgns., 2000—05; bd. mem. Partnership for Nonprofit Excellence, 2007—11. Capt. US Army, 1966—68. Recipient Lifetime Achievement award, The American Lawyer mag., 2009. Fellow Va. Law Found., Pro Brono Task Force Local Svc. Corp.; mem. ABA(commr. Commn. Lawyers Assn. Program 2008-11), Va. Bar Assn. (chmn. substance abuse com. 1995-96), Va. State Bar, Richmond Bar Assn. (chmn. pro bono com. 1998-2001). Republican. Episcopalian. Office: Hunton & Williams LLP Riverfront Plz East Tower 951 E Byrd St Richmond VA 23219-4074 Home Phone: 804-364-5612; Office Phone: 804-788-8324. Office Fax: 804-788-8218. Business E-Mail: ghettrick@hunton.com.

HETZER, G. SCOTT, energy executive; BBA, U. Richmond, Va., 1978; MBA, U. Va., 1984. Mng. dir. Wheat First Butcher Singer; v.p., treas. Dominion, Richmond, 1997—99; sr. v.p., treas. Dominion Resources, Inc., 1999—, sr. v.p., treas., Va. Power and Consol. Natural Gas Co., 2000—; pres., Dominion Capital Dominion; sr. v.p., treas., va. power and consol. Natural Gas Co., 2000. Office: Dominion Resources Inc 120 Tredegar St Richmond VA 23219 Office Phone: 804-819-2000. Office Fax: 804-819-2233. Business E-Mail: Scott_Hetzer@dom.com.

HEUER, ROBERT MAYNARD, II, retired opera company executive; b. Detroit, Nov. 27, 1944; s. Robert Maynard and May Elizabeth (Quinn) Heuer. Student, Capital U., Columbus, Ohio; BA in Speech and Theater, Wayne State U., Detroit, 1976. Youth dir. Grace Luth. Ch., Detroit, 1964-66; costume designer, prodn. mgr. U. Windsor, Ont., Canada, 1967-69; program coord. Detroit Youth Theatre/Detroit Inst. Arts, 1970-71; founding mng. dir. Mich. Opera Theatre, Detroit, 1971-79; dir. prodn. Fla. Grand Opera (formerly Greater Miami Opera), 1979-83, asst. gen. dir., 1983—85, gen. dir., CEO, 1985—2012. Apptd. mem. Fla. Alliance Arts Edn., 1988; bd. dirs. and v.chmn. OPERA America; chmn. & mem. Opera/Music Theatre Grants Panel, Nat. Endowment for the Arts, Fla. State Music Grants Rev. Panel. Recipient Grand Decoration of Honor, Republic of Austria, 1990, Narot Humanitarian award, Temple Israel Greater Miami, 2001, Arts Mgmt. Excellence award, Arts & Bus. Coun., 2007. Mem.: Greater Miami C. of C.

HEUSINKVELD, DICK G., corporate financial executive; BSME, Queen's U., Kingston, Ont., Can. Registered profl. engr., Ont., Alta. Application engr. Dresser-Rand Group, Inc., Toronto, Canada, 1976, gen. mgr., packaging operation Canada, gen. mgr., svc. ctr., gas engine project mgr. Painted Post, NY, dir., power recovery and power turbines Olean, NY, Can. sales dir., new equipment, v.p., gen. mgr., Asia Pacific ops., 2007—. Office: Dresser-Rand Group Inc W8 TowerSte 1000 10205 Westheimer Rd Houston TX 77042 Office Phone: 713-973-5497. Office Fax: 713-354-6110.

HEWITT, LESTER L., lawyer; b. Houston, Mar. 11, 1942; BSME, U. Houston, 1965, LLB cum laude, 1968. Bar: Tex. 1968; Ct. admissions US Ct. Appeals 5th, 11th and Fed. Cir., US Dist. Ct. (No., So. and Western)Tex. Examiner U.S. Patent Office, 1968-69; atty. Pravel, Hewitt, Kimball & Krieger, Houston, 1971-98; ptnr., co-head intellectual property practice nationally Akin Gump, Strauss, Hauer & Feld LLP, Houston, 2003—06, ptnr., 2006—. Assoc. prof. engring. law U. Houston, 1973-80; spkr. in field. Named The Best Lawyers in America, Tex. Super Lawyer, 2004, 2005. Mem. Am. Intellectual Property Law Assn. (treas. 1985-88), Houston Intellectual Property Law Assn. (pres. 1991-92), Houston Bar Assn. (former bd. dirs.), Order of the Barons, Phi Delta Phi, Pi Tau Sigma, Tau Beta Pi, Omicron Delta Kappa. Office: Akin Gump Strauss Hauer & Feld LLP 44th fl 1111 Louisiana St Houston TX 77002 Office Phone: 713-220-5851. Office Fax: 713-236-0822. Business E-Mail: lhewitt@akingump.com.

HEWITT, LLEYTON GLYNN, professional tennis player; b. Adelaide, Australia, Feb. 24, 1981; s. Glynn and Cherilyn; m. Bec Cartwright, July 21, 2005; children: Mia Rebecca, Cruz. Profl. tennis player (ATP), 1998—. Mem. Australian Davis Cup Team, 1999—. Global amb. Special Olympics, 2002—. Named Most Popular South Australian Athlete, 2001—03, Male Athlete of the Yr., Australian Sports Awards, 2002, Sportsman of the Yr., GQ (Australia), 2003, Young Australian of Yr., 2003. Achievements include winning US Open, 2001, Wimbledon, 2002; winning doubles (with Max Mirnyi),

US Open, 2000; winner of 26 career singles titles, 2 doubles titles, ATP Tour; being a member of Australian Davis Cup Championship Team, 1999. Avocations: golf, Australian Rules Football. Office: Octagon 1751 Pinnacle Dr Ste 1500 Mc Lean VA 22102

HEWITT, PAUL HARRINGTON, men's college basketball coach; b. Jamaica, May 4, 1963; m. Dawnette Hewitt; 3 children. BA in Journalism and Econs., St. John Fisher Coll., 1985. Jr. varsity head coach Westbury HS, LI, NY, 1985—88; asst. coach C.W. Post U. Pioneers, NY, 1988—89, U. So. Calif. Trojans, 1989—90, Fordham U. Rams, 1990—92, Villanova U. Wildcats, 1992—97; head coach Siena Coll. Saints, 1997—2000, Georgia Inst. Tech. Yellow Jackets, 2000—11, George Mason U. Patriots, 2011—. Recipient Coaches vs. Cancer Champion award, Nat. Assn. Basketball Coaches, 2011. Achievements include coached Georgia Tech to NCAA Final Four appearance, 2004. Office: George Mason University Mens Basketball Office PC 1090 Mail 1D4 440 University Dr MS 3A5 Fairfax VA 22030

HEWITT, THOMAS FRANCIS, hotel executive; b. Marblehead, Mass., Dec. 7, 1943; s. Ralph Augustine and Shirley Elizabeth (Morris) H.; m. Sharyn Ann Holleran, June 11, 1968; 1 son, Sean Thomas. BBA, Bryant Coll., 1967; D (hon.), Johnson and Wales U. Gen. mgr. Sheraton LaGuardia, NYC, 1973-74; gen. mgr. Sheraton Heights Hotel, Hasbrouck Heights, N.J., 1974-75, Sheraton Plaza Hotel, Chgo., 1975-78; v.p., gen. mgr., area mgr. The Sheraton-Boston Hotel (The Sheraton Corp.), Boston, 1978-81; v.p., gen. mgr. Sheraton New Orleans Hotel, 1981, sr. v.p., gen. mgr., area mgr., 1983—; pres. Sheraton Corp. N.Am., 1983-85; exec. v.p. through pres., COO The Continental Cos., 1985—98; chmn., CEO Interstate Hotels Inc., 1999—2002; dir. Interstate Hotels & Resorts, 2002—05, CEO, 2005—. Chmn. Interstate Hotels Corp., Pitts., 1999. Mem. aviation com. New Orleans C. of C.; mem. Coconut Grove C. of C., Dade County's Beacon Coun. Recipient Lawson A. Odde award, Am. Hotel and Lodging Assn., 2001. Mem. Hotel Sales Mgrs. Assn., Greater New Orleans Hotel-Motel Assn. (dir.), Am. Hotel and Motel Assn. (vice chmn. internat. travel com.). Roman Catholic. Office: Interstate Hotels & Resorts 4501 N Fairfax Dr Arlington VA 22203

HEY, WAYNE ALBERT, urologic surgeon, medical association executive; b. Upper Darby, Pa., Jan. 20, 1950; s. Warren Albert and Doris Elanore Hey; m. Margaret Ann Davies, Mar. 17, 1972 (div. July 1993); children: Wayne, Lauren; m. Paula Jean Hey, May 26, 1994; children: Sarah, Zach, Joshua, Bethany. BA with honors, Temple U., 1971; DO, Phila. Coll. Osteo. Medicine, 1975. Cert. Am. Coll. Osteo. Surgeons. Intern Detroit Osteo. Hosp. Corp., 1975-76, resident urology, 1976-80; asst. prof. surgery Tex. Coll. Osteo. Medicine, Ft. Worth, 1980—, founder, dir. urology residency, 1986-94. Pres. DFW Urology Consultants, Ft. Worth, 1982—, Imaging Resources, Inc., Ft. Worth, 1984—; mng. gen. ptnr. Dallas Ft. Worth Imaging Partnership, 1984—. Deacon Bloomfield Hills (Mich.) Bapt. Ch., 1978-80; elder Pantego Bible Ch., Arlington, Tex., 1988-90. Recipient Meade Johnson award Meade Johnson Pharms., 1977. Fellow Am. Coll. Osteo. Surgeons; mem. Am. Urol. Assn., Tex. Osteo. Med. Assn. Republican. Avocations: jogging, singing, raising six children. Office: Dfw Urology 1101 University Dr Fort Worth TX 76107-3012 E-mail: wahfacos@airmail.net.

HEYBURN, JOHN GILPIN, II, federal judge; b. Boston, 1948; m. Martha Keeney, 1976. BA, Harvard U., 1970; JD, U. Ky., 1976. Ptnr. Brown, Todd & Heyburn, Louisville, 1976-92; judge US Dist. Ct. (we. dist.) Ky., Louisville, 1992—2001, 2008—, chief judge, 2001—08. Chmn. US Jud. Panel on Multidistrict Litig., 2007—. Mem. Budget Com. Jud. Conf.of US, 1994-04, chmn. 1997-04; chair Jefferson County Crime Commn.; mem. vis. com. U. Ky., 1980; active Leadership Louisville Found. With USAR, 1970-76. Mem. ABA, Ky. Bar Assn., Louisville Bar Assn., U. Ky. Coll. Law Alumni Assn. Office: US Dist Ct Gene Snyder US Courthouse 601 W Broadway Ste 239 Louisville KY 40202-2227

HEYER, STEVEN JAY, former hotel and beverage company executive; b. NYC, June 13, 1952; s. Harold and Ethel Heyer; m. Margaret Tobin, Feb. 13, 1989. BA, Cornell U., 1974; MBA, NYU, 1976. Various position including sr. v.p., mng. ptnr. Booz Allen & Hamilton, 1976—92; pres., COO Young & Rubicam Advt. Worldwide, 1992—94, Turner Broadcasting System, Inc., 1994—2001, Coca-Cola Co., Atlanta, 2002—04; CEO Starwood Hotels & Resorts Worldwide, Inc., White Plains, NY, 2004—07; chmn., co-CEO Electric Eye Entertainment Corp., Atlanta. Bd. dirs. Internet Security Systems Inc., 2004—, Starwood Hotels & Resorts Worldwide, Inc., 2004—07, Omnicare, Inc., 2008—, Lazard Ltd., 2005—, lead dir., 2009—. Bd. advisors Amos Tuck Sch., Dartmouth Coll.; bd. dirs. Piedmont Hosp., Atlanta, Trinity Sch., Atlanta; bd. visitors Emory U., Atlanta; ret. chmn. bd. dirs. Cable Advt. Bur.; bd. dirs. Ad Coun. Office: Electric Eye Entertainment Corp 1800 Peachtree St NW Ste 250 Atlanta GA 30309

HEYMAN, JOHN H., information technology executive; BBA in Acctg., U. Ga.; MBA, Harvard U. With Arthur Andersen, LLP, 1983—87; v.p., acquisitions Forsch Corp., 1989—91; v.p., CFO Phoenix Comm., Inc., 1991—95; exec. v.p. Radiant Systems, Inc., 1995—2001, pres., CFO, 1995—2003, bd. dirs., 1996—, CEO, 2002—. Office: Radient Systems Inc 3925 Brookside Pky Alpharetta GA 30022 Office Phone: 770-754-7790. Business E-Mail: john.heyman@radiantsystems.com.

HIAASEN, CARL, journalist, writer; b. Plantation, Fla., Mar. 12, 1953; s. Kermit Odel and Patricia Hiaasen; m. Connie Lyford (div. 1996); m. Fenia Clizer, 1999. BA in Journalism, U. Fla., 1974. Reporter Cocoa Today, Fla., 1974—76, Miami Herald, Fla., 1976—79, investigative reporter, 1979—85, weekly columnist, 1985—. Author: (novels) Tourist Season, 1986, Double Whammy, 1987, Skin Tight, 1989, Native Tongue, 1991, Strip Tease, 1993, Stormy Weather, 1995, Lucky You, 1997, Sick Puppy, 2000, Basket Case, 2002, Hoot, 2002 (Newbery Honor, Assn. Libr. Svc. to Children), Skinny Dip, 2004, Flush, 2005, Nature Girl, 2006, Scat, 2009, Star Island, 2010, Bad Monkey, 2013, (non-fiction) Team Rodent: How Disney Devours the World, 1998, Kick Ass, 1999, Paradise Screwed: Selected Columns, 2001, The Downhill Lie, 2008; co-author: Naked Came the Manatee, 1998, (novels with Bill Montalbano) Powder Burn, 1981, Trap Line, 1982, A Death in China, 1984. Recipient Damon Runyon award, Denver Press Club, 2003—04, Rebecca Caudill Young Reader's Book award, 2005. Avocations: music, guitar. Mailing: c/o Alfred A Knopf Books Random House 1745 Broadway New York NY 10019 Office: c/o The Miami Herald 3511 NW 91st Ave Doral FL 33172-1216*

HIATT, JANE CRATER, arts agency administrator; b. Winston-Salem, NC, May 26, 1944; d. Howard Rondthaler Jr. and Irene (Sides) Crater; m. K.W. Everhart Jr. (div. June 1973); m. Wood Coleman Hiatt, May, 1978; 1 child, Jonathan David. BA, U. N.C., 1966; MA, Wake Forest U., 1972. Eng. tchr. Winston-Salem (N.C.)/Forsyth County Schs., 1966-70; exec. dir. Tenn. Com. for the Humanities, Nashville, 1973-77; cons. various ednl. and cultural agys. Ocean Springs, Miss., 1978-80; asst. dir. Miss. Humanities Coun., Jackson, Miss., 1981-85; exec. dir. Arts Alliance of Jackson and Hinds County, Miss., 1985-89, Miss. Arts Commn., Jackson, 1989-95; interim dir. Miss. Mus. Art, 2001. Participant Arts Leadership Inst. of Humphrey Inst. for Pub. Affairs, Mpls., 1986, Leadership, Jackson, 1987; interim exec. dir. Miss. Mus. Art, 2001. Co-editor Peoples of the South, 1976; exec. producer (TV series) The South with John Siegenthaler, 1976; host, reporter Miss. Ednl. TV, Jackson, 1981-87. Active Miss. Econ. Coun., 1986—87, Miss. R&D Coun., 1984—88; pres. Mental Health Assn. of Hinds County, Jackson, 1986; treas. Miss. for Ednl. Broadcasting, 1987, 1988, 1989, Premier Class Leadership, Jackson, 1987, 1988; cmty. adv. coun. Jr. League of Jackson, 1995—; mem. representing Miss. Friends of Art and Preservation in Embassies Millennium Com.; bd. dirs. Miss. Mus. Art, 2000—09, Friends of Univ. Press, 2004—; bd. dirs. Miss. state com. Nat. Mus. Women in Arts. Recipient Heritage award City of Biloxi, 1984. Mem.: Women's Fund (benefactor and bd. dirs. 2002—09), Greater Jackson Found. (bd. dirs. 1996—2009, chmn. 2002—03), Pub. Edn. Forum (bd. dirs. 1993—95), Miss. Ctr. for Nonprofits (vice chmn., bd. dirs. 1993—96, adv. bd. 1997—), So. Arts Fedn. (bd. dirs. 1989—95), Nat. Assembly State Arts Agys. (bd. dirs. 1992—95, 2d v.p. 1995), Nat. Coun. on Arts, Nat. Assembly Local Arts Agys., Phi Beta Kappa. Home: 4 Waterstone Pl Jackson MS 39211-5987 E-mail: hiattw@bellsouth.net.

HICKEY, JOSEPH MICHAEL, investment banker; b. Greenburgh, Pa., June 6, 1940; s. Joseph Michael and Margaret (Nelson) H.; m. Suzanne Klempay, July 2, 1970. BS, Ind. U. Pa., 1963. Sales rep. 3M Co., St. Paul, 1967-69; acct. exec. Hornblower & Weeks, Helphill, Noyes, Cleve., 1970-75; pres. Prescott, Ball & Turben, Cleve., 1976-88; dist. chmn. Nat. Assn. Security Dealers, Cleve., 1979-81; mem. mktg. com. SIA, NYC, 1982-86, mem. regional firms com., 1989; chmn. bd. Canregie Capital Mgmt. Co., Cleve., 1983-86; pres. J.W. Charles Group, Boca Raton, Fla., 1988-90; chmn. Pierman Golf Co., North Palm Beach, Fla., 1991-92; pres. Greyfriar Capital Corp., North Palm Beach, Fla. S.E. region adv. bd. No. Trust. Capt. US Army, 1963—67. Mem. Loxahatchee Club, Lost Tree Club, Cleve. Clinic Fla. Health & Wellness Ctr. (leadership bd. mem. 2008-).

HICKEY, SUSAN OWENS, federal judge; b. Dallas, 1955; m. Hickey Joseph; children: Raymond Patrick, Michael Andrew, Joseph Bartholomew. BA, U. Ark., 1977; JD, U. Ark. Sch. Law, 1980. Staff atty. Murphy Oil Corp., El Dorado, Ark., 1981—84; judicial law clk. to Hon. Harry F. Barnes US Dist. Ct. (western dist.) Ark., 1997, 1998, 2003—10; cir. judge Thirteenth Judicial Cir., Ark., 2010—11; judge US Dist. Ct. (western dist.) Ark., El Dorado, 2011—. Office: US District Court 219 US Post Office & Courthouse 101 South Jackson Ave El Dorado AR 71730

HICKMAN, CLEVELAND PENDLETON, JR., biology professor; b. Greencastle, Ind., Oct. 29, 1928; m. Ethel Rae Rickenbacher, Aug. 19, 1950; children: Andrew Richard (dec.), Diane Elaine. AB, DePauw U., 1950; MS, U. N.H., 1953; PhD in Zoology (B.C. Elec. scholar), U. B.C., 1958. Fishery researcher U. Wash., Seattle, 1954-55; asst. prof. U. Alta., 1958-63, asso. prof., 1963-67; assoc. prof. biology Washington and Lee U., Lexington, Va., 1967-70, prof., 1970-93, prof. emeritus, 1993—. Author: (with L.S. Roberts and A. Larson) Animal Diversity, 1995, 3rd edit., 2003, (with L.S. Roberts) Biology of Animals, 7th edit., 1998, (with L.S. Roberts, S.I. Keen, A. Larson, H. I'Anson and D. Eisenhour) Integrated Principles of Zoology, 14th edit., 2008, A Field Guide to Sea Stars and Other Echinoderms of Galápagos, 1998, A Field Guide to Marine Molluscs of Galápagos, 1999, A Field Guide to Crustaceans of Galapagos, 2000, A Field Guide to Corals and Other Radiates of Galapagos, 2008, (with William S. Hoar) A Laboratory Companion for General and Comparative Physiology, 3d edit., 1983; contbr. numerous articles to profl. jours. Nat. Rsch. Coun. Can. grantee, 1959-67; sr. rsch. fellow, 1965-66; NIH grantee, 1962-65; NSF grantee, 1970-74 Office: Washington and Lee U Dept Biology Lexington VA 24450 Personal E-mail: hickman.c@rockbridge.net. Business E-Mail: hickmanc@wlu.edu.

HICKMAN, ELIZABETH PODESTA, retired counselor; b. Livingston, Ill., Sept. 30, 1922; d. Louis and Della (Martin) Podesta; m. Franklin Jay Hickman, Mar. 17, 1944 (dec.); children: Virginia Hickman Hellstern, Franklin. BEd summa cum laude, Ea. Ill. State U.; MA, George Washington U., 1966, EdD, 1979; postgrad., U. Chgo., 1945, U. Va., 1964-66; postgrad. (fellow), Northeastern U., 1967-68; exxon, Found.Raskob Found. grantee. Lic. counselor, Va. Tchr. pub. schs., Ill., Ohio, Va., Naples, Italy, 1944-64; dir. coll. transfer guidance Maymount Coll. Va., Arlington, 1964-67, dir. Counseling Ctr., 1974-81, assoc. dean counseling and residence life, 1981-84; cmty. counselor Divsn. Mass. Employment Security, Newton, 1968-69; tchr. English conversation, Fuchu, Japan, 1969-73; placement dir., career counselor Coll. of Gt. Falls, Mont., 1973-74. Lectr. Far East divsn. U. Md., Fuchu, 1971-73; spl. advisor Internat. Ranger Camps, Denmark and Switzerland, 1974-81; spl. cons. Internat. Quaker Sch., Werkhoven, The Netherlands, 1959-63; mem. steering com. Pres.'s Com. on Employment of Handicapped, 1974-95. Vol., ARC, 1967-68, Family Svcs., 1954-75, White House Agy. Liaison, 1986—, Kennedy Ctr. Adminstrn., Washington, 1984—, Arlington Free Clinic, 2000-02. With WAVES, 1943-44. Recipient Disting. Alumnus award Ea. Ill. U., 1984, Pres.'s Vol. Svc. award Washington DC, 2007-, White House vol. award, 2008. Mem. Brent Soc., Rose Soc., Potomac (Ill) Soc., Italian Am. Soc., Marymount U. Angels Soc., Women's Com. Nat. Symphony Orch., Washington Opera Guild, Square Sigma Sigma, Pi Lambda Theta, Am. League. Roman Catholic.

HICKMAN, JEFFREY W., state legislator; b. Alva, Okla., Nov. 28, 1973; s. Steve and Cathy (Leamon) Hickman; m. Jana Harris; children: Taylor, Ashley, Austin. BA in Journalism with Distinction, Univ. Okla., 1996. Bd. mem. Okla. Centennial Commn.; press sec. U. Okla., project coord., office pres., 2000—03; vice pres. Omni Media Group, Woodward, Okla., 2003—04; owner, farmer in Alfalfa and Wood Counties; mem. Dist. 58 Okla. House of Representatives, 2004—. Former Alfalfa Co. EMS Vol. 1st responder. Recipient Farm Bureau Meritoris Svc. award, 2007; named Hon. Prospector, Selemite Crystal Festival. Mem.: Woodward United Way, 101 Classic Bowl Found. (bd. mem.), Okla. Summer Art Inst. (bd. mem.), Woodward Rotary Club. Republican. Methodist. Office: 2300 N Lincoln Blvd Rm 411 Oklahoma City OK 73105 Address: RR 1 Box 7 Dacoma OK 73731 Fax: 405-962-7612. Business E-Mail: jwhickman@okhouse.gov.

HICKMAN, TRAPHENE PARRAMORE, retired library director, consultant, storyteller; b. Dallas, Jan. 31, 1933; d. Redden Travis and Stella (Moore) P.; m. John Robert Hickman, June 9, 1950; children: Lynn Kleifgen, Laurie Ward AA, Mountain View C.C.; BA, U. Tex-Arlington; MLS, U. North Tex. Cert. libr., Tex. Libr. Cedar Hill (Tex.) Pub. Libr., 1959-77, interim dir., 2009—10; dir. Dallas County Libr. Sys., Dallas, 1977-93; libr. cons. Dallas County, 1993-95; libr. High Pointe Elem. Sch. Cedar Hill Ind. Sch. Dist., 2003—05. Chair leadership coun. and family ministries FUMC of Cedar Hill, pres. Cedar Hill C. of C., 1984. Editor: History and Directory of Cedar Hill, 1976; editor News and Views newsletter Dallas county Employees, 1986-92. Chmn. Bicentennial Com., Cedar Hill, 1976; del. Dem. Nat. Conv. 9th Senate Dist., Tex., 1976; chmn. Sesquicentennial Com., Cedar Hill, 1984-86; Dallas County Dem. Forum; mem. Electoral Coll., 1988; chairperson Women's Bd. Northwood Inst., Cedar Hill; active Dallas County Sesquicentennial Com., 1996-; lay speaker United Methodist Ch., 2004-13. Recipient Newsmaker of Yr. award Cedar Hill Chronicle, 1976; named Amb. of Goodwill, State of Tex., 1976 Mem. ALA, Tex. Libr. Assn. (legis. com. 1984-95, councillor 1982-83, trustee com. 1987-95, pub. info. com. 1987-95), Pub. Libr. Adminstrs. of North Tex. (sec., v.p., pres. 1980, 87), Dallas County Libr. Assn., N.E. Tex. Libr. Sys. (legis. commn. 1978-95, Libr. of Yr. 1987), U. North Tex. Sch. Libr. and Info. Scis. Alumni Assn. (pres. 1987-88), Cedar Hill C. of C., Cedar Summit Book Club (pres.), Dallas Area Storytelling Guild (pres. 1995-99, speaker, 2004-, trainer 2008-, program organizer 2011). Democrat. Methodist. Avocations: writing, reading, storytelling, gardening, bridge, travel, square dancing. Home and Office: 421 Lee St Cedar Hill TX 75104-2697

HICKS, JEFF J., advertising executive; BA, Amherst Coll., Mass.; MBA, Harvard U. With Leo Burnett, Chgo., 1987—97, v.p., 1994—97; pres., ptnr. Crispin Porter & Bogusky, Miami, 1997—, CEO, 2004—10, vice chmn., 2010—. Office: Crispin Porter + Bogusky 3390 Mary St Ste 300 Miami FL 33133 Office Phone: 305-859-2070.

HICKS, MARION LAWRENCE, JR., (LARRY HICKS), lawyer; b. Bethlehem, Pa., Sept. 5, 1945; s. Marion Lawrence and Martha (McCracken) H.; m. Beverly Brickman, Nov. 28, 1970; children: Yale McCracken, Hadley Brook, Kelley Hayden. BA in History, Duke U., 1967; JD with honors, U. Tex., 1970. Bar: Tex. 1970. Law clk. 9th cir. US Ct. Appeals, LA, 1970-71; assoc. Thompson, Knight, Simmons & Bullion, Dallas, 1971-77; adminstrv. ptnr. Thompson & Knight LLP, 1977—; mng. ptnr. Dallas Office. Spkr. in field. Editor Tex. Law Rev.; contbr. articles to profl. jour. Named one of Tex. Super Lawyers; named to Best Lawyers in Am., Chambers USA and other publs. Mem. ABA (real property, trust and probate sects.), Am. Coll. Mortgage Atty. (past. pres.), State Bar Tex., Dallas Bar Assn. (past chmn. real property sect., legal aid and legal svc. com.), Coll. State Bar Tex., Order of Coif, Petroleum Club, Phi Delta Phi. Avocations: sports, hunting, fishing. Home: 4310 Throckmorton St Dallas TX 75219-2240 Office: Thompson & Knight LLP 1722 Routh St Ste 1500 Dallas TX 75201 Home Phone: 214-219-4450; Office Phone: 214-969-1627. Business E-Mail: larry.hicks@tklaw.com.

HICKS, S. MAURICE, JR., federal judge; b. New Orleans, 1952; BA, Tex. Christian U., 1974; JD, La. State U., Baton Rouge, 1977. Law clk., staff atty. La. Legis. Coun., 1975—77; pvt. practice atty. Shreveport, La., 1977—2003; judge US Dist. Ct. (we. dist.) La., Shreveport, 2003—. Office: US Dist Ct 300 Fannin St Shreveport LA 71101-3083 Office Phone: 318-676-3055.

HICKS, TERRELL COHLMAN, surgeon, educator, health facility and academic administrator; b. Seminole, Okla., 1949; MD, U. Tex., 1977. Diplomate Am. Bd. Surgery, Am. Bd. Colon and Rectal Surgery. Intern U. Louisville, 1977-78, resident in surgery, 1979-82; fellow in colon and rectal surgery Ochsner Clinic, New Orleans, 1982-83, now surgeon, assoc. chmn. dept. colon and rectal surgery, 1983—, program dir. colon & rectal surgery tng. fellowship program; assoc. clin. prof. surgery Sch. Medicine La. State U. Mem. AMA, Am. Soc. Colon and Rectal Surgery (pres.), So. Med. Assn. Office: Ochsner Clinic 1514 Jefferson Hwy New Orleans LA 70121-2483 E-mail: tchbknight@aol.com.

HICKS, TOM (THOMAS OLLIS HICKS SR.), professional sports team executive, real estate developer; b. Dallas, Feb. 7, 1946; s. John H. Hicks Jr.; m. Cinda Hicks, 1990; 6 children. BBA, U. Tex., 1968; MBA, U. So. Calif., 1970. Investment officer Morgan Guaranty Trust Co., NYC, 1968-74; pres. First Dallas Capital Corp., Dallas, 1974-77; co-mng. ptnr. Summit Ptnrs., Dallas, 1977-83; co-chmn., co-CEO, Hicks & Haas Inc., Dallas, 1983-89; chmn., CEO, Hicks, Muse, Tate & Furst Inc., Dallas, 1989—2004; owner, chmn. Dallas Stars, 1995—2011, Tex. Rangers, Arlington, 1998—2010; CEO, chmn. Southwest Sports Group Inc., Hicks Holdings LLC, 2005—; co-owner, co-chmn. Liverpool F.C. (English Premier League), 2007—. Bd. dirs. MLB Advanced Media; vice chair bd. govs. NHL, 2007—. Contbr. United Way, Goodwill, Dallas Art Mus., Dallas Symphony Orchestra, Sci. Place at Fair Park. Recipient Henry Cohn Humanitarian Award, Anti-Defamation League, 2000, Marshall Trojan Award, U. So. Calif. Marshall Sch. Bus., 2005. Achievements include being the owner of the Stanley Cup Champion Dallas Stars, 1999. Avocation: golf. Office: Hicks Holdings LLC 100 Crescent Ct Ste 1200 Dallas TX 75201 Office Phone: 214-615-2300.

HICKSON, GERALD BENNETT, pediatrician; b. Tifton, Ga., Apr. 22, 1952; BS, U. Ga.; MD, Tulane U. Sch. Medicine, 1978. Cert. Am. Bd. Pediat. Resident, pediat. Vanderbilt U. Med. Ctr., Nashville, 1978—81; fellow, gen. academic pediat. Vanderbilt U. Med. Ctr./Metro Nashville Gen. Hosp., Tenn., 1981—83; chief, pediat. Vanderbilt Clinic, Nashville, 1990—2003; health policy fellow Vanderbilt Inst. Pub. Policy Studies, Nashville, 1991; instr., pediat. Vanderbilt U. Sch. Medicine, Nashville, 1982—83, assoc. prof., 1997, prof., pediat., 1998, assoc. prof., pediat., 1990—98, prof., psychiatry, 2001, assoc. dean, clin. affairs, 2003—, prof., pediat., 2003—, dir., Ctr. for Patient and Profl. Advocacy; asst. prof. Vanderbilt Sch. Nursing, Nashville, 1990—92, assoc. prof., family and health sys. nursing, 1994—; dir., clin. risk and loss prevention Vanderbilt U. Med. Ctr. Vis. prof., pediat. U. Carabobo, Valencia, Venezuela, 1985; rsch. investigator Peabody Coll., Vanderbilt U., Tenn., 1988; bd. gov. Nat. Patient Safety Found.; chairperson, quality care com. Nat. Assn. Children's Hosp. and Related Inst. Mem.: Am. Acad. Pediat. (mem. com. on quality improvement). Office: Ctr for Patient & Profl Advocacy Vanderbilt U Med Ctr 405 Oxford House Nashville TN 37232-4200 Office Phone: 615-343-4500. Office Fax: 615-343-8580. Business E-Mail: gerald.hickson@vanderbilt.edu.

HICKSON, RICHARD G., bank executive; Exec. v.p. Tex. Commerce Bancshares, Houston; chmn., CEO TCB, El Paso, pres.; with Citizens and Southern Nat. Bank, Atlanta, 1971; pres., CEO South-Trust Bank of Georgia, N.A., 1997; chmn. Trustmark Corp., 2002—, Trustmark Nat. Bank, 2002—. Office: Trustmark Corp 248 E Capitol St Jackson MS 39201 Office Phone: 601-208-5111. Office Fax: 601-208-6684. Business E-Mail: rhickson@trustmark.com.

HIDRON, ALICIA, internist, medical educator; b. Feb. 15, 1975; MD, CES Inst. Healt Scis., Columbia, 1999. Diplomate Am. Bd. Internal Medicine. Resident internal medicine Emory U. Sch. Medicine, Atlanta, 2002—05, chief resident, 2005—06, fellow divsn. infectious disease, 2006, asst. prof. medicine, 2007—. Contbr. articles to profl. jours. Mem.: ACP, Alpha Omega Alpha Honor Med. Soc. Office: 69 Jesse Hill Jr Dr SE Atlanta GA 30303 Office Phone: 404-616-7027. Business E-Mail: ahidron@emory.edu.

HIERS, RICHARD HYDE, lawyer, educator, writer; s. Glen and Mildred H.; m. Jane Gale, 1954; children: Peter, Rebecca. BA, Yale U., 1954, BD, 1957, MA, PhD, 1959-61; JD, U. Fla., 1983. Bar: Fla. 1984, Fla. Eigth Judicial Cir. Bar Assn., US Dist. Ct. (we. dist.) Tex. 1988, US Ct. Appeals (5th cir.) 1988. Instrn. asst. Yale Divinity Sch., 1958—61; asst. prof. Coll. Liberal Arts and Scis., U. Fla., Gainesville, 1961-66, assoc. prof., 1966-72, prof., 1972—2003, prof. emeritus, 2003—, affiliate prof. law Coll. Law, 1994—2003, affiliate prof. law emeritus, 2003—. Pres. Am. Acad. Religion, Southeastern Region,

1969-70; pres. Soc. Biblical Literature, Southeastern Region, 1982-83; jud. law clk. US Ct. Appeals, 5th cir., 1987-88, disting. fellow Eckerd Coll. Ctr. Spiritual Life, 2003-06; chmn. adv. com., Jour. Law and Religion, 2006-11. Author (book) Women's Rights and the Bible, 2012; several books; contbr. numerous articles to profl. jours., chpts. to books. Former mem. Danforth Assocs. Tchg.; former pres. Gainesville Coun. Human Relations, Gainesville /Alachua County Housing Assn.; bd. dirs. Fla. Free Speech Forum, 2009—13. Recipient Disting. Faculty award, Fla. Blue Key Orgn., 1998. Mem. Soc. Christian Ethics, Yale Whiffenpoofs of 1954, Mory's Assn., Order of the Coif, Phi Beta Kappa (pres. U. Fla. chpt., 1975-76), Phi Kappa Phi (pres. U. Fla chpt., 1995-96), League of Conservation Voters, Natural Resources Def. Coun., Save-the-Redwoods League, Sierra Club, Wilderness Soc. Democrat. Presbyterian. Avocations: hiking, reading, singing. Office: University Fla Box 117410 107 Anderson Hall Gainesville FL 32611-7410 Business E-Mail: hiers@law.ufl.edu.

HIGDON, JIMMY, state legislator; b. 1953; BS, Morehead State U., Ky. Mcht. Higdon's Foodtown; state rep. Dist. 24 Ky. Legislature, 2003—09, state senator Dist. 14, 2009—. Served with USAR. Mem.: Lebanon-Marion County Indsl. Found., Ky. Grocers Assn., Marion County Econ. Devel. Republican. Roman Catholic. Mailing: 507 W Main St Lebanon KY 40033 Office: Capitol Annex Rm 204 702 Capitol Ave Frankfort KY 40601 Office Phone: 270-692-3881, 502-564-8100 ext. 623. Office Fax: 270-692-1111. Business E-Mail: jimmy.higdon@lrc.ky.gov.

HIGGINBOTHAM, JOHN BURNELL, information technology executive; b. Conway, SC, Oct. 18, 1955; s. Walter G. and Sara B. (Brown) H.; m. Carrie E. Kidwell, Dec. 17, 1984; children: Robert, Sarah, John David. BS in Civil Engring. with honors, Va. Tech., 1977; MBA, Harvard U., 1979. Product mktg. mgr. Hewlett Packard Co., Corvallis, Oreg., 1979-81; satellite systems analyst Corroon & Black Inspace, Bethesda, Md., 1981; co-founder, dir., v.p. International Technologies Underwriters, Bethesda, 1981-89, sr. v.p., 1989—91; pres., mng. dir. Spacevest Mgmt. Group, Washington, 1991—2006; pres., CEO Integral Systems, Inc., 2008—09; chmn., CEO Blue Ridge Networks, Inc., Va., 2010—. Mem. bd. dirs. Houselife, Inc., Great Falls, Va., Space Commerce Editorial Bd., Washington, Integral Sys., Inc., 2008-2009. Contbr. articles to profl. jours. Mem. bd. dirs. Va. Tech. Alumni Assn., Blacksburg, 1977-79, No. chpt., Blacksburg, 1989—; mem. bd. dirs., pres. Falcon Ridge Homeowners Assn., Great Falls, 1989-90, Telephone Condiminium Assn., Washington, 1990-91. Presdl. scholar Va. Polytech. Inst. & State U., 1986. Mem. AIAA (sr.), IEEE, ASCE, Washington Space Bus. Roundtable (bd. dirs. 1988—, vice chmn. 1990-91). Office: Blue Ridge Networks 14120 Parke Long Ct Ste 103 Chantilly VA 20151 Office Phone: 703-631-0700.

HIGGINBOTHAM, PATRICK ERROL, federal judge; b. McCalla, Ala., Dec. 16, 1938; Student, U. Ala., 1956, Arlington State Coll., 1957, North Tex. State U., 1958, U. Tex., 1958; BA, U. Ala., 1960, LLB, 1961; LLD (hon.), So. Meth. U., 1989. Bar: Ala. 1961, Tex. 1962, US Supreme Ct. 1962. Assoc. to ptnr. Coke & Coke, Dallas, 1964—75; judge US Dist. Ct. (no. dist.) Tex., Dallas, 1976—82, US Ct. Appeals (5th cir.), Dallas, 1982—2006, sr. judge, 2006—. Adj. prof. So. Meth. U. Law Sch., 1971—, adj. prof. constl. law, 1981—, U. Tex. Sch. Law, 1998; M.D. Anderson pub. svc. prof. in residence Tex. Tech. U. Sch. Law, 1999; John Sparkman jurist-in-residence U. Ala. Sch. Law, 1995, 1997, 1999; vis. prof. St. Mary's Law Sch., 2006—07; conferee Am. Assembly, 1975, Pound Conf., 1976; bd. suprs. Inst. Civil Justice Rand. Contbr. articles to profl. jours. With JAG USAF, 1961—64. Recipient Dan Meador award, U. Ala., Samuel E. Gates Litigation award, Am. Coll. Trial Lawyers, 1997, A. Sherman Christensen award, 2002, Fifth Cir. Profl. award, Inns Ct. Found., 2006, Justice Lewis Powell award, Presdl. US Sect., 2008, Chief J. John Marshall award, JAL Assn., WNSAC, 2010, Sir Thomas More award, St. Mary's Law Sch., 2011, Judge of Yr. 2006, Tex. Ann. Bd. Trial Advs.; named Outstanding Alumnus, U. Tex., Arlington, 1978, One of Nation's 100 Most Powerful Persons for the 80's, Next Mag. Fellow: Am. Bar Found.; mem.: ABA, Ctr. for Am. and Internat. Law (bd. dirs. 1998—, chmn.), Am. Inns of Ct. Found. (pres. 1996—2000), Farrah Law Soc., Patrick E. Higginbotham Inn of Ct., Nat. Jud. Coun. State and Fed. Cts., Am. Judicature Soc., Am. Law Inst., Dallas Bar Found., Dallas Bar Assn., Bench and Bar, Order of Coif (hon.), Omicron Delta Kappa. Office: US Ct Appeals Rm 400 903 San Jacinto Blvd Austin TX 78701

HIGGINBOTHAM, WENDY JACOBSON, political advisor, freelance writer; b. Salt Lake City, Oct. 23, 1947; d. Alfred Thurl and Virginia Lorraine (LaCom) Jacobson; m. Keith Higginbotham, July 12, 1969; children: Ann Elizabeth Morley, Ryan Keith, Laura Carol Hoopes. Student, Occidental Coll., 1965—66, U. Grenoble, France, 1967; BA cum laude with highest honors, Brigham Young U., 1969. Tchg. instr. Brigham Young U., Provo, Utah, 1969-70, editor univ. press, 1970-71; freelance editor Camarillo, Calif., 1971-78; freelance newspaper writer Vienna, Va., 1983-85; mem. profl. staff US Senate Labor Com., Washington, 1985—88, legis. asst.; legis. dir. U.S. Senator Orrin G. Hatch, Washington, 1988-91, chief of staff, 1991-94, chief policy adviser, 1994-95, communications advisor, 2000—07; polit. adviser, freelance writer Washington, 1996. Mem. Profl. Rep. Women, Phi Kappa Phi. Republican. Mem. Lds Ch. Avocations: travel, hiking. Home: 2022 Willow Branch Ct Vienna VA 22181-2972

HIGGINBOTTOM, SAMUEL LOGAN, retired air transportation executive; b. North Lawrence, Ohio, Oct. 5, 1921; s. Samuel Bradlaugh and Vera Abbie (Gutchess) H.; m. Fair Steinschneider, Aug. 30, 1947 (dec. May 1997); children: Samuel Logan, Marie Fair, Michele Rowan Maclaren; m. Janaina Dornelles, Aug. 4, 1998. BS in Civil Engring, Columbia, 1943; grad. Advanced Mgmt. Program, Harvard U. Design engr. Parsons, Brinckerhoff, Hogan & McDonald, NYC, 1945-46; v.p. engring., flight, test and inspection Trans World Airlines, Inc., 1946-64; v.p. engring. and maintenance Eastern Air Lines, Inc., 1964-67, v.p. operations group, 1967-69, sr. v.p., 1969, exec. v.p., 1969-70, pres., chief operating officer, 1970-73; chmn., pres., chief exec. officer Rolls-Royce Inc., NYC, 1974-86. Bd. dirs. Heico Corp. Emeritus chmn. bd. trustees Columbia U.; mem. adv. bd. Taub Inst. Capt. USAAF, WWII, ETO. Decorated hon. comdr. Order Brit. Empire; recipient Egleston medal Columbia U. Engring. Sch., 1977 Fellow AIAA; mem. Soc. Automotive Engrs., Conquistadores del Cielo, Wings Club (pres.1980-81), Deering Bay Yacht and Country Club, Tau Beta Pi, Psi Upsilon, Theta Tau. Roman Catholic. Personal E-mail: samhiggi@bellsouth.net.

HIGGINS, BRADFORD ROBERT, humanitarian organization executive, former federal agency administrator; b. 1952; m. Kimberly Rossetter; 1 child, Schuyler. BS, Columbia U., 1974, JD, 1978. Assoc. Simpson Thacher & Bartlett, 1978—80; mng. dir. Bear Sterns Asset Mgmt., 1980—87; CFO Coalition Provisional Authority, Iraq; chief of planning, Iraq reconstruction mgmt. office US Dept. State, CFO, sr. advisor office asst. sec. resource mgmt., sr. advisor to US amb. Iraq, asst. sec. for resource mgmt., CFO, 2006—09; mng. ptnr. SOSventures, LLC, 2009—; pres., chmn. JumpStart Internat., 2009—. Bd. dirs. Capital Growth Systems Inc., 2010—. Office: JumpStart International PO Box 868 Decatur GA 30031 Office Phone: 404-607-8153.

HIGGINS, KEVIN, food service executive; B in Engring., U. Coll. Dublin, Ireland, M in Engring. Sci.; MBA, Henley Mgmt. Coll., England. Various positions M&M Mars Inc., Pepsico Restaurants, London; dir. devel., franchisee devel. and fin., UK Yum! Brands, 2001—04, gen. mgr., Europe and Russia Franchise Bus. Unit Geneva, 2004—09; pres., EMEA Burger King Corp., Zug, Switzerland, 2009—. Office: Burger King Corp 5505 Blue Lagoon Dr Miami FL 33126 Office Phone: 305-378-3000.

HIGGINS, ROD (RODERICK DWAYNE HIGGINS), professional sports team executive, retired professional basketball player; b. Monroe, La., Jan. 31, 1960; m. Concetta Higgins; children: Rick, Cory. Student, Calif. State U., Fresno. Profl. basketball player Chgo. Bulls, 1982—85, 1986, Seattle SuperSonics, 1985, San Antonio Spurs, 1985, NJ Nets, 1986, Golden State Warriors, 1986—92, 1994—95, Sacramento Kings, 1992—93, Cleve. Cavaliers, 1993—94; asst. coach Golden State Warriors, 1994—2000; asst. gen. mgr. Washington Wizards, 2000—03; gen. mgr. Golden State Warriors, 2004—07, Charlotte Bobcats, 2007—11, pres. basketball ops., 2011—. Office: Charlotte Bobcats 333 E Trade St Charlotte NC 28202

HIGGINS, VINCENT, mining executive; Undergraduate degree in Physics Summa Cum Laude, U. Dallas, Tex., 1986; PhD in High Energy Physics, Purdue U., West Lafayette, Ind., 1989; degree in Philosophy & Theology, Pontifical U., Rome, Italy, 1993. V.p., mktg. and investor rels. Chancery Resources, Inc., bd. dirs., 2009—. Bd. advisor Exec. Edge Inc., 2009—. Bd. dirs. Lumen Inst., 2004—08; pres., founder Inst. for Effective Leadership, 2008—. Office: Chancery Resources Inc 4553 Jimmy Doolittle Dr Ste 5 Addison TX 75001-5456 Office Phone: 214-288-9897. Office Fax: 972-930-7202.

HIGGINSON, STEPHEN ANDREW, federal judge, former federal prosecutor; b. Boston, Apr. 1961; m. Collett Creppell. AB summa cum laude, Harvard U., 1983; M in Philosophy, Cambridge U., 1984; JD, Yale U., 1987. Law clk. to Hon. Patricia M. Wald US Ct. Appeals (DC Cir.), 1987—88; law clk. to Justice Byron R. White US Supreme Ct., 1988—89; asst. US atty. Dist. Mass., Criminal Divsn. US Dept. Justice, Boston, 1989—93, asst. US atty. (eastern dist.) La., 1993—2011, chief of appeals, 1995; assoc. prof. law Loyola U. New Orleans Coll. Law, 2004—11; judge US Ct. Appeals (5th Cir.), New Orleans, 2011—. Dep. dir. spl. projects Presdl. Rule of Law Initiative US Dept. State, 1997—98. Harvard Scholar, Cambridge U. Office: US Court Appeals 600 Camp St Rm 244 New Orleans LA 70130*

HIGHSMITH, SHELBY, federal judge; b. Jacksonville, Fla., Jan. 31, 1929; s. Isaac Shelby and Edna Mae (Phillips) H.; m. Mary Jane Zimmerman, Nov. 25, 1972; children: Holly Law, Shelby, Jr. AA, Ga. Mil. Coll., 1948; BA, JD, U. Kansas City, 1958. Bar: Fla. 1958. Trial atty., Kansas City, Mo., 1958-59, Miami, Fla., 1959-70; circuit judge Dade County, Fla., 1970-75; sr. ptnr. Highsmith, Strauss, Glatzer & Deutsch, P.A., Miami, 1975-91; judge US Dist. Ct. Fla. Southern Dist., Miami, 1991—2008. Chief legal adviser Gov.'s War on Crime Program, 1967-68; spl. counsel Fla. Racing Commn., 1969-70; mem. Inter-Agy. Law Enforcement Planning Coun. Fla., 1969-70. Served to capt. AUS, 1949-55. Decorated Bronze Star; recipient Outstanding Alumni Achievement Law award, U. Mo., 1998, Korean War Svc. medal, Pres. South Korea on 50th Anniversary of Korean War, Disting. Alumnus award, Ga. Mil. Coll., 2002. Fellow Internat. Soc. Barristers; mem. ABA, Dade County Bar Assn., Bench and Robe, Torch and Scroll, Wildcat Cliffs Country Club, (Highlands, N.C.), Omicron Delta, Phi Alpha Delta. Republican. Roman Catholic.

HIGHTOWER, DUSTIN, state legislator, lawyer; B, U. West Ga.; JD, John Marshall Sch. Law, Atlanta. Cert.: (mediator). Prosecutor Carroll County Solicitor's Office, Ga.; ptnr. Miller & Hightower, Douglasville, Ga.; mem. Dist. 68 Ga. House of Reps., Atlanta, 2011—. Republican. Office: Miller & Hightower 8424 Adair St Douglasville GA 30134 also: Ga House of Reps Coverdell Legis Office Bldg Atlanta GA 30334 Office Phone: 770-884-1862.

HIGLEY, BRUCE WADSWORTH, retired orthodontist; b. Iowa City, Dec. 1, 1928; s. Lester Bodine and Harriet (Wadsworth) H.; m. Marta Beatriz Velasco, Sept. 23, 1966. D.D.S., State U. Iowa, 1952, MS, 1953; student, Grinnell Coll., 1946-48, orthodontic certificate, 1953. Diplomate Am. Acad. Pain Mgmt. Research, instr. Iowa Dental U., 1952-53; practice dentistry, specializing in orthodontics South Miami, Fla., 1955—; Owner, chmn. bd. M.B.H. Enterprises, Inc., Miami, Fla., 1960—. Vice chmn. dist. coun. Boy Scouts Am., 1959-62; Mem. Personnel Bd., South Miami, 1959. 1st lt. Dental Corps AUS, 1953-55 Fellow Internat. Coll. Cranio-Mandibnlar ORthopaedics, World Fedn. Orthodontists; mem. Am. Assn. Orthodontics, Fla. Orthodontic Soc., So., Miami socs. orthodontists, Fla., Am. socs. dentistry for children, Fla., Fla. East Coast, Miami dental socs., Am., S. Dade dental assns., Fedn. Dentaire Internat., English Royal Acad., C. of C. (past dir., sec., treas.), Psi Omega, Omicron Kappa Upsilon. Presbyn. (deacon). Clubs: Rotarian (pres. 1961-62), Elk, Coral Reef Yacht, Coral Gables Country, Royal Palm Tennis; Bankers, Executive (Miami); Army-Navy. Home: 2000 Brickell Ave Miami FL 33129-1721 Office: 7210 S Red Rd Miami FL 33143-5321 Personal E-mail: drhigley@higleyorthodonticspecialist.com, brucehigley@att.net.

HILDEBRAND, JEFFREY D., oil industry executive; married; 3 children. B, U. Tex., Austin, M in Petroleum Engring. Petroleum geologist, engr. Dan A. Hughes Co., Beeville, Tex.; with Am. Energy Capital Corp., 1988; geologist Exxon; co-founder Hilcorp Energy Co., 1989, pres., CEO. Named one of Forbes 400: Richest Americans, 2006—. Mem.: Tex. Ind. Petroleum Royalty Owners Assn., La. Oil and Gas Assn., Houston Geol. Soc., Soc. Petroleum Engrs., Ind. Petroleum Assn. Am. Office: Hilcorp Energy Co 1201 Louisiana Ste 1400 Houston TX 77002

HILDEBRAND, PHILLIP J., insurance company executive; b. Prineville, Oreg., 1952; BA, Northern Ariz. U., 1974. Sr. v.p. New York Life Insurance Co., 1997—2001, exec. v.p., 2001—06, chief dist. officer, life annuity, 2001—06, vice chmn., 2006—08; pres., CEO HealthMarkets, Inc., Richland Hills, Tex., 2008—. Office: HealthMarkets Inc 9151 Blvd 26 North Richland Hills TX 76180 Office Phone: 817-255-5200. Business E-Mail: phillip.hildebrand@healthmarkets.com.

HILDERBRAN, HARVEY, state legislator; b. Uvalde, Tex., Feb. 9, 1960; m. Tracy Hilderbran; 2 children. Grad., Tex. Tech U., Lubbock, 1983. Real estate, ranching, advt., bus. mgmt. profl.; legis. asst. for agr. and small bus. issues US Congress, Washington; asst. dir. state affairs Tex. Farm Bur.; v.p. mktg. engring. firm Kerrville, Tex.; mem. Dist. 53 Tex. House of Representatives, 1988—. Recipient of several awards and honors. Republican. Office: 125 Lehmann Dr Kerrville TX 78028 also: Room CAP GW.12 Capitol PO Box 2910 Austin TX 78768 Office Phone: 830-257-2333, 512-463-0536.

HILDRETH, JAMES ROBERT, retired air force officer; b. Pine Bluff, Ark., May 4, 1927; s. William Wilson and Martha Leah (Chidester) H.; m. Beth Dixon Baker, July 12, 1955; children: John Baker, William Reid, Margaret Leah, Mark Dixon, Amy Beth. BA cum laude, La. Poly. Inst., 1952. Commd. 2d lt. USAF, 1952, advanced through grades to maj. gen., 1976; ret., 1981; comdr. 1st Air Commando Sqdn., 1967, Army War Coll., 1969—70; comdr. 4th Tactical Fighter Wing, 1970—72; dep. dir. ops. Office of Joint Chiefs of Staff, 1972—73; dep. comdr. 13th Air Force, 1973—75; sr. Air Force rep. Weapons Systems Evaluation Group, Office of Sec. Def., 1975—76; comdr. Tactical Fighter Weapons Center, 1976—79; comdr. 13th Air Force, 1979—81. Pres. So. Nev. Fed. Exec. Agy., 1975-76; mem. adv. bd. United Way, Las Vegas, Nev., 1975-79; bd. dirs. Las Vegas C. of C., 1976-79; dist. chmn. Boy Scouts Am., 1979-81. Decorated D.S.M., Silver Star, Def. Superior Svc. medal, Legion of Merit (3), D.F.C. (3), Bronze Star, Air medal (14), Meritorious Svc. Medal, Air Force Commendation medal (3), Purple Heart, Cross of Gallantry (Vietnam), Rep. Phillipines Legion of Honor. Mem. Kappa Sigma, Phi Kappa Phi, Omicron Delta Kappa, Sigma Tau Delta. Clubs: DAV. Methodist. Home: 315 E Branch St PO Box 897 Spring Hope NC 27882-0897 Personal E-mail: cbhild@yahoo.com.

HILER, EDWARD ALLAN, agricultural and engineering educator; b. Hamilton, Ohio, May 14, 1939; s. Earl and Thelma (Kolb) H.; m. Patricia Burke; children: Karen, Richard, Scott. BS in Agrl. Engring., MS in Agrl. Engring., Ohio State U., 1963, PhD in Agrl. Engring., 1966. Registered profl. engr., Tex. Asst. prof. Tex. A&M U., College Station, 1966-69, assoc. prof., 1969-73, prof., 1973—, head dept. agrl. engring., 1974-88, dep. chancellor for acad. program planning and rsch., 1989-91, interim chancellor, 1991, exec. dep. chancellor, 1991, dep. chancellor for acad. and rsch. programs, 1991-92; vice chancellor, dean agrl. and life scis., dir. Tex. Agrl. Expt. Sta., 1992—2004; dir. Tex. Coop. Ext., 1998—2002, Ellison chair in internat. floriculture, depts. hort. scis. and biol. and agrl. engring., 2005—07. Cons. on water conservation, environ. quality, energy and biol. processes and future agrl. engring. Office Tech. Assessment, U.S. Congress, Office of Water Rsch. and Tech., Dept. Interior, others. Contbr. over 100 articles to profl. jours. Recipient numerous ednl. and rsch. awards. Fellow AAAS, Instn. Agrl. Engrs. Eng., Am. Soc. Engring. Edn., Am. Soc. Agrl. Engrs. (bd. dirs., pres. 1991-92, trustee Found.); mem. NAE, CNH Glabal(bd. dirs.,) Riley meml. Found. (bd. dirs., 2000-) Presbyterian. Avocations: golf, photography, reading. Home Phone: 940-575-9242. Business E-Mail: e-hiler@tamu.edu.

HILGERS, JOHN JACK WILLIAM, management, transportation and veterans consultant; b. Carmel-by-the-Sea, Calif., Nov. 17, 1934; s. Rudolph Joseph and Eleanor Maude (King) H.; m. Sharon Ann Hilgers, Dec. 15, 1968; children; Jon Marc, John Jack William Jr. BA in Psychology, San Jose State U., 1956; BA in Criminology, U. Calif., Berkeley, 1963; MS in Sys. Mgmt., U. So. Calif., 1984; MS in Urban Studies, Old Dominion U., 1995, PhD in Urban Svcs., 1998. Enlisted USMC, 1957, advanced in grades to col., ret. Norfolk, 1988; rsch. asst. Bur. Rsch. Old Dominion U., Norfolk, 1988-90, program mgr. Coll. Bus. and Pub. Adminstrn., 1991-98, assoc. dir. Internat. Maritime Ports and Logistics Inst., 1993—98; exec. asst. Va. Legislature, 1999—2007; dir. devel. Va. Dept. Vet. Svcs., 2007—; exec. dir. Va. Vets. Svc. Found., 2008—. Dir., mem. exec. com. Atlantic Rim Network, Boston, 1995-2001; exec. sec. Maritime Adv. Coun., Norfolk, 1991-2005; mem. tech. com. Met. Planning Orgn., Hampton Roads, Va., 1996-98; internat. maritime com. chmn. Conf. of World Regions, 1997-03. Editor (newsletter) Bullets and Cannonballs, 1993-98, (mag.) Bus. and Econ. Quar., 1992-96. Divsn. dir. United Way, Norfolk, 1996, 97, Virginia Beach Sister City Group, 1995-2000; trustee Norfolk Sister City Assn., 1992-, Old Dominion U., 1998-2002, Old Dominion U. Rsch. Found. Bd., 2001-11, Norfolk Sister City Assn., 1992- Recipient Va. Commerce Builder award, 1999, Va. Patrick Henry award, Commonwealth of Va., 2001. Mem.: ASPA (exec. com. transp. policy and adminstrn. com. 1997—2001), Internat. Bus. Coun., Econs. Club (Hampton Roads), Propeller Club U.S. (dir. Port of Norfolk 1996—2003), Pepper Lovers Club Va. Internat. (dir. 1994—96), Hampton Roads Fgn. Commerce Club (pres. 1996), Rotary (pres. Sunrise Norfolk chpt 1997—98, asst. gov. Dist. 7600 2002—04, Paul Harris fellow 1996, 2002, 2008), Phi Alpha Alpha, Phi Kappa Phi. Avocation: antiques. Home and Office: 1309 Lakeview Dr Virginia Beach VA 23454 Office Phone: 804-382-3715. Personal E-mail: jackhilgers@earthlink.net.

HILL, ALLEN EDWARD, delivery service executive; b. Decatur, Ala., Sept. 9, 1955; BA, David Lipscomb U., Nashville, 1977; JD, Nashville Sch. Law, 1984. Bar: Tenn. 1984. Joined as package loader and sorter United Parcel Service of America, Inc. (UPS), 1976, joined legal dept., 1988, v.p., dept. mgr. corp. legal group, 1995—2003, sr. v.p. legal and pub. affairs, gen. counsel, corp. sec., 2004—06, sr. v.p. human resources, 2005—. Bd. vis. Ga. State U. Coll. Law. Mem.: ABA, Tenn. Bar Assn., Am. Corp. Counsel Assn. Office: United Parcel Svc Inc 55 Glenlake Pkwy NE Atlanta GA 30328

HILL, ANGELA BURKS, state legislator; b. Picayune, Miss., Aug. 14, 1965; m. Richard Byron Hill; children: Andrew Byron, Kelly Gray. Attended, Pearl River CC, Poplarville, Miss., U. So. Miss., Hattiesburg. Former sci. tchr.; mem. Dist. 40 Miss. State Senate, Jackson, 2012—. Republican. Office: Miss State Senate PO Box 1018 Jackson MS 39215 Business E-Mail: ahill@senate.ms.gov.

HILL, BRYCE DALE, school administrator; b. Seminole, Okla., Mar. 5, 1930; s. Charles Daniel and Ollie (Nichols) Hill; m. Wilma Dean Carter, Aug. 16, 1956; children: Bryce Anthony, Brent Dale. BS, East Ctrl. State Coll., 1952, M in Tchg., 1957; postgrad., U. Okla., 1959—70; profl. adminstrs. cert., 1969. Tchr. pub. schs., New Lima, Okla., 1952—56; supt. pub. schs., 1956—95; owner New Lima Gas Co., 1958—82. Mem. Seminole County Bd. Health, 1985—95, v.p., 1986—88, chmn., 1988—95; edn. leader com. Okla. Farmers Union, 1990—93; exec. com. Okla. Commn. for Ednl. Leadership, 1993—95; chmn. Seminole County Dem. Ctrl. Com., 1962—64, 1970—95; chmn. bd. dirs. Seminole County chpt. ARC, 1969—90; v.p. bd. dirs. Redland Cmty. Action Program, 1968—71; mem. Seminole County Rural Devel. Coun.; v.p. bd. dirs. Okla. Assn. Acad. Competition, 1991—95. Named to Seminole Jr. Coll. Hall of Fame, 1995. Mem.: NEA, Seminole County Sch. Adminstrs. Assn. (chmn. 1969—70, 1993—95), Seminole County Tchrs. Assn. (pres. 1971—72, 1979—80, 1990—91), Orgn. Rural Okla. Schs. (bd. dirs. 1986—92, pres. 1993—94, Pioneer award 1998), Okla. Assn. Sch. Adminstrs. (exec. com. 1976—78, 1979—81, bd. dirs. 1979—81, 1993—95, Dist. 8 Adminstr. of Yr. 1983, 1994, Lifetime Achievement award 1996), Am. Assn. Sch. Adminstrs., Okla. Edn. Assn. (Friend of Edn. award Zone 6 1996), Okla. Assn. Svc. Impact Schs. (bd. dirs. 1987—95), Seminole Hist. Soc. (v.p. 1971—73, 1974—76), Seminole County Ret. Tchrs. Assn. (pres. 1996—2003), Okla. Ret. Educators Assn. (steering com. to legis. com. 2000—05, legis. com. 2000—, budget com. 2006, polit. action com. 2006—), Seminole County Schoolmasters Club (pres. 1963—64, 1969—70, 1977—78). Baptist. Home: 2736 E 16th Pl Tulsa OK 74104-5927 Home Phone: 405-273-4092. Personal E-mail: bryce.wilma@charter.net.

HILL, CALVIN, state legislator; b. Sierra, Nev., Apr. 9, 1947; State rep. Dist. 21, Ga., 2002—. Republican. Office: 611 Legis Off Bldg Atlanta GA 30334 Mailing: 145 Mountain Brook Dr Woodstock GA 30188 Office Phone: 404-656-0314. Business E-Mail: chill@legis.state.ga.us.

HILL, CHARLYNANN, information systems specialist; b. Cin., Jan. 24, 1956; d. Campbell Clay and Buena Irene (Mack) b.; m. Steven Wayne Hill, May 4, 1974 (dec. 1987); children: Jonathan, Daniel, David, Adam. Student, Toronto U., Can., 1983, Miami U., Oxford, Ohio, 1984-86, Truett-McConnell, Cleveland, Ga., 1988, U. Cin., 1991. Info. specialist Advanced Data Cons., Inc., Cin., 1978-88, Mead Imaging Corp., Dayton, Ohio, 1989-91, Senco Products, Inc., Cin., 1991—. Info. cons. Lebanon (Ohio) Congregation, 1989—. Author: Impressions of Gyotaku, 1985, From Basho to America, 1990; contbr. articles to profl. jours. Video cataloger Lebanon City Schs., 1988-89. Recipient Community award Lions Assn., 1983. Mem. NAFE, Spl. Librs. Assn., Coun. Internat. Bus. Mgmt., Japan Am. Soc., Bus. and Profl. Women's Clubs, U. Cin. Alumni. Avocations: scuba, whitewater rafting, oriental art. Office: Citrus Libraries 425 W Roosevelt Blvd Beverly Hills FL 34465 Home: PO Box 2072 Crystal River FL 34423

HILL, DEWEY L., state legislator; b. Whiteville, NC; m. Muriel Hill; children: Dewey Jr., Cheryl Ward. State rep. Dist. 14, NC, 1993—2002; state rep. Dist. 20 NC, 2003—; chmn. Hills Super Markets Inc.; pres. Hillcrest Corp., Home Run Food Marts. Contbr. columns in newspapers. Recipient Grand Marshall award, Winston Motor Speedway, 1988, America Statesman award, Nat. Grocers Assn., 1990. Mem.: NC Retail Merchants Assn., NC Food Dealers Assn., Columbus County Com. 100, Food Merchandising Industry, America Legion, Masons (32 degree), Nash-Finch Centennial Club, Asparagus Club. Democrat. Baptist. Address: PO Box 723 Whiteville NC 28472 Office: NC House of Reps 16 W Jones St Rm 1309 Raleigh NC 27601-1096 Office Phone: 919-733-5830, 910-642-6044. Business E-Mail: Dewey.Hill@ncleg.net.

HILL, DONALD DEE, former managing director, management consultant, educator, writer, engineer; b. Moultrie, Ga. s. Thomas Dee and Vivan Mae (Monk) H. BCE, Ga. Tech., State. Bd. cert. civil engr., Ala., Ga. Structural engr. Patchen & Zimmerman Cons. Engrs., Augusta, Ga.; asst. dir. F.S.D. Am. Plywood Assn., Tacoma; mng. dir., CEO Internat. Gas Turbine Inst. Cons., lectr. to Czech Republic; lectr., Vietnam, 1997, Ctr. for Pvt. Enterprise, US Chamber; lectr. advanced mgmt. course Asian execs. Kennesaw State U.; lectr. and spkr. in field. Columnist Convene Mag. V.p. Letterman's Club; 1st lt. U.S. Army. Named Eagle of the Acropolis, Palais de Congres, Nice, France; named to Coll. of 17 Gentlemen, Netherlands Congress Bur.; named Ark. Traveler, Gov. of Ark.; recipient R. Tom Sawyer Gas Turbine award ASME, 1996. Mem.: Ga. Tech. Alumni Assn., Am. Soc. Assn. Execs., Kappa Sigma. Home and Office: 5108 Parkside Dr Roswell GA 30075-7654

HILL, DOROTHY SUE, state legislator; b. Mittie/Dry Creek, La., Apr. 23, 1939; m. Herman Hill; 1 child, Craig. BS in Home Economics Edn., McNeese State U., 1960. Home economics tchr. Allen Parish Sch. Bd., 1960—69, Beauregard Parish Sch. Bd., 1969—92; owner/operator T&H Hereford Farms; mem. Dist. 32 La. House of Reps., 2008—, mem. health and welfare com., mcpl., parochial and cultural affairs com., transp., hwys. and pub. works com. Democrat. Baptist. Office: State Capitol Po Box 44486 Baton Rouge LA 70804 Mailing: 529 Tramel Rd Dry Creek LA 70637 Office Phone: 225-342-6945, 800-259-2118. Office Fax: 337-639-4045. Business E-Mail: hilld@legis.state.la.us.

HILL, GREGORY PAUL, oil industry executive; b. Springfield, Ill, Mar. 2, 1961; s. James Isaac and Bonnie Lee (Ball) Hill; 1 child, Justin Gregory. BSME, U. Wyo., Laramie, 1983. Divsn. engring. mgr. Shell Calif. Prodn., Inc., Bakersfield, Calif., 1988-90; strategic planning mgr. Shell Oil Co., Houston, 1991-92; mgr. petroleum engring. Shell Western E&P, Houston, 1992-93; area mgr. LA Basin Calresources, LLC, Bakersfield, 1994-95, v.p. oper., 1996, Aera Energy, LLC, Bakersfield, 1996—97; v.p. planning exec. strategy/affairs Shell Internat., London, 1998; sr. v.p. innovation and breakthrough performance Aera Energy LLC, Bakersfield, 1999, sr. oper. v.p., 1999—2002; CEO Enterprise/Shell, Shell Internat. E&P, London, 2002—03; v.p. prodn. Europe Shell E&P Internat., 2003—06, exec. v.p. Asia divsn., 2006—08; exec. v.p., pres. worldwide exploration & production Hess Corp. (formerly Amerada Hess), NYC, 2009—. Lobbyist Shell Oil Co., Calif., 1987; chmn. bd. dirs. Terrain Tech., LLC, 1999—2002; chmn. Enterprise Oil PLC, 2002—03, U. Wyo. Found. Bd., 2012—. Mem.: Tau Beta Pi (treas. 1982—83), Pi Tau Sigma, Phi Kappa Phi. Republican. Roman Catholic. Avocations: mountain climbing, skiing, fishing, hunting, investing. Office: Hess Corp Hess Tower 1501 McKinney Houston TX 77010 Business E-Mail: ghill@hess.com.*

HILL, HOWARD DARNELL, professor, consultant; b. May 4, 1942; s. Howard Jr. and Della Mae (Williams) H.; m. Clemmie Faye Coulter, Dec. 24, 1963; children: Ray Darnell, Edith Renee (dec.). BA in Social Studies, Philander Smith Coll., 1964; MSE in Secondary Sch. Adminstrn., Ark. State U., 1968; PhD in Curriculum and Instrn., Kans. State U., 1973; postdoctoral study in edn1. adminstrn., U. SC, 1983—85. Secondary sch. tchr. Jonesboro Pub. Sch., Ark., 1964—66; supr. instrn. Marion Sch., 1966—69; asst. prin. West Memphis Schs., 1969—70; secondary sch. tchr. Tunica Pub. Sch., Miss., 1970—71; asst. prof. edn. U. Houston, 1973—77; assoc. prof. Miss. Valley State U., Itta Bena, 1977—78; prof., chmn., program coord. dept. edn. SC State U., Orangeburg, 1978—87; dir. chpt. programs Phi Delta Kappa Hdqs., Bloomington, Ind., 1987—97; dean Sch. Grad. Studies SC State U., 1997—98, dir. doctoral program, chair ednl. leadership/counselor edn., 1998—2001; v.p. acad. affairs Claflin U., Orangeburg, SC, 2001—05; pres., CEO Assocs. in Edn. & Bus., 2006—; loaned exec. SC United Way of the Midlands, 2006—07; vis. prof. edn. SC State U., 2007—08, dissertation specialist, 2010—; dir. planned giving Claflin U., 2008—09. Contbr. articles to profl. jours., chapters to books, columns in newspapers. Chmn. Regional Med. Ctr. Found., 2007—08, trustee emeritus, 2011; chair Orangeburg Consolidated Sch. Dist. 5, Charter Sch. Healthcare Professions. Bush-Hewlett scholar Harvard U., 2002. Mem.: ASCD, United Way Midlands (bd. dirs. 2010—), Am. Studies Assn., SC Assn. Sch. Adminstrs., SC Coun. Social Studies, Nat. Soc. Study of Edn., Nat. Assn. Secondary Sch. Prins., Assn. Tchr. Educators, Nat. Alliance Black Sch. Educators, Nat. Coun. Social Studies, Orangeburg Rotary Club-Morning (Rotarian of Yr. 2007), Rotary (scholarship programs com. Dist. 7770 2000—07, coord. vocat. awareness 2003—05), Orangeburg C. of C. (bd. dirs. 2000—02, v.p. 2001—02), Phi Delta Kappa. Home: 1186 Pruitt Dr Orangeburg SC 29118-4024 Home Phone: 803-534-5568. Business E-Mail: educationconsultant@sc.rr.com.

HILL, JACK, state legislator; b. Reidsville, Ga., July 15, 1944; m. Ruth Ann; children: Dawn, Amy, Lance. BBA, Ga. So. Coll., 1966. Grocer; mem. Dist. 4 Ga. State Senate, 1990—. Served 37 years Ga. Air Nat. Guard and USAFR, Inspector Gen. & unit comdr. Ga. Air Nat. Guard, 1998—2000. Named Citizen of Yr., Georgia Air Nat. Guard, 1979. Mem.: Rotary Club, Grocers Assn. (former pres.), C. of C., Reidsville Lions Club (former pres.). Republican. Baptist. Mailing: PO Box 486 Reidsville GA 30453 Office: 234 State Capitol Atlanta GA 30334 Office Phone: 404-656-5038, 912-557-3811. Office Fax: 912-557-3522. Business E-Mail: jack.hill@senate.ga.gov.

HILL, JENNIFER, bank executive; BA in Govt., French, Hamilton Coll., 1983—87; MBA in Fin., Columbia U., 1992—94. Mng. dir. Goldman Sachs, 1996—2006; CFO Tisbury Capital, 2006—07; group dir., strategy and corp. fin. The Royal Bank of Scotland (RBS), 2008; CFO Bank of Am. Merrill Lynch Investment Banking Group, 2011—. Office: Bank of America 100 N Tryon St Charlotte NC 28202

HILL, JUDSON, state legislator; m. Shelly Hill; 3 children. BA, Emory Uiv.; JD, Mercer Univ. Asst. U.S. Atty. No. Ga. Dist.; spl. asst. to Gen. Counsel USAID, US State Dept., Washington; atty. Allen & Ballard PC; mng. dir. Day Capital LLC; mem. Dist. 32 Ga. State Senate, 2004—. Republican. Mailing: 3102 Raines Ct Marietta GA 30062 Office Phone: 770-565-0024. Office Fax: 770-234-5378. Business E-Mail: judson.hill@senate.ga.gov.

HILL, MATTHEW, state legislator; State rep. Dist. 7, Tenn., 2005—. Mem.: Nat. Fedn. Ind. Bus., Wash. County Rep. Party, Nat Rifle Assn., Contact Ministries (bd. dir.), Morrison City Mission Ch. (mem. bd. trustees), Telfold Ruritan Club. Republican. Office: 216 Mockingbird Pl Jonesborough TN 37659 also: G-24 War Memorial Bldg Nashville TN 37243 Office Phone: 615-741-2251. Business E-Mail: rep.matthew.hill@capitol.tn.gov.

HILL, MELISSA A., real estate company executive; B in Bus., Ball State U. Pres. LandAmerica OneStop Inc., 2002—03; exec. v.p., prodn. and process improvement LandAmerica Fin. Group Inc., 2004—06, pres., residential svcs. customer channel, 2007—09; exec. v.p., ops. LandAmerica Financial Group, Inc., 2009—. Office: LandAmerica Financial Group Inc 201 Concourse Blvd Ste 200 Glen Allen VA 23059-5640 Office Phone: 804-267-8000. Office Fax: 804-267-8850. Business E-Mail: mhill@landam.com.

HILL, MICHAEL, professional sports team executive; m. Vivian Hill; children: Donovan, Xavier. B, Harvard U., Cambridge, Mass. Minor league baseball player Tex. Rangers, 1993—94, Cin. Reds, 1995; scouting and player devel. asst. Tampa Bay Devil Rays, 1995—97, asst. dir. scouting, 1998—99; dir. player devel. Colo. Rockies, 1999—2001; v.p., asst. gen. mgr. Miami Marlins (formerly Fla. Marlins), 2002—07, v.p., gen. mgr., 2007—. Named to Hot List, Black Enterprise mag., 2003. Office: Miami Marlins 501 Marlin Way Miami FL 33125

HILL, MIKE, state legislator; b. Birmingham, Ala., Mar. 3, 1949; m. Carol Hill; children: Hayden Jeffries, Hunter, Jon Michael(dec.). BS, Auburn U., Ala.; attended Sch. Banking, La. State U.; attended Comml. Lending Sch., Okla. State U. Mem. Dist. 41 Ala. House of Reps., Montgomery, 1986—. Chmn. Ala. Sight Lions Club; deacon First Bapt. Ch., Columbiana; mem. state bd. dirs. Ala. Easter Seals; bd. dirs. Birmingham Occupational Rehab. Ctr. Mem.: Inverness Lions Club, Columbiana Kiwanis Club (life). Republican. Baptist. Office: 114 Arlington Ave Columbiana AL 35051 also: Ala House of Reps Ala State House 11 S Union St Rm 628-D Montgomery AL 36130 Office Phone: 334-242-7715. Business E-Mail: mhillcolum@aol.com.

HILL, RALPH A., energy executive; B in Fin., U. Mo., Columbia, 1981; MBA, U. Tulsa, 1984. Fin. planning analyst Williams Companies, Inc., 1981; v.p., gen. mgr. Williams Field Svcs. Gas and Liquids Resources, Williams Prodn. Co.; v.p. Williams Gas Mktg.; v.p., gen. mgr., gas resources Williams Field Svcs. Group LLC; pres., Williams Exploration and Prodn. Unit Williams Companies, Inc., various positions, 1993, v.p., Exploration and Prodn. Unit, 1993—98, sr. v.p., petroleum svcs., 1998—2003, sr. v.p., exploration and prodn., 1998; chmn., CEO Apco Oil and Gas International, Inc., 2002—. Bd. dirs. Petrolera Entre Lomas S.A., 2003, Apco Oil and Gas Internat. Inc. Mem. Tulsa Boys Home and Children's Hosp., United Way, 1995-96, St. Dunstan's Episcopal Ch. Vestry, 1996-99, St. Nicholas Club of Tulsa, Am. Petroleum Inst., Ind. Petroleum Assn. of America, Colo. Oil & Gas Assn., Ind. Petroleum Assn. Mountain States; bd. dirs. Petroleum Club of Tulsa, 1998-01, Thomas Gilcrease Mus. Assn.; mem., exec. com. Midcontinent Oil & Gas Assn. Office: Apco Oil and Gas International Inc One Williams Ctr Mail Drop 35 Tulsa OK 74172 Office Phone: 918-573-2164. Office Fax: 918-588-2296.

HILL, SCOTT A., stock exchange executive; BBA in Finance, U. Tex.; MBA, NYU. Head IBM strategic account team Cirrus Logic, Inc.; v.p. sales Alliance Semiconductor; sr. mgmt. sales position Micro Linear, Silicon Motion; v.p. North Am. sales ARC Internat.; joined IBM Corp., 1991, asst. contr. fin. strategy and budgets, 2002—03, v.p. sales IC Media Corp., 2003—05, asst. contr. fin. forecasts and measurements, 2005—07; sr. v.p., CFO IntercontinentalExchange, Inc., 2007—. Office: InterContinental Exchange Inc 2100 Riveredge Pkwy Ste 500 Atlanta GA 30328*

HILL, SUSAN SLOAN, safety engineer; b. Quincy, Mass., June 1, 1952; d. Ralph Arnold and Grace Elenore (Sloan) Crosby; m. William Loyd Hill, Dec. 16, 1973 (div. July 1982); m. William Joseph Graham, Sept. 10, 1983 (div. Feb. 1985). AS in Gen. Engring., Motlow State C.C., Tullahoma, Tenn., 1976; BS in Indsl. Engring., Tenn. Technol. U., Cookeville, 1978. Intern, safety engr. Intern Tng. Ctr., US Army, Red River Army Depot, Tex., 1978-79, Field Safety Activity, Charlestown, Ind., 1979, sys. safety engr. Comm.-Electronics Command Ft. Monmouth, NJ, 1979-84, gen. engr., 1984-85; chief sys. safety Arnold Air Force Sta., USAF, Tullahoma, 1984; sys. safety engr. US Army Safety Ctr., Ft. Rucker, Ala., 1985-91; medically ret.; ind. cons. sys. safety, 1991—. Former realtor, NJ, Ala.; founder Fibromyalgia Support Group; leader Arthritis Found. Support Group; active Arthritis Found. Recipient 5 letters of appreciation, U.S. Army, letter of appreciation, Arthritis Found. Mem. NAFE, Assn. Fed. Safety and Health Profls. (regional v.p. 1980-84), Soc. Women Engrs., Nat. Safety Mgmt. Soc., Am. Soc. Safety Engrs., Sys. Safety Soc., Order Engr. Republican. Episcopalian. Avocations: reading, gardening, walking, cooking, golf. Home and Office: 1307 Bel-Aire Dr Tullahoma TN 37388

HILL, THAD (JOHN B. HILL), energy executive; BA magna cum laude, Vanderbilt Univ.; MBA, Tuck Sch. Bus. Dartmouth Coll. Cons. positions through v.p. & dir. No. Am. energy practice Boston Consulting Group, Inc., 1995—2005; exec. v.p. bus. develop. Texas Genco, 2005—06; sr. mgmt. positions NRG Energy, Inc., 2006—07, pres. Texas, 2007—08; exec. v.p., chief comml. officer Calpine Corp., 2008—10, exec. v.p., COO, 2010—. Named an Edward Tuck Scholar. Office: Calpine Corp 717 Texas Ave Houston TX 77002

HILL, VONCIEL JONES, councilwoman; b. Hattiesburg, Miss. BA in Hist. & English, U. Tex., Austin, 1969; MLS, Clark Atlanta U., 1971; MA in Hist., Rice U., Houston, 1976; JD, U. Tex. Sch. Law, Austin, 1979; MDiv., Perkins Sch. Theology-SMU, 1990; LHD (hon.), Paul Quinn Coll., 2003. Bar: Tex., cert.: (civil & family mediator), (atty. ad litem). Tchr. Atlanta Pub. Schools, Ga.; asst. law libr. Tex. Southern U., Houston; asst. circulations libr. Prairie View A & M U.; staff atty. Pub. Utility Commn. Tex., 1979; asst. city atty. City of Dallas, 1980—86, mcpl. ct. judge, 1987—2004, dist. ct. adminstr., 2004—05; owner Law Office of Vonciel Jones Hill, 2005—; interim mcpl. judge City of The Colony, Tex., 2005—07; councilwoman, Dist. 5 Dallas City Coun., 2008—. Mem. Interim Jud. Nominating Commn., 1989—91, Mcpl. Ct. Task Force, 1989, Coll. State Bar Tex., Fin., Audit & Accountability, Housing, Transp. & Environ. coms.; vice chmn. Quality of Life & Govt. Svcs. com.; evidence tchr. Tex. Mcpl. Ct. Edn. Ctr.; guest lectr. Queen's Theol. Coll., Birmingham, England, Perkins Sch. Theology-SMU. Bd. dirs. & chmn. Methodism's Breadbasket; bd. trustees Paul Quinn Coll.; bd. dirs. Cable Access of Dallas, Inc., 1989—91; faculty search com. Perkins Sch. Theology-SMU, 1990; bd. visitors Mus. African-American Life & Culture; sr. pastor Brit. Meth. Ch., England, Mt. Zion African Meth. Episcopal Ch.; asst. & assoc. pastor St. Luke Cmty. United Meth. Ch.; elder African Meth. Episcopal Ch.; deacon United Met. Ch. North Tex. Ann. Conf. Recipient Honoree, Met. Bus. & Profl. Women Org., 2005, Pres. award, Dallas Interdenominational Ministerial Alliance, 2005, Dallas Urban League, 2006. Mem.: Tex. Mcpl. Ct. Assn. (bd. mem.), Dallas Bar Found. (former fellow), William "Mac" Taylor Am. Inn of Ct. (chmn. mem. com.), J.L. Turner Legal Assn. (sec.), Dallas Bar Assn. (libr. com., co-chmn Bench Bar com., chmn. admissions & mem. com., Task Force on Racial Bias in the Courtroom), State Bar Tex. (Women & Law Section treas.), NAACP, Nat. Coun. Negro Women, Mothers Against Teen Violence (former adv. bd. mem.), Rice U. Alumni Assn., U. Tex. Law Sch. Alumni Assn. (exec. com.). Office: City Hall 1500 Marilla St Rm 5FN Dallas TX 75201 Office Phone: 214-670-0777. Office Fax: 214-670-5117.

HILL, WALTER A., agricultural sciences and chemistry educator, researcher, chemistry educator, researcher; b. New Brunswick, NJ, Aug. 9, 1946; s. Henry Solomon and Tessie Paisley H.; m. Jill Karen Harris; children: Shaka W.T., Askia A.H., Osei J.E. BA in Chemistry, Lake Forest Coll., 1968; MAT in Chemistry, U. Chgo., 1970; MS in Soil Chemistry, U. Ariz., 1973; PhD in Agronomy, U. Ill., 1978. Asst. prof. to prof. dept. agrl. scis. Tuskegee (Ala.) U., 1978-84, adminstr. USDA Cooperative Extension Program, 1987-91, rsch. dir. USDA Cooperative State Rsch. Program, 1986—, dir. G.W. Carver Agrl. Experiment Sta., 1986—, dean Coll. Agriculture, Environ. & Natural Scis., 1996—. Bd. dirs. AVEC, 1990-2005; chair 1890 Coun. Deans, 1992—, Profl. Agrl. Workers Conf., 1988—, Internat. Symposium Sweetpotato Tech. for 21st Century, 1991; co-dir. Nat. Sweetpotato Info. Ctr., 1991—; dir. NASA Ctr. Food and Environ. Sys. Human Exploration of Space, 1991—2006, So. Food Systems Edn. Consortium, 1994-2007; mem. various coms. Nat. Rsch. Coun.; mem. adv. bd. NSF, 97, NAJA, 1992—2004; USAID sci. liaison Asian Vegetable Rsch. and Devel. Ctr., Taiwan, 1989—; mem. agrl. biotech. rsch. adv. com. USDA, 1992—; vis. sci. NASA Kennedy Space Ctr., 1987, Internat. Inst. Tropical Agriculture, Nigeria, 1985, Dept Agronomy Purdue U., summer 1981; chair elect Assn. Rsch. Dirs., 1992-96. Founder Tuskegee Horizons Mag./Jour., 1990—; editor Sweetpotato Technology for the 21st Century, 1993; contbr. numerous articles, books, book chpts., procs., abstracts; patentee in field. Trustee Lake Forest Coll., Ill., 1989—2001; vol. Boy Scouts Am., Tuskegee, 1990—; steward Washington Chapel A.M.E. Recipient Outstanding Rsch. and Teaching award Ala. Soil & Water Conservation Soc., 1992, Futurist in Sci. and Tech. award Black Enterprise Mag., 1990, Faculty award execellence in sci. & tech. White House Initiative on HBCU, 1988, Disting. Alumni Svc. citation Lake Forest Coll., 1986, Hon. Doctorate, 2001, Faculty Achievement award Tuskegee (Ala.) U., 1985, Diversity award Coun. on Chem. Rsch., 2004, Irving Leadership award ADEC, 2004, Cultural award ALFA, 2005, Award of Honor Credit Bank of Tex., 2005, Humanitarian award, 2007, Lifetime Svc. award, 2007; named Exec. of Yr. by Profl. Secs. Internat., 1991, Danforth assoc. for excellence in undergrad. teaching Danforth Found., 1980; Kellogg fellow, 1988; USDA grantee, NASA grantee, U.S. Dept. Edn. grantee, USAID grantee, NSF grant others. Fellow Am. Soc. Agronomy (Outstanding Minority Educator award 1990); mem. Am. Soc. Horticultural Sci., Crop Sci. Soc. Am., Internat. Soil Sci. Soc., Internat. Soc. Tropical Root Crops (Plucknett Outstanding Rsch. Paper award 1983), Internat. Soc. Horticultural Sci., Soil Sci. Soc. Am., Phi Beta Kappa, Sigma Xi, Gamma Sigma Delta. Office: Tuskegee Univ Carver Agrl Expt Sta Campbell Hall Rm 100 Tuskegee Institute AL 36088

HILLELSON, RUTH LEANNA, plastic surgeon; b. Providence, USA; m. Terr L. Whipple. Attended, Johns Hopkins U., 1971—75, U. Vt., 1975—77, Harvard U., 1977—79. Diplomate Am. Bd. Plastic Surgery, 1987. Intern Univ. Va., 1979—80, resident gen. surgery, 1980—81, fellow plastic, maxillofacial, and craniofacial surgery, 1981—82; resident gen. surgery John Hopkins Univ., 1982; resident plastic and maxillofacial surgery Univ. of Kans. Med. Ctr., 1983—85; project dir. NSF; hospital appointments include Johnston-Willis Hosp., Saint Mary's Hosp., Southside Regional Hosp.; co-founder Am. Self Ctr. for Cosmetic, Plastic and Orthopedic Surgery, dir. aesthetics and plastic surgery. Author: (publs.) Plastic and Reconstructive Surgery, Microangiographic Study of Hematoma-associated Flap, Necrosis and Salvage with Isoxsuprine. Recipient Best Meeting Presentation, Internat. Soc. of Plastic and Reconstructive Surgery-Brazil, 2006, Nat. Pinnacle award, Non-Invasive Radiofrequency, 2006—07. Mem.: Southeastern Soc. of Plastic and Reconstructive Surgery, Richmond Acad. of Medicine, Med. Soc. of Va., Am. Soc. of Plastic Surgeons, Am. Soc. of Laser Medicine and Surgery, Am. Soc. for Aesthetic Plastic Surgery, ACS, German Club. Achievements include research in Induced osteogenesis; Microangiographic study of hematoma-associated flap necrosis; Fascial tensile strength; Microangiographic study on pharmacologic skin flap delay; Radiofrequency on dorsal hand. Avocations: horseback riding, water-skiing, guitar, piano. Office: American Self PLC 9900 Independence Pk Dr Richmond VA 23233 Office Phone: 804-290-0060. E-mail: hillelson@americanself.com.

HILLEN, JOHN FRANCIS, think-tank executive, former federal agency administrator; b. Feb. 3, 1966; s. John Francis and Lisa (Grassi) Hillen. BA in Pub. Policy Studies & History, Duke U., 1988; MA in War Studies, King's Coll.; MBA, Cornell U.; Ph.D in Internat. Rels., Oxford U. COO Island ECN; head def. and intelligence practice Am. Mgmt. Sys. Inc.; def. policy adv. & speechwriter to Pres. The White House, Washington, 2000; asst. sec. for polit. military affairs US Dept. State, Washington, 2005—07; pres. Global Strategies Group (USA) LLC, Washington, 2007—. Cons. ABC News; trustee Internat. Inst. Strategic Studies, London; trustee, dir. program on nat. security Fgn. Policy Rsch. Inst.; trustee Phila. U.; mem. exec. com. The Internat. Inst. for Strategic Studies; spkr. in field. Contbg. editor: Nat. Law Review; co-editor: (book) Future Visions for U.S. Defense Policy, 1999; author: Blue Helmets: The Strategy of UN Military Operations, 1997; contbr. articles to profl. jours. and newspapers. Reconnaissance and spl. ops officer US Army, 1988—2000. Mem.: Veterans of Fgn. Wars (life), Coun. Fgn. Rels. (life). Office: Global Strategies Group Usa Llc 1501 Farm Credit Dr Ste 2400 Mc Lean VA 22102-5011

HILLENMEYER, HENRY REILING, JR., restaurant company executive; b. Temple, Tex., Nov. 13, 1943; s. Henry Reiling and Lucy Carolyn (Taylor) H.; m. Sallie Long Sigler, Oct. 30, 1976; children: Henry Reiling, Edward Ferriday, Taylor Jennings, Morgan Andrew, Hunter Taverner. BA, Yale U., 1965. Trainee Kanawha Valley Bank, Charleston, W.Va., 1965-67, asst. sec., 1967-68; v.p. CBM, Inc., Cleve., 1968-70, pres., 1970-72, chmn., dir., 1972-74; pres., dir. Ireland's Restaurants, Inc., Nashville, 1974-78; exec. v.p. Womco, Inc., Nashville, 1978-82; pres., dir. So. Hospitality Corp., Nashville,

1983-89, chmn., pres., dir., 1989-94; chmn., CEO, dir. Skillsearch Corp., Nashville, 1995-99, Cooker Restaurant Corp., 1995—2004; cons. Compass Execs., LLC, 2006—; pres. Music City Flats, LLC, 2008—. Bd. dirs. Jr. Achievement, Nashville, 1985—, chmn., 1991-92, 97-99; bd. dirs. Tenn. Spl. Olympics, Nashville, 1986-90; trustee Harding Acad., Nashville, 1985-90; nat. assoc. Boys Clubs of Am., N.Y.C., 1986-90, bd. dirs. Genetic Assays INC., 2007-. Mem. World Pres. Orgn., Belle Meade Country Club, Scroll and Key Soc., Fence Club, Yale Club of Middle Tenn. (pres. 1983-88). Republican. Episcopalian. Home: 218 Cantrel Ave Nashville TN 37205 Office: 1300 Division St Ste 106 Nashville TN 37203 Office Phone: 612-256-9009. Personal E-mail: hilly615@bellsouth.net.

HILLIARD, ROBERT GLENN, insurance company executive, lawyer; b. Anderson, SC, Jan. 18, 1943; s. Baz Robert and Louise (Holcombe) H.; m. Heather Ann Prevost, Apr. 1, 1966; children: Kathryn Louise Stuart, Nancy Ann, Mary Elizabeth Glenn. BA, Clemson U., 1965; JD, George Washington U., 1968. Bar: S.C. 1969. Gen. counsel Liberty Life Ins. Co., Greenville, SC, 1965-82, 1975-82; v.p., gen. counsel, sec. Liberty Life Ins. Co., Greenville, SC, 1975-82; pres., chief exec. officer Liberty Life; pres. Liberty Life Ins. Co., Greenville, SC, 1982-88, chmn. bd., 1988-89; dir. Liberty Corp., 1982-89; pres., CEO, Security Life of Denver ING Americas, Atlanta, 1989—92, pres., CEO ING America Life, 1992—93, CEO, pres., chmn., 1993—2003; chmn. CNO Financial Group, Inc. (formerly Conseco, Inc.), Carmel, Ind., 2003—. Bd. dirs. Carolina First Corp., Security Life; founder, chmn. emeritus Foothills Trail Conf.; chmn. Netherlands Ins. Co., ING Can., N.Am. Investment Centre, NN Fin. Bd. dir. Piedmont Hosp., Atlanta; vice chmn., fin., High Mus.; chmn. investment com., Clemson Univ. Found.; former chmn. bd. dirs. S.C. Gov.'s Sch. for Arts, Perception, Inc. Recipient Jim Kern award Am. Hiking Soc. Mem. ABA, S.C. Bar Assn., Am. Coun. Life Ins., Assn. Life Ins. Counsel, INternat. Ins. Soc., Org. for Internat. Investment, Internat. Bus. Fellows, Bare Minimum Track Club (co-founder, bd. dirs.), Greenville Country Club, Poinsett Club (S.C.), Colo. Concern, Colo. Forum, Denver Athletic Club, Univ. Club. Presbyterian. Office: CNO Fin Group 11825 N Pennsylvania St Carmel IN 46032

HILLIARD, ROBERT L., emeritus communications professor, author, playwright; b. NYC, June 25, 1925; children: Mark, Mara. BA, U. Del., 1948; MA, Western Res. U., 1949, MFA, 1950; PhD, Columbia U., 1959; postgrad., Tchrs. Coll., 1959-60. Profl. in theatre, radio and TV, newspaper reporter, editor, 1943-64; instr. Bklyn. Coll., 1950-56; asst. prof. Adelphi U., 1956-60; assoc. prof. U. N.C., Chapel Hill, 1960-64; chief Ednl./Pub. Broadcasting Br., FCC, Washington, 1964-80; chmn. Fed. Interagency Media Com., Washington, 1965-78; dean grad. studies, dean contbg. edn. Emerson Coll., Boston, 1980—84, prof., 1984—2007. Cons. and lectr. in field. Author: Surviving the Americans: The Continued Struggle of the Jews After Liberation, 1997, Media, Education, and America's Counter-Culture Revolution, 2001, Writing for Television and Radio, 10th edit., 2011, Hollywood Speaks Out: Pictures that Dared to Protest Real World Issues, 2009, also included 40 books; co-author: (with Michael Keith) Waves of Rancor: Tuning in the Radical Right, 1999, The Broadcast Century and Beyond, 5th edit., 2010, The Quieted Voice: The Rise and Demise of Localism in Radio, 2005, Dirty Discourse: Sex and Indecency in Broadcasting, 2nd edit., 2007, (novel) Phillipa, 2010, The Greener Trees, 2011; contbr. articles to profl. jours. and newspapers; artist (plays) The Hounds of God, Miracle at St. Ottilien, Breakfast at Starbucks, 48th Parallel, When Do We Shoot Them?, Encounter in Jerusalem. Pres. adv. congress Cambridge (Mass.) Cmty. Cable TV, 1986-90; bd. dirs. Armstrong Meml. Rsch. Found., 1994—98, Toda Inst., 1996-2009; trustee New Eng. Inst. for Peace, 1987-90; commr. Mass. Telecomm. Commn., 1981-82. U.S. Army, Europe, 1944-46. Decorated Purple Heart, Combat Inf. Budge, Commendation Ribbon, others; recipient award Ohio Med. Edn. Network, Broadcast Preceptor award, Kappa Delta Pi, World Comm. Yr. award, Phi Delta Kappa, Ann. award, Cambridge Cmty. TV, Lifetime Achievement award, Emerson Coll., Columbia Disting. Alumni award; Goethe Inst. fellowship. Mem. Nat. Instrs. TV Fixed Svc. Assn. (bd. dirs., exec. vice chair), Actors Equity Assn., Am. Fed. TV & Radio Artists, Internat. Univ. Comm. (founder, 1st pres.). Home: PO Box 1144 Sanibel FL 33957

HILLIARD, SAM BOWERS, geography educator; b. Hart County, Ga., Dec. 21, 1930; s. Asa Farris and Flora Elizabeth (Bowers) H.; m. Joyce Collier, June 4, 1955; children— Steven Glen, Anita Joy. AB, U. Ga., 1960, MA, 1962; MS, U. Wis., 1963, PhD, 1966. Electrician Savannal River Valley plant Dupont Co., Aiken, SC, 1954-59; teaching asst. U. Wis., 1961-65, instr. Milw., 1965-67; asst. prof. geography So. Ill. U., 1967-71; prof. La. State U., Baton Rouge, 1971-82, alumni prof., ret., 1983-93, chmn. dept. geography, 1976-79, 85-86, dir. Sch. Geosci., 1977-79. Columnist The Hartwell Sun newspaper; historian Hart County. Author: Hog Meat and Hoecake: Food Supply in the Old South, 1972, An Atlas of Antebellum Southern Agriculture, 1984; co-author: Louisiana: Its Land and People, rev. edit., 1987, The South Revisited: Forty Years of Change, 1992, Vignettes of Hart, vol. 1, 2001, vol. 2, 2002, A Century of Rural Education: Hart County, 1860-1960, A Calling of Churches: Sketches of Hart County Churches, 2003; contbr. articles to profl. jours. County historian, 1998. Served with U.S. Navy, 1950-54. Mem. Nat. Geog. Soc., Agrl. History Assn.

HILLIARD, WES, state legislator; s. Don and Allene (Moss) Hilliard; m. Melissa Cottrell; 1 child, Weston. BA in Polit. Sci., Okla. State Univ.; MEd, East Central Univ. Adult prog coord. Southern Oklahoma Tech. Ctr.; lending officer Landmark Bank, N.A., Davis; mem. Dist 22 Okla. House of Representatives, 2005—. Democrat. Mailing: PO Box 886 Sulphur OK 73086 Office: Oklahoma House of Representatives 2300 N Lincoln Blvd Rm 540 Oklahoma City OK 73105 Office Phone: 405-557-7412. E-mail: weshilliard@okhouse.gov.

HILLIS, JOHN DAVID, broadcast executive, television producer, newswriter; b. Washington, Dec. 28, 1952; s. Willard E. and Holly M. Hillis; m. Catherine H. McQuaig, Nov. 21, 1975; children: Faith Courteney, David Esten, Elizabeth Nicole. BA in Journalism, cum laude, U. Ga., 1975. Film editor Sta. WSB-TV, Atlanta, 1973-74, asst. producer, 1974-76, news producer, 1976; exec. news producer Sta. KOTV-TV, Tulsa, 1976-79; news producer Sta. WRAL-TV, Raleigh, N.C., 1979-80, Cable News Network, Inc., Atlanta, 1980-81, exec. producer, Newswatch, 1981-83, exec. producer, 1983-84, spl. events producer, 1984; news dir. Cablevision Systems Corp., Woodbury, N.Y., 1984-86; gen. mgr. Rainbow News 12 Co., Woodbury, 1986-89; pres., CEO Allnewsco, Inc., Washington, 1989—2002, Newschannel 8 Cable Svc., Springfield, Va., 1991—2002; pres., prin. Equinox Media Internat., LLC, Fairfax, Va., 2002—. Contbr. articles to profl. jours. Mem. strategic com. Greater Washington Bd. of Trade; bd. dirs. Va. Cmty. Found. Recipient Radio Newscast award Ga. AP Broadcasters, 1973, TV Newscast award Okla. AP Broadcasters, 1978, TV Series award News Acad. Cable Programming, 1985, Washington Region Emmy award, 1997, Cable Ace awards, 1996, 97, 98, Cmty. Spirit award NCTA, 1999, Scripps-Howard award, 1999. Mem. NATAS (Bd. of Govs. award Washington chpt.), Soc. Profl. Journalists (disting. svc. award 1998), Radio TV News Dirs. Assn., Nat. Press Club, Assn. Regional News Channels (founder, chmn. 1993), Nat. Cable TV Assn. (satellite network com.). Methodist. Office: Equinox Media Internat LLC PO Box 41 Round Hill VA 20142-0041 Business E-Mail: mail@equinox-media.com.

HILLIS, WILLIAM DANIEL, biology professor; b. Paris, Ark., June 12, 1933; s. Charles Raymond Hillis and Carra Elizabeth (Daniel) Coffee; m. Argye Idell Briggs, Dec. 23, 1952; children: William Daniel Jr., David Mark, Argye Elizabeth Trupe. BS, Baylor U., 1953; MD, Johns Hopkins U., 1957. Lic. in medicine and surgery Md., Tex. Asst. prof. pathobiology Johns Hopkins U. and Sch. Hygiene and Pub. Health, Balt., 1965-68, assoc. prof., 1968-72; asst. prof. Johns Hopkins U. Sch. Medicine, Balt., 1972-76, assoc. prof., 1976-82; prof., chmn. dept. biology Baylor U., Waco, Tex., 1982-85, Cornelia Marshall Smith prof. biology, 1985-98, disting. prof. biology, 1995—2012, exec. v.p., 1985-89, v.p. student affairs, 1989-98. Cons. Nat. Cancer Inst., Bethesda, Md., 1965-68, Nat. Heart and Lung Inst., Bethesda, 1977-82; dir. Health Professions Rsch. Tng. Program, Balt., 1979-82, Out-Patient Clin. Rsch. Ctr., Balt., 1975-82. Contbr. articles to profl. jours. Pres. Bapt. Home Md., Balt., 1972-81; Md. rep. exec. com. So. Bapt. Conv., NAshville, 1977-82; bd. dirs. Food for Hungry, Glendale, Calif., 1972-82, Caritas, Waco, Tex., chair, 1989-95. Col. USAF, 1960-65, USAFR, 1965-85. Recipient Louis Livingston Seaman award, Assn. Mil. Surgeons U.S., 1978, Disting. Alumnus award, Baylor U., 1998, Collins Prof. award, 2010, U. Prof. of Yr. award, Cornelia Marshall Smith, 2009; named Outstanding Prof., Baylor U., 1985. Mem. Am. Assn. Immunologists, Soc. for Exptl. Biology and Medicine, Am. Soc. for Microbiology, N.Y. Acad. Sci., McLennan County Med. Soc., Waco C. of C. (bd. dirs. 1987), Johns Hopkins Soc. of Scholars, Mortar Bd., Phi Beta Kappa, Alpha Omega Alpha, Omicron Delta Kappa. Clubs: Johns Hopkins (Balt.). Democrat. Avocations: gardening, carpentry, stamp collecting/philately, music. Office Phone: 254-710-2091. Business E-Mail: william_hillis@baylor.edu.

HILLKIRK, JOHN M., newspaper editor; b. 1955; BA in English, Allegheny Coll., Meadville, Pa., 1978. Bus. reporter Times-Union, Rochester, NY, Valley Dispatch, Tarentum, Pa.; reporter, editor USA Today, Gannett Co. Inc., McLean, Va., 1982—, mng. editor Money sect., 1995—2004, exec. editor USA Today, 2004—09, editor-in-chief, 2009—11, sr. editor investigative journalism and nat. enterprise reporting, 2011—. Co-author: (with Gary Jacobson) Xerox: American Samurai, 1986 (one of Ten Best of Yr., Businessweek, 1986), Grots Guts and Genius, 1990, (with Donald E. Peterson) A Better Idea: Redefining the Way Americans Work, 1991. Office: USA Today 7950 Jones Branch Dr Mc Lean VA 22108 Office Fax: 703-854-2139.

HILLS, JOHN MERRILL, educational association administrator, consultant, public relations executive, researcher; b. Wethersfield, Conn., May 6, 1944; s. Merrill Clarke and Elizabeth (Tarrant) H.; m. Irene Jeanne Lavallee, Oct. 7, 1974 (div.); children: John M. Jr., Sara Clarke; life ptnr. Scott R. Beach, Jun. 22, 2009. Student, U. Hartford, 1963; BBA, Nichols Coll., 1969; postgrad., U. Md., 1976. Salesman Peter A Frasse and Co., Inc., Hartford, Conn., 1963-64; dir. alumni relations, asst. dir. admissions Nichols Coll., Dudley, Mass., 1969-72; regional dir. Georgetown U., Washington, 1972-74; dir. devel. cen. adminstrn. U. Md., College Park, 1974-77; v.p. Roanoke Coll., Salem, Va., 1977-86, The Brookings Instn., Washington, 1986-98; pres. JMH Assocs., 1998—. Pres. J.M.H. Assocs., Washington, 1979—; cons. Am. Assn. Univ. Cons., Inc., Washington, 1975-77; mgmt., pub. relations and fund raising cons. Trustee, mem. exec. com. Nichols Coll., Dudley, Mass., 1993-2000, Higher Edn. Roundtable, Lamplighters; judge U.S. Steel Alumni Award, Pitts., 1979-86; bd. dirs. Mill Mountain Theater, Roanoke, 1983-86, Roanoke ARC, 1984-86, Roanoke Valley C. of C., 1983-86; mem. adv. bd. Phoenix Soc. Georgetown U. Sch. Law.; nat. bd. equality forum, 2007-; mem. Little Theater of Alexandria. With U.S. Army, 1965-67, N.G. Guard USN, 1964—67. Recipient Alumni Achievement award Nichols Coll., 1991; named one of Outstanding Young Men Am., U.S. Jaycees, 1980, Outstanding Nat. Advisor, Pi Lambda Phi, Conn., 1983, 86. Mem. Nat. Soc. Fund Raiser Execs., Coun. for Advancement and Support of Edn. (faculty chmn.), Alexandria Sportsman's Club (mem. exec. com.), Hunting Hills Club, Jefferson Club (Roanoke), Met. Club Washington, Paul Hill Choral Soc. (mem. corp. bd.). Roman Catholic. Avocations: sailing, jogging. Home (Summer): 17 Josephine St Rehoboth Beach DE 19971-2017 Home and Office: JMH Assocs 5801 Bayview Dr Fort Lauderdale FL 33308 Office: JMH Assocs 2613 3rd St NE Washington DC 20002 also: JMH Assocs 6 Whittier Pl 10 D Boston MA 02114 Office Phone: 954-267-9155, 202-262-9299. Personal E-mail: jackhills@jackhills.com.

HILLSTRAND, KRIS W., energy executive; BS in Computer Hardware Engring. cum laude, U. Conn., MBA cum laude. Officer Accenture (formerly known as Andersen Consulting), Deloitte Consulting, Sci. Applications International Corp.; sr. v.p., ops. TXU Energy (subs. of Energy Future Holdings Corp.), 2008—; chief info. officer Energy Future Holdings Corp. (formerly TXU Corp.), 2008—. Recipient Eta Kappa Nu, U. Conn., Tau Beta Pi. Office: Energy Future Holdings Corp 1601 Bryan St Dallas TX 75201 Office Phone: 214-812-4600.

HILTON, CLAUDE MEREDITH, federal judge; b. Scott County, Va., Dec. 8, 1940; s. Claude Swanson and Edna (Fletcher) H.; m. Joretta Cabaniss, June 16, 1963; children: John, Rachel. BS, Ohio State U., 1963; JD, Am. Univ., 1966. Bar: Va. 1966, US Ct. Appeals (4th cir.) 1967, US Supreme Ct. 1981. Dep. clk. of cts. Arlington County, Va., 1964-66, asst. commonwealth atty. Va., 1967-68, commonwealth atty. Va., 1974; sole practice Arlington, 1968—73, 1976—85; judge US Dist. Ct. (ea. dist.) Va., Alexandria, 1985—2005, chief judge, 1997—2004, sr. judge, 2005—; judge Fgn. Intelligence Surveillance Ct., 2000—. Commr. in chancery U.S. Ct. Appeals (4th cir.), 1976-85; bd. govs. criminal law sect. Va. State Bar, 1979-84, chmn., 1982-83, mem. ins. com., 1981-85. Mem. ABA, Va. Bar Assn., Arlington County Bar Assn. Lodges: Masons, Alexandria Lodge of Perfection, Kena Temple. Republican. Methodist. Office: US Dist Ct 401 Courthouse Sq Alexandria VA 22314-5704

HILTON, MARK KELLY, state legislator; b. Valdese, NC, Apr. 18, 1966; Police officer; state rep. Dist. 45 NC, 2001—02; state rep. Dist. 88 NC, 2003—04; state rep. Dist. 96 NC, 2005—. Mem. Appropriations com., Appropriations Subcom. on Edn., Edn. com., Edn. Subcom. on Universities, Homeland Security, Military and Veterans Affairs com., Ways and Means/Broadband Connectivity com.; vice chmn. Transp. com. Republican. Office: North Carolina House of Representatives 16 W Jones St Rm 1227 Raleigh NC 27601-1096 Home: 1351 Northern Dr NW Conover NC 28613 Office Phone: 919-733-5988. E-mail: Mark.Hilton@ncleg.net.

HIMELBLAU, JACK JOSEPH, Latin-American literature and culture educator; b. Chgo., Feb. 6, 1935; m. Divorced; children: two BA, U. Chgo., 1958, MA, 1959; PhD, U. Mich., 1965. Asst. prof. U. Mich., Ann Arbor, 1965-72; assoc. prof. Columbia U., NYC, 1969-72, Mills Coll., Oakland, Calif., 1972-76; prof. U. Tex., San Antonio, 1976—. Author: Alejandro O. Deustua: Philosophy in Defense Man, 1979, Quiche Worlds in Creation: Popol Vuh as a Narrative Work Art, 1989, Indian in Spanish America: Two Centuries Removal, Survival and Integration, 1993, Indian in Spanish America: Centuries Removal, Survival, and Integration. A Critical Anthology Vol. I: The Discovery and The Colonial (Pre-RePub.an) Yrs., 1994, Vol. II: RePub.an and Post-Repub.an Periods, 1995; Indian in Spanish America. Centuries Removal, Survival, and Integration. A Critical Anthology. Edited, with a Critical Introductory Study and Commentary Notes, by Jack J. Himelblau. Augmented Second Edition. Vol. 1. Lancaster, Calif.: Labyrinthos, 2006; Morphology the Cantar de Mio Cid. Potomac, Maryland: Scripta Humanistica, 2010. SH 164; contbr. numerous articles to profl. jours. Ford Found. postdoctoral fellow, 1966-67. Fellow Miembro Correspondiente Extranjero de la Academia Venezolana de la Lengua, Correspondente de la Real Española; mem. Am. Assn. Tchrs. Spanish and Portuguese. Avocation: hiking. Home: 5410 Rolling Wood Dr San Antonio TX 78228-1042 Business E-Mail: jack_himelblau@utsa.edu. E-mail: jack_himelblau@yahoo.com.

HIMELSTEIN, PHILIP NATHAN, psychology professor; b. Isidore and Martha H.; m. Peggy Donn, June 1, 1952; children: Steven Mark, Carol Sue, Roger Alan. AB, NYU, 1949, AM, 1950; PhD, U. Tex., 1955. Diplomate Am. Bd. Profl. Psychology. Clin. psychologist Salem (Va.) VA Hosp., 1955-56; rsch. psychologist USAF, 1956-58; mem. faculty U. Ark., Fayetteville, 1958-63; assoc. prof. N.Mex. State U., Las Cruces, 1963-65; prof. psychology U. Tex., El Paso, 1965-90, prof. emeritus, 1990—, chmn. dept., 1966-71; ret., 1990. Clin. psychologist El Paso Psychiat. Clinic, 1971-78; clin. assoc. prof. psychiatry Tex. Tech. U. Sch. Medicine, 1978-80; adj. prof. Sch. Psychology, Fla. Inst. Tech., Melbourne, 1977-90; chief psychologist El Paso State Ctr., 1995-98. Co-editor: Readings on the Exceptional Child, 1962, 2nd edit., 1972, Handbook of Gestalt Therapy, 1976. With USAAF, WWII. Mem. Fellow APA, Soc. Personality Assessment, Acad. Clin. Psychology; mem. El Paso Psychol. Assn. (pres. 1971-72), El Paso County Psychol. Soc. (pres. 1990-91), Sigma Xi, Phi Kappa Phi. Home: 331 Rainbow Cir El Paso TX 79912-3717

HIMMELBLAU, DAVID MAUTNER, chemical engineer; b. Chgo., Aug. 29, 1923; s. David and Roda (Mautner) H.; m. Betty H. Hartman, Sept. 1, 1948; children: Andrew, Margaret Ann. BS, MIT, Cambridge, 1947; MBA, Northwestern U., Evanston, Ill., 1950; PhD, U. Wash., Seattle, 1957. Cost engr. Internat. Harvester Co., Chgo., 1946-47; cost analyst Simpson Logging Co., Seattle, 1952-53; mgr. Excel Battery Co., Seattle, 1953-54; tchg. asst., instr. U. Wash., Seattle, 1955-57; successively asst. prof., asso. prof., prof. chem. engring. U. Tex., Austin, 1957—, chmn. dept., 1973-77. Pres. RAMAD Corp.; Univ. Fed. Credit Union, 1964-68; exec officer CACHE Corp. of Mass., 1984-2000. Author: Basic Principles and Calculations in Chemical Engineering, 1962, 7th edit., 2004, Process Analysis and Simulation, 1968, Process Analysis by Statistical Methods, 1970, Applied Nonlinear Programming, 1974, 2d edit., 1999, Optimization of Chemical Processes, 1989, 2d edit., 2000; contbr. articles to profl. jours. Served with US Army, 1943-46, 51-52. Grantee, NSF, 1953—94, NATO Sci. Com., 1969. Mem. Am. Inst. Chem. Engrs. (dir. 1973-76), Am. Chem. Soc., Am. Math. Soc., Ops. Rsch. Soc. Am., Soc. Indsl. and Applied Math., Sigma Xi, Delta Mu Delta. Clubs: Headliners (Austin). Office: Univ Texas Coll Engring Austin TX 78712 Home: 4024 Walnut Clay Dr Austin TX 78731-3932 Office Phone: 512-471-7445. Business E-Mail: himmelblau1@che.utexas.edu.

HIMMELRIGHT, ROBERT JOHN, JR., rubber company executive; b. Canton, Ohio, Mar. 29, 1926; s. Robert John and Katherine Dewees (Nusly) H.; m. Suzanne Hadley, Mar. 11, 1950; children: Robert John III, Christina S., George H., Anne D. BA, U. N.Mex., 1951; LLD (hon.), Kenyon Coll., 1987. With Teledyne Monarch Rubber Co., Hartville, Ohio, 1950-84, asst. to pres., then v.p., 1955-62, pres., 1963-84; chmn. Monarch South Seas Ltd., Delray Beach, Fla., 1984—. Alt. del. Rep. Nat. Conv., 1972, 76; trustee Kenyon Coll., Gambier, Ohio. With USNR, 1944-46, 50-51. Lutheran. Home and Office: 178 777 E Atlantic Ave Ste C2 Delray Beach FL 33483-5352 Personal E-mail: redhjr@aol.com.

HINCHEY, JOHN WILLIAM, lawyer; b. Knoxville, Tenn., June 18, 1941; s. Roy William and Ruth (Ownby) H.; m. Sherie Paulette Archer, May 12, 1968; children: Paul William, Meredith Marie, John Oliver. AB, Emory U., 1964, LLB, 1965; LLM, Harvard U., 1966; MLitt., Oxford U., 1980. Bar: Ga. 1965, U.S. Dist. Ct. (no., mid. and so. dists.) Ga. 1968, U.S. Ct. Appeals (11th cir.) 1968, U.S. Supreme Ct. 1970. Asst. atty. gen. State of Ga., Atlanta, 1968-72; ptnr. McConaughey & Hinchey, Decatur, Ga., 1972-76, Phillips & Mozley, Atlanta, 1976-84, Phillips, Hinchey & Reid, Atlanta, 1984-92, King and Spalding, Atlanta, 1992—2010; ret., 2011. Contbr. articles to profl. jours.;, author numerous books. Fellow: Canadian Coll. Construction Lawyers, Coll. Comm. Arbitrator; mem.: ABA (chair Forum on Constrn. Industry), JAMS Global Engring. and Constrn. Panel, CPR Inst., Alternative Dispute Resolution Counsel, Chartered Inst. Arbitrators, London Ct. Internat. Arbitration, Atlanta Bar Assn. (chair constrn. law sect. 1999—2000), Ga. Bar Assn., Am. Coll. Constrn. Lawyers (bd. govs. 2001—04, sec. 2005—, pres. 2008—09, immediate past pres. 2009—, past pres. 2009—). Independent. Methodist. Office Phone: 404-572-4922, 404-933-0821. Business E-Mail: jhinchey@jamsadr.edu.

HINES, ANDREW HAMPTON, JR., utilities executive; b. Lake City, Fla., Jan. 28, 1923; s. Andrew Hampton and Louise Dixie (Howland) H.; m. Ann Groover, June 28, 1947' children: Andrew Hampton III, Elizabeth Renee, John Bradford, Daniel Howland. BME with high honors, U. Fla., 1947; degree (hon.), Stetson U., 1987, U. South Fla., 1989, Rollins Coll., 1989, Fla. So. Coll., 1994; degree (hon.), U. Fla., 2007. Registered profl. engr., U. Fla., 2007. With R&D depts. GE, 1947-51; pres. Fla. Power Corp., 1972-82; chmn. bd. Fla. Progress Corp., St. Petersburg, 1982-91, Precise Power Corp., Bradenton, Fla., 1990-97. Cons. Triangle Cons. Group; past chmn. N.Am. Electric Reliability Coun.; exec.-in-residence Eckerd Coll., 1990-2001. Life trustee Asbury Theol. Sem.; bd. dirs. U. Fla. Found., Sunday sch. tchr. Christian Missionary Alliance Ch.; chmn. Pinellas County Cmty. Reuse Orgn., 1994-97; chmn. No Casinos in Fla., Inc., 1994-1998. 2d lt. USAAF, 1943-45. Decorated Air medal, Prisoner of War medal. Fellow ASME; mem. U.S. Energy Assn., Blue Key, St. Petersburg Yacht Club, Sigma Tau, Phi Kappa Phi, Tau Beta Pi, Beta Gamma Sigma. Personal E-mail: ahh@tampabay.rr.com.

HINES, ANGUS IRVING, JR., petroleum marketing executive; b. Suffolk, Va., Aug. 7, 1923; s. Angus Irving and Lois E. (Howell) Hines; m. Genevieve Hopkins McCollum, Nov. 24, 1949 (div. 1977); children: Ann Russell Hines Mauer, Marilyn N. Hines Stulb, A. McCollum, Angus Irving III. Pres. Angus I. Hines, Inc., Suffolk, 1945—. With Angus Hines, Inc., Svc. Gas Co., Inc. With Maritime Svc. US Army, 1943—45, with, ETO. Mem.: Quiet Birdmen, Rotary Club (past pres.), Va. Petroleum Jobbers Assn. (past pres.). Methodist. Office: Angus I Hines Inc 1220 Holland Rd Suffolk VA 23434-6313 Home Phone: 757-627-4488; Office Phone: 757-539-0832. Personal E-mail: angushines@aol.com.

HINES, DONALD E., state legislator; b. Nov. 14, 1933; m. Jacqueline Ewing Jackie. Diplomate America Bd. Family Practice. Mem. Avoyelles Parish Sch. Bd., La., 1972—93, pres., 1973—76, 1984—86; mem. La Wildlife & Fisheries Commn., 1984—90; state senator Dist. 28, 1992—; vice chmn. Health & Welfare Com.;

Physician Family Practice, New Iberia, La., 1964—66; with Bunkie, La., 1966—; senate pres.; mem. Agr. & Natural Resources; vice chmn. La State Senate. Recipient Citizen of Yr., Bunkie Rotary Club, 1980. Mem.: America Acad. Family Physicians, America Med. Assn., LA State Med. Soc., La Acad. Family Practice, Eighth Dist. Med. Soc, Avoyelles Parish Med. Soc., Avoyelles Parish Cancer Soc. (pres.), Bunkie Quarterback Club, Bunkie Lions Club (Citizen of Yr.). Democrat. Baptist. Address: 109 N Lexington Bunkie LA 71322 Mailing: PO Box 262 Bunkie LA 71322 Fax: 318-346-2301.

HINES, JOHN W., SR., state legislator, private investigator; b. Greenville, Miss., Apr. 6, 1966; m. Sherrie B. Gregory. Attended, Miss. Valley State U. Ins. agent & investigator McTeer Assocs.; mem. Dist. 50 Miss. House of Reps., 2001—. Mem. Conservation & Water Resources, Fees & Salaries Pub. Officers, Juvenile Justice & State Libr. coms., 2001—. Democrat. Home: PO Box 114 Greenville MS 38701 Office: PO Box 1018 Rm 400F-NC Jackson MS 39215-1018 Office Phone: 601-359-3374, 662-334-9444. Business E-Mail: jhines@house.ms.gov.

HINES, MACK T., state legislator; b. Florence, SC, Dec. 2, 1946; s. Mack T. and Susana Gregg Hines; m. Gladys Jackson, 1971; children: Mack T. III, Michael T., Gregory J. Chmn. Ministerial Com.; former chmn. Relig Com., SC Legislature Black Caucus, SC; former mem. Mil. Com., Pub. Com., Munic Affairs Com.; state rep. Dist. 59 SC, 1995—2005; vice moderator Florence County & Affiliated Countys Union, 1989—, Pee Dee Baptist Assn., 2002—; trustee Morris Coll., 1989—93; asst. sec. Nat. Baptist Conv., USA Inc., 1994—; founder, chmn. Pee Dee Investor's Group, 1998—. Exec. bd. mem. Pee-Dee Baptist Assn., 1984—; founder Wilsonian Clergy, vice chmn., 1988, chmn., 2001; pastor St. Paul Baptist Ch., 1984—. Recipient Masters award, SC Gen. Baptist Conv., 1994; named Key to City, Mullins, SC, 1985, Sommerset, NJ, 1987. Mem.: NAACP (life), Mullins Area Ministerial Alliance (founder, pres. 1986—). Democrat. Baptist. Address: 1414 Aaron Cir Florence SC 29506 Home: 310 E Pocket Rd Florence SC 29506 Home Phone: 843-662-5435; Office Phone: 843-678-3410, 803-734-2965. Home Fax: 803-678-3412.

HINES, PRESTON HARRIS, state supreme court justice; b. Atlanta, Sept. 6, 1943; s. James Reuben and Edith (Hawkins) Hines; m. Helen Holmes Hill; children: Mary Margaret, James Harris. AB in Polit. Sci., Emory U., 1965, JD, 1968. Bar: Ga. 1968, U.S. Dist. Ct. Ga. 1973. Law clk. Civil Ct. Fulton County, 1968-69; pvt. practice Marietta, Ga., 1969-74; judge State Ct. of Cobb County, 1974-82, Superior Ct. of Ga., 1982—95; justice Ga. Supreme Ct., 1995—, presiding justice, 2013—. Chmn. attys. divsn. Cobb County United Appeal, 1972; participant Leadership Ga., 1975, Leadership Atlanta, 1978-79; pres. YMCA Cobb County, 1976; co-treas. Cobb Landmarks Soc., 1976-77; former bd. dirs. Cobb County Emergency Aid Assn., Cobb-Marietta Girls Club, Ga. chpt. Leukemia Soc. Am., Cobb County Children's Ctr., Met. Atlanta Red Cross, First Presbyn. Day Kindergarten; mem. cmty. adv. com. Marietta-Cobb County LWV; bd. dirs. Kennesaw Coll. Found.; trustee Cobb Cmty. Symphony. Named Outstanding Young Man of Yr., Ga. Jaycees, 1975, Boss of Yr., Cobb County Legal Secs. Assn., 1975-76, 83-84. Mem. ABA, State Bar Ga. (chmn. Law Day com. 1975, mem. exec. com. younger lawyers sec. 1974-76), Cobb Jud. Cir. (sec. 1972-73, chmn. Law Day com. 1972), Joseph Henry Lumpkin Inn of Ct. Ga., Atlanta Lawyers Club, Kiwanis (bd. dirs. Marietta chpt., chmn. Key Club com., past chmn. spiritual aims com., past pres.), Cobb County C. of C., Sigma Alpha Epsilon (Atlanta and Marietta chpts.). Office: Georgia Supreme Court 244 Washington St Atlanta GA 30334*

HINES, WILLIAM H., lawyer; AB, Princeton U., NJ, 1978; JD, U. Va., 1982. Bar: La. 1982, US Dist. Ct. (ea., mid. dists.) La., US Ct. Appeals (5th cir.). Ptnr. Jones, Walker, Waechter, Poitevent, Carrère & Denègre LLP, New Orleans, mng. ptnr. of firm, 2006—. Bd. dirs. Ochsner Clinic Found., 2003—, chmn. nominating com., 2009—. Contbr. articles to profl. jours. Bd. dirs. La. State Mus. Found., 1998—, sec., 1999—2002; bd. trustees United Way Greater New Orleans, 2002—, mem. exec. com., 2002—07, 2009—, vice chmn. bd. trustees, 2004—05, chmn. bd. trustees, 2005—06; bd. dirs. New Orleans Jazz Orch., 2003—, chmn. bd. dirs., 2006—; bd. dirs. New Orleans Art Coun., 2003—, vice chmn., mem. exec. com., 2005—06, chmn. bd. dirs., 2007—09; bd. trustees World War II Mus., 2007—; hon. consul to Portugal State of La., 2000; mem. econ. growth adv. coun., bus. retention and recruitment panel Office of Gov. Bobby Jindal, La., 2007—; mem. econ. devel. transition task force Office of Mayor Mitch Landrieu, New Orleans, 2010; commr. Downtown Devel. Dist. of City New Orleans, 2010—; mem. internat. bus. com. World Trade Ctr. New Orleans, 1994—2004, vice chmn. internat. bus. com., 1995, 1999, bd. dirs., 1998—2009, mem. exec. com., 2000—01, 2008—09, vice chmn. govt. affairs com., 2007, chmn. govt. affairs com., 2008—09, sec., 2009, mem. adv. bd. dirs., 2010; mem. vis. com. Loyola U. Coll. Bus. Adminstrn., 2000—; mem. bus. coun. Metairie Pk. Country Day Sch., 2000—; mem. cmty. adv. bd. Teach for America, 2000—, chmn. cmty. adv. bd., 2004—06; mem. adv. bd. Bus. Coun. New Orleans and the River Region, 2001—; bd. dirs. Greater New Orleans Sports Found., 2001—, U. New Orleans Found., 2002—, Assn. Corp. Growth, La., 2004—, New Orleans Regional Med. Ctr., 2006—, The Horizon Initiative, 2007—, La. Appleseed, 2008—, Bayou Dist. Found., 2009—, Coun. for Better La., 2002—, chmn. bd. dirs., 2009; bd. dirs. The Idea Village, 2002—, mem. exec. com., 2008—, vice chmn., 2010—; bd. dirs. Greater New Orleans Inc., The Regional Econ. Alliance, 2004—09, chmn. bd. dirs., 2004—05, mem. exec. com., 2004—07, bd. dirs. emeritus, 2009—; mem. Tulane U. Pres. Coun., 2004—; mem. adv. bd. U. New Orleans Coll. Bus. Adminstrn., 2005—; mem. Com. of 100 for Econ. Devel., 2006—, mem. exec. com., membership chmn., 2007—, chmn., 2010—; hon. chmn. Justice for All Ball of Pro Bono Project for Greater New Orleans Region, 2007. Named one of The Best Lawyers in America, Banking, Corp. and Internat. Trade & Fin. Law, 1999—; named to La. Super Lawyers, Bus./Corp., 2007—. Fellow: American Bar Found., La. Bar Found.; mem.: ABA (mem. pub. adv. bd. 1994—96), La. State Bar Assn., New Orleans Bar Assn. (mem. exec. com., young lawyers divsn. 1984—85), Maritime Law Assn. of US (mem. marine financing com., mem. maritime legislation com.). Office: Jones Walker Waechter Poitevent Carrere & Denegre LLP 201 St Charles Ave New Orleans LA 70170-5100 Office Phone: 504-582-8272. Office Fax: 504-582-8583. Business E-Mail: bhines@joneswalker.com.

HINICH, MELVIN J., economics professor; b. Pitts., Apr. 29, 1939; s. Joseph and Sara (Rubinstein) Hinich; m. Sonje Gregg, Sept. 14, 1966; 1 child, Amy Sara. BS, Carnegie Inst. Tech., 1959, MS in Math, 1960; PhD in Statistics, Stanford, 1963. Asst. prof. indsl. adminstrn. Carnegie Inst. Tech., 1963-68; assoc. prof. indsl. adminstrn., statistics, 1968-70; prof. statistics, polit. economy Carnegie Mellon U., 1970-73; prof. econs. dept. Va. Poly. Inst. and State U., Blacksburg, 1973-82; prof. govt. and econs. U. Tex., Austin, 1982—, Frank Erwin prof. govt., 1984-86, Mike Hogg prof. govt. and econs., 1986—, with Applied Rsch. Labs., 1985—. Fairchild disting. scholar Calif. Inst. Tech. Inc., Pasadena, 1975-76; cons. Teledyne-Isotopes, Inc., Internat. Research & Tech., Inc., FDA, Air Pollution Control-Allegheny County Health Dept., U.S. Naval Coastal Systems Center, Tracor Applied Scis., Inst. Macroeconomics, Fed. Res. Bank of Mpls.; cons. task force on regulatory reform U.S. Senate Govt. Ops. Com., NATO Saclant Research Ctr., La Spezia, Italy, devel. program UN; editl. bd. Pub. Choice. Author: Introduction to Continuous Probability, 1969, Consumer Protection Legislation and the U.S. Food Industry, 1980, The Spatial Theory of Voting: An Introduction, 1984, Advances in the Spatial Theory of Voting, 1990, Political Economy: Institutions, Competition and Representation, 1993, Ideology and the Theory of Political Choice, 1994, Analytical Politics, 1997, Empirical Studies in Comparative Politics, 1998, Topics in Analytical Political Economy, 2007; assoc. editor: Macroeconomic Dynamics, Studies in Nonlineat Dynamics & Econometrics; contbr. articles to profl. jours. Fellow: Am. Statis. Assn., Pub. Choice Soc. (pres. 1992—94), Inst. Math. Stats.; mem.: Sigma Xi. Home: 3902 Cresthill Dr Austin TX 78731-3808 Office: University Tex Batts Hall Austin TX 78712-1087 Office Phone: 512-835-3278. Business E-Mail: hinich@austin.utexas.edu.

HININGER, DAMON, private sector financial services company executive; BS, Kansas State U., 1991; MBA, Jack Massey Grad. Sch. Bus., Belmont U., Nashville, 2000; attended, U. Pa.-Wharton Sch., 2009. Correctional officer Leavenworth Detention Ctr., Kans., 1992—94; tng. mgr. Ctrl. Ariz. Detention Ctr., 1994; mgr., facility start-up Corrections Corporate of America, 1995—98, v.p., bus. analysis, 2000, v.p., fed. and local customer relations, 2002, sr. v.p., fed. and local customer relations, 2007—08, pres., 2008—, COO, 2008—09, CEO, 2009—. Bd. dirs. Corrections Corp. of America, 2009—. Office: Corrections Corporation of America 10 Burton Hills Blvd Nashville TN 37215 Office Phone: 615-263-3000.

HINKLE, ROBERT LEWIS, federal judge; b. Apalachicola, Fla., Nov. 7, 1951; s. Jene L. and Lena (Chauncey) H.; m. Marylou Bevis, June 8, 1974. BA magna cum laude, Fla. State U., 1972; JD magna cum laude, Harvard U., 1976. Bar: Fla. 1976. Law clk. to judge US Ct. Appeals (5th cir.), Dallas, 1976-77; assoc. Sutherland, Asbill & Brennan, Atlanta, 1977-78; ptnr. Hinkle & Battaglia, Tallahassee, 1979-82, Wadsworth, Davis & Hinkle, Tallahassee, 1982-84, Holland & Knight, Tallahassee, 1984-85, Aurell, Fons, Radey & Hinkle, Tallahassee, 1985-89, Aurell, Radey, Hinkle & Thomas, Tallahassee, 1989-91, Aurell, Radey, Hinkle, Thomas & Beranek, Tallahassee, 1991-94, Radey Hinkle Thomas & McArthur, Tallahassee, 1994—96; judge US Dist. Ct. (no. dist.) Fla., Tallahassee, 1996—2004, 2009—; chief judge US Dist. Ct. (No. Dist.) Fla., 2004—09. Adj. prof. law Fla. State U., Tallahassee, 1981. Active Leadership Fla., 1990-91. Office: US District Courthouse 111 N Adams St Tallahassee FL 32301-7730 Office Phone: 850-521-3601.

HINLICKY, PAUL RICHARD, minister; b. Portchester, NY, Sept. 4, 1952; s. William Paul and Marie Maxine (Novotny) H.; m. Ellen Irene Christiansen, Aug. 17, 1974; children: Sarah Ellen, William Alfred. BA, Concordia Coll., Fort Wayne, Ind., 1974; MDiv, Seminex, St. Louis, 1978; PhD, Union Theol. Sem., 1983. Ordained to ministry Evang. Luth. Ch. Am., 1978. Asst. pastor Mount Zion Luth. Ch., Harlem, N.Y., 1978-80; resch. assoc. Dept. Ch. in Soc. Luth. Ch. in Am., 1982-85; pastor Immanuel Luth. Ch., Delhi, 1985—93; editor, exec. dir. Luth. Forum Am. Luth. Publicity Bur., 1988—93. Author: Paths not Taken of Luther and the Beloved Community; contbr. articles to jours. in field. Office: Roanoke Coll 221 College Ln Salem VA 24153 E-mail: hinlicky@roanoke.edu.

HINMAN, ALAN RICHARD, public health physician, epidemiologist; b. New Orleans, Mar. 23, 1937; s. E. Harold and Katharine Ellen (Fradenburgh) H.; m. Donna Virgene Graham, Dec. 21, 1959 (div. 1962); m. Lucy Winkler Householder, May 30, 1965; children: Johanna Mary, Katharine Emily. BA, Cornell U., 1957; MD, Western Res. U., 1961; MPH, Harvard U., 1969. Intern Cleve. Met. Hosp., 1961—62, resident in internal medicine, 1962—64, chief resident, 1964-65; with USPHS, 1965-70, 77-96; advanced through grades to asst. surgeon gen., 1988; epidemic intelligence svc. officer Ctr. for Disease Control, Calif. State Dept. Health, 1965-66; regional evaluation officer malaria eradication program Ctrs. for Disease Control, Atlanta, 1966-67, San Salvador, El Salvador, 1967-68, asst. chief viral diseases br. epidemiology program Atlanta, 1969-70; dir. Bur. Epidemiology, N.Y. State Dept. Health, Albany, 1970-71, asst. commr. epidemiology and preventive health svcs., 1971-75; asst. commr., dir. Bur. Preventive and Med. Svcs., Tenn. Dept. Pub. Health, Nashville, 1975-77; dir. divsn. immunization Ctr. for Prevention Svcs., Ctrs. for Disease Control, Atlanta, 1977-88; coord. nat. vaccine program Office of Asst. Sec. for Health, 1987-90; asst. surgeon gen. USPHS, 1988-96; dir. Nat. Ctr. for Prevention Svcs. Ctrs. for Disease Control, 1988-95; sr. advisor to dir. Ctrs. for Disease Control and Prevention, 1995-96; coord. CDC World Bank collaboration on immunizations Task Force Global HealthDecatur, Atlanta, 1996—2000; sr. pub. health scientist Task Force Child Survival and Devel., Atlanta, 1996—; prin. investigator All Kids Count, 2000—04; coord. PARTNERS TB ctrl. program, 2001—02; progarm dir. Uganda Immunization Tng. Program, 2008—. Adj. asst. prof. preventive and cmty. medicine Albany Med. Coll., Union U., 1970-75; adj. asst. prof. pub. health Rensselaer Poly Inst., 1971-75; assoc. clin. prof. dept. preventive medicine Vanderbilt U., 1975-77; clin. asst. prof. dept. cmty. medicine Divsn. Healthcare Svcs., U. Tenn., 1975-77; clin. asst. prof. dept. family and cmty. health Meharry Med. Coll., 1975-77; clin. assoc. prof. dept. preventive medicine-cmty. health Emory U. Sch. Medicine, Atlanta, 1978-90; vis. prof. Case Western Res. U. Sch. Medicine, 1984; adj. prof. Emory U. Sch. Pub. Health, 1990—; vis. lectr. Shanghai 1st Med. Coll., 1981; sr. pub. health scientist The Task Force for Child Survival and Devel., 1996—. Contbr. over 300 articles to profl. jours. Decorated D.S.M.; recipient Indian Health Svc. Dir. Spl. Excellence award, 1992. Fellow ACP, APHA (mem. gov. coun. 1975-77, mem. program devel. bd. 1984-86, mem. nominating com. 1984-86, chair 1985-86, chair-elect epidemiology sect. 1985-87, chair sect. 1987-89, past chair 1989-91, mem. exec. bd. 1991-95, spkr. governing coun. 1995-2007), Am. Acad. Pediat., Am. Coll. Epidemiology (mem. exec. bd. 1990-94, v.p. 1991-92, pres. 1992-93), Am. Coll. Preventive Medicine (regent 1974-75, 77-81, v.p. for pub. health 1975-76); mem. AMA, Am. Epidemiol. Soc., Am. Soc. Tropical Medicine and Hygiene, Am. Venereal Disease Assn. (bd. dirs. 1972-75, sec.-treas. 1975-77), Assn. Tchrs. Preventive Medicine, Infectious Diseases Soc. Am., Internat. Epidemiol. Assn., Physicians for Social Responsibility, Soc. Epidemiol. Rsch., Soc. Med. Decision Making. Home: 2194 Creek Park Rd Decatur GA 30033-2714 Office Phone: 404-687-5636. Business E-Mail: ahinman@taskforce.org.

HINOJOSA, FEDERICO GUSTAVO, JR., retired judge; b. Edinburg, Tex., Apr. 16, 1947; s. Federico Gustavo and Zulema (Trevino) H.; m. Yolanda Silva, 1970 (div. 1977); children: Cynthia, Zelda Cassandra; m. Magdalena Garza, Oct. 30, 1992. BA, Pan Am. U., 1969; JD, U. Houston, 1977. Bar: Tex. 1977, U.S. Dist. Ct. (so. dist.) Tex. 1977, U.S. Ct. Appeals (5th cir.) 1980, U.S. Supreme Ct. 1980. Assoc. Clark, Lowes & Carrithers, Houston, 1977-79; ptnr. Clark & Hinojosa, Houston, 1979-81; child support atty. Tex. Dept. Human Resources, McAllen, 1981-83; asst. dist. atty. Hidalgo County, Edinburg, 1983-84; assoc. Atlas & Hall, McAllen, 1984-87; ptnr. Lewis, Pettitt & Hinojosa, McAllen, 1987-91; justice Tex. Ct. Appeals for 13th Dist., Corpus Christi, 1991—2006, ret., 2006. Sgt. USAF, 1970—74. Fellow Tex. Bar. Found. (life); mem. State Bar Tex., Mexican-Am. Bar Tex., Mexican-Am. Bar Assn. Coastal Bend (dir. 1993-94), Hidalgo County Bar Assn. (dir. 1986-90), Corpus Christi Bar Assn., Cameron County Bar Assn., Am. Judicature Soc. Democrat. Office: 710 Laurel Ave Mcallen TX 78501 Office Phone: 956-687-8203. Personal E-mail: judgehinojosa@gmail.com.

HINOJOSA, GILBERTO, political organization administrator; b. Tex. m. Cyndi Hinojosa; children: Gina, Xochitl, Miguel, Diego, Maya. B, Pan American U. (now U. Tex.-Pan American); JD, Georgetown U., Washington, DC. Atty. Migrant Legal Action Program; dir. Migrant Farm Worker Program Colo. Rural Legal Svcs.; mng. atty. Tex. Rural Legal Aid Inc., Brownsville; mem. bd. trustees Brownsville Ind. Sch. Dist., 1984, v.p. bd. trustees; presiding judge Cameron County Ct. at Law No. 2; judge 107th Dist. Ct., Cameron County, Tex., 1987; justice 13th Ct. Appeals, Tex.; mem. Tex. Bd. Criminal Justice; Cameron County judge Tex.; chair Cameron County Dem. Party, 2007; chmn. Tex. Dem. Party, Austin, 2012—. Democrat. Office: Texas Democratic Party 4818 E Ben White Blvd Ste 104 Austin TX 78741 Office Phone: 512-478-9800.

HINOJOSA, JUAN J., state legislator; b. McAllen, Tex., Mar. 7, 1946; s. Juan de Dios and Esperanza Hinojosa; m. Irma Hinojosa. BS in Polit. Sci. with honors, U. Tex. Pan Am.; JD, Georgetown U., Washington. Staff atty. Legal Aid Soc. of Nueces County, Tex.; former asst. atty. gen. Office of Atty. Gen., Tex.; mem. Dist. 41 Tex. House of Representatives, 1981—91, mem. Dist. 40, 1997—2002; apptd. interim county judge Hidalgo County, Tex., 1995; ptnr. Hinojosa & Powell; mem. Dist. 20 Tex. State Senate, Tex., 2002—. Adv. coun. mem. Fed. Res. Bd.; mem. bd. trustees McAllen Meth. Hosp. Squad leader USMC, 1966—68, Vietnam. Recipient Appreciation award, Hidalgo County, Tex. State Tech. Inst., McAllen, 1984, Holy Spirit Parish Cub Scouts, 1985; named Legislator of Yr., Tex. Chpt. Nat. Orgn. Mem.: Tex. State Bar, Nat. Fedn. Ind. Bus., McAllen 100, McAllen Jaycees. Democrat. Roman Catholic. Office: 612 Nolana Ste 410B Mcallen TX 78504 also: PO Box 12068 Capitol Station Austin TX 78711 also: 2820 S.P.I.D. Ste 291 Corpus Christi TX 78415 Office Phone: 956-972-1841, 512-463-0120, 361-225-3576. Office Fax: 956-664-0602.

HINOJOSA, MICHAEL, school system administrator; m. Kitty Hinojosa; 3 children. BA, Tex. Tech U., Lubbock; MA, U. North Tex., Denton; EdD, U. Tex., Austin. Tchr., coach L.V. Stockard Mid. Sch., Dallas, W.H. Adamson HS, Dallas; campus and ctrl. office adminstr., assoc. supt. Grand Prairie Ind. Sch. Dist., Tex.; supt. Fabens Ind. Sch. Dist., Tex., 1994—97, Hays Consolidated Sch. Dist., Tex., 1997—2002, Spring Ind. Sch. Dist., Houston, 2002—05, Dallas Ind. Sch. Dist., Tex., 2005—11, Cobb County Sch. Dist., Ga., 2011—. Exec. dir. Region 19 Edn. Svc. Ctr., El Paso, Tex., 1997. Recipient Golden Deeds Award, Tex. Assn. Mid-Size Sch.; named Tex. Supt. Yr., Tex. Assn. Sch. Bds., 2002, Supt. Yr., Coop. Supt. Program, U. Tex. Austin. Mem.: Tex. Assn. Sch. Adminstrs. (past pres.). Office: Cobb County School District 514 Glover St Marietta GA 30060 Office Phone: 770-426-3452. E-mail: michael.hinojosa@cobbk12.org.

HINOJOSA, RICARDO H., federal judge; b. Rio Grande City, Tex., 1950; BA, U. Tex., 1972; JD, Harvard U., 1975. Law clk. Tex. Supreme Ct., Austin, 1975-76; assoc. Ewers & Toothaker, McAllen, Tex., 1976-79, ptnr., 1979-83; judge US Dist. Ct. (southern dist.) Tex., McAllen, Tex., 1983—2009, chief judge, 2009—. Mem. Pan American U. Bd. Regents, 1979—83, chmn., 1981—83; commr. US Sentencing Commn., 2003—, chair, 2004—09, acting chair, 2009, vice chair, 2013—; adj. prof. U. Tex. Sch. Law. Recipient Disting. Svc. award, Pan-Am. U. Alumni Assn., 1986, Disting. Alumnus award, U. Tex. Ex-Students Assn., 2001. Office: US Dist Ct Southern Dist Tex 1701 W Bus Hwy 83 Ste 1011 Mcallen TX 78501 Office Phone: 956-618-8100.*

HINOJOSA, RUBÉN, United States Representative from Texas; b. Edcouch, Tex., Aug. 20, 1940; m. Martha Lopez; 5 children. BBA, U. Tex., Austin, 1962; MBA, U. Tex.-Pan Am., Edinburg, 1980. Mem. Tex. State Bd. Edn., 1974—84; pres., CFO H & H Foods; mem. US Congress from 15th Tex. Dist., 1997—; chmn. Congressional Hispanic Caucus, 2012—13. Founding chmn. bd. trustees South Tex. Cmty. Coll., 1993—96. Recipient Lifetime Achievement award, Hispanic Bus. Mag.; named Rio Grande Valley Hispanic Man of Yr., 1994. Democrat. Office: US House of Representatives 2262 Rayburn House Office Bldg Washington DC 20515 also: 2864 W Trenton Rd Edinburg TX 78539 Office Phone: 202-225-2531.*

HINSHAW, CARROLL ELTON, economics professor; b. Texarkana, Ark., Aug. 2, 1936; s. Curtis Tillman and Loma Dean (Roberts) H.; m. Jane A. Simpson, Aug. 11, 1957; children: Stephen, Rebecca, Carroll. BBA, Baylor U., 1958; PhD, Vanderbilt U., 1966. Assoc. prof. La. Coll., 1962-64; from asst. prof. econs. to prof. emeritus Vanderbilt U., Nashville, 1966—2000, prof. emeritus, 2000—, asst. dean Coll. Arts and Sci., 1970-72, assoc. dean, 1972-74. Vis. asst. prof. Getulio Vargas Found., Rio de Janeiro, Brazil, 1967-69; CEO Shiloh Paper, Inc.; CFO Farmhouse Foods, Inc.; cons. in field. Author: Forecasting and Recognizing Business Cycle Turning Points, 1968; Contbr. articles to profl. jours. H.B. Earhart fellow, 1965-66 Mem. Am. Econ. Assn. (sec. 1976-93, treas. 1988-96, sec., treas. emeritus, 2000), Beta Alpha Psi, Omicron Delta Epsilon, Immanuel Baptist Church (dir.). Baptist. Office: Am Econ Assn 2014 Broadway Ste 305 Nashville TN 37203-2425 also: Dept Econs Vanderbilt Univ Nashville TN 37232-0001

HINSHAW, CHESTER JOHN, lawyer; b. Sacramento, Mar. 10, 1941; s. Chester Edward and Gertrude Lorraine (Miller) H.; m. Karen Forbes Breakey, Feb. 19, 1977. AB, Stanford U., 1963; JD, U. Calif., Berkeley, 1966. Bar: Calif. 1966, U.S. Dist. Ct. (no. dist.) Calif. 1967, U.S. Ct. Appeals (9th cir.) 1967, N.Y. 1968, U.S. Dist. Ct. (so. dist.) N.Y. 1972, U.S. Dist. Ct. (ea. dist.) N.Y. 1974, U.S. Ct. Appeals (2d cir.) 1974, U.S. Dist. Ct. (no. dist.) N.Y. 1980, U.S. Dist. Ct. (ea. dist.) Mich. 1982, U.S. Dist. Ct. (no. dist.) Tex. 1983, Tex. 1984, U.S. Ct. Appeals (5th cir.) 1984, U.S Supreme Ct. 1991. Assoc. Chadbourne & Parke, NYC, 1967-74, ptnr., 1974-83, Jones Day, Dallas, 1983-99. Lectr. U. Calif., Berkeley, 1966. Mem. ABA, Tex. Bar Assn., Calif. Bar Assn. Home: 5510 Park Ln Dallas TX 75220-2158 Office Phone: 214-368-4332.

HINSHAW, JUANITA H., board member; BA in Jr. Acctg., U. NC, 1967, BS in Economics & Bus. Adminstrn., 1972. Sr. v.p., CFO & bd. dirs. Graybar Electric Co., Inc., 2000—05; pres., CEO H&H Advisors, 2005—. Bd. dir. Ipsco Inc.; bd. mem. KETC/Channel 9; bd. dir. Insituform Technologies, Inc, 2000—, Commerce Bank, 2002—; bd. dirs. The Williams Companies, Inc., 2004—, Synergetics USA, Inc., 2005—. Bd. dirs. Grand Ctr., Md. U., United Way. Office: The Williams Companies Inc Bd Directors 1 Williams Ctr Tulsa OK 74172 Office Phone: 918-573-2000. Office Fax: 918-573-6714. Business E-Mail: juanita.hinshaw@williams.com.

HINSHAW, MARILYN L., retired library director; d. Leland E. Baker and Sybil G. Zook-Baker; m. S'Lee Bud Hinshaw, Oct. 25, 1964; children: S'Lee Arthur, Bethanie Anna. BA, Emporia State U., Kans., MLS, 1970; MS in Pub. Adminstr., U. Mo., Columbia, 1982. Cert. pub. libr. Okla. Dept. Librs., 1997. Cons., continuing edn. coord. State Libr. Kans., Topeka, 1970—73; br. ext. coord., libr. sys. adminstr. El Paso Pub. Libr., Tex., 1973—77; asst. dir. Daniel Boone

Regional Libr., Columbia, Mo., 1977—82; exec. dir. Ea. Okla. Dist. Libr. Sys., Muskogee, ret., 2008. Recipient Distinguished Svc. award, Mountain Plains Libr. Assn., Okla. Libr. Assn., 2008; named Outstanding New Libr., Tex. Libr. Assn. Mem.: ALA (pres. 1975—76), Tex. Libr. Assn. (chair pub. libr. divsn.), Mountain Plains Libr. Assn. (pres. 1999—2000), Pub. Libr. Assn. (pres. Met. libr. sect. 1984—85), Okla. Libr. Assn. (pres. 1986—87). Avocations: gardening, reading, writing. Home: 3506 University Muskogee OK 74403

HINSON, H. DOUGLAS, lawyer; b. Staunton, Va., June 27, 1960; s. Harold D. and Betty M. (Morris) H.; m. Michelle R. Olsen, Aug. 9, 1986. BA magna cum laude, Emory U., 1982; JD cum laude, Georgetown U., 1986. Bar: Ala. 1986, Ga. 1989, US Dist. Ct. (no. and so. dists.) Ala. 1986, US Ct. Appeals (11th cir.) 1987, US Dist. Ct. (no. dist.) Ga. 1989, DC 2011. Assoc. Bradley, Arant, Rose & White, Birmingham, Ala., 1986-88; assoc. Alston & Bird, Atlanta, 1988-94, ptnr., litig., 1994—. Active Salvation Army. Mem. Phi Beta Kappa. Avocations: golf, travel. Office: Alston & Bird 1 Atlantic Ctr 1201 W Peachtree St NW Atlanta GA 30309-3424 Office Phone: 404-881-7590. Office Fax: 404-881-7777. Business E-Mail: doug.hinson@alston.com.

HINSON, JACK ALLSBROOK, research toxicologist, educator; b. Mullins, SC, Aug. 18, 1944; s. Layton Liston and Will (Allsbrook) H.; m. Joanne Edwards Kidd; children: Edward Thomas, Richard William. BS, Coll. of Charleston, 1966; MS, U. S.C., 1968; PhD, Vanderbilt U., 1972. Postdoctoral fellow Nat. Inst. of Health, Bethesda, Md., 1972-75, sr. staff fellow, 1975-80; rsch. toxicologist Nat. Ctr. Toxicological Rsch., Jefferson, Ark., 1980-90, chief biochem. mechanisms br., 1989-90; adj. prof. U. Ark. Med. Sci., Little Rock, 1980-90, prof., dir. div. toxicology. Dir. interdisciplinary toxicology program U. Ark. Med. Sci., 1990—; chmn. Ark. Toxicology Symposium, 1992-99; adj. assoc. prof. U. Tenn. Ctr. for Health Scis., Memphis, 1982-90; vis. fellow Middlesex Hops. Med. Sch., London, 1982; vis. prof. U. Leiden, The Netherlands, 1986. Editor Drug Metabolism Revs., 1997—, mem. editl. bd., 1995-97; mem. editl. bd. Toxicology and Applied Pharmacology, 1980-89, 96—, Jour. Toxicology and Environ. Health, 1991—; contbr. chpts. to books and articles to profl. jours. Mem. Soc. Toxicology (pres. South Ctrl. chpt. 1990-92), Am. Soc. Pharmacology and Exptl. Therapeutics, Internat. Soc. for Study of Xenobiotics. Episcopalian. Home: 8 Piedmont Ln Little Rock AR 72223-2232 Office: U Ark Med Sci Divsn Toxicology 4301 W Markham St # 638 Little Rock AR 72205-7101 Home Phone: 501-225-5671. Business E-Mail: HinsonJackA@uams.edu.

HINSON, JEFFREY T., corporate financial executive; BBA, U. Tex., Austin, 1977, MBA, 1979. Sr. v.p., CFO Hispanic Broadcasting Corp. (acquired by Univision), 1997—2003, Univision Radio, 2003—04; exec. v.p., CFO Univision Comm., Inc., 2004—05, cons., 2005; pvt. fin. cons. Live Nation, Inc., 2005—07; pres., CEO Border Media Partners, LLC, 2007—. Former bd. dirs. Alltel Holding Corp., 2006; bd. dirs. Border Media Partners, Live Nation, Inc., 2005—, Windstream Corp., 2006—, TiVo, Inc., 2007—. Office: Border Media Partners LLC Ste 650 750 N Central Expressway Dallas TX 75231 Office Phone: 214-692-2000. Office Fax: 214-361-0563. Business E-Mail: jhinson@tivo.com.

HINSON, ROBERT WILLIAM, advertising executive, consultant; b. Neptune, NJ, Nov. 30, 1944; s. Herbert William and Bernice (Stadelhofer) H. AB in Econs. and Sociology, Boston Coll., 1966. Media planner Benton & Bowles, Inc., NYC, 1968—70; v.p., assoc. media dir. SSC&B: Lintas Worldwide, NYC, 1970—74, sr. v.p., dir. media ops., 1976—80; v.p., assoc. media dir. Foote Cone & Belding, Inc., LA, 1974—76; exec. v.p., chmn. mgmt. com., chmn. ops. com., dir. media svcs. Rosenfeld, Sirowitz & Lawson, Inc., NYC, 1980—85, exec. v.p., dir. mktg. and media svcs., chief adminstrv. officer, 1986—87; pres., CEO Hinson and Assocs., Inc., NYC, 1987—91. Cons. in field, 1991—. Author: Media Leverage, 1985. Media dir. Tuesday Team, Reagan-Bush '84 campaign, 1984; sustaining mem. Rep. Nat. Com.; mem. Ronald Reagan Presdl. Libr. Found., Monmouth County (N.J.) Rep. Orgn.; bd. dirs. Monmouth Symphony Orch.; mem. nat. campaign com. Boston Coll. Mem. NATAS, Nat. Assn. TV, Arts and Scis., Internat. Radio and TV Soc., Media Dirs. Industry Coun., Am. Assn. Advt. Agys. (media policy com. 1980-87), Am. Rsch. Found. (media com. coun. 1983-86), Boston Coll. Alumni Assn., Wagner Soc. N.Y., Monmouth County Hist. Soc., Alliance Francaise of NY County, Met. Opera, NY, Vieux Carre Property Owners Assn., Hist. New Orleans Collection, N.Y. Athletic Club, Deal (N.J.) Golf and Country Club, Allenhurst (N.J.) Beach Club. Roman Catholic. Home: 921 Chartres St New Orleans LA 70116 also: 60 Sutton Pl S #2MN New York NY 10022

HINTON, JAMES FORREST, JR., lawyer; b. Gadsden, Ala., Nov. 19, 1951; s. James Forrest Sr. and Juanita Grey (Weems) H. BA, Vanderbilt U., 1974; JD, U. Ala., 1977. Bar: Ala. 1977, D.C. 1979, U.S. Dist. Ct. (so. dist.) Ala. 1979, U.S. Ct. Appeals (5th cir.) 1980, U.S. Ct. Appeals (11th cir.) 1981, La. 1982, U.S. Dist. Ct. (ea. and mid. dists.) La. 1982, U.S. Dist. Ct. (no. dist.) Ala 1982, U.S. Supreme Ct. 1982, U.S. Dist. Ct. (we. dist.) La. 1983, U.S. Dist. Ct. (no. dist.) Ohio 1983, U.S. Ct. Appeals (D.C. cir.) 1984, U.S. Ct. Appeals (fed. cir.) 1985, U.S. Dist. Ct. (so. dist.) Tex. 1987, U.S. Dist. Ct. (no. dist.) Tex. 1991, Tex. 1992, Tenn. 1992, U.S. Dist. Ct. (ea. and we. dists.) Ark. 1992, U.S. Ct. Appeals (6th and 8th cirs.) 1992, U.S. Dist. Ct. (ea. and we. dists.) Tex. 1993, U.S. Dist. Ct. (mid. dist.) Ala. 1993, U.S. Dist. Ct. (ea. and mid. dist.) Tenn. 1994, U.S. Dist. Ct., Colo. 2000. Law clk. to chief judge U.S. Dist. Ct. (so. dist.) Ala., Mobile, 1977-79; ptnr. Darby, Myrick & Hinton, Mobile, 1979-82; dir. McGlinchey Stafford Lang, New Orleans, 1982-93; ptnr. Adams & Reese, New Orleans, 1993-97; shareholder Berkowitz, Lefkovits, Isom & Kushner, Birmingham, 1997—2003, Baker, Donelson, Bearman, Caldwell & Berkowitz, 2003—13. Contbr. articles to profl. jours. Mem. ABA (antitrust, intellectual property, litigation sects.), FBA, Order of Coif, Phi Beta Kappa. Office: 124 Oak Cir Gadsden AL 35901-5814 Office Phone: 205-585-2781. Business E-Mail: jforresthinton@yahoo.com.

HIOTT, DAVID R., state legislator; b. Easley, SC, Oct. 20, 1960; Mem. Dist. 4 SC House of Reps., 2004—, second vice chair Agr., Natural Resources and Environ. Affairs Com., mem. Rules Com. Republican. Mailing: 419B Blatt Bldg Columbia SC 29201 Home: PO Box 997 Pickens SC 29671 Office Phone: 803-734-3323. Business E-Mail: HiottD@scstatehouse.net.

HIRSCH, ERIC DONALD, JR., language educator; b. Memphis, Mar. 22, 1928; s. Eric Donald and Leah (Aschaffenburg) H.; m. Mary Monteith Pope, June 15, 1958; children: Eric, John, Frederick, Elizabeth. BA, Cornell U., 1950; MA, Yale U., 1955, PhD (Fulbright fellow), 1957; LittD (hon.), Williams Coll., 1989, Rhodes Coll., 1993, Rollins Coll., 1994, Marietta Coll., 1997. Instr. Yale, 1956-61, asst. prof. English, 1961-64, assoc. prof., 1964-66; prof. U. Va., Charlottesville, 1966—, chmn. dept. English, 1968-71, 81-83, dir. composition, 1971—, Kenan prof. English, 1973—, Linden Kent prof. English Charlottesville, 1989-94, Univ. prof. edn. and humanities, 1994; founder, chmn. Core Knowledge Found., Charlottesville, 1986—. Bd. dirs. U. Press; lectr. in field; supervising com. English Inst., 1972-74; mem. nat. adv. coun. N.Y. Regent's Competency Tests in Writing, 1979; advisor Nat. Coun. Ednl. Rsch., 1983; bd. dirs. Founds. Literacy Project, 1985—; pres. Cultural Literacy Found., 1987, Core Knowledge Found., 1990; dir. Albert Shanker Inst., 1997—. Author: Wordsworth and Schelling: A Typological Study of Romanticism, 1960, Innocence and Experience: An Introduction to Blake, 1964 (Explicator award), Validity in Interpretation, 1967, The Aims of Interpretation, 1976, The Philosophy of Composition, 1977, Cultural Literacy: What Every American Needs to Know, 1987; co-author: A Dictionary of Cultural Literacy, 1993, 2002; editor: A First Dictionary of Cultural Literacy, 1989, 2004, The Core Knowledge Series, Book I: What First Graders Need to Know, 1991, Book II: What Second Graders Need to Know, 1991, Book III: What Third Graders Need to Know, 1992, Book IV: What Fourth Graders Need to Know, 1992, Book V: What Fifth Graders Need to Know, 1993, Book VI: What Sixth Graders Need to Know, 1993, The Schools We Need and Why We Don't Have Them, 1996, The Knowledge Deficit, 2006, The Making of Americans, 2009; mem. adv. bd. Jour. Basic Writing, Blake Studies, Critical Inquiry, Genre New Lit. History, Lit. in Performance; contbr. articles to profl. jours. Pres. Coalition for Core Curriculum, 1989—, 1989—. With USNR, 1950—52. Recipient Fordham award 2003; Morse fellow, 1961-62, Guggenheim fellow, 1964-65, sr. fellow NEH, 1971, 80-81, fellow Center for Humanities Wesleyan U., 1973, fellow Council Humanities Princeton U., 1976, fellow Center for Advanced Study in Behavioral Scis., 1980-81, fellow Humanities Research Ctr., Australian Nat. U., 1982; Bateson lectr. Oxford U., 1983 Fellow: Internat. Acad. Edn. in Royal Acad. Sci. Lit. and Arts (Brussels); mem.: MLA, Am. Fedn. Tchrs. (Biennial Quest award 1997), Am. Acad. Arts and Scis. (supervisory com. 1981—86), Byron Soc. Home: 200 Garrett St Unit 505 Charlottesville VA 22902-5670 Personal E-mail: edh9k@aol.com. Business E-Mail: edh9k@virginia.edu.

HIRSCH, JEFFREY ALLAN, lawyer; b. Chgo., June 14, 1950; m. Lennie Sue Henderson, June 16, 1979; children: Lea, Ashley. BSBA, U. Fla., 1972, JD with honors, 1975. Bar: Fla. 1975, U.S. Dist. Ct. (so. and mid. dists.) Fla. 1975. Assoc. Swann & Glass, Coral Gables, Fla., 1975-76, Glass, Schultz, Weinstein & Moss, Coral Gables, 1976-80; ptnr. Holland & Knight, Ft. Lauderdale, Fla., 1980-93; prin. shareholder Greenberg, Traurig, P.A., Ft. Lauderdale, Fla., 1993—. Exec. dir. Govtl. Research Ctr., Gainesville, Fla., 1975. Active Leadership Broward, Ft. Lauderdale, 1986—, Leadership Fla., 1994—. Mem. ABA, Fla. Bar Assn., Broward County Bar Assn. Avocations: reading, travel. Office: Greenberg Traurig PA 401 E Las Olas Blvd Ste 2000 Fort Lauderdale FL 33301-2278 Office Phone: 954-765-0500. Business E-Mail: hirschj@gtlaw.com.

HIRSCH, LAURENCE ELIOT, private equity firm executive, lawyer; b. NYC, Dec. 19, 1945; s. S. Richard and Lillian (Avenet) H.; m. Susan Judith Creskoff, Dec. 23, 1967; children: Daria Lee, Bradford Richard. BS in Economics, U. Pa., 1968; JD cum laude, Villanova U., 1971; MS in Internat. Pub. Policy, Johns Hopkins Sch. Internat. Studies, 2005. Bar: Pa. 1972, Tex. 1973. Assoc. Wolf, Block, Schorr & Solis Cohen, Phila., 1971-73, Bracewell & Patterson, 1973-76, ptnr., 1976-78; pres. Southdown, Inc., 1977-85, CEO, 1984-85; pres. Centex Corp., 1985-88, CEO, 1988—91, chmn., 1991—2004, Eagle Materials, Inc., 1994—97, 1999—, interim CEO, 2003; chmn. Highlander Partners, LP, Dallas, 2004—. Bd. dirs. Centex Corp., 1985-91, Belo Corp., 1985-2008, Luminex Corp., 1996-2008, A.H. Belo Corp., 2008-11, Freddie Mac (Federal Home Loan Mortgage Corp.), 2008-12, Chmn. Ctr. for European Policy Analysis, Washington, 2005—; bd. cons. Villanova U. Law Sch. With USAR, 1968—75. Office: Highlander Partners LP 3811 Turtle Creek Blvd Ste 250 Dallas TX 75219 Office Phone: 214-245-5000. Office Fax: 214-245-5015. Business E-Mail: lhirsch@highlander-partners.com.

HIRSCH, PHILIP FRANCIS, pharmacologist, educator; b. Stockton, Calif., June 24, 1925; s. Harold and Elsa (Frohman) H.; m. Eugenia Isaeff, Sept. 21, 1956; children: Steven, Lisa, Ken, Nancy. BS in Chemistry, U. Calif., Berkeley, 1950, PhD in Physiology, 1954. Lectr. physiology U. Calif., Berkeley, 1954-55; instr. pharmacology Sch. Dental Medicine, Harvard U., Boston, 1955-57, asso. in pharmacology, 1957-63, asst. prof. pharmacology, 1964; physiologist Lawrence Livermore Lab., 1964-66; asso. prof. pharmacology Sch. Medicine, U. NC, Chapel Hill, 1966-70, prof., 1970-92; dir. dental research ctr. U. NC, 1975-83, prof. dental ecology Sch. of Dentistry, 1988-92, U. N.C., 1992—. Mem. gen. medicine B study sect. NIH, 1974-78, clin. scis. study section, 1981-85. Contbr. articles to profl. jours. Bd. dirs. YMCA, Chapel Hill, 1981-83. Served with AUS, 1943-46. Mem. Endocrine Soc., Am. Soc. Pharmacology and Exptl. Therapeutics, Sigma Xi. Achievements include research in calcium metabolism, parathyroid hormone and calcitonin. Home: 135 Carolina Meadows Villa Chapel Hill NC 27517-8512 Personal E-mail: pfhirsch@med.unc.edu.

HIRSCH, ROBERT LOUIS, energy analyst, consultant; b. Evanston, Ill., Mar. 6, 1935; s. Louis Aaron and Dorothy Jean (Block) H.; m. Barbara Palmer, 2006, Evelyn Podhouser, Feb. 1, 1959 (div. 2000); children: Allen, Lauri, Scott. BS, U. Ill., Champaign-Urbana, 1958, PhD, 1964; MS, U. Mich., Ann Arbor, 1959. Rsch. engr. Atomics Internat., 1959-60; physicist, later dir. ITT Indsl. Labs., Fort Wayne, Ind., 1964-68; sr. physicist controlled thermonuclear rsch. AEC (now Dept. Energy), Washington, 1968-72, divsn. dir., 1972—76; asst. adminstr. solar, geothermal and advanced energy sys. ERDA (presdl. appointment), 1976-77; dep. mgr. sci. and tech. dept. Exxon Corp., 1977; gen. mgr. exploratory petroleum rsch. Exxon Rsch. and Engring. Co., 1977-80, mgr. Synthetic Fuels Rsch. Lab. Baytown, Tex., 1980-83; v.p., mgr. rsch. and tech. svcs. dept. Arco Oil and Gas Co., Dallas, 1983-91; CEO ARCO Power Techs., Inc., 1986-91; v.p. Washington office Electric Power Rsch. Ins., 1991-94; cons. in tech. and mgmt., 1994—; exec. advisor Advanced Power Technologies, Washington, 1997—2001; pres. The Energy Tech. Collaborative, Inc., 1995-97; sr. energy analyst Rand, 2001—02; chmn. bd. on energy and environ. sys. NRC, 1996—2003; sr. energy program advisor SAIC, 2003—07; sr. energy advisor MISI, 2007—. Mem. bds. Annapolis Ctr. and Fusion Power Assocs.; participant in Atlantic Coun. Studies; mem. LDRD Bd. Lawrence Livermore Nat. Lab., 1993-95; mem. U.S.-USSR Joint Commn. on Peaceful Uses of Atomic Energy, 1970s; chmn. US del. US-USSR Joint Fusion Power Coord. Com., 1970s; mem. Internat. Fusion Rsch. Coun., 1970s, Dept. Energy Rsch. adv. bd., 1980s; vice chmn. com. on sci., engring. and tech. Fed. Coord. Coun. for Sci. Engring. and Tech., 1976; adv. bd. Princeton Plasma Physics Lab., 1980s, Oak Ridge Nat. Lab., 1993-97; rsch. coord. coun. Gas Rsch. Inst., 1980s. Contbr. articles to profl. jours; patentee in field. Elected nat. assoc. Nat. Acads., 2001. Recipient Meritorious award William Jump Found., 1971, Disting. Svc. award AEC, 1974, spl. achievement award Fusion Power Assocs., 1982, spl. Achievement award ERDA, 1976, 77, commendation NASA, 1982, merit award U. Mich. Engring. Alumni Soc., 1997; AEC Spl. fellow, 1960-63. Fellow AAAS; mem. Am. Nuc. Soc. (chmn. fusion tech. group, dir. 1975-76, 78-79, outstanding tech. achievement award 1983), Tau Beta Pi (U. Ill. Alumni Honor award), Phi Epsilon Pi. Home and Office: 723 Fords Landing Way Alexandria VA 22314 Personal E-mail: rlhirsch@comcast.net.

HIRSCH, STEVEN NEAL, pharmaceutical executive; B in Engring. Sci., Johns Hopkins U., 1972; MS in Indsl. Adminstrn., Purdue U., 1973. With Pfizer, Inc. (Howmedica divsn.); various positions, including v.p., sales and mktg., orthopedic bus. Pfizer, Inc.; various positons, Orthopedics divsn. Smith & Nephew plc, 1996—2005, sr. v.p., gen. mgr., Reconstructive divsn., 2003—05, pres., orthopedic bus., European, 2005; with BioMimetic Therapeutics, Inc. (formerly Biomimetic Pharmaceuticals, Inc.) (corp. comm.); exec. v.p., orthopedics, COO BioMimetic Therapeutics, Inc., 2005—. Office: BioMimetic Therapeutics Inc 389 Nichol Mill Ln Franklin TN 37067 Office Phone: 615-844-1280. Office Fax: 615-844-1281. Business E-Mail: shirsch@biomimetics.com.

HIRSCHBERG, JOSEPH GUSTAV, physicist, educator; b. Chgo., Apr. 13, 1921; s. Joseph Gustav and Lillian Hirschberg; m. Delores Dietrich, Jan. 1944 (div. Apr. 1946); m. Ginette Henriette Tetard, Apr. 26, 1947 (dec. Aug. 12, 1992); children: Dorothy Jean Pixomatis, Joseph Gerald, Anne Marie Smith, Lynn Susan Sontag; m. Judith Klausner Mintz, Apr. 2, 1996. AB magna cum laude with distinction in Physics, Dartmouth Coll., 1943; MS, U. Wis., 1951, PhD, 1952. Rsch. assoc. U. Wis., 1953—57; head optical group, rsch. physicist Plasma Physics Lab., Princeton, 1958—65; prof. d'Echange U. Paris, 1963; prof. physics U. Miami, Fla., 1965—85, chmn. dept., 1965—72, dir. optical physics lab., 1968—, prof. emeritus physics, 1986—. Pres. Fed. Engring. Corp., 1953—58; contractor Langley Rsch. Ctr., NASA, 1966—69; vis. rsch. faculty Oak Ridge Nat. Lab., Tenn., 1966; vis. rsch. physicist Princeton U., NJ, 1976, sr. rsch. faculty, 1986—89; leader solar eclipse expdns., Mexico, 1970, Canada, 1972, Kenya, 1973; vis. astronomer Sacramento Peak Obs., 1977; vis. scientist Inst. de Pathologie Cellulaire, Paris, 1980, Chercheur d'Echange, Mus. d'Histoire Naturel, Paris, 1983, Chercher d'Echange, Hosp. Henri Mondor, Creteil, France, 1985; vis. sr. scientist Max Planck Inst. Biophys. Chemistry, Göttingen, Germany, 1996, Göttingen, 1997, Göttingen, 2002. Co-author: Spectroscopic Measurements, 1962; author: Physics of Music, 1974; co-author: Cell Structure and Function by Microspectrofluorometry, 1989, Photobiology, 1995; contbr. articles to sci. jours.; author: Physics for the Arts, 2001; co-editor: Fluorescent Probes in Oncology, 2002; co-author (with E. Kohen, R. Santus and N. Ozkutuk): Atlas of Cell Organelles Fluorescence, 2004. Served Pvt. to capt. USAAF, 1943—47, weather forecaster & weather equipment engr. Fellow: Papanicolaou Cancer Rsch. Inst., European Acad. Scis., Arts and Letters, Optical Soc. Am., Am. Phys. Soc.; mem.: AAAS, Fla. Acad. Scis., Am. Soc. Photobiology, Sigma Xi, Phi Beta Kappa, Omega Delta Kappa, Sigma Pi Sigma. Achievements include co-discoverer of telluric sodium absorption in solar radiation; invention of several optical spectroscopic devices; infrared turbidity meter; Brillouin laser ocean probe; nonlinear optical interference microscope; microfluorospectrometers; x-ray microscopy; solar and tidal energy systems; compact triangular interferometer; hydrogen economy devices; photoacoustic microscope; combination fluorescence and phase microscope with large working space. Home: 1046 Alfonso Ave Coral Gables FL 33146-3302 E-mail: jhirshberg@aol.com.

HIRSCHMAN, KAREN L., lawyer; b. York, Pa., Dec. 15, 1952; BA, U. Del., 1973; MA, U. Tex., 1980, JD with honors, 1983. Bar: Tex. 1983, DC 2002, NY 2003. Ptnr., co-head Litig. Sect. Vinson & Elkins LLP, Dallas, 1999—. Fellow: American Coll. Trial Lawyers, Tex. Bar Found.; mem.: ABA, Am. Law Inst. Office: Vinson & Elkins LLP Trammell Crow Ctr 2001 Ross Ave, Ste 3700 Dallas TX 75201*

HIRSHBERG, ALAN J., oil industry executive; BS in Mech. Engring., Rice U., Houston, 1982, MS in Mech. Engring., 1983. With ExxonMobil Corp., 1983—2009, numerous positions of increasing responsibility in planning, engring and prodn. ops., Exxon and affiliate companies, including sr. dept. head upstream planning, analysis and fin. reporting Exxon Co. USA, then various mgmt. positions in offshore and deep water projects, ExxonMobil Devel. Co., 2000—04, project exec., deepwater Africa projects, 2004—06, v.p. established areas projects, 2006—08, v.p. worldwide deepwater projects, 2008—09, v.p. worldwide deepwater and Africa projects, 2009—10; sr. v.p. planning & strategy ConocoPhillips, Houston, 2010—. Office: ConocoPhillips PO Box 2197 Houston TX 77252

HIRT, JIM (JAMES R. HIRT), professional society administrator; MBA, Nat. U., La Jolla, Calif., 1994. Dir. DC Svc. Corps, Washington; dep. dir. Nat. Assn. Mortgage Brokers, 1995—2000; dep. exec. dir. Pub. Risk Mgmt. Assn., 2000—01, exec. dir., 2001—06, Am Assn. Poison Control Centers, Alexandria, Va. Office: Am Assn Poison Control Centers 515 King St Ste 510 Alexandria VA 22314 Office Phone: 703-894-1858. Office Fax: 703-683-2812. Business E-Mail: hirt@aapcc.org.

HISE, RALPH E., JR., state legislator; m. Linn Hise; children: Deren Hise, Thomas Hise. B in Stats., Appalachian State U.; M in Higher Edn. Adminstrn., NC State U. Mayor, Spruce Pine, NC; instl. planning & assessment officer Md. Cmty. Coll.; chmn. Mitchell County Rep. Party; mem., NC Victory Campaign NC Rep. Party, 2004, 2006; mem. Dist. 47 NC State Senate, 2011—. Republican. Mailing: 44 Hemlock Ave Spruce Pine NC 28777 Office: NC Senate 16 W Jones St Room 1026 Raleigh NC 27601-2808 Office Phone: 919-733-3460, 828-766-8329. Business E-Mail: ralph@ralphwise.com, Ralph.Hise@ncleg.net.

HITCHCOCK, JOANNA, publisher; b. London; BA, Oxford U., Eng., 1960, MA in Modern History, 1965. Asst. publicity dept. Oxford U. Press, London, 1962-66; asst. promotion mgr. Princeton (N.J.) Univ. Press, 1966-68, advt. and exhibits mgr., 1968-69, staff editor, 1970-72, mng. editor, 1972-80, exec. editor, 1980-84, asst. dir., 1985-87, exec. editor for humanities, 1988-92; dir. U. of Tex. Press, Austin, 1992—. Mem. Princeton U. Libr. Coun., 1986-95; adv. com. Tex. Book Festival, 1996-. Mem. Am. Assn. Univ. Presses (bd. dirs. 1984-87, chair equal opportunities com. 1985-86, ann. program planning com. 1986-87, pres. 1997-98, past pres. 1998-99). Home: 1507 Preston Ave Austin TX 78703-1903 Office: Univ of Texas Press PO Box 7819 Austin TX 78713-7819 Office Phone: 512-232-5704.

HITTNER, DAVID, federal judge; b. Schenectady, NY, July 10, 1939; s. George and Sophie (Moskowitz) H.; children: Miriam, Susan, George. BS, NYU, 1961, JD, 1964. Bar: N.Y. 1964, Tex. 1967. Pvt. practice, Houston, 1967-78; judge Tex. 133rd Dist. Ct., Houston, 1978-86, US Dist. Ct. (so. dist.) Tex., Houston, 1986—2004, sr. judge, 2004—. Author 2 books; contbr. articles to profl. jours. Mem. Nat. coun. Boy Scouts Am. Capt. inf., paratrooper U.S. Army, 1965-66. Recipient Silver Beaver award Boy Scouts Am., 1974, Silver Antelope award Boy Scouts Am., 1988, Samuel E. Gates award Am. Coll. Trial Lawyers. Mem. ABA (Merit award), State Bar Tex. (Outstanding Lawyer in Tex. award), Houston Bar Assn. (Pres.'s and Dirs.' award), Am. Law Inst., Masons (33d degree), Order of Coif (hon.). Office: US Courthouse 515 Rusk St Ste 8509 Houston TX 77002-2603 Office Phone: 713-250-5711.

HITZ, FREDERICK PORTER, public and international affairs educator; b. Washington, Oct. 14, 1939; s. Frederick Porter and Elizabeth (Hume) H.; m. Mary Buford Bocock, Sept. 7, 1963; 1 child, Eliza. AB, Princeton U., 1961; JD, Harvard U., 1964. Bar: Mass.

1965, Va. 1966, DC 1976, US Supreme Ct. 1988. Asst. lectr., law dept. U. IFE, Ibadan, Nigeria, 1964-65; fgn. svc. officer US Dept. State, Abidjan, Cote d'Ivoire, 1963—73, congl. rels. officer Washington, 1974-75, dep. asst. sec. legis. affairs, 1975-77; mem. energy policy and planning staff Exec. Office of Pres., Washington, 1977; dir. congl. affairs U.S. Dept. Energy, Washington, 1977-78; legis. counsel CIA, Washington, 1978-81; ptnr. Schwabe, Williamson & Wyatt, Washington, 1982-90; inspector gen. CIA, Washington, 1990-98; lectr. in pub. and internat. affairs Princeton U. Woodrow Wilson Sch., NJ, 1998—2006, Weinberg prof. of pub. policy, 1999—2006; sr. fellow Princeton U. Butler Coll., 2000—; lectr. U. Va. Sch. Law, Charlottesville, Va., 2004—, Frank W. Batten Sch. Leadership and Pub. Policy, 2008—; lectr. Woodrow Wilson dept. politics U. Va., Charlottesville, 2004—. Mem. Coun. Fgn. Rels., 2003—, Miller Ctr. Pub. Affairs Governing Coun., 2009; mem., bd. trustees Charlottesville U. Symphony Orch., 2009. Author: The Great Game: The Myth and Reality of Espionage, 2004; prodr.: Why Spy: Espionage in an Age of Uncertainty, 2008. Trustee Potomac Sch., McLean, Va., 1989-95, chmn. bd. trustees, 1992-94; vestry St. Paul's Ch., Alexandria. Mem. ABA, Wash. Nat. Cathedral, Protestant Episcopal Cathedral Found., Deer Isle Yacht Club (Maine), Met. Club (Washington, bd. govs. 1994-99, sec. 1995-96, pres. 1998-99), Ivy Club (Princeton, N.J., grad. bd. 2001-). Democrat. Episcopalian. Avocations: sailing, skiing, squash. Personal E-mail: fphitz@aol.com.

HITZMAN, DONALD OLIVER, microbiologist; b. Milw., Dec. 2, 1926; s. Walter John and Irene (Smith) H.; m. Mary Elizabeth Neumann, Aug. 20, 1952; children: Murray W., Daniel C. AB, Carleton Coll., Northfield, Minn., 1948; MS, U. Ill., 1950, PhD, 1954. Resident microbiologist Texaco Co., Long Beach, Calif., 1951; sr. rsch. assoc. Phillips Petroleum Co., Bartlesville, Okla., 1954-85; v.p. rsch. Geo-Microbial Tech., Inc., Ochelata, Okla., 1985—. Contbr. articles to sci. publs. With USAAF, 1944-45. Fulbright scholar, Australia, 1951. Mem. Soc. Microbiology, Soc. Indsl. Microbiology, Am. Chem. Soc. Republican. Episcopalian. Achievements include over 60 patents; numerous fgn. patents. Office: Geo-Microbial Tech East Main St Ochelata OK 74051 Home Phone: 918-333-1717; Office Phone: 918-535-2281. E-mail: gmtgeochem@aol.com.

HIXON, JAMES A., lawyer, rail transportation executive; BS, Va. Polytechnic Inst., 1976; JD, Coll. William & Mary, 1979, ML&T, 1980. Asst. tax counsel Norfolk Southern Corp., 1985, gen. tax atty., asst. v.p., tax counsel, v.p. taxation, 1993—99, sr. v.p. employee rels., 1999, sr. v.p. adminstrn., sr. v.p. legal and govt. affairs, 2003, exec. v.p. fin. and pub. affairs, 2004, exec. v.p. law and corp. rels., 2005—. Office: Norfolk So Corp Three Commercial Pl Norfolk VA 23510-2191 Office Phone: 757-629-2680, 757-629-2370.

HIXON, WILLIAM M., state legislator; b. Sept. 6, 1957; s. John L. and Elizabeth C. Hixon. Bd. dirs. Augusta Southern Nationals Drag Boat Races; mem. North Augusta C. of C., North Augusta Area Med. Ctr., Aiken County Home Builders; bd. dirs., Aiken County Commn. Higher Edn. U. of SC, Aiken; mem. NRA; treas. Interstate Cooperation; mem. Aiken County Rep. Party, Edgefield County Rep. Party; chmn. Aiken Tech. Coll. Commn.; vice chmn. Economic Development Partnership for Aiken and Edgefield Counties; v.p., region 3 SC Assn. of Realtors; bd. dirs. The Ind. Ins. Agents, SC; bd. adv. Wachovia Bank, North Augusta; mem. SC Assn. of Realtors, Edgefield County Devel. Bd.; bd. dirs. Augusta-North Augusta M.L.S. Svc.; mem. First Bapt. Ch., North Augusta, bd. trustees; state constable SC; bd. adv. Security Fed. Bank, North Augusta; bd. dirs. Edgefield County C. of C.; mem. SC Electric & Gas Co.; bd. adv. SCANA Regional Adv. Bd.; mem., exec. com. Commn. of the Future of Aiken County; mem. Agr., Natural Resources & Environ. Affairs Com.; pres. Hixon Ins. Inc.; pres., owner Hixon Realty Co.; vol. fireman North Augusta, 1973—; pres. North Augusta Bd. of Realtors, 1988, 1997, 1998, 2005, 2006; amb. SC Econ. Devel., 1999; mem. Dist. 83 SC House of Representatives, 2011—. Recipient Realtor of the Yr., North Augusta Belvedere Bd. of Realtors, 1989, Legis. Grassroots Realtor of the Yr., SC Associations of Realtors, 1997, Realtor of the Yr., North Augusta Belvedere Bd. of Realtors, 1997, Accredited Land Cons. Designation award, 2010. Republican. Office: South Carolina House of Representatives District 83 416A Blatt Bldg Columbia SC 29201 Address: PO Box 7927 North Augusta SC 29861 Office Phone: 803-212-6898.

HIXSON, ELMER L., retired engineering educator; Prof. emeritus dept. elec. engring. U. Tex., Austin. Recipient Fellow Mems. award Am. Soc. Engring. Educators, 1992. Fellow Acoustical Soc. Am.; mem. IEEE (life), Inst. for Noise Control Engring. (founding mem.). Office: U Tex Dept Elec & Computer Engring Austin TX 78712 E-mail: ehixson@mail.utexas.edu.

HJORT, HOWARD WARREN, economist, consultant; b. Plentywood, Mont., Dec. 20, 1931; BS, Mont. State U., 1958, MS, 1959; postgrad., N.C. State U. Staff economist Office of Sec. Agr., Washington, 1963-65, spl. asst. to under sec., 1965; dir. staff for program planning and analysis Office of Sec., 1965-69; planning and mgmt. adviser with Ford Found., India, 1969-72; dir. Office of Econs., Policy Analysis and Budget, 1977-81; co-founder Schnittker Assocs. (agrl. cons.), Washington, 1972-77; ptnr. EPI (McLean), Va., 1981-84; dir. policy analysis div. FAO, Rome, 1984-90, dir. liaison office for N.Am. Washington, 1990-91, dep. dir. gen. Rome, 1992-97; cons., 1998—. Home: 700 Park Ave Falls Church VA 22046-3211 Home Phone: 703-536-1810; Office Phone: 703-536-1810. Personal E-mail: howardhjort@aol.com.

HLOZEK, CAROLE DIANE QUAST, finance company executive; b. Dallas, Apr. 17, 1959; d. Robert E. and Bonnie (Wootton) Quast. BS, BBA, Tex. A&M U., 1982. CPA Tex.; cert. securities prin. FINRA. Internal auditor Brown & Root Inc., Houston, 1982-84; asst. contr. Wilson Supply Co., Houston, 1984-86; sr. acctg. supr. Hydro Conduit Corp., Houston, 1986-87; fin. analyst Am. Capital, Houston, 1989-94; dir. adminstrn. Am. Gen. Securities, Inc., Houston, 1994-98; CFO 1st Fin. Group Am., Houston, 1998-2000; contr. Clearworks, 2000-01; dir. Ornate Holdings Inc., Houston, 2001—02; full time cons. Robert Half Internat., 2002—03; contr., v.p. finance eLinear Techs., 2003—04; interim CAO Quantlab, 2004—07, dir. acctg., 2004—10, cons., 2011—. Chmn. bd. dirs. On Our Own, Inc., 1987-91; mentor CPA's Helping Schs.; treas. Sampson Elem. PTO, 2002-04. Mem. Mensa, Houston Livestock Show and Rodeo (life), Ticket Svcs. Com. Home: 17811 Safe Haven Dr Cypress TX 77433-3595 Business E-Mail: cdhlozek@gmail.com.

HO, JAMES C., lawyer; b. Taiwan; BA in Pub. Policy with honors, Stanford U., Calif., 1995; JD with high honors, U. Chgo., 1999. Bar: Va., Tex., DC. Legis. aide to Quentin Kopp Calif. State Senate; law clk. to the Honorable Jerry E. Smith US Ct. Appeals 5th Cir.; law clk. to the Honorable Clarence Thomas US Supreme Ct., Washington; chief counsel to John Cornyn US Senate, Washington; atty., civil rights divsn. US Dept. Justice, Washington; atty., office legal counsel The White House, Washington; of counsel Gibson Dunn and Crutcher, Dallas, ptnr., 2010—; solicitor gen. State of Tex., 2008—10. Adj. prof. law U. Tex. Law Sch. Contbr. articles to profl. jours. Bd. dirs. Dallas Holocaust Mus., Human Rights Initiative North Tex., Inc., The Tony Patiño Fellowship, Inc., Asian Pacific American Bar Assn. Ednl. Fund; bd. governors Dallas Symphony Orch. Named a Rising Star, Tex. Super Lawyers, 2008, Law360, 2011; named one of 35 Under 35, The Hill, 2005, 25 Extraordinary Minorities in Tex. Law, Tex. Lawyer, 2009, Minority 40 Under 40, The Nat. Law Jour., 2011. Fellow: Dallas Bar Found., Tex. Bar Found., American Bar Found.; mem.: ABA, Dallas Asian American Bar Assn. (sec.), Nat. Asian Pacific American Bar Assn. (co-chmn. judiciary com., Best Lawyers Under 40 2006, Presdl. award 2009), State Bar Tex., American Law Inst., The Federalist Soc. Law and Pub. Policy Studies. Office: Gibson Dunn & Crutcher 2100 McKinney Ave Ste 1100 Dallas TX 75201 Business E-Mail: jho@gibsondunn.com.

HOAGLUND, JOHN ARTHUR, philosophy educator, editor; b. June 15, 1936; s. Rudolph Arthur and Doris Antoinette (Barker) H.; m. Lilian Nilsson, June 18, 1966; children: Glen Arthur, Larissa Ann. Student, Ludwig Maximilians U., Munich, 1957—58, U. Vienna, 1958—59; PhD, Free U., Berlin, 1967. Lectr. Padagogische Hochschule, Berlin, 1966—67, Free U., Berlin, 1967—72; prof. Christopher Newport U., Newport News, Va., 1972—; editor Vale Press, Newport News, 1982—. Lectr., Europe and N.Am., 1972—. Author: Critical Thinking, 2004. With USMC, 1953—55. Recipient grant, Am. Coun. Learned Socs., 1975, NEH, 1977, Fulbright fellowship, 1980—81. Mem.: AAUP (chpt. v.p. 1977—79, pres. 1979—80, chpt. v.p. 1983—87), Am. Philos. Assn., Assn. for Informal Logic and Critical Thinking (exec. com. 1983—89, pres. 1985—87, exec. com. 2001—03, founding mem., exec. com 2005—07). Democrat. Home: 13 Cherbourg Dr Newport News VA 23606-1538 Office: Christopher Newport U 1 University Pl Newport News VA 23606-2998 Home Phone: 757-930-3002; Office Phone: 757-594-7085. Business E-Mail: hoaglund@cnu.edu.

HOANG, AL, councilman, lawyer; m. Diane Hoang; 3 children. BA in Philosophy, U. Houston, 1989; JD, Tex. So. U. Criminal defense atty., Houston; councilman, Dist. F Houston City Coun., 2010—. Mem.: Vietnamese Cmty. in Houston and Vicinity (pres.). Avocations: bicycling, jogging. Office: City Hall Annex 900 Bagby, 1st Fl Houston TX 77002 Office Phone: 832-393-3002. E-mail: districtf@cityofhouston.net.

HOBAR, P. CRAIG, plastic surgeon, educator; b. Pitts., Oct. 21, 1954; MD, U. Miami, 1982. Cert. Am. Bd. Plastic Surgery. Resident gen. surgery Parkland Meml. Hosp., Dallas, 1982—87; resident plastic surgery U. Tex. Southwestern Health Sci. Ctr., Dallas, 1987—89; fellowship craniofacial surgery NYU Med. Ctr., NYC, 1989—90; pvt. practice Dallas, 1990—; founding ptnr. Dallas Plastic Surgery Inst.; head craniofacial surgery Children's Med. Ctr., Dallas; clin. assoc. prof. plastic surgery U. Tex. Southwestern Med. Ctr. Founder, med. dir. LEAP; affiliate plastic surgeon Dallas Stars. Named Dallas Cmty. Hero of 2000, Dallas Bus. Jour. Mem.: Christian Med. and Dental Soc., Am. Acad. Anti-Aging Medicine, Am. Assn. Plastic Surgeons, Am. Soc. Plastic and Reconstructive Surgeons, Am. Soc. Aesthetic Plastic Surgery (In Chul Song Award). Office: 411 N Washington Ave, Ste 6000 Dallas TX 75246 Office Phone: 214-832-8423. E-mail: chobar@earthlink.net.

HOBAUGH, CHARLES OWEN, astronaut; b. Bar Harbor, Maine, Nov. 5, 1961; s. Jimmie and Virginia Hobaugh; m. Corinna Lynn Leaman; 4 children. BSc in Aerospace Engring., U.S. Naval Acad., 1984. Commd. 2d lt. USN, 1984; advanced through grades to maj. USMC, various assignments, 1984—87, with marine attack squadron, 1987—91; project officer, 1992—94; student Naval Test Pilot Sch., 1991—92, instr., 1994—96; astronaut NASA, Houston, 1996—. Pilot STS-104 mission to Internat. Space Station, 2001, STS-118 Mission (Endeavour) to Internat. Space Station, 2007; comdr. STS-129 Atlantis Mission, 2009. Decorated Strike/Flight Air medal USN, Combat Action ribbon, Unit Commendation, Marine Corps Achievement medal. Mem.: U.S. Naval Acad. Alumni Assn. Achievements include logging over 3,000 flight hours in more than 40 different aircraft and has over 200 V/STOL shipboard landings. Avocations: weightlifting, volleyball, boating, water-skiing, snow skiing, soccer, bicycling, running, triathlons. Office: Astronaut Office CB NASA Johnson Space Center Houston TX 77058

HOBBS, DEBRA, state legislator; b. Hershing, Austria, July 8, 1955; m. Ray Hobbs; children: Amanda, Jonathan. BS in Sci. Composite, U. Ozarks, 1977; MS in Counseling Edn., U. Ark., 1987. Mem. Dist. 96 Ark. House of Reps., 2009—. Republican. Office: State Capitol Rm 350 Little Rock AR 72201 also: 3901 Arnold Ave Rogers AR 72758 Office Phone: 501-682-6211, 501-682-7771, 479-636-3982. Business E-Mail: dhobbs55@sbcglobal.net.

HOBBS, HELEN HASKELL, medical geneticist; b. Boston, May 5, 1952; m. Dennis Keith Stone; children: Langdon Gundry, Hunter Hobbs. BA in Human Biology, Stanford U., 1974; MD, Case Western Reserve U., 1979. Cert. Am. Bd. Internal Medicine, 1983, Endocrinology & Metabolism, 1986. Intern, internal medicine Columbia-Presbyn. Med. Ctr., NYC, 1979—80; resident, internal medicine Parkland Meml. Hosp., Dallas, 1980—82; chief resident, internal medicine U. Tex. Southwestern, 1982—83, postdoctoral fellow in endocrinology & molecular genetics, 1983—87, asst. prof., 1987—90, assoc. prof., 1991—94, prof. internal medicine & molecular genetics, 1995—; chief med. genetics divsn. U. Tex. Southwestern Med. Ctr., Dallas, 1995—, dir. McDermott Ctr. Human Growth & Devel., 2000—; investigator Howard Hughes Med. Inst., Dallas, 2002—. Bd. dirs. Pfizer, Inc., 2011—. Consulting editor Circulation, 2002—. Recipient Heinrich Wieland prize, 2005. Fellow: American Acad. Arts & Sciences; mem.: NAS, American Soc. Human Genetics, American Heart Assn. (est. investigator 1990—95), American Soc. Clin. Investigation (nat. coun. 1992—94, v.p. 1996—97), Assn. American Physicians, Inst. of Medicine. Office: UT Southwestern Med Ctr at Dallas 5323 Harry Hines Blvd Dallas TX 75390-9046 Office Phone: 214-648-6724. Office Fax: 214-648-7539. E-mail: helen.hobbs@utsouthwestern.edu.

HOBBS, LANDEL C., former broadcast executive; b. Tex., 1962; married; 2 children. BBA, Angelo State U., San Angelo, Tex., 1984. Sr. v.p., audit dir. Banc One Ill. Corp.; sr. mgr. KPMG Peat Marwick, 1984—90; with Turner Broadcasting Sys., Inc. (TBS), 1993—2000, various positions, including sr. v.p., pres., contr., chief acctg. officer, 1996—2000; v.p., fin. analysis & ops. support Time Warner, Inc., 2000—01; exec. v.p., CFO Time Warner Cable, Inc., 2001—05, COO, 2005—10. Bd. dirs. Nat. Cable Satellite Corp., 2005—. Mem. High Mus. of Art, Atlanta; bd. dirs. Big Brothers, Springfield, Ill., Women in Cable & Telecom., Atlanta Symphony Orch, CTAM Edn. Found., C-SPAN; alumni Angelo State U.

HOBBS, MICHAEL EDWIN, retired broadcast executive; b. Washington, Nov. 26, 1940; s. Robert Boyd and Barbara Alberta (Davis) H.; m. Ann Reed, Sept. 16, 1989. AB cum laude, Dartmouth Coll., 1962; JD, Harvard U., 1965. Bar: Mass. 1966. Staff counsel, asst. to gen. mgr. Sta. WGBH Ednl. Found., Boston, 1966-67; exec. asst. ednl. TV stas. Nat. Assn. Ednl. Broadcasters, Washington, 1967-70; sec. PBS, Washington, 1970-87, gen. counsel, 1970-71, dir. adminstrn., 1970-73, v.p., 1973-76, sr. v.p., 1976-87, sr. v.p. for policy and planning, 1987-91; sr. fellow Hartford Gunn Inst., Alexandria, Va., 1991—2007. Active Alexandria Rep. City Com., 1997—, chmn. 1998-2000; bd. dirs. Old Town Civic Assn., 2001-10, 2012-, pres., 2004-06; bd. dirs. Agenda: Alexandria, 2005—, treas., 2006-10, vice chair, 2010-11, chair 2011-12; bd. dir. Friends Carlyle House, 2010-, Alexandria Fedn. Civic Assns., 2006—, co-chair, 2006-08, Hist. Alexandria Resources Commn., 2010-. Mem.: ABA, Nat. Acad. TV Arts and Scis., George Town Club, Phi Beta Kappa. Home: 419 Cameron St Alexandria VA 22314-3221 Personal E-mail: mhobbs27@comcast.net.

HOBBS, TRUMAN MCGILL, federal judge; b. Selma, Ala., Feb. 8, 1921; s. Sam F. and Sarah Ellen (Greene) H.; m. Joyce Cummings, July 9, 1949; children— Emilie C. Reid, Frances John Rose, Dexter Cummings, Truman McGill. AB, U. NC, 1942; LLB, Yale U., 1948. Bar: Ala. 1948. Practiced in, Montgomery, 1951-80; law clk. US Supreme Ct., 1948-49; ptnr. Hobbs, Copeland, Franco & Screws, 1951-80; judge US Dist. Ct. (mid. dist.) Ala., Montgomery, 1980—84, sr. judge, 1991—. Chmn. Ala. Unemployment Appeal Bd., 1952-58 Pres. United Appeal Montgomery; pres. Montgomery County Tb Assn.; v.p. Ala. Com. for Better Schs.; Chmn. Montgomery County Exec. Democratic Com., 1970. Served to lt. USNR, 1942-46, ETO, PTO. Decorated Bronze Star medal. Fellow Am. Coll. Trial Lawyers; mem. Internat. Acad. Trial Lawyers, Ala. Plaintiffs Lawyers Assn. (past pres.), Ala. Bar Assn. (pres. 1970-71), Montgomery County Bar Assn. (past pres.) Home: 2301 Fernway Dr Montgomery AL 36111-1603

HOBBY, SCOTT M., lawyer; b. Phila., Mar. 24, 1945; BA, Emory U., 1967; JD cum laude, U. Ga., 1973. Bar: Ga. 1973. Mem. Powell, Goldstein, Frazer & Murphy, Atlanta, 1973—96; ptnr. in charge of Outsourcing and Sys. Integration Practice Hunton & Williams, Atlanta, 1996—2005, Paul, Hastings, Janovsky & Walker, 2005—07; ptnr. Outsourcing and Sys. Integration Practice Sutherland Asbill & Brennan, Atlanta, 2007—. Mem. editorial bd. Ga. Law Review, 1968-69, 73. Lt. (j.g.) USN, 1969-72. Mem. ABA, State Bar Ga., Atlanta Bar Assn., Phi Sigma Alpha, Phi Kappa Phi, Phi Delta Phi. Office: Sutherland Asbill & Brennan 999 Peachtree St NE Atlanta GA 30309-3996 Office Phone: 404-853-8051. Business E-Mail: scott.hobby@sutherland.com.

HOBBY, WILLIAM PETTUS, retired broadcast executive; b. Houston, Jan. 19, 1932; s. William Pettus and Oveta (Culp) H.; m. Diana Poteat Stallings, Sept. 11, 1954; children: Laura Poteat Beckworth, Paul William, Andrew Purefoy, Katherine Pettus Gibson. BA, Rice U., 1953. Pres. H & C Communications, Inc., 1979-83, chmn. bd., chief exec. officer, 1983-96; lt. gov. Tex., 1973-91; chancellor Univ. of Houston Sys., 1995-97. Sid Richardson prof. Lyndon B. Johnson Sch. Pub. Affairs, U. Tex., Austin, 1990-97; Radoslav Tsanoff prof. Rice U., Houston, 1991—. Served to lt. (j.g.) USNR, 1953-57. Office: Hobby Comm LLC 2131 San Felipe Houston TX 77019-5620 Office Phone: 713-521-0960.

HOBEROCK, LAWRENCE LINDEN, mechanical engineer, educator; b. Wichita, Kans., Oct. 21, 1939; s. Lawrence H. and Teresa B. (Gornick) H.; m. Judith L. Anderson, June 6, 1964; children: Michael Jo, Barbara T., Timmothy M. BSME, U. Mo., Rolla, 1961; MSME, Purdue U., W. Lafayette, 1963, PhD, 1966. Registered profl. engr., Tex., Okla. Asst. prof., then assoc. prof. U. Tex., Austin, 1968-78; rsch. assoc. Amoco Prodn. Co., Tulsa, 1978-81, rsch. supr., 1981-85; v.p. rsch. Derrick Mfg. Corp., Buffalo, 1985-86; pvt. practice engring. cons. Buffalo, 1986-87; prof., head mech. and aero. engring. Okla. State U., Stillwater, 1987—2012, prof. & head emeritus, 2012—. Cons. Amoco Prodn. Co., 1977-78, 88, Shell Devel. Co., Houston, 1989-91, Conoco, Ponca City, Okla., 1990, Cagle Oilfield Svcs., Tulsa, 1990; Dean U. Kans. Eng., Manhattan, 1998, Schlumberger & Halliburton, Houston 2003, HarnesS, Dickey, & Pierce, PLC, Troy, Mich., 2008. Contbr. articles to profl. publs. Capt. U.S. Army, 1966-68, pres. Stillwater Frontier Rotary Club, 2013-14 Fellow ASME (life)(dedicated svc. award, chair dynamic sys., v.p. sys. and design, assoc. editor); mem. Am. Soc. Engring. Edn. Roman Catholic. Avocations: carpentry, hunting, birdwatching. Office: Okla State U Sch Mech and Aero Engring 218 En Stillwater OK 74078-5016 Office Phone: 405-744-5900.

HOCHBERG, SCOTT, state legislator; b. Oct. 2, 1953; m. Kathryn Elek Hochberg. MSEE, Rice U.; LLD (hon.), Houston Bapt. U. Co-founder electronic mfg. firm; operator software devel. firm; mem. Dist. 132 Tex. House of Representatives, 1993—2002, mem. Dist. 137, 2003—. Recipient Frankie award, Harris County Dem., 1993, Good Guy award, Women's Polit Caucus Houston, 1993—94; named Legislator of Yr., Tex. Coun. Adminstr. Special Edn.; named to Outstanding Tex. Legislator, Tex. Parent Tchr. Assn. Democrat. Office: Room CAP 4N.08 PO Box 2910 Austin TX 78768 also: 6000 Reims Rd Apt 2605 Houston TX 77036-3052 Office Phone: 832-252-7336, 512-463-0492. Office Fax: 832-201-9388.

HOCTOR, JAMES JOSEPH, lawyer; b. Biddeford, Maine, Dec. 4, 1963; s. Michael James and Lorraine Belair Hoctor; m. Lynn Marie Hoctor, May 3, 1997; children: Michael James, James Lawrence. BS in Acctg., U. Fla., Gainesville, 1985, MA in Acctg., 1986; JD, Duke U., NC, 1990. CPA Fla., 1987; bar: Fla. 1990. Acct. Ernst & Whinny, Orlando, Fla., 1986—87; lawyer Lowndes Drosdick Doster, Orlando, 1990—. Bd. dirs. Friends Mennello Mus., Orlando, 2002—. Home: 1891 Winchester Dr Winter Park FL 32789 Office: Lowndes Drosdick Doster 215 N Eola Dr Orlando FL 32801 Office Phone: 407-418-6254, 407-843-4444. Business E-Mail: jim.hoctor@lowndes-law.com.

HOCUTT, MAX OLIVER, retired philosophy educator; b. Berry, Ala., July 3, 1936; s. Harry Juell and Edith Pauline (Skelton) H.; m. Dorothy Lois Etheredge, Nov. 22, 1957; children: James Max, Cassandra Diane. BA in Philosophy with honors, Tulane U., 1957, MA, 1958; PhD, Yale U., 1960. Instr. U. South Fla., Tampa, 1960-62, asst. prof., chmn. dept. philosophy, 1962-65; assoc. prof. U. Ala., 1965-70, prof., 1970—2001, chmn. dept., 1978-91; ret., 2001. Vis. fellow, Oxford U., 1971, Princeton U., 1979, St. Andrews U., 1987; bd. dirs. ACLU, University, 1969. Author: The Elements of Logical Analysis and Inference, 1979, First Philosophy, 1980, Grounded Ethics, 2000; editor: Behavior and Philosophy, 1992-96; contbr. articles to profl. jours. Honors scholar, Tulane U., 1957, So. Fellowships Career Tchg. fellow, Yale U., 1958—60. Mem. Ala. Philos. Soc. (pres. 1967), So. Soc. Philosophy and Psychology, Am. Philos. Assn., Phi Beta Kappa. Home: 5510 Golden Pond Ave Northport AL 35473-1529 Office: U Ala Dept Philosophy Tuscaloosa AL 35487-0001

HODEL, MARY ANNE, library director; b. St. Louis, Aug. 12; d. William George and Florence Marie (Betz) H.; children: Courtney Hodel Denham, Christian Hodel Denham. BA, U. Wis., 1972; MLS, Cath. U., 1973. Project libr. TRACOR-JITCO, Rockville, Md., 1973—74; project mgr. to database mgr. Nat. Resources Libr. US Dept. Interior, Washington, 1974—77; cataloger USAF Base Libr., Ramstein, Germany, 1977—79; project libr. to automation libr. Law Libr. Georgetown U., Washington, 1984—85, automation libr. Law Libr., 1985—91; chief state libr. resource ctr. Enoch Pratt Free Libr., Balt., 1991—95; dir. Ann Arbor Dist. Libr., Mich., 1995—2001; dir., CEO Orange County Libr. Sys., Orlando, Fla., 2002—. Network coord. Coun. Md. Librs., 1991-95; mem. Sailor Implementation group, 1992-95, grants and devel. task force liaison, 1993-95; v.p. Mich. Libr. Consortium, 1998-99, bd. pres., 1999-2000, bd. dirs., bd. mem. Fla. Humanities Coun., 09-, mem. com. Urban Librs. Coun., 2009-11; spkr. in field, mag. reviewer, Fla. Librs. Mag., 2011-. Mem. exec. com. Ann Arbor Hands On Mus., 1998—2002. Recipient Libr. of Yr. award Libr. Jour., 1997-98, Fla. Libr. of Yr. award, 2010, Innovation award Urban Liibr. Coun., 2010, 2011, Award for Dem. Govt. & Innovation, Ash Ctr., 2010. Mem.: LLAMA (mgmt. practice com. chairperson 2006—10, SASS exec. com. mem. 2011—), ALA (local arrangements chmn. ann. conf. Orlando 2004, coun. mem. 2011—, Libr. of Yr. award 1998—99, Libr. of Future award 2011, Program award Office Info. Tech. 2011, Office Tech. award 2011—13), Fla. Libr. Assn. (legis. com. mem. 2011—, treas. 2012—, exec. com. mem. annual conf. com. 2012—, Libr. Innovation award 2011), Fla. Libr. Network Coun., Law Librs. Soc. Washington (pres. acad. spl. interest sect. 1988—89, prog. coord. 1989, chair innovative interfaces users workshop 1989, rec. sec. 1989—91, prog. coord. 1990), Md. Libr. Assn. (del. to ALA legis. day 1992, conf. planning com. 1993—94, co-chair tech. interest group 1994, prog. coord. 1994), Md. Assn. Profl. Libr. Adminstrs., Pub. Libr. Assn. (sys. sect. v.p./pres.-elect 1994—95, pres. 1995—96, chair Leonard Wertheimer award com. 2000—01, award com mem. 2000—01, sys. & svcs. sect. esec. com. mem. 2007—09, mem. exec. bd. 2008—11, bd. dirs. 2008—11, sys. & svcs. sect. esec. com. mem. 2011—, chair 2011—, nominating com. mem. 2012—, Demco New Leaders Travel grant 2008—10), Mich. Libr. Consortium (v.p. 1999, pres. 1999—2000), Am. Assn. Law Librs. (prog. coord. ann. meeting 1987, chair innovative interfaces users com. 1988—89, editor innovative interfaces users com. 1989), Mich. Libr. Assn. (chair pub. libr. divsn. 2001—). Avocations: travel, photography. Office: Orlando Pub Libr 101 E Central Blvd Orlando FL 32801 Office Phone: 407-835-7601. E-mail: hodel.maryanne@ocls.info.

HODGE, BOBBY LYNN, mechanical engineer, manufacturing executive; b. Yadkinville, NC, Oct. 14, 1956; s. Robert Henry and Betty Jean (Martin) H.; m. Robin Mayhue Renegar, June 8, 1979; children: Andrew, Adam. AAS with honors, Forsyth Tech. Inst., Winston-Salem, NC, 1976; BS in Engring. Tech., U. NC, Charlotte, 1978. Design engr. Clark/Gravely Corp., Clemmons, NC, 1978-79, project engr., 1979-80; design engr. Ingersoll-Rand, Davidson, NC, 1980-83, devel. engr., 1983-85; sr. applications engr. INA Bearing Co., Ft. Mill, SC, 1985-87, mgr. automotive driveline engring. group, 1987-88, mgr. automotive applications engring., 1988-89, dir. automotive applications engring., 1989-96, dir. automotive engring., 1996-99; v.p. engring./product devel. The Setco Group, Cin., 1999—2002, v.p. engring/quality, 2002—. Internat. spkr. on design and application of rolling element bearings and machine tool spindles. Contbr. articles to profl. jours. Mem. adv. coun. U. NC-Charlotte Coll. Engring. Mem. ASME, SAE, Soc. Mfg. Engrs., Soc. Tribologists and Lubrication Engrs., Am. Soc. Metals. Republican. Baptist. Achievements include 10 patents in field. Avocations: golf, hunting, woodworking. Home: 1518 Jolee Dr Hebron KY 41048-9514 Office: The Setco Group 5880 Hillside Ave Cincinnati OH 45233-1599 Home Phone: 859-689-2642. Personal E-mail: hodge1518@aol.com. Business E-Mail: bhodge@setcousa.com.

HODGE, RHYS S., territorial supreme court chief justice; b. Anguilla; m. Jean Dalmida, 1973; 4 children. Attended, Coll. VI; BSc, Kans. State U, Manhattan, 1971; JD, Rutgers U. Sch. Law, Camden, NJ, 1977. Bar: VI, Commonwealth of Pa., Ct. of Appeals (3rd cir.), Ct. of Appeals (fed. cir.). Law clerk, Hon. Almeric L. Christian Dist. Ct. the VI, 1977—79; pvt. practice atty. The Law Offices of Rhys S. Hodge, 1979—2000; judge Superior Ct. the VI, 2000—06, presiding judge, 2006; chief justice Supreme Ct. the VI, 2006—. Past pres. VI Bar; mem. lawyers adv. com. Dist. Ct. the VI; mem. Com. Bar Examiners the VI, VI Jud. Coun. Mem. exec. bd. VI Coun. the Boy Scouts of America, 1981—2000, pres., 1991—92; bd. dirs. VI Coun. the Girls Scouts of the USA; v.p., bd. trustees VI Montessori Sch. Mem.: ABA, Conf. Chief Justices, Am. Judges Assn., Nat. Bar Assn., VI Bar Assn. (chmn. ethics and grievance com., chmn. continuing legal edn. com.). Office: Supreme Ct the VI PO Box 590 St Thomas VI 00804*

HODGES, ANN, retired television editor, columnist; b. McCamey, Tex., Sept. 7, 1928; d. Ernest Cornelius and Margaret Isabel (Wood) Haynes; m. Cecil Ray Hodges, July 2, 1954 (div. Nov. 1974); children: Craig McNeley, Elizabeth Ann. BJ, U. Tex., 1948. Reporter Houston Chronicle, 1948-51; soc. editor The News, Mexico City, 1951-52, TV editor, columnist, TV critic Houston Chronicle, 1962—2003; ret., 2003. Mem. adv. bd. U. Miami TV Ctr. for Advancement of Modern Media, 1994—; U.S. juror Banff TV Festival, 1995. Mem.: Houston Press Club (pres. 1967), TV Critics Assn. (founder, exec. bd., v.p., pres.), Critics Consensus (dir. 1965—75). Personal E-mail: 1ahodges@comcast.net.

HODGES, DEWEY HARPER, aerospace engineer, educator; b. Clarksville, Tenn., May 18, 1948; s. Plummer Maxwell Sr. and Etha Maude (Harper) H.; m. Margaret Elin Jones, Aug. 14, 1971; children: Timothy, Jonathan, David, Philip, Benjamin. BS in Aerospace Engring., U. Tenn., 1969; MS in Aero. and Astro. Engring., Stanford U., 1970, PhD in Aero. and Astro. Engring., 1973. Rsch. scientist U.S. Army Aeroflight Dynamics Directorate, Ames Rsch. Ctr., Moffett Field, Calif., 1970-80, sr. rsch. scientist, theoretical group leader, 1980-86; prof. aerospace engring. Ga. Inst. Tech., Atlanta, 1986—. Instr. No. Calif. Bible Coll., San Jose, 1974-86; lectr. Stanford U., 1980-86; guest rsch. scientist DLR Inst. Structural Mechanics, Braunschweig, Fed. Republic of Germany, 1984. Author: Nonlinear Composite Beam Theory, 2006; co-author (with G. Alvin Pierce): Introduction to Structural Dynamics and Aeroelasticity, 2002, 2nd edit., 2011; co-author: (with George J. Simitses) Fundamentals of Structural Stability, 2006; contbr. more than 350 articles to profl. jours. & conf. procs., seven chpts. to books. Elder Christian Comty. Ch., San Jose, 1980-86, Mt. Paran Ch., Atlanta, 1992-94, Chalcedon Presbyn. Ch., Cumming, Ga., 2003-. Capt. US Army, 1973—77. Recipient R & D Achievement award, US Army, 1979, Fed. Aviation Adminstrn. Spl. Recognition award, Dept. Transp., 1996, Sustained Rsch. award, Ga. Tech. Sigma Xi, 2011, Holt Ashley Award for Aeroelasticity, AIAA, 2013, Alexander A. Nikolsky Hon. Lectureship award, Am. Helicopter Soc. Internat., 2014. Fellow AIAA, Am. Helicopter Soc., Am. Acad. Mechanics; mem. ASME, Tau Beta Pi, Pi Tau Sigma. Republican. Presbyterian. Achievements include patents for hingeless helicopter rotor with improved stability; real-time missile guidance system. Avocations: piano, singing, squash, theology. Home: 1172 Branch Water Ct Atlanta GA 30338-4026 Office: Ga Inst Tech Sch Aerospace Engring Atlanta GA 30332-0150 Office Phone: 404-894-8201. Business E-Mail: dhodges@gatech.edu.

HODGES, KENNETH F., state legislator; b. Feb. 11, 1952; s. Benjamin F. and Lydia Whaley Hodges; m. Patricia Few; children: Kendrea, Kenyatta, Kenithea. BA, Clark Coll., Vancouver, Wash., 1977; MDiv, Morehouse Sch. Religion Interdenominational Theol. Ctr., Atlanta, 1986. Pastor Shiloh Bapt. Ch., Bennettsville, SC, 1986—95; mem., exec. bd. Marlboro County br. NAACP, 1987—93; commr. Bennettsville Housing Authority, 1989—93; councilman Bennettsville City Coun., 1989—95; chmn. Bennettsville Housing Authority, 1991—93; faculty mem. SC Bapt. Congress Christian Edn., 1994—; mem., exec. bd. Bapt. Edn. & Missionary Conv., 1995—2001; mem. Beaufort County Econ. Devel. Bd., 1998—2001; mem. Dist. 121 SC House of Reps., 2005—. Bd. dirs. Beaufort Area Boys & Girls Club, 1997—2002. Mem.: Old Ashley Bapt. Assn. (vice moderator 1994—2004, moderator 2004—), Main St. Beaufort USA, Beufort Dist. Old Ashley Assn. (vice chmn. 1997—2000). Democrat. Address: PO Drawer 355 Green Pond SC 29446 Home: 14906 Bennetts Point Rd Green Pond SC 29446 Office: 434B Blatt Building Columbia SC 29201 Home Phone: 843-844-8756; Office Phone: 843-525-9006. Business E-Mail: HodgesK@schouse.org.

HODGES, M. KEITH, state legislator; b. Richmond, Va., May 6, 1966; m. Shelley Gaye Williams; children: Chloe, Ella. BS, Med. Coll. of Va., 1989. Mem. Dist. 98 Va. House of Delegates, 2012—, mem. Counties Cities and Towns Com. & Health Welfare and Institutions Com. Bd. dirs. Riverside Walter Reed Hosp., EPIC Pharmacies. Mem.: Rsch. and Edn. Found. Bd., Va. Pharmacists Assn., Nat. Cmty. Pharmacists Assn. (bd. dirs.). Republican. Office: General Assembly Building PO Box 406 Richmond VA 23218 also: PO Box 928 Urbanna VA 23175 Office Phone: 804-698-1098. Office Fax: 804-698-6798. E-mail: DelKHodges@house.virginia.gov.

HODGES, MARLANE FAIRLEIGH, retired management educator; b. Three Rivers, Mich., Feb. 28, 1939; d. Ronald Edward and Evelyn May (Roth) Paxson; m. James Parkinson Fairleigh, June 25, 1960 (dec.); children: William P. Fairleigh, Karen Hofferber; m. Bob Shiver Hodges, Sept. 17, 2006 (dec.). MusB, U. Mich., 1960; MBA, Jacksonville State U., 1986. Cert. econ. devel. fin. profl. Nat. Devel. Coun., 1989. Mem. adj. faculty Providence Coll., 1976-80, R.I. Coll., Providence, 1978-80; grad. asst. news bur. and info. ctr. Jacksonville (Ala.) State U., 1983-84, grad. asst. Coll. Commerce, 1984-85; bus. cons. Jacksonville State U. Small Bus. Devel. Ctr., 1985-96. Presenter in field. Contbr. articles to profl. jours.; soprano soloist (songs) Coll. Music Soc. Internat. Conf., Berlin, Germany, 1995, Vienna, Austria, 1997, (chamber music recitals) Auburn U., Jacksonville State U., 1998, Gadsden, Ala., 2001, lectr.-recitalist (songs) U. Ala., Tuscaloosa, 1997, U. Ctrl. Fla., Orlando, 1999, Jacksonville State U., 1999, State U. West Ga., 1998, Valdosta State U., 2001, U. South Fla., Tampa, 2003, recitalist (chamber music) Colonial Dames Am., Gadsden, Ala., 2001, Gadsden Music Club, 2001. Chair Jacksonville State U. campus United Way Calhoun County, 1986-87. Mem. Sigma Beta Delta. Avocations: vocal performing, water-skiing, swimming, hiking. Home: 13116 Janda Rd Seneca SC 29672

HODGES, VALARIE, state legislator; Attended, Bob Brooks Sch. Real Estate, Baton Rogue, La. State U. Accountant, v.p. Straightway Ministries; co-pastor Destiny Internat.; mem. Dist. 64 La. House of Reps., Baton Rogue, 2012—. Republican. Office: 35055 Louisiana Hwy 16 Ste 2A Denham Springs LA 70706 also: La House of Reps 900 N 3rd St Baton Rouge LA 70804 Office Phone: 225-791-2199. Business E-Mail: hodgesv@legis.la.gov.

HODGES, WILLIAM TERRELL, federal judge; b. Lake Wales, Fla., Apr. 28, 1934; s. Haywood and Clara Lucy (Murphy) H.; m. Peggy Jean Woods, June 8, 1958; children: Judson, Daniel, Clay. BSBA, U. Fla., 1956, JD, 1958, LLD (hon.). Bar: Fla. 1959. Mem. firm Macfarlane, Ferguson, Allison & Kelly, Tampa, 1958-71; instr. bus. law U. South Fla., Tampa, 1961-66; judge US Dist. Ct. (mid. dist.) Fla., Tampa, 1971—82, 1989—99, chief judge, 1982—89, sr. judge, 1999—. Mem. com. on ops. jury system Jud. Conf., 1982-87, cir. coun., 11th cir., 1981-86; mem., adv. com. on criminal rules procedure and evidence Jud. Conf., 1987-93, chmn., 1990-93; ad hoc com. on habeas corpus reform; chmn., bench book com. Fed. Jud. Ctr., 1987-93; chmn., Ad Hoc Com. of the Jud. Conf. to study relations within the Fed. Jud. Ctr., 1997-98; chmn., US Jud. Panel on Multidistrict Litig., 2000-07. Exec. editor, U. Fla. Law Rev., 1957-58. Mem. Am., Tampa-Hillsborough County bar assns., Fla. Bar (chmn. grievance com. 1967-70, chmn. uniform comml. code com. 1970-71), Dist. Judges Assn. 5th Circuit (co-chmn. com. on pattern jury instrn. 1977-81), Dist. Judges Assn. 11th Circuit (chmn. jury instrns. com. 1982—, pres. 1981-82) Am. Judicature Soc. Office: US Dist Ct Golden Collum Meml Fed Bldg 207 N W 2nd St Rm 330 Ocala FL 34475-6666 Office Phone: 352-380-2422.

HODGSON, ERNEST, toxicologist, educator; b. Durham, Eng., July 26, 1932; arrived in U.S., 1955; s. Ernest Victor and Emily (Moses) Hodgson; m. Mary Kathleen Devlin, Dec. 21, 1957 (dec.); children: Mary Elizabeth, Audrey Catherine, Patricia Emily Devlin, Ernest Victor Felix. BSc with honors, Kings Coll. U., Durham, Eng., 1955; PhD, Oreg. State U., 1959. Rsch. fellow Oreg. State U., Corvallis, 1955-59, U. Wis., Madison, 1959-61; asst. prof. N.C. State U., Raleigh, 1961-63, assoc. prof., 1963-65, prof. toxicology, 1965—, William Neal Reynolds prof., 1977—, chmn. toxicology dept., 1982-97, Disting. Alumni Rsch. prof., 1987-90; disting. prof. emeritus NC State U. Mem. adv. panel U.S. EPA, Washington, 1982—85; mem. toxicology study sect. NIH, Washington, 1985—89; mem. study sect. NIEHS, 1992—96, chmn., 1994—96; pres. Toxicology Comm., Raleigh, 1982—; vis. scientist U. Wash., Seattle, 1975; exec. dir. Found. Toxicology & Agromedicine. Author, editor: Introduction to Biochemical Toxicology, 1980, 4th edit., 2008, Modern Toxicology, 1987, 4th edit., 2010, Dictionary of Toxicology, Molecular and Biochemical Toxicology, 4th edit., 2008; editor: Revs. Biochemical Toxicology, 1979—, Revs. Environ. Toxicology, 1984—, Jour. Biochemical and Molecular Toxicology; mem. editl. bd. Chemico-Biol. Interactions; contbr. articles to profl. jours. Chmn. policy rev. com. Gov.'s Waste Mgmt. Bd., Raleigh, 1984. Grantee, NIH, 1962—, U.S. Army, 2000—. Mem.: AAAS, Internat. Soc. Study Xenobiotics (mem. coun. 1986—89, sec.-elect 1990—92, sec. 1992—94, pres.-elect 1996—97, pres. 1998—99, Disting. Svc. award 2004), Am. Chem. Soc. (Sterling Hendricks award USDA 1997, Burdick and Jackson Internat. award in pesticide chemistry), Am. Soc. Pharmacology (mem. drug metabolism com. 1981—84), Soc. Toxicology (pres. N.C. chpt. 1984—85, mem. edn. com. 1984—, pres. mechanisms sect. 1991—92, historian, archivist 2005—09, Edn. award 1984, Merit award 1994), Sigma Xi (chpt. pres. 1974). Democrat. Avocations: history, writing, travel. Office: NC State U Dept Toxicology PO Box 7633 Raleigh NC 27695-0001 Office Phone: 919-515-5295. Business E-Mail: ernest_hodgson@ncsu.edu.

HOE, RICHARD MARCH, securities consultant, writer; b. Plainfield, NJ, June 16, 1939; s. Arthur James Hoe and Marjorie (Vandergrift) Beeson; m. Lynne Hovell, Sept. 26, 1964; children: Joshua Blake, Susan Brooke, Seth Jamieson. Student, Pace U., 1964-67, U. Tenn., 1976. CLU. Asst. to controller, fleet mgr., asst. purchasing agt. Hoe & Co. Inc., Bronx, NY, 1962—66; pres. OJS Mfg. Co., Bklyn., 1966-68, Fresh Impressions Inc., NYC, 1968; agt. Fidelity Mut. Life, NYC, 1968—72; asst. mgr. Fin. Life, NYC, 1972—73; brokerage mgr. Am. Life N.Y., NYC, 1973—75; exec. Provident Life & Accident Ins. Co., Chattanooga, 1975—78; br. mgr. Jefferson Standard, Tulsa, Okla., 1978—81; pres. Hoe & Co. Inc., Tulsa, 1981—93; fin. planner, designer, cons. Tulsa, 1978—99; specialist Am. Citizens Fin. Svcs., Tulsa, 1989—99; exec. v.p. Summit Fin. Group, Tulsa, 2000—05; fin. planner Richard Hoe Investments, LLC, 2005—. Lectr. project bus. Tulsa Pub. Schs., 1983, 85, cons., 1984-86; faculty mem., Calif. Inst. Fin., Calif. Luth. U. Grad. Sch., Thousand Oaks, Calif., 2007—; lectr. in field; founder employee and exec. benefit plans, residual split-dollar, money purchase flexible spending plans, pvt. sector social security alternative portable plans, satellite split-dollar, satellite supplemental pensions, lifetime income nontaxable retirement plans, balanced funding plans. Author: Love in Pasadena, 1996; columnist (monthly) Broker World, 1985-86, 87-88, Probe, Life Assn. News, Life Insurance Selling, 2000—13, Retirement Advisor, 2014-; contbr. articles to profl. jours., novelist. Chmn. fund raising Grimes Elem. Sch., Tulsa Pub. Schs., 1984-87; mem. gifted and talented com. Tulsa Pub. Schs., 1982; bd. dirs. Nat. ALS Found., N.Y.C., 1971-82. Fellow: Life Underwriter Tng. Coun. (moderator 1979—86, chartered fin. cons., chartered life underwriter, accredited estate planner); mem.: Tulser Chap. Fin. Planning Assn., Soc. Fin. Svcs. Profl. (bd. dir. 2007—, treas. 2008—09, pres. 2010—12), Tulsa Estate Planning Forum (treas. 2005—09), Okla. Planned Giving Coun., Reach Across Divisions. Republican. Episcopalian. Avocations: writing, chess, bicycling, jazz. Home: 5843 E 50th St Tulsa OK 74135-6885 Office: Richard Hoe Investments LLC 5801 East 41st St Ste 108 Tulsa OK 74135-5629 Office Phone: 918-398-7200. E-mail: richardhoe@richardhoe.com.

HOEVELER, WILLIAM MARCELLIN, federal judge; b. Paris, Aug. 23, 1922; m. Mary Griffin Smith, 1950; 4 children. Student, Temple U., 1941-42; BA, Bucknell U., 1947; LLB, Harvard U., 1950. Bar: Fla. 1951. Pvt. practice atty., Miami, Fla., 1951-77; judge US Dist. Ct. (so. dist.) Fla., Miami, 1977—91, sr. judge, 1991—. Lectr. in field. Incorporator, bd. dirs. Youth Industries, Inc.; mem. vestry St. Stephens Episcopal Ch., 1973-75, chancellor, 1973. Served to lt. USMC, 1942-46. Mem. Am. Judicature Soc., Fla. Bar (personal injury and wrongful death adv. com. 1976), Phila. Bar Assn., Dade County (Fla.) Bar Assn. (chmn. charity drives com. 1966), Am. Bar Assn. (chmn. com. on products, profl. and gen. liability law 1972-73, program chmn. sec. ins., negligence and compensation law 1975, mem. sect. governing council 1975-78, mem. governing com. of forum com. on constrn. industry), Omicron Delta Kappa. Office: US Dist Ct 301 N Miami Ave Fl 9 Miami FL 33128-7702

HOFF, GERHARDT MICHAEL, lawyer, insurance company executive; b. Vienna, June 12, 1930; came to U.S., 1951, naturalized, 1955; s. Erich Theodor and Vilma (Frank) Klockenhoff; m. Lisa Decristoforo, June 1, 1970; children: Michael, Elisabeth, Anne-Christine. Student, U. Munich Law Sch., Germany, 1948-51, Columbia U., 1951-52; LL.B., NYU, 1958; LL.M. in Taxation, Emory U., 1982; C.L.U., 1961. Bar: Mass. 1959, D.C. 1968, Ga. 1984. With Mass. Mut. Life Ins. Co. and Variable Annuity Life Ins. Co., 1958-67; v.p. Variable Annuity Life Ins. Co. Am., Washington, 1967-68; mem. staff fin. services group ITT Corp., 1968-69; pres. ITT Hamilton Life Ins. Co., also ITT Variable Annuity Ins. Co., St. Louis, 1970-72, Sun Life Ins. Co. Am., Balt., 1972-78, 81-83, chief exec. officer, 1972-83; pres. Sun Life Group Am., Inc., Atlanta, 1978-83. Chmn. law practice Bus. Planning Corp. Am., Atlanta, 1983—; founder (with Lisa Hoff) Cities in Color, Inc., 1985—. Served with AUS, 1955-57. Decorated Commendation ribbon with pendant. Mem. Am. Soc. C.L.U.'s, ABA Clubs: Capital City (Atlanta). Presbyterian. Office: 12 Braemore Dr NW Atlanta GA 30328-4845 Office Phone: 404-255-1185. E-mail: gmhoff2@aol.com.

HOFFER, JOHN LEE, anesthesiologist, medical educator and anesthesia, parioperative systems developer; BS, LeTourneau U., 1955; PhD in Biomed. Engring., U. NC, Chapel Hill; MD, U. NC, 1976. Diplomate Am. Bd. Anesthesiology, Am. Bd. Quality Assurance and Utilization Rev. Physicians. Resident anesthesiology U. N.C. Hosps.; assoc. prof. anesthesiology Ohio State U., 1979—83, assoc. prof. biomed. engring., 1979—83; assoc. prof. anesthesiology and physiology Northeastern Ohio U. Coll. Medicine, 1984—92; prof. engring. Tex. A&M U., 1992—2009; prof. anesthesiology Tex. A&M U. Health Sci. Ctr., Coll. Medicine, 1992—2009, emeritus prof., 2009—. Chmn. dept. anesthesiology libr. com., Scott & White Clinics, mem. quality assurance com., mem. instnl. rev. bd., mem. tenure and faculty promotion com. predoctoral. Predoctoral fellow, NIH. Office: Dept Anesthesiology 2401 S 31st St Temple TX 76508

HOFFHEIMER, MICHAEL HARRY, law educator; b. Cin., Dec. 21, 1954; s. Harry Max and Charlotte (O'Brien) H.; m. Luanne Buchanan; children: Joseph Allen, Jean Sarah. BA with gen. honors, Johns Hopkins U., 1977; MA, U. Chgo., 1978, PhD in History, 1981; JD cum laude, U. Mich., 1984. Bar: Ohio 1984, U.S. Dist. Ct. (ea. dist.) Ky. 1984, U.S. Ct. Appeals (6th cir.) 1984, U.S. Dist. Ct. (so. dist.) Ohio 1985, D. C. Ct. Appeals 1985, U.S. Supreme Ct. 1987, U.S. Ct. Appeals (5th cir.) 1987. Intern Office of State Appellate Defender, Ottawa, Ill., summer-fall 1982; summer assoc. Frost & Jacobs, Cin., 1983, assoc., 1984-87; asst. prof. law U. Miss., Oxford, 1987-90, assoc. prof. law, 1990-97, prof. law, 1997—, Miss. Def. Lawyers Assn. Disting. lectr., 1998—2013, Leonard B. Melvin disting. lectr., 2013—. Adj. faculty U. Cin. Coll. Law, 1985-87; panel mem. Hamilton County Pub. Defender, Cin., 1985-87. Author: Conflict of Laws: Examples and Explanations, 2010, Justice Holmes and the Natural Law, 1992, Eduard Gans and the Hegelian Philosophy of Law, 1995, Directory of Law Reviews, 6th edit., 2005, Fiddling for Viola, 2000; Fiddle Care & Setup, 2008; articles editor U. Mich. Jour. Law Reform, 1983; contbr. articles to profl. jours. Kunstader fellow, U. Chgo., 1978—79. E-mail: mhoffhei@olemiss.edu.

HOFFMAN, KARLA LEIGH, mathematician, educator; b. Paterson, NJ, Feb. 14, 1948; d. Abe and Bertha (Guthaim) Rakoff; m. Allan Stuart Hoffman, Dec. 26, 1971; 1 child, Matthew Douglas. BA, Rutgers U., 1969; MBA, George Wash. U., Washington, DC, 1971, DSc in Ops. Rsch., 1975. Ops. rsch. analyst IRS, Washington, 1970-72; rsch. asst. George Washington U., 1972-75, assoc. profl. lectr., 1978-85; NSF postdoctoral rsch. fellow NAS, Washington, 1975-76; assoc. prof. sys. engring. dept. George Mason U., Fairfax, Va., 1985-86, assoc. prof. ops. rsch. and applied stats., 1986-89, prof. ops. rsch., 1990—, disting. prof., 1989, interim dept. chmn., 1996-97, chmn., 1997-98, chmn. sys. engring. and ops. rsch., 1998—2000. Mathematician Nat. Bur. Stds., Washington, 1976—84; vis. assoc. prof. ops. rsch. U. Md., 1982; mng. ptnr. Optimization Software Assocs.; cons. Govt. Agys., Airline, Telecom. and Def. Industries; bd. dirs. Parkinsons Found. Nat. Capital Area, 2006. Assoc. editor Internat. abstracts of Ops. Rsch., 1991—96, The Math. Programming Jour., Series B, 1987—, The Ops. Rsch. Soc. Jour. on Computing, 1991—96, Jour. Computational Optimization and Applications, 1992—98, mem. editl. bd. Annals of Ops. Rsch., 2000—; contbr. articles to profl. jours. Bd. dirs. Nat. Capital Region Parkinsons Found., 2006. Recipient Applied Rsch. award, Nat. Inst. Stds. and Tech., 1984, Silver medal, U.S. Dept. Commerce, 1984, Disting. Prof. award, 1989, Kimball medal, Inst. Ops. Rsch. & Mgmt. Svc., 2005, Omega Rho Lectureship award, 2008, Harvey Greenberg Svc. award, Inform Computing Soc., 2009, Outstanding Rsch. award, Sch. Engring., 2010. Fellow: Inst. Ops. Rsch. and Mgmt. Sci. (treas. 1995—96, exec. com. 1995—99, pres. 1998, fellow 2003); mem.: Math. Programming Soc. (editor newsletter 1979—82, chmn. com. algorithms 1982—85, coun. 1985—88, exec. com., chmn. membership com. 1988—89), Ops. Rsch. Soc. Am. (sec.-treas. Computer Sci. Tech. sect. 1979—80, vis. profl. lectr. 1980—, vice chmn. sect. 1981, chmn. sect. 1982, chmn. tech. sect. com. 1983—86, coun. 1985—88, chmn. Lanchester Prize com. 1989, treas. 1993—94). Home: 6921 Clifton Rd Clifton VA 20124-1525 Office Phone: 703-993-1679.

HOFFMAN, LARRY J., lawyer; b. NYC, Aug. 20, 1930; s. Max and Pauline (Epstein) H.; m. Deborah E. Alexander, Oct. 2, 1954; children: Lisa, Ken, Heidi, Mark. AA, U. Fla., Gainesville; JD, U. Miami. Bar: Fla. 1954. Chmn. Greenberg, Traurig, PA, Miami, 1968—. Mem. ABA, Fla. Bar Assn., Dade County Bar Assn. Avocations: art, computers, photography, golf. Office: Greenberg Traurig LLP 333 Ave Am Ste 4400 Miami FL 33131-3238 Business E-Mail: hoffmanl@gtlaw.com.

HOFFMAN, MARGUERITE STEED, former art gallery director; m. Robert Kenneth Hoffman; 1 child, Katherine. Positions with Dallas Mus. Art; former dir. Gerald Peters Gallery. Bd. trustees Dallas Mus. Art, 1999—, chmn. bd.; bd. dirs. Tex. Freedom Network; mem. coun. Dallas Women's Found.; donated contemporary art collection and a $20 million endowment Dallas Mus. Art, 2005. Named one of Top 200 Collectors, ARTnews mag., 2003—08. Avocation: Collector postwar Am. and European art, Chinese monochromes. Office: Dallas Mus Art 1717 N Harwood Dallas TX 75201

HOFFMAN, RANDALL G., marketing executive; BS in Liberal Studies, U. Md., 1974, BSBA, 1980, M in Adminstrn., 1989. Mktg. mgr., White and New Idea product lines AGCO Corp., gen. mktg. mgr., 1995—98, mgr., Distrbn. Devel., N.Am., 1998—2000, dir., Distrbn. Devel., N.Am., 2000, v.p., Dealer Ops., 2000—01, v.p., Mktg., N.Am., 2001, v.p., Sales and Mktg., N.Am., 2001—02, v.p., Worldwide Challenger Divsn., 2002—04, gen. mgr., Worldwide Challenger Divsn. Worldwide, 2002—05, sr. v.p., Challenger Divsn. Worldwide, 2004—05, sr. v.p. global sales, mktg. and product mgmt., 2005—. Office: AGCO Corp 4205 River Green Pky Duluth GA 30096 Office Phone: 770-813-9200. Office Fax: 770-813-6118. Business E-Mail: Randy.Hoffman@agcocorp.com.

HOFFMAN, RONALD, historian, educator; b. Balt., Feb. 10, 1941; s. Emanuel and Ethel (Lubin) H.; m. Sandra Zalma Rudman, Aug. 28 (div. Feb. 24, 2009), 1965; children: Maia, Barak. AA, Balt. C.C., 1963; BA, George Peabody Coll., 1964; MA, U. Wis., 1965, PhD, 1969. Asst. prof. history U. Md., College Park, 1969—74, assoc. prof., 1974—92, prof., 1992—95; dir. Omohundro Inst. Early Am. History and Culture, Williamsburg, Va., 1992—2013; prof. Coll. William and Mary, Williamsburg, 1993—2013; project dir. Charles carroll, 1978—. Cons. Office Sec. Def., Washington, 1975—2007; symposia dir. U.S. Capitol Hist. Soc., Washington, 1977-93. Author: A Spirit of Dissension, 1973, Princes of Ireland, Planters of Maryland: A Carroll Saga, 1500-1782, 2000, (Libr. Va. Book Literary award non-fiction, So. Hist. Assn. Frank L. and Harriet C. Owsley award, Md. Hist. Soc. book prize 2002); co-author: The Pursuit of Liberty: A History of the American People, 1983; editor: Dear Papa, Dear Charley: The Papers of Charles Carroll of Carrollton, 3 vols. (J. Franklin Jameson award Am. Hist. Assn.); co-editor: Diplomacy and Revolution, 1971, Sovereign States in an Age of Uncertainty, 1982, Slavery and Freedom in the Age of the American Revolution, 1983, Arms and Independence: The Military Character of the American Revolution, 1983, An Uncivil War: The Southern Backcountry during the American Revolution, 1985, Peace and Peacemakers: The Treaty of 1783, 1985, The Economy of Early America: The Revolutionary Period, 1763-1790, 1989, We Shall Overcome: Martin Luther King, Jr., and the Black Freedom Struggle, 1990, To Form a More Perfect Union: The Critical Ideas of the Constitution, 1992, Religion in a Revolutionary Age, 1994, Of Consuming Interests: The Style of Life in the Eighteenth Century, 1994, The Transforming Hand of Revolution, 1996, Launching the Extended Republic: The Federalist Era, 1996, The Bill of Rights: Government Proscribed, 1997, Native Americans and the New Republic, 1999; contbr. articles to profl. jours. 3d class petty officer USNR, 1959-61. Fellow Ford Found., 1967, Eleutherian Mills-Hagley Found., 1978; grantee NEH, 1977, 2004, 2006-, Nat. Hist. Publs. and Records Commn., 1979-. Mem. Am. Hist. Assn., Orgn. Am. Historians, Assn. Documentary Editing, So. Hist. Assn., Va. Hist. Soc., Md. Hist. Soc. Democrat. Jewish. Home: 430D E Duke Of Gloucester St Williamsburg VA 23185-4250 Office: 806 Settlement Dr Williamsburg VA 23188 Business E-Mail: rxhoff@wm.edu.

HOFFMANN, FRANK A., state legislator; BA, EdM, EdD, U. La., Monroe. Ret. asst. supt. Ouachita Parish sch. sys.; mem. Dist. 15 La. House of Reps., 2008—, vice chair edn. com., mem. retirement com., ways and means com., joint legis. com. on capital outlay. Republican. Office: State Capitol PO Box 44486 Baton Rouge LA 70804 Mailing: 204 N3rd St Ste A West Monroe LA 71291 Office Phone: 225-342-6945, 318-362-4130. Office Fax: 318-362-4131. Business E-Mail: hoffmanf@legis.state.la.us.

HOFFNER, JOHN F., food service executive; m. Jean Hoffner; children: John, Robert. BS in Indsl. Mgmt., Purdue U., 1970; MBA, Xavier U., 1974. With Procter & Gamble Co.; asst. contr. Federated Dept. Stores; contr., dir., fin. svcs., Mervyn's Divsn. Dayton Hudson Corp.; v.p., CFO Pic N Save Stores; sr. v.p., fin. and adminstrn. Wherehouse Entertainment Inc.; exec. v.p., CFO Sweet Factory, Inc.; exec. v.p., adminstrn., CFO & sec. Cost Plus, Inc., 1998—2001; exec. v.p., CFO Jack in the Box, Inc., 2001—05. Bd. dirs. AFC Enterprises, Inc., 2006—. Former bd. dirs., Krannert Mgmt. Sch. Purdue U.; former bd. dirs. Jr. Achievement of LA and San Diego; bd. dirs. St. Joseph's East Ga. (subs. Saint Joseph's Health System of Atlanta). Office: AFC Enterprises Inc Bd Directors 400 Perimeter Center Ter NE Ste 1000 Atlanta GA 30346-1234 Office Phone: 404-459-4450. Business E-Mail: jhoffner@afce.com.

HOFMEISTER, JOHN D., not-for-profit organization executive, retired oil industry executive; b. 1948; m. Karen O. Hofmeister. BA in Polit. Sci., Kans. State U., 1971, MA in Polit. Sci., 1973. Human resources mgmt. Gen. Eletric Co., 1973—82, gen. mgr., motor rels. op. Fort Wayne, Ind., 1982—88; asst. v.p. human resources Northern Telecom Inc., Raleigh, NC, 1988—99, v.p. US human resources Nashville, 1989—92; v.p. aerospace human resources AlliedSignal Inc., LA, 1992—95, v.p. internat. human resources Hong Kong, Paris, 1995—97; group human resources dir. Royal Dutch/Shell Group of Companies, London, 1997—2005, US chair, 2005—08; pres. Shell Oil Co., Houston, 2005—08; founder, CEO Citizens for Affordable Energy, Inc., Washington, 2008—. Bd. visitors NC State U. Agriculture Tech., Greenville, 1993—99; bd. govs. Internat. Inst. Mgmt. Devel., 1999—2005; bd. mem. Cornell U. Sch. Indsl. Labor Relations, Ithaca, NY, 2001—06; chmn. adv. bd. Cornell U. Ctr. Advanced Human Resource Studies, 2004—06; bd. dirs. US Energy Assn., 2005—06, NAM, 2005—06; bd. mem., exec com. American Petroleum Inst., 2005—06, Greater Houston Partnership, 2005—06; vice chmn. Nat. Urban League, 2005—06, chair, 2009—. Author: Why We Hate the Oil Companies: Straight Talk from an Energy Insider, 2010. Bd. dirs. Jobs for America's Graduates, Wash., DC, 1993—2000. Recipient Corp. Leadership award, Minority Supplier Devel. Coun., 2008; fellow, Nat. Acad. Human Resources, 2003. Fellow: Foreign Policy Assn. Office: Citizens for Renewable Energy 1015 15th St NW Ste 802 Washington DC 20005

HOGAN, JOHN DONALD, retired college dean, finance educator; b. Binghamton, NY, July 16, 1927; s. John D. and Edith J. (Hennessy) H.; m. Anna Craig, Nov. 26, 1976; children: Thomas P., James E. AB, Syracuse U., 1949, MA, 1950, PhD, 1952. Registered prin. Nat. Assn. Securities Dealers. Prof. econs., chmn. dept. Bates Coll., Lewiston, Maine, 1953-58; dir. edn. fin. research State of N.Y., 1959, chief mcpl. fin., 1960; staff economist, dir. research Northwestern Mut. Life Ins. Co., Milw., 1960-68; v.p. Nationwide Ins. Cos., Columbus, Ohio, 1968-76; dean Sch. Bus. Adminstrn. Central Mich. U., Mt. Pleasant, 1976-79; v.p. Am. Productivity Ctr., Houston, 1979-80; pres., chmn., chief exec. officer Variable Annuity Life Ins. Co., Houston, 1980-83; sr. v.p. Am. Gen. Corp., Houston, 1983-86; dean, prof. fin. Coll. Commerce U. Ill., Champaign, 1986-91; dean, prof. fin. and econs. Coll. Bus. Adminstrn. Ga. State U., Atlanta, 1991-97, prof. fin. and econs., 1998—2001, dean and prof. emeritus, 2002—. Bd. dirs. Sinfonia da Camera, Champaign, Ga. Coun. on Econ. Edn., Pvt. Industry Coun., World Trade Ctr., Atlanta; vis. prof. fin. Poznan (Poland) U. Econs., Caucasus Sch. Bus., Tbilisi, Georgia; cons. in field. Author: American Social Legislation, 1965, U.S. Balance of Payments and Capital Flows, 1967, School Revenue Studies, 1959, Fiscal Capacity of the State of Maine, 1958, American Social Legislation, 1973; editor: Dimensions of Productivity Research (2 vols.), 1981; contbr. articles to jours., abstracts to profl. meetings. Bd. dirs. Goodwill Industries, Columbus, 1972-76, chmn. capital fund drive, 1974-75; mem. Houston Com. on Fgn. Rels., 1980—, Chgo. Coun. on Fgn. Rels., 1986—, Chgo. com., 1987—; mem. dean's coun. Maxwell Grad. Sch., Syracuse U., 2003—. Served with U.S. Army, 1944-46, ETO; capt. (ret.) USAR. Maxwell fellow Syracuse U., 1950-52; recipient Best Article award Jur. Risk and Ins., Alumni Appreciation award U. Ill., 1991, 1964, Medal of Merit Poznan U., Poland, 1999; Maxwell Centennial lectr. Maxwell Grad. Sch., Syracuse U., 1970. Mem.: Inst. Rsch. in Econs. of Taxation (dir. 1984—), Nat. Tax Assn. (dir. 1981—85, treas., exec. com. 1988—2001), Nat. Assn. Bus. Economists, Inst. Mgmt. Scis., Am. Econ. Assn., Acad. Mgmt., Columbus C. of C. (chmn. econ. policy com. 1972—76), World Trade Club (Atlanta, bd. dirs. 1993—99), Columbus Athletic Club, Heritage Club (Houston), Commerce Club (Atlanta), Lincolnshire Fields Country Club (Champaign), Univ. Club (Chgo.), Beta Gamma Sigma, Phi Kappa Phi. Office: Ga State U Coll Bus Adminstrn Univ Plaza Atlanta GA 30303-3083 also: 3892 Byrnwyck Pl NE Atlanta GA 30319-1654

HOGAN, MARK T., automotive executive; b. Chgo., May 15, 1951; BSBA in Fin., U. Ill., 1973; MBA, Harvard U., 1977. Factory analyst, electro-motive divsn. GM Corp., Chgo., 1973—77, fin. staff Detroit, 1977—80, sr. adminstr. fisher body divsn. through dir., treas. office, 1981—84, group dir., pub. affairs staff Chevrolet-Pontiac-GM Can. group, 1984—86; gen. mgr., comptr. New United Motor Mfg., Inc., 1986—88; group dir., bus. planning truck and bus group GM Corp., Detroit, 1988—92, exec. dir., planning N.Am. ops., 1992; pres., mng. dir. GM do Brasil, 1992—97; gen. mgr., N.Am. car group, small car ops. GM Corp., Detroit, 1997—98; group v.p. through pres. e-GM, Detroit, 1999—2002; group v.p., advanced vehicle devel. GM Corp., 2002; pres. Magna Internat. Inc., 2004; lead gen. mgr. exec. The Vehicle Prodn. Group LLC, pres., CEO. Fellow, GM. Office: The Vehicle Production Group LLC 1395 Brickell Ave Miami FL 33131 Office Phone: 786-425-1505.

HOGLUND, FORREST EUGENE, retired petroleum company executive; b. Lawrence, Kans., July 1, 1933; s. Roy A. and Edna M. (McMichael) H.; m. Sally Sue Roney, June 19, 1956; children: Kelly M., Shelly L., Kristan K. BS in Mech. Engring, U. Kans., 1956. With Exxon Corp., 1957-1977; v.p. ops. Exxon Corp. (Middle East), NYC, 1973-75, v.p. gas, 1976-77; pres., COO Tex. Oil and Gas, Dallas, 1977-83, pres., CEO, 1983-87; dir. USX Corp., Pitts., 1986-87; chmn., CEO EOG Resources, Houston, 1987—99; chmn. Forest Oil, 2003—08; chmn., CEO Arctic Resources, Houston, 1999—2004, SeaOne Maritime Corp., Houston, 2004—; CEO SeaOne Corp. Former chmn. bd. visitors Univ. Cancer Found.--M.D. Anderson; former chmn. Houston Mus. Natural Sci. With C.E., U.S. Army, 1957-58. Mem. Am. Petroleum Inst., AIME, Soc. Petroleum Engrs., Ind. Petroleum Assn. Am., Tex. Ind. Producers and Royalty Assn., Petroleum Club, Dallas Country Club, River Oaks Country Club, Tau Beta Pi, Pi Tau Sigma, Sigma Tau, Omicron Delta Kappa. Office: Hoglund Interests 5910 N Central Expressway Ste 250 Dallas TX 75206 Office Phone: 214-987-4924.

HOGUE, CAROL JANE ROWLAND, epidemiologist, educator; b. Springfield, Mo., Dec. 11, 1945; d. Perry Albright and Lois Virginia (Spencer) Rowland; m. L. Lynn Hogue, May 28, 1966; 1 child, Elizabeth Rowland. AB summa cum laude, William Jewell Coll., Liberty, Mo., 1966; MPH, U. N.C., 1971, PhD, 1973. From rsch. assoc. to asst. prof. U. N.C. Sch. Pub. Health, Chapel Hill, 1969-77; asst./assoc. prof., dir. epidemiology prog. divsn. biometry U. Ark. for Med. Scis., Little Rock, 1977-82; br. chief pregnancy epidemiology br. Ctrs. Disease Control, Atlanta, 1983-88, dir. divsn. reproductive health, 1988-92; Terry prof. maternal and child health, prof. epidemiology Rollins Sch. Pub. Health, Emory U., Atlanta, 1992—. Cons. FDA, Washington, 1978-80, EPA, Washington, 1980-81; vis. scientist Ctrs. Disease Control, Atlanta, 1982-83; fellow Environ. Health Inst., Pittsfield, Mass., 1990-97; mem. com. on unintended pregnancy Inst. Medicine, 1994-96; mem. regional adv. panel human reprodn. program WHO, 1991-2000, chmn., 1997-2000, mem. sci. tech. adv. group, 1998-2000. Contbr. articles to profl. jours., chpts. to books. Mem. nat. perinatal health promotion com. March of Dimes, White Plains, N.Y., 1990-93; priority one adv. coun. Kiwanis Internat., 1990-91. Fellow Am. Coll. Epidemiology (pres., 2002-03); mem. Soc. Epidemiologic Rsch. (pres. 1988-89), Am. Epidemiological Soc., Am. Pub. Health Assn. (program devel. bd. 1976-78), Population Assn. Am., Internat. Epidemiol. Assn., Nat. Med. Com., Planned Parenthood Fedn. Am. Democrat. Episcopalian. Avocations: sailing, hiking, reading. Office: 1518 Clifton Rd NE Atlanta GA 30322-4201 Home Phone: 404-876-6067; Office Phone: 404-727-8095. E-mail: chogue@sph.emory.edu.

HOGUE, W. DENNIS, real estate company executive; BS in Psychology, Fla. State U., 1974. V.p., sales E3 Corp., 1996—97, pres., N.Am., 1997—99, pres., CEO, 1999—2000; CEO Global Food Exch., 2001—02; pres., CEO Mercari Technologies Inc., 2002—03; CEO Datatrac Corp., 2003—05, Hogue Enterprises, Inc., 2005—; pres. American Durahomes, 2007—. Bd. dirs. Am. Software, Inc., 2001—. Office: American Durahomes Ste 1940 3 Ravinia Dr Atlanta GA 30346-2118 Office Phone: 678-990-4911.

HOHLT, RICHARD FREDERICK, lobbyist; b. Indpls., Dec. 4, 1947; s. Edgar F. and Mabel F. Hohlt; m. Deborah Lee Messick, Sept. 25, 1993. BS, Milliken U., 1970. Internal auditor, systems analyst, Indpls.; asst. to treasurer Marion County, Indpls.; asst. to Mayor Richard G. Lugar City of Indpls., 1975—76; dep. campaign mgr. Richard Lugar for Senate Com., 1976—77; exec. asst. to US Senator Richard G. Lugar US Senate, 1977—80; asst. v.p., govt. affairs US League Savings Institutions, 1980—82, v.p., govt. affairs, 1982—84, sr. v.p., govt. affairs, 1984—90; pres. Hohlt & Associates, Alexandria, Va., 1990—. Mem. Peace Corps. Adv. Coun., 1983—84; mem. bd. dirs. overseas Pvt. Investment Corp., 1985—88, Student Loan Mktg. Assn., 1990—94. Served in USAF Res., 1970—76.

HOKE, SHEILA WILDER, retired librarian; b. Greensboro, NC; d. Herbert Bruce Wilder and Virginia Dare (Caylor) Wilder-Dell; m. Robert Edward Hoke, Nov. 22, 1958 (dec.); children: Raymond Fellow, Philip Wilder. Student, Montclair Coll., 1948; BA in History, U. Kans., 1950, postgrad., 1951, BS in Edn., 1952; postgrad., John Hopkins U., 1955; MLS, U. Wis., 1955; MS in Edn., Southwestern Okla. State U., 1977; postgrad., Johns Hopkins U., Montclair State Coll. Tchr. history Fredonia (Kans.) High Sch., 1952-54; student asst. U. Wis., Madison, 1954-55; children's libr. BR Enoch Pratt Libr., Balt., 1955-58; libr. dir. U.S. Army Spl. Svcs., Bavaria, Fed. Republic Germany, 1958-59; libr. U.S. Army Dependent Schs., Straubing, Fed. Republic Germany, 1959-60; cataloger Southwestern Okla. State U. Libr., Weatherford, 1963-69, libr. dir., 1969-93; ret., 1993. Mem. spl. projects com. Okla. Dept. Edn., 1974, adv. com. Okla. State Regents Libr., 1975-77. Mem. Okla. State Regents for Higher Edn. Libr. Networking, 1989-93; vol. with children Agape Med. Clinic; reading tutor to 1st grade student Weatherford Pub. Schs.; vol. helper for home-bound; active sr. citizens groups., student asst. Med. Libr., U Wis. Named Vol. of Yr., Pioneer Citizens Weatherford Group, 2010. Mem. AAUW (pres., state bd. dirs. 1980, Weatherford br. 1981-83), Nat. Assn. Ret. Fed. Employees, Okla. Libr. Assn. (chmn. tech. svcs. divsn. 1969-70, chmn. coll. and univ. divsn. 1972-73, chmn. adminstrs. workshop 1973, chmn. libr. edn. divsn. 1975-76, chmn. recruitment com. 1978, archives com. 1980), Okla. Ret. Tchrs. Assn., Weatherford C. of C. (edn. com. 1974-75, cert. meritorious achievement from Gov. Nigh 1985), Custer County Hist. Soc., western Okla. Hist. Soc., Higher Edn. Alumni Coun. Okla., Delta Kappa Gamma (pres. Lambda chpt. 1980-82), Phi Alpha theta, Kappa Kappa Iota (pres. Lambda chpt. 1984-85, 2005-06). Republican. Baptist. Avocation: travel. Personal E-mail: swhoke@att.net.

HOLBERT, JIM, pilot, retired military officer; b. Knoxville, Tenn., July 10, 1952; m. Cindy Holbert; 3 children. B, U. Tenn., 1975. Cert. secondary sch. tchr. in sci. and math. Part-time laborer, 1970—75; inf. and aviation staff officer US Army, 1975—81; aviator, staff officer Army NG, 1981—82, US Coast Guard, 1982—96; profl. pilot, 1996—. Independent. Office: 189 Clay Lucas Dr London KY 40744 Office Phone: 606-682-9337. Business E-Mail: contact@jimholbert2008.com.

HOLCOM, KAREN J., corporate financial executive; BS in Acctg., Clemson U., 1991; Exec. MBA, Ga. State U. CPA. Various fin. acctg., reporting functions Nat. Svc. Industries, Inc., 1998; fin mgmt. positions through sr. v.p., fin. Acuity Brands, Inc., 1998—, interim CFO, 2004—05, v.p., contr., 2004—06; sr. v.p., fin Acuity Brands Lighting, Inc., 2006—. Office: Acuity Brands Inc Ste 2400 1170 Peachtree St NE Atlanta GA 30309-7676 Office Phone: 404-853-1400. Office Fax: 404-853-1411.

HOLCOMB, SCOTT, state legislator; b. Nov. 02; m. Kathleen Holcomb; children: Carter, Kirsten. BA, U. Conn.; JD, W.Va. U. Atty. Sutherland Absill & Brennan, LLP; gen. counsel J.P. Turner & Co., LLC, 2007—11; atty. The Holcomb Law Firm, LLC, 2011—; mem. Dist. 82 Ga. House of Representatives, 2011—. Part time tchr. Ga. Inst. Tech. Sam Nunn Sch. Internat. Affairs. Capt., JAG US Army. Democrat. Avocations: swimming, bicycling, running. Office: 2306 Briarcliff Commons NE Atlanta GA 30345 also: Ga House of Reps 511 Coverdell Legis Office Bldg Atlanta GA 30334 Office Phone: 404-656-6372. Business E-Mail: scott@repscottholcomb.com.

HOLCOMB, STEPHEN NORRIS, music educator; b. Waco, Tex., June 7, 1952; s. Frank Norris and Mae Jean Holcomb; m. Patricia Lyster, Jan. 13, 1973; children: Rachel Ann Simpson, Patrick Stephen. MusB in Edn., Baylor U., Waco, 1974; MusM, Baylor U., 1981; PhD in Musical Arts, Southwestern Bapt. Theol. Sem., Ft. Worth, 1993. Min. of music Highland Bapt. Ch., Waco, 1974—88; prof. music Dallas Bapt. U., 1988—; min. of music Pk. Cities Bapt. Ch., Dallas, 2003—04. Composer: (choral anthems) Love Came Down at Christmas, Holy is the Lord, Let Us Come Before the Lord. Named Piper Outstanding Prof., Dallas Bapt. U., 2001; named one of Outstanding Young Men of Am., 1989. Mem.: Music Educators Nat. Conf., Tex. Music Educators Assn., Tex. Choral Dirs. Assn., Am. Choral Dirs. Assn. Office: Dallas Baptist Univ 3000 Mountain Creek Pky Dallas TX 75211

HOLCOMBE, RANDALL GREGORY, economics professor; b. Bridgeport, Conn., June 4, 1950; s. Lynn Montanye Holcombe and Gloria Gabriel (Rita) Ledbetter; m. Lora Hunt Pritchett, June 18, 1983. BS, U. Fla., 1972; MA, Va. Tech., 1974, PhD, 1976. Asst. prof. Tex. A&M U., College Station, 1975-77; prof. Auburn (Ala.) U., 1977-88, Fla. State U., Tallahassee, 1988—. Sr. fellow James Madison Inst., Tallahassee, 2004—, mem. rsch. adv. com., 1987-2004, chmn., 1991-2004; mem. editl. bd., Rev. Austrian Econs., 1987-97, 2013-, Pub. Fin. Rev., 1995-2003, Quar. Jour. Austrian Econs., 1998—; adj. scholar Ludwig Von Mises Inst., 1982-; mem. Fla. Gov.'s Coun. Econ. Advisors, 2000-06; contbg. editor Independent Rev., 2004—. Author: Public Finance and the Political Process, 1983, An Economic Analysis of Democracy, 1985, Economic Models and Methodology, 1989, The Economic Foundations of Government, 1994, Public Policy and the Quality of Life, 1995, Public Finance: Government Revenues and Expenditures in the United States Economy, 1996, (with R. Sobel) Growth and Variability in State Tax Revenue, 1997, Writing Off Ideas, 2000, From Liberty to Democracy: The Transformation of American Government, 2002, Public Sector Economics, 2007, Entrepreneurship and Economic Progress, 2006, Producing Prosperity, 2013; Liberalism and Cronyism, 2013; The Austrian School of Economics, 2014; book rev. editor Pub. Choice, 2005-2012, mem. editl. bd., 2004—; contbr. articles to profl. jours. Mem. Fla. Gov. Coun. Econ. Adv., 2000—06. Scaife Found. fellow, 1972-73, H.B. Earhart Found. fellow, 1973-75; research grantee Earhart Found., 1979-80, 83, 89, 90, 98. Mem. Am. Econ. Assn., Pub. Choice Soc. (pres. 2006—08), So. Econ. Assn., Soc. Devel. Austrian Econs. (pres. 2007). Home: 3514 Limerick Dr Tallahassee FL 32309-3139 Office: Fla State U Dept Econs Tallahassee FL 32306 Business E-Mail: holcombe@fsu.edu.

HOLDEN, E. WAYNE, research and development company executive, psychologist; PhD. Assoc. prof. & dir. pediatric psychology, dept. pediat. U. Md. Sch. Medicine; v.p., sr. v.p. & pres. ORC Macro, 1998—2005; exec. v.p. social & statis. sciences RTI Internat., Research Triangle Pk., NC, 2005—12, pres., CEO, 2012—. Adj. prof., dept. psychiatry & behavioral sciences Duke U. Sch. Medicine, 2006—; bd. dir. Ziptronix, Inc. Contbr. chapters to books, articles to profl. jours. Bd. dirs. NC Methodist Home Children, Inst. for Ages, Sarasota, Fla.; bd. advisors Emily Krzyzewski Ctr.; trustee Triangle U. Ctr. Advanced Studies, Inc. Fellow: American Psychol. Assn. Office: RTI International 3040 E Cornwallis Rd PO Box 12194 Research Triangle Park NC 27709-2194+

HOLDEN, JOHN WILLIAM, III, utilities executive; b. Atlanta, Feb. 16, 1961; s. John William H. Jr. and Ann Morris; m. Donna G., Aug. 15, 1992; children: Carson Leigh, Mary Reeves. BS in Economics and Political Sci., Vanderbilt U., 1983; MBA, Emory U., 1985. Mgr., fin. analysis So. Co. Svcs., Inc., Atlanta, 1989—92, dir., corp. fin., 1992—94; v.p., bus. devel., Asia-Pacific region Mirant Corp., Atlanta, 1994—96, v.p., ops. & bus. devel., S.Am., 1996—99, v.p., treas., 1999—2001, sr. v.p., 2002—, CFO, 2009—10; exec. v.p., CFO GeOn Energy (merger of Reliant & Mirant Corp.), 2011—. Office: GeOn Energy 1000 Main St Houston TX 77002 Office Phone: 678-579-5000. Business E-Mail: john.holden@mirant.com.

HOLDEN, MELVIN LEE, mayor-president, Baton Rouge, Louisiana; b. New Orleans, La, Aug. 12, 1952; m. Lois Holden; children: Melvin II, Angela, Monique, Myron, Brian Michael. BA in Journalism, La. State U., Baton Rouge, 1974; MA in Journalism, Southern U., Baton Rouge, 1982; JD, Southern U. Sch. Law, 1985; D in Pub. Policy (hon.), Southern U. New dir. WXOK Radio, Baton Rouge, 1975—77; reporter WWL Radio, New Orleans, 1977—78, WBRZ Channel 2, Baton Rouge, 1978—79; pub. relations specialist Census Bur., 1980; pub. info. officer Baton Rouge City Police, La., 1981—83; councilman, Dist. 2 City of Baton Rouge, 1984—88; legal clerk La. Dept. Labor Office Workers' Compensation, Baton Rouge, 1986—87; mem. La. State Senate from Dist. 63, 1988—2001, La. State Senate from Dist. 15, 2003—04; atty. Melvin Holden & Assocs.; mayor-pres. City of Baton Rouge, La., 2005—. Adj. prof. law Southern U. Sch. Law, Baton Rouge, 1991—. Mem. Environ. & Joint Capital Outlay Com., Gt. Baton Rouge Airport Commn., Fedn. Fleet Task Force; chair, mem. Nat. League of Cities Coun. for Youth, Edn. and Families, 2007; mem. City Parish Capital Improvement Com. Recipient UGS Innovative Leadership award, Brown Pelican award, Environmental Legislators of Louisiana, Nat. Environ. Justice Adv. Coun. Svc. award, U.S. Environ. Protection Agency & Office of Environ. Justice, 2002, Dedicated Elected Official award, Scotland HS Alumni Assn., 2002, Fleur de Lis Leadership award in Healthcare, 2002, Econ. Devel. Champion award, Econ. Devel. Partnership, 2003, Friend of Sch. Psychology award, La. Sch. of Psychol. Assn., 2003, Senator of Yr. award, La. Fedn. of Teachers, 2003, Meritorious Svc. award, Alpha Phi Alpha Frat., 2003, Legis. Yr. Award, Assn. Retarded Citzens La., 2003, La. Cmty. & Technical Coll. System award, 2003, Cmty. Against Drugs & Violence, Inc. award, 2003, Disting. Svc. award, Phi Beta Sigma Fraternity, Inc. Gulf Coast Region, 2004, Outstanding Svc. award Track & Field, Southern U., 2004, Friend of Edn. award, La. Fedn. Teachers, 2004, Blues Found. Slim Harpo award-Blue Amb., 2005, Network Legend award, 2005, Nat. Conf. Black Mayors Valiant award for Balanced Govt., 2006, 225 Mag. Best of Awards-Best Politician, 2006, Nat. Conf. Black Mayors Valiant award for Balanced Govt., 2006, UGS Innovative Leadership award, 2006, award winner- academic distinction fund, 2006, Am. Planning Assn., La. Chpt. Disting. Leadership award, 2006, Military Order of the Purple Heart Disting. Svc. award, 2007, Quality of Life award for Outstanding Contributions, Community and Public Service, Baton Rouge Growth Coalition, 2007, La. Emergency Preparedness Dedication award, 2007, BREC Trailblazer award, 2007, Internat. Black Broadcasters Assn. Leadership award, 2007, Brotherhood / Sisterhood award, 2007, Rear Admiral Isaac C. Kidd Meritorious Svc. award, 2007, Baton Rouge Growth Coalition, Quality of Life award for Outstanding Contributions, Cmty. and Pub. Svc., 2007, Meritorious Svc. award, Internat. Union of Police Assns., 2008, Centikor Cmty. award, 2008, Lambda Alpha Chapter, Omega Psi Phi Fraternity Citizen of Yr. award, 2008, Internat. Union Police Associations Meritorious Svc. award; named Outstanding Alumni of Century, Southern U., Outstanding Legislator, Sierra Club; named to La. State U. Alumni Hall of Distinction, La. State U. Manship Sch. Comm. Hall of Fame, Southern U. Law Ctr. Hall of Fame, La. Justice Hall of Fame, La. Polit. Hall of Fame, La. 4-H Hall of Fame. Mem.: La. Trial Lawyers, Am. & Nat. Bar Assn. Democrat. Baptist. Achievements include becoming the first African-American Mayor-President in parish of East Baton Rouge history on January 1, 2005. Office: Off of the Mayor 222 Saint Louis St Third Fl Baton Rouge LA 70802 Office Phone: 225-389-3100. Office Fax: 225-389-5203. Business E-Mail: mayor@brgov.com.*

HOLDER, ANGELA RODDEY, retired law educator; b. Rock Hill, SC, Mar. 13, 1938; d. John T. and Angela M. (Fisher) Roddey; 1 child, John Thomas Roddey Holder. Student, Radcliffe Coll., 1955-56; BA, Newcomb Coll., 1958; postgrad., Faculty of Law-King's Coll., London, 1957-58; JD, Tulane U., New Orleans, 1960; LLM, Yale U., New Haven, Conn., 1975. Bar: La. 1961, S.C. 1960, Conn. 1981. Counsel Roddey, Sumwalt & Carpenter, Rock Hill, SC, 1960-91; atty. criminal div. New Orleans Legal Aid Bur., 1961-62; counsel York County Family Ct., SC, 1962-64; asst. prof. polit. sci. Winthrop Coll., Rock Hill, 1964-74; research assoc. Yale U. Law Sch., 1975-77, exec. dir. program in law, sci. and medicine, 1976-77; lectr. dept. pediatrics Yale U. Sch. Medicine, 1975-77, asst. clin. prof. pediatrics and law, 1977-79, assoc. clin. prof., 1979-83, clin. prof., 1983-2001; prof. practice of med. ethics Duke U. Med. Ctr., Durham, NC, 2001—07, prof. emerita med. ethics and humanities, 2007—09. Trustee Am. Bd. Pediatrics, 2003—07; mem. com. on pediat. palliative care Inst. Medicine, 2001—02, mem. com. on clin. rsch. with children, 2002—04. Author: The Meaning of the Constitution, 1968, 3d edit., 1997, Medical Malpractice Law, 1975, 2d edit. 1978, Legal Issues in Pediatrics and Adolescent Medicine, 1977, 3d edit., 1997; contbg. editor: Prism mag., AMA; mem. editl. bd.: IRB, 1976-2000, Medicine and HealthCare, 1978-2000, Jour. Philosophy and Medicine; contbr. articles to profl. jours. Mem. Rock Hill Sch. Bd., 1967—68; chmn. bd. dirs. Family Planning Clinic, 1970—73; bd. trustees Ednl. Commn. for Fgn. Med. Grads., 1990—97, exec. com., 1997; bd. dir. Conn. Planned Parenthood, 1993—99, exec. com., 1996—99; mem. lawyers' rev. group Health Care Task Force, The White House, 1993; bd. trustees Cushing/Whitney Med. Libr. at Yale U., 1996—2001; ethics com. Leeway AIDS Hospice, New Haven, 1996—2001; alumnae bd. visitors Nat. Cathedral Sch., Washington, 2000—; cons. Artificial Reproductive Techs. Com., Ct. Ho. of Reps.; mem. adv. bd., grad. health programs Sarah Lawrence Coll., 2004—. Mem. Conn. Bar Assn., S.C. Bar Assn. (medico-legal com. 1973—), La. Bar Assn., New Haven County Bar Assn., Am. Soc. Law and Medicine (treas. 1981-83, sec. 1983-85, pres. 1986-88, bd. dirs. 1977-91). Democrat. Episcopalian. Home: 9210 Ravenwing Dr Charlotte NC 28262-2406 Home Phone: 919-419-1594. Business E-Mail: angela.holder@duke.edu.

HOLDER, DOUG, state legislator; b. Marietta, Ga., Dec. 7, 1966; m. Shannon Holder; children: Channing, Chase. BS in Polit. Sci., Mid. Tenn. State U., Murfreesboro, 1990. Real estate broker; mem. Dist. 70 Fla. House of Reps., Tallahassee, 2006—, vice chair criminal and civil justice policy coun., mem. criminal and civil justice appropriations com., fin. and tax coun., govtl. affairs policy com., pub. safety and domestic security policy com. Mem. NRA (life), Fla. Assn. Realtors, Nat. Assn. Realtors, Sarasota Assn. Realtors, Sarasota C. of C. (trustee). Republican. Episcopalian. Office: 8486 S Tamiami Trail Sarasota FL 34238-2953 also: 410 House Office Bldg 402 S Monroe St Tallahassee FL 32399-1300 Office Phone: 941-918-4028, 850-488-1171.

HOLDER, JANICE MARIE, state supreme court justice; b. Canonsburg, Pa., Aug. 29, 1949; d. Louis V. and Sylvia (Abraham) H.; m. George W. Loveland II, June 5, 1976 (div. Mar. 1987). Student, Allegheny Coll., 1967-68, Sorbonne, 1970; BS summa cum laude, U. Pitts., 1971; JD, Duquesne U., 1975. Bar: Pa. 1975, US Supreme Ct. 1983, Tenn. 1979, DC 1988. Sr. law clk. to chief judge U.S. Dist. Ct. for Western Dist. Pa., Pitts., 1975-77; assoc. Catalano & Catalano, P.C., Pitts., 1977-79, Holt, Batchelor, Spicer & Ryan, Memphis, 1980-82; pvt. practice Memphis, 1982—87; assoc. James S. Cox & Assocs., Memphis, 1987-89; pvt. practice law Memphis, 1989-90; judge 30th Jud. Dist., Memphis, 1990-96; justice Tenn. Supreme Ct., 1996—, chief justice, 2008—10. Solicitor Borough of McDonald (Pa.), 1978-79. Bd. dirs. Alliance for Blind and Visually Impaired, Memphis, 1985—94, Midtown Mental Health Ctr., 1995—97; trustee Memphis Bot. Garden Found., 1995—2002; mem. state coordinating coun. Tenn. Task Force Against Domestic Violence, 1994—96. Recipient W.J. Michael Cody Pro Bono Attorney of Yr. award, Memphis Area Legal Svcs., 2009. Fellow: Tenn. Bar Found. (trustee 1995—99); mem.: ABA, Southeastern Region Am. Bd. Trial Advs. (named Jurist of Yr. 2009), Coalition Mediation Awareness Tenn. (Grayfred Gray Pub. Svc. Mediation award 2008), Tenn. Trial Judges Assn. (exec. com. 1994—96), Tenn. Lawyers' Assn. for Women (founding mem.), Memphis Trial Lawyers Assn. (bd. dirs. 1988—90), Am. Inns Ct., Tenn. Jud. Conf. (treas. 1993—94, exec. com. 1993—96), Assn. for Women Attys. (treas. 1989, v.p. 1991, Marion Griffin-Frances Loring award 1999), Memphis Bar Assn. (bd. dirs. 1986—87, editor Memphis Bar Forum 1987—91, sec. 1993, bd. dirs. 1993—94, editor Memphis Bar Forum 1993—94, treas. 1994, Sam A. Myar award 1990, Judge of Yr. divorce and family law sect. 1992, Chancellor Charles A. Rond award Outstanding Jurist 1992), Tenn. Bar Assn., Am. Bar Found. Office: Tennessee Supreme Court 50 Peabody Pl Ste 209 Memphis TN 38103-3665*

HOLDING, FRANK B., JR., board member, bank executive; BA in Bus., U. NC, Chapel Hill, 1982; MBA, U. Pa., 1986. Chief adminstrv. officer First Citizens Bank & Trust Co., area exec. Raleigh, NC, 1992—94, pres., 1994—2008, pres., CEO, 2008—09, chmn., pres., CEO, 2009—; CEO IronStone Bank, chmn., CEO, 2009—; chief adminstrv. officer First Citizens Bancshares, Inc., pres., 1994—2009, chmn., CEO, 2008—. Bd. dirs. Mount Olive Pickle Co., First Citizens BancShares Inc., 1993—, NC Natural Gas (divsn. Piedmont Natural Gas), 1995—, Piedmont Natural Gas Co., 2003—. Dir. The Bapt. Retirement Homes of NC, Triangle Fellowship Christian Athletes; trustee Providence Bapt. Church, Raleigh; past dir. Mecklenburg chpt. Am. Heart Assn; chmn. Mecklenburg chpt. NC Vet. Med. Found., Econ. Devel. Coun. of the Charlotte C. of C.; mem. exec. com. Greater Raleigh C. of C.; dir. Inst. for Defense & Bus., BlueCross BlueShield NC; past dir. Charlotte Mchts. Assn., NC Global Transpark Authority, Wake Med. Ctr., Raleigh, WTVI Pub. Broadcasting Authority; past chmn. WTVI Auction; past mem. cmty. adv. coun. Jr. League of Raleigh. Office: First Citizens Bancshares 4300 Six Forks Rd Raleigh NC 27609 Office Phone: 919-716-7000. Office Fax: 919-716-7074. Business E-Mail: frank.holding@firstcitizens.com.

HOLDING, GEORGE E.B. (GEORGE EDWARD BELL HOLDING), United States Representative from North Carolina, former federal prosecutor; b. Raleigh, NC, Apr. 17, 1968; m. Lucy E. Herriott; children: Beatrice Elizabeth, Alice Margaret, Louisa Maggie. BA in Classical Studies with honors, Wake Forest U., 1991; JD, Wake Forest U. Sch. Law, 1996. Law clk. to Hon. Terrence Boyle US Dist. Ct. (eastern dist.) NC, 1996—97; assoc. Kilpatrick Stockton LLP, Raleigh, NC, 1997—98; legislative counsel to Senator Jesse Helms US Senate, 1999—2001; atty. Maupin Taylor, Raleigh, 2001—02; first asst. US atty. (eastern dist.) NC US Dept. Justice, 2002—06, US atty., 2006—11; mem. US Congress from 13th NC Dist., Washington, 2013—, US House Fgn. Affairs Com., 2013—, US House Judiciary Com., 2013—. Republican. Southern Baptist. Office: US House of Representatives 507 Cannon House Office Bldg Washington DC 20515 also: 3725 National Dr Ste 101 Raleigh NC 27612 Office Phone: 202-225-3032, 919-782-4400. Office Fax: 919-782-4490.*

HOLDITCH, STEPHEN ALLEN, petroleum engineering educator, consultant; b. Corsicana, Tex., Oct. 20, 1946; s. Damon and Marjorie Elenor (Stephens) H.; m. Ann Friddle, Jan.9, 1971; children: Katie Jean Holditch Rowe, Abbie Diane Holditch Walsh. BS in Petroleum Engring., Tex. A&M U., 1969, MS in Petroleum Engring., 1970, PhD in Petroleum Engring., 1976. Registered profl. engr., Tex. Engr. Pan Am. Petroleum Corp., Tyler, Tex., 1968-69; prodn. engr. Shell Oil Co., New Orleans, 1970-74; consulting engr. pvt. practice, College Station, Tex., 1974-76; from asst. prof. to prof. Tex. A&M U., College Station, 1976—; pres. S.A. Holditch & Assocs., College Station, 1977—97. Bd. dirs. Wells Fargo, Bryan/College Station, Tex. Author: (with others) Recent Advances in Hydraulic Fracturing, 1989; contbr. numerous articles to profl. jours.; collaborated on over 100 presentations to profl. groups. 2d lt. U.S. Army, 1971, res., 1971-77. Elected to Nat. Acad. Engring., 1995; appointed to Shell Disting. Chair in Petroleum Engring., Tex. A&M U., 1983-87; recipient Lester C. Uren award Soc. Petroleum Engrs., 1995. Mem. Soc. Petroleum Engrs. (pres. 2002, numerous coms. 1974— chmn. unconventional gas tech. symposium, 1986, gas tech. symposium, 1988, reprint series com. 1992-93; editor Coalbed Methane reprint, 1990-91, Disting. Svc. award for petroleum engring. faculty 1981, Disting. Lectr. 1982-83, Disting. Mem. 1989, Lester C. Uren award 1994), Am. Assn. Petroleum Geologists, Soc. Profl. Well Log Analysts, Soc. Petroleum Evaluation Engrs., Pi Epsilon Tau, Sigma Xi. Republican. Methodist. Avocations: golf, hunting, fishing. Office: Texas A&M University Petroleum Engineering 3116 TAMU College Station TX 77843 Business E-Mail: holditch@tamu.edu.

HOLGORSEN, DANA, college football coach; b. June 21, 1971; children: McClayne, Logan, Karlyn. B, Iowa Wesleyan Coll., Mount Pleasant, 1993; M in Health and Phys. Edn., Valdosta State U., Ga., 1995. Quarterbacks, wide receivers, spl. teams coach Valdosta State U. Blazers, 1993—95, Miss. Coll. Choctaws, 1996—98; quarterbacks, wide receivers coach Wingate U. Bulldogs, 1999; inside receivers coach Tex. Tech U. Red Raiders, 2000—04, co-offensive coord., 2005—06, offensive coord., quarterbacks coach, 2006—07, U. Houston Cougars, 2008—09, Okla. State U. Cowboys, 2010; offensive coord., quarterbacks coach, head coach W.Va. U. Mountaineers, 2011—. Office: West Va University Football c/o Dept Athletics PO Box 0877 Morgantown WV 26507-0877 Office Phone: 304-293-4194.

HOLIFIELD, BROOKS E., history professor; BA, Hendrix Coll., Conway, Ark., 1963, Dlitt, 1985; BD, Yale U., New Haven, 1966, PhD, 1970. Ordained elder The United Methodist Church. Sr. fellow ctr. for the study of law and religion Emory Univ., prof. Am. church history Candler Sch. of Theology. Author: A History of Pastoral Care in America, 1983, Health and Medicine in the Methodist Tradition, 1986, Theology in America: Christian Thought from the Age of the Puritans to the Civil War, 2003, Era of Persuasion: American Thought and Culture, 2004, God's Ambassadors: A History of the Christian Clergy in America, 2007, numerous others. Recipient Univ. Scholar-Tchr. award, Emory Univ., 2010; named Outstanding Theological Educator, Assn. Theol. Schs. Fellow: Am. Acad. Arts & Sciences. Office: Emory University Candler School of Theology 1531 Dickey Dr Atlanta GA 30322 Office Phone: 404-727-6319. Office Fax: 404-727-2494.

HOLIFIELD, E. BROOKS, theology educator emeritus; b. Little Rock, Jan. 5, 1942; s. E. J. and Irene (French) H.; m. Vicky Lee Thompson, June 22, 1963; children: Erin, Ryan. BA, Hendrix Coll., 1963, DLitt (hon.), 1985; BD, Yale U., 1966, MA, 1968, PhD, 1970. Asst. prof. Candler Sch. Theology, Emory U., Atlanta, 1970-75, assoc. prof., 1975-80, prof., 1980-83, Charles Howard Candler prof., 1983—. Author: The Covenant Sealed, 1974, The Gentlemen Theologians, 1978, A History of Pastoral Care in America, 1983, Health and Medicine in the Methodist Tradition, 1986, Era of Persuasion, 1989, Theology in America, 2003, God's Ambassadors: A History of the Christian Clergy in America, 2007. NEH fellow, 1976, 83, 91. Fellow. AAAS; mem. Am. Soc. Ch. History. Democrat. Methodist. Home: 3214 Bolero Pass Atlanta GA 30341-5765 E-mail: eholifi@emory.edu.

HOLIFIELD, MARK, retail executive; BBA with honors, U. Tex., Austin; MBA, Baylor U. Various logistics positions H-E-B Grocery Co., 1977—86; mem. staff, logistics through traffic mgr. Frito-Lay Inc., 1986—88; supply chain sys. positions, including dir., consulting projects Dallas Sys. Corp., 1988—94; arch. Office Depot, Inc., Delray Beach, dir., transp. & traffic, 1994—96, v.p., transp. & logistics, 1996—97, sr. v.p., supply chain mgmt., 1997—2003, exec. v.p., supply chain, 2003—06; sr. v.p., global supply chain Home Depot, Inc., 2006—. Office: The Home Depot Inc 2455 Paces Ferry Rd NW Atlanta GA 30339-4024 Office Phone: 770-433-8211. Office Fax: 770-384-2356. Business E-Mail: mark_holifield@homedepot.com.

HOLLAND, BRUCE, state legislator; Student in chem. engring., U. Ark., Fayetteville. Cattleman and rancher, Ark.; mem. Dist. 6 Ark. State Senate, 2011—. Former chmn. Farm Svc. Agency County Com.; former pres. Sebastian County Farm Bur.; mem. Van Buren Farmers Co-op; mem. governance coun. Land O' Lakes Corp. Mem. Sebastian County Fair Bd. & Assn.; bd. mem. Sebastian County Hist. Soc. Mem.: NRA, Nat. Wild. Turkey Fedn. Republican. Mailing: PO Box 2387 Greenwood AR 72936 Office Phone: 479-996-4520. Business E-Mail: bruce.holland@senate.ar.gov.

HOLLAND, COREY N., state legislator; b. Duncan, Okla., Jan. 1, 1970; m. Kim Holland; children: Chisholm, Walker. B, Okla. Bapt. U. Educator Marlow pub. schs., 1994—; mem. Dist. 51 Okla. House of Representatives, 2008—. Deacon First Bapt. Ch., Marlow. Republican. Baptist. Office: 2300 N Lincoln Blvd Rm 537 Oklahoma City OK 73105 Home: 14 NW Millcreek Rd Lawton OK 73505-9548 Office Phone: 405-557-7405. Business E-Mail: corey.holland@okhouse.gov.

HOLLAND, DANIEL STEPHEN (STEVE), state legislator; b. Tupelo, Miss., Nov. 5, 1955; m. Gloria Temple; children: Ashley, Emily, McKinley. Former staff aide to congressman Jamie Whitten & Senator Thad Cochran; mem. Dist. 16 Miss. House of Reps., 1984—, chair pub. health and human svcs. com., mem. appropriations com., congl. redistricting com., judiciary A com., judiciary en banc com., legis. budget com., legis. reapportionment com., mem. Medicaid com.; dir. Regional Rehab. Ctr. & Spl. Olympics; co-owner Lee Mem. Funeral Home; farmer. Mem.: Shriner, Tombigbee Elec. Power Assn., Miss. Soybean Assn., Farm Bur., Cmty. Devel. Found., Miss. Funeral Dir. Assn., Civitan Club, Verona Mason Lodge. Democrat. United Methodist. Mailing: PO Box 2 Plantersville MS 38862 Office Phone: 601-359-3320. Business E-Mail: sholland@house.ms.gov.

HOLLAND, GEORGE EDISON, JR., (ED), lawyer, utilities executive; b. Rutherfordton, NC, Dec. 2, 1952; m. Elizabeth (Betsy) Bird; children: Laura E., Caroline S. BA in Polit. Sci., Auburn U., Ala., 1975; JD, U. Va., 1978. Bar: Fla. 1978, US Dist. Ct. (no. dist. Fla.) 1978, US Ct. Appeals (11th cir.) 1981, US Ct. Appeals (5th cir.) 1986, US Ct. Appeals (DC cir.) 1988, US Supreme Ct. 1990. Ptnr., also served as gen. counsel to Gulf Power Beggs & Lane; v.p., corp. counsel concurrently served as system compliance officer Southern Co., subsidiary of Gulf Power, Atlanta, 1992—95, exec. v.p., gen. counsel, corp. sec., also chief compliance officer, 2001—13; v.p. power generation and transmissions, corp. counsel Gulf Power, Pensacola, Fla., 1995—97; pres., CEO Savannah Electric (was merged with Georgia Power in 2007), Savannah, Ga., 1997—2001, Mississippi Power (subsidiary of Southern Co.), Gulfport, Miss., 2013—. Chmn. Energy Ins. Mutual; mem. Gulf Coast Bus. Council; bd. dirs. Miss. Economic Council, Miss. Energy Inst., Miss. Partnership for Economic Development; mem., former chmn. legal com. Edison Electric Inst.; former dir. Inst. for Legal Reform, US Chamber of Commerce. Bd. dirs. Georgia Aquarium. Mem.: Escambia-Santa Rosa Bar Assn. (pres. 1987—98), Fla. Bar (mem. adminstrv. law sect.), ABA (mem. pub. utility, communications and transportation law sect.), United Way de Tocqueville Soc. Avocations: golf, boating, hunting. Office: Mississippi Power 2992 W Beach Blvd Gulfport MS 39501*

HOLLAND, GREGORY D., consulting company executive; With McGuire Woods, LLP, Jacksonville, Fla., Coffman, Coleman, Andrews & Grogan, Jacksonville, Fla.; assoc. gen. counsel MPS (Modis Professional Services) Group, Inc. (acquired by Adecco), 1997, v.p., 2001—04, chief legal officer, sec., 2002—, sr. v.p., 2004—. Office: MPS Group Inc 10151 Deerwood Park Blvd Ste 200-400 Jacksonville FL 32256-0557 Office Phone: 904-360-2000.

HOLLAND, JAMES RICHARD, JR., bank executive; b. Conway, Ark., Nov. 22, 1943; s. James R. and D. Mildred Holland; 1 child, Jeff D. BS in Chem. Engring., Okla. State U., 1966; MS in Indsl. Adminstrn., Carnegie-Mellon U., 1969. Assoc. Booz, Allen & Hamilton, Inc., Chgo., 1969-72; v.p. Texas Industries, Inc., Dallas, 1972-77; pres. KSA Industries, Inc., Houston, 1977—80, Western Svcs. Internat., Inc., Ft. Worth, 1980—85; exec. v.p. TGI Friday's, Inc., Dallas, 1985—87, Coast Am. Corp., Denver, 1987—88; chmn., CEO Nedinco, Inc., Houston, 1989—91; pres. Unity Hunt Resources, Inc., Dallas, 1991; pres., CEO Unity Hunt, Inc., 1991—; chmn. Texas Capital Bancshares, Inc., 2008—. Bd. dirs. Placid Oil Co., Dallas, Cryomec, Inc., Anaheim, Calif.; Nat. CineMedia, Inc., 2007-. Author: Information for Marketing Management, 1971. Mem. Leadership Ft. Worth, 1982, Forum Ft. Worth, 1983—; vice chmn. Grad. Sch. Indsl. Adminstrn., Pitts., U. Denver, 1984, allocations United Way, Ft. Worth, 1983; chmn. pension trust 1982-84, investment com. 1984-85, WCNA, Ft. Worth. Mem. Planning Forum. Clubs: Windsor, Shady Oaks, Houston, Tower. Office: Texas Capital Bancshares Inc 2000 McKinney Ave Ste 700 Dallas TX 75201-1985 Office Phone: 214-932-6600. Office Fax: 214-932-6604. Business E-Mail: james.holland@texascapitalbank.com.

HOLLAND, JAMES TULLEY, retired plastics company executive; b. Pikeville, Ky., May 24, 1940; s. Thomas Joseph and Mary Alta (Tulley) Holland; m. Susan Ellen Joy; children: James Christopher, Kathleen Holland Wiesel. BA in Econs., U. Va., 1962; MBA, Am. U., 1969. With br. banking ops. United Va. Bank, Alexandria, 1965-67; with Booz Allen & Hamilton, Washington, 1967-76; treas., chief fin. officer O'Sullivan Corp., Winchester, Va., 1976-84, exec. v.p., COO, 1984-86, pres., COO, 1986—95, CEO, 1995-98, ret., 1998, also bd. dirs.; bd. dirs. Mus. Shenandoah Valley. Bd. dirs. Va. Nat. Bank. Author: (novel) Moneybags, 2007. Trustee Glass Glen Burnie Found. Capt. US Army, 1963—65. Mem. Winchester Country Club, Farmington Country Club (Charlottesville, Va.), St. Andrews Club (Alexandria). Roman Catholic. Avocations: golf, reading, writing. Home: 261 Merrifield Ln Winchester VA 22602-2306 Personal E-mail: tullyholland@comcast.net.

HOLLAND, JOHN BEN, clothing manufacturing company executive; b. Scottsville, Ky., Mar. 26, 1932; s. Elbridge Winfred and Lou May (Whitney) H.; m. Margaret Irene Pecor, Jan. 31, 1954; children: John Sandra, Robert. BS in Acctg., Bowling Green U., 1959. With Union Underwear Co., Inc., Bowling Green, Ky., 1961—2001, v.p. adminstrn., 1972-74, vice chmn., 1975, chmn., CEO, 1976-96; cons.,

1996—99; pres. Fruit of the Loom, Inc., CEO, 2002—11; chmn., CEO, Russell Corp., 2006—11. Bd. dirs. Farmers Nat. Bank, bd. mem., NY Cotton Exchange, 1989-92. Bd. dirs. Ky. Coun. Econ. Edn., Louisville, 1981-90, Ky. Advocates for Higher Edn. Inc., 1985-93, Ky. C. of C., 1987-88, NY Cotton Exchange, 1989-92, Camping World Inc., 1985-97, Associated Industries of Ky., Ireland-Am. Econ. Adv. Bd., Tech. Corp. Inc.; chmn. corp. coun. Western Ky. U., devel. steering com., 1985-96; vice-chmn. West Point Pepperial, Inc., 1989-92; chmn. Intermodal Transp. Authority, 1998-2000. Mem. Bowling Green-Warren County C. of C. (bd. dirs. 1981-85), Am. Arbitration Assn. (panel 1985-93). Office: Dunree Capital Inc 1111 Shive Ln Ste 105 Bowling Green KY 42103

HOLLAND, KEVIN R., human resources specialist; B in Economics, U. RI. Human resources mgmt. positions Frito-Lay Co., Abbott Labs., Inc., Gateway, Inc.; v.p., human resources Kinko's; chief people officer Coors Brewing Co., 2003—05; joined Chiquita Brands International, Inc., 2005, sr. v.p., human resources, 2005—07, sr. v.p., chief people officer, 2007—. Capt. US Army, Germany, US. Office: Chiquita Brands International Inc 550 S Caldwell St Ste 1010 Charlotte NC 28202-2681 Office Phone: 513-784-8000. Office Fax: 513-784-8030. Business E-Mail: kholland@chiquita.com.

HOLLAND, LYMAN FAITH, JR., lawyer; b. Mobile, Ala., June 17, 1931; s. Lyman Faith and Louise (Wisdom) H.; m. Leannah Louise Platt, Mar. 6, 1954; children: Lyman Faith III, Laura. BS in Bus. Adminstrn, U. Ala., 1953, LLB, 1957. Bar: Ala. 1957, U.S. Supreme Ct. 1992. Assoc. Hand, Arendall & Bedsole, Mobile, 1957-62; ptnr. Hand, Arendall, Bedsole, Greaves & Johnston, 1963-94, mem., 1995, Hand Arendall LLC, 1996—2011; ret., 2012. Mem. Mobile Jr. C. of C. (Jaycees), 1957-1968, bd. dirs., 1963-68; mem. Mobile Hist. Devel. Com., 1965-69, v.p., 1967-68; bd. dirs. Mobile Azalea Trail, Inc., 1963-68, chmn. bd., 1963-65; bd. dirs. Mobile Mental Health Ctr., 1969-76, v.p., 1972, pres., chmn. bd., 1973; bd. dirs. Mobile chpt. ARC, 1969-97, vice-chmn., 1975-77, exec. vice-chmn., 1978-80, chmn., 1980-82, life bd. dirs. emeritus, 1997—; bd. dirs. Deep South coun. Girl Scouts U.S., 1965-71, Gordan Smith Ctr. Inc., 1973, Bay Area Coun. on Alcoholism, 1973-76, Cmty. Chest Coun. Mobile County, Inc., 1976-81, Greater Mobile Mental Health-Mental Retardation Bd., Inc., 1975-81, pres., 1975-77; active Mobile Estate Planning Coun., 1981—2011, exec. com., 1988-97, pres., 1994-95. Lt. col. USAF, ret. Recipient Bar Register of Preeminent Lawyers; named to Best Lawyers in America. Mem.: ABA, Ala. Law Found., Am. Coll. Trust and Estate Counsel Found. (bd. dirs. 1990—96), Am. Coll. Trust and Estate Counsel, Mobile County Bar Assn., Ala. State Bar (chmn. sect. corp., banking and bus. law 1978—80), Ala. Law Inst. (life), Camellia Club of Mobile (pres. 2012—13), Country Club of Mobile, Athelstan Club (Mobile), Lions, Phi Delta Phi, Pi Kappa Alpha. Baptist (deacon, ch. trustee 1968-73, chmn. trustees 1971-73). Home: 3606 Provident Ct Mobile AL 36608-1534 Office: Hand Arendall LLC PO Box 123 Mobile AL 36601-0123 Office Phone: 251-694-6228, 251-432-5511. Business E-Mail: lholland@handarendall.com.

HOLLAND, PAUL V., medical products executive; b. Toronto, Ontario, Can. m. Patricia Holland; 4 children. BA, U. Calif. Riverside, 1958; MD, U. Calif. LA, 1962. Lic. Calif., N.Y. Clin. assoc. prof. pathology Uniformed Svcs. U. Health Scis. and Georgetown U., 1977—83; clin. prof. medicine and pathology U. Calif. Davis, 1984—; transfusion medicine and blood bank cons. ABO-to-GO, 2004—. Bd. dirs Immucor, Inc., 2008—; med. dir. Pacificord, Irvine, Calif., 2008—. Mem. editl. bd., co-review editor Vox Sanguins, 2004—, mem. editl. bd. Blood Banking and Transfusion Medicine, 2003—. Med. dir., CEO Sacramento Med. Found. Blood Ctr.; chief, blood bank dept. NIH, 1974—83; med. dir., CEO BloodSource, Sacramento, 1983—2004; sci. dir. Delta Blood Bank, Stockton, Calif., 2004—. Recipient Nobel Prize in Medicine and Physiology. Mem.: Am. Soc.Histocompatibility and Immunogenetics, Calif. Blood Bank Soc., Am. Soc. Hemotology, Am. Assn. Blood Banks. Mailing: Immucor Inc PO Box 5625 Norcross GA 30071 Office: Immucor Inc 3130 Gateway Dr Norcross GA 30071 also: ABO-to-Go 6403 Horsemans Canyon Dr Walnut Creek CA 94595 Office Phone: 770-441-2051. Office Fax: 770-441-3807. Business E-Mail: pholland@immucor.com.

HOLLAND, ROBERT, JR., retired food products executive; b. 1940; Married; 3 children. BSME, Union Coll.; MBA in Internat. Mktg., Baruch Coll. Assoc. McKinsey & Co., 1968-81; chmn., CEO Rokher-J, White Plains, NY and, Mich., 1984-87, 91-95; chmn. Gilreath Mfg., 1987-91; pres., CEO Ben & Jerry's Homemade, Inc., Waterbury, Vt., 1995—96; CEO WorkPlace Integrators, 1997—2001. Chmn. West Africa Fund; bd. dirs. Lexmark Internat. Inc., 1998-, Carver Bancorp, Neptune Orient Lines, Yum Brands!, Inc. Chmn. bd. trustees Spelman Coll.; trustee Atlanta Univ. Ctr.; dir. Lincoln Ctr. Theater, Harlem Jr. Tennis Program. Office: Lexmark Internat Inc Bd Directors 740 New Circle Rd NW Lexington KY 40550

HOLLANDER, GILBERT P., retail executive; Various mgmt. positions Piercing Pagoda, 1997—2000, sr. v.p., mdse., 2000—03, v.p., divisional mdse., 2003—05, pres., 2005—06, pres., corp. sourcing, group sr. v.p., 2006—07; exec. v.p., chief sourcing & supply chain officer Zale Corp, 2007—. Office: Zale Corp 901 W Walnut Hill LnMS 5B-12 Irving TX 75038-1003 Office Phone: 972-580-5266. Office Fax: 972-580-5523.

HOLLANDER, WILLIAM H., lawyer; AB cum laude, Harvard Coll., Cambridge, Mass., 1975; JD summa cum laude, Ind. U., Bloomington, 1984. Bar: Ind., Ky. Mem. intellectual property protection and litig. svc. team Wyatt, Tarrant & Combs LLP, Louisville, mng. ptnr. of firm, chmn. exec. com. Contbr. articles to profl. jours. Bd. dirs. Libr. Found., Fund for Arts, Leadership Louisville, 2009—; vice chair Maryhurst. Named one of The Best Lawyers in America, Woodward/White, 2005—, America's Leading Bus. Lawyers, Intellectual Property, Chambers USA, 2007—; named to Ky. Super Lawyers, Intellectual Property, 2007—; Bingham fellow, Leadership Louisville, 1995—96. Mem.: Ky. Bar Assn., Louisville Bar Assn., Internat. Trademark Assn. Office: Wyatt Tarrant & Combs LLP PNC Plz 500 W Jefferson St Louisville KY 40202 Office Phone: 502-562-7318. Office Fax: 502-589-0309. Business E-Mail: whollander@wyattfirm.com.

HOLLANS, IRBY NOAH, JR., retired trade association administrator; b. Christiansburg, Va., Nov. 3, 1930; s. Irby Noah and Annie May (Lester) H.; m. Frances Jo Cox, June 21, 1957; children: Susan Frances, Carol Leigh, Irby Neil. BS in Gen. Bus. Adminstrn., Va. Poly. Inst. and State U., 1953. Mgr. promotion Sta. WRVA-Radio, Richmond, Va., 1956-64, editor bus. news, 1956-64; dir. travel devel. Va. State C. of C., 1964-70, asst. exec. dir., 1970-72; exec. dir. Optical Labs. Assn., Washington, 1972-96. Instr. bus. Va. Commonwealth U., Richmond, 1965-71 Mem. Dulles (Va.) Internat. Airport Devel. Commn., 1968-76; mem. Va. Nat. Capital Airports Acquisition Study Commn., 1968-76; bd. dirs. Va. Thanksgiving Festival Inc., 1965-70, Keep Va. Beautiful, Inc., 1965-73, Central Va. Ednl. TV, 1970-72, Va. Travel Coordinating Com., 1964-72. Served to maj. USAF, 1953-72, Korea. Recipient Service award Va. Profl. Photographers Assn., 1966; Nat. award Profl. Photographers Assn. Am., 1970 Mem. Am. Soc. Assn. Execs. (cert.), Va. Pub. Rels. Conf., Nat. Assn. Wholesaler-Distbrs.-Pros Group, Am. Nat. Stds. Inst. (med. devices stds. mgmt. bd. 1973-80), Washington Soc. Assn. Execs., Va. C. of C., Vienna (Va.) Photog. Soc. (pres. 1990-92), Greater Washington Coun. Camera Clubs (exec. v.p. 1988-93), Rotary Internat. (exec. dir. 1996—). Home and Office: 5339 Cristfield Ct Fairfax VA 22032-3809 Office Phone: 703-503-9788. E-mail: ihollans@earthlink.net.

HOLLENSHEAD, TODD, computer game company executive; BS in Acctg. magna cum laude, U. North Tex., MS in Tax, 1991. Internat. tax mgr. Deloitte & Touche; acct., tax mgr., mfg. industry group Arthur Andersen, mgr., Mfg. & High Tech, 1991—96; CEO id Software, LLC, Mesquite, Tex., 1996, co-owner, pres., 2004—. Office: id Software LLC 1500 N Greenville Ave Ste 700 Richardson TX 75081-2271 Office Phone: 972-613-3589. Office Fax: 972-686-9288. E-mail: toddh@idsoftware.com.

HOLLEY, CHARLES MURPHY, JR., retail company executive; b. Dallas, July 9, 1956; s. Charles Murphy Sr. and Patricia Lucille (Biel) H.; m. Shannon Spence, Apr. 27, 1996. BBA in Acctg., U. Tex., 1979; MBA in Fin., U. Houston, 1980. CPA, Tex. Sr. mgr. Ernst & Young LLP, Ft. Worth, 1980-90; dir. internat. fin. Tandy Corp., Ft. Worth, 1991-92; mng. dir. Europe Memorex Consumer Products, London, 1992-94; v.p., CFO Wal-Mart Internat., Bentonville, Ark., 1994—2003, sr. v.p., contr., 2003—05, sr. v.p. fin., 2005—07, exec. v.p. fin., treas., 2007—10; exec. v.p., CFO Wal-Mart Stores, Inc., Bentonville, Ark., 2010—. Bd. dirs. Easter Seal Soc., Tarrant County, Tex., 1987-90. Mem. AICPA, Tex. Soc. CPAs. Avocations: tennis, travel, reading. Office: Wal-Mart Stores Inc 702 SW 8th St Bentonville AR 72716-6299

HOLLEY, IRVING BRINTON, JR., historian, educator; b. Hartford, Conn., Feb. 8, 1919; s. Irving B. and Mary L. (Sharp) H.; m. Janet Carlson, Oct. 9, 1945; children: Janet Turner Holley Wegner, Jean Carlson Holley Schmidt, Susan Sharp Holley. BA cum laude, Amherst Coll., 1940; MA (Brooker scholar), Yale U., 1942, PhD, 1947; student, Oxford U., summer, 1937. Instr. dept. history Duke U., Durham, N.C., 1947-51, asst. prof., 1952-54, asso. prof., 1955-61, prof., 1962-89, prof. emeritus, 1989—; vis. prof. U.S. Mil. Acad., 1974-75, Nat. Def. U., 1978-79; cons. to Army Research Office, 1963-73; mem. U.S. Commn. on Mil. History, 1974—. Occasional lectr. Army War Coll., USAF Acad., Inf. Sch., Air War Coll., Command and Gen. Staff Coll.; chmn. adv. com. on history Sec. Air Force, 1970-79; mem. adv. com. on history NASA, 1974-81 Author: Ideas and Weapons, 1953, Buying Aircraft, 1964, Development of Aircraft Gun Turrets in the AAF, 1917-1944, Evolution of the Liaison Type Airplane, 1917-1944, 1946, An Enduring Challenge: The Problem of Air Force Doctrine, 1974, General John M. Palmer, Citizen Soldiers, and the Army of a Democracy, 1982, Technology and Military Doctrine, 2004, The Highway Revolution: 1895-1925, 2008; contbr. articles on mil. history to scholarly publs.; editor: The Transfer of Ideas: Historical Essays, 1968, editorial adviser various jours. Trustee Air Force Hist. Found., 1973—. With USAAF, 1942—47, capt. USAF, 1947—81, reserves, maj. gen. USAF, 1981, reserves. Decorated D.S.M., Legion of Merit; recipient Outstanding Civilian Service to the Army medal, 1975, Exceptional Civilian Service to the Air Force medal., 1979 Fellow AIAA (assoc.); mem. Am. Hist. Assn., Soc. History of Tech., Soc. Mil. History, Phi Delta Theta. Episcopalian. Home: 2701 Pickett Rd Durham NC 27705-5688 E-mail: ibholley@duke.edu.

HOLLEY, JIMMY W., state legislator; b. Coffee County, Ala., July 30, 1944; m. Mary Harmon; children: John, Jason. BS, East Tenn. State U., Johnson City, 1967, MA, 1973. Elem. sch. tchr. Glenwood Elem. Sch., Greenville, Tenn., 1968; tchr., coach Elba HS, Ala., 1968—69, Goodman Jr. HS, Enterprise, Ala., 1969—71; dir., Title III pre-sch project Elba City Schs., 1971—74; mem. Dist. 91 Ala. House of Reps., Montgomery, 1974—94; prin. New Brockton HS, Ala., 1974—75; prin. owner, pres. Elba Tractor Co., Inc., 1975—83; br. mgr., loan officer The Peoples Bank, New Brockton, Ala., 1983—84; employee Southeast Pharmaceuticals, Inc., Elba; mem. Dist. 31 Ala. State Senate, Montgomery, 1999—. Commr. Edn. Commn. the States; mem. Ala. Soil & Water Conservation Commn.; dir. Ctr. Environ. Rsch. & Svc. Troy State U., Ala., chmn. Arboretum Com.; mem. vocat. adv. coun. MacArthur State Tech. Coll., Ala. & Coffee County Vocat. Edn. Coun. Mem. College Ave. Ch. of Christ, Enterprise, Ala.; bd. mem. Southeast Ala. Regional Inservice Ctr. Mem. Elba & Enterprise C. of C. Democrat. Church Of Christ. Office: Ala State Senate Ala State House 11 S Union St Rm 731-C Montgomery AL 36130 Office Phone: 334-242-7845.

HOLLIDAY, CHARLES O. (CHARLES OTIS HOLLIDAY JR.), bank executive; b. Nashville, Mar. 9, 1948; s. Charles O. Sr. and Ann (Hunter) H.; m. Ann Blair, June 27, 1970; children: Scot, Chad. BS in Indsl. Engring., U. Tenn., 1970; DSc (hon.), Washington Coll., Chesterton, Md., 1988, Polytechnic U., Bklyn., NY, 2005. Registered profl. engr., Tenn. Engr. E.I. du Pont de Nemours & Co., 1970—74, bus. analyst, fibers to product planner, 1974—78, various mfg. assignments, fibers dept. Seaford, Del., 1978—84, Martinville, Va., 1978—84, Charleston, SC, 1978—84, corp. plans mgr., 1984—86, global bus. dir., Nomex, 1986, global bus. dir., Kevlar, 1987, dir. mktg., chemicals and pigments, 1988—90, v.p. then pres., Asia Pacific Tokyo, 1990—92, sr. v.p., 1992—95, exec. v.p., mem. Office Chief Exec., chmn. Asia-Pacific, 1995—97, pres., 1997—98, CEO, 1998—99, 1998—2008, chmn., 2009—10, Bank of America Corp., 2010—. Bd. dirs. CH2M HILL Companies, Ltd.; vice-chmn. Bus. Coun., 2001; bd. dirs. HCA, Inc., 2002—06, Deere & Co., 2007—. Co-author (with Stephan Schmidheiny): Walking the Talk: The Business Case for Sustainable Development, 2002. Mem. Nat. Acad. of Engring., Vice chmn. John F. Kennedy Ctr. Performing Arts; active Alliance Global Sustainability, Del. Bus./Pub. Edn. Coun., U. Tenn., Winterthur Mus., founding mem. Internat. Bus. Coun., chmn. World Bus. Coun. Sustainable Devel. 2000; chmn. World Bus. Coun. 2002, chmn. The Bus. Coun., Environ. Task Force Bus. Roundtable 2004. Named Tomorrow's CEO, Fortune, 1996. Mem. Japan Am. Soc. Del., Soc. Chem. Industry (vice-chmn., 2000, chmn., Am. Sect., 2002), Inst. Indsl. Engrs. (sr.), Soc. Chem. Inter-Am. Sect, NAE., chmn. emeritus Catalyst, chmn. US Coun. on Competitiveness, mem. Singapore-U.S. Bus. Coun. Office: Bank of America Corp 100 N Tryon St Charlotte NC 28255 Office Phone: 704-386-5681. Office Fax: 704-386-6699. Business E-Mail: charles.o.holliday@bankofamerica.com.*

HOLLIDAY, RONALD STURGIS, lawyer; b. Wichita, Kans., Dec. 11, 1947; s. Robert Dwight and Mary Irene (Smith) H.; m. Deborah June Winship, Aug. 29, 1975; children: Brian Joseph, Kathryn June. BA with honors, U. Kans., 1969; JD magna cum laude, U. Mich., 1972. Bar: Mich. 1972, U.S. Dist. Ct. (ea. dist.) Mich. 1972, U.S. Dist. Ct. (we. dist.) Mich. 1977, U.S. Ct. Appeals (6th cir.) 1982, Fla. 1986, U.S. Dist. Ct. (mid. dist.) Fla. 1987. Assoc. Dykema Gossett, Detroit, 1972-80, ptnr., 1980; mng. ptnr. Tampa office DLA Piper (formerly DLA Piper Rudnick Gray Cary). Served to lt. JAGC, USN, 1973-76. Recipient Leadership Detroit award Greater Detroit C. of C., 1980. Fellow Mich. State Bar Found. (mem. antitrust law sect.); mem. ABA, Mich. Bar Assn., Detroit Bar Assn., Fla. Bar Assn., Sarasota County Bar Assn., Hillsborough County Bar Assn. Office: DLA Piper Ste 2000 101 N Tampa Tampa FL 33602-5809 Office Phone: 813-222-5926. Office Fax: 813-371-1160. Business E-Mail: ronald.holliday@dlapiper.com.

HOLLIEN, HARRY FRANCIS, communications engineer; b. Brockton, Mass., July 16, 1926; s. Henry Gregory and Alice Bernice (Coolidge) H.; m. Patricia Ann Milanowski, Aug. 26, 1969; children: Karen Ann, Kevin Amory, Keith Alan, Brian Christopher, Stephanie Ann, Christine Ann. BS, Boston U., 1949, MEd, 1951; MA, U. Iowa, 1953, PhD, 1955. Asst. prof. Baylor U., 1955-58, U. Wichita, 1958-62; assoc. prof. speech U. Fla., Gainesville, 1962-68, prof., 1968-98, prof. linguistics, 1976-98, prof. criminal justice, 1979-98, assoc. dir. comm. scis. lab., 1962—65, dir. comm. scis. lab., 1965—75, dir. Inst. Advanced Study Comm. Processes, 1975—84; prof. emeritus, rsch. scientist Inst. Advanced Study of Communication Processes, 1998—, assoc. dir. linguistics, 1989-91; founding dir. Inst. Advanced Study Comm. Processes U. Fla., 1984—. Vis. prof. Inst. Telecomm. and Acoustics, Wroclaw Tech. U., Poland, 1974; adj. prof. Juilliard Sch. Music, NYC, 1973—84; rsch. assoc. Gould Rsch. Lab., 1958; vis. scientist Speech Transmission Lab., Royal Inst. Tech., Stockholm, 1970; Fulbright prof. U. Trier, Germany, 1987; fencing coach U. Iowa, 1953—55; mem. comm. sci. study sect. NIH, 1963—67; mem. neurobiology merit rev. bd. VA, 1969—74; mem. Credibility Assessment Rsch. Summit, Dept. Def., 2006—; pres. Hollien Assocs., 1966—; cons. in field. Author: Current Issues in Phonetic Sciences, 1978, Acoustics of Crime, 1990, Forensic Voice Identification, 2002; assoc. editor Jour. Speech and Hearing Rsch., 1967-69, Jour. Voice, 1987—; editor The Phonetician, 1975-92; mem. edtl. bd. Jour. Comm. Disorders, 1980-91, Jour. Rsch. in Singing, 1980-83, Jour. Phonetics, 1982-85, Studia Phonetica Posnan, 1985—, Speech, Language and the Law, 1993-2002. Chmn. bd. Unitarian Fellowship, Waco, Tex., 1956-58; chmn. bd. Wild Animal Retirement Village, 1981-90. Served with USN, 1944-46; with USNR, 1946-75. Recipient Garcia/Sandoz prize Internat. Assn. Logopedics and Phoniatrics, 1971, Gould award Wm. and Harriett Gould Found., 1975, Gutzmann medal Union European Phoniatrists, 1980, Professorial Excellence award U. Fla., 1996; NIH career fellow, 1965-70, Fulbright scholar, 1987. Fellow: AAAS, Inst. Acoustics, Am. Acad. Forensic Sci. (John R. Hunt award 1988), Internat. Soc. Phonetic Scis. (sec.-gen. 1975—89, exec.v.p. 1983—89, pres. 1989—98, Kay Elemetrics prize 1987, S. Smith prize 1991, Soc. Honors 1998, hon. pres. 1999—), Am. Speech and Hearing Assn., Acoustical Soc. Am.; mem.: SAR (regional v.p. 2000—04, pres. local chpt. 2001—03, state rec. sec. 2001—03, sr. v.p. 2004—05, pres. 2005—06, Patriot medal 2003), Jamestowne Soc. (NFC treas. 2010—), Internat. Assn. Forensic Phonetics, Voice Found. (sci. bd., merit awards 1981, 1993), World Congress Phoneticians (permanent coun.), Japan Soc. Phonetic Scis. (hon. v.p. 1989—97), Am. Assn. Phonetic Scis. (pres. 1973—75, editor 1976—79, exec. com. 1979—82, assn. honors 2007), Order Found. Patriots (chaplain, state soc. 2004—09, coun. gen. 2007—10, treas. 2011—), Mayflower Descs. (capt. state soc. 1999—2002, gov. local chpt. 2002—05), Sigma Xi. Republican. Achievements include patent for apparatus using radiation sensitive switch for signalling and recording data. Home: 229 SW 43rd Ter Gainesville FL 32607-2270 Office: U Fla Inst Advanced Study Comm Processes 63 Dauer Hall Gainesville FL 32611 Office Phone: 352-377-8622. Business E-Mail: hollien@ufl.edu.

HOLLIER, LARRY HAROLD, hospital administrator, vascular surgeon; b. Crowley, La., Apr. 18, 1943; s. Villere Joseph and Agnes (Guidry) H.; m. Diana Gayle Johnson, Jan. 25, 1964; children: Larry Jr., Michelle Ann. BS, La. State U., 1965, MD, 1968. Diplomate Am. Bd. Surgery, spl. qualifications in vascular surgery. Intern Charity Hosp. La., New Orleans, 1968-69, gen. surgery resident, 1969-75; vascular surgery fellow Baylor U. Med. Ctr., Dallas, 1973-74; chief vascular surgery La. State U. Med. Sch., New Orleans, 1975-80, Mayo Clinic, Rochester, Minn., 1980-87; chmn. dept. surgery Ochsner Clnic, New Orleans, 1987-93; med. dir. HCI Internat. Med. Centre, Glasgow, Scotland, 1993—96; Julius H. Jacobson II MD prof. surgery Mount Sinai Sch. Medicine, NYC, 1996—2003, chmn. dept. surgery, 1996—2003; surgeon-in-chief Mount Sinai Med. Ctr., NYC; pres. The Mount Sinai Hosp., NYC, 2002—03; dean, Sch. Medicine La. State U. Health Sci. Ctr., New Orleans, 2004—05, chancellor, 2005—. Founder divsn. vascular surgery Mayo Clinic, Rochester, 1983; bd. mgmt. Ochsner Clinic, New Orleans, 1989-93. Editor: Vascular Surgery - Basic Science in Clinical Correlations, 1994, Haimovici's Vascular Surgery, 1995. Maj. USAF, 1970-72. Fellow ACS (young surgeons rep. 1979, pres. La. chpt. 1989); mem. Soc. Vascular Surgery (chmn. membership com. 1985-86), Soc. Clin. Vascular Surgery (pres. 1995), So. Assn. Vascular Surgery (pres. 1995), Midwestern Vascular Soc. (pres. 1988). Avocations: sailing, scuba diving. Office: LSU Med Sch 433 Bolivar New Orleans LA 70112 Office Phone: 504-568-4800.

HOLLINGER, F. BLAINE, physician, educator; s. Lloyd L. and Kora M. Hollinger; m. Judith B. Hollinger, June 17, 1978; children: Jeffrey K., Cynthia M. Hollinger Cassity, Jed W. Keys, Alan A. Keys. BA, U. Kans., Lawrence, 1957; MD, U. Kans. Sch. Medicine, Kans. City, 1962. Cert. Tex. Med. Bd. Physician. Exch. fellow U. Southampton, England, 1957—58; fellow Rockefeller Found., China Med. Bd. NY, Inc., Manila, Philippines, 1961—62; internship/residency tng. U. Calif SF, Various Locations, 1962—66, U. Wash Seattle, U. Kans., 1962—66; asst. chief, arbovirus infections unit Ctrs. Disease Control and Prevention, Atlanta, 1966—68; asst., assoc. prof. virology & epidemiology Baylor Coll. Medicine, Houston, 1970—78, prof. medicine, molecular virology & epidemiology, 1978—, dir., Eugene B. Casey Hepatitis Rsch. Ctr., 1988—. Cons., transfusion transmitted diseases com. Am. Assn. Blood Banks, Bethesda, Md., 1985—; chmn., blood products adv. com., CBER US FDA, Bethesda, 1996—2000, 2010—12; past assoc. editor Jour. Infectious Diseases, European Jour. Clin. Microbiology & Infectious Diseases, Jour. Viral Hepatitis; editl. bd. mem. Hepatobiliary & Pancreatic Diseases Internat., 2010—; cons. editor, numerous jour. hosp. appointments Baylor, St. Luke's Med. Ctr., 2005—, Veterans Affairs Med. Ctr., 1988—, Ben Taub Gen. Hosp., 1984—2014, Methodist Hosp., Houston, 1982—; advisor, cons. NIH & FDA program projects, grants & contracts related to viral hepatitis and drug therapy. Editor: (book) Viral Hepatitis, 1985, 1991, 2002; contbr. to over 265 articles in profl. jours, chapters to books. Active, choir St. Luke's United Meth. Ch., Houston, 1977—. Lt. cdr USPHS, 1966—68, Atlanta. Recipient Award, Am. Men and Women Sci., Adv. Com. Svc. award, FDA, 2000, 2012; named Physician of Yr., Am. Liver Found., South Tex. Chpt., 2005; fellowships, NIH, DoD. Fellow: Am. Coll. Gastroenterology; mem.: Asian Pacific Assn. Study of the Liver, European Assn. for the Study of the Liver, KU Med. Ctr. Alumni Assn., KU Alumni Assn., European Assn. Study Liver, Am. Assn. Study Liver Diseases, Infectious Disease Soc., Am. Gastroent. Assn., Internat. Assn. Study Liver, K Club, Omicron Delta Kappa, Phi Beta Kappa, Alpha Omega Alpha, Internat. Assn. Study Liver. Methodist. Avocations: basketball, golf, tennis, travel. Office: Baylor Coll Medicine One Baylor Plaza BCM-385 Houston TX 77030 Office Phone: 713-798-3008. Business E-Mail: blaineh@bcm.edu.*

HOLLINSHEAD, ARIEL CAHILL, oncologist, educator, researcher; b. Allentown, Pa., Aug. 24, 1929; d. Earl Darnell and Gertrude Loretta (Cahill) H.; m. Montgomery K. Hyun, June 12, 1957; children: William C., Christopher C. Student, Swarthmore Coll., 1947-48; AB, Ohio U., 1951, DSc (hon.), 1977; MA, George Washington U., 1955, PhD, 1957, MD, 1977. Asst. prof., fellow in virology Baylor U. Med. Ctr., 1958-59; asst. prof. pharmacology George Washington Med. Ctr., 1959-61, asst. prof. medicine, 1961-64, assoc. prof. medicine, head lab. virus and cancer rsch., 1964-73, prof., dir. lab. virus and cancer rsch., 1974-89; on sabbatical leave 1990, prof. medicine emeritus, 1991—; rschr. HI Virus and Cancer Rsch., 1991—2006. Mem. bd. Neogenix; clin. rschr. trials in oncology and virology; cons. to biotech. cos.; panelist FDA and NIH. Contbr. over 280 articles on active immunotherapy and immunochemotherapy of cancer and virus diseases to sci. jours. Bd. dirs. Nat. Women's Econ. Alliance, Ohio U., Med. Coll. Pa., 1980-2003, Women's Inst., 1995-97. Named Bicentennial Med. Woman of Yr., Joint Bd. Am. Med. Colls., 1976, one of Outstanding Woman of Am., 1987, Outstanding Alumnus of Yr., Ohio U., 1990; recipient Cert. Merit Med. Coll. Pa., 1975-76, Marion Spencer Fay Med. Woman of Year award Med. Coll. Pa.; decorated Star of Europe, 1980. Fellow AAAS (med. sci. com. 1993-96, 99—), Washington Acad. Sci. N.Y. Acad. Scis.; mem. Grad. Women in Sci. (nat. pres. 1985-86, bd. dirs. 1986-92, nat. liaison to Washington, 1992—), Internat. Soc. Preventive Oncology, Nat. Soc. Exptl. Biology and Medicine (Disting. Scientist award 1985, Disting. Scientist emeritus award for Outstanding Career in Tchg. and Rsch. in Medicine 1996, past pres. Greater Washington chpt.), Am. Soc. Microbiology, Am. Assn. Cancer Research, Am. Assn. Immunologists, Women in Cancer Rsch., Vet. Females Am., Clin. Immunology Soc., Internat. Soc. Antiviral Research, Am. Soc. Clin. Oncology, Internat. Assn. Study Lung Cancer, Internat. Union Against Cancer, Am. Med. Writers Assn., Soc. Profs. George Washington U. Emeriti, Blue Ridge Mountain Country Club, Twin Isles Country Club, Washington Forum (pres. 1987, 91), Phi Beta Kappa (Mother of Immunotherapy award 2010). Achievements include identification of antiviral drugs and vaccines; discovering resistance to antiviral drugs; being first to purify, develop and test cancer gene products, including peptides and to study activities; first to invent field called proteomics; peptides were studied and identified for the ability to induce long-lasting cell-mediated immunity; developed proteomics technology and pioneered clinical testing and monitoring epitope activity during seventeen clinical trials; patentee in field, having five volumes of medical research papers availible for review at the National Library of Medicine in Bethesda, Maryland as well as other institutions. Home: 23465 Harborview Rd #622 Punta Gorda FL 33980-2162

HOLLIS, CHARLES EUGENE, JR., finance company executive; b. Daytona Beach, Fla., Sept. 14, 1948; s. Charles Eugene and Betty Lou (Beech) H.; m. Carol Repass, Mar. 20, 1971 (div. Nov. 1993); children: Stephanie Dyane, Charles Preston, Robin Jene. AA, Dayton Beach Jr. Coll., 1968; BA, U. South Fla., 1972. CPA Fla. Asst. Deloitte Haskins & Sells, Tampa, Fla., 1972—73, sr. asst., 1973—75, sr., 1975—78, mgr., 1978—82; audit mgr. Jack Eckerd Corp., Clearwater, Fla., 1982—85; v.p. fin., contr. Freedom Savs. and Loan Assn., Tampa, 1985—87, sr. v.p., CFO, treas., 1987—88, exec. v.p., 1988—89, CenTrust Fed., Miami, Fla., 1990; supervisory fin. instn. specialist Resolution Trust Corp., Atlanta, 1990—95; exec. v.p. Beech Mgmt. Group, Inc., 1996—; portfolio mgr. GMAC Comml. Mortgage Corp., 2000—06, Capmark Finance, Inc., 2006—08, regions bank v.p., spl. asset officer, 2008—. Chmn. fin. and taxation com. Fla. League Cities, Tallahassee, 1979—81; mem. fin. com. Nat. League Cities, Washington, 1980—86; code enforcement bd. City of Temple Terrace, 1986—91; trustee Univ. Community Hosp., 1987—91; charter mem., treas. Northeast Sertoma, 1989—90; City councilman City of Temple Terrace, Fla., 1976—86, vice mayor Fla., 1981—82; treas. Christ Our Redeemer Luth. Ch., 1984—86, pres., 1987—88; treas. Fla. Synod-Evangelical Luth. Ch. in Am., 1988—92; pres. Oaks of Dunwordy Condominium Assn., 2005—. Recipient Disting. Service award, U. South Fla. Coll. Bus., 1972, Outstanding Alumnus award, Beta Alpha Psi, 1983. Mem.: Tampa C. of C. (Leadership Tampa 1987—88), Fin. Mgrs. Soc., Fla. Soc. CPAs, Am. Inst. CPAs, Beta Alpha Psi. Republican. Home: 11251 Campfield Dr Unit 2203 Jacksonville FL 32256-3918 Office Phone: 770-673-5965. Business E-Mail: charles.hollis@regions.com.

HOLLIS, JESSE KENDRICK (KEN), state legislator; b. Alexandria, La., Mar. 13, 1942; m. Barbara Jones. Parish councilman, 1980—82; state senator, Dist. 9 La., 1982—; vice chairman Spkrs. Bur. Nat Health Care Act; gen. agent Mass. Mutual Life Insurence Co.; president & chief exec. officer Hollis Co.; mem. Jefferson Parish County, 1980—82. Recipient Man of Yr. award, Assn. Builders & Contractors, 1984, Senator of Yr. award, Alliance Good Govt., 1985, 1987, SE Region Man of Yr. award, Mass. Mutual Life Insurence Co. Mem.: Employee Benefit Planning Assn. La (pres.), America & New Orleans Soc. Charter Life Underwriters. Republican. Presbyterian. Address: 4717 Shores Dr Metairie LA 70006 Mailing: 2800 Veterans Memorial Blvd Suite 365 Metairie LA 70002 Home Phone: 504-456-2068; Office Phone: 504-838-8979. Fax: 504-831-8325.

HOLLIS, PAUL B., state legislator; b. 1972; m. Ashley Hollis; 1 child, Brec. BA in Polit. Sci., La. State U. Mem. Dist. 104 La. State Senate, 2012—, mem. Commerce Com., Edn. Com. & Retirement Com. Founder Paul Hollis Rare Coins. Republican. Office: District Office 2000 Preserve Lake Dr, Suite B Covington LA 70433 Office Phone: 985-871-4680. Office Fax: 985-871-4682. E-mail: hollisp@legis.la.gov.

HOLLIS, TIMOTHY MARTIN, bank executive; b. Marietta, Ga., Nov. 13, 1962; s. Milton Joel and Mary Sylvia (Skanner) Hollis. BSBA in Mgmt., Shorter U., Rome, Ga., 1986. Desk supr. front desk Wyndham Hotel Co., Atlanta, 1986-87; personal banker C&S/Sovran Corp., Atlanta, 1987-90, sr. personal banker, 1990-91; asst. br. mgr., banking officer NationsBank Ga., N.A., Atlanta, 1991-92, banking ctr. mgr., 1992-95; sales mgr. Wachovia Bank, NA (formerly First Union Nat. Bank Ga.), Atlanta, 1995—97; fin. specialist, v.p. Wachovia Diversity Coun.-Ga. Gen. Bank, 1997—2005; v.p., relationship mgr. Wachovia Pvt. Adv. Banking, Atlanta, 2006—07; writer, 2007—; mem. Downtown Atlanta Devel. Review Com., 2013—. Treas., mktg. chair, mem. fin. com., trustee Choral Guild Atlanta, 1991; bd. dirs. Artcare, Inc., Atlanta, 1991—94; docent, vol. mem. Friends of Zoo Atlanta; mem. steering com. First Night Atlanta, 1993—99, 1994 Class Atlanta Midtown Leadership Program, Atlanta Midtown Alliance, 1992—, Human Rights Campaign Fund, 1992—2004, GAPAC, 1993—95, AIDS Walk Atlanta, 1995—97; mem. adv. bd. Atlanta Exec. Network, 1993—96, co-chair young profls., 1996—98; mem. adv. bd. Joining Hearts Inc., 1994—99; bd. dirs. Positive Impact, 1996—97, Pets are Lovin Support, Inc., 1997—99; conf. chair First Night Internat., 1998; bd. dirs. AIDS Treatment Initiative, 1997—99, pres., 1998—99, Renaissance Pk. II Condominiums Assn., 2011—; vol., mem. Friends of Ctrl. and Renaissance Pk., 2011—, v.p., 2013—; mem. Downtown Atlanta Devel. Review Com., 2013—; vol. Pres. Obama Election Campaign, 2008. Mem.: Ctrl. Atlanta Neighbors (pres. 2013—), Renaissance Pk. Roundtable (chairperson 2011—12). Methodist. Avocations: exercise, volunteering, travel. Home: 28 Finch Trail NE Atlanta GA 30308-2418 Personal E-mail: timholli321@ahoo.com.

HOLLO, MARK W., state legislator; b. Litchfield, Ill., July 24, 1958; m. Barbara Hollo; children: Scott Hollo, Robbie Hollo. BS, Southern Ill. U., Edwardsville, 1980; grad., Wakeforest U., 1983. Physican asst. Litchfield Family Care Ctr., 1983—90, Family Care Ctr., 1990—; former mem. Soc. of Air Force Physician Assistants, Alexander County Edn. Blue Ribbon Study Com., Soc. of Air Force Physician Assistants, Litchfield Chpt. Bd., Am. Red Cross, Alexander County Head Start Program Policy Bd, Alexander County Cmty. Child Protection Team; mem. Ill. Acad. of Physician Assistants Bd., 1983—90, Am. Acad. of Physician Assistants, 1983—, Litchfield Cmty. Bd. of Edn., 1987—90; sec., mem., bd. edn. Ill. Cmty. Sch. Dist., Litchfield, 1987—90; mem. NC Acad. of Physician Assistants, 1990—; precinct chmn. Alexander County Rep. Party, 2002—03; mem. Dist. 88 NC House of Representatives, 2010—. Capt. UA Air Reserve. Republican. Lutheran. Office: 432 Westwood Lane Taylorsville NC 28681 Address: North Carolina House of Representatives 300 N Salisbury St Room 633 Raleigh NC 27603-5925 Office Phone: 919-715-8361, 828-632-1728. Business E-Mail: Mark.Hollo@ncleg.net.

HOLLOWAY, BRYAN R., state legislator; m. Misti Holloway. History tchr., farmer; state rep. Dist. 91 NC, 2005—. Mem. Agrl. com., Appropriations com., Appropriations Subcom. on Edn., Edn. com., Edn. Subcom. on Presch., Elem. and Secondary Edn., Commerce, Small Bus. and Entrepreneurship com.; vice chmn. Pensions and Retirement com. Republican. Mailing: Dist Off 1165 Sterling Pointe Dr King NC 27021 Office: North Carolina House of Representatives 300 N Salisbury St Rm 502 Raleigh NC 27603-5925 Office Phone: 919-733-5609, 336-985-0826. Business E-Mail: Bryan.Holloway@ncleg.net.

HOLLOWAY, CLYDE CECIL, state commissioner, former United States Representative from Louisiana; b. Lecompte, LA, Nov. 28, 1943; s. James Cecil Holloway & Ever Christina (Barker) H.; m. Catherine Kohlhepp, 1967; children: Tim, Mark, Rebecca, Sara. Grad. high sch., Forest Hill, La.; student, Nat. Aeronautics Sch., Kansas City, Kans. With sales and promotion dept. Pan American Airways; owner, operator Holloway's Nursery; mem. US Congress from 8th La. Dist., Washington, 1987—93; state dir. Office Rural Devel. USDA, La., 2006—09; commr. Dist. 4 La. State Public Svc. Commn., 2009—. Mem. Cenla C. of C., La. Farm Bur., La. Nursery Assn., Nat. Fedn. Ind. Bus., Regional Nursery Assn. Republican. Baptist. Office: Louisiana Public Service Commission (PSC) PO Box 91154 Baton Rouge LA 70821 Office Phone: 225-342-4404. Office Fax: 225-342-2831.*

HOLLOWAY, GREGORY L., state legislator; b. Hazlehurst, Miss. m. April Singleton; children: Gregory L. II, Joshalyn. Mem. Dist. 76 Miss. House of Reps., 2000—, chair forestry com., mem. agr. com., conservation and water resources com., edn. com., municipalities com., oil, gas and other minerals com., univs. and colls. com. Democrat. Mem. Church Of Christ. Mailing: 115 Edgewood Dr Hazlehurst MS 39083 Office Phone: 601-359-3305. E-mail: gholloway@house.ms.gov.

HOLLOWAY, PAUL FAYETTE, retired aerospace transportation executive; b. Hampton, Va., June 7, 1938; s. Eldridge Manning and Minnie Powell H.; m. Barbara Jane Menetch, June 23, 1956(dec. Nov. 22, 2012); children: Paul Manning (dec.), Eric Scott. BS, Va. Poly. Inst. and State U., 1960; postgrad., U. Va., 1961, Coll. William and Mary, 1962-63; grad. advanced mgmt. program, Harvard U., 1988; PhD (hon.), Old Dominion U., 1994. With NASA Langley Rsch. Ctr., Hampton, Va., 1960-97, aerospace technologist, 1960-69, space shuttle task group, 1969, chief space sys. divsn., 1972-75; acting dep. assoc. adminstr. Office Aeronautics and Space Tech., 1977, dir. for space, 1975-85, dep. dir., 1985-91, dir., 1991-96, acting dep. adminstr., 1992-93, ret., 1997. Cons. in field. Mem. editl. bd. Jour Spacecraft and Rockets, 1972-77, editor in chief, 1978-80; contbr. articles to profl. jours. Mem. Poquoson (Va.) Planning Commn.; v.p. local PTA; mem. coll. bd. Thomas Nelson C.C., 1997-2001. Recipient Outstanding Leadership medal NASA, 1980, Exceptional Svc. medal, 1981; Presdl. Rank award for meritorious exec., 1981, Presdl. Rank award for disting. exec., 1987, 93, Equal Opportunity medal, 1992, Disting. Svc. medal, 1992; named Peninsula Engr. of Yr., Peninsula Engrs. Club, 1996; elected to Va. Tech. Acad. Engring. Excellence, 2002. Fellow AIAA (v.p. publs. 1991-94), Am. Astronautical Soc.; mem. Internat. Acad. Astronautics, Sigma Gamma Tau. Methodist. Home: 16 N Westover Dr Poquoson VA 23662-1424

HOLLYFIELD, JOHN SCOGGINS, lawyer; b. Harlingen, Tex., Aug. 20, 1939; m. Penny Pounds, Dec. 27, 1962; children: Jon Scott, Courtney. Bar: Tex. 1968. Assoc. Fulbright & Jaworski, Houston, 1968—75, ptnr., 1975—2001, of counsel, 2001—. Lt. USNR, 1961-65. Recipient Pres.'s award Houston Bar Assn., 1986. Mem. ABA (coun. real property sect. 1986-93, sec. 1993-94, vice chair real property divsn. 1994-96, chair 1997-98, ho. of dels. 1999—2004), Am. Coll. Real Estate Lawyers (pres. 1990-91), Anglo-Am. Real Property Inst. (chair 2001). Office: Fulbright & Jaworski LLP 1301 Mckinney St Houston TX 77010-3095 Office Phone: 713-651-3717. Business E-Mail: jhollyfield@fulbright.com.

HOLM, GEORGE L., food products executive; BS, Grand Canyon Univ. Sr. mgmt. positions Alliant Foodservice Inc., US Foodservice Inc., Sysco Corp.; CEO Roma Food Enterprises; pres., CEO Vistar Corp., Centennial, Colo., 2002—08, Performance Food Group, Richmond, Va., 2008—. Office: Performance Food Group 12500 West Creek Pkwy Richmond VA 23238

HOLMAN, EDWIN J., retail executive; b. Kans. City, Mo., 1947; BSBA, Rockhurst U., 1976, MBA, 1980. Various positions, Midwest Macy's, Inc. (formerly Federated Dept. Stores Inc.), 1971—76, v.p., contr., Midwest, 1976—81; sr. oper. exec. The Neiman Marcus Group, v.p., contr., 1981—82, sr. v.p., ops., 1982—85; vice chmn., COO The Carter Hawley Hale Stores, 1985—94; pres., COO Woodward & Lothrop, Inc., 1994—96; chmn., CEO Petrie Retail, Inc., 1996—99; COO, Rich's, Lazarus and Goldsmiths divsns. Federated Dept. Stores, Inc., 1999—2000; pres., COO, Bloomingdale's divsn. Federated Dept. Stores Inc., 2000—03; pres., CEO and COO Galyan's Trading Co., Inc., 2003—04, bd. dirs., 2003—05, chmn., 2004—05; chmn., CEO, Macy's Ctrl. divsn. Macy's, Inc., 2004—09; chmn. Pantry, Inc., 2009—, interim pres., CEO, 2011—12. Bd. dirs. Circle Internat. Inc., 1994—2000, Office Max, Inc., 1995—2003, La-Z-Boy Inc., 2010—. Office: The Pantry Inc 305 Gregson Dr Cary NC 27511 Office Phone: 919-774-6700. Office Fax: 919-774-3329. Business E-Mail: eholman@thepantry.com.

HOLMAN, JAMES, allergist; b. Jacksonville, Tex., Aug. 13, 1921; MD, U. Tex. Southwest, 1945. Diplomate Am. Bd. Allergy and Immunology. Intern Parkland Meml. Hosp., Dallas, 1945-46; resident in allergy U. Va., Charlottesville, 1947-48; fellow in medicine U. Tex. Southwest, Dallas, 1946-47, 48-50; with Presbyn. Hosp., Dallas, 1966—. Asst. clin. prof. pharmacology U. Tex. Southwest Med. Sch., 1950-83, clin. assoc. prof. internal medicine, 1981-88. Fellow Am. Acad. Allergy, Asthma and Immunology, Am. Coll. Allergy, Asthma and Immunology, Am. Coll. Clin. Pharmacology and Chemotherapy.

HOLMEN, ORRIE JEFFREY, electronics company executive; b. Denver, Mar. 17, 1953; s. Orrie Joel and Eunice May (Thompson) H.; m. Mary Jane Wenzel, Apr. 21, 1984; children: Elizabeth Anne, Orrie Joel, Paul Abraham. Student, U. Colo., 1972-75, No. Ill. U., 1971. Lic. 1st class radiotelephone/gen. radiotelephone; cert. netware engr. Mgr. repair La Marche Mfg. Co., Des Plaines, Ill., 1971-72; technician Motorola Corp., Schaumburg, Ill., 1972-74; asst. mgr. Shakey's, Broomfield, Colo., 1973-75; salesman Mktg. Dept., Inc., Broomfield, Colo., 1976; pres. CBTS, Inc., Denver, 1976-78; chmn. U.S. Telephone, Denver, Dallas, Salt Lake City, Chgo. and N. Bridgton, Maine, 1978—. Cons. Marcom, Inc., Salt Lake City, 1983-84; chmn., chief exec. officer Modulex, Inc., 1989—. Author: Operations Manual, 1986, Universal Twisted Pair Wiring, 1988. Supporter Salt Lake City Rescue Mission, 1985-86; active Rep. Presdl. Task Force, 1989—; mem. Rep. Senatorial Inner Circle, 1992—; del. Rep. Conv., 1992, 94. Recipient Rep. Senatorial Medal of Freedom, 1994. Mem. Full Gospel Men's Fellowship Internat. (v.p. 1983-84), Internat. Christian Bus. Leaders, Prosperity Golf Club (Tulsa), Collin County Rep. Men's Club (v.p. 1993). Avocations: reading, scuba diving, skiing, tennis, programming. Office: US Telephone 2201 Waterview Pkwy Richardson TX 75080-2210 also: Modulex 2201 Waterview Pky MD 1 606 Richardson TX 75080-2256

HOLMES, ALVIN A., state legislator; b. Oct. 26, 1939; 1 child, Veronica. BS, MEd, MA, LLD, Rochester Bus. Inst., Ala. State U., Atlanta U., U. Pa., U. Ala., Jones Sch. Law. Mem. Dist. 78 Ala. House of Reps., Montgomery, 1974—; lic. real estate broker; asst. prof. Ala. State U., Montgomery. Alt. del. Dem. Nat. Convention, 1976, del., 1980—96; mem. State Dem. Exec. Com., Hutchinson Missionary Bapt. Ch. Mem.: NAACP, SCLC, Montgomery Improvement Assn., Kappa Alpha Psi. Democrat. Baptist. Office: PO Box 6064 Montgomery AL 36106 also: Ala House of Reps Ala State House 11 S Union St Rm 525-A Montgomery AL 36130 Office Phone: 334-264-7807, 334-242-7706.

HOLMES, ANNA-MARIE, ballerina; b. Mission City, BC, Can., Apr. 17, 1942; arrived in U.S., 1981; d. George Henry and Maxine Marie (Botterill) Ellerbeck; m. David Holmes; 1 child, Lian-Marie. Diploma, Royal Conservatory of Music. Tchr. Royal Ballet, London, 2005, Danish Ballet, Denmark, 2005, Toulous Ballet, 2005, Oslo Ballet, Norway, 2006, Royal Ballet Flanders, 2006, Atlanta Ballet, 2006, N.C. Sch. of Arts, 2006; artistic dir. Jacobs Pillow Ballet Program, 2000—10, Internat. Ballet Sch., Italy, 2006; lectr. in field. Dancer (ballets) Swan Lake, Cinderella, Romeo and Juliet, Sleeping Beauty, Bayadere, Laurencia, Paquita, Graduation Ball, Les Sylphides, Prince Igor, Giselle, Nutcracker, Firebird, Raymonda; guest appearances at numerous theatres Berlin Staarts Opera, Royal Albert Hall, London, Roy Alex, Toronto, Ont., Royal Festival Hall, London, Teatro Colon, Buenos Aires, Covent Garden, London; dancer Kirov Ballet, Leningrad, 1963, (films) Tour En L'Air, Ballet Adagio, Don Juan, Chinese Nightingale, numerous appearances on European N.Am. TV; artistic dir., prin. choreographer Tenn. Festival Ballet, Oak Ridge, 1981—, staged ballets Am. Ballet Theatre, —, Theatre of Harlem, —, Boston Ballet, 1984—, Ramonda, Am. Ballet Theatre, Met. Opera House, NYC, 2005, Corsaire, Am. Ballet Theatre, 2006, ballet mistress Ballet Theatre Francais, 1985—, tchr. Boston Ballet Co., 1985—, set Giselle Boston Ballet, 1987—; dancer Don Quixote, 1989—; mng. dir. Performing Arts/Dance Ctr., Oak Ridge, 1982—85; co-dir.: (ballets) Massimo Opera Theatre, 1993; asst. to artistic dir. Boston Ballet, 1989, dean, assoc. dir. Ctr. for Dance Edn., 1993, artistic dir., 1997—2001, guest tchr. Nervi Festival, Genoa, Italy; prodr.(film documentation): Kirov Vagonova Tchg. Sys.; artistic dir. Jackson Internat. Competition Sch., 1990, Internat. Ballet Competition Sch., 1994; choreographer Swan Lake, Tokyo, 1991, Norwegion Nat. Ballet, 1998, Sleeping Beauty Act III, Boston Ballet, 1991, Giselle, 1991, Sleeping Beauty, Boston Ballet, 1993, 1996, Tokyo, 1996, Le Corsaire, Boston Ballet, Am. Ballet Theatre, 1998, Great Performances, 1999, Met. Opera House, N.Y.C., 1999, Don Quixote, Boston Ballet, 2000, (ballets) Don Q-Washington Ballet, 2009, NuTcrackw for City of Vancouver, Can., 2009, Corsaire for Buenos Aire, 2010; co-prodr.: Raymonda Finnish Nat. Ballet, 2003, Premier Am. Ball Theater, 2004; artistic dir. La Bayadere, Flanders-Antwerp Belgium, 2004; dir.: Jacob's Pillow Ballet Program, 2006, Ballet Adriatico, Italy, 2006. Recipient Emmy award, 2000. Home: 2458 Maplewood Ave Winston Salem NC 27103-3535 Office Phone: 917-365-5311. Personal E-mail: aellerbeck@aol.com.

HOLMES, BERT OTIS E., JR., retired editor; b. Milan, Tenn., Sept. 20, 1921; s. Otis E. and Mary (Lassiter) H.; m. Marian Bush, June 10, 1942 (dec. Nov. 1964); children: Bert Otis E., Richard Bush; m. Helen Hankins, July 24, 1965; children: Chris, David. AA, Magnolia A. and M. Jr. Coll., 1940; BS, So. Meth. U., 1942. Successively copy reader, makeup editor, state editor, city staff reporter, city editor Dallas Times Herald, 1946-56, news editor, 1956-60, asst. mng. editor, 1960-64, exec. editor, 1964-65, assoc. editor, 1965-90. Pres. Family Svc. Agy., 1963-68, Tex. United Community Svcs., 1970-72, Sr. Citizens of Greater Dallas, 1995-96; bd. dirs. Dallas United Fund, Dallas Community Coun.; mem. City of Dallas Sr. Affairs Commn., 2005. With AUS, 1942-46, PTO. Mem. Dallas Assembly, Sigma Delta Chi, Dallas Press Club (pres. 1957, 78-79) Methodist. Home: 4515 W Lawther Dr Dallas TX 75214-1935

HOLMES, BROOX GARRETT, lawyer; b. Mobile, Ala., Nov. 15, 1932; s. Williams Coghlan and Philomene (Boogaerts) H.; m. Laura Claire Hays, Feb. 21, 1955 (dec. 2000); children: Broox Garrett, Dupree Hays, Williams Coghlan II; m. Elsie Crain Lyons, June 5, 2004. BA, U. Ala., 1954, JD, 1960. Bar: Ala. 1960. Since practiced in, Mobile; mem. firm Armbrect Jackson LLP, 1960—. Trustee St. Paul's Episcopal Sch., chmn. bd., 1980-83. Capt. USMCR, 1954-58. Fellow Am. Coll. Trial Lawyers (state chmn. 1991-92), Am. Bar Found.; mem. ABA, Ala. State Bar (bd. commrs. 1987-93, chmn. litigation sect. 1991, pres. 1994-95), Ala. Bar Found., Mobile Bar Assn. (exec. com. 1987-93), Nat. Assn. R.R. Trial Counsel, Internat. Assn. Def. Counsel, Am. Law Inst., Ala. Law Inst., Ala. Def. Lawyers (pres. 1977-78, named one of Best Lawyers in Am. bus. and personal injury litigation), Mobile Country Club (pres. 1983-84), Mobile Touchdown Club, Athelstan Club, Delta Kappa Epsilon, Phi Delta Phi. Episcopalian. Home: 5 Holland Park Mobile AL 36608 Office: Armbrecht Jackson LLP PO Box 290 Mobile AL 36601-0290 Office Phone: 251-405-1300. Personal E-mail: bgh308@aol.com. Business E-Mail: bgh@ajlaw.com.

HOLMES, GRACE B., energy executive; Attended, U. Tex., Austin, 1973; BBA summa cum laude, U. St. Thomas, Houston, Tex., 1998. Lic. Tex. real estate broker. Various positions including dir., cmty. affairs, asst. corp. sec. Transco Energy (acquisition of The Williams Companies, Inc.); asst. corp. sec. Cameron International Corp., 1995, ethics and compliance officer, 2003—08, corp. sec., governance officer, 2008—. Mem. Nat. Assn. Stock Plan Professionals, Greater Houston Bus. Ethics Roundtable, Ethics and Compliance Officers Assn., Soc. Corp. Secretaries and Governance Professionals, bd. dirs.

Better Bus. Bur. Houston. Avocations: sailing, golf. Office: Cameron International Corp 1333 W Loop S Ste 1700 Houston TX 77027 Office Phone: 713-513-3300. Office Fax: 713-513-3421. Business E-Mail: grace.holmes@c-a-m.com.

HOLMES, JACK A., trucking executive; Various ops., engring., and safety assignments positions United Parcel Service of America, Inc. (UPS), Utah, Ga., Ala., part time employee West Chester, Pa., 1979—82, package car driver, 1982—83, mgmt. positions, 1983; sr. v.p., ops. UPS Ground Freight, Inc. (subs. of United Parcel Svc., Inc.), 2006—07, pres., 2007—. Office: UPS Ground Freight Inc 1000 Semmes Ave Richmond VA 23224-2246 Office Phone: 804-231-8000. Office Fax: 804-231-8504. Business E-Mail: jholmes@ups.com.

HOLMES, J(AMES) LEON, federal judge; b. Hazen, Ark., 1951; BA, Ark. State U., 1973; MA, Northern Ill. U., 1976; PhD, Duke U., 1979; JD, U. Ark., 1982. Law clk. to Hon. Frank Holt Ark. Supreme Ct., 1982—83; pvt. practice atty. Little Rock, 1983—90, 1992—2004; tutor, prof. Thomas Aquinas Coll., 1990—92; judge US Dist. Ct. (ea. dist.) Ark., Little Rock, 2004—05, chief judge, 2005—. Adj. faculty polit. sci. dept. U. Ark., 1983, adj. faculty Sch. Law, 2002. Office: US Dist Ct Ea Dist Ark 500 W Capitol Ave Little Rock AR 72201

HOLMES, JEROME A., federal judge; b. Washington, Nov. 18, 1961; BA cum laude, Wake Forest U., 1983; JD, Georgetown U., 1988; MPA, John F. Kennedy Sch. Govt., Harvard U., 2000. Bar: Washington, DC 1991, Okla. 1997, Pa. 1988, US Supreme Ct. 1998, US Dist. Ct (we. dist.) Okla. 1999, US Dist. Ct (no. dist.) Okla., US Dist. Ct (ea. dist.) Okla. 2005. Law clk. to Hon. Wayne E. Alley US Dist. Ct. (we. dist.) Okla., 1988—90; law clk. to Hon. William J. Holloway US Ct. Appeals (10th Cir.), 1990—91; assoc. Steptoe & Johnson LLP, 1991—94; asst. US atty. (we. dist.) Okla. US Dept. Justice, 1994—2005; dir. Crowe & Dunlevy, PC, Oklahoma City, 2005—06; judge US Ct. Appeals (10th cir.), 2006—. Recipient John McTigue Essay award, 1988, Am. Jur award in Consumer Protection, 1988. Mem.: Okla. Bar Assn. Bd. Govs. (v.p.). Office: US Ct Appeals 333 W 4th St Ste 4-562 Tulsa OK 74103

HOLMES, MICHAEL, performing arts company executive, educator; b. Palestine, Tex., June 29, 1939; s. George Washington and Marion Rebecca Holmes. Student, U. Tex. Austin, 1957—60. Tchr. Debbie Reynolds Studio, N. Hollywood, Calif., 1979—87; artistic dir. The Chandler Studio, N. Hollywood, Calif., 1988—. Prof. UCLA, 1989—93; pres., CEO Action/Reaction Theater Corp., LA, 1994—, artistic dir., 1994—, Glendale, Calif., 2003—. Actor(adapter - director): (play) Acting: The First Six Lessons (3 Drama-Logue Awards, 1990, LA Times Outstanding prodn. of the yr. in smaller theater, 1988); author (director - producer): (play) Ryder (L. A, Valley Theater League, Best Play; Best Dir., 1992), The Ring (4 Drama-Logue Awards; Valley Theater League Best Dir., Best Play, 1994, L.A. Times Recognition of the 10 Most Memorable Prodns. of the Yr., 1995), The Cleaning Man (Critics Choice: The LA Times, 2000); touring (one-man shows) Keep a-Goin!, 2007—. Dir. summer theater Glendale Hist. Soc., 2001—04. Recipient Pick of the Week: Infinite Cages, Hollywood Complex, The L.A Weekly, 2000, Drama-Logue award, Drama - Logue Industry newspaper, 1990—96, Artistic Dir. awards, The Valley Theater League, 1992—95, Pick of the Week: Infinite Cages, Hollywood Complex, The LA Weekly, 2002. Mem.: AFTRA, SAG, Actors Equity Assn. Achievements include Many articles in the Los Angeles Times and other publications including a picture and story on the front page of the Los Angeles Times; featured on Broadway, films and television Beverly August: Osage County at the Zachary Scott Theatre Austin, Texas. Home and Office: 2601 Penny Ln Apt 204 Austin TX 78757-7612 Personal E-mail: mholmes204@att.net.

HOLMES, PAUL KINLOCH, III, (P.K. HOLMES), federal judge, former federal prosecutor; b. Newport, Ark., Nov. 10, 1951; s. Paul K. Jr. and Virginia (Harrison) H.; m. Katherine Hewitt, July 28, 1978; children: Christopher, Stephen. BA, Westminster Coll., 1973; JD, U. Ark., Fayetteville, 1978. Bar: Ark. 1978. Ptnr. Warner & Smith, Ft. Smith, Ark., 1978—80, Warner, Smith & Harris, Ft. Smith, Ark., 1980—93; US atty. (western dist.) Ark US Dept. Justice, Ft. Smith, Ark., 1993—2001; ptnr. Warner, Smith & Harris PLC, 2001—09, of counsel, 2009—11; judge US Dist. Ct. (western dist.) Ark., 2011—, chief judge, 2012—. Mem. Ark. Supreme Ct. Com. on Model Jury Instructions-Civil, 2006—. Fellow: Ark. Bar Found.; mem.: ABA, Ark. Bd. Trial Advocates, Ark. Bar Assn. (mem. House of Delegates 1983—86, chmn. Natiral Resources Law Section 1988—89), Sebastian County Bar Assn. (pres. 1994—95). Office: US District Court PO Box 1547 Fort Smith AR 72902 Office Phone: 479-783-1466. Office Fax: 479-783-6308.*

HOLMES, ROBERT ALEXANDER, state legislator; b. Shepherdstown, W.Va., July 13, 1943; s. Clarence and Priscilla H.; div.; children: Donna Lee Vaughn, Darlene Marie Jackson, Robert A., Jr. BS in Polit. Sci., Shepherd Coll., 1964; MA in Pub. Law and Govt., Columbia U., 1966, PhD in Polit. Sci., 1969. Dir. summer studies program Harvard-Yale-Columbia, 1968-69; assoc. prof. So. Univ., 1969-70; dir. SEEK CUNY, 1970-71; disting. prof. polit. sci. Atlanta U., 1971—, dir. Ctr. Studies Pub. Policy, 1989—; Ga. State Representative, Dist. 39 Ga. Ho. of Reps., Atlanta, 1974—82, Ga. State Representative, (redistrict) Dist. 28, 1982—93, Ga. State Representative, (redistrict) Dist. 53, 1993—2002, Ga. State Representative, Dist. 48, Ga. State Representative, Dist. 61, 2004—, chmn. edn. com. Atlanta, mem. appropriations, rules coms. Bd. dirs. Capital City Bank and Trust; past pres. Rsch. Atlanta, Inc. Author, co-author, editor more than 25 monographs and books; contbr. more than 70 articles to profl. jours. Chmn. bd. dirs. JOMANDI Theater Co., Sickle Cell Found., Metro-Atlanta YMCA; pres. S. Fulton Running Ptnrs.; bd. dirs. Shepherd Coll. Found. Named Outstanding Young Man of Yr., Atlanta Jaycees, Layman of Yr., Metro Atlanta YMCA, Vol. of Yr., S.W. Atlanta YMCA, Legis. of Yr., Am. Assn. Adult Educators, Ga. Environ. Coun., Lobbying Network Hall of Fame, Atlanta NAACP; recipient Legis. Svcs. award Ga. Mcpl. Assn., Tchg. Excellence award Amoco Found., Torchbearer award Sickle Cell Found., Cmty. Svc. award Fannie Lou Hamer. Mem. Nat. Conf. Black Polit. Scientists (pres. 1973-74), Assn. Social Behavioral Scientists (pres. 1976-77), Am. Polit. Sci. Assn. (exec. com. 2000-02). Democrat. Methodist. Office: State Capitol Rm 226 Atlanta GA 30334 also: PO Box 110009 Atlanta GA 30311-0909 also: Clark-Atlanta U So Ctr Studies Pub Policy 223 James P Brawley Dr Atlanta GA 30314 Office Phone: 404-880-8089. E-mail: bholmes@cau.edu.

HOLMES, SUSAN D., state legislator; b. Jasper County, Ga., Oct. 08; m. Paul Holmes; children: Sam, John, Cammie McCook. BS in Bus. Edn., U. Ga. Educator, postmaster, legal asst., ins. co. exec., lic. real estate agent; mayor City of Monticello; mem. Dist. 125 Ga. House of Representatives, 2011—. Republican. Presbyterian. Office: PO Box 151 Monticello GA 31064 also: Georgia House of Reps 501 Coverdell Legis Office Bldg Atlanta GA 30334 Office Phone: 404-656-0177. Business E-Mail: susan.holmes@house.ga.gov.

HOLMES, WALTER MICHAEL, biology professor; b. Little Rock, Ark., Sept. 23, 1942; s. Carmac Holmes and Freda Lou Holmes-Ross; m. Zendra Elizabeth Zehner, May 17, 1985; children: Michael Stuart, Lesli Paige. BS, U. Memphis, 1964, MS, 1966; PhD, U. Tenn., Memphis, 1973. Postdoctoral fellow U. Calif., Irvine, 1974—77; prof. microbiology Va. Commonwealth Univ. Sch. Medicine, Richmond, 1977—. Microbial genetics study panel NIH, Bethesda, Md., 1984—87; panel cons. FDA, DC, 1984—89; editl. bd. Gene, Netherlands, 1989—94; study sect. ad hoc mem. Am. Cancer Soc. Grant Review, Atlanta, 1991—95; chercheur assoc. CNRS, Strasbourg, Alsace, France, 1995—96; rsch. cons. Glaxo Smith Kline, Swedeland, Pa., 2001—03; vis. prof. U. Calif., Berkeley, 2005. Grantee Rsch. grant, NIH, 1978—98, NSF, 1995—2003. Independent. Achievements include research in mechanisms of RNA modification. Avocation: jazz. Home: 1803 Idlebrook Ct Richmond VA 23238 Office: Va Commonwealth Univ ISBDD 800 E Leigh St Ste 212 Richmond VA 23298 Office Fax: 804-827-3664. Business E-Mail: holmes@vcu.edu.

HOLMQUIST, LARS, marketing executive; BA, Colgate U., Hamilton, NY, 1983; MBA, NYU Leonard N. Stern Sch. Bus., 1989. Formerly with American Express Co., US, Swenen, Brierley & Partners; v.p. loyalty consulting svcs. MasterCard Worldwide (subs. of Mastercard, Inc.); exec. v.p. bus. devel. & consulting ESC Loyalty, Total Sys. Svcs., Inc., Columbus, Ga., 2002—06, pres., 2006—08; chief mktg. officer Vesdia Corp., Atlanta, 2008—. Office: Vesdia Corp Tower Place 200 3348 Peachtree Rd NE Ste 300 Atlanta GA 30326 E-mail: lars.holmquist@vesdia.com.

HOLNESS, GORDON VICTOR RIX, engineering executive, mechanical engineer; b. London, Sept. 6, 1939; arrived in US, 1969, naturalized, 1989; s. Ernest Arthur and Ivy A. (Rix) H.; m. Susan F. Sage (dec.); m. Audrey A. Bezz, Apr. 18, 1984. Cert., Croydon Tech. Coll., Surrey, Eng., 1962; diploma in environ. engring., Nat. Coll., London, 1964. Registered profl. engr. Mich., Minn., Tex., Conn., Calif., Kans., Colo., Fla., Ariz., NY, DC, Ala., NC, Ky., Ohio, Mo., Tenn., Ill., Ont., Can. Design engr. West Sussex County Coun., Chichester, Sussex, Eng., 1956-59, C. McKechnie Jarvis & Ptnrs., London, 1959-64, Barlow Leslie & Ptnrs., Croydon, 1964; sr. engr. R. J. Tamblyn & Ptnrs., Toronto, Ont., Canada, 1964-66; asst. chief engr. Giffels Assocs., Windsor, Ont., Canada, 1966-69; from asst. chief engr. to chmn. and CEO, bd. dirs. Albert Kahn Assocs. Inc., Detroit, 1969—2001, also bd. dirs.; ret. chmn. emeritus, 2001. Contbr. articles to profl. jours. Bd. dirs. YMCA, Mt. Clemens, Mich., 1980-82; commr. Grosse Pointe Shores Planning Commn.; trustee Grosse Pointe Shores Improvement Found. Fellow ASHRAE (chmn. energy mgmt. com. 1987, chmn. govt. affairs com. 1989, chmn. bd. policy com., bd. dirs. 2002-04, v.p. 2004-06, treas. 2007-08, pres. elect. 2008-09, pres., 2009-10); mem. NSPE, Am. Cons. Engrs. Coun., Chartered Inst. Bldg. Svcs. of Eng., Engring. Soc. Detroit, Mich. Soc. Profl. Engrs. (v.p. 1986, fellow 1998), Detroit Econ. Club (bd. dirs.). Republican. Presbyterian. Avocations: golf, tennis, chess, sailing. Home: 7573 Hawks Landing Dr West Palm Beach FL 33412-3140 Personal E-mail: gholness@comcast.net.

HOLROYD, SUZANNE, geriatrician, psychiatrist, educator; MD, U. Va., 1986. Diplomate Nat. Bd. of Med. Examiners, 1987, Am. Bd. Psychiatry and Neurology, 1992, Am. Bd. Psychiatry and Neurology-geriatric psychiatry, 2004. Resident psychiatry Johns Hopkins Hosp., 1987—90, fellow geriatric psychiatry, 1990—91; hosp. affiliation includes: Univ. Va. Med. Ctr.; prof. psychiatry Univ. Va. Sch. of Medicine. Office: University of Virginia Medical Center 1215 Lee St Charlottesville VA 22908-0001 Office Phone: 434-924-0211.

HOLSAPPLE, CLYDE WARREN, decision and information systems educator; b. Raleigh, NC, Nov. 1, 1950; s. Van Warren and Jeanne (Rickert) H.; m. Carol Eades; children: Christiana, Claire. BS in Math., Purdue U., 1972, MS in Computer Sci., 1975, PhD in Mgmt., 1977. From asst. prof. to assoc. prof. bus. adminstrn. U. Ill., Urbana, 1978-83; vis. asst. prof. mgmt. Purdue U., West Lafayette, Ind., 1977-78, from assoc. prof. to prof. mgmt., 1983-89; prof. decision sci. and info. systems U. Ky., Lexington, 1988—, Rosenthal endowed chair in mgmt. info. systems, 1988—, chmn. dept. decision sci. and info. systems, 1993-94. Adj. prof. U. Tex., Austin, 1989—94. Co-author: Foundations of Decision Support Systems, 1981, Micro Database Management, 1984, Manager's Guide to Expert Systems, 1986, The Information Jungle, 1988, Operations Research and Artificial Intelligence, 1994, Decision Support Systems: A Knowledge-Based Approach, 1996; editor: Handbook on Knowledge Management, 2003; editor-in-chief Jour. Orgnl. Computing and Electronic Commerce, Taylor & Francis, Phila., 2005-; assoc. editor Mgmt. Sci., Providence, 1991-98, Decision Scis., Hoboken, NJ, 2008; area editor Decision Support Systems, Amsterdam, 1992—, sr. editor Infomation Sys. rsch., 2007-10; contbr. over 125 articles to profl. jours. Recipient Pres.'s Acad. award Purdue U., 1970, 71, 72, Computer Educator of Yr. award Internat. Assn. for Computer Info. Systems, 1993. Recipient U. Ky. Chancellor's award outstanding tchr., 1995, R&D Excellence Program award, Ky. Sci. and Engring. Found., 2002, U. Ky. Robertson Faculty Rsch. Leadership award, 2005, AIS SIGDIS Best Jour. Paper award, 2005. Fellow Decision Scis. Inst.; mem. IEEE, Internat. Soc. for Decision Support (co-founder, co-dir. 1989—2004), Assn. for Computing Machinery, Inst. for Operations Rsch. Mgmt. Scis., Assn. for Info. Systems, Decision Sci. Inst., Phi Beta Kappa, Phi Kappa Phi. Office: Univ Ky Gatton Coll Bus & Economics Lexington KY 40506-0034 Business E-Mail: cwhols@uky.edu.

HOLSINGER, JAMES WILSON, JR., cardiologist, physician; b. Kansas City, Kans., May 11, 1939; s. James Wilson and Ruth Leona (Reitz) H.; m. Barbara Jenn Craig, Dec. 28, 1963; children: Anna Elizabeth, Martha Ruth, Sarah Frances, Rachel Catherine. Student, Duke U., 1957-60, MD, 1964, PhD, 1968; MS, U. S.C., 1981; BA, U. Ky., 1997; DS (hon.), Pikeville Coll., 1996; MA in Bibl. Studies, Asbury Theol. Seminary, 2004, DMin in New Testament Studies, 2009. Intern Duke U. Hosp., Durham, NC, 1964, resident in surgery, 1965, fellow in thoracic surgery, 1966, fellow in anatomy, 1966-68; resident in surgery U. Fla., Gainesville, 1968-70, fellow in cardiology, 1970-72; with VA, 1969-94; chief of staff VA Med. Ctr., Augusta, Ga., 1978-81, dir. Richmond, Va., 1981-90, Lexington, Ky., 1993-94; chief med. dir. US Dept. Vets. Affairs, Washington, 1990-93, under sec. health, 1992-93; prof. medicine and anatomy Med. Coll. Ga., Augusta, 1978-81; prof. med. and health admin. Med. Coll. of Va., Richmond, 1981-93; asst. v.p. health scis. VA Commonwealth U., Richmond, 1985-90; chancellor U. Ky. Med. Ctr., Lexington, 1994—2003, Wethington chair in health scis., 2001—, chancellor emeritus, 2003—; prof. medicine, surgery and anatomy U. Ky. Coll. Medicine, 1994—; profl. health care adminstrn. U. Ky. Coll. Allied Health Profls., 1994—2006; sr. v.p. U. Ky., Lexington, 2001—03; sec. Cabinet Health and Family Svcs. Commonwealth of Ky., Frankfort, 2003—05; prof. preventive medicine and health svcs. mgmt. U. Ky. Coll. Pub. Health, 2006—. Mem. com. evangelism N. Ga. conf. United Meth. Ch., 1980-81, com. 80, World Meth. Coun., 1981—2011, bd. discipleship Va. conf., 1982-86, lay mem., 1984-93, assoc. dist. lay leader, 1983-84, dist. lay leader, 1984-86, conf. lay leader, 1986-92, conf. chmn. health and welfare ministries, Ky., 1996-2000, Ky. conf. lay mem., 1996-00, del. gen. conf., 1988, 92, 96, 2000, del. S.E. jurisdictional conf., 1988, 92, 96, 2000; exec. com. World Meth. Coun., 1986—2011, order jerusalem, 2011, treas., 1993—2011, gen coun. on ministries United Meth. Ch., 1988-2000, Gen. Bd. Pubs., 1992-96, bd. dirs. United Meth. Pub. House, 1996-2000, jud. council, 2000-08, pres. 2004-08; commr. Joint Commn. on the Accreditation of Healthcare Orgns., 1996-2002. Contbr. articles to profl. jours.; editor: Contemporary Public Health: Principles, Practice and Policy, 2012. Major gen. M.C., Aus-Ret, 2004-, bd. dirs., Africa U., 2012-. Master ACP; fellow Am. Coll. Cardiology, Am. Coll. Healthcare Execs. (Gold medal award 1993); mem. Am. Assn. Anatomists, Am. Heart Assn. (fellow clin. coun.), Soc. Med. Adminstrs., Internat. Brotherhood Magicians (order of Merlin with shield), Ky. Inst. Medicine, Ret. Officers Assn. (bd. dirs. 1998-2000), Assn. Theol. Schs. (bd. dirs. 2006—). Republican. Office: 111 Washington Ave Ste 107 Lexington KY 40506-0003

HOLSTEAD, JOHN BURNHAM, retired lawyer; b. Dallas, Mar. 5, 1938; s. J.B. and Maurice (Cook) H.; m. Marilyn Morris, Nov. 23, 1963; children: Will, Rand, Scott. BA, La. Tech. U., 1959; LL.B., U. Tex.-Austin, 1962. Bar: Tex., US Dist. Ct. Tex. 1965, US Ct. Appeals (5th cir.), US Ct. Appeals (10th cir.), US Supreme Ct. 1974. Briefing clk. Tex. Sup. Ct., 1962-63; assoc. Culton, Morgan, Britton & White, Amarillo, Tex., 1963—65, Vinson and Elkins, Houston, 1965—71, assoc. ptnr., 1972—2002, comml. litig. atty.; ret., 2002. Mem. bd. advisors Biology Inflamation Ctr., Baylor Coll. Medicine; spkr. on civil litigation and bus. disputes. Bd. dirs., trustee Goodwill Industries Houston, Inc. Recipient Centennial Outstanding Alumni award, La. Tech. U., 1998. Fellow Internat. Soc. Barristers, Houston Bar Found., Tex. Bar Found.; mem. ABA, Tex. Bar Assn., Houston Bar Assn., River Oaks Country Club, Houston Club, Watercolor Art Soc.(Houston) Episcopalian. Office: Vinson & Elkins 1001 Fannin St Houston TX 77002-6706 Home Phone: 713-960-8282; Office Phone: 713-758-2432. Business E-Mail: jholstead@velaw.com.

HOLSTEIN, WILLIAM KURT, business administration educator; b. Stamford, Conn., Nov. 19, 1936; s. Kurt Edward and Doris Christiana (Werner) H.; m. Audrey Louise Bedford, Aug. 15, 1959; children: Kurt Edward II, William Kurt Jr., Catherine Louise. BChE, Rensselaer Poly. Inst., Troy, NY, 1958; MS in Indsl. Mgmt., Purdue U., 1959, PhD in Econs., 1964. Instr., then asst. prof. indsl. mgmt. Purdue U., 1959-64; asst. prof., then assoc. prof. Harvard U. Grad. Sch. Bus. Adminstrn., 1964-72; prof. SUNY, Albany, 1972-99, disting. svc. prof., 1991-99, dean sch. of bus., 1972-81, 86-87, exec. dir. Inst. for Study of Info. Sci., 1988-96, prof. emeritus, 1999—; dir. Ctr. for Pvt. Enterprise Devel., Budapest, Hungary, 1991-93; D. Hollins Ryan prof. bus. adminstrn. Coll. William and Mary, Williamsburg, Va., 1999—2005, adj. prof., 2005—; prof. Lorange Inst. Bus. Zurich (formerly Grad. Sch. Bus. Adminstrn.), 1996—. Dir. exec. devel. programs in Singapore, Taiwan, Argentina, Switzerland, Eng. and Ctrl. Am., 1969—, cons. to industry and govt.; vis. prof. IMEDE, Lausanne, Switzerland, 1983-85. Co-author: Production Planning and Control, 1963, Casebooks in Production Management, 1968, BASIC: Concepts and Applications, 1987; author articles in field. Trustee Upsala Coll., 1969-72; mem. accreditation com., editorial adv. com., visitation teams Am. Assembly of Collegiate Schs. of Bus., 1972-81; mem. exec. com. Middle Atlantic Assn. Schs. Bus. Adminstrn., 1976-81, pres., 1980; bd. dirs. Albany Symphony Orch., 1976-99, Seagle Music Colony, 1998—2005; bd. dirs., treas., v.p. adminstrn. Parsons Child and Family Center, Albany, 1977-94, pres., 1989-92; chmn. Metro 2000 Project, 1979; mem. com. on computer-aided mfg. Nat. Acad. Scis., 1980-83. Mem. Inst. Mgmt. Scis., Am. Prodn. and Inventory Control Soc. (hon.), Delta Sigma Pi, Beta Gamma Sigma. Lutheran. Home: 3104 Parkside Ln Williamsburg VA 23185-7696 Office: Coll William and Mary Mason Sch Bus Williamsburg VA 23187-8795

HOLSTI, OLE RUDOLF, political scientist, educator; b. Geneva, Aug. 7, 1933; came to U.S., 1940, naturalized, 1954; s. Rudolf Waldemar and Liisa (Franssila) H.; m. Ann Wood, Sept. 20, 1953; children: Eric Lynn, Maija. BA with highest honors, Stanford U., 1954, PhD, 1962; MAT., Wesleyan U., Middletown, Conn., 1956. Instr., asst. prof. polit. sci., research coordinator Stanford U., 1962-67; assoc. prof. U. B.C., Vancouver, Can., 1967-71, prof., 1971-74; George V. Allen prof. polit. sci. Duke U., 1974—2010, emeritus prof., 2010—, chmn. dept. polit. sci., 1977-83; prof. Dept. Polit. Sci. U. Calif., Davis, 1978-79. Mem. adv. com. on hist. diplomatic documentation U.S. Dept. State, 1983-86; mem. oversight com. NSF, 1981-84; co-dir. Triangle Univs. Security Sem. Duke U., 1983-98. Author (with D.J. Finlay and R. R Fagan): Enemies in Politics, 1967; author: Analysis of Communication Content: Development in Scientific Theories and Computer Techniques, 1969, Content Analysis for Social Sciences and Humanities, 1969, Crisis Escalation War, 1972, Unity and Disintegration in International Alliances: Comparative Studies, 1973, Change in the International System, 1980, American Leadership in World Affairs: The Vietnam and Breakdown of Consensus, 1984, Pub. Opinion and Am. Fgn. Policy, 1996, 2004, To See Ourselves as Others See Us: How Publics Abroad View the US Since 9/11, 2009, American Public Opinion on the Iraq War, 2011; co-author: International Crises, 1972, Content Analysis: Handbook with Application for the Study of Internat. Crisis, 1963, Political Science Annual, 1975, Thought and Action in Foreign Policy, 1975, The Behavior of Nations, 1976, World Politics, 1976, Diplomacy, 1979, Challenges to America, 1979, Containment, 1986, Behavior, Society and Nuclear War, 1989, Soviet-American Relations after the Cold War, 1991, Explaining the History of American Foreign Relations, 1991, 2d edit., 2004, Psychological Dimensions of War, 1991, Diplomacy, Force and Leadership, 1993, Encyclopedia of US Foreign Relations, 1997, Pondering Postinternationalism, 2000, The New International Studies Classroom, 2000, Soldiers and Civilians: The Civil-Military Gap and American National Security, 2001, Millennial Reflections on International Studies, 2002, On The Cutting Edge of Globalization, 2005; author: Making American Foreign Policy, 2006, To See Ourselves as Other See Us: How Publics Abroad View the US Since 9/11, 2008, American Public Opinion on the War in Iraq, 2011, US Public Opinion on the Iraq War, 2011; co-prodr.: American Democracy Promotion, 2000; author: Public Participation in Foreign Policy, 2012, Public Opinion and International Intervention, 2012; co-prodr.: Eagle Rules?: Foreign Policy and American Primacy in the 21st Century, 2001; assoc editor Western Polit. Quar., 1970—79, Jour. Conflict Resolution, 1967—72, bd. editors Computer Studies in the Humanities and Verbal Behavior, 1968—76, Am. Jour. Polit. Sci, 1975—80, Internat. Interaction assoc., Am. Review of Politics, editor then bd. editors Internat. Studies Quar., 1970—75, Jour. Politics, 1991—2000, Internat. Studies Perspectives, 1999—, adv. bd. Univ. Press Am., 1976—, corr. editor Running Jour., 1984—2010, corr. Racing South, 1983—87; contbr. articles to profl. jours, chapters to books. With 4th Inf. Divsn. US Army, 1956—58. Recipient Nevitt Sanford award, 1988, Disting. Tchrs. award Howard Johnson, 1990, Runner of Yr. award CGTC, 1985, Alumni Disting. Undergrad. Tchg. award, 1995, All-Am. award U.S. Masters Track & Field, 2000, 02; GE Found. Owen D. Young fellow, 1960-61, Haynes Found. Rsch. fellow, 1961-62, Can. Coun. Leave fellow, 1970-71, Ctr. Advanced Study in Behavioral Sci. fellow, 1972-73, Ford Found. Faculty Rsch. fellow, 1972-73, Guggenheim fellow, 1981-82, Pew Faculty fellow Harvard U., 1990; grantee Can. Coun. Rsch., 1969, NSF, 1975-77, 79-81, 83-85, 88-90, 92-95, 96-98; mem. Nat. Champion Cross Country Team (men 50-59), 1985, 88, champion, 1988; champion Tar Heel Running Tour, 1987, champion, Triple Crown Race, 1992-93; named Runner Yr., 1993, Carolina Godiva Track Club, Dave Smith award, Carolina Godiva Track Club, 2007. Mem. Internat. Studies Assn. (pres. west region 1969-70, south region 1975-77, nat. pres. 1979-80,

Tchr.-Scholar award Internat. Studies Assn. 2000, Ole Holsti Disting. award, 2014), Internat. Soc. Polit. Psychology (coun. 1990-92, v.p. 1993-95, Nev. H. Sanford award 1988), Internat. Peace Sci. Soc. (pres. so. sect. 1975-76), Am. Polit. Sci. Assn. (coun. 1982-84, adminstrn. com. 1982-85, Disting. Lifetime Achievement award 1999, Best Fgn. Policy Paper award 2004), Can. Polit. Sci. Assn., Western Polit. Sci. Assn. (exec. coun. 1971-74), USA Track and Field (N.C. Racewalk chair 1999-2002), Phi Beta Kappa, Duke Master Runners Club, Carolina Godiva Track Club (Runner of Yr. award 1985, 93). Avocation: running. Office: Duke U Dept Polit Sci PO Box 90204 Durham NC 27708-0204 Home: 1878 Harvard Ave Salt Lake City UT 84108 Home Phone: 801-906-0515. Business E-Mail: holsti@duke.edu.

HOLT, DOUGLAS, state legislator; b. July 11; Mem. Dist. 112 Ga. House of Reps., 2005—, mem. energy, utilities & telecom., health & human svcs., and transp. coms., vice chmn. interstate cooperation and spl. rules coms., sec. ins. com. Republican. Mailing: 401 A Coverdell Legis Off Bldg Atlanta GA 30334 Office Phone: 404-656-0152. Business E-Mail: doug@dougholt.org.

HOLT, EDWIN JOSEPH, counseling and psychology educator; b. Shreveport, La. s. James S. and Sammie L. (Draper) H.; m. Essie Williams; children: Lisa Michelle, Rachelle Justine. BA, Cen. State U., Wilberforce, Ohio, 1958; MS, Ind. U., 1962; EdD, U. Ark., 1972; postgrad., U. Tenn., 1976. Cert. lic. profl., La. Tchr. Caddo Parish Sch. System, Shreveport, 1959-67, guidance counselor, 1967-68, asst. prin., 1968-71, prin., 1971-74, dir. spl. services, 1974-80, asst. supt., 1980-90; assoc. prof. psychology La. State U., Shreveport, 1990-2000; clin. mgr., therapist Success Insite, Bossier City, LA, 2000—. Adj. asst. prof. La. State U., Baton Rouge, 1972, N.E. La. U., Monroe, 1973, La. Tech. U., Ruston, 1974, Grambling (La.) State U., 1974-84. Vice-pres. N.W. La. United Way, 1987; dir. Summer Youth Program, Trinity Bapt. Ch., 1980-90; active Shreveport Clean Cmty. Commn., 1981-85, Shreveport Youth Enrichment Program, 1986-90, La. Parental Involvement Task Force, 1987, Shreveport Task Force on Housing, 1984, Caddo Cmty. Coun. of Parents and Educators, 1984-90; bd. dirs. Am. Heart Assn., 1991-92, Norwella Coun. Boy Scouts Am., 1983-87; fin. chmn. Carver br. YMCA Bd. Mgmt., 1983-88; cultural arts chmn. Caddo Dist. PTA Bd. Mgrs., 1981-90; chmn. bd. trustees Trinity Bapt. Ch., pres. Trinity Devel. Corp., 2007-. Nat. Sci. Found. fellow, So. Fund fellow, NDEA fellow; recipient Nat. Council of Negro Women's award, 1984, 85, Nat. Univ. Women's Council award, 1984, 85. Mem. NEA, ACA, La. Edn. Assn., Am. Assn. Sch. Adminstrs., Ctrl. State U. (life), NAACP (life), Nat. Alliance Black Sch. Educators, Caddo Assn. Educators, Kappa Delta Pi, Sigma Pi Phi. Avocations: bowling, swimming, jogging, reading. Home: 208 Plano St Shreveport LA 71103-2057 Office: Cognitive Inst Inc 6007 Financial Plz Ste 207 Shreveport LA 71129 Office Phone: 318-621-0910.

HOLT, GERALD SIDNEY, US marshal; b. 1943; AA in Adminstrn. of Justice, Va. Western Cmty. Coll., 1989; BA in Criminal Justice and Psychology, Radford U., Va., 1995. Jailer Roanoke County Sheriff's Office, Va., 1970, numerous positions including corrections dep., uniform patrol officer, uniform patrol supr.-lt. & crime prevention officer Va., then dep. sheriff Va., 1977—91, sheriff Va., 1992—2010, ret. Va., 2010; US marshal (we. dist.) Va. US Dept. Justice, 2010—. Chmn. Western Va. Regional Jail Authority Bd.; advisor Roanoke County Criminal Justice Acad. Office: US Marshal 247 Federal Bldg 210 Franklin Rd SW Roanoke VA 24009 Office Phone: 540-857-2230.

HOLT, JEFFREY THOMAS, federal marshal; b. 1955; BS in Criminal Justice, U. Tenn., Martin, 1977. Chief of police City of Bolivar, Tenn.; chief investigator Fayette County Sheriff's Office; trooper Tenn. Highway Patrol; criminal investigator Office of Dist. Atty., 29th Judicial Dist. Tenn.; sheriff Dyer County, 1994—2010; US marshal (we. dist.) Tenn. US Marshals Svc., US Dept. Justice, Memphis, 2010—. Office: US Marshals Service Federal Building 167 N Main St, Room 1029 Memphis TN 38103 Office Phone: 901-544-3304.

HOLT, PETER M., professional sports team owner, agricultural products executive; b. Peoria, Ill. s. B.D. Holt; m. Julianna Hawn. Investment banker, restaurateur, Calif.; pres., CEO Holt Machinery Co., San Antonio, 1983—; owner, chmn. bd., CEO NBA San Antonio Spurs, 1996—. Commr. Tex. Dept. Parks & Wildlife; bd. dir. Free Trade Alliance-San Antonio, San Antonio Econ. Devel. Found.; corp. bd. mem. Chase Bank, San Antonio. Past chmn. United Way, San Antonio; chmn. bd. St. Mary's Hall Sch. Served to sgt. E5 US Army, Vietnam. Decorated Purple Heart, Silver Star, three Bronze Stars; named to Tex. Bus. Hall of Fame, 2004. Mem.: World Presidents' Orgn. Office: San Antonio Spurs 1 AT&T Ctr San Antonio TX 78219

HOLT, RAY, councilman; m. Nanette Holt. BA in Criminal Justice, Fla. State U.; MA in Pub. Adminstrn., U. South Fla. Councilman, Dist. 11 Jacksonville City Coun., Fla., 2007—. Mem. Land Use & Zoning, Pub. Health & Safety Coms.; vice chmn. Recreation & Cmty. Devel. Com.; coun. liaison Jacksonville Aviation Authority; mem. Jacksonville Waterways Commn., Tower Rev. Com., Value Adjustment Bd. Chap. Jacksonville City Coun. Mem.: Baden Powell Dist. Boy Scouts (chmn.). Republican. Office: 117 W Duval St Ste 425 Jacksonville FL 32202 Office Phone: 904-630-1386, 904-630-1684. Business E-Mail: holt@coj.net.

HOLTON, MARTIN L., III, (MARK HOLTON), lawyer, tobacco products manufacturing company executive; b. High Point, NC; BA in Econ., Univ. NC, Chapel Hill; JD with honors, Univ. NC, 1982. Assoc. Ford & Harrison, Atlanta, 1982, Womble Carlyle Sandridge & Rice, PLLC, 1984, ptnr., 1990; joined R.J. Reynolds Tobacco Co. (subs. Reynolds American Inc.), 2002, v.p., dep. gen. counsel, 2002, sr. v.p., gen. counsel, sec.; exec. v.p., gen. counsel R.J. Reynolds Tobacco Co. & RAI Services Co. (subs. Reynolds American Inc.), 2011—; exec. v.p., gen. counsel, asst. sec. Reynolds American Inc., 2011—. Mem. Rotary Club, Winston-Salem; bd. dirs. U. NC Law Alumni Assn. Office: Reynolds American Inc 401 N Main St Winston Salem NC 27102 Office Phone: 336-741-2000. Office Fax: 336-741-4238. Business E-Mail: holtonm@rjrt.com.*

HOLTON, WALTER CLINTON, JR., lawyer; b. Winston-Salem, NC; s. Walter Clinton and Mabel (Hartsfield) H.; m. Lynne Rowley. BA in Polit. Sci., U. N.C., 1977; JD, Wake Forest U., 1984. Bar: N.C. 1984, U.S. Dist. Ct. (mid. dist.) N.C. 1986, U.S. Ct. Appeals (4th cir.) 1990, U.S. Supreme Ct., 1996. Asst. dist. atty. Office 21st Jud. Dist. Atty., Winston-Salem, 1985-87; assoc. White & Crumpler, Winston-Salem, 1987-88; pvt. practice Winston-Salem, 1989; ptnr. Holton & Menefee, Winston-Salem, 1989-92, Tisdale, Holton & Menefee, PA, Winston-Salem, 1992-94; U.S. atty. Office U.S. Atty. Mid. Dist. N.C., Greensboro, NC, 1994-2001; pvt. practice Grace Holton Tisdale & Clifton PA, Winston-Salem, 2001—06, Walter C. Holton Jr. PLLC, 2006—. Democrat. Office: 301 N Main St Ste 804 Winston Salem NC 27101 Home Phone: 336-924-0557; Office Phone: 336-777-3480. Fax: 336-722-3478. Business E-Mail: wholton@walterholton.com.

HOLTON, WILLIAM COFFEEN, electrical engineering executive; b. Washington, July 24, 1930; s. William B. and Esther (Coffeen) H.; m. Mary Schaeffer, Aug. 5, 1953; children: Elizabeth Ashe, William Andrew, Sarah Anne. BS in Physics, U. N.C., 1952; PhD in Physics, U. Ill., 1960. Tech. staff corp. rsch. lab. Tex. Instruments, Dallas, 1960-65, mgr. quantum electronics, 1965-72, dir. advanced components lab., 1972-78, dir. R & D semicondr. group, 1978-82, mgr. strategic planning, 1982-83; dir. Semiconductor Rsch. Corp., Research Triangle Park, NC, 1984-88, sr. dir., 1989-90, v.p., 1990-95; rsch. prof. NC State U., Raleigh, 1996—; adj. prof. U. NC, Chapel Hill, 2004—. Lt. (j.g.) USN, 1952-54. Union Carbide fellow, 1959; recipient Dept. of Energy award, 1997, Nat. Medal Tech., US Govt. 2005. Fellow IEEE (life, mem. awards bd. 1999-2009, chair tech. field awards coun. 2005-07, Phillips award 1998), APS, Electron. Device Soc. of IEEE (governing bd. 1975-98, chmn. internat. electron device meeting 1975); mem. Phi Beta Kappa, Phi Eta Sigma. Presbyterian. Office: NC State Univ Box 8617 234B Monteith Engring Rsch Ctr Raleigh NC 27695-8617 Home: 361 Carolina Meadows Chapel Hill NC 27517 Business E-Mail: holton@ncsu.edu.

HOLTZ, LOU (LOUIS LEO HOLTZ), sportscaster, retired college football coach; b. Follansbee, W.Va., Jan. 6, 1937; m. Beth Barcus, July 22, 1961; children: Luanne, Skip, Kevin Richard, Elizabeth. BA, Kent State U., 1959; MA, U. Iowa, 1961. Asst. football coach U. Iowa Hawkeyes, Iowa City, Coll. William and Mary, Williamsburg, Va., head football coach, 1969-71; asst. football coach U. Conn. Huskies, Storrs, U. SC Gamecocks, Columbia, head football coach, 1998—2004; asst. football coach Ohio State U. Buckeyes, Columbus; head football coach NC State U. Wolfpack, Raleigh, 1972-75, NY Jets, 1976, U. Ark. Razorbacks, Fayetteville, 1977-83, U. Minn. Golden Gophers, Mpls., 1983-85, Notre Dame U. Fighting Irish, South Bend, Ind., 1986-96; analyst Coll. Football Today CBS, NYC, 1997—98; coll. football analyst ESPN, 2005—. Motavational spkr. Author: The Offensive Side of Lou Holtz, 1978, The Kitchen Quarterback: Basics for Beginning Football Fan, 1980, Fighting Spirit: A Championship Season at Notre Dame, 1990, Teen's Game Plan for Life, 2002, Wins, Losses and Lessons: An Autobiography, 2006; co-author (with Harvey MacKay) Winning Every Day: The Game Plan for Success, 1999 Named NCAA Dist. Coach of Yr., 1973, Nat. Coach of Yr. Football Writers, Sporting News, 1977, AP, 1988, Atlantic Coast Conf. Coach of Yr., 1972, Southwest Conf. Coach of Yr. AP, UPI, 1979, Southeast Conf. Coach of Yr., 2000; named to College Football Hall of Fame, 2008; recipient Paul "Bear" Bryant award Nat. Sportscasters & Sportswriters Assn., 1988, Living and Giving award Juvenile Diabetes Rsch. Found., 2001. Roman Catholic. Achievements include coaching the NCAA National Championship winning University of Notre Dame team, 1988.

HOLTZ, SKIP (LOUIS LEO HOLTZ JR.), college football coach; b. Willimantic, Conn., Mar. 12, 1964; s. Louis Leo and Beth (Barcus) Holtz; m. Jennifer Fitzgerald; children: Louis Leo III, Chad Fitzgerald, Hailey Elizabeth. Attended, Holy Cross Jr. Coll., South Bend, Ind., 1982—84; B in Bus. Mgmt., U. Notre Dame, South Bend, Ind., 1986. Grad. asst. coach Fla. State U. Seminoles, Tallahassee, 1987—88; wide receivers coach Colo. State U. Rams, Ft. Collins, 1989, U. Notre Dame Fighting Irish, South Bend, Ind., 1990—91, offensive coord., 1992—93; head football coach U. Conn. Huskies, East Hartford, 1994—98; asst. head coach, offensive coord. U. SC Gamecocks, Columbia, 1999—2003, asst. head coach, quarterbacks coach, 2004; head football coach East Carolina U. Pirates, Greenville, NC, 2005—09, U. South Fla. Bulls, Tampa, 2010—12, La. Tech Bulldogs, Ruston, La., 2013—. Hon. chmn. Camp Courant, Hartford, Conn.; hon. chmn., mem. bd. trustees Am. Diabetes Assn.; mem. ethics com. Nat. Football Found. Recipient St. Francis award, Franciscan Life Ctr., 1995, Man of Yr. award, Nat. Football Found., 1996; named Asst. Coach of Yr., All-American Football Found., 2001, Conf. USA Coach of Yr., The Sporting News, 2008. Office: Louisiana Tech Bulldogs Po Box 3046 Ruston LA 71272 Office Phone: 318-257-4111.

HOLTZMAN, GARY YALE, retired diversified financial services company executive; b. NYC, Aug. 7, 1936; s. Abram and Pearl (Kashetsky) H.; m. Alice A. Lang, Sept. 5, 1958; children: Bruce, Sheri, Michele. BBA, CCNY, 1958. Buyer, ops. mgr. Bloomingdale's, NYC, 1966; exec. v.p. control and ops. Jordan Marsh Co., Miami, Fla., 1967-87; sr. v.p. ops. and stores L. Luria & Sons Inc., Miami, 1987-93; exec. dir. Mar Jewish Community Ctr., Greater Miami, Fla., 1993-95; agt. Social Security Adminstrn.-TSR, 1995—2002; ret., 2002. Bd. advisers Universal Nat. Bank. Bd. dirs. Dade County Safety Coun., Miami, 1978-85, Jewish Cmty. Ctr. Greater Miami, 1983-88, Fla. Bus. Roundtable, 1975-80, Anti-Defamation League of B'nia B'rith, 1983-87; bd. advisers Opportunities Industrialization Ctr., 1982-84; pres. Michael Ann Russell Jewish Cmty. Ctr., 1984-86, bd. dirs., 1980—; life bd. dirs. Temple Beth Torah Adath Yeshurun, 1969-94, Temple B'nai Aviv, 1994-98; mem. fin. com. Temple Dor Dorim, 1998—, fin. com., 1999-, sr. adult pres. club, 2005-, bd. dirs. 2005-; active Jewish Fedn. Broward County and Greater Miami, Miami Jewish Fedn.; com. chmn. United Way of Dade County. Lt. U.S. Army, 1958-59; capt. USAR, 1959-67. Recipient Americanism award Anti-Defamation League, 1983; recipient Adath Yeshurun Man of Yr. award, 1978 Mem. Greater Miami C. of C., Fla. Retail Fedn. Democrat. Home: 2019 Cove Ln Weston FL 33326-2336 E-mail: algari@bellsouth.net.

HOLTZMAN, WAYNE HAROLD, psychologist, educator; b. Chgo., Jan. 16, 1923; s. Harold Hoover and Lillian (Manny) H.; m. Joan King, Aug. 23, 1947; children: Wayne Harold, James K., Scott E., Karl H. BS, Northwestern U., Evanston, Ill., 1944, MS, 1947; PhD, Stanford U., Calif., 1950; LHD (hon.), Southwestern U., Georgetown, Tex., 1980. Asst. prof. psychology U. Tex., Austin, 1949-53, assoc. prof., 1953-59, prof., 1959—2003, dean Coll. Edn., 1964-70, Hogg prof. psychology and edn., 1964—2003, prof. emeritus, 2003—. Assoc. dir. Hogg Found. Mental Health, 1955-64, pres., 1970-93, spl. counsel, 1993-2003; dir. Social Sci. Rsch. Coun., 1957-63, Centro de Investigationes Sociales, Mex., 1960-70; cons. USAF, sci. adv. bd., 1969-71; basic rsch. com. NRC, 1968-71; behavioral sci. study sect. USPHS, 1957-59, mem. mental health study sect., 1960, chmn. personality and cognition rsch. rev. com., 1968-72; rsch. adv. panel Soc. Security Adminstrn., 1961-62; L.Am. adv. bd. IBM, 1985-89; dir. WHO Collaborating Ctr. in Mental Health for Tex. and Mex., 1993-2003; pres. Austin Project, 2001-03; bd. dirs. Menninger Clinic, 1982-2010. Author: (with B.M. Moore) Tomorrow's Parents, 1964, Computer Assisted Instruction Testing and Guidance, 1971, (with R. Diaz-Guerrero and J. Swartz) Personality Development in Two Cultures, 1975, Introduction to Psychology, 1978; (with K.A. Heller and S. Messick) Placing Children in Special Education, 1982, (with T. Bornemann) Mental Health of Immigrants and Refugees, 1990, School of the Future, 1992, Holtzman Inkblot Technique Research Guide, 1999, (with M.R. Rozenweig, Michel Sabourin and David Belanger) History of the International Union of Psychological Science, 2000; editor: Jour. Ednl. Psychology, 1966-72. Trustee Ednl. Testing Service, Princeton, 1972-74, 77-80, 83-86, J.W. and Cornelia Scarborough Found., 1977-82, Ctr. for Applied Linguistics, 1978-80, Salado Inst. Humanities, 1980-85, Population Inst., 1979-85, Population Resource Ctr., 1980-2006, chmn. bd. dirs.; dir. Sci. Rsch. Assocs., 1975-88; pres., bd. dirs. S.W. Ednl. Devel. Lab., 1974-75; mem. adv. com. computing activities NSF, 1970-73; mem. computer sci. and engring. bd. NAS, 1971-73, chmn. panel on selection and placement of mentally retarded students, 1979-82; chmn. interdisciplinary cluster on social and behavioral devel. Pres.'s Biomed. Research Panel, 1975-76; bd. dirs. Found.'s Fund for Rsch. in Psychiatry, 1973-77, chmn., 1976-77; dir. Conf. of S.W. Found., 1976-84, pres., 1978-79; mem. nat. adv. mental health coun. Alcohol, Drug Abuse, and Mental Health Adminstrn., 1978-81; mem. acad. info. sys. adv. coun. IBM, 1982-85; bd. trustees Menninger Found., 1982-2010; bd. dirs. Menninger Clinic 1988-2010; chmn., 1994-97, dir. emeritus, 2010-. Commd. ensign USNR, 1944, Northwestern U. NROTC, anti-aircraft gunnery officer USNR, Pacific, lt. (jg.) USNR, 1945, flag lt. to admiral oscar badger to admiral roper USNR. Faculty Rsch. fellow, Social Sci. Rsch. Coun., 1953—54, Ctr. Advanced Study Behavioral Scis., 1962—63. Fellow APA, AAAS; mem. Tex. Psychol. Assn. (pres. 1957), S.W. Psychol. Assn. (pres. 1958), Am. Statis. Assn., InterAm. Soc. Psychology (pres. 1966-67), Am. Ednl. Rsch. Assn., Internat. Union Psychol. Scis. (sec.-gen. 1972-84, pres. 1984-88, exec. com. 1972-92), Philos. Soc. Tex. (pres. 1982-83), Sigma Xi. Methodist. Avocations: photography, gardening, travel, swimming. Home: 2500 Barton Creek Blvd Apt 1504 Austin TX 78735 E-mail: wayne.holtzman@utexas.edu.

HOLZ, ROBERT KENNETH, retired geography educator; b. Kankakee, Ill., Nov. 3, 1930; s. Harry H. and Margaret (Conway) H.; m. Joyce F. Harpin, May 19, 1951; 1 child, Eric R. BA in Zoology, So. Ill. U., Carbondale, 1958, MA in Geography, 1959; PhD in Geography, Mich. State U., East Lansing, 1963. Asst. prof. U. Tex., Austin, 1962-67, assoc. prof., 1967-72, prof., 1972—, dir. ctr. for Middle Eastern Studies, 1991-99, Eric W. Zimmerman Regents prof., 1991-99, Eric W. Zimmerman Regents prof. emeritus, 1999—; ret., 1999. Cons. in field. Co-author: Mendes I, 1980; author, editor: The Surveillant Science, 2d edit., 1985. Staff sgt. USAF, 1951-55. Recipient Group Achievement award NASA, 1974, Urban Achievement award L.B.J. Sch. Pub. Affairs, 1984. Mem. Assn. Am. Geographers (chmn. remote sensing specialty group 1980-82, chmn. southwest div. 1971-72, medal for outstanding contbns. to remote sensing Remote Sensing Specialty Group 1998), Am. Soc. Photogrammetry, Tex. Assn. Coll. Tchrs., Am. Congress of Surveying and Mapping. Roman Catholic. Avocations: hunting, fishing, squash. Office: U Tex Dept Geography Austin TX 78712 Home: 14320 Tandem Blvd Apt 4409 Austin TX 78728-6672 Home Phone: 512-452-6574. Personal E-mail: holzrj@aol.com, holzrj@gmail.com.

HOMAN, EDWARD S., state legislator; b. Oklahoma City, Okla., Aug. 10, 1943; m. Carol Homan; children: John, David, Mark. BS in Biochemistry, La. State U., 1964; MD, La. State U. Med. Sch., 1968. Orthopedic surgeon ES Homan, Jr. MD, PA, 1975—; chief of staff Univ. Cmty. Hosp., 1997—98; asst. prof., orthopedics U. South Fla. Med. Sch.; mem. Dist. 60 Fla. House of Reps., Tallahassee, 2002—, chair health and family svcs. policy coun., mem. health care appropriations com., policy coun., state univs. and pvt. colls. policy com. Served with USN, 1970—72, Guantanamo, Cuba. Mem. Hillsborough County Med. Assn. (pres. 1999-2000), West Ctrl. Fla. Health Coun., Temple Terrace C. of C. Republican. Methodist. Office: 9385 N 56th St Ste 311 Temple Terrace FL 33617-5505 also: 1302 The Capitol 402 S Monroe St Tallahassee FL 32399-1300 Office Phone: 813-983-3330, 850-488-3087. Business E-Mail: homan.ed@myfloridahouse.com.

HOMAN, RICHARD V., dean, physician; m. Rita Homan; 3 children. BS in Biomedical Sci., Brown U., 1978; MD, SUNY, Buffalo, 1982. Diplomate Nat. Bd. Med. Examiners, American Bd. Family Practice, cert. in geriatric medicine American Boards of Family Practice and Internal Medicine, in sports medicine American Boards of Family Practice, Internal Medicine, Pediat. and Emergency Medicine. Resident in family medicine Milton S. Hershey Med. Ctr. Pa. State U., 1982—85, chief resident Dept. Family and Cmty. Medicine, 1984—85; physician USPHS Whiteriver Indian Health Svc. Hosp., Ariz., 1985—87; clin. asst. prof. Pa. State U. Sch Medicine, 1987—89; asst. prof. Dept. Family and Cmty. Medicine Tex. Tech U. Health Sciences Ctr., Lubbock, 1989—93, assoc. prof., 1993—2001, Paul and Eva Braddock chair Dept Family and Cmty. Medicine Lubbock, El Paso, Amarillo and Odessa, 1994—2001, prof. Lubbock, 2001, assoc. dean clin. affairs and fin., 2001, dean Grad. Sch. Biomedical Sciences, 2001—03, dean Sch. Medicine, 2001—05, v.p. clin. affairs, 2003—05; sr. v.p. health affairs, Annenberg dean Drexel U. Coll. Medicine, Phila., 2005—11, pres., Annenberg dean, 2010—11; provost, dean Ea. Va. Med. Sch., Norfolk, Va., 2012—. Office: Eastern Virginia Medical School Lewis Hall PO Box 1980 Norfolk VA 23501 Office Phone: 757-446-5800.*

HONAMAN, J. CRAIG, health facility administrator; b. Montclair, NJ, June 15, 1943; s. Richard Karl and Gloria (McElwain) H.; m. Dee Dee Toerpe, Dec. 31, 1971; children: Justin Craig Jr., Garman Grayson. BS, N.C. State U., 1965; MS, U. Ala., Birmingham, 1971. Sr. v.p. Bapt. Hosp., Pensacola, Fla., 1970-79; exec. v.p. Tallahassee (Fla.) Meml. Hosp., 1979-89; adminstr. Quorum Health Resources/Leesburg (Fla.) Regional Med. Ctr., 1989-91; v.p., adminstrn. home health care Meth. Med. Ctr., Jacksonville, Fla., 1991-92; pres. Kellogg Healthcare, Inc., Jacksonville, 1992-93, KNH Healthcare, Jacksonville, 1993-95; exec. dir. HomeCare Alliance of Ga., Inc., Atlanta, 1994-98; sr. v.p. Haney & Assocs., Atlanta, 1998—2001; prin. H&H Cons. Ptnrs., LLC, Atlanta, 2001—. Cons. in field, Atlanta, Ga., 1991—. Contbr. articles to profl. jours. Active Boy Scouts Am., ARC, Am. Cancer Soc., Ronald McDonald House. Capt. U.S. Army, 1966-69, Vietnam. Recipient Nat. Golden Hour award MBB Helicopter, 1988, Pub. Benefit Flying award Nat. Aeronautic Assn., 2004. Fellow Am. Coll. Healthcare Execs. (cert. health care mgr.; regent for north Ga.; cert. retirement coach), Rotary. Methodist. Avocations: golf, running. Office: H&H Cons Ptnrs LLC 560 Cambridge Way NE Ste 101 Atlanta GA 30328-1007 Personal E-mail: Careerdir1@aol.com.

HONEYCUTT, DEBORAH ANN, physician; b. Chgo., Aug. 8, 1947; m. Andrew Honeycutt. BS, Univ. Ill., 1969, MA, 1972, MD, 1991. Med. dir. Clayton State Univ. Managed Health Clinic; instr. Emory Univ. Family Practice Residency Program; physician Ga. Baptist Tenet Atlanta Med. Ctr., 1994—99; faculty mem. Atlanta Med Ctr. Family Practice Residency Program, 1994—2004; med. dir. D. Ann Travis MD LLC, 1999—; owner, physician Five Points Family Practice, 2002—05; med. dir. Good Shepherd Free Clinic, 2005—06; physician Eagle's Landing Family Practice, 2007—. Co-chair Dept. Cmty. Health Minority Health Adv. Council, 2006—. Fellow: Am. Acad. Family Physicians; mem.: Ga. Acad. Family Physicians, Nat. Med. Assn., Alpha Kappa Alpha Sorority. Republican. Christian. Mailing: 118 North Ave Jonesboro GA 30236 Office Phone: 404-895-2765.

HONEYWELL, CHARLENE VANESSA EDWARDS, federal judge; b. Deerfield Beach, Fla., Nov. 17, 1957; BA in Polit. Sci., Howard U., Washington, 1979; JD, U. Fla., Gainesville, 1981. Pub. defender Leon County Pub. Defender's Office, Tallahassee, 1982—85; asst. pub. defender Hillsborough County Pub. Defender's Office, Tampa, 1985—87; asst. city atty. City of Tampa Bay, 1987—94; sr. atty. Hill, Ward & Henderson, Tampa, 1995—97, ptnr., 1997—2000; judge Fla. Thirteenth Jud. Cir. Ct., 2001—09, US Dist.

Ct. (mid. dist.) Fla., Ft. Myers, 2009—. Past mem. Fla. Fed. Jud. Nominating Commn. Office: US Dist Ct US Courthouse 2110 First St Rm 6-186 Fort Myers FL 33901 Office Phone: 239-461-2170. Office Fax: 239-461-2179.

HONG, DENNIS WONSUH, engineering educator, researcher; b. Torrance, Calif., Jan. 24, 1971; s. Yong Shik and Byung Hee Hong; m. So-Young Kim, Dec. 20, 1996. BS, U. Wis., Madison, 1994; MS, Purdue U., West Lafayette, Ind., 1999, PhD, 2002. Vis. asst. prof. Purdue U., 2002—03; asst. prof. Va. Tech., Blacksburg, 2003—09; assoc. prof. Va. Tech. Blacksburg, 2009—. Cons. TruFlex, West Lebanon, Ind., 1998—2000; dir. RoMeLa, Robotics & Mechanisms Lab., Blacksburg, Va., 2003—. Recipient Freudenstein, Gen. Motors Young Investigator award, ASME Mechanisms and Robotics Com., 2005, 2008, Best Paper award, 13th Internat. Conf. Advanced Robotics, 2007, Career award, NSF, 2007, Best Paper award, Nat. Instruments, 2007, Editor's Choice award, 2007, Outstanding New Asst. Prof. award, Coll. Engring., Va. Tech., 2007, Forward award, Wis. Alumni Assn., 2008, Excellence in Robotics Edn. award, Maxon, 2008, SAE Tector award, 2009, 1st Pl., CAGI Innovation award, Compressed Air and Gas Inst., 2008, 2009. Mem.: IEEE, ASME, Korean-Am. Scientists and Engrs. Assn., Soc. Mfg. Engrs., Assn. Unmanned Vehicle Sys. Internat., Soc. Automotive Engrs., Am. Soc. Engring. Edn., Tau Beta Pi. Achievements include invention of self-excited tripedal dynamic experimental robot; intelligent mobility platform with actuated spoke system; climbing inspection robot with compressed air; development of autonomous vehicle for the DARPA urban challenge; first to whole skin locomotion; patents pending for tripedal locomotion robot or walking machine and simulation of a dynamic gait for single or multiple steps; a novel compliant revolute joint with high radial stiffness and planar topology; an apparatus for propulsion using a helical chain of oscillating joints; a device for clamping and cutting umbilical cords; design of multi appendage robotic system. Home: 1213 Brook Cir Blacksburg VA 24060 Office: Va Tech Mech Engring 0238 Blacksburg VA 24061-0238 Office Fax: 540-231-9100. Business E-Mail: dhong@vt.edu.*

HONG, JAE-DONG, industrial engineering educator; b. Daegu, South Korea, Mar. 20, 1954; arrived in U.S., 1981; s. Hyun-Tae and Kyung-Hee (Kim) H.; m. Bong-Sun Lee, Sept. 25, 1981; children: Thomas, Christina, James. BS, Korea U., Seoul, 1979; MS, Pa. State U., 1985, PhD, 1988. Quality and process engr. Daewoo Heavy Indsl., Anyang, South Korea, 1979-81; from asst. prof. to assoc. prof. indsl. engring. tech. S.C. State U., Orangeburg, 1988-97; prof., Gov.'s disting. prof. S.C. State U. Sch. Engring. Tech. and Scis., Orangeburg, 1997—. Contbr. articles to profl. jours. Named Disting. prof., Gov. S.C., 1993. Home: 106 Fox Run Ct Orangeburg SC 29118-9791 Office: SC State U 102 Lewis Lab Orangeburg SC 29117-7722 Office Phone: 803-536-8861. E-mail: jdhong@earthlink.net.

HONORÉ, RUSSEL L., retired military officer; b. Lakeland, La., 1947; s. Lloyd Honoré and Marie Udell St. Amant; m. Beverly Honoré; children: Michael, Stephen, Stephanie, Kimberly. BS in Vocational Agrl., So. U. & A&M Coll., 1971, D (hon.) in Pub. Adminstrn.; MA in Human Resources, Troy State U.; LLD (hon.), Stillman Coll. Advanced through grades to lt. gen. U.S. Army, 2004; dep. commdg. gen./asst. commandant U.S. Army Infantry Ctr. and Sch., Fort Benning, Ga.; vice dir. ops. (J-3) The Joint Staff, Washington; commdg. gen., 2nd Infantry Divsn. 8th Army Eighth U.S. Army, Republic of Korea, 2000—02; comdr. Standing Joint Force Hdqs. Homeland Security U.S. No. Command, 2002—04; commdg. gen. First U.S. Army, Fort Gillem, Ga., 2004—08; comdr. Joint Task Force Katrina, 2005—06. Co-author (with Ron Martz): Survival: How A Culture of Preparedness Can Save You and Your Family From Disaster, 2009. Decorated Def. Disting. Svc. Medal, DSM, Def. Superior Svc. Medal, Legion of Merit with four oak leaf clusters, Bronze Star Medal, Def. Meritorious Svc. Medal, Meritorious Svc. Medal with three oak leaf clusters, Army Commendation Medal with three oak leaf clusters, Army Achievement Medal, Nat. Def. Svc. Medal with two bronze svc. stars, Armed Forces Expeditionary Medal, S.W. Asia Svc. Medal with one bronze svc. star, Global War on Terror Svc. Star, Korean Def. Svc. Medal, Armed Forces Svc. Medal, Humanitation Svc. Medal, Army Svc. Ribbon, Overseas Svc. Ribbon (4), Kuwait Liberation Medal (Saudi), Kuwait Liberation Medal (Kuwait), Joint Meritorious Unit Award; recipient Omar N. Bradley Spirit of Independence award, 2005.

HONROÉ, DALTON W., state legislator; BS, So. U., La.; attended, La. State U., Law Enforcement Inst. Ret. law enforcement, La.; businessman La.; mem. Dist. 63 La. House of Reps., Baton Rouge, 2010—. Democrat. Office: La State House of Reps 900 N Third St Baton Rouge LA 70804 also: 8776 Scenic Hwy Baton Rouge LA 70807 Office Phone: 225-771-5674. Office Fax: 225-771-5673. Business E-Mail: honored@legis.state.la.us.

HOOD, HENRY J., lawyer, energy executive; b. 1960; m. Laura Hood; children: Sydney, Emory. AB, Duke U., 1982; JD, U. Okla. Coll. Law, 1985. Bar: 1985. With Watson & McKenzie, 1987—92; assoc. White, Coffey, Galt & Fite, 1992—95; v.p. land & legal Chesapeake Energy Corp., Oklahoma City, 1995—97, sr. v.p. land & legal, 1997—2006, sr. v.p. land & legal, gen. counsel, 2006—. Cons. Chesapeake Energy Corp., 1995—97. Mem.: Tex. Bar Assn., Okla. Bar Assn. Office: Chesapeake Energy Corp PO Box 18496 Oklahoma City OK 73154-0496

HOOD, JIM (JAMES MATTHEW HOOD), state attorney general; b. New Houlka, Miss., May 15, 1962; m. Debra Lynn Hood; 3 children. BA, U. Miss., 1984; JD, U. Miss. Sch. Law, 1988. Law clk. Miss. Supreme Ct.; dist. atty. Third Jud. Dist. Cir. Ct., North Miss.; asst. atty. gen. State of Miss., Jackson, atty. gen., 2004—. Recipient Justice Achievement award, Crime Victim's Compensation Program, 2003. Mem.: Nat. Assn. of Attorneys General (pres.-elect 2013—). Democrat. Baptist. Achievements include the 2005 prosecution of Edgar Ray Killen for the 1964 triple murders of Miss. civil rights workers Andrew Goodman, James Chaney and Michael Schwerner (with dist. atty. Mark Duncan). Office: Office of the Attorney General Department of Justice PO Box 220 Jackson MS 39205-0220 Office Phone: 601-359-3680. Business E-Mail: msag05@ago.state.ms.us.*

HOOD, JOEY, state legislator; m. Cynthia Hood; children: Jonah, Owen. BA in Polit. Sci. and History, Miss. State U.; JD, Miss. Coll. Aide to Trent Lott US Senate; law clk. Miss. Ct. Appeals; atty. Choctaw County Med. Found., Town of French Camp, Miss.; pvt. practice atty. Ackerman, Miss.; mem. Dist. 35 Miss. House of Reps., Jackson, 2012—. Mem., former exec. chmn. Choctaw County Rep. Party; mem. Enon Cumberland Presbyn. Ch.; vol. fireman, bd. mem. Simpson Vol. Fire Dept. Republican. Office: Miss House of Reps PO Box 1018 Jackson MS 39215 Business E-Mail: jhood@house.ms.gov.

HOOD, JOHN D., state legislator; b. Mar. 24, 1931; married; 3 children. State rep. Dist. 48, Tenn., 1997—; with bank mktg.; treas. Rutherford County Emergency Comm. Dist.; ret. Recipient Disting. Alumnus award, Middle Tenn. State U., 1976. Mem.: Middle Tenn. State U. Alumni Assn. (pres.), Tenn. Sch. Bd. Assn. (pres.), C. of C., South Tenn. Advisor Bd., Murfreesboro Cable TV Commn., Murfreesboro-Rutherford County Cultural Arts Commn., Exch. Clubs America (nat. pres.), AAA Auto Club South (bd. dir.), Clubs America, Exch. Club Murfreesboro (charter mem.). Democrat. Office: 402 Olympia Pl Murfreesboro TN 37130-4643 Mailing: Tenn State Legis Rm 110 War Mem Bldg Nashville TN 37243-0148 Office Phone: 615-893-4651. Fax: 615-893-2068. E-mail: rep.john.hood@legislature.state.tn.us.

HOOD, JOSEPH MARTIN, federal judge; b. Ashland, Ky., 1942; BS, U. Ky., 1965, JD, 1972. Laborer Ashland Oil, Inc., Ashland, Ky., 1965; bricklayer's helper Armco Steel Corp., Ashland, Ky., 1966; bus driver Fayette County Schs., Lexington, Ky., 1971—72; law clk. to Hon. H. David Hermansdorfer US Dist. Ct. (ea. dist.) Ky., Catettsburg, Ky., 1972-76, magistrate, 1976-90, judge, 1990—2005, chief judge, 2005—07, sr. judge, 2007—. Active United Cerebral Palsy Ea. Ky.; bd. trustees Alice Lloyd Coll. Served to capt. US Army, 1966—70, (Vietnam, 1968-69). Decorated Bronze Star with V device and 4 oak leaf clusters, Ky. Bar Assn. Outstanding Judge, 1999. Mem. Ky. Bar Assn., Fayette County Bar Assn., Fed. Judges Assn, Phi Delta Phi, YMCA, Rotary, Bellefonte Country Club. Office: US Dist Ct Ste 306 101 Barr St Lexington KY 40507

HOOD, MARY BRYAN, museum director, painter; d. Irving B. and Mary Louise (Anderson) Cayce; m. Ronnie L. Hood. Student, Ky. Wesleyan Coll., 1956-59, 69-72. Exec. dir. Owensboro (Ky.) Arts Commn., 1974-76; founding dir. Owensboro Mus. Fine Art, 1976—; pres. Owensboro Mus. Fine Art Found., Inc., 1996—. Curator exhbns. on Ky. and regional art. Author, editor: exhbn. catalogs. Chair Owensboro Mayor's Arts Com., 1970—75, Owensboro Sculpture Pk., Mayor's Sculpture Pk. Commn., 1998; mem. exec. com. Ky. Arts Coun., 1974—76, Ky. Citizens for Arts, 1980—86, Owensboro Arts Commn., 1996—97, chmn., 2003—; mem. Cmty. Appearance Planning Bd., 1988—90, Daviess County Bicentennial Commn., 1990—92; mem. steering com. Yr. of the Am. Craft, Ky., 1991—93; mem. Mayor's Adv. Coun. Arts, 1996, Davies County Millennium, 1999; chmn. Owensboro Pub. Art Commn., Owennsboro, 2003—; bd. dirs. Theatre Workshop Owensboro, 1968—70, Owensboro Mus. Sci. & History, 1970—72, Owensboro Symphony, 1975—76, Japan-Am. Soc. Ky., 1987—89. Named Mary Bryan Hood Day in her honor, 1974. Mem.: Fall Art Soc. (Distin. award 2007), Ky. Assn. Mus. (pres. 1980—82), Am. Assn. Mus., Southeastern Mus. Conf. Office: Owensboro Mus Fine Art 901 Frederica St Owensboro KY 42301-3052 Business E-Mail: info@omfa.us.

HOOFMAN, CLIFF, state supreme court justice, former state legislator; b. June 23, 1943; m. Deborah L. Dodds; 1 child, Regan. BS, U. Ctrl. Ark., 1968; JD, U. Ark., 1972. Bar: Ark., U.S. Supreme Ct. City atty. City of North Little Rock, 1973—74; mem. Ark. House of Reps., 1975—82, Ark. State Senate, 1983—2002; asst. atty. gen. State of Ark., 2003—06, hwy. commr., 2007—11; judge Ark. Ct. Appeals, 2011; sr. ptnr. Hoofman & Bingham, North Little Rock; assoc. justice position 7 Ark. Supreme Ct., Little Rock, 2013—. Mem. Big Bros. Assn., Area Agy. on Aging; guest as polit. leader Am. Haus Rissen Inst., Hamburg, German. Recipient Outstanding Young Man award Ark. Jaycees, 1978, Outstanding Young Man of North Little Rock, Rose City Jaycees, Outstanding Sen. award Ark. Fraternal Police Assn., 1998; named Sen. of Yr. Ark. Sherifs Assn., 1990, also Ark. Chiefs of Police Assn., 1990. Mem. Ark. Bar Assn., Ark. Trial Lawyers Assn., North Pulaski County Bar Assn., North Little Rock C. of C. (past bd. dirs.). Democrat. Office: Arkansas Supreme Ct 625 Marshall St Little Rock AR 72201

HOOGENDOORN, BENNO, food products executive; Mng. dir., Mars Snack Foods-Continental Europe Mars, Inc., regional pres., snacks Europe, pres., Marsh Europe, CEO, co-pres. McLean, Va., 1999—. Office: Mars Inc 6885 Elm St Mc Lean VA 22101 Office Phone: 703-821-4900. Office Fax: 703-448-9678.

HOOK, LISA A., telecommunications industry executive; b. Pitts., Feb. 28, 1958; d. Melvin E. and Patricia R. (Reiser) H.; m. George S. Springsteen, Oct. 5, 1993. AB, Duke U., 1980; JD, Dickinson Sch. Law, Pa. State U., 1983. Bar: D.C. 1983. Assoc. Hogan & Hartson LLP, Washington, 1983-85; sr. counsel Viacom Internat. Inc., NYC, 1985-87; legal advisor to chmn. FCC, Washington, 1987-89; spl. adv. to vice chmn. & v.p. Time Warner Inc., NYC, 1989-91; exec. v.p., COO Time Warner Telecom., Washington, 1991—96; ptnr. Brera Capital Partners LLC, 1998—2000; sr. v.p., COO AOL Mobile, Dulles, Va., 2000—01, pres., 2001—02, AOL Broadband, Premium & Developer Services, 2002—05; pres., CEO SunRocket, Inc., Vienna, Va., 2006—07; pres., COO NeuStar, Inc., Sterling, Va., 2008—10, pres., CEO, 2010—. Bd. dirs. Covad Comm. Group, Inc., 2005-06; non-exec. dir. Reed Elsevier PLC and Reed Elsevier NV, 2006-; mng. dir. Alpine Capitol Group LLC Bd. trustee, Nat. Pub. Radio Mem. Fed. Comm. Bar Assn., Personal Comm. Industry Assn. (bd. dirs. 1993—). Avocations: tennis, painting. Office: NeuStar Inc 46000 Center Oak Plaza Sterling VA 20166

HOOKS, GEORGE BARDIN, state legislator, insurance company executive; b. Americus, Ga., May 9, 1945; s. Thomas Bardin III and Rose Mary (Fay) H.; m. Gail Ann Goen, Aug. 30, 1975 (deceased); children: George Bardin Jr., Mary Ann. BA, Auburn U., 1970; postgrad., Princeton U.; LLD (hon.), Mercer U. V.p. southeast region Alliance of Am. Insurers, Atlanta, 1972-77; pres. Hooks Agy. Inc., Americus, Ga., 1977—; mem. Ga. House Reps., 1980-90; mem. Dist. 14 Ga. State Senate, 1990—. Floor leader for Gov. Ga. House Reps., 1988-90, chair rules com., 1992-93, chair appropriations com., 1993—. Active bd. dirs. Ft. Valley State U., 1992—, Mercer U., 1997—. Named Legislator of Yr., Mcpl. Assn., 1992, County Com. Assn., 1993. Mem. Ga. Assn. Ins. Agts. (bd. dirs 1978-80. legis. dir. 1974, Pres. Citation 1974, 80), Ga. C. of C. (leadership Ga. 1982), Americus C. of C. (legis. chmn.), Rotary, Kappa Alpha. Democrat. Baptist. Office: PO Box 928 Americus GA 31709-0928 Office Phone: 229-924-2924. Office Fax: 229-924-2091. Business E-Mail: george.hooks@senate.ga.gov.

HOOKS, VENDIE HUDSON, III, surgeon; b. Metter, Ga., Nov. 1, 1948; s. Vendie Hudson Jr. and May (Jones) H.; m. Carolyn Anderson Braithwaite, Nov. 1, 1974; children: Hudson, Susanna, David, Katherine. BS, U. Ga., 1970; MD, Med. Coll. Ga., 1974. Diplomate Am. Bd. Surgery, Am. Bd. Colon and Rectal Surgery. Intern surgery Med. Coll. Ga. Hosps., Augusta, 1974-75, resident gen. surgery, 1975-78, chief resident gen. surgery, 1978-79; G.I. surgery fellow gen. infirmary U. Leeds (Eng.), 1979-80; colon and rectal surgery fellow U. Minn. Hosps., 1982-83; asst. prof. surgery, asst. chief sect. GI surgery Med. Coll. Ga., Augusta, 1980-85, dir. colon/rectal surgery clinic, 1980-85; attending in surgery VA Hosp., Augusta, 1980-85; from asst. clin. prof. surgery to assoc. clin. prof. Med. Coll. Ga., Augusta, 1985-2001, clin. prof., 2001—; staff surgeon Univ. Hosp., Augusta, 1985—, St. Joseph Hosp., Augusta, 1985—; attending colon/rectal surgery endoscopy Univ. Hosp., Augusta, 1986—. Dir. Southeastern Familial Polyposis Registry; bd. dirs. Richmond-Columbia County unit Am. Cancer Soc., v.p. medicine, 1985-91; mem. Ethicon Colon and Rectal Adv. Panel, 1988, Panel Specialist-Surgery, Vocat. Rehab., 1980—; mem. interview com. for med. sch. admissions Med. Coll. Ga., 1981-82, 84-85, mem. tissue com., 1983-85; chmn. familial polyposis registry com. U. Hosp. Augusta, 1986—; assoc. examiner Am. Bd. Colon and Rectal Surgery, 1995-98, mem., 1998—2006, v.p., 2005, pres., 2006. Contbr. articles to profl. jours.; book reviewer and abstractor in field; reviewer Gastrointestinal Endoscopy, 1985-88. Pres. med. staff U. Hosp., Augusta, Ga., 1999, Richmond County Hosp. Authority, Augusta, 1998. Recipient Continuing Med. Edn. award Am. Soc. Colon and Rectal Surgeons, 1984, 87, Spl. award for colorectal cancer control Am. Cancer Soc., 1987, Cert. of Appreciation, Am. Cancer Soc., 1991-92, Award of Excellence, Am. Cancer Soc., 1992-93; grantee Am. Soc. Hosp. Pharmacists, 1981, Smith Kline & French Labs., 1981, Merck Sharp & Dohme, 1984. Fellow ACS, Southeastern Surg. Congress, Am. Soc. Colon and Rectal Surgeons; mem. AMA (Physician Recognition award 1984-89, 1990-93, 93-96, 97-2000, 04), Med. Assn. Ga., Richmond County Med. Soc. (sec.), So. Med. Assn., Moretz Surg. Soc., Assn. for Acad. Surgeons, Ga. Gastroenterologic and Endoscopy Soc., Am. Soc. for Gastrointestinal Endoscopy, Soc. Am. Gastrointestinal Endoscopic Surgeons, Ga. Surg. Soc., Piedmont Soc. Colon and Rectal Surgeons (pres. 1992-94), Soc. Surgery Alimentary Tract, Phi Beta Kappa, Alpha Omega Alpha, Phi Kappa Phi. Methodist. Avocations: golf, hunting. Office: 1348 Walton Way Ste 6500 Augusta GA 30901-5111 Office Phone: 706-722-2118.

HOOPER, ED, state legislator; b. Statesville, NC, Aug. 5, 1947; m. Lee Ellen Hooper; children: Brian, Ann Hall. Student in fire sci. and emergency medicine studies, St. Petersburg Jr. Coll., Fla. Ret. fire lt.; ptnr. Consus Group, LLC; mem. Dist. 50 Fla. House of Reps., Tallahassee, 2006—, majority dep. whip, 2008—10, vice chair econ. devel. and cmty. affairs policy coun., pub. safety and domestic security policy com., mem. econ. devel. policy com., govt. ops. appropriations com. Commr. City of Clearwater, 1996—2000; mem. Pinellas Planning Coun., 1998—99, Pinellas County Met. Planning Orgn., 1999—2000. Bd. dirs., trustee Long Ctr. Found., 1997—; apptd. chmn. Pinellas Fire & EMS Task Force; apptd. Clearwater Cmty. Devel. Bd. Named Firefighter of Yr., State of Fla., 1999. Mem.: Clearwater Regional C. of C., Florida Profl. Firefighters. Republican. Methodist. Office: 2963 Gulf to Bay Blvd Ste 206 Clearwater FL 33759-4259 also: 410 House Office Bldg 402 S Monroe St Tallahassee FL 32399-1300 Office Phone: 727-724-3000, 850-488-1540.

HOOPER, KAY, writer; b. Merced, Calif., Oct. 30, 1957; d. James Henry and Martha Raye (Robbins) Hooper. Attended, Isothermal Cmty. Coll., Spindale, NC. Co-owner Fireside Books & Gifts, Forest City, NC. Author: (novels) Lady Thief, 1981, Mask of Passion, 1982, Return Engagement, 1982, Breathless Surrender, 1982, Taken by Storm, 1983, On Wings of Magic, 1983, Elusive Dawn, 1983, Kissed by Magic, 1983, CJ's Fate, 1984, Moonlight Rhapsody, 1984, Something Different, 1984, Pepper's Way, 1984, If There Be Dragons, 1984, Illegal Possession, 1985, Eye of the Beholder, 1985, Rebel Waltz, 1986, Belonging to Taylor, 1986, Time After Time, 1986, The Shamrock Trinity: Rafe, the Maverick, 1986, On Her Doorstep, 1986, The Delaney's of Killaroo: Adelaide, the Enchantress, 1987, Summer of the Unicorn, 1988, Delaney Historicals: Golden Flames, 1988, Delaney Historicals II: Velvet Lightning, 1988, Enemy Mine, 1989, Crime of Passion, 1991, The Haviland Touch, 1991, House of Cards, 1991, The Wizard of Seattle, 1993, Masquerade, 1994, The Haunting of Josie, 1994, Amanda, 1996, After Caroline, 1997, Finding Laura, 1998, Haunting Rachel, 1999, (Hagen series) In Serena's Web, 1987, Raven On the Wing, 1987, Rafferty's Wife, 1987, Zach's Law, 1987, The Fall of Lucas Kendrick, 1988, Unmasking Kelsey, 1988, Outlaw Derek, 1988, Shades of Gray, 1988, Captain's Paradise, 1988, It Takes a Thief, 1989, Aces High, 1989, (Once Upon a Time series) Golden Threads, 1989, The Glass Shoe, 1989, What Dreams May Come, 1990, Through the Looking Glass, 1990, The Lady and the Lion, 1990, Star-Crossed Lovers, 1990, The Matchmaker, 1991, (Men of Mysteries Past series) The Touch of Max, 1993, Hunting the Wolfe, 1993, The Trouble with Jared, 1993, All for Quinn, 1993, (Bishop/Special Crimes Unit series) Stealing Shadows, 2000, Hiding in the Shadows, 2000, Out of the Shadows, 2000, Touching Evil, 2001, Whisper of Evil, 2002, Sense of Evil, 2003, Hunting Fear, 2004, Chill of Fear, 2005, Sleeping with Fear, 2006, Blood Dreams, 2007, Blood Sins, 2008, Blood Ties, 2010, (Quinn/Thief series) Once a Thief, 2002, Always a Thief, 2003, (Compilations) Enchanted, 2003, Elusive, 2004, The Real Thing, 2004. Office: PO Box 370 Bostic NC 28018-0370 Mailing: Fireside Books & Gifts 2270 US Hwy 74A Byp Ste 509 Forest City NC 28043 Office Fax: 828-245-1805. E-mail: kay@kayhooper.com.

HOOTMAN, HARRY EDWARD, retired educator, nuclear engineer, consultant; b. Oak Park, Ill., June 5, 1933; s. Merle Albert and Rachel Edith (Atkinson) Hootman; m. Linda P. Smith, Nov. 23, 1963; children: David, Holly, John. BS in Chemistry, Mich. Technol. U., 1959; MS in Nuc. Engring., 1962; LLB, LaSalle Ext. U., 1971; MA in English Lit., U. SC, 1999; PhD in English and Am. Lit., 2004. Registered profl. engr., SC. Rsch. assoc. Argonne Nat. Lab., Ill., 1959—62; process engr. Savannah River Plant, Aiken, SC, 1962—65; rsch. assoc. reactor physics group, nuclear engring. divsn. Savannah River Lab., Aiken, 1965—87; with New Reactor Devel. Group, 1987—92; adv. engr. Planning, Studies and Analysis, 1992—95; ret., 1995; cons. transuranic waste disposal and incineration, radioisotope prodn., separation and shielding; instr. dept. math. and engring. U. SC, Aiken, 1979—80, 1990—94, instr. dept. English, 2004—09; mem. US/UK Transuranic Waste Tech. Exch., 1976—78. Adv. editor The Poetess Archive, 2005—06; bd. dirs. Ctrl. Savannah River Area Sci. and Engring. Fair, Inc., Augusta, Ga., 1972—91. Author: Index to British Literary Annuals and Giftbooks, 1823-61. Sgt. USAF, 1953—57. Mem.: NSPE (local chmn. 1978—79), Am. Phys. Soc., Am. Nuclear Soc. (local chmn. 1979—80), Am. Acad. Environ. Engrs., Phi Lambda Upsilon, Sigma Tau Delta, Sigma Xi. Baptist. Achievements include invention of alpha waste incinerator. Personal E-mail: hehootman@gmail.com.

HOOVER, JEFFREY H., state legislator, lawyer; b. Albany, Ky., Jan. 18, 1960; m. Karyn Hoover; children: Blair, Ryan, Evan. JD, Centre Coll., Danville, Ky. Atty.; city atty. Jamestown, Ky., 1990—, Liberty, Ky., 1996—; mem. Dist. 83 Ky. House of Reps., 1997—, minority caucus chmn., 1999—2000, minority fl. leader. Mem.: Russell County Jaycees. Republican. Baptist. Mailing: PO Box 985 Jamestown KY 42629-0985 Office: Ky Legislature Annex Rm 314 702 Capitol Ave Frankfort KY 40601 Office Phone: 270-343-5588, 502-564-0521, 502-564-5391. Business E-Mail: Jeff.Hoover@lrc.state.ky.us.

HOOVER, JOHN ELWOOD, former military officer, consultant, writer, educator; b. Timberville, Va., Apr. 28, 1924; s. Saylor Cornelius and Ruby Mae (Brill) H.; m. Mary Jo Cox, May 17, 1953; children: M. Kathryn, Holly H. Bullock. Student, Bridgewater Coll., Va., 1941-43, Amherst Coll., Mass., 1943-44; BS, U.S. Mil. Acad., 1947; MA, Georgetown U., 1955; postgrad., Columbia U., 1955-56, U.S. Army Command and Gen. Staff Coll., Ft. Leavenworth, Kans., 1958-59, U.S. Army War Coll., Carlisle Barracks, Pa., 1962-63. Commd. 2d lt. U.S. Army, 1947, advanced through grades to maj. gen., 1971; with 24th Inf. Div., Japan and Korea, 1948-51, Ft. Gordon, Ga., 1951-53; faculty dept. social scis. U.S. Mil. Acad., 1955-58; bn. comdr. U.S. Army, Germany, 1959-60, Hdqrs. U.S. Army Europe, Germany, 1961-62; with Office Asst. Sec. Def. for Internat. Security Affairs, Washington, 1963-66; chief communications plans Hdqrs. Pacific Command, Hawaii, 1966-69, group comdr. Vietnam, 1969-70;

exec. officer, then dir. communications systems, then dep. asst. chief staff for communication-electronics Hdqrs. Dept. Army, Washington, 1970-73; dep. comdg. gen. U.S. Army Communications Command, Ft. Huachuca, Ariz., 1973-74; dir. Joint Tactical Communications Office, Office Sec. Def., Ft. Monmouth, NJ, 1974-78; ret., 1978. Cons. command, control, comms. and mgmt.; historian emeritus U.S. Army Signal Rgt.; author and spkr. on U.S. mil. comms. history. With USAR, 1943. Decorated D.S.M., Legion of Merit with oak leaf cluster, Bronze Star with oak leaf cluster, Meritorious Svc. medal, Air medal with oak leaf cluster, Joint Svc. Commendation medal, Army Commendation medal, Good Conduct medal, Armed Forces Honor medal Republic of Vietnam, Staff Svc. medal (Republic of Vietnam), Vietnam Gallantry Cross with palm, Presdl. Unit citation, Meritorious Unit citation, Presdl. Unit citation Republic of Korea, Republic of Korea Order of Mil. Merit. Mem. Assn. Grads. U.S. Mil. Acad., Signal Corps Assn., Mil. Heritage Found., Silver Order Mercury, U.S. Army Signal Regiment (Disting. mem). Home Phone: 706-863-6318.

HOPE, PATRICK ALAN, state legislator, lawyer, lobbyist; b. San Antonio, Tex., Mar. 6, 1972; s. James Ernest and Sylvia Carol Hope; m. Kristen Ann Satariano, Aug. 23, 1972; 3 children. BA (hon.), St. Mary's U., Tex., 1993; MA, Cath. U. America, Washington, 1996; JD, Cath. U. America Columbus Sch. Law, Washington, 2001. Bar: Va. (U.S. Ct. Appeals, 4th cir.) 2001, Va. (Supreme Ct.) 2001. Legislative asst. The Hon. Henry B. Gonzalez, US. Ho. Representatives, Washington, 1995—98; lobbyist/congl. rels. Med. Advocacy Services, Inc, Washington, 1998—99; mgr. fed. affairs Am. Med. Group Assn., Alexandria, Va., 1999—2000; assoc. Mintz Levin Cohn Ferris Glovsky & Popeo, Pc, Washington, 2000—01; legis. counsel, dir. legis. policy Am. Coll. Physicians, Washington, 2001—; mem. Dist. 47 Va. House of Delegates, Richmond, 2010—. Adj. prof. Johns Hopkins U. Bloomberg Sch. Pub. Health. Commr. Arlington County Commn. on Aging, 2002—; coach Spl. Olympics, Arlington, 2002—; pres. Buckingham Cmty. Civic Assn., Arlington, 2003—; chmn. Arlington County Cmty. Svs. Bd., Va., 2004—; precinct capt. Arlington County Dem. Com., 2002—; pres./founder Hope for Kids, Inc., Arlington, 2002—; dir. DC Health Law Sterring Com., 2006—; bd. dirs. No. Va. Health Edn. Recipient Civic Hero award, Arlington Civic Fedn., 2005, James B. Hunter Cmty. Hero Recognition award, 2007, Joseph V. Gartlan award, Va. Assn. Cmty. Svc. Boards, 2007, Arlington Recognition award, Nat. Assn. Mentally Ill, 2008, Russell Garth "You Are Change" award, ARC No. Va., 2008. Democrat. Roman Catholic. Avocation: basketball. Office: Amer Coll Cardiology 2400 N St NW 7th Fl Washington DC 20037-1153 also: Va House of Dels Gen Assembly Bldg Rm 712 PO Box 406 Richmond VA 23218 also: PO Box 3148 Arlington VA 22203 Office Phone: 804-698-1047, 703-486-1010. Office Fax: 804-698-6747, 703-772-0120. Business E-Mail: delphope@virginia.house.gov.

HOPE, WILLIAM DUANE, retired zoologist, curator; b. Ft. Collins, Colo., June 7, 1935; s. William Earl and Lois Howe (Burnett) H.; m. Colleen Bryan, Dec. 23, 1956 (div.); children: Pam Hope Herbert, Karen Hope Van Zandt, Linda Hope. BS, Colo. State U., 1957, MS, 1960; PhD, U. Calif., Davis, 1965. Systematic zoologist. dept. invertebrate zoology Nat. Mus. Natural History, Smithsonian Instn., Washington, 1964—69, curator, 1969—75, chmn. dept., 1976—81, emeritus rsch. zoologist, 2006—. Contbr. articles to profl. jours. Vol. Rocky Mountain Nat. Pk. Democrat. Avocations: hiking, bicycling, fly fishing, birdwatching. Personal E-mail: wdhope@aol.com.

HOPKINS, ANTONY GERALD, history professor; b. London, Eng., Feb. 21, 1938; s. George Henry and Queenie Ethel Hopkins; m. Wendy Beech, Aug. 15, 1964; children: William Edward, John Arthur. BA with honors, U. London, 1960, PhD, 1964; DU (hon.), U. Stirling, Scotland, 1996; DLitt (hon.), U. Birmingham, Eng., 2013. Prof. econ. history U. Birmingham, England, 1977—88; prof. internat. history U. Geneva, 1988—94; Smuts prof. commonwealth history U. Cambridge, England, 1994—2002; Walter Prescott Webb chair history U. Tex., Austin, 2002—. Mem. Inst. Advanced Study, Princeton, NJ, 1974—75; fellow Pembroke Coll., Cambridge, 1994—2002, emeritus fellow, 2002—; spkr. in field. Author: (books) An Economic History Of West Africa, 1973; co-author (with P.J. Cain): British Imperialism 1688-1990 2 vols., 1993; editor: Jour. African History, 1972—79, Econ. History Rev., 1980—85, Cambridge Imperial and Post Colonial Studies, 1994—2003. Recipient Forkosch prize, Am. Hist. Assn., 1995; fellow, Brit. Acad., London, 1996. Avocations: running, opera. Office: Univ Tex Dept History 1 University Sta Campus Code B7000 Austin TX 78712

HOPKINS, FRANK E., oil and gas company executive; BS in Bus. Adminstrn., Pa. State U.; grad. exec. edn. program, Northwestern U. Kellogg Sch. Mgmt. Various positions including mgr., investor rels., fin. & strategic comm. and asst. contr. Mobil; dep. mgr. investor rels., then gen. mgr. strategic planning global shared svcs. group, Exxon-Mobil Corp.; v.p. investor rels. Pioneer Natural Resources Co., 2005—. Office: Pioneer Natural Resources Co Ste 200 5205 N O Connor Blvd Irving TX 75039 Office Phone: 972-444-9001. Office Fax: 972-402-7023. Business E-Mail: frank.hopkins@pxd.com.

HOPKINS, GROVER PREVATTE, lawyer; b. Jacksonville, Fla., Sept. 2, 1933; s. John Taylor and Capitola (Prevatte) H.; m. Ann Hutchinson, Oct. 16, 1965 (dec.); children: John, George, James, Corbin; m. Connie Jefferys, June 7, 1973. AB, Fla. State U., 1958; JD, U. N.C., 1971. Bar: N.C. 1971, Fla. 1972, D.C. 1981, U.S. Dist. Ct. (ea. dist.) N.C. 1971, U.S. Ct. Appeals (4th cir.) 1974, U.S. Supreme Ct. 1974; cert. mediator N.C. Cts., 1997. Announcer Sta. WTAL, Tallahassee, 1951-54; pub. rels. dir. Inter-Am. U., San German, PR, 1958-60; pers. mgr. Northridge Knitting Mills, San German, 1960-62; cons. bus and pers. Mayaguez, PR, Miami, Fla., 1963-69; mem. Weeks & Muse, Tarboro, NC, 1971-73, Hopkins & Assocs., Tarboro, 1973—. Served with U.S. Army, 1954-57. Mem. Inter-Am. Bar Assn. (sec. gen. 1989-91). Republican. Office: Hopkins & Geoffrion Attys Sherwood Bldg 212 N Main St Tarboro NC 27886-5008 Business E-Mail: jack@jackhopkins.com.*

HOPKINS, JOHN DAVID, lawyer; b. Memphis, Feb. 8, 1938; s. John and Helen (Sweeney) H.; m. Evelyn Harry, June 8, 1963 (div. Feb. 1985); children: John David III, Katharine Jane, Matthew Foster Joseph; m. Laurie Eileen House, June 3, 1987. BA, Vanderbilt U., 1959; LLB, U. Va., 1965. Bar: Ga. 1966, D.C. 1979. From assoc. to ptnr. King & Spalding, Atlanta, 1965-93; exec. v.p., gen. counsel Jefferson-Pilot Corp., Greensboro, NC, 1993—2003; of counsel Womble Carlyle Sandridge & Rice, PLLC, Atlanta, 2003—09; ptnr. Taylor English Duma, LLP, Atlanta, 2009—. Bd. dirs., mem. exec. com. RockTenn Co., Atlanta, 1989-2011; mem. bd. visitors Guilford Coll., 1994-2000; bd. dirs. U. NC, Greensboro Excellence Found., 1995-2003. Bd. dirs. Atlanta Ballet, 1991-93, Greensboro United Arts Coun., 1994-97, Ea. Music Festival, 1998—2005, Highlands NC Cmty. Found., 2012-; mem. alumni coun. U. Va. Law Sch. Alumni Assn., 2000-03; trustee Children's Sch., Inc., Atlanta, 1971-79, 88-89, Nat. Assn. Children's Hosps. and Related Instns., Alexandria, Va., 1973-79. Lt. USN, 1959-62. Mem. Ga. Bar Assn. (chmn. corp. code revision com., corp. and banking sect. 1970-79), D.C. Bar Assn., Cherokee Town and Country Club (Atlanta), Highlands Country Club N.C., Amelia Island Club, Order of Coif, Omicron Delta Kappa. Episcopalian. Office: 1600 Parkwood Cir Ste 400 Atlanta GA 30339 Office Phone: 678-336-7187.

HOPKINS, JOHN L., engineering company executive; Completed Advanced Mgmt. Program; BBA, U. Tex., Austin. Pres., CEO TradeMC Inc., 2000—01; joined Fluor Corp., 1984, mgmt. positions, govt. unit, various sr. mgmt., sales and ops. positions, including pres., chemicals, plastics & fibers, group pres., corp. sales and mktg., corp. devel. and project fin., pres., chemicals & life sciences; sr. exec. mem. Fluor United Kingdom, Fluor Netherlands; group exec. Fluor Global Svcs. (subs. Fluor Corp.), 2001—02; group exec., sales, mktg. and strategic planning Fluor Corp., 2002—03, group pres., govt., 2003—09, group exec., corp. devel., 2009—. Bd. dirs. Bus. Coun. for Internat. Understanding, U.S. C. of C. Office: Fluor Corp 6700 Las Colinas Blvd Irving TX 75039 Office Phone: 469-398-7000. Office Fax: 469-398-7255. Business E-Mail: john.hopkins@fluor.com.

HOPKINS, LAURA, public health service officer; BS in Gerontology, Western Mich. U., 1979. Mktg. mgr. Harris Methodist Health System, 1995—2000; CEO, Cmty. Care New Mex. Amerigroup Corp., 2000—. Office: Amerigroup Corp 4425 Corporation Ln Virginia Beach VA 23462 Office Phone: 757-490-6900. Office Fax: 757-518-3600.

HOPKINS, LEE BENNETT, writer, educator; b. Scranton, Pa., Apr. 13, 1938; s. Lee Hall and Gertrude (Thomas) H. BA, Kean Coll., 1960, LLD (hon.), 1980; MS, Bank St. Coll., 1964; profl. diploma, Hunter Coll., 1966. Elem. tchr. Fair Lawn Pub. Schs., 1960—66; lang. arts supr. Bank St. Coll., NYC, 1966-68; curriculum specialist Scholastic, Inc., NYC, 1968-75; author Scarborough, NY, 1975—. Cons., vis. prof. various US and Can. colls. and univs.; bd. dirs. Soc. Sch. Librs. Internat.; lit. cons. Random House Achievement Program in Lit.; chmn. Nat. Coun. Tchrs. English poetry award com. Author: Been to Yesterdays: Poems of a Life, 1996 (The Christopher Book award and Golden Kite Honor Book award), numerous children's and junior books, poetry (awards include Nat. Coun. Tchrs. English, Tchrs. Choice award, Pa. Keystone to Reading award, Am. Inst. Graphic Arts award); contbr. articles, texts, and curriculum materials to mags., profl. jours. Recipient Lasting Contbn. to Field Children's Lit. awad U. So. Miss., 1989, Manhattan Coun. Literacy award Internat. Reading Assn., 1983, Ednl. Leadership award Phi Delta Kappa, 1980; named Keystone Author of Yr., Pa.; established Lee Bennett Hopkins Poetry award in conjunction with Children's Lit. Coun. Pa. State U., 1993—, Lee Bennett Hopkins Promising Poet award in conjunction with Internat. Reading Assn., 1995-, Excellence in Poetry for Children award, Nat. Coun. Tchrs. Eng., 2009. Mem.: Soc. Children's Book Writers and Illustrators, Internat. Reading Assn., Nat. Coun. Tchrs. of English. Avocations: reading, travel. Home and Office: 4923 Agualinda Blvd Cape Coral FL 33914 Office Phone: 239-549-9514. E-mail: lbhcove@aol.com.

HOPKINS, MARTHA ANN MARKLINE, artist; b. Meridian, Miss., Feb. 4, 1940; d. Hugh Wallace Markline and Martha Lou Morton; m. Harry L. Hopkins, Aug. 19, 1961; children: Peter Ashley, Caroline Baker. BA in Spanish, U. So. Miss., 1961; BA in Visual Art, U. Montevallo, 1982; BFA in Sculpture, U. Ala., 2004. Exec. sec., engr. asst. Humble Oil & Refining Co., New Orleans, 1961—65; modern lang. tchr. Meridian HS, 1967—71. Arts camp tchr. Birmingham (Ala.) Mus. Art, 1999, sculpture tchr. hs students, 2000. Prodr.: (films, demonstration video for Pub. TV) Found Object Sculpture, 2000; exhibitions include Celebrating Women Artists of Ala., 2001, Nat. Small Sculpture Exhbn., 2000, Three Rivers Arts Festival, Pitts., 1999, Gadsden (Ala.) Cultural Arts Ctr., 1998, Meridian Mus. Art, 1995, Meridian (Miss.) Cmty. Coll., 2004, Large Format Painting Exhbn., Montgomery, Ala., Minimalism in the 21st Century, Chgo., 2012, Contemporary Women Artists, St. Louis U. Mus. Art, "Bound" at Phoenix Gallery, NYC, 2012, prin. works include Ala. Vets. Meml. sculpture, Red Tide sculpture, U. Ala., Birmingham, 1991, Wild Blue sculpture, Meridian Miss. Airport, 2003, (book) Carousels Abound, 2003, Wheel for Lilith sculpture, Hardin Ctr. Cultural Arts, Gadsden, Ala., 2010, Stories WeTell. Phoenix Gallery, NYC, 2013, The Story of the Creative, NYC, 2013, Equilibrium, Chgo., 2014, Meridian Mus. Art, 2014. Bd. dirs. Planned Parenthood Ala., Birmingham, 1998—2001. Mem.: Ala. Designer/Craftsmen (pres. 1978—2001), Birmingham Doll Club (past pres.). Avocations: antiques, doll collecting, sculpting. Office: 3611 Oak Glen Dr Tuscaloosa AL 35406*

HOPKINS, VIRGINIA EMERSON, federal judge; b. Anniston, Ala., 1952; m. Chris Hopkins, 1978. Student, Agnes Scott Coll.; BA, U. Ala., 1974; JD, U. Va., 1977. Assoc. Lange, Simpson, Robinson & Somerville, Birmingham, Ala., 1977—78; mem. Taft, Stettinius & Hollister, Washington, 1978—91, ptnr., 1986—91, Campbell & Hopkins, Anniston, 1991—2004; judge US Dist. Ct. (no. dist. Ala.), 2004—. Office: US Dist Ct No Dist Ala Hugo Black Courthouse 1729 5th Ave N Birmingham AL 35203 E-mail: Virginia_Hopkins@alnd.uscourts.gov.

HOPPER, JACK RUDD, chemical engineering professor; b. Highlands, Tex., May 12, 1937; s. Bonnie Preston and Rosa Mae Hopper; m. Marilyn Joyce Spears, May 30, 1958; children: Connie, Bradley. Student, Lee Coll., 1957; BSChemE, Tex. A&M U., 1959; MChemE, U. Del., 1964; PhD, La. State U., 1969. Rsch. engr. Esso Rsch. and Engring., Baytown, Tex., 1959-67; asst. prof. chem. engring. Lamar U., Beaumont, Tex., 1969-72, assoc. prof. chem. engring., 1972-75, prof. chem. engring., 1975—, chair chem. engring. dept., 1974—99, dir. engring. grad. studies, 1989-99, liaison hazardous waste alternatives ctr., 1987-88, dean coll. engring., 1999—, interim assoc. provost for rsch., 2006—, provost rsch., 2007—07, exec. asst. econ. devel. and indsl. rels., 2007—, pres. econ. devel. and indsl. rels.; interim dir Gulf Coast Rsch. Ctr., 1993-94, assoc. dir., 1995-97, dir., 1997-99, Tex. Hazardous Waste Rsch. Ctr., 1993—, Tex. Ctr. Tech. Incubation, 2004—. Cons. J. M. Montgomery, New Orleans, 1991-92, Texaco Chem., Port Arthur, Tex., 1989-90, Star Enterprise, 1990-93, Tex. Internat. Ednl. Consortium, Austin, 1991-93, Mobil Chem., 1993. Mem. editl. bd. Waste Mgmt., 1992-96, co-editor 1996-2001; contbr. articles to profl. publs. Recipient Dow Outstanding Faculty award Am. Soc. for Engring. Edn., 1971, Outstanding Alumni award Lee Coll., 1981; named Hall of Distinction, LSU Coll. Engring., 2009. Fellow AIChE; mem. Tex. Soc. Profl. Engs. (Engr. of Yr. award Sabine chpt. 2004). Lutheran. Achievements include inventions in field. Office: Lamar U 4400 MLK Pkwy Beaumont TX 77705

HOPPER, KAREN, state legislator; m. Fred Waddell. BS in Journalism & Mktg., Murray State U. Assoc. vice chancellor rsch., spl. projects & distance learning Ark. State U., Mountain Home; former sr. dist. rep. Office US Congressmen Tim Hutchinson; mem. Dist. 81 Ark. House of Reps., 2009—. Bd. dirs. Mountain Home C. of C. Recipient Opal award, Mountain Home C. of C. Mem.: NRA. Republican. Office: State Capitol Rm 350 Little Rock AR 72201 also: PO Box 864 Mountain Home AR 72654 Office Phone: 501-682-6211, 501-682-7771, 870-431-8934. Business E-Mail: hopperk@arkleg.state.ar.us.

HOPPER, LYN, strategic planning consultant, retired librarian; Master of Edn., U. West Ga., 1978; Master of Librarianship, Emory U., 1984; Specialist's Degree in Library and Information Studies, Fla. State U., 2010. Lic. as Librarian Grade 5B by Georgia State Bd. for the Certification of Librarians. Asst. state librarian for library development, Ga., 2006—10; planning cons., 1986—2010; strategic planning consultant Lyn Hopper Consulting, 2009—. Taught library administration and management U. Ala. Graduate Program in Library and Information Services, 1999; consultant on LYRASIS project with Pa. libraries, 2011; faculty coordinator, supervised fieldwork, Master of library Administration Valdosta State U., instr. spl. topics - Master of Library and Information Sci., 2011—; dir. for two multi-county Georgia Public Library Systems. Author: Tools for Trustees: The Georgia Public Library Trustee Manual, 2006; contbr.; reviewer for Professional Reading column, Library Journal, initiator, coordinator We Love Libraries column, Georgia Library Quarterly. Mem.: Assn. for Rural and Small Libraries, Ga. Library Assn., Public Library Assn., American Library Assn. (Elizabeth Futas Catalyst for Change award 2012), Friends of Ga. Libraries, Beta Phi Mu. Office: Lyn Hopper Consulting 263 Lucy Lane Dahlonega GA 30533 Office Phone: 706-864-7163. Business E-Mail: lyn@lynhopper.com.

HOPPMANN, RICHARD ANTHONY, dean, physician, educator; b. Charleston, SC, Aug. 20, 1950; s. Harry Joseph and Dorothy Gadsen (Couturier) H.; m. Anne Griffin Harman, May 331, 1975; children: Emily, Karla, Nicholas. BS, U. S.C., 1972; MS, U. Ga., 1978; MD, Med. U. S.C., 1982. Diplomate Am. Bd. Internal Medicine, subspeciality rheumatology. Resident internal medicine East Carolina U. Sch. Medicine, Greenville, N.C., 1982-85; rheumatology fellow Bowman Gray Sch. Medicine, Wake Forest U., Winston-Salem, N.C., 1985-87; ast. prof. medicine East Carolina U. Sch. Medicine, Greenville, 1987-90; chief rheumatology med. svcs. Dorn Vets. Hosp., Columbia, S.C., 1990—; prof. medicine, dir. divsn. allergy, immunology U. SC Sch. Medicine, Columbia, 1990—, assoc. dean med. edn. and academic affairs, 2000—06, dean, 2006—. Mem. editorial bd. Med. Problems of Performing Artists, 1992—; contbr. articles to profl. jours. Recipient VA Commendation-Profl. Leadership, 1993. Fellow ACP, Am. Coll. Rheumatology; mem. AMA, Internat. Arts Medicine Assn., Nat. Assn. VA Physicians and Dentists, Performing Arts Medicine Assn. (mem. policy com.), S.C. Rheumatology Assn. Avocations: gardening, running, music, reading. Office: University SC Sch Medicine Office of Dean Bldg 3 6311 Garners Ferry Rd Columbia SC 29209

HOPSON, CHUCK, state legislator; b. Sept. 18, 1941; m. Billie Hopson; 3 children. Degree in pharmacy, U. Houston. Owner, operator, ind. pharmacist May Drugs, Jacksonville, Tex., 1973—; mem. Jacksonville Sch. Bd., Jacksonville City Coun.; mem. Dist. 11 Tex. House of Reps., 2000—. Mem.: NRA, Ctrl. East Tex. Pharmacy Assn., Tex. Soc. of Hosp. Pharmacists, Tex. Pharmacy Assn., Tex. State Rifle Assn. Democrat. Avocations: hunting, fishing. Office: Room GW.06 Capital PO Box 2910 Austin TX 78768 also: PO Box 2286 Jacksonville TX 75766-0067 Office Phone: 903-541-2250, 512-463-0592. Office Fax: 903-586-0823.

HOPSON, EDWIN SHARP, lawyer; b. Louisville, Apr. 23, 1945; s. Henry Dockins and Martha (Linton) H.; m. Jane Mayo Fitzpatrick, July 20, 1968; children: Edwin Hopson Jr., Martha. BSL, U. Louisville, 1967, JD, 1969; LLM, George Washington U., 1971. Bar: Ky. 1969, Fla. 1969, U.S. Supreme Ct. 1972, U.S. Dist. Ct. (we. dist.) Ky. 1974, U.S. Ct. Appeals (6th cir.) 1977. Atty. Solicitor's Office, U.S. Dept. Labor, Washington, 1969-72; field atty. NLRB, Balt., 1972-74; assoc. Tarrant, Combs, Blackwell & Bullitt, Louisville, 1974-77; ptnr. Tarrant, Combs & Bullitt, Louisville, 1977-80, Wyatt, Tarrant & Combs, L.L.P., Louisville, 1980—. Mem. Labor and Employment Practice Group. Co-author: The Developing Labor Law, 2002, 5th edit., 2006; editor: (chpt.) How Arbitration Works, 1989, 2nd edit., 2001—; chpt. editor: Discipline and Discharge in Arbitration, 1998, supplement, 2001. Bd. dirs. Bellewood Presbyn. Children's Home, Louisville, 1988-96, pres., 1991-93; bd. dirs. Louisville Ballet, 1991-92, v.p., 1992-93, pres., 1993-94; bd. dirs. Bellewood Children's Found., 1995-02, pres., 1995-96. Fellow Coll. Labor and Employment Lawyers, Inc.; mem. ABA (co-chmn. pub. of arbitration awards subcom. 2000-03, adr. com. of labor and employment sect. 1985—), FBA (chpt. pres. 1991-92), Louisville Bar Assn. (co-chmn. labor and employment law sect. 1982-83), Ky. Bar Assn. (co-chmn. labor and employment law sect. 1987-89, mem. ho. of dels. 1996-02, chair pub. com. 1989-91, 01—09, editor Bench and Bar Mag.). Republican. Presbyterian. Avocations: flying, various sports, reading. Home: 3003 Lightheart Rd Louisville KY 40222-6138 Office: Wyatt Tarrant & Combs LLP 2800 PNC Plz Louisville KY 40202-2823 Office Phone: 502-562-7360. Business E-Mail: ehopson@wyattfirm.com.

HOPSON, MARY LOUISE CARSTENS, marketing consultant; d. Carl Rand and Sally Carstens; m. David Carlisle Hopson, 1982. BA in Journalism, La. State U., 1978; Grad. Mktg. Cert., So. Meth. U., 2000. Corp. law cert. Inst. for Paralegal Tng., 1978. Corp. legal asst. Tex. Instruments Inc., Dallas, 1979-81; legal asst. Natural Resource Mgmt. Corp., Dallas, 1981-84; mgr. bus. devel. Haynes & Boone, Dallas, 1984-90; dir. practice devel. Calhoun, Gump, Spillman & Stacy, Dallas, 1990-93; pvt. practice profl. svcs. mktg. cons. Dallas, 1993—; prin. Marketing for the Professions, Dallas, 1993—; free-lance writer, editor, 1993—. Lectr. in field. Contbr. articles to profl. jours. Mem.: Jr. League Dallas (sustaining mem.). Home: 6626 Northwood Rd Dallas TX 75225-2534

HOPSON, W. BRIGGS, III, state legislator; b. Memphis, Oct. 10, 1965; m. Alison Quaid; children: Liam, Walt, Jane. Attended, U. Miss. Atty.; adjunct prof. Miss. coll. Law sch.; mem. Dist. 23 Miss. State Senate, 2008—. Republican. United Methodist. Office: PO Box 1018 Jackson MS 39215 Home: 306 Madison Ridge Rd Vicksburg MS 39180-3337 Office Phone: 601-359-3211. E-mail: bhopson@senate.ms.gov.

HOQUE, AKM MANSURUL, chemistry professor; PhD, Tex. Tech U., Lubbock, 1990. Assoc. prof. Ln. Coll., Jackson, Tenn., 1990—95; prof. Dyersburg State CC, Tenn., 1996—. Office: Dyersburg State CC 1510 Lake Rd Dyersburg TN 38024

HORAN, KEVIN, state legislator; m. Clarissa DeHart. B, U. Miss.; JD, Miss. Coll., Clinton. Atty.; CFO Milestone Hospice, Inc.; mem. Dist. 24 Miss. Hosue of Reps., Jackson, 2012—. Democrat. Office: Miss House of Reps PO Box 1018 Jackson MS 39215 Business E-Mail: khoran@house.ms.gov.

HORAN, RICHARD T., JR., lawyer; b. Washington, Dec. 24, 1961; BA summa cum laude, James Madison U., Harrisonburg, Va., 1984; JD, U. Va. Sch. Law, 1987. Bar: Va. 1988. Law clk. to Hon. James C. Cacheris US Dist. Ct. (ea. dist.) Va., 1987—88; ptnr. exec. com. Hogan Lovells US LLP (formerly Hogan & Hartson LLP), Mc Lean, Va., 1988—95, ptnr., 1996—, mem. exec. com., 2005—07, dir. corp., securities & fin. practice group, 2003—. Named a Va. Super Lawyer, Law & Politics mag., 2006—09, Washington, DC Super Lawyer, 2007—09; named one of America's Leading Lawyers for Bus., Chambers USA, 2005—10. Mem.: ABA, Fairfax Bar Found. (bd.

dirs.), Va. Bar Assn. Office: Hogan Lovells US LLP Park Pl II Ninth Fl 7930 Jones Branch Dr Mc Lean VA 22102-3390 Office Phone: 703-610-6111. Office Fax: 703-610-6200. Business E-Mail: richard.horan@hoganlovells.com.

HORCHOW, S. ROGER, theater producer; b. Cin., July 3, 1928; m. Carolyn Pfeifer, Dec. 29, 1960 (dec. Jun. 15, 2009); children: Regen Horchow Fearon, Elizabeth Horchow Routman, Sally Horchow McCauley. BA, Yale U., 1950, DLHD (hon.), 1999. Buyer Foley's, Houston, 1953-60; v.p. Neiman-Marcus, Dallas, 1960-68, 69-71; pres. Design Research, Cambridge, Mass., 1968-69, Kenton Collection, Dallas, 1971-73; chmn. Horchow Collection, Dallas, 1973-90. Author: Elephants in Your Mailbox, 1979, Living in Style, 1981; prodr. Crazy for You, 1991-95; co-prodr. Kiss Me Kate, 1999. (Broadway) Curtains, 2006, Gypsy, 2008; co-author: The Art of Friendship, 2005. Bd. dirs. Jefferson Award for Pub. Svc., Yale Art Galley, Found. Art and Preservation of Embassies, Dallas Mus. Art. Mem. Dallas Theater Ctr., Yale Club (N.Y.C.), Nantucket Yacht Club, Knickerbocker Club. Office: 5722 Chatham Hill Rd Dallas TX 75225-3208 Office Phone: 214-692-1954. E-mail: rhorchow@gmail.com.

HORCOFF, SHAWN, professional hockey player; b. Trail, BC, Canada, Sept. 17, 1978; s. John and Bruna Horcoff; m. Cindy Horcoff, 2003; children: Jade, Will. Grad., Mich. State U., 2000. Center Edmonton Oilers, 2000—13, Dallas Stars, 2013—; capt. Edmonton Oilers, 2010—13. Mem. Team Canada, World Hockey Championships, 2003, 2004, 2005. Named to NHL YoungStars Game, 2003, NHL All-Star Game, 2008; finalist Hobey Baker award, 2000. Office: Dallas Stars American Airlines Ctr 2500 Victory Ave Dallas TX 75201*

HORFORD REYNOSO, ALFRED JOEL (AL HORFORD), professional basketball player; b. Puerto Plata, Dominican Republic, June 3, 1986; s. Tito Horford and Arelis Reynoso. Attended, U. Fla., Gainesville, 2004—07. Forward, center Atlanta Hawks, 2007—. Named to NBA All-Rookie First Team, 2008, Ea. Conf. All-Star Team, NBA, 2010, 2011; finalist NBA Rookie of Yr. award, 2008. Achievements include being a member of back-to-back NCAA Division I National Championship University of Florida Gators teams, 2006, 2007. Office: Atlanta Hawks Centennial Tower 101 Marietta St NW Ste 1900 Atlanta GA 30303

HORGAN, CORNELIUS OLIVER, applied mathematics and mechanics professor, engineering educator; m. Myra O'Callaghan; children: Olivia, David. BS, Univ. Coll., Cork, 1964, MS, 1965; PhD, Calif. Inst. Tech., 1970; DSc, Nat. U. Ireland, 1983. Lectr. U. Mich., Ann Arbor, 1970-72; sr. research assoc. U. East Anglia, Norwich, U.K., 1972-74; assoc. prof. U. Houston, 1974-78; prof. applied mechanics and math. Mich. State U., East Lansing, 1978-88; prof. applied math. and applied mechanics U. Va., Charlottesville, 1988-94, Wills Johnson prof., 1994—. Vis. prof. Northwestern U., Evanston, 1977-78, Calif. Inst. Tech., Pasadena, 1984-85, U. Pisa, Italy, 1996, 97, U. Lecce, Italy, 2001, 03, U. Ferrara, Italy, 2001, 03, U. Politecnica de Catalunya, Terrassa, Spain, 2001, 03, Dublin City U., 2007. Contbr. over 200 publs. in field of theoretical mechanics and applied math. to profl. publs. Fellow ASME (chmn. tech. com. 1981-86), Am. Acad. Mechanics; mem. Soc. Engring. Sci. (bd. dirs. 1993-99, Eringen Medal 2005), Soc. Indsl. and Applied Math., Soc. Nat. Phil., Internat. Soc. Interaction of Mechanics and Maths. (exec. com. 2000-07). Home: 2820 Meadow Vista Dr Charlottesville VA 22901-9559 Office: U Va Dept Civil & Env Engring Thornton Hall Charlottesville VA 22904 Business E-Mail: coh8p@virginia.edu.

HORGER, EDGAR OLIN, III, retired obstetrics and gynecology educator; b. Eutawville, SC, May 30, 1937; s. Edgar Olin Jr. and Frances Durant (Jordan) H.; m. Polly Jo Collins, May 29, 1960; children: Edgar Olin IV, David Collins, Patricia Bowen. BS, Furman U., 1959; MD, Med. Coll. S.C., 1962. Cert. Am. Bd. Obstetrics and Gynecology, 1971, Am. Bd. Obstetrics and Gynecology Dvsn. Maternal-Fetal Medicine, 1974. Intern Med. U. Hosp., Charleston, SC, 1962-63, resident in ob-gyn, 1963-67; NIH fellow U. Pitts., 1967-68, asst. prof., 1968-69, Med. U. S.C., Charleston, 1969-71, assoc. prof., 1971-76, prof., 1976-90, dir. maternal-fetal medicine, 1973-90; prof. ob-gyn. U. S.C. Sch. Medicine, Columbia, 1990-2001, disting. prof., chmn., 1993-99, disting. prof. emeritus, 2001—. Mem. S.C. Bd. Med. Examiners, 1985-87, disting.prof. emeritus, U. SC, Sch Medicine, 2001 Contbr. articles to profl. jours. Adv. bd. Charleston chpt. March of Dimes, 1984-90. Capt. USAR, 1963-66. Recipient Disting. Alumnus award Med. U. S.C., 1995; USPHS fellow, 1967-68. Mem. AMA, S.C. Med. Assn., Am. Coll. Ob-Gyn. (Outstanding Faculty award dist. IV 1988, vice chmn. S.C. sect. 1993-96, chmn. 1996-98, treas. dist. IV 1997-2000, Outstanding Dist. Svc. award 2001), Coun. Res. Edn. ObGyn, South Ctrl. Ob-Gyn. Soc., South Atlantic Assn. Ob-Gyn. (exec. com. 1983-94, sec. 1987-90, v.p. 1990-91, pres.-elect 1991-92, pres. 1992-93; Lifetime Achievement award 2007), So. Perinatal Assn. (dir. Mid-Atlantic region 1974-76), Soc. Perinatal Obstetricians (dir. 1977-78), Am. Gynecol. Obstet. Soc., Am. Assn. Ob-Gyn., S.C. Ob-Gyn. Soc. (pres. 1991-92), Columbia Med. Soc., Assn. Profs. Gynecology and Obstetrics (Excellence in Tchg. award 1992), S.C. State Bd. Med. Examiners (bd. dirs. 1985-87), Wild Dunes Club, Alpha Omega Alpha. Episcopalian. Avocations: tennis, scuba diving, skiing, genealogy. Home: 17 Beach Club Ct Isle Of Palms SC 29451 Personal E-mail: ehorger@aol.com.

HORHN, JOHN, state legislator; b. Goodman, Miss., Feb. 8, 1955; m. Lydia Gale Cole; children: Siraj, Charla. Mem. Dist. 26 Miss. State Senate, 1993—; mem. Pub. Access Adv. Bd., Jackson City; cons., cmty. devel.; bd. trustees Ctr. Coll.; exec. com. mem. Jackson Arts Alliance; bd. mem. S. Art Fedn.; mem., adv. bd. Ctr. Study S. Cult, Woodhaven Neighborhood Assn., Milsaps Arts & Lecture Series; motivational spkr. Mem.: NAACP, Miss. Inst. Arts & Letters, Sci. & Tech. Com., Duke Govs. Ctr., A. Philip Randolph Inst., Screen Actors Guild, 100 Black Men of Jackson, Leadership Jackson Alumni Assn. Democrat. Baptist. Mailing: PO Box 2030 Jackson MS 39225-2030 Home Phone: 601-362-1045; Office Phone: 601-366-4285, 601-359-6217. Fax: 601-366-4293; Office Fax: 601-359-2879. Business E-Mail: jhorhn@senate.ms.gov.

HORKEY, WILLIAM RICHARD, retired oil industry executive; b. Tulsa, Apr. 22, 1925; s. William Edward and Clara Doris (Rice) H.; m. Barbara Jeanne Williamson, Oct. 18, 1952; m. Celia Ann Rosenberger, Jan. 8, 2008.; children: Elaine Gail, Edward Richard, Ellen Beth. BA, State U. Iowa, 1947; JD, U. Okla., 1950; grad., Advanced Mgmt. Program, Harvard U., 1962. Bar: Okla. 1950. With Gulf Oil Corp., 1950-51, Skelly Oil Co., 1951-55, Helmerich & Payne, Inc., Tulsa, 1955-90, sec., legal counsel, 1955-64, v.p., 1960-64, exec. v.p., 1964-87, sr. v.p., 1987-90, bd. dirs., 1957-90. Chmn. Grand River Dam Authority, Okla. Ordnance Works Authority, Woolslayer Cos. Inc., EnviroFuels Inc.; bd. dirs. Asbury Group. Bd. dirs. Tulsa United Way, 1978-88; chmn. S.E. Tulsa YMCA, 1970-72; pres. Met. Tulsa YMCA, 1972-73, Tulsa Bus. Health Group 1978-96; chmn. Tulsa chpt. ARC, 1987-88; bd. dirs. Emergency Med. Svcs. Authority, 1977-95, chmn., 1981-95; pres. Tulsa Cmty. Found. for Indigent Health Care, 1980—. Mem. ABA, Okla. Bar Assn., Tulsa County Bar Assn., Order of Coif, So. Hills Country Club, Mid-Continent Harvard AMP (Tulsa) (pres. 1969-75), Phi Delta Phi, Phi Delta Theta. Republican. Presbyterian. Home: 7310 Aberdeen Pkwy E Tulsa OK 74132-2140 Home Phone: 918-388-3865. Personal E-mail: william.horkey@cox.net.

HORLANDER, DENNIS, state legislator; Attended, U. Louisville. Mfrs. rep.; mem. Dist. 40 Ky. House of Reps., 1996—. Mem.: Barkley & Shive, Manufacturer's Assn., Hardware Retail Assn., Marydale Club, Shively Area Bus. Assn., Dixie Post 220 (assoc.). Democrat. Catholic. Mailing: Suite 6 1806 Farnsley Rd Shively KY 40216 Office: Capitol Annex Rm 351D Frankfort KY 40601 Office Phone: 502-442-2498, 502-564-8100 ext 636. E-mail: dennis.horlander@lrc.ky.gov.

HORN, CARL, III, retired federal judge, lawyer, mediator, arbitrator, law educator; b. 1951; BA with honors, U. Va., 1973; JD, U. S.C., 1976. Bar: N.C. 1976. Assoc. Grier, Parker, Poe, Thompson, Bernstein, Gage & Preston, Charlotte, NC, 1976-79; legal counsel, instr. Wheaton Coll., 1979-82; spl. asst. civil rights divsn. U.S. Dept. Justice, Charlotte, 1982-83, chief asst. U.S. atty. for western dist. N.C., 1987-93; ptnr. Horn & Conrad and predecessor, Charlotte, 1984-87; US magistrate judge for western dist. NC US Dist. Ct., Charlotte, 1993—2009; of counsel Anderson & Terpening PLLC, Charlotte, NC, 2009—10, Law Offices of Carl Horn, III, PLLC, 2010—. Author: Fourth Circuit Criminal Handbook, 1994—, Horn's Federal Criminal Jury Instructions for the Fourth Circuit, 1997, LawyerLife: Finding a Life and a Higher Calling in the Practice of Law, 2003; editor: Michie's Fourth Circuit Criminal Reporter, 1995—, Federal Civil Practice in the Fourth Circuit, 1997, Law for Physicians, 1999; co-author and editor: The Battle for Morality in Pluralistic America, 1985; contbr. articles to law jours. Office: 2810 Wamath Dr Charlotte NC 28210 Office Phone: 704-591-6398. Business E-Mail: ch@carhornlaw.com.

HORN, CHARLES L., credit services company executive; BBA, Abilene Christian U., Tex.; MBA, U. Tex., Austin. CPA. Audit mgr. PricewaterhouseCoopers; exec. v.p., CFO Conquest Industries, 1992—94; v.p. fin. and treasury, retail ops. Pier 1 Imports, Inc., 1994—99; v.p. fin., contr. Builders FirstSource Inc., Dallas, 1999—2000, sr. v.p., CFO, 2000—09; sr. v.p. Alliance Data Sys., Inc., 2009; exec. v.p., CFO Alliance Data Systems Corp., 2009—. Office: Alliance Data Systems, Inc 7500 Dallas Pky Ste 700 Plano TX 75024 Office Phone: 214-494-3000. Personal E-mail: charles.horn@alliancedata.com.

HORN, DWIGHT CRAIG, state legislator; Mem. Dist. 68 NC House of Representatives, 2011—. Republican. Office: 5909 Bluebird Hill Ln Weddington NC 28104 Address: North Carolina House of Representatives 16 W Jones St Room 1010 Raleigh NC 27601-1096 Office Phone: 704-844-9960, 919-733-2406. Business E-Mail: craig@hornfornchouse.com, Craig.Horn@ncleg.net.

HORN, J. STACY, energy executive; BS in Geology, Sam Houston State U., 1981, MBA in Bus. Mgr. gas supply Delhi Gas Pipeline, 1988—95; dir. bus. devel. Teco Pipeline Co., 1995—97, PG&E Tex. Pipeline Co., 1997—2000; comml. mgr., dir. bus. devel., mgr. gas supply El Paso Field Svcs., L.P., 2000—04; mgr. gas supply Enterprise Products Co., 2004; v.p. comml. devel. Eagle Rock Energy, Inc., 2004—05, Eagle Rock Pipeline, LP, 2005—, Eagle Rock Energy G&P, LLC, 2006—, Eagle Rock Energy Partners, LP, 2006—. Office: Eagle Rock Energy Partners LP PO Box 2968 Houston TX 77252-2968 Office Phone: 281-408-1200. Office Fax: 281-408-1399. Business E-Mail: s.horn@eaglerockenergy.com.

HORNBACK, PAUL, state legislator; b. Shelbyville, Ky. m. Patricia Hornback; children: Amanda, Stephanie. Farmer, 1977—; mem. Dist. 20 Ky. State Senate, Frankfort, 2011—. Mem.: Ky. Bankers Assn., Shelby County C. of C., Shelby County Farm Bur. Republican. Roman Catholic. Office: Kentucky State Senate Annex Rm 203 702 Capitol Ave Frankfort KY 40601 Office Phone: 502-564-8100 ext. 648. Business E-Mail: paul.hornback@lrc.ky.gov.

HORNBAKER, RENEE JEAN, wholesale distribution executive; b. Gary, Ind., Aug. 6, 1952; d. Charles James and Paula (Augustinovich) Westbay; m. Gordon Lee Hornbaker, May 17, 1975. BA in English, Ind. U., 1974, MBA, 1977. CPA, Ariz., Ill. Staff acct. Deloitte, Haskins & Sells (now Deloitte & Touche Tohmatsu), Phoenix, 1977—79, sr. acctg. positions Chgo., 1980—83, mgr., 1983—85, sr. mgr., 1986; asst. contr. Southwest Forest Industries, Phoenix, 1986—87; v.p., asst. treas., v.p., info. svcs. Cir. K. Corp., Phoenix, 1987; v.p., bus. devel. Flowserve Corp., 1986—96, v.p., CFO, 1997—2004; CEO, cons. CompuCom Sys., Inc., 2005—06; CFO Shared Technologies, Inc. Bd. dirs. Eastman Chem. Co., 2003—. Chmn. corp. com. UCP, 1988—. Mem. Am. Inst. CPA's, Ariz. CPA Soc., Beta Gamma Sigma. Lodges: Soroptimist. Republican. Roman Catholic. Avocations: golf, art, antiques. Office: Shared Technologies Inc 2425 Gateway Dr Irving TX 75063 Office Phone: 972-462-5800. Business E-Mail: renee.hornbaker@stfi.com.

HORNBECK, LARRY J., physicist, researcher; b. Mo. m. Laura Hornbeck; children: Jason, David. BS, MS in Physics, Case Western Res. U., Cleve., PhD in Solid State Physics, 1973. Mem. tech. staff Ctrl. Rsch. Labs., Tex. Instruments, Dallas, 1973—83, sr. mem. tech. staff, 1983—93, Tex. Instruments fellow, 1993—. Contbr. articles to sci. jours. Recipient Tech. award, Eduard Rhein Found., Germany, 1995, Emmy Engring. award, Acad. TV Arts & Scis., 1998, Karl Ferdinand Braun prize, Soc. Info. Display, 1999, David Sarnoff Medal award, Soc. Motion Picture & TV Engineers, 2002, Best of Small Tech. Lifetime Achievement award, Small Times Mag., 2004, Progress medal, Photographic Soc. America, 2006, Royal Photographic Soc., 2007, Indsl. Applications of Physics prize, Am. Inst. Physics, 2007; named to Nat. Inventors Hall of Fame, 2009. Fellow: IEEE (Daniel E. Noble award 2004), Internat. Soc. Optical Engring. (Electronic Imaging Honoree of Yr. award 2001); mem.: NAE. Achievements include invention of the Digital Micromirror Device, an optical semiconductor with as many as 2 million hinged, tiltable and individually controllable micromirrors integrated on a chip; development of CCD image sensors, uncooled IR detectors and reflective spatial light modulators; patents in field. Fax: 214-567-5454. E-mail: l-hornbeck@ti.com.

HORNBY, SARA ANN, metallurgical engineer, marketing professional; b. Plymouth, Devon, Eng., Apr. 17, 1952; came to U.S., 1986; d. Foster John and Joanna May (Duncan) Hornby; m. John Victor Anderson, Sept. 2, 1978 (div. May 1987). BSc in Metallurgy with honors, Sheffield City Poly., Eng., 1973, PhD in Indsl. Metallurgy, 1980. Chartered engr. Metallurgist Joseph Lucas Rsch., Solihull, England, 1970, William Lee Malleable, Dronfield, 1972; tech. sales specialist Applied Rsch. Labs, Luton, Beds, 1973—74; quality assurance metallurgist Firth Brown Tools, Sheffield, 1974—75, rsch. metallurgist high speed steel, 1975; lectr. Sheffield City Poly., 1975—78; grad. metallurgist, strip devel. metallurgist British Steel Corp., Rotherham, 1978—80; program mgr. Can. Liquid Air, Montreal, Canada, 1980—85; group mktg. mgr. Liquid Air Corp., Countryside, Ill., 1986—90, tech. mgr. Walnut Creek, Calif., 1990—93; bus. devel. mgr.-metals and materials Can. Liquid Air, Toronto, Ont., 1993—97, N.Am. steel tech. mgr., 1995—97; dir. steelmaking tech. Goodfellow Techs. Inc., Mississauga, Ont., Canada, 1997, dir. ops., 1997—99, mgr. bus. devel., 1999; product mgr. steel making/ melting Midrex Techs., Inc., Charlotte, NC, 1999—2003; pres. Global Strategic Solutions, Inc., Charlotte, NC, 2003—06; process innovation specialist Linde Gas LLC, Cleve., 2006—07; pres. Global Strategic Solutions, Inc., Charlotte, 2007—08; v.p. sales & mktg. Process Tech. Internat. Inc., Tucker, Ga., 2008—10; prin. Global Strategic Solution Inc., 2010—11, 2013—; dir. optimization group Tube City IMS LLC, 2011—13. Bd. dirs., chmn. R & D com., mem. publs. com., chmn. promotions and mktg. com. Investment Casting Inst., Dallas; presenter to confs. in field. Contbr. articles to profl. jours.; patentee in field of metallurgy. Vol. Charlotte Police Dept. Mem. AIME, Inst. Metals (young metallurgists com. 1974-80), Sheffield Metall. Soc. Inst. Metals (sec. 1978-80), Am. Foundry Soc., Iron and Steel Soc. (steering com. 1987-91, chmn. topics com. 1988-89, sec. 1992, vice chair 1993, chmn. process tech. divsn. 1994, bd. dirs., strategic planning com. 1995-98, internat. affairs com. 1998-2004, bd. dirs. ad hoc com. on internat. affairs 1998-99, univ. rels. com. 1998-2004), Assn. Iron and Steel Tech. (ironmaking com. 2004—08). Avocations: scuba diving, horseback riding, swimming, gardening. Office Phone: 219-730-2798, 704-488-7969. Business E-Mail: shornby@tubecityims.com. E-mail: shornbyanderson@carolina.rr.com.

HORNE, JENNY ANDERSON, state legislator; b. Summerville, SC, Oct. 12, 1972; d. John D. and Cynthia W. Anderson; m. Marc F. Horne, May 11, 1996; children: Marc Nicholas, Margaret. BA in English, U. SC, 1994, JD, 1997. Law clk. to hon. Margaret Beane Seymour US Dist. Ct. SC, 1998—2000; mem. Dist. 94 SC House of Reps., 2008—. Mem.: SC Women Lawyers Assn., Summerville Oakbrook Rotary Club. Republican. Meth. Home and Office: Dist/Home Office 102 Perry Ln Summerville SC 29483 Office: Capitol Office 308D Blatt Bldg Columbia SC 29201 Home Phone: 843-821-6496; Office Phone: 843-873-1721, 803-212-6871. E-mail: jennyhorne@schouse.org.

HORNE, NATHAN E., air transportation executive; B in Bus. Mgmt., Miss. State U.; participated in Postgraduate & Exec. Edn. Programs, Ga. State U., Harvard U., Ga. Tech. U. Various bus. devel. and product mgmt. AT and T; co-founder Jet Black Oil, Inc., Las Vegas, Nev., v.p., COO; chmn. CEO Legend Constrn. Inc., Nev.; founder NEH Enterprises, LLC, 2001, mgmt. postions; mng. ptnr., exec. dir. WiFi2Go, LLC, Ga., 2003—; exec. v.p., energy and tech. Air Transport Group Holdings, Inc., 2009—. Office: Air Transport Group Holdings Inc 7453 Woodruff Way Stone Mountain GA 30087-6137 Office Phone: 404-671-9253.

HORNE, STEPHEN (STEVE) A., state legislator; b. Meridian, Miss., June 10, 1958; m. Suzy Coker Horne. Ins. asst. adminstr.; mem. Dist. 81 Miss. House of Reps., 2004—, mem. county affairs com., forestry com., univs. and colls. com., wildlife, fisheries and pks. com. Mem.: NRA, Masons. Republican. Baptist. Address: 5904 Causeyville Rd Meridian MS 39301 Office Phone: 601-482-1456. Business E-Mail: shorne@house.ms.gov.

HORNER, CARL MATTHEW, chemistry professor; b. Cicero, NY, June 4, 1930; s. Oscar Wendell and Gladys Cecilia (Horner) H. BS, LeMoyne Coll., 1952; MS, Syracuse U., 1958, PhD, 1965. Asst. prof. analytical chemistry SUNY-Oneonta, 1958-61, assoc. prof., 1961-64, prof., 1964—97, prof. emeritus, 1998—. Coord. ann. instrumental chemistry workshops, 1986-95; docent Edison Botanic Rsch. Lab., Ft. Myers, Fla., 2006—, cons., Edison Botanic Rsch. Lab., 2011-. NSF CAUSE grantee, 1979-82; NSF CSIP grantee, 1986-88; Walter B. Ford Found. grantee, 1980, 83. Mem. AAAS, Am. Chem. Soc. Achievements include research in infrared spectroscopy and laboratory robotics. Avocations: scuba diving, photography. Home: 230 SE 10th Ave Cape Coral FL 33990-1241 also: 24 Suncrest Ter Oneonta NY 13820

HORNER, MIKE, state legislator; b. Jacksonville, Fla., Jan. 8, 1968; m. Abby Horner; 1 child, Lawson. BA, U. Fla., 1989; MPA, U. Central Fla., 1995. Mem. Dist. 79 Fla. House of Reps., 2008—, dep. whip, 2008—09, vice chair transp. and econ. devel. appropriations com., mem. econ. devel. and cmty. affairs policy coun., energy and utilities policy com., health care regulation policy com. Chmn. Osceola Legis. Delegation. Bd. mem. Cmty. Health Improvement Coun., Cmty. Vision, Good Samaritan Retirement Village, Osceola Regional Med. Ctr. With Fla. Nat. Guard US Army, 1992—96. Recipient Compadre award, Hispanic Bus. Coun., 2002, Outstanding Svc. to Srs. award, Osceola County Coun. on Aging, 2004, Outstanding Cmty. Leader, Cmty. Vision, 2005, Golden Eagle award, Osceola Boy Scouts, 2006; named Person of Yr., Osceola Veterans Coun., 2004. Mem.: NRA (life), Osceola County Rep. Exec. Com. (Rep. Man of Yr. 2006). Republican. Baptist. Office: House Office Bldg 402 S Monroe St Rm 300 Tallahassee FL 32399-1300 also: 323 Pleasant St Kissimmee FL 34741-5763 Office Phone: 850-488-8992, 407-943-3077. Business E-Mail: mike.horner@myfloridahouse.gov.

HORSLEY, DONALD R., telecommunications industry executive; b. Birmingham, Ala. BSEE, MBA, U. Ala., Tuscaloosa. Various positions with Ala. Power including engr., asst. to the exec. v.p. for customer svc., human resources gen. mgr. and Birmingham divsn. mgr. Southern Co., 1978—2001, gen. mgr. transmission lines for power delivery, 2001—05, v.p. transmission, 2005—06, v.p. customer services and retail mktg. for Miss. Power, 2006—11, pres., CEO SouthernLINC Wireless and Southern Telecom, 2011—. Bd. dirs. Miss. Energy Policy Inst.; chmn. Shelby County Econ. and Indsl. Devel. Authority; mem. power delivery & utilization coun. Electric Power Rsch. Inst. Bd. dirs. Jefferson County Schools Pub. Edn. Found.; bd. chmn. United Way South Miss.; mem. engring. found. coun. U. Ala. Sch. Engring., Birmingham; mem. diversity adv. coun. Miss. State U. Bagley Coll. Engring. Office: SouthernLINC Wireless 5555 Glenridge Connector Ste 500 Atlanta GA 30342

HORSLEY, WALLER HOLLADAY, retired lawyer; b. Richmond, Va., July 2, 1931; s. John Shelton Jr. and Lilian (Holladay) H.; m. Margaret Stuart Cooke, Dec. 3, 1955; children: Margaret Terrell, Stuart W., John Garrett. BA with distinction, U. Va., 1953, LLB, 1959. Bar: Va. 1959, U.S. Dist. Ct. (ea. dist.) Va. 1959, U.S. Tax Ct. 1959, U.S. Ct. Appeals (4th cir.) 1959, U.S. Supreme Ct. 1969. Ptnr. Hunton & Williams, Richmond, 1965-92, Horsley & Horsley, Richmond, 1992—2005. Lectr. taxation U. Va. Law Sch., 1961-65, 69. Mem. editorial bd. Taxation for Lawyers, 1975-86, Probate Lawyer, 1976-87, Probate Notes, 1976-87, editor, 1986-87; bd. advisors Va. Tax Rev., 1981—2001; contbr. articles to legal jours. Mem. adv. coun. Sch. Bus., Va. Commonwealth U., 1983-91; sr. warden St. Stephen's Episcopal Ch., 1977-79; gen. conv. dep. Diocese of Va., 1979, 85; pres. Richmond Tennis Patrons Assn., 1969, Va. Silver Star Found., 1985-86; mem. bd. visitors U. Va., 1988-92; sec. bd. govs. The Cmty. Found., 2000-03. With USN, 1953-56; to lt. comdr. USNR, 1956-62. Recipient Algernon Sydney Sullivan award, 1953; named Outstanding Young Man of Yr., Richmond Jr. C. of C., 1965. Fellow Am. Bar Found., Va. Bar Found.; mem. ABA, Va. State Bar (pres. 1982-83), Va. Bar Assn., Am. Coll. Trust and Estate Counsel (pres. 1990),

Country Club of Va., Westwood Club, Omicron Delta Kappa, Phi Beta Kappa, Order of Coif. Democrat. Episcopalian. Home: 6161 River Rd # 48 Richmond VA 23226-3334 Office Phone: 804-359-9596. E-mail: whhorsley@comcast.net.

HORSMAN, DAVID A. ELLIOTT, writer, finance company executive, educator; b. Calvert County, Md., June 28, 1932; s. Alvin W. and Bessie L. (Elliott) H. Student, U. Chgo.; BA, San Francisco State U., 1964; MA, NYU, 1967, PhD, 1970; MDiv, Episc. Div. Sch., 1984. Ordained priest, consecrated bishop Jurisdiction of Orthodox Ch. of Far Isles, 2000. Fl. dir., stage mgr. WTOP-TV, Washington, 1959-61; TV writer/producer Insight, Nat. Coun. Chs., Washington, 1961-62; English master, dir. studies Searing Sch., NYC, 1965-67; asst. prof. humanities Acad. Aeros., Flushing, N.Y., 1967-68; instr. humanities Rensselaer Poly. Inst., Troy, N.Y., 1969-70; assoc. prof., founder and coord. film sequence U. South Fla., Tampa, 1970-80; headmaster All Hallows Acad., Alexandria, Va., 1985-87; pres. Elliott Horsman & Assocs., 1988-89; fin. cons. Shearson Lehman Hutton, Inc., Balt., 1989-91; investment broker RAF Fin. Corp., Atlanta, 1991-92; exec. Josepthal, Lyon & Ross, Atlanta, 1992-93; v.p. Meyers, Pollock & Robbins, Atlanta, 1992-97; pres. Horsman Bros., Inc., 1998—. Chmn. bd. of fellows All Hallows Hall, 1998—; founder Horsman Hedge Fund, 1999 Author: The Liturgy as Communication, 1970, Introduction to Structural Description of Liturgical Dromena, 1979, (novel and screenplay) Pilgrims on Strange Strands, 1979, The Hovering Mercy and the Outstretched Hand, 2003, The Briar Patch, 2003, Christus Via, 2004, (novel) The Cosmopolitan Club Dossier, 2011. With US Army, 1957—59. Recipient Founders Day award NYU, 1971. Personal E-mail: allhallowshall@att.net.

HORTON, DONALD R., construction executive; b. Ark., 1950; married; 2 children. B, U. Ctrl. Ark. Pres. D.R. Horton, Inc., Fort Worth, Tex., 1991—98, chmn., 1991—. Bd. dirs. D.R. Horton, Inc., 1991—. Named one of World's Richest People, Forbes mag., 2007. Office: DR Horton DR Horton Tower 301 Commerce St Ste 500 Fort Worth TX 76102 Office Phone: 817-856-8200.

HORTON, JOSEPH JULIAN, JR., economics and finance educator; b. Memphis, Tenn., Nov. 7, 1936; s. Joseph Julian and Nina (Williams) H.; m. Linda Anne Langley, May 30, 1964; children: Joseph Julian, Anne Adele, David Douglas. AA, Lon Morris Jr. Coll., 1955; BA, N.Mex. State U., 1958; MA, So. Meth. U., 1965, PhD, 1968; postgrad., Harvard U., 1970—71. Claims examiner Social Security Adminstrn., Kansas City, Mo., 1958-60, claims authorizer, 1960-61; with FDIC, Washington, 1967-71, fin. economist, 1967-69, coord. merger analysis, 1969-71; prof., chmn. dept. econs. and bus. Slippery Rock (Pa.) State Coll., 1971-81; vis. fin. economist Fed. Home Loan Bank Bd., Washington, 1978-79; prof., chmn. commerce divsn. Bellarmine (Ky.) Coll., 1981-82, dean W. Fielding Rubel Sch. Bus., 1982—86; dean Sch. Mgmt. U. Scranton, Pa., 1986-96; prof. Coll. Bus. Adminstrn. U. Ctrl. Ark., Conway, 1996—2001, prof. econ. and fin., 2001—. Asst. prof. George Washington U., Washington, 1968-69, U. Md., College Park, 1969-70; pres. Pa. Conf. Economists, Internat. Acad. Bus. Disciplines, Congress of Polit. Economists, U.S.A. Bd. editors Ea. Econ. Jour.; contbr. articles to profl. jours. Recipient Cokesbury award So. Meth. U., 1965; NSF Grad. fellow, 1964-66, Ford Found. Dissertation fellow, 1966-67, Harvard U. Rsch. fellow, 1970-71, Bank Adminstrn. Inst. Clarence Lichtfeldt fellow, 1981, Burk fellow. Mem. Am. Econ. Assn., Am. Fin. Assn., Internat. Acad. Bus. Disciplines (pres.), N.Am. Econs. and Fin. Assn. (bd. dirs., v.p., pres.), Ea. Econ. Assn. (v.p.). Office: U Cen Ark Dept Econ and Fin Coll Bus Adminstrn Conway AR 72035-0001 Office Phone: 501-450-5310. Business E-Mail: jhorton@uca.edu.

HORTON, THOMAS EDWARD, JR., mechanical engineering educator; b. Houston, Jan. 12, 1935; s. Thomas Edward and Minnie Tolula (Sloan) H.; m. Bobbie Jean Newcomb, June 8, 1963; children— Holly Anne, Thomas Edward. BS, U. Tex., 1957, PhD, 1964; MS (Caterpillar rsch. fellow), Stanford U., 1958. Jr. mech. engr. Shell Devel. Co., Houston, 1957-58; tchg. asst., rsch. asst., rsch. scientist U. Tex., Austin, 1959-62; rsch. engr. Jet Propulsion Lab. Calif. Inst. Tech., Pasadena, 1962, sr. rsch. engr., 1963-66; asso. prof. mech. engring., rsch. engr. U. Miss., 1966-71, prof., rsch. engr., 1971-94, emeritus prof., 1994—. Dir. U.S. Army Laser Sci. Lab., Redstone Arsenal, Ala., 1975-76, Reiton Corp. of Houston; cons. Army Research Office, Jet Propulsion Lab., Marathon Oil Co., Shell Devel. Co., Exxon, Chevron, Mobil, Texaco. Contbr. articles to profl. jours.; patentee in field. Fellow AIAA (assoc.; mem. tech. coms.); mem. ASME (life; mem. tech. coms.), Am. Phys. Soc., Am. Soc. Engring. Edn. (research award Southeastern sect. 1971), Sigma Xi (pres. local chpt.), Tau Beta Pi (student adviser), Pi Tau Sigma, Phi Eta Sigma. Republican. Methodist. Home: 5100 San Felipe Rd 97E Houston TX 77056

HORTON, TOM (THOMAS W. HORTON), air transportation executive; b. Hampton, Va., May 24, 1961; m. Janet Horton, 1983; 2 children. BBA magna cum laude, Baylor U., 1983; MBA, Southern Methodist U., 1985. CPA. Staff mem. finance dept. American Airlines, Inc., 1985—88, mgr. financial planning, 1988—90, mng. dir. treasury, 1990—92, mng. dir. corporate acctg., 1992—94, v.p., controller, 1994—98, v.p. Europe London, 1998—2000, sr. v.p. finance, CFO, 2000—02, exec. v.p., finance & planning, CFO, 2006—10, pres., 2010—11, chmn., pres., CEO, 2011—; sr. v.p. finance, CFO AMR Corp., 2000—02, exec. v.p., finance & planning, CFO Ft. Worth, 2006—10, pres., 2010—11, chmn., pres., CEO, 2011—13; chmn. American Airlines Group, Inc., 2013—; sr. exec. v.p., CFO AT&T Corp., 2002—05, vice chmn., CFO, 2005—06. Bd. dirs. ExpressJet Holdings, Inc., 2005—06, Qualcomm, Inc., 2008—, AMR Corp., 2010—13, American Airlines, Inc., 2010—13, American Airlines Group, Inc., 2013—. Bd. govs. United Way of Tri State; mem. exec. bd. Southern Methodist U., Cox Sch. Bus.; chmn. Oneworld Alliance, 2011—. Office: American Airlines Group Inc 4333 Amon Carter Blvd Fort Worth TX 76155*

HORUZSKO, ANATOLIJ, medical researcher; b. Pinsk, Belarus, Oct. 10, 1953; s. Pavel Horuzsko and Anna Juskevich; m. Vera Portik-Dobos, Mar. 30, 1981; children: Julia Szonja, Daniel David. MD (hon.), Pediat. Med. Sch., Leningrad, Russia, 1976; PhD in immunology and allergy, Inst. of Exptl. Medicine, Russian Acad. of Sci., Leningrad, Russia, 1980; MD, Semmelweis U. of Medicine, Budapest, Hungary, 1986; PhD in clin. immunology and allergy, Hungarian Acad. of Sci., Budapest, Hungary, 1987. Lectr., sr. lectr. Pediatric Med. Sch., Leningrad, Russia, 1979—86; sr. lectr. Nat. Inst. of Hematology and Blood Transfusion, Budapest, Hungary, 1986—92; non-clin. scientist, grade 1 Nat. Inst. for Med. Rsch., London, 1992—95; sr. rsch. scientist Med. Coll. of Ga., Augusta, 1995—98, instr., 1998—2002, asst. prof., 2002—06, assoc. prof., 2006—. Author: (over 40 studies) Dealing With Issues In Transplantation Medicine And Immunobiology. Recipient Prize of George Soros, George Soros Found., 1988, Internat. Rsch. award, Wellcome Trust, U.K., 1992—95, Internat. Human Frontier Sci. Program Orgn., Strasbourg, France, 1998, Internat. Union Against Cancer, Geneva, Switzerland, 1999, Roche Organ Transplantation Rsch. Found., Switzerland, 2001. Mem.: European Fedn. for Immunogenetics (assoc.), Hungarian Soc. for Immunology (assoc.), Brit. Soc. for Immunology (assoc.), AAAS (assoc.), Am. Assn. of Immunologists (assoc.). Office: Med Coll of Ga 1410 Laney Walker Blvd Augusta GA 30912-2615 Personal E-mail: horuzsko@netzero.net. Business E-Mail: ahoruzsko@mcg.edu.

HORVITZ, PAUL MICHAEL, economist; b. Providence, Aug. 6, 1935; s. Abraham and Rose (Gershkoff) H.; m. Carol Broomfield, Nov. 17, 1955; children: Marcia Ellen Cohen, Steven Jay. BA, U. Chgo., 1954; MBA, Boston U., 1956; PhD in Econs., MIT, 1958. Fin. economist Fed. Reserve Bank of Boston, 1957-60; asst. prof. Boston U., 1960-62; sr. economist, compt. of currency Washington, 1963-66; dir. rsch., dep. to chmn. FDIC, 1967—77; prof. banking and fin. U. Houston, 1977—2001, emeritus, 2001—. Author: Management of Bank Funds, 1981, Monetary Policy & the Financial System, 6th edit., 1987; founding co-editor Jour. Fin. Svcs. Rsch.; contbr. articles to profl. jours. Mem. Shadow Fin. Regulatory Com., Beta Gamma Sigma. Jewish. Home: 150 Sugarberry Cir Houston TX 77024-7244 Home Phone: 713-780-3771; Office Phone: 713-780-3771. Personal E-mail: paulmhorvitz@gmail.com.

HORWITZ, KENNETH MERRILL, lawyer, accountant; b. Atlanta, Oct. 11, 1943; s. Sidney A. and Lillian Ann (Rappaport) H.; m. Barbara Lynn Smith, June 23, 1968; children: Seth A., Lisa E. BS in Psychology, Ga. Inst. Tech., 1965; JD, Emory U., 1968; LLM, George Washington U., 1972. Bar: Ga. 1968, D.C. 1969, Tex. 1974. Sr. tax specialist IRS, Washington, 1969-74; assoc. McDonald, Sanders et al, Ft. Worth, 1974-76; ptnr. Laventhol & Horwath, Dallas, 1978-83, Coopers & Lybrand, Dallas, 1989, Washington, 1983-89; ptnr. gen. bus. & taxation Vial, Hamilton, Koch & Knox, Dallas, 1989—. Contbr. articles to profl. jours. Mem. ABA, AICPA, Tex. Bar Assn., Tex. Soc. CPAs (bd. dirs., bd. govs. CPE Found.),, Dallas Bar Assn. (past chair internat. law sect.), Internat. Trade Assn. Dallas Ft. Worth (former treas.), Dallas Coun. World Affairs (bd. dirs.), Internat. Tax Assn. (chmn. Dallas chpt.).

HOSEMANN, DELBERT (CHARLES DELBERT HOSEMANN JR), state official; b. Vicksburg, Miss., June 30, 1947; s. Charles D. and Patricia H. Hosemann; m. Mary Lynn Lagen; children: Kristen Cullen, Charles Delbert III, Mark Mansfield. BBA, U. Notre Dame, Ind., 1969; JD, U. Miss. Law Sch., 1972; LLM in Taxation, NYU, 1973. Assoc. Dossett, Magruder & Montgomery, Jackson, Miss., 1973-78; ptnr. Magruder, Montgomery, Brocato & Hosemann, Jackson, 1978-88, Phelps Dunbar, LLP, Jackson, 1988—2008; sec. of state State of Miss., Jackson, 2008—. Mem. Leadership Jackson, 1991—92, bd. dirs., 1995—96; pres. Miss. Blood Svcs., Inc., 1994—95; trustee Jackson State U. Devel. Found.; bd. dirs. First Comml. Bank. Recipient J. Tate Thigpen award for exemplary leadership, support, and commitment to Am. Red Cross, 1992, George L. Phillips Cmty. Svc. award, US Dept. Justice, 2006. Mem.: NRA, ABA, Nat. Fedn. Ind. Businesses, Jackson Young Lawyers Assn. (pres. 1977—78), Miss. State Bar Assn. (dir. young lawyers sect. 1976—78), Hinds County Bar Assn. (sec. 1980), Delta Wildlife Found., Miss. Wildlife Fedn., Home Builders Assn. Miss., Ducks Unlimited. Republican. Avocation: hunting. Office: Office of the Secretary of State PO Box 136 Jackson MS 39205 Office Phone: 601-359-1350. Office Fax: 601-359-6700. E-mail: delbert.hosemann@sos.ms.gov.*

HOSEY, LONNIE, state legislator; b. Dunbarton, SC, Dec. 1, 1946; s. Quille and Eva Hosey Hosey; m. Doris Creech; 1 child. AA, Voorhees Coll., Denmark, SC, 1975, BS, 1978. Chmn. Barnwell County Dem. Com., 1994; mem. Dist. 91 SC House of Reps., 1999—. Bd. dirs. Barnwell County Cmty. Activities Ctr., Inc. Svc. with USMC, 1966—69. Mem.: NAACP, VFW, Greenbranch Christian Benevolent Soc. (pres.), Cmty. Svc. Club Williston, Inc., Salkethatchie Vietnam Vets. (bd. dir.), Am. Legion (post comdr. Harley-Butler Post 246). Democrat. Baptist. Mailing: 404A Blatt Bldg PO Box 11867 Columbia SC 29201 also: PO Box 423 Barnwell SC 29812 Home Phone: 803-259-1178; Office Phone: 803-734-2829, 803-536-8903. E-mail: LH1@scstatehouse.net.

HOSHIDE, AKIHIKO, astronaut; b. Tokyo, 1968; BEE, Keio U., 1992; MS in Aerospace Engring., U. Houston Cullen Coll. Engring., 1997. With Nat. Space Develop. Agy. Japan (NASDA), 1992—94, astronaut support engr., astronaut office, 1994—99; astronaut Nat. Space Develop. Agy. Japan (NASDA) (now JAXA-Japan Aerospace Exploration Agy. because of merge Inst. Space & Astronautic Sci. and Nat. Aerospace Lab. Japan), 2001—; completed Soyuz TMA Flight Engr.-1 tng. Yuri Gagarin Cosmonaut Tng. Ctr., Star City, Russia, 2004; astronaut NASA, 2004—. Mission specialist STS-124 Mission (Discovery), mission to Internat. Space Station to launch components to complete Japanese Kibo Lab., 2008. Mem.: Japan Soc. Aero. and Space Scis. Avocations: flying, rugby football, swimming, snow skiing, travel. Office: Astronaut office/CB NASA Lyndon B Johnson Space Ctr 2101 NASA Pwky Houston TX 77058

HOSKIN, CHUCK, state legislator; b. Claremore, Okla., Jan. 29, 1952; m. Stephanie (Reichert) H; children: Amy, Charles. AA, Northeastern Okla. A&M Coll.; MEd, Northeastern State Univ. Former rep. Cherokee Nation Tribal Coun.; former adminstrs. Locust Grove Pub. Sch.; former tchr. Vinita Pub. Sch.; tchr. America History And Govt. Sch.; rep. Craig and Nowata Counties; mem. Dist. 6 Okla. House of Representatives, 2007—. Served USN. Democrat. Address: PO Box 941 Vinita OK 74301 Office: Oklahoma House of Representatives 2300 N Lincoln Blvd Room 509 Oklahoma City OK 73105 Office Phone: 405-557-7319. E-mail: chuck.hoskin@okhouse.gov.

HOSKINS, CRAIG, food products executive; BS in Bus. Adminstrn., U. No. Colo., Greeley; MS in Mktg., U. Colo., Denver. With NW Transport, Lange Sales; various positions of increasing responsibility in mktg., merchandising/purchasing, sales and ops. Vistar Corp., 1990—2008; sr. v.p. sales Performance Food Group, 2008—. Office: Performance Food Group 12500 W Creek Pky Richmond VA 23238

HOSKYNS, WILLIAM A., dentist; b. Sept. 1962; m. Susan Hoskyns; 4 children. DDS, U. Nebr., 1990. Resident Erie County Med. Ctr., Buffalo; cosmetic dentist Smile Sanctuary of Scottsdale, Goodyear, Ariz.; ptnr. Atlanta Ctr. for Cosmetic Dentistry, 2007—. Cosmetic dentist Phoenix Coyotes, NHL, 2001, Miss USA Pageant; dental cons. MTV True Life, I Want a Famous Face. Featured on Deutche TV, 2004. Named one of Best Dentists in Am., Consumer Rsch. Coun. Am. Mem.: Am. Acad. Cosmetic Dentistry. Office: PO Box 673006 Marietta GA 30006-0051

HOSMAN, LAWRENCE ANDREW, communications educator; s. Robert Harold and Martha Havens Hosman; m. Susan Ann Siltanen, Apr. 5, 1980; children: Sarah Siltanen Hosman, Laura Siltanen Hosman. BA in Comm., U. Mo., Kansas City, 1973; MA in Speech and Dramatic Arts, U. Iowa, Iowa City, 1975, PhD in Speech and Dramatic Arts, 1978. Asst. prof. comm. U. Ala., Birmingham, 1978—80; prof. speech comm. U. So. Miss., Hattiesburg, 1980—. Recipient Golden Anniversary Prize Fund award, Nat. Comm. Assn., 1979. Mem.: Nat. Comm. Assn., So. States Comm. Assn. (life; pres. 1992—93, Excellence in Tchg. award 1999). Office: Univ So Miss 118 College Dr #5131 Hattiesburg MS 39406-0001 Personal E-mail: lhosman3@comcast.net. Business E-Mail: lawrence.hosman@usm.edu.

HOSTETLER, JEFF (WILLIAM JEFFREY HOSTETLER), high school football coach, retired professional football player; b. Johnstown, Pa., Apr. 22, 1961; s. Norm & Dolly Hostetler; m. Vicky Nehlen; children: Jason, Tyler, Justin. Attended, Pa. State U., 1979—80; BS in Finance, W.Va. U., 1984. Quarterback NY Giants, 1984-92, L.A. Raiders, 1993—96, Wash. Redskins, 1997; owner construction co. Morgantown, W.Va.; head coach Trinity Christian Sch., Morgantown, 2013—. Founder The Hoss Found., 1991—. Named to The American Football Conf. Pro Bowl Team, 1994. Office: Trinity Christian School 200 Trinity Way Morgantown WV 26505 Office Phone: 304-291-4659.

HOTZ, V. JOSEPH, economics professor; s. Vincent Joseph Hotz and Ora Jane Coultas; m. Diane Schumacher; children: Simon, Andrew. BS, U. Notre Dame, Ind., 1972; MS, U. Wis., Madison, 1977; PhD, U. Wis., 1977. Prof. economics U. Calif., LA; prof. pub. policy U. Chgo.; asst. prof. economics Carnegie Mellon U., Pitts.; arts & scis. prof. economics Duke U., Durham, NC, 2007—. Dir. pop. rsch. ctr. U. Chgo., 1990—96; cons. RAND, Santa Monica, Calif., 1997—. Recipient Borden Freshman prize, U. Notre Dame, 1969. Fellow: Econometric Soc.; mem.: Phi Beta Kappa. Office: Duke Univ Dept Economics Durham NC 27708 Business E-Mail: hotz@econ.duke.edu.

HOUCK, CHARLES WESTON, federal judge; b. Florence, SC, Apr. 16, 1933; s. William Stokes and Charlotte Barnwell (Weston) H.; children from previous marriage: Charles Weston, Charlotte Elizabeth. Grad., U. N.C., 1954; LLB, U. S.C., 1956. Bar: S.C. Mem. firm Willcox, Hardee, Houck, Palmer & O'Farrell, 1956, 58-70; ptnr. Houck, Clarke & Johnson, 1971-79; judge US Dist. Ct. SC, Florence, 1979—93, 2000—03, chief judge, 1993—2000, sr. judge, 2003—. Mem. S.C. Ho. of Reps., 1963-66; chmn. Florence City-County Bldg. Commn., 1968-76. Served with AUS, 1957-58. Mem. ABA, S.C. Bar Assn. Episcopalian. Office: US Dist Ct PO Box 2317 Florence SC 29503-2317

HOUCK, MARK HEDRICH, engineering educator; b. Balt., May 14, 1951; s. Walter C. and Ruth Houck; m. Margaret Ann Nolan, Sept. 1, 1972; children: Timothy Daniel, Megan Hillary, Brigid Elyse BES, Johns Hopkins U., Balt., 1972, PhD, 1976. Registered profl. engr., Ind., Md., diplomate, Am. Acad. Water Resources Engrs., cert. profl. hydrologist, Am. Inst. Hydrology, 2005, bd. cert., Am. Acad. Environ. Engr. Rsch. asst. prof. dept. civil engring. U. Wash., Seattle, 1975—77; from asst prof. to prof. sch. civil engring. Purdue U., West Lafayette, Ind., 1977—92; dr. of univ. Johns Hopkins U., Balt., 1989—90; prof. civil, environ. and infrastructure engring. Volgenau Sch. Engring., George Mason U. Fairfax, Va., 1992—; chair CEIE dept. George Mason U. Fairfax, 1998—2002. Pres. Omtek Engring., Inc., West Lafayette, 1983-1991, MHH Engring. LLC, Ellicott City, Md., 2008-; v.p. Water Resources Mgmt., Inc., Columbia, Md., 1988-89; vis. prof. Heriot-Watt U., Edinburgh, Scotland, 2003 Assoc. editor Water Resources Rsch. Jour., 1981-85; co-editor Jour. Civil Engring. & Environ. Sys., 2004-06. Fellow ASCE (chmn. water resources sys. com. 1984, chmn. emerging techs. com. 1986-88, Huber Rsch. prize 1988); mem. Am. Geophys. Union, Inst. Ops. Rsch. and Mgmt. Sci., Chi Epsilon, Sigma Xi, Omega Rho. Office: George Mason U Volgenau Sch Engring Dept Civil Enviro and Infrast Eng MS 6C1 Fairfax VA 22030 Office Phone: 703-993-1737. Business E-Mail: mhouck@gmu.edu.

HOUCK, WILLIAM RUSSELL, bishop emeritus; b. Mobile, Ala., June 26, 1926; Attended, St. Mary's Sem. Coll.; STL, St. Mary's U., Balt., 1951; MA, Cath. U. of Am., 1954. Ordained priest Archdiocese of Mobile, Ala., 1951; ordained bishop, 1979; aux. bishop Diocese of Jackson, Miss., 1979—84, bishop, 1984—2003, bishop emeritus, 2003—. Roman Catholic. Office: PO Box 2248 237 E Amite St Jackson MS 39225 Office Phone: 601-969-1880. Office Fax: 601-960-8455.

HOUGH, DEREK, dancer, choreographer, musician, actor; b. Salt Lake City, May 17, 1985; s. Bruce Robert Hough and Mari Anne (Heaton). Attended, Italia Conti Acad. Theatre Arts, London, 1998—2004. Actor, dancer (plays) Footloose, 2006—07, Top Cat: The Musical, Chitty Chitty Bang Bang, Fosse Tribute, Jack & the Beanstalk, Cabaret, Jesus Christ Superstar, Master Thief, (Broadway plays) Burn the Floor, 2010, (films) Make Your Move, 2013; actor(guest appearance): (TV series) Better With You, 2011; dancer, panelist (TV series) Dance X, BBC, 2007—; dancer (TV series) Dancing With the Stars, 2007— (Season 7 winner, with ptnr. Brooke Burke-Charvet, 2008, Season 10 winner, with ptnr. Nicole Sherzinger, 2010, Season 11 winner, with ptnr. Jennifer Grey, 2010, Season 16 winner, with ptnr. Kellie Pickler, 2013, Emmy award for Outstanding Choreography, 2013); musician, co-founding mem. Ballas Hough Band (formerly Almost Amy); musician: (albums) Ballas Hough Band, 2009. Recipient Outstanding Dancer of Yr. award, LA Underground, Outstanding Dancer award, NY Dance Alliance; named World Youth Latin Champion for Poland (with Aneta Piotrowska), Internat. Dance Sport Fedn., 2002, winner, Under 21 Latin Am. Championship, Brit. Open Championship, Blackpool, Internat. Open to the World Championship, US Open Championship. Office: Learning2Dance Ste 550/424 11807 Westheimer Rd Houston TX 77077*

HOUGHTALING, PAMELA ANN, strategic communications consultant, writer, public speaker; b. Catskill, NY, July 8, 1949; d. Stanley Kenneth and Mildred Edythe (Fyfe) H. BA, Princeton U., 1971; M in Internat. Affairs, Russian Inst., Columbia U., 1974. Internat. rels. analyst Libr. of Congress, Washington, 1974-75, US GAO, Washington, 1976-77; pub. affairs specialist IBM Corp., 1977-81; sr. external programs analyst IBM World Trade Americas/Far East Corp., North Tarrytown, NY, 1981-82; mgr. labor affairs/bus. practices US Coun. Internat. Bus., NYC, 1982-84; comms. specialist-advt. IBM Corp., Boca Raton, Fla., 1984-86, staff comms. specialist White Plains, NY, 1986-88, comms. cons., 1988-90; sr. mktg. specialist Wang Labs., Bethesda, Md., 1990-93; pub. rels. dir. STG Mktg. Comm., 1993-94; mgr. mktg. comm. Cable & Wireless, Inc., Vienna, Va., 1994-95; tech. comms. cons., journalist Falls Church, Va., 1995—98; contractor to Applied Physics Lab. Johns Hopkins University, 1998-99; mktg. mgr. Info. Tech. Lab. Nat. Inst. Stds. and Tech., Gaithersburg, Md., 2000—03, 2005, comm. mgr. Mfg. Ext. Partnership, 2005—06; fellow US Dept. Commerce Sci. and Tech., 2003—04; with Office Def. Rsch. and Engring. US Dept. Def., 2003—04, stragic com. cons. writer, 2008; pub. officers con. Office Naval Rsch. Dept. Navy, 2007; stragic com. cons. writer US Dept. Homeland Security, 2009—; project mgr. Teracore Inc., 2010—12; cons. stragic com. Adayana Govt. Group, 2013—. Mem. AAAS, Nat. Assn. Sci. Writers, Toastmasters Internat.

HOUSEL, DAVID, emeritus athletic director; b. York, Oct. 18, 1946; m. Susan McIntosh. BA, Auburn U., 1969. News editor Huntsville (Ala.) News, 1969-70; from adminstrv. asst. athletic office Auburn (Ala.) U., 1970-72, instr. journalism, advisor newspaper, 1972-80, asst. dir. sports info., dir., asst. athletic dir., 1980-94, athletic dir., 1994—2005, athletic dir. emeritus, 2006—. Author: Saturdays to Remember, From the Desk of David Housel--A Collection of Auburn Stories, Auburn University Football Vault, Alabama-Auburn Rivvalry Vault, The Complete Aubie Story, Tigresses, Tigerettes and Lady Tigers-A Story of Women's Athletic of Auburn. Mem. Phi Gamma Delta. Home: 813 Moores Mill Dr Auburn AL 36830-7567

HOUSKAMP, MELISSA, energy executive; married; 1 child, Connor. B in Economics, U. of Florida. With World Bank, Washington; v.p. JPMorgan Investment Banking Group; CFO NTE Energy, 2011—. Office: NTE Energy LLC 24 Cathedral Place Suite 303 Saint Augustine FL 32084 Office Phone: 866-992-3670. Office Fax: 904-814-8022.

HOUSMAN, BRENT, state legislator; b. June 10, 1973; BS in Mgmt. & Mktg., Union U.; MBA, Murray State U. Mem. Dist. 3 Ky. House of Reps., 2009—. Republican. Baptist. Office: 702 Capitol Ave Rm 413B Frankfort KY 40601 Home: 465 Ashcreek Rd Paducah KY 42001-5879 Office Phone: 502-564-8100 Ext. 634, 270-366-6611. Office Fax: 270-442-6394.

HOUSTON, FRANK MATT, dermatologist; b. New Orleans, Dec. 15, 1939; s. Matt Francis and Amanda Vallie (Welch) H.; m. Helen Butler, Apr. 24, 1965; children: F. Matt, Catherine E.C., Amanda J.B. BS, La. State U., 1960, MD, 1964. Diplomate Am. Bd. Dermatology. Intern Johns Hopkins U., Balt., 1964—65, resident, fellow, 1967—70; physician, dermatologist Greensboro Dermatology Assocs., NC, 1970—. Cons. Cath. Cone Health (formerly Moses H. Cone Hosp. Sys.), Greensboro, NC, 1970—; adj. asst. clin. prof. dermatology U. NC Sch. Medicine, Chapel Hill, 1980—. Bd. dirs. Greensboro Hist. Mus., Greensboro Preservation Soc., Greensboro Symphony Soc., Greensboro Opera Co. Capt. U.S. Army, 1965-67. Recipient Army Commendation medal, 1967. Fellow: Am. Acad. Dermatology; mem.: Dermatology Found., NC Dermatology Soc., Pennybyrn Maryfield High Point, NC (adv. bd., chair adv. bd.), Friends Homes Inc. (chair bd. visitors), Am. Skin Assn. (sci. adv. com. to bd. dirs.), Royal Society Medicine, NC Soc. Medicine, Surf Club (Wrightsville Beach, NC), Greensboro Country Club. Republican. Episcopalian. Avocations: travel, aerobics, music. Office: Greensboro Dermatology 2704 Saint Jude St Greensboro NC 27405-3670 Office Phone: 336-954-7546. Personal E-mail: f_houston@bellsouth.net.

HOUSTON, JAMES GORMAN, JR., retired state supreme court justice; b. Eufaula, Ala., Mar. 11, 1933; s. James Gorman and Mildred (Vance) H.; m. Martha Martin, Dec. 3, 1955; children: Mildred Vance, J. Gorman III. BS, Auburn U., 1955; LLB, U. Ala., 1956, JD, 1969. Bar: Ala. 1956. Law clk. to chief justice Ala. Supreme Ct., Montgomery, 1956-57; ptnr. Houston & Martin, P.C., Eufaula, 1960-85; assoc. justice Ala. Supreme Ct., Montgomery, 1985—2003, acting chief justice, 2003—04; ret., 2005; of counsel Lightfoot, Franklin & White, LLC, Birmingham, Ala., 2005—. County atty. Barbour County, Clayton, Ala., 1961-79. Contbr. numerous opinions to So. Reporter; contbr. articles to profl. jours. Mayor pro tem, alderman City of Eufaula, 1964-70; pres. Heritage Assn., Eufaula, Ala., 1979-82; mem. Ala. Commn. on Uniform State Laws. 1st lt. JAGC, USAF, 1957-60. Named Citizen of Yr., City of Eufaula, 1979; recipient Alumni Achievement in Humanities award Auburn Univ., 1993. Fellow Am. Bar Found.; mem. ABA, Ala. Bar Assn., Ala. State Bar (examiner 1979-82, disciplinary commn. 1984-85, state bar commr. 1982-85), Barbour County Bar Assn. (pres. 1975), Eufaula C. of C. (pres. 1974). Republican. Methodist. Office: Lightfoot Franklin & White LLC The Clark Bldg 400 20th St N Birmingham AL 35203-3200 Home Phone: 334-834-4414; Office Phone: 334-834-4417. Business E-Mail: ghouston@lfwlaw.com.

HOUSTON, JAMIE GILES, III, lawyer, accountant; b. Greenwood, Miss., June 11, 1952; s. Jamie Giles Jr. and Joan (Miller) H.; m. Katherine Elise Smith, Dec. 29, 1979; children: Jamie G. IV, Andrew Phillips. BBA, U. Miss., 1974, JD, 1976; LLM in Taxation, NYU, 1978. Bar: Miss. 1976, U.S. Dist. Ct. (no. dist.) Miss. 1976, U.S. Dist. Ct. (so. dist.) Miss. 1978, U.S. Tax Ct. 1979, U.S. Ct. appeals (5th cir.) 1983; CPA, Miss. Assoc. Knight, Ballew & Van Slyke, Jackson, Miss., 1976-79; ptnr. Van Slyke & Houston, Jackson, 1979; assoc. Watkins & Eager, PLLC, Jackson, 1979-82, mem., 1983—. Spkr. Miss. Tax Inst., Jackson, 1980, chmn. bd. trustees, 1983-84; mem. estate planning coun. Millsaps Coll., Jackson, 1987-93. Mem. adminstrv. bd. Galloway United Meth. Ch., Jackson, 1983-88, 92-94; bd. dirs. Goodwill Industries, 1992-94, U. Miss. Found., 1996—, chmn., 2004—06, Comm. Found. Greater Jackson Area, 2013-. Named Best Lawyers in America, 1997—, Leading Lawyers, Chamber USA, 2008—13, Super Lawyers, Mid South, 2007—. Mem. ABA, AICPA, Miss. State Bar (chmn., estates and trusts sect. 2000-01), Hinds County Bar Assn., Miss. Estate Planning Coun., Miss. Soc. CPA's, Am. Coll. Trust and Estate Counsel (state chair 2002-07), Miss. Bar Found. Avocation: golf. Office: Watkins & Eager PLLC 400 E Capitol St Jackson MS 39201-2610 Office Phone: 601-948-6470, 601-965-1900. E-mail: jhouston@watkinseager.com.

HOUSTON, KEN, energy executive; Region safety dir. Key Energy Svcs., Inc., v.p. health, safety, security & environ. Office: Key Energy Services Inc 1301 McKinney Ste 1800 Houston TX 77010 Office Phone: 713-651-4434. Office Fax: 713-652-4005. Business E-Mail: khouston@keyenergy.com.

HOUSTON, PENNY, state legislator; children: N G Bo IV, lowery, Adam. Former mem. Berrien County Bd. Edn.; former dir. Ga. Sheriff'S Youth Homes; former state rep. Dist. 139 Ga.; former state rep. Dist. 170 Ga., 2004—; state rep. Dist. 166 Ga., 1999—2002; mem. Agr. & Consumer Affairs Coms., Edn. & State Planning & Cmty. Affairs Com.; house rep. Ga., 1999; bd. trustees Ga. Sheriff Ranch. Mem.: Nashville Women's Club. Democrat. Methodist. Mailing: 507 Legis Off Bldg Atlanta GA 30334 Office: 1115 Ray City Rd Nashville GA 31639

HOUTZ, DUANE TALBOTT, hospital administrator; b. Kansas City, Mo., Apr. 28, 1933; s. Dudley and Helen (Talbott) H.; m. Margaret McNiel; children: Erik Siegfried, Jamie Houtz Harvey. BS, U. Kans., 1955; MHA, Washington U., St. Louis, 1960. Asst. dir. Shands Teaching Hosp. and Clinics, Gainesville, Fla., 1961-65; asst. prof. Ctr. for Health and Hosp. Adminstrn., U. Fla., Gainesville, 1964-65; adminstr., exec. v.p. Baptist Med. Ctr., Montclair-Birmingham, Ala., 1965-75; hosp. dir. Alton Ochsner Med. Found., New Orleans, 1975-77; pres. Morton F. Plant Hosp., Clearwater, Fla., 1977-92, pres. emeritus, 1992—; nat. advisor to the health care industry Pershing Yoakley & Assocs., P.C., 1995-99; ptnr. Corrigo Health Care Solutions, 2000—. Chmn. Southeastern Hosp. Conf., 1986-87; chmn., pres. SunHealth Care Plans Fla., 1986-87; bd. dirs. SunHealth Enterprises Inc., SunHealth Corp.; advisor Corrigo Health Care Solutions, LLC, 1998—; bd. mem. Madonna Ptak Alzheimer's Rsch. Ctr., 2007-. Contbr. articles to profl. jours. Bd. dirs. Cmty. Svc. Coun., Birmingham, 1972-75, United Way of Pinellas County, 1987-93, campaign chmn. med. divsn., 1992-94; bd. dirs. Fla. League for Nursing, 1989-98, Bay Area Hosp. Coun./Tampa Bay Hosp. Coun., 1990-95, Morton Plant Found., 1990-96; mem. Fla. Geriatric Rsch. Bd., 1993-98; adv. bd. Jr. League Pinellas County, 1993-94; active Vets. Affairs Mgmt. Assistance Coun., 1996—2010; vice-chmn. Sun Coast Health Coun., 1998-2003; mem. fundraising bd. Magic Found., 2005. Capt. USAF, 1955-58. Recipient Acad. award USAF Basic Flight Sch., 1956, award of merit Fla. Hosp. Rsch. and Edn. Found., 1993, Washington U. Hosp. Adminstrn. Program Alumni of Yr. award, 1996; fellow Birmingham Bapt. Hosp. Found., 1985. Fellow Am. Coll. Healthcare Execs. (Regents award 1992); mem. Nat. League Nursing (bd. dirs.), Am. Hosp. Assn. (vice-chmn. council nursing 1983, rsch. com.), Assn. Voluntary Hosps. Fla. (bd. dirs. 1979-83, pres. 1979-80), Fla. Hosp. Assn. (trustee, bd. dirs. 1979-82), Greater Clearwater C. of C. (Outstanding Citizen selection com. 1982, bd. govs. 1984-87, bd. govs. 1987-88), Pinellas Suncoast C. of C. (adv. coun. 1984-87), Kiwanis (pres. Birmingham chpt. 1970-71), Phi Delta Theta. Office Phone: 727-631-0110. Personal E-mail: dhoutz1@tampabay.rr.com.

HOVEE, MARK JOHN, psychologist; b. Portland, Oreg., Feb. 20, 1954; s. Harry Juel and Janene Arden Hovee; m. Judy Lynn Pratt, Sept. 23, 2005; children: Nathanael James, Maris Alise, Claire Marie. BA in Polit. Sci., Seattle U., 1979; MA in Political Philosophy, Boston Coll., 1983; MA in Clin. Psychology, George Fox U., 1994, PsyD in Clin. Psychology, 1997; advanced cert. in peace studies, European Peace U., Stadtschlaining, Austria, 2007. Lic. psychologist Ky. Pvt. practice psychologist, Paintsville, Ky., 2002—; psychologist ARH Psych. Ctr., Hazard, Ky., 2003—04. Adj. faculty Union Inst., Cin., 1999—2003, Morehead State U., Prestonsburg, Ky., 2005—05; supr. U. Ky., Prestonsburg, 2001—04; psychologist Highlands Regional Hosp., Prestonsburg, 2001—04, 2007—, Corrections Corp. Am., Wheelwright, Ky., 2002—04, 2005—07, 2008—, US Penitentiary Big Sandy, Ky.; psychologist Landstuhl (Germany) Reg. Med. Ctr. U.S. Army, 2004—05; presenter Transylvania U., Lexington, 2005. Contbr. articles to profl. jours.; author: Wayward Soldier: A Reserve Psychologist's Memoir and Analysis During the Second American-Iraqi War, 2007. Sgt. US Army, 1973—76, sgt. USAR, 1983—2001, capt. USAR, 2001—. Mem.: APA, Assn. Conflict Resolution, Brit. Psychol. Soc., Internat. Soc. Polit. Psychology (presenter 2004), Ky. Psychol. Assn. (presenter 2005), Rotary (presenter 2005, 2007). Democrat. Methodist. Achievements include development of cross-border food supply deliveries at Thai-Cambodian border; lobbied on behalf of Cambodian refugees with US congressional members and Geneva Conference on Refugees. Avocations: skiing, swimming, tennis, boating, travel. Home and Office: PO Box 51 Paintsville KY 41240 Office Phone: 606-297-7315. Personal E-mail: markhovee@yahoo.com.

HOVEN, ARDIS DEE, epidemiologist, medical educator; b. Cin., Aug. 1, 1944; m. Ronald L. Sanders. BS in Microbiology, U. Ky., Lexington, 1966; MD, U. Ky. Coll. Medicine, 1970. Diplomate American Bd. Internal Medicine, cert. in pediatric infectious diseases. Internal medicine intern U. NC, Chapel Hill, 1970-71, infectious disease resident, 1971-73, fellow, 1973-75; prof. medicine, divsn. infectious diseases U. Ky. Coll. Medicine, med. dir. Bluegrass Care Clinic. Apptd. Nat. Adv. Coun. Healthcare Rsch. & Quality. Recipient Alumni Svc. award, U. Ky. Coll. Medicine, 1993, Bluegrass Health Heroes award, 1994, Physician Hero award, American Coll. Med. Staff Devel., 1995. Fellow: ACP, Infectious Disease Soc. America; mem.: AMA (bd. trustees 2005—, sec. 2009—10, chair bd. trustees 2010—11, immediate past chair 2011—), Ky. Med. Assn. (pres. 1993—94, Ednl. Achievement award 1991, Disting. Svc. award), American Soc. Internal Medicine, Alpha Omega Alpha. Republican. Christian. Mailing: Univ Kentucky Chandler Med Ctr Office MN668 A 138 Leader Ave Lexington KY 40506 Office Phone: 859-323-8178. Office Fax: 859-323-8926. E-mail: adhove2@uky.edu.

HOVING, JOHN HANNES FORESTER, consulting firm executive; b. NYC, July 18, 1923; s. Hannes and Mary Alma (Gilbert) H.; m. Anne Fisher Spiers, Feb. 1, 1958; children: Christopher, Karen Anne, Katherine Jean. BA in History, U. Chgo., 1947. Radio news editor, reporter Milw. Jour., Capital Times, Madison, Wis., 1947-51; asst. to chmn. Democratic Nat. Com., 1952-54; exec. positions Kefauver, Stevenson, Johnson, Humphrey, Sanford presdl. campaigns; asst. to presdl. asst. for trade policy 1962; v.p. exec. action Air Transp. Assn. Am., Washington, 1956-64; propr. cons. firm Washington, 1964-72; sr. v.p. Federated Dept. Stores, Inc., Cin., 1972-82; pres. The Hoving Group (cons. firm), Washington, 1982—. Chmn. Washington Theol. Consortium, 1993-96; mem. adv. bd. Fashion Inst. Design Merchandising; past dep. chmn. planning Dem. Nat. Com. With AUS, 1943-46. Decorated Purple Heart, Bronze Star Mem. Am. Assn. Polit. Cons., Met. Club, Nat. Press Club, Nat. Capital Dem., Queen City Club (Cin.), Lotos Club (N.Y.C.). Home: 415 Dogleg Dr Williamsburg VA 23188

HOVLAND, ERIC JEFFREY, retired dean, endodontics educator; b. Oct. 9, 1946; Student, Lehigh U., Bethlehem, Pa.; BS, U. Md., 1968; DDS, U. Md. Balt. Coll. Dental Surgery, 1972; MS in Adult Edn., Va. Commonwealth U., 1977; MBA in Health Care, Loyola Coll., Balt., 1980. Clin. instr. dept endodontics Med. Coll. Va., Sch. Dentistry, 1975-77; asst. prof. endodontics U. Md., Balt. Coll. Dental Surgery, 1977-82, dir. undergrad. clinics, Office Clin. Affairs, 1980—84, acting assoc. dean clin. affairs, 1981, assoc. prof. endodontics, 1982-89, chmn. dept. endodontics, 1985—93, dir. advanced splty. edn. in endodontics, 1986—87, prof. endodontics, 1989-93, acting v.p. academic affairs, 1991; prof. dept. endodontics La. State U. Med. Ctr. Sch. Dentistry, New Orleans, 1993—2008, dean, 1993—2008. Cons. U. Md. Hosp., 1978—82, Johns Hopkins Hosp., Balt., 1980—85, Northeast Regional Bd. Dental Examiners, 1990—93; mem. cons. med. staff VA Hosp., New Orleans. Mem. editorial bd. Oral Surgery, Oral Medicine, Oral Pathology, Oral Radiology, Endodontics Jour.; contbr. articles to profl. jours., chapters to books. Served with USAF, 1973—75. Fellow: Am. Coll. Dentists, Internat. Coll. Dentists; mem.: ADA, Am. Dental Edn. Assn. (pres. 2005—06), Loyola Coll. Alumni Assn., Balt. Coll. Dental Surgery Alumni Assn., Am. Assn. Endodontists (pres. 1993—94), So. Conf. Deans & Dental Examiners (pres. 1995—96), Internat. Assn. Dental Traumatology, Endodontic Soc. South Africa (hon.), Am. Assn. Dental Rsch, Internat. Assn. Dental Rsch., New Orleans Dental Assn, La. State Dental Assn. (house dels. 1994—95), Md. State Dental Assn., Am. Assn. Dental Schools. Office Phone: 504-619-8500. Business E-Mail: ehovla@lsuhsc.edu.

HOWARD, ALAN D., environmental science professor; b. Evanston, Ill., Mar. 30, 1939; s. Alan S. and Mary L. Howard; m. Marlowe Martin, Mar. 7, 1949. BS, Yale U., New Haven, 1961; MS, Harvard U., Cambridge, Mass., 1962; PhD, Johns Hopkins U., Balt., 1970. Asst. prof. U. Va., Charlottesville, 1970—73, assoc. prof., 1973—84, prof., 1984—. Vis. prof. U. Coll., London, 1991, UFR Sci. Physiques de la Terre, Paris, 1999; sci. advisor Grand Canyon Rsch. and Monitoring Ctr., Flagstaff, Ariz., 2001—06. Assoc. editor: Caves and Karst, 1969—74, Water Resources Rsch., 1975—79, 1995—97, mem. editl. bd.: Earth Surface Processes and Landforms, 1998—2003. Sp5 US Army, 1961—65. Recipient G.K. Gilbert award, Assn. Am. Geographers, 1991, G.K. Warren prize, NAS, 2010. Fellow: Am. Geophys. Union; mem.: Geol. Soc. Am. Office: Dept Environ Scis U Va PO Box 400123 Charlottesville VA 22904-4123 Office Fax: 434-982-2137. Business E-Mail: ah6p@virginia.edu.

HOWARD, ALEX T., JR., federal judge; b. 1924; Student, U. Ala., 1942, student, 1946, Auburn U., 1942-44; JD, Vanderbilt U., 1950. U.S. probation officer, Mobile, Ala., 1950-51; ptnr. Johnstone, Adams, Howard, Bailey & Gordon, Mobile, 1951-86; U.S. commr. U.S. Dist. Ct. (so. dist.) Ala., Mobile, 1956—70, judge, 1986—, chief judge, 1989-94, sr. judge, 1996—. Assoc. editor Am. Maritime Cases for Port of Mobile. Served to 2d lt. U.S. Army, 1943-46. Mem. ABA, Internat. Soc. Barristers, Internat. Assn. of Ins. Counsel, Maritime Law Assn. of U.S., Southeastern Admiralty Law Inst. (dir. 1978-80), Ala. Bar Assn., Ala. Def. Lawyers Assn. (dir. late 1950's), Mobile Bar Assn. (pres. 1973). Home: 901 Somerby Dr Apt 108 Mobile AL 36695-3492

HOWARD, ARTHUR ELLSWORTH DICK, law educator; b. Richmond, Va., July 5, 1933; s. Thomas Landon and Marie Antoinette (Dick) H. BA, U. Richmond, 1954; LLB, U. Va., 1961; BA with honors, Oxford U., 1960, MA, 1965; LLD (hon.), James Madison U., 1983, U. Richmond, 1984, Campbell U., 1986, Coll. William and Mary, 1991, Wake Forest U., 2000. Bar: Va., D.C. 1961. Asso. Covington & Burling, Washington, 1961-62; law clk. to Supreme Ct. Justice Hugo L. Black, Washington, 1962-64; assoc. prof. law U. Va., Charlottesville, 1964-67, prof., 1967-76, White Burkett Miller prof. law and public affairs, 1976—, assoc. dean, 1967-69, dir. Ctr. for Pub. Svc., 1988-89, Earle K. Shawe rsch. prof., 2006—. Bd. dirs. Am. Ditchley Found.; counsel sessions Gen. Assembly Va., 1969—70. Author: Commentaries on the Constitution of Virginia, 2 vols., 1974 (Phi Beta Kappa prize), The Road from Runnymede: Magna Carta and Constitutionalism in America, 1968, (with Baker and Derr) Church, State and Politics, 1982, Democracy's Dawn, 1991, Constitution-Making in Eastern Europe, 1993, Magna Carta: Text and Commentary, 1998; bd. editors The American Oxonian, 1968—, The Wilson Quar., 1977—. Chmn., exec. dir. Va. Commn. on Constl. Revision, 1968—69; chmn. Va. Commn. on Bicentennial of US Constn., 1985—92; mem. Va. Ind. Bicentennial Commn., 1966—83; vice chmn. Magna Carta Commn. Va., 1965—66; Va. sec. Rhodes Scholarship Trust, 1970—; counselor to Gov. of Va., 1982—86; vis. scholar Nat. Constn. Ctr., 2009—; bd. dirs. Am. Ditchley Found., 2003—, James Madison Meml. Found., Jamestown-Yorktown Found., 2003—; hon. mem. High Table Christ Ch., Oxford, 2002—. With US Army, 1954—56. Recipient Disting. Prof. award U. Va., 1981, Randa medal Czech Republic, 1996, George C. Marshall award internat. law and diplomacy World Affairs Coun., 2004; fellow Woodrow Wilson Internat. Ctr. for Scholars, Smithsonian Instn., Washington, 1974-75, 76-77; fellow Ctr. Advanced Studies U. Va., 1970-71, 76-77, 82-83; Rhodes scholar Oxford U., 1958-60; Disting. Vis. scholar in residence Rhodes Ho., Oxford U., 2001. Mem. Va. Bar Assn. (v.p. 1970-71), Va. Acad. Laureates (chmn. 1981-92), Lit. Soc. (Washington), Cosmos Club (Washington), Oxford and Cambridge Club (London). Episcopalian. Home: 627 Park St Charlottesville VA 22902-4654 Office: U Va Sch Law 580 Massie Rd Charlottesville VA 22903-1738 Office Phone: 434-924-3097. E-mail: adh3m@virginia.edu.

HOWARD, AYANNA MACCALLA, electrical and robotics engineer, educator; b. Providence, 1972; married. BSEE, Brown U., 1993; MSEE, U. So. Calif., 1994, PhD in Elec. Engring., 1999. Computer scientist, advanced tech. sect. NASA Jet Propulsion Lab., Pasadena, Calif., 1993—96, info. sys. engr., info. technologies rsch. sect., 1997—99, robotics researcher, telerobotics rsch. and applications group, also cognizant engr., prin. investigator, and task mgr., 1999—2002, dep. mgr., strategic u. rsch. partnership office, Office of Chief Scientist, also task mgr., cognizant engr., 2003—05, sr. robotics researcher, mobility sys. concept develop. sect., 2002—05; assoc. prof., sys. and controls, sch. elec. and computer engring. Ga. Inst. Tech., Atlanta, 2005—, with sys. and controls group, 2005—, dir., founder, Human-Automation Sys. (HumAns) Lab., 2005. Mem. spkr. bur. NASA Jet Propulsion Lab., 1998—2005, coun. mem., director's adv. coun. for women, 1999—2001, technical recruiter, 1999—2005, bd. mem. minority edn. initiatives adv. bd., 2002—05, technical reviewer, director's R&D fund, 2003, 2004, proposal reviewer, grad. student rsch. program, 2004, mem., Nat. Soc. Black Engineers Convention Planning Team, 2003—04; reviewer NASA NRA Cross Enterprise Tech. Develop. Program (CETDP), 2000, La. Bd. Regents R&D Grants Program, 2002, NASA Small Bus. Innovative Rsch. Proposals, 2002—04, La. Bd. Regents R&D Grants Program, 2003, NASA Faculty Awards for Rsch. (FAR) Program, 2002; mem. adv. panel NSF Artificial Intelligence and Cognitive Sci., 2004; NASA Small Bus. Innovation Rsch. sub-topic mgr. Mars In-situ Robotics Tech., 2003—05; mem. Ga. Electronic Design Ctr., 2005—; rep., Ga. Tech Engring. and Computing Career Conf. Sch. Elec. and Computer Engring., Ga. Inst. Tech., 2005, mem. undergraduate com., 2005, rep., Family Affair, 2006, mem., Ga. Tech Women Talk on Grad. Schs., 2005; cons. WonderPlanet, Inc., LA, 1999, Bitstar Internat., Seattle, 2001, Veritouch Ltd., NY, 2003; vis. scholar, elec. engring. dept. U. Wash., 2004; selected participant NAE Symposium on Frontiers in Engring., 2004; selected presenter NAS Frontiers of Sci. Symposium, 2005; invited presenter in field. Contbr. several articles to profl. jours., chapters to books; referee for profl. publs. and conf. publs., assoc. editor Internat. Jour. Intelligent Automation and Soft Computing, 2000—, media coverage includes TIME Mag. Innovators/Artificial Intelligence: Forging the Future, 2004, NASA Space Sci. and Tech., Robots with Brains, 2004, and several others. Computer tutor Restore, Inc., 1998—2002; engring. advisor FIRST, 2001—02; founder Pasadena Delta Acad., 2001—04; space expert Challenger Ctr. for Space Sci. Edn., Space Day, 2002; co-founder JUMP (Jet Propulsion Lab Undergraduate Mentoring Program for Women), 2001—05. Recipient Lew Allen award of Excellence for significant technical contbns., 2001, NASA Honor award for Safe Robotic Navigation Task, 2002, Best Paper award, 9th Internat. Symposium on Robotics and Applications, 2002, NASA Space Act award for Path Planning Graphical User Interface, 2003, Engr. of Yr. award, LA Coun. Engr. and Scientists, 2004, NASA Space Act Award for Fuzzy Logic Engine for Space Applications, 2004, Calif. Women. in Bus. award for Sci. and Tech., 2005; named San Francisco Airport Mus. Honoree, African-Am. Tech. Trailblazers in Calif., 2002, Allstate Ins. Disting. Honoree for Achievement in Sci., 2004; named one of Top 100 Young Innovators of 2003, MIT Tech. Review Jour. Mem.: Am. Assn. Artificial Intelligence, IEEE (sr. mem. robotics and automation soc. 1999—, IEEE Early Career award in Robotics 2005), Soc. Women Engineers (sr.). Achievements include patents pending in field. Office: Sch Elec and Computer Engring Ga Inst Tech Van Leer Elec Engring Bldg 77 Atlantic Dr NW Office TSRB 444 Atlanta GA 30332-0250 Office Phone: 404-385-4824. Business E-Mail: ayanna.howard@ece.gatech.edu.

HOWARD, CECIL BYRON, retired pediatrician; b. Wallins, Ky., Apr. 16, 1927; s. William Knott and Maggie (Cawood) H.; m. Rebekah Ann Buckley, Mar. 4, 1931; children: Mark Byron, Sally Ann Howard Truxal, Maggie Elizabeth Howard Ray. BA, Vanderbilt U., 1949, MD, 1953. Intern U. Va. Hosp., Charlottesville, 1953-54; resident U. Tex. Med. Br., Galveston, 1954-56; pediatrician pvt. practice, Maryville, Tenn., 1956—2006. Dir. Christian Ch. Found. Handicapped, 1983—; elder 1st Christian Ch., Maryville, 1961-2003; scoutmaster Boy Scouts Am., 1964-79, chmn. Tuckaleechee Dist. Great Smoky Mountain Coun., 1973-75; mem. Blount County D.H.S. Child Abuse Rev. Team, 1965-2002. With U.S. Army, 1945-47.

Fellow Am. Acad. Pediatrics; mem. Blount County Med. Soc. (pres. 1973), Maryville Optimist Club (pres. 1973). Republican. Avocations: hiking, piano, reading. Office: 1220 S Dogwood Dr Maryville TN 37804-5214

HOWARD, CHARLIE F., state legislator; b. Wheeler Don, Ala., May 30, 1942; s. Charles Edward Robert and Gladys Franklin Howard; m. Alma Jo Edmondson; children: Chad Joseph Rivers, Julie. BSEE, Auburn U., Ala.; MBA, Harvard U.; grad. student in engring., U. Ala. Contract telecommunications worker NASA, 1964—68; exec. v.p., operating officer Sugar Land Properties, Inc., 1973—86; pres. Howard/Turner Co., Inc., 1986—92; exec. v.p. Titus Constrn. Co., Inc., 1986—92; pres. C. Howard Co., 1993—; mem. Dist. 26 Tex. House of Representatives, 1995—. Deacon Sugar Creek Baptist Ch., 1989—; trustee Houston Baptist U.; advisor Wharton County Jr. Coll.; dir. Fort Bend Mus., 1983—88, Econ. Devel. Coun., 1984—88. Recipient Eagle award, Eagle Forum, Leadership God, Family & Country award, VFW, Tex. Families First award, Concerned Women America, Leader Excellence award, Free Mkt. Enterprise, Key Leadership award, Tex. Home Sch. Coalition; named Outstanding Legislator of Yr., Am. Family Assn., 1997. Mem.: Rose Rich C. of C., Fort Bend Assn. Realtors (life), Soc. Indsl. Realtors (life), Am. Legislature Exch. Coun. (life), Fort Bend C. of C. (life; former pres.), Fort Bend County Fair (life), Rotary Club, Oyster Club. Republican. Southern Baptist. Office: 1 Flour Daniel Bldg Sugar Land TX 77478 also: Room CAP 4S.05 Capitol PO Box 2910 Austin TX 78768 Office Phone: 281-565-9500, 512-463-0710. Office Fax: 281-565-1579.

HOWARD, DONNA, state legislator; b. Austin, Tex. m. Derek Howard; 3 children. BN, U. Tex., M in Health Edn. Former critical care nurse, patient edn. coord. Brackenridge Hosp., Seton Hosp.; patient edn. coord. Austin; former health edn. instr. U. Tex.; former mem. Eanes Ind. Sch. Bd., West Austin, Tex., 1996—99; mem. Dist. 48 Tex. House of Representatives, 2006—. Former bd. mem. Tex. Freedom Network; bd. mem. Expanding Horizons Found. Mem.: Tex. Nurses' Assn. (former pres. Dist. 5). Democrat. Office: PO Box 2910 Austin TX 78768 Address: Room E2.418 Capitol Extension PO box 2910 Austin TX 78768 Office Phone: 512-463-0631.

HOWARD, DWIGHT DAVID, II, professional basketball player; b. Atlanta, Dec. 8, 1985; s. Dwight David and Sheryl Howard. Center, forward Orlando Magic, 2004—12, LA Lakers, 2012—13, Houston Rockets, 2013—. Mem. US Men's Sr. Nat. Basketball Team, 2006, Beijing, 2008. Co-founder Dwight D. Howard Found., Inc., Coll. Pk., Ga., 2004. Recipient Morgan Wooten HS Player of Yr. award, 2004, Gatorade Nat. Player of Yr. award, 2004, Rich and Helen De Vos Cmty. Enrichment award, 2005, Gold medal, men's basketball, Beijing Olympic Games, 2008; named McDonald's Nat. HS Player of Yr., 2004, Co-MVP, McDonald's HS All-Am. Game, 2004, Mr. Basketball, State of Ga., 2004, 1st Team All-Rookie, NBA, 2005, 1st Team All-NBA, 2008—12, NBA Defensive Player of Yr., 2009, 2010, 2011; named to Ea. Conf. All-Star Team, NBA, 2007—12, NBA All-Defensive 1st Team, 2009—12, We. Conf. All-Star Team, 2013. Achievements include being the first overall pick in the NBA Draft, 2004; leading the NBA in: rebounding, 2006-10, 2012, 2013; blocked shots, 2009, 2010; winning the NBA All-Star Weekend Slam Dunk Contest, 2008; the first player in NBA history to lead the league in blocked shots and rebounds in the same season, 2008-09. Office: Houston Rockets 1510 Polk St Houston TX 77002*

HOWARD, FRANK A., state legislator; Graduate, Nat. Sheriff's Inst. Ret. Sheriff Vernon Parish; mem. Dist. 24 La. House of Reps., 2008—, mem. adminstrn. of criminal justice com., agr., forestry, aquaculture, and rural devel. com., transp., hwys. and pub. works com. Republican. Office: State Capitol PO Box 44486 Baton Rouge LA 70804 Mailing: 1601 Texas Hwy Many LA 71449 Office Phone: 225-342-6945, 318-256-4135. Office Fax: 318-256-4137. Business E-Mail: howardf@legis.state.la.us.

HOWARD, GENE CLAUDE, lawyer, retired state senator; b. Perry, Okla., Sept. 26, 1926; s. Joe W. and Nell L. (Brown) Howard; m. Belva J. Prestidge, Dec. 28, 1979; children: Jean Ann, Joe Ted, Belinda Janice. JD, U. Okla., 1951. Bar: Okla. 1950, US Ct. Mil. Appeals 1956, US Supreme Ct. 1956. Ptnr. Howard & Widdows PC (and predecessors), Tulsa, 1952—; mem. Okla. Ho. of Reps., 1958-62, Okla. Senate, 1964-82, pres. pro tem, 1974-81. Mem. exec. com. Coun. State Govts., 1974—76; chmn. Okla. State and Edn. employees Group Ins. Bd., 1990—98; bd. dirs. Cubic Energy Corp., Local Okla. Bank, 1992—2004; trustee Phila. Mortgage Trust, Okla. Coll. Savs. Plan, 1998—2002. Mem. So. Growth Policy Bd., 1972—76; pres. Okla. Jr. Dems., 1954; del. Dem. Nat. Conv., 1964. With US Army, 1944—46, PTO, lt. col. USAF, 1961—62. Mem.: Okla. Mil. Acad. (disting. alumni), Phi Delta Phi, Tulsa County Bar Assn. (Outstanding Young Atty. 1953), Okla. Bar Assn. Democrat. Mem. Disciples Of Christ. Home: 2404 E 29th St Tulsa OK 74114-5619 Office: Howard Widdows PC 2066 Nations Bank Ctr 15W6 Tulsa OK 74119 Home Phone: 918-744-1119; Office Phone: 918-744-7440. Personal E-mail: howardgc@b-htulsalaw.com.

HOWARD, HARRY CLAY, lawyer; b. Rockwood, Tenn., May 1, 1929; s. Harry Clay and Julia Roe (Cannon) H.; m. Mary Helen Harrison, June 12, 1951 (dec. Dec. 1997); children: Helen Howard Porter (dec.), Anne Howard Ames; m. Telside Matthews Strickland, Dec. 15, 1998. BA, Vanderbilt U., 1951; LLB, Emory U., 1955. Bar: Ga. 1955. Sr. ptnr. King & Spalding, Atlanta, 1956-92, ret. ptnr., 1993—. Mem. coun. Emory Law Sch., 1975-85, chmn., 1976-77; bd. dirs. Cen. Atlanta Progress Inc., 1981-85, Wesley Woods Geriatric Hosps., 1987-93, chmn., 1988-92; trustee Wesley Homes Inc., 1961-93, chmn., 1981-86; past trustee Oglethorpe U., The Lovett Sch. 1st lt. USMC, 1951-53. Mem. Am. Law Inst., State Bar Ga., Atlanta Bar Assn., Lawyers Club Atlanta, Piedmont Driving Club, Peachtree Golf Club, Highlands Country Club, Phi Beta Kappa, Omicron Delta Kappa. Office: King & Spalding 1180 Peachtree St Ste 1700 Atlanta GA 30309 Office Phone: 404-572-4835. E-mail: harrychoward@aol.com.

HOWARD, JAMES KENTON, academic administrator, journalist; b. June 30, 1943; s. Arthur R. and Dora G. (Utt) H.; m. Lynn M. Marsh, Sept. 23, 1982; children: Lara L., James M. BA, U. Okla., 1965, MA, 1979; Inst. Edml. Mgmt., Harvard U., 1991. Asst. dean students U. Okla., Norman, 1965-67, asst. to pres., 1967-68, asst. to v.p. for univ. rels. and devel., 1978; editor Northland Press, Flagstaff, Ariz., 1972-77; cons. Okla. Dept. Public Safety, Oklahoma City, 1977; asst. dean student affairs Northeastern State U., Tahlequah, Okla., 1978-79, dir. univ. svcs., 1979-82, asst. prof. journalism, 1979—2004, v.p. adminstrn., 1982-91, v.p. bus. and devel., 1991—2004, trustee NSU Found., 1981—, chair investment com., 1988—, v.p. emeritus, 2004—. Mem. Coun. Bus. Officers, Okla. State Regents for Higher Edn., 1982-04; adv. dir. BancFirst, 1995—; mem. bd. dirs. Cherokee County Edml. Facilities Found., 2003-07. Author: Ten Years With the Cowboy Artists of America, 1976. Bd. dirs. Friends of Mus. No. Ariz., 1974-77; chmn. No. Ariz. campaign March of Dimes, 1973-74; founding chmn. Cherokee County Cmty. Sentencing Coun., 1997—2009; No. Ariz. coord. Babbit for Atty. Gen. Campaign, 1974; trustee Flagstaff-Coconino County Pub. Libr., 1976-77, chmn. bd. trustees, 1976-77; pres. Indian Nations Soccer Coun., 1981-82; bd. dirs. Indian Nations coun. Boy Scouts Am., 1990-94, Okla. Found. for Excellence, 1996—; trustee Tahlequah Pub. Schs. Found., 1990-2000, founding chair, 1990-98; bd. dirs. Leadership Okla., 1990—, mem. exec. com., 1990-98, pres., 1994-95, mem. Class II, 1988-89; bd. dirs. Okla. Assn. of Coll. and Univ. Bus. Officers, 1993-98, pres., 1996-97; bd. dirs. Okla. Acad. for State Goals, 1993—, chair, 1999-2000; founding pres. Boys and Girls Club of Tahlequah, 1996-2000; pres., Coll. Assn. Liability Mgmt., 1996-98, 2002-2004; bd. dirs. Okla. Arts Inst., 1997-2005, Okla. Music Hall of Fame, 2000-2004, Communities Found. Okla., 2000-02, bd. govs., 2002—; founding pres. Tahlequah Comty. Found., 2003—09. With USAF, 1968-72. Recipient Eason Book Collection award, 1965, Book Design award Rounce and Coffin Club of L.A., 1974-75, Citation of Profl. Merit Northeastern State U., 1991, Excellence in Okla. Leadership award, 1995, Disting. Leadership award Nat. Assn. Cmty. Leadership, 1995-96; named Outstanding Citizen, Tahlequah Area C. of C., 2005, Centurion award, Northeastern State U., 2009. Mem. U. Okla. Assn. (life), Nat. Cowboy and Western Heritage Mus. (life), Tahlequah Area C. of C. (bd. dirs. 1985-88), Mensa, Rotary (past pres., Paul Harris fellow), Sigma Delta Chi, Kappa Tau Alpha, Lambda Chi Alpha. Address: 714 Brentwood Dr Tahlequah OK 74464

HOWARD, JEFFREY A., psychologist, educator; m. Janet Howard; children: Jonathan, David. PhD in Psychology, Kans. State U., 1981. Prof. psychology Eckerd Coll., St. Petersburg, Fla., 1981—. Exec. coach Leadership Devel. Inst., St. Petersburg, 1993—. Pres. Carlton Manor, St. Petersburg, 1987—2007. Office: Eckerd Coll 4200 54th Ave S Saint Petersburg FL 33711 Business E-Mail: howardja@eckerd.edu.

HOWARD, JULIA CRAVEN, state legislator; b. Salisbury, NC, Aug. 20, 1944; d. Allen Leary and Ruth Elizabeth Snider Craven; m. Abe N. Howard Jr., 1962; children: Amedia Paige, Abe N Howard III. Chmn., bd. trustees Davie County Hosp., 1978—85; chmn. Coun. Ministries, 1979—81; commr. town Mocksville NC, 1981—88; state rep. Dist. 74 NC, 1987—2002; state rep. Dist. 79 NC, 2003—; v.p. Davie Builders Inc.; pres. Howard Realty & Ins. Agency Inc. Mem. Youth Coun., First United Methodist Ch., 1974—84. Mem.: Sertoma, Realtors Assn. (pres., Davie county bd. 1972, state dir. 1973—75). Republican. Methodist. Address: 330 S Salibury St Mocksville NC 27028 Office: North Carolina House of Representatives 16 W Jones St Rm 1106 Raleigh NC 27601-1096 Home Phone: 336-751-3538; Office Phone: 919-733-5904. E-mail: Julia.Howard@ncleg.net.

HOWARD, KENNETH B., museum director; b. Dunn, NC; m. Martha Howard. B in Bus. Adminstrn., U. NC, Chapel Hill, 1976; JD, Wake Forest U., 1982. Sr. v.p., sales Medic Computer Sys., 1983—96, Misys Healthcare Sys., 1996—99; exec. v.p., acute care A4 Health Sys., 2000—06; interim dir. NC Mus. History, 2007, dir., 2007—. Office: NC Mus History 4650 Mail Service Ctr Raleigh NC 27699-4650 also: 5 E Edenton St Raleigh NC 27601-1011 Office Phone: 919-807-7878. Office Fax: 919-733-8655. Business E-Mail: ken.howard@ncmail.net, ken.howard@ncdcr.gov.

HOWARD, LEON, state legislator; s. Wilbert and Minnie Howard. AD, Midland Tech. Coll. Pres. Howard's Garage, Paint and Body Shop, and Wrecker Svc.; mem. Dist. 76 SC House of Reps., 1995—, chair Med., Mil., Pub. and Mcpl. Affairs Com., mem. Subcommittee on Other Occupational Regulation and Licensing Bds. Chair SC Legis. Black Caucus, 2007—08; chair bd. sch. commrs. Richland County Sch. Dist. One. Democrat. Baptist. Mailing: 2425 Barhamville Rd Columbia SC 29204 Office: 425 Blatt Bldg Columbia SC 29201 Home Phone: 803-254-1216; Office Phone: 803-734-3046, 803-254-9468. Business E-Mail: LH@schouse.org.

HOWARD, MALCOLM JONES, federal judge; b. Kinston, NC, June 24, 1939; s. Clayton and Thelma (Jones) H.; m. Eloise McGinty, Nov. 24, 1964; children: Shannon Lea, Joshua Brian. BS, U.S. Mil. Acad., 1962; JD, Wake Forest U., Winston Salem, NC, 1970. Bar: NC 1970, US Ct. Appeals (4th cir.) 1973. Sec. Judge Adv. Gen. Sch., Charlottesville, Va., 1970-71; legis. counsel to sec. US Army, Washington, 1971-72; asst. US atty. Ea. Dist. NC, Raleigh, 1972-73; judge US Dist Ct. (ea. dist.) NC, Greenville, 1988—2005, sr. judge, 2005—; dep. spl. counsel to Pres. U.S. Washington, 1974; sr. ptnr. Howard Browning Sams & Poole, Greenville, SC, 1974-88; judge Fgn. Intelligence Surveillance Ct. (FISC), 2005—. With US Army, 1962-82. Office: US Dist Ct PO Box 5006 Greenville NC 27835-5006

HOWARD, MARCIA MORALES, federal judge; b. Jacksonville, Fla., 1965; BS, Vanderbilt U., 1987; JD with honors, U. Fla., 1990. Bar: Fla. 1990, US Supreme Ct., US Ct. Appeals (11th cir.), US Dist. Ct. (middle and no. dists.) Fla. Assoc. Commander, Legler, Werber, Dawes, Sadler & Howell, 1990—91, Foley & Lardner, 1991—94, McGuireWoods LLP, 1994—98, ptnr., 1998—2003; magistrate judge US Dist. Ct. (mid. dist.) Fla., Jacksonville, 2003—07, judge, 2007—. Bd. mem., sec. Jacksonville Transp. Authority, 1999—2003. Office: US Dist Ct Simpson US Courthouse 300 N Hogan St Ste 11-350 Jacksonville FL 32202-4244 Office Phone: 904-301-6750.

HOWARD, MELVIN, financial executive; b. Boston, Jan. 5, 1935; s. John M. and Molly (Sagar) H.; m. Beverly Ruth Kahan, June 9, 1957 (dec. 2003); children: Brian David, Marjorie Lyn; m. Vivien K. Weissman, Oct. 6, 2005. BA, U. Mass., 1957; MS, Columbia U., 1959. Fin. exec. Ford Motor Co., Dearborn, Mich., 1959—67; v.p. adminstrn. Shoe Corps. of Am., Columbus, Ohio, 1967-70; contr., sr. v.p. fin., chief fin. officer Xerox Corp., 1970—82, exec. v.p., chmn. fin. svcs., 1982—86, vice chmn. of bd., 1986-90, bd. dirs., 1982-90; pres., CEO Ehrlich Bober Fin. Corp., 1990-92; mng. dir. Taurus Adv. Group, 1993—95. Bd. dirs. Gould Pumps, Inc., Sector Mgmt., Inc. Trustee Nursing and Home Care, U. Mass, Amherst, chmn., Commonwealth Coll. 1st lt. US Army, 1957. Mem. Birchwood Country Club, La Gorce Country Club, Beta Gamma Sigma. Home: 5500 Collins Ave Apt 404 Miami Beach FL 33140-5530 Personal E-mail: mhhoward@aol.com.

HOWARD, RALPH, state legislator; m. Yolande Howard; children: Makaila, Keonna, Trey. BA in Criminal Justice, U. Ala. Adult edn. instr. Shelton State CC, Tuscaloosa; mem. Dist. 72 Ala. House of Reps., Montgomery, 2005—. Mem. Ala. Dem. Conf., Pleasant Grove Missionary Bapt. Ch. Served with USMC. Mem.: DAV, Friendship Lodge 228. Democrat. Baptist. Office: 700 NW Rollins Ln Greensboro AL 36744 also: Ala House of Reps Ala State House 11 S Union St Rm 527-D Montgomery AL 36130 Office Phone: 334-624-1887, 334-242-7759.

HOWARD, THOMAS JOSEPH, SR., editor; b. Georgetown, SC, Aug. 9, 1948; s. Lawrence Edgar Howard, Sr. and Claudia Wolf Howard; m. Ruthann M. Oberly, Nov. 4, 1967; 1 child, Thomas Joseph Howard, Jr. BA in Journalism, U. SC, Columbia, 1966—69, grad. work in journalism, 1969—70, grad. work in journalism, 1978—80. Co. clk. US Army, Ft. Benning, Ga., 1970—72; news dir. WACA Radio, Camden, SC, 1972—73; editor Wing Publs., Cayce, SC, 1973—77; pres., owner Forest Pub. Co., Columbia, 1977—80; asst. mgr. The Print Shop, Columbia, 1980—86; sr. dist. exec. Indian Waters Coun., Boy Scouts Am., Columbia, 1986—92; darkroom technician Palmetto State Printing, Columbia, 1992—93; adminstrv. asst., field inventory auditor SC Jud. Dept., Columbia, 1993—94; claims assoc. III Blue Cross and Blue Shield, Surfside Beach, SC, 1994—97; customer svc. rep. Healthcare Bus. Resources, Pawleys Island, SC, 1997—99; state editor The Times, Georgetown, 2000—. Editor: (book) Looking Through the Window, An Informal History of the Family of Henry Richardson Howard Sr. & Alice May Baker Howard, 2005. Vol. leader Boy Scouts Am., Georgetown, Columbia, Garden City Beach, Charlston, 1980—2012; tng. chmn. Boys Scout Dist., 1995—; precinct pres. Richland County Rep. Party, Columbia, 1975—84; eucharistic min., lector various cath. chs., Georgetown, Garden City Beach, Columbia, 1965—2006; mem. KC, Georgetown, Columbia, 1976—2013; dist. commr., 2005—07. Specialist 4th class US Army, 1970—72, Ft. Jackson, SC & Ft. Benning, Ga. Recipient Wood Badge Tng. award, Boy Scouts Am., 1983, Scouter's Tng. award, 1985, Dist. Merit award, 1986, Boys' Life award, 1986—92, Nat. Quality Dist. award, 1987—91, Pilot Dist., New Scout Program award, 1989—90, Writing award, SC Press Assn., 2002, 2005; named to Chief Scout Exec. Winner's Cir., Boy Scouts Am., 1987—92. Mem.: Am. Mensa (bd. mem. 1984—2006), Georgetown Breakfast Rotary Club (bd. dirs. 2000—09, pres. 2005—06). Roman Cath. Avocations: computers, reading, camping, hiking, coin collecting/numismatics. Home: 1704 Pringles Ferry Rd Georgetown SC 29440 Office: The Times 615 Front St Georgetown SC 29440 Personal E-mail: tjhowardsr@aol.com. Business E-Mail: thoward@gtowntimes.com.

HOWARD-HILL, TREVOR HOWARD, language educator; b. Wellington, New Zealand, Oct. 17, 1933; came to U.S. 1972; s. Roland Henry and Dulcie Helena (Howard) Hill; children: Miranda Caroline, Victoria, Penelope Anne Din, Christopher John, Dorothy Disterheft. BA, Victoria U., Wellington, New Zealand, 1955; MA, Victoria U., 1957, PhD, 1960; DPhil, U. Oxford, Eng., 1971. Head cataloguing Alexander Turnbull Libr., Wellington, 1961-63; sr. rsch. fellow Oxford U. Computing Lab., 1965-70; lectr. English Univ. Coll., Swansea, Wales, 1970-72; assoc. prof. English U. S.C., Columbia, 1972-77, prof English, 1977-90, chmn. dept. English, 1990-91, C. Wallace Martin prof. English, 1990-99, Disting. prof. emeritus, 1999—, sr. rsch. fellow, Thomas Cooper Libr., 1999—. Coll. dir. S.C. Coun. Tchrs. English, 1982-85; bibliography/access panelist NEH, 1984, 86. Author: Ralph Crane, 1972, Literary Concordances, 1979, Middleton's Vulgar Pasquin: Essays on a Game of Chess, 1995, editor: Sir John van Olden Barnavelt, 1980, The Book of Sir Thomas More: Essays, 1989, A Game of Chess, 1990, Thomas Middleton's A Game of Chess, 1993, Middleton's Bridgewater Manuscript of A Game of Chess, 1995; mem. editl. bd. Lit. Rsch., 1986-94, Rev., 1992-2000, Shakespeare Notes, 1996—; compiler: Oxford Shakespeare Concordances, 1969-73, Index to British Literary Bibliography, 9 vols., 1969—, British Book Trade Dissertations to 1980, 1998, Shakespearian Bibliography and Textual Criticism, 2000; editor Papers of the Bibliog. Soc. Am., 1994—; co-editor Renaissance Papers, 1996-2000. Recipient Russell award for rsch. U. S.C., 1988; U. New Zealand fellow, 1958-59, NIRNS fellow Oxford U., 1966-67, fellow H.E. Huntington Libr., 1975, NEH, 1979, Guggenheim fellow, 1989, fellow Folger Shakespeare Libr., 1993, Brit. Libr. Ctr. for Book, 1994-95, Edinburgh U. Ctr. for Book, 1999, David Laing fellow IASH Edinburgh U., 2003, Foxcraft lectr. State Libr. Victoria, 2007, editl. bd. The Libr., 2007. Mem. Soc. for Textual Scholarship, Shakespeare Assn. Internat., Bibliog. Soc. London, Bibliog. Soc. Am. (coun. 1994-2000). Home: 823 Poinsettia St Columbia SC 29205-2039 Office: U SC Thomas Cooper Libr 107 Columbia SC 29208-0001 E-mail: ralphcrane@msn.com.

HOWARD-PEEBLES, PATRICIA N., clinical cytogeneticist; b. Lawton, Okla., Nov. 24, 1941; d. J. Marion and R. Leona (prestidge) Howard; m. Thomas M. Peebles, Aug. 16, 1975. BSEd, U. Ctrl. Okla., 1963; student, Randolph-Macon Coll. Women, 1964; PhD in Zoology (Genetics), U Tex. at Austin, 1969. Diplomate Am. Bd. Med. Genetics; cert. clin. cytogeneticist, med. geneticist. Sci. and history tchr. Piedmont (Okla.) Pub. Schs., 1963-64; biochem. technician biochemistry sect. biology divsn. Oak Ridge (Tenn.) Nat. Lab., 1964-66; instr. rsch. pediatrics dept. pediatrics, instr. cytotech. U. Okla. Health Scis. Ctr., Oklahoma City, 1971-72; asst. prof., dir. Cytogenetics Lab. U. So. Miss., Hattiesburg, 1973-77, assoc. prof., dir. Cytogenetics Lab., 1977-80; assoc. prof. dept. pub. health, staff Lab. Med. Genetics U. Ala., Birmingham, 1980-81; assoc. prof., dir. Cytogenetics Lab. dept. pathology U. Tex. Health Sci. Ctr., Dallas, 1981-85, prof., dir. Cytogenetics Lab., 1985-87; prof. dept. human genetics Med. Coll. Va., Richmond, 1987—; clin. cytogeneticist, dir. postnatal lab. Genetics & IVF Inst., Fairfax, Va., 1987-98, co-dir. cytogenetics lab., 1998-2000; genetic, cytogenetic cons., 2000—. Am. Cancer Soc. postdoctoral fellow dept. human genetics U. Mich. Med. Sch., Ann Arbor, 1969-70, dept. human genetics and devel. Coll. Physicians and Surgeons, Columbia U., N.Y.C., 1970-71; genetic cons. Ellisville (Miss.) State Sch., 1973-80; attending staff dept. pathology Parkland Meml. Hosp., Dallas County Hosp. Dist., 1981-87; mem. sci. adv. com. Fragile X Found., 1985-2002; mem. Internat. Standing Com. on Human Cytogenetic Nomenclature, 1991-96. Contbr. articles to profl. jours., chpts. to books; reviewer Am. Jour. Human Genetics, Am. Jour. Med. Genetics, Clin. Genetics, Human Genetics. Fellow Am. Coll. Med. Genetics (founding mem.); mem. Am. Soc. Human Genetics, Assn. Genetic Technologists, Tex. Genetics Soc. (chmn. planning com. ann. meeting 1984), Am. Cytogenetics Conf., Delta Kappa Gamma, Sigma Xi. Bapt. Office Phone: 214-893-8635. Personal E-mail: phpeebles@yahoo.com.

HOWARDS, STUART S., urologist, educator; b. Milw., Mar. 29, 1937; s. Harvey H. and Anne (Levin) H.; m. Carter N. Howards, Aug. 20, 1966; children: Penelope P., Hugh N. BA, Yale U., 1959; MD, Columbia U., 1963. Cert. Am. Bd. Urology, 1975. Intern in surgery Peter Bent Brigham Hosp., Boston, 1963-64, resident in urology, 1968-71; resident in surgery Childrens Hosp., Boston, 1964-65; rsch. assoc. NIH, Bethesda, Md., 1965-68; asst. prof. urology and physiology U. Va., Charlotteville, 1971-74, assoc. prof., 1974-76, prof., 1976—, chief divsn. pediat. urology, 1986—. Chmn. exam com. Am. Bd. Urology, 1985-91, trustee, 1986-92, pres., 1992-93, exec. sec., 1997—2012; sr. sci. advisor to the dir. of urology. NIDDK/NIH, 2002—. Editor: Infertility in the Male, 1991, 3d edit., 1997, Adult and Pediatric Urology, 1991, 4th edit., 2010; editor Jour. Urology, 1983-2000. Maj. USPHS, 1965-68. Recipient Career Investigation award NIH, 1973-78. Fellow Am. Acad. Pediats.; mem. Am. Urol. Assn. (Golden Cystoscope award 1981, Scott award 1990, Hugh Young award 1991, Disting. Svc. award 2001), Clin. Soc. Genitourinary Surgeons, Am. Soc. Reproductive Medicine (bd. dirs. 1994-96, treas. 1996—), Soc. Andrology, Genitourinary Surgeons, Am. Assn. Genito-Urinary Surgeons (sec.-treas. 1992-97), Nat. Bd. Med. Examiners. Office Phone: 434-924-9559. Business E-Mail: ssh4e@virginia.edu.

HOWE, JOHN PRENTICE, III, health foundation president, physician; b. Jackson, Tenn., Mar. 7, 1943; s. John Prentice and Phyllis (MacDonald) H.; m. Tyrrell Flawn; children: Lindsey Warren, Brooke Olmsted, John Prentice IV. BA, Amherst Coll., 1965; MD, Boston U., 1969. Diplomate Am. Bd. Internal Medicine, internal medicine and cardiovascular disease. Research assoc. cellular physiology Amherst Coll., 1963-64; research assoc. cardiovascular physiology Boston U. Sch. of Medicine, 1966-67; lectr. medicine Boston U. Sch. Medicine, 1972-73; intern Boston City Hosp., 1969-70, asst. resident, 1970-71;

rsch. fellow in medicine Harvard U., 1971-73, Peter Bent Brigham Hosp., 1971-73; survey physician Framingham Cardiovascular Disease Study, Nat. Heart and Lung Inst., 1971; asst. clin. prof. medicine U. Hawaii, 1973-75; from asst. prof. medicine to assoc. prof. U. Mass., 1975-85, assoc. prof., 1977-85, vice-chmn. dept. medicine, 1975-78, asst. dean continuing edn. for physicians, 1976-78, assoc. dean profl. affairs and continuing edn., 1978-80, acad. dean, 1980-85, vice chancellor, 1980-85, acting chmn. dept. anatomy, 1982-85; pres. U. Tex. Health Scis. Ctr., San Antonio, 1985-2000; pres., CEO Project HOPE, Millwood, Va., 2001—. Prof. medicine, U. Tex. Health Sci. Ctr., San Antonio, 1985-2005; chief of staff, U. Mass. Hosp., 1978-80. Mem. editl. bd. Archives Internal Medicine, 1991—2004; contbr. articles to profl. jours., chpts. to books. Trustee S.W. Found. for Biomed. Rsch., S.W. Rsch. Inst. Maj. M.C, U.S. Army, 1973-75; bd. trustees, Boston U., 2007. Alfred P. Sloan scholar Amherst Coll., 1962-65; recipient Ruth Hunter Johnson award Boston U. Sch. of Medicine, 1969 Fellow: Am. Coll. Chest Physicians, Am. Coll. Cardiology, ACP; mem.: Bexar County Med. Soc. (exec. com. 1985—2000, 1985—2000, pres. 1996), Tex. Soc. Biomed. Rsch. (past pres.), Tex. Med. Soc. (coun. med. edn. 1986—2001, ho. of dels. 1989—2001, pres.-elect 1997—98, pres. 1998—99), Am. Heart Assn. (fellow coun. clin. cardiology), AMA (coun. on sci. affairs 1993—2001, del. ho. dels. 1995—2001), Omicron Kappa Epsilon, Alpha Omega Alpha. Avocations: tennis, skiing. Business E-Mail: jhowe@projecthope.org.*

HOWE, LYMAN HAROLD, III, chemist, researcher; b. Wilkes-Barre, Pa., Nov. 5, 1938; s. Lyman Harold and Esther Madeline (Smith) H.; m. Mary Louise Reinhart, June 16, 1962; 1 child, Jennifer. BS, Duke U., 1960; MS, Emory U., 1961; PhD, U. Tenn., 1966. Rsch. assoc. Emory U., 1960-61; rsch. and teaching assoc. U. Tenn., 1962-66; rsch. chemist water mgmt. TVA, Chattanooga, 1966-97. Co-author publs. in field. Fellow ASTM (water com. results advisor 1976-97, Max Hecht award 1985, Award of Merit 1993); mem. Am. Chem. Soc., Am. Contact Bridge League (reviewer environ. sci. and tech. 1989, Ace of Clubs award, 3d pl. Chattanooga Club Master of Yr. award 1989, N.Am. Bridge Championship master 2005), U.S. Chess Fedn. Clubs: Torch (1st v.p. chpt. 1981, pres. 1982-83, 2d v.p. 1984-88). Presbyterian. Home: 1241 Mountain Brook Cir Signal Mountain TN 37377-2127 Personal E-mail: lhowe007@comcast.net.

HOWELL, BOBBY B., state legislator; b. Dec. 23, 1941; m. Charmayne Killebrew; children: Gary Brian, Haley Marten. Mayor, Kilmichall, 1969—91; mem. Dist. 46 Miss. House of Reps., 1969—91; pharmacist. Mem.: Am. Legislature Exchange Coun., Galen Order, Gideon, Cattlemen's Assn., Miss. Munic Assn., Montgomery County Econ. Coun., Miss. Pharmacist Assn. (pres.), Lions. Republican. Baptist. Mailing: PO Box 213 Kilmichael MS 39747 Office Phone: 601-359-2420. Fax: 662-262-4397. Business E-Mail: bhowell@house.ms.gov.

HOWELL, DONALD LEE, lawyer; b. Waco, Tex., Jan. 31, 1935; s. Hilton Emory and Louise Howell; m. Gwendolyn Avera, June 13, 1957 (dec. July, 2012); children: Daniel Liege, Alison Avera, Anne Turner. BA cum laude, Baylor U., 1956; JD with honors, U. Tex., 1963. Bar: Tex. 1963. Assoc. Vinson & Elkins, Houston, 1963-70, ptnr., 1970—2007, mem. mgmt. com., 1980-99; of counsel Andrews Kurth, 2008—. Capt. USAFR, 1956—59. Fellow Am. Bar Found., Tex. Bar Found., Houston Bar Found., Am. Law Inst.; mem. ABA, Am. Coll. Bond Counsel, Houston Bar Assn., Nat. Assn. Bond Lawyers (pres. 1981-82, bd. dirs. 1979-83), Attys. Liability Assurance Soc. (Bermuda bd. dirs. 1992-2005, chmn. 2000-02, US bd. dirs. 1992-2005, chmn. 2000-02), Houston Club, Order of Coif, Phi Delta Phi. Democrat. Episcopalian. Office Phone: 713-220-3892. Personal E-mail: don.howell@gmail.com. Business E-Mail: dhowell@andrewskurth.com.

HOWELL, GEORGE COOK, III, lawyer; b. New Orleans, June 27, 1956; s. George C. Jr. and Billie Grace (Webb) H.; m. Cynthia M. Howell; children: Margaret Sloan, George C. IV. AB magna cum laude, Princeton U., 1978; JD, U.Va., 1981. Bar: Va. 1981, U.S. Dist. Ct. (ea. dist.) Va. 1982, U.S. Ct. Appeals (4th cir.) 1982. Law clk. U.S. Dist. Ct. (ea. dist.) Va., Alexandria, 1981—82; assoc. Hunton & Williams, Richmond, Va., 1982—89, ptnr., 1989—, team head tax & employee benefits, 1989—. Contbr. Va. Law Rev., 1980; editor-in-chief Va. Tax Rev., 1980-81; articles editor The Tax Lawyer, 1983-86, mng. editor, 1987-89. Participant Leadership Metro Richmond, 1987-88. Mem. ABA (taxation sect. chmn. remic task force 1987-88, chmn. mini-program on mortgage-backed securities 1988, chmn. subcom. on asset securitization 1988-90, corp. tax shelters tax force 2000-2001, vice chmn. com. on fin. trans. 1990-92, chmn. com. on fin. trans. 1992-94, sec. taxation 1995-97, sect. taxation coun., 1997-2000, vice chmn. comm. 2001-2003), Princeton Assn. Va. (treas. 1987-89, pres. 1989-91), Va. State Bar, Am. Coll. Tax Counsel (chair 2011-), Order of Coif, Phi Beta Kappa. Republican. Avocations: golf, running, stock market. Office: Hunton & Williams 951 E Byrd St Ste 200 Richmond VA 23219-4074 Office Phone: 804-788-8793. Office Fax: 804-788-8218.

HOWELL, JANET DENISON, state legislator; b. Washington, May 7, 1944; m. Hunt Howell. Former chmn. State Bd. Soc. Svc.; mem. Dist 32 Va. State Senate, Va., 1992—; mem. Courts of Justice com., Edn. & Health com., Fin. & Privileges & Elections Com. Recipient Citizen of Year, Reston Times, 1984, Va. Citizen of Year, Nat. Assn. Social Workers, 1991. Mem.: Reston County Parent-Tchr. Assn. (former pres.), Reston Cmty. Assn. (former pres., Restonian of Yr. 1989). Democrat. Unitarian. Mailing: PO Box 2608 Reston VA 20195-0608 Fax: 703-435-1995. E-mail: senhowell@aol.com, district32@sov.state.va.us.

HOWELL, JOHN E., lawyer; b. Texarkana, Tex., Sept. 9, 1946; BA, Rice U., 1968; JD with honors, U. Tex., 1974. Law clerk Supreme Ct. Tex., 1974-75; ptnr. Hughes & Luce, LLP (merged with K&L Gates), Dallas; ptnr., corp. practice K&L Gates LLP, Dallas, 2008—. Bd. trustees Dallas Theater Ctr., Dallas Theater Ctr. Endowment Fund; bd. dir. AT&T Performing Arts Ctr. Mem. ABA, State Bar Tex., Dallas Bar Assn., Order of Coif. Office: K&L Gates LLP Ste 2800 1717 Main St Dallas TX 75201 Office Phone: 214-939-5461. Office Fax: 214-939-5849. Business E-Mail: john.howell@klgates.com.

HOWELL, LLOYD W., JR., management consultant; BSEE, U. Pa.; MBA, Harvard U. Assoc., investment banking divsn. Goldman Sachs; client svc. officer, civil market clients, fin. svcs. Booz Allen Hamilton Holding Corp., cons., 1988—91, mem., strategy & orgn., 1995—2000, v.p., 2000—05, capability leader, strategy & orgn., 2005—09, exec. v.p., 2005—. Former chmn. Friends of the Nat. Zoo (FONZ); former bd. dirs. Children''s Nat. Med. Ctr.; bd. dirs. United Negro Coll. Fund (UNCF). Recipient Black Engr. of the Yr. award, 2010. Office: Booz Allen Hamilton Holding Corp 8283 Greensboro Dr Mc Lean VA 22102 Office Phone: 703-902-5000. Office Fax: 703-902-3333. Business E-Mail: lloyd_howell@bah.com.

HOWELL, RALPH RODNEY, pediatrician, geneticist, educator; b. Concord, NC, June 10, 1931; s. Fred Lee and Grace Mary (Blackwelder) H.; m. Sarah Vosburg Esselstyn, Nov. 19, 1960 (dec.); children: Grace Meyer, Elizabeth Eriksson, John Esselstyn. BS, Davidson Coll., 1953; MD, Duke U., 1957. Cert. Am. Bd. Pediatrics, Am. Bd. Med. Genetics/Clin. Biochem. Genetics. Intern Duke U., 1957—58, resident in pediat., 1958—59, rsch. fellow in pediat. and medicine, 1959—60; clin. assoc. and staff NIH, Bethesda, Md., 1960—64; assoc. prof. pediat. Johns Hopkins U., Balt., 1964—72; pediatrician-in-chief U. Children's Hosp. at Hermann, Houston, 1972—87, chmn. med. bd., 1972—87; David Park prof. U. Tex. Med. Sch., Houston, 1972—89, chmn. dept. pediat., 1972—87; prof., chmn. dept. pediat. U. Miami Sch. Medicine, 1989—2003, chmn. emeritus, prof., 2003—; sec. med. staff Jackson Meml. Hosp., Miami, 1992—93; sr. advisor dir. Eunice Kennedy Shriver Nat. Inst. Child Health & Human Devel., Bethesda, Md., 2003—11; v.p. med. staff Jackson Meml. Hosp., Miami, 1993—97, pres. med. staff, 1997—99; mem. Hussman Inst. Human Genomics U. Miami, 2011—. Cons. pediat. M.D. Anderson Hosp. and Tumor Inst., 1972-89; metabolism study sect. NIH, 1973-77, chmn. maternal and child health adv. com., 1983-86; exec. com. Nat. Practitioner Data Bank, 1995-98; nat. clin. adv. com. Nat. Found. March of Dimes, 1973-79; chmn. sci. adv. bd. Muscular Dystrophy Assn., 1989-2007, bd. dirs. chmn., 2007-; vis. prof. Inst. Molecular Genetics, Baylor Coll. Medicine, Houston, 1988; chief pediat. Holtz Childrens Hosp., U. Miami-Jackson Meml. Med. Ctr., 1989-2003; nat. adv. coun. Nat. Inst. Child Health and Human Devel., 1999-2003; chair HHS Sec.'s Adv. Com. on Hereditary Disorders in Children and Newborns, 2004—2011. Author: (with G.H. Thomas) Selected Screening Tests for Genetic Metabolic Diseases, 1973, (with F.H. Morriss, L.K. Pickering) Role of Human Milk in Infant Nutrition, 1986; contbr. articles to profl. jours. Trustee Jackson Lab. Bar Harbor, Maine, 1985-2003; dir. Rip van Winkle Found., Claverack, N.Y., 1987-92, pres., 1992—; bd. dirs. Congl. Ch. Found., Coconut Grove, Fla., 2003-2005, Dr. John T. Macdonald Found., Coral Gables, Fla., 2003-. Served to sr. surgeon, 1960—64, USPHS. Recipient Klauber Lectureship, Greenwood Genetic Ctr., 2004, Lifetime Achievement award, Duke Med. Sch., 2007, Butterfield Lectr. award, NICHD, U. Colo., 2009, Lifetime Achievement award, Am. Coll. Med. Genetics Found., 2012, award, Birdsong Lectr. U. Va., 2012, March Dimes Col. Harland Sanders Lifetime Achievement award, 2013, Lifetime Achievement award, March of Dimes, 2013; named Jimmy Simon Hon. Lectr., Wake Forest U., 2005; named one of 30 Rare Diseases Heroes, US FDA, 2013; Joseph P. Kedy Jr. Sr. Rsch. scholar in Mental Retardation. Fellow AAAS, Am. Acad. Pediat. (com. on genetics); mem. AMA (ho. of dels. 1998—), Am. Pediat. Soc., Soc. Pediat. Rsch., Houston Pediat. Soc. (pres. 1978-79), Tex. Med. Assn., Soc. Inborn Errors of Metabolism (pres. 1981), Miami Pediat. Soc., Fla. Med. Assn., Am. Coll. Med. Genetics (bd. dirs., treas. 1995-96, pres.-elect 1997-98, pres. 1999—2000), Am. Coll. Med. Genetics (found. pres. 2003—12), Nat. Adv. Coun. (liaison mem. 2006-2012), Nat. Human Genome Rsch. Inst. (chmn. ethical, social and legal issues rev. group 1996-2003), Pi Kappa Alpha, Cosmos Club (Washington). Congregationalist. Avocations: flying, classic auto collector. Office: University Miami Sch Medicine Dept Pediatrics 626 Biomed Rsch Bldg 1501 NW 10th Ave Miami FL 33136 Office Phone: 305-243-1073. Business E-Mail: rhowell@miami.edu.

HOWELL, ROBERT EDWARD, hospital administrator; b. Marietta, Ohio, Jan. 19, 1949; married; 3 children. BS, Muskingham Coll., 1971; MS in Hosp. and Health Svcs. Adminstrn., Ohio State U., 1977. Assoc. dir. U. Minn. Hosps. and Clinics, Mpls., 1980-86; exec. dir. Med. Coll. Ga. Hosps. and Clinics, Augusta, 1986-94; dir., CEO, U. Iowa Hosps. and Clinics, Iowa City, 1994—. Mem. exec. com. Accreditation Coun. for Grad. Med. Edn. Mem. Coun. Tchg. Hosps. (past chmn.), Am. Assn. Med. Colls. (exec. com.), Am. Hosp. Assn. (coord. com. med. edn.), Univ. Health System Consortium (exec. com.). Office: U VA Med Ctr 3007 McKim Hall PO Box 800809 Charlottesville VA 22908-0809

HOWELL, TERRY ALLEN, agricultural engineer; b. Dallas, Sept. 7, 1947; s. Levi Lowe III and Lila Lee (Allen) H.; m. Mary Sue Parkerson, Feb. 22, 1969; children: Terry A. Jr., Lisa H. Dreibrodt, Michael S. BS, Tex. A&M U., 1969, MS, 1970, PhD, 1974. Rsch. asst. Tex. A&M U., College Station, 1969-70, rsch. assoc., 1971-74; asst. prof. N.Mex. State U., Las Cruces, 1975, Tex. A&M U., College Station, 1976-79; agr. engr. USDA ARS, Fresno, Calif., 1979-83, Bushland, Tex., 1983—92, rsch. leader, 1992—2009, lab. dir., 2009—. Co-author: Modification of the Aerial Environment Crops, 1979, Design and Operation of Farm Irrigation Systems, 1980, Limitations to Effective Water Use in Crop Production, 1983, Irrigation of Agricultural Crops, 1991, Agricultural System Models, 2002, Encyclopedia of Water Science, 2003; co-editor, co-author: Management of Farm Irrigation Systems, 1991. Tchr. Paramount Bapt. Ch., Amarillo, 1985-94, deacon, 1987—; troop com. chmn. Boy Scouts Am., Amarillo, 1991-93. Recipient Tex. Environ. Excellence award in agr. Tex. Natural Resource Conservation Commn., 1999, Fed. Energy and Water Mgmt. award U.S. Dept. Energy, 199, Tech. Transfer award ARS, 1999, Sr. Scientist Yr. ARS, So. Plains area, 2000, Mid-Continent Regional Lab. award, 2000, Blue Ribbon award Am. Soc. Agrl. and Biol. Engrs., 2006, John Deere Gold medal, 2008, Heermann Sprinkler Irrigation award, 2008; named Agrl. Engr. of Yr. Tex. Sect. Am. Soc. Agrl. and Biol. Engrs., 2005. Fellow ASAE (chmn. soil and water divsn. 1987-88, Paper award 1972, 74, 80, 2010, soil and water divsn. editor 1993-97, Hancor award 2000 (Heermann Sprinkler Irrigation award 2008, John Deere Gold medal 2008), Tex. sect. Engr. of Yr. 2005), Am. Soc. Agronomy (A-3 divsn. chair 1999-2000), ASCE (chmn. irrigation water requirements com. 1990-93, Tipton award 1997), Am. Acad. Water Resource Engrs. (diplomate 2007), Soil Sci. Soc. America; mem Irrigation Assn. (life; Person of Yr. award 1995), Coun. for Agrl. Sci. and Tech., Tex. Agrl. Irrigation Assn. Office: USDA ARS PO Box 10 Bushland TX 79012-0010 Business E-Mail: terry.howell@ars.usda.gov.

HOWELL, WILLIAM ASHLEY, III, lawyer; b. Raleigh, NC, Jan. 2, 1949; s. William Ashley II and Caroline Erskine Greenleaf; m. Esther Holland, Dec. 22, 1973. BS, Troy State U., 1972; postgrad., U. Ala., Birmingham, 1974-75; JD, Birmingham Sch. Law, 1977. Bar: Ala. 1977, U.S. Dist. Ct. (no. dist.) Ala. 1977, U.S. Ct. Appeals (5th cir.) 1977, U.S. Supreme Ct. 1982, U.S. Ct. Appeals (11th cir.) 1983, U.S. Dist. Ct. (mid. dist.) Ala. 1987. Atty. pub. defender divsn. Legal Aid Soc. of Birmingham, 1977—78, civil divsn. Legal Aid Soc. of Birmingham, 1978—81; dist. office atty. SBA, Birmingham, 1980—82, supervising atty. Ala. Dist., 1982—; spl. asst. U.S. Atty. (mid. dist.), Ala., 1988—, U.S. Atty. (so. dist.), Ala., 2002—. Part-time instr. legal and social environ. and human resources mgmt. Jefferson State C.C., Birmingham, 1993. Contbr. articles to profl. jours. Vol. reader Radio Reading Svc. Network for Blind, 1991—93; mem. Shelby County Econ. Devel. Coun., 1993—94, Hispanic Outreach Commn., 2000—01, Highland Crest Homeowners Assn., 2002—; del. state conv. Episc. Ch. of Ala., various yrs.; bd. dirs. Hoover Homeowners Assn., 1977—81, Southside Ministries, Inc., 1990—91, v.p. bd. dirs., 1990—91; bd. dirs. SafeHouse of Shelby County, Inc., 1990—93, vice chmn., 1991—93. Recipient Am. Jurisprudence Criminal Procedure Book award. Mem. ABA (sect. corporation, banking and bus. law), Nat. Parks and Conservation Soc. (life), Fed. Bar Assn. (sec. Birmingham chpt. 1980-81, del. nat. conv. 1993, 94, del. mid yr. meeting, 1994-95), Ala. Bar Assn. (com. on future of the profession 1978-81, 83-84, com. on quality of life 1992-93, sect. bankruptcy and corp. law, sect. bankruptcy and comml. law, sect. corp. counsel, sect. banking and bus. law), Nature Conservacy (life), Birmingham Bar Assn., Birmingham Venture Club, Sierra Club (life), Sigma Delta Kappa (v.p., Outstanding Sr. award 1977). Episcopalian. Office: US Small Bus Adminstrn 801 Tom Martin Dr Ste 201 Birmingham AL 35211-4436 Fax: 205-290-7443. E-mail: william.howell@sba.gov.

HOWELL, WILLIAM JAMES, state legislator; b. Washington, May 8, 1943; m. Cecelia Stump; children: William F., Leland J. BBA, U. Richmond, Va., 1964; JD, U. Va. Sch. Law. Trust and estate atty., Va.; sr. v.p. Nat. Bank Fredericksburg, Va.; mem. Dist. 28 Va. House of Delegates, Va., 1988—, house spkr., 2003—. Bd. dirs. Rappahannock Hospice; former vice chmn. bd. dirs. Mary Washington Hosp. Mem. YMCA Rappahannock; active Young Life. Mem.: American Legis. Exch. Coun. (bd. dirs. 2001—, nat. chmn. 2009), Va. State C. of C. (former dir.), Stafford C. of C., Fredericksburg C. of C. (past pres.), Spotsylvania C. of C. (past pres.). Republican. Bapt. Office: PO Box 8296 Fredericksburg VA 22404-8296 also: Capitol Office Gen Assembly Bldg Rm 635 PO Box 406 Richmond VA 23218 Office Phone: 540-371-1612, 804-698-1028. Office Fax: 540-371-7449, 804-698-6728. Business E-Mail: delWhowell@house.virginia.gov.

HOWELLS, JEFFREY P., computer company executive; B in Acctg., Stetson U. CPA. With Price Waterhouse, 1979—91, sr. audit mgr.; v.p. fin. Tech Data, 1991-92; CFO Tech Data Corp., 1992-93, sr. v.p. fin., CFO, 1993-97, exec. v.p., CFO, 1997—. Mailing: PO Box 6260 Clearwater FL 33758-6260 Office: Tech Data Corp 5350 Tech Data Dr Clearwater FL 33760-3122 Office Phone: 727-539-7429, 727-539-7429. E-mail: jeffery.howells@techdata.com.

HOWER, FRANK BEARD, JR., retired banker; b. Louisville, Ky., Nov. 26, 1928; s. Frank Beard and Katharine (Coffman) H.; m. Virginia W. Barker, Dec. 30, 1954; children: Frank Beard III, William. AB, Centre Coll., Danville, Ky., 1950. With Liberty Nat. Bank, Louisville, 1950-90, exec. v.p., 1967-71, pres., 1971-90, CEO, chmn. bd. dirs., 1973-90, ret., 1990. Bd. dirs. Falls City Industries, Inc., Louisville, Bank One, Ky., Norton Health Sys., Inc., Am. Life and Accident Ins. Co., Churchill Downs Inc., Anthem Inc.; chmn. Norton Kosair Childrens Hosp., Inc., 1983-84. Trustee J. Graham Brown Found., U. Louisville; chmn. regional adv. bd. Comptr. of Currency, 1976; mem. Ky. Registry of Election Finance, 1966-70, Ky. Econ. Progress Commn., 1964-70; vice chmn. Ky.-Tenn. Export Coun.; gen. chmn. United Appeal, 1969; chmn. Greater Louisville Fund for the Arts, 1976; v.p. Louisville Philharm. Orch., 1974-75; chmn. Regional Airport Authority of Louisville and Jefferson County, Louisville Devel. Com.; bd. dirs., chmn. U. Louisville; trustee, chmn. Ky. Ind. Coll. Found.; trustee Centre Coll.; mem. Actors Theatre Bd. Maj. USMCR, 1951-52, Korea. Mem. Am., Ky. bankers assns., Robert Morris Assos., Assn. Res. City Bankers, Louisville C. of C. (pres. 1973) Republican. Episcopalian.

HOWES, JAMES GUERDON, communication and transportation executive; b. Balt. s. James Harold and Edna Esther (Lowman) H. BS, U. Md., 1967, MBA, 1969. Staff asst. U.S. Senate, Washington, 1965-68; regional mktg. adminstrn. Hertz Corp., Balt., 1972-75; commr. aviation Dutchess County, Poughkeepsie, NY, 1975-80; airport dir. St. Petersburg-Clearwater (Fla.) Internat. Airport, 1980-2001; CEO Atlas Comm., Balt., 2001—; cons. Bermuda Govt., 2002—. Prodr. radio programs Choral Masterpieces, 1985-95, King of Instruments, 1983-95, Sacred Classics, 1995—, other CD's and concerts. Committeeman Rep. Nat. Com. Campaign, Washington, 1974-84, Riverside Ch., N.Y.C., 1976-80; v.p. Boy Scouts Am., Largo, Fla., 1987-91, nat. coun. rep., 1992-96. Capt. USAF, 1969-72. Recipient So. divsn. Airport of Yr. Safety award, 1998; named Man of Yr., Bermuda Hotel Assn., 2004. Mem. Am. Assn. Airport Execs., Southeastern Airport Mgrs. Assn. (pres. 1993-94), Belleair Country Club. Methodist. Avocations: flying, scuba diving, classical music, photography, white water rafting. Home: 41 Pinewood Cir Safety Harbor FL 34695-5421 Office: PO Box 42231 Baltimore MD 21284 E-mail: jimhowes@sacredclassics.com.

HOWEY, JOHN RICHARD, architect, writer; b. New Haven, Jan. 13, 1932; s. Joseph Herman and Dorothy Pauline (Good) H.; m. Maria Andrea Hatges, Sept. 8, 1968; children: John Michael, Dorothy Anne. Student, Wooster Coll., 1951-52; BS, Ga. Inst. Tech., 1956, BArch, 1957. Registered architect Fla. With various archtl. firms, Fla., 1958—65, John Howey, Architect, AIA, Tampa, Fla., 1965—73, John Howey Assocs., Tampa, Fla., 1973—. Pres. Baypark, Inc., Tampa, 1988—. Prin. works include coll. bldgs. U. So. Fla., 1975, Louis Pappas Restaurant, Tarpon Springs, Fla., 1975 (honor design award AIA 1976), office bldg. 101 S. Franklin St., Tampa, 1980 (Fla. Preservation award 1984), Williers Residence, Tampa, 1980 (honor design award AIA 1981), modular urban transit shelters, 1977 (U.S. patent 1980, honor design award AIA 1985), Tehran, Iran Libr. Project, 1978, Baypark Pl. apt. bldgs., Tampa, 1989 (honor design award AIA 1989, Millenium Award of Honor, 2000), others; author: The Sarasota School of Architecture, 1995; co-author: Florida Architecture, A Celebration, 2000, As Architecture Florida Modern, 2004, Selected and Current Works, John Howey Associates, 2006. With C.E., U.S. Army, 1957-58. Fellow AIA (Fla./Caribbean region Design Excellence Honor award 1985, Fla. ctrl. chpt. Medal of Honor 1986); mem. Sertoma Club (bd. dirs. 1970-73), Economic Club. Episcopalian. Avocations: photography, painting. Home: 1507 Bay Villa Pl Tampa FL 33629 Address: John Howey Assocs 121 E Whiting St Tampa FL 33602-5136 Business E-Mail: jhoweyarch@tampabay.rr.com.

HOWZE, JOSEPH LAWSON EDWARD, bishop emeritus; b. Daphne, Ala., Aug. 30, 1923; s. Albert Otis and Helen Artamesa (Lawson) Howze. BS, Ala. State U., 1948; postgrad., Phillips Coll., Gulfport, Miss., 1980; LLD (hon.), U. Portland, 1974, St. Bonaventure U., 1977, Manhattan Coll., NYC, 1979; HHD (hon.), Sacred Heart Coll., Belmont, NC, 1977, Lift Bible Crusade Coll., 1987, Belmont Abbey Coll., 1999, Christ the King Sem., 2002. Ordained priest, 1959; pastor chs. Charlotte, Southern Pines, Durham, Sanford, Asheville, NC, 1959—72; ordained bishop, 1973; aux. bishop Diocese of Natchez-Jackson, Miss., 1972—77; bishop Diocese of Biloxi, Miss., 1977—2001, bishop emeritus, 2001—. Mem. Miss. Health Care Commn.; mem. adminstrv. bd., vacation com. NOCB/USCC; mem. edn. com. USCC, mem. social devel. and world peace com.; liaison com. to Nat. Office of Black Catholics NCCB; trustee Xavier U., New Orleans; bd. dirs. Biloxi Regional Med. Ctr. Recipient Star of the Sea award, U.S. Conf. Cath. Bishops, 2002. Mem.: Knights of St. Peter Claver, KC. Democrat. Roman Catholic. Mailing: Diocese of Biloxi 1790 Popps Ferry Rd Biloxi MS 39533-1189

HOY, MARJORIE ANN, entomology educator; b. Kansas City, Kans., May 19, 1941; d. Dayton J. and Marjorie Jean (Acker) Wolf; m. James B. Hoy; 1 child, Benjamin Lee AB, U. Kans., 1963; MS, U. Calif., Berkeley, 1966, PhD, 1972. Asst. entomologist Conn. Agrl. Expt. Sta., New Haven, 1973-75; rsch. entomologist U.S. Forest Svc., Hamden, Conn., 1975-76; asst. prof. entomology U. Calif., Berkeley, 1976-80, assoc. prof. entomology, 1980-82, prof. entomology, 1982-92, prof. emeritus, 1992—; Fischer, Davies and Eckes prof., dept. entomology and nematology U. Fla., Gainesville, 1992—; chmn. Calif. Gypsy Moth Sci. Adv. Panel, 1982—; mem. genetics resources adv. com. USDA, 1992—, mem. adv. com. agrl. biotech., 2000—02; mem. com. on biol. threats to agrl. plants and animals NRC and NAS, 2001—02. Chmn. Calif. Gypsy Moth Sci. Adv. Panel, 1982—; mem. genetics resources adv. com. USDA, 1992—, mem. adv. com. agrl. biotech., 2000—01; F.E. Guyton disting. lectr. Auburn (Ala.) U., 1997; mem. com. on biol. threats to agrl. plants and animals NRC and NAS, 2001—02; sci. cons. transgenic insects Pew Initiative Food and Biotech. Editor, co-editor: Genetics in Relation to Insect Managment, 1979, Recent Advances in Knowledge of the Phytoseiidae, 1982, Biological Control of Pests by Mites, 1983, Biological Control in Agricultural IPM Systems, 1985, Insect Molecular Genetics, 1994, 2d edit., 2003, The Phytoseiidae as Biological Control Agents of Pest Mites and Insects: A Bibliography, 1996, Managing the Citrus Leafminer, 1996; mem. editl. bd. Internat. Jour. Pest Mgmt., Biol. Control, Biocontrol Sci. and Tech., Environ. Biosafety Rsch.; contbr. articles to profl. jours. Mem. Sec. Agr.'s adv. com. agrl. biotech.; cons. Pew Charitable Trust. Recipient citation for outstanding achievments in regulatory entomology Fla. Divsn. Plant Industry, 1995, USDA honor award Sec. of Agr., 1996, award for sci. Nat. Agri-Mktg. Assn., 1998, sr. faculty award U. Fla. chpt. Gamma Sigma Delta, 1998, Biol. Control Scientist of Yr., Internat. Orgn. Biol. Control, 2004. Fellow AAAS, Royal Entomol. Soc. London, Entomol. Soc. Am. (mem. Pacific br. governing bd. 1985, Bussart award 1986, Founder's Meml. award 1992), Coun. Agr. Sci. and Tech. (Charles Black award 2004); mem. Nat. Acad. Scis. (com. on biol. threats to agr. plants and animals), NY Acad. Scis., Am. Genetic Assn., Internat. Orgn. Biol. Control (v.p. 1984-85, Disting. Scientist award 2004), Am. Inst. Biol. Scis. (adv. coun. 1996-98, governing bd. 1999-2001), Acarological Soc. Am. (governing bd. 1980-84, pres. 1992), Soc. for Study of Evolution, Fla. Entomological Soc. (Team Rsch. award 1997, Outstanding Tchg. award 1999), Phi Beta Kappa, Sigma Xi (chpt. sec. 1979-81, Sr. Faculty Rsch. award 1996). Avocations: hiking, gardening, snorkeling. Home: 4320 SW 83rd Way Gainesville FL 32608-4131 Office: U Fla Dept Entomology and Nematology PO Box 110620 Gainesville FL 32611-0620 Home Phone: 352-335-7839; Office Phone: 352-273-3961. Business E-Mail: mahoy@ifas.ufl.edu.

HOYE, ROBERT EARL, systems science educator; b. Warwick, RI, Jan. 12, 1931; s. S. Earl and Alice (Landry) H.; m. Patricia Buswell, Aug. 20, 1955 (dec. May 22, 2002); children: Robert Earl Jr., Joanne D., Peter M., Kathleen B. BA, Providence Coll., 1953; MS, St. John's U., NYC, 1955; PhD, U. Wis., Madison, 1973. Instr. St. John's U., 1953-55; dir. guidance Middleboro (Mass.) Pub. Schs., 1955-56, Rutland (Vt.) Pub. Schs., 1956-57; dean Champlain (Vt.) Coll., 1957-58; supt. Frontier Regional Sch. Dist., Deerfield, Mass., 1958-60; New Eng. dir. Sci. Rsch. Assocs. subs. IBM, Chgo., 1960-65; nat. dir. Learning Systems div. Xerox Corp., NYC, 1965-66; dir. Instrnl. Media Lab. U. Wis., Milw., 1966-73; asst. v.p. U. Louisville, 1974-81, prof. cmty. health Sch. Medicine, 1981-92, prof. urban policy, coord. grad. program in health systems, 1981-95, prof. edn., 1992-95, prof. emeritus, 1995—. Cons. to mgmt., Louisville, 1966—; mem. faculty health svcs. Walden U., 1988—; vis. prof. exec. leadership U. Sarasota, 1995-2001 Author: Index to Computer Based Learning, 1973; co-author: Home Health, 1996; editor Edn. Jour., 1968-73; also articles. Recipient cert. of merit San Diego State U., 1983, Grad. Teaching Excellence award U. Louisville, 1984, gold medal Project Innovation, 1984, Outstanding Faculty Mem. award Walden U., 2000. Fellow Am. Acad. Med. Adminstrs. (diplomate, chmn. editl. bd. 1986-94, dir. Ky. chpt. 2006—), Royal Soc. Health (Statesman in Healthcare Adminstrn. award 1992). Democrat. Roman Catholic. Personal E-mail: rehoye@att.net.

HOYNES, LOUIS LENOIR, JR., lawyer; b. Indpls., Sept. 23, 1935; s. Louis L. and Catharine (Parker) H.; m. Judith E. Kass, Oct. 12, 1958 (div. 1979); children: Thomas M., William D., Ellen B.; m. Virginia Devin, Dec. 9, 1979. AB, Columbia U., 1957; JD cum laude, Harvard U., 1962. Bar: NY 1963, US Supreme Ct. 1967, US Dist. Ct. (so. dist.) NY, US Ct. Appeals (2d, 7th and 9th cirs.). Assoc. Willkie Farr & Gallagher, NYC, 1962-68, ptnr., 1969-90; counsel Nat. League Profl. Baseball Clubs, 1970-90; sr. v.p., gen. counsel Wyeth (formerly) Am. Home Products Corp., 1990-2000; exec. v.p. gen. counsel Am. Home Products Corp. (now Wyeth), 2000—03. Lectr. law Columbia U., N.Y.C., 1982-91; bd. dirs. Cytec Industries Inc., 1994-, US C. of C. Inst. for Legal Reform, 2002-07; trustee Food and Drug Law Inst., 1994-2002. Served to lt. USNR, 1957-59, PTO. Mem. ABA, N.Y. State Bar Assn., Assn. of City of Bar of N.Y., The Assn. Gen. Counsel. Home: 220 Sundial Ct Vero Beach FL 32963 Home Phone: 516-759-1396.

HOYT, CLARK FREELAND, editor; b. Providence, Nov. 20, 1942; s. Charles Freeland and Maude Leslie (King) H.; m. Jane Ann Hauser, Sept. 30, 1967 (div. Jan. 1978); m. Linda Kauss, Aug. 22, 1988. AB, Columbia Coll., 1964. Research asst. to U.S. Senator, Washington, 1964-66; reporter Lakeland (Fla.) Ledger, 1966-68; politics writer Detroit Free Press, 1968-70; Washington corr. Miami Herald, 1970-73; nat. corr. Knight Newspapers, Washington, 1973-75, news editor Washington bur., 1975-77; bus. editor Detroit Free Press, 1977-79, conv. editor, 1979-80, asst. to exec. editor, 1980-81; mng. editor Wichita Eagle-Beacon, Kans., 1981-85; news editor Washington Bur., Knight-Ridder Newspapers, 1985-87, bur. chief, 1987-93, v.p. news, 1993-99, Washington editor, 1999—2006; cons. The McClatchy Co., Reston, Va., 2006—07; public editor The NY Times, 2007—10; cons. Bloomberg News, 2010—. Recipient Pulitzer Prize for Nat. Reporting, 1973. Mem. Nat. Press Club (fin. sec., bd. govs. 1975), Gridiron Club.

HOYT, KENNETH M., federal judge; b. San Augustine County, Tex., 1948; AB, Tex. So. U., 1969, JD, 1972. Mem. firm Wickliff, King, Hoyt & Jones, 1972-75, Anderson, Hodge, Jones & Hoyt, 1975-79, Webster & Andrews, 1979-81; presiding judge 125th Civil Dist. Ct., 1981-82; pvt. practice law Kenneth M. Hoyt & Assocs., 1983-85; justice U.S. Ct. Appeals (1st cir.), 1985-88; judge US Dist. Ct. (so. dist.) Tex., Houston, 1988—. Faculty trial advocacy program South Tex. Coll., 1981-82; adj. prof. Thurgood Marshall Sch. Law, 1983-84. Contbr. articles to profl. jours. Former bd. dirs. Bus. and Profl. Men's Club; judge trial advocacy program U. Houston, 1982-84, 87-88; former mem. Juvenile Justice & Delinquency Prevention Adv. Bd., Blue Ribbon Commn., Rev. Criminal Justice Corrections System, Referendum Force, Selection of Judges; former mem. adv. bd. Parents of Murdered Children and Coalition of Victims Rights; formerly active Salvation Army; former chmn. Capital Devel. Com., Wheeler Ave. Bapt. Ch.; past dir. Houston Lawyer's Referral Svc. With USNG, 1972-78. Decorated Am. Spirit medal; recipient Outstanding Community Svc. award Kendleton, Tex., Ethel Ranson Art & Literary Club award, Outstanding Acheivement award Thurgood Marshall Sch. Law Alumni Assn., 1986; named one of Most Outstanding Black Rep. South Tex. Mem. Nat. Bar Assn., State Bar Tex. (task force, minimum continuing legal edn.). Office: US District Courthouse Suite 11144 515 Rusk Ave Houston TX 77002-2605

HOYT, MONT POWELL, arbitrator; b. Oklahoma City, Apr. 3, 1940; s. Lester Dean and Paula (Powell) H.; m. Alice Nathalie Ryan, June 15, 1974; children: Mont Powell Jr., Kathleen, Michael, Caroline. BA, Northwestern U., 1962; JD, Okla. Law Sch., 1965; M in Comparative Law, U. Chgo., 1968. Bar: Okla. 1965, Tex. 1968. Law clk. U.S. Dist. Ct., Oklahoma City, 1965; stagiaire to French advocat Paris, 1967-68; assoc. Baker & Botts, Houston, 1968-75, ptnr., 1975-92; shareholder Verner, Liipfert, Bernhard, McPherson & Hand, Houston, 1993-94; ptnr. Hughes & Luce, Houston, 1994-2001, Shook, Hardy & Bacon, Houston, 2001—04, Munsch, Hardt, Kopf & Harr P.C., Houston, 2004—06, Hoyt & Assocs., Houston, 2006—. Adj. prof. law U. Houston, 1970—76; sec. Houston Com. Fgn. Rels., 1993—; hon. consul gen. for Malaysia in Tex., 2003—. Contbr. articles to profl. jours. Bd. dirs. French Am. Found., N.Y.C., 1979-85, Mexican Cultural Inst., 1991-95, Fgn. Policy Assn., 1991-93; mem. Latin Am. adv. bd. Americas Soc., 1992—2005, adv. panel to ALI Restoturnat, US Law of Comml. Arbitration, 2009-. Mem.: ABA (chmn. sect. internat. law and practice 1984—85), Arbitration Medicine & Energy Com., Chartered Inst. Arbitrators, InterAm. C. of C. (bd. dirs. 1991—99, chmn. 1996—98), German Am. C. of C. (bd. dirs. 1978—94), Am. Arbitration Assn., Am. Soc. Internat. Law, Am. Law Inst., Internat. Bar Assn. (coun. sect. of energy and nat. resources law 1983—86), Coun. on Fgn. Rels. (chmn. Houston 1991—92), U. Chgo. Law Sch. Alumni Assn. (v.p. 1990—91), Houston Internat. Arbitration Club, Met. Club (Washington), Houston Country Club. Avocations: languages, running, international dispute resolution, amateur radio. Office: PO Box 131026 Houston TX 77219-1026

HOZA, JEFFREY S., construction executive; Grad., Pa. State U.; MBA, U. Pitts. With General Electric Co.; joined Wachovia Securities, 1995, dir. Real Estate Divsn.; v.p. treas. Beazer Homes USA, Inc., 2008—. Office: Beazer Homes USA Inc Ste 1200 1000 Abernathy Rd NE Ste 260 Atlanta GA 30328-5648 Office Phone: 770-781-6430. Office Fax: 770-481-2808.

HSU, MING-YU, engineering educator; b. Kweiyang, Kweichow, China, Dec. 4, 1925; s. Pei-Kung and Wan-Ju (Hsiao) H.; m. Chih-Ju Yao, Jan. 1, 1952; children: Chi-Hsing, Chi-Yun, Chi-En, Chi-Che, Chi-Cheng. BE, Nat. Kweichow U., 1948; Dipl.Engr., Delft Tech. U., The Netherlands, 1959. Registered profl. engr., Ill., Ga., Fla., S.C. Prof. Cheng-Kung U., Tainan, Taiwan, 1960-68; dir. Land Devel. Commn., Taipei, 1960-68; engring. cons. Ministry of Housing & Utilities, Sehba, Libya, 1968-71; sr. engr. Philipp Holzmann Ag., Hamburg, Fed. Republic of Germany, 1971-74, Weber, Griffith & Mellican, Galesburg, Ill., 1974-80; chief engr. Chatham Engring. Co., Savannah, Ga., 1980-82; sr. cons. Hussey, Gay, Bell & DeYoung, Inc., Savannah, 1982—96; prof. Savannah Coll. of Art and Design, 1987—2000. Designed and constructed numerous indsl. office, apt. and comml. bldgs., marine structures including docks, loading platforms, marinas, shipyards and water and waste water treatment structures. Contbr. articles on structural engring. to profl. jours. Mem. Nat. Soc. Profl. Engrs., ASCE. Home: 1115 Wilmington Island Rd Savannah GA 31410-4508 Office: Hussey Gay Bell & DeYoung PO Box 14247 Savannah GA 31416-1247

HSU, STEPHEN DE, medical educator; b. Tianjin, China, June 11, 1955; arrived in US, 1982, naturalized, 2000; s. Xukai Hsu and YunLian Qian; m. Yan Ping Wang, Dec. 5, 1995; children: Alexander, Andrew. BS, Wuhan U., China, 1982; MA, Montclair State U., 1985; PhD, U. Cinn., 1990. Fellow Sloan-Kettering Inst., NYC, 1991—95; sports anchor ESPN Internat., Bristol, Conn., 1995—98; asst. prof. Nat. U. Singapore, Singapore, 1997—98; rsch. fellow N.Y. U., NYC, 1998—99; asst. prof. Med. Coll. Ga., Augusta, 1999—2004, assoc. prof., 2004—, rschr., 2007—. Contbr. articles to profl. jours. Recipient Ruth L. Kirstein Rsch. Svc. award, Nat. Cancer Inst., 1998, innovation award, 2006; Rsch. grant, Nat. Cancer Inst., 2003. Mem.: Soc. Investigative Dermatology, Am. Assn. Dental Rsch., Am. Assn. Cancer Rsch. Independent. Buddhist. Achievements include invention of mega-t green tea chewing gum and mints; green tea skin care and nail care lines; helped train military dentists. Avocations: travel, sports, history. Home: 4476 Woodberry Ct Evans GA 30809 Office: Med Coll Ga AD1443 Sch Dentistry Augusta GA 30912 Office Phone: 706-721-2317.

HSU, SYLVIA, dermatologist, educator; arrived in US, 1968; d. Mao Yang and Chih Jean Hsu; m. Tien Pei Wong, Dec. 27, 1986; children: Michael Gregory Wong, Kenneth Jason Wong. BA, Rice U., 1985; MD, Baylor Coll. Medicine, Houston, 1989. Cert. Am. Bd. Dermatology, 1994. Clin. asst. prof. dermatology Jefferson Med. Coll., Phila., 1994—97; asst. prof. dermatology Baylor Coll. Medicine, Houston, 1997—2000, assoc. prof. dermatology, 2000—05, prof. dermatology, 2005—. Chief dermatology Ben Taub Gen. Hosp., Houston, 2000—. Mem.: Houston Dermatol. Soc. (pres. 2006), Phi Beta Kappa. Office: Baylor Coll Medicine 1977 Butler Blvd Ste E6 200 Houston TX 77030 Office Fax: 713-798-3250, 713-798-3252. Business E-Mail: shsu@bcm.edu.

HSU, THOMAS TSENG-CHUANG, civil engineer, educator; b. Swatow, China, July 28, 1933; came to U.S., 1958; s. Benjamin D.H. and Lucy S.K. (Ma) Zi; m. Laura H.N. Ling, July 20, 1963; children: Lynne Ling, Mia Ming. BS, Harbin Inst. Tech., China, 1957; MS, Cornell U., 1960, PhD, 1962. Engr. structural rsch. lab. Portland Cement Assn., Skokie, Ill., 1962-68; assoc. prof. structural engring. U. Miami, Coral Gables, Fla., 1968-73, prof., 1973-79, dept. chmn., 1974-78; vis. prof. dept. civil engring. Nat. Taiwan U., Taipei, 1979-80; prof. structural engring. U. Houston, 1980—, chmn., 1980-84, Moores univ. prof., 1998—. Eshbach disting. vis. prof. Tech. Inst., Northwestern U., 1991-92; prin. investigator NSF, Washington, 1970—; cons. Kaiser Transit Group, Dade County, Fla.; 1977-79. Author: Torsion of Reinforced Concrete, 1984, Unified Theory of Reinforced Concrete, 1993; contbr. articles to profl. jours. Recipient Rsch. medal Am. Soc. Engring. Edn., 1969, Award of Excellence, Halliburton Found., 1990; named Hon. Disting. Prof., Harbin Inst. Civil and Archtl. Engring., China, 1993. Fellow ASCE (Walter L. Huber Rsch. prize 1974), Am. Concrete Inst. (Leonard C. Wason medal 1965, Arthur R. Anderson award 1990, Arthur J. Boase award 2007). Home: 5034 Glenmeadow Dr Houston TX 77096-4212 Office: U Houston Dept Civil Environ Engring Houston TX 77204-0001 Office Phone: 713-743-4268. Business E-Mail: thsu@uh.edu.

HUBAND, FRANK LOUIS, corporate officer, general counsel, electrical engineer, lawyer; b. Washington, July 12, 1938; m. Carol Singer. BS, Cornell U., 1961, PhD, 1967; JD, Yale U., 1975. Bar: DC 1975, US Patent Office, 1977; registered prof. engr., Tex. Asst. prof. elec. engring. and math. scis. Rice U., Houston, 1966—72; owner, pres. Engring. Systems, Houston, 1972—73; atty., adv. FEA, Washington, 1975—76; divsn. dir. NSF, Washington, 1976—90; exec. dir. Am. Soc. Engring. Edn., Washington, 1990—2010; former sec. gen. Internat. Assn. Continuing Engring. Edn.; v.p., gen. counsel World Tech. Evaluation Ctr., 2010—. Cons. Tex. Instrument, 1968-75; lectr. George Mason U., Fairfax, Va., George Washington U. Author: Protection of Computer Systems and Software, 1986. Mem. IEEE, ABA, NSPE, Am. Chem. Soc., Am. Inst. Physics. Office: 4600 N Fairfax Dr Arlington VA 22203 Office Phone: 202-480-9832. Business E-Mail: frank@huband.org.

HUBBARD, JON, state legislator; b. Camden, Ark., Dec. 12, 1946; m. Regina Hubbard; children: Rus Hubbard, Shane Hubbard. Tchr. Ark. and Tenn. Schs.; ins. agent Ind. and Co. Employee, 1975—; tchr. Walnut Ridge High Sch., 1991—95; owner, agent Ark. First Stop Ins., Inc., 1995—2006; mktg. rep Equity Ins. Co., 2006—; mem. Dist. 75 Ark. House of Representatives, 2011—. Republican. Baptist. Office: 2104 White Ln Jonesboro AR 72404 Office Phone: 870-919-4507. Business E-Mail: hubbard_jon@yahoo.com.

HUBBARD, JOSEPH LISTER, state legislator, lawyer; m. Ashley Hubbard; children: Hill, Hattie. BA cum laude, Huntingdon Coll., Montgomery, Ala., 2003; JD, Cumberland Sch. Law, 2002. Bar: US Ct. Appeals (11th cir.), US Dist. Ct. (no., mid., so. districts Ala.), Ala. Law clk. to Justice Champ Lyons, Jr. Ala. Supreme Ct.; ptnr. Hubbard Coleman, PC, Montgomery, Ala.; mem. Dist. 73 Ala. House of Reps., 2011—. Vestry Episc. Ch. of Ascension; bd. dirs. Ascension Day Sch., Holy Cross Episc. Sch., Ala. Nat. Fair. Mem.: American Inns Ct., Hugh Maddox Chpt., Montgomery Bar Assn., Leadership Montgomery, Montgomery Kiwanis. Democrat. Office: Ala House of Reps Rm 630-A 11 S Union St Montgomery AL 36130 also: PO Box 781 Montgomery AL 36101-0781 also: Hubbard Coleman PC 418 Scott St Montgomery AL 36104 Office Phone: 334-242-7707, 334-832-1001. Business E-Mail: joe@hubbardcoleman.com.

HUBBARD, MIKE, state legislator; b. Hartwell, Ga., Feb. 11, 1962; m. Susan Hubbard; children: Clayte, Riley. Degree in Radio and TV, U. Ga., 1983. Lic. Pilot. Assoc. sports info. dir. Auburn U. Athletic Dept.; gen. mgr. Auburn Network, 1990—94; pres., owner Auburn Network, Inc., 1994—2003; mem. Dist. 79 Ala. House of Reps., Montgomery, 1999—, minority leader, 2004—; pres. Auburn Project Internat. Sports Properties; chmn. Ala. Rep. Party, 2007—11. Mem. bd. dirs. Regions Bank of Lee County, 1998—, Bus. Coun. Ala., 2004—, Ala. Wireless Telecom.; mem. Lee County Rep. Exec. Com., 1999—; del. Rep. Nat. Conv., 2000, 2004; chmn. Ala. Gov. Inaugural Com., 2003, 2007. Chmn. Heroes Campaign Lee County Red Cross, 2006; mem. adv. bd. Auburn/Opelika Airport, 2005—. Recipient Legis. Leadership award, Coun. for Leaders in Ala. Schools, 2001; named Young Bus. Person of Yr., Auburn C. of C., 1998, Ala. Lawmaker of Yr., Ala. Ind. Ins. Agents Assn., 2001, Rep. of Yr., Lee County Rep. Party, 2003. Mem.: Ala. Broadcasters Assn. (mem. bd. dirs. 2006—). Republican. Office: Ala State House Rm 519 A 11 S Union St Montgomery AL 36130 Office Phone: 334-826-9946, 334-242-7739. Office Fax: 334-826-9151. E-mail: hubbard@mikehubbard.com.

HUBBARD, TYLER, musician; b. Monroe, Ga. Degree, Belmont U., Nashville. Co-founder, band mem. Florida Georgia Line, 2011—. Musician: (albums) Here's to the Good Times, 2012, (songs) Cruise, 2012 (Duo Video of Yr., Breakthrough Video of Yr., CMT Music Awards, 2013, Single of Yr., Country Music Assn. Awards, 2013, Single of Yr. (version featuring Nelly), American Music Awards, 2013). Named New Vocal Duo or Group of Yr., Acad. Country Music Awards, 2013, New Artist of Yr., 2013, Vocal Duo of Yr., Country Music Assn. Awards, 2013, Acad. Country Music Awards, 2014. Office: Big Machine Records 1219 16th Ave South Nashville TN 37212*

HUBBARD, WILLIAM C., lawyer; b. Florence, SC, Apr. 8, 1952; BA magna cum laude in History, U. SC, 1974, JD, 1977, LLD (hon.), 2010. Bar: SC 1977, US Ct. Appeals (4th cir.) 1978, US Dist. Ct. SC 1979, US Supreme Ct., DC. Law clk. to Judge Robert F. Chapman US Dist. Ct. SC, Columbia, 1977-78; ptnr., chair bus. litig. and employment group Nelson, Mullins, Riley & Scarborough, Columbia. Permanent mem. US Fourth Cir. Jud. Conf. Mem. bd. trustees U. SC, 1986—, vice chmn. bd., 1992, chmn. bd. 1996-2000; chair bd. dirs., The World Justice Project Recipient Algernon Sydney Sullivan Award, 1974, Order of the Palmetto, State of SC, 2002, Professionalism Award, Am. Inns of Ct., 2007, John F. Williams award, Richland County Bar, 2008, U. SC Disting. Alumni award, 2009, Inaugural recipient of the Leadership in Law award, SC Lawyers Weekly, 2009, U. SC Sch. of Law Compleat Lawyer Platinum award, 2010; named a Carolina Scholar, 1970—74; named one of Men of the Decade, Columbia Met. mag., 2000. Fellow American Coll. of Trial Lawyers; mem. ABA (mem. spl. coord. com. on professionalism 1988-90, American Bar Endowment bd. 1988—, house dels. 1988—, chmn., 2008-10, ALI-ABA com. on continuing profl. edn. 1988-89, resource devel. coun. 1988—, chair young lawyer's divsn. 1987-88, chair-elect 1986-87, sec. 1985-86, dir. 1984-85, select com. of house, 1990—, mem. bd. of govs., 1991, chmn. standing com. on assn. communications, 1992—, SC state del. to house dels., chair house rules and calendar com., mem. standing com. on fed. judiciary, pres.-elect, 2013-, bd. mem. American Bar Found., chair house dels. 2008-10, pres. American Bar Found. 2010-12, past pres.), SC Bar Assn. (SC Young Lawyer of Yr. award, 1986, chmn. profl. responsibility com., 1990-91, chmn. profl. com. 1991-92, chmn. SC bar long range planning com. 1986-87), American Bd. Trial Advocates, Richland County Bar Assn., Columbia Young Lawyers (v.p. 1980-81), SC Def. Trial Attys. Assn., John Belton O'Neall Inn of Ct., American Judicature Soc., Phi Beta Kappa, Omicron Delta Kappa, Phi Delta Phi. Office: Nelson Mullins Riley & Scarborough 1320 Main St Meridian 17th Fl Columbia SC 29201 Office Phone: 803-255-9418. Office Fax: 803-255-9440.*

HUBBARD, WILLIAM JAMES, library director; b. Grand Rapids, Mich., July 17, 1941; s. Willard Wright and Sara (Rast) H.; m. Barbara Ockun, Sept. 8, 1962; children: William, Thomas, James, Gregory. AB, Dartmouth Coll., 1963; MLS, SUNY, Geneseo, 1972. Engr., supr. Rochester (N.Y.) Telephone Corp., 1963-71; contract libr. Xerox Corp., Webster, NY, 1971-72; libr. circulation SUNY, Fredonia, 1973-75; libr. user svcs. Va. Tech., Blacksburg, 1975-80; dir. libr. svcs., dir.automation-networks, act. state libr. Va. State Libr., Richmond, 1980-88; univ. libr. Jacksonville (Ala.) State U., 1988—2008, univ. libr. emeritus, 2009—. Bd. visitors Jacksonville State U. Author: Stack Management, 1981; Editor: Faculty Trends; contbr. articles to profl. jours. Mem. Ala. Libr. Assn., Nat. Assn. Scholars. Office: State U Univ Libr Jacksonville AL 36265 Business E-Mail: bhubbard@jsu.edu. E-mail: williamj@hubbards.org.

HUBBELL, RICHARD A., oil industry executive; b. 1944; BA, Westminster Coll., 1966. With Rollins Comm., Inc., 1970—87; COO RPC Inc., 1987—2004; pres., bd. dirs. RPC, Inc., 1987—; CEO RPC Inc., 2003—; pres., CEO & bd. dirs. Marine Products Corp., 2001—. With USN, 1966-70. Office: RPC Inc 2170 Piedmont Rd NE Atlanta GA 30324 Office Phone: 404-321-2140. Office Fax: 404-321-5483. Business E-Mail: rhubbell@rpc.net.

HUBER, DONALD SIMON, physician; b. Clarendon, Pa., Apr. 18, 1929; s. Walter Casper and Mary Agnes (Earley) H.; m. Mary Hanks, Sept. 6, 1958; children: Donald Scott, Mark Walter, Mary Lisa. BA, Duke U., 1951, MD, 1954. Diplomate Am. Bd. Internal Medicine, Am. Bd. Allergy and Immunology. Intern Charity Hosp., New Orleans, 1954-55; resident internal medicine Tulane U. Hosp., New Orleans, 1955-56, 58-60; pvt. practice Huntsville, Ala., 1960-96 (ret. 1996); clin. assoc. prof. medicine Sch. Primary Med. Care, Huntsville, 1985—. Med. dir. Cmty. Free Clinic., 1998—. Lt. commdr. USN, 1956-58, USNR, 1958-60. Fellow Am. Coll. Allergists; mem. AMA, Am. Acad. Allergy and Immunology, Ala. Soc. Allergy and Immunology (pres. 1985), Huntsville Rotary Club (bd. dirs. 1978). Republican. Methodist. Avocation: travel. Home: 507 Holmes Ave Huntsville AL 35801 E-mail: donhuber@comcast.net.

HUBER, LIEZEL, professional tennis player; b. Durban, South Africa, Aug. 21, 1976; arrived in US, 1992, naturalized, 2007; d. Jan and Sica; m. Tony Huber, Feb. 19, 2000. Profl. tennis player WTA, 1993—. Mem. South African nat. team Summer Olympic Games, Sydney, 2000, mem. US nat. team, Beijing, 2008, London, 2012; mem. South African nat. team Fed Cup, 2003, mem. US nat. team, 2008. Founder Liezel's Cause, 2005—, Huber Tennis Ranch, 2008—. Recipient Humanitarian award, Stars for Stars, 2006, 2008; named South African Sportswoman of Yr., 2005, 2007 Doubles Team of Yr. (with Cara Black), 2008; named to Tour Player's Coun., 2003—04. Achievements include winning 52 career WTA Tour doubles titles; winning 11 career ITF doubles titles; winner Grand Slam doubles titles: Wimbledon, 2005, 2007; Australian Open, 2007; US Open, 2008, 2011; winner Grand Slam mixed doubles titles: French Open, 2009; US Open, 2010. Office: WTA Corp Hdqs 100 Second Ave S Ste 1100 S Saint Petersburg FL 33701

HUBERDEAU, JONATHAN, professional hockey player; b. Saint-Jérôme, Quebec, Can., June 4, 1993; Center Saint John Sea Dogs (QMJHL), 2009—12, Fla. Panthers, 2011—. Recipient Calder Meml. Trophy, 2013. Achievements include being a member of the QMJHL First Team All-Stars, 2010-11. Office: Florida Panthers BankAtlantic Center One Panther Parkway Sunrise FL 33323*

HUBERMAN, JEFFREY ALLEN, architect; b. Boston, Jan. 2, 1942; s. Sidney H. and Miriam (Walker) H.; m. Barbara Kemp, May 16, 1964 (div.); children: Amy Beth, Marc Walker. BArch, U. Fla., Gainesville, 1964. Designer Odell Assocs., Charlotte, NC, 1964-67, Wolf-Johnson Assocs., Charlotte, 1967-69; designer, arch. Wolf Assocs., Charlotte, 1970-71; ptnr. Gantt Huberman Archs., Charlotte, 1971—. Mem. NC Bd. Architecture, 1995-2005, sec., 1996-97, treas., 1997-98, v.p., 1999-2001, pres., 2001-03. Chmn. ann. fund drive Charlotte-Mecklenburg Arts and Sci. Coun., 1975-81, v.p., 1977-78, bd. dirs., 1977; bd. dirs. Charlotte Opera Assn., 1966-82, pres., 1979-81; bd. dirs. Opera Carolina, 2008-; pres. Children's Theatre, 1984-85, bd. dirs., 1981-87; bd. dirs. Temple Beth El, 1968-83, Charlotte-Mecklenburg Cmty. Rels. Com., 1974-84, Planned Parenthood of Greater Charlotte, 1978-80, Charlotte Jr. Soccer Found., 1978-82, Tarradiddle Players, 1986-87; chmn. Charlotte Clean City Com., 1975-77; youth soccer coach, 1975-84; com. mem. Performing Arts Ctr. Adv. Ctr., 1983-85; adv. com. Charlotte/Douglas Internat. Airport, 1987-88, art adv. com., 1992-94; bd. dirs. Green Hill Ctr. for NC Arts, 2000-05. Fellow AIA (NC) (chmn. honor awards com. 1972, treas. Charlotte, NC sect. 1976-77, chmn. audit com. 1987, bd. dirs. 1987-92, long range planning com. 1990, component resources com. 1992, pres. NC chpt. 1991, NC Archtl. Found. 1994, NC Gold medal 2002, NC Firm of Yr. 2006, licensing com. 2005-07, jury of fellows 2009-11), Nat. Coun. Archtl. Registration Bd. (juror divsns. B and C archtl. registration exam. 1984-86, chmn. divsn. B graphic 1989, master jurors com. 1986, archtl. registration exam. com. 1996-97, intern devel. program com. 1998-2002, chair, 2000-02, procedures and documents com. 2000-05, 2007-08, chmn. 2004-05, chair reciprocity impediment task force 2002-04, So. region sec. 2003-04, bd. dirs. 2005—08, exec. bd. com. 2006-08, 2d v.p. 2007-08, NCARB prize jr. 2008-10). Office: Gantt Huberman Architects 500 N Tryon St Charlotte NC 28202-2232 Office Phone: 704-334-6436. Office Fax: 704-342-9639. Business E-Mail: jhuberman@gantthuberman.com.

HUCH, RONALD KIND, historian, educator; s. Emory Wallace and Anna Ophelia Huch; m. Margo Lynn Laskowski; children: Diane, Anita, Jocelyn, Elanor. BA, Thiel Coll., 1962; MA, Pa. State U., 1964; PhD, U. Mich., 1971. Asst. prof. Murray State U., Ky., 1967—68; from instr. to prof. U. Minn., Duluth, 1968—86; prof. Dickinson State U., ND, 1986—92; chmn. history U. Papua New Guinea, Port Moresby, 1992—2000; prof., chmn. dept. history Ea. Ky. U., Richmond, 2000—. Cons. Ednl. Testing Svc., Princeton, NJ, 1988—. Author: The Radical Lord Radnor, 1977, Henry, Lord Brougham: Later Years, 1993, From Blacksmith Shop to Modern Hospital, 1985; co-author: Joseph Hume: The People's M.P., 1985; contbr. articles to profl. jours. Founder History Scholarships for Papua New Guineans, Port Moresby, 1996; v.p. NC chpt. AAUP, 1990—91. Recipient Solon Buck award, Minn. Hist. Soc., 1981; fellow, Am. Philos. Soc., 1971, 1975, 1977, 1981, Am. Coun. Learned Socs., 1973; summer fellow, NEH, Washington, 1988. Mem.: Anglo-Am. Historians, N.Am. Conf. Brit. Studies, Am. Hist. Assn. Avocation: horse racing. Office: Ea Ky U Dept History 521 Lancaster Ave Richmond KY 40475 Fax: 859-622-1357. Business E-Mail: ron.huch@eku.edu.

HUCK, PAUL C., federal judge; b. Covington, Ky., 1940; BA, U. Fla., Gainesville, 1962, JD, 1965. Assoc. Frates, Fay, Floyd & Pearson, 1965—69; shareholder Quinton, Lieb, Parks & Aurell, 1969—73, Aurell & Huck, 1973—75, Mahoney, Hadlow & Adams, 1975—81, Proenza, White, Huck & Roberts, 1986—93, Kozyak, Tropin & Throckmorton, 1994—2000; ptnr. Fleming & Huck, 1981—86; judge US Dist. Ct. (so. dist.) Fla., Miami, 2000—10, sr. judge, 2010—. Mem. US Army, 1965—72. Office: US Dist Ct Ferguson US Courthouse 400 N Miami Ave Rm 13-2 Miami FL 33128 Office Phone: 305-523-5520.

HUCKABEE, MIKE (MICHAEL DALE HUCKABEE), political commentator, former Governor of Arkansas; b. Hope, Ark., Aug. 24, 1955; s. Dorsey Willis and Mae (Elder) Huckabee; m. Janet McCain, May 25, 1974; children: John Mark, David, Sarah. BA in Religion, Ouachita Bapt. U., Arkadelphia, Ark., 1976; LLD (hon.), Ouachita Baptist U., Arkadelphia, Ark., 1992; attended, Southwestern Bapt. Theol. Sem., Ft. Worth; HHD (hon.), John Brown U., 1991. Ordained Southern Bapt. min. Pastor Walnut St. Bapt. Ch., Arkadelphia, 1974-75, Immanuel Bapt. Ch., Pine Bluff, Ark., 1980-85, Beech St. 1st Bapt. Ch., Texarkana, Ark., 1986—96; pres. KBSC-TV, Texarkana, Ark., 1987—92, Cambridge Comm., Texarkana, Ark., 1992—96; lt. gov. State of Ark., Little Rock, 1993-96, gov., 1996—2007; polit. commentator Fox News Channel, 2008—, host, Huckabee, 2008—; host, Cumulus Media Network The Huckabee Report, 2009—; host, syndicated radio program, Cumulus Media Network The Mike Huckabee Show, 2012—. Pres. Ark. Bapt. Conv., 1989—91; founder, past pres. American Christian TV Sys., Pine Bluff, Ark.; state chmn. Delta Regional Authority; mem., past chmn. Interstate Oil & Gas Compact Commn. Author: Living Beyond Your Lifetime: How to be Intentional About the Legacy You Leave, 2000, Quit Digging Your Grave With a Knife and Fork: A 12-Stop Program to End Bad Habits and Begin a Healthy Lifestyle, 2005, From Hope to Higher Ground: 12 STOPS to Restoring America's Greatness, 2007, Do the Right Thing: Inside the Movement That's Bringing Common Sense Back to America, 2008 (NY Times bestseller), A Simple Christmas: Twelve Stories That Celebrate the True Holiday Spirit, 2009 (Publishers Weekly bestseller), Can't Wait Til Christmas, 2010, A Simple Government: Twelve Things We Really Need From Washington (and a Trillion We Don't!), 2011, Dear Chandler, Dear Scarlett, 2012; co-author (with John Perry): Character is the Issue: How People With Integrity Can Revolutionize America, 1997; co-author: (with George Grant) Kids Who Kill: Confronting Our Culture of Violence, 1998; musician: (cover band) Capitol Offense. Chancellor Victory Univ. Found., 2010—; candidate Republican Presdl. Nomination, 2007—08. Named Man of Yr., American Sportfishing Assn., 1997; named one of the 25 Most Influential People for Conservation, Outdoor Life Mag. Mem.: Nat. Governors Assn. (chmn. 2005—06), Southern Internat. Trade Coun., Southern Tech. Coun. Republican. Baptist. Office: c/o The Huckabee Report Cumulus Media 261 Madison Ave New York NY 10016*

HUCKABY, GARY CARLTON, lawyer; b. Lanett, Ala., July 12, 1938; s. Carl Walker and Mary Evelyn (Meriwether) H.; m. Jeanne Davey Huckaby, Feb. 23, 1963; children: Gary Jr., John Stephen, Michael Stewart. BA, U. Ala., 1960, JD, 1962. Bar: US Supreme Ct. 1963, US Ct. of Mil. Appeals 1963, US Ct. Appeals (5th and 11th cirs.) 1963, US Dist. Ct. (no., middle and so. dists) Ala. 1963. Law clk. to chief justice Ala. Supreme Ct., Montgomery, 1962-63; asst. US Sen. Lister Hill, Washington, 1963; ptnr. Smith, Huckaby & Graves, Huntsville, Ala., 1966-85; dir. Ala. Ctr. for Law & Civic Edn., 1992—2001; ptnr. Bradley, Arant, Rose & White, Huntsville, 1985—2007; ret. Dir. coun. Internat. Visitors of Huntsville-Madison County, 1983-89, Tenn. Valley Boy Scouts Am., 1975-79, Mental Health Assn. Madison County, 1970-78, Ala. Law Sch. Found., 1981—; pres. Huntsville-Madison County Mental Health Bd., 1977-80, Madison County Heart Assn., 1968; active Citizens Com. on Higher Edn. of Ala. Legis., 1976, judicial sect. of Huntsville-Madison County Local Govt. Study Com., 1969. Capt. USAF, 1963-66. Fellow Am. Bar Found., Am. Coll. Trial Lawyers; mem. ABA (bd. govs. 1990-91, house of delegates, chmn. standing com. on lawyer referral and info. services 1982-85, chmn. spl. com. on delivery of legal services 1976-79, standing com. on lawyers pub. service responsibility 1987-90, consortium on legal services and the pub. 1976-79, task force on pub. edn. 1978, standing com. on lawyers in the armed forces 1971-73), Ala. State Bar (pres., bd. commrs. 1981-87, exec. com. 1982-83, 84-85, 87-88, chmn. governance com. 1986-87, action group on professionalism, disciplinary bd. 1981-87; recipient award of merit 1986), Huntsville-Madison County Bar Assn. (pres. 1977-78, chmn. grievance com. 1976, bench and bar relations 1981, convention host com. 1971, law day com. 1968), Am. Judicature Soc. (former bd. dirs.), Rotary. Democrat. Episcopalian. Office Phone: 256-534-9693. Personal E-mail: ghuckabysr@aol.com.

HUCKINS, HAROLD AARON, engineering executive consultant; b. Cambridge, Mass., Nov. 28, 1924; s. Harold Aaron and Julia E. (Nugent) Huckins; m. Elizabeth L. Kearns, Nov. 15, 1952; children: Richard W., Robert M., Christopher N., Patricia A., Leslie K. BSChemE, Northeastern U., Boston, 1945; ASME, Lowell Inst., 1946; degree in Bus. Adminstrn., Boston U., 1947—49; degree in Chem. Engring., U. Pitts., 1950—52. Chem. process engr., asst. project mgr. Monsanto Chem. Co., Boston-Everett, Mass., 1945—49; sr. process engr., project mgr. Koppers Co. Chem. Divsn., Pitts., 1949—53; mgr. pilot plants, project mgr., dir. v.p. project evaluation-process design Sci. Design Co., Inc., NYC, 1953—69; tech. dir., v.p. tech. ops. Oxirane Chem. Co., Tex., Princeton, NJ, 1969—74; v.p., tech. assessment Halcon SD Group, NYC, 1974—85; founder, pres., internat. cons., firm for chem. processing, materials, environ., multi-client reports, tech. legal cases expert witness Princeton Advanced Tech., Inc., 1985—; chmn. World's 1st Elec. Car Conf. with Princeton U., 1978; initiative chmn. World's 1st Advanced Materials Conf. with 29 Tech. Socs., 1984. Dir. Assn. Cons. Chemists and Chem. Engrs., NYC, 1985-93; dir. Materials Tech. Inst., St. Louis, 1976-85; dir., chair, Joint Engring. Coun. John Fritz Engring. entreprenuer medal award commn., 1979-89, AIChE mem., 1947, fellow, 1977-; nat. spkr. bur., 1977-94, chmn., Ctrl. Jersey Sect., 1976-77, dir. mgmt. divsn, 1980-82, dir. chmn. materials engring. sci. divsn., 1977-90, New Tech. Comm., 1985-93, chmn. entrepreneurial Forum, 1994-99, 1947-. Co-author: The Chemical Plant, 1966; contbr. articles to profl. jours. Spkr. local groups/TV global energy trends, congressmen Proposed Nat. Energy Policy, 2007—. Recipient AIChE Highest Indsl. award, 1979, Chem. Engring. Practice award, 1994, NASTAR Racing award. Mem. Am. Chem. Soc., Nat. Assn. Corrosion Engrs., Comml. Devel. Assn., Mensa Internat., Hilton Head Ski Club (bd. dirs.). Achievements include 13 US patents for chemical process technology, four of which are for a proprietary hydrogen peroxide process plus energy consulting. Avocations: skiing, golf, gardening, travel, photography. Home and Office: Princeton Advanced Tech Inc 4 Bertram Pl Hilton Head Island SC 29928-3936 Office Phone: 843-689-2311. Office Fax: 843-689-2311. Personal E-mail: hhuckins1@roadrunner.com.

HUDAK, CHERYL C., travel company executive; Cert. travel counselor Inst. Cert. Travel Agts., 1989. Founder, owner Travel Dimensions, Boardman, Ohio, 1985—. Adv. bd. mem. Alamo Car Rental, Royal Caribbean Cruise Line, Travel Agt. Mag., Thrifty/Dollar Car Rental's. Travel radio show host. Named one of Most Powerful Women in Travel, Travel Agt. Mag., 1999, 100 Most Powerful Women in Travel, 2000. Mem.: Am. Soc. Travel Agts. (chair World Travel Congress 2000, pres., CEO 2006—, past. nat. v.p., area 7 bd. dirs., chair allied mktg. com., mem. budget and fin. com., mem. future planning com., co-chair Super Regional Conf. 1994). Office: Travel Dimensions 725 Boardman Canfield Rd # S Youngstown OH 44502 also: Am Soc Travel Agents 1101 King St Ste 200 Alexandria VA 22314 Office Phone: 703-739-2782, 330-726-2801. Office Fax: 703-684-8319.

HUDAK, THOMAS F(RANCIS), finance company executive; b. Donora, Pa., Jan. 29, 1942; s. Thomas Joseph and Ann Marie (Petrus) Hudak; m. Dorothy Ann Palko, July 27, 1963 (dec. Mar. 2006); children: Diana Lynn, Debra Ann, Thomas David; m. Carol F. Ethier, Nov. 28, 2009. BS, St. Vincent Coll., 1963; MBA, Ohio State U., 1968. CPA Ohio. Accountant Coopers & Lybrand, Columbus, Ohio, 1963-65; dept. mgr., data processing Western Electric Corp., Columbus, 1965-66; fin. controls mgr. Indsl. Nucleonics Co., Columbus, 1966-69; sr. v.p. fin., chief fin. officer G.C. Murphy Co., McKeesport, Pa., 1969-85, chmn. bd., 1981-85; pres. Hudak & Assocs. Treas. Mack Realty Co., McKeesport, Murphy Devel. Corp., Court House Village Co., Spotsylvania Realty Co.; bd. dirs., pres. Terry Farris Stores, Inc.; mem. adv. bd. Liberty Mut. Ins. Co.; corp. comptr. PPG Industries, Inc., Pitts., 1986—89; chmn. bd. dirs., pres. Continental Plastics, Inc., 1989—95; bd. dirs. RXI Corp. Bd. dirs., pres. G. C. Murphy Co. Found. Mem.: AICPA, Nat. C. of C. Taxation & Final Policy Com., Peanut Butter and Nut Processors Assn., Assn. Dressings and Sauces, Assn. Spice Traders, Machinery and Allied Products Inst. (mem. fin. coun.), Nat. Assn. Corp. Dirs., Nat. Retail Mchts. Assn. (dir. fin. divsn. 1982—85), Risk and Ins. Mgmt. Soc., Fin. Execs. Inst. (bd. dirs. Pitts. chpt. 1982—85).

HUDDLESTON, MAC, state legislator; b. Sept. 16, 1943; m. Flavia Hutchinson. BS, DVM, Auburn U.; grad. Certified Investigator Program, MDPS. Veterinarian; criminal investigator; mem. Dist. 15 Miss. House of Reps., 2008—, vice chair enrolled bills com., mem. agr. com., apportionment and elections com., mil. affairs com., univs. and colls. com. Republican. Baptist. Home: PO Drawer 300 Pontotoc MS 38863 Office: PO Box 1018 Jackson MS 39215 Home Phone: 662-489-5157. E-mail: mhuddleston@house.ms.gov.

HUDDLESTON, ROBERT E., state legislator; b. Sumner, Miss., Feb. 22, 1955; m. Chirito Bowie Huddleston; children: Anthony, Tina, Marguetta, Robert Jr., Mamie. Former pres. Tallahatchie County Union Progress; former sch. bd. mem.; mem. Dist. 30 Miss. House of Reps., 1996—; constrn. supr. Mem.: NAACP, Aaron Henry Help Ctr., West Tallahatchie Utility Assn. (vice chmn.). Democrat. Baptist. Mailing: PO Box 426 Sumner MS 38957 Office Phone: 601-359-3363. Business E-Mail: rhuddleston@house.ms.gov.

HUDNALL, JARRETT, JR., management consultant, educator, marketing professional; b. Rhome, Tex., Oct. 6, 1931; s. Jarrett and Katherine (Wilson) H.; m. Sarah Ruth Warren, Nov. 24, 1955; children: Jarrett Joseph, William Warren, Katherine Lee, Thomas Wilson. Student, Arlington State Coll., Tex., 1948-50; BBA, U. Tex., Austin, 1953, MBA, 1956; PhD, U. Ala., 1966. Lectr. U. Tex., 1955-56; asst. prof. Arlington State Coll., 1956-58; instr. U. Ala., 1958-61; asst. prof. La. Tech. U., 1961-62, assoc. prof. mktg., 1962-67, prof., head dept. bus., 1967-77; exec. Superior Supply Co., Inc., 1978-83, P&A div. Ciba-Geigy, 1983-84; v.p. Rohcar, Inc., 1984-90; prof. mgmt. and mktg. Stephen F. Austin State U., Nacogdoches, Tex., 1985-92; dean coll. bus. and commerce U. West Ala., Livingston, 1992-94; prof. mktg. Miss. U. for Women, Columbus, 1994—2002; emeritus; emeritus designee Assn. Collegiate Bus. Schs. & Programs, 2002—. Vice pres. Ctrl. Asian Cons., LLC; bd. dirs. SBI; cons. firms in chem. fertilizer, petroleum, farm equipment mfg., bus.; cons. agrl. and econ. devel. products W. Republic of Uzbekistan, 1995; vis. prof. mktg. Huron U., London, 2000, 2002. Author: (with A.L. Seeyle) Compensation of Retail Department Store and Specialty Store Salesman in Major Texas Cities, 1957, Attitudes of Gulf Service Station Dealers Toward Minor Tuneup and Repair Work, 1963, An Economic Analysis of Income and Employment in a Four-State Deep South Region, 1950-60, 1966. Lt. AUS, 1953-55. Gulf Oil Corp. fellow, 1963. Mem. VFW, Am. Mktg. Assn., So. Mktg. Assn., S.W. Fedn. Allied Disciplines, Am. Collegiate Retailing Assn., So. and Southwestern Bus. Dean's Assn., Small Bus. Inst. Dirs.' Assn., Allied Acads., Kiwanis Internat., Sigma Iota Epsilon, Beta Gamma Sigma, Alpha Kappa Psi, Kappa Delta Pi, Delta Mu Delta. Democrat. Baptist. Home: 1003 Lakeview Dr Ruston LA 71270-5233 Personal E-mail: jhud95@gmail.com.

HUDSON, BILLY, state legislator; b. June 16, 1938; m. Barbara Lee; children: Trudy, Bill, Ben. Attended, U. Ariz., 1957, U. Southern Miss. Rancher; mem. Dist. 45 Miss. State Senate, 2008—. Republican. Baptist. Office: PO Box 1018 Jackson MS 39215 Home: 27 Troon Hattiesburg MS 39401-8821 Home Phone: 601-794-0606; Office Phone: 601-359-4090. E-mail: bhudson@senate.ms.gov.

HUDSON, CELESTE NUTTING, retired education educator, consultant, reading clinic administrator; b. Nashville, Sept. 18, 1927; d. John Winthrop Chandler and Hilda Bass (Alexander) Nutting; m. Frank Alden Hudson III, Dec. 30, 1948 (dec.); m. Robert Daniel Quartell, June 3, 1989; children: Frank Alden Hudson IV (dec.), Jo Ann Hudson Algermissen (dec.), Celeste Jane Hudson Norman, Jack Winthrop N. Hudson. BS, Western Oreg. State U., Monmouth, 1952; MA, So. Ill. U., Edwardsville, 1963; PhD, So. Ill. U., Carbondale, 1973. Cert. tchr., Tenn., Oreg., Mo. Iowa. Tchr. pub. schs., Crossville, Tenn., 1949—51, Salem, Oreg., 1952—53, West Walnut Manor, Mo., 1953—54, Normandy Sch. Dist., St. Louis County, Mo., 1954—66; reading coord. Sikeston Pub. Schs., Mo., 1966—69, Charleston, Mo., 1969—72; traveling cons. Ednl. Devel. Labs., Huntington, NY, 1970—71; mem. clin. staff So. Ill. U. Reading Ctr., 1972; asst. prof. edn. St. Ambrose Coll., 1972—75, U. Tenn., Chattanooga, 1975—76; dir. children's reading clinic St. Ambrose U. (formerly St. Ambrose Coll.), 1973—94; project dir. Learning Skills Ctr. St. Ambrose U., 1976—80, from asst. prof. edn. to prof., 1976—94, prof. emeritus, 1995—. Dir. elem. edn. St. Ambrose U., 1972-94, chmn. dept. edn., 1980-84, divsn. chmn., 1984-87, faculty vice-chair, 1989-90, faculty chair, 1990-91; staff cons. Chandler Acad., 2002; cons, 2004- Author: Handbook for Remedial Reading, 1967, Cognitive Listening and the Reading of Second Grade Children, 1973, The Effect of Visual Fatigue on Reading, 1990, Longitudinal Study of Children in Clinical Reading, 1994. Active Kimberly Village Bd., Davenport, Iowa, 1976-93, Trinity Hosp. Aux., 2001-04; chmn. worship com., Asbury Meth. Ch., 1985-90, choir, 1978-98, 2005-08 bell choir, 1995-97; co-chmn. Sarah Cir., 1996-9; choir St. Johns Meth. Ch., Georgetown, Tex. Mem.: AARP, DAR (Hist. Soc.), AAUW (Lit. club), AAUP, Mo. ret. Tchr. Assoc., NC Club (lit. group), Phi Delta Kappa, Ret. Tchrs. Assn. Garfield Sch., Normandy Ret. Tchrs. Assn., Davenport Area Ret. Tchrs. Assn., Internat. Reading Assn. (Scott County coun. 1976—2003), Iowa Assn. Colls. Tchr. Edn. (exec. bd. 1989—92), Red Hat Soc., United Daus. of the Confederacy (3rd v.p. 1966—70), New Eng. Women (pres.-elect 1994—95, pres. 1996—2003, yearbook chmn. 2004—05), Georgetown New Comers Club (recipe group), United Daughters of Confederacy Real Granddaughters Club, Ret. Tchrs. Club, Quad City Women's Investment Club (treas. 2001—05), Tripoly Club, Original Music Students Club (corr. sec. 1995—96), Bettendorf Lionels (treas. 1998—2002), Kappa Delta Pi (sponsor 1974—96), Phi Delta Kappa (life; internat. emeritus staus), Alpha Delta Kappa (life; past pres., Golden Sister award 2011). Personal E-mail: drhcnhq@aol.com.

HUDSON, HELEN (SISTIE) G., state legislator; m. Robert Hudson. Former state rep. Dist. 120, Ga.; former state rep. Dist. 95 Ga.; state rep. Dist. 124 Ga., 2004—; vice chmn. Govt. Affairs Com.; mem. Health & Ecol. Com., Agr. & Consumer Affairs Com.; house rep. Ga.; businesswoman & cons. Democrat. Mailing: PO Box 58 Sparta GA 31087 Office: 612 Legis Office Bldg Decatur GA 30034 Home Phone: 706-444-7247; Office Phone: 706-444-6545. E-mail: hhudson@legis.state.ga.us.

HUDSON, HENRY E., federal judge; b. Washington, July 24, 1947; BA, American U., 1969; JD, American U. Washington Coll. Law, 1974. Asst. commonwealth atty. Office Commonwealth Atty., Arlington County, Va., 1974—79, commonwealth atty., 1980—86; asst. US atty. (eastern dist.) Va. US Dept. Justice, Alexandria, 1978—79; pvt. law practice, 1979, 1991—92, 1994—98; US atty. US Dept. Justice, Alexandria, 1986—91, dir. US Marshals Svc. Washington, 1992—93; cir. ct. judge 19th Judicial Cir. Ct., Fairfax County, Va., 1998—2002; judge US Dist. Ct. (eastern dist.) Va., Richmond, 2002—. Office: US District Court 701 East Broad St Richmond VA 23219 Office Phone: 804-916-2290.

HUDSON, J. CLIFFORD, hotel executive, federal agency administrator; m. Leslie Hudson; children: Stuart, Bennett. BA, U. Okla.; JD Phi Delta Phi, Georgetown U., 1979. With presidential, 1994—2001; chmn. Securities Investor Protection Corp., Washington, 1994; officer Sonic Corp., Oklahoma City, 1984, pres., 2004—08, CEO, chmn. Oklahoma City, 2008—. Lectr. in field. Editor Internat. Law Jour. novels; contbr. articles Assn. of Student Internat. Law Socs. Mem. econ. policy com. U.S. C. of C.; mem. Okla. Gov.'s Econ. Adv. Task Force, 1990's; mem. State Bd. for Property and Casualty Rates, State of Okla., 1980's., chmn., Okla. City Sch. Bd., 2001-2008, trustee, Ford Found., NY, chmn., Nat. Trust for Historic Preservation, mem., Georgetown U. Pres.'s Leadership scholar., Golden Chain award, Multi-Unit Foodservice Operators, 200, International Foodservice Mfrs. Assn., Foodservice Operator award, 2004, U. Regents award, 2001., Paul Dean award, 2006. Mem. Phi Beta Kappa. Avocations: swimming, music, wine collecting. Office: Sonic Corp 300 Johnny Bench Dr Oklahoma City OK 73104 Office Phone: 405-225-5000. Office Fax: 405-280-7696. Business E-Mail: jhudson@sonicdrivein.com.

HUDSON, JOHN LESTER, chemical engineering professor; b. Chgo., 1937; s. John Jones and Linda Madeline (Panozzo) H.; m. Janette Glenore Caton, June 29, 1963; children: Ann, Barbara, Sarah. BS, U. Ill., 1959; MS in Engring., Princeton U., 1960; PhD, Northwestern U., 1962. Registered profl. engr., Ill. Asst. prof. chm. engring. U. Ill.-Urbana, 1963-69, assoc. prof., 1969-75; prof., chmn. dept. chem. engring. U. Va., Charlottesville, 1975-85, mem. Ctr Advanced Studies, 1985-86, prof., 1986-88, Wills Johnson prof., 1988—. Mgr. Ill. Div. Air Pollution Control, Springfield, 1974-75; cons. to various industires and govt. agys., 1966— Contbr. articles to profl. jours., Nat. Acad. of Engring, 2008. Recipient sr. Humboldt prize, 1989; NSF fellow, 1962, Fulbright fellow, 1961-63, 82-83. Mem. AIChE (Wilhelm award 1991), Am. Chem. Soc. Home: 1920 Thomson Rd Charlottesville VA 22903-2419 Office: U Va Dept Chem Engring 102 Engineers Wy Box 400741 Charlottesville VA 22904-4741 Business E-Mail: hudson@virginia.edu.

HUDSON, MATT, state legislator; b. Columbus, Ohio, July 9, 1966; m. Susan Hudson; 5 children. Grad., Mantee Cmty. Coll., 1987, Edison Coll., 1992; grad, Barry U., 2007. Store mgr. Walgreen Drug Store Co., 1982—2002; broker VIP Realty Group, 2002—; fire commr. Golden Gate Fire Dist., 2002—06; instr. Naples Sch. Real Estate, 2003—; mem. Dist. 101 Fla. House of Reps., 2007—, vice chair health and family svcs. policy coun., mem. econ. devel. policy com., energy and utilities policy com., health care appropriations com., health care regulation policy com., mem. joint legis. com. on Everglades oversight, select policy coun. on strategic and econ. planning. Mem. State Exec. Com. Fla. Rep. Party, Collier County Land Trust Adv. Com., 1993—2002, Golden Gate Land Trust Adv. Coun., 1993—2002, Golden Gate Master Plan Restudy Com., 2003, Collier County Revenue Commn., 2003—05, Collier County Productivity Com., 2004—06; sheriff & clerk Courts Innovation Group, 2006—07; chmn. Collier County Legis. Delegation, Golden Gate Fire Commn., 2003—06. Mem.: Fla. Assn. Realtors (dir. 2004—07), Naples Area Bd. Realtors (dir. 2005—07, treas. 2007), Homeowners Assn. Golden Gate Estates (charter mem.), Golden Gate CERT, Golden Gate Estates Civic Assn. (former dir.), Collier Rotary Club of Naples (pres. 2007). Republican. Catholic. Office: 1302 The Capitol 402 S Monroe St Tallahassee FL 32399-1300 also: Adminstrn Bldg 3301 E Tamiami Tr Ste 212 Naples FL 34112-3972 also: 10100 Pines Blvd Bldg B 3rd Fl Pembroke Pines FL 33026-6037 Office Phone: 850-488-1028, 239-417-6270, 954-704-2990. Business E-Mail: matt.hudson@myfloridahouse.gov.

HUDSON, RICHARD LANE, JR., United States Representative from North Carolina, former legislative staff member; b. Franklin, Va., Nov. 4, 1971; m. Renee Howell, May 21, 2010. BA, U. NC, Charlotte, 1996. Field dir. Richard A. Vinroot for Gov., NC, 1996; dep. campaign mgr. Steve Arnold for Lt. Gov., NC, 1996; customer svc. Carolina Power & Light Co., 1997; comm. dir. NC Republican Party, 1997—99; dist. dir. to Rep. Robin Hayes US House of Representatives, Washington, 2000—05, chief of staff to Rep. Virginia Foxx, 2005—06, chief of staff to Rep. John R. Carter, 2006—08, chief of staff to Rep. Mike Conaway, 2009—11; campaign mgr. Pat McCrory for Gov., NC, 2008; founder Cabarrus Mktg. Group, Concord, 2011—12; mem. US Congress from 8th NC Dist., Washington, 2013—, US House Agrl. Com., 2013—, US House Edn. & the Workforce Com., 2013—, US House Homeland Security Com., 2013—. Chapt. sec. Jaycees, 2000—04; bd. govs. U. NC Charlotte Alumni Assn., 1999—2002; mem. Phi Eta Sigma, Omicron Delta Kappa, Order of Omega; bd trustees Rowan-Cabarrus CC, 2001—05. Named Man of Yr., NC Fedn. of Young Reps., 1999. Mem.: F.A.A.M., Magnolia Lodge No. 53, NC State Soc. Washington, Tex. State Soc. Washington, RAMS, House Chief of Staff Assoc., Republican Club Capitol Hill, Kappa Alpha Order (pres. U. NC Charlotte Alumni chapt. 1998—). Republican. Methodist. Avocation: hunting. Office: US House of Representatives 429 Cannon House Office Bldg Washington DC 20515 also: 325 McGill Ave NW Ste 500 Concord NC 28027 Office Phone: 202-225-3715, 704-786-1612. Office Fax: 704-782-1004.*

HUDSON, ROBIN E., state supreme court justice; b. Ga., 1952; married; 2 children. BA, Yale U., New Haven, 1973; JD, U. NC Sch. Law, 1976. Bar: NC 1976. Atty., Raleigh, Durham, NC, 1976—2000; judge NC Ct. Appeals, 2001—06; assoc. justice Supreme Ct. NC, 2007—. Founding steering com. mem. NC Assn. Women Attys., 1978; mem. NC Acad. Trial Lawyers, 1978—2001, bd. govs., 1993—99, chair workers' compensation sect., 1993—98; mem. Family Ct. Adv. Com., 2001—. Mem. adv. coun. NC Indsl. Commn., 1994—2000; chair NC OSHA Rev. Bd., 1994—2006. Mem.: NC Jud. Conf. (treas. 2002—), ABA Appellate Judges Conf., Nat. Assn. Women Judges, NC Assn. Black Lawyers, Wake County Bar. Assn., NC Bar Assn., Wake Women Attys., Women's Forum NC (mem. 2001—, bd. mem. & sec. 2004—05). Office: Supreme Ct NC PO Box 2170 Raleigh NC 27602-2170 also: 5417 Olde South Rd Raleigh NC 27606 Office Phone: 919-733-3723.*

HUDSON, ROY DAVAGE, retired pharmaceutical executive; b. Chattanooga, June 30, 1930; s. Roy and Everence (Wilkerson) H.; m. Constance Joan Taylor, Aug. 31, 1956; children: Hollye Lynne, David Kendall. BS, Livingstone Coll., 1955; MS, U. Mich., 1957, PhD, 1962; MA, Brown U., 1968; LL.D., Lehigh U., 1974, Princeton, 1975. Asst. prof. pharmacology U. Mich. Sch. Medicine, 1961-66; assoc. prof. med. sci. Brown U. Sch. Medicine, 1966-70, assoc. dean grad. sch., 1966-69; pres. Hampton U., 1970-76; dir. rsch. planning and coordination Parke, Davis Pharm. Co., Ann Arbor, Mich., 1976; v.p. rsch. planning Warner Lambert/Parke-Davis Pharm. Rsch. Divsn., Ann Arbor, 1977-79; mgr. sci. liaison Upjohn Co., Kalamazoo, 1979-81, mgr. CNS diseases rsch., 1981—85, dir. CNS diseases rsch., 1985-87; v.p. pharm. rsch. divsn. Europe Upjohn Co., Brussels, 1987-90; corp. v.p. pub. rels. Upjohn Co., Kalamazoo, 1990-92, ret., 1992. Adj. prof. Black Americana studies Western Mich. U., Kalamazoo, 1993; interim exec. dir., CEO Guidance Clinic, Kalamazoo, 1993; interim pres. Livingstone Coll., Salisbury, N.C., 1995-96; dir. Parke-Davis & Co., United Va. Bank-Citizens and Marine, United Va. Bankshares, Comerica Bank-Mich., Chesapeake and Potomac Telephone Co. of Va. Contbr. articles to profl. jours., chpts. to books. Mem. screening com. Danforth Grad. Fellowships, 1962-78; mem. adv. council Danforth Grad. Fellows program Danforth Found., 1972-79; chmn. Va. Com. on Selection Rhodes Scholars, 1973; mem. Commn. on Fed. Relations, Am. Council on Edn., 1972-76, bd. dirs., 1973-76; mem. adv. council to dir. NIH, 1974—; Mem. R.I. Commn. Econ. Devel., 1967-69, R.I. Urban League scholarship com., 1966-70; mem. inst. policy commn. So. Regional Edn. Bd.; bd. dirs. Afro-Am. Soc. Conn. Coll., Kalamazoo Area Math and Sci. Ctr., Kalamazoo Area Academic Achievement Program, ARC; bd. dirs., v.p. Nat. Assn. Equal Opportunity in Higher Edn.; trustee Brown U., Livingstone Coll., Peninsula United Community Services, Spelman Coll. Served with USAF, 1948-52. Recipient Disting. Alumni award Livingstone Coll.; Outstanding Civilian Service award U.S. Army.; Danforth Grad. fellow, 1955-61 Mem. Am. Soc. Pharmacology and Exptl. Therapeutics, Peninsula C. of C., NAACP (life, 1st v.p., Golden Heritage), AAAS, N.Y. Acad. Scis., Sigma Xi, Phi Kappa Phi, Phi Sigma, Beta Kappa Chi, Kappa Delta Pi, Omega Psi Phi, Gamma Alpha, Alpha Kappa Mu. Home: 201 Brookview Pl Woodstock GA 30188 Personal E-mail: r.d.hudson@att.net.

HUDSON, SHERRILL W., energy executive; m. Mary Ann Hudson; 3 children. Mng. ptnr. Deloitte and Touche, LLP, Fla., 1965—2002; bd. dir. TECO Energy, Inc., Tampa, Fla., 2003—; chmn., CEO TECO Energy, Tampa, Fla., 2004—10; exec. chmn. TECO Energy, Inc., Tampa, Fla., 2010—. Bd. dir. Publix Super Markets, Lennar Corp., 2008—; past bd. dir. Standard Register, A. Duda & Sons. Treas., chmn. develop. com. Cmty. Partnership for Homeless; vice-chmn. Goodwill Industries Miami-Dade County; past chmn. Fla. Internat Univ. Found., Greater Miami C. of C., Dade Cmty. Found., Jackson Meml. Found., Am. Cancer Soc.; past pres. Orange Bowl Com., Zoological Soc. Fla. Mem.: Fla. Inst. CPAs (Outstanding CPA in Bus. & Industry 2006). Office: TECO Energy 702 N Franklin St Tampa FL 33602

HUDSON, STEVEN J., surgeon; b. Wilkinsburg, Pa., Dec. 27, 1968; m. Lori Hudson; children: Alaina, Brennan, Chloe, Avery. BS in Neuroscience, U. Pa., 1990; MD in Medicine and Surgery, Uniformed Svcs. U. Sch. Medicine, 1994; JD in Law and Health Care, U. Md., 2001; MPA, Marist Coll., 2008. Med. officer USN Res. Med. Corps, 1990—; eye surgeon Willis-Falkenberg Eye Care, Fredericksburg, Va. Mem.: AMA. Republican. Home: 13253 Blue Heron Hills Dr King George VA 22485-2433 Office Phone: 540-371-2777. Office Fax: 703-666-9143. Business E-Mail: steven.hudson@williseye.com.

HUDSON, TIM, professional baseball player; b. Columbus, Ga., July 14, 1975; m. Kim Bruner; 3 children. Grad., Auburn U., Ala. Pitcher Oakland Athletics, Calif., 1999—2004, Atlanta Braves, 2005—. Recipient Hutch award, 2010; named Rookie Pitcher of Yr., Maj. League Baseball, 1999, Nat. League Comeback Player of Yr., Maj. League Baseball Players Assn., 2010; named to Am. League All-Star Team, Maj. League Baseball, 2000, 2004, Nat. League All-Star Team, 2010, Ala. CC Conf. Hall of Fame, 2001. Achievements include leading the American League in: wins, 2000; starts, 2001; shutouts, 2003, 2004; leading the National League in: starts, 2006. Office: Atlanta Braves Turner Field 755 Hank Aaron Dr Atlanta GA 30315

HUDSON, WILLIAM L., conductor; Studies with Anthony Gigliotti, Max Rudolph, Erich Leindorf; grad., Phila. Mus. Acad., U. Pa., Yale U.; conducting student, Tanglewood Music Festival, Curtis Inst. Music, Phila. Conservatory. Condr., music dir. Fairfax Symphony Orch., Annandale, Va. Prof. music, condr. opera prodns. and symphony orch. U. Md.; faculty mem. Conducting Inst. Am. Symphony Orch. League; music dir. Shenandoah Valley Music Festival, 1979—. Bd. dirs. No. Va. Youth Symphony, Fairfax (Va.) Chorale Soc.; mem. adv. panel Fairfax County Coun. Arts; hon. chmn. Fairfax Spotlight on Arts, 1990. Recipient Outstanding Music Dir./Condr. award Washington Area Music Assn., 1985. Office: 3905 Railroad Ave STE 202N Fairfax VA 22030-3931

HUDSPETH, CHALMERS MAC, lawyer, educator; b. Denton, Tex., Oct. 18, 1919; s. Junia Evans and Ethel (Burns) H.; m. Demaris Eleanor De Lange, Jan. 30, 1945; children: Albert James, Thomas Richard, Helen Demaris. BA, Rice U., Houston, 1940; JD, U. Tex., Austin, 1946. Bar: Tex. 1946. Pvt. practice, Houston, 1947—; of counsel De Lange Hudspeth McConnell and Tibbets LLP, 1988—; asst. prof. law U. Tex. at Austin, 1946-47; lectr. govt. Rice U., 1947—, bd. govs., 1980—82, trustee, 1982-89, trustee emeritus, 1989—. Bd. dirs. Stewart Title Guaranty Co., ret. Contbr. articles to profl. jours. Mem. bi-racial com. Houston Ind. Sch. Dist., 1955-56; trustee, v.p. Brown Found., 1983-89. Served to lt. USNR, 1942-45. Fellow Am. Bar Found., Tex. Bar Found.; mem. ABA, Tex. Bar Assn., State Bar Tex. (dir. 1966-68, v.p. 1968-69), Houston Philos. Soc. (pres. 1964-65), Chancellors, Order of Coif, Phi Delta Phi. Office: De Lange Hudspeth McConnell & Tibbets LLP 1177 W Loop S Ste #1700 Houston TX 77027 Office Phone: 713-871-2000. Personal E-mail: hhanddh@sbcglobal.net. Business E-Mail: hank@dhmtlaw.com, hank.hudspeth@rice.edu.

HUDSPETH, HARRY LEE, federal judge; b. Dallas, Dec. 28, 1935; s. Harry Ellis and Hattilee (Dudney) H.; m. Vicki Kathryn Round, Nov. 27, 1971; children: Melinda, Mary Kathryn. BA, U. Tex., Austin, 1955, JD, 1958. Bar: Tex. 1958. Trial atty. Dept. Justice, Washington, 1959-62; asst. U.S. atty. Western Dist. Tex., El Paso, 1962-69; assoc. Peticolas, Luscombe & Stephens, El Paso, 1969-77; U.S. magistrate El Paso, 1977-79; judge US Dist. Ct. (we. dist.) Tex., El Paso, 1979—92, US Dist. Ct. (we. dist) Tex., 1999—2001, chief judge El Paso, 1992-1999, sr. judge Austin, Tex., 2001—. Bd. dirs. Sun Carnival Assn., 1976, Met. YMCA El Paso, 1980-88. Mem. U. Tex. Ex-students Assn. (exec. coun. 1980-86), Chancellors, Order of Coif, Phi Beta Kappa. Democrat. Mem. Christian Ch. (Disciples Of Christ). Office: US Dist Ct We Dist Tex 903 San Jacinto Ste 440 Austin TX 78701 Office Phone: 512-916-5837.

HUEBNER, SCOTT C., health insurance company executive; BA in Mktg., Tex. A&M U. Cert. in internat. bus. Sr. adminstr. N.Am. Med. Mgmt.; v.p. network ops. Texas HealthSpring, 2000—06, pres., 2006—; sr. v.p. HealthSpring, Inc., 2000—06, pres. GulfQuest mgmt. ops., 2006—, exec. v.p., 2009—. Pres. Ctrl. Houston Ind. Physician Orgn., Met. Ind. Physician Orgn. Office: HealthSpring Inc Ste 501 9009 Carothers Pky Franklin TN 37067 Office Phone: 615-291-7000. Office Fax: 615-401-4566.

HUECHTKER, EDWARD DARRELL, professor; b. Louisville, May 24, 1937; s. Charles Edward and Hazel Irene (Munkers) H.; m. Sandra Wallace Dunning, Apr. 16, 1960 (dec. Feb. 23, 2006); children: Tracie, Tara, Edward, Trent; m. Betty Gravitt Holcomb, Oct. 25, 2008. Cert. physician assoc., Duke U., 1975; BA, Marymount Coll., 1979; MPA, L.I. U., 1981; cert. physician asst. leadership tng., St. Francis Coll., 1994; PhD, Kennedy We. U., 2004. Cert. Nat. Commn. Physician Assts. With USN, 1955—71, USCG, 1971—87, physician asst., 1975—87; assoc. dean Tampa Coll., Clearwater, Fla., 1982—87, dean, 1987—88; internat. recruiter Sperry Internat., Clearwater, 1988—90; asst. prof., assoc. dir. physician asst. program Med. Coll. Ga., Augusta, 1990—96; chair, dir. physician asst. program East Carolina U., Greenville, NC, 1996—2002; assoc. prof. U. Ala., Birmingham, 2002—12, chmn. Depts. Critical Care and Diagnostic and Therapeutic Sci., 2002—10. Med. examiner Phys. Measurements, Inc., Newport News, Va., 1975-78, Tricorps of Tenn., Spring, 1990-94; physician asst. Med. Ctr. Ctrl. Ga., Macon, 1992-96, various hosps. and clinics, Ga. and N.C., 1990—; sec., bd. dirs. Ala. Grief Support Svcs., 2006-10, bd. dir., chmn., 2010-. Contbr. articles to profl. jours., chpts. to books. Chair adv. com. VA Hosp., Bay Pines, Fla., 1988-90; chair adv. bd. A.R. Johnson Med. H.S., Augusta, 1991-96; deacon 1st Bapt. Ch., Seminole, fla., 1984-90. Fellow Am. Acad. Physician Assts.; mem. Assn. Physician Asst. Programs (co-chair conf. planning), Ala. Soc. Physician Assts., N.C. Acad. Physician Assts., Ret. Officers Assn., Ky. Col. Republican. Avocations: travel, reading, motorcycling. Office: Univ Alabama Birmingham Health Professions Clin and Diagnostic Scis SHPB 431 1530 3rd Ave S Birmingham AL 35294-1212 Home: 30969 Peninsula Dr Ono Island Orange Beach AL 36561 Business E-Mail: huechtker@gmail.com.

HUETT, GREG, food products executive; m. Jamie Huett; 4 children. BA in Agrl. Bus., Ark. Tech. U. Joined Tyson Foods, Inc., 1983, various positions, including gen. mgr., Tyson de Mex., sr. v.p., pres., Tyson Internat. Springdale, Ark., 2002—. Office: Tyson Foods Inc 2200 Don Tyson Pky Springdale AR 72762-6999 Office Phone: 479-290-4000. Office Fax: 479-290-4061. Business E-Mail: greg.huett@tyson.com.

HUETTEMAN, SUSAN ANN BICE, writer, reviewer; b. Crossville, Ill., Jan. 24, 1934; d. John Oren Fulkerson and LaVerne Brown, adopted d. Francis Joseph Bice; m. Albert George Huetteman, June 12, 1956; children: Scott Christopher, Mark Bice. AA in Voice, Colby-Sawyer U., 1953; MusB in Voice, New Eng. Conservatory, 1956; MA in Comms., Goddard Grad. Sch., 1979. Owner Huetteman Studio, Iowa, Ohio, Nebr., Ill., and Mass., 1958—98, author, cons., 1966—; lectr., dir. arts, mgmt. cons. and tchr. voice Performing Arts Divsn. U. Mass., Amherst, Mass., 1977—98. Cons. mgmt. Nat. Guild Cmty. Sch. of the Arts, Englewood, N.J., 1995-98; Web site cons. Hallinan Consulting, Venice, Calif., 1998-2004, Am. Collection Masterpiece Theatre, Nat. Coun. Tchrs. English. Author: (poetry set to music) The Seasons, 1966 (Ohio State Archives 1973), (book, lyrics) The Hatch, Jeff Holmes composer, 1999, Mary and Four Songs, Ind. State U. Archives; editor: Iowa Music Tchr., 1974-75; columnist: Valley Advocate, Amherst Bull., 1986-87; contbr. essays, articles, and poetry to anthologies and Web sites. Coord. Bike Safety U. Mass., Town of Amherst, 1977-79, judge Global eBook Awards, 2012. Named Woman of Yr., Optimists, 1980s. Mem.: Internat. Women's Writing Guild, Theatre Comm. Group, Soc. Children's Writers and Book Illustrators, Nat. Assn. Tchrs. Singing (pres. Western chpt. 1996), Fla. Writers Assn. Avocations: walk races, golf. Home (Summer): 82 E Quail Run Charlestown RI 02813-2808 Home (Winter): 222 N Brockfield Dr Sun City Center FL 33573 E-mail: shuett@cox.net.

HUEY, WARD L(IGON), JR., retired media executive; b. Dallas, Apr. 26, 1938; s. Ward Ligon and Irene Helen (Freeman) H.; m. Marian Kennedy Powell, Oct. 28, 1961; children: Ward L. III, David Powell. BA, So. Meth. U., 1960. Successively with dept. prodn., sales svc. mgr. local sales, regional sales mgr., gen. sales mgr. Sta. WFAA-TV, Dallas, 1960-67, sta. mgr., 1972-75; v.p., gen. mgr. Belo Broadcasting Corp., Dallas, from 1975; vice chmn. bd. dirs., pres. broadcast div. A. H. Belo Corp., Dallas, 1987—2001. Chmn. affiliate bd. govs. ABC-TV, 1981-82; chmn. bd. TV Operators Caucus, 1989. Mem. exec. com. So. Meth. U. Meadows Sch. Arts, 1986—, Goodwill Industries Dallas, 1978-79, State Fair Tex., 1992—; bd. dirs. Children's Med. Found. Tex., Dallas, 1985-94, Dallas Found., 1993—; trustee So. Meth. U., 1996—2008. Recipient Disting. Alumni award, So. Meth. U., 2000; named Disting. Alumni, Highland Park H.S., 1998, Pioneer of Yr., Tex. Broadcasters, 2000; named to, Broadcasting and Cable Hall of Fame, 1999, Nat. TV Acad. Mgmt. Hall of Fame, 2004. Mem. Maximum Svc. TV Assn. (vice chmn. 1988-94), TV Bur. Advt. (past bd. dirs., exec. com. 1984-88), Assn. Broadcast Execs. Tex. (bd. dirs. 1977-78), Dallas Advt. League (bd. dirs. 1975-76), Salesmanship Club Dallas (pres. 1992-93), Dallas Country Club. Methodist. Avocations: skiing, boating, swimming, golf, music.

HUFF, JOHN ROSSMAN, energy executive; b. Oxford, Miss., Mar. 14, 1946; s. William Jennings and Frances (Rossman) H.; m. Karen Keohane; children: Christopher Travis. Attended, Rice U., 1966; BCE, Ga. Inst. Tech., 1968; PMD, Harvard U., 1977. Engr. Offshore Co., Houston, 1968-70; chief engr. Zapata Off-Shore Co., Houston, 1970-72; mgr. engring. Western Oceanic, Inc., Houston, 1972-75, v.p., tech. svcs., 1975-76, v.p., sales, 1976-78, v.p, ops., 1978-80, chmn., pres., 1980-86; mng. ptnr. Falcon Ptnrs., Inc., 1986; CEO Oceaneering International, Inc., 1986—2006, chmn., 2006—. Bd. dirs. BJ Svcs.Co., KBR, Inc., Suncor Energy Inc., Houston Triton Energy, Dallas Suncor, Calgary. Contbr. articles to mags. Bd. govs. Miss. Boys State, 1963; bd. dirs. overseas edn. coun. Dept. State, 1981-84, U.S. Coast Guard Found., 1982—, Strake Jesuit Prep. Acad., Houston, 1983-95. Recipient career achievement award ASME/U. Houston, 1994, Rhodes award 1997; sr. fellow Am. Leadership Forum; NSF grantee Ind. U., 1963; named CEO of yr. Fin. World, 1994. Mem. Am. Bur. Shipping (bd. dirs. 1984—), Nat. Ocean Industries Assn. (bd. dirs.), Young Pres. Orgn., Mensa. Clubs: River Oaks Country (Houston). Republican. Episcopalian. Avocations: scuba diving, gardening. Office: Oceaneering International Inc 11911 Fm 529 Rd Houston TX 77041 Office Phone: 713-329-4500. Office Fax: 713-329-4951. Business E-Mail: jhuff@oceaneering.com.

HUFF, ROLLA P., Internet company executive; b. Sept. 26, 1956; BS in Mgmt., Purdue U., 1979. CPA. Various positions NCR Corp.; fin. v.p., merger & acquisitions AT&T Corp., 1994—95; sr. v.p., CFO AT&T Wireless Svcs., Inc., 1994—97, pres., ctrl. US region, 1997—98; exec. v.p., CFO Frontier Corp., 1998—99, pres., COO, 1999; chmn., CEO Mpower Comm. Corp., 1999—2006; pres., CEO & chmn. EarthLink, Inc., 2007—. Office: Earthlink Inc 1375 Peachtree St Atlanta GA 30309 Office Phone: 404-815-0770. Office Fax: 404-815-8805.

HUFFINGTON, ANITA, sculptor; b. Balt., Dec. 25, 1934; d. Norris Jackson and Agnes (Hook) H.; m. Manuel Rubin Duque, Sept. 17, 1957 (div. Nov. 1964); 1 child, Lisa Huffington Duque; m. Henry Sutter, Dec. 4, 1964. BA, CCNY, 1973, MFA, 1975. Resident La Napoule Art Found., France, 1996. One-woman exhbns. include U. Ark., Fayetteville, 1982, Valley House Gallery, Dallas, 1986, Benton Gallery, Southampton, NY, 1989, Ark. Art Ctr., Little Rock, 1990, O'Hara Gallery, NYC, 1994, 96, 99, 2001, 04, 06, 07, 08, U. Ctrl. Ark., Conway, 1997, Triangle Gallery, San Francisco, 1998, Lisa Kurts Gallery, Memphis, 1999, 2003, 05, 07, 08, Morris Mus., Augusta, Ga., 2004, 06, 08, Walton Art Ctr., Fayetteville, Ar., 2004, Fayetteville Pub. Libr.Sculpture Lecture 2008; artist, book, Anita Huffington Sculpture, 2007, Jonathon O'Hara Gallery, 2006; 2-person show Lisa Kurts Gallery, 1995; 3-person shows Louis Stern Gallery, West Hollywood, Calif., 1996, Triangle Gallery, San Francisco, 1996; group exhbn. include Internat. Women's Art Festival, NYC, 1976, U. Ark., Fayetteville, 1978, 92, Ark. Arts Ctr., Little Rock, 1979-81, Territorial Restoration Gallery, Little Rock, 1981, Harris Gallery, Houston, Tex., 1981-93, Sculptural Arts Mus., Atlanta, 1982, Benton Gallery, Southampton, NY, 1988, Kornbluth Gallery, Fair Lawn, NJ, 1989, The Art Show, 7th Regiment Armory, NYC, 1989-2008, Art of the 20th Century 7th Regiment Armory, NYC, 2003-04, LA Art Show, Santa Monica, Calif., Ft. Smith Art Ctr., Ark., 1990, Salon de Mars, Paris, 1992, U. Pa., Phila. US Artists Art Fair, Pa. Acad., 1992-2002, 2003, ARTexas, Dallas, 1993-94, Art Fair Seattle, 1995-97, Art Miami, 1996, 98, Triangle Gallery, San Francisco, 1996, 99, 2000, Am. Acad. Arts and Letters, NYC, 1997, Columbus Mus., Ga., and Miss. Mus. Art, Jackson, 1997, Am. Acad. Arts and Letters, 1997, Two Sculptors, Inc., NYC, 1998, Valley House Gallery, Dallas, 1998, Art Palm Beach, 1998, 99, 2000, 01, Dallas Internat. Art and Antiques Fair, 2000-02, 50th Anniversary Show, Valley Ho. Gallery, Dallas, Hist. Ark. Mus., Little Rock, 2001, Art Santa Fe, 2005, 06, 07, 08, The Art Show, Haverstraw, 2006, 07, 08, Telfair Mus., Savannah, Ga., 2006; permanent collections include Met. Mus. Art, NYC, 2002, Morris Mus., 2008, others; featured in various profl. publ., mag., newspapers, and videos. Recipient Jimmy Ernst award Am. Acad. Arts and Letters, 1997, Residency award La Lapoule Art Found., 1997, Individual Artist award Gov., Little Rock, Ark., 2005, others; Visual arts fellow Ark. Arts Coun.

HUFFMAN, DELTON CLEON, JR., pharmacy association executive; b. St. Louis, Feb. 18, 1943; s. Delton Cleon and Kathryn (Saegesser) H.; m. Judy Hill, Aug. 11, 1962; children: Kimberly Lea, Jeffrey Keith. BS in Pharmacy, U. Ark., 1966; PhD, U. Miss., 1971. Pharmacist Crank Drug Co., Inc., Little Rock, 1966—67; asst. prof., dir. divsn. pharmacy adminstrn. U. Tenn. Coll. Pharmacy, Memphis, 1970—73, asso. prof., chmn. dept. pharmaceutics, 1973—74; exec. v.p. Am. Coll. Apothecaries, 1971—2010, also prof., chmn. dept. pharmacy, 1974—89, vice chancellor adminstrn., 1984—89; exec. dir. Nat. Cmty. Pharmacists Assn. Mgmt. Inst., Alexandria, Va., 1989—99, sr. v.p. practice and mgmt., 1992—99. Contbr. articles to profl. lit. Recipient Lederle Faculty award, 1971; NDEA fellow, 1967-70; Am. Found. for Pharm. Edn. fellow, 1967-70; Archer Drug Co. scholar, 1966. Fellow Am. Coll. Apothecaries; mem. AAAS, Am. Assn. Colls. Pharmacy, Am. Pharm. Assn., Nat. Cmty. Pharmacists Assn., Tenn. Pharm. Assn., Okla. Pharm. Assn. (hon.), Ark. Pharm. Assn. (hon., life), Am. Soc. Assn. Execs., Kappa Psi, Rho Chi. Home: 240 Lewis Fairway Cir Oakland TN 38060 Office: 2830 Summer Oaks Dr Bartlett TN 38134-3811

HUFFMAN, GERALD P., science administrator, educator; b. Steubenville, Ohio, Sept. 12, 1938; s. Sherwood John and Anne Virginia Huffman; m. Shelby-Jean Walker; children: Scott Bradley, Brad Christopher, Kirsten Ahn Rowland. PhD, W.Va. U., 1965. Rsch. scientist Fundamental Rsch. Lab., U.S. Steel Corp., Monroeville, Pa., 1965—85; pres. MacroAtom, Inc., Monroeville, 1985—86; dir. Consortium for Fossil Fuel Sci. U. Ky., Lexington, 1986—, prof. depts. chem. and materials engring. and physics, 1986—. Editor: (jour.) Fuel Processing Technology, numerous conf. procs.; contbr. 300 sci. papers to profl. jours. and books. Recipient 46 rsch. grants and contracts, various govt. agys. and industry, 1972—2004, Henry Marion Howe medal, Am. Soc. Metals, 1984, Best Fundamental Paper award South Tex. sect., AIChE, 1995, Wall of Honor award, West Liberty U., 2004, Crystal Flame award Innovation in Rsch., FuelCellSouth, 2007. Fellow: Am. Phys. Soc., Am. Chem. Soc. (chair divsn. fuel chemistry 1997—98, cert. of merit divsn. environ. chemistry 1998). Achievements include research in catalysis; conversion of coal, natural gas, and waste plastics into clean liquid fuels,lube oil, hydrogen; catalytic dehydrogenation, C1 chemistry; XAFS and Mössbauer spectroscopy; electron microscopy; toxic trace metals, respirable quartz and fine airborne particulate matter; patents in field. Home: 908 Belmere Dr Lexington KY 40509 Office Fax: 859-257-7215. Personal E-mail: gphuffmanasfe@gmail.com. Business E-Mail: gphuffman@uky.edu.

HUFFMAN, GREGORY SCOTT COMBEST, lawyer; b. Austin, Tex., Dec. 19, 1946; s. Calvin Combest and Olive Agnes (Weaver) H.; m. Mary L. Murphy, Feb. 1, 1986. Student, Stanford U., France, 1966—67; BA in History with great distinction, Stanford U., 1969; postgrad., London Sch. of Econs., 1971—72; JD, Harvard U., 1973. Bar: Tex. 1973, U.S. Dist. Cts. Tex. 1974, U.S. Ct. Appeals (5th cir.) 1975, U.S. Supreme Ct. 1976. From assoc. to sr. ptnr. Thompson & Knight, Dallas, 1973—, also dir. Chief editor (monographs) Texas Free Enterprise and Antitrust Act, 1984-90, Texas Antitrust and Related Statutes, 1991—. Pres. Northern Hills Neighborhood Assn., 1980; bd. dirs. Common Cause of Tex., 1979-81, Love Field Citizens Action Commn., 1980-83, Appleseed Found., 1996-2001; adminstrv. chmn., bd. dirs. Tex. Appleseed, 1996-2014; active Tex. Supreme Ct. Adv. Com. on Professionalism. Named Best lawyers in America, 2010, 2012; named one of Top Ten Antitrust lawyers, 2007—13. Fellow Tex. Bar Found., Dallas Bar Found.; mem. ABA (antitrust and litigation sect.), Am. Coll. Trial Lawyers, Tex. Bar Assn. (antitrust and litigation sect., chmn. unlawful practice law com. 1981-83, chmn. lawyer referral svc. com. 1982-83, bd. legal specialization 1974-77, chmn. antitrust and bus. litigation sect. 1991-92, bd. dirs. 1983—, task force on unauthorized practice of law, author of reports, presdl. citation 2000, cert. of merit 2001), Am. Bd. Trial Advocates, Dallas Bar Assn. (antitrust sect., sec.-treas. 1981, chmn. unauthorized practice law com. 1979, chmn. lawyer referral svc. com. 1980-81, chmn. profl. svcs. com. 1986-87, chmn. spkrs. com. 1999-2000, chmn. CLE com. 2001, bd. dirs. antitrust sect. 1981, 89-2002, bd. dirs. litigation sect. 1988), Harvard Law Sch. Assn. Tex. (pres. 1987-88), Phi Beta Kappa, Sigma Alpha Epsilon. Methodist. Office: Thompson & Knight 1722 Routh St Ste 1500 Dallas TX 75201 Office Phone: 214-969-1144. Business E-Mail: huffmang@tklaw.com.*

HUFFMAN, JOAN, state legislator; m. Keith Huffman; 1 child, Luke. BA, La. State U.; JD, South Tex. Sch. Law. Former sec. Harris County Dist. Atty.'s Office, Tex., former chief felony prosecutor, former spl. crimes gang prosecutor, former legal counsel, organized crime narcotics task force; judge 183 Criminal Dist. Ct.; mem. Dist. 17 Tex. State Senate, 2008—. Republican. Office: 129 Circle Way Ste 101 Lake Jackson TX 77566 also: PO Box 12068 Capitol Station Austin TX 78711 also: 6217 Edloe Houston TX 77005 Office Phone: 979-480-0994, 512-463-0117, 713-662-3821.

HUFFMAN, JOAN BREWER, history professor; b. Springfield, Ohio, Aug. 18, 1937; d. James Clarence and Berniece (Notter) Brewer; m. James Russell Huffman, Aug. 21, 1959; children: Jill Elizabeth, Jean Elaine. AB, Ohio U., 1959; MA, Ga. State U., 1968, PhD, 1980. Adj. prof. Wesleyan Coll., Macon, Ga., 1981-82; instr. history Macon State Coll., 1968-72, asst. prof., 1972-81, assoc. prof., 1981-86, prof., 1986-2000, prof. emerita, 2000—; owner The Printed Page, Macon, Ga., 1993-97, Picture Perfect, 1995—, PB and Jellie, 2008—. Chmn. History adv. com. U. Sys. Ga., 1986—87. Contbr. articles to profl. jours. Mem., bd. dirs. Oklahatchee Pk., Perry, Ga., 1966-68, Macon State Coll. Found., 1985-90, Ga. Humanities Coun., Atlanta, 1983-87. Katharine C. Bleckley scholar English-Speaking Union, 1977; recipient Gov.'s award in the humanities, 1998. Mem. N.Am. Conf. on Brit. Studies, Am. Hist. Assn., Southern Hist. Assn. (membership com. 1988-89), Ga. Assn. Historians (pres. 1982-83), Phi Beta Kappa, Phi Alpha Theta (award 1978). Home: 281 Wesleyan View Dr Macon GA 31210 Office Phone: 478-746-6365. Business E-Mail: huffmanj@bellsouth.net.

HUFFMAN, JOHN WILLIAM, chemist, educator; b. Evanston, Ill., July 21, 1932; s. John W. and Florence (Kearns) H.; m. Eunice Marie Taylor, June 19, 1954 (div. Aug. 1973); children: Paul W., James R., George R., John E.; m. Dana Alayne Holderby, Dec. 5, 1975 (div. May 1997); m. Hollye Kay Moss, Dec. 13, 1997. BS, Northwestern U., 1954; AM, Harvard U., 1956, PhD, 1957. Asst. prof. chemistry Ga. Inst. Tech., 1957-60, Clemson (S.C.) U., 1960-62, assoc. prof., 1962-67, prof., 1967—2005, rsch. prof., 2006—10, prof. emeritus, 2010—. Contbr. articles to profl. jours. NIH Career Devel. awardee, 1965-70, NIDA Sr. Sci. award, 2002-05; grantee NIH, NIDA, 1958—2010. Mem. Am. Chem. Soc., Internat. Cannabinod Rsch. Soc. Democrat. Roman Catholic. Avocations: stamp collecting/philately, model railroad. Home Phone: 828-631-3339. Business E-Mail: huffman@clemson.edu.

HUFFMAN, WALTER B., retired army officer, dean, law educator; b. Keesler AFB, Miss., Oct. 8, 1944; m. Anne Robison; children: Burl, Becky, Ross. BS, Tex. Tech U., 1967, MEd, 1968, JD with highest honors, 1977. Commd. 2d lt. U.S. Army, 1968, advanced through grades to maj. gen.; judge adv. in various assignments including Desert Shield/Desert Storm, 1977-97; judge advocate gen. U.S. Army, 1997—2002; ret., 2002; dean, prof. law Sch. Law Tex. Tech. U., Lubbock, 2002—. Editor-in-chief Tex. Tech Law Rev. Decorated Legion of Merit with one oak leaf cluster, Bronze Star medal with 2 oak leaf clusters, Hungarian Disting. Svc. medal. Office: Tex Tech Univ Sch Law 18th and Hartford Lubbock TX 79409

HUFFSTETLER, PALMER EUGENE, lawyer; b. Shelby, NC, Dec. 21, 1937; s. Daniel S. and Ethel (Turner) H.; m. Mary Ann Beam, Aug. 9, 1958; children: Palmer Eugene, Ben Beam, Brian Tad. BA, Wake Forest U., 1959, JD, 1961. Bar: N.C. 1961. Practiced in, Kings Mountain, NC, 1961-62, Raleigh, NC, 1962-64; with State Farm Ins. Co., Orlando, Fla., 1962; gen. legal counsel Carolina Freight Corp., Cherryville, NC, 1964-93, sec., 1969-90, sr. v.p., 1969-89, exec. v.p., 1985-93, pres., 1993-95; ret., 1995; pres., CEO Blue Chip Inc., 1997-99. Author, composer: Senior Man on Carolina Line, Fifty Years Ago. Chmn. Cherryville Zoning Bd. Adjustment, 1967-70; active N.C. Gasoline and Oil Insp. Bd., 1974-76; class chmn. Wake Forest Coll. Fund, 1971-79, decade chmn.Wake Forest Law Sch. Law Adv. Com., 1981-82; governing body, chmn. adminstrv. com. So. Piedmont Health Systems Agy., 1975-77; mem. Cherryville Econ. Devel. Commn., 1982-87, Cherryville Econ. Devel. Com., 1995-97; pres. Cherryville Devel. Corp., 1986—; bd. dirs. C. Grier Beam Truck Mus., 1982-2002, pres. 1982-96; bd. dirs. Schiele Mus., Gastonia, N.C., 1985-88, Gaston Meml. Hosp., 1990-93, vice-chmn. bd.; active N.C. Gov.'s Hwy. Safety Commn., 1985-88, Gov.'s Bus. Com., N.C., 1993-95; v.p. Ctrl. and So. Rate Bur., 1984-89; trustee Brevard Coll., 1987-93, fin. com. mem. Ctrl. United Math. Ch., King Mt., 2011-. Mem. N.C. State Bar, N.C. Bar Assn. (mem. adminstrv. bd. 1965-69, 71-72, chmn. adminstrv. bd., trustee 1970-73, fin. com. 1994-2002, Fin. Com. Ctrl. United Methodist, 2011-), mem. Moorings HOA (bd. dirs. 2007-2008), First United Meth. Ch. (coun. 2002-2004). Methodist. Home: 2141 Fairways Dr Cherryville NC 28021-2115

HUG, CARL CASIMIR, JR., pharmacology and anesthesiology educator, medical ethics educator; b. Canton, Ohio, Dec. 20, 1936; s. Carl Casimir and Aimee Cecelia (McArdle) H.; m. Marilyn Ann France, May 12, 1956; children: Patricia Ann DeStephano, Michael Stephen, Joan Marie Daniel, Mary Lynn Higgins, Lori Renee Mauldin. BS in Pharmacy summa cum laude, Duquesne U., 1958; PhD in Pharmacology, U. Mich., 1963, MD with distinction, 1967. Diplomate Am. Bd. Anesthesiology 1975, recert., 1993. From instr. to assoc. prof. pharmacology U. Mich., Ann Arbor, 1963-71; from assoc. prof. anesthesiology and pharmacology to emeritus prof. Emory U. Sch. Medicine, Atlanta, 1972—, dir. cardiothoracic anesthesiology, 1982—98, dep. chmn. for rsch., 1987-95, dep. chmn. for acad. affairs, 1995—2001; faculty affiliate Emory U. Ctr. for Ethics, 1999—. Vis. rsch. prof. U. Leiden, The Netherlands, 1982, dir. Am. Bd. Anesthesiology, 1984-96, v.p. 1990-92, pres. 1992-93; bd. dirs. Found. Anesthesia Edn. Rsch. 1993-2002, v.p. 1995-98, pres. 1998-2001; councilor-at-large Assn. U. Anesthesiologists 1980-83, pres. 1984-86; vis. prof., lectr. in field, grantee in field. Author: Alfentanil: Pharmacology and Uses in Anesthesia, 1984; New Developments in Drugs Used in Anaesthesia, 1991; editor Pharmacokinetics of Anaesthesia, 1984; editor Anesthesiology, 1979-88; contbr. articles to profl. jours. Chmn. St. Francis Sch. Bd., Ann Arbor, Mich., 1967—71; coach Little League, Ann Arbor, 1967—71; active Corpus Christi Cath. Ch., Stone Mountain, Ga., 1972—96, St. John Neumann Cath. Ch., Liburn, Ga., 1997—. Recipient Lifetime Achievement award Am. Soc. Critical Care Anesthesiologists, 2002; Ralph M. Waters, MD award Ill. Soc. Anesthesiologists, 2004; named Tchr. of Yr. Emory U. Anesthesiology, 1989, Excellence in Cardiothoracic Anesthesiology award, 1998. Fellow Royal Coll. Anaesthetists (Eng., hon.), Australian and New Zealand Coll. Anaesthetists (hon.), Am. Coll. Anesthesiologists; mem. Belgian Soc. Anesthesia and Reanimation (hon.), Am. Soc. Anesthesiologists (chmn. various coms. 1976—, named Emery A. Rovenstine lectr. 1999, Disting. Svc. award 2006), Assn. Cardiac Anesthesiologists, Soc. Cardiovasc. Anesthesiologists, Am. Soc. Clin. Pharmacology and Therapeutics, Am. Soc. Pharmacology and Expl. Therapeutics. Roman Catholic. Avocations: bicycling, walking, racquetball, piano. Office: Emory Univ Hosp Dept Anesthesiology 1364 Clifton Rd NE Atlanta GA 30322-1104 Office Phone: 404-778-3917. Business E-Mail: chug@emory.edu.

HUGGINS, BOB, college basketball coach; b. Morgantown, W.Va., Sept. 21, 1953; s. Charles Huggins; m. June Ann Fillman; children: Jenna Leigh, Jacqueline. BS magna cum laude, U. W.Va., 1977, MA in Health Adminstrn., 1978. Grad. asst. basketball coach W.Va. U., Morgantown, 1977—78, head coach, 2007—; asst. basketball coach Ohio State U., Columbus, 1978-90; head coach Walsh Coll., Canton, Ohio, 1980-83; asst. basketball coach U. Ctrl. Fla., Orlando, 1983-84; head basketball coach U. Akron, Ohio, 1984-89, U. Cin., 1989—2005, Kans. State U., 2006—07. Mem. basketball coaching staff U.S. World Univ. Games team, 1993. Founder Bob Huggins Found., 1997-98. Named Coach of the Yr. dist. 22 NAIA, 1981-82, 1982-83, area 6, 1982-83, Mid-Ohio Conf., 1981-82, 1982-83, Ohio Valley, 1984-85, Metro Conf., 1989-90, Dapper Dan Man of Yr., 1986-87, dist. 4 USBWA, 1991-92, Conf. USA, 1996-98, 98-99, 99-2000, Mideast Coach of Yr. Basketball Times, 1991-92, 95-96, Co-Nat. Coach of Yr., 1991-92 Hoop Scoop mag., finalist for AP Coach of Yr., 1991-92, Ohio Coll. Coach of Yr. Columbus Dispatch, 1991-92, 1995-96, Nat. Coll. Coach of Yr., Playboy Mag., 1992-93, Midseason Coach of Yr. USA Today, 1991-92 season, Mideast Coach of Yr. Basketball Times, 1995-96 season, Nat. Coach. of Yr. Basketball Times, 1997-98 season, The Sporting News, 1999-2000 season, ESPN.com, 2001-02 season; recipient Ray Meyer award Gt. Midwest conf., 1991-92, 92-93, Ray Meyer award Conf. USA Coach of Yr, 1997-98, 1998-99, 1999-2000. Achievements include his 517-184 record (.738) amassed during his 22 seasons as a head coach ranks him sixth in winning percentage and 18th in victories among active Division 1 mentors; his string of 12 consecutive NCAA tournament appearances is the third-longest active streak; his teams have won over 20 games in all but three of his 22 campaigns and he has averaged 23.5 victories a season, 26.3 wins per campaign over the past eight years; he has compiled a 349-112 record (.757) in his 14 years at Cincinnati, making him the most winning coach in terms of victories and percentage in the school's rich basketball history. Office: West Virginia U PO Box 6201 Morgantown WV 26506 Home Phone: 513-677-0446; Office Phone: 513-556-5847. Business E-Mail: herouxmm@email.uc.edu.

HUGGINS, CHIP, state legislator; b. Columbia, SC, Nov. 30, 1961; s. Cecil and Kathleen Wood Huggins; m. Ginger Huggins; children: Hiller, Laine. BS, Winthrop U., 1987. Realtor, broker in charge Century 21 Bob Capes Realtors; mem. Dist. 85 SC House of Reps., 2000—, chair Subcommittee on Bus. and Commerce, mem. Labor, Commerce and Industry Com. Mem.: SC Assn. Realtors, Avalon Homeowner's Assn., Greater Columbia Assn. Realtors (grievance com. mem., PEP award), St. Andrews Rotary Club, Million Dollar Club (life). Republican. Presbyterian. Office: 323B Blatt Bldg PO Box 11867 Columbia SC 29201 Mailing: 308 Wayworth Ct Columbia SC 29212 Home Phone: 803-732-4418, 803-250-4416; Office Phone: 803-734-2971, 803-779-4503. E-mail: ch@schouse.org.

HUGHES, ALFRED CLIFTON, archbishop emeritus; b. Boston, Dec. 2, 1932; s. Alfred Clifton and Ellen Cecelia (Hennessey) Hughes. AB, St. John's Sem. Coll., 1954; STL, Gregorian U., Rome, 1958, STD, 1961. Ordained priest Archdiocese of Boston, 1957; asst. pastor St. Stephen's Parish, Framingham, Mass., 1958—59, Our Lady Help of Christians, Newton, Mass., 1961—62; lectr. St. John's Sem., Brighton, 1962—65, spiritual dir., 1965—81, rector, 1981—86; ordained bishop, 1981; aux. bishop Archdiocese of Boston, 1981—93, regional bishop of Merrimack, 1986—90, vicar for adminstrn., 1990—93; bishop Diocese of Baton Rouge, La., 1993—2001; coadjutor archbishop Archdiocese of New Orleans, 2001—02, archbishop, 2002—09, archbishop emeritus, 2009—. Chmn. com. on doctrine US Cath. Conf. Bishops, 1991—94, com. on use of catechism, 1995—. Author: Preparing for Church Ministry, 1979, Spiritual Masters, 1999, Towards a Civilization of Life and Love, 2004; chmn. editl. bd.: Nat. Dir. for Catechesis; contbr. articles to profl. jours. Recipient Mellon and Davis Founds. grant, 1976. Mem.: Catholic Theol. Soc. America. Roman Catholic. Office: Archdiocese of New Orleans 7887 Walmsley Avenue New Orleans LA 70125-3496

HUGHES, ANN HIGHTOWER, retired economist; b. Birmingham, Ala., Nov. 24, 1938; d. Brady Alexander and Juanita (Pope) H. BA, George Washington U., 1963, MA, 1969. Asst. U.S. trade rep. Exec. Office of Pres., Washington, 1978-81; dep. asst. sec. trade agreements Dept. Commerce, Washington, 1981-82, dep. asst. sec. Western Hemisphere, 1982-95; dir. C & M Internat., Washington, 1995-97; ret. Recipient meritorious exec. award Pres. of U.S., 1982, 88, disting. exec. award, 1993. Avocation: dog breeding.

HUGHES, BARBARA ANN, dietitian, public health administrator, nutritionist; b. McMinn County, Tenn., July 22, 1938; d. Cecil Earl and Hannah Ruth (Moss) Farmer; m. Carl Clifford Hughes, Oct. 13, 1962. BS in Home Econs. cum laude, Carson Newman Coll., Jefferson City, Tenn., 1960; MS in Instl. Mgmt., Ohio State U., Columbus, 1963; MA (Adonarium Judson scholar), So. Bapt. Theol. Sem., 1968; MPH, U. N.C., Chapel Hill, 1972; postgrad. in nutrition, U. Iowa, 1974, U. N.C., 1975-85, Case Western Res. U., 1979, Walden U.; PhD, 1988; grad. Inst. Polit., NC, 1994. Registered, lic. nutritionist, dietitian, cert. Tng. adult weight mgmt., 2004, in child & adlecent weight mgmt, 2010. Instr., clin. dietitian Riverside Meth. Hosp., Riverside Whitecross Sch. Nursing, Columbus, Ohio, 1963-66; consulting dietitian Mount Holly Nursing Home, Ky. Dept. Mental Health, 1966-68, Eastern Region N.C. Bd. Health, Raleigh, 1968-73; dir. Nutrition and Dietary Svcs. br. Divsn. Health Svcs. N.C. Dept. Human Resources, Raleigh, 1973-89; instr, U. tenn., 1988—90; also dir. Women-Infants-Children Program N.C. Dept. Human Resources, Raleigh; pres. B.A. Hughes and Assocs., 1990—; dir. adult nutrition Inst. Lifestyle and Weight Mgmt., 2006—07; intern. Ohio State U. Instr. Wake Tech. C.C., 1996—97; med. nutrition therapist CIGNA Health Care of N.C., Inc., United Behavioral Health, Blue Cross, Blue Shield N.C., NC State Health Plan, Aetna Ins., Medicaire Ins.; asst. to rep. Karen Gottovi 14th dist. N.C. Ho. of Reps., Gen. Assembly N.C., 1994; adj. instr. Case Western Res. U., Cleve., 1988—89; adj. asst. prof. dept. nutrition Sch. Public Health U. N.C., Chapel Hill, 1975—89; adv. bd. Hospitality Edn. program NC Dept. Cmty. Colls., 1974—80; adv. com. Ret. Senior Vol. Program, Raleigh and Wake County, NC, 1975—79, N.C. Network Coordinating Coun. for End-Stage Renal Disease, 1975, Nat. Adv. Coun. on Maternal, Infant and Fetal Nutrition, Spl. Supplemental Food Program for Women, Infants and Children, Dept. Agr., 1976—79; adv. com. Nutrition Edn. and Tng. program N.C. Dept. Pub. Instrn., 1978—80; chmn. adv. leadership coun. N.C. Cooperative Ext. Svc., 1997—99, advisor com. to Wake County, 1992—, chair adv. coun., 1994—96; coord. undergrad. program in gen. dietetics East Carolina U.; apptd. rep. Coll. of Agrl. and Life Scis. N.C. State U. to Nat. Coun. for Agrl. Rsch. Extension and Tchg., 1996—2000; apptd. mem. strategic planning and new directions com. Wake County Bd. Commrs. to Wake County Human Svcs. Bd., 1996—2006, new dirs. strategic planning com., children's com., bd. liaison, partnership com., 2001—04, agy. performance com., 1998—2000; chmn. agy. svcs. com., exec. com. Wake County Human Svcs. Bd., 2004, cmty. health comm., 2005—; apptd. to adv. bd. Agromedicine Program East Carolina and N.C. State Univs., 1996—99; apptd. N.C. Dept. Human Resources Sec.'s Adv. Coun. Alternative/Contemporary Medicine Consortium Natural Medicine and Pub. Health, 2000; adv. coun. N.C. Gov.'s Office Citizen Affairs; cons. dietitian Augusta Victoria Hosp. and Jerusalem (Israel) Crippled Childrens Ctr., 1968; witness U.S. congressional and Senate hearings in field; mem. planning com. NC Summit on Natural Med. Products, 2002; dietitian, dir. food svcs. archaeol. expedition, Israel, 1968; mem. Ralugh Human Rels. Comm., 2006—11. Co-author: Diet and Kidney Disease, Assn. for N.C. Regional Med. program, 1969, Ohio State U., Alumni Assoc., sec. Triangle chpt.; contbr. numerous papers, articles to symposia, periodicals in field, vol. areas. Trustee Gardner-Webb Coll., Boiling Springs, NC, 1978—82, chmn. curriculum com., 1981—82; chmn. adv. bd. dept. home econ. Carson-Newman Coll., 1975—78; chmn. Edn. and Cmty. Com., 1992; pres. NC Coun. on Spl. Teens, 1993—94; appt. mem. NC Dept. Health & Human Svc. Accreditation Bd., 2010; mem. Race Rels. Commn., 2006—11; chair Bylaws, Police Affairs & Awards & Celebrations Commn., 2006—11; v.p. Wake County Literacy Coun., 1986—87, bd. dirs., 2004; with Wake Co. Bd. & Health, Wale Co. Human Svcs. Bd.; treas., 2011—; del. various Dem. Convs., 1981—, precinct sec.-treas., 1981—, 1st vice chmn., 1983—85, 2nd vice chmn., 1993—96, 1998—, chair, 1985—87, 1998—2000, 2005—; adv. bd., del. NC Dem. Party Exec. Com., 1998—2002, 2008—; elected mem. NC Dem. Party Coun. Review Representing 4th Congl. Dist.; active edn. program Pullen Meml. Bapt. Ch., Raleigh; area ministry capt. Raleigh, 1977—78; personnel com. Pullen Meml. Bapt. Ch., Raleigh, Raleigh, 1978—80; bd. dirs. Cmty. Outreach, 1989—92, futuring com., 1995—96, coordinating coun. vice-chair, 1996—97, chmn., 1997—98; bd. dirs. NC Literacy Assn., 1978—83, 1993, 1995, pres., 1981—83. Named Woman of Yr., Wake County, 1975, N.C. Outstanding Dietitian of Yr., 1976, N.C. Outstanding Dietitian, Southeastern Hosp. Conf. Dietitians, 1978; recipient Disting. Alumna award Carson-Newman Coll., 1983, Eleanor Roosevelt Humanitarian award Altrusa Internat., 1995, S.E. Trustee award Nat. Assn. Local Bd. Health, 2002, Women in Bus. award Triangle Bus. Jour., 2002, Power of Prevention award, NC Health and Wellness Trust Fund leadership in Obesity award, 2007, Nutrition-Entrepreneurs DPG, 2006, Excellence Practice award, 2005, 08, Medallian award, 2004, Excellence Practice Cons. Bus. Practice award, 2005 Fellow: Am. Dietetic Assn. (mem., commn. on dietetic registration), N.C. Inst. Polit. Leadership; mem.: APHA (mem. nutrition sect. 1969—, chmn. nominating com. 1975—77, chair pub. policy com. 1977—79, mem. pub. policy com. 1977—79, chair award com. food and nutrition sect., other offices 1995—96, Catherine Cowell award 1994), AAUW Raleigh Wake Co Br. (life; pres. Raleigh/Wake County br. 1971—75, pres. N.C. divsn. 1978—80, area rep. 1980—82, mem. Program Com. Legis./Pub. Policy Com. 1980—82, ednl. founder 1980—82, nat. bd. dirs. 1980—92, nat. edn. found. bd. dirs. 1987—91, mem. found. 1987—91, pres. Raleigh/Wake County br. 1991—93, ednl. equity roundtable 1992, coord. Wake Women Celebrate 1995, coord. ptnrs. for heart disease and stroke prevention 1995, treas. 2011—, 2011—, pres. Raleigh/Wake County br. 2013—14), Interfaith Food Shuttle, Raleigh (bd. mem. 2007—08, mem. bd. affiliate 2009—10), Women's Forum N.C. (young leadership award com. 1989—90, newsletter editor bd. dirs. 1992—2013, young leadership award com. 1992—, adminstr. 1995—2003), N.C. Acad. Pub. Health (pres.-elect 2001, pres. 2002), Nutrition Today Soc., Soc. Nutrition Edn., Am. Acad. Health Adminstrn., N.C. Coun. Women's Orgns. (Wellness in State Employees adv. bd. 1989—91, mem. at large bd. dirs. 1989—92, leadership com.

1991—, chair nutrition subcom.), N.C. Coun. Foods and Nutrition (chmn. membership 1975, dir. 1976—78, nominating com. 1979), N.C. Assn. Bds. of Health (dir. 1994—98, nominating com. 1998—2000, treas. 1999—2000, mem. com. 1999—2005, awards com. 1999—2006, pres. 2002—03, immediate past pres. 2004—06, pres. 2012—), Assn. State and Territorial Pub. Health Nutrition Dirs. (pres. 1977—79, dir. 1981—89, chair legis. and pub. policy com. 1984—89, liaison to Assn. Faculties Grad. Program in Pub. Health Nutrition, Commendation award 1989), So. Health Assn. (pres. 1982—83, chair nominating com. 1985—86, 1991—92, awards com. 1992—93, Spl. Meritorious award 1989), Greater Raleigh C. of C. (mem. Alumni Assn. 1995, mem. west area bus. coun., chair legis. com. rep. leadership Raleigh Alumni Assn.), Altrusa Internat. Found. (1st v.p. 1985—87, chmn.-elect 1990—92, chmn. 1992—, bd. dirs. 1993—97), U.N.C. Pub. Health Alumni Assn. (life), U.N.C. Gen. Alumni Assn. (life), Ohio State U. Alumni Assn. (life), Altrusa Internat. (pres. Raleigh club 1973—74, 1973—74, dir. 1976—78, Internat. vocat. svcs. chmn. 1977—79, 1st vice gov. 1978—79, dist. Three gov. 1979—81, chmn. nomination com. 1980—82, 1st v.p. 1985—87, 1st v.p. 1985—87, pres.-elect 1987—89, pres. 1989—91, 1989—91, past pres. 1991—92, pres. 1991—93, pres. Raleigh club 2005—08, 2010—11, chmn. nomination com. 2010—11, 2010—, internat. nominating comm. mem. 2012—, Triangle Bus. Jour. Women in Bus. award 2002), Kappa Omicron Nu. Achievements include olympic torchbearer, 1996. Home and Office: 4208 Galax Dr Raleigh NC 27612-3714 Home Phone: 919-787-2949. Business E-Mail: barbara-ann@bahughes.com.

HUGHES, BILL, lobbyist, former legislative staff member; b. Aberdeen, SD, Apr. 15, 1959; BS, Augustana Coll., Sioux Falls, SD, 1981; MA, Lyndon B. Johnson Sch. Public Affairs, U. Tex., 1983. Budget examiner, transp. br. Office Mgmt. & Budget (OMB), Exec. Office of the Pres., 1983—85; sr. analyst US Senate Budget Com., 1985—90; profl. staff mem. US Senate Subcommittee on Aviation, 1993—94; Republican staff dir. US Senate Commerce, Sci. & Transp. Com., 2009; Republican profl. staff mem. US House Public Works & Transp. Com., 1995—99, profl. staff mem. budget & economic devel., 1999—2001; spl. asst. for policy, then policy dir., Office of Spkr. US House of Representatives, 2001—07; staff dir. US Senate Republican Policy Com., 2007—08; chief of staff to Senator Kay Bailey Hutchison US Senate, 2010—13; sr. v.p. govt. affairs Retail Industry Leaders Assn. (RILA), Washington, 2013—. Republican. Office: Retail Industry Leaders Assn (RILA) 1700 N Moore St Ste 2250 Arlington VA 22209 Office Phone: 703-600-2012. Office Fax: 703-841-1184. E-mail: bill.hughes@rila.org.*

HUGHES, BRYAN, state legislator; b. July 21, 1961; Attended, Tyler Jr. Coll., Tex., U. Tex., Tyler; JD, Baylor U. Sch. Law, 1995. Briefing atty. to Judge William M. Steger US Dist. Ct.; pvt. practice atty. Marshall, Tex., Mineola, Tex.; mem. Dist. 5 Tex. House of Representatives, 2002—. Bd. trustee Steward's Found. Mem.: NRA, Rotary Club of Mineola. Republican. Office: 701 N Pacific Ave PO Box 450 Mineola TX 75773 also: Room E1.404 Capitol Extension PO Box 2910 Austin TX 78768 also: Harrison County Annex PO Box 2910 Austin TX 78768-2910 Office Phone: 903-935-1141, 903-569-8880, 512-463-0271.

HUGHES, DAN, professional basketball coach; m. Mary Hughes; children: Sara, Bryce. Grad. in Phys. Edn. and Hist., Muskingum Coll., New Concord, Ohio, 1977; MEd, Miami U., Ohio, 1978. Grad. asst. Miami U., Ohio, 1977—78; asst. coach men's basketball Mt. Union Coll., 1982—84, 1985—91, Baldwin-Wallace Coll., 1984—85, U. Toledo, 1991—96, asst. coach women's basketball, 1996—97; asst. coach Charlotte Sting, 1999, head coach, 1999, Cleve. Rockers, 2000—03; asst. commr. men's basketball ops. Mid-Am. Conf.; head coach, gen. mgr. San Antonio Silver Stars, 2005—. Named Coach of Yr., WNBA, 2001, 2007. Office: San Antonio Silver Stars One AT&T Ctr San Antonio TX 78219

HUGHES, DAVID MICHAEL, rancher; b. Knoxville, Tenn., Mar. 20, 1939; s. Cleo L. and Lucille (Farmer) H.; m. Louise Love, Mar. 17, 1960 (div. 1971); children: David Michael Jr., Sheryl Lynn; m. Elizabeth Grove, Mar. 16, 1974; children: Christopher Grove, Andrew Carter. BCE, U. Tenn., 1962. Founder, owner World Wide Divers, Inc., Morgan City, La., 1962-69; founder, past chmn. bd. Oceaneering International, Inc., Houston, 1969-90; founder, owner Broken Arrow Ranch, Ingram, Tex., 1975—; founder, pres. Tex. Wild Game Coop., Ingram, 1981, Game Ranching, Inc., Ingram, 1986. Founder, former chmn. Oceaneering Internat., Inc., 1969—1990, bd. dirs. 1969-. Author: Broken Arrow Ranch Cookbook, 1984; patentee underwater corrosion meter, underwater camera and a device for identifying a characteristic of an object or the contents of a container. Chmn. Hist. Preservation Com., Ingram, 1986—; mem. Adv. Coun. Tex. Marine Sci. Inst., 1980-91; hon. chmn. Hunters for the Hungry, 1991—, nat. chmn. Named "Who's Who in Tex. Food and Wine", Dallas Morning News Poll, 1992; named industry pioneer Offshore Energy Hall of Fame, 1999. Mem. Assn. Diving Contractors (pres. 1967-71, Galletti award 1981), Exotic Wildlife Assn. (pres. 1987-89), Chi Epsilon (nat. conv. del. 1961). Republican. Avocations: woodworking, cooking. Home: Broken Arrow Ranch Inc PO Box 530 Ingram TX 78025-0530 Office: Broken Arrow Ranch Inc 3296 Junction Hwy Ingram TX 78025 Business E-Mail: dhughes@oceaneering.com.

HUGHES, GRACE-FLORES, federal agency administrator; b. Taft, Tex., June 11, 1946; d. Adan Flores and Catalina San Miguel; m. Harley Arnold Hughes, May 25, 1980. BA, U. D.C., 1977; MPA, Harvard U., 1980. Sec. Dept. Air Force Kelly AFB, San Antonio, 1967-70, Pentagon-Office Sec. of Def., Washington, 1970-72; program asst., social sci. analyst HEW, Washington, 1972-78; social sci. analyst, acting dir. Office Hispanic Ams. HHS, Washington, 1978-81; vis. prof. Nebr. Wesleyan U., Lincoln, 1982-83, U. Nebr., Omaha, 1984; spl. asst. SBA, Washington, 1985-88, assoc. adminstr. for minority small bus., 1988; dir. community rels. Dept. Justice, Washington, 1988-92; pres. Grace, Inc., Alexandria, Va., 1996—98; v.p. for intergovtl. affairs USTAK, LLCcs., Inc.; v.p. TFS & Assoc., 2002—08. Spl. asst. Reagan/Bush '84 Campaign, Nebr. and Washington, 1984, 50th Presdl. Inaugural, Washington, 1984-85, Office Pub. Liaison, The White House, 1985. Author: The Bureaucrat, Categorized Workforce, 1992; co-author: New Book of Knowledge, 1980; chair adv. bd. Harvard Jour. Hispanic Policy, 1989—; The Use and Abuse of Diversity Mag., 1994, Hispanic Mag., 1996. Adv. mem. U.S. Senate Rep. Task Force, Washington, 1988-91; alumni exec. bd. J.F. Kennedy Sch. Govt., Harvard U., Cambridge, Mass., 1989-93; mem. Rep. Hispanic Assembly, 1984—; apptd. by Gov. Allen of Va. to Bd. for Profl. and Occpl. Regulations, 1994—, Bd. for Agr. and Consumer Svcs., 1997—; bd. dirs. Hispanic Found. for Arts; apptd. by Pres. Bush Fed. Svc. Impasses Panel, 2000. Recipient Excellence award Nev. Econ. Devel. Corp., 1988, Leadership award Am. GI Forum, Omaha, 1989; named one of 100 Most Influential Hispanics in U.S. Hispanic Bus. Mag., 1988. Mem. Assn. Pub. Adminstrs. (Outstanding Pub. Svc. award 1990), Hispanic Bus. Roundtable, Coun. in Excellence in Govt. (prin.), Fedn. Rep. Women, Mex.-Am. Women's Nat. Assn., Univ. Club (Washington). Episcopalian. Avocations: tennis, jogging, aerobics, equestrian. Home and Office: 5208 Bedlington Ter Alexandria VA 22304-3551 Office Phone: 703-395-2863. E-mail: harley45@aol.com.

HUGHES, JAMES R., marketing executive; Various mgmt. positions Belden Wire & Cable, 1983—95; sr. v.p., North Am. Broadband Sales and Mktg. CommScope Inc., 1997—2005; exec. v.p., Broadband Sales and Mktg. CommScope, Inc., 2005—. Office: CommScope Inc 1100 CommScope Pl SE Hickory NC 28602 Mailing: CommScope Inc PO Box 339 Hickory NC 28602 Office Phone: 828-324-2200. Office Fax: 828-982-1708. Business E-Mail: jhughes@commscope.com.

HUGHES, JEFFERSON D., III, state supreme court justice; BA with honors in history, La. State U., JD. Law clk. to Judge Frank Polozola; atty. Adcock, Dupree, and Shows, Baton Rouge; pvt. practice atty. Walker, La.; judge 21st Jud. Dist. Ct., 1990—2004, La. Ct. Appeal, First Cir., Baton Rouge, 2004—12; assoc. justice La. Supreme Ct., New Orleans, 2013—. Mem. Shady Bower Ch., Walker, La. Office: Louisiana Supreme Ct 400 Royal St New Orleans LA 70130

HUGHES, JOHN W., lawyer, mediator; b. Tyler, Tex., Dec. 18, 1941; BBA in Acctg., Tex. Christian U., Fort Worth, 1965; JD, Baylor U. Sch. Law, Waco, Tex., 1967. Bar: Tex., Tex. Supreme Ct. 1967, US Dist. Ct. (no. dist.) Tex. 1970, US Dist. Ct. (ea. dist.) Okla. 1971, US Ct. Appeals (5th cir.) 1972, US Ct. Appeals (10th cir.) 1974, US Supreme Ct. 1975, US Dist. Ct. (so. dist.) Tex. 1976, cert.: Dispute Resolution Services Tarrant County, Tex. (in family law mediation) 1992. Atty. Hardwick & Pope, Kelly Jacobs and Simon & Simon, Fort Worth, Tex., 1967—80; founder, ptnr. Hughes & Langston, 1980—84; oil & gas, real estate and mfg. businessman, 1984—91; atty. Simon, Anisman, Doby, Wilson & Skillern, 1991—96; mediator Garrison & Hughes, 1996—2000; sole practitioner in mediation and arbitration Fort Worth, 2000—. Named Attorneys of Excellence by Fort Worth Bus. Press, 2003—10, Best Lawyers in Fort Worth, 2003—13, Best Lawyers in America, 2008—13, America's Most Honored Professionals, 2012, Tex. Lawyers' Tex. Best, 2012; named a Tex. Super Lawyer, Tex. Monthly, 2003—12; named one of Top 100 in the State of Tex.: Super Lawyers, 2009; named to Nat. Acad. of Disting. Neutrals. Fellow: Tex. Bar Found., Tarrant County Bar Found.; mem.: Tarrant County Young Lawyers Assn. (past-pres. 1970—71), American Arbitration Assn., Assn. Atty.-Mediators (pres. 2010—11), Tex. Assn. Mediators, Tarrant County Assn. Mediators, Tex. State Bar Assn., Tarrant County Bar Assn. Office: John W Hughes PC 4524 Knoll Ridge Fort Worth TX 76008 Office Phone: 817-377-4800. Office Fax: 817-291-4147. Business E-Mail: jwhughes@mediatortexas.com.*

HUGHES, KAREN PARFITT, public relations executive, former federal agency administrator; b. Paris, Dec. 27, 1956; m. Jerry L. Hughes; 1 child, Robert. BA in English, So. Meth. U., 1977, BFA in Journalism, 1977. Television reporter KXAS-TV, Dallas/Ft. Worth, Tex., 1977—84; Tex. media coord. Reagan/Bush Campaign, 1984; media cons. Rep. Party of Tex., 1985—91, exec. dir., 1991—94; dir. comm. to Gov. George W. Bush State of Tex., 1994—2001; dir. comm. Bush-Cheney campaign, 2000, adv., 2004; counselor to Pres. The White House, Washington, 2001—02; under sec. for pub. diplomacy & pub. affairs US Dept. State, Washington, 2005—07; global vice chair Burson-Marsteller, Austin, Tex., 2008—. Author: Ten Minutes From Normal, 2004. Office: 98 San Facinto Ste 1450 Austin TX 78701 Office Phone: 512-372-6363. Office Fax: 512-372-6360.

HUGHES, KEITH WILLIAM, insurance company executive; b. Cleve., July 1, 1946; s. Delmar Vern and Margaret Virginia Hughes; m. Cheryl Foster, Aug. 30, 1969; 1 child, Amy. BS, Miami U., Oxford, Ohio, 1968, MBA, 1969. Mktg. mgr. Continental Bank, 1970-73; v.p., mktg. Northwestern Nat. Bank, 1974-76; sr. v.p. Crocker Bank, 1976-81; exec. v.p., broker & dealer subs. Assocs. Corp., 1973-74, exec. v.p., dir., 1981-85, sr. exec. v.p., 1985-88, vice-chmn., 1988-91, pres., chmn & CEO, 1995-96; chmn., CEO Assocs. First Capital Corp., 1995—2000; vice chmn. Citigroup, Inc., 2000—01. Bd. dir. Fidelity Nat. Info. Svcs. Inc., Pilgrim's Pride Corp.; bd. dirs. Carreker, 2003—; bd. dir. Tex. Industries Inc., 2003—. Bd. dir. Cancer Found., Dallas Mus. of Art, Southwestern Med. Found., Children's Med. Ctr. of Dallas, Salvation Army, Dallas, United Way of Met. Dallas; chmn. Dallas campaign United Way; bd. dir. Certegy Inc., Proudfoot Consulting, Majesco; bd. dir. Cox Sch. Bus. So. Meth. U. Mem. Am. Bankers Assn., Bank Mktg. Assn., Consumers Bankers Assn., Nat. Consumer Fin. Assn., Olympic Club (San Francisco), Los Colinas Country Club (Tex.), Crescent Club (Dallas), Ocean Reef Club (Key Largo). Office: Fidelity National Information Services Inc Bd Directors 601 Riverside Ave Jacksonville FL 32204 Office Phone: 904-854-5000. Office Fax: 904-357-1105. Business E-Mail: keith.hughes@fisglobal.com.

HUGHES, LYNN NETTLETON, federal judge; m. Olive (Allen). BA, U. Ala., 1963; JD, U. Tex., 1968; LLM, U. Va., 1992. Bar: Tex., 1966. Pvt. practice, Houston, 1966-79; judge Dist. Ct. Tex., Houston, 1979-85, US Dist. Ct., Houston, 1985—. Adj. prof. South Tex. Coll. Law, 1973-03, U. Tex., 1990-91, 00-01, mem. bd. visitors, 2006-; Tex. del. Nat. Conf. State Trial Judges, 1983-85; cons. Tex. Jud. Budget Bd., 1984; lectr. Tex. Coll. Judiciary, 1983; mem. task force on revision rules of civil procedure Supreme Ct. Tex., 1993-94; cons. on constrn., European Cmty. and Eastern European Certain, 1994-97; mem. jud. adv. bd. Law and Econs. Ctr., George Mason U., 1999—, lectr. ethics, Am. Assoc. Petroleum Geologists, 2007-09. Mem. adv. bd. Houston Jour. Internat. Law, 1981—, chmn., 1989-99. Trustee Rift Valley Rsch. Mission, 1978—; mem. St. Martin's Episcopal Ch., 1951-; dir. World Affairs Coun. Houston, 1997—, co-chair 1999-2000. Mem.: FBA (bd. dirs. Houston chpt. 1986—89), Am. Inns of Ct. XV (pres. 1986—92), Houston Philos. Soc. (exec. com. 2000—03), Am. Anthrop. Assn., Am. Soc. Legal History, Tex. State Bar (selection, compensation and tenure state judges com. 1981—85, ct. cost, delay and efficiency com. 1981—90, vice chmn. 1982—83, nominations com. jud. sect. 1983, vice chmn. 1984—86, liaison with law schs. com. 1987—92, plain lang. com. 1989—96), Houston Bar Assn., Am. Law Inst., Coun. on Fgn. Rels., Houston Com. Fgn. Rels. (chmn. 2003—04). Office: US Courthouse 11122 515 Rusk Ave Houston TX 77002-2605 Home: PO Box 61565 Houston TX 77208 Office Phone: 713-250-5900. Business E-Mail: lnh@txs.uscourts.gov.

HUGHES, MIKE, advertising executive; b. Washington, May 27, 1948; s. James Richard and Ann Marie (Lucas) Hughes; m. Ginny Lee Ferguson, Apr. 12, 1975; children: Preston Ferguson(dec.), Jason Christopher. BA, Washington & Lee U., Lexington, Va., 1970. Copy editor, reporter Richmond News Leader, Va., 1965—70; reporter Richmond Times Dispatch, 1967-70; copywriter Clinton E. Frank Advt., 1971-72, Martin & Woltz Advt., Richmond, 1973; creative dir. Lawler & Ballard, Richmond, 1974; founder, ptnr. Hughes Wynne, Richmond, 1975-78; exec.v.p., creative dir. The Martin Agy., Inc., Richmond, 1978-99, vice chmn., 1986-99; pres., creative dir. Martin Agency, Inc., Richmond, 1999—. Contbr. articles to profl. jours. Mem.: Advt. Club Richmond (bd. dirs.), One Club for Copy & Art. Office: The Martin Agency Inc One Shockoe Plz Richmond VA 23219-4132 Office Phone: 804-698-8000. Office Fax: 804-698-8001. Business E-Mail: mike.hughes@martinagency.com.

HUGHES, RALPH EUGENE, management educator; BA, Lenoir Rhyne Coll., 1964; MS in Bus. Adminstrn., U. NC Greensboro, 1971; DBA in Bus. Adminstrn., U. Ky., 1975. Asst. prof. U. Wis. Oshkosh, 1974—76; assoc. prof. Miss. State U., Starkville, 1976—79; prof. W.Va. U., Morgantown, 1979—85, East Carolina U., Greenville, NC, 1985—2012, ret. prof. emeritus. Contbr. articles to profl. jours. E-4 USAF, 1958—62. E-mail: hughesr@ecu.edu.

HUGHES, SUE MARGARET, retired librarian; b. Cleburne, Tex. d. Chastain Wesley and Sue Willis (Payne) H. BBA, U. Tex., Austin, 1949; MLS, Tex. Woman's U., Denton, 1960, PhD, 1987. Sec.-treas. pvt. corps., Waco, Tex., 1949-59; asst. in public svcs. Baylor U. Libr., Waco, 1960-64, acquisitions libr., 1964-79, acting univ. libr., summer 1979, dir. Moody Libr., 1980-89; interim univ. libr. Baylor U., Waco, 1989-91, spl. materials cons., 1991-92; ret., 1992. Bd. advs. Baylor U. Libr., 2006—08. Mem. AAUP, ALA, Tex. Libr. Assn., AAUW, Brazos Forum, Hist. Waco Found., Altrusa Club, Delta Kappa Gamma, Beta Phi Mu, Beta Gamma Sigma. Methodist.

HUGHES, THOMAS JOSEPH ROBERT, mechanical engineering educator, consultant; b. Bklyn., Aug. 3, 1943; s. Joseph Anthony and Mae (Bland) H.; m. Susan Elizabeth Weh, July 1, 1972; children: Emily Susan, Ian Thomas, Elizabeth Claire. B.M.E., Pratt Inst., Bklyn., 1965; M.M.E., Pratt Inst., 1967; MA in Math., U. Calif.-Berkeley, 1974, PhD in Engring. Sci., 1974; Doctorate (hon.), U. Catholique de Louvain, Belgium, 2003, U. Pavia, Italy, 2007, U. Padua, 2007, Nat. U. Sci. & Tech., Norway, 2009, Northwestern U., 2010. Mech. design engr. Grumman Aerospace, Bethpage, NY, 1965-66; R & D Gen. Dynamics, Groton, Conn., 1967—69; lectr., asst. rsch. engr. U. Calif., Berkeley, 1975-76; assoc. prof. structural mechanics Calif. Inst. Tech., Pasadena, 1976-80; assoc. prof. mech. engring. Stanford U., Calif., 1980-82, prof. Calif., 1983—, chmn. divsn. applied mechanics, 1984-88, 94—, chmn. dept. mech. engring., 1988-89; founder, chmn. CENTRIC Engring. Sys., Inc., 1990-99; prof. aerospace engring. & engring. mechanics, computational & applied math., chair III U. Tex., Austin, 2002—. Galileo vis. prof. Scuola Normale Superiore, Pisa, Italy, 1999; Eshbach vis. prof. Northwestern U., 2000; cons. in field. Author: A Short Course in Fluid Mechanics, 1976, Mathematical Foundations of Elasticity, 1983, The Finite Element Method: Linear Static and Dynamic Finite Element Analysis, 1987, Computational Inelasticity, 1998, Isogeometric Analysis: Toward Integration of CDA and FEA, 2009; editor: Nonlinear Finite Element Analysis of Plate and Shells, 1981, Computational Methods in Transient Analysis, 1983; editor Jour. of Computer Methods in Applied Mechanics and Engring., 1980—; contbr. numerous articles to profl. jours. Recipient Computational Mechanics prize Japan Soc. Mech. Engrs., 1993. Fellow AAAS, ASME (Melville medal 1979, Worcester Reed Warner medal 1998, Timoshenko medal 2007), NAS, AIAA, ASCE (Huber prize 1978, Von Karman medal 2009), Internat. Assn. Computational Mechanics (pres. 1998-2002, Gauss-Newton medal), Am. Acad. Mechanics, U.S. Assn. Computational Mechanics (pres. 1990-92, von Neumann medal 1997), Nat. Acad. Engring, Am. Acad. Arts & Scis. (Humboldt Sr. Scientist award 2009), Inst. Lombardo, Austrian Acad. Scis.; mem. Sigma Xi, Phi Beta Kappa. Office: U Tex at Austin 1 University Sta C0200 201 E 24th St ACES 6 412 Austin TX 78712-0027 Business E-Mail: hughes@ices.utexas.edu.

HUGHES, THOMAS MORGAN, III, circuit judge; b. Racine, Wis., June 14, 1949; s. Thomas Morgan and Rosemary (Navratil) Hughes; m. Teresa Lee Cloud, Aug. 10, 1974; 1 child, Gwyneth Leigh. BBA, U. Wis.-Madison, 1971; JD, St. Louis U., 1974. Bar: Ark. 1974, US Dist. Ct. (ea. dist.) Ark. 1974. Sole practice, Beebe, Ark., 1974—78; ptnr. Hughes & Hughes, Searcy, Ark., 1978—2008; instr. Ark. State U., Beebe, 1975; city atty. City of Beebe, 1975—76; treas. Beebe Indsl. Devel. Corp., 1983—; judge City Ct., Beebe, 1985—87, Beebe Mcpl. Ct., 1987—2002, White County dist., 2002—04. Mem.: Beebe C. of C. (pres. 1984—), White County Bar Assn. (pres. 1996), Kiwanis (pres. 1981—82, bd. dirs. 1979—). Independent. Office: Circuit Judge 17 Divsn 1 Wilbur D Mills Courts Bldg 301 W Arch Ave Searcy AR 72143 Office Phone: 501-279-6219.

HUGHES, WALTER THOMPSON, pediatrician, educator; b. Cleve., May 16, 1930; s. Walter Thompson and Millie Hasentine (Collette) H.; m. Frances J. Skinner, Nov. 24, 1957; children: Carla, Gregory, Christopher. MD, U. Tenn., 1954. Diplomate Am. Bd. Pediatrics. Resident in pediatrics U. Tenn. Coll. Medicine, Memphis, 1955-57, prof. pediatrics and microbiology, 1969-77, prof. pediatrics, 1981—; mem. St. Jude Children's Rsch. Hosp., Memphis, 1969-77, mem., chair dept. infectious diseases, 1981-95; mem. staff Walter Reed Army Med. Ctr., Ft. Detrick, Md., 1957-59; pvt. practice pediatrics Cleve., 1959-61; instr. to prof. U. Louisville Sch. Medicine, 1961-69; Eudowood prof. pediatrics, dir. div. infectious diseases Johns Hopkins U. Sch. Medicine, Balt., 1977-81; Arthur Ashe chair in pediat. AIDS rsch. St. Jude Children's Rsch. Hosp., Memphis, 1993-98, emeritus mem., 1998—. Capt. U.S. Army, 1957-59. Fellow Am. Acad. Pediatrics; mem. Am. Pediatric Soc., Infectious Diseases Soc. Am., Soc. Pediatric Rsch., Pediatric Infectious Diseases Soc. (pres. 1983-85). Republican. Methodist. Home: 854 River Park Dr Memphis TN 38103-0804 Office: Saint Jude Childrens Rsch Hosp 262 Danny Thomas Pl Memphis TN 38105-3678 Home Phone: 901-528-9460; Office Phone: 901-495-3485. Personal E-mail: fhu5774238@aol.com. Business E-Mail: walter.hughes@stjude.org.

HUGHES ABRAMSON, LISABETH, state supreme court justice; m. Leslie W. Abramson; 3 children. B with highest honors, U. Louisville, 1977; JD magna cum laude, U. Louisville Sch. Law, 1980. Pvt. practice, bus. and comml. litig.; judge Ky. Ct. of Appeals, 1997—98, 2006—07, Ky. 30th Jud. Cir., 1999—2006; assoc. justice Ky. State Supreme Ct., 4th Dist., 2007—. Lectr. Ky. Cir. Judges Jud. Coll. Past pres. U. Louisville Brandeis Sch. Law Alumni Coun.; trustee Ky. Jud. Form Retirement Sys. Bd. Mem.: ABA, Louisville Bar Assn., Ky. Bar. Assn. Office: Kentucky Supreme Ct Jefferson County Jud Ctr 700 W Jefferson St Ste 1000 Louisville KY 40202-4737 also: 4th Supreme Ct Dist State Capitol 700 Capitol Ave Frankfort KY 40601 Office Phone: 502-595-3199.*

HUGHES HALLETT, ANDREW, economist, educator; b. London, Nov. 1, 1947; permanent resident, USA, 2006; s. Charles and Joyce (Cobbold) Hughes Hallett; m. Claudia Becker, July 22, 1982; children: David, James, Nicola. BA with honors, U. Warwick, Eng., 1969; MS in Econs., London Sch. Econs., 1971; DPhil, U. Oxford, 1977. Lectr. U. Bristol, Eng., 1973-77; assoc. prof. Erasmus U., Rotterdam, Netherlands, 1977-85; prof. U. Newcastle-upon-Tyne, Newcastle, Eng., 1985-89, Princeton U., 1992-94, U. Strathclyde, Glasgow, Scotland, 1989—2001, Vanderbilt U., 2001—06, George Mason U., Fairfax, Va., 2006—, U. St. Andrews, Scotland, 2007—, Harvard U., 2012—13. Consul European Cmty., Brussels, 1982—, World Bank, Washington; fellow Ctr Econ Policy Research, London, 1985—2010; scholar, consul IMF, Washington, 1994—2001; consul on policy to various govts and nat banks; council econ. advisors Govt. Scotland. Author economic framework for independence, (book) Stabilising Speculative Commodity Markets, 1987; author: (editor) Fiscal Aspects of European Monetary Union, 1999, Challenges for Economic Coordination in European Monetary Union, 2001, The Theory of Economic Policy in a Strategic Context, 2013; editor: Scottish Jour.

Polit. Economics, 1998—2011; mem. editl. bd. 6 acad./profl. jours.; contbr. articles to profl. jours. Expert witness Ho. of Parliament, 1997, 2003, 2010, HM Treasury, 2003; selector Govt Econ Svc, London, 1988—2000; advisor UK Govt. Commn. Devolution, 2008—09. Fulbright scholar, 1992, 1993, sr. assoc., St. Anthony's Coll., Oxford U., sr. fellow, U. Bonn, 2000. Fellow: Royal Soc. Edinburgh (chmn. econ. panel); mem.: Royal Econs. Soc., European Econ. Assn., Am. Econ. Assn., Scottish Econ. Soc. (mem coun 1999—). Avocations: history, hiking. Office: George Mason University Sch Pub Policy 3351 Fairfax Dr MS 3B1 Arlington VA 22201 Office Phone: 703-993-2280. Business E-Mail: ahughesh@gmu.edu.*

HUGLEY, CAROLYN F., state legislator; b. Forrest City, Ark., May 2, 1958; m. Isaiah Hugley; children: Isaiah Jr., Kimberly. Student, U. Ark.; BA in Polit. Sci., Miss. State U., MPA. Former mem. Dist. 113 Ga. House of Reps., mem. Dist. 133, 1993—, minority whip, mem. ethics com., ins. com., rules com., appropriations com. Chair Lower Chattahoochee Area Workforce Investment Bd. Bd. dirs. Liberty Theatre, Greater Ga. Chpt. Alzheimer's Assn. Democrat. Baptist. Mailing: 614 Legis Off Bldg Atlanta GA 30334 Office: 4019 Steam Mill Rd Columbus GA 31907 Office Phone: 706-687-4327, 404-656-3947. E-mail: chugley@legis.state.ga.us.

HUGO, TIMOTHY D., state legislator; b. Norfolk, Va., Jan. 7, 1963; m. Paula Mary Goggin; children: Katie, Christopher, Jackie. BA in Govt. Rels., Coll. William & Mary, Va., 1986. Tech. govt. rels. profl.; mem. Dist. 40 Va. House of Delegates, 2004—. Served with USAR, 1990—98. Republican. Office: PO Box 893 Centreville VA 20122 Office Phone: 703-968-4101. Business E-Mail: DelTHugo@house.virginia.gov.

HUITT, JIMMIE L., rancher, oil and gas industry executive, real estate developer; b. Gurdon, Ark., Aug. 21, 1923; s. John Wesley and Almedia (Hatten) H.; m. Janis C. Mann, Oct. 30, 1945; children—Jimmie L., Jr., Allan Jerome BS in Chem. Engring., La. Tech. U., 1944; MS in Chem. Engring., U. Okla., 1948, PhD, 1951. Research engr. Mobil Oil Corp., Dallas, 1951-56, Gulf Research Co., Pitts., 1956-67; ops. coordinator Kuwait Oil Co., London, 1967-71; gen. mgr. Gulf Oil-Zaire, Kinshasa, 1971-74; mng. dir. Gulf Oil-Nigeria, Lagos, 1974-76; sr. v.p., exec. v.p. Gulf Oil Exploration and Prodn. Co., Houston, 1976-81, pres., CEO, 1981—85; rancher Four Jays Ranch, Industry, Tex., 1986—. Contbr. articles to profl. jours.; patentee in field Served to 1st lt. U.S. Army, 1944-47 Mem. Soc. Petroleum Engrs. (chmn. various coms. 1956—), Masons, Shriners. Republican. Office: Four Jays Ranch PO Box 236 Industry TX 78944-0236

HUIZENGA, WAYNE (HARRY WAYNE HUIZENGA), entrepreneur, professional sports team owner; b. Evergreen Park, Ill., Dec. 29, 1939; s. G. Harry and Jean (Riddering) Huizenga; m. Martha Jean Pike, Apr. 17, 1972; children: H. Wayne Jr., H. Scott, Ray, Pamela Ann. Student, Calvin Coll., 1957-58. Vice chmn., pres., COO Waste Management, Inc., Oak Brook, Ill., 1968-84; chmn. Huizenga Holdings, Inc., Ft. Lauderdale, Fla., 1984—; chmn., CEO Blockbuster Entertainment Corp., Ft. Lauderdale, 1987-94; co-owner Miami Dolphins, 1990—93, 2008—09, owner, 1993—2008, minority owner, 2009—; owner Fla. Marlins, Miami, 1992-99, Fla. Panthers, Sunrise, Fla., 1993—2001; chmn. Boca Resorts, Inc., Boca Raton, Fla., 1996—2004, AutoNation, Inc., Ft. Lauderdale, 1994—2002. Mem. Fla. Victory Com., 1988-89, Team Repub. Nat. Com., Washington, 1988-90; organizer Broward Victory 90 PAC, Ft. Lauderdale, 1989-90. Recipient Entrepreneur of Yr. award Wharton Sch. U. Pa., 1989, Excalibur Award Bus. Leader of Yr. News/Sun Sentinel, 1990, Silver Medallion Brotherhood award Broward Region Nat. Conf. Christians and Jews, 1990, Laureates award Jr. Achievement Broward and Palm Beach Counties, 1990, Jim Murphy Humanitarian Award The Emerald Soc., 1990, Entrepreneur of Yr. award Disting. Panel Judges Fla., 1990, Man of Yr. Billboard/Time Mag., 1990, Man of Yr. Juvenile Diabetes Found., 1990, Fla. Free Enterpriser of Yr. award Fla. Coun. on Econ. Edn., 1990, commendation for youth restricted video State of Fla. Office of Gov., 1989, Hon. Mem. Appreciation award Bond Club Ft. Lauderdale, 1989; named one of Forbes 400: Richest Americans, 2006-; honored with endowed teaching chair Broward Community Coll., 1990. Mem. Lauderdale Yacht Club, Tournament Players Club, Fisher Island Club, Ocean Reef Club, Cat Cay Yacht Club, Coral Ridge Country Club, Linville Ridge Country Club. Avocations: golf, collecting antique cars. Office: Huizenga Holdings 450 E Las Olas Blvd Ste 1500 Fort Lauderdale FL 33301-4212

HUKILL, DOROTHY L., state legislator; b. NYC, Sept. 20, 1946; 1 child, Jonathan. BA, CUNY: Hunter Coll., NYC, 1967; MA, Columbia U., NYC, 1970; JD, St. John's U., Queens, NY, 1978. Atty.; councilwoman Town of Ponce Inlet, Fla., 1992—94; vice mayor, councilwoman City of Port Orange, 1998—99, mayor, 2000—04; mem. Dist. 28 Fla. House of Reps., Tallahassee, 2005—, chair mil. and local affairs policy com., mem. econ. devel. and cmty. affairs policy coun., health care regulation policy com., policy coun., select policy coun. on strategic & econ. planning, mem. transp. and econ. devel. appropriations com. Vice chair, past chair Volusia County Legis. Del., 2005—06. Mem.: Volusia Coun. Govts., Volusia League of Cities, Volusia/Flagler Assn. Women Lawyers, Volusia County Bar Assn., Fla. Bar Assn. Republican. Protestant. Office: 1398 Dunlawton Ave Ste 1-A Port Orange FL 32127-8915 also: 200 House Office Bldg 402 S Monroe St Tallahassee FL 32399 Office Phone: 386-322-5111, 850-488-6653.

HULBERT, MARK J., columnist; B, Haverford Coll., Pa., 1977. Fin. columnist New York Times Co.; founder, pres. Hulbert Fin. Digest Inc., Annandale, Va., 1983—2002; columnist MarketWatch-.com (acquired Hulbert Financial Digest, Inc.), 2002—, Barron's Online, 2004—. Co-author: Interlock: The Untold Story of American Banks, Oil Interests, the Shah's Money, Debts & the Astounding Connections Between Them, 1982, Hulbert Guide to Financial Newsletters, 1993. Bd. trustees Sidwell Friends Sch. Office: Hulbert Financial Digest Inc MarketWatch 8001 Braddock Rd Ste 107 Springfield VA 22151-2110 Office Phone: 703-750-9060. Office Fax: 703-770-9210. Business E-Mail: mhulbert@marketwatch.com.

HULBERT, STEPHEN THOMPSON, academic administrator; BS in Edn., Worcester State Coll., Mass., 1966; MEd, U. Mass., Amherst, 1968; DEd, SUNY, Albany, 1972. Dir. student activities and residence life Western New England Coll., Springfield, Mass., 1968-70; cons. Univ. Assocs. Inc., Washington, 1971-72; exec. asst. to the pres. Mansfield (Pa.) U., 1972-77; v.p. for fin. and adminstrn. Slippery Rock (Pa.) U., 1977-88; v.p. adminstrv. svcs., treas. bd. trustees U. Northern Colo., Greeley, 1988-91, interim pres., 1991, sr. v.p., 1992-94, provost, v.p. for acad. affairs, 1994-96; commr. higher edn., CEO R.I. Bd. of Govs. for Higher Edn., Providence, 1996-99; chancellor U. Mont.-Western, Dillon, 1999—2003; pres. Nicholls (La.) State U., 2003—. Bd. dirs. La. Campus Compact; bd. chair Marm Sura Consotorium. Mcpl. coun. Grove City, Pa., 1986-88; adv. bd. Franklin Regional Hosp., Franklin, Pa., 1985-88; mem. exec. bd. Longs Peak coun. Boy Scouts Am., 1991-96, disting. citizen com. chair, 1992, others; mayor's adv. task force City of Greeley, 1992-96, U. No. Colo. Found., Inc., 1991-96, R.I. Children's Crusade Higher Edn., 1996-99, U. No. Colo. Rsch. Corp., Inc., 1988-96, chair 1994-96, vice chair 1992-94, corp. treas. 1988-92; steering com. Edn. Comms., 1988—99; bd. govs. Colo. Alliance for Sci., 1995-96. Mem. Nat. Assn. Intercollegiate Athletics (coun. pres.), Frontier Athletic Conf. (chair coun. pres. 2000-03), Southland Conf. (bd. dirs. 2003-, bd. chair 2008-). Office: Nicholls State U PO Box 2001 Thibodaux LA 70310 Home: 111 Acadia Dr Thibodaux LA 70301 Office Phone: 985-448-4003. Business E-Mail: stephen.hulbert@nicholls.edu.

HULET, RANDALL GARDNER, physics professor; b. Walnut Creek, Calif., Apr. 27, 1956; s. Ervin Kenneth and Betty Jo (Gardner) H.; m. Lourdes Teresa Hernandez, Aug. 16, 1980; children: Benjamin Hernandez, Gabriella Alison. BS in Physics, Stanford U., 1978; PhD in Physics, MIT, 1984; PhD (hon.), Utrecht Univ., 2002. Rsch. asst. MIT, Cambridge, Mass., 1978-84, rsch. assoc., 1984-85; Nat. Rsch. Coun. postdoctoral fellow Nat. Inst. Standards and Tech., Boulder, Colo., 1985-87; asst. prof. physics Rice U., Houston, 1987-92, assoc. prof. physics, 1992-96, prof., 1996-99, Fayez Sarofim prof. physics, 1999—. Contbr. articles to profl. jours. Alfred P. Sloan fellow, 1988; Nat. Inst. Standards and Tech. grantee, 1988-91; recipient Presdl. Young Investigator's award NSF, 1989, Exceptional Sci. Achievement medal NASA, 2004, Willis Lamb award, Laser Sci. & Quantum Optics, 2011. Fellow: AAAS, Am. Phys. Soc. (I.I. Rabi prize 1995); mem.: Am. Acad. Arts and Scis. Office: Rice U Dept Physics and Astronomy MS61 Houston TX 77251 Business E-Mail: randy@rice.edu.

HULKA, JAROSLAV FABIAN, obstetrician, gynecologist; b. NYC, Sept. 29, 1930; s. Jaroslav Hugo and Milada (Touskova) H.; m. Barbara E. Sorenson, Nov. 13, 1954; children— Carol Ann, Gregory Fabian, Bryan Herbert. BA, Harvard U., 1952; MD, Columbia U., 1956. Diplomate: Am. Bd. Ob-Gyn. Intern Roosevelt Hosp., NYC, 1956-57; resident Sloane Hosp. for Women, Columbia-Presbyn. Med. Center, NYC, 1957-60; Josiah Macy, Jr. fellow Columbia-Presbyn. Med. Center, 1960-61; practice medicine specializing in Ob-Gyn, 1961—; asst. prof. Ob-Gyn U. Pitts. Sch. Medicine, 1961-66, asso. mem. grad. faculty, 1962-66, acting chmn. dept. ob-Gyn, 1963-64; assoc. prof. dept. ob-Gyn Sch. Medicine, U. N.C., Chapel Hill, 1967-76, prof. dept. ob-Gyn and dept. maternal and child health, 1976-96, prof. emeritus dept. ob-gyn.; prof. emeritus dept. maternal and child health U. N.C. Sch. Pub. Health, Chapel Hill. Author: Textbook of Laparoscopy, 1985, 3d edit., 1997; patentee in field. Assoc. dir. Carolina Population Center, 1967-74. Recipient Excel award Soc. of Laparoendoscopic Surgeons, 1994. Fellow ACOG; mem. Soc. for Gynecol. Investigation, Am. Assn. Gynecol. Laparoscopists (pres. 1980), Am. Fertility Soc., Soc. Reproductive Surgeons (founding), N.C. State Bar (bd. legal specialization 1990-96), Planned Parenthood Fed. Am. (chair nat. med. com. 1991-94), Soc. Physicians for Reproductive Choice and Health (founding). Achievements include development of and teaching of worldwide use of clips for female sterilization by laparoscopy; demonstration of local anesthesia for safer procedures. Home: 2317 Honeysuckle Rd Chapel Hill NC 27514-1716 Personal E-mail: jhulka@unc.edu.

HULL, CHARLES WILLIAM, retired special education educator; b. East St. Louis, Ill., Feb. 23, 1936; s. William Semple Hull and Jessie Marie (Brennan) Poole; m. Beverly Kay Julian, Aug. 19, 1967; 1 child, William Kenneth. BA in Econs., Cen. Meth. Coll., 1964; MEd, Olivet Nazarene Coll., 1974; AA (hon.), Joliet Jr. Coll., 1987. Tchr. elem. grades Taft Sch., Lockport, Ill., 1965-67; tchr. spl. edn. S.W. Cook County Coop. Assn. Spl. Edn., Oak Forest, Ill., 1967-99; ret., 1999. Represented in permanent collections Tchr.'s Ret. Office Bldg., Springfield, Ill. Mem. Nat. Trust Hist. Preservation; past bd. dirs., v.p., chmn. fund raising Easter Seals Will and Grundy Counties; dist. leader Am. Cancer Soc., 1984, residential campaign chmn., 1985; vol., mem. adv. bd. Big Bros.-Big Sisters Will County; mem. Cub Scouts com. Boy Scouts Am., 1980—81, commr. Rainbow coun., bd. dirs. troop 61; Will County walkathon chmn. March of Dimes, 1979; chmn. Canal Days events Will County Hist. Soc., 1987, pres., 1989; mem. Lockport Area Geneal. Hist. Soc.; bd. dirs. Joliet Project Pride, Will G. Project Pride, 2000—06; life mem. Friends Ill. and Mich. Canal; mem. Pleasant Hill Hist. Soc., Cumberland County Farm Bur., Tenn., 2005—06; choir, past trustee Faith United Meth. Ch. With USMC, 1955—58. Recipient Congl. medal of Merit, 1985, Frederick Bartleson Meml. award, Will County Hist. Soc., 1985, Citizen of the Week award, Sta. WBBM, Chgo., 1985, Leadership award, Am. Cancer Soc., 1985, Outstanding Svc. award, Big Bros.-Big Sisters Will County, letter of commendation, Pres. of U.S., 1986, 1989, Disting. Svc. award, Joliet Jr. Coll., 1987, Citizen of the Month award, Southtown Economist; named to Joliet/Will County Hall of Pride, 2002. Mem.: KC (plaque), Tenn. Hist. Soc., Ill. Ret. Tchrs. Assn., Will County Old-Timers Baseball Assn., Coalition Citizens with Disabilities Ill. (life), White County Hist. Soc. (life), 1st Marine Divsn. Assn., Joliet Area Ret. Tchrs. Assn., Royal Order Scotland, Lions (pres. Manhattan club 1984, chmn. youth and fgn. exch. dist. 1986—87, bd. dirs. Lockport chpt.), Scottish Rite Club, Medina Temple, Shriners (pres. Joliet club 1983, Shriner of the Yr. 1989), Am. Legion, Masons (life 32 degree). Republican. Methodist. Home: PO Box 429 Pleasant Hill TN 38578 E-mail: chull@frontier.com.

HULL, DAVID GEORGE, aerospace engineering educator, researcher; b. Oak Park, Ill., Mar. 27, 1937; s. John Lawrence Hull and Elizabeth Christine (Carstensen) Meyer; m. Meredith Lynn Kiesel, June 2, 1962 (div. July 1980); children: David, Andrew, Matthew; m. Vicki Jan Poole, June 30, 1983; children: Katherine, Emily. BS, Purdue U., 1959; MS, U. Wash., 1962; PhD, Rice U., 1967. Staff assoc. Boeing Sci. Research Labs., Seattle, 1959-64; research assoc. Rice U., Houston, 1964-66; asst. prof. U. Tex., Austin, 1966-71, assoc. prof., 1971-77, prof., 1977-85, M.J. Thompson Regents prof., 1985—. Cons. several aerospace cos. Co-editor-in-chief: JOTA; author: Optimal Control Theory for Applications, 2003; author: Fundamentals of Airplane Flight Mechanics, 2007; reviewer several engring. jours.; contbr. over 61 articles to profl. jours. Recipient/co-recipient more than 50 grants and contracts; recipient award Best paper, AAS/AIAA Space Flt. Mechanics Conf., Albuquerque, 1995. Fellow AAS, AIAA (assoc., atmospheric flight mechanics tech. com. 1974-77, guidance and control tech. com. 1984-87); mem. Delta Tau Delta (treas. Purdue U. 1958-59) Office: U Tex ASE/EM C0600 Austin TX 78712-0235 Office Phone: 512-471-4908. Business E-Mail: dghull@mail.utexas.edu.

HULL, ELAINE MANGELSDORF, psychology neuroscience professor; b. Houston, Aug. 15, 1940; d. Paul August and Mary Eleanor (Stephens) Mangelsdorf; m. Richard Thompson Hull, May 30, 1962; 1 child, Geoffrey Alaric (dec.). BA, Austin Coll., Sherman, Tex., 1963; PhD, Ind. U., 1967. Asst. prof. psychology SUNY, Buffalo, 1967-73, assoc. prof., 1973-86, prof., 1986—2004, dir. biopsychology grad. program, 1996—2004; prof. psychology Fla. State U., Tallahassee, 2004—. Contbr., articles to sci. jours., chapters to books. Recipient Chancellor's award for excellence in teaching SUNY, Buffalo, 1975, Tchg. award, SUNY Students Assn., 1986, N.Y. State Union Univ. Profls. Excellence award 1990, Disting. Alumna award Austin Coll., 2004; grantee NIMH, 1974, 80, 84, 86, 93, 96, 2000, 01, 07, NSF, 1992. Mem. APA, AAAS, Am. Psycol. Soc., Internat. Acad. Sex Rsch., Soc. Neurosci., Internat. Soc. Psychoneuroendocrinology, NY Acad. Scis., Phi Beta Kappa. Democrat. Avocations: jogging, classical music. Office: Fla State Univ Psychol Tallahassee FL 32306 Home Phone: 850-893-6539; Office Phone: 850-645-2389. E-mail: hull@psy.fsu.edu.

HULL, FRANK MAYS, federal judge; b. Augusta, Ga., Dec. 9, 1948; d. James M. Hull Jr. and Frank (Mays) Pride; m. Antonin Aeck, Apr. 16, 1977; children: Richard Hull Aeck, Molly Hull Aeck. AB, Randolph-Macon Women's Coll., 1970; JD cum laude, Emory U., 1973. Bar: Ga. 1973, US Ct. Appeals (5th cir.) 1973, US Dist. Ct. (no. dist.) Ga. 1974, US Ct. Appeals (11th cir.) 1982. Law clk. to Hon. Elbert P. Tuttle US Ct. Appeals (5th cir.), Atlanta, 1973—74; assoc. Powell, Goldstein, Frazer & Murphy, Atlanta, 1974—80, ptnr., 1980—84; judge State Ct. Fulton County, Atlanta, 1984—90, Superior Ct. Fulton County, Atlanta, 1990—94, US Dist. Ct. (no. dist.) Ga., 1994—97, US Ct. Appeals (11th cir.), 1997—. Mem. commn. on family violence State of Ga., 1992—94, commn. on gender bias in jud. sys., 1988—90. Mem. Leadership Atlanta, 1986—, program co-chair criminal justice com., 1988—89; Sunday sch. tchr. Cathedral St. Philip, Atlanta, 1983—88, children's com., 1981—82, outreach com., 1989—91; bd. dirs. Met. Atlanta Mediation Ctr., Inc., 1976—79, Atlanta Vol. Lawyers Assn., 1988—91. Fellow, AAUW, 1973—. Mem.: ABA (fin. sec. long range planning com. tort and ins. practice sect. 1979—82, chmn. contract documents divsn., forum com. on constrn. industry 1983—85, editl. staff jour. 1981—85, vice chmn. fidelity and surety law com. 1978—85), Nat. Assn. Women Judges, Ga. Assn. Women Lawyers, Atlanta Bar Assn., Am. Judicature Soc. (bd. dirs. 1990—96), Ga. Bar Assn., Order of Coif. Office: US Ct of Appeals 56 Forsyth St NW Rm 300 Atlanta GA 30303-2289

HULL, ROBERT F., JR., (BOB HULL), consumer products company executive; B in Acctg., U. N.C., Charlotte, BBA. CPA. Controller Side Show, Inc., 1997—99; v.p. fin. planning and analysis Lowe's Companies, Inc., 1999—2003, sr. v.p., CFO, 2003—04, exec. v.p., CFO, 2004—. Office: Lowes Cos Inc 1605 Curtis Bridge Rd Wilkesboro NC 28697

HULL, ROBERT JOE, lawyer; b. Ft. Monmouth, NJ, Dec. 16, 1944; s. Thurman Beuford and Helen Louise (Bracey) H.; m. Susan Diane Hull, Mar. 12, 1966; 1 child, Robert Steven. BA, U. Tex., 1966, JD, 1969. Bar: Tex. 1969, Calif. 1970, U.S. Dist. Ct. (ctrl. dist.) Calif. 1970, U.S. Ct. Appeals (9th cir.) 1970, U.S. Tax. Ct. 1971, U.S. Supreme Ct. 1992. Assoc. Sheppard, Mullin, Richter & Hampton, LA, 1969-76, ptnr., 1976-98, Bracewell & Giuliani LLP, Houston, 1998—. Co-author: Representing Start-Up Companies, 1992, (annual) ABA Sales & Use Tax Handbook; mem. editorial bd., contbr. Jour. Multistate Taxation, 1991—. Mem. Tex. Found., Club at Escondido. Republican. Episcopalian. Home: 7800 SW Pk Way Unit 712 Austin TX 78735 Office: Bracewell & Giuliani LLP 111 Congress Ave Ste 2300 Austin TX 78701 Office Phone: 512-494-3611. Business E-Mail: joe.hull@bgllp.com.

HULL, WILLIAM EDWARD, theology studies educator; b. Birmingham, Ala., May 28, 1930; s. William Edward and Margaret (King) H.; m. Julia Wylodine Hester, July 26, 1952; children: David William, Susan Virginia. BA, Samford U., 1951; MDiv, So. Bapt. Theol. Sem., Louisville, 1954, PhD, 1960; postgrad., U. Gottingen, Germany, 1962—63, Harvard U., 1971; Doctor of Letters (hon.), Samford U., 2008. Ordained to ministry Bapt. Ch., 1950. Pastor Beulah Bapt. Ch., Wetumpka, Ala., 1950-51, Cedar Hill Bapt. Ch., Owenton, Ky., 1952-53, 1st Bapt. Ch., New Castle, Ky., 1953-58; from instr. to assoc. prof. So. Bapt. Theol. Sem., Louisville, 1954-67, prof., 1967-75, dean theology and provost, 1969-75; pastor 1st Bapt. Ch., Shreveport, La., 1975-87; provost Samford U., Birmingham, 1987-96, Univ. prof., 1987-2000; theologian in residence Mountain Brook Baptist Ch., Birmingham, 1991; rsch. prof. Samford U., Birmingham, 2000—. Author: Gospel of John, 1964, Broadman Bible Commentary, 1970, Beyond the Barriers, 1981, Love in Four Dimensions, 1982, The Christian Experience of Salvation, 1987, Southern Baptist Higher Education: Retrospect and Prospect, 2001, The Quest for Spiritual Maturity, 2004, The Four-Way Test: Core Values of the Rotary Movement, 2004, Strategic Preaching: The Role of the Pulpit in Pastoral Leadership, 2006, The Meaning of the Baptist Experience, 2007, Harbingers of Hope: Claiming God's Promises in Todays World, 2007, Seminary in Crisis: The Strategic Response of the Southern Baptist Theological Seminary to the SBC Controversy, 2010; (with others) Professor in the Pulpit, 1963, The Truth That Makes Men Free, 1966, Salvation in Our Time, 1978, Set Apart for Service, 1980, Celebrating Christ's Presence Through the Spirit, 1981, The Twentieth Century Pulpit, Vol. II, 1981, Minister's Manual, 1983-87, 2000, 5th edit., 2005, Biblical Preaching: An Expositor's Treasury, 1983, Preaching in Today's Biblical World, 1984, Heralds to a New Age, 1985, Getting Ready for Sunday: A Practical Guide for Worship Planning, 1989, Best Sermons 2, 1989, The University Through the Eyes of Faith, 1998, Putting Women in Their Place: Moving Beyond Gender Stereotypes in Church and Home, 2003, Distinctively Baptist: Essays on Baptist History, 2005, Gladly Learn, Gladly Teach: Living Out One's Calling in the 21st Century Academy, 2005, The Future of Baptist Higher Education, 2006, Bound on Earth: A Festschrift for Edmon Lewin Rowell Jr., 2006; contbr. articles to profl. jours. Mem. Futureshape Shreveport (La.) Commn., 1985-87. Recipient Denominational Svc. award Samford U., 1974, Liberty Bell award Shreveport Bar Assn., 1984, Brotherhood and Humanitarian award NCCJ, 1987, Charles D. Johnson Outstanding Educator award Assn. So. Bapt. Colls. and Schs., 1999, Samford U. Alumnus Yr., 2005, Vocat. Svc. award Rotary Dist. 6860, 2009. Mem. Nat. Assn. Bapt. Profs. Religion (pres. 1967-68), Am. Acad. Religion, Soc. Bibl. Lit., The Club (Birmingham), Vestavia Country Club (Birmingham), Rotary, Phi Kappa Phi, Phi Eta Sigma, Omicron Delta Kappa. Baptist. Home: 2850 Saddletree Blvd NE Huntsville AL 35811-2622 Office Phone: 205-726-4030. Business E-Mail: wehull@samford.edu.

HULSE, RUSSELL ALAN, physicist; b. NYC, Nov. 28, 1950; s. Alan Earle and Betty Joan (Wedemeyer) Hulse. BS, Cooper Union, 1970; MS, U. Mass., 1972, PhD, 1975. Rsch. assoc. Nat. Radio Astronomy Observatory, Charlottesville, Va., 1975—77; mem. tech. staff Princeton U. Plasma Physics Lab., 1977—80, staff rsch. physicist, 1980—84, rsch. physicist, 1984—92, prin. rsch. physicist, 1992—. Vis. prof. physics, math., sci. edn. U. Tex., Dallas, 2004—07, assoc. v.p. for rsch. and econ. devel., 2005—07, regental prof., assoc. v.p. for strategic initiatives, 2007—; bd. dirs. Battelle Meml. Inst. Contbr. articles to profl. jours. Recipient Nobel prize in physics, 1993. Fellow: AAAS, Inst. Physics, Am. Phys. Soc.; mem.: Am. Astron. Soc. Achievements include discovery of first binary pulsar - a twin star system that provides a rare natural laboratory in which to test Albert Einstein's prediction that moving objects emit gravitational waves. Avocations: target shooting, birdwatching, canoeing, hiking, hunting. Office: University of Texas Dallas Rm AD 3.204D 800 W Campbell Rd Richardson TX 75080 Office Phone: 972-883-4573. Business E-Mail: russell.hulse@utdallas.edu.

HULSEY, THOMAS C., epidemiologist, researcher; BS in Biology, Bapt. Coll., Charleston, SC, 1975; MPH, U. SC, 1977; DSc, Johns Hopkins U., Balt., 1988. Prof. Med. U. SC, Charleston, 1987—. Fellow: Am. Coll. Epidemiology; mem.: Am. Pediatric Soc., Soc.

Pediatric Rsch. Lutheran. Office: Med Univ South Carolina PO Box 250566 135 Ashley Ave Charleston SC 29425 Home: 424 Rice Hope Dr Mount Pleasant SC 29464 Business E-Mail: hulseytc@musc.edu.

HULTMAN, CHARLES WILLIAM, economics professor; b. Oelwein, Iowa, Apr. 6, 1930; s. John William and Alma (Loeb) H.; m. Irene Oliver, June 7, 1957; children: Susan, Gregory. BA, Upper Iowa U., 1952; MA, Drake U., 1957; PhD, U. Iowa, 1960. Asst. prof. U. Ky., Lexington, 1960-64, prof. econs., 1967-98, chmn. dept., 1969-71, CSX prof. bus. and pub. policy, 1988-98, assoc. dir. Ctr. for Devel. Change, 1971-73, assoc. dean for rsch., 1976-85, prof. emeritus, 1998—; tchr. English, Luth. Ch., Pingxiang, China, summer 1999. Vis. assoc. prof. U. Calif., 1964-65, prof. of banking and fin. Univ. Coll., Dublin, Ireland, 1990; fall sememster Ford Found. prof. Fudan U., Shanghai, China, 1989. Author: International Finance, 1963, American Business and the Common Market, 1964, Problems of Economic Development, 1967, Ireland in the World Economy, 1969, (with M. Wasserman, R. Ware) International Economics, 1969, Comparison of Projected Unemployment Insurance Costs, 1973, The Environment of International Ban King, 1990; book rev. editor: Internat. Devel. Rev.; mem. editorial adv. bd. Sage Papers in Internat. Studies; assoc. editor internat. econs. Wall Street Rev. Books; acting editor: Jour. Growth and Change, 1979-86. Chmn. Ky. Coun.Econ. Advisors, 1976-85; mem. So. Growth Policies Bd., 1976-90. With U.S. Army, 1952-55. Fulbright lectr., Ireland, 1967—68. Mem. Eastern Econ. Assn. (exec. bd. 1980-84) Lutheran. Home: 3341 Crown Crest Rd Lexington KY 40517-2809

HULTSTRAND, CHARLES JOHN, architect; b. Mt. Vernon, Ohio, Dec. 26, 1951; s. Donald M. and Marjorie R. (Richter) H.; m. Kathi, Brooke, Andrew, Caroline, Clay, Kristi, Scott. BSE, Princeton U., 1974; MArch, Rice U., 1977. Registered architect, S.C. Assoc., project designer Golemon & Rolfe Architects, Houston, 1977-83; prin., exec. v.p., dir. of design The Boudreaux Group, Inc., Columbia, SC, 1983—2003; ptnr., dir. design Neal-Prince & Ptnrs., Greenville, SC, 2003—. Guest lectr. Clemson (S.C.) U. Coll. Architecture, 1993-2007, Cornerstone Nat. Conf. 2005; mem. steering com. Onions & Orchids Award Program, Columbia, 1988, jury mem., 1989; mem. steering com. Columbia R/UDAT Commn., 1987; v.p. Terrace Lake, Inc.; bd. dirs. Columbia Devel. Corp. Pres. parent tchr. fellowship Ben Lippen Sch., Columbia, 1991-94, mem. bd. mgrs., 1991-2000, v.p. bd., 1995-2000; mem. fundraising com., 1993-2002; deacon Cornerstone Presbyn. Ch., Columbia, 1988-91, First Presbyn. Ch., Columbia, 1997-99, 2000-03, vice chmn., 2001-02, chmn., 2003; mem. bd. Faith & Form, 2005-, bd. sec., 2006—, v.p., 2009; pres. Yokemen Svc. Orgn., 1982-83; vol. ARC Hurricane Hugo Relief, 1990, SCETV Fundraising, Columbia, 1991; mem. sch. com. Princeton Alumni Assn., 2000-08. Recipient AIA SC Honor Award, Columbia Internat. U. Prayer Towers, 1988, St. Francis of Assisi Episcopal Ch., 1988, Brick Assn. of Carolinas Pres. Award, St. Christopher's Episcopal Ch., 1996, Merit Award Columbia Chpt. AIA, 1996, SC Conservatory, 1996, Clemson U. Student Housing, 1996, Honor Award Brick Assn. of Carolinas, 1998, Honor Award, USC Athletic Practice Faculty, 1999, Historic Columbia Found. Preservation Award, Flinn Hall Classroom Bldg., 2000, Bldg. of Yr. Award for Archtl. Steel, The Berkeley Bldg., Con/Steel Alliance, 2003, Design award, Upstate Masonry Assn., 2007; named Columbia Small Bus. Person of Yr., Greater Columbia C. of C., 2003; finalist US Bldg. awards, CEMEX, 2007. Mem. AIA (pres. S.C. chpt. 1996, v.p./pres.-elect S.C. chpt. 1995, sec.-treas. S.C. chpt. 1993-94, chmn. spkrs. bur. 1988-90, dir. Columbia sect. 1988-90, chmn. govt. affairs commn. S.C. chpt. 1990-93, bd. dirs., advisor intern devel. program 1990-94, state engr.'s com. 2002-03, 2005), S.C. Archtl. Soc. (bd. dirs./sec. 1997-99), Columbia Design League (bd. dirs. 1997-98), Columbia Coun. Archs. (pres. 1986-87, bd. dirs. 1984-87), Princeton Alumni Assn. S.C. (treas. 1990-94), Architecture Ministry (bd. mem. 2008-), SC Archipac (bd. mem. 2009-, sec. 2009), Greater Columbia C. of C. Avocations: reading, walking, tennis, golf. Office: Neal-Prince & Ptnrs Ste 300 110 W North St Greenville SC 29601 Office Phone: 864-235-0405. E-mail: chuck@neal-prince.com.

HULTSTRAND, DONALD MAYNARD, bishop; b. Apr. 16, 1927; s. Aaron Emmanuel (H.) and Selma Avendla (Liljegren) Hultstrand; m. Marjorie Richter, June 11, 1948; children: Katherine Ann, Charles John; m. Lenorg Ann Haselwood, Feb. 18, 2006. BA summa cum laude, Macalester Coll., 1950; BD summa cum laude, Colgate-Rochester Theol. Sem., 1974; DD (hon.), Nashotah Divinity Sch., 1986, Bexley Hall Sem., 2003. Ordained priest Episcopal Ch., 1953, consecrated bishop Episcopal Ch., 82. Vicar St. John's Episcopal Ch., Worthington, Minn., 1953—57; rector Grace Meml. Ch., Wabasha, Minn., 1957—62, St. Mark's Episcopal Ch., Canton, Ohio, 1962—68, St. Paul's Episcopal Ch., Duluth, Minn., 1969—75; assoc. rector St. Andrew's Episcopal Ch., Kansas City, Mo., 1968—69; exec. dir. Anglican Fellowship of Prayer, 1975—79; rector Trinity Episcopal Ch., Greeley, Colo., 1979—82; bishop Episcopal Diocese of Springfield, Ill., 1982—91; exec. bd. Episcopal Radio (TV Found.), Atlanta, 1982—87, Anglican Fellowship of Prayer, 1968—93; adv. bd. Episcopal Boys' Homes, Salinas, Kans., 1983—91; com. of execs. Ill. Conf. Chs., 1982—91; mem. House of Bishops, 1982—, mem. Minn. Standing Com., 1970—73. Chmn. Minn. Examining Chaplains, 1954—61; chaplain Pewsaction Fellowships U.S.A., 1983—92; pres. Living Ch. Found., 1992—2002; advisor Diocesan Youth of Minn., 1956—60. Author: The Praying Church, 1978, And God Shall Wipe Away All Tears, 1968, Intercessory Prayer, 1972, Upper Room Dialogues, 1980, Revelations of Effective Prayer, 1995; co-author: The Parish as a Center of Prayer, 1996, Life in The Spirit, 2008. Bd. dirs. Sr. Citizens Housing, Duluth, Minn., 1972—75, St. Luke's Hosp., Duluth, 1969—75; pres. Low-Rent Housing Project, Greeley, 1979—82. With USNR, 1945—46. Recipient Disting. Svc. award, Young Life Minn., 1974; named hon. canon, Diocese of Ohio, Cleve., 1967. Mem.: Pi Phi Epsilon. Episcopalian.

HUMANN, L. PHILLIP, retired bank executive; b. Nov. 8, 1945; BA, Auburn U., Ala., 1967, MS, 1969. Chmn., CEO Trust Co. Bank, Atlanta, 1985—89; exec. v.p. SunTrust Banks, Inc., Atlanta, 1989—90, sr. v.p., 1990—91, pres., 1991, CEO, 1998—2006, chmn., 1998—2006, exec. chmn., 2007—08, cons., 2008—. Mem. bd. dirs. Coca-Cola Enterprises Inc., Equifax Inc., Haverty Furniture Cos., Inc. Office: SunTrust Banks Inc PO Box 4418 Atlanta GA 30308-4418 Office Phone: 404-588-7711. Office Fax: 404-827-6173.

HUMBLE, MONTY GARFIELD, lawyer; b. Cameron, Tex., Dec. 20, 1951; s. Don Garfield Humble and Betty Sue (Maedgen) French; m. Donell Lou Moss, Mar. 12, 1976 (div. June 1981); m. Macy A. Melton, Oct. 23, 1993; children: Megan Elizabeth, John Marshall, Nicole Marie, Crawford Melton. BA, U. Tex., 1974, JD, 1976. Assoc. Clark, Thomas, Winters and Shapiro, Austin, Tex., 1972-82, Vinson & Elkins, Houston, 1982-86, ptnr. Dallas, 1986—2008; sr. v.p., gen. coun. Mesa Power Group LLC, 2008—. Bd. dirs. Ft. Worth Ballet, 1990-94, Dallas Opera, 1987-92, Tex. Gen. Counsel Forum, 2001-2003, Tex. Nanotech. Initiative, 2002—, Am. Wind Energy Assn., 2009-, chair transmission com., 2009; gen. counsel Superconducting Super Collider Devel. Authority, 1987-94; active Leadership Dallas, 1988, Greater Dallas Planning Coun.; legal adv. Dallas City Charter Revision Com., 1990; adv. coun. U. Tex. Dallas External Rsch., 2002—. Fellow Dallas Bar Found., Tex. Bar Found.; mem. ABA, State Bar Tex., Nat. Assn. Bond Lawyers (steering com. 1985-87, 94-96, bd. dirs. 2001-06, treas. 2002-03, pres.-elect 2003-04, pres. 2004-05, past pres. 2005-06), Am. Coll. Bond Coun., Dean's Roundtable, U. Tex. Sch. Law, Health Care Fin. Mgrs. Assn. (bd. dirs. 1990-92), Crescent Club, Bent Tree Country Club, Phi Beta Kappa. Republican. Office: Masa Power Group LLC 8117 Preston Rd Ste 260 Dallas TX 75225 Office Phone: 214-265-4161. Business E-Mail: mhumble@bpsap.net. E-mail: mhumble@velaw.com.

HUML, DONALD SCOTT, manufacturing executive; b. Lake Geneva, Wis., May 8, 1946; s. Robert Francis and Shirley (Roberts) H.; m. Joyce Cora Featherstone, Oct. 2, 1965; children: Tiffany Lynn, Alison Michelle, Andrew Scott. BBA, Marquette U., 1969; MBA, Temple U., 1980. Mgr. treasury ops. Allis-Chalmers Corp., West Allis, Wis., 1970-73; dir. fin. services CertainTeed Corp., Valley Forge, Pa., 1973-75, asst. treas., 1975-78, v.p., treas., 1978-81, v.p., comptroller, 1981-83, v.p., div. pres., 1983-86, v.p., group pres., 1986-89, v.p., chief fin. officer, 1989-90; v.p., CFO Saint-Gobain Corp., Valley Forge, Pa., 1990-94; sr. v.p., CFO Snap-on, Inc., Kenosha, Wis., 1994—2002; exec. v.p., CFO Greif, Inc., Delaware, Ohio, 2002—10; ret. Mem. adv. bd. Marquette U. Sch. Bus. Adminstrn. Mem. Am. Mgmt. Assn., Fin. Execs. Inst., Conf. Bd. CFO Coun., Leading CFOs, Beta Gamma Sigma. Republican. Roman Catholic. Avocations: tennis, running, reading. Home: PO Box 346 Boca Grande FL 33921

HUMPHREY, JOHN, corporate financial executive; MBA, U. Mich. Various prodn. mgmt. positions Detroit Diesel; various fin. positions AlliedSignal, Honeywell Internat., 1994—2000; v.p. fin. Honeywell Aerospace, 2000—01, v.p., CFO engines, systems and services, 2001—03, v.p., CFO, 2003—06, Roper Industries, Inc., 2006—. Office: Roper Industries Inc 6901 Professional Pky E Ste 200 Sarasota FL 34240 Office Phone: 941-556-2601. Office Fax: 941-556-2670.

HUMPHREYS, DONALD D., oil industry executive; BS in Indsl. Engring. and Mgmt., Okla. State U., 1971; MBA, U. Pa. Wharton Sch. Bus., 1976. Sys. analyst Exxon Corp., 1976, sr. fin. advisor contr.'s dept. NYC, 1986—88, v.p., contr., 1997—99, asst. treas., 1997, v.p., contr., 1997—99; fin. reporting mgr. Exxon Co. Internat., 1988, asst. gen. auditor; upstream contr. Exxon Co., USA, 1990; fin. dir. Exxon Cos., Kuala Lumpur, Malaysia, 1993—97; v.p., contr. ExxonMobil Corp., Irving, Tex., 1999—2004, v.p., treas., 2004—06, sr. v.p., treas., mem. mgmt. com., 2006—. Bd. gov. Okla. State U. Found. Served in US Army, 1972—74. Mem.: Conf. Bd. Coun. Fin. Execs., Am. Petroleum Inst., Fin. Execs. Internat. Office: Exxon Mobil Corp 5959 Las Colinas Blvd Irving TX 75039-2298 Office Phone: 972-444-1000.

HUMPHREYS, KENNETH KING, engineer, professional society administrator, educator, pastor; b. Pitts., Jan. 19, 1938; s. Meredith Harold and Olga (Adamitis) H.; m. Harriet Elizabeth Moss, May 6, 1961; children: Kenneth King, Keith Alan, Kevin James, Karen Elizabeth. BS, Carnegie Inst. Tech., 1959, postgrad., 1961-62, U. Pitts., 1965; MS, W.Va. U., 1967; PhD, Kennedy Western U., 1990. Registered profl. engr., Pa., N.C., W.Va.; cert. cost engr. U.S., Mex., Internat. Tech. asst. Applied Research Lab.-U.S. Steel Corp., 1959-60, tech. assoc. Monroeville, Pa., 1960-62, asst. technologist Universal, Pa., 1962-63, assoc. research engr., 1963-65; cost engr. W. Va. U. Coal Research Bur., Morgantown, 1965-67, sr. staff and cost engr., 1967-71, asst. dir., 1971-81; asst. prof. Coll. Mineral and Energy Resources-W. Va., Morgantown, 1970-73; assoc. prof. Coll. Mineral and Energy Resources-W. Va. U., Morgantown, 1973-76, prof., 1976-82, adj. prof., 1982-92, asst. to dean, 1971-77, chmn. minerals program, 1978-81, asst. dean acad. affairs, 1979-82; exec. dir. Am. Assn. Cost Engrs., 1971-92. Engring. cons. metallurgy and fuel tech., 1963—82; engring. cons. cost engring. and project mgmt., 1993—. Author: Basic Cost Engineering, 1981, 2d edit., 1986, 3d edit., 1996, What Every Engineer Should Know About Ethics, 1999; editor: Control and Management of Capital Projects, 2d edit., 1992, reprint edit., 1998; co-author, co-editor: Basic Mathematics and Computer Applications for Coal Preparation and Mining, 1983; co-author, assoc. editor: Coal Preparation, 4th edit., 1979; co-author, editor: Project and Cost Engineers' Handbook, 4th edit., 2005; co-author, co-editor: Mechanical Estimating Guidebook, 5th edit., 1987, 6th edit., 1995; co-author, editor: Jelen's Cost and Optimization Engineering, 3d edit., 1991; editor: Effective Project Management Through Applied Cost and Schedule Control, 1996; contbr. articles to prof. jours.; patentee in field. Leader Allegheny Trails, Piedmont and Mountaineer area couns. Boy Scouts Am., 1961—, dist. commr. Mountaineer area coun., 1969-72, dist. tng. chmn., 1972-74, 90, chmn. coun. tng., 1975-77, exec. bd., 1987-89, leadership devel. com., area 6 East Cen. region, 1977-79, dist. commr. Piedmont coun., 1996-97, rechartering com., 1997-99, asst. dist. commr., 1999-2002, asst. coun. commr., 2003-07, internat. rep., 2001-; deacon 1st Presbyn. Ch., Morgantown, W.Va., 1968-70, ruling elder, 1972-75, 90-92, pres. congregation, 1975-77; deacon Waldensian Presbyn. Ch., Valdese, N.C., 1995-97, treas., 1995-96; ruling elder Fairview Presbyn. Ch., Lenoir, N.C., 2007—09; co-pastor 1st Presbyn. Ch., Bessemer City, NC, 2010-11, pastor, Conley Meml. Presbyn. Ch., Marion, NC, 2012-. Recipient Silver Beaver award Mountaineer Area Coun. Boy Scouts Am., 1973, Disting. Silver Beaver award Boy Scouts Am., 1990; recipient dist. award of merit Mountaineer Area Coun. Boy Scouts Am., 1969, Woodbadge award Mountaineer Area Coun. Boy Scouts Am., 1971, 50-Year Vets. award Boy Scouts Am., 1998, Het Schaap mit vijf Poten award Royal Netherlands Industries Fair, 1977; named Hon. West Virginian Gov. West Virginia, 1974. Fellow NSPE (life mem.), Assn. Cost Engrs. U.K. (Tony Jarvis Outstanding Paper award 2006), Assn. Advancement Cost Engring. Internat. (nat. chmn. 1969-71, 1998-2004, Mem. of Moment, nat. bd. dirs. 1971, exec. dir. 1971-92, award of merit 1993, award recognition 1979, Brian Dunfield Edn. award 2007, pub. Cost Engring. mag. 1981-92, co-editor trans. 1982-92, pres. No. W.Va. sect. 1989-91, pres. Catawba Valley, Charlotte, N.C. sect. 1994-96, regional rep. 1996-2009), Profl. Engrs. N.C. (ethics steering com. 1995-2005, coun. fellows 2005-, chmn. ethics com. 1999-2001, Engr. of Yr. award 1999, Ctrl. Piedmont chptr., dir. 2007-), Assn. Italiana di Ingegneria Economica; mem. Soc. Mexicana de Ingenieria Economica Financiera y de Costos (Mex.), So. African Project Control Inst. (hon. life, regional rep. 1996—), Internat. Cost Engring. Coun. (sec.-treas. 1976-2006, asst. sec. 2006-08, disting. internat. fellow, Outstanding Paper awards 1996, 98), W.Va. Soc. Profl. Engrs. (bd. dirs. 1971-76, 83-92, v.p. 1980-81, pres. 1982-83, W.Va. Engr. of Yr. 1986), Morgantown Chptr. Profl. Engrs. (W.Va.) (pres. 1969-70, bd. dirs. 1970-76), Am. Assn. Engring. Socs. (bd. govs. 1979-83), Coun. Engring. Splty. Bds. (pres.-elect 1990-92, pres. 1992-93), Sigma Xi, Beta Theta Pi (asst. gen. sec. 1987-91), Alpha Phi Omega. Democrat. Home and Office: 1168 Hidden Lake Dr Granite Falls NC 28630-8592

HUMPHREYS, PAUL WILLIAM, philosophy educator, consultant; b. London, Jan. 17, 1950; came to U.S., 1971; s. William Edward and Florence C. (Didcock) H.; m. Diane Gail Snustad, July 14, 1984; children: Emily Victoria, Alexandra Elizabeth. BSc, U. Sussex, UK, 1971; MA, MS, Stanford U., 1974, PhD, 1976. From asst. to assoc. prof. philosophy U. Va., Charlottesville, 1978-91, prof., 1991—, chmn., 1996—97, 1999—2004; v.p. Assn. for Founds. Sci., 1995-99. Seminar dir. NEH, Va., 1991, 95; cons. EPA, CDC, BCG; vis. prof. CNRS, Paris, France, 2005, ENS, Paris, 2008. Author: Chances of Explanation, 1989, Extending Ourselves, 2004; editor: Synthese, 1991—98, Foundations of Science, 1993—98, Oxford Studies in the Philosophy of Science, 1999—. Recipient Fulbright travel award, 1971, Scholars award NSF, 1984, 2006; ACLS fellow, 2008. Mem.: Philosophy Sci. Assn. (gov. bd. 1997—2000), Am. Philos. Assn. (chmn. com. internat. cooperation 2007—10, bd. officers 2007—10), Keswick Soc. (chmn. 2000—08). Home: 323 Kent Rd Charlottesville VA 22903-2409 Office: U Va Dept Philosophy PO Box 400780 Charlottesville VA 22903-4780

HUMPHRIES, JOHN O'NEAL, cardiologist, educator, dean; b. Columbia, SC, Oct. 22, 1931; s. Arthur Lee and Helen Elliott (O'Neal) H.; m. Mary Ellen Cregan, Mar. 13, 1954; children: Arthur Thomas, Ellen Cregan, John Elliott. BS, Duke U., 1952; MD, Johns Hopkins U., 1956. Diplomate Am. Bd. Internal Medicine (mem. bd. subsplty. cardiovascular disease 1974-79). Intern Johns Hopkins Hosp., 1957; asst. resident Osler Med. Service, Osler Med. Svc., 1958-60, resident physician pvt. med. svc., 1962-64, staff physician, 1962-79; rsch. fellow in cardiology U. London, St. George's Hosp., 1960-61, Johns Hopkins U. Med. Sch., 1956-57, 61-62, mem. faculty, 1964-79, Robert L. Levy prof. cardiology, 1975-79, prof. medicine, 1976-79; O.B. Mayer Sr. and Jr. prof. medicine U. S.C., Columbia, 1979-86, prof. medicine, 1979-96; disting. prof. medicine, dean emeritus, 1997—; chmn. dept. medicine U. S.C., Columbia, 1979-87, dean Sch. Medicine, 1983-94. Contbr. articles to med. publs.; mem. editl. bd. various jours. Bd. dirs. Md. Ballet, Balt., 1975-78. Master ACP (bd. govs. for S.C. chpt. 1986-90), Am. Coll. Cardiology (bd. govs. for Md. chpt. 1973-76); mem. Am. Fedn. Clin. Rsch., Am. Heart Assn. (fellow coun. clin. cardiology, chmn. postgrad. edn. com., exec. com. 1972-75), Cen. Md. Heart Assn. (pres. 1972-73), Md. Heart Assn. (pres. 1976-77), Assn. Univ. Cardiologists, Am. Clin. and Climatol. Assn., Alpha Omega Alpha. Office: U SC Sch Medicine Columbia SC 29208-0001

HUND, THOMAS N., rail transportation executive; BA in Bus. Adminstrn., Loyola U.; MBA, U. Chgo., 1988. Acct. Burlington Northern Santa Fe Corp., 1983-89, asst. v.p., contr., 1989-90, v.p., contr., 1990-95, sr. v.p., CFO, 1999-2000, exec. v.p., CFO, 2001—10, Burlington Northern Santa Fe LLC (subs. Berkshire Hathaway), 2010—. Mem.: AICPA. Office: Burlington Northern Santa Fe Corp PO Box 961056 Fort Worth TX 76161-0056 Office Phone: 817-867-6100.

HUNSAKER, BARRY, JR., aerospace engineer, lawyer; b. Mesa, Ariz., May 4, 1950; BS in Aerospace Engring., Tex. A&M U., 1972, MS in Aerospace Engring., 1973, PhD in Aerospace Engring., 1976; JD, U. Tex., 1979. Bar: Tex. 1979. Ptnr. Vinson & Elkins, LLP, 1979—96; sr. v.p., gen. counsel EOG Resources, Inc., 1996—2007; treas. Bill White for Tex. Campaign, 2008—. Bd. dirs. Houston Pub. Libr. Mem.: State Bar Tex., Order of Coif, Tau Beta Pi, Sigma Gamma Tau, Phi Kappa Phi. Office: Bill White for Texas Campaign 1415 Louisiana St Ste 3200 Houston TX 77002-7353 Office Phone: 713-659-9000. Office Fax: 713-659-9004. Business E-Mail: bhunsaker@billwhitefortexas.com.

HUNSPERGER, ELIZABETH JANE, educator; b. Phila., Aug. 30, 1938; d. Francis Charles and Elizabeth Julia Thorpe; m. Robert George Hunsperger, Sept. 13, 1958; 1 child, Lisa Marie. AA in Design, Santa Monica Coll., Calif., 1974; student, UCLA, 1975-76; BA in Art History, U. Del., Newark, 1978; postgrad., Rutgers U., 1978-81; MA in Edn., Del. State Coll., 1993; EdD in Ednl. Tech., U. Del., Newark, 2006. Designer Huntingdon Mills, Phila., 1960-63, Rothschild's, Ithaca, NY, 1963-65, Cornell U., Ithaca, 1965-67; freelance designer Malibu, Calif., 1967-76; art and design cons., lectr. Art & Sci. Assocs., Newark, Del., 1980—2001, Galena, Md., 2001—; adj. prof. edn. St. Josephs U., Phila., 2011—. Art tchr. Cath. Diocese of Wilmington, 1988-95, Kent County HS, Md., 2002-04; art and spl. edn. tchr., Capital Sch. Dist. Dover HS, 2006-, Red Clay Consolidated Sch. Dist. A.I. duPont HS, Greenville, Del., 1995-97, Shorehaven Sch., Chesapeake City, Md., 1997-99, A.I. duPont Inst., Wilmington, Del., 1999—; with Leech Sch., 1994; cons. Arts and Sci. Assocs., ceo; cons. Ednl. and Design Svcs., Newark, Del., 1995—; coord. Delmarva Edn. Action Learning Project; educator Kent County Pub. Schs., Md., 2002-04. Exhbns. include Malibu Art Assn. Show, 1973-74, Newark Art Show, 1987-88. Founding mem. bd. dirs., v.p. Newark Housing Ministry, Inc., 1983-94, pres., 1989-91; social concerns com. and drug and alcohol task force Del.; active Coun. Exceptional Children. Recipient Outstanding Svc. award YWCA, Santa Monica, Calif., 1972, award of recognition Missionhurst, 1982, Gov.'s Vol. of the Yr. award State of Del., 1990. Mem. Nat. Art Edn. Assn., Am. Craft Coun., Art Educators of Del. (bd. dirs., pres.), Soroptimist Internat., Debutante Assembly Club (N.Y.C.). Episcopal. Home: 3723 SE 18th Ave Cape Coral FL 33904 Personal E-mail: elizabeth_hunsperger@usa.net. Business E-Mail: ehunsper@sju.edu.

HUNSTAD, JOSEPH PAUL, plastic surgeon, educator; b. Detroit, Mar. 14, 1955; s. Norman Allan and Freda Mae Hunstad; m. Sherry Sue Sietsema, July 11, 1987; children: Lauren Grace Marie, Megan Alexandra Ann. MD, Mich. State U., East Lansing, Michigan, 1981. Diplomate The Am. Bd. Plastic Surgery, 1989. Intern gen. surgery Butterworth Hosp., Grand Rapids, Mich., 1981—82, resident plastic surgery, 1982—84, Grand Rapids Area Med. Edn. Ctr., 1984—86, resident, 1985—86; fellowship reconstructive microsurgery MECOM Microsurgical Inst., Baylor Dept. Plastic Surgery, Houston, 1986—87; staff mem. Carolinas Med. Ctr U., 1987—95, Presbyn. Hosp., U. Hosp., Charlotte, 1995—; asst. clin. prof. Sch. Medicine Dept. Surgery U. NC, Chapel Hill, NC, 1987—95; asst. consulting prof. plastic surgery Med. Ctr. Dept. Surgery Duke U., Durham, NC, 2001—; pvt. practice Charlotte. Contbr. chapters to books. Mem. bd. dirs. Team Staffing Internat., Charlotte, NC, 2001—06. Named one of Charlotte Top Doctors, Charlotte Mag., 2005, America's Top Physicians, Consumer Rsch. Coun. Am., 2005, 2006. Fellow: ACS; mem.: Internat. Soc. Asthetic Plastic Surgery, Southeastern Soc. Plastic and Reconstructive Surgeons, Mecklenburg County Med. Soc., Lipoplasty Soc. N.Am. (bd. dirs. 1992—2001), NC Med. Soc., NC Soc. Plastic Surgeons (pres. 2004—05, Presdl. award 2005), Am. Soc. Aesthetic Plastic Surgery, Am. Soc. Plastic Surgeons. Independent. Presbyn. Avocations: woodworking, hunting, water sports, skiing, tennis. Office: 8605 Cliff Cameron Dr Suite # 100 Charlotte NC 28269 Office Fax: 704-549-1511, 704-549-1511. E-mail: jph1@hunstad.com.

HUNSTEIN, CAROL, state supreme court justice; b. Miami, Fla., Aug. 16, 1944; AA, Miami-Dade Jr. Coll., 1970; BS, Fla. Atlantic U., 1972; JD, Stetson U., 1976, LLD (hon.), 1993. Bar: Ga. 1976; U.S. Dist. Ct. 1978; U.S. Ct. Appeals 1978; U.S. Supreme Ct. 1989. Atty. Hunstein & Hunstein, Atlanta, 1976-84; judge Superior Ct. of Ga. (Stone Mt. cir.), 1984-92; justice Supreme Ct. of Ga., Atlanta, 1992—, presiding justice, 2005—09, 2012, chief justice, 2009—12, 2012—13. Chair Ga. Commn. Access and Fairness; pres. Coun. of Superior Ct. Judges of Ga., 1990-91; adj. prof. Sch. Law Emory U., 1991—; former chair State Commn. on Child Support, 1992, 1993, 2000; Supreme Court Liaison, Chief Justice's Commn. on Professionalism. Adv. Ga. Campaign Adolescent Pregnancy Prevention, 1992-2001. Recipient Clint Green Trial Advocacy award 1976, Women Who Made A Difference award Dekalb Women's Network 1986, Outstanding Svc. commendation Ga. Legislature, 1993, Cmty. Svc. award Emory U. Legal Assn. for Women Students., 1993, Gender Justice award Ga. Commn. Family Violence, 1999, Margaret Brent award ABA, 1999; inducted to Fla. Atlantic U. Hall of Fame, 1993, Shining Star award, Atlanta Womens Found., Kathleen Kessler award, Ga. Assn. Women, Leadership award Atlanta Bar, 2009, Women of Excellence award Bus. to Bus. Mag., 2009, Wayne ShaeKleForo Excellence award Assn. Ct. Commrs. Ga., 2010; named Possible Women of Yr., 2007, Tradition of Excellence award, Gen. Practice and Trial Sect. State. Mem. Ga. Assn. of Women Lawyers, Nat. Assn. of Women Judges (dir. 1988-90), Bleckley Inn of Ct., State Bar Ga. (mem. com. women and minorities in profession 2006, Commitment to Equality award), Nat. Consortium Racial and Ethnic Fairness in the Cts., Stetson U. Sch. Law Bd. Oerseers, Supreme Ct. Com. Unauthorized Practice Law(chair), Atlanta Bar Assn. Pub. Perceptions Com., John Marshall Law Sch.(bd. dirs.) Office: Supreme Ct Ga 244 Washington Street Atlanta GA 30334-9007 Office Phone: 404-656-3475. Business E-Mail: hunsteic@gasupreme.us. E-mail: hunsteic@supreme.courts.state.ga.us.*

HUNT, ANGELA, councilwoman; BA, Rice U., Houston, 1994; JD, U. Tex. Sch. Law, 1998. Former comml. litigator McKool Smith PC; councilwoman, Dist. 14 Dallas City Coun., 2005—; chair Commn. Jud. Appts.; co-chair Bicycle Plan Commn. Exec. v.p. Dallas Homeowners League; founder, chair M Streets Conservation Dist., Dallas. Mem. exec. bd. Preservation Dallas; mem. pres. adv. coun. Dallas Ctr. Performing Arts; bd. dirs. Dallas Black Dance Theatre. Recipient Dream award, Greater Dallas Planning Coun., 2004, Graffiti Hurts award, Keep America Beautiful, 2006, Marshall Meml. Fellowship, German Marshall Fund of US, 2008, Va. Macdonald Leadership award, 2010; named Best City Coun. Mem., Dallas Observer, 2006—08, Dallas Voice, 2008—10, Dallas League of Woman Voters. Mailing: Dallas City Hall 1500 Marilla St Rm 5FS Dallas TX 75201 Office Phone: 214-670-5415. Office Fax: 214-670-5117. Business E-Mail: angela.hunt@dallascityhall.com.

HUNT, EARL STEPHEN, independent consultant; b. Chattanooga, Nov. 28, 1948; s. Earl Gladstone, Jr. and Mary Anne (Kyker) Hunt; m. Edeltraut Gilgan, Sept. 6, 1986. BA with honors, Emory and Henry Coll., 1971; MA, Am. U., 1973; PhD, U. Va., 1979; MLS, CAS, Syracuse U., 2000. Instr. Fla. So. Coll., Lakeland, 1980-81; edn. cons. Nashville, NYC, 1980-82; editor, cons. Washington, 1982-86; sr. rsch. analyst US Dept. Edn., Washington, 1986—94, sr. internat. rels. specialist internat. affairs staff Office Sec., 2002—10; planning dir. Nat. Libr. Edn., 1995—2002; mgr. US Network Edn. Info., 1997—. Mem. drug prevention task force US Dept. Edn., Washington, 1986—89; cons. US Dept. Labor, Washington, 1990—, NSF, Washington, 1990—, US Trade Rep., Washington, 1999—, US Dept. Homeland Security, Washington, 2001—; mgr. US network for edn. info. UNESCO, Coun. Europe, 1997—; US expert, adviser G8 Negotiations, 2005—06; independent cons. internat. edn., 2010—. Co-editor: (book) The Apocalyptic Premise: Nuclear Arms Debated, 1982; author: Drug Prevention Curricula, 1993, Mapping the World of Education: The Comparative Database System, 1994, Professional Workers as Learners, 1992, A Guide to the International Interpretation of U.S. Education Program Data, 1993; co-author: Classification of Instructional Programs (CIP), 1990, 2000; prin. tech. advisor (book) Classification of Instructional Programs (CIP); contbr. articles to profl. jours.; co-author: Developed Attitude to Recognition: Sucstantial Differences in an age Globalisation, 2010. Mem. Sangamore-Brooks Ln. Citizens' Assn., Bethesda, Md., 1990—. Grantee, USIA, 1982. Mem.: Nat. Assn. Fgn. Student Advisers-Assn. Internat. Edn., European Assn. Internat. Edn., Nat. Contract Mgmt. Assn., Phi Delta Kappa, Blue Key, Phi Gamma Mu, Alpha Phi Omega (life). Methodist. Avocations: reading, travel, gardening, cooking. Office: USNEI 168 Ginger Quill Cir Candler NC 28715

HUNT, JAMES CALVIN, physician, academic administrator; b. Lexington, NC, Sept. 11, 1925; s. James Lee and Sarah Della (Frank) Hunt; m. Irene Kivett, Sept. 17, 1949; children: James Calvin, Michael S., Cynthia Irene. AB, Catawba Coll., 1949; MD, Bowman Gray Sch. Medicine, 1953; MS, U. Minn., 1958; ScD, Wake Forest U., 1992. Diplomate Am. Bd. Internal Medicine. Intern N.C. Bapt. Hosp., Winston-Salem, 1953-54; resident, fellow Mayo Grad Sch. Medicine, Rochester, Minn., 1954-58; practice medicine, specializing in internal medicine (cardiovasc.-renal diseases) Rochester, 1958-78; cons., instr. to asst. prof. dept. medicine Mayo Clinic and Mayo Med. Sch., 1958-63, assoc. prof., chmn. divsn. nephrology, 1963-72, prof., chmn. dept. medicine, 1973-78; prof., assoc. dean clin. ednl. programs Mayo Med. Sch., 1972-74; prof. medicine U. Tenn., Memphis, 1978—, dean Coll. Medicine, 1978-81, v.p. health affairs, chancellor Univ. Health Scis. Ctr., 1981-93, univ. disting. prof., dir. clin. scholars program, 1993—2001, v.p. health affairs, chancellor emeritus, 2001—. Adv. coun. Nat. Heart, Lung and Blood Inst. NIH, 1976—81. Contbr. articles to profl. jours. Pres. Nat. Kidney Found., 1973—76; mem. Congl. Tech. Adv. Coun., 1987—96; bd. dirs. Memphis Downtown Neighbors Assn., 1995—99, pres., 1997—98; mem. adv. bd. Goals for Memphis, 1987—95; bd. dirs. YMCA, Memphis, Memphis Riverfront Devel. Corp., 1999—, sec., 2000—02; trustee Le Bonheur Children's Med. Ctr., 1981—93, Christian Bros. Coll., 1983—96; mem. cmty. adv. bd. Bapt. Meml. Hosp., 1986—; bd. dirs. Bapt. Meml. Coll. Health Scis., 1995—2005, chair acad. affairs com., 1998—2005; mem. adv. bd. Rhodes Coll. With USAAF, 1943—46, ETO. Recipient Disting. Svc. award, Bowman Gray Sch. Medicine, Wake Forest U., 1975, Disting. Alumnus award, Catawba Coll., 1974, Educator of the Yr. award, Memphis State U., 1986, Outstanding Alumnus award, Mayo Found., 1991, Gift of Life award, Nat. Kidney Found., 1991. Fellow: ACP, Am. Heart Assn. (mem. coun. circulation), Am. Coll. Cardiology; mem.: AMA, Am. Soc. Clin. Pharmacology and Therapeutics, Am. Soc. Internal Medicine, Coun. High Blood Pressure Rsch., Soc. Nuc. Medicine, Internat. Soc. Hypertension, Internat. Am. Socs. Nephrology, Sigma Xi, Phi Rho Sigma, Alpha Omega Alpha. Home: 504 Shannondale Way Maryville TN 37803-5967

HUNT, JAMES KELSO, finance company executive; b. El Paso, Tex., Oct. 1, 1951; s. J. Kelso and Laurette (Macdonald) h.; m. Margaret Fellner, July 23, 1983; children: Lindsay, Charlotte. BBA, U. Tex., El Paso, 1972; MBA, U. Pa., 1975. V.p., sr. credit officer Citicorp/Citibank, NYC, Chgo., San Francisco, L.A., Jakarta, 1975-89; v.p., acquisitions Davis Cos., LA, 1989-90; exec. v.p. Sun Am. Investments, LA, 1990; pres. Sun Am. Corp. Fin., Century City, Calif., 1994. Bd. dirs. Lender Processing Svcs. Inc. Dir. Jr. Achievement So. Calif., L.A., 1989—. Mem. Olympic Club, Jonathan Club, Bel Aire Club. Home: 1221 Ocean Ave Apt 601 Santa Monica CA 90401-1045 Office: Lender Processing Services Inc Bd Directors 601 Riverside Ave Jacksonville FL 32204 E-mail: james.hunt@lpsvcs.com.

HUNT, JOHN EDWIN, insurance company executive, consultant; b. Ozark, Ala., Jan. 13, 1918; s. Tim Atticus and Ada (Arnold) H.; m. Winnifred Prichard; children: Jacqueline, John Edwin Jr., Geoffery, Scott, Richard; md. 2d Leona Snowden. Student, Columbus U., Washington, 1938-40, Pace U., 1940-41; diploma in banking, Am. Inst. Banking, 1942; diploma in ins., Travelers Ins. Co., 1944. Aide to regional adminstr., chief auditor Fed. Housing Adminstrn., Washington, 1938-40; with trust dept. Riggs Nat. Bank, Washington, 1940-42; asst. trust officer Fla. Nat. Bank, Jacksonville, 1942-44; asst. mgr. Travelers Ins. Co., Jacksonville, 1944-45, gen. agt. regional br., 1945-58; pres. John E. Hunt & Assocs., Tallahassee, 1972-84; chmn. bd. dirs. Hunt Ins. Group-Spl. Law Enforcement Agy. and Self-Ins. Fund Adminstrn., Tallahassee, 1984-97; pres. John Hunt & Assocs., Miami, Fla., 1958-72; chmn. emeritus Hunt Ins. Group, Tallahassee, 1997—; elected hon. sheriff Fla. Sheriff Assn., 2009. Pres. Ins. Cons. and Analysts, Tallahassee, 1972-95. Past chmn. pvt. industry coun. Pres. Reagan's Job Tng. Partnership Act; past mem. Gov's Adv. Coun. for Ins.; founder Fla. Police Chiefs Edn. & Rsch. Found., Inc.; trustee, mem. pres.'s coun. Fla. So. Coll., Lakeland, 1986-97. trustee emeritus, 1997—. Named Hon. Sheriff Fla.; Hall of Fame. Mem. Fla. Assn. Surplus Lines, Fla. Assn. Ins. Agts., Com. of 99 (past pres., bd. dirs., law enforcement com. 1984-85), Greater Miami Mortgage Brokers Assn. (pres. 1964-65), Fla. Jr. C. of C. (nat. dir., state v.p. 1950-52), Fla. Police Chiefs Assn. (hon., life), Fla. Sheriffs Assn. (hon., life), Killearn Golf and Country Club, Fla. Econ. Club, Tiger Bay Club, Govs. Club, Masons, Shriners, Elks (life). Republican. Avocation: yachting. Home: PO Box 14015 Tallahassee FL 32317-4015 Office: Hunt Ins Group Inc 3606 Maclay Blvd S Tallahassee FL 32312 Office Phone: 850-385-3636.

HUNT, JOHNELLE, transportation executive; b. Heber Springs, Ark. m. Johnnie Hunt (dec. 2006); 2 children. Attended, Univ. Central Ark. Co-founder JB Hunt Transport Services, 1969—, credit mgr., 1969—86, corp. sec., 1969—2008. Adv. bd. mem. Bernice Jones Eye Inst.; adv. coun. mem. Susan G. Komen Breast Cancer Found. Ozark Affiliate. Recipient Worthen Prof. Women of Distinction award, 1992; named one of Forbes 400: Richest Americans, 2009; named to Ark. Bus. Hall of Fame, 2001. Mem.: Wash. County United Way Alexis de Tocqueville Soc. (founding chmn.). Office: 333 Pinnacle Hills Pkwy Ste 602 Rogers AR 72758

HUNT, MARK A., state legislator; b. Charleston, Jan. 23, 1960; m. Tracy Conard; children: Andrew(dec.), Mark Jr., Jackie. BA, U. Charleston, 1982; MA, Marshall U., 1984; JD, U. DC, 1994. Analyst W.Va. Legis. Svcs., 1984—90; atty. W.Va. State Auditor, 1993—94, Hunt and Serreno, 1995—; mem. W.Va. House of Delegates, 1994—2000, 2004—06, mem. Dist 30, 2008—, mem. Banking and Ins. Com., Constitutional Revision Com. & Judiciary Com. Mem.: Am. Trial Lawyers Assn., W.Va. Trial Lawyers Assn., W.Va. Bar Assn., Kanawha County Bar Assn. Democrat. Protestant. Office: State Capitol Complex Rm 208E, Bldg 1 Charleston WV 25305 Mailing: 901 Edgewood Rd Charleston WV 25302 Home Phone: 304-346-9561; Office Phone: 304-340-3392, 304-344-1800. E-mail: mhunt@markahunt.com.

HUNT, NEAL KEMP, state legislator, real estate company executive; b. Thomasville, NC, Sept. 17, 1942; s. Walter Skellie and Miriam Hall Hunt; m. Frances Campbell, Nov. 14, 1963; children: Eleanor Scott, Kemp Neal. BS, Hampden-Sydney Coll., 1964; MBA in Mktg. and Fin., U. Pa., 1968. Real Estate Broker State of NC, 1991. Asst. v.p. Wachovia Bank, Releigh, NC, 1968—72, head of regional income property loans, 1970—72; gen. ptnr. Hunt-Austin Assocs., 1973—80; pres. Hunt Properties, Inc., 1980—90, HMC Corp., 1991—. At-large coun. mem. Raleigh City Coun., 2001—04; mem. Dist. 15 NC State Senate, 2004—. Adv. bd. Raleigh Rescue Mission, 1999—2006, treas. bd. dirs., 2000—02; mem. Friends of Lake Johnson Bd., 2004—06; adv. bd. Camp Oak Hill, 2003—, NC Mus. Natural Sci.; vice chair Wake County Open Space Task Force, 1996—98; mem. Raleigh Planning Commn., 1995—2001, chair, 1998—2001, City Coun. Comprehensive Planning Com., 2001—04. Mem.: Raleigh Home Builders Assn. (dir. 1980—84), Kappa Sigma (Epsilon Chpt.) (pres. 1964). Republican. Christian. Avocations: golf, travel, reading, politics, exercise. Office: HMC Corp 2600 Fairview Rd Raleigh NC 27608 also: NC Senate 16 W Jones St Rm 308 Raleigh NC 27603-5925 Office Phone: 919-781-3464, 919-733-5850. E-mail: Neal.Hunt@ncleg.net.

HUNT, RAY LEE, petroleum company executive; b. Apr. 6, 1943; s. H. L. and Ruth (Ray) Hunt; m. Nancy Ann Hunt; 5 children. B in Econs., So. Meth. U., Dallas, 1965. With Hunt Oil Co., Dallas, 1958—, CEO, 1976—, former chmn.; chmn., pres., CEO Hunt Consolidated Inc., Dallas, 1994—. Pres. Domestic Petroleum Coun., 1980—81; bd. dirs. PepsiCo, Inc., 1996—, Halliburton Co., 1998—2007, King Ranch, Inc., Bessemer Venture Patnrs., Electronic Data Sys., Dallas; chmn. bd. dirs. Fed. Res. Bank, Dallas; mem. Fgn. Intelligence Adv. Bd., Washington, 2001—, Nat. Petroleum Coun., Washington, chmn., 1991—94. Former chmn. Dallas Citizens Coun., North Tex. Commn., Ctrl. Dallas Assn.; bd. trustees Ctr. Strategic & Internat. Studies, Washington, So. Meth. U., The Cooper Inst., Dallas; chmn. bd. trustees Dallas Med. Resource; mem. exec. com. Southwestern Med. Found., Dallas. Named one of Forbes 400: Richest Americans, 1999—, World's Richest People, Forbes mag., 2001—; named to Tex. Bus. Hall of Fame, 1992. Mem.: Am. Petroleum Inst. (chmn. 1991—94, pub. policy com., bd. dirs.). Office: Hunt Consolidated Inc 1445 Ross Ave Ste 1400 Dallas TX 75202

HUNT, RONALD J., dean, dental educator; DDS, U. Iowa, 1973, MS in Dental Pub. Health, 1982. Diplomate Am. Bd. Dental Pub. Health. Assoc. prof. dental ecology U. NC Sch. Dentistry, Chapel Hill, 1986—88, prof. dental ecology, 1990—92, asst. dean, 1992—98, assoc. dean academic affairs, 1992—98; Harry Lyons Prof., dean Va. Commonwealth U. Sch. Dentistry, Richmond, Va., 1999—. Disting. vis. scholar U. Adelaide, Australia, 1990. Fellow: Am. Coll. Dentists, Am. Assn. Dental Schools; mem.: Va. Dental Saan., Am. Ass. Dental Rsch., Am. Dental Edn. Assn. (pres.-elect 2008—09, pres. 2009—10, William J. Gies Ednl. Fellowship 1997). Office: VCU Sch Dentistry 520 N 12th St Box 980566 Richmond VA 23298 Office Phone: 804-827-2077. Business E-Mail: rjhunt@vcu.edu.

HUNT, TERRY H., fuel company executive; BS in Mechanical Engring., U. Saskatchewan; MBA, Southern Methodist U. With, various positions Texas Oil & Gas Corp.; various positions Atlantic Richfield, ARCO; v.p., project devel. Delhi Gas Pipline Corp., Dallas; chmn., pres. Carnegie Natural Gas Co., Apollo Gas Co., Pitts., 1992—99; pres., CEO Penn Fuel Gas, Oxford, 1998—2000; sr. v.p., strategic planning, PP&L Resources PPL Corp., 1998. Bd. dirs. UTI Energy Corp., 1994—2001, Patterson-UTI Energy, Inc., 2003—. Office: PP&L Resources Inc 2 N 9th St Allentown PA 18101-1139 also: Patterson-UTI Energy Inc Bd Directors 450 Gears Rd Ste 500 Houston TX 77067 Office Phone: 281-765-7100. Office Fax: 281-765-7113. Business E-Mail: huntt@patenergy.com.

HUNT, THOMAS R., III, hand surgeon, educator; MD, Vanderbilt U., 1986. Cert. orthopedic surgery 2006, hand surgery 2006. Resident in orthopedic surgery Univ. Kansas Med. Ctr., Kansas, 1987—92; fellow in hand surgery Hosp. U. Pa., Phila., 1992—93; prof. in surgery Univ. Ala.; hosp. affiliation includes Univ. Ala. Hosp., Birmingham. Office: University of Alabama Hospital 619 19th St S Birmingham AL 35249 Office Phone: 205-934-4011.

HUNT, WILLIAM B., pulmonologist; b. Lexington, NC, Sept. 27, 1927; s. William B. and Maxine (Cox) H.; married; children: William B., III, Anne, Alex, Sarah. BS, Wake Forest U., 1948; MD, Bowman Gray Sch. Medicine, Winston Salem, NC, 1953. Diplomate Am. Bd. Internal Medicine, Am. Bd. Allergy and Immunology. Intern, resident U. Va., Charlottesville, 1953-55, resident, fellow, 1957-59, assoc. prof., 1960-75, asst. dean Sch. Medicine, 1972-75; fellow gastroenterology Bowman Gray Sch. Medicine, Winston Salem, 1959-60; instr. internal medicine N.Y. Med. Coll., NYC, 1959-60; from clin. assoc. prof. medicine to clin. prof. medicine East Carolina Sch. Medicine, Greenville, NC, 1975—; staff physician Craven Regional Med. Ctr., New Bern, NC, 1975—, med. dir. cardiopulmonary svcs., 1975-95. Cons. N.C. Health Dept., TB Control Br., 1997-2000; TB control physician Craven County Health Dept., 1999—; mem. N.C. TB Peer Rev. Com., 1996-2000. Pres. Ea. Area Health Edn. Ctr., 1990-95. Recipient Douglas Southhall Freeman award Va. Lung Assn., 1975, Disting. Alumnus award Bowman Gray Sch. Medicine, 1973, Robert Bageant award Va. Soc. Respiratory Care, 1987. Fellow Am. Coll. Chest Physicians, Am. Thoracic Soc., Am. Coll. Physicians; mem. N.C. Med. Soc. (councillor 1978, exec. com. 1981), Va. Thoracic Soc. (pres. 1974), N.C. Thoracic Soc. (pres. 1984), N.C. Lung Assn. (pres. 1986), Craven Pamlico Jones Med. Soc. (pres. 1984). Democrat. Episcopalian. Avocations: skiing, golf, flying, sailing, tennis. Home: 80 Bishops Ridge Dr Charlottesville VA 22901

HUNT, WILLIS B., JR., federal judge; LLB, Emory U., Atlanta, 1954; LLM, U. Va., 1990. Former judge Houston, Superior Ct. Ga.; justice Ga. Supreme Ct., Atlanta, 1986-95, chief justice, 1994-95; judge US Dist. Ct. (no. dist.) Ga., Atlanta, 1995—2005, sr. judge, 2005—. Office: US Dist Ct No Dist Ga 1756 US Courthouse 75 Spring St SW Atlanta GA 30303-3309

HUNTER, BEVERLY CLAIRE, research scientist, educator; b. Pitts., Apr. 19, 1941; d. Eldon Clare and Ethel Mae (Kamer) Roberts m. Harold G. Hunter, Jan. 7, 1966; children: Cynthia Claire, Gregory Shawn. BA cum laude (Nat. Merit scholar), U. Pitts., 1963. Cert. Geographic Info. Sys. George Mason Univ., 2003. Computer programmer U.S. Navy, 1964-65; systems engr. IBM Corp., 1965-66; dir. instructional programming Human Resources Rsch. Orgn., Alexandria, Va., 1966-68, sr. staff scientist, 1970-87; staff scientist Matrix Rsch., Alexandria, 1969; lead scientist BBN Corp., 1993-98, NSFf, program mgr. rsch. on tchg. and learning, 1989—93; scientist Boston Coll., 1998-99; pres. Piedmont Rsch. Inst., Amissville, Va., 1999—. Cons. U.S. Congress, U.S. Office Edn., Bell Labs., Telenet Comms.: pres. Targeted Learning Corp., 1983-89; adj. prof. U. San Francisco, 1985-86; v.p. Piedmont Rsch. Ctr., 1979-80; peer reviewer. Co-author: Learning Alternatives in U.S. Education: Where Student and Computer Meet, 1975, Computer Literacy, 1982; Author: My Students Use Computers, 1984 Guide to Learning Resources for Users of IBM Personal Computers, Scholastic U.S. History Data Bases, 1985, Scholastic U.S. Government Data Bases, 1985, Scholastic Life Science Data Bases, 1985, Scholastic Physical Sciences Data Bases, 1985, Scholastic World Geography Data Bases, 1986, Scholastic Poetry and Mythology Data Bases, 1986, Scholastic Literature Data Bases, 1986, Scholastic Constitution Then and Now Data Files, 1987, Scholastic Weather and Climate Data Files, 1987, Working with the U.S. Congress, 1988, Online Searching in the Curriculum, 1989; Scientists at Work hypermedia data base; editor Edn. and Computing Internat. Jour.; contbr. articles to publs. Grantee, N.S.F., 1979—2003. Mem.: Va. Natural Resources Leadership Inst., Rappahannock Friends and Lovers of Our Watershed (bd. dir., pres.), Rappahannock League Environ. Protection (Lifetime Env. Achievement award 2007), Nature Conservancy. Office: 130 Mossie Ln Amissville VA 20106-4152*

HUNTER, BYNUM MERRITT, retired lawyer; b. Greensboro, NC, June 13, 1925; s. Hill McIver and Annie (Merritt) H.; m. Ann Fulenwider, June 22, 1957 (div. 1968); children: Ann Shirley, Mary Parker; m. Mary Lane Yancey, Aug. 7, 1969 (div. 1978); m. Mary Bonneau McElveen, June 13, 1980; 1 son, Bynum Jr. AB, U. N.C., 1945, JD, 1949. Bar: N.C. 1949. Ptnr. Smith Moore LLP, 2005; ret., 2005. Served with USNR, 1943-46, 51-53. Fellow Am. Coll. Trial Lawyers, Am. Bar Found. (life mem.); mem. ABA, Internat. Assn. Def. Counsel, Am. Judicature Soc., Greensboro Bar Assn. (pres. 1965-66) 4th Cir. Jud. Conf., N.C. Bar Assn., Zeta Psi, Phi Delta Phi. Clubs: Rotary. Home: 710 Country Club Dr Greensboro NC 27408-5714 Office: Smith Moore Leatherwood, LLP Ste 1400 PO Box 21927 300 N Green St Greensboro NC 27420-1927 Office Phone: 336-378-5200. Business E-Mail: bynum.hunter@smithmoorelaw.com.

HUNTER, JACK E., retired senior district judge; b. Alexandria, La., May 24, 1945; s. William A. and Lucy A. Hunter; m. Marciela Sanchez, Aug. 12, 1989 (div. Dec. 2001). BBA, U. Houston, 1969; JD, South Tex. Coll. Law, Houston, 1974. Bar: Tex., bd. cert. criminal law: Tex. 1st asst. dist. atty., acting dist. atty. Nueces County Dist. Atty.'s Office, Corpus Christi, Tex., 1977—83; chief judge Corpus Christi Mcpl. Ct., Corpus Christi, Tex., 1983—86; state dist. judge 94th Dist. Ct., Corpus Christi, Tex., 1987—2006; ret., 2006. Adv. com. legal asst. program Del Mar Coll., Corpus Christi, 1990—; past adj. prof. arts and humanities Tex. A&M C.C., Corpus Christi. Author: From The Bench, 2005, Osaka Spa Murders, 2005, Drug Running, 2007, Three Men in A Boat Murder a cold case, 2008; contbr. articles to legal jours. Past chmn. Nueces County Gang Task Force; past adv. chair Leadership Corpus Christi XXII; past adminstrv. judge Nueces County Bd. Judges; past chmn. Nueces County Juvenile Bd.; founder Texans Against Gangs; past dist. chmn. Boy Scouts Am.; of counsel IAN Firm, McLemore, Reddell, Ardoin, & Story PLLC. Vet. US Army, 1970—71. Recipient Spirit of Benevolence award, Coastal Bend Coun. Alcohol and Drug Abuse, 1998, Citizen of Yr. award, Arthritis Found. Corpus Christi, 2000; fellow, Tex. Bar Found. Mem.: Corpus Christi Bar Assn. (chmn. continued legal edn. 1989—, Cecil Burney Humanitarian award 1990), Teen Ct. Inc. (co-founder, pres. 1990—). Democrat. Roman Catholic. Avocations: reading, travel, exercise. Personal E-mail: jhunter4010@att.net.

HUNTER, JON BLAIR, state legislator; b. Richwood, W.Va., Dec. 25, 1938; s. John Patrick and Johnie Holifield Hinkleman Hunter; m. Judy Raught; children: Greg, Beth. Former vice chmn. Mil. Com.; former founder & pres. Coalition On Legislature For Elderly; state senator 14th Dist. W.Va., 1996—; mem. Mil. Com., Edn., Health & Human Resources Com., Energy Com., Industry & Mining Com., Judiciary Labor Com., Adv. Coms. Social Work & Ctr. On Aging; adj. faculty W.Va. U.; adv. bd. W.Va. Rural Devel. Coun.; exec. dir. W.Va. Coun. Home Health Agys. Mem.: VFW, 4-H Rd. Cmty. Assn. Democrat. Catholic. Address: 1265 4H Camp Rd Morgantown WV 26508 Mailing: State Capitol Rm 225W Charleston WV 25305 Office Phone: 304-292-5826.

HUNTER, JUSTIN, healthcare services company executive, lawyer; b. Mo. m.Caroline Hunter; children: Vivian Hunter, Helena Hunter. BA in Polit. Sci., Miss. State U., 1992; JD, U. Memphis, 2000. Served to former Congressman Ed Bryant, Capitol Hill; legal clk. Methodist HealthCare; with Powers Pyles Sutter & Verville PC, Wash., DC; sr. v.p., govt. & regulatory affairs HealthSouth Corp., 2004—. Office: HealthSouth Corp 3660 Grandview Pky Ste 200 Birmingham AL 35243 Office Phone: 205-967-7116. Office Fax: 205-969-4740. Business E-Mail: justin.hunter@healthsouth.com.

HUNTER, MARCUS L., state legislator; BS in Sociology, So. U., Baton Rogue, JD. Atty., La.; mem. Dist. 17 La. House of Reps., Baton Rogue, 2012—. Democrat. Office: La House of Reps 900 N 3rd St PO Box 94062 Baton Rouge LA 70804 Business E-Mail: hunterm@legis.la.gov.

HUNTER, TODD AMES, state legislator; b. Bartlesville, Okla., Aug. 26, 1953; s. Richard A. and Patricia L. (Ames) H.; m. Alexis Taylor, May 24, 1981; children Todd Jr., Michael, Christina BA, U. Kans., 1975; JD, So. Meth. U., 1978. Bar: Tex. 1978, US Dist. Ct. (So., No & We. dist.) Tex., US Ct. Appeals (5th cir.), US Supreme Ct, bd cert. Civil Trial Law Tex. bd Legal Specialization, attended atty-Mediators Inst. Inc. (November 1991) and Advanced tng. (April 1992). Assoc. Meredith & Donnell, Corpus Christi, Tex., 1978-81; ptnr. Kleberg and Head, Corpus Christi, 1981-88; mem. Dist. 36 Tex. House of Representatives, 1988—91, mem. Dist. 32, 1992—; mem. Redford, Wray and Woolsey, Corpus Christi, 1989—; sr. ptnr. Hunter & Handel, P.C., Corpus Christi, Tex. Bd. dirs. Falfurrias (Tex.) State Bank. Chmn. civil svc. bd. Civil Svc. Commn., Corpus Christi, 1982-87, Leadership Corpus Christi, 1984, Charter Rev. Com., Corpus Christi, 1986-87; hon. bd. mem. Consumer Credit Counseling Svc.; past dir., adv. bd. mem. Corpus Christi Bend Boy Scouts. Best of Best legislators by Harte-Hanks newspapers, cited one of five legislators who had a career year by Tex. Monthly magazine, Outstanding Alumni of year by Leadership Corpus Christi Alumni 1995, Harry Gibson Statesmanship award by Golden Crescent Regional Planning Commn., recognized Texas Medicines Best Legislators by Texas Medical Assn. and Friend of Business by Tex. Bus. magazine 1995., a rising star in Tex. Legislature by Corpus Christi Caller Times and Dallas Morning News, Newsmaker Of Year by Corpus Christi Caller Times 1996. Fellow Tex. Bar Found.; mem. Tex. Bar Assn., Nueces County Bar Assn. (pres. 1986-87), Nueces County Young Lawyers Assn. (Outstanding Young Lawyer 1985), Phi Beta Kappa. Lodges: Rotary, ABA., Corpus Christi Bar Assn (past pres.), Corpus Christi Young Lawyers Assn. (past pres.), mem. Greater Corpus Christi Bus. Alliance, Corpus Christi Hispanic, Rockport-Fulton, Port Lavaca-Calhoun County, Port O'Connor, Seadrift, Port Aransas and Jackson County C.of C., mem. Corpus Christy Rotary Club. Episcopalian. Avocations: tennis, travel. Office: Hunter & Handel PC Ste 1600 Tower II 555 N Carancahua Corpus Christi TX 78478 Address: 15217 S.P.I.D. Ste 205 Corpus Christi TX 78418 Office: Room E2.808 Capital Extension PO Box 2910 Austin TX 78768 Office Phone: 361-884-8777, 512-463-0672, 361-949-4603. Office Fax: 361-884-1628. Business E-Mail: lawyers@hunterhandel.com.

HUNTLEY, ROBERT EDWARD ROYALL, retired academic administrator; b. Winston-Salem, NC, June 13, 1929; s. Benjamin F. and Elizabeth (Royall) H.; m. Evelyn Whitehurst, 1954; children: Martha Royall Huntley Rodes, Catherine Winslow Huntley McConnel, Jane Whitehurst. BA, Washington and Lee U., 1950, LLB, 1957; LLM, Harvard U., 1962. Bar: Va. 1957. Assoc. Boothe, Dudley, Koontz and Boothe, Alexandria, Va., 1957-58; asst. prof. law Washington & Lee U., Lexington, Va., 1958-59, assoc. prof. law, 1959-64, prof. law, 1964-68, pres., 1968-83, dean Sch. Law, 1967-68; pres., COO Best Products Co., Inc., Richmond, Va., 1984-87, chmn., pres., CEO, 1987-88; counsel Hunton & Williams LLP, Richmond, Va., 1988-95. Bd. dirs. Philip Morris Companies, Inc., 1976-2003, Altria Group, Inc., 2003- Mem. Va. Bd. Edn., 1970-74; mem. Va. Found. for Ind. Colls., 1968—, pres., 1974-76, chmn., 1982-83; pres. Coun. Ind. Colls. in Va., 1977-78; trustee Union Theol. Sem., Richmond, 1981-88, chmn. bd. trustees, 1983-88; mem. Gov.'s Com. on Future of Va., 1983-84; vice chmn. Gov.'s Policy Adv. Commn. on High Tech., 1984-85; pres. So. U. Conf., 1981-82; staff dir., cons. Gov.'s Task Force on Sci. and Tech., 1983-84; trustee Va. Hist. Soc., 1984-91, treas., 1988-91; trustee Stonewall Jackson Found., 1996—. With USN, 1950-53. Mem. ABA, Va. Bar Assn., Order of Coif, Phi Beta Kappa, Omicron Delta Kappa, Phi Delta Phi, Delta Tau Delta.

HUNTLEY, WILLIAM THOMAS, III, private investor, consultant; b. Greensboro, North Carolina, Mar. 13, 1935; s. William Thomas Jr. and Lillian H.; m. Gladys Louise (Bowden), Aug. 11, 1953; children: David C., William Thomas IV, Charlton A., Kimberly Patrick. BA in Econ., Davidson Coll., NC, 1958. CPCU. Field rep. Aetna Casualty and Surety Co., Atlanta, 1958—62; marine dept. mgr. Chubb and Son, Inc., Atlanta, Dallas, 1962—67; sr. v.p. Pritchard and Jerden, Inc., Atlanta, 1967—96; mng. gen. ptnr. Huntley-Bradley, Ltd., Partnership, Roswell, Ga., 1995—. Com. chmn. Peach Bowl, 1969-75. Mem. Coun. of Ins. Agt. and Brokers (pres. 1990-91), Atlanta Assn. Ind. Ins. Agt. (pres. 1979-80), Ind. Ins. Agt. Ga. (bd. dirs. 1979-81), Atlanta C. of C. (chair sports com. 1969), Atlanta Athletic Club, Golf Club Amelia Island. Republican. Presbyterian. Avocations: golf, numismatics. Home: 1807 Atlantic Pl Amelia Island FL 32034-5818 Office: Huntley-Bradley LP 2030 Riverside Rd Roswell GA 30076-4026

HUPPE, ALEX, public relations executive; b. Princeton, NJ, June 18, 1947; s. Bernard F. and Mary Lois (McMaster) Huppe. BA with honors, Harpur Coll., 1969; MA, U. Va., Charlottesville, 1971. Prof. English Western Piedmont C.C., Morganton, NC, 1971-79, asst. to pres., 1979-80; asst. dean Boston U., 1980-85; dir. news Dartmouth Coll., Hanover, NH, 1985-95; dir. pub. affairs Harvard U., Cambridge, Mass., 1995—99, v.p., cons., 1999—. Rschr. Smith/Huppe Rsch., Boston, 1980—85; adj. prof. English Maine Maritime Acad., 2002—04; adv. bd. Harpur Coll., 1998—. Co-author: (book) Alaska National Communication Program, 1982; mem. editl. bd.: Binghamton U., Binghamton Mag., 2006—. Pres. River City Arts, 1993—95; U.S. election observer Gabon, 2005; chmn. bd. dirs. Celo Health and Edn. Corp., Burnsville, NC, 1973—78; bd. dir. Assocs. Boston Pub. Libr., 1997—2002, Castine Hist. Soc., 2001—04, SUNY Binghamton Alumni, 2003—; elect. Binghamton Found. Bd., 2009. Recipient Disting. Alumni award, 2009. Mem.: NATAS (New Eng. chpt. gov. 1983—87, dir., Disting. Svc. award 1987), Slow Spokes Touring Club (elect. v.p. 2012), Ivy League News Dirs. (sec. 1988—91), Pub. Rels. Soc. Am. (exec. bd. counselors higher edn. 1998). Avocations: sailing, skiing, auto restoration. Home (Winter): 750 N Tamiami Trail 1508 Sarasota FL 34236 Personal E-mail: alexhuppe@aol.com.

HURLBURT, HARLEY ERNEST, ocean modeling and prediction scientist; b. Bennington, Vt., Apr. 12, 1943; s. Paul Rhodes and Evelyn Arlene (Lockhart) H.; m. Cheryl Elaine Finch, Jan. 10, 1998. BS in Physics, Union Coll., Schenectady, NY, 1965; MS, Fla. State U., 1971, PhD in Meteorology, 1974. NASA trainee Fla. State U., 1970-72; postdoctoral fellow advanced studies program Nat. Ctr. Atmospheric Rsch., Boulder, Colo., 1974-75; staff scientist JAYCOR, Alexandria, Va., 1975-77; oceanographer Naval Rsch. Lab. and related orgns., Stennis Space Ctr., Miss., 1977—2011; ret.; br. head Naval Rsch. Lab. and related orgns., Stennis Space Ctr., Miss., 1983-85, sr. scientist ocean modeling and prediction, 2000—11. Adj. faculty marine sci. U. So. Miss., Stennis Space Ctr., 1993-2010, part time rsch. scientist Fla. State U., 2011-; adj. faculty meteorology Fla. State U., Tallahassee, 1995—; nat. adv. panel satellite surface stress working group NASA, 1981-84, Minerals Mgmt. Svc. interagy. adv. group, 1982-89, world ocean circulation experiment working group on numerical modeling, 1984-96, USN space oceanography working group, 1986-89; co-chmn. working group on global prediction sys., ocean prediction workshop, 1986; internat. working group on acoustic monitoring of world ocean Sci. Com. Oceanic Rsch., 1991-98; internat. working group on modelling subarctic North Pacific circulation North Pacific Marine Sci. Orgn., 1994-95; sci. steering team Internat. Global Ocean Data Assimilation Experiment, 1998—2008; lectr. summer sch., Perth, Australia, 2010; mem. NASA High Resolution Ocean Topography Sci. Working Group, 2001, NASA Wide Swath Ocean Altimeter Sci. Working Group, 2002-03; project leader eddy-resolving global ocean prediction model devel. USN, NRL layered ocean model, 1987-03, later using the Hybrid Coordinate Ocean Model (HYCOM), 1999-2008; mem. steering team Philippine Straits Dynamics Experiment Office Naval Rsch., 2007-2010. Contbr. numerous articles to profl. jours. V.p. Burgundy Citizens Assn., 1976—77. Weather officer USAF, 1965—69. Scholar Union Coll., 1961-65; recipient Disting. Scientist medal 13th Internat. Colloquium, Liege, Belgium, 1981, Publ. award for best basic rsch. paper Naval Ocean R & D Activity, 1980, 90; grantee Office Naval Rsch., 1975-77, 1984-2011, Dept. Energy, 1975-78, Tex. A&M U., 1976, Office of Naval Tech., 1987-93, Space Warfare Sys., 1989-94, Advanced Rsch. Projects Agy., 1993-95, Strategic Environ. Rsch. and Devel. Program, 1994-95, Def. Dept. High Performance Computing Challenge, 1997-2011, Nat. Ocean Partnership Program, 1997—2008; case study on Eddy-resolving Global Ocean Modeling and Prediction included in 2000 Computerworld Smithsonian Collection archived in Smithsonian's Nat. Mus. Am. History's permanent rsch. collection, Excellence Partnering award Nat. Ocean Partnership Program, 2008. Mem. Am. Meteorol. Soc., Am. Geophys. Union, Oceanography Soc., Phi Sigma Kappa, Sigma Xi (Kaminski Publ. award 1991), Sigma Tau, Chi Epsilon Pi. Methodist. Achievements include research on the theory of El Nino oceanic onset and the dynamics of loop current eddy shedding in the Gulf of Mexico; discovery of the impact of upper ocean-topographic coupling via flow instabilities on upper ocean current pathways, including the Gulf Stream in the Atlantic and the Kuroshio in the Pacific; dynamical explanation of Gulf Stream separation from the coast and its pathway to the east, resolving a 60-year conundrum in oceanography; transition of the world's first eddy-resolving global ocean prediction system to the Naval Oceanographic Office for operational use. Home: 507 Hermitage Ct Pearl River LA 70452-3903 Office: Naval Rsch Lab Bay Saint Louis MS 39529 Personal E-mail: hehurlburt@gmail.com. Business E-Mail: harley.hurlburt.ctr@nrlssc.navy.mil.

HURLEY, ALFRED FRANCIS, historian, academic administrator emeritus, retired air force officer; b. Bklyn., Oct. 16, 1928; s. Patrick Francis and Margaret Teresa (Coakley) H.; m. Joanna Helen Leahy, Jan. 24, 1953; children: Alfred F., Thomas J., Mark P., Claire T., John K. BA summa cum laude, St. John's U., 1950; MA, Princeton U., 1958, PhD, 1961. Enlisted USAF, 1950, commd. lt., 1952, tng. officer, instr. navigator, 1952—56; from instr. to asst. prof. history USAF Acad., 1958—63, prof., head dept. history, 1966—80, prof. emeritus, 1990—; navigator, exec. officer USAF Hdqrs., Germany, War Plans Staff, Joint Chiefs of Staff, 1963—66; bd. mem. Acad. Bd., 1977-80; advanced through grades to brig. gen. USAF, ret., 1980; v.p. adminstrv. affairs U. North Tex. (formerly North Tex. State U.), Denton, 1980-82, pres., chancellor, 1982-2000, prof. history, 1981—; chancellor U. North Tex., 2000—02, emeritus chancellor, pres., prof. history, 2002—. Mem. adv. com. USAF hist. program sect. USAF, Washington, 1982-86, chmn., 1984-86; mem. bd. visitors Air U., 1993-97. Author: Billy Mitchell, Crusader for Air Power, 1964, (rev. edit.), 1975; contbg. author: Winged Shield, Winged Sword: A History of the USAF, 1997; co-editor: Air Power and Warfare, 1979; pub. Air Power History, 2006—. Decorated Legion of Merit (2), 1972, 1980; USAF Commendation medal, 1963, 1966; Republic of Vietnam Gallantry Cross, 1968; Guggenheim fellow, 1971-72, Eisenhower Inst., Smithsonian fellow, 1976-77; recipient Pres.'s medal St. John's U., 1990; Founders medal, U. North Tex. Health Sci. Ctr., 2006. Mem.: Tex. Philos. Soc. (pres. 2003—04, bd. dirs. 2004—), Dallas Citizens Coun. (bd. dirs. 2000—02), North Tex. Commn. (bd. dirs. 1986—2000, chmn. 1995—97, bd. dirs. 2004—), Alliance for Higher Edn. of North Tex. (trustee 1983—89, chmn. coun. of pres. 1989—90), Tex. Coun. Pub. Univ. Pres. and Chancellors (chmn. 1987—89), Coalition Urban and Met. Univs. (co-chair 1993—2002, mem. exec. com. 2002—04), Am. Hist. Assn. (chmn. NASA fellowship com. 1993—94), Am. Coun. Edn. (commn. leadership 1993—96), Am. Assn. State Colls. and Univs. (coun. state reps. 1989—92), Air Force Hist. Found. (trustee 1980—), Am. Mil. Inst. (trustee 1973—78, 1981—85). Roman Catholic. Home: 3505 Turtle Creek Blvd Apt 6-A Dallas TX 75219-5566 Business E-Mail: hurley@unt.edu.

HURLEY, DANIEL T. K., federal judge; b. Fitchburg, Mass., Feb. 24, 1943; AB cum laude, St. Anselm's Coll., 1964; JD, George Washington U., 1968. Bar: Fla. 1969, DC 1969, Calif. 1979. Asst. county solicitor Palm Beach County, Fla., 1970—73; exec. asst. state atty. 15th Jud. Cir., Fla., 1973—75, judge, 1977—79, 1986—94, chief judge, 1988—93; judge Palm Beach County Ct., 1975—77, US Dist. Ct. Appeals (4th dist.) Fla., West Palm Beach, 1979—86, US Dist Ct. (so. dist.) Fla., West Palm Beach, 1994—2009, sr. judge, 2009—. Office: US Courthouse 701 Clematis St Rm 352 West Palm Beach FL 33401-5111

HURLEY, DOUGLAS G., pilot; b. Endicott, NY, Oct. 21, 1966; BSE in Civil Engring., Tulane U., La., 1988. Entered flight tng., Tex., 1989; designated a naval aviator, 1991; reported Marine Fighter/Attack Tng. Squadron 101 for F/A-18 tng. Marine Corps Air Station, El Toro, Calif.; assigned to Marine All Weather Fighter/Attack Squadron 225; attended a number of tng. courses; F/A-18 project officer, test pilot Naval Strike Aircraft Test Squadron, VX-23, 1997; pilot NASA, 2000—. Lead astronaut support personnel for Shuttle Missions STS-107 and STS-121; worked Shuttle Landing and Rollout; served on the Columbia Reconstruction Team Kennedy Space Ctr.; with the Exploration Br. in support of the selection of the Orion Crew Exploration Vehicle; NASA dir. ops. Gagarin Cosmonaut Tng. Ctr., Star City, Russia; pilot STS-127 Mission (Endeavour), 2009, STS-135-Atlantis-The Final Space Shuttle Mission, 2011. Decorated Meritorious Svc. medal, two Navy and Marine Corps Commendation medals; recipient NASA Superior Accomplishment award, 2004, 2005, 2006, 2007. Achievements include first ever Marine pilot to fly the F/A-18 E/F Super Hornet. Avocations: hunting, bicycling, attending NASCAR races. Office: NASA Johnson Space Ctr 2101 NASA Parkway Houston TX 77058

HURLEY, FRANK THOMAS, JR., realtor; b. Washington, Oct. 18, 1924; s. Frank Thomas and Lucille (Trent) H.; m. Betty Guisinger, Aug. 9, 1997. AA, St. Petersburg Jr. Coll., 1948; BA, U. Fla., 1950. Reporter St. Petersburg Evening Independent, Fla., 1948-53; editor Arcadia Tribune, Calif., 1956-57; reporter Los Angeles Herald Express, 1957; v.p. Frank T. Hurley Assocs., Inc. Realtors, 1958—, pres., 1964—. Author: Surf, Sand and Post Card Sunsets, 1977, Pass-a-Grille Vignettes, 1999. Elected St. Petersburg Beach Bd. Commrs., 1965—69; chmn. Pinellas County Traffic Safety Coun., 1968—69; apptd. mem. Pinellas County Hist. Commn., 1993—, chmn., 2003; pres. Pass-A-Grille Cmty. Assn., 1963; mem. St. Petersburg Mus. Fine Arts, St. Pete Beach Aesthetic and Hist. Rev. Bd., chmn., 1994—96; apptd. mem. Pinellas County Sesquicentennial Coord. Com., 1995; pres. Gulf Beach Bd. Realtors, 1969; bd. govs. Palms of Pasadena Hosp., 1979—86. With USAAF, 1943—46. Recipient St. Petersburg Beach Vol. of Yr. award, 2006, Disting. Svc. award, Fla. Trust for Hist. Preservation, 2007; named Nat. Assn. Realtors. Mem.: Fla. Assn. Realtors (dir., dist. v.p. 1971), St. Petersburg Suncoast Assn. Realtors (life, Ambassadors award 1994), St. Petersburg Beach C. of C. (dir., pres. 1975-76, Citizen of Yr. award 1983), Fla. Hist. Soc., Ky. Col., Am. Legion, Pass-A-Grille Yacht Club (bd. govs.), Sigma Delta Chi, Sigma Tau Delta. Home: 2808 Sunset Way Saint Petersburg Beach FL 33706-4133 Office: 2506 Pass A Grille Way Saint Petersburg Beach FL 33706-4160 Home Phone: 727-360-7229; Office Phone: 727-367-1949.

HURLEY, GRADY SCHELL, lawyer; b. New Orleans, Nov. 29, 1954; s. Daniel Patrick and Joycelyn Mary (Schell) H.; children: Joshua, Benjamin, Mary Elizabeth, William, John. BA, Tulane U., 1976, JD, 1979, LLM, 1981. Bar: La. 1979, U.S. Dist. Ct. (ea., mid. and we. dists.) La. 1979, U.S. Ct. Appeals (5th and 11th cirs.) 1980, U.S. Supreme Ct. 1986. Assoc. Jones, Walker, Waechter, Poitevent, Carrere and Denegre, New Orleans, 1979-84, ptnr., 1984—. Bd. dirs. Tulane Admiralty Law Inst., 2006—. Editor: Damages Recoverable in Maritime Matters, 1984, Briefly Speaking, 1993. Mem. ABA (House of Delegates, 2003-06, chmn. subcom. on wrongful death and workers compensation 1990-94), Fed. Bar Assn., La. Bar Assn. (dist. rep. young lawyers sect. 1986, La. Bar examiner 1989—, elected Bar Found. appt. jud. liasion comm., 2005), New Orleans Bar Assn. (chmn. maritime law com. 1990-92, exec. bd. 1994-2003, pres.-elect 2001, pres. 2002), New Orleans Bar Found. (v.p. 2006, pres. 2007), Am. Inns of Court (chpt. pres. 2004-06), Maritime Law Assn. (maritime pers. com., proctor, chmn. offshore industires com., bd. dirs.), S.E. Admiralty Law Inst. (bd. dirs. 2004-06), Tulane U. Alumni Assn. (bd. dirs. 1986-96, pres. 1995, chmn. 35th ann. ednl. conf.), Mariner Club, Tulane Admiralty Law Inst. (bd. dirs. 2006-), EJGH Found. (bd. mem. 2006-). Republican. Roman Catholic. Avocations: sports, reading, painting, movies. Office: Jones Walker Waechter Poitevent Carrère & Denègre 201 St Charles Ave Ste 5000 New Orleans LA 70170-5100 Office Phone: 504-582-8225.

HURLEY, PAT B., state legislator; Dep. clerk Superior Ct.; state rep. Dist. 70 NC, 2007—. Mem. Appropriations com., Appropriations Subcom. on Justice and Pub. Safety, Edn. com., Edn. Subcom. on Cmty. Colleges, House Select Com. on Civil Custody Guardians, Judiciary II com., Mental Health Reform com.; vice chmn. Pensions and Retirement com. Republican. Office: North Carolina House of Representatives 300 N Salisbury St Rm 532 Raleigh NC 27603-5925 Office Phone: 336-625-9210, 919-733-5865. Business E-Mail: Pat.Hurley@ncleg.net.

HURLEY, REBECCA, lawyer; Grad. summa cum laude, U. Tex., Austin, 1976; JD summa cum laude, So. Meth. U., 1982. Law clk. to Hon. Irving L. Goldberg, US Ct. Appeals (5th cir.), 1982—83, Hon. Warren E. Burger, US Supreme Ct., 1983—84; atty. Dallas; chmn., Bus. Transactions Practice Group Patton Boggs, LLP, 2000—02; chief compliance officer Triad Hospital, Inc., v.p., compliance Plano, Tex., 2002—04, assoc. gen. counsel, chief compliance officer & asst. sec., 2004—05, sr. v.p., gen. counsel & sec., 2005—. Office: Triad Hospitals Inc 4000 Meridian Blvd Franklin TN 37067-6325 Office Phone: 214-473-7000. Business E-Mail: rebecca.hurley@triadhospitals.com.

HURNEY, MARTY (MARTIN RUSSELL HURNEY), former professional sports team executive; b. Wheaton, Md., 1955; m. Jeannie Hurney; children: Joe, James. BA in Gen. Studies, Cath. U., Washington, 1993. Journalist Montgomery Jour., Silver Springs, Md., Washington Star, 1978—81; Washington Redskins beat writer Washington Times, 1981—86; pub. rels. dept. Washington Redskins, 1988—90; asst. to the gen. mgr. San Diego Chargers, 1990—98; dir. football ops. Carolina Panthers, 1998—2002, gen. mgr., 2002—12.

HURST, MICHAEL KENNETH, otolaryngologist, educator; DDS, W.Va. U., 1977; MD, Marshall U., 1988. Diplomate Am. Bd. Otolaryngology, 1994, lic. to practice Pa., 1993. Resident otolaryngology Univ. W.Va. Hosps., Morgantown, W.Va., 1989—93, resident head and neck surgery, 1989—93, intern, 1989; assoc. prof. otolaryngology W.Va. Univ.; hosp. affiliation includes Monongalia Gen. Hosp. Office: West Virginia University Hospitals Medical Center Dr Morgantown WV 26506-4749 Office Phone: 304-598-4000.

HURST, STEVE, state legislator; m. Linda Hurst; children: Michael, Kenneth, Vance. Businessman; employee Ga. Pacific Corp.; commr. Talladega County, Ala.; mem. Dist. 35 Ala. House of Reps., Montgomery, 1998—. Mem. Calhoun County C. of C., Talladega County C. of C. Democrat. Office: 155 Quail Run Rd Munford AL 36268 also: Ala House of Reps Ala State House 11 S Union St Rm 630-A Montgomery AL 36130 Office Phone: 334-353-9215.

HURT, ROBERT (BOB HURT), United States Representative from Virginia, former state legislator; b. NYC, June 16, 1969; m. Kathryn Raine Heithaus; children: Charles Hallam, Clement Nolting, John. BA in English, Hampden-Sydney Coll., Va., 1991; JD, Miss. College Sch. Law, 1995; grad., Sorensen Inst. Political Leadership, Charlottesville, Va., 2000. Chief asst. commonwealth's atty. Pittsylvania County, Va., 1996—99; atty. H. Victor Millner, Jr. P.C., Chatham, Va., 1999—2008; mem. Dist 16 Va. House of Delegates, Richmond, 2002—07; mem. Dist 19 Va. State Senate, Richmond, 2008—10; pvt. law practice Chatham, 2008—; mem. US Congress from 5th Va. Dist., Washington, 2011—, US House Financial Services Com., Washington, 2011—. Councilman Chatham Town Coun., 2000—01. Mem. adv. bd. Hampden-Sydney Wilson Ctr.; elder Chatham Presbyn. Ch.; bd. dirs. New Coll. Inst., Martinsville, Va., Roman Eagle Meml. Home, Danville, John Marshall Found. Mem.: Va. Bar Assn. (bd. governors), Va. State Bar, Chatham Rotary. Republican. Presbyterian. Office: US House of Representatives 125 Cannon House Office Bldg Washington DC 20515 Office Phone: 202-225-4711. Office Fax: 202-225-5681.*

HURT, WADE, state legislator; b. Feb. 20, 1967; m. Lara Hurt; children: Christian, Joseph, Jeremiah. Conceal-carry instr.; lic. real estate agt.; mem. Dist. 37 Ky. House of Reps., Frankfort, 2011—. Mem. Epiphany United Meth. Ch. Named a Ky. Col. Republican. Methodist. Office: Kentucky House of Reps Annex Rm 324E 702 Capitol Ave Frankfort KY 40601 Home Phone: 502-424-1544; Office Phone: 502-564-8100 ext. 629. Business E-Mail: wade.hurt@lrc.ky.gov.

HURWITZ, SHEPARD RAPHAEL, orthopaedic surgeon, educator, medical association administrator; b. NYC, Aug. 19, 1950; s. Paul A. and Beatrice T. H.; m. Margretta Kristine Manser, Apr. 11, 1992; children: Zoe, Leah. BA, Columbia Coll., 1972; MD, Columbia U., 1976. Internship U. Va., 1976—77, residency, 1977—78, N.Y. Orthopaedic Hosp., 1978—81; asst. prof. George Washington U., Washington, 1984-88; assoc. prof. U. Rochester, NY, 1989-94; assoc. prof. orthop. surgery U. Va., Charlottesville, 1994—2000, prof. orthop. surgery, 2000—08, S. Ward Casscells prof. orthop. surgery, 2001—08; exec. dir. American Bd. Orthop. Surgeons, 2008—; prof. orthop. surgery U. NC Sch. Medicine, 2008—. Cons. NIH Clin. Ctr., Bethesda, Md., 1983-2001. Author, editor: Foot and Ankle Pain, 2nd edit., 2000. Mem. American Orthopaedic Assn. (mem. nominating com. 1997-98), American Assn. Orthop. Surgeons (leadership devel. com., dir. 2005). Jewish. Avocations: fishing, hunting, tennis. Office: American Bd Orthop Surgery 400 Silver Cedar Ct Chapel Hill NC 27514 Office Phone: 919-929-7103. Business E-Mail: shurwitz@abos.org.*

HUSA, KAREL, composer, conductor, educator; b. Prague, Czech Republic, Aug. 7, 1921; came to U.S., 1954, naturalized, 1959; s. Karel and Bozena (Dongresova) H.; m. Simone Perault, Feb. 2, 1952; children: Catherine, Anne-Marie, Elizabeth, Caroline. M summa cum laude, Conservatory and Acad. Music, Prague, 1945, M summa cum laude, 1947; lic. for conducting, Ecole Normale de Paris, 1947; grad., Conservatoire de Paris, 1948; MusD (hon.), Coe Coll., 1976, Cleve. Inst., 1985, Ithaca Coll., 1986, Baldwin-Wallace Conservatory, 1991, Hartwick Coll., 1997, New Eng. Conservatory, 1998, Acad. Musical Arts, Capital U., 2006; DHL (hon.), Coll. St. Vincent, 1996; ArtsD (hon.), Masaryk U., Czech Republic, 2000, Acad. Musical Arts, 2000; DFA (hon.), U. Ctrl. Ark., 2006; attending, U. Fla., 2011—. Guest condr. Czechoslovak Radio, Prague, 1945-46; guest condr. orchs. in Hamburg, Germany, Brussels, Paris, Zurich, Switzerland, Suisse Romande, London, Manchester, England, Prague, Stockholm, Hong Kong, Singapore, Japan, Cin., Buffalo, NYC, Boston, Rochester, NY, Balt., San Diego, Syracuse, NY; faculty Cornell U., Ithaca, NY, 1954—, prof. music, 1954—, dir. univ. symphony and chamber orchs., 1972-92, Kappa Alpha prof. music emeritus. Composer: Symphony, 1953, Fantasies for Orchestra, 1957, Divertimento for Brass, 1959, Poem for Viola and Orchestra, 1959, Elegy and Rondeau for Saxophone and Orchestra, 1961, Divertimento for String Orchestra, 1948, String Quartet No.1, 1942, String Quartet No. 2, 1952, Portrait for String Orch., 1953, Mosaiques for Orch., 1961, Fresque for Orchestra, rev. 1964, Sonatina for Piano, 1943, Sonatina Violin and Piano, 1945, Sonata for Piano, 1949, Evocations of Slovakia for Clarinet, Viola and Cello, 1951, Eight Duets for Piano, 1955, Twelve Moravian Songs, 1956, Poem for Viola and Orchestra, 1962, Serenade for Woodwind Quintet and Orch., 1963, Concerto for Brass Quintet and Orch., 1965, Two Preludes; flute, clarinet, bassoon, 1966, Music for Percussion, 1966, Concerto for alto saxophone, concert band, 1967, String Quartet No. 3, 1968 (Pulitzer prize 1969), Music for Prague; for Band, 1968, for Orch., 1969, Apotheosis of this Earth for Winds, 1970, Concerto for Percussion and Winds, 1971, Two Sonnets from Michelangelo for Orch., 1971, Concerto for Trumpet and Wind Orch., 1973, Apotheosis of this Earth for Chorus and Orch., 1973, Sonata for Violin and Piano, 1972-73, The Steadfast Tin Soldier; for narrator and orch., 1974, Sonata for Piano, No. 2, 1975, Monodrama, ballet for orch., 1975, An American Te Deum; for mixed chorus, baritone solo, band and organ, 1976, for orch., 1978, Landscapes for Brass Quintet, 1977, Fanfare for Brass Ensemble, 1980, Pastoral for Strings, 1980, Three Moravian Songs, 1981, The Trojan Women, ballet for orch., 1981, Sonata a Tre, 1982, Concerto for Wind Ensemble, 1982 (Sudler award 1983), Cantata, 1983, Smetana Fanfare for Wind Ensemble, 1984, Variations for Violin, Viola, Cello and Piano, 1984 (Friedheim award 1986), Symphonic Suite for Orch., 1984, Intrada for Brass Quintet, 1984, Concerto for Orch., 1986, Concerto for Organ and Orch., 1987, Frammenti for Organ solo, 1987, Concerto for Trumpet and Orch., 1987, Concerto for Violoncello and Orch., 1988 (Grawemeyer award 1993), String Quartet No. 4, 1990, String Quartet No. 0, 1943, Singanietta for Orchestra, 1943, Suica for Viola & Piano, 1945, Youth Overture, 1991, Cayuga Lake (Memories), 1992, Concerto for Violin and Orch., 1993, Five Poems for Wood-Wind Quintet, 1994, Les Couleurs Fauves, 1995, Midwest Celebration Fanfare, 1996, Celebration for Orch., 1997, Postcard from Home, 1997, Song, for Mixed Chorus, 2000, Sonatina for Flute and Piano, 2003, Cheetah for Wind Ensemble, 2006, Three Studies for Clarinet 2007, 4 Bohemian Sketches, 2009, others; commns. from, UNESCO, Koussevitsky Found., Nat. Endowment for Arts, Friends of Music at Cornell, Fine Arts Found. Chgo., Ithaca Coll., U. Ga., Chgo. Symphony Orch., Butler U., Washington Music Soc., Coe Coll., NY Philharm., U. So. Calif., Kerze Found., Prague Spring Festival, also others.; editor: French Baroque Music: Reconstructions of Old French Baroque works by Lully and Delalande, 1961-68. Recipient prize Prague Acad. Arts, 1948, French Govt. award, 1946-47, L. Boulanger award, 1952, Pulitzer prize in music, 1969, Acad. Inst. Arts and Letters award, 1989, Grawemeyer award U. Louisville, 1993, Serge Koussevitzky Music Found. award, 1993, Czech Republic's medal of merit of 1st degree Pres. V. Havel, 1995, medal of Honor, City of Prague, 1998; Guggenheim fellow, 1964-65. Mem. Internat. Inst. Arts and Letters (life), AAAL, Belgian Royal Acad. Arts and Scis., Am. Music Ctr., Internat. Soc. Contemporary Music, French Soc. Composers, Am. Fedn. Musicians, Kappa Gamma Psi (hon.), Kappa Kappa Psi (hon.), Delta Omicron (hon.), Phi Mu Alpha (hon.). Avocations: painting, sports. Home: 3417 Foy Glen Ct Apex NC 27539-3681 Office: Karel Husa Archive & Gallery Sch Music Ithaca Coll Ithaca NY 14850

HUSSAM, ABUL, chemistry professor; BSc with honors in Chemistry, U. Dhaka, Bangladesh, 1975, MSc in Chemistry, 1976; PhD in Analytical Chemistry, U. Pitts., 1982. Prof. dept. chemistry and biochemistry George Mason U., Fairfax, Va. Contbr. articles to sci. jours. Recipient Grainger Challenge Gold award, NAE, 2007. Achievements include invention of the SONO filter, a household water treatment system for eliminating arsenic. Office: Dept Chemistry and Biochemistry George Mason U 4400 University Dr Fairfax VA 22030 Office Phone: 703-993-1085. E-mail: ahussam@gmu.edu.

HUSSEY, WAYNE A., retail executive; Grad., Drake U. Sr. v.p., properties & store devel. Neiman Marcus stores, 1999—2007; sr. v.p., properties and store devel. Neiman Marcus, Inc., 2007—; sr. v.p., properties & store devel. Neiman Marcus Group, Inc., 2007—. Office: Neiman Marcus Inc 1618 Main St Dallas TX 75201 Office Phone: 214-743-7600. Business E-Mail: wayne_hussey@neimanmarcus.com.

HUSSMAN, WALTER E., JR., publishing executive; b. Texarkana, Tex., 1947; s. Walter E. Sr. and Betty (Palmer) Hussman; m. Robena Kendrick; 3 children. BA in Journalism, U. NC, Chapel Hill, 1968; MBA, Columbia U., NYC, 1970. Gen. mgr. Camden News, Ark.; from v.p. & gen. mgr. to pres, CEO WEHCO Media, Inc. (formerly Palmer Newspapers), Little Rock, 1973—; pub., owner Ark. Democrat, 1974—91, Ark. Democrat-Gazette, 1991—. Bd. visitors U. NC, Chapell Hill. Recipient Disting. Alumnus award, U. NC Chapel Hill, 2009; named Pub. of Yr., Editor & Pub. mag., 2008. Office: Ark Dem Gazette 121 E Capitol Ave Little Rock AR 72201 also: WEHCO Media Inc PO Box 2221 Little Rock AR 72203 Office Phone: 501-378-3400.

HUSTON, DANIEL CLIFF, geophysicist; b. Anchorage, June 29, 1955; s. Arthur Cliff and Allie Mae (Ogden) H.; m. Holly Hunter, Oct. 10, 1992; children: Lana Marie, Hayley Allison. BS in Geology and Geophysics, U. Hawaii, 1980, marine option program cert., 1980; MA in Geological Scis., U. Tex., 1987. Surveyor Trans Alaska Pipeline, 1975-78; geologist R&M Cons., Anchorage, 1980; geophysicst U.S. Minerals Mgmt. Svc., Anchorage, 1981-83; rsch. asst. Miss. Canyon Project, Austin, 1983-84; project SEER U. Tex. Inst. Geophysics, Austin, 1983-87; geophys. intern Sohio Petroleum Co., San Francisco, summer 1984; geophysicist leader advanced seismic methods group Unocal Sci. and Tech. Divsn., Brea, Calif., 1987-90; sr. geophysicist Unocal Oil and Gas Divsn., Houston, 1991-96; founder, v.p. Hunter 3-D Inc. (geophys. consulting firm), 1996—, Creekside Exploration, Inc. (oil and gas exploration firm), 1999—. Pres. Creekside Exploration, Inc., 1999—; presenter in field. Contbr. articles to profl. jours. Fellow U. Tex. Indsl. Assocs., 1983. Mem. Am. assn. Petroleum Geologists, Soc. Exploration Geophysicists (presenter workshop 1984, ann. conv. 1986, regional conv. 1989, presenter workshop Melbourne, Australia, 2006). Methodist. Avocations: travel, scuba diving, skiing, weightlifting, reading, boating. Home: 1635 Creekside Dr Sugar Land TX 77478-4203

HUSZAGH, FREDRICK WICKETT, lawyer, information technology executive, educator; b. Evanston, Ill., July 20, 1937; s. Rudolph LeRoy and Dorothea (Wickett) H.; m. Sandra McRae, Apr. 4, 1959; children: Floyd McRae, Fredrick Wickett II, Theodore Wickett II. BA, Northwestern U., 1958; JD, U. Chgo., 1962, LLM, 1963, JSD, 1964. Bar: Ill. 1962, U.S. Dist. Ct. D.C. 1965, U.S. Supreme Ct. 1966. Market rschr. Leo Burnett Co., Chgo., 1958-59; internat. atty. COMSAT, Washington, 1964-67; assoc. Debevoise & Liberman, Washington, 1967-68; asst. prof. law Am. U., Washington, 1968-71; program dir. NSF, Washington, 1971-73; assoc. prof. U. Mont., Missoula, 1973-76, U. Wis., Madison, 1976-77; exec. dir. Dean Rusk Ctr., U. Ga., Athens, 1977-82; prof. U. Ga., 1982—2003, prof. emeritus, 2004—. Chmn. TWH Corp., Athens, 1982—; chmn. Profession Mgmt. Techs., Inc., Athens, 1993-96; cons. TWH Scv. Corp.; cons. Pres. Johnson's Telcommunications Task Force, Washington, 1967-68; co-chmn. Nat. Gov.'s Internat. Trade Staff Commn., Washington, 1979- 81. Author: International Decision-Making Process, 1964, Comparative Facts on Canada, Mexico and U.S., 1979; editor Rusk Ctr. Briefings, 1981-82; contbr. articles to publs. Mem. Econ. Policy Coun., N.Y.C., 1981-89. NSF grantee, 1974-78. Republican. Presbyterian. Office: U Ga Law Sch Athens GA 30602 Home Phone: 706-255-4536. Business E-Mail: huszagh@uga.edu.

HUTCHENS, J. JUSTIN, investment company executive; BS in Human Services, U. No. Colo.; MS in Mgmt., Regis U. Sr. v.p., COO Summerville Sr. Living, 2003—07; exec. v.p., COO Emeritus Sr. Living, 2007—09; pres., COO Nat. Health Investors, Inc., 2009—11, pres., CEO, 2011—. Named one of America's 20 Most Powerful CEOs 40 and Under, Forbes mag., 2012. Office: National Health Investors, Inc 222 Robert Rose Dr Murfreesboro TN 37130 Office Phone: 615-890-9100. Office Fax: 615-225-3030.

HUTCHEON, WALLACE SCHOONMAKER, retired historian; b. NYC, June 27, 1933; s. Wallace Schoonmaker and Dorothy Mae (Tate) Hutcheon; m. Margaret Marie Crossen, Apr. 27, 1963; children: Dorothy Lee, Hillary Ann. BS in Agrl. Econs., Pa. State U., 1954; MA in History, George Washington U., 1969, MPhil in History, 1971, PhD in History, 1975. Commd. ensign USNR, 1955, advanced through grades to comdr., 1970; comm. officer Fawtulant Naval Air Sta., Key West, Fla., 1955-59; edn. officer USS Kitty Hawk, 1962-64; air intelligence officer CVW-2, 1964-66, intelligence analyst DIA, 1966-70; released to inactive duty, 1970; lectr. George Mason U., Fairfax, Va., 1970; instr. St. Marys Coll., Md., 1971; from asst. prof. to assoc. prof. history No. Va. CC, Annandale, 1971—80, prof., 1980—2008, head dept., 1974—2008, asst. chmn. divsn. social scis. and pub. svcs., 1979—2003, asst. dean Liberal Arts, 2003—08, prof. emeritus, 2009—. Mgmt. tng. cons. Health Resources Adminstn., HEW, Hyattsville, Md., 1978; cons. mil. evaluations program Am. Coun. Edn., Washington, 1980; cons. coll. history textbooks Houghton-Mifflin Co., Boston, 1992—; pub. spkr. Mariners Mus., DC Historian Luncheon, others. Mem. adv. bd. ann. edits. Dushkin Pub. Co.; author: Robert Fulton: Pioneer of Undersea Warfare, 1981; contbr. manuscripts collection to U.S. Navy History Divsn. Mem. History of City of Fairfax Roundtable, 1995—98; history day judge George Mason U., 1990—2002. Recipient Outstanding Contbns. to Edn. award, Alumni Fedn. No. Va. CC, 1993, 1995, 2003, 2008, Golden Apple award, Student Govt., 1999—2000, Constn. Day Spkr., Northern Vr. CC, 2009. Mem.: U.S. Capitol Hist. Soc., No. Va. Assn. History (bd. dirs. 1994, v.p. 1994), U.S. Naval Inst., 1885 Club, Delta Chi. Democrat. Episcopalian. Avocations: swimming, reading, music, theater. Home: 4425 Village Dr Fairfax VA 22030-5642 Personal E-mail: mhutch70@cox.net.

HUTCHESON, JACK ROBERT, hematologist, medical oncologist; b. Rock Hill, SC, Dec. 26, 1946; s. Jack Robert and Lillian Massey (Dunlap) H.; m. Charlene Marie Dixon, Sept. 14, 1974; children: Gregory Allen, Julia Lynn. BS in Biology, Wake Forest U., 1969; MD, Med. U. S.C., 1973. Diplomate in internal medicine, hematology, oncology Am. Bd. Internal Medicine. Straight med. intern U. Md. Hosp., Balt., 1973-74, resident in medicine, 1974-76; fellow in hematology Med. U. S.C., Charleston, 1976-78; fellow in oncology Emory U., Atlanta, 1978-79; oncologist, hematologist Oncology and Hematology Assocs. SW Va. Inc., Roanoke, 1979—2007; med. dir. Carilion Health Sys. Oncology Svc. Line, Roanoke, 1996—2003. Instr., assoc. investigator in hematology Med. U. S.C./VA Hosp., Charleston, 1977-78; assoc. prof. medicine U. Va., Roanoke. Contbr. articles to med. jours. Pres. Scottish Soc. Va. Highlands, Roanoke, 1996, 2000, 01; chair com. on smoking cessation Va. br. Am. Cancer Soc., Roanoke, 1980; mem. Vets. Corps. of Artillary, N.Y. Decorated Comdr. Most Venerable Order of Hosp. of St. John of Jerusalem, Caballero Grand Cruz Order Don Carlos I (Portugal); recipient Berson Yalow award, Soc. Nuclear Medicine, 1977; grantee for hematology, VA Career Devel., 1977—78. Fellow ACP; mem. Am. Soc. Clin. Oncology, Am. Soc. Hematology, St. Andrews Soc. Presbyterian. Avocations: Jaguar auto restoration, genealogy, Scottish/Celtic activities, bagpipes. Home: 2860 S Jefferson St Roanoke VA 24014-3320 Personal E-mail: auldpyper@aol.com.

HUTCHESON, JAMES STERLING, retired physician, allergist; b. Richmond, Va., Apr. 17, 1936; s. James P. and Daisy-Clarke (Lorentz) H.; m. Nancy Montgomery Sanders, May 20, 1961; children: Anne Farrar McCausland, Betsy Dulaney Hutcheson Harvey. Student, Roanoke Coll., Va., 1953-55; BA, U. Va., 1955-57; MD, The Johns Hopkins U., 1957-61. Diplomate Am. Bd. Allergy and Clin. Immunology. Intern in medicine U. Va., Charlottesville, Va., 1961-62; resident in medicine Med. Coll. Va., Richmond, Va., 1962-64; fellow in allergy and immunology U. Va., Charlottesville, Va., 1964-65; asst. prof. medicine Med. Coll. Va., 1967-68; staff Nalle Clinic, Charlotte, 1968-89; pvt. practice Carolina Asthma and Allergy Ctr., 1990—2005, ret., 2005. Founder Allergy Clinic USAF Acad. Hosp., Colo., 1965-67; cons. Blue Cross/Blue Shield of NC, 1985-2002; adj. assoc. prof. pediats. U. NC Sch. Medicine, Carolinas Med. Ctr., Charlotte, 1997-2000. Bd. trustees Charlotte County Day Sch., 1974-85; bd. dirs. Friends of Music Queens Coll., 1994-96. Capt. USAF M.C. Fellow Am. Acad. Allergy, Asthma and Immunology, Am. Coll. Allergy, Asthma and Immunology; mem. Southeastern Allergy Assn., NC Soc. Allergy and Clin. Immunology (former pres.). Episcopalian. Avocations: gardening, hiking, classical music, reading. Home: 334 Green Cove Rd Sugar Mountain Banner Elk NC 28604 Personal E-mail: sthutch@skybest.com.

HUTCHESON, TAD, air transportation executive; b. Lookout Mountain, Tenn. BS in French Lit. & Bus. Adminstrn., King Coll.; MBA, Wake Forest U. Planning & mktg. positions Delta Air Lines, Inc.; dir. strategic planning, v.p. mktg. KIWI Internat. Air Lines; joined AirTran Airways, 1971, dir. mktg., 2005; v.p. mktg. and sales AirTran Airways, Inc., 2005—. Mem. Am. Assn. of Advt. Agencies, Atlanta Symphony Orchestra, Church of Apostles, Emory U., Fla. Gov.'s Conf. on Tourism, Ga. C. of C., IEG Sponsorship Conf., Jr. Achievement of Ga., Metro Atlanta C. of C., Pub. Rels. Soc. America Conf., Travelers' Aid of Metropolitan Atlanta, Wharton Sch. Bus. Recipient Rising Star awards, Travel Agent Mag. Office: AirTran Holdings Inc 9955 AirTran Blvd Orlando FL 32827 Office Phone: 407-318-5600. Office Fax: 407-318-5900. Business E-Mail: tad.hutcheson@airtran.com.

HUTCHINGS, ROBERT L., dean, former ambassador; m. Susan Schwartz, June 7, 1969. BS, US Naval Acad., 1969; MA, Coll. William & Mary, 1975; PhD, U. Va., 1979. Fellow & dir. internat. studies Woodrow Wilson Internat. Ctr. Scholars, Washington, 1993—97; dir. European affairs NSC, Washington, 1989—92; spl. adviser sec. US Dept. State, Washington, 1992—93; chmn. US Nat. Intelligence Coun., Washington, 2003—05; asst. dean Woodrow Wilson Sch. Pub. and Internat. Affairs Princeton U., NJ, 1997—2002, diplomat-in-residence, 2005—10; dean Lyndon B. Johnson Sch. Pub. Affairs, U. Tex., Austin, 2010—. Lt. USN, 1969—74. Office: Lyndon B Johnson Sch Pub Affairs University of Texas at Austin PO Box Y Austin TX 78713-8925 Home: 3709 Weather Hill Love Austin TX 78730 Business E-Mail: hutchngs@princeton.edu.*

HUTCHINSON, DONNA, state legislator; b. New Bern, NC; MA, Univ. Ark. Mediator DJ Consulting; mem. Dist. 98 Ark. House of Reps., 2007—. Republican. Address: 24 Rillington Dr Bella Vista AR 72714 Office Phone: 479-876-6011. Business E-Mail: hutchinsond@arkleg.state.ar.us.

HUTCHINSON, LESLIE JULIAN, preventive medicine physician; b. Cin., June 22, 1957; s. Joseph Edward and Evelyn (Moss) H.; m. Stephanie Ellyn Leffingwell, Dec. 22, 1989. BS, Xavier U., 1978; MD, U. Cin. Coll. of Medicine, 1984; MPH, The Johns Hopkins U., 1990. Diplomate in occupl. medicine Am. Bd. Preventive Medicine; MD, Calif., Ga.; registered hazardous substances profl. Chemist EPA, Cin., 1982; Ctrs. for Disease Control vis. program staff fellowship Nat. Inst. for Occupl. Safety and Health, Cin., 1984; resident in internal medicine Wright State U., Dayton, Ohio, 1984-85; med. officer Agy. for Toxic Substances and Disease Registry, Atlanta, 1986-92; occupl. medicine resident Emory U., Atlanta, 1992-93; adj. assoc. prof. environ. and occupl. health Emory U. Sch. Pub. Health, Atlanta, 1990—; pres. HLM Consultants, Atlanta, 1993—. On-site peer reviewer Tex. Air Control Bd., Galveston, 1987-88; mem. Emory U. Acad. Adv. Coun. on Occupl. and Environ. Health, Atlanta, 1989—; v.p., chief med. officer Internat. Inst. Environ. Risk Mgmt., U. S.W. Tex., San Marcos, 1997—. Contbr. articles to profl. jours. Instr. med. coll. admission text preparation program for minority students Atlanta U., 1987-90. Recipient Performance Mgmt. and Recognition System award Dept. Health and Human Svcs., 1989, Spl. Act or Svc. award Dept. of Health and Human Svcs., 1992, Xavier U. Achievement and Nat. Merit scholarships, Xavier Biology prize. Mem. Nat. Environ. Health Assn., Delta Omega, Alpha Omega Alpha, Sigma Pi Sigma. Avocations: photography, oriental philosophy. Office: HLM Consultants 214 Wynfield Way Auburn GA 30011-2849 Business E-Mail: hlm@hlmconsultants.com.

HUTCHINSON, SCOTT, energy executive; BA in Mktg., U. Ctrl. Fla., 1977. Sr. buyer Fluor Corp., 1979—84; various positions Grant Supply Co., 1984; various positions, Grant Supply Unit McJunkin Red Man Corp., 1984, outside sales rep., Grant Supply Unit Houston, regional mgr., Northern and Southern Calif., 1990—98, sr. v.p., Midwest region, 1998, sr. v.p., Eastern region, 2009, exec. v.p., N.Am. ops., 2009—. Office: McJunkin Red Man Corp 2 Houston Ctr 909 Fannin Ste 3100 Houston TX 77010-1011 Office Fax: 713-655-1477. Business E-Mail: shutchinson@mcjunkin.com.

HUTCHISON, KAY BAILEY (KATHRYN ANN BAILEY HUTCHISON), lawyer, former United States Senator from Texas; b. Galveston, Tex., July 22, 1943; d. Allan Abner & Kathryn Ella (Sharp) Bailey; m. John Pierce Parks, April 8, 1967 (div. 1969) m. Elton Ray Hutchison, March 16, 1978 (dec, March 30, 2014); children: Kathryn, Houson, Brenda, Julie BA, U. Tex., 1992, LLB, 1967. Bar: Tex. 1967, US Supreme Ct., 1977. TV news reporter, Houston, 1969-71; pvt. law practice, 1969-74; press sec. to co-Chair Anne Armstrong Republican Nat. Com. (RNC), 1971; vice chair Nat. Transp. Safety Bd. (NTSB), Washington, 1976-78; asst. prof. U. Tex., Dallas, 1978-79; sr. v.p., gen. counsel Republic Bank Corp., Dallas, 1979-81; pntr. Boyd-Levinson, Ltd., Houston and Dallas, 1981-91; mem. Tex. House of Reps., 1972-76; treas. State of Tex., 1991—93; US Senator from Tex. Washington, 1993—2013; chair US Senate Republican Conf., 2001—07, US Senate Republican Policy Com., 2007—09; vice chmn. US Senate Com. on Commerce, Sci. & Transp., 2009—13; sr. counsel Bracewell & Giuliani LLP, Dallas, 2013—. Mem. internat. advisory bd. FleishmanHillard, 2013—; mem. advisory coun. Ctr. for Strategic & Internat. Studies (CSIS), 2013—; mem. global advisory coun. Bank of America Corp., 2013—; mem. Campaign to Fix the Debt's Congressional Fiscal Leadership Coun., 2013—. Co-author: Nine and Counting: The Women of the Senate, 2000; author: American Heroines: The Spirited Women Who Shaped Our Country, 2004, Leading Ladies: American Trailblazers, 2007, Unflinching Courage: Pioneering Women Who Shaped Texas, 2013. Recipient Eagle award for Valued Commitment to Our Nation's Hispanic Cmty., 1993, Silver Ingot Ward Coastal Conservation Assn, 1997, CLEAT award, 2000, Nat. Family Mil. Assn. award, 2001, Nat. Leadership award Hispanic Assn. Coll. and U., 2002, Congl. Leadership award Women's Fgn. Policy Grp., 2004, Disting. Public Svc. award Alliance for Aging Rsch., 2004, Adam Smith Fed. Elected Official medal Bus. Industry Polit. Action Com., 2004, Wetland Sponser of Yr. award Ducks Unlimited, 2005, Disting. Public Svc. award American Legion Nat. Comdr., 2006, Outstanding Legislator award Assn. US Army, 2006, Charles Dick Medal of Merit Nat. Guard Assn. Tex., 2006, Sewall-Belmont House & Museum's Alice award, 2007, Air Force Assn. Disting. American award, 2008, US Hispanic Chamber of Commerce Lifetime Achievement award, 2012; named Republican Woman of Yr. Nat. Fedn. Republican Women, 1995, Outstanding U. Tex. Alumnus, 1995, Texan of Yr. Tex. Legis. Conf., 1997, Mr. South Tex. Washington's Birthday Celebration Assn., 2005, Legislator of Yr. Deep East Tex. Coun. of Govt., 2005; named to The Tex. Women's Hall of Fame, 1997, named one of The 100 Most Influential Texas Women of the Century Tex. Women's Chamber of Commerce, 1999, The 30 Most Powerful Women in America, Ladies Home Jour., 2001, 100 Most Powerful Women in World, Forbes mag., 2005. Fellow, U. Tex. Law Alumni Assn. (pres. 1985-86). Republican. Episcopalian. Office: Bracewell & Giuliani LLP 1445 Ross Ave Ste 3800 Dallas TX 75202 Office Phone: 214-758-1042. Office Fax: 800-404-3970.*

HUTCHISON, LARRY M., lawyer, insurance company executive; b. Des Moines, Iowa, Jan. 29, 1954; BBA, U. Iowa, 1976; JD, Drake U., 1979. Bar: Iowa 1979. Joined Torchmark Corp., Birmingham, Ala., 1986, v.p., 1997—99, exec. v.p., 1999—, gen. counsel, 1999—, co-CEO, 2012—. Mem.: Iowa Bar Assn. Office: Torchmark Corp 3700 S Stonebridge Dr PO Box 8080 Mc Kinney TX 75070-8080 Office Phone: 972-569-4000. Business E-Mail: lhutchison@torchmarkcorp.com.

HUTCHISON, VICTOR HOBBS, biologist, educator; b. Blakely, Ga., June 15, 1931; s. Joseph Victor and Veva (Hobbs) H.; m. Theresa Dokos, Dec. 14, 1952; children: Victoria Ann, John Christopher, David Michael (dec.), Kenneth Hobbs (dec.). BS, N. Ga. Coll., 1952; MA, Duke U., 1956, PhD, 1959; grad., U.S. Army Command and Gen. Staff Coll. Instr. Duke U., 1957-58, faculty fellow, So. Fellowship Fund fellow, 1958-59; mem. faculty U. R.I., 1959-70, prof. biology, 1968-70; dir. Inst. Environ. Biology, 1966—70; prof., chmn. dept. zoology U. Okla., Norman, 1970-80, George Lynn Cross rsch. prof. zoology, 1979-2001, rsch. prof. emeritus, 2001—; col. med. svc. corp. USAR, 1954—82. Rsch. prof. Universidad de Los Andes, Bogotá, Colombia, 1965-66; prin. investigator Nat. Geog. Soc.-U. R.I. herpetological expdn. to Colombia, 1964-65, Nat. Geog. Soc.-U. Okla. expdns. to Lake Titicaca, 1975, Cameroon, 1981. Editor Animal Natural History series, 1991—; rsch. and articles on heat tolerances of lower vertebrates, effects of day-length on metabolism and temperature tolerance of lower vertebrates, physiology of lower vertebrates, physiol. ecology of amphibians and reptiles, respiration in amphibians, behavioral thermoregulation. Founder, past pres. Oklahomans for Excellence in Sci. Edn. With US Army, 1952—54. Decorated Army Commendation medal, Meritorious Svc. medal; Guggenheim fellow, 1965-66; Friend of Darwin award Nat. Ctr. Sci. Edn., 2008, Constl. Heritage award, Okla. Chpt. Americans United for Separation of Ch. and State, 2000, Disting. Svc. to Okla. Sci. Edn. award, Okla. Sci. Tchrs. Assn., 2011, Merit award Okla. Acad. Sci. Fellow: AAAS; mem.: Am. Inst. Biol. Sci., Am. Soc. Ichthyologists and Herpetologists (pres. 1988), Am. Physiol. Soc., Ecol. Soc. America, Herpetologists League (exe. com. 1968-71), Soc. Study Amphibians and Reptiles (bd. govs. 1986-88, pres. 1998-99), Explorers Club, Sigma Xi, Phi Sigma, Phi Kappa Phi. Achievements include demonstration of facultative endothermy in brooding pythons; research on role of skin in amphibian respiration; development of standardized method for determination of critical thermal maximum in animals. Home: 2010 Crestmont Ave Norman OK 73069-6414 Office Phone: 405-325-6721.

HUTTO, CHARLES BRADLEY (BRAD HUTTO), state legislator; b. Orangeburg, SC, Aug. 6, 1957; s. Charles L. and Harriet Lancaster Hutto; m. Macpherson Teresa Dawn Hutto; 1 child, Skyler Bradley. BA, U. SC, 1978; JD, Georgetown U., 1981. Atty. Williams & Williams, Orangeburg, SC, 1982—; mem. Dist. 40 SC State Senate, 1996—; mem. Agr. & Natural Resources Com., Fish, Game and Forestry Com., Med. Affairs Com., Judiciary, & Rules Com. Named one of Young Dem. Yr., SC Young Dems., 1982, Young Lawyer of Yr, SC Bar Assn., 1992. Mem.: Palmetto Legal Svcs. (bd. mem.). Democrat. Mailing: PO Box 1084 Orangeburg SC 29116-1084 Office: 510 Gressette Bldg PO Box 142 Columbia SC 29201 Home Phone: 803-536-1808; Office Phone: 803-212-6140. Fax: 803-212-6299. Business E-Mail: cbh@scsenate.org.

HUTTON, GEORGE N., JR., wire and cable manufacturing company executive; B in Econs., U. NC. Bd. dirs. Centel Corp., M/A-Com, Inc., 1980, Sprint Corp., First National Bank Catawba County, CommScope, Inc., 1997—. Office: CommScope Inc 1100 CommScope Pl SE Hickory NC 28602 Office Fax: 828-982-1708. Business E-Mail: ghutton@commscope.com.

HUTTON, KEITH A., energy executive; BS in petroleum engring., Tex. A&M Univ. Engr. Sun Oil Co., 1982—87; mgmt. positions through exec. v.p. ops. XTO Energy, Fort Worth, Tex., 1987—2005, pres., 2005—08, pres., CEO, 2008—10; CEO XTO Energy, Inc. (subs. ExxonMobil), 2010—. Bd. dir. XTO Energy, 2005—. Office: XTO Energy 810 Houston St Fort Worth TX 76102-6298

HUVAL, MIKE, state legislator; Attended, U. La., Lafayette. Ind. insurance agency owner, La.; mem. Dist. 46 La. House of Reps., Baton Rogue, 2012—. Republican. Office: 391 Cannery Rd Breaux Bridge LA 70517 also: La House of Reps 900 N 3rd St Baton Rouge LA 70804 Office Phone: 337-332-3331. Business E-Mail: huvalm@legis.la.gov.

HUVAL, TIM, human resources specialist; A in Bus. Mgmt., Salt Lake CC; B in Mktg., Weber State U.; M in Pub. Adminstrn., Brigham Young U.; doctorate in Humane Letters (hon.), Salt Lake CC, 2007. Chief info. officer, Global Wealth & Investment Mgmt. Bank of America Corp., sr. human resources exec., pres., Del. Market, 2009—. Bd. dirs. Del. Bus. Roundtable, Del. Children's Museum, United Way Del. Office: Bank America Corp 100 N Tryon St Charlotte NC 28255 Office Phone: 704-386-8486. Office Fax: 704-386-6699. Business E-Mail: tim.huval@bankofamerica.com.

HUYNH, PHAN TUONG, diagnostic radiologist, educator; MD, U. Va., 1989. Diplomate Am. Bd. Radiology-diagnostic radiology, 1994. Resident diagnostic radiology Univ. of Va. Med. Ctr., Charlottesville, 1990—94; fellow mammography Univ. of Va., 1994—95; assoc. clin. prof. radiology Baylor Med. Coll.; hosp. affiliations include St. Luke's Episcopal Hosp. Office: St Luke's Episcopal Hospital St Luke's Tower Womens Ctr Fl 10 6624 Fannin St Houston TX 77030 Office Phone: 832-355-8130.

HWU, PATRICK, oncologist; BA, Lehigh U., 1983; MD, Med. Coll. Pa., 1987. Cert. med. oncology 1993. House officer Johns Hopkins Hosp., 1987—89; fellow & clinical assoc. Nat. Inst. Health, 1989—93; chmn. dept. melanoma med. oncology U. Tex. MD Anderson Cancer Ctr., 2003—, assoc. dir. Ctr. for Cancer Immunology Rsch. Office: MD Anderson Cancer Center Dept of Melanoma Medical Oncology 1515 Holcombe Blvd #207 Houston TX 77030-4017 Office Phone: 713-563-1728. Office Fax: 713-745-1046. E-mail: phwu@mdanderson.org.

HYATT, LAWRENCE ELIOT (LARRY HYATT), restaurant chain company executive; b. NYC, Oct. 12, 1954; s. Arnold Jan and Sylvia (Koral) H.; m. Carol Lynn Marcus, Dec. 30, 1978; children: Seth, Rebecca. BA in Economics, Williams Coll., 1976; MBA, Harvard U., 1980. Financial analyst US Dept. Energy, Washington, 1976-78; sr. cons. ICF, Inc., Washington, 1980-81; sr. staff auditor Marriott Corp., Bethesda, Md., 1981-82, sr. financial analyst, 1982-83, mgr. financial analysis, 1983-84, dir. planning, analysis, 1984-86, v.p. ops. planning & control, 1986-88; sr. v.p. finance & planning Marriott Mgmt. Services, Bethesda, Md., 1989—99; exec. v.p., restructuring officer, CFO PSINet, Inc., 2000—02; exec. v.p., CFO Cole Nat. Corp., 2002—04; treas., CFO O'Charley's, Inc., Nashville, 2004—10, interim pres., CEO, 2009; sr. v.p., CFO Cracker Barrel Old Country Store, Inc., Lebanon, Tenn., 2011—. Contbg. editor Harcourt,Brace, Jovanovich Co. Cons., tchr. Jr. Achievement bus. project, Montgomery County, Md., 1983-85; treas. Citizens for Claypoole for Sch. Bd., Montgomery County, 1984, chmn. citizen' adv. bd. State Senator Bainvm, Montgomery County, 1984—; chmn. campaign com. State Del. Kirchenbauer, Montgomery County, 1985—. Democrat. Jewish. Avocations: jogging, reading. Office: Cracker Barrel Old Country Store Inc 305 Hartmann Dr Lebanon TN 37087

HYDE, BARRY, state legislator; Comml. builder Hydco Inc.; mem. Dist. 40 Ark. House of Reps., 2007—. Democrat. Roman Catholic. Address: 208 N Beech St North Little Rock AR 72114 Office Phone: 501-371-0255. Office Fax: 501-371-0020. Business E-Mail: bhyde@hydco.com.

HYDE, KEVIN E., lawyer, former councilman; m. Kathi Hyde; children: Virginia, Michal. BA magna cum laude, U. South Fla., 1984; JD with honors, U. Fla., 1988. Bar: Fla., Va. Councilman-at-large Group 4 Jacksonville City Coun., 2003—11, v.p., 2004—05, pres., 2005—06; mng. ptnr. Jacksonville office, vice chair labor & employment practice, mem. automotive industry team Foley & Lardner LLP. Vice chmn. Rules Com.; former chmn. Fla. Bar Labor & Employment Section; mem. Pub. Health & Safety Com., Joint Planning Com., Spl. Com. on City Pension Reform. Liaison Jacksonville Journey Oversight Com.; alt. Transp. Planning Org.; mem. Prosperity Scholarship Fund Governing Coun.; bd. mem. Youth Crisis Ctr., Northeast Fla. Safety Coun.; deacon Lakeshore Ch. Christ, 1992—. Named a Leading Atty., Jacksonville Mag., 2001, Up & Comer, Jacksonville Bus. Jour., 2001, Leading Employment Atty., Fla. Trend Mag., 2005. Mem.: Zoological Soc. (bd. dirs.), Fla. 4-H Found. (former pres.). Republican. Office: Foley & Lardner LLP 1 Independent Dr Ste 1300 Jacksonville FL 32202-5017 Office Phone: 904-359-8786. E-mail: khyde@foley.com.

HYDER, MARCIE, travel company executive; BBA in Acctg., Tex. A&M U., 1989—93. CPA. Audit KPMG (Klynveld Peat Marwick Goerdeler), 1993—96; fin. reporting analyst Brinker Internat., 1996—98; dir.- fin. reporting and investor rels. Builders FirstSource, 2005—07; dir corp. acctg. Pegasus Solutions, 2007—08, v.p. and contr., 2008—11, exec. v.p. and CFO, 2011—. Mem.: Alpha Kappa Psi. Office: Pegasus Solutions 8350 N Ctrl Expy Suite 1900 Campbell Centre I Dallas TX 75206 Office Phone: 214-234-4000. Office Fax: 214-234-4040.

HYDE-SMITH, CINDY, state agency administrator, former state legislator; b. Brookhaven, Miss. married; 1 child. AA, Copiah-Lincoln CC; B, U. So. Miss. Farmer; Congl. affairs cons.; mem. Dist. 39 Miss. State Senate, 2000—12; commr. Miss. Dept. Agr. and Commerce, 2012—. Mem.: Miss. Cattleman's Assn., Miss. Wildlife Fedn., Am. Cancer Soc. Republican. Baptist. Office: Miss Dept Agriculture & Commerce 121 N Jefferson St Jackson MS 39201 Office Phone: 601-359-1100.

HYLAND, GREGORY E., water transportation executive; BA, MBA, Univ. of Pitts. Various positions Rockwell Internat.; v.p., mktg. sales Anderson, Greenwood & Co., 1991—93, exec. v.p., 1993—94; various positions to group pres., corp. officer Keystone Internat. (acquired by Tyco Internat., Inc.), pres., Anderson, Greenwood & Co., 1994—97; pres., engineered products group, flow control disn. Tyco Internat., Inc., 1997—2000; chmn., CEO, Textron golf, turf & specialty products Textron, Inc., 2000—02, pres., indsl. products segment, 2002; exec. v.p., US fleet mgmt. solutions Ryder Sys. Inc., 2004—05; chmn., pres. & CEO Walter Industries, Inc. (now Walter Energy, Inc.), 2005—06; chmn. Mueller Water Products, Inc., 2005—, pres., CEO, 2006—. Office: Mueller Water Products Inc 1200 Abernathy Rd Atlanta GA 30328 Office Phone: 770-206-4200. Office Fax: 770-206-4235. Business E-Mail: ghyland@muellerwp.com.

HYNES, THOMAS N. (TOBY), automotive company executive; BBA, Hillsdale Coll.; MBA, Stanford U. Various key positions in sales and ops. Ford Motor Co., 1969, regional mgr. Ford and Lincoln-Mercury divsns., pres., COO Primus Fin. divsn., 1995-99; pres., gen. mgr. Gulf States Toyota Inc., Houston, 1999—. Office: Gulf States Toyota 1355 Enclave Pkwy Houston TX 77077-2026

HYSLOP, NEWTON EVERETT, JR., infectious disease specialist; b. Newton, Mass., 1935; AB, Harvard U., 1957, MD, 1961. Diplomate Am. Bd. Allergy and Immunology, Am. Bd. Internal Medicine, Am. Bd. Infectious Disease. Intern Mass. Gen. Hosp., Boston, 1961-62, resident in medicine, 1962—63, fellow in infectious disease, 1966—68; rsch. assoc. lab. immunology Nat. Inst. Allergy and Immunology, Bethesda, Md., 1963—65; resident in medicine Peter Bent Brigham Hosp., Boston, 1965—66; with Tulane U. Med. Ctr., New Orleans, 1984—; prof. medicine Tulane U., 1984—2006, prof. emeritus, 2006—. Instr. to asst. prof. Harvard Med. Sch., 1965—85; asst. to assoc. physician Mass. Gen. Hosp., 1965—85; Moseley traveling fellow and vis. scientist dept. biochemistry U. Oxford, 1968—69; chief infectious disease sect. Tulane Sch. Medicine, 1984—2006; founder and prin. investigator Tulane-La. State U. AIDS Clin. Trials unit, 1987—96, co-prin. investigator, 1996—2006; med. dir. HIV/AIDS/TB In-Patient unit, Charity Hosp., 1991—2006; clin. head HIV disease mgmt. initiative, health care svcs. divsn. La. State U. Health Scis. Ctr., 1999—2007. Fellow ACP, Infectious Dis. Soc.; mem. Am. Assn. Immunologists, Am. Soc. Microbiology, Assn. Subspecialty Professors. Office: Tulane U Sch Medicine Infectious Diseases Sect SL87 1430 Tulane Ave New Orleans LA 70112-2699 Home Phone: 504-891-1541; Office Phone: 504-988-7316. Business E-Mail: nhyslop@tulane.edu.

IANNI, MARK, telecommunications industry executive; B, McGill U., Can.; MBA, Queen's U., Can. Gen. mgmt. positions, sales, ops. and bus. devel. General Electric Capital, Canada, General Electric Co., Canada; v.p., emerging markets GE Equipment Svcs. (subs. GE); v.p., sales FPL FiberNet, LLC (subs. of FPL Group, Inc.), 2005—05, pres., 2005—, NextEra Energy Resources, LLC (subs. FPL Group, Inc.), Gexa Energy GP, LLC (subs. FPL Group, Inc.). Office: FPL FiberNet LLC 9250 W Flagler St Miami FL 33174 Office Phone: 305-552-3539. Office Fax: 305-229-5959.

IAQUINTO, SALVATORE R., state legislator; b. Manhasset, NY, Mar. 1, 1968; m. Stephanie Jane Tomlinson; children: Nicholas, Alex. State del. Dist. 84, Va., 2006—; mem. Ct of Justice Com., Transportation Com., Counties, Cities & Towns Com., 2006—; house del. Va. Mem. Forefront Church. Mem.: Norfolk-Portsmouth Bar Assn., Va. Beach Bar Assn. Republican. Office: PO Box 6888 Virginia Beach VA 23456 Home Phone: 757-430-2882; Office Phone: 757-430-0102. Business E-Mail: DelSIaquinto@house.state.va.us.

IBAKA, SERGE (SERGE JONAS IBAKA NGOBILA), professional basketball player; b. Brazzaville, Republic of Congo, Sept. 18, 1989; naturalized, Spain, 2011; s. Desire Ibaka and Amadou Djonga. Power forward CB L'Hospitalet, Spain, 2007—08, Ricoh Manresa, Spain, 2008—09, Oklahoma City Thunder, 2009—, Real Madrid, Spain, 2011. Mem. Spanish nat. team FIBA European Championships, Lithuania, 2011, Summer Olympic Games, London, 2012. Recipient Gold medal, FIBA European Championship, 2011, Silver medal, men's basketball, Summer Olympic Games, 2012; named to NBA All-Defensive 1st Team, 2012, 2013. Achievements include leading the NBA in: blocked shots, 2012, 2013. Office: Oklahoma City Thunder 100 W Reno Rd Oklahoma City OK 73102*

IBANEZ, MANUEL LUIS, academic administrator, biologist, educator; b. Worcester, Mass., Sept. 23, 1935; s. Ovidio Pedro and Esperanza Fe (Perez) I.; m. Jane Marie Bourquard, Oct. 16, 1970; children: Juana Lia Cristina, Vincent Ovidio, William Dayan, Marc Albert BS cum laude, Wilmington Coll., 1957; MS, Pa. State U., 1959, PhD, 1961. Asst. prof. Bucknell U., Lewisburg, Pa., 1961-62; postdoctoral fellow UCLA, 1962; sr. biochemist IICA de la OEA, Turrialba, Costa Rica, 1962-65; assoc. prof., chmn. dept. U. New Orleans, 1965-70, prof., 1977-90, assoc. dean grad. sch., 1978-82, assoc. vice chancellor acad. affairs, 1982-83, acting vice chancellor, 1983-85, vice chancellor acad. affairs, provost, 1985-89, prof. emeritus, 1990—; pres. Tex. A&M U., Kingsville, 1989-98, named disting. prof. biology, 1998, pres., prof. emeritus; ret., 2000. Bd. regents Smithsonian Instn.; adj. prof. biology Delmar CC, 2000—. Author: Basic Biology of Microorganisms, 1972; contbr. articles to profl. jours. Regent Smithsonian Inst., 1994-2006, regent emeritus, 2006—; mem. Alliance for Good Govt., New Orleans, 1980. NSF coop. fellow, 1958-61 Mem. Am. Assn. State Colls. and Univs., Kingsville C. of C. (pres. 1991), Rotary, KC, Sigma Xi Democrat. Roman Catholic. Avocations: chess, tennis, bicycling, collections.

IBARGUEN, ALBERTO, foundation administrator, former publishing executive; b. Rio Piedras, PR, Feb. 29, 1944; s. Albert E. and Angelica (Bigas) I.; m. Susana E. Lopez, Jan. 8, 1969; 1 child, Diego. BA in History, Wesleyan U., Middletown, Ct., 1966; JD, U. Pa., 1974. Bar: Conn. 1974. Atty. Legal Aid Soc., Hartford, Conn., 1974-76; dir., counsel Conn. Election Commn., Hartford, 1976-77; ptnr. Cloud & Ibarguen, Hartford, 1977-78; atty. Updike, Kelly & Spellacy, Hartford, 1978-79; dep. gen. coun., v.p. public affairs, v.p. pvt banking Connecticut National Bank, Hartford, 1979-84; sr. v.p. Hartford Courant, 1984-86; exec. v.p. ops. Newsday/N.Y. Newsday, NYC, 1986-95; pub. El Nuevo Herald, Miami, Fla., 1995-98; v.p. The Miami Herald, 1995-98, pub., 1998—2004; chmn. Miami Publishing Co., 1998—2005; pres., CEO John S. & James L. Knight Foundation, Miami, 2005—. Bd. dirs. AMR Corp., 2008—. Bd. dirs. Lincoln Ctr. for Performing Arts, N.Y.C., 1990-96, Dade County Found., Com. to Protect Journalists, Fla. Philharm., Pub. Broadcasting Sys., 1997—; trustee Wesleyan U., 1992-95, Smith Coll., 1995-97; mem. bus. commn. Met. Mus. Art, 1990-95. Mem. N.Y. Athletic Club. Office: John S & James L Knight Foundation Wachovia Fin Ctr Ste 3300 200 S Biscayne Blvd Miami FL 33131

ICAHN, CARL CELIAN, investor; b. Queens, NY, Feb. 16, 1936; m. Liba Icahn, 1979 (div. 1999); children: Brett, Michelle; m. Gail Golden, 1999. BA in Philosophy, Princeton U., NJ, 1957; student, NYU Sch. Medicine. Apprentice broker Dreyfus Corp., NYC, 1960-63; options mgr. Tessel, Patrick & Co., NYC, 1963-64, Gruntal & Co., 1964-68; chmn., pres. Icahn & Co., NYC, 1968—2005; bd. chmn. Starfire Holding Corp. (formerly Icahn Holding), 1984—; chmn. ACF Industries, Inc., St. Charles, Mo., 1984—; chmn., pres., CEO Trans World Airlines Inc., NYC, 1985—93; founder Icahn Capital, Inc., 1987—; bd. chmn. American Property Investors, Inc., 1990—, American Railcar Industries, Inc., 1994—, Maupintour Holdings, LLC, 1998—2002; pres. Stratosphere Corp., 1998—2004; bd. chmn. GB Holdings, 2000—07, XO Holdings, Inc. (formerly XO Communications), 2003—, ImClone Systems Inc., 2006—08. Bd. dirs. Starfire Holding Corp., 1984—, Cadus Pharm. Corp., 1993—, American Railcar Industries Inc., 1994—, Blockbuster Inc., 2005—, WestPoint Internat., Inc., 2005—, ImClone Systems Inc., 2006—08, WCI Communities, Inc., 2007—, Yahoo! Inc., 2008—09, Motricity, Inc., 2008—, Federal-Mogul Corp., 2007—, non-exec. chmn., 2008—. Founder Icahn House, NYC, Carl C. Icahn Charter Sch., NYC. Served in US Army, 1960—61. Named one of Top 200 Collectors, ARTnews mag., 2004, Forbes 400: Richest Americans, 2006—, World's Richest People, Forbes Mag., 2007—, 50 Most Influential People in Global Fin., Bloomberg Markets, 2013. Jewish. Avocation: Collector Old Masters and Impressionist art. Office: Icahn Capital LP 767 Fifth Ave 47th Fl New York NY 10153*

ICE, CARL R., rail transportation executive; b. 1956; married; 2 children. BS in Indsl. Engring., Kans. State U., 1979. With indsl. engring. dept. Santa Fe Rlwy., 1979, positions in ops., financial & info. systems, v.p. adminstrn., 1992—94, v.p. carload bus. unit, 1994, v.p. exec., 1994—96; v.p., chief mech. officer Burlington Northern Santa Fe Corp., 1996—99, v.p. ops. north, 1999, sr. v.p. ops., 1999—2000, exec. v.p., COO, 2000—10; pres., COO Burlington Northern Santa Fe LLC (subs. Berkshire Hathaway), 2010—13, pres., CEO, 2014—. Bd. dirs. Transp. Tech. Ctr. Inc. Mem. engring. adv. bd. Kans. State U. Coll. Engring. Mem.: Inst. Indsl. Engrs. Office: Burlington Northern Santa Fe LLC PO Box 961056 Fort Worth TX 76161-0056 Office Phone: 817-867-6100.*

IFILL, GWEN, moderator, political reporter; b. NYC, Sept. 29, 1955; d. Oliver Urcille and Eleanor Ifill. BA in Comm., Simmons Coll., Boston, 1977. Food columnist Boston Herald, 1977—80; staff Balt. Evening Sun, 1981—84, Washington Post, 1984—91; White House corr., journalist NY Times, 1991—94; chief congl., polit. corr. NBC News, 1994—99; moderator, mng. editor Washington Week (formerly Washington Week in Review) PBS, 1999—, sr. corr., back-up anchor NewsHour with Jim Lehrer, 1999—. Moderator Vice Presdl. debates, 2004, 2008; bd. dirs. Harvard U. Inst. Politics, Com. to Protect Journalists; bd. dir. Mus. of TV & Radio, U. Md. Philip Merrill Coll. Journalism. Author: Breakthrough: Politics and Race in the Age of Obama, 2009; co-host with Kaitlyn Adkins (Hist. Channel spl.) Jamestown LIVE!, 2007. Named one of The 100 Most Powerful Women in DC, Washingtonian mag., 2009. Fellow: Am. Acad. Arts & Sciences. Methodist. Office: Washington Week PBS 2775 S Quincy St Arlington VA 22206 Address: The NewsHour with Jim Lehrer PBS 3620 27th St S Arlington VA 22206 Office Phone: 703-998-2600, 703-998-2137.

IHLENFELD, WILLIAM J., II, federal prosecutor; b. 1972; married. BA, Ohio U., 1994; JD, W.Va. U., 1997. Ptnr. Ihlenfeld Law Office, PLLC, Wheeling, W.Va., 1997—2010; asst. prosecuting atty., chief asst. prosecutor Ohio County, W.Va., 1997—2007, mem. Ohio Valley Drug and Violent Crimes Task Force W.Va.; asst. prosecuting atty. Brooke County, W.Va., 2007—10; US atty. (northern dist.) W.Va. US Dept. Justice, Wheeling, W.Va., 2010—. Vol. Legal Aid of W.Va. Vice-chmn. Seeing Hands Assn., Inc.; mem. Ohio County Schs. Comprehensive Ednl. Facilities Plan Com. Avocation: running. Office: US Attorney's Office US Courthouse & Federal Bldg 1125 Chapline St, Ste 1125 Wheeling WV 26003 Office Phone: 304-234-0100.*

IKARD, FRANK NEVILLE, JR., lawyer; b. Wichita Falls, Tex., June 26, 1942; s. Frank Neville and Jean (Hunter) I.; children: Frank III, Jean, Charles; m. Kathleen P. Ikard, Feb. 14, 1998. BA, U. Tex., 1965, JD, 1968. Bar: Tex. 1968; cert. Tex. Estate Planning and Probate Law Bd. of Legal Specialization. Assoc. then ptnr. Clark, Thomas, Winters, & Shapiro, Austin, Tex., 1968-84; mng. ptnr. Jenkens & Gilchrist, Austin, 1985-88; ptnr. Johnson & Gibbs, Austin, 1988-92, Ikard & Golden, Austin, 1992—. Bd. dirs. Paramount Theatre, Austin, 1988-89, pres. bd. dirs., 1991-92; mem. Greater Austin Crime Commn. Fellow Am. Coll. Probate Counsel, Tex. Bar Found.; mem. Am. Coll. Trust and Estate Coun. (fiduciary litigation com. 1991-2001), Tex. Acad. Real Estate (pres. probate and trust law coun. 1988-89), State Bar Tex. (chmn., sec.-treas. legis. com. real estate, probate trust law sect. 1983-84, coun. chmn.), Travis County Bar Assn., Tarry House, Headliners, U. Tex. Club. Avocations: fly fishing, photography. Home: 1102 Claire Ave Austin TX 78703 Office: Ikard and Golden 400 W 15th St 975 Austin TX 78701-1600 Office Phone: 512-472-2884. Business E-Mail: fni@ikardgolden.com.

IKEDA, ROBIN M., public health service officer; BA, Stanford U., Calif.; MD, Cornell U. Med. Coll., NY; MPH in Epidemiology, Emory U., Ga. Cert. in internal medicine, in preventive medicine. Epidemic intelligence officer NY State Dept. Health Bur. Communicable Disease Control; various positions including team leader and staff epidemiologist Centers Disease Control and Prevention, Atlanta, 1993—2006, assoc. dir. sci. Nat. Ctr. Injury Prevention and Control, 2003—06, acting dir. Nat. Ctr. Injury Prevention and Control, 2010, dep. dir., 2010—, dir. Office Communicable Diseases, Injury and Environ. Health, 2010—. Capt. US Pub. Health Svc. Office: Centers Disease Control and Prevention Office NC Diseases Injury Environ Health 1600 Clifton Rd Atlanta GA 30333

ILDSTAD, SUZANNE T., transplant surgeon, immunologist, educator; b. Mpls., May 20, 1952; m. David J. Tollerud, Dec. 19, 1971; children: David J. II, Suzanne K. BS in Biology summa cum laude, U. Minn., 1974; MD, Mayo Med. Sch., 1978. Diplomate Am. Bd. Surgery. Resident in gen. surgery Mass. Gen. Hosp., Boston, 1978-82, 85-86; med. staff fellow, immunology Nat. Cancer Inst., NIH, Bethesda, Md., 1982-85; clin. fellow pediatric surgery Children's Hosp. Med. Ctr., Cin., 1986-88, prof., chief dept. surgery, 1994; asst. prof. dept. surgery U. Pitts., 1988—92, assoc. prof. dept. surgery, 1992—95, prof., chief, divsn. cellular therapeutics, 1995—96; dir., Inst. for Cellular Therapeutics, prof. surgery, dept. surgery Allegheny U. Health Scis., Phila., 1996—98; Jewish Hosp. Disting. Prof. Transplantation, prof. surgery U. Louisville, Ky., 1998—, dir., Inst. for Cellular Therapeutics Ky., 1998—. Mem. Affirmative Action com., resident adv. com. dept. surgery U. Pitts., 1988-91; mem. instl. animal care and use com., 1991-94; mem. coord. com. rsch. integrity, 1992; mem. lab. usage com., oncology com., GCRC adv. com., residency coord. dept. surgery Children's Hosp., Pitts., 1988-91; vis. prof. U. Minn., 1991, Children's Meml. Hosp., U. Chgo., 1992; mem. various coms. Children's Cancer Study Group; founder, Med. Sch. Sickle Cell Project, 1999; lectr., rschr. in field. Mem. editorial bd. Jour. Transplantation, 1992, Transplantation Sci., 1992, Jour. ACS and others; mem. adv. bd. Clin. Transplantation Procs., 1992; editor Chimerism and Tolerance; contbr. articles to profl. jours., also numerous abstracts, letters and presentations in field, chpts. to books; work has been covered by CNN, CBS, Time Mag., US News and World Report, Discover, People, NY Times, Washington Post and USA Today. Recipient James A. Shannon Dirs.'s award for rsch. excellence, NIH, 1991; Instl. grantee Am. Cancer Soc., 1990-91; grantee U. Pitts., 1989-90, 91-92, Children's Hosp. Pitts. Rsch. Adv. Com., 1990-91, NIH - RO1, 1991-96, 92-95, U. Pitts. Med. Ctr., 1991-92, Juvenile Diabetes Found., 1991-92, Nat. Kidney Found., 1991-92, Am. Heart Assn., 1992-95, Am. Diabetes Assn., 1992-94, E. Donnall Thomas Lectr. award for rsch. contbn. to the field of bone marrow transplantation; named Mayo Med. Sch. Alumnus of the Decade, 2001. Fellow ACS (Pediatric Surg. Forum award 1990, Young Investigator award 1990-92, fellowship award 1990-92, sec. Pediatric Surgery Biology Club 1989-91); mem. AAAS, AMA, Inst. Medicine, Am. Acad. Pediatrics, Am. Assn. Cancer Rsch., Am. Assn. Immunologists, Am. Fedn. Clin. Rsch., Am. Soc. Clin. Rsch., Am. Soc. Transplant Surgeons (program com. 1991-94), Am. Soc. Transplant Physicians, Mass. Med. Soc., Pediatric Transplant Study Group, Soc. Clin. Immunology, Soc. Head and Neck Surgeons (Resident/Fellow award 1983), Soc. Univ. Surgeons, Surg. Infection Soc. (travel grantee XII Internat. Congress, Sydney, Australia, 1988), Assn. Acad. Surgeons (program com. 1989-91), Cell Transplant Soc. (adv. bd. 1991, counselor-at-large 1992—), Internat. Soc. for Hematotherapy and Graft Engring., Internat. Soc. for Heart and Lung Transplantation, Pa. Med. Soc., Phila. County Med. Soc., Transplantion Soc., NY Acad. Scis., Am. Soc. for Blood and Marrow Transplantation. Achievements include discovery of the facilitating cell in bone marrow, which allows marrow transplants to take hold and grow, even when donor and recipient are poorly matched; one of only 5 women pediatric transplant surgeons in the US; first women to ever receive a Mayo Clinic Distinguished Alumnus award; patents in field. Office: U Louisville 570 S Preston St Baxter Bldg Ste 404 Louisville KY 40202 Office Phone: 502-852-2080. Office Fax: 502-852-2085. E-mail: stild01@gwise.louisville.edu.

ILER, FRANK, state legislator; m. Jackie Iler. Diploma in Business, Campbell U. Cost acct.; budget supr.; owner fast food franchise; various positions in sales and mktg.; chmn. 7th Congl. Dist. Rep. Party, Brunswick County Rep. Party, 2006—09; state rep. Dist. 17 NC, 2009—. Named to NC Rep. Party Hall of Fame, 2009. Republican. Office: North Carolina House of Representatives 300 N Salisbury St Rm 632 Raleigh NC 27603-5925 Office Phone: 919-301-1450. E-mail: Frank.Iler@ncleg.net.

IMBEAU, STEPHEN ALAN, allergist; b. Portland, Oreg., Nov. 25, 1947; s. David A. and Marjory Anne (Jacobsen) I.; m. Shirley Ruth Burke, Aug. 18, 1979; children: Stephanie Frances, Andrew Paul, Charles Burke. BA, U. Calif., Berkeley, 1969; MD, U. Calif., San Francisco, 1973. Diplomate Am. Bd. Internal Medicine, Am. Bd. Allergy. Intern U. Wis., Madison, S.C., 1973-74, resident in internal medicine, 1974-75, resident in allergy, 1976-78, resident in infectious diseases, 1978-79; pvt. practice Florence, S.C., 1980—. Budget and control bd. S.C. Data Oversight Coun., 1993—98; founder Coastal Growth Ptnrs. (a Venture Capital Co.), 1997—2003; bd. dirs. Joint Coun. Allergy and Immunology, 1998—; gen. ptnr. Trelys Investments, Venture Capital Co., 2005—; mem. practicing physicans adv. coun. U.S. HHS Health Care Financing Adminstrn., 2000—03; commr. S.C. Dept. Mental Health, 2003—05; chair elect AMA SE Del., 2013—. Contbr. articles to profl. jours. Chmn. Florence Symphony Orch., 1985-91; bd. dirs. Big Bros., 1989-92, Am. Lung Assn., 1982-86, Florence County Progress, chmn. 1993-95; mem. SC Mental Health Commn., 2003-05; trustee SC Venture Capital Fund, 2005—10. Fellow: ACP; mem.: AMA (S.C. alt. del. 1992—98, SE del., vice chair to chair 2011—, chair SE del. 2013—), Florence Rotary Club, Florence County Med. Assn. (pres. 1984—85), Joint Coun. Allergy Immunology (bd. mem. 2000, sec. 2002—04, treas. 2004—06, pres. 2008—10), Am. Acad. Allergy, Asthma, Immunology (alt. del. to AMA 1999—2004), SC Med. Soc. (trustee 1988—90, sec. bd. 1990—94, treas. 1995—97, pres. elect 1997, pres. 1998—99, del to AMA 2004—, chair SCMA AMA Del 2007—, Amb. of Yr. 1995), Am. Acad. Allergists, Rotary Club, Lions (pres. Florence chpt. 1987—88). Avocations: reading, hunting, stamp collecting/philately. Home: 950 Park Ave Florence SC 29501-5734 Office: 800W E Cheves St Ste 420 Florence SC 29506-2769 Office Phone: 843-679-9335. Personal E-mail: stephenimbeau@yahoo.com.

IMHOFF, KATHLEEN RUTH TOSTRUD, library administrator; b. Superior, Wis. d. Gerhard Lars Oliver Tostrud and Dorothea Henrietta (Panzenhagen) Tostrud Stream; m. Clement T. Imhoff; children: Ethan Charles, Eliot Clifford. BA in English, Valparaiso U., Ind.; MA, U. Wis. Dir. Horseshoe Bend Regional Libr., Dadeville, Ala.; head mobile info. svcs. Atlanta Pub. Libr.; cons. libr. svcs. State Libr. Wis., Madison, 1974—75; dir. Bur. Pub. and Coop., Madison, 1975—77, Chattahoochee Regional Libr., Columbus, Ga., 1977—80, Broward County Libr. Sys., 1980—83, Head Office Planning Evaluation, 1983—87; head Cmty. & Regional Libr., 1987—90; head pub. svcs. Broward County Libr., Ft. Lauderdale, Fla., 1993—96; dir. Harrison Regional Libr., Columbiana, Ala., 1996—2003; asst. dir. Broward County Libr., Ft. Lauderdale, Fla., 2003—09; exec. dir., CEO Lexington Pub. Libr., Ky., 2003—09; libr. cons., 2010—; pres. Royal Crown Kathleen, Online Fine Arts Gallery, 2011—. Bd. Solinet, Atlanta, 1988-91; instr. Auburn U., Ala., 1971-73. Author: Making the Most of New Technology, 1996, Library Contests, 2009; contbr. chpts. to books: Bibliographic Access in Europe, 1990, Interlending and Document Supply, 1991; contbr. numerous articles to profl. jours. Pres. Montevallo HS PTA, Ala., 1993-94; bd. trustees OCLC Inc., 2009-. Recipient John Cotton Dana award, 1972, Internat. Study award ALA/Pub. Libr. Assn., 1989, Bumblebee Cannot Fly award Omnisystems Internat., 1992, Disting. Svc. award SE Fla. Libr. Info. Network, 2003, Rothrock award Southeastern Libr. Assn., 2009; named One of 15 Leading Woman Ctrl. Ky., 2009. Mem. AAUW, ALA (councilor chpt. 1989—), Lexington Directions (pres. 2008-10), Southeastern Libr. Assn. (pres. 2008-10), Shelby County Art Assn. (historian 1992-93), Optimist Club (2nd v.p. 1984-85, coord. cmty. cupbd., 2011-), Westmoreland Homeowner's Assn. (bd. mem. 2010-), Realtor Sales Assoc.

INABINET, GEORGE WALKER, JR., retired state agency administrator; b. Cameron, SC, Sept. 24, 1927; s. George Walker and Elizabeth (Wolfe) I.; m. Helen Ruth Davis, Sept. 27, 1947; children: Pamela Ruth, Jeffrey Walker. Cert. EE, S.C. Area Trade Sch., Columbia, 1949; Bus. Mgmt. degree, U. S.C., 1951; electronics engr. cert., Nat. Radio Inst., Washington, 1967. Asst. dir. S.C. Dept. Hwys., Columbia, 1951-53; adminstr. transp. S.C. Dept. Edn., Columbia, 1953-90. Chmn. Boy Scouts Am., Sandy Run, S.C., 1965-70; pres. Sandy Run Cmty. Club, 1966-70, pres., S.C. Football Ofcls. Assn., Columbia, 1971-72; mem. White House Coun. on Youth, Washington, 1972-76; chmn. Calhoun County Tri-Centennial Commn., 1970; chmn. adminstrn. bd. Mt. Zion United Meth. Ch., Sandy Run, 1952-75; mem. Gov.'s Com. on Comm., 1976-1980; vice chmn. Calhoun County Planning Commn., 1996—, Calhoun County Planning Com.; pres. ch. coun. Sandy Run Luth. Ch. Named to S.C. Football Ofcls. Hall of Fame, 2000. Mem. Assn. Pub. Safety Communications Officers (pres. 1979-81), Assn. Pub. Communications Officers (v.p. 1979-80, pres. 1980-81), S.C. Assn. Pupil Transp. (v.p. 1981-82, pres. 1982-83), Columbia Civitan Club (pres.), Am. Legion (chmn. state oratorical com. 1989-97, mem. nat. commn. on Americanism), Masons, Shriners. Avocations: golf, fishing, swimming, sports. Home: Windy Hill 2496 Old State Rd Swansea SC 29160-9350 Office Phone: 803-465-3753.

INAGAMI, TADASHI, biochemistry professor; b. Kobe, Japan, Feb. 20, 1931; m. Masako Araki, Nov. 12, 1961 BS, Kyoto U., 1953, DSc, 1963; MS, Yale U., 1955, PhD, 1958. Rsch. staff Yale U., New Haven, 1958—59, rsch. assoc., 1962—66; rsch. staff Kyoto U., Japan, 1959—62; instr. biochemistry Nagoya City U., Japan, 1962; asst. prof. biochemistry Vanderbilt U., Nashville, 1966—69, assoc. prof., 1969—74, prof. biochemistry, 1975—91, dir. hypertension rsch. ctr., 1979—95, Stanford Moore prof. biochemistry, 1991—, prof. medicine, 1992—. Contbr. numerous articles to profl. jours. Fulbright fellow, 1954-55; recipient Roche Vis. Prof. award, 1980, Humboldt Found. award, 1981, Spa award Belgium Nat. Funds Sci. Rsch., 1985, Ciba award High Blood Pressure Res Coun., 1986, Sutherland prize Vanderbilt U., 1990, Charles Park award for Excellence in Rsch., 2002, Okamoto Internat. award Japan Vascular Disease Rsch. Found., 1994. Res Achievement award Am. Heart Assn., 1995, award for excellence in cardiovascular rsch. Bristol Meyers Squibb, 1996, award Japan Acad., 1996, Jokichi Takamine award Japan Cardiovasc. Endocrine-Metabolism Soc., 1998, Merit award NHLBI, 2000, Distng. Scientist award, Am. Heart Assn., 2009 Fellow: Am. Soc. Advancement Sci., Japan Soc. Cardiovascular Endocrinol. Metabolism; mem.: Japan Soc. Biochemistry, Japan Soc. Hypertension, Internat. Soc. Hypertension, Am. Soc. Hypertension, Soc. Neurosci., Japan Soc. Agrl. Chemistry (hon.), Japan Endocrine Soc. (hon.), Am. Soc. Cell Biology, Am. Soc. Pharmacology and Therapeutics, Am. Chem. Soc., Endocrine Soc., Am. Physiol. Soc., Am. Soc. Biol. Chemists and Molecular Biologists. Office: Vanderbilt U Sch Medicine Ste 212 Oxford House Nashville TN 37232 Office Phone: 615-936-0719. Business E-Mail: tadashi.inagami@vanderbilt.edu.

INCH, MORRIS ALTON, theology educator; b. Wytopitlock, Maine, Oct. 21, 1925; s. Clarence Sherwin and Blanche (Mix) I.; m. Joan Parker, Dec. 16, 1950; children: Deborah, Lois, Thomas, Joel, Mark. AB, Houghton Coll., 1949; MDiv, Gordon Div. Sch., 1951; PhD, Boston U., 1955. Ordained to ministry Bapt. Ch., 1951. Pastor South Boston Bapt. Ch., 1951-55, Union Sq. Bapt. Ch., Somerville, Mass., 1955-61; prof., dean students, dean of coll. Gordon Coll., Wenham, Mass., 1955-62; prof., chmn. dept. Biblical, religious and archeol. studies Wheaton (Ill.) Coll., 1962-86; pres. The Inst. of Holy Land Studies, 1986-90. Vis. prof. Instnl. Biblic Baptiste de Oradea, 1991-93. Author: Psychology in the Psalms, 1969, Christianity Without Walls, 1972, Paced By God, 1973, Celebrating Jesus as Lord, 1974, Understanding Bible Prophecy, 1977, The Evangelical Challenge, 1978, My Servant Job, 1979, Doing Theology Across Cultures, 1982, Saga of the Spirit: A Biblical, Systematic and Historical Theology of the Holy Spirit, 1985, Making the Gospel Relevant, 1986, Revelation Across Cultures, 1995, Charting a Good Church Trip, 1995, Exhortations of Jesus According to Matthew and Up From the Depths: Mark as Tragedy, 1997, A Case for Christianity, 1997, Sage Sayings, 1997, In Tune with God: A User-Friendly Theology, 1998, The Chaos Paradigm: A Theological Exploration, 1998, Man: The Perennial Question, 1999, Devotions With David: A Christian Legacy, 2000, Demetrius the Disciple, 2000, Casey and Tonka, 2000, Scripture As Story, 2000, Two Gospel Motifs, 2001, The High God, 2001, Why Take the Bible Seriously?, 2001, Whispers of Heaven, 2002, Two Mosaic Motifs, 2003, 12 Who Changed the World, 2003, Why Take Jesus Seriously?, 2003, The Elder Brother: A Christian Alternative to Anti-Semitism, 2003, God's Design and Man's (Politically Correct) Disorder, 2005, Signature of the Spirit, 2005, Matthew in the Messianic Tradition, 2006, Why Take the Church Seriously?, 2006, Service Is As Service Does, 2006, In Christ & On Track, 2008, Potpourri, 2008, Pain As A Means of Grace, 2009, Space-Time Odyssey, 2009, The Wonder of It All, 2009, Thumbs Up for the Family;, 2010, Enigms of Justice, 2010, Potpourri 2, 2011, Echoes of the Shema and Our Fathers Footprints, 2012, Holy Sprit in Cross-Cultural Perspective, 2012, editor: (with Samuel Schultz) Interpreting the Word of God, 1976, (with C. Hassell Bullock) The Literature and Meaning of Scripture, 1981, (with Ronald Youngblood) The Living and Active Word of God, 1983; contbr. articles to profl. jours. With USAAF, 1943-46. Named Sr. Tchr. of Year Wheaton Coll., 1971; recipient Centennial award Houghton Coll., 1983; ann. lectureship established Wheaton Coll., 1986. Mem. Evang. Theol. Soc. Home: 349 Cagle Rock Cir Russellville AR 72802-1921 Personal E-mail: minch@centurytel.net. Business E-Mail: mainok@cenyurytizzk.net.

INGE, MILTON THOMAS, American literature and culture educator, author; b. Newport News, Va., Mar. 18, 1936; s. Clyde Elmore and Bernice Lucille (Jackson) I.; m. Betty Jean Meredith, 1958 (div. 1977); 1 child, Scott Thomas; m. Tonette Long Bond, 1982 (div. 1991); 1 stepchild, Michael Gordon Bond; m. Donaria Romeiro Carvalho, 1998. BA, Randolph-Macon Coll., 1959; MA, Vanderbilt U., 1960, PhD, 1964. Instr. English Vanderbilt U., 1962-64; asst. prof. Am. thought and lang. Mich. State U., 1964-68, assoc. prof., 1968-69; assoc. prof. English Va. Commonwealth U., Richmond, 1969-73, prof., 1973-80, chmn. dept. English, 1974-80; prof., chmn. dept. English, Clemson U., SC, 1980-84; resident scholar in Am. studies USIA, Washington, 1982-84; prof. humanities Randolph-Macon Coll., Ashland, Va., 1984—. Reader English Composition Test Coll. Entrance Exam Bd., 1967, 1969, 1977, 1980; Va. Cultural Laureate, 1992; dir. USIA Summer Inst. in Am. Studies, 1993—95; liberal studies disting. scholar-in-residence U. Louisville, 2003; vis. disting. prof., English and Am. Studies Palacky U., Olomouc, Czech Republic, 2012—. Author: Donald Davidson: Essay and Bibliography, 1965, (with T.D. Young) Donald Davidson, 1971, The American Comic Book, 1985, Comics in the Classroom, 1989, Great American Comics: 100 Years of Cartoon Art, 1990, Comics as Culture, 1990, Faulkner, Sut, and Other Southerners, 1992, Perspectives on American Culture: Essays on Humor, Literature, and the Popular Arts, 1994, Anything Can Happen in a Comic Strip: Centennial Reflections on an American Art Form, 1995, William Faulkner: Overlook Illustrated Lives, 2006, The Incredible Mr. Poe: Comic Book Adaptations of the Works of Edgar Allan Poe, 2008, Mark Twain in the Comics, 2009; editor: (books) Sut Lovingood's Yarns, 1966, 2d edit. 1987, High Times and Hard Times, 1967, 2nd Edit., 2013, Agrarianism in American Literature, 1969, A.B. Longstreet, 1969, Faulkner: A Rose for Emily, 1970, Wm. Byrd of Westover, 1970, Studies in Light in August, 1971, Frontier Humorists: Critical Views, 1975, Ellen Glasgow: Centennial Essays, 1976,(with J. Bryer and M. Duke) Black American Writers: Bibliographic Essays, 2 vols., 1978, Handbook of American Popular Culture, Vol. I, 1978, Vol. II, 1980, Vol. III, 1981, 3 vols. rev. and expanded edits., 1989, Concise Histories of American Popular Culture, 1982, (with E.E. MacDonald) James Branch Cabell: Centennial Essays, 1983, (with J. Bryer and M. Duke) American Women Writers: Bibliographical Essays, 1983, Huck Finn Among the Critics: A Centennial Selection, 1984, rev. edit., 1985, Truman Capote: Conversations, 1987, Naming the Rose: Essays on Umberto Eco's "The Name of the Rose", 1988, 2nd Edit., 2011, Handbook of American Popular Literature, 1988, A Nineteenth Century American Reader, 1988, The Comics, 1991, (with Sergei Chakovsky) Russian Eyes on American Literature, 1992, Dark Laughter: The Satiric Art of Oliver W. Harrington, 1993, Why I Left America and Other Essays of Oliver W. Harrington, 1993, William Faulkner: The Contemporary Reviews, 1994, 2nd edit., 2008, (with James E. Caron) Sut Lovingood's Nat'ral Born Yarnspinner: Essays on George Washington Harris, 1996, Mark Twain's A Connecticut Yankee in King Arthur's Court, 1997, 2nd edit., 2008, The Achievement of William Faulkner: A Centennial Tribute, 1998; Conversations with William Faulkner, 1999, "Co. Aytch," or a Side Show of the Big Show and Other Sketches by Samuel R. Watkins, 1999, Charles M. Schulz: Conversations, 2000, (with Ed Piacentino) The Humor of the Old South, 2001, (with Dennis Hall) Greenwood Guide to American Popular Culture, 4 vols., 2002, The New Encyclopedia of Southern Culture: Literature, vol. 9, 2008, My Life with Charlie Brown, 2010, (with Ed Piacentino) Southern Frontier Humor: An Anthology, 2010, Will Eisner: Conversations, 2011; (with Marcel Arbeit) The (Un)Popular South, 2011, The Dixie Limited: Writers on Faulkner and His Influence, 2013; editor Resources for American Literary Study, 1971-79, American Humor: An Interdisciplinary Newsletter, 1974-79, Studies in American Humor, 2004-08, Studies in Comics, 2010-; gen. editor Greenwood Press Bio-Bibliographies and Reference Guides in Popular Culture, Cambridge U. Press Am. Critical Archives, U. Press Miss., Great Comic Artists and Conversations with Comic Artists Series; book reviewer: Nashville Tenneseean, Richmond Times-Dispatch. Bd. dirs. Friends of Richmond Pub. Libary; bd. dirs. San Francisco Acad. Comic Art, James Br. Cabell Libr. Assocs., Va. Commonwealth U.; bd. dirs., exec. com. Edgar Allen Poe Mus. Recipient Bd. Govs. award Am. Cultural Assn., 1999, Disting. Prof. award, Randolph Macon Coll, 2004; fellow So. Fellowship Fund, 1959-62, Newberry Libr., 1987, Va. Found. Humanities, 1987, 93; grantee Fulbright-Hays, 1967-68, 71, 79, 88, 94, Mich. State U., 1965, 66, 68, Am. Philos. Soc., 1970, Clemson U., 1981, NEH, 1986, 91, 92; recipient Disting. Alumnus award Randolph-Macon Coll., 1995, Lifetime award Soc. for the Study of Southern Lit., 2008. Mem. MLA (hon. life, del. assembly 1976-78, 2001-03, chmn. elections com. 1980), South Atlantic MLA (program com. 1982-85, chmn. 1986, v.p. 1987, pres. 1988-89), Am. Studies Assn., Popular Culture Assn., Am. Humor Studies Assn. (pres. 1978, 88, Charlie award 1996), Soc. Study So. Lit. (exec. coun. 1971-73, 78-80, 86-88), Melville Soc., Ellen Glasgow Soc. (exec. coun. 1974-84, pres. 1987-88), Mus. Cartoon Art (nominating com. Hall of Fame 1975-95), European Assn. Am. Studies, So. Studies Forum (founder, exec. coun. 1988—), Popular Culture Assn. in South (v.p. 1987-88, pres. 1988-89), Mark Twain Cir. (chmn. nominating com. 1987-88), Mark Twain Cir. Am. (hon.), Cosmos Club, Omicron Delta Kappa, Phi Beta Kappa (key reporter), Pi Delta Epsilon, Lambda Chi Alpha. Mailing: PO Box 129 Ashland VA 23005-0129 Office Phone: 804-752-7282. Business E-Mail: tinge@rmc.edu.

INGLE, DAN W., state legislator; Former chief of police; former commr. Alamance County Bd. of Commrs., NC; state rep. Dist. 64, 2009—. Mem. Agrl. com., Appropriations com., Appropriations Subcom. on Capital, Judiciary I com., Transp. com., Wildlife Resources com. Republican. Office: North Carolina House of Representatives 300 N Salisbury St Room 530 Raleigh NC 27603-5925 Office Phone: 919-733-5905. Business E-Mail: Dan.Ingle@ncleg.net.

INGLE, ROBERT P., II, retail executive; Various mgmt. positions Ingles Markets, Inc., 1985—96, v.p. ops., 1996—2011, chmn., 2004—11, chmn., CEO, 2011—. Office: Ingles Markets Inc 2913 US Hwy 70 W Black Mountain NC 28711-9103 also: Ingles Markets Inc PO Box 6676 Asheville NC 28816

INGMIRE, TERRY, state legislator; b. Ponca City, Okla., Sept. 8, 1956; s. Donald Dean Ingmire and Booth McConnell I. Peggy; m. Fawn B. Lamb, 1984; children: Blake, Kalli. State rep. Dist. 34, Okla., 1997—; bus. cons. Okla. Natural Gas County, 1989—. Mem.: Nat. Youth Sports Coaches Assn., Nat. Exchange Club. Republican. Mailing: 523 Wedgewood Dr Stillwater OK 74075 Office: PO Box 6263 Edmond OK 73083-6263 Fax: 405-377-2991.

INGRAM, CHARLES CLARK, JR., energy executive; b. Dec. 10, 1916; s. Charles Clark and Winnie (Edwards) I.; m. Maxine Waterbury, Jan. 29, 1939; children: James C., Jack R. BS, U. Okla., 1940; LLD, Oral Roberts U., 1983. Registered profl. engr., Okla. With Oneok Inc., Tulsa, 1940—, pres., 1966-71, CEO, 1966-81, chmn., 1966-87, chmn. emeritus, 1987—. Former chmn. bd. trustees Frontiers of Sci. Found. of Okla., Inc., 1973-74; former adv. bd. Downtown Tulsa Unlimited; former bd. govs. Am. Citizenship Ctr., Oklahoma City; mem. pres.'s bd. visitors, chmn. Tulsa Engring. Coun., U. Okla. Maj. AUS, WWII, 1941-46. Named to Okla. Hall of fame, 1982. Mem. AIME, Am. Assn. Petroleum Geologists, Am. Gas Assn. (chmn. 1979-80), So. Gas Assn. (past pres.), Engrs. Soc. Tulsa, Okla. State C. of C. (pres. 1981), Oklahoma City C. of C., Tulsa C. of C., Nat. Alliance Businessmen (chmn. Ea. Okla. and Tulsa 1973-74), Propeller Club U.S., Summit Club, So. Hills Country Club (gov., past pres.), Cedar Ridge Country Club (Tulsa), Masons, Sigma Tau, Sigma Gamma Epsilon. Baptist. Office: Oneok Inc 100 W 5th St PO Box 871 Tulsa OK 74102-0871

INGRAM, CLAY, state legislator; b. Pensacola, Fla., Feb. 5, 1978; m. Leslie Cagle. BA in Gen. Comm., Fla. State U., Tallahassee, 2000. Former tchr.; real estate profl.; mem. Dist. 2 Fla. House of Representatives, 2011—. Paul Harris fellow, Cantonment Rotary Club. Republican. Office: Fla House of Reps 1301 The Capitol 402 S Monroe St Tallahassee FL 32399-1300 also: 11000 University Pkwy Pensacola FL 32514-5732 Office Phone: 850-494-7330, 850-488-8278.

INGRAM, JACK, musician; b. Nov. 15, 1970; Student, So. Methodist U., Dallas. Signed to Big Machine Records, Nashville, 2005—. Singer: (albums) Jack Ingram, 1995, Live at Adair's, 1995, Lonesome Question, 1995, Livin' or Dyin', 1997, Flutter, 1997, Hey You, 1999, Electric, 2002, Live at Billy Bob's Texas, 2003, Live at Gruene Hall: Happy Happy, 2004, Acoustic Motel, 2005, Live Wherever You Are, 2006, This is It, 2007, (songs) Wherever You Are, 2006, Love You, 2006 (Wide Open Country Video of Yr., Country Music TV awards, 2007). Recipient Top New Male Vocalist award, Acad. Country Music, 2008. Office: Big Machine Records 1219 16th Ave S Nashville TN 37212 Office Phone: 615-324-7777. E-mail: artistinfo@bigmachinemail.com.

INGRAM, KEITH, state legislator; Mem. Dist. 53 Ark. House of Reps., 2009—. Democrat. Office: State Capitol Rm 350 Little Rock AR 72201 also: PO Box 1028 Little Rock AR 72201 Office Phone: 501-682-6211, 501-682-7771, 870-735-9580. Business E-Mail: ingramk@arkleg.state.ar.us.

INGRAM, KENNETH FRANK, retired state supreme court justice; b. Ashland, Ala., July 7, 1929; s. Earnest Frank and Alta Mary (Allen) I.; m. Judith Louise Brown, Sept. 3, 1954; children: Jennifer Lynn Ingram, Kenneth Frank Jr. BS, Auburn U., 1951; LLB, Jones Law Sch., 1963. Bar: Ala. 1963, U.S. Dist. Ct. (no. dist.) Ala. 1965, U.S. Dist. Ct. (mid. dist.) Ala. 1966. City councilman City of Ashland, Ala., 1956-58; mem. Ho. of Reps., Ala., 1958-66; presiding judge 18th Jud. Cir. Ct., Ala., 1968-87; judge Ala. Ct. Civil Appeals, Montgomery, 1987-89, presiding judge, 1989-91; assoc. justice Ala. Supreme Ct., Montgomery, 1991-97. Mem., chmn. Ala. Jud. Inquiry Commn., 1979-87. Contbr. articles on jud. ethics to profl. pubs. With USMC, 1952-54. Mem. Ala. Bar Assn., Masons. Democrat. Meth. Avocations: woodworking, metalcrafting, tennis, swimming. Home: 264 1st St N PO Box 729 Ashland AL 36251-0729

INGRAM, MARK, JR., professional football player; b. Flint, Mich., Nov. 4, 1988; s. Mark and Shonda Ingram. Attended, U. Ala., Tuscaloosa, 2008—11. Running back U. Ala. Crimson Tide, Tuscaloosa, 2008—11, New Orleans Saints, 2011—. Recipient Heisman Meml. Trophy, Heisman Trophy Trust, 2009; named Offensive Player of Yr., Southeastern Conf., 2009, 1st Team All-SEC, 2009, 1st Team All-American, American Football Coaches Assn., 2009, AP, 2009. Achievements include member of the BCS National Championship winning University of Alabama Crimson Tide, 2010. Office: New Orleans Saints 5800 Airline Dr Metairie LA 70003

INGRAM, MARTHA RIVERS, publishing executive; b. Charleston, SC, Aug. 20, 1935; m. E. Bronson Ingram (dec. 1995), Oct. 4, 1958; children: Orrin Henry III, John Rivers, David Bronson, Robin. BA in History, Vassar Coll., 1957. V.p., pub. affairs Ingram Industries Inc., Nashville, 1979—95, mem., bd. directors, 1981—, chmn. bd. dirs., 1995—. Bd. dirs. Baxter Internat., Weyerhaeuser Co., Ashley Hall, Vassar Coll., Harpeth Hall Sch., Ingram Micro Inc.; mem. adv. bd. Kennedy Ctr. for Performing Arts, Washington. Chmn. Tenn. Bicentennial Commn., 1996; bd. dirs. Tenn. Performing Arts Ctr., Nashville Ballet, Nashville Opera, Nashville Inst. for Arts, Nashville Symphony, Nashville Cmty. Found.; past chmn. United Way's Alexis de Tocqueville Soc.; founder, bd. dirs. Tenn. Repertory Theater; chmn. bd. trustees Vanderbilt U., 1999-; co-founder Ingram Charitable Fund, 1995. Recipient Mary Harriman Cmty. Leadership award, Jr. League Internat., Inc., 1999, Golden Plate award, Acad. Achievement, 2004, Joe Kraft Humanitarian award, Cmty. Found., 2006; named one of Richest Americans, Forbes, 2001—, World's Richest People, 2001—; named to Jr. Achievement Nat. Bus. Hall of Fame, 1999, SC Bus. Hall of Fame, 1999. Mem. Nashville Area C. of C. Office: Ingram Industries Inc One Belle Mead Pl 4400 Harding Rd Nashville TN 37205-2244

INGRAM, RILEY EDWARD, state legislator; b. Halifax County, Va., Oct. 1, 1941; m. Mary Ann Brinkley (dec.); children: Tracy Crowder, Stacy Hansen, Riley Jr. Real estate broker, Va.; councilman Hopewell City Coun., Va., 1986—91; mayor City of Hopewell, 1988—91; mem. Dist. 62 Va. House of Delegates, Va., 1992—. Inf., Co. E Nat. Guard, 1959—60, inf., Co. E Nat. Guard, 1961—62, active duty US Army, 1960, served with 80th divsn. band USAR, 1962—68. Named Realtor of Yr., Southside Va. Assn. Realtors, Soldier of Yr., USAR Band. Mem.: NRA, Hopewell-Prince George C. of C. (former pres.), American Hellenic Edn1. and Progressive Assn., Ducks Unlimited, Wild Turkey Fedn., T.E. Peterson Chpt., Hopewell-Prince George Rotary, Hopewell Jaycees (life Boss of Yr.), Acca Temple Shrine, Scottish Rite, American Legion, Moose, AF&AM Masons Lodge 289. Republican. Church Of Nazarene. Office: 3302 Oaklawn Blvd Hopewell VA 23860 Office Phone: 804-458-9873. Office Fax: 804-458-0621. Business E-Mail: DelRIngram@house.virginia.gov.

INGRAM, ROBERT ALEXANDER, pharmaceutical executive; b. Dec. 6, 1942; BS in Bus. Adminstrn., Ea. Ill. U., 1965. Various positions including sales rep., sales mgr. and v.p. pub. affairs Merrell Dow Pharms.; v.p. govt. affairs Merck & Co., Inc. (formerly Schering-Plough Corp.), 1985—88, pres. Merck Frosst Can. Inc., 1988-90; exec. v.p. adminstrv. and regulatory affairs Glaxo Inc., 1990—93, exec. v.p., 1993, pres., COO, 1993—94, pres., CEO, 1994—97; CEO Glaxo Wellcome plc, 1997—2000; chmn. Glaxo Wellcome Inc., 1999—2000; pres., COO pharm. ops. GlaxoSmithKline plc, 2001—03, vice chmn. pharmaceuticals, 2003—09, advisor to CEO, 2010—; gen. ptnr. Hatteras Venture Partners, 2007—. Bd. dirs. Lowe's Companies, Inc., 2001—, Edwards Lifesciences Corp., 2003—, Valeant Pharmaceuticals Inc., 2003—, chmn., 2010—; bd. dirs. Allergan, Inc., 2005—, Cree, Inc., 2008—, Elan Corp. plc, 2010—, chmn., 2011—, OSI Pharmaceuticals, Inc., 2003—. Mailing: Hatteras Venture Partners 280 S Mangum St Ste 350 Durham NC 27701 also: OSI Pharmaceuticals Inc 41 Pinelawn Rd Melville NY 11747 Office Phone: 631-962-2000. Office Fax: 631-752-3880. Personal E-mail: ringram@osip.com.

INGRASSIA, ANTHONY FRANK (TONY), human resource specialist; b. Middletown, NY, Sept. 22, 1926; s. Joseph and Mary (Dina) I.; m. Eleanor Mae Birkholz, Aug. 9, 1952 (dec.); children: Micki Dee, Mary, Steve, Laura, Anne, Jane, Lisa, Timothy. BA, U.Wis., 1948. Reporter, acting editor Wis. News, West Bend, 1946—47; sports writer Milw. Sentinel, 1948-62; exec. v.p. Milw. Newspaper Guild, 1952-62; asst. dir. Dist. Coun. 48 Am. Fedn. State, County, Mcpl. Employees, AFL-CIO, Milw., 1962-64; labor rels. specialist, labor rels. dir. US P.O. Dept., Washington, 1964-69; dir. office labor-mgmt. rels. US CSC, Washington, 1970-78; asst. dir. labor-mgmt. rels. US Office Pers. Mgmt., Washington, 1979-82, asst. dir. agy. compliance and evaluation, 1982-86, dep. assoc. dir. pers. sys. and oversight, 1986-90, chmn. fed. prevailing rate adv. com., 1990-96; vice chmn., acting chmn. (presdl.) Fed. Salary Coun., Washington, 1992—95, vice chmn. (presdl.), 1995—2000. US del. ILO Pub. Employee Conf., Geneva, 1975-77, 86; spkr. seminar on collective bargaining U. Tel Aviv, 1979; cons. civil svc. reform Govt. Hungary and Poland, Budapest and Warsaw, 1991; cons. civil svc. Govt. of Saudi Arabia, Riyahd, 1986. Vol. Arlington (Va.) Food Assistance Ctr., 1992-97, Hospice, 1996-2002; ombudsman No. Va. Long Term Care Program, 1999-2003. Recipient presdl. rank awards Disting. Govt. Exec., 1980, Meritorious Govt. Exec., 1988. Mem. Soc. Fed. Labor Rels. Profl. (outstanding contbn. to fed. labor rels. award 1983-87), KC. Roman Catholic. Avocations: gardening, golf. Home: 12206 Cathedral Dr Lake Ridge VA 22192

INGWERSEN, MARTIN LEWIS, water transportation executive; b. Sandusky, Ohio, Nov. 5, 1919; s. John Christian and Irene Catherine (Hinkey) Ingwersen; m. Blanche Robinson, Apr. 26, 1947; children: Brenda, Richard Charles, Martin Lewis. BS, U. Notre Dame, 1941; postgrad., Western Res. U., 1941, Princeton U., 1943. Asst. to hull supt. Gt. Lakes Engring. Works, Ashtabula, Ohio, 1941-43, asst. supt., 1946-49; supt. plant Am. Ship Bldg. Co., Buffalo, 1948-50; mgr. plant Toledo, 1950-52, Lorain, Ohio, 1952-53; v.p. ops., 1954-58; v.p., works mgr. Ingalls Shipbldg. Corp., Pascagoula, Miss., 1958-65, v.p. ops., 1965-67; pres. Md. Shipbldg. and Drydock Co., Balt., 1967-68; exec. v.p. Lockheed Shipbldg. Co., Seattle, 1968-73; pres. Lockheed Shipbldg. and Constrn. Co., Seattle, 1973-76, exec. v.p. office of pres., 1976-86, trustee, 1973-86; cons. shipbldg. and ship repair, 1986—. Bd. dirs. Puget Sound Bridge and Dry Dock Co., Colby Crane & Mfg. Inc. Served to lt. USNR, 1943—46. Mem.: Am. Soc. Naval Engrs., Soc. Naval Archs. and Marine Engrs., Am. Bur. Shipping, Navy League, Notre Dame Club Vero Beach, Propeller Club U.S. Roman Catholic. Home and Office: 940 Turtle Cove Ln #304 Vero Beach FL 32963 Home Phone: 772-492-5075; Office Phone: 772-492-5075. Personal E-mail: mingwersen@aol.com.

INHOFE, JIM (JAMES MOUNTAIN INHOFE), United States Senator from Oklahoma; b. Des Moines, Nov. 17, 1934; s. Perry and Blanche Mountain Inhofe; m. Kay Kirkpatrik; children: James, Perry(dec.), Molly, Katy. BA, U. Tulsa, 1973. Pres. Quaker Life Ins. Co.; mem. Okla. House Reps., 1967—69, Okla. State Senate, 1969—77; mayor City of Tulsa, 1978-84; mem. US Congress from 1st Okla. Dist., 1987-94; US Senator from Okla., 1994—; chmn. US Senate Environment & Public Works Com., 2003—07, ranking minority mem., 2007—. Author: The Greatest Hoax: How the Global Warming Conspiracy Threatens Your Future, 2012. Mem. Tulsa Airport Authority, Tulsa Area Safety Coun. Served in US Army, 1955—56. Recipient Democracy award, Internat. Found. Election Systems, 1996, William S. Lee award leadership, Nuclear Energy Inst., 2001, Nat. Guardian award, Lincoln House Heritage Inst., 2002. Mem.: Friends of American Diabetes Assn. Republican. Presbyterian. Office: US Senate 205 Russell Senate Office Bldg Washington DC 20510-0001 also: District Office Ste 530 1924 South Utica Ave Tulsa OK 74104-6511 Office Phone: 202-224-4721, 918-748-5111. Office Fax: 202-224-6008, 918-748-5119. E-mail: jim_inhofe@inhofe.senate.gov.*

INMAN, BOBBY RAY, retired military officer, former dean; b. Rhonesboro, Tex., Apr. 4, 1931; s. Herman H. and Mertie F. (Hinson) I.; m. Nancy Carolyn Russo, June 14, 1958; children: Thomas, William. BA, U. Tex., 1950; grad., Nat. War Coll., 1972. Commd. ensign US Navy, 1952, advanced through grades to adm., 1981, asst. naval attache Stockholm, 1965-67, exec. asst., sr. aide to vice chief naval ops. Washington, 1972-73, dir. Naval Intelligence, 1974-76; asst. chief of staff for intelligence US Pacific Fleet (USPACFLT), 1973-74; vice dir. Def. Intelligence Agy. (DIA), 1976-77; dir. Nat. Security Agy. (NSA), Ft. Meade, Md., 1977-81; dep. dir. CIA, 1981-82; chmn., pres., chief exec. officer Microelectronics and Computer Tech. Corp., Austin, Tex., 1983-86; chmn. bd., chief exec. officer Westmark Systems, Inc., Austin, 1986-89; pvt. investor Austin, 1990—; prof., Lyndon B. Johnson Centennial chair in nat. policy University of Texas, Austin, 2001—, interim dean Lyndon B. Johnson Sch. Pub. Affairs, 2005, 2009—10. Chmn. Fed. Reserve Bank of Dallas, 1987—90; bd. dirs. Massey Energy Co. (formerly A.T. Massey Coal), 1985—, non-exec. chmn., 2010—. Decorated Def. D.S.M., Navy D.S.M., Legion of Merit, Def. Superior Service medal, Meritorious Service medal, Nat. Security medal, Joint Services Commendation medal. Office: 301 Congress Ave Ste 1350 Austin TX 78701 also: Lyndon B Johnson Sch Pub Affairs U Tex at Austin PO Box Y Austin TX 78713-8925 Office Phone: 512-471-6716.

INMAN, MARIANNE ELIZABETH, retired academic administrator; b. Berwyn, Ill., Jan. 9, 1943; d. Miles V. and Bessee M. (Hejtmanek), Plzak; m. David P. Inman; Aug 1, 1964. BA, Purdue U., 1964; AM, Ind. U., 1967; PhD, U. Tex., 1978. Dir. Comml. Div. World Instruction and Translation, Inc., Arlington, Va., 1969-71; program staff mem. Ctr. for Applied Linguistics, Arlington, 1972-73; lectr. in French No. Va. Community Coll., Bailey's Crossroads, 1973; faculty mem., linguistic researcher Tehran (Iran) U., 1973-75; intern mgmt. edn. rsch. & devel. S.W Ednl. Devel. Lab., Austin, Tex., 1977-78; asst. prof., program dir. Southwestern U., Georgetown, Tex., 1978; dir. English lang. inst. Alaska Pacific U., Anchorage, 1980-87, chairperson all-U. requirements, 1984-88, assoc. dean acad. affairs, 1988-90; v.p. dean of coll. Northland Coll., Ashland, Wis., 1990-95; pres. Ctrl. Meth. U., Fayette, Mo., 1995—2013, emeritua pres., 2013—. Contbr. Pres. Commn. Foreign Lang. and Internat. Studies, Washington, 1978-79; manuscript evaluator The Modern Lang. Jour., Columbus, Ohio, 1979-84; cons. Anchorage Sch. Dist., 1984-90; cons., evaluator The Higher Learning Commn. of N. Cen. Assn. Colls. and Schs., Chgo., 1990—; mem. dean's task force Coun. of Ind. Colls., 1993-95; pres. Ind. Colls. and Univs. Mo., 1996-00, 2010-12. Co-author: English for Medical Students, 1976; co-author and editor: English for Science and Engineering Students, 1977; contbr. articles to profl. jours. Treas. Alaska Humanities Forum, Anchorage, 1982-87; mem. Anchorage Matanuska-Susitna Borough Pvt. Industry Coun., 1983-86, Sister Cities Commn., Anchorage, 1984-90; mem. Multicultural Edn. Adv. Bd., Anchorage, 1987-90; with speakers bur. Wis. Humanities Com., 1992-95, Mcpl. Libr. Bd., 1993-95; active Mo. Humanities Coun., 1997-03, 04—12, vice chmn., 2005—07, chmn., 2007-09; bd. dirs. Mo. Colls. Fund, mem. bd. Great Rivers Coun. Boy Scouts Am., 1996—2013; mem. Howard County Economic Devel. Coun., 2007-13; mem. presdl. adv. com. Mo. Coordinating Bd. for Higher Edn., chair, 2008-09; mem. U. Senate, United Meth. Ch., pres. 2009-12; trustee, Garrett-Evangelical Theol. Seminary, Evanston, Ill., 2013-. Named Fellow of Grad. Sch., U. Tex. Austin, 1977-78, Nat. Teaching Fellow, Alaska Pacific U., Anchorage, 1980-81, Bus. Leader of Yr. Fayette Rotary, 2009; recipient Pub. Svc. award Sister Cities Commn., Anchorage, 1987, Kellogg Found. Nat. fellowship, Battle Creek, Mich., 1988-91. Mem. LWV, Nat. Assn. Women Edn., Nat. Assn. Ind. Colls. and Univs. (bd. dirs. 2005-08, chair policy and pub. rels. com. 2007-08), Am. Assn. Higher Edn., Am. Coun Tchg. Fgn. Langs., Nat. Assn. Schs. and Colls., United Meth. Ch. (bd. dirs., mem., Univ. Senate 2005-12, pres 2009-12), Tchrs. English to Speakers Other Langs., Nat. Coun. Tchrs. English, Gold Peppers, Mortar Board, Alpha Chi, Alpha Lambda Delta, Delta Rho Kappa, Kappa Delta Pi, Omicron Delta Kappa, Phi Kappa Phi, Pi Delta Phi, Pi Lambda Theta, Sigma Delta Pi, Sigma Epsilon Pi, Sigma Kappa. Methodist. Avocations: community theater, hiking, camping, fishing. Home: 102 Aster Cir Georgetown TX 78633 Business E-Mail: minman@centralmethodist.edu.*

INMAN, SCOTT, state legislator; BA, JD, Univ. Okla. Mem. Dist. 94 Okla. House of Representatives, 2007—. Democrat. Address: PO Box 55532 Del City OK 73155 Office: 2300 N Lincoln Blvd Rm 548 Oklahoma City OK 73105 Office Phone: 405-557-7370. E-mail: scott.inman@okhouse.gov.

INNES, DAVID LYN, university official, educator; b. Cleve., Dec. 19, 1941; s. Harry Donald and Mildred Marie (Svozil) I.; m. Janet Lynn Koons, Sept. 5, 1964; children: Debra Lynn, Jonathan Lyn. BS, Ohio Wesleyan U., 1964; MS, U. Cin., 1966; PhD, Ohio State U., 1969; JD, Mercer U., 2005. Instr. Ohio State U., Columbus, 1969-70; asst. to assoc. prof. Temple U., Phila., 1970-80; prof. Sch. Medicine, Mercer U., Macon, Ga., 1980—, assoc. v.p. grants and founds., 1982-84, asst. to the provost for med. affairs, 1985-88, asst. provost for med. affairs, 1988-93, asst. v.p. for health and biosafety, 1993-96, assoc. v.p. for univ. rsch. and biosafety, 1996—. Contbr. articles and abstracts to profl. jours. Mem. bd. Edn., Willow Grove, Pa., 1973-79, Mental Health Adv. Com., Abington, Pa., 1979-80. Grantee NIH, 1978, constrn. grantee NIH, 1987. Mem. Am. Assn. for Lab. Sci., Am. Gastroenterology Assn., Am. Physiol. Soc., Fedn. Am. Socs. for Exptl. Biology, Ga. Assn. for Biomed. Rsch. (treas., bd. dirs. 1988-98), Ga. Higher Edn. Network Environ. Health and Safety (v.p. 1994-96, pres. 1996-97), Sigma Xi (rsch. grantee), Phi Kappa Phi. Republican. Methodist. Avocations: swimming, biking. Home: 201 Rocky Creek Ct Forsyth GA 31029-5354 Office: Mercer U 1400 Coleman Ave Macon GA 31207-1500 Office Phone: 478-752-4075.

INNES, DEBORAH, bank executive; 3 children. V.p., treasury mgmt. Amegy Bank of Tex.(subsidiary SW Bancorp. of Tex., Inc.), 1992—94, exec. v.p., treasury mgmt., 1994—, exec. v.p., retail banking, 2005—. Bd. secy. and chair of volunteer services I Have a Dream, Houston; bd. mem. ESCAPE Family Resource Ctr., Juvenile Diabetes Rsch. Found., Houston. Named one of 25 Women to Watch, US Banker mag., 2005, 25 Most Powerful Women in Banking, US Banker, 2006. Office: Amegy Bank of Texas 4400 Post Oak Pky Houston TX 77027-7459 Office Phone: 713-235-8800. Office Fax: 713-439-5949.

INOUE, HIROSHI, broadcast executive; b. Japan, 1940; Mng. dir. Toppan Printing Co., Ltd.; joined Tokyo Broadcasting System Inc., 1963, v.p., 2001—02, pres. & CEO, 2002—. Bd. dirs. Tokyo Electron America Inc. Office: Tokyo Electron America Inc 2400 Grove Blvd Austin TX 78741-6500 Office Phone: 512-424-1000. Office Fax: 512-424-1001. Business E-Mail: hiroshi.inoue@tel.com.

INSALACO, VINCENT, political organization administrator; b. NY; m. Sally Riggs Insalaco (dec. 2006); children: Elizabeth, Vincent III. B in History and Polit. Sci., U. Ark. at Little Rock. Asst. sec. of state State of Ark., 1981—84; host "Vince Insalaco Show" KARN and Ark. Radio Network, 1985—91; campaign mgr. North Little Rock Mayor Patrick Hays, 1988; founder Family Entertainment; co-founder, artistic dir. Argenta Cmty. Theater, North Little Rock; chair Dem. Party of Ark., 2013—. Prodr.: (films) War Eagle, Arkansas, 2007 (Charles B. Pierce Award for Best "Made in Arkansas" film, 2008). Recipient Cmty. Engagement Award, Argenta Cmty. Devel. Corp., 2012, Ed Fry Dem. of Yr., 2013. Democrat. Office: Democratic Party of Arkansas 1300 W Capitol Ave Little Rock AR 72201 Office Phone: 501-374-2361.

INSKO, VERLA C., state legislator; b. 1936; m. Chester Chet. Bd. edn. mem., Carrboro, 1977—85; chmn. Orange County Dem. Party, 1983—85, Orange County Women's Ctr., 1987—90; mem., bd. commr. Orange County, 1990—94; mem. NC Sickle Cell Found., 1993—96; vis. bd. mem. U. NC, Chapel Hill, 1999—; mem. L.Am. Resource Ctr., 2000—; former state rep. Dist. 24 NC; state rep. Dist. 56 NC, 2003—. Recipient Legislator of Yr. award, NAMI, 2000—01, Valand award, Mental Health Assn. NC, 2000. Mem.: NC Women's Forum. Democrat. Protestant. Office: North Carolina House of Representatives 300 N Salisbury St Rm 603 Raleigh NC 27603-5925 Office Phone: 919-733-7208. E-mail: Verla.Insko@ncleg.net.

INTERIAN, ALBERTO, JR., cardiac electrophysiologist, educator; MD, U. Miami, 1982. Diplomate Am. Bd. Internal Medicine, 1985, Am. Bd. Internal Medicine-cardiovasc. disease, 1987, Am. Bd. Internal Medicine-clin. cardiac electrophysiology, 2000. Resident internal medicine Jackson Meml. Hosp., 1983—85, fellow cardiovasc. disease, 1986—88; prof. medicine and cardiology Univ. of Miami; med. dir. Arrhythmia Syncope Ctr.; hosp. affiliations include Mercy Hosp., Jackson Meml. Hosp. Author numerous book chapters, co-author more than 50 articles. Recipient numerous honors and awards. Office: Mercy Arryhthmia and Syncope Center 3641 S Miami Ave Ste 221 Bayside Pavillion Bldg Miami FL 33133 Office Phone: 305-285-2685.

IRBY, HOLT, lawyer; b. Dodge City, Kans., July 4, 1937; s. Jerry M. and Virgie (Lorean) I.; m. LaVerne Smith, May 27, 1956; children: Joseph, Kathy, Kay, Karon, James. BA, Tex. Tech. U., 1959; JD, U. Tex., 1962. Bar: Tex. 1962, U.S. Dist. Ct. (no. dist.) Tex. 1963. Asst. city atty. City of Lubbock, Tex., 1962-63; assoc. Hugh Anderson, Lubbock, 1963-66; gen. counsel, sec. Merc. Fin. Corp., Dallas, 1966-69; gen. counsel, v.p. Ward Food Restaurants, inc., Dallas, 1969-71; pvt. practice, Garland, Tex., 1971—. Mem. lawyer referal com. State Bar Tex., 1977, 78. Mem. bd. deacons First Bapt. Ch., Garland, 1979-90, chmn., 1976-77; bd. dirs. Garland Assistance Program, 1980, Habitat for Humanity of Greater Garland, Inc., 1997-2001, Dallas Life Found., 1980-90, Toler Children's Cmty., 1983-85; bd. dirs. Garland Civic Theatre, 1986—, pres., 1990-91, 92-93, v.p., 1991-92; mem. Garland Drug Task Force, 1990; deacon South Garland Bapt. Ch., 1992—, chmn., 1993-94, 98-99, 2002-03. Mem. Tex. Trial Lawyers Assn., Tex. Assn. Bank Counsel, Tex. Bar Assn., Garland Bar Assn. (bd. dirs. 1986-96, sec. 1992-93, v.p. 1993-94, pres. 1995-96), Dallas Bar Assn., Praetor Legal Frat. (named outstanding mem. 1962), Lubbock Jaycees (dir. 1963-65), Kiwanis (dir. 1973-74). Office: Bank of Am Tower 705 W Avenue B Ste 110 Garland TX 75040-6241 Business E-Mail: holt@irby-spencer.com.

IRBY, MARK, marketing executive; V.p. mktg. and advt. Publix Supermarkets, Lakeland, Fla. Office: Publix Supermarkets 1936 George Jenkins Blvd Lakeland FL 33815-3760

IRONS, TAMMY, state legislator, lawyer; BS in Acctg., U. North Ala., Florence; JD, U. Memphis. Jud. law clk. Tenn. Ct. of Appeals; bus. atty. Irons Law Firm; mem. Dist. 1 Ala. House of Reps., Montgomery, 2006—11, Ala. State Senate, 2011—. Mem. pres. coun. U. North Ala.; mem. Sherrod Ave. Church of Christ; bd. mem. Shoals Entrepreneurial Ctr., Shoals Econ. Devel. Authority, SafePlace, Inc., Boys and Girls Clubs. Mem.: Lauderdale County Bar Assn. (past pres.). Democrat. Office: Irons Law Firm 219 N Court St Florence AL 35630 also: State House 11 S Union St Montgomery AL 36130 Office Phone: 256-766-9201, 334-353-9032, 334-242-7800. Business E-Mail: tammy@ironslawfirm.com.

IRONS, WILLIAM LEE, lawyer; b. Birmingham, Ala., June 9, 1941; s. George Vernon and Velma (Wright) Irons. BA, U. Va., 1963; JD, Samford U., 1966. Bar: Ala. 1966, U.S. Dist Ct. (no. dist.) Ala. 1966, U.S. Ct. Appeals (5th cir.) 1966. Dir. mil. justice Maxwell AFB, Ala., 1963—69; law clk. Speir, Robertson & Jackson, Birmingham, 1964—66; asst. judge adv. Whiteman AFB, Mo., 1966, Gunter AFB, 1967—68; ptnr. Speir, Robertson, Jackson & Irons, 1970—71, Speir & Irons, 1971—72, William L. Irons & Assoc., 1972—. U.S. trustee, 1964—86; instr. sr. officers Judge Adv. Gen.'s Sch. Air War coll. Air U. Maxwell AFB; chief inspector city, state and fed. elections Jefferson County, Ala., 2002—. Author: (magazine articles on Am. Revolution era) Colonial Navy, 1992 (U.S. Senate commendation), Chronicles of the Am. Revolutionary War, 1995 (N.Y. State Senate commendation). Candidate Ala. Ho. Reps., 1966; exec. com. Jefferson County Rep. Party; mem. steering com. Jefferson City Rep. Party, 2004; deacon Mountain Brook Bapt. Ch., Sunday sch. supt. Capt. Strategic Air Command USAF. Decorated Commendation medal and citation USAF, Congl. medal of honor project Freedom's Found., Valley Forge, Pa.; named Outstanding Jr. Officer Vietnam War, USAF, 1969; DuPont Regional scholar, U.Va. Mem.: SAR (pres. Ala. chpt., Taylor award 1990), ABA, Nat. Res. Officer Assn., Fed. Bar Assn., Nat. Assn. Cert. Judge Advs., Assn. Trial Lawyers Am., Birmingham Bar Assn., Descendants of Washington's Army at Valley Forge (capt. of the guard, adm. state of Md. 1995), Birmingham Exec. Club (pres. 1978—79), Nat. Lawyers Club, St. Andrews Soc., Newcomen Soc., Sigma Delta Kappa. Republican. Baptist. Home: 3855 Cove Dr Birmingham AL 35213-3801

IRWIN, JOHN DAVID, electrical engineering educator; b. Mpls., Aug. 9, 1939; s. Arthur Fowle and Virginia I.; m. Patricia Edith Watson, Aug. 26, 1961; children: Geri Marie, John David, Laura Lynne. BEE, Auburn U., Ala., 1961; MS, U. Tenn., 1962, PhD, 1967. Mem. tech. staff Bell Labs., Holmdel, NJ, 1967—68; supr. Bell Labs, Holmdel, 1968—69; asst. prof. elec. engring. Auburn U., 1969—72, assoc. prof., 1972—73, assoc. prof., head dept., 1973—76, prof., head dept., 1976—, Earle C. Williams Eminent Scholar and dept. head, 1993—; pres. Southeastern Ctr. for Elec. Engring. Edn., Orlando, Fla., 1983—84. Hon. prof. Chinese Acad. Sci., Inst. for Semiconductors, Beijing, 2004. Author: (with Nelson and Carroll) Introduction to Computer Logic, 1975, (with E.R. Graf) Industrial Noise and Vibration Control, 1979, Basic Engineering Circuit Analysis, 1984, 9th edit. (with R.M. Nelms), 2008, (with V.P. Nelson, H.T. Nagle, B.D. Carroll, J.D. Irwin) Digital Logic Circuit Analysis and Design, 1995, (with D.V. Kerns) Introduction to Electrical Engineering, 1995, On Becoming An Engineer, 1997; editor-in-chief The Industrial Electronics Handbook, 1997, Emerging Multimedia Computer Communication Technologies. Recipient Robert M. Janowiak Outstanding Leadership and Svc. award, ECE Dept. Heads Assn., 2010, James H. Mulligan Jr. Edml. medal, IEEE, 2013. Fellow IEEE (editor jour. Indsl. Electronics 1982-83, Centennial medal 1984, A.H. Hornfeck Svc. award Indsl. Electronics Soc. 1986, Region III Outstanding Educator award 1989, Meritorious award Edn. Soc. 2005, Ednl. Activities Bd. V.P.'s Recognition award, 2006), Am. Soc. Engring. Edn. (Elec. and Computer Engring. Disting. Educator award 2001); mem. IEEE Edn. Soc. (pres. 1989-90, IEEE-Indsl. Electronics Soc. Achievement award 1991, IEEE Edn. Soc. award 1991, IEEE Edn. Soc./Soc. McGraw Hill Jacob Millman award 1993, Undergrad. Tchg. award 1998, Third Millennium medal 2000, Richard M. Emberson award 2000). Roman Catholic. Home: PO Box 2740 Auburn AL 36831-2740 Office: Auburn U Dept Engring Auburn AL 36849 Business E-Mail: irwinjd@auburn.edu.

IRWIN, JOHN ROBERT, retired public company executive, educator, director; b. Melbourne, Australia, July 24, 1945; came to U.S., 1969; s. Robert L. and Daisy O. I.; m. Margo E. Mayon, 1979; children: Joshua R., Elizabeth J. BE with honors, U. Melbourne, M Engring. Sci., 1969; MS in Indsl. Adminstrn., Purdue U., 1970; AMP, Harvard Bus. Sch., 1990. Registered profl. engr., Australia. Mgmt. program Kerr-McGee Corp., Wis., Tex., Okla., 1970-72, Transworld Drilling Co. (sub. Kerr-McGee Corp.) La. Wales, Denmark, Singapore Myanmar, Scotland, 1972—75; mng. dir., mgr. ops. Transworld Drilling Co., Sharjah, Nigeria and La., 1975—79; mgr. ops. Atwood Oceanics, Inc., Houston, 1979-80, gen. mgr., 1980, v.p., 1980-88, exec. v.p., 1988-92, pres., CEO, 1992—2009, bd. dirs., 1992—2010; Halsey disting. vis. prof. U. Va., 2011. Bd. dirs. Offshore Tech. Conf., 1999-2007; dir. U. Melbourne USA Found., 2009-, Internat. Assn. Drilling Contractors, 1980-2010, chmn., 2000. Bd. dir. McCoy Corp., 2012—. Recipient Entrepreneur of Yr. award, Gulf Coast, Ernst & Young, 2006. Fellow: Inst. Engrs. Australia; mem.: Am. Bur. Shipping. Avocations: history, reading, Australian football, learning.

IRWIN, PETER JOHN, orthopaedic surgeon; b. East St. Louis, Ill., July 7, 1934; s. Peter and Anne (Sokalski) Iwasyszyn; m. Kathryn Swanson, June 15, 1960; children: Kathryn Linda, Mary Elizabeth, Amy Marie, Kenneth John, James Patrick. BS in Biology, St. Louis U., 1955, MD, 1959. Diplomate Am. Bd. Orthopedic Surgery. Intern Creighton Meml. St. Joseph Hosp., Omaha, 1959-60; resident in orthop. surgery U. Ark. Med. Ctr., Little Rock, 1961-65, tchg. staff, 1965—77; pvt. practice Fort Smith, Ark., 1965-97; mem. staff St. Edward Mercy Med. Ctr., 1965-97; ret., 1997. Mem. staff Sparks Regional Med. Ctr., 1965—97, chief staff, 1979, bd. dirs., 1980—87. Lt. comdr. M.C. USN, 1966—68. Fellow: ACS, Am. Acad. Orthop. Surgeons (councillor 1983—89); mem.: AMA, Am. Soc. Sports Medicine, Am. Orthop. Soc. Sports Medicine, So. Orthop. Assn., Mid-Ctrl. States Orthop. Soc. (pres. 1979—80), Clin. Orthop. Soc., Mid-Am. Orthop. Assn. (founding mem., pres. 1993—94), Ark. Orthop. Assn. (pres. 1976—77), Sebastian County Med. Soc. (pres. 1997), So. Med. Assn., Ark. Hand Club.

ISAAC, JASON, state legislator; m. Carrie Crain; 2 children. Grad. in Bus., Stephen F. Austin State U., 1996. Transportation cons.; mem. Dist. 45 Tex. House of Representatives, 2011—. Founder Stephen F. Austin State U. Lacrosse Team; co-founder, dir. Stephen F. Austin State U., Assn. of Sports Club; pres. Ctrl. Tex. Chapter US Lacrosse; bd. dirs. Dripping Springs Youth Sports Assn. Republican. Office: Room E1.410 Capitol Extension PO Box 2910 Austin TX 78768 Office Phone: 512-850-5524, 512-463-0647. Business E-Mail: jason.isaac@house.state.tex.us.

ISAAC, WILLIAM MICHAEL (BILL ISAAC), brokerage house executive, retired federal official; b. Bryan, Ohio, Dec. 21, 1943; s. Charles R. and Ruth L. (Hallberg) I.; m. Carma Sue Dunbar, Aug. 15, 1965 (div. 1993); m. Christine Verney, Nov. 16, 1997; children: David M., Stephanie A., Lennon G., Quinn V. BS, Miami U. Oxford, Ohio, 1966, LLD (hon.), 1984; JD summa cum laude, Ohio State U., 1969. Bar: Wis. 1969, Ky. 1974, D.C. 1986. Atty. Foley & Lardner, Milw., 1969-74; v.p., gen. counsel, sec. First Ky. Nat. Corp., Louisville, 1974-78; chmn. FDIC, Washington, 1978-85; ptnr. Arnold & Porter LLP, Washington, 1985-93; chmn. The Secura Group, Washington, 1985—2007, Secura Burnett Co. LLC, San Francisco, 1992—2007; mem. Depository Institutions Deregulation Com., 1981-85, Bush Task Group, 1982-85; chmn. Fed. Fin. Instns. Exam. Coun., 1983-85, Isaac Property Companies, 1992—, LECG Global Financial Services, 2007—, Secura Group of LEGC, LLC, 2007—, Fifth Third Bancorp, 2010—. Bd. dirs. Fifth Third Bancorp., 2010—. Co-author: Bank Holding Companies: A Practical Guide to Bank Acquisitions and Mergers, 1972; author: Senseless Panic: How Washington Failed America, 2010; contbr. articles on banking to profl. jours. Mem. nat. coun. Coll. Law, Ohio State U., Columbus, 1980—; mem. bus. adv. coun. Miami U., Oxford, Ohio, 1982—; trustee Miami U. Found., 1988-96; bd. dirs. Ohio State U. Found., The Cmty. Found. of Sarasato County; chmn.-elect Goodwill Ind.; chmn. Isaac Properties Group. Mem. ABA, Wis. Bar Assn., Ky. Bar Assn., Fed. Nat. Mortgage Assn. (adv. bd. 1989-90). Republican. Office: LECG Global Financial Services 1725 Eye St NW Ste 800 Washington DC 20006 Office Phone: 941-388-0088. Office Fax: 941-388-1211. Personal E-mail: billisaac@comcast.net. E-mail: bissac@legc.com.

ISAACS, GERALD WILLIAM, retired agricultural engineering educator, consultant; b. Crawfordsville, Ind., Sept. 3, 1927; s. William Paul and Verna Ethel (Johnson) I.; m. Phyllis Joyce Seaton, Aug. 22, 1948; children: Joyce Irene (dec.), David Gerald, Donald Phillip, Joseph Lee (dec.), Susan Verna, Linda Kay. BSEE, Purdue U., 1947, MSEE, 1949; PhD in Agrl. Engring., Mich. State U., 1954. Grad. asst. agrl. engring. dept. agrl. engring. Mich. State U., E. Lansing, 1952-54; instr. agrl. engring. Dept. Argl. Engring, Purdue U., W. Lafayette, Ind., 1948-52, from asst. prof. agrl. engring to prof. agrl. engring., 1954-1964, prof., head dept. argl. engring., 1964-81; prof., chmn. dept. agrl. engring. U. Fla., Gainesville, 1981-91, prof. emeritus, 1991—. Cons. engr. various mfg. and legal firms, 1958—. Contbr. articles to profl. jours. Recipient Massey Ferguson Gold medal Am. Soc. Agrl. Engrs., 1991, Silver medal Max Eyth Gesselschaft, Germany, 1979. Mem. Polish Acad. Sci., Rotary Internat. (dir. 1976-78, Paul Harris fellow 1993), Am. Soc. Agrl. Engrs. (nat. pres. 1982-83), Soc. German Engrs. (hon. corr. mem.); Verien Deutscher Ingeneurs (corr.). Lutheran. Avocations: photography, travel, music. Office: U Fla Dept Agrl and Biol Engring Frazier Rogers Hall Gainesville FL 32611 Personal E-mail: isaacsg@bellsouth.net. Business E-Mail: isaacs@ufl.edu.

ISAACS, HAROLD, history professor; b. Newark, Dec. 19, 1936; s. Albert Lewis and Bertha (Wohl) I.; m. Doris Carolne Mack, Apr. 25, 1974 (dec. Jan 31, 2011); m. Susan Blomberg, Dec. 29, 1959 (div. May 15, 1964), children Debra Marlene, Sherri Darlene. BS in History, U. Ala., University, 1958, MA in History, 1960, PhD in History, 1968. Grad. tchg. fellow U. Ala., Univ., 1959—62; instr. hist. Memphis State U., 1962-65; asst. prof. hist. Ga. Southwestern State U., Americus, 1965-70, assoc. prof. hist., 1970-79, prof. hist., 1979—2005, prof. emeritus hist., 2006. Bd. dirs. World Communities Theater, Ctr. Third World Studies, 2005—; bd. advs. Ency. Developing World; scholar cons. Jimmy Carter Residency Program, Author: Jimmy Carter's Peanut Brigade, 1977; founder, editor Jour. of Third World Studies, 1984—. Advisor Young Dems., Ga. Southwestern State U., 1965-80, chmn. faculty capital campaign, 2003; founder, coord. Third World in Perspective Program Seminar Series, 1981—; coord. Black Leaders Lecture Series, 1981. Recipient Tchr. of Yr. award Alpha Phi Alpha, 1982, Outstanding Svc. award Americus Early Bird Civitan Club, 1983, Outstanding Historian and Humanitarian award SABU, 1994, Presdl. Citation for Disting. Svc., 1995, Outstanding Svc. to African Am. and Third World Studies SABU 1996-97, Harold Isaacs 3rd World Studios Collection, All-Africa award African Studies and Rsch. Forum, 2001, Africa Excellence in Scholarship and Svc. award, 2006, Internat. Lincoln Ctr. Disting. Leadership and Scholarship award, 2003, African Studies and Rsch. Forum Presdl. award, 2007-08, faculty award Univ. Sys. Ga. Regents' Hall of Fame, 2004, Grand Marshal Spl. Svc. award, Ga. Southwestern State U., 1994-2005, award, 2002-, Presdl. Medallion award, 2006. Mem. Assn. Third World Studies, Inc. (founder, pres., exec. dir., 1983-91, treas. 1983-97, proceedings editor 2002—, Presdl. award 1992, Harold Isaacs Grad. award, 2001, ATWS Appreciation award, 2008). Democrat. Jewish. Home: 180 Lakeshore Dr Americus GA 31719-8233 Office: Ga Southwestern State 800 GSW State University Dr Americus GA 31709-4376 Office Phone: 229-931-2078. Business E-Mail: haroldisaacs2@bellsouth.net.

ISAKSON, JOHNNY (JOHN HARDY ISAKSON), United States Senator from Georgia; b. Atlanta, Ga., Dec. 28, 1944; m. Dianne (Davison) Isakson; children John, Kevin, Julie BBA, U. Ga., 1966. Pres. Northside Realty, Atlanta, 1979—98; CEO Fairgreen Capital LP, Atlanta, 1996—99; mem. Ga. House of Reps., 1976—90, Republican leader, 1983—90; mem. Ga. State Senate, 1994—96, US Congress from 6th Ga. Dist., 1999—2005; US Senator from Ga., 2005—; vice chmn. US Senate Select Com. on Ethics, 2009—. Chmn. Ga. State Bd. Edn., 1996—99. Winner spl. election to succeed Rep. Newt Gingrich, who resigned, 1999; represented Cobb County in the Ga. legislature 17 yrs.; Rep. candidate for gov. of Ga., 1990, Rep. primary candidate for US Senate, 1996; Sunday sch. tchr. Mt. Zion Meth. Ch., 1978—; adv. bd. Fed. Nat. Mortgage Assn.; bd. trustees Kennesaw State U., Ga.; bd. dirs. Ga. Club, Metro Atlanta C. of C., Ga. C. of C., Riverside Bank. Served with USAF, 1966—67, served as SSG with Ga. Nat. Guard, 1967—72. Recipient Best Legis. in Am. award, Rep. Nat. Com., 1989, Disting. Svc. award, Ga. Mcpl. Assn., Guardian Small Bus. award, Nat. Fedn. Independent Bus., Hero of Taxpayers award, Americans for Tax Reform, Tax fighter award, Nat. Tax Limitation Com., Blue Key award, U. Ga., 1998. Mem.: Realty Alliance (pres.), Nat. Assn. Realtors (exec. com.). Republican. Methodist. Office: US Senate 131 Russell Senate Office Bldg Washington DC 20510 also: One Overton Park Ste 970 3625 Cumberland Blvd SE Atlanta GA 30339-6406 Office Phone: 202-224-3643, 770-661-0999. Office Fax: 202-228-0724, 770-661-0768.*

ISAKSON, MICHAEL M., furniture manufacturing company executive; V.p., franchise sales The ServiceMaster Co., 1990—92, COO, Merry Maids, 1992, pres., Merry Maids, 1992—98, pres., Consumer Svcs. Franchise Svcs. Group, 1994—95; pres., COO, Franchise Svcs. Group Servicemaster Co., Servicemaster Global Holdings, 1995—; pres., COO Furniture Medic, 2007—, AmeriSpec, 2007—. Chmn., former bd. dirs., co-chmn., franchisor forum Internat. Franchise Assn., mem., exec. com. Recipient Marion E. Wade award, The ServiceMaster Co. Office: The ServiceMaster Co 860 Ridge Lake Blvd Memphis TN 38120 Office Phone: 901-597-1400. Office Fax: 630-663-2001. Business E-Mail: misakson@amerispec.com.

ISBELL, JERI L., human resources specialist; BBA in Acctg., Eastern Ky. U., 1975; MBA, Xavier U. CPA; cert. mgmt. acct. Various staff and mgmt. positions IBM Corp.; joined Lexmark International, Inc., 1991, v.p., fin., mgr., mfg. fin. planning, bus. printer divsn., US contr., v.p., worldwide compensation and resource programs, human resources, 2001—03, v.p., human resources, 2003—. Bd. dirs. Commerce Lexington. Bd. dirs. Lexington Metro YMCA. Office: Lexmark International Inc 740 W New Cir Rd Lexington KY 40550 Office Phone: 859-232-2000. Office Fax: 859-232-2403. Business E-Mail: JIsbell@lexmark.com.

ISDELL, NEVILLE (EDWARD NEVILLE ISDELL), retired beverage company executive; b. Downpatrick, County Down, Ireland, June 8, 1943; came to U.S., 1989; s. Edward Neville and Margaret (Smith) I.; m. Pamela Anne Gill, Jan. 10, 1970; 1 child, Cara Anne. BA in Social Sci., Cape Town U., Republic of South Africa, 1965; PMD, Harvard Bus. Sch.; DSci. (hon.), U. Ulster, 2007. Mgmt. trainee Edgars Stores Ltd., Johannesburg, 1966, Copperbelt Bottling Co., Kitwe, Zambia, 1966-68; various positions Coca-Cola Co., Atlanta, Zambia, South Africa, 1968—80, regional mgr. Sydney, 1980—81; pres. Coca-Cola Bottlers Philippines, Inc., Manila, 1981—85; pres., Central European div. Coca-Cola Co., Essen, West Germany, 1985—89, sr. v.p., pres. Northeast Europe and Africa group Atlanta, 1989-92, sr. v.p., pres. Northeast Europe and Middle East group, 1993—95, pres., Greater Europe Group, 1995—98; chmn., CEO Coca-Cola Beverages plc, England, 1998—2000; CEO Coca-Cola Hellenic Bottling Co. S.A., 2000—01, vice chmn, 2001; sr. internat. cons. to CEO Doug Daft Coca-Cola Co., 2001—04, chmn., CEO, 2004—08, chmn., 2008—09. Bd. dirs. The Coca-Cola Co., 2004—, Sun Trust Bank, 2004—08, Gen. Motors Co., 2008—09, 2009—, Grocery Manufacturers Assn.; trustee US Council for Internat. Bus.; chmn. US-Russian Bus. Coun. Trustee Ctr. for Strategic & Internat. Studies; vice-chmn. corp. fund. bd. John F. Kennedy Ctr. for the Performing Arts, 2005—07, chmn. corp. fund. bd., 2007—; trustee Emory Univ. Mem. Ch. of Ireland. Office: The Coca-Cola Co PO Box 1734 Atlanta GA 30301

ISKANDRIAN, AMI EDWARD, cardiologist; b. Baghdad, Iraq, Oct. 21, 1941; arrived in US, 1971, naturalized, 1971; s. Simon and Marian Iskandrian; m. Greta P. Iskandrian, Mar. 18, 1967; children: Basil, Susan, Kristen. MD, U. Baghdad, 1965. Diplomate Am. Bd. Internal Medicine, Am. Bd. Cardiovasc. Diseases; Bd. cert. in nuc. cardiology. Intern, then resident Hahnemann U. Hosp., Phila., 1971-73, cardiology fellow, 1973-75, from asst. prof. medicine to prof., 1975-86; clin. prof. medicine U. Pa. Sch. Medicine, Phila., 1987-96; William Penn Snyder III prof. medicine Med. Coll. Pa./Hahnemann U. Med. Sch., Phila., 1996—, chief sect. nuc. cardiology, dir. cardiovasc. rsch. ctr., 1996—; sect. chief nuc. cardiology U. Ala., Birmingham, 1999—, disting. prof. medicine and radiology, 1999—; chair, imaging com. Am. Heart Assn.; past chair Cert. Bd. Nuc. Cardiology; mem., editl. bd., reviewer, several jours. Co-dir. Phila. Heart Ins., 1987-96. Author, co editor: Nuclear Cardiac Imaging: Principles and Applications, 1985, 4th edit., 2009; co-editor: Cardiac Output, 1993, Myocardial Viability, 1994, Nuclear Atlas Companion to Braumwald Textbook of Cardiology;editor in chief, Jour. Nuclear Cardiology, author and co-author over 1000 papers, abstracts, and book chpts. Recipient Leonard Tow Humanism Medicine award, Numerous Tchg. awards. Master: Am. Coll. Cardiology (chair, imaging com.); fellow: Am. Soc. Nuc. Cardiology (past pres.). Presbyterian. Avocations: classical music, nature, reading, history. Office: UAB/TKC Clinic 1530 3rd Ave Birmingham AL 35294*

ISMAIL, RASHIT, consumer products company executive; Attended, Iowa State U. Product brand mgr., European brand mgr. SC Johnson; European product devel. mgr. Procter & Gamble Co., tech. brand mgr., product coord., North Africa & Middle East; v.p., mktg. and bus. devel., Europe, Africa and the Middle East, corp. officer Tupperware Brands Corp., v.p., global product mktg., 2007—08, sr. v.p., global product mktg., 2008—. Office: Tupperware Brands Corp 14901 S Orange Blossom Trail Orlando FL 32837 Office Phone: 407-826-5050. Office Fax: 407-826-8268.

ISON, JAMIE, state legislator; m. M. Harland Ison; children: Philip, Wyatt. BA in Speech Pathology, U. Miss., M in Communicative Disorders. Regional dir. Ala. Inst. Deaf and Blind; mem. Dist. 101 Ala. House of Reps., Montgomery, 2002—. Alumnus Leadership Ala.; mem. All Saints Episc. Ch.; bd. mem. Leadership Mobile, Habitat for Humanity, Mobile Adv. Commn. for the Disabled, Ala. Dept. Sr. Services. Mem.: Mobile Sunrise Rotary Club (past pres.). Republican. Episcopalian. Office: 104 S Lawrence St Mobile AL 36602 also: Ala House of Reps Ala State House 11 S Union St Rm 527-B Montgomery AL 36130 Office Phone: 251-208-5480, 334-242-7711. Business E-Mail: isonfor101@comcast.net.

ISONAKA, JUN, insurance company executive; Grad., Kwansei Gakuin U., 1980. Joined Aflac Inc, 1980; gen. mgr., group mktg., mktg. and sales promotion depts. AFLAC, Inc., 1999—2001; v.p., Customer Svc., Info. and Ops. Divsn. Aflac Japan (subs. Aflac Inc.), 2002—05; v.p AFLAC, Inc., 2002—07; v.p., ter. dirs., Northeast Ter. Aflac Japan (subs. Aflac Inc.), 2005—06, v.p., contact ctr., 2006—07, sr. v.p., sales, 2007—09; sr. v.p., policy data adminstrn., contact ctr. mgmt. and customer svc. AFLAC, Inc., 2007—; sr. v.p., dep. chief adminstrv. officer AFLAC Japan, 2009—. Office: Aflac Inc 1932 Wynnton Rd Columbus GA 31999 Office Phone: 706-323-3431. Office Fax: 706-324-6330. Business E-Mail: jisonaka@aflac.com.

ISRAEL, KIMBERLY HELD, lawyer; b. Jacksonville, Fla., Aug. 7, 1969; d. Edwin W. and Leslie (Edwards) Held; m. Jonathan Bruce Israel, Apr. 2, 1995; children: Eliza, Allie, Ayden. BA, Vanderbilt U., 1991; JD, U. Fla., 1994. Assoc. Moseley, Warren, Prichard & Parrish, Jacksonville, 1995—99, ptnr., 2000—04, Held & Israel, 2004—. Mem. editl. bd. SEALI, Ga., 2002—04. Bd. dirs. Jewish Cmty. Alliance, 2002—04; chmn. editl. bd. Jacksonville Jewish News, 2004—06; bd. dirs. Jacksonville Jewish Fedn., 2004—06. Recipient Young Leadership Award, Jax Jewish Fedn., 2000. Mem.: FBA, ABA, Chester Bedell Inn Ct., Women Bus. Owners of North Fla., Comml. Law League Am., ABC Women Coun., Fed. Bar Assn. (treas. Jacksonville chpt. 2003—04, sec. 2004—05, v.p. programs 2005—06, v.p. 2006—07, pres. 2008—, 2008—), Jacksonville Women Lawyer's Assn., Jacksonville Bar Assn., Fla. Bar. Jewish. Office: Held & Israel 6320 St Augustine Rd Ste 2 Jacksonville FL 32217 Office Phone: 904-398-7038. Office Fax: 904-398-4283. Business E-Mail: khisrael@hilawfirm.com.

ISRAILI, ZAFAR HASAN, pharmacologist, educator; came to U.S., 1961, naturalized, 1977; s. Siddiq Hasan and Zahida Khatun I.; m. Sally Jean Smith, Oct. 24, 1970; children: Shahnaz Joy, Taj Hasan, Rana Shereen. BSc, Aligarh M. U., 1951, MSc, 1953; PhD, U. Kans., 1968. Lectr. chemistry Aligarh M. U., 1953-54, sr. rsch. scholar, 1954-57; rsch. asst., jr. sci. officer AEC India, 1957-61; rsch. assoc. U. Kans., 1968-69; sr. rsch. chemist Alza Corp., Lawrence, Kans., 1969-70; asst. prof. medicine and chemistry Emory U., Atlanta, 1970-75, assoc. prof. chemistry, 1975-78, assoc. prof. medicine, 1975—, prof. chemistry, 1978—. Rsch. pharmacologist Atlanta VA Med. Ctr., Decatur, 1979-87; sci. staff Grady Hosp., Atlanta, 1974—; adj. prof. chemistry Ga. Perimeter Coll., 2004—. Editor Ethnicity and Disease, 1997—; assoc. editor Drug Metabolism Revs., 1974—, Venezuelan Jour. Hypertension, 2005-, Revista Latino Americana Hipertension, 2006—; guest editor Internat. Jour. Hypertension, 2010-12, lead guest editor, 2013-; mem. editl. bd. Drug Devel. Rsch., 1979—, Archives Venezuelan Pharm. Ter., 1983—, Am. Jour. Ther., 2003-, Diabetes Internat., 2009-; contbr. articles to profl. jours., chpts. to books. Recipient Asia Found. award, 1962; Merit scholar Aligarh M. U., 1953; Merck Sharpe & Dohm grantee, 1977, 85, 87, NIH grantee, 1978-83, VA grantee, 1979-87, Am. Heart Assn. grantee, 1989-91. Mem. Am. Soc. Clin. Pharmacology and Therapeutics, Am. Soc. Pharmacology and Exptl. Therapeutics, Soc. Exptl. Biology and Medicine, Am. Assn. Cancer Rsch., Am. Aging Assn., Am. Chem. Soc., Am. Soc. Hypertension, Chem. Soc. London, Internat. Soc. for Study Xenobiotics, Interam. Soc. Clin. Pharm. Therapeutics (pres.-elect 1997-2000, pres. 2000—), Internat. Soc. on Hypertension in Blacks, Am. Heart Assn., Sigma Xi, Rho Chi, Phi Lambda Upsilon.

Independent. Muslim. Home: 3567 Cloudland Dr Stone Mountain GA 30083-4005 Office: Emory Univ Sch Medicine Dept Medicine 69 Jesse Hill Jr Dr Atlanta GA 30303-2607 Personal E-mail: israilgpc@yahoo.com.

ITKIN, IVAN, nuclear scientist, mathematician; b. NYC, Mar. 29, 1936; s. Abraham Aaron and Eda (Kreger) I.; m. Judith Ann Weiss, Aug. 19, 1962 (div. 1975); children: Marc Eric, Laurie Rachel; m. Joyce Lee Hudak, July 12, 1975; 1 child, Max Eugene. BSChemE, Poly. Inst., Bklyn., 1956; M in Nuclear Engring., NYU, 1957; PhD in Math., U. Pitts., 1964; D of Pub. Svc. (hon.), Chatham Coll., 1994. Assoc. scientist Bettis Atomic Power Lab. Westinghouse Electric Corp., Pitts., 1957-59, scientist, 1959-64, sr. scientist, 1964-71, fellow scientist, 1971-73; mem. Pa. Ho. of Reps., Harrisburg, 1973-98; dir. Office Civilian Radioactive Waste Mgmt. U.S. Dept. Energy, Washington, 1999-2001. Majority caucus chmn. Pa. Ho. of Reps., 1982-90, majority whip, 1990-92, majority leader, 1993-94, Democratic whip, 1995-98; Dem. nominee for Pa. gov., 1998; chmn. sci., tech., and resource planning com. Nat. Conf. State Legislators, Denver, 1988; del. Dem. Nat. Conv., 1984, 96; U.S. presdl. elector, 1992, 96. Election judge 19th Dist., 14th Ward, Pa., 1966-68; chmn. 14th Ward Dem. Com., Pitts., 1970-72. Recipient Keystone award Alcoholism and Addiction Assn., 1983, Award of Appreciation, Nat. Fedn. Blind, 1983, Disting. Svc. award Pa. Coll. Optometry, 1986; named House Mem. of Yr., Pa. Jewish Coalition, 1983. Mem. ACLU, AIPAC, Am. Nuclear Soc., Am. Jewish Congress, B'nai B'rith, Sierra Club. Home: 3200 N Ocean Blvd Unit 606 Fort Lauderdale FL 33308-7155 Personal E-mail: iitkin@bellsouth.net.

IVENS, MARY SUE, microbiologist, medical mycologist; b. Maryville, Tenn., Aug. 23, 1929; d. McPherson Joseph and Sarah Lillie (Hensley) Ivens. BS, East Tenn. State U., Johnson City, 1949; MS NIH rsch. trainee, Tulane U. Sch. Medicine, New Orleans, 1963; PhD, La. State U. Sch. Medicine, New Orleans, 1966; postgrad., Emory U. Sch. Medicine, Atlanta, 1960. Diplomate Am. Bd. Microbiology. Dir. microbiol. and mycol. labs. Lewis-Gate Hosp., Roanoke, Va., 1953—56; rsch. mycologist Ctrs. Disease Control, Atlanta, 1957—60; rsch. assoc. La. State U. Sch. Medicine, New Orleans, 1963—66; instr. medicine La. State U., 1966—72, instr. microbiology, 1966—72, clin. prof., 1972—. Dir. micology lab. La. State U. Sch. Medicine, 1963—72, lectr. sch. dentistry, 1968—70; assoc. prof. natural scis. Dillard U., New Orleans, 1972—; assoc. Marine Biol. Lab., Woods Hole, Mass., 1978—; cons. in field; mem. exec. bd. Trinity Dental Assn., 2006. Contbr. articles to profl. jours. Commr. conf. on ctr. Mycotic sera WHO, 1969; mem. La. assn. def. counsel expert witness bank, 1985—; bd. dirs. La. coun. Girl Scouts US, Cmty Relationships Greater New Orleans, Zoning Bd. River Ridge, La.; mem. exec. bd. River Ridge Civic Assn., 1982—98, sec., 1982—84; chmn. pers. bd. Riverside Bapt. Ch., River Ridge; dir. outreach First Bapt. Ch., New Orleans, 1989—97; chmn. gold medal award com. Sigma Xi, 1978. Recipient Rosicrucian Humanitarian award, 1981; grantee NSF, NIH; fellow Macy, MBL, 1978—79. Mem.: Nat. Inst. Sci., AAAS, Am. Soc. Microbiology (Nat. com. on membership 1983—87), Med. Mycological Soc. Am., Internat. Soc. Human and Animal Mycology, Sigma Xi. Office: Dillard U Div Natural Sci New Orleans LA 70122 Home: 809 Prestwick Dr Maryville TN 37803-6757

IVESTER, TOM, state legislator; b. Sayre, Okla., 1969; m. DeAun Ivester; children: Joseph, Jackson. B, Tex. Christian Univ.; JD, Univ. Okla. Atty.; mem. Dist. 26 Okla. State Senate, 2006—. Mem.: Okla. Bar Assn., Beckham County Bar Assn. Democrat. Office: PO Box 1950 Elk City OK 73648 also: 2300 N Lincoln Blvd Rm 529 Oklahoma City OK 73105 Home: 1816 N Randall Ave Elk City OK 73644-1414 Home Phone: 580-928-5322; Office Phone: 405-521-5545. E-mail: invester@oksenate.gov.

IVEY, DENISE HASSELL, retired publishing executive; b. 1950; m. Michael Ivey; children: Forest, Scott. BS, La. State U., 1978. CPA. With Gannet Co., Inc., 1983—2008, v.p. East regional group, v.p. South newspaper group, 1991—94, pres. Gulf Coast newspaper group, 1994—2006, pres. Mid-South group, 2006—08; asst. contr. Gainesville (Ga.) Times, 1983-84, contr., 1984, pres., pub., 1986, Herald-Dispatch, Huntington, W.Va., 1989; v.p. & pub. Pensacola (Fla.) News Jour., 1991—94, pres. & pub., 1994—2006, Louisville Courier-Jour., 2006—08; ret., 2009. Bd. dirs. IMPACT 100 Pensacola Bay Area, 2003—05, 2008—, Leadership Louisville Ctr., 2007—08. Mem.: Southern Newspaper Pubs.' Assn., Ky. Press Assn. Office: c/o IMPACT 100 Pensacola Bay Area PO Box 13304 Pensacola FL 32591-3304

IVEY, KAY ELLEN, Lieutenant Governor of Alabama, former state treasurer; b. Repton, Ala., Oct. 15, 1944; d. Boardman Nettles and Barbara Elizabeth Ivey. BS, Auburn U., 1967; cert. in Mktg., U. Colo., 1975; cert. in Banking, U. South Ala.; cert. in Strategic Leadership for State Execs., Duke U., 1989. Tchr., coach forensics Rio Linda HS, Calif., 1968-69; asst. v.p. Mchts. Nat. Bank, Mobile, Ala., 1970-79; cabinet officer Office of the Gov., State of Ala., Montgomery, 1979-81; reading clk. Ala. House of Reps., 1981-82; exec. v.p. St. Margaret's Hosp. Found., 1982-85; dir. govt. affairs Ala. Commn. Higher Edn., 1985—98; treas. State of Ala., 2003—11, lt. gov., 2011—. Owner, cons. Ivey Enterprises, Montgomery, 1982—; speaker in field. Editor (audio-visual presentation) What Price Freedom (award of Excellence), 1976, St. Margaret's Hosp. Heart tabloid, 1983. Mem. adv. bd. Sch. Bus. Auburn U., 1980-83; candidate Ala. State Auditor, 1982; sec. Ala. div. Am. Cancer Soc., 1985—; bd. dirs. Ala. Girl's State Sch., 1983-85, Stetson Hoedown Rodeo Queen's Pageant, Montgomery, Montgomery YMCA; bd. trustees Sheriff's Boys and Girls Ranches.; charter trustee, Ala. Banking Sch. Mem. Indsl. Developers Ala., Young Men's Bus. Orgn., Pub. Relations Council Ala. (bd. dirs. 1976-82), DAR (state chmn. 1985-86), Ala. Young Bankers (past pres.), Ala. Bankers Assn. (chmn. edn. com., cons.), Ala. Forestry Assn., Alpha Gamma Delta (disting. citizen award 1986), Montgomery Rotary Club (dir., Paul Harris award), Homemakers Am. (hon.), Future Farmers Am. Republican. Presbyterian. Avocations: horseback riding, public speaking. Office: Office of Lieutenant Governor Suite 725 11 S Union St Montgomery AL 36130 Office Phone: 334-242-7900. Office Fax: 334-242-4661.*

IVEY, MICHAEL WAYNE, mortgage broker; b. Albany, Ga., Nov. 27, 1964; s. Samuel Warlick and Barbara Ann (Norton) I. BBA, U. Ga., 1986. Cert. mortgage broker. Mortgage broker First So. Mortgage, Atlanta, 1986-87, Fed. Savs. Bank, Atlanta, 1987-88, Paragon Mortgage Corp., Atlanta, 1988-94; regional v.p. Mortgage.com, Atlanta, 1994-97; CEO, pres., cert. mortgage broker Capital City Mortgage Corp., Atlanta, 1997—. Bd. dirs. Powers Ridge Office Park, 1998—, Govs. Ridge Office Park, 2003—, Marietta Tree Keepers, 2003—; pres. bd. dirs. Ctr. for Children and Young Adults, 2003—, chmn., 2003. Mem. Cobb C. of C. (Leadership Cobb Class 1996-97, Ernest Barrett award, Hon. Comdrs. 1998), Marietta Kiwanis. Methodist. Office: Capital City Mortgage Corp Bldg 7 Ste 200 1827 Powers Ferry Rd NW Atlanta GA 30339-5621 Home: 5505 Glen Errol Rd NW Atlanta GA 30327-4851

IVEY, SUSAN M., corporate board member, retired tobacco company executive; b. Schenectady, NY, Oct. 31, 1958; m. Trevor Ivey, 1997. BS, U. Fla., Gainesville, 1980; MBA, Bellarmine U., Louisville, 1987. Trade mktg. repr. Brown & Williamson Tobacco Corp., 1981—83, dist. sales mgr., 1983, dir. Far East mktg., then head internat. brands London, 1990—94, dir. mktg., Brit. American Tobacco Hong Kong, 1994—96, mgr. internat. brands London, 1996—99, sr. v.p. mktg. Louisville, 1999—2000, pres., CEO, 2001—04; chmn. RJ Reynolds Tobacco, Winston-Salem, NC, 2004—08; pres., CEO Reynolds American, Inc., Winston-Salem, NC, 2004—06, 2010—11, chmn., pres., CEO, 2006—10. Bd. dirs. Reynolds American Inc., 2004—11, R.R. Donnelley & Sons Co., 2009—. Mem. women's leadership initiative United Way America; bd. dirs. United Way Forsyth County, Winston-Salem YWCA, Sr. Svcs. Inc., Winston-Salem, Salem Coll., U. Fla. Found. Named one of The 100 Most Powerful Women, Forbes mag., 2005—10, The 50 Most Powerful Women in Bus., Fortune mag., 2006—10. Home: 3081 NE 39Th St Fort Lauderdale FL 33308-5827

IVORY, BENNIE L., newspaper editor; b. Hot Springs, Ark., June 19, 1951; Grad., Henderson State U., Arkadelphia, Ark. Staff Sentinel-Record, Hot Springs, 1969—79, Gannett Co. Inc., 1979—; mng. editor Clarion-Ledger, Miss., 1989—93; exec. editor Fla. Today, 1993—95, News Jour., Del., 1995—97; v.p. news, exec. editor The Courier-Jour., Louisville, 1997—. Mem. journalism adv. bd. Fla. A&M U. Mentor exec. leadership program Asian American Journalists Assn. Recipient Pres.'s Ring award (10-time winner), Gannet Co., 1994—2004, Signet award, 2005, Robert G. McGruder award for Diversity Leadership, Freedom Forum, 2004; named Editor of Yr., 1994. Mem.: American Soc. Newspaper Editors, Nat. Assn. Black Journalists. Office: The Courier Journal 525 W Broadway Louisville KY 40201-7431 Mailing: Courier Journal PO Box 740031 Louisville KY 40201-7431 Office Phone: 502-582-4295. E-mail: bivory@courier-journal.com.

IVY, JOAN CAROL, data processing executive; b. Port Chester, NY, Mar. 1, 1939; d. John Henry and Molly Elizabeth (Gates) Daugherty; m. Stanley Donald McIntyre, Aug. 24, 1957 (div. Jan. 1986); children: Michael Stanley McIntyre, David John McIntyre, Sharon Lynne McIntyre; m. James Morrow Ivy IV, June 1, 1988. Student, Northwestern U., 1956-57, U. Ill., 1957-58. Assoc. editor Writer's Digest, Cin., 1966-68; instr. creative writing U. Ala., Huntsville, 1974-75; editor Strode Pubs., Huntsville, 1974-75; paralegal Smith, Huckaby & Graves (now Bradley, Arant, Rose & White), Huntsville, 1976-82; exec. v.p. Micro Craft, Inc., Huntsville, 1982-85, pres., 1985-89, ceo, chmn. bd., 1989—; also bd. dirs., co-owner. Author: numerous computer operating manuals for law office software, 1978—; co-author: Alabama and Federal Complaint Forms, 1979; editor: Alabama Law for the Layman, 1975; contbr. numerous articles to profl. jours. and short stories to mags. and lit. mags. Hon. scholar Medill Sch. Journalism Northwestern U., 1956. Mem. Huntsville Literary Soc. (bd. dirs. 1976-77). Republican. Methodist. Office: 123 Fairington Rd NW Huntsville AL 35806-2249 Office Phone: 256-830-9746. Personal E-mail: jivy546@gmail.com.

IYER, SHANTHI, electrical engineering and nanoengineering educator, researcher; d. Mangalam Arunachalam and Visalakshi Ekambaram; m. Nathan Padmanabha Iyer; children: Soumya N., Padma V. BSc with honors, Delhi U., New Delhi, 1974, MSc, 1976; PhD, Indian Inst. Tech., New Delhi, 1983. Adj. asst. prof. elec. engring. N.C. A&T State U., Greensboro, 1981-85, asst. prof. elec. engring., 1986-91, assoc. prof. elec. engring., 1991-97, prof. elec. engring., 1997—; vis. scientist Wright Patterson Lab., Ohio, 1991—; rsch. prof. Dept. Electrical & Computer Engineering, 2006—, Dept. ECE Dept. & Nanoengineering Joint Sch. Nanosci. & Nanoengring., 2010—. Dir. NCA & TSU Mol. Beam Epitaxy Lab., 1994—, NCA & TSU Ctr. Excellence ARO, 2004—11. Missile Def. Agy. HBCU MI Program Elbow Grease & Ingenuity. Recipient Outstanding Sr. Rschr. award, NCA & TSU Coll. Engring., 2006—07, Excellence Rsch. Coll. Engring. award, 1993; DoD Nat. HBCU MI Com. grant, 2010. Mem. IEEE (sr.; faculty advisor N.C. A&T State U. student br. 1991-95), Materials Rsch. Soc. (treas. N.C. sect. 1994-95, v.p. 1995-96). Office: NC A&T State U 536 McNair Hall 1601 E Market St Greensboro NC 27401-3209*

JACINTO, GEORGE ANTHONY, social worker, counselor, educator, consultant; b. Gilroy, Calif., Dec. 21, 1949; s. George Peter and Isabelle Agnes (Joseph) J. BS in Criminology-Corrections, Calif. State U., Fresno, 1974; postgrad., Wash. Theol. Union, 1975, U. Wis., 1980, Boise State U., 1981; MEd in Guidance and Counseling Svcs., Albertson Coll. of Idaho, 1982; MSW in Clin. Social Work, Fla. State U., 1990; PhD, Barry U., 2007. LCSW; cert. profl. coach. Youth min. Ch. St. Michael, Olympia, Wash., 1976-77; dir. youth ministry St. James Congregation, Franklin, Wis., 1977-80; diocesan youth dir. Cath. Diocese of Boise, Idaho, 1980-83; dir. religious edn. St. Andrew Ch., Orlando, Fla., 1983-84; vocat. rehab. counselor DLES State of Fla., Orlando, 1984-88, vocat. rehab. cons., 1988-89; social worker Fla. Hosp./Rebound, Orlando, 1989-91; vocat. program specialist Fla. Hosp. Med. Ctr., Orlando, 1991-92; mental health specialist Orange County Cmty. Corrections Dept., Orlando, 1992-96; adj. faculty Fla. State Univ. Sch. Social Work, Orlando, 1994-95, U. Ctrl. Fla., Orlando, 1994-96; clin. instr. Sch. Social Work, 1996—2007; assoc. prof. dept. social work Ark. State U., Jonesboro, 2007—11, St. Leo U., Fla., 2011—12; assoc. prof., MSW program coord. U. Ctrl Fla., Orlando, 2012—. Home health social worker Olsten Health Svcs., Winter Park, Fla., 1991-92; fair hearings officer Orange County Dept. of Social Svcs. Orlando, 1991-92; founder Am. Life Planning Assocs., Orlando, 1985—; profl. coach Grow Tng. Inst., Inc., San Diego; cons. in field. Active diversion program Union St. Ctr., Olympia, Wash.; campaign leader for children's toys Indo-China Refugee Relief, Milw.; adv. cmty. agys. concerned with youth issues, U. Ctrl. Fla., 1991-92. Mem. NASW (chair Ctrl. Fla. unit 1990-92, bd. dirs. Fla. chpt. 1990-92, Nat. HIV task force Fla. chpt. liaison, ctrl. unit social worker of yr. 1993, del. assembly 1993, 96, 99, NEAR br. chair Ark. 2008-09, v.p. Ark. chpt. 2009-11). Office: University Ctrl Fla Sch Social Work PO Box 163358 Orlando FL 32816 Home: PO Box 677007 Orlando FL 32867-7007 Personal E-mail: drgeorgejacinto@aol.com.

JACK, JANIS GRAHAM, federal judge; b. LA, 1946; RN, St. Thomas Sch. Nursing, 1969; BA, U. Balt., 1974; JD summa cum laude, South Tex. Coll., 1981. Pvt. practice, Corpus Christi, Tex., 1981-94; judge US Dist. Ct. (so. dist.) Tex., Corpus Christi, 1994—. Jud. mem. The Maritime Law Assn. U.S. Mem. ABA, Fed. Judges Assn., Fifth Cir. Dist. Judges Assn., Nat. Assn. Women Judges, Jud. Conf. Com. Info. Tech., Tex. Bar Found., State Bar Tex., The Philos. Soc. Tex., Order of Lytae, Phi Alpha Delta. Office: US Dist Ct 1133 N Shoreline Blvd Corpus Christi TX 78401

JACKSON, ALAN, musician; b. Newnan, Ga. s. Eugene and Ruth Jackson; m. Denise Jackson; children: Mattie Denise, Ali Jane, Dani Grace. Student, W. Ga. Coll. Musician: (albums) Here in the Real World, 1990, Don't Rock the Jukebox, 1991 (Album of Yr., Acad. Country Music), A Lot About Livin' (and a Little 'Bout Love), 1992, Honky Tonk Christmas, 1993, Who I Am, 1994, The Greatest Hits Collection, 1995, Everything I Love, 1996, High Mileage, 1998, Under the Influence, 1999, When Somebody Loves You, 2000, Drive, 2002, What I Do, 2004, Like Red on a Rose, 2006, Live at Texas Stadium, 2007, Good Time, 2008, Freight Train, 2010, Thirty Miles West, 2012, Precious Memories, 2012, Precious Memories Volume II, 2013, (songs) Don't Rock the Jukebox, 1991 (Single Record of Yr., Acad. Country Music, 1991, ASCAP Country Song of yr., 1992, Single & Music Record of Yr., Country Music Assn., 1993), Chattahoochee, 1993 (Single Record of Yr., Acad. Country Music, 1993), Where Were You (When the World Stopped Turning), 2002 (Best Country Song, Grammy Awards), As She's Walking Away, 2010 (Vocal Event of Yr. award, Acad. Country Music, 2011). Recipient Triple Play award, Country Music Assoc., 1990, 1991, 1992, Star, Hollywood Walk of Fame, 2010; named Country Songwriter of Yr., ASCAP, 1992, Male Vocalist of Yr., Acad. Country Music, 1994, 1995, Entertainer of Yr., Country Music Assoc., 1995. Office: Alan Jackson Fan Club PO Box 121945 Nashville TN 37212-1945 also: Arista Records 7 Music Cir Nashville TN 37203*

JACKSON, ALPHONSO ROY, public policy educator, former United States Secretary of Housing and Urban Development; b. Marshall, Tex., Sept. 9, 1946; s. Arthur Todd and Henriette (Green) Jackson; m. Marcia A. Jackson, June 18, 1988; children: Annette Watkins, Lesley Jackson. BS, Truman State U.(formerly Northeast Mo. State), 1968, MA, 1969; JD, Washington U., St. Louis, 1973. Asst. prof. criminal justice & polit. sci. U. Mo., St. Louis, 1973—77; dir. pub. safety City of St. Louis, 1977—81, dep. exec. dir. housing authority, 1981—82; dir. cons. services Laventhol & Horwath, St. Louis, 1982-87; CEO DC Dept. Pub. & Assisted Housing, Washington, 1987-89; pres., CEO housing authority City of Dallas, 1989-96; pres. American Electric Power-TEXAS, 1996—2001; dep. sec. US Dept. Housing & Urban Devel. (HUD), Washington, 2001—04, acting sec., 2003—04, sec., 2004—08; Disting. U. prof., dir. Ctr. for Pub. Policy & Leadership Hampton U., Hampton, Va., 2008—. Adj. prof. U. Mo., St. Louis; bd. commissioners Planned Indsl. Expansion City of St. Louis, 1978—; bd. dirs. St. Louis Local Devel. Co., 1978—. Mem. Mo. Governor's Task Force on Edn., 1975-76, Sister Cities Internat., 1976-81; bd. dirs. Zale-Lipshy Hosp., Dallas, 1992, Children's Med. Ctr., Dallas, 1994 Truman State U., 1995, Tex. Southern U., 1998; chmn. Tex. Gen. Svcs. Commn., Austin, 1998 Recipient Chairman's award Nat. Boys & Girls Clubs of America, 1997; fellow Kellogg fellow Ctr. Biology Nat. Sys., Washington U., 1970-71, U. Oxford, 1977, Danforth Found., 1981, The Aspen Inst. Fellow: Kappa Alpha Psi; mem.: Nat. Bar. Assn., Anniversary Club. Democrat. Roman Catholic. Avocations: jogging, golf, reading. Office: Hampton University Wigwam Bldg Ste 100 Hampton VA 23668 Office Phone: 757-727-5426. Office Fax: 757-728-4913.

JACKSON, BARBARA, state supreme court justice; b. Dec. 25, 1961; d. Kenneth W. and Phyllis S. Jackson. BA, U. NC, Chapel Hill, 1984, JD with honors, 1990. Rsch. asst. to Hon. Burley B. Mitchell, Jr. NC Supreme Ct.; asst. legal counsel to gov. State of NC, assoc. gen. counsel to gov.; dep. gen. counsel NC Gov.'s Advocacy Coun. for Persons with Disabilities; assoc. Holt York McDarris, LLP, Raleigh; gen. counsel NC Dept. Labor; assoc. justice NC Supreme Ct., 2010—. Recipient Order of Long Leaf Pine; fellow NC Inst. Polit. Leadership; Thomas J. Watson Nat. Merit Scholar. Mem.: NC Assn. Women Attys., Wake County Bar Assn. (bd. dirs.), NC Bar Assn., Zeta Tau Alpha. Office: Supreme Court of NC PO Box 2170 Raleigh NC 27602-2170 Office Phone: 919-831-5700.*

JACKSON, BARBARA ANN GARVEY, music educator, publisher; b. Normal, Ill., Sept. 27, 1929; d. Neil Ford and Eva Burkhart Garvey; m. Robert Seagrave, 1953 (div. 1958); m. Kern C. Jackson, Mar. 29, 1970; stepchildren: Kern, Ross, Bruce, Paul. MusB, U. Ill., 1950; MusM, Eastman Sch., 1952; PhD in Musicology, Stanford U., 1959. Spl. music tchr. LA Pub. Sch., 1956—57; asst. prof. music Ark. Poly. Coll., Russellville, 1957—61; prof. music U. Ark, Fayetteville, 1954—56, 1961—91, prof. emerita, 1991—. Co-author (with others): Practical Beginning Theory, 1962, 8th edit., 2000; editor (publisher): ClarNan Editions, 1984—. Mem.: Phi Kappa Phi, Pi Kappa Lambda, Sigma Alpha Iota (hon.). Democrat. Episcopalian. Avocations: gardening, photography. Office Phone: 479-442-7414. Business E-Mail: clarnan@sbcglobal.net.

JACKSON, BOBBY RAND, minister; b. Wilson, NC, Dec. 14, 1931; s. Joel John and Bessie Francis (Mayo) J.; m. Martha Jane Ketteman, May 30, 1953; children: Stephen Rand, Philip Wayne. BA, Free Will Bapt. Bible Coll., Nashville, 1954; MA, Bob Jones U., Greenville, SC, 1955. Ordained to ministry Free Will Baptists Ch., 1951. Evangelist Free Will Baptists Ch., Nashville, 1955—; asst. moderator Nat. Assn. Free Will Baptists, Nashville, 1972-77, moderator, 1978-87, mem. exec. com., 1972-87, chmn. exec. com., 1978-87, presiding officer of gen. bd., 1978-87. Author: Messages That Matter, 1960, Six Steps to Successful Living, 1962, Awakening in the Wilderness, 1965, Beyond the Stars, 1966; soloist: record albums Softly and Tenderly, 1968, Then Sings My Soul, 1969, Fill My Cup, Lord, 1970, My God and I, 1978, Songs from Two Generations, 1985. Mem. Free Will Bapt. Bible Coll. Alumni Assn., Bob Jones U. Alumni Assn. Home: 1412 E 14th St Greenville NC 27858-4734 E-mail: bjea@suddenlink.net.

JACKSON, BRENT (WILLIAM BRENT JACKSON), state legislator; m. Debbie Jackson; children: Rodney, Adam, Josh. Attended, NC State U. Founder, pres., CEO Jackson Farming Co., Inc., 1981—; state senator Dist. 10 NC, 2010—. Republican. Baptist. Mailing: 2905 Ernest Williams Rd Autryville NC 28318 Office: NC Senate 300 N Salisbury St Room 525 Raleigh NC 27603-5925 Office Phone: 919-733-5705, 910-567-2202. Business E-Mail: Brent.Jackson@ncleg.net.

JACKSON, BRIAN ANTHONY, federal judge; b. New Orleans, 1960; BS, Xavier U. La., 1982; JD, Southern U., 1985; LLM, Georgetown U., 2000. Gen. atty. LA Dist. Office US Immigration & Naturalization Svc., US Dept. Justice, 1985—87, asst. gen. counsel Washington, 1987—88; spl. asst. US atty. (ea. dist.) La. US Dept. Justice, New Orleans, 1988—92, asst. US atty., 1990, asst. dir. evaluation and review staff Exec. Office for US Attys. Washington, 1992—94, first asst. US atty. (middle dist.) La. Baton Rouge, 1994—2002, interim US atty., 2001, assoc. dep. atty. gen. Washington, 1998—99; ptnr. Liskow & Lewis, New Orleans, 2002—10; judge US Dist. Ct. (middle dist.) La., Baton Rouge, 2010—, chief judge, 2013—. Office: US Distict Court Russell B Long Fed Bldg & US Courthouse 777 Florida St, Ste 139 Baton Rouge LA 70801 Office Phone: 225-389-3500.*

JACKSON, CARLTON LUTHER, history professor, writer; b. Blount, Ala. s. Luther Harrison and Winnie Forrestor Jackson; m. Patricia Ann Dow, Jan. 30, 1954; children: Beverly, Daniel, Matthew, Hilary. BA, Birmingham Southern Coll., Ala., 1958, MA, 1959; PhD, U. Ga., Athens, 1963; degree (hon.), U. Argentina, Buenos Aires, 1976. From mem. staff to disting. prof. We. Ky. U., Bowling Green, Ky., 1961—96, disting. prof. history, 1996—. Mem. selection com. Fulbright Found., Washington, 1991—96. Author: Hattie: The Life of Hattie McDaniel, 1996. Sgt. USAF, 1951—55. Fellow, Fulbright

Found., 1989—90. Mem.: Fulbright Assn. (life). Episcopalian. Office: Western Ky Univ Dept History Bowling Green KY 42101 Office Phone: 270-745-5730. Business E-Mail: carlton.jackson@wku.edu.

JACKSON, DARRELL, state legislator; b. Columbia, SC, Feb. 1, 1957; s. Andrew C. and Janie Lumpkin Jackson; m. Willie Mae Rooks, 1980; children: Darrell Jr., Antoine Joseph. BA, Benedict Coll., 1979. Founder, pres. Sunrise Enterprise of Columbia, Inc.; mem. Dist. 21 SC State Senate, 1993—, mem. Banking and Ins. Com., Edn. Com., Fin. Com., Gen. Com. & Med. Affairs Com. Sr. pastor Bible Way Ch. Atlas Rd. Columbia Inc., SC. Recipient Thanks for Making Difference award, WOIC, 1995, SC Bus. Vision Influence award, Vision Mag., 1997, Modjeska Monteith Simkins Polit. Courage award, NAACP, 2000, Recognition Outstanding Legislature Support Child Victims Crime award, 2000, SC Dept. Edn. award, 2004; named Legislator of Yr., SC Victims Asst. Network, Birchwood Inst. Cert. Appreciation, 1993, Outstanding Legislature award, Richland One Sch, 1999. Mem.: Am. Cancer Soc. (mem. pub. relations com.), Nat. Assn. Market Developers (bd. dir.), Columbia C. of C., Am. Lung Assn., Nat. Assn. Advancement Colored People, Columbia Visitors Bur. (bd. mem.), United Way (former trustee), Big Brothers Big Sisters (former bd. mem.), SC Coalition Black Chs. (exec. dir.). Democrat. Office: 612 Gressette Bldg Columbia SC 29201 Mailing: 608 Motley Rd Hopkins SC 29061 Office Phone: 803-771-0325, 803-212-6048. Business E-Mail: 610@legis.lpitr.state.sc.us. E-mail: DJ1@scsenate.org.

JACKSON, DARREN G., state legislator; Mem. Dist. 39 NC House of Reps., 2009—. Mem. Aging com., Alcholic Beverage Control com., Edn. com.; vice chmn. State Govt./State Personnel com.; chmn. House Select Com. on Civil Custody Guardians. Democrat. Office: 16 W Jones St Rm 1019 Raleigh NC 27601-1096 Home Phone: 919-733-5974; Office Phone: 919-733-5974. Business E-Mail: Darren.Jackson@ncleg.net.

JACKSON, DARREN RICHARD, automotive parts company executive; b. Detroit, Nov. 13, 1964; s. Richard Dennis and Connie May (Ellis) J.; m. Terry Ann Hall, May 28, 1988; children: Ryan David, Bridget Caffrey. BS in Acctg., Marquette U., 1986. CPA, Wis. Supr. KPMG Peat Marwick, Milw., 1985-89; dir. fin. reporting Carson, Pirie, Scott & Co., Milw., 1989-90, dir. treasury svcs., 1990-91, v.p., treas., CFO, 1992-1998; CFO, Full-line Store Div. Nordstrom, Inc.; sen. v.p. fin. & treas. Best Buy Co., Inc., Mpls., 2000-2001, sr. v.p., CFO, 2001—02, exec. v.p., CFO, 2002—07; exec. v.p. customer operating groups Best But Co., Inc., Mpls., 2007—08; pres., CEO Advance Auto Parts, Inc., Roanoke, Va., 2008—09, CEO, 2009—. Bd. dirs. Advance Auto Parts, Inc., 2004—. Bd. trustees Marquette U.; bd. dirs. Cristo Rey Network Schools. Office: Advance Auto Parts Inc 5008 Airport Rd Roanoke VA 24012

JACKSON, DAVID R., electrical engineer, educator; b. St. Louis, Mo., Mar. 28, 1957; s. Max T. and Joann C. Jackson; m. Christine A. Allen; 1 child, Alex Alan. BSEE, U. Mo., Columbia, 1979, MSEE, 1981; PhD, UCLA, 1985. Prof. U. Houston, 1985—. Office: Univ Houston 4800 Calhoun Rd Houston TX 77204-4005 Office Fax: 713-743-4444. Business E-Mail: djackson@uh.edu.

JACKSON, DESEAN WILLIAM, professional football player; b. Long Beach, Calif., Dec. 1, 1986; s. Bill and Gayle Jackson. Student in Social Welfare, U. Calif., Berkeley, 2005—08. Wide receiver, punt returner Phila. Eagles, 2008—13, Washington Redskins, 2014—. CEO Jaccpot Records. Founder The DeSean Jackson Found. for Pancreatic Cancer. Named 1st Team All-Conf., Pac-10 Conf., 2007, 1st Team All-American, AP, Walter Camp Found., Football Writers Assn. America, The Sporting News, 2007, American Football Coaches Assn., 2008; named to The Nat. Football Conf. Pro Bowl Team, NFL, 2009, 2010, 2013. Office: Washington Redskins 21300 Redskin Park Dr Ashburn VA 20149*

JACKSON, DONALD WILSON, political science professor, lawyer; b. Houston, May 15, 1938; s. Enoch Wilson and Ozella Rae J.; m. Joanne Shea, Apr. 20, 1985; children: Daniel Wilson, Michael Oden. BA, So. Meth. U., Dallas, 1959; JD, So. Meth. U., 1962; PhD in Polit. Sci., U. Wis., Madison, 1972. Bar: Tex. 1962, Supreme Ct. 75. Assoc. Storey, Armstrong & Steger, Dallas, 1962—66, ptnr., 1966—67; instr. polit. sci. So. Meth. U., 1967—68; asst. prof. polit. sci. Idaho State U., Pocatello, Idaho, 1970—74; jud. fellow Supreme Ct. U.S., Washington, 1974—75; Herman Brown prof. polit. sci. Tex. Christian U., Ft. Worth, 1975—, dir. Ctr. for Civic Literacy, 2006—. Author: An Introduction to Political Analysis: The Theory and Practice of Allocation, 1978, Even the Children of Strangers: Equality Under the U.S. Constitution, 1992 (Oustanding Book on Human Rights, Gustavus Myers Center for Human Rights, 1993), The United Kingdom Confronts the European Convention on Human Rights, 1997; editor: Presidential Leadership and Civil Rights Policy, 1995; co-editor: Comparative Judicial Review and Public Policy, 1992, Globalizing Justice: Critical Perspectives on Transnational Law and the CrossBorder Migration of Legal Norms, 2009; editor (assoc.): Governments of the World: A Global Guide to Citizens' Rights and Responsibilities, 2006. Bd. dirs. ACLU, NYC, 2000—01, Quaker United Nat. Com., NYC, 1997—2000; mem. adv. bd. Am. United for Separation of Ch. and State, Washington, 1995—2001, bd. trustees, 2005—09, exec. com. mem., 2006—09; bd. dirs. Tex. affil. ACLU, Austin, 1992—2001. Recipient Citizenship Participation: Bill of Rights award, Tarrant County LWV, 1995, Silver Spur award, Planned Parenthood of North Tex., 1997; named Outstanding Prof. in North Tex., N. Tex. Assn. Phi Beta Kappa, 1984, Tex. Piper Prof., Minnie Stevens Piper Found., 2003. Mem.: We. Polit. Sci. Assn., Internat. Polit. Sci. Assn. (sec.-treas. 1997—2000, mem. rsch. com. comparative jud. studies), Am. Polit. Sci. Assn. (sec. treas. law and cts. sect. 1996—99), Phi Beta Kappa. Avocations: backpacking, golf. Office: Tex Christian U TCU Box 297021 Fort Worth TX 76129-0001 Office Phone: 817-257-5914. Office Fax: 817-257-7397; Home Fax: 817-763-5364. Personal E-mail: djj1955@sbcglobal.net.

JACKSON, GARY, state legislator; b. Starkville, Miss., Sept. 11, 1950; m. Dianne Poss Jackson. Mem. Dist. 15 Miss. State Senate, 2004—. Mem.: NRA, Farm Bur. Republican. Baptist. Address: PO Box 40 French Camp MS 39745 Home: PO Box 40 French Camp MS 39745-0040 Home Phone: 662-262-9273; Office Phone: 601-359-3221. Fax: 662-262-9273; Office Fax: 601-359-2437. E-mail: gjackson@senate.ms.gov.

JACKSON, GIROD, III, state legislator; Gen. contractor; mem. Dist. 87 La. House of Reps., 2008—, mem. house and govtl. affairs com., mcpl., parochial and cultural affairs com., ways and means com., joint legis. com. on capital outlay, mem. house com. on homeland security, joint com. on homeland security. Democrat. Office: State Capitol PO Box 44486 Baton Rouge LA 70804 also: 2010 Woodmere Blvd Unit G Harvey LA 70058 Office Phone: 504-349-0030, 225-342-6945. Office Fax: 504-349-0032. Business E-Mail: jacksong@legis.state.la.us.

JACKSON, JEFFERY M., transportation executive; BS in Economics & Govt., Dartmouth Coll.; MS in Mgmt., Northwestern U. V.p., corp. devel., treas., v.p. & contr. Am. Airlines, Inc., sr. fin. analyst, 1984—88; sr. v.p. Sabre, Inc. (subs. of Sabre Holdings Corp.), Southlake, Tex., 1998—99, CFO, 1998—, exec. v.p. Southlake, Tex., 1999—. Bd. dirs. Travelocity.com, 2002, Rent-A-Ctr. Inc., 2007—. Office: Sabre Holdings Corp 3150 Sabre Dr Southlake TX 76092 Office Phone: 682-605-1000. Business E-Mail: jeffery.jackson@sabre-holdings.com.

JACKSON, JIMMY LEE, state legislator; b. Floydada, Tex., Mar. 20, 1939; s. Vernon Lester and Vivian (Inez) J.; m. Sue Ellen Jackson, June 6, 1959; children: Stephen Bradley, Deborah LeAnne. BA, U. North Tex., Denton, 1962. Orgnl. dir. Dallas County Rep. Party, 1965-69, exec. dir., 1972-74; ptnr. Jackson-Terry Ins. Agy., Dallas, 1970-73; county commr. Dallas County, 1974—2004; mem. Dist. 115 Tex. House of Representatives, 2004—. Chmn., vice-chmn. Nat. Assn. Counties Large Urban County Caucus, Washington, 1995-96; chmn. Nat. Assn. Counties Deferred Compensation Adv. Com., Washington, 2002; vice-chmn. Nat. Assn. Counties Transp. and Telecomms. Policy Steering Com., Washington, 1995-2000. Exec. bd. North Ctrl. Tex. Coun. of Govts., Arlington, 1992-99, 2002-03, pres. 1997-98; bd. dirs., chmn. Dallas Ctrl. Appraisal Dist., 1988-95; bd. dirs. Tex. Assn. Regional Couns., 1996-99; chmn. Tex. Conf. Urban Counties, 1981; mem. Congl. Dist. Rep. Nat. Del. Selection Com., 1992, 96; del. Rep. Nat. Conv., 1992; arrangements chmn., 1986, congl. and senatorial dist. caucus chmn., 1990, 92, 94, 96, Rep. State Conv.; pres. Irving Rep. Club, 1979, Rep. Assembly, 1986-87, Metrocrest Rep. Club, 1991-92; mem. Tex. Commission on Jail Standards 1999-2004, chair 2004-05. Recipient of several awards and honors. Republican. Avocations: fishing, travel. Office: 1120 Metrocrest Dr Ste 107 Carrollton TX 75006 also: Room E2.718 Capitol Extension PO Box 2910 Austin TX 78768 Office Phone: 972-416-7698, 512-463-0468. Business E-Mail: Jim.Jackson@house.state.tx.us.

JACKSON, JOHN E., energy executive; Grad. in Bus. Adminstrn. cum laude, Baylor U., Waco. CPA. Staff acct. Arthur Young & Co., Ft. Worth, 1979; various treasury, contr. & acctg. positions, including CFO Gathering, Processing & Mktg. divsn. Union Pacific Resources, 1981—99; v.p., contr. Duke Energy Field Svcs., 1999—2001, v.p., CFO, 2001—02; chmn., CEO & pres. Price Gregory Svcs., Inc., 2008; gen. ptnrs. Encore Energy Partners, LP, 2008—. Bd. dirs. Encore Energy Ptnrs. GP LLC; CFO, sr. v.p. Exterran Holdings, Inc. (formerly Hanover Compressor Co.), 2002—04, pres., CEO, 2004—07, bd. dirs., 2004—, Seitel, Inc., 2007—. Office: Encore Energy Partners LP 5847 San Felipe Ste 3000 Houston TX 77057 Office Phone: 832-327-2255. Office Fax: 832-327-2260. Business E-Mail: john.jackson@exterran.com.

JACKSON, JUDY FAYE, academic administrator; b. Robersonville, NC; d. S. T. and Estella Jackson. BA in French Lang. and Lit., U. N.C., Greensboro; M in Francophone African Lit., Geography and Fgn. Policy, Bucknell U.; PhD in Adminstn., Planning and Social Policy, Harvard U. Mem. faculty English dept. Susquehanna U., 1981—85; various positions Cornell U. Coll. Engring., 1985—89, asst. dir. for advising and counseling, asst. dean for minority programs, asst. dean for advising counseling and minority programs; various positions MIT, 1989—2000, assoc. dean undergrad. edn. and student affairs, dir. minority edn., ombudsman Pres. Office, staff mem. Provost Office, spl. adviser to provost on faculty diversity; exec. asst. to pres., clk. of the corp. Babson Coll., Babson Park, Mass.; assoc. provost for instnl. engagement NYU, NY, 2002—04; dean Vassar Coll., Poughkeepsie, NY, 2004—08; v.p. institutional diversity U. Ky., 2008—. Office: U Ky 2099 Newtown Pike Lexington KY 40506 E-mail: jj@uky.edu.

JACKSON, KATRINA R., state legislator; b. Monroe, La. BA, U. La., Monroe; JD, So. U., Baton Rogue, 2004. Tchr. Carroll HS, La.; atty. Law Offices of Willie Hunter, Jr., La.; atty. to the labor and indsl. rels com. La. House of Reps., Baton Rogue, exec. dir. La. Legis. Black Caucus, mem. Dist. 16, 2012—. Mem.: La. State Bar Assn. Democrat. Office: La House of Reps 900 N 3rd St PO Box 94062 Baton Rouge LA 70804 Business E-Mail: jacksonk@legis.la.gov.

JACKSON, LARRY ARTOPE, retired college president; b. Florence, SC, Feb. 7, 1925; s. Arthur Edward and Rosa (Gilbert) J.; m. Barbara Atwood, June 27, 1953; children: Elizabeth Jackson Eble, Arthur Edward, Barbara Jackson Allen, Charles Rhett. AB, Wofford Coll., 1947, DLitt (hon.), 1976; MDiv, Union Theol. Sem., 1953; MA, U. Pacific, 1973, DD (hon.), 1961; D in Humanities (hon.), Clemson U., 1991. Prin. Santiago (Chile) Coll., 1959-64; provost Callison Coll. of U. Pacific, Stockton, Calif., 1964-70; v.p. for adminstrn. U. Evansville, 1970-73; pres. Lander Univ. (formerly Lander Coll.), Greenwood, SC, 1973-92, ret., 1992. Vis. fellow Wolfson Coll., Cambridge U., 1985; appointed by Gov. to serve as mem. S.C. Commn. on Higher Edn., 2000-2003. Mem. Fulbright Commn. for Chile, 1961-64; mem. Commn. on Black Colls. Related to the Meth. Ch., 1973-76. With USAAF, 1943-45; with Am. Friends Svc. Com., 1948-49. Decorated Air medal with 2 oak leaf clusters. Mem. Rotary. Democrat. Home: 604 Cambridge Ave W Greenwood SC 29649-1967 Personal E-mail: ljack@embargmail.com.

JACKSON, LAWRENCE V., manufacturing executive, former retail executive; b. 1953; m. Kimberly J. Jackson; 3 children. BA in Economics, Harvard U., 1975, MBA. With Bank of Boston, 1975—79, McKinsey & Co., 1979—80, PepsiCo., 1980—97; sr. v.p. supply ops. Safeway, Inc., Pleasanton, Calif., 1997—2003; pres., COO Dollar General Corp., 2003—04; exec. v.p., human resources divsn. Wal-Mart Stores, Inc., 2004—06, pres., CEO global procurement divsn., 2006—07; chmn., CEO SourceMark, LLC. Bd. dirs. Parsons Corp., Allied Waste, Assurant, Inc., 2009—, RedPrairie, 2010—. Named one of 50 Most Powerful Black Execs., Fortune mag., 2002. Office: SourceMark, LLC 100 Winners Circle, Ste 250 Brentwood TN 37027 Office Phone: 615-269-6010. Business E-Mail: ljackson@newmountaincapital.com.

JACKSON, LES, professional sports team executive; b. Manning, Alta., Can., Dec. 1952; children: Brock, Drake, Reid. Head coach Great Falls Americans, 1979—80, Brandon Wheat Kings, 1980—82; asst. coach Minn. North Stars, 1985—87; asst. gen. mgr. Dallas Stars, 1993—98, asst. gen. mgr., dir. hockey ops., 2000—07, interim co-gen. mgr., 2007—08, co-gen. mgr., 2008—09, dir. scouting and player devel., 2009—; asst. gen. mgr. Atlanta Thrashers, 1998—2000. Office: Dallas Stars 2601 Avenue of the Stars Frisco TX 75034 Office Phone: 214-387-5500.

JACKSON, LESTER G., III, state legislator, dentist; m. Lorna Jackson; 4 children. DDS, Meharry Med. Coll., Nashville, Tenn. Family dentistry practice, Savannah, Ga.; mem. Dist. 148 Ga. House Reps., 1999—2008; mem. Dist. 2 Ga. State Senate, 2009—. Served USN. Democrat. Office: 1501 Abercorn St Savannah GA 31401 Office Phone: 912-233-7970. Office Fax: 912-201-0431. Business E-Mail: lester.jackson@senate.ga.gov.

JACKSON, MACK, state legislator; b. Tennille, Ga., July 15; m. Valarie Jackson; 1 child, Michael; 1 child, Daryl. Attended, Albany State Coll.; grad. in Polit. Sci., Ga. Coll. & State U. Former employee Ga. Dept. Juvenile Justice, Ga., Ga. Dept. Labor, Ga.; former office mgr. Sandersville Probation Office; ptnr. Benchmarck Ptnrs. LLC; pastor St. James Christian Fellowship Inc.; mem. Dist. #142 Ga. House of Reps., Ga., 2008—. Named Hon. award, Ga. C. of C., 2009. Mem.: Tennille Optimist Club, Sandersville Club. Democrat. Christian. Achievements include elected to the Georgia House of Representatives November 2008. Office: Capitol Address 611-F Coverdell Legislative Office Bldg Atlanta GA 30334 also: District Office 733 Evelyn St Sandersville GA 31082 Office Phone: 404-656-0314. Personal E-mail: mack.jackson@house.ga.gov.

JACKSON, MICHAEL J., automotive retail company executive; Technician Mercedes-Benz dealership, Cherry Hill, N.J.; mng. ptnr. Euro Motorcars, Bethesda, Md.; dist. mgr. Mercedes-Benz N.Am.; sr. mktg. exec. Mercedes-Benz USA, Inc., pres., CEO, responsible for N.Am. bus., until 1999; chmn., CEO AutoNation, Inc., Ft. Lauderdale, Fla., 1999—. Former chmn. Mercedes-Benz Nat. Dealer Coun. Recipient All-Star Dealer award Sports Illustrated, 1990; mem. automotive execs. Dream Team, Automotive News, 2 times; recognized mem. of Mktg. 100, Advt. Age, 4 times; named to Automobile Hall of Fame, 2003; named Automotive Industry Leader of Yr., 2003. Office: AutoNation Inc 110 SE 6th St Fort Lauderdale FL 33301-5000

JACKSON, MICHAEL PETER, security technologies industry executive, former federal agency administrator; b. Apr. 28, 1954; married; 1 child. BA in Polit. Sci., U. Houston, 1977; PhD in Govt., Georgetown U., 1985. Asst. prof. University of Georgia, 1985—86; various positions US Dept. Edn., Washington, 1986—88; spl. asst. to Pres. for cabinet liaison The White House, 1989—91; chief of staff to sec. of transp. US Dept. Transp., 1992—93, dep. sec., 2001—03; sr. v.p. American Trucking Associations, 1993—97; COO transp. systems and svcs., IMS bus. divsn. Lockheed Martin, 1997—2001; sr. v.p. AECOM Technology Corp., Fairfax, Va., 2003—05; dep. sec. US Dept. Homeland Security, Washington, 2005—07; founder, pres. Firebreak Partners, LLC, McLean, Va., 2008—. Mem. President's Commn. Implementation of US Space Exploration Policy, 2004; bd. dirs. AirTran Holdings, Inc., 2009—, VidSys, Inc., 2009—. Republican. Mailing: AirTran Airways 9955 AirTran Blvd Orlando FL 32827 Office Phone: 407-318-5600. Office Fax: 407-318-5900. Business E-Mail: m.jackson@fbpart.com.

JACKSON, MIKE, state legislator; b. Baton Rouge, Aug. 20, 1953; m. Vickie Jackson Wolf; children: Vic, Michelle. Student, La. Tech. U., La. State U. Pres. Force Corp., La Porte, Tex.; mem. Tex. House of Representatives, Austin, 1989-98; mem. Dist. 11 Tex. State Senate, Austin, 1999—. Tex. del. Energy Coun.; bd. counselors St. John Hosp.; mem. La Porte Mayor's Adv. Coun.; mem. mgmt. devel. adv. com. San Jacinto Coll. Recipient of several awards and honors. Mem. La Porte-Bayshore C. of C., Pasadena C. of C., Rotary. Republican. Methodist. Office: PO Box 12068 Capitol Station Austin TX 78711 also: 2225 CR90 Ste 107 Pearland TX 77584 also: PO Box 12068 Austin TX 78711-2068 Office Phone: 713-948-0111, 512-463-0111, 281-485-3117. Business E-Mail: mike.jackson@senate.state.tx.us.

JACKSON, MIKE, state legislator; b. Kiowa, Kans., Mar. 6, 1978; s. Duane and Sherill Jackson; m. Caralyn Jackson; 1 child, Candence. BS in Agricultural Sciences and Natural Resources in Agricultural Communications, Okla. State Univ. Former dir. mktg. for the call monitoring divsn. Cadcom Telesystems; pub. info. officer Okla. Dept. Agrl.; former field rep. to Senator Jim Inhole; mem. Dist 40 Okla. House of Representatives, 2005—. Republican. Mailing: 2906 Cellar Door Ln Enid OK 73703 Office: 2300 N Lincoln Blvd Rm 441 Oklahoma City OK 73105 Office Phone: 405-557-7317. E-mail: mikejackson@okhouse.gov.

JACKSON, RAYMOND A., federal judge; b. 1949; BA, Norfolk State U., 1970; JD, U. Va., 1973. Capt. U.S. Army JAGC, 1973-77; asst. U.S. atty. Ea. Dist. Va., Norfolk, 1977-93, chief criminal divsn., civil divsn., exec. asst.; judge U.S. Dist. Ct. (ea. dist.) Va., Norfolk, 1993—. Mem. jud. conf. U.S. Ct. Appeals (4th cir.); adj. faculty Marshall Wythe Sch. of Law, Coll. of William and Mary, 1978—93; mem. com. on admistrn. Magistrate Judges Sys., 1998—2004. Active Day Care and Child Devel. Ctr., Tidewater, 1980—86; mem. exec. com. Va. State Bar, 1991—93; bd. dirs. Peninsula Legal Aid Ctr., 1977. Col. Res. USAR, ret. 1998. Fellow: Va. Law Found.; mem.: Maritime Law Assn., Am. Inn Ct. (Hoffman-l'Anson chpt. pres. 2000—02), South Hampton Rds. Bar Assn., Norfolk-Portsmouth Bar Assn., Old Dominion Bar Assn. (pres. 1984—86), U.S. Dist. Judges Assn. Office: 600 Granby St Norfolk VA 23510-1915

JACKSON, ROBERT L., state legislator; b. Lambert, Miss., Aug. 15, 1955; Mem. Dist. 11 Mis. State Senate, 2004—, vice chair vets. and mil. affairs com. Democrat. Baptist. Address: PO Box 383 Marks MS 38646 Home Phone: 662-326-3637; Office Phone: 662-326-4000, 601-359-3211. Fax: 662-326-3904; Office Fax: 601-359-3935. E-mail: rjackson@senate.ms.gov.

JACKSON, ROBERT WILLIAM, retired utilities executive; b. Beaumont, Tex., June 22, 1930; s. Robert and Elizabeth (Watler) J.; m. Theta Ann Watt, Aug. 14, 1959; 1 child, Robert W. Jr. BBA, U. Tex.; MBA, U. Ill. With Gulf States Utilities Co., Beaumont, Tex., 1955-79, sec., chief fin. officer, 1972-74, sec., treas., chief fin. officer, 1974-75, v.p. fin., chief fin. officer, sec., 1975-79, Cen. Ill. Pub. Svc. Co., Springfield, 1979—95, sr. v.p. fin., chief fin. officer, corp. sec., 1980-95, also bd. dirs.; pres., chief exec. officer CIPSCO Investment Co., Springfield, 1990-95, also bd. dirs.; sr. v.p. CIPSCO Inc., Springfield, 1990—95; ret., 1995. Bd. dirs. 1st Bank of Ill. Co., Springfield, 1st Nat. Bank Springfield, Sangamon State U. Found.; bd. govs. Econs. Am. Mem. bus. adv. coun. U. Ill.; pres., bd. dirs. Springfield Symphony Orch., pres., bd. dirs. Montgomery County Performing Arts Soc., Conroe, Tex., bd. dirs. Conroe Symphony Orch., United Way of Sangamon County; adv. bd. St. John's Hosp., Springfield. Served with U.S. Army, 1953-55, USAR, 1955-61. Mem. Am. Soc. Corp. Secs., Fin. Execs. Inst., Edison Electric Inst. (fin. exec. com.). Methodist.

JACKSON, SAMPSON, II, state legislator; b. Preston, Miss., Jan. 30, 1953; m. Patricia Hayes Jackson; children: Kalvin B., Kieth K., Sampson III. Mem. Dist. 32 Miss. State Senate, 1992—; with Miss. State Tax Commn.; farmer businessman; weight enforcement officer. Mem.: Farm Bureau, Miss. Cattlemen's Assn., Kemper Co. Black Caucus, NAACP. Democrat. Baptist. Mailing: 749 Matthew Jackson Rd Preston MS 39354 Home Phone: 601-677-2305; Office Phone: 601-743-5900, 601-359-3172. Office Fax: 601-359-5957. Business E-Mail: sjackson@senate.ms.gov.

JACKSON, STEPHEN JESSE, professional basketball player; b. Houston, Apr. 5, 1978; Attended, Butler County CC, Eldorado, Kans. Forward NJ Nets, 2000—01, San Antonio Spurs, 2001—03, 2012—13, Atlanta Hawks, 2003—04, Ind. Pacers, 2004—07, Golden State Warriors, 2007—09, Charlotte Bobcats, 2009—11, Milw. Bucks, 2011—12.*

JACKSON, STEVEN RASHAD, professional football player; b. Las Vegas, July 22, 1983; Attended, Oreg. State U., Corvallis. Running back St. Louis Rams, 2004—12, Atlanta Falcons, 2013—. Spokesman Susan G. Komen Race, 2006, 2008. Named to The Nat. Football Conf.

Pro Bowl Team, NFL, 2006, 2009, 2010. Achievements include leading the NFL in: all-purpose yards/yards from scrimmage (2334), 2006. Office: Atlanta Falcons 4400 Falcon Pky Flowery Branch GA 30542

JACKSON, THOMAS E., state legislator; b. Thomasville, Ala., Aug. 24, 1950; m. Dorothy Jackson; children: Kimberly, Terence, Thomas III, Trumaine. BS in Psychology, Knoxville Coll.; MA in Edn. & Counseling, Ala. State U. Dir. Upward Bound Program Ala. So. Coll.; assoc. pastor Ch. of God in Christ; mem. Dist. 68 Ala. House of Reps., Montgomery, 1994—. Past pres. Clarke County Edn. Assn.; past vice chmn. Clarke County Dem. Conf.; coord. Thomasville Precinct-ADC; bd. dirs. Southwest Ala. Boys and Girls Club. Mem.: NEA, Ala. Edn. Assn., Nat. Black Caucus State Legislators, Kiwanis, Kappa Alpha Psi. Democrat. Methodist. Office: Ala House of Reps Ala State House 11 S Union St Rm 522-C Montgomery AL 36130 Home: PO Box 636 Thomasville AL 36784-0636 Office Phone: 334-246-3597, 334-242-7738.

JACKSON, VINCENT, professional football player; b. Ft. Polk, La., Jan. 14, 1983; s. Terence and Sherry Jackson; m. Lindsey VanDeweghe. BBA, U. No. Colo., Greeley, 2005. Wide receiver San Diego Chargers, 2005—11, Tampa Bay Buccaneers, 2012—. Active San Diego Food Bank, Guide On. Named Offensive Player of Yr., Great West Conf., 2004, 1st Team Divsn. I-AA All-American, AP, 2004; named to American Football Conf. Pro Bowl Team, NFL, 2009, 2011, Univ. No. Colo. Athletic Hall of Fame, 2011. Office: Tampa Bay Buccaneers One Buccaneer Pl Tampa FL 33607

JACKSON, WANDA LAVONNE, country western musician; b. Maud, Okla., Oct. 20, 1937; m. Wendell Goodman; children: Gregory Jackson, Gina Gail. Signed to Capital Records, 1954—73; toured with Hank Thompson's Band, 1954, Elvis Presley, 1955—56. Songs include You Can't Have My Love, 1954, I Gotta Know, 1956, Let's Have a Party, 1958, Right or Wrong, 1961, In the Middle of a Heartache, 1961, If I Cried Every Time You Hurt Me, 1962, Fujiyama Mama; albums include Wanda Jackson, 1958, There's a Party Goin' On, 1959, Rockin' with Wanda!, 1960, Right or Wrong, 1961, Lovin' Country Style, 1962, Wonderful Wanda, 1962, Love Me Forever, 1963, Blues in My Heart, 1964, Wanda Jackson Sings Country Songs, 1966, Closer to Jesus, 1967, Reckless Love Affair, 1967, Wanda Jackson Salutes the Country Music Hall of Fame, 1967, You'll Always Have My Love, 1967, Cream of the Crop, 1968, The Happy Side of Wanda Jackson, 1969, The Many Moods of Wanda Jackson, 1969, Wanda Jackson in Person, 1969, A Woman Lives for Love, 1970, Country, 1970, I've Gotta Sing, 1971, I Wouldn't Want You Any Other Way, 1972, Praise the Lord, 1972, Country Keepsakes, 1973, When It's Time to Fall in Love Again, 1973, Country Gospel, 1974, Now I Have Everything, 1974, My Testimony, 1982, Rock & Roll Away Your Blues, 1984, 2 Sides of Wanda, 1987, Queen of Rockabilly, 2000, Live and Still Kickin', 2003, Heart Trouble, 2003, I Remember Elvis, 2006, Hold What You Got, 2008. Named to Rock & Roll Hall of Fame, 2009. Office: Wendell Goodman/Wanda Jackson Enterprises PO Box 891498 Oklahoma City OK 73189-1498 Office Phone: 405-692-7719. E-mail: wandajent@aol.com.

JACKSON, WESLEY, publishing executive; b. Louisville; BA in Comm., U. Ky., Lexington. Various positions including v.p. interactive sales, pres./gen. mgr. interactive media and corp. sr. v.p. Belo Corp., 2000—07; ptnr. Maroon Ventures, LLC; pres., COO VuPal Networks; founder Mastery Mavens, LLC; v.p. sales & mktg. The Courier-Jour, Louisville, 2011—12, pres., pub., 2012—. Bd. dirs. Classified Ventures, Colo. Real Estate Online. Active Big Brothers America; youth baseball & football coach; mem. devel. com. Denver Better Bus. Bur. Recipient Digital Edge award, 1998. Mem.: Online Publishers Assn. (bd. dirs.). Office: The Courier Journal 525 W Broadway PO Box 740031 Louisville KY 40201-7431 Office Phone: 502-582-4101. Business E-Mail: wjackson@courier-journal.com.

JACKSON, WILLIAM DAVID, research and development company executive; b. Edinburgh, May 20, 1927; came to U.S., 1955, naturalized, 1968; s. Joseph and Margaret (Johnston) Jackson; children: Margaret Eleanor, David Foster. BSc, U. Glasgow, 1947, PhD, 1960; postgrad., U. Strathclyde, 1948. Apprentice English Electric Co., Stafford, 1945—47; rsch. asst. elec. engring. dept. U. Strathclyde, Glasgow, 1948—51; lectr. elec. engring. U. Manchester, England, 1951—55, 1957—58; vis. lectr. dept. elec. engring. MIT, 1955—57, asst. prof., 1958—62, assoc. prof., 1962—66, lectr. elec. engring., 1968—73; vis. prof. Tech. U., Berlin, 1966; prof. elec. engring., dept. energy engring. U. Ill., Chgo., 1966—67; prin. rsch. scientist, dir. tech. edn. Avco-Everett Rsch. Lab., Mass., 1967—72; prof. elec. engring. U. Tenn. Space Inst., Tullahoma, 1972—73; mgr. Electric Power Rsch. Inst., Palo Alto, Calif., 1973—74; mgr. office coal rsch. Interior Dept., Washington, 1974—75; dir. magnetohydrodynamic divsn. ERDA, Washington, 1975—77; dir. tech. analysis divsn. Office Energy Rsch., Dept. Energy, Washington, 1977—79; pres. Energy Cons., Inc., 1979—84, HMJ Corp., 1982—. Professorial lectr. George Washington U., 1979—91, vis. prof., 1986—87, adj. prof., 1991—2009, faculty in residence Wise program, 2007; edn. coord. HOSC, 2010; bd. dirs. Hexogon Inc., prodn. v.p., 1999—2001; bd. dirs. Clean Energy Combustion, Inc., 2001—03; mem. Internat. Magnetohydrodynamic Liaison Group, 1966—, chmn., 1969—74, sec., 1986—2002; coord. coop. program magnetohydrodynamic power generation U.S.-USSR, 1974—79; mem. numerous govt. and internat. coms. and panels; cons. numerous indsl. firms and govt. agencies, 1948—; adj. prof. Tenn. State U., 2012—, Dream Tullahoma Com., 2011—. Editor: Electricity From MHD, 1968; edtl. bd.: Internat. Jour. Elec. Engring. Edn, 1962-70; editor-in-chief Magnetohydrodynamics: An Internat. Jour., 1987-92. U.K. Fulbright scholar, 1955-57; recipient ILG award Internat. Magnetogydrodynamic Liaison Group, 2005. Fellow Instn. Engring. & Tech. (past com. sec., chmn.), IEEE (sec.-treas. prof. group biomed. electronics Boston sect. 1962-63, energy devel. subcom. 1973—, chmn. 1988-98, energy devel. and power gen. com. 1986-99, steering com. intersoc. energy conversion engring. conf. 1988—2002, conf. program chair 1989, conf. gen. chair 1996, 2002), ASME (past chmn. adv. energy sys. divsn., energy com. 1986-90), AIAA (assoc., Energy Sys. award 1995); mem. AAUP, AAAS, Am. Phys. Soc., Am. Soc. Engring. Edn., Sigma Xi, Nat. Model Rail Soc. Office: 710 N College St Tullahoma TN 37388-2552 Office Phone: 931-563-7654. Business E-Mail: hmjcorpwdjackson@aol.com.

JACKSON, WILLIAM PAUL, JR., lawyer; b. Bexar, Ala., July 7, 1938; s. William Paul and Evelyn Mabel (Goggans) J.; m. Barbara Anne Seignious, Sept. 30, 1966; children: Jennifer Anne, Susan Barrett, William Paul III. BS in Physics, U. Ala., 1960, JD, 1963. Bar: Ala. 1963, DC 1969, Va. 1975. Law clk. to judge Ala. Ct. Appeals, Montgomery, 1965; assoc. Bishop and Carlton, Birmingham, Ala., 1965-68, Todd, Dillon and Sullivan, Washington, 1968-70; founding ptnr. Jackson & Jessup, Washington, 1970-75, Arlington, Va., 1975—76; pres., sr. atty. Jackson & Jessup, PC, Arlington, 1976—2001, McLean, Va., 2002—. Advisor Oren Harris chair of transp. U. Ark., 1974-91. Comments editor U. Ala. Law Rev., 1962, leading articles editor, 1963; contbr. articles to profl. jours. French horn. U. Ala. Million Dollar Band, 1960-63, City Fairfax Band, Va., 72-77; V.p. McLean Hunt Homeowners Assn., Va., 1974, pres., 1975-76; bd. dirs. McLean Citizens' Assn., 1976-78; pres. McLean Legal Action Fund, Inc., 1977-81; session mem. Lewinsville Presbyn. Ch., 1981-84; v.p., Clan Marjoribanks Soc., 1994-96, pres., 1996-98; active The Alexandria Chorale, 1985-94. 1st lt. Signal Corps, US Army, 1963-65. Recipient Pub. Service awards Am. Radio Relay League, 1958, Merit award Armed Forces Comm. and Electronics Assn., 1963; Sigma Delta Kappa scholar, 1963; chevalier, La Confrérie de la Chaîne des Rôtisseurs. Mem. ABA, Ala. State Bar, Va. State Bar, DC Bar, Bar Assn. DC (chmn. computer tech. com. 1998-2000, chmn. mem. com. 2000-01, treas. 2001-02, bd. dirs. 2002-03, chmn. website com. 2004, Presdl. award 2000), Transp. Lawyers Assn. (chmn. legis. com. 1989-90), Bar Assn. DC Found. (bd. dirs. 1999-2001), Assn. Transp. Law Profls. (nat. pres. 1991-92, chmn. nominating com. 1992-93, chmn. membership com. 1993-99, chmn. DC chpt. 1989-90, com. govtl. rels. 1975-90, motor editor Assn. Highlights 1992-98, Presdl. award 1994, 99), So. Transp. Logistics Assn. (exec. dir. 1970-99), Ea. Indsl. Traffic League (exec. dir. 1978-88), Bench and Bar Legal Honor Soc. (pres. 1963), Farrah Law Soc. (trustee 2000—, sec.-treas. 2006-2008, vice chair 2008-10, chmn. 2010-12), Coll. Arts & Scis., U. Alabama (leadership bd. 2008-), Nat. Soc. DAR (bd. advisors to pres. gen. 2004-07), St. Andrews Soc., Omicron Delta Kappa. Presbyterian (elder). Office: Jackson & Jessup PC PO Box 4030 Mc Lean VA 22103 Home: PO Box 4030 West McLean VA 22103-4030 Business E-Mail: wpj@translaw.com.

JACKSON, WILLIAM S., state legislator; b. Dec. 30; children: William, Paula. Owner Tile Center Inc., 1961—; former chmn. Columbia Bd. Ed.; mem. Ga. House of Reps., 1979—84, 1987—90, 1997—2002, State Bd. Corrections, 2006—07; mem. Dist. 24 Ga. State Senate, 2007—; sec. Transp. Com. Mem. Columbia Co. C of C, Shiloh Meth. Ch. Republican. Methodist. Office: 319-A Coverdell Legislative Office Bldg Atlanta GA 30334 also: PO Box 528 Appling GA 30802 Office Phone: 404-656-5114, 706-863-5818. Office Fax: 404-657-0797, 706-541-0197. Business E-Mail: bill.jackson@senate.ga.gov.

JACKSON, YVONNE RUTH, human resources specialist; b. L.A., June 30, 1949; d. Giles B. Jackson and Gwendolyn (Battle); m. Frederic Jackson, Jr., Mar. 24, 1989; children: Cortney, Douglass. BA in Hisotry & Bus. Adminstrn., Spelman Coll., 1970; MA, Harvard U., 1985. Asst. dept. mgr. Sears, Roebuck & Co., Torrance, Calif., 1970—71, dep. mgr., 1971—72, asst. buyer, asst. retail sales mgr. NYC, 1972—77, pers. mgr., 1977—79; exec. recruiter employee rels.mgr., dir., human resources Avon Products, Inc., 1979—85, v.p. human resources, 1979—93, dir. mfr., redeployment, dir., human resources internat., 1985—87, v.p. internat., 1987—93; sr. v.p., worldwide human resources Burger King Corp., 1993—99; sr. v.p., orgn. & human resources Compaq Computer Corp., Houston, 1999—2002; sr. v.p., human resources Pfizer, Inc., NYC, 2003—05; founder, pres. BeecherJackson, Coral Gables, Fla., 2005—. Bd. trustees Spelman Coll., 1996—, chmn. bd. trustees, 2004—; bd. dirs. Inst. Women's Policy Rsch., Girls, Inc., Winn-Dixie Stores, Inc., 2006—, AGB, 2007—10, Spartan Stores, Inc., 2010—; mem. advisory bd. Catalyst, 1993—. Recipient Bus. Achievement award, Spelman Coll. Alumnae Assn., 1993; named a Black Achiever, YMCA, 1986, Woman Achiever, YMCA of Greater NY, 1992. Office: BeecherJackson 13633 Deering Bay Dr Ste 235 Coral Gables FL 33158 Office Phone: 305-255-1983. Business E-Mail: yvonnej@beecherjackson.com.

JACKSON LEE, SHEILA, United States Representative from Texas; b. Queens, NY, Jan. 12, 1950; d. Erica Shelwyn and Jason Cornelius Bennett; m. Elwyn C. Lee; children: Erica, Jason. BA in Polit. Sci., with honors, Yale U., New Haven, 1972; JD, U. Va. Sch. Law, Charlottesville, 1975. Bar: Tex. Sr. counsel select com. on assassinations US Congress, 1977—78; trial atty. Fulbright & Jaworski, 1978-80; sr. atty. United Energy Resources, Inc., 1980; assoc. judge City of Houston Mcpl. Ct., 1987-89; councilwoman Houston City Coun., 1990-94; mem. US Congress from 18th Tex. dist., 1995—, founder Congl. Children's Caucus. Recipient Top Women in Sci. award, Nat. Tech. Assn. Scientists & Engineers, 1998, Phillip Burton Immigration & Civil Rights policy award, Immigrant Legal Resource Ctr., 2006; named one of 100 Most Influential Black Americans, Ebony mag., 2006; named to Power 150, 2008. Mem.: Tex. Mcpl. Judges Assn., State Bar Assn. Justice Com. Democrat. Office: US House Representatives 2160 Rayburn House Office Bldg Washington DC 20515 also: 1919 Smith St Ste 1180 Houston TX 77002 Office Phone: 202-225-3816.*

JACOB, BRUCE ROBERT, law educator; b. Chgo., Mar. 26, 1935; s. Edward Carl and Elsie Berthe (Hartmann) J.; m. Ann Wear, Sept. 8, 1962; children: Bruce Ledley, Lee Ann, Brian Edward. BA, Fla. State U., 1957; JD, Stetson U., 1959; LLM, Northwestern U., 1965; SJD, Harvard U., 1980; LLM in Taxation, U. Fla., 1995. Bar: Fla. 1959, Ill. 1965, Mass. 1970, Ohio 1972. Asst. atty. gen. State of Fla., 1960-62; assoc. Holland, Bevis & Smith, Bartow, Fla., 1962-64; asst. to assoc. prof. Emory U. Sch. Law, 1965-69; rsch. assoc. Ctr. for Criminal Justice, Harvard Law Sch., 1969-70; staff atty. Cmty. Legal Assistance Office, Cambridge, Mass., 1970-71; assoc. prof. Coll. Law, Ohio State U., 1971-73, prof., dir. clin. programs, 1973-78; dean, prof. Mercer U. Law Sch., Macon, Ga., 1978-81; v.p., dean, prof. Stetson U. Coll. Law, St. Petersburg, Fla., 1981-94, dean emeritus, prof., 1994—. Contbr. articles to profl. jours. Mem. Fla. Bar, Sigma Chi. Democrat. Home: 1946 Coffee Pot Blvd NE Saint Petersburg FL 33704-4632 Office: Stetson U Coll Law 1401 61st St S Saint Petersburg FL 33707-3246 Office Phone: 727-562-7866.

JACOBS, ANDREW F., mortgage company executive; V.p., control, treasurer Capstead Mortgage Corp., Dallas, 1989—91, sr. v.p., control, treasurer, 1991—98, sec., 1992—98, exec. v.p., asset & liability, 1998, exec. v.p., finance, treasurer, sec., 1998—99, CFO, sr. v.p., finance, 1998—2003, sec., 2000—03, pres., CEO, 2003—. Office: Capstead Mortgage Corp 8401 N Central Expressway Ste 800 Dallas TX 75225-4410

JACOBS, BENJAMIN FRANKLIN, cardiologist; b. St. Louis, Oct. 2, 1942; MD, Tulane U., 1968. Intern Barnes Hosp., St. Louis, 1968-69, resident, 1969-70, VA Hosp., St. Louis, 1972-73; fellow in cardiology Ochsner Found. Hosp., New Orleans, 1973-75, staff cardiologist, 1975—78; with East Jefferson Gen. Hosp., Metairie, La., 1978—. Fellow Am. Coll. Cardiology. Office: 4200 Houma Blvd Metairie LA 70006-2970 Office Phone: 504-454-4102. E-mail: bfj3@aol.com.*

JACOBS, GEORGE BRAUN, neurosurgeon; b. Poland, Jan. 9, 1934; naturalized US citizen, 1954; s. Maurice and Lena J.; m. Rosanne Wille, 1980; children: Leigh, Steven, Alec, Jeffrey. Student, NYU, 1952-54; MD, SUNY, Syracuse, 1958; postgrad. in general surgery, Bronx Mcpl. Hosp., 1958-59; postgrad. in neurological surgery, Albert Einstein Coll. of Medicine, 1959-64. Cert. airline transport pilot, flight instr., sr. aviation med. examiner, FAA accident counselor. Attending neurosurgeon Hackensack Med. Ctr., NJ, 1965-86, sr. attending neurosurgeon, 1986—, chief neurosurgery sect., 1981-86; attending surgeon Holy Name Hosp., Teaneck, NJ, 1965, chief neurosurgery, 1976-81, 90-94; chief sect. neurosurgery Hackensack U. Med. Ctr., 1970-86, chief spine surgery, 1986—2001, chmn. dept. neurosurgery, chief spine surgery, 1986—2001; dir. spine svcs. Montefiore Med. Ctr. Albert Einstein Coll. Medicine, Bronx, 1992-93; prof. neurological surgery U. Pitts. Sch. Medicine, 1993-94; dir. spine ctr., spine surgery U. Pitts., 1993-94; prof. neurosurgery U. Medicine and Dentistry NJ, Newark, 1994—; sr. cons. neurosurgery and spine surgery VA, 2011—. Vis. prof. neurosurgery, U. Saigon, Vietnam, 1965-66; clin. asst. prof. neurosurgery, NJ Coll. Medicine, Newark, 1970-73; asst. prof. clin. neurosurgery, Albert Einstein Coll. Medicine, 1973-75; assoc. prof. clin. neurosurgery, 1975-89; prof. clin. neurosurgery, 1989-92, prof. neurosurgery, 1992-93; prof. neurosurgery, 1993-1994, prof. surgery NJ Med. Sch., UMDNJ, 1994-; sr. cons. neurosurgeon VA, 2010-; spkr. numerous convs./cons. in field. Author: (novels) A Simple Twist of Fate, Freedom Quest, (textbooks) Medical Malpractice: A Guide to Medical Issues, 1986, Textbook of Operatives Spine Surgery, 1999; contbr. numerous articles to profl. jours. and publs. Fellow US Public Health Svc., 1959-60; bd. trustees Lehman Coll. Art Gallery, 1986-87; bd. dirs. Hackensack U. Med. Ctr. Found., 1997-2003, gov. bd. govs., 1979-2002; mem. Hillcrest Found. Bd., 1980-2002; bd. dirs. Lehman Coll. Art Gallery, 1986-87; hon. surgeon Police Dept. City of NY Decorated Army Commendation medal for Vietnam Svc., 1966; Disting. Svc. cert. of Merit Bd. of Chosen Freeholders of Bergen County, 1971. Fellow USPHS, Am. Coll. Surgeons, Am. Coll. Angiology, Internat. Coll. Angiology, Internat. Coll. Surgeons, Scoliosis Rsch. Soc., Cervical Spine Rsch. Soc., N.Am. Spine Soc.; mem. AMA, Internat. Soc. Pediatric Neurosurgery, Internat. Health Policy and Mgmt. Inst., Am. Pain Soc., Am. Assn. Neurol. Surgeons (chmn. liaison com. 1976-78), Bergen County Med. Soc. (trustee 1976, mem. judicial com. 1977-82, chmn. legis. com. 1980), Congress of Neurol. Surgeons, Assn. of Mil. Surgeons of US, NY Soc. Neurosurgery, Acad. Medicine NJ, NJ Neurosurg. Soc. (mem. exec. com. 1973, chmn. peer review com., 1974, pres. 1989-90), Fla. Med. Assn., Fla. Physicians Assn., Soc. Surgeons of NJ, Med. Soc. NJ, San Francisco Neurosurg. Soc. (corr.), others. Avocations: golf, aviation, boating, cooking. Address: 5506 Harbour Preserve Cir Cape Coral FL 33914

JACOBS, GORDON WALDEMAR, surgeon, educator; b. Cuero, Tex., May 30, 1933; s. Elmer Waldemar and Clara Esther Jacobs; m. Lorraine Maria Maguire, Oct. 24, 1970; children: Mary Lou Baker, Kristen Clara Goodman, Damien Gordon, Melanie Anne. BA, U. Iowa, 1955, MD, 1958; diploma in Tropical Medicine and Hygiene, U. Liverpool, 1983; diploma in French, Tng. Inst. for Execs., 1984. Diplomate Am. Bd. Surgery, 1972. Resident in surgery Loma Linda U., Riverside, Calif., 1959; intern U. Calif., Sacramento, 1958—59; locum tenens family practice Santa Barbara County Hosp., Calif., 1962; locum tenens gen. surgery Kaiser Permanente Hosp., Santa Clara, Calif., 1966, 1969; resident gen. surgery U. Calif., Oakland-Martinez, Calif., 1962—66; fellow gen. surgery Lahey Clinic, Boston, 1969—70; gen. surgeon Somerville (Mass.) Surg. Assocs., 1970—75; pvt. practice gen. surgeon Gordon W. Jacobs, Md, Vallejo, Calif., 1975, Berkeley, Calif., 1975—83, Lancaster, SC, 1986—88, Gordon W. Jacobs, Md Facs Pa, Charlotte, NC, 1989—2003, gen. surgeon locum tenens, 2003—. Missionary gen. surgeon Evang. Covenant Mission Hosp., Karawa, 1984—86; missionary gen. surgeon, instr. in surgery Evangelical Covenant Mission Hosp. & N.W. Teams Internat., Karawa, 2005, Bongolo Hosp., Pan African Acad. Christian Surgeons and N.W. Med. Teams Internat., Lebamba, Gabon, 2005—08, Bongolo Hosp., Pan African Acad. Christian Surgeons Cameroon, 2008—09; missionary gen. surgeon Luth. Mission Hosp., Madang, Papua New Guinea, 1966—69; missionary surgeon, instr. surgery Haile Selassie U. Med. Sch., Addis Ababa, Ethiopia, 1973—74, Pan African Acad. Christian Surgeons Ngaoundéré Protestant Hosp., Cameroon, 2009—10; with SIM, 2008—10. Contbr. articles to profl. jours. Pres. Oakland (Calif.) Uptown Toastmasters, 1980—81; active Big Bros., Boston, 1970—73; vol, med. dir. SIM (Serving in Missions); with Kibogora Hosp. Cyangugu Rwanda World med. Mission, 2010; vol. missionary surgeon Kibogora Hosp., 2010, Ngaoundere Protestant Hospital, 2010—; pres. Trinity Luth. Ch., Oakland, 1979—81; troop physician Boy Scouts Am., Charlotte, Calif., 1995; vol. Pioneer Hosp. Imfound. Republic of Congo, 2011, Global Outreach Mission; vol. instr. Missionary Surgeon; vol. missionary surgeon Kibaye Burundi Hope Med. Sch., 2012. Capt. med. corp. US Army, 1960—62, Germany. Recipient Vol. Presdl. Svc. award, Northwest Med. Teams, 2007; named Presdl. Vol., 2009; named one of Notable Americans, Am. Biog. Inst., 1978, Cmty. Leaders & Noteworthy Americans, 1978, Personalities Of West & Midwest, 1978; named to Book Of Honor, 1978, Personalities Of Am., 1978, Men Of Achievement, Internat. Biog. Centre, 1979. Fellow: ACS, Am. Soc. Gen. Surgeons, S.E. Surg. Congress; mem.: AMA (chmn. com. medicine and religion Calif. chpt. 1980—81), Christian Med. & Dental Assn., Mecklenburg County Med. Soc., Charlotte Surg. Soc., N.C. Med. Soc. Republican. Avocations: woodworking, french studies, flying, exercise, gardening. Home and Office: Gordon W Jacobs Md Facs Pa 14920 Wyndham Oaks Drive Charlotte NC 28277 Business E-Mail: gordonjacobsmd@pol.net.

JACOBS, HARRY MILBURN, JR., advertising executive; b. July 23, 1928; s. Harry Milburn and Nina (Gibbs) J.; m. Barbara Ann Mills; children: Kathryn, Christopher, Letitia. Student, East Carolina U., 1947-49; BFA, Corcoran Coll. Design, 1951. Art dir. The Hecht Co., Washington, 1951-53, Bradham & Co., Greensboro, N.C., 1953-54, sr. art dir., 1956-59; art dir. Cargill, Wilson & Acree, Richmond, Va., 1959—61, creative dir. Charlotte, N.C., 1961-68, corp. creative dir. Atlanta, 1969-74, pres., 1970-74, Martin Agy., Richmond, Va., 1977-83, 1983-86, chmn. bd., 1993—97, CEO, 1993, chmn. emeritus, 1997. Scoutmaster Boy Scouts Am., 1956—58, mem. exec. coun. Robert E. Lee coun., 1987—89; bd. visitors Sch. Journalism U. N.C., Chapel Hill, Va. Commonwealth U. Found.; bd. visitors East Carolina U., 2001—; bd. overseers Corcoran Coll. Design, Washington; bd. dirs., exec. com. Richmond Renaissance, Tryon Palace Comm.; trustee Woodberry Forest Sch., 1986—2001, St. Mary's Coll., 1986—2001; bd. dirs. Meml. Guidance Clinic, Richmond Children's Mus., Marymount Park, Goodwill Industries, Richmond Sch. Ballet, Virginians in Support of Guard and REs., Downtown Presents. With US Army, 1954—56. Recipient numerous advt. awards, Disting. Eagle Scout award, Boy Scouts Am., 1988; named Advt. Man of Yr. Silver medal, Am. Advt. Fedn., 1972; named to Va. Comm. Hall of Fame, 1986, N.C. Advt. Hall of Fame, 1991, One Club Creative Hall of Fame, N.Y., 2001, Am. Advt. Fedn. Hall of Fame, 2004. Mem. One Club Art & Copy NY, Art Dirs. Club of NY, Commonwealth Club. Republican. Office: Martin Agy One Shockoe Plaza Richmond VA 23219-4132 Office Phone: 804-698-8310, 804-698-8000. Personal E-mail: hjacobs2@comcast.net. Business E-Mail: harry.jacobs@martinagency.com.

JACOBS, JOEY A., healthcare service company executive; Asst. v.p., Salt Lake City Divsn., asst. v.p. Ctrl. group, v.p. Western group, pres. Western group HCA Inc. (formerly Hosp. Corp. of America), pres., Tennessee Divsn.; co-founder, pres., CEO Psychiatric Solutions, Inc., 1997—, chmn., 2002—. Office: Psychiatric Solutions Inc Ste 500 800 Crescent Centre Dr Ste 200 Franklin TN 37067-7285 Office Phone: 615-312-5700. Office Fax: 615-312-5711. Business E-Mail: joey.jacobs@psysolutions.com.*

JACOBS, LOUIE A., state banking agency administrator; Commr. banking SC State Bd. Fin. Instns. Office: SC State Board of Financial Institutuions Office of the Commissioner of Banking 1205 Pendleton St Ste 305 Columbia SC 29201 Office Phone: 803-734-2001. Office Fax: 803-734-2013. Business E-Mail: louie.jacobs@banking.sc.gov.

JACOBS, M. CHRISTINE (M. CHRISTINE JACOBS), medical products company executive; b. Columbus, Ohio, 1950; Grad., Rosary Hill Coll., 1972, Ga. State U., 1991. Regional mgr. Amersham; v.p. sales & mktg. Theragenics Corp., Norcross, Ga., pres., COO, 1992—93, pres., CEO, 1993—97, 2005—07, pres., CEO, co-chmn., 1997—98, chmn., pres., CEO, 1998—2005, 2007—. Adv. bd. NY Stock Exch.; bd. dirs. McKesson Corp., 1999—. Bd. dirs. Am. Coun. Capital Formation; bd. councilors Carter Ctr.; mem. Dem. Senatorial Campaign Com.; bd. dirs. Friends Centers Disease Control and Prevention; mem. Nat. Rep. Senatorial Com.; bd. dirs. The Ga. State U. Found. Mem.: Ga. Aquarium (trustee). Office: Theragenics Corp 5203 Bristol Industrial Way Buford GA 30518-1799 Office Phone: 770-271-0233. Office Fax: 678-482-4909. Business E-Mail: mjacobs@theragenics.com.

JACOBS, MARK M., energy executive; b. 1962; BBA, So. Methodist U.; MBA, Northwestern U. Mng. dir. natural resources group Goldman, Sachs and Co., Houston, 1989—2002; exec. v.p., CFO Reliant Energy, Inc., Houston, 2002—07, pres., CEO, 2007—10; pres., COO GenOn Energy (merger of Reliant & Mirant Corp.), Houston, 2010—11; chmn., CEO, pres. GeOn Mid Atlantic LLC; CEO, pres. GeOn Americas Generation, LLC. Mem. bd. dirs. Theatre Under the Stars. Office: GenOn Energy 1000 Main St Houston TX 77002 Office Phone: 832-357-3000.

JACOBS, MIKE, state legislator; b. May 15; Atty. Altson & Bird; mem. Dist. 80 Ga. House of Reps., 2005—, chmn. MARTOC, mem. budget & fiscal affairs oversight, ins., judiciary, juvenile justice, and transp. coms. Democrat. Office: 131 State Capitol Atlanta GA 30334 Office Phone: 404-656-5116. E-mail: repjacobs@gmail.com.

JACOBS, PHILIP C., marketing executive; BS, U. Tenn., Knoxville; MS, Vanderbilt U., Nashville. Formerly with Valentine Radford Inc., Kansas City, Mo.; dir. strategic devel. DDB Needham Dallas, 1996—2000, mng. ptnr., 1998—2000; v.p. mktg. Data Return LLC, Dallas, 2000—02; exec. v.p., chief mktg. officer Publicis Mid America, Dallas, 2002—04, CompUSA, Inc., 2004—07; sr. v.p., chief mktg. officer Service Corp. International, 2007—. Office: Service Corp International 1929 Allen Pky Houston TX 77019 Office Phone: 713-522-5141. Office Fax: 713-525-5586.

JACOBS, SAM GALLIP, bishop; b. Greenwood, Miss., Mar. 4, 1938; BA, Cath. U. of Am., 1959, MA, 1960, MA, 1964. Ordained priest Diocese of Lafayette, La., 1964; ordained bishop, 1989; bishop Diocese of Alexandria, 1989—2003, Diocese of Houma-Thibodaux, 2003—. Roman Catholic. Office: Diocese of Houma-Thibodaux PO Box 505 2779 Highway 311 Schriever LA 70395 Office Fax: 985-850-3124, 985-850-3229.

JACOBSEN, DIANE DEMELL, foreign policy specialist; b. NYC, Sept. 21, 1944; d. A. Leonard and Lizette DeMell; m. Thomas H. Jacobsen, June 15, 1985 (dec. July 20, 2002). Bachelors Degree, CUNY, 1965; M in Liberal Arts, Washington U., 1995, M in Internat. Affairs, 2000, PhD in Internat. Affairs, 2003. Sr. exec. Internat. Bus. Machine, Armonk, NY, 1965-86; sr. v.p. Bapt. Health Inc., Jacksonville, Fla., 1987-88; pres., CEO Dependable Ins. Group, Jacksonville, 1988-91; pres. DeMell Group, Ponte Vedra Beach, Fla., 1991—2001, Polartic Enterprises LLC, 2007—. Conflict resolution specialist Ctr. for Internat. Understanding, St. Louis; adv. dir. internat. leadership program Washington U., St. Louis, 1998—; mem. Coun. Fgn. Rels. Women and Fgn. Policy Adv. Group, 2002-; chmn. Thomas H. and Diane DeMell Jacobsen PhD Found., 2011-. Creator, lender (exhibitions) The Art of Seating: 200 Yrs. Am. Design, 2011—, Thirteen Mus. in US and Can. Adv. commr., hon. trustee St. Louis Art Mus., 1992—; bd. dirs. World Affairs Coun. of Jax, 2005—10, mem. adv. bd., 2010—. Recipient Allison Atlas award, Nat. Marrow Donor Program, 2003, Joint Civilian Orientation Conf. 73, 2007; named Arts & Scis. Disting. Alumna of Yr., Washington U., 2005, Disting. Alumna of Yr. award, Wash. U. St. Louis, 2012. Avocations: bicycling, art, woodworking. Home and Office: Polartic Enterprises LLC 830 A1A N Ste 13 PMB 411 Ponte Vedra Beach FL 32082

JACOBSON, ANTONE GARDNER, retired zoology educator; b. nr. Salt Lake City, May 22, 1929; s. Rufus Ingman and Marvell (Gardner) J.; m. Jacqueline James, July 26, 1962; children: Lauren, Eric. AB, Harvard U., 1951; PhD, Stanford U., 1955. Mem. faculty dept. zoology U. Tex., Austin, 1957—, assoc. prof., 1961-68, prof., 1968-97, prof. emeritus, 1997—; instr. Marine Biol. Lab., Woods Hole, Mass., 1969-70; ret., 1997. Contbr. articles to profl. jours. Harvard Nat. scholar, 1947-51, Henry Newell Honors scholar, 1951-55. Mem. Soc. Devel. Biology, Soc. Integrative & Comparative Biology, Am. Assn. Anatomists, Sigma Xi. Home: 201 Skyline Dr West Lake Hills TX 78746-3610 Office: Univ Tex MCDB Pat Labs 1 University Sta C1000 Austin TX 78712-0253 Office Phone: 512-471-5403. Business E-Mail: antone@mail.utexas.edu.

JACOBSON, HARRY RUDOLF, hospital administrator, physician; MD, U. Ill., 1972. Resident, internal medicine Johns Hopkins University; resident, nephrology U. Tex. Health Sci. Ctr.; chief, nephrology U.S. Army Surg. Rsch. Ctr., Brooke Army Med. Ctr., 1976—78; faculty mem. U. Tex. Southwestern Med. Sch., Dallas, 1978—81; prof., medicine, dir., nephrology divsn. Vanderbilt Med. Sch., 1981—97, CEO, vice chancellor, health affairs, 1997—. Bd. dirs. Nashville Health Care Coun., Mid. Tenn. Coun., Boy Scouts Am., Health Gate, Inc., CSA, Inc., Renal Care Group, Kinetic Concepts, Inc. Contbr. articles to profl. jours.; co-editor: The Principles and Practice of Nephrology. Mem.: Inst. Medicine, Soc. Med. Adminstrs. (pres.), Assn. Am. Physicians, Am. Soc. Clin. Investigation. Office: Vanderbilt University Medical Center 21st Ave S and Medical Center Dr Nashville TN 37232 Office Phone: 615-322-5000. Business E-Mail: hjacobson@vanderbilt.edu.

JACOBSON, LAWRENCE ALBERT, professional society administrator, lawyer; b. Rockville Ctr., NY, May 27, 1948; BA, Wheaton Coll., Ill., 1970, MA in History, 1972; JD, John Marshall Law Sch., Chgo., 1984. Bar: Ill. 1984. Mgr. Servicemaster Industries, Downers Grove, Ill., 1972-84; v.p. Mktg. Bldg. Owners and Mgrs. Inst., Annapolis, Md., 1984-88, pres., 1988-92, CEO, 1992-93; exec. dir. Nat. Assn. Search and Rescue, Chantilly, Va., 1994, exec. v.p., 1994; exec. dir. Assn. Specialists in Cleaning & Restoration, MATHCOUNTS Found., Alexandria, Va., NSPE, Alexandria, 2007—. Mem.: Am. Nat. Stds. Inst., Am. Soc. Assn. Execs. Office: NSPE 1420 King St Alexandria VA 22314 Office Phone: 703-684-2800. Office Fax: 703-836-4875.

JACOBSON, LEONARD I., psychologist, educator; b. Bklyn., Aug. 9, 1940; s. Harry L. and Violet (Natkin) J. AB cum laude, CUNY, 1961; PhD, SUNY-Buffalo, 1966. Research psychologist Children's Hosp., Buffalo, 1965-66; asst. prof. psycholgy U. Miami, Coral Gables, Fla., 1966-71, assoc. prof., 1971-76, prof., 1976—. Adj. asst. prof. Guidance Ctr.-U. Miami, Coral Gables, 1969-70; prof. pediatrics U. Miami Sch. Medicine, 1980—; cons. Miami Mental Health Ctr., 1968-79, Sunland Tng. Ctr. at Miami, Opa-Locka, 1969-72, Camarillo State Hosp. (Calif.), 1970, Mailman Ctr. for Child Devel.-U. Miami Sch. Medicine, 1972-75, Miami Lighthouse for the Blind, 1975—; mem. outcome study panel Dade-Monroe Mental Health Bd., 1980; cons. Metro-Dade Pub. Safety Dept., 1982; mem. panel of psychologists, State of Fla., 1982—; dir. psychology Psychol. Specialists, P.A., 1987—. Contbr. articles to profl. jours. USPHS clin. fellow, 1962-63; grantee NSF, 1966-68, NIMH, 1967-68, NIH, 1968, Soc. Psychol. Study Social Issues, 1969, NASA, 1969-71 Fellow Am. Assn. Med. Psychotherapists (diplomate); mem. Am. Psychol. Assn., Southeastern Psychol. Assn., Western Psychol. Assn., Fla. Psychol. Assn., AAAS, Assn. Advancement of Behavior Therapy, Am. Assn. Workers for the Blind, Soc. Research in Child Devel., Psychonomic Soc., Soc. Psychotherapy Research, InterAmerican Assn. Psychology, Internat. Assn. Applied Psychology, Sigma Xi, Psi Chi Republican. Office: Univ Miami 7000 SW 62d Ave PH-L South Miami FL 33143 Personal E-mail: lijacobson@aol.com.

JACOBSON, MELVIN JOSEPH, mathematician, educator; b. Providence, Nov. 25, 1928; s. Charles and Rose (Chusmir) J.; m. Dorothy Troup, June 8, 1952 (div. Aug. 1985); children: Deborah Lynn, Donald Bruce; m. Gertrude R. Ackerman, Jan. 27, 2002. AB, Brown U., 1950; MS, Carnegie Inst. Tech., Pitts., 1952, PhD, 1954. Instr. Carnegie Inst. Tech., 1953-54; mem. tech. staff Bell Tel. Labs., Whippany, NJ, 1954-56; asst. prof. math. Rensselaer Poly. Inst., Troy, NY, 1956-58, assoc. prof., 1958-63, prof., 1963-90, prof. emeritus, rsch. cons., 1991—; prin. investigator and cons. Office Naval Rsch. Contracts, 1957-96; contract Unisys. Corp., 1985-88; prin. investigator NSF grant, 1962-67; contract Inst. for Naval Oceanography, 1987-91, NASA, 1988-91, U.S. Mil. Acad. (for U.S. Army Atmospheric Sci. Lab.), West Point, NY, 1989-91. Vis. prof. Rosenstiel Sch. Marine and Atmospheric Sci., U. Miami, Fla., 1963-64, adj. prof., 1969-72; cons. to industry, NRC. Contbr. articles to numerous publs. Fellow Acoustical Soc. Am.; mem. AAUP, Sigma Xi, Phi Kappa Phi, Pi Mu Epsilon. Home: 4705 Chandlers Forde Sarasota FL 34235-7120 Home Phone: 941-379-3251. Personal E-mail: melgeet@comcast.net.

JACOBUS, ARTHUR, performing company executive; b. 1940; Artist's diploma, Academia di Musica, Italy, 1976; BBA, Columbia Coll., 1978; MA in Arts Adminstrn., Golden Gate U., 1982, MBA, 1984; MA in Human Resources Mgmt., Pepperdine U., 1980; Grad. Exec. Mgmt. Program, U. Wash., 1986; Grad. Strategic Perspectives Program, Harvard U., 1995. Bandleader, chief musician US Navy 6th Fleet, 1966—69; instr., chief musician US Navy Sch. Music, Little Creek, Va., 1969—71; bandleader, master chief musician CinC South Band, 1971—76; bandmaster, chief warrant officer US Navy Band San Francisco, 1976—79; founder, dir. NATO Internat. Band, Naples, 1973-79; pres., gen. mgr. Oakland Symphony, 1979-84; pres., CEO Pacific N.W. Ballet, Seattle, 1984-93; exec. dir. San Francisco Ballet, 1993—2002; pres. Ky. Ctr. for the Performing Arts, 2002—05, The American Ctr. for Wine Food & the Arts, 2005—08; exec. dir. The Atlanta Ballet, Inc., 2010—. Mem. Dance/USA. Office: The Atlanta Ballet Inc 1695 Marietta Blvd NW Atlanta GA 30318-3644 Office Phone: 404-873-5811. Office Fax: 404-874-7905.

JACOBUS, CHARLES JOSEPH, lawyer, writer; b. Ponca City, Okla., Aug. 21, 1947; s. David William and Louise Graham Jacobus; m. Heather Jeanne Jones, June 6, 1970; children: Mary Helen, Charles J. Jr. BS, U. Houston, 1970, JD, 1973. Bar: Tex. 1973; cert. specialist residential and commercial real estate law Tex. Bd. Legal Specialization. Pvt. practice, Houston, 1973-75; staff counsel Tenneco Realty, Inc., Houston, 1975-78, v.p., gen. counsel, 1979—83; chief legal counsel Speedy Muffler King, Deerfield, 1978-79; v.p. Commerce Title Co., Houston, 1983-85; exec. v.p. Charter Title Co., Houston, 1986—; ptnr. Jacobus & Melamed PC, Houston, 1988-97; shareholder Jenkens & Gilchrist, Houston, 1998-99; pvt. practice Bellaire, Tex., 1999—; advisory title officer Fidelity Nat. Title Insurance Co., 2010—. Adj. faculty Tex. A&M U., 1986-90; mem. exec. adv. com., adj. prof. U. Houston Law Ctr., U. H. Bauer Sch. Bus., Houston C.C., Champions Sch. Real Estate; course dir. State Bar Tex., 1990; chmn. Tex. Land Title Inst., 2001; co-chmn. broker-lawyer com. Tex. Real Estate Commn. Author: Real Estate Law, 2d edit., 1996, Texas Real Estate Law, 11th edit.; co-author: Mastering Real Estate Titles and Title Insurance in Texas, 1996, Georgia Real Estate, 2007, Ohio Real Estate, 2d edit., 1990, Tex. Real Estate, 11th edit., 2008, Calif. Real Estate, 1989, Keeping Current with Texas Real Estate, updated annually, Real Estate Principles, 11th edit., 2009, Real Estate, An Introduction to the Profession, 11th edit., 2009, Texas Title Insurance, updated annually, Texas Real Estate Brokerage and the Law of Agency, 2008-; co-author: Real Estate Brokerage Law and Practice; editor: Building Blocks of a Commercial Transaction, 1992, Building Blocks of a Residential Real Estate Transaction, 1994, Texas Real Estate Law Deskbook, 1995; editor-in-chief Tex. Forms Manual. Chmn. Planning and Zoning Commn., Bellaire, Tex., 1976-77; bd. dirs. Tax Increment Fin. Dist., Bellaire, 1984-91; chmn. task force on edn. Tex. Real Estate Commn.; chmn. profl. adv. com. dept. urban and regional planning Tex. A&M U., 1988-89; 1st asst. scoutmaster Boy Scout World Jamboree, Holland, 1995, scoutmaster, Chile, 1999; scoutmaster Nat. Boy Scout Jamboree, 1997, 1st asst. scoutmaster, 2001; mayor City of Bellaire, 1998-2000; sec.-treas. Harris County Mayors and Coun. Assn. 1999. Recipient Peggy Hayes Tchg. Excellence award TLTA, 1993, Don Roose award of excellence in real estate edn., 2001. Mem. ABA (acquisitions editor books and pubs. com. 1994-2001, chmn. brokers and brokerage com. 1986-93), Internat. Wine Food Soc. (pres. Houston chpt. 1993-94), Am. Coll. Real Estate Lawyers, Tex. Land Title Assn. (chmn. forms manual com., TREC earnest money contract task force), State Bar Tex. (mem. coun. of real estate, probate and trust law sect. 2002-06, chmn. title ins. com., 2006-2007, Disting. Tex. Real Estate atty. Lifetime Achievement award Probate Trust Law Sect. State Bar Tex. 2012, Disting. Eagle Scout award, 2013), Tex. Real Estate Ctrs. MCE Writing Com., Tex. Real Estate Tchrs. Assn. (Outstanding Real Estate Educator 1986, treas. 2007, pres. 2009), Houston Real Estate Lawyers Coun., Real Estate Educator's Assn. (pres. 1987-88, bd. dirs., 2009-, Real Estate Educator of Yr. 1986, 2000, Disting. Career award 2004), Houston Bar Assn. (chmn. real estate sect. 1987-88), Internat. Wine and Food Soc. (bd. dirs.), South Ctrl. Educator's Group (pres. 2000-02, treas. 2007-09), Bellaire/S.W. Houston C. of C. (Outstanding Businessman of Yr. 1990, chmn. Tex. Real Estate Commns. Edn. Task Force, 1999-2000), U. Tex. Mortgage Lending Inst. (faculty), U. Houston Law Alumni Assn. (bd. dirs. 1999-2005), Les Amis Escoffier. Republican. Roman Catholic. Home: 5223 Pine St Bellaire TX 77401-4820 Office: Ste 615 6750 West Loop S Bellaire TX 77401-4525 Office Phone: 713-839-8800. E-mail: jacobusbellaire@aol.com.

JACOBY, LOWELL EDWIN (JAKE JACOBY), information technology executive; b. Aug. 28, 1945; m. Celia L. Williams, Dec. 9, 1975. BS in Economics, U. Md.; M in Nat. Security Affairs, Naval Postgrad. Sch.; grad., Aviation Officer Can. Sch., 1969; attended, Navy Postgrad. Sch., 1975. Head, naval ops. br. Navy Field Operational Intelligence Office, dir. Naval Surveillance Info. Ctr.; asst. chief of staff, intelligence carrier group eight USS Nimitz Battle Group, Mediterranean; intelligence placement officer, jr. officer assignment officer Naval Mil. Personnel Command, 1979—81; asst. chief of staff, intelligence carrier group eight USS SC, North Atlantic, 1985; asst. chief of staff intelligence for comdr. in chief U.S. Pacific fleet, 1990—92; commdg. officer Joint Intelligence Ctr. Pacific, 1992—94; dir. intelligence U.S. Pacific Command, 1994—97; rear admiral USN, 1997; comdr. Office Naval Intelligence, 1997—99; dir., Joint Staff J-2 The Pentagon, Washington, 1999—2002; exec. v.p., strategic intelligence opportunities CACI International, Inc., Arlington, Va., 2006—. Bd. dirs. Def. Intelligence Agy. Decorated Def. Disting. Svc. medal, Navy Disting. Svc. medal, Def. Superior Svc. medal, 3 Meritorious Svc. medals, 2 Legion of Merit medals, 2 Navy Commendation medals, Navy Achievement medal, Nat. Intelligence Medal for Achievement Dir. Ctr. Intelligence, Australian Chief of Def. Commendation. Office: CACI International Inc 1100 N Glebe Rd Arlington VA 22201 Office Phone: 703-841-7800. Office Fax: 703-841-7882. E-mail: ljacoby@caci.com.

JACOBY, WILLIAM JEROME, JR., retired military officer, internist; b. Mt. Carmel, Pa., Aug. 9, 1925; s. William Jerome and Florence Marie Jacoby; m. Joeann J. Powroznick, May 5, 1956; children: William Jerome, Teresa Marie. AB, Emory U., 1946; MD, Jefferson Med. Coll., 1950. Diplomate Am. Bd. Internal Medicine. Commd. lt. (j.g.) M.C., USN, 1950, advanced through grades to rear adm., 1972; intern Jefferson Med. Coll. Hosp., Phila., 1950-51, resident in internal medicine, 1951-52, 55-56; Am. Heart Assn. fellow, 1956-57; chmn. dept. medicine U.S. Naval Hosps. Gt. Lakes, Ill., 1964-69, Phila., 1969-72; chmn. dept. medicine, dir. edn. and rsch. Nat. Naval Med. Ctr., Bethesda, Md., 1972-75; comdg. officer Naval Regional Med. Ctr., Portsmouth, Va., 1975-78; dir. med. svcs. VA Cen. Office, Washington, 1978-80, dep. chief med. dir., 1980-83. Assoc. clin. prof. Jefferson Med. Coll., 1969—; prof. medicine George Washington U. Med. Sch., 1972, Eastern Va. Sch. Medicine, Norfolk, 1976-78; mem. adv. coun. Nat. Heart, Lung and Blood Inst., NIH, 1972-75. Contbr. articles to profl. jours. Decorated Legion of Merit, Meritorious Svc. medal. Fellow ACP (Laureate award 1996); mem. Assn. Mil. Surgeons (Founders medal 1974), Alpha Omega Alpha, Phi Beta Pi. Roman Catholic. Home: 737 E Tazewells Way Williamsburg VA 23185-6521

JACQUEMIN, JOHN MICHAEL, hotel executive, equipment leasing company executive; b. Paris, Sept. 20, 1946; came to U.S., 1952; s. Claude and Jeanine (Frantz) J.; m. Tracie Ann Jensen, June 18, 1988; 1 child, Juliana Morgan. BA, Pa. State U., 1968; MBA, Dartmouth Coll., 1973. Fin. analyst Radnor Assocs., King of Prussia, Pa., 1973-74; mgmt. cons. Coopers & Lybrand, Phila., 1974-77; v.p. finance CFC Corp., Reading, Pa., 1977-82; pres. MTV Leasing Corp., Arlington, Va., 1982—; pres., CEO Mooring Financial Corp., 1995—. Bd. dirs. George Washington U. Health Plan, Washington, 1988—. Chmn. D.C. legis. com. Greater Washington Bd. Trade, 1986—; vol. Mentors, Inc., Washington, 1988—; mem. finance com. D.C. Mayoral campaign, Washington, 1990. Mem. Potomac Club (chmn. bd. dirs. 1985-88), Toastmasters, Washington Area Sailing Soc. (bd. dirs. 1986-88). Republican. Avocations: sailing, scuba diving, tennis, skiing, triathalons. Office: MTV Leasing Corp 2000 14th St N Ste 710 Arlington VA 22201-2539 also: Mooring Financial Corp 8614 Westwood Ctr Dr Vienna VA 22182-2233 Office Phone: 703-917-0707. Business E-Mail: john.jacquemin@pngaming.com.

JAEGER, INA CLAIRE, music educator, violinist; b. Ashtabula, Ohio, July 18, 1929; d. Norman Clare and Vivien Elizabeth (Cole) Burlingham; m. Gerald Byrd Forbes, Aug. 28, 1954 (div. 1967); 1 child, David; m. Marc Jules Jaeger, June 23, 1973; children: Dominic, Olivia. MusB with distinction, Eastman Sch. Music, 1952, MusM, 1955. Violinist Rochester (N.Y.) Philharm. Orch., 1953-54, Fla. String Quartet, Gainesville, 1963-66, New Orleans Philharm. Orch., 1966-67; prof. music, violinist U. Fla., Gainesville, 1967-92, prof. emeritus, 1992—. Author: Basic Elements in Music Theory: A Modular Program of Instruction, 1976, Harmonic Dictation Exercises, Progressions, Answers, and Cassette Tapes: Neapolitan Sixth Chords and Augmented Sixth Chords, 1990, Harmonic Dictation Exercises, Progressions, Answers, and Cassette Tapes: Secondary Dominant Chords and Secondary Leading Tone Chords, 1991, (with C. White) Fundamentals of Music Theory, 1973; contbr. articles to profl. jours.; performer various recordings 1972, 74, 76, 78, 87. Faculty rsch. grantee U. Fla., 1970, 73, 75, 80-81, 89, 90, 91; named Tchr. of Yr., 1991. Mem. Sigma Alpha Iota (Sword of Honor award 1952). Avocations: gardening, reading, travel. Home: 5915 SW 36th Way Gainesville FL 32608-5150

JAEGER, RICHARD CHARLES, electrical engineer, educator, science association director; b. NYC, Sept. 2, 1944; s. O. Fred and Mary Jane (Shatzer) J.; m. Joan Carol Hill, Dec. 28, 1964; children: Peter, Stephanie. BSEE with high honors, U. Fla., 1966, M in Elec. Engring., 1966, PhD in Elec. Engring., 1969. Staff engr. IBM Corp., Boca Raton, Fla., 1969—72, adv. engr., 1972-74, 77-79, rsch. staff Yorktown Heights, NY, 1974—76; assoc. prof. Auburn (Ala.) U., 1979—82, prof. elec. engring. dept., 1982—90, alumni prof., 1983—88, disting. prof., 1990—2007; prof. emeritus Auburn U., Ala., 2008—; dir. Ala. Microelectronics Ctr., Auburn, 1984—2000, dir. wireless engring., 2001—03. Program com. Internat. Solid State Circuits Conf., San Francisco and N.Y.C., 1978-93, program vice-chmn., 1992, program chmn., 1993; program co-chmn. Internat. VLSI Cirs. Symposium, Kyoto, Japan, 1989, conf. chmn., Honolulu, 1990, exec. comm. chair, 2000-06. Author: Introduction to Microelectronic Fabrication, 1988, 2d edit., 2002, Microelectronic Circuit Design, 1997, 4th edit., 2010, Computerized Circuit Analysis Using SPICE Programs, 1997 (IEEE Edn. Soc. McGraw Hill/Jacob Millman award 1998); editor: IEEE Jour. Solid State Cirs., 1995-98; contbr. over 200 articles to profl. jours.; patentee in field. Grantee NSF, Semicondr. Rsch. Corp., Dept. Def., Ala. Rsch. Inst. Fellow IEEE (pres. solid state cirs. coun. 1990-91, v.p. 1988-89, sec. 1984-87, Inst. Level award 2004); mem. Computer Soc. IEEE (bd. govs. 1985-86, Outstanding Contbn. award 1984, Golden Core award 1996), IEEE Solid-State Cirs. Soc. (adcom mem. 1996—, v.p. 2004-05, pres. 2006-07, past pres. 2008-09, Outstanding Contbn. award 1998, Millenium medal 2000, Outstanding Svc. award 2004, 2010). Home: 2160 Estate Dr Auburn AL 36830 Office: Auburn U Elec and Computer Engring 200 Broun Hall Auburn AL 36849-5201 Office Phone: 334-844-1871. Business E-Mail: rj@jaegerengineering.com.

JAFFE, BARBARA GEFEN, finance company executive; b. Jacksonville, Fla., Mar. 21, 1948; d. Sidney J. and Lois (Isaac) Gefen; m. Lawrence L. Jaffe, Nov. 30, 1980; children: Bradley, Sanford. Student, U. Fla., 1966—68, Jacksonville U., 1968—70. Newspaper reporter Fla. Times Union, Jacksonville, 1966—74; vice-chair Jacksonville Mayor's Adv. Com. Status of Women, 1976—80; sr. v.p. investments, asst. mgr. Prudential-Bache Securities, Jacksonville, 1979; sr. v.p. investments Wachovia Securities, Jacksonville; coun. pres. Jacksonville; bd. mem., bd. chair; mem. coun. Jacksonville U., 1983—; founding bd. mem. Jacksonville Jewish Found., 1996—. Chair Women and the Law, 1978; mem. bd. govs. Jacksonville C. of C. Recipient Endowment Achievement award, United Jewish Cmtys., 2007; named one of Top 100 Women Fin. Advisors Barron's, 2008. Mem.: Hadassah Lodge (pres. 1976). Democrat. Jewish. Avocations: art, golf. Office: Morgan Stanley Smith Barney 50 N Laura St Ste 2000 Jacksonville FL 32202-3623 Business E-Mail: barbara.g.jaffe@smithbarney.com.

JAFFE, JEFF HUGH, retired food products executive; b. Washington, Dec. 25, 1920; s. Henry A. Jaffe and Mildred (Loewenberg) Auslander; m. Natalie Rubin, Dec. 31, 1945; children: Bonita Jaffe Berens, Holly Anne. BS in Archtl. Engring., Va. Poly. Inst. and State U., 1943. Chmn. bd. dirs., pres. The Chunky Corp. (now Ward Candy, Inc.), 1950-69; pres., CEO candy, chocolate and biscuit group Ward Foods Inc., 1969-71, pres., COO, 1971-72; also bd. dirs. Ward Foods, Inc., 1972-74; chmn. bd. dirs., pres. Schutter Candy Co., 1958-67, Klotz Confection Co., 1960-67; pres., CEO The Schrafft Candy Co., 1974-78; v.p. consumer products group Gulf and Western Industries, 1974-78; pres., CEO Bernan Foods, Inc., 1980-85, ret., 1985. Bd. dirs. Cmty. Nat. Bank of S.I., N.Y., Ward Foods, Inc., Ward Candy Co., Oxford Energy Co.; guest lectr. Harvard Bus. Sch., 1970-84. Bd. dirs., nat. treas. Young Pres.'s Orgn., Woodmere Acad., Martin County (Fla.) Libr. Found.; bd. dirs. Village Hewlett Bay Park; sponsor and patron Fla. Laws of Life Essay Contest for H.S. Students, Martin County, 1999-. Mem. Assn. Mfrs. of Confectionery and Chocolate (past chmn.), Candy Execs. Club, Property Owners Assn. (Sailfish Point, Fla., pres., chmn. transition com., chmn. emeritus, CEO). Home: 128 Via Mariposa Palm Beach Gardens FL 33418-6211

JAFFE, JONATHAN M., construction executive; Grad., U. Fla., Gainesville; student in Architecture, Ga. Inst. Tech. Joined Lennar Corp., Miami, Fla., 1983, regional pres. homebuilding divsn., v.p., 1994—, head Western Region ops. Calif., 1996—2004, bd. dirs., 1997—2004, COO, 2004—. Bd. dirs. HomeAid Am. Named to Calif. Bldg. Industry Found. Hall of Fame. Office: Lennar Corp 700 NW 107th Ave Ste 400 Miami FL 33172 Office Phone: 305-559-4000. Office Fax: 305-226-4158.

JAFFE, RUSSELL MERRITT, pathologist, research director; b. Albany, NY, Jan. 1, 1947; AB cum laude, Boston U., 1972, MD with honors, 1972, PhD in Biochemistry, 1972. Diplomate Am. Bd. Pathology (clin., chem.), Nat. Bd. Med. Examiners. Med. intern Boston U. Med. Ctr., 1972-73; resident in clin. pathology NIH, Bethesda, Md., 1973-75, sr. staff physician clin. pathology dept., 1973-79, chief resident tng. program clin. chemistry sect., 1976-79; fellow health rsch., practice, policy devel. Health Studies Collegium, 1979—; dir. ELISA/ACT Biotech., Sterling, Va., 1987—, Princeton BioCenter, 1989-92. Prin. faculty Oriental Med. Strategy in Western Med. Practice, HSC, N.Y.C., 1980-85. Assoc. editor The New Physician, 1971-72, sr. assoc. editor, 1972-73. Bd. govs. Light Found., 1980-99. Comdr. USPHS, 1973-79. Recipient Nat. Rsch. award Am. Acad. Med. Preventics, 1979, J.D. Lane award USPHS, 1975, Excellence in Rsch. award Mead Johnson, 1969, Man of Yr. award Hillel Found., 1967. Fellow Am. Coll. Nutrition, Am. In-Vitro Allergy/Immunology Soc., Am. Soc. Clin. Pathologists; mem. APHA, Am. Assn. Clin. Chemists, Health Studies Collegium (founding chmn. 1990-2012). Achievements include patents in biotechnology and nutritional metabolism; research in fundamental mechanisms measuring, monitoring, and evoking human healing responses; novel delivery systems for better functional bioavailability of essential nutrients delivering safer predictive results. Office: Health Studies Collegium 44621 Guilford Dr #150 Ashburn VA 20147

JAFFE, STEPHEN L., neurologist, educator, researcher; b. NYC; s. Walter and Pearl Jaffe; m. Nancy Marie Holman; children: Adam Byron, Emily Blythe. BA in Philosophy, Purdue U., W. Lafayette, Ind., 1964; MD, Cornell U. Méd. Coll., NY, 1968. Lic. Va. Bd. Med. Examiners, 1969, Ill. Dept. Registration & Edn., 1972, diplomate Nat. Bd. Med. Examiners, 1969, Am. Bd. Psychiatry & Neurolgy, 1974, cert. Fed. State Méd. Bbs. US, 2001; lic. La. State Bd. Med. Examiners, 2001. Externship neurology Inst. Neurology, Queen Square, London, 1967; externship psychiatry Payne Whitney Clinic, Cornell U. Méd. Coll., 1968; intern straight medicine U. Va. Hosp., Charlottesville, 1969, house staff executive, 1970, v.p., 1971, resident neurology, 1972; asst. prof. medicine neurology, neurosci. curriculum coord. Southern Ill. U. Sch. Medicine, 1972—75, acting dir., family practice residency program, 1974—75; clin. prof. neurology Méd. Coll. Va., 1999—2001; Joanna Gunning Magale prof. neurology La. State U., Sch. Medicine-Shreveport, 2001—; course dir., active staff La. State U., Health Sci. Ctr., 2003—. Clin. practice, 1972—; lectr., paper presenter at numerous internat. & nat. neurosci. meeting; editl. bd. mem. J. Pédiatric Neurology, Turkey, J. Pediatric Epilepsy, Turkey. Contbr. articles to profl. jours. & publs. With 29th Inf. Divsn., 94th Combat Support Hosp., US Army, 1994—2006. Col. RC US Army, 2002—06. Decorated Meritorious Svc. medal, 2 Army Commendation medals. Fellow: Am. Acad. Neurology; mem.: N.Am. Ménopause Soc., Am. Clin. Neurophysiology Soc., Internat. Brain Rsch. Orgn., Am. Epilepsy Soc., Soc. Neuroscie., Delta Rho Kappa. Achievements include research in neurophysiologic correlates of behavior, neurotransmission/neuromodulation; neuromuscular disease, headache, epilepsy, stroke, MS, clinical/basic neurophysiology, molecular genetics, médical éducation, curriculum development. Avocations: languages, horseback riding. Office: La State University Health Sci Ctr Dept Neurology 1501 Kings Hwy PO Box 33932 Shreveport LA 71103 Office Phone: 318-675-4941. Office Fax: 318-675-6382. Business E-Mail: sjaffe1@lsuhsc.edu.*

JAFFE, SUSAN, dean, ballerina; b. Washington, 1962; Student, Md. Sch. Ballet, Sch. American Ballet, American Ballet Theatre Sch.; D of Arts (hon.), Tex. Christian U., 2010. With American Ballet Theatre II, 1978-80; with American Ballet Theatre, 1980—, soloist, 1981-83, prin. dancer, 1983—2002; faculty mem. Jacqueline Kennedy Onassis Sch., 2002—12, ballet mistress, 2010—12; co-founder Princeton Dance & Theatre Studio, Princeton, NJ, 2003—; dean Sch. Dance U. NC Sch. Arts, Winston-Salem, 2012—. Repertoire includes: Le Corsaire, The Merry Widow (by Ronald Hynd), Apollo, Eugene Onegin (by John Cranko), La Bayadere, Bouree Fantastique, Carmen, Cinderella, Concerto, Duets, Giselle, The Guards of Amager, Push Comes to Shove, Symphonie Concertante, Ballet Imperial, Coppelia, Etudes, Giselle, Jardin auxLilas, Romeo and Juliet, The Sleeping Beauty, Other Dances, Theme and Variations, Swan Lake, La Sylphide, Undertow, Voluntaries, Dim Lustre, Manon, Gala Performance, Don Quioxte, Cruel World, Sextet, The Snow Maiden, Fall River Legend, Grande Pas Classic, Stepping Stones, Without Words (by Nacho Duato), Anastasia, others; created role Lynne Taylor-Corbett's Great Galloping Gottschalk, Bruch Violin Concerto No. 1, Serious Pleasures; appeared Spoleto in An Evening of Jerome Robbins Ballets, 1982, Known by Heart (Twyla Tharp); appeared with Kirov Ballet, 1988; guest appearances with The Royal Swedish Ballet, The Royal Danish Ballet, The English Nat. Ballet, La Scala Ballet, Milan, 1997, 98, The Royal Ballet, 1998, 2000, Stuttgart Ballet, 1998, 2000, The Munich Opera Ballet, The Vienna State Opera Ballet; dir. (movie) Angie, by Martha Koolidge; author: (children's books) Becoming A Ballerina, 2003 Recipient N.Y. Woman-Lancome Paris Woman of Yr. award, 1989, Dance Mag. award, 2003 Office: University North Carolina School of Dance 1533 South Main St Winston Salem NC 27127 Office Phone: 336-770-3399.

JAFFEE, MICHAEL SCOTT, neurologist, military officer; b. Silver Spring, Md., Oct. 6, 1966; BS in Economics, U. Pa., Phila., 1988; MD, U. Va. Sch. Medicine, Charlottesville, 1992. Diplomate Am. Bd. Psychiatry & Neurology, Nat. Bd. Med. Examiners. Resident psychiatry/neurology Wilford Hall USAF Med. Ctr., Lackland Air Force Base, San Antonio, 1992—98, assoc. neurology program dir., 2002—04, neurology program dir., 2004—07; clin. assoc. prof. psychiatry & family pactice U. Nebr. Med. Ctr., Omaha, 1998—2001; chief neurology svc., mental health med. dir. Ehrling-Bergquist Med. Ctr., Omaha, 1998—2001; assoc. clin. prof. psychiatry & neurology U. Tex. Health Sci. Ctr., San Antonio, 2001; nat. dir. Def. & Vets. Brain Injury Ctr., Washington, 2007—. Asst. prof. neurology Uniformed Svcs. Univ. Health Scis., Bethesda, Md. Contbr. articles to profl. jours., chapters to books. Officer commd. as 2nd Lt. USAF, 1988, capt. 1992, maj. 1998, lt. col. 2002, chief med. staff., dep. comdr. med. svcs. Air Force Theater Hosp., 332nd Expeditionary Med. Group, Balad Air Base, Iraq 2006-07. Decorated Achievement Medal USAF, Commendation Medal, Meritorious Svc. Medal; recipient US Surgeon Gen.'s Cert. of Appreciation, 2003. Mem.: Am. Neuropsychiatric Assn., Acad. Psychosomatic Medicine (William Webb Rsch. Fellowship 1997—98), Am. Acad. Neurology, Am. Pyschiat. Assn. Office: Def & Vets Brain Injury Ctr Bldg 1 Rm B209 Walter Reed Army Med Ctr 6900 Georgia Ave NW Washington DC 20307

JAHNCKE, MICHAEL LEE, professor director; BS, U. Wis. Stevens Point, 1975; MS, Cornell U., Ithaca, NY, 1979, PhD, 1986. Prof., dir. Va. Tech, Blacksburg, Va., 1977; program coord. Nat. Marine Fisheries Svc., Pascagoula, Miss., 1992—97, dep. dir., 1992—97, lab. coord. Food technologist Nat. Marine Fisheries Svc., Charleston, SC, 1985—90. Recipient award, USDA, FDA. Mem.: Nat. Adv. Com. (award 1995—2002, 2005—), Aquatic Food Products (chair 1998—99), Va. Sea Grant (rsch. ext. adv. com. 1999—), Global Cold Chain Alliance (sci. advisor 2001—), Seafood HACCP Alliance (steering com. 2000—), Gamma Sigma Delta. Achievements include research in development of a fatty acid analytical method to distinguish wild from cultured fish; development and use HACCP principles to control disease and use of chemicals in aquaculture. Office: VA Tech 102 S King St Hampton VA 23669 Business E-Mail: mjahncke@vt.edu.*

JAKES, T.D. (THOMAS DEXTER JAKES), bishop, author; b. So. Charleston, WV, June 9, 1957; s. Ernest Jakes, Odith Jakes; m. Serita Jakes; 5 children. Founder, CEO Potter's House of Dallas, Inc., 1996—; founder Clay Acad., South Dallas, Tex., 1998—, Metroplex Econ. Devel. Corp., 1998—; founder, CEO TDJ Enterprises, LLC. Host numerous conferences and speaking tours. Author: Can You Stand To Be Blessed?, 1994, The Lady, Her Lover, and Her Lord, 2000, Experiencing Jesus: The Workmanship of the Believer, 2000, God's Leading Lady, 2003, Follow the Star, 2003, HeMotions: Even Strong Men Struggle, 2004, Promises From God for Single Women, 2005, Mama Made the Difference, 2006 (Quills award religion/spirituality The Quills Literacy Found., 2006, NAACP Image award best instructional book, 2007), Promises from God for Parents, 2006, His Lady: Sacred Promises for God's Woman, 2006, Not Easily Broken: A Novel, 2006, Reposition Yourself: Living Life Without Limits, 2007, T.D. Jakes Speaks to Men, 3-in-1, 2007, Before You Do: Making Great Decisions That You Won't Regret, 2008 (Publishers Weekly bestseller), Power for Living, 2009, The Memory Quilt: A Christmas Story for Our Times, 2009, Making Great Decisions Reflections: For a Life Without Limits, 2009, Wisdom from T.D. Jakes, 2010, 64 Lessons for a Life Without Limits, 2011, Let It Go: Forgive So You Can Be Forgiven, 2012, Healing Wounds of the Past, So You Call Yourself a Man?, Loose That Man and Let Him Go, Anointing Fall On Me: Accessing the Power of the Holy Spirit, Your Harvest Without Limits, God's Trophy Woman, Beside Every Good Man, 10 Commandments of Working in a Hostile Environment, Woman Thou Art Loosed!: Healing the Wounds of the Past, Why? Because You Are Anointed, Reposition Yourself: Living Life Without Limits, Overcoming the Enemy: The Spiritual Warfare of the Believer, Strength to Stand: Overcoming, Succeeding, Thriving, Advancing, Winning, Maximize the Moment: God's Action Plan for Your Life, Cover Girls, Release Your Anointing 40-Day Devotional Journal: Tapping the Power of the Holy Spirit in You, From the Cross to Pentecost: God's Passionate Love for Us Revealed, Water in the Wilderness, Healing, Blessings, and Freedom: 365-Day Devotional & Journal, Life Overflowing: 6 Pillars for Abundant Living, Life Overflowing: The Spiritual Walk of the Believer, Intimacy with God: The Spiritual Worship of the Beliver, Release Your Destiny, Release Your Anointing, Help I'm Raising My Children Alone: A Guide for Single Parents and Those Who Sometimes Feel They Are Single, Loved By God: The Spiritual Wealth of the Believer, The Great Investment: Balancing Faith, Family and Finance to Build a Rich Spiritual Life, God's Leading Ladies Workbook: Taking Your Place on Life's Center Stage, Celebrating Marriage: The Spiritual Wedding of the Believer, The Harvest, Naked and Not Ashamed: We've Been Afraid to Reveal What God Longs to Heal, When Shepherds Bleed: A Study Guide for Wounded Pastors; co-author: The Leadership Gap: How to Build, Motivate and Organize a Great Ministry Team; prodr.: gospel albums (Grammy award, Best Gospel Choir or Chorus Album, 2004). Named one of 100 Most Influential Black Americans, Ebony mag., 2006; named to Power 150, 2008. Office: TD Jakes Ministries Inc PO Box 5390 Dallas TX 75208

JAKUBS, DEBORAH, university librarian; BA, U. Wis. Madison; MLIS, U. Calif. Berkeley; PhD in Latin Am. History, Stanford U., 1986. Joined Duke U., Durham, NC, 1983, various positions including libr. for Latin Am. & Iberia, head internat. and area studies dept. and dir. collections svc., Rita DiGiallonardo Holloway univ. libr., vice provost libr. affairs, 2005—. Assoc. dir. U. NC-Duke U. Consortium in Latin Am. Studies, 1995—97, 2000—02, dir., 1997—99; chair Area Studies Coun. of Ctr. for Rsch. Libr.; mem. steering com. Program for Latin Am. Libr. & Archival Collections Harvard U.; adj. prof. history Duke U. Mem.: Assn. Rsch. Libraries (vis. program officer 1996—2002). Office: Duke University Libraries Perkins Libr 112 PO Box 90193 Durham NC 27708-0193 Office Phone: 919-660-5800. Business E-Mail: deborah.jakubs@duke.edu.

JAMAIL, JOSEPH DAHR, JR., lawyer; b. Houston, Oct. 19, 1925; s. Joseph Dahr and Marie (Anton) Jamail; m. Lillie Mae Hage, Aug. 28, 1949 (dec.); children: Joseph Dahr III, Randall Hage, Robert Lee. BA, U. Tex., 1950; LLB, U. Tex. Sch. Law, 1953. Bar: Tex. 1952. Asst. dist. atty., Harris County, Tex., 1953—55; founder, owner Jamail & Kolius, Houston, 1953—. Author: (autobiography) Lawyer: My Trials and Jubilations, 2003; contbr. articles to profl. jours. Grand marshall Martin Luther King Day Parade, Houston, 1989; co-chair Tex. Access to Justice Commn. Recipient Jurisprudence award, Anti-Defamation League B'nai B'rith, 1989, Brotherhood award, Nat. Conf. Christians & Jews, 1993, War Horse award, Southern Trial Lawyers Assn., 1993, Outstanding Alumnus award, U. Tex. Sch. Law, 1996; named Trial Lawyer of Century, Calif. Trial Lawyers, 1999; named one of Forbes 400: Richest Americans, 2006—. Fellow: Internat. Acad. Trial Lawyers, Internat. Soc. Barristers, Internat. Acad. Law & Sci., Tex. Bar Found. (life); mem.: ABA, World Jurist Assn., World Assn. Lawyers, American Judicature Soc., Assn. Trial Lawyers America, Inner Circle Advocates (Outstanding Fifty Yr. Lawyer award 2003), State Bar Tex., Houston Bar Assn., American Coll. Trial Lawyers, U. Tex. Ex-Students' Assn. (life), Delta Theta Phi, Order of Barristers. Achievements include recognition as one of the country's leading trial lawyers; represented Pennzoil Co. in a lawsuit against Texaco Inc. in 1985, receiving the largest jury verdict upheld on appeal in legal history; has tried more than 500 jury and bench trials, which resulted in more than $13 billion in judgments for his clients; has given large donations to th University of Texas, having a swim-ming center, a law school pavilion and the foot-ball field named for him. Office: Jamail & Kolius 500 Dallas St, Suite 3434 Houston TX 77002-4793 Office Phone: 713-574-9419. Office Fax: 713-651-1957.

JAMEEL, HASAN, chemical engineering professor; BS, Tex. A&M U., 1975; PhD in Chem. Engring., Princeton U., 1980. With International Paper Co., 1979—87; prof. Dept. Wood & Paper Sci. College Natural Resources, NC State University, 1987—, Ellis Signe Olsen prof. pulp and paper tech. Bd. dirs. Packaging Corp. of America (PCA), 2008—. Contbr. articles to profl. jours. Recipient Bd. Gov.'s Coll. Award for Excellence in Tchg., Coll. Natural Resources, NC State Coll., 2009. Fellow: TAPPI (Johan C.F.C. Richter Prize 2005, David Wetherhorn Award 1994), Internat. Acad. Wood Sci.; mem.: AIChE. Office: Department of Forest Biomaterials NC State University Box 8005 Raleigh NC 27695 Office Phone: 919-515-7739. Office Fax: 919-515-6302.

JAMES, ALLIX BLEDSOE, retired university president; b. Marshall, Tex., Dec. 17, 1922; s. Samuel Horace and Tannie Etta (Judkins) James; m. Sue Nickens, Feb. 14, 1945; children: Alvan Bosworth, Portia Veann. AB, Va. Union U., 1944, MDiv, 1946; ThM, Union Theol. Sem. Va., 1949, ThD, 1957; postgrad., Boston U., summer 1951, Pa. State U., summer 1957; LLD, U. Richmond, 1970; DD, St. Paul's Coll., 1980. Ordained to ministry Bapt. Ch., 1942. Moderator No. Neck Bapt. Assn., 1950-52; minister Union Zion Bapt. Ch., Gloucester, Va., 1944-53, Mt. Zion Bapt. Ch., Downings, Va., 1945-57, 3d Union Bapt. Ch., King William, Va., 1953-70; dean students Va. Union U., Richmond, Va., 1950-57, dean Sch. Theology, 1957-70, Henderson-Griffith prof. pastoral theology, v.p., 1960-70, pres., 1970-79, ret., 1979, pres. emeritus, 1975—85, chancellor, 1985-93, pres. emeritus, 1993—. Author: Calling a Pastor in a Baptist Church, Threescore and Ten Plus-the Pilgrimage of an African-American Educator, 1922-, 1997; contbg. editor: The Continuing Quest, 1970. Chmn. Richmond City Planning Commn., 1969—75; dir. Va. Electric and Power Co., Dominion Resources, Inc., Consol bank and Trust Co.; mem. Commn. on Ch. Family Fin. Planning; mem. scholarship selection com. Philip Morris, Inc.; mem. Mayor's Commn. on Human Rels., 1963—65; pres. Norrell Sch. PTA, 1963—65; mem. exec. com. Ctrl. Va. Ednl. TV; mem. Richmond Independence Bicentennial Commn., Richmond Downtown econ. and Devel. Commn.; co-chmn. Northside Cmty. assn., 1964—68; chmn. Univ. Ctr. in Va.; mem. State Bd. Edn. Va., 1975—85, pres., 1980—82; bd. dirs. NCCJ, Va. Inst. Pastoral Care, Task Force for Renewal Urban Strategy and Tng., Richmond chpt. ARC, 1974—75, Better Richmond, Inc., Richmond Downtown Devel. Unltd., Am. Coun. on Edn., 1970—72, Richmond renaissance, Inc., Met. Richmond Leadership; mem. adv. bd. Inst. for Bus. and Cmty. Devel. U. Richmond; bd. fellows Interpreters House, Lake Janaluska, NC; trustee Richmond Meml. Hosp., Nat. Assn. for Equal Opportunity in Edn., v.p.; pres. Richmond Gold Bowl Sponsors, Inc., Nat. Conf. Richmond and Jews, Inc., 1987—90; nat. co-chair Nat. Conf. Christians and Jews, Inc., 1994; chmn. bd. dirs. Cosol. Bank and Trust Co., chmn./bd. dirs., 2001—. Recipient Disting. Svc. award, Links, Inc., 1971, Ednl. Achievement award, 1985, Good Govt. award, Richmond First Club, 1985, Brotherhood award, NCCJ, 1975, Mozelle E. Manuel Outstanding Svc. award, Met. Bus. League, 1991, Exemplary Vision award, Fullwood Foods, Inc., 1992, Flame Bearers Edn. award, United Negro Coll. Fund, 1997, Excellence in Leadership award, Dominion Va. Power, 2000, Disting. Cmty. Svc. award, Sigma Pi Phi, 2003; named Citizen of Yr., Astoria Beneficial Club, 1971, Omega Psi Phi, 1972, Univ. chapel named Allix B. James Chapel in his honor, 1992. Mem.: Clergy Assn. Richmond Area (pres.), Bapt. Gen. Conv. Va. (exec. bd.), Soc. for Advancement Continuing Edn. for Mins. (exec. bd.), Am. Bapt. Conv. (pres. coun. on theol. edn. 1969—72), Am. Assn. Theol. Schs. (pres. 1970—72), Greater Richmond C. of C. (bd. dirs.), Kiwanis (honoree Richmond area Appreciation Dinner 1993), Alpha Phi Alpha (Achievement award 1981, 1985), Alpha Kappa Mu.

JAMES, DONALD M., construction materials executive; b. 1949; BS, MBA, U. Alabama; JD, U. Virginia. Pres. so. divsn. Vulcan Materials, 1994-96, sr. v.p. south constrn. materials group, 1995-96, pres., COO, 1996-97, pres., CEO, 1997; chmn., CEO Vulcan Materials Co., 1997—; also bd. dir. Bd. dirs. Protective Life Corp., So. Co., SouthTrust Corp., Wells Fargo, 2009-. Office: Vulcan Materials 1200 Urban Center Dr Birmingham AL 35242

JAMES, DONZELLA, state legislator; b. Atlanta, May 03; m. Elmo James; children: Brian, Kerry (dec.). Attended, Morris Brown Coll., Atlanta, Ga. State U.; HHD (hon.), Emmanuel Bible Coll., Macon, Ga. Mem. Nat. Alliance Postal and Fed. Employees; tchr. cmty. schs. program Atlanta Pub. Schs.; senator Dist. 35 Ga. State Senate, 1995—2002, 2009—. Former polit. cons.; vice chair state and local govt. ops. com., sec. youth, aging and human ecology com., sec. consumer affairs com., mem. ethics and agr. coms., mem. policy com. of senate Dem. caucus, former chair senate study com. on solid waste reduction, chair senate recycling and econ. devel. study com., 1996, mem. senate young drivers study com., 1996, Ga. State Senate. Del. 2 nat. Dem. convs.; mem. South Fulton (Ga.) 2002, Vision 2000, Atlanta Women's Polit. Caucus, Nat. Polit. Congress of Black Women, Nat. Assn. Negro Bus. and Profl. Women; chair edn. com. Tri-Cities cluster Atlanta Project; co-founder, chair Task Force for Good Govt.; mem. adv. coun. Benjamin E. Mays H.S.; bd. dirs. adv. com. Atlanta Job Corp.; mem. pastoral coun. Blessed Sacrament Ch. Atlanta. Recipient Legis. Svc. award Ga. Mcpl. Assn., Assn. County Commrs. of Ga., award Nat. Alliance Postal and Fed. Employees, Ga. Hwy. Safety Mgmt. Sys. Democrat. Office: 3800 Pittman Rd College Park GA 30349-1435 also: Ga State Senate 313-B Coverdell Legis Office Bldg Atlanta GA 30334 Office Phone: 404-463-1379. Office Fax: 404-656-6579. Business E-Mail: donzella.james@senate.ga.gov.

JAMES, EDWARD C., II, (TED JAMES), state legislator; BS in Acctg., Southern U., JD. Policy advisor housing, social services and cmty. devel. State of La.; spl. counsel to sec. La. Dept. Revenue; staff atty. La. House of Reps., atty. Com. on Labor, mem. Dist. 101, 2012—, mem. Appropriations Com., Judiciary Com., Natural Resources and Environment Com. & Joint Legislative Com. on the Budget. Democrat. Office: District Office 246 Ship Dr Baton Rouge LA 70806 E-mail: jamest@legis.la.gov.

JAMES, ELIZABETH R. (LEE LEE JAMES), bank executive; b. Columbus, Ga., June 11, 1961; m. David M. (Sandy) James Jr.; children: David, Parker. BA in Polit. Sci., Auburn U., 1983; grad., Cannon Fin. Inst. Trust Sch., 1988; grad, Duke U., 1990. Mem. staff, Trust Dept., Columbus Bank and Trust Co. Synovus Fin. Corp., Columbus, Ga., 1986—89, dir., training TSYS, 1989—90, v.p., human resources dir., TSYS, 1990—94, sr. v.p., human resources dir., TSYS, 1994—95, sr. v.p., human resources divsn. officer, Synovus Svc. Corp., 1995—96, pres., Synovus Svc. Corp., 1996—2000; chief people officer Synovus Financial Corp., Columbus, Ga., 1996—, vice chmn., chief info. officer, 2000—. Mem., tech. secretariat adv. group Banking Industry. Chmn. staff parish St. Paul United Meth. Ch., mem. adminstrv. bd.; chmn. The Alexis de Tocqueville Soc. of United Way; bd. dir. Columbus (Ga.) Symphony, Ronald McDonald House; mem.

YMCA Task Force Com.; chmn. Leadership Devel. Task Force Gov.'s Comm. for a New Ga. Named Woman of Yr. in Tech., Tech. Assn. of Ga., 2002; named one of The 25 Most Powerful Women in Banking, US Banker mag., 2003, 2004. Mem.: Alexis deTocqueville Soc. United Way (past chmn.), Library Found., Fin. Svcs. Roundtable. Office: Synovus Financial Corp 1111 Bay Ave Ste 500 Columbus GA 31901 Business E-Mail: ejames@synovus.com.

JAMES, FRANCIS MARSHALL, III, anesthesiologist; b. Phila., Dec. 22, 1935; MD, Hahnemann U., 1961. Intern Phila. Gen. Hosp., 1961—62; resident Hosp. U. Pa., Phila., 1964—67, attending anesthesiologist, 1967—68, NC Bapt. Hosp., Winston-Salem, 1968—2000; assoc. dean grad. med. edn. Wake Forest U., NC, 1999-2000, faculty Sch. Medicine NC, 1968—2000, chair dept. anesthesiology NC, 1983—98, prof. emeritus NC, 2001—. Dir. Am. Bd. Anesthesiology, 1988-2000, pres., 1999-2000. Office: Wake Forest U Sch Medicine Dept Anesthesiology Medical Ctr Blvd Winston Salem NC 27157-1009 Personal E-mail: fmj111@aol.com.

JAMES, KATHI, construction executive; V.p., sales & mktg. Morrison Homes, Inc.; sr. v.p., chief mktg. officer Beazer Homes USA, Inc. Office: Beazer Homes USA Inc 1000 Abernathy Rd NE Ste 260 Atlanta GA 30328-5648 Office Phone: 770-829-3700. Office Fax: 770-481-2808.

JAMES, KAY COLES, think-tank executive, former federal agency administrator; b. Portsmouth, Va., June 1, 1949; d. Susie Armistead Coles; m. Charles Everett James; children: Charles Jr., Elizabeth, Robert III. BS, Hampton Inst., Va., 1971; LLD (hon.), Pepperdine U. Traffic svc. advisor C&P Telephone, Roanoke, Va., 1971-72, group supr., 1973, force mgr., 1974; conf. coord. devel. disabilities project State of Virginia, Richmond, Va., 1978-79; asst. to housing coord. Housing Opportunities Made Equal, Richmond, Va., 1980-81, dir. cmty. edn. & devel., 1981-83; pers. dir. Cir. City Stores, Beltsville, Md., 1983-85; dir. pub. affairs Nat. Right to Life Com., Washington, 1985-88; asst. sec. for pub. affairs US Dept. Health & Human Services, Washington, 1989—90; assoc. dir. Office Nat. Drug Control Policy, Washington, 1991—93; sr. v.p. Family Rsch. Coun., 1993—94; sec. Va. Dept. Health & Human Resources, Richmond, Va., 1994—96; dean Robertson Sch. Govt. Regent U., Virginia Beach, Va., 1996—99; sr. fellow Citizenship Project Heritage Foundation, Washington, 1999—2001; dir. US Office Pers. Mgmt., Washington, 2001—05; sr. exec. v.p. Athena Innovative Solutions, Inc., 2005—; pres., founder Gloucester Institute, Gloucester, Va., 2008—. Pres. Black Americans for Life, Washington, D.C., 1985-88; mem. White House Com. on Children, Washington, D.C., 1988, White House Task Force on Blacks, Washington, D.C., 1988, Nat. Coalition on Pro-Family Issues, Washington, D.C., 1988; co-founder Nat. Family Inst., Washington, D.C., 1987; chair, Nat. Gambling Impact Study Com., 1999-2001; bd. dirs. Amerigroup Corp., 1999-2001, 2005-, The PNC Financial Services Group Inc., 2006- Contbr. numerous articles to jours. and newspapers; author: Never Forget, 1993, Transforming America From the Inside Out, 1995, What I Wish I'd Known Before I Got Married, 2001 Recipient Disting. Fed Svc. award, Nat Assn. Hispanic Fed. Executives, 2004, Publius award for Pub. Svc., U. Va., Spirit of Democracy award for Pub. Policy Leadership, Nat. Coalition on Black Civic Participation. Republican. Presbyterian. Avocations: reading, walking, cooking. Office: The Gloucester Institute 6496 Allmondsville Rd Gloucester VA 23061

JAMES, LEBRON RAYMONE, professional basketball player; b. Akron, Ohio, Dec. 30, 1984; s. Gloria James and McClelland Anthony; m. Savannah Brinson, Sept. 14, 2013; children: LeBron Jr., Bryce Maximus. Forward Cleve. Cavaliers, 2003—10, Miami Heat, 2010—; co-founder, ptnr. LRMR Innovative Mktg. & Branding, Cleve. Mem. US nat. team Summer Olympic Games, Athens, Greece, 2004, Beijing, 2008, London, 2012. Co-host: ESPY Awards show, 2007; guest host: (TV series) Saturday Night Live, 2007; featured on cover Vogue, 2008, appeared in (documentaries) More Than A Game, 2008, (TV series) Entourage, 2009; co-author (with Buzz Bissinger): Shooting Stars, 2009. Founder, bd. dirs. LeBron James Family Found., 2004—. Recipient Bronze medal, men's basketball, Summer Olympic Games, 2004, Gold medal, men's basketball, 2008, 2012, Best Male Athlete award, Black Entertainment TV (BET), 2006—07; named Nat. HS Player of Yr., USA Today, 2003, NBA Rookie of Yr., 2004, NBA All-Star Game MVP, 2006, 2008, NBA Player of Yr., The Sporting News, 2006, 2009, NBA MVP, 2009, 2010, 2012, 2013, NBA Finals MVP, 2012, 2013, Sportsman of Yr., Sports Illus., 2012, Male Athlete of Year, AP, 2013; named one of The 100 Most Influential People in the World, TIME mag., 2005, 2013, The 100 Most Powerful Celebrities, Forbes.com, 2008, The Most Influential People in the World of Sports, Bus. Week, 2007, 2008, The 100 Agents of Change, Rolling Stone mag., 2009, The 40 Under 40, Fortune mag., 2010, The 10 Most Fascinating People of 2010, Barbara Walters Special; named to NBA All-Rookie First Team, 2004, Ea. Conf. All-Star Team, NBA, 2005—13, All-NBA 1st Team, 2006, 2008—13, The Power 150, Ebony mag., 2008, NBA All-Defensive 1st Team, 2009—13. Achievements include being the first overall pick in the NBA Draft, 2003; leading the NBA in: minutes, 2005, 2007; field goals, 2005, 2008; free throws, 2009; points per game, 2008; member of NBA Finals championship winning Miami Heat, 2012, 2013; the youngest player in NBA history to score 20,000 points, 2013. Office: Miami Heat 601 Biscayne Blvd Miami FL 33132*

JAMES, LYNMORE, state legislator; b. Aug. 28, 1937; m. Faye James; children: Lynorris, Mack Carlton, Jeffery James. Former state rep. Dist. 114, Ga.; vice chmn. Agr. & Consumer Affairs Com.; chmn., gen. govt. subcom.; mem. Appropriations Com., Spl. Policy Rules Com.; house rep. Ga.; bd. dir. Flag Bank; gov. bd. Flint River Cmty. Hosp.; adv. bd. Ga. Ctr. For Youth; state rep. Dist. 140 Ga., 1992—2002; state rep. Dist. 135 Ga., 2005—; sec., natural resources & environment com.; mem. Agr. & Consumer Affairs Com., Banks & Banking Com., U. Ga. Rsch. Adv. Bd.; farmer; bd. mem. Fort Valley State Coll. Found., West Ctrl. Ga. Cmty. Action Coun. Mem.: Ga. AgriLeaders Forum, Five-Point Cmty. Club. Democrat. Baptist. Office: 401 Legis Office Bldg Atlanta GA 30334 Home: 1897 Willie James Rd Montezuma GA 31063-6140 Office Phone: 404-657-8441, 478-472-5064. Business E-Mail: ljames@legis.state.ga.us.

JAMES, MATTHEW, state legislator; b. Norfolk, Va., Sept. 11, 1955; m. Karen Scott; children: Lauren, Kelly. Attended, US Naval Acad., Annapolis, Md., 1973—75; BA in Economics, Hampton U., Va., 1978; MBA, Northwestern U., Ill., 1981. With Kraft Foods, Chgo.; asst. econ. devel. dir. Chesapeake, Va.; econ. devel. dir. Portsmouth, Va.; pres., CEO Peninsula Coun. Workforce Devel., Newport News, Va.; house del. Dist. 80 Va. House of Dels., Richmond, 2010—. Peninsula region adv. bd. mem. BB&T. Mem. Main St. Bapt. Ch.; bd. mem. Mary Immaculate Hosp. Mem.: Va. Econ. Developers Assn. (former pres., v.p., treas., sec.), Civic Leadership Inst., Eureka Club, Inc., Sigma Pi Phi. Democrat. Office: Va House of Dels Gen Assembly Bldg Rm 814 PO Box 406 Richmond VA 23218 also: PO Box 7487 Portsmouth VA 23707 Office Phone: 804-698-1080. Office Fax: 804-698-6780. Business E-Mail: delmjames@house.virginia.gov.

JAMES, ROBERT D., JR., prosecutor; b. Murfreesboro, Tenn. s. Robert D. and Barbara James; m. Karria James; 1 child, Brookelyn M. BA in History, Middle Tenn. State U., Murfreesboro; JD, Ga. State U., Atlanta, 1999. Asst. dist. atty. Rockdale County, Ga.; prosecutor, crimes against children unit DeKalb County, Ga., solicitor-gen., 2007—10, dist. atty., 2010—. Apptd. mem. Ga. State Judicial Nominating Com., 2011—; mem. Ray of Hope Christian Ch., Decatur, Ga. Named one of Minority 40 Under 40, The Nat. Law Jour., 2011. Office: DeKalb County Dist Attorneys Office 556 N McDonough St Adminstrn Bldg Ste 700 Decatur GA 30030 Office Phone: 404-371-2561.

JAMES, ROBERT GILLESPIE, federal judge; b. Ruston, La., 1946; BA, La. Tech U., 1968; JD, La. State U., Baton Rouge, 1971. Pvt. practice atty., Ruston, 1971—98; judge Ruston City Ct., 1985—98, US Dist. Ct. (we. dist.) La., 1998—2009, chief judge, 2009—. Bus. law instr. La. Tech U., 1992—98. Office: US Dist Ct PO Drawer 3107 Monroe LA 71210 Office Phone: 318-322-6230.

JAMES, ROBERT LEO, retired advertising executive; b. NYC, Sept. 23, 1936; s. Leo Francis and Mildred Virginia (Schaffa) James; m. Anne Krapp, Feb. 2, 1968; children: Robert Leo, Victoria, Jeffrey. AB, Colgate U., Hamilton, NY, 1958; MBA, Columbia U., NYC, 1961. Field rschr. Farm Jour., Inc., Cleve., 1956-57; salesman Procter & Gamble Co., Schenectady, NY, 1958-59, sales mgr., office head Syracuse, NY, 1959—; product mgr., new product devel. Colgate Palmolive Co., NYC, 1961-64; sr. v.p., mgmt. svc. dir. Ogilvy & Mather Worldwide, Inc., NYC, 1964-68, Marschalk Co., Inc., NYC, 1968, dir., 1968-80, exec. v.p., 1970, gen. mgr., 1971, pres., 1974, chmn. bd. dirs., CEO, 1975-80; dir. Interpublic Group of Cos., Inc., 1975—95, vice chmn., 1980-81; vice chmn. US ops. McCann-Erickson Worldwide, 1981-85, chmn. bd. dirs., pres., CEO, 1985-95, ret., 1995—. Adj. assoc. prof. mktg. Fordham U., NYC, 1968—69; chmn. corp. adv. coun. Nat. Captioning Inst., 1990—94. Trustee Fordham Prep. Sch., 1977—83, NY Presbyn. Hosp., 1988—, South Street Seaport Mus., NYC, 1990—2002, Worldship Trust; coun. mem. Internat. Exec. Svc. Corps, 1988—92; trustee, mem. exec. com. Woods Hole Oceanog. Instn., 1995—, chmn. life trustees, 2013; dir. Am. Cruise Lines, 2001—; bd. dirs. March of Dimes NYC, 1981—88; chmn. bd. dirs. Nat. Air & Space Mus., 1999—2002; nat. bd. dirs. Smithsonian Instn. Recipient Cecil B. Green award, Woods Hole Oceanog. Inst., 2012; named to Advt. Hall of Fame, Am. Advt. Fedn., 2010. Mem.: Naval War Coll. Nat. Security Conf., Nat. Security Seminar US Army War Coll., World Pres. Orgn., Advt. Coun. (bd. dirs. 1992), Am. Assn. Advt. Agencies (chmn. 1992—93), YPO/WPO (life), Young Pres. Orgn., NY Yacht Club (commodore 1997—99).

JAMES, SHERMAN ATHONIA, epidemiologist, educator; b. Hartsville, SC, Oct. 25, 1943; s. Jerome and Helen Genese (Bachus) J.; m. Vera Lucia Moura; children: Sherman Alexander, Scott Anthony. AB, Talladega Coll., 1964; PhD, Washington U., 1973. Prof. epidemiology U. N.C., Chapel Hill, 1973-89, U. Mich., Ann Arbor, 1989—2003, assoc. dean acad. affairs Sch. Pub. Health; prof. pub. policy Duke U., Durham, NC, 2003—. Cons. NIMH, NIH, Bethesda, Md., 1979-83, Nat. Heart, Lung and Blood Inst., 1985—, Nat. Inst. Environ. Health Sci., 1990—; cons. NAS, Washington, 1994—. Contbr. articles to profl. jours. Capt. USAF, 1964-69. Fellow Soc. of Fellows, U. Mich., 1993—. Fellow Am. Heart Assn., Acad. Behavioral Medicine Rsch., Soc. Behavioral Medicine, Am. Coll. Epidemiology; mem. Am. Men and Women of Sci. Inst. Medicine. Avocations: travel, photography, tennis, nature walks. Office: Duke Univ 213 Sanford Inst 90245 Durham NC 27708

JAMES, THOMAS A., investment company executive; BA magna cum laude, Harvard Coll., 1964; MBA with high distinction, Harvard Bus. Sch., 1966; JD, Stetson Coll. Law, 1969. Joined Raymond James & Associates, Inc., St. Petersburg, Fla., 1966; CEO Raymond James Financial, Inc., St. Petersburg, Fla., 1969—87, chmn., CEO, 1987—2010, exec. chmn., 2010—. Bd. dir. Cora Health Services, 1997—; chmn. Fin. Services Roundtable, 2007—; past. chmn. Securities Industry Assn. Pres. bd. trustees Salvador Dali Mus.; chmn. Fla. Council of 100; mem. bd. Dean's advisors Harvard Bus. Sch.; bd. mem. Internat. Tennis Hall of Fame; chmn. Chi Chi Rodriguez Youth Found. Baker Scholar. Office: Raymond James Fin Inc 880 Carillon Pkwy Saint Petersburg FL 33716-1100

JAMIL, DHIAA M., energy executive; b. 1956; m. Hope Robertson; 3 children. BS in Elec. Engring., U. NC, Charlotte; completed sr. nuc. plant mgmt. course, Inst. Nuc. Power Ops. Registered profl. engr., NC, SC; tech. nuc. cert. Duke Energy. Design engr. to electrical systems engring. supr., Oconee Nuc. Station Duke Energy Corp., 1981—94, electrical systems engring. mgr., 1994—97, maintenance supt., McGuire Nuc. Station, 1997—99, station mgr., 1999—2002, site v.p., McGuire Nuc. Station, 2002—03, site v.p., Catawba Nuc. Station and sr. v.p. nuc. support, 2003—08, group exec., chief nuc. officer, 2008—. Former mem. Coun. Nat. Acad. Nuc. Tng., Dominion Energy Mgmt. Safety Rev. Adv. Com., TVA Nuc. Safety Rev. Bd., Pacific Gas & Elec. Nuc. Safety Oversight Com.; mem. new plant oversight com. Nuc. Energy Inst., mem. nuc. strategic issues adv. com. steering group; mem. exec. adv. group Inst. Nuc. Power Ops.; bd. dirs. Charlotte Rsch. Inst.; mem. adv. bd. U. NC Charlotte Sch. Engring. Bd. dirs. York County C. of C., SC. Mem.: IEEE (sr.). Office: Duke Energy 526 S Church St Charlotte NC 28202-1904 Office Phone: 704-594-6200.

JANEWAY, RICHARD, retired academic administrator; b. LA, Feb. 12, 1933; s. VanZandt and Grace Ellen (Bell) Janeway; m. Katherine Esmond Pillsbury, Dec. 23, 1955 (dec. Jan. 7, 2010); children: Susan Kent, David VanZandt, Elizabeth Anne; m. Nancy Hirsman Harper Janeway, May 28, 2011. AB, Colgate U., 1954; MD, U. Pa., 1958. Diplomate Am. Bd. Psychiatry and Neurology. Intern Hosp. U. Pa., 1958—59; resident N.C. Baptist Hosp., Winston-Salem, 1963—66; mem. faculty Bowman Gray Sch. Medicine (now Wake Forest Sch. Medicine), Winston-Salem, 1966—, dean, 1971—85, exec. dean, 1985—94, v.p. health affairs, 1983—90, exec. v.p. health affairs, 1990—97, ret., 1997—; prof. neurology Wake Forest U., Winston-Salem, 1971—2003, prof. medicine and mgmt., 1997—2003, prof. emeritus, 2003—, dir. Cerebral Vascular Rsch. Ctr., Bowman Gray Sch. Medicine, 1969—71; pres. emeritus Wake Forest Health Scis., 2011. Mem. exec. com. So. Nat. Bank, Winston-Salem, NC, 1982—95; dir. BB&T Corp., 1995—2003, bd. dirs., mem. exec. com., chmn., 2001—03; mem. nat. adv coun. regional med. programs HEW, 1974—77; mem. -at-large Nat. Bd. Med. Examiners, 1979—87; mem. N.C. Joint Conf. Com. on Med. Care, Inc., 1983—2003; dir. N.C. Inst. Medicine. Mem. Winston-Salem Forsyth Co. Bd. Edn., 1970—73; trustee Winston-Salem State U., 1991—95, Colgate U., 1988—95, Sr. Svcs. Inc., 2007—; mem. investment com. Episcopal Diocese NC, 2000—06, chmn., 2004, 2005; bd. dirs. Nat. Assn. for Biomed. Rsch., 1993—96, Ams. for Med. Progress, Inc., 1993—97, Winston-Salem Found., 1994—2002, chmn., 1997, 1998. Capt. USAF, 1959—63, flight surgeon, 1962—63. Recipient fellow, USPHS, 1956, Markle scholar, 1968—73, Medallion of Merit, Wake Forest U., 1998, Maroon Citation, Colgate U., 2004. Fellow: ACP, Am. Heart Assn. (coun. on stroke), Am. Acad. Neurology; mem.: AMA, Soc. Med. Adminstrs., Greater Winston-Salem C. of C. (bd. dirs. 1985—89, 1991—95, chmn. 1992), Inst. Medicine of NAS, Am. Clin. and Climatol. Assn., Assn. Am. Med. Colls. (exec. coun. 1977—86, mem. accreditation coun. on grad med. edn. 1981—85, chmn. coun. of deans 1982—83, exec. com. 1982—86, chmn. 1984—85), Am. Neurol. Assn., Rotary (dir. 1977—80, v.p. 1981—82, pres. 1982—83), Alpha Omega Alpha, Sigma Xi, Phi Beta Kappa. Republican. Episcopalian. Avocations: photography, golf, flower arranging, reading, gardening. Personal E-mail: rjaneway@triad.rr.com.

JANG, JEONG, professional golfer; b. Taejeon, Korea, June 11, 1980; Attended, JoongBoo U. Profl. golfer LPGA, 2000—. Mem. Korea Women's Nat. Team, 1997—98, World Amateur Championship Team, 1998. Achievements include winning LPGA Tour major championship: Weetabix Women's British Open, 2005; winning LPGA Tour event: Wegmans LPGA, 2006; winning LPGA of Japan Tour event: Japan Women's Open, 2006. Avocations: skiing, nintendo. Office: c/o LPGA 100 International Golf Dr Daytona Beach FL 32124-1092

JANG, NA RA, singer; b. Seoul, South Korea, Mar. 18, 1981; Grad. in Theatre and Atrs, Chungang U., South Korea. Tourism amb., Seoul, Republic of Korea, 2011—. Assoc. prof. Beijing Huajia Univ., 2010—. Actor: (TV films) Non Stop 2, 2001, Oh! Happy Day, 2003, Girl's Revolution, 2007; (TV series) Iron Masked Singer, 2010, Diao Man Qiao Yu Yi, 2011, Baby-faced Beauty, 2011; singer: (songs) Burying My Face In Tears, April Story, (albums) The First Story, 2001, Sweet Dream, 2002. With Family Health Internat. Charity Orgn. Recipient, MBC Singer Award, 2002, KBS Music Awards, 2002; named Singer of the Year (Korea), CCTV-MTV Music Honors, 2003, Asia's Best Woman Singer, Asia-Pacific Music Chart Award, 2004—05. Avocations: counted cross stitch, dance, flute. Office: Family Health International Headquarters 2224 E NC Hwy 54 Durham NC 27713 Office Fax: 919-544-7261, 919-544-7040.

JANICKI, ROBERT STEPHEN, retired pharmaceutical executive; b. Manette, Wash., Dec. 7, 1934; s. Stephen Walter and Elizabeth Caroline (Gorman) J.; m. I. Jane Betcher, Aug. 18, 1956; children: Robert, Beth, David. BS, Grove City Coll., 1956; MD, Temple U., 1961. Diplomate Nat. Bd. Med. Examiners. Intern U.S. Naval Hosp., Phila., 1961-62; resident in occupl. medicine USN, 1962-63; assoc. dir. clin. rsch. Dow Pharms., Indpls., 1966-68; assoc. med. dir. Neisler divsn. Union Carbide Corp., Sterling Forest, NY, 1968-69; assoc. med. dir. regulatory affairs Abbott Labs., North Chicago, Ill., 1969-70, dir. clin. rsch. pharm. products divsn., 1970-71, v.p. med. affairs pharm. products divsn., 1971-79, v.p. research pharm. products divsn., 1979-83, corp. v.p. R & D pharm. products divsn., 1983-89, sr. v.p., 1989-90. Cons. New Drug Devel. Contbr. articles to profl. jours. Trustee Grove City (Pa.) Coll., 1995-99. Lt. comdr. M.C., USN, 1961-66. Fellow Am. Coll. Clin. Pharmacology; mem. Am. Soc. Clin. Pharmacology and Therapeutics, Sigma Xi, Alpha Omega Alpha. Home: 138 Anchor Dr Vero Beach FL 32963-2941 Personal E-mail: rsjanicki@aol.com.

JANKE, KENNETH S., JR., insurance company executive; BS in Polit. Sci., U. Mich.; MBA, Oakland U., Rochester, Mich. Dir. corp. svcs. Nat. Assn. Investors Corp., chmn. corp. adv. com., bd. dirs. Investment Edn. Inst.; with AFLAC, Inc., Columbus, Ga., 1985, sr. v.p. investor rels., chair corp. disclosure com. Mem. sr. investor rels. roundtable Nat. Investor Rels. Inst. Office: AFLAC Inc 1932 Wynnton Rd Columbus GA 31999 Office Phone: 706-323-3431.

JANKOVIC, JELENA, professional tennis player; b. Belgrade, Serbia, Feb. 28, 1985; d. Veselin and Snezana. Named Most Improved Player, WTA 2006 Player Awards. Achievements include winning 12 career singles titles, 1 career doubles title, WTA; winning (singles) Budapest, 2004, ASB Classic, Auckland, 2007, Family Cir. Cup, 2007, Campionati Internazionali d Italia, 2007-08, DFS Classic, 2007, China Open, 2007, Porsche Tennis Grand Prix, 2008; winning Kremlin Cup, 2008, Western & Southern Financial Group Women's Open, 2009; winning (doubles) Birmingham (with Li), 2006, WTA; mem. Serbian Fed Cup Team, 2001-05; mem. Serbia and Montenegro Olympic Team, 2004. Avocations: basketball, swimming. Office: c/o WTA Hdqs One Progress Plz Ste 1500 Saint Petersburg FL 33701

JANKOVIC, JOSEPH, neurologist, educator; b. Teplice, Czechoslovakia, Mar. 1, 1948; came to U.S., 1965; m. Cathy Sue Inselberg, May 26, 1973; children: Jason, Daniel, Zachary. MD, U. Ariz., 1973. Diplomate Am. Bd. Neurology. Med. intern Baylor Coll. Medicine, Houston, 1973-74, asst. prof. neurology, 1977-84, assoc. prof., 1984-88, prof., 1988—; resident in neurology Columbia U., NYC, 1974-76, chief resident in neurology, 1976-77. Dir. Parkinson's Disease Ctr. and Movement Disorder Clinic, Houston, 1977—; sr. attending physician Meth. Hosp., Houston, 1988—. Author over 700 articles and book chpts. in field; editor/co-editor 40 med. books; mem. editorial bd. jours. Movement Disorders, Clin. Neuropharmacology, Neurology Jour., Jour. Neurology Psychiatry. Chmn. sci. adv. bd. Blepharospasm Rsch. Found.; mem. adv. bd. Dystonia Med. Rsch. Found., Internat. Tremor Found., Tourette's Syndrome Med. Adv. Bd. Grantee disease rsch. founds., pharmaceutical cos., NIH Fellow Am. Acad. Neurology (Rsch. award); mem. AMA, Am. Neurol. Assn. (hon.), Soc. for Neurosci., Movement Disorders Soc. (pres.-elect 1991-94, pres. 1994-96). Avocations: tennis, music. Office: Baylor College Of Medicine Dept Neurology Smith Tower 6550 Fannin STE 1801 Houston TX 77030

JANNEY, DONALD WAYNE, lawyer; b. Clinton, NC, Jan. 9, 1952; s. Wayne Columbus and Bernice (Talley) J.; m. Sydney Louise Rhame, May 28, 1977; children: Taylor Columbus, Camden St. Clair. BA, Furman U., 1974; JD, U. Va., 1978. Bar: Ga. 1978, US Dist. Ct. (no. dist.) Ga. 1978, US Ct. Appeals (11th cir.) 1982. Assoc. Troutman Sanders, Atlanta, 1978-85; ptnr. Troutman Sanders and predecessor firm, Atlanta, 1985—. Bd. dirs. State YMCA Ga., Atlanta, 1980-91. Mem. State Bar of Ga., Atlanta Bar Assn., Phi Beta Kappa. Baptist. Home: 705 E Morningside Dr Atlanta GA 30324-5220 Office: Troutman Sanders Ste 5200 600 Peachtree St NE Atlanta GA 30308-2216 Office Phone: 404-885-3000. E-mail: donald.janney@troutmansanders.com.

JANNEY, OLIVER JAMES, lawyer; b. NYC, Feb. 11, 1946; s. Walter Coggeshall and Helen Jennings (James) Janney; m. Suzanne Elizabeth Lenz, June 21, 1969; children: Elizabeth Flower, Oliver Burr. BA cum laude, Yale U., 1967; JD, Harvard U., 1970. Bar: Mass. 1970, N.Y. 1971, Fla. 1991. With Walston & Co., Inc., NYC, 1970—73, asst. v.p., 1971-73; assoc. Cleary Gottlieb, Steen & Hamilton, NYC, 1973-76; with RKO Gen., Inc., NYC, 1976-90, sec., gen. counsel, 1985-89; exec. v.p., gen. counsel, sec. Uniroyal Tech. Corp., Sarasota, Fla., 1990—2003; ptnr. Janney & Curd, LLP, 2005—06, Robbins Equitas, 2006—10; gen. counsel, asst. sec. Uniroyal Engineered Products LLC, 2010—. 1st lt. USAR, 1969—77. Mem.: ABA, Deer Creek Cmty. Assn. (dir., sec.), Fla. Bar, Sarasota County Bar Assn., N.Y. State Bar Assn., Am. Corp. Counsel Assn., St. Boniface Episcopal Ch. (chancellor), Yale Club Suncoast (dir. former pres.), Sarasota Ivy League Club (gov., former pres.). Republican. Home: 8555 Woodbriar Dr Sarasota FL 34238-5664 Office: Uniroyal Engineered Products LLC Suite 970 1800 2nd St Sarasota FL 34236 Office Phone: 941-906-8580 314. Business E-Mail: ojanney@nauga.com.

JANNUZI, F. TOMASSON, economics professor; b. Pitts., Apr. 23, 1934; s. Frank Humbert and Angela Mary (Tomasson) J.; m. Barbara Lucille Gallagher, Sept. 15, 1957; children: Buell Tomasson, Frank Sampson. AB, Dartmouth Coll., 1955; PhD in Econ., U. London, London Sch. Economics, 1958. Field rep. for So. Asia, E. Africa Found. For Youth and Student Affairs, NYC, 1959-61; asst. rep. The Asia Found., NYC, 1961-62, program officer for So. Asia div. San Francisco, 1962-65, asst. rep. for India, 1965-68; vis. lectr. in econs. U. Tex., Austin, 1968-72, dir. at the Ctr. for Asian Studies, Nat. Resource Ctr. for So. Asia, 1972-86, assoc. prof. of econs., 1973-79, prof. of econs. and Asian studies, 1979-98, assoc. chmn. dept. econs., 1995-97, prof. emeritus econs., 1998—. Pres. Asia Rsch. Assoc. Inc., Austin, Tex., 1985-99; vis. fellow Internat. Devel. Ctr. U. Oxford, Eng., 1989-92; sr. assoc. St. Antony's Coll. Oxford, 1989; vis scholar Ctr. for South Asian Studies, U. Va., 1999—; cons. USAID, Dept. State, DRF. Intelligence Agy., World Bank, 1973—. Author: Agrarian Crisis in India: The Case of Bihar, 1974, India in Transition: Issues of Political Economy in a Plural Society, 1988; India's Persistent Dilemma: The Political Economy of Agrarian Reform, 1994; co-author: (with James T. Peach) The Agrarian Structure of Bangladesh, 1980; contbr. articles to profl. jours. Dir. Austin Coun. on Fgn. Affairs Inc., Tex., 1987-98; mem. Inst. of Current World Affairs, Hanover, N.H., 1987—98; trustee Am. Inst. of Indian Studies, Chgo., 1973-87, chmn. 1979-81. Ford Found. fellow. Mem.: Phi Beta Kappa. Democrat. Avocation: travel. Home: 3 Dogwood Cir Blacksburg VA 24060-6298 Personal E-mail: ftjannuzi@msn.com.

JANSEN, DONALD ORVILLE, lawyer; b. Odessa, Tex., Nov. 17, 1939; s. Orville Charles and Dolores Elizabeth J.; m. E. Janice Law; children: Donald Orville, Lauren, Christine, David, Margaret. BBA magna cum laude, Loyola U., New Orleans, 1961, JD cum laude, 1963; LLM, Georgetown U., 1966. Bar: La. 1963, Tex. 1965. Sr. ptnr. Fulbright and Jaworski, Houston, 1966—2005; sr. tax counsel U. Tex. Sys., 2007—. Served to capt. JAGC US Army, 1963—66. Mem. ABA, Fed. Bar Assn. State Bar Tex., La. Bar Assn., Am. Coll. Trust and Estate Counsel, Am. Coll. Tax Coun. Roman Catholic. Home: 5137 Doliver Dr Houston TX 77056 Office: U Tex Sys Office Gen Counsel 201 W 7th St Austin TX 78701 Office Phone: 512-499-4493. Business E-Mail: donald.jansen@nortonrcsffulbright.com.

JANSEN, MICHAEL JOHN, health facility administrator; b. Swannanoa, NC, July 24, 1945; s. Edward John and Mary Bernadette (Haughian) J.; m. Roxanne Shellenberger, June 27, 1970 (div. May 1992); m. Linda Kathryn Hughes, Aug. 21, 1993; children: Kathryn Anne, Victoria Elizabeth. BS in BA, U. S.C., 1967; M. Health Adminstrn., Duke U., 1976. Adminstrv. asst. Watts Hosp., Durham, NC, 1976-77; asst. dir. Durham County Gen. Hosp., 1977-80; asst. adminstr. St. Joseph's Hosp., Atlanta, 1980-83, sr. v.p., COO, 1983-89; group v.p. SunHealth, Charlotte, NC, 1989-90; sr. assoc. adminstr., COO Cape Fear Valley Health Sys., Fayetteville, NC, 1991-2001; CEO MedAccom, Research Triangle Park, NC, 2001—03; adminstr. Breezewood Family Healthcare, Fayetteville, NC, 2003—08, Linda K. Hughes MD, PA, Fayetteville, 2008—. Bd. dirs. St. Joseph's Hosp., Atlanta, 1985-89, Fayetteville Symphony Orch., 1993-95, United Way of Cumberland County, Fayetteville, 1993-95; chmn. bd. dirs. Shared Svcs. for So. Hosps., Atlanta, 1986-87. Capt. USAF, 1967-72, Col. USAFR, 1990-96. Recipient Falcon award/Spaatz award Civil Air Patrol, 1967. Fellow Am. Coll. Healthcare Execs. Office: Linda K Hughes MD PA 2149 Valleygate Dr Ste 001 Fayetteville NC 28304-3666

JANSON, JULIA S., energy executive; m. Chip Janson; children: Jennifer, Rachel. BA in Am. Studies, Georgetown Coll., Ky.; JD, U. Cin., 1988. Bar: Ohio 1988, Ky. Law clk. Adams, Brooking, Stepner, Wolterman & Dusing, Covington, Ky., Cin. Gas & Electric Co., 1987—88, supr. securities processing, transfer agt. common and preferred stock, 1988—93; corp. atty., key mem. legal team responsible for completing merger of Cin. Gas & Electric Co. and PSI Energy Cinergy Corp., 1993—94, mgr. investor rels., 1995—96, counsel, 1996—98, sr. counsel, 1998—2004, corp. sec., 2000—06, chief compliance officer, 2004—06; sr. v.p. ethics and compliance, corp. sec. Duke Energy Corp., Charlotte, NC, 2006—08, pres. Duke Energy Ohio & Ky., 2008—. Bd. dirs. Lighthouse Youth Svcs., 2000—01. Office: Duke Energy 526 S Church St Charlotte NC 28202-1904 Office Phone: 704-594-6200.

JANUS, MICHAEL W., municipal official, former state legislator; b. Charleston, SC, Nov. 27, 1966; m. Nathalie Cousins Janus. Former econ. devel. mgr., Biloxi, Miss.; mem. Dist. 117 Miss. House of Reps., 1996—2009; pres. Tenix Holdings Inc.; city mgr. City of D'Iberville, Miss., 2009—. Mem.: KC, Am. Legislature Exch. Coun., C. of C., Boys & Girls Club, Kiwanis Club. Republican. Catholic. Office: City Mgr 10383 Automall Pky Diberville MS 39540 Home Phone: 228-388-5686; Office Phone: 601-359-2439, 228-594-6800. Fax: 228-594-6887. Business E-Mail: mjanus@house.ms.gov.

JARMAN, MARK FOSTER, language educator; b. Mt. Sterling, Ky., June 5, 1952; s. Donald Ray and Bo Dee (Foster) J.; m. Amy Lynn Kane, Dec. 28, 1974; children: Claire Marie, Zoe Anne. BA, U. Calif., Santa Cruz, 1974; MFA, U. Iowa, 1976. Instr. Ind. State U., Evansville, 1976-78; vis. lectr. U. Calif., Irvine, 1979-80; asst. prof. English Murray State U., Ky., 1980-83, Vanderbilt U., Nashville, 1983-86, assoc. prof. English, 1986-92, prof. English, 1992—2007, Centennial prof. English, 2007—. Mem. Associated Writing Programs, Norfolk, Va., 1980—, Poets' Prize Com., NYC, 1988—2002. Author: Iris, 1992, The Black Riviera, 1990, 2d edit., 1995, Far and Away, 1985, The Rote Walker, 1981, North Sea, 1978, 2d edit., 1989, The Reaper Essays, 1996, Questions for Ecclesiastes, 1997, Unholy Sonnets, 2000, The Secret of Poetry, 2001, Body and Soul: Essays on Poetry, 2002, To the Green Man, 2004, Epistles, 2007; editor: Rebel Angels: 25 Poets of the New Formalism, 1996. Winner Poets' prize, 1991, Lenore Marshall Poetry prize, Acad. of Am. Poets and The Nation Mag.,1998; John Simon Guggenheim Meml. Found. poetry fellow, 1991-92, Robert Frost fellow, Bread Loaf Writer's Conf., 1985: NEA grantee, 1977, 83, 92; recipient Joseph Henry Jackson award SF Found., 1974. Mem.: Nat. Book Critics Cir. Mem. Christian Ch. Office: Vanderbilt U Dept English Nashville TN 37235

JARQUIN VALDIVIA, ADRIAN ALBERTO, internist, neurologist, researcher; b. Jinotepe, Nicaragua, June 16, 1966; s. Alberto Jarquin Bonilla and Yolanda Valdivia Quijano; m. Tonya Jarquin Valdivia, May 1, 2004; 1 child, Isabella G. Jarquin-Valdivia. MD, Universidad Nacional Autonoma de Honduras, 1993. Diplomate Am. Bd. Internal Medicine, 1997, Neurology ABPN, 2004, Critical Care Am. Bd. Internal Medicine, 2005, Vascular Neurology ABPN, 2005, ARDMS, 2003, Ct/Mri ASN, 2004, Neurosonology ASN, 2002. Asst. prof. neurology, anesthesiology and internal medicine Vanderbilt U. Med. Ctr., Nashville, 2002—. Dir., neurology clerkship Vanderbilt U. Med. Ctr., Nashville, 2004—. Recipient CANDLE Tchg. Award, Vanderbilt Med. Sch., 2004. Mem.: AMA. Achievements include research in new ultrasound sign for non-invasive intracranial pressure determination - the angle of deceleration.

JARRARD, LEONARD EVERETT, psychologist, educator; b. Waco, Tex., Oct. 23, 1930; s. Thomas Ivan and Levis Everett (Lasswell) J.; m. Janet Grier Shoop, Aug. 16, 1958; children: Alice Grier, David Frazier, Hugh Everett. BA, Baylor U., Waco, 1955; MS, Carnegie Inst. Tech., Pitts., 1957, PhD, 1959. Asst. to asso. prof. psychology Washington and Lee U., 1959-66; assoc. prof. to prof. psychology Carnegie-Mellon U., 1966-71; Robert L. Telford prof. psychology Washington and Lee U., Lexington, Va., 1971-2001, prof. emeritus, 2001—. Vis. lectr., prof. exptl. psychology U. Oxford, Eng., 1975-76; interim assoc. prof. anatomy U. Fla., 1965-66; acad. visitor Inst. Psychiatry, U. London, 1988-89. Editor: Cognitive Processes of Nonhuman Primates, 1971; cons. editor: Jour. Comparative and Physiol. Psychology, 1970-75, Behavioral Neurosci. Psychology, 1995-2001, Hippocampus, 03-. Served with USAF, 1952-54. Fellow AAAS, APA, APS; mem. Soc. for Neurosci., Psychonomics Soc., Va. Acad. Sci. So. Soc. Philosophy and Psychology, Phi Beta Kappa, Omicron Delta Kappa, Sigma Xi. Home: PO Box 5 1067 Lexington VA 24450 Office: Washington and Lee U Dept Psychology Lexington VA 24450 Business E-Mail: jarrardl@wlu.edu.

JARRELL, CHARLES MICHAEL, bishop; b. Opelousas, La., May 15, 1940; BA in Philosophy, Cath. U. Am., Washington, 1962, MA in Philosophy, 1963; DD. Ordained priest Diocese of Lafayette, La., 1967; ordained bishop, 1993; bishop Diocese of Houma-Thibodaux, 1993—2002, Diocese of Lafayette, 2002—. Roman Catholic. Office: Diocese of Lafayette 1408 Carmel Dr Lafayette LA 70501-5290 Office Phone: 337-261-5613. Office Fax: 337-261-5603.

JARRETT, DALE (ARNOLD), commentator, retired professional race car driver; b. Conover, NC, Nov. 26, 1956; s. Ned Jarrett; m. Kelley Jarrett; children: Jason, Natalee, Karsyn, Zachary. Profl. race car driver NASCAR, 1987—2008, Joe Gibbs Racing, 1992—96, Robert Yates Racing, 1996—2006, Michael Waltrip Racing, 2007—08; ret., 2008; co-owner PayTheFan.com; lead analyst Sprint Cup ESPN, 2008—. 1st pl. Champion Spark Plug 400 Mich. Internat. Speedway, 1991, 1st pl. GM Goodwrench Dealer 400, 1996, 1st pl. Kmart 400, 1999, 1st pl. Pepsi 400, 2002; 1st pl. Daytona 500 Daytona Internat. Speedway, 1993, 1996, 2000, 1st pl. Pepsi 400, 1999; 1st pl. Mello Yello 500 Charlotte Motor Speedway, 1994, 1st pl. Coca-Cola 600, 1996, 1st pl. UAW-GM Quality 500, 1997; 1st pl. Miller Genuine Draft 500 Pocono Raceway, 1995, 1st pl. Pa. 500, 1997, 1st pl. Pocono 500, 2002; 1st pl. Brickyard 400 Indpls. Motor Speedway, 1996, 1999; 1st pl. Primestar 500, Ga., 1997; 1st pl. TranSouth Fin. 400 Darlington Raceway, 1997, 1998, 1st pl. Carolina Dodge Dealers 400, 2000; 1st pl. Goody's Headache Powder 500 Bristol Motor Speedway, 1997; 1st pl. Exide NASCAR Select Batteries 400 Richmond Internat. Raceway, 1997, 1st pl. Pontiac Excitement 400, 1999; 1st pl. Dura Lube 500 Phoenix Internat. Raceway, 1997; 1st pl. MBNA Platinum 400, Del., 1998; 1st pl. Winston 500 Talladega Superspeedway, 1998, 1st pl. UAW Ford 500, 2005; 1st pl. Pop Secret Microwave Popcorn 400 NC Speedway, 2001, 1st pl. Subway 400, 2003; 1st pl. Harrah's 500 Tex. Motor Speedway, 2001; 1st pl. Va. 500 Martinsville Speedway, 2001. Co-founder Dale Jarrett Found., 2002. Named NASCAR Winston Cup Series Champion, 1999; named one of NASCAR's 50 Greatest Drivers, 1998; named to Ct. of Legends, Lowe's Motor Speedway, 2008. Achievements include becoming the second driver in NASCAR history to place first two times in the Brickyard 400, 1996 and 1999. Avocations: golf, sports, basketball. Office: PO Box 279 Conover NC 28613-0279 Office Phone: 828-464-8818 ext. 304. Office Fax: 828-465-5088.

JARVIS, BILLY BRITT, lawyer; b. Amarillo, Tex., Jan. 9, 1943; s. Billy and Francis Olivia (Beck) J.; m. Linda Jean Holt, Feb. 26, 1965; children: William Britt, Anne Marie, Bonnie Lea. BS in Agrl. Econs., Tex. A&M U., 1965; JD, So. Meth. U., 1968. Bar: U.S. Dist. Ct. (no. dist.) Tex. 1972, U.S. Supreme Ct. 1975. Asst. county atty. Hutchinson County, Borger, Tex., 1968-69; pvt. practice law Spearman, Tex., 1971—. Contbr. articles to profl. jours. Leader Hansford County 4-H, 1976-91; scout master Troop 551, Boy Scouts Am., troop com. chmn., 2006-, Spearman, Tex. Capt. U.S. Army, 1969-71, Vietnam. Decorated Bronze Star. Mem. ABA, Tex. Bar Assn., Panhandle Bar Assn., Tex. Conf. Bar Pres., Phi Delta Phi, Masons, Shriners. Avocation: camping. Office: 124 W Kenneth St PO Box 515 Spearman TX 79081-0515 Home Phone: 806-659-2444; Office Phone: 806-659-2554. E-mail: bbjarvis@ptsi.net.

JARVIS, MIKE, men's college basketball coach; b. Cambridge, Mass. m. Connie Jarvis; children: Mike II, Dana Shaiyen. Grad., Northeastern U., Boston, 1968. Tchr., head basketball coach Cambridge Rindge and Latin HS, Cambridge, 1968—85; head coach Boston U. Terriers, 1985-90, George Washington U. Colonials, 1990-98, St. John's U. Red Storm, 1998—2003, Fla. Atlantic U. Owls, 2008—. Asst. coach USA Olympic Trials, 1980, 88, World Games, 1998; head coach East Squad, USA Olympic Festival, 1993; asst. coach to head coach USA Basketball 22 and under Team, 1993. Named North Atlantic Conf. Coach of Yr. 1990, Met. Writers Assn., 1999, Dist. One Eastern Region, 1999, Sun Belt Conf. Coach of Yr., 2011; named to Mass. HS Hall of Fame, 1991, Cambridge Rindge and Latin HS Hall of Fame, 1996. Mem.: Nat. Assn. Basketball Coaches (former pres.). Achievements include coaching three programs to the NCAA men's basketball tournament, Boston University 1988, 90, George Washington University, 1993-96, St. John's University, 1999. Office: Fla Atlantic Univ Tom Oxley Athletic Ctr 777 Glades Rd Boca Raton FL 33431

JARVIS, RICHARD S., academic administrator; b. Nottingham, Eng., Feb. 13, 1949; came to U.S., 1974; s. John Leslie and Mary Margaret (Dodman) J. BA in Geography, Cambridge U., Eng., 1970, MA, 1974, PhD in Geography, 1975. Lectr. Durham (Eng.) U., 1973-74; assoc. prof. SUNY, Buffalo, 1975-87, asst. to pres., 1986-87, v.p. acad. Fredonia, 1987-90, prof. geoscis., 1987-90; vice provost SUNY Sys., Albany, 1990-94; chancellor Univ. and C.C. Sys. Nev., Reno and Las Vegas, 1994-99, U.S. Open U., Aurora, Colo., 1999—2002, Oreg. U. Sys., 2002—04; provost U. Tex., El Paso, 2005—. Editor: River Networks, 1983; contbr. articles to profl. jours. Office: U Tex El Paso 500 W University Ave El Paso TX 79968 Home Phone: 915-307-6383; Office Phone: 915-747-7885. Business E-Mail: rsjarvis@utep.edu.

JARVIS, ROBERT MARK, law educator; b. NYC, Oct. 17, 1959; s. Rubin and Ute (Hacklander) J.; m. Judith Anne Mellman, Mar. 3, 1989. BA, Northwestern U., 1980; JD, U. Pa., 1983; LLM, NYU, 1986. Bar: N.Y. 1984, Fla. 1990. Assoc. Haight Gardner Poor & Havens, NYC, 1983-85, Baker & McKenzie, NYC, 1985-87; asst. prof. law ctr. Nova Southeastern U., Ft. Lauderdale, Fla., 1987-90, assoc. prof., 1990-92, prof., 1992—. Chmn. bd. dir. Miami Maritime Arbitration Bd., 1993—94; vice chmn. bd. dir. Miami Internat. Arbitration and Mediation Inst., 1993—94; mem. adv. bd. Carolina Acad. Press, 1996—; book review editor Am. Jour. Legal History, 2009—10, chair adv. bd., 2010—. Author: Careers in Admiralty and Maritime Law, 1993, An Admiralty Law Anthology, 1995; co-author: AIDS: Cases and Materials, 1989, 3d edit., 2002, AIDS Law in a Nutshell, 1991, 2d edit., 1996, Notary Law and Practice: Cases and Materials, 1997, Travel Law: Cases and Materials, 1998, Sports Law: Cases and Materials, 1999, Art and Museum Law: Cases and Materials, 2002, Gaming Law: Cases and Materials, 2003, Theater Law: Cases and Materials, 2004, Admiralty: Cases and Materials, 2004, Aviation Law: Cases and Materials, 2006, Out Of the Muck: A History of the Broward Sheriff's Office, 1915-2000, 2010, Fla. Legal Malpractice and Atty. Ethics, 2013; editor: Maritime Arbitration, 1999, Law of Cruise Ships, 2000, Teaching Legal History: Comparative Perspectives, 2014; co-editor: Prime Time Law: Fictional Television as Legal Narrative, 1998, Bush v. Gore: The Fight for Florida's Vote, 2001, Amicus Humoriae: An Anthology of Legal Humor, 2003; mem. editl. bd. Washington Lawyer, 1988—94, Jour. Maritime Law and Commerce, 1990—92, 2001—, Gaming Law Rev. & Econ., 2006—, assoc. editor Jour. Maritime Law and Commerce, 1993—95, editor, 1996—2000, Maritime Law Reporter, 1991—99, Hospitality Law, 1999—2001, adv. bd. World Arbitration and Mediation Review, 1990—; Transnat. Lawyer, 1991—2004, U. San Francisco Maritime Law Jour., 1992—95, 2002—06, contbg. editor Preview US Supreme Ct. Cases, 1990—95, 1999—2002. Mem.: ABA (vice chmn. admiralty law com. young lawyers divsn. 1992—93, chair 1993—94), Phi Delta Phi (province pres. 1989—91, coun. 1991—93), Assn. Am. Law Schs. (chmn.-elect maritime law sect. 1991—93, chmn. 1993—94), Fla. Bar Assn. (admiralty law com. 1988—95, vice chmn. 1991—92, chmn. 1992—93, exec. coun. internat. law sect. 1992—96), Acacia, Northwestern U. Club South Fla. (v.p. 1992—93, pres. 1993—95), Phi Beta Kappa. Democrat. Jewish. Office: Nova Southeastern U Law Ctr 3305 College Ave Fort Lauderdale FL 33314-7721 Home: 5473 Wiles Rd Apt 101 Coconut Creek FL 33073 Office Phone: 954-873-9173. Business E-Mail: jarvisb@nsu.law.nova.edu.

JARVIS, WILLIAM ROBERT, epidemiologist, educator; s. John James and Mattie Belle (Steele) J.; m. Janine M. Jason, July 4, 1982; children: Danielle Kristin, Ashley Alana. BS in Psychology with honors, U. Calif., Davis, 1970; MD, U. Tex., Houston, 1974. Intern U. Tex. Med. Ctr., Houston, 1974-75; resident in pediat. Children's Hosp., LA, 1975-77; pediatric infectious disease fellow Toronto Hosp. for Sick Children, 1977-78; fellow pediat. infectious diseases, virology, pub. health Yale U. Sch. Med., 1978-80; commd. med. officer USPHS, 1980, advanced through grades to capt., 1990, ret., 2003; asst. chief Nat. Nosocomial Infections Surveillance Systems Ctrs. for Disease Control, Atlanta, 1981-90, asst. chief epidemiology br., 1984-87, chief epidemiology br. hosp. infections program, 1987-91, chief investigation, prevention br. hosp. infections program, 1991-2000, acting dir. hosp. infections program, 1996-98, assoc. dir. program devel. Divsn. Healthcare Quality Promotion, 2001—02; dir. Office Extramural Rsch. Nat. Ctr. for Infectious Diseases, Atlanta, 2002—03; pres. Jason and Jarvis Assoc., LLC, 2003—. Asst. prof. pediat. infectious disease and immunology Emory U., Atlanta, 1985-96, assoc. prof., 1996-2009; asst. prof. Rollins Sch. Pub. Health, 1999-2003, pvt. cons., 2003-2004; pres Jason & Jarvis Assocs., 2003—. Editor: ICHE, 2004—07, Hosp. Infections Book, 2005—; contbr. articles to profl. jours., chapters to books. Capt. Commn. Corps, US Public Health Service. Mem. Infectious Diseases Soc. Am., Am. Soc. Microbiology, Soc. Hosp. Epidemiologists Am. (pres. 2001-02). Roman Catholic. Avocations: stock market, gardening, tennis, travel. Office: Jason &Jarvis Assoc 135 Dune Ln Hilton Head Island SC 29928 Home: 135 Dune Ln Hilton Head Island SC 29928-6527 Office Phone: 404-512-4777. Personal E-mail: wrjmj@aol.com.

JASEK, JOHN H., oil and gas company executive; BS in Petroleum Engring., Tex. A&M U. With Anadarko Petroleum Corp., Amoco Prodn. Co.; joined Newfield Exploration Co., 2000, petroleum engr. Western Gulf of Mex., gen. mgr., v.p. Gulf of Mex., 2005—07, v.p. Gulf Coast, mgr. onshore Gulf Coast ops., 2007—08, v.p. Gulf of Mex., 2008—. Mem.: Am. Petroleum Inst., Soc. of Petroleum Engrs. Office: Newfield Exploration Co 363 N Sam Houston Pky E Ste 2020 Houston TX 77060 Office Phone: 281-847-6000. Office Fax: 281-405-4242.

JASPERSE, RICK, state legislator; b. July 22; m. Marcia Rowlett. B in Food Sci., U. Ga. Farmer; asst. county agent Bartow County, Ga.; county agent, educator Pickens County, Ga.; educator U. Ga. Coll. Agr.; mem. Dist. 12 Ga. House of Reps., Atlanta, 2010—. Bd. mem. Mountain Conservation Trust, Chattahoochee Tech. Coll., Appalachian Cattleman's Assn.; pres. Picken's HS Tip-Off Club. Mem.: Jasper Lion's Club. Republican. Office: 89 Apple Valley Farm Ln Jasper GA 30143 also: Ga House of Reps 504 Coverdell Legis Office Bldg Atlanta GA 30334 Office Phone: 404-656-0188. Business E-Mail: rick.jasperse@house.ga.gov.

JASSO, DELIA D., councilwoman; m. Juan Jasso; children: Eric, Laura. BA, So. Meth. U. Mem. Dallas Park and Recreation Bd., 2002—09, v.p., 2005; councilwoman, Dist. 1 Dallas City Coun., 2009—, mem. Pub. Safety Com., Budget, Fin. and Audit Com., Trinity River Corridor Project, Transp. and Environ. Com., 2009—. Bd. mem. Dallas Convention and Visitors Bur., North Ctrl. Tex. Coun. of Govts. Emergency Preparedness Planning Coun. Vol., mem. bd. dirs. Tex. Can! Academies. Office: Dallas City Hall 1500 Marilla St, Rm 5FN Dallas TX 75201 Office Phone: 212-670-4052. Office Fax: 214-670-5117.

JASTROW, KENNETH M., forest products, real estate and financial company executive; Pres., CEO Lumbermen's Investment Corp.; chmn. Capital Mortgage Bankers; CFO Temple-Inland, Inc., Austin, Tex., 1991—99, group v.p., 1995—98, pres., COO, 1998—99, chmn., CEO, 2000—07; non-exec. chmn. Guaranty Financial Group, Austin, Tex., 2008—. Bd. dir. MGIC Investment Corp., KB Home. Office: Guaranty Fin Group 400 N Saint Paul St Ste 600 Dallas TX 75201-6805

JASZCZAK, RONALD JACK, physicist, researcher, consultant; b. Chicago Heights, Ill., Aug. 23, 1942; s. Jacob and Julia J.; m. Nancy Jane Bober, Apr. 15, 1967; children: John, Monica. BS with highest honors, U. Fla., 1964, PhD, 1968. Staff physicist Oak Ridge Nat., 1969-71, AEC postdoctoral fellow, 1968-69; prin. rsch. scientist Searle Diagnostics, Inc., 1971-73, sr. prin. rsch. scientist, 1973, rsch. group leader, 1973-77, chief scientist, 1977-79; assoc. prof. radiology Duke U. Med. Ctr., Durham, NC, 1979-89, prof., 1989—2010, assoc. prof. biomed. engring., 1986-91, prof., 1992—2010, emeritus prof., 2010—. Rsch. prof. Inst. of Stats. and Decision Scis., 1991-93; founder, chmn. bd. dirs. Data Spectrum Corp., Hillsborough, N.C.; investigator Nat. Cancer Inst. Grant, 1983-2008, Dept. Energy Grant, 1989-99. Contbr. articles to profl. jours.; patentee in field. Recipient Outstanding Alumni award U. Fla. Dept. Physics, 2004; named Edward J. Hoffman Med. Imaging Scientist award IEEE Nuc. and Plasma Scis. Soc., 2006; NASA fellow, 1964-67, U. Fla. fellow, 1967-68; RCA scholar, 1963-64. Fellow IEEE; mem. IEEE Nuc. and Plasma Scis. Soc. (pres. 1997-98), AAAS, Soc. Nuc. Medicine (Paul C. Aebersold award 2000), Am. Phys. Soc., Am. Assn. Physicists in Medicine, Soc. Photo-Optical Instrumentation Engrs., Sigma Xi, Phi Beta Kappa, Phi Kappa Phi, Tau Sigma, Sigma Pi Sigma. Office: Duke U Med Ctr Dumc 3949 Durham NC 27710-0001

JAVITS, ERIC MOSES, ambassador, lawyer; b. NYC, May 24, 1931; s. Benjamin A. and Lily Javits; m. Margaretha Espersson, May 24, 1979; children from previous marriage: Jocelyn Ingrid, Eric Jr. Student, Stanford U., 1948-49; AB, Columbia U., 1952, JD, 1955. Bar: NY 1955, US Supreme Ct. 1959. Temp. cons. Office Def. Moblzn., Washington, 1951; assoc. firm Javits & Javits, NYC, 1955-58, mem. firm to ptnr., 1958-82; sr. ptnr. Javits, Robinson, Brog,

Leinwand & Reich, P.C. (and successor firms), 1984-89; cons. to Dept. State, amb.-designate to Venezuela, 1989-90; sr. counsel Robinson, Brog, Leinwand, Reich, Genovese & Gluck, P.C. (and successor firms), 1993—2001; U.S. perm. rep. & amb. UN Conf. on Disarmament, Geneva, 2001—03, Orgn. Prohibition Chem. Weapons, The Hague, 2003—09; mem. adv. com. to dir. gen. Open Future Chem. Weapons Conv., 2010—11. Ind. gen. ptnr. ML Venture Ptnrs., 1982-96; spl. dep. to NY Atty. Gen. Elections Frauds Bur., 1958-59; counsel NY Senate Com. on Affairs of City NY, 1959; mem. NYC Commn. for Protocol, 1994-2001; bd. dirs. NY State Conv. Ctr. Oper. Corp., 1995-2001; past dir. NY Stock Exch., Am. Stock Exch., over the counter cos. Author: SOS New York, 1961, Twists and Turns. Mem. numerous charitable coms.; bd. govs. NY Young Rep. Club, 1955-58, v.p., 1957-58, bd. advisors, 1958-64; mem. Nat. Inst. Soc. Scis., 1958-; trustee French Inst./Alliance Francaise, 1995-2001, Cardozo Law Sch., 1997-2001; mem. exec. com. Jacob K. Javits campaigns, 1954-80; mem. NY Rep. County Com., 1960-64; mem. exec. com. Nat. Rep. Club, 1962-70; exec. sec. US Paper Exporters Coun., Inc., 1964-72; mem. bd., sec., counsel Am. Health Fdn., 1971-85; mem. bd. Spain-USA C. of C., 1993-2001, mem. bd. 1979-1989, pres. 1981-1987, chmn. 1987-1989; mem. bd. Spanish Inst., NYC, 1979-89, pres., 1981-87, chmn., 1987-89, chmn. emeritus, 1989-2001; bd. dir. Fair Return League, Inc., pres., 1975-2006, Eric Javits Family Fdn., 2006—, pres., 2006—, Nat. Inst. Soc. Sci., 1958-; chmn. Republican Eagles, 1999-2001. Decorated Order of Isabel La Catolica (Spain), 1981, 89; recipient Spanish Inst. Gold medal, 1994. Mem.: Beta Theta Pi Oxford Group, Nacoms, U. Club NYC, Phi Alpha Delta, Beta Theta Pi (Oxford Cup 2013), Phi Beta Kappa. Jewish. Personal E-mail: javits@me.com.

JAYAKAR, PARUL, clinical geneticist; MD, India, 1978. Cert. Am. Bd. Med. Genetics-clin. biochemical genetics, 2005, Am. Bd. Med. Genetics-clin. genetics, 2010, Am. Bd. Med. Genetics-clin. cytogenetics, 2010. Resident internal medicine Lady Hardinge Med. Sch., Bombay, 1979—80; resident clin. genetics Jackson Meml. Hosp., 1988—92; hosp. affiliation include Univ. Miami Hosp.; physician Baptist Hosp. Office: Baptist Hospital M C H Genetics & Metabolism 3100 SW 62 Ave Fl 3 Miami FL 33155 Office Phone: 786-624-4717. Office Fax: 786-624-4704. E-mail: Parul.jayakar@mch.com.

JAYSON, MELINDA GAYLE, lawyer; b. Dallas, Sept. 29; d. Robert and Louise Adelle (Jacobs) J. BA, U. Tex., 1977, JD, 1980. Bar: Tex. 1980, U.S. Dist. Ct. (no. dist.) Tex. 1980, U.S. Ct. Appeals (5th and 11th cirs.) 1981, U.S. Dist. Ct. (so. dist.) Tex. 1989, U.S. Ct. Appeals (8th cir.) 1990, U.S. Supreme Ct. 1991. Assoc. Akin, Gump, Strauss, Hauer & Feld, Dallas, 1980-86, ptnr., 1987-96, Melinda G. Jayson, P.C., 1987—; gen. counsel Hall Fin. Group, Dallas, 1999—2008. Comml. arbitrator, large complex case arbitrator, internat. arbitrator, mediator Am. Arbitration Assn.; arbitrator ICC Ct. Arbitration, mediator, CPR Inst. Dispute Resolution; mediator U.S. EEO Commn., 1999-2000. Named Outstanding Young Women Am., 1983, Top Rated Lawyers Alternative Dispute Revolution, 2012-14. Fellow: Chartered Inst. Artbitrators; mem.: Inst. Transnational Arbitration (mem. adv. bd.), Am. Health Lawyers Assn. (arbitrator, mediator), Dallas Bar Assn., State Bar of Tex. (mem. dist. 6A grievance com. professionalism enhancement com. 1997-99). (mem. coun. ADR sect. 2012—). Office: Ste 2015 5445 Caruth Haven Ln Dallas TX 75225-8166 Personal E-mail: jgmelinda@yahoo.com.

JEDLOVEC, GARY, meteorologist; b. Berwyn, Ill., Oct. 21, 1957; s. Robert Frank and Lois Marie Jedlovec; m. Kathleen Caragher, Mar. 15, 1980; children: Benjamin, Phillip, Dylan. BS, St. Louis U., Mo., 1979; MS, St. Louis U., 1981; PhD, U. Wis., Madison, 1987. Atmospheric scientist NASA Marshall Space Flight Ctr., Huntsville, Ala., 1985—. Mem.: Am. Meteorologic Soc. Achievements include discovery of innovative techniques to use NASA satellite data to improve weather forecasting. Office: NASA /MSFC Earth Science Office 320 Sparkman Dr Huntsville AL 35805 Business E-Mail: gary.jedlovec@nasa.gov.

JEFFARES, RICK, state legislator; b. Griffin, Ga. m. Leslie Jeffares; 4 children. BS in Tech. Mgmt., Clayton Coll. and State U., Ga. Owner J&T Environ. Svcs.; city mgr. City of Locust Grove, Ga., 2001—08; mem. Dist. 2 Henry County Bd. Commissioners, Ga., 2008—10; mem. Dist. 17 Ga. State Senate, 2011—. Mem.: Ga. Rural Water Assn. (v.p.). Republican. Avocation: baseball. Office: 300 Lester Mill Rd Ste 200-E Locust Grove GA 30248 also: Ga State Senate 320A Coverdell Legis Office Bldg Atlanta GA 30334 Office Phone: 678-432-7676, 404-656-0503. Business E-Mail: rick.jeffares@senate.ga.gov.

JEFFERSON, AL, professional basketball player; b. Monticello, Miss., Jan. 4, 1985; Grad., Prentiss HS, Miss., 2004. Forward Boston Celtics, 2004—07, Minn. Timberwolves, 2007—10, Utah Jazz, 2010—13, Charlotte Bobcats, 2013—. Named McDonald's All-Am., 2004. Office: Charlotte Bobcats 333 E Trade St Charlotte NC 28202*

JEFFERSON, JOSEPH H., state legislator; b. Pineville, SC, May 30, 1947; BS, Claflin U., Orangeburg, SC, 1970; grad., SC Criminal Justice Acad. Magistrate Sch., 1999. Spl. asst. to congressman Mendel Davis, 1972—80; mem., chmn. Berkeley County Sch. Bd., 1982—93; mem. SC Dept. Transp. Commn., 1994—98; magistrate judge Berkeley County; mem. Dist. 102 SC House of Reps., 2004—. Democrat. Mailing: 304D Blatt Bldg Columbia SC 29201 Home: 1375 Colonel Maham Dr Pineville SC 29468 Home Phone: 803-734-2936. Business E-Mail: JeffersonJ@scstatehouse.net.

JEFFERSON, PATRICK O'NEAL, state legislator; BA in English summa cum laude, Dillard U., 1990; student, U. Heidelberg, Germany, 1991-92, Somerville Coll., Oxford, Eng., 1991; JD, Ohio State U., 1994. Dir. Daniel C. Thompson-Samuel DuBois Cook honors program, adminstrv. asst. Dillard U., New Orleans; atty.; mem. Dist. 11 La. House of Reps., Baton Rogue, 2012—. Pres. Coun. Ind. Colleges / United Negro Coll. Fund. Woodrow Wilson fellow Princeton U., 1988, Dorothy Danforth Compton fellow Ohio State U., Faculty Devel. fellow Coun. Ind. Colleges / United Negro Coll. Fund, 1995; Budeskanzler scholar Alexander von Humboldt Found. and Govt. of Germany, 1991-92, Dean's scholar Ohio State U. Mem. Nat. Assn. African-Am. Honors Programs (mem. Constn. rev. com.), Nat. Collegiate Honors Coun., Alpha Kappa Mu, Phi Alpha Theta, Alpha Phi Alpha. Democrat. Office: 700 Main St Homer LA 71040 also: La House of Reps 300 N 3rd St Baton Rouge LA 70802 Office Phone: 318-927-2519. Business E-Mail: jeffersonpo@legis.la.gov.

JEFFERSON, WALLACE B., former state supreme court justice; s. William and Joyce Jefferson; m. Rhonda Jefferson; 3 children. BA in Political Philosophy, 1985, JD U. Tex., 1988. Cert.: Tex. Bd. Legal Specialization (in civil appellate law). With Groce, Locke & Hebdon, San Antonio, 1988—91; ptnr. Crofts, Callaway & Jefferson, San Antonio, 1991—2001; justice Tex. Supreme Ct., Austin, 2001—04, chief justice, 2004—13; atty. Alexander Dubose Jefferson & Townsend, Austin, 2013—. Mem. Tex. Supreme Ct. Adv. Com., Tex. State Commn. on Jud. Conduct; chair host com. Fifth Circuit Jud. Conf., 2000. Mem. bd. dirs. San Antonio Pub. Libr. Found., Alamo Area Big Bros./Big Sisters.; mem. edn. com. San Antonio Area Found. Named 40 Under 40 Rising Star, San Antonio Bus. Jour., 1996, Texas Lawyer, 2001, Outstanding Young Lawyer, San Antonio Young Lawyers Assn., 1997. Mem.: William S. Sessions Am. Inns of Ct. (past pres.), San Antonio Bar Assn. (pres. 1998—99, President's award 2000). Office: ADJT 515 Congress Ave Ste 2350 Austin TX 78701-3562 E-mail: wjefferson@adjtlaw.com.

JEFFERY, GEOFFREY MARRON, medical parasitologist; b. Dundee, NY, May 13, 1919; s. Joseph Ewart and Augusta (Knapp) J.; m. Jane Wicker, Aug. 16, 1941; children: Janet A. Harrison, Thomas W., Sarah V. Houghton, Susan E. Tosh. AB, Hobart Coll., 1940; MA, Syracuse U., 1942; ScD, Johns Hopkins U., 1944; MPH, Yale U., 1961. Biol. aide health and safety dept. TVA, 1944; commd. officer USPHS, 1944, scientist dir., 1960; tech. aid, cons. malaria control in war areas TVA, 1944-45; assigned divsn. lab. svcs. Communicable Disease Ctr., 1945-46, charge br. lab. Sch. Tropical Medicine San Juan, 1946-47; asst. prof. biology U. Bridgeport, Conn., 1947-48; charge Malaria Rsch. Lab., NIH, Milledgeville, Ga., 1948-54; mem. staff Lab. Tropical Diseases-Lab. Parasite Chemotherapy, NIAID, NIH, Columbia, SC, 1954-63, head sect. epidemiology, 1961-63; asst. chief Lab. Parasite Chemotherapy, NIAID, NIH, Bethesda, 1963-66, acting chief, 1966, chief, 1967-69, C.Am. Malaria Rsch. Sta., San Salvador, El Salvador, 1969-74; asst. dir. Bur. Tropical Diseases, Ctr. Disease Control, Atlanta, 1974-75; dir. vector biology and control div. Bur. Tropical Diseases, 1975-81; asst. dir. divsn. parasitic diseases Ctr. for Infectious Diseases, Ctrs. for Disease Control, 1982-84. Mem. expert adv. panel on malaria WHO, 1963—99; assoc. mem. commn. malaria Armed Forces Epidemiol. Bd., 1965-69, mem., 1969-73; Del. Internat. Congress Tropical Medicine and Malaria, Lisbon, 1958, Rio de Janeiro, 1963, Teheran, Iran, 1968; Del. Internat. Congress Parasitology, Rome, Italy, 1964, Washington, 1969; Del. Internat. Conf. on Protozoology, London, 1965, Latin Am. Congress Parasitology, Medellin, Colombia, 1973; mem. sci. group on chemotherapy of malaria WHO, Geneva, 1967, mem. sci. group on parasitology, Teheran, 1968; cons. on status of malaria in Africa AID, 1979; mem. sci. working group on applied field rsch. in malaria WHO, Geneva, 1979, mem. steering com., 1981-86; cons. on malaria U.S.-China Health Agreement, 1980; del. Asia and Pacific Conf. on Malaria, Honolulu, 1985; temp. advisor meetings WHO, Kuala Lumpur, 1981, Albuquerque, 1982, Nairobi, 1983, Bangkok, 1984; invited participant concerted action 1st plenary meeting on malaria modelling European Union, Tuebingen, Germany, 1998. Contbr. numerous articles to sci. jours. tropical medicine and parasitology. Recipient Pub. Health Svc. Commendation medal, 1966, Dept. Army cert. of appreciation patriotic civilian svc., 1973 Fellow Royal Soc. Tropical Medicine (local sec. 1984-89); mem. Am. Soc. Tropical Medicine and Hygiene (sec.-treas. 1961-67, v.p. 1971, pres. 1975, Bailey K. Ashford award 1959), Am. Soc. Parasitologists, Assn. Southea. Biologists (editor bull. 1959-60, exec. com. 1962-66), Tropical Medicine Assn. Washington, Southea. Soc. Parasitologists, S.C. Acad. Sci. (mem. council 1960, 62, Jefferson award 1952, 56, 60), Commd. Officers Assn. USPHS, Sigma Xi, Kappa Sigma. Presbyterian. Home: 1800 Clairmont Lake Apt 513 Decatur GA 30033-4039 Personal E-mail: gjeffery2@comcast.net.

JEFFERY, WILLIAM JEREMY, insurance company executive; Grad. in Polit. Sci., Yale U., New Haven. Exec. dir. Fixed Income Instl. Sales Morgan Stanley; sr. v.p., investments, chief investment officer AFLAC, Inc., 2005—. Chmn. Annual Fund Rippowam/Cisqua Sch., Bedford, NY; bd. mem. Friends of the John Jay Homestead, NY. Office: AFLAC Inc 1932 Wynnton Rd Columbus GA 31999 Office Phone: 706-323-3431. Office Fax: 706-324-6330.

JEFFRESS, HARMON (GENE), state legislator; b. Crossett, Ark., Oct. 18, 1948; m. Cynthia Jeffress; 3 children. BME, Univ. Ark., 1971. Ret. tchr.; mem. Dist. 38 Ark. House Reps., 1999—2002; mem. Dist. 25 Ark. State Senate, 2003—. Democrat. Southern Baptist. Address: 1483 Ouachita 47 Louann AR 71751 Mailing: Ark Senate State Capitol, Rm 320 Little Rock AR 72201 Office Phone: 870-689-3537. Business E-Mail: gjeffress@arkleg.state.ar.us.

JEFFRESS, JIMMY LANE, state legislator; b. Monticello, Ark., Sept. 19, 1947; m to Candace; children: Melody, Whitney, Summer & Leslie. BME, Univ. Ark., 1971; MME, Univ. La., 1986. Tchr. Crossett Pub. Schools, 1971—99; mem. Crossett City Coun., 1987—93; justice of the peace Ashley County Quorum Ct., 1995—96; mem. Dist. 83 Ark. House of Reps., 1997—2000; mem. Dist. 24 Ark. State Senate, 2001—. Mem.: NEA, Am. Cattlemen's Assn., Am. Choral Directors Assn., Crossett Lions Club. Democrat. Southern Baptist. Home: 711 Maple St Crossett AR 71635-3519 Office Phone: 870-364-8291. E-mail: jjeffress@arkleg.state.ar.us.

JEFFRIES, JOHN CALVIN, JR., law educator, former dean; b. 1948; BA, Yale U., 1970; JD, U. Va., 1973. Bar: Va. 1973, D.C. 1974. Law clk. to Hon. Justice Powell US Supreme Ct., 1973-74; asst. prof. law U. Va. Sch. Law, Charlottesville, 1975-79, assoc. prof. law, 1979-81, prof. law, 1981—, Emerson Spies prof. law, 1986—2001, acad. assoc. dean, 1994—99, Arnold H. Leon prof. law, 2001—08, dean, 2001—08, David & Mary Harrison Disting. prof. law, 2008—. Prof. FBI Acad., Quantico, Va., 1976—; vis. asst. prof. Stanford U., fall 1977; vis. prof. Yale U., 1981-82, So. Calif. U., fall 1986, 89, 93; John V. Ray rsch. prof. 1989-1991; Horace W. Goldsmith rsch. prof. 1992-1995; William L. Matheson & Robert M. Morgenthau Disting. prof. 1996-2001. Author: Justice Lewis F. Powell, Jr.: A Biography, 1994, (with Low) Model Penal Code and Commentaries, 3 vols., 1980, (with Karlan, Low and Rutherglen) Civil Rights Actions: Enforcing the Constitution, 2000, Federal Courts and the Law of Federal-State Relations, 4th edit., 1998, (with Low and Bonnie) Cases and Materials on Criminal Law, 1982, 2d edit., 1986; editor-in-chief Va. Law Rev. 2nd lt. gen. US Army. Mem. American Law Inst., Va. State Bar (com. for oversight of bar activities); fellow American Acad. Arts & Sciences Office: U Va Sch Law WB315 580 Massie Rd Charlottesville VA 22903-1738 Office Phone: 434-924-3436. Business E-Mail: jjeffries@virginia.edu.

JEFFRIES, MCCHESNEY HILL, JR., lawyer; b. Atlanta, Dec. 25, 1954; s. McChesney Hill Sr. and Alice Elizabeth (Mitchell) J.; m. Virginia Lee Hartley, Aug. 2, 1980; children: Virginia Hartley, McChesney Hill III. BA with high distinction, U. Va., 1977, JD, 1980. Bar: Ga. 1980, U.S. Dist. Ct. (no. dist.) Ga. 1980, U.S. Ct. Appeals (11th cir.) 1980. Ptnr. Long, Aldridge & Norman LLP, Atlanta, 1988—95, Alston & Bird, Atlanta, 1995—, head capital markets group, 2000—05, co-head of corp. practice, 2005—08. Contbr. articles to profl. jours. Mem.: ABA, Atlanta Bar Assn. (founding dir. bus. and fin. law sect., trustee Westminister Schs., Atlanta & Vassar Woolley Fdn.), Ga. Bar Assn. (Ga. Bus. Corp Code Revision com. mem.), Piedmont Driving Club (Atlanta). Presbyterian. Avocation: sports. Home: 7 Austell Way Atlanta GA 30305 Office: Alston & Bird LLP One Atlantic Ctr 1201 W Peachtree St NW Atlanta GA 30309-3424 Office Phone: 404-881-7823. Office Fax: 404-253-8348. Business E-Mail: hill.jeffries@alston.com.

JEFFUS, MARGARET (MAGGIE) M., state legislator; b. Oct. 22, 1934; m. Charles Jeffus (dec.); m. Ted J. Thompson, 1991; children: Edward Dane, Holly Ann. State rep. Dist 89, NC, 1990—94, NC, 1996—2002; state rep. Dist 59 NC, 2003—; former educator. Mem.: League of Women Voters, Altrusa Club of Greensboro Inc. Democrat. Presbyterian. Office: North Carolina House of Representatives 16 W Jones St Rm 1307 Raleigh NC 27601-1096 Home Phone: 336-275-4762; Office Phone: 919-733-5191. E-mail: Maggie.Jeffus@ncleg.net.

JEHN, CHRISTOPHER, economist, think-tank executive, computer company executive, federal official; b. Chgo., Mar. 12, 1943; s. Mark and Pearl Jehn; m. Mary Ellen Jehn, Dec. 26, 1967; 1 child, Andrea Jehn Kennedy. Student, Reed Coll., 1960—62; BA in Economics, Beloit Coll., 1964; MA in Economics, U. Chgo., 1969. Instr. economics U. Ill., Chgo., 1969—70; asst. prof. economics George Wash. U., Washington, 1970—72; project dir. Ctr. Naval Analyses, Arlington, Va., 1972—77, dir. inst. naval studies, 1977—79, dir. marine corps ops. analysis group, 1979—89, v.p., 1981—89; asst. sec. def. U.S. Dept. Def., Washington, 1989—93; dir. strategy forces and resources divsn. Inst. Def. Analyses, Alexandria, Va., 1993—95; sr. v.p. ICF Kaiser Internat., Vienna, Va., 1995—97; exec. dir. Nat. Def. Panel, Washington, 1997—98; asst. dir. nat. security Congl. Budget Office, Washington, 1998—2001; v.p. govt. programs Cray Inc., Seattle, 2001—08; mem. Spectrum Group, 2009—13. Commr. Commn. Servicemembers and Veterans Transition Assistance, Arlington, 1996—98. Mem., bd. dirs. N.G. Youth Found., Alexandria, 2007; mem. bd. advisors Nat. Mil. Family Assn., Alexandria, Va., 2003. Recipient Benjamin Hooks Disting. Svc. award, NAACP, 1991, Meritorious Police Cross, Red Category, Govt. of Spain, 1992, Disting. Pub. Svc. medal, U.S. Dept. Def., 1993. Mem.: AAAS. Republican. Home: 6508 Lakeview Dr Falls Church VA 22041 Office: 11 Canal Center Plz Ste 103 Alexandria VA 22314 Office Phone: 571-216-1380. Personal E-mail: cjehn@cox.net. Business E-Mail: cjehn@spectrumgrp.com.

JELKS, MARY LARSON, retired pediatrician; b. Galva, Ill., 1929; MD, U. Nebr., 1955. Diplomate Am. Bd. Pediats., Am. Bd. Allergy and Immunology. Intern Johns Hopkins Hosp., Balt., 1955-56, resident, 1956-57, 58-60, Grace-New Haven Hosp., 1957; fellow U. Fla. Tchg. Hosp., 1960-61; clin. asst. prof. U. South Fla.; ret.; active aerobiology, 1985—. Fellow Am. Acad. Allery and Immunology, Am. Acad. Pediats.; mem. AMA. Achievements include active research in aerobiology. Home: 1930 Clematis St Sarasota FL 34239-3813

JELLICORSE, JOHN LEE, communications and theatre educator; b. Bristol, Tenn., Nov. 1, 1937; s. Harold Lee and Kathleen J.; m. Lenah Mary Lawrence, July 21, 1961 (div. 1980); 1 child, Jennifer Lee; m. Delayna Maxine Jordan, June 28, 1992; 1 child, John Adam. AB, U. Tenn., 1959; PhD, Northwestern U., 1967. From instr. to assoc. prof. Northwestern U., Evanston, Ill., 1962-69; assoc. prof. U. Tenn., Knoxville, 1969-74; prof., head dept. communication and theatre U. N.C., Greensboro, 1974-88, dir. theatre divsn., 1988-90, dir. broadcasting/cinema divsn., 1990-91, prof., 1994—2009, head dept. broadcasting and cinema, 2001—06, dir. entrepreneurial innovation in the arts, 2007—09; dean Sch. Comm. Hong Kong Bapt. U., 1991-94. Cons. Wroclaw Tech. U., Poland. Contbr. chapters to books, articles to profl. jours. Recipient Outstanding Tchr. award Northwestern U., 1968; So. Fellowship Fund fellow, 1959-62. Mem. Nat. Comm. Assn. Office: U NC Greensboro 308 McIver PO Box 26170 Greensboro NC 27402 Home Phone: 336-312-5095. Business E-Mail: jljellic@uncg.edu.

JELLISON, BRIAN D., manufacturing executive; BS, Indiana U.; MS, Columbia U. Mgmt. positions with Ingersoll-Rand Co., Woodcliff Lake, NJ, 1985—94, corp. v.p., 1994—98, corp. exec. v.p., 1998—2001; pres., CEO Roper Industries, Sarasota, Fla., 2001—03; chmn., pres., CEO Roper Industries, Inc., Sarasota, Fla., 2003—. Bd. dir. Champion Enterprises. Office: Roper Industries Ste 200 6901 Professional Pkwy E Sarasota FL 34240

JEMISON, MAE CAROL, physician, engineer, entrepreneur, philanthropist, educator, former astronaut; b. Decatur, Ala., Oct. 17, 1956; d. Charlie and Dorothy (Green) J. BS in ChemE, BA in African-Am. Studies, Stanford U., 1977; MD, Cornell U., 1981. Physician Peace Corps, Sierra Leone, Western Africa, 1983—85; pvt. practice LA; mission specialist NASA, Houston, 1987—93, astronaut on space shuttle Endeavor, 1992; prof. Dartmouth Coll., 1995—2002. Founder, pres. The Earth We Share Internat. Sci. Camp; A.D. White prof.-at-large Cornell U.; bd. dirs. Valspar Corp.; founder, pres. BioSentient Corp.; bd. dirs. Kimberly-Clark Corp.; mem., bd. dirs. Scholastic, Inc., 1993—; founder, pres. The Jemison Group, Inc., 1993—, The Dorothy Jemison Foundation for Excellence, 1994—; national sci. literary advocate Bayer Corp., 1995—. Author: Find Where The Wind Goes, 2001; TV host Discovery Channel, World of Wonder, 1994—95. Named one of World's 50 Most Beautiful People, People Mag., 1993. Mem.: NAS Inst. Medicine. Achievements include being first woman of color to fly in space. Office: Jemison Group Inc PO Box 591455 Houston TX 77259 Business E-Mail: mae.jemison@scholastic.com.

JENKINS, ALBERT FELTON, JR., lawyer; b. Madison, Ga., Jan. 18, 1941; s. A. Felton and Jimmie Lucille (Davis) J.; m. Julie Richardson Green, Apr. 16, 1966; children: A. Felton III, Emily Green, Alan Davis. AB, U. Ga., 1963, LLB, 1965. Bar: Ga. 1965, U.S. Dist. Ct. (no. dist.) Ga. 1965, U.S. Ct. Appeals Ga. 1965, U.S. Ct. Appeals (4th cir.) 1981, U.S. Ct. Appeals (5th cir.) 1966, U.S. Ct. Appeals (11th cir.) 1981, U.S. Ct. Appeals (D.C. cir.) 1987, U.S. Supreme Ct. 1968. Assoc. King & Spalding, Atlanta, 1965-70, ptnr., 1971-92, ret. ptnr., 1992—. Chmn. bd. visitors U. Ga. Law Sch., Athens, 1974; mem. Gov.'s Appellate Jud. Selection Com., Atlanta, 1972-73, Gov.'s Jud. process Rev. Com., Atlanta, 1984-85, Ga. Joint Study Commn. on Revenue Structure, 1992-95, Ga. Agrl. Exposition Authority, 1998-2006. Co-author: (2 vol. treatise) Georgia Civil Procedure Forms-Practice, 1988. Sec. bd. trustees U. Ga. Found., 1979-85; chmn., pres. Atlanta unit Am. Cancer Soc., 1982-83; trustee, vice-chmn. Atlanta Fulton Pub. Libr. Sys., 1995-97; regent Univ. Sys. of Ga., 2006—. Sgt. Air N.G., 1965-71. Fellow Am. Bar Found.; mem. State Bar of Ga. (pres. Young Lawyers 1972-73, bd. govs. 1983-91), Piedmont Driving Club (Atlanta), Phi Beta Kappa, Omicron Delta Kappa. Methodist. Office: King & Spalding 1180 Peachtree St NW Atlanta GA 30309-3521 Office Phone: 706-342-3564.

JENKINS, BENJAMIN P., III, bank executive; b. May 8, 1944; BS in Textile Chemistry, NC State U.; MBA, U. Ala. Pres. First Union, Md., DC, Va., Fla., 1999; pres., Gen. Bank Wachovia Corp., Charlotte, NC, 1999, sr. exec. v.p., 2001—05, vice chmn., 2005, interim COO, 2008; vice chmn., Retail Banking Group Morgan Stanley, 2010—. 2002 campaign chmn. Mecklenburg Arts & Sci. Coun.; bd. dirs. Presbyn. Hosp. Healthcare/Novant; trustee Queens U.; bd. advisors N.C. State U., POST; bd. visitors N.C. State U. Office: Morgan Stanley 1900 Selwyn Ave Charlotte NC 28274-0001 Office Phone: 212-761-4000. Office Fax: 212-761-0086. Business E-Mail: benjamin.jenkins@morganstanley.com.

JENKINS, CHARLES H., JR., retail company executive; m. Dorothy Chao; children: Jennifer, Anthony. BBA, Emory U., Ga., 1964, MBA, 1965; PhD, Havard Bus. Sch., Mass. Asst. to real estate v.p. Publix Super Markets, Inc., Lakeland, Fla., 1969, v.p., 1974, exec. v.p., 1988, chmn. exec. com., 1990—2000, COO, 2000, CEO,

2001—08, chmn., 2008—. Pres. Lakeland C. of C. Mem.: Boston Symphony Orch. Bd. of Overseers. Office: Publix Super Markets PO Box 407 Lakeland FL 33802-0407

JENKINS, CLARK, state legislator; State senator Dist. 3, NC, 2002—; mem. W.S. Clark Farms. Mem. Appropriations on Dept. of Transp. com., Appropriations/Base Budget com., Commerce com., Judiciary I com., Pensions and Retirement and Aging com.; vice chmn. Transp. com.; co-chmn. Fin. com. Democrat. Mailing: Dist Off PO Box 310 Tarboro NC 27886 Office Phone: 919-715-3040, 252-823-7029. Business E-Mail: Clark.Jenkins@ncleg.net.

JENKINS, DOROTHY C., chemicals executive; Grad., Wellesley Coll.; BS in Math., U. South Fla. Bd. dirs. A-Group Holdings, Westlake Chem. Corp., 2003—. Bd. dirs. Polk Museum of Art, John and Mable Ringling Museum of Art Found. Office: Westlake Chemical Corp 2801 Post Oak Blvd Houston TX 77056 Office Phone: 713-960-9111. Office Fax: 713-963-1590. Business E-Mail: djenkins@westlake.com.

JENKINS, EVAN H., state legislator; b. Huntington, W.Va., Sept. 12, 1960; s. John E. and Dorothy C. Jenkins; m. Elizabeth Weiler; children: Evan Jr., Charles, Olivia. Atty. Jenkins Fenstermaker PLLC, 1987—92; with W. Va. State C. of C., 1992—99; exec. dir. W. Va. Med. Assn., 1999—; mem. W. Va. House of Dels., 1994—98; mem. Dist. 5 W. Va. State Senate, 2002—. Former bus. law instr. Marshall U.; mem. US Delegation to Taiwan, Am. Coun. Young Polit. Leaders. Past pres. Big Brothers/Big Sisters of the Tri-State; bd. dir. Cabell County Cmty. Svcs. Orgn., Huntington Main St., Riverview Manor, W. Va.Coun. on Economics in Edn., W. Va. EPSCORE; pres. bd. dir. Leadership W. Va., Operation Bus. and Edn. Succeeding Together; past. mem., bd. dirs. Western W. Va. Chpt. Am. Red Cross; organizer W. Va. Health Initiative Inc. and W. Va. Ctr. for Patent Safety; mem. cmty. adv. com. YMCA Activate America. Recipient Med. Exec. Meritorious Achievement award, AMA, 2006. Mem.: W. Va. Bar Assn., Cabell County Bar Assn., ABA, Dem. Leadership Coun. (adv. bd.). Democrat. Presbyterian. Office: State Capitol, Rm 216 W Bldg 1 Charleston WV 25305 Home: 121 Oak Ln Huntington WV 25701-4762 Office Phone: 304-357-7956. E-mail: evan.jenkins@wvsenate.gov.

JENKINS, HOWARD M., supermarket executive; b. 1951; MBA, Emory U. Joined Publix Super Markets, Inc., Lakeland, Fla., 1966, v.p. rsch., exec. v.p., 1976-90, CEO, 1990—2001, chmn., 1990—2008, chmn. exec. com., 2008—. Pres., chmn. Jenkins Clinic. also: 1936 George Jenkins Blvd Lakeland FL 33815-3760

JENKINS, JAMES STEPHEN, internist; b. Little Rock, Jan. 24, 1961; MD, U. Ark., 1987. Diplomate Am. Bd. Internal Medicine. Intern U. Mo. Hosp., Columbia, 1987-88, resident in medicine, 1988-90, fellow in cardiology, 1991-93; fellow in interventional cardiology Oschner Clin., New Orleans, 1993-94; assoc. sect. head, interventional cardiol. Ochsner Med. Inst., New Orleans, and dir. interventional cardiology rsch. Named one of Top Doctors La., La. Life mag., 2007. Fellow Am. Coll. Cardiology (La. chpt.), mem. Coll. Physicians. Office: Ochsner Med Inst 1514 Jefferson Hwy New Orleans LA 70121-2429 Office Phone: 504-842-3786.

JENKINS, JOHNIE NORTON, research geneticist, research administrator; b. Barton, Ark., Nov. 3, 1934; married, 1959; 2 children. BSA, U. Ark., 1956; MS, Purdue U., 1958, PhD in Genetics, 1960. Rsch. assoc. in agronomy U. Ill., Urbana, 1960-61; rsch. geneticist Agrl. Rsch. Svc., USDA, 1961-80, dir. Crop Sci. Rsch. Lab. Mississippi State, Miss., 1980—. Prof. crop sci. and mem. grad. faculty Miss. State U., 1964—. Recipient Mobay Cotton Rsch. Recognition award, Verdant Crop Genetics award of yr., 2000. Fellow AAAS, Am. Soc. Agronomy, Crop Sci. Soc. Am. Achievements include research on host plant resistance to cotton insects and nematodes; investigations of basic causes of insect and nematode resistance in cotton plants and development of factors which will confer resistance. Office: USDA-ARS Crop Sci Rsch Lab PO Box 5367 Mississippi State MS 39762-5367

JENKINS, JONI L., state legislator; b. Dec. 6, 1958; Comm. specialist; mem. Dist. 44 Ky. House of Reps., 1995—. Mem.: Jefferson County Young Dem., America Soc. Tng. & Devel., Shively & Jackson Dem. Clubs. Democrat. Mailing: 2010 O'Brien Court Shively KY 40216 Home Phone: 502-447-4324; Office Phone: 502-564-8100 ext. 692. Business E-Mail: jonijenkins@aol.com.

JENKINS, KENT, JR., communications executive; Attended, U. NC, Chapel Hill, 1973. Comm. mgr. Redback-Ericsson, 1999—2000, Real Networks, 1999—2000, Microsoft, 1999—2000, Cisco, 1999—2000; mng. dir. Burson-Marsteller, 2002—04; sr. v.p., corp. comm. Amerigroup Corp. Office: Amerigroup Corp 4425 Corporation Ln Virginia Beach VA 23462 Office Phone: 757-490-6900. Office Fax: 757-518-3600. Business E-Mail: kjenkins@amerigroupcorp.com.

JENKINS, MARSHALL, internet consultant, entrepreneur; b. Dayton, Ohio, Apr. 8, 1952; s. Bobbie Whitfield and Louise (Stafford) J.; m. Catherine Fogle. AA, Brevard C.C., Cocoa, Fla., 1972; BA, U. South Fla., 1975; MS, Fla. State U., 1978. Program analyst Planning Rsch. Corp., Cocoa Beach, Fla., 1978-81; assoc. engr. Martin Marietta Aerospace, Kennedy Space Ctr., Fla., 1982-83; software project and software quality assurance engr., mgmt. system analyst Lockheed Space Ops. Co., Titusville, Fla., 1983-91; founder, owner Quaylor Comm., Melbourne, Fla., 1991—2010; pres., LLC mgr. Quaylor.Com LLC; founder, pres. Quaystar Corp., 2010. Software design strategist internet website developer, communication strategies, mgmt. sys. cons., pub. rels. Vol. Spl. Olympics Dist. Competitions, Merritt Island, Fla., 1983. Mem. Am. Mgmt. Assn., Space Coast Seminole Boosters Inc. (pres. Melbourne, Fla. 1986-87, bd. dirs. 1987-88), Fla. State U. Seminole Boosters Inc. (Brevard County, Fla. area chmn. 1987-88), Fla. State U. Alumni Assn., Tau Kappa Epsilon. Republican. Methodist. Avocations: tennis, golf, travel. Home: 4365 Windover Way Melbourne FL 32934-8518 Business E-Mail: marshje@outlook.com.

JENKINS, MICHAEL AUSTIN, corporate executive; b. Dallas, Feb. 1, 1942; s. Berniece (Pollard) J.; m. Bee Lyn Sterett; children: Delanie Carol, Michael Angus, Tiffany Lyn. M in Theater, Bus. and Journalism, Baylor U., 1963. V.p. Six Flags Over Tex., Arlington, 1970; pres. Leisure and Recreation Concepts, Inc., Dallas, 1970—. Bd. dirs. Internat. Broadcasting Corp., Mpls.; mem. recreational devel. coun. Urban Land Inst., Washington, bd. dirs. Silverleaf Resorts, Inc., 1997-2002, bd. dirs. Silverleaf Resorts, Inc., 2009-. Mem. pres.'s task force State Fair of Tex., Dallas; bd. dirs. Dallas Summer Mus., 1989—, Dallas Theater Ctr., Dallas Shakespeare Festival, YMCA, Dallas, 1989—. Republican. Mem. Internat. Assn. Amusement Pks. and Attractions (bd. dirs., Fred W. Sweepstakes award 1980, Dudley S. Humphrey award 1977, Hon. Mention 1976, N.S. Alexander award 1969), Internat. Assns. Fairs and Exhibitions, Am. Recreational Equipment Assn. Home: 1805 Burr Oak St Arlington TX 76012-5602 Office: Leisure & Recreation Concepts 2151 Fort Worth Ave Dallas TX 75211-1812 Office Fax: 214-941-5157. Business E-Mail: MJenkins@silverleafresorts.com.

JENKINS, RICHARD LEE, manufacturing executive; b. Lynchburg, Va., July 20, 1931; s. Robert Julian and Beulah Vivian (Crews) J.; m. Doris E. Rucker, Dec. 24, 1958; children: Terena M., Richard C. BA, Lynchburg Coll., 1957; MBA, U. Mass., 1970. Various fin. mgmt. positions Gen. Electric Co., Lynchburg, Schenectady, NY, and Pittsfield, Mass., 1957-72; controller, mgr. Mfg. Transformer div. Allis-Chalmers, Pitts., 1972-75; gen. mgr. Indsl. Pump div. Allis-Chalmers, Cin., 1975-79; sr. v.p. Lynchburg Foundry, 1979-81; gen. mgr. service div. Siemens-Allis, Inc., Atlanta, 1981-84; sr. v.p. adminstrn. and internat. ops., chief fin. officer Diversified Products Corp., Opelika, Ala., 1984—. Treas., bd. dirs. Micah Corp. of Berkshire County, Pittsfield, 1968-72; bd. dirs. Va. Nat. Bank, Lynchburg, 1979-81. Auditor ARC, Pittsfield, 1966; bd. dirs., exec. on loan United Community Services, Pittsfield, 1972; campaign chmn. Piedmont Heart Assn., Lynchburg, 1980. Served with USN, 1950-54, Korea. Mem.: Cherokee Country (Atlanta), Saugahatchee Country (Opelika). Office: Diversified Products Corp 309 Williamson Ave Opelika AL 36804-7313 Home: 1820 E University Dr Auburn AL 36830-5230 E-mail: richardjenkins@charter.net.

JENKINS, ROGER W., oil industry executive; B in Petroleum Engring., La. State U., 1983; MBA in Finance, Tulane U., 1994. Drilling mgr. Murphy Oil Corp., Kuala Lumpur, Malaysia, 2001—02, ops. mgr. Sabah, 2002—04, sr. ops. mgr., 2004—06, gen. mgr., 2006—07, v.p., gen. mgr., 2007, sr. v.p. North America Houston, 2007—09, pres., Exploration and Production Company, 2009—12, COO, 2012—13, pres., CEO, 2013—. Bd. dirs. Murphy Oil Corp., 2013—. Office: Murphy Oil Corporation 200 Peach St PO Box 7000 El Dorado AR 71731-7000*

JENKINS, RUBEN LEE, chemicals executive; b. Beggs, Okla., Nov. 27, 1929; s. William Arnold and Myrtle (Kimble) J.; m. Sylvia Griffin, July 17, 1956; children: Amy, Kimble Lee, William Griffin. BA, U. Okla., 1952, LLB, 1956; LLM, NYU, 1959. Bar: Okla. 1956. Law clk. to presiding justice U.S. Dist. Ct. (we. dist.) Okla., Oklahoma City, 1956; clk. U.S. Ct., Oklahoma City, 1956-58; research asst. in internat. law NYU, NYC, 1958-59; assoc. Allende & Brea, Buenos Aires, 1959-60; exec. v.p., gen. counsel White Eagle Internat., Midland, Tex., 1960-65; v.p. corp. devel. Plough, Inc., Memphis, 1965-71, dir, 1970, sr. v.p. hdqrs., 1972-73, exec. v.p., 1973-76, pres., 1976-89; dir. Schering-Plough Corp., Madison, NJ, 1971-89, sr. v.p., 1976-80, exec. v.p., 1980-89. Bd. dirs. Chickasaw coun. Boy Scouts Am., Memphis; hon. trustee Memphis U. Sch. Capt. USMC, 1952-54. Mem. ABA, Tenn. Bar Assn., Okla. Bar Assn., Non-Prescription Drug Mfrs. Assn. (bd. dirs. 1976-89), Palm Beach Polo and Country Club. Methodist. Address: 2886 Winding Oaks Ln West Palm Beach FL 33414 Personal E-mail: rljenkins1@comcast.net.

JENKINS, SHEILA ALNITA, psychologist; b. Inverness, Fla., Sept. 28, 1963; d. Peggy Ann Gary. BS, U. Houston, 1985, MEd, 1987; PhD, U. Ga., 1992. Psychologist Tex., registered Nat. Register Health Svc. Providers in Psychology. Psychologist Houston Ind. Sch. Dist., 1992—2003; psychologist, owner Sheila A. Jenkins, PhD & Associates, Houston, 1993—. Bd. dirs. Tex. Psychol. Found., 2004—08, pres., 2007, Houston Psychol. Found., 2004—; active Delta Academic, Artistic, and Philanthropic Found., Inc., Houston, 2004—08. Named Leadership Honoree, Heman Sweat Found., 2004; grad. scholar, U. Ga., 1989. Mem.: APA, Houston Psychol. Assn. (pres. 1999—2000, President's award 1997, 2004), Tex. Psychol. Assn. (trustee 2000—01), Delta Sigma Theta (chpt. pres. 2004—06). Office: 5821 Southwest Fwy Ste 380 Houston TX 77057-7539 Business E-Mail: drjenkins@drsheilajenkins.com.*

JENKINS, WILLIAM L., academic administrator; b. South Africa; arrived in US, 1978; m. Peggy Jenkins; children: Sharon, Gwynn, Anthea, Warren. Professional vet. medicine degree, U. Pretoria, South Africa, 1958, vet. specialist credentials, 1968; PhD, U. Missouri, Columbia, Mo., 1970; D (hon.), U. Pretoria, 2004. Various positions over several years to prof. and head, Dept. of Vet. Physiology, Pharmacology and Toxicology U. Pretoria, South Africa, 1971—78; faculty, Dept. of Vet. Physiol. and Pharmacology Texas A&M U., College Station, Tex., 1978—88; dean of Sch. of Vet. Medicine La. State U., Baton Rouge, 1988—93, provost and vice chancellor, 1993—96, chancellor, 1996—99, acting chancellor, 2008—; pres. La. State U. Sys., Baton Rouge, 1999—2007, pres. emeritus, 2007—. Mem. NIH's Alcohol Abuse and Misuse on Coll. Campuses Com., La. Blue Ribbon Commn. for Teacher Quality. Pub. more than 60 scientific articles and 15 textbook chapters; co-author: vet. pharmacology textbook. Bd. dir. Greater Baton Rouge C. of C., Baton Rouge Ctr. for World Affairs, Coun. for a Better La., Arts Coun. of Greater Baton Rouge, La. Endowment for the Humanities, Academic Distinction Fund; bd. dirs. Nature Conservancy of La., Teach for America South La.; mem. Baton Rouge board of Nat. Conf. for Cmty. and Justice. Recipient Communication and Leadership award, Toastmasters Internat., 1999, Vision of Excellence award, New Orleans Regional C. of C., 2000; named Communicator of Yr., PublicRelations Assn. of La., 1997, Disting. Alumnus, U. Mo., 1997. Mem.: Am. Academy of Vet. Nutrition, Internat. Assn. of Forensic Toxicologists, World Assn. of Vet. Physiologists, Pharmacologists and Biochemists, Am. Coll. Vet. Clin. Pharmacology, Am. Vet. Medical Assn. Office: Office of Chancellor La State Univ 156 Thomas Boyd Hall Baton Rouge LA 70803 Office Phone: 225-578-6977. E-mail: chancellor@lsu.edu.

JENNE, EVAN, state legislator; b. Hollywood, Fla., Sept. 4, 1977; s. Kenneth C. Jenne. BS in Polit. Sci., Fla. State U., 1999, MPA, 2002. Banker; mem. Dist. 100 Fla. House of Reps., Tallahassee, 2006—, Dem. floor leader, 2008, Dem. whip, 2006—, ranking mem. transp. and econ. devel. appropriations com., mem. ins., bus. and fin. affairs policy com., mil. and local affairs policy com., policy coun., rules and calendar coun. Mem. Child Net Adv. Bd.; bd. mem. Susan B. Anthony Recovery Ctr. Mem.: Optimist Club, Cooper City. Democrat. Episcopalian. Office: 3107 Stirling Rd Ste 207 Fort Lauderdale FL 33312-8502 also: 1401 The Capitol 402 S Monroe St Tallahassee FL 32399-1300 Office Phone: 954-321-2760, 850-488-0245.

JENNEWEIN, JAMES JOSEPH, architect; b. New Rochelle, NY, July 20, 1929; s. Carl Paul and Gina (Pirra) J.; m. Edith Joan Wilson, Nov. 28, 1953; children: James Christopher, Gina Louise, Donald Andrew, Jonathan Paul. BArch, Syracuse U., 1952. Fulbright scholar Stuttgart U. (Technische Hochschule), Federal Republic of Germany, 1955-56; draftsman McCoy & Blair Architects, White Plains, NY, 1956-57; designer Harrison & Abramovitz Architects, NYC, 1957-60; prin./ptnr. Jennewein Architects, NYC, 1961-62; prin. McElvy, Jennewein, Stefany & Howard, Architects, Tampa, Fla., 1962-84, Jennewein, Archtl. Planning, Tampa, 1984; prin., ptnr. Jennewein Schemmer and Assocs., Tampa, 1985-91; ptnr. JDR Archs., PA, Tampa, 1992—. Pres. Fla. State Bd. Architecture, 1969-72. Trustee Brookgreen Gardens, Murrells Inlet, S.C., 1983-05, trustee emeritus, 2006—; chmn. Gasparilla Art Show, Tampa, 1977, Tampa C. of C. Environ. Com., 1987; pres. Tampa Bay Art Ctr., 1975, Tampa Mus. Art, 1985. Lt. (j.g.) USN, 1952-55. Recipient House of Yr. award Archtl. Record, N.Y.C., 1963, Ybor Sta. P.O. award Hillsborough County Planning Commn., Tampa. 1989. Fellow AIA; mem. Fla. Assn. AIA (pres. 1985-86, Pullara award 1985), Fla. Cen. Chpt. AIA (pres. 1967-68, Honor medal 1985), Nat. Sculpture Soc. (bd. dirs. 2004-, Honor medal 2013), Tampa Yacht Club, Ye Mystic Krewe of Gasparilla, Tampa. Republican. Episcopalian. Avocations: fishing, sailing. Home: 4710 W Clear Ave Tampa FL 33629-5512 Office: JDR Archs 3333 W Kennedy Blvd Ste 203 Tampa FL 33609-2959 Office Phone: 813-879-6633. E-mail: rdjmail@rdjarchitects.com.

JENNINGS, CHRISTINE LOUISE, retired bank executive; b. New Boston, Ohio, Nov. 26, 1945; d. Kenneth Franklin and E. Louise Jennings. Student, Ea. Ky. U., Franklin U., Columbus, Ohio. Asst. v.p. Huntington Nat. Bank, Columbus, 1970-84; v.p. S.E. Bank, Sarasota, Fla., 1984-85, NCNB, Sarasota, 1985-87; sr. v.p. Liberty Nat. Bank, Bradenton, Fla., 1987-90; founder, pres., CEO Sarasota Bank, Bradenton, Fla., 1990—2004; ret., 2004. Apptd. chair Real Property-Lease Procurement Task Force, Fla. Past pres. John & Mable Ringling Mus. Art, Sarasota, Sarasota Film Festival, Mental Health Assn. Sarasota County, Sarasota Ballet, Downtown Assn. Sarasota; active Big Brothers/Big Sisters, All Faiths Food Bank, Cmty. AIDS Network; exec. com. United Way Manatee County, 1988—90. Mem.: Fla. Bankers' Assn. (state chair polit. action and legis. coms.), Sarasota C. of C., Fla. Women's Network. Democrat. Avocations: reading, music, public speaking, golf, walking, biking. Home: Apt 510 988 Boulevard Of The Arts Sarasota FL 34236-4835 Mailing: Campaign Address 1549 Ringling Blvd Ste 601 Sarasota FL 34236 Office Phone: 941-366-8121.

JENNINGS, HENRY SMITH, III, cardiologist; b. Atlanta, May 16, 1951; s. Henry Smith Jr. and Elizabeth (Martin) J.; m. Polly Cooper; 1 child, Mary Bailey. BS summa cum laude, Davidson Coll., 1973; MD, Vanderbilt U., 1977. Diplomate Am. Bd. Internal Medicine, subspecialty cardiovascular diseases and interventional cardiology, Nat. Bd. Med. Examiners; lic. physician and surgeon, Tenn., Ky. Intern internal medicine Vanderbilt U. Affiliated Hosps., Nashville, 1977-78, resident internal medicine, 1978-80; fellow clin. cardiology divsn. cardiology dept. medicine Vanderbilt U., 1980-82; clin. instr. medicine Vanderbilt U. Sch. Medicine, 1982-89, asst. clin. prof. medicine, 1989-97, assoc. clin. prof. medicine, 1997—2007, asst. prof. medicine, 2007—; med. dir. Cardiac Rehab. Ctr. St. Thomas Hosp., Nashville, 1984—2001, assoc. chief cardiac scis., 2001—05, pres.-elect med. staff, 2005—06; chmn. steering com. St. Thomas Heart Inst., 2002—04; med. dir. Network Develop. Vanderbilt Heart & Vascular Inst., 2007—10. Mem. active staff Vanderbilt U. Med. Ctr.; mem. courtesy staff Centennial Med. Ctr., Nashville, St. Thomas Hosp.; mem. cons. staff Bapt. Hosp., Nashville. Contbr. articles to profl. jours. Bd. dirs. Heart Inst., St. Thomas Hosp., Nashvile, 1992-94, Tenn. Heart Inst., 1989-91. Justin Potter med. scholar Vanderbilt U. Sch. Medicine, Nashville, 1973-77. Fellow ACP, Am. Coll. Cardiology, Am. Coll. Chest Physicians, Coun. Clin. Cardiology Am. Heart Assn., Soc. Cardiac Angiography and Interventions; mem. AMA, Am. Assn. Cardiovasc. and Pulmonary Rehab., Internat. Soc. Heart Transplantation, Am. Heart Assn., So. Med. Assn., Tenn. Med. Assn., Nashville Acad. Medicine, Gottlieb Friesinger Soc. (pres.-elect 2001, pres. 2002), Canby Robinson Soc. Bd. Methodist. Home: Northumberland 3 Castle Rising Nashville TN 37215-4126 Office: Vanderbilt Heart and Vascular Inst Ste 5209 MCE South Tower 1215 21st Ave S Nashville TN 37232-8802 Home Phone: 615-665-0860; Office Phone: 615-322-2318. Office Fax: 615-936-7365. Business E-Mail: henry.jennings@vanderbilt.edu.

JENNINGS, JOSEPH ASHBY, banker; b. Richmond, Va., Aug. 12, 1920; s. Joseph Ashby and Leone (Bishop) J.; m. Anne Barrow Hatcher, Oct. 29, 1960; children: Joseph Ashby III, Ashby Anne. BS, U. Richmond, 1949, DSc (hon.), 1980; grad. certificate, Rutgers U., 1952; LLD (hon.), Va. Union U., 1991. With United Va. Bank, Richmond, 1949-85, v.p., 1956-66, sr. v.p., 1966-67, exec. v.p., 1967-71, pres., 1971, chmn. bd., 1972-85; also dir.; vice chmn. bd. United Va. Bankshares, Inc., 1972-75, pres., 1975-76, chief adminstrv. officer, 1972-76, chmn. bd., chief exec. officer, 1976-85, chmn. bd., 1985-86. Served with USAAF, 1942-46. Mem. Fin. Analysts Fedn. (past exec. v.p., dir.), Phi Beta Kappa, Omicron Delta Kappa, Phi Delta Theta, Beta Gamma Sigma. Presbyterian.

JENNINGS, MICHAEL C., oil industry executive; BA, Dartmouth Coll.; MBA, Univ. Chgo. Fin. mgmt. positions U.S. Trust Co., NYC, British Petroleum; dir. acquisitions & corp. fin. Cooper Cameron Corp., 1995—98; v.p. fin. & corp. develop. Unimin Corp., 1998—2002; v.p., treas. Cooper Cameron Corp., 2000—05; exec. v.p., CFO Frontier Oil Corp., Houston, 2005—08, pres., CEO, 2009—10, chmn., pres., CEO, 2010—11; pres., CEO HollyFrontier Corp., Dallas, 2011—. Office: HollyFrontier Corp Ste 1300 2828 N Harwood Dallas TX 75201 Office Phone: 214-871-3555.

JENNINGS, ROBERT BURGESS, experimental pathologist, medical educator; b. Balt., Dec. 14, 1926; s. Burgess Hill and Etta (Crout) J.; m. Linda Lee Sheffield, June 28, 1952; children: Carol L., Mary G., John B., Anne E., James R. BS, Northwestern U., 1947, MS, B.M., 1949, MD, 1950. Diplomate Am. Bd. Pathology (trustee 1976-87, pres. 1986-87). Intern Passavant Meml. Hosp., Chgo., 1949—50, resident pathology, 1950—51; mem. faculty Northwestern U. Med. Sch., 1953—75, prof. pathology, 1963—75, chmn. dept., 1969—75, Magerstadt prof., 1969—75; prof., chmn. dept. pathology Duke U. Med. Sch., Durham, NC, 1975—89, James B. Duke prof., 1980—2003, prof. emeritus, 2003—. Vis. scientist Middlesex Hosp. Med. Sch., London, 1961-62; cons. VA Rsch. Hosp., Chgo.; mem. attending staff Northwestern Meml. Hosp., Chgo., 1963-75; mem. pathology A Study sect. USPHS, 1960-65; mem. clin. cardiology adv. com. NIH, 1976-80, mem. cardiovasc. and renal study sect., 1992-95. Mem. editl. bd. Lab. Investigation, 1967-95, Archives Pathology, 1970-80, Jour. Molecular and Cellular Cardiology, 1972-89, Exptl. and Molecular Pathology, 1973-99, Circulation, 1988-91, 93-96, Circulation Rsch., 1976-82, Histopathology, 1977-92, Am. Jour. Pathology, 1983-92, Jour. Applied Cardiology, 1986-90, Cardiosci., 1990-95, Trends in Cardiovasc. Medicine, 1991-92, Cardiovasc. Pathology, 1991-95, Heart Failure Revs., 1996-. Served as lt. (j.g.) USNR, 1951—53. Recipient Peter Harris award, Internat. Soc. Heart Rsch., 1992, Disting. Leader award, 2009, Disting. Achievement award, Soc. Cardiovasc. Pathology, 1996, Discovery Health Channel Am. Med. Honors award, AHA, 2004, Medal of Merit award, Internat. Acad. Cardiovasc. Scis., 2005, Gold-Headed Cane award, Am. Soc. Investigative Pathology, 2007; Markle scholar med. scis., 1958—63. Office: Duke U Med Ctr Dept Pathology Durham NC 27710-0001 Home: 7 Silver Maple Ct Durham NC 27705-5642 Office Phone: 919-684-3776. Business E-Mail: jenni004@mc.duke.edu.

JENNINGS, THOMAS PARKS, lawyer; b. Alexandria, Va., Nov. 16, 1947; s. George Christian and Ellen (Thompson) J.; m. Shelley Corrine Abernathy, Oct. 30, 1971; 1 child, Kathleen Eayre. BA in History cum laude, Wake Forest U., 1970; JD, U. Va., 1975. Bar: Va. 1975. Assoc. Lewis, Wilson, Lewis & Jones, Arlington, Va., 1975-78; atty. First Va. Banks, Inc., Falls Church, 1978-80, gen. counsel, 1980—2003, sec., 1993-99, sr. v.p., 1995—2003; sr. atty. advisor Fed. Housing Fin. Agy., 2004—09. Adj. prof. George Mason U. Sch. Law, Arlington, 1987—88. Trustee Arlington Cmty. Found., 1998-2003, treas., 2001-03; dir. Rixey St. Found., Inc., 1997—; deacon Georgetown Presbyn. Ch., Washington, 1980-82, elder, 1983-85, 95-97, 2006-08, trustee, 1988-90, dir. Bd. Pensions, Presbyn. Ch. USA,

2001—2010, Com. Ministry Nat. Capital Presbyn., 2010-. With US Army, 1970—71. Mem.: Va. State Bar Assn. Presbyterian. Avocations: bridge, kayaking. Personal E-mail: stkj123@aol.com.

JENNINGS, WANDA TAYLOR, state legislator; b. Feb. 9, 1946; m. Terry Lee Jennings. Mem. Dist. 7 Miss. House of Reps., 1999—, vice chair state libr. com., mem. apportionment and elections com., appropriations com., congl. redistricting com., edn. com., ethics com., legis. reapportionment com., rules com.; sec. DeSoto County Rep. Com.; businesswoman; dir. Olive Br. Cmty. Theatre. Mem.: DeSoto Rep. Club (bd. dir.), Southaven C. of C., DeSoto Area Rep. Women. Republican. Mailing: 1535 Sherwood Lane Southaven MS 39531 Office Phone: 601-359-9465. E-mail: wjennings@house.ms.gov.

JENRETTE, THOMAS SHEPARD, JR., music educator, choral director; b. Roanoke, Va., Feb. 1, 1946; s. Thomas Shepard and Virginia Catherine (Harris) J. BA, U. N.C., 1968, MusM, 1970; D of Mus. Arts, U. Mich., 1976. Choral dir. Cummings H.S., Burlington, NC, 1969—72; dir. cultural arts Burlington City Schs., NC, 1972—73; dir. choral activities S.W. State U., Marshall, Minn., 1976—79, East Tenn. State U., Johnson City, 1979—2012; emeritus prof., music, 2012—. Dir. music First Christian Ch., Johnson City, 1981-84, Covenant Presbyn. Ch., Johnson City, 1991—; dir. East Tenn. State U. Chorale European Tour, 1985, 98, 2001, 06, 09, 11-12; guest condr. choral festival N.C. High Sch., Raleigh, 1987, 2002, Govs. Sch. for Arts, Murfreesboro, Tenn., 1987, Nat. Seminar of Intercollegiate Men's Choruses, Inc., 1992, 2004, 2010; guest condr. N.C. All-State Male Choir, 1997, All-East Tenn. H.S. Male Choir, 1998, Tenn. All-State H.S. Male Choir, 2001, S.C. All-State Male Choir, 2002, Ga. All-State H.S. male choir, 2003, We. Carolina Choral Festival, 2005, 2008, All East Tenn. HS Mixed Choir, 2008, Wis. All-State male Choir., 2010, Nat. Condrs. Conf., U. So. Miss., 2000. Grantee East Tenn. State U., 1988, 90, 96, 99; recipient Marshall Bartholomew award, 2012. Mem. Am. Choral Dirs. Assn. (life; condr. 1986, 88, 94, 2000, 04, so. divsn. convs., 89, 99, 2007, nat. conv., so. divsn. repertoire and stds. chair for male choirs 1999-2005; Tenn. Lifetime Achievement award, 2012), Tenn. Music Educators Assn. (conductor state convs. 1990, 91, 94, 2000, dir. White House, Christmas 1989, 2001, Canticum Novum Festival, Caracas, Venezuela, 1996), Internat. Fedn. Choral Music, Nat. Assn. Tchrs. Singing, Coll. Music Soc. (life), Music Educators Nat. Conf. (condr. so. divsn. conv. 1997), Phi Mu Alpha (hon.), Sigma Alpha Iota Nat. Arts Assoc., Omicron Delta Kappa, Pi Kappa Lambda Home: 2734 E Oakland Ave Apt C-25 Johnson City TN 37601-1887 Office Phone: 423-341-5228. Business E-Mail: jenrette@etsu.edu.

JENSEN, KENNETH R., private equity firm executive; AB in Economics, Princeton U., NJ, 1965; MBA, U. Chgo., 1968, PhD in Acctg., Economics and Fin., 1974. Co-founder, CFO Catallactics Corp., 1968—82; CFO Market Rsch. Corp. America, 1974—80, SunGard Data Systems, Inc., 1983; exec. v.p. Fiserv, Inc., 1984—86, sr. exec. v.p., CFO, Treas., 1986—2006; gen. ptnr. Welsh, Carson, Anderson & Stowe, 2006—. Bd. dirs. Fiserv, Inc., 1984—2007, Alliance Data Sys. Corp., 2001—. Office: Welsh Carson Anderson & Stowe 320 Park Ave Ste 2500 New York NY 10022 Mailing: Alliance Data Systems Inc 7500 Dallas Pky Ste 700 Plano TX 75024 Office Phone: 214-494-3000. Personal E-mail: ken.jensen@alliancedata.com.

JENSEN, RON, mayor, Grand Prairie, Texas, manufacturing executive; m. Rebecca Hyde; children: Eric, Jennifer, Nichole. Grad., U. Tex., Arlington, 1973. From saw shop worker to owner, pres. & CEO Control Products Corp., 1972—; councilman Grand Prairie City Coun., Tex., mayor pro tem, 2003, 2010, 2012; mayor City of Grand Prairie, 2013—. Sunday sch. tchr., trustee Matthew Rd. Bapt. Ch.; bd. mem., past pres. YMCA; pres. Dickinson Elem. PTA, South Grand Prairie Cheerleader Booster; bd. mem. DFW Hosp. Mem.: Grand Prairie C. of C. (bd. mem.), Grand Prairie Rotary Club (past pres.). Office: City of Grand Prairie 317 College St Grand Prairie TX 75050 also: Control Products Corporation 1513 W Jefferson St Grand Prairie TX 75051 Office Phone: 972-314-8014. Business E-Mail: ronj@cpctexas.com.*

JENSEN, THOMAS LEE, lawyer, state legislator; b. Cincinnati, OH, Dec. 29, 1948; s. Carl and Martha Jensen; m. Nannette Curry; children: Natalie, Laura. Student, Cumberland Coll., 1972, No. Ky. U., 1978. Minority floor leader, 1991-94; pvt. practice Jensen Cessna & Benge, London, Ky., 1978—; mem. Dist. 21 Ky. House of Reps., 2005—. Active Just Say No to Drugs Program; del. Mexico for Am. Coun. Young Polit. Leaders; chmn. Laural County Rep. Com.; legal counsel Mem. Rep. Ho. of Reps., 1988; chmn. Ky. State Rep. Party; bd. dirs. Cumberland River Comprehensive Care. Mem. C. of C. (local bd. dirs.), Masons, Shriners. Republican. Presbyterian. Office: Jensen Cessna & Benge 303 S Main St London KY 40741-1906

JENSON, PAUL MARTIN, healthcare services company executive; m. Gay Jenson; 4 children. Various positions HCA, Inc.; CEO Brunswick Cmty. Hosp., 2002—05, St. Luke's Med. Ctr., 2005—07, Biltmore Surgery Ctr., Phoenix, Ariz., 2005—07, St. Luke's Behavioral Health Ctr., 2005—07; pres., Nev. market IASIS Healthcare, LLC, 2007, pres., Ariz. market, 2007—08, exec. v.p., Western region, 2008—. Office: IASIS Healthcare LLC Dover Ctr Bldg E 117 Seaboard Ln Franklin TN 37067 Office Phone: 615-844-2747. Office Fax: 615-846-3006.

JEPSON, ROBERT SCOTT, JR., bank executive; b. Richmond, Va., July 20, 1942; m. Alice Finch Andrews, Dec. 28, 1964; children: Robert Scott, John Steven. BS, U. Richmond, 1964, M of Commerce, 1975; JD (hon.), Gonzaga U., 1986; DCS (hon.), U. Richmond, 1987; DH (hon.), Hamline U., 1988; LLD (hon.), Tusculum Coll., 1989, Ashland U., 1990, Elmhurst Coll., 1991; DSC in Bus. Adminstrn., Franklin U., 1996; D in Bus. (hon.), Fla. So. Coll., 2006, Lees Inerae, 2013; LittD (hon.), Savannah Coll. Art and Design, 2013. With Va. Commonwealth Bankshares, Richmond, 1966-68; v.p. corp. fin. Birr Wilson & Co., Inc., San Francisco, 1968-69; pres. Calif. Capital Mgmt. Corp., Irvine, 1970-73; v.p., dir. corp. fin. Cantor Fitzgerald & Co., Beverly Hills, Calif., 1973-75; dir. corp. planning and devel. Campbell Industries, San Diego, 1975-77; v.p., mgr. merger and acquisition divsn. Continental Ill. Bank, Chgo., 1977-82; sr. v.p., group head U.S. Capital Markets Group, 1st Nat. Bank Chgo., 1982-83; chmn., CEO The Jepson Corp., Chgo., 1983-89, Jepson Assoc. Inc., Savannah, Ga., 1989—. Chmn. Jepson Vineyards Ltd., Ukiah, Calif., 1985—, Coburn Optical Industries Inc., Tulsa, 1992-98; chmn., CEO Kuhlman Corp., Savannah, Ga., 1993-99; bd. advisors Jepson Found., Chgo., 1988—; bd. dirs. AGL Resources, Inc., Atlanta, 1999-2003, Dominion Resources, Inc., Richmond, Va., 2003-; asst. prof. fin. Nat. U., 1976; lectr. U. Richmond, U. Chgo., Northwestern U., Kansas U., Luther Coll., Wake Forest U Bd. trustees Gonzaga U., Spokane, Wash., 1982—86, Hamline U., St. Paul, 1987—92; bd. trustees, vice rector U. Richmond, 1992—95; mem. bd. advisors Franklin U., Columbus, 1996—; chmn., bd. dirs. Ga. Cancer Coalition, 2004—06; chmn., bd. visitors Savannah Coll. of Art and Design, 2001—; bd. dirs. Ga. Ports Authority, Savannah, 2008—; bd. trustees Ga. Hist. Soc., Savannah, 2010—, Lees-Morrae Coll., Banner Elk, NC, 2010—. 1st lt. US Army, 1964—66. Recipient Citation Honor Founders medal Elmhurst Coll., Ill., 1994, Volunteerish and Philanthropy award, Coun. Ind. Colls., 1997. Mem. Commonwealth Club (Richmond), Oglethorpe Club (Savannah), Chatham Club (Savannah), Plantation Club (Savannah), Omicron Delta Kappa (Laurel Crowned Cir. award 2008), Alpha Kappa Psi, Beta Gamma Sigma (Entrepreneur of Yr. medallion 1996), Savannah Tech. Coll. (Cmty. Star award 2007), Omicron Delta Kappa Soc. Inc., Nat. Leadership Honor Soc., Phi Gamma Delta. Republican.

JERGER, EDWARD WILLIAM, engineering educator, dean; b. Milw., Mar. 13, 1922; s. Nickolaus and Ann (Huber) J.; m. Dorothy Marie Post, Aug. 2, 1944 (dec. 1981); children: Betty Ann Murphy, Barbara Lee Smyth; m. Elizabeth Cordiner Sweitzer, Mar. 27, 1982. BS in Mech. Engring, Marquette U., 1946; MS, U. Wis., 1948; PhD, Iowa State U., 1951. Registered profl. engr., Iowa, Ind. Process engr. Wis. Malting Co., Manitowoc, 1946-47; asst. prof. mech. engring. Iowa State U., 1948-55; asso. prof. mech. engring. U. Notre Dame, 1955-61, prof., head mech. engring., 1961-68, asso. dean, 1968-82, prof. mech. engring., 1982-97, prof. emeritus, 1989—. Cons. U. Madre De Maestra Santiago, Dominican Republic, 1965-71 Bd. dirs. Beaufort County Schoolbook Fund. Served with USAAF, 1943-46. Mem. ASME, Am. Soc. Engring. Edn., Nat. Soc. Profl. Engrs., Nat. Fire Protection Assn., Sigma Xi, Phi Kappa Phi, Pi Tau Sigma (nat. v.p. 1969-74, pres. 1974-78), Tau Beta Pi. Home: 16 Freshwater Ln Hilton Head Island SC 29928 Personal E-mail: ejerger@sc.rr.com.

JERGUSON, SEAN, state legislator; b. Feb. 03; m. Kate Jerguson; children: Claire, Eli. Mem Holly Springs City Coun., 2001—; acting mayor Holly Springs, 2003; state rep. Dist. 22 Ga., 2007—; mem. Game Com., 2007—, Fish and Pks. Com., 2007—, Health and Human Svcs. and Regulated Industries Com., 2007—; sec. Children and Youth Com., 2007—. Republican. Methodist. Office: Ga State Assembly Suite 607 Coverdell Legl Office Bldg Atlanta GA 30334 Home Phone: 770-401-2490. E-mail: sean@electsean.com.

JERNIGAN, DONALD, hospital administrator; BS in chemistry, U. Tex., Arlington; PhD, Baylor U. Former pres. Metroplex Hosp., Killeen, Tex., Tennessee Christian Med. Ctr.; CEO, Multi-State Hosp. Divsn. Adventist Health Sys., sr. v.p.; CEO, pres. Fla. Hosp. Ctr., 1999—2006; exec. v.p. Adventist Health Sys., pres., CEO, 2006—. Diplomat Am. Coll. Healthcare Execs. Office: 111 N Orlando Ave Winter Park FL 32789

JERNIGAN, WYATT E., energy executive; Attended in Sociology, Va. Wesleyan Coll. Trainee, petroleum fundamentals University of Texas; various positions, crude oil supply, petroleum mktg. and asset devel. El Paso, Coastal Corp.; mng. dir., petroleum markets originations Coastal Corp. (merged with El Paso), 2001; mng. dir. Prudentia Energy, 2004—05; exec. v.p., crude oil acquisition and petroleum mktg. CVR Energy, Inc., 2006—; exec. v.p., crude and feedstocks Coffeyville Resources, LLC., 2005—07; exec. v.p., crude oil acquisition and petroleum mktg. Coffeyville Acquisition, LLC, 2007—. Office: CVR Energy Inc 2277 Plz Dr Ste 500 Sugar Land TX 77479 Office Phone: 281-207-3200. Business E-Mail: wjernigan@coffeyvillegroup.com.

JERRY, ROBERT HOWARD, II, dean, law educator; b. Lafayette, Ind., July 11, 1953; s. Robert Howard and Marjorie (Collings) J.; m. Lisa Nowak, Sept. 4, 1982; children: John Robert, James Martin, Elizabeth Catherine. BS magna cum laude, Ind. State U., 1974; JD cum laude, U. Mich., 1977. Bar: Ind. 1977, U.S. Ct. Appeals (D.C. cir.) 1978, U.S. Ct. Appeals (7th cir.) 1980, U.S. Ct. Appeals (10th cir.) 1989. Law clk. to Hon. George MacKinnon U.S. Ct. Appeals (DC cir.), Washington, 1977-78; assoc. Barnes, Hickam, Pantzer & Boyd, Indpls., 1978-81; assoc. prof. law U. Kans., Lawrence, 1981-85, prof., 1985-94, dean Sch. Law, 1989-94; prof., Herbert Herff chair of excellence law Cecil C. Humphreys Sch. Law U. Memphis, 1994—98; Floyd R. Gibson Mo. endowed prof. law U. Mo.-Columbia Sch. Law, 1998—2003; dean, Levin Mabie & Levin prof. law Fredric G. Levin Coll. Law, U. Fla., Gainesville, 2003—. Co author: Understanding Insurance Law (with Douglas R. Richmond), 1987, 2d edit., 1996, 3rd edit., 2002, 4th edit. 2007; (with Roger C. Henderson) Insurance Law: Cases and Materials, 2d edit., 1996, 3rd edit., 2001; contbr. numerous articles to profl. jours., chpts. to books. Recipient Bodman-Longley Award, Mich. Law Review, 1976, Coblentz Prize, 1977, Disting. Alumnus Award, Ind. State U., 1992, Dean Sina Award, U. Fla., 2005. Fellow Am. Bar Found.; mem. ABA, Am. Law Inst. Democrat. Episcopalian. Office: U Florida Office of the Dean Fredric G Levin College of Law 264 Holland Hall Spessard L Holland Law Ctr PO Box 117620 Gainesville FL 32611 Office Phone: 352-273-0609. Office Fax: 352-392-8727. Business E-Mail: jerryr@law.ufl.edu.*

JESSEN, DAVID WAYNE, retired accountant; b. Albuquerque, Jan. 13, 1950; BBA in Acctg., U. N.Mex., 1972. CPA N.C., N.Mex., S.C. Staff acct. local CPA firm, Albuquerque, 1971-74, jr. ptnr., 1974-75; mgr. in charge Santa Fe office Ernst & Young, 1975-80, prin. in charge Santa Fe office, 1980—86, dir. taxes N.Mex. offices Albuquerque, 1980-86, tax ptnr. N.Mex. offices, 1986, ptnr. Raleigh, NC, 1987-89, mng. ptnr. office, 1987—89. Mem. Arthur Young Nat. Real Estate Com., 1988, mem. nat. hightech com., 1988—94; ptnr. Ernst & Young, Raliegh, 1975—2008, ptnr., dir. entrepreneurial svcs., 1989—2002, S.E. region dir. entrepreneurial svcs., 1992—94, dir. tax dept., 1995—2008, dir. tax entrepreneurial svcs., 1998—2002; bd. dirs. WakeMed Health & Hosps., chair audit com., 2007—; exec. in residence, faculty accountancy & bus. law dept. U. NC, Wilmington, 2008—. Asst. scoutmaster Boy Scouts Am.; bd. dirs. St. Joseph Hosp. Health Care Found., 1986—87, NC Mus. Art Found., 1992—, treas., 1994—2001, Kiwanis Found. Eagle Scout, Bus. Friends Coun., NC Soc. Prevent Blindness; chmn. pres.'s cir. Wake Med. Ctr. Found., 1996—2001, bd. dirs., 1996—2006; bd. dirs., chmn. fin. com., exec. com. WakeMed, 2005—06, treas., 2005—; bd. dirs. Food Bank NC, 2001—, chmn. fin. com., treas.; mem. parents coun. U. NC, Chapel Hill, 2000—03; bd. trustees WakeMed Health & Hosp. Sys., 2006—; mem. bus. sch., acctg./MSA adv. bd. U. NC, Wilmington; treas. NC Mus. Art, 1994—2001, bd. dirs., 2002—. Mem.: AICPA, NC Assn. CPAs, N.Mex Soc. CPAs, N.Mex Estate Planning Coun., Nat. Assn. Accts., Coun. Entrepreneurial Devel., Albuquerque Jaycees, Albuquerque C. of C., Santa Fe C. of C., Raleigh C. of C., Santa Fe Jaycees, West Raleigh Rotary, Kiwanis, Elks, Alpha Kappa Psi. Home: 8840 Mariner Dr Raleigh NC 27615 Office Phone: 919-345-7675, 910-962-7142. Business E-Mail: jessende@uncw.edu.

JESTER, GUY EARLSCOURT, engineering consultant; b. Oct. 20, 1929; s. Guy Earlscort Jester; m. Babbette Sale, Oct. 24, 1993; children: Mark, Robin, Elaine, Guy Leigh. BS in Engring., U.S. Mil. Acad., 1951; MS in Civil Engring., U. Ill., 1958; postgrad., Columbia U., 1963-65, U.S. Army War Coll., 1968; PhD, U. Ill., 1969; postgrad., U. Pitts., 1973. Registered profl. engr., Tex. Commd. 2d lt. U.S. Army, 1951, advanced through grades to col., 1971; dep. dir. and acting dir. Corps. of Engrs., Waterways Expt. Sta., 1965-67, divsn. engr. 9th Inf. Divsn., 1968-69, office chief R&D, asst. to chief R&D, chief info. system, 1968-71; dist. engr. Corps. of Engrs., St. Louis, 1971-73, ret., 1973. V.p., bd. dirs. J.S. Alberici Constrn. Co., Inc., St. Louis, 1973-94; bd. dirs. Alberici Corp.; dir. Alberici Engring.; pres. Internat. Constrn. Ltd., St. Louis, gen. mgr., B.G. Properties, LLC, 1995—; past mem. exec. com. engring. accreditation com. Accrediting Bd. Engring. and Tech.; past vice chmn. bd. St. Louis Regional Commerce and Growth Assn.; past chmn. bd. and pres. Assn. for Improvement of Miss. River. Contbr. articles to profl. jours. Former sr. warden St. Timothy's Episcopal Ch.; former vice chmn. coun. Diocese of Mo., Episcopal Ch.; former chmn. bd. trustees St. Louis Coll. Pharmacy. Recipient Cert. of Appreciation, U.S. Army, C.E., 1974, Spl. Svc. award Fed. Exec. Bd., 1972, 73; named St. Louis Contrn. Man of Yr., 1980. Fellow Am. Soc. Mil. Engrs. (past pres. St. Louis Post, past regional v.p., dir., Appreciation award 1983); mem. ASCE (past pres. St. Louis sect., Presdl. citation, 1979), Associated Gen. Contractors (former chmn., code and environ. coms.), Engrs. Club of St. Louis (Merit award 1981), U. Ill. Civil Engr. Alumni Assn. (former pres., bd. dirs.), West Point Soc. St. Louis (former pres.), Engrs. Club (former bd. dirs.), Am. Def. Preparedness Assn. (bd. dirs.), Nat. Bldg. Sersmic, Safety Coun. (mem. com. case studies project), Sigma Xi, Phi Kappa Phi. Avocations: reading, golf, bridge. Home: 12229 Pecan Forest Dr Dallas TX 75230 Home Phone: 972-392-2804. Office Fax: 972-392-2824. Personal E-mail: guy.jester@sbcglobal.net.

JETER, FRANCES, gas industry executive; Grad. in Internat. Affairs, U. NC. Dir. planned giving Univ. of Houston System, Tex., 1994—96; asst. v.p. devel. Rice Univ., Houston, 1996—2000; v.p. pub. affairs Duke Energy Gas Transmission, NC, 2000—06; mgr. energy mktg. Bracewell & Giuliani LLP, Houston, 2007—08, chief mktg. officer, 2008—11; group v.p. internal and external affairs Spectra Energy Corp., Houston, 2011—. Recipient YWCA Outstanding Woman, 2004, Outstanding Young Woman of America, 2004, Woman on the Move, Tex. Exec. Women, 2005. Mem.: Legal Mktg. Assn. (southeastern chpt.), Phi Beta Kappa Alumni (Houston). Office: Spectra Energy Corporation 5400 Westheimer Ct Houston TX 77056-5310 Office Phone: 713-627-5400.

JETT, STEPHEN CLINTON, geography and textiles educator, researcher, editor; b. Cleve., Oct. 12, 1938; s. Richard Scudder Jett and Miriam Ida (Horn) Jett Greene; m. Mary Frances Manak, Aug. 7, 1971 (div. 1977); 1 child, Jennifer Frances Jett; m. Lisa Sue Roberts, June 17, 1995. AB, Princeton U., 1960; postgrad., U. Ariz., 1962—63; PhD, Johns Hopkins U., 1964. Instr. geography Ohio State U., Columbus, 1963-64; asst. prof. geography U. Calif., Davis, 1964-72, assoc. prof., 1972-79, prof., 1979—2000, prof. textiles and clothing, 1996—2000, prof. emeritus geography, textiles and clothing, 2000—, chmn. geography dept., 1978-82, 87-89. Author: Navajo Wildlands, 1967 (1 of 50 Books of Yr., Am. Inst. Graphic Arts 1967, 1 of 20 Merit Award Books, Western Book Pubs. Assn. 1969), House of Three Turkeys, 1977, Navajo Architecture, 1981 (1 of Outstanding Acad. Books, Choice mag. ALA 1981), Navajo Placenames and Trails of the Canyon de Chelly System, Arizona, 2001, France, 2004; (monograph) Tourism in the Navajo Country, 1966; editor jour. Pre-Columbiana; curator textile exhbns.; contbr. numerous articles to profl. jours. and chpts. to books. Mem. Hist. and Landmarks Commn., Davis, 1969-73; vice chmn. Gen. Plan Noise Element Study Com., Davis, 1974-76, chmn. ad hoc citizens noise com., 1997-98; mem. exec. com. Univ. Farms Unit Number 1 Neighborhood Assn., Davis, 1987-90. Fellow: Explorers Club; mem.: AAAS, Friends Wash. County Pub. Libr. (v.p. 2009—11), Found. Rsch. Ancient Maritime Explorations (bd. dirs. 2002—, treas. 2006—), Inst. for Study of Am. Cultures (bd. dirs. 1996—), Epigraphic Soc. (bd. dirs. 1996—, v.p. 2005—), Soc. Am. Archaeology, Assn. Am. Geographers (chair Am. Indian splty. group 1989—91, rep. to sec. anthropology). Avocations: travel, photography, textiles and other ethnographic arts, French language and culture. E-mail: scjett@hotmail.com.

JEU, JOSEPH H., federal agency administrator; BBA, Coll. William and Mary, Williamsburg, Va.; grad. sr. officials in nat. security program, Harvard U. Kennedy Sch. Govt., Cambridge, Mass. Commissary officer & specialist, European commissary region US Army Troop Support Agency, Heidelberg and Zweibruecken, Germany, 1978—81; commissary mgmt. specialist, directorate transp., energy and troop support US Dept. of Army, Washington, 1981—84; commissary program mgr. USMC Hdqs. Facilities and Services Divsn., Installations and Logistics Dept., Washington, 1984—87, head services br., 1987—2000; asst. commr. office transp. and property mgmt. US GSA Fed. Supply Svc., Arlington, Va., 2000—04, asst. commr. office global supply, 2004—06; asst. commr. gen. supplies and services portfolio US GSA Fed. Acquisition Svc., 2006—10; dir., CEO Def. Commissary Agy., Fort Lee, Va., 2011—. Recipient Navy Superior Civilian Svc. award, 1987, Navy Disting. Civilian Svc. award, 2001, Presdl. Rank Award for Meritorious Exec., 2009. Office: Defense Commissary Agency 1300 E Avenue Fort Lee VA 23801-1800*

JEWELL, ROBERT V., lawyer; b. Houston, 1954; BBA in Fin., U. Tex., 1975; JD, So. Meth. U., 1978. Bar: Tex. 1978. Ptnr. corp./securities dept. Andrews & Kurth LLP, Houston, mem. mgmt. com., mng. ptnr., chmn. exec. com., 2007—. Editor: Southwestern Law Jour., 1978. Recipient CEO Legal Diversity award, Diversity Best Practices, 2008; named a Tex. Super Lawyer in Securities and Corp. Fin. and Mergers & Acquisitions, Tex. Monthly, 2003—10; named one of Leading Lawyers Bus., Corp./M&A in Tex., Chambers USA, 2001—11, Best Lawyers in America, Corp., 2006—11. Mem.: ABA, Tex. Bus. Law Found., State Bar Tex. (corp. law com., Corp. Banking & Bus. Law Sect.), Houston Bar Assn., Phi Delta Phi. Office: Andrews & Kurth LLP 600 Travis St Ste 4200 Houston TX 77002-3090 Office Phone: 713-220-4358. Office Fax: 713-238-7135. Business E-Mail: bjewell@andrewskurth.com.

JIMENEZ, MARCOS DANIEL, lawyer, former prosecutor; b. Havana, Cuba, Dec. 15, 1959; came to U.S., 1961; s. Frank T. and Daisy (D'Clouet) J. BA magna cum laude, U. Miami, Fla., 1980, JD magna cum laude, 1983. Bar: Ill. 1983, U.S. Dist. Ct. (northern dist.) Ill. 1983, Fla. 1984, U.S. Dist. Ct. (southern dist.) Fla. 1984, U.S. Ct. Appeals (11th cir.) 1985. Assoc. Phelan, Pope and John, Ltd., Chgo., 1983-84, Greenberg, Traurig et al, Miami, 1984-89; asst. US atty. (southern dist.) Fla. US Dept. Justice, Miami, 1989—92, US atty., 2002—05; ptnr. White & Case LLP, 1992—2002, Kasowitz Benson Torres & Friedman LLP, Miami. Contbr. articles to profl. jours. Named one of The Nation's Top Litigators, The Nat. Law Journal, 2011. Mem. ABA, Fla. Bar Assn. (com. mem.), Dade County Bar Assn. (com. mem.), Hurricane Club. Republican. Baptist. Avocations: basketball, saxophone. Office: Kosowitz Benson Torres & Friedman LLP The Four Seasons Tower 1441 Brickell Ave, Ste 1420 Miami FL 33131 Office Phone: 305-377-1666. Office Fax: 305-377-1664. E-mail: mjimenez@kasowitz.com.

JINDAL, BOBBY (PIYUSH JINDAL), Governor of Louisiana; b. Baton Rouge, La., June 10, 1971; s. Amar and Raj Jindal; m. Supriya Jolly; children: Selia, Shaan, Slade Ryan. BS in Biology, Brown U., Providence, 1991; MLitt in Politics, Oxford U., Eng., 1994. Assoc. McKinsey & Co., Washington, 1994—96; sec. La. Dept. Health & Hospitals, Baton Rouge, 1996—98; exec. dir. Nat. Bipartisan Commn. Future of Medicare, Washington, 1998—99; pres. U. La. Sys., Baton Rouge, 1999—2001; asst. sec. for planning & evaluation US Dept. Health & Human Services, Washington, 2001—03; mem. US Congress from 1st La. Dist., Washington, 2005—08; gov. State of La., 2008—. Bd. dirs. Our Lady of Lake Hosp., Baton Rouge, 2000—01,

Edn. Commn. of States, 2000—01. Bd. dirs. Salvation Army, Baton Rouge, 1986—87; bd. dirs. Baton Rouge chpt. Teach for America, 1997—98, Nat. Conf. Cmty & Justice, 2000—01. Recipient Jefferson award, Nat. Inst. Pub. Svc., 1998; named La.'s Most Outstanding Young Man, Jr. C. of C., 1995; named one of The Politics 40 Under 40, TIME Mag., 2010; named to All-USA First Acad. Team, USA Today, 1992; scholar, Rhodes Trust, 1992—94. Mem.: Phi Beta Kappa. Republican. Roman Catholic. Avocation: tennis. Office: Office of the Governor PO Box 94004 Baton Rouge LA 70804-9004 Office Phone: 225-342-7015. Office Fax: 225-342-7099.*

JINRIGHT, CHARLES W., councilman; m. Martha Jinright; 1 child, Bo. BS in Bus., Troy U., Ala., 1968. Councilman City of Montgomery from Dist. 9, Ala., 1995; pres. City of Montgomery Coun., Ala.; acting mayor City of Montgomery, Ala., 2009; current chmn. Securance Group, Inc. Pres. Capital City Jaycees, 1974, East Montgomery Optimist Club, 1983; bd. dirs. Boy Scouts, Goodwill Industries, Montgomery Area Food Bank, Montgomery YMCA, Met. Planning Orgn. With USAR, 1966—72. Named Citizen of Yr., March of Dimes River Region, 2008. Avocations: golf, boating. Office: City Hall 103 N Perry St Rm 206 Montgomery AL 36104 Business E-Mail: cjinright@montgomeryal.gov.

JNEID, HANI, interventional cardiologist, researcher; BS, Am. U. Beirut, 1994, MD, 1998. Diplomate in internal medicine Am. Bd. Medicine, 2002, Am. Soc. Nuc. Cardiology, 2004, Am. Bd. Cardiovasc. Medicine, 2006, Am. Bd. Interventional Cardiology, 2008. Intern Cleveland Clinic Found.; fellow in cardiology U. Louisville; fellow in interventional cardiology Mass. Gen. Hosp. Harvard Med. Sch.; asst. prof. medicine Baylor Coll. Medicine, Houston, 2008—; asst. dir. interventional cardiology Michael E. DeBakey VA Med. Ctr., Houston. Mem. leadership com. Nat. Am. Heart Assn., Dallas. Recipient Fellow of Yr. Award, Divsn. Cardiology-U. Louisville, 2004; named Sr. Med. Resident of Yr., Cleve. Clinic Found., 2002. Fellow: Am. Coll. Cardiology; mem.: Am. Heart Assn. Office: Micheal E DeBakey Med Ctr 2002 Holcombe Blvd Houston TX 77030 Office Phone: 713-794-7300. Office Fax: 713-794-7134.

JOANNOU, JOHNNY SAVAS, state legislator; b. Bklyn., Apr. 22, 1940; m. Chris Paul Kolantis; 1 child, Stephanie. Former mem. Portsmouth Dem. Com.; former pres. Dist. 4 Young Dem.; state del. Va., 1976—84; state del. Dist. 79, 1979, 1998—; state senator, Dist. 13 Va., 1984—91; atty-at-law Joannou, Knowles & Assocs. Named Legislator of Yr., Sheriff's Assn. Mem.: Scottish Rite, Trial Lawyers Assn. (founding mem.), Am. Bar Assn. (founding mem.), Portsmouth Bar Assn. (founding mem.), Va., Norfolk-Portsmouth, Va. Trial Lawyers Assn. (founding mem.), AF&AM, Aiding Leukemia-Stricken Am. Children (past dir.), Citizens Against Pollution (past legal advisor), Portsmouth Naval Lodge. Democrat. Greek Orthodox. Mailing: 709 Court St Portsmouth VA 23704

JOBE, LARRY ALTON, finance company executive; b. Knox City, Tex., Jan. 12, 1940; s. Lloyd Alton and Georgia (Swift); m. Suzanne Marie Storch, Aug. 2, 1980; 1 dau., Jennifer Marie; children by previous marriage: Lorrie Aileen, Lezlie Amee, Lowell Alton, Lloyd Alan, Leland Austin, Llewyn. BBA, U. North Tex., 1961, postgrad., 1961-65. CPA, Tex. Joined Grant Thornton, Dallas, 1961, mgr., 1967-69, ptnr., 1968-69, mng. ptnr., mem. exec. com. Dallas, 1973—, S.W. regional mng. ptnr., 1983-91; chmn. Legal Network, Inc., 1991—; pres. PI Resources LLP, 1997—; chmn. Ind. Bank Tex., 2002—; asst. sec. commerce Washington, 1969-72; v.p. fin. Dart Industries, 1972-73. Mem. acctg. adv. bd. U. North Tex., U. Tex.; bd. dirs. Ind. Nat. Bank, US Home Sys., Inc., SWS Group, Inc., Mannatech, Inc. Contbr. articles to profl. jours. Bd. dirs. Dallas Citizens Coun., Eisenhower World Affairs Inst.; chmn. bd. trustees Dallas Theol. Sem.; mem. Chief Execs. Roundtable; chmn. bd. Dallas Alliance for Minority Enterprise, Dallas Minority Bus. Ctr., Profl. Devel. Inst. of U. North Tex.; mem. pres.'s coun. North Tex. State U. Recipient Excellence in Acctg. award Haskins and Sells Found., 1960; Outstanding Alumni award U. North Tex., 1965, Pres.' Svc. award, 1986; U.S. Interagy. Audit Tng. award, 1970, Outstanding Svc. award, 1st Place Author's award Fed. Govt. Accts. Assn., 1970. Mem. AICPA, Tex. Soc. CPAs, Fed. Govt. Accts. Assn., Dallas C. of C. (dir., vice chmn.), Blue Key, Phi Eta Sigma, Alpha Chi, Alpha Lambda Pi, Beta Alpha Psi. Office: 600 N Pearl St Ste 2100 Dallas TX 75201-2825 E-mail: ljobe@legaljobnet.com.

JOBE, TONY BRYSON, air transportation executive, lawyer; b. Washington, Aug. 29, 1943; s. William Theodore and Marguerite (Hendrickson) Jobe. BA in English, Southwestern U., Memphis, 1966; JD, Tulane U., 1974. Bar: La. 1975. Prin. Jobe & Assocs., New Orleans, 1975—; pres., CEO Air New Orleans, 1981—98; with Olsen, Gilman & Pangia, Washington, 1988—; of Counsel Ryon & Willeford. Bd. dirs. New Orleans Ballet, 1981—83. Capt. USMC, 1967—71. Decorated DFC. Mem.: AAJ, ABA, Attys. Info. Exch. Group (exec. bd. 1979—), Assn. Bar City NY, NTSB Bar Assn. (past-pres.), Internat. Soc. Air Safety Investigators. also: 14465 Settlers Landing Way Gaithersburg MD 20878-4304 Office: Law office Tony B Jobe 500 Water St Madisonville LA 70447

JOEL, WILLIAM LEE, II, interior and lighting designer; b. Richmond, Va., Feb. 23, 1933; s. J. Alton and Dorothy Joel; m. Merry Pick, June 5, 1955; children: Taryn, Dana, Wendy, Holly. Student, R.I. Sch. Design, 1953-55; AB, Brown U., 1955; postgrad., N.Y. Sch. Interior Design, 1956, Pratt Inst., 1958-61. Cert. interior designer Commonwealth of Va. Draftsman Mills Denmark Inc., NYC, 1957-58; with sales and interior design Lord & Taylor's Inc., NYC, 1958-61; pres., interior designer Richmond (Va.) Art Co. Inc. Instr. Va. Commonwealth U. (formerly Richmond Profl. Inst.), 1963-67; set designer Barksdale Theatre, Hanover, Va., 1977-88; mem. adv. bd. interior design program Va. Poly. Inst and State U., 1986-90; speaker numerous orgns., radio and TV programs. Prin. works include Culpepper (Va.) Hosp., The Curles Neck Pl., Richmond, Dominion Nat. Bank, Richmond, Gary, Stoch, Walls offices, Richmond, Gov.'s Exec. Mansion, Commonwealth Va., 1976, Hello Inc., Richmond, Hill Bldg., Richmond, Hunter House Mus., Norfolk, Va., Richmond, Fredericksburg and Potomac R.R. Co. corp. hdqrs., Rolph Clark Stone Packaging Co. offices, Straub and Dalch office complex, Westminster Canterbury House, Richmond, Wickham Valentine House, Willow Oaks Country Club, Continental Cablevision, Richmond, St. Paul Episcopal Ch., Richmond, numerous residences; author: articles published bi-monthly in Rich Art website. Co-chmn. com. for cert. Va. Interior Designers, 1982-90; mem. Downtown Mktg. Com., chmn. subcom. Xmas Sound and Lighting, Richmond, 1988-91, mem. prodn. Richmond Forum sets and lighting design, 1989-95; bd. visitors Found. for Interior Design Edn. and Rsch., 1977-84, mem. accreditation com., 1984-88; mem. Va. Mus. Fine Arts, City of Richmond Christmas Candlelight Com., edn. com. Retail Mchts. Assn., 1980-85; mem. urban design com. Ctrl. Richmond Assn., 1993. 1st lt. USMC, 1952-57. Recipient award Va. Mus. Fine Arts, Richmond, 1970, Cert. Distinction, 1973; named contest winner Richmond Symphony Orch., 1975. Fellow Am. Soc. Interior Designers (cert., pres. Va. chpt. 1970-72, 80-81, mem. nat. bd. 1972-74, 76-77, regional v.p. 1976-77, nat. com. 1976); mem. Nat. Fire Protection Assn. Avocations: sailing, canoeing. Home: Richmond Art Co 8905 Sierra Rd Richmond VA 23229-7828 Business E-Mail: rich@richartco.com.

JOERGER, DAVID, professional basketball coach; s. Joe Joerger; m. Kara Joerger; children: Alli, Kiana. Attended, Concordia Coll., Minn., Minn. State U., Moorhead, 1995—97. Gen. mgr. & asst. coach Dakota Wizards, Internat. Basketball Assn., 1997—2000, head coach, 2000—01, Dakota Wizards, Continental Basketball Assn., 2001—04, Sioux Falls Skyforce, Continental Basketball Assn., SD, 2004—06, Dakota Wizards, NBA D-League, 2006—07; asst. coach Memphis Grizzlies, 2007—13, head coach, 2013—. Named Coach of Yr., Continental Basketball Assn., 2002, 2004. Office: Memphis Grizzlies 191 Beale St Memphis TN 03810*

JOHN, LEWIS GEORGE, retired political science educator; b. Waco, Tex., Nov. 25, 1936; s. Lewis Hervin and Margaret Reese J.; m. Annette Louise Church, June 3, 1961; children: Andrew Lewis, Christopher Donald. BA, Washington & Lee U., 1958; M in Pub. Affairs, Princeton U., 1961; PhD, Syracuse U., 1973. Asst. dean students, dir. fin. aid and placement Washington & Lee U., Lexington, Va., 1963-66, assoc. dean students, 1968-69, dean students, prof. politics and adminstrn., 1969-90, prof. politics, 1969—2006. Leader workshops and seminars, various colls., 1981-85; presenter symposia and confs. Contbr. articles to profl. jours. and chpts. to books. Chmn. Lexington Sch. Bd. 1979-80; pre-law adviser, 1993-2001; rep. NCAA Faculty Athletics, 1998-2001. Served to 1st lt. US Army, 1961-63. Recipient Disting. Alumni award, Washington-Lee U., 2013; Woodrow Wilson fellow Princeton U., 1959-60; Fulbright scholar U. Edinburgh, 1958-59. Mem. ASPA, Nat. Assn. Student Personnel Adminstrs. (bd. dirs. 1977-79, 87-89, region III exec. bd. 1980-85, chmn. career devel. and profl. standards div. 1987-89, Disting. Svc. award 1982), Va. Assn. Student Personnel Adminstrs. (pres. 1975, Outstanding Profl. award 1983), Am. Polit. Sci. Assn., Phi Beta Kappa, Beta Gamma Sigma, Omicron Delta Kappa (faculty sec. Washington and Lee chpt. 1987-90, faculty advisor 1990-98), Inst. For Honor (chair campus com. 2009-12), Omicron Delta Epsilon, Pi Sigma Alpha. Democrat. Presbyterian. Avocation: sports. Home: 8 Edmondson Ave Lexington VA 24450-1904 E-mail: johnl@wlu.edu.

JOHNS, JOHN D., insurance company executive, lawyer; BA, U. Ala.; MBA, JD, Harvard U. Ptnr. Cabaniss, Johnston, Gardner, Dumas & O'Neal; founding ptnr. Maynard Cooper & Gale; v.p., gen. counsel Sonat Inc., 1988—93; exec. v.p., CFO Protective Life Corp., Birmingham, Ala., 1993—96, pres., COO, 1996—2001, chmn., pres., CEO, 2001—. Bd. dir. John H. Harland Co., Ala. Nat. Bancorporation, Genuine Parts Co. Office: Protective Life Corp 2801 Hwy 280 S Birmingham AL 35223

JOHNS, RONNIE, state legislator; b. July 14, 1949; m. Michelle Servat Johns; 1 adopted child, Claire Broussard. Pharmacist, 1972—82; city councilman, 1978—82; ins. agent, 1982—; mem. La. Mineral Bd., 1988—92; mem. Dist. 33 La. House of Reps., 1996—2007; mem. Dist. 27 La. State Senate, 2012—. Mem.: W Calcasieu Assn. Commerce, Chamber SW, Rotary Club. Republican. Roman Catholic. Office: 1011 Lakeshore Dr Ste 515 Lake Charles LA 70601 also: La State Senate 900 N 3rd St Baton Rouge LA 70804 Office Phone: 337-491-2016. Business E-Mail: johnsr@legis.la.gov.

JOHNSON, ANDRE LAMONT, professional football player; b. Miami, Fla., July 11, 1981; Student in liberal arts, U. Miami, Coral Gables, Fla. Wide receiver Houston Texans, 2003—. Named Player of Yr., Touchdown Club, 2004, 2006, Wide Receiver of Yr., NFL Alumni, 2006, 1st Team All-Pro, AP, 2008, 2009; named to Am. Football Conf. Pro Bowl Team, NFL, 2004, 2006, 2008—10, 2012. Achievements include leading the National Football League in: receptions 2006, 2008; receiving yards per game, 2007; receiving yards, 2008, 2009. Office: The Houston Texans Two Reliant Pk Houston TX 77054

JOHNSON, ANTHONY O'LEARY (ANDY JOHNSON), meteorologist, consultant; b. Tampa, Fla., Apr. 19, 1957; s. Paul Bryan and Katie Hobbs (Nunez) J. BS in Meteorology, Fla. State U., 1979. Courthouse runner Gregory, Cours, et. al., Tampa, 1977; water resources planner S.W. Fla. Water Mgmt. Dist., Brooksville, 1978; staff meteorologist Sta. WTVT-TV, Tampa, 1979-82, systems mgr., 1982-89, weather office mgr., 1989—. Meterol. cons. Gulf Coast Weather Svc.-Weather Vision, Tampa, 1979—; software devel. mgr. TTI Techs. Inc., Tampa, 1989-92; site coord. Space Sci. and Engring. Ctr. U. Wis., Madison, 1989—. Active capital improvements com. Plantation Homeowners Assn., Tampa, 1991; judge Hillsborough Regional Sci. Fair, Tampa, 1990, 91, 92, 96; fundraiser Dunedin Youth Guild, 1992, Northside Mental Health Hosp. Aux., 1993, 94, Children's Home, Pinellas Aux., 1993, 94, 95; vol. Sch. Enrichment Vols. in Edn. (SERVE), 1992. Mem. AAAS, Am. Meteorol. Soc. (Seal of Approval for TV weathercasting 1982—, v.p. West Fla. chpt. 1984-85, pres. 1989-92, 94—2010, cert. meteorologist), Internat. Platform Assn., Phi Beta Kappa, Pi Mu Epsilon, Chi Epsilon Pi. Republican. Achievements include development of quantitative predictive methods of energy delivery interruption in severe Florida freezes; research on temporal and spatial climatological anomalies on landfalling hurricanes in West Central Florida. Office: Sta WTVT-TV Weather Svc 3213 W Kennedy Blvd Tampa FL 33609-3006 Home: 3912 W Dale Ave Tampa FL 33609-4405 Home Phone: 813-878-2929. Personal E-mail: andyccm@aol.com.

JOHNSON, ARNOLD JOSEPH, lawyer, energy executive; b. Des Moines, Iowa, Aug. 2, 1955; m. Mary Le. BS in Pub. Adminstrn., Northwest Mo. State U., 1977; JD, Creighton U., 1980. With ARCO, 1980—89; asst. gen. counsel. Vastar Resources Inc., 1997—2000; sr. counsel BP America, Inc., 2000—01; assoc. gen. counsel, asst. sec. Noble Energy, Inc., 2001—04, v.p., gen. counsel, sec., 2001—. Chmn. La. Mineral Law Inst., 2006—07. Mem.: Houston Bar Assn. (chair oil, gas & mineral law section 1994—95). Office: Noble Energy Inc 100 Glenborough Dr Ste 100 Houston TX 77067 Office Phone: 281-872-3100. Office Fax: 281-872-3111. Business E-Mail: ajohnson@nobleenergyinc.com.

JOHNSON, ARTHUR E., gas industry executive; b. 1946; BA, Morehouse Coll., 1968. Joined IBM Corp., 1969, pres., IBM Fed. Sys., 1992; group v.p., Fed. Sys. Group Loral Corp., 1994—96; v.p., pres., LM Fed. Sys. Lockheed Martin, 1996—97; v.p., corp. strategic devel. Lockheed Martin Corp., 1996—2001, pres., Sys. Integration Group, 1997; pres., COO, Info. & Svc. Sector Lockheed Martin Corp, 1997—99; sr. v.p., strategic devel. Lockheed Martin Corp., 2001—09. Bd. dirs. IKON Office Solutions, Inc., 1999, Delta Air Lines, Inc., 2005—07, Eaton Corp., Calcomp Tech., Inc., 1997—, AGL Resources Inc., 2002—. Trustee Fidelity Mutual Funds. Office: AGL Resources Inc 10 Peachtree Pl NE Atlanta GA 30309 Office Phone: 404-584-4000. Office Fax: 404-584-3714. Business E-Mail: Ajohnson@aglresource.com.

JOHNSON, BEN SIGEL, music educator; b. Springfield, Mo., Aug. 8, 1929; s. Ben W. and Florence (Owen) J.; m. Bonnie Kay Blackport, Nov. 5, 1940; children: Jennifer Ann, Kristian Marvin, Ben Jerome. BA, U. Mo., 1950; student, Juilliard Sch. of Music, 1950-52; MA, Columbia U., 1951, EdD, 1964; student, Akademie für Musik und Darstellende Kunst, Vienna, Austria, 1968-69. Baritone soloist Riverside Ch., NYC, 1950-51; dir. music Wellsville Pub. Schs., Mo., 1951-53; assoc. prof. music William Carey Coll., Hattiesburg, Miss., 1953-56; minister of music First Bapt. Ch., Hattiesburg, 1953-56, Wake Forest Bapt. Ch., N.C., 1956-80; prof. music Southeastern Theol. Sem., Wake Forest, N.C., 1956—; instr. of music Columbia U., NYC, 1962-63; organist, choirmaster Cen. Meth. Ch., Yonkers, N.Y., 1962-63, Millbrook Methodist Ch., Raleigh, N.C., 1983—. Vis. prof. music U. N.C., Chapel HIll, 1990-91; adjudicator State Choral Festival, Mo., 1951-53, Atlanta, 1960-86; condr. State Choral Festival, Winston-Salem, 1958-59. Contbr. articles to ch. publs., condr. (album) Christmas at S.E., 1966; composer Choral Overtones, 1970. Am. Assn. Theol. Schs. Fellowship, 1968-69; Brit. Library Scholar, 1975. Mem. AAUP, Am. Choral Dirs. Assn. Baptist. Avocations: golf, swimming, bridge. Home: 204 W Juniper Ave Wake Forest NC 27587-2314

JOHNSON, BENJAMIN F., VI, economist, consultant; b. Kingston, NY, Sept. 17, 1952; s. Benjamin F. and Alice (Terry) J. BA in Econs., U. South Fla., 1974; MS in Econs., Fla. State U., 1977, PhD in Econs., 1982. Sr. utility analyst Office of Pub. Counsel, State of Fla., 1974-77; pres., cons. economist Ben Johnson Assocs., Inc., Tallahassee, Fla., 1977—. Contbr. articles to N.Y. Times, Pub. Utilities Fortnightly, profl. jours. Mem. Am. Econ. Assn. Office Phone: 850-893-8600.

JOHNSON, BENJAMIN FRANKLIN, III, retired lawyer; b. Atlanta, Aug. 20, 1943; s. Benjamin Franklin Jr. and Stella Byrd (Darnell) J.; m. Ann Armistead, Aug., 6, 1966; children: Benjamin Franklin IV, James Leslie Armistead. BA magna cum laude, Emory U., 1965; JD, Harvard U., 1968. Bar: Ga. 1968, U.S. Ct. Appeals (5th cir.) 1973, U.S. Ct. Appeals (11th cir.) 1982, U.S. Dist. Ct. (no. dist.) Ga. 1969, U.S. Dist. Ct. (so. dist.) Ga. 1978, U.S. Dist. Ct. (mid. dist.) Ga. 1981. Law clk. to judge Griffin B. Bell U.S. Ct. Appeals (5th cir.), Atlanta, 1968-69; assoc. Alston, Miller & Gaines, Atlanta, 1971-76; ptnr. Alston & Bird and predecessor firm Alston, Miller & Gaines, Atlanta, 1976—97; mng. ptnr. Alston & Bird LLP, Atlanta, 1997—2008. Mem. faculty Stonier Grad. Sch. Banking, Newark, Del., 1982-91. Co-author: Problem Loan Strategies, 1985. Chmn. governing bd. Woodward Acad., College Park, Ga., 1982-95; chmn. bd. trustees Atlanta Leadership Devel. Found., 1994-95; trustee Emory U., 1995, Charles Loridans Found., 1991-95; pres. Rsch. Atlanta, 1988. 1st lt. U.S. Army, 1969-71, Vietnam. Recipient Disting. Alumnus award Woodward Acad., 1981, Law Firm Disting. Leader award, The American Lawyer mag., 2010 Mem. Ga. Bar Assn., Atlanta Bar Assn. (chmn. litigation sect. 1980), Atlanta Lawyer's Club, Commerce Club, Ansley Golf Club. Democrat. Avocations: reading, music, politics, exercise. Office: Alston & Bird LLP 1 Atlantic Ctr 1201 W Peachtree St NW Atlanta GA 30309-3400 Office Phone: 404-881-7297. Office Fax: 404-881-8797. Business E-Mail: bjohnson@alston.com.

JOHNSON, BERNETTE JOSHUA, state supreme court chief justice; b. Ascension Parish, La. d. Frank Joshua Jr. and Olivia W. Johnson. BA, Spelman Coll., Atlanta, 1964; JD, La. State U., 1969; LLD (hon.), Spelman Coll., 2001. Bar: La. Law intern Civil Rights Divsn. US Dept. Justice; judge La. Civil Dist. Ct., 1984-94, chief judge, 1994; assoc. justice La. Supreme Ct., New Orleans, 1994—2013, chief justice, 2013—. Legal svc. atty. New Orleans Legal Assistance Corp.; community organizer NAACP Legal Defense & Educational Fund, NYC; chair New Orleans Chapter So. Christian Leadership Conference. Bd. dirs. YMCA, New Orleans; chmn. bd. Learning Ctr., Greater St. Stephen Full Gospel Bapt. Ch.; bd. dirs. NOLAC, 1992-99. Named Woman of Yr., LaBelle chpt. American Bus. Women's Assn., 1994; Named one of The Outstanding Women on Bench New Orleans Assn. Black Women Attorneys; recipient Ernest N. Morial award NOLAC, Daniel Byrd award NAACP, A.P. Tureaud Citizenship award NAACP, Margaret A. Brent Women Lawyers of Achievement award ABA., President's award for Exceptional Svc. Louis A. Matinet Legal Soc., 1997, 2008, Nat. Nobel Women award Org. Black Elected Legislative Women, 2005, Disting. Jurist award La. Bar Found., 2009, Disting. Civil Rights Advocate award Lawyers' Com. for Civil Rights Under Law, 2010 Office: La Supreme Ct 400 Royal St New Orleans LA 70130*

JOHNSON, CALVIN M., otolaryngologist, educator, facial plastic surgeon; Attended, Yale U.; MD, Tulane U., 1967. Cert. Am. Acad. of Facial Plastic and Reconstructive Surgery, Am. Acad. of Otolaryngology Head and Neck Surgery. Resident surgery Tulane Univ. Sch. of Medicine, New Orleans, 1970—71, resident otolaryngology, 1971—74; fellow facial plastic and reconstructive surgery; clin. prof. dept. of otolaryngology head and neck surgery Tulane Sch. of Medicine; founder Hedgewood Surg. Ctr., New Orleans. Author (sr.): (textbooks) Open Structure Rhinoplasty, The Aging Face, A Case Approach to Open Structure Rhinoplasty. Named one of the Top 5 Rhinoplasty Surgeons in the world, W Mag. Mem.: AMA, ACS, Am. Acad. of Facial Plastic and Reconstructive Surgery, La. State Med. Soc., Am. Acad. of Otolaryngology Head and Neck Surgery. Office: Hedgewood Surgical Center 2427 St Charles Ave New Orleans LA 70130 Office Phone: 504-895-7642.

JOHNSON, CHARLES LAVON, JR., clinical neuropsychologist, consultant; b. Raleigh, NC, Aug. 31, 1954; s. Charles Lavon Sr. and Edna Louise (Schaaf) J.; m. Janet Andrews, June 23, 1990. BA, N.C. State U., 1976, MS in Sociology, 1979, MS in Psychology, 1983; PhD, Fielding Inst., Santa Barbara, Calif., 1989. Lic. practicing psychologist. Instr., sch. psychologist N.C. State U., Raleigh, 1983-84; contractual psychologist Wake County Pub. Sch. System, Raleigh, 1985-86; clin. psychology intern John Umstead Hosp., Butner, N.C., 1988, staff psychologist, 1989; cons. psychologist Springmoor Life Care Retirement Community, Raleigh, 1988-90; sr. psychologist Dorothea Dix Hosp., Raleigh, 1989-91; contractual psychologist Cumberland County Pub. Sch. System, Fayetteville, N.C., 1989-91; cons. psychologist Disability Determination Svcs., Raleigh, 1991—2002; pvt. practice, 1990—2002. Cons. clin. neuropsychologist Coastal Plan Hosp., Rocky Mount, 1991-93, Tenth Jud. Dist. Juvenile Ct., Raleigh, 1990-91, Dartmouth Clinic, Southern Pines, N.C., 1990-92), clin. instr. dept. psychiatry U. N.C. Sch. Medicine, Chapel Hill, 1990-94. Contbr. articles to profl. jours. Mem. West Raleigh Citizens Adv. Coun., Raleigh, 1985-90. Avocations: music, golf, antiques.

JOHNSON, CHRISTINE A., former state legislator; b. Dec. 25; life ptnr. Lorie Hutchison Johnson; 1 child, Olivia. Mem. Dist. 25 Utah House of Reps., Utah, 2007—10; mem. Higher Edn. Appropriations Subcommittee, Judiciary Com., Revenue & Taxation Com.; exec. dir. SC Equality, 2010—. Mem.: Stonewall Dems. (former vice chair), Equality Utah, East Ctrl. Cmty. Coun. (former chair), Salt Lake City Human Rights Comn. (vice chair). Democrat. Home: 701 Whaley St Ste 202 Columbia SC 29201-5900 Office: SC Equality PO Box 544 Columbia SC 29202 Office Phone: 803-256-6500. Office Fax: 866-532-1223. E-mail: hristine@scequality.org.

JOHNSON, CONSTANCE N., state legislator; b. Holdenville, Okla., 1952; BA in French, Univ. Pa. Former mem. Cmty. Action Dir. Assn., Okla.; former employment coord. Comprehensive Employment And Training Act; staff mem. Okla. State Senate, 1981—2005, mem.

Dist. 48, 2005—. Democrat. Address: PO Box 61241 Oklahoma City OK 73146 Office: 2300 N Lincoln Blvd Rm 534B Oklahoma City OK 73105 Office Phone: 405-521-5531. Fax: 405-521-5580. Business E-Mail: johnsonc@oksenate.gov.

JOHNSON, CRAIG A., tobacco company executive; BBA in Acctg., U. Mich. CPA. Acctg. positions Price Waterhouse LLP (now PricewaterhouseCoopers LLP), 1984—88; mgmt. positions Procter & Gamble Co., Frito-Lay Inc.; v.p. Philip Morris USA Inc. & subs., 1991—2005; sr. v.p., ops., CFO MitoKor, Inc., 1994—2004; v.p, fin., CFO, prin. acctg. officer., sec. TorreyPines Therapeutics, 2004—05; exec. v.p., sales & brand mgmt. Philip Morris USA Inc., 2005—08, pres., 2008—09; exec. v.p. Altria Group, Inc., 2009—11, pres., CEO Altria Group Distbn. Co., 2011—. Bd. dirs. Ardea Biosciences Inc., 2008—. Bd. dirs. St. Christopher's Sch., The First Tee Richmond & Chesterfield, Va., Peter Paul Devel. Ctr. Mem.: Assn. Bioscience Fin. Officers (past pres.). Office: Altria Group Inc 6601 W Broad St Richmond VA 23230 Office Phone: 804-274-2200. Business E-Mail: Craig.Johnson@altria.com.

JOHNSON, CURTIS, state legislator; b. 1952; married; 3 children. State rep. Dist. 68, Tenn., 2005—. Mem. Clarksville County Coun., 1994—2002. Named Boss of Yr., Clarksville Jaycees. Mem.: Assn. of US Army TN/KY Chpt. (former pres.), Austin Peay Alumni Assn. (former pres.), Austin Peay Gov.'s Club (former pres.), Clarksville Shrine Club (former pres.). Republican. Presbyterian. Office: 2599 Memorial Dr Clarksville TN 37043 also: 212 War Memorial Bldg Nashville TN 37243-0168 Office Phone: 931-358-3719, 615-741-4341. Office Fax: 615-253-0269. Business E-Mail: rep.curtis.johnson@capitol.tn.gov.

JOHNSON, CYNDA ANN, physician, educator; b. Girard, Kans., July 16, 1951; BA in Biology and German with honors, Stanford U., 1973; MD, UCLA, 1977; MBA, U. Mo., Kansas City, 1999. Diplomate Am. Bd. Family Medicine (bd. dirs., pres. 1999-2000). Tchg. fellow U. N.C., Chapel Hill, 1980-81; intern U. Kans. Med. Ctr., Kansas City, 1977-78, 1978-80, prof., acting chair dept. family medicine, 1998—99; prof., head dept. family medicine U. Iowa Coll. Medicine, Iowa City, 1999—2003; dean Brody Sch. Medicine East Carolina U., Greenville, NC, 2003—06, sr. assoc. vice chancellor for clin. and translational rsch., 2007—08; pres. and dean Va. Tech. Carilion Sch. Medicine, 2008—. Mem. Am. Acad. Family Physicians, Soc. Tchrs. Family Medicine, Va. Acad. Family Physicians, Va. Med. Soc. Office: Va Tech Carilion Sch Medicine PO Box 13727 Roanoke VA 24036 Office Phone: 540-853-0432. Office Fax: 540-983-1190. E-mail: cajohnson@carilion.com.

JOHNSON, DANIEL, lawyer; b. Hickory, NC; m. Creecy Johnson; 1 child, Bowen. BA, JD, U. NC, Chapel Hill. Staffer US Senator Max Cleland; felony prosecutor State of NC; atty. Sigmon, Clark, Mackie, Hutton, Hanvey and Ferrell, PA, Hickory. Mem. First Presbyn. Ch., Hickory. Officer USS Blue Ridge USN. Decorated Navy and Marine Corps Medal. Democrat. Office: Sigmon Clark Mackie Hutton Hanvey and Ferrell PA 420 3rd Ave NW # B Hickory NC 28601 Office Phone: 828-328-2596.

JOHNSON, DAVID E., state legislator, lawyer; b. Nashville, Tenn. BA, Georgetown Univ., 1991; JD, Univ. Ark., 1997. Bar: Ark. 1997. Staff asst. Com. on Small Bus. US Senate, 1991—94; dep. prosecuting atty. Office of Pulaski County Atty., 1998—2004; prin. David E. Johnson PLLC, 2005—06; assoc. James & House PC, 2006—07, Wright, Lindsey & Jennings LLP, Little Rock, 2007—; mem. Dist. 38 Ark. House of Reps., 2005—08; mem. Dist. 32 Ark. State Senate, 2009—. Bd. dir., past v.p. Tree Streets Inc.; vice-chair First United Methodist Church, 2006—08. Mem.: ABA, Ark. Bar Assn., Pulaski County Bar Assn., Ark. Trial Lawyers Assn., William R. Overton Inn of Ct., Phi Delta Phi. Democrat. Methodist. Office: 2511 Valley Park Dr Little Rock AR 72212 also: Wright Lindsey & Jennings Ste 2300 200 W Capitol Ave Little Rock AR 72201 also: State Capitol Rm 320 Little Rock AR 72201 Business E-Mail: johnsond@arkleg.state.ar.us.

JOHNSON, DAVID HORTON, oncologist; b. Dalton, Ga., Apr. 19, 1948; BS in Zoology, U. Kentucky, MS in Physiology; MD, Med. Coll. Ga., 1976. Intern, medicine U. South Ala. Med. Ctr., Mobile, Ala., 1977, resident, medicine, 1977—79; resident Med. Coll. Ga. Hosp., Augsuta, Ga., 1979—80, Vanderbilt U. Med. Ctr.; dir. divsn. oncology, hematology Vanderbilt U., Nashville, Cornelius Abernathy Craig Prof. Med. and Surgical Oncology; dep. dir. Vanderbilt-Ingram Cancer Ctr., Nashville. Investigator in field. Contbr. articles to profl. publications. Recipient Frank Moran Clinical Leadership award, U. Mich., 2000. Mem.: Am. Soc. Clinical Oncology. Office: Vanderbilt U 777 Preston Research Bldg Hematology/Oncology Nashville TN 37232-6307 also: 1903 The Vanderbilt Clinic Nashville TN 37232-5536 Office Phone: 615-343-9454, 615-322-6053. Office Fax: 615-343-8668.

JOHNSON, DAVID L., computer company executive; BA in English, Boston Coll., MBA in Fin. Various positions IBM Corp.; sr. v.p., corp. strategy Dell, Inc., 2009—. Office: Dell Inc One Dell Way Round Rock TX 78682 Office Phone: 512-338-4400. Office Fax: 512-728-3653.

JOHNSON, DENNIS, state legislator; b. July 22, 1953; m. Susan Johnson; children: Bryan, Laura, Caroline. BS in Mktg., Weber State U. Small bus. owner; mayor City of Duncan, 1996—2003; mem. Duncan City Coun., 1996—99; mem. Dist. 50 Okla. House of Representatives, 2007—. Republican. Address: 3512 Spencer Rd Duncan OK 73533 Office: 2300 N Lincoln Blvd Rm 435 Oklahoma City OK 73105 Office Phone: 405-557-7327. E-mail: dennis.johnson@okhouse.gov.

JOHNSON, DONALD LEE, retired agricultural materials company executive, bio-process and product consultant; b. Aurora, Ill., Mar. 9, 1935; s. Leonard F. and Fern J. (Johnson) J.; m. Virginia A. Wesoloski, Sept. 3, 1960; children: Joyce E., Janis M., Jolene G., Jay R. AS, Joliet Jr. Coll., 1959; BS, U. Ill., 1962; DSc, Washington U., 1966. Devel. engr. Petrolite Corp., Webster Groves, Mo., 1962-64; sr. devel. engr. A.E. Staley Co., Decatur, Ill., 1965-67, rsch. mgr. chem. div., 1967-75, dept. dir. rsch. div., 1975-87; v.p. product and process tech. Grain Processing Corp., Muscatine, Iowa, 1987-2000, Biobased Indsl. Products Consulting, 2000—. Adv. coun. adult vocat. edn. State of Ill., Springfield, 1983—87; mem. organizing com. Ann. Symposium on Biotech. for Fuels and Chems., 1985—97; departmental vis. com. botany dept. U. Tex., Austin, 1986—99; mem. applied sci. adv. coun. Miami U., Oxford, Ohio, 1987—97; chmn. rev. com. Solar Energy Rsch. Inst., Golden, Colo., 1988—89; mem. Sci. and Industry Adv. Bd., Nat. Renewable Energy Lab., Golden, Colo., 1993—99; mem. Bd. on Higher Edn. in the Workforce NRC, 2001—08; mem. sci. adv. bd. Mascoma Corp., 2006—. Contbr. sci. papers to profl. jours.; patentee in field. Staff sgt. USAF, 1953-57. Mem. AAAS, AIChE, Am. Chem. Soc., Nat. Acad. Engring., Rotary. Avocation: sailboat racing. Home: 106 Cape Fear Dr Hertford NC 27944-9239 Office Phone: 252-619-7217. Personal E-mail: dljgov1011@embarqmail.com.

JOHNSON, DOUGLAS WILLIAM, radiologist; b. Westpoint, NY; s. Andrew Larson and Barbara Joan (Rosborough) J.; m. Susan Mary Friedman, July 23, 1977; children: Danielle, Michael. BS in Biology, Va. Tech., Blacksburg, Va., 1976; MD, Med. Coll. Va., Richmond, 1979. Chmn. radiation oncology David Grant USAF Med. Ctr., Travis AFB, Calif., 1983-87; ptnr. Fla. Radiation Oncology Group, Jacksonville, Fla., 1987—. Asst. prof. radiation-oncology Stanford Med. Ctr., Stanford U., Calif., 1983-87; asst. prof. oncology Mayo Clinic Med. Sch., Rochester, Minn., 1995—; fellow Am. Coll. Radiology, Phila., 1995. Patentee in field. Col. USAF, 1975-. Fellow Am. Coll. Radiology; mem. Am. Soc. Therapeutic Radiology & Oncology. Avocation: aviation. Office: Baptist Cancer Inst 1235 San Marco Blvd Ste 100 Jacksonville FL 32207-8560 Office Phone: 904-202-7020.

JOHNSON, EDDIE BERNICE, United States Representative from Texas; b. Waco, Tex., Dec. 3, 1935; d. Lee Edward and Lillie Mae (White) Johnson; m. Lacy Kirk Johnson, July 5, 1956 (div. Oct. 1970); 1 child, Dawrence Kirk. Diploma in Nursing, St. Mary's Coll., U. Notre Dame, South Bend, Ind., 1955; BSN, Tex. Christian U., 1967; MPA, So. Meth. U., Dallas, 1976; LLD (hon.), Bishop Coll., 1979, Jarvis Coll., 1979, Tex. Coll., 1989, Houston-Tillotson Coll., 1993, Paul Quinn Coll., 1993. Chief psychiat. nurse Vets. Adminstrn. Hosp., Dallas, 1956-72; mem. Dist. 33 Tex. House of Reps., 1973—77; Dallas regional dir. Dept. Health, Edn. and Welfare, 1977-79, exec. asst. to adminstr. for primary health care policy Washington, 1979-81; v.p. Vis. Nurse Assn. Tex., Dallas, 1981-87; mem. Dist. 23 Tex. State Senate, 1987—93; mem. US Congress from 30th Tex. dist., 1993—. Exec. asst. pers. divsn. Neiman-Marcus, Dallas, 1972—75; cons. divsn. urban affairs Zales Corpn., Dallas, 1976—77; pres. Eddie Bernice Johnson & Assocs., Inc. Recipient Citizenship award, Nat. Conf. Christians & Jews, 1985, Heroes award, Tex. NAACP, 2000, Pres.'s award, Nat. Conf. Black Mayors, 2001, Visionary award, Nat. Orgn. Black Elected Legis. Women, 2001, Woman of Yr. award, 100 Black Men of America, Inc., 2001, 25th Anniversary Outstanding Achievement award, Nat. Black Caucus State Legislators; named one of The Most Influential Black Americans, Ebony mag., 2006; named to Power 150, 2008. Mem.: Alpha Kappa Alpha. Democrat. Office: US House Representatives 2468 Rayburn House Office Bldg Washington DC 20515 also: 3102 Maple Ave Ste 600 Dallas TX 75201 Office Phone: 202-225-8885.*

JOHNSON, EDGAR MCCARTHY, psychologist; b. Jacksonville, Fla., Oct. 29, 1941; s. James Mack and Dorothy (Vickers) Johnson; m. Fatima Nunes, Sept. 9, 1967; children: Victoria C., David M. BS in Applied Psychology, Ga. Inst. Tech., 1964; MS in Exptl. Psychology, Tufts U., 1967, PhD in Exptl. Psychology, 1969. Rsch. psychologist U.S. Army Rsch. Inst., Alexandria, Va., 1970-78, chief human factors sect., 1978-80, dir. systems rsch. lab., 1980-82, tech. dir., 1982-93, dir., 1993—2002; chief psychologist U.S. Army, 1982—2002; mem. rsch. staff Inst. Def. Analyses, Alexandria, Va., 2002—. Bd. trustees Amelia Island Mus. History, 2007—. Served to capt. US Army, 1968—70. NDEA fellow, 1965—67. Fellow: APA, Washington Acad. Sci. (Sci. Achievement award 1980), Human Factors and Ergonomics Soc., Am. Psychol. Soc.; mem.: Cosmos Club (Washington), Sigma Xi. Home: 1384 Mission San Carlos Dr Amelia Island FL 32034 Personal E-mail: emj1@sigmaxi.net.

JOHNSON, ERIC, architect, former state legislator; b. New Orleans, La., Aug. 20, 1953; m to Kathryn; children: Marcus & Righton. MA, Tulane Univ., 1976. Arch., v.p. Hussey, Gay, Bell & Deyoung; arch. North Point Real Estate; mem. Ga. House Reps., 1992—94; mem. Dist. 1 Ga. State Senate, 1995—2009, minority leader, 1999—2000, former pres. pro tempore. Georgia's Young Republican of Year, 80. Mem. Am. Inst. Architects Republican. Christian. Office: 128 Baymeadow Point Dr Savannah GA 31405 Office Phone: 912-443-1577.

JOHNSON, ERIC, state legislator; m. Nakita Johnson. Degree in History, Harvard U., 1998; JD, U. Pa.; M in Public Affairs, Princeton U., 2003. Of counsel Sandler Law Firm PLLC; mem. Dist. 100 Tex. House of Representatives, 2010—. Bd. mem. Boys and Girls Club of Greater Dallas, Inc., Martin Luther King, Jr. Cmty. Ctr., Educational Opportunities, Inc., Metro Dallas Homeless Alliance, Dallas County Historical Commission & The Arts Cmty. Alliance, Dallas Arboretum. Avocations: reading, sports. Office: 1409 S Lamar St Ste 9 Dallas TX 75215 Address: Room E1.306 Capitol Extension PO Box 2910 Austin TX 78768 Office Phone: 214-565-5663, 512-463-0586.

JOHNSON, ERNIE, JR., sportscaster; b. Milw. s. Ernie and Lois Johnson; m. Cheryl Johnson; 4 children. Grad., U. Ga. News and sports dir. WAGQ-FM, Athens, Ga., 1977—78; news anchor WMAZ-TV, Macon, Ga., 1979—81; news reporter WSPA-TV, Spartanburg, SC, 1981; gen. assignment news reporter WSB-TV, Atlanta, 1982—83, weekend sports anchor, reporter, 1983—89; studio host Turner Sports, 1989—; studio host NFL coverage TNT, 1990—94, game host NFL coverage, 1995—96, hole-by-hole announcer PGA Grand Slam of Golf coverage, 1999—2000, 2002—03, co-host Listen Up, 2002—03, co-host Inside the NBA, host NBA and PGA coverage; host Pacific-10 and Big-12 Coll. Football TBS, studio host, Maj. League Baseball, 2007—. Recipient UPI award, Sportscasting, 1984, Ga. Associated Press award, Sports Reporting, 1988, Ga.-area Emmy award, Outstanding Achievement-TV News Excellence/Sports Reporting, 1989, Emmy award, Outstanding Sports Personality - Studio Host, 2001, 2007, John Wooden Keys to Life award, 2007. Office: Turner Sports One CNN Ctr 13 South Tower Atlanta GA 30303

JOHNSON, FRANKLYN ARTHUR, academic administrator; b. Rochester, NY, Nov. 6, 1921; s. Robert Barnes and Olyve Cole (Eckler) J.; m. Emily Bernetta Lingle, Aug. 15, 1945 (div. Aug. 1978); children: Franklyn Arthur Jr.(dec.), Terri A. Cochran, Sandra C. Fox; m. Elena Senese, Sept. 27, 1991. BA, Rutgers U., 1947; MA, Harvard U., 1949, PhD, 1952; LHD (hon.), Jacksonville U., 1961; DLitt (hon.), Mt. Senario Coll., Ladysmith, Wis., 1971; LLD (hon.), Flagler Coll., St. Augustine, Fla., 1976; DCL (hon.), Drury Coll., Springfield, Mo., 1976; HHD (hon.), Mo. Valley Coll., 1978. Intelligence officer CIA, Washington, 1949-51; asst., assoc. prof. govt. Rollins Coll., Winter Park, Fla., 1952-56; pres., prof. govt. Jacksonville U., Fla., 1956-63, Calif. State U., Los Angeles, 1963-65; asst. sec., dir. Job Corps OEO, Washington, 1965-67; pres., chmn., trustee Wm. H. Donner Found., NYC, 1967-70; dir. Arthur Vining Davis Founds., Coral Gables, Fla., 1970-78; prof. adminstrn. Fla. Atlantic U., Boca Raton, 1970-87; pres., prof. mgmt. S.W. Fla. Coll., Naples, 1987—90. Trustee Inst. for Am. Univs., Aix-en-Provence, France, 1967—97, Eckerd Coll., St. Petersburg, Fla., 1978—90, Milt. Order of Purple Heart, 2007; chmn. S.E. Coun. Founds., Atlanta, 1975—77. Author: Defence by Committee, 1960, Defence by Ministry, 1980, 81, One More Hill, 1949, rev. edits., 1982, 88, 2010, Santori, 1990, Castro: The Last Hurrah, 1992, The Periled Presidency, 1995, Here and There, 1995, After Thoughts, 1996, D. S. Nemenoff, Maestro, 1996, A Chance Encounter, 1996, Odds and Ends, 1996, The Gods That Failed, 1997, Pearls Are a Girl's Best Friend, 1997, The 22nd Amendment, 1998, The Reluctant Presidents, 1999, Santori Island of Evil, 1999, Key West to Cuba, 2000, The Mismated, 2001, Triangle of Terror: Trauma in Everglades City, 2003, Dynasty of Deceit: 2015, The Last of the 3 Castros, 2004, Eyes Only: Countdown to Chaos, 2005; contbr. articles to profl. jours. Mem. U.S. Com. United World Colls., NYC, 1975-85, Fla. Gov.'s Coun. on Indian Affairs, Tallahassee, 1975-80, exec. adv. coun. Fla. Atlantic U., chmn.; bd. dirs. Collier Cultural and Ednl. Ctr., Naples; v.p., dir. Beachwood Assn., Inc., 1992-94; pres. Francobollo Press, 1998-2006. Lt. U.S. Army, 1942-45, ETO. Decorated Disting. Svc. medal, Jubilee of Liberty, Legion of Honor (France), Croix deGuerre, Diplome de la Liberation de Normandie (France); Prisoner of War medal, Silver Star, 5 Bronze Stars, 3 Purple Hearts, Conspicuous Svc. Cross, Combat Infantryman's Badge; Fulbright Scholar, London Sch. Econ., 1951-52; recipient George Washington honor medal Freedoms Found., Valley Forge, 1956, Profl. Achievement award Barry U., Miami, Fla., Eric Fenby lectr., 1991; named Champion Ind. Higher Edn. in Fla., Ind. Colls. Fla., 1992 Svc. Medallion, N. Fla. Jr. Coll., Madison, Fla., Disting. Dolphin award, Jacksonville U. Fellow Inter-U. Seminar on Armed Forces and Soc.; mem. Delius Assn. Am. (life, founding pres.), Can. Inst. Strategic Studies, Phi Beta Kappa, Phi Alpha Theta, Pi Alpha Alpha (pres.), Phi Kappa Phi. Republican. Presbyterian. Avocation: classical music. Home: PO Box 1873 Bonita Springs FL 34133-1873 Home Phone: 239-992-5190.

JOHNSON, GERARD, retail executive; Attended, Fla. Met. U., 1986. Adj. CIS faculty Fla. Met. U., 1989—2001; sr. cons. Resource Solutions, 1997—99; dir., tech. HSN, Inc., 1999—. Office: HSN Inc 1 HSN Dr Saint Petersburg FL 33729 Office Phone: 727-872-1000. Office Fax: 727-872-6615. Business E-Mail: gerard.johnson@hsn.net.

JOHNSON, GLORIOUS J., public relations executive, former councilwoman; 1 child, Stephanie. MusB, Jacksonville U.; MA in Sch. Adminstrn., Nova U., Ft. Lauderdale; MA in Ednl. Adminstrn., Columbia U. Tchrs. Coll. Former tchr. Duval County Sch. Sys.; master admissions rep. Everest U.; instr. bus. adminstrn. Jones Coll., admissions rep., West Campus; councilwoman-at-large Group 5 Jacksonville City Coun., 2003—11; v.p. bus. comm. The McCormick Agy., Jacksonville, 2011—. Chmn. Value Adjustment Bd.; vice chmn. Pub. Health & Safety Com.; mem. Rules, Transp., Energy & Utilities Coms., Victim Assistance Adv. Coun.; coun. liaison Duval County Sch. Bd. Vol. DAWN Prison Program; mem. Fla. Commn. on the Status of Women, US Dist. Ct. Fla. Fed. Jud. Nomination Commn.; bd. mem. Naval Ship Mus. Recipient Equal Justice award, Jacksonville Area Legal Aid, Inc., 2008, Grad. Cert., Citizens Police Acad.; fellow Women in Pub. Policy, Rockefeller Grad. Sch. Pub. Affairs & Policy. Mem.: Women Elected in Mcpl. Govt., Fla. League Cities (Northeast bd. mem.), Fla. Parent-Teacher Assn. (life), Sister to Sister Heart Found. (cmty. coun.), Nat. Coun. Negro Women, Jacksonville Hist. Naval Ship Assn., Northeast Fla. Sickle Cell Assn., MADDADS (pres. Women's Div.), Zeta Phi Beta, Phi Delta Kappa-Alpha Gamma Chpt. Democrat. Office: The McCormick Agency 2579 Oak St Jacksonville FL 32204-4559 Office Phone: 904-630-1387, 904-630-1386. Business E-Mail: gloriousj@coj.net.

JOHNSON, GORDON SELBY, consulting electrical engineer; b. Petersburg, Ind., July 25, 1918; s. Basil Orvil and Lillian May (Selby) J.; m. Frances Marie Overstreet, June 15, 1940; children: Lowell, Anne, Judith, Martha, Carol, Gordon, Mary; m. Alice Woods, 2002. BSEE, Purdue U., 1939. Registered profl. engr., Wis. Engr. Sunbeam Electric Mfg. Co., Evansville, Ind., 1939-41, Kohler (Wis.) Co., 1941-48, dept. head, 1948-55, chief engr., 1955-65, mgr. engring., 1965-76, sr. staff engr., 1976-85, cons. engr., 1985-87; pvt. practice cons. Winter Haven, Fla., 1987—. Dir. communications and tech. assistance Elec. Generating Systems Assn., Boca Raton, Fla., 1986-92, tech. dir., 1993-99, pres., 1983-84. Author: Kohler Tech. Series, 1976-85; editor: Elec. Grounding, 1992, On-Site Power Generation, 1990, 2d edit., 1993, 3rd edit., 1998; editor Powerline mag., 1986-92, tech. editor, 1993-99; contbr. numerous articles to profl. jours. Pres. Sheboygan County Coun. of Chs., 1965-67; lay leader N.E. Wis. Dist. United Meth. Ch., 1975-76; chmn. adv. com. Lakeshore Tech. Coll., Sheboygan, 1970-80; adv. high sch. sci. seminars. With U.S. Mcht. Marine, 1944-45, ETO, NATOUSA. Recipient L.H. Carpenter Outstanding Svc. award Elec. Generating Systems Assn., 1973; named Athlete of Yr., Fla. Sr. Games, 1999. Fellow IEEE (sect. chmn. 1953-54); mem. NSPE, Soc. Automotive Engrs., Nat. Fire Protection Assn. Avocations: running, bicycling, gardening. Home and Office: 421 Flagler Rd SE Winter Haven FL 33884 Office Phone: 863-324-3711. E-mail: johnsonjogs@aol.com.

JOHNSON, GREGORY HAROLD, career officer, astronaut, experimental test and fighter pilot; b. South Ruislip, Middlesex, England, May 12, 1962; came to the U.S., 1964; s. Harold Cumings and Marion Joyce (Frye) J.; m. Cari Michele Harbaugh Johnson, July 8, 1989; children: Matthew, Joseph, Rachel. BS, U.S. Air Force Acad., 1984; MS, Columbia U., 1985; MBA, U. Tex., Austin, 2005. cert. USAF pilot, F-15E fighter pilot, test pilot. Air Force pilot, Reese AFB, Tex., 1986; T-38A instr. pilot 54 Flying Training Squadron, Reese AFB, Tex., 1986-89; F-15E Eagle fighter pilot 335th Fighter Squadron, Seymour Johnson AFB, NC, 1990-93; deployed to Al Kharj, Saudi Arabia, flying 34 combat missions in support of Operation Desert Storm, 1990; deployed to Saudi Arabia, flew an additional 27 combat missions in support of Operation Southern Watch, 1992; test pilot, flew and tested F-15C/E, NF-15B and T-38A/B aircraft 445th Flight Test Squadron, Edwards AFB, Calif., 1994—97; with astronaut corps. Johnson Space Ctr., Houston, 1998—; technical asst. to dir., Flight Crew Ops. Directorate (FCOD) NASA. Technical asst. to dir., Flight Crew Ops. Directorate (FCOD), 2000; assigned to Shuttle Cockpit Avionics Upgrade Coun. (CAU), 2000-; various positions including direct support to the crews of STS-100 and STS-108, chief of shuttle abort planning and procedures fro contigency scenarios, and ascent procedure develop, Space Shuttle Br., 2001; key mem., "tiger teams" during the investigation into the cause of the Columbia accident in 2003; astronaut rep. to the External Tank (ET)foam impact test team, eventually proved that ET foam debris on ascent could critically damage the shuttle's leading edge thermal protection sys.; dep. chief, Astronaut Safety Br., 2004; crew rep. supporting the design and testingof NASA's Crew Exploration Vehicle, 2005; pilot, mission to deliver the Japanese Logistics Module and the Canadian Spl. Purpose Dexterous Manipulator to the Internat. Space Station (ISS), STS-123 Mission (Endeavour), 2008; pilot STS-134-Final Flight of Endeavour, 2011. Eagle Scout, Boy Scouts Am., 1978. Decorated DFC, Saudi Arabia, 1991, Lt. Gen. Bobby Bond award top test pilot USAF, 1996, NASA Superior Performance award, Disting. Flying Cross, Meritorious Svc. medal (two), Air medals (four), Aerial Achievement medals (three), USAS Commendation medal, USAF Achievement medals (two), Stephen D. Thorne Top Fox Safety award, 2005, Dean's award for Academic Excellence-McCombs Sch. Bus., 2005; Guggenheim fellow Columbia U., 1984, Legion of Merit Mem. AIAA, Planetary Soc., Optimist Club. Republican. Methodist. Avocations: bridge, golf, woodworking, chess, backgammon, travel, bicycling, music. Office: NASA/JSC Cobe CB 2101 Nasa Rd 1 Houston TX 77058-3691 Home: 2109 Riverside Dr League City TX 77573-5892

JOHNSON, HENRY C., JR., (HANK JOHNSON), United States Representative from Georgia, lawyer; b. Washington, DC, Oct. 2, 1954; m. Mereda Davis; children: Randi, Alex. BA, Clark U., 1976; JD, Tex. So. U., 1979. Judge Magistrate Ct, DeKalb County, Ga., State Ct. of Ga.; ptnr. Johnson & Johnson Law Group LLC, Decatur, Ga.; mem. US Congress from 4th Ga. Dist., 2007—. Mem. DeKalb County Bd. Commrs., chmn. Budget Com. Named to Power 150, Ebony mag.,

2008. Mem.: State Bar Ga., Ga. Lawyers Found., Ga. Assn. Criminal Defense Attys., DeKalb County Law Libr. Democrat. Office: US House of Representatives 2240 Rayburn House Office Bldg Washington DC 20515 also: 5700 Hillandale Dr, Ste 120 Lithonia GA 30058 Office Phone: 202-225-1605.*

JOHNSON, HERBERT ALAN, historian, lawyer; b. Jersey City, Jan. 10, 1934; Son of Harry Oliver and Magdalena Gertrude (Diemer) J.; m. Barbara Arlene (Balcerak), Sept. 24, 1955 (dec. Nov. 1980); children: Amanda Blair, Vanessa Paige Smiley, m. Jane (McCue), June 4, 1983. AB, Columbia U., 1955, MA, 1961, PhD (Schiff fellow), 1965; LLB, N.Y. Law Sch., 1960; postgrad., Luth. Theol. So. Sem., 1981-84. Bar: N.Y. 1960; U.S. Supreme Ct. 1965; D.C. 1967; S.C. 1983; ordained vocat. deacon, The Episcopal Ch., 1991. Jr. clk. First Nat. City Bank of N.Y., NYC, 1955; adminstrv. asst. Chase Manhattan Bank, NYC, 1957—60; practiced law in NYC, 1960—67; rsch. asst. Papers of John Jay, Columbia U., 1961—63; lectr. Hunter Coll., NYC, 1964—65, asst. prof. history, 1965—67; assoc. sem. on history of legal polit. thought Columbia U., 1966—77, assoc. sem. on early Am. history, 1967—77; assoc. editor Papers of John Marshall, Inst. Early Am. History and Culture, Williamsburg, Va., 1967—70, co-editor, 1970—71, editor, 1971—77; prof. law and history U. S.C., Columbia, 1977—90, Ernest F. Hollings prof. constl. law, 1991—2002, disting. prof. law emeritus, 2002—; first lt, USAF, 1955—57; col. USAFR, 1958—87. Lectr. Coll. William and Mary Williamsburg, 1967-77; Bostick vis. rsch. prof. So. studies program U. S. C., 1976, 77; mem. com. rsch., publ. Heritage '76 Com. Am. Revolution Bicentennial Commn., 1972-73; mem. bd. adjustments, appeals, Williamsburg, 1970-77; trustee Fund for Preservation of John Marshall House, 1972-74; Fund Coop. Editl. Rsch. Am. Antiquarian Soc., 1972-76; mem. profl. adv. bd. Angel Home Health & Hospice, 2002-06. Author: The Law Merchant and Negotiable Instruments in Colonial New York, 1664-1730, 1963; John Jay, 1745-1829, 1970; Imported Eighteenth Century Law Treatises in Am. Libraries 1700-1799, 1978; Essays on New York Colonial Legal History, 1981; History of Criminal Justice, 1988, 3d edit., 2002; John Jay: Colonial Lawyer, 1989, 2006; The Chief Justiceship of John Marshall, 1997; Wingless Eagle: U.S. Army Aviation Through World War I, 2001, Gibbons v. Ogden: John Marshall, Steamboats and The Commerce Clause, 2010; co-author: Historical Courthouses of New York State-18th and 19th Century Halls of Justice Across the Empire State, 1977; Foundations of Power, John Marshall, 1801-15, vol. 2, History of the Supreme Court of the U.S., 1981; editor: The Papers of John Marshall, Vol. 1, 1974, Vol. II, 1977; South Carolina Legal History, 1980; Am. Legal and Constitutional History: Cases and Materials, 1994, 2d edit., 2000; gen. editor Chief Justiceships of the U.S. Supreme Court Series, 1989—; contbg. articles to profl. jour. Chaplain assoc. Bapt. Med. Ctr., Columbia, 1983-2002; hospice legal svc. vol., 1986-2000; chaplain Angel Hospice, Franklin, N.C., 2002-2004; mem. ethics com. S.C. Episcopal Home, Still Hopes, 1989-99 Recipient: William P. Lyons Masters' Essay Award Loyola U., 1962; Paul S. Kerr History prize NY State Hist. Assn., 1970, Rsch. award Faculty Law U. SC, 2001; U. SC Edn. Found. Rsch. Award profl. sch., 2000; Am. Council Learned Soc. Fellow, 1974-75; Inst. Humane Studies Fellow, 1981, 85; vis. fellow Centre for Comparative Constl. Studies, U. Melbourne Law Faculty, 1992; vis. rsch. scholar U. Toronto Law Faculty, 1995; vis. prof. U. Birmingham, Eng., 1998, Vis. faculty, Western Carolina U., 2007; fellow Gilder-Lehrman Inst. Am. History, 2006, Folger Shakespeare Libr., 2009-10, Nat. Soc. Cin., 2013. Fellow Soc. Cin. Libr.; mem. Am. Hist. Assn. (Littleton-Griswold com. 1976-81, interim com. Bicentennial era 1976-77), Selden Soc. (state corr. for S.C. 1988-2002), Air Force Assn., Am. Law Inst., Assn. Am. Law Sch. (chmn. legal history sect. 1979), Am. Soc. Legal History (pres. 1974-75, del. Am. Coun. Learned Soc. 1977-80, bd. dirs. 1999-2001), Assn. Episcopal Deacons, Libr. Co. Phila., N.Am. Conf. Brit. Studies, U. South Caroliniana Soc., Res. Officers Assn., Nat. Eagle Scout Assn. Episcopalian. Home: 5 Williamette Cir Weaverville NC 28787-9405 Personal E-mail: janeherb@charter.net.

JOHNSON, INGE PRYTZ, federal judge; b. Svendborg, Denmark, 1945; CJuris, U. Copenhagen, 1969; MCLaw, U. Ala., 1970; JD, U. Ala., 1973. Pvt. practice atty., Copenhagen, 1970—71, Tuscumbia, Ala., 1973—79; adj. faculty U. Copenhagen Sch. Law, 1970—71; mcpl. judge Muscle Shoals City Ct., 1978—79; judge 31st Jud. Cir. Ct. Ala., 1979—98, presiding cir. judge, 1980—99; judge US Dist. Ct. (northern dist. Ala.), 1998—2012, sr. judge, 2012—. Office: US District Ct Hugo Black Courthouse 1729 5th Ave N Birmingham AL 35203*

JOHNSON, I.S. LEEVY, social services administrator; b. Columbia; BSBA, Benedict Coll.; JD, U. SC. Founder Carolina Nat. Bank (merged with First Nat. Bank); owner Leevy Johnson Funeral Home, Inc.; atty. Johnson, Toal & Battiste, P.A., 1976—. Bd. dirs. First Nat. Bancshares, Inc., 2008—, First Nat. Bank of the South, 2008—. Office: Johnson Toal & Battiste PA First Fl Centre Orangeburg SC 29115 Office Phone: 803-536-9610. Office Fax: 803-536-3926.

JOHNSON, J. MITCHELL, communications executive; b. Dallas, May 12, 1951; s. J. Edward and Blanche (Dabney) J.; 1 child, Philip Louis. BS, U. Tex.; MS, U. So. Calif. Prodn. asst. Guggenheim Prodns., Washington, 1975-77; pres. Ft. Worth Prodns., 1977—; CEO J. Mitchell Johnson Prodns., Ft. Worth, 1986—; publisher Fodor's Video Guides, Ft. Worth, 1986-93; CEO Abamedia, LP, Ft. Worth and Moscow, 1995—; pres. Archive Media Project, Ft. Worth and Moscow, 1996—. Ofcl. trade rep. Russian State Film and Photo Archives, Krasnogorsk. Producer 14 films for Fodor's, 1986-93; 20 TV programs for Ostankino Russian TV; Co-production ABC News N.Y. 1994-95; prodr., dir. TV films including Gymnast, Pub. Broadcasting System, 1980 (JQ award 1981), Artist and Athlete, ABC, 1980; producer TV films Moses Pendleton Presents Moses Pendleton, ABC, 1983 (1st place award San Francisco Film Festival 1984), Mondale for America, 1984, Yanks for Stalin (History Channel) 1999, Red Files (PBS Series) 1999, World Without Waves (Santa Fe Film Festival Best of S.W), 2004. Exec. producer Mondale for Am.-Cons. '84, Washington, 1984; chmn. Budapest, Hungary-Ft. Worth Sister Cities Internat. Com., chmn. media panel Tex. Commn. for Arts and Humanities, Austin, 1986, chmn. Citizens Cable Bd., City of Ft. Worth, 1990-91; bd. dirs. Mental Health Assn. Tarrant County. Recipient Gold award N.Y. TV Film Festival, 1981, Golden Eagle award Council on Internat. Nontheatrical Events, Washington, 1983, Best Documentary and Film awards N.Mex. Film Festival, Albuquerque, 1984, Best Documentary award USA Film Festival, Dallas, 1984. Mem. Internat. Music Ctr. (pres. 1987-88), Motion Picture Producers Tex. (pres. 1987-88), Found. for Social Innovations Moscow-N.Y. (bd. dirs.), Lone Star Film Soc., Ft. Worth Club. Democrat. Methodist. Avocations: travel, music, electronics. Office: J Mitchell Johnson Prodns Inc PO Box 125 Fort Worth TX 76101-0125

JOHNSON, JACK C., state legislator; b. Amarillo, Tex., July 25, 1968; m. Deanna Johnson; 3 children. Sec. Transp. Com.; mem. Govt. Ops. Com., Gen. Welfare & Human Resources Com.; asst. fl. leader Rep. Caucus; sr. v.p. Pinnacle Fin. Ptnrs., fin. advisor; state senator Dist. 23 Tenn., 2007—. Republican. Office: 330 Franklin Rd, Ste 135-A-178 Brentwood TN 37027 also: 10A Legislative Plz Nashville TN 37243-0023 Office Phone: 615-741-2495. Office Fax: 615-253-0321. Business E-Mail: sen.jack.johnson@capitol.tn.gov.

JOHNSON, JAMES TERENCE, lawyer, writer, minister, educator; b. Springfield, Mo., Oct. 25, 1942; s. Clifford Lester and Margaret Jeanne (Wallace) Johnson; m. Martha Susan Mitchell, May 2, 1964; children: Jennifer Jeanne Clark, Emily Jill Brown. BA, Okla. Christian Coll., 1964; JD, So. Meth. U., 1967; LLD (hon.), Pepperdine U., 1980. Min., Okla., 1961—2000; staff counsel, asst. prof. Okla. Christian Coll., Oklahoma City, 1968-72; pvt. law practice Oklahoma City, 1969—2000; v.p. Okla. Christian U., 1972-73, exec. v.p., 1973-74, pres., 1974-95, chancellor, 1996—2000. Co-founder Enterprise Sq., 1982, Cascade Coll., 1993. Chmn. Highland Lakes Family Crisis Ctr., 2006—07; elder Marble Falls (Tex.) Ch. Christ, 2004. Named to Okla. Higher Edn. Hall of Fame, 2000, Okla. Pub. Author, 2006, Mo. Sports Hall of Fame, Am. Legion Baseball Team, 2009. Mem.: Okla. Bar Assn., Phi Delta Theta.

JOHNSON, JIMMIE KENNETH (JAMES KENNETH JOHNSON), race car driver; b. El Cajon, Calif., Sept. 17, 1975; s. Gary and Cathy Johnson; m. Chandra Johnson; 1 child. Race car driver NASCAR Hendrick Motorsports, 2002—; driver, Truck Series Randy Moss Motorsports, 2008; co-founder The Jimmie Johnson Found., 2006—. 1st pl. NAPA Auto Parts 500 Calif. Speedway, 2002, 1st pl. Sharp AQUOS 500, 2007, 1st pl. Pepsi 500, 2008, 2009, 1st pl. Auto Club 500, 2010; 1st pl. MBNA Platinum 400 Dover Internat. Speedway, 2002, 1st pl. MBNA All-Am. Heroes 400, 2002, 1st pl. MBNA RacePoints 400, 2005, 1st pl. Dover 400, 2009, 2009, 1st pl. AAA 400, 2010, 1st pl. FedEx 400, 2012; 1st pl. Coca-Cola 600 Lowes Motor Speedway, 2003, 2004, 2005, 1st pl. UAW-GM Quality 500, 2004, 1st pl. UAW GM-Quality 500, 2005, 1st pl. Bank of America 500, 2009; 1st pl. New Eng. 300 NH Internat. Speedway, 2003, 1st pl. Sylvania 300, 2003, 1st pl. Lenox Indsl. Tools 301, 2010; 1st pl. Carolina Dodge Dealers 400 Darlington Raceway, 2004, 1st pl. Mountain Dew Southern 500, 2004, 1st pl. Bojangles' Southern 500, 2012; 1st pl. Pocono 500 Pocono Raceway, 2004, 1st pl. Pa. 500, 2004; 1st pl. Subway 500 Martinsville Speedway, 2004, 2006, 2007, 1st pl. Goody's Cool Orange 500, 2007, 1st pl. TUMS QuikPak 500, 2008, 1st pl. Goody's Fast Pain Relief 500, 2009, 1st pl. Tums Fast Relief 500, 2012; 1st pl. Bass Pro Shops/MBNA 500 Atlanta Motor Speedway, 2004, 1st pl. Kobalt Tools 500, 2007, 1st pl. Pep Boys Auto 500, 2007; 1st pl. UAW DiamlerChrysler 400 Las Vegas Motor Speedway, 2005, 1st pl. UAW-DaimlerChrysler 400, 2006, 1st pl. UAW-DiamlerChrysler 400, 2007, 1st pl. Shelby Am., 2010; 1st pl. Daytona 500 Daytona Internat. Speedway, 2006, 2013; 1st pl. Allstate 400 at The Brickyard Indpls. Motor Speedway, 2006, 2008, 2009, 1st pl. Crown Royal Curtiss Shaver 400, 2012; 1st pl. Crown Royal 400 Richmond Internat. Raceway, 2007, 1st pl. Chevy Rock-n-Roll 400, 2007, 2008; 1st pl. Dickies 500 Tex. Motor Speedway, 2007, 1st pl. AAA Tex. 500, 2012; 1st pl. Checker O'Reilly Auto Parts 500 Phoenix Internat. Raceway, 2007, 2008, 2009, 1st pl. Subway Fresh Fit 500, 2008; 1st pl. Camping World RV 400 Kansas Speedway, 2008, 1st pl. Hollywood Casino 400, 2011; 1st pl. Food City 500 Bristol Motor Speedway, 2010; 1st pl. Toyota/Save Mart 350 Infineon Raceway, Sonoma, Calif., 2010; 1st pl. Aaron's 499 Talladega Superspeedway, 2011. Commentator ESPN, spokesperson Chevrolet divsn. GM; host: (weekly radio show) Not What You Expected; appeared in (documentaries) 24/7 Jimmie Johnson: Race to Daytona, 2010. Co-founder Jimmie Johnson Found., 2006—. Recipient ESPY award, Best Driver, ESPN, 2008; named Pat Schauer Meml. Rookie of Yr., American Speed Assn., 1998, NASCAR Driver of Yr., 2006—07, 2009—10, NASCAR Athlete of Decade, 2000's, The Sporting News, 2009, NASCAR Nextel Cup Champion, 2006, 2007, 2008, 2009, 2010, 2013, Male Athlete of Yr., AP, 2009. Achievements include being the first driver in history to win four consecutive NASCAR Cup Series championships, 2006-09. Office: c/o Hendrick Motorsports 4400 Papa Joe Hendrick Blvd Charlotte NC 28262*

JOHNSON, JOHN H., lawyer; b. Raleigh, NC, 1948; BA, Univ. NC, 1970, JD, 1976. Bar: NC 1976, Ga. 1987. Staff atty., legal br., enforcement divsn., region 4 EPA, 1977—80, chief, air and toxics law br., office of regional counsel, region 4, 1980—83, chief, hazardous waste law br., office of regional counsel, region 4, 1983—86; assoc. Troutman Sanders LLP, Atlanta, 1986—90, ptnr., environ., natural resources, 1990—, and practice group leader, environ. and natural resources. Exec. com. bd. dir. Piedmont Park Conservancy. Named a Super Lawyer, Atlanta Mag., 2004, 2005, 2006, 2007, 2008, 2009; named one of Am.'s Leading Lawyers for Environ. Law, Chambers USA, 2005, 2006, 2007, 2008, 2009, Best Lawyers in Am. for Environ. Law, 2006, 2007, 2008, 2009. Mem.: ABA, NC State Bar, State Bar Ga. Office: Troutman Sanders LLP Bank of America Plz Ste 5200 600 Peachtree St NE Atlanta GA 30308-2216 Office Phone: 404-885-3166. Office Fax: 404-962-6594. Business E-Mail: john.johnson@troutmansanders.com.

JOHNSON, JOHNNY RAY, retired mathematics professor; b. Chatham, La., Dec. 19, 1929; s. Dave Ernest and Bessie (Morris) J.; m. Betty Ann Moore, Oct. 21, 1960 (div. May 1982); children: Todd Michael, John Fitzgerald, Shauna Renee; m. Barbara F. Kennedy, June 1, 1990. BS, La. Tech U., 1951; MS, Auburn U., 1953, PhD, 1959. Registered profl. engr., La. Asst. prof. math. La. Tech U., 1958-62; assoc. prof. math. Appalachian State U., 1962-63; prof. elec. engring. La. State U., Baton Rouge, 1963-83, prof. emeritus, 1983—; prof. math. U. North Ala., 1984-95, prof. emeritus, 1995—. Adj. prof. elec. engring. U. Fla., Gainesville, 1976-77; mem. staff Combat Ops. Research Group, Ft. Monroe, Va., summer 1957; mathematician Boeing Co., New Orleans, summer 1965; engring. specialist Gen. Dynamics, 1983-84 Author: (with David E. Johnson) Mathematical Methods in Engineering and Physics, 1965, Graph Theory with Engineering Applications, 1972, Introductory Electric Circuit Analysis, 1981, Linear Systems Analysis, 1975; (with David E. Johnson and John L. Hilburn) Basic Electric Circuit Analysis, 1978, 3d edit., 1986, 4th edit., 1990, (with David E. Johnson, John L. Hilburn and Peter D. Scott) 5th edit., 1995, (with David E. Johnson and Harry P. Moore) A Handbook of Active Filters, 1980, (with David E. Johnson) A Funny Thing Happened on the Way to the White House, 1983, revised edit., 2004, 2007, (with David E. Johnson and John L. Hilburn) Electric Circuit Analysis, 1989, 2d edit., 1991, Introduction to Digital Signal Processing, 1989, (with David E. Johnson, John L. Hilburn & Peter D. Scott) Electric Circuit Analysis, 3d edit., 1997. Pres. Wildwood PTA, 1973-74. Served with US Army, 1954—56. Mem. IEEE (sr. 1968-93, Centennial medal 1984), U. North Ala. Inst. for Learning in Retirement (v.p., chmn. curriculum com. 1997-98, treas. 1998-99), Sigma Xi, Tau Beta Pi, Phi Kappa Phi, Eta Kappa Nu, Pi Mu Epsilon, Kappa Mu Epsilon. Home: 209 Wesley Ct Florence AL 35630-1486 Personal E-mail: jjohnson66@att.net.

JOHNSON, JOSEPH CLAYTON, JR., retired lawyer; b. Vicksburg, Miss., Nov. 15, 1943; s. Joseph Clayton and Rose Butler (Levy) J.; m. Cherrian Frances Turpin, Oct. 24, 1970; children: Mary Clayton, Erik Cole. BS, La. State U., Baton Rouge, 1965; JD, La. State U., 1969. Bar: La. 1969, U.S. Dist. Ct. (ea. and mid. dists.) La. 1969, U.S. Dist. Ct. (we. dist.) La. 1979, U.S. Ct. Appeals (5th cir.) 1982. Ptnr. Taylor, Porter, Brooks & Phillips, Baton Rouge, 1969—2012; ret., 2012. Mem. civil justice reform act com. U.S. Dist. Ct. (mid. dist.) La., 1995-97, chmn. 1996-97; mem. La. Atty. Disciplinary Bd., 1997-99. Bd. editors Oil and Gas Reporter, 1988—2005. Pres. Baton Rouge area Am. Cancer Soc., 1987—88; mem. adv. bd. Ctr. for Energy Law, 2000—05; bd. dirs., Capital Area chpt. Am. Red Cross, 2005—, chair, 2010—12. With US Army, 1969—75. Recipient John Rogers award, 1999, Ctr. for Am. and Internat. Law. Mem.: Ctr. for Am. and Internat. Law (bd. editors Oil and Gas Reporter 1987—2005), Baton Rouge Bar Assn., La. State Law Inst. (mineral code com.), La. Bar Assn. (mem. ho. of dels. 1979—92, coun. rep. mineral law sect. 1986—94, chmn. mineral law sect. 1992—93). Republican. Methodist. Office: PO Box 2471 Baton Rouge LA 70821-2471 Office Phone: 225-387-3221. Business E-Mail: clay.johnson@taylorporter.com.

JOHNSON, JOSEPH PICKETT, state legislator; b. Washington, Va., Dec. 12, 1931; m. Mary Ann Allison; children: Mary Jo Neal, Joseph P., Sage B. III. House del. atty. Johnson, Scyphers & Austin, Va., 1960—; substitute judge Gen. Dist. Ct., Va., 1971—89; mem. Dist. 4 Va. House of Dels., Va., 1990—; mem. Ct. Justice Com., Agrl. Com., Fin. & Coorps. Com., Inst. Banking Com. Bd. dirs. First Va. Bank, Damascus. Chmn. bd. govs. Emory & Henry Coll. Named Young Man of Yr., Abingdon Jaycees, 1967. Mem.: America Legion (past post cmdr.), Shrines, Masons (past master), VFW (post & dist. cmdr., dept. judge adv., former dept. chief staff), Va. State Bar Assn., Wash. County Bar Assn. (former pres.), Abington Civitan. Democrat. Baptist. Office: 164 E Valley St Abingdon VA 24210 Office Phone: 276-628-9940. Business E-Mail: DelJJohnson@house.virginia.gov.

JOHNSON, KAREN C., physician, epidemiologist, researcher; MD, U. Tenn., Memphis, 1985; MPH, Johns Hopkins U., Baltimore, 1989. Prof. Dept. Preventive Medicine, Memphis, 1990—, vice chair, 1996—2010, interim chair, 2010—. Office: Univ Tennessee Health Sci C 66 N Pauline Ste 633 Memphis TN 38163

JOHNSON, KELLY OVERSTREET, lawyer; b. Tallahassee, May 3, 1958; m. Hal Johnson; 2 children. BS in Real Estate and pre-Law, Fla. State Univ., 1979, JD with honors, 1982. Civil litigator Fla. Dept. of Legal Affairs, 1983—85; atty. Ervin, Varn, Jacobs, Odom & Kitchen, 1985—88; pvt. practice, 1988—90; ptnr. Broad and Cassel, Tallahassee, 1990—. Mem.: Cert. Cir. Civil Mediator, ABA Sect. Litigation (co-chair), Nat. Conf. Bar Presidents (exec. coun.), Am. Bar Assn. (Ho. of Del. 1992—94, 2003—06), Tallahassee Women Lawyers (pres.), Tallahassee Bar Assn. (pres. 1990—91), Fla. Bar (young lawyers divsn. bd. gov. 1986—90, bd. govs. 1997—2004, pres. 2004—05), Leadership Fla. Class XXIV, Legal Aid Found. Office: Broad & Cassel 215 S Monroe St Ste 400 PO Box 11300 Tallahassee FL 32302-1300 Office Phone: 850-681-6810. Business E-Mail: kjohnson@broadandcassel.com.

JOHNSON, KEN, state legislator; Registered rep. Trinity Fin. Group; owner Global Sourcing Svc. Inc.; mem. Dist. 7 Ala. House of Reps., Montgomery, 2011—. Republican. Office: 12001 Hwy 157 Ste 6 Moulton AL 35650 also: Ala House of Reps Rm 526-E 11 S Union St Montgomery AL 36130 Office Phone: 256-974-5175, 334-242-7754. Business E-Mail: kenjohnsonrep@gmail.com.

JOHNSON, KEVIN B., pediatrician, biomedical researcher; BS in Biology, Dickinson Coll., Carlisle, Pa.; MS in Med. Informatics, Stanford U. Sch. Medicine, Calif.; MD, Johns Hopkins U. Sch. Medicine, Balt. Diplomate American Bd. Pediat. Resident dept. pediat. Johns Hopkins Hosp.; postdoc. rsch. fellowship U. Calif., San Diego; mgmt. of perioperative services fellowship Stanford U.; faculty pediat. and biomedical info. scis. Johns Hopkins U. Sch. Medicine, 1992—2002; pediatric chief resident Johns Hopkins Hosp., 1992—2002; faculty Vanderbilt U. Sch. Medicine, Nashville, 2002—, prof. pediat., vice chair biomedical informatics. Mem. med. adv. bd. PatientKeeper, Inc., 2001—. Asst. editor JAMIA-Jour. American Med. Informatics Assn., mem. editl. bd. Ambulatory Pediat.; contbr. numerous articles to profl. jours., chapters to books. Harold Amos Med. Faculty Devel. Program scholar, Robert Wood Johnson Found., 1998—2002. Mem.: American Pediatric Soc., Inst. Medicine, American Acad. Pediat., American Med. Informatics Assn. Achievements include research in the uses of advanced computer technologies, including the Worldwide Web, personal digital assistants, and pen-based computers in medicine; development of computer-based documentation systems for the point of care. Office: Vanderbilt U Rm 428 Eskind Biomedical Library 2209 Garland Ave Nashville TN 37232 Office Phone: 615-936-3596. Office Fax: 615-936-1427. E-mail: kevin.b.johnson@vanderbilt.edu.

JOHNSON, KEVIN L., state legislator; b. Sept. 27, 1960; s. Willie L. and Sallie M. Johnson; m. Gloria R. Johnson, July 5, 1987; children: Kimberly, Kenneth, Kyndra. BS, U. SC, 1982. Chmn. Black River Healthcare, Inc., 1988—2004; mem. Dist. 2 Clarendon Sch., 1988—2000; mem. Manning City Coun., 1994—2000; mayor City of Manning, 2000—11; mem. Dist. 64 SC House of Representatives, 2011—. Mem. Leadership SC, 1995, Nat. Conf. of Black Mayors, 2003—09; pres. SC Conf. of Black Mayors, 2004—10; mem. SC Exec. Inst., 2006, Santee-Lynches Coun. of Governments, 2000—11, SC Assn. of Regional Councils, 2002—11. Democrat. Home: PO Box 156 Manning SC 29102 Office: 422A Blatt Bldg Columbia SC 29201 Office Phone: 803-212-6929, 803-435-8117.

JOHNSON, LINDA P., state legislator; Former state rep. Dist. 90, NC; state rep. Dist. 83 NC, 2005—. Mem. Appropriations com., Edn. com., Edn. Subcom. on Presch., Elem. and Secondary Edn., Judiciary II com., Pub. Utilities com., Sci. and Tech. com.; vice chmn. Appropriations Subcom. on Edn. Republican. Office: North Carolina House of Representatives 300 N Salisbury St Room 301D Raleigh NC 27603-5925 Home: 1205 Berkshire Dr Kannapolis NC 28081 Office Phone: 919-733-5861. Business E-Mail: Linda.Johnson2@ncleg.net.

JOHNSON, LOCH KINGSFORD, political science educator, researcher; b. Auckland, New Zealand, Feb. 21, 1942; arrived in USA, 1946; s. Roland and Kathleen Winifred (Frost) Johnson; m. Leena Sepp, Mar. 22, 1969; 1 child, Kristin Elizabeth. BA, U. Calif., Davis, 1965; PhD, U. Calif., Riverside, 1969. Staff aide US Senate, Washington, 1969—70, 1975—77; asst. prof. Ohio U., 1971—75; staff dir. US House Reps. Subcom., Washington, 1977—79; from assoc. prof. dept. polit. sci. to Regents prof. polit. sci. U. Ga., Athens, 1979—. Cons. Nat. Security Coun., Washington, 1980, US House Reps. Fgn. Affairs Com., 1980, US Dept. State, Washington, 1972. Author: The Making of International Agreement, 1984, Season of Inquiry, 1985, Bombs, Bugs, Drugs, and Thugs, 2000, Seven Sins of American Foreign Policy, 2006; co-author: American Foreign Policy: History, Politics, and Policy, 2004; editor: Intelligence and Nat. Security; contbr. articles to profl. jours. Issues dir. Frank Church for Pres., Washington, 1976; debate advisor Jimmy Carter for Pres., Washington, 1980. Recipient Josiah Meigs prize, U. Ga., Owens award; named Outstanding Tchr., Pi Sigma Alpha, U. Ga., 1980, 1981, Outstanding Honors Prof., U. Ga., 1981, 1982, 1985; fellow, Haynes Found., 1966; vis. scholar, Yale U., 2005. Mem.: Legis. Studies Group, Ctr. Nat. Policy (mem. adv. bd. 1980—85), Ga. Polit. Sci. Assn., Internat. Studies Assn., Am. Polit. Sci. Assn. Presbyterian. Office: Univ Ga 305 Candler Hall Herty Dr Athens GA 30602 Office Phone: 706-542-6705. Office Fax: 706-583-8266. Business E-Mail: johnson@uga.edu.*

JOHNSON, LOYD, agricultural engineer, researcher; b. Mar. 18, 1927; s. Iley Benford and Ruth (Humphrey) J.; m. Ester Banegas, Dec. 24, 1952 (dec. July 19, 2003); children: Theresa Ann, Thomas Patrick,

Loyd Carl; m. Collean Turney Lemmord, Sept. 16, 2005. BS, Auburn U., 1950, MS, 1954. Registered profl. engr., Calif. Sr. project engr. United Fruit Co., Tiquisate, Guatemala, La Lima, Honduras, Almirante, Panama, 1951—60; agrl. engr. Rockefeller Found., 1960-82; mem. rsch. staff Internat. Rice Rsch. Inst., Los Banos, Philippines, 1960-68, Centro Internacional de Agricultura Tropical, Cali, Columbia, 1968-77, Internat. Agrl. Devel. Svc., Guayaquil, Ecuador, 1977-81, Internat. Fertilizer Devel. Ctr., Florence, Ala., 1981-82. Cons. agrl. engr. Internat. Agrl. Devel. Svcs., Dhaka, Bangladesh, 1982-83, Bogor, Indonesia, 1984-85, WINROCK, Pyinmana, Myanmar, 1986-88, Islamabad, Pakistan, 1990, 94. With USNR, 1945-46. Mem. Am. Soc. Agrl. Engrs. (Kishida Internat. award), Indian Soc. Agrl. Engrs. (life), Bangladesh Soc. Agrl. Engrs. Roman Catholic. Achievements include development of agricultural experimental station fields and research support facilities. Home: 308 College ST NW Hartselle AL 35640-2354

JOHNSON, MARGARET M., critical care specialist; MD, Thomas Jefferson U., 1990. Diplomate Am. Bd. Internal Medicine, 2003, Am. Bd. Internal Medicine- pulmonary disease, 2006, Am. Bd. Internal Medicine- critical care medicine, 2007. Intern Thomas Jefferson Univ., Phila., resident in internal medicine; fellow in pulmonary critical care medicine Wake Forest Baptist Hosp., Winston- Salem, NC, 1993; asst. prof. Bowman Gray; chair allergy and pulmonary medicine Mayo Clinic. Co-author: Amoxicillin therapy of poultry flocks: effect upon the selection of amoxicillin-resistant commensal Campylobacter spp, 2009, Predictors of poor neurologic outcome after induced mild hypothermia following cardiac arrest, 2009, Postmenopausal estrogen and progestin effects on the serum proteome, 2009, Upfront, randomized, phase 2 trial of sorafenib versus sorafenib and low-dose interferon alfa in patients with advanced renal cell carcinoma: clinical and biomarker analysis, 2010, Bordetella bronchiseptica pneumonia in a kidney-pancreas transplant patient after exposure to recently vaccinated dogs, 2010, 73-year-old woman with progressive shortness of breath, 2010, Distribution and abundance of anthropogenic marine debris along the shelf and slope of the US West Coast, 2010, Facial nerve hemangiomas: vascular tumors or malformations?, 2010, Case records of the Massachusetts General Hospital. Case 6-2010. A 37-year-old man with a lesion on the tongue, 2010, Use of electron microscopy in core biopsy diagnosis of oncocytic renal tumors, 2010, Single-dose palifermin prevents severe oral mucositis during multicycle chemotherapy in patients with cancer: a randomized trial, 2010, Detection of elevated plasma levels of epidermal growth factor receptor before breast cancer diagnosis among hormone therapy users, 2010, Clinical correlates of NRAS and BRAF mutations in primary human melanoma, 2011, CAN-mediated oxidations for the synthesis of xanthones and related products, 2010, various publs. Office: Mayo Clinic 4500 San Pablo Rd S Jacksonville FL 32224 Office Phone: 904-953-7290.

JOHNSON, MARK, construction executive; V.p., gen. mgr., Midwest divsn., Alden dist. Martin Marietta Materials, Inc. Office: Martin Marietta Materials Inc 2710 Wycliff Rd Raleigh NC 27607-3033 Office Phone: 919-781-4550. Office Fax: 919-783-4535.

JOHNSON, MARK COLWELL, biology professor; b. Denver, Colo., May 7, 1953; s. Richard F. and Claire Colwell Johnson; m. Wanda Baber, Oct. 20, 1984; children: Bethany, Micah. BS, Colo. State U., Fort Collins, 1975; PhD, U. Ky., Lexington, 1980. Rsch. assoc. USDA, Agrl. Rsch. Svc., Lexington, 1981—85; prof. Georgetown Coll., Ky., 1985—. Contbr. jour. articles. Recipient Cawthorne Excellence Tchg., Georgetown Coll., 2007. Mem.: Am. Soc. Microbiology. Office: Georgetown Coll 400 East Coll Georgetown KY 40324 E-mail: mjohnson@georgetowncollege.edu.

JOHNSON, MARK MATTHEW, museum director, curator; b. Rochester, Minn., Dec. 10, 1950; s. Charles Michael Jr. and Jean Lee (Reid) J.; m. Amy Joy Schneider, March 10, 1984; children: Rachel Amelia, Sarah Jean. BA in Art History, U. Wis., Whitewater, 1974; MA in Art History, U. Ill., Urbana-Champaign, 1976. Cert. in art mus. studies U. Ill., 1976. Rsch. assoc. Krannert Art Mus., Champaign, Ill., 1975, asst. dir., curator, 1981-85; lectr., dept. mus. edn. Art Inst. Chgo., 1975-77; curator, dept. art history and edn. Cleve. Mus. Art, 1977-81; dir., Muscarelle Mus. Art. Coll. William and Mary, Williamsburg, Va., 1985-94, lect. dept. fine arts, 1985-94; dir., chief curator Montgomery Mus. Fine Arts, Ala., 1994—. Author: Idea to Image: Preparatory Studies from the Renaissance to Impressionism, 1980, Romeyn de Hooghe, 1989, Literacy Through Art, 1990, Nissan Engel: Nouvelles Dimensions, 1994, Hans Grohs: An Ecstatic Vision, 1996, (English and French edits.) Nissan Engel, 1998, Ginny Ruffner, 2003, American Painting Collection: Montgomery Museum of Fine Arts, 2006, Cappy Thompson, 2006, Sonja Blomdahl, 2007, (photograph) Karsh, 2010; organized, curated numerous exhbns., 1980—. Rsch. and travel grantee various mus. Mem. Assn. Art Mus. Dirs. (edn. com.), Internat. Coun. Mus. (exhbns. com.), Coll. Art Assn., Am. Alliance Mus. (accreditation vis. com., mus. assessment program reviewer). Office: Montgomery Museum Fine Arts PO Box 230819 One Museum Dr Montgomery AL 36123-0819 Office Fax: 334-240-4384. Business E-Mail: mjohnson@mmfa.org.

JOHNSON, MARSHA SAMPSON, utilities executive; b. Jacksonville, Fla. BA in Polit. Sci. and Govt., Jacksonville U., Fla.; grad. advanced mgmt. program, Harvard U., Cambridge, Mass., 1999. Assoc. Westinghouse Elec. Corp., United Way Met. Atlanta, Coleman Mgmt. Consultants; mgmt. devel. analyst Southern Co., personnel mgr., asst. to divsn. v.p., divsn. mgr. bus. office ops., v.p. customer svc., v.p. Ala. Power Co. Birmingham divsn., v.p. diversity, chief diversity officer. Bd. dirs. Atlanta Symphony Orchestra; mem. Edward Lee Norton bd. advisors, mgmt. and profl. edn. Birmingham-Southern Coll. Named to Women Worth Watching, Profiles in Diversity Jour., 2007; fellow Am. Polit. Sci. Assn. and Nat. Inst. Mental Health, Fla. State U. Office: Southern Co 30 Ivan Allen Jr Blvd NW Atlanta GA 30308 Office Phone: 404-506-5000.

JOHNSON, MARSHALL HARDY, investment company executive; b. Raleigh, NC, Sept. 7, 1923; s. William Thompson and Evie (Barnes) J.; m. Mary Lynn Lewis, June 24, 1947 (div. 1977); children: Marshall Hardy (dec.), Lynn Lewis Johnson-Titchener, Carter Johnson Overton; m. Beverly Ray Johnson, June 2, 1984. Student, U. N.C., 1942—43, student, 1945—46; grad. in banking, U. Pa., 1957. Reporter, analyst Dunn & Bradstreet, Raleigh, 1946-47; chmn., pres., CEO McDaniel Lewis & Co., Greensboro, NC, 1947—; v.p. Scott & Stringfellow, Inc., Richmond, Va., 1993-96. Mem. Midwest Stock Exch., Chgo., 1960-77; chmn., dir. emeritus First Citizen Bank & Trust, Greensboro, Mcpl. Coun., Raleigh; adv. dir. Friends Home, 1985-; freelance writer. Contbr. articles to profl. jours. Dir. Young Dems., Greensboro, 1962-66, Jr. C. of C., Greensboro, 1964-70; deacon, tchr. First Bapt. Ch., Greensboro. With USNR, 1942-46, WWII USS Grapple Pacific Theater of Operations, 1945-1946. Fellow: Fin. Fedn. Am.; mem.: Securities Dealers of Carolinas (pres. 1976), Securities Industries Assn. (Mid-Atlantic exec. com. 1986—93), Boys Scouts America (life), Nat. Assn. Securities Dealers, Am. Arbitration Assn., Greensboro Country Club, Odd Fellows, Magna Charta Barons, Kiwanis (life Hixon award 1998), VFW, Alpha Tau Omega. Avocations: tennis, golf, swimming, walking. Home and Office: McDaniel Lewis & Co 310 Kimberly Dr Greensboro NC 27408-5018

JOHNSON, MARTIN ALLEN, publishing executive, artist; b. Bklyn., Aug. 20, 1931; s. Ellis A. and Estelle (Rudnick) Johnson; m. Suzanne Cornbleet, Dec. 12, 1964 (div. Feb. 1979); 1 child, Sarah; m. Diane Schlesinger Krull, Aug. 19, 1981. AB, Bard Coll., 1954. Assoc. editor Am. Printer and Lithographer mag., NYC, 1956-57, mng. editor, 1957-58, editor, 1958; mng. editor Printing Impressions mag., Phila., Delaware Valley Printing Impressions, 1958-61; pub. PTM mag., Chgo., 1959-67; v.p. Ednl. Screen and Audio Visual Guide, Chgo., 1962-67; pres. Trade Periodical Co., Chgo., 1967—, Pub. Dynamics, Inc., Stamford, Conn., 1968—, U.S. Indsl. Publs., Inc., Stamford, 1971—, U.S. Graphics Corp., Stamford, 1974—, Landmark Comms. Corp., Stamford. Spl. coor. Sun-Sentinal, Chgo. Tribune. Contbr. articles to profl. jours. With US Army, 1954—56. Recipient Justin P. Allman award, Wallcoverings Assn., 1993. Mem.: ArtSource, Cornell Mus. Art Guild, Fla. Watercolor Soc. (signature mem.), Boca Raton Mus. Artist Guild (signature mem.), Am. Watercolor Soc. (sustaining), Am. Soc. Interior Designers, Typophiles (N.Y.C.), Norton Mus. Art, Am. Music Libr. Israel, Wellington Club (London), Landmark Club (Stamford), Exec. Club (Chgo.), Chgo. Press Club. Jewish. Avocations: poetry, objective biblical history, painting. Office: 9506 Lantern Bay Cir West Palm Beach FL 33411 Office Phone: 561-204-3883. Personal E-mail: mjtalk2me@aol.com.

JOHNSON, MICHAEL R., civil engineer, academic administrator, retired military officer; BCE, Univ. Colo., 1970; B in bus., Chapman Coll., 1975; MCE, Univ. Pitts., 1978. PE. Advanced through grades to rear adm. Civil Engr. Corps US Navy, 1970—2004; dir. shore installation mgmt. Staff of Comdr. in Chief Atlantic Fleet; comdr. 2d Naval Constrn. Brigade; comdr. Atlantic divsn. Naval Facilities Engring. Command (NAVFAC), chief civil engr., 2000—03, comdr., 2003—04; assoc. vice chancellor for facilities Univ. Arkansas, Fayetteville, 2004—. Bd. dirs. Moffat & Nichol Engineers. Fellow: ASCE (OPAL award 2005); mem.: Nat. Acad. Engring. Office: Univ Arkansas Facilities Mgmt 1 Univ Arkansas Fayetteville AR 72701-1201 Office Phone: 479-575-6601. Business E-Mail: mrj03@uark.edu.

JOHNSON, PAUL, college football coach; b. Newland, NC, Aug. 20, 1957; m. Susan Johnson; 1 child, Kaitlyn. BS in Phys. Edn., Western Carolina U., Cullowhee, NC, 1979; MS in Health and Phys. Edn., Appalachian State U., Boone, NC, 1982. Offensive coord. Avery County HS, NC, 1979—80, Lees-McRae Jr. Coll., 1981—82; defensive line coach Ga. Southern U. Eagles, 1983—85, offensive coord., 1985—86, head football coach, 1997—2001; offensive coord. U. Hawai'i Rainbow Warriors, 1987—94, US Naval Acad. Midshipmen, 1995—96, head football coach, 2002—07, Ga. Inst. Tech. Yellow Jackets, 2008—. Recipient Eddie Robinson award, 1998; named Coach of Yr., Southern Conf., 1997, 1998, I-AA Coach of Yr., Am. Football Coaches Assn., 1997—2000, Bobby Dodd Coach of Yr., 2004, ACC Coach of Yr., Atlantic Coast Sports Media Assn., 2008, 2009, Sporting News, 2008. Office: Ga Tech Athletic Assn 150 Bobby Dodd Way NW Atlanta GA 30332-0455

JOHNSON, PAULA ANN, lawyer; b. 1963; BA, U. Okla., 1985, JD, 1988. Ptnr. Fulbright & Jaworski LLP, Houston; sr. counsel litigation group ConocoPhillips, 2002—06, mng. counsel for litigation & claims, 2006—09, dep. gen. counsel corporate, 2009—10, dep. gen. counsel corporate, chief compliance officer, 2010—12; exec. v.p., legal, gen. counsel, corporate sec. Phillips 66, 2012—. Office: Phillips 66 3010 Briarpark Dr Houston TX 77042*

JOHNSON, PHILIP MCBRIDE, lawyer; b. Springfield, Ohio, June 18, 1938; BA with honors, Ind. U., 1959; LLB, Yale U., 1962. Bar: Ill. 1962, DC 1983, NY 1984. Ptnr. Kirkland & Ellis, Chgo., 1962-81; chmn. Commodity Futures Trading Commn., Washington, 1981-83; ptnr. Wiley, Johnson & Rein, Washington, 1983-84; ptnr., of counsel, commodities, futures and options Skadden, Arps, Slate, Meagher & Flom, Washington, 1984—2011; lectr., commodities regulation U. Va. Law Sch., 1993—2011. Spkr. panelist on Commodity Exch. Act Fed. Bar Assn., others; mem. adv. com. definition and regulation Commodity Futures Trading Commn., adv. com. state jurisdiction and responsibility; adv. com. regulatory coordination, adv. com. fin. products, adv. com. tech., adv. com. global markets Commodity Futures Trading Commn.; chair, Commodity Futures Trading Commn., 1981-83 Author: Derivatives Regulation, 3 vols., 1997, Derivatives: A Manager's Guide to the World's Most Powerful Financial Instruments, 1999-; mng. editor Yale U. Law Jour, 1962, Agrl. Law Jour; bd. editors, International Financial Law Review; contbr. articles to legal jours. Named to Futures Industry Assn. Hall of Fame. Mem. ABA (founder, first chmn. com. on regulation of futures and derivative instruments 1976-81, mem. governing coun. sect. on bus. law 1981-83), Futures Industry Assn. (bd. dirs. 1980-81, 86-87, Hall of Fame), Internat. Bar Assn. (founder, first chmn. subcom. on commodities, futures and options law 1987-90), NY Stock Exch. (mem. regulatory adv. com. 1989—2004). Home: 5/89 Village Way Fernandina Beach FL 32034 Personal E-mail: philipmcbridejohnson@gmail.com.

JOHNSON, PHILIP WAYNE, state supreme court justice; b. Greenwood, Ark., Oct. 24, 1944; s. John Luther and Flora (Joyce) J.; m. Carla Jean Newsom, Nov. 6, 1970; children: Betsy, Carl, Jeff, Laura, Philip. BA, Tex. Tech. U., 1965, JD, 1975. Bar: Tex. 1975, U.S. Dist. Ct. (no. and we. dists.) Tex. 1976, U.S. Ct. Appeals (5th cir.) 1984, U.S. Supreme Ct. 1984; cert. in civil trial and personal injury trial law, Tex. Bd. Legal Specialization. Assoc. Crenshaw Dupree & Milam, Lubbock, Tex., 1975-80, ptnr., 1980-98; justice Tex. State Ct. of Appeals (7th dist), Amarillo, 1999—2002, chief justice, 2003—05; justice Tex. Supreme Ct., Austin, Tex., 2005—. Bd. dirs., pres. Lubbock County Legal Aid Soc., Tex., 1977-79; bd. dirs., chmn. Trinity Christian Schs., Lubbock, 1978-83, 85-89; bd. dirs., pres. S.W. Lighthouse for Blind, Lubbock, 1978-85. Served to capt. USAF, 1965-72. Decorated Silver Star, D.F.C.; Cross of Gallantry (Vietnam); Disting. Alumnus award Tex. Tech. U. Sch. Law Fellow: Tex. Bar Found. (life), Am. Bar Found. (life); mem.: Am. Law Inst., Austin (Tex.) Bar Assn., Lubbock County Bar Assn. (pres. 1984—85), Amarillo Bar Assn., Order of Coif, Phi Delta Phi. Mailing: PO Box 12883 Austin TX 78711 Home: 5604 Southwest Pkwy Apt 412 Austin TX 78735 Office: Texas Supreme Ct 201 W 14th St Rm 104 Austin TX 78701

JOHNSON, PHILLIP (MAX PHILLIP JOHNSON), state legislator; b. Texarkana, Tex., Mar. 26, 1961; m. Allison Johnson; children: Beau, Cannon. BS in Bus. Admin., U. Ark. Owner/ operator Beaumont Bldg. Inspections, 1996—; mem. Dist. 78 Tenn. House of Reps., 2003—. Mem. Cheatham County Republican Party; Williamson County Republican Party; rev. bd. Cheatham County Foster Care; mem. Cheatham County C. of C., Leadership Cheatham County; asst. coach South Cheatham Little League. Mem.: Am. Soc. Home Inspectors, Tenn. Farm Bur. Republican. Christian. Mailing: 4050 Beverly Hills Dr Pegram TN 37143 Office: 104 War Memorial Bldg Nashville TN 37243-0178 Office Phone: 615-741-7477. Business E-Mail: rep.phillip.johnson@capitol.tn.gov.

JOHNSON, PHILLIP EUGENE, mathematics professor; b. Bostic, NC, Feb. 25, 1937; s. Lin Joe and Gertrude (Pitman) J.; m. Carolyn Roberta Long, Dec. 23, 1959; 1 son, Philip Marc. BS, Appalachian State U., 1959; MA, Am. U., 1966, Vanderbilt U., 1963, PhD, 1968; postgrad., N.C. State U., 1971, Cambridge U., 1973. Tchr. math., Fredericksburg, Va., 1960-61, Fairfax County, Va., 1961-63; faculty U. Richmond, 1963-65, Vanderbilt U., 1966-71; prof. math. U. N.C., Charlotte, 1971—2004; prof. math. & dir. Appalachian State U., Math and Sci. Ctr., Boone, NC, 2004—. Author: A History of Set Theory, 1972; Contbr. articles to profl. jours. Served with USMCR, 1960. Grantee NSF, 1960-63, summers 1961-63; Grantee Ga. U. summer, 1965 Mem. Math. Assn. Am., Nat., N.C. councils tchrs. math., AAUP, Pi Mu Epsilon. Home: 336 Beaver Creek Estate Dr West Jefferson NC 28694-0977 Office: ASU Math and Science Edn Ctr Boone NC 28608-2091 Office Phone: 828-262-3185. Business E-Mail: johnsnpe@appstate.edu.

JOHNSON, R. MILTON, corporate financial executive; b. Dec. 15, 1956; m. Denice Johnson; children: Lindsay, Tyler. BBA, Belmont U. CPA 1981. Acct. Ernst & Young LLP; tax mgr., rsch. & planning area HCA, Inc., 1982—87; dir., tax HealthTrust (merged with HCA, Inc.), 1987—95; v.p., tax HCA, Inc., 1995—98, sr. v.p., contr., 1998—2004, exec. v.p., 2004—11, CFO, 2004—, bd. dirs., 2009—, pres., 2011—. Bd. trustees, bd. regents Belmont U.; bd. dir. HCA Found., McNeilly Ctr. for Children; bd. dirs. Siloam Family Health Ctr., Sarah Cannon Rsch. Inst.; mem., conf. bd. Coun. of Fin. Execs. Office: HCA Inc 1 Park Plz Nashville TN 37203 Office Phone: 615-344-9551. Business E-Mail: r.johnson@hcahealthcare.com.

JOHNSON, ROBERT A., state legislator; BA in Polit. Sci., Loyola U., 1997; attended Internat. Legal Sys. Studies, U. Vienna Law Sch., Austria, 1999; JD, Loyola U. Sch. Law, 2000. Atty.; mem. Dist. 28 La. House of Reps., 2008—, mem. agr., forestry, aquaculture and rural devel. com., civil law and procedure com., health and welfare com. Democrat. Office: State Capitol PO Box 44486 Baton Rouge LA 70804 Mailing: PO Box 467 Marksville LA 71351 Office Phone: 225-342-6945, 318-253-8891. Office Fax: 318-253-6377. Business E-Mail: johnsoro@legis.state.la.us.

JOHNSON, ROBERT D., board member; m. DeDe Johnson; 3 children. BA in Economics & Math., Miami U., Oxford, Ohio. Pres., mng. dir. GE Aircraft Engines, 1983—93; v.p., gen. mgr., mfg. and svcs. AAR Corp., 1993—94; v.p., gen. mgr., global repair and overhaul operations AlliedSignal Aerospace, 1994—96, v.p., gen. mgr., aerospace svcs., 1996—97, pres., CEO, mktg., electronic and avionics systems, 1997—99, pres., CEO, mktg., sales, & svcs., 1997—99, pres., CEO, 1999—2001; Honeywell Aerospace, Phoenix, 1999—2004, chmn., 2005—06; CEO Dubai Aerospace Enterprise Ltd, 2006—08. Bd. trustee Ariz. State U. Pres. Club; bd. dirs. Aviation Safety Alliance, Entrada Software; bd. trustee Embry-Riddle Aeronautical U., 2002—; bd. dirs. Phelps Dodge Corp., 2003—07, Roper Industries Inc., 2005—, Spirit AeroSystems, 2005—, Ariba, Inc., 2005—. Bd. dirs. Scottsdale Home Nat. Bank, The Zanesville, Ohio. Mem.: Aerospace Inductries Assn. (exec. com.), Devel. and Flight Safety Edu. Com., U. Ariz. (adv. bd.), Miami U. of Ohio (adv. bd.), Conquistadores Del Cielo. Office: Roper Industries Inc Bd Directors 6901 Professional Pky E Ste 200 Sarasota FL 34240 Office Phone: 602-365-3099, 973-445-2000, 941-556-2601. Office Fax: 973-455-4807, 941-556-2670. Business E-Mail: rjohnson@roperind.com.

JOHNSON, ROBERT JEROME, JR., (BOB JOHNSON), lawyer; b. Dayton, Ohio, 1972; m. Julie Johnson; children: Logan, Riley, Olivia. BS in Psychology summa cum laude, Miami U., Ohio, 1994; JD with honors, Ohio State U. Michael E. Moritz Coll. Law, 1997. Assoc. Squire, Sanders & Dempsey LLP, Cleve., 1997—2004; atty. BB&T Corp., Winston-Salem, NC, 2005—08, dep. gen. counsel, mgr. corporate, securities & tax practice, 2008—10, gen. counsel, corporate sec., chief corporate governance officer, 2010—. Avocation: golf. Office: BB&T Corp 200 W 2d St Winston Salem NC 27101*

JOHNSON, ROBERT L., III, state legislator; b. Natchez, Miss., Nov. 29, 1958; m. Evelyn Joiner; 1 child, Kai Alexandra Diane. Mem. Dist. 38 Miss. State Senate, 1993—2003; mem. Dist. 94 Miss. House of Reps., 2005—; mem. Adams County Devel. Bd.; atty. Mem.: Adams County Voters League (pres.), Miss. Trial Lawyers Assn., Miss. Bar Assn. Democrat. African Methodist Episcopal. Mailing: PO Box 1678 Natchez MS 39121 Home Phone: 601-445-5690; Office Phone: 601-359-9485. Business E-Mail: rjohnson@house.ms.gov.

JOHNSON, ROBERT LOUIS, professional sports team owner, former broadcast executive; b. Hickory, Miss., Apr. 8, 1946; s. Archie and Edna Johnson; m. Sheila Crump, Jan. 19, 1969 (div. 2002); 2 children. BA in Hist., U. Ill., 1968; MA in Pub. Affairs, Princeton U., 1972. Press sec. Hon. Walter E. Fauntroy, Congl. del., Washington, 1973—76; v.p., govt. rels. Nat. Cable TV Assn., 1976—79; founder Black Entertainment TV, Washington, 1979, pres., 1979—93; founder, pres. Dist. Cablevision, Inc., 1980; chmn., pres., CEO BET Holdings, Inc. (formerly Black Entertainment TV sold to Viacom), Washington, 1993—2001; CEO BET Holdings, Inc., 2001—05, chmn., 2005; founder, chmn. RLJ Companies, LLC, 2001—; majority owner Bobcats Basketball Holdings, LLC, 2003—; owner Women's NBA Charlotte Sting, 2003—. Former bd. dirs. US Airways, Inc.; bd. dirs. Gen. Mills, Inc., 1999—2004, Hilton Hotels Corp., 1994—2006; bd. govs. Rock and Roll Hall of Fame; bd. dirs. Strayer Edn., Inc., 2003—, Lowe's Companies, Inc., 2005—, KB Home, 2008—. Bd. dirs. United Negro Coll. Fund, Am. Film Inst.; bd. govs. The Grammy Found.; bd. dirs. Jazz at Lincoln Ctr., Strayer Edn., Inc., Johns Hopkins U. Recipient Image award, NAACP, 1982, Bus. of Yr. award, DC C. of C., 1985, Exec. Leadership Coun. award, Turner Broadcasting, 1993, 20/20 Vision award, Cablevision Mag., 1995, Hall of Fame award, Broadcasting and Cable Mag., 1997, Good Guys award, Nat. Women's Polit. Caucus, 1998, Disting. Alumni award, Princeton U., 1998; named one of Most Influential Black Ams., Ebony mag., 2006, 400 Richest Ams., Forbes mag., 2006, Most Influential People in the World of Sports, Bus. Week, 2008; named to Advt. Hall of Fame, 2006, Power 150, Ebony mag., 2008. Democrat. Office: Lowe's Companies Inc Bd Directors 1000 Lowe's Blvd Mooresville NC 28117 Office Phone: 704-758-1000. Office Fax: 336-658-4766. Business E-Mail: rjohnson@bobcats.com.

JOHNSON, ROGER WARREN, chemical engineer; b. Huntsville, Ala., Oct. 25, 1960; s. Frederic Allen and Joan (Bickum) J.; m. Margaret Jane Major, June 16, 1984. BChemE, Auburn U., 1984. Process engr. fibers divsn. E.I. DuPont de Nemours & Co., Waynesboro, Va., 1984-86, devel. engr. imaging systems Brevard, N.C., 1986-87; R & D engr. Hercules Inc.-A&TP, Oxford, Ga., 1987-92; account mgr. Hercules Inc.-Absorbents and Textile Products, Oxford, Ga., 1992-95; product mgr. Hercules Inc.-A&TP, Oxford, Ga., 1995-96; staple II plant mgr. FiberVisions LLC, Oxford, Ga., 1997-98; fiber and film tech. svc. mgr. Ineos Olefins and Polymers, LaPorte, Tex., 1998—. Mem. Auburn Alumni Assn., Phi Kappa Phi. Home: 1410 Mclendon Ave NE Atlanta GA 30307-2129 Office: Ineos Olefins and Polymers 1410 McLendon Ave NE Atlanta GA 30307 E-mail: roger.johnson@innovene.com.

JOHNSON, RONALD G. (RON JOHNSON), state legislator; b. Bonifay, Fla., Sept. 21, 1943; m. Susan Johnson; 1 child, Stephanie Lee. BS, Fla. State U., Tallahassee; BSc in Pharm., Auburn U., Ala. Mem. Dist. 33 Ala. House of Reps., Montgomery, 1978—; ptnr. Med. Care Equipment, Inc. Mem. Sylacauga C. of C. Mem.: Nat. Fedn. Ind. Bus., Sylacauga Retail Merchants Assn., Ala. Pharm. Assn., South Talladega Pharm. Assn., Md. Pharm. Assn., Am. Pharm. Assn., Auburn Kiwanis Club, Talladega Kiwanis Club. Republican. Baptist. Office: 3770 Sylacauga-Fayette Hwy Sylacauga AL 35151 also: Ala House of Reps Ala State House 11 S Union St Rm 627-D Montgomery AL 36130 Office Phone: 256-249-3558, 334-242-7777.

JOHNSON, SAMUEL ROBERT, United States Representative from Texas; b. San Antonio, Oct. 11, 1930; m. Shirley L. Melton; children: James R., Gini Mulligan, Beverly Briney. BBA, So. Meth. U., Dallas, 1951; MA in Internat. Affairs, George Washington U.; grad., Armed Forces Staff Coll., Nat. War Coll. Career mil. officer USAF, 1950—79, fighter pilot, prisoner of war, 1966-73, dir. Air Force Fighter Weapons Sch., mem. Thunderbirds, wing commdr., air divsn. commdr.; mem. Tex. House of Reps., 1984-91, US Congress from 3rd Tex. dist., 1991—. Decorated 2 Silver Stars, 4 Air medals, 2 Purple Hearts, 2 Legions of Merit, Bronze Star with Valor. Republican. Office: US House of Representatives 1211 Longworth House Office Bldg Washington DC 20515 also: 2929 N Central Expy Ste 240 Richardson TX 75080-2000 Office Phone: 202-225-4201.*

JOHNSON, SHEILA CRUMP, entrepreneur; b. Pa. m. Robert L. Johnson (div. 2002); children: Paige, Brett; m. William T. Newman, 2005. Music tchr. Sidwell Friends Sch., Washington, 1973—89; former cultural liaison to Middle East U.S. Info. Agency; co-founder Black Entertainment TV; owner Salamander Farms, Middleberg, Va.; developer Salamander Inn and Spa, Middleberg, Va.; co-owner Lincoln Holdings, LLC; owner, team pres. WNBA Wash. Mystics; designer of luxury linens; CEO Salamander Hospitality, LLC. Bd. dirs. Parsons Sch. Design; pres. Washington Internat. Horse Show; established first Nat. Music Conservatory, Amman, Jordan. Named one of The 100 Most Powerful Women in DC, Washingtonian mag., 2009; named to Power 150, Ebony mag., 2008. Achievements include first Black female to be certified as billionaire. Avocations: horseback riding, music, violin. Office: Salamder Hospitality LLC 100 West Washington St Middleburg VA 20118

JOHNSON, STEPHEN L., air transportation executive; BA, Calif. State Univ., Sacramento; MBA, JD, Univ. Calif., Berkeley. Assoc. Bogle & Gates, Seattle; legal & mgmt. positions through sr. v.p. & gen. counsel GPA Group plc, 1989—94; legal mgmt. positions through sr. v.p. legal & exec. v.p. corp. America West Holdings Corp., 1995—2003; co-founder, ptnr. Indigo Partners LLC, Phoenix, 2003—09; exec. v.p. corporate & govt. affairs, gen. counsel US Airways Group, Inc., Tempe, Ariz., 2009—13; exec. v.p. corporate affairs American Airlines Group Inc., Forth Worth, Tex., 2013—. Office: American Airlines Group Inc 4333 Amon Carter Blvd Fort Worth TX 76155*

JOHNSON, TERRY, state legislator; b. Jan. 9, 1950; m. Nancy Johnson; children: Patrick, Brett. Grad., Realtors Inst. Multi-state broker Terry Johnson Realty; former state rep. State 35 Ga.; former mem. Def & Vets. Affairs, Industry Com., Natural Resources & Environ. Com.; state rep. Dist. 37 Ga., 2005—. Democrat. Office: 570 Shay Dr Marietta GA 30060 Office Phone: 404-656-0341. Business E-Mail: terryjonson@cobb.net.

JOHNSON, THOMAS H., investment company executive; BS In Indsl. Engring., Ga. Inst. of Tech.; MBA, Harvard U. Chmn., CEO Canal Corp.; various mgmt. and exec. positions Mead Corp., 1976—89; pres., CEO Riverwood Internat., 1989—2007, Chesapeake Corp., 1997—2005, chmn. Richmond, Va., 2000—04, 2000—05; mng. ptnr. THJ Investments, LP, 2005—. Vice chmn. Chesapeake Corp., 2005—06; bd. dirs. Superior Essex, 2005—08, Coca-Cola Enterprises Inc., Universal Corp., 2001—, Mirant Corp., 2006—, ModusLink Global Solutions, Inc., 2006—. Mem. Acad. of Distinguished Engring. Graduates Ga. Inst. of Tech. Commissioned officer US Navy, 1971-74. Recipient Sybron Fellowship, Harvard U., Marco Polo award, People's Rep. of China, 1999. Office: The Taffrail Group LLC Ste 1670 300 Galleria Pky Atlanta GA 30339 Office Phone: 678-281-0949. Business E-Mail: thjoh@taffrailgroup.com.

JOHNSON, TIM, pastor, retired professional football player; b. Sarasota, Fla., Jan. 29, 1965; m. Le'Chelle Johnson; 4 children. BA in Mktg. & Speech Comm., Pa. State U., 1987. Defensive tackle Pittsburgh Steelers, 1987—89, Washington Redskins, 1990—95, Cin. Bengals, 1996; ret. NFL, 1997; sr. assoc. pastor Bethel World Outreach Ctr., Nashville, 2000—05, sr. pastor, 2005—06; founder, sr. pastor Orlando World Outreach Ctr., Fla., 2006—. Tchr. Every Nation Leadership Inst. Co-founder Good Samaritan Found., 1992. Achievements include member of NCAA Football National Championship winning Pennsylvania State University Nittany Lions, 1986; member of NFL Super Bowl XXVI championship winning Washington Redskins. Office: Orlando World Outreach Center 800 N Highland Ave Orlando FL 32803*

JOHNSON, TRENT, men's college basketball coach; b. Berkeley, Calif., Sept. 12, 1956; m. Jackie Johnson; children: Tinishia, Terry. BS in Phys. Edn., Boise State U., Idaho, 1983. Basketball player Wash. Lumberjacks, We. Basketball Assn., Kennewick, 1978—79; head coach Boise HS, 1980—85; asst. coach U. Utah Utes, 1986—89, U. Wash. Huskies, 1989—92, Rice U. Owls, 1992—96, Stanford U. Cardinal, 1996—99, head coach, 2004—08, U. Nev. Wolf Pack, 1999—2004, La. State U. Fighting Tigers, 2008—12, Tex. Christian U. Horned Frogs, 2012—. Named Western Athletic Conf. Coach of Yr., 2003, Pacific-10 Conf. Coach of Yr., 2008, Southeastern Conf. Coach of Yr., 2009, Dist. VII Coach of Yr., US Basketball Writers Assn., 2012. Office: Tex Christian University Basketball Program 3500 Bellaire Dr N PO Box 297600 Fort Worth TX 76129 Office Phone: 225-578-8217.

JOHNSON, VICTOR S., III, (TORRY JOHNSON), prosecutor; married; 3 children. AB, Hamilton Coll.; JD, Vanderbilt Univ. Bar: Tenn. 1974. Law clk. US Ct. Appeals; asst. dist. atty. Office of Dist. Atty. Gen. 20th Judicial Dist., Nashville, 1975; atty., pvt. practice, 1983; dist. atty. gen. 20th Judicial Dist., Nashville, 1987—. Founding pres. Nashville Child Advocacy Ctr. Mem.: Nat. Dist. Atty. Assn. (v.p.), Tenn. Bar Assn. (bd. dir.), Nashville Bar Assn. (bd. dir.). Office: Dist Atty Gen Washington Sq Ste 500 222 2d Ave N Nashville TN 37201 Office Phone: 615-862-5500. Office Fax: 615-862-5599.

JOHNSON, WAYNE, state legislator; children: Trent, Jeremy. Dep. sheriff, criminal investigator Madison County, Ala.; bailiff Madison County Ct.; sub. tchr.; mem. Dist. 22 Ala. House of Representatives, 2011—. Mem. Chase Bapt. Ch. Served with US Army. Named Madison County Dep. of Yr., 1997. Republican. Office: Ala House of Reps Rm 527-C 11 S Union St Montgomery AL 36130 Office Phone: 334-242-7492.

JOHNSON, WAYNE D., gas industry executive; b. Winterset, Iowa, Sept. 20, 1932; s. Leslie E. and Ruth N. J.; m. Lynne Alice Brouwer, June 15, 1963; children: Christopher W., Kevin B. BA, U. Nebr., 1954; LLB, Harvard U., 1959. Bar: Ill. bar 1959. Assoc., then ptnr. Ross, Hardies, O'Keefe, Babcock & Parsons, Chgo., 1959-72; asst. gen. counsel Peoples Gas Co., Chgo., 1972-75; sr. v.p., gen. counsel Entex, Inc., Houston, 1975-78, pres., 1978-86, utility cons., 1986-87; pres. UnitedTex. Transmission Co., 1987-93, Am. Natural Gas Power, Inc., Houston, 1993-97; utility cons., 1997—. Dir. Simmons & Co., Internat., 1980—2011. Past chmn. Galveston Bay Found.; exec. comm. Sam Houston Area Coun., Boy Scouts Am.; mem. data integration team and demand task force Nat. Petroleum Coun., Com. on Natural Gas, 1998-2000. With U.S. Army, 1954-56. Woodrow Wilson fellow, 1954 Mem. Am. Gas Assn., So. Gas Assn. (past chmn.), Lawyer's Club (Chgo.). Home: 5517 Cedar Creek Houston TX 77056

JOHNSON, WILLIAM DEAN (BILL JOHNSON), federal agency administrator, former energy executive; b. Pa., Jan. 9, 1954; BA in History, Duke U., 1978; JD, U. N.C., 1982. Law clk. to Hon. J.D. Philips Jr. US Ct. Appeals (4th Cir.), 1982-83; assoc. Hunton & Williams LLP, 1983-90, ptnr., 1990-92; assoc. gen. counsel Carolina Power & Light, Raleigh, NC, 1992-95, v.p., corporate sec., 1995-1999, sr. v.p., corporate sec., 1999-2001; pres., CEO Progress Energy Svc. Co., Raleigh, NC, 2002—03; exec. v.p., gen. counsel, sec. Progress Energy, Inc., Raleigh, NC, 2001—02, group pres. energy delivery, 2004—05, pres., COO, 2005—07, chmn., pres., CEO, 2007—12; pres., CEO Duke Energy Corp., Charlotte, NC, 2012, Tenn. Valley Authority, Knoxville, 2012—. Mem. ABA, N.C. Bar Assn. Office: Tennessee Valley Authority 400 W Summit Hill Dr Knoxville TN 37902 Office Phone: 865-632-2101.*

JOHNSON, YVONNE J., former Mayor, Greensboro, NC; b. Oct. 26, 1942; d. Vernon and Ruby Jeffries; m. Walter T. Johnson; 4 children. BA in Psychology, Bennett Coll., Greensboro, 1964; MS in Guidance & Counseling, NC A&T Univ., 1978. Exec. dir. One Step Further, Greensboro, 1983—; councilwoman City of Greensboro, 1993—99, 2005—07, mayor pro tem., 1999—2005, mayor, 2007—09. Coun. liaison Greensboro Housing Devel., S Elm-Lee St Devel. Project, Hope VI-Willow Oaks; exec. bd. mem. Malachi House; pres. emeritus Bd. Women's Resource Ctr.; bd. trustees Bennett Coll.; bd. mem. Justice Fellowship Task Force, 1993. Recipient Nat. Alumnae Achievement award, Bennett Coll., 2003; named African Am. Woman of Distinction, African Am. Atelier, 1993. Office Phone: 336-373-2396. Office Fax: 336-574-4003. Business E-Mail: yvonne.johnson@greensboro-nc.gov.

JOHNSON, ZACH (ZACHARY HARRIS JOHNSON), professional golfer; b. Iowa City, Iowa, Feb. 24, 1976; s. Dave Johnson; m. Kimala Barclay, Feb. 8, 2003. Grad. in Bus. Mgmt. and Mktg., Drake U., Des Moines, 1998. Profl. golfer, 1998—; mem. Prairie Golf Tour, 1998, PGA Tour, 2004—. Mem. US team Ryder Cup, 2006, 2010, 2012, Presidents Cup, 2007, 2009. Named Hooters Tour Player of Yr., 2001, Nationwide Tour Player of Yr., 2003. Achievements include winning Nationwide Tour events: the Rheem Classic, 2003, Envirocare Utah Classic, 2003; winning PGA Tour events: the BellSouth Classic, 2004, AT&T Classic, 2007, Texas Open, 2008, 2009, Sony Open, 2009, Crowne Plaza Invitational at Colonial, 2010, 2012, John Deere Classic, 2012; winning The Masters Tournament, 2007. Mailing: PGA Tour 112 PGA TOUR Blvd Ponte Vedra Beach FL 32082

JOHNSON EFFINGER, NAOMI BOWERS, nursing and health facility administrator; b. Ft. Benning, Ga., Aug. 17, 1954; d. Bob and Henrietta Violet (Hoomalu) Bowers; m. James William Johnson, Dec. 7, 1973 (div.); children: Amelia, Melissa, Charity, James-William; m. Bobby L. Effinger, Mar. 19, 2005; stepchildren: Wilson, Margaret, Gloria. ADN, Troy State U., Montgomery, Ala., 1974. Office supr., lab. supr., nursing coord. physician's office, Selma, Ala.; patients care coord. West. Ala. Home Health Agy., Selma; discharge planning/social svcs., SOBRA and clin. case mgmt. coord. Vaughan Regional Med. Ctr. Hosp., Selma; DON Dunn Nursing Home, Selma, Capitol Hill Health Care Ctr.; dir. mktg. and admissions Mariner Post Acute Health Care Network, Montgomery, Ala.; DON Ball Healthcare-Lighthouse, Selma. Author (poet): Publish America/International Poet Society, 2002—03. Personal E-mail: hoomalu@bellsouth.net, nululani@yahoo.com.

JOHNSTON, GREGORY L., retail executive; Hourly assoc., asst. mgr., gen. mgr. Wal-Mart Stores, Inc., Bentonville, Ark., 1982—93, dir. ops., Sam's Club, 1993—97, regional v.p., 1997—2005, exec. v.p. ops., Sam's Club, 2005—. Recipient World Class Leadership award, Wal-Mart Stores, Inc., 2005. Office Phone: 479-277-7000.

JOHNSTON, JAMES WESLEY, retired consumer products company executive; b. Chgo., Apr. 11, 1946; s. Ted and Irma (Hacker) J.; m. Angela Johnston; children: Amanda E., Emily S. BS in Accountancy, U. Ill., 1967; MBA, Northwestern U., 1971. C.P.A., Ill. Fin. analyst Ford Motor Co., 1967-69; with N.W. Industries, 1969-79, dir. corp. devel., 1973-75, v.p. mktg., 1975-79; exec. v.p. Asia/Pacific R.J. Reynolds Tobacco Internat. Inc., 1979, pres., chief exec. officer Asia/Pacific Hong Kong, 1979-81; exec. v.p. R.J. Reynolds Tobacco Co., 1981-84; divsn. exec. consumer banking N.E. U.S. Citicorp, NYC, 1984-89; chmn. CEO R.J. Reynolds Tobacco Co., Winston-Salem, NC, 1989-95; chmn. R.J. Reynolds Tobacco Worldwide, Winston-Salem, NC, 1993-96; vice chmn. RJR Nabisco, Inc., 1995-96, ret., 1996. Bd. dirs. Sealy Corp., Trinity, NC, Lance, Inc., Charlotte, NC, 2008. Treas., trustee, pres. Village of Bolingbrook, Ill., 1973-75; bd. dirs. Winston-Salem Bus. Inc., 1989—96; active N.C. Bus. Coun. Mgmt. and Devel., Raleigh, 1989—96; trustee Wake Forest U., Winston-Salem, 1991—; mem. bd. visitors Wake Forest U. Bapt. Med. Ctr., Winston-Salem, 1991—. Mem.: Old Town Club. Office: 111 S Longfellow Ln Mooresville NC 28117

JOHNSTON, JOSH, state legislator; b. Little Rock, Ark., Nov. 13, 1974; Mem., deacon Clearview Baptist Ch. Heber Springs; owner Quality Rock, Inc., 2003—; mem. Dist. 59 Ark. House of Representatives, 2011—. Republican. Baptist. Office: 970 Lone Star Rd Rose Bud AR 72137 Office Phone: 501-556-1951. Personal E-mail: josh.johnston@arkansashouse.org.

JOHNSTON, KEITH P., professor of chemical engineering; BS, U. of Michigan, 1977; MS, U. of Illinois, Urbana, 1979, PhD, 1981. Prof. dept. of chem. engring. Univ. of Texas, Austin, 1982—, holds m. c. (bud) and mary beth baird endowed chair, dept. of chem. engring. Co-author: (rsch. publs.) Ordering in Asymmetric Block Copolymer Films by a Compressible Fluid, 2007, Contact Angle of Water on Polystyrene Thin Films: Effects of CO2 Environment and Film Thickness, 2007, Supercritical CO2-based solvents in next generation microelectronics processing, 2007, Flocculated Amorphous Nanoparticles for Highly Supersaturated Solutions, 2008, and numerous others. Recipient Univ. of Texas Engring. Found. Faculty Excellence award, 1990, 1995, Allan P. Colburn award, Am. Inst. of Chem. Engrs., 1990, Indsl. Gas award, 2004, Inst. award for Excellence in Indsl. Gases Tech., 2004; named one of 100 Chem. Engrs. of the Modern Era, Centennial, 2008; finalist Discover Mag. awards for Technol. Innovation, 2001; scholar, Camille and Henry Dreyfus Found., 1987. Mem.: NAE. Office: University of Texas Department of Chemical Engineering 1 University Sta C0400 Austin TX 78712-0231 Office Phone: 512-471-4617. Office Fax: 512-471-7060. E-mail: kpj@che.utexas.edu.

JOHNSTON, KENNETH C., lawyer; b. Gulfport, Miss., June 9, 1966; BA in Banking and Fin., U. Miss., 1988, JD, 1991. Bar: Miss. 1991, Tex. 1995, US Dist. Ct. (no., so., ea. and we. dists.) Tex., US Dist. Ct. (no. and so. dists.) Miss., US Ct. Appeals (5th cir.). Intern US Dept. Justice, Washington; atty. Byrd & Wiser, Biloxi, Miss.; shareholder, dir Kane Russell Coleman & Logan PC, Dallas, 1994—. Contbr. articles to profl. jours. Bd. advisors U. NC Sch. Law Ctr. Banking & Fin.; bd. dirs. SMU Athletic Forum, Dallas, Dallas Providence Homes, Inc. Named an Outstanding Young Lawyer, Law & Politics/Tex. Rising Stars mag., 2004, 2006; named one of Best Lawyers Under 40, D Mag., 2006, The Top 15 Bus. Def. Attorneys in North Tex., Dallas Bus. Jour., 2008, America's Leading Lawyers for Bus., Chambers USA, 2009, 2010. Mem.: American Law Inst., Dallas Assn. Young Lawyers, Tex. Young Lawyers Assn., Tex. Assn. Bank Counsel, American Bankruptcy Inst., Dallas Bar Assn., Pro Bono Coll. of State Bar Tex. Office: Kane Russell Coleman & Logan PC 1601 Elm St Ste 3700 Dallas TX 75201 Office Phone: 214-777-4222. Office Fax: 214-777-4299. E-mail: kjohnston@krcl.com.

JOHNSTON, LARRY L., JR., motor and generator manufacturing company executive; BS in Acctg., U. Ark., Little Rock, 1991. CPA Okla., Ark. Mgr., audit KPMG, 1996—2000; acct. Ernst & Young LLP, sr. mgr., audit, 2000—07; integration specialist Baldor Electric Co., 2007—08, v.p., audit svcs., 2008—. Vet. USMC. Office: Baldor Electric Co 5711 R S Boreham Jr St Fort Smith AR 72901 Office Phone: 479-646-4711. Office Fax: 479-648-5792. Business E-Mail: ljohnston@baldor.com.

JOHNSTON, THOMAS E., judge; b. Charleston, W.Va., 1967; BA, W.Va. U., 1989; JD, W.Va. U. Coll. Law, 1992. Atty. Schrader, Byrd & Companion, Wheeling, W.Va., 1994—96; assoc. Flaherty, Sensabaugh and Bonasso, Charleston, 1996—98; ptnr. Bailey, Riley, Buch & Harmon, Wheeling, 1998—2001; US atty. (no. dist.) W.Va. US Dept. Justice, Wheeling, 2001—06; judge US Dist. Ct. (so. dist.) W.Va., 2006—. Office: 6610 Robert C Byrd US Courthouse 300 Virginia St E Charleston WV 25301-0011 Office Phone: 304-347-3217.

JOHNSTONE, DOUGLAS INGE, retired state supreme court justice, lawyer; b. Mobile, Ala., Nov. 15, 1941; s. Harry Inge and Kathleen (Yerger) J.; m. Mary Frances Jayne (div.); 1 child, Francis Inge. BA, Rice U., 1963; JD, Tulane U., 1966. Bar: Ala. 1966, U.S. Dist. Ct. Ala. 1966, U.S. Ct. Appeals (5th cir.) 1968, U.S. Supreme Ct. 1969. Pvt. practice, Mobile, 1966—84, 2005—; dist. judge Ala. Dist. Ct., Mobile, 1984—85, presiding dist. judge, 1985, cir. judge, 1985—99; justice Supreme Ct. Ala., Montgomery, 1999—2005; ret., 2005. Mem. House of Reps. State of Ala., 1974-78. Mem. bd. advisors Salvation Army, Mobile, 1989—; bd. dirs. Mental Health Assn., Mobile, 1990-92; chmn. Appellate Sect. Mobile Bar Assn., Ala. Pattern Jury Instrn. Com., 2008-. Capt. U.S. Army, 1963-72. Elected Outstanding Freshman Rep., Capital Press Corps., 1975; recipient Meritorious Svc. award Mobile County Bd. of Health, 1968, Humanitarian Svc. award Mobile Cerebral Palsy Assn., 1973. Mem. Am. Judges Assn., Ala. Bar Assn., Mobile Bar Assn., Internat. Acad. Trial Judges, Exptl. Aircraft Assn. Democrat. Episcopalian. Avocations: hunting, boating, flying. Office Phone: 251-973-1947.

JOINES, ALLEN, mayor, Winston-Salem, North Carolina; BS, Appalachian State University; MPA U. Ga. Asst. to city mgr. City of Winston-Salem, NC, dir. evaluation NC, pub. safety coord. NC, dir. devel. NC, dep. city mgr. NC, 1971—2000, mayor NC, 2001—; pres. Winston-Salem Alliance, NC, 2000—01. Chmn. Triad March of Dimes, vice chmn.; bd. dirs. Salvation Army Boys' Club; program chmn. Leadership Winston-Salem; past chmn. Winston-Salem Arts Coun.; chmn. United Way Campaign, 2004; former mem. bd. deacons Wake Forest Baptist Church, mem.; pres. N.C. Devel. Assn.; bd. dirs. Children's Mus., chmn. cmty. adv. bd., 2006; bd. dirs. Housing Authority of Winston-Salem; v.p. and past pres. Sertoma West; past mem. Tourism Devel. Authority; past bd. dirs. NC League Municipalities; chmn. NC Metropolitan Coalition. Recipient Legacy award, Winston-Salem Found., 2002, Dare to Dream award, Martin Luther King, Jr. Commemoration, 2005, Lifetime Achievement award, Arthritis Found. NC, 2007, Marvin Collins Planning award for Disting. Leadership of an Elected Ofcl., NC Chpt., Am. Planning Assn., 2007; named Man of Yr., Winston-Salem Chronicle, 2003; named one of The Triad's Most Influential People, The Business Journal, 2006, 2007, 2008. Democrat. Achievements include creating new jobs; rebuilding the econonomy. Office: Suite 150 City Hall 101 N Main St Winston Salem NC 27101 Mailing: PO Box 2511 Winston Salem NC 27102-2511 Office Phone: 336-727-2058. Office Fax: 336-748-3241. Business E-Mail: allenj@cityofws.org.*

JOKLIK, WOLFGANG KARL, biochemist, virologist, educator; b. Vienna, Nov. 16, 1926; s. Karl F. and Helene (Giessl) J.; m. Judith Vivien Nicholas, Apr. 9, 1955 (dec. Apr. 1975); children: Richard G., Vivien H.; m. Patricia Hunter Downey, Apr. 23, 1977. B.Sc. with 1st class honors, U. Sydney, Australia, 1948, M.Sc., 1949; D.Phil. (Australian Nat. U. scholar), U. Oxford, Eng., 1952. Australian Nat. U. research fellow, Copenhagen, 1953, Canberra, Australia, 1954-56; fellow, 1957-62; assoc. prof. cell biology Albert Einstein Coll. Medicine, Bronx, NY, 1962-65, prof. cell biology, 1965-68, Siegfried Ullmann prof. biochem. virology, 1966-68; prof., chmn. dept. microbiology and immunology Duke U. Med. Ctr., Durham, NC, 1968-92, James B. Duke Disting. prof. microbiology and immunology, 1972-92, James B. Duke prof. microbiology, 1992-96, James B. Duke prof. emeritus, 1996—. Sr. author: Zinsser Microbiology, 15th, 16th, 17th, 18th, 19th, 20th edits.; editor-in-chief Virology, 1975-93, Microbiological Rev., 1991-95; contbr. articles to profl. jours. Recipient Sr. US award Alexander Humboldt Found., 1985, ICN Internat. prize for virology, 1991. Mem. NAS, Inst. Medicine of NAS, Am. Soc. Virology (pres. 1982-83), Am. Soc. Microbiology, Am. Soc. Biol. Chemists. Address: Duke U Med Ctr Dept Molecular Genetics and Microbiology PO Box 3020 Durham NC 27710-0001 Office Phone: 919-748-8793. Office Fax: 919-489-4433. Business E-Mail: joklikb@aol.com.

JOLAS, PAUL M., lawyer, energy executive; BA, Northwestern U.; JD, Duke U. Mem., Corp. Securities Group Haynes and Boone, LLP; exec. v.p., gen. counsel, corp. sec. Radiologix, Inc.; sr. regional counsel, Tex. Div. KB Home Corp.; v.p., dep. gen. counsel Trinity Industries, Inc., Dallas, 2006—09, corp. sec., 2007—09; exec. v.p., chief legal officer & sec. Regency Energy Partners LP, 2009—. Office: Regency Energy Partners LP 2001 Bryan St Ste 3700 Dallas TX 75201 Office Phone: 214-750-1771. Office Fax: 214-750-1749.

JOLIBOIS, MARCUS, professional sports team executive; m. Diane Jolibois; children: Andrew, Connor, Scott, Luke. Grad., Gonzaga U., Spokane, Wash., 1981. Acct. Peterson, Sullivan and Co., Seattle, 1981—84; operational and fin. auditor San Diego, 1984—86; audit mgr. Levitz, Zacks and Ciceric, San Diego, 1986—94; CFO, mem. sr. exec. com. Houston Rockets, 1994—. Office: Houston Rockets 1730 Jefferson St Houston TX 77003-5028

JOLLEY, CLARK, state legislator, lawyer; m. Verlyne Jolley; children: Alex, Lauren. BA, BME, Okla. Baptist Univ., 1992; JD, Univ. Okla., 1995. Atty. Jolley & Jolley, 1995—; mem. Dist. 41 Okla. State Senate, 2004—. Bd. dir. Fine Arts Inst., Edmond, Okla. Acad. for State Goals; mem. Okla. Sci. & Tech. Rsch. Bd. Republican. Office: 2300 N Lincoln Blvd Rm 425 Oklahoma City OK 73105 Home: 3016 Thornbrook Blvd Edmond OK 73013-6070 Office Phone: 405-521-5622. Business E-Mail: jolley@oksenate.gov.

JOLLEY, SAMUEL DELANOR, JR., academic administrator; b. Ft. Valley, Ga., Feb. 1, 1941; s. Samuel Delanor Sr. and Mary Louise (Breazele) J.; m. Jimmye Christine Hambry, Dec. 24, 1963; children: Terena, Samuel III. BS, Ft. Valley State Coll., 1962; MS, Atlanta U., 1965; EdD, Ind. U., 1974. Tchr. math. Ballard Hudson Sr. H.S., Macon, Ga., 1962-67; instr. math. Ft. Valley (Ga.) State Coll., 1967-70, asst. prof. math., 1970-75, assoc. prof. math., 1975-82, coord. student teaching, 1980-83, chmn. divsn. edn., 1983-85; prof. math. Fort Valley (Ga.) State Coll., 1982-93, dean Sch. Arts and Scis., 1985-93; exec. dir., CEO, Atlanta Univ. Ctr., Inc., 1998—2004; pres. Morris Brown Coll., Atlanta, 1993—97, 2004—. Mem. adv. bd. Salvation Army, Atlanta, 1995-97; bd. dirs. AUC Coun. Pres.'s, Atlanta, 1993—, Atlanta Paralympics Organizing Com., 1994-97, Univ. Ctr. Ga., Atlanta, 1993—97, Univ. Cmty. Devel. Corp., Atlanta, 1993—2004; nat. bd. dirs. Fund for Improvement of Post Secondary Edn. Mem. NAACP, Am. Assn. Higher Edn., Omega Psi Phi, Sigma Pi Phi. Democrat. Methodist. Avocations: chess, swimming, tennis. Office: Morris Brown Coll 643 Martin Luther King Jr Dr N Atlanta GA 30314-4140 Office Phone: 404-739-1010. E-mail: sjolleyjr@aol.com.

JOLLY, DAVID WILSON, United States Representative from Florida; b. Dunedin, Fla., Oct. 31, 1972; m. Carrie Jolly (div. Jan. 16, 2014). BA in History, Emory U., 1994; JD cum laude, George Mason U. Sch. Law, 2001. Assoc. Fried, Frank, Harris, Shriver, & Jacobson, 2001; adv., gen. counsel to Rep. Bill Young US House of Representatives, 1995—2013; lobbyist Van Scoyoc Associates Inc., Washington; founder, owner Three Bridges Advisors, 2008—14; v.p. Boston Finance Group, Clearwater, 2012—14; CEO Olympus Found. Mgmt., 2013—14; mem. US Congress from 13th Fla. Dist., Washington, 2014—, US House Transp. & Infrastructure Com., 2014—, US House Veterans' Affairs Com., 2014—. Founder Fla. Fed. Contractors Assn. Named one of The 40 Under 40, Gulf Coast Bus. Review, 2009. Republican. Office: US House of Representatives 2407 Rayburn House Office Bldg Washington DC 20515 also: 9210 113th St Seminole FL 33772 Office Phone: 202-225-5961, 727-392-4100. Office Fax: 202-225-9764.*

JOLLY, E. GRADY, federal judge; b. Oct. 3, 1937; BA, U. Miss., 1959, LLB, 1962. Trial atty. NLRB, Winston-Salem, NC, 1962—64; asst. U.S. atty. No. Dist. Miss., 1964—67; trial atty. Dept. Justice Tax Div., Washington, 1967—69; pvt. practice Jolly, Miller & Milam, Jackson, Miss., 1969—82; judge US Ct. Appeals (5th cir.), Jackson, 1982—. Office: James O Eastland US Courthouse 245 E Capitol St Rm 202 Jackson MS 39201

JOLLY, RUSSELL, state legislator; b. Aug. 15, 1955; m. Rhonda Brand; children: Greg, Brandon. Cattleman, Miss.; mem. Dist. 8 Miss. State Senate, Jackson, 2012—. Mem.: Gideons, Masons, Shriners. Democrat. Baptist. Office: Miss State Senate PO Bix 1018 Jackson MS 39215 Business E-Mail: rjolly@senate.ms.gov.

JONES, ANITA KATHERINE, retired computer scientist; b. Ft. Worth, Mar. 10, 1942; d. Park Joel and Helene Louise (Voigt) Jones; m. William A. Wulf, July 1, 1977; children: Karin, Ellen. AB in Math., Rice U., Houston, 1964; MA in English, U. Tex., 1966; PhD in Computer Sci., Carnegie Mellon U., Pitts., 1973, PhD (hon.) in Sci. and Tech., 2000; PhD (hon.), U. Southern Calif., 2009; DSc (hon.), Carnegie Mellon U., Pitts., Duke U. Programmer IBM, Boston, Washington, 1966-69; assoc. prof. computer sci. Carnegie-Mellon U., Pitts., 1973-81; founder, v.p. Tartan Labs. Inc., Pitts., 1981-87; freelance cons. Pitts., 1987-88; prof., head computer sci. dept. U. Va., Charlottesville, 1988-93, prof. computer sci. dept., 1997—, univ. prof. computer sci. dept., 1998—2010, univ. prof. emerita computer sci. dept., 2010—, Lawrence A. Quarles prof. engring. & applied sci., 1999; dir. def. rsch. & engring. US Dept. Def., Washington, 1993-97. Mem. Def. Sci. Bd., US Dept. Def., 1985-93, 98—; mem. sci. adv. bd. USAF, 1979-84; mem. adv. coun. for Policy and Global Affairs Divsn., Nat. Rsch. Coun. 1997-2006; governing bd. NSF, vice-chair governing bd., 1998-2004; bd. dirs. Sci. Applications Internat. Corp., 1998-, BBN Techs., 2006-09, ATS Corp., 2010-; trustee Mitre Corp., 1989-93, InQTel; chair Va. Rsch. and Tech. Adv. Commn., 1999-2002; mem. corp. Charles Stark Draper Labs., 1999-; mem. Nat. Sci. Bd. 1999-2004, vice chair; ind. dir. SAIC, Inc. McLean, Va. Editor: Perspectives on Computer Science, 1977, Foundations of Secure Computation, 1971. Recipient Air Force Meritorious Civilian Svc. award, 1985, Medal for Disting. Pub. Svc. US Dept. Def., 1996, Disting. Svc. award Computing Rsch. Assn., 1997, Augusta Ada Lovelace award, Assn. Women in Computing, 2004. Fellow IEEE (Founders medal 2007), AAAS, Assn. Computing Machinery (editor-in-chief Transactions on Computer Sys. 1983-91), Am. Acad. Arts and Scis., Am. Philos. Soc.; mem. NAE(Arthur M. Bueche award, 2010), MIT Corp. (Corp. Exec. Com. 2007-10), Sci. Found. Ireland (bd. dirs. 2000-03), Sci. Found. Ariz. (bd. dirs. 2006—), Am. Philos. Soc., Sigma Xi. Avocation: gardening. Office Phone: 434-982-2224. Business E-Mail: jones@virginia.edu.

JONES, BERT, state legislator; b. Reidsville, NC, May 26, 1962; m. Susan Jones; children: David Jones, Caroline Jones. BA, U. NC, Chapel Hill, 1983; DDS, U. NC, 1988. Mem. Eden C. of C., Reidesville C. of C., Am. Dental Assn., Rockingham County Com. of 100, Boy Scouts of America; legis. contact NC Dental Soc.; bd. dirs. Rockingham Coun. of Bible Edn.; pres. Rockingham County Dental Soc., 1991—93; chmn. First Congl. Christian Ch. of Reidsville Bd. of Deacons, 1994—96; chmn., pres. Rockingham County Rep. Party, 1995—99; del. Rep. Nat. Convention, 1996; pres. Kiwanis, 1996—97; newsletter editor Rotary Club, 2000; candidate NC House of Representatives, 2000; fellow NC Inst. of Polit. Leadership, 2000; mem. Dist. 65 NC House of Representatives, 2011—. Office: 299 Fairfield Rd Reidsville NC 27320 Address: North Carolina House of Representatives 300 N Salisbury St 306A1 Raleigh NC 27603-5925 Office Phone: 336-342-6171, 919-733-5779. Business E-Mail: Bert.Jones@ncleg.net.

JONES, BOISFEUILLET, JR., (BO JONES), broadcast executive; b. Atlanta, Nov. 14, 1946; s. Boisfeuillet and Laura (Coit) Jones; m. Barbara Frost Pendleton, Sept. 13, 1969; children: Lindsay Farmer, Theodore Boisfeuillet. AB, Harvard U., 1968; DPhil in Modern History, Exeter Coll., Oxford U.; JD, Harvard Law Sch., 1974. Law clk. Judge Levin H. Campbell, US Ct. Appeals (1st cir.), Boston, 1974-75; atty. Hill & Barlow, Boston, 1975-80; v.p., gen. counsel The Washington Post, 1980—95, pres., gen. mgr., 1995-2000, assoc. pub., 2000, pub., CEO, 2000—08, chmn., 2008—11; vice chmn. The Washington Post Co., 2008—11; pres., CEO MacNeil/Lehrer Productions, 2012—. Bd. dirs. Bowater Mersey Paper Co., AP, Robinson Terminal Warehouse Corp., Alexandria, Va. Bd. dirs. Eugene & Agnes E. Meyer Found., Washington, Cmty. Found. Nat. Capitol Area, Cooperative Assistance Fund, Fed. City Coun., Washington, Econ. Club Washington; chmn. Newspaper Assn. America, 2006—07. Rhodes scholar, Oxford U., 1968. Episcopalian. Office: MacNeil/Lehrer Productions 2700 Quincy St Ste 250 Arlington VA 22206

JONES, BRADLEY E., healthcare service company executive; BS in Pub. Adminstrn., Va. Tech, 1988; M in Health Fin. & Mgmt. and Health Policy & Mgmt., The Johns Hopkins U., 1992. Exec. positions, Ala., Fla., DC, Md., Tex. Triad Hospital, Inc., Universal Health Services, Inc., Cmty. Health Sys., Inc., The Johns Hopkins Hosp., Ala.; CEO Crestwood Med. Ctr., 2001—07; sr. v.p., pres., Divsn III Health Management Associates, Inc., 2007—. Office: Health Management Associates Inc Ste 500 5811 Pelican Bay Blvd Naples FL 34108 Office Phone: 239-598-3131. Business E-Mail: bradley.jones@hma.org.

JONES, BUTCH (LYNN ALLEN JONES), college football coach; b. Saugatuck, Mich., Jan. 17, 1968; m. Barbara Jones; children: Alex, Adam, Andrew. B, Ferris State U., Big Rapids, Mich., 1990. Intern Tampa Bay Buccaneers, 1987—89; grad. asst. coach Rutgers U. Scarlet Knights, NJ, 1990—92; offensive coord. Wilkes U. Colonels, Pa., 1993—94; running backs coach Ferris State U. Bulldogs, Mich., 1995, offensive coord., 1996—97; asst. football coach Ctrl. Mich. U. Chippewas, 1998—2004, offensive coord., 2001—03, head football coach, 2007—09; asst. football coach W.Va. U. Mountaineers, 2005—06; head football coach U. Cin. Bearcats, 2010—12, U. Tenn. Volunteers, 2013—. Named Big East Conf. Coach of Yr., 2011. Achievements include coaching the Central Michigan University Chippewa football program to its first-ever Top 25 AP national ranking, 2009. Office: University of Tennessee Football Program 1704 Johnny Majors Dr Knoxville TN 37996

JONES, CAROLYN ELLIS, retired employment agency owner; b. Marigold, Miss., Feb. 21, 1928; d. Joseph Lawrence and Willie Decelle (Forrest) Peeples; m. David Wright Ellis, May 30, 1945 (div. 1966); children: David, Lyn, Debbie, Dawn; m. Frank Willis Jones, Jan. 1, 1980. Student, La. State U., 1949. Owner, mgr. Personnel and Bus. Svc., Inc., Greenwood, Miss., 1962-88; owner Honor Pub. Co., 1988—2005; ret. ESL tchr. at a Spanish Mission, nr. Sunflower, Miss., 2004—. Author: The Lottie Moon Storybook, 1985, The John Wesley Storybook, 2003; editor: An Old Soldier's Career, 1974; contbr. articles to religious and gen. interest publs. Mem. adv. bd. career edn. Greenwood Pub. Schs., 1975-76, mem. adv. bd. vocat.-tech. dept., 1975-88; conf. leader Miss. Bapt. Convention Singles Retreat, 1980; Mission Svc. Corps del. Home Mission Bd., So. Bapt. Conv., Hawaii, 1979; team mem. United Meth. Vols. in Mission, Estonia/Russia, 1996 Mem. Greenwood C. of C. (edn. com. 1980—, guest spkr. career day program local high sch.), Mothers Against Drunk Drivers, Altrusa Internat., Nat. Fedn. Ind. Bus., Miss Delta Rose Soc., Miss. Native Plant Soc., Gideon Aux. (pres. 1986-88). Avocations: writing, rose exhibitions, wildflowers. Office: 802 W President Ave Greenwood MS 38930-3326 Home Phone: 662-458-8731.

JONES, CHARLES E., JR., public relations executive; b. 1944; BA in Acctg. & Economics, Vanderbilt U., Nashville; MBA, Emory U., Ga. Securities analyst, dir. rsch. J.C. Bradford & Co.; founder, pres., prin. Corporate Communications, Inc., 1975—. Bd. dirs. CBRL Group, Inc., 1981—. Mem.: Nat. Assn. Security Dealers (former mem. issuer affairs & mktg. coms.). Office: Corporate Communications Inc 523 Third Ave S Nashville TN 37210 Office Phone: 615-254-3376. Office Fax: 615-254-3420.

JONES, CHARLES HILL, JR., banker; b. July 14, 1933; s. Charles Hill and Susan Roy (Johnston) J.; m. Hope Haskell, Jan. 28, 1961; children: Hope H., Charles Hill III, Henry M.T. Grad., Groton Sch., Mass., 1952; BA in Econs., U. Va., 1956. With Wood, Struthers & Winthrop, Inc., NYC, 1956-73, gen. ptnr., 1968-69, v.p., dir., dir. rsch., 1969-73; sr. v.p., chief investment officer Midlantic Nat. Bank, Edison, 1974-87; gen. ptnr. Edge Ptnrs., 1987—; chmn, pres. NJ Title Insurance Co., 2000—01. Chmn., bd. dirs. NJT Holdings, 2000—. Author: (with Joseph D. Davis) Toll Road Bonds, 1959, The Growth Rate Appraiser, 1968. Treas. N.Y. chpt. R.E. Lee Meml. Found., 1964-69; trustee, chmn. fin. com. Monmouth Med. Ctr., 1975-81; pres. bd. trustees Rumson (N.J.) Country Day Sch., 1982-85; trustee Hampden-Sydney Coll., 1995-99, 2002-03. Mem. Inst. Chartered Fin. Analysts Office Phone: 732-389-3600 ext. 219.

JONES, D. PAUL, JR., lawyer, retired bank executive; b. Birmingham, Ala., Sept. 26, 1942; s. D. Paul and Virginia Lee (Mount) J.; m. Charlene Dale Angelich, Aug. 1964; children: Holly, Allison, Paul, III. BS, U. Ala., 1964, JD, 1967; LL.M., NYU, 1968. Bar: Ala. Mem. firm Balch, Bingham, Baker, Hawthorne, Williams & Ward, Birmingham, 1970-78, of counsel, 1978-86; exec. v.p., gen. counsel, dir. Compass Bancshares, Inc., Birmingham, 1978-84, vice chmn., 1984-89, pres., COO, 1989-91, chmn., CEO, 1991—2007; of counsel Balch & Bingham LLP, Birmingham, 2008—. Bd. dirs. Compass Bancshares, Inc., 1978-2008, Fed. Rs. Bank Atlanta, 1994-2000, Bank of America Corp., 2009- Chmn. Ala. Bus. Charitable Trust Fund; mem. adv. bd. Better Bus. Bur. Birmingham; adv. bd. Salvation Army, Birmingham; bd. visitors Sch. Commerce and Bus. Adminstrn., U. Ala.; mem. pres.'s coun. U. Ala., Birmingham, Ala. Inst. Deaf and Blind; ptnr. Econ. Devel. Partnership Ala.; grad. bd. trustees Leadership Birmingham; grad. Leadership Ala.; mem. adv. bd. Juvenile Diabetes Found., Ala., corp. chmn. Walk to Cure Diabetes, 1999; co-chmn. Advantage 21 Leadership Coun.; mem. adv. coun. Nat. Multiple Sclerosis Soc.; bd. dirs. Region 2020, Inc.; dinner chmn. 32d ann. awards dinner Nat. Conf. for Cmty. and Justice, 2000; adv. bd. Svc. Corp. Ret. Execs. Mem. ABA, Ala. Bar Assn. (chmn. sect. corp., banking and bus. law 1973-75, bd. bar examiners 1975-78), Birmingham Bar Assn., Am. Bankers Assn. (mem. govt. rels. coun. 1985-88), Ala. Bankers Assn. (pres. 1989-90, chmn. fin. com. 1990-91, exec. coun.), Fin. Svcs. Roundtable (bd. dirs., banking and fin. markets com.), Soc. Internat. Bus. Fellows, Newcomen, Birmingham C. of C., Birmingham C. of C. Found., Birmingham Bus. Leadership Group, Svc. Corps Ret. Execs. (adv. bd.), The Club, Old Overton, Country Club Birmingham, Willow Point Golf and Country Club (Alexander City), Rotary. Office: Balch & Bingham LLP 1901 Sixth Ave N Ste 1500 Birmingham AL 35203 Office Phone: 205-226-8708. Office Fax: 205-488-5903. E-mail: pjones@balch.com.

JONES, DAN BRIGMAN, ophthalmologist, educator; b. Raleigh, NC, June 12, 1936; m. Marilyn Woodall; children: Danny Brigman Jr., Allen Walker. BA, Duke U., 1958, MD, 1962. Diplomate Am. Bd. Ophthalmology. Intern Duke Hosp., Durham, NC, 1962-63; resident in ophthalmology Bascom Palmer Eye Inst., U. Miami (Fla.) Sch. Medicine, 1965-69; fellow in cornea and external disease Moorfields Eye Hosp., Inst. Ophthalmology, London, 1967-68; asst. prof. then assoc. prof. ophthalmology dept. surgery Vanderbilt U. Sch. Medicine, Nashville, 1969-71; assoc. prof. then prof. ophthalmology Cullen Eye Inst., Baylor Coll. Medicine, Houston, 1972-78, Sid W. Richardson prof., chmn. dept. ophthalmology, 1981—, Margarett Root Brown chair ophthalmology, 1991—, Disting. Svc. prof., 2003—; mem. staff, then chief ophthalmology svc. Ben Taub Gen. Hosp., 1972—; mem. staff, then chief ophthalmology Meth. Hosp., Houston, 1972—2009; mem. staff St. Luke's Episcopal Hosp., Houston, 1973—. Chief ophthalmology sect. VA Hosp., Houston, 1973-78; mem. sci. adv. com. Knights Templar Eye Found., Inc., 1984-2002; mem. various coms. and couns. Nat. Eye Inst., 1975-76; mem. adv. panel on ophthalmology U.S. Pharmacopeial Conv., 1980-84; mem. ophthalmic drugs adv. com. FDA, 1975-78; cons. in field; vis. prof. to numerous schs., including Johns Hopkins U., Balt., 1975, 79, Washington U., St. Louis, 1975, Tipler Army Hosp., Honolulu, 1974, Yale U., New Haven, 1988, others; lectr. in field. Contbr. numerous articles to profl. jours. Bd. dirs. William C. Connor Found., Tex. Christian U., 1981—, Tex. Soc. to Prevent Blindness, 1981—; bd. dirs. The Lighthouse of Houston, 1981-89, mem. adv. coun., 1989—; mem. exec. med. com. Lions Eye Bank of Tex., 1981—, bd. dirs., 1989—. Epidemic intelligence officer USPHS, 1963-65. Recipient Honor award in Edn. Am. Acad. Ophthalmology and Otolaryngology, 1976; grantee NIH, 1978—, Sid W. Richardson Found., 1977-82. Mem. AMA (mem. program com. sect. ophthalmology 1970-73), Am. Acad. Ophthalmology (mem. faculty of basic and clin. sci. course 1970-76, mem. ophthalmology knowledge assessment com. 1972-80, mem. adv. com. 1973-77, mem. long range planning com. 1976-80, mem. program adv. com. 1986-89, sec. instrn. 1989—, trustee 1989-93, Sr. Honor award 1986, Life Achievement award, 2003, Spl. Recognition award, 2003), Am. Ophthalmol. Soc., Am. Soc. for Microbiology, Assn. for Rsch. in Vision and Ophthalmology, Assn. Univ. Profs. Ophthalmology (chmn. resident and fellowship edn. com. 1986-88, chmn. edn. com. 1988-93, trustee 1988-93, pres. bd. trustees 1993-94), Harris County Med. Soc., Houston Ophthal. Soc. (pres. 1979-80), Ocular Microbiology and Immunology Group, Inc. (exec. sec. 1973-89, bd. dirs. 1989-93), Pan Am. Assn. Ophthalmology, Tex. Ophthal. Assn. (mem. bd. councillors 1982-85), Tex. Soc. Infectious Diseases, Baylor Ophthalmology Alumni Assn., Inc., Bascom Palmer Alumni Assn., Phi Beta Kappa, Phi Eta Sigma, Alpha Omega Alpha. Office: Cullen Eye Inst 6565 Fannin NC 205 Houston TX 77030 Home Phone: 713-668-0219; Office Phone: 713-798-5951. Business E-Mail: dbj@bcm.tmc.edu.

JONES, DANIEL WAYNE, academic administrator, physician, educator; b. Morton, Mar. 19, 1949; married; 2 children. BS in Chemistry, Miss. Coll., Clinton, 1971; MD, U. Miss. Sch. Med., Jackson, 1975. Pvt. practice Internal Medicine Clinic of Laurel, 1978—85; staff physician Jones County Cmty. Hosp.; dir. hypertension clin. Wallace Mem. Bapt. Hosp., Pusan, Republic of Korea, 1985—92; asst. prof. medicine, dir. clin. hypertension U. Miss. Med. Ctr., Jackson, 1992, assoc. dean Med. Sch., dean Med. Sch., 2003—09, vice chancellor health affairs, 2003—09, Herbert G. Langford prof. medicine (cardiovascular disease); chancellor U. Miss., 2009—. Contbr. articles to profl. jours. Mem.: Am. Heart Assn. (bd. dirs. 2003—, pres. 2007—08). Office: University of Mississippi Office of Chancellor 123 Lyceum University MS 38677 Office Phone: 662-915-7111. E-mail: djones@ovc.umsmed.edu, chancllr@olemiss.edu.*

JONES, DARILYN, gas industry executive; BBA, MBA, U. Houston. Sr. mgr., global energy strategy consulting practice Accenture; exec. positions, risk mgmt. El Paso Energy; with Exxon; exec. positions, risk mgmt. Koch Energy Trading; with Mobil Oil; exec. positions, risk mgmt. PG&E Energy Trading; with Tenneco; v.p., risk control Sequent Energy Management, LP, 2003—. Mem. Global Assn. Risk Profls. (GARP). Office: Sequent Energy Management Two Allen Ctr 1200 Smith St Houston TX 77002 Office Phone: 832-397-1700. Office Fax: 832-397-1722. Business E-Mail: drjones@sequentenergy.com.

JONES, DAVID, mining executive; B in Bus. Mgmt., Okla. State U., 1984. Sales mgr. CSR Rinker Materials, 1988—2001; v.p., gen. mgr. South Ctrl. divsn., Ala. dist. Martin Marietta Materials, Inc., Birmingham, 2001—. Office: Martin Marietta Materials Inc South Ctrl Divsn Ala Dist 1800 International Park Dr Birmingham AL 35243 Office Phone: 205-969-2629.

JONES, DAVID A., JR., venture capital firm executive, former insurance company executive; s. David A. Jones. BA in History magna cum laude, Yale U., 1980, JD, 1988. English tchr. Hunan Med. Coll., Changsha, China; with internat. divsn. First Nat. Bank Boston; atty.-adviser Bur. East Asian and Pacific Affairs U.S. Dept. State, 1988-92; assoc. Hirn Reed & Harper, Louisville; chmn., mng. dir. Chrysalis Ventures, LLC, Louisville, 1993—; vice chmn. Humana, Inc., Louisville, 1996—2005, chmn., 2005—10. Bd. dir. Humana, Inc., 1993-; adj. prof. Georgetown U. Law Ctr., Washington; former chmn. Greater Louisville Health Enterprises Network; mem. adv. com. Brookings Ctr. on Health Policy; bd. mem. Nat. Com. on US-China Relations. Office: Chrysalis Ventures LLC 1650 Nat City Tower 101 S Fifth St Louisville KY 40202 also: Humana Inc 500 W Main St Louisville KY 40202

JONES, DAVID ALLEN, retired health benefits company executive; b. Louisville, Aug. 1931; m. Betty L. Ashbury, July 24, 1954. BS, U. Louisville, 1954; JD, Yale U., 1960. Bar: Ky. 1960. Founder Humana Inc. (formerly Extendicare Inc.), Louisville, 1961, CEO, 1961—97, chmn., dir. Louisville, 1997—; ptnr. Greenebaum, Doll and McDonald and predecessor, Louisville, 1965—69, of counsel, 1969—74; ret. Lt. (j.g.) USN, 1954—57.

JONES, DAVID MEREDITH, retired communications educator; b. Anderson, Ind., Mar. 14, 1940; s. Harry Paul and Ruby A. (Hiday) J.; m. Mary Joan Croft, Feb. 12, 1993; children: Vincent Arno, Yann Christophe. BS in Journalism, Ball State U., 1971, MA in Journalism, 1974; PhD in Higher Edn., U. Pitts., 1978. Cert. with marine survey Va. Marine Inst. Reporter Anderson (Ind.) Daily Bull., 1965-74; prof. journalism Point Park U., Pitts., 1974-2001, chmn. dept. journalism and comms., 1987-91, dir. grad. program, 1981—87, 1996-2000. Contbr. articles to profl. jours. Mem. Am. Legion; vol. Wilmington NC Vets. Adminstrn. Med. Clinic. Sgt. US Army, 1961—65. Mem. Am. Boat and Yacht Coun. Democrat. Avocations: boating, boat surveying, woodworking. Home: 7821 Cypress Island Wilmington NC 28412 Office Phone: 910-612-8976.

JONES, DAVID P., corporate financial executive; BSBA, U. Tenn, Knoxville. CPA. Sr. audit KPMG Peat Marwick; supr. Pershing, Yoakley and Assocs.; pres. Team Health Fin. Svcs., Inc.; CFO, prin. acctg. officer, v.p., treas. Health Financial Corp.; v.p., treas., prin. acctg. officer Team Financial, LLC, CFO, 1996—; v.p., asst. sec., treas., prin. acctg. officer Team Health Inc., contr., 1994—96; CFO Team Health Holdings, Inc., 1996—; v.p., treas. Team Health Holdings, Inc (formerly Team Health Holdings LLC), contr., 1994—96; CFO Team Health Holdings, Inc., 1996—, exec. v.p., 2010—. Office: Team Health Holdings Inc 265 Brookview Ctr Way Ste 400 Knoxville TN 37919 Office Phone: 865-693-1000. Office Fax: 865-539-3073. Business E-Mail: david.jones@teamhealth.com.

JONES, DENNIS L., state legislator; b. Erie, Pa., Apr. 5, 1942; Student, St. Petersburg Jr. Coll., Lincoln Chiropractic Ctr., 1963. Chiropractic physician N.E. Chiropractic Ctr.; mem. Fla. House of Reps., Tallahassee, 1978—2000, minority floor whip, 1984-86, spkr.

pro tem, 1999—2000; v.p. econ. devel. and innovative programs St. Petersburg Coll.; mem. Dist. 13 Fla. State Senate, Tallahassee, 2002—, majority leader, 2002—04, chair policy and steering com. on govtl. ops., regulated industries com., mem. policy and steering com. on commerce and industry, criminal and civil justice appropriations com., environ. preservation and conservation com. Chair Com. on Health Care Stds. and Regulatory Reform Govt. Svcs. Coun., 1996-97; mem. Com. on Real Property and Probate Justice Coun., 1996-97, Com. on Health and Human Svcs. Appropriations Fiscal Responsibility Coun., 1996-97, Com. on Regulated Svcs. Econ. Impact Coun., 1996-97; vice chmn. Pinellas County Legis. Del., 1984-85, chmn., 1985-87; chmn. House Rep. Campaign Com., 1985-90; chmn. Rep. Caucus, 1990-94; mem. Joint Exec. and Legis. Commn. on Postsecondary Edn., 1979, House Rep. Policy Com., House Rep. Leadership; dean House Rep. Caucus; mem. Fla. Chiropractic Adv. Coun., 1977-79. Mem. Pinellas County Rep. Exec. Com.; mem. exec. com. legis. mem. Fla. Rep. Party; bd. trustees U. Gen. Hosp., Women's Hosp., Med. Ctr. Recipient Legis. Svc. award Fla. Assn. Cmty. Colls., 1981, Fla. Alcohol and Drug Abuse Assn., 1981, First Annual Champion of Small Bus. award St. Petersburg C. of C., 1984, Legis. of Yr. award Fla. Health Care Assn., 1984, 91, Friend of Edn. award FTP-NEA, 1986, Gulf Beaches Libr. Appreciation award, 1988, Friend of Fla. Boating award Marine Industries Assn., 1988, Legis. Humanitarian award Boley Inc., 1988, Svc. to Mankind award Seminole Evening Sertoma Club, 1989, PACE award Pinellas Emergency Mental Health Svc., 1988, Guardian of Small Bus. award Nat. Fedn. Ind. Bus., 1988, First Annual Outstanding Legislator award Pinellas County Coun. of Firefighters, 1990, Legis. Leadership award Fla. Restaurant Assn., 1992, Disting. Svc. award Fla. Literary Coalition, 1993, award State Long-Term Care Ombudsman Coun., 1994. Fellow Internat. Chiropractic Colls.; mem. Am. Legis. Exch. Coun., AARP, Fla. Chiropractic Assn. (pres. 1971-72, Chiropractor of Yr. 1982, D.J. Rainey Legis. award 1984, 88), Pinellas County Chiropractic Soc. (pres. 1965-66), Gtr. Seminole Area C. of C., Gtr. Largo Area C. of C., Treasure Is. C. of C., Gulf Beaches C. of C., St. Petersburg Rep. Club (pres. 1977-78), St. Petersburg Young Reps. Club (pres. 1974), Rep. Club Gtr. Largo, Rep. Club Gtr. Seminole, Ivory Club, Suncoast Tiger Bay Club, Breakfast Optimist Club, Pinellas Marine Inst. (bd. trustees, Friend of Fla. Boating award 1988, Contbn. to Ednl. and Scientific Programs award 1989), Masons, Shriners, Royal Order of Jesters, Sigma Phi Kappa. Republican. Methodist. Avocations: sailing, softball, skiing, fishing, chess. Office: 408 Senate Office Bldg 404 S Monroe St Tallahassee FL 32399-1100 Office Phone: 727-549-6411, 850-487-5065. Business E-Mail: jones.dennis.web@flsenate.gov.

JONES, DONNIE, men's college basketball coach; b. July 7, 1966; m. Michelle Gibson; children: Madisyn Michelle, Donald Isaac, Sofie Louise. B in Bus. Edn., Pikeville Coll., Ky., 1988; M in Sports Mgmt., Marshall U., Huntington, W.Va., 1992. Asst. basketball coach, admissions adminstr. Pikeville Coll. Bears, Ky., 1988—90; grad. asst. Marshall U. Thundering Herd, W.Va., 1990—92, asst. coach, 1992—96, head basketball coach, 2007—10; asst. coach U. Fla. Gators, Gainesville, 1996—2006, assoc. head coach, 2006—07; head basketball coach U. Ctrl Fla. Golden Knights, 2010—. Named to Pikeville Hall of Fame, 2004. Office: University Ctrl Fla Basketball c/o UCF Athletics Assn Inc 4000 Central Florida Blvd Orlando FL 32816

JONES, DWIGHT CLINTON, mayor, Richmond, Virginia; b. Phila., Feb. 3, 1948; m. Gertrude A. Davis; children: Dwight Brenton, Drick Elton, Nichole Dannille. Former chmn. Richmond City Sch. Bd., 1982—85; hon. mem. Va. House Delegates from Dist. 70, 1994—2008; mayor City of Richmond, 2008—. Rep. Richmond Commn. on Human Rels., Va Commn. on Immigration; chmn. Va Legis. Black Caucus. Former chmn. Richmond Renaissance; co-founder South Richmond Sr. Ctr., Imani Intergenerational Cmty. Devel. Corp.; bd. dir. Met. Richmond Conv. & Visitors Bur.; bd. mem. MCV Hosp. Authority, YMCA. Named one of Richmond's 100 Most Outstanding Citizens, 1985. Mem.: Nat. Bapt. Conv. (bd. dirs.), Nat. Coun. Churches (gov. bd.), Richmond Red Cross. Democrat. Baptist. Office: 900 E Broad St Ste 201 Richmond VA 23219 Office Phone: 804-233-7679, 804-646-7970. Office Fax: 804-646-7987. E-mail: Del_DJones@house.state.va.us.*

JONES, EDITH HOLLAN, federal judge; b. Phila., Apr. 7, 1949; m. Sherwood (Woody) Jones; 2 children. BA Cornell U., 1971; JD with honors, U. Tex., 1974. Bar: Tex. 1974, US Supreme Ct. 1979, US Ct. Appeals (5th & 11th circuits), US Dist. (southern & northern districts) Tex. Assoc. Andrews & Kurth, Houston, 1974—82, ptnr., 1982—85; judge US Ct. Appeals (5th Cir.), Houston, 1985—, chief judge, 2006—12. Gen. counsel Republican Party of Tex., 1981—83. Mem. bd. dir. Boy Scouts of America. Master: ABA; mem.: Garland Walker American Inns of Ct., Houston Bar Assn., State Bar Tex. Republican. Presbyterian. Office: US Courthouse 515 Rusk Ave Rm 12505 Houston TX 77002-2655 Office Phone: 713-250-5484.*

JONES, EDITH IRBY, internist; b. Conway, Ark., Dec. 23, 1927; d. Robert and Mattie (Buice) Irby; m. James Beauregard Jones, Apr. 16, 1950 (dec. Oct. 1989); children: Gary Ivan, Myra Vonceil Jones Romain, Keith Irby. BS, Knoxville Coll., 1948; MD, U. Ark., 1952; Doctorate (hon.), Mo. Valley Coll., Mary Holmes Coll., Knoxville Coll. Intern Univ. Hosp., Little Rock, 1952-53; gen. practice medicine Hot Springs, Ark., 1953-59; resident in internal medicine Baylor Coll. Medicine, Houston, 1959-62; pvt. practice medicine specializing in internal medicine Houston, 1962—; mem. staff Meth. Hosp., Houston, Hermann Hosp., Houston, St. Elizabeth Hosp., Houston, St. Anthony Ctr., Houston, St. Joseph Hosp., Houston, Thomas Care Ctr., Houston, Town Pk., Houston, chief of staff; chief med. staff Riverside Gen. Hosp., Houston, 2006—. Clin. asst. prof. medicine Baylor Coll. Medicine, U. Tex. Sch. Medicine, Houston; dir. Prospect Med. Lab.; bd. dirs., sec. Mercy Hosp. Comprehensive Health Care Group; ptnr. Jones, Coleman and Whitfield; grad. med. examiner Ct. Calanthe Jurisdiction, Tex.; cons. Social Security Agy., Tex. Pub. Welfare Dept., Vocat. Rehab. Assn., Tex. Rehab. Commn.; bd. dirs. Std. Savs. Assn., others. Contbr. articles to profl. jours. Bd. dirs. Drug Addiction Rehab. Enterprise, March of Dimes, Houston, Odessey House, Houston; adv. bd. Houston Coun. Alcoholism; mem. com. revising justice code Harris County, Tex.; impartial hearing officer Houston Ind. Sch. Dist.; mem. Cmty. Welfare Planning Assn., Friends of Youth, Human Svcs. Adv. Coun., Houston, PTA, YMCA; founder Edith Irby Jones Found.; bd. dirs. Houston Internat. U.; chmn. bd. trustees Knoxville Coll.; trustee Must. Assn. Profl. Svc.; bd. visitors U. Houston, others. Recipient proclamation, Houston City Coun., 1985, Mayor of Houston, 1986, cert. of citation, Tex. Ho. of Reps., 1986, commendation, Calif. Senate, 1989, Volunteerism and Cmty. Svc. award, Tex. Acad. internal Medicine, 2000, Scroll of Merit award, Nat. Med. Assn., 2001, Silas Hunt Legacy award, U. Ark., Fayetteville, 2006; named Dr. Edith Irby Jones Day in her honor, State of Ark., 1985, NYC, 1986, Disting. Alumna, J. William Fulbright Coll. Arts and Scis., 2005, a clinic in her honor, Veracruz, Mex., Most Influential People of 1986, Ebony mag.; named one of 30 Most Influential Black Women Houston, 1984, 100 Leading Black Physicians, Black Enterprise mag., 2001; named to Tex. Black Women's Hall of Fame, 1986, Hall of Fame, U. Ark. Sch. Med. Scis., 2004. Master: ACP; fellow: Am. Soc. Internal Medicine (Oscar E. Edward award 2001), Am. Coll. Medicine; mem.: NAACP, AMA, Physicians for Human Rights, Bus. and Profl. Women, Tex. Assn. Disability Examiners, Houston Med. Forum, Harris County Med. Assn., Lone Star Med. Assn., Nat. Med. Assn. (first female past pres., Scroll of Merit 2001, Living Legend), Am. Med. Women's Assn. (v.p. Houston chpt.), Nat. Coun. Negro Women (v.p. Dorothy Height chpt.), Women of Achievement (Hall of Fame 1985), Girl Friends, Tops Ladies of Distinction, Links, Order Eastern Star, Eta Phi Beta, Delta Sigma Theta, Alpha Kappa Mu. Democrat. Achievements include being first African American to graduate from the University of Arkansas School for Medicine Sciences. Avocations: travel, walking, swimming. Home: 3402 S Parkwood Houston TX 77021 Office: 2601 Prospect St Houston TX 77004-7737 Home Phone: 713-747-5116; Office Phone: 713-529-3145. Business E-Mail: eijones@advmed.com.

JONES, ELI, III, academic administrator; b. Houston, Nov. 24, 1961; s. Eli Jones, II and Elvira Jones; m. Fern Cecilia Walker; children: Necia, Tracia , Christopher, Elicia. BS in Journalism, Tex. A&M U., College Station, 1982, MBA, 1986, PhD in Mktg., 1997. Key account mgr. Quaker Oats Co., Houston, 1986—88, zone sales planning mgr. Jacksonville, Fla., 1988—89, key accounts exec. Charlotte, NC, 1989—90; sales mgr. Nabisco, Houston, 1990—92; zone mgr. Frito-Lay, Houston, 1992—93; instr. Texas A&M University, 1993—97; asst. prof. C.T. Bauer Coll. Bus., U. Houston, 1997—2002, exec. dir. Program for Excellence in Selling, 1997—2007, assoc. prof. mktg., 2002—07, exec. dir. Sales Excellence Inst., 2004—07, prof. mktg., assoc. dean, 2007—08; Ourso disting. prof. bus., dean E.J. Ourso College Business, Louisiana State University, Baton Rouge, 2008—. Bd. dirs. Administaff, 2004—; mem. adv. bd. La. Bus. & Tech. Ctr., 2008—. Co-author: (textbook) Selling ASAP: Art, Science, Agility, Performance, 2005—, Strategic Sales Leadership: Breakthrough Thinking for Breakthrough Results, 2006; mem. editl. rev. bd. Indsl. Mktg. Mgmt., 2001—08, Jour. Personal Selling & Sales Mgmt., 2001—, Jour. Acad. Mktg. Sci., 2006—; contbr. articles to profl. jours. Instr. Seeds of Life Ministry Workshop, Houston, 1999; guest spkr. Sales & Mktg. Execs. Assn., Houston, 1999—2000. Mem.: Southwestern Mktg. Assn., Acad. Mktg. Sci. (Outstanding Mktg. Tchr. 2001), American Mgmt. Assn., Alpha Mu Alpha. Avocations: Contemporary Christian Music Ministry, A/V technology, travel, basketball. Office: LSU EJ Ourso College of Business 3304 Patrick F Taylor Hall Baton Rouge LA 70803 Mailing: Administaff Bd Directors 19001 Crescent Springs Dr Kingwood TX 77339-3802 Office Phone: 281-358-8986. Personal E-mail: eli-fern-jones@msn.com. Business E-Mail: eli-jones@uh.edu. E-mail: eli_jones@administaff.com, elijones@lsu.edu.

JONES, EMANUEL, state legislator, automotive executive; b. Atlanta, Ga. m. Gloria Jones; children: Emanuel, Elam, Emani. BSEE, Univ. Pa., 1981; MBA, Columbia Univ., 1986. Mgmt. positions IBM, 1981—84, Arthur Anderson & Co., 1986—88; owner, pres. Legacy Ford McDonough, 1992—, Legacy Goodyear Tire McDonough, 1995—, Legendary Ford-Mercury, Marion, NC, 1998—, Legacy Toyota Union City, 1998—, ANSA Automotive Macon & LA, 2002—; mem. Dist. 10 Ga. State Senate, 2005—. Served to capt. Corps of Engineers US Army. Democrat. Baptist. Mailing: PO Box 370224 Decatur GA 30037 Office Phone: 770-964-8888. Office Fax: 770-964-7162. Business E-Mail: emanuel.jones@senate.ga.gov.

JONES, FRANCES BROOKS, lawyer, bank executive; b. 1962; AB in Govt., Dartmouth Coll., Hanover, NH, 1984; JD, Vanderbilt U. Sch. Law, Nashville, 1987. Bar: Ky. 1987. Corp. banking counsel., documentation mgr. Bank of Louisville, 1996—2002; assoc. gen. coun. BB&T Corp. (Branch Banking and Trust Co.), Winston-Salem, NC, 2001—07, gen. counsel, corp. sec., chief corp. governance officer, 2008—10, dep. gen. counsel, practice group mgr., 2010—. Mem.: ABA, Louisville Bar Assn., Ky. Bar Assn. Office: BB&T Corp 401 Main St Ste 400 Louisville KY 40202*

JONES, FRANK GRIFFITH, lawyer; b. Houston, Sept. 11, 1941; s. A. Gordon and Grace (Griffith) Jones; m. Deborah Ann Young, July 5, 1969; children: Russell G., Sarah G., Christopher Y. BS, Rice U., 1963; JD, U. Tex., 1966. Bar: Tex. 1966, U.S. Dist. Ct. (so., no. and ea. dists.) Tex., U.S. Ct. Appeals (5th cir.), cert.: (civil trial specialist). Of counsel, ptnr. Fulbright & Jaworski, LLP, Houston, 1974—2006, co-ptnr. in charge Houston office, 2001—06. Chmn. Fulbright & Jaworski Employment Commn., 1988—92. Chmn. troop com. Boy Scouts Am., Houston, 1986—88; chair Environ. Adv. Com., 2004—05, Govtl. Rels. Com., 2005—06; bd. dirs. exec. com. Greater Houston Partnership, 2004—06; bd. dirs. Friends Fondren LIbr.; bd. mem. Friends of Harris County Court House; bd. dirs., chmn. Houston Forum; cmty. adv. bd. mem. Edn. Found. Houston; mem. Rice U. Fund Coun., Houston, 1987—93; pres. Baker Coll. Rice U., 1962—63. Lt. (j.g.) USNR, 1967—72. Keeton Fellow, U. Tex. Law Sch., 1993—. Fellow: Internat. Acad. Trial Lawyers, Am. Coll. Trial Lawyers (ADR com. 1986—96, chmn. 1992—94, ethics com. 1996—2001, nat. moot ct. competition com. 2004—07, chmn. 2005—07); mem.: ABA, Def. Rsch. Inst., Tex. Assn. Def. Counsel, Am. Bar Found., Houston Bar Found. (chmn. 2003), Tex. Bar Found., Tex. Bar Assn., Houston Young Lawyers Assn. (pres. 1972—73), Phi Delta Phi (past pres.). Avocation: travel. Office: Fulbright & Jaworski LLP Fulbright Twr 1301 Mckinney St Ste 5100 Houston TX 77010-3095 Home Phone: 713-621-3340; Office Phone: 713-651-5473.

JONES, FRANKIE T., SR., consulting firm executive; m. Alease Jones; children: Frankie Jr., Anthony. Degree in Div., Duke U., Va. U. Several positions including exec. v.p. B & C Associates, Inc., High Point, NC, 1993, COO, pres., 2000—. Bd. dirs. Piedmont Natural Gas Co., 2007—. Bd. dirs. NC Citizens For Bus. & Industry, Internat. BookSmart Found. Inc., High Point United Way; bd. visitors The Wake Forest U. Div. Sch.; bd. mem. Va. U., Lynchburg, Northeastern Piedmont Regional Small Bus. and Tech. Develop. Ctr., High Point Cmty. Found., Tougaloo Coll.; mem. entrepreneurship adv. bd. NC A&T State U. Ret. USAF, spl. assignments USAF. Recipient Roy Wilkins Meritorious Svc. award, Nat. NAACP, 1990, Chairman's award, Nat. Newspaper Publishers Assn., 2007. Office: B & C Associates Inc 6727 N Nc Highway 62 Burlington NC 27217-8645 Office Fax: 336-884-0744, 336-884-5311. Business E-Mail: fjones@bandcassociates.com.

JONES, FRANKLIN ROSS, writer, educator; b. Charlotte, NC, Jan. 3, 1920; s. William Morton and Olive Ruth (Moser) J.; divorced; children: Franklin Ross, Clarence Morton, Susan Noel. AB, Lenoir Rhyne Coll., 1941; MA, U. NC, 1951; DEd, Duke U., 1960. Tchr., NC, 1944-48; prin. Jr. HS, Henderson, NC, 1948-54; dist. sch. prin. Wake County, NC, 1954-56; dist. supt. Roxboro schs., NC, 1956-58; chmn. dept. edn. Randolph-Macon Coll., Ashland, Va., 1959-64; interim dean U. Richmond, Va., 1962; vis. prof. U. Va., Richmond Va. Ctr., 1956—64; dean Sch. Edn. Old Dominion U., 1964-69, Eminent prof., 1974-94; founder Child Study Ctr., 1965, disting. prof., 1969—, social founds. program leader, 1973-77, doctoral program liaison rep., 1974-77, faculty chmn., 1981—. Dir. Forest Ridge Corp., 1985; vis. rsch. scholar Duke U., 1967; cons. HEW, State Sch. Sys. and Colls.; lectr. in field; mem. com. White house Conf. Children and Youth, 1968-71, Ea. regional chmn., 1968-71; mem. Va. Gov.'s Com. Implementation, 1971-73; spkr. 25th Internat. Congress of Psychology, Brussels, 1992; symposium chmn. European Congress of Psychology, Athens, Greece, 1995; cons. to dean on test score stats., Old Dominion U., 1995—; adj. prof. U. Va., 1959-64. Author: Psychology of Human Development, 1969, 2nd edit., 1985, 3d edit. 1992, Handbook on Testing, 1972, Understanding the Middlescent Years, 1978, Theory of Adult Development, 1980, How to Survive Middle Age, 2005; Radio series Sta. WTAR, Norfolk, 1973-75; test item writer for NY Regency exams, 1987, Ednl. Testing Svc., 1989; guest editor Education, 1990—, Jack, 2002. Mem. Norfolk Urban Coalition, 1969-73; chmn. March of Dimes, Person County, NC, 1956-57; mem. adv. bd. Tidewater Rehab. Ctr., 1967-69; chmn. Hull Scholarship Fund, 1983-85; coord. U. Joy Fund Drive, 1974-95; univ. chmn. United Fund, 1982, 84; chmn. assessment com. Va. Reading to Learn Program, 1990-91; cons. to sch. systems, ETS, HEW, Coll. 1966—; dir. Praxis Ctr., 1965-2005; adminstr. Nat. Bd. for Cert. Counselors Ctr., Nat. Lang. and Music Bd. of Certification; chmn. scholarship fund Brewton Parker Coll., Mt. Vernon, Ga., 1999-2004; chmn. drive for low-paid faculty Old Dominion U., 2002-. Recipient Heritage Found. award, 1996, Football recognition and scholar Brewton Parker Coll., Ga., 1999, Hon. Chmn., 2007, Hon. Alumnus, 2007; Va. Golden Olymnpics tennis doubles champion, 1982-84, 880 meter run Gold medal, 1983, 100 meter dash Silver medal, 1984; named to Football Hall of Fame Brenton Parker Coll., Mt. Vernon, Ga., 2008. Mem. Am. Psychol. Soc. (charter), S.E. Psychol. Assn., Va. Assn. U. Profs. (dir. 1962-64), South Atlantic Philosophy Edn. Soc. (pres. 1966-69, dir. 1969—), Va. Assn. Rsch. in Edn. (Disting. Rsch. awards 1972, 73, 78), NC Edn. Assn. (pres. North Ctrl. chpt. 1951, pres. North Ctrl. Prins. 1956), Ea. Ednl. Rsch. Assn., Nat. Urban Edn. Assn., Alpha Tau Kappa, Kappa Delta Pi, Phi Delta Kappa, Phi Kappa Phi, Pi Gamma Mu (sec. 1962-64), Harbor Club (Norfolk), Lions, Rotary. Achievements include being member of Bicycle Relay Jr. Marathon World's Record team, 1933; organizing the the 1st off-campus courses for college and teaching the 1st television course at Old Dominion U. Home: 9810 Woodbay Dr Tampa FL 33626-2425 Personal E-mail: drfrjones@aol.com.

JONES, GARY, former political organization administrator; b. Ft. Sill, Okla., Aug. 1954; m. Mary Jane Jones; children: Kelly, Chris. BBA, Cameron U., Lawton, Okla., 1978. CPA Okla. With Southwestern Bell Tel. Co.; vice-chmn., commr. Comanche County, Okla.; chmn. 4th Dist. Rep. Party, Okla.; chmn. & exec. dir. Okla. Rep. Party, Oklahoma City, 2003—10; state auditor & inspector State of Okla., 2011—. Mem.: Okla. Farm Bur., Okla. Cattlemen's Assn., Nat. Cattlemen's Assn. Republican. Office: Okla State Auditor Rm 100 State Capitol Oklahoma City OK 73105 Office Phone: 405-521-3495. Office Fax: 405-521-3426.

JONES, GENE PAUL, food products executive; b. Rensselaer, Ind., Oct. 2, 1951; s. Emmett Earl and Dora Angeline J.; m. Mary Olga Remminton, June 3, 1984; children: Leslie Ann, Lauren Amanda. BS, St. Joseph Coll., 1973; MS, Ind. U., Ft. Wayne, 1976. Sr. mgr. KPMG Peat Marwick, San Antonio, 1976-85; v.p., treas. Nat. Bancshares Corp. of Tex., San Antonio, 1985-88; chief accounting officer Am.'s Favorite Chicken Co., San Antonio, 1988-91; exec. v.p. First Fla. Bank, Tampa, 1991-92; sr. v.p. fin., treas. America's Favorite Chicken Co., Atlanta, 1992—; CFO, treas. Vital Link Bus. Sys., Inc., 2002—03; co-founder, sec., treas. Encore Legal Solutions, Inc., 2003—06; ptnr. Tatum, LLC, 2006—; sec., treas., CFO Vaughan Foods, Inc., 2007—. Mem. AICPA, Tex. Soc. CPAs, Fin. Execs. Inst. Home: 3845 Winters Hill Dr Atlanta GA 30360-1330 Office: Vaughan Foods Inc 216 NE 12th St Oklahoma City OK 73160 Office Phone: 405-794-2530. Office Fax: 405-985-6596.

JONES, GEORGE FLEMING, international consultant; b. San Angelo, Tex., June 27, 1935; s. George Fleming and Cora (Brewer) J.; m. Maria Rosario Correa, Apr. 23, 1960; children: George III, Robert, Michael, Mary Louise. AB magna cum laude, Wabash Coll., 1955; AM, Tufts U., 1956; MA, Stanford U., 1967; LLD, Wabash Coll., 2000. Joined Fgn. Svc., Dept. State, 1956; with Econ. Bur., Dept. State, Washington, 1956-58; with Am. Embassy Ecuador, 1958-60, Ghana, 1961-63, Venezuela, 1963-66; officer in charge Venezuelan affairs Dept. State, Washington, 1967-69, officer in charge Colombian affairs, 1969-71; polit. advisor U.S. Mission to IAEA, Vienna, 1971-74; counselor for polit. affairs Am. Embassy, Guatemala, 1974-77; student Nat. War Coll., Washington, 1977-78; Latin Am. adviser U.S. del. U.S.-Soviet Conventional Arms Talks, 1978; dep. dir. office Latin Am. regional polit. affairs Dept. State, 1978-80, dir., 1980-82; dep. chief of mission Am. Embassy Costa Rica, 1982-85, Chile, 1985-89; sr. adviser for Latin Am. and Caribbean affairs U.S. del. UN Gen. Assembly, NYC, 1990, 95; amb. to Republic of Guyana, 1991-95; dir. programs for the Ams., Internat. Found. for Election Sys., Washington, 1996-99. Dir. Democracy and Governance Ctr. Devel. Assocs., Inc., 2000-05; mem. editl. bd. Fgn. Svc. Jour., 2007-. Recipient Superior Honor award Dept. State, 1987. Mem. Am. Fgn. Svc. Assn. (v.p. 1989-90, 2003-05, bd. dirs. 1999-2001), Sr. Fgn. Svc. Assn. (bd. dirs. 1990-92), Washington Inst. Fgn. Affairs. Home: 3804 Acosta Rd Fairfax VA 22031-3804 E-mail: georgejones@cox.net.

JONES, GEORGE W., museum director, military officer; b. Chatearoux, France; married; 1 child. BAS, The Citadel, 1979; MA in Teaching, Webster U., St. Louis, 1987. Joined USAF, advanced through ranks to lt. col.; squadron comdr. Maj. 32d Fighter Wing, Soesterberg Air Base, Netherlands, 1992—93; lt. col. 46 Test Wing Logistics Group, Eglin AFB, Fla., 1997—99; comdr. 46 Maintenance Squadron, Eglin AFB, Fla., 1997—99; lt. col. 46 Test Wing Maintenance Grp., Eglin AFB, Fla., 1999—2003; dep. comdr. 46 Maintenance Grp., Eglin AFB, Fla., 1999—2003; dir. Air Force Armament Mus., Eglin AFB, Fla., 2003—. Decorated 4 Meritorious Svc. medals, 5 Air Force Commendation medals, 4 Air Force Achievement medals; recipient Maintenance Effectiveness award, Air Combat Command, 1995, Maintenance Effectiveness/Daedalian award, 1998—2002, Team Excellence award, Air Force CSAF, 1997, Lt. Gen. Leo Marquez Field Grade Officer of Yr. award, Air Force Materiel Command, 1998, Civilian Notable Achievement award, 2004—05, Civilian Performance awards, 2005—07, Staff Civilian of Yr., 96 Air Base Wing, 2007. Mem.: Mil. Officers Assn. Am., Logistics Officer Assn., Citadel Alumni Assn. Office: Air Force Armament Mus 100 Museum Dr Eglin AFB FL 32542 Office Phone: 850-651-1808. E-mail: george.jones2@eglin.af.mil.

JONES, GLOWER WHITEHEAD, lawyer; b. Atlanta, May 4, 1936; s. Samuel L. and Alma (Powell) Jones; m. Joanna Dayvault, Apr. 5, 1980; children: Jeff, Tom, Frank, Michael, Mark. Grad., Dartmouth Coll., Hanover, NH, 1958; JD, Emory U., Atlanta, 1963. Bar: Ga. 1962, US Dist. Ct. Ga. 1963, US Ct. Appeals (5th and 11th cirs.), US Ct. Claims, US Supreme Ct. Assoc. Smith, Swift, Currie, McGhee & Hancock, Atlanta, 1963—65; ptnr. Smith Currie & Hancock, Atlanta, 1967—99, of counsel, 2000—. Author: Legal Aspects of Doing Business in North America and Canada, 1987, Alternative Clauses to Standard Construction Contracts, 1990; editor: 2d edit., Construction Subcontracting: A Legal Guide for Industry Professionals, 1991, Wiley Construction Law Update, 1992, 1993, 1994, Construction Contractors: The Right To Stop Work, 1992, Remedies for International Sellers of Goods, 1993; mem. editl. bd. Ga. State Bar Jour.; contbr. articles to profl. jours. Exec. bd. Met. Atlanta Boys' & Girls' Clubs, Inc., asst. sec., 1973—80, sec., 1980—83; trustee, past pres. Atlanta Florence Crittendon Svcs., Inc.;

trustee IBA Found.; bd. dirs. Samuel L. Jones Boys' & Girls' Club, Inc., So. Region Boys Clubs Am., Carrie Steele Pitts Home, Gate City Day Nursery Assn. Recipient Golden Boy award, Met. Atlanta Boys' Club, 1971; named Ga. Superlawyer in Constrn. Law, 2004. Fellow: Chartered Inst. Arbitrators; mem.: ABA, Fed. Bar Assn., Internat. Bar Assn. (chmn. internat. sales com., chmn. UNCITRAL subcom., chmn. membership com., mem. governing coun. sect. bus. law), Ga. Bar Assn. (elected Ga. Superlawyer for Constrn. Law 2004), State Bar Ga., Atlanta Bar Assn. (former chmn. prepaid legal svcs. com., engr. lawyers rels. com.), Lawyers Club Atlanta, Am. Judicature Soc., Assn. Trial Attys. Am., Ga. Assn. Trial Lawyers, Dartmouth Coll. Alumni Club, Emory U. Alumni Club, Ansley Park Golf Club, World Trade Club, Dartmouth Club, Atlanta Athletic Club, Baylor Alumni Club, Phi Delta Theta. Home: 195 14th St NE PH401 Atlanta GA 30309-2680 Office: Smith Currie & Hancock 2700 Marquis One Tower 245 Peachtree Center Ave Atlanta GA 30303-1227

JONES, HOUSTON GWYNNE, archivist, history professor; b. Yanceyville, NC, Jan. 7, 1924; s. Paul Hosier and Lemma Sue (Fowlkes) J. BS, Appalachian State Coll., Boone, NC, 1949; MA, George Peabody Coll., Nashville, 1950; postgrad., NYU, 1951—52; cert. archival adminstrn., Am. U., Washington, 1957; PhD, Duke U., Durham, NC, 1965. Prof. history Oak Ridge Mil. Inst., NC, 1950-53; chmn. div. soc. scis. West Ga. Coll., Carrollton, 1955-56; state archivist of N.C. State Dept. Archives & Hist., Raleigh, NC, 1956-68; dir. State Dept. Archives & History, Raleigh, NC, 1968-74; adj. prof. history U. NC, Chapel Hill, 1974-94, dir. NC Coll., 1974-94, Thomas W. Davis rsch. historian, 1994—. Mem. Nat. Hist. Publs. and Records Commn., Washington, 1978—86, NC Hist. Commn., Raleigh, 1977—. Author: Books For History's Sake, 1966, The Records of a Nation, 1969, Local Government Records, 1980, North Carolina Illustrated, 1983, North Carolina History: An Annotated Bibliography, 1995, Historical Consciousness in the Early Republic, 1995, Scoundrels, Rogues and Heroes of the Old North State, 2004, The Sonarman's War, 2010; editor-in-chief NC Hist. Rev., 1968-74; gen. editor: North Caroliniana Society Imprints, 1978—2011. Chmn. Am's. 400th Anniversary Com., Chapel Hill, 1978-80; founder, sec.-treas. North Caroliniana Soc., Chapel Hill, 1975—2011; sec. Joint Commn. on Status of Nat. Archives, Washington, 1967-68. With USN, 1942—46. Recipient Disting. Alumnus award Appalachian State U., 1971, Cannon Cup hist. preservation NC Soc. for Preservation of Antiquities, 1971, Univ. Svc. award U. NC Gen. Alumni Assn., 1990, Disting. Svc. award in documentary publ. and preservation Nat. Hist. Publs. and Records Commn., Washington, 1990, John Tyler Caldwell award in humanities NC Humanities Coun., 2001, NC awrd State of NC, 2002. Fellow Soc. Am. Archivists (pres. 1968-69, Waldo G. Leland prize 1967, 81), Soc. North Caroliniana (sec. 1975-2011, Soc. award 1994); mem. NC Literary and Hist. Assn. (sec. 1969-75, pres. 1975-76, Crittenden Meml. award 1977), NC Writers Conf. (chmn. 1982, Conf. award 1994), Am. Assn. for State and Local History (sec. 1978-82, award of merit 1968, award of distinction 1989), Nat. Assn. State Hist. Preservation Officers (com. chmn. 1972-74), Hist. Soc. NC (pres. 1979-80, R.D.W. Connor award 1956), Soc. History Discoveries (coun. 2003-05) Office: U NC Libr NC Collection Chapel Hill NC 27599-3930 Home: 3000 Galloway Ridge C-307 Pittsboro NC 27312-8662*

JONES, HUGH WILLIAMS, JR., internet and travel company executive; b. 1963; BS in Geology, U. Wis.; MBA, So. Meth. U., Dallas. Joined Am. Airlines, Inc., 1988, various positions including fin. controller European & Pacific airport sales and reservations ops., fin. controller food & beverage svcs., mgr. fin. analysis; mng. dir. fin. Sabre Travel Info. Network, Sabre Holdings, sr. v.p., controller, 2001—03, sr. v.p. N.Am. Sabre Travel Network, 2003, sr. v.p., COO Sabre Travel Network/Sabre Airline Solutions, then pres., CEO Travelocity Global, 2009—. Office: Sabre Holdings Worldwide Hdqs 3150 Sabre Dr Southlake TX 76092 Business E-Mail: hugh.jones@sabre.com.

JONES, J. LARRY, food service executive; Dir. ops. adminstrn. Cracker Barrel Old Country Store, Inc., v.p. innovation. Office: Cracker Barrel Old Country Store Inc 305 Hartmann Dr Lebanon TN 37088-0787 Office Phone: 615-444-5533. Office Fax: 615-443-9476.

JONES, JAMES BEVERLY, retired mechanical engineering educator, consultant; b. Kansas City, Mo., Aug. 21, 1923; BS, Va. Poly. Inst., 1944; MS, Purdue U., 1947, PhD in Mech. Engring., 1951. Asst. mech. engr. engr. bd. U.S. War Dept., Va., 1944-45; from asst. instr. to assoc. prof. mech. engring. Purdue U., 1945-57, prof., 1957-64; svc. engr. Babcock & Wilcox Co., 1948; devel. engr. Gen. Electric Co., 1951-52; sr. project engr. Allison divsn. Gen. Motors Corp., 1953; prof., head dept. mech. engring. Va. Poly. Inst. & State U., Blacksburg, 1964-83, cons., 1994—. Author: (with R.E. Dugan) Engineering Thermodynamics, 1996. NSF faculty fellow Swiss Fed. Inst. Tech., 1961-62. Mem. ASME (James Harry Potter Gold medal 1991), AIAA, Am. Soc. Engring. Edn., Sigma Xi. Achievements include research in fluid mechanics, thermodynamics. Home: 1500 Hollyhill Pl Blacksburg VA 24060-6200 Business E-Mail: jbjones@vt.edu.

JONES, JAMES LOGAN, JR., consulting firm executive, former national security advisor, retired military officer; b. Kansas City, Mo., Dec. 19, 1943; BS Sch. Fgn. Svc., Georgetown U., 1966; student, Amphibious Warfare Sch., Quantico, Va., 1973-74; Grad., Nat. War Coll., 1985; LittD (hon.), Georgetown U., 2002. Commd. 2d lt. USMC, 1967, advanced through grades to gen., 1999, ret., 2007; platoon and co. comdr. Vietnam, 1967-68; co. comdr. Camp Pendleton, Calif., 1968-70, Marine Barracks, Washington, 1970-73, 3d Marine Divsn., Okinawa, Japan, 1974-75; served in officer assignments sect. Marine Hdqrs., Washington, 1976-79; liasion officer to U.S. Senate Washington, 1979-84; comdr. 3d bn. 9th Marines 1st Marine Divsn., Camp Pendleton, 1985-87; from sr. aide to comdt. to mil. sec. to comdt. Hdqrs. Marine Corps., Washington, 1987-89; comdg. officer 24th Marine Expeditionary Unit, Camp Lejeune, NC, 1990-92; dep. dir. US European Command (USEUCOM), Stuttgart, Germany, 1992-94; comdg. gen. 2d Marine Divsn., Camp Lejeune, 1994-96; dep. chief of staff plans, policies, and ops. USMC, Washington, 1996-99; sr. mil. aide to sec. US Dept. Def., Washington, 1997-99; comdt. USMC, Washington, 1999—2003; comdr. US European Command (USEUCOM), Brussels, 2003—06; supreme allied comdr. NATO, Europe (SACEUR), Brussels, 2003—06; pres., CEO Inst. for 21st Century Energy, Washington, 2007—09; spl. envoy for Middle East security US Dept. State, Washington, 2007—08; asst. to the Pres. for nat. security affairs NSC, Washington, 2009—10; pres. Jones Group Internat. (JGI), Vienna, Va., 2011—. Chmn. Independent Commn. on the Security Forces of Iraq, 2007; bd. dirs. Invacare Corp., 2007—09, 2011—, General Dynamics Corp., 2011—. Decorated D.S.M., Silver Star, Legion of Merit with 3 gold stars, Bronze Star with Combat V, Can. Meritorious Svc. Cross Office: Jones Group International 8000 Towers Crescent Dr Ste 1350 Vienna VA 22182 Office Phone: 703-760-4498. Office Fax: 703-917-7907.

JONES, JAMES PARKER, federal judge; b. Tampa, Fla., July 3, 1940; s. Edmund Leroy and Nellie (Parker) J.; m. Mary Duke Trent, June 24, 1964; children: J. Trent, Benjamin P., Jonathan E. AB, Duke U., 1962; LLB, U. Va., 1965. Bar: Va. 1965. Asst. atty. gen. Va. Atty. Gen., Richmond, 1965-66; law clk. US Ct. Appeals, Richmond, 1966-68; atty. Penn, Stuart, Eskridge & Jones, Abingdon and Bristol, Va., 1968-96; judge US Dist. Ct. (We. Dist.) Va., Abingdon, 1996—2004, 2004—, chief judge, 2004—10. Bd. dirs. Va. Ctr. for Innovative Tech., Reston, Va., 1987-90. State senator Commonwealth of Va., 1983-88; mem. Dem. Nat. Com., 1982-92; mem. State Bd. Edn., 1990-96, pres., 1992-96. Fellow Am. Coll. Trial Lawyers (mem. Va. state com. 1995-96); mem. The Nature Conservancy (trustee Va. chpt. 1988-96). Democrat. Espicopalian. Office: US Dist Ct 180 W Main St Abingdon VA 24210-2844 Business E-Mail: jamesj@vawd.uscourts.gov.

JONES, JAN, state legislator; b. Warner Robins, Ga. m. Kalin Jones; children: Tramell, Peyton, Shelby, Griffin. BA in Journalism and English, U. Ga.; MBA in Fin., Ga. State U. Former auditor, analyst, mktg. dir. HBO, Inc.; mem. Dist. 38 Ga. House of Reps., 2002—04, mem. Dist. 46, 2004—, majority whip, 2009—10, spkr. pro tempore, 2010—. Apptd. mem. Land Conservation Partnership. Active Northpoint Cmty. Ch. Republican. Office: 13765 Brittle Rd Alpharetta GA 30004 Office Phone: 404-656-0137, 770-346-9667. Business E-Mail: jan.jones@house.ga.gov.

JONES, JANE D., human resources specialist; b. 1956; BA in Acctg., So. Meth. U., Dallas. Cert. compensation profl. V.p. total rewards Dynegy, Inc.; exec. dir. human resources Svc. Corp. Internat., Inc., 2003—05; v.p. human resources Service Corp. International, 2005—. Mem.: Soc. Human Resource Mgmt., WorldatWork. Office: Service Corp International Inc 1929 Allen Pky Houston TX 77019 Office Phone: 713-522-5141. Office Fax: 713-525-5586.

JONES, JEANNE PITTS, retired pre-school administrator; b. Richmond, Va., Oct. 19, 1938; d. Howard Talliaferro and Anne Elizabeth Pitts; children: Jack Hunter Jr., Judith Anne, James Howard, Jon Martain. BA, Marshall U., 1961, postgrad., 1962, Presbyn. Sch. Christian Edn., Richmond, 1974—94; MEd in Early Childhood Edn., Va. Commonwealth U., 2000. Cert. tchr. Va. Tchr. Richmond Pub. Schs., 1961-65; founder Bon View Sch. Early Childhood Edn., Richmond, 1971, tchr., 1971-91, dir., 1971—2011. Acad. affairs chmn. Good Shepherd Episcopal Sch. Bd., Ricmond, 1985—88; mentor Ecumenical Child Care Network Nat. Coun. Chs., Washington, 1990—92; ednl. cons., mentor Success By Six, 2002. Chmn. rm. parents Crestwood Sch. PTA Bd., Richmond, 1974—80; vol. mentor Cmtys. in Schs. Chesterfield County, 2011—; children's coord. Bon Air United Meth. Ch., Richmond, 1985—93; v.p. Bon Air United Meth. Ch. Women, Richmond, 1991—94; dir. Camp Friendship Bon Air United Meth. Ch., Richmond, 1992—2004; rep. Va. Conf. United Meth. Ch., 1993—95, weekday com., 1992—94; publicity chmn. Va. Swimming, Richmond, 1978—88; rep. Va. Children's Action Network. Recipient Spl. Mission recognition, Bon Air United Meth. Women, 1987. Mem.: Nat. Assn. Edn. for Young Children (validator 1993—2005, mentor 1994—98), Va. Assn. for Early Childhood Edn. (affiliate pres. 2002—04, 3d v.p. liaisons 2004—05, accreditation chair 2005—06, conf. treas. 2011), Chesterfield Coalition Early Childhood Educators (bd. dirs. 1993—97), Presch. Assn. Ch. Ednl. Dirs. (pres. 1993—95), Richmond Early Childhood Assn. (mem.-at-large 1994—96, rec. sec. 1996—98, 1998—2000, v.p. membership 2000—02, pres.-elect 2001—02, pres. 2002—04, past pres. 2004—06, accreditation chair 2006—07, historian 2007—, tres. 2009—14, bd. mem., v.p. programs 2014—, Richmond Early Childhood Adv. of the Yr. 2002, Educator of Yr. 2013). Avocations: tai chi, reading. Home: 9103 Whitaker Cir Richmond VA 23235-4053 Personal E-mail: jeannepjones@verizon.net.

JONES, JEFFREY ALLEN (JEFF JONES), men's college basketball coach; b. Owensboro, Ky., June 29, 1960; s. Bob Jones; m. Danielle Jones; children: Meghann, Madison Perry, Jeffrey Robert. BS in Psychology, U. Va., 1982. Part-time asst. coach U. Va. Cavaliers, 1982—86, asst. coach, 1986—90, head basketball coach, 1990—98; assoc. head coach U. RI Rams, 1999—2000; head basketball coach Am. U. Eagles, 2000—13, Old Dominion U. Monarchs, 2013—. Named Coach of Yr., Patriot League, 2009; named to Apollo HS Hall of Fame, Owensboro. Office: Old Dominion University Basketball Program Intercollegiate Athletics Jim Jarret Athletic Administration Bldg Norfolk VA 23529-0201*

JONES, JERRY (JERRAL WAYNE JONES), professional sports team owner; b. LA, Oct. 13, 1942; m. Gene Jones; children: Stephen, Charlotte, Jerry Jr. Grad., U. Ark., 1965, MBA, 1970. Exec. v.p. Modern Security Life, Springfield, Mo., 1965-69; founder Jones Oil and Land Lease, Okla.; owner, pres., gen. mgr. Dallas Cowboys, 1989—. Mem. mgmt. coun. exec. com. Nat. Football League, mem. broadcast com., mem. spl. com. on league econs., mem. bus. ventures com., mem. LA stadium working group. Appeared in (TV series) Entourage, 2010. Active Children's Med. Ctr. of Dallas, Happy Hill Farm Acad./Home, Kent Waldrep Paralysis Found., The Family Pl., The Rise Sch. of Dallas; co-founder Gene and Jerry Jones Family Charities, Gene and Jerry Jones Family Ctr. for Children, 1998; mem. nat. bd. Boys and Girls Club of Am.; mem. nat. adv. bd. Salvation Army, 1998—. Co-recipient Evangeline Booth award, Salvation Army, 1999, Chmn.'s award, Boys and Girls Club of Am., 2001, Children's Champion award for philanthropy, Dallas for Children Orgn., 2002, Annette G. Strauss Humanitarian award, Family Gateway Orgn., 2003, Hope award, Nat. Multiple Sclerosis Soc., 2005; named Ptnr. of Yr., Salvation Army, 1999; named one of Forbes 400: Richest Americans, 2006—, 50 Most Influential People in Sports Bus., Street & Smith's SportsBus. Jour., 2007—09, The Most Influential People in the World of Sports, Bus. Week, 2007, 2008. Mem.: Salvation Army William Booth Soc. Avocations: hunting, fishing, tennis, water-skiing, skiing. Office: Dallas Cowboys 1 Cowboys Pky Irving TX 75063-4999

JONES, JERRY, JR., professional sports team executive; b. Sept. 27, 1969; s. Jerral Wayne and Gene Jones; m. Lori Jones; children: James, Mary Chambers. BA, Georgetown U., Washington, 1992; JD, So. Meth. U., Dallas, 1995. Assoc. Godwin Pappas Ronquillo, LLP, 1995—96; v.p., gen. counsel Dallas Cowboys, 1996—, exec. v.p., chief sales and mktg. officer, 2001—; gen. mgr., pres., CEO Dallas Desperados, 2000—; pres. Dallas Cowboys Merchandising Ltd., 2001—. Mem. mktg. execs. com. NFL. Named one of Forty Under 40, Street & Smith's SportsBus. Jour., 2009. Office: Dallas Cowboys One Cowboys Pky Irving TX 75063

JONES, JERRY LEE, computer educator; b. Glade Spring, Va., Nov. 24, 1947; s. William and Mary (Waugh) Jones. BS, Va. State U., Petersburg, 1969, MEd, 1973; EdD, Va. Poly. Inst. and State U., Blacksburg, 1979; postgrad., East Tenn. State U., Johnson City, 1969—71, Morgan State U., Balt., 1970—71, U. Memphis, 1982—86, Va. Commonwealth U., Richmond, 1974, Purdue U., West Lafayette, Ind., 1995—2005, Ind. U., Bloomington, 2006—09. Tchr. H.S. Balt. City Pub. Schs., 1969—74; prof. J. Sargeant Reynolds C.C., Richmond, Va., 1974—2001. Part-time instr. Marymount Cath. HS, Richmond, Va., 1987—89; vis. prof. Emory and Henry Coll., Va., 2001—; adj. prof. Va. Highlands C.C., Abingdon, Va., 2001—02. Author: (textbook) Structured Programming Logic, 1985. Mem. Glade Spring Town Coun., Va., 2006—10. Methodist. Avocations: piano, organ. Office: Emory and Henry College PO Box 947 Emory VA 24327-0947 Home: PO Box 183 Glade Spring VA 24340-0183 Home Phone: 276-429-5104; Office Phone: 276-944-6697. Business E-Mail: jjones@ehc.edu.

JONES, JOE KENLEY, journalist; b. Greenville, SC, Feb. 24, 1935; s. J. Clyde and Mildred Idel (Smith) J.; m. Margaret Jean McPherson, Dec. 11, 1965; children— Stephanie, Jason, Eleanor. Student, Furman U., 1953-55; BS in Speech, Northwestern U., 1957, MS in Journalism, 1963; postgrad., Columbia U., 1964-65. Reporter City News Bur. of Chgo., 1962; reporter, cameraman KRNT-TV, Des Moines, 1963-64, WSB-TV, Atlanta, 1965-69; fgn. corr. NBC News, Asia, 1969-72; corr. NBC News (Southeast Bur.), Atlanta, 1972-98. Served with USNR, 1958-61. Recipient Overseas Press Club award for best television reporting from abroad, 1970 Mem. AFTRA, Nat. Acad. Television Arts and Scis. Presbyterian.

JONES, JOHNNY, men's college basketball coach; B, La. State U., Baton Rogue, 1985. Asst. coach La. State U. Fighting Tigers, 1984—94, assoc. head coach, 1994—97, head basketball coach, 2012—; asst. coach U. Memphis Tigers, 1997—99, assoc. head coach, 1999—2000; asst. coach U. Ala. Crimson Tide, 2000—01; head basketball coach U. North Tex. Mean Green, 2001—12. Office: Louisiana State University Basketball Program LSU Athletics Administration Bldg Baton Rouge LA 70803 Office Phone: 225-578-8217.

JONES, JOSEPH SEYMOUR, small business owner, poet; b. Gadsden, Ala., July 4, 1962; s. Jimmie and Sallie Carstarphen Jones. AS in Bus., Bishop State Jr. Coll., Mobile, Ala., 1983; BS in Bus., U. Mobile, 1986; MA in Tchg., Spring Hill Coll., 1994. Cert. elem. tchr. Ala. Dept. Edn., 1994. Acctg./engring. support staff U.S. Army Corps Engrs., Mobile, 1979—87; parts clk. Mobile County Pub. Schs., 1988—90, fuel specialist, 1990—94, cert. elem. tchr., 1994—98; owner, mng. founder Believe Enterprises, LLC, Mobile, 2001—. Author: A Poet's Poetic Expressions: Mustard Seeds, 2001, Lady! The World Forever Thanks You!, 1998, Lady! Le Monde à Jamais Vous Remercie!, 1999, numerous poems. Recipient Poet of Merit awards, Internat. Soc. Poets, Washington, 1998—2000; nominee Pulitzer prize, 2008. Avocations: restoring classic cars and antique homes, fishing, photography. Office: Believe Enterprises LLC PO Box 40216 Mobile AL 36640-0216

JONES, JUNE SHELDON, III, college football coach; b. Portland, Oreg., Feb. 19, 1953; 4 children. Attended, U. Oreg., 1971—72, U. Hawaii, 1973—74, Portland State U., 1975—76. Quarterback Atlanta Falcons, 1977—81, Toronto Argonauts, Can. Football League, 1982; quarterbacks coach U. Hawaii Warriors, 1983, head coach, 1999—2007; wide receivers coach Houston Gamblers, US Football League, 1984; offensive coord. Denver Gold, US Football League, 1985, Ottawa Roughriders, Can. Football League, 1986; quarterbacks coach Houston Oilers, 1987—88; quarterbacks and receivers coach Detroit Lions, 1989—90; offensive coord. Atlanta Falcons, 1991—93, head coach, 1994—96; quarterbacks coach, interim head coach San Diego Chargers, 1998; head coach So. Methodist U. Mustangs, 2008—. Founder June Jones Found. Named Nat. Coach of Yr., The Sporting News, 1999, CNN/Sports Ill., 1999, Western Athletic Conf. Coach of Yr., 1999, 2006, 2007. Office: So Methodist U PO Box 750216 Dallas TX 75275

JONES, KENNETH B., JR., retired surgeon, ER physician; b. Shreveport, La., 1940; MD, Tulane U., 1966. Diplomate Am. Bd. Surgery. Intern Confederate Meml. Med. Ctr., Shreveport, 1966—67; resident gen. surgery La. State U. and affiliated Hosp., Shreveport, 1969—73; fellow pediat. surgery Ala. Children's Hosp., 1973; chief staff Christus Schumpert Med. Ctr., Shreveport, 1999—2001; clin. asst. prof. surgery La. State U. Med. Ctr., 1984—. Presenter, lectr. in field. Co-author: Obesity Surgery: Principles and Practice, 2008; contbr. articles to profl. med. jours., chapters to books; edtl. bd. mem. Obesity Surgery and Surgery Obesity and related Diseases, 2007—12, assoc. editor Obesity Surgery, 2010—12. Fellow: ACS, Am. Soc. Metabolic and Bariatric Surgery (chmn. surg. access com. 1997—2000, sec. treas. 1998—2000, pres. 2001—02, chmn. surg. access com. 2002—06); mem.: AMA, Internat. Fedn. Surgery Obesity, Surg. Assn. La., Brazilian Soc. Bariatric Surgery (hon.), Am. Soc. Gen. Surgeons (nomination com. 2004), Southeastern Surg. Congress. Achievements include research in bariatric surgery. Home and Office: 6121 Fern Ave #112 Shreveport LA 71105 Personal E-mail: pbsurgkj@aol.com.

JONES, KENNETH BRUCE, surgeon; b. Scottsville, Ky., Apr. 17, 1953; s. Kenneth C. and Betty (Miller) J.; m. Carol Jean Munger, June 28, 1980; children: Daniel, Christopher, Elizabeth. BS, U. Ky., 1974; MD, Vanderbilt U., Nashville, 1978. Diplomate Am. Bd. Surgery; cert. advanced trauma life saving. Surg. intern and resident U. Louisville Med. Sch., 1978-80; resident in surgery East Tenn. U. Med. Sch., Johnson City, 1980-82, chief resident, 1983; surgeon Claiborne Surg. Group, Tazewell, Tenn., 1983-84, NEA Bapt. Clinic, Jonesboro, Ark., 1984—; sec. med. staff Meth. Hosp., 1986-87, chief of surgery, 1988-90, vice chief of staff, 1989-91, chief of staff, 1992-94; chief of surgery St. Bernard's Regional Med. Ctr., 1996-97; mem. hosp. bd. Regional Med. Ctr. N.E., 1997, NEA Baptist Hosp. Bd., 2010—, chmn. bd., 2014. Asst. clin. prof. surgery U. Ark. Area Health Edn. Ctr., Jonesboro, 1985—; cancer liaison of ACS Commn. on Cancer to St. Bernard's, 1996-2006; alumni bd. Vanderbilt Med. Sch., 2005—12; cons. Am. Bd. Surgery, 2005-07; pres. Ark. chpt. Am. Coll. Surgeons, 2009-10. Contbr. articles to profl. jours. Active sch. bd., 1993-98; deacon So. Bapt. Ch.; bd. dirs. N.E. Ark. Clinc Found, 2005-08, mem. bd. NEA Baptist Med. Clinic, 2000-, bd. mem., Operation New Life Surg. Missions to Honduras. Justin Potter med. scholar, 1974-78. Fellow: ACS (pres., Ark. chpt. 2009—10); mem.: NRA, Am. Soc. Bariatric and Metabolic Surgery, Soc. Am. Gastrointestinal Endoscopic Surgeons, Am. Cancer Soc. (pres. Craighead County unit 2000—01), Nat. Wild Turkey Fedn., Ducks Unltd., Phi Beta Kappa. Baptist. Avocations: hunting, jogging, toy trains, target shooting. Home: 2600 Nix Lake Dr Jonesboro AR 72404-0917 Office: NE Ark Surg Clinic 800 S Church St Ste 104 Jonesboro AR 72401-4154 Home Phone: 870-972-6895; Office Phone: 870-932-4875.

JONES, KENNETH H., JR., finance company executive; BA, Rice U., 1957, BS, 1958; LLB, U. Tex., 1961. Pvt. practice, Fort Worth, Tex.; shareholder Decker, Jones, McMackin, McClane, Hall & Bates, P.C., Fort Worth, Tex. Vice chmn. KBK Capital Corp. (formerly Marquette Comml. Fin., Inc.), 1995—99; bd. dirs., chmn. audit com. AmeriCredit Corp., 1988—. Bd. trustees Tex. Wesleyan U., 1988—, chmn. bd. trustees, 2010—; chmn. bd. Tex. Health Harris Methodist Found., First United Methodist Ch. Fort Worth Found.; past pres. YWCA Found. Forth Worth. Office: AmeriCredit Corp Bd Directors 801 Cherry St Ste 3900 Fort Worth TX 76102 Office Phone: 817-302-7000. Office Fax: 817-302-7101. Business E-Mail: kenneth.jones@americredit.com.

JONES, KENNETH WAYNE, state legislator; b. Canton, Miss., Mar. 3, 1966; m. Bobby Ann Jenkins; children: Kennedy, William. Attended, Jackson State U. Bus. owner; candidate Dist. 21 Miss. State Senate, 2003, mem. Dist. 21, 2008—. Democrat. Baptist. Home: 232

Boyd St Canton MS 39046 Office: PO Box 1018 Jackson MS 39215 Home Phone: 601-859-3438; Office Phone: 601-859-8844, 601-359-3232. E-mail: kjones@senate.ms.gov.

JONES, MIA L., state legislator; b. Jacksonville, Fla., Apr. 26, 1968; BS in Acctg., Fla. A&M U., Tallahassee, 1991, MBA, 1992. Dir. minority bus. affairs Duval County Pub. Schs.; councilwoman, dist. 10 Jacksonville City Coun., 2003, 2007; mem. Dist. 14 Fla. House of Reps., Tallahassee, 2008—, mem. edn. policy coun., elder and family svcs. policy com., preK-12 policy com., select policy coun. on strategic and econ. planning, mem. state univs. and pvt. colls. appropriations com. Bd. dirs. Essential Capital; JAC adv. com. The Fourth Jud. Cir.; mem. adv. bd. Healthy Start Coalition. Mem.: NAA-Fla. A&M U. (life), Alpha Kappa Alpha. Democrat. Baptist. Office: 3890 Dunn Ave Ste 901 Jacksonville FL 32218 also: 1402 The Capitol 402 S Monroe St Tallahassee FL 32399-1300 Office Phone: 904-924-1615, 850-488-6893.

JONES, MIKE, JR., state legislator; BS with honors, Birmingham Southern U.; JD, U. Ala. Mem. Andalusia City Coun., Ala., 2000—08, mayor pro-tem, 2004—08; mem. Dist. 92 Ala. House of Reps., 2011—. Mem. Andalusia Downtown Redevel. Authority, Ala. Easter Seals, First Bapt. Ch. Andalusia. Mem.: NRA, Ala. State Bar Assn., Andalusia C. of C. Republican. Office: Ala House of Reps Rm 536-A 11 S Union St Montgomery AL 36130 Office Phone: 334-242-7739. Business E-Mail: mike.jones@alhouse.gov.

JONES, MILTON H., JR., bank executive; m. Sheila Jones; children: Milton C., Tiffany. BS in Acctg., U. Notre Dame, Ind. Sr. planning analyst Bank of America Corp., various positions, fin. grp., 1977—90, exec. v.p., grp. mgr., fin. and adminstrn. of the Ga. bank, 1990—97, chmn., diversity adv. coun., mem., mgmt. ops. com., grp. exec., tech. & ops., tech. solutions exec., quality and productivity exec., consumer and comml. bank, quality and productivity exec., 2003, pres. Ga., fin. svcs. exec., pres. GA and Atlanta, 2007—; fin. exec. NationsBanc Svcs., Greensboro, NC, 1994—97, pres., dealer fin. svc. grp., 1997. Mem. Leadership Atlanta, Leadership Ga.; mem. exec. com. YMCA of Metro. Atlanta, Charlotte YMCA, Metro. Atlanta C. of C., Charlotte Ctr. City Ptnrs.; mem. bd. trustees Meharry Med. Coll., Nashville; bd. dirs. First Tee Charlotte; vice chmn. Ga. Coun. Econ. Edn. Recipient Career Achievement award, Nat. Assn. of Black Accts., Corp. Trailblazer award, Dollars and Sense Mag., Best and Brightest award, Pioneer award, Atlanta Urban Banker's Assn. Office: Bank of Am Corp 100 N Tryon St Charlotte NC 28255

JONES, PAUL, lawyer; BA, Washington & Lee U.; JD, Emory U. Sch. Law. Atty. Ford & Harrison, Atlanta; sr. counsel Fed. Express Corp., 1997—2007; mng. dir., assoc. gen. counsel US Airways Group, 2007—09, v.p. legal affairs, 2009—13; sr. v.p., gen. counsel American Airlines Group, Inc., 2013—. Office: American Airlines Group Inc 4333 Amon Carter Blvd Fort Worth TX 76155 Office Phone: 817-963-1234.*

JONES, PHILIP KIRKPATRICK, JR., lawyer; b. Baton Rouge, June 26, 1949; s. Philip Kirkpatrick and Mary Jane (Kincade) J.; m. Serena Catherine Cockayne, Apr. 5, 1980; children: Veronica Cockayne, Nicola Kincade, Clare Kirkpatrick, Philip Carruth Elliot. BA in Govt., Dartmouth Coll., 1971; JD, La. State U., 1974; LLB, diploma in legal studies, Cambridge U., Eng., 1976. Bar: La. 1974, U.S. Dist. Ct. (ea. and we. dist.) La. 1980, U.S. Ct. Appeals (5th and 11th cirs.) 1981, U.S. Dist. Ct. (mid. dist.) La. 1987, U.S. Supreme Ct. 1992. Law clk. to John A. Dixon Jr. Supreme Ct. La., New Orleans, 1974-75; staff atty. Presdl. Clemency Bd., Washington, 1975; lectr. U. Singapore, 1977-79; from assoc. to ptnr. Liskow & Lewis PC, New Orleans, 1980—. 1st lt. USAFR, 1975. Republican. Presbyterian. Office: Liskow & Lewis PC 50th Fl One Shell Square New Orleans LA 70139 Home Phone: 504-861-0672; Office Phone: 504-556-4132. Business E-Mail: pkjones@liskow.com.

JONES, RAY S., state legislator; b. Oct. 6, 1969; Mem. Banking & Ins. oms., Ky. Senate, Judiciary & Transp. Com.; atty. ones & Friend, PSC. Democrat. Baptist. Mailing: PO Drawer 3850 Pikeville KY 41502 Office: Capitol Annex Rm 214 Frankfort KY 40601 Office Phone: 606-432-5777, 502-564-8100 ext 681. Fax: 606-432-5154.

JONES, RONALD E., pastor, former mayor, Garland, Texas; b. Dallas; m. Peggy Jones; children: Ronald E. II, Daryl L. BA, Dallas Baptist U.; MS in Mgmt. and Psychology, Abilene Christian U. Lic. clinical pastoral counselor; cert. temperament counselor Nat. Christian Counselors Assn., mediator Dallas Mediation Services of Dallas, Inc, grad. Leadership Garland Class, 1981. Asst. city mgr. City of Garland, Tex., several exec. mgmt. positions Tex., parliamentarian to mayor and city coun. Tex., mayor Tex., 2007—13. Adj. prof. El Centro Coll., Dallas. Former scoutmaster, pack 501 Boy Scouts of America; sr. pastor New Hope Baptist Ch., Dallas, 2013—; bd. dir. Garland Civic Theater, Achievement Ctr. Recipient Outstanding Cmty. Svc., East Garland Cmty. Concerned Citizens, 1977, Achievement award, 1989, Outstanding Cmty. Svc., KRLD, 1977, Outstanding Svc., Phi Delta Kappa, 1997, Dallas Chpt. Jack and Jill of America, 2000, Mark of Excellence award, Nat. Form for Black Pub. Adminstrn., 2004, Outstanding Leadership award, 2005. Mem.: NAACP (life), PTA (life), Nat. Assn. Parliamentarians, Am. Tract Soc., Nat. Christian Counselors Assn. (profl. clin. mem.), Garland Citizens Police Acad. Alumni Assn., Kiwanis Club of Garland. Office: New Hope Baptist Ch 5002 S Central Expressway Dallas TX 75215*

JONES, RUSSEL CAMERON, civil engineer, educator; b. Tarentum, Pa., Oct. 18, 1935; s. Frederick Russel and Helena Doris (Elliot) Jones; m. Bethany S. Jones; children: Amy Sue, Kimberly Nicole, Tamara Melissa. BS, Carnegie Inst. Tech., 1957, MS, 1960, PhD, 1963; MALS, U. Del., 1994. Structural engr. Hunting, Larsen & Dunnels, Pitts., 1957-59; asst. prof. civil engring. MIT, 1963-66, assoc. prof., 1966-71; prof., chmn. dept. civil engring. Ohio State U., Columbus, 1971-76; dean Sch. Engring., U. Mass., Amherst, 1977-81; v.p. acad. affairs Boston U., 1981-87, v.p. acad. devel., 1985-87; pres. U. Del., Newark, 1987-88, univ. rsch. prof., 1988-95; exec. dir. NSPE, Alexandria, Va., 1995-98; mng. ptnr. World Expertise LLC, Falls Church, Va., 1998—; pres. Masdar Inst. Sci. and Tech., Abu Dhabi, United Arab Emirates, 2007—08; advisor Khalifa U., Abu Dhabi, United Arab Emirates, 2008—10. Recipient Collingwood prize, ASCE, 1966, Edmund Friedman profl. recognition award, 1981, Internat. medal for disting. contbns. to engring. edn., Australasian Assn. Engring. Edn., 1993, Chair's award, Am. Assn. Engring. Socs., 2005; named Del. Engr. of Yr., 1994; fellow, NDEA, 1959—62, ASCE, 1962—63. Fellow AAAS, ASCE (hon.; bd. dirs. 1969-71, 72-75, v.p. 1976-77), NSPE, Am. Soc. Engring. Edn., Accreditation Bd. Engring. and Tech. (bd. dirs. 1983-86, pres. 1987-88), Royal Soc. for Encouragement of Arts, Mfrs. and Commerce, Instn. of Engrs. of Ireland; mem. IEEE, Am. Assn. Higher Edn., Nat. Assn. for Sci., Tech. and Soc. (bd. dirs. 1992-95), Sigma Xi, Tau Beta Pi, Phi Kappa Ph, Chi Epsilon, Sigma Nu. Office: 2001 Mayfair Mclean Ct Falls Church VA 22043-1761 Personal E-mail: rcjonespe@aol.com.

JONES, SAM, state legislator; BA in History, Nicholls State U., 1975. Sheriff dep. St. Mary Parish, 1971—78; office mgr. Intracoastal Pipeyard and Oilfield, 1978—81; tchr. St. Joseph Cath. Sch. of Jeanerette, Jeanerette, La., 1981—82; mayor City of Franklin, Franklin, 1982—2004; sr. mem. Govs. Office, 2004—; contractor; real estate/investments agt.; mem. Dist. 50 La. House of Reps., 2008—, mem. mcpl., parochial and cultural affairs com., natural resources and environment com., transp., hwys. and pub. works com. Democrat. Office: Capitol Office State Capitol PO Box 44486 Baton Rouge LA 70804 also: 733 Main St Franklin LA 70538 Office Phone: 337-828-4100 370, 337-828-7778, 225-342-6945. E-mail: joness@legis.state.la.us.

JONES, SHEILA, state legislator; b. Feb. 16; Mem. Dist. 44 Ga. House of Reps., 2006—. Recipient Freshman Legislator of Yr., Cobb Democratic Women. Mem.: AFL-CIO, Internat. Assn. Machinists & Aerospace Workers. Democrat. Office: 611 Coverdell Legislative Office Bldg Atlanta GA 30334 Mailing: PO Box 784 Smyrna GA 30081-0784 Office Phone: 404-656-0323. E-mail: info@sheilajones.org.

JONES, SHERRY STONER, state legislator; b. Nashville, Tenn., Apr. 3, 1947; d. Charles L. and Jean Moss Stoner; m. Richard L. Jones, 1965; children: Richard Michael, Summer Michelle. Mem. Children & Youth Com.; owner Wholesale Jewelry Distbr., 1976—85; office mgr. Hosp. Corp. America, 1985—87; metro councilman Nashville, 1987—95; cons., 1987—; metro planning commr., 1991—94; state rep. Dist. 59 Tenn., 1995—; chmn. Davidson County Del., 1996—, Consumer Affairs Cmty., 1998—; majority caucus treas. Recipient Leadership award, Tenn. AFL-CIO, 1997, Legislator of Yr. award, Tenn. Podiatric Assn., 2000, Vanderbilt U. Law Sch., 2000, Family & Children's Svcs., 2000, AARP, 2000; named Tenn. Trial Lawyers, 1997. Mem.: Davidson County Dem. Women, Davidson County Women's Polit. Caucus. Democrat. Presbyterian. Office: 4947 Sherman Oaks Dr Nashville TN 37211 also: 26 Legislative Plz Nashville TN 37243-0159 Office Phone: 615-741-2035, 615-832-4211. Office Fax: 615-741-4322, 615-253-0290. Business E-Mail: rep.sherry.jones@capitol.tn.gov.

JONES, STEPHEN, lawyer; b. Lafayette, La., July 1, 1940; s. Leslie William and Gladys A. (Williams) J.; m. Virginia Hadden (dec.); 1 child, John Chapman; m. Sherrel Alice Stephens, Dec. 27, 1973; children: Stephen Mark, Leslie Rachael, Edward St. Andrew. Student, U. Tex., 1960—63; LLB, U. Okla., 1966. Sec. Rep. Minority Conf., Tex. Ho. of Reps., 1963; personal asst. to Richard M. Nixon NYC, 1964; adminstrv. asst. to Congressman Paul Findley, 1966-69; legal counsel to gov. of Okla., 1967; spl. asst. U.S. Senator Charles H. Percy and U.S. Rep. Donald Rumsfeld, 1968; mem. U.S. del. to North Atlantic Assembly NATO, 1968; staff counsel censure task force Ho. of Reps. Impeachment Inquiry, 1974; spl. U.S. atty. No. Dist. Okla., 1979; spl. prosecutor, spl. asst. dist. atty. State of Okla., 1977; judge Okla. Ct. Appeals, 1982; civil jury instrn. com. Okla. Supreme Ct., 1979—81; adv. com. ct. rules Okla. Ct. Criminal Appeals, 1980; now mng. ptnr. Stephen Jones & Assoc., Enid, Okla. Adj. prof. U. Okla., 1973—76; instr. Phillips U., 1982—90; bd. dirs. Coun. on the Nat. Interest Found.; mem. adv. con. Ctr. Am. History U. Tex., Austin, 2007—; sr. coun. Okla. Commr. Ins., 2011—. Author: Oklahoma and Politics in State and Nation, 1907-62, 1974, Others Unknown: The Oklahoma City Bombing Case and Conspiracy, 1998; co-author: France and China, The First Ten Years, 1964-74, 1991, Vernon's Oklahoma Forms 2d Criminal Practice & Procedure Vols. I, II, 1999; contbr. articles to profl. jours. Bd. dirs., coun. mem. Nat. Interest Found.; acting chmn. Rep. State Com., Okla., 1982; Rep. nominee Okla. atty. gen., 1974, US Senate, 1990; mem. Rep. State Fin. Com., 2006—10; spl. counsel to Gov. Okla., 1995; apptd. chief def. counsel by US Dist. Ct., Oklahoma City, US vs. Tim McVeigh, Oklahoma City Bombing Case, 1995-97; mem. vestry St. Matthews Episc. Ch., 1974, sr. warden, 1983-84, 89-90; mem. adv. bd. Ctr. for Am. History U. Tex., Austin, 2007-10, mem. Rep. State Fin. Com., 2010, sr. counselor Okla. Comm. Ins., 2011- Mem.: Okla. Bar Assn., Garfield County Bar Assn., Beacon Club. Office: PO Box 472 Enid OK 73702-0472 Office Phone: 580-242-5500. Business E-Mail: sjones@stephenjoneslaw.com.

JONES, STEPHEN, professional sports team executive; b. Little Rock, June 21, 1964; s. Jerry and Gene Jones; m. Karen Jones; children: Jessica, Jordan, Caroline, John Stephen Jr. BS in Chem. Engring., U. Ark., Fayetteville, 1988. Engr. JMC Exploration, 1988—89; joined as v.p. Dallas Cowboys, Irving, Tex., 1989, COO, exec. v.p., dir. player devel.; pres. Tex. Stadium, Arlington. Mem. Young Pres. Organ., Dallas Citizens Coun.; bd. dirs. Episc. Sch. Dallas, Kent Waldrep Nat. Paralysis Found., SMU Athletic Forum, Cotton Bowl Athletic Assn., Cir. Ten Coun. of Boy Scouts America. Office: Dallas Cowboys 1 Cowboys Pky Irving TX 75063

JONES, STEVE CARMICHAEL, federal judge; b. Athens, Ga., 1957; m. Lillian Kincey. BBA, U. Ga., 1978, JD, 1987. Bar: Ga. 1987, Superior Cts. Ga. 1987, Supreme Ct. Ga. 1988, Ga. Ct. Appeals 1988, US Dist. Ct. (middle dist.) Ga. 1994, US Supreme Ct. 2007. Asst. dist. atty. Western Judicial Cir. Dist. Atty.'s Office, Athens, Ga., 1987—93; judge Athens-Clarke County Mcpl. Ct., Ga., 1993—95; superior ct. judge Tenth Superior Ct. (western judicial cir.) Ga., 1995—2011; judge US Dist Ct (northern dist.) Ga., Altanta, 2011—. Bd. dirs. Athens Area Cmty. Found., 2007—, chmn., 2007—10. Bd. dirs. U. Ga. Alumni Assn., 2007—, pres., 2011—; bd. visitors Riverside Mil. Acad., 2009—. Recipient Chief Justice Robert Benham Award for Cmty. Svc., 1998, Vol. of Yr. Award, Jr. League of Athens and Athens First Bank & Trust, 2007, Heart of Gold Award, St. Mary's, 2007. Mem.: Nat. Football Found. (2nd v.p. 2009), State Bar of Ga. Office: Richard B Russell Federal Building and Courthouse 75 Spring St, SW Atlanta GA 30303-3361 Office Phone: 404-215-1228.

JONES, STEVEN CHRISTOPHER, state legislator; b. Suffolk, Va., June 23, 1958; m. Karen Hope Harrison; 1 child, Kaitlin. City councilman, Suffolk, 1986—98; v. mayor, 1986—90; mayor, 1992—96; state del. Dist. 76, 1999—; mem. Privileges & Elections Com., Counties, Cities & Towns Com., Agr. Com., Sci. & Tech. Com., 1999—; house del. Va.; chmn. Western Tidewater Regional Jail Authority; mem. bd. dir. Forward Hampton Rds. Recipient Alumni Star award, Sch. Pharmacy, Med. Coll. Va., 1992; named Va. Retailer of Yr., Retail Merchants Assn., 1995. Fellow: Mt. Zion; mem.: North Suffolk Rotary Club. Republican. Mailing: Gen Assembly Bldg Off 419 PO Box 406 Richmond VA 23218

JONES, TODD, retail executive; Front svc. clerk to various store level positions Publix Super Markets, Inc., New Smyrna Beach, Fla., 1980—88, store mgr. Jacksonville, Fla., 1988—97, dist. mgr., 1997—99, regional dir., 1999—2003, v.p. Jacksonville divsn., 2003—05, sr. v.p. product bus. devel. Lakeland, Fla., 2005—07, pres., 2007—. Office: Publix Super Markets Inc 3300 Publix Corporate Pky Lakeland FL 33811 Office Phone: 863-688-1188.

JONES, TOM, construction executive; BA in Edn., U. Northern Iowa. Sales mgr. Des Moines Dist. Martin Marietta Materials, Inc., 1999—2000, v.p., gen. mgr. Des Moines Dist., 2000—05, v.p., gen. mgr. Western Divsn. Lewisville, Tex., 2005—06, pres. Western Divsn., 2006—. Office: Martin Marietta Materials Inc Western Division 1825 Lakeway Dr, Ste 300 Lewisville TX 75057 Office Phone: 972-350-8200.

JONES, VIRGINIA MCCLURKIN, retired social worker; b. Anniston, Ala., Mar. 13, 1935; d. Louie Walter and Virginia Keith (Beaver) McClurkin; m. Charles Miller Jones, Jr., Mar. 16, 1957; children: Charles Miller III, V. Grace. BA, Agnes Scott Coll., 1957; MA, U. Tenn., 1965, MSSW, 1979. English instr. U. Tenn., Knoxville, 1967-71; religious edn. dir. Oak Ridge Unitarian Ch., 1972-73, 76-78; co-owner, mgr. The Bookstore, 1973-76; English instr. Roane State C.C., 1975-80; pvt. practice clin. social work Oak Ridge, 1980-98. Cons. Mountain Cmty. Health Ctr., Coalfield, Tenn., 1980-83, Valley Ridge Hospice, 1987-89. Contbr. articles to newspapers. Elected mem. Oak Ridge Charter Comm., 2008—. Mem.: NASW, AAUW, Rotary (Svc. award 2000—01). Democrat. Episcopalian. Office: 969 Oak Ridge Turnpike Oak Ridge TN 37830-6554

JONES, W. S. (STEVE JONES), management educator, former dean; b. Elkin, NC; m. Lisa Jones; 4 children. BA in Economics, U. NC, 1974; MBA, Harvard Bus. Sch., 1978; PhD (hon.), Queensland U. Tech., 2002. Worked in drive systems divsn. GE; mgmt. cons. McKinsey & Co., Atlanta, 1984—88, Melbourne, Australia, 1988—90; joined as cons. ANZ Banking Group, Australia, 1990, mng. dir. retail ops., 1993—95, New Zealand mng. dir., 1995—96; CEO Suncorp Metway Ltd., Brisbane, Queensland, Australia, 1996—2002; dean Kenan-Flagler Bus. Sch., U. NC, Chapel Hill, 2003—07, prof. mgmt. & organizational behavior, 2003—. Recipient Centenary Medal for svc. to bus. and commerce through banking and fin, Australian Govt., 2003; named one of Top 50 CEOs in Australia, The Bulletin mag., 2001. Office: Kenan-Flagler Bus Sch U NC Chapel Hill Campus Box 3490 McColl 4417 Chapel Hill NC 27599-3490 Office Phone: 919-962-4456. E-mail: wsj@unc.edu.

JONES, WALTER BEAMAN, JR., United States Representative from North Carolina; b. Pitt County, NC, Feb. 10, 1943; s. Walter Beaman Jones; m. Joe Anne Jones; 1 child. BA in Hist., Atlantic Christian Coll., Wilson, NC, 1967. Mgr. Walter B. Jones Office Supply Co., 1967-73; salesman Dunn Assoc., 1973-82; pres. Benefit Reserves, Inc., 1989-94, Judson Co., 1990-94; mem. NC House of Reps., 1983-92, US Congress from 3rd NC Dist., 1995—, US House Armed Services Com., 1995—, US House Financial Services Com., 1995—2012. With NC Nat. Guard, 1967—71; mem. adv. bd. Disabled Children's Relief Fund. Recipient George (Buck) Gillispie Congl. award, Meritorious Svc., Blinded Am. Vets. Found., 2004, George L. Murphy award, United Seniors Assn., Golden Bulldog award, Watchdogs of the Treasury, Inc., Pro-Nat. Security award, Ctr. Security Policy, Spirit of Enterprise award, US C. of C.; named Taxpayer Hero, Coun. Citizens against Govt. Waste, Guardian of Small Bus., Nat. Fedn. Ind. Bus.; named a Friend of the Family, Christian Coalition, Friend of the Farmer, Am. Farm Bur. Fedn. Republican. Roman Catholic. Office: US House of Representatives 2333 Rayburn House Office Bldg Washington DC 20515 also: 1105-C Corporate Dr Greenville NC 27858-4211 Office Phone: 202-225-3415, 252-931-1003. Office Fax: 252-931-1002.*

JONES, WALTER F., civilian military employee, director; BSME, Clemson U., PhD, MS in Engring. Mechanics; MS in Natural Resource Strategy, Indsl. Coll. of the Armed Forces, Ft. Lesley J. McNair, Washington, DC. Dep. for rsch. sciences Office if the Asst. Sec. of the Air Force Acquisition US Air Force, dep. for sci. and technology, Office of the Nat. Security Space Architect; sr. program analyst, Office of the Deputy Dir. Central Intelligence for Cmty. Management; dir. aerospace and materials sciences Air Force Office of Scientific Rsch., Arlington, Va.; dir. plans and programs Air Force Rsch. Laboratory, Wright-Patterson AFB, Ohio; exec. dir. Office of Naval Rsch., 2007—. Faculty position U. Fla., U. Tennessee, Clemson U. Office: Office of Naval Research One Liberty Ctr 875 N Randolph St Ste 1425 Arlington VA 22203-1995*

JONES, WARREN A., councilman; BA in Polit. Sci., U. Fla. Councilman, Dist. 9 Jacksonville City Coun., Fla., 1979—99, 2007—, coun. pres., 1991—93. Mem. Fin., Recreation, Cmty Devel. & Rules Coms.; ex-officio mem. Jacksonville Econ. Devel. Commn.; vice chmn. Spl. Com. on City Pension Reform. Democrat. Office: 117 W Duval St Ste 425 Jacksonville FL 32202 Office Phone: 904-630-1386, 904-630-1395. Business E-Mail: wajones@coj.net.

JONTZ, JEFFRY ROBERT, lawyer; b. Stuart, Iowa, May 28, 1944; s. John Leo Jontz and Leora Burnette (Pittman) Myers; m. Sharyn Sue Kopriva, June 8, 1968; 1 child, Eric Barrett. BA, Drake U., 1966; JD with distinction, U. Iowa, 1969. Bar: Iowa 1969, Fla. 1971, U.S. Dist. Ct. (mid. dist.) Fla. 1971, Ohio 1972, U.S. Ct. Appeals (5th cir.) 1972, U.S. Ct. Appeals (11th cir.) 1981, U.S. Tax Ct. 1983. Law clk. to Hon. Charles R. Scott U.S. Dist. Ct. (mid. dist.) Fla., Jacksonville, 1969-70; to Hon. Bryan Simpson U.S. Ct. Appeals (5th cir.), Jacksonville, 1970-71; assoc. Jones, Day, Cockley & Reavis, Cleve., 1971-72; asst. U.S. atty. U.S. Dist. Ct. (mid. dist.) Fla., Orlando, 1972-74; pvt. practice Orlando, 1974—; ptnr. Young, Turnbull & Linscott, Orlando, 1974-79, Baker & Hostetler, Orlando, 1979, DeWolf, Ward & Morris, Orlando, 1979-84, Jontz, Russell & Hull, Orlando, 1985-86, Holland & Knight, 1986-96, Carlton Fields, Orlando, 1996—2005, Swann & Hadley, Winter Pk., Fla., 2005—; mem. State of Fla. Statewide Nominating Com., 2012—. Contbr. articles to profl. jours.; mem. editl. bd. Iowa Law Rev., 1968. Chmn. Fed. Jud. Rels. Com., 2001—04; past bd. dirs. Door Drug Rehab. Ctr. Ctrl. Fla.; bd. dirs. Fla. Symphony Orch., 1985—93, Jr. Achievement Ctrl. Fla., 1997—2005; mem. code enforcement bd. City of Maitland, Fla., 1990—92; chmn bd. adjustment City of Winter Park, Fla., 1995—2005, 2012—; mem. parents com. Dartmouth Coll., 1995—99; trustee Winter Pk. Libr., 2013—; mem. long range planning com., former county commiteeman Orange County Reps., Fla.; elder Winter Pk. Presbyn. Ch., 2012—; past chmn. bd. trustees First Congl. Ch., Winter Park. Recipient Outstanding Individual Cmty. Leadership award, Vol. Ctr. Ctrl. Fla., 1991. Mem.: ABA (mem. comml. transactions litig. com., others), Winter Pk. Library Bd., Am. Arbitration Assn. (comml. arbitrator 2005—), Orange County Bar Assn. (chmn. jud. rels. com. 1995—97, mem. bankruptcy com.), Iowa State Bar Assn., Fla. Bar (mem. 9th cir. grievance com. 1979—82, chmn. comml. litig. com. 1981—82, mem. com. jud. adminstrn., selection and tenure 1985—86, mem. jud. nominating procedures com. 1995—96, mem. bankruptcy and creator's rights com., lectr. seminars), Ctrl. Fla. Bankruptcy Lawyers Assn., Am. Bankruptcy Inst., U. Iowa Alumni Assn. (bd. dirs. 2003—09), Drake U. Nat. Alumni Assn. (bd. dirs. 1981—93, past chmn. ctrl. Fla. chpt., pres.'s cir. coun.), Citrus Club, Winter Park Racquet Club (pres. 1989—94, 1996—98, bd. govs., sec., v.p.), Order of Coif, Phi Delta Phi, Tau Kappa Epsilon, Omicron Delta Kappa. Office: Swann Hadley Stump Dietrich & Spears PA PO Box 1961 Winter Park FL 32790-1870 also: 1031 W Morse Blvd Winter Park FL 32789 Office Phone: 407-647-2777. Business E-Mail: jjontz@swannhadley.com.

JOOST, STEPHEN C., councilman; b. Jacksonville, Mar. 19, 1962; m. Nicole Joost; children: Emma, Christopher. BS in Acctg., Tulane U., 1984. CPA Fla. Acct. Deloitte & Touch, 1984—89; controller Loop Restaurants, 1990—93; v.p. & CFO Firehouse Subs, Inc., 1994—; v.p., CFO, co-dir. franchise ops. Firehouse Restaurant Group, Inc., 1995—; councilman-at-large, Group 3 Jacksonville City Coun. Vice chmn. Land Use & Zoning Com.; mem. Seaport & Airport Spl. Com., Spl. Com. on City Pension Reform; chmn. Tower Rev. Com.;

treas. Transp. Planning Org.; coun. liaison JEA. Chmn. Muscular Dystrophy Assn. Tennis Tournament; hon. chmn. Nat. Rep. Congl. Com. Bus. Adv. Coun.; bd. mem. Justice Coalition; mem. Fla. Hospitality Inst.-Fresh Ministries, Mayor Peyton's Transition Subcommittee for Adminstrn. & Fin.; former treas. & sec. Salvation Army Adv. Bd. Northeast Fla. Area Command. Mem.: Jacksonville Sister Cities Assn. (coun. liaison), Tulane Acctg. Honor Soc. Republican. Office: 117 W Duval St Ste 425 Jacksonville FL 32202 Office Phone: 904-630-1386. Business E-Mail: joost@coj.net.

JORDAHL, RONALD IVAN, librarian, educator; b. Buffalo Ctr., Iowa, May 29, 1936; s. George Harry and Leota Eola (Yost) Jordahl; m. Faye Lorraine Bixby, Aug. 29, 1964; children: Philip, Ronald, Rebekah. BA, Luther Coll., 1958; MLS, U.S.C., 1988. Libr., tchr. Prairie Bible Coll. and Gad. Sch., Three Hills, Alta., Canada, 1966—98; libr. Southern Evangelical Seminary, 1998—. Contbr. articles to profl. jours.;, editor The Christian Libr. Mem.: ALA, Assn. Christian Libr. (bd. dirs. 1975—92, pres. 1981—82), Can. Librs. Assn. Office: Southern Evangelical Seminary 3000 Tilley Morris Rd Matthews NC 28105 Home: 2500 Farecroft Way Monroe NC 28110 Business E-Mail: rjordahl@ses.edu.

JORDAK, JOHN A., JR., lawyer; b. Saginaw, Mich., Dec. 9, 1967; AB cum laude, Duke U., 1990; JD with distinction, Emory U., Atlanta, 1993. Bar: Ga. 1993. Ptnr., chmn., securities litig. group Alston & Bird LLP, Atlanta. Writes and lectures frequently on securities litig. and regulation. Alumni Admissions Adv. Com. Duke U. Recipient NC Scholars Scholarship, Duke U., Am. Jurisprudence award in Contracts; named a Ga. Super Lawyer, Atlanta Mag., 2006, 2007. Office: Alston & Bird LLP One Atlantic Ctr 1201 W Peachtree St Atlanta GA 30309-3424 Office Phone: 404-881-7868. Office Fax: 404-253-8358. Business E-Mail: john.jordak@alston.com.

JORDAN, ADALBERTO JOSE, federal judge; b. Havana, Cuba, 1961; m. Esther Jordan. BA, U. Miami, 1984, JD, 1987. Law clk. to Hon. Thomas Alonzo Clark US Ct. Appeals (11th cir.), 1987—88; law clk. to Justice Sandra Day O'Connor US Supreme Ct., Washington, 1988—89; assoc. Steel, Hector & Davis, Miami, 1989—94, ptnr., 1994; asst. US atty. (southern dist.) Fla. US Dept. Justice, Miami, 1994—99, dep. chief appellate divsn., 1996—98, chief appellate divsn., 1998—99; judge US Dist. Ct. (southern dist.) Fla., Miami, 1999—2012, US Ct. Appeals (11th Cir.), Miami, 2012—. Adj. prof. U. Miami Sch. Law, 1990—. Office: US Court Appeals 99 NE 4th St #1212 Miami FL 33132 Office Phone: 305-579-4430.

JORDAN, CARMEN ANGELLE, bank executive; m. Matt Jordan; children: Kelsey, Carmen. BBA in Fin., Lamar U., Beaumont, Tex. Br. mgr. First Interstate Bank; comml. lender Amegy Bank Tex., Houston, 1997—2002, founder energy services lending divsn., sr. v.p., mgr. corp. energy services divsn., 2002—. Active Big Brothers/Big Sisters. Named one of 25 Women to Watch, US Banker, 2007, 2008. Office: Amegy Bank Tex PO Box 4837 Houston TX 77210-4837 Office Phone: 713-888-4610.

JORDAN, CHARLES MILTON, lawyer; b. Houston, Apr. 3, 1949; m. Jeanette Jordan; children: Nicole, John, Rebecca. BBA, U. Tex., 1971, JD, 1975. Bar: Tex. 75, U.S. Dist. Ct. (so. dist.) Tex. 76, U.S. Supreme Ct. 78, U.S. Ct. Appeals (5th cir.) 79, U.S. Dist. Ct. (no. dist.) Tex. 82, U.S. Dist. Ct. (we. and ea. dists.) Tex. 83. Assoc. Troutman, Earle & Hill, Austin, 1975, Simpson & Burwell, Texas City, 1976—78, Smith & Herz, Galveston, Tex., 1978—80; ptnr. Dibrell & Greer, Galveston, 1980—85, Barlow, Todd, Crews & Jordan PC, Houston, 1986—88, Barlow, Todd, Jordan & Oliver, LLP, Houston, 1988—99, Barlow, Todd, Jordan & Jones, LLP, Houston, 1999—2002, Daughtry & Jordan, P.C., Houston, 2003—. Commr. Commn. Texas City/Galveston Ports, 1984. 1st lt. USAF, 1971—77. Recipient Outstanding Young Man Am. award, U.S. Jaycees, 1980. Mem. Tex. Bar Assn., Galveston County Bar Assn. (pres. 1981-82, bd. dirs. 1985-88), Tex. Young Lawyers Assn (bd. dirs. 1982-85, Outstanding Dir. award 1983-84), Galveston County Young Lawyers Assn. (pres. 1979-80, Outstanding Young Lawyer award 1981). Office: Daughtry & Jordan PC 17044 El Camino Real Houston TX 77058-2630 Business E-Mail: cmjordan@daughtryjordan.com.

JORDAN, D. BRYAN, bank executive; BA in Fin. & Acctg., Catawba Coll. With KPMG, Wachovia Corp. (formerly First Union Corp.), Charlotte NC; exec. v.p., corp. contr. Regions Financial Corp., Birmingham, Ala., 2000—02, exec. v.p., CFO, 2000—07; CFO First Horizon Nat. Corp., 2007—08, chmn., pres., CEO, 2008—. Mem.: Regions Asset Mgmt. Co., Rebsamen Ins. Inc. (dir.). Office: First Horizon National Corp 165 Madison Ave Memphis TN 38103 Office Phone: 901-523-4444. Business E-Mail: djordan@firsthorizon.com.

JORDAN, DANIEL PORTER, JR., foundation administrator, historian, educator; b. Phila., Miss., July 22, 1938; s. Daniel Porter and Mildred M. (Dobbs) J.; m. Lewellyn Lee Schmelzer, Dec. 18, 1961; children: Daniel P., Grace Dobbs, Katherine Lewellyn. BA, U. Miss., 1960, MA, 1962; PhD, U. Va., Charlottesville, 1970; PhD (hon.), Drake U., Des Moines, Iowa, 2005. Various tchg. positions overseas divsn. U. Md., 1962-65, Richmond, Va., 1968-69, U. Va., summers 1970-72; prof. history Va. Commonwealth U., Richmond, 1969-84, Ariz. State, 1995; dir. Stratford Hall Summer Sem., 1981-91; exec. dir. Thomas Jefferson Found. (Monticello), 1985—, pres., 1994—2008; founding ptnr. Bryan & Jordan Consulting LLC, 2008—. Scholar in residence U. Va., 1985—. Author: Political Leadership in Jefferson's Virginia, 1983, A Richmond Reader, 1733-1983, 1983, Tobacco Merchant: The Story of Universal Leaf Tobacco Company, 1995. Mem. adv. com. Papers of Thomas Jefferson, Princeton U.; mem. Sec. of Interior's adv. bd. Nat. Pk. Sys., 1984-88, chmn., 1987-88; mem. Jeffersonian Restoration Adv. Bd., U. Va., 1985—; mem. rev. bd. Va. Hist. Landmarks Commn., 1981-92, chmn., 1989-92; mem. Nat. Pks. and Conservation Bd., 1989-92, Ea. Nat. Bd., 1991-2001; pres. Richmond Civil War Roundtable, 1983; trustee Nat. Trust for Hist. Preservation, 1999—, vice chair, 2008-; bd. dirs. Fund for the U.S. Capitol Visitor Ctr., 2000—; mem. adv. bd. Freedom Forum Mus., 2002—, Eudora Welty Found., 2002—; mem. curatorial adv. bd. US Senate, 2004—, Gilder Lehrmen Inst. Am. History, 2008-, Focused Ultrasound Found., 2008-. Served with inf. US Army, 1962-65. Thomas Jefferson Found. fellow, 1965-68; recipient award of merit Am. Assn. for State and Local History, 1977, 88, Pub. Svc. award US Dept. of Interior, 1990, Medal for Va. Svc., AIA, 1993; named Outstanding Virginian, 2006. Mem. Am. Antiquarian Soc., Va. Hist. Soc. (bd. dirs. 1986-91), Mass. Hist. Soc., So. Hist. Assn. (life), Orgn. Am. Historians (life), Walpole Soc., Phi Beta Kappa (pres. Alpha of Va. 1995-98), Omicron Delta Kappa, Sigma Chi., Am. Acad. in Rome(James Marston Fitch Resident 2009, vis. scholar 2012) Methodist. Home and Office: 3625 Raleigh Mountain Trail Charlottesville VA 22903 Business E-Mail: dpjordan@live.com.

JORDAN, DANIEL PORTER, III, federal judge; b. Ft. Bragg, NC, 1964; BBA, U. Miss., 1987; JD, U. Va., 1993. Bar: Miss. 1993. Assoc. Butler, Snow, O'Mara, Stevens & Cannada, PLLC, 1993—99, equity mem., 2000—06; judge US Dist. Ct. (so. dist.) Miss., 2006—. Office: 245 E Capitol St Ste 110 Jackson MS 39201 Office Phone: 601-965-4418.

JORDAN, DARRYL, state legislator; Former state rep. Dist. 96, Ga.; former mem. Children & Youth Com., Edn. Com., Game Com., Fish & Pks. Com.; state rep. Dist. 83 Ga., 2003—04; state rep. Dist. 77 Ga., 2004—. Democrat. Office: 316 Herring Way Riverdale GA 30274 Business E-Mail: djordan@legis.state.ga.us.

JORDAN, DAVID, state legislator; b. Leflore Co, Miss., Apr. 3, 1933; m. Christine Bell Jordan; children: David Jr., Joyce, Donald, Darryl. Former city councilman, Greenwood, Miss.; former vice chmn. Pub. Property Com.; former sci. tchr.; mem. Dist. 24 Miss. State Senate, 1993—; mem. State Dem. Exec. Com.; ret. Mem.: NAACP, MMA, NBC-LEO, Nat. & Miss. Edn. Assns., Greenwood Voters League (pres.). Democrat. Baptist. Mailing: PO Box 8173 Greenwood MS 38930 Home Phone: 662-453-5361; Office Phone: 601-359-3244. Fax: 662-455-7636; Office Fax: 601-359-9210. Business E-Mail: djordan@senate.ms.gov.

JORDAN, FRED, state legislator; Mem. Dist. 69 Okla. House of Representatives, 2007—. Republican. Address: 121 W 124 Jenks OK 74037 Office: Oklahoma House of Representatives 2300 N Lincoln Blvd Rm 333 Oklahoma City OK 73105 Office Phone: 405-557-7331. E-mail: fred.jordan@okhouse.gov.

JORDAN, HILARY PETER, lawyer; b. Mineola, NY, July 30, 1952; s. Thomas F. and Clorinda G. Jordan; m. Judith Lynn Spencer, Sept. 7, 1984. BA, U. Ariz., 1974; JD, Harvard U., 1977. Bar: Ga. 1977, US Dist. Ct. (no. dist.) Ga. 1977, US Ct. Appeals (5th cir.) 1978. Assoc. Kilpatrick Stockton LLP, Atlanta, 1977-84, ptnr., chair, Leveraged Fin. Team, 1984—2010; ptnr. McGuireWoods LLP, 2010—. Co-author: Georgia Jurisprudence: Uniform Commercial Code, 1995. Mem.: ABA, Ga. Fin. Lawyer Assn. (bd. dirs.), State Bar of Ga. Office: McGuireWoods LLP 1230 Peachtree St NE Ste 2100 Atlanta GA 30309-3534 Office Fax: 404-541-3256. Business E-Mail: hjordan@mcguirewoods.com.

JORDAN, JAMES RANDALL, plastic surgeon, educator; b. Mobile, Ala., Jan. 21, 1955; m. Allison Jordan. MD, U. Fla. Coll. Medicine, Gainseville, 1986. Diplomate Am. Bd. Otolaryngology, 1992, Am. Bd. Facial Plastic and Reconstructive Surgery, 1995. Prof. U. Miss. Med. Ctr., Jackson, 2002—, vice chmn. dept. otolaryngology, 2003—. Contbr. scientific papers, articles to profl. jours. Recipient Resident Book award, 1989—91; named Tchr. of Yr., U. Miss. Med. Ctr., 2003. Mem.: Am. Bd. Facial Plastic and Reconstructive Surgery (guest bd. examiner 2013, mem. publs. com.), Am. Acad. Otolaryngology (chmn. edn. subcom. 2013), Am. Acad. Plastic and Reconstructive Surgery (chmn. continuing med. edn. com. 2010), Am. Acad. Facial Plastic and Reconstructive Surgery. Methodist. Achievements include patents pending for malar implant with dual-plane adhesion. Office: University Miss Med Ctr Dept Otolaryngology and Comm Jackson MS 39216 Business E-Mail: jrjordan@umc.edu.*

JORDAN, JONATHAN CHRISTIAN, state legislator; m. Tracie McMillan Jordan; children: Landon Jordan, Lily Grace. BA in Economics & Politics, magna cum laude with Honors, Wake Forest U., 1990; MBA, Vanderbilt U., 1992; MPA, JD, U. N.C., Chapel Hill. Mem. Ashe County Bd. of Realtors; mem., bd. dirs. Ashe Pregnancy Care Ctr.; mktg., svcs., mktg. concentration; chmn.; human resource, org. mgmt. concentration; rsch. assistantship in Pub. adminstrn.; mem. Internet News and Polit. Commentary Website; legal Counsel Fifth Congressional District Rep. Exec. Com.; mem., bd. dirs. High Country Bus. Network; editor in chief Old Gold and Black student newspaper; mem., adv. coun. Legal Aid of NC, Inc.; mem. NC Rep. Party Exec. Com.; editor in chief The Bottom Line student newspaper; dir., rsch. The John Locke Found., 1997—99; human resources mgr. Acting Legal Counsel, Enterprise Network Svc., Inc., 1999—2000; pres., editor Network Carolina News Co., LLC, 2000—01; comm. dir. N.C. Republican Party, 2001—03; atty. Stokes County, NC, 2003—06; mem. Jordan and Jordan Law Offices, PLLC, 2005—, NC Rep. State Conv., 2007—10; vice chmn. Ashe County Rep. Party, 2007—10; mem. Dist. 93 NC House Of Representatives, 2011—. Bd. dirs. Ashe County Home Builders Assn., Ashe County Free Med. Clinic, Ashe County C. of C. Recipient gold scholarship recipient, NC law lic., 1997. Mailing: PO Box 744 Jefferson NC 28640 Office: North Carolina House of Representatives 300 N Salisbury St Room 418C Raleigh NC 27603-5925 Office Phone: 336-846-7777, 919-733-7727, 336-846-1657. Business E-Mail: jonathan@jordan4nchouse.com, Jonathan.Jordan@ncleg.net.

JORDAN, LEWIS H., airline executive; b. Griffin, Ga. BS in Aerospace Engring., Ga. Inst. Tech., 1967. Asst. v.p. So. Airways; sr. v.p., ops. Flying Tiger Line, Inc., pres., COO, resigned, 1986; exec. v.p. Continental Airlines, Inc., Houston, 1986-91, pres., dir. and COO, 1991-93; COO ValuJet Airlines, Inc., Atlanta, 1993—96; owner, prin. Wingspread Enterprises, 1997—. Bd. dirs. AirTran Airways, 1993—, RARE Hospitality Internat., Inc., 1998—. Office: AirTran Airways Bd Directors 2702 Love Field Dr Dallas TX 75235-1908 Office Phone: 407-318-5600. Office Fax: 407-318-5900. Business E-Mail: lewis.jordan@airtran.com.

JORDAN, MICHAEL JEFFREY, professional sports team executive, retired professional basketball player; b. Bklyn., Feb. 17, 1963; s. James and Deloris Jordan; m. Juanita Vanoy, Sept. 2, 1989 (div. Dec. 29, 2006); children: Jeffrey Michael, Marcus James, Jasmine; m. Yvette Prieto, Apr. 27, 2013; children: Victoria, Ysabel. Student, U. NC, 1981—84. Guard Chgo. Bulls, 1984—93, 1995—98; minor league baseball player Chgo. White Sox AA Team, 1994-95; pres. basketball ops. Washington Wizards, 1999—2000, guard, 2001—03; ret. player NBA, 2003; minority owner, mng. mem. basketball ops. Charlotte Bobcats, 2006—10, majority owner, chmn., 2010—. Owner Michael Jordan's: The Restaurant, 1993—; founder Jordan Brand Clothing, 1997—, MJ Basketball Holdings, LLC. Author: RareAir: Michael on Michael, 1993; co-author (with Tinker Hatfield): Driven From Within, 2005; actor: (films) Space Jam, 1996, He Got Game, 1998. Recipient Naismith award, 1984, Wooden award, 1984; named First Team All-Am., Sporting News, 1983—84, NBA Rookie of Yr., 1985, Seagram's NBA Player of Yr., 1987, Slam-Dunk Championship winner, 1987, 1988, NBA All-Star Game MVP, 1988, 1996, 1998, NBA Def. Player of Yr., 1988, NBA MVP, 1988, 1991, 1992, 1996, 1998, Male Athlete of Yr., AP, 1991, 1992, 1993, NBA Finals MVP, 1991—93, 1996—98; named one of Most Influential People in the World of Sports, Bus. Week, 2007, 2008, The 100 Most Powerful Celebrities, Forbes.com, 2008; named to Eastern Conf. All-Star Team, NBA, 1985—93, 1996—98, 2002—03, All-NBA First Team, 1987—93, 1996—98, NBA All-Def. Team, 1988—93, 1996—98, Naismith Meml. Basketball Hall of Fame, 2009. Achievements include member of the NCAA Division I Men's Basketball Championship winning University of North Carolina Tar Heels, 1982; member of the Gold Medal winning US Olympic basketball team, 1984, 92; leading the NBA in: points, 1985, 1987-93, 1996-98; scoring average, 1987-93, 1996-98; minutes, 1987-89; steals, 1988, 1990, 1993; holding the record for most points in an NBA playoff game (63), 1986; member of the NBA Championship winning Chicago Bulls, 1991, 92, 93, 96, 97, 98. Office: Charlotte Bobcats 333 E Trade St Charlotte NC 28202*

JORDAN, RANDALL WARREN, optometrist; b. Camilla, Ga., May 19, 1952; s. Billie Howard and Sara Ann (Richards) Jordan; m. Angela Marie Farmer, May 15, 1982; 1 child, Samantha Marie. BS in Biology, So. Coll. Optometry, 1987, OD, 1989. Diplomate So. Coun. Optometrists. Supply and distbn. mgr. Phoebe Putney Meml. Hosp., Albany, Ga., 1981-85; ophthalmic technician Omni Eye Svcs., Memphis, 1987; optometrist Albany Retinal-Eye Ctr., Albany, 1989-90, Eyecare Assocs. Ga., Brunswick, 1990-91, Eye Med, Chamblee, 1992-95, Drs. Shelton, Spooner, and Jordan, 1995-2000, Jordan Eye Care, 2000—. Optometrist Dougherty County Health Dept., Albany, 1989-90, Dept. Children's Med. Svcs., Albany, 1989-90, Lion's Club Vision Screening, Montezuma, Ga., 1989; mem. Emory Vision Correction Ctr. With U.S. Army, 1972-74. Mem. Am. Optometric Assn., Ga. Optometric Assn., Kiwanis, Beta Sigma Kappa, Omega Delta, Phi Theta Upsilon. Avocations: water-skiing, scuba diving, photography, reading, music. Home: PO Box 5103 Cordele GA 31010-5103 Office: PO Box 5103 Cordele GA 31010-5103 Home Phone: 229-271-0347; Office Phone: 229-273-0018.

JORDAN, ROBERT E., air transportation executive; m. Kelly Jordan; children: Sheryl, Soren. BS in Computer Sci., Tex A&M U., MBA. Tech. mgmt. positions Hewlett-Packard; programmer analyst, mgr. & dir. sales acctg., dir. revenue acctg., contr. SW Airlines Co., 1988—2002, v.p., tech., 2002—04, sr. v.p., enterprise spend mgmt., 2004—06, exec. v.p., strategy & tech., 2006—08, exec. v.p., chief comml. officer, 2008—; pres. AirTran Airways, Inc., 2011—. Office: Southwest Airlines Co 2702 Love Field Dr Dallas TX 75235 Office Phone: 214-792-4000. Office Fax: 214-792-5015. Business E-Mail: rjordan@southwest.com.

JORDAN, ROBERT LEON, federal judge; b. Woodlawn, Tenn., June 28, 1934; s. James Richard and Josephine (Broadbent) J.; m. Dorothy Rueter, Sept. 8, 1956; children: Robert, Margaret, Daniel. BS in Fin., U. Tenn., 1958, JD, 1960. Atty. Goodpasture, Carpenter, Dale & Woods, Nashville, 1960-61; mgr. Frontier Refining Co., Denver, 1961-64; atty. Green and Green, Johnson City, Tenn., 1964-66; trust officer 1st Peoples Bank, Johnson City, 1966-69; v.p., trust officer Comml. Nat. Bank, Pensacola, Fla., 1969-71; atty. Bryant, Price, Brandt & Jordan, Johnson City, 1971-80; chancellor 1st Jud. Dist., Johnson City, 1980-88; judge US Dist. Ct. (ea. dist.) Tenn., Knoxville, 1988—2001, sr. judge, 2001—. Mem. adv. com. U. Tenn. Law Alumni, 1978-80; sec. Tenn. Jud. Conf., 1987-88, mem. exec. com., 1988; del. Tenn. State-Fed. Judicial Coun., 1993—. Bd. dirs., v.p. Tri-Cities estate Planning Coun., Johnson City, 1969; bd. dirs. Washington County Tb Assn., Rocky Mount Hist. Assn., High Rock Camp, Johnson City, Jr. Achievement of Pensacola Inc.; bd. dirs., treas. N.W. Fla. Crippled Children's Assn., Pensacola; chancellor's assoc. U. Tenn. With U.S. Army, 1954-56. Named Boss of Yr. Legal Secs. Assn., Washington, Carter County, Tenn., 1982. Mem. Tenn. Bar Assn., Tenn. Bar Found., Knoxville Bar Assn. (bd. govs. 1999), Washington County Bar Assn. (pres.-elect 1980), Johnson City C. of C., Hamilton Burnett Am. Inn of Ct. (pres. 1993-94), 6th Cir. Dist. Judges Assn. (pres. 2005), Kiwanis (pres. Met. Johnson City Club 1969, Kiwanian of Yr. award 1986-87). Republican. Mem. Ch. Of Christ. Office: Howard H Baker US Courthouse 800 Market St Ste 141 Knoxville TN 37902-2303 Office Phone: 423-545-4224.

JORDAN, ROBERT SMITH, political science professor, civilian military employee; b. LA, June 11, 1929; s. Ralph Burdette and Mary Wright (Smith) J.; m. Sara Jane Hatch, Sept. 19, 1961; children: Sara Jane, Mary Rebecca Leming, Robert Hatch, David Thomas. AB, UCLA, 1951; MS, U. Utah, 1955; MA, Princeton U., 1957, PhD, 1960; PhD (Fulbright scholar), St. Antony's Coll., Oxford U., Eng., 1960; Henry P. DuBois fellow, Princeton U., 1956—57. Instr. dept. politics Princeton U., 1956—57; asst. prof. pub. and internat. affairs, exec. asst. to dean Grad. Sch. Pub. and Internat. Affairs, U. Pitts., 1959—60; assoc. professorial lectr. George Washington U., 1960—62; asst. dir. Army War Coll. Center, 1960—61; dir. Air U. Center, 1961—62, assoc. prof. polit. sci. and internat. affairs, 1962—70, asst. to pres., 1962—64; dir. Ford Found. Fgn. Affairs Intern Program, Sch. Pub. and Internat. Affairs, 1968—70; dean faculty econ. and social studies, head dept. polit. sci. Fourah Bay Coll., U. Sierra Leone, 1965—67; prof. polit. sci. State U. NY at Binghamton, 1970—76, chmn. dept., 1970—74; dir. rsch. UN Inst. for Tng. and Rsch., NYC, 1975—79; Dag Hammarskold vis. prof. internat. rels. U. SC, Columbia, 1979—80; prof. polit. sci., rsch. prof. U. New Orleans, 1980—2002, dean Grad. Sch., 1980—82; rsch. prof. Coll. Urban Affairs, 2002—04, emeritus, 2004—. Disting. vis. prof. Naval War Coll., 1984-86; Fulbright prof. Cen. Study of Arms Control and Internat. Security, U. Lancaster, Eng., Jan.-June, 1988; vis. prof. internat. rels. US Air War Coll., 1992-94, U. Wis. sys., 2007-11. Author: The NATO International Staff/Secretariat, 1967, Government and Power in West Africa, 1970, rev. edit., 1977, Political Leadership in NATO, 1979, Norstad: Cold War NATO Supreme Commander, 2000, A Diasporan Mormon's Life: Essays of Rememberence, 2009, A Newsman Remembered: Ralph Burdette Jordan and His Times, 2011; co-author: Europe and the Superpowers, 1971, rev. edit., 1990, The World Food Conference and Global Problem Solving, 1976, Changing Role and Concepts in the International Civil Service, 1980, Dag Hammarskjold Revisited: The UN Secretary-General as a Force in World Politics, 1983, Europe in the Balance: The Changing Context of European International Politics, 1986, International Organizations: A Comparative Approach of the Management of Cooperation, 2001, Musings: Of My Early Life, 2011; editor and contbr.: International Administration, 1971, Multinational Cooperation, 1972, Generals in International Politics: NATO's Supreme Allied Commander, Europe, 1987, co-editor and contbr.: Maritime Strategy and the Balance of Power: Britain and America in the Twentieth Century, 1989; author: Unsung Soldier: The Life of General Andrew of Goodpaster, 2013. With USAF, 1951—53. Decorated Bronze Star; named Disting. Alumnus, Hinckley Inst., U. Utah, 1964; NATO rsch. fellow, 1969—70, 1990, Hooper postdoctoral fellow, U.S. Naval Hist. Ctr., 1987, 1997. Mem. ASPA (chmn. sect. on internat. and comp. adminstrn.), Assn. Princeton Grad. Alumni (pres.), Internat. Studies Assn. (v.p., chmn. sect. internat. orgn.), Acad. Coun. UN, Internat. Inst. Strategic Studies (London), Royal Inst. Internat. Affairs (London), Cosmos Club (Washington), Plimsoll Club (New Orleans), Sigma Chi (UCLA and Utah). Democrat. Mem. Lds Ch. Home: 12312 Wadsworth Way Woodbridge VA 22192 Home Phone: 608-302-2563. Personal E-mail: smitty192982@gmail.com.

JORDAN, W. CARL, lawyer; b. Mobile, Ala., Apr. 7, 1949; s. William Cecil and Lois Elizabeth (Smith) J.; m. Lisa Anne Gagne, Aug. 17, 1974; children: Kimberly Gardner, Hillary Elizabeth, William Christopher, Clement Nicholas. BA, Baylor U., 1971; JD, Harvard U., 1974. Bar: US Dist. Ct. (so., no. and ea. dists.) Tex. 1975, US Ct. Appeals (5th cir.) 1975, US Ct. Appeals (9th cir.), Tex. 1984, US Supreme Ct. 1984. Assoc. Vinson & Elkins, LLP, Houston, 1974-81, ptnr., 1981—, co-head Employment Litig. and Labor Sect. Gen. counsel Tex. Employment Law Coun., Austin, 1984—. Author: Developing and Enforcing Drug and Alcohol Work Rules: A Primer for Tex. Employers, 1986; editor: Employment Discrimination Law, supplement, 1998; contbr. articles to profl. jours. Mem. ABA (labor and employment law sect., equal employment opportunity law com., subcom. chmn. 1983-86). Home: 3722 Farber St Houston TX 77005-3714 Office: Vinson & Elkins 1st City Tower 1001 Fannin St Ste 2300 Houston TX 77002-6706 Business E-Mail: cjordan@velaw.com.

JORDAN, WILLIAM DAVIS, lawyer; b. Palestine, Tex., Aug. 5, 1940; s. Henry Latimer and Evelyn (Davis) J.; m. Toby Stall Feb. 8, 1964; children: Russell Stall Jordan, Stephen Monnig Jordan. BBA with honors, U. Tex., 1963, LLB with honors, 1964. Bar: Tex. 1964; cert. estate planning and probate law Tex. Bd. Legal Specialization. Assoc., then ptnr. Jackson and Walker, Dallas, 1964—97; shareholder Johnson, Jordan, Nipper & Monk, P.C., Dallas, 1997—. Chmn. U. Tex. Tax Conf., 1977, also planning com.; spkr. in field. Contbr. articles to profl. jours. Active Dallas Estate Planning Coun.; chmn. Southwestern Legal Found. Oil and Gas Tax Inst., 1981-86, planning com.; dir., past chmn. Dallas Met. YMCA; past dir. Baylor U. Med. Ctr. Found., YMCA Rockies, Colo.; past chmn. YMCA Found.; adv. dir. Cmtys. Found. Tex., Dallas Found.; past mem. Rotary, found. trustee Dallas, 1985-91. Mem. Tex. Bar Assn. (co-chmn. peer com. 1967-68), Dallas Bar Assn. (chmn. tax sect. 1977), Dallas Estate Planning Coun. (past bd. dirs.), Dallas Country Club, Beta Theta Pi. Presbyterian. Office: Johnson Jordan Nipper Monk 17300 Dallas Pkwy Dallas TX 75248-1145 Office Phone: 972-392-1123.

JORDEN, JAMES ROY, oil industry executive, consultant; b. Oklahoma City, Apr. 16, 1934; s. James Roy and Gordon (Peeler) J.; m. Shirley Ann Swan, Nov. 17, 1956; children: Philip Taylor, David Emerson. BS in Petroleum Engring., U. Tulsa, 1957; MA in Theol. Studies, Austin Presbyn. Theol. Sem., 2004. Engr. Shell Oil Co., various locations, 1957, 1960-81, petrophys. engr. advisor Houston, 1981-85; mgr. petroleum engring. rsch. Shell Devel. Co., Houston, 1985-88, mgr. head office prodn., tech. tng., 1988-93; mgr. CPI tng. Shell Oil Co., Houston, 1993-95; retired, 1995; cons. Quicksilver Resources, Inc., 1998—. Mem. industry adv. bd. petroleum engring. U. Tulsa, 1987-92, chmn., 1988; vis. com. petroleum engring. Colo. Sch. Mines, Golden, 1988-95. Co-author: Well Logging I., 1984, Well Logging II, 1986; co-inventor in field. 1st lt. USAF, 1957—60. Named to Hall of Fame, Petroleum Engring. Dept. U. Tulsa, 1985. Mem. Am. Inst. Mining, Metall. and Petroleum Engrs. (trustee 1983-85, 2000-02, 2004-08, pres., 2006-07), Soc. Petroleum Engrs. (hon., pres. 1984, Disting. Svc. award 1988, DeGolyer Disting. Svc. medal 1991, bd. dirs. 1975-85, dir. svc. corps. 1984-90, life trustee found., treas. found. 1991-92, sr. v.p. found. 1993-95, pres. found. 1995-97), United Engring. Found. (trustee, 2005-09), Kappa Alpha. Republican. Presbyterian. Avocations: golf, reading, wine. Home: PO Box 8111 Horseshoe Bay TX 78657-8111

JORDEN, YON YOON, board member; B in Acctg., Calif. State U. V.p., contr. FHP Internat. Corp.; sr. v.p., CFO Blue Cross Calif., Aera Energy LLC, WellPoint Health Networks, Inc., 1990—97; exec. v.p., CFO Oxford Health Plans, Inc., Norwalk, Conn., 1998—. Bd. dirs. Maxwell Tech., Inc., 2004—, Magnetek, Inc., 2004—, US Oncology Inc., 2004—, Meth. Health System, 2009—. Office: US Oncology Inc Bd Directors 10101 Woodloch Forest The Woodlands TX 77380 Office Phone: 281-863-1000. E-mail: yon.jorden@usoncology.com.

JORDON, ROBERT EARL, physician; b. Buffalo, May 7, 1938; s. James Wallace and Helen Viola (Sampson) J.; m. Mary Ann Michels, July 12, 1969; children: James H., Kathryn L., Marie H. BA, Hamilton Coll., 1960; MD, SUNY-Buffalo, 1965; MS, U. Minn., 1970. Diplomate: Am. Bd. Dermatology, Dermatological Immunology Diagnostic and Laboratory Immunology. Intern straight medicine Buffalo Gen. Hosp., 1965-66; resident, fellow in dermatology Mayo Clinic and Mayo Found., Rochester, Minn., 1966-69, asso. cons., 1971-73, cons. dermatology, 1973-77; instr. pathology U. Minn. Hosps., Mpls., 1971-73; Nat. Inst. Arthritis and Metabolic Diseases spl. research fellow U. Minn., Mpls., 1972-73; asst. prof. dermatology Mayo Grad. Sch. Medicine, Rochester, 1971-73, Mayo Sch. Medicine, Rochester, 1973-76, asst. prof. immunology, 1974-77, asso. prof. dermatology, 1976-77; prof. medicine, chmn. dermatology Med. Coll. Wis., Milw., 1977-82; med. career investigator VA, 1978-82; chief dermatology Froedtert Meml. Luth. Hosp., Milw., 1980-82; chmn. dept. dermatology U. Tex. Health Sci. Ctr., Houston, prof., 1983—; chief dermatology Hermann Hosp., Houston, 1983—2003; mem. study sect. NIH, 1983-86. Mem. nat. arthritis adv. bd. Nat. Inst. aRthritis and Metabolic Diseases, NIH; mem. nat. adv. bd. Arthritis, Musculoskeletal and Skin Diseases, 1989-91, chmn. 1992-93. Mem. editl. bd. Jour. Investigative Dermatology, 1977-82, Jour. Clin. and Lab. Immunology, 1977—, Archives of Dermatology, 1978-87, sect. editor Am. Jour. Dermatopathology, 1981-83, Clin. Aspects Autoimmunity, 1989-92. Elder Grace Presbyn. Ch., Houston, 1987—; bd. dirs. CAnCare of Houston, 1991-2001, pres. bd. dirs., 1997-99, chmn. bd., 1999-2001. Lt. comdr. M.C., USN, 1965-71. Recipient Bacelli Research award SUNY, Buffalo, 1965, Med. Spltys. Outstanding Achievement award Mayo Found., 1969, Marion B. Sulzberger award Am. Soc. Dermatologic Allergy and Immunology, 1983, award Am. Skin Assn., 1999, JB & Blanche Earthman award 2002. Mem. AAAS, AMA, Soc. Investigative Dermatology (com. nominations 1986—, dir. 1977-82, v.p. 1993-94), Am. Acad. Dermatology (co-chmn. com. lab. proficiency and quality control in immunodermatology 1980-83, dir. Immunopathology Symposium 1981-86, bd. dirs. 1993-98), Am. Assn. Immunologists, Am. Dermatol. Assn., Am. Fedn. Clin. Research, Am. Soc. Clin. Investigation, Assn. Profs. Dermatology (bd. dirs. 1987-89), Central Soc. Clin. Research, Dermatology Found. (chmn. med. and sci. com. 1980-81, trustee 1993-98, discovery award 2000), Soc. Exptl. Biology and Medicine, Lupus Erythematosus Soc. Wis. (mem. med. adv. bd. 1977-83), Wis. Dermatol. Soc. (pres. 1979-80), Wis. State Med. Soc., Chgo. Dermatol. Soc., Tex. Med. Assn., Houston Dermatol. Soc., Lupus Soc. Houston (adv. bd. 1986—90), Sigma Xi. Home: 376 Green Cove Dr Montgomery TX 77356-8267 Office: U Tex Health Sci Ctr Houston TX 77030 Office Phone: 713-500-8336. Business E-Mail: robertejordon@uth.tmc.edu.

JORIZZO, JOSEPH L., dermatology educator; b. Rochester, NY, Oct. 6, 1951; s. Joseph Lucius and Margaret R. (Volpe) J.; m. Susan MacLeod, Aug. 23, 1975 (div.); children: John Joseph, Michael Wesley; m. Irene Carros, Dec. 30, 1995; 1 child, Melina Margaret. AB, Boston U., 1972, MD magna cum laude, 1975. Diplomate Am. Bd. Dermatology. Intern in internal medicine N.C. Meml. Hosp., Chapel Hill, 1975-76, resident in dermatology, 1976-78, chief resident, 1978-79; overseas registrar Dermatology Inst. St. John's Hosp. for Diseases of the Skin, London, 1979-80; clin. asst. prof. dept. dermatology U. Tex. Med. Br., Galveston, 1979-80, from asst. prof. dept. dermatology to assoc. prof. dept. dermatology, 1980-86; prof. Sch. Medicine of Wake Forest U., Winston-Salem, NC, 1986—, prof. and founding chair dept. dermatology, 1986—2002. Cons. VA Clinic, Winston-Salem, 1986—, Forsyth Meml. Hosp., Winston-Salem, 1989—, VA Hosp., Salisbury, N.C., 1991—; mem. med. adv. bd. Am. Behcet's Disease Assn., 1988—, Winston-Salem/Forsyth County Lupus Found., 1989—; co-chmn. Southeastern Consortium for Dermatology, 1990, steering com., 1987—; mem. internat. steering com. Bechet's Disease, 1989—; mem. adv. com. Nat. Student Rsch. Forum, 1981-86; speaker more than 100 meetings, symposia, U.S. and Europe; vis. prof. Cath. U. Rome Med. Sch., 1981, U. Ark. Med. Scis., Little Rock, 1982, Brooke Army Med. Ctr., San Antonio, 1982, U. Louisville, 1982, U. N.Mex., Albuquerque, 1985, U. Mich., Ann Arbor, 1985, Duke U. Med. Ctr., 1986, U.Va., Charlottesville, 1986, Emory U., Atlanta, 1986, 92, U. South Fla., Tampa, 1987, Brown U. Med. Ctr., Providence, R.I., 1990, U. Ind., Indpls., 1991, NYU Med. Ctr., 1991, Columbia U., N.Y.C., 1993, U. Pitts., 1993, many others; invited speaker numerous meetings including Chapel Hill Alumni Dermatology Conf., 1981, Immunology Club Meeting, Galveston, 1984, Fla. Dermatol. Soc. Ann. Meeting, Ft. Lauderdale, 1984, Stetson lectr. N.Mex. Dermatol. Soc., Albuquerque, 1985, Mich. Dermatological Soc., Shanty Creek, 1985, Charlotte Dermatol. Soc., 1986, Greensboro Dermatopathology/Dermatology Semiann. Meeting, 1987, N.C. Med. Soc., 1987, Richmond-Tidewater Dermatologic Soc., Williamsburg, Va., 1988, AARP, Winston-Salem, 1988, No. Calif. Dermatologic Assn., North Lake Tahoe, Calif., 1989, Stiefel Can. Symposium, Key Biscayne, Fla., 1990, Dermatologic Soc. Greater N.Y., 1990, Westwood Conf. Clin. Dermatology, Hilton Head, S.C., 1990, Westwood Conf., Charleston, S.C., 1991, Charlotte Dermatol. Soc. Meeting, 1992, N.C. Med. Soc. Dermatology Sect., 1992, Charlotte Family Practice Soc., 1993. Co-author: Dermatological Signs of Internal Disease, 1988; contbr. chpts. to books, more than 90 articles to profl. jours.; author abstracts in field; reviewer Archives of Dermatology, 1981—, Jour. Am. Acad. Dermatology, 1981—, Pediatric Dermatology, 1986—, Jour. Investigative Dermatology, 1986—, Internat. Jour. Dermatology, 1984—, JAMA, 1988—, others; mem. editorial bd. Clin. and Exptl. Dermatology, 1988—, Jour. Am. Acad. Dermatology, 1988-93, Archives of Dermatology, 1990—, Jour. European Acad. of Dermatology and Venereology, 1992—, Current Problems in Dermatology, 1992—, Practical Cases in Dermatology, 1993—, others. Trustee Forsyth Country Day Sch., Winston-Salem, 1990-94, chmn. devel. com., 1991-92, coord. new parent's bldg. fund, 1987-88; participant med bowl fund raiser for Crisis Control, Winston-Salem, 1990. William Reed traveling fellow, 1979, Am. Acad. Dermatology fellow, 1982, 84, Dermatology Found. fellow, 1983, Upjohn Pharm. Co. Spl. grantee, 1982, Ital. Dermatology Soc. grantee, 1981, Italian Found. Rsch. Dermatology grantee, 1981, Wellcome Trust/Royal Soc. Medicine grantee, 1993, Dermatology Found. grantee, 1984, 86, 87, Noah Worcester Dermatologic Soc. grantee, 1986, Nat. Inst. Dental Rsch. grantee, 1985-86, Neutrogena grantee, 1986, Am. Cyanamid Co. grantee, 1987, Hoechst-Roussel grantee, 1988, numerous other grants including Herbert Labs., Genderm, Dermik Labs., R.W. Johnson Pharms., Stiefel Labs., Pfizer Labs., Curatek Pharms., Allergan Herbert, Bristol-Myers Squibb, Hoffman LaRoche Dermatologics, Glaxo Pharm. Co., RJR Nabisco, Ortho-McNeil Pharms. Fellow ACP; mem. AMA, Soc. Investigative Dermatology (sec.-treas. So. sect. 1984-85, v.p. So. sect. 1985-86, pres. So. sect. 1986-87, membership com. 1987-90, chmn. membership com. 1989-90), Am. Acad. Dermatology (mem. numerous coms. including internat. affairs 1981-84, summer session com. 1989—, chmn. clin. studies session 1990, nominating com. 1993—, v.p.-elect 2002--, chmn. various awards coms., media tng. recipient 1984), Am. Coll. Cyrosurgery, Dermatology Found. (dir. membership subcom. 1983-85, devel. com. 1983-86), So. Med. Assn., Forsyth County Med. Soc. (Membership Task Force 1989-90), N.C. Med. Soc., N.C. Dermatology Soc., Am. Fedn. Clin. Rsch., Psoriasis Found., Noah Worcester Dermatologic Soc., N.Am. Clin. Dermatological Soc., Pacific Dermatologic Assn. (hon.), Am. Dermatologic Assn., Am. Bd. Dermatology (Part I test com.), Societe Francaise de Dermatologie et de Venereologie, Am. Skin Assn., Internat. Soc. Tropical Dermatology, St. John's Dermatological Soc. (U.K.), Sir James Saunders Soc., Academia Medicorum Litteratorum (Italy), South Ctrl. Dermatological Soc. (organizing com. 1981-84, program com. 1984-86),Italian Soc. Dermatology and Venereology (corr.), Brit. Assn. Dermatologists (overseas mem.), Assn. Profs. Dermatology (internal medicine com. 1984-86), Dowling Club (U.K.), Phi Beta Kappa, Sigma Chi Rsch. Soc., Alpha Omega Alpha. Home: 4424 Bent Tree Farm Rd Winston Salem NC 27106-4252 Office: Wake Forest U Sch Med Dept Dermatology Med Ctr Blvd Winston Salem NC 27157-0001

JOSEPH, JAMES ALFRED, retired ambassador, political scientist, educator; b. Opelousas, La., Mar. 12, 1935; s. Adam and Julia Lee (Jones) J.; m. Mary Braxton; children: Jeffrey, Denise. BA, So. U., 1956; MDiv, Yale U., 1963; degree (hon.), Loyola U. Chgo., U. Md., Winthrop Coll., Southeastern U., Fla. Meml. U., Shaw U., Ind. U., Pomona Coll. Ordained to ministry United Ch. Christ, 1963. Asso. dir. Assn. of Founds., Columbus, Ind., 1967-69; chaplain Claremont (Calif.) Colls., 1969-70; exec. dir. Irwin-Sweeney-Miller Found., Columbus, 1970-72; v.p. Cummins Engine Co., 1972-77, 81-82; also pres. Cummins Found., Columbus, 1972-77, 81-82; ambassador to So. Africa, U.S. Dept. State, 1996-99; prof. practice of pub. policy studies Duke U., Durham, NC, 2000—, exec. dir. U.S./So. Africa Ctr. for Leadership and Pub. Values. Under sec. U.S. Dept. Interior, Washington, 1977-81; chmn. Commn. on No. Mariana Islands, 1980-86; pres., CEO, Coun. on Founds., 1982-95; mem. faculty Stillman Coll., Tuscaloosa, Ala., 1963-64, Pitzer Coll., Claremont, 1966, Claremont Sch. Theology, 1970, Yale U., 1981-82; mem. adv. com. nat. Sci. Acad., Agy. Internat. Devel. Author: The Charitable Impulse, 1990, Remaking America, 1995; co-editor: Three Perspectives on Ethnicity, 1976; contbr. articles to profl. publs. Chmn. Spl. Commn. on Racism and Devel., World Council Chs., Geneva, chmn., U.S. del. to UN Conf. in Kenya, Bilateral Consultation with Mex. Pres. Claremont Intercultural Coun., 1965-67; chmn. nat. bd. NCCJ; mem. City Park and Recreation Commn., Claremont, 1965-67, apptd. by Pres. Clinton chmn. bd. dirs. Corp. for Nat. Svc., chmn. ofcl. U.S. govt. dels. to Mex., Micronesia, Canada; pres. Nat. Black United Fund; bd. dirs. Pitzer Coll., Brookings Inst., Nat. Endowment for Democracy, Points of Light Found., Colonial Williamsburg Found., Africare, Opportunity Funding Corp., Union Theol. Sem., N.Y.C., African-Am. Inst. N.Y., Children's Def. Fund, New Transcentury Found.; bd. visitors Inst. Policy Scis., Duke U. Served to 1st lt., Med. Service Corps U.S. Army, 1956-58. Fellow Met. Applied Research Center, N.Y.C., 1958; vis. fellow Nuffield Coll., Oxford U. Mem. Assn. Black Found. Execs. (chmn. 1970-76), Council Fgn. Relations, Hague Club, Alpha Phi Alpha. Office: Terry Sanford Inst Pub Policy Duke Univ Box 90239 Durham NC 27708-0239

JOSEPH, MICHAEL J., media company executive; Formerly with Pioneer Press Newspapers, Ill.; various positions in advt.sales, distbn., mfg., fin., info. systems & human resources Cox Ohio Pub., 1995—2008, pres., CEO, 2008—09, pub. Dayton Daily News, 2008—09; pres., gen. mgr. Atlanta Jour.-Constn., 2009, pub., 2009—12; exec. v.p. Cox Media Group, Atlanta, 2012—. Office: Cox Media Group 6250 Peachtree Dunwoody Rd Atlanta GA 30328

JOSEPH, PAMELA A., bank executive; m. Hank; 3 children. BBA, U. Ill., Urbana-Champaign. Sr. sales & mktg. positions Wells Fargo Bank; dir. new market devel. VISA Internat., 1991—94; pres. mktg. Nova Info. Systems, 1994—95, sr. v.p. bus. devel., 1995—97, chief info. officer, 1997—2001, pres., COO, 2001—04; chmn., pres., CEO Nova Info. Systems (now Elavon), 2004—05; vice chmn. US Bancorp Payment Services, 2004—. Bd. dir. Paychex, 2005—, Centene Corp., 2007—; adv. bd. mem. Electronic Transfer Assn. Hon. chair Gift for a Child; active Habitat for Humanity. Named one of 25 Most Powerful Women in Banking, US Banker, 2006—10, American Banker, 2011. Avocation: golf. Office: Elavon 2 Concourse Pkwy Ste 800 Atlanta GA 30328-5588 Office Phone: 678-731-5000.

JOSEPH, ROBERT G., public policy educator, former federal agency administrator; b. Williston, ND, 1949; BA, St. Louis U., 1971; MA, U. Chgo., 1973; PhD, Columbia U., 1978. Asst. for negotiations, Office Asst. Sec. for Internat. Security Affairs US Dept. Def., Washington, 1978, asst. for gen. purpose forces, 1979, asst. for nuclear policy Office Under Sec., 1980—81, chief nuclear policy/plans section, 1982—84, acting prin. dep. asst. sec. for internat. security policy, 1987, prin. dep. asst. sec. for internat. security policy, 1987—89, dep. asst. sec. nuclear forces & arms control policy, 1989—91, amb. U.S.-Russian consultative commn. nuclear testing; prof. nat. security studies Nat. Def. U., Washington, 1992—2001, founder, dir., Ctr. Counterproliferation Rsch., 1992—2001; spl. asst. to Pres., sr. dir. proliferation strategy, counterproliferation & homeland def. NSC, Washington, 2001—05; under sec. for arms control & internat. security US Dept. State, Washington, 2005—07; dir. theater nuclear forces policy, US Mission NATO, Brussels, 1985—87. Sr. scholar, dir. of studies Nat. Inst. Pub. Policy (NIPP), 2004—05, sr. scholar, 2007—; prof. defense & strategic studies Mo. State U., 2005—; mem. Def. Policy Bd. Advisory Com., 2007—. Recipient Pres. Award for Individual Achievement, Nat. Def. U., 2004, Gold Medal for Disting. Svc., Nat. Nuclear Security Adminstrn., 2004, Medal for Disting. Civilian Svc., US Dept. Def., Ronald Reagan award, 2006. Office: National Institute for Public Policy (NIPP) 9302 Lee Highway Ste 750 Fairfax VA 22031 Office Phone: 703-293-9181. Office Fax: 703-293-9198.

JOVANOVSKI, ED, professional hockey player; b. Windsor, Ont., Canada, June 26, 1976; s. Kostadin and Lilja Jovanovski; m. Kirstin Jovanovski; children: Kylie, Kyra, Cole, Coco. Defenseman Fla. Panthers, 1995—98, 2011—, capt., 2013—; defenseman Vancouver Canucks, 1998—2006, Phoenix Coyotes, 2006—11. Mem. Can. World Cup Team, 1996, 2004, Can. Olympic Hockey Team, Salt Lake City, 2002. Named to NHL All-Rookie Team, 1996, NHL All-Star Game, 2001—03, 2007, 2008. Achievements include being a member of gold medal Canadian Hockey team, Salt Lake City Olympic Games, 2002; being a member of World Cup Champion Team Canada, 2004. Office: Florida Panthers BankAtlantic Center One Panther Parkway Sunrise FL 33323

JOWERS, GAYLON, JR., finance company executive; B in Mktg., Troy State U., M in Mgmt. Worked Merck; pres., CEO DotsConnect (subs. Total System Svcs., Inc.); various mgmt. positions Total System Svcs., Inc., 1991, pres., internat., exec. v.p., M&A & Emerging Markets, exec. v.p.; pres. TSYS Internat. Bd. dirs. China UnionPay Data Svcs., Ltd., GP Network Corp., Japan, TSYS Managed Svcs. EMEA, Japan. Office: Total System Services Inc 1 TSYS Way Columbus GA 31902-2567 Office Phone: 706-649-2310. Office Fax: 706-649-4266. Business E-Mail: gaylo.jowers@tsys.com.

JOYCE, EDWARD ROWEN, retired chemical engineer, educator; b. St. Augustine, Fla., Oct. 20, 1927; s. Edward Rowen and Annie Margaret (Cobb) J.; m. Leland Livingston White, Sept. 11, 1954; children: Leland Ann, Julia, Edward Rowen III, Theo, Adele. BS in Chem. Engring., U. Miss., 1950; M of Engring., U. Fla., 1969; MBA, U. North Fla., 1975. Registered profl. engr., Fla. Petroleum engr. Texaco, Harvey, La., 1953-55; project engr. Freeport Sulphur Co., New Orleans, 1955-59; chem. engr. SCM Corp., Jacksonville, Fla., 1959-81; profl. engr. Jacksonville Electric Authority, 1981-93, ret., 1993. Adj. prof. U. North Fla., Jacksonville, 1977-2002, Jacksonville U., 1989-2001; newspaper columnist Fla. Times Union, Jacksonville, 1970-87. Co-author: Sulfate Turpentine Recovery, 1971; author booklet; patentee in field. Sci. fair judge Duval County Sch. System, Jacksonville, 1960-92; co-chmn. adv. com. U. North Fla., 1981-85; merit badge advisor Boy Scouts Am., Jacksonville, 1960—; advisor Jr. Achievement, Jacksonville, 1963; vestryman, lay Eucharistic min., sr. warden, Diocesan Conv. del. local Episcopal ch. Comdr. USN, 1950-53, Korea, 1960-61, Europe. Fellow Fla. Engring. Soc. (pres. Jacksonville chpt. 1983); mem. AICE (pres. Peninsular Fla. chpt. 1963-64), Phi Kappa Phi, Alpha Pi Mu, Gamma Sigma Epsilon. Republican. Avocations: stamp collecting/philately, coin collecting/numismatics, water sports, camping. Home: 9601 Southbrook Dr Villa N106 Jacksonville FL 32256 Personal E-mail: EdwardRJoyce@aol.com.

JOYCE, RENE R., energy executive; Pres. Acadian Gas Corp., 1990—96; sr. exec. v.p. Tejas Gas, 1996—98; pres. Transok Inc. (subs of Tejas), 1996—98; pres. energy services Coral Energy LLC, 1998—99; energy ind. cons., 2000—04; CEO Targa Resources Corp., Houston, 2004—11, exec. chmn., 2012—. Presiding supervising dir. Core Laboratories NV, 2000—; bd. dirs. Targa Resources Corp., 2005—. Office: Targa Resources Corp Ste 4300 1000 Louisiana Houston TX 77002

JOYNER, ARTHENIA LEE, state legislator, lawyer; b. Lakeland, Fla., Feb. 3, 1943; BS in Polit. Sci., Fla. A & M U., 1964, JD, 1968. Tchr. Hillsborough County Bd. of Pub. Instructions, Tampa, Fla., 1964; adminstrv. asst., Rep. Joe Lang Kershaw Fla. House of Reps., Tallahassee, 1969, mem., 2000—06; sole practice Tampa, 1969—; mem. Dist. 18 Fla. State Senate, Tallahassee, 2006—, minority whip, 2006—10, vice chair comm., energy and pub. utilities com., judiciary com., mem. criminal and civil justice appropriations com., ethics and elections com., transp. com., policy and steering com. on commerce and industry. Bd. dirs. Travellers Aid Inc.; nat. legal advisor Delta Sigma Theta Sorority, Inc., 1985—. Bd dirs. Bay Area Legal Services, Inc., 1979-86, pres. 1983; bd. dirs. Helping Hand Day Nursery; pres. Charmettes Inc. Named one of Am.'s Top 100 Black Bus. and Profl. Women, Dollars and Sense mag., 1985, one of 100 Most Influential Black Ams., Ebony mag., 1985; recipient Outstanding Achievement and Community Service award Eastgate Community Ch., 1985, Tampa br. NAACP Human Rights award, 1985. Mem. ABA (house of dels. 1981-82), Nat. Bar Assn. (pres. 1984-85), Fla. Bar Assn., Hillsborough County Bar Assn., Nat. Assn. Women Lawyers, Hillsborough County Assn. Women Lawyers, Am. Judicature Soc. Democrat. Avocations: collecting gold coins, pub. speaking, reading. Office: 508 W Dr Martin Luther King Jr Blvd Tampa FL 33603-3415 also: 210 Senate Office Bldg 404 S Monroe St Tallahassee FL 32399-1100 Office Phone: 813-233-4277, 850-487-5059. Business E-Mail: joyner.arthenia.web@flsenate.gov.

JOYNER, CHARLIE, state legislator; b. Rose Hill, NC, July 22, 1940; m. Gwen Joyner; 4 children. Ops. mgr. Tony's Caesar's Flowers & Green Houses; ret. fire chief Midwest Fire Dept.; vice mayor Midwest City; mem. Dist. 95 Okla. House of Representatives, 2007—. Mem.: Midwest City C. of C., Midwest City Rotary Club (pres.). Republican. Avocations: golf, travel. Address: 3500 Bella Vista Dr Midwest City OK 73150 Office: Okla House of Reprs 2300 N Lincoln Blvd Rm 336 Oklahoma City OK 73105 Office Phone: 405-557-7314. Business E-Mail: charlie.joyner@okhouse.gov.

JOYNER, GARY KELTON, lawyer; b. Rocky Mount, NC, Apr. 22, 1957; s. George Andrew and Mary Marjorie (Bone) J. BA, U. N.C., 1979; JD, Wake Forest U., 1982. Bar: NC 1982, US Dist. Ct. (ea. and mid. dists.) NC 1982, US Ct. Appeals (4th cir.) 1983. Assoc. Bailey, Dixon, Wooten, McDonald, Fountain & Walker, Raleigh, NC, 1982-86, ptnr., 1986; assoc. Petree, Stockton & Robinson, Raleigh, NC, 1986-89; ptnr. Petree Stockton LLP, Raleigh, NC, 1990—97, Kilpatrick Stockton LLP, Raleigh, NC, 1997—. Bd. dirs. Wake Edn. Partnership, 1993—. Chmn. allocations panel United Way, Wake County, NC, 1985-91; lt. membership YMCA, Raleigh, 1985-88; mem. NC Legis. Forum, 1986-89; chmn. Campership drive Wake County Boys Club, Raleigh, 1986—; bd. dirs. Boys and Girls Club Wake County, 1990-96; exec. bd. dirs. NC Mus. Natural Scis. Soc., Raleigh, 1985-90; bd. dirs. Downtown Housing Improvement Corp., Triangle Cmty. Coalition, 2000-03, Rsch. Triangle Reg. Partnership. Mem. ABA (chmn. environ. law com. young lawyers divsn. 1989-91, state co-chmn. Fund for Justice and Edn. 1989-90, chmn. real property com. 1991-93, liaison real property probate and trust law sect. 1993-94), NC Bar Assn. (chmn. law day com. 1985-86, spl. projects com. 1986-87, sec. 1986-87, chmn. young lawyers divsn. 1988-89, co-chair long range plan coordinating com., chmn. real property curriculum com. 1994-96, Young lawyers divsn., chair, 1988-89), Wake County Bar Assn. (bd. dirs. 1993-95, chmn. real property lawyers 1993), NC Bankers Assn., Greater Raleigh C. of C. (exec. com. mem. 2001-02, mem. bd. adv. 2003-04), NC Chamber(bd. dirs., 2008-10), NC Bankers Assn., Rsch. Triangle Regional Partnership(bd. dirs., 2004-10), Boys & Girls Club Wake County(NC area chmn., 2005-07, pres., 2003-04, bd. dirs., 1997-), Greater Releigh C. of C.(chair, 2010-11, exec. com. 2009-10, bd. advs., 2003-08, chmn. edge II, 2003-04, v.p. econ. devel., 2001-02, exec. com., 2001-02, chmn. sucess task force com., 2000-04), Habitat Humanity(bd. dirs., 2005-07), Triangle Cmty Coalition(bd. dirs, 2000-08), Wake County Real Property Lawyers Assn.(pres., 1993), Wake County Bar Assn. (bd. mem., 1992-94), WakeMed Found.(bd. mem., 2004-10) Democrat. Home: 308 Marlowe Rd Raleigh NC 27609-7064 Office: Kilpatrick Stockton LLP 4208 Six Forks Rd Ste 1400 Raleigh NC 27609-5764 Office Phone: 919-420-1750. Office Fax: 919-510-6119. E-mail: GJoyner@KilpatrickStockton.com.

JOYNER, LEON FELIX, retired university administrator; b. Savannah, Ga., Nov. 20, 1924; s. Leon Felix and Sarah (Thompson) J.; m. Margaret Ruth Barrett, June 28, 1944; children-Leon Stephens, Barrett Ray. Student, Harvard, 1944-45; AB, Berea Coll., 1947; postgrad., Univs. Ala., Tenn., Ky., 1947-48. Mem. budget staff Ky. State Govt., 1948-55; mem. field staff Pub. Adminstrn. Service, Chgo., 1956-60; commr. personnel Ky. State Govt., 1960-62, health welfare adminstr., 1962-63, commr. fin., 1963-67; v.p. fin. U. N.C., 1968-95. Cons. Govts. of Burma, Thailand, 1956-59, Auditor-Gen., Pakistan, 1968 Chmn. Commn. on Reorganization of Exec. Br. State Govt. Ky., 1962; Bd. dirs. Research Triangle Found., N.C., 1970-94. Served to lt. (j.g.), Supply Corps USNR, 1943-46. Named Pub. Adminstr. of Year Ky. chpt. Am. Soc. Pub. Adminstrn., 1961, Univ. award U. N.C. Bd. Govs., 1996. Mem. Nat. Assn. State Budget Officers (past mem. exec. com. 1950-56), Internat. Bridge, Tunnel and Turnpike Assn. (past dir. 1962-68), Phi Kappa Phi. Democrat. Presbyterian. Home: 616 Churchill Dr Chapel Hill NC 27517-2505 Personal E-mail: fjoyner919@aol.com.

JOYNER, OSCAR A., communications executive; s. Tom Joyner. MBA, Fla. A&M U., Tallahassee. Pres., COO REACH Media, Inc., Dallas. Sr. v.p. Tom Joyner Found.; co-founder, prin. Educational Development Corp. America. Named to Power 150, Ebony mag., 2008. Mem.: Nat. Black MBA Assn. (mem. bd. dirs. 2008—). Office: Reach Media Inc 13760 Noel Rd Ste 750 Dallas TX 75240

JOYNER, TOM, radio personality; b. Tuskegee, Ala., 1949; m. Donna Richardson; children from previous marriage: Thomas Jr., Oscar. BA, Tuskegee Inst. Disc jockey WRMA, Montgomery, WLOK, Memphis, KWK, St. Louis, KKDA, Dallas, morning disc jockey; afternoon disc jockey WGCI, Chgo.; host The Tom Joyner Morning Show ABC Radio Networks, 1994—. Original mem. The Commodores. Co-author: I'm Just a DJ but... It Makes Sense to Me, 2005. Founder Tom Joyner Found., HBCU Scholarship Relief Fund, 1998. Recipient Joe Loris Award, Impact Mag., Best Urban Contemporary Air Personality award, Billboard, Most Influential Black Americans, Ebony mag., 2006; named to Power 150, 2008. Office: Tom Joyner Found 13760 Noel Rd Dallas TX 75240

JOYNER, WALTON KITCHIN, lawyer; b. Raleigh, NC, Apr. 1, 1933; s. William Thomas and Sue (Kitchin) J.; m. Lucy Holmes Graves, Sept. 23, 1955; children: Sue Carson Clark, Walton K. Jr., James Y. II. AB in Polit. Sci., U. N.C., 1955, JD with honors, 1960. Bar: N.C., cert. mediator:; lic. comml. pilot. Ptnr. Joyner & Howison, Raleigh, 1960-80, Hunton & Williams, Raleigh, 1980—. Sec., treas. N.C. R.R. Co., Raleigh, 1966; bd. dirs. United Title Ins. Co., Raleigh; bd. mgrs. Wachovia Bank, N.C., 1969-98; bd. govs. U.S. Power Squadrons, 1974-81. Assoc. editor U. N.C. Law Rev. Pres. Rehab. and Cerebral Palsy Ctr. Wake County, Raleigh, 1974; trustee St. Mary's Coll., 1990-91; vice chmn., bd. dirs. Peace Coll. Found., 2001—. Mem.: Law Alumni Assn. U. N.C. (bd. dirs.), Wake County Bar Assn. (chmn., bd. dirs. 1977), N.C. Bar Assn. (treas. probate sect. 1983), Carolina Country Club (pres. 1983—84, 2000—01), Order of Coif, Phi Beta Kappa. Presbyterian. Avocation: flying. Home: 815 Marlowe Rd Raleigh NC 27609-7022 Office: Hunton & Williams 1 Hannover Sq PO Box 109 Fl 14 Raleigh NC 27602-0109

JOYNES, BARBARA COLE, marketing executive; b. Rahway, NJ, Sept. 4, 1960; d. Clayton Eugene and Margaret (Fitzgerald) Cole; m. Matthew Thomas Thornhill, Oct. 15, 1983 (div. 1996); children: Allison, Clark; m. Stanley Knight Joynes III, June 24, 2000; stepchildren: Elizabeth, Alexandra. BBA in Mktg., Coll. of William and Mary, 1982. Asst. account exec. March Direct/McCann Direct, NYC, 1983-84, account exec., 1984-86, account supr., 1986-87; dir. comml. client divsn. Huntsinger & Jeffer Direct, Richmond, Va., 1987-89; v.p., account supr. The Stenrich Group, Richmond, 1989-90, sr. v.p., dir. account mgmt., 1990-92, exec. v.p., dir. account mgmt., bd. dirs., 1992-95; exec. v.p. for integrated mktg. comm., mem. exec. com. The Martin Agy., Richmond, 1995-96, exec. v.p., chief adminstrv. officer, 1996—99, pnr. integrated svcs., 2000—. Mem. profit sharing com. The Martin Agy., Richmond, 1993—2003, chair mgmt. com., 1999—2002. Exec. com. bd. trustees Richmond Children's Mus., 1992-99, dir. bd. trustees, 1991-92; area coord. William and Mary Alum Admissions Network, Richmond, 1988-98; co-chair William and Mary Class of 82 Reunion com., 1992-97, mem. class gift com., 2002-07; mem. Leadership Metro Richmond Class of 1997; book fair chair Maybeury Elem. Sch., 1997—2000; cookie chair Brownie Troop #292, Girl Scouts U.S., 1996-98, bd. dirs. Commonwealth Girl Scouts Coun., 1999-2002; bd. dirs. Arts Coun. Richmond, 1998-2002; bd. dirs. Leadership Metro Richmond, 1998—2004, mem. exec. com., 1999-2004, chair devel. com., chair mem. programs com., sec. awareness/pub. rels. com., mem. recruitment com.; bd. dirs. YWCA of Richmond, 2001-08, v.p., 2003-05, pres. 2005-07, past pres. 2007-08; mem. Direct Mktg. Agy. Leaders Coun., mem. bd. dir. ChildFund Internat., 2008-, co-chair fundraising and devel. com., 2009-; mem. bus. ptnrs. bd., William and Mary Sch. Bus., 2006-, mem. exec. com., 2010-; bd. dirs. William and Mary Alumni Assn., 2009-. Recipient Silver Echo award Direct Mktg. Assn., 1991, 94, Gold Echo award, 2003, 05, Richmond Area Marketer of Yr. award Am. Mktg. Assn., 1992, 93, 94, Gold Effie award, 1992, Silver Effie award, 2000, YWCA Outstanding Woman award, 1999. Mem. Greater Richmond C. of C. (mem. exec. com. 2002-04, bd. dirs. 2000—06, chmn's cir. 2006-), Va. League Planned Parentwood (mem. bd. dir.), Willow Oaks Country Club, Farmington Country Club. Avocations: travel, reading, golf. Office: The Martin Agy One Shockoe Plz Richmond VA 23219-4132

JUANES, (JUAN ESTEBAN ARISTIZÁBAL VÁSQUEZ), musician; b. Medellin, Colombia, Aug. 9, 1972; m. Karen Martínez, Aug. 6, 2004; children: Luna, Paloma. Founding band mem. Ekhymosis, Colombia, 1988—98; solo career, 1998—. Musician: (albums) Fíjate Bien, 2000 (Best Rock Solo Album and Best Rock Song, Latin Grammy Awards, 2001), Un Día Normal, 2002 (Album of Yr., Best Rock Solo Vocal Album, Latin Grammy Awards, 2003), Mi Sangre, 2004 (Best Rock Solo Album, Latin Grammy Awards, 2005), La Vida...Es un Ratico, 2007 (Album of Yr., Best Male Pop Vocal Album, Latin Grammy Awards, 2008, Best Latin Pop Album, Grammy Awards, 2009), P.A.R.C.E., 2010, Juanes MTV Unplugged, 2012 (Best Latin Pop Album, Grammy Awards, 2013), (songs) A Dios le Pido, 2002 (Best Rock Song, Latin Grammy Awards, 2002), Es por ti, 2002 (Record of Yr., Song of Yr., Latin Grammy Awards, 2003), Mala Gente, 2002 (Best Rock Song, Latin Grammy Awards, 2003), Nada Valgo Sin Tu Amor, 2004 (Best Rock Song, Latin Grammy Awards, 2005), Volverte a Ver, 2004 (Best Music Video, Latin Grammy Awards, 2005), Me Enamora, 2007 (Record of Yr., Song of Yr., Best Music Video, Latin Grammy Awards, 2008). Founder Mi Sangre Found., Colombia. Recipient Best New Artist award, Latin Grammy Awards, 2001; named a Chevalier, Ordre des Arts et des Lettres, France, 2006; named one of 100 Most Influential People, Time Mag., 2005. Office: c/o Fernan Martinez Communications 4141 NE 2nd Ave Ste 106C Miami FL 33137-3500

JUDD, GEORGE R., wholesale distribution executive; B mktg., We. Conn. State Univ., 1984. V.p. sw region Georgia-Pacific Corp., 1999—2000, v.p. no. & midwest regions, dist. div., 2000—02, v.p. sales & ea. region ops., 2002—04; pres., COO BlueLinx Holdings, Atlanta, 2004—08, CEO, 2008—09; pres., CEO BlueLinx Holdings, Inc., Atlanta, 2009—. Past chmn. Nat. Lumber & Bldg. Materials Dealers Assn. Office: BlueLinx Holdings 4300 Wildwood Pkwy Atlanta GA 30339

JUDD, WYNONNA ELLEN (CHRISTINA CLAIRE CIMINELLA), musician; b. Ashland, Ky., May 30, 1964; d. Charles Jordan and Naomi Judd, Michael Ciminella (Stepfather); m. Arch Kelly, Jan. 21, 1996 (div. 1998); children: Elijah, Grace; m. Dan R. Roach, Nov. 22, 2003 (separated Feb. 2007); 1 child, Zac; m. Cactus Moser, June 17, 2012. Vocalist, musician, entertainer (country duo) The Judds, 1979-1991, 2010-, signed with RCA, 1984; formed Wynonna & The Big Noise, 2011; songs include Had a Dream, 1983, Mama, He's Crazy, 1984, Why Not Me, 1984, Girls Night Out, 1985, Love Is Alive, 1985, Have Mercy, 1985, Rockin' with the Rhythm, 1986, Grandpa, 1986, Let Me Tell You About Love, 1989, She Is His Only Need, 1992, No One Else on Earth, 1992, and many others; albums include Wynonna & Naomi, 1983, Why Not Me, 1984, Rockin' With the Rhythm, 1986, Heartland, 1987, Greatest Hits, 1988, River of Time, 1989, Love Can Build a Bridge, 1990, Greatest Hits Vol. 2, 1991, (video) Their Final Concert, 1992, The Judds Collection, 1983-1990, 1992, Classic Gold, 1992, This Country's Rockin', 1993, (video) Naomi & Wynonna-The Farewell Tour, 1993, Christmas With The Judds & Alabama, 1994, In Concert, 1995, The Judds Reunion: Live, 2000, Number One Hits, 2000, Christmas Time with the Judds, 2003; (solo albums) Wynonna, 1992, Tell Me Why, 1993, Revelations, 1996, Collection, 1997, The Other Side, 1997, New Day Dawning, 2000 (also co-prodr.), What the World Needs Now Is Love, 2003, (CD and DVD) Her Story: Scenes From a Lifetime, 2005, A Classic Christmas, 2006, Sing: Chapter 1, 2009, Love Heals, 2010; solo duet (with Clint Black) A Bad Goodbye, 1993; co-author: (with Naomi Judd) Love Can Build a Bridge, 1993 (NY Times Best Seller)(also TV film, 1995), Coming Home to Myself: A Memoir, 2005 (NY Times Best Seller); host Am. Music Awards, 1993, CBS TV Spl., 1996, Nashville Star, 2007; (TV appearances) Touched By An Angel, 1999, Hope & Faith, 2005, Army Wives, 2010; performer for the Pope, 1993, Superbowl, 1994, Daytona 500, 1998, MTV-Music In High Places, Italy, 2000, Opening Ceremonies 2002 Paralympic Games, Salt Lake City, MusiCares Person of Yr, 2004, Predident Bush, 2001, The White House and Pentagon, 2004, Good Morning America Songs for Tsunami, 2005; (voice-soundtrack) Prince of Egypt (song Freedom), 1998, Lilo & Stitch (Burnin' Love), 2002; co-writer, prodr., recorder (film soundtrack) Someone Like You (song-You Are), 2001; recorded song with others, Heart of America, Habitat for Humanity, 2005; reality TV personality, The Judds, 2011; performer: Dancing With the Stars, 2013. Charitable efforts for Nashville Oasis Ctr., St. Jude Children's Hosp., Am. Red Cross, and Habitat for Humanity; chair, celebrity auction Am. Liver Found., 1998; amb. YouthAIDS, 2003—; nat. spokesperson Power to Change Program, 2000; spokesperson Kmart Corp., 2000. Recipient (with Naomi Judd) Horizon award, Country Music Assn., 1984, five Grammy awards, nine Country Music Assn. awards and eight Billboard Music awards; named with Naomi Judd 40 Greatest Women of Country Music, Country Music TV (CMT), 2002; recipient Female Vocalist of the Yr. award, Acad. of Country Music, 1994, Connie B. Gay award, Country Music Assn., 2004, USO Merit award, 2005; co-recipient with husband Dan R. Roach, Turn for Peace award, ANASAZI Found., 2005; nominee for Humanitarian of Yr., Academy of Country Music, 2003; named Grand Marshall, Indy 500 Festival and Race (first country artist), 2003.; named to Nashville Music City Walk of Fame, 2007. Office: Big Enterprises LLC 819 18th Avenue South Nashville TN 37203

JUDGE, JONATHAN J., information technology executive, former financial services company executive; BA, Harvard Univ. Sales, mktg. & ops. mgmt. positions IBM Corp., 1976—98, mgr. sales, svc. & support, personal computing div., mem. mgmt. com., 1998—2001, gen. mgr. personal computing div., 2001—02; pres., CEO Crystal Decisions Inc., Vancouver, BC, 2002—03, Paychex Inc., Rochester, NY, 2004—10; CEO First Data Corp., Atlanta, 2010—. Bd. dirs. PMC-Sierra Inc., Dun & Bradstreet Corp., Paychex Inc., 2004—10. Office: First Data Corp 5565 Glenridge Connector NE Atlanta GA 30342

JUDGE, KATHLEEN W., dermatologist; MD, La. State U. Med. Ctr. Diplomate Am. Bd. Dermatology. Resident La. State Univ. Med. Ctr.; hosp. affiliations include Orlando Regional Healthcare, Fla. Hosp., Health Ctrl. Mem.: AMA, Leader Soc. Dermatology Found., Am. Acad. of Anti-Aging Medicine, Am. Soc. for Dermatologic Surgery, Fla. Med. Assn., Am. Soc.of Cosmetic Dermatology & Aesthetic Surgery, Orange County Med. Soc., Am. Soc. for Laser Medicine & Surgery, Women's Dermatologic Surgeon's Interest Group, Women's Dermatology Soc., Fla. Soc. of Dermatology and Dermatologic Surgeons, Ctrl. Fla. Soc. of Dermatology, Am. Acad. of Dermatology. Office: Central Florida Dermatology Associates 700 E Michigan St Orlando FL 32806 Office Phone: 407-481-2620.

JUDSON, PATRICIA LYNN, obstetrician, gynecologist, oncologist; 2 children. BS, Hamline U., St. Paul, 1987; MD, U. Minn., 1998. Assoc. prof. U. Minn., Mpls., 1999—2011, dir. gyn. oncology, 2011—, fellowship dir. Mpls., 2003—11; dir. gyn. oncology North Meml. Med. Ctr., Robbinsdale, Minn., 1999—2009; assoc. prof. Moffitt Cancer Ctr., 2011—. Med. adv. bd. Minn. Ovarian Cancer Alliance, St. Louis Park, 1999—. Reviewer: Jour. Ob-Gyn., 1987—, Jour. Gyn. Oncology, 2000—; contbr. articles to profl. jours., chapters to books. Sci. adv. com. Gyn. Oncology Group, 2005—06. Named one of America's Top Obstetricians and Gynecologists, Consumers' Rsch. Coun. of Am., 2004—12, Top Twin Cities Doctors for Women, Minn. Monthly Mag., 2006—10. Fellow: ACS (life); mem.: Soc. Gynecol. Oncologist (edn. com. 2006), Minn. Women Physicians, Minn. Soc. Clin. Oncology, Deborah E. Powell Ctr. for Women's Health, Am. Coll. Ob-Gyn. (life; program com. 2001—05). Lutheran. Office: Moffitt Cancer Ctr 12902 Magnolia Dr Tampa FL 33612*

JUGIS, PETER JOSEPH, bishop; b. Charlotte, Mar. 3, 1957; BA, U. NC, Charlotte, 1978; STB, Pontifical Gregorian Univ., Rome, 1982, JCL, 1984; JCD in Canon Law, Cath. U. Am., Washington, 1993. Ordained priest Diocese of Charlotte, 1983; asst. pastor St. Leo the Great Cath. Ch., Winston-Salem, 1984—85; parochial vicar St. John Neumann Cath. Ch., Charlotte, 1985—87, Sacred Heart Cath. Ch., Salisbury, NC, 1988—89, St. Leo the Great Cath. Ch., 1991—93; pastor Holy Infant Cath. Ch., 1993—96, Queen of Apostles Cath. Ch., Belmont, NC, 1996—97; residency St. Patrick Cathedral, 1997—98; pastor Our Lady of Lourdes Ch., Monroe, NC, jud. vicar; adminstr. Holy Spirit, Denver; ordained bishop, 2003; bishop Diocese of Charlotte, 2003—. Roman Catholic. Office: Diocese of Charlotte 1123 S Church St PO Box 36776 Charlotte NC 28236 Office Phone: 704-370-6299. Office Fax: 704-370-3378.

JULIAN, JIM LEE, lawyer; b. Osceola, Ark., Dec. 14, 1954; s. John Roland and Lucille Angela (Potts) Julian; m. Patricia Lynn Roberts, Jan. 26, 1980; 1 child, Kathryn Elizabeth. BA, Ark. State U., 1976; JD, U. Ark., 1979. Bar: Ark. 1979, US Dist. Ct. (eastern and western dists.) Ark. 1979, US Ct. Appeals (8th cir.). Assoc. Skillman & Durrett, West Memphis, Ark., 1979-82; staff atty. Ark. Power and Light Co., Little Rock, 1982-84; assoc. House, Wallace & Jewell, Little Rock, 1984-85, ptnr., 1986-89, Chisenhall, Nestrud & Julian, P.A., Little Rock, 1989—. Pres. Crittenden County Young Dems., Ark., 1980—82; chmn. bd. dirs. Northside YMCA, 1992—96. Mem.: ABA, Ark. Assn. Def. Counsel, Pulaski County Bar Assn., Internat. Assn. Def. Counsel, Ark. Bar Assn. (pres. 2010—11, Outstanding Lawyer-Citizen award 2000—01), Major Sports Assn., Pleasant Valley Country Club. Avocation: golf. Home: 3711 Lochridge Rd North Little Rock AR 72116-8328 Office: Chisenhall Nestrud & Julian 400 W Capitol Ave Ste 2840 Little Rock AR 72201-3467 Office Phone: 501-372-5800. Office Fax: 501-372-4941. E-mail: jjulian@cnjlaw.com.

JULIEN, JEFFREY P., investment company executive; BS in Mgmt. Sci., Duke U., Durham, NC, 1978. CPA Price Waterhouse (now PricewaterhouseCoopers); Joined Raymond James Financial, Inc., St. Petersburg, Fla., 1983, sr. v.p., CFO, 1987, exec. v.p. fin., CFO; chmn. bd. Raymond James Trust Co., Raymond James Bank. Office: Raymond James Fin Inc 880 Carillon Pkwy Saint Petersburg FL 33716-1100

JULIEN, JOHN PATRICK, state legislator; b. Port-au-Prince, Haiti, July 22, 1963; m. Julie Julien; 5 children. BS in Acctg., SUNY, Old Westbury, 1985. Councilman North Miami Beach City Coun., Fla., 2005—10; mem. Dist. 104 Fla. House of Representatives, 2011—. Democrat. Office: 633 NE 167th St Ste 600 North Miami Beach FL 33162-2444 also: Fla House of Reps 1401 The Capitol 402 S Monroe St Tallahassee FL 32399-1300 Office Phone: 305-650-0022, 850-488-7088.

JUM'AH, ABDALLAH, oil industry executive; b. al-Khobar, Saudi Arabia; BA in Polit. Sci., Am. U., Beirut, 1968; completed Program for Mgmt. Devel., Harvard U., Cambridge, Mass. Joined Saudi Aramco, Saudi Arabia, 1968, v.p., power sys., 1984, v.p., employee rels., 1988, sr. v.p., indsl. rels., 1991, sr. v.p., internat. ops., 1992, bd. dirs., 1994, exec. v.p., internat. ops., 1995, pres., CEO, 1995. Bd. dirs. Halliburton Co., 2010—. Mem. Coun. of Eastern Province of Saudi Arabia, Saudi Arabian Supreme Coun. for Petroleum and Mineral Affairs; mem. bd. trustees Am. U. Cairo, 2001—. Recipient Petroleum Exec. of Yr. Award, Energy Intelligence, 2005. Office: Halliburton Co 3000 N Sam Houston Pky E Houston TX 77032 Office Phone: 281-575-3000.

JUMPER, JOHN PHILLIP, retired military officer, aerospace and defense company executive; b. Paris, Tex., Feb. 4, 1945; s. Jimmy Jumper and Maree Loretta (Jumper) J.; m. Ellen Elizabeth McGhee, Mar. 29, 1969; children: Catherine, Janet, Melissa. BSEE, Va. Mil. Inst., 1966; MBA, Golden Gate U., 1978; postgrad., Air Command and Staff Coll., Maxwell AFB, Ala., 1977-78, Nat. War Coll., Washington, 1981-82. Commd. 2d lt. USAF, 1966, advanced through grades to gen., 1997, ret., 2005; instr. pilot 414th Fighter Weapons Squadron, Nellis AFB, Nev., 1974-77; action officer Directorate for Ops. and Tng., Washington, 1978-81; comdr. 430th Tactical Fighter Squadron, Nellis AFB, Nev., 1983; exec. officer to comdr. Hdqrs. Tactical Air Command, Langley AFB, Va., 1983-86; comdr. 33d Tactical Fighter Wing, Eglin AFB, Fla., 1986-87, 1987-88, 57th Fighter Weapons Wing, Nellis AFB, 1988-90; dep. dir. politico-mil. affairs Joint Staff, Washington, 1990-92; sr. mil. asst. for sec. def. Office Sec. Def., Washington, 1992-94; comdr. 9th AF, Shaw AFB, 1994-96; dep. chief of staff, air & space HAF, Washington, 1996-97; commdr. Allied Air Forces Ctrl. Europe, Ramstein AB, Germany, 1997-2000, HQ Air Combat Command, Langley AFB, 2000—01; chief of staff, USAF US Dept. Def., Washington, 2001—05; pres., CEO Science Applications International Corp. (SAIC), 2012—. Adv. bd. PlatinumSolutions, Reston, Va.; bd. dirs. Goodrich Corp., 2005—, Rolls-Royce North Am. Holdings, Inc., 2005—, TechTeam Global, Inc., 2006—, Vought Aircraft Industries, Inc., 2006—, Jacobs Engrg. Group Inc., 2007—, Science Applications International Corp. (SAIC), 2007—, Somanetics Corp. Contbr. articles to mil. pub. Bd. dirs. The George C. Marshall Found., The Air Force Village Charitable Found., American Air Mus. in Britain; bd. visitors Va. Mil. Inst. Decorated Def. DSM with oak leaf cluster, Legion of Merit DSM with oak leaf cluster, DFC with 2 oak leaf clusters, Air medal with 17 oak leaf clusters. Mem. Air Force Assn., Air Force Village Charitable Found. Roman Catholic. Avocations: racquet ball, jogging, piano, guitar, golf, sports cars. Office: Science Applications International Corp 1710 SAIC Drive Mc Lean VA 22102 Office Phone: 703-676-4300.*

JUNEAU, TED, academic administrator; m. Judy Juneau; 1 child, Whitney. BA, Ft. Hays State U., Kans., 1972; MA, U. Kans., 1992. Spl. edn. tchr. Topeka HS, Kans., 1972—81, head coach women's basketball and track, asst. coach football and men's basketball; social studies tchr. Lawrence HS, Kans., 1981—89, asst. prin., 1989—94, head coach women's cross country, golf, men's basketball; prin. Lawrence Ctrl. Jr. HS, 1994—2005; project dir. U. Kans. Inst. Edn. Rsch. and Pub. Svc., 2005—07; instr. U. Kans. Sch. Edn., 2005—07; cons. to the pres. on athletics Haskell Indian Nations U., Lawrence, 2007, athletic dir., 2007—10; head basketball coach Haskell Indian Nations U. Indians, 2007—10; academic coord. U. Tulsa Athletics

Dept., Okla., 2012—. Named Kans. Coach of Yr., women's basketball, 1981, Kans. Coach of Yr., men's basketball, 1983, Kans. Coach of Yr., women's golf, 1985. Office: Univerity of Tulsa Athletics 800 S Tucker Dr Tulsa OK 74104

JUNELL, ROBERT ALAN, lawyer, federal judge; b. El Paso, Tex., Jan. 27, 1947; s. Robert Frank and Maxine (Simmons) J.; m. Beverly Ann Singley, Dec. 26, 1968; children: Ryan, Keith, Elizabeth, Clay. AA, N.Mex. Mil. Inst., 1967; BS, Tex. Tech U., 1969, JD, 1976; MA, U. Ark., 1974. Bar: Tex. 1977, U.S. Dist. Ct. (no. dist.) Tex. 1979, U.S. Dist. Ct. (we. dist.) Tex. 1984. Assoc. Scott, Hulse, Marshall & Feuille, El Paso, 1977-79, Webb, Stokes & Sparks, San Angelo, Tex., 1979—; judge US Dist. Ct. (we. dist.) Tex., 2003—03. Mem. Tex. Tech Found., Lubbock. Served to capt. U.S. Army, 1970-73. Mem. Tex. Bar Assn. (cert.), Tom Green County Bar Assn. (bd. dirs.), Tex. Trial Lawyers Assn. (assoc. bd. dirs.), Tex. Tech Law Sch. Alumni Assn. (bd. dirs.). Democrat. Avocations: steer roping, skiing. Office: Webb Stokes Sparks Parker 314 W Harris Ave San Angelo TX 76903-6339 also: 200 E Wall Midland TX 79701

JUNG, PETER MICHAEL, lawyer; b. Ossining, NY, May 12, 1955; s. Peter Joseph and Paula June (Moyer) J.; m. Gretchen Lee Megowen, June 19, 1976. SB in Math., Earth and Planetary Sci., MIT, 1975; JD magna cum laude, Harvard U., 1979. Bar: Tex. 1979, US Dist. Ct. (no. dist.) Tex. 1979, US Ct. Appeals (5th cir.) 1980, US Dist. Ct. (ea. dist.) Tex. 1981, US Ct. Appeals (10th cir.) 1984, US Ct. Appeals (6th cir.) 1992, US Supreme Ct. 1988, US Dist. Ct. (so. and we. dists.) Tex. 1989; cert. civil appellate law Tex. Bd. Legal Specialization, US Cts. of Appeals (8th cir., 9th cir.), 2004, US Cts. of Appeals (11th cir., 1996). Tech. staff C.S. Draper Lab., Cambridge, Mass., 1975-76; law clk. to hon. Patrick E. Higginbotham US Dist. Ct. (no. dist.) Tex., Dallas, 1979-80; assoc. Strasburger & Price, Dallas, 1980-85, ptnr., 1986—. Lectr. El Centro Cmty. Coll., Dallas, 1980-82; instr. So. Meth. U., Dallas, 1984-86, com. Qualified Judiciary 1992-, Dallas Ethics Rev. Task Force 1999, Dallas Charter Rev. Commn. 2002-03, adv. com. Dallas Comprehensive Plan 2004-06. Co-author: An Alternative Entry-Through-Landing Guidance Scheme for the Space Shuttle Orbital Flight Test, 1976, Introduction to the American Legal System, Texas Edition, 1982; contbg. editor Legal Asst. Today Mag., 1983-88. Sec. Dallas Homeowners League, 1984-86, 1st v.p., 1986-87, pres., 1987-88, treas., 1988-89, 92—97, bd. dirs. 1984-90, 91-02; pres. White Rock Neighborhood Assn., Dallas, 1984-85, v.p., 1994—2011, pres., 2011-; mem. adv. com. Dallas Zoning Ordinance, 1985-2005, Leadership Dallas, 1985-86, Dallas City Plan and Zoning Commn., 1987-89, 91; bd. dirs. Friends of Fair Park, 1990-96, mem. exec. com., 1991-96; bd. dirs. Tex. Neighborhoods Together, 1989-95, sec., 1989-91, pres. 1991-95, Harvard Law Sch. Assn; bd. dir. Tex. Land Conservancy, 2000-; exec. bd. dirs. Tex. Creative Problem Solving Orgn., 2003-, bd. dirs. White Rock Lake Mus., 2004-, sec., 2004-, congregation coun., King & Glory Lutheran Ch., 2008-11, v.p., 2009, pres., 2010. Recipient Pres.'s award, 1992, 1997, Super Lawyers, Tex. Monthly's top 100, 2003—09, Best Lawyers in Dallas, D Mag.'s, Best Lawyers in Am., 2001—10; named Top 10 Lawyers, 2010. Mem. Tex. Bar Assn. (com.) 1995-1996, Dallas Bar Assn.(chmn.) 1995,2003, Bar Assn. 5th Fed. Cir., Tex. Assn. Def. Counsel (vice-chmn. 1985-87, chmn. amicus curiae com. 1991-1997, regional v.p. 1993-95, adminstrv. v.p. 1995-97), (nominating com., 1998, 2000, 2001), chair Strasburger's Appellate and Zoning & Land Use practices,mem. Govtl. Law practice grp., fellow Am. Acad. Appellate Lawyers, Supreme Ct.Tex. Task Force Jury Charge 1991-94. Republican. Lutheran. Avocations: theater, travel. Office: Strasburger & Price 901 Main St Ste 4400 Dallas TX 75202 Office Phone: 214-651-4724. Office Fax: 214-659-4022. Business E-Mail: michael.jung@strasburger.com.

JUNG, RODNEY C., internist, academic administrator; b. New Orleans, Oct. 9, 1920; s. Frederick Charles and Clara (Cuevas) J. BS in Zoology with honors, Tulane U., 1941, MD, 1945, MS in Parasitology and Microbiology, 1950, PhD, 1953. Diplomate: Am. Bd. Internal Medicine. Intern Charity Hosp. La., New Orleans, 1945-46; dir. Hutchinson Meml. Clinic, 1948; asst. parasitology Tulane U., 1948-50, instr. tropical medicine, 1950-53, asst. prof., 1953-57, assoc. prof. tropical medicine, 1957-63, prof. tropical medicine, 1963-73, clin. prof. internal medicine, 1973-91, clin. prof. tropical medicine, 1983-92, prof. emeritus tropical medicine, 1992—, head div. tropical medicine, 1960-63; health dir. City of New Orleans, 1963-70, 79-82; internist in charge Ill. Central Hosp., New Orleans, 1956-70. Sr. vis. physician Charity Hosp., 1959—; mem. study sect. on tropical medicine and parasitology Nat. Inst. Allergy and Infectious Disease, 1963-67; mem. Commn. on Parasitic Diseases Armed Forces Epidemiol. Bd., 1967-73; chief communicable disease control, City of New Orleans, 1978; sr. in internal medicine Touro Infirmary. Co-author: Animal Agents and Vectors of Disease and Clinical Parasitology; editl. bd. Am. Jour. Tropical Medicine and Hygiene, 1972-94; contbr. articles to profl. jours. Pres. Irish Cultural Soc. New Orleans, 1980-92, pres. emeritus 1992—; officer res. div. New Orleans Police Dept., 1977-84; chmn. New Orleans Mosquito and Termite Control Bd. John and Mary Markle Scholar in med. sci. Fellow ACP; hon. fellow Brazilian Soc. Tropical Medicine; mem. Am., Royal socs. tropical medicine and hygiene, Am. Soc. Parasitologists, La. State Med. Soc., Orleans Parish Med. Soc., Nat. Rifle Assn., Irish Georgian Soc., La. Mosquito and Termite Control Assn., La. Soc. Internal Medicine, Am. Soc. Internal Medicine, New Orleans Acad. Internal Medicine, Am. Def. Preparedness Assn., Irish-Am. Cultural Inst., Nat. Trust. Historic Preservation, La. Landmarks Soc., Naval Inst., New Orleans Mus. Art, New Orleans Opera Assn., La. Wildlife Fedn., Phi Beta Kappa, Sigma Xi, Delta Omega, Alpha Omega Alpha. Presbyterian.

JUNKER, BOBBY RAY, research and development company executive, physicist; b. San Antonio, Tex., Aug. 29, 1943; s. Richard Eugene and Alice Emma (Gruetzmacher) J.; m. Judith Lynne Combs, Sept. 12, 1968 (div. Aug. 1974); 1 child, Bryce Allyn; m. Sheryl Ann Watson, Oct. 8, 1976 (div. July 1995); children: Melissa Sheryl, Evan Ryan; m. Virginia C. Katt, July 13, 1996. BS, U. Southwestern La., 1965; MA, U. Tex., 1967, PhD in Chemistry, 1969. Instr. chemistry U. Tex., Austin, 1969-70; rsch. assoc. physics U. Pitts., 1970-72; asst. prof. physics U. Ga., Athens, 1972-76; sci. officer Office Naval Rsch., Arlington, Va., 1977-84, dir. physic. divsn., 1983-86, dir. math. and phys. scis. dept., 1986-93, head electronics, info. and surveillance dept., 1993—2005, head C4I3R dept., 2006—. Contbr. chpts. to books. Treas. PTA, Fairfax, Va., 1988-89, county rep., 1990-92; treas. Fairfax Christian Ch., 1982-87, 92-95. Recipient Presdl. Meritorious Rank award U.S. Govt., 1989, 99, 2008, Presdl. Disting Rank award U.S. Govt., 2003. Mem. AAAS, Am. Phys. Soc., Sigma Xi. Achievements include rsch. theoretical atomic physics, including electron-atom and ion-atom collisions. Office: Office Naval Rsch Info Electronics and Surveillance Dept 800 N Quincy St Arlington VA 22203

JURGENS, JULIE GRAHAM, retired mathematics professor; b. Washta, Iowa, Mar. 8, 1950; d. Albert Harm and Thelma Ann (Johnson) Haenfler; m. Dennis Dean Graham, Mar. 16, 1969 (div. Oct. 17, 1988); children: Tracy Ann Graham-Lester, Tricia Jean Graham-Banta; m. David Dallas Jurgens, Apr. 17, 1998. Undergrad., Morningside Coll., Sioux City, Iowa, 1968—69; BA in Math. Edn./Phys. Edn., Wayne State Coll., 1969—72; MS, Marycrest Coll., Davenport, Iowa, 1985; PhD, U. Iowa, 1997. Prof. math. and computer sci. Marycrest U., 1985—97; dept. chair math., sci., and tech. Flagler Coll., St. Augustine, Fla., 1997—. Mem.: AAUP, Fla. Coun. Tchrs. Math., Fla. Assn. Computer in Edn., Nat. Coun. Tchrs. Math., Math. Assn. Am., Phi Delta Kappa. Home: 18297 W Spencer Dr Surprise AZ 85374 Office: Flagler Coll Saint Augustine FL 32085

JURGENSEN, WARREN PETER, retired psychiatrist, educator; b. Sioux City, Iowa, June 30, 1921; s. Matthias Peter and Dagmar J.; m. Gwenda Doris Downey, Mar. 30, 1946 (dec. May, 2011); children—Gail, Karen, Timothy BS, Northwestern U., 1945; MD, Creighton U., 1950. Diplomate: American Bd. Psychiatry. Intern Edward W. Sparrow Hosp., Lansing, Mich., 1950—51; regional health dir., then asst. chief U.S. Health Mission to Iran, 1951—54; psychiat. resident USPHS Hosp., Lexington, Ky., 1955—57, Cin. Gen. Hosp., 1957—58; with USPHS, 1951—70; chief Clin. Research Center, NIMH, Ft. Worth, 1969-70; dir. student health services U. Tex.-Arlington, 1970-77, also adj. prof. biology; psychiatrist Tarrant County Mental Health Mental Retardation Svcs., Ft. Worth, 1977-86; psychiat. cons., 1984—96; ret., 1996. Clin. asst. prof. U. Ky. Med. Sch., 1962—66; clin. asst. prof. psychiatry U. Tex. Southwestern Med. Sch., 1966—72; vis. rsch. scientist Inst. Behavorial Rsch. Tex. Christian U., 1967—72; vis. lectr. Regional Tng. Ctr. North Ctrl. Tex. Council Govts., 1967—77; cons. Alive and Well Program U. Tex. Southwestern Med. Sch., 1974—79. Mem. Gov.'s Adv. Council on Drug Abuse, 1973-79. Served with USNR, 1942-45. Fellow American Pub. Health Assn.; mem. American Psychiat. Assn. (Disting. Life fellow) Episcopalian. Office: Warren & Jurgensen 5100 Randoll Mill Rd Apt 1116 Fort Worth TX 76112-1523*

JURICIC, DAVOR, engineering educator; b. Split, Croatia, Aug. 2, 1928; arrived in U.S., 1968; s. Mate and Slavka (Franceschi) J.; m. Milesa L. Harris, Mar. 10, 1984; 1 child, Ivanna Albertin. Dipl.Ing., U. Belgrade, Yugoslavia, 1952, DSc, 1964. Stress analyst Icarus Aircraft Industries, Zemun, Yugoslavia, 1953-58; rsch. engr. Inst. Aeronautics, Belgrade, 1958-63; asst. prof. U. Belgrade, 1963-65, assoc. prof., 1965-68, S.D. State U., Brookings, 1968-73, prof., 1973-75; vis. prof. Stanford (Calif.) U., 1975-78; prof. mech. engring. U. Tex., Austin, 1978-98, prof. emeritus, 1998—. Contbr. numerous articles to profl. jours. Rsch. grantee various agencies, 1962—. Mem. Am. Soc. Engring. Edn. (Chester F. Carlson award 1993). Achievements include research in a suspension system for railway vehicles; patent in field. Business E-Mail: juricic@mail.utexas.edu, dmj@austin.utexas.edu.

JURKA, EDITH MILA, psychiatrist, researcher; b. NYC, Dec. 4, 1915; d. Charles Anton and Edith Dorothy (Schevcik) J. BA, Smith Coll., Northampton, Mass., 1936; postgrad., Charles U., Prague, Czechoslovakia, 1936-38; MD, Yale U., New Haven, Conn., 1944. Diplomate Am. Bd. Psychiatry and Neurology. Intern in children's med. svc. Bellevue Hosp., NYC, 1944-45, asst. alienist, 1947-49; rotating intern Gallinger Hosp., Washington, 1945-46; intern NY State Psychiat. Inst., NYC, 1946-47; asst. psychiatrist Mt. Sinai Hosp., NYC, 1949-51; pvt. practice NYC, 1949—; asst. psychiatrist Roosevelt Hosp., NYC, 1954-57; chief psychiatrist Pleasantville Cottage Sch., NY, 1961-74. Bd. dirs. intuition network Inst. Noetic Scis.; founder Wind Song Inst. Sec. Jane Coffin Childs Fund, 1938—41. Fellow Am. Orthopsychiat. Assn.; mem. Am. Psychiat. Assn., NY Coun. Child and Adolescent Psychiatry, NY County Med. Soc., NY State Med. Soc. (psychiat. medicine com.), Westchester Psychiat. Soc. Avocations: architecture, parapsychology, travel, gardening, theater. Home: 1548 S Hillcrest Ave Clearwater FL 33756-2258 also: 1692 Ashton Abbey Rd Clearwater FL 33755-1301 Office Phone: 212-737-0591.

JURRJENS, JAIR F., professional baseball player; b. Willemstad, Curaçao, Jan. 29, 1986; s. Carl Jurrjens. Pitcher Detroit Tigers, 2007, Atlanta Braves, 2008—. Mem. Dutch nat. team World Baseball Classic, 2006. Named to Nat. League All-Star Team, Maj. League Baseball, 2011. Achievements include leading the National League in: starts (34), 2009. Office: Atlanta Baraves 755 Hank Aaron Dr Atlanta GA 30315

JUSKOWIAK, TERRY EUGENE, career military officer, information technology executive; s. Joe Leon and Betty; m. Susan K. Renn, Sept. 15, 1974; children: John, Christopher, Jennifer. BA, The Citadel, Charleston, SC, 1973; MS, Fla. Inst. Technology, Melbourne, 1981. Commd. 2d lt. U.S. Army, 1973, advanced through ranks to major gen., 1999, contract cost mgmt. analyst Army Mat. Ctr. Alexandria, Va., 1980-84, aide-de-camp Sec. Army Washington, 1984-85, dep. V Corps logistics officer Frankfurt, Germany, 1986-88, exec. officer 122 Main 3d Armored Divsn. Hanau, Germany, 1988-89, from divsn. staff to battalion cmdr. 82d Airborne Divsn. Ft. Bragg, NC, 1989-92, spl. asst. to chief of Staff Washington, 1992-94, brigade cmdr. 10th Mtn. Divsn. Ft. Drum, NY, 1994-96, asst. divsn. cmdr. support 10th Mtn. Divsn., 1996—; dep. comdg. gen. NATO SFOR Spt Cmd, 1996-98; dir. logistics 14 U.S. Atlantic comd. Norfolk, Va., 1997-98; comdr. 1st Corps Support Command (Airborne), Ft. Bragg, NC, 1998-2000; dir. logistics U.S. Forces Command, Ft. McPherson, Ga., 2000-01; quartermaster gen., comdt. Quartermaster Sch., 2001—02; comdr. Combined Arms Support Command, 2002—04; lead ptnr. Army acct. IBM Global Svcs., 2004—. Decorated DSM, Def. Superior Svc. medal, Legion of Merit, Bronze Star, Def. Meritorious Svc. medal. Mem. Assn. Citadel Men, Assn. U.S. Army, Quartermaster Assn., 82d Airborne Assn., 10th Mtn. Divsn. Assn. Presbyterian. Avocations: reading, running, skiing. Office Phone: 678-546-6407. Personal E-mail: tjuskowiak@aol.com. Business E-Mail: tjuskowiak@us.ibm.com.

JUSTICE, CAROLYN H., state legislator; b. Wilmington, NC, May 13, 1946; m. William Justice; children: William Jr., Robert. Bookkeeper Ashland Oil Ky Warren Bros, 1970—73; owner Pier 1 Clothing, 1976—78; bus. mgr. Condo and Patio Assns.; state rep. Dist. 16 NC, 2002—. Mem.: Greater Hampstead C. of C. (founding bd. mem.), Greater Hampstead Civic Assn. (founding bd. mem.), Lions Club (program chair 2000—). Republican. Methodist. Mailing: Dist Off PO Box 296 Hampstead NC 28443 Office: North Carolina House of Representatives 300 N Salisbury St Rm 420 Raleigh NC 27603-5925 Office Phone: 910-270-4604, 919-715-9664. E-mail: Carolyn.Justice@ncleg.net.

JUSTICE, MADELINE CAROL, education educator; b. Beaumont, Tex., Nov. 5, 1950; d. Frank and Rosie Lee Molo; m. James Henry Justice, June 29. BA, Tex. Woman's U., 1972, MA, 1977; EdD, East Tex. State U., 1987. Cert. tchr. English, history, education, mid-mgmt. Tex. English tchr. Plano (Tex.) Ind. Sch. Dist., 1972—92; prof., asst. dept. chair Coll. Edn. Tex. A&M U., Commerce, 1992—. Proposal reviewer S.W. Ednl. Rsch. Conf., 2000—02; chpt. reviewer Wadsworth-Thomson Learning, 2003; grant proposal reviewer Fund for the Improvement of Postsecondary Edn., 2004; presenter and cons. in field. Contbr. articles to profl. jours.; mem. editl. bd.: Contemporary Issues in Technology and Teacher Education: Current Practices, 2000—. Recipient Neil Humfield Disting. Faculty award, Tex. A&M U., 1999. Mem.: Am. Assn. Colls. for Tchr. Edn., Soc. for Info. Tech. and Tchr. Edn. (mem. program com. 1999—), Phi Delta Kappa (Pres. award 1996, 1998). Democrat. Avocations: singing, reading, research. Office: Tex A&M Univ Commerce PO Box 5011 Commerce TX Office Phone: 903-886-5582. Business E-Mail: madeline_justice@tamu-commerce.edu.

JUSTICE, ROCKLEN R., automotive executive; Regional v.p. ctrl., NE group Genuine Parts Co., v.p. Southern divsn. Office: Genuine Parts Co 2999 Cir 75 Pky Atlanta GA 30339 Office Phone: 770-953-1700. Office Fax: 770-956-2211. Business E-Mail: rocklen_justice@genpt.com.

JUSTICE, RON, state legislator; BS, M, Okla. State Univ. Ret. Okla. State Univ. extension agt.; mem. Dist. 23 Okla. State Senate, 2004—. Republican. Office: 2300 N Lincoln Blvd Rm 423 Oklahoma City OK 73105 also: 2209 County St 2880 Chickasha OK 73018 Office Phone: 405-521-5537. Business E-Mail: justice@oksenate.gov.

JUSTINIANI, FEDERICO ROBERTO, retired internist, educator; b. Havana, Cuba, Aug. 15, 1929; came to U.S., 1964, naturalized, 1969; s. Federico Luis and Margarita (Longa) J.; m. Maria Suarez, Nov. 29, 1955. BS, De La Salle Coll., Havana, 1947; MD, Havana U., 1954. Diplomate Am. Bd. Internal Medicine (recognized for advanced achievement 1987). Intern, resident in internal medicine Havana U. Hosp., 1955-61; practice medicine Havana, 1961-64; intern St. Francis Hosp., Miami Beach, Fla., 1965; resident in internal medicine Mt. Sinai Hosp., Miami Beach, 1966-69, program coord. residency in internal medicine, 1969-74; dir. med. edn. Mt. Sinai Med. Ctr., Miami Beach, 1974—2002; instr. medicine U. Miami, 1969-72, asst. prof., 1972-82, assoc. prof., 1982-90, prof., 1990—2010. Contbr. articles to profl. jours. Master ACP; mem. AMA (Physicians Recognition awards), Fla. Med. Assn., So. Med. Assn., Dade County Med. Assn., Am. Geriatrics Soc., Cuban Med. Assn. in Exile, Nat. Assn. Cuban-Am. Educators (pres. 2004—08). Home Phone: 305-444-6845. Personal E-mail: fjustin@bellsouth.net.

KAAT, JIM, sportscaster, retired professional baseball player; b. Zeeland, Mich., Nov. 7, 1938; s. John Kaat; m. MaryAnn Montanaro (dec. 2008); 4 children; m. Margie Bowes Mather, 2009. Attended, Hope Coll., Holland, Mich. Pitcher Washington Senators, 1959—60, Minn. Twins, 1961—73, Chgo. White Sox, 1973—75, Phila. Phillies, 1976—79, NY Yankees, 1979—80, St. Louis Cardinals, 1980—83; analyst, minor league games Home Team Sports Network, 1981; ret. Maj. League Baseball, 1983; pitching coach Cin. Reds, 1984—85; chief correspondent, Good Morning America WABC-TV, 1984, 1985; analyst, play-by-play announcer WPIX-TV, NYC, 1986; analyst, Olympic baseball WNBC-TV, 1988; analyst, Minn. Twins broadcasts WCCO-TV, 1988—93; analyst, Coll. World Series, Maj. League Baseball ESPN, Bristol, Conn., 1988, chief analyst, Baseball Tonight, 1994; analyst WTBS-TV, Atlanta, 1988; analyst, play-by-play announcer WSB-AM Radio, Atlanta, 1988; primary analyst, Maj. League Baseball CBS Sports, 1989—93; analyst, NY Yankees/Seattle Mariners playoff series Baseball Network, ABC Sports, 1995; pregame analyst, Yankees Score Card Madison Sq. Garden Network, NYC, 1995, analyst, NY Yankees broadcasts, 1995—2002, YES Network, NYC, 2002—06, blogger, Kaat's Korner; color commentator, Thursday Night Baseball Maj. League Baseball Network, 2009—. Founder Southpaw Enterprises, Inc., Ft. Pierce, Fla. Author: Still Pitching: Musings from the Mound and the Microphone, 2003. Founder MaryAnn Kaat Meml. Fund, 2008. Recipient Gold Glove award, 1962—77, Emmy award, Outstanding Live Sports Coverage, 1997, Emmy award, Outstanding Live Sports Coverage-Single Program, 1997, 2004, Emmy award, Outstanding Live Sports Coverage-Series, 1997, 1999, Emmy award, On-camera Achievement, 2004, Emmy award, Talent, 2005; named Am. League Pitcher of Yr., The Sporting News, 1966; named to Am. League All-Star Team, Maj. League Baseball, 1962, 1966, 1975. Achievements include leading the American League in: shutouts, 1962; starts, 1965, 1966; innings pitched, complete games, wins, 1966; member of the World Series championship winning St. Louis Cardinals, 1982. Office: PO Box 1130 Port Salerno FL 34992 also: c/o MLB Advanced Media 75 Ninth Ave 5th Fl New York NY 10011

KACHERGIS, JOYCE W., book designer; b. Omaha, Feb. 9, 1925; d. Lawrence Benjamin Webster and Olga Agnes Olsen; m. George J. Kachergis, July 6, 1946 (dec. Aug. 1974); children: Peter W., Karl George, Anne Olga; m. Jess G. Bell, 1986 (dec. Apr. 2001). AA, Stephens Coll., 1945; BFA, Sch. of the Art Inst., Chgo., 1947. Prodn. design mgr. U. N.C. Press, Chapel Hill, 1963-77; prodn. and design mgr. Stanford U. Press, Palo Alto, Calif., 1977-80; founder, pres., designer Kachergis Book Design, Pittsboro, NC, 1980—. Vis. prof. Radcliffe Sch. Pub., Cambridge, Mass., 1979-82. Grantee, Kresge Found., 1974. Mem. Am. Assn. Univ. Presses (bd. dirs. 1978-80). Office: Kachergis Book Design 14 Small St N Pittsboro NC 27312-5453 Personal E-mail: jwkb@mindspring.com.

KADANE, SHEFFIELD A., councilman, investment company executive, real estate agent; m. Deborah Kadane; 7 children. Grad., U. Tex., Arlington. Pres. PICS Investment Co., Dallas, 1963—; agent/broker Ebby Halliday, Dallas, 1995—; councilman, Dist. 9 Dallas City Coun., 2007—, vice-chair transp. & environ. com., mem. pub. safety com., econ. devel. com., judicial appts. com., quality of life & govt. svcs. com. Mng. ptnr. K-B Oil Co., Dallas, 1978—; mem bd. adjustments City of Dallas, 1995—2003; mem. White Rock Lake Task Force. Vice-chmn. planning/design Dallas Park & Recreation Bd., 2003—06; bd. dirs. Disciples of Trinity, Dallas. Mem.: Nat.Assn. Realtors, MetroTex Assn. Realtors (mem. govt. affairs com.), Dallas NE C. of C., Dallas Arboretum, Dallas Rotary Club. Office: Dallas City Coun 1500 Marilla St Rm 5FS Dallas TX 75201 Office Phone: 214-670-4069. Office Fax: 214-670-5115. Business E-Mail: sheffield.kadane@dallascityhall.com.

KADENYUK, LEONID K., astronaut; b. Chernivtsi region, Ukraine, Jan. 28, 1951; m. Vera Kosolapinkova; 2 children. Grad. pilot-engr., Chernihiv Higher Aviation Sch., Ukraine, 1971; grad. test pilot, State Sci. Rsch. Inst. of Russian Air Forces Ctr., 1977; grad., Yuri Gagarin Cosmonaut Tng. Ctr., 1978; MSME, Moscow Aviation Inst., 1989. Cert. test pilot 1st class, mil. pilot 2d class, pilot instr. Trainee USSR Cosmonaut Team Yuri Gagarin Cosmonaut Tng. Ctr., Star City, Russia, 1976—, test cosmonaut, pilot multiple usage space sys. group, 1978—83; test pilot GLIC VVS Russia Russian Air Force, 1984—88; comdr. Ukrainian space crew, 1990—96; sci. investigator Ukrainian-Am. expt. in space biology Inst. Botany, Nat. Acad. Scis. Ukraine, Kiev, 1996; mem. astronaut group Nat. Space Agy. of Ukraine, 1996—; prime payload specialist STS-87 Columbia Nat. Space Agy. Ukraine, NASA, 1997. Chmn. State Com. on SU-275M cockpit design, 1985. Achievements include logging over 2400 hours flying time in 54 different types of aircraft; over 15 days, 16 hours in space, 252 Earth orbits. Avocations: running, athletics. Office: NASA Johnson Space Ctr Astronaut Office/CB Houston TX 77058

KADING, KELLY, food products executive; Sr. prodn. mgr. The Southland Corp., 1980—87; v.p., ops., Model Dairy Suiza Foods, 1987—97, pres., Model Dairy, 1997—2000, sr. v.p., ops., 2000; sr. v.p., ops., Diary Group Dean Foods Co., 2007—. Office: Dean Foods Co 2515 McKinney Ave Ste 1200 Dallas TX 75201 Office Phone: 214-303-3400. Office Fax: 214-303-3499. Business E-Mail: kelly_kading@deanfoods.com.

KADOW, JOSEPH J., lawyer, food service executive; b. Scranton, Pa., 1956; BS in Acctg., U. Scranton, 1978; JD, Pa. State U., 1981. Bar: Pa. 1981, Fla. 1983. Ptnr. Baker & Hostetler LLP, 1990—94; v.p. OSI Restaurant Ptnrs., Inc. (formerly Outback Steakhouse, Inc.), Tampa, Fla., 1994—2001, gen. counsel, sec., 1994—2005, sr. v.p. Tampa, Fla., 2001—05; exec. v.p., chief legal officer OSI Restaurant Partners, LLC, Tampa, Fla., 2005—. Trustee Florida TaxWatch, 2000. Office: OSI Restaurant Partners Inc 5th Fl 2202 N W Shore Blvd Tampa FL 33607 Office Phone: 813-282-1225. Office Fax: 813-282-1209. Business E-Mail: joekadow@outback.com.

KAESTNER, H. TODD, hospital and healthcare company executive; BA in Economics & Bus. Adminstrn., Vanderbilt U.; MBA, U. Louisville. Exec. v.p., corp. devel. Am. Retirement Corp., 1993—2006, Brookdale Senior Living, Inc., 2006—. Office: Brookdale Senior Living Inc 111 Westwood Pl Ste 200 Brentwood TN 37027 Office Phone: 615-221-2250. Office Fax: 615-221-2289. Business E-Mail: TKaestner@brookdaleliving.com.

KAFOURE, MICHAEL D., food products executive; married; 3 children. BS in Mgmt. & Adminstrn., Ind. U. Pres. Merico, Inc.; joined Campbell Taggart, 1967, pres., COO, bakery ops., 1990; pres., COO Interstate Brands Corp. (subs. Interstate Bakeries Corp.), Interstate Brands West Corp. (subs. Interstate Bakeries Corp.); sr. v.p. Hostess Brands, Inc. (formerly Interstate Bakeries Corp.), Kansas City, Mo., 1995, pres., COO, 1995—. Office: Hostess Brands Inc 6031 Connection Dr Irving TX 75039 Office Phone: 972-532-4500. Office Fax: 972-892-7694. Business E-Mail: michael_kafoure@interstatebrands.com.

KAGLE, JOSEPH LOUIS, JR., artist, administrator, historian; b. Pitts., May 2, 1932; s. Joseph Louis and Edith (Marcellus) K.; m. Anne Cornelia Schiller, Jan. 19, 1957; children: Samantha Anne, Christopher Yung Wook. Student, Carnegie Mus. Sch. Art, 1938-51; BA in English, Dartmouth Coll., 1955; MFA in Art and Art History, U. Colo., 1958; MEd in Gifted and Talented Edn., U. Ark., Little Rock, 1984. Cert. tchg. K-12 Bridgewater State U. Instr. Wis. State U., Whitewater, 1958-60; head dept. art, asst. prof. Washington and Jefferson Coll., Pa., 1960-64; head dept. art, assoc. prof. Keuka Coll., 1964-68; artist in residence Chapman Coll., World Campus Afloat, 1968-69; prof., head dept. fine arts, visual arts, dance, music and theatre U. Guam, 1970-76; prof. art Community Coll. Finger Lakes, 1976-78; exec. dir. S.E. Ark. Arts and Sci. Center, Pine Bluff, 1978-84; dir. Brockton (Mass.) Art Mus., 1984-86, The Art Ctr., Waco, Tex., 1987—2000, Bridgewater State Coll., 1986-87, McLennan CC, 1987—2005; hon. prof. Tbilsi Acad. Fine Arts, 2001—03; vis. scholar Mongolian State U., 2004, Lone Star Coll., Kingwood, Tex., 2005—. Artist in residence Wash. State U., Spokane, 1965—66, Naples Mill Sch., 1976—2001, Internat. Plentary of Artists, Kutaisi, Georgia, 2001; bd. contbrs. Waco Tribune-Herald Opinion Editls.; lectr. USIS, Taiwan, 1970—76; critic Pine Bluff (Ark.). Work exhibited in over 750 nat. and internat. exhbns. including Nat. Gallery, Washington, Nat. Mus., Tiblisi, Georgia, Upstream People Gallery 2009-, dir. 50 TV shows on art; muralist, Hafa Adai Theatre, Bank of Guam, Fine Arts Bldg. U. Guam; author: Death Is All the Time, 1976; contbr. articles to profl. publs.; 2010-2013;curator for world tour exhibition, My Peace Journey by Ryofu Pussel, Japan, 2007-, Open the Door; author of 100 essays and two major works on Peace, Rotary Global History Fellowship, 2006-07. Mem. planning bd. Pine Bluff Com. Gifted and Talented, 1979-80; mem. adv. bd. Sta. KCTF, 1989-92; bd. dirs. Greater Waco Coun. on the Arts, 1989—; bd. dirs. Assn. for Retarded Citizens., chmn., 1990-92, 93-94. Recipient Fulbright specialist, Mongolia, 2003, Darmouth Coll. Alumni award for Outstanding Svc., Class of 1955, 2006, Nat. Vol. of Yr., Arc, 1993, Artist of Yr., Am. Inst. Archs., 1975, Outstanding Alumni, Dartmouth Coll., 2006, Sys. Pub. award, Lone Star Sys., 2009; named Fulbright scholar, Taiwan, 1965, Georgia, 2001—03, Fulbright specialist, Mongolia, 2004, Smithsonian Instn. Kellog Found. Project scholar, 1983, artist of yr., Pacific chpt. AIA, 1976—77; named one of 12 Am. Artists, Houston, 2013. Mem. Am. Mus. Assn., Coll. Art Assn., Tex. Assn. Mus., Coll. Art Assn., Am. Assn. Mus., Waco Assn. Mus. (chmn. bd. dirs. 1995-97), Waco C. of C. (bd. dirs. 1994-97), Rotary Global History Fellowship (pres. 2007-10), Rotary, E-Club SW USA (pres. 2010-11), Rotarians Internet. Democrat. Avocations: travel, art, writing. Home: 3758 Glade Forest Dr Houston TX 77339-1739 Home Phone: 281-360-7355; Office Phone: 281-360-7355. Personal E-mail: joe_kagle@hotmail.com.

KAHAN, BARRY DONALD, surgeon, educator; b. Cleve., July 25, 1939; s. Jacob Marvin and Pearl (Schultz) Kahan; m. Rochelle Liebling, Sept. 22, 1963 (dec.); 1 child, Kara; m. Marsha Capen, Dec. 3, 2005. BS, U. Chgo., 1960, PhD, 1964, MD, 1965. Intern Mass. Gen. Hosp., Boston, 1965-66, resident in surgery, 1968-72; staff asso. in immunology NIH, 1966-68; asst. prof. surgery and physiology Northwestern U. Sch. Medicine, Chgo., 1972-74, asso. prof., 1975-76; prof. surgery U. Tex. Med. Sch., Houston, 1977—2008, emeritus dir., divs. organ transplantation dept. surgery, dir. program immunology, grad. sch., 1998—2008. Editor in chief Transplantation Proceedings, 2002—. Bd. dirs. Ill. Kidney Found., 1974—76. Mem. ACS, AAAS, Soc. Univ. Surgeons, Am. Soc. Clin. Investigation, Am. Soc. Transplant Surgeons (pres. 1989—), Am. Surg. Assn., Internat. Transplantation Soc. (charter, treas. 1990—), Am. Surg. Assn., Am. Assn. Immunologists, Am. Assn. Cancer Rsch., Am. Physiol. Soc.

KAHN, BERND, radiochemist, educator; b. Pforzheim, Baden, Germany, Aug. 16, 1928; US1938; s. Eric Herman and Alice Dora (Meyer) K.; m. Gail Pressman, Aug. 6, 1961; children: Jennifer, Elizabeth. BSChemE, N.J. Inst. Tech., 1950; MS in Physics, Vanderbilt U., 1952; PhD in Chemistry, MIT, 1960. Commd. officer USPHS, 1954, advanced through grades to capt., 1970, health physicist, radiochemist, Oak Ridge (Tenn.) Nat. Lab., 1951-54, engr. various facilities Tenn., Mass., Ala., Ohio, 1954-74, ret., 1974; prof. nuc. engring. and health physics Ga. Inst. Tech., Atlanta, 1974-96, prof. emeritus, 1996—, assoc. dir. Environ. Resources Ctr., 1974—. Editor: Radioanalytical Chemistry, 2006; co-author: Radioanalytical Chemistry Experiments, 2007; co-editor: Management of Low-Level Radioactive Waste, 1979. Mem. Nat. Coun. Radiation Protection and Measurments (hon.), Am. Chem. Soc., Am. Phys. Soc., Health Physics Soc. Achievements include research in radiochemistry and environmental radioactivity; co-inventor recovery of magnesium salts from sea water. Office: Ga Tech Rsch Inst Atlanta GA 30332-0841 Business E-Mail: bernd.kahn@gtri.gatech.edu.

KAHN, ELLIS IRVIN, lawyer; b. Charleston, SC, Jan. 18, 1936; s. Robert and Estelle Harriet (Kaminski) Kahn; m. Janice Weinstein, Aug. 11, 1963; children: Justin Simon, David Israel, Cynthia Kahn Nirenblatt. AB in Polit. Sci., Citadel, 1958; JD, U. S.C., 1961. Bar: S.C. 1961, U.S. Ct. Appeals (5th cir.), U.S. Ct. Appeals (4th cir.), US Supreme Ct., US Claims Ct., diplomate: Nat. Bd. Trial Advocacy, Am. Bd. Profl. Liability Attys., cert.: (civil ct. mediator). Law clk. U.S. Dist. Ct. S.C., 1964—66; prin. Kahn Law Firm, Charleston; bd. trustees Nat. Bd. Legal Splty. Cert., 2007—. Adj. prof. med.-legal jurisprudence Med. U. S.C., 1978—87; mem. rules com. US Dist. Ct., 1984—96. Mem. nat. coun. Am. Israel Pub. Affairs Com., 1982—88, Hebrew Benevolent Soc., pres., 1994—96; mem. S.C. Organ Procurement Agy., 1989—94, Hebrew Orphan Soc., pres., 2011—12; chmn. campaign Charleston Jewish Fedn., 1986—87, pres., 1988—90. Capt. JAG USAF, 1961—64. Fellow: Internat. Soc. Barristers; mem.: DC Bar, ABA, AAJ (state committeeman 1970—74), Am. Bd. Profl. Liability Attys. (trustee 1989—, treas. 2006—10), S.C. Trial Lawyers Assn. (pres. 1976—77), 4th Cir. Jud. Conf. (life), SC Bar. Home: 316 Confederate Cir Charleston SC 29407-7431 Office: PO Box 31397 Charleston SC 29417-1397 Office Phone: 843-577-2128.*

KAHN, JACK MERRILL, television producer; b. Boston, Nov. 25, 1952; s. David Lowell and Shirley Kahn; m. Diana Burlant; 2 children. B of Hebrew Lit., Hebrew Coll., 1974; BS, Boston U., 1974; MA, Am. U., 1975. Reporter James Srodes News Svc., Washington, 1975-76, WCIX-TV, Miami, Fla., 1976-78, exec. prodr., 1978-79; prodr. Nightly Bus. Report WPBT-TV, Miami, 1979-90; sr. prodr. spl. projects NBR Enterprises/WPBT, Miami, 1990-95, dir. program devel., 1996—. Prodr.: (videotapes) How Wall Street Works, 1991, 2007 (AFVA 1991, Worldfest Houston Spl. Jury award, 2008), NBR Guides to Retirement Planning, Buying Insurance, 1992 (AFVA 1992), Stock Market Strategies, 1992, 2003 (WorldFest Houston Platinum award 2003), How to Find the Right College, 1992, 2001 (NY Festivals award 1992, WorldFest Houston Gold award 2001), How to Plan Your Estate, 1993 (N.Y. Festivals award 1993, Silver Gavel award ABA 1994), How to Invest in Mutual Funds (N.Y. Festivals award 1994, Gold award Worldfest Houston, 2006), How to Find The Right Franchise (Silver Cindy award 1997), Making Your Company a Better Place for Employees (Silver Cindy award 1999), Careers for the 21st Century (Bronze Cindy award 1999), NBR Guide to Buying Bonds (WorldFest Houston Platinum award 2002), (DVD), You're Retired: Now What? (World Fest Houston Plantinum award, 2010), Get Your Finances Ready for Retirement (World Fest Houston Platinum award, 2009), (CD-Rom) Encyclopedia of Personal Finance, NBR Edition (Dalton Pen award Multi-media 2005, Grand award Worldfest Houston, 2006). Bd. dirs. Beth David Congregation, Miami, 1980-2002; pres. Young Israel Adventura, 2006-07. Recipient Excellence in Fin. Writing award Pannell Kerr Forster, 1989, Excellence in Fin. Journalism award N.Y. State Soc. CPA's, 1991, 2002, Journalism award for excellence in personal fin. reporting Investment Co. Inst. Edn. Found., The Am. U., 1992, Gracie Allen award Am. Women Radio TV, 1998, Silver award, Platinum, Gold Remi award World Fest, Houston, 2005, 06, 07, 09. Mem. Soc. Am. Bus. Editors and Writers Inc. Jewish. Office: NBR Enterprises/WPBT 14901 NE 20th Ave Miami FL 33181-1121 Personal E-mail: jsharjoel@aol.com. Business E-Mail: jack_kahn@nbr.com.

KAHN, ROBERT ELLIOT, engineer, computer scientist; b. Bklyn., Dec. 23, 1938; BEE, CCNY, 1960; MA, Princeton U., NJ, 1962, PhD in Elec. Engring., 1964. Mem. tech. staff Bell Labs.; asst. prof. elec. engring. MIT; sr. scientist Bolt, Beranek & Newman, Cambridge, Mass.; dir. info. processing techniques Def. Advanced Rsch. Projects Agy. (DARPA), Arlington, Va., 1972—86; founder, pres. Corp. Nat. Rsch. Initiatives (CNRI), Reston, Va., 1986—, also chmn., CEO. Mem. adv. com. on internat. comm. and info. policy US Dept. State; past mem. Pres.'s Adv. Coun. on Nat. Info. Infrastructure. Recipient Marconi award, Internet Soc., 1994, Nat. Medal Tech., 1997, Prince of Asturias award, 2002, Digital ID World award, 2003, Townsend Harris medal, CCNY Alumni Assn., 2005, Presdl. Medal of Freedom, 2005, Computer & Comm. prize, KEC Found., Tokyo, 2005, Webby Lifetime Achievement award, Internat. Acad. Digital Arts & Scis., 2006, Japan prize, 2008, Harold Pender award, U. Pa., 2010, Harry Goode Meml. award, Am. Fedn. Info. Processing Soc., Computerworld/Smithsonian Leadership award, Pub. Svc. award, Computing Rsch. Bd., US Sec. of Def. Civilian Svc. award; named to Nat. Inventors Hall of Fame, 2006. Fellow: AAAS, IEEE (Koji Kobayashi award, Alexander Graham Bell medal, Third Millennium medal), Assn. Computing Machinery (Pres.'s award 1985, SIGCOMM award 1993, A.M. Turning award 2004, Software Systems award), Am. Assn. Artificial Intelligence, Soc. Tech. Comm. (hon.); mem.: NAE (Charles Stark Draper prize 2001). Achievements include system design of the Arpanet, the first packet-switched network; co-invention of the TCP/IP Internet network protocol. Office: Corp for Nat Rsch Initiatives 1895 Preston White Dr Ste 100 Reston VA 20191-5434

KAHNE, KASEY (KENNETH), race car driver; b. Enumclaw, Wash., Apr. 10, 1980; s. Kelly and Tammy Kahne. Race car driver NASCAR Gillett Evernham Motorsports, 2004—08, Richard Petty Motorsports, 2009—10, Red Bull Racing USA, 2010—. 1st pl. Chevy Am. Revolution 400 Richmond Internat. Raceway, 2005; 1st pl. Samsung/Radio Shack 500 Tex. Motor Speedway, 2006; 1st pl. 3M Performance 400 Mich. Internat. Speedway, 2006; 1st pl. Sony HD 500 Calif. Speedway, 2006; 1st pl. Golden Corral 500 Atlanta Motor Speedway, 2006; 1st pl. Bank of America 500 Lowe's Motor Speedway, 2006, 1st pl. Coca-Cola 600, 2006, 2008; 1st pl. Pocono 500 Pocono Raceway, 2008; 1st pl. Toyota/Save Mart 350 Infineon Raceway, Sonoma, Calif., 2009; 1st pl. Kobalt Tools 500 Phoenix Internat. Raceway, 2011; 1st pl. Coca-Cola 600 Charlotte Motor Speedway, 2012; 1st pl. Lennox Indsl. Tools 301 NH Motor Speedway, 2012. Founder Kasey Kahne Found., 2005. Named NASCAR Nextel Cup Rookie of Yr., 2004. Address: Kasey Kahne Found 296 Cayuga Dr Mooresville NC 28117 Office: Red Bull Racing USA 136 Knob Hill Rd Mooresville NC 28117-6847

KAINE, TIM (TIMOTHY MICHAEL KAINE), United States Senator from Virginia, former Governor of Virginia; b. St. Paul, Feb. 26, 1958; s. Albert A. & Mary Kathleen (Burns) K.; m. Anne Bright Holton, Nov. 24, 1984; children: Annella, Woody, Nat. AB summa cum laude, U. Mo., 1979; JD cum laude, Harvard Law Sch., 1983. Law clk. to Hon. R. Lanier Anderson III US Ct. Appeals (11th cir.), 1983—84; pvt. law practice Richmond, 1984—2001; mem. city council City of Richmond, 1994—98, mayor, 1998—2001; lt. gov. State of Va., 2002—06, gov., 2006—10; chmn. Democratic Nat. Com., Washington, 2009—11; US Senator from Va., 2013—; mem. US Senate Budget Com., 2013—, US Senate Fgn. Rels. Com., 2013—, US Senate Armed Services Com., 2013—. Prof. law U. Richmond Law Sch.; chmn. Southern Governors Assn., 2008-09 Contbr. articles to profl. jours. Bd. dirs. Historic Jackson Ward Found. Recipient Pro Bono Public award, Richmond Bar Assn., 1995. Mem. ABA, Va. Bar Assn., Richmond Bar Assn. Democrat. Roman Catholic. Office: US Senate 388 Russell Senate Office Bldg B40C Washington DC 20510 Office Phone: 202-224-4024. Office Fax: 202-224-6363.*

KAISER, ALBERT FARR, manufacturing executive; b. NYC, May 14, 1933; s. Albert Louis and Lucille (Daggett) K.; m. Joy E. White, Sept. 16, 1961; children— Elizabeth Ann, Albert Farr. BA, Hamilton Coll., Clinton, NY, 1955; MBA, Harvard U., 1960. With acquisitons dept. AMF Inc., 1960-61; with data processing div. IBM Corp., 1961-84; with Sperry and Hutchinson Co., 1974-82; pres. The Gunlocke Co., Inc., 1977-79, pres. promotional services div., also chmn. motivation and travel div., 1979-80; corp. exec. v.p. Sperry and Hutchinson, Inc., NYC, 1980-82; investment banker J.J. Lowrey & Co., NYC, 1983-84; pres. ABB Power Distbn. Inc., 1984-92; ret., 1992—. Served to lt. (j.g.) USNR, 1955-58. Mem.: Hamilton Coll. Alumni Assn. (former pres. Westchester County chpt.), Key Royale Club (Holmes Beach, Fla.), Champlain Country Club (St. Albans, Vt.). Republican. Mem. Reformed Ch. Am. Home: 105 Sunset Ln Holmes Beach FL 34217 Home (Summer): 25 Camp Rich Rd Milton VT 05468

KAISER, ALLEN BERNARD, health facility administrator; b. Columbia, SC, 1942; BA, MD, Vanderbilt U., 1967. Intern Johns Hopkins Hosp., Balt., 1967—68, resident internal medicine, 1968—69, Vanderbilt U. Hosp., 1971—72, fellow, 1972—74; (former) hosp. epidemiologist St. Thomas Hosp., chief divsn. infectious diseases, chief dept. medicine; vice-chmn. clin. affairs Vanderbilt U. Hosp., prof. medicine, chief of staff, 2004—, vice chair med. affairs; assoc. chief med. officer Vanderbilt U. Med. Ctr., 2004—. Mem.: Soc. Healthcare Epidemiology Am. (past pres.). Office: Vanderbilt Med Ctr D 3100 Med Ctr N Nashville TN 37232

KAISER, GEORGE B., corporate financial executive; b. 1943; s. Herman George Kaiser; m. Betty Eudene, 1965 (dec. 2002); 3 children; m. Myra Kaiser. BS, MBA, Harvard U. Chmn. BOK Fin., Tulsa; prin. owner Fountains Continuum of Care, Inc., Kaiser-Francis Oil Co., 1969—. Founder Tulsa Cmty. Found., 1998, George Kaiser Family Found. Named one of Forbes 400: Richest Americans, 1995—, World's Richest People, Forbes Mag., 2001—. Office: Kaiser Francis Oil Co Hdqs 6733 S Yale Ave Tulsa OK 74136

KAISER, THOMAS GRIFFETH, insurance company executive; b. Schenectady, NY, Feb. 11, 1947; s. Ofrville H. and Norma (Griffeth) K.; m. Diane L. Hanna, Nov. 22, 1970. A in Arts & Sciences, SUNY, Alfred, 1967; BS, SUNY, Albany, 1970; MS, SUNY, Plattsburgh, 1975. CPCU; assoc. Risk Mgmt. Account rep. Arkwright-Boston Ins. Co., Greenwich, Conn., 1975-77, mgr., field sales, 1977-79, mgr., regional sales Greenwich, 1979-83, regional mgr. San Mateo, Calif., 1983; various positions, including v.p., AIG Fgn. Gen., pres., AIU Energy divsn. and Star Tech. Risk Agy. American International Group, Inc. (AIG), 1993—98; pres., CEO Zurich Corp. Solutions, 1999—2002; exec. v.p., pres., Marine, Energy and Aviation Spl. Risks Divsn. Arch Ins. Group, 2002—08; pres. Houston Casualty Co. (subs. of HCC Insurance Holdings, Inc.), 2008—, US Specialty Insurance Co. (subs. HCC Insurance Holdings, Inc.), 2008—. Instr. Ins. Edn. Assn., 1984—. Served to capt. USAF, 1970-75. Mem. No. Calif. Assn. CPCU's, San Francisco C. of C. Clubs: Banker (San Francisco). Avocations: walking, reading. Office: Houston Casualty Co 13403 NW Fwy Houston TX 77040-6006 Office Phone: 713-462-1000. Business E-Mail: tkaiser@ussic.com.

KAISERLIAN, PENELOPE JANE, publishing executive; b. Paisley, Scotland, Oct. 19, 1943; came to U.S., 1956; d. W. Norman and Magdalene Jeanette (Houlder) Hewson; m. Arthur Kaiserlian, June 29, 1968; 1 child, Christian. BA, U. Exeter, Eng., 1965. Copywriter, sales rep. Pergamon Press, Elmsford, NY, 1965-68; exhibits mgr. Plenum Pub., NYC, 1968-69; asst. mktg. mgr. U. Chgo. Press, 1969-76, mktg. mgr., 1976-83, assoc. dir., 1983-2001; dir. U. Va. Press, 2001—. Mem. Assn. Am. Univ. Presses (pres. 2006—07), Assn. Documentary Editing, Colonnade Club. Office: Univ Va Press PO Box 400318 Charlottesville VA 22904-4318

KAISERMAN, DAVID J., construction executive; Mem., co-founder, mcht. banking group Saybrook Capital LLC; pres. Strategic Holdings, Inc., 2005; mem., Supervisory Bd. Lennar Corp., pres., Lennar Ventures, 2005—; sr. v.p., bus. devel. Lenner Fin. Svcs. LLC. Rep., govt. affairs and green coms., High Prodn. Builders Coun. Nat. Assn. of Homebuilders. Office: Lennar Corp 700 NW 107th Ave Miami FL 33172 Office Phone: 305-559-4000. Office Fax: 305-226-4158. Business E-Mail: david.kaiserman@lennar.com.

KAKKAR, AMAN K., cardiologist; married; 3 children. MD, U. Delhi, 1993. Diplomate Am. Bd. Internal Medicine-cardiovasc. disease, 2004, Am. Bd. Internal Medicine-interventional cardiology, 2005. Intern NY Med. Coll., Valhalla, resident internal medicine, 1994—97; fellow cardiovasc. disease La. State Univ., Shreveport, 2001—04; fellow interventional cardiology Univ. of Rochester, NY, 2004—05; founding mem. and physician Heart and Vascular Care Inc., Ga.; dir. cardiac cath lab. Northside Forsyth Hosp.; physician Emory Johns Creek Hosp. Author: numerous articles in interventional cardiology. Recipient multiple nat. awards. Fellow: Soc. of Coronary Angiography and Intervention, Am. Coll. of Cardiology. Avocations: participating in cmty. functions, travel, family time. Office: Heart and Vascular Care Inc 1505 Northside Blvd Ste 4000 Cumming GA 30041 Office Phone: 678-513-2273. Office Fax: 678-513-8869.*

KALAFUT, GEORGE WENDELL, retired distribution company executive, retired naval officer; b. Chgo., Feb. 21, 1934; s. George Andrew and Ann Catherine (Panak) K.; m. Alice Quinn, Nov. 9, 1957; children: Katherine, Tracy. AB in Econs., St. Joseph's Coll., Rensselaer, Ind., 1955; MBA, Harvard U., 1969. Commd. USN, 1956, advanced through grades to capt., 1976; asst dir. air equipment purchasing divsn. Naval Air Systems Command, Washington, 1969-71, dep. dir. F14/Grumman rev. team Washington and Bethpage, NY, 1971, dir. airframes purchasing div. Washington, 1972-73; supply officer USS Ranger CV61, San Francisco, 1973-75; dir. plans and budget Naval Supply Systems Command, Washington, 1976-78; retired USN, 1978; dir. inventories Motion Industries, Birmingham, Ala., 1979, v.p., 1980-83, v.p. fin., chief fin. officer, 1983-85, sr. v.p., 1985-89, also bd. dirs.; sr. v.p. fin. and adminstrn. Genuine Parts Co., Atlanta, 1989-91, exec. v.p. fin. and adminstrn., chief fin. officer, 1991—2001, exec. v.p., 2001—04; ret., 2004. Baker scholar Harvard Bus. Sch., 1969. Home: 1755 Spalding Dr Atlanta GA 30350-4321

KALBFLEISCH, JOHN MCDOWELL, retired cardiologist; b. Lawton, Okla., Nov. 15, 1930; s. George and Etta Lillian (McDowell) K.; m. Jolie Harper, Dec. 30, 1961. AS, Cameron A&M U., Lawton, 1950; BS, U. Okla., 1952, MD, 1957. Diplomate Am. Bd. Internal Medicine, Am. Bd. Cardiovascular Disease. Intern U. Va. Hosp., 1957-58; resident and fellow U. Okla. Med. Ctr., 1958-62, instr. medicine, 1964-66, asst. prof., 1966-69, assoc. clin. prof., 1970-78, clin. prof. Tulsa br., 1978—2007; pvt. practice Tulsa, 1969—2007; founder, chmn. bd., CEO Cardiology of Tulsa, Inc., 1969—2007; dir. cardiovascular svcs. St. Francis Hosp., Tulsa, 1975—2005. Physician adv. bd. City of Tulsa, 1978-81; bd. dirs. St. Francis Hosp., exec. com., 1987-97, 2001-06; exec. v.p., chief med. officer St. Francis Health Sys., 1998-99; treas. Tulsa Med. Edn. Found., 1988-89, v.p., 1990-92, pres., 1992-94; med. dir., chmn. bd. Warren Clinics, 1990-97; mem. Okla. Ctr. for Advancement of Sci. and Tech., 1989-95; mem. adv. com. Ctr. for Lasser Devel. and Applications, Okla. State U. Contbr. articles to profl. jours. With USPHS, 1962-64. Recipient Lifelong Svc. award, Tulsa Med. Edn. Found./U. Okla. Coll. Medicine, 2002; named Okla. Profl. Health Care Champion, Partnership Blue Cross Blue Shield Okla., Okla. State Dept. Health, Okla. Hosp. Assn., Okla. Osteo. Assn., 2005; named to, St. Francis Health Sys. Hall of Fame, 2003. Master ACP (gov.-elect Okla. 1990-91, gov. 1991-95, Okla. Laureate award 1995), Am. Coll. Cardiology (gov. Okla. 1978-81); mem. AMA, AAAS, Tulsa County Med. Soc., Okla. State Med. Assn., Am. Heart Assn. (Fellow coun. on clin. cardiology), tchg. scholar 1967-69), Okla. Soc. Internal Medicine v.p., pres.-elect 1983-84, pres. 1985-86), Am. Soc. Internal Medicine, Am. Fedn. Clin.

Rsch., Am. Inst. Nutrition, U. Okla. Med. Alumni Assn. (Physician of Yr. in Pvt. Practice 1999), Delta Upsilon. Republican. Presbyterian. Home: 6528 E 101st St Ste D-1 # 367 Tulsa OK 74133 Personal E-mail: jmkalbfleisch@aol.com.

KALDER, FRANK M., JR., federal agency administrator; b. 1952; married; 4 children. BS in Forensic Sci. & Psychology, Ind. U., 1974; MPA, Mich. State U., 1983. Presdl. mgmt. intern Office Mgmt. & Budget Exec. Office of the Pres., 1983, examiner, 1983—89, dir. budget & liaison Office Nat. Drug Control Policy, 1989—93; from asst. dir. to dep. dir. US Dept. Justice, 1993—97, dep. dir. Exec. Office US Attorneys, 1997—2000; CFO Drug Enforcement Adminstrn., Alexandria, Va., 2000—. Recipient Disting. Exec. Presdl. Rank award, 2002. Office: Drug Enforcement Admin 8701 Morrissette Dr Springfield VA 22152-1080

KALIN, ROBERT, retired mathematics professor; b. Everett, Mass., Dec. 11, 1921; s. Benjamin and Celia (Kraff) K.; m. Shirley Sharney, Oct. 22, 1944; children: Susan Leslie, John Benjamin; m. 2d Madelyn Pildish, Aug. 17, 1962; 1 child, Richard Dean. Student, Northeastern U., 1940-43; BS, U. Chgo., 1947; MAT, Harvard U., 1948; PhD, Fla. State U., 1961. Tchr. math. Holten H.S., Danvers, Mass., 1948-49, Beaumont H.S., Hadley Tech. Sch., Soldan-Blewitt H.S., St. Louis, 1949-52; ednl. statistician Naval Air Tech. Tng. Ctr., Norman, Okla., 1952-53; test specialist, assoc. in research Ednl. Testing Svc., Princeton, NJ, 1953-55; exec. asst. Commn. on Math. of Coll. Entrance Exam. Bd., 1955-56; instr. dept. math. edn. Fla. State U., Tallahassee, 1956-61, asst. prof., 1961-63, assoc. prof., 1963-65, prof., 1965-90, prof. emeritus Tallahassee, 1990, assoc. dept. head, 1968-73, program chmn., 1975-78. Co-author: Elementary Mathematics, Patterns and Structure, 11 vols., 1966, (with George Green) Modern Mathematics for the Elementary School Teacher, 1966, (with E.D. Nichols) Analytic Geometry, 1973, Holt School Mathematics, 9 vols., 1974, rev. 1978, Holt Mathematics, 9 vols., 1981, rev., 1985, (with M.K. Corbitt) Prentice Hall Geometry, 1990, rev. edit., 1993. Mem., treas. Brownsville-Haywood County Libr. Bd., 1991-95, chmn., 1995-97; bd. dirs. Friends of Tenn. Librs., 1995-2002, sec., 1996-97, pres.-elect, 1997-99, pres., 1999-2000, past pres., 2000-02; pres. Temple Adas Israel, 1992-94, treas., 1994-2000; bd. dirs. Jewish Hist. Soc. of Memphis and the Mid-South, 1998-2001, sec., 2000-01. Mem. Math. Assn. Am. (sec.-treas. Fla. sect. 1985-91, Svc. award Fla. sect. 1991), Fla. Coun. Tchrs. Math. (pres. 1960-61), Fla. Assn. Math. Educators (pres. 1984-86), Nat. Coun. Tchrs. Math. (chmn. external affairs com. 1972-73), Nat. High Sch. and Jr. Coll. Math. Clubs (gov. 1972-75, pres. 1978-80). Home: 7 Stoneleigh Pl Brownsville TN 38012-2463

KALKWARF, KENNETH LEE, dean, dental educator; b. Lincoln, Nebr., Apr. 12, 1946; s. Robert G. and Grace L. (Beck) K.; m. Sharon R. Moore, July 6, 1974; children: Kyle J., Kevin J. Student, U. Nebr., 1964-66, DDS, 1970, MS, 1973. Diplomate Am. Bd. Periodontology. Asst. prof. U. Nebr., Lincoln, 1973-78, prof., 1980-87; assoc. prof. U. Okla., Oklahoma City, 1978-80; prof., assoc. dean U. Tex. Health Sci. Ctr. Dental Sch., San Antonio, 1987-88, prof., dean, 1988—2012, interim pres., 2012—13. Contbg. author textbooks, 1978—; contbr. articles to profl. jours., rsch. abstracts. Bd. dirs. McAllister Park Little League, San Antonio, 1990-94, mem. Leadership San Antonio, 1989-90. Recipient Alumni Achievement award U. Nebr., 1990, Outstanding Tchr. award U. Okla., 1980, Distinguished Svc. award, Am. Dental Assn., 2009, U. Tex., 2013. Fellow Internat. Coll. Dentists, Am. Coll. Dentists (bd. regents, 2007-11, pres. 2013-; mem. ADA (chmn. Commn. Dental Accreditation, 2003-04), Am. Acad. Periodontology, S.W. Soc. Periodontology (bd. dirs. 1984-97, pres. 1993-94), Tex. Soc. Periodontists (bd. dirs. 1988-95), Am. Dental Edn. Assn. (pres 2006-07). Republican. Methodist. Avocations: spectator sports, jogging, reading. Office: Univ Tex Health Sci Ctr 7703 Floyd Curl Dr San Antonio TX 78284-6200 Office Phone: 210-567-3166. Office Fax: 210-567-6721. Business E-Mail: kalkwarf@uthscsa.edu.*

KALLEBERG, ARNE LINDEMAN, sociologist, educator; b. Larvik, Norway, Feb. 9, 1949; came to U.S., 1954; s. Theodor F. and Solveig Kalleberg; m. Judith Lynn Johansen, June 3, 1972; children: Kathryn, Jonathan, Kari. BA, Bklyn. Coll., 1971; MS, U. Wis., 1972, PhD, 1975. From asst. prof. to prof. sociology Ind. U., Bloomington, 1975-85; prof. sociology U. N.C., Chapel Hill, 1986-94, Kenan prof., 1994—. Author: The Mismatched Worker, 2007, Good Jobs, Bad Jobs, 2011; co-author: Work and Industry, 1987, Culture, Control and Commitment, 1990, Organizations in America, 1996, Manufacturing Advantage, 2000. Guggenheim fellow, 1984, fellow NSF, 1982, 84, 87-89, 95; recipient Bklyn. Coll. Disting. Alumni award. Fellow: AAAS. Democrat. Lutheran. Avocations: basketball, reading, boating. Office: U NC Dept Sociology Hamilton Hall CB # 3210 Chapel Hill NC 27599-3210 Office Phone: 919-962-0630. Business E-Mail: arnekal@email.unc.edu.*

KALLON, ABDUL KARIM, federal judge; b. Freetown, Sierra Leone, Apr. 5, 1969; AB, Dartmouth Coll., Hanover, NH, 1990; JD, U. Pa. Law Sch., 1993. Bar: Pa. 1994, Ala. 1995. Law clk. to Hon. U.W. Clemon US Dist. Ct. (no. dist.) Ala., 1993—94, judge, 2009—; atty. Bradley Arant Boult Cummings LLP, Birmingham, Ala., 1994—2009. Articles editor U. Pa. Jour. Internat. Bus. Law, 1992—93. Mem.: ABA. Office: Hugo L Black US Courthouse 1729 Fifth Ave N Birmingham AL 35203

KALOS, ALAN V., health planning administrator; b. NYC, July 10, 1946; s. Sol and Anne Kalos; m. Mary F. Brogan, Nov. 23, 1977; children: James A., Elizabeth A. BA in Psychology, U. Fla., Gainesville, 1969; MEd, U. Cin., 1982. Health planning adminstr. Northern Ky. Health Dept., Edgewood, 1987—; with process devel. com. Pub. Health Accreditation Bd., 2009, site reviewer, 2010. Com. mem. Nat. Assn. County and City Health Ofcls., Washington, 1997—2010; co-developer Protocol for Assessing Cmty. Excellence in Environ. Health, 1997—2000, Mobilizing for Action through Planning and Partnerships, 2000—08; reviewer NACCHO Project Pub. Health Ready, Nat. Assn. County & City Health Offcls., 2010; apptd. mem. NACCHO Accrediation Spkr.'s Bur., 2012. Contbr. article to Pub. Health Mgmt. and Practice, chapters to books. Participant Nat. Pub. Health Performance Standards, 2006—07. Mem.: Ky. Pub. Health Assn. Avocation: stamp collecting/philately. Office: Northern Kentucky Health Department 610 Medical Village Dr Edgewood KY 41017-3416 Office Fax: 859-578-3689. Business E-Mail: alan.kalos@nkyhealth.org.*

KAMBURY, STUART A., automotive executive; Attended, Ohio State U., 1982. Regional v.p. South, Midwest group Genuine Parts Co., v.p. Southwest divsn., US automotive parts group. Office: Genuine Parts Co 2999 Cir 75 Pky Atlanta GA 30339 Office Phone: 770-953-1700. Office Fax: 770-956-2211. Business E-Mail: stuart_kambury@genpt.com.

KAMEL, HOSAM KAMAL, medical educator, researcher, geriatrician; b. Cairo, May 18, 1965; married; 1 child. MB, BChir, Kuwait U., 1989; MPH, Med. Coll. Wis., 2004. Cert. Am. Bd. Internal Medicine, Am. Bd. Geriatric Medicine, Cert. Bd. Nutrition Specialists, Nat. Bd. Wound Mgmt. Asst. prof. medicine SUNY, Stony Brook, 1998—99; chief divsn. geriatric medicine Nassau U. Med. Ctr., East Meadow, NY, 1999—2001; asst. prof. medicine St. Louis U. Sch. Medicine, 1999—; asst. prof. geriatrics Med. Coll. Wis., 2001—03; dir. geriatrics and extended care St. Joseph's Mercy Health Ctr., Hot Springs, Ark., 2003—; asst., assoc. clin. prof. geriatric U. Ark. Med. Sci., 2004—. Dir. edn. and rsch., geriatrics Nassau U. Med. Ctr., East Meadow, 1999; mem. physician adv. panel Divsn. Aging, Dept. Social Svcs., Jefferson City, Mo., 2000—; pres. Ark. Med. Dirs. Assn., 2006—; bd. dirs. Mo. Assn. Long-Term Physicians, Mo. Fellow: Am. Coll. Nutrition; mem.: ACP, Gerontol. Soc. Am., Am. Geriatric Soc., Ctrl. Soc. for Clin. Rsch. Democrat. Muslim. Office: Mission Clin Svc 1 Mecy Ln Ste 405 Hot Springs AR 71913 Home: 120 Dellmere Dr Hot Springs National Park AR 71913-7399 Personal E-mail: kamel@pol.net.

KAMINKOW, BETH ANN, marketing executive; married. B in Journalism & Advt., Syracuse U., NY; MBA, Boston U. Market rschr. Hasbro; mktg. profl. ClarkeGowardFitts and Clarke & Co., Boston, Brodeur & Partners, Brodeur Porter Novelli, Brodeur Worldwide, Brodeur; pres., COO TracyLocke, 2006—11, pres., CEO, 2011—. Named a Woman to Watch, Advertising Age, 2011. Office: TracyLocke 1999 Bryan St Ste 2800 Dallas TX 75201

KAMINSHINE, STEVEN J., dean, law educator; BA summa cum laude, NYU; JD, DePaul U. Ptnr. labor and employment law practice, NYC; atty. Nat. Labor Rels. Bd., Washington, DC; mem. law faculty Ga. State U., Coll. Law, 1985—, assoc. prof., assoc. dean academic affairs, interim dean, 2004—05, dean, 2005—. Contbr. articles to law jours. Mem.: Atlanta Bar Assn. (chair Labor and Employment Sec.), Ga. Bar Assn. Office: Georgia State University College of Law 140 Decatur St Rm 422 Atlanta GA 30303 Office Phone: 404-431-9035. Office Fax: 404-413-9227. Business E-Mail: skaminshine@gsu.edu.*

KAMINSKI, PAUL GARRETT, former federal agency administrator, investment banker; b. Cleve., Sept. 16, 1942; s. Theodore Albert and Eleanor Marie (Dobranski) K.; m. Julia Kent Crafts, Oct. 8, 1966; children: Laura Denise, Garrett Kent. BS, USAF Acad., 1964; MS in Aerospace and Astronautics, MIT, 1966, MSEE, 1966; PhD in Aeronautics and Astronautics, Stanford U., 1971. Commd. 2d lt. USAF, 1964, advanced through grades to col., 1979, spl. asst. to under sec. of def. Washington, 1977-81; dir. low observables tech. Office Dep. Chief Staff for R&D, Dept. Air Force, 1981-84; ret., 1984; pres., COO, Tech. Strategies & Alliances, Burke, Va., 1985-93, chmn., CEO, 1993-94; under sec. of def. for acquisition and tech. Dept. Def., Washington, 1994-97; chmn., CEO Technovation, Inc., 1997—; sr. ptnr. Global Tech. Ptnrs. LLC, 1998—. Chmn. Def. Sci. Bd., Washington, 1993-94, 2009-; dir., Atlantic Coun. US, General Dynamics; mem. Senate Select Com. on Intelligence Technical Adv. Group, Nat. Reconnaissance Office Adv. Coun.; chmn. RAND; cons. Office of Sec. Def./Def. Sci. Bd. Contbr. articles to sci. jours. Bd. mem. USAF Acad. Endowment; dir. Spl. Olympics, Palos Verdes HS, Calif., 1971-73; hon. trustee, Am. Tech. Alliances; chmn. Def. Svc. Bd.; mem. Pres.'s Intelligence Adv. Bd., Dir. Nat. Intelligence Sr. Adv. Group, FBI Dirs. Adv. Bd. Ret. col. USAF. Decorated Legion of Merit, French Republic Legion d'Honneur, Medal of Merit in Gold Netherlands Ministry Def., Disting. Pub. Svc. DOD medal; recipient Nat. Tech. medal, 2006, SPIE Lifetime Achievement award, Missile Def. Reagan award. Fellow: IEEE, AIAA; mem.: NAE, AAAS, Sigma Gamma Tau, Tau Beta Pi, Sigma Xi. Avocations: golf, tennis, jogging, cross country skiing. Office Phone: 703-430-2160. E-mail: pgkaminski@aol.com.

KAMP, ARTHUR JOSEPH, JR., lawyer; b. July 22, 1945; s. Arthur Joseph and Irene Catherine (Ehrstein) K.; m. Barbara Hays, Aug. 24, 1968; children: Sara, Nathaniel. BA, SUNY, 1968, JD, 1970. Bar: N.Y. 1971, U.S. Dist. Ct. (we. dist.) N.Y. 1971, Va. 1973, U.S. Dist. Ct. (ea. dist.) Va. 1973. Atty. Neighborhood Legal Svcs., Buffalo, 1971; assoc. Diamonstein & Drucker, Newport News, 1972-77; ptnr. Diamonstein, Drucker & Kamp, Newport News, 1977-84, Kamp & Kamp, Newport News, 1984-87, Kaufman & Canoles, 1987-96, David, Kamp & Frank, L.L.C., 1996—; v.p. Peninsula Legal Aid Ctr., Inc., 1978-92. Newport News Planning Commn., 1990-97, chmn., 1994-96; mem. bd. visitors Ea. Va. Med. Sch., 1997-2003, vice rector, 2001, rector, 2002; trustee Ea. Va. Med. Sch. Found., 2004—09; mem. local bd. dirs. Thomas Nelson C.C., 2005-07. Lt. USAF, 1971-72. Mem. Va. State Bar Assn., Newport News Bar Assn. (past bd. dirs., chmn. legal aid com.), Va. Bar Assn., Va. Peninsula C. of C. (bd. dirs., exec. com., chmn. 1997, gen. counsel 1999-2001). Democrat. Office: David Kamp & Frank LLC 739 Thimble Shoals Blvd Ste 105 Newport News VA 23606 Office Phone: 757-595-4500. Business E-Mail: ajkamp@davidkampfrank.com.

KANAS, JOHN ADAM, bank executive; b. Southampton, NY, Nov. 16, 1946; s. George & Barbara Kanas; m. Elaine Kanas; children: Melissa, Allison, Adam, John. BA in History, Southampton Coll., 1968; postgraduate student, C.W. Post Coll. Long Island U., 1970, Rutgers U., NJ, 1976. Mgmt. trainee North Fork Bank & Trust Co., Mattituck, NY, 1971, various sr. mgmt. positions, 1971—77, chmn., pres., CEO, 1977—2006, North Fork Bancorporation, Inc., Melville, NY, 1987—2006; pres. banking Capital One Financial Corp., McLean, Va., 2006—07; chmn., pres., CEO BankUnited Inc., Miami, 2009—. Bd. dirs. BankUnited Inc., 2011—. Recipient Tree of Life award, Jewish Nat. Fund, 2003. Mem. NY State Ind. Bankers Assn. (chmn., pres. 1980-81), Long Island Bankers Assn. (pres., dir. 1980), NY State Bankers Assn. (pres.). Office: BankUnited Inc 14817 Oak Lane Miami Lakes FL 33016

KANDT, RAYMOND S., neurologist; b. Rochester, NY, July 8, 1950; m. Irene Kandt; children: Melanie, Lauren. AB cum laude, U. Va., 1972; MD, U. Va. Sch. Medicine, 1976. Diplomate Am. Bd. Med. Examiners, Am. Bd. Pediatrics, Am. Bd. Psychiatry & Neurology with spl. competence in child neurology and with added qualifications in clin. neurophysiology; cert. neurovascular & pediat. neurosonologist; cert. MRI/CT. Intern, resident in pediatrics Johns Hopkins Hosp., Balt., 1976-78, resident in pediatric neurology, fellow in devel. pediatrics, 1978-81; instr. depts. neurology, pediatrics U. Mich., Ann Arbor, 1981-82, asst. prof. depts. neurology & pediatrics, 1982-84; asst. prof. pediatrics div. pediatric neurology Duke U. Med. Ctr., Durham, NC, 1984-89, assoc. prof. pediatrics div. pediatric neurology, 1989-92, asst. prof. medicine div. neurology, 1990-92; assoc. prof. neurology, pediatrics Bowman Gray Sch. Medicine, Winston-Salem, NC, 1992-97; clin. assoc. prof. pediatrics Wake Forest U./Bapt. Med. Ctr., Winston-Salem, 1997—2011; prof. neurology Wake Forest U. Health Scis. Chief sect. child neurology Bowman Gray Sch. Medicine, 1992-97, grad. med. edn. com. 1993-97, clin. faculty adv. coun., 1993-97; faculty advisor pediatric house staff U. Mich., 1981-84, faculty advisor med. students, 1983-84, com. on edn., 1982-84; pediatric rep. continuing med. edn. com. Duke U. Med. Ctr., 1985-92; mem. gen. clin. rsch. ctrs. com. nat. ctr. for rsch. resources NIH, 1991-95; cons. and reviewer in field. Reviewer: Am. Jour. Human Genetics, 1995, Jour. Neurol. Scis., 1993—97, Nature Genetics, 1993, Annals of Neurology, 1998—2002; contbg. editor: Annals of Behavioral Medicine, 1991—93. Adv. bd. My Father's House Group Homes, 1993; med. adv. com. Children's Ctr. for the Physically Handicapped, Winston-Salem, N.C., 1993—97, sec., treas. NC Neurol. Soc., 2012-13, mem. com. Am. Soc. Neuroimaging, 1999-2012, postal care com. High Point Regional Hosp., NC, 1997-98, dir. Child Neurology Residency Program, Bowman Gray Sch. of Medicines, 1992-97. Grantee NIH, 1986-91, 89-92, Nat. Tuberous Sclerosis Assn., 1992-93, grantee Glaxo, 1995-96; recipient Merck award, 1976.Samuel L. Katz Pediat. Faculty Tchg. award Duke U. Med. Ctr., Durian, NC, 1991-92. Golden Hammer neurology Faculty Tchg. award, Wake Forest U. Health Scis., Winston, 2013-14 Mem.: Profs. Child Neurology, Tuberous Sclerosis Alliance (chmn. med. adv. com. N.C. chpt. 1988—, mem. profl. adv. bd. 1990—2011, chmn. clin. care adv. bd. 1995—97, scientific adv. bd. 1995—2011, scientific grant rev. com. 1995—2007), Child Neurology Soc., N.C. Med. Soc., Am. Neurol. Assn., Phi Sigma, Alpha Omega Alpha. Office: Johnson Neurologic Clinic 606 N Elm St High Point NC 27262-4336 Home: 1630 Whetstone Way Apt 313 Baltimore MD 21230-5152 Office Phone: 336-889-8877.

KANE, ANNETTE PIESLAK, religious organization executive; b. Trenton, NJ, May 2, 1933; d. Theodore P. and Stella (Mackiewicz) Pieslak; m. Joseph P. Kane, Sept. 6, 1958; children: Paula M., Stephen J., Brian P., Christine A. BA, Trinity Coll., Washington, 1954; MA, U. Pa., 1956. Asst. prof. Rosemont (Pa.) Coll., 1955-58, Trinity Coll., Washington, 1958-61, editor alumni jour., 1973-79; program dir. Nat. Coun. Cath. Women, Washington, 1979-86, exec. dir., 1986—. Bd. dirs. Nat. Coun. Aging, Washington, 1985-87, CARA-Ctr. for Applied Rsch. in Apostolate, Washington, 1989—, Nat. Relig. Partnership for Environ., 1993—, commn. women, Fairfax County, 2003—. Roman Catholic. Office: Nat Coun of Cath Women 200 N Glebe Rd Ste 703 Arlington VA 22203-3728 Personal E-mail: annettekane@verizon.net.

KANE, JIM, retail executive; Attended, Duquesne U., Pitts. Asst. store mgr. Home Depot, Inc., 1987, various positions, store mgr., dist. mgr. and merchandising v.p., regional v.p., Ohio Valley, pres., Northern Divsn., 2008—. Office: The Home Depot Inc 2455 Paces Ferry Rd NW Atlanta GA 30339 Office Phone: 770-433-8211. Office Fax: 770-384-2356. Business E-Mail: Jim_Kane@homedepot.com.

KANE, MICHAEL G., publishing executive; BA, Va. Tech., 1981. Asst. exec. dir. Internat. Newspaper Mktg. Assn., 1982—88; mgr. mktg. & promotion Balt. Sun, 1988—92; with Gannett Co. Inc., 1992—, mgr. mktg. svcs. The News Jour. Wilmington, Del., 1992—93, dir. mktg. devel. Poughkeepsie Jour. NY, 1993, pres., pub. Lansing State Jour. Mich., v.p. Midwest Newspaper Group, then regional v.p. East Newspaper Group Rochester, NY, 2005—08, 2010—, pres., pub. Rochester Dem. & Chronicle, 2005—08, 2010—, interstate group pres., pub. Indpls. Star, 2008—10. Office: Gannett Co Inc 7950 Jones Branch Dr Mc Lean VA 22107-0150 also: Rochester Democrat & Chronicle 55 Exchange Blvd Rochester NY 14614 Business E-Mail: michael.kane@indystar.com.

KANE, ROBERT HILARY, philosophy educator; b. Boston, Nov. 25, 1938; s. Hilary Thomas and Vivian Lenzi Kane; m. Claudette Marcile Drennan, Jan. 23, 1965; children: Russell Hilary, Nathan Robert. BA, Holy Cross Coll., 1960; MA, Yale U., 1962, PhD, 1964. Asst. prof. philosophy Fordham U., NYC, 1964-67; Alfred E. Sloan asst. prof. philosophy Haverford (Pa.) Coll., 1967-70, assoc. prof., 1974-85; prof. philosophy U. Tex., Austin, 1985-95, univ. disting. teaching prof. philosophy, 1995—. Author: Free Will and Values, 1985, Through the Moral Maze, 1994, The Significance of Free Will, 1996 (R.W. Hamilton Faculty Book award 1997), A Contemporary Introduction to Free Will, 2005, Ethics and The Quest For Wisdom, 2010; editor: The Oxford Handbook of Free Will, 2002. Recipient Quality of Life award Alliance for Mentally Ill., Tex., 1993; Woodrow Wilson fellow Yale U. and Woodrow Wilson Found., 1961-64. Office: U Tex 1 University Sta Dept Philosophy (C3500) Austin TX 78712 Office Phone: 512-471-6753.

KANET, ROGER EDWARD, political science professor; b. Cin., Sept. 1, 1936; s. Robert George and Edith Mary (Weaver) K.; m. Joan Alice Edwards, Feb. 16, 1963; children: Suzanne Elise Zelle, Laurie Alice Burhart. PhB, Berchmanskolleg, Pullach-bei-München, Ger., 1960; AB, Xavier U., Cin., 1961; MA, Lehigh U., 1963; AM, Princeton U., 1965, PhD, 1966. Asst. prof. polit. sci. U. Kans., Lawrence, 1966-69, assoc. prof., 1969-74; joint sr. fellow Russian Inst. and Rsch. Inst. Communist Affairs, Columbia U., NYC, 1972-73; from vis. assoc. prof. to assoc. prof. to prof. U. Ill., Champaign-Urbana, 1973—97, prof. emeritus, 1997—, head dept. polit. sci., 1984—87, assoc. vice chancellor for acad. affairs, dir. internat. programs and studies, 1989—97; prof. dept. internat. studies U. Miami, Fla., 1997—, dean Sch. Internat. Studies, 1997—2000, dir. undergrad. studies, 2002—04. Partipant exch. with Hungary and Poland, Internat. Rsch. and Exchs. Bd., 1976; cons. Inst. Pub. Policy Devel., Washington, 1977-79; assoc. Ctr. Advanced Study, U. Ill., 1981-82; mem. Coun. on Fgn. Rels., NY, 1991—; mem. Chgo. Coun. on Fgn. Rels., 1993-97; chair internat. edn. panel Com. Instl. Coop. Big 10 & Chgo., 1993-96; co-founder Ill. Consortium for Internat. Edn. Editor, co-editor: The Behavioral Revolution and Communist Studies, 1971, On the Road to Communism, 1972, The Soviet Union and the Developing Countries, 1974, Soviet and East European Policy, 1974, Soviet Economic and Political Relations with the Developing World, 1975, Background to Crisis: Policy and Politics in Gierek's Poland, 1981, Soviet Foreign Policy and East-West Relations, 1982, Soviet Foreign Policy in the 1980s, 1982, The Soviet Union, Eastern Europe and the Third World, 1987, Asia in Soviet Global Strategy, 1987, The Limits of Soviet Power in the Developing World: Thermidor in the Revolutionary Struggle, 1989, The Cold War as Cooperation: Superpower Cooperation in Regional Conflict Management, 1991, Soviet Foreign Policy in Transition, 1992 (paperback reprint, 2008), Regional Conflicts and Conflict Resolution, 1995, Coping with Conflict After the Cold War, 1996, Foreign Policy of the Russian Fed., 1997, Resolving Regional Conflicts, 1998, The New Security Environment. The Impact on Russia, Ctrl. and Ea. Europe, 2005, Russia: Re-Emerging Great Power, 2007, From Superpower to Besieged Global Power: Restoring World Order After the Failure of the Bush Doctrine, 2008, Identities, Nations and Politics after Communism, 2008, The United States and Europe in a Changing World, 2009, A Resurgent Russia and the West: The European Union, NATO, and Beyond, 2009, Key Players and Regional Dynamics in Eurasia: The Return of the Great Game, 2010, Russian Foreign Policy in the 21st Century, 2010, Russia and its Near Neighbours, 2012, Russia and European Security, 2012, Competing for Influence: The Eu and Russia in Post Soviet Eurasia, 2012, Shifting Priorities in Russian Foreign & Security Policy, 2014; gen. editor, series of 12 vol. on Eastern Europe & USSR, Slavica and Praeger, 1975-77, series of 9 vol. on Eastern Europe & USSR; Unwin, Praeger, Pergamon and Russica, 1982-84; guest editor spl. issue jour. Nationalities Papers, 2007, spl. issues of journal, Internat. Politics, 2008, 12, general editor series, Ctrl. & Eastern Europe, 13 vol., Palgrave-Macmillan, 2007-08; contbr. more than 340 chpts. & articles to scholarly jours. and books. Co-founder, pres. Kans. Parents Assn. Hearing-Handicapped Children, 1968-70. Recipient US Dept. State Rsch. award, 1976, Excellence in Undergrad. Teaching award U. Ill., 1981, 84, Faculty Achievement award Burlington No. Found., 1989, US Inst. Peace award, 1991; fellow NDEA, 1963-66, NATO, 1976, Internat. fellow Fed. Inst. for East European and Internat. Studies, Cologne, Fed. Republic of Germany, 1988; Am. Coun. Learned Socs. grantee, 1972-73, 78. Mem. Am. Assn. Advancement of Slavic Studies, Assn. Internat. Studies Assn. (chmn. Am.-Soviet rels. sect. 1990-92), Internat. Coun. for Ctrl. and

Ea. European Studies (program chmn. 1st World Congress 1974, mem. program com. and gen. editor conf. publs. 1st World Congress 1974, 2nd World Congress 1980, 7th World Congress 2005). Liberal. Roman Catholic. Home: 9225 SW 142d St Miami FL 33176 Office Phone: 305-284-3407. Business E-Mail: rkanet@miami.edu.

KANFER, JULIAN NORMAN, biochemist, educator; b. Bklyn., May 23, 1930; s. Benjamin N. and Clara (Lichtenberger) K.; m. Beverly Kanfer; children— Brian, Rachel, Addison Slaeton Cressa. BSc, Bklyn. Coll., 1954; MSc, George Washington U., 1958, PhD, 1961. Biochemist Mass. Gen. Hosp., Boston, 1969-75; dir. biochem. research E.K. Shriver Center, Waltham, Mass.; also dir. research W.E. Fernald State Sch., Waltham, 1969-75; adj. asso. prof. biochemistry Brandeis U., Waltham, 1969-75; asso. prof. neuropathology Harvard, 1969-75, prin. research assoc., 1974-75; prof. U. Man., Winnipeg, Can., 1975—, head dept. biochemistry, 1975—. Cons. Health Scis. Centre, Winnipeg, 1976—; mem. med. adv. bd. Nat. Tay-Sachs Found., N.Y.C., 1970—; mem. study sect. on pathobiol. chemistry NIH, 1974—; postdoctoral fellowship com. NRC, 1983—; mem. Grant Commn. Nutrition and Metabolism Med. Rsch. Coun., Can., 1992—; vis. prof. dept. psychiatry U. Pitts. Med. Ctr., 1993-94; vis. prof. Stetson U., Deland, Fla., 1998—; adj. Daytona Beach C.C. Contbr. articles to profl. jours. Bd. dirs. Winnipeg chpt. Multiple Sclerosis Soc. Can., 1976. Named Hon. Citizen of New Orleans, 1997, Fellow Inst. de la Sante et de la Recherche Medicale (France); mem. Am. Soc. Biol. Chemistry, Am., Internat. neurochemistry socs., Am. Chem. Soc., AAAS, Soc. for Complex Carbohydrates, Fedn. Am. Socs. for Exptl. Biology, Can. Fedn. Biol. Socs., Canadian Biochem. Soc. Office: 1415 Ocean Shore Blvd Ormond Beach FL 32176-3673

KANG, JIMIN, professional golfer; b. Republic of Korea, Jan. 28, 1980; Attended, Ariz. State U., Tempe. Profl. golfer Futures Tour, 2002—04, LPGA Tour, 2003—. Named Futures Tour Player of Yr., 2004. Achievements include winning Futures Tour events: M&T Bank Loretto Golf Classic, 2002; Graetere Tampa Duramed Futures Classic, Betty Puskar Golf Classic, 2004; winning LPGA Tour events: LPGA Corning Classic, 2005; Sime Darby LPGA Malaysia, 2010. Office: c/o LPGA 100 International Golf Dr Daytona Beach FL 32124-1092

KANGAS, EDWARD A., healthcare company executive; b. 1942; m. Catherine Elizabeth Stephens, Sept. 17, 1994. BBA, U. Kansas, 1967, MBA. CPA NY, Conn. CPA, staff acct. Touche Ross & Co., Kansas City, 1967-74, ptnr., 1975-76, dir. mgmt. consulting ops., 1976-81, nat. dir. mgmt. consulting, 1981-85, mng. ptnr., CEO NYC, 1985-89; mng. ptnr. Deloitte and Touche USA LLP, NYC, 1989-94; global chmn, chief exec. Deloitte Touche Tohmatsu International, 1989—2000; cons. Deloitte Touche, Wilton, Conn., 2000—; non-exec. chmn. Tenet Healthcare Corp., Dallas, 2003—. Bd. dirs. Electric Data Systems Corp., 2004—, Intuit Inc., 2007—, United Technologies Corp., 2008—, Eclipsys Corp., Hovnanian Enterprises, Inc., Com. for Econ. Develop.; chmn. Oncology Therapeutics Networks. Bd. dirs., mem. fin. com., mem. and chmn. fund raising com. Nat. Multiple Sclerosis Soc.; trustee Com. Econ. Devel., U. Kansas Endowment Assn.; bd. overseers The Wharton Sch.; mem. U. Kansas Bus. Sch. Advisors Office: Tenet Healthcare Corp 13737 Noel Rd Dallas TX 75240

KANIPE, M. TODD, bank executive; BS in Fin., Western Ky. U.; grad., Cannon Personal Trust Sch., Ky. Sch. Banking Comml. Lending. Interim pres., interim CEO Citizens First Corp.; v.p., trust relationship mgr. Citizens First Bank, Inc. (subs. of Citizens First Corp.), 1999—2003; exec. v.p., chief credit officer Citizens First Corp., 2004—07, Citizens First Bank, Inc. (subs. of Citizens First Corp.), 2004—07, exec. v.p., credit adminstrn., fin., 2008, Citizens First Corp., 2008; exec. v.p., credit adminstrn. Citizens First Bank, Inc. (subs. of Citizens First Corp.), 2008, Citizens First Corp., 2008; pres., CEO, bd. dirs. Citizens First Bank, Inc., 2009—, Citizens First Corp., 2009—. Office: Citizens First Corp 1805 Campbell Ln Bowling Green KY 42104 Office Phone: 270-393-0700. Office Fax: 270-393-0716. Personal E-mail: tkanipe@citizensfirstbank.co.

KAO, CHANGQING CHRIS, medical educator, director; b. Meihekou, Jilin, China, May 18, 1955; s. Deyuan Kao and Guilan Sun; m. Xiaoren Sharon Lu, Aug. 6, 1981; children: Ying-ying Julia, Crystal Jing. MD, Bethune Med. U., Changchun, China, 1980; PhD, Va. Commonwealth U., Richmond, 1994. Dir., deep brain stimulation Vanderbilt Sentient Med. Sys., Nashville, 2001—. Rsch. assoc. prof. Vanderbilt U., Nashville, 2001—. Contbr. articles to profl. publs. Recipient Nat. Intro-operative Electrophysiology award, 2008. Achievements include patents for neurosurgical instrumentation. Office: Vanderbilt Med Ctr T-4224 Med Ctr North Nashville TN 37232-2380 Home: 554 Lester Ct Brentwood TN 37027 Business E-Mail: chris.kao@vanderbilt.edu.*

KAPLAN, ALAN LESLIE, gynecology educator, oncologist, department chairman; b. Atlanta, Sept. 10, 1930; children: John, Robert; m. Cissie Rauch Kaplan, Feb. 13, 2004. AB, Washington and Lee U., 1951; MD, Columbia U., 1955. Diplomate Am. Bd. Ob-Gyn. Intern Jackson Meml. Hosp., Miami, Fla., 1955-56; resident in ob-gyn Columbia-Presbyn. Med. Ctr., NYC, 1956-59, 61-63; prof. dept. ob-gyn, dir. divsn. gynecologic oncology Baylor Coll. Medicine, Houston, 1963—2005; prof. dept. ob-gyn Cornell U., 2005—; chmn. dept. ob-gyn The Meth. Hosp., Houston, 2005—. Med. dir. gynecologic oncology program Meth. Hosp., Houston, 1989—. Capt. M.C., U.S. Army, 1959-61. Mem. ACS, AMA, Am. Coll. Obstetricians and Gynecologists, Am. Cancer Soc., Am. Soc. Clin. Oncology, Soc. Gynecol. Oncology, Houston Gynecol. and Obstet. Soc. Office: Smith Tower Ste 901 6550 Fannin Houston TX 77030 Office Phone: 713-441-3193. Business E-Mail: akaplan@tmhs.org, akaplan@houstonmethodist.org.

KAPLAN, HENRY JERROLD, ophthalmologist, educator; b. NYC, Dec. 29, 1942; s. Ralph and Henrietta (Davis) K.; m. Adele Lotner, June 26, 1966; children: Wendi Suzanne, Todd Daniel, Ariane Dev. AB, Columbia U., 1964; MD, Cornell U., 1968. Diplomate Am. Bd. Ophthalmology. Intern in medicine Lakeside Hosp., Univ. Hosps. Cleve., Case-Western Res. U., 1968-69; surg. resident Bellevue Hosp., NYU Med. Ctr., 1969-70; NIH rsch. fellow in immunology U. Tex. (Southwestern) Med. Sch., Dallas, 1972-74, asst. prof. dept. cell biology, 1974-75; resident in ophthalmology U. Iowa Hosps. and Clinics, Iowa City, 1975-78; retina-vitreous fellow dept. ophthalmology Med. Coll. Wis., Milw., 1978-79; assoc. prof. dept. ophthalmology Emory U. Sch. Medicine, Atlanta, 1979-84, prof., dir. rsch., 1984-88, assoc. prof. dept. microbiology, 1985-88; prof. dept. ophthalmology and visual scis. Washington U. Sch. Medicine, St. Louis, 1988-2000, chmn. dept. ophthalmology and visual scis., 1988-98; prof., chmn. dept. opthalmology and visual scis. U. Louisville (Ky.) Sch. Medicine, 2000—, William H. and Blondina F. Evans Prof. Ophthalmology, 2000—. Ophthalmologist in chief Barnes-Jewish Hosp., Washington U. Med. Ctr., 1988-98; affiliate scientist in pathology and immunology Yerkes Regional Primate Rsch. Ctr., Atlanta, 1981—; adj. prof. dept. small animal medicine U. Ga., Athens, 1985—; assoc. chief ophthalmology Emory U. Hosp., 1985-88; mem. visual scis. study sect. A-1 NIH, Bethesda, Md., 1985-89, chmn., 1987-89; pres. Barnes Eye Care Network, 1994-98; dir. Ky. Lions Eye Ctr., Louisville, 2000—; pres. Eye Specialists Louisville, Ky.,2000—; chmn. U. Physician Assocs., 2004—06, bd. dirs. exec. com. U. Phys. Assocs., 2004-11, bd. dirs.; chair exec. compensation com. U. La. Physicians, 2011-, bd. dirs., exec. com. fin. com. Author, co-author or editor, co-editor more than 250 med. textbooks, chpts. and articles on uveitis and macular degeneration and retinal degeneration pub. in refereed sci. and med. jours., 1974—; mem. sci. jour. rev. bds. Archives Ophthalmology, 1978—, Retina, 1982—, Am. Jour. Ophthalmology, 1983—, Ophthalmology, 1983—, Current Eye Rsch., 1986—, Exptl. Eye Rsch., 1986—; mem. sci. rev. bd. Investigative Ophthalmology and Visual Sci., 1983—, mem. editorial bd., 1990-92; co-editor Ocular Immunology and Inflammation, 1994-98; editor: Ocular Immunology and Inflammation, 1999—2009. Maj. M.C., USAF, 1970-72. Recipient sci. award Alcon Rsch. Inst., 1987; Olga Keith Weiss rsch. scholar to Prevent Blindness, Inc., N.Y.C., 1984. Fellow ACS, Am. Acad. Ophthalmology (Honor award 1984, Sr. Honor award 1994); mem. AMA, Assn. for Rsch. in Vision and Ophthalmology, Am. Assn. Immunologists, Macula Soc., Am. Uveitis Soc. (pres. 1997-99), Retina Soc., Louisville Ophthal. Soc., Ky. Acad. Eye Physicians and Surgeons. Jewish. Office: U Louisville Sch Medicine Dept Opthalmol & Visual Sci 301 E Muhammad Ali Blvd Louisville KY 40202-1511 Office Phone: 502-852-3716. Business E-Mail: hank.kaplan@louisville.edu.

KAPLAN, JOEL D., electric power industry executive, lawyer; B in Govt., Harvard Coll.; JD, Harvard U. Policy advisor, Bush-Cheney presdl. campaign, Austin, Tex.; artillery officer US Marine Corp.; law clk., justice Antonin Scalia US Supreme Ct.; law clk., judge J. Michael Luttig US Ct. Appeals Fourth Cir.; editor Harvard Law Rev.; joined White House, 2001, dep. dir., mgmt. and budget office, spl. asst., policy, pres., 2003—06, dep. chief staff, pres., George W. Bush, 2006—08; exec. v.p., pub. policy and external affairs Energy Future Holdings Corp. (formerly TXU Corp.), 2009—. Bd. dirs. Electric Drive Transp. Assn. Arty. officer USMC. Office: Energy Future Holdings Corp 1601 Bryan St Dallas TX 75201-3411 Business E-Mail: joel.kaplan@energyfutureholdings.com.

KAPLAN, JOHN, photojournalist, educator, consultant; b. Wilmington, Del., Aug. 21, 1959; s. Ralph Benjamin and Ruth Jillya (Denkin) Kaplan. BJ cum laude, Ohio U., Athens, 1982; MS in Journalism, Ohio U., 1998. Photojournalist, designer Spokesman Rev./Chronicle, Spokane, Wash., 1983—84; photojournalist, picture editor Pitts. Press, 1984—90; photojournalist Pitts. Post-Gazette, 1990—92; spl. corr. Block Newspapers, 1992—94. Tchr., lectr. numerous univs., seminars, profl. groups U.S., Can., 1984—; vis. lectr. Bradley U., Peoria, Ill., 1989; adj. prof. Syracuse U., London campus, 1993; assoc. prof. U. Fla., Gainesville, 1999—; dir. Media Alliance, cons., Pitts., 1990—2000; mem. Pulitzer Prize jury, 1994, 1995; photojournalism mem. Ball State U., Muncie, 1998—99. Author: Mom and Me, 1996; contbr. to book series The Best of Photojournalism, Vols. 6, 7, 9, 10, 11, 14, 18, 1981-93; work in permanent collection Carnegie Mus. Art, Pitts.; author: Photo Portfolio Success, 2003. Recipient Golden Quill Journalism award, Pitts. Press Club, 1986, 1989, Robert F. Kennedy Journalism award, Kennedy Found., 1989, 2003, Pulitzer prize for feature photography, 1992, 2003, Matrix Mag. award, Women in Comm., 1992, Ohio U. Disting. Grad. award, 1993, award for feature photography, Overseas Press Club, 2003, Harry Chapin award, 2003; named Pitts. Photographer of Yr., News Photographers Assn. Greater Pitts., 1986, 1989, 1992, Photographer of Yr., Pa. Photographers Assn., 1989, No. Photographer of Yr., 1992; named to, Ohio U. Coll. Comm. Hall of Fame, 1993; Knight fellow, Ohio U., 1997—98. Mem.: Soc. Newspaper Design (Gold award 1989), Nat. Press Photographers Assn. (contest chmn. Region 3 1987—89, Regional Photographer of Yr. award 1985, 1986, 1987, 1989, Nat. Newspaper Photographer of Yr. award 1989, Nikon Documentary Sabbatical award 1990, Harry Chapin award 2023, others), Amnesty Internat. Avocations: racquet sports, furniture design, wines. Home: 4509 NW 53rd St Gainesville FL 32606 Personal E-mail: kaplan@writeme.com

KAPLAN, LEONARD EUGENE, accountant; b. Chgo., Mar. 3, 1940; s. David Solomon and Faye Gertrude (Grossman) K.; m. Myrna Dee Shellist, Dec. 20, 1959; children: Sheri Kaplan Mayes, Jodi Kaplan Hoffman, Jeffrey. Student, U. Ill., Chgo., 1958-59; BSc in Acctg., De Paul U., 1961. CPA, Tex., Ill.; cert. ins. counselor; cert. global mgmt. acct. Staff acct. Goldstein, Engerman & Shane, Chgo., 1960-63, BDO Seidman, Chgo., 1963-72, ptnr., 1972-79, Houston, 1979-95, regional tech. dir. region III, 1982-84, mng. ptnr., 1984-89, nat. dir. industry specialization, 1990-92; also bd. dirs.; exec. v.p., sec., CFO Delta Ins. Group Corp., Houston, 1995—, dir. Mem. adv. coun. dept. acctg. U. Tex., 1989-95. Contbr. articles to various publs. Mem. WYO Standards Com., FEMA, 2003-09; chmn. bd. dirs Surplus Lines Stamping Office, Tex., 2011, chmn. Fin. Com. Ill. State scholar, 1958-61, Jack Clator Meml. scholar, 1998. Mem.: AICPA, Property Casualty Insurers Assn. Am., Tex. Surplus Lines Assn. (pres. 2006—07, Pres. award 2005, Don King award 2001), Bus. and Profl. Soc. of Jewish Fedn., Am. Assn. Mng. Gen. Agts., Soc. of Cert. Ins. Counselors, Tex. Soc. CPAs (vice chmn. com. on rels. with attys. Houston chpt. 1984—85), B'nai B'rith (newsletter editor 1971—72), Royal Oaks Country Club (fin. com.). Jewish. Avocations: golf, tennis, crossword puzzles. Business E-Mail: lenk@deltains.com.

KAPLAN, ROBERT N., foundation administrator; BA in Pub. Policy Analysis, U. NC, Chapel Hill, 1983; MPA in Devel. Policy, Princeton U., NJ, 1988. Vol. Peace Corps, Paraguay; work on edn. & environ. projects and sector studies World Bank, 1988—97; chief environ. and natural resources mgmt. divsn. Inter-American Devel. Bank, 1998—2007, chief advisor to the exec. v.p., 2007—10; pres., CEO Inter-American Found., 2010—. Office: Inter American Found 901 N Stuart St 10th Fl Arlington VA 22203 Office Phone: 703-306-4301. Office Fax: 703-306-4365. Business E-Mail: rkaplan@iaf.gov.

KAPLOWITZ, LISA GLAUSER, physician, educator; b. Phila., Apr. 18, 1951; d. Felix E. and Charlotte Glauser; m. Paul Bernard Kaplowitz, Dec. 28, 1970; children: Joshua Michael, Daniel Steven. BS, U. Mich., 1970; MD, U. Chgo., 1975; MS in Health Adminstrn., Va. Commonwealth U., 2002. Diplomate Am. Bd. Internal Medicine; Am. Bd. Infectious Diseases. Resident U. N.C., Chapel Hill, 1976—78, post grad. fellow, 1978—80, instr. dept. medicine, 1980—82; asst. prof., dept. medicine Med. Coll. Va., Richmond, 1982—89, assoc. prof., 1989—; dir. HIV/AIDS Ctr., Va. Commonwealth U., Richmond, 1993—2002, asst. v.p. fed. health policy; med. dir. ambulatory care Va. Commonwealth U. Health Sys., Richmond, 2000—02; dep. commr. for emergency preparedness and response Va. Dept. Health, Richmond, 2002—08; dist. health dir. Alexandria Health Dept., 2008—. Bd. dirs. AIDS Action Coun., Washington, 1995-96; mem., 1999-2000 class Exec. Leadership in Acad. Medicine Program for Women, MCP Hahnemann U. Contbg. (book chpt.) Conn's Current Therapy, 1985, 2d rev. edit., 1988, 3d edit., 1998; Principles of Critical Care Medicine, 1992. Mem. adv. bd. Va. League for Planned Parenthood, Richmond, 1993—, Richmond AIDS Ministry, 1988—92; mem. Leadership Metro Richmond, 1992—93; grad. Exec. Leadership in Acad. Med. for Women, MCP-Hahnemann U., 2000, Nat. Pub. Health Leadership Inst., U. N.C., 2003—04. Named Woman of Yr. Va. Commonwealth U., 1995; mem. Va. Women's Hall of Fame; fellow Inst. Medicine, 1996-97, Office of Senator Jay Rockefeller, 1997; recipient Local Legend award Nat. Libr. Medicine, 2004. Fellow ACP, Infectious Disease Soc. Am.; mem. APHA; Am. Soc. Microbiology. Avocation: piano. Office: Dist Dir Alexandria Health Dist 4480 King St Alexandria VA 22302 Home Phone: 703-535-5988; Office Phone: 703-838-5058. Business E-Mail: Lisa.Kaplowitz@vdh.virginia.gov.

KAPNICK, S. JASON, oncologist, surgeon; b. Providence, Mar. 28, 1949; s. I.H. and Martha (Shaulson) K.; children: Senta Marie-Rose, Isrel Berndt-Stefan, Sesselja Edda, Finn MacCumaill. BLS summa cum laude, boston U., 1974; MD, Harvard Med. Sch., 1981. Surg. rsch. assoc. Harvard Med. Sch., Boston, 1976—79, assoc. in ob/gyn., lectr., 1981-85; intern, resident in ob-gyn. Brigham & Women's Mass. Gen. Hosp., Boston, 1981—85; adminstrv. chief resident Mass. Gen. Hosp./Brigham Hosps., 1985; instr. in gynecology, fellow tumor surgery Harvard Med. Sch., Boston, 1985—87; cons. in gynecologic oncology Dana Farber Cancer Inst., Boston, 1985-87; clin. fellow Am. Cancer Soc., Boston, 1985-87; attending oncologic surgeon, gynecologic oncologist West Palm Beach, Fla., 1989—. Asst. cons. prof. Duke U. Med. Ctr., Durham, NC, 1994—; reviewer rsch. submissions Cancer med. jour., Bethesda, Md., 1995—; invited lectr. Am. Cancer Soc., Bethesda, 1995, also Switzerland, Germany, France and Eng., 1990-, bus. advisory bd. Admiralty Bank 1992-99. Contbr. articles to profl. jours. Vol., contbr. Ctr. for Family Svcs., West Palm Beach, 1992—; mem. Mass. Gen. Hosp., Bulfinch Soc.; trustee, founder Helga Helgason BSRN Meml. Fund; dean's coun. and John Warren Fellow Med. Sch., Harvard U.; donor Covenant House Children's Shelter, 2004—; founder, dir. Kapnick Meml. Cancer Ctrl. Consortium, 2006; founder, Clin. Care Initiative Theresa Pratt RN Meml., 2006—; active Cath. Diocese children's programs, 1998—; mem., donor First Unitarian Ch., North Palm Beach, Fla., 1991—; bd. dirs. Palm Beach Opera, 1992—2007. Henry Merritt Wriston scholarship Brown U. Mem. Ezekial Hersey Soc., Harvard Med. Sch., Legacy Soc., Brigham Women's Hosp., Harvard Club of Palm Beach. Achievements include research in ovarian colon, breast, and abdominal cancers which changed patient management. Avocations: philosophy, music. Office: 335 Leeward Dr Jupiter FL 33477 Home Phone: 561-743-4599; Office Phone: 561-622-3810. Personal E-mail: jasonkapnickmd@gmail.com.

KAPOOR, KAY, telecommunications industry executive; b. 1963; BS in Info. Sys., U. Md.; MS in Bus., Johns Hopkins U., 1996. Dep. to pres. civil programs bus. unit Lockheed Martin IS&GS, 1990—2010, v.p., 1990—2010, ITT Corp., 2010—11, gen. mgr., 2010—11; mng. dir. Accenture, 2011—13, chief exec. Accenture Fed. Services NY, 2011—13; pres. AT&T Govt. Solutions, Oakton, Va., 2013—. Recipient numerous awards. Mem.: Asian American Govt. Execytives Network, Women in Tech., Soc. of Women Engineers, Coun. for Fgn. Rels., TechAmerica, American Coun. for Tech.-Industry Adv. Coun. Office: AT&T Govt Solutions 3033 Chain Bridge Rd Oakton VA 22185

KAPP, JOHN PAUL, lawyer, physician, educator; b. Galax, Va., Feb. 22, 1938; s. Paul Homer and Jesse Katherine (Vass) Kapp; m. Emily Lureese Evans, June 23, 1961; children: Paul Hardin, Emily Camille. MD, Duke U., 1963, BS, 1966, PhD in Anatomy, 1967; JD, Wake Forest U., 1990. Bar: NC 1990, Va. 1991, Fla. 1991. Intern Med. Coll. Va., Richmond, 1963; resident in surgery Duke U., Durham, NC, 1964, resident in neurosurgery, 1964-69; asst. prof. neurosurgery U. Tenn., Memphis, 1971-72; attending neurosurgeon Bay Meml. Med. Ctr., Panama City, Fla., 1972-80, Gulf Coast Cmty. Hosp., 1977-80; assoc. prof. neurosurgery U. Miss., Jackson, 1980-83, prof., 1983-85; prof., chmn. dept. neurosurgery SUNY, Buffalo, 1985-87; pvt. practice as lawyer Galax, 1990—, Winston-Salem, NC, 1990—, Panama City, Fla., 1990—. Editor: The Cerebral Venous System and Its Disorders, 1984; contbr. articles to profl. jours. and chpts. to books; patentee arterial pressure control system, prosthetic vertebral body, cranial sensor attaching device. Major US Army, 1969-71. Recipient Rsch. award, Am. Acad. Neurol. Surgery, 1967; fellow USPHS Neurosurgy fellow, 1965—67. Republican. Methodist. Avocation: hunting. Office: 105 W Grayson St Galax VA 24333 Business E-Mail: kapp@ls.net.

KAPP, MICHAEL KEITH, lawyer; b. Winston-Salem, NC, Nov. 28, 1953; s. William Henry and Betty Jean (Minton) K.; m. Mary Jo Chancy McLean, Aug. 13, 1977; children: Mary Katherine, Kapp Muto. AB with honors, U. NC, 1976, JD with honors, 1979. Bar: NC 1979, US Dist. Ct. (ea. dist.) NC 1980, US Ct. Appeals (4th cir.) 1982, US Dist. Ct. (mid. dist.) NC 1986, US Supreme Ct. 1988. Law clk. to presiding judge NC Ct. Appeals, Raleigh, 1979—80; assoc. justice NC Supreme Ct., 1980—81; assoc. Maupin, Taylor & Ellis, Raleigh, 1981—85; ptnr. Williams, Mullen (formerly Maupin, Taylor & Ellis, P.A.), 1985—, mng. dir., 2002—07, v.p., 2007—, vice chair bd., 2011—. Research editor U. NC Jour. Internat. Law and Comml. Regulation, 1978-79; editor Survey of Significant Decisions of North Carolina Court of Appeals and North Carolina Supreme Court, 1979-81, 2d vol., 1981-82. NC Teen Dem. advisor, 1983-85; mem. exec. coun. NC Dem. Party, 1983-85; founding dir. NC Vol. Lawyers for Arts, Raleigh, 1982-85; counsel Moravian Music Found., Winston-Salem, 1982-85, trustee, 1985-90, pres., 1990-92; counsel Raleigh Little Theatre, 1996-98, bd. dir., pres., 2003; bd. dir. Moravian Ch. Archives, Winston-Salem, 1984-89, Carolina Charter Corp., dir. 1995-, v.p., 2011-; co-chair Raleigh First Night, 2000; bd. dirs. Soc. for Preservation of Historic Oakwood, Raleigh, 1981-83, Moravian Ministries Found., Inc., 2006-, chair, 2010-12, bd. dir. Capital City Club, 2009-. Morehead scholar U. NC, 1972. Mem.: ABA, NC Bar Assn. (bd. govs. 1983-86), NC State Bar (ethics com. 1981-91, jud. dist. councilor 2001-10, chair ethics com. 2007, 2008, v.p. 2010-11, pres. elect. 2011-12, pres. 2012-13), Wake County Bar Assn. (bd. dirs. 1988-90, pres.-elect 1995, pres. 1996), Raleigh Execs. Club (pres. 1998), Kiwanis (Raleigh Kiwanis Found. dir., 1996-98, 2008-10), Phi Beta Kappa, Phi Delta Phi, Pi Lambda Phi. Democrat. Avocations: historic preservation, hiking, gardening. Office: Williams Mullen PA 301 Fayetteville St Ste 1700 PO Box 1000 Raleigh NC 27601 Office Phone: 919-981-4000, 919-981-4024. Business E-Mail: kkapp@williamsmullen.com.

KAPPITT, MICHAEL, food service executive; Attended, Fla. Internat. U. Sr. dir. revenue mgmt. Vanguard Car Rental Group Inc. (ANC Rental, Nat. Car Rental, Alamo Rent A Car), 1989—2002; dir. field mktg. Burger King Corp., 2002—03, dir. nat. promotions, 2003—04, sr. dir. performance analysis, 2004, v.p. consumer insights & performance analysis, 2004—07, sr. v.p. global bus. intelligence & strategy, 2007—10, chief mktg. officer, 2010—. Office: Burger King Corp 5505 Blue Lagoon Dr Miami FL 33126 Office Phone: 305-378-3000. E-mail: mkappitt@whopper.com.

KAPPLOW, JON, marketing executive; b. Miami, Fla. BS, U. Ala.; MBA, Ga. Inst. Tech. Founder, customer picks HSN, Inc., 2005, dir., multichannel mktg., 2004—06; v.p., multichannel mktg. HSN.com, 2006—. Office: HSN Inc 1 HSN Dr Saint Petersburg FL 33729 Office Phone: 727-872-1000. Business E-Mail: jon.kapplow@hsn.com.

KAPRIELIAN, VICTORIA SUSAN, medical educator; d. Walter and Julia (Hachigian) Kaprielian; m. Jonathan R. Luis. BA in Human Biology magna cum laude, Brown U., 1981; MD, UCLA, 1985. Diplomate Am. Bd. Family Practice. Resident Duke-Watts Family Medicine, Durham, NC, 1985-88; fellow UCLA Family Medicine,

LA, 1988-89; asst. clin. prof. Duke U. Med. Ctr., Durham, NC, 1989-98, chief, divsn. predoctoral edn. and faculty devel., dept cmty and family medicine, 1994-96, assoc. clin. prof., 1998—2003, clin. prof., 2003—06, prof., 2006—12; fellowship dir., dept. cmty. and family medicine Duke U., Durham, NC, 1994—99, 2000—04, dir. predoctoral edn. and faculty devel., 1996-99, vice chair for edn., dept. cmty. and family medicine, 2006—12; interim chief Phys. Therapy Program, Duke U., 2009—11, prof. emeritus, 2012—; fellow Am. Coun. Edn., 2009—10; prof., family medicine Campbell U., 2012—; assoc. dean Faculty Devel. & Med. Edn., Campbell U. Sch. Osteopathic Medicine, 2013—. Medical dir. WellPath Cmty. Health Plans, 1998. Fellow Am. Acad. Family Physicians (pub. com. 1985, mental health com. 1986-88, commission on continuing profl. devel., 2006-09); mem. NC Acad. Family Physicians (bd. dirs. 1998-2002, 2005—09 edn. com. 1989-90, med. sch. affairs 1990—2001, chair of com. 1991-97, CME coun. 2006-), Soc. Tchrs. Family Medicine (steering com., predoc. dir. working group 1995-98, chair 1998, Bishop fellow 2009-10), Nat. Commn. Certification Physician Assts. (bd. dirs. 2008-, bd. sec. 2012-), Alpha Omega Alpha 1984-, Phi Beta Kappa 1980-. Avocations: singing, yoga, ethnic cooking. Office: Campbell University Sch Osteopathic Medicine PO Box 4280 Buies Creek NC 27506 Office Phone: 910-893-1783. Business E-Mail: kaprielianv@campbell.edu.

KAPUT, JIM L., lawyer; b. Toms River, NJ, May 28, 1960; BS, U Pa., 1982; JD, Cornell U., 1986. Bar: Ill. 1987. Assoc. Sidley & Austin (now Sidley Austin Brown & Wood), Chgo., ptnr., 1994—2000; sr. v.p., gen. counsel The ServiceMaster Co., Downers Grove, Ill., 2000—. Avocation: running. Office: Servicemaster 860 Ridge Lake Blvd Memphis TN 38120-9434

KARAKOSTAS, TASOS, engineer, director; s. Klimentini Karakostas; m. Alexia Sarantos, Aug. 18, 2001. PhD, Ohio State U., Columbus, 2001. Dir. motion analysis lab. Tex. Tech U. Health Scis. Ctr., Lubbock, 2001—05, U. SC, Charleston, 2006—. Achievements include research in bioengineering and rehabilitation. Office: Med Univ SC 77 President St Charleston SC 29425

KARAOGLAN, ALAIN MAURICE, insurance company executive; b. 1962; BS, BA in Economics, Pepperdine U., 1983; MBA in Finance, Dartmouth Coll., 1987. Investment banker The First Boston Corp., 1988—92; mng. dir. Bear, Stearns & Co., Inc., 1992—97; equity rsch. analyst Donaldson, Lufkin, & Jenrette Securities Inc., 1997—2000; mng. dir., North American Equity Rsch. Deutsche Bank Securities, Inc., 2000—07; mng. dir., Equity Rsch. Banc of America Securities LLC, 2007—09; sr. v.p., Divestiture American International Group, Inc. (AIG), 2009—11; exec. v.p. finance & strategy ING Ins. America, 2011—. Office: ING America Insurance 5780 Powers Ferry Rd NW Atlanta GA 30327

KARBHARI, VISTASP M., engineering educator, researcher; b. Dec. 21, 1961; BCE, U. Poona, India, 1984, M in Structural Engring., 1985; PhD, U. Del., Newark, 1991. Rsch. asst. prof., scientist U. Del., Newark, 1991—95; asst. prof. U. Calif., San Diego, 1995—97, assoc. prof., 1997—2001, prof., 2001—08, U. Ala., Huntsville, 2008—, Dept. Mech. & Aerospace Engring., Dept. Civil & Environ. Engring.; exec. v.p. Academic Affairs and Provost. Mem. editl. bd. Internat. Jour. Sustainable Materials and Structural Sys.; assoc. editor Jour. Civil Structural Health Monitoring. Am. editor: Internat. Jour. Materials and Product Tech., mem. editl. bd.: Composite Structures; mem. editl. bd. ASTM Jour. Testing and Evaluation, Structural Engring. & Mechanics, Recent Patents Materials Sci.; contbr. 23 chapters to books, over 260 conf. proceedings, over 200 articles to profl. jours.; editor: Durability of Composites for Civil Structural Applications, Structural Health Monitoring of Civil Infrastructure Systems, Service Life Estimation and Extension of Civil Engineering Structures. Recipient Best Paper award Engring. Soc. Detroit, 1992, CIICE, 1999, ASC, 2000, Charles Pankow award for innovation in design Civil Engring. Rsch. Found., 1996, Career award NSF, 1997, Faculty award Am. Soc. Nondestructive Testing, 2003, International Institute for FRP in Construction (IIFC) Pres. award, 2006, Best Paper award European Workshop on Structural Health Monitoring, 2006; Powell Faculty fellow, 1997-99, IIFC fellow, 2006. Fellow: ASM Internat.; mem.: ASCE, Soc. Materials and Process Engring., Internat. Inst. FRP in Contrn. (exec. com., v.p. award 2006), Internat. Soc. Structural Health Monitoring of Intelligent Structures (coun. mem.), Am. Concrete Inst., Am. Soc. Metals (Best Paper award 1992). Office: University Ala Huntsville 366 Shelbie King Hall Huntsville AL 35899 Office Phone: 256-824-6335. Business E-Mail: vmk0001@uah.edu, vistasp.karbhari@uah.edu.

KARFF, SAMUEL EGAL, rabbi; b. Phila., Sept. 19, 1931; s. Louis and Reba (Margalit) K.; m. Joan Mag, June 29, 1959; children: Rachel Karff Weissenstein, Amy Karff Halevy, Elizabeth Karff Kampf. AB magna cum laude, Harvard U., 1953; MAHL, DHL, Hebrew Union Coll., 1956. Rabbi Congregation Beth Israel, Hartford, Conn., 1958-60, Temple Beth El, Flint, Mich., 1960-62, Chgo. Sinai Congregation, 1962-74; sr. rabbi Congregation Beth Israel, Houston, 1975-99, rabbi emeritus, 1999—; vis. prof. soc. and health U. Tex. Health Sci. Ctr., Houston, 1999—. Lectr. U. Chgo. Divinity Sch., 1968-75; vis. assoc. prof. U. Notre Dame, 1966-67; adj. prof. religious studies Rice U., Houston, 1976—; assoc. dir. McGovern Ctr. for Health, Humanities, and Human Spirit, U. Tex. Med. Sch., Houston, 2004-, vis. prof. family medicine, 2004-. Author: Agada: The Language of Jewish Faith, 1970, Permissions to Believe Finding Faith in Troubled Times, 2005; editor Centennial Vol. Hebrew Union Coll.-Jewish Inst. of Religion, 1981-84; contbr. chpts. Judaism Religions of the World, 1982. Bd. dirs. United Way, Houston, 1991—, Inst. Religion, Houston, 1990—. Recipient Homiletics award HUC-JIR, Cin., 1956; John Harvard scholar Harvard U., 1951-52. Mem. Cen. Conf. Am. Rabbis (pres. 1989-91), Houston Philos. Soc., Phi Beta Kappa, Kiwanis. Jewish. Avocations: tennis, walking, movies, reading. Office: Congregation Beth Israel 5600 N Braeswood Blvd Houston TX 77096-2901 E-mail: skarff@sph.uth.tmc.edu.

KARGER, HOWARD JACOB, finance educator; b. Bklyn., Nov. 9, 1948; s. Samuel and Frieda Karger; m. Anna Janette Conaty; children: Aaron Abraham, Saul Leon, Raphael Efraim. MS in Counseling, U. Wis., Superior, 1974; MSW, U. Minn., Duluth, 1978; PhD, U. Ill., Urbana-Champaign, 1985. Prof. La. State U., Baton Rouge, 1989—94, U. Houston, Houston, 1994—. Author: (book) Shortchanged: Life and Debt in the Fringe Economy (Economics, Fin. and Investment award, Ind. Book Publs., 2006). Dir. Policy America, DC, 1990—2008. Office: Univ Houston 231 Social Work Bldg Houston TX 77096 Business E-Mail: hkarger@uh.edu.

KARI, ROSS JAY, mortgage company executive; b. 1958; BA in Math., U. Oreg., 1980, MBA in. Fin., 1983. Analyst in fin. Wells Fargo & Co., 1983, v.p., 1987, sr. v.p. fin. & planning, gen. auditor, exec. v.p., 1995, head fin., mgr. controller's divsn./corp. tax., 1997, v.p., CFO, 1998—2001; CFO myCFO; exec. v.p., COO Fed. Home Loan Bank of San Francisco, 2002—07; exec. v.p., CFO Safeco Corp., Seattle, 2006—08, Fifth Third Bancorp, Cin., 2008—09; CFO Freddie Mac - Federal Home Loan Mortgage Corp., McLean, Va., 2009—. Office: Freddie Mac 8200 Jones Branch Dr Mc Lean VA 22102

KARIM, MOHAMMAD ATAUL, electrical engineering educator, researcher; b. Sylhet, Bangladesh, June 1, 1953; came to U.S., 1976; s. Muhammad Abdus and Anwara (Nuri) Shukur; m. Setara Karim, Dec. 20, 1977; children: Lutfi, Lamya, Aliya. BS in Physics with honors, U. Dacca, Bangladesh, 1976; MS in Physics, U. Ala., 1978, MS in Elec. Engring., 1979, PhD in Elec. Engring., 1981. Asst. prof. elec. engring. U. Ark., Little Rock, 1981-83, Wichita (Kans.) State U., 1983-86; dir. electro-optics program U. Dayton, Ohio, 1990-98, chair elect. and computer engring. dept. Ohio, 1994-98; head Elec. Engring. Dept. U. Tenn., Knoxville, 1998—2000; dean, engring. City Coll. of NY, NYC, 2000—04; v.p. rsch. Old Dominion U., Norfolk, Va., 2004—. Author: Digital Design, 2007,Continous Signals and Systems with Matlab, 2008, 1988, EO Devices and Systems, 1990, Optical Computing, 1992, Electro-Optical Displays, 1992, A Pragmatic Approach, 1987; N.Am. editor Jour. Oprics and Laser Tech.; contbr. over 325 articles to profl. jours. and conf. procs.; editor 23 jour. spl. issues; holder 2 patents. Recipient Outstanding Scientist award Engring. and Sci. Found. (Dayton), 1994, Outstanding Engring. Scholarship award, 1998, Alumni award U. Dayton, 1991, NASA Tech Brief award 1990, Up-Comers award Muse-Machine, Dayton, 1990. Fellow IEEE, Optical Soc. Am., Soc. Photo-Instrumentation Engrs., Inst. Physics, Instn. Engring. and Tech., Am. Soc. Engring. Edn., Bangladesh Acad. Scis. Muslim. Office: Old Dominion U Innovation Rsch Park 4111 Monarch Way Suit 203 Norfolk VA 23529 Home Phone: 757-463-0224. E-mail: mkarim@odu.edu.

KARIM, MUHAMMAD BAZLUL, political scientist, educator; b. Mymensingh, Bangladesh, Dec. 26, 1949; arrived in U.S., 1975; s. Abdul and Akika Khatoon Bari; m. Jean Ellickson, July 26, 1975. BA with honors, Dhaka U., Bangladesh, 1972, MA in Geography, 1973, Western Ill. U., 1978; cert. in computer programming, Strayer Coll., Washington, 1981; MA in Internat. Studies, U. Denver, 1984, cert. in devel. studies, 1985, PhD in Internat. Studies, 1991. Asst. dir. Integrated Rural Devel. Program, Dhaka, 1973-74; rsch. asst. Rajshahi (Bangladesh), 1974-75; rsch. assoc. Ethikos Rsch., Inc., Silver Spring, Md., 1980-81; rsch. asst. Internat. Food Policy Rsch. Inst., Washington, 1981; owner Asian Am. Net., 1996—; instr. Spoon River Coll., Macomb, 1991-95; asst. prof. Western Ill. U., Macomb, 1994—98; web content editor and rschr. Mayer, Brown LLP, Chgo., 2000—10. Cons. Ill. Dept. Human Rights, 1998-99; presenter in field. Author: A Farmer's Market in America, 1981, The Green Revolution: An International Bibliography, 1986, Structural Constraints to Participatory Development: An Examination of Social Stratification System in Rural Bangladesh, 1992, Participation, Development and Social Structure: An Empirical Study in a Developing Country, 1994; editor Who's Who of Asian Ams., 1998-; contbr. articles and rsch. reports to profl. jours. Vol. flood victims, Kampsville, Ill., 1993; election judge primary and gen. election Macomb City Precinct 7, McDonough County, Ill., 1990. Rsch. fellow Shell Cos. Found., 1987; grad. rsch. assistantship U. Denver, 1984-85, stipend and tuition scholar, 1983-84. Mem. Assn. Third World Studies (life, web master 1996—2000). Home Phone: 863-496-1570. Business E-Mail: info@asianamerican.net.

KARMAN, JAMES ANTHONY, retired manufacturing executive; b. Grand Rapids, Mich., May 26, 1937; s. Anthony and Katherine D. Karman; m. Carolyn L. Hoehn, Aug. 29, 1959; children: Robb Thomas, Janet Ellen, Edward John, Christopher James. BS cum laude, Miami U., Oxford, Ohio, 1959; MBA, U. Wis., 1960. Instr. corp. fin. University of Wisconsin, Madison, 1960-61; asst. mgr. investment dept. Union Bank & Trust Co., Grand Rapids, 1961-63; treas. RPM, Inc., Medina, Ohio, 1963-69, v.p., treas., 1969-72, v.p., sec.-treas., 1972-73, exec. v.p., sec.-treas., 1973-78, pres., 1978—99, also bd. dirs., CFO, 1982-93, 2001, vice chmn. Medina, Ohio, 1999—2002. Instr. Am. Inst. Banking, 1962; mem. bd. dirs. Metro. Fin. Corp., Shiloh Industries, Inc., A. Schulman, Inc., RPM Internat. Inc., 2002-. Trustee Trinity Cathedral, Cleve., Western Res. Hist. Soc., Boys & Girls Club, Cleve., The Leelanau Sch., Glen Arbor, Mich.; past bd. trustees Cleve. Orch., Boys Hope, Cleve., Cleve. Playhouse; mem. adv. coun. Miami U. Sch. Bus. Adminstrn.; mem. bd. visitors U. Wis.; mem. corp. coun., fin. com. Cleve. Mus. Art.; mem. Bluecoats, Inc., Cleve. Mem. US Power Squadron, Gt. Lakes Hist. Soc., Mayfield Country Club, Cleve. Playhouse Club, Pine Lake Trout Club, Union Club (Cleve.), St. Louis Club, Order of Artus, Phi Beta Kappa. Home: 110 Seaspray Ave Palm Beach FL 33480-4227 Office Fax: 330-225-8743. Business E-Mail: jkarman@rpminc.com.

KARNER, STEPHEN LESLIE, geophysicist; s. Garry David and Lois Gwenda Karner; m. Karen Ann Davies, Jan. 18, 1992. BS, Flinders U. of South Australia, 1986, BS with honors, 1987; MA, CUNY, Flushing, 1993; PhD, MIT, Cambridge, Mass., 1999. Intern Delhi Petroleum Inc., Adelaide, South Australia, Australia, 1986—87; geologist So. Australian Oil and Gas, Adelaide, Australia, 1987—88; geophysicist Wiltshire Geol. Svcs. Inc., Adelaide, South Australia, Australia, 1988—89; tchg. and rsch. asst. Queens Coll., CUNY, Flushing, NY, 1989—93; rsch. asst. Lamont-Doherty Earth Obs. of Columbia U., Palisades, NY, 1993; tchg. and rsch. asst. MIT, Cambridge, 1993—99, post-doctoral rsch. scientist, 1999—2000; post-doctoral rschr., rsch. scientist Tex. A&M U., Coll. Sta., 2000—04, adj. rsch. scientist, 2004—07; post-doctoral rsch. scientist Wash. State U., Pullman, 2004—06; geomechanicist, geothermal energy Idaho Nat. Lab., Idaho Falls, 2004—06; geomechanicist Exxon Mobil Upstream Rsch. Co., Houston, 2006. Cons. Quantitative Basin Analysis Inc., Ramsey, NJ, 2004; steering com. Phys. Properties of Earth Materials, 2004—07; attendee and spkr. UN Internat. Decade on Natural Disaster Reduction, Beijing, 1997—97. Author: (family history website) Blackadder - The Whole Damn Dynasty, (family history articles) 1804 First Settlers Association Newsletter; contbr. articles to profl. jours. County coord. FreeCen UK Census Project (freecen.rootsweb.com), 2001—04; dancer George Tomov Folkdance Ensemble, NYC, 1981—93; choreographer and dancer Adelaide Traditional Dancers, Adelaide, South Australia, Australia, 1984—89, Jedinstvo Folkdance Ensemble, Adelaide, 1986—89, KUD Biljana Folkdance Ensemble, Adelaide, 1984—86, Queanbeyan Folkdance Ensemble, Queanbeyan, New South Wales, Australia, 1983—83, Canberra Internat. Folkdance Assn., Canberra, Australian Capital Territory, Australia. Grantee Keith Runcorn Travel award, European Geophys. Soc., 1997, Rsch. grantee, NSF, 2004—05; fellow David B. Harris Post-Doctoral fellow, Tex. A&M U., Coll. Sta., TX USA, 2003—04. Mem.: Seismol. Soc. of Am, Am. Geophys. Union, Am. Assn. of Petroleum Geologists, 1804 First Settlers Assn., Borders Family History Soc., Herefordshire Family History Soc. Avocations: folklore, cultural heritage, dance, family history. Office: Exxon Mobil URC-URC N209 PO Box 2189 Houston TX 77252-2189 Home: 3118 Junegrass Ct Kingwood TX 77345 Business E-Mail: stephen.l.karner@exxonmobil.com.

KARP, HERBERT RUBIN, neurologist, educator, geriatrician; b. Atlanta, Apr. 13, 1921; s. Louis and Sadie (Fischer) K.; m. Hazel Berman, June 16, 1948; children: Eleanor Beth, Miriam Sarah, Benjamin Chaim. BA, Emory U., Atlanta, 1943, MD, 1951. Diplomate Am. Bd. Psychiatry and Neurology. Intern then resident in internal medicine Grady Meml. Hosp., 1951-54; resident in neurology Duke U. Med. Ctr., 1954-56; clin. and rsch. fellow in neurology and neuropathology Harvard U.-Mass. Gen. Hosp., 1956-58; asst. prof. neurology Emory U., Atlanta, 1958-63, prof., 1963-91, prof. emeritus, 1991—, disting. emeritus prof., 2006—, prof. medicine, 1983-91, chmn. dept. neurology, 1974-83, dir. geriat. program dept. medicine, 1983-90; dir. med. svcs. Wesley Woods Geriatric Ctr., 1983-91, med. dir. emeritus, 1991—. Med. dir. medicare svcs. Ga. Med. Care Found.; med. dir. for Medicare quality improvement, 2005-11; trustee Atlanta Symphony Orch., 1975-95, bd. counselors 1996—, sec., 1979-80; pres. Ahavath Achim Synagogue, 1980-82; trustee Nat. Found. Jewish Culture, 1976-84, mem. bd. overseers, 1984-90. With USNR, 1943—46, with U.S. Public Health Svc. Reserve, 1946—. Recipient Thomas Jefferson award Emory U., 1984, Outstanding Med. Alumnus award, 1986, Disting. Med. Achievement award, 2001; Eternal Light award Jewish Theol. Sem. Am., 1985, Civic Endeavor award Med. Assn. Ga., 1989, Myrtle Wreath award Hadassah, 1990, Wakeman award Duke U., 1990; spl. fellow Nat. Inst. Neurol. Diseases, 1956-58; Herbert R. Karp Leadership award established in his name Dept. of Neurology, Emory U., 1999. Fellow Am. Acad. Neurology; mem. Am. Neurol. Assn. (mem. coun.), Assn. Univ. Profs. Neurology, Atlanta Interfaith Broadcasters (bd. dirs. 1991—2009, sec. 1997-2005, chair 2005-08), Alpha Omega Alpha. Democrat. Jewish. Home: 880 Somerset Dr NW Atlanta GA 30327-3732 Personal E-mail: hkarp02@emory.edu.

KARSTAEDT, NOLAN, diagnostic radiologist; MD, South Africa, 1971. Diplomate Am. Bd. Radiology-diagnostic radiology, 1979. Resident pediat. Baragwanath Hosp., 1972—73, resident radiation oncology, 1974—77; fellow radiation oncology Mallinckrodt Inst., St. Louis, 1977—79; hosp. affiliation includes St. Luke's Hosp. Office: St Luke's Hospital 4201 Belfort Rd Jacksonville FL 32216 Office Phone: 904-296-3700.*

KARTSOTIS, KOSTA N., consumer products company executive; V.p. mktg. Fossil, Inc., 1988—91, bd. dirs., 1990—, pres., 1991—2006, COO, 1991—2000, CEO, 2000—. Office: Fossil Inc 901 S Central Expy Richardson TX 75080-7302 Office Phone: 972-234-2525. Office Fax: 972-234-4669. Business E-Mail: kosta@fossil.com.

KASBAR, MICHAEL J., energy executive; Co-founder, officer, dir. TransTec New York, 1985—94; CEO marine fuel svc. World Fuel Services, Inc. (subs. World Fuel Services Corp.), Miami, Fla., 1995—2002, bd. dirs., 1995—, pres., COO, 2002—12, pres., CEO, 2012—. Office: World Fuel Services Corp Ste 400 9800 NW 41st St Miami FL 33178

KASH, DON ELDON, political science professor; b. Macedonia, Iowa, May 29, 1934; s. Albert W. and Blanche Opal (Smith) K.; m. Elizabeth Gunn; children: Kelli Denise, Jeffrey Paul. BA, U. Iowa, Iowa City, 1959, MA, 1960, PhD, 1963. Instr. Tex. Tech. U., 1960-61; asst. prof. Ariz. State U., 1963-65, U. Mo., Kansas City, 1965-66; assoc. prof. Purdue U., West Lafayette, Ind., 1966-70; prof. polit. sci. U. Okla., Norman, 1970-91, George Lynn Cross rsch. prof. polit. sci., 1975-91, dir. Sci. and Pub. Policy Program, 1970-78; John T. Hazel Sr. and Ruth D. Hazel chair in pub. policy George Mason U., Fairfax, Va., 1991—. Vis. assoc. prof. Ind. U., 1969-70; chief conservation div. U.S. Geol. Survey, 1978-81; mem. Assembly Engring., Marine Bd. NRC; prof. Tsinghua U., Beijing. Author: The Politics of Space Cooperation, 1967, Energy Under the Oceans: A Technology Assessment of Outer Continental Shelf Oil and Gas Operations, 1973, North Sea Oil and Gas: Implication for Future U.S. Development, 1973, Energy Alternatives: A Comparative Analysis, 1975, Our Energy Future, 1976, U.S. Energy Policy: Crisis and Complacency, 1983, Perpetual Innovation: The New World of Competition, 1989, The Complexity Challenge: Technological Innovation in the 21st Century, 1999; contbr. articles to profl. jours. With AUS, 1952-54. Recipient Disting. Alumni award, U. Iowa, 1988. Fellow AAAS. Office: George Mason U Sch Public Policy 4400 University Dr Fairfax VA 22030-4444 Business E-Mail: dkash@gmu.edu.

KASHDIN, GLADYS SHAFRAN, painter, educator, volunteer; b. Dec. 15, 1921; d. Edward M. and Miriam P. Shafran; m. Manville E. Kashdin, Oct. 11, 1942 (dec.). BA magna cum laude, U. Miami, 1960; MA, Fla. State U., 1962, PhD, 1965. Photographer, NYC and Fla., 1938-60; tchr. art Fla. and Ga., 1956-63; from asst. prof. to prof. humanities U. South Fla., Tampa, 1965-87, prof. emerita, 1987—. Lectr., adv. bd. Hillsborough County Mus., 1975—84. Exhibitions include The Everglades, 1972—75, Aspects of the River, 1975—80, Processes of Time, 1981—2006, Retrospective, 1941—96, Tampa Mus. Art, 1996, Appleton Mus. Art, Ocala, 1999, 2001—02, Mus. Sci. and Industry, Tampa, 2003, Represented in permanent collections Columbus Mus. Arts, LeMoyne Art Found., Tampa Internat. Airport, Tampa Mus. Art, Appleton Mus. Art, Ocala, Mus. Sci. and Industry, Tampa, Miss. Mus. Art, Jackson, Jan Kaminis Platt Libr., Tampa, U. So. Fla. Spl. Collections Libr., Coll. Bus., Tampa Water Dept. Mem. U.S. Fla. Status of Women Com., 1971-76, chmn., 1975-76; nat. bd., Mus. Sci. and Industry, Tampa, 2003—; founder Dr. Gladys Shafran Kashdin Welcome Ctr., 2004 Recipient Women Helping Women in Art award Soroptomist Internat., 1979, Citizens Hon. award Hillsborough Bd. County Commrs., 1984, Mortar Bd. award for tchg. excellence, 1986, Recognition award for lifetime achievement in arts and scis. So. Acad. Letters, Arts and Scis., 2002. Mem. AAUW (1st v.p. Tampa br. 1971-72), Phi Kappa Phi (chpt.-pres. 1981-83, artist/scholar award 1987). Home: 600 S Magnolia Ave Ste 125 Tampa FL 33606-2751 Office Phone: 813-988-3011.

KASINATH, BALAKUNTALAM S., medical researcher; b. Nov. 9, 1951; m. Uma Kasinath; children: Manasa, Vivek. MBBS in Medicine, Bangalore Med. Coll., India, 1975. With internal medicine Ill. Masonic Med. Ctr., Chgo., 1977-80; with nephrology U. Chgo. Hosps. and Clinics, 1980-83; asst prof. Rush-Presbyn.-St. Luke's Med. Ctr., Chgo., 1983-90; assoc. prof. dept. medicine divsn. nephrology U. Tex. Health Sci. Ctr., San Antonio, 1990-98; chief renal sect. Audie Murphy Meml. VA Hosp., San Antonio, 1991—2005, staff physician, 1991—. Prof. dept. medicine U. Tex. Health Sci. Ctr., San Antonio, 1998—. Contbr. articles to profl. jours., chpts in books; lectr. in field. Recipient Henry Christian award for excellence in rsch. Am. Fedn. for Clin. Rsch., 1994, Rsch. award Am. Diabetes Assn., 1995, 99, 2002, 05, Rsch. award VA, 1993, 97, 2002, 07, Rsch. award NIH, 1986, 90, 2003, 07. Mem. AAAS, Am. Soc. Nephrology, Internat. Soc. Nephrology, Indian Soc. Nephrology. Achievements include research in metabolic regulation of extracellular matrix molecules in diabetic renal disease. Office: U Tex Health Sci Ctr Dept Medicine-Nephrology Mail Code 7882 7703 Floyd Curl Dr San Antonio TX 78229-3900 Office Phone: 210-567-4707. Business E-Mail: kasinath@uthscsa.edu.

KASKINEN, BARBARA KAY, composer, musician, educator; d. Norman Ferdinand and Martha Agnes (Harju) Kaskinen. AA, Broward C.C., Coconut Creek, Fla., 1978; BA with honors, Fla. Atlantic U., 1981, MA, 1995; D in Mus. Arts, U. Miami, 2006. Studio musician, composer/arranger Electric Rize Prodns., Margate, Fla., 1982—; ind. instr. piano, electronic keyboard and guitar. Margate, 1979—; music tchr. Sam Ash Music, 2013—. Co-founder Oasis Coffee House, Boca Raton, Fla., 1990—92; co-owner Electric Rize Publ, 1991; asst dir TOPS Piano Camp, 1994—96; mem. adj faculty Fla. Atlantic U., 1995—97, Broward C.C., Coconut Creek, 1996—, Miami Dade Coll., 2003—08; adj instr., accompanist Palm Beach Atlantic U., West Palm Beach, Fla., 2003—09. Musician (bass, keyboard player): Electric Rize Band, 1982—; composer: Hansen House, 1987—88; author: Adult Electronic Keyboard Course Book I, 1988, Adult Electronic Keyboard Course Books II and III, 1989. Mem.: ASCAP, Broward County Music Tchrs. Assn. (treas, composition contest chmn., recording sec.), Fla. State Music Tchrs. Assn., Nat. Guild Piano Tchrs. Personal E-mail: neniksa@aol.com.

KASLOW, FLORENCE WHITEMAN, psychologist, educator, family business consultant, executive, life transitions and relationship coach; b. Phila., Jan. 06; d. Irving and Rose (Tarin) Whiteman; m. Solis Kaslow; children: Nadine Joy, Howard Ian. AB in Sociology with distinction, Temple U., 1952; MA, Ohio State U., 1954; PhD, Bryn Mawr Coll., 1969. Lic. psychologist, Fla.; bd. cert. psychologist Am. Bd. Clin. Psychology, Am. Bd. Forensic Psychology, Am. Bd. Couple & Family Psychology, Am. Bd. Profl. Psychology. Pvt. practice, Palm Beach Gardens, Fla., 1964—; dir. Fla. Couples and Family Inst., Palm Beach Gardens, 1982—2009; pres. Kaslow Assoc., Palm Beach Gardens, 1985—. Cons. USN Dept. Psychiatry Residency Tng. Programs, San Diego, Portsmouth, Va., Phila., 1976-88, Palm Beach Inst., 1983-90; adj. prof. med. psychology Duke U. Med. Ctr., Durham, N.C., 1982-2002; disting. vis. prof. psychology Fla. Inst. Tech., Melbourne, 1985-; disting. vis. prof. Calif. Grad. Sch. Family Psychology, 1989-92; vis. prof. psychiatry & behavioral sci. Mercer Med. Coll., Macon, Ga., 2007-10; weekly radio guest Voice of Am., Focus on Families, 1993-2003; pres. Am. Bd. Forensic Psychology, 1977-80, Am. Bd. Family Psychology, 1996-2000. Editor: Voices in Family Psychology, 1990, The Military Family in Peace and War, 1993, Handbook of Relational Diagnoses and Dysfunctional Family Patterns, 1996, Handbook of Family Business and Family Business Consultation: A Global Perspective, 2006; editor: (with F. Shapiro and L. Maxfield) EMDR & Family Therapy Processes, 2007; editor: (with L.L. Schwartz) Dynamics of Divorce: A Life Cycle Perspective, 1987; editor: Painful Partings: Divorce and Its Aftermath, 1997, Handbook of Couple and Family Forensics, 2000, Comprehensive Handbook of Psychotherapy, 4 vols., 2002; author (with L.L. Schwartz): Welcome Home: an International and Non Traditional Adoption Reader, 2004, Divorced Fathers and Their Families: Legal, Economic, and Emotional Dilemmas, 2012; mem. editl. bd. Jour. Marital and Family Therapy, 1976—, Jour. Family Psychology, 1987—, Jour. Sex and Marital Therapy, 1984—2002, Jour. Clin. Child Psychology, 1986—2002, Jour. Psychotherapy, 1988—2004, Profl. Psychology, 2002—07, Jours. Couple Family Psychology, 2011—, assoc. editor Jour. Family Psychotherapy, 1990—; contbr. chapters to books, articles to profl. jours. Recipient Outstanding Family Therapy Contbn. award, Am. Assn. Marriage and Family Therapy, 1991, NIMH trainee, 1969, Interdisciplinary Achievement award, Family Firm Inst., 2007, Life Achievement award in Practice of Psychology, Am. Psychol. Found., 2008, Russell J. Bent award, American Bd. Profl. Psychology, 2010. Mem. APA (divsn. family psychology pres. 1987, sec. 1983-85, com. mem. 1987—, pres. divsn. media psychology 1993, coun. rep. 2002-08, co-chair, Com. on Internat. Rels. in Psychology 2011, Disting. Lifetime Contbn. to Media Psychology award, 2000, Outstanding Conbtn. Internat. Advancement Psychology, 2002), Internat. Acad. Family Psychology (pres. 1998-2002, Pres. award 2006), Am. Assn. Marital and Family Therapy, Am. Bd. Profl. Psychologists (trustee 2002-2010, Disting. Psychology Contbn. award 1994, Russell Bent award 2010), Am. Family Therapy Acad., Coalition Family Diagnosis (chmn. 1989-93), Internat. Family Therapy Assn. (founding pres. 1987-90), Acad. Family Mediators (bd. dir. 1982-88, treas. 1985-87), Family Therapists Without Borders (hon. chair 2007-10), Am. Bd. Profl. Psychology Found. (pres. elect, 2012-14). Jewish. Avocations: travel, writing, dance, ballet, opera, theater. Office Phone: 561-625-0288. Personal E-mail: drfkaslow@bellsouth.net.

KASTIN, ABBA JEREMIAH, endocrinologist, researcher; b. Cleve., Dec. 24, 1934; s. Isadore I. and Ruth (Urdang) K. AB, Harvard U., 1956, MD, 1960; doctorate (hon.), U. Nacional Federico Villerarreal, Lima, Peru, 1980; DSc (hon.), U. New Orleans, 1984; PhD (hon.), Uppsala U., Sweden, 2008. Hon. prof. Peking U. Health Sci. Ctr., Beijing, Lanzhou U., China; intern Vanderbilt U. Hosp., Nashville, 1960-61, resident in internal medicine, 1961-62; clin. assoc. USPHS, NIH, 1962-64; clin. investigator VA Hosp., New Orleans, 1965-68; chief endocrinology sect. VA Med. Ctr., 1968—2004; prof. dept. medicine Tulane U. Sch. Medicine, New Orleans, 1974—2004; grad. faculty U. New Orleans, 1976—2006; prof. and endowed chair Pennington Biomed. Rsch. Ctr., Baton Rouge, 2004—. Cons. prof. dept. psychology U. New Orleans, 1986-2006, FDA, 1979; mem. visual arts vis. com. Loyola U., New Orleans, 2004-11; mem. med. adv. bd. Nat. Pituitary Agy., 1974-77; Wellcome vis. prof., 1990; pre-reviewer in endocrinology, mem. residency com. for internal medicine Accreditation Coun. for Grad. Med. Edn., 1984-95; vis. sr. scientist Japan Soc. Promotion Sci., 1997; spkr., lectr. in field. Editor-in-chief: Peptides, an Internat. Jour., 1980—; editor: Handbook of Biologically Active Peptides, 2006, 2nd edit., 2013; mem. editl. bd. Jour. Clin. Endocrinology and Metabolism, 1976-80, Brain Rsch. Bull., 1986-95, Neurosci. and Biobehaviorial Rev., 1977-95, New Trends Exptl. Clin. Psychiatry, 1985-2001, Progress in Neuroendocrinimmunology, 1988-90, Pharmacology, Biochemistry and Behavior, 1989-1995, Molecular and Cellular Neuroscis., 1990-95, Physiology and Behavior, 1993-95, Endocrine Practice, 1994-2004, Neuroimmunomodulation, 1995-2000, Current pharm. Design, 2003—, Medicinal Chemistry, 2004—, Clinical Medical Insights: Endocrinology and Diabetes, 2007-; sect. editor Endocrine anf Metabolic Agents; contbr. more than 900 articles to profl. jours. Advisory bd. La. Philharmonic Orch., 1997—; bd. dirs. Baton Rouge Symphony Orch., 2007—, Opéra Louisiane, 2007—13; bd. dirs. vis. com. Loyola U., 2004—13. Recipient Edward T. Tyler Fertility award Internat. Fertility Soc., 1975, Eagle award Fed. Bus. Assn., 1975, Copernicus medal Med. Faculty Krakow, Poland, 1979, William S. Middletown award VA, 1982, Strand award 2001; named in top 100 Most Cited Scientist List, Inst. for Scientific Info. Fellow Am. Coll. Endocrinology; mem. Am. Physiol. Soc., Am. Peptide Soc., Endocrine Soc., Soc. Exptl. Biol. Medicine, Soc. Neurosci., Internat. Soc. Psychoneuroendocrinology (introductory hon. scientific lectr. XVth Congress), Internat. Soc. Neuroendocrinology, Internat. Behavioral Neuroscience Soc. (keynote speaker first meeting, mem. adv. coun.), Internat. Neuropeptide Soc. (pres. 1993—) hon. mem. Brazilian Soc. Toxinology, Indian Soc. Comparative Endocrinology, La Soc. de Dermo-Chimie, Chilean Soc. Endocrinology, Phillippine Soc. Endocrinology and Metabolism, Peruvian Ob-Gyn Soc., Peruvian Endocrine Soc., Polish Endocrine Soc., Hungarian Endocrine Soc., Harvard Club LA (pres. 1991-95), Green Wave Masters Swim Club (pres. 1978-84). Jewish. Office: Pennington Biomed Rsch Ctr 6400 Perkins Rd Baton Rouge LA 70808-4124 Business E-Mail: peptides@pbrc.edu.

KATONA, PETER GEZA, biomedical engineer, educator; b. Budapest, Hungary, June 25, 1937; came to U.S., 1956, naturalized, 1962; s. Stephan and Irene (Renner) K.; m. Jaroslava Blanar, Aug. 27, 1966; children— Catherine Iris, Andrew George. BS in Elec. Engring, U. Mich., 1960; S.M. in Elec. Engring. (Sloan fellow, 1960-62), M.I.T., 1962, Sc.D. in Elec. Engring, 1965. Asst. prof. elec. engring. M.I.T., 1965-69; assoc. prof. biomed. engring. Case Western Res. U., Cleve., 1969-78, prof., 1978-92, chmn. dept., 1980-87. Program dir. biomed. engring. and aiding the disabled NSF, 1989—91; v.p. biomed. engring. The Whitaker Found., 1991—95, exec. v.p. biomed engring., 1995—98, pres. biomed. engring., 1998—2000, pres., CEO, 2000—06; prof. elec. and computer engring. George Mason U., 2006—; prof. bio-engring. Mem. editl. bd. Am. Jour. Physiology, 1975-81; contbr. articles on cardio-respiratory control and automated drug delivery to profl. jours. Recipient Alexander von Humboldt award, 1987-88, Disting. Achievement award, BMES, 2005, Pierre Galletti award, AIMBE, 2006. Fellow AAAS, Am. Inst. Med. & Biol. Engring. (founding); sr. mem. IEEE, Am. Physiol. Soc., Biomed. Engring. Soc. (bd. dirs. 1977-80, pres. 1984-85), Am. Soc. Engring. Edn. Office Phone: 703-993-9347. Business E-Mail: pkatona@gmu.edu. E-mail: peter@katonaconsulting.org.

KATRANA, DAVID JOHN, retired plastic and reconstructive surgeon; b. Moline, Ill., Oct. 16, 1945; s. Nicholas John and Marilyn Ann Katrana; m. Carol; children: Nicole Elaine, Kimberly Ann. BA in Biology, Northwestern U., Evanston, Ill., 1967; DDS, Northwestern U., Chgo., 1971, MD, 1974. Diplomate Am. Bd. Plastic and Reconstructive Surgery. Resident oral surgery Northwestern U. Dental Sch., Chgo., 1971-72; intern surgery Northwestern U. McGraw Med. Ctr., Chgo., 1974-75, resident gen. surgery, 1975-77, resident plastic and reconstructive surgery, 1977-79; assoc. Houston Plastic Surgery Assocs., 1979-91; pvt. practice plastic surgery, 1991—; asst. clin. prof. plastic surgery Baylor Coll. Medicine, Houston, 1980—; dir. wound & hyperbaric Unit Meml. Herm & Rahab. Hosp.; coord. wound and hyperbaric unit Meml. Hosp. meml. Cirt, Houston, 2013; co-dir., wound & hyperbark unit Herman Meml. City Hosp., 2012—. Pres. Hyperbaric Mgmt. Assocs. Inc., 1997-2000; dental cons. The Chgo. Bulls, 1977-79; instr. surgery, dental cons. Northwestern U. Med. Sch., Chgo., 1978-79; dir. burn unit Humana Hosp. Southmore, Pasadena, Tex., 1982-88; div. chief surgery Rosewood Hosp., Houston, 1984-86, pres. med. staff, 1988-89; plastic surg. cons. Houston Gamblers Profl. Football Team, 1984; mem. Meml. Hermann Rehab. Hosp.-Katy, West Houston Med. Ctr., Meml. Hosp. at Memorial City, also others; lectr. various univs. and hosps. Contbr. articles to profl. jours. Trustee Rosewood Med. Ctr., Houston, 1989—96, chmn. bd., 1995—2000; dir. Ctr. Wound Care and Hyperbaric Medicine, Spring Br. Med. Ctr., 2000—01. Fellow ACS; mem. Internat. Soc. Burn Injuries, Am. Burn Assn., Am. Soc. Plastic and Reconstructive Surgeons, Tex. Soc. Plastic Surgeons, Tex. Med. Assn., Harris County Med. Soc., Houston Soc. Plastic Surgeons, Wound Healing Soc. Home: 5001 Woodway #1204 Houston TX 77056 Office: PO Box 79427 Houston TX 77279-9427 E-mail: davidkatrana@yahoo.com.

KATTWINKEL, JOHN, pediatrician, educator; b. Newton, Mass., June 24, 1941; s. Egon Emil and Dorothy Lucile (Fish) K.; m. Phyllis Ann Denton, Sept. 14, 1963; children: Susan, Linda. BS, Rensselaer Poly. Inst., 1964; B in Med. Sci., Dartmouth Coll., 1966; MD, Harvard U., 1968. Diplomate Am. Bd. Pediatrics, Am. Bd. Neonatology (bd. dirs. 1981-86). Resident in pediatrics Duke Med. Ctr., Durham, NC, 1968-70; clin. assoc. NIH, Bethesda, Md., 1970-72; neonatology fellow Case Western Res. U., Cleve., 1972-74; asst. prof. pediatrics U. Va., Charlottesville, 1974-78, assoc. prof., 1978-84, prof., 1984—, dir. neonatology, 1974—, Charles Fuller chair in neonatology, 1998—2012, prof. emeritus, 2013—. Founder Perinatal Edn. Ctr., Charlottesville, 1976—; Poland and China cons. Project HOPE, Milwood, Va., 1979-92; hon. prof. Zhejiang Med. U., Hangzhou, People's Republic of China, 1985. Editor: American Heart Association and American Academy of Pediatrics Neonatal Resuscitation Program, 1998-2011; mem. editl. bd. Pediatrics, 1999—2005; contbr. articles on newborn respiration and med. edn. to profl. jours.; inventor device for nasal ventilation of infants; founder Perinatal Continuing Edn. Program; co-developer physiologic predictive monitoring system for neonatal apnea. Lt. comdr. USPHS, 1970-72. Recipient Discovery Health Channel Med. Honor, 2004, Outstanding Faculty award, State Coun. Higher Edn. Va., 2008, Charles H. Hudson award for Cardiopulmonary Pub. Health, Am. Found. Respiratory Care, 2009; named Disting. prof., U. Va. Alumni Assn., 2007; named one of Ams. Top Doctors, 2004—13. Fellow: Am. Acad. Pediat. (fetus and newborn com. 1983—89, neonatal resuscitation program steering com. 1989—98, Task Force on Sudden Infant Death Syndrome, chair 1991—2009, chair 1994—98, editor 1999—2012, Ross Profl. Edn. award 1989, Apgar award 2008); mem.: Soc. Pediat. Rsch., Am. Pediat. Soc. Avocation: tennis. Home: 500 Rocks Farm Dr Charlottesville VA 22901 Office: U Va Dept Pediatrics Charlottesville VA 22908-0001 Office Phone: 434-924-5428.

KATZ, JOEL ABRAHAM, lawyer; b. Bronx, NY, May 27, 1944; s. Harry and Hilda (Weezenthal) K.; Kane Swims, 1994; children from previous marriage: Leslie Helaine, Jeni Michelle. BA in Econs., Hunter Coll., 1966; JD, U. Tenn., 1969. Bar: Tenn. 1969, Ga. 1971, US Dist. Ct. (ea. dist.) Tenn. 1970, US Dist. Ct. Appeals (11th cir.) 1971. Founding ptnr. Katz, Smith & Cohen; founding shareholder, co-mng. shareholder emeritus Atlanta office, chair global entertainment & media practice Greenberg Traurig LLP, Atlanta; mem., music adv. bd. Hunter Coll. Gen. counsel, bd. dirs. Farm Aid Inc.; spl. counsel Country Music Assn.; former vice chmn. Gibson Found., Gibson Guitar Corp., Baldwin Piano Corp.; state music industry rep. State of Ga.; chmn. USO Entertainment Adv. Coun. Mem. bd. T.J. Martell Found. for Leukemia Rsch., NYC; bd. dirs. Very Spl. Arts, TouchTunes, Kiz Toys Inc., Luxure Media Group, MultiplyLive, Charity Ptnrs. LLC; Bd. govs. Buckhead Club; spl. council Rock and Roll Hall Fame; mem., bd. reps. Sony-ATV Music Pub. LLC. Named one of The 100 Power Lawyers in Entertainment, The Hollywood Reporter, 2007—12; named to Ga. Music Hall of Fame, 1995. Fellow Royal Soc. for Encouragement Arts, Manufacturers, and Commerce; mem. NARAS (gen. counsel, past v.p., past nat. trustee, dir. found. bd., nat. chmn. bd. trustees, trustee Atlanta chpt., chmn. emeritus), Bar Assn., Ga. Bar Assn., Tenn. Bar Assn. Office: Greenberg Traurig LLP Terminus 200 3333 Piedmont Rd NE Ste 2500 Atlanta GA 30305 Office Phone: 678-553-2100. Office Fax: 678-553-2212. Business E-Mail: katzj@gtlaw.com.

KATZ, KAREN W., retail executive; b. 1957; m. Alan J. Katz; 1 child. BA, U. Tex., 1979; MBA, U. Houston, 1982. Asst. buyer, dept. mgr., buyer Foley's Dept. Stores; merchandise mgr. Neiman Marcus Town & Country, Houston, 1985—87; v.p., divsnl. merchandise mgr., handbags, designer accessories Neiman Marcus Stores, 1987—91, v.p., gen. mgr., NorthPark Dallas, 1991—96, sr. v.p., dir. stores, 1996—98, exec. v.p., 1998—2000, pres., CEO, 2002—10, Neiman Marcus Direct Catalog, e-commerce bus., Dallas, 2000—02; exec. v.p. Neiman Marcus Group, Inc., 2007—10, pres., CEO, 2010—. Bd. dirs. Pier 1 Imports, 2001—. Bd. dir. Dallas Theater Ctr., Charter 100. Named one of Next 20 Female CEOs, Pink Mag. & Forté Found., 2006. Mem.: Dallas Jewish Comty. Ctr. (bd. dir.). Office: The Neiman Marcus Group Inc 1618 Main St Dallas TX 75201-4720 Office Phone: 214-741-6911. Office Fax: 214-573-5789. Business E-Mail: karen_katz@neimanmarcus.com.

KATZ, SAMUEL LAWRENCE, pediatrician, researcher; b. Manchester, NH, May 29, 1927; s. Morris and Ethel (Lawrence) Katz; m. Betsy Jane Cohan, June 27, 1950; children: Samuel Lawrence Jr.(dec.), John S.L., David L., Deborah Susan, William L., Susan Johanna, Penelope Jennifer; m. Catherine Minock Wilfert, July 23, 1971; stepchildren: Rachel Ann, Katie Claiborne. AB magna cum laude, Dartmouth Coll., 1948; MD cum laude, Harvard U., 1952; DSc (hon.), Georgetown U., 1996, Dartmouth Coll., 1998. Intern Beth Israel Hosp., Boston, 1952—53; resident Children's Hosp., Boston, 1953—54, 1955—56, Mass. Gen. Hosp., 1954—55; from rsch. fellow to asst. prof. Harvard Med. Sch., 1956—68; prof., chmn. dept. pediat. Duke Med. Sch., 1968—90, Wilburt C. Davison prof., 1972—97. Mem. sci. adv. bd. Hasbro Children's Found., St. Jude Children's Rsch. Hosp.; rschr. on virology, virus vaccines and immunization NIH couns. and study sects. WHO; chmn. India-US Vaccine Action Program, 1999—2004; chmn. adv. com. immunization practice Ctrs. for Disease Control, Atlanta, 1985—93. Developer (with John F. Enders) attenuated live measles-virus vaccine; contbr. chapters to books, articles to profl. jours. Chmn. bd. trustees Internat. Vaccine Inst., Seoul, Republic of Korea, 2003—07. With USNR, 1945—46. Recipient Rsch. Career Devel. award, NIH, 1965—68, Presdl. medal of achievement, Dartmouth Coll., 1991, Sabin Gold medal, Albert Sabin Vaccine Inst., 2003, Duke U. Founder's medal, 2004, Alfred duPont award Pediat. Rsch., Nemours Found., 2006, Pollin prize Pediat. Rsch., 2007; fellow, Nat. Found., 1956—58. Mem.: APHA (Needleman medal and award 1997), Inst. Medicine NAS, Pediat. Infectious Diseases Soc. (Disting. Physician award 1991), Assn. Med. Sch. Pediat. Dept. Chmn. (pres. 1977—79), Am. Acad. Pediat. (Grulee award 1975, Jacobi award 1986), Am. Assn. Immunologists, Infectious Diseases Soc. Am. (co-chmn. vaccine initiative 1998—99, co-chmn. nat. network for immunization info. 1999—2003, Bristol award 1988, Soc. citation 1993), New Eng. Pediat. Soc., Am. Pediat. Soc. (pres. 1986—87, St. Geme award 1988, Howland award 2000), Soc. Pediat. Rsch., Am. Soc. Clin. Investigation, Am. Fedn. Clin. Rsch. Home: 1917 Wildcat Creek Rd Chapel Hill NC 27516-9786 Office: Duke U Med Ctr PO Box 2925 Durham NC 27710-0001 Office Phone: 919-668-4852, 919-684-3734. Office Fax: 919-668-4859.

KATZ, SANDRA, educational consultant, psychologist, educator; d. Victor Benaim and Anita de Benaim; m. Gabriel Katz, Aug. 14, 1977; children: Valerie Katz-Seibald, Alan, Denise. BA in Psychology, U. Tenn., 1978, MS in Ednl. and Counseling Psychology, 1980; lic. in Psychology, U. Catolica Andres Bello, Caracas, 1983. Sch. intervention specialist Invedin: Venezuelan Inst. Child Devel., Caracas, 1980—81; pvt. practice child psychology Unit Psychoednl. Intervention, Caracas, 1981—95; head sch. psychologist Eutimio Rivas Pub. Sch. Sys., Miranda, Venezuela, 1984—89; mem. faculty dept. sch. psychology U. Catolica Andres Bello, Caracas, 1984—; mem. grad. faculty Andres Bello Cath. U., Caracas, 1991—2001, interim head grad. program on child devel., 1998; CEO, co-funder, sr. cons. Proyecto Armonia, Caracas, 1994—. V.p. bd. dirs. Ctr. Rsch. and Edn., Caracas, 1995—2000; mem. adv. bd. Retorno: Addiction Prevention Ctr., Caracas, 2001—02; mem. jury Tchr. Excellence Award, Caracas, 2002; presenter, leader workshops in field. Author: Armonia por la Paz, 2003, 100 Icebreakers for Harmony (in Spanish), 2005, Armonia in Preschool, 2006; contbr. numerous articles to profl. pubs. Staff trainer Atenea's Found. for Abandoned Children and Youth, Caracas, 1996—98, Fundana Found. for Abandoned Children, Caracas, 2004—05, UCAB Cmty. Outreach Program, 2004—05; advisor, cons. Venezuelan Camping Assn., 2000—05; advisor, cons., staff trainer Crecer con Valores program, 1997—2001; bd. dirs. Cmty. Edn. Sys.-Fundasec, Caracas, 2005. Recipient Teaching Excellence award, Herzl-Bialik Cmty. Edn. Sys., 2003, Recognition award, Ctr. Rsch. and Edn., CIEPI, Venezuela, 2000, Contbn. award, Venezuelan Camping Assn., 2000; named Top Contbr., Jewish Cmty.'s Edn., Caracas, 2003—04. Mem.: Miranda Assn. Psychologists, Venezuelan Psychol. Assn. (honor award), Nat. Assn. Sch. Psychologists, Venezuelan Fedn. Psychologists (hon.), U. Tenn. Alumni Assn., Women Internat. Zonist Orgn. Achievements include development of ednl. programs in field. Office: Proyecto Armonia POBA Internat 158P-025255 Miami FL 33102-5255 Business E-Mail: sandra@proyectoarmonia.com.

KATZEN-GUTHRIE, JOY, performance artist, engineering executive; b. Memphis, Nov. 11, 1958; d. Eli and Bess (Bloomfield) Katzen; m. Mark C. Guthrie, Aug. 7, 1983. BFA in Music cum laude, Stephens Coll., Columbia, Mo., 1980, BA in Comms. magna cum laude, 1980. Traffic dir. WPLP News/Talk Radio, Pinellas Park, Fla., 1981-83, ops. mgr., 1982-83; traffic reporter WUSA-FM and WDAE-AM, Tampa, Fla., 1985-86; announcer, programmer, pub. rels. mgr. WXCR-FM Classics 92, Safety Harbor, Fla., 1983-87; v.p., dir. Katzen and Guthrie Assocs., Inc., Palm Harbor, Fla., 1987—; pres. Tune-of-the-Century Music, 1989—. Creator, designer, owner website www.JoyfulNoise.net, 1998—. Co-author, composer musical comedy Once Around Manhattan, 1985; author: (one-act play) A Murder in Pine County, 1987; composer, lyricist some 750 songs; performance artist CD/Cassette albums Seasons of Joy, 1989, Heart of Ancient Promise, 1993, New State of Mind, 1993, How Good and Pleasant, 1996, Passages, 1998, SoulStream, 1998, Favorite Melody, 2005, A Steadfast Bridge, ltd. edit., 2005, Favorite Melody vol. 2, 2006; studio vocalist Jeff Arthur Prodns., St. Petersburg, Fla., 1985, 86, Studio C. Prodns., Tampa, 1991-92; studio vocalist, jingle writer West End Rec., Tampa, 1989, 90; session musician Hurricane Pass Studios, Clearwater, Fla., 1993—. Music dir. religious sch. Temple B'nai Israel, Clearwater, 1988-89; music dir. Perry-Mansfield Performing Arts Camp, Steamboat Springs, Colo., 1987; cantorial soloist B'nai B'rith Hillel Found., Tampa, 1990-93, Temple Shir Shalom, Gainesville, 1994-99, Congregation B'nai Emmunah, Tarpon Springs, 1996-99, Congregation Aliyah, Clearwater, 1999-2000, Temple B'nai Israel, Clearwater, 2000-2002, 2005, Temple Beth El, Sarasota, 2002-2004. Recipient 1st and 3d place awards Memphis Songwriters Assn. Competition, 1988, others; Pinellas County Arts Coun. grantee, 1997, 2004. Mem. Songwriters Guild Am., Dramatists Guild Inc., Hadassah (life). Democrat. Jewish. Avocations: photography, travel, music, theater, films, books. Home and Office: 2487 Indian Trl E Palm Harbor FL 34683-2806 Home Phone: 727-785-4568; Office Phone: 727-785-4568, 800-354-1302. Personal E-mail: joyfulnoise@earthlink.net.

KAUFMAN, DANIEL J., lawyer; b. Wilmington, Del., 1959; m. Cathy Kaufman; children: Michael, Matthew, Andrew. BA in Econs., Rutgers U., 1981; JD, U. Va., 1984. With Richard Layton & Finger, Wilmington, Del.; assoc. White & Case, NYC; with Robinson Silverman Pearce Aronsohn & Berman, NYC, 1988—90; asst mktg. dir. Resolution Trust Corp., Phila., 1990—93; gen. counsel Zelenkofske, Axelrod & Co., Jenkintown, Pa., 1993—94; gen. counse Zany Brainy Inc.; v.p., gen. counsel Electronics Boutique Holdings Corp., 2002—05; sr. v.p., gen. counsel GameStop Corp., Grapevine, Tex., 2005—. Office: GameStop Corp 625 Westport Pkwy Grapevine TX 76051

KAUFMAN, DAVID GORDON, medical educator; s. James and Perle Kaufman; m. Jane Ann Atlanta, June 25, 1966; children: Cheryl Lynn Isley, Jamie Catherine. BA, Reed Coll., Portland, Oreg., 1965; MD, Wash. U., St. Louis, 1968, PhD, 1973. Cert. Nat. Bd. Med. Examiners, 1969. Prof. U. NC, Chapel Hill, 1980—, vice chair, 2000—10. Contbr. articles to numerous sci. jours. Surgeon USPHS, 1970—75, Bethesda, Md. Recipient Support of Cancer Rsch. Elliott Osserman award, 2009; Several Rsch. Support and Tng. grant, NIH, 1975—2013. Mem.: Soc. Toxicology (pres., Carcinogenesis Splty. Sect. 1993—94), Am. Soc. Investigative Pathology (pres. 1996—97), Am. Assn. Cancer Rsch., Fedn. Am. Socs. Exptl. Biology (pres. 1999—2000, bd. dirs. 1995—99). Achievements include research in DNA replicated in early S phase and reconstruction of human endometrial tissue in Vitro; discovery of progesterone ameliorates carcinogenic effects of estrogens used in hormone replacement therapy, cells are exceptionally vulnerable to chemical induction of cancer when treated when cells are entering S phase of cell cycle. Office: Univ NC School of Medicine CB 7525 Chapel Hill NC 27599*

KAUFMAN, GLEN FRANK, retired art educator; b. Fort Atkinson, Wis., Oct. 28, 1932; s. Eli J. and Elynor B. (Jensik) K. BS with honors, U. Wis., 1954; MFA, Cranbrook Acad. Art, 1959; cert., State Sch. Arts and Crafts, Copenhagen, 1960. Head fibers dept. Cranbrook Acad. Art, Bloomfield Hills, Mich., 1961-67; assoc. prof. art U. Ga., Athens, 1967-72, prof. art, 1972—, prof. in charge, fabric design, 1967—, grad. faculty, 1969—. Staff designer Dorothy Liebes Design Studio, N.Y.C., 1960-61; designer Regal Rugs, Inc., North Vernon, Ind., 1966-82; vis. artist Sch. Textiles, Royal Coll. Art, London, 1976; juror The Albuquerque (N.Mex.) Mus., 1981, Midland (Mich.) Art Coun., 1985, Itami Craft Ctr., Osaka, Japan, 1991, others; panelist Visual Artists Fellowship/Crafts, Nat. Endowment for the Arts, Washington, 1992—; cons. in field; lectr. and workshop presenter in field. One-man shows include Gallery Maronie, Kyoto, Japan, 1984, Sembikiya Gallery, Tokyo, 1985, Arrowmont Sch. Arts and Crafts, Gatlinburg, Tenn., 1986, Fiberworks, Berkeley, Calif., 1987, Madison (Ga.)-Morgan Cultural Ctr., 1988, Fuji Gallery, Osaka, Japan, 1988, Wacoal Ginza Art Space, Tokyo, 1989, Allrich Gallery, San Francisco, 1990, Azabu Mus. of Arts and Crafts, Tokyo, 1991, Lamar Dodd Art Ctr., LaGrange (Ga.) Coll., 1992, Gallery Gallery, Japan, 1992, Wacoal Ginza Art Space, Tokyo, 1994, Gallery Nouveau, Pusan, Korea, 1994, Ba Tang Gol Arts Ctr., Seoul, Korea, 1994, Wacoal Ginza Art Space, Tokyo, 1996, Gallery Gallery, Kyoto, Japan, 1996, others; exhibited in group shows at Columbia Mus. Art, SC, 1980, No. Ill. U., DeKalb, 1981, Visual Arts Ctr. Alaska, Anchorage, 1982, Robert L. Kidd Gallery, Birmingham, 1983, Am. Craft Mus., NY, 1986, Denki Kaikan Gallery, Nagoya, Japan, 1987, Gayle Wilson Gallery, Southampton, NY, 1988, Sch. Visual Arts, NY, 1989, Itami Craft Ctr., Osaka, 1989 (Silver prize), Farrell Collection, Washington, 1991, Allrich Gallery, San Francisco, 1991, Nagoya Trade and Industry Ctr., 1991, New Visions Gallery Contemporary Art, Atlanta, 1992, Mus. Kyoto, 1992, Smithsonian Instn., Washington, 1992-93, Atlanta (Ga.) Fin. Ctr., 1993, Nat. Mus. Modern Art, Kyoto, Japan, 1993, Art Inst. Chgo., 1993, Brenau U. Gallery, Gainesville, Ga., 1993, Mus. Kyoto, 1994, Asian Arts Ctr. Towson (Md.) State U., 1994, Am. Craft Mus., NY, 1995, Nogaya and Trade Industry Ctr., Japan, 1995, Gallery, Gallery, Kyota, Japan, 1995, Harbourfront Ctr., Toronto Can., 1995, Musée Marsil, Montreal, Can., 1995, Brown/Grotta Gallery, Wilton, Conn., 1995, NJ Ctr. for Visual Arts, Summit, 1997, Georgia State U. Gallery, Atlanta, 1997, Brown/Grotta Gallery, Wilton, Conn. 12997, Vanderbilt U. Sarratt Gallery, Nashville, 1997, Georgia Mus. Art, Athens, 1997, others; represented in permanent collections Am. Craft Mus., NYC, Juraku Mus, Kyoto, Cleve. Mus. Art, Art Inst. Chgo., U. Wis., Madison, Itami City Craft Ctr., Hyogo Prefecture, Japan, Ithaca (NY) Coll. Mus. Art, Long House Found., L.I., NY, Nat. Mus. Modern Art, Kyoto, Smithsonian Instn., Rockford Art Assn., Ill., S.C. Johnson Collection, U.S.A. Collection Contemporary Crafts, SUNY, Oneonta, Wichita Art Assn., Kans., pvt. collections; works illustrated in many books; contbr. articles to jours. Recipient Fulbright grant to Denmark, 1959-60, Grant for rsch. and travel to Europe, U. Ga., Dept. Art, 1973, Nat. Endowment for the Arts Craftsmen's Fellowship grant, 1976, Nat. Endowment for the Arts Svcs. to the Field grant, 1980-81, 81-82, Faculty Rsch. grant U. Ga. Athens Office of V.P. for Rsch., 1983-96, Nat. Endowment for the Arts Visual Artist's Fellowship grant, 1990, Ga. Coun. for the Arts Individual Artist grant, 1991, Sr. Faculty Rsch. grant U. Ga. Athens Rsch. Found., 1992, others. Fellow Am. Craft Coun.; mem. World Craft Coun., Surface Design Assn. (S.E. regional rep. 1977-80, pres. 1980-82, named hon. life mem. 1983), Phi Beta Delta. Office: Sch of Art Univ Ga Athens GA 30602

KAUFMAN, HERBERT EDWARD, ophthalmologist, educator; b. NYC, Sept. 28, 1931; s. Benjamin and Claire (Krinsky) K.; m. Maija H. Uotila; children: Stephen, Joshua, Claire. AB magna cum laude, Princeton U., 1952; MD magna cum laude, Harvard U., 1956. Intern Mass. Gen. Hosp., Boston, 1956-57; resident Mass. Eye and Ear Infirmary, Boston, 1959-62; assoc. prof., chief div. ophthalmology Coll. Medicine, U. Fla., 1962-64, prof., chmn. dept., 1964-77, prof. pharmacology, 1970-77; acting dean Coll. Medicine, U. Fla. (Coll. Medicine), 1972; prof., head dept. ophthalmology La. State U. Med. Ctr., 1978—, Boyd prof., ophthalmology, pharmacology, and exceptional therapeutics, 1985—; med. dir. Eye, Ear Nose and Throat Hosp. La., 1978-84. Chmn. tng. com. Nat. Eye Inst., 1970-71, mem. nat. eye adv. council, 1978-82, 1993-96; Pocklington lectr. Royal Coll. Surgeons, 1979; Jackson Meml. lectr., 1979, Maxwell K. Bochner Meml. lectr., 1978, Proctor lectr., 1981, Thorpe Meml. lectr., 1982, Jack S. Guyton lectr., 1982, Dunphy Meml. lectr., 1983, Waldert Meml. lectr., 1983, First Wohl Meml. lectr., 1983, Glover-Lisman lectr., 1983, G. Victor Simpson lectr., 1984, Peter Kronfield Meml. lectr., 1984, Irvine lectr., 1986, Earl Padfield Meml. lectr., 1987, Montgomery lectr., 1987, 1st Claes Dohlman lectr., 1991; adv. bd. Dry Eye Inst., 1985—; gen. com. revision U.S. Pharmocopeial Conv., 1985. Editorial bd. Am. Jour. Ophthalmology; editor: Investigative Ophthalmology, 1972-77; contbr. articles profl. jours. Served with USPHS, 1957-59. Recipient Lions Humanitarian award, 1968; R. Townley Payton award, 1983, Lacrima award Dry Eye Inst., 1984, Sr. Honor award Am. Acad. Ophthalmology, 1984, Castroviejo award, 1987, Physician's Recognition award, 1987, Montgomery medal, 1987, Innovator's award Am. Soc. Cataract and Refractive Surgery, 1990. Fellow AAAS, A.C.S., Am. Coll. Clin. Pharmacology; mem Am. Assn. Immunologists, Am. Assn. Ophthalmology, Am. Fedn. Clin. Research, AMA, Am. Soc. Microbiology, Am. Soc. Clin Investigation, Assn. Research Vision and Ophthalmology (pres. 1975), Assn. U. Profs. Ophthalmology (trustee, pres. 1980), Pan Am. Assn. Ophthalmology (mem. council), Am. Soc. Contemporary Ophthalmology (pres.), Am. Acad. Ophthalmology and Otolaryngology, Eye Bank Assn. Am. (dir.), N.Y. Acad. Scis., Eye Bank Assn. Am. (bd. dirs. 1985—), Com. Study Nat. Needs for Biomed. and Behavioral Research Personnel, Contact Lens Assn. Ophthalmologists (pres. 1979), Soc. Exptl. Biology and Medicine, Royal Soc. Medicine, Can. Implant Assn. (hon.), Ophthal. Soc. Finland (hon.) Sigma Xi. Office: La State U Eye Center 2020 Gravier St Suite B New Orleans LA 70112

KAUFMAN, JANICE HORNER, French and ESL instructor, interpreter; b. Mattoon, Ill., Apr. 30, 1949; d. Daniel Ogden and Julia Betty (McDermid) Horner; m. Richard Boucher Kaufman, June 24, 1972 (div. Mar. 27, 2002); children: Julia Kaufman Nussdorfer, Richard Pearse. AB in French, Duke U., 1971; MA in Liberal Studies, Hollins Coll., 1979; PhD in French, U. Va., Charlottesville, 1997. Tchr. in French Roanoke (Va.) City Pub. Schs., 1971-72, North Cross Sch., Roanoke, Va., 1974-82; instr. French Va. Tech. U., Blacksburg, 1984-86, 88, 90, 94, 98, 2010—11, asst. dir. fgn. lang. camps, 1984-85, administrv. dir., 1986; French, English interpreter, translator Coll. Architecture and Urban Studies, Va. Tech., Blacksburg, 1988; instr. ESL U. Cmty. Internat. Coun., Cranwell Internat. Ctr., Blacksburg, 1987-89; instr. French Hollins Coll., Roanoke, Va., 1989-90, Radford (Va.) U., 1989-90; grad. tchg. asst. U. Va., Charlottesville, 1992; adj. assoc. prof. French No. Va. C.C., Woodbridge and Alexandria, 1997-99; asst. prof. French and women's and gender studies SUNY-Oneonta, 2000—06, chair, women's and gender studies, 2003—06; tchr. French Roanoke Cath. Sch., 2007—08; vis. asst. prof. French Roanoke Coll., 2008—10. Student counselor Am. Inst. Fgn. Study, Greenwich, Conn., 1977; session leader Russell County Pub. Schs., Lebanon, Va., 1985, Va. Assn. Ind. Schs., Richmond, 1986; asst. tchr. Am. Coun. for Internat. Studies, 1995; faculty cons. advanced placement exam in French, Ednl. Testing Svc., Trenton State Coll., 1991-95, 97-98; adj. prof. French, George Mason U., Fairfax, Va., 1999-2000, French Ferrum Coll., 2011, ESL instr., Nat. Coll., Roanoke Valley, Va.Spring, 2012-; acad. dir. study abroad in Strasbourg, France, George Mason U. Ctr. for Global Edn., summer 2000; presenter in field, co-moderator, Le Bon mot, French Table Roanoke, mem., Saint Lo Sister City Assn., bd. mem., assoc. prof. French, Va. Western CC, Roanoke, Va., 2012, French/English interpreter Commonwealth Catholic Charities, French/English interpreter Star City Reporting 2014-. Contbr. articles to profl. jours. Recipient Knight of the Order of Academic Palms, French Republic. Mem. MLA, Pi Delta Phi, Phi Sigma Iota. Avocations: reading, travel, exercise. Office Phone: 540-986-1800 ext 4169.

KAUFMAN, MARK DAVID, lawyer; b. St. Louis, Feb. 24, 1949; s. Rudolf Ernst and Edith (Greiderer) K.; m. Margaret Taylor James, June 1, 2002; children: Mark, Thomas. BA, Northwestern U., 1971; JD, Duke U., 1974. Bar: Ga. 1974, U.S. Ct. Appeals (11th cir.) 1974, U.S. Dist. Ct. (no. dist.) Ga. 1974. Assoc. Sutherland Asbill & Brennan LLP, Atlanta, 1974-81, ptnr., 1981—, exec. com., 1996-2000. Contbr. articles to profl. jours. Named to Best Lawyers in Am., 2005, Am. Leading Lawyers Bus., Chamber US, 2004. Mem. ABA, Ga. Bar Assn., Atlanta Bar Assn. (legal counsel 1979-2000, Exceptional Svc. award 1987, Pres.'s Disting. Svc. award 1979-80, Charles E. Watkins Jr. award 1989), Atlanta Bar Found. (legal counsel 1985-2000), Order of Coif. Lutheran. Home: 3181 Habersham Rd NW Atlanta GA 30305 Office Phone: 404-853-8107. Business E-Mail: mark.kaufman@sablaw.com.

KAUFMAN, MARK STUART, lawyer; b. Binghamton, NY, June 16, 1947; s. Leonard and Edith (Levinson) K.; m. Chris Kestle, Feb. 13, 1981; children: Olivia, Dylan (dec.). BS with high distinction, Cornell U., 1969; JD cum laude, Harvard U., 1973. Bar: Ga. 1973, US Dist. Ct. (no. dist.) Ga. 1973, US Ct. Appeals (5th cir.) 1973, US Ct. Appeals (11th cir.) 1981, US Ct. Appeals (6th cir.), US Ct. Appeals (9th cir.), 2001. Assoc. Troutman, Sanders, Lockerman, Ashmore, Atlanta, 1973-79, ptnr., 1979-87, McKenna Long & Aldridge (formerly Long, Aldridge & Norman), Atlanta, 1987—; chair Mcpl. Reform and Innovation Practice Group; counsel City of Harmsburg, 2011—. Chmn. Chpt. 11 Bankruptcy Bench and Bar Conf., Ga. and Atlanta Bars, 1991; spkr., Mcpl. Distress Conf., Am. Bankruptcy Inst. Jour., 2013; symposium spkr. Emory U. Mcpl. Distress, 2013. Contbr. articles to profl. jours. Chmn. Atlanta Mcpl. Ct. Task Force, 1985; organizing com. Citizens Conf. on Judiciary, 1982; participant Leadership Ga., 1977; moderator Turnaround and Mgmt. Assn., 2012. Recipient Legal Elite, Ga. Trend Mag., 2003—; named one of Best Lawyers in America, 2006—, Top Lawyers, Corp. Coun., 2008—; named to Chambers Guide to Am.'s Leading Lawyers for Bus., 2003—. Mem. Southeastern Bankruptcy Law Inst. (bd. dirs. 1994—, pres. 2006-07, chmn. 2007-08), Atlanta Bar Assn. (bd. dirs. bankruptcy sect. 1990—, sec. 1993, pres. 1996). Office: McKenna Long & Aldridge 303 Peachtree St NE Ste 5300 Atlanta GA 30308 Office Phone: 404-527-4120. Office Fax: 404-527-4198. Business E-Mail: mkaufman@mckennalong.com.

KAUFMAN, RICHARD STUART, conductor; b. LA, Nov. 20, 1947; s. Walter S. and Margye L. (Whisler) Kaufman; m. Gayle Kaufman; 1 child, Whitney Claire. BA in Music, Calif. State U., Northridge, 1970. Condr. for various performers including Burt Bacharach, Juliet Prowse, Andy Williams, John Denver; music dir., condr. LA Civic Light Opera, 1975—80; music assoc. 20th Century Fox Studios, LA, 1982—84; music coord. Metro Goldwyn Mayer/United Artists Comm., Culver City, Calif., 1984-87, dir. music/TV, 1988—2002; condr. Pacific Symphony, Orange County, 1990—; prin. pops condr., pops condr. laureate Dallas Symphony Orch., 1997—. Mem. music adv. bd. Young Musicians Found. Composer: Alma Mater and Fight Song for Calif. State U., 1969. Recipient Best Pop Instrumental Performance, Grammy Awards, 1993; fellow, Berkshire Music Festival, 1969, Tanglewood, 1969. Mem.: Phi Mu Alpha. Avocations: baseball, racquetball. Office: MGM/UA Communications Inc 10000 Washington Blvd Suite 2091 Culver City CA 90232 also: Dallas Symphony 2301 Flora St Dallas TX 75201 also: Pacific Symphony Ste 100 3631 S Harbor Blvd Santa Ana CA 92704

KAUFMAN, STEPHEN LAWRENCE, radiologist, educator; b. Phila., Nov. 7, 1942; s. Abraham S. and Genevieve (Finestone) Kaufman. BA, U. Pa., 1963, MD, 1967. Resident in radiology, then fellow cardiovasc. radiology Johns Hopkins Med. Ctr., Balt., 1970-75, asst. prof. radiology, 1975-79, assoc. prof., 1980-88; prof. radiology, dir. cardiovasc. and interventional radiology Emory U., Atlanta, 1988—2003, prof. emeritus radiology, 2003—; attending radiologist Asheville VA Med. Ctr., 2003—12. Author: Techniques in Interventional Radiology, 1982; editor: Billiary Radiology, 1992; contbr. articles to profl. jours. Lt. comdr. USPHS, 1968—70. Fellow: Am. Heart Assn., Soc. Interventional Radiology; mem.: Am. Coll. Radiology, Radiol. Soc. N.Am. Avocations: hiking, white-water rafting, golf, computers. Personal E-mail: kauf8727@bellsouth.net.

KAUGER, YVONNE, state supreme court justice; b. Cordell, Okla., Aug. 3, 1937; d. John and Alice (Bottom) K.; 1 child, Jonna Kauger Kirschner. BS magna cum laude, Southwestern State U., Weatherford, Okla., 1958; JD, Oklahoma City U., 1969, LLD (hon.), 1992. Cert. med. technologist, St. Anthony's Hosp., 1959. Med. technologist Med. Arts Lab., 1959-68; assoc. Rogers, Travis & Jordan, 1970-72; jud. asst. Okla. Supreme Ct., Oklahoma City, 1972-84, justice, 1984-94, 1998—, vice chief justice, 1994-96, chief justice, 1997-98. Mem. appellate divsn. Ct. on Judiciary; mem. State Capitol Preservation Commn., 1983-84; mem. dean's adv. com. Oklahoma City U. Sch. Law; lectr. William O. Douglas Lecture Series, Gonzaga U., 1990. Founder Gallery of Plains Indian, Colony, Okla., Red Earth (Down Towner award 1990), 1987; active Jud. Day, Girl's State, 1976-80; keynote speaker Girl's State Hall of Fame Banquet, 1984; bd. dirs. Lyric Theatre, Inc., 1966—, pres. bd. dirs., 1981; past mem. bd. dirs. Civic Music Soc., Okla. Theatre Ctr., Canterbury Choral Soc.; mem. First Lady of Okla.'s Artisans' Alliance Com. Recipient Herbert Harley award, 1999, Gov.'s Arts award, 2005; named Panhellenic Woman of Yr., 1990, Woman of Yr., Red Lands Coun. Girl Scouts, 1990; named one of 10 Most Notable Women in Okla., OKC Orch. League, 2005; named to Washita County Hall of Fame, 1992, Okla. Women's Hall of Fame, 2001. Mem. ABA (law sch. accreditation com.), Okla. Bar Assn. (law schs. com. 1977—, Jud. Excellence award 1999), Washita County Bar Assn., Washita County Hist. Soc. (life), St. Paul's Music Soc., Iota Tau Tau, Delta Zeta (Disting. Alumna award 1988, State Delta Zeta of Yr. 1987, Nat. Woman of Yr. 1988). Episcopalian. Office: Oklahoma Supreme Ct Okla Judicial Ctr 2100 N Lincoln Blvd Ste 4 Oklahoma City OK 73105-4907 Office Phone: 405-521-3841. E-mail: yvonne.kauger@oscn.net.*

KAUSHAL, GUR PRASAD, biochemist, educator; s. Chandu Lall and Bhagvati Kaushal; m. Varsha Dhingra, Nov. 20, 1979; children: Megha, Sarah. BS, Punjab Agrl. U., Ludhiana, India, 1969, MS, 1971, PhD, 1976. Asst. prof. Punjab Agrl. U., 1977—83; postdoc. fellow U. Tex. Health Sci. Ctr., San Antonio, rsch. instr., 1987—91; asst. prof. U. Ark. Med. Scis., Little Rock, 1992—98, assoc. prof., 1998—2005, prof., dept. biochemistry and medicine, 1998—; rsch. scientist Ctrl. Ark. Vets. Healthcare Sys., Little Rock, 1992—2007, rsch. career scientist, 2008—. Contbr. scientific papers to rsch. jours. (Rsch. Career Scientist award, 2008). Reviewer NIH, Career Devel. Awards, Washington, 2001—08. Recipient Herbert L. Thomas, Sr. award, U. Ark. Med. Scis., 2007; grant, NIH, 2001—, VA Merit grant, Dept. Vets. Healthcare, 2004—. Mem.: Am. Heart Assn., Am. Soc. Nephrology, Am. Soc. Biochemistry and Molecular Biology. Achievements include research in biochemistry, medicine-nephrology. Home: 73 Valley Estate Cove Little Rock AR 72212 Office: Univ Ark Med Scis 4301 W Markham Little Rock AR 72205 Office Phone: 501-257-5834. Office Fax: 501-257-5827. Business E-Mail: kaushalgurp@uams.edu.*

KAUTEN, JAMES RICHARD, cardiothoracic surgeon; b. Neosho, Mo., Nov. 26, 1952; MD, U. Health Scis. Chgo. Med. Sch., 1978. Cert. Am. Bd. Thoracic Surgery, Am. Bd. Surgery. Intern, gen. surgery So. Ill. Sch. Medicine, Springfield, Ill., 1978—79, resident, cardiothoracic surgery, 1979—83; fellow Emory U., Atlanta, 1983—86, mem. chief surgical donor cardiectomy team, 1984—85, mem., cardiac transplant team, surgery, 1984—85; clin. assoc. prof., surgery So. Ill. U., 1987—88; asst. prof. Emory U., Ga., 1988—90; with Peachtree Cardiovasc and Thoracic Surgeons, PA, Ga., 1986—. Hosp. appointments include St. Joseph's Hosp., Atlanta, Northeast Ga. Med. Ctr., Gainesville. Office: Peachtree Cardiovasc and Thoracic Surgeons 95 Collier Rd NW Ste 2055 Atlanta GA 30309 Address: 5665 Peachtree-Dunwoody Rd Ste 150 Atlanta GA 30342 Office Phone: 404-252-6104, 404-355-9515. Office Fax: 404-257-1808, 404-355-9537.

KAVALEK, LUBOMIR, chess expert; b. Prague, Czechoslovakia, Aug. 9, 1943; came to U.S., 1970; s. Lubomir and Stepanka (Kavalkova) K.; m. Irena Koritsanska, Nov. 24, 1971; 1 child, Steven. Student, Faculty of Transp., U. Zilina, 1960-65, Faculty of Journalism, Charles U., Prague, 1967-68, George Washington U., 1970-71. Journalist Voice of Am., USIA, 1971-72; chief editor RHM Chess Pub., Great Neck, NY, 1973-89; mem. German chess team, Solingen, 1969-89, U.S. chess team in chess Olympiad, 1972, 74, 76, 78, 82, 84, 86; reporter world chess championship, chess columnist Washington Post, 1986—2010; xc Huffington Post, 2010—; exec. dir. Grandmaster Assn., Brussels, 1987-91, key organizer world cup, 1988-89; coach Bobby Fischer World Championship, 1972, world championship Challenger, N. Short, 1990—93. Author: Wijk aan Zee 1975 - Grandmaster Chess Tournament, 1976, World Cup Chess, 1990, Tilburg, 1977; author: (with Efim Geller, Svetozar Gligoric and Boris Spassky) The Najdorf Variation - Sicilian Defense, 1976; author: (with Nastimil Hort, Vitezslar Houstea and Pavel Matocho) Karel Opocensky. Recipient Cramer award, 1999, Best Newspaper Chess Column award Chess Journalists Am., 2003, 06, 07, 08, Gallery of Distinguished Chess Journalists, 2006; inductee World and U.S. Chess Hall of Fame, 2001. Mem. Internat. Assn. Chess Journalists Am., U.S. Chess Fedn. Achievements include being the German chess team champion, 1969, 71, 72, 73, 74, 75, 80, 81, 86, SS Dutch Open champion, 1969, Czechoslovakian champion, 1962, 68, Internat. Grandmaster, 1965-, U.S. co-champion, 1972, 73; U.S. champion, 1978, European Cup team champion, 1976, Olympic champion, 1976, German Internat. champion, 1981; winner 30 internat. all-play-all tournaments; most Olympiad medals of any U.S. player (1 gold and 5 bronze medals) since 1924. E-mail: lkavalek@att.net.

KAVANAUGH, FRANK JAMES, film producer, educator; b. Chgo., Sept. 12, 1934; s. Kenneth James and Carol Mae (Wilkey) K.; m. Barbara Ann Barrett, Nov. 16, 1957; children: Franklin James Jr., Christopher Barrett, Kenneth Wilkey. BA, Lake Forest Coll., Ill., 1956; PhD, Union Inst., Cin., 1982. Prodr., dir., exec. ABC-TV, Chgo., NYC, 1956-67; pres. Ravens Hollow Ltd., Warrenton, Va., 1967-69; exec. prodr. Airlie Prodns., Warrenton, 1979-89; prof. comm., prof. med. and pub. affairs, comm. chair George Washington U., Washington, 1983-89. V.p. Airlie Found., 1979-2006; adj. prof. Union Inst. Grad. Sch., 1987—; pres. Kavanaugh Assocs., Inc., 1989—; mentor Capella U.; emeritus chair Internat. Acad. for Preventive Medicine; v.p. Cooper Inst. for Advanced Studies in Medicine and the Humanities, 1989-90. Asst. dir. TV Kukla, Fran & Ollie, 1958; prodr. (film) The Saving of the President, 1982 (Emmy award 1982); prodr. dir. films A Moveable Scene, 1968 (Emmy award nominee 1969), Flowers of Darkness, 1969 (Emmy award 1969), Bridge From No Place, 1970 (Emmy award 1970), The Possible Dream, 1970 (Emmy award 1970), More Than a Paycheck, 1978 (Emmy award nominee 1978), others; prodr., dir., writer film Each Child Loved, 1972 (Emmy award 1972), others. Bd. dirs. Performing Arts Trust. Recipient Cup of Italy Italian Film Festival, Salerno, 1982, highest award Edinburgh Film Festival, Scotland, 1982, Blue Ribbon Am. Film Festival, NYC, 1983, Gold medal Houston Internat. Film Festival, 1983. Mem. Nat. Acad. TV Arts and Scis. (life), C.I.N.E., Inc. (life), Dirs. Guild Am., Radio and TV Dirs. Guild, Mensa, Nat. Assn. TV Program Execs. (Iris award 1983), Broadcast Pioneers. Avocations: photography, scuba, boating, motorcycling.

KAVANDI, JANET LYNN, astronaut aerospace power engineer, chemist; b. Springfield, Mo., July 17, 1959; d. William Winfred and Wanda Ruth (Garner) Sellers; m. Farhad John Kavandi, June 5, 1982. BS magna cum laude, Mo. So. State Coll., 1980; MS, U. Mo., Rolla, 1982; PhD, U. Wash., 1990. Project engr. Eagle-Picher Industries, Joplin, Mo., 1982-84; prin. engr. power systems tech. Boeing Def., Seattle, 1984—95; Astronaut NASA, Houston, 1995—, dep. dir. Flight Crew Ops. Mem. ASE, Am. Chem. Soc. Avocations: skiing, horseback riding, windsurfing, sailing, camping. Office: Astronaut Office NYC CA Lyndon B Johnson Space Center Houston TX 77058

KAW, AUTAR KRISHEN, mechanical engineer, educator; b. Srinagar, India, Feb. 15, 1960; came to U.S., 1982; s. Radha Krishen and Chuni Devi (Mattoo) K.; m. Sherrie Lynn Phillips, May 16, 1986; children: Candace Sandhya, Angelie Kristen. BE with honors, Birla Inst. Tech. & Sci., Pilani, India, 1981; MS, Clemson U., 1984, PhD, 1987. Student trainee Nat. Thermal Power Corp., New Delhi, 1980; maintenance engr. Escorts Tractors Ltd., Faridabad, India, 1981-82; grad. rsch. asst. Clemson (S.C.) U., 1982-83, prin. grad. asst., 1984-87; asst. prof. mech. engring. U. South Fla., Tampa, 1987-92, assoc. prof., 1992-96, prof., 1996—. Author: Mechanics of Composite Materials, 1997; contbr. articles to profl. publs. Recipient Ralph Teetor award Soc. Automotive Engrs., 1991, Tchg. Incentive Program award State of Fla., 1994, 96. Mem. ASME (assoc., chpt. exec. com. 1989-90), Mech. Engring. Assn. India (pres. local chpt. 1982), Am. Soc. Engring. Edn. (New Mechanics Educator award 1992, Archie Higdon Mechanics Educator award 2003, Fla. Prof. Yr., 2004, Nat. Outstanding Tchg. award, 2011, US Prof. of Yr., 2012). Avocations: music, bicycling, movies. Office: U South Fla Mech Engring ENB 118 4202 E Fowler Ave Tampa FL 33620-5350 Business E-Mail: kaw@usf.edu.

KAY, BRUCE A., insurance company executive; BA in Economics, Colgate U.; M in Commerce, U. Richmond. V.p. investor rels. and real estate Markel Corp., mng. dir. investor rels. Bd. dirs. Richmond

Workforce Investment Bd., Henrico Bus. Coun.; sec. bd. dirs. Pocahontas Parkway Assn., 2001. Bd. dirs. Maymont Found., Innsbrook Found. Office: Markel Corp 4521 Highwoods Pky Glen Allen VA 23060 Office Phone: 804-747-0136. Office Fax: 804-965-1600. Business E-Mail: bkay@markelcorp.com.

KAY, JOEL PHILLIP, lawyer; m. Marilyn Soltz, July 9, 1961 BS in Econs., Wharton Sch., U. Pa., 1958; LLB, U. Tex., 1961; LL.M., Georgetown U., Washington, 1967. Bar: Tex. 1961, U.S. Dist. Ct. (so. and we. dists.) Tex., U.S. Dist. Ct (so. dist.) Ala., U.S. Ct. Appeals (5th cir.), U.S. Supreme Ct. Trial atty. tax div. Dept. Justice, 1963-67; U.S. atty. So. Dist. Tex., 1967-69; ptnr. Sheinfeld, Maley & Kay, P.C., Houston, 1969—2001; of counsel Hughes, Watters & Askanase, LLP, Houston, 2001—11. Mem. Tex. Bd. Pub. Accountancy, 1984-85, quality rev. oversight bd., 1992-93; speaker at numerous institutes on comml. and bankruptcy law. Dir. Am. Coll. Bankruptcy Found., 2002—08. Capt. AUS, 1961—63. Recipient Banco Rotto award, Bankruptcy Law Sect., State Bar Texas, 2007. Fellow Am. Bar Found., Am. Coll. Bankruptcy (5th cir. regent 1998-2003); mem. ABA, Tex. Bar Assn. (dir. 1979-81, chmn. bd. 1981-82), Houston Bar Assn., Tex. Bar Found. (trustee 1983-86), Houston Bar Found. (dir. 1995-98), Tex. Supreme Ct. (grievance oversight com. 1987-94). Office Phone: 713-723-6984. Personal E-mail: twokays836@gmail.com.

KAY, THOMAS OLIVER, agricultural consultant; b. Anderson, SC, Sept. 29, 1929; s. Thomas Crayton and Gertrude (Whitworth) K.; m. Rebecca Moore, Aug. 29, 1954 (div. 1965); children— Michael (dec.), Mitchell; m. Bette Hutto, Oct. 1, 1966 (dec. Nov. 1991); stepchildren— Dallon Weathers, Bruce Weathers BA, Furman U., 1950; LL.D. (hon.), John Marshall Law Sch., Atlanta, 1960. Adminstrv. asst. U.S. Congress, Washington, 1966-73; legis. officer USDA, Washington, 1973-77; exec. asst. U.S. Senate, Washington, 1977-79; lobbyist Nat. Assn. Realtors, Washington, 1979-80; asst. to adminstr. Fgn. Agrl. Service USDA, Washington, 1981-82, dir. congl. relations, 1982-83, dep. asst. sec. govtl. and pub. affairs, 1983-85, dep. undersec. internat. affairs and commodity programs, 1985-86, adminstr. fgn. agrl. svc., 1986-90; pres. Kay Assoc., 1990—94. Mem. Litchfield Country Club (Pawleys Island, S.C.). Avocations: golf, swimming. Home: 17 Goodson Loop Pawleys Island SC 29585-8037

KAYE, RICHARD WILLIAM, retired labor economist; b. Chgo., May 14, 1939; s. Albert Louis and Helen (Beckman) K.; m. Betty Ann Terry, Aug. 7, 1964; children: Ronald, William, Richard, Timothy. AB, Cornell U., 1960; MBA, Columbia U., 1962. Various fin. positions Inland Steel Co., Chgo., 1964-81; dir. info. svcs. No. Ind. Pub. Svc. Co., Hammond, 1981-86, dir. econ. analysis, 1986-88. Vis. dir. Purdue U., 1988; ct.-appointed receiver, 1989—92; mgmt. and fin. cons., 1993—97; labor market economist, 1998—. Advisor Calumet Coll., Whiting, Ind., 1985—; active Village Planning Commn., village trustee. Lt. (j.g.) USNR. Mem. Am. Mgmt. Assn., Cornell U. Alumni Assn., Columbia U. Alumni Assn., Rotary. Avocations: tennis, golf. Home: 12415 McGregor Woods Cir Fort Myers FL 33908-2443 Personal E-mail: rwk.assoc@comcast.net.

KAYE, WILLIAM A., endocrinologist, educator; b. July 13, 1951; married; 2 children. BA, Brown U., 1973, MD, 1976. Diplomate American Bd. Internal Medicine, 1981, American Bd. Internal Medicine-nephrology, 1983, American Bd. Internal Medicine-endocrinology, diabetes and metabolism, 1983, lic. RI, 1978, Calif., 1978, Mass., 1982, Fla., 1985. Intern (PGY I) internal medicine Roger Williams Hosp., Providence, 1976, resident (PGY II, III) internal medicine, 1977—79; fellow nephrology Univ. Hosp., San Diego, 1979, Meml. Sloan-Kettering Cancer Ctr., NYC, 1980—81; fellow nephrology/transplant immunology Rogosin Kidney Ctr., NY Hosp., NYC, 1981—82; attending physician and rsch. assoc., rsch. divsn. Joslin Diabetes Ctr., Cambridge, Mass., 1982—86; staff physician Brookline Hosp., Mass., 1982—85, New Eng. Baptist Hosp., Boston, 1982—85, New Eng. Deaconess Hosp., Boston, 1982—86; instr. medicine Harvard. Med. Sch., Boston, 1983—86; pres. Palm Beach Diabetes and Endocrine Specialists, PA, Fla., 1985—; staff physician JFK Med. Ctr., Lake Worth, Fla., 1986—, St. Mary's Hosp., West Palm Beach, Fla., 1986—, chief, endocrinology, 1990—98; staff physician Good Samaritan Med. Ctr., West Palm Beach, Fla., 1986—, chief, endocrinology, 1990—98; clin. asst. prof. Univ. of Miami Sch. of Medicine, Fla., 1987—94; staff physician Palm Beach Gardens Med. Ctr., Fla., 1988—, Jupiter Med. Ctr. Fla., 1988—; co-dir. Metabolic Rsch. Inst., Inc., West Palm Beach, Fla., 1996—. Author: (publs.) Understanding Kidney Disease, 1987, Latest Advances in Diabetic Kidney Disease, 1988, Diabetes and Hypertension, 1989, When the Pressure Gets to be Too Much, 1993, and numerous other publs. Recipient Rsch. Grant award, Shering Plough and Upsula, 1979; named one of The Best Doctors in America, 1996; grantee Rsch. Support Grant, NIH Biomedical, 1983, Sandoz Pharmaceuticals, 1985. Fellow: ACP; mem.: Brown Univ. Med. Soc., American Soc. of Nephrology, Pan American Med. Assn. (v.p. (Nephrology) 1986—90), American Diabetes Assn. (Palm Beach chpt.) (pres. 1987—88, 1988—96), Diabetes and Wellness Found. (med. adv. bd. 1999—). Office: Metabolic Research Institute Inc Ste 440 1515 N Flagler Dr West Palm Beach FL 33401 Office Phone: 561-802-3060.*

KAZA, GREG JOHN, economist, educator; b. Wyandotte, Mich., Nov. 11, 1960; s. John J. and Mary A. Kaza. BA in Econs., U. Detroit, 1989; MSF in Internat. Fin., Walsh Coll., Troy, Mich., 1998. V.p. policy rsch. The Mackinac Ctr., Midland, Mich., 1989-91; adj. prof. Northwood Inst. and Walsh Coll., Troy, Mich., 1998—00; state rep. State of Mich., 1993-98; exec. dir. Citizen Legislators' Caucus Found., Washington, 1999-2000, Ark. Policy Found., Little Rock, 2001—. Author 9 state laws. Contbr. articles to profl. jours. Mem.: Highpointers Club. Republican. Roman Catholic. Office: Ark Policy Found Stephens Bldg 111 Center St Ste 1200 Little Rock AR 72201 Office Phone: 501-537-0825.

KAZEM, ISMAIL, radiation oncologist, educator, health facility administrator; b. Cairo, Feb. 28, 1931; came to U.S., 1966; s. Mohamed and Khadiga A. (Abou-Hadid) K.; m. Barbara Jean Whitelock; children: Farid, Mohamed, Karen, Ramsey. MB, BChir, Ein Shams U., Cairo, 1955; diploma in radiotherapy, Royal Coll. Radiologists, London, 1960. Diplomate Am. Bd. Nuclear Medicine, Am. Bd. Radiology. Intern Demerdach U. Hosp., Cairo, Egypt, 1955-56; clin. demonstrator radiology dept. Ein Shams U. Faculty Medicine, 1956-59; trainee Meyerstein Inst. Radiotherapy Middlesex Hosp., London, England, 1959, 60; IAEA fellow Strahlen Klinik, Czerny Krankenhaus U. Heidelberg, Germany, 1959; sr. registrar dept. radiotherapy St. Bartholomew's Hosp., London, England, 1960-61; lectr., then asst. prof. radiation therapy U. Alexandria, Egypt, 1962-65; sr. rschr. Inst. Nuclear Medicine German Cancer Rsch. Ctr., Heidelberg, 1965-66; from instr. to asst. prof. radiology Hahnemann Med. Coll. and Hosp., Phila., 1966-70; prof., chmn. dept. radiation therapy and nuclear medicine Sint Radboud Acad. Hosp., Cath. U., Nijmegen, The Netherlands, 1970-83; dir. dept. radiation therapy and Regional Cancer Ctr. Mercer Med. Ctr., Trenton, NJ, 1983-92; dir. divsn. radiation oncology U. Medicine Dentistry-NJ Univ. Hosp., Newark, 1992-94; dir. dept. radiation oncology Geisinger Med. Ctr., Danville, Pa., 1994-2000; chief radiation oncology svc. James A. Haley VA Hosp., Tampa, Fla., 2000—. Clin. prof. radiation oncology Temple U., Phila., 1985-91, Thomas Jefferson U., 1995—; prof. clin. radiology U. Medicine and Dentistry N.J., Newark; presenter in field. Author: (poetry) An Anthology of My Own Thing, 1975, Reflections and Definitions, 1978, Conversations with My Thoughts, 1992, Introduction to Oncology (in Dutch), 1983; mem. editorial bd. N.J. Medicine; editor Mercer County Medicine. Exec. com. Mercer County unit Am. Cancer Soc., pres., 1992-94; mem. pilot project task force for breast cancer screening in Mercer County, N.J. Dept. Health, Trenton, also mem. reaction group licensure reform project; mem. adv. coun. N.J. Office Pub. Guardian for Elderly. WHO fellow, 1963, Disting. fellow Am. Coll. Nuclear Medicine, 1993. Fellow Royal Soc. Medicine (London), Royal Coll. Radiologists (London), Acad. Medicine N.J., Am. Coll. Nuclear Medicine (disting., charter), Am Coll. Radiology; mem. AMA, Soc. Nuclear Medicine, Am. Soc. for Therapeutic Radiology and Oncology, Netherlands Soc. Radiotherapy, European Soc. Therapeutic Radiology and Oncology, Am. Assn. Cancer Edn., Am. Soc. Clin. Oncology, Pan Am. Med. Assn., Am. Endocurietherapy Soc., Pa. Med. Soc., N.J. Med. Soc., N.Y. Acad. Scis., Mercer County Med. Soc. (pres. 1993-94). Office: James A Haley VA Hosp Radiation Oncology Svc 13000 Bruce B Downs Blvd Tampa FL 33612 Office Phone: 813-972-7667. E-mail: ismailkazem@aol.com.

KAZEN, GEORGE PHILIP, federal judge; b. Laredo, Tex., Feb. 29, 1940; s. Emil James and Drusilla M. (Perkins) K.; m. Barbara Ann Sanders, Oct. 27, 1962; children: George Douglas, John Andrew, Elizabeth Ann, Gregory Stephen. BBA, U. Tex., 1960, JD with honors, 1961. Bar: Tex. 1961, US Supreme Ct., US Ct. Claims, US Ct. Appeals (5th cir.), US Dist. Ct. (so. dist.) Tex. Briefing atty. Tex. Sup. Ct., 1961-62; founder, first pres. Laredo Legal Aid Soc., 1966-69; assoc. Mann, Freed, Kazen & Hansen, 1965-79; judge US Dist. Ct. (so. dist.) Tex., Laredo, 1979-96, 2003—09, chief judge, 1996—2003, sr. judge, 2009—; founder, first pres. Laredo Legal Aid Soc., 1966-69; judge Fgn. Intelligence Surveillance Ct. (FISC), 2003—. Mem. Jud. Conf. Com. Criminal Law, 1990-96, chair com., 1996-99; mem. 5th Cir. Jud. Coun., 1991-94, 96-2003; adj. prof. law St. Mary's U. Sch. Law, 1990-2004. Pres. Laredo Civic Music Assn.; chmn. St. Augustine-Ursuline Consol. Sch. Bd.; bd. dirs. Boys' Clubs Laredo; trustee Laredo Jr. Coll., 1972-79; bd. dirs., v.p., pres. Econ. Opportunities Devel. Corp., 1968-70; past bd. dirs. D.D. Hachar Found. With USAF, 1962-65. Decorated Air Force Commendation medal; named Outstanding Young Lawyer, Larado Jaycees, 1970. Mem. ABA, Tex. Bar Found., Tex. Bar Assn., Tex. Criminal Def. Lawyers Assn., Tex. Assn. Bank Counsel, Tex. Assn. Def. Counsel, Laredo C. of C. (bd. dirs. 1975-76), 5th Cir. Dist. Judges Assn. (v.p. 1984-85, pres. 1986-88), U. Tex. Law Sch. Alumni Assn. (bd. dirs. 1976-77). Roman Catholic. Office: US Dist Ct PO Box 1060 Laredo TX 78042-1060

KAZOR, LISA, apparel executive; Mdse. mgr. Prestonwood Store; dept. mgr. NorthPark Store; exec. trainee The Neiman Marcus Group, Inc., 1983, asst. buyer, Galleria, 1983, v.p., divsn. mdse. mgr., designer sportswear, 1995, sr. v.p., gen. mdse. mgr., Neiman Marcus stores. Office: Neiman Marcus Group Inc One Marcus Sq1618 Main St Dallas TX 75201 Office Phone: 214-741-6911. Office Fax: 214-741-6857. Business E-Mail: liza_kazor@neimanmarcus.com.

KEAHEY, GEORGE M. (MARC KEAHEY), state legislator; s. Ronnie Keahey; m. Lara Keahey; 1 child, George Marshall II. Indigent def. contract counsel Clarke County, Ala.; pvt. practice atty.; mem. Dist. 65 Ala. House of Reps., Montgomery, 2006—09; mem. Dist. 22 Ala. State Senate, Montgomery, 2009—. Democrat. Office: Ala State Senate Ala State House 11 S Union St Rm 731 Montgomery AL 36130 also: 128 Main St PO Box 297 Grove Hill AL 36451 Office Phone: 251-275-3127, 334-242-7743.

KEAM, MARK LEE, state legislator, lawyer; b. Seoul, Republic of Korea, May 10, 1966; m. Alex Seong; children: Tyler, Brenna. BS in Polit. Sci., Univ. Calif., Irvine; JD, Univ. Calif., San Francisco. Intern Dem. Nat. Com., Washington; trial atty., enforcement Wireless Telecom. Bur., FCC, Washington; asst. chief counsel, Office of Advocacy SBA, Washington; chief counsel to Senator Richard J. Durbin US Senate Com. on Judiciary, Washington, 2001—07; v.p., counsel fed. govt. rels. Verizon Comm., 2007—; mem. Dist. 35 Va. House of Delegates, Richmond, 2010—. Sr. editor Hastings Law Journal. Active in DC Hate Crimes Task Force, DC Mayor's Neighborhood Adv. Coun., Building One Neighborhood Project, Coalition of Asian Pacific Am., Va.; grad. Leadership Washington, 2001; den parent Boy Scouts Vienna Pack 1139, Va.; apptd. Va. Gov. Asian Am. Adv. Bd. Named one of Best Lawyers Under 40, Nat. Asian Pacific Am. Bar Assn., 2004. Mem.: ABA, Asian Pacific Am. Bar Assn., Greater Washington DC (past pres.), DC Bar, Calif. Bar, Korean Am. Coalition-DC, Vienna-Tysons Regional C. of C., Rotary Club Vienna. Democrat. Office: VA House of Dels Gen Assembly Bldg Rm 717 PO Box 406 Richmond VA 23218 also: PO Box 1134 Vienna VA 22183-1134 Office Phone: 804-698-1035, 703-350-3911. Office Fax: 804-698-6735. Business E-Mail: delmkeam@house.virginia.gov.

KEAN, STEVEN J., energy executive; BA, Iowa State U., Ames; JD, U. Iowa, Iowa City. With El Paso Natural Gas, Utilicorp, Enron; v.p. strategic planning Natural Gas Pipeline group Kinder Morgan, Inc., 2002, pres. Intrastate Pipeline Group Kinder Morgan Energy Ptnrs., L.P., 2002—05, exec. v.p. ops., 2005—06, exec. v.p., COO Houston, 2006—. Office: Kinder Morgan 500 Dallas St Ste 1000 Houston TX 77002 Office Phone: 713-369-9000.

KEANE, DENISE F., lawyer, food products executive; JD. Atty. and various mgmt. and leadership positions Philip Morris USA, Inc., 1977—95, sr. v.p., gen. counsel, 1995—97, sr. v.p. worldwide regulatory affairs, assoc. gen. counsel Philip Morris Companies, Inc., 1997—2001, gen. counsel, 2001—08; exec. v.p., gen. counsel Altria Group, Inc., 2008—. Bd. mem. ArtsFund Ctrl. Va., Va. Opera. Mem.: ABA, Assn. of the Bar the City of NY. Office: Altria Group Inc 6601 W Broad St Richmond VA 23230 Office Fax: 804-274-2200.*

KEANE, MARGARET E., lawyer; BA with high honors, U. Louisville, 1979, JD magna cum laude, 1982. Bar: Ky. 1982, US Dist. Ct. (western dist.) Ky. 1982, US Dist. Ct. (eastern dist.) Ky. 1983, US Ct. Appeals (6th cir.) 1984, US Ct. Fed. Claims 1991, US Ct. Appeals (federal cir.) 1992, US Supreme Ct. 1993. Mem. Litig. and Dispute Resolution Practice Group, co-chair Beverage Alcohol Team Greenbaum Doll & McDonald PLLC. Mem. Ky. Access to Justice Commn., 2011. Master: Louis D. Brandeis American Inn Ct. at Louisville (pres. 2003—05, past pres. 2005—07, sec.-treas. 2007—); mem.: ABA, Trual Attys. America, Northern Ky. Bar Assn., Fayette County Bar Assn., Louisville Bar Assn. (v.p., treas. 1995, pres.-elect 1996, pres. 1997, past. pres. 1998), Ky. Def. Coun., Def. Rsch. Inst., Ky. Bar Assn. (v.p. 2009—10, pres.-elect 2010—11). Office: Greenbaum Doll & McDonald PLLC 3500 National City Tower 101 S Fifth St Louisville KY 40202-3140 Office Phone: 502-587-3641. Office Fax: 502-540-2203. E-mail: mek@gdm.com.

KEANE, PETER J., construction executive; Pres. PulteGroup, Inc. (formely Pulte Homes Inc.), Ill., pres., Gt. Lakes area; Joined PulteGroup, Inc., 1993; sr. v.p., homebuilding ops. & sr. v.p., project mgmt. PulteGroup, Inc. (formely Pulte Homes Inc.), 2006—10; sr. v.p., project mgmt. office PulteGroup, Inc., 2010—. Office: Pulte-Group Inc 4901 Vineland Rd Ste 500 Orlando FL 32811-7383 Office Phone: 352-291-7300. Business E-Mail: peter.keane@pulte.com.

KEANEY, THOMAS ADDIS, academic administrator, management consultant, military officer; b. Boston, June 14, 1940; s. James Francis and Anna Catherine (Keefe) K.; m. Mary Beth Martin, June 22, 1963; children: Thomas M., Kathleen P., Maura E., Anna C. BS, USAF Acad., Colo., 1962; MA, U. Mich., 1971, PhD, 1975. Commd. 2d lt. USAF, 1962, advanced through grades to col., 1982; assoc. prof. history USAF Acad., Colo., 1973-77; flight comdr., ops. officer 7th Bomb Wing USAF, Fort Worth, 1977-79, squadron comdr. B-52, 43rd Strategic Wing Andersen AFB, Guam, 1980-81, dep. base comdr., 1981-82, mil. planner air staff Washington, 1983-85, base comdr. Wurtsmith AFB, Mich., 1985-86; chmn. dept. mil. strategy Nat. War Coll., Washington, 1986-91; rschr., author Dept. Air Force, Washington, 1991-92; prof. mil. strategy Nat. War Coll., Washington, 1993-98; exec. dir. Fgn. Policy Inst. Nitze Sch. Advanced Internat. Studies, Johns Hopkins U., Washington, 1998—2007, exec. dir. Merrill Ctr. Strategic Studies, 2004—, assoc. dir., sr. adj. prof. strategic studies program. Author: Strategic Bombers and Conventional Weapons, 1984, Gulf War Air Power Survey, 2 vols., 1993, Revolution in Warfare?, 1995, U.S. Allies in a Changing World, 2000, Armed Forces in the Middle East: Politics and Strategy, 2001, War in Iraq: Planning and Execution, 2007, Understanding Counter in surgency, 2010. Roman Catholic. Home: 3047 Holly St Falls Church VA 22044-2617 Office: Nitze Sch Advanced Intl Studies 1619 Massachusetts Ave NW Washington DC 20036-2213 E-mail: tkeaney@jhu.edu.

KEARFOTT, JOSEPH CONRAD, lawyer; b. Martinsville, Va., Sept. 24, 1947; s. Clarence P. and Elizabeth (Kelly) K.; m. Mary Jo Veatch, Feb.10, 1969; children: Kelly, David. BA, Davidson Coll., 1969; JD, U. Va., 1972. Bar: Va. 1972, US Dist. Ct. (ea. and we. dists.) Va. 1973, US Ct. Appeals (4th cir.) 1973, US Tax Ct. 1979, US Ct. Appeals (1st cir.) 1981, US Ct. Appeals (5th cir.) 1982. Law clk. to presiding judge U.S. Dist. Ct. (ea. dist.) Va., Richmond, 1972-73; assoc. Hunton & Williams, Richmond, 1973-80, ptnr., 1980—. Lectr. NITA program, Washington and Lee U., 1982-83, Va. Com. on Continuing Legal Edn., 1984-2005; mem. 4th Cir. Jud. conf. Co-author: Virginia Evidentiary Foundations, 1998. Mem. Richmond Bd. Housing, 1977-85, Richmond Dem. Com., 1978-82; trustee Libr. Va. Found., 1994-, chmn., 2004-06, William Byrd Cmty. House, 1978-84, chmn., 1982-84; trustee United Way Svcs., Richmond, 1989-95, treas., 1993-95; trustee Libr. Va., 1989-94, vice chmn., 1990-91, chmn., 1991-92; trustee Trinity Episcopal Sch., 1986-94, treas., 1989-92, chmn., 1993-94; mem. Richmond Regional Bd., Thomas C. Sorensen Inst. Polit. Leadership, chmn., 2004-06; treas. St. Paul's Episcopal Ch., 2003—09. Fellow: Va. Law Found.; mem.: ABA, Richmond Bar Assn., Va. Bar Assn. (Boyd Graves conf. chmn. 1999—2001), Order of Coif, Country Club Va. Avocations: golf, skiing. Home: 4436 Custis Rd Richmond VA 23225-1012 Office: Hunton & Williams East Tower Riverfront Pla 951 E Byrd St Richmond VA 23219-4074

KEARNEY, CHRISTOPHER J., manufacturing executive, lawyer; b. Mount Pleasant, Pa., 1955; BA, U. Notre Dame, 1977; JD, DePaul U. Law Sch., 1981. Sr. atty. Borg-Warner Chems.; sr. counsel, global materials bus. General Electric Co.; sr. v.p., gen. counsel Grimes Aerospace Co., 1995—97; v.p., sec., gen. counsel SPX Corp., Charlotte, NC, 1997—2004, pres., CEO, dir., 2004—07, chmn., pres., CEO, 2007—. Office: SPX Corp 13515 Ballantyne Corp Pl Charlotte NC 28277

KEARNEY-NUNNERY, ROSE, nursing administrator, educator, consultant; b. Glen Falls, NY, July 8, 1951; d. James J. and Helen F. (Oprandy) K.; m. Jimmie E. Nunnery (dec.). BS, Keuka Coll., 1973; M of Nursing, U. Fla., 1976, PhD, 1987. Asst. prof. La. State U. Med. Ctr., New Orleans, 1976-87; project coord., indigent health care U. Fla., Gainesville, 1984-85; asst. prof. U. South Fla., Tampa, 1987-88; dir. nursing programs SUNY, New Paltz, NY, 1988-94; project dir. MS in gerontol. nursing advanced nursing edn. grant U.S. Health Resources and Svc. Adminstrn. Div. Nursing, 1992-94; head nursing dept. Tech. Coll. of the Low Country, Beaufort, SC, 1995-97, v.p. acad. affairs, 1997—2005, cons., adj. instr., 2005—08, interim v.p. acad. affairs, 2007; dean Coll. Nursing South U., 2009—10; adj. prof. Armsstong Alantic State U., 2010. Prof. chair dept. nursing U. SC Beanfort, 2011—. Author: Advancing Your Profession Concepts for Profl. Nursing, 5th edit., 2012, Making the Transition from LPN to RN, 2010. Bd. dirs. Beaufort Co. First Steps, 2000-01; Ulster County unit Am. Cancer Soc., 1991-94; nursing edn. com., 1990-92; bd. dir. Mid-Hudson Consortium for Advancement Edn. for Health Profl., 1988-94; nursing edn. com., 1988-92; scholarship com., 1989-93; com. chmn., 1990-93, treas., 1992-94; prof. devel. program SUNY, Albany, 1989-92; adv. coun. Ulster CC, 1989-94; adv. regional planning group for early intervention svc. United Cerebral Palsy Ulster County Inc., Children's Rehab. Ctr., 1989-91; mem. Ulster County adv. com. Office for Aging, 1991-94; state del. S.C. Conf. on Aging, 1995; bd. dir. Beaufort County Coun. on Aging, 1995; cmty. adv. bd. Hilton Head Med. Ctr. and Clinics, 1996-2000; mem. SC Bd. Nursing, 2000—, pres. 2001-03; accreditation evaluator So. Assn. Coll. and Sch. Commn. on Coll., 2000-05. Mem. ANA, Nat. League Nursing, S.C. Nurses Assn. (editl. bd. 1994-99, chair 1996-99), Nat. Coun. State Bds. of Nursing (mem. practice, regulation and edn. com. 2001-05, area III dir. 2005-07, chair Model Act & Rules Comm., 2010-), Sigma Theta Tau. Roman Catholic. Home: 66 Windjammer Ct Hardeeville SC 29927-2939 Office Phone: 843-208-8310. Personal E-mail: rosekn@hargray.com.

KEATS, BRONYA JOY BEVERIDGE, medical educator, department chairman; b. Adelaide, Australia, Mar. 15, 1951; d. Reynold Gilbert and Joy Keats; m. Joseph Foard Gettrust, Jan. 4, 1978; 1 child, Patrick Joseph Keats Gettrust. BSc, Australian Nat. U., Canberra; PhD, Australian Nat. U. Lic. clin. molecular geneticist Am. Bd. Med. Genetics, 1993. Asst. rschr. U. Hawaii, Honolulu, 1976—82; prof., chair genetics La. State U., Health Scis. Ctr., New Orleans, 1999—. Office: La State Unic Health Scis Ctr 533 Bolivar St New Orleans LA 70112 Home: 1300 Lark St New Orleans LA 70122-2238 Office Fax: 504-568-8500. Business E-Mail: bkeats@lsuhsc.edu.

KECK, DONALD BRUCE, physicist; b. Lansing, Mich., Jan. 2, 1941; s. William G. and Zelda Divine Keck; m. Ruth A. Moilanen, July 10, 1965; children: Lynne Ann Vaia, Brian William. BS, Mich. State U., East Lansing, 1962, MS, 1964, PhD, 1967; DSc (hon.), Rensselaer Poly. Inst., Troy, NY, 2004. With Corning Glass Works, NY, 1968-76, mgr. applied physics NY, 1976-86; dir. optics and photonics Corning, Inc., 1986-91, v.p., dir. optics and photonics, 1997—2000, v.p., exec. dir. rsch., 2000—02; chief tech. officer Infotonic Tech. Ctr., 2002—04; cons. Big Flats, NY, 2004—. Bd. dirs. PCO, Inc., LA, 1985-90; bd. chmn. Opto-Electronics Inds. Develop. Assn., 1999-2002; mem. Nat. Inst. Standards and Tech. vis. com. advanced tech., 2003-06; lectr. in field. Editor: Jour. Lightwave Tech., 1989—94, co-author (5 books on optical fibers); contbr. more than 150 to profl. jours. Chmn. planning bd. Town of Corning, 1990—2007; mem. adv. bd. Corning Salvation Army; mem. Nat. Medal Tech. Nomination Evaluation Com., 2009—; moderator 1st Congl. Ch., Corning, 1986—87, 1991—92; bd. dirs. ARC-Corning chpt., 1995—2007, Cmty. Found., 2000—06; chmn. troop com. Boy Scouts Am., Corning, 1968—71; pres. Civic Music Assn., Corning, 1971—75; bd. dirs. Nat. Inventors Hall of Fame Found., 1994—, pres., 2001—02; bd. dirs. Nat. Inventors Hall of Fame, 2000—06, sec., 2002—04, vice chair, 2003—. Recipient Tech. Achievement award Internat. Soc. Optical Engring., 1981, IR-100 award Indsl. Rsch., 1981, Engring. Achievement award Am. Soc. Metals, 1983, Am. Innovator award, 1995, John Tyndall award IEEE/Optical Soc. Am., 1992, Disting. Alumni award Mich. State U., 1996, Lauren Publishing, "Distinction in Photonics" award, 2002, Nat. medal of Tech., U.S. Pres., 2000, Macbeth award Greater Steuben Chpt. Am. Red Cross, 2007; inductee Nat. Inventors Hall of Fame, 1993; Paul Harris fellow Rotary Internat., 1998, Hon. Mem. award OSA, 2013. Fellow IEEE OSA, Optical Soc. Am. (bd. dirs. 1994-96), Nat. Acad. Engring., World Innovation Found.(hon.). Achievements include 36 patents in field; invention of optical telecommunications fiber that enabled the Internet. Avocations: skiing, music, woodworking, piano, photography. Home: 20151 Cheetah Ln Estero FL 33928 Home Phone: 607-562-3695. Personal E-mail: keckdb@gmail.com.

KEE, TOMMY, corporate financial executive; BS in Acctg., U. Tenn.; MBA, U. Memphis. CFO Allied Interstate, Inc., West Palm Beach; chief acctg. officer Bravo! Brands, Inc.; CFO, treas. Hearx Ltd., West Palm Beach, Fla.; internat. contr., fin. dir. Holiday Inns Inc, Orlando; CFO Attitude Drink Co., Inc. (subs. of Attitude Drinks, Inc.), 2007—. Office: Attitude Drinks Inc Ste 101 712 US Highway 1 Ste 200 North Palm Beach FL 33408-4521 Office Phone: 561-799-5053.

KEEDY, CHRISTIAN DAVID, lawyer; b. Worcester, Mass., Jan. 9, 1945; BBA, Tulane U., 1967, JD, 1972. Bar: Fla. 1972; bd. cert. in admiralty and maritime law, Fla. Pvt. practice Christian D. Keedy, P.A., Miami, Fla., 1981—. Mem. Maritime Law Assn. US, Southeastern Admiralty Law Inst. (dir. 1982-83), The Fla. Bar (chmn. 1981-82, 03-04, admiralty law com.). Office: Christian D Keedy PA 7931 SW 59th Ave South Miami FL 33143-5513 Office Phone: 305-669-4478. E-mail: ckeedy@bellsouth.net.

KEEGAN, JANE ANN, retired insurance executive, consultant; b. Watertown, NY, Sept. 1, 1950; d. Richard Isidor and Kathleen (McKinley) K. BA cum laude, SUNY, Potsdam, 1972; MBA in Risk Mgmt., Golden State U., 1986. CPCU. Comml. lines mgr. Lithgow & Rayhill, San Francisco, 1977-80; risk mgmt. account coord. Dinner Levison Co., San Francisco, 1980-83; ins. cons. San Francisco, 1983-84; account mgr. Rollins Burdick Hunter, San Francisco, 1984-85; account exec. Jardine Ins. Brokers, San Francisco, 1985-86; ins. cons. San Francisco, 1986-87; ins. adminstr. Port of Oakland, 1987—, risk mgr., 1989—, mgr. accts. payable, 1996—2010. Vol. San Francisco Ballet vol. orgn., 1981-96, Bay Area Bus., Govt. ARC disaster conf. steering com., 1987-88, 89, 90, 91-92; mem. Nob Hill Neighbors Assn., 1982—, City of Oakland Emergency Mgmt. Bd., 1990—. Named Industry Ceader award, Risk & Ins. Mag., 2009. Mem. Safety Mgmt. Soc., CPCU Soc. (spl. events chairperson 1982-84, continuing profl. devel. program award 1985, 88, chair loss prevention), Calif. Assn. of Port Authorities (ins. chair 1998—), Risk and Ins. Mgr. Soc. (dep., sec. 1990—, dir. legis. 1993, dir. conf.). Democrat. Roman Catholic. Home: 548 NE Alice St Jensen Beach FL 34957 Personal E-mail: ja.keegan@sbcglobal.net.

KEEL, JEFFERSON, Native American tribal leader; m. Carol Keel; children: Thomas, Jeff, Kristen. AA, Murray State Coll., Tishomingo, Okla.; B, East Ctrl. U., Ada, Okla., 1978; MS, Troy U., Ala. Joined US Army, 1966, infantryman, 1st Cavalry Divsn. Vietnam, infantryman, 101st Airborne Divsn., mem. Army Rangers, stationed Hawaii, 1973—74, 2d lt. field arty. Ft. Sill, 1978, arty. divsn. comdr., hdqs. comdr. Ft. Carson, Colo., 1980, nuc. targeting officer, corps arty. plans and ops. staff officer Frankfurt, Germany, fire support and combined arms instr. Ft. Rucker, Ala., 1985—89, ret., 1989; social services and tribal health profl.; lt. gov. Chickasaw Nation Okla.; first v.p. Nat. Congress of Am. Indians, Washington, 2005—09, pres., 2009—. Decorated Purple Heart, Bronze Star, Army Commendation medal, Meritorious Svc. medal, Air medal, Combat Infantryman Badge; recipient Gen. George C. Marshall award, East Ctrl. U.; named Disting. Alumnus, 2008. Office: Chickasaw Nation PO Box 1548 Ada OK 74821 also: Nat Congress of Am Indians 1516 P St NW Washington DC 20005 Office Phone: 580-436-7232. Office Fax: 580-436-7209.*

KEELER, JAMES LEONARD, food products executive; b. Richmond, Va., Jan. 31, 1935; s. Joseph McCauley and Nora Elizabeth (Thomas) Keeler; m. Joan Sandra Barnhart, Aug. 14, 1954; children: Mark Leonard, Tracy Ann, Steven James, Gregory Wayne. JD, U. Va., 1983; BS, Bridgewater Coll., 1957, LLD honorary causa, 2010. CPA Va., 1958; bar: Va. 1983. Ptnr., acct. Hueston & Keeler, CPAs, Harrisonburg, Va., 1958-63; mng. ptnr., acct. Keeler, Phibbs & Co., CPAs, Harrisonburg, 1963-80; ptnr., atty. Wharton, Aldhizer & Weaver, Harrisonburg, 1983-88; CEO WLR Foods, Inc., Broadway, Va., 1988—2001, pres., 1990—2001, Wampler Foods, Inc., Broadway, 1997—2001. Mem. Va. Bus. Coun., 1995—2001, Gov.'s Adv. Com. Va.'s Strategy, 1998; bd. dir. Massanutten Regional Libr., 2001—02; mem. exec. com. and trustee Bridgewater (Va.) Coll., 1974—2010, vice chmn. bd. trustees, 1974—91, chmn. bd. trustees, 2003—10, life trustee, 2010; exec. adv. coun. Coll. Bus. James Madison U., Harrisonburg, 1989—95; bd. dir. Rockingham Meml. Hosp., 1994—98, Va. Econ. Devel. Partnership, 1995—2001, Valley Va. Partnership Edn., 2000—04. Recipient Disting. Alumnus award, Bridgewater Coll., 1990, Outstanding Bus. Person award, Harrisonburg-Rockingham C. of C., 1995. Fellow: Va. Soc. CPAs (pres. 1970—71, Outstanding Mem. award); mem.: AICPA (mem. governing coun. 1969—70, 1974—75, 1976—77), ABA, Va. Bar Assn., Va. C. of C. (vice chmn. 1994—96, chmn. 1997—98, mem. exec. com., bd. dirs. 1994—98). Republican. Presbyn. Avocation: boating.

KEELEY, IRENE PATRICIA MURPHY, federal judge; b. Bklyn., 1944; BA, Coll. Notre Dame of Md., Balt., 1965; MA, W.Va. U., 1977; JD, W.Va. U. Coll. Law, 1980. Bar: W.Va. 1980. Atty. Steptoe & Johnson, Clarksburg, W.Va., 1980-92; judge US Dist. Ct. (no. dist.) W.Va., 1992—, chief judge, 2001—08. Adj. prof. W.Va. U. Coll. Law, 1990—91; mem. exec. com. Nat. Conf. Fed. Trial Judges. Mem.: ABA, W.Va. U. Alumni Assn. (v.p. 1997—98, bd. dirs.), Harrison County Bar Assn., W.Va. Bar Assn., Oral Lake Fishing Club, Clarksburg Country Club. Office: US Courthouse PO Box 2808 500 W Pike St Rm 202 Clarksburg WV 26302-2808 Office Phone: 304-624-5850. Office Fax: 304-622-1928.

KEELY, CHESTER MARTIN, federal marshal; b. LA; AS, Jefferson State Coll.; B in Law Enforcement Mgmt., Samford U., Birmingham, Ala.; JD, Birmingham Sch. Law; grad., FBI Nat. Acad., Quantico, Va. Police officer Mountain Brook Police Dept., Ala., 1969—87, chief of police, 1987—2002; US marshal (no. dist.) Ala. US Marshals Svc., US Dept. Justice, 2002—. Past pres. exec. bd. FBI Nat. Acad. Associates, Inc. Past pres. United Cerebral Palsy, Birmingham, Ala.; alumnus Leadership Birmingham, 1993—94. Recipient Law Enforcement Officer of Yr. award, US Marshals Svc., 1990. Mem.: Ala. Assn. Police Chiefs (past pres.), Met. Criminal Justice Exec. Assn. (past pres.), Rotary (Vocational Svc. award). Office: No Dist Ala US Marshal 1729 N 5th Ave Rm 240 Birmingham AL 35203 Office Phone: 205-776-6200.

KEEN, RACHEL, psychology professor; b. Burkesville, Ky., Oct. 5, 1937; d. James Em and Regina Elizabeth (Simpson) Keen; m. Charles E. Clifton, Aug. 20, 1965 (div. 2002); children: Ramona Clifton, Catherine Ferrando. BA, Berea Coll., Ky., 1959; MA, U. Minn., 1960, PhD, 1963; Degree (hon.), Uppsala U., Sweden, 2009. Fellow U. Wis., Madison, 1963-65; rsch. assoc. U. Iowa, Iowa City, 1966-68; from asst. prof. to assoc. prof. U. Mass., Amherst, 1968-76, prof., 1976—2007, U. Va., Charlottesville, 2007—12, prof. emeritus, 2012. Vis. prof. Stanford U., Palo Alto, Calif., 1975—76, U. Sussex, Brighton, England, 1981—82, U. Cambridge, England, 1989—90, Harvard U., 2002—04, U. Edinburgh; mem. rsch. rev. com. NIMH, 1983—87; mem. human devel. study sect. NIH, 1990—94. Recipient Rsch. Scientist award, NIMH, 1981—2001, Disting. Faculty award, U. Mass., 1988, Merit award, NICHD, 1999—2009, Disting. Sci. Contbn. award, Soc. Rsch. Child Devel., 2005; named Disting. Alumna, Berea Coll., 1994; grantee, NIMH, NIH, NSF, 1968—; NIMH fellow, U. Minn., 1961—63. Fellow: AAAS, APA, Am. Acad. Arts and Scis., Acoustical Soc. Am.; mem.: Internat. Soc. Infant Studies (pres. 1998—2000), Soc. Psychophysiol. Rsch. (assoc. editor jour. 1972—75, bd. dirs. 1975—78), Fedn. Behavioral, Psychol. and Cognitive Scis. (sec. 1987—90), Soc. Rsch. Child Devel. (assoc. editor jour. 1977—79, sec. 1979—85, editor Monographs 1993—99). Democrat. Presbyterian. Avocations: playing piano, reading.

KEENAN, ANTHONY LEE, trucking executive; b. Greenwood, SC, Mar. 18, 1949; s. Arthur Lee and Betty (Hart) K.; m. Cheryl Toney, Dec. 31, 1985; children: Andrew Lee, Anthony LeBrett, Aric Lane. BA, W.Ga. Coll., 1973; postgrad., Woodrow Wilson Coll. Law, 1975-79. Pres. Keenan, Inc., Decatur, Ga., 1975—; v.p. All Day Leasing Co., Decatur, 1977—; pres. United Trucker's Svcs., Conyers, Ga., 1978—; exec. dir. Ind. Trucker's United Co., Conley, Ga., 1979-80; pres. Southeastern Gen. Agy., Inc., 1983—; CEO Getaway Travel, 1996—. Pres. Am. Risk Reduction, Inc.; CEO, Am. Commerce and Shipping Assn., 1991-; mem. adv. bd. Rockdale Nat. Bank. Mem. White House Task Force To Develop Motor Carrier Act of 1980, 1979-80; com. chmn. Am. Mem. Profl. Truck Svcs. Assn., pres. 1987-89, chmn. bd. 1990; com. chmn. 354 Cub Scouts Am. Mem.: Ga. Surplus Lines Assn. (com. chmn. 1982—), Assn. Transp. Practitioners (com. chmn. 1992—), Aircraft Owners and Pilots Assn. (com. chmn.). Office Phone: 770-922-6200. E-mail: acsa@utsinfo.com.

KEENAN, BARBARA MILANO, federal judge, former state supreme court justice; b. Vienna, 1950; BA, Cornell U., 1971; JD, George Washington U., 1974; LLM, U. Va., 1992. Asst. commonwealth atty. Fairfax County, Va., 1974—76; pvt. law practice, 1976—80; judge Fairfax County Gen. Dist. Ct., 1980-82, Fairfax County Cir. Ct., 1982-85, Va. Ct. Appeals, 1985-91; assoc. justice Va. Supreme Ct., Richmond, 1991—2010; judge US Ct. Appeals (4th Cir.), 2010—. Recipient American Jurisprudence award, Fairfax Bar Assn., 1995. Office: US Court Appeals 1100 E Main St Richmond VA 23219

KEENE, DEBORAH M., law librarian; b. Nashville, Sept. 29, 1952; BA, Vanderbilt U., 1974, MLS, 1975; JD, U. Tenn., 1980. Assoc. dean libr. and tech. George Mason U. Sch. Law, Arlington, Va. Contbr. articles to profl. jours. Office: George Mason University School Law Rm 243 3301 Fairfax Dr Arlington VA 22201 Office Phone: 703-993-8110. E-mail: dkeene@gmu.edu.

KEENE, DENNIS, state legislator; b. Aug. 17, 1956; Mem. Wilder City Coun.; mem. Dist. 67 Ky. House of Reps., 2005—. Republican. Address: 1040 Johns Hill Rd Newport KY 41076 Office: Ky Legislature Capitol Annex Rm 358 702 Capitol Ave Frankfort KY 40601 Office Phone: 502-564-8100 ext. 626.

KEENE, JACK DONALD, molecular genetics and microbiology educator; b. Jacksonville, Fla., June 21, 1947; s. Jack Donald and Stella Collene (Ellis) Keene; m. Judy May Keene, Sept. 6, 1969; children: Mike, Lisa E. Dugan. AB, U. Calif., Riverside, 1969; PhD, U. Wash., 1974. Staff fellow NINDS/NIH, Bethesda, Md., 1974-78; asst. prof. microbiology and immunology Duke U. Med. Ctr., Durham, NC, 1979-84, assoc. prof., 1984—88, prof., 1988—92, chmn., 1992—2002, James B. Duke disting. prof., 1997—, founder Duke Ctr. RNA Biology, 1999—. Exptl. virology study sect. NIH, 1984—88, mem. molecular biology study sect., 1991—95, chmn., 1993—95; mem. nat. sel. and adv. bd. PEW Scholars in the Biomed Scis., 1991—96; co-chmn. Diversity Biotech. Consortium, Santa Fe, 1994—; dir. basic sci. rsch. Duke U. Comprehensive Cancer Ctr., 1995—2003; with program in genetics and genomics and molecular and cellular biology Duke U.; dir. combinatorial scis. ctr. Duke U. Med. Ctr., 1994—2000; biotech. cons. LipoGen, Inc., BioWhittaker, Inc., Med. and Biol. Labs., Inc., Nagoya, Japan; co-founder SARCO, Inc., Combinatorial Sci. Systems, Inc., ChemCodes, LLC; founder Ribonomics, Inc., Research Triangle Park, NC; bd. dirs. Alpha Vax, Inc.; chmn. bd. sci. counselors NIEHS, NIH; mem. forum on drug disc., devel. & translation Inst. Med. Nat. Acad. Sci. Assoc. editor Virology, 1983-2007, RNA Biology, 2005-; mem. editl. bd. Jour. of Virology, 1985-95, Molecular and Cellular Biology, 1991—2008, Alliance Cellular Signaling; editor Microbiology and Molecular Biology Revs., 1992-2000, editor-in-chief, 2000-05; editor Molecular Diversity, 1995-2003, Jour. Biol. Chemistry, 2003—2008; primary reviewer Jour. Immunology, 1996—. Mem. fellowship com. Arthritis Found., 1990-92, mem. rsch. com., 1990-92. Recipient Faculty Rsch. award Am. Cancer Soc., 1981-86, Devil's Bag award Arthritis Found., 1985-91; Nanaline Duke Faculty Scholar, 1981-84, PEW Scholar in the Biomed. Scis., 1986-90. Fellow Am. Acad. Microbiology; mem. Am. Soc. Virology, Am. Soc. Biochemistry and Molecular Biology, Am. Soc. Microbiology (mem. pub. bd. 2000-05), Ribonucleic Acid Soc., The Henry Kunkel Soc., Ny Acad. Scis. Office: Duke Univ Med Ctr Box 3020 Mol Gen and Microbiol Dept Research Dr/414 Jones Bldg Durham NC 27710 Office Phone: 919-684-5138.

KEENER, GAITHER MCDONALD, JR., lawyer, consumer products company executive; b. Newton, NC, June 15, 1949; BA, Western Carolina U., 1972; JD, Wake Forest U., 1977. Bar: N.C. 1977, U.S. Supreme Ct. 1982. Assoc. counsel McElwee, Hall, & McElwee, 1977-86; sr. corp. counsel Lowe's Companies, Inc., North Wilkesboro, NC, 1986—98, v.p., asst. gen. counsel, sec., 1998—2004, sr. v.p., gen. counsel, sec., 2004—06, sr. v.p., gen. counsel, sec., chief compliance officer, 2006—11, exec. v.p., gen. counsel, sec., chief compliance officer, 2011—. Commr. Wilkes Regional Med. Ctr. With U.S. Marines, 1968-71. Named to N.C. Baseball Hall of Fame, 1995. Mem. N.C. Bar Assn. Office: Lowe's Companies Inc 1000 Lowe's Blvd Mooresville NC 28117*

KEENER, LARRY H., construction executive; Divsn. pres. Palm Harbor Homes, Inc., 1989—94, COO, 1994—97, pres., 1994—, CEO, 1997—, chmn., 2005—. Bd. dirs. Palm Harbor Homes Inc., 1980—94. Office: Palm Harbor Homes Inc Ste 800 15301 Spectrum Dr Ste 500 Addison TX 75001-6425 Office Phone: 972-991-2422. Office Fax: 972-991-5949. Business E-Mail: lkeener@palmharbor.com.

KEESLING, JAMES EDGAR, mathematics professor; b. Indpls., June 26, 1942; s. Fred Edgar and Martha Belle (Grimes) K.; m. Marian Ellen Calley, Jan. 26, 1963; children: James Jr., Marian Esther, Timothy Carl, Ruth Emily. BS in Indsl. Engring., U. Miami, 1964, MS in Math., 1966, PhD in Math., 1968. Asst. prof. math. U. Fla., Gainesville, 1967-71, assoc. prof. math., 1971-75, prof. math., 1975—, chair dept. math., 2008—; pres. pro-tempore Coll. of Liberal Arts and Scis., U. Fla., 1989-90, parliamentarian, 2006—11, chair faculty assembly, 2010—. Vis. faculty U. Ga., 1976-77, U. Utah, 1991-92; vis. lectr. Soc. Indsl. and Applied Math., 1992—; lectr. numerous nat. and internat. conf. in math., 1969—. Mng. editor: Topology and its Applications, 2000—09, bd. advisors: adv. bd. Topology & Its Application, 2009—; editor: Revista Matemática Complutense, 2003—; contbr. articles to profl. jours. Elder, ch. chmn. Creekside Community Ch. (Evangelical Free Ch. of Am.), Gainesville, 1987-90, 94-97, 2001-2003. Recipient Tchg. award U. Fla., 1994, 98. Mem. Am. Math. Soc., Math. Assn. Am., Soc. Indsl. and Applied Math., Tau Beta Pi, Phi Kappa Phi. Home: 710 NE 6th St Gainesville FL 32601-5566 Office: U Fla Dept Math Gainesville FL 32611-8105 Business E-Mail: kees@ufl.edu.

KEETON, JAMES E., dean, surgeon, educator; BA, U. Miss., 1961, MD, 1965. Cert. American Bd. Urology. Residency in gen. surgery and urology U. Miss. Med. Ctr., Jackson, prof. surgery and pediat., various adminstrv. appointments including interim vice chancellor, chief of staff to the vice chancellor and assoc. vice chancellor clin. affairs, vice chancellor health affairs, dean sch. medicine, 2010—; residency in pediatric urology London; pvt. practice Miss., 1970—. Lt. col. med. corps USN. Fellow: American Acad. Pediat. Office: University Miss Med Ctr Sch Medicine LRC Rm U-016 2500 North State St Jackson MS 39216 Office Phone: 601-984-1010. Office Fax: 601-984-1013. Business E-Mail: jkeeton@umc.edu.*

KEEVER, PATRICIA R., state legislator; b. Charlotte, NC, Dec. 20, 1947; children: Jenny Peterken, Betsy Keever. BA, Duke U., 1969; MEd, Western Carolina U., 1979. Mem. Health Ptnrs., Mountain Ctr. for Substance Abuse Prevention; tchr. Fort Bragg Fort Benning, 1969, Matthews Elem. Sch., 1970, Asheville Country Day, 1971—72, Glen Arden Elem. Sch., 1979—81, Carrington Jr. High Sch., 1981—82, Valley Springs Mid.Sch., 1982—83, Venable Elem. Sch., 1983—86, Enka Mid.Sch., 1986—2002; pres. Asheville-Buncombe League of Women Voters, 1977—79; pres., dist. and local chpt. NC Assn. of Educators, 1987—89; county commr., Buncombe County, 1992—2004; chmn. Criminal Justice Partnership Program, 1995—; bd. advisor Canary Coalition, 2003—; bd. dirs. Buncombe County Bd. of Health, 1993—, Regional Water Authority, 2003—, C. of C. Legis. Task Force, 2003—04, United Way, Juvenile Crime Prevention Coun.; mem. Dist. 115 NC House of Representatives, 2011—. Democrat. Unitarian Universalist. Office: 17 Braddock Way Asheville NC 28803 Address: North Carolina House of Representatives 16 W Jones St Room 1317 Raleigh NC 27603-1096 Office Phone: 828-274-0114, 919-733-5746. Business E-Mail: Patsy.Keever@ncleg.net.

KEFFER, JAMES L. (JIM KEFFER), state legislator; b. San Angelo, Tex., Jan. 20, 1953; m. Leslie Bradley Keffer; 3 children. Grad., Tex. Tech U., Lubbock. Republican County Chmn. for Eastland County; pres. EBBA Iron Sales, Inc., Eastland, Albany, Tex., 1988—; mem. Dist. 60 Tex. House of Representatives, 1997—. Recipient Leader Excellence award, Free Market Com., Free Enterprise Polit. Action Com., and several others. Mem.: Am. Waterworks Assn., Am. Foundry Soc., Eastland C. of C., Tex. Assn. Bus., Tex. Cast Metal Assn. (former chmn.). Republican. Office: PO Box 857 Eastland TX 76448 also: Room 1N.12 Capitol PO Box 2910 Austin TX 78768 Office Phone: 800-586-4515, 512-463-0656. Office Fax: 512-478-8805.

KEGEL, WILLIAM GEORGE, mining company executive; b. Pitts., Mar. 15, 1922; s. William G. and Gertrude (Holl) K.; m. Jacqueline Treacy, Feb. 17, 1942; children: Kathy, Danyele, Janice, Jacqueline, William, Madeline, Colleen, Lisa, Brian. Student elec. engring, U. Pitts., 1940-43; LLD (hon.), Ind. U. of Pa., 1986. Mgr. mech. and elec. depts. Lee Norse Co., 1941-50; with Jones & Laughlin Steel Corp., Pitts., 1950-76, gen. mgr. raw materials and traffic, 1975-76; pres. Cerro Marmon Coal Group, 1976-79; pres., chief exec. officer Rochester & Pitt. Coal Co., Indiana, Pa., 1979-88, chmn. bd., 1988-98. Dir. emeritus Savs. and Trust Co. Pa., Indiana. Mem. Indiana (Pa.) Airport Authority, 1980-2001; bd. dirs. Brownsville Gen. Hosp., 1964-71; mem. Centerville Borough Council, 1952-60. Mem. AIME, Coal Mining Inst. Am., Am. Mining Congress (dir.), Pitts. Coal Mining Inst., Duquesne Club, Ind. Country Club, Laurel Valley Country Club. Republican. Roman Catholic. Home: 61 Duck Woods Dr Southern Shores NC 27949 Home Phone: 252-255-1918. E-mail: wgkegel@charter.net, wgk@charter.net.

KEGLEVIC, PAUL, corporate financial executive; married; 3 children. BS in Acctg., Northern Ill. U., 1976. Acctg. positions, mng. ptnr, pacific region & leader N. Am. utilities industry practice Arthur Anderson, 1976—2002; ptnr., leader US utility sector and clients & sector assurance leader PricewaterhouseCoopers, 2002—08; exec. v.p., CFO Energy Future Holdings Corp. (formerly TXU Corp.), Dallas, 2008—. Office: Energy Future Holdings Corp Energy Plz 1601 Bryan St Dallas TX 75201 Office Phone: 214-812-4600. Business E-Mail: paul.keglevic@energyfutureholdings.com.

KEGLEY, CHARLES WILLIAM, JR., political science professor; b. Evanston, Ill., Mar. 5, 1944; s. Charles William Kegley and Elizabeth Euphemia Meck; m. Ann Curry Taylor, Apr. 1, 1966 (div.); 1 child, Mrs. Suzanne, Mitchell Douglas; m. Pamela Ann Holcomb, July 2, 1975 (div.); m. Debra Annette Jump, July 6, 2002. BA, Sch. Internat. Svc. America, 1966; PhD, Syracuse U., 1971. Asst. prof. Sch. Fgn. Svc., Georgetown U., 1971-72, assoc. prof., 1974, prof., 1979; prof., chmn. dept. polit. sci. U. SC, Columbia, 1981—85, dir. Byrnes Internat. Ctr., 1986—88, holder Pearce endowed chair in internat. rels., 1985—2005, disting. Pearce prof. internat. rels. emeritus, 2006—; founding ptnr. Kegly Internat., Inc., 2006—. Vis. prof. U. Tex., 1976; Moses Back Peace prof., Rutgers U., New Brunswick, N.J., 1989, People's U. China, Beijing, 1996, Grad. Inst. Internat. Studies & Devel., Geneva, 2004, bd. trustees, Carnegie Coun. Ethics Internat. Affairs, NY, 1989-; faculty fellow Moynihan Global Affairs Inst., Maxwell Sch., Syracuse U., 2006—. Author: A General Empirical Typology of Foreign Policy Behavior, 1973, El Desafío Multipolar la Política de las Grandes Potencias en el Siglo XXI, 2008; co-author, co-editor (with William Coplin): A Multi-Method Introduction to International Politics: Observation, Explanation and Prescription, 1971, Analyzing International Relations: A Multi-Method Introduction, 1975; co-author: (with Eugene R. Wittkopf) American Foreign Policy: Pattern and Process, 1979, (with Eugene R. Wittkopf and Christopher Jones) 7th edit., 2007, World Politics: Trend and Transformation, 1981, 12th edit., 2009, (with Shannon Lindsey Blanton) 14th edit. rev., 2011, Svetska Politika, 2005; (with Gregory A. Raymond) When Trust Breaks Down: Alliance Norms and World

Politics, 1990, A Multipolar Peace? Great-Power Politics in the 21st Century, 1994, How Nations Make Peace, 1999, From War to Peace: Fateful Decisions in International Politics, 2002, Exorcising the Ghost of Westphalia: Building World Order in the New Millennium, 2002, The Global Future, 2006, 4th edit. 2011, After Iraq: The Imperiled American Imperium, 2007; co-editor: (with Robert W. Gregg) After Vietnam: The Future of American Foreign Policy, 1971; (with Gregory A. Raymond, Robert M. Rood, Richard A. Skinner) International Events and the Comparative Analysis of Foreign Policy, 1975; (with Patrick J. McGowan) Challenges to America: U.S. Foreign Policy in the 1980's, 1979, Threats, Weapons, and Foreign Policy, 1980, The Political Economy of Foreign Policy, 1981, Foreign Policy: USA/USSR, 1983; (with Eugene R. Wittkopf) Perspectives on American Foreign Policy, 1983, The Global Agenda: Issues and Perspectives, 1984, 6th edit., 2001 (with Patrick McGowan) Foreign Policy and the Modern World System, 1983; (with Eugene R. Wittkopf) The Nuclear Reader: Strategy, Weapons, War, 1985, 2nd edit., 1989; (with Charles F. Hermann and James N. Rosenau) New Directions in the Study of Foreign Policy, 1987, (with Eugene R. Wittkopf) The Domestic Sources of American Foreign Policy, 1988, (with Kenneth Schwab) After the Cold War: Questioning the Morality of Nuclear Deterrence, 1991, (with Eugene R. Wittkopf) The Future of American Foreign Policy, 1992, 2nd edit., 1994; editor: The Long Postwar Peace: Contending Explanations and Projections, 1990, International Terrorism: Characteristics, Causes, Controls, 1990, Controversies in International Relations Theory: Realism and the Neoliberal Challenge, 1995, The New Global Terrorism, 2003; contbr. chpts. to books, articles to profl. jours. Bd. trustees Carnegie Coun. for Ethics in Internat. Affairs, 1992-98, 2000-. Recipient Disting. Alumni award Am. U., 1984; R.M. Davis scholar, 1962-66; Maxwell fellow, 1968-69, 70-71; NY State Regents fellow, 1969-70, Moynihon Faculty Rsch. fellow Syracuse U., 2006-; Fulbright sr. scholar, 1978, Russell rsch. awardee in humanities and social scis., 1982. Mem. Am. Polit. Sci. Assn., Am. Soc. Internat. Law, Am. Soc. Advancement Sci., Internat. Polit. Sci. Assn., Internat. Studies Assn. (assoc. dir. 1980-84, pres. 1993-94), Peace Sci. Soc., Peace Rsch. Soc., So. Polit. Sci. Assn., Pi Sigma Alpha, Omicron Delta Kappa, Delta Tau Kappa, Alpha Tau Omega. Home: 35 Veranda Ln Blythewood SC 29016-7602 Office: Kegley Internat Inc 1289 Rose Hill Rd Wytheville VA 24382-4650 Office Phone: 803-743-7834, 803-743-7834. Personal E-mail: jumpkegs@aol.com.

KEHLBECK, JOSEPH H., software developer, consultant; b. Clifton, NJ, Sept. 14, 1926; s. Joseph John and Elizabeth Harriet (Lockhoff) K.; m. Mary Kathryn Russell, Nov. 15, 1957; 1 child, Keith Alan. BS in Engring., State U. Iowa, 1950; MBA in Fin., Rutgers U., 1954. Registered profl. engr., Calif. Various positions Gen. Electric, 1952-69, mgr. mfg. engring. Louisville, 1969, mgr. mfg. Trenton, N.J., 1969-72, Louisville, 1972-77, mgr. material resource ops., 1977—87, gen. mgr. internat. purchasing Bridgeport, Conn., 1988; cons., software developer Kehlbeck & Assocs., Prospect, Ky., 1988—2005; v.p. Strategies Skyway USA, 2007—09. Mem. adv. bd. On Display, San Ramon, Calif., 1998-99, Skyway USA, Louisville, 2007; bd. dirs. Philippine Appliance Co., Manila, 1979-85; mayor City of Prospect, 2006-. Author: Production Leveling, 1959. Mem. Mayor's adv. bd. City of Prospect, Ky., 2003, ordinance bd., 2004; bd. dirs. Mercer City Hosp., NJ, 1970—71. Paratrooper US Army, 1943—45, lt. res. Corps. of Engrs. US Army, 1946—52. Recipient award Order of Engrs., 1977, Craigmyle Pub. Svc. award City of Prospect, Ky., 2006. Fellow Inst. Indsl. Engrs. (pres. 1977), Hunting Creek Country Club (bd. dirs.), Home Owners Assn., Shriners, Tau Beta Pi. Avocations: golf, tennis. Office: 7812 Cedar Ridge Ct Prospect KY 40059-9491 Personal E-mail: kehlbeck@aol.com.

KEIG, LOWELL ADAMS, lawyer; b. Dallas, Sept. 5, 1962; s. Edward Quincy Adams and LoRita Jane (Stevens) K.; m. Elizabeth Brophy Johnson, May 13, 1989; children: Logan Edward, Eden Katherine, Trevor BS, Trinity U., San Antonio, 1985; JD, U. Tex., 1988. Bar: Tex. 1988, U.S. Dist. Ct. (we. dist.) Tex. 1989, U.S. Dist. Ct. (so. dist.) Tex. 1992. Assoc. Law Offices of Elliott Flood, Austin, 1988-89, Smith, Barship, Stoffer & Millsap, San Antonio, 1989-92; asst. dist. atty. Bexar County Dist. Atty.'s Office, San Antonio, 1992-94; ptnr. Keig & Thomas, LLP, San Antonio, 1994; pvt. practice San Antonio, 1994-97; of counsel Sessions & Sessions, L.C., San Antonio, 1997—2000; dep. chief Antitrust & Civil Medicaid Fraud divsn. Office Atty. Gen., State of Tex., Austin, 2000—05; gen. counsel Youth & Family Centered Services Inc. (YFCS), Austin, 2005—. Barrister Am. Inns Ct. Contbr. articles to profl. jours. Pres.-elect nat. alumni bd. Trinity U., 1997-98. Mem. Tex. Young Lawyers Assn. (dir. 1993-95, 96-98, Pres.'s award of merit 1992-93, 96-97, Outstanding Dir. 1993-94), San Antonio Young Lawyers Assn. (pres. 1993-94, Outstanding Young Lawyer award 1994), San Antonio Bar Assn. (dir. 1994-96). Episcopalian. Office: Youth & Family Centered Services Inc (YFCS) 1120 Capital of Texas Highway S Bldg 1 Ste 200 Austin TX 78746 Office Phone: 512-327-1119. Office Fax: 512-327-4576.

KEILLER, JAMES BRUCE, clergyman, dean; b. Racine, Wis., Nov. 21, 1938; s. James Allen and Grace (Modder) Keiller; m. Darsel Lee Bundy, Feb. 8, 1959; 1 child, Susanne Elizabeth. Diploma, Beulah Heights Bible Coll., 1957; BA, William Carter Coll., 1963, EdD (hon.), 1973; LLB, Blackstone Sch. Law, 1964; MA, Evang. Theol. Sem., 1965, BD, 1966, ThD, 1968; MA in Ednl. Adminstrn., Atlanta U., 1977; degree, Nat. Tax Tng. Sch., Monsey, NY, 1986; EdS, Ga. State U., 1987; DD, Heritage Bible Coll., 2001; postgrad., Atlanta Law Sch., Harvard U., 2001—03, North Ctrl. U., Ariz., 2005—09. Ordained to ministry Internat. Pentecostal Assemblies, 1957, advanced studies in higher edn. leadership,Northcentral U. 2009. Pastor Maranatha Temple, Boston, 1957-58, Midland Full Gospel Ch., Mich., 1958-64; v.p. acad. dean Beulah Heights U., Atlanta, 1964—, trustee, 1964—92, v.p., acadmic dean, 1964—2013; nat. dir. youth and Sunday sch. dept. Internat. Pentecostal Assemblies, 1958-64, sr. advisor to pres., Instl. and Corp. Affairs, 2014—, dir. world missions Atlanta, 1964-76; missionary editor Bridegroom's Messenger, 1964—2007; dir. global missions Internat. Pentecostal Ch. of Christ, 1976—2007, mem. exec. com., 1976—2007; mem. exec. bd. Mt. Paran Christian Sch., 1980-91; ordained min. Evang. Ch. Alliance, 2008—. Named Alumnus of Yr., William Carter Coll., 1965. Mem.: ASCD, Kappa Delta Pi, Assn. Coll. Adminstrv. Profls., Acad. Polit. Sci., Assn. Coll. Adminstrn. Profls., Nat. Assn. Alternative Cert., Intercollegiate Studies Inst., Am. Bd. Master Educators (cert.), Am. Inst. Parliamentarians, Coll. of Tchrs., Little Mountain Village Condo Assn. (bd. dirs. 1994—), So. Accrediting Assn. Bible Colls. (exec. sec. 1970—93), Evang. Theol. Soc., Kiwanis (lt. gov. Ga. dist. 1986—87, chmn. human values state com. Ga. dist. 1989—90). Republican. Home: 21A Little Mountain Vlg Ellenwood GA 30294-3337 Office: Beulah Heights Univ 892 Berne St SE Atlanta GA 30316-1873 Office Phone: 404-627-2681 ext. 102. Business E-Mail: james.keiller@beulah.org.

KEISER, BERNHARD EDWARD, engineering executive, communications engineer, consultant; b. Richmond Heights, Mo., Nov. 14, 1928; s. Bernhard and Helen Barbara Julia (Buerkle) K.; m. Florence Evelyn Keiser, Jan. 22, 1955; children: Sandra, Carol, Nancy, Linda, Paul. BSEE, Washington U., St. Louis, 1950, MSEE, 1951, DScEE, 1953. Registered profl. engr., Va. Mgr. plans and programs RCA, Cape Canaveral, Fla., 1964-67, adminstr. advanced system planning Moorestown, NJ, 1967-69; v.p., tech. dir. Page Communication Engring., Washington, 1969-70; dir. advanced engring. Atlantic Rsch. Corp., Alexandria, Va., 1971-72; dir. anaylsis Fairchild Space & Electronics Co., Germantown, Md., 1972-75; pres. Keiser Engring., Inc., Vienna, Va., 1975—2003. Author: EMI Control in Aerospace Systems, 1979, Principles of Electromagnetic Compatibility, 1979, rev. edit. 1987, Broad band Coding, Modulation and Transmission Engineering, 1989, rev. edit. 1994; co-author: Digital Telephony and Network Integration, 1985, rev. edit. 1995. Fellow IEEE (chmn. No. Va. sect. 1980-81), Washington Acad. Scis., Radio Club Am. Republican. Lutheran. Home and Office: 2046 Carrhill Rd Vienna VA 22181-2917

KEISER, EDMUND DAVIS, JR., biologist, educator; b. Appalachia, Va., Feb. 18, 1934; s. Edmund Davis and Ora Elizabeth (Wade) K.; m. Alice Sue Tucker, Sept. 10, 1982; children: Mark Edmund, Julie Ann; stepchildren: Louis King III, Jenifer King. BA, So. Ill. U., Carbondale, 1956, MS, 1961; PhD in Zoology, La. State U., Baton Rouge, 1967. Tchr. sci. Kinmundy High Sch., Ill., 1956-57, Mt. Vernon Twp. Sch. Dist., Ill., 1957-58; dist. sci. coordinator Freeburg Sch. Dist. 70, Freeburg, Ill., 1958-62; instr. biology La Salle-Peru-Oglesby Jr. Coll., La Salle, Ill., 1962-64; teaching asst. La. State U., Baton Rouge, 1964-66; asst. prof. U. Southwestern La., Lafayette, 1966-70, assoc. prof., 1970-75, prof. biology, 1976, mem. coun. grad. coords., 1973-76; prof. biology U. Miss., Oxford, 1976—2005, 2007—, chmn. dept. University, 1976-87, prof. emeritus, chmn. emeritus, 2005—. Rsch. assoc. Gulf South Rsch. Inst., 1972—74; mem. Atchafalaya River Basin Rsch. Coun., 1972—74; exec. coun., state dir. sci. tchg. La. Acad. Scis., 1972—74; exec. coun. Gopher Tortoise Soc., 1979—81; commr. Miss. Dept. Wildlife Conservation, 1978—79, 1980—84, chmn., 1983—84; cons. U.S. Fish and Wildlife Svc., 2001—, U.S. Army Corps of Engrs., 2001—, Mississippi Dept. Wildlife, Fisheries and Parks, 2007—; owner and cons. Ecol. Cons., Field Assoc. Miss. Mus. Natural Sci., 2007—. Mem. Miss. Wildlife Heritage Com., 1980—84, Gov.'s Select Com. on Radioactivity and Radioactive Waste Depository, 1979—80; field assoc. Miss. Mus. Natural Sci., 2001—. Recipient numerous grants; Disting. Prof. award U. Southwestern La., 1973; Govs. Meritorious Service award State of Miss., 1979; citation for outstanding sci. teaching Nat. Sci. Tchrs. Assn.-Ill. Supt. Public Instrn., 1962 Fellow Explorers Club; mem. Soc. for Study Amphibians and Reptiles, Golden Key Honor Soc., Sigma Xi (chpt. pres. 1976, 79-80), Beta Beta Beta, Phi Eta Sigma, Phi Kappa Phi. Home and Office: Ecological Consulting 211 Saint Andrews Cir Oxford MS 38655-2518 Business E-Mail: bykeiser@olemiss.edu.

KEISER, PETER B., food service executive; Attended, Babson Coll., Babson Pk., Mass., 1989—93. Mktg. profl. Friendly's; sr. mktg. mgr. Bob Evans Farms, Inc.; v.p. mktg. Cracker Barrel Old Country Store, Inc., 2005—. Bd. dirs. Jr. Achievement Mid. Tenn. Office: Cracker Barrel Old Country Store Inc 305 Hartmann Dr Lebanon TN 37087 Office Phone: 615-444-5533. Office Fax: 615-443-9818.

KEITH, TOBY (TOBY KEITH COVEL), musician, producer; b. Clinton, Okla., July 8, 1961; s. H.K. and Joan Covel; m. Tricia Keith, Mar. 24, 1984; children: Shelly Reeve, Krystal, Stelen Keith Covel. Degree (hon.), Villanova U., Pa. Worked in oil industry; mem. The Easy Money Band; defensive end Okla. City Drillers, minor league, semi-pro football team, Okla. Outlaws, US Football League (USFL) team; signed with Mercury Records, Nashville, 1984—99, DreamWorks, Nashville, 1999; founder Show Dog Nashville Records, 2005—. Singer: (albums) Toby Keith, 1993, Christmas to Christmas, 1995, Boomtown, 1995, Blue Moon, 1996, Dream Walkin', 1997, Greatest Hits, Vol. 1, 1998, How Do You Like Me Now?, 1999 (Album of Yr., Acad. Country Music Awards, 2000), Pull My Chain, 2001, Unleased, 2002 (Favorite Country Album, American Music Awards, 2003), 20th Century Masters- The Millennium, 2003, Shock 'n Y'all, 2003 (Album of Yr., Acad. Country Music Awards, 2003, Best Country Album, Am. Music Awards, 2004), Greatest Hits 2, 2004, Honkytonk University, 2005, White Trash with Money, 2006, Big Dog Daddy, 2007, A Classic Christmas, 2007, Love Me If You Can, 2007, That Don't Make Me a Bad Guy, 2008, American Ride, 2009, Bullets in the Gun, 2010, Clancy's Tavern, 2011, Hope On the Rocks, 2012, Drinks After Work, 2013, (songs) Should've Been A Cowboy, 1993 (Most Played Song of Decade in the 90's, Billboard), How Do You Like Me Now?, 2000 (Named Most Played Song of 2000, Billboard), Whiskey Girl, 2003 (Hottest Video of Yr., Country Music TV Music Awards, 2005), As Good As I Once Was, 2005 (Music Video of Yr., Country Music Assn. Awards, 2005), Red Solo Cup, 2011 (Music Video of Yr., Country Music Assn. Awards, 2012, Video of Yr., Acad. Country Music Awards, 2012); actor: (films) Broken Bridges, 2006; writer, prodr., actor: Beer for My Horses, 2008 (Tex Ritter award, Acad. Country Music, 2009). Recipient Country Album Artist of Yr., Country Music Assn., 2005; named Entertainer of Yr., Acad. Country Music Awards, 2002, 2003, Top Male Vocalist, 2000, 2003, Favorite Male Country Artist, Am. Music Awards, 2004, 2006, Country Artist of Yr., Billboard Music Awards, 2005. Achievements include invited by George W. Bush to addresss at MacDill Air Force Base in Tampa, Fla., site of US Cent. Command and headquarters of Gen. Tommy Franks; a super-patriotic response to Sept. 11th that became one of country's most highly charged political statements; songwriting, 12 of his 16 #1 hits have been self-penned; radio airplay, 8 Billboard country #1's and eight R&R country #1's from his DreamWorks Records alone; sales of more than $13.5 million. Office: c/o TKO Artist Management 2303 21st Ave South 3rd Fl Nashville TN 37212 Office Phone: 615-383-5017.*

KEITT, ANDREW WANNAMAKER, history professor; b. Boston, July 2, 1962; s. Alan Seaver and Ruth Morris Keitt; m. Aileen Elizabeth Guerrero, Nov. 16, 2001; 1 child, Kurtis Joens. BA cum laude, Duke U., 1985; MA, U. Calif., Berkeley, 1992, PhD, 1998. Assoc. prof. U. Ala., Birmingham, Ala., 1999—. Named Ala. Prof. of Yr., Carnegie Found. for Advancement of Tchg. and Coun. for Advancement and Support of Edn., 2010. Office: University of Alabama at Birmingham HHB 360N 1401 University Blvd Birmingham AL 35294-1152 Office Phone: 205-934-7083, 205-934-7083. E-mail: akeitt@uab.edu.

KELEHEAR, CAROLE MARCHBANKS SPANN, legal assistant; b. Morehead City, NC, Oct. 2, 1945; d. William Blythe and Gladys Ophelia (Wilson) Marchbanks; m. Henry M. Spann, June 5, 1966 (div. 1978); children: Lisa Carole Spann, Elaine Mabry Spann; m. Zachariah Lockwood Kelehear, Sept. 15, 1985. Student, Winthrop Coll., 1963-64; grad., Draughon's Bus. Coll., 1965; cert. in med. terminology, Greenville Tech. Edn. Coll., 1972; grad., Millie Lewis Modeling Sch. Office mgr. S.C. Appalachian Adv. Commn., Greenville, 1965-68, Wood-Bergheer & Co., Newport Beach and Palm Springs, Calif., 1970-72, Dr. James B. Knowles, Greenville, 1977-78, Constangy, Brooks & Smith, Columbia, 1978-83; asst. to Dr. J. Ernest Lathem Lathem & McCoy, P.A., Greenville, 1972-75; asst. to Gov. Robert E. McNair, McNair, Konduros, Corley, Singletary and Dibble Law Firm, Columbia, SC, 1975-77; legal asst. to sr. ptnr. William L. Bethea Jr., Bethea, Jordan & Griffin, P.A., Hilton Head Island, 1983—88; legal asst. Rajko D. Medenica, MD, PhD, 1988—95; adminstr. Dibble Law Offices, Columbia, 1995-96; asst. to mng. dir. Steve A. Matthews and COO Larry B. Mack Haynsworth Sinkler Boyd, P.A., Columbia, 1997—2007; v.p., sec. H.A.P.I. Place Tree Farm, Estill, SC. Notary pub.; vol. Ladies aux. Greenville Gen. Hosp., 1966—72, S. Coast Hosp., Laguna Beach, Calif., 1973, St. Francis Hosp., Greenville, 1974—76, Hilton Head Hosp., 1983—92. Mem.: NAFE, Am. Soc. Notaries, Am. Bus. Women's Assn., Profl. Women's Assn. Hilton Head Island, Hilton Head Hosp. Aux., Beta Sigma Phi.

KELLEHER, HERBERT DAVID, retired air transportation executive, board member; b. Camden, NJ, Mar. 12, 1931; s. Harry and Ruth (Moore) Kelleher; m. Joan Negley, Sept. 9, 1955; children: Julie, Michael, Ruth, David. BA cum laude, Wesleyan U., Middletown, Conn., 1953; LLB cum laude, NYU, 1956. Bar: NJ 1957, Tex. 1962. Clk. NJ Supreme Ct., 1956—59; assoc. Lum, Biunno & Tompkins, Newark, 1959—61; ptnr. Mathews, Nowlin, Macfarlane & Barrett, San Antonio, 1961—69; sr. ptnr. Oppenheimer, Rosenberg, Kelleher & Wheatley, Inc., San Antonio, 1969—81; co-founder, gen. counsel, chmn. Southwest Airlines Co., Dallas, 1967—81, chmn., pres., CEO, 1981—2001, exec. chmn., 2001—08, chmn. emeritus, 2008—. Bd. dirs. Fed. Res. Bank Dallas, 2007—, dep. chmn., 2009—10, chmn., 2011—. Recipient Tony Jannus award for outstanding leadership in comml. aviation industry, Tony Jannus Disting. Aviation Soc., 1993, Bower award for Bus. Leadership, Franklin Inst., 2003, L. Welch Pogue award for lifetime achievement in aviation, Aviation Week & Space Tech. mag., 2005, Disting. Pub. Svc. Medal, US Dept. Homeland Security, Wings Club Disting. Achievement award; named CEO of the Century, Tex. Monthly mag.; named one of History's Top Three CEOs, Chief Exec. mag.; named to US Bus. Hall of Fame, Jr. Achievement Worldwide, 2004, Advt. Hall of Fame, American Advt. Fedn., 2011, San Diego Aerospace Hall of Fame, Tex. Labor Mgmt. Hall of Fame, Nat. Aviation Hall of Fame, Southwest Advt. Hall of Fame, Dallas Bus. Hall of Fame, Tex. Bus. Hall of Fame. Mem.: Transport Workers Union (hon. life), Delta Kappa Epsilon.

KELLEHER, PATRICK B., insurance company executive; B, Franklin & Marshall Coll. Fin. mgmt. positions Sun Life Assurance Canada, 1980—92; fin. mgmt. positions through CFO Manulife Fin., 1992—98; exec. v.p., CFO Transamerica Reinsurance, Charlotte, NC, 1998—2006; sr. v.p., CFO Genworth Financial, Inc., Richmond, Va., 2007—11, exec. v.p. retirement & protection segment, 2011—. Fellow: Canadian Soc. Actuaries, Soc. Actuaries; mem.: CGA Assn. Canada. Office: Genworth Fin Inc 6620 W Broad St Richmond VA 23230

KELLER, ANDREW, advertising executive; Grad., Washington & Lee U., Lexington, Va. Art. dir. Crispin Porter & Bogusky, Miami, Fla., 1998—2000, assoc. creative dir., 2000—03, v.p., 2001—10, creative dir., 2003—05, exec. creative dir., 2005—08, co-creative dir., 2008—10, CEO, 2010—. Office: Crispin Porter & Bogusky 3390 Mary St Miami FL 33133

KELLER, GARY, real estate company executive, writer; m. Mary Pfluger; 1 child, John Christian. BBA in Mktg. and Real Estate, Baylor U., 1979. Realtor JB Goodwin Co., Houston, 1979—83; founder Keller Williams Realty Inc., Austin, Tex., 1983—; chmn. bd. Keller Williams Realty Internat. Mem. Austin Bd. Realtors, Tex.; bd. dir. Austin Multiple Listing Svc., Tex.; invited spkr. in the field. Author: Your First Home: The Proven Path to Home Ownership, 2008, Shift: How Top Real Estate Agents Tackle Tough Times, 2008 (named to The Wall Street Journal Business, New York Times, and USA Today Bestseller Lists); co-author: The Millionaire Real Estate Agent, 2004 (named to BusinessWeek Best Seller List), The Millionaire Real Estate Investor, 2005 (named to The New York Times and BusinessWeek Best Seller Lists), Flip: How to Find, Fix, and Sell Houses for Profit, 2007, The One Thing: The Surprisingly Simple Truth Behind Extraordinary Results, 2013. Bd. dir. Jaycees, Austin, Austin (Tex.) Ctr. Battered Women. Named Ernst & Young's Entrepreneur of the Year for Central Texas, Second Most Influential Person in Real Estate Industry, REALTOR Mag., 2003; named one of Five Most Admired People, REAL Trends Magazine, 2000, 100 Most Influential Real Estate Leaders, Inman News, 2006; finalist Inc. Magazine's Entrepreneur of the Year award, 2004. Mem.: Tex. Assn. Realtors, Nat. Assn. Realtors (bd. dirs. 2000—). Avocations: guitar, piano, reading, hiking, travel, snow skiing, horseback riding, fly fishing, going to movies and rock concerts, football, basketball. Office: Keller Williams Realty Inc 1221 South Mopac Expressway Ste 400 Austin TX 78746 Office Phone: 512-327-3070.

KELLER, JOHN WARREN, lawyer; b. Niagara Falls, Aug. 6, 1954; s. Joseph and Edith Lilian (Kilvington) K.; m. Sandra D. Hubbard, Dec. 18, 1981; children: Sean, Christopher. BA, Rider U., 1976; JD, Coll. William and Mary, 1979. Bar: Ky. 1980. Staff atty. Appalachian Rsch. & Def. Fund Ky., Inc., Barbourville, 1979-82; assoc. F. Preston Farmer Law Offices, London, Ky., 1982-88; ptnr. Farmer, Keller & Kelley, London, 1988-91, Taylor, Keller, Dunaway & Tooms, London, 1991—2010, Lexington, Ky., 1991—2010, Taylor, Keller, Oswald, 2010—. Mem. Fla. Adv. Com. on Arson Prevention, 1990—; chmn. bd. dirs. Appalachian Rsch. & Def. Fund Ky., 1994-96; founder, chmn. bd. dirs. Ky. Lawyers for Legal Svcs. to the Poor. Contbg. editor: ABA Annotations to Homeowner's Policy, 3rd edit., 1995, ABA Bad Faith Annotations, 2d edit., 2001. Pres. Access to Justice Found., 1996—; bd. dirs. Christian Ch. in Ky., 1994—98; elder First Christian Ch., London, 1994—97, 2002—, chmn. bd. elders, 2002—03. Recipient Access to Justice award Ky. Legal Svcs. Programs, 1995, Outstanding Svc. award Ky. chpt. Nat. Soc. Profl. Ins. Investigators, 2000. Fellow: Ky. Bar Found. (bd. dirs. 2000—, pres. 2006—07); mem.: ABA (vice chair property ins. law com. 1992—97), Nat. Soc. Profl. Ins. Investigators (bd. dirs. 2001—05, pres. 2004, F. Lee Brininger award 2004), Laurel County Bar Assn. (pres. 1992—93), Ky. Bar Assn. (bd. govs. 1996—2002, Donated Legal Svcs. award 2001), The Honorable Order of Ky. Cols. Office: Taylor Keller & Oswald 1306 W 5th St London KY 40741-1615 also: Hamburg Place Office Park 1795 Alysheba Way Ste 2102 Lexington KY 40509 Home Phone: 859-264-1181; Office Phone: 606-878-8844.

KELLER, MICHELLE M., state supreme court justice; d. Richard Meier; m. James Keller; children: Brenna, Olivia. Grad. in psychology, Northern Ky. U., 1985, JD, 1990. Bar: Ky., US Dist Ct. (ea. dist. Ky.), US Supreme Ct. Asst. county pros.; atty. Arnzen, Wentz, Molloy, Laber and Storm; judge divsn. 1 Ky. Ct. Appeals, 2006—13; justice 6th dist. Ky. Supreme Ct., 2013—. Chairwoman emeritus Ky. Pers. Bd. Named an Outstanding Woman of Northern Ky., 2012. Mem.: ABA (mem. ethics and profl. responsibility judges adv. com.). Office: Kentucky Supreme Ct Kenton County Justice Ctr 230 Madison Ave Ste 821 Covington KY 41011 Office Phone: 859-291-9966.

KELLER, NADYA CLARK, retired biochemistry educator, researcher; b. St. Francis, Kans., July 28, 1933; d. Albert Vernon and Lois Beatrice (Needles) Clark; m. Karl Ernest Keller, Feb. 13, 1954 (div. Oct. 1965); children: Karen Sue Keller Searight, Kevin Dean. AB, Ft. Hays U., 1965; PhD, U. Okla., 1970. Dir. metabolic lab. Cornell U. Med. Ctr./N.Y. Hosp., NYC, 1970—73; prof. biochemistry Northwestern State U., Natchitoches, La., 1973—2000, Richard Lounsbery prof. of chemistry, 1994-2000; ret., 2000. Founding mem. La. Scholar's Coll. for Academically Gifted Students, Northwestern State Univ. La., Natchitoches, United States, 1987—. Contbr. articles to profl. jours. Mem. AAAS, Am. Chem. Soc., La. Acad. Scis. (pres-elect 1992-93, pres 1993-95, editor newsletter 1995-97), Sigma Xi (pres. local chpt. 1974). Personal E-mail: nlckeller@suddenlink.net.

KELLER, RANDAL JOSEPH, toxicology educator; b. Salem, Ind., Nov. 22, 1957; s. Frank Joseph and Virginia Francis (Barrett) K.; m. Pamela Marie Stroman, Sept. 17, 1994. BA, Eisenhower Coll., Seneca Falls, NY, 1979; MS, Utah State U., 1984, PhD, 1988. Cert. indsl. hygienist; cert. safety profl.; diplomate Am. Bd. Toxicology. Postdoctoral fellow Nat. Ctr. Toxicology Rsch., Jefferson, Ark., 1988-90; instr. U. Ark. for Med. Scis., Little Rock, 1990-91, coord. occupl. and environ. health program, 1991-96; assoc. prof. dept. occupl. safety and health Murray (Ky.) State U., 1996—. Peer reviewer Ctr. for Indoor Air Rsch., 1995—. Contbr. articles to profl. jours. Rsch. grantee U.S. EPA, Washington, 1993-96, NIOSH, Morgantown, W.Va., 1993-95. Fellow Am. Acad. Indsl. Hygiene; mem. Am. Indsl. Hygiene Assn. (pres. elect. Ark. sect. 1993-94, pres. 1994-95), Am. Conf. Govt. Indsl. Hygienists, Am. Soc. Safety Engrs., Am. Soc. Toxicology (1st pl. award metals splty. sect. 1986). Republican. Avocations: running, reading. Office: Murray State U Dept Occupl Safety and Health 157 Industry and Tech Ctr Murray KY 42071-3347 Home: 1305 Olive Blvd Murray KY 42071 Office Phone: 270-809-6655. Business E-Mail: randal.keller@murraystate.edu.

KELLER, SARA LEE, communications executive; BA cum laude, Wells Coll.; JD, Villanova U., LLM in Taxation. Ptnr. Wolf Block Solis-Cohen; dep. gen. counsel DVI Fin. Solutions; assoc. gen. counsel Express Fin. Solutions, 2001—05; ptnr. corp. practice Freeborn and Peters LLP, 2005—07; sr. v.p., gen. counsel, sec. The Trustmark Companies, Chgo., 2007—11; exec. v.p., gen. counsel Clear Channel Outdoor, 2011—. Bd. dirs. Health Fitness Corp. Mem.: ABA. Office: Clear Channel Outdoor 200 E Basse Rd San Antonio TX 78209 Office Phone: 210-832-3700.

KELLER, THOMAS FRANKLIN, business administration educator; b. Greenwood, SC, Sept. 22, 1931; s. Cleaveland Alonzo and Helen (Seago) K.; m. Margaret Neel Query, June 15, 1956; children: Thomas Crafton (dec.), Neel McKay, John Caldwell. AB, Duke U., 1953; MBA, U. Mich., 1957, PhD, 1960; HHD (hon.), Clemson U., 1987. CPA, N.C. Mem. faculty Fuqua Sch. Bus. Duke U., Durham, N.C., 1959—, assoc. prof., 1962-67, prof., 1967-74, R.J. Reynolds prof., 1974—2004, chmn. dept. mgmt. scis., 1974-96, vice provost, 1971-72, dean Fuqua Sch. Bus., 1974-96; dean Fuqua Sch. Bus. Europe, Frankfurt, 1999-2001; dean emeritus Fuqua Sch. of Bus., 2004—; prof. emeritus R.J. Reynolds, 2004—. Mem. editl. bd. Duke U. Press, 1970-87; vis. assoc. prof. Carnegie Mellon U., 1966-67, U. Wash., Seattle, 1963-64; cons. to govt. and industry; Fulbright-Hays lectr., Australia, 1975; bd. dirs. Wendy's Internat., Dublin, Ohio, Biogen Idec, Cambridge, Mass, 2008; dir. Ft. Dake, Mus. Life & Sci., Durham Libr. Found., NC Mus. Life Sci., The Forest at Duke. Author: Accounting for Corporate Income Taxes, 1961, Intermediate Accounting, 1963, 68, 74, Advanced Accounting, 1966, Financial Accounting Theory vol. 1, 1964, 73, 84, vol. 2, 1969, Earnings or Cash Flows: An Experiment on Functional Fixation and the Valuation of the Firm, 1979; editor: monographs Financial Information Needs of Security Analysts, 1977, The Impact of Accounting Research on Practice and Disclosure, 1978; contbr. articles to profl. jours. Elder Presbyn. Ch.; With AUS, 1953-55. Recipient Outstanding Educator award, N.C. Assn. CPA's, 1997, Univ. medal, Duke Univ., 2001; fellow Haskins and Sells Found., U. Mich., 1959, Ford Found., Duke U., 1960, 1961. Mem. AICPA, Am. Acctg. Assn. (v.p. 1967-68, editor jour. 1972-75), N.C. Assn. CPAs, Fin. Execs. Inst., University Club, Phi Beta Kappa, Phi Kappa Sigma, Beta Gamma Sigma, Alpha Kappa Psi. Avocations: hiking, fishing, reading, sailing. Office: Duke U Fuqua Sch Bus Box 90120 Durham NC 27708-0120 Office Phone: 919-660-8045. Business E-Mail: tfk1@duke.edu.

KELLERMANNS, FRANZ WILLI, management consultant, educator; PhD, U. Conn., Storrs, 2003. Assoc. prof. mgmt. Miss. State U., 2003—. Assoc. editor, family bus. rev. Contbr. articles to profl. jours.

KELLEY, ALLEN CHARLES, economist, educator; b. Everett, Wash., Sept. 5, 1937; s. Charles Edward and Velma L. (Allen) K.; m. Patty Ann Cochran, June 20, 1959; children: Brian Allen, Mark Andrew, Michael Charles. Student, Linfield Coll., 1955-57; AB, Stanford U., 1959, PhD, 1964. Vis. research fellow Australian Nat. U., 1962-63; cons. Rand Corp., 1962-67; acting asst. prof. Stanford U., 1963-64; faculty U. Wis., Madison, 1964-72, prof., 1970-72; prof. econs. Duke U., Durham, NC, 1972-81, James B. Duke prof., 1981—, chmn. dept., 1973-80; asso. dir. Center for Demographic Studies, 1973—. Vis. prof. Monash U., Melbourne, Australia, 1970-71; Esmee Fairbairn research prof. Herriot Watt U., Edinburgh, Scotland, 1978; research scholar Internat. Inst. Applied Systems Analysis, Laxenburg, Austria, 1979 Author: (with J.G. Williamson and R.J. Cheetham) Dualistic Economic Development, 1972, (with B.A. Weisbrod et al.) Disease and Economic Development, (with J.G. Williamson) Lessons from Japanese Development - An Analytical Economic History, 1974, The Professor's Guide to TIPS, 1975, (with R.M. Schmidt) The User's Guide to TIPS, 1975, TIPS Program Manual, 1976, (with J.G. Williamson) Modeling Urbanization and Economic Growth, 1980, (with A. Khalifa and M.E. El-Khorazaty) Population and Development in Rural Egypt, 1982; mem. editorial bd. Jour. Econ. Edn, 1973—; Contbr. articles, revs. to profl. jours. Scholar, fellow Weyerhaeuser Co., 1955-59; Scholar, fellow Ford Found., 1961-62; Scholar, fellow Earhart Found., 1959-61; Scholar, fellow Social Sci. Research Council, 1962-63; Richard I. Downing fellow econs. U. Melbourne, 1987-88; grantee Carnegie Found., 1964-65; grantee Exxon Edn. Found., 1965-67, 68-70, 71-74; grantee Ford Found., 1973-79; grantee Nat. Inst. Edn., 1974-75; grantee NSF, 1966-68; grantee Rockefeller Found., 1967-69; grantee Sloan Found., 1969-73, 79—; co-recipient Arthur Cole prize Econ. History Assn., 1972. Mem. Am. Econ. Assn. (chmn. com. econ. edn. 1978—), So. Econ. Assn. (v.p. 1981-82), Internat. Union for Sci. Study Population, Population Assn. Am., Joint Council on Econ. Edn. (trustee 1978—, exec. com. 1978—), Phi Beta Kappa. Office: Duke U Econs Dept Durham NC 27708 Home: 328 Cedar Club Cir Chapel Hill NC 27517-7211

KELLEY, BRIAN, musician; b. Ormond Bch., Fla. m. Brittney Marie Cole, Dec. 16, 2013. Attended, Fla State U., Daytona State Coll.; degree, Belmont U., Nashville. Co-founder, band mem. Florida Georgia Line, 2011—. Musician: (albums) Here's to the Good Times, 2012, (songs) Cruise, 2012 (Duo Video of Yr., Breakthrough Video of Yr., CMT Music Awards, 2013, Single of Yr., Country Music Assn. Awards, 2013, Single of Yr. (version featuring Nelly), American Music Awards, 2013). Named New Vocal Duo or Group of Yr., Acad. Country Music Awards, 2013, New Artist of Yr., 2013, Vocal Duo of Yr., Country Music Assn. Awards, 2013, Acad. Country Music Awards, 2014. Office: Big Machine Records 1219 16th Ave South Nashville TN 37212*

KELLEY, CHARLES, singer, musician; b. Augusta, Ga., Sept. 30, 1981; m. Cassie McConnell, June 2009. Grad., U. Ga., 2004. Founding band mem. Lady Antebellum, 2006—. Singer: (albums) Lady Antebellum, 2008, A Merry Little Christmas, 2010, Need You Now, 2010 (Best Country Album, Record of Yr., Grammy Awards, 2011), Own the Night, 2011 (Best Country Album, Grammy Awards, 2012), On This Winter's Night, 2012, Golden, 2013, (songs) I Run to You, 2009 (Single of Yr., County Music Assn. Awards, 2009, Best Country Performance by Duo or Group with Vocals, Grammy Awards, 2010), Need You Now, 2009 (Single Record of Yr., Song of Yr., Acad. Country Music Awards, 2010, Group Video of Yr., CMT Music Awards, 2010, Single of Yr., Country Music Assn., 2010, Best Country Performance by Duo or Group with Vocals, Song of Yr., Grammy Awards, 2011, Top Country Song, Billboard Music Awards, 2011), Hello World, 2010 (Group Video of Yr., CMT Music Awards, 2011), We Owned the Night, 2011 (Group Video of Yr., CMT Music Awards, 2012), Downtown, 2013 (Group Video of Yr., CMT Music Awards, 2013). Named Top New Duo or Group, Acad. Country Music, 2008, Top Vocal Group of Yr., 2010, 2011, 2012, New Artist of Yr., Country Music Assn., 2008, Vocal Group of Yr., 2010, 2011, Favorite Country Band, Duo or Group, American Music Awards, 2010, 2011, 2012, 2013, Top Country Artist, Billboard Music Awards, 2012. Office: c/o Capitol Records Nashville 3322 W End Ave #11 Nashville TN 37203*

KELLEY, CRAIG I., lawyer, educator; b. Detroit, July 14, 1963; s. Hilliard Leonard and Barbara Lee Kelley; m. Melissa Held; children: Jacob, Marina. BSBA, U. Fla., Gainesville, 1985; JD (hon.), U. Miami, Fla., 1988. Bar: Fla. 1988, US Dist. Ct. (so. dist.) Fla. 1990, US Dist. Ct. (mid. dist.) Fla. 1995, US Dist. Ct. (no. dist.) Fla. 2000, US Bankruptcy Ct. 1990. Assoc. Ackerman, Bakst, Lauer & Scherer, West Palm Beach, Fla., 1989—91, Grazi, Gianino & Cohen, Stuart, Fla., 1992—96; ptnr. Ward, Damon & Posner, West Palm Beach, 1996—2001, Kelley & Fulton, P.A., West Palm Beach, 2001—. Adj. prof. Palm Beach C.C., Palm Beach Gardens, Fla., 1990—; lectr. in field. Contbr. articles to profl. jours. Pro bono atty. Legal Aid Soc. Palm Beach, 1989—2006; team sponsor, coach baseball and basketball JTAA, Jupiter, Fla., 2001—06. Mem.: Am. Bankruptcy Inst., Bankruptcy Bar Assn. So. Dist. Fla., Inns Ct. (pres. 2007—08, bd. dirs. 2002—06, Inns Cup). Avocations: boating, baseball, classic cars, wave runners, bicycling. Office: Kelley & Fulton PA 1665 Palm Beach Lakes Blvd Suite 1000 West Palm Beach FL 33401 Office Fax: 561-684-3773. Business E-Mail: craig@kelleylawoffice.com.

KELLEY, JAMES FRANCIS, lawyer; b. Milw., Dec. 30, 1941; s. James O'Connor and Marcella Cecilia (Salb) Kelley; m. Anne H. Morgan; children: Sarah, Leah stepchildren: Morgan Baker, Curtis Baker. AB, Yale U., 1963; JD, U. Chgo., 1966. Bar: NY 1967, Tex. 1981. Assoc. Breed, Abbott & Morgan, NYC, 1967—75; dep. gen. counsel United Tech. Corp., Hartford, Conn., 1975—81; sr. v.p., gen. counsel Maxus Energy Corp., Dallas, 1981—88; ptnr. Jones, Day, Reavis & Pogue, Dallas, Paris, 1988—93; sr. v.p., gen. counsel Georgia-Pacific Corp., 1993—2000, exec. v.p., gen. counsel, 2000—05. Gov. Dallas Symphony Assn., 1985—89; bd. dirs. North Tex. Pub. Broadcasting Found., Dallas, 1983—91, mem. exec. com., 1988—91; bd. dirs. Altanta Symphony Orch., 1994—, mem. exec. com., 1996—2007, chair fin. com., 2002—07; mem. bd. visitors Emory U., 1999—2001; bd. dirs. Piedmont Healthcare Inc., 2003—12; chair Audit & Compliance Com., 2008—12. Mem.: Assn. Gen. Counsel, Piedmont Driving Club, Chattooga Club.

KELLEY, MICHAEL, internal medicine and pediatric physician; b. NYC, Jan. 7, 1966; m. Gretchen Kelley; 4 children. BA, Harvard U., 1989; MD, U. Louisville, 1993; grad. in Internal Medicine and Pediat., East Carolina U., 1997. Pvt. practice, Crestwood, Ky., 1997—. Democrat. Home: 1710 Cedar Point Rd La Grange KY 40031-9766 Business E-Mail: info@kelley08.com.

KELLEY, PATRICIA HAGELIN, geology educator; b. Cleve., Dec. 8, 1953; d. Daniel Warn and Virginia Louise (Morgan) Hagelin; m. Jonathan Robert Kelley, June 18, 1977; children: Timothy Daniel, Katherine Louise. BA, Coll. of Wooster, 1975; AM, Harvard U., 1977, PhD, 1979. Instr. New Eng. Coll., Henniker, NH, 1979; asst. prof. U. Miss., University, 1979-85, assoc. prof., 1985-89, acting assoc. vice chancellor acad. affairs, 1988, prof., 1989-92, assoc. dean, 1989-90; program dir. NSF, Washington, 1990-92; prof., chmn. dept. geology U. N.D., Grand Forks, 1992-97; prof. U. NC, Wilmington, 1997—, chmn. dept. earth scis., 1997—2003. Editor several books; contbr. articles to profl. jours. Deacon Bethel Presbyn. Ch., Olive Branch, Miss., 1985-90. Rsch. grantee NSF, 1986-89, 90-99, 2000-03, 2008-; NSF fellow, 1976-79. Fellow AAAS, Geol. Soc. Am., Paleontol. Soc. (coun. 1984-85, 95-96, 98-2004, chair S.E. sect. 1984-85, chair N.C. sect. 1995-96, pres.-elect 1998-2000, pres. 2000-02, past pres. 2002-04); mem. Assn. Women Geosci. (Outstanding Educator award 2003), Paleontol. Rsch. Inst. (trustee 2003-, pres. bd. trustees 2004-06), Soc. Econ. Paleontologists and Mineralogists, Nat. Assn. Geosci. Tchrs. (disting. spkr. 2006-09), Sigma Xi, Phi Beta Kappa. Presbyterian. Avocations: writing, music, travel. Office: Dept Geography and Geology Univ NC Wilmington NC 28403-5944 Office Phone: 910-962-7406. Business E-Mail: kelleyp@uncw.edu.

KELLEY, PATRICK G., human services administrator; m. Jill Kelley; children: Katelyn, Mason. MS in Social Work, U. Louisville. Regional v.p. ResCare, Inc., v.p. ops. Ctrl. Region, 1999—2003, sr. v.p., 2003—06, pres. Cmty. Svcs. Group, 2008—09, COO, 2009—. Divsn. pres. Rawlings Co., 2006—08. Office: Res-Care Inc 9901 Linn Station Rd Louisville KY 40223 Office Phone: 502-394-2100. Office Fax: 502-394-2206. Business E-Mail: pkelley@rescare.com.

KELLGREN, GEORGE LARS, manufacturing executive; b. Boras, Sweden, May 23, 1943; came to U.S., 1979; s. Lars Anders and Ann-Marie (Fröberg) Kjellgren; m. Rubi Caridad Godoy, Nov. 6, 1982; children: Adrian Anders, Derek Lars, Viveka Victoria. BS, Umea U., Sweden, 1967. Researcher, developer Husquarna (Sweden) Arms Factory, Husquarna, 1968; tech. officer Council for Sci. and Industrial Research, Pretoria, Republic of South Africa, 1969-74; mng. dir. Interdynamic Forsknings AB, Stockholm, 1975-79; tech. dir. Intratec U.S.A., Inc., Miami, 1979-83; pres. Grendel, Inc., Cocoa, Fla., 1983-95; CEO Kel-Tec CNC Industries, Inc., Cocoa, 1995—. Contbr. articles to profl. jours.; inventor firearms. Republican. Lutheran.

KELLISON, STEPHEN GEORGE, actuarial consultant; b. Ord, Nebr., Mar. 20, 1942; s. Orin Albian and Sarah Viola (Crouch) K.; m. Chery Le Wagner, June 14, 1963 (div. Jan. 1970); m. Erica Elizabeth Bowers, Jan. 27, 1978 (div. June 1985); m. Maureen Antoinette Gage, Nov. 15, 1986. AB, U. Nebr., Lincoln, 1963, MS, 1967. CFP. Actuarial supr. Occidental Life Ins. Co., LA, 1963-65; actuary Lincoln Liberty Life Ins. Co., Lincoln, Nebr., 1965-66; prof. U. Nebr., 1966-75; consulting actuary G.V. Stennes & Assocs., Dallas, 1975-76; exec. dir. Am. Acad. Actuaries, Washington, 1976-88; chmn. Dept. Risk Mgmt. and Ins. Ga. State U., Atlanta, 1989-93; sr. v.p. instnl. svcs. Am. Gen. Retirement Svcs., Houston, 1994—2001. Chmn. tech. panel Social Security Adv. Coun., 1989—91; pub. trustee Social Security and Medicare, 1995—2000; mem. task force on interest methods Fin. Acctg. Stds. Bd., 1989—95; sec. Actuarial Edn. and Rsch. Fund, 1989—92; mem. tech. panel Social Security Adv. Bd., 2003—04; vis. prof. U. Ctrl. Fla., Orlando, 2005—. Author: The Theory of Interest, 1970, 2d edit., 1991, 3d edit., 2008, Fundamentals of Numerical Analysis, 1975. Fellow Soc. Actuaries (bd. dirs. 1973-75, 90-93, v.p. 1999-2001, pres. 2003-05); mem. Nat. Acad. Social Ins., Am. Acad. Actuaries (bd. dirs. 1975-76), Internat. Actuarial Assn., Actuarial Standards Bd. (chair 2008-)Phi Beta Kappa. Home and Office: 9301 Wickham Way Orlando FL 32836-5518 Office Phone: 407-909-0853. Personal E-mail: sgkellison@aol.com.

KELLMAN, STEVEN G., literature educator, author; b. Bklyn., Nov. 15, 1947; s. Max and Pearl (Pomerantz) Kellman. BA, SUNY, Binghamton, 1967; MA, U. Calif., Berkeley, 1969, PhD, 1972. Asst. prof. Bemidji State U., Minn., 1972—73; lectr. Tel-Aviv U., 1973—75; vis. lectr. U. Calif., Irvine, 1975—76; asst. prof. U. Tex., San Antonio, 1976—80, assoc. prof., 1980—85, prof. comparative lit., 1995—, Ashbel Smith prof., 1995—2000. Vis. assoc. prof. U. Calif. Berkeley, 1982; columnist, critic The San Antonio Light, 1983-93; fiction critic Gettysburg Rev., 1991-93; editor lit. scene USA Today mag., Valley Stream, N.Y., 1985—2010; film critic San Antonio Current, 1986-89, 98—; NEH seminar, U. Natal, South Africa, 1996 Author: The Self-Begetting Novel, 1980, Loving Reading: Erotics of the Text, 1985, The Modern American Novel, 1991, The Plague: Fiction and Resistance, 1993, Perspectives on Raging Bull, 1994, The Translingual Imagination, 2000, Redemption: The Life of Henry Roth, 2005; editor: Approaches to Teaching Camus's The Plague, 1985, (lit. mag.) Occident, 1969-70, Switching Languages: Translingual Writers Reflect on their Craft, 2003, M.E. Ravage, An Am. in the Making, 2009; co-editor: Into the Tunnel, 1998, Leslie Fiedler and American Culture, 1999, Torpid Smoke: Vladimir Nabokov's Short Fiction, 2000, Magill's Literary Annual, 2000—, UnderWords: Perspectives on Don DeLillo's Underworld, 2002; contbg. writer The Tex. Observer, 1989—. Pres. bd. dir. Gemini Ink, 1998-2002, bd. editors Jewish Jour. San Antonio, 1987-, chmn., 1991-95; adv. humanities Inter-Am. Book Fair, San Antonio, 1987-94; adv., judge Tex. Film Festival, San Antonio, 1986-87, Cine Festival, San Antonio, 1985-90; v.p., bd. dir. Tex. Humanities Resource Ctr., 1991-92; del. Dem. Nat. Conv., 1992 Recipient H.L. Mencken award, Balt. Sun, 1986, Arts and Letters award, San Antonio Libr. Found., 2005, award, NY Soc. Libr. Bd., 2005, First Pl. in Arts Criticism, Assn. Alternative Newsweeklies, 2006, Fulbright lectr. Tbilisi State U., Georgia, U.S. Govt., 1980, Nona Balakian Citation for Excellence in Reviewing, Nation Book Critics Cir., 2006, Gemini Ink award Lit. Excellence, 2008; named lectr. Peru, Ptnrs. of Ams., 1988, Ptnrs. of Ams., Washington, 1995, Fulbright Disting. prof. U. Sofia, Bulgaria, 2000; grantee People's Republic of China, Fulbright Found., 1995; Sawyer fellow, Harvard U., 1997. Mem. MLA, Nat. Book Critics Cir. (bd. dir. 1996-2002, 2009-, v.p. 2010-), PEN Am. Ctr., Tex. Inst. Letters Home: 302 Fawn Dr San Antonio TX 78231-1519 Office: U Tex Dept English San Antonio TX 78249-0643 Office Phone: 210-458-5216. E-mail: steven.kellman@utsa.edu.

KELLMANSON, MARY, retail executive; BA in Govt., Franklin & Marshall Coll., 1989; attended, U. Rochester, 1994. Various positions, v.p., advt. & mktg. Wegmans Food Market, Inc., 1994—2007; v.p., mktg. Winn-Dixie Stores, Inc., 2008—. Office: Winn-Dixie Stores Inc 5050 Edgewood Ct Jacksonville FL 32254-3699 Office Phone: 904-783-5000. Office Fax: 904-370-7224. Business E-Mail: marykellmanson@winn-dixie.com.

KELLNER, LARRY (LAWRENCE WESLEY KELLNER), private equity firm executive, retired air transportation executive; b. 1959; m. Susan Kellner; 4 children. BS in Bus. Adminstrn., magna cum laude, U. SC, 1981. Exec. v.p., CFO The Kohl Co., American Savings Bank F.A., 1992—95; sr. v.p. Continental Airlines Inc., Houston, 1995—96, CFO, 1995—2001, exec. v.p., 1996—2001, pres., 2001—04, COO, 2003—04, chmn., CEO, 2004—09; founder, pres. Emerald Creek Group, LLC, 2010—. Bd. dirs. Air Transport Assn., Continental Airlines Inc., 2001—09, Marriot Internat. Inc., 2002—, Row 44, Inc., 2010—, The Chubb Corp., 2011—, The Boeing Co., 2011—. Mem. nat. exec. bd. Boy Scouts of America; mem. adv. bd. March of Dimes, Teach for America; bd. dirs. YMCA Greater Houston Area; vice chmn. Greater Houston Partnership; bd. dirs. Spring Br. Edn. Found., Ctrl. Houston Inc.; mem. devel. bd. U. Tex. Health Sci. Ctr.; bd. dirs. Methodist Hosp. Recipient Disting. Alumni award, U. SC, 1998, Tony Jannus award for outstanding achievement in comml. air transp., Tony Jannus Disting. Aviation Soc., 2008. Office: Emerald Creek Group LLC 8901 Gaylord Dr Ste 200 Houston TX 77024-3042 Office Phone: 713-468-4050. Office Fax: 713-468-4919. E-mail: larry.kellner@emeraldcreek.com.

KELLOGG, DAVID WAYNE, agricultural studies educator, researcher; b. Seymour, Mo., Aug. 19, 1941; s. Martin David and Lula May (Spurlock) K.; m. Mary Sue Powell, June 7, 1964; children: Kirk David, Susan Joann Franz, Kimberley Annelle Van Vacter, Gregory William. BS, U. Mo., 1963, MS, 1964; PhD, U. Nebr., 1968. Profl. animal scientist. Asst. prof. agriculture N.Mex. State U., Las Cruces, 1967-71, assoc. prof., 1971-78, prof., 1978-81; prof., dept. head U. Ark., Fayetteville, 1981-86, prof., 1986—. Cons. AID-N.Mex. State U. Mission, Asuncion, Paraguay, 1971; spkr. Ark. Farm Bur., Little Rock, 1981-90, ORFFA Seminar, Rennes, France, 1995, Breda, Holland, 1996, San Jose, Costa Rica, 1999; Brenen and Leipsig, Germany, 2002, Bergano and Piedmont, Italy, 2002, Santa Cruz, Bolivia, 2002, 04, Belo Horizonte, Brazil, 2004. mem. adv. com Ark. Livestock and Poultry Commn., 1989-94; reviewer rsch. proposals USDA, Small Bus. Innovation. Mem. editl. bd.: Jour. Dairy Sci., 1978—84, nutrition sect. editor:, 2000—06, editor-in-chief: Profl. Animal Scientist, 2006—; contbr. chapters to books, articles to profl. jour. Mem. Fellowship Bible Ch.; vice chmn. US Bd. African Christian U., Zambia, 2009—. Fellow: Am. Dairy Sci. Assn. (sec. so. sect. 1991, v.p. 1992, pres. 1993, awards com. 1996—98, spkr. symposium on highest producing dairy herds 2000, Disting. Svc. award 2005); mem.: Ark. Nutrition Coun., Ark. Registry Profl. Animal Scientists (sec., treas. 1989—93, charter), So. Assn. Agrl. Sci. (bd. dir. 1993—94), Am. Grassland and Forage Coun., Am. Soc. Animal Sci. (awards com. 1990—92, spkr. symposium on chelated trace minerals 1996), Am. Registry Profl. Animal Sci. (bd. dir. 1989—91, pres.-elect 1993—94, pres. 1994—95, nominating com. 1996—98), Gideons Internat. (trustee 1975—81). Office: U Ark Dept Animal Sci Fayetteville AR 72701 Business E-Mail: wkellogg@uark.edu.

KELLOUGH, J. EDWARD, political science professor, department chairman; BA, Berea Coll., 1977; MA, Miami U., 1982, PhD in Polit. Sci., 1987. Tchg. asst. Miami U., 1981—85, vis. instr., 1985—86; instr. Tex. A&M U., 1986—88; asst. prof. Dept. Polit Sci. U. Ga., 1988—94, assoc. prof., 1994—2006, assoc. prof. Dept. Pub. Adminstrn. and Policy, 2002—06, prof., 2006—; head Dept. Pub. Adminstrn. and Policy, 2008—. Contbr. articles to profl. jours. Mem.: Pub. Mgmt. Rsch. Assn., Am. Polit. Sci. Assn., Am. Soc. Pub. Adminstrn. Office: Dept Pub Adminstrn and Policy U Ga Sch Pub and Internat Affairs 204 Baldwin Hall Athens GA 30602-1615 Office Phone: 706-542-0488. Office Fax: 706-542-9660. E-mail: kellough@uga.edu.

KELLY, ALAN J., oil industry executive; b. Iserlohn, Germany; Degree, Bristol U., England. Joined ExxonMobil Corp., 1981, regional dir. North America ExxonMobil Lubricants & Petroleum Specialties Co., 2001—03, gen. mgr. corp. planning, 2003—07, v.p., pres. ExxonMobil Lubricants & Petroleum Specialties Co., 2007—. Project dir. global oil and gas study Nat. Petroleum Coun., 2006. Office: Exxon Mobil Corp Hdqs 5959 Las Colinas Blvd Irving TX 75039-2298

KELLY, ANTHONY ODRIAN, textiles executive; b. Dublin, June 12, 1935; s. John Peter and Delia Mary (Finnegan) K.; m. Sheila Josephine Clancy, Sept. 4, 1963; children— Barbara Anne, Adrienne Elizabeth, Damian Anthony. Grad., Coll. Commerce, Dublin, 1958; MBA, Columbia U., 1965, doctoral degree, 1971. Adj. asst. prof. Columbia U., NYC, 1968-69; dir. econ. studies Sperry & Hutchinson Co., 1969-71, asst. to pres. furnishings divsn., 1975; dir. mktg. Irish Agrl. Devel. Co., 1971-74; sr. v.p. mktg. Bigelow-Sanford, Inc., Greenville, SC, 1976-79, exec. v.p., COO, 1979-85, pres., CEO, 1985-86; pres., chief ops. officer Mannington Mills Inc., 1992, pres., CEO, 1993-2000, ret., 2000. Ford Found. fellow; Samuel Bronfman fellow. Mem. Inst. Cost and Mgmt. Accts., Kiawah Island Club, Beta Gamma Sigma. Personal E-mail: aok-sjk@att.net.

KELLY, DAN, judge, former state legislator; b. Aug. 29, 1950; m. Darlene Kelly; 5 children. BS in Zoology, Tex. A&M U.; JD, U. Louisville. Former city atty., Springfield, Ky.; state senator Dist. 14 Ky. Legislature, 1991—2009, minority fl. leader, 1995—98; judge Ky. 11th Jud. Cir. Ct., Springfield, 2009—. Lt. col. US Army. Decorated Meritorious Svc. medal, Army Commendation medal, Nat. Def. medal; recipient Pres. award, BSA. Mem.: U. Louisville Brandeis Soc., J. Ruben Clark Soc., Ky. & Louisville Bar Assn. Republican. Latter-Day Saints. Office: Ky 11th Jud Cir Ct 102 W Main St PO Box 388 Springfield KY 40069 Office Fax: 859-336-0670.

KELLY, EDWARD JOHN, V, counselor; b. Saratoga Springs, NY, July 10, 1936; s. Edward John IV and Blanch Marie (O'Connor) K.; children: Edward J. VI, Patrick J., Kevin J., Michael J., Kathleen M. Student, Union Coll., Schenectady, NY, 1954-56; MEd in Guidance and Counseling, Campbell U., Buies Creek, NC, 1990; student, U. Dayton, 1967; BA in History, N.C. Wesleyan Coll., 1982. Commd. USAF, 1956, advanced through grades to lt. col., 1975; instr. navigation Strategic Air Command USAF, various locations, 1958-69; scheduler KC-135 USAF, Castle AFB, Calif., 1970-71, chief bomber ops., 1972-73, chief KC-135 planner Anderson AFB, Guam, 1973-74; 8AF chief of tng. Anderson AFB, Guam, 1974-75; dir. ops. and tng. USAF, Seymour Johnson AFB, N.C., 1977-78, ret., 1979; job developer, counselor Wayne C.C., Goldsboro, N.C., 1979-80, dir. coop. edn., job placement and apprenticeship, 1980-97. Chmn. County Workforce Devel. Coun., Goldsboro, 1980-97; com. chmn. N.C. Internship Coun., 1985-93, N.C. trails com. chmn. 1989-92. Author: Canoeing the Neuse River, 1983, Your Move Into the World of Work, 1988. Chmn. task force Waynesborough State Pk., 1983-86, 90-94, 95-2002; scoutmaster Boy Scouts Am., Merced., Calif. and Guam, Goldsboro, 1971-86, coun. commr., Goldsboro, 1976-81, 84-88, dist. chmn., 1982-84, coun. commr., 2012-; cand. Rep. Party, Wayne County, 1982, 84, 86; bd. dirs. Sr. Inst., Ctrl. Fla. C.C., 2003—07, pres., 2003-05; v.p. Silver Springs Shores Residents Assn., 2003, pres., 2004-10; bd. dirs. Pub. Policy Inst., 2005-; chair, citizen adv. com. Cmty. Transp. Orgn., 2008-. Recipient Yaddo medal Saratoga HS, 1954, Boy Scouts Am., 1951, Eagle award, Silver Beaver award, 1973. Mem. DAV, VFW, Coop. Edn. Assn., N.C. Coop. Edn. Assn. (bd. dirs. 1985-97, pres. 1994, Outstanding Profl. 1994), N.C. Placement Assn. (program co-chmn. 1990, Outstanding Profl. 1994), Neuse Trails Assn., Air Force Assn. (pres. 1980-82, 90-91, v.p. 2004, pres. 2004-07, Merit medal 1989), County Pers. Assn. (pres. 1992). Avocations: organic gardening, horticulture, recreational vehicles, canoeing, fishing. Home: 2 Emerald Ct Ocala FL 34472- Personal E-mail: ejk5@embarqmail.com.

KELLY, GARY CLAYTON, air transportation executive; b. Mar. 12, 1955; s. Clayton Kelly; m. Carol G. Kelly; children: Caroline, Elizabeth. BBA in Acctg., U. Tex., 1977. CPA, Tex. Audit mgr. Arthur Young & Co., Dallas; controller Sys. Ctr. Inc., Irving, Tex., Southwest Airlines Co., Dallas, 1986-89, v.p. fin., CFO, 1989—2001, exec. v.p., CFO, 2001—04, vice chmn., CEO, 2004—08, chmn., CEO, 2008, chmn., pres., CEO, 2008—. Bd. dirs. Southwest Airlines Co., 2004—, Air Transport Assn. America, Jefferson-Pilot Corp. Mem. advisory council McCombs Sch. Bus., Univ. Tex., Austin. Named one of 25 Most Influential Executives, Business Travel News, 2004. Avocation: guitar. Office: Southwest Airlines Co 2702 Love Field Dr Dallas TX 75235

KELLY, HUGH RICE, lawyer, retired energy executive; b. Austin, Tex., Dec. 16, 1942; s. Thomas Philip and Cecilia Elizabeth (Rice) Kelly; m. Marguerite Susan McIntosh, Dec. 27, 1971; children: Susan McIntosh, Cecilia Rice. BA, Rice U., 1965; JD, U. Tex., 1972. Bar: Tex. 1972, U.S. Dist. Ct. (so. dist.) Tex. 1974, U.S. Ct. Appeals (5th cir.) 1975, U.S. Supreme Ct. 1975. Assoc. Baker Botts, Houston, 1972-78, ptnr., 1979-84; exec. v.p., gen. counsel Reliant Energy (formerly Houston Lighting & Power Co.), Houston, 1984—2003; gen. counsel Texans for Lawsuit Reform, 2003—. 1st lt. US Army, 1966—69. Fellow: ABA Found., Houston Bar Found., Tex. Bar Found.; mem.: ABA, Am. Law Inst., Houston Bar Assn., State Bar Tex., Coronado Club. Republican. Home and Office: 1936 Rice Blvd Houston TX 77005-1635 E-mail: hkelly00@gmail.com.

KELLY, JAMES MICHAEL, plant and soil scientist; b. Knoxville, Feb. 2, 1944; s. Woodrow Wilson and Thelma Lucille (Miller) K.; m. Susan Kay Morris, Aug. 9, 1969; children: John Kip, Christopher Kenneth. BS, E. Tenn. State U., 1966; MS, U. Tenn., 1968, PhD, 1973. Cert. profl. soil scientist. Assoc. ecologist NUS Corp., Pitts., 1973-74; rsch. assoc. Forestry Dept. Purdue U., West Lafayette, Ind., 1975-76; program mgr. Tenn. Valley Authority, Oak Ridge, 1977-88, sr. rschr., 1990-94; sr. tech. specialist, team leader, 1994-95; prof., chair dept. forestry Iowa State U., Ames, 1995—2001, chair dept. natural resource ecology and mgmt., 2002—04; dean Coll. Natural Resources Va. Tech. U., Blacksburg, 2004—. Vis. prof. agronomy Purdue U., 1988-89; adj. prof. U. Tenn., Knoxville, 1980-95, forestry dept. Purdue U., 1985-95. Author: Carbon Forms and Functions in Forest Soils, 1995; assoc. editor Soil Sci. Soc. Am. Jour., 1989-95, Forest Sci., 1998-01; editl. bd. Forest Ecology and Management, 2001-05; contbr. more than 100 articles to profl. jours. Head referee Ayso Youth Soccer, Oak Ridge, 1985-88; troop com. Boy Scouts Am., Oak Ridge, 1989-95. Oak Ridge Assoc. Univ. fellow, 1970-72; Elec. Power Rsch. Inst. grantee, 1978, 82, 89, 91, 95, NSF grantee, 1995; recipient Rsch. Champion award Elec. Power Rsch. Inst., 2002. Fellow Soil Sci. Soc. Am. (chmn. divsn. S7 1986-87, bd. dirs. 1988-89, awards com. 1992-93, fellows com. 1997-99, profl. svc. com. 2000-02); mem. AAAS, Ecol. Soc. Am., Soc. Am. Foresters, Exptl. Aircraft Assn. (chpt. pres. 1991-93), Trees Forever (bd. dirs. 1995-05), Sigma Xi, Gamma Sigma Delta, Xi Sigma Pi. Achievements include research and application of environmental science. Office: Va Tech Univ Coll Natural Resources Blacksburg VA 24061 Office Phone: 540-231-5481. Business E-Mail: jmkelly@vt.edu.

KELLY, JAMES PATRICK, lawyer; b. Twin Falls, Idaho, Mar. 25, 1946; s. James Patrick Sr. and Ynes Mary (Alastra) K.; m. Carol Louise White, June 6, 1968; children: Mary Louise, Christopher John. AB, Harvard U., 1968, JD, 1975. Bar: Ga. 1975, U.S. Dist. Ct. (no. and so. dists.) Ga. 1976, U.S. Ct. Appeals (5th cir. 1976, 6th cir. 1996, 1st cir. 1997, 11th cir.), U.S. Supreme Ct. 1999. Assoc. Kilpatrick & Cody, Atlanta, 1975-80; ptnr. Morris & Manning, Atlanta, 1980-83, Smith, Gambrell & Russell, Atlanta, 1983-85, Asbill, Porter & Churchill, Atlanta, 1985-86; sr. ptnr. Kelly Law Firm, P.C., Atlanta, 1986—. Bd. dirs. Sr. Citizen Services of Met. Atlanta, 1980-83. Served to capt. U.S. Army, 1968-72. Named Ga. Super Lawyer, 2007—, Leading Lawyers for Bus., Chambers USA; named one of Best Lawyers in America, 2008—. Mem. ABA (corp. and banking law sect., health law forum), Ga. Bar Assn., Atlanta Bar Assn., Ga. Acad. Healthcare Attys. (bd. dirs. 1987-89), Am. Health Lawyers Assn. (bd. dirs. 1993-99, arbitrator, mediator 2005-, fellow 2005-), Internat. Network Boutique Law Firms, Lawyers Club Atlanta, Harvard Alumni Assn. (bd. dirs. 1983-84), Harvard Law Sch. Assn. Ga. (v.p. 1988-89, pres. 1989-91), Harvard Club (pres. 1982-83, bd. dirs. 1990—), Harvard Club Ga. (pres. 1980-81), Bar Register Pre-Eminent Lawyers, Capital City Club, Kiwanis (pres.). Episcopalian. Avocations: public speaking, travel, horseback riding, swimming, bicycling, running. Office: One Securities Ctr 3490 Piedmont Rd Ste 340 Atlanta GA 30305 Office Phone: 404-446-2300. Business E-Mail: jpkelly@kellylawfirm.com.

KELLY, JANET LANGFORD, oil industry executive, lawyer; b. Kansas City, Mo., Nov. 27, 1957; m. John Kelly; children: Jack, Kate. BA, Grinnell Coll., 1979; JD, Yale U., 1983. Bar: NY 1985, Ill. 1989, Mich. 2004. Law clk. to Hon. James J. Hunter III US Ct. Appeals (3rd cir.), 1983-84; ptnr. Sidley & Austin LLP, Chgo., 1984-89; sr. v.p., sec., gen. counsel Sara Lee Corp., Chgo., 1995-99; exec. v.p. corp. devel., gen. counsel, sec. Kellogg Co., Battle Creek, Mich., 1999—2001, exec. v.p. corp. devel. & adminstrn., gen. counsel, sec., 2001—06; dep. gen. counsel ConocoPhillips, Houston, 2006—07, sr. v.p. legal, gen. counsel, corp. sec., 2007—. Sr. editor Yale Law Jour., 1983. Bd. dirs. Am. Arbitration Assn., Constl. Rights Found.; mem. adv. bd. Chgo. Vol. Legal Svcs. Found. Mem.: ABA. Office: ConocoPhillips 600 N Dairy Ashford Rd PO Box 2197 Houston TX 77079 Office Phone: 281-293-1000. E-mail: janet.l.kelly@conocophillips.com.*

KELLY, JOHN B., pain management specialist; MD, U. Colo., 1986. Diplomate American Bd. Psychiatry and Neurology, 1991. Intern NC Bapt. Hosp., resident; resident neurology Wake Forest Univ., 1987—90; asst. dir. Univ. Cin.; hosp. affiliations include St. Luke Hosp. East, St. Elizabeth Med. Ctr. Covington; physician St. Elizabeth Edgewood. Office: St Elizabeth Edgewood 1 Medical Village Dr Bromley KY 41017-3403 Office Phone: 859-301-2000.*

KELLY, JOHN FRANCIS, career military officer; b. Boston, 1950; married; children: John, Robert Michael(dec.). BS, U. Mass., 1976; Grad., US Army Infantry Advanced Courses, Ft. Benning, 1980, Marine Corps Command & Staff Coll., Sch. for Advanced Warfare, Nat. War Coll., 1995. Served in USMC, 1970—72, 2nd lt., 1976, advanced through ranks to gen., 2012; rifle & weapons platoon comdr 2nd Marine Divsn., 1976—80, 1984—87, battalion ops. officer, 1987; assignment monitor USMC Headquarters, 1981—84; head Offensive Tactics Section then dir. Infantry Officer Course Basic Sch., Quantico, Va., 1987—90; commdg. officer 1st Light Armored Reconnaissance Battalion 1st Marine Divsn., 1992—94; commandant's liaison officer to the US House of Reps. USMC, 1995—98; spl. asst. to Supreme Allied Comdr. Europe (SACEUR) NATO, Mons, Belgium, 1999—2001; asst. chief of staff (G-3) 2nd Marine Divsn., 2001—02; asst. divsn. comdr. 1st Marine Divsn., 2002—04; legislative asst. to comdt. USMC, 2004—07; commdg. gen. I Marine Expeditionary Force (Forward), 2007—08, Multi-Nation Force-West, Baghdad, Iraq, 2008—09; comdr. Marine Forces Reserve & Marine Forces North, 2009—11; sr. mil. asst. to sec. US Dept. Def., Washington, 2011—12; comdr. US Southern Command (USSOUTHCOM), Doral, Fla., 2012—. Decorated Defense Disting. Svc. medal, Defense Superior Svc. medal, Legion of Merit (2) with Valor V, Meritorious Svc. medal, Navy & Marine Corps Commendation medal, Navy & Marine Corps Achievement medal, Joint Meritorious Unit award, Marine Corps Expeditionary medal, Global War on Terrorism Expeditionary medal, Global War on Terrorism Svc. medal, Kuwait Liberation medal. Office: US Southern Command (USSOUTHCOM) 9301 NW 33rd St Doral FL 33172*

KELLY, JOHN HUBERT, diplomat; b. Fond du Lac, Wis., July 20, 1939; s. James Daniel and Clarice L. Kelly; m. Helena Marita Ajo; children: David Snowdon, Maria Louise. BA, Emory U., 1961; advanced studies cert., Georgetown U., 1982. Vice consul Am. Consulate, Adana, Turkey, 1965-66; 3rd sec. Am. Embassy, Ankara, Turkey, 1966-67, 2nd sec. Bangkok, 1968-69; consul Am. Consulate, Songkhla, Thailand, 1969-71; 1st sec. Am. Embassy, Paris, 1976-80; fgn. svc. U.S. Dept. of State, Washington, 1972-76, dep. exec. sec., 1980-81, dep. asst. sec. of state, 1982-85, asst. sec. state for Near East and South Asia, 1989-91; U.S. amb. Am. Embassy, Beirut, 1986-88, amb. Helsinki, Finland, 1991-94; pres. John Kelly Cons., Conyers, 1994—; mng. dir. Internat. Equity Ptnrs., Atlanta, 1995-98. Mem. adv. coun. Una Chapman Cox Found., 1982-86; trustee Lebanese Am. U., 1996-2005. Mem. Coun. on Fgn. Rels., Mid. East Inst. Office: John Kelly Consulting 3027 Hanover Ln Se Conyers GA 30094-3249

KELLY, JOHN WILLIAM, JR., academic administrator; b. Greenville, SC, Jan. 5, 1955; s. John William and Betty (Kelly) K.; children: Christopher, Kimberly. BS, Clemson U., 1977; MS, Ohio State U., 1979, PhD, 1982. Asst. prof. Tex. A&M U., 1982-85, Clemson (S.C.) U., 1985-89, assoc. prof., 1989-91, prof., dept. head, dir. bot. garden, 1991-96, sch. dir., interim v.p. pub. svc. and agr., 1996-97, v.p. pub. svc. and agr., dir. S.C. Bot. Garden, 1997—. Cons. in field. Contbr. more than 50 articles to profl. jours. Bd. govs. S.C. BIO; chmn. bd. dirs. Am. Distance Edn. Corp., Pate Found., Forestry Assn. Recipient Outstanding Contbr. award S.C. Nurseryman's Assn., 1991. Fellow Am. Soc. Hort. Sci. (v.p. 1995-99, pres. 1999, chmn. bd. dirs. 2000, Outstanding Rschr. 1994, Outstanding Adminstr. 1995, So. region Outstanding Educator 1989); mem. So. Assn. Agrl. Scientists (past pres.), S.C. Greenhouse Growers Assn. (life, exec. sec. 1991). Avocations: gardening, nature. Office: Clemson U Pub Svc and Agr 130 Lehotsky Hall Clemson SC 29634-0101

KELLY, KATHLEEN S(UE), communications educator; b. Duluth, Minn., Aug. 6, 1943; d. Russell J. and Idun N. Mehrman; m. George F. Kelly, Apr. 29, 1961; children: Jodie A., Jennifer L. AA, Moorpark Coll., Calif., 1971; BS in Journalism, U. Md., College Park, 1973, MA in Pub. Rels., 1979, PhD in Pub. Communication, 1989. Accredited pub. rels.; cert. fundraising exec. Dir. pub. info. Bowie (Md.) State U., 1974-77; asst. to dean, instr. Coll. Journalism U. Md., College Park, 1977-79, assoc. dir. devel., 1979-82; v.p. Mt. Vernon Coll., Washington, 1982-83; dir. devel. U. Md., College Park, 1983-85, assoc. dean, lectr. Coll. Journalism, 1985-88, asst. dean Coll. Bus. and Mgmt., 1988-90; prof. U. La., Lafayette, 1991—2003; prof., chair dept. pub. rels. U. Fla., Gainesville, 2003—06, prof. dept. pub. rels. Cons. NASA, NIH, Mt. St. Marys Coll., 1986—; lectr. CASE, Pub. Rels. Soc. Am., 1987—. Author: Fund Raising and Public Relations: A Critical Analysis, 1991, Building Fund-Raising Theory, 1994, Effective Fund-Raising Management, 1998. Named PRIDE Book award winner Speech Comm. Assn., 1991, article award winner 1994, John Grenzebach award winner for rsch. on philanthropy CASE and Am. Assn. Fund-Raising Coun., 1991, 98, PRIG award winner for outstanding dissertation Internat. Comm. Assn., 1990, winner 1995 Pathfinder award Inst. for Pub. Rels. Rsch. and Edn., Staley/Robeson/Ryan/St. Lawarence prize for rsch. on fund raising and philanthropy Nat. Soc. Fundraising Execs., 1998, Jackson, Jackson & Wagner Behavioral Sci. prize, Pub. Relations Soc. Am. Found., 1999, Outstanding Educator award Pub. Rels. Soc. America, 2004; fellowship APR. Fellow Pub. Rels. Soc. Am. (chmn. ednl. and cultural orgn. sect. 1989, pres. Md. chpt. 1986-87, Pres.' Cup 1981, nat. bd. dirs. 1994-96, mem. Nat. Soc. Fund Raising Execs. (mem. rsch. coun.), Coun. Advancement and Support of Edn. (women's forum 1983), Phi Kappa Phi. Democrat. Avocations: travel, reading. Office: U Fla Dept Pub Rels PO Box 118400 Gainesville FL 32611-8400 Office Phone: 352-392-9359. Business E-Mail: kskelly@jou.ufl.edu.

KELLY, LUCIE STIRM YOUNG, retired nursing educator; b. Stuttgart, Germany, May 2, 1925; came to U.S., 1929; d. Hugo Karl and Emilie Rosa (Engel) Stirm; m. J. Austin Young, Aug. 30, 1946 (div. Feb. 1971); m. Thomas Martin Kelly, 1972 (dec. Aug. 2003); 1 child by previous marriage, Gay Aleta (Mrs. Donald Meyer). BS, U. Pitts., 1947, MLitt, 1957, PhD, 1965; D in Nursing Edn. (hon.), U. RI, 1977; LHD (hon.), Georgetown U., 1983; DSc (hon.), Widener U., 1984; D of Pub. Svc. (hon.), Am. U., 1985; DSc (hon.), U. Mass., 1989; DHL (hon.), SUNY, 1996. Instr. nursing McKeesport (Pa.) Hosp., 1953-57, asst. adminstr. nursing, 1966-69; asst. prof. nursing U. Pitts., 1957-64, asst. dean, 1965; prof., chmn. nursing dept. Calif. State U., LA, 1969-72; co-project dir. curriculum rsch. Nat. League for Nursing, 1973-74; project dir. patient edn., office consumer health edn., also adj. assoc. prof. cmty. medicine Coll. Medicine and Dentistry N.J.-Rutgers Med. Sch., 1974-75; prof. pub. health and nursing Sch. Pub. Health and Sch. Nursing Columbia U., NYC, 1975-90, prof. emeritus Sch Pub. Health, Sch. Nursing, 1990—, assoc. dean acad. affairs Sch. Pub. Health, 1988-90, hon. prof. nursing edn. Tchrs. Coll., 1977-93, acting head divsn. health adminstrn. Sch. Pub. Health, 1980-81, 86-88; on leave as exec. dir. Mid-Atlantic Regional Nursing Assn., 1981-82. Cons. U. Nev., Las Vegas, 1970-72, Ball State U., Ind., 1971, Long Beach (Calif.) Naval Hosp., 1971-72, Travis AFB, Calif., 1972, Brentwood VA Hosp., LA, 1971-72, Ctrl. Nursing Office VA, Washington, 1971-94, NJ Dept. Higher Edn., 1974-78, John Wiley Pub., 1974-76, Sch. Nursing and Sch. Pub. Health Am. U. Beirut accreditation visit, 1978; spl. med. adv. group VA Dept. Medicine and Surgery, Washington, 1980-84; cons. nursing com. AMA, 1971-74, Citizen's Com. for Children, NYC; v.p. Pa. Health Coun., 1968-69; adv. com. physicians assts. Calif. Bd. Med. Examiners, adv. com. Cancer Soc. LA, 1970-72, com. nursing VA, Washington, 1971-74, chair 1975-90, regional med. programs, Pa., 1967-69, Calif. 1970-72; spl. adv. com. on med. licensure and profl. conduct N.Y. State Assembly, 1977-79, nat. adv. com. Encore (nat. YWCA post-mastectomy group rehab. project), 1977-83; assoc. mem. NY Acad. Medicine, 1988-90; ethics com. Palisades Med. Ctr., 1993-05, bd. govs., 1995-05, mem. profl. and quality rev. com., 1995-05, chair, 1998-05, exec. com., 1998-99; 2d vice chair N.Y. Presbyn. Healthcare Sys., Palisades Med. Ctr., 1999-03, 1st vice chair 2003-05; lectr., cons., guest Beijing Med. Coll., China, 1982, Aga Khan U., Pakistan, 1990; bd. visitors U. Pitts. Sch. Nursing, 1986-93; editl. adv. bd. Am. Jour. Pub. Health, 1992, chair, 1993-97; chair adv. com. grad. program in pub. health U. Medicine and Dentistry NJ, 1995-00; vol. cert. mediator for Hudson County mcpl. cts., 2004-05; lectr. in field Author: (textbooks) Dimensions of Profl. Nursing, 8th edit., 1999, The Nursing Experience: Trends, Challenges, Transitions, 4th edit., 2002; contbg. editor: Jour. Nursing Adminstrn., 1975—82; columnist: jour. Nursing Outlook, editor-in-chief, 1982—91; mem. bd. advisors (jour.) Nurses Almanac, 1978, Nurse Manager's Handbook, 1979, Nursing Administration Handbook, 1992; editor (editl. bd.): (jour.) Am. Health, 1981—91; mem. editl. bd. Nursing and Health Care, 1991—95, Internat. Nursing Index, 1997—2001. Bd. dirs. ARC, LA, 1971-72; bd. dirs. Vis. Nurse Svc. N.Y., 1980-01, mem. exec. com., chmn. human resources, 1989-01; bd. dirs. Concern for Dying, 1983-89; bd. trustees Calif. State Coll. LA Found., 1971-72, U. Pitts., 1984-90, mem. exec. com. 1988-90; chair bd. visitors U. Pitts. Sch. Pub. Health, 1988-90; bd. visitors U. Miami Sch. Nursing, 1996-05; mem. health svcs. com. Children's Aid Soc., N.Y., 1978-84; v.p. Am. Nurses Found., 1980-82; mem. nat. adv. coun. on nurse tng. HRA, 1981-85; mem. nurses leadership coun. Chlorine Chemistry Coun., 1999-03; hon. bd. dirs. NOVA Found., 1998—, Health Professions Panel, Am. Legacy Found., 2000—. Named Outstanding Alumna U. Pitts. Sch. Nursing, 1966, Pa. Nurse of Yr., 1967, Roll of Honor N.J. State Nurses Assn., 1990; named to Tchrs. Coll. Columbia U. Nursing Edn. Alumni Hall of Fame, 1999; recipient Disting. Alumna award U. Pitts. Sch. Edn., 1981, Shaw medal Boston Coll., 1985, Bicentennial Medallion of Distinction, U. Pitts., 1987, R. Louise McManus Medallion for Disting. Svc. to Nursing, Tchrs. Coll. Columbia U., 1987, Dean's Disting. Svc. award Columbia Sch. Pub. Health, 1995, Second Century award in health care, Columbia U. Sch. Nursing, 1996; fellow HEW, 1965. Fellow Am. Acad. Nursing (named Living Legend 2001); mem. ANA (dir. 1978-82, Hon. Recognition award 1992), APHA (Ruth Freeman Pub. Health Nursing award 1993), Pa. Nurses Assn. (pres. 1966-69), Nat. League Nursing (bd. govs. 1991-95), Nurses Ednl. Funds Bd., U. Pitts. Sch. Nursing Alumni (pres. 1959), Vis. Nurse Assn. Ctrl. Jersey (bd. dirs. 1999-2001, mem. bd. trustees), Am. Hosp. Assn. (com. chmn. 1967-68), Assn. Grad. Faculty Cmty. Health/Pub. Health Nursing (v.p. 1980-81), Sigma Theta Tau (sr. editor Image 1978-81, pres.-elect 1981-83, pres. 1983-85, nat. campaign chair Ctr. for Nursing Scholarship 1987-89, chair devel. com. 1989-95, spl. advisor 1995-97, planned giving task force 1998-2001, Mentor award 1985, 93, 97, Spirit of Philanthropy award 1997), Pi Lambda Theta, Alpha Tau Delta (Cert. of Merit 1968). Achievements include collection of papers in Mugar Library, Boston U. Personal E-mail: stormwebr@gmail.com.

KELLY, MICHAEL J., broadcast executive; Ill., U.Ill. Urbana-Champaign. Pres. AOL Media Networks, 2004—07; pres., CEO The Weather Channel Co. (TWC), 2009—12, spl. advisor, 2012—, Bain Capital, 2012—. Former bd. advisor Contextweb; former bd. dirs. Visible World, Eyeblaster. Bd. dirs. Am. Town Network, CEO; founder Am.Town Network, 2000; adv. Veronis Suhler Stevenson, 2007—. Office: The Weather Channel Co (TWC) 300 Interstate North Parkway Atlanta GA 30339 Office Phone: 770-226-0000. Office Fax: 770-226-2390. Business E-Mail: mkelly@weather.com.*

KELLY, RAYMOND BOONE, III, lawyer; b. Ft. Worth, Oct. 12, 1947; s. Raymond Boone Jr. and Martha (Morehead) K.; m. Ellen McCarthy; children: Alice Katherine, Anne Rowan. BA, Tulane U., 1970; JD, So. Meth. U., 1974. Bar: Tex. 1974. Ptnr. Decker, McMackin & McClane, Ft. Worth, 1974—. Dir. William E. Scott Found., Ft. Worth, 1978—, pres., 2005-. Bd. dirs., past pres. Goodwill Industries Ft. Worth, 1975-94; bd. dirs. Arts Coun. Ft. Worth and Tarrant County, 1980-91, 95-97, Conf. of S.W. Founds., Dallas, 1986-89, 97-2000, Davey O'Brien Found., 2001—, Ft. Worth Mus. Sci. and History, 2003-, Big Bros./Bis Sisters, Ft. Worth, 1987-94, Intercultura, Inc., Ft. Worth, 1989-96, chmn., 1992-94, Funding Info. Ctr., 1993-97, Ft. Worth Dallas Ballet, 1996-97, Cmty. Found. North Tex., 1996-2002, Bishop Davies Ctr, 1999-2005, Baylor All Saints Med. Ctr., 1997—; trustee All Saints Health Found., 1987-, chmn. 1991-2002; trustee Modern Art Mus. Ft. Worth, 1981—, Fort Worth Country Day Sch., 1996-2002, Goodwill Industries Ft. Worth Found., 1997-, Ft. Worth Club, 1999-2002. Mem. ABA, State Bar Tex., Tarrant County Bar Assn., Tex. Bar Found. (life fellow), Tarrant County Bar Found., Ft. Worth Club, Exchange Club, Rivercrest Country Club, Steeplechase Club, Ind. Petroleum Assn. Am., Tex. Oil and Gas Assn. Republican. Episcopalian. Avocations: running, skiing, golf, travel. Home: 301 Virginia Pl Fort Worth TX 76107-1611 Office: Decker, McMackin & McClane 801 Cherry St Ste 2000 Fort Worth TX 76102-3812

KELLY, ROBERT DONALD, management consultant; b. Chgo., Sept. 14, 1929; s. Donald Francis and Irene Sarah (Gardner) K.; m. Kay R. Black, Apr. 25, 1959; children: Kim Robert, Kris Donald, Candis Elizabeth. BS in Indsl. Engring., Iowa State U., 1951; MS, Purdue U., 1955, PhD, 1957. Cert. mgmt. cons.; lic. inds. psychologist, Ill. Mem. faculty Purdue U., West Lafayette, Ind., 1953—57; from assoc. prin. to ptnr., dir. Kearney Mgmt. Cons., Chgo., 1957—79; mng. ptnr. pers., internat. pers. ptnr. Arthur Andersen World Hqtrs., Chgo., 1979—90; sr. internat. cons. Watson Wyatt Co., Chgo., 1990—2003; freelance cons. Chgo., 2003—. Bd. dirs. Allied Farm Equip., Duff Truck Line, Smith, U.S. Contbr. articles to profl. jours. Chmn. bd. trustees Clarendon Hills Presbyn. Ch., 1969-72; chmn. bd. deacons, 1966-69; pres. Bd. Edn. Hinsdale Sch. Dist. 1975-83; trustee and chmn. bd. Coll. DuPage, 1985-91; trustee, bd. dirs. Village of Hinsdale, 1995-99; chmn. Hist. Preservation Commn., Village of Hinsdale, 2001-03; bd. dirs. Hideaway Beach Assn., 2006-09, Governance Com., 2010-. With USAF, 1951-53. Mem. Am. Inst. Mgmt. Cons., Am. Compenstion Assn., Am. Psychol. Assn., Univ. Club, Econs. Club Chgo., Sigma Xi. Office: Unit 837 5000 Royal Marco Way Marco Island FL 34145 Home: 120 S Elm St Hinsdale IL 60521-4227 Personal E-mail: kelly80369@aol.com.

KELLY, SCOTT J., astronaut, military officer; b. Orange, NJ, Feb. 21, 1964; s. Richard and Patricia Kelly; m. Leslie Yandell; 2 children. BSEE, SUNY Maritime Coll., 1987; MS in Aviation Sysems, U. Tenn., Knoxville, 1996. Commd. ensign SUNY Maritime USN, 1987; advanced through grades to lt. comdr.; student pilot USN, Naval Air Sta. Beeville, Tex., 1987—89; naval pilot USN Fighter Squadron 101, Oceana, Va., 1989—90; pilot USN, Fighter Squadron 143, USS Dwight D. Eisenhower, 1990—93; test pilot student USN Test Pilot Sch., 1993—94; test pilot USN, Patuxent River, Md., 1994—96; astronaut NASA Johnson Space Ctr., Houston, 1996—. Served as NASA's dir. ops., Star City, Russia; back-up crew mem. ISS Expedition-5; astronaut office space station branch chief NASA; pilot STS 103 Mission, 1999; comdr. STS-118 Mission (Endeavour) to Internat. Space Station, 2007; flight engr. Internat. Space Station-Expedition 25, 2010; comdr. Internat. Space Station-Expedition 26, 2011. Decorated Def. Superior Svc. medal, Navy Commendation medal, Navy Achievement medal, (2) Navy Unit Commendations Nat. Def. Svc. medal, Southwest Asia Svc. medal, Kuwait Liberation medal, Sea Svc. Deployment Ribbon; recipient NASA Space Flight medal, NASA Exceptional Svc. medal, Korolev Diploma, Fedn. Aeronautique Internationale, 1999. Fellow: Soc. Exptl. Test Pilots (assoc.); mem.: Assn. Space Explorers. Achievements include being the first flight pilot to fly an F-14 with an experiment digital flight control system installed and performed subsequent high angle of attack and departure testing; Logged over 3,700 flight hours in more than 30 Different aircraft and has over 250 carrier landings. Avocations: running, weightlifting. Office: Astronaut Office Johnson Space Ctr Houston TX 77058

KELLY, STANHOPE A., bank executive; b. Nov. 25, 1957; BA in Bus., NC State U. Various positions including regional exec., head consumer fin. svcs. Wachovia Corp. (now Wells Fargo & Co.), Forsyth county exec. Winston-Salem, NC, mgmt. assignments, dealer fin., retail banking & corp. banking, sr. exec. v.p., banking & wealth mgmt. divsn., 2000—01, sr. exec. v.p., pres., wealth mgmt. Charlotte, NC, 2001—. Co-chair capital campaign drive Children's Mus., Winston-Salem; active Forsyth County Heart Gala, Wachovia Arts and Sci.; trustee Forsyth County Day Sch.; mem. bd. visitors Wake Forest U., Bapt. Med. Ctr. Mem.: Fin. Svcs. Roundtable. Office: Wachovia Corp 301 S College St Ste 400 Charlotte NC 28288 Office Phone: 704-335-5878.

KELLY, TIMOTHY MICHAEL, newspaper publisher; b. Ashland, Ky., Nov. 28, 1947; s. Robert John and Pauline Elizabeth (Henneman) K.; m. Carol Ann Knight, Aug. 2, 1969; children: Kimberly, Kevin. BA, U. Miami, Fla., 1970. Sports copy editor, writer The Courier-Jour., Louisville, 1970-71; exec. sports editor The Phila. Inquirer, 1971-75; dep. mng. editor Dallas Times Herald, 1975-81; mng. editor The Denver Post, 1981-84; exec. editor Dallas Times Herald, 1984; editor Daily News, LA, 1984-87; mng. editor The Orange County Register, Santa Ana, Calif., 1987-89; editor, sr. v.p. Lexington (Ky.) Herald-Leader, 1989-96, pub., 1996—. Juror Pulitzer Prize, 1987-88. Bd. dirs. YMCA of U.S.A., 2004—, nat. sec., 2005—07. Recipient Excellence Cmty. Svc. award Knight Ridder, 1995, Ida B. Wells award, 1999, Ky. Journalism Hall of Fame award, 2000, Byron B. Harless award Knight Ridder, 2003. Roman Catholic. Office: Lexington Herald Leader 100 Midland Ave Lexington KY 40508-1999 Office Phone: 859-231-3257. Business E-Mail: tkelly@herald-leader.com.

KELLY, WILLIAM WATKINS, retired educational foundation executive; b. Asheville, NC, Sept. 21, 1928; s. John Jackson and Trula (Watkins) K.; m. Lura Jane Kelly, Feb. 14, 1953 (div. Jan. 14, 1983); children: William Watkins (Jr.), Robert Jackson, Blair Massey, Gregory Clark.; m. Catherine Messer Penney, Jan. 22, 1983. BA, Va. Mil. Inst., 1950; A.M., Duke U., 1955, PhD, 1957. Commandant cadets, tchr. English John Marshall High Sch., Richmond, Va., 1950-52; instr. English Va. Mil. Inst., 1952-53, English Air Force Acad., 1957-58, asst. prof., 1958-60, English Va. Mil. Inst., 1960-62; asst. prof. Am. thought and language Mich. State U., 1962-65, assoc. prof., 1965-69; assoc. dir. The Honors Coll., 1965-68, dir., 1968-69; pres. Mary Baldwin Coll., 1969-76, Transylvania U., Lexington, Ky., 1976-81; sr. assoc. Univ. Assos., 1981-82; exec. v.p. L.Q.C. Lamar Soc., 1981-82; pres. Ala. Assn. Ind. Colls. and Univs., 1982-88, Ga. Found. for Ind. Colls. Inc., Atlanta, 1988-96; pres. emeritus, 1996—; pres. Assn. Pvt. Colls. and Univs. in Ga., Atlanta, 1990-96; sr. v.p. Jon McRae & Assocs. Inc., Atlanta, 1996—2001; dir. coll. and unv. rels. Connexxia, 2001—05; sr. adv. higher edn. divsn. James Tower, 2005—07; sr. assoc. Jon McRae and Assocs., 2007—09; v.p. of sr. advisor Myers McRae, 2010—. Mem. Va. Commn. on Status of Women, 1973-76, Ky. Commn. on Status of Women, 1977-81; chmn. Ky. Rhodes Scholar Selection Com., 1978-79; pres. Coun. Ind. Ky. Colls. and Univs., 1978-80; bd. dirs. Ala. Humanities Found., 1983-88, chmn. bd. dirs., 1985-87; bd. dirs., exec. com. Ga. Humanities Coun., 1989-96, vice chair, 1991-93, chair, 1994-96. Author: Ellen Glasow: A Bibliography, 1964. Trustee ODK Lifetime Found., 2010—; with ODK Five Star Soc., 2010; bd. dirs. ODK Found., 2002—10, Ky. State C. of C., 1980—82; trustee Greensboro Coll., 1993—2000, 2002—09. Ret. lt. col. USAF, 1950—82. Ellis L. Phillips Found. intern Rutgers U., 1964-65; Ala. recipient IBM Disting. Performance award Ind. Coll. Funds Am., 1986, Outstanding Ala. Fund Raising Exec. award Nat. Soc. Fund Raising Execs., 1986, Leadership award Brunswick Pub. Charitable Found., 1993; Danforth fellow, 1953-57; Duke scholar, 1954-55; William Watkins Kelly Endowed Scholarship in the Humanities established Ga. Found. Ind. Colls., 1996. Fellow Found. Ind. Higher Edn. (nat. presiding officer 1992-94, Disting. Performance award 1996); mem. MLA, Am. Studies Assn., Soc. Values in Higher Edn., Am. Assn. Higher Edn., Ellen Glasgow Soc. (pres. 1973-75), Newcomen Soc. N.Am., Rotary (Paul Harris fellow), Phi Beta Kappa, The Fellows of Phi Beta Kappa (bd. dirs. 2000—), Omicron Delta Kappa (Found. bd. dirs. 2002—10, lifetime found. trustee 2010-), Rotary. Home: 4015 Brockton Close Marietta GA 30068-4931 Personal E-mail: drkelly@bellsouth.net.

KELSEY, BRIAN, state legislator; b. Memphis, Dec. 22, 1977; Atty. Martin, Tate, Morrow & Marston; mem. Dist. 83 Tenn. House of Reps., Tenn., 2005—09, minority floor leader, 2007—09; mem. Dist. 31 Tenn. State Senate, 2009—. Recipient Top 40 Under 40 award, Memphis Bus. Jour., 30 Under 30 award, Bus. Tenn. Mag. Fellow: Memphis Ch.; mem.: Memphis Bar Assn., Tenn. Bar Assn., Christian Legal Soc., Rep. Nat. Lawyers Assn., Shelby County Young Rep. Exec. Bd., Shelby County Rep. Party Steering Com., Federalist Soc., Lester Cmty. Ctr. Vol. Children's Reader, Lester Legal Soc. Republican. Office: Martin Tate Morrow & Marston 6410 Poplar Ave Ste 1000 Memphis TN 38119 also: 110 War Memorial Bldg Nashville TN 37243-0183 Office Phone: 901-522-9000.

KELSO, LINDA YAYOI, retired lawyer; b. Boulder, Colo., 1946; d. Nobutaka and Tai Ike; m. William Alton Kelso, 1968. BA, Stanford U., 1968; MA, U. Wis., 1973; JD, U. Fla., 1979. Bar: Fla. 1980. Assoc. Mahoney, Hadlow & Adams, Jacksonville, Fla., 1979-82, Commander, Legler, Werber, Dawes, Sadler & Howell, Jacksonville, 1982-86, ptnr., 1986-91, Foley & Lardner, L.L.P., Jacksonville, 1992—. Mem. ABA (bus. law sect.), Jacksonville Bar Assn., Phi Beta Kappa, Order of Coif. Avocations: music, gardening, cooking.

KELSON, RICHARD B., consumer products company executive; b. Pitts., Nov. 20, 1946; B in Polit. Sci., U. Pa.; JD, U. Pitts. Atty. Alcoa, Inc., Pitts., 1974-77, gen. atty., 1977—83, mng. gen. atty., 1983—84, asst. sec., mng. gen. atty., 1984—89, asst. gen. counsel, 1989—91, sr. v.p., environ. health and safety, 1991—94, exec. v.p., environ., health and safety, gen. counsel, 1994—97, exec. v.p., CFO, 1997—2006, chmn.'s counsel, 2006; oper. advisort Pegasus Capital Advisors, LP, 2006—09; pres., CEO Servco Holdings, LLC, 2009—, Servco, LLC, 2009—. Bd. dirs. MeadWestvaco Corp., 2002—. Bd. dirs. Alcoa Found., U. Pitts. Law Sch. Bd. Visitors, Pitts. Civic Light Opera; mem. Fin. Exec. Inst. the Officers Conf. Group, The Pvt. Sector Coun.'s CFPs; mem. bd. trustees Carnegie Mellon. Mem. ABA. Office: MeadWestvaco Corp Bd Directors 501 S 5th St Richmond VA 23219-0501 Office Phone: 804-444-1000. Business E-Mail: richard.kelson@meadwestvaco.com.

KEMP, BRIAN PORTER, state official; b. Athens, Ga., Nov. 2, 1963; m. Marty Argo; children: Jarrett, Lucy, Amy. BS in Agrl., U. Ga., 1987. Pres. Kemp Devel.; mem. Dist. 46 Ga. State Senate, Atlanta, 2002—06; sec. of state State of Ga., Atlanta, 2010—. Past pres. Athens Area Home Builders Assn.; bd. dirs. St. Mary's Hosp., Athens. Republican. Episcopalian. Office: Office of the Secretary of State 214 State Capitol Atlanta GA 30334 Office Phone: 404-656-2881. Office Fax: 404-656-0513. Business E-Mail: sos@sos.ga.gov.*

KEMP, CHARLES C., engineering educator; married. BS in Computer Sci. and Engring., MIT, 1997, MEng in Electrical Engring. and Computer Sci., 1998, PhD in Electrical Engring. and Computer Sci., 2005. Rsch. asst., Artificial Intelligence Lab and Computer Sci. and Artificial Intelligence Lab MIT, 1998—2005, postdoctoral researcher, Computer Sci. and Artificial Intelligence Lab, 2005—06; sr. rsch. scientist Health Sys. Inst. and Wallace H. Coulter Dept. Biomedical Engring., Ga. Tech and Emory U., 2006—07; dir. Ctr. for Healthcare Robotics in the Health Systems Inst., 2006—; asst. prof. Wallace H. Coulter Dept. Biomedical Engring. at Ga. Tech and Emory U., 2007—. Adj. asst. prof. Sch. of Interactive Computing, 2008—; mem. NSF Review Panel, 2008; presenter in field. Referee for several publications; contbr. several articles to profl. jours., chapters to books. Mem.: Eta Kappa Nu, Sigma Xi, Tau Beta Pi. Avocation: music. Office: Health Systems Inst Wallace H Coulter Dept Biomedical Engring Ga Inst Tech and Emory U 313 Ferst Dr Atlanta GA 30332-0535 Business E-Mail: charlie.kemp@hsi.gatech.edu.

KEMP, STEPHEN FRANK, pediatric endocrinologist, educator, composer; b. Newport, Oreg., Mar. 21, 1947; s. Frank Shirley and Charla Mae (Wait) Kemp. BA, U. Oreg., 1969; PhD in Biochemistry, U. Chgo., 1974, MD, 1976. Diplomate Am. Bd. Pediat. Intern Stanford U., 1976-77, resident in pediat., 1977-78, fellow in pediat. endocrinology, 1978-80; asst. prof. pediat., chief pediat. endocrinology U. South Ala., Mobile, 1980-84; asst. prof. pediat. U. Ark. for Med. Sci., 1984-86, asst. prof. biochemistry, 1985-95, assoc. prof. pediat., 1986-95, chief pediat. endocrinology, 1987—2001, prof. pediat., 1995—. Composer (various choir, organ and orchestral works); contbr. V.p. Ala. affiliate Am. Diabetes Assn., 1982—84, pres., 1986—88, chmn. youth com. Ark. affiliate, mem. camp com.; bd. dirs. Human Growth Found., v.p., 1999—2000, pres., 2000—06; chief editor Endrocrinology in WebMD Pediat., 2007—. Recipient Postdoctoral Nat. Rsch. Svc. award, NIH, 1978—80. Fellow: Am. Coll. Endocrinology; mem.: Ark. Med. Soc., Med. Assn. State Ala., So. Pediat. Soc., Endocrine Soc., Am. Fedn. Clin. Rsch., Am. Pediat. Soc. Democrat. Episcopalian. Home: 8 Victoria Cir Maumelle AR 72113-6423 Office: Univ Ark Med Sci Dept Pediat 1 Children's Way Little Rock AR 72202-3591 Business E-Mail: kempstephenf@uams.edu.

KEMPER, ROBERT VAN, anthropologist, minister, educator; b. San Diego, Nov. 21, 1945; s. Ivan L. and Roberta (King) K.; m. Sandra L. Kraft, Sept. 9, 1967 (dec. June 25, 2010); 1 child, John Kraft, m. Julie Adkins, Feb. 26, 2011. BA, U. Calif., Riverside, 1966; MA, U. Calif., Berkeley, 1969, PhD, 1971; MDiv, So. Meth. U., 1999. Ordained to ministry Presbyn. Ch., 1999. Postdoctoral fellow U. Calif., Berkeley, 1971-72; asst. prof. So. Meth. U., Dallas, 1972-77, assoc. prof., 1977-83, prof., 1983—, chmn., 1992-94, 2004—08, pres. faculty senate, 2005—06, trustee, 2005—06. Vis. rsch. scholar U. Iberoamericana, Mexico City, 1970, 79-80, Ctr. U.S.-Mex. Studies, La Jolla, Calif., 1983, U. Nat. Autónoma Mex., Mexico City, 1990-91, El Colegio de Michoacán, Zamora, Mex., 1991, 2000; sec. Inst. Study of Earth and Man, Dallas, 1989-92; Coun. Preservation Anthrop. Records; founding chair Commn. Anthropology Tourism, Internat. Union Anthrop. and Ethnol. Scis., 1993-96. Author: Migration and Adaptation, 1977, Tzintzuntzan, 2010; co-author: History of Anthropology, 1977; co-editor: Anthropologists in Cities, 1974, Migration Across Frontiers, 1979, (series) Contemporary Urban Studies, 1990-2008, Chronicling Cultures, 2002, Translated as Cronicas Culturales, 2010, Urban Life, 2010; editor Socio Cultural Anthropology, Am. Anthropologist, 1985-90, Human Orgn., 1995-98; mem. editl. bd. Ency. World Cultures, 1990-96, Ency. Urban Cultures, 1999—2002. Elder North Pk. Presbyn. Ch., Dallas, 1987-89, 95-97; parish assoc. Trinity Presbyn. Ch., 1999-2008; mem. Mcpl. Libr. Adv. Bd., Dallas, 1975-79; bd. dir. Oasis Housing Corp., 2000-04, Presbyn. Assn. Cmty. Transformation, 2003-04. Fulbright fellow, 1979-80, 91-92, Wenner-Gren fellow, 1974-76, 79-83, Woodrow Wilson fellow, 1966-67. Fellow AAAS, Am. Anthrop. Assn. (bd. dir. 1990-92), Soc. Applied Anthropology (chmn. Malinowski award com. 1979-80, bd. dir. 1995-98); mem. Latin Am. Studies Assn. (co-chmn. XI Internat. Congress 1983), Soc. Urban Anthropology (pres. 1988-90), Soc. Latin Am. Anthropology (pres. 1981-82), Phi Beta Kappa (pres. chpt. 1987-88). Office: So Meth Univ Dept Anthropology 3225 Daniel Ave Dallas TX 75205-1437 Home: 103 Brooke Ln Waxahachie TX 75165 Home Phone: 972-923-0226; Office Phone: 214-768-2928. Business E-Mail: rkemper@smu.edu.

KEMPF, DONALD G., JR., retired lawyer; b. Chgo., July 4, 1937; s. Donald G. and Verginia (Jahnke) K.; m. Nancy Kempf, June 12, 1965; children: Donald G. III, Charles P., Stephen R. AB, Villanova U., 1959; LLB, Harvard U., 1965; MBA, U. Chgo., 1989. Bar: Ill. 1965, U.S. Supreme Ct. 1972, N.Y. 1986, Colo. 1992. Assoc. Kirkland & Ellis, Chgo., 1965-70, ptnr., 1971-2000; exec. v.p., chief legal officer, sec. Morgan Stanley, NYC, 2000—05; ret., 2005. Adj. law prof., 2006—; sr. adv. Gleacher & Co., 2007—12, Blaqwell Inc., 2007—12. Trustee Chgo. Symphony Orch., 1995—, Am. Inns of Ct., 1997-2006, v.p., 2002-06; bd. govs. Chgo. Zool. Soc., 1975-2008, Art Inst. Chgo., 1984—2010; bd. dirs. United Charities Chgo., 1985-2003, chmn. bd., 1991-93; trustee NYC Opera, 2002-05; commr. Antitrust Modernization Commn., 2004-07. Capt. USMC, 1959-62. Recipient Stephen E. Banner award, 2004. Fellow Am. Coll. Trial Lawyers; mem.ABA, Chgo. Club, Econ., Saddle and Cycle Club (Chgo.), Snowmass (Colo.) Club, Roaring Fork Colo. Club, Country Club Fla. Roman Catholic. Address: 14 Country Rd Village Of Golf FL 33436 Personal E-mail: dkempf@kempflaw.com.

KEMPF, STEVEN J., federal agency administrator; BA in History, Marquette U., Milw.; MBA, JD, George Wash. U., Washington. Intern to the office tech. assistance US Gen. Services Adminstrn., technical chmn. for ANSWER and project mgr. Calif., 1996—2000, various positions including dir. ops. to the fed. systems integration & mgmt. ctr. and dep. asst. commr. office integrated tech. services, 2000—08; asst. commr. office acquisition mgmt. US Gen. Services Adminstrn. Fed. Acquisition Svc., 2008, acting dep. commr., 2008—09, dep. commr., 2009—10, acting commr., 2010, commr., 2010—. Office: Office of Commissioner Federal Acquisition Svc 2200 Crystal Dr 11th Fl Arlington VA 22202 Office Phone: 703-605-5400. Business E-Mail: steve.kempf@gsa.gov.

KENAGY, CHERI LYNN, nurse; b. Houston, Nov. 12, 1958; d. Kenneth Leigh and Mary Louise Kenagy; m. William J. Balan, July 30, 1982 (dec. Jan. 15, 1991). Student, San Jacinto Coll., 1980. Lic. vocat. nurse, cert. pediat. advanced life support. Hosp. staff relief Ace Med. Staffing, Houston, 1998—, AHA, Houston, 1998—. Conservative. Presbyterian. Avocations: travel, scuba diving. Home: Box 5885 Pasadena TX 77508-5885 Personal E-mail: txauburn2002@yahoo.com.

KENDER, WALTER JOHN, horticulturist, educator; b. Camden, NJ, Dec. 20, 1935; s. Walter and Martha K.; m. Carole Holm, May 26, 1957; children: David, Lily BS, Del. Valley Coll., 1957, DSc (hon.), 1993; MS, Rutgers U., 1959, PhD, 1962. From asst. prof. to assoc. prof. horticulture U. Maine, Orono, 1962-69; mem. faculty Cornell U., N.Y. State Agrl. Expt. Sta., Geneva, 1969-82, prof. pomology, 1975-82, head dept. pomology and viticulture, 1972-82; chmn. dept. pomology Cornell U., Ithaca, 1975-82; dir. citrus rsch. and edn. ctr. U. Fla., Lake Alfred, 1982-96, prof., 1982-2001, prof. emeritus, 2001—. Co-chmn. task force fruit rsch. N.E. USDA State Exptl. Stas., 1973-75; sec. Internat. Working Group Juvenility Woody Plants, 1974-82; cons. Winrock Internat. (USAID) Pakistan, 1989, Indonesia, 1992, P.R. Dept. Agr., 1996; disting. scientist Agrl. U., Wageningen, Netherlands, 1974; mem. adv. bd. Archbold Biol. Sta., 1991-2001. Contbg. author: Blueberry Culture, 1966; contbr. articles to profl. jours. Bd. dirs. Green Horizon Land Trust, 2004. Fellow AAAS, Am. Soc. Hort. Sci. (dir. 1975-85, trustee endowment fund 1982-87); mem. N.Y. State Hort. Soc., Internat. Soc. Hort. Sci., Internat. Citriculture Soc. (corr.), Am. Pomological Soc. (mem. adv. com.), Fla. Inst. Food Tech., Coun. Agrl. Sci. and Tech., Fla. State Hort. Soc. (hon. mem. 2000, pres. 1996, chmn. of bd. 1997), N.Y. State Fruit Testing Assn. (sec.-treas. 1972-82), Farm Bur. Adv. Com., Haines City Citrus Growers Assn. (bd. dirs. 1991-96), Fla. Citrus Showcase (bd. dirs. 1996-2000), Sigma Xi (past chpt. pres.). Office: Citrus Rsch & Edn Ctr 700 Experiment Station Rd Lake Alfred FL 33850-2243 Office Phone: 863-956-1151. Personal E-mail: kenderw@aol.com.

KENDLE, CANDACE, pharmaceutical executive; b. 1947; m. Christopher C. Bergen; 2 children. BS in Pharmacy, U. Cin., 1970, PhD in Pharmacy, 1972. Resident Cincinnati Children's Hospital Medical Center, 1972; epidemiology fellow U. N.C. Sch. Pub. Health; dir. pharmacy The Children's Hosp. Phila., 1979—81; clin. asst. prof. Phila. Coll. Pharmacy & Sciences, 1979—81; clin. assoc. prof. pediat. U. Pa. Sch. Medicine., 1979—81; co-founder, CEO Kendle International, Inc., Cin., 1981, CEO, 1981—91, chmn., CEO, 1991—2011. Adj. assoc. prof. U. Cin. Sch. Pharmacy, 1982—84; bd. dirs. H.J. Heinz Co., 1998—, United Parcel Svc., Inc. (UPS), 2011—. Contbr. articles to profl. jours. Recipient Entrepreneur of Yr. award, Cin. Mag., 1998, Disting. Alumni award, U. Cin. Dept. Women's Studies, 1999, Arthur C. Glasser Disting. Alumni award, U. Cin., Coll. Pharmacy, 2001, William Howard Taft medal for notable achievement, U. Cin., 2002; named one of The Nations Top 25 Female CEO's, Worth mag., 2001. Mem.: Com. of 200, Assn. Clin. Rsch. Orgns. (founder).

KENDLER, KENNETH SEEDMAN, psychiatrist, medical educator; b. NYC, July 12, 1950; BA in Biology and Religion, U. Calif., Santa Cruz, 1972; MD, Stanford U. Sch. Medicine, Calif., 1977; DSc (hon.), U. Birmingham, Eng., 1999. Diplomate Am. Bd. Psychiatry & Neurology. Intern, resident psychiatry Yale U., New Haven, 1977-78; asst. prof. dept. psychiatry Mt. Sinai Sch. Medicine, NYC, 1980-83; assoc. prof. depts. psychiatry and human & molecular genetics Va. Commonwealth U., Richmond, 1983—87, prof. depts. psychiatry and human genetics, 1987—, Rachel Brown Banks disting. prof. psychiatry, 1991—, dir. Va. Inst. Psychiat. & Behavioral Genetics, 1996—. Biol. scientist tng. program fellow Yale U. Sch. Medicine, 1978—80; rsch. assoc. Bronx VA Med.l Ctr., NYC, 1981—83; Thomas William Salmon lectr. NY Acad. Medicine, 2001; Fritz Redlich fellow Ctr. Advanced Study in Behavioral Scis., Stanford, Calif., 2003—04. Mem. editl. bd. Archives Gen. Psychiatry, Bipolar Disorders, Current Psychiatry Reports, Neuropsychiat. Genetics, Schizophrenia Rsch., Social Psychiatry & Psychiat. Epidemiology, Brit. Jour. Psychiatry, mem. internat. adv. panel Indian Jourl. Psychiatry; contbr. articles to profl. jours., chapters to books. Recipient Lieber prize for outstanding rsch. in schizophrenia, Nat. Alliance Rsch. Schizophrenia & Depression, 1995, Stanley R. Dean award, Am. Coll. Psychiatrists, 1998, Kurt Schneider Sci. award, 1998, Edward Strecker award for outstanding contbn. to psychiat. care and treatment, 2000, Edward J. Sachar award for outstanding contbn. to psychiat. rsch., 2001, Rema Lapouse award, Am. Pub. Health Assn., 2002, Erik Stromgren medal, Stromgren Found., Denmark, 2003. Fellow: Am. Psychiat. Assn.; mem.: AAAS, Behavior Genetics Assn., Genetic Epidemiology Soc., Am. Soc. Human Genetics. Office: Va Commonwealth U Dept Psychiatry PO Box 980126 Richmond VA 23298-0126 Office Phone: 804-828-8590. Office Fax: 804-828-1471. Business E-Mail: kendler@hsc.vcu.edu.

KENDRICK, DAR'SHUN, state legislator; b. Atlanta, Ga., Aug. 28; d. Ricky and Daisy Kendrick. BA in Polit. Sci. & Comm., Oglethorpe U., Atlanta, 2004; JD in Law, U. Ga., 2007; MBA, Kennesaw State U.,

Ga., 2011. Owner, pvt. practice atty. Kendrick Law Practice, Lithonia, Ga., 2010—; mem. Dist. 94 Ga. House Of Representatives, 2011—. Democrat. Office: PO Box 630 Lithonia GA 30058 also: Georgia House of Reps 404 Coverdell Legis Office Bldg Atlanta GA 30334 Office Phone: 678-323-7887, 404-656-0109. Business E-Mail: dkendrick@kendrickforgeorgia.com.

KENDRICK, DAVID ANDREW, economist, educator; b. Gatesville, Tex., Nov. 14, 1937; s. Andrew Green and Nina Alice (Murray) K.; m. Gail Tidd, July 4, 1964; children— Ann, Colin. BA, U. Tex., 1960; PhD (Woodrow Willson fellow 1961-62), MIT, 1965. Asst. prof. Harvard U., Cambridge, Mass., 1966-70; vis. scholar Stanford U., Calif., 1969-70; vis. prof. MIT, Cambridge, 1978-79; prof. econs. U. Tex., Austin, 1970—. Author (with A. Stoutiesdijk): The Planning of Industrial Investment Programs, 1978; author: (with P. Dixon and S. Bowles) Notes and Problems in Microeconomic theory, 1980; author: Stochastic Control for Economic Models, 1981, Feedback: A New Framework for Macroeconomic Policy, 1988, Models for Analyzing Comparative Advantage, 1990; author: (with P.R. Mercado and H.M. Amman) Computational Economics, 2006. Served with U.S. Army, 1960-61. Ford faculty fellow, 1969-70. Fellow AAAS; mem. Econometric Soc., Am. Econs. Assn., Soc. Econ. Dynamics and Control. (pres. 1980), Soc. Computational Econs. (pres. 1998, Kendrick award 2010, Disting. Svc. award 2010). Home: 7209 Lamplight Ln Austin TX 78731-2119 Office: U Tex Dept Econs ECB 3-134E Austin TX 78712

KENELLY, JOHN WILLIS, JR., mathematician, educator; b. Bogalusa, La., Nov. 22, 1935; s. John Willis and Erma (Whittom) K.; m. Charmaine Voss, Aug. 12, 1956(Dec. Dec 23, 1999); children: Deidre Ammie, John Trent. BS, Southeastern La. U., 1957; MS, U. Miss., 1957; PhD, U. Fla., 1961. Instr. U. Fla., 1959-61; asst. prof. U. Southwestern La., 1961-63; assoc. prof. Clemson U., SC, 1963-68, prof. math., 1969-85, Alumni Disting. prof. math., 1985—94, head dept., 1969-77; prof. math., chmn. dept. U. New Orleans, 1968-69; vis. prof. US Mil. Acad., 1982-83; research investigator NASA; mem. com. undergrad. programs Math. Consultant's Bur., 1968—; chief reader advanced placement program in math. Ednl. Testing Service, 1975-79; chmn. calculus devel. com. Coll. Bd., 1979-83, chmn. acad. affairs council, 1985-87, chmn. math. sci. adv. com., 1983-86, dir. advanced placement reading, 1985-91, interim dir. advanced placement program, 1989-90; program dir. NSF, 1988. Nat. pres. Mu Alpha Theta, 1989-91; bd. dirs. Clemson aea 1st Nat. Bank, S.C. Nat. Bank, Wachovia Bank; treas. Clemson Hotels, Inc. Author: Informal Logic, 1967, Explorations on the Texas Instruments TI-85, 1993, Calculus Concepts-4ed, 2008; prodr. Video Visit: Mathematics in a New Era, 1992; contbr. articles to profl. jours.; referee: Pacific Jour. Math. Mem. Math. Assn. Am. (vis. lectr. 1969-92, chmn. com. placement exam. 1985-89, bd. govs. 1985—2011, fin. com. 1988—2011, prodr. several videos, treas. 2002-11), Am. Math. Soc., Nat. Coun. Tchrs. Math. Pres., Clemson Unitarian Fellowship. Lodge: Rotary. Home: 1000 Keystone Ln Clemson SC 29631 Office Phone: 864-508-1070.

KENKEL, JEFFREY MILLER, plastic surgeon, educator; b. Washington, July 15, 1963; s. John Bonaventure and Grace Marie Kenkel; m. Suzanne Marie Kenkel, May 9, 1992; children: Matthew Miller, Ashley Marie. BS, Boston coll., 1985; MD, Georgetown U., 1989. Diplomate Am. Bd. Plastic Surgery. Resident gen. surgery Georgetown U. Sch. Med., Washington, 1989—94; resident plastic surgery U. Tex. Southwestern Med. Ctr., Dallas, 1994—96, faculty mem., 1996—2000, assoc. prof. to prof., vice chmn. Dept. Plastic Surgery, 2000—, dir. Clin. Ctr. Cosmetic Laser Treatment, Rod J. Rohrich, MD Disting. Professorship wound healing and plastic surgery; dir. Clin. Ctr. Cosmetic Laser Treatment, chief plastic surgery VA Med. Ctr., Dallas. Attending staff mem. Baylor U. Med. Ctr., Children's Med. Ctr., Dallas, Parkland Meml. Hosp., St. Paul U. Med. Ctr., Zale Lipshy Univ. Hosp.; plastic surgeon, team physician Dallas Stars, 1996—. Co-author: Ultrasound-Assisted Liposuction; editor: Body Contouring After Massive Weight Loss; contbr. articles to med. jours. Named one of Best Doctors in Dallas, D Mag., 2005, Best Doctors in America, 2006; grantee Am. Soc. Aesthetic Surg. Rsch. Found., 1997, Plastic Surgery Ednl. Found., 1998, 1999. Fellow: ACS; mem.: AMA, Aesthetic Surgery Edn. and Rsch. Found. (treas.), Am. Soc. Laser Medicine and Surgery, Dallas Soc. Plastic Surgeons (past pres.), Tex. Soc. Plastic Surgeons, Am. Soc. Plastic and Reconstructive Surgeons, Am. Soc. Aesthetic Plastic Surgery (bd. mem.). Avocations: golf, ice hockey, rollerblading, music. Office: U Tex Southwestern Med Ctr Outpatient Bldg 1801 Inwood Rd, 5th Fl Dallas TX 75390-9132 Office Phone: 214-645-2353, 214-645-3112. Office Fax: 214-645-2354. E-mail: jeffrey.kenkel@utsouthwestern.edu.

KENNA, THOMAS H., rail transportation executive; 3 children. BS, Fla. State U.; MBA, Nova Southeastern U. Worked CMA CGM, Hapag-Lloyd AG; dir., mktg. Panama Canal Railway Co., 2000—08, pres., dir. gen., 2008—. Office: Panama Canal Railway Co PO Box 527948 Miami FL 33152 Office Phone: 507-317-6070. Office Fax: 507-317-6061. Business E-Mail: tkenna@panarail.com.

KENNE, LESLIE FARR, consulting firm executive, retired military officer; b. 1947; BS in Aerospace Engring., Auburn U., 1970; Grad., Squadron Officer Sch., 1975; M in Procurement Mgmt., Webster Coll., 1979; Grad., Armed Forces Staff Coll., 1981, Nat. War Coll., 1986, Def. Sys. Mgmt. Coll., 1988; advanced mgmt. program, U. N.H., 1993; nat. and internat. security mgmt., Harvard U., 1995. Cert. level III program mgmt., level III test and evaluation. Commd. 2d lt. USAF, 1971, advanced through grades to lt. gen., 2002, ret., 2003; maintenance supr. 474th Orgnl. Maintenance Squadron, Takhli Royal Thai AFB, Thailand, 1973-74; project mgr., dep. test dir. range measurement sys. jt. test Tactical Fighter Weapons Ctr., Nellis AFB, Nev., 1975-78; program mgr. Office of Sec. of Def.-directed joint tests Air Force Test and Evaluation Ctr., Kirtland AFB, N.Mex., 1978-81; chief airborne sys. test br., chief elec. sys. test divsn. 324th Test Wing, Eglin AFB, Fla., 1982-85; dir. ops. and support Airborne Warning and Control Sys. Program Officer, Hanscom AFB, Mass., 1986-88; chief spl. projects divsn. directorate spl. programs Office of Asst. Sec. of Air Force for Acquisitions, Washington, 1988-90; dir. LANTIRN Sys. Program Office Aero. Sys. Divsn., Wright-Patterson AFB, Ohio, 1993-94; dep. dir. fighters and C2 and weapons programs Office of Asst. Sec. of Air Force for Acquisition, Washington, 1992-93; dir. F-16 Sys. Program Office Aero. Sys. Ctr., Wright-Patterson AFB, 1993-94, vice comdr., 1994-95, Sacramento Air Logistics Ctr., McClellan AFB, Calif., 1995-96; dep. dir. Joint Strike Fighter Program, Arlington, Va., 1996-97, dir., 1997-99; comdr. Electronics Sys. Ctr., Hanscom AFB, Mass., 1999—2002; chief of staff for warfighting integration USAF, Washington, 2002—03; pres. LK Associates, Fairfax, Va. Bd. dirs. EDO Corp., 2004—07, Harris Corp., 2004—, Unisys Corp., 2006—, Oshkosh Corp., 2010—. Decorated Legion of Merit, Bronze Star, Meritorious Svc. medal with 2 oak leaf clusters.

KENNEDY, ANDY, men's college basketball coach; b. Louisville, Miss., Mar. 13, 1968; m. Kimber Kennedy; children: Meagan, Kaitlyn. Attended, NC State U., Raleigh, 1986—87; BA, U. Ala., Birmingham, 1991. Forward Charlotte Hornets, 1991, Greece, Spain, The Netherlands, PR, 1991—94; asst. basketball coach U. South Ala. Jaguars, 1994—95; comml. real estate broker, 1995—96; asst. basketball coach U. Ala. Birmingham Blazers, 1996—2001; asst. basketball coach, recruiting coord. U. Cin. Bearcats, 2001—04, assoc. head basketball coach, recruiting coord., 2004—05, interim head basketball coach, 2005—06; head basketball coach U. Miss. Rebels, 2006—. Finalist Clair Bee award, 2009. Office: Univ Miss Mens Basketball 908 All-American Dr PO Box 1848 University MS 38677 Office Phone: 662-915-7534, 662-915-7617. Business E-Mail: kennedya@olemiss.edu.

KENNEDY, BILLY, men's college basketball coach; b. Metairie, La., Feb. 2, 1964; m. Mary Ethridge; children: Will, Lexie, Brooks, Anna Cate. AA in Gen. Studies, Delgado CC, New Orleans, 1984; BA in Social Studies, Southeastern La. U., Hammond, 1986. Student asst. coach Southeastern La. U. Lions, 1985—86, head basketball coach, 1999—2005; vol. asst. coach U. New Orleans Privateers, 1986—87; grad. asst. coach U. Wyoming Cowboys, 1987—88; asst. coach Northwestern State U. Demons, La., 1988—89, Tulane U. Green Wave, La., 1989—90, Tex. A&M U. Aggies, 1990—91, head basketball coach, 2011—; asst. coach Creighton U. Bluejays, Omaha, 1991—93, U. Calif. Golden Bears, Berkeley, 1993—97; head basketball coach Centenary Coll. Gents, La., 1997—99; asst. coach U. Miami Hurricanes, Fla., 2005—06; head basketball coach Murray State U. Racers, Ky., 2006—11. Recipient John Lotz "Barnabas" award, Fellowship Christian Athletes, 2011; named Southland Conf. Coach of Yr., 2004, Dist. 8 Coach of Yr., Nat. Assn. Basketball Coaches, 2004, 2005, Dist. 19 Coach of Yr., 2010, Coach of Yr., La. Assn. Basketball Coaches, 2004, 2005, La. Sports Writers Assn., 2004, 2005, Ohio Valley Conf. Coach of Yr., 2010, 2011; finalist Hugh Durham award, 2010, Skip Prosser Man of Yr. award, 2010. Office: Tex A&M University Athletics Dept Men's Basketball PO Box 30017 College Station TX 77842-3017 Office Phone: 979-845-4531.

KENNEDY, JAMES COX, publishing and media executive; b. Honolulu, Nov. 1947; two sons, one daughter. BBA, U. Denver, 1970; LHD (hon.), Kennesaw State U., 2003. With Atlanta Newspapers, 1972-79, prodn. asst., 1972-76, exec. v.p., gen. mgr., reporter, copy editor, advt. salesman and bus. mgr., 1976-79; pres. Grand Junction Newspapers, 1979-80; pub. Grand Junction Daily Sentinel, 1980-85; v.p. Cox Newspapers (subs. of Cox Enterprises Inc.), Atlanta, 1985-86; exec. v.p. Cox Enterprises Inc., Atlanta, 1986-87, pres., chief oper. officer, exec. v.p., 1986-87, chmn., CEO, 1988—. Hon. chmn. Tour de Cure cycling event, Am. Diabetes Assn., 1997, Ga. chapter Nat. Multiple Sclerosis Soc. Bike Tour, 1993—95; bd. mem. Ducks Unlimited, PATH Found.; pres. Wetlands Am. Trust. Named Philanthropists of the Yr. (with wife Sarah), Greater Atlanta chapter Assn. Fund-raising Professionals, 2003; named one of Forbes 400: Richest Americans, 2009; named to J. Mack Robinson Coll. Bus. Hall of Fame, Ga. State Univ., 2004. Past Masters Nat., Pan-Am. & World champion, 3000 meter pursuit cycling race; capt. of four man cycling team, winning Race Across America in 1992, setting a world record, and finished 2d in 1994, setting an Am. record; named to U.S. Cycling Fedn. Master's All-American team. Mailing: Cox Enterprises Inc 6205 Peachtree Dunwoody Rd Atlanta GA 30328 Office Phone: 678-645-0000. Office Fax: 678-645-1079. Business E-Mail: james.kennedy@cox.com.

KENNEDY, JOE DAVID, JR., (JOEY KENNEDY), editor; b. Dayton, Tex., Mar. 28, 1956; s. Joe David Sr. and Patricia Ann (Harper) K.; m. Veronica Elaine Pike, Feb. 2, 1980. BA, U. Ala., Birmingham, 1988, MA, 2003. Reporter gen. assignments Houma Daily Courier, La., 1974-76; dir. news, sports Sta. KJIN-AM/KCIL-FM, Houma, 1976-77; reporter gen. assignments Cullman Times, Ala., 1977-78; asst. sports editor Anniston Star, Ala., 1978-81; sports copy editor Birmingham News, 1981-83, asst. editor lifestyle, 1983-85, editor photography, 1985-86, Sunday editor, 1986-89, editor book revs., 1986-95, editl. writer, columnist, 1989—. Adj. prof. dept. English, U. Ala., Birmingham, 2001—. Contbr. Redbook mag., 1997, 98, Iron Horse Lit. Rev., 2004, Aura Lit. Rev., 2005. Mem. Houma-Terrebonne Bicentennial Commn., 1975-76; press sec. rep. gubernatorial candidate Guy Hunt, Ala., 1978; tutor literacy Birmingham Pub. Schs. Adult Learning Ctr., 1990-91; judge J.C. Penney Golden Rule Awards for Vols., 1992; lectr. Lee Coll. Springs Art Festival, Baytown, Tex., 1992; mem. adv. bd. Sch. Journalism, U. Miss., 1992-98, Dept. Comm. Studies U. Ala. Birmingham, 2005-; bd. dirs. So. Mus. Flight, 1992-93; mem. Leadership Birmingham Class, 1994-95, AIDS Care Team, 1994-00; bd. dirs. A Baby's Place, 1996-97, PATH Orgn. for Homeless, 1997-99, Childcare Resources, 2004-05, Bridges Found., 2006—08, Baptist Jt. Com. Religious Freedom, 2008-; mem. Ct. Appointed Spl. Advocates for Children, 1996—; mem. bd. deacons Southside Bapt. Ch.; reading tutor 4th graders Birmingham Pub. Schs., 1999. Recipient various awards, La. Press Assn., 1974—77, Ala. Press Assn., 1989—2001, Best Commentary award, 1992, 2000, 2004, 2008, Ala. Sportswriters Assn., 1978—81, Hector award, Troy State U., 1991, 1992, 1994, 1995, Pulitzer prize for edtl. writing, 1991, Nat. Edn. Writers Assn., 1994, Ed. Press Award, John S. Coley award as Outstanding Graduate Student, U. Ala.-Birmingham, 2003, Nat. Headliner award, 2006; named Comm. Alumnus of Yr., U. Ala., Birmingham, 1991, One of the Top 20 Grads., 1994, Champion Justice, Nat. Assn. Criminal Def. Lawyers, 2008; nominee Pulitzer prize, 1994, Pulitzer prize, 2006; scholar Howton Scholarship in Creative Writing, U. Ala.-Birmingham, 2002—03. Mem. U. Ala. Birmingham Nat. Alumni Soc. (life; bd. dirs. 1999-2004, v.p. 2002-04), Outstanding Grad. Student Sch. Arts and Humanities 2003. Avocations: reading, writing. Home: 1635 11th Pl S Birmingham AL 35205-5907 Office: Birmingham News 2200 4th Ave N Birmingham AL 35203-3840 Home Phone: 205-324-7111; Office Phone: 205-325-2466. Business E-Mail: jkennedy@bhamnews.com, joekennedy@me.com.

KENNEDY, JOHN EDWARD, lawyer; b. Mpls., Feb. 18, 1947; s. John Edward and Margaret (Greathouse) K.; m. Linda Bagwell, June 22, 1968; children: John Harlan, Elizabeth. AB cum laude, Harvard U., 1968, JD magna cum laude, 1971. Bar: Tex. 1971, US Dist. Ct. (so. dist.) Tex. 1972, US Ct. Appeals (5th cir.) 1972, US Supreme Ct. 1975, US Ct. Appeals (DC cir.) 1984. Assoc. Vinson & Elkins LLP, Houston, 1971-80, ptnr., 1980—2012. Served to 2d lt. USAR, 1972. Mem. ABA, Houston Bar Assn., Energy Bar Assn. Presbyterian. Home: 2617 Pemberton Dr Houston TX 77005-3441 Office: Vinson & Elkins LLP 2500 First City Tower 1001 Fannin St Houston TX 77002-6760 Office Phone: 713-758-2550.

KENNEDY, KAREN SYENCE, advertising agency executive; b. Bklyn., May 7, 1943; d. Bruno Weinschel and Pearl Heyman; first marriage: Michael Syence; children: Sherry, Scott; m. Peter Kennedy, Aug. 25, 1979. BS, Boston U., 1963. Cert. in comml. photography Germain Sch. Photography, NY, 1961. Advt. mgr. Weinschel Engring., Gaithersburg, Md., 1965-68; mktg. svcs. mgr. Rixon Electronics, Silver Spring, Md., 1968-70; pres. Comm. Unltd., Chevy Chase, Ltd., 1970-74; v.p. Ehrlich Manes & Assocs., Bethesda, Md., 1974-77; pres. Rainbow Tree, St. Croix, V.I., 1978-80; advt. programs dir. GE, McLean, Va., 1980-81; pres. Karen Syence Kennedy Assocs., Fairfax, Va., 1981-83; pres., CEO, KSK Comm., Inc., Vienna, Va., 1983—2002; ptnr. EPB Comms., NYC, 1999—2002; pres. Karen Syence Kennedy Assocs., Gt. Falls, Va., 2002—. Pres., chmn. Treasure Beach Found., Inc., 2000—. Treas. Beach Found.; vol., founder, pres., bd. chmn. Personal E-mail: karen@kennedy101.biz.

KENNEDY, LAURENCE, endocrinologist, educator; b. Belfast, Northern Ireland, Jan. 24, 1948; m. Sarah Louise; children: Christopher, Jonathan. MD, Queens U., Ireland, 1972. Jr. house officer (intern) Royal Victoria Hosp., Belfast, Northern Ireland, 1972—73, sr. registrar endocrinology and diabetes, 1976—78, cons. physician endocrinology, diabetes, medicine, 1980—92; gen. med. tng. (resident) Belfast Tchg. Hosps., Northern Ireland, 1973—76; cons. physician gen. medicine, diabetes Ards Hosp., Northern Ireland, 1992—94; cons. physician endocrinology, diabetes, medicine Dr. Gray's Hosp., Elgin, Scotland, 1994—96; clin. assoc. prof. medicine Univ. NC, Chapel Hill, 1996—97; rsch. fellow and clin. instr. endocrinology Univ. Fla., Gainesville, 1978—80, interim chief, divsn. endocrinology and metabolism, 1999—2001, assoc. prof. and dir. clin. svcs., 1997—, chief, divsn. endocrinology and metabolism, 2001—. Mem.: Am. Diabetes Assn., Assn. of Physicians of Great Britain and Ireland, Soc. for Endocrinology (UK), Endocrine Soc., European Assn. for the Study of Diabetes, Irish Endocrine Soc., Brit. Diabetic Assn. Office: University of Florida Division of Endocrinology, Department of 1600 SW Archer Rd Gainesville FL 32610 Office Phone: 352-846-2230. Office Fax: 352-846-2231.

KENNEDY, LEANNE P., diversified financial services company executive; BBA in Fin., Columbus State U., Ga.; grad., Ga. Sch. Banking. Joined Synovus Fin. Corp., 1991, sr. v.p. product mgmt. Columbus Bank and Trust, dir. credit portfolio mgmt.; dir. enterprise risk mgmt. Synovus Financial Corp., 2005—. Office: Synovus Financial Corp 1111 Bay Ave Ste 500 Columbus GA 31901 Office Phone: 706-649-5220. Office Fax: 706-641-6555.

KENNEDY, LEE A., finance company executive; Pres. Telecredit Svc. Ctr. (now Equifax, Inc.), 1981—90; exec. v.p. Equifax, Inc., Atlanta, 1990—99, pres., COO & bd. dirs., 1999—2001; chmn., pres., CEO Certegy Inc., 2001—02; pres., CEO Fidelity National Information Services, Inc., Jacksonville, Fla., 2002—09; chmn. Lender Processing Services, Inc., Jacksonville, Fla., 2009—; interim chmn., CEO Ceridian Corp., 2010—. Office: Lender Processing Services 601 Riverside Ave Jacksonville FL 32204 Office Phone: 904-854-5100. E-mail: lee.kennedy@lpsvcs.com.

KENNEDY, MARC J., lawyer; b. Newburgh, NY, Mar. 2, 1945; s. Warren G. K. and Frances F. (Levinson) K.; m. Karen Karatsu; children: Kayla R., Shawna D. BA cum laude, Syracuse U., NY, 1967; JD, U. Mich., 1970. Bar: NY 1971. Assoc. Davies, Hardy, Ives & Lawther, NYC, 1971-72, London, Buttenweiser & Chalif, NYC, 1972-73, Silberfeld, Danziger & Bangser, NYC, 1973; counsel Occidental Crude Sales, Inc., NYC, 1974-75; v.p., gen. counsel Internat. Ore & Fertilizer Corp., NYC, 1975-82; asst. gen. counsel Occidental Chem. Corp., Houston, 1982; v.p., gen. counsel Occidental Chem. Agrl. Products Inc., Tampa, Fla., 1982-87; v.p., gen. counsel agrl. products group Occidental Chem. Corp., Tampa, 1987-91, assoc. gen. counsel Dallas, 1991—. Contbr. articles to profl. jours. Mem. governing bd. Ctr. for Brain Health U. Tex. Dallas, 2001—2005; trustee Bar Harbor Festival Corp., NYC, 1974-87; bd. dirs. Am. Opera Repertory Co., 1982-85; mem. com. planned giving NY Foundling Hosp., 1977-88; Explorer post advisor Boy Scouts Am., 1976-78. Mem. ABA (vice-chmn. com. internat. law liaison young lawyers sect. 1974-75, chmn. sub-com. proposed trade barriers to the importation of products into US 1985-88, vice chmn. corp. counsel com. 1992-93, co-chmn. corp. counsel com. 1993-98), NY State Bar Assn., Assn. Corp. Counsel, Tex. Bar Assn., Dallas Bar Assn. Office: Occidental Chem Corp PO Box 809050 Dallas TX 75380-9050

KENNEDY, MICHAEL D., executive recruiter, federal agency administrator; BA in History & Polit. Sci., U. NC, Chapel Hill; MBA, Harvard U., Mass. Investment mgr. JP Morgan and Co., NYC; v.p. corp. group Wachovia Corp.; v.p. corp. fin. group GE Capital Corp.; venture capital cons.; sr. client ptnr., fin. Korn/Ferry Internat., Atlanta. Bd. dirs. Fed. Retirement Thrift Investment Bd., Washington, 2010—, chmn., 2011—. Former mem. bd. trustees Phillips Exeter Acad., NH; bd. trustees Ga. Employees Retirement Sys. Pension Fund; bd. visitors U. NC. Mem.: Atlanta Venture Forum, Leadership Atlanta, Harvard Bus. Club Atlanta. Office: Korn/Ferry International 1201 W Peachtree St NW Ste 2500 Atlanta GA 30309 Office Phone: 404-222-4009. Business E-Mail: michael.kennedy@kornferry.com.*

KENNEDY, TOM, corporate financial executive; BS in Economics summa cum laude, Tulane U.; MBA, Harvard U. CFO, sr. v.p., exec. v.p. Vanguard Car Rental USA, Inc; with Merrill Lynch Capital Markets, Bank of Yokohama, Chiquita Brands International; v.p., fin., planning and analysis Northwest Airlines Corp; sr. v.p. Northwest Airlines, Inc., 1992—2003; contr. Northwest Airlines Corp., 1992—2005, sr. v.p., 2007—08; exec. v.p., CFO Hilton Worldwide, Inc., 2008—. Office: Hilton Worldwide 7930 Jones Branch Dr Mc Lean VA 22102 Office Phone: 703-883-1000. Business E-Mail: thomas_kennedy@hilton.com.

KENNON, ROZMOND HERRON, retired physical therapist; b. Birmingham, Ala., Dec. 12, 1935; m. Gloria Oliver; children: Shawn, Rozmond Jr. BA, Talldega Coll., 1956; cert., U. Colo., 1957. Asst. chief phys. therapist St. John's Hosp., St. Paul, 1957-58, Creigthon Meml. St. Joseph's Hosp., Omaha, 1958-61; asst. chief, phys. therapist Sister Kenny Inst., Mpls., 1962, chief phys. therapy, 1962-64; cons. in phys. therapy Mt. Sinai Hosp., Mpls., 1963-70; pvt. practice, 1964-98. Contbr. articles to profl. jours. Bd. dirs. Southdale YMCA, Edina Human Rights, Southside Med. Ctr., Mpls., Boy Scouts Am.; trustee Talladega (Ala.) Coll.; pres., CEO Daniel Kennon and Verna Herron Kennon Family Found.; pres. Talladega Bd. Trustees; exec. bd. dirs. Greater Ala. Coun. Boy Scouts Am. Mem. Am. Phys. Therapy Assn., Am. Registry Phys. Therapists, Ala. Phys. Therapy Assn. (mem. social-econ. com., past chmn. profl. practice com., bd. dirs., past sec.). Home: 6108 Waterside Ct Birmingham AL 35244-4158

KENNY, DAVID W., internet professional services executive; b. 1961; BS, Gen. Motors Inst. (Kettering Univ.); MBA, Harvard Bus. Sch. Ptnr. Bain & Co., 1987—96; vice-chmn. Bronner, Slosberg, Humphrey, Inc., 1996—97, ptnr., CEO Boston, 1997—99; chmn., CEO Digitas, Inc., Boston, 1999—2007; co-founder, mng. ptnr. VivaKi, 2008—10; pres. Akamai Technologies, Inc., Cambridge, Mass., 2010—11; chmn., CEO The Weather Co., 2012—. Bd. dirs. Digitas, Inc., 1999—2007, Publicis Groupe, 2007—10, Akamai Technologies Inc., 2007—, Yahoo! Inc., 2011—12, SessionM, 2012—, The Ad Council. Bd. dirs. Teach for America. Office: The Weather Channel 300 Interstate North Parkway Atlanta GA 30339 Office Phone: 617-444-3000.

KENNY, GREGORY B., industrial equipment executive; BS, Georgetown Univ.; MBA, George Washington Univ.; MPA, Harvard Univ. Fgn. svc. officer US Dept. State, 1975—82; from v.p. corp. devel. to group exec. for tech. prod. and svcs. Penn Central Corp., 1982—94; exec. v.p. General Cable, 1994—97, bd. dir., 1997—, exec. v.p., COO, 1997—99, pres., COO, 1999—2001, pres., CEO, 2001—. Bd. dir. IDEX Corp., 2002—07, Corn Products Internat., Cardinal Health, 2007—. Office: c/o General Cable 4 Tesseneer Dr Highland Heights KY 41076 Office Phone: 859-572-8000. Office Fax: 859-572-8458.

KENSETH, MATT ROY, race car driver; b. Madison, Wis., Mar. 10, 1972; m. Katie Martin, 2000; one child Ross (previous relationship). Race car driver Roush Fenway Racing, 1999—. Winner Rockingham Speedway, NC, 1998, Pikes Peak Internat. Raceway, Colo., 1998, Dover Internat. Speedway, 1998, 2000, 2011, Darlington Raceway, 1999, 2005, Auto Club Speedway, Fontana, Calif., 1999, 2000, 2003, 2007, 2009, Nazareth Speedway, Pa., 1999, Bristol Motor Speedway, 1999, 2006, Daytona Internat. Speedway, 2000, 2009, 2012, Charlotte Motor Speedway, 2000, 2003, 2011, Tex. Motor Speedway, Ft. Worth, 2001, 2004, 2011, NH Motor Speedway, Loudon, 2004, Atlanta Motor Speedway, 2004, 2008, Phoenix Internat. Raceway, 2006, Homestead-Miami Speedway, 2006, Talladega Superspeedway, 2012, Kans. Speedway, 2012. Named Winston Cup Rookie of Yr., 2000, NASCAR Winston Cup Champion, 2003, NASCAR Driver of Yr., The Sporting News, 2003. Office: 4101 Roush Pl Concord NC 28027 also: Matt Kenseth Fan Club 700 Kenseth Way Cambridge WI 53523

KENT, BARTIS MILTON, retired physician; b. Terrell, Tex., June 23, 1925; s. Bartis William and Annie (Smalley) K.; m. Ann L. Kiel, July 6, 1954; children: Susan Ruth, Martha Lucille, Bartis Michael. Student, So. Meth. U., 1942-44; MD, Baylor U., 1948. Diplomate Am. Bd. Internal Medicine. Intern Jefferson Davis Hosp., Houston, 1948-49; resident pathology Mass. Meml. Hosps., Boston, 1951; resident in internal medicine Baylor U., 1953-56; indsl. physician Humble Oil Co., Houston, 1949-51; instr. dept. medicine U. Iowa, 1956-58; staff physician Iowa City VA Hosp., 1956-58; practice medicine specializing in internal medicine Muskogee, Okla., 1958—2002. Cons. Muskogee VA Hosp.; clin. asst. prof. medicine U. Okla. Sch. Medicine, 1975-98. Chmn. Muskogee County chpt. Am. Nat. Red Cross, 1963-65. With USAF, 1951—53. Decorated Air medal. Fellow A.C.P.; mem. Indsl. Med. Assn., Soc. Nuclear Medicine, Am. Fedn. Clin. Research, Am. Heart Assn., Aerospace Medicine Assn., Am., Okla. socs. internal medicine, Muskogee C. of C. Methodist. Mason (Shriner). Avocations: fishing, gardening. Home: 800 N 45th St Muskogee OK 74401-1505

KENT, DAVID CHARLES, lawyer; b. Shreveport, La., July 23, 1953; s. Keith C. and Louise (Goode) Kent; m. Carol Elizabeth Hittson, July 3, 1976; children: John, Meredith, Robert. BA, Baylor U., 1975, JD, 1978. Bar: Tex. 1978, U.S. Dist. Ct. (no. dist.) Tex. 1980, U.S. Ct. Appeals (5th cir.) 1980, U.S. Dist. Ct. (so. and we. dists.) Tex. 1981, U.S. Dist. Ct. (ea. dist.) Tex. 1981, bd. cert. civil trial law, personal injury trial law:. Briefing atty. Supreme Ct. Tex., Austin, 1978-79, Hughes & Luce L.L.P., Dallas, 1979-2000, Diamond McCarthy Taylor Finley Bryant & Lee, LLP, 2000—03, Sedgwick LLP, 2003—. Editor: Managing Scarce World Resources, 1975, Crime and Justice in America, 1976, Medical Care and Health in America, 1977, Meeting America's Energy Needs, 1978; contbr. articles to profl. jours. Mem. nat. exploring com. Boy Scouts Am., Irving, Tex., 1982—92; coord. employee campaign United Way, Dallas, 1981—90; teamwalk March of Dimes, Dallas, 1981—87; mem. Baylor Parents League, pres. North Dallas area chpt., 1999—2001; pres. Twin Bridge Homeowners Assn., 2000—02; bd. dirs. High Adventure Treks Dads and Daus., Inc., chmn., 2005—; bd. dirs. Law Focused Edn. Inc., 1997—2006, pres., 2004—06. Recipient Cert. Recognition, United Way, 1983, Baylor Law Sch. Alumnus of North award, 2011; named Outstanding Young Lawyer Dallas, Dallas Assn. Young Lawyers, 1989. Fellow: Tex. Bar Found., Dallas Bar Found.; mem.: ABA (life fellow ABA Young Lawyer Divsn.), Hugh O'Brian Youth Leadership North Tex. (mem., bd. dirs. 1999—2013, sec. 2000—06, pres. 2006—08, Vol. of Yr. award 2010), State Bar of Tex. (mem., dist. 6 grievance Com. 2009—), Dallas Bar Assn. (chair, Tex. HS Mock Trial Program 1994—99, chair law day com. 2000—01, chair spkrs. com. 2002, dir. tort and ins. practice sect. 2005—10, sec./treas. tort and ins. practice sect. 2006, co-chair Bench Bar conf. com. 2006, bd. dirs. 2007, vice chair tort and ins. practice sect. 2007, co-chair, admissions & membership com. 2008, chair tort. and ins. practises sect. 2009, mem. bus. litigation sect. leadership coun. 2010, bus. litigation sect. treas. 2011, mem. bd. dirs., trial skills sect. 2014, chair pub. forum com. 2014, chair bus. litigation sect. 2013, Outstanding Com. Chair award 1998, Outstanding Sect. award 2007, 2010), Baylor U. Alumni Assn. (scholarship com. 1980—81). Methodist. Office: Sedgwick Detert Moran & Arnold LLP 1717 Main St Ste 5400 Dallas TX 75201 Business E-Mail: david.kent@sdma.com.*

KENT, JEFF (JEFFREY FRANKLIN KENT), business owner, retired professional baseball player; b. Bellflower, Calif., Mar. 7, 1968; s. Alan and Sherry Kent; m. Dana Kent; children: Lauren Elizabeth, Hunter Franklin, Colton Ryan, Kaeden Thomas. Attended, U. Calif., Berkeley. Second baseman Toronto Blue Jays, 1992, NY Mets, 1992-96, Cleve. Indians, 1996, San Francisco Giants, 1997—2002, Houston Astros, 2003—04, LA Dodgers, 2005—09; ret., 2009; owner Kent Powersports, LP, Selma, Tex. Contestant: Survivor, 2012. Co-founder, Women Driven Scholarship Program U. Calif. Recipient Silver Slugger award, 2000—02, 2005; named Nat. League MVP, 2000; named to Nat. League All-Star Team, 1999—2001, 2004—05. Achievements include tying the San Francisco Giants grand slam record (3) in 1997; hitting 128 RBI in the 1998 season, the most by a second baseman since Roger Hornsby hit 149 in 1929 with the Chicago Cubs; becoming the all-time leader in home runs as a second baseman, 2004. Avocations: hunting, fishing. Office: Kent Powersports 15664 IH 35 Selma TX 78154 Office Phone: 210-655-2625. Office Fax: 210-655-2820.

KENT, MUHTAR, beverage company executive; b. Ayvalik, Turkey, 1952; m. Defne Kent; 2 children. BS in Economics, Hull U., 1975; MS in Adminstrv. Sciences, London City U. Various mktg. and operations roles Coca-Cola Co., Atlanta, 1978—85, gen. mgr. Coca-Cola Turkey & Ctrl. Asia, 1985—89, sr. v.p. internat., pres. East Ctrl. Europe divsn., 1989—95, mng. dir. Coca-Cola Amatil-Europe, 1995—98; pres., CEO Efes Beverage Group, Istantbul, Turkey, 1999—2005; pres, CEO North Asia, Eurasia & Middle East Group Coca-Cola Co., 2005—06, exec. v.p., 2006; pres. Coca-Cola Internat., 2006; pres., COO Coca-Cola Co., 2006—08, pres., CEO, 2008—09, chmn., CEO, 2009—. Bd. dirs. The Coca-Cola Co., 2008—. Mem. internat. bd. dirs. Special Olympics, 2007—. Office: The Coca-Cola Co One Coca-Cola Plz Atlanta GA 30313 Office Phone: 404-676-2121. Office Fax: 404-676-6792.*

KENT, PHIL (PHILIP I. KENT), broadcast executive; b. 1954; BA in Economics, Lehigh U., 1976. With sales team Blair Television, 1975; co-founder subs. Blair Entertaiment John Blair & Co., 1981, v.p. program develop., 1984; packaging agent TV dept. Creative Artist's Agency (CAA), 1986—93; pres. Turner Home Entertainment, Atlanta, 1993—96, Turner Broadcasting Systems Internat. Inc., Atlanta, 1996—2000; pres., COO CNN News Group, 2000—01; chmn., CEO Turner Broadcasting System, Inc, 2003—13, chmn., 2014—. Bd. dirs. Ad Coun., Atlanta Braves; mem. dean's exec. bd. UCLA Sch. Theater, Film & TV. Bd. dirs. Woodruff Arts Ctr., Atlanta, Ctrl. Atlanta Progress. Named to The Broadcasting & Cable Hall of Fame, 2007. Mem.: Metro Atlanta Chamber of Commerce (bd. dirs.), Nat. Cable & Telecommunications Assn. (bd. dirs.). Office: Turner Broadcasting System Inc 1 CNN Ctr Atlanta GA 30348-5366*

KENT, THOMAS ANDREW, neurologist, educator; MD, U. Kans., 1979. Diplomate American Bd. Psychiatry and Neurology-psychiatry, 1993, American Bd. Psychiatry and Neurology-neurology, 2006. Resident in psychiatry Univ. Kans. Affiliated Hosp., Kans., 1980—83; fellow in psyhopharmacology Univ. Kan. Affiliated Hosp., 1982—83; resident in neurology Univ. Tex. Affiliated Hosp., Galveston, 1984—85; prof. in neurology Baylor Coll.; hosp. affiliation includes Michael E. DeBakey VA Med. Ctr. Office: Michael E DeBakey VA Medical Center 2002 Holcombe Blvd Houston TX 77030-4298 Office Phone: 713-791-1414.*

KEOUGH, DONALD RAYMOND, investment company executive; b. Maurice, Iowa, Sept. 4, 1926; s. Leo H. and Veronica (Henkels) K.; m. Marilyn Mulhall, Sept. 10, 1949; children: Kathleen Anne, Mary Shayla, Michael Leo, Patrick John, Eileen Tracey, Clarke Robert. BS, Creighton U., 1949, LLD (hon.), 1982, U. Notre Dame, 1985, Emory U., 1993, Trinity U., Dublin, Ireland, 1993, Clarke U., 1994. With Butter-Nut Foods Co., Omaha, 1950-61; with Duncan Foods Co., Houston, 1961-67; v.p., dir. mktg. foods divsn. The Coca-Cola Co., Atlanta, 1967-71, pres. foods divsn., 1971-73; exec. v.p. Coca-Cola USA, Atlanta, 1973-74, pres., 1974-76; exec. v.p. The Coca-Cola Co., Atlanta, 1976-79, sr. exec. v.p., 1980-81, pres., COO, 1981-93, advisor to bd., 1993-98; chmn. Coca-Cola Enterprises, Inc., Atlanta, 1986-93, Allen & Co., LLC, Atlanta, 1993—, DMK Internat. Bd. dirs. The Coca Cola Co., 1981-93, 2004-13, Interactive Corp. (IAC), 1998-, Convera Corp., 2002-08, Berkshire Hathaway Inc., 2003-Served in USNR, 1944-46. Named to The Advt. Hall of Fame, 2006, The Irish American Hall of Fame, 2010. Mem. American Acad. Arts & Sciences, Capital City Club, Piedmont Driving Club, Commerce Club, Peachtree Golf Club. Office: DMK International 200 Galleria Pky NW Ste 970 Atlanta GA 30339-5945

KEOUGH, PHILIP J., IV, retail executive; married; 3 children. BS in Pharmacy, Auburn U., 1989. Dist. mgr., registered pharmacist, store mgr. Reliable Drug Stores, Inc., 1990—93; various positions Revco Drug Stores, Inc., Twinsburg, Ohio, 1993—97; regional sales mgr. CVS Corp., 1997—99, dir., pharmacy ops. Woonsocket, RI, 1999—2002; sr. v.p., pharmacy ops. Rite Aid Corp., Camp Hill, Pa., 2002—08; owner, pres. Keoco, LLC, 2008—; chief strategy officer FlavoRx, 2009—; chief bus. devel. officer Learnsomething, 2009—. Office: LearnSomething 2457 Care Dr Tallahassee FL 32308 Office Phone: 850-385-7915. Office Fax: 850-385-7964. Business E-Mail: pkeough@learnsomething.com.

KERCHEVAL, ALEC NORTON, mathematician; s. Basyl Hurley Kercheval and Edwina Simi Norton; m. Lilian Garcia-Roig, May 7, 1995; children: Claire Elizabeth Kercheval-Roig, Olivia Anne Kercheval-Roig. BS, Harvey Mudd Coll., 1980; MA, Merton Coll., U. Oxford, 1982; PhD, U. Calif., Berkeley, 1987. Asst. prof. Math., Univ. Tex., Austin, 1989—98; sr. cons. Barra, Inc., Berkeley, 1999—2001; prof. Math., Fla. State U., Tallahassee, 2001—. Marshall scholarship, Marshall Aid Commn., Brit. Govt., 1980-1982, Postdoctoral fellowship math. scis., NSF, 1989-1992. Mem.: Am. Math. Soc. Office: Dept Math Florida State U Tallahassee FL 32306-4510 Business E-Mail: kercheva@math.fsu.edu.

KERCHEVAL, JOHN WILLIAM, III, vulture capitalist, philanthropist, finance professor, former aerospace and defense executive; b. Arlington, Va., Aug. 21, 1965; s. John William Kercheval II and Carolyn Ann Booth Kercheval. BS in Chemistry, U. Calif., Berkeley, 1987, MBA in Fin. and Ops. Rsch., 1993. Rsch. assoc. Genentech, Inc., South San Francisco, Calif., 1986—88; assoc. tech. corp. fin. Hambrecht & Quist, LLP, San Francisco, 1988—91, assoc. v.p., corp. fin. dept., 1991—93; v.p. merchant banking Pierce Group, Arlington, 1993—95; dir. fin. planning and analysis Orbital Scis. Corp., Dulles, 1995—97; v.p., treas. Orbital Scis. Corp. / ORBCOMM, Dulles, Va., 1997—2001, European Aeronautic Def. and Space Co., N.V., Amsterdam, 2001—03; exec. v.p., CFO AeroAstro, Inc., Ashburn, Va., 2003—05; sr. mng. dir. Mid-Atlantic Vulture Capital Fund, Century City, Calif., 2004—; fin. prof. Georgetown U., Washington, 2004—. Dir. ORBCOMM Global, LP, Dulles, 1997—2000, ORBCOMM Internat., LP, London, 1997—2000. Mem. St. John's Episcopal Ch., McLean, Va. Alumni scholar, U. Calif., Berkeley, 1984—87. Mem.: Anubis Soc. (dir.), Calif. Alumni Soc., Skull and Keys Soc., The Tuckahoe Club, Order of Golden Bear, Phi Beta Kappa (sec. Washington chpt. 1999—2002). Democrat. Episcopalian. Avocations: swimming, weightlifting, stereo and sound reproduction. Office: The Vulture Capital Fund 1350 Beverly Rd Ste 115 Mc Lean VA 22101 Personal E-mail: johnwkercheval@aol.com. Business E-Mail: john.kercheval@vulture-capital.net.

KERGER, PAULA ARNOLD, broadcast executive; b. Dec. 20, 1957; m. Joseph Kerger. BS, U. Balt., 1979. Program devel. officer US Com. UNICEF, Washington, 1979—84; dir. devel. Internat. House, NYC, 1984—89; dir. principle gifts Met. Opera, NYC, 1989—93, WNET-TV, NYC, 1993—2006, v.p., dir. devel. and Govt. affairs, 1993—2002, sta. mgr., 2002—04, exec. v.p., COO, 2004—06; pres., CEO PBS, Arlington, Va., 2006—. Bd. dirs. PBS, Internat. Acad. TV Arts & Scis., Smithsonian Nat. Mus. Natural History. Recipient Woman of Achievement award, WID, NYC, 2008; named one of 100 Most Powerful Women in Entertainment, Hollywood Reporter, 2006—09, 2012—13. Mem.: Elizabeth Glaser Pediat. AIDS Found. Bd. Office: PBS 2100 Crystal Dr Arlington VA 22202-3785*

KERN, BERNARD DONALD, retired physicist; b. New Castle, Ind., Oct. 31, 1919; s. William Bernard and Cecile McDonald (Hudson) K.; m. Nedda Wisler Burdsall, Aug. 20, 1946; children: Richard B., Jonathan K., Arthur R. BS, Ind. U., 1942, MS, 1947, PhD, 1949. Physicist Signal Corps and Manhattan Project, Chgo., 1942-43; sr. physicist Oak Ridge Nat. Lab., 1949-50; faculty U. Ky., 1950-85, prof. physics, 1958-85, chmn. dept. physics and astronomy, 1967-69, prof. emeritus, 1985—. Physicist U.S. Naval Radiol. Def. Lab., San Francisco, 1957-58, cons., 1957-69; prof. Inst. Teknologi Bandung, Indonesia, U Ky., State Dept. Ednl. Assistance Program, 1961- 62 Author articles on nuc. physics. Served to lt.(jg) USNR, 1943-46. Fellow Am. Phys. Soc.; mem. Am. Inst. Physics, Am. Assn. Physics Tchrs. Home: 441 S Ashland Ave Lexington KY 40502-2114 Personal E-mail: slrcamera@aol.com.

KERN, JOHN WORTH, III, retired judge; b. Indpls., May 25, 1928; s. John Worth and Bernice (Winn) K.; children: John, Stephen. BA, Princeton U., 1949; LLB, Harvard U., 1952. Bar: D.C. 1953, U.S. Ct. Appeals (D.C. cir.) 1955. With CIA, 1952-54; law clk. to chief judge U.S. Ct. Appeals D.C. Cir. Ct., 1954-55; asst. U.S. atty. D.C. Dist. Dept. Justice, Washington, 1955-59; assoc. Kilpatrick, Ballard & Beasley, Washington, 1959-65; with Dept. of Justice, Washington, 1965-68; judge D.C. Ct. Appeals, Washington, 1968-84, sr. judge, 1987—2011. Dean Nat. Jud. Coll., Reno, 1984-87; chair Annual Harold R. Medina Seminar for State and Fede. Judges on Humanities & Sci., Princeton U. Mem. D.C. Bar. Presbyterian.

KERN, PAUL JOHN, manufacturing executive, retired military officer; b. West Orange, NJ, June 16, 1945; s. Bruno Michael and Marjorie (Bolan) K.; m. Dolores I. Mercaldo, Aug. 28, 1971; children: Paul John Jr., Alexander Matthew. BS, US Mil. Acad., 1967; MS in Mech. and Civil Engring., U. Mich., 1973; fellow in Nat. Security, Harvard U., 1986-87. Registered profl. engr., Va. Advanced through grades from commdg. 2nd lt. to gen. US Army, 1967—2001, platoon leader, staff mem., 1967-69, troop comdr. 11th Armored Cavalry Regiment Vietnam, 1969-70, ret., 2004; asst. prof., course dir. dept. engring. US Mil. Acad., West Point, NY, 1973-76; ops. officer 2nd bn., 33rd Armor, 3rd Armor Divsn., Kirch Goens, Germany, 1976-78; br. chief Bradley Prog. Mgmt. Office, Warren, Mich., 1979-82; team chief rsch. and devel. US Army Staff, Pentagon, Washington, 1982-84; bn. comdr. 5th bn., 32nd Armor, 24th Inf. Divsn., Ft. Stewart, Ga., 1984-86; mil. asst. to under sec. US Dept. Def., Washington, 1987-89, mil. asst. to sec., 1993-96; comdr. 2nd brigade, 24th Inf. Divsn., Saudi Arabia and Iraq, 1989-91; dir. requirements Army staff, 1991-92; asst. divsn. comdr.-maneuver, 24th Inf. Divsn. Ft. Stewart, Ga., 1992-93; commdg. gen. 4th Inf. Divsn., Ft. Hood, Tex., 1996-97; mil. dep. to asst. sec. acquisition, logistics & tech. US Army, Washington, 1997—2001; commdg. gen. US Army Materials Command, Alexandria, Va., 2001—04; sr. counselor The Cohen Group, Washington, 2005—; pres., COO AM General LLC, South Bend, Ind., 2008—. Head internal investigation into abuses at Abu Ghraib prison US Army, 2004; bd. dirs. EDO Corp., 2005—07, iRobot Corp., 2006—. Co-author: Acquisition Managers - Role and Reality, 1987. Decorated Bronze Star with 3 oak leaf clusters, Silver Star, Purple Heart with 2 oak leaf clusters, Def. Disting. Svc. medal, Army Disting. Svc. medal, Def. Superior Svc. medal, Legion of Merit, German Cross of Honor Fed. Armed Forces; recipient Alumni Soc. medal U. Mich., Teeter award Soc. Automotive Engineers Mem. NAE, Soc. Automotive Engrs. (Teetor award 1975), Armor Assn., Assn. US Army, Coun. Fgn. Rels., US Naval Inst., Chi Epsilon. Roman Catholic. Avocations: sailing, woodworking, computers. Office: AM General LLC 105 N Niles Ave PO Box 7025 South Bend IN 46617 also: The Cohen Group 500 Eighth St NW Ste 200 Washington DC 20004 Office Phone: 202-863-7200, 574-237-6222. Office Fax: 202-863-7800. E-mail: pkern@cohengroup.net.

KERN, RONALD PAUL, dean, consultant; b. Chickasha, Okla., Sept. 2, 1947; s. John Edward Kern and Winona Briscoe Kern; m. Stephanie Perry, May 30, 1970; children: Stephanie Rachel Nelson, Jayson Paul. BS, U. Ctrl. Okla., 1970; MA, U. Tex., San Antonio, 1977; PhD, U. North Tex., 1990. Computer info. sys. Wideband Gigabit Network Engr. Dept. chair, tchr. Permian HS, Odessa, Tex., 1981-84; prof. Odessa Coll., Tex., 1984-85, dean, curriculum dir. Tex., 1990-97; curriculum dir. Maypearl Ind. Sch. Dist., Tex., 1985-88; coord. Collin County CC, Plano, Tex., 1988-90; v.p. acad. affairs We. Okla. State Coll., 1997-99; dir. Tex. Tech Univ.-Acad. 2000, Plano, 1999—2002; prin., owner Xstream Computers, 2002—06; tchr. AP computer sci. Highland Park HS, 2004—06; dean graduate sch. Kaplan U., 2005—09; dean Nova U., 2009—13; chief academic officer Concorde Career Coll., 2013—. Cons. Tex. colls. and univs., 1988—; tech. field reader Tex. Higher Edn. Coord. Bd., chair, standing com. on univ. transfer and dispute resolutions. Contbr. articles to profl. jours. Recipient Tchg. Excellence award, Nat. Inst. Staff and Orgnl. Devel., 1991; named Tchr. of Yr., Samuel Clemens HS, 1976, Disting. Bandmaster of Am., State of Ariz., 1981, Disting. Prof. Bus. and Industry Divsn., Collin County CC, 1989; finalist Educator of Yr., Tex. Computer Edn. Assn., 1987. Mem. Tex. Assn. Instructional Adminstrs., Tex. Assn. Tech. Educators, Tex. Tech. Soc., Am. Indian Sci. and Engring. Soc., Odessa Optimist Club (bd. dirs. 1991-93), Phi Kappa Phi. Personal E-mail: rk429@nova.edu.

KERN, SALLY, state legislator; b. Jonesboro, Ark., Nov. 27, 1946; m. Steven Kern; children: Jesse, Nathan. BA in Sociology, Univ. Tex., 1971. Teacher; mem. Dist. 84 Okla. House of Representatives, 2005—. Mem. Olivet Baptist Church. Mem.: Tricity Rep. Women's Club, Frontier County Republican Women, Am. Legislative Exchange Coun., Heart & Hand, Northwest C. of C., Eagle Forum. Republican. Baptist. Mailing: 2713 Sterling Ave Oklahoma City OK 73127 Office: 2300 N Lincoln Blvd Rm 433 Oklahoma City OK 73105 Office Phone: 405-557-7348. Business E-Mail: sallykern@okhouse.gov.

KERN, TERRY C. (TERENCE C. KERN), federal judge; b. Clinton, Okla., Sept. 25, 1944; s. Elgin L. and Lora Lee (Miller) Kern; m. Charlene Heinen, Dec. 26, 1970 (dec. Feb. 2002); children: Lauren, Suzanne, Justin Hunter; m. Jeanette Martin, Dec. 31, 2004. BS, Okla. State U., Stillwater, 1966; JD, U. Okla., Norman, 1969; LLM, U. Va., Charlottesville, 2004. Bar: Okla. 1969, US Dist. Ct. (eastern dist.) Okla. 1974, US Dist. Ct. (western dist.) Okla. 1979, US Dist. Ct. (northern dist.) Okla. 1993, US Ct. Appeals (10th cir.) 1979. Gen. atty. FTC, Washington, 1969—70; ptnr. Fischl, Culp, McMillin, Kern & Chaffin, Ardmore, Okla., 1971—86; founding ptnr., pres. Kern, Mordy & Sperry, Ardmore, 1986—94; judge US Dist. Ct. (northern dist.) Okla., Tulsa, 1994—2010, chief judge, 1996—2003, sr. judge, 2010—. Mem. Jud. Conf. Com. on Security and Facilities, 10th Cir. Jud. coun. Chmn. bd. dirs. Southern Okla. Meml. Hosp., Ardmore, 1982—92, chmn., 1989—91. With USAR, 1970—75. Recipient Leadership Legacy award, Okla. State U., 2000, Disting. Alumnus award, 2001; named to, Beta Theta Pi Hall of Fame, 2000. Fellow: Okla. Bar Found. (pres. 1991, Disting. Svc. award 1992), American Bar Found.; mem.: ABA, Tulsa County Bar Assn. (bd. dirs.), Fed. Judges Assn., U. Okla. Coll. Law Assn., Okla. Bar Assn., American Bd. Trial Advocates (Okla. chpt.), Coun. Oak/Johnson-Sontag Inns of Ct. (master of bench, pres. 2008—09). Democrat. Methodist. Office: US Dist Courthouse 333 W 4th St Tulsa OK 74103-3839

KERNAN, JOSEPH D., career military officer; b. Travis AFB, Calif., Feb. 4, 1955; m. Jan Kernan; children: Sean, Shannon. Grad., US Mil. Acad., 1977; attended, Surface Warfare Officer Sch. Advanced through grades to vice admiral USN, 2009; engring. officer USS Horne, San Diego; designated Naval Spl. Warfare Officer, 1981; platoon comdr. Underwater Demolition Team 12, SEAL Delivery Vehicle Team 1, SEAL Delivery Vehicle Team 5; dep. comdr. Naval Spl. Warfare Task Force, Middle East Force; exec. officer Naval Spl. Warfare Unit 1, Subic Bay, Philippines; cmty. mgr., dep./chief staff officer Naval Spl. Warfare Devel. Group; chief of staff and dep. Naval Spl. Warfare Command; dir. Navel Spl. Warfare Br.; dep. dir. and dir. ops. Joint Spl. Ops. Command, Fort Bragg, NC; dir. ops. Ctr. Spl. Ops., US Spl. Ops. Command (USSCOCOM), MacDill AFB; comdr. Naval Spl. Warfare Command, 2007—08, US Fourth Fleet & US Naval Forces Southern Command, 2008—09; sr. mil. asst. to sec. US Dept. Def., Washington, 2009—11; mil. dep. comdr. US Southern Command (USSOUTHCOM), Miami, 2011—. Office: US Southern Command (USSOUTHCOM) 3511 NW 91st Ave Miami FL 33127

KERNELL, MICHAEL LYNN, state legislator; b. Memphis, Dec. 20, 1951; s. Sam Houston Kernell and Ima Irene Park K.; children: David Christopher, Isabelle Marie. Pres. Shelby Comunity Young Dem., Tenn., 1970—72; state rep., Dist. 93 Tenn., 1974—; chmn. Govt. Oper Com. & Special Study Com. Earthquake Preparedness; mem. Conservation & Environ. Com., Environ, Wildlife & Parks Subcom., Tourism Subcom.; mem., calendar & rules com.; house rep. Tenn. Democrat. Office: 3583 Allandale Ln Memphis TN 38111-5601 also: 38 Legislative Plz Nashville TN 37243-0193 Office Phone: 901-454-1113, 615-741-3726. Office Fax: 615-253-0320. Business E-Mail: rep.mike.kernell@capitol.tn.gov.

KERNER, JON D., staffing and recruiting company executive; BS in Indsl. & Sys. Engring., Ga. Tech.; MBA, Ga State U., MS in Computer Info Sys. Cons. Coopers & Lybrand Consulting; ptnr. Scott, Madden & Assocs.; chief info. officer EarthLink, Inc., 2000—08; sr. v.p., chief info. officer MPS (Modis Professional Services) Group, Inc. (acquired by Adecco), 2008—. Office: MPS Group Inc 10151 Deerwood Park Blvd Ste 200-400 Jacksonville FL 32256-0557 Office Phone: 904-360-2000. Office Fax: 904-360-2972.

KERNS, VIRGINIA B., anthropologist, writer; b. San Diego, 1948; m. Ronald Adam Hallett. BA in Anthropology, Coll. William and Mary, 1970; PhD in Anthropology, U. Ill., 1977. Vis. asst. prof. Coll. William and Mary, Williamsburg, Va., 1977—78, from asst. prof. to prof., 1985—, rsch. prof., 2010—, chair dept. anthropology, 1988—93; asst. prof. Va. Tech, Blacksburg, Va., 1978—83; vis. asst. prof. U. Iowa, Iowa City, 1981; rsch. anthropologist UN Food and Agr. Orgn., Rome, 1984. Author: Women and the Ancestors: Black Carib Kinship and Ritual, 1983, 2d edit., 1997, Scenes from the High Desert, 2003 (William P. Clements prize for Best Nonfiction Book on Southwestern Am., 2004, Evans Biography award, 2004), Journeys West, 2010; editor: In Her Prime, 1985, 2d edit., 1992; mem. editl. bd.: Am. Ethnologist, 1979—84. Recipient Faculty award for Advancement of Scholarship, Phi Beta Kappa, Alpha of Va., 1988, Thomas Jefferson Tchg. award, Coll. William and Mary, 1989, Outstanding Faculty award, State Coun. of Higher Edn. in Va., 1991; named Writer-in-residence, Mesa Refuge, 2005, 2007; grantee, Wenner-Gren Found. for Anthrop. Rsch., 1974—75, 1976; fellow, Fulbright-Hays Commn., 1974—75, Va. Found. for Humanities, 1989; Hon. fellow, Woodrow Wilson Found., 1974. Fellow: Am. Anthrop. Assn.; mem.: Jury (Evans Biography award 2008—12), U. Press Va. (bd. dirs.), Phi Beta Kappa. Office: Coll William and Mary Dept Anthropology PO Box 8795 Williamsburg VA 23187-8795 Business E-Mail: vbkern@wm.edu.

KERR, ALICE FORGY, state legislator; b. Aug. 30, 1954; State senator Dist. 12, Ky., 1999—; mem. Edn. Com., Energy Com., Judiciary Com., Licensing & Occupations Com., Local Govt. Com., State Govt. Com., 1999—; state senate Ky.; bd. dir. Ky. Baptist Homes Children. Mem.: Women Leadership, United Way Bluegrass. Republican. Baptist. Mailing: 3274 Gondola Dr Lexington KY 40513 Office: Capitol Annex Rm 209 Frankfort KY 40601 Office Phone: 859-223-3274, 502-564-8100 ext 625. Business E-Mail: alice.kerr@lrc.ky.gov.

KERR, ALLEN, state legislator; b. Little Rock, Ark., Nov. 19, 1956; s. Virgil and Frieda; m. Marliese Kerr. Owner & operator Allen Kerr Insurance; mem. Pulaski County Quorum Ct., 2006—; budget chmn. Pulaski County, 2007—, justice of the peace; mem. Dist. 32 Ark. House of Reps., 2009—. Republican. Office: State Capitol Rm 350 Little Rock AR 72201 also: 1429 Merrill Dr Little Rock AR 72211 Office Phone: 501-682-6211, 501-682-7771, 501-225-3170. Business E-Mail: kerra@arkleg.state.ar.us.

KERR, CRISTIE, professional golfer; b. Miami, Fla., Oct. 12, 1977; m. Erik Stevens, 2006. Profl. golfer LPGA Tour, 1997—. Mem. US nat. team Curtis Cup, 1996, Solheim Cup, 2002, 2003, 2005, 2007, 2009. Achievements include winner LPGA tournaments: Longs Drugs Challenge, 2002, LPGA Takefuji Classic, 2004, ShopRite LPGA Classic, 2004, State Farm Classic, 2004, Michelob ULTRA Open at Kingsmill, 2005, 2009, Wendy's Championship for Children, 2005; Franklin American Mortgage Championship, 2006, CN Canadian Women's Open, 2006, John Q. Hammons Hotel Classic, 2006, Safeway Classic, 2008, LPGA State Farm Classic, 2010; winner major championships: US Women's Open, 2007; LPGA Championship, 2010. Avocations: fishing, baking. Office: c/o LPGA 100 International Golf Dr Daytona Beach FL 32124-1092

KERR, DONALD MACLEAN, JR., physicist, former federal official; b. Phila., Apr. 8, 1939; s. Donald MacLean and Harriet (Fell) K.; m. Alison Richards Kyle, June 10, 1961; 1 dau., Margot Kyle. B.E.E. (Nat. Merit scholar), Cornell U., 1963, MS, 1964, PhD (Ford Found. fellow, 1964-65, James Clerk Maxwell fellow 1965-66), 1966. Staff Los Alamos Nat. Lab., 1966-76, group leader, 1971-72, asst. div. leader, 1972-73, asst. dir., 1973-75, alt. energy divsn. leader, 1975-76; dep. mgr. Nev. ops. office US Dept. Energy, Las Vegas, 1976-77, dep. asst. sec. for def. programs, 1977-79, acting asst. sec. for def. programs Washington, 1978, dep. asst. sec. for energy tech., 1979; dir Los Alamos Nat. Lab., 1979-85; sr. v.p. EG&G, Inc., Wellesley, Mass., 1985-88, exec. v.p., 1988-89, pres., bd. dirs., 1989-92; exec. v.p., bd. dirs. Sci. Applications Internat. Corps., San Diego, 1993-96, Info. Sys. Labs., San Diego, 1996-97; asst. dir. FBI, Washington, 1997—2001; dep. dir. sci. & tech. CIA, Washington, 2001—05; dir. Nat. Reconnaissance Office, 2005—07; prin. dep. dir. Office Dir. Nat. Intelligence, 2007—09; rsch. prof. George Mason U. Volgenau Sch. Info. Engring., 2009—. Mem. Navajo Sci. Com., 1974-77, Def. Sci. Bd., 1993-98, 2010-; mem. sci. adv. panel U.S. Army, 1975-78; mem. engring. adv. bd. U. Nev., Las Vegas, 1976-78, Cornell U., 1985—; chmn. com. R&D Internat. Energy Agy., 1979-85; mem. nat. security adv. coun. SRI Internat., 1980-89; mem. adv. bd. U. Alaska Geophys. Inst., 1980-85; mem. sci. adv. group Joint Strategic Planning Staff, 1981-91; mem. adv. bd. Georgetown U. Ctr. Strategic Internat. Studies, 1981-87; mem. adv. com. Naval Rsch., 1982-85; mem. corp. Draper Lab., 1982-97; mem. DCI Nonproliferation Adv. Panel, 1993-98; mem. bd. San Diego Tech. Coun., 1994-97; bd. dirs. Resources for the Future, Washington, 1990-99; bd. trustees Mitre Corp., McLean, Va., 2009-; bd. dirs. US Space LLC, 2009- Published research on plasma physics, microwave electronics, ionospheric physics, energy and nat. security. Trustee New Eng. Aquarium, 1989-93. Recipient Outstanding Services award, US Dept. Energy, 1979, Disting. Intelligence Medal, CIA, 2005, Nat. Intelligence Disting. Svc. medal, 2009, Sec. of Def. medal for Outstanding Pub. Svc., US Dept. Def., 2009. Fellow AAAS, Am. Phys. Soc.; mem. Am. Geophys. Union, Nat. Assn. Mfrs. (bd. dirs. 1986-92), Southwestern Assn. Indian Affairs, World Affairs Coun. Boston (bd. dirs. 1988-92), Atlantic Coun. (bd. dirs. 1991-97), Cosmos Club (Washington), Sigma Xi, Tau Beta Pi, Eta Kappa Nu.

KERR, JAMES YANCEY, II, lawyer, utilities executive; b. Goldsboro, NC, Mar. 8, 1964; BA Politics cum laude, Washington & Lee U., 1986; JD, U. N.C., 1992. Bar: U.S. Dist. Ct. (we., mid., ea. dists. N.C.). With First Union Corp., Charlotte, Atlanta, 1986—89; ptnr. Smith, Anderson, Blount, Dorestt, Mitchell & Jernigan, LLP; mem. N.C. Utilities Commn., 2001—08; ptnr. McGuireWoods LLP, 2008—14; sr. advisor McGuire Woods Consulting LLC, 2008—14; gen. counsel, chief compliance officer, exec. v.p. Southern Company, 2014—. Delegate 6th European Union-US Energy Regulatory Roundtable, Athens, Greece, 2007; bd. dirs. Electric Power Research Inst. Bd. dirs. Triangle Divsn. March of Dimes. Named Bonbright Honoree, James C. Bonbrights Utilities Ctr. of the Terry Coll. of Business, U. Ga., 2005. Mem.: Southeastern Assn. of Regulatory Utility Commissioners (pres. 2002—03), Nat. Assn. of Regulatory Utility Commissioners (pres. 2007—08), N.C. Assn. Def. Attys., N.C. Bar Assn., ABA. Democrat. Office: Southern Company 30 Ivan Allen Jr Blvd NW Atlanta GA 30308*

KERR, JOHN H., III, state legislator; b. Richmond, Va., Feb. 28, 1936; s. John H. and Mary Hinton Kerr; m. Sandra Edgerton, 1960; children: John H. IV, James Y. II. Former pres. Wayne County Young Dem., NC; former ptnr. Warren, Kerr, Walston & Hollowell, Goldsboro, NC; former bd. dir. & chmn. Southern Nat. Bank, NC; former bd. dir. Mt. Olive Coll. Area Found.; state senate NC; atty., 1961—; chmn. Wayne County Dem. Exec. Com., 1980—85; state rep. NC, 1987—92; state senator Dist. 8 NC, 1993—2002; state senator Dist. 7, 2003—04; state senator Dist. 5 NC, 2005—; vice chmn., judiciary I Environ. & Natural Resources Com., Pub. Utilities Com.; mem. NC Retail Mchts. Assn. Recipient Legislator award, Sch. Counselors Assn., 1991; named Boss of Yr., Am. Bus. Women's Assn. Goldsboro Chpt., 1978. Mem.: Lawyers NC Inc. (former pres.), Wayne County C. of C., Wayne County Bar Assn. (former pres.), NC Bar Assn., Wayne County Red Cross, Goldsboro Jaycees (v.p. 1962—71, Key Man award), Rotary Club. Democrat. Baptist. Mailing: 526 Legis Bldg Raleigh NC 27601-2808 Address: PO Box 1616 Goldsboro NC 27533 Office Phone: 919-733-5621. Fax: 919-733-3113. E-mail: johnk@ncleg.net.

KERR, ROBERT B., astronomer, atmospheric scientist; BS in Physics, Ohio U., 1979; MS in Atmospheric Sci., U. Mich., 1981, PhD in Atmospheric Sci., 1986. Mem. tech. staff Aerospace Corp., El Segundo, 1987; prof. astronomy Boston U., 1988—97; dir. rsch. Sci. Solutions Inc., North Chelmsford, Mass., 1997, CEO, 2000—; with Dartmouth Coll., U. Mich.; prog. dir. aeronomy NSF; dir. Arecibo Obs., PR, 2007—. Mem. sci. adv. com. Arecibo Obs. Recipient Presdl. Young Investigator award. Office: Arecibo Obs HC03 Box 53995 Arecibo PR 00612 Office Phone: 787-878-2612. Office Fax: 787-878-1861.

KERR, STEVE (STEPHEN DOUGLAS KERR), sportscaster, retired professional basketball player, former professional sports team executive; b. Beirut, Sept. 27, 1965; m. Margot Kerr; children: Nicholas, Matthew, Madeleine. Grad., U. Ariz. Guard Cleve. Cavaliers, 1989—92, Chgo. Bulls, 1993—98, San Antonio Spurs, 1998—2001, 2002—03, Portland Trail Blazers, 2001—02; NBA analyst Turner Sports, 2003—07, 2010—; pres. basketball ops., gen. mgr. Phoenix Suns, 2007—10. Participant NBA All-Star Weekend, 1994, 95, 96, 97. Named to NBA All-Interview Second Team, 1997-98, 98-99. Achievements include member of NBA Final championship winning Chicago Bulls, 1996-98; San Antonio Spurs, 1999, 2003; winner NBA All-Star Weekend's 3-Point Shootout, 1997. Office: Turner Sports One CNN Ctr 13 S Tower Atlanta GA 30303

KERR, THOMAS ROBERT, lawyer, state legislator; b. Covington, Ky., July 25, 1950; s. Thomas Hoover and Joann (Moffett) K.; m. Janice Duncan, May 26, 1973; children: Julie Ann, Jennifer Suzanne, Jill Mackenzie. BBA, U. Ky., 1972; JD, Chase Coll. Law, 1977. Bar: Ky. 1977, U.S. Dist. Ct. (ea. dist.) Ky. 1977. Sole practice, Covington, 1977—; mem. Dist. 64 Ky. House of Reps., 1985—. Mem. pro-bono panel, Covington, 1980—; pub. defender Kenton County Pub. Defender's Office, Covington, 1977—. State rep. Ky. Gen. Assembly, Frankfort, 1985—; dir. Community Coun. on Religious Edn., Covington, 1985—; dir. Victims Assistance Network, Frankfort, 1985—, Calvary Christian Sch., Covington, 1981-87; deacon Calvary Bapt. Ch., Latonia, Ky., 1982; bd. dirs. No. Ky. Area Devel. Dist., 1988-93, Good Will, 1993—. With Air NG, 1971-77. Named One of Outstanding Young Men of Am., 1980, 83. Mem. Ky. Bar Assn., No. Ky. Bar Assn., Am. Trial Lawyers Assn., Ky. Acad. Trial Attys., Covington Christian Businessmans Assn. Clubs: Taylor Mill (Ky.) Swim (bd. dirs. 1983-87). Democrat. Baptist. Avocations: tennis, reading, various sports. Office: 732 Scott St Covington KY 41011-2418 also: Ky Legislature Annex Rm 457E 702 Capitol St Frankfort KY 40601 Office Phone: 859-431-2222, 502-564-8100 ext. 694. Business E-Mail: thomas.kerr@lrc.ky.gov.

KERR, WILLIAM T., publishing and broadcast executive; b. Seattle, Apr. 17, 1941; m. Mary Lang, Oct. 15, 1966; 1 child, Susannah Gaskill Kerr Adler. BA, U. Wash., 1963, Oxford U., Eng., 1965; MA, Harvard U., 1967, MBA, 1969. V.p. Dillon Read & Co., NYC, London, 1969—73; cons. McKinsey & Co., NYC, 1973-79; v.p. New York Times Co., NYC, 1979-91; pres. The NY Times Mag. Group, NYC, 1985-91; exec. v.p., pres. mag. group Meredith Corp., Des Moines, 1991-94, pres., COO, 1994-96, pres., CEO, 1997-98, chmn., CEO, 1998—2006, chmn., 2006—; interim pres., CEO Arbitron, Inc., Columbia, Md., 2010—. Bd. dirs. Meredith Corp., 1994—, The Prin. Fin. Group, Inc., 2001—, Whirlpool Corp., 2006—, Interpublic Group of Companies, Inc., 2006—, Arbitron, Inc., 2007—; trustee Oxford U. Press, Harvard Bus. Sch. Publs., Internat. Fedn. Periodical Press. Bd. dirs. Bus. Com. for Arts. Mem.: Lost Tree Club, Reform Club, Wakonda Club, Quogue Field Club, The Brook Club, Union Club, Century Assn. Roman Catholic. Office: Meredith Corp 1716 Locust St Des Moines IA 50309-3023

KERRIGAN, SYLVIA J., lawyer; b. Vitoria da Conquista, Brazil, 1965; m. Matt Kerrigan. BA in Philosophy, Polit. Economy & English cum laude, Southwestern U., 1986; JD, U. Tex., 1990. Clk. to Justice Eugene Cook Tex. Supreme Ct., 1990; atty. Clann, Bell & Murphy, Houston, 1990—95, Marathon Oil Corp., Houston, 1995—2003, asst. gen. counsel, litig., human resources & environ. law, 2003—09, v.p., 2009—12, gen. counsel, sec., 2009—, exec. v.p., 2012—; sr. legal officer, & team leader UN Compensation Commn.; with pvt. practice UN Security Council's Commn. d'Indemnisation, Geneva. Bd. dirs. Nat. Assn. Minority & Woman-Owned Law Firms, Houston Bar Assn., Tex. Accountants & Lawyers for the Arts, Am. Leadership Forum; past chmn., internat law sect. State Bar of Tex.; fellow Tex. Bar Found. Recipient Major Litigation Magna Stella award, Tex. Gen. Counsel Forum, 2007. Fellow: Tex. Bar Found. (life). Office: Marathon Oil Corp 5555 San Felipe Rd Houston TX 77056-2723 Office Phone: 713-629-6600. Office Fax: 713-296-2952. Business E-Mail: skerrigan@marathonoil.com.*

KERSCH, MICHELLE, finance company executive; BA in Comm., U. North Fla., MBA. Cert. accredited pub. rels. profl. Sr. v.p., corp. comm. Fidelity National Information Services, Inc.; sr. v.p., mktg. & corp. comm. Lender Processing Services, Inc., 2009—. Office: Lender Processing Services Inc 601 Riverside Ave Jacksonville FL 32204 Office Phone: 904-854-5100. Office Fax: 904-854-4124. Business E-Mail: michelle.kersch@lpsvcs.com.

KERSHNER, RUTH, healthcare educator; MS, EdD, W.Va. U. Cert. in sch. health, health edn. specialist; RN. Mem. cmty. health promotion divsn. W.Va. U. Sch. Medicine, 1991—, assoc. prof. cmty. medicine; vis. assoc. prof. W.Va. U. Coll. Phys. Activity and Sports Scis.; faculty assoc. W.Va. U. Ctr. Women's Studies. Faculty student liaison W.Va U., sch. health coord. Named Univ. Prof. of Yr., Am. Assn. Health Edn., W.Va. Prof. of Yr., Carnegie Found. for Advancement of Tchg. and Coun. for Advancement and Support of Edn., 2009. Office: WVa University Sch Medicine 3009 HSN PO Box 9190 Morgantown WV 26506 Office Phone: 304-293-7440. Office Fax: 304-293-6685. Business E-Mail: rkershner@hsc.wvu.edu.

KERSTETTER, WAYNE ARTHUR, law educator, artist; b. Chgo., Dec. 1, 1939; s. Arthur Edward and Lillian (Asplund) K. BA, U. Chgo., 1964, JD, 1967. Bar: Ill. 1968. Gen. counsel Ill. Drug Abuse Treatment Program, 1968—70; admin. and rsch. assoc. Ctr. Studies in Criminal Justice U. Chgo. Law Sch., 1970—72; asst. commr. N.Y. Police Dept., NYC, 1972—73; supt. Ill. Bur. Investigation, Chgo., 1973—76; assoc. dir. Ctr. Studies in Criminal Justice U. Chgo., 1976—78; assoc. prof. criminal justice dept. criminal justice U. Ill., Chgo., 1978—2000. Sr. rsch. fellow Am. Bar Found., Chgo., 1982-93, fellow, 1993—; cons. U.S. Civil Rights Commn., U. Chgo., ABT Assoc., Univ. Rsch. Assoc., Police Found. Contbr. articles to profl. jours. Mem. transition team Mayor Washington, Chgo., 1983, Criminal Justice Project of Cook County, 1987. Served with USNR, 1962-64. Rsch. grantee Nat. Inst. Justice, 1976, Chgo. Bar Found., 1979-80, Am. Bar Found., 1983; fellow Ctr. for Studies in Criminal Justice, U. Chgo. Law Sch., 1978-82. Home: 1070 S Collier Unit 702 Marco Island FL 34145 Office Phone: 239-642-4960. Personal E-mail: wkerstett2@aol.com.

KESELOWSKI, BRAD, race car driver; b. Rochester Hills, Mich., Feb. 12, 1984; s. Bob Keselowski. Owner Brad Keselowski Racing, 2007—; race car driver, NASCAR Penske Racing, Mooresville, NC, 2009—. 1st pl. Aaron's 499 Talladega Superspeedway, Ala., 2009, 2012; 1st pl. STP 400 Kans. Speedway, Kansas City, 2011; 1st pl. Good Sam RV Ins. 500 Pocono Raceway, Long Pond, Pa., 2011; 1st pl. Irwin Tools Night Race at Bristol Bristol Motor Speedway, Tenn., 2011, 1st pl. Food City 500, 2012; 1st pl. Quaker State 400 Ky. Speedway, 2012; 1st pl. Geico 400 Chicagoland Speedway, Ill., 2012; 1st pl. AAA 400 Dover Internat. Speedway, 2012. Founder Checkered Flag Found., 2010—. Named Nationwide Series Most Popular Driver, NASCAR, 2008—10, Nationwide Series Champion, 2010, Sprint Cup Series Champion, 2012. Office: c/o Sports Mgmt Network Inc 1668 Telegraph Rd Ste 200 Bloomfield Hills MI 48302 also: Penske Racing 200 Penske Way Mooresville NC 28115

KESHA, (KESHA ROSE SEBERT), singer; b. LA, Mar. 1, 1987; d. Pebe Sebert. Singer: (albums) Animal, 2010, Cannibal, 2010, I Am the Dance Commander + I Command You to Dance: The Remix Album, 2011, Warrior, 2012, (with the Flaming Lips) Lipsha, 2013, (songs) Tik Tok, 2009, (featuring 3OH!3) Blah Blah Blah, 2010, Your Love Is My Drug, 2010, We R Who We R, 2010, Blow, 2011; author: (autobiography) Kesha: My Crazy Beautiful Life, 2012; reality TV personality Kesha: My Crazy Beautiful Life, 2013. Named Best New Act, MTV Europe Music Awards, 2010. Office: c/o Vector Management PO Box 120479 Nashville TN 37212

KESSELMAN, MARC L., lawyer; b. 1971; married; 2 children. BA in Govt., Cornell U., 1993; JD, U. Pa., 1996. Bar: 1997. Law clk. to Hon. Julia S. Gibbons US Dist. Ct., Memphis, 1996—97; assoc. Ropes & Gray, LLP, 1997—2000; trial atty. fed. programs bur. US Dept. Justice, 2000—03, sr. counsel Office Legal Policy Washington, 2003; assoc. gen. counsel office Office Mgmt. & Budget (OMB), Exec. Office of the Pres., 2003—04; dep. gen. counsel Office Mgmt. & Budget (OMB), Exec. Office of the Pres., 2004—06; gen. counsel USDA, 2006—09; v.p., gen. counsel Frito-Lay North America, Inc., Dallas. Office: Frito-Lay PO Box 660634 Dallas TX 75266 Office Phone: 202-720-3351. Office Fax: 202-720-8666.

KESSLER, EDWIN, meteorology educator, consultant; b. Bklyn., Dec. 2, 1928; s. Edwin and Marie Rosa (Weil) K.; m. Lottie Catherine Menger; children: Austin Rainier, Thomas Russell. AB, Columbia Coll., 1950; MS in Meteorology, MIT, 1952, ScD in Meteorology, 1957. Chief synoptic meteorology sect. Weather Radar br. Air Force Cambridge Rsch. Lab., Bedford, Mass., 1954-61; sr. rsch. scientist Travelers Rsch. Ctr., Hartford, Conn., 1961-62, dir. atmospheric physics div., 1962-64; dir. Nat. Severe Storms Lab., NOAA, Norman, Okla., 1964-86; adj. prof. U. Okla., 1964—. Vis. prof. MIT, 1975-76, McGill U., Can., 1980; bd. dirs. N.Am. Transp. Inst., Noman Sustainability Network. Editor: Thunderstorms, A Social Scientific and Technological Documentary, 3 vols., 1982, 2d edits., 1983-88, paperback edits., vol. 1, 1988, vol. 2, 1992; contbr. articles to profl. jours., chapters to books. State chair Common Cause, Okla., 1993-99, vice chair, 1999-. With U.S. Army, 1946-47. Recipient award for outstanding authorship, NOAA, 1971, Lifetime Achievement Award, Common Cause, 2005, Red Earth Sierra Club, 2008. Fellow AAAS, Am. Meteorol. Soc. (nat. councilor 1966-69, past mem. coms. on hurricanes, atmospheric electricity, agr. and forestry, cloud and precipitation physics, severe local storms, past chmn. com. on weather radar, cert. cons. meteorologist, Cleveland Abbe award for disting. svc. 1988); mem. AIAA (sr. mem.), LWV, Royal Meteorol. Soc. (fgn.), Am. Geophys. Union, Sigma Xi (founding editor-in-chief Energies, online jour. 2008-09). Achievements include research in agriculture and energy; manager of 350 acres of pasture, streams and wilderness in central Oklahoma, donated to Oklahoma University in 1989 and 1998. Personal E-mail: kess3@swbell.net.

KESSLER, JEFFREY VINCENT, state legislator, lawyer; b. Wheeling, W. Va., Nov. 16, 1955; s. George Henry & Rosemary Krupica Kessler; m. Gretchen Kessler; children Jacob, Lauren, Jackson. BA, West Liberty State Coll.; JD, W.Va. U. Bar: W.Va. Asst. prosecuting atty., Marshall County, 1985—2000; city solicitor City of Brentwood, 1983—97; municipal court judge City of McMechen, 1982—89; mem. Dist. 2 W.Va. State Senate, 1998—, pres., 2011—. Mem. Ohio Valley Indsl. and Bus. Devel. Corp. Recipient Marshall County Dem of Yr. award, 1994, Family Violence Prevention Program Legislator of Yr. award YWCA, 199; named Legislator of Yr., W.Va. Trial Lawyers Assn., 1999, 2005, W.Va. American Trauma Soc., 1994, American Acad. of Nurse Practitoner, 2011, W.Va. Nurses Advanced Nurse Practitioner, Marshall County Democrat of the Yr. award, 1994 Democrat. Roman Catholic. Office: Senate President Room 227M Bldg 1 State Capitol Complex Charleston WV 25305 Home: 607 Wheeling Ave Glen Dale WV 26038-1641 Home Phone: 304-843-1386; Office Phone: 304-357-7801.*

KESSLER, MURRAY S., tobacco manufacturing company executive; BSBA, Villanova U.; MBA in Mktg. & Fin., NYU. Various positions Clorox; vice chmn. Altria Group, Inc.; gen. mgr., Swanson divsn. Campbell Soup Co., 1997—98, v.p., exec. officer, Vlasic Internat. Foods, & pres., Swanson Frozen Foods divsn., 1998—99; sr. v.p. U.S. Smokeless Tobacco Co., 2000, pres., 2000—05; pres., CEO UST LLC; COO UST, Inc. (acquired by Altria Group, Inc.), Greenwich, Conn., 2005—06, pres., 2005—09, CEO Greenwich, Conn., 2007—09, chmn., 2008—09; pres., CEO Lorillard, Inc., 2010—, chmn., 2011—. Office: Lorillard Inc 714 Green Valley Rd Greensboro NC 27408-7018 Office Phone: 203-622-3549, 336-335-7000. Office Fax: 203-622-3520, 336-335-7550. Business E-Mail: mkessler@lorillard.com.

KESSLER, RICHARD PAUL, JR., lawyer; b. Latrobe, Pa., July 11, 1945; s. Richard Paul Sr. and Dorothy Henrietta (Comp) K.; m. Kathleen Jane Parker, June 17, 1973 (dec. May 11, 1996); 1 child, Grace Elizabeth; m. Susan Kessler, Oct. 2000. BA, Fairfield U., Conn., 1968; JD, Emory U., 1971. Bar: Ga. 1971, U.S. Dist. Ct. (no. dist.) Ga. 1973, U.S. Ct. Appeals (5th cir.) 1974, U.S. Ct. Appeals (11th cir.) 1981, U.S. Supreme Ct. 1995. Law clk. to presiding justice U.S. Dist. Ct. (no. dist.) Ga., 1971-73; of counsel Macey, Wilensky, Kessler & Hennings, LLC and predecessor firm, Atlanta, 1973—. Lectr. Practising Law Inst., 1981, 83, Fin. Svc. Corp. Career Conf., Atlanta, 1986, Ga. and Ala. Insts. of Continuing Legal Edn., 1993-95;

panelist Credit Union Nat. Assn., Inc. League Attys. Conf., 1980-82, 87, 88-93, ABA, 1990-91; participant Nat. Conf. Commrs. on Uniform State Laws Drafting Com. on U.C.C. Articles, 3, 4, 4A, 1985-90; chair corp. and banking law sect. State Bar Ga., 1995-96, Bus. Law Sect. Author: What You Should Know About the New Bankruptcy Code, 1979, Guide to the Bankruptcy Laws: The Bankruptcy Reform Act of 1978, 79, Guide to the Bankruptcy Laws: The Bankruptcy Reform Act of 1978 (Bankruptcy Code) as Amended by the Bankruptcy Amendments and Federal Judgeship Act of 1984, The Bankruptcy Judges, U.S. Trustees and Family Farmer Bankruptcy Act of 1986; contbg. editor Banking and Lending Instn. Forms, 1996-2011; contbr. articles to profl. jours. Mem.: East Lake Golf Club. Office: Ste 4420 303 Peachtree St NW Atlanta GA 30303 Office Phone: 404-584-1200. Business E-Mail: rkessler@maceywilensky.com.

KESSLER, RONALD BOREK, journalist, writer; b. NYC, Dec. 31, 1943; s. Ernest Borek and Minuetta Kessler; m. Pamela Johnson Whitehead; children: Greg, Rachel. Student, Clark U., Worcester, Mass. Reporter Worcester Telegram, 1964; investigative reporter, editl. writer Boston Herald, 1965—68; NY bur. reporter Wall St. Jour., 1968-70; investigative reporter Washington Post, 1970-85; journalist/author, 1985—. Author: (nonfiction) The Life Insurance Game, 1985, The Richest Man in the World: The Story of Adnan Khashoggi, 1988, Spy vs. Spy: Stalking Soviet Spies in America, 1989, Moscow Station: How the KGB Penetrated the American Embassy, 1990, The Spy in the Russian Club: How Glenn Souther Stole America's Nuclear War Plans and Escaped to Moscow., 1992, Escape from the CIA: How the CIA Won and Lost the Most Important Spy Ever to Defect to the U.S., 1992, The FBI: Inside the World's Most Powerful Law Enforcement Agency, 1994, Inside the CIA: Revealing the Secrets of the World's Most Powerful Spy Agency, 1994, Inside the White House: The Hidden Lives of the Modern Presidents and the Secrets of the World's Most Powerful Institution, 1996 (NY Times bestseller), The Sins of the Father: Joseph P. Kennedy and the Dynasty He Founded, 1996, Inside Congress: The Shocking Scandals, Corruption, and Abuse of Power Behind the Scenes on Capitol Hill, 1997, The Season: Inside Palm Beach and America's Richest Society, 1999, The Bureau: The Secret History of the FBI, 2003, The CIA at War: Inside the Secret Campaign Against Terror, 2004, A Matter of Character: Inside the White House of George W. Bush, 2004 (NY Times bestseller), Laura Bush: An Intimate Portrait of the First Lady, 2006 (NY Times bestseller), The Terrorist Watch: Inside the Desperate Race to Stop the Next Attack, 2008, In the President's Secret Service: Behind the Scenes With Agents in the Line of Fire and the Presidents They Protect, 2009 (NY Times bestseller, 2014), The Secrets of the FBI, 2011. Recipient Pub. Affairs Reporting award, Am. Polit. Sci. Assn., 1965, 1st prize in newswriting, UPI, 1967, Sevellon Brown Meml. award, AP, 1967, George Polk Meml. award for cmty. svc., LI Univ., 1972, George Polk Meml. award for nat. reporting, 1979, Bill Pryor Meml. Reporting award, Washington-Balt. Newspaper Guild, 1973, 1st pl. in investigative reporting, Assn. Area Bus. Publs., 1987; named Robert Hovak Journalist of Yr. award, 2010; named a Washingtonian of Yr., Washingtonian mag., 1972. Home Phone: 301-279-5818. Personal E-mail: KesslerRonald@gmail.com.

KESSLER, WALTER BRUCE, dean, mathematics professor; b. Greensburg, Ky., Dec. 7, 1967; s. Malcolm Wayne and Connie Lobb Kessler; m. Heather Webb Webb, June 6, 1992; children: Todd Alexander, Evan Thomas, Sarah Brooke, Emily Lauren. AB, Western Ky. U., Bowling Green, 1989; MS, Vanderbilt U., Nashville, 1991, PhD, 1997. Instr. math. Western Ky. U., 1991—97, asst. prof. math., 1997—2002, assoc. prof. math., 2002—07, asst. dean, Ogden Coll. Sci. & Engring., 2004—, prof. math., 2007—. Contbr. articles to profl. jours. Mem.: Am. Math. Soc., Ky. Acad. Sci., Pi Mu Epsilon, Math. Assn. Am. Office: Western Kentucky Univ 1906 College Heights Blvd Bowling Green KY 42101 Home: 1818 Bent Tree Ct Bowling Green KY 42103-0900 Office Fax: 270-745-6471. Business E-Mail: bruce.kessler@wku.edu.

KESTERSON, DAVID BERT, language educator, academic administrator; b. Springfield, Mo., Feb. 19, 1938; s. Homer Russell and Dorothy (Mace) K.; m. Cheryl Renee Monk; children: A. Todd, Chad Russell. BSE, Mo. State U. (formerly SW Mo. State U.), 1959; MA, U. Ark., 1961, PhD, 1965. NDEA fellow, 1959-62; grad. teaching asst. U. Ark., Fayetteville, 1962-64; asst. prof. English N.C. State U., Raleigh, 1964-68; from asst. prof. to prof. English North Tex. State U. (name now U. North Tex.), Denton, 1968—2007, disting. Alumni prof., 1979, chmn. dept. English, 1981-86, assoc. dean Coll. Arts and Scis., 1986-92; sr. Fulbright lectr. U. Würzburg (Germany), 1985; interim dean Coll. Arts and Scis. U. North Tex., Denton, 1992-93, vice provost, 1993-98, v.p. for acad. affairs, 1998-2000, provost, v.p. acad. affairs, 2000—03, prof. English, 2003—07, spl. asst. to pres. for humanities, 2003—06; prof., English, 2007; ret., 2008. Cons. presses on manuscripts in Am. lit Author: Josh Billings, 1973, Bill Nye, 1980; monograph Bill Nye: The Western Writings, 1976; editor: Studies in the Marble Faun, 1971, Critics on Poe, 1973, Critics on Mark Twain, 1973, Critical Essays on Hawthorne's The Scarlet Letter, 1988; founding editor: Hawthorne Soc. Newsletter (now Nathaniel Hawthorne Rev.), 1974-82; adv. editor: Studies in the Novel, 1970—, Nathaniel Hawthorne Jour., 1980-82. With USAR, 1956-60. Recipient Mortar Bd. Outstanding Educator award, 1980; Outstanding Alumnus award S.W. Mo. State U., 1986, Disting. Grad. Alumnus award Dept. English U. Ark., 1988. Mem. Nathaniel Hawthorne Soc. (co-founder, 1st pres. 1974-76), Am. Humor Studies Assn. (pres. 1980-81), South Ctrl. MLA (exec. com. 1976-77), MLA (del. assembly 1977-80, 84-87), Melville Soc., Soc. Study So. Lit. (pres. 1999-01), Mark Twain Circle, Thoreau Soc., Thomas Wolfe Soc., Fulbright Assn., POE Studies Assn., Phi Kappa Phi, Phi Beta Delta, Golden Key. Office: 2719 Hartlee Ct Denton TX 76208 Personal E-mail: kestersondavid@yahoo.com.

KETCHAND, ROBERT LEE, lawyer; b. Shreveport, La., Jan. 30, 1948; s. Woodrow Wilson and Attie Harriet (Chandler) K.; m. Alice Sue Adams, May 31, 1969; children: Peter Leland, Marjory Attie. BA, Baylor U., 1970; JD, Harvard U., 1973. Bar: Tex. 1973, Mass. 1973, DC 1981. Assoc., ptnr. Butler & Binion, Houston, 1976-85, Washington, 1981-82; shareholder Brodsky & Ketchand, Houston, 1985-88; ptnr. Webster & Sheffield, Houston, 1988-90; atty. pvt. practice, Houston, 1990-92; ptnr. Short & Ketchand, Houston, 1992-2001; dir. Boyer & Ketchand, P.C., Houston, 2001—09; owner Ketchand Law Firm PLCC, 2010—, mng. mem., 2011—. Founder, chmn. bd. dirs. Rolling Waters, d/b/a Houston Legal Clinic. Pres. Prisoner Svcs. Com. Houston, 1986; deacon South Houston Bapt. Ch., 1976—; gen. counsel, dir. Houston Met. Ministries, 1986-88; dir. Interfaith Ministries Greater Houston, 1996-98; gen. counsel Houston Bus. Roundtable, 1988—. Lt. USNR, 1973-76. Mem. ABA, Tex. Bar Assn., Houston Bar Assn. (chmn. dispute com. 1989-90). Avocations: reading, writing. Home: 2707 Carolina Way Houston TX 77005-3423 Office: Ketchand Law Firm PLLC 2726 Bissonnet #240-242 Houston TX 77005-1352 Office Phone: 713-598-1885. Office Fax: 713-588-2558. Business E-Mail: ketchand@gmail.com.*

KETCHUM, MENIS E., II, state supreme court justice; b. Huntington, W.Va., 1943; m. Judy Varnum, 1966; children: Kelli Morgan, Bert ketchum, Chad. Grad., Ohio U., Athens; JD, W.Va. U., 1967. Assoc. Green, Ketchum & Baker, sr. ptnr.; justice W.Va. Supreme Ct. of Appeals, 2008—. Bd. mem. pub. defender corporations W.Va. 6th Jud. Cir., W.Va. 24th Jud. Cir. Mem. bd. governors Marshall U., 2002—08, vice chmn., bd. chmn.; mem. Huntington Urban Renewal Authority. Named to Best Lawyers in Am. Mem.: Leading Honoraries, Am. Bd. Trial Advocates, Am. Coll. Trial Lawyers. Office: Supreme Ct of Appeals Capitol Complex Bldg 1 Rm E-306 Charleston WV 25305 Office Phone: 304-558-2604.*

KETNER, KENNETH LAINE, philosopher, educator; b. Mountain Home, Okla., Mar. 24, 1939; s. Louis Elaine and Johnnie Lucille (Hannah) K.; m. Berti Gabriella Zehetmeier, Aug. 24, 1964 (dec. Oct. 1996); 1 child, Kenneth Laine Jr. BA in Philosophy, Okla. State U., 1961, MA, 1967; MA in Folklore, UCLA, 1968; PhD in Philosophy, U. Calif., Santa Barbara, 1972. Part-time instr. Okla. State U., 1964-67; tchg. asst. U. Calif., Santa Barbara, 1969-70; mem. faculty Tex. Tech U., Lubbock, 1971—, prof. philosophy, 1977-98, chmn. dept., 1979-81; founder, dir. Inst. Studies in Pragmaticism, 1972—, Charles Sanders Peirce prof. philosophy, 1981-98, Charles Sanders Peirce interdisciplinary prof., 1998—, Paul Whitfield Horn prof., 1999—. Asst. prof. philosophy and folklore UCLA, summers, 1972, 74; co-organizer C.S. Peirce Bicentennial Internat. Congress, Amsterdam, Netherlands 1976; Peirce Sesquicentennial Internat. Congress, Harvard U., 1989. Author: A Critical Study of Stephen C. Pepper's Approach to Metaphysics, 1967, An Essay on the Nature of World Views, 1972, An Emendation of R.G. Collingwood's Doctrine of Absolute Presuppositions, 1973; editor, compiler: Charles Sanders Peirce: Contributions to the Nation, 4 parts, 1975, 78, 79, 87, Comprehensive Bibliography of Works of C.S. Peirce, 1977, rev. edit., 1986, Reasoning and the Logic of Things, 1993, A Thief of Peirce, 1995, His Glassy Essence: an Autobiography of C.S. Peirce, 1998; founder, gen. editor Peirce Studies, 1979—, Philosophical Inquiries, 1989—, more. Capt. USAR, 1962-64. Grantee NSF, Nat. Endowment Humanities, Am. Coun. Learned Socs. Fellow Charles S. Peirce Soc. (pres. 1983); mem. Am. Philos. Assn., Freemason, Tau Kappa Epsilon. Democrat. Home: PO Box 65135 Lubbock TX 79464-5135 Office: Texas Tech Univ Library 305 Lubbock TX 79409-0002

KETNER, LINDA, consulting company executive, civic worker; b. Faith, NC, May 12, 1950; d. Ralph Ketner and Ruth Hope. BA in English, U. NC, Chapel Hill, 1972; MA in Sociology, U. NC, Greensboro; D in Sociology (hon.), Columbia Coll. Pub. HS tchr.; dir. orgn. devel. Food Lion, Inc.; exec. SmithKline Corp., Ctr. for Creative Leadership; founder KSI Corp., 1980—. Pres. Coastal Cmty. Found., established Women's Fund, established Ketner Fund, established Fund for Social Justice; pres. Charleston Interfaith Crisis Ministries; chair Mayor's Coun. on Homelessness and Affordable Housing, SC Housing Trust Fund; founder SC Citizens for Housing, Alliance for Full Acceptance, Charleston Affordable Housing, SC Equality Coalition; bd. mem. Hollings Cancer Ctr., Health Scis. Found., YWCA of the USA, Riley Pub. Policy Inst., Coll. Charleston Women Studies Program. Recipient Nat. Salute to Citizenship award, SC Woman Valor award, Girl Scout Woman Distinction award, SC Housing Achievement award, Malcolm D. Haven award for Cmty. Svc., African Am. Life and History Trailblazer award, Lifetime Achievement award, YWCA, Ctr. for Women an Florence Crittenton Found awards, J. Arthur Brown award for Outstanding Svc., NAACP, Friend of Distinction award, Arthur J. Clement award for Race Rels., Urban League; named Woman of Yr., SC Hosp. Assn. Democrat. Episcopalian. Home: 12 Church St Charleston SC 29401-2744 Office Phone: 843-937-4901. Office Fax: 843-937-4903. Business E-Mail: info@lindaketner.com.

KETRON, BILL, state legislator; b. Sept. 4, 1953; m. Theresa Ketron; 1 child, Kelsey. Repub. floor leader; sec. State & Local Govt. com.; mem. Edn. com., Govt. Op. com.; state senate Tenn.; commr. Rutherford Co. Commn., 1990—98; chmn. Health & Edn. com.; mem. Budget com., Pub. Works com., Pub. Safety com.; state senator Dist 13 Tenn., 2003—; owner Universal Int. Ins., Murfreesboro, Tenn. Mem.: Leadership Rutherford Alumni Assn., Bradley Acad, Rutherford Co. Conv. & Visitors Bureau, Shriner, Mason, Eagle Scout, Co-founder Mid. Tenn. State U Blue Raider Athletic Assn., Rutherford Vol. Fire Dept., Prof. Ins. Agts. Tenn., Found for Prevention Child Abuse, Nat. Exchange Club. Republican. Methodist. Office: 12 Jefferson Sq 805 South Church St Murfreesboro TN 37130 also: 13 Legislative Plz Nashville TN 37243-0213 Office Phone: 615-741-6853. Office Fax: 615-741-7200. Business E-Mail: sen.bill.ketron@capitol.tn.gov.

KETTELKAMP, DONALD BENJAMIN, retired orthopedist; b. Anamosa, Iowa, Jan. 21, 1930; s. Enoch George and Elsie (Norden) K.; m. Alice June Mencke, Dec. 30, 1954; children: Karen June, Lisa Marie, Suzanne D., Jonathan B.; m. Clemencia Oliveros Brandon, Apr. 28, 1989. BA, Cornell U., Mt. Vernon, Iowa, 1952; MD, U. Iowa, 1955, MS, 1960. Diplomate Am. Bd. Orthop. Surgery. Intern Thomas D. Dee Meml. Hosp., Ogden, Utah, 1955—56; resident orthopedic surgery U. Iowa, Iowa City, 1958—61; practice medicine specializing in orthopaedic surgery Anchorage, 1961—64; asst. prof. Albany (N.Y.) Med. Coll., 1964—66, assoc. prof., 1966—68, U. Iowa, Iowa City, 1968—71, prof., 1971; prof., chmn. dept. orthopaedic surgery U. Ark., Little Rock, 1971—74, Ind. U., Indpls., 1974—84; assoc. dean Tex. Tech. U., El Paso, 1984—87; exec. dir. Am. Bd. Orthop. Surgery, Chgo., 1986—94. Trustee: Jour. Bone and Joint Surgery, 1991—96. With USPHS, 1956—58. Mem.: ACS, Knee Soc., Assn. Orthopaedic Chairmen (pres. 1981), Am. Orthopaedic Assn. (pres. 1989—90), Am. Soc. Surgery of Hand, Am. Acad. Orthopaedic Surgeons.

KEULMAN, KENNETH PAUL, international relations & ethics educator; b. Chgo., Jan. 23, 1942; Student, U. Santa Clara, 1960-61; AB, Maryknoll Coll., 1964; MDiv, St. Patrick's Sem. & U., Menlo Pk., Calif., 1968, MA, 1969; PhD, U. Toronto, 1979. Lectr. Harvard Divinity Sch., Cambridge, Mass., 1981; Rockwell lectr. U. Houston, 1983; sr. rsch. assoc., lectr. Rice U., Houston, 1984-85; prof. Loyola U., 1986—. Vis. scholar Harvard Divinity Sch., Cambridge, 1979-81, Harvard Law Sch., Cambridge, 1990-91, Stanford (Calif.) Law Sch., 1996-97, Weatherhead Ctr. Internat. Affairs Harvard U., 2004-05, assoc. 2005-06; assoc., Cetr. Govt. and Internat. Studies, Harvard U., 2011-12; with Berkeley/Harvard Project in Comparative Ethics, Harvard U., Cambridge, 1980-83, rsch. assoc. Harvard U., Ctr. European Studies, 1981-86, chmn. seminar on nuclear politics and soc., 1982-85; vis. fellow Woodrow Wilson Sch. Pub. & Internat. Affairs, Ctr. Internat. Studies, Princeton U., NJ, 1993-94, chmn. seminar comparative democratization; assoc. Atlantic Coun.; reviewer in field. Author: The Nuclear Age: Strategies for Survival, 1989, The Balance of Consciousness, 1990, Critical Moments in Religious History, 1993, Horizons of Value Conceptions: Axiological Discourses for the 21st Century, 2007, European Identity, 2014; rev. editor: Human Rights Rev., 2003—10; contbr. chapters to books, articles to profl. jours. Mem. Amnesty Internat., Oxfam, Internat. Rescue Com., Cultural Survival. With Res. Officers' Tng. Corps. Pershing Rifles. Recipient award, Raskob Found., 1960, Faculty Devel. award, Apple Computer, 1988; named Provost Disting. Prof., Loyola U., 2013; fellow, Atlantic Coun., 2002; grant, Rockwell Found., 1983, Scanlon Found., 1984—85, Collegium fellowship, 1994. Mem.: Assn. Study Nationalities, Asia Soc., Atlantic Coun., Internat. Studies Assn., Am. Polit. Sci. Assn. Office: Loyola University Campus Box 81 6363 St Charles Ave New Orleans LA 70118 Office Phone: 504-865-2652. Business E-Mail: kkeulman@loyno.edu, kkeulman@wcfia.harvard.edu.*

KEVORKIAN, RICHARD, artist; b. Dearborn, Mich., Aug. 24, 1937; s. Kay and Stana (Bedeian) K.; m. Salpy Bouroujian; children: Anna, Raffi, Soseh and Ellina (twins), Salpi Serar. BFA, Richmond Profl. Inst., 1961; MFA in Painting, Calif. Coll. Arts and Crafts, 1962. Instr. drawing and painting Richard Bland Coll., Petersburg, Va., 1961-64; instr. dept. fine arts Va. Commonwealth U., Richmond, 1962-66, asst. prof. dept. painting and printmaking, 1967-69, assoc. prof., 1969-77, prof., 1967-93, prof. emeritus, 1993, chmn. dept., 1969-81; ret. One-man exhbns. include Aaron Gallery, Washington, Marita Gilliam Gallery, Raleigh, N.C.; exhbns. include Birmingham Mus. Art, Ala., 1977, Greenville County Mus. Art, S.C., 1977, Southeastern Ctr. Contemporary Art, Winston-Salem, N.C., 1977, 78, Hunter Mus. Art, Chattanooga, 1978, Va. Mus. Fine Art, 1983, U. Tenn., Knoxville, 1983, Lee Hansley Gallery, Raleigh, N.C. Mem. selection bd. for visual arts Va. Ctr. for Creative Arts, Sweet Briar. Served with N.G., 1955-63; guest curator Retrospective Exhib. Maurice Bonds Anderson Gallery, 2003. NEA individual sr. artists grantee, 1972, Va. Commonwealth U. Sch. Arts faculty creative research grantee, 1974, Nat. Endowment for Arts, Southeastern Ctr. Contemporary Arts grantee, 1976; Guggenheim fellow, 1978 Home: 7909 Rock Creek Rd Henrico VA 23229-6643

KEY, CHARLES DANIEL, state legislator; b. Lubbock, Tex., Apr. 18, 1954; s. Bill P. and Catherine L. Taylor Key; m. Janice J. Key; children: Kyan, Joshua, Jacob, Chelsea. Ins. businessman; mem. Dist. 90 Okla. House of Representatives, 1987—98, 2007—. Named Friend of Taxpayer, Okla. Taxpayers Union. Mem.: South Okla. City C. of C., Bethany C. of C., Lions Club. Republican. Church Of Christ. Mailing: 700 Manchester Lane Oklahoma City OK 73127 Office: Oklahoma House of Representatives 2300 N Lincoln Blvd Room 405 Oklahoma City OK 73105 Office Phone: 405-557-7354. E-mail: charles.key@okhouse.gov.

KEY, JOHNNY R., state legislator; b. Arkadelphia, Ark., Dec. 9, 1968; m Shannon Key; children: Ryan & Rachel. BSChE, Univ. Ark., 1991. Engr.; owner Open Arms Learning Ctr.; Justice of the Peace Baxter County, Ark., 1997—2002; mem. Ark. House of Reps., 2003—09, minority leader; mem. Dist. 1 Ark. State Senate, 2009—. Mem. Am. Soc. Quality, Mountain Home C. of C., Mountain Home Lions Club. Republican. Assembly Of God. Address: 1030 Hwy 62 E Mountain Home AR 72653 Office Phone: 870-425-5200. Office Fax: 870-424-7437. Business E-Mail: keyj@ark.leg.state.ar.us.

KEYES, DANIEL, author; BA in Psychology, Bklyn. Coll., 1950, MA in English, 1961. Assoc. fiction editor Magazine Mgmt. Co., NYC, 1950-52; v.p. Fenko and Keyes Photography, Inc., 1952-53; tchr. English N.Y.C. Bd. Edn., 1955-62; instr. English Wayne State U., Detroit, 1962-66; mem. faculty Ohio U., Athens, 1966—, prof. English and creative writing, 1972-97, prof. emeritus, 2000—; agt. William Morris Agy., NYC, Calif. Author: (novels) Flowers for Algernon (Hugo award 1959, Nebula award 1966, movie version: Charly, 1968 (Acad. award), The Touch, 1968, The Fifth Sally, 1980, (nonfiction) The Minds of Billy Milligan, 1981 (Spl. award Mystery Writers Am., Kurd Lasswitz award, 1st prize Best Fgn. Book award 1986), Unveiling Claudia, 1986, Daniel Keyes Collected Stories, 1993 (Japan), The Milligan Wars, 1994 (Japan), Daniel Keyes Reader, 1995 (Japan), Until Death Do Us Part: The Sleeping Princess, 1998 (Japan), (TV movie) Flowers for Algernon, 2000, (non-fiction) Algernon, Charlie and I: A Writer's Journey, 2000; (13 episode TV series) flowers for Algernon (Japan), 2002, The Touch, revised 2003; supervising prodr. (TV movie) The Mad Housers, 1990. With U.S. Maritime Svc., 1945—47. Ohio Arts Council Individual Artist fellow, 1986-87; recipient Baker Fund award 1986-87, Disting. Alumnus Honor award Bklyn. Coll. CUNY, 1988. Mem.: PEN, Sci. Fiction Writers Am. (Author Emeritus award 2000), Mystery Writers Am., Dramatists' Guild. Office: 7491 N Federal Hwy C5-110 Boca Raton FL 33487-1625 Personal E-mail: dankeyes@usa.net.

KEYES, DAVID R., lawyer; b. NYC, Jan. 9, 1940; AB, Princeton U. Woodrow Wilson Sch. Pub. & Internat. Affairs, NJ, 1965; JD with high honors, U. Tex. Sch. Law, 1968. Bar: Tex. 1968, NY 2009. Law clk. to Hon. Walter Ely US Ct. Appeals (9th cir.), 1968—69; atty. Vinson & Elkins LLP, Houston, 1969—2006; ptnr. Kelly Hart & Hallman LLP, Austin, Tex., 2009—. Adj. prof. South Tex. Coll. Law, 2007—11, mem. adv. bd. Transactional Practice Ctr., 2007—. Contbr. articles to profl. jours. Named one of America's Leading Bus. Lawyers, Chambers USA, 2003—10, Tex. Super Lawyers in Banking Law, Tex. Monthly mag., 2004—10. Fellow: American Bar Found. (life), Tex. Bar Found. (life), Houston Bar Found. (life); mem.: ABA (governing coun. mem. Bus. Law Sect. 2008—, vice chair 2011—), Tex. Assn. Bank Counsel, State Bar Tex. (mem. bus. law sect.), American Law Inst., Phi Delta Phi, Order of the Coif. Office: Kelly Hart & Hallman LLP 301 Congress Ave Ste 2000 Austin TX 78701 Office Phone: 512-495-6455. Office Fax: 512-495-6933. E-mail: david.keyes@kellyhart.com.

KEYES, JAMES WILLARD (JIM KEYES), film rental company executive; b. Worcester, Mass., Mar. 17, 1955; s. Harold L. and Dorothy M. (Anderson) K.; m. Margo Bernadette Ramirez, Apr. 20, 1991. BA, Coll. Holy Cross, 1977; postgrad., U. London; MBA, Columbia U., 1980. Dir. corp. planning Gulf Oil Corp., Pitts., 1980-85; v.p. nat. gasoline The Southland Corp., Dallas, 1985-93; sr. fin. officer The Southland Corp. subs. 7-Eleven, Inc., CFO, 1996—98, exec. v.p., COO, 1998—2000, pres., CEO, 2000—05; chmn., CEO Blockbuster, Inc., Dallas, 2007—11. Founder Education is Freedom Found. Bd. govs. Dallas Symphony Assn., Inc., chmn.; bd. govs. ARC; trustee The Cooper Inst.; bd. mem. Edwin L. Cox Sch. Bus., So. Methodist U. Recipient Horatio Alger award, 2005. Mem. Phi Beta Kappa. Avocations: pilot, musician.

KEYES, MICHAEL J., food products executive; 3 children. BA in History, U. Mich., 1979. Category mgr. Allied Lyons, Hiram Walker; sales and mktg. positions Stroh Brewery Co.; sr. v.p., mng. dir. Brown-Forman Corp., gen. mgr., Korbel brand, 1991, dir., Jack Daniel's brand, 1997—98, v.p., Jack Daniel's brand, 1998, pres., N.Am. region, 2008—. Office: Brown Forman Corp 850 Dixie Hwy Louisville KY 40210 Office Phone: 502-585-1100. Office Fax: 502-774-7876. Business E-Mail: michael_keyes@b-f.com.

KHABBAZ, RIMA, public health service officer; BS, Am. U. Beirut, 1975, MD, 1979. Cert. in internal medicine. Internal medicine tng. Am. U. Beirut Med. Ctr., Lebanon, 1978—80; fellowship in infectious diseases U. Md.; resident internal medicine Union Meml. Hosp., Balt.; epidemic intelligence officer Centers for Disease Control, 1980; dep. dir. Divsn. Viral and Rickettsial Diseases Nat. Ctr. Infectious Diseases, Centers for Disease Control, assoc. dir. epidemiologic sci., acting dep. dir., dir., 2005—08; dir., Nat. Ctr. Preparedness, Detection and Control Infectious Diseases Centers for Disease Control and Prevention, dep. dir., dir. Office Infectious Diseases. Blood product adv. com. US Food & Drug Adminstrn., 1995—99. Contbr. chapters to books, articles to profl jours. Fellow: Infectious Disease Soc. Am.

(scientific program com. 1999—2002); mem.: Am. Soc. of Tropical Medicine and Hygiene, Am. Bd. for Microbiology, Am. Epidemiologic Soc. Office: Nat Ctr Infectious Diseases CDC Bldg 1 Rm 6013 1600 Clifton Rd NE Atlanta GA 30333 Business E-Mail: rima.khabbaz@cdc.hhs.gov.

KHACHATURIAN, JON, civil engineer, manufacturing executive; s. Narbey and Margaret Khachaturian; m. Bobbi Baker; children: Matthew, Sara, Bethany. BSCE, Univ. Ill., 1978. PE. Founder, pres., CEO Versabar, Houston, 1981—. Named one of Top 25 Newsmakers, Engring. News Record. Mem.: ASCE, Nat. Acad. Engring. Achievements include patents in field; invention & development of "Bottom Feeder" underwater heavy lifting system. Office: Versabar 11349 FM 529 Rd Houston TX 77041 also: Versabar 1111 Engineers Rd Belle Chasse LA 70037 Office Phone: 713-937-3100, 504-392-3200.

KHACHATURIAN, MARK HAIG, systems engineer, consultant; b. Royal Oak, Mich., Nov. 16, 1979; s. Arek and JoAnn Diane Khachaturian. BSE in Engring. Physics, U. Mich., Ann Arbor, 2001; BSE in Nuc. Engring., 2001; MSE, MIT, Cambridge, 2003; PhD in Nuc. Sci. & Engring., 2007. Sys. engr. Fermi II Power Plant, Monroe, Mich., 1999—99; core engr. Westinghouse Electric Co., Monroeville, Pa., 2000—00; rsch. asst. U. Mich. Dept. Nuc. Engring., Ann Arbor, Mich., 2001—01, Athinoula A. Martinos Ctr. Mass. Gen. Hosp., Charlestown, 2002—07; sole propr. owner MHK MRI Consulting, Florence, SC, 2007—; sys. engr. GE Healthcare, Florence, 2008—. Tutor Wylie E. Groves HS, Beverly Hills, Mich., 1996—97. Mem.: Tau Beta Pi, Alpha Delta Phi (historian, sports chair 2000—01). Achievements include development of method to accurately quantify the white matter structure in the human brain using MRI hardware to improve the resolution of primate imaging studies; research in to understand the functional interaction between nodes in the visual system using MRI; development of technology to understand the functional interaction of nodes in the visual system and a method to quantify the electrostatic potential in high resolution gamma ray detectors; design of a system to measure the vibration of piping inside nuclear reactors to predict mechanical failure and Participated in the design of multiple nuclear reactor fuel loading patterns. Home: 9999 W North Ave Apt 118 Milwaukee WI 53226-2517 Personal E-mail: mkhachat@hotmail.com. Business E-Mail: mark.khachaturian@med.ge.com.

KHAN, ALI S., federal agency administrator; b. Bklyn., June 14, 1963; MD, Downstate Med. Ctr., NY, 1987; MPH, Emory U., Ga., 2000. Diplomate Nat. Bd. Med. Examiners. Joint residency in internal medicine and pediatrics U. Mich., Ann Arbor; joined as an epidemic intelligence svc. officer Ctrs. Disease Control and Prevention and the US Health Svc. Commd. Corps, 1991; dep. dir. nat. ctr. emerging zoonotic infectious diseases Ctrs. Disease Control and Prevention, 2006—10, asst. surgeon gen., dir. office pub. health preparedness and response, 2010—. Cons. NASA, Ministries of Health, WHO; adj. prof. Emory U., 2005—11. Decorated Meritorious Svc. medal US Pub. Health Svc., Commendation medal, Outstanding Svc. medal; recipient Outstanding Unit Citation award, Sec.'s award. Fellow: ACS, Am. Acad. Physicians; mem.: Delta Omega, Alpha Omega Alpha. Office: 1600 Clifton Rd MS D44 Atlanta GA 30329 Business E-Mail: ask0@cdc.gov.

KHAN, MUSHFIQUDDIN, neuropharmacologist, researcher; s. Noor Mohammad Khan and Aqila Begum; m. Salma Ansar, June 15, 1966 (dec.); children: Tooba, Talha, Hamza. BSc with honors, Aligarh Muslim U., India, 1976, MSc, 1978, MPhil, 1980. Postdoctoral rschr. Ehime U., Matsuyama, Shikoku, Japan, 1984—86; rsch. scientist-pool officer Aligarh Muslim U., Uttar Pradesh, India, 1986—88; lectr. Shibli Nat. Postgraduate Coll., Azamgarh, Uttar Pradesh, India, 1988—90; postdoctoral rschr. Med. U. SC, Charleston, 1994—98, asst. prof., 2002—. Scientist Modern Foam Industries, Janupur, 1990—94; sr. scientist Ariz. Inst. for Biomedical Rsch., Scottsdale, 1999—2001; grant reviewer NIH, Washington. Mem. AMU Rsch. Student's Assn., Aligarh, 1980—82. Recipient Mitchell I. Rubin rsch. award, Children's Hosp., MUSC; grantee, NINDS, NIH, Bethesda, MD, 2000—05; Monbusho fellow, Govt. of Japan, jr. rsch. fellow, CSIR, Govt. of India, sr. rsch. fellow. Mem.: AAAS, Indian Soc. for Mass Spectrometry, Am. Soc. for Neurochemistry, Am. Assn. for Biochemistry and Molecular Biology. Avocations: travel, classical music, humor, handball. Home: 3529 Ashwycke St Mount Pleasant SC 29466 Office: Med Univ SC 173 Ashley Ave 508 CRI Charleston SC 29425 Business E-Mail: khanm@musc.edu.

KHAN, SHAH-NAZ HAYAT, neurosurgeon; d. Muhammad Jalal and Mehrunisa Jalat Khan. BSc, U. Punjab, Rawalpindi, Pakistan, 1987, MBBS, 1989. Cert. in neurosurgery Coll. Medicine, U. Sask., Can., 2005. Endovascular neurosurgeon Marshfield Clinic, 2008—09; asst. prof. endovascular neurosurgeon St. Louis U., St. Anthony's Med. Ctr., 2009—10, U. N.Mex, Albuquerque, 2010—12; dir. neurosurgery, endovascular neurosurgery and stroke intervention St. Francis Hosp., Columbus, 2013. Clin. fellow NYU Med. Ctr., 1994—96; neurotrauma fellow U. Conn., Hartford Hosp., Farmington, 1996—97; postdoc. stroke rsch. fellow Sask. Stroke Rsch. Ctr., U. Sask., Saskatoon, Canada, 1998—2000; fellow cerebrovascular and endovascular neurosurgery U. Cin., Mayfield Clinic, 2006—08; reviewer Neurosurgery Jour. Congress Neurol. Surgery, 2012. Grant, Royal U. Hosp. Found. Fund, Saskatoon, 2002. Fellow: RCS, Am. Assn. Neurol. Surgeons; mem.: Am. Stroke Assn., Soc. Neurointervetional Surgeons, Can. Neurol. Scis. Fedn., Am. Heart Assn., Congress Neurol. Surgeons. Avocations: bicycling, hiking, writing.*

KHARGONEKAR, PRAMOD PRABHAKAR, engineering professor, former dean; b. Indore, India, Aug. 24, 1956; s. Prabhakar K. and Leela P. Khargonekar; m. Seema P. Pai, Apr. 7, 1983; children: Aditya, Shivangi. BTech. in elec. engring., Indian Inst. Tech., Bombay, 1977; MS in math., U. Fla., 1980, PhD in elec. engring., 1981. Asst. prof. elec. engring. U. Fla., Gainesville, 1981-84; assoc. prof. elec. engring. U. Minn., Mpls., 1984-88, prof. elec. engring., 1988-89; prof. elec. engring. and computer sci. U. Mich., Ann Arbor, 1989—2001, Arthur F. Thurnau Prof., 1995—98, assoc. chair elec. engring. and computer sci., 1995-97, chair elec. engring. and computer sci., 1997—2001, Claude E. Shannon Prof. Engring. Sci., 2000—01; dean Coll. Engring. U. Fla., Gainesville, 2001—08, assoc. v.p. Engring. and Indsl. Experiment Sta., 2001—09, Eckis prof. elec. & computer engring., 2001—09, prof., Eckis chair elec. & computer engring., 2009—. Contbr. articles to profl. jours. Recipient Sigma Xi award for Outstanding Rsch. on Math. Sys. Theory, U. Fla., 1982, Best Faculty Paper award, Dept. Elec. Engring., 1983, Presdl. Young Investigator award, NSF, 1985, George Taylor award for Rsch., U. Minn. Inst. Tech., 1987, Donald Eckman award, Am. Automatic Control Coun., 1989, O. Hugo Schuck Best Paper award, 1993, Tchg. Excellence award, Elec. Engring. and Computer Sci. Dept., U. Mich., 1992, Rsch. Excellence award, U. Mich. Coll. Engring., 1994, Disting. Alumnus award, Indian Inst. Tech., 1997. Fellow: IEEE (Control Systems Soc. George S. Axelby Best Paper Award 1990, W.R.G. Baker Prize Paper Award 1991). Avocations: reading, music. Office: University of Florida Dept Elec & Computer Engring PO Box 116130 Gainesville FL 32611-6130 Office Phone: 325-392-0918, 352-392-0918. Business E-Mail: ppk@ufl.edu.

KHATENA, JOE, psychology professor; b. Singapore, Oct. 25, 1925; came to U.S., 1966, naturalized, 1972; s. Jacob J. and Rachel (Rahmin) K.; m. Nelly Joshua, Dec. 17, 1950; children— Annette, Jacob Allan, Moshe, Serena BA with honors, U. Malaya, Singapore, 1960-61; M.Edn., U. Singapore, 1964; PhD, U. Ga., 1969. Tchr. Govt. of Singapore, 1950-57; lectr. English, Singapore Tchrs. Coll., 1961-66; asst. prof. psychology East Carolina U., Greenville, NC, 1968-69; assoc. prof. Marshall U., Huntington, W.Va., 1969-72, prof., 1972-77; prof., head ednl. psychology Miss. State U., Mississippi State, 1977-91, prof., head emeritus, 1991—; pres. Nat. Assn. Gifted Children, 1977—79. Author: Creatively Gifted Child, 1978, Educational Psychology of the Gifted, 1982, Imagery and Creative Imagination, 1984, Gifted: Challenge and Response for Education, 1992, Enhancing Creativity of Gifted Children, 2000, others; co-author: Khatena-Torrance Creative Perception Inventory, 1976, rev., 1998, Thinking Creatively with Sounds and Words, 1973, rev., 1998, Khatena-Morse Multitalent Perception Inventory, 1992, (with Nelly Khatena) Developing Creative Talent in Art, 1999; mem. editorial bd. Gifted Child Quar., 1975—, assoc. editor Jour. Mental Imagery, 1981—; contbr. articles to profl. jours. Recipient Book prize U. Malaya, 1957, Rsch. award Marshall U., 1976, Disting. Svc. award Nat. Assn. Gifted Children, 1983, Rsch. award Phi Delta Kappa Miss. State U., 1989; Nat. Assn. Gifted Children Disting. scholar, 1982, Fulbright sr. lectr., 1985, 90. Fellow Am. Psychol. Assn.; mem. Internat. Psychol. Assn., Am. Ednl. Research Assn., N.Y. Acad. Scis., Phi Kappa Phi, Kappa Delta Pi.

KHATOR, RENU, academic administrator, political science professor; b. June 29, 1955; m. Suresh Khator; 2 children. BA, Kanpur U., 1976; MA, Purdue U., 1975, PhD in Polit. Sci., 1985. Vis. asst. prof. polit. sci. U. South Fla., Tampa, 1985—87, asst. prof., 1987—91, dir. grad. program Dept. Govt. & Internat. Affairs, 1990—93, assoc. prof. govt. & internat. affairs, 1991—95, prof., 1995—, faculty asst. to pres., 1995—97, dir., chair Environ. Sci. and Policy Dept., 1997—2000, dean Coll. Arts and Scis., 2000—03, provost, sr. v.p., 2003—07; chancellor U. Houston Sys., 2008—; pres. U. Houston, 2008—. Mem. Nat. Adv. Coun. on Environ. Policy and Mgmt., 2004—07. Author: Environment, Development and Politics in India, 1991; co-editor: Public Administration in the Global Village, 1994; co-author: Managing Development in a Global Context, 2007; contbr. articles to profl. jours. Mem. City of Tampa's Environ. Task Force, 1999—, City of Clearwater Brownfield Adv. Bd., 1999—, U. South Fla. Found. Bd., 1998—, U. South Fla. Rsch. Found. Bd., 2003—, Univ. Area Cmty. Devel. Bd., 2004—, Hillsborough Edn. Found Bd., 2005—; bd. dirs. Moffitt Cancer Hosp., 2000—, Lowry Park Zoo Bd., 2001—; bd. pres. Kiran C. Patel Charter Sch., 2003—. Recipient Outstanding Am. by Choice Award, US Citizenship and Immigration Svcs., 2006, Outstanding Educator Award, Am. Found. for Greek Language and Culture, 2006, Hind Rattan Award, 2007. Mem.: Internat. Polit. Sci. Assn. Office: U Houston 4800 Calhoun Rd Houston TX 77204 Office Phone: 713-743-2255.

KHIM, JAY WOOK, information technology executive; b. Taegu, Korea, Oct. 22, 1940; came to U.S., 1965; s. Joon Mook and Soon E. (Lee) K. BS in Agrl. Econs., Kyung Pook U., Korea, 1963, MA in Agrl. Econs., 1966; postgrad. PhD program in Econs., U. Md., 1965-69; LLD (hon.), Randolph-Macon Coll., 1988; PhD (hon.), Kyungpook Nat. U., Republic of Korea, 1990. Mem. rsch. staff Brookings Instn., Washington, 1967-69; sr. economist NAB, Dept. of Labor, Washington, 1969-72; sr. assoc. Planning Rsch. Corp., Washington, 1972-74; chmn., CEO JWK Internat. Corp., Washington, 1974—, Internat. Trade and Investment Corp., Washington, 1977—. Bd. dirs. Millennium Bank. Author: The Third Eye, 1998; author, editor more than 100 research reports, articles for fed. govt. in fields of health, energy, def., transp., housing and internat. affairs Bd. dirs. Fulbright Found., 1999—, Asia Soc., Washington, 1999—, George Mason Inst., George Mason U., Fairfax, Va., 1983—, United Bank, 1997—, No. Va. Cmty. Found., 1998—, Worf Trap Found. for Performing Arts, 1998—; mem. World Presidents Orgn., 1992—, chmn. Washington Met. chpt., 1994-2000; bd. govs. U. Md. Alumni Assn.; bd. trustees Fairfax Hosp. Assn., 1986-2001; candidate for U.S. Congress from 11th Va. dist., 1992; chmn. fin. com. Rep. Party, Va.; commr. Small and Minority Bus. Commn., Fairfax County, 1992. Fulbright scholar, 1965, 66; recipient Sam Ill Found. award Korea, 1962, 63 Mem. Young Pres.'s Orgn., Pres. Club of Am. Mgmt. Assn., Nat. Security Assn., Am. Def. Preparedness Assn., Am. Econ. Assn., Fairfax C. of C. (bd. dirs. 1984-87), World Pres.'s Orgn. (chmn. Washington Met. chtp. 1994-95), City Club, Tower Club, Robert Trent Jones Club, Tournament of Players Club, Internat. Club (D.C.), River Bend Country Club, Fairbanks Golf and Country Club (San Diego). Office: JWK Internat Corp Ste 1040 7617 Little River Tpke Annandale VA 22003-2689 also: 10900 Tara Rd Potomac MD 20854-1342

KHONSARI, MICHAEL M., mechanical engineering educator; b. Aug. 17, 1957; m. Karen Sue Troy, Sept. 1, 1990. BS in Mech. Engring. with honors, U. Tex., Austin, 1978, MS in Mech. Engring., 1979, PhD in Mech. Engring., 1983. Rsch. and tchg. asst. U. Tex., Austin, 1978-83; asst. prof. Ohio State U., Columbus, 1984-87, U. Pitts., 1988-90, assoc. prof., 1990-96; prof. So. Ill. U., Carbondale, 1996-99, prof., chmn. dept. mech. engring. and energy processes, 1996-99; Dow Chem. endowed chair, prof. mech. engring. La. State U., Baton Rouge, 1999—, Dow Chem. endowed chair in rotating machinery, 1999—. Apptd. project dir. and assoc. commr. Sponsored R&D at La. Bd. Regents, Exptl. Program to Stimulate Competitive Rsch., 2003—; mem. mech. engring. grad. com. U. Pitts., 1988-90, design interest group, 1988-96; mem. faculty ctr. motion control U. Pitts.; reviewer NSF, NASA, Am. Chem. Soc. Books, McGraw Hill Books, Addison Wesley Books, Prentice-Hall Books, Holt Rinehart and Winston Books; lectr. in field. Assoc. editor ASME Jour. Tribology, 1997—, STLE Tribology Transactions, 1990—; assoc. editor, Jour. Engring. Tribology, editl. bd., Tribology Internat.; mem. editl. bd., reviewer Jour. Engring. Design Graphics, 1987—; contbr., reviewer, mem. editl. bd. adv. com. CRC Handbook of Lubrication, vol. III, 1991-93; reviewer Lubrication Engring. Jour., Wear Jour., Rheology Jour., Heat Transfer Jour., Tribology Jour., Applied Mechanics Jour.; co-author: Applied Triology, 2001; pub. abstracts and reports; referee various jours.; contbr. articles to profl. jours. Recipient Found. award ALCOA, 1990, 91. Fellow Soc. Tribology Lubrication Engrs. (bearings com. 1985—, chmn. 1988-91, assoc. editor, rev. Tribology Transactions 1990—, assoc. editor Jour. Tribology 1997—, Presdl. Rsch. Coun. award 1993), ASME (conf. planning com. 1989-96, reviewer Jour. Tribology and conf. papers, chmn. ASME/Soc. Tribology and Lubrication Engrs. Internat. Conf. in Tribology 1996, Burt L. Newkirk award 1990). Achievements include research in thermal effects in hydrodynamic bearings, thermal effects in wet clutches, hot spot prediction in mechanical components, Thermoclastic instability, powder lubrication, multi-phase flows in bearings, friction associated with instrument pointing mechanisms operating under ultra low speeds. Office: La State U Dept Mech Engring 2508 Ceba Baton Rouge LA 70803-0001 Office Phone: 225-578-9192. Business E-Mail: khonsari@me.lsu.edu.

KHOOBEHI, KAMRAN, plastic surgeon; married. MD, St. Louis U., 1986—90. Diplomate Am. Bd. Surgery, 1999, Am. Bd. Plastic Surgery, 2000. Gen. surgery La. State Univ. Health Sci. Ctr., New Orleans, 1990—95, clin. prof. surgery; plastic surgeon Solo Practitioner, Metairie, La., 1997—; hosp. affiliations include Tulane-Lakeside Hosp., East Jefferson Gen. Hosp., Univ. Med. Ctr., Lakeview Regional Med. Ctr., Ochsner Baptist Med. Ctr. Recipient Tchg. Excellence in Aesthetic Surgery, 2005. Fellow: Am. Coll. of Surgeons; mem.: Am. Soc. of Reconstructive Microsurgery, La. Soc. of Plastic Surgeons, Am. Soc. for Aesthetic Plastic Surgery, Am. Soc. of Plastic Surgery. Avocations: deep sea fishing, swimming, spending time with his children. Office: 3901 Veterans Blvd Metairie LA 70002 Office Phone: 504-273-7267.

KHOURIE, BILL, aerospace transportation executive; BS, U. Okla., Norman; MA, Murray State U., Ky., 1975. Program mgr., crew mem. Hist. DC-3 Ship 41 Restoration Project Delta Air Lines; with Okla. Space Industry Devel. Authority, Burns Flat, 2002—, exec. dir., 2004—. Mem. Gov.'s Aerospace and Edn. Taskforce, Okla. Aeronautics and Space Commn., Nat. Transonic Wind Tunnel Taskforce, Gov.'s Taskforce in New Airline Svc. for Okla. Bd. trustees Delta Air Lines Mus. Mem.: Aerospace States Assn. (nat. chmn. aeronautics com.). Office: Okla Space Industry Devel Authority PO Box 689 Burns Flat OK 73624 Office Phone: 580-562-3500. Office Fax: 580-562-3499. E-mail: bill.khourie@okspaceport.state.ok.us.

KHOURY, AMIN J., aerospace product and parts manufacturing executive; BS in Chemistry, MS in Chemistry, Northeastern U., MBA with distinction. Founder, chmn. Applied Extrusion Technologies, 1986—2005, pres., 1988—92; CEO Applied Extrusion Technologies, Inc., 2002—; co-founder BE Aerospace, Inc., 1987, chmn., 1987—, CEO, 1987—96, 2005—; co-founder, CEO Advanced Thermal Technologies. Bd. dirs. Synthes, Inc., 1986—, BE Aerospace, Inc., 1987—, Brooks Automation Inc., 1994—2006, Aerospace Ind. Assn. Bd. mem. Brigham & Women's Hosp., Kravis Ctr. for Performing Arts, Biomotion Found., Boys & Girls Club Martin County, Boys & Girls Club Palm Beach County, Dana Farber Cancer Rsch. Inst. Mem.: Phi Kappa Phi, Beta Gamma Sigma. Office: BE Aerospace Inc 1400 Corp Ctr Way Wellington FL 33414 Office Phone: 561-791-5000. Office Fax: 561-791-7900.

KHOURY, KENNETH F., lawyer, air transportation executive; b. NY, July 17, 1951; BA with honors, Rutgers Coll., NJ, 1972; JD, Fordham U., 1977. Bar: NY 1978, NJ 1979, Ga. Assoc. White & Case, 1977—82; sr. counsel THE BOC Group Inc., 1982—83; asst. v.p., assoc. counsel The Continental Corp., 1983—88; sr. v.p., assoc. gen. counsel Shearson Lehman Hutton, Inc., 1988—90; assoc. gen. counsel to v.p., dep. gen. counsel, sec. Georgia-Pacific Corp., Atlanta, 1990—2005; sr. v.p., gen. counsel Weyerhaeuser Co., 2006; exec. v.p., gen. counsel Delta Air Lines, Inc., Atlanta, 2006—08, Beazer Homes USA, Inc., Atlanta, 2009—. Office: Beazer Homes USA 1000 Abernathy Rd NE Atlanta GA 30328

KHURI, ANDRE ILIAS, statistician, educator; b. Damascus, Syria, Mar. 1, 1940; arrived in US, 1966; s. Elias Boulos and Rosette (Khalil Shami) Khuri; m. Ronnie Lee Gross, Oct. 11, 1970; children: Marcus, Roxanne. BS in Math., Damascus U., 1963; MS in Math., Am. U. Beirut, Lebanon, 1966; PhD in Math., U. Fla., Gainesville, 1969; MS in Stats., Va. Poly. Inst., Blacksburg, 1974, PhD in Stats., 1976. Asst. prof. math. Middle East Tech. U., Ankara, Turkey, 1970—71, Beirut U. Coll., 1971—73; asst. prof. stats. U. Fla., Gainesville, 1976—82, assoc. prof. stats., 1982—88, prof. stats., 1988—2007, prof. emeritus, 2007—. Assoc. editor Technometrics, Washington, 1983—92. Contbr. articles to profl. jours.; author (with J.A. Cornell): Response Surfaces, 2nd edit., 1996; author: Advanced Calculus with Applications in Statistics, 2nd edit., 2003; author: (with T. Mathew and B. K. Sinha) Statistical Tests for Mixed Linear Models, 1998; author: Linear Model Methodology, 2010; editor: Response Surface Methodology and Related Topics, 2006. Recipient Boyd Harshbarger award, Va. Poly. Inst., 1974. Fellow: AAAS, Am. Statis. Assn.; mem.: Internat. Statis. Inst. (elected mem.), Phi Kappa Phi. Greek Orthodox. Avocations: fishing, reading. Home: 5827 NW 54th Way Gainesville FL 32653 Business E-Mail: ufakhuri@stat.ufl.edu.

KIAR, MARTIN DAVID (MARTY KIAR), state legislator; b. Pembroke Pines, Fla., June 19, 1977; s. Monroe Kiar; m. Kelly Kiar. BA, Palm Beach Atlantic U., 1999; JD magna cum laude, Nova Southeastern U., Ft. Lauderdale, Fla., 2002. Atty.; mem. Dist. 97 Fla. House of Reps., Tallahassee, 2006—, ranking mem. preK-12 appropriations com., mem. edn. policy coun., govt. accountability act coun., preK-12 policy com. Mem.: Weston Area C. of C., Parkland C. of C., Davie/Cooper City C. of C., Coral Springs C. of C., Weston Dem. Club, Parkland/Coral Springs Dem. Club, Davie/Cooper City Dem. Club. Democrat. Roman Catholic. Office: 6600 University Dr Parkland FL 33067-2500 also: 1003 The Capitol 402 S Monroe St Tallahassee FL 32399-1300 Office Phone: 954-346-2813, 850-487-1588.

KIBLER, JAMES EVERETT, JR., naturalist, writer, preservationist; b. Prosperity, SC, June 24, 1944; s. James Everett Kibler, Sr. and Juanita Connelly. BA cum laude in English (hon.), U. S.C., Columbia, 1966, PhD, 1970. Prof. English U. Ga., Athens, 1970—2009. Author: (social history) A Carolina Dutch Fork Calendar (Confederation of Local S.C. Hist. Socs. award, 1988), (poetry) Poems From Scorched Earth (So. Heritage Soc.'s Lit. Achievement award, 2000), (short story cycle) Child to the Waters, (novel) Walking Toward Home, Our Fathers' Fields (Fellowship of So. Writers award, 1999), Memory's Keep, The Education of Chauncey Doolittle, Tiller; editor: (poetry collection) Selected Poems of William Gilmore Simms, New edit., expanded & rev., (biographical dictionary) American Novelists Since World War II, (short story collection) Fireside Tales, The Poetry of William Gilmore Simms: An Introduction and Bibliography; founding editor The Simms Review, 1993—, John Punterick Poetry and the Practical Literature and Civilization; author: William Gilmore Simms: A Reference Guide, William Gilmore Simms's Selected Reviews on Literature & Civilisation. Mem.: Pres. Soc. U. SC, Thomas Cooper Soc., Ballylee Nature Conservancy (bd. chmn. 2012—), Palmetto Trust Hist. Preservation (adv. bd. mem. 2012—), SC Hist. Soc., Abbevil Inst. (faculty), League of South (founding mem.), Hist. Columbia Found., William Gilmore Simms Soc. (life; sec. 1993—2008, mem. exec. com. 2009—), Tyger River Alliance, South Caroliniana Soc. (life), Southern Garden History Soc., Delta Phi Alpha (life), Sigma Pi Kappa (life), Phi Beta Kappa (life). Independent. Lutheran. Avocations: farming, gardening. Home: Ballylee Plantation Ballylee Heritage Preserve 211 Peters Creek Rd Whitmire SC 29178 Home Phone: 803-276-4337.

KIBLER, WILLIAM BENJAMIN, orthopedist, surgeon; b. Kingsport, Tenn., Sept. 29, 1946; s. Jacob B. and Della M. Kibler; m. Elizabeth Fay Mugler, June 20, 1970; children: B. Chase, David. BA, Vanderbilt U., 1968, MD, 1972. Cert. Am. Bd. Orthopedic Surgery, 1978. Intern, surgery Parkland Hosp., Dallas, 1972—73; resident, orthop. surgery Vanderbilt U., Nashville, 1973—77; staff physician Lexington Clinic, Ky., 1977—, head sect. orthop surgery, 1998—2007, med. dir. Sports Medicine Ctr., 1984—; med. dir. Shoulder Ctr. Ky., 2006—; bd. dirs. Vanderdict Med. Alumni Assn., 2010—. Bd. dirs. Am. Coll. of Sports medicine, Indpls., 1990—96; pres. Soc. Tennis Medicine and Sci., NYC, 1990—99; lectr. various national and internat. orthop. soc. Author: The Athletic Preparticipation Exam, 1990, Functional Rehabilitation of Sports Injuries, 1998;

contbr. articles various profl. jours. Recipient Citation award, Am. Coll. of Sports Medicine, 1998, Plagenhof Sci. award, Profl. Tennis Registry, 1998, Hughston award, Am. Physical Therapy Assn., 2008, Edn. Merit award, Internat. Tennis Hall of Fame, 2010; named Best Dr. America Inc., 2004—. Fellow: Am. Acad. Orthop. Surgeons; mem.: Womens Tennis Assn. (cons.), US Tennis Assn. Sports Sci. Com., Arthoscopy Assn. America, Internat. Soc. Arthroscopy, Knee Surgery and Orthopedic Sports Medicine, Am. Orthopedic Assn., Am. Coll. Sports Medicine, Am. Shoulder and Elbow Surgeons, Am. Orthop. Soc. for Sports Medicine. Methodist. Avocations: sports, travel, hiking, bible study. Home: 240 Mkt St Lexington KY 40507 Office: Lexington Clinic 1221 S Broadway Lexington KY 40504 Office Phone: 859-258-8575. Office Fax: 859-258-8562. Personal E-mail: wkibler@aol.com. Business E-Mail: bkibl@lexclin.com.

KIBSGAARD, PAAL, oil industry executive; M in Petroleum Engring., Norwegian Inst. Tech., Trondheim. petroleum engr. With ExxonMobil Corp., 1992—97; reservoir engr. through mgr., GeoMarket, Caspian region Schlumberger Ltd., Saudi Arabia, 1997—2003, pres., drilling and measurements, Oilfield Svcs. divsn., 2003—06, v.p., pers., 2006—07, v.p., engring., mfg. and sustaining, 2007—09, pres., Reservoir Characterization Group, 2009—10, COO, 2010—11, CEO, 2011—. Office: Schlumberger Ltd 17th Fl 5599 San Felipe Houston TX 77056 Office Phone: 713-513-2000. Business E-Mail: pkibsgaard@slb.com.

KIDD, JANE V., former political organization administrator, state legislator; b. Atlanta, Ga., Feb. 12, 1953; d. Ernest Vandiver; m. David Kidd; children: Elizabeth, Alex. Grad., U. Ga. Grady Coll. Journalism & Mass Comm. Former mem. Lavonia City Coun.; campaign mgr., then dist. dir. to Ga. state senator Don Johnson; mem. Clarke County Dem. Com., 1998—; mem. from 115th Dist. Ga. State House of Reps., Athens, 2005—06; chairwomen Dem. Party of Ga., 2007—11. Alumni dir. Grady Coll. Journalism and Mass Comm., 1999; v.p. univ. rels. Clemson U., SC. Mem.: Clarke County Dem. Women. Democrat. Office: Dem Party of Ga Ste 408 1100 Spring St NW Atlanta GA 30309 E-mail: janekidd@georgiademocrat.org.

KIDD, RUSTY (E. CULVER KIDD), state legislator; b. May 10, 1946; Rep. Dist. 141 Ga. House of Reps., Atlanta, 2009—. Office: 102 S Wayne St Milledgeville GA 31061 also: Ga Gen Assembly 612 Coverdell Legis Office Bldg Atlanta GA 30334 Office Phone: 478-452-1354, 404-656-0325. Office Fax: 478-452-3493. Business E-Mail: rusty.kidd@house.ga.gov.

KIEFABER, CLAY H., pump and motor manufacturing company executive; BA in Polit. Sci., Miami U., 1978; MBA in Fin. & Info. Sys., U. Colo., Boulder, 1981. Sr. mgr., Advanced Mfg. Group Price Waterhouse LLP; sales rep. Digital Equipment Corp., 1981—83; mfg. sales rep. Hewlett-Packard Co., 1983—85; materials mgr., corp. mgr., mfg. planning Harris Corp., 1985—87; dir., JIT Planning Merillat Industries LLC (subs. Masco Corp.), 1989—94, bd. dirs. Adrian, 1990—92, dir., assembly mfg., 1992—94, v.p., mfg., 1994—96, v.p., ops., 1996—97, exec. v.p., 1997—98, pres., 1998—2003; various sr. exec. positions Masco Corp., group v.p., Builder Cabinet Group, 2004—05, group pres., 2006—07; bd. dirs. Colfax Corp., 2008—, pres., CEO, 2010—. Mem. Jr. Achievement; pres. Boys & Girls Club of Lenawee County. Office: Colfax Corp 8730 Stony Point Pky Ste 150 Richmond VA 23235 Office Phone: 804-560-4070. Office Fax: 804-560-4076. Business E-Mail: clay.kiefaber@colfaxcorp.com.

KIEFFER, JAROLD ALAN, publishing executive, writer; b. Mpls., May 5, 1923; s. Charles O. and Edith Ida (Feinberg) K.; m. Frances Clarfield, Aug. 13, 1949; children: Edith Charlotte, Charles Edward, Philip William. BA, U. Minn., 1947, PhD, 1950. Tchg. asst. polit. sci. dept. U. Minn., 1949, tchg. asst. social sci. program, 1950-51; rsch. asst., world affairs program Mpls. Star, 1949-50; exec. sec. def. moblzn. manpower coms. Office of Def. Moblzn., Exec. Office of Pres., 1951-52, staff asst. to exec. sec., 1951—52, staff sec., 1952, asst. to exec. officer, 1953, exec. sec., Borrowing Authority Rev. Bd., 1953, spl. asst. to dir., 1955-56, acting dep. asst. dir. nat. security affairs, 1956-57; cons., exec. asst. to dir. orgn. and pers. US Atomic Energy Commn.; exec. sec. AEC Pers. Adv. Com., 1952—53; mem. Commn. Orgn. Exec. Br. Fed. Govt. (Hoover Commn.), 1953—55; asst. to Arthur Flemming, mem. Nat. Security Coun., 1953—56; mem., pres. adv. com. Govt. Orgn. PACGO, 1953—61; cons., US overseas broadcasting reports Nat Security Coun., 1958; Herbert Hoover's laison to Hoover Commn. Task Force Pers. & Civil Svc., 1953—55; adviser to Meyer Kestnbaum Hoover Commn. & Intergovtl. Rels. Commn. Matters, White House, 1957—58; asst. to Nelson Rockefeller for policy and issues devel., NY gubernatorial campaign, 1957—58; asst. Arthur Flemming US Nat. Security Coun., 1953—56; mem. Commn. Orgn. Exec. Br. Fed. Govt., 1953—55, Pres. Adv. Com. Govt. Orgn., 1953—61; cons. US Nat. Security Coun. US Overseas Broadcasting Requirements, 1958; white house staff asst. meyer Kestnbaum; spl. asst. to pres. Eisenhower Hoover Commn. & Intergovernmental Rels. Matters, 1956—57. Cons. to sec. HEW, Washington, 1958, asst. to sec., 1958-59, asst. to sec. for program analysis, 1959-61; sec. bd. trustees Nat. Cultural Ctr., 1959-63, exec. dir., 1961-63; renamed John F. Kennedy Ctr. for Performing Arts; assoc. prof. polit. sci. U. Oreg., 1963-67, acting chmn. polit. sci. dept., 1964, asst. to pres., 1963-67; chmn. pub. affairs and adminstrn. programs, prof. pub. policy and adminstrn. Lila Acheson Wallace Sch. Cmty. Svc. and Pub. Affairs, 1967-69; U. Oreg. chmn. Interdisciplinary Masters Program on Pub. Affairs, 1965-69; dir. Macalester Found. for Higher Edn., 1969-70; exec. officer bd. trustees Macalester Coll., 1970-71, also adj. prof. polit. sci., 1969-71; dir. Office Internat. Tng., AID, US State Dept., 1971-72, asst. adminstr. for population and humanitarian assistance, 1972-75; adj. prof. internat. rels. Am. U., Washington, 1975, staff dir. pres.' panel on biomed. rsch., 1975-76. Dep. commr. social security U.S. Dept. HHS, 1976-77; staff dir. Task Force on House Adminstrv. Sys., Commn. on Adminstrv. Rev., U.S. Ho. Reps., 1977; dir. Nat. Com. on Careers for Older Ams., Acad. Edn1. Devel., Inc., 1978-80, staff dir., 1981 White Ho. Conf. on Aging, 1980-82; vice chmn. Gov. Planning Coun. Arts and Humanities, State of Oreg., 1965-67; chmn. Project 70's Task Force on State Govt. Reorgn., Oreg. Gov.'s Office, 1968-69; chmn. task force on Strategic Perspectives on Aging, Fairfax, Va., 1986; cons. Office High Speed Ground Transp., U.S. Dept. Transp., 1971; cons. U.S. Office Edn., 1971; officer, mem. exec. com. Lane County Auditorium Assn., Oreg., 1963-69; exec. com. United Way, Fairfax, 1985-88; bd. dirs. World Population Soc., 1983-2002 pres., 1990-92; bd. dirs. Fairfax Vol. Action Ctr., 1967-91, hon. bd. mem., 1991-93; mem. Gov.'s Job Tng. Coordination Coun., Commonwealth Va., 1987-94, chmn. older worker and youth com., 1989-94, mem. exec. com., 1990-94; mem., chmn. transp. com. Fairfax Area Commn. on Aging, 1991-95, exec. com., 1993-95; bd. dirs., sec. No. Va. Coalition of Vol. Interfaith Caregivers, Inc., 1991-94; mem. Fairfax Alliance for Human Svcs., 1996—2011, chmn., 2001-04; bd. dirs.,2005-09, officer, mem. exec. com., 2007-08, Fairfax Symphony Orch., mem. exec. com. 2007-08, With AUS, 1942-46. Mem. ASPA (life), Am. Polit. Sci. Assn., Advanced Transit Assn. (dir. 1976—2009, chmn. 1983-84, sec.-treas. 1985-95, chmn. 1995-2000), Sr. Employment Resources Inc. (chmn. 1985-2008,chmn. emeritus, 2008, bd. dirs., 1984-, editor SER Publs., 1989-97), Kieffer Publs. (pres., editor 1998-2008). Home: 7414 Spring Village Dr Apt 106 Springfield VA 22150-4498

KIEHART, DANIEL P., biophysicist, educator; PhD, U. Pa., Phila., 1979. Postdoctoral fellow Johns Hopkins U. Med. Sch., Balt., 1982—84; asst. prof. dept. cellular and devel. biology Harvard U., Cambridge, Mass., 1984—88, assoc. prof. dept. cellular and devel. biology, 1988—92; assoc. prof. dept. cell biology Duke U. Med. Ctr., 1992—2000, prof. dept. cell biology, 2000—; prof. dept. biology Duke U., 2000—, chair dept. biology, 2007—. Invited spkr. in field. Mem. editl. bd.: Human Frontiers in Sci. Jour., 2006—; contbr. articles to sci. jours. Mem.: Marine Biol. Lab. Corp. (life). Office: Duke University Dept Biology Rm 4330 French Family Sci Ctr Box 90338 Durham NC 27708 Office Phone: 919-613-8157. Business E-Mail: dkiehart@duke.edu.

KIEL, JEFF E., former publishing executive; b. 1959; m. Gayle Kiel; children: Ryan, Alexa. BS, U. Fla., 1981. CPA. Acct. Ernst & Young, 1981—87, Kauffman, Rossin & Co., 1987; with Miami Herald, 1988—2002, v.p. fin., CFO, 1999—2002; v.p. advt. San Jose Mercury News, Calif., 2002—07, pub. Calif., 2007—08. E-mail: jkiel@mercurynews.com.

KIELTY, THOMAS J., manufacturing executive; V.p., traffic and distbn. Massey Energy Co., 2006—. Office: Massey Energy Co PO Box 16429 Bristol VA 24209-6429 Office Phone: 804-788-1864. Office Fax: 804-788-1870. Business E-Mail: tom.kielty@masseyenergyco.com.

KIELY, DAN RAY, fund manager, real estate company executive, consultant; b. Ft. Sill, Okla., Jan. 2, 1944; s. William Robert and Leona Maxine (Ross) K. BA in Psychology, U. Colo., 1966; JD, Stanford U., 1969. Cert. property mgr. Assoc. Holme, Roberts and Owen, Denver, 1969—70; pres. DeRand Equity Group, Arlington, Va., 1973-89; pres., chmn. bd. Bankwest Corp and related banks, Denver; ptnr. Starlin & Kiely, P.C., 1989-94; trustee DeRand Real Estate Investment Trust, 1974—; pres. Strategy Corp. Internat., 2005—. Chmn. Pace Holdings, Inc., Washington, 1988—93, Washington Capital Corp., 1989—; pres. Catelyst Comm. Inc., Palm Beach, Fla., 2001—10, Strategy Corp. Internat., 2005—; spkr., lectr. in field. Deacon, McLean Bapt. Ch., Va., 1977-80. Officer USAR, 1969-73. Decorated Legion of Merit. Mem. ABA, Nat. Bd. Realtors, Inst. Real Estate Mgmt., Nat. Assn. Rev. Appraisers, Internat. Coun. Shopping Ctrs., Nat. Assn. Real Estate Investment Trusts, Internat. Inst. (cert. valuer), Colo. Indsl. Bankers Assn. (bd. dirs. 1985-87). Home: 301 Clematis St Ste 3000 West Palm Beach FL 33401 Business E-Mail: dkiely@scifunds.com.

KIER, ANN B., pathology educator; b. Littlefield, Tex., June 26, 1949; d. Robert Merlin and Martha (Bond) Yarbrough; m. Friedhelm Schroeder, Dec. 9, 1978; 1 child, Hilary. BA, U. Tex., 1971; BS, Tex. A&M U., 1973, DVM, 1974; PhD, U. Mo., 1979. Diplomate, Am. Coll. Lab. Animal Medicine. NIH fellow U. Mo., Columbia, 1976-79, asst. prof., 1979-84, assoc. prof., 1984-87; assoc. prof. dept. pathology U. Cin. Med. Sch., 1987-91, prof., dir. divsn. comparative pathology, dept. pathology, 1991-93; prof., head dept. pathobiology Tex. A&M U., College Station, 1994—2005. Cons. NIH, Washington, 1983—, Comparative Pathology, Frann Sci., Cin., 1987—. Contbr. articles to profl. jours. NIH grantee, 1980—. Mem. AAAS, Am. Assn. Pathologists. Avocations: scuba diving, reading. Home: Tex A & M University PO Box 500 Wellborn TX 77881-0500 Office: Tex A&M Univ Dept Pathobiology College Station TX 77843-0001 Office Phone: 979-862-1509. Business E-Mail: akier@cvm.tamu.edu.

KIESLING, ERNST WILLIE, civil engineering educator; b. Eola, Tex., Apr. 8, 1934; s. Alfred William and Louise (Kern) K.; m. Juanita Haseloff, Aug. 25, 1956; children: Carol, Chris, Max BSME, Tex. Tech. Coll., 1955; MS in Applied Mechanics, Mich. State U., 1959, PhD, 1966. Registered profl. engr. Asst. prof. Tex. Tech. Coll., 1959—63; sr. rsch. engr. S.W. Rsch. Inst., San Antonio, 1966—69; prof. civil engring. Tex. Tech U., Lubbock, 1969—, chmn. dept. civil engring., 1969—88, assoc. dean engring., 1988—93; prof. civil engring. Tex. Tech. U., Lubbock, 1993—2004, sr. assoc. dean, 2004—06. NSF faculty fellow, 1963-64 Fellow ASCE; mem. NSPE (life), Am. Soc. Engring. Edn., Nat. Storm Shelter Assn. (exec. dir. 2001—), Sigma Xi, Chi Epsilon, Tau Beta Pi Achievements include pioneering work in storm shelter research and utilization. Home: 5111 97th St Lubbock TX 79424-4867 Office: Tex Tech U Dept Civil Engring Lubbock TX 79409

KIFFIN, LANE, college football coach; b. Bloomington, Minn., May 9, 1975; s. Monte and Robin Kiffin; m. Layla Kiffin; children: Landry, Pressley. BA in Leisure Svc. Mgmt., Fresno State U., 1998. Grad. asst. Fresno State U. Bulldogs, 1997—98; offensive line asst. Colo. State U. Rams, 1999—2000; def. quality control coach Jacksonville Jaguars, 2000; tight ends coach U. Southern Calif. Trojans, 2001, wide receivers coach, 2002—05, passing game coord., 2004, offensive coord., 2005—06, recruiting coord., 2005—06, head football coach, 2010—13, Oakland Raiders, 2007—08, U. Tenn. Volunteers, 2008—10; offensive coord. U. Ala. Crimson Tide, Tuscaloosa, 2014—. Office: University Alabama Crimson Tide Box 870393 Tuscaloosa AL 35487*

KIKER, BILLY FRAZIER, economics professor; b. Elkin, NC, 1936; s. William James and Ruby Lucille K.; m. Martha Jane Parker, Aug. 4, 1962; children: Todd, Jonathan, David. AB, Lenoir-Rhyne U., 1961; PhD, Tulane U., 1965. From asst. prof. to prof. dept. econs. U. S.C., Columbia, 1965—2006, disting. prof. emeritus, 2006—, chmn. dept., 1973-87, dir. Ctr. Studies in Human Capital, 1972-75. Vis. prof. U. Edinburgh, Scotland, 1973, U. Minho, Portugal, 1995-96, Wirtschafts U., Vienna, Austria, 1997; cons. in field. Author: Human Capital in Retrospect, 1968, Macroeconomic Analysis, 1974; editor: Investment in Human Capital, 1971; contbr. articles to profl. jours. Fulbright scholar U. Porto, Portugal, 1988. Methodist. Avocations: boating, fishing. Office: Univ SC Moore Sch Bus Columbia SC 29208

KILBERG, BOBBIE GREENE, trade association administrator; b. NYC, Nov. 25, 1944; m. Bill Kilberg; 5 children. BA, Vassar Coll., 1965; MA, Columbia U., 1966; LLB, Yale U., 1969. Atty. Arnold & Porter, Washington, 1971—73; v.p. academic affairs Mount Vernon Coll., 1973; assoc. counsel to Pres. Gerald Ford The White House, 1975—76, dep. asst. to Pres. US., dir. pub. liaison, 1989—92, dir. office intergovernmental affairs, 1992, mem. Pres.'s Coun. Advisors on Sci. and Tech., 2001; with Aspen Inst., 1978; v.p., gen. counsel Roosevelt Ctr. for American Policy Studies, 1982; pres., CEO Northern Va. Tech. Coun., 1998—. Bd. dirs. Luna Innovations Inc., 2006—09. Recipient Women of Achievement award, Anti-Defamation League, 2001, Cmty. Champion award, Vol. Fairfax, 2003, DC Celebration Honoree award, Girls Inc., 2003, Lifetime Achievement award, Women in Tech., 2004, Women Who Mean Bus. award, Washington Bus. Jour., 2005; named one of The 100 Most Powerful Women in DC, Washingtonian mag., 2009. Office: Northern Va Tech Coun 2214 Rock Hill Rd Ste 300 Herndon VA 20170 Office Phone: 703-904-7878 ext. 204. Business E-Mail: bkilberg@nvtc.org.

KILBERG, JAMES ANTHONY, real estate company executive; b. Balt., Feb. 26, 1956; s. Albert and Hilary (Zieve) K.; m. Lori Jill Eisenberg, Jan. 7, 1979; children: Jonathan Ross, Thomas Mathew, Kathryn Maura. BS in Bus., Washington U., St. Louis, Mo., 1978; M in Bus. Mgmt., Ga. State U., 1983; M in Corp. Real Estate, Nat. Assn. Corp. Real Estate. Various mktg. positions IBM Corp., mktg. rep. St. Louis, 1977-78; various mktg. positions AT&T Inc. (merger of SBC Communications & AT&T Corp.), indsl. cons., 1978-83; officer, v.p., Pizza Hut Divsn. PepsiCo, Inc., sr. dir., Pizza Hut Divsn., 1992; pres. Ga. Ventures, 1992; v.p., real estate Pep Boys - Manny, Moe & Jack, 1995—98; exec. v.p., asset mgmt., SouthEastern US Trammell Crow Co. (subs. CB Richard Ellis Group, Inc.), various positions, devel. bus., 1983—87, divisional ptnr., 1987, prin., 1998—2001, mng. dir., global svcs. bus., 2001—03; v.p., land mgmt. Plum Creek Timber Co., Inc., 2003—06, sr., v.p., real estate, 2006—. Bd. dirs. Fulton County Developers Assn., Atlanta, 1987—, Ga. ICSC Govt. Affairs, Atlanta, 1990—. Bd. govs. Washington U., St. Louis, 1978-85; chmn. Washington U. Alumni, Atlanta, 1978-85; bd. dirs. Ga. C. of C., Alliance Theater, Atlanta Chamber Players, Atlanta, 1989-91; exec. com. Bus. vols. for the Arts, Atlanta, 1990—; mem. cultural affairs bd. City of Atlanta. Mem. Internat. coun. Shopping Ctrs. (panelist 1983—), Urban Land Inst., Nat. Assn. Indsl. Office Parks, Building Owners, Leadership Bucklead, Ga. Hospitality and Trade (panelist 1980-83). Avocations: tennis, theater, baseball coach. Office: Plum Creek Timber Co Inc 601 Union St Ste 3100 Seattle WA 98101-1374 Office Phone: 206-467-3600. Business E-Mail: jim.kilberg@plumcreek.com.

KILBY, TOMMY, state legislator; b. Jan. 27, 1964; m. Rachel Kilby; children: Latisha, stepchildren Tyler; 1 child, Noah. Former vice chmn. East Human Resource Agency, Tenn.; former dir. Morgan County Medical Ctr.; vice chmn. East Devel. Dist., Tenn.; co. commr. Morgan Co., 1982—90; sec. treas. Dem. Caucus; state senator Dist 12 Tenn., 2004—; currentlymem Judiciary Com., 2004—; mem. transp. com., 2004—, Dem. Caucus Sec.,Treas., Govt. Op's Com., 2004—; state senate Tenn.; appraiser Real Estate. Recipient Morgan Co. News "Best Elected Off". Mem.: Nat. Rifle AssN., Morgan Co. C. of C. (former bd. dir.). Democrat. Baptist. Office: 11A Legislative Plaza Nashville TN 37243-0212 Office Phone: 615-741-1449. Fax: 615-253-0237. E-mail: sen.tommy.kilby@legislature.state.tn.us.

KILGORE, TERRY GENE, state legislator; b. Kingsport, Tenn., Aug. 23, 1961; m. Debbie Sue Wright; children: Kayla Wright, Kyle Bellamy. Mem. Dist. 1 Va. House of Dels., 1994—; mem. Militia & Police, Sci. & Tech., Corp. & Ins. & Banking, Cts. Justice & Mining & Mineral Resource, Commerce & Labor. Republican. Methodist. Office: PO Box 669 Gate City VA 24251 Office Phone: 276-386-7011. Office Fax: 276-386-2377. Business E-Mail: DelTKilgore@house.virginia.gov.

KILLIAN, JAMES M., medical educator; b. Evanston, Ill., Jan. 1934; s. James E. and Florence M. Killian; m. Marjorie V. Voskuil, Sept. 8, 1958; children: James P., Michael E., John S., Moira A., Sheila M. MD, Wis. U., Milw., 1958. Lic. Am. Bd. Neurology and Psychiatry, 1969. Prof. neurology Baylor Coll. Medicine, Houston, 1979—. Interim chair, dept. neurology Baylor Coll. Medicine, 2005—06. Contbr. articles to profl. jours. Lt. USNR, 1961—63, Pensacola, Fla. Fellow: Am. Acad. Neurology. Home: 10215 Sugar Hill Houston TX 77042 Office: Baylor Coll Medicine 6501 Fannin St Houston TX 77030 Personal E-mail: jmkmvk@aol.com.

KILLIAN, RIC, state legislator; State rep. Dist. 105, NC, 2007—. Mem. Appropriations com., Appropriations Subcom. on Capital, Environ. and Natural Resources com., State Govt./State Personnel com., Transp. com.; vice chmn. Homeland Security, Military and Veterans Affairs com. With US Army, with USAR, 1991—. Republican. Office: North Carolina House of Representatives 16 W Jones St Room 2219 Raleigh NC 27601-1096 Office Phone: 919-733-5886. Business E-Mail: Ric.Killian@ncleg.net.

KILLIAN, WILLIAM CHARLES (BILL KILLIAN), federal prosecutor; b. Jasper, Tenn., 1949; BS, U. Tenn., Knoxville, 1971, JD, 1974. Bar: Tenn. 1975, Tenn. Supreme Ct. 1975, US Ct. Appeals (6th cir.) 1987, US Supreme Ct. 1988, US Dist. Ct. (northern dist.) Ala. 1993, US Ct. Appeals (11th cir.) 1996, US Dist. Ct. (middle dist.) Tenn., US Dist. Ct. (northern dist.) Fla. 2008, US Dist. Ct. (northern dist.) Ga. 2008. Asst. dist. atty. Twelfth Judicial Dist. Tenn., Dayton, 1976—79, 1988—90; pvt. practice Jasper, Tenn., 1979—2010; city atty. Town of Monteagle, Tenn., 1981—88, Tenn., 1996—2010; US atty. (eastern dist.) Tenn. US Dept. Justice, Knoxville, 2010—. Prof. civil & criminal justice NE State Jr. Coll., Rainsville, Ala., 1979—80, Edmondson Jr. Coll., Chattanooga, 1979—80; adj. prof. trial advocacy U. Tenn. Sch. Law, 2003. Contbr. articles to law jours. Mem. City of South Pittsburg, Tenn. Water Bd. and Marion Nat. Gas Bd., 1979—83; bd. mem. Am. Red Cross, Chattanooga Chap., 2009; mem. Bd. SE Tenn. Legal Svcs., 1986—91, Tenn. Ct. Reporting Bd., 2009—10. Served in US Army, 1970—73. Master: American Inns of Ct. (Ray L. Brock and Robert E. Cooper Chap.); fellow: Tenn. Bar Found. (Mem. House of Del.); mem.: Tenn. Trial Lawyers Assn. (membership chmn. 1984—86), Tenn. Bar Assn. (chmn. Solo & Small Practice 1995—96), Nat. Assn. Criminal Def. Lawyers, Tenn. Criminal Def. Lawyers Assn., American Trial Lawyers Assn., Fed. Ct., Eastern. Dist. Hist. Soc., Fed. Bar Assn., Sierra Club. Office: Office of US Attorney Suite 301 1110 Market St Chattanooga TN 37402 Office Phone: 423-752-5140. Office Fax: 423-752-5150.*

KILLIAN, WILLIAM PAUL, manufacturing executive; b. Sidney, Ohio, Apr. 26, 1935; s. Ray and Erie K.; m. Beverly Ann Buchanan, Sept.7, 1957; children: William, Katherine, Michael B in Chem. Engring. with honors, Ga. Inst. Tech., 1957; M in Engring. Adminstrn. with honors, U. Utah, 1968. Chem. engr. Esso, Baton Rouge, 1957—58; mgr. research and devel. mfg. engring., then plant mgr. Thiokol Corp., Brigham City, Utah, 1958—68; mgr. corp. project mgmt. Masonite Corp., Chgo., 1968—70, mgr. new bus. ventures, 1970—73; mgr. strategic planning, chem. and metall. group Gen. Electric Co., Pittsfield, Mass. and Columbus, Ohio, 1973—77; v.p. corp. planning and devel. Hoover Universal Inc., Ann Arbor, Mich., 1977—85; v.p. corp. devel. Johnson Controls Inc., Milw., 1985—87, v.p. corp. devel. and strategy, 1987—2000. Bd. dirs. Cleaver-Brooks, Inc., Milw., RBC Bearing Corp. (NASDQ Roll), Oxford, Conn., Premix Inc., North Kingsville, Ohio; chmn., bd. advisors iNUX, Inc., Tampa. Bd. advisors Salvation Army, Sarasota; bd. dirs. All Faiths Food Bank, Sarasota, Fla. Mem.: Coun. Strategy Planning & Devel., Strategic Leadership Forum, Mfrs. Alliance (past chmn.), Coun. Strategic Planning Execs. of Conf. Bd. (past chmn.), Assn. for Corp. Growth Internat. (past nat. pres., past pres. Wis. chpt.), Mensa Soc, Koseme Soc., Tau Beta Pi, Phi Eta Sigma, Pi Delta Epsilon, Phi Kappa Phi, Omicron Delta Kappa. Personal E-mail: wkillian@comcast.net.

KILLINGER, CLAYTON, energy executive; B in Acctg., U. Tex., San Antonio. CPA. Ptnr. Arthur Andersen LLP, San Antonio; asst. contr. Valero Energy Corp., San Antonio, 2001—03, v.p. to sr. v.p., contr., 2003—. Office: Valero Energy Corpn PO Box 696000 San Antonio TX 78269-6000

KILLION, THEO, retail executive; b. 1957; m. Dana Killion; 4 children. BA, MEd, Tufts U. Sportswear buyer, exec. trainee, labor rels. mgr. R.H. Macy & Co., 1974—83, dir. human resources, 1984—94; sr. v.p. human resources divsn. Home Shopping Network, Inc., 1995—96; v.p. human resources Lane Bryant, 1997—99; v.p.

human resources, store ops. Ltd. Brands, Inc., Columbus, Ohio, 1999—2004; exec. v.p. human resources Tommy Hilfiger U.S.A., Inc., 2004—05, Tommy Hilfiger Corp.; with Berglass + Associates; exec. v.p. human resources, legal & corp. strategy Zale Corp., Irving, Tex., 2008, pres., 2008—10, CEO, 2010—. Recipient Benjamin E. Mays award, A Better Chance, Inc., 2000. Office: Zale Corp 901 W Walnut Hill Ln Irving TX 75038

KILLORIN, ROBERT WARE, lawyer; b. Atlanta, Nov. 12, 1959; s. Edward W. and Virgina (Ware) K. AB cum laude, Duke U., 1980; JD, U. Ga., 1983. Bar: Ga. 1984, US Dist. Ct. (no. dist.) Ga. 1984, US Ct. Appeals (11th cir.) 1984. Ptnr. Killorin & Killorin, Atlanta, 1984—2006, Chitwood, Harley & Harnes, LLP, Atlanta, 2006—. Mem.: ATLA, State Bar Ga. (chair SCOPE com. 1986, young lawyers sect. legis. affairs com. 1989—91, instr. mock trial program 1989—), Atlanta Bar Assn., Ga. Trial Lawyers Assn., Fed. Bar Assn., 11th Cir. Hist. Soc., Mil. Order of Carabao, Nat. Speliological Soc., Nat. Assn. Underwater Instrs., Explorers Club, U. Ga. Pres.'s Club, Ga. C. of C. (govtl. affairs com.). Avocations: forestry, scuba diving. Personal E-mail: rwk@bellsouth.net.

KIM, ANTHONY, professional golfer; b. LA, June 19, 1985; s. Paul Kim. Attended, U. Okla., Norman. Profl. golfer, 2006—. Mem. US team Ryder Cup, 2008, Presidents Cup, 2009. Recipient Charlie Coe award, Univ. Okla., 2004, 2005; named All-Am., NCAA, 2004—06, Player of Yr., Big 12 Conf., 2005. Achievements include winning PGA Tour events: Wachovia Championship, AT&T National, 2008, Shell Houston Open, 2010; being a member of the Ryder Cup winning US team, 2008. Office: PGA Tour 100 PGA TOUR Blvd Ponte Vedra Beach FL 32082

KIM, HONG NACK, political science professor; b. Youngchun, Korea, Aug. 20, 1933; came to U.S., 1956, naturalized, 1973; s. Sang Do and Nam Jo (Sung) K.; m. Boohi Suh, Mar. 26, 1967; children: Michael, Jeffrey, Brian Kim. BA, Seoul Nat. U., Korea, 1956; MA, Georgetown U., 1960, PhD, 1965. Lectr. Georgetown U., Washington, 1965-66; asst. prof. North Tex. State U., Denton, 1966-67, 1967-72, assoc. prof., 1972-77; prof. polit. sci. W.Va. U., Morgantown, 1977—. Author: Scholars Guide to Washington, D.C. for East Asian Studies, 1979; editor-in-chief: Internat. Jour. of Korean Studies, 2000—2005; editor: Asian Forum, 1972-74, Polit. Studies Rev., 1984-87; co-editor: Essays in Political Science, 1972, Korean Reunification: New Perspectives and Approaches, 1984, North Korea: The Politics of Regime Survival, 2006; contbr. articles to various publs. Pres. Korean Assn. W.V., 1981-82, Assn. Korean Polit. Scientists N.Am.83-85, Internat. Coun. on Korean Studies, Washington. Fulbright-Hays Faculty Rsch. Abroad grantee U.S. Dept. Edn., 1979, 82; Fulbright Lecturing/Rsch. grantee U.S. Info. Agy., 1990; recipient Outstanding Rsch. award W.Va. U., 1985. Mem. Am. Polit. Sci. Assn., Assn. Asian Studies. Democrat. Presbyterian. Home: 1270 Braewick Dr Morgantown WV 26505-3339 Office: W Va U Dept Polit Sci Morgantown WV 26505 Business E-Mail: Hongkim@wvu.edu.

KIM, HYUNGGUN, biomedical engineer, educator; b. Jeju, Republic of Korea, Mar. 26, 1975; PhD, U. Iowa, 2005. Rsch. asst. U. Iowa, 2000—05, adj. asst. prof., 2007—11; rsch. engr. Northwestern U., 2005—06; asst. prof. U. Tex. Health Sci. Ctr., Houston, 2006—. Adj. asst. prof. U. Tex., Austin, 2007—11, U. Tex. Grad. Sch. Biomed. Scis., Houston, 2008—, Sungkyunkwan U., Republic of Korea, 2010—; chair Korea-Am. Biomed. Scientists Symposium, 2011. Contbr. numerous articles to profl. publs., chapters to books. Recipient Pilot Project award, U. Tex. Ctr. Clin. and Translational Scis., 2010; Govtl. scholarship, Korea Advanced Inst. Sci. and Tech., 1993—97, R01 Rsch. Project grant, NIH, 2011—, Internat. Collaboration Rsch. Project grant, Ministry Knowledge Economy Republic of Korea, 2012—. Mem.: Biomed. Engr. Soc., Am. Soc. Mech. Engr., Korean-Am. Scientists and Engrs. Assn. (pub. dir. 2011—12), Am. Heart Assn. Achievements include development of novel diagnostic and treament strategies in cardiovascular disease research. Avocations: skiing, golf, racquetball, tennis, basketball. Office: 6431 Fannin St MSB 1246 Houston TX 77030 Business E-Mail: hyunggun.kim@uth.tmc.edu.*

KIM, IN-KYUNG, professional golfer; b. Republic of Korea, June 13, 1988; Profl. golfer LPGA Tour, 2007—, Ladies European Tour, 2010—. Mem. Team Asia Lexus Cup, 2007. Named Rookie of Yr., Ladies European Tour, 2010. Achievements include winning LPGA Tour events: Longs Drug Challenge, 2008; LPGA State Farm Classic, 2009; Lorena Ochoa Invitational, 2010; winning Ladies European Tour event: Dubai Ladies Masters, 2009. Office: LPGA 100 International Blvd Daytona Beach FL 32124-1092

KIM, MI HYUN, professional golfer; b. Inch'on, South Korea, Jan. 13, 1977; m. Won Hee Lee. Student, Yongin U., Korea, Sun Gkyun Kwan U. Profl. golfer Korean LPGA, LPGA, 1999—. Named Rookie of Yr., LPGA, 1999. Achievements include winning 11 tournaments on the LPGA of Korea Tour, 1997-1999; winning LPGA Tour events: State Farm Rail Classic, First Union Betsy King Classic, 1999; Safeway LPGA Golf Championship, 2000; Giant Eagle LPGA Classic, Wendy's Championship for Children, 2002; Ginn Clubs & Resorts Open, Jamie Farr Owens Corning Classic, 2006; Sem Group Championship, 2007. Avocations: shopping, pool, piano. Office: LPGA 1000 International Golf Drive Daytona Beach FL 32124-1092

KIM, SHANE, computer software company executive; m. Dana Kim; 2 children. B in Economics and Internat. Rels., Stanford U.; MBA, Harvard Bus. Sch., 1990. Intern Workgroup Applications team Microsoft Corp., Redmond, Wash., 1989—90, product mgr. Workgroup Applications, mgr. internat. mktg. group, 1993—95, dir. bus. devel. Microsoft Game Studios, 1995, gen. mgr., COO Microsoft Game Studios, corp. v.p. Microsoft Game Studios, 2004—08, corp. v.p. global mktg., interactive entertainment bus., 2008, corp. v.p. strategy and bus. devel., interactive entertainment bus., 2008—09. Ptnr. Social Venture Ptnrs.; bd. dirs. GameStop, 2011—. Office: GameStop 625 Westport Parkway Grapevine TX 76051

KIMBALL, CURTIS ROLLIN, financial analyst; b. Grand Rapids, Mich., Dec. 21, 1950; s. Rollin Hibbard and Jane Ann (Walterman) K.; m. Marilyn M. Quaderer; 1 child, Neil Curtis. BA, Duke U., 1972; MBA, Emory U., 1984. Comml. lending and trust portfolio mgr. Wachovia Bank and Trust Co. N.A., Winston-Salem, N.C., 1972-81; v.p., trust mgr. bus. owner svcs. group Citizens and So. Bank, Atlanta, 1981-88; prin., nat. dir. Willamette Mgmt. Assocs., Inc., Portland, Oreg., 1988—, mng. prin. Atlanta office Atlanta, 1995—2012. Chair activities coun. Portland Art Mus., 1993-94; bd. dirs. Cmty. Action Ctr.; founding mem. Ga. Shakespeare Festival, 1986. Fellow CFA Inst. (coun. of examiners 1997, mem. disciplinary rev. com. 2000, Atlanta chpt. bd. trustee, 2012-); mem. Am. Soc. Appraisers (sr. mem., pres. Atlanta chpt. 1985-86, treas. 1996-98, treas. Portland chpt. 1993-94, bus. valuation com., 2001-04), Nat. Assn. Bus. Economists (pres. Portland chpt. 1992-93), Atlanta Econs. Club (treas. 2004-06), Inst. Mgmt. Accts., Employee Stock Ownership Plan Assn., Indian Hills Country Club. Republican. Episcopalian. Avocations: running, tennis. Office: Willamette Mgmt Assocs Inc 1355 Peachtree St NE Ste 1470 Atlanta GA 30309-3274 Office Phone: 404-475-2307.

KIMBALL, DAN B., parks director; b. Mich. married; 1 child. BA in Earth Sciences, Denison U., Granville, Ohio, 1971; MS in Water Resources Adminstrn., U. Ariz., Tucson, 1974. Environ. cons.; positions with US Office Surface Mining, US EPA; asst. to the dep. dir. US Nat. Park Svc., Washington, acting supt. Zion Nat. Pk. Utah, chief water resources divsn., 1993—2005, supt. Everglades Nat. Pk. Homestead, Fla., 2005—. Recipient Superior Svc. award, US Dept. Interior, 1989, Stephen Tyng Mather award, Nat. Parks Conservation Assn., 1995, Pacific NW Regional Director's Profl. Excellence in Natural Resources award, 2002. Office: Everglades Nat Park 40001 State Rd 9336 Homestead FL 33034-6733 Office Phone: 305-242-7707. Office Fax: 305-242-7711.

KIMBALL, MOLLY, dietician, nutritionist; BS in Dietetics, magna cum laude, La. State U. Agrl. & Mech. Coll., 1998, BS in Food. Sci. and Tech., magna cum laude, 1999. Registered dietician, cert. specialist in sports dietetics. Dietetic internship Touro Infirmary Hosp., New Orleans, 1999; sports & lifestyle nutritionist, mgr. nutrition program Elmwood Fitness Ctr., Ochsner Health Found., New Orleans. Nutrition columnist The Times-Picayune, New Orleans; host weekly segment 'Get Fit with Molly' ABC 26's Good Morning New Orleans. Regular appearances as nutritional expert NY Times, Vogue, Newsweek, Shape, Fitness, Runner's World, Cosmopolitan, ABCNews-.com, WebMD, CNN.com. Mem.: Am. Dietetic Assn. Office: Elmwood Fitness Ctr 1200 S Clearview Pkwy Ste 1200 New Orleans LA 70123 Office Phone: 504-842-9572. Business E-Mail: molly@mollykimball.com.

KIMBERLIN, SAM OWEN, JR., financial consultant; b. Wichita Falls, Tex., Feb. 4, 1928; s. Sam Owen and Mary Ruth (Crowell) K.; m. Alison Gray, Dec. 20, 1955; children: S. Scott, David Winston. BBA, U. Tex., Austin, 1951, LLB, 1953; grad. in banking, Rutgers U., 1972. Bar: Tex. 1953. First asst. Office Dist. Atty., Austin, 1953-54; asst. atty. gen. Office Atty. Gen. State Tex., Austin, 1955; gen. counsel Tex. Dept. Banking, Austin, 1956-62; exec. dir. Assn. State Chartered Banks in Tex., Austin, 1962-64; exec. v.p. Tex. Bankers Assn., Austin, 1964-88; mng. dir. TBA Svcs. Co., Inc., Austin, 1988-90; cons. Austin Trust Co., 1990—, Thornhill Securities, Inc., Austin, 1990—. Chmn. devel. bd. Austin Trust Co., 1991—; mem. Third Age Coun., U. Tex., Austin Author: Banking in Texas, 1972 (honors award 1972); co-author: Fight Your Texas Tax Appraisal and Win, 1997. Adv. coun. on property tax cons. Tex. Dept. Licensing and Regulation, 1996-2005; chmn. appraisal rev. bd. Travis Ctrl. Appraisal Dist., 1995-96; trustee S.F. Austin High Continuing Edn. Found. With USMC, 1946-48. Mem. Am. Soc. Assn. Execs. (co-founder Tarry House). Methodist. Avocation: tennis. Home: 3503 Scenic Hills Dr Austin TX 78703-1044 Office: PO Box 5930 Austin TX 78763-5930 Office Phone: 512-477-2255. Personal E-mail: samkim@austin.rr.com.

KIMBERLY, ROBERT PARKER, medical educator; b. New Haven, July 29, 1946; s. John Taylor and Beatrice Eileen (Branch) K.; m. Susan Johnson Alesbury, June 17, 1972; children: Christopher, Taylor, Sarah, Michael, Thomas. AB, Princeton U., 1968; MA, New Coll., Oxford, Eng., 1970; MD, Harvard U., 1973. Diplomate Am. Bd. Internal Medicine. Intern Hosp. of U. Pa., Phila., 1973—74, resident in medicine, 1974—75; fellow in rheumatology Applied Rsch. Br., NIAMDDK, NIH, Bethesda, Md., 1975-77, Hosp. Spl. Surgery-Cornell Med. Ctr., NYC, 1977-79; asst. prof. medicine Cornell U. Med. Coll., NYC, 1979-84, assoc. prof. medicine, 1984-91, prof. medicine, 1991—96; dir. biomedical component and program dir. Cornell Arthritis Ctr., 1988—96; prof. immunology Cornell Grad. Sch. Med. Sciences, 1991—96; Howard L. Holley Prof. Medicine U. Ala. Sch. Medicine, Birmingham, 1996—; program dir. and sr. scientist U. Ala. Arthritis Ctr., 1996—; prof. microbiology and sr. scientist U. Ala. Comprehensive Cancer Ctr., 1996—, sr. assoc. dean rsch., 2007—. Andrew Mellon Found. tchr., scientist, 1980; sci. adv. bd. Alliance for Lupus Rsch.; trustee Arthritis Found. Contbr. numerous articles to profl. jours. Lt. comdr. USPHS, 1975-77. Rhodes Trust scholar, 1968. Fellow ACP, Am. Coll. Rheumatology (pres. N.E. chpt. 1990-91); mem. NY Rheumatism Assn. (pres. NYC chpt. 1992-93), Am. Assn. Immunologists, Am. Soc. Clin. Investigation. Office: Univ Ala Dept Rheumatology Immunology 1530 3rd Ave S Shelby 172D Birmingham AL 35294 Office Phone: 205-934-5306.

KIMBLER, DELBERT LEE, JR., retired industrial engineering educator; b. Whitman, W.Va., Sept. 8, 1945; s. Delbert and Jewell (Browning) K.; m. Elisabeth Moore Davidson, May 18, 1967. BS Engrng. with distinction, U. South Fla., 1976; PhD in Indsl. Engrng. and Ops. Rsch., Va. Poly. Inst. and State U., 1980. Registered profl. engr., S.C. Asst. prof. dept. indsl. and mgmt. sys. engrng. U. South Fla., Tampa, 1980—84, assoc. prof. dept. indsl. mgmt. sys. engrng., 1984—86; assoc. prof. dept. indsl. engrng. Clemson U., SC, 1986—90, head dept. indsl. engrng., 1989—90, prof. dept. indsl. engrng., 1990—, chair dept. indsl. engrng., 1995—2000, emeritus prof., 2008—; ret.; bd. mem. Emeritus Coll., 2013—. Acad. adviser Systems Modeling Corp., State College, Pa., 1983-86; cons. engr. CIBA Vision Corp., Ga., 1992-93, Indsl. Engrng. Accrediation, 2000-; coun. mem. Coll. Industry Coun. for Material Handling Edn., Charlotte, N.C., 1984-87; program evaluator Accreditation Bd. for Engrng. and Tech., 1997—; photography instr. project dir. Art Ctr. Clemson,SC. Author: TQM-Based Project Planning, 1996, (editor) Seasons of Clemson, 2010; editor: (procs.) 19th Annual Simulation Symposium, 1986, (std.) ANSI Z94.17 in Industrial Engineering Terminology, 1990, (newsletter) Comms. of SIM-IIE, 1989-90; sr. editor Jour. Mfg. Sys., 1991-2001; area editor Computers in Ind. Engring. 2002—11. Mem., chmn. Zoning Bd. Ajustment, Clemson, 1989-92; unit commr. Boy Scouts Am., Clemson, 1990-92; mem. Planning Commn., Clemson, 1994-2000, bd. mem. Zoning Appeals, 2010-, Arts & Cultural Commn., 2013-. With U.S. Army, 1966-70. Grantee 19 different sponsors, 1980-2003; named Engrng. Educator of Yr., S.C. Soc. Profl. Engrs., Piedmont chpt. 1992. Fellow Inst. Indsl. Engrs. (sr., pres. SIM 1988-90, Mfg. System award 1988); mem. Tau Beta Pi, Alpha Pi Mu. Democrat. Achievements include research in quality and in I.E. edn. Office: Clemson U 110 Freeman Hl Clemson SC 29634-0920 Home Phone: 864-654-7322; Office Phone: 864-650-3822, 864-656-4716. Personal E-mail: kimbler.kai@earthlink.net. Business E-Mail: kimbler@clemson.edu.

KIMBROUGH, ROBERT S., astronaut; b. Killeen, Tex., June 4, 1967; s. Robert W. Kimbrough and DeAnn Johnson; m. Robbie Lynn Nickels; 3 children. BS in Aerospace Engring., US Mil. Acad., West Point, NY, 1989; MS in Ops. Rsch., Ga. Inst. Tech., 1998. Assigned to 24th Infanrry Divsn. (Mechanized), Fort Stewart, Ga.; deployed to Southwest Asia to serve in Operation Desert Storm; helicopter platoon leader, aviation liaison officer, attack helicopter battalion ops. officer 24th Infantry Divsn.; commanded an Apache helicopter co., regimental hdqrs. co. 229th Aviation Regiment (Attack) (Airborne), Fort Bragg, NC, 1994; asst. prof. dept. math. scis. US Mil. Acad., 1998; flight simulation engr., Shuttle Tng. Aircraft (STA) NASA Aircraft Ops. Divsn., Ellington Field, Houston, 2000; mission specialist, astronaut NASA, 2004—. Crew mem., mission specialist (first spaceflight, will perform two spacewalks) STS-126 Endeavour Mission, 2008. 2nd lt. US Army, Army aviator, 1990. Mem.: Assn. US Army, West Point Soc. Greater Houston, Army Athletic Assn., US Mil. Acad. Assn., Army Aviation Assn. Am. Graduates. Avocations: baseball, golf, weightlifting, running. Office: NASA Johnson Space Center 2101 NASA Pkwy Houston TX 77058

KIMBROUGH, WALTER MARK, academic administrator; b. Apr. 22, 1967; s. Walter L. and Marjorie L. Kimbrough; m. Adria Nobles Kimbrough; 1 child, Lydia Nicole. BS, U. Ga., 1989; MS, Miami U., Oxford, Ohio, 1991; PhD, Ga. State U., 1996. Coord. Greek life Emory U., Atlanta, 1992-95; dir. new student programs Ga. State U., Atlanta, 1995-96; dir. student activities Old Dominion U., Norfolk, Va., 1997-2000; v.p. Albany State U., Albany, Ga., 2000—04; pres. Philander Smith Coll., Little Rock, 2005—. Spkr. in field. Bd. dirs. Heart Ark. United Way. Named one of people who made a difference in Ark., Ark. Times, 2005, 25 influential African Americans in Arkansas, Powerplay mag., 2006. Mem.: Little Rock C. of C. (bd. dir.), Brothers of Acad., Assn. Fraternity Advisors, Nat. Assn. Student Profl. Adminstrs. Office: Philander Smith College Office of President 900 Daisy Bates Dr Little Rock AR 72202 Office Phone: 501-370-5314. Office Fax: 501-370-5277.

KIMEL, JACOB DANIEL, physics professor; b. Winston-Salem, NC, Aug. 11, 1937; s. Jacob Daniel and Emily Nell (Davis) K.; m. Carol Ann Allen, Feb. 27, 1965 (div. Feb. 1990); children: Leslie Ann, Kristine Lynn, Jacob Daniel III, Karen Elizabeth; m. Laura Gale Gunter, May 4, 1991. BS in Physics, U. N.C., 1959; MS in Physics, U. Wis., 1960, PhD in Physics, 1965. Rsch. assoc. U. Wis., Madison, 1965—66, Fla. State U., Tallahassee, 1966—67, asst. prof., 1967—73, assoc. prof., 1973—88, prof., 1988—2003, emeritus prof., 2003—. Dir. grad. affairs Dept. Physics, Fla. State U., 1989-91. Contbr. article to profl. jours. Fellow Woodrow Wilson Found., 1959, NSF, 1960-63; High Energy Physics Rsch. grantee Dept. Energy, 1966-90. Mem. Am. Phys. Soc., Sigma Xi. Lutheran. Achievements include research on double-scattering models and Chew-Low extrapolations, uniqueness of the interaction involving spin 3/2 particles, parton transverse momentum effects and QDC, higher order QCD calculations, Monte Carlo study of spin 1 Blume-Capel model. Home: 2043 Owenby Dr Tallahassee FL 32308-4337 Office: Fla State U Dept Physics Tallahassee FL 32306 Home Phone: 850-656-2950; Office Phone: 850-644-4014. Business E-Mail: kimel@physics.fsu.edu.

KIM JOO, PILJU, agronomist; b. Northern Korea, Sept. 9, 1937; came to US, 1962; d. Myung Ryun and Ockjin (Chu) Kim; m. Young Don Joo, Nov. 27, 1963; children: Michael Wuchung, Thomas Wuil, Eungie. BS in Agronomy, Seoul Nat. U., Suwon, Korea, 1960; MS in Agronomy, Seed Tech., Miss. State U., Starkville, 1964; PhD in Agronomy, field Crops, Cornell U., 1970. Ext. specialist Rural Adminstrn. Office, Suwon, 1960-62; grad. rsch. asst. Miss. State U., Korea, 1962-64, rsch. asst. State College, 1964-65; grad. rsch. asst. Cornell U., Ithaca, NY, 1965-67, rsch. asst., assoc., 1969-75; rsch. asst. Pa. State U., University Park, 1967-69; mgr. and dir. seed sci. rsch. Northrup King Co., Mpls., 1975-84; dir. seed sci. rsch. Stauffer Chem. Corp., Richmond, Calif., 1984-85; tech. svcs. dir. Pioneer Hi-Bred Internat., 1986-92; from v.p. to CEO Agglobe Services Internat., Inc. (formerly Agglobe Technologies), Fairfax, Va., 1992—. Chmn. ad hoc com., editor Seed Vigor Handbook, AOSA-SCST, 1980-82; chmn. corn rsch. working groups Internat. Seed Testing Assn., 1983-86, 89-92; hon. scientist Rural Adminstrn. Office, Suwon, 1992—; lectr. in field; adj. prof. U. Minn., 1995—. Contbr. articles to profl. jours. Named one of 150 Women Who Shake the World, Newsweek, 2011. Mem. AAAS, Am. Soc. Agronomy, Crop Sci. Soc. Am., Soc. Comml. Seed Technologist, Am. Forage and Grassland Coun., Am. Seed Trade Assn., Minn. Forage and Grassland Coun., Korean Am. Scientists and Engrs. Assn., Korean Soc. for Hort. Sci. Presbyterian. Avocations: creative writing, reading, travel and cultural study, skiing, golf. Office: Agglobe Services International 3901 Fair Ridge Dr Ste 211 Fairfax VA 22033 Office Phone: 703-591-6400. Office Fax: 701-591-6401.

KIMMEL, ELLEN BISHOP, psychologist, educator; b. Knoxville, Tenn., Sept. 16, 1939; d. Archer W. and Mary Ellen (Baker) Bishop; divorced; children: Elinor, Ann, Jean, Tracy. BA summa cum laude, U. Tenn., 1961; MA, U. Fla., 1962, PhD, 1965. Asst. prof., rsch. assoc. Ohio U., 1965-68; asst. prof. U. South Fla., Tampa, 1968-72, assoc. prof., dean Univ. Studies Coll., 1972-73, prof. psychology and ednl. psychology, 1975-95, chair, 1992-94, disting. prof., 1996—2003, prof. emerita, 2003—. Disting. vis. prof. psychology Simon Fraser U., Vancouver, B.C., Can., 1980-81; cons. numerous sch. systems, bus. and govt. Author books; contbr. articles to profl. jours., chpts. to books. Mem. Fla. Blue Ribbon Task Force on Juvenile Delinquency, 1976-77; mem. Fla. Gov.'s Commn. on Women, 1979-83; mem. adv. bd. Stop Rape, Good Govt., Inc.; bd. dirs. NCCJ. Recipient Outstanding Svc. award State of Fla., 1975, Outstanding Tchg. award U. South Fla., 1978, Career Achievement award U. Tenn., 1983, Professorial Excellence award Fla. State U. Sys., 1997, Disting. Sr. Scholar Spl. Commendation of Honor, AAUW, 2001; 17 rsch. grants. Fellow: APA (governing coun. 1982—85, pres. divsn. 1986—88, Disting. Leadership award 1993), Am. Assn. Applied and Preventive Psychology (bd. dirs. 1994—97, charter fellow, program chair 1991, Disting. Edn. award 1994), Am. Psychol. Soc. (charter fellow, conf. chair 1990); mem.: Southeastern Psychol. Assn. (pres. 1977—79), Assn. Women in Psychology (Disting. Publ. award 2000), Athena Soc., Omicron Delta Kappa, Delta Kappa Gamma, Sigma Xi. Democrat. Office: U South Fla EDU 162 Tampa FL 33620 Business E-Mail: ekimmel@usf.edu.

KIMMET, PAMELA O., beverage company executive; b. May 16, 1958; BS in Industrial and Labor Rels., Cornell U.; MBA, Mich. State U. With human resources dept. GM Corp.; with Citigroup Inc., 1996—2000, v.p., dir. compensation and benefits; v.p. compensation, benefits and health svc. Lucent Technologies, sr. v.p. human resources, 2001—06; sr. mng. dir., head global human resources adminstrn. Bear, Stearns & Co., 2006—08; sr. v.p. human resources Coca-Cola Enterprises Inc., Atlanta, 2008—. Office: Coca-Cola Enterprises Inc 2500 Windy Ridge Parkway, Ste 700 Atlanta GA 30339

KIMMONS, JOHN F., career military officer, former federal official; BA in History, The Citadel, Mil. Coll. of SC, 1974; MBA, U. Okla.; attended, US Army Comd. & Gen. Staff Coll., US Army War Coll. Commd. as 2d lt. US Army, 1974, advanced through ranks to maj. gen., 2003, assignments include platoon leader C Co., 1st Bn., 77th Armor Ft. Carson, Colo., 1974—75, S-2, 1st Bn., 77th Armor, 4th Inf. Divsn., 1975—77, S-2, 2d Brigade, 4th Inf. Divsn., 1977—78, analyst Intelligence Ctr. Pacific Camp H.M. Smith, Hawaii, 1979—82, electronic warfare officer/G-3, 82d Airborne Divsn. Ft. Bragg, NC, 1982—83, comdr. B Co., 313th Mil. Intelligence Bn., 82d Airborne Divsn., 1983—84, S-3, 313th Mil. Intelligence Bn., 82d Airborne Divsn., 1984—85, intelligence officer, 1st Spl. Forces Operational Detachment-DELTA, 1985—87, dep. G-2, 8th Inf. Divsn. (mechanized) Bad Kreuznach, Germany, 1988—91, comdr. 519th Mil. Intelligence Bn. Ft. Bragg, 1991—93, dir. ops., US Security Coordination Detachment Ft. Belvoir, Va., 1993—94, dir. intelligence, (J-2), joint spl. ops. comd. Ft. Bragg, 1995—97, comdr., 1997—99, dep. dir. ops., Nat. Mil. Comd. Ctr. Washington, 1999—2001, dir. intelligence (J-2), US Ctrl. Comd. (USCENTCOM) MacDill Air Force Base, Fla., 2001—03, commdg. gen., US Intelligence & Security Command Ft. Belvoir, 2003—05, dep. chief of staff for intelligence (G-2) Washington, 2005—09; dir. intelligence staff Office Nat. Intelligence,

2009—10; v.p. Booz Allen Hamilton, 2011—. Decorated Def. Superior Svc. medal with 3 Oak Leaf Clusters, Legion of Merit, Bronze Star medal, Def. Meritorious Svc. medal with 2 Oak Leaf Clusters, Meritorious Svc. medal with 2 Oak Leaf Clusters, Joint Svc. Commendation medal, Army Commendation medal with Oak Leaf Cluster; recipient Disting. Svc. meadl. Office: Booz Allen Hamilton 8283 Greensboro Dr Mc Lean VA 22102*

KIMYAI-ASADI, ARASH, surgeon; s. Taghi Kimyai-Asadi and Fatemeh Milani; m. Ming Hewy Jih, May 24, 2003; children: Leila, Zane. BA, Johns Hopkins U., Balt., 1995, MD, 1999. Diplomate Am. Bd. Dermatology. Mohs surgeon DermSurgery Assocs., Houston, 2004—. Contbr. Fellow: Am. Coll. Mohs Surgery; mem.: Am. Acad. Dermatology, Am. Soc. for Dermatologic Surgery, Phi Beta Kappa. Office: DermSurgery Assocs 7515 Main Ste 290 Houston TX 77030 Home: 6615 Belmont St Houston TX 77005 Office Phone: 713-791-9966. Office Fax: 713-791-9927. Personal E-mail: akimyai@yahoo.com.

KINCHEN, THOMAS ALEXANDER, college president; b. Thomasville, Ga., Dec. 28, 1946; s. George H. and Annie L. (Castleberry) K.; m. Ruth Ann Hunter, Aug. 27, 1967; children: Alex, Lisa Ann. AB summa cum laude, Ga. So. Coll., 1969; MEd, U. Ga., 1975; MDiv, New Orleans Bapt. Theol. Sem., 1979, PhD, 1982. Pastor several chs., 1972-76; v.p. New Orleans Bapt. Theol. Sem., 1982-86; exec. dir., treas. W.Va. Conv. So. Bapt., Scott Depot, 1986-90; pres. The Bapt. Coll. of Fla., Graceville, 1990—. Editor Laos: All the People of God, 1984; contbr. articles to profl. jours. Bd. dirs. Area Devel. Coun., Graceville, 1991; mem. edn. commn. So. Bapt. Conv., 1992—; pres. bd. dirs. Jackson County Devel. Coun., 1996. Mem. So. Bapt. Adult Edn. Assn. (pres. 1996-98, v.p. 1994-96), Assn. Southern Bapt. Colls. and Schs.(bd. dir. 2000-03), Graceville C. of C. (pres. 1993), Kiwanis, Jackson County C. of C. (bd. dir. 2003-06, vice chmn. 2004, chmn. 2005), New Orleans Bapt. Theol. Sem. (Outstanding Alumnus 2000), Phi Kappa Phi, Alpha Psi Omega. Avocations: golf, fishing, woodworking. Office: Bapt Coll Fla 5400 Coll Dr Graceville FL 32440-1831 Office Phone: 850-263-3261. E-mail: takinchen@baptistcollege.edu.

KINDBERG, SHIRLEY JANE, pediatrician; b. Newark, Feb. 4, 1936; d. John Bertil and Mabel Jacoba (deJonge) Kindberg; m. Charles Dale Coln, May 12, 1962; children: Sara Goldstein, Eric Coln, Lois Thompson, Ruth Skipper, Mary Mielenz. BS, Wheaton Coll., 1957; MD, Baylor U., 1961. Intern Tex. Children's Hosp., Houston, 1961-62; resident Children's Med. Ctr., Dallas, 1962-63; fellow in pediat. pulmonary disease U. Tex. S.W. Med. Sch., Dallas, 1963-64, fellow in pediat. infectious disease, 1965-67; pvt. practice gen. pediat. Dallas, 1969-81; pvt. practice newborns, 1981—2004. Active Park Cities Presbyn. Ch.; mem. Dallas Symphony Assn. Republican. Avocations: cooking, travel, music, exercise. Personal E-mail: colnoma@sbcglobal.net.

KINDER, RICHARD DAN, natural gas pipeline, oil and gas company executive; b. Cape Girardeau, Mo., Oct. 19, 1944; s. Luke Frazelle and Edna (Corbin) Kinder; m. Anne Lamkin; 1 child, Kara; m. Nancy McNeil, 1997. BA, U. Mo., 1966, JD, 1968. Sole practice, Cape Girardeau, Mo., 1972—80; sr. atty. Continental Resources/Fla. Gas Cos., Winter Pk., 1981—82, v.p., gen. counsel Winter Park, 1982—84; sr. v.p., gen. counsel Houston Natural Gas Corp., 1985, HNG/InterNorth Inc., Houston, 1985—86; exec. v.p. law and corp. devel. Enron Corp., Houston, 1986—87, exec. v.p., chief of staff, 1987—88, vice chmn. bd., 1988—89, pres., COO, 1989—96; chmn., CEO Kinder Morgan, Inc., Houston, 1997—. Bd. dirs. Soc. Performing Arts, Houston, 1986—, Mus. Fine Arts, Houston, 1987—. Capt. US Army, 1968—72. Named one of Forbes 400: Richest Americans, 2006—. Mem.: Houston Bar Assn., Mo. Bar Assn., ABA, Nat. Bd. of Smithsonian Instn., Petroleum Club, Houston Racquet. Methodist. Office: Kinder Morgan Inc 500 Dallas St, Ste 1000 Houston TX 77002

KING, ALAN, school system administrator; CPA. With Harlingen Sch. Dist., Tex.; asst. supt. Goose Greek Sch. Dist.; dep. supt. Lewisville Independent Sch. Dist.; chief of staff, CFO Dallas Independent Sch. Dist., 2011—12, interim supt., 2011—12, internal auditor, 2013—. Office: Dallas Independent School District 3700 Ross Ave Dallas TX 75204 Office Phone: 972-925-3400.*

KING, BERNICE ALBERTINE, minister, advocate; b. Atlanta, Mar. 28, 1963; d. Martin Luther, Jr. and Coretta (Scott) King. BA in Psychology, Spelman Coll., Atlanta, 1985; JD, MDiv, Emory U., Atlanta, 1990. Ordained Bapt. min. 1990. Intern City Atty.'s Office, Atlanta; asst. min. Ebenezer Bapt. Ch., Atlanta, 1990—93; assoc. to asst. min. Greater Rising Star Bapt. Ch., Atlanta, 1994; min. New Birth Missionary Bapt. Ch., Lithonia, Ga.; pres. So. Christian Leadership Conf. (SCLC), 2009—11. Author: Hard Questions, Heart Answers, 1996. Founder Be A King Scholarship, Spelman Coll., 2007. Recipient Commitment to Cmty. award, Ga. Alliance African Am. Attorneys, 2007; named a Woman of Strength & Courage, Am. Legacy Mag., 2005; named one of Ten of Tomorrow, Ebony mag. Mem.: State Bar Ga., Alpha Kappa Alpha. Mailing: c/o First Kingdom Mgmt PO Box 110277 Atlanta GA 30311

KING, BRYAN, state legislator; Poultry & cattle farmer; mem. Dist. 91 Ark. House of Reps., 2007—. Republican. Assembly Of God. Address: 871 County Rd 814 Green Forest AR 72638 Office Phone: 870-438-4565. Business E-Mail: kingb@arkleg.state.ar.us.

KING, CAROLYN DINEEN, federal judge; b. Syracuse, NY, Jan. 30, 1938; d. Robert E. and Carolyn E. (Bareham) Dineen; m. Thomas M. Reavley; children: James Randall, Philip Randall, Stephen Randall. BA summa cum laude, Smith Coll., 1959; LLB, Yale U., 1962. Bar: D.C. 1962, Tex. 1963. Assoc. Fulbright & Jaworski, Houston, 1962—72; ptnr. Childs, Fortenbach, Beck & Guyton, 1972—78, Sullivan, Bailey, King, Randall & Sabom, 1978—79; judge US Ct. Appeals (5th Cir.), 1979—2013, chief judge, 1999—2006, sr. judge, 2013—. Mem. US Jud. Conf., 1999—2006, exec. com., 2000—05, chmn. exec. com., 2002—05. Trustee, exec. com., treas. Houston Ballet Found., 1967—70; Houston dist. adv. coun. SBA, 1972—76; Dallas regional panel President's Commn. White House Fellowships, 1972—76, mem. commn., 1977; bd. dirs. Houston chpt. American Heart Assn., 1978—79; nat. trustee Palmer Drug Abuse Program, 1978—79; trustee, sec., treas., chmn. audit com., fin. com., mgmt. com. United Way Tex. Gulf Coast, 1979—85; coun. mem., exec. com. treas. American Law Inst., 1991—; trustee, exec. com., chmn. audit. com., finance com., gov. com. Baylor Coll. Medicine, 2007—; trustee, exec. com., chmn. bd. trustees U. St. Thomas, 1988—98; dir. South Texas Coll. Law, 2005—10. Recipient Smith Coll. medal, 1997, Outstanding Alumnus award, Phi Beta Kappa Alumni of Greater Houston, 1998, Margaret Brent Women Lawyers of Achievement award, ABA, 2005, Edward J. Devitt Disting. Svc. Justice award, American Judicature Soc., 2007; Rsch. fellow, Ctr. for American & Internat. Law, 1989—. Mem.: ABA, Philos. Soc. Tex., Houston Bar Assn., State Bar Tex., Fed. Bar Assn., Phi Beta Kappa. Roman Catholic. Office: US Ct Appeals 11020 US Courthouse 515 Rusk Avenue Houston TX 77002-2694*

KING, DAVID A., aerospace engineer; m. Lisa King; 2 children. BS in Mech. Engring., U. S.C., 1983; MS in Bus Adminstrn., Fla. Inst. Tech., 1991. Space shuttle main propulsion sys. engr. NASA, 1983—93, flow dir. Space Shuttle Discovery, 1993—95, dep. dir. shuttle processing, 1996—97, shuttle launch dir., 1997—99, dep. dir. Marshall Space Flight Ctr., 2002—03, dir. Marshall Space Flight Ctr., 2004—09; exec. v.p. Dynetics, Inc., 2009—. Recipient Exceptional Svc. medal, NASA, 1996, Oustanding Leadership medal, 2000, 2004, Presdl. Rank award for Meritorious Execs., 2001, Presdl. Rank award for Disting. Execs., 2005. Fellow: Am. Inst. Aeronautics & Astronautics Found. (assoc.). Office: Dynetics Inc 1002 Explorer Blvd SW Huntsville AL 35806-2806 Office Phone: 256-964-4000.

KING, DAVID PAUL, health services executive, lawyer; b. Washington, June 20, 1956; s. Ivan Robert and Alice King. AB, Princeton U., 1977; JD, U. Pa., 1982. Bar: Ga. 1984. Law clk. to Hon. Alvin B. Rubin, US Ct. Appeals (5th cir.), Baton Rouge, 1982-83; assoc. Rogers & Hardin, Atlanta, 1983-85, Covington & Burling, LLP, Washington, 1985-87, Hogan & Hartson, L.L.P., Balt., 1990-92, ptnr., 1992—2001; asst. US atty. Dept. Justice, Balt., 1987-90; sr. v.p., gen. counsel, chief compliance officer Lab. Corp. Am. Holdings, 2001—04, exec. v.p. strategic planning and corp. devel., 2004—05, exec. v.p., COO, 2005—06, pres., CEO, 2007—09; chmn., pres., CEO Laboratory Corp. of America Holdings, 2009—. Adj. prof. U. Md. Law Sch., Balt. Mem. ABA, Md. Bar Assn., DC Bar Assn., Ga. Bar Assn. Office: Lab Corp Am Holdings 358 S Main St Burlington NC 27215

KING, EMILY, school librarian; MSLS, U. NC, Chapel Hill, 2008. Coord. e-learning services U. NC, Chapel Hill. Named to Movers & Shakers, Libr. Jour., 2011. Office: University NC at Chapel Hill Undergraduate Libr CB# 3942 203 South Rd Chapel Hill NC 27515-8890 Office Phone: 919-962-1355. Business E-Mail: emking@unc.edu.

KING, JAMES C., retired military officer; b. Mar. 18, 1946; BS in Polit. Sci., Utah State U.; MS in Pub. Adminstrn., U. Mo., Kansas City; grad., Command and Gen. Staff Coll., Army War Coll. Commd. 2d lt. U.S. Army, 1968, advanced through grades to lt. gen., 1998, various assignments U.S. and overseas, 1968-88; chief mil. intelligence br. U.S. Total Army Personnel Command, Alexandria, Va., 1988-89; chief intelligence, electronic warfare and reconnaissance Office of Dep. Chief of Staff for Ops. and Plans, Washington, 1989-90; comdr. 66th Mil. Intelligence Brigade, Europe and Germany, 1990-92; exec. officer to dep. chief of staff for intelligence U.S. Army, Washington, 1992; chief of ops. and targeting group Nat. Security Agy., Ft. Meade, Md., 1993-94; dir. intelligence U.S. Ctrl. Command, MacDill AFB, Fla., 1994-96; dir. for intelligence The Joint. Staff, Washington, 1996—98; dir. Nat. Geospatial-Intelligence Agy. (formerly Nat. Imagery and Mapping Agy.) US Dept. Def., Bethesda, Md., 1998—2001; sr. exec. v.p. for nat. security affairs MZM, Inc., Washington, 2001—05, pres., 2005; pres., CEO Athena Innovative Solutions, Inc. (formerly MZM, Inc.), Washington, 2005—. Office: Athena Innovation Solutions INC 901 N Glebe Rd Ste 810 Arlington VA 22203-1853

KING, JAMES LAWRENCE, federal judge; b. Miami, Fla., Dec. 20, 1927; s. James Lawrence and Viola (Clodfelter) K.; m. Mary Frances Kapa, June 1, 1961; children— Lawrence Daniel, Kathryn Ann, Karen Ann, Mary Virginia BA in Edn., U. Fla., Gainesville, 1949, JD, 1953; LHD (hon.), St. Thomas U., Miami, 1992. Bar: Fla. 1953. Assoc. Sibley & Davis, Miami, Fla., 1953-57; ptnr. Sibley Giblin King & Levenson, Miami, 1957-64; judge 11th Jud. Cir. Dade County, Miami, 1964-70; temp. assoc. justice Supreme Ct. Fla., 1965; temp. assoc. judge Fla. Ct. Appeals (2nd, 3rd and 4th dist.), 1965-68; judge US Dist. Ct. (so. dist.) Fla., Miami, 1970-84, 1991—92, chief judge, 1984-91, sr. judge, 1992—. Temp. judge US Ct. Appeals 5th cir., 1977-78; mem. Jud. Conf. US, 1984-87, mem. adv. commn. jud. activities, 1973-76, mem. joint commn. code jud. conduct, 1974-76, mem. commn. to consider stds. for admission to practice in fed. cts., 1976-79, chmn. implementation com. for admission attys. to fed. practice, 1979-85, mem. com. bankruptcy legis., 1977-78; mem. Jud. Conf. US, 1984-87; mem. Jud. Coun. 11th Cir., 1989-92; pres. 5th cir. U.S. Dist. Judges Assn., 1977-78; chief judge US Dist. Ct. C.Z., 1977-78; long range planning commn. Fed. Judiciary, 1991-95. Mem. state exec. council U. Fla., 1956-59; mem. Bd. Control Fla. Governing State Univs. and Colls., 1964. Served to 1st lt. USAF, 1953-55 Recipient Outstanding Alumnus award U. Fla. Law Rev., 1980, Lifetime Achievement award Greater Miami Jewish Fedn. Commerce and Professions Attys. Divsn., 1992, 18th Annual Edward J. Devitt Disting. Svc. to Justice award, 2000; The James Lawrence King Fed. Justice Bldg. named in his honor U.S. Congress, 1996. Mem. Fla. Bar Assn. (pres. jr. bar 1963-64, bd. govs. 1958-63, Merit award young lawyer sect. 1967), ABA, Am. Law Inst., Inst. Jud. Adminstrn., Fla. Blue Key, Pi Kappa Tau, Phi Delta Phi Democrat. Office: US Dist Ct James Lawrence King Fed Justice Bldg 99 NE 4th St Rm 1127 Miami FL 33132-2139 Office Phone: 305-523-5000.

KING, JOHN R., state legislator; b. Chester, SC, June 25, 1976; s. Chris C. and Margie (Buckson) King. Attended, Morehouse Coll., 1997, Gupton-Jones Coll. Funeral Svcs., 1998; MEd, Strayer U., 2006. Mem. Chester City Coun., Chester, SC, 1999, Chester Co. Coun., Chester, SC, 2000—06, SC Funeral Dirs. Assn., SC, SC Funeral Dirs. & Morticians Assn., SC, Nat. Funeral Dirs. Assn., Nat. Funeral Dirs. & Morticians Assn.; former gov. 5th Dist. Funeral Dirs. & Morticians Assn.; mem. Dist. 49 SC House of Reps., 2008—. Democrat. Office: Dist/Home Office Post Office Box 11555 Rock Hill SC 29731 also: Capitol Office 328B Blatt Building Columbia SC 29201 Home Phone: 803-980-5454; Office Phone: 803-377-1144, 803-212-6873. E-mail: johnking@schouse.org.

KING, KELLY S., bank executive; b. Raleigh, NC, Sept. 12, 1948; married; 2 children. BSBA, East Carolina U., 1970, MBA, 1971; grad., Rutgers U., 1981. Mktg. prof. East Carolina U., Greenville, NC, 1971-72; Joined BB&T Corp. (Branch Banking and Trust Co.), Winston-Salem, NC, 1972, mgmt. positions inc. mgr. ctrl & met. regions, city exec., bus. services mgr., consumer loan mgr., mktg. officer, & branch network mgr., 1988—2004, COO, 2004—08, pres., CEO, 2009, chmn., CEO, 2009—. Past vice-chmn. Am. Bankers Council; past bd. mem. Am. Bankers Assn. Chair, Piedmont Triad Leadership Group, United Way Tocqueville Leadership Campaign & United Way Tocqueville Leadership Soc.; mem., Financial Services Roundtable & Triangle Cmty. Found. Leadership Coun.; bd. mem., N.C. Chamber of Commerce; bd. trustees, St. Augustine's Coll., Mission Emanuel, N.C. Ctr. for Non-Profits, N.C. Econ. Devel. Commn., NC Child Advocacy Inst., NC Cmty. Coll. Found. & Winston-Salem Downtown Church Ctr., NC Bankers Assn. Mem. Raleigh C. of C. (econ. devel. adv. council). Clubs: Capital City (Raleigh) (bd. govs.). Office: BB&T Corp BB&T Financial Center 200 W 2nd St Winston Salem NC 27101-4019

KING, KIM, state legislator; b. Sept. 26, 1962; m. Cary King; 2 children. BA in Fitness and Wellness Mgmt., Ea. Ky. U., Richmond, 2004. Farmer; fitness trainer; mem. Dist. 55 Ky. House of Reps., Frankfort, 2011—. Mem. wellness com. Mercer County Bd. Edn. Republican. Office: Kentucky House of Reps Annex Rm 429J 702 Capitol Ave Frankfort KY 40601 Home Phone: 859-734-2173; Office Phone: 502-564-8100 ext. 763.

KING, LESLIE D., state supreme court justice; m. Patricia Smith; 2 children. BA, U. Miss., 1970; JD, Tex. So. U., 1973. Pvt. practice, Greenville, Miss., 1973; mem. Miss. House of Reps., 1980—84, vice-chmn. Ways and Means Com., 1988—91, vice-chmn. Conservation and Water Resources Com., 1992; judge Miss. Ct. Appeals, 1995—2004, chief judge, 2004—11; assoc. justice Miss. Supreme Ct., 2011—. Youth ct. counselor Washington County, Miss.; pub. defender, youth ct. prosecutor, mcpl. ct. judge Town of Metcalfe, Miss. Chmn. Miss. Black Legis. Caucus, 1988. Office: Mississippi Supreme Court 450 High St PO Box 117 Jackson MS 39205 Office Phone: 601-359-3697. Office Fax: 601-359-2443.*

KING, MARTHA JANE, state legislator; b. Apr. 13, 1955; m. Stephen King; children: Steven, Michael. BA, Western Ky. U. Lic. realtor. Transp. agent.; tchr. Head Start; mem. Dist. 16 Ky. House of Reps., 2009—. Chmn. & former vice chmn. Logan County Dem. Exec. Com. Democrat. Office: 702 Capitol Ave Rm 329J Frankfort KY 40601 also: Lake Malone 633 Little Cliff Estates Lewisburg KY 42256 Office Phone: 502-564-8100 Ext. 618, 270-657-2707. Office Fax: 270-657-2755. Business E-Mail: MarthaJane.King@lrc.ky.gov.

KING, PHIL S., state legislator; b. Lubbock, Tex., Feb. 29, 1956; m. Terry Lynn; 6 children. BA, MBA, Dallas Bapt. U.; JD, Tex. Wesleyan U. Capt. Ft. Worth Police Dept., 1974—89; instr. Dallas Bapt. U.; justice of peace Parker County, Tex.; ptnr. Snakard, Gambil & King, Eggleston Flowers & King, LLP; mem. Dist. 61 Tex. House of Representatives, 1999—. Lt. col. in Tex. State Guard. Recipient of several awards and honors. Mem.: Parker County Bar Assn., Tex. State Bar, Rotary. Republican. Office: 2110 Ft Worth Hwy Weatherford TX 76086 also: Room CAP 1N.7 Capitol PO Box 2910 Austin TX 78768 Office Phone: 817-596-4796, 512-463-0738.

KING, PRESTON THEODORE, social sciences educator, writer, political philosopher; b. Albany, Ga., Mar. 3, 1936; s. Clennon Washington and Margaret (Slater) K.; children: Akasi Peter, Oona, Slater. BA, Fisk U., Nashville, 1956; DLitt (hon.), Fisk U., 1999; MS in Econ., London Sch. Econ., 1958, PhD, 1966. Tutor London Sch. Econ., 1958-60; lectr. Keele U., Eng., 1961-62, U. Ghana, 1963-66, U. Sheffield, Eng., 1966-68; reader U. East Africa, Nairobi, 1968-70; sr. rsch. fellow Acton Soc. Trust, London, 1970-72; prof. U. Nairobi, 1972-76, U. New South Wales, Sydney, Australia, 1976-86, Lancaster (Eng.) U., 1986—2001; vis. prof. dept. philosophy U. East Anglia, England, 2002—. Vis. prof. McGill U., Montreal, Can., 1981, Auckland U., New Zealand, 1995, Australian Nat. U., Canberra, 1997, Birkbeck Coll., U. London, 2000-2003, Emory U. & Morehouse Coll., Atlanta, 2002-05, Fisk U., Nashville, 2006, Macquarie U., Sydney, Australia, 2007; chair Polit. Philosophy Rsch. Commn. of Internat. Polit. Sci. Assn., 2006-. Author: Fear of Power, 1967, Politics and Experience, 1968, The Ideology of Order, 1974, 1999, Toleration, 1976, 2d edit., 1998, The Study of Politics, 1977, Federalism & Federation, 1982, The History of Ideas: An Introduction to Method, 1983, An African Winter, 1986, A Constitution for Europe, 1991, Thomas Hobbes: Critical Assessments, 4 vols., 1993, Socialism and the Common Good: New Fabian Essays, 1996, Thinking Past a Problem, 2000, The Challenge to Friendship in Modernity, 2000, Trusting in Reason, 2003, Black Leaders and Ideologies in the South: Resistance and Nonviolence, 2005, Friendship in Politics, 2007; author, narrator documentary; founder, editor, Critical Rev. Internat. Social and Polit. Philosophy. Past convenor Fabian Soc. Socialist Philosophy Group; past trustee Nat. Museums and Galleries on Merseyside. Mem. Internat. Polit. Sci. Assn., Am. Philos. Assn., Am. Polit. Sci. Assn., Polit. Studies Assn., Phi Beta Kappa. Mem. Labour Party. Avocation: walking. Office: Morehouse Coll 830 Westview Dr SW Atlanta GA 30314 Office Phone: 404-507-8651. Business E-Mail: pres.king@morehouse.edu.

KING, REATHA CLARK, retired energy executive; b. Ga. m. N. Judge King Jr.; children: N. Judge III, Scott. BS in Chemistry & Math., Clark Coll., 1958; PhD in Chemistry, U. Chgo., 1960; MBA, Columbia U., 1977; PhD (hon.), Smith Coll., 1993, S.C. State U., 1995. Rsch. chemist Nat. Bur. Standards, Washington, 1963-68; mem., chemistry faculty York Coll. CUNY, Jamaica, 1968-77, assoc. dean, divsn. natural scis. & math., 1970-74, assoc. dean, acad. affairs, 1974-77; pres. Met. State U., St. Paul, Mpls., 1977-88; v.p. General Mills, Inc., 1988—2002; pres., exec. dir. Gen. Mills Found., 1988, chmn., 2002—03. Bd. dirs. Minn. Mut. Ins. Co., St. Paul, H.B. Fuller Co., St. Paul, N.W. Corp., Mpls., Exxon Mobil Corp., Lenox Group; cons., spkr. in field. Contbr. numerous articles to profl. jours. Bd. dirs. Coun. on Founds., Washington, Minn. Coun. on Found., H.B. Fuller Co. Found., St. Paul, Corp. Nat. and Cmty. Svc., vice-chair; chair corp. adv. coun. ARC; bd. overseers Clark Atlanta U.; mem. ministers and missionaries benefit bd. Am. Bapt. Ch., N.Y.C. Recipient Sisterhood award for disting. humanitarian svc. Nat. Conf. Christian and Jews, 1993, Woman of Distinction award St. Croix Valley Girl Scouts, 1995. Mem. NAACP (cmty. svc. award in edn. 1994), Delta Sigma Theta. Home: 110 Bank St SE Apt 2005 Minneapolis MN 55414-3905 Office: Exxon Mobil Corp Bd Directors 5959 Las Colinas Blvd Irving TX 75039-2298 Office Phone: 972-444-1000. Office Fax: 972-444-1350. Business E-Mail: reatha.king@exxonmobil.com.

KING, ROBERT BRUCE, federal judge; b. White Sulphur Springs, W.Va., Jan. 29, 1940; m. Julia Kay Doak, Apr. 16, 1965. BA, W.Va. U., 1961; JD, W.Va. Coll. of Law, 1968. Bar: W.Va. 1968, US Dist. Ct. (so. dist.) W.Va. 1968, US Ct. Appeals W.Va. 1968, US Ct. Appeals (4th cir.) 1970, US Dist. Ct. (no. dist.) W.Va. 1972, US Supreme Ct. 1974, US Dist. Ct. (ea. dist.) Ky. 1975, US Claims Ct. 1985, US Tax Ct. 1991. Asst. mgr. Sam Snead All-Am. Golf Course, Sharpes, Fla., 1965; rsch. asst. State and Cmty. Planning Office, Office of R&D, W.Va. U., Morgantown, W.Va., 1966—68; law clk. Chief Judge John A. Field, Jr. US Dist. Ct. (so. dist.) W.Va., Charleston, 1968—69; assoc. Haynes and Ford, Lewisburg, W.Va., 1969—70; asst. US atty. So. Dist. of W.Va., Charleston, 1970—74; assoc. Spilman, Thomas, Battle and Klostermeyer, Charleston, 1975, ptnr., 1976—77, 1981; US atty. So. Dist. of W.Va., Charleston, 1977—81; ptnr. King Allen Guthrie & McHugh, 1981—98; judge US Ct. Appeals (4th cir.), Richmond, Va., 1998—. Mem. Jud. Investigation Commn. of W.Va., 1990—94; vis. com. Coll. of Law of W.Va. U., 1997—; mem. 4th Cir. Jud. Coun. Mem., W.Va. N.G., 1957—59, mem. USAF, 1961—64. Scholar Patrick Duffy Koontz. Fellow: Am. Bar Found., Am. Coll. Trial Lawyers; mem.: ABA, Am. Bd. Trial Advocates (W.Va. chpt. pres. 1986—90), Jud. Conf. of 4th Cir. Ct. Appeals, W.Va. Law Sch. Assn., W.Va. U. Alumni Assn., Greenbrier County Bar Assn., Kanawha County Bar Assn., W.Va. Bar Assn., W.Va. Golf Assn., US Golf Assn., Order of the Coif, Phi Alpha Delta, Pi Sigma Alpha. Presbyterian. Office: Ste 7602 300 Virginia St Charleston WV 25301

KING, ROBERT LEROY, business administration educator; b. Decatur, Ga., Jan. 22, 1931; s. John Todd and Charlotte (Stringer) K.; m. Helen Butler Leaptrott, Mar. 25, 1956; children: Robert Todd, Keith Alan, John Christopher. BBA, U. Ga., 1952; MA, Mich. State U., 1953, PhD, 1960; Dr honoris causa, Wroclaw U. Economics,

Poland, 1992. Asst. prof. mktg. U. S.C., Columbia, 1957-61, assoc. prof., 1961-65; prof. mktg. Va. Poly. Inst. and State U., Blacksburg, 1965-82, head dept., 1969-76; prof. bus. adminstrn., head dept. The Citadel, Charleston, SC, 1982-85, Robert A. Jolley chair bus. adminstrn., 1985-90; dir. internat. bus. studies, prof. mktg. U. Richmond, 1990-96, prof. emeritus, 1996—. Cons. in field; vis. rsch. Warsaw Tech. U., Acad. Econs. in Wroclaw; overseas tchr. in field. Author: An Annotated Index to the Procs. of the Am. Mktg. Assn. Educators Confs., 1973, 90, Procs.: So. Mktg. Assn. 1973 Conf., 1974, Marketing and the New Science of Planning, 1969, Retailing: Theory and Practice for the 21st Century, 1985, Marketing in an Environment of change, 1986, Minority Marketing: Issues and Prospects, 1987, Retailing: Its Present and Future, 1988, Procs. of the 1988 Conf. of the Acad. of Internat. Bus. S.E. U.S. Region, Mktg.: Positioning for the 1990s, 1989, Marketing: Toward the 21st Century, 1991, Retailing: Reflections, Insights and Forecasts, 1991, Developments in Marketing Science, Vol. XIV, 1991, Marketing: Perspectives for the 1990s, 1992, Minority Marketing: Research Perspectives for the 1990s, 1993, Retailing: Theories and Practices for Today and Tomorrow, 1994, Retailing: End of a Century and a Look to the Future, 1997, Internat. Conf. Procs. of Am. Acad. Advt.: 2001 Asia-Pacific Conf., 2001, Internat. Conf. Procs. of Am. Acad. Advt., 2003, Asia-Pacific Conf., 2003; contbr. numerous articles to profl. jours. With AUS, 1953-55, maj. Res., 1955-76. Grantee Ford Found., 1964-65, Va. Poly. Inst. and State U., 1979-82, Citadel Devel. Foun., 1982-90. Mem. Am. Acad. Advt. (exec. sec. 1986-2002, dir. conf. svcs. 2002-10, book rev. editor Jour. Advt. 1983-94, Disting. Svc. award), Am. Mktg. Assn., Acad. Mktg. Sci. (bd. govs. 1988-94, chmn. bd. govs. 1988-90, v.p. fin., treas. 1986-88), Assn. for Consumer Rsch., Acad. Internat. Bus., Am. Ass. for Advancement of Slavic Studies, Decision Scis. Inst., So. Conf. Slavic Studies, So. Mktg. Assn. (pres. 1972-73), Delta Sigma Pi, Omicron Delta Epsilon, Omicron Delta Kappa, Beta Gamma Sigma. Baptist. Avocations: classical music, history, travel, photography, genealogy. Home: 2440 Edgeview Ln Midlothian VA 23113-9618

KING, SPENCER BIDWELL, III, cardiologist, educator, medical educator; b. Asheville, SC, May 12, 1937; s. Spencer B. and Caroline Paul King; m. Judith Gail Hayes; children: Spencer B., Susan Gail. AB, Mercer U., Macon, Ga., 1959; MD, Med. Coll. Ga., Augusta, 1963. Diplomate in internal medicine, cardiovasc. disease and interventional cardiology Am. Bd. Internal Medicine. Intern, internal medicine Walter Reed Army Med. Ctr., Washington, 1963—64; capt. M.C., U.S. Army, Honolulu and Vietnam, 1964—66; med. resident, cardiology Emory U. Sch. Medicine, Atlanta, 1966—68, cardiology fellow, 1968—70, dir., cardiac catheterization labs., 1972—90, dir. interventional cardiology, 1985—2000, prof. medicine; cardiologist St. Luke's Hosp. / U. Colo., Denver, 1970—72; dir. Andreas Cardiovasc. Ctr., Atlanta, 1986—2000; Fuqua chair interventional cardiology Fuqua Heart Ctr., Piedmont Hosp., Atlanta, 2000—08; exec. dir., academic affairs St. Joseph's Heart Vascular Inst., 2008—, pres., 2008—. Bd. dirs. Surgivision, Inc., Columbia, Md.; chair interventional cardiology bd. Am. Bd. Internal Medicine, 1997—. Co-author: (book) Coronary Angiography and Angioplasty, Atlas of Interventional Cardiology, Hurst's the Heart; author and co-author of other books., editor-in-chief JACC: Cardiovasc. Interventions, mem. editl. boards for several publications, editl. cons. The New England Journal of Medicine; contbr. several articles to profl. jours. Trustee Mercer U., Macon, Ga., 1982—2002, 2007—; bd. of visitors Mercer U. Sch. Medicine, Macon, Ga., 1982—84. Capt. US Army, 1963—66. Decorated Bronze Star; recipient Disting. Alumnus award, Med. Coll. Ga., 1992, RO1 Rsch. award, NHLBI, 1987-1997. Fellow: Am. Coll. Physicians, European Soc. Cardiology (Ethica Award 2000), Soc. Cardiac Angioplasty and Interventions (pres. 1990—91, First Founders Lecture 1990), Am. Coll. Cardiology (pres. 1998—99, Master). Achievements include development of multipurpose coronary arterography and invetion of beta radiation catheter endovascular brachytherapy. Avocation: golf. Office: St Joseph Hosp Heart and Vascular Inst 5665 Peachtree Dunwoody Rd NE Atlanta GA 30342 Office Fax: 404-851-7339. Business E-Mail: sbking@sjha.org.

KING, SUSAN, state legislator; m. Austin King; children: Helen Adair King Stockstill, Lewis Austin, Martha Jourdan. BSN with honors, U. Tex., Austin. Lic. Tex. Bd. Nursing; pvt. pesticide applicator Tex. Dept. Agr. Former co-dir. surg. unit Tex. Heart Inst., St. Luke's Episc. Hosp., Tex. Children's Hosp.; co-owner, co-dir., practicing surg. nurse Elm Place Ambulatory Surg. Ctr.; owner Windy Bluff Ranch, Taylor County, Tex.; mem. Dist. 71 Tex. House of Representatives, 2006—. Performer: Young Audiences Abilene. Former bd. mem. Abilene Philharmonic, Abilene Ballet Theatre, Abilene Cmty. Theatre. Mem.: Farm Bureau, Nat. Rifle Assn. Republican. Presbyterian. Office: PO Box 2376 Abilene TX 79604 also: Room E2.422 Capitol Extension PO Box 2910 Austin TX 78768 Office Phone: 325-670-0384, 512-463-0718.

KING, TERESA L., career military officer; b. 1961; Specialist US Army, 1980, advanced through grades to command sgt. maj., postal clk. Germany, drill sgt.; aide to sec. of def. US Dept. Defense, Washington; first sgt. 18th Airborne Corps US Army, Fort Bragg, NC, with NATO Hdqs., mem. 369th Adj. Gen. General Bn., comdt. Drill Sgt. Sch. Fort Jackson, SC, 2009—. Office: US Army Drill Sergeant Sch 4394 Strom Thurmond Blvd Columbia SC 29207

KING, TRACY O., state legislator; b. Baytown, Tex., Nov. 9, 1960; m. Cheryl Baker; children: Katelyn Marie, Clayton Baker. Attended, SW Tex. Jr. Coll., Sul Ross State U.; BS in Agrl. Engring., Tex. A&M U. Employee Beltone Hearing Aid Ctr., San Antonio, 1983—87, owner, operator Uvalde, Tex., 1987—; mem. Dist. 43 Tex. House of Representatives, 1994—2002, mem. Dist. 80, 2004—. Bd. trustees First United Meth. Ch., Uvalde. Mem.: Tex. Hearing Aid Assn. (former pres.), Kiwanis Club. Democrat. Office: 1995 Williams St Eagle Pass TX 78852 also: Room GW.07 Capitol PO Box 2910 Austin TX 78768 Office Phone: 830-773-0860, 512-463-0194. Office Fax: 830-757-0317.

KING, VANIA, professional tennis player; b. Monterey Park, Calif., Feb. 3, 1989; Profl. tennis player WTA, 2006—. Achievements include winning (doubles) Tokyo, 2006, 2008, Bangkok, 2006, Fes, 2007, Kolkata, 2007, Quebec City, 2008, 2009, Brisbane, 2009, Memphis, 2010, Strasbourg, 2010, US Open, 2010, Wimbledon, 2010; winning (singles) Bangkok, 2006. Office: c/o WTA Tour One Progress Plz Ste 1500 Saint Petersburg FL 33701

KING-LAVINDER, JOYCE, consumer products company executive; Attended, Emory U. Treasury positions RJR Nabisco, Wachovia Bank; mgr. cash and banking Coca-Cola Enterprises, Inc., 1990—98, asst. treas., 1998—2003, v.p., asst. treas., 2003—04, v.p., treas., 2004—. Office: Coca Cola Enterprises Inc 2500 Windy Ridge Pky Atlanta GA 30339 Office Phone: 770-989-3000. Office Fax: 770-989-3363. Business E-Mail: jking-lavinder@cokecce.com.

KINGSBURY, ELLEN ANN DAGON, anesthesiologist, general practitioner; b. Balt., Feb. 3, 1936; d. Emmett Paul and Annie (Sollers) Dagon; m. Lyle Jordan Millan IV, Dec. 21, 1963; children: Lyle Jordan V, Elizabeth Lyle, Ann Sheridan Worthington.; m. T. Marshall Duer, Jr., Aug. 23, 1985; m. Milton D. Kingsbury, Oct. 13, 2006. AB, George Washington U., 1959; MD, U. Md., 1964; postgrad., Johns Hopkins U., 1965—68. Intern Union Meml. Hosp., Balt., 1964—65; resident in anesthesiology Johns Hopkins Hosp., Balt., 1965—68, fellow in surgery, 1965—68; practice medicine specializing in anesthesiology Balt., 1968—; faculty Ch. Home and Hosp., Balt., 1969—; attending staff Union Meml. Hosp., Ch. Home and Hosp., Franklin Sq. Hosp., Children's Hosp., James Lawrence Kernan Hosp., Balt., 1982—94; co-chief anesthesiology James Kernan Hosp., 1983—94, med. dir. out-patient surgery dept., 1987—94; med. dir. Northern Neck Free Health Clinic, 2009. Affiliate cons. emergency room Ch. Home and Hosp., Balt., 1969—, med. audit and utilizaions com., 1970-72, mem. emergency and ambulatory care com., 1973-74, chief emergency dept., 1973-74; cons. anesthesiologist Md. State Penitentiary, 1971; fellow in critical care medicine Md. Inst. Emergency Medicine, 1975-76; infection control com. U. Md. Hosp., 1975—; instr. anesthesiology U. Md. Sch. Medicine, 1975—; staff anesthesiologist Mercy Hosp., 1978—, audit com., 1979-80, 82; asst. prof. anesthegiology U. Md. Med. Sch., 1989-94; med. exec. com. Kernan Hosp., 1990-94, v.p. 1990, chief of staff, 1992—; active Tappahannock Family Practice, 1994-96, Rappahannock Gen. Hosp. Family Practice, 1996—, Rappahannock Gen. Hosp., 1996—, ethics com., 1997—; med. examiner No. Neck of Va., 1996—; active Commonwealth of Va. Med. Bd. Mem. AMA, Am. Coll. Emergency Physicians, Am. Acad. Gen. Practitioners, Met. Emergency Dept. Heads Am., Md. Soc. Anesthesiologists, Balt. County Med. Soc., Mid. Peninsula Med. Soc., No. Neck Med. Soc., Med. Soc. Va., Med. and Choir Faculty Med., Chirurg. Soc., Internat. Congress Anaesthesiologists, Internat. Anesthesia Rsch. Soc. Anglican. Home: 244 Oak Hill Rd Lancaster VA 22503 Office Phone: 804-435-0575.

KINGSBURY, KLIFF, college football coach; b. San Antonio, Tex., Aug. 9, 1979; Attended, Tex. Tech U. Quarterback Tex. Tech U. Red Raiders, Lubbock, Tex., 1998—2002, New Eng. Patriots, 2003, New Orleans Saints, 2004, NY Jets, 2005, Cologne Centurions, 2006, Winnipeg Blue Bombers, 2007; asst. coach U. Houston Cougars, 2008—09, co-offensive coord. & quarterbacks coach, 2010—11; offensive coord. Tex. A & M U. Aggies, College Station, 2012; head football coach Tex. Tech. U Red Raiders, 2013—. Recipient Sammy Baugh Trophy, 2002. Office: Texas Tech Athletics Jones AT&T Stadium Box 43021 6th & Boston Lubbock TX 79409

KINGSOLVER, BARBARA ELLEN, writer; b. Annapolis, Md., Apr. 8, 1955; d. Wendell and Virginia (Henry) Kingsolver; m. Steven Hopp, 1994; 1 child, Lily; 1 child from previous marriage, Camille. BS in Biology, DePauw U., Greencastle, Ind., 1977, LittD (hon.), 1994; MS in Ecology and Evolutionary Biology, U. Ariz., 1981; LHD (hon.), Duke U., 2008. Sci. writer U. Ariz., Tucson, 1981-85; free-lance journalist Tucson, 1985-87; novelist, 1987—. Founder Bellwether Prize for fiction, 2000; book reviewer NY Times, LA Times. Author: (novels) The Bean Trees, 1988, Animal Dreams, 1990, Pigs in Heaven, 1993 (LA Times Times Book prize, 1993), High Tide in Tucson, 1995, The Poisonwood Bible, 1998 (Patterson Fiction prize, The Poetry Ctr., 1999, Nat. Book award of South Africa), Prodigal Summer, 2000, The Lacuna, 2009 (Orange prize for fiction, 2010), Flight Behavior, 2012, (non-fiction) Holding the Line: Women in the Great Arizona Mine Strike of 1983, 1989, Animal, Vegetable, Miracle: A Year of Food Life, 2007, (short story collections) Homeland and Other Stories, 1989, (poetry collections) Another America, 1992, (essay collections) Small Wonder: Essays, 2002, Last Stand: America's Virgin Lands, 2002. Recipient Award for Outstanding Feature Writing, Ariz. Press Club, 1986, Nat. Humanities Medal, 2000, Gov.'s Nat. Award in the Arts, State of Ky., 2002, Frank Waters Writing award, 2002; named one of 100 Best Writers of the 20th Century, Writers Digest, 1999. Mem.: Nat. Writers Union (Andrea Egan award 1998), Phi Beta Kappa. Avocations: gardening, history. Office: PO Box 160 Meadowview VA 24361 Mailing: c/o Harper Collins 10 E 53rd St New York NY 10022-5244 Address: c/o Judy Carmichael Office of Barbara Kingsolver PO Box 160 Meadowview VA 24361

KINGSTON, JACK (JOHN HEDDENS KINGSTON), United States Representative from Georgia; b. Bryan, Tex., Apr. 24, 1955; m. Libby Kingston; children: Betsy, John, Ann, Jim. BA in Economics, U. Ga.; attended, Mich. State U., 1973—74. Salesman, v.p. Palmer & Cay Carswell Ins. Co., 1979-92; mem. Ga. State Ho. Reps., 1985-93, US Congress from 1st Ga. dist., 1993—. Mem. Ways & Means Com., 1985-93, Appropriations Com., Congl. Rural Caucus Exec. Bd., 1993—, chmn. Theme Team (house Rep. comm. team). Vol. Hospice, United Way; mem. Atlantic Coast Conservation Assn., Isle of Hope Community Assn. Recipient Guardian Small Bus. award, Nat. Fed. Ind. Bus. 103, 104, 105, 106, 1992, Sound Dollar award Free Cong. Found., 1994, Golden Bulldog award mems. 103rd, 104th, 105th, 106th cong., 1994, 96, Golden Eagle award Nat. Security Caucus, 1994, cert. recognition inspector. gen. Criminal Investigator Acad., 1994, plaque of appreciation Camden county bd. realtors, 1995, disting. cit. award Armstrong state coll., 1996, merit award the Seniors Coalition, 1996, comm. police award city of Statesboro, 1997, numerous others. Mem. Am. Legislative Exchange Coun., Soc. Chartered Property & Casualty Underwriters, Solomon's Lodge F&AM, Rotary (Paul Harris fellow). Republican. Episcopalian. Office: US House of Representatives 2372 Rayburn House Office Bldg Washington DC 20515*

KINGTON, BARRY CLARK, investor, consultant; b. Sept. 2, 1942; s. William Hayes and Margret Elisabeth (Clark) K.; children: Barry Clark, Paige Dawson. BS, Murray State U., 1969, MSAE, 1990. Owner coal and oil rights; investor stocks and commodities; bus. cons., pres. Point One Adv. Group, Inc., Am. Soc. Farm Mgrs. and Rural Appraisers. Fellow Internat. Soc. Philos. Enquiry (sr.); mem. AAAS, N.Y. Acad. Scis., Triple Nine Soc. (past regent), Appoloosa Horse Club, Archaeol. Inst. Am., Mensa (pres. Evansville area 1986-88), Am. Angus Assn., Prometheus Soc (past treas.)., Am. Soc. Agr. Cons., Internat. Soc. Agr. Cons., Aircraft Owners and Pilots Assn., Exptl. Aircraft Assn., Masons, Shriners, KT. Home: Kilmarnock Ln Madisonville KY 42431 Office: PO Box 1111 Madisonville KY 42431-0022

KINKEADE, JAMES E. (ED KINKEADE), federal judge; b. Denton, Tex., 1951; BA, Baylor U., 1973, JD, 1974; LLM, U. Va., 1998. Law clk., Tex., 1974—75; pvt. practice atty. Tex., 1975—80; assoc. mcpl. judge City of Irving, Tex., 1976—80; judge Dallas County Criminal Ct. #10, 1981, Tex. 194th Dist. Ct., 1981—88; justice 5th Dist. Ct. Appeals, Tex., 1988—2002; judge US Dist. Ct. (no. dist.) Tex., Dallas, 2002—. Adj. prof. Tex. Wesleyan Sch. Law, 1981—2002. Office: US Dist Ct 1100 Commerce St Rm 1625 Dallas TX 75242-1003 Office Phone: 214-753-2720.

KINNAIRD, ELEANOR GATES, state legislator, lawyer; b. Rochester, Minn., Nov. 14, 1931; d. E. Vernon and E. Madge (Pollock) Gates; m. Richard W. Kinnaird, July 27, 1954 (div. June 1982); children: Robinson S., Michael G., Paul N.; m. Daniel N. Pottitt, Apr. 26, 2009. BA, Carleton Coll., 1953; MM, U. N.C., 1973; JD, N.C. Ctrl. U., 1992. Bar: N.C. 1992, U.S. Dist. Ct. (ea. and mid. dists.) N.C. 1992, U.S. Ct. Appeals (4th cir.) 1992. Staff atty. N.C. Prisoner Legal Svcs., Inc., Raleigh, 1993—2004; mem. Dist. 23 NC State Senate, 1997—; pvt. practice, 2004—09. Mayor, Town of Carrboro, 1987-95. Mem.: Phi Alpha Delta. Democrat. Episcopalian. Avocations: political and civic activities, movies, reading, gardening. Office: NC Senate 300 N Salisbury St Room 628 Raleigh NC 27603-5925 Office Phone: 919-733-5804. Business E-Mail: Ellie.Kinnaird@ncleg.net.

KINNE, FRANCES BARTLETT, academic administrator; b. Story City, Iowa; d. Charles Morton and Bertha (Olson) Barlett; m. Harry L. Kinne, Jr. (dec.); m. M. Wothington Bordley, Jr. (dec.). Student, U. No. Iowa; B of Music Edn., M of Music Edn., Drake U., degree (hon.); PhD cum laude, U. Frankfurt, Fed. Republic of Germany, 1957; LHD (hon.), Wagner Coll., NY; LLD (hon.), Lenoir Rhyne Coll.; DHL (hon.), Jacksonville U., 1995; LLD (hon.), Flagler Coll.; DFA (hon.), Drake U., 1981. Tchr. music Kelley (Iowa) Consol. Sch.; supr. music Boxholm Consol. Sch., Des Moines, Des Moines pub. schs.; sr. army hostess Camp Crowder, Mo.; dir. recreation VA, Wadsworth, Kans.; lectr. music, English and Western culture Tsuda Coll., Tokyo; cons. music U.S. Army Gen. McArthur's Hdqrs., Tokyo; mem. faculty Jacksonville (Fla.) U., 1958—, Disting. Univ. prof., 1961-62, prof. music and humanities, 1963—, dean, founder Coll. Fine Arts, interim pres., 1979, pres., 1979-89, chancellor, 1989-94; chancellor emeritus, 1995—. Past chmn. Ind. Colls. and Univs. Fla.; mem. adv. coun. Nat. Soc. Arts and Letters; hon. mem. staff Mayo Clinic, Jacksonville; corporator Charles Schepens Eye Rsch. Inst. Havard U., Cambridge, Mass., mem. adv. bd. Women's Eye Task Force. Author: A Comparative Study of British Traditional and American Indegenous Ballads, 1958, Iowa Girl: The President Wears a Skirt, 2000, (CD) Memories (in memory of friend, Bob Hope), 2004; contbr. chapters to books, articles to profl. jours. Mem., chmn. adv. bd. Ronald McDonald House; bd. dirs., life mem. Jacksonville Symphony Assn.; bd. dirs., mem. exec. com. Eye Rsch. Found.; trustee Drake U.; past mem. bd. govs. Jacksonville C. of C., past v.p.; mem. pres.'s adv. coun. Flagler Coll. Recipient hon. awards, Bus. and Profl. Women's Clubs, 1962, Disting. Svc. award, Drake U., 1966, 1st Fla. Gov.'s award for achievement in arts, 1972, EVE award in edn., 1973, Arts Assembly Individual award, 1978—79, Roast award, Soc. for Prevention of Blindness, 1980, Brotherhood award, NCCJ, 1981, Top Mgmt. award, Jacksonville Sales and Mktg. Execs., 1981, Alumni Achievement award, U. No. Iowa, Ann. Burton C. Bryan award, Pub. Svc. award, Physicians Edn. Network, Freedom Found. Valley Forge, Disting. Svc. award, Fla. Soc. Ophthalmology, Women of Achievement award, 1st Coast Bus. and Profl. Women's Club Jacksonville, Disting. Educator award, Internat. Longshoremen's Assn., Hope award, Nat. Multiple Sclerosis Soc., Disting. Am. award, Nat. Football Fedn., Fla. State Mus. Tchrs. award, Outstanding Civic Leader award, Civic Roundtable of Jacksonville, Vol. Jacksonville 2d Ann. Bernard Gregory Servant Leader award, Elaine Gordon Lifetime Achievement award, Fla. Fedn. Bus. and Profl. Women, 1996, Order of the South award, So. Acad. Letters, Arts and Scis., Nat. Soc. Arts and Letters, Lifetime Achievement award, Arthritis Found., 2004, Davis award for Lifetime Achievement, Vision award, Schepen's Eye Rsch. Inst., Women Vision Hon. award, Academics Area Girls Inc., 2011; named Eve of Decade, hon. mem., 3d Armored Divsn., U.S. Army, Woman of Achievement, Ponte Vedra Woman's Club, 2005, Outstanding Philanthropist, 2005, Hall of Fame, Jacksonville U. Sports, 2011, Mayor Alvin Brown, Frances Bartlett Kinne Day Jacksonville; named to Jacksonville U. Sports Hall of Fame, 2011; inducted into Fla. Women's Hall of Fame, Outstanding Svc. to Theatre Edn. Fla. Assn. for Theatre Edn., day named in her honor, Women's Club of Jacksonville and other orgns., one of six women featured on History Week posters apptd. by Mayor Jacksonville, bldgs. named in honor, Frances Bartlett Kinne Univ. Ctr. Jacksonville U., Frances Bartlett Kinne Alumni and Devel. Ctr. Drake U., Frances Bartlett Kinne Auditorium at Mayo Clinic, Jacksonville, north wing of Bertha Bartlett Pub. Libr., Kinne Garden (Wilma's Little People Sch.), Jacksonville. Mem.: AAUW, PEO, Nat. Soc. Arts and Letters (adv. coun.), Internat. Coun. Fine Arts Deans (past chmn.), So. Acad. Letters, Arts and Scis., Ind. Colls. and Univs. Fla. (past chmn.), Nat. Assn. Schs. Music (past chmn. region 7), Fla. Coll. Music Edn. Assn. (past pres., v.p.), Friday Musicale, Assn. Am. Colls. (past bd. govs., mem. exec. com.), Fla. Music Edn. Assn. (past bd. dirs.), Music Educators Nat. Conf., Fla. Music Tchr. Assn., Nat. Music Tchrs. Assn., Fine Art Forum (hon.), Jacksonville Women's Network Inner Wheel, Fla. Women's Hall of Fame (Gov.'s 1st award), Delius Assn. Fla. (life), Ret. Officers Assn. (hon.), River Club (first women mem.), Exch. Club (Golden Deeds award), St. John's Dinner Club (past pres., first women pres.), Rotary (pres. 2000, pres. Jacksonville 2000—, bd. dirs. Jacksonville chpt., first woman mem. and pres., restoring sight internat. adv. bd., Paul Harris fellow), Green Key (hon.), Alpha Xi Delta (Woman of Distinction award), Beta Gamma Sigma, Mu Phi Epsilon (Elizabeth Mathias award), Alpha Xi Delta, Omicron Delta Kappa (hon.), Alpha Kappa Psi (hon.), Alpha Kappa Pi (hon.), Alpha Psi Omega (hon.). Home: 5817 Fleet Landing Blvd Atlantic Beach FL 32233

KINNEAR, PETER D., retired energy executive; b. 1947; BSCE, Vanderbilt U., 1969; MBA, U. Chgo., 1971. Joined FMC Corp., 1971, mgr. bus. develop., 1972—75, mgr. Far East wellhead bus. Singapore, 1975—79, other mgmt. positions, 1979—82, global wellhead ops. mgr., 1982—85, div. mgr. fluid control & wellhead equip., 1982—94, gen. mgr. petroleum equip. & systems, 1994—2001, v.p., 2001, FMC Technologies, Inc., Houston, 2001—04, exec. v.p. energy systems, 2004—06, pres., COO, 2006—07, pres., CEO, 2007—08, chmn., pres., CEO, 2008—10, chmn., CEO, 2010—11, chmn., 2011. Bd. dirs. FMC Technologies, Inc., 2006—11, Stone Energy Corp., 2008—, Superior Energy Services, Inc., 2011—.

KINNEBREW, JACKSON METCALFE, lawyer; b. Oklahoma City, June 29, 1941; s. Jackson A. and Mary Lucille (Metcalfe) K.; m. Carole A. Vadner, Sept. 23, 1967; children: Scott, Sarah. BBA in Acctg., U. Okla., 1963; JD, So. Meth. U., 1967, LLM in Taxation, 1973. Bar: Tex. 1968, U.S. Dist. Ct. (no. dist.) Tex. 1968, U.S. Tax Ct. 1970, U.S. Ct. Appeals (5th cir.) 1971, U.S. Supreme Ct. 1971; CPA, Tex. Assoc. Strasburger & Price, Dallas, 1968-74, ptnr., 1975—98, of counsel, 1999—. Lectr. Wills and Probate Inst., 1980, 81, 83, 89, Practicing Law Inst., 1983; bd. trustees Ctr. Am. and Internat. Law (formerly Southwestern Legal Found.), 1987-2012; dir. exec. bd. Southern Meth. U. Sch. Law, 2002-. Contbr. legal articles to profl. jours. Fund raising chmn. Boy Scouts Am., Dallas, 1984—86; chmn. legacy com. Am. Cancer Soc., Dallas, 1978—82; outside gen. counsel Cmtys. Found. of Tex., Dallas, 1987—2005; interim exec. dir. Cmtys. Found. Tex., Dallas, 2001—05; trustee Cmtys. Found. of Tex., Dallas, 2005—. Lt. US Army, 1963—65. Recipient Disting. Alumni award Pub. Interest, So. Meth. U. Sch Law, 2002. Fellow Am. Coll. Trust and Estate Counsel (state chmn. 1984-89, bd. regents 1988-94, membership selection com. 1993-99), Internat. Acad. Estate and Trust Law (academician 1990—); mem. ABA (subcom. chmn. 1979), State Tex. Bar Assn. (lectr. 1981, 82), Dallas Bar Assn. (chmn. probate sect. 1985), Tex. Soc. CPAs, Dallas Estate Planning Coun. (pres. 1985, program v.p. 1984, treas. 1982, sec. 1981), Tex. Bd. Legal Specialization (cert.). Avocations: golf, sports, bridge. Office: Strasburger & Price LLP Bank Am Plz 901 Main St Ste 4400 Dallas TX 75202-3724

KINNEY, THOMAS J. JOHN, finance educator; b. Dansville, NY, Jan. 31, 1946; m. Linda G. Gates, Dec. 12, 1970; children: Matthew, Andrew. BA in Psychology, Syracuse U., 1968; MSW in Mgmt., SUNY, Albany, 1974; DPA in Adminstrn. & Mgmt., U. Albany, NY,

1981; PhD in Sci. (hon.), Russian Acad. Edn., Moscow, 1995; degree in Adult Edn., Nova Southeastern U., Fla., 1999. Case worker Livingston County Social Svc., Geneseo, NY, 1969—72; tng. specialist N.Y. State Dept. Social Svcs., Albany, 1974—76; dir. continuing edn. U. Albany, SUNY, 1976—82, dir. profl. development program, Nelson A. Rockefeller coll. pub. affairs and policy, 1983—99, spl. asst. to provost, 1997-99; chief learning officer, v.p. edn. Premier Health Alliance, Chgo., 1999—2001; CEO Kinney and Assoc., 2000—; faculty Keller Grad. Bus. Sch. Mgmt., 2002—, U. Phoenix Sch. Bus., 2001—; CEO Kinney Gallary Visual Arts, Ocala, Fla. Bd. dirs. Synquest Technologies, Inc.; mem. Task Force N.Y. State Work Force 21st Century; mem. SUNY 2000 Task Group Social Svcs.; dir. Ctr. Profl. Devel. and Continuing Edn. Rsch., chmn. quality forum Rockefeller Coll. Press; prof. Russian Acad. Edn.; co-founder Russian-Am. Ctr. Adult and Continuing Edn., Moscow; mem. task force employee assistance programs N.Y. State Assembly; mem. implementation adv. com. WorkKeys project Am. Coll. Testing; presenter in field. Editor Jour. Continuing Social Work Edn.; sculptor and master woodcarver 1-2 shows. Named Continuing Educator of Yr., Continuing Edn. Assn. N.Y., 1988; named to Internat. Adult and Continuing Hall of Fame, 1996 Fellow N.Y. State Acad. Pub. Adminstrn.; mem. Am. Assn. Adult and Continuing Edn. (treas., past chair commn. continuing profl. edn., Outstanding Svc. medallion 1994, pres. 1998-2000), Nat. Univ. Continuing Edn. Assn. (chair divsn. continuing edn. professions, mem. fin. com., mem. task force displaced profls.), Internat. Wood Collectors Soc. (bd mem, trustee) Avocation: wood carving. Office Phone: 630-667-8468. Business E-Mail: thomaskinney@msn.com.

KINNEY, WILLIAM LIGHT, JR., editor, publishing executive; b. Bennettsville, SC, Oct. 26, 1933; s. William Light and Annie Laurie (Mayer) K.; m. Margaret Rene Pegues, Mar. 21, 1964; children: Elisabeth Mayer Kinney McNiel, William Light III (dec.). BS, Wofford Coll., 1954, DHL, 1999; BA in Journalism, U. S.C., 1977. With Wofford College ROTC, 1951—53, US Army Res., 1954—56, 1958—62, US Army, 1956—58; copy editor The State, Columbia, SC, 1955-58; reporter Marlboro Herald-Advocate, Bennettsville, 1958-59, advt. mgr., 1959-60, bus. mgr., 1960-65, mng. editor, 1965-70, editor, pub., 1970—; pres. Marlboro Pub. Co. Inc., 1970—. Sec. Marlboro Savs. & Loan Assn., Bennettsville, 1970-82, First Nat. Bank SC, Bennettsville, 1973-84; adv. bd. SC Nat. Bank, Bennettsville, 1984-94, Wachovia Bank, 1994-2000; sec., adv. bd. Security Fed. Savs. & Loan, 1982-90, bd. dirs., 1986-89; pres. Greater Pee Dee Press Inc., 1972-82, Bennettsville Parking and Devel. Co., 1964; v.p. Hamlet (NC) News Inc., 1973-82 Editor, pub.: Three Who Dared, 1960, Sherman's March—A Review, 1961, The Story of the Sculpture Light, 2001. Pres. United Fund, Bennettsville, 1963-64; chmn. Marlboro County com. SC Tricentennial, 1970, US Bicentennial, 1974—81; councilman, mayor pro tem City of Bennettsville, 1967-69; mem. Marlboro County Devel. Bd., 1958-81; bd. dir. Kinney Found., 1971-99, emeritus, 1999-, chmn. bd. dir., 1975-99; bd. dir. Indian Mus. of Carolinas, 1972-2005; trustee Whipple Found., 1979—2009, chmn., 1981—2009; pres., S.C. Press Assn. 1972-73; trustee, S.C. Press Assn. Found., 1978-93, 2000-, vice-chmn., 1985-92, chmn., 1992-93; trustee Neil Monroe Trust Fund, 1965-91, chmn., 1977-91; adv. bd. SBA, 1962-64; chmn. fin. com. 1st Meth. Ch., 1985-87, staff parish com. chmn., 1990-92; active Chancel Choir, 1948—; trustee SC Meth. Adv., 1968-78, SC Meth. Archives Commn., 2010-, chmn., 2010-; SC Official Hall of Fame, 1980-88, 2005—, v.p., 1980-82; dir. SC Confedn. Local Hist. Socs., 1974-75, treas., 1975-78, v.p., 1979, pres., 1980-82; warden 1777 St. David's Soc., 1978-80, pres., 1980-81; chmn. Jennings-Brown House Restoration, 1974-76, Bennettsville Downtown Commn., 1977-82; v.p. Bennettsville Downtown Devel. Assn., 1993—; trustee Am. Folklife Ctr., Libr. Congress, Washington, 1982—2012, chmn. 1987, 92-93, 98-2000, vice-chmn., 1990-92, 94-2012; mem. SC Archives and History Commn., 1987—, vice-chmn., 1988-90, 98—, chmn., 1990-93; SC rev. bd. Nat. Register of Hist. Places, 1988—, chmn., 1990—, SC State Devel. Bd., 1993; bd. dir. Friends Brookgreen Gardens, 1991-97, 2001-, pres., 1993-96, trustee, 1993-96; bd. visitors Coker Coll., 1986-89; bd. dirs. SC Com. for Humanities, 1981-85, Pawleys Island Civic Assn., 1979—, dir., 2004—; dir. Palmetto Trails, 1993-97; trustee Scotia Village Retirement Cmty., 1995—2014, v.p. 2010-12; v.p. Marlboro Civic Ctr. Found., 1994—2012, chmn., 2012-; bd. mgrs. SC Hist. Soc., 2005—, v.p. 2007-14. pres., 2014-. Named Bennettsville and SC Young Man of Yr., 1961, SC Amb. for Econ. Devel., 1990, Knight of Justice of the Order of St. John, Knights of Malta, Sovereign Order of St. John of Jerusalem, 1995—; recipient Govs. award Hist. Preservation 1996, Robert M. Pryor Volunteer Svc. award, Confederation SC Local Hist. Socs., 1985, 2008; Elizabeth O'Neill Verner Gov.'s award for the arts 2002, Jean Laney Harris Folk Heritage award SC Gen. Assembly, 2003. Mem. SAR, Nat. Trust for Historic Preservation (bd. advisors So. Region 1997-2006, chmn., 2000-02, nat. exec. com. 1999-2002), S.C. Press Assn. (pres. 1972-73), Palmetto Conservation Found. (dir. 1997-2001), Palmetto Trust Hist. Preservation (trustee 2002-09), Marlboro County Hist. Preservation Com. (chmn. 1986-96), S.C. C. of C. (bd. dir. 1964-68, 75-78), Bennettsville C. of C. (bd. dir. 1964-67, 75-78), Bennettsville Jaycees (pres. 1962), S.C. Jaycees (v.p. 1963, nat. dir. 1964), Marlboro Hist. Soc. (bd. dir. 1967-79, 2000-, pres. 1975-79), U. S.C. Soc. (bd. dir. 1972-82, vice chmn. 1977-82), Wofford Coll. Alumni Assn. (bd. dir. 1968-72), Marlboro Country Club, Marlboro Cotillion Club (pres. 1984-86, 2004-06), Nat. Debutante Cotillion (sponsor 1987-95), Sans Souci Club (pres. 1980-82), Rotary (bd. dir. 1968-70, 99-2001, pres. 1970-72), McLeod Med. Ctr. Found. (trustee 1997-2007, 2008-), Phi Beta Kappa, Sigma Alpha Epsilon, Sigma Delta Chi. Avocations: history, gardening, walking. Office: Marlboro Herald-Adv Shiness PO Box 656 Bennettsville SC 29512 Business E-Mail: wlkinneyjr@mecsc.net.

KINSER, CYNTHIA D., state supreme court chief justice; b. Pennington Gap, Dec. 20, 1951; d. Morris and Velda (Myers) Fannon; m. H. Allen Kinser, Jr., March 17, 1974; children: Charles Adam, Terah Diane. Student, Univ. of Ga., 1970-71; BA, Univ. of Tenn., 1974; JD, Univ. of Va., 1977. Bar: Va. 1977, U.S. Dist. Ct. (we. dist.) Va. 1977, U.S. Ct. Appeals (4th cir.) 1977, U.S. Supreme Ct. 1988. Law clk. to Judge Glen M. Williams U.S. Dist. Ct., 1977-78; pvt. law practice, 1978-90; commonwealth's atty. Lee County, Va., 1980-83; magistrate judge US Dist. Ct. (western dist.) Va., Abingdon, 1990-98; justice Va. Supreme Ct., Richmond, 1998—, chief justice, 2011—. Trustee Chapter 7 Panel, U.S. Bankruptcy Ct., 1979-90. Mem. Va. Bar Assn., Va. Trial Lawyers Assn., ABA Methodist. Office: Va Supreme Ct PO Box 1315 Richmond VA 23218-1315*

KINSEY, JAMES LLOYD, chemist, educator; b. Paris, Tex., Oct. 15, 1934; s. Lloyd King and Elaine Mills K.; m. Berma McDowell, July 28, 1962; children: Victoria, Samuel, Adam. BA, Rice U., 1956, PhD, 1959; NSF fellow, U. Uppsala, Sweden, 1959-60; postdoctoral fellow, U. Calif., Berkeley, 1960-62. Asst. prof. dept. chemistry M.I.T., 1962-67, asso. prof., 1967-74, prof., 1974-88, chmn. dept., 1977-82; D.R. Bullard-Welch Found. prof. sci. Rice U., Houston, 1988—2007; D.R. Bullard-Welch Found. prof. emeritus sci., 2008—; dean natural scis., 1988-98; interim provost Rice U., Houston, 1993-94. Cons. Los Alamos Nat. Labs., external rev. com. chemistry and laser sci. divsn., 1983—89; Miller rsch. fellow, 1960—62; bd. chem. scis. NAS-NRC, 1980—83, 2004—08, co-chmn. bd. chem. scis., 1981—83; steering com. U.S. Army Basic Sci. Rsch.-NRC, 1981—86; oversight rev. com. chemistry divsn. NSF, 1989; vis. com. divsn. chemistry and chem. engring. Calif. Inst. Tech., 1999—2004; com. of chemistry facilities and infrastructure U. Calif., Berkeley, 1992—93; corp. vis. com. dept. chemistry MIT, 1994—2004; vis. com. for chemistry Stanford U., 1993—96; external rev. com. chemistry U. Pa., 2000; adv. com. rsch. projects State of Tex. Higher Edn. Coordinating Bd., 2000—02; adv. bd. for engring. and scis. Internat. U. Bremen, Germany, 2000—04. Assoc. editor Jour. Chem. Physics, 1981-84; mem. editorial adv. bd. Jour. Phys. Chemistry, 1984-88, Ann. Rev. Phys. Chemistry, 1985-89; mem. adv. editorial bd. Chem. Physics Letters, 1992-97; mem. Coun. of Am. Acad. of Arts and Scis., 1997-2001; contbr. articles to profl. jours. Chmn. sci. adv. bd. Robert A. Welch Found., 2006—11. Recipient E.O. Lawrence award U.S. Dept. Energy, 1987; Alfred P. Sloan fellow, 1964-68, Guggenheim fellow, 1969-70. Fellow AAAS, Am. Phys. Soc. (exec. com. divsn. chem. physics 1985-88, Earle K. Plyler prize 1995), Am. Acad. Arts and Scis.; mem. NAS, Am. Chem. Soc. (chmn. divsn. phys. chemistry 1985, Nobel Laureate Signature award for grad. edn. 1990), Acad. Medicine, Engring. and Sci. Tex.(bd. dirs. 2009-11), Houston Philos. Soc. (pres. 2006-07), Sigma Xi, mem. Chem. Heritage Bd. of Overseers, 2008-. Office: Rice U MS-600 PO Box 1892 Houston TX 77251-1892 Business E-Mail: jlkinsey@rice.edu.*

KINSMAN, FRANK ELLWOOD, engineering executive; b. Westfield, Pa., Oct. 2, 1932; s. Ellwood L. and Josephine I. (Champney) K. m. Ednamae J. Reuter, June 12, 1954; children: Patricia Ash, Beverly Armstrong, Cheryl Gray, Lora Moriconi. BSEE, John Brown U., Siloam Springs, Ark., 1958. Cert. energy mgr. Tech. staff Cornell Aero. Lab., Buffalo, 1958-61; sr. engr. Tex. Instruments, Dallas, 1961-79; v.p. Bywaters & Assocs., Cons. Engrs., 1980-86; pres. Kinsman & Assocs., Cons. Engrs., 1986—2002, 2003—08, v.p., 2009—. Pres. ops. rsch. Cornell Aero. Lab., Buffalo, 1958-61; energy resources mgr. Tex. Instruments, Dallas, 1974-79; energy sys. analysis and design Bywaters & Assocs., also Kinsman & Assocs., Dallas, 1980—; mem. engring. adv. bd. John Brown U., Siloam Springs, Ark., 1970-72, 94-2003; vis. lectr. So. Meth. U., Dallas, 1984-85; energy cons. to univs., schs., hosps. and fed. and state agencies, 1987—. Contbr. articles to profl. jours. Bd. chmn. Grace Bible Ch., Dallas, 1990. With USN, 1950-53. Selected Alumnus of the Yr., John Brown U., 1994. Mem.: ASHRAE, Assn. Energy Engrs. (sr.). Achievements include devel. of material signatures at long infrared wavelengths; rsch. include airborne and satellite data interpretations. Home Phone: 972-233-5262. Personal E-mail: fek@sbcglobal.net.

KINZEY, CARA D., retail executive; BA in Economics & Fin., Ark. Tech U. Various positions Wal-Mart Stores, Inc., including cashier, v.p. store, specialty & treasury sys., v.p. human resources, fin. & corp. sys., v.p. membership, mem. svcs. & credit Sam's Club chain; sr. v.p. info. tech. RadioShack Corp., 2006—08; sr. v.p. info. tech., store, field & corp. support Home Depot, Inc., 2008—. Office: The Home Depot Inc 2455 Paces Ferry Rd NW Atlanta GA 30339-4024 Office Phone: 770-433-8211. Office Fax: 770-384-2356. E-mail: Cara_Kinzey@homedepot.com.

KINZIG, DENNIS R., healthcare company executive; Cert. info. sys. auditor, fraud examiner., fin. svcs. auditor. Sr. v.p. Equicor, Inc.; gen. auditor, v.p., corp. governance Prudential Financial, Inc.; chief risk mgmt. officer Amerigroup Corp., 2008—. Office: Amerigroup Corp Ste 100 4425 Corporation Ln Virginia Beach VA 23462 Office Phone: 757-490-6900. Office Fax: 757-518-3600. Business E-Mail: dkinzig@amerigroupcorp.com.

KIRBY, C. EUGENE, JR., bank executive; Exec. v.p., head retail banking SunTrust Banks, Inc., exec. v.p., dir. internat and e-bus. svcs. Atlanta, 1999—2002, corp. exec. v.p. retail line of bus. and corp. mktg. Office: SunTrust Banks Inc PO Box 4418 Atlanta GA 30302-4418 Office Phone: 404-588-7711. Office Fax: 404-827-6173.

KIRBY, DAN, state legislator; b. Apr. 18, 1958; 2 children. BS in Theology, ABI. Real estate; mem. Dist. 75 Okla. House of Representatives, 2008—. Republican. Office: 2300 N Lincoln Blvd Rm 334 Oklahoma City OK 73105 Address: 12208 E 38th PL Tulsa OK 74146 Office Phone: 405-557-7356. Business E-Mail: dan.kirby@okhouse.gov.

KIRBY, JAMES EDMUND, JR., theology educator; b. Wheeler, Tex., June 24, 1933; s. James Edmund and Mamie (Helton) K.; m. Patty Ray Boothe, July 22, 1955; children: David Edmund, Patrick Boothe. BA in English with cum laude, McMurry Coll., Abilene, Tex., 1954; BD with honor, Perkins Sch. Theology, Dallas, 1957, STM with high honors, 1959; PhD in Am. Ch. History, Drew U., Madison, NJ, 1963; postgrad., Cambridge U., Eng., 1957-58. Ordained to ministry United Meth. Ch., 1959; pastor First Meth. Ch., Roby, Tex., 1958-59, Milford (Pa.) Meth. Ch., 1960-61; asst. prof. Bible, McMurry Coll., Abilene, Tex., 1959-60; asst. prof. religion Sweet Briar Coll., Va., 1963-67; prof. religion, head dept. religion Okla. State U., Stillwater, 1967-70; head Sch. Humanistic Studies, 1970-76; dean, Prof. Ch. History Sch. Theology, Drew U., Madison, N.J., 1976-81; dean Perkins Sch. Theology Southern Meth. U., Dallas, 1981—94, pres. ad interim, 1994—95, prof. ch. history, 1995—, prof. emeritus, 2005. Teaching asst. Drew Theol. Sem., Madison, N.J., 1960-61; cons. bd. missions United Meth. Ch., South Africa, 1968 Co-author: The Methodists, 1996; author: Brother Will, 2000, The Episcopacy in American Methodism, 2000; contbr. articles to profl. jours.; bd. dirs., pres. Wesley Works Editl. Project. Vol. Dallas Olympics 2012 Ethics Com.; distingmem. bd. trustees McMurry U., 1999—2008. Recipient Disting. Svc. award, Okla. State U., 1976, Disting. Alumnus award, McMurry U., 1982; John M. Moore fellowship, 1957-58, Dempster fellowship, 1962. Mem. Am. Acad. Religion, Am. Soc. Ch. History, Alpha Chi, Omicron Delta Kappa. Home: 9235 Windy Crest Dr Dallas TX 75243-6222

KIRBY, MURRELL DEAN, state legislator; b. Lake City, Ark., Nov. 21, 1946; m. Jean Latham Kirby; children: Chris, Tara, Tina. Mem. Dist. 30 Miss. State Senate, 1992—; adv. bd. mem. River Oaks Hosp. Mem.: America Legislature Exchange Coun., Nat. Fedn. Independent Bus., Independent Ins. Agents America & Miss., C. of C., Scottish Rite Mason (32 degree), Nat. Conf. State Legislators, Kiwanis, Exchange Club. Republican. Baptist. Mailing: PO Box 54099 Pearl MS 39288 Home Phone: 601-932-1966; Office Phone: 601-359-3246. Fax: 601-939-0194; Office Fax: 601-359-3063. Business E-Mail: dkirby@senate.ms.gov.

KIRCHNER, ERIC W., delivery service executive; b. Chillicothe, Ill. B, Ind. U.; grad., Stanford U. Exec. Program, Calif. Assoc. in sales, field ops. and aircraft scheduling Menlo Worldwide Forwarding, Inc., Redwood City, Calif., COO; dir. N.Am. freight forwarding United Parcel Svc. America, Inc., pres. freight forwarding, 2008—. Trustee Internat. Air Cargo Assn. Office: United Parcel Svc America Inc 55 Glenlake Pky NE Atlanta GA 30328

KIRGIS, FREDERIC LEE, law educator; b. Washington, Dec. 29, 1934; s. Frederic Lee Sr. and Kathryn Alice (Burrows) K.; children: Julianne, Paul Frederic. BA, Yale U., 1957; JD, U. Calif.-Berkeley, 1960. Bar: Colo. 1961, Va. 1983. Atty. Covington & Burling, Washington, 1964-67; from asst. prof. to prof. law U. Colo., Boulder, 1967-73; prof. law UCLA, 1973-78; from prof. law to prof. emeritus Washington & Lee U., Lexington, Va., 1978—2005, prof. emeritus, 2005—, dir. Frances Lewis Law Ctr., 1978-83, dean law sch., 1983-88. Author: International Organizations in their Legal Setting, 1977, 2d edit. 1993, Prior Consultation in International Law, 1983, The American Society of International Law's First Century: 1906-2006, 2006; contbr. articles to profl. jours. Pres. Maury River Soccer Club, Lexington, 1978-85, pres. Rockbridge Area Transp. System, 2011-. Served to capt. USAF, 1961-64 Recipient Deak award 1974; research fellow NATO, Brussels, 1978 Mem. Am. Soc. Internat. Law (v.p. 1985-87, sec. 1994—2010), Am. Law Inst., Internat. Law Assn. (Am. br.), Am. Jour. Internat. Law (bd. editors 1984-96, 98-2003, hon. editor 2003—), State Bar Va., Order of Coif. Democrat. Presbyterian. Home: 15 Grey Dove Rd Lexington VA 24450-2269 Office: Washington and Lee U Sch of Law Lexington VA 24450 Office Phone: 540-458-8532. Business E-Mail: kirgisr@wlu.edu.

KIRK, RONALD, lawyer, former federal official, former mayor; b. Austin, Tex., June 27, 1954; m. Matrice Ellis; children: Elizabeth Alexandria, Catherine Victoria. BA with honors in Polit. Sci. & Sociology, Austin Coll., 1976; JD, U. Tex., 1979; LHD (hon.), Austin Coll., 2006. Legislative asst. to Senator Lloyd Bentsen US Senate, Washington, 1981-83; asst. city atty., chief lobbyist City of Dallas, 1983-89; shareholder Johnson & Gibbs, P.C., Dallas, 1989-94; ptnr. Gardere & Wynne LLP, Dallas, 1994—2005; sec. of state State of Tex., Austin, 1994-95; mayor City of Dallas, 1995—2001; ptnr. Vinson & Elkins LLP, Dallas, 2005—09; US Trade Rep. Office US Trade Rep., Exec. Office of the Pres., Washington, 2009—13; sr. of counsel Gibson Dunn & Crutcher LLP, Dallas, 2013—. Mem. Gen. Services Commn. Tex., 1992-94, chmn., 1993; bd. dirs. Brinker Internat., 1997-2009, Dean Foods Co., 2003-09, PetSmart, Inc., 2003-09 Active Big Bros./Big Sisters of Dallas, 1986-92; adv. trustee Schreiner Coll., 1988-90; chair South Dallas/Fair Park Trust Fund Adv. Bd., 1990-91; bd. trustees Austin Coll., 1991—; mem. exec. com. Dallas Regional Mobility Coalition, 1992-94; bd. dirs. State Fair of Tex., 1993—; active North Tex. Food Bank, 1985-90, Leadership Dallas Alumni Assn., 1986—, Dallas Assembly, 1990—, Dallas Democratic Forum, 1990-93, Dallas Helps, 1990-91, Mus. African-American Life & Culture, 1991—, St. Luke Community United Meth. Ch., Dallas. Recipient Vol. of Yr. award Big Bros./Big Sisters Met. Dallas, 1992, Disting. Alumni award, Austin Coll. Alumni Assn., 1992, CB Bunkley Cmty. Svc. award, JL Turner Legal Assn., 1994, Mickey Leland Leadership award, Woodrow Wilson Ctr. award, 2000, Jurisprudence award, Anti-Defamatoin League, 2004, Justinian award, The Dallas Lawyers Auxiliary, 2008; named Citizen of Yr., Omega Psi Phi, 1994; named one of The 50 Most Influential Minority Lawyers in America, The Nat. Law Jour., 2008. Mem. ABA, Nat. Bar Assn., State Bar Tex., J.L. Turner Legal Assn. (C.B. Bunkley Cmty. Svc. award 1994), Austin Coll. Alumni Assn. (Disting. Alumni award 1992), U. Tex. Alumni Assn. (pres. elect, 2008-09) Democrat. Methodist. Achievements include being the first African American to be elected mayor of the city of Dallas, 1994. Office: Gibson Dunn & Crutcher LLP 2100 McKinney Ave Ste 1100 Dallas TX 75201 Office Phone: 214-698-3295. Office Fax: 214-571-2933. E-mail: rkirk@gibsondunn.com.*

KIRK, SUSANNE SMITH, editor; b. Washington; d. Harold Clair and Theodora Smith; m. Donald Kirk, 1965 (div. 1985); m. Samuel Alexander Tomlinson III, 1989. Student, Kaiserin-Theophanu Sch., Cologne, W.Ger., 1958; AB, Smith Coll., 1963; cert., Goethe Inst., Berlin, 1963; MS, Columbia U., 1965. Reporter South China Morning Post, Hong Kong, 1965-67; corr. German News Agy., Saigon, Vietnam, 1968-69; editor Charles Tuttle Pubs., Tokyo, 1972-74; freelance journalist, 1965-74; asst. editor Charles Scribner's Sons (now Scribner div. Simon & Schuster), NYC, 1975, editor, 1976-80, asst. v.p., 1977-98, fgn. rights dir., 1978-82, sr. editor, 1980-85, exec. editor, 1985—2004, v.p., exec. editor, 1998—2004, editl. cons., 2004—. Spkr. various writers' confs. Contbr. articles to newspapers. Mem. Mystery Writers Am. (Ellery Queen award 2000), Crime Writers Assn. (U.K.), Internat. Assn. Crime Writers, Snarks Ltd. (N.Y.C., v.p. 1983-84, pres. 1985-86), Columbia Club, Pilgrimage Garden Club (Natchez), Smith Coll. Club (N.Y.C.). Home: 28 Homochitto St Natchez MS 39120-3996 Personal E-mail: suskirk@aol.com.

KIRKENDALL, BILL, professional golfer; Grad., Ill. State U. CEO Orlimar, Puma, Tretorn; v.p. Golden Bros. Inc., 1976—82; CEO Etonic Inc., sales rep., 1982—85, nat. sales mgr., 1985—86, v.p., 1986—88, sr. v.p., 1988—89, exec. v.p., 1989—91, pres., 1991—98; pres., CEO Tretorn of N.A., Inc., 1998—99, Orlimar Golf Co., 1999—2002; ind mgmt. cons., 2002—; gen. ptnr. D.A. Weibring/Golf Resources Group, 2006; CEO Pure Motion, Inc., 2007—. Bd. dirs. Finish Line Inc., 2001—. Office: D A Weibring Golf Resources Group 5601 W Spring Creek Pky Plano TX 75024-3577 Office Phone: 972-378-6631. Office Fax: 972-378-6632. Business E-Mail: bkirkendall@finishline.com.

KIRKLAND, JAMES BRYANT, III, chief financial officer; b. Greensboro, NC, June 5, 1965; s. James Bryant Jr. and Evelyn Caroline (Johnson) K.; m. Susan McKay, Jan. 11, 1992. BS in Bus. Adminstrn., U. N.C., 1987; MBA, Barry U., 2006. Tax mgr. Coopers & Lybrand, Raleigh, N.C., 1987-92; dir. fin. planning control Liggett Group, Inc., Durham, N.C., 1992-94; dir. fin. rsch. and analysis New Valley Corp., Miami, Fla., 1994, v.p., treas., CFO, 1998—2006, v.p., CFO, dir., CDSI Holdings Inc., 1998; v.p. Vector Group Ltd., 2001—, CFO, treas., 2006. Spkr. in field. Bd. dirs. N.C. State U. Coll. Edn. and Psychology Found., Raleigh, 1991—2006, bd. visitors NC State U., 2002-06 Office: New Valley Corp 100 SE 2nd St Miami FL 33131-2100

KIRKLAND, RONALD E., retired insurance company executive; children: Michael S., Jonathan S. Sales assoc. AFLAC, Inc., Ga., 1975, dist. sales coord. to regional sales coord. to state sales coord., state sales coord. Mo., v.p., West Territory dir., 2004—05, sr. v.p., dir., US sales, 2005—09.

KIRKPATRICK, MARK A., biology professor; BA in Biology, magna cum laude, Harvard U., 1978; PhD in Zoology, U. Wash., 1983. T.S Painter Centennial Prof. Integrative Biology U. Tex., Austin. Contbr. articles to profl. jours. Bd. dirs. Save Our Springs Alliance, Austin. Named a Presdl. Young Investigator, Nat. Sci. Found., 1987—92, Guggenheim Fellow, 1997—98; grantee Nat. Sci. Found. Fellowship, 1978—82. Fellow: Am. Acad. Arts & Scis.; mem.: Am. Genetic Assn., Am. Soc. Naturalists (Young Investigators award 1986, President's award 1998). Office: U Tex Ctr Computational Biology and Bioinformatics PAT 652 Austin TX 78712 Office Phone: 512-471-3760. Office Fax: 512-471-3878. Business E-Mail: kirkp@mail.utexas.edu.

KIRSHNER, ALAN I., insurance company executive; Grad., Vanderbilt U. Dir. Markel Corp., Glen Allen, Va., 1978—, pres., 1979—92, chmn., CEO, 1986—. Office: Markel Corporation 4521 Highwoods Pkwy Glen Allen VA 23060

KIRWIN, THOMAS F., prosecutor; Interim US atty. (no. dist.) Fla. US Dept. Justice, 2001, first. asst. US atty. (no. dist.) Fla., 2003—, acting US atty. (no. dist.) Fla., 2008—10. Office: US Attys Office 111 N Adams St 4th Fl Tallahassee FL 32301 Office Phone: 850-942-8430. Office Fax: 850-942-8429.

KISER, JACKSON L., federal judge; b. Welch, W.Va., June 24, 1929; m. Carole Gorman; children: Jackson, William, John Michael, Elizabeth Carol. BA, Concord Coll., 1951; JD, Washington and Lee U., 1952. Bar: Va. Asst. US atty. Western Dist. Va., 1958-61; assoc., then ptnr. R.R. Young, Young, Kiser, Haskins, Mann, Gregory & Young P.C., Martinsville, Va., 1961-82; judge US Dist. Ct. (we. dist.) Va., 1982-93, chief judge, 1993-97, sr. judge, 1997—. Mem. Martinsville City Sch. Bd., 1971-77. With JAGC U.S. Army, 1952-55, capt. Res., 1955-61. Mem. Am. Coll. Trial Lawyers (state com.), Va. Bar Assn. (exec. com.), Va. State Bar, Va. Trial Lawyers Assn., 4th Cir. Jud. Conf. (permanent), Martinsville-Henry County Bar Assn., Order of Coif.

KISHNANI, PRIYA SUNIL, medical geneticist; arrived in U.S., 1991; MB, BChir, Bombay U., 1985, MD, 1990; DCH, Coll. Physicians and Surgeons Bombay, 1989. Cert. Am. Bd. Pediat., Am. Bd. Med. Genetics, Am. Bd. Clin. Biochem. Genetics. Co-dir. Down Syndrome Clinic Duke U. Med. Ctr., Durham, NC, 1996—, dir. Lysosomal Storage Disease Program, 1997—, dir. biochem. genetics, 1997—, dir. Metabolic Clinic, 1998—, assoc. prof. pediat., dir. clin. trials, 2002—, chief, 2007—. Contbr. articles to profl. jours. Recipient Spl. Recognition Honors, Triangle Down Syndrome Network, 2001, Exceptional Parent Maxwell J. Schleffer Disting. Svc. award, Exceptional Parent, 2005. Mem.: Am. Glycogen Storage Disease Assn. (sci. adv. bd. for pompe disease 1997—), Itnernat. Collaborative Gaucher Group (adv. bd. 2005—), Assn. for Glycogen Storage Diseases (chairperson 2005—), Soc. for the Study Inborn Errors Metabolism, Am. Coll. Med. Genetics, Am. Soc. Human Genetics. Achievements include involvement in clinical trials for treatment of cognitive deficits in Down Syndrome and for enzyme replacement therapy of infantile and late onset Pompe disease. Avocations: singing, cooking, writing. Office: Duke Univ Med Ctr Pediat Med Genetics 595 Lasalle St GSRB1 Box 103856 Durham NC 27710

KISS, ELIZABETH, academic administrator, philosophy educator; d. Sandor and Eva Ilona Kiss; m. Jeffrey Holzgrefe, Mar. 18, 1989. BA magna cum laude, Davidson Coll., NC, 1983; B of Philosophy, Oxford U., UK, 1985, D. Philosophy, 1990. Instr. in politics Princeton U., 1988—89, asst. prof., 1990—96; vis. prof. of humanities Deep Springs Coll., Deep Springs, Calif., 1990—91; fellow, ethics prog. Harvard U., Cambridge, Mass., 1992—93; fellow Nat. Humanities Ctr., NC, 1995—96; vis. prof. Deep Springs Coll., Deep Springs, Calif., 1999; assoc. prof. Duke U., Durham, NC, 1997—, Nannerl O. Keohane dir. Kenan Inst. for Ethics, 1997—2006; pres. Agnes Scott Coll., Decatur, Ga., 2006—. Bd. of directors Ctr. for Documentary Studies, Durham, NC, 1997—2003; dean's adv. com. on svc. learning Duke U., Durham, NC, 1997—, bd. trustees, 2007—; co-chair Academic Integrity Assessment Com., Durham, NC, 1999—. Author: (article) Moral Ambition within and beyond Political Constraints: Reflections on Restorative Justice, Democracy and the Politics of Recognition, In Praise of Eccentricity: Character, Moral Education, and Democracy, Alchemy or Fools Gold: Assessing Feminist Doubts and Rights; editor: (book) Debating Moral Education, Rethinking the Role of the Modern University, 2010. Represented Hungarian Human Rights Found. Conf. on Non-Governmental Organizations and Human Rights, UN, Geneva, 1987—87; Martin Luther King day planning com. Duke U., Durham, NC, 2000—01; interpreter at Hungarian elections Alliance of Free Democrats, Budapest, Hungary, 1990—90. Recipient Bowen Presdl. Preceptorship, Princeton U., 1994-1997; grantee Postdoctoral grant, Am. Coun. of Learned Societies, 2000-2001; scholar Rhodes Scholarship, Oxford U., 1983-1986. Mem.: Womens Coll. Coalition (bd. trustees 2009—), Woodruff Arts Ctr. Atlanta (bd. dirs. 2008—), Assn. Practical and Profl. Ethics (exec. com. mem. 2002—10), Dist. VI Rhodes Scholarships (selection com. mem. 2007—), N. Am. Soc. for Social Philosophy, NAS (treas.), Ctr. for Academic Integrity (bd. of directors 1997—2003), Davidson Coll. (bd. of trustees 1997—2003), NC Rhodes Scholarships (sec., selection com. 1998—2003). Office: Agnes Scott College Office of President 141 E College Ave Decatur GA 30030 Office Fax: 404-471-6067. E-mail: president@agnesscott.edu.*

KISS, MARY CATHERINE CLEMENT, writer; b. Johnson City, Tenn., July 28, 1928; d. Hugh Wilfred and Ruby Pearl (Sammons) Clement; m. Alvin Ferencz Josef Kiss, Feb. 27, 1954 (dec. 1998); children: Tony, Stephen, Mary Margaret. Student, St. Mary-of-the-Woods Coll., 1946—47; BA in Journalism, U. Mich., 1950. Staff writer Kingsport Times News, Tenn., 1950—90; video co-prodr., script writer, cons. Get The Picture, Kingsport, 1990—93; owner Mary Kiss Media Svcs., Kingsport, 1990—; staff writer The Independent, Bluff City, Tenn., 1994—95; freelance writer, rschr., cons., 1996—. Recipient 1st Pl. award Best Local Feature Tenn. Press. Assn., 1970, 1st Pl. award Pub. Svc. Features, 1978. Mem. Investigative Reporters and Editors. Avocation: social service. Home and Office: Mary Kiss Media Svcs 100 Edmond Cir Kingsport TN 37663-2612 Office Phone: 423-239-8986, 423-817-3333. E-mail: mckiss_1999@yahoo.com.

KISSAM, LUTHER C., IV, (LUKE KISSAM), lawyer, chemicals executive; B in English summa cum laude, The Citadel, 1986; JD magna cum laude, U. SC, 1989. Assoc. gen. counsel Monsanto Co.; v.p., gen. counsel & sec. Merisant Co.; v.p., gen. counsel, sec. Albemarle Corp., Richmond, Va., 2003—05, sr. v.p., mfg. and law, 2005—09, exec. v.p., 2009—10, pres., 2010—11, dir., CEO, 2011—. Office: Albemarle Corp 330 S 4th St Richmond VA 23219 Office Phone: 804-788-6000. Business E-Mail: luke_kissam@albemarle.com.

KISSELL, FELISE GLANTZ, retail executive; BA in Govt., Colby Coll., 1991; Exec. MBA, Fordham U., 2001. Adj. prof., mgmt. inst. sch. continuing and profl. studies NYU; mng. dir., ptnr. The Carson Group; sr. advisor Thomson Fin.; v.p., investor rels. and fin. AFC Enterprises, Inc., 2002—05; joined Maidenform Brands, Inc., 2005, v.p., investor rels. & corp. devel.; sr. v.p., investor rels. & strategy HSN, Inc., 2008—. Bd. dirs., NY chpt. Nat. Investor Rels. Inst. Office: HSN Inc 1 HSN Dr Saint Petersburg FL 33729 Office Phone: 727-872-1000. Office Fax: 727-872-6615. Business E-Mail: felise.kissell@hsn.net.

KISSLING, FRED RALPH, JR., publishing and insurance agency executive; b. Nashville, Feb. 10, 1930; s. Fred Ralph and Sarah Elizabeth (FitzGerald) K.; m. Mary Jane Gallaher (dec. 1999); children: Sarah FitzGerald, Jayne Kirkpatrick. BA, Vanderbilt U., 1952, MA, 1958. Spl. agt. Northwestern Mut. Life Ins. Co., Nashville, 1953-58, gen. agt. Lexington, Ky., 1962-80, New Eng. Mut. Life Ins. Co., 1981-87, Bennett & Edwards, Kingsport, Tenn., 1958-62; pres. Employee Benefit Cons., Inc., Lexington, 1961—. Owner Lexington House, Inc., 1966—, Kennington Assocs., 1967—; prin. Kissling Orgn., 1980—, pub. Leader's mag., 1967-2006, editor, 1996—; owner, editor Fin. and Estate Planners Quar., 1993-2003; owner and pub. Fin. Svcs. Advisor, 1993—2007, Fraternal Monitor, 1999-2008; owner, pub., editor Probe Pub. Inc., 1997—; pub. Estate Rsch. Inst. Inc. Author: Sell and Grow Rich, 1966; editor: Questionnaire in Pension Planning, 1970, Questionnaire in Estate Planning, 1971. Adv. bd. Salvation Army, Lexington, 1971—, chmn., 1988-91, bd. mem. Boys & Girls Club, 2009-; gen. chmn. United Way of Blue Grass, 1975, bd. dir., 1975-78, 80-83; trustee, chmn. bd. Lexington Children's Theatre, 1979-81, pres., 1981-83; mem. Iroquois Hunt Club, 1984-2009, Ea. Ky. U. Friends Libr. Bd., 2007—. Mem. Am. Soc. CLU's (chpt. pres. 1969-70, 80-81, 2001-02, regional v.p. 1971-73), Ky. Gen. Agts. and Mgrs. Assn. (pres. 1965-66), Million Dollar Round Table (life mem., v.p., program chmn. 1976), Assn. for Advanced Underwriting (bd. dirs. 1976-84, pres. 1982-83), Am. Soc. Pension Actuaries (bd. dir. 1971-78, pres. 1974-), U. Akron Sales Insts. (adv. dir. 1996-2010), Am. Philatelic Soc., Ea. Ky. Friends of Libr. (bd.), Sigma Chi, Spindletop Hall, Masons, Shriners, Thoroughbred Club Am., Boys & Girls Club (bd. mem. 2009-). Avocations: horse breeding, horse racing. Office Phone: 859-277-6135. Business E-Mail: fred@kisslingorganization.com.

KISTLER, MATT, retail executive; BA in Mktg., Mich. State U., East Lansing; MBA, Northwestern U., Evanston, Ill. Various mgmt. mgmt. positions Kraft Foods, Inc., Oscar Mayer, Gen. Foods Corp.; dir. pvt. brands Sam's Club (subs.) Wal-Mart Stores, Inc., 2003—04, v.p. product devel., pvt. brands, packaging and quality testing, 2004—06, v.p. product and packaging innovation, 2006—07, sr. v.p., mktg., rsch. and insights, 2007; v.p., corp. strategy and sustainability Wal-Mart Stores, Inc., 2007—08, sr. v.p. sustainability, 2008—10, sr. v.p. mktg. ops., 2010—. Office: Wal Mart Stores Inc 702 SW 8th St Bentonville AR 72716 Office Phone: 479-273-4000. Office Fax: 479-277-1830. Business E-Mail: Matt.Kistler@wal-mart.com.

KITCH, EDMUND WELLS, law educator; b. Wichita, Kans., Nov. 3, 1939; s. Paul R. and Josephine (Pridmore) K.; m. Joanne Steiner, 1966 (div. 1976); 1 child, Sarah; m. Alison Lauter, Jan. 29, 1978 (div. 2000); children: Andrew, Whitney; m. Gail Lettwich Apr. 26, 2003. BA, Yale U., 1961; JD, U. Chgo., 1964. Bar: Kans. 1964, Ill. 1966, US Supreme Ct. 1973, Va. 1986. Asst. prof. law Ind. U., 1964-65; mem. faculty U. Chgo., 1965-82, prof., 1971-82, dir. law & economics program, 1980—82; mem. Ctr. Advanced Studies U. Va., Charlottesville, 1982-85; prof. U. Va. Sch. Law, 1982—85, Joseph M. Hartfield prof., 1985—2003, Sullivan and Cromwell rsch. prof., 1996-99, Mary and Daniel Loughran prof. law, 2003—, E. James Kelly, Jr. - Class of 1965 rsch. prof., 2003—06, chair faculty senate, 2008—09. Vis. prof. Bklyn. Law Sch., 1995, Northwestern U., 1996, Georgetown U., 2002, U. Nebr., 2002; spl. asst. to solicitor gen. US Dept. Justice, 1973-74; exec. dir. Adv. Com. on Procedural Reform CAB, 1975-76; reporter Com. on Pattern Jury Instruction, Ill. Supreme Ct., 1966-69; mem. com. on pub.-pvt. sector rels. in vaccine innovation Inst. of Medicine, NAS, 1982-85, mem. com. on evaluation polio vaccine, 1987-88. Co-author: (with Harvey Perlman) Intellectual Property and Unfair Competition, 5th edit., 1997, (with Paul Goldstein) Selected Statutes and International Agreements on Unfair Competition, Trademarks, Copyrights and Patents, 2008. Mem. ABA, Va. Bar Assn., Am. Law Inst., Order of Coif, Phi Beta Kappa. Office: U Va Sch Law 580 Massie Rd Charlottesville VA 22903-1789 Office Phone: 434-924-7047. E-mail: ewk@virginia.edu.

KITCHENS, JAMES W., state supreme court justice; b. Crystal Springs, Miss., Apr. 29, 1943; m. Mary Tooke Kitchens; 5 children. BS, Univ. So. Miss., 1964; JD, Univ. Miss., 1967. Bar: Miss. 1967, US Dist. Ct. No. & So. Miss. Districts, US Ct. Appeals 5th cir., US Supreme Ct. Dist. atty. Copiah, Lincoln, Pike & Walthall counties, Miss., 1972—83; atty., private practice, 1984—2008; assoc. justice Miss. Supreme Ct., 2009—. Office: Miss Supreme Ct 450 High St Jackson MS 39201 Office Phone: 601-359-2180.*

KITCHENS, WILLIAM H., lawyer; b. Newnan, Ga., Aug. 3, 1948; m. Ellen Parker Kitchens; children: William H. Jr., Nathan P., Madison H., Claire C. BA with high honors, Emory U., 1970; JD, U. Ga., 1973. Bar: Ga. 1973, US Dist. Ct. (no. dist.) Ga. 1974, US Ct. Appeals (1st. cir.) 1981, US Ct. Appeals (5th cir.) 1974, US Ct. Appeals (11th cir.) 1981, US Supreme Ct. 1977. Mng. ptnr. Arnall Golden Gregory, LLP, Atlanta, 1996—2008. Adj. prof. food and drug law Emory U. Sch. Law, 1979—; bd. dirs. Ga. Biomed. Partnership; mem. Metro Atlanta Biosci. Leadership Coun.; mem. S.E. task force Med. Tech. Leadership Forum; Acad. Programs Com., Acad. Audit Com., Food and Drug Law Inst. Notes editor Ga. Law Review, 1972-73; mem. editl. adv bd. Food and Drug Law Jour., 1981-87, 96-2001; author: Tactical Approaches to Common Problems FDA-Regulated Companies in Inside The Minds Food and drug Law Settlements and Negotiations, 2006,Georgia Jurisprudence Environmental Law, 1995, 96, The Georgia Environmental Law Handbook, 1996, FDA Regulation of Tissue Engineering in Synthetic Biodegradable Polymer Scaffolds, 1997, FDA Inspections and Enforcement in Fundamentals US Regularity Affiars, 2011; contbr. articles to profl. jours. Mem. Leadership Atlanta; trustee Profl. Assn. Ga. Educators Found.; bd. dir. Met. Atlanta C. of C. Recipient Biomed. Cmty. award, Ga. Biomed. Partnership, 2006; named one of Best Lawyers in Am., FDA, & Biotech., 2007, Ga. Super Lawyers. Mem. ABA, State Bar Ga., Lawyers Club Atlanta, Atlanta Bar Assn, Food and Drug Law Inst., Lawyers Club Atlanta, Omicron Delta Kappa; fellow Lawyers Found. Ga., Atlanta Bar Found. Office: Arnall Golden & Gregory LLP 171 17th St NW Ste 2100 Atlanta GA 30363-1031 Office Phone: 404-873-8500.

KITCHIN, CAMERON (L. CAMERON KITCHIN), museum director; b. Norfolk, Va., 1969; BA in fine arts, Harvard U.; MBA, Coll. William and Mary. Sr. assoc. Econ. Rsch. Associates, Washington, 1998—2002; exec. dir. Contemporary Art Ctr. Va., 2002—08; dir. Memphis Brooks Mus. Art, 2008—. Mem.: Am. Assn. Museums (mgr. strategic planning, head of polit. campaign). Office: Memphis Brooks Mus Art 1934 Poplar Ave Memphis TN 38104 Office Phone: 901-544-6200. Office Fax: 901-725-4071.

KITTELBERGER, LARRY E., retired engineering executive; b. 1949; BS in Computer Sci., Pa. State U., Univ. Park; MBA in Fin. and Quantitative Analysis, Old Dominion U., Norfolk, Va. Various leadership positions in engring. and info. systems Tenneco, Inc.; sr. v.p., chief info. officer AlliedSignal, Inc., 1994—99, Lucent Technologies, Inc., 1999—2001; sr. v.p. adminstrn., chief info. officer Honeywell Internat., Inc., Morristown, NJ, 2001—06, sr. v.p. tech. & ops., 2006—10.

KITTLESON, HENRY MARSHALL, lawyer; b. Tampa, Fla., May 13, 1929; s. Edgar O. and Ardath (Ayers) K.; m. Barbara Clark, Mar. 20, 1954; 1 dau., Laura Helen. BS with high honors, U. Fla., 1951, JD with high honors, 1953. Bar: Fla. 1953. Ptnr. Holland & Knight, Lakeland and Bartow, Fla., 1955—. Mem. adv. bd. Fla. Fed. Savs. & Loan Assn., 1974-86; mem. Fla. Law Revision Commn., 1967-76, vice chmn., 1969-71; mem. Gov.'s Property Rights Study Commn., 1974-75, Nat. Conf. Commrs. Uniform State Laws, 1982—. Mem. coun. U. Fla. Law Ctr., 1974-77. Served to maj. USAF, 1953-55. Fellow Am. Bar Found.; mem. ABA (chmn. standing com. on ethic and profl. responsibility 1980-81), Am. Law Inst., Am. Coll. Real Estate Lawyers, Fla. Bar (chmn. standing com. profl. ethics 1965-66, tort litig. rev. commn. 1983-84), Blue Key, Sigma Phi Epsilon, Phi Delta Phi, Phi Kappa Phi, Beta Gamma Sigma. Presbyterian. Home: 1111 S Lakemont Ave Apt 511 Winter Park FL 32792

KITTLITZ, RUDOLF GOTTLIEB, JR., chemical engineer, researcher; b. Waco, Tex., Apr. 19, 1935; s. Rudolf Gottlieb and Lena Hulda (Landgraf) Kittlitz; children: Lenell, Theresa, Liesel, Rolf. BSChemE, U. Miss., 1957; MS in Engring., U. Ala., 2003. Registered profl. engr., Calif. Engr., polychems. rsch. E.I. du Pont de Nemours & Co., Wilmington, Del., 1957-60, engr., textile fibers dept. Seaford, Del., 1960-62, sr. engr., textile fibers dept., 1962-67, Chattanooga, 1967-68, sr. research engr., 1968-83, sr. research engr. textile fibers Seaford, 1983-87, research assoc. textile fibers, 1987-92, sr. rsch. assoc. fibers, 1992-94, Chattanooga, 1995—2000; statis. cons. Rudy Kittlitz & Assocs., Alpine, Tex., 2001—10, Waco, Tex., 2011—. Lectr. in field; adj. prof. U. Tenn.-Chattanooga, 1980—82, Sul Ross State U., 2001—09; math. adj. prof. ITT Tech. Inst., Waco, 2011; Citizen Am. Program del. to Russia, 1991. Co-author: Quality Assurance for the Chemical and Process Industries--A Manual of Good Practices, 1987, 2d edit., 1999, ANSI/ASQC Q90/ISO 9000: Guidelines for Use by the Chemical and Process Industries, 1992, Specifications for the Chemical and Process Industries--A Manual for Development and Use, 1996, Glossary and Tables for Statistical Quality Control, 4th edit., 2004. Vice chmn. Cmty. Action Com., Seaford, 1966; mem. Alp Par Bd., 2001—10, chmn., 2005—10; mem. US Tech Adv. Group, 1995—2010, chmn., 2001—10. Fellow: Am. Soc. for Quality (chmn. Chattanooga sect. 1975—76, councilor region 11 chem. divsn. 1975—80, chmn. Del. sect. 1984—85, regional dir. 1986—87, exec. regional dir. 1987—91, dir.-at-large 1991—93, parliamentarian 1993—99, 2000—05, cert. quality and reliability engr., W.G. Hunter award 1989); mem.: Am. Nat. Inst. Standards, Internat. Orgn. for Standardization Geneva, Am. Statis. Assn., Nat. Assn. Parliamentarians. Democrat. Baptist. Home and Office: 213 Village Cir Waco TX 76710-2574 E-mail: rgkjr75@gmail.com.

KITTREDGE, JOHN WILLIAMSON, state supreme court justice; b. Greenville, SC, Sept. 28, 1956; s. Elwyn Herbert and Marian (Jeffries) K.; m. Lila Hewell, June 20, 1981; children: Lila Marian, John Williamson Jr., Zay Jeffries II. BS in Criminal Justice, summa cum laude, U. SC, 1979, JD, 1982. Bar: SC 1982, US Dist. Ct. SC 1983, US Ct. Appeals (4th cir.) 1983, DC 1986, US Ct. Mil. Appeals 1986, US Supreme Ct. 1986. Law clk. to Hon. William W. Wilkins, Jr. US Dist. Ct., SC, Greenville, 1982-84; asst. solicitor County of Greenville, 1984-85; ptnr. Wilkins, Nelson & Kittredge, 1984-91; judge Family Ct., 13th Jud. Cir., Greenville, 1991-96, SC Cir. Ct., 1996—2003, SC Ct. Appeals, 2003—08; assoc. justice SC Supreme Ct., 2008—. Mem. Crimestoppers Greenville, 1984-91, pres. 1990-91; commr. civil svc. City of Greenville, 1987-91, chmn., 1991. Recipient Lee Connor Williams scholarship US Coll. Criminal Justice, 1978. Mem. SC Bar Assn., Order of Coif, Order of Wig and Robe, Phi Beta Kappa. Presbyterian. Office: Supreme Court of South Carolina PO Box 11330 Columbia SC 29211 Office Phone: 803-734-1080.*

KIVISTO, THOMAS L., former energy executive; s. Ernie Kivisto; m. Julie Lienhard. BS in Pre-Med/Psychology, U. Kans., Lawrence. Exec. v.p. crude oil mktg. Koch Industries; pres., CEO Eaglwing Trading, 1993—2000; co-founder, pres., CEO SemGroup, LP, 2000—08; dir. SemGroup Energy Partners G.P., LLC. Bd. dirs. BOK Fin. Corp., St. Francis Health Sys., Tulsa Cmty. Found., Project Single Parent; bd. trustees U. Tulsa, Kans. U. Endowment Assn. Named to Ill. Basketball Hall of Fame. Office: SemGroup LP Two Warren Pl 6120 S Yale Ave Ste 700 Tulsa OK 74136-8100 Office Phone: 918-524-8100.

KJELLMARK, ERIC WILLIAM, JR., management consultant, performing company executive; b. New Rochelle, NY, May 14, 1928; s. Eric William and Anna Sophia (Fogelstrom) K. BCE, Cornell U., 1950. Mgr. mktg. planning E. I. DuPont de Nemours, Wilmington, Del., 1980-87, dir. Far East task force, 1987-89; gen. dir. Opera Del., Inc., Wilmington, 1985-95; cons. Condux, Inc., Wilmington, 1985-94; rsch., nylon, flurocarbon and acetals E.I. Dupont Nemours, 1952—87. Cons. Monkman-Rumsey, Inc., Wilmington, 1986-92. Treas., v.p. Grand Opera House, Inc., Wilmington, 1971-91, bd. trustees 1992-95; panelist Del. State Arts Coun., Wilmington, 1987-89, 96, 97; sec.-treas. Opera Del., 1994-96, bd. dirs., 1956-04, Wilmington Waterways, Inc., 1985-89; chmn. oversight com. Delaware Art Stabilization, 1993-96, chmn. level IV cos. Opera Am., 1989-91, bd. dirs., 1991-94; panelist Mid-Atlantic States Arts Consortium, 1990, NEA, 1991-94; pres. Opera for Youth, 1997-00; bd. dirs. Nat. Opera Assn., 1998, 99. Chem. corps US Army, 1950—52. Recipient W.W. Laird award DE, 1992, Partners in Excellence award Opera Guild Internat., 1994. Mem. Am. Chem. Soc., Am. Inst. Chem. Engrs., Alpha Chi Sigma. Republican. Episcopalian. Office: 3300 NE 36th St #821 Fort Lauderdale FL 33308

KLAES, JAMES GRAHAM, III, advertising executive; b. Mt. Vernon, NY, Nov. 21, 1945; s. James Graham, Jr. and Frances Imelda (Barker) K.; m. Geraldine Margaret Romitti, Jan. 27, 1968 (div. Dec. 1984); children: Ian Christopher, Brian Jeremy. BA in English, U. San Francisco, 1968. Writer, prodr. White & Shuford Advt., El Paso, Dallas, 1971-73, Mithoff Advt., El Paso, 1973-75, Chapman Advt., El Paso, 1976-78; creative dir., prodr. Paragon Advt., El Paso, 1978-79; prodr., news reporter KDBC-TV, El Paso, 1980-83; creative dir., prodr. Knight & Co. Advt., El Paso, 1983-84; freelance writer and prodr., 1984-95; mgr., prodr. RXL-Pulitzer, Spokane, Wash., 1995-97; writer El Paso Inc., 1997—99; assignment editor KVIA-TV News, El Paso, 1999—2000; gen. mgr. Results video, El Paso, 2000—02; exec. dir. Insights, El Paso Sci. Mus., 2003—05; with El Paso Police Dept., Crime Stoppers, 2006—. Dir., prodr. (TV show) Contact, KDBC-TV, El Paso, 1980-82; prodr., writer (video) The Murals of El Paso, 1993, Carlos Callejo Fresco, 1995; host (TV show) Mayor's Spotlight, Paragon TV, El Paso, 1997-99. Bd. dirs. El Paso Tourist Attractions Promotions, 1983-88, Mexican Food Capitol of World, El Paso, 1985-90, Goodwill Industries, 1990-96, El Paso Ctr. Children, 1991-97. With U.S. Army, 1968-70, Germany. Mem. Advt. Fedn. El Paso (Topps award 1973, Vision award 1993). Avocations: rock climbing, archaeology, local history, arts. Office Phone: 915-564-7124. Business E-Mail: klaesjg@elpasotexas.gov.

KLAMON, LAWRENCE PAINE, lawyer; b. St. Louis, Mar. 17, 1937; s. Joseph Martin and Rose (Schimel) K.; m. Jo Ann Karen Beatty, Nov. 1957 (div. Feb. 1974); children: Stephen Robert, Karen Jean, Lawrence Paine; m. Frances Ann Estes, Mar. 1980. AB, Washington U., St. Louis, 1958; JD, Yale U., 1961. Bar: N.Y. 1964, Ga. 1992. Confidential asst. Office Sec. Def., Washington, 1961-62, spl. asst. to gen. counsel, 1962-63; asso. Cravath, Swaine & Moore, NYC, 1963-67; v.p., gen. counsel Fuqua Industries, Inc., Atlanta, 1967-73, sr. v.p. fin. and adminstrn., 1971-81, pres., 1981-89, chief exec. officer, 1989-91; chmn., 1991; sr. counsel Alston & Bird, Atlanta, 1991-95; pres., CEO Fuqua Enterprises, Inc., Atlanta, 1995-97. Chmn. Gov.'s Internat. Adv. Coun., 1992-95. Mem. bd. editors Yale Law Jour., 1959-61. Mem. State Bar Ga., Order of Coif, Phi Beta Kappa, Omicron Delta Kappa.

KLASKO, STEPHEN KENT, dean, obstetrician, gynecologist; b. Phila., Dec. 23, 1953; MD, Hahnemann U., Phila.; MBA, U. Pa. Diplomate Am. Bd. Ob-Gyn. Resident in ob-gyn. Allentown Hosp., Pa.; chmn. residency program, dir. ob-gyn. Lehigh Valley Hosp., Allentown, Pa.; prof. clin. ob-gyn., assoc. chmn. dept. ob-gyn. Pa. State U.; dean Coll. Medicine Drexel U., Phila., prof. ob-gyn., dean grad. med. edn.; CEO, medicine, nursing and public health U. South Fla., Tampa, 2009—, dean Coll. Medicine, 2004—. Pres. bd. dirs. Lehigh Valley Physician's Group; dir. Trexlertown Women's Health Mall. Fellow Am. Coll. Ob-Gyn., Am. Fertility Soc.; mem. Am. Assn. Gynecol. Laparoscopists, Am. Inst. Ultrasound in Medicine, Gynecol. Laparoscopy Soc. Office: Office of Dean College Medicine Univ South Fla 12901 Bruce B Downs Blvd Tampa FL 33612

KLEBE, TERRY A., corporate financial executive; Ptnr. Ernst and Young LLP; v.p., contr. Cooper Industries, plc., 1995—99, sr. v.p., strategic sourcing, 1999—2002, CFO, 2002—10, sr. v.p., 2003—10, vice chmn., 2010. Office: Cooper Industries Inc 600 Travis St Ste 5400 Houston TX 77002-2909

KLECKER, BEVERLY MCCAULEY, education educator; d. Robert Francis and Dorothy (Camden) McCauley. MA in Counseling, Ohio State U., Columbus, 1966; PhD, Ohio State U., 1996. Lic. Profl. Clin. Counselor Ky., 2005. Grad. rsch. assoc. Ohio State U., Columbus, Ohio, 1992—95; asst. prof. Ea. Ky. U., Richmond, Ky., 1996—99; team leader Divsn. Validation & Rsch., Office Assessment & Accountability, Ky. Dept. Edn., 1999—2000. Rschr., evaluator, grants Morehead State U., Morehead, Ky., 2001—; prof., coord. Coll. Edn. Assessment, 2007—; internal evaluator US Dept. Edn., prin. rschr.; faculty rsch. fellow Coun. Postsecondary Edn. KY, prof. Contbr. articles to profl. jours., scientific papers. Pres. Nat. Assessment Edn. Progress, 2013—14; Ky. rep. Mid-South Ednl. Rsch. Assn., Gatlinburg, Tenn., 2003—05; bd. mem. Cath. Social Svcs., Columbus, Ohio, 1987—90. Recipient Outstanding Dissertation, Phi Delta Kappa, 1996, Disting. Rschr. award, Morehead State U., 2008—09. Mem.: NAEP SIG, Am. MENSA, Soc. Info. Tech. & Tchr. Edn., Mid-Western Ednl. Rsch. Assn., Mid-South Ednl. Rsch. Assn., ADHL & Classroom Assessment SIG, Am. Ednl. Rsch. Assn., Ohio State U. Alumni Assn. (life), Pi Lambda Theta. Office: Morehead State U 503 Ginger Hall Morehead KY 40351*

KLECKLEY, CHARLES E. (CHUCK KLECKLEY), state legislator; m. Laurie Pitman Kleckley; 3 children. Former pres. Calcasieu Parish Police Jury, mem.; owner Four Corners Market, Lake Charles, La.; mem. Advisor Bd, First Nat. Bank Lake Charles; mem. Dist. 36 La. House of Reps., 2005—, chair ins. com., mem. house exec. com., legis. audit adv. coun. Mem.: Profit & Loss Bus. Assn. (bd. mem.), Southwest La Partnership Econ. Develop (exec. bd. mem.), Kiwanis Club(South Lake Charles) (bd. mem.). Republican. Mailing: 130 Jamestown Rd Lake Charles LA 70605 Fax: 337-475-3018.

KLEEBERGER, KENT A., corporate financial executive; CPA. V.p., contr., Victoria's Secret Catalogue The Limited, Inc., 1991—95, corp. contr., 1995—98; various positions, including exec. v.p., CFO, sec., treas., prin. acctg. officer Too Inc. (now Tween Brands, Inc.), 1998—2004, bd. dirs., 2000, exec. v.p., logistics and sys., 2001—02, COO, 2002—04; sr. v.p., CFO, prin. acctg. officer Dollar Tree Stores, Inc., 2004—07; exec. v.p., fin., CFO, treas. Chico's FAS, Inc., 2007—, prin. acctg. officer, 2009—. Bd. dirs. Shoe Carnival, Inc., 2003—. Office: Chico's FAS Inc 11215 Metro Pky Fort Myers FL 33966 Office Phone: 239-277-6200. Office Fax: 239-274-4018. Business E-Mail: kent.kleeberger@chicos.com.

KLEFFNER, GREGORY WILLIAM, retail executive, accountant; b. St. Louis, Nov. 21, 1954; s. Francis R. and Charlotte P. (Petersen) Kleffner; m. Renee A. Drake, June 10, 1993; children: Patricia Elaine, Laura Elizabeth, Michael Gregory. BS in Bus. Adminstrn., Washington U., St. Louis, 1977. Various positions Arthur Andersen & Co., St. Louis, 1977-79, sr. acct., 1979-81, mgr., then ptnr., head audit dept., 1981—2002; v.p. Kellwood Co., St. Louis, 2002—05, contr., 2002—07, corp. v.p. fin., 2005—06, sr. v.p. fin., 2006—07, CFO, 2007—09; sr. v.p., CFO Stein Mart, Inc., 2009—10, exec. v.p., CFO, 2010—. Bd. mem. Grand Center, Inc., St. Louis County Indsl. Develop. Authority, St. Louis County Bus. Fin. Co. Mem.: St. Louis County Econ. Devel. Assn. (mem. loan rev. com. 1986—87), AICPA, Am. Y-Flyer Yacht Racing Assn. (sec.-treas.). Avocations: sailing, golf. Office: Stein Mart Inc 1200 Riverplace Blvd Jacksonville FL 32207

KLEIDERER, KARL, aerospace and defense parts manufacturing company executive; BS, U. Notre Dame, Ind.; MBA in Fin. & Orgnl. Behavior, Northwestern U., Ill. NASDAQ trader, ptnr. William Blair and Co.; NASDAQ trader Morgan Stanley; dir., bus. devel. Goodrich Corp., 2005—09, v.p., acquisitions & divestitures, 2009—. Flight officer USN. Office: Goodrich Corp Four Coliseum Ctr 2730 W Tyvola Rd Charlotte NC 28217-4578 Office Phone: 704-423-7000. Office Fax: 704-423-7002. Business E-Mail: Karl.Kleiderer@goodrich.com.

KLEIN, BENJAMIN GARRETT, mathematics professor, consultant; b. Durham, NC, Jan. 24, 1942; s. James Raymond and Lenetta Mae (Garrett) K.; m. Rosemary Therese McAndrew, June 19, 1971; children: David Garrett, Peter Raymond. BA, U. Rochester, 1963; MA, Yale U., 1965, PhD, 1968. Lectr., asst. prof. NYU, NYC, 1967-71; asst. prof. to prof. math. Davidson Coll., NC, 1971—, vice chmn. faculty NC, 1985-88, appt. Dana prof. math. NC, 1990-93, appt. Dolan prof. math. NC, 1993—, chair dept. math. NC, 1994-98, mem. advanced placement calculus devel. com., 1999—2003; gov. southeastern sect. Math. Assn. Am., 2003—06. Cons. N.C. Dept. Pub. Instrn., Raleigh, 1981-85, 90—. Mem. editl. bd. The Coll. Math. Jour. Elder Davidson Coll. Presbyterian Ch., 1981-83, 87-89, 94-96. Recipient Thomas Jefferson award, 1990, Hunter-Hamilton Love of Tchg. award, 2004; named NC Prof. of Yr., Coun. Advancement and Support Edn., 1991. Mem.: N.C. Assn. Advanced Placement Math. Tchrs., N.C. Coun. Tchrs. Math. (W.W. Rankin award 2007), Nat. Coun. Tchrs. Math., Math. Assn. Am. (chair S.E. sect. 1993—95, gov. S.E. sect. 2003—06, Sect. Disting. Tchg. award 1999, Sect. Disting. Svc. award 2008), Am. Math. Soc. Democrat. Office: PO Box 1713 Davidson NC 28036 Home Phone: 704-892-8306; Office Phone: 704-894-2318. Business E-Mail: beklein@davidson.edu.

KLEIN, BERNARD, publishing executive; b. NYC, Sept. 20, 1921; s. Joseph J. and Anna (Wolfe) K.; m. Betty Stecher, Feb. 17, 1946; children: Cheryl Rona, Barry Todd, Cindy Ann. BA, CCNY, 1942. Founder, pres. U.S. List Co., Boca Raton, Fla., 1946—; founder, pres., chief editor B. Klein Publs., Boca Raton, Fla., 1953—. Cons. in field. Author: all biennials Ency. of American Indian, 1954—; Guide to American Directories. Served with AUS, 1942-45, ETO. Mem. Direct Mail Advt. Assn. Lodges: Masons. Home: 11579 Orange Blosom Ln Boca Raton FL 33428 Office Phone: 561-367-3799. Personal E-mail: bkleinpub@aol.com.

KLEIN, GORDON LESLIE, pediatrician, educator; b. NYC, Aug. 26, 1946; s. Hyman David and Ruth Harriet (Katz) K.; m. Joann Pamela Schulz, July 1, 1973; children: Andrew Howard (dec.), Adrienne Lindsay. BA, Columbia U., 1967; postgrad., Cambridge U., 1970-71; MD, Albert Einstein Coll. Medicine, 1971; MPH, UCLA, 1980. Cert. Am. Bd. Pediat., 1976, in pediat. gastroenterology and nutrition Am. Bd. Pediat., 1990. Intern, resident in pediat. Stanford U. Med. Ctr., Calif., 1971-74, Internat. Ctr. Med. Rsch. and Tng., Colombia, 1973; postdoctoral fellow pediat. nutrition Johns Hopkins U. Med. Sch., Balt., 1976-78, Nutrition Rsch. Inst., Lima, Peru; postdoctoral fellow in pediat. gastroenterology UCLA, 1978-80, adj. asst. prof. pediat., 1980-82; asst. prof. pediat. Tulane U. Med. Sch., New Orleans, 1982-84; pediat. gastroenterologist City of Hope Med. Ctr., Duarte, Calif., 1984-86; assoc. prof. pediat. and preventative medicine U. Tex. Med. Br., Galveston, 1986-95, prof. pediat., 1995—2009, clin. prof. orthop. surgery, 2010—, mem., med. staff, 2010—12, sci. staff, Shriners Burns Hosp., 2010—; prof. pediat., dir. pediat. nutrition U. Ky., Coll. Medicine & Ky. Pediat. Rsch. Inst., Lexington, 2009—10. Mem. com. revision US Pharmacopeia, Rockville, Md., 1990-2000, chmn. gastroenterology adv. panel, 1990-2005, exec. com. rev., 1995-2000; cons. on malnutrition Nicaraguan Ministry Health, 1992, FDA, NICHD aluminum toxicity in infants, 1996; mem. spl. rev. panel osteoporosis NIH, 1997; spl. govt. cons., FDA, 1998-2006, evaluator NICHD Best Pharm. Children Act, 2010, Best Pharm. Children Act, NICHD, Hematology Working Group, 2011, Rheumatology Working Group, 2012, cons. Abbott Labs, 2002, Novartis, 2012; vis. prof. Okayama U., Kyushu U., Japan, 1996, Baylor Coll. Medicine, Houston, 1999, U. Sheffield, Eng., 2000, Sanjay Gandhi Postgrad. Inst. Med. Scis., Lucknow, India, 2009, Cin. Children's Hosp., U. Cin., 2009, U. Pitts., 2010, Hosp. U. d'Etat Haiti, Port-au-Prince, 2010; invited lectr. Hosp. Necker, Paris, 1991, Columbia U., 1988, 1997, 2014, Harvard U., 1994, 99, 2009, U. Melbourne, U. Sydney, Australia 1995, Japan, 1996, 2003, 2013, China, 1997, 99, 2002, 2009, 2012, 2013 Asian Pacific Osteoporosis Conf. & Internat. Soc. Clin. Densitometry, Beijing, 2009, mem. sci. adv. com. 10th Internat. Conf. Bone & Mineral Rsch. Xian, China, 2012, 11th Internat. Conf. Bone & Mineral Rsch., Guangzhou, China, 2013, Cambridge U., 1981, 2004, 06, Am. Soc. Bone and Mineral Rsch., 2004, 2012, Pediat. Acad. Soc., 2005, NIH, 2005, Oxford U., 2005, 09, 12, Johns Hopkins U., 2000, 2006, 4th Internat. Conf. on Children's Bone Health, 2007, sci. adv. com., 2007, All India Inst. Med. Scis., New Delhi, 2009, 7th Asia Pacific Burn Congress, New Delhi, 2009, Sanjay Gandhi Postgrad. Inst. Med. Scis., King George V Med. Coll., Lucknow, 2009, Internat. Soc. Clin. Densitometry, Beijing, 2009, Asia Pacific Osteoporosis Conf., Beijing, 2009, Red Cross Hosp., U. Cape Town, South Africa, 2010; mem. sci. adv. com. Internat. Osteoporosis Conf., Shanghai, 2002, 10th Internat. Conf. Bone & Mineral Rsch. Xian, 2012, 11th Internat. Confacerer Bone & Mineral Rsch. Guangzhou, Nanchang Third Hosp. Endocrine Conf. Guangdong Pharm. U., China, 2013, US Army Inst. Surg. Rsch., 2006, 2008, 2011, Ajou U. Med. Ctr. Suwon, Republic of Korea, 2013; organizing com. pharmacology and pediat. bone workshop NIH and Am. Soc. for Bone and Mineral Rsch., 2005-, sr. editor proceedings, 2007; combined expert adv. panel Internat. Conf. Children's Bone Health and Internat. Soc. Clin. Densitometry, 2007, mem. editl. bd. F 1000 Rsch., 2012-. Editor: Bone Drugs in Pediatrics, 2014; co-editor: Metabolic Bone Disease in Total Parenteral Nutrition, 1985; co-editor: Current Opinion in Pharmacology: Endocrine and Metabolic Diseases, 2005; mem. internat. adv. bd. Jour. of Bone and Mineral Metabolism, 2005-, mem. editl. bd. Jour. Burns and Wounds, 2006-08, Jour. Bone and Mineral Rsch., 2008-12; contbr. articles to profl. jours. Lt. comdr. USN, 1974—76. Named Clin. Assoc. Physician NIH, 1980-82; recipient Nat. Rsch. Svc. award, 1979-80, Travel award Internat. Conf. Calcium Regulating Hormones, Melbourne, 1995; nominee Howard Hughes Investigatorship in Translational Rsch., 2001; Nutrition Program fellow Project HOPE Nicaragua, 1992, Commdg. Gen. Medallion of Exellence, US Army, 4th Inf. Divsn., San Antonio, Tex, 2006. Fellow Am. Acad. Pediat., Am. Gastroent. Assn.; mem. N.Am. Pediat. Bone and Mineral Working Group (founder, sec.-treas. 1984-85), Soc. for Pediat. Rsch., Am. Soc. Bone and Mineral Rsch. (lectr. 2004, 12, edn. com., 2013-), Am. Soc. Nutrition, Am. Gastroent. Assn., Am. Pediat. Soc., Princeton Club NY, English Speaking Union (mem. exec. bd. Houston br., 2011-14, v.p., 2012). Achievements include development of the Pediatric Bone Disease Initiative with the American Society for Bone and Mineral Research and the NIH; FDA rule governing aluminum contamination of intravenous solutions used for nutrition of hospitialized patients; characterization of the toxic damage of aluminum to bones and liver; characterization of bone loss following burn injury including abnormalities in vitamin D, calcium, parathyroid hormone, prevention of the bone loss; collaborative studies with US Army Institute for surgical research on the effects of combat injury on calcium and bone metabolism; introduction of bone density determinations into the routine diagnostic management of severely burned children. Avocations: travel, reading, horseback riding, music. Personal E-mail: gordonklein@ymail.com.

KLEIN, JERRY LEE, SR., minister, philosophy and religion professor; b. Walters, Okla., Oct. 25, 1947; s. Rudolf Anton and Mable Eula (Elliott) K.; m. Jane Ellen Keeth, Apr. 20, 1969; children: Jerry, Jr., John. AA, Cameron U., 1967; BA, Okla. Christian Univ. of Sci. and Arts, 1969; MA, Harding U., 1974; postgrad., N.Y. Inst., 1988-91, Tex. Tech U., 1994. Instr. Bible, Henderson State Coll., Arkadelphia, Ark., 1970-71; pulpit min. Ch. of Christ, Comanche, Okla., 1971-75; instr. Greek Prairie Hill Sch. of Bible, Comanche, 1974-75; pulpit minister Main St. Ch. of Christ, Lockney, Tex., 1975-82; prof. religion Amarillo (Tex.) Coll., 1982-95, instr. part-time, Philosophy Dept., 1995—2013; dir. Amarillo Bible Chair, 1982-94; min. Comanche Trail Ch. of Christ, Amarillo, 1995—2013; tchr. Bible, Caprock H.S., Amarillo, 1995—96, 2001—02; philosophy & religion prof. Amarillo Coll., 2013—. Edn. dir. Mountain Terrace Ch. of Christ, Memphis, Tenn., 1969-70, San Jacinto Ch. of Christ, Amarillo, 1984-89; campus coun. Amarillo Coll., 1982-94, chaplain, 1990-91; steering com. Amazing Grace Campaign, Amarillo, 1990. Author: (children's songs) Bible Teachers Mailbox, 1988, True Worship, 1989, Training Leaders for Christ II, 1998, rev. edit., 2010, Improve Your English: A Class for Immigrants, 2004; contbr. articles to religious jours. Dir. vols. Ark. Children's Colony, Arkadelphia, 1970-71; bd. dirs. VICA, Tascosa H.S., 1983-94; city chmn. Heart Fund and Kidney Found., Comanche, 1974-75; cubmaster Boy Scouts Am., Lockney, 1978-82; coach Little League Baseball, Lockney, 1978-82; mem. child welfare bd., Floyd County, Tex., 1980-82; bd. dirs. Samaritan Pastoral Counseling Ctr., 1998-99; vol. chaplain Northwest Tex. Hosp., 2005—09; mem. ethics com. Jan Werner Adult Day Care Ctr., Amarillo, 2006—. Recipient spl. citation Ark. Children's Colony, 1971, certs. appreciation Tex. Dept. Health, 1982, Tex. Dept. Human Resources, 1983; named Favorite Prof. Bapt. Student Union, Amarillo Coll., 1989, 93. Mem. Christian Edn. Assn., Soc. Bibl. Lit., Am. Acad. Religion, Lions (pres. Comanche 1974-75), Rotary, Kappa Chi. Republican. Home: 5614 Purdue St Amarillo TX 79109-5823 Office: Comanche Trail Ch of Christ 2700 E 34th Ave Amarillo TX 79103-4700 Personal E-mail: jj_klein@sbcglobal.net.

KLEIN, JOHN E., academic administrator; b. 1945; married. BA, Princeton U., 1967; JD, U. Mich., 1971. Assoc. Sullivan & Cromwell, 1971—75; with Bunge Corp., 1976, v.p., 1981—83, exec. v.p., 1983—85, pres., N.Am., 1985—2004; exec. vice chancellor, adminstrn. Washington U., 2004—07; pres. Randolph College, Lynchburg, Va., 2007—. Bd. dir. Energizer Holdings Inc., 2003—. Office: Randolph College Inc Office of Pres 2500 Rivermont Ave Lynchburg VA 24503-1555 Office Phone: 434-947-8000. Office Fax: 434-947-8134. Business E-Mail: jklein@rmwc.edu.

KLEIN, LINDA ANN, lawyer; d. Gerald Ira Klein and Sandra Florence Fishman; m. Michael S. Neuren. BA cum laude, Union Coll., 1980; JD, Washington and Lee U., Lexington, Va., 1983. Bar: Ga. 1983, 1985, DC 1984, US Dist. Ct. (no. and mid. dist.), US Ct. Appeals (11th cir.) 1986. Assoc. Nall & Miller, Atlanta, 1983—86, Martin, Cavan & Andersen, Atlanta, 1986—90, ptnr., 1990—93; mng. ptnr. Gambrell & Stolz, 1993—2007, Mng. Shareholder Baker Donelson, 2007—. Mem.: ABA (editor Trial Techniques newsletter 1989, vice chmn. trial techniques com. 1989—90, chair 1991—92, vice chair fidelity and surety com. 1994—97, chair ann. meeting 1996—97, coun. tort and ins. practice sect. 1998—2005, chair tort and ins. practice sect. 2003—04, chair com. rules & calendar 2006—08, chair coalition for justice 2006—10, chair House of Dels. 2010—12, mem., Coun. Sect. Internat. Law 2012—, chair ABA Day Com. 2012—14, Margaret Brent Women Lawyers of Achievement award 2004, Edmond Muskie Pro Bono 2009), Am. Law Inst., Coun. of Superior Cts. Judges (ex-officio uniform rules com.), Atlanta Bar Assn. (chair commn. on uniform rules of ct. 1986, bd. dirs. Atlanta Coun. on Young Lawyers 1986—89), Inst. for CLE (chair Ga. br. 1998—2000), Nat. Conf. Bar Pres. (exec. coun. 1998—2001), State Bar Ga. (chair study com. on rules of practice 1987—94, bd. govs. 1989—, exec. com. 1992—99, sec. 1994—96, pres. 1997—98, vice chair profl. liability com., Randolph Thrower Diversity award 2009, Marshall Professionalism award 2011), Pi Sigma Alpha, Phi Alpha Delta. Office Phone: 404-577-6000. Business E-Mail: lklein@bakerdonelson.com.

KLEIN, MARTIN P., insurance company executive; BA in math & bus. adminstrn., Hope Coll., 1981; MS in statistics & actuarial sci., Univ. Iowa, 1983. CFA. Ins. mgmt. positions Providian Corp., 1983—90; mng. dir. capital mgmt. ICH Corp., 1990—92; exec. v.p., CFO ARM Fin. Group, 1992—94; mng. prin. Zurich Ins. Group, 1994—96, mng. dir., 1996—98; sr. v.p. Lehman Bros., 1998—2003, mng. dir. ins. solutions group, 2003—05, pres. Lehman Re subs., 2004—06, mng. dir., head ins. & pension solutions group, 2005—08; mng. dir., sr. relationship mgr. Barclay's Capital, 2008—11; sr. v.p., CFO Genworth Financial, Inc., 2011—, acting pres. & CEO, 2012—. Fellow: Soc. of Actuaries; mem.: Am. Acad. of Actuaries. Office: Genworth Financial 6620 W Broad St Richmond VA 23230

KLEIN, MICHAEL L., oil industry executive; m. Jeanne Klein. BS in petroleum engring., U. Tex., Austin, 1958, LLB, 1963. Founder ind. oil and gas exploration and prodn. co., Midland, Tex. Devel. bd. U. Tex., Austin, mem. press adv. coun.; bd. dirs. Site Santa Fe, Humanities Tex., 2007—; bd. trustees Hirshhorn Mus. and Sculpture Garden, Washington; mem. Longhorn Found. Named one of top 200 collectors, ARTnews Mag., 2003—12. Avocation: postwar and contemporary art collection. Office: Michael L Klein Ste 1230 500 W Texas Midland TX 79701 Office Phone: 432-684-8442. E-mail: mlk@michaellklein.com.

KLEIN, RUSSELL B., marketing executive; m. Lori Klein; 3 children. Grad., Harvard Bus. Sch. Advanced Mgmt. Program. Sr. v.p., exec. officer Dr. Pepper/Seven Up, Inc.; exec. v.p., mng. dir. Foote Cone & Belding Advt., Inc., Chgo.; prin. Whisper Capital, Chgo., 1999—2003; chief mktg. officer 7-Eleven Inc., 2002—03, Burger King Corp., 2003—06, exec. v.p., pres. global mktg., strategy & innovation, 2006—09; chief mktg. officer Arby's Restaurant Group, Inc., 2012—. Bd. dirs. Jackie Robinson Found., Jesse Owens Found. Recipient Distinctive Alumni award, Ohio State U. Max M. Fisher Coll. Bus.; named a Top-100 Marketer, Advt. Age mag. Office: Arbys Restaurant Group 1155 Perimeter Center W Atlanta GA 30338

KLEIN, SCOTT RICHARD, acting and directing educator; b. Aberdeen, SD, June 2, 1959; s. Richard Lewis and Jalois Mae (Janisch) K. BA, Gustavus Adolphus Coll., 1981; MFA, Minn. State U., Mankato, 1983. Actor, tchr. Ark. Arts Ctr., Little Rock, 1983-84; assoc. dir. Permian Playhouse, Odessa, Tex., 1984-89; instr. acting and directing, coach Cameron Univ., Lawton, Okla., 1989-92, asst. prof., 1992, chmn., 1994—, assoc. prof., 1997—2004, prof., 2004—. Directed plays including Echoes, 1983; Vanities, 1985; A.B.C., 1986; Wiley and the Hairy Man, 1988; Night of January 16th, 1988; The Foreigner, 1989; The Barber of Seville, 1991; The Lion in Winter, 1992; Seascape, 1993; Betty the Yeti, 1995; Night Sky, 2002 (ACTF OK I Respondent's Choice Award), A Midsummer Night's Dream, 2006; Almost, Maine, 2010, Grease, 2012; appeared in plays The Glass Menagerie, 1989; Anything Goes, 1989; A Funny Thing Happened, 1989; Charley's Aunt, 1986; The Crucible, 1991; Christopher Columbus: The Gypsy's Fortune, 1992; Guys and Dolls, 2000, 1776, Fiddler on the Roof, 2006, Suesical the Musical!, 2008; The 25th Ann. Putnam County Spelling Bee, 2010; comml. for Kent Kwik, 1987 (Addy Award). Rep., United Way, Lawton, Okla., 1989-2000. Recipient Excellence in Direction award ACTF region V north, 1983; Best Dir. award Kaleidoscope Co., 1988; Alpha Psi Omega, 1990; Outstanding Rsch. Performance, C.U. Sch. Fine Arts, 1994; OK I Excellence in Direction award ACTF, 2001, Okla. Speech Theatre Comm. Theatre Educator of the Yr., 2004; named Vol. of Yr. Arts for All S.W. Okla. Opera Guild, 1997; Vol. of Yr. S.W. Theatre Assn., 2000; Lawton Arts and Humanities Educator in the Arts, 2002, 2013. Mem. Okla. Speech Theatre Comm. Assn. (Theatre Arts Educator Yr. 2004), Okla. Cmty. Theatre Assn. (Jean C Wray award 2011), Tex. Non-Profit Theatres (cons. 1984—, adjudicator 1995, 97-99, 2005, 07, 09), Theatre N. Mex., Am. Assn. Cmty. Theatres(Nat. 2011), Assn. Theatre in Higher Edn., S.W. Theatre Assn. (v.p. promotions 1997-2000, webmaster 2000-05), Okla. Cmty. Theatre Assn., Arts for All, Inc. (bd. dirs. 1996-99), Lawton Cmty. Theatre (bd. dirs. 1995-), Phi Kappa Phi. Avocations: music, dance, reading, movies. Home: 717 N W 36th St Lawton OK 73505-5123 Office: Cameron University 2800 W Gore Blvd Lawton OK 73505-6377 Office Phone: 580-581-2346, 580-581-2480. Business E-Mail: sklein@cameron.edu, srk@fidnet.com.

KLEIN, STEPHEN THOMAS, performing arts executive; b. Cleve., Mar. 9, 1947; s. Howard B. and Lilly (Gatchell) Klein; m. Mary Ussery, Nov. 19, 1972; children: William Howard, Sarah Katherine. BFA, Boston U., 1970. Orch. mgr. Cleve. Orch., 1978—82; exec. dir. Denver Symphony Orch., Colo., 1982—85, Nat. Symphony Orch., Wash., 1985—94; mng. dir. Pitts. Pub. Theater, 1994—2003, Shakespeare Theatre, NJ, 2004—05. Office Phone: 502-562-0100.

KLEINLEIN, KATHY LYNN, training and development executive; b. S.I., NY, May 2, 1950; d. Thomas and Helen Mary (O'Reilly) Perricone; m. Kenneth Robert Kleinlein, Oct. 30, 1983. BA, Wagner Coll., 1971, MA, 1974; MBA, Rutgers U., 1984; MA in Theology, Barry U., 1998; EdD, Grad. Theol. Found., 2004. Cert. secondary tchr., N.Y., N.J., Fla. Tchr. English N.Y.C. Bd. Edn., SI, 1971-74, Matawan (N.J.) Bd. Edn., 1974-79; instr. English Middlesex County Coll., Edison, NJ, 1978-81; med. sales rep. Pfizer/Roerig, Bklyn., 1979-81, mgr. tng. ops. NYC, 1981-86; dir. sales tng. Winthrop Pharms. divsn. Sterling Drug, NYC, 1986-87; dir. tng. Reuters Info. Sys., NYC, 1987—90; pres., dir. tng. Women in Transition, 1990—98; pastoral min., dir. religious edn. St. Raphael's Ch., 1998—2001;

diocesan dir. catechesis & diocesan dir. Safe Environment Tng. & Awareness Diocese of Venice, Fla., 2001—. Pres. Kleinlein Cons.; pers. mgmt. officer USAR, NJ, 1981-86; cons. Concepts & Prodrs., NYC, 1981-85; bd. regents Blessed Edmund Rice Sch. for Pastoral Ministry; bd. dirs. Campaign for Human Devel. Trainer United Way, 1982-83, polit. action com., 1982—85; mem. Rep. Presdl. Task Force, Washington, 1983—; chair Sarasota Library Adv. Bd.; sec. Intracoastal Civic Assn.; reinventing govt. coun. Sarasota County Planning Commn., exec. bd. Edn. Found., St. Joseph Bon Secours Hosp.; grievance com. Fla. Bar; bd. regents Blessed Edmund Rice Sch. for Pastoral Ministry; exec. bd. mem., bd. dirs., Nat. Conf. Catechetical Leaders, 2009-. Mem. Sarasota County Sch. Bd., 2002—10. Capt. US Army, 1974—78. First woman in N.Y. N.G., 1974; first woman instr. Empire State Mil. Acad., Peekskill, N.Y., 1976. Mem.: Sarasota Women's Alliance, Rep. Women's Club, Alpha Omicron Pi. Republican. Roman Catholic. Office Phone: 941-484-9543. Business E-Mail: kleinlein@dioceseofvenice.org.

KLEINMAN, MARK H., oil and gas company executive, lawyer; BA in Govt., U. Tex., 1983, JD, 1986. Bar: Tex. 1986. Asst. gen. counsel Sterling Software, Inc., 1996—2000; v.p. legal Inet Technologies Inc, 2000—01; v.p., gen. counsel, sec. Inet Technologies, Inc., 2001—09; v.p., corp. sec., chief compliance officer Pioneer Natural Resources Co., 2009—. Office: Pioneer Natural Resources Co Ste 200 5205 N O'Connor Blvd Irving TX 75039 Office Phone: 972-444-9001. Office Fax: 972-402-7023.

KLEINSCHMIDT, TIM, state legislator; s. A.P. Kleinschmidt; m. Anna Kleinschmidt; 3 children. Rancher; mem. Lee County Farmers Co-op, Tex.; city atty. Giddings, Tex., Lexington, Tex.; atty. Lee County; mem. Dist. 17 Tex. House of Representatives, 2008—. Mem.: Tex. & Southwestern Cattle Raisers Assn., Lee Co. Bar Assn. (pres.), Tex. Wildlife Assn. Republican. Office: Room E2.814 Capitol Extension PO Box 2910 Austin TX 78768 Address: PO Box 868 Lexington TX 78947 Office Phone: 512-463-0682, 979-542-8037. Office Fax: 512-463-9955.

KLEMM, WILLIAM ROBERT, scientist, educator; b. South Bend, Ind., July 24, 1934; s. Lincoln W. and Helen (DeLong) K.; m. Doris Isabell Mewha, Aug. 27, 1957 (dec.); children: Mark, Laura. DVM, Auburn U., Ala., 1958; PhD, Notre Dame, Ind., 1963. Assoc. prof. dept. physiology and pharmacology Iowa State U., Ames, 1963-66; interim head, prof. dept. biology Tex. A&M U., College Station, 1966-80, neurosci. rschr., 1966—, prof. dept. integrative bioscis., 1980—; K-12 sci. edn. and tchr. tng., 2000—. Mobilization augmentee Human Systems Div. USAF, San Antonio, 1981-89. Author: Animal Electroencephalography, 1969, Science, The Brain & Our Future, 1972; editor: Discovery Processes in Modern Biology, 1977, Brainstem Mechanisms of Behavior, 1990, Understanding Neuroscience, 1995, Dillos, 2007, Core Ideas in Neurosci., 2008, 2013, Blame Game, 2008, Better Grades, Less Effort, 2010, Atoms of Mind, 2011, Memory Power 101, 2012, Mental Biology, 2014. Capt. USAF, 1958-60, Col. Res. ret. Recipient Disting. Alumnus award, 2011. Mem. AAAS (regional pres. 2006-07), Soc. Neurosci., Sigma Xi (pres. Tex. A&M U. chpt. 1990-91, nat. bd. dir. 1997-2000, 2007-10), Nat. Disting (mem. lectr. 2011, disting. mem. 2011). Avocations: jazz, writing. Office: Tex A&M U Dept Vet Integrative Bioscis College Station TX 77843-4458

KLEMPA, ORPHY M., state legislator; b. Wheeling, W.Va., Oct. 9, 1951; m. Mary Jo K. Gray; children: Orphy Michael Jr., Jeremy John, Justin Joseph, Ricki Jo Thompson. AD, W.Va. No. CC, 2004. Coal miner N.Am. Coal, 1970—73; union carpenter for various contractors, 1973—95; union carpenter foreman Eastley and Rivers, Inc., 1980, LM Construction Inc., 1991; bus. rep. Mid-Atlantic Regional Coun. of Carpenters, 1995—; mem. Dist. 3 W.Va. House of Delegates, 2007—10; mem. Dist. 1 W.Va. State Senate, 2011—. Democrat. Roman Catholic. Office: WVa State Senate Rm 204W Bldg 1 State Capitol Complex Charleston WV 25305 also: 5 Locust Ave Wheeling WV 26003 Office Phone: 304-242-9200, 304-357-7918. Business E-Mail: orphy.klempa@wvsenate.gov.

KLEPPINGER, ERIKA L., pharmacist, educator; b. Allentown, Pa., Sept. 11, 1977; PharmD, U. Scis. Phila., 2001. Bd. cert. pharmacotherapy specialist; cert. diabetes educator. Assoc. clin. prof. Auburn U. Harrison Sch. Pharmacy, 2003—. Pharmacy practice resident Temple U. Hosp., 2001—02; ambulatory care pharmacy resident Phila. Coll. Pharmacy, 2002—03. Recipient Preceptor of Excellence, Auburn U. Harrison Sch. Pharmacy, 2005—06, 2009—10, Outstanding Faculty, 2010. Mem.: Am. Edn1. Rsch. Assn., Am. Coll. Clin. Pharmacy, Am. Pharmacists Assn., Am. Diabetes Assn., Am. Assn. Colls. Pharmacy. Office: Auburn University Dept Pharmacy 2131 Walker Bldg Auburn AL 36849 Office Fax: 334-844-4410. Business E-Mail: kleppel@auburn.edu.*

KLESIUS, PHILLIP HARRY, microbiologist, researcher; b. Phila., Mar. 1, 1938; s. Phillip M. and Mary Hoagen (Plummer) K.; m. Patricia Ann Wood, Oct. 31, 1969; children— Stephen, Patrick BS, Fla. So. U., Lakeland, 1961; MS, Northwestern State U., Natchitoches, La., 1963; PhD, U. Tex., Austin, 1966; postgrad., U. Calif.-San Francisco, 1967. Hon. diplomate Am. Coll. Vet. Microbiologists. Asst. prof. microbiology U. Tex., Austin, 1967-68; asst. prof microbiology U. Ariz., Tucson, 1968-72; asst. chief strep sect. USPHS, Fort Collins, Colo., 1972-73; research microbiologist U.S. Dept. Agr., Auburn, Ala., 1973-82, dir., 1982—. Adj. prof. Auburn U., 1974—; adj. assoc. prof. Med. Coll. S.C., Charleston, 1975—; visting prof. Tuskegee Inst., Ala., 1974— Contbr. articles to profl. jours. Recipient Technology Transfer award USDA, 1999; named USDA Scientist of Yr., 1994, 99. Fellow Am. Acad. Microbiology, Am. Assn. Vet. Immunologists (dir. 1985—), Am. Assn. Vet. Pathologists, Am. Assn. Vet. Parasitologists, Am. Soc. Microbiologists. Office: Aquatic Animal Disease Rsch Lab PO Box 952 Auburn AL 36831-0952 Home: 2009 Hillbrook Cir Auburn AL 36830-7657 Business E-Mail: klesiph@vetmed.auburn.edu. E-mail: klesiph@charter.net, pklesius@ars.usda.gov.

KLESSE, WILLIAM R. (BILL KLESSE), energy executive; BS in Chemical Engring., U. of Dayton, 1968; MBA, West Texas State U., 1973. Joined Diamond Shamrock Corp., 1969, sr. v.p./Group Executive, 1989—95, exec. v.p., 1995—96; exec. v.p., Refining, Product Supply and Logistics Ultramar Diamond Shamrock Corp., San Antonio, 1996—98, exec. v.p., operations, 1999—2001; chmn. Shamrock Logistics GP, LLC, 1999—2001; exec. v.p., COO Valero Energy Corp., 2001—05, vice chmn., CEO, 2006—07, chmn., CEO, 2007—08, chmn., pres., CEO, 2008—.*

KLESSEL, LEWIS, investment company executive, retail executive; BS, U. Pa.; MBA, Harvard U. CPA. Sr. auditor Ernst & Young LLP; strategy cons. McKinsey & Co.; various positions, pres. maintenance warehouse, pres., supply's facilities maintenance bus., divisional merchandise mgr., head strategic bus. devel. Home Depot, Inc., 1997—2005; v.p. Guitar Center Holdings, Inc., 2005; operating to managing ptnr. Bain Capital, LLC and Bain Capitol Private Equity, 2005—; interim COO Michael's Stores, Inc., 2012—, interim Office of CEO, 2012—. Bd. dirs. Guitar Center Holdings, Inc. and Guitar Center, Inc., Micheals Stores, Inc., 2006—, Home Depot Supply, Inc., 2009—. Recipient Baker Scholar, Harvard Bus. Sch. Office: Bain Capital LLC 200 Clarendon St Fl 37 Boston MA 02116-5042 Address: Michaels Store Inc 8000 Bent Branch Dr Irving TX 75063-6023 Office Phone: 617-516-2000. Office Fax: 617-516-2010. Business E-Mail: lklessel@baincapital.com.

KLIEFOTH, A. BERNHARD, III, neurosurgeon; b. San Antonio, Nov. 1942; S. Arthur Bernhard, Jr. and Pauline (Gray) K.; m. Ingrid R. Kunde, Apr. 22, 1968; children: Karena, Tanya. AB in Chemistry, Princeton U., 1965; MD, U. Tex. Med. Br., Galveston, 1970. Diplomate Am. Bd. Neurol. Surgery, 1980. Intern Naval Hosp., Oakland, Calif., 1970-71, resident gen. surgery San Diego, 1972-73; neurosurg. tchr. Washington U., St. Louis, 1973-78, chief resident, 1976—77, instr. in neurosurg., 1976—78, rsch. fellow dept. radiation scis., 1977-78; commd. ensign USN, 1969, advanced through grades to comdr., 1977; staff neurosurgeon Naval Regional Med. Ctr., Oakland, 1978-81; capt. USNR, 1985; practice medicine specializing in neurosurgery Knoxville, Tenn., 1981—; mem. staff U. Tenn. Hosp., St. Mary's Hosp., Tennova Regional Med. Ctr.; chmn. dept. surgery, 1989-90; clin. assoc. prof. surgery U. Tenn.; chmn. IRB St Marys, 1984—2008, sec. med. staff, 1990. Bd. dirs. Tenn. Donor Svcs., Cole Neurosci. Found., Knoxville Donor Svcs., Epilepsy Found. Ea. Tenn., vis. prof. Bethesda Naval Hosp./Nat. Naval Med. Ctr. Pres., treas/ Princeton Alumni Assn. Knoxville and Ea. Tenn.; mem. exec. com. West Hills Assn.; treas. Westborough Assn. Commd. ensign USN, 1969, med. officer, radiation safety officer USS Bainbridge DLG (N)-25 USN, 1971—81, with USNR, 1981—96, med. officer in charge reserve unit drs. & nurses PRIMUS. Recipient Disting. Southern Neurosurgeon award, So. Neurosurgery Soc., 2003—. Fellow ACS, Stroke Coun. Am. Heart Assn.; mem. AMA, Am. Assn. Neurol. Surgeons, Am. Soc. Stereotactic and Functional Neurosurgery, Tenn. Neurosurg. Soc., World Soc. Stereotactic and Functional Neurosurgery, Congress Neurol. Surgeons, So. Neurosurg. Soc., So. Med. Assn., Tenn. Med. Assn., Knoxville Acad. Medicine, San Francisco Neurol. Soc., Soc. Med. Cons. to Armed Forces, Assn. Mil. Surgeons U.S., Soc. Neurosci., N. Am. Neuromodulation Assn., Internat. Neuromodulation Assn. Avocations: photography, coin collecting/numismatics, stamp collecting/philately, computers, travel, scuba diving. Office: 6901 Office Park Cir Knoxville TN Address: PO Box 51648 Knoxville TN 37950-1648 Office Phone: 865-524-9400.

KLICER, MILTON RICHARD, diversified financial services company executive; b. NYC, Sept. 26, 1922; s. David and Sadie (Zelikow) K.; m. Ruth Salkind, Jan. 30, 1944 (dec. July 1991); children: Alan S., Sandra F.; m. Gladys Duarte, Sept. 26, 1992. BBA, Bernard Baruch Coll., 1947. Acct. Shipowners Agy. Inc., NYC, 1946-48; chief acct. Am.-Israeli Shipping Co. Inc., NYC, 1948-53; exec. v.p. Maritime Overseas Corp., NYC, 1953-87, also bd. dirs.; CFO, sr. v.p., treas. Overseas Shipholding Group Inc., NYC, 1970-87, also bd. dirs.; pres. OSG Internat. Inc., 1980-87; sr. v.p. Argent Group, Ltd., NYC, 1988-89; pres. Milton Kliger Mgmt. Svcs., Inc., NYC, 1989-93, Marine Equity Corp., NYC, 1990—. Home: 7000 Island Blvd Apt 909 Aventura FL 33160

KLINE, JOHN ALVIN, distinguished professor of leadership; b. Marshalltown, Iowa, July 24, 1939; s. Laurence Alvin Kline and Kathryn White; m. Ann Kline; children: Teri, David, Marc, Nanette, Melissa. BS in English and Speech, Iowa State U., 1967; MS in Speech Comm., U. Iowa, 1968, PhD in Speech Comm., 1970. Sr. exec. service, U.S. Govt. Asst. prof. speech U. N.Mex., Albuquerque, 1970-71; assoc. prof. speech communication U. Mo., Columbia, 1971-75; dean communication skills Air U., Maxwell AFB, Ala., 1975-82, ednl. advisor, 1982-86, sr. exec. provost, 1986—2000, Havard U. JFK Sch. Gov. & Nat. Security Program, 1994; prof. edn. Troy State U., 2000—03, dir. Inst. Leadership Devel., 2003—. Conf. leader; motivational spkr. Author: Guide to Air Force Speaking, 1980, Speaking Effectively, 1989, Listening Effectively, 1996, Listening Effectively: Achieving High Standards in Communication, 2003, Speaking Effectively: Achieving Excellence in Presentations, 2004; contbr. articles to profl. jours. Named Outstanding Tchr. Ctrl. States Speech Assn., 1972, Fed. Employee of Yr. Montgomery Fed. Adminstrs., 1979; recipient Award for Meritorious Civilian Svc., 1985, Decoration for Exceptional Civilian Svc., 1988, Outstanding Civil Svc., 2000, Career Civilian Svc. award, 2000, Internat. Toastmasters award, 2001, Sr. Achievement award, 2004, Ingalls Outstanding Tchrs. award, Troy U., 2009-10, Higher Edn. Partnership award State Ala., 2011, Multistate Toastmasters award, 2011; NDEA Title IV fellow U. Iowa, 1967-70. Mem. Internat. Listening Assn., Speech Comm. Assn., Air Force Assn., Rotary, Phi Delta Kappa, Phi Kappa Phi. Methodist. Office: Inst Leadership Development Troy Univ 260 Smith Hall Troy AL 36082 Business E-Mail: jkline@klinespeak.com, jkline@troy.edu.

KLINE, JOHN WILLIAM, retired military officer, management consultant; b. Zanesville, Ohio, June 26, 1919; s. Gerry William and Lillian Elizabeth (Scheiderer) K.; m. Katherine Edmond Winton, Oct. 24, 1942 (dec. May 23, 2008); children: Susan Isabel (Mrs. John Farris Morehead), Flora Edmond (Mrs. Richard Crandall Creighton), Elizabeth Gerry (Mrs. Paul Sweeney). Student, Ohio U., 1937-40; grad., Primary, Basic and Advanced Flying Schs., 1941, Air Command and Staff Sch., 1949, Air War Coll., 1959; BA, La. Tech. U., 1971. Commd. 2d lt. USAAF, 1941; advanced through grades to maj. gen. USAF, 1968; comdr. (2d Bomb Wing), Hunter AFB, Ga., 1961-63, (397th Bomb Wing), Dow AFB, Maine, 1963-64; dir. operations, chief staff Hdqrs. 8th Air Force, Westover AFB, Mass., 1964-66; vice comdr. 3d Air Div., Andersen AFB, Guam, 1966-68; asst. dep. chief staff ops. Hdqrs. SAC, Offutt AFB, Nebr., 1968-69; vice-comdr. 2d Air Force, Barksdale AFB, La., 1969-72; ret., 1972; v.p., mgmt. cons. Paul R. Ray, Inc., Ft. Worth, 1972—; pres. Mapotec, Inc., Daytona Beach, Fla., 1974, Precision Aerial Surveys, Inc., 1975-85; v.p. ops. Aero Service, Houston, 1976-80, v.p. new ventures and planning, 1980-82. Decorated D.S.M., Legion of Merit with 3 oak leaf clusters, Air medal with oak leaf cluster, Air Force Commendation medal; Air Force Distinguished Service Order Republic Vietnam). Mem. Ft. Sam Houston Golf Club, Guadalajara Golf Club, Beta Theta Pi. Presbyterian. Home: One Towers Park Ln # 912 San Antonio TX 78209-

KLINEDINST, DUNCAN STEWART, lawyer; b. Washington, July 10, 1952; s. David Moulson and Mary Stewart (Coxe) Klinedinst; m. Mary Rose Bartelloni, June 29, 1990; children: Catherine Anne, Caroline Stewart. BA, Washington & Lee U., Lexington, Va., 1974; JD, U. Va. Sch. Law, 1978. Bar: DC 1978, Va. 1987. Investment analyst Riggs Nat. Bank, Washington, 1974-75; assoc. Hogan Lovells US LLP (formerly Hogan & Hartson LLP), Washington, 1978-86, ptnr. McLean, Va., 1987—. Mem. vestry St. John's Episcopal Ch., McLean. Named one of Legal Elite, Va. Bus. Mag., 2005, 2006. Mem.: U. Va. Alumni Assn., Washington & Lee U. Alumni Assn. (chair admissions com. 1983—90, v.p. fraternity coun. 1991—93), Va. Bar Assn., Phi Kappa Psi, Omicron Delta Epsilon, Phi Beta Kappa. Episcopalian. Office: Hogan Lovells US LLP Park Place II Ninth Fl 7930 Jones Branch Dr Mc Lean VA 22102 Office Phone: 703-610-6102. Office Fax: 703-610-6200. E-mail: duncan.klinedinst@hoganlovells.com.

KLINEFELTER, ANNE, law librarian, educator; BA in English and Spanish, U. Ala., 1981, MLS, 1986, JD, 1992. With Law Libr. U. Ala., Boston U.; acting dir. Law Libr. U. Miami; asst. dir. pub. svcs. Katherine R. Everett Law Libr., U. NC Sch. Law, Chapel Hill, 1999—2000, assoc. dir., 2000, dir., 2007—; clin. asst. prof. law U. NC Sch. Law, Chapel Hill, 1999—2005, clin. prof. law, 2005—07, assoc. prof. law, 2007—. Contbr. articles to law jours. Mem.: American Assn. Law Libraries, American Assn. Law Schs. (chair Sect. on Law Libraries). Office: University of North Carolina School Law 3030 Van Hecke-Wettach Hall 160 Ridge Rd, CB #3385 Chapel Hill NC 27599-3385 Office Phone: 919-962-1049. Office Fax: 919-962-1193. E-mail: klinefel@email.unc.edu.

KLINEFELTER, JAMES LOUIS, retired lawyer; b. LA, Oct. 8, 1925; s. Theron Albert and Anna Marie (Coffey) K.; m. Joanne Wright, Dec. 26, 1957 (div.); children: Patricia Anne, Jeanne Marie, Christopher Wright; m. Mary Lynn S. Klinefelter, Aug. 19, 1971; 1 child, Mary Katherine. BA, U. Ala., Tuscaloosa, 1949, LLB, 1951. Bar: Ala. 1951, US Dist. Ct. (no. dist.) Ala. 1959, US Ct. Appeals (11th cir.) 1983. Regional claims rep. State Farm Mut. Auto Ins. Co., Anniston, Ala., 1951-54; ptnr. Burnham & Klinefelter, Anniston, 1954—2003; mem. Sides, Oglesby, Held and Dick, Anniston, 2003—08. Mem. adv. com. Supreme Ct. Ala. Mem. Svc. Core of Retired Execs., Ala. Dem. Exec. Com., 1964—, chmn. legis. rev. com., 1964—; past chmn. Calhoun County Dem. Exec. Com., 1964—; mem. Anniston City Sch. Bd. Lt. (j.g.) USNR, 1943-46. Mem. ABA, Assn. Def. Trial Attys., Ala. Bar Assn. (mem. task force on jud. selection, mem. long-range planning task force), Calhoun County Bar Assn., Ala. Def. Lawyers Assn. (past pres.), Ala. Law Inst. (bd. dirs.), Ala. Sch. Bd. Attys. (past pres.), Internat. Assn. Def. Counsel, Kiwanis (past pres.), Anniston Country Club, Phi Kappa Sigma, Phi Alpha Theta. Avocations: tennis, swimming, reading. Home: 1412 Christine Ave Anniston AL 36207-3924 Personal E-mail: jlk1412@cableone.net, jlk1412@yahoo.com.

KLINGES, VINCENT C., information technology executive; BBA, St. Bonaventure U. Various positions including contr., sales technologies Dun & Bradstreet, Inc., 1986—95; contr. Indus Internat. Inc. (formerly known as TSW Internat. Inc.), 1995—98; v.p., fin. American Software, Inc., 1998—99, CFO, 1999—, Logility, Inc. (subs. of American Software, Inc.), 1999—. Office: American Software Inc 470 E Paces Ferry Rd Atlanta GA 30305 Office Phone: 404-261-4381. Office Fax: 404-264-5514. Business E-Mail: vklinges@amsoftware.com.

KLINGMAN, JOHN PHILIP, architect, educator; b. Phila., July 31, 1947; s. John Philip and Ethel Iva (Serfas) K. BSCE, Tufts U., 1969; postgrad., Stanford U., 1969-70; MArch, U. Oreg., 1983. Registered architect, La. Constrn. coord., project mgr. Payette Assocs., Inc., Boston, 1972-81; mem. design team Fairchild Biochemistry Bldg. Harvard U., 1977—78; project architect LaBouisse & Waggonner Inc. Architects, New Orleans, 1986-89; cons. architect Waggonner & Ball, Inc. Architects, New Orleans, 1990-96; design, planning and preservation U.S. Customhouse, New Orleans, 1996—. Asst. prof. Sch. Architecture Tulane U., New Orleans, 1983-90, assoc. prof., 1990-96, prof., 1996—, Favrot prof., 2002—10, Richard Koch chair, 2010-, assoc. dean, 1991-93; chmn. archtl. rev. com. Historic Dists. Landmarks Commn., 1995—; mem. sustainability subcom., urban planning com. Mayor's Bring New Orleans Back Commn., 2005-06. Author: New New Orleans Architecture, New Orleans Mag., annually, 1997-; co-editor: (with Waggonner & Ball Archs.) Talk About Architecture: A Century of Architectural Education at Tulane, 1993. Recipient GSA Honor award, 1996. Avocation: wood sculpture. Home: 1309 Harmony St New Orleans LA 70115-3424 Office: Tulane U Sch Architecture New Orleans LA 70118 Office Phone: 504-314-2339. Business E-Mail: jklingm@tulane.edu.

KLINKOV, IVO, hotel executive; M in Automation Control Sys., Tech. U., Sofia. Chief engr. Hilton Worldwide, Inc. Office: Hilton Worldwide Inc 7930 Jones Branch Dr Ste 1100 Mc Lean VA 22102 Office Phone: 703-883-1000. Business E-Mail: ivo.klinkov@hilton.com.

KLIPPEL, JOHN H., medical association administrator, physician; BA in Chemistry and Math., magna cum laude, Bowling Green State U., Ohio; MD, U. Cin. Coll. Medicine. Diplomate Am. Bd. Internal Medicine, cert. in rheumatology. Resident internal medicine Yale-New Haven Hosp.; rheumatology fellow NIH, U. Calif., San Diego; clin. dir. Nat. Inst. Arthritis & Musculoskeletal & Skin Diseases, NIH; med. dir. Arthritis Found., Atlanta, 1999—2003, pres., CEO, 2003—. Contbr. articles to profl. jours. Recipient Burroughs-Wellcome Vis. Prof. award, Royal Soc. Medicine, London, Surgeon Gen.'s Exemplary Svc. award, Borden Rsch. award. Fellow: ACP, Am. Coll. Rheumatology; mem.: Omicron Delta Kappa, Phi Eta Sigma, Alpha Omega Alpha. Office: Arthritis Found PO Box 7669 Atlanta GA 30357-0669 Office Phone: 404-965-7671. Business E-Mail: jklippel@arthritis.org.

KLOCK, JOSEPH PETER, JR., lawyer; b. Phila., Mar. 14, 1949; s. Joseph Peter and Mary Dorothy (Fornace) K.; children: Susan Elizabeth, Kathleen Marie, Robert Charles, Peter Joseph II. BA in Philosophy with honors, LaSalle Coll., 1970; JD cum laude, U. Miami, Fla., 1973; DHL (hon.), LaSalle U., 1999. Bar: Fla. 1973, Pa. 1973, D.C. 1978. Ptnr. Steel, Hector & Davis LLP, Miami, Fla., 1977-79, adminstrv. ptnr., 1978-82, chmn., mng. ptnr., 1982—2004, chmn., 2004—05; gen. counsel, chief legal officer Fanjul Corp., 1991—; shareholder Epstein Becker Green, PC, 2007—09; ptnr. Rasco Klock Perez Nieto, 2009—. Adj. prof. U. Miami Law Sch., 1974-84; bd. dirs. Nat. Beverage Corp., 1995-2012, Premier Hotel Corp.; chmn. bd. dirs. Baypoint Sch., Inc.; mem. Fed. Jud. Nominating Com. of Fla., 1993-97. Trustee Belen Jesuit Prep. Sch., St. Joseph's Preparatory Sch., 1998-04, Barry U., Friends of Drug Court Inc., Fundacion Mir, New Hope Charities, Inc.; chmn. bd., trustee Carrollton Sch., 1982-98. Fellow Am. Bar Found.; mem. ABA (chmn. Caribbean law com. internat. law sect. 1991-92), Fla. Bar (chmn. civil procedure rules com. 1979-82), Am. Law Inst., Am. Assn. Sovereign Mil. Order Malta, Iron Arrow Honor Soc., Miami City Club (pres. 1994-97), Phi Alpha Delta, Phi Kappa Phi, Omicron Delta Kappa, Miami Art Mus. (mem. bd. 1995-2004). Democrat. Roman Catholic. Home: 5095 SW 82nd St Miami FL 33143-8503 also: Ste 200 One North Clematis St West Palm Beach FL 33401 Office: 283 Catalonia Ave Coral Gables FL 33134 Office Phone: 305-476-7111, 305-577-2877. Office Fax: 305-675-7707. Business E-Mail: jklock@rascoklock.com.

KLOER, PHILIP BALDWIN, journalist; b. Honolulu, Sept. 13, 1955; s. Baldwin Ernest and Betty Louise (Burger) K.; m. Heather Ann Windsor, May 14, 1976; 1 child, Amanda Cynthia. BA, Ind. U., 1976. Writer Stillwater (Okla.) News-Press, 1976-78; film critic, columnist Fla. Times-Union, Jacksonville, 1978-85; arts editor Atlanta Constitution, 1985—87, TV critic, 1987—2001, pop culture critic, 2001—. Recipient Olive Br. award Ctr. for War, Peace & Media, NYU, 1991, finalist Green Eyeshade award Sigma Delta Chi, 1986, Feature Writing award Am. Assn. Sunday and Feature Editors,

2004; named TV Critic of Yr., Nat. TV Movie Festival, 1990, Critic of Yr., Fla. Soc. Newspaper Editors, 1985. Office: Atlanta Constitution 223 Perimeter Center Pkwy NE Atlanta GA 30346-1301 E-mail: pkloer@ajc.com.

KLOTMAN, PAUL, academic administrator, physician; BS, U. Mich., 1972; MD, Ind. U., 1976. Tng. in medicine and nephrology, faculty mem., assoc. prof. medicine Duke U. Med. Ctr., 1976—83; chief molecular medicine sect. NIH Lab. Devel. Biology, 1988—98; chief NIDR/NIH Viral Pathogenesis Lab., 1993—94; Irene and Dr. Arthur M. Fishberg prof. medicine, chief nephrology divsn. Mt. Sinai Sch. Medicine, 1994—2001, chmn. Samuel Bronfman dept. medicine, 2001—10; pres., CEO Baylor Coll. Medicine, 2010—. Chmn. study sections NIH, Am. Heart Assn., Nat. Kidney Found, VA Rsch. Svc.; bd. mem. on various sci. adv. boards to biotech., pharm. and healthcare companies. Contbr. more than 200 publs. Mem.: Assn. Am. Physicians, Am. Soc. Clin. Investigation. Office: Baylor College Medicine One Baylor Plz Houston TX 77030 Office Phone: 713-798-4951.

KLOTSCHE, CHARLES MARTIN, real estate company executive, photographer, writer, financial columnist; b. Milw., Jan. 30, 1941; s. J.M. and Roberta; m. Christine Klotsche, Feb. 13, 1972; children: Lyna, Kelly, Kay. BA in Econs., Babson Coll., 1962; postgrad., U. Wis., Madison, 1963—64; grad., NY Inst. Finance, 1965; MBA in Fin., U. Wis., Milw., 1968. Account exec. Harris-Upham and Co., 1963-65; head, mgr. Real Estate Comml. Divsn., 1966—68; cons. N.Mex. Dept. Indsl. Devel., 1975—77; chmn. bd. First Equity Corp., 1980—; pres. N.Am. Yachtshares, Inc., 1981—, Pan Am. Publs., Inc., 1982—, Trans Pacific Investments, Inc., 1986—; chmn. bd., CEO Klotsche Properties, Inc., 1983—; pres., CEO Pacific Continental Holdings, Inc., 1992—, Blue Moon Charter Co., 1992—; CEO Pan Am. Press, Inc., 1996—. Adv. dir. Bank of Santa Fe; bd. dirs. Visa Internat. Bank, Granada; lectr. Marquette U., 1967, U. New Mex., 1986, Babson Coll., 1991, U. Calif., Irvine, 1992, Santa Monica Coll., 1993, Fla. Atlantic U., 2002, Explorers Club, 2001, Barnes and Noble Bookstores, Palm Beach, 2001-2003, Four Arts Soc., 2003; featured on NBC Evening News, Dateline, Hardcopy, Voice of Am; exe. dir. Rain Forest Adventures. Author: The Encumbered Perceptive and the Intrepid, 1978, The Real Estate Revolution, 1979, Real Estate Investing, A Practical Guide to Wealth Building Secrets, 1980, Real Estate Syndications, the Complete Handbook, 1983, Real Estate Development and Fin. Handbook, 1986, The 49th Vibration, 1989, Color Vibrational Healing, 1993, Omega Point, 1993, Delta Raven Four, 1994, The Silent Victims, 1997, Continents in the Mist, 1997, How Wall Street Makes Money the Old Fashion Way: They Steal it-, 2004; (screenplays) Capture, 1996, Providence, 1997; (travel) Journeys, 1999, Crossings, 2000, Passages, 2002, Travels with Charlie, 2003, 2d edit., 2005, Good Time Charlie, 2006-, The Predicter Dire Events, 2007, Amazing Voyages, 2008; travel writer Christian Sci. Monitor, 1988, Gannet and Cox Newspapers; fin. columnist Cox Newspapers; featured in popular mags. Bd. dirs. N.Mex. Spl. Olympics for Mentally Retarded, Orch. Santa Fe, Santa Fe Assn. Retarded Citizens, St. Elizabeth Shelter, UN Assn., Fla., U. Wis.-Milw. Found.; pres. Santa Fe Bus. Cmty. for Arts, 1986—, Palm Beach Sailing for the Disadvantaged, Inc., 2003; active Arthritis Found., Mayors for Peace, Music at Bethesda, Voice for the Children, Inc., Palm Beach, Palm Beach Crime Watch, Adopt-A-Minefield, Palm Beach Symphony; active Boys and Girls Club Palm Beach; exec. dir. Globetrotter Marathon Program, Achilles Found., Freedom Team. With Officer Corps USMC, 1964-67. Recipient 3 nat. awards for excellence Nat. Assn. Homebuilders, US Mil. award, Nat. Defense Svc. medal, US Marine Corps Commemorative medal, Frontier Pro Patria Medal. Mem. US Mortgage Brokers Assn., Nat. Assn. Realtors, Fla. Assn. Realtors, Urban Land Inst., N.Mex. Gen. Contractors Assn., Rocky Mountain Outdoor Writers and Photographers Assn., Nat. Gallery Art, Smithsonian, Memorial Sloan, Internat. Assn. Resort Developers, Timesharing Internat., Rotary, Gentlemen of the Garden Soc., Palm Beach Zool. Soc., Palm Beach Civic Assn., Palm Beach Preservation Soc., Vets. for Peace, Am. Vets. Disabled for Life, UN Assn. (pres. Palm Beach chpt.), Circumnavigators Club Internat.(pres. Palm Beach chpt.), Palm Beach Sailing Club, Palm Beach Yacht Club, Palm Beach Theater Guild, Southshore Yacht Club, Milw. Athletic Club, Palm Beach Pundits Club, Sons of Civil War Vets. Club, Soc. of Colonial Wars, World Affairs Coun. of Palm Beach, Fla. Cracker Trail Assn., Humane Farming Assn., Nat. Vets. Found., Iraq and Afghanistan Vets. Am., Miami Press Club, South Fla. Internat. Press Club, Palm Beach Maritime Mus., The Lord's Place of Palm Beach, Habitat for Humanity, Marines Palm Beaches, Boys and Girls Club Palm Beach County, Explorers Club, Sierra Club, Audubon Soc., Nat. Inst. Social Scis., Sci. Mus. Palm Beach, Mental Health Assn. Palm Beach, Arthur Marshall Found., Miami Internat. Press Club, Everglades Found., Heifer Project Internat., Hospice of Palm Beach County, Scripps Inst. Fla, Palm Beach Writers Club. Republican. Lutheran. Office: PO Box 2603 Palm Beach FL 33480-2603 Office Phone: 561-803-0000. Personal E-mail: charlesklotsche@gmail.com.

KLOTTER, JAMES C., historian, educator; b. Lexington, Ky., Jan. 17, 1947; s. John Charles K. and Marjorie Virginia (Gibson) Gabbard; m. Freda Jean Campbell, Dec. 28, 1966; children: Karen, Christopher, Katherine. BA, U. Ky., 1968, MA, 1969, PhD, 1975; LittD, Ea. Ky. U., 1997, Union Coll., 1998. Rsch. analyst Ky. Hist. Soc., Frankfort, 1973-75, asst. editor, 1975-78, mng. editor, 1978-80, state historian, 1980-88, asst. dir., 1988-90, dir., state historian, 1990-98; state historian, prof. history Georgetown Coll., 1998—. Chmn. bd. dir. Farmers State Bank, Booneville, Ky.; bd. dir. Hyden Middlefork Fin., Ky., Ky. Mansion Preservation Found. Author: William Goebel: Politics of Wrath, 1977, co-author: A New History of Kentucky, 1997; editor: Our Kentucky: Study of Blue Grass State, 2000. Sec. Ky. Civil War Roundtable, Lexington, 1984-94, pres. 1994-2007. Mem. So. Hist. Assn., Ky. Assn. Tchrs. History (pres. 1986-87), Ky. Coun. on Archives (chmn. 1980-81), Ky. Oral History Commn. Bd. Office: 400 E College St # 244 Georgetown KY 40324-1628 Business E-Mail: james_klotter@georgetowncollege.edu.

KLUKA, DARLENE ANN, dean, researcher; b. Berwyn, Ill., Oct. 6, 1950; d. Aloysius Louis and Lillian (Malkovsky) K. BA, Ill. State U., 1972, MA, 1976; PhD, Tex. Woman's U., 1985; DPhil, U. Pretoria, South Africa, 2008. Educator, coach Fenton HS, Bensenville, Ill., 1972-73, New Trier East HS, Winnetka, Ill., 1973-80; coach Bradley U., Peoria, Ill., 1980-82; grad. tchg. asst. Tex. Woman's U., Denton, 1982-85; prof. Newberry Coll., SC, 1985-86; prof., rschr., dir. Human Performance Ctr. Grambling State U., La., 1986-90, prof., coord. kinesiology and sport studies, 1997—2005; asst. prof. human studies and sport adminstrn. U. Ala., Birmingham, 1990-94, rschr., dir. Motor Behavior and Sports Vision Lab., 1990-94; dir. grad. program U. Ctrl. Okla., Edmond, 1994-97; dir. Internat. Acad. Women's Leadership Kennesaw State U., Ga., 2006—07; prof. U. Pretoria, 2008—13, extraordinary prof., 2010—13; prof. Barry U., 2008—, dean Sch. Human Performance and Leisure Scis., 2010—. Head del. Internat. Olympic Acad., Olympia, Greece, 1990; dep. del. US Olympic Com., 1996-2000; adv. bd. Women's Sports Found., 1992—; USA Volleyball Sports Medicine and Performance Commn., 1994—; bd. dirs. USA Volleyball, v.p. rels. and human resources, 1996-2000. Author: Visual Skill Enhancement for Sport Exercises, 1989, Volleyball Drills, 1990, Volleyball, 4th edit., 2000, Motor Behavior: From Learning to Performance, 1999; founding co-editor: Internat. Jour. Sports Vision, 1991-97; founding editor: Internat. Jour. Volleyball Rsch., 1997—2007, mem. editl. bd. Coaching Volleyball Jour., 1988-2005. Dir. Internat. Coun. Health, Phys. Edn., Recreation, Sport and Dance Girls and Women in Sport Commn., 1993—2001; mem. La. Gov.'s Coun. on Phys. Fitness and Sports, 2003—05; mem. La. advocacy com. Am. Heart Assn., 2005—06, mem. Ga. advocacy com., 2006—08. Recipient Rsch. award So. Assn. Phys. Edn. Coll. Women, 1994, USA Volleyball Leader award, 1998, Joseph Andera Rsch. award Internat. Acad. of SportsVision, 1999, Disting. Svc. award AAALF Internat. Rels. Coun., 1999, Disting. Achievements award Ill. State U. Alumni Assn., 1997, named to Hall of Fame, Ill. State U., 2010, TWU Disting. Alumni award, 2008, named to NASPE Hall of Fame, 2010; LAHPERD scholar, 1999-2000, Honor award 2002, So. Dist. Honor award 2003; AAHPERD Honor award, 2004; Disting. Scholar in Sport award 1995, Internat. Coun. of Health Physical Edn., Recreation, Sport and Dance. Mem. AAHPERD (rsch. fellow, bd. govs. 1993-96, So. dist. scholar 2001, Ethnic Minority award 2005), AAUP (Disting. scholar award 1997), JOPERD (editl. bd. 2002-05, chair 2004-04), Nat. Assn. for Girls and Women in Sport (bd. dirs., exec. com. 1989-92, 93-96, pres. 1990-91, Honor award 1996), Internat. Coun. for Sport Sci. and Phys. Edn. (exec. bd. 1997-02, treas. 2002-04, editl. bd. 1998-2008, editl. bd. advisor, 2008-, editl. bd. chmn., 2005—08, mem. pres.' com. 2002—08, mem. exec. bd., 2012-, Philip Noel Baker Rsch. award, 2008), Internat. Acad. Sports Vision (adv. bd. 1989-98, v.p. 1993-01), Am. Volleyball Coaches Assn. (mem. editl. bd. Coaching Volleyball Jour., 1988-2004, bd. dirs. 2003—06, chmn. edn. and publs. com. 2003—06, Excellence in Edn. award 1999), IAPESGW (Kluka/Love Young Rsch. Award named in her honor 2001), Am. Volleyball Coaches Assn. (Hall of Fame inductee 2003), Women's Sports Found. (internat. coun. 1993—2012, edn. and rsch. coun. 1995—2012, Pres.'s award 1996, Darlene A. Kluka rsch. award named in her honor 2001), Internat. Assn. Phys. Edn. and Sports Girls and Women, Girls and Women in Sport (bd. cons. 2000—06, 09-13, exec. bd. mem., 2013-, pres. 2005—09, chair), Commn. Sport Mgmt. Accreditation (bd. commr. 2013-). Roman Catholic. Avocation: photography. Office: Sch Human Performance and Leisure Scis Barry University 11300 NE 2nd Ave Miami Shores FL 33161 Office Phone: 305-899-3549. Business E-Mail: dkluka@barry.edu.

KLUTZ, ANTHONY ALOYSIUS, JR., health, safety and environmental manager; b. Wilkes-Barre, Pa., Dec. 2, 1954; s. Anthony A. Klutz and Matilda (Konopka) Weigand; m. LetaMarie A. Rydzewski, July 15, 1978; children: Athena Marie, Anthony A. III. BS, Kings Coll., Wilkes-Barre, 1976; MS, Rensselaer Poly. Inst., 1978; MBA, Clemson U., 1988. Material devel. engr. Sangamo Capacitor-Schlumberger, Pickens, S.C., 1978-87, product devel. engr., 1986-87; mgr. process engring. Sangamo Weston-Schlumberger, West Union, S.C., 1987-90; safety and environ. mgr. Schlumberger Industries, West Union, 1990-94, health, safety and environ. mgr. Electricity N.Am., 1994-98, health, safety environ. N. Am., 1998—; health, safety, environ. and main tenance dir. Itron, Spokane, Wash., 2005—. Vice chmn. Oconee County Local Emergency Planning Com., Walhalla, S.C., 1988—; mem. coun. Holy Cross Parish, Pickens, 1986-87. Mem. Am. Vacuum Soc., Electro Chem. Soc., Am. Soc. Materials, S.C. C. of C. (tech. com.), Mgmt. Club (pres. 1985, 92, v.p. 1991), KC (Knight of Mo. award Pickens 1988, Grand Knight 1994-97). Avocations: reading, computing, travel. Office: Sangamo Weston-Schlumberger Hwy 11 West Union SC 29696-9610 Home: 26705 E Maddie Ln Newman Lake WA 99025-8527

KNAPP, CHARLES BOYNTON, economist, former university president, educator; b. Ames, Iowa, Aug. 13, 1946; s. Albert B. and Anne Marie (Taff) K.; m. Lynne Vickers, Aug. 25, 1967; 1 dau., Amanda. BS, Iowa State U., 1968; MA, PhD, U. Wis., 1972. Asst. prof. econs., research assoc. Ctr. for Study of Human Resources, U. Tex., Austin, 1972-76; spl. asst. to Sec. of Labor Dept. Labor, Washington, 1977-79, dep. asst. sec. labor, 1979-81; assoc. prof. pub. policy George Washington U., 1981-82; assoc. prof. econs. Tulane University, New Orleans, 1982-87, sr. v.p., 1982-85, exec. v.p., 1985-87; pres., prof. econs. University of Georgia, Athens, 1987-97, pres. emeritus, 2005—; pres. Aspen Inst., 1997-99; ptnr. Heidrick & Struggles International, Inc., Atlanta, 2000—04; dir. ednl. devel. CF Found., Inc., Atlanta, 2004—. Bd. dirs. AFLAC Inc. Contbr. articles to profl. jours. Office: CF Found Inc 3445 Peachtree Rd NE Ste 175 Atlanta GA 30326 Business E-Mail: cknapp@cffdn.org.

KNAPP, MARK LANE, communications educator, consultant; b. Kansas City, Mo., July 12, 1938; s. Herbert H. and Mary Ellen (Coleman) K.; m. Cynthia Lackie Dennis, Jan. 27, 1963 (div. Aug. 1974); children: Hilary A. Cellard, Eric C.; m. Lillian J. Davis, Aug. 8, 1975 (div. July 2002; 1 child, Avery K. Davis. BS, U. Kans., 1962, MA, 1963; PhD, Pa. State U., 1966. From instr. to asst. prof. U. Wis., Milw., 1965-70; from assoc. prof. to prof. Purdue U., West Lafayette, Ind., 1970-80; prof. SUNY, New Paltz, NY, 1980-83; disting. vis. prof. U. Vt., Burlington, 1983; vis. prof. U. Tex., Austin, 1983-85, sr. lectr., 1985-87, prof., 1987-89, Jesse H. Jones Centennial prof. in comm., 1989—, U. Tex. Disting. Tchg. prof., 1999—2007, prof. emeritus, 2007—. Cons., lectr. in field. Author: Nonverbal Communication in Human Interaction, 1972, 6th edit. (with J. Hall), 2005, Japanese edit., 1979, Spanish edit., 1980, Chinese edit., 1999, Portuguese edit., 1999, Polish edit., 2000, Russian edit., 2004, Social Intercourse: From Greeting to Goodbye, 1978, Essentials of Nonverbal Communication, 1980, Interpersonal Communication and Human Relationships, 1984, 6th edit. (with A. Vangelisti), 2009, (with J.C. McCroskey and C.E. Larson), An Introduction to Interpersonal Communication, 1971; editor: (with G.R. Miller) Handbook of Interpersonal Communication, 1985, 2d edit., 1994, 3d edit. (with J.A. Daly), 2002, Lying and Deception in Human Interaction, 2007, (with M. McGlone) The Interplay of Truth and Deception, 2009; contbr. articles to profl. jours., chpts. to books. With U.S. Army, 1957-59. Recipient Outstanding Young Tchr. award Ctrl. States Speech Assn., 1969; Ea. Comm. Assn. scholar, 1982-83. Fellow Internat. Comm. Assn. (pres. 1975-76); mem. Nat. Comm. Assn. (pres. 1989-90, Golden Anniversary award 1974, Disting. Scholar award 1993, Robert J. Kibler Meml. award 1993, Ecroyd award 2004), Assn. Comm. Adminstrs. (pres. 1997), Coun. Comm. Assns. (vice chair 1997). Achievements include research in interpersonal communication, nonverbal communication, communication in developing and deteriorating relationships, lying and deception, communication and the process of aging, communication behavior in organizational settings. Office: U Tex Dept Comm Studies Austin TX 78712 Office Phone: 512-471-3787. Business E-Mail: mlknapp@mail.utexas.edu.

KNAPP, RICHARD DAVID, psychiatrist, educator; BS in Biology, Fairleigh Dickinson U., NJ, 1967; DO, Phila. Coll. Osteo. Medicine, 1971. Lic. Fla., 1978, diplomate Am. Bd. Psychiatry and Neurology-psychiatry, 1985, Am. Bd. Psychiatry and Neurology-addiction psychiatry, 1993. Intern Tri-County Hosp., 1972; resident psychiatry Belmont Behavioral Health (formerly Phila. Psychiat. Ctr.), Phila., 1972—75; pvt. practice gen. medicine Miami, Fla., 1979—82; clin. dir. adolescent substance abuse program Humana Hosp. South Broward, Hallandale, Fla., 1982—86; pvt. practice gen., geriatric and addictions psychiatry Miami, Fla., 1982—86; asst. assoc. clin. prof. Coll. Osteo. Medicine Nova Southeastern Univ., Miami, Fla., 1983—94; pvt. practice gen., geriatric and addictions psychiatry Hollywood, Fla., 1986—2001; prin. investigator Fla. Clin. Rsch. Ctr. LLC, 2001—; hosp. affiliations includes Meml. Regional Hosp. Office: Memorial Regional Hospital 3501 Johnson St Hollywood FL 33021 Office Phone: 954-961-1500.

KNAUSS, ROBERT LYNN, corporate financial executive; b. Detroit, Mar. 24, 1931; s. Karl Ernst and Loise (Atkinson) K.; m. Angela Tirola Lawson, Feb. 21, 1973; children by previous marriage: Robert B., Charles H., Katherine E.; 1 stepson, Ian T. Lawson. AB, Harvard U., 1952; JD, U. Mich., 1957. Bar: Calif., Tenn., Tex. Assoc. Pillsbury, Madison & Sutro, San Francisco, 1958-60; prof. law U. Mich., 1960-72, v.p. student svcs., 1970-72; dean, prof. law Vanderbilt U., Nashville, 1972-79; dean U. Houston Law Ctr., 1981-93, disting. univ. prof. Vis. prof. Vt. Law Sch., South Royalton, Amos Tuck Sch. Bus. Adminstrn., Dartmouth Coll., Hanover, NH, 1979—81; chmn., CEO Baltic Internat. USA/Inc., 1994—2003; chmn., prin. exec. officer Phillips Svcs. Corp., 2002—03; dir., non-exec. chmn. Equus Total Return, Inc., 2010—, Wild Life Mgmt., 1998—; former dir. Nine Pub. Cos. Editor: Small Business Financing, 4 vols., 1966, Securities Regulation Sourcebook, 1970-71, (with others) Cases and Materials on Enterprise Organizations, 1987; contbr. articles to profl. jours. Regent Nat. Coll. Dist. Attys., 1981-95. Lt. (j.g.) USN, 1952-55. Fellow Tex. Bar Found., Am. Bar Found; mem. Calif. Bar Assn., Tenn. Bar Assn., Tex. Bar Assn. (chmn. corp. coun. sect. 1991), Am. Law Inst. (life), Order of Coif. Home: PO Box 40 5580 FM 1697 ThreeCreek Ranch Burton TX 77835-0040 Office Phone: 979-289-4000. Personal E-mail: bobknauss@cs.com.

KNEDLIK, RONALD W., retail grocery distributing executive; b. Charlotte, NC, Feb. 20, 1949; m. Anita T. Knedlik; children: Courtney, Nathan. BS in Acctg., U. N.C., 1971; MBA, Wake Forest U., 1982. Staff acct. Strand, Skees, Jones & Co., Greensboro, N.C., 1971-74; contr. Mchts. Distbrs., Inc., Hickory, NC, 1974—80, v.p., fin., 1980—87, sr. v.p. fin., adminstrn., 1987—92, Alex Lee, Inc., Hickory, NC, 1992, exec. v.p., CFO, 1992—. Bd. dirs. Instn. Food House, Inc., Hickory, Lowe's Food Stores Inc., Winston-Salem, N.C., Mchts. Distbrs., Inc., Hickory. Bd. dirs. Family Guidance Ctr., Hickory, 1993-95, Catawba Sci. Ctr., Hickory, 1995—. Mem. AICPA, N.C. Assn. CPAs, N.C. Real Estate Brokers, Catawba County C. of C. (bd. dirs. 1988-90). Office: Alex Lee Inc 120 4th St SW Hickory NC 28602 Office Fax: 828-725-4435. Business E-Mail: rknedlik@alexlee.com.

KNEE, STANLEY LA MOYNE, security firm executive, former police chief; married; 4 children. B in Criminal Justice, Calif. State U., Fullerton, 1977; grad., FBI Nat. Acad., 1982, Calif. Peach Officers Stds. and Tng. Command Coll., 1986; M in Criminal Justice, Calif. State U., Long Beach, 1987. From patrol officer to field sgt. Garden Grove Police Dept., Calif., 1969-78, lt., 1978-81, capt., 1981-88, chief police, 1992-97, Nat. City Police Dept., Calif., 1988-92, Austin Police Dept., Tex., 1997—2006; head security Seton Family of Hospitals, 2010—. Instr. Calif. State U., Fullerton, 1993-97; guest lectr. in field; cons. to various orgns. Lt. U.S. Army, 1967-69, Vietnam. Decorated 2 Bronze Stars; recipient Svc. Appreciation award Orange County Korean C. of C., 1992, Outstanding Pub. Adminstr., Orange County chpt. Am. Soc. Pub. Adminstrn., 1994, Humanitarian award Orange County Human Rels. Commn., 1995, Cmty. Svc. award Orange County chpt. 100 Black Men, 1996, Cmty. Svc. Support award Garden Grove Interfaith Coun., 1997. Mem. Internat. Assn. Chiefs of Police, Police Exec. Rsch. Forum, Major City Chiefs Assn., FBI Nat. Acad., Tex. Police Chief's Assn., Command Coll. Alumni Assn., Law Enforcement Intelligence Unit. Office: Seton Family of Hospitals 601 E 15th St Austin TX 78701 Fax: 512-480-5279.

KNEISEL, EDMUND M., lawyer; b. Atlanta, Feb. 21, 1946; s. John F. and Mary E. (Moore) K.; m. Leslie A. Jones, June 19, 1976; 1 child, Mary Kathleen. AB, Duke U., 1968; JD, U. Ga., 1974. Bar: Ga. 1974, U.S. Dist. Ct. (no. and mid. dists.) Ga., U.S. Ct. Appeals (1st, 2d, 4th, 5th, 6th and 11th cirs.), U.S. Supreme Ct. 1984. Law clk. to Hon. R.C. Freeman U.S. Dist. Ct. (no. dist.) Ga., Atlanta, 1974-76; assoc. Kilpatrick & Cody, Atlanta, 1976-82; ptnr. Kilpatrick Townsend & Stockton LLP, 1982—2013, of counsel, 2014—. Mng. editor Ga. Law Rev., Athens, 1973-74; contbr. articles to profl. jours. Lt. USNR, 1968-71. Mem. ABA, Lawyers Club Atlanta, Druid Hills Golf Club. Office: Kilpatrick Townsend & Stockton LLP 1100 Peachtree St NE Ste 2800 Atlanta GA 30309-4530 Office Phone: 404-815-6500. Business E-Mail: ekneisel@kilpatricktownsend.com.

KNELLER, MICHAEL K., transportation services executive; m. Andrea DeFlorio. BA, Yale U., 1996; JD, Stanford U., 2000. V.p., gen. counsel, sec. Landstar System, Inc., Jacksonville, Fla., 2005—. Mem.: ABA, Fla. Bar Assn., NY State Bar Assn. Office: Landstar Sys Inc 13410 Sutton Pk Dr S Jacksonville FL 32224 Office Phone: 904-398-9400. Office Fax: 904-306-2539.

KNESEK, MICHAEL JOHN, energy executive; b. Corpus Christi, Tex., July 11, 1954; s. Johnny Louis and Peggy Lou (Rektorik) K.; m. Ellen Clarissa Waters, June 19, 1976; children: Brian Michael, Kristin Marie. CPA Tex. Acctg. supr. Union Tex. Petroleum Corp., Houston, 1976-81; acctg. mgr. to contr. Enterprise Cos., Inc., Houston, 1981—90, v.p., contr., 1990; v.p., contr., prin. acctg. officer Enterprise Products GP and EPCO, Houston, 2000—05, sr. v.p., contr., prin. acctg. officer, 2005—, Enterprise GP Holdings, LP, Houston, 2005—. Freelance acct., Houston, 1986. Mem. AICPA, Tex. Soc. CPAs. Republican. Lutheran. Avocations: water-skiing, skiing, jogging, racquetball. Office: Enterprise GP Holdings LP PO Box 4323 Houston TX 77210-4323 Office Phone: 713-381-6500.

KNESEL, ERNEST ARTHUR, JR., health facility administrator, chemicals executive; b. New Orleans, Dec. 11, 1945; s. Ernest Arthur and Catherine Charlotte (Maier) K.; m. Lavina Lynn Menge, June 2, 1968; children: Eric Ernest, Tami Lynn, Bradley William. Student, Armstrong Coll., 1963—64; BS, Fairleigh Dickinson U., 1968, MS, 1970. Cert. clin. chemist. Technologist Am. Biol. Control Lab., Tenefly, NJ, 1966—68; sr. technologist Englewood Hosp., NJ, 1968—69; founder, v.p. Biomed. Reference Labs., Inc., Burlington, NC, 1969—82; sr. v.p. Roche Biomed. Labs., Inc., Burlington, 1982—95; pres., founder Roche Image Analysis Sys., Inc., Elon College, NC, 1989—96; exec. v.p., founder Autocyte, Inc., Elon College, 1996—99; v.p., founder TriPath Imaging, 1999—2000; cons. True North Group, 2000—01; founder, pres. Select Diagnostics Inc., 2001—11; co-founder, pres. Select Lab. Ptnr., 2003—10. Founder, mgr. CellSolutions LLC, 2007—, Select Labs. SC, 2007—; chmn., pres. Select Labs. Ptnrs., Inc., 2010—. Inventor serum filter/dispenser vial, automated aliquoting system, cyto-rich automated cytology preparation system and simultaneous machine and human interactive cytology evaluation system, Cell Solution 120 high capacity thin-layer cytology preparation system, Cell Solution 30 and BestCyte Imaging System. Mem. Am. Assn. Clin. Chemistry, Am. Soc. Clin. Pathologists (assoc.). Roman Catholic. Avocation: magic. Office: Select Lab Ptnrs Inc 1100 Revolution Mill Dr # 1 Greensboro NC 27405

KNEUER, JOHN M.R., information technology executive, former federal agency administrator; b. 1968; BA, JD, Cath. U. Am. Bar: DC. Atty. advisor comml. wireless divsn. wireless telecomm. bur. FCC,

1996—97; dir. govt. rels. Indsl. Telecomm. Assn., 1997—98; sr. assoc. DLA Piper Rudnick, LLP; dep. asst. sec. for comm. & info. US Dept. Commerce, 2004—05, acting asst. sec. for comm. & info., 2006, asst. sec. for comm. & info., 2006—08; counselor to asst. sec. Nat. Telecom. & Info. Adminstrn. (NTIA), 2003—04, dep. adminstr., 2004—05; adminstr. Nat. Telecom. & Info. Adminstrn., 2006—07; v.p. for strategic planning & external affairs Rivada Networks, Washington, 2007—. Office: Rivada Networks PO Box 76 Centreville VA 20122-0076 Office Phone: 202-482-1840. Office Fax: 202-501-0536.

KNICKEL, CARIN S., oil industry executive; b. Powell, Wyo., 1956; BA in Mktg. & Statistics, U. Colo., 1978; M in Mgmt., MIT. Mktg. account mgr. ConocoPhillips, 1979—87, area dir. light oil sales product supply and trading, 1987, gen. mgr. bus. develop. for refining and mktg. in Europe London, gen. mgr. refining, mktg., and transp., pres. specialty bus. divsn., 2001—03, v.p. human resources, 2003—. Chmn. rodeo run com. ConocoPhillips; bd. dirs. Colo. Spl. Olympics. Office: ConocoPhillips 600 N Dairy Ashford Rd PO Box 2197 Houston TX 77079

KNIFFEN, BENNIE G., corporate financial executive; BBA in Acctg., Hardin-Simmons U.; MBA in Acctg., U. of North Tex. CPA. Dir., auditing Southland Royalty Co., 1976—86; sr. v.p., contr. XTO Energy, Inc., 1986—. Office: XTO Energy Inc 810 Houston St Fort Worth TX 76102-6298 Office Phone: 817-870-2800. Office Fax: 817-870-1671. Business E-Mail: Bennie_Kniffen@xtoenergy.com.

KNIGHT, BARRY D., state legislator; b. Sept. 26, 1954; m. Paula Jane Whitehurst; children: K. Hunter, Kyle, Forrest. Farmer; v.p. Virginia Beach Farm Bur.; mem. Dist. 81 Va. House of Delegates, 2009—. Recipient Chowan River Basin Clean Water Farm Award, 1999; named Virginia Beach Man of the Year in Agr., 1998. Republican. Office: 1852 Mill Landing Rd Virginia Beach VA 23457 also: General Assembly Bldg PO Box 406 Richmond VA 23218 Office Phone: 757-426-6387, 804-698-1081. Fax: 804-698-6781. E-mail: DelBKnight@house.virginia.gov.

KNIGHT, DAVID, state legislator; m. Marie Harvey. Degree in Acctg., U. Ga.; attended, Augusta Coll. State rep. Dist. 126, Ga., 2005—. Republican. Baptist. Mailing: 411 Legis Off Bldg Atlanta GA 30334

KNIGHT, GARY, lawyer, writer, educator; b. St. Joseph, Mo., Dec. 8, 1939; s. Herbert S. and Iris (Crawford) K.; m. Rebecca Emelie Forrester, Nov. 24, 1962; children: Kevin Crawford, David Forrester, Jonathan Gary. Student, Westminster Coll., 1957-59; AB in Polit. Sci., Stanford U., 1961; JD, So. Meth. U., 1964. Bar: Calif. 1965. Assoc. Nossaman, Thompson, Waters and Moss, LA, 1964-68; mem. faculty La. State U. Law Center, Baton Rouge, 1968-85, assoc. prof., 1971-75, prof. law, 1975-85, Campanile prof. marine resources law, 1971-85; owner Jonathan Pub. Co., 1981—2010. Adv. com. on law of sea Nat. Security Council Inter-Agy. Law of Sea Group, 1972-81; cons. CIA, 1977-85; mem. Gulf of Mex. Fishery Mgmt. Coun., 1981-84. Author: The Future of International Fisheries Management, 1975, Managing the Sea's Living Resources, 1977, The International Law of the Sea: Cases, Documents and Readings, 1991, Marine Fisheries Management Reporter, 1981-94; assoc. editor: Ocean Development and International Law: A Jour. of Marine Affairs, 1972-85. Trustee Wimberley Village Libr. Dist., 2005—, pres., 2007—; bd. dirs. Wimberley Edn. Found., 2006—10, pres., 2007—08. Mem. ABA (com. on law of sea 1971-80, com. marine resources 1967-71), Am. Soc. Internat. Law (bd. rev. and devel. 1975-80, panel on law of sea 1972-80), Internat. Law Assn. (com. on law of sea 1974-81), Law of Sea Inst. (exec. bd. 1975-81), Order of Coif, Phi Alpha Delta, Omicron Delta Kappa, Beta Theta Pi.

KNIGHT, JOHN F., state legislator; b. June 7, 1945; children: Tamara, Tehrik. BS in Bus. Adminstrn. with honors, Ala. State U., Montgomery, 1974. Dir. comm. & pub. affairs Ala. State U., spl. asst. to the pres.; mem. Dist. 77 Ala. House of Reps., Montgomery, 1993—. Chmn. Montgomery County Dem. Conf.; mem. Montgomery County Dem. Exec. Com.; bd. dirs. Kershaw YMCA, Cleveland Ave. YMCA, Montgomery Housing Authority, Ret. Sr. Vol. Program, Montgomery Improvement Assn., Family Sunshine Ctr., Southern Devel. Coun., Inc. Served with US Army, Vietnam. Mem.: NAACP, Leadership Ala. & Montgomery. Democrat. Methodist. Office: PO Box 6300 Montgomery AL 36106 also: Ala House of Reps Ala State House 11 S Union St Rm 516-A Montgomery AL 36130 Office Phone: 334-229-4286, 334-242-7660.

KNIGHT, PAT (PATRICK KNIGHT), men's college basketball coach; b. Sept. 21, 1970; s. Robert Montgomery and Nancy Lou Knight; m. Amanda Shaw, May 10, 2002. Grad. in Sports Mgmt., Ind. U., Bloomington, 1995. Adminstrv. asst., scout Phoenix Suns, 1995—97; asst. coach Conn. Pride, 1997; head coach Wis. Blast, 1998; asst. coach Ind. U. Hoosiers, 1999—2000, U. Akron Zips, 2000—01, Tex. Tech. U. Red Raiders, 2001—08, head coach, 2008—11, Lamar U. Cardinals, 2011—. Office: Lamar University Mens Basketball 211 Redbird Ln Beaumont TX 77710 Office Phone: 409-880-8301.

KNIGHT, PATSY G., state legislator; b. Conway, SC, Dec. 09; d. B. C. and Margaret Anderson Gleaton; m. Roy Al (dec.); children: Mary Margaret Riser, Laura Ann Schipmann. Treas. Dorchester County, SC, 1981—2006; mem. Dist. 97 SC House of Reps., 2007—. Recipient L.H. "Sonny" Siau award, 2004. Mem.: Women League Voters, Tri-County C. of C., Summerville Dorchester C. of C., America Bus. Women's Assn. St. George, Dorchester Ducks Unlimited, Indian Field United Methodist Ch. Democrat. Mailing: PO Box 673 Saint George SC 29477 Office: 306B Blatt Building Columbia SC 29201 Office Phone: 803-734-2960. E-mail: KnightP@schouse.org.

KNIGHT, WALKER LEIGH, publishing executive, minister; b. Henderson, Ky., Feb. 6, 1924; s. Cooksey Bennett and Rowena (Henderson) K.; m. Iva Nell Moseley, Nov. 10, 1943; children: Walker Leigh, Kenneth Wayne, Nelda Denise, Emily Jill. BA, Baylor U., 1949. Ordained min. Bapt. Ch., 1948. Reporter Henderson Gleanor and Jour., 1942; pastor in Dale, Tex., 1948-49; editor Falls County Record, Marlin, Tex., 1948-49; assoc. editor Bapt. Std., Dallas, 1950-59; editl. dir. So. Bapt. Home Mission Bd., Atlanta, also editor Missions U.S.A. mag. and Atlanta bur. chief Bapt. Press News Service, 1959-83; editor, pub. Bapts. Today (formerly SBC Today), 1983-89, pub., 1989-93, pub. emeritus, 1994—. Author: Panama, The Land Between, 1965, Struggle for Integrity, 1969, See How Love Works, 1971, Seven Beginnings, 1976, Chaplaincy, Love on the Line, 1978, Tell the People, 1986, From Zion to Atlanta Memories, 2013; contbr.: Southern Baptists Observed, 1992, Struggle for the Soul of the SBC, 1993; editor: The Whitsitt Jour., 1995-98. With USAAF, 1943-45. Home: 341 Winn Way Apt 211 Decatur GA 30030-2107 Personal E-mail: wleighknight@comcast.net.

KNOLL, JEANNETTE THERIOT, state supreme court justice; b. Baton Rouge; m. Jerold Edward Knoll; children: Triston Kane, Eddie Jr., Edmond Humphries, Blake Theriot, Jonathan Paul. BA in Polit. Sci., Loyola U., 1966; JD, Loyola U. Sch. of Law, 1969; LLM in Jud. Process, U. Va. Sch. of Law, 1996; studied with Maestro Adler, Mannes Coll. of Music, 1962-63. Criminal defense atty., first asst. dist. atty. Twelfth Jud. Dist. Ct. Avoyelles Parish, 1972-82; gratuitous atty., advisor U.S. Selective Svc., Marksville, La.; judge (3d cir.) U.S. Ct. of Appeal, 1982-93; assoc. justice La. Supreme Ct., 1997—. Instr. La. Jud. Coll.; chair CLE La. Ct. of Appeal Judges; former mem. state bd. of La. Commn. on Law Enforcement & Criminal Justice; former mem. Past pres. Bus. and Profl. Women's Club; Marksville C. of C.; active Am. Legion Aux.; dir. Arts & Humanities Council of Avoyelles, Inc.; former chmn. La. March of Dimes. Recipient Met. Opera Assn., New Orleans Opera Guild Scholarship, Outstanding Jud. award, Victims & Citizens Against Crime, Inc., 1995, 2002; named La. Crimefighters' Outstanding Jurist of Yr., 2000; named to La. Political Hall of Fame, 2000. Mem.: La. State Bar Assn. Office: La Supreme Ct 400 Royal St New Orleans LA 70130*

KNOTTS, JOHN MILTON, JR., (JAKE KNOTTS), state legislator; b. West Columbia, SC, Dec. 12, 1944; s. John Milton (Stepmother) and Dovereen Jessie Williams Knotts; m. Betty Lee Bodie, 1989; children: Michelle Nicole, Tara Marie. BA, U. SC, 1982. Officer, detective & investigator Columbia Police Dept., 1968—96; certified firearms instr., 1996—; mem. Dist. 88 SC House of Reps., 1995—2002; mem. Dist. 23 SC State Senate, 2003—, chair Invitations Com. Mem.: 40 & 8 Legionnaire, Mason, America Legion, Boy Scouts (chmn.). Republican. Address: 500 W Dunbar Rd West Columbia SC 29169 Office: 303 Gressette Bldg PO Box 142 Columbia SC 29201 Home Phone: 803-755-6350; Office Phone: 803-212-6350. E-mail: SIV@scsenate.org.

KNOUS, PAMELA K., apparel executive, former food service company executive; b. Minn., 1954; Student, Carleton Coll.; BA in Math., U. Ariz., 1976, BS in Bus. Adminstrn., 1976. With KPMG Peat Marwick, L.A., Calif., 1977—89, ptnr., 1989—91; v.p. finance, contr. The Vons Companies, Inc., 1991—94, group v.p. finance, contr., 1994, sr. v.p., CFO, 1994—95, exec. v.p., CFO, treas., 1995—97; exec. v.p., CFO Supervalu Inc., Eden Prarie, 1997—2010; exec. v.p., CFO, chief acctg. officer Chico's FAS, Inc., Fort Myers, Fla., 2011—. Bd. dirs. Tennant Co., 1998—2007. Office: Chico's FAS Inc 11215 Metro Pkwy Fort Myers FL 33966

KNOWLES, BEYONCÉ GISELLE, singer, actress; b. Houston, Sept. 4, 1981; d. Matthew and Tina (Beyincé) Knowles; m. Shawn Corey Carter (Jay Z), Apr. 4, 2008; 1 child, Blue Ivy Carter. Mem. Destiny's Child, 1997—2005; solo artist, 2003—. Spokesperson L'Oreal, Pepsi, Nintendo, Vizio; launched Tommy Hilfiger's True Star fragrance, 2004, True Star Gold, 2005, Emporio Armani Diamonds, 2007, women's fragrance Beyoncé Heat, 2010; launched (with Tina Knowles) House of Dereon fashion line, 2005, Sasha Fierce for Deréon, 2009, Deréon by Beyoncé for C&A clothing stores, 2010. Singer: (albums with Destiny's Child) Destiny's Child, 1998, The Writing's on the Wall, 1999, Survivor, 2001 (Best R&B Performance by a Duo or Group with Vocals (for title track), Grammy Awards, 2002), 8 Days of Christmas, 2001, Destiny Fulfilled, 2004, #1's, 2005, (solo albums) Dangerously in Love, 2003 (Best Contemporary R&B Album, Grammy Awards, 2004, Best Female R&B/Soul Album, Soul Train Music Awards, 2004), Live at Wembley, 2004, B'day, 2006 (Best Contemporary R&B Album, Grammy Awards, 2007), I Am-...Sasha Fierce, 2008 (Album of Yr., Soul Train Music Awards, 2009, Best Contemporary R&B Album, Grammy Awards, 2010), 4, 2011 (Top R&B Album, Billboard Music Awards, 2012), Beyoncé, 2013 (Outstanding Female Artist, NAACP Image Awards, 2014), (songs) Dangerously in Love 2, 2003 (Best Female R&B Vocal Performance, Grammy Awards, 2004), (featuring Jay-Z) Crazy in Love, 2003 (Best Female Video, Best R&B Video, MTV Video Music Awards, 2003, Best Collaboration, BET Awards, 2004, Best R&B Song, Best Rap/Sung Collaboration, Grammy Awards, 2004), (with Luther Vandross) The Closer I Get to You, 2004 (Best R&B Performance by a Duo or Group with Vocals, Grammy Awards, 2004), (with Stevie Wonder) So Amazing, 2005 (Best R&B Performance by a Duo or Group with Vocals, Grammy Awards, 2006), Irreplaceable, 2006 (Video of Yr., BET Awards, 2007, Best Female R&B/Soul Single, Soul Train Music Awards, 2007), Single Ladies (Put A Ring On It), 2008 (Song of Yr., Soul Train Music Awards, 2009, Best R&B Song, Teen Choice Awards, 2009, Best Choreography, Video of Yr., MTV Video Music Awards, 2009, Video of Yr., BET Awards, 2009, Best Female R&B Vocal Performance, Best R&B Song, Song of Yr., Grammy Awards, 2010), Halo, 2009 (Best Female Pop Vocal Performance, Grammy Awards, 2010), (with Lady Gaga) Telephone, 2010 (Best Collaboration, MTV Video Music Awards, 2010), Love on Top, 2011 (Best Traditional R&B Performance, Grammy Awards, 2013), (songs with Destiny's Child) Say My Name, 2000 (Best R&B Song, Best R&B Performance by a Duo or Group with Vocals, Grammy Awards, 2001); actress: (films) Austin Powers in Goldmember, 2002, The Fighting Temptations, 2003, The Pink Panther, 2006, Dreamgirls, 2006, Cadillac Records, 2008, Obsessed, 2009, Epic (voice), 2013; exec. prodr., dir. (documentaries) Life Is But a Dream, 2013, appeared as cover model Sports Illustrated Swimsuit Issue, 2007. Recipient Sammy Davis Jr. award for Entertainer of Yr., Soul Train Music Awards, 2004, Internat. Artist award, American Music Awards, 2007, Award for Outstanding Contbn. to the Arts, World Music Awards, 2008, Millennium award, Billboard Music Awards, 2011, New York Assn. of Black Journalists Writing award for a story titled Eat, Play, Love written in July 2011 issue of Essence Mag., 2012; named Best Internat. Female Solo Artist, Brit. Phonographic Industry (BRIT) Awards, 2004, Favorite Female Performer, People Choice Awards, 2004, 2008, Entertainer of Yr., NAACP Image Awards, 2004, Outstanding Female Artist, 2009, Female R&B/Hip-Hop Artist of Yr., Billboard Music Awards, 2006, Best Female R&B Artist, Black Entertainment TV (BET) Awards, 2006, 2007, 2008, 2012, Video Dir. of Yr. (with Alan Ferguson), 2012, Favorite Female Soul/R&B Artist, American Music Awards, 2009, 2011, 2012, Best Female R&B/Soul Artist, Soul Train Music Awards, 2009, Choice Female Hottie, Teen Choice Awards, 2009, Choice Music: R&B Artist, 2010, World's Most Beautiful Woman!, People mag., 2012; named one of The 50 Most Influential African-Americans, Ebony mag., 2004, The 50 Most Powerful Women in NYC, NY Post, 2007, 2008, The 100 Most Powerful Celebrities, Forbes mag., 2008—12, The 100 Most Powerful Women, 2010—13, The 100 Most Influential People in the World, TIME mag., 2013—14, The 100 Most Powerful Women in Entertainment, Hollywood Reporter, 2013. Office: Music World Entertainment 1505 Hadley St Houston TX 77002*

KNOWLES, HARRY JAY, Internet personality, blogger, film critic; b. May 12, 1971; s. Jay and Helen Knowles; m. Patricia Jones, July 15, 2007. Founder, owner website Ain't It Cool News, 1996—. Salesman vintage film memorabilia. Author: Ain't It Cool?: Hollywood's Redheaded Stepchild Speaks Out, 2003; film critic, Penthouse mag., 2006-; film appearances: Ballad of the Sad Cafe, 1991, Colin Fitz, 1997, The Faculty, 1998, Monkeybone, 2001, Ghosts of Mars, 2001, Texas Chainsaw Massacre, 2003, No Pain, No Gain, 2005, Pathogen, 2006, Fanboys, 2009. Named No. 82 of 100 Best Things to Happen to Hollywood, Movieline mag., 1997, No. 25 on Forbes Power List, 2000, No. 1 Entertainment News Site in World, London Times, 2005; named one of Top 25 Web Celebs, Forbes mag., 2006, 2007, named to Top 50 Influence List of high impact media players, Brill's Content, 2000. Mem.: Austin Film Critics Assn. Office: PO Box 180011 Austin TX 78718-0011 Business E-Mail: harry@aintitcool.com.

KNOWLES, JULIE NALL, secondary school educator; b. Webb, Ala., Nov. 5, 1941; d. Ealie Edward and Creola (Carter) Nall; m. William Durwood Knowles, Jan. 17, 1970. BS in Edn. magna cum laude, Troy State U., Ala., 1965; MA in English, Samford U., Birmingham, Ala., 1969; PhD in English, Auburn U., Ala., 1980; AA in Music, Chattahoochee Valley CC, Phenix City, Ala., 1999. Cert. tchr. Ala., Ga., Fla. Tchr. Ahrens H.S. Jefferson County Schs., Louisville, 1975—76; instr. Auburn U., Ala., 1981—82; assoc. prof. Stillman Coll., Tuscaloosa, Ala., 1983—85; asst. prof. Mercer U., Macon, Ga., 1986—87; prof. Troy State U., Phenix City, Ala., 1987—99; tchr. Camden County HS Camden County Schs., Kingsland, Ga., 1999—2000; tchr. Paxon Sch. Advanced Studies Duval County Sch. Sys., Jacksonville, Fla., 2000—04; prof., chair Bapt. Coll. of Fla., Graceville, 2005—09. Editor, creator: The Chariot, 1988-91, Scarecrow's Children, 2014; contbr. articles to mags. Ch. pianist Turners Station Bapt Ch., Ky., 1973—76, Union Grove Bapt. Ch., Opelika, Ala., 1976—82, Hatchechubbee Bapt. Ch., Ala., 1988—95; mem. choir Folkston Bapt. Ch., Ga., 2000—4. Rsch. grantee Troy State U., 1992; recipient Woodrow Hale Meml. Prize # 1 Green River Writers, 1996. Mem. Profl. Assn. Ga. Educators, Phi Theta Kappa, Phi Kappa Phi, Kappa Delta Pi (counselor Rho Phi chpt. 1989-92, Point of Excellence award 1993). Democrat. Southern Baptist. Avocations: motorcycling, piano, fishing. Personal E-mail: knowleswebb@centurylink.net.

KNOWLES, MARJORIE FINE, retired law educator, dean; b. Bklyn., July 4, 1939; d. Jesse J. and Roslyn (Leff) Fine; m. Ralph I. Knowles, Jr., June 3, 1972. BA, Smith Coll., 1960; LLB, Harvard U., 1965. Bar: Ala., N.Y., D.C. Teaching fellow Harvard U., 1963-64; law clk. to judge U.S. Dist. Ct. (so. dist.), NY, 1965-66; asst. U.S. atty. U.S. Atty.'s Office, NYC, 1966-67; asst. dist. atty. N.Y. County Dist. Atty., NYC, 1967-70; exec. dir. Joint Found. Support, Inc., NYC, 1970-72; asst. gen. counsel HEW, Washington, 1978-79; insp. gen. U.S. Dept. Labor, Washington, 1979-80; assoc. prof. U. Ala. Sch. Law, Tuscaloosa, 1972-75, prof., 1975-86, assoc. dean, 1982-84; law prof., dean Ga. State U. Coll. Law, Atlanta, 1986-91, law prof., 1986—2011, ret., 2012; trustee Tchrs. Ins. and Annuity Assn., 2002—09. Cons. Ford Found., NYC, 1973-98, 2000-03, trustee Coll. Retirement Equities Fund, NYC, 1983-2002; exec. com. Conf. on Women and the Constn., 1986-88; com. on continuing profl. edn. Am. Law Inst.-ABA, 1987-93; bd. dirs. Internat. Corp. Governance Network, 2007. Contbr. articles to profl. jours. Am. Council Edn. fellow, 1976—77, Aspen Inst. fellow, Rockefeller Found., 1976. Mem. ABA (chmn. new deans workshop 1988), Ala. State Bar Assn., N.Y. State Bar Assn., D.C. Bar Assn., Am. Law Inst., Tchrs. Ins. Annuity Assn. (trustee 2003-). Home: 145-15 St NE Apt 104 Atlanta GA 30309 Office Phone: 404-413-9181.

KNOWLES, MARK, professional tennis player; b. Nassau, Bahamas, Sept. 4, 1971; m. Dawn Knowles, Dec. 7, 2003; 1 child, Graham. Profl. tennis player ATP, 1992—. Mem. ATP Player Coun., 2002—04, v.p. Named ATP Doubles Team of Yr. (with Nestor), 2002, 2004. Achievements include winning 50 career doubles titles, ATP; mem. Davis Cup team, 1989-; Grand Slam Championships: (mixed doubles) Wimbledon, 2009. Avocations: golf, spearfishing, free diving. Office: 201 ATP Tour Blvd Ponte Vedra Beach FL 32082

KNOWLES, MICHAEL RAY, medical educator, researcher; m. Marilyn Goodman; children: Joshua, Rachel. AB, U. NC, Chapel Hill, 1967, MD, 1971. Diplomate Am. Bd. Internal Medicine, 1974, Pulmonary Disease Subspecialty Bd. Medicine, 1980. Chief internal medicine USAF Malcolm Grow Med. Ctr., Andrews AFB, DC, 1975—78; instr. dept. medicine U. NC, Chapel Hill, 1980—82, asst. prof. medicine, 1982—87, assoc. prof. medicine, 1987—94, prof. medicine, 1994—. Prin. investigator primary ciliary dyskinesia Nat. Consortium to Study Genetic Disorders of the Lung, 2003—. Author: (textbook) Cystic Fibrosis in Adults; contbr. articles to profl. med. jours. Maj. USAF, 1975—78, Andrews AFB. Recipient Jefferson Pilot award, U. NC, Chapel Hill, 1983—87, Paul de St. Agy. award, 22nd Ann. CF Conf., 2008, Doris Tulcin CF award, UAB, 2011; named one of Best Doctors Am., 1992—2011; Rsch. Sabbatical, Cambridge, Eng., 1988—89. Mem.: Alpha Omega Alpha. Office: UNC Chapel Hill 7019 Thurston Bowles Bldg CB7248 Chapel Hill NC 27599-7248 Business E-Mail: knowles@med.unc.edu.

KNOWLES, RICHARD NORRIS, chemist; b. Wilmington, Del., Aug. 8, 1935; s. Francis and Dorothy Edith Knowles; m. Alice Keith Pfohl, Aug. 30, 1957 (div. May 1987); children: Elizabeth Nelson, Dorothy Lawrence, Cynthia Norris; m. Claire Elaine Frerichs, Dec. 31, 1988; 1 stepchild, Christine J. Stoelting. MBA, Oberlin Coll., 1957; PhD, U. Rochester, 1961. With DuPont Co., Wilmington, Del., 1960-96; asst. works mgr. Chambers Works, NJ, 1980-83; mgr. Niagara Falls Plant, NY, 1983—87, Belle Plant, W.Va., 1987-95; dir. cmty. awareness emergency response & industry outreach Wilmington, 1995-96; with Chem. Mfrs. Assn. in Responsible Care, 1985—96; assoc. Dalmau Network; prin. Richard N. Knowles & Assocs.; advisor to mayor Niagara Falls, 1999—2004; founder, dir. Ctr. Self-Orgnl. Leadership, 2001—. Adj. instr. Medaille Coll., Buffalo. Author: The Leadership Dance, Pathways to Extraordinary Organizational Effectiveness, 2002, Partnering for Safety and Business Excellence, 2012; (feaures include) The New Pioneers, 1998, The Soul at Work, 2000; contbr. articles to profl. jours., chapters to books. Mem. adv. bd. Inst. Sustainable Enterprise at Fairleigh Dickinson U.; elder Presbyn. Ch.; bd. dirs. Du Versity, Inst. for the Study of Coherence and Emergence, World Bus. Acad. Recipient Chem. Emergency Planning and Preparedness Ptnr. award, EPA, 1995, 1996. Mem.: Almost Heaven Hammered Dulcimer Soc., Nature Conservancy (DuPont Agrl. Products Crystal award 1991). Achievements include 40 patents in field. Personal E-mail: rnknowles@aol.com.

KNOWLES, SOLANGE, singer, model; b. Houston, June 24, 1986; d. Mathew and Tina Knowles; m. Daniel Smith, Feb. 2004 (div. 2007); 1 child, Daniel Julez Jr. Spokesmodel Rimmel London, 2011—; model House of Deréon; launched jr. apparel collection Déreon; guest blogger vogue.com, 2012—; with Next Model Mgmt., 2012—. Singer: (albums) Solo Star, 2003, Sol-Angel and the Hadley St. Dreams, 2008, True, 2012; actress: (films) Johnson Family Vacation, 2004, Bring It On: All or Nothing, 2006. Office: Music World Entertainment 1505 Hadley St Houston TX 77002

KNOWLES, TRACY, chemistry professor; BS in Chemistry, U. Tenn., Chattanooga, 1992; MS in Environ. Sci., Ind. U., Bloomington, 1998. Environ. analytical chemist Oak Ridge Nat. Lab.; tchr. Ind. U. Sch. Pub. and Environ. Affairs; assoc. prof. chemistry and environ. sci. tech. Bluegrass Cmty. and Tech. Coll., Lexington, Ky. Mem. State Small Bus. Stationary Source Compliance Adv. Panel. Named Ky. Prof. of Yr., Carnegie Found. for Advancement of Tchg. and Coun. for Advancement and Support of Edn., 2009. Office: Bluegrass Cmty & Tech College Cooper Campus 234 H Oswald Bldg 470 Cooper Drive Lexington KY 40506 Office Phone: 859-246-6460. Business E-Mail: Tracy.Knowles@kctcs.edu.

KNOWLING, ROBERT E., JR., management consultant; BA in Theology, Wabash Coll., Crawfordsville, Ind.; MBA, Northwestern U., Ill. Joined Indiana Bell, 1977, various positions in ops., engring. and mktg.; v.p. network ops. Ameritech, 1994—96, US West, 1996—97, exec. v.p. ops. and technologies, 1997—98; chmn., pres., CEO Covad Comm., 1998—2001; chmn., CEO SimDesk Technologies, Inc., 2001—03; CEO NYC Leadership Acad., 2003—05, Telewares, 2005—09; chmn. Eagles Landing Partners, 2009—. Bd. dirs. Aprimo, Inc., Heidrick & Struggles Internat., Inc., Ariba, Inc., Roper Industries, Inc., 2008—. Chmn. nat. svcs. group YMCA; mem. bd. adv. Northwestern U. Kellogg Grad. Sch. Mgmt. Office: c/o Roper Industries Inc 6901 Professional Pkwy E Ste 200 Sarasota FL 34240 Office Phone: 941-556-2601. Office Fax: 941-556-2670.

KNOX, BOONE A., bank executive; b. 1929; Pres., CEO Allied Bank of Ga. (subs. Allied Bankshares Inc.), Thomson, 1975—86, chmn.; CEO Allied Bankshares, Inc., 1984—97, chmn., 1984—, Merry Land LLC (formerly, Merry Land & Investment Co.), 1996—98, Regions Bank of Central Georgia, 1997—; bd. dirs. InterCept, Inc., 1998—2002, vice chmn., 2002. Former bd. dirs. Merry Land Properties Inc., (MRYP); bd. dirs. Cousins Properties Inc., 1969—, Equity Residential, 1998—2010. Bd. trustee Knox Found. Office: Allied Bankshares Inc 1700 Market Pl Blvd Cumming GA 30041-7928 Office Phone: 770-888-0063. Business E-Mail: booneknox@cousinsproperties.com.

KNOX, ROGER, zoological park administrator; b. Ark., Sept. 28, 1937; BA in Psychology, U. Ark., 1961. With Foley's Depart. Stores, Houston; chmn., CEO Federated Dept. Stores Foleys, Houston, 1963-83; COO and pres. Goldsmith Dept. Stores, Houston, 1983-87; pres., emeritus, CEO Memphis Zoo Soc., 1989—2003; chmn., CEO Goldsmith's Depart. Stores, 1987—89. Bd. dirs. Hancock Fabrics, Inc., Fred's, Inc., 1992—. Office: Fred's Inc Bd Directors 4300 New Getwell Rd Memphis TN 38118 Office Phone: 901-365-8880. Office Fax: 901-328-0354. Business E-Mail: rknox@fredsinc.com.

KNOX, WYCK AUSTIN, JR., board member, lawyer; b. Augusta, Ga., Nov. 1, 1940; s. Wyckliffe Austin Knox Sr. and Byrnece (Purcell) Swanson; m. Shell Hardman, Apr. 15, 1967; children: Wyckliffe Austin III, Dorothy Shell, John Hardman, Davis Purcell. BBA, U. Ga., 1962, JD, 1964. Bar: Ga. 1964, U.S. Dist. Ct. (so. dist.) Ga. 1964, U.S. Ct. Appeals (5th cir.) 1966, U.S. Ct. Claims 1973, U.S. Supreme Ct. 1973, U.S. Ct. Appeals (11th cir.) 1981, U.S. Ct. Appeals (4th cir.) 1983. Assoc. Hull, Towill & Norman, Augusta, 1964-67; ptnr. Hull, Towill, Norman, Barrett & Johnson, Augusta, 1967-76; chmn., CEO Knox Rivers Constrn. Co., 1976—95; ptnr. Knox & Zacks, Augusta, 1976-77, pres., 1977—94; ptnr., chmn. Kilpatrick Stockton LLP, Augusta & Atlanta, 1976—2007; ptnr. Kilpatrick & Cody, 1994—97. Chmn. bd. dirs. 1st Union Nat. Bank of Ga., Augusta, Knox-Rivers Constrn. Co., Thomson, Ga. Mem. bd. visitors sch. law U. Ga., Athens, 1973-76, bd. dirs. athletic assn., 1975-85, emeritus dir. 1985-; mem. jud. com. Bus. Council Ga., Atlanta, 1986—; pres. Ga. council Boy Scouts Am., Augusta, 1974-75; pres.Richmond/Columbia County unit Am. Cancer Soc., Augusta, 1985, chmn. bd. dirs. 1986—; trustee Richard B. Russell Found., Atlanta, 1971—; pres. Georgians for Better Transp.; founding dir. & past chmn. Ga. Lottery Corp.; mem Met. Atlanta Olympic Games Auth.; mem. Commn. for a New Ga.; dir. Ga. C. of C. Fellow Am. Bar Found., Ga. Bar Found; mem. Augusta Bar Assn. (pres. 1984), Ga. Bar Assn., Ga. Acad. Hosp. Attys. (bd. dirs. 1979-80), Am. Acad. Healthcare Attys., Ga. Def. Lawyers Assn. (bd. dirs. 1973-76), YPO. Clubs: Piedmont Driving (Atlanta), Augusta Country (pres. 1988), Pinnacle (Augusta). Lodges: Rotary (pres. local club 1979-80). Methodist. Avocations: fishing, skiing, golf. Office: Kilpatrick Stockton LLP Ste 1400 Wachovia Bank Bldg 699 Broad St Augusta GA 30901-1453 also: Kilpatrick Stockton LLP Ste 2800 1100 Peachtree St Atlanta GA 30309-4530 also: AGL Resources Inc Bd Directors 10 Peachtree Pl NE Atlanta GA 30309 Office Phone: 404-584-4000. Office Fax: 404-584-3714. Business E-Mail: wknox@kilpatrickstockton.com.

KOBDISH, GEORGE CHARLES, lawyer; b. Casper, Wyo., June 30, 1950; s. Richard Matthew and Jo Earl (Uttz) K.; m. Mary Ellen Griffith, Jan. 24, 1969; children: George Charles, Jr., Kelly Rebecca, Kimberlee Nelle. BBA with honors, U. Tex., 1971, JD, 1974. Bar: Tex. 1974, U.S. Dist. Ct. (no. dist.) Tex. 1975. Asst. atty. gen. State of Tex., Austin, 1974—76; assoc. McCall, Parkhurst & Horton LLP, Dallas, 1976—80, ptnr., 1981—. Bd. dirs. North Dallas Shared Ministries, 1993—2000, pres., 1996—98; lay gen. chairperson Cath. Cmty. Appeal, 2000—01; bd. dirs. Notre Dame of Dallas Schs, Inc., 2000—06, pres., 2004—06; mem. adv. coun. Cath. Found., 2006—08, bd. dir., 2008—13. Mem. Am. Coll. Bond Counsel, Nat. Assn. Bond Lawyers, Tex. Bar Assn., Dallas Bar Assn., Royal Oaks Country Club, Serra Internat. (Dallas bd. dirs., pres. 1998-99, USA coun., gov. Dist. 46, 2002-03), Phi Delta Theta. Roman Catholic. Office: McCall Parkhurst & Horton LLP 717 N Harwood St Ste 900 Dallas TX 75201-6586 Office Phone: 214-754-9236. Business E-Mail: ckobdish@mphlegal.com.

KOBECK, JO KAREN, artist, writer; b. Lawrenceburg, Tenn., Apr. 10, 1944; d. William Horatio and Ethel Marie (Hendrix) Kobeck; m. J.R. Benson, 1963 (div. 1974); children: Pamela Jo Benson Robinson, Anita Marie Benson Bosaw Cert. in drafting, Miss. Gulf Coast Jr. Coll., 1974; cert. in engring. graphics, U. Tenn., 1975; cert. in drafting, Mountain Empire C.C., 1980. Advt. asst. Rogers, Inc., Florence, Ala., 1966-67; drafter Litton Industries, Pascagoula, Miss., 1972-74; drafter, illustrator Cities Svc. Co., Copperhill, Tenn., 1974-78; design drafter Westmoreland Coal Co., Big Stone Gap, Va., 1978-88; design drafter, neon designer and illustrator Designs by Jo, East Stone Gap, Va., 1983—97. Mem. Copper Basin Redevel. Design Coun., 1975-77; lectr. Take off Pounds Sensibly, Appalachia, Va., 1985-87, 93-94, Coeburn, Va., 1999-2006, 2010-13; active Friends of Libr., Big Stone Gap, 1988; bd. dirs. H.E.L.P. Ctr., Big Stone Gap, 1988; Va. Family and Cmty. Edn., 1991-98; election officer Dist. 3, Wise County, 1996, 97; mem. Christian Ch. Avocations: photography, wildlife rehabilitation, decorative artist. Home: 122 Green Meadow Dr W Gahanna OH 43230-2749 Personal E-mail: artistjok@yahoo.com.

KOBER, JOHN A., lawyer; b. LaCrosse, Kans., 1957; s. John B. and Dotty Kober; m. Norma Kober, Sept. 28, 1985; children: Kersten, Colin. BS, Kans. State U., 1980; JD, Washburn U. Sch. Law, Topeka, 1982; LLM, U. Mo., 1984. Bar: Tex., Nebr., Kans., DC, US Dist. Ct. (no. dist.) Tex. Ptnr. Employee Benefits & Exec. Compensation practice Morgan, Lewis & Bockius LLP, Dallas, 2004—, mng. ptnr. Dallas. Contbr. articles to profl. jours. Chair North Tex. Family Firm Inst. Named one of Best Lawyers in Dallas, D Mag., 2005. Mem.: AICPA, ABA, Dallas Bar Assn., Tex. Soc. CPAs, Atty.-CPA Assn., Tarrant County Bar Assn., Tex. Bar Assn., Employee-Owned S Corp. America, Nat. Ctr. Employee Ownership (bd. dirs.), Employee Stock Ownership Plan Assn. Office: Morgan Lewis & Bockius 1717 Main St Ste 3200 Dallas TX 75201 Office Phone: 214-466-4105. Office Fax: 214-466-4001. Business E-Mail: jkober@morganlewis.com.

KOCH, JAMES VERCH, academic administrator, economist; b. Springfield, Ill., Oct. 7, 1942; s. Elmer O. and Wilma L. K.; m. Donna L. Stickling, Aug. 20, 1967; children: Elizabeth, Mark. BA, Ill. State U., 1964; PhD, Northwestern U., 1968. From asst. prof. to prof. econs. Ill. State U., 1967-78, chmn. dept., 1972-78; dean Faculty Arts and Scis., R.I. Coll., Providence, 1978-80; prof. econs., provost, v.p. acad. affairs Ball State U., Muncie, Ind., 1980-86; pres. U. Mont., Missoula, 1986-90, Old Dominion U., Norfolk, Va., 1990-2001, prof. econs., 2001—. Author: Industrial Organization and Prices, 2d edit, 1980, Microeconomic Theory and Applications, 1976, The Economics of Affirmative Action, 1976, Presidential Leadership, 1996, The Entrepreneurial President, 2003, Born, not Made, 2008, America for Sale, 2009 Mem. Am. Econ. Assn. Lutheran. Office: Old Dominion U Dept Econs Norfolk VA 23529 Home Phone: 757-683-3458; Office Phone: 757-683-3458. Business E-Mail: jkoch@odu.edu.

KOCH, STEVEN EDWARD, federal official, meteorologist; b. Cin., July 21, 1950; s. Edward Ralph and Jean (Rulison) K.; m. Sioux Ann Hawkins, Jan. 20, 1972 (div. May 25, 1979); m. Lois Vivian Kopke, Sept. 20, 1980; children: Christina Marie, Brian Edward. BS, U. Wis., 1972, MS, 1974; PhD, U. Okla., 1979. Postdoctoral fellow Cooperative Inst. for Mesoscale Meteorol. Studies, U. Okla., Norman, 1979-80; rsch. meteorologist NASA/Goddard Space Flight Ctr., Greenbelt, Md., 1980-93; assoc. prof. N.C. State U., Raleigh, NC, 1993—2000; chief Forecast Rsch. Divsn. Forecasts Systems Lab (FSL) NOAA, US Dept. Commerce, 2000—06, acting dir. then dir. Global Systems Divsn. Earth System Rsch. Lab Boulder, Colo., 2006—11, dir. Nat. Severe Storms Lab Washington, 2011—. Chmn. Storm I Systems Integration Com., 1991-93. Assoc. editor: Jour. of the Atmospheric Sciences, 1983; contbr. articles to profl. jours.; editor: Weather and Forecasting. Mem. Handgun Control, Inc., Washington, 1988—, Sierra Club. Recipient NASA Goddard Exceptional Achievement award, 1991, NASA Goddard Certificate of Outstanding Performance, 1992, Nat. Weather Svc. award for Applied Svc., 1998, Nat. Weather Assn. Rsch. Achievement award, 1998. Mem. American Meterol. Soc., Nat. Weather Assn., American Geophysical Union Achievements include development of remote sensing and modeling of gravity waves and frontal scale contraction processes, assimilation of satellite-derived products into mesoscale models; assisted in development of GEMPAK meteorological analysis and visualization systems. Office: National Severe Storms Lab National Weather Center 120 David L Boren Blvd Norman OK 73072 Office Phone: 405-325-3620. E-mail: Steven.Koch@noaa.gov.

KOCH, WILLIAM C., JR., state supreme court justice; b. Honolulu, Sept. 12, 1947; married. BA, Trinity Coll., Hartford, Conn., 1969; JD, Vanderbilt U., Nashville, 1972; LLM, U. Va., Charlottesville, 1996. Asst. atty. gen. State of Tenn., 1972—76, sr. asst. atty. gen., 1976—77, dep. atty. gen., 1977—78, counsel to Gov. Lamar Alexander, 1981—84; commr. Tenn. Dept. Pers., 1979—81; judge Tenn. Ct. Appeals, 1984—2007; assoc. justice Tenn. Supreme Ct., 2007—. Adj. instr. Vanderbilt U., 1988—95; instr. constl. law Nashville Sch. Law, 1997—. Mem. Harry Phillips Am. Inn of Ct., 1990—, Am. Inns of Ct. Found., 2000—; bd. trustees United Way Met. Nashville, 1981—; mem. instl. rev. com. Baptist Hosp., 1991—94, mem. ethics com., 1994—2003; co-chair Tenn. Supreme Ct. Adv. Commn. Tech., 1997—2001; bd. trustees Cmty. Found. Mid. Tenn., 2005—. Mem.: ABA, Scribes, Am. Judicature Soc., Nashville Bar Found., Tenn. Bar Found., Nashville Bar Assn., Tenn. Bar Assn., Nashville Rotary. Episcopalian. Office: Tenn Supreme Ct 203 Supreme Ct Bldg 401 Seventh Ave N Nashville TN 37219*

KOCH, WILLIAM I, energy executive; b. Wichita, Kans. m. Bridget Rooney-Koch; 6 children. Grad., Culver Mil. Acad.; BCE, MCE, MIT, PhD in Chem. Engring. Founder, CEO Oxbow Carbon LLC (formerly Oxbow Carbon & Minerals LLC), West Palm Beach, Fla. Founder Oxbridge Acad. of Palm Beach. Named one of Forbes Richest Americans, 2006. Office: Oxbow Corp 1601 Forum Pl Ste 1400 West Palm Beach FL 33401 Office Fax: 561-640-8740. Business E-Mail: william.koch@oxbow.com.

KOCHER, BRIAN W., food products executive; BBA in Acctg., Ohio U., 1987. CPA. Auditor Price Waterhouse; v.p., fin. and adminstrn. CONXUS Comm., Inc.; various positions GE Co.; v.p., fin. GE Capital Internat. Fin. Holding Co.; v.p., global contr. GE Capital Global Consumer Fin.; global contr. GE Capital Info. Tech. Systems, 1999—2002; joined Hill-Rom, Inc., 2002, exec. dir., comml. fin., v.p., nat. accts., 2003—04, v.p., sales for svcs., 2004—05; v.p., fin. Chiquita Brands International, Inc., 2005, v.p., contr., 2005—07, chief acctg. officer, 2005—08, pres., N.Am., 2007—. Mem.: Health Industry Group Purchasing Assn.(former bd. dirs.). Office: Chiquita Brands International Inc 550 S Caldwell St Ste 1010 Charlotte NC 28202-2681 Office Phone: 513-784-8000. Office Fax: 513-784-8030. Business E-Mail: bkocher@chiquita.com.

KOCHER, KENNETH J., retail executive; BBA in Acctg, U. N.D. CPA. Accountant Edie Bailley; contr. Hat World Corp. (subs. of Genesco, Inc.), pres., 2005—; sr. v.p. Genesco, Inc., 2006; CFO Hat World Corp. (subs. of Genesco, Inc.), 1997. Bd. dirs. Indiana Bulls Youth Baseball. Office: Genesco Inc 1415 Murfreesboro Rd Ste 264 Nashville TN 37217 Office Phone: 615-367-7000. Office Fax: 615-367-8278. Business E-Mail: kkocher@genesco.com.

KOCI, KEITH, metal products executive; CPA Tex. CFO, contr. Optimum Nutrition Inc., 1996—98; regional contr. Flat Rolled Group Metals USA, Inc., 1998—2003, corp. dir. budgeting, 2003—04, v.p., corp. contr., 2004—05, sr. v.p. bus. devel., 2005—, Metals USA Holdings Corp., 2006—. Office: Metals USA Inc 2400 E Commercial Blvd Ste 905 Fort Lauderdale FL 33308-4059 Office Phone: 713-965-0990. Office Fax: 713-965-0067.

KOEDEL, JOHN GILBERT, JR., retired metal products executive; b. Pitts., June 25, 1937; s. John Gilbert and Elizabeth Marie (Kramer) K.; m. Fay Birren, Dec. 21, 1963; 1 son, John III. BS in Commerce, Washington and Lee U., 1959. V.p. Pitts. Nat. Bank, 1960-68; various positions up to pres. Nat. Forge. Co., 1968-95. Served to sgt., U.S. Army, 1960-65. Mem. Fishing Bay Yacht Club, Conenango Club, Masons. Republican. Presbyterian. Avocations: sailing, woodworking. Home: PO Box 87 Deltaville VA 23043-0877

KOEN, BILLY VAUGHN, mechanical engineering educator; b. Graham, Tex., May 2, 1938; s. Ottis Vaughn and Margaret (Branch) Koen; m. Deanne Rollins, June 3, 1967; children: Kent, Douglas. BA in Chemistry, U. Tex., 1961, BS in Chem. Engring., 1961; S.M. in Nuclear Engring., MIT, 1962, Sc.D. in Nuclear Engring., 1968; Diplome d'ingenieur en Genie Atomique, L'institut National des Scis. et Techniques Nucleaires, France, 1963. Registered profl. engr., Tex. Asst. prof. mech. engring. U. Tex., Austin, 1968-71, assoc. prof., 1971-80, Minnie S. Piper prof., 1980, prof., 1981—2008, emeritus prof., 2008—; dir. Bur. Engring. Teaching U. Tex.-Austin, 1973-76. Prof. Ecole Centrale, Paris, 1983; undergrad advisor mech. engring., 1988-92; vis. prof. Tokyo Inst. Tech., 1994 (summer), 1998-99, 2001 (summer); cons., lectr. in field. Author: Definition of the Engineering Method, 1985, Discussion of the Method, 2003; contbr. articles to profl. jours. Bd. dirs. Oak Ridge Associated Univs., 1975-76. Recipient Standard Oil Ind. award, 1970, W. Leighton Collins Distinguished and Unusual Service awd., Am. Soc. for Engineering Education, 1992. Fellow Am. Soc. Engring. Edn. (v.p. 1987-93, Chester Carlson award 1980, Ben Dasher best paper award 1985, 86, Helen Plants award 1986, William Elgin Wickenden best paper award 1986, Olmsted award, dir. 1982-84, W. Leighton Collins award 1992, Centennial medallion 1993), Am. Nuc. Soc.; mem. N.Y. Acad. Sci., Association des Ingenieurs en Genie Atomique, Rotary Club (Austin; Internat. fellow 1962), Phi Beta Kappa, Sigma Xi (disting. lectr. 1981-83), Tau Beta Pi. Mem. Soc. Of Friends. Achievements include development of computer algorithm for calculation of nuclear system reliability. Office: U Tex Dept Mech Engring Etc 5160 Austin TX 78712 Business E-Mail: koen@uts.cc.utexas.edu.

KOENIG, ADAM, state legislator; b. Feb. 22, 1971; BA, Miami U. Owner MAK Consulting, Inc.; former pres. Northern Ky. Area Planning Coun.; mem. Dist 69 Ky. House of Reps., 2007—. Mem.: Vision 2015, Northern Ky., Telecom. Bd., Covington Salvation Army. Republican. Catholic. Home: 170 Herrington Ct Apt 12 Erlanger KY 41018-1995 Home Phone: 859-578-9258; Office Phone: 502-564-8100 ext. 689. Business E-Mail: adam.koenig@lrc.ky.gov.

KOENIG, RODNEY CURTIS, lawyer, rancher; b. Black Jack, Tex., Nov. 21, 1940; s. John Henry and Elva Marguerite (Oeding) K.; m. Mary Mishler, May 1, 1993; children: Erik Jason, Jon Todd. BA, U. Tex., 1962, JD with honors, 1969; postgrad., Auburn U., 1965-67. Bar: Tex. 1969, U.S. Dist. Ct. (so. dist.) Tex. 1970, U.S. Ct. Appeals (5th cir.) 1970, U.S. Tax Ct. 1980, U.S. Ct. Mil. Appeals 1986. Ptnr. Fulbright & Jaworski, LLP, Houston, 1969—. Asst. prof. Auburn U., 1965-67; lectr. in field Contbr. articles to profl. jours. Pres. Houston Navy League, 1979-81; mem. Battleship Texas Commn.; bd. dirs. Houston divsn. Am. Heart Assn., Fayette Heritage Mus., St. Mark's Med. Ctr. Found.; dir. Advanced Estate Planning and Probate Course, 1988, Crawford & Hattie Jackson Found.; trustee James Dick Found. Performing Arts, Luck and Loessin Collection Trust, Harold Williams Found., Alice Taylor Gray Found., John and Allie Orton Found., Luth. Found. of the S.W., treas., exec. com.; active Tex. Luth. U. Corp.; co-chair Planned Giving Adv. Coun., U. Tex., 2005-08; Midshipmans Found. Bd.; Bach Soc. Houston Bd.; Houston-Leipzig Sister City Assn. Bd.; U. Texas Health Houston Adv. Bd. With USN, 1962—67, capt. JAGC USNR, 1967—89. Recipient Fed. Republic of Germany Order of Merit, 1994, Named Best Lawyers in America, trusts and estates, Best Lawyers, 1989 - 2010, Texas Super Lawyer, Thomson Reuters, 2003 - 2009, Texas Top Rated Lawyer, LexisNexis Martindale-Hubbell, 2013 Fellow Am. Coll. Trust and Estate Counsel, Coll. State Bar Tex. (charter); mem. ABA, Internat. Acad. Estate and Trust Law (academician, exec. com.), German Texan Heritage Soc. (pres. 1997-2000), Tex. German Soc. (founding dir.), Res. Officers Assn., Sons of Republic of Tex., Wednesday Tax Forum (past chmn.), German Gulf Coast Assn. (pres. 1989-93), Bach Soc. (bd. dirs., v.p. 2005—), English Speaking Union (bd. dir., v.p.), Houston Early Music (pres. 2000-04), Houston Karneval Verein (prince 1994-95), USS San Jacinto Com. (treas.), Houstonian Club, Frisch Auf Valley Country Club, Order of Coif, US Naval Order, U.T. NROTC Alumni Assn. (pres. 2000-02), Houston Saengerbund (pres. 2006—), Phi Delta Phi, Omicron Delta Kappa. Lutheran. Home: 2720 University Blvd Houston TX 77005-3440 Office: Norton Rose Fulbright 1301 Mckinney St Fl 51 Houston TX 77010-3031 Home Phone: 713-667-9566; Office Phone: 713-651-5333. Business E-Mail: Rodney.Koenig@NortonRoseFulbright.com.

KOENIGER, ALFRED CASH, history professor; b. Little Rock, Mar. 16, 1949; s. Alfred William and Mary Tom Koeniger; m. Rachel Lynn Flora, July 5, 1980; 1 child, Anderson Cash. AB with honors, Washington & Lee U., 1971; MA, Vanderbilt U., 1974, PhD, 1980. Vis. instr. Murray (Ky.) State U., 1979—80; vis. asst. prof. Miss. State U., Starkville, 1980—81; asst. prof. U. So. Miss., Natchez, 1981—86; assoc. prof. Va. Mil. Inst., Lexington, 1986—90, prof., 1990—. Coord. social studies U. So. Miss., Natchez, 1981—86; vis. prof. Washington & Lee U., Lexington, Va., 2003—04; exec. dir. Alumni Coll. at Va. Mil. Inst., Inc., Lexington, 1996—2007, pres. bd. dirs., 2004—07. Contbr. articles to profl. jours., chapters to books. Mem. adv. com. Brownsburg Mus., Va., 2006—; elder New Providence Presbyn. Ch., Brownsburg, 1991—. Rsch. grantee, Am. Philos. Soc., 1982, AASLH/NEH, 1984. Mem.: So. Hist. Assn., Sigma Chi (v.p. bd. dirs. ho. corp. Zeta chpt. 1995—2006). Avocation: gardening. Office: Dept History Va Mil Inst Lexington VA 24450 Office Phone: 540-464-7470. Office Fax: 540-464-7246. E-mail: koenigerac@vmi.edu.

KOEPPEL, PETER STAFFORD, advertising executive; m. Deborah Koeppel; 2 children. BA in Psychology magna cum laude, SUNY, Albany, 1975; MBA, U. Pa., Phila., 1980. Assoc. product mgr. H.J. Heinz, Pitts., 1980—82; product mgr. Ben Hogan Co., Ft. Worth, 1982; account supr. Richards Group, Dallas, 1983—86; ptnr. Joiner Rowland Serio Koeppel, Dallas, 1986—95; pres. Koeppel Direct, Dallas, 1995—. Adv. bd. mem. Electronic Retailing mag., Washington, 2004—; columnist Electronic Retailer Mag., 2005—; spkr. ERA D2C Conv., 2009, 2012—13; mem. editl. adv. bd. Response Mag., 2011—; spkr. Response Expo., 2012—13. Contbr. articles to profl. jours. Sole sponsor FBLA Invention Showcase Scholarship Program for Young Inventors, Washington, 2006; plan competition mentor Wharton Sch. Bus., 2007—08; judge bus. plan competition Wharton Sch., 2007—08; hon. com. mem. Wheelchair Found., 2007; chmn. meeting and convention com. Electronic Retailers Assn., 2007—08, bd. mem., 2009, spkr., ann. conf., 2012—13; author for adotas, leading online advt. website, 2007—. Mem.: Electronic Retailer Assn. (membership com. mem. 2011), Direct Mktg. Assn. (broadcast coun. 2005—08, pharm. coun. 2005—08). Avocations: golf, reading, travel. Office: Koeppel Direct 16200 Dallas Pkwy 270 Dallas TX 75248 Office Phone: 972-732-6110. Business E-Mail: pkoeppel@koeppelinc.com.

KOETTER, DIRK J., professional football coach; b. Pocatello, Idaho, Feb. 5, 1959; m. Kim Koetter; children: Kaylee, Kendra, Derek, Davis. BS in Physical Edn., Idaho State U., 1981, MA in Athletic Adminstrn., 1982. Offensive coord. San Francisco State U. Gators, 1985; offensive coord., quarterbacks coach U. Tex.-El Paso Miners, 1986—88, U. Mo. Tigers, 1989—93, Boston Coll. Eagles, 1994—95, U. Oreg. Ducks, 1996—97; head football coach Boise State U. Broncos, 1998—2000, Ariz. State U. Sun Devils, 2000—06; offensive coord. Jacksonville Jaguars, 2007—11, Atlanta Falcons, 2012—. Named Big West Conf. Coach of Yr., 1999, 2000. Office: Atlanta Falcons 4400 Falcon Pky Flowery Branch GA 30542*

KOFF, SHIRLEY IRENE, writer; b. Oakland, Calif., Aug. 31, 1948; d. Lawrence Ray and Stella Pauline (Durham) Butler; m. Robert Allen Koff, June 12, 1971; children: Jennifer, Katherine. BA, Calif. State U., 1971, MA, 1972. Adj. prof. Pellissippi State U., Knoxville, 1989-93; asst. mgr. Adolfo II, Pigeon Forge, Tenn., 1994-98; mgr. Jackson-Hewitt Tax Svc. Franchise Office, 1998—. Poet, writer; tchr. adult religious edn. classes and seminars; expert info. provider internet resource AskAnything.com. Tchr., lay min., bd. dirs. First Assembly of God Ch., Sevierville, 1996-99; core group leader, founding mem. Wellspring Congregation, United Meth. Ch., 1999-2001. Mem.: AAUW, Knoxville (Tenn.) Writers Guild, Tenn. Writers Alliance, Appalachian Writers Assn., Mensa. Democrat. Avocations: writing, speaking, teaching. Home: 1214 Amber Ln Sevierville TN 37862-6101 E-mail: sikoff@chartertn.net.

KOFORD, JONÉ LAW, healthcare services company executive; Various ops. positions Altius Health Plans, Arcon Healthcare, Inc., HealthTrust, Inc., HCA, Inc.; v.p., devel. LifePoint Hosps., Inc., 2001, divsn. pres., 2001—08; group pres., organic growth LifePoint Hospitals, Inc., 2008—. Office: LifePoint Hospitals Inc Ste 200 103 Powell Ct Brentwood TN 37027 Office Phone: 615-372-8500. Office Fax: 615-372-8575. Business E-Mail: jone.koford@lifepointhospitals.com.

KOHELET, GREGORY, painter; b. Fergana, Uzbekistan, 1954; married; 2 children. Grad., Tashkent Inst. of Performing and Fine Arts, 1981. With Tashkent Inst. of Performing and Fine Arts, 1986—89. Exhibitions include, Jerusalem, Dusseldorf, Paris, Madrid, Geneva and several others; author: Kabbalah and Art. Mailing: c/o Silka Gallery 7117 Enterprise Ave Mc Lean VA 22101

KOHLENBERGER, GERALD L., energy executive; BCE, MCE; MBA in fin., U. So. Calif. Project engr. Mobil Oil Corp., Torrance, Calif., 1974, gen. mgr., global info., gen. mgr. bus. resources corp., chief info. officer, 1998—2000; pres. ExxonMobil Lubricants and Petroleum Spltys. Co., 2002—07, ExxonMobil Global Svcs. Co., 2000—01; v.p., global info. svcs. ExxonMobil Corp., Fairfax, Va., 2000—01, v.p., 2002—. Office: Exxon Mobil Corp 5959 Las Colinas Blvd Irving TX 75039-2298 Office Phone: 972-444-1000. Office Fax: 972-444-1350. Business E-Mail: jerry.kohlenberger@exxonmobil.com.

KOHLER, MATTHEW F., gynecologic oncologist, educator; BA in Biochemistry, Yale U., New Haven, 1983; MD, Duke U., 1987. Diplomate Am. Bd. Ob-Gyn, Am. Bd. Ob-Gyn-gynecologic oncology. Intern ob-gyn. dept. Duke Univ. Med. Ctr., 1988, resident ob-gyn. dept., 1987—91, fellow gynecologic oncology, 1991—94; assoc. prof. ob-gyn. dept. Med. Univ. SC, dir. gynecologic oncology dept. Named one of the Best Doctors, 2011—12. Office: Medical University of South Carolina 171 Ashley Ave Charleston SC 29403 Office Phone: 843-792-1414. Business E-Mail: kohlermf@musc.edu.

KOHLER, PETER OGDEN, academic administrator, internist, educator; b. Bklyn., July 18, 1938; s. Dayton McCue and Jean Stewart (Ogden) K.; m. Judy Lynn Baker, Dec. 26, 1959; children: Brooke Culp, Stephen Edwin, Todd Randolph, Adam Stewart. BA, U. Va., 1959; MD, Duke U., 1963; PhD in Pub. Svc. (hon.), U. Portland, 2003; PhD (hon.), Oreg. Health Sci. U., 2006. Diplomate Am. Bd. Internal Medicine and Endocrinology. Intern Duke U. Hosp., Durham, NC, 1963-64, fellow, 1964-65; clin. assoc. Nat Cancer Inst., Nat Inst. Child Health and Human Devel., NIH, Bethesda, Md., 1965-67, sr. investigator, 1968-73, head endocrinology service, 1972-73; resident in medicine Georgetown U. Hosp., Washington, 1969-70; prof. medicine and cell biology, chief endocrinology divsn. Baylor Coll. Medicine, Houston, 1973-77; prof., chmn. dept. medicine University of Arkansas, 1977-86, interim dean, 1985-86; chmn. Hosp. Med. Bd., 1980-82, chmn. council dept. chmn., 1979-80; prof., dean Sch. Medicine, U. Tex., San Antonio, 1986-88; pres. Oreg. Health & Sci. U., Portland, 1988—2006, pres. emeritus, 2006; vice chancellor NW U. Ark. for Med. Scis., 2007—. Cons. endocrinology merit rev. bd. VA, 1985—86; mem. bd. sci. counselors NICHD, 1987—92, chair, 1990—92; chair task force on health care delivery AAHC, 1991—92, Inst. Medicine, 1994—; bd. dirs. Stancorp Fin. Group, 1990—2011; bd. dirs., Portland br. Fed. Res. Bank San Francisco, 2002—06; chair IOM Task Force on Improving Quality of Long-Term Care, 2004; mem. adv. bd. Loaves and Fishes, 1989—99; mem. Gov.'s adv. com. Commn. on Tech. Edn., 1989—92; chair Oreg. Health Coun., 1993—95; various positions Am. Bd. Internal Medicine, 1987—93, NIH; mem. numerous bd. dirs. and adv. bds. Editor: Current Opinion in Endocrinology and Diabetes, 1994-97, Diagnosis and Treatment of Pituitary Tumors, (with G. T. Ross), 1973, Clinical Endocrinology, 1986; assoc. editor: Internal Medicine, 1983, 87, 90, 94, 98; contbr. articles to profl. jours. Mem. campaign cabinet United Way, 1999—2004. With USPHS, 1965-68. NIH grantee, 1973—; Howard Hughes Med. Investigator, 1976-77; recipient NIH Quality awrds, 1969, 71, Disting. Alumnus award Duke Med. Sch., 1992, MRF Mentor award, Med. Rsch. Found., 1994, Humanitarian award Am. Lung Assn., 1996, Jewish Nat. Fund Tree of Life award, 1998, Internat. Citizens award Oreg. Consular Corps., 1999, Human Rels. award Am. Jewish Com., 2002, Leadership award Coun. for Advancement and Support of Edn., 2004; named Honored Citizen, Archl. Found. Oreg., 2002; named one of Twenty Leaders of Change, The Bus. Jour., 2004, Nat. Multiple Sclerosis Soc. Hope award, 2005, Oregon Health Forum Lifetime Leadership award, 2007 Master: ACP; mem.: AMA (William Beaumont award 1988), Inst. Medicine, Am. Soc. Clin. Investigation, Am. Fedn. Clin. Rsch. (nat. coun. 1977-78, pres. so. sect. 1976), So. Soc. Clin. Investigation (coun. 1979-82, pres. 1983, Founder's medal 1987), Am. Soc. Cell Biology, Assn. Acad. Health Ctrs. (chmn. 1998-99, bd. dirs.), Assn. Am. Physicians, Am. Diabetes Assn., Endocrine Soc. (coun. 1990-93), Raven Soc., Phi Beta Kappa, Alpha Omega Alpha, Omicron Delta Kappa, Phi Eta Sigma. Methodist. Office: UAMS NW 1125 N College Ave Fayetteville AR 72703 Office Phone: 479-713-8000. Business E-Mail: pkohler@uams.edu.

KOHLMEIER, LOUIS MARTIN, JR., newspaper reporter; b. St. Louis, Feb. 17, 1926; s. Louis Martin and Anita (Werling) K.; m. Barbara Anne Wilson, Nov. 15, 1958; children— Daniel Kimbrell, Ann Werling. B.Journalism, U. Mo., 1950. Staff writer Wall St. Jour., St. Louis and Chgo., 1952-57, Washington, 1960—; staff writer St. Louis Globe-Democrat, 1958-59. Author: The Regulators Watchdog Agencies and the Public Interest, 1969. Served with AUS, 1950-52. Recipient Nat. Headliners Club award nat. reporting, 1959, Sigma Delta Chi award Washington corr., 1964, Pulitzer prize nat. reporting, 1964 Home: 12819 Hazelbrook Ln Cornelius NC 28031-8254

KOHN, RICHARD H., historian, educator; b. Chgo., Dec. 29, 1940; s. Henry L. and Kate K.; m. Lynne Holtan, Aug. 15, 1964; children: Abigail, Samuel. AB, Harvard U., 1962; MS in History, U. Wis., 1964, PhD in history, 1968. Asst. prof. history CCNY, 1968-71; from asst. prof. to prof. Rutgers U., New Brunswick, NJ, 1971-84; Harold Keith Johnson vis. prof. mil. history U.S. Army Mil. History Inst., Army War Coll., Carlisle Barracks, Pa., 1980-81; chief of Air Force history USAF, Washington, 1981-91; adj. prof. Nat. War Coll., Washington, 1985-90; from assoc. prof. to prof. history U. NC, Chapel Hill, 1991—2011, emeritus prof., 2011—, chair curriculum in peace, war and defense, 1992—2006; Omar N. Bradley chair strategic leadership US Army War Coll. Dickinson Coll, 2006—07; ind. review panel Quadrennial Defence Review, 2010; bd. trustee Nat. History Ctr., 2010—. Expert witness U.S. Indian Claims Commn., Washington, 1974; cons. to various def. and hist. agys. and orgns., 1972—; vis. scholar strategic studies Johns Hopkins U. Sch. Advanced Internat. Studies, 1991; dir. Triangle Inst. for Security Studies, 1992-2000; bd. visitors Air Univ. USAF, 1996-2001. Author: Eagle and Sword: The Federalists and the Creation of the Military Establishment in America, 1783-1802, 1975; co-author: The Exclusion of Black Soldiers from the Medal of Honor in World War II, 1997; editor (reprint series) The American Military Experience, 1979; editor: The U.S. Military under the Constitution of the United States, 1789-1989, 1991; co-editor: (books) Air Superiority in World War II and Korea, 1983, Air Interdiction in World War II, Korea, and Vietnam, 1986, Strategic Air Warfare, 1988, Soldiers and Civilians, 2001; contbr. articles to profl. jours., chpts. to books. Recipient cert. for patriotic civilian service Dept. of Army, 1981, 96, Orgnl. Excellence award Dept. Air Force, 1990, Exceptional Civilian Svc. award Dept. Air Force, 1991, Edward F. Miller History prize Naval War Coll., 2005. Mem. Air Force Hist. Found. (Pres.' award 1987), Am. Antiquarian Soc., Am. Hist. Assn. (coun. 1986-89, Herbert Feis award 2008, Herbert Feis Award Com., 2010-13), Orgn. Am. Historians (Binkley-Stephenson award 1973, pub. history com. 1989-92, chair 1991-92), Soc. for Mil. History (trustee 1981-89, 95-99, parliamentarian 1982-89, pres. 1989-93, chair nom. com. 2000-2003, Victor Gondos Meml. Svc. award 1996, Samuel Eliot Morison prize 2009), World War II Studies Assn. (bd. dirs. 1985-88, 91-97, 2000-06).

KOHUT, ROBERT IRWIN, otolaryngologist, educator; b. Chgo., Nov. 29, 1932; s. Emil and Ruth Irene Kohut; m. Joanne Kay Hughes, Dec. 26, 1953 (dec. Oct. 1982); children: James, Paul, Robert, John; m. Frances Irene Speas, June 6, 1983 (div. 1999). BA, Wittenburg Coll., 1956; MD, U. Chgo., 1960. Diplomate Am. Bd. Otolaryngology (bd. dirs. 1979). Intern U. Chgo., 1961—62, resident in otolaryngology, 1962—65, NIH fellow, 1965—66, instr. in otolaryngology, 1965—66; asst. prof. U. Fla., Gainesville, 1966—68, assoc. prof., 1968-71, assoc. prof., acting chmn., 1971—72; prof., chief otolaryngology U. Calif., Irvine, 1972—79; prof., chmn. otolaryngology Wake Forest U. Sch. Medicine, Winston-Salem, NC, 1979—99, emeritus prof., chair, 1999—. Mem. study sect. Nat. Insts. Neurol. and Communicative Disorders and Stroke/NIH, Bethesda, Md., 1981—86; cons. NASA, 1982—84; mem. adv. bd. Nat. Inst. Deafness and Other Comm. Disorders, 1991—94; exec. v.p. med. affairs, med. dir. Deafness Rsch. Found., 1999—2001. Contbr. numerous chpts. to books and articles to profl. jours.; editor otology divsn. Head and Neck Surgery-Otolaryngology; mem. editorial bd. Am. Jour. Otology, 1992-2000, Am. Jour. Otolaryngology, 1982-2000, Archives of Otolaryngology, 1980-2000, Laryngoscope, 1976-2000. With USAF, 1950-53. Recipient Norvel Pierce award Chgo. Laryngological Soc., 1965, Basic Rsch. award Acad. Ophthalmology and Otolaryngology, 1968. Fellow ACS, mem. AMA (rep. residency review com. otolaryngology 1975-80), Soc. Univ. Otolaryngologists (pres. 1978-79), Barany Soc., Am. Laryngological, Rhinological and Otological Soc. (exec. coun. 1987-90, Edmund Fowler award 1974, Guest of Honor, So. sect. 1996), Am. Broncho-Esophagological Ass., Am. Neurotology Assn., Otosclerosis Study Group, Am. Otological Soc. (sec.-treas. 1987-92, pres.-elect 1992-93, pres. 1993-94), Assn. Acad. Depts. Otolaryngology, Pacific Coast Oto-Ophthalmol. Soc., Forsyth County Med. Soc., N.C. Med. Soc., N.C. Soc. Otolaryngology Head and Neck Surgery (v.p. 1985, pres. 1986-87), Assn. for Rsch. in Otolaryngology, Am. Acad. Otolaryngology-Head and Neck Surgery, Am. Soc. Head and Neck Surgery, Internat. Fedn. Oto-Rhino-Laryngological Soc. (chmn. emeritus standing com. edn. 2004), others. Avocations: fishing, hunting, sailing. Office: Wake Forest U Sch Medicine Dept Otolaryngology Medical Center Blvd Winston Salem NC 27157-0001 Personal E-mail: rikohut@att.net.

KOK, HANS GEBHARD, consulting engineer; b. Potshausen, Germany, Apr. 5, 1923; came to U.S., 1951, naturalized, 1959; s. George J. and Anitina K. (Janssen) K.; m. Roselle V. Venier, June 22, 1960; Children: George H., Karen R. Student, Suderburg Engring. Coll., Germany, 1940-42, Hamburg Engring Coll., 1945-46; Dipl.Ing, Technische Hochschule, Aachen, Germany, 1950. Registered profl. engr., N.Y., Pa., Ind., Mich., Calif., Fla., N.J., Ariz., Md. Design engr. Lummus Co., NYC, 1951-53; structural engr. M.H. Treadwell Co., NYC, 1953-56, head structural engring. sect., 1956-62, chief structural engr., 1962-63; mgr. plant design divsn. Treadwell Corp., NYC, 1963-69, asst. v.p. engring., 1969-73, v.p. engring., 1973-83; pres. Treadwell Corp. Mich., Inc., 1974-83; dir. BassetMiller Treadwell Pty. Ltd., 1973-83; cons. engr., 1983—. Chmn. exec. com. Coun. Engring. Laws, 1976. Contbr. articles to profl. jours. Recipient 1st award James F. Lincoln Arc Welding Found., 1966. Fellow ASCE; mem. Nat. Soc. Profl. Engrs., N.Y. State Soc. Profl. Engrs., Am. Inst. Mining, Metall. and Petroleum Engrs. (chmn. materialshandling com.), Am. Mining congress, Am. Mgmt. Assn. Home: 4438 Meager Cir Port Charlotte FL 33948-9495

KOLB, CHARLES CHESTER, foundation administrator; b. Erie, Pa., Sept. 4, 1940; s. John Christian and Edna Lucille (Church) Kolb; m. Joy Bilharz, June 3, 1972 (div. Mar. 1991); 1 child, Nancy Gwenyth; m. P. Jean Drew, July 20, 1991; 1 child, Catherine Claire Fraley. BA in History, Pa. State U., 1962, PhD in Archaeology and Anthropology, 1979. Instr. anthropology Pa. State U., University Park, 1966-69, Bryn Mawr (Pa.) Coll., 1969-73; from instr. to asst. prof. anthropology Pa. State U., Erie, 1973-84; dir. rsch. and grants Mercyhurst Coll., 1984-89, asst. dir. Hammermill Libr., 1989; humanities adminstr. program officer divsn. state programs NEH, Washington, 1989-91, program officer divsn. preservation and access, 1991-96, sr. program officer, 1997—, Recovering Iraq's Past Initiative, 2003—, Rediscovering Afghanistan Initiative, 2004—. Manuscript reviewer Holt, Rinehart and Winston, Inc., 1977—89, Prentice-Hall, Inc., 1979—85, William C. Brown, Pubs., 1982—85, U. Tex. Press, 1988—, U. Utah Press, 1991—, U. Press Fla., 1994—, AltaMira Press/Sage, 1995—, U. Pa. Mus. Applied Sci. Ctr. Archaeology, 1996—, Dover Pub., 1996—, U. Press Colo., 2003—, Centro de Estudios Arqueológicos el Colegio de Michoacán, Mexico, 2004—, U. Ariz. Press, 2005—; grant proposal reviewer NEH, 1981—89, NSF, 1982—, Wenner-Gren Found. Anthropol. Rsch., 1987—89, Social Sci. Humanities Rsch. Coun. Can., Canada, 2003—, Can. Found. Innovation, 2004—, Nat. Geog. Soc. Rsch., Conservation and Exploration Grants, 2005—; co-founder, ann. symposium co-organizer Ceramic Studies Interest Group, 1986—. Author: Marine Shell Trade and Classic Teotihuacan, 1987; editor: A Pot for All Reasons, 1988, Ceramic Ecology, 1988, 1989, 1997; contbr. articles to profl. jours., chapters to books; book and film reviewer: Sci. Books and Films, 1977—, manuscript reviewer: Am. Antiquity, 1978—, Current Anthropology, 1979—, Ancient Mesoamerica, 1990—, Ethnohistory, 1995—, Jour. Material Culture, 1995—, Hist. Archaeology, 1995—, L.Am. Antiquity, 1995—, H-Net Revs., 1996—, Jour. Archeol. Sci., 1998—, Jour. Am. Inst. Conservation, 2001—, The Historian, 2005—, Geoarchaeology, 2007—, Jour. Archaeological Method and Theory, 2008—, abstractor: Ceramic Abstracts, 1990—96, Art and Archaeology Tech. Abstracts, 1996—, regional editor: La Tinaja: Newsletter Archeol. Ceramics, 1991—, N.Am. corr.: Old Potter's Almanack, 1992—, reviewer: CHOICE, 1992—, ScienceNETLinks, 1999—, Transoxiana: E-Jour. de Estudios Orientales, 2003—, Ctrl. Asian Rsch. Rev., 2003—; co-author: Ency. Modern Asia, 2002, Ency. World's Minorities, 2003, Dictionary Am. History, 2002, Ency. Modern Mid. East and N. Africa, 2d edit., 2004, Ency. Developing World, 2005, Ency. World Geography, 2005, Ency. China, 2008, World History Encyclopedia, 2009. Mem. Commonwealth of Pa., Gov.'s Conf. Librs. and Info. Sys., 1989. Fellow: AAAS (Panelist Sci. Journalism awards 2003—), Am. Anthrop. Assn., Royal Anthrop. Inst. Gt. Britain and Ireland; mem.: ALA, Assn. Asian Studies, Soc. S.W. Archivists, Mid-Atlantic Regional Archives Conf. Archivists, Assn. Recorded Sound Collections, Soc. Clay Pipe Rsch., Am. Inst. Afghanistan Studies, Ctrl. Eurasian Studies Soc., Naval Hist. Found., Assn. Moving Image Archivists, Paleopathology Assn., NY State Archeol. Assn., Soc. Pa. Archeology, Register Profl. Archeologists, Soc. Am. Archivists, Soc. Hist. Archeology, Soc. Am. Archeology, Prehistoric Ceramic Rsch. Group, Soc. Archeol. Scis. (life; assoc. editor Archeol. Ceramics Bull. 1997—, bd. dirs. 1998—), Pearl Harbor History Assocs. (life), Materials Rsch. Soc., Coun. Mus. Anthropology, Assn. Field Archaeology, Archeol. Inst. Am., Am. Soc. Ethnohistory, Am. Ethnological Soc., Am. Chem. Soc., Am. Ceramic Soc., Internet 2: Archaeology Spl. Interest Group, US Naval Inst. (life), Sigma Xi, Pi Gamma Mu, Phi Kappa Phi, Alpha Kappa Delta. Home: 1005 Pruitt Ct SW Vienna VA 22180-6429 Office: NEH Divsn Preservation & Access 1100 Pennsylvania Ave NW Washington DC 20506-0001 Office Phone: 202-606-8250. Business E-Mail: ckolb@neh.gov.

KOLB, HAROLD HUTCHINSON, JR., language educator; b. Boston, Jan. 16, 1933; BA in English with honors, Amherst Coll., 1955; MA in Am. Studies, U. Mich., 1960; PhD in British and Am. Lit., Ind. U., 1968. Instr. English Valparaiso U., 1960-62; teaching assoc. Ind. U., 1962-65; from asst. prof. to prof. English U. Va., Charlottesville, 1967-99, prof. emeritus, 2000—, dir. Ctr. for Liberal Arts, 1984-99. Project dir. NEH, 1972-76, 85-99; dir. Canadian Judicial Writing Program, 1981-84; guest prof. Am. studies U. Bonn, 1982; chmn. MLA Delegate Assembly Steering Com., 1984-85. Author: The Illusion of Life-American Realism as a Literary Form, 1969, A Field Guide to the Study of American Literature, 1976, A Writer's Guide: The Essential Points, 1980; co-author: A Handbook for Research in American Literature and American Studies, 1994; contbr. articles to scholarly and other publs. Naval aviator USN, 1955—59. Recipient Armstrong prize in English, Amherst Coll., 1952, James A. Work prize, Ind. U., 1965, Guggenheim fellowship, 1970-71, Faculty Leadership award Am. Assn. Higher Edn., Carnegie Found. for Advancement of Teaching and Change mag., 1986, Citation for Leadership in Rejuvenation of Secondary and Elem. Edn., Va. Bd. Edn., 1987, Phillip E. Frandson award for Innovation and Creative Programming, Nat. U. Continuing Edn. Assn., 1988, Outstanding Faculty award, Va. Coun. Higher Edn., 1988. Business E-Mail: hhk6s@virginia.edu.

KOLB, JERRY WILBERT, accountant; b. Chgo., Dec. 22, 1935; s. Herman and Myrtle (Richter) K.; m. Marlene Joyce Tipp, Feb. 3, 1957 (div. July 1986); children: Bradley, Steven, Lisa; m. Carol Ann Fleming, Dec. 14, 1986. BS in Acct. with high honors, U. Ill., 1957; MBA, DePaul U., 1962. CPA Ill., NY, Iowa. Acct. Deloitte Haskins & Sells CPAs, Chgo., 1957-68, ptnr., 1968-76, ptnr.-in-charge Chgo. Office, 1976-83; ptnr.-in-charge profl. svcs. Deloitte & Touche CPAs (formerly Deloitte Haskins & Sells), NYC, 1983-86, CFO, 1986-92, vice-chmn., 1992-98; dir. New Skies Satellites N.V., 1998—, Mid America Group, 2002—, Walter Industries, Inc., 2003—. Lectr. DePaul U., Chgo., 1962-76, mem. adv. council dept. acctg., 1981-83; mem. profl. adv. bd. dept. accountancy U. Ill., Urbana, 1979-82; mem. adv. council Sch. Accountancy, Northwestern U., Evanston, 1980-83. Recipient Disting. Alumni award DePaul U., 1970. Mem. AICPA (Sells Gold Medal award 1957), Ill. CPA Soc. (bd. dirs. 1973-77, v.p. 1976-77), Am. Acctg. Assn., NY Yacht Club, Tampa Yacht and Country Club. E-mail: nquest1@aol.com.

KOLBAS, ROBERT MICHAEL, electrical engineering educator; b. Syracuse, NY, Nov. 13, 1953; s. John Michael and Frances C. Kolbas; children: Michael Thomas, Daniel Robert, Sarah Anne, Mary Chen; m. Yan Wang. BS in Engring., Cornell U., 1975; MS in Physics, U. Ill., 1977, PhD, 1979. Rsch., teaching asst. U. Ill., Urbana, 1975-79; prin. rsch. scientist Honeywell, Inc., Bloomington, Minn., 1979-83, sr. prin. rsch. scientist, 1983-85; assoc. prof. N.C. State U., Raleigh, 1985-90, prof. elec. and computer engring., 1990—, head elec. and computer engring. dept., 1995-2000, 2008—09. Contbr. articles to profl. publs.; patentee in field. Mentor to high sch. students, N.C. Sch. Sci. and Math., Durham, 1988-91. Kodak doctoral fellow U. Ill./Kodak, 1978. Fellow IEEE; mem. Tau Beta Pi, Sigma Xi. Office: N C State U PO Box 7911 Raleigh NC 27695-0001 Home Phone: 919-821-4676; Office Phone: 919-515-5257. Business E-Mail: kolbas@ncsu.edu.

KOLINSKY, MICHAEL ALLEN, emergency physician; b. Phila., Dec. 23, 1947; BA, U. Wis., 1970; MD, Rush U., 1979. Diplomate Am. Bd. Emergency Medicine. Staff physician emergency dept. River Parishes Hosp., LaPlace, La., 1982-85, Rutland Regional Med. Ctr., Vt., 2005—; co-med. dir. emergency dept. Meadowcrest Hosp., Gretna, La., 1985-92; co-med. dir. City of New Orleans Emergency Med. Svcs., 1987—2004; med. dir. emergency dept. Tulane U. Med. Ctr., New Orleans, 1992—2008, staff physician, 2008—; staff physician emergency dept. Bapt. Hosp., New Orleans, 2009—. Office: Ochsner Bapt Hosp Emergency Dept 2700 Napoleon Ave New Orleans LA 70115 E-mail: kolinsky@tulane.edu.

KOLKHORST, LOIS W., state legislator; m. Jim Kolkhorst; children: Lois Kate, Jake. BS in Advt. and Pub. Rels., Tex. Christian U., 1998. Athletic adminstr. Tex. Christian U., 1988—96; owner, operator Kolkhorst Petroleum, Navasota, Tex.; CEO Wash. C. of C. and the Econ. Devel. Found., Brenham; mem. Dist. 13 Tex. House of Representatives, 2000—. Served on Tex. Economic Develop. Coun., Brazos Valley Workforce Commission; appointed to One-Call Bd. of Tex. Republican. Avocations: golf, hunting, fishing. Office: PO Box 1867 Brenham TX 77834 also: Room GN.09 Capitol PO Box 2910 Austin TX 78768 Office Phone: 979-251-7888, 512-463-0600.

KOLLAER, JIM C., real estate executive, architect; b. Amarillo, Tex., Jan. 5, 1943; s. Walter W. and Margaret M. Kollaer; 1 child, Andrew N. Student, Amarillo Coll., 1960-62, La. State U., 1962-65; BArch, Tex. Tech. U., 1969. Lic. architect, Tex.; lic. broker, Tex. V.p., dir. urban design RKA Inc. Assoc., Dallas, 1969-75; with CRS Inc., Houston, 1975—80, v.p., dir. mktg., 1977-80; pres. Houston divsn. Henry Miller Co., Houston, 1980-85; pres. Henry S. Miller/Grubb & Ellis, 1985-89, Kollaer Internat., 1989-90; pres., CEO Greater Houston Partnership, 1990—2005; exec. v.p., ptnr. Staubach Co. Houston, Corp. Svc., 2005—07; mng. dir. Kollaer Advisors, LLC, 2007—. Past chmn. Tex. Bus. Hall of Fame; past bd. dirs. Ctr. Houston's Future; cons. and lectr. in field. Sr. fellow Am. Leadership Forum. Fellow AIA; mem. Tex. Soc. Archs., Urban Land Inst., Tex. Assn. Realtors, Nat. Assn. Realtors, Houston Wilderness (bd. dirs.), U.S. C. of C. (bd. dirs. 1999-2005), Chamber Found. (bd. dirs.), Coronado Club, Houston Realty Breakfast Club. Republican. Presbyterian. Home Phone: 713-523-6339; Office Phone: 713-542-9075. E-mail: jim.kollaer@kollaeradvisors.com.

KOLODEY, FRED JAMES, lawyer; b. LaCoste, Tex., Mar. 5, 1936; s. Raymond and Mamie V. (Newman) K.; children: Trecia Anne Dilger, Michele Leigh Winn; m. Helen Gable McIntosh, June 10, 1989. BA, Tex. Christian U., Ft. Worth, 1962; LLB, So. Meth. U., Dallas, 1964. Bar: Tex. 1964. Since practiced in, Dallas; ptnr. Kolodey & Thomas, 1975-83, of counsel, 1983-94, Thomas, Sheehan & Culp, 1994—2001, Kolodey, Thomas & Blackwood, 2001—05; prin. Law Office Fred Kolodey, Dallas, 2005—08, Rockwall, Tex., 2008—; of counsel Thomas & Blackward, LLP, 2008—. Pres. Dallas Jr. Bar Assn., 1969 Comments editor: Southwestern Law Jour, 1963-64. Mem. dist. hearing office panel Dallas Community Coll., 1974, Democratic precinct chmn., 1968-73. Mem. Tex., Rockwall Bar Assns., Delta Theta Phi (pres. 1963, Nat. award 1964), Alpha Chi, Pi Sigma Alpha. Business E-Mail: fred@kolodeylaw.com.

KOLODNY, STANLEY CHARLES, oral surgeon, retired military officer; b. NYC, Feb. 22, 1923; s. Aaron and Lea (Stern) K.; m. Mary Kathryn Leigh, Feb. 22, 1947; children: Kathleen Susan, Carter Leigh, Stanley Charles. BA, U. Tex., 1944; D.D.S., Baylor U., 1947; MS, U. Ill., 1961. Diplomate: Am. Bd. Oral and Maxillofacial Surgery. Commd. 1st lt. USAF, 1951, advanced through grades to maj. gen., 1981; cons. in oral surgery Surgeon Gen. U.S. Air Force, 1966; chmn. dept. oral surgery Wilford Hall USAF Med. Center, San Antonio, 1969-75, dir. dental services, 1975-77; asst. surgeon gen. for dental services Bolling AFB, Washington, 1979-82. Clin. prof. dept. surgery U. Tex. Dental Br., Houston, 1969-77; clin. asso. prof. dept. surgery U. Tex. Med. Sch., San Antonio, 1969-77 Contbr. chpt. to book, articles to profl. jours. Bd. dirs. Am. Cancer Soc., 1970-77. Decorated D.S.M., Legion of Merit with oak leaf cluster, Air Force Commendation medal; recipient cert. of achievement for outstanding oral surgery USAF. Fellow Am. Coll. Dentists, Am. Assn. Oral and Maxillofacial Surgeons; mem. ADA, Soc. Air Force Clin. Surgeons. Home: USAF 6401 Red Bud Dr Flower Mound TX 75022-5859

KOLODZIESKI, ED, retail executive; CEO and rep. exec. officer Seiyu Ltd., Japan, 2005—10; CEO Walmart Japan Holdings G.K.; sr. v.p. Wal-mart Stores Inc., 2000, sr. v.p. and COO of Wal-Mart internat., 2004—, exec. v.p. global sourcing, 2010—. Office: Wal-Mart Stores, Incorporated 702 SW 8th St Bentonville AR 72716 Office Phone: 479-273-4000. Office Fax: 479-273-4053.

KOLSKI, STEPHEN J., air transportation executive, lawyer; b. Newark, Jan. 3, 1941; s. Stefan and Jean (Dejewski) K.; m. Lois Ann Hyland; children: Stephen Jr., Mark, Kristi. BA in Economics, U. Notre Dame, 1963; JD, U. Miami, Coral Gables, 1971. Dir. labor rels. Nat. Airlines, Miami, Fla., 1966—75, staff v.p. flight ops., 1975-80; v.p. ops. NY Air, NYC, 1980-87; v.p. regulation compliance Ea. Airlines, Miami, 1987-88, v.p. base mgmt., 1988-89; pres., COO Continental Express, 1990—93; dir., pres., COO ATX, Inc., 1993—95; cons. aerospace industry, 1995—99; exec. v.p. corp. affairs AirTran Airways, Inc., 1999—, exec. v.p., corp. affairs, 2010—. Bd. dirs. CHRIS Kids, Inc, Atlanta. Capt. U.S. Army, 1965. Republican. Roman Catholic. Avocation: boating. Office: AirTran Airways 2702 Love Field Dr Dallas TX 75235-1908 Office Fax: 407-318-5900. Business E-Mail: stephen.kolski@airtran.com.

KOLTHOFF CARABALLO, ERICK V., territorial supreme court justice; b. San Juan, Sept. 15, 1961; m. Betsy Morales Cintron; 1 child, Johann Gabriel. BBA, Interamerican Univ., MS in criminal justice summa cum laude; JD, Univ. PR, 1988. Atty. private practice, 1989; examiner PR Pub. Svc. Commn., 1990—92; legal adv. PR Courts Adminstrn. Office, 1992—93; atty. private practice, 1993—98; examiner PR Telecommunications Regulatory Bd., 1998—2000, dir. legal div., 2000—01; legal specialist regulatory affairs PR Telephone Co., 2001—05; exec. dir. office of tech. assessment PR Senate, 2005—07; judge PR Superior Ct., 2007—09; assoc. justice PR Supreme Ct., 2009—. Mailing: Rama Judicial de Puerto Rico PO Box 9022392 San Juan PR 00902-2392 Office Phone: 787-723-6033.*

KOMAN, ALAN JAMES, lawyer, educator; b. Atlanta, Ga., Nov. 28, 1950; s. Albert James and Marjorie (Morgan) Koman. BA, Cornell U., 1972; JD, Duke U., 1975; LLB, U. Munich, 1981. Bar: Ga., N.Y., Washington D.C., U.S. Supreme Ct., U.S. Cir. Ct. (all), U.S. Ct. Appeals for Armed Forces, U.S. Ct. Fed. Claims, U.S. Ct. Internat. Trade, cert.: Hague Acad. Internat. Law 1978. Pvt. practice, Atlanta; chmn. Ga. Law & Nat. Security Inst. Guest lectr. Air U. USAF; guest lectr. Duke U., Harvard U., Johns Hopkins U., U. Munich, Swarthmore Col., U. Va., U. Pa.; instr. nat. security issues and mil. history Emory U., Atlanta. Contbr. articles to profl. jours.; author: A Who's Who of Your Ancestral Saints. Mem.: ABA (Internat. law and practice sect., standing com. on law and nat. security), Soc. of War of 1812, USA Dance, SOR, St. Thomas More Soc., St. Andrews Soc., Royal Soc. St. George, Order of St. Gregory the Great, Order of Crown Charlemagne, Mil. Order Crusades, Inter-U. Seminar Armed Forces & Soc., Heraldry Soc. (Scotland), Hagiography Soc., Baronial Order of Magna Charta, Atlanta Coun. Internat. Rels., Antebellum Planters, Internat. Soc. Mil. Law and Law of War, Fgn. Policy Rsch. Inst., Order of St. Gregory the Great, Winston Churchill Meml. and Libr., Templars, Am. Friends of Vatican Libr., Medieval Acad. Am., First Families of Ga., Colonial and Antebellum Bench and Bar, Am. of Royal Descent, Descendants of Knights of Garter, Gen. Soc. Colonial Wars, So. Acad. Letters, Arts and Scis., Most Venerable Order of St. John, Inquiry Club, Phi Beta Kappa. Office: 1770 Indian Trail Rd Ste 200 Norcross GA 30093

KOMECHAK, MARILYN GILBERT, retired psychologist, writer; b. Wabash, Ind., Aug. 28, 1936; d. Russell and Evelyn Georgianna (Snyder) Gilbert; m. George J. Komechak, Aug. 23, 1958; children: Kimberly Ann, Gilbert Matthew. BS, Purdue U., Ind., 1958, Tex. Christian U., Ft. Worth, 1966, MEd, 1968; PhD, North Tex. State U., 1975. Grad. asst. Tex. Christian U., 1967—68; counselor clin. staff Child Study Ctr., Ft. Worth, 1968—74; assoc. dir. Behavioral Ctr. Cmty. Svc., North Tex. State U., Denton, 1974—77; pvt. practice psychology Ft. Worth, 1977—96. Adj. prof. Tex. Christian U., U. Tex., Arlington; dir. Jon Pierce, Inc.; mem. Sanger-Harris Adv. Bd. Dallas, Ft. Worth, 1983; mem. chancellor's alumni adv. com. U. North Tex., 1987, bd. dirs., dance theater arts dept., 1989—96; cons. to schs. mgmt.; presenter in field; coord. Centennial Celebration, Ft. Worth, Tex Poetry Soc., 2010. Author: Getting Yourself Together, 1982, 2nd edit., 2002, 3rd edit., 2013, The Prairie Tree, 1987, Morals and Manners for the Millennium, 2002 (Finalist Judy and A.C. Greene Lit. Pub. Festival Anthology), 2nd edit., 2013, Paisano Pete: Snake-Killer Bird, 2003 (named Best Juvenile Book, Okla. Writers Fedn., 2004), Aries Lit. Jour., Tex. Wesleyan U., 2005; contbr. poetry to lit. jours.; author: (short stories) The Least He Could Do, 2013; contbr. articles counseling and psychology to profl. jours., poetry to anthologies; co-author: Pronto Pete Screenplay (Okla. Writers Fedn. award, 2007); author: Flash Fiction story, 2009, Tex. Poetry Calendar Poems, 2002—03, 2008—09; presenter with painter Kim Komechak Ekphrastic Poetry with Abstract Paintings, 2009—; contbr. poetry to anthology; author: Deborah Sampson: The Girl Who Went to War, 2012. Co-coord. Pen Women's Artist's Gallery Night, Ft. Worth, 2011. Recipient Outstanding Alumnus award, La Fontaine HS, Ind., 2004, Fiction award, Weatherford Coll., Tex., Canis Latran Writing Contest, 2012; named one of Notable Women of Tex., 1984—85. Mem.: DAR, Ft. Worth Song Writers, Ft. Worth Writers Anthology (fiction, poetry mem.), Nat. League Am. Pen Women, Ft. Worth Writers, Inc., Ft. Worth Poetry Soc. (Mem.'s Contest award 1999, 2002, 2006), Tex. State Poetry Soc., Ft. Worth Women's Club (judge, lit. divsn. 2005—13), Psi Chi, Delta Gamma. Episcopalian.

KOMISAREK, MIKE, professional hockey player; b. West Islip, NY, Jan. 19, 1982; s. Roman and Kathy Komisarek. Attended, U. Mich., 2000—02. Defenseman Hamilton Bulldogs (Am. Hockey League), 2002—05, Montreal Canadiens, 2002—09, Toronto Maple Leafs, 2009—13, Carolina Hurricanes, 2013—. Named to All-Rookie Team, Am. Hockey League, 2003, NHL All-Star Game, 2009. Office: Carolina Hurricanes RBC Ctr 2 1400 Edwards Mill Rd Raleigh NC 27607*

KONDONASSIS, ALEXANDER JOHN, economist, educator; b. Greece, Feb. 8, 1928; arrived in US, 1948, naturalized, 1960; s. John I. and Eve (Hatzistylianou) K.; m. Patricia Mundorff, Feb. 2, 1956; children: John, Yolanda. AB with distinction, DePauw U., 1952; MA, Ind. U., 1953, PhD, 1961. Teaching assoc. Ind. U., 1954-56, lectr., 1956-58; mem. faculty U. Okla., 1958—, prof. econs., 1964—, David Ross Boyd prof. econs., 1970—, chmn. dept., 1961-71, dir. div. econs., 1979-86, dir. advanced program in econs. bus. coll., 1971—, chmn. faculty senate, 1976-77, Regents prof., 1993. Lectr. Am. participant program U.S. Info. Agy., Iceland, Greece, Yugoslavia, 1986; Fulbright prof. Athens (Greece) Sch. Econs. and Bus. Sci., 1965-66, vis. prof., 1971; assocs. disting. lectureship U. Okla., 1988; bd. dirs. Am. Bank of Commerce; mem. Gov. Okla. Adv. Coun. Export Expansion, 1964-65;adv. council Inst. E. Mediterranean Affairs, 1967-68; chmn. editorial policies com. S.W. Soc. Sci. Quar., 1974-77. Author: Concepts of Economic Development with Special Reference to Underdeveloped Countries, 1963, Monetary Policies of the Bank of Greece, 1949-1951, Contributions to Monetary Stability and Economic Development, 1961, (with others) An Economic Base Study of Lawton, Oklahoma, 1963, Economic Planning and Free Enterprise, 1966, The Role of Agriculture in a Developing Economy, 1973, The EEC and Her Association with Israel, Spain, Turkey and Greece, 1972, Some Recent Trends in Development Economics, 1972, Contributions of Agriculture to Economic Development: The Cases of U.K., U.S.A., Japan and Mexico, 1973, Mediterranean Europe and the Common Market, 1976, The European Economic Community in the Mediterranean: Developments and Prospects on a Mediterranean Policy, 1976, The European Economic Community and Greece: Toward a Full Membership, 1977, The Greek Inflation and the Flight from the Drachma: 1940-48, 1977, The Greek Economy: The Old and the New, 1979, The Bank of Greece, 1949-51: Credit Control Changes in An Inflationary Environment, 1979, The European Economic Community: Toward a Common Development Policy, 1980, Recent Trends in Development Assistance Committee Aid Programs, 1981, Economic and Non-Economic Aspects of Economic Development, the Less Developed Countries: A Synthesis, 1983, Some Internal Problems of Social Sciences with Special Emphasis on the Economics of Development, 1985, Agricultural Productivity and Economic Development: A Note on Japan and Taiwan, 1987 Approaches to Economic Development: Some Swings of the Pendulum, 1988, The European Economic Community and the Single European Act, 1989, The European Economic Community in 1992, 1991, The Economy of Cyprus, 1991, Major Issues of Global Development, 1991, German Unification: Problems and Prospects, 1993, Monetary Union and Economic Integration: The Less Developed Areas of the European Community. 1993, Toward Monetary Union of the European Community: History and Experiences of the European Monetary System, 1994, NAFTA: Old and New lessons from Theory and Practice with Economic Integration, 1996, The European Monetary Union in Transition, 1998, Strengthening the Global Financial Stability, 2001. Bd. dirs. Am. Friends Wilton Park, N.Y., 1967-68. Recipient U. Okla. Regents award excellence teaching, 1964, Merrick Found. Teaching award, 1977, DePauw U. Rector Scholar Alumni Achievement award, 1977; inducted Okla. Higher Edn. Hall of Fame, 1998. Mem. Am. Econ. Assn., So. Econ. Assn., Southwestern Econ. Assn. (pres. 1993-94), Mo. Valley Econ. Assn. (dir., exec. com. 1980—, pres. 1983-84), Southwestern Social Sci. Assn. (v.p. 1980-83, pres. 1983-84, disting. svc. award, 2003), AAUP (pres. 1977-78), Phi Beta Kappa, Omicron Delta Epsilon (pres.-elect internat. exec. bd. 1985-89, pres. 1989-92), Beta Gamma Sigma. Home: PO Box 695 Norman OK 73070-0695 Office Phone: 405-325-2861. Business E-Mail: ajk@ou.edu.

KONE, BRUCE C., medical educator, nephrologist, scientist, former dean; b. Frankfurt, Germany, Jan. 29, 1958; s. Kenneth M. and Dorothy Kone; m. Daisy Linda Waller, June 10, 1992; children: Natalie Audrey, Justine Dorothy, Lindsey Jane. AB, Princeton U., NJ, 1979; MD, U. Fla., Gainesville, 1983. Internal Medicine Am. Bd. Internal Medicine, 1984, Nephrology Am. Bd. Internal Medicine, 1994; cert. nephrology Am. Bd. Internal Medicine, 2004. Resident Johns Hopkins Hosp., Baltimore, Md., 1983—86; renal fellow Brigham and Women's Hosp., Boston, 1986—88; instr. medicine Johns Hopkins U. Sch. Medicine, Baltimore, Md., 1989—91; asst. prof. medicine U. Fla. Coll. Medicine, Gainesville, 1991—95, dean, 2007—08, Folke H. Peterson/deans disting. professorship, prof. medicine and biochem. & molecular biology, 2007—09; assoc. prof. medicine U. Tex. Med. Sch., Houston, 1995—99, prof. medicine, 2000—07, dir., divsn. renal diseases and hypertension, 2000—07, vice chair, dept. internal medicine, 2000—04, James T. and Nancy B. Willerson chair, 2001—07, chmn. internal medicine, 2004—07, vis. prof. medicine, 2009—10, prof. medicine, 2010—; chief, sect. nephrology U. Tex. M.D. Anderson Cancer Ctr., Houston, 2000—07; pres. chmn. Fla. Proton Therapy Inst., Inc., 2008; dir. Shands Healthcare Bd., 2007—08, U. Tex. Physicians Bd., 2005—07, vice chair, 2006—07; dir. Meml. Hermann Hosp. Sys. Physicians Tex. Bd., 2007, Med. Svc., R. & D. Plan Bd., U. Tex. Health Sci. Ctr. Houston, 2002—05. Gov. Tobacco Edn. & Use Prevention Adv. Coun., Fla. Dept. Health, 2007—08. Recipient RO1 Individual Rsch. awards, 2010, 2013, World #1 Ranking, FINA Masters Swimming, 2013, US Masters Champion, Nat. Age Group, 2012; named Best Dr. in America, 2005—; grantee Clin. Investigator award, NIH; fellow Nat. Rsch. Svc. award. Fellow: Am. Soc. Nephrology, AAAS, Am. Coll. Clin. Pharmacology, ACP, Am. Heart Assn. (Established Investigator award); mem.: So. Soc. Clin. Investigation (councilor 2003—07, pres. 2007—08, adv. coun. 2009—), Alpha Omega Alpha Honor Med. Soc. Avocation: swimming. Office: Univ Tex-Houston Divsn Renal Diseases MSB 5 124 6431 Fannin St Houston TX 77030 Home: 1104 Berthea Houston TX 77006

KONES, RICHARD, cardiologist, medical services company executive; b. Joseph Irwin and Ruth (Winkler) K. BSChemE, NYU, 1960, MD, 1964; DSc in Physiology, Somerset U., Eng., 1988, PhD in Exercise Physiology and Nutrition, 1990. Diplomate Am. Bd. Internal Medicine, Nat. Bd. Med. Examiners. Intern Kings County Hosp., Bklyn., 1964-65; resident in surgery Bronx Mcpl. Hosp., NYC, 1965-66; resident in medicine Lenox Hill Hosp., NYC, 1966-68; fellow cardiology VA Hosp., New Orleans, 1969—71; physician in charge CCU Arthur Logan Hosp., 1968—69; USPHS-NIH fellow in cardiology, chief resident Sch. Medicine, Tulane U., New Orleans, 1969-71; asst. prof. cardiology N.Y. Med. Coll., NYC, 1971, chief CCU, 1971-75; cons. and chief CCU CCU Midtown Hosp.-NYU, Cmty. Hosp., NYC, 1971—79; chief exec. officer Community Med. Offices, Inc., Houston and NYC, 1974—; asst. physician, dir., ECG conf. coord. Cornell Med. Ctr. Park City Hosp., Bridgeport, Conn., 1975-78; sr. cardiologist Cabrini Med. Ctr.-NYU, NYC, 1978—88; physician and cons. in cardiology SW Meml. Hosp., 1979-81, Alief Gen. Hosp., Houston, 1979—81; lectr. medicine U. Tex., 1979; faculty Inst. Spirituality & Health Tex. Med Ctr., 2009—; editor Medpedia Project, Cardiovasc. Disease, 2009—; editor-in-chief Rsch. Reports Clin. Cardiology, Dove Med. Pres, 2010—. Asst. prof. to assoc. prof. medicine NY Med.Coll., 1971—; vis. rsch. cardiologist, Tulane U. Sch. Medicine, New Orleans, 1969-1992; med. dir., chief Nutrition, Sports, Health Clinic, Houston,1989—; lectr. medicine & cardiology U. Tex. Health Sci. Ctr., Houston Med. Ctr.; CCU Nursing CME lect., Spring Branch Hosp., Houston, 2007-9; Med. Dir., Cardiometabolic Rsch. Inst. & Found., Houston, 2006-, internat. mentor, AHA, mentor, Am. Coll. Pharmacology, Am Soc. Clin. Pharmacology & Therapeutics, Endocrine Soc., Com. Publ. Ethics COPE, 2010-, bd. mem., Cardiovascular Com., Internal Medicine Com., Medpedia Project, 2008-, Credentials & Publs. Coms., Am. Coll. Clin. Pharmacology 2008—; Quality Care & Outcomes Rsch., Working Group, AHA, 2006—; Coun. Metabolism, Am. Coll. Nutrition 2006—; Coun. Clin. Cardiology Practice, European Soc. Cardiology 2008—; Sci. Program Com., Am. Soc. Clin. Pharmacology & Therapeutics 2008—. Author, editor books on biochemistry, physiology, cardiology, nutrition, metabolism, nutrition and sports medicine; contbr. rsch. papers to profl. pubs., Academic peer reviewer, numerous medical jour. & publs., 1972-. Sponsorer US Olympic Com., 2008; advocacy, "You're the Cure" program Am. Heart Assn., 2009; spkr's bur., 2020 CV Mortality Goals Am. Heart Assn. Life's Simple 7, 2011—; lectr. Parkinson's Soc., 2007—. Recipient Faculty Excellent Recognition award, Academic Congress Internat. China, 2011, Outstanding Contribution Clin. Rsch. Key Investigator, NY Med. Coll. & Sandoz, 1994, Physicians Recognition awards, AMA, 1993, Best Doctors in America Plaque, Best Doctors in America, 1981, Advances in Molecular Cardiology Plaque, Sec. Health, Hosp. Juarez, 1980, Appreciation Biol. Edn. award, Am. Inst. Biol. Scis., 1978, Investigator award, Dobutamine study excellence, NY Med Coll, 1976, Appreciation Outstanding Voluntary Svc. award, Hosp. & Cmty. Svc. Plaque, Arthur Logan Hosp. Harlem, NY, 1969, Faculty Excellence Recognition award, Academic Congress Intlernat. China, 2011, award, Internat. Conf. Pharmaceuticals, 2011, Colegio de Medicina Interna Mex., 2011, Editl. Excellence award, Medpedia, 2010. Fellow AHA, European Soc. Cardiology, Royal Soc. Medicine, Royal Soc. Health, NY Cardiological Soc., Am. Coll. Pharmacology, Am. Geriatric Soc., Am. Coll. Angiology, Internat. Coll. Angiology, Am. Soc. Angiology, Am. Coll. Nutrition, Internat. Coll. Nutrition, Internat. Soc. Noninvasive Monitoring Electrocardiography; mem. Am. Heart Assn., Am. Soc. Clin. Pharmacology Exptl. Therapeutics, Am. Soc. Clin. Pharmacology Therapeutics, World Heart Fedn., European Atherosclerosis Soc., Am. Physiol. Soc., Am. Soc. Cardiovasc. and Pulmonary Rehab., Physiological Soc. (London); Nutrition Soc. (London), French Soc. Cardiology (Paris), NY Acad. Scis., Coun. Clin. Cardiology, Am. Soc. Preventive Cardiology, Heart Rhythm Soc., European Heart Rhythm Soc., Am. Coll. Sports Medicine, Soc. Gen. Internal Medicine, Am. Soc. Nutrition, Heart Failure Soc America, Am. Soc. Hypertension, European Soc. Cardiac Prevention and Rehab, Am. Assn. Clin. Chemistry, Am. Chem. Soc., European Soc. Clin. Nutrition and Metabolism, Am. Med. Athletic Assn., Inflammation Rsch. Assn., Nutritional Rsch. Coun., Am. Fedn. Clin. Rsch., Am. Dietetic Assn., Am. Soc. Internal Medicine, Am. Thoracic Soc., Am. Diabetes Assn., Am. Pub. Health Assn., So. Med. Assn., Brit. Soc. Nutritional Medicine, Mitochondrial Rsch. Soc. Avocations: tennis, electronics, music.

KOONCE, PAUL D., energy executive; b. 1960; Grad., U. Tenn., 1982. With Transcontinental Gas Pipeline, Sonat Energy Svcs., Consol. Natural Gas; sr. v.p., comml. ops. Dominion Resources, Inc., Richmond, sr. v.p., portfolio mgmt. Va. Power, 2000—02, exec. v.p., 2007; exec. v.p., CEO Dominion Energy, 2006—09; CEO, transmission Dominion Virginia Power, 2003, pres., COO, 2004—06, CEO, 2009—. Office: Dominion 120 Tredegar St Richmond VA 23219 Office Phone: 804-819-2000. Office Fax: 804-819-2233. Business E-Mail: paul_koonce@dom.com.

KOONS, KENNETH EDWARD, historian, educator, consultant; b. Waynesboro, Pa., Oct. 10, 1954; s. John Henry and Doris Elaine Koons; m. Deborah Jean Kocher, July 2, 1955; children: Jacob Wesley, Elizabeth Marie. BA in History, Shippensburg State Coll., 1976, MA in History, 1978; ArtsD in History, Carnegie Mellon U., 1982. Asst. prof. history Va. Mil. Inst., Lexington, 1982—88, assoc. prof. history, 1988—92, prof. history, 1992—, Gen. Edwin Cox '20 Inst. prof. history, 2002—, assoc. head history dept. Scholar/curator Mus. Shenandoah Valley, Winchester, Va., 2000—05; guest lectr./cons. Frontier Culture Mus., Staunton, Va., 1990—2004; mem. nat. adv. coun./cons. Stonewall Jackson Ho., Lexington, 2004—; cons./editor Va. Cattlemen's Found. and Dairy Found. Va., Daleville, 2002—04; cons. McGraw Hill Pub., New York, NY, 2003—04; scorer advance placement examinations in world history Ednl. Testing Svc., Princeton, NJ, 2002. Editor: (collection essays) After the Backcountry: Rural Life in the Great Valley of Virignia, 1800-1900; contbr. essay; editor: (book) Virginia's Cattle Story: The First Four Centuries; contbr. articles to profl. jours. Wrote essay in support of hist. photog. and artifact display Augusta County Cultural and Hist. Commn., Verona, Va., 1994—95; rec. sec./mem. books com. Augusta County Hist. Soc., Staunton, 2003—06. Recipient Maury Rsch. Award, Va. Mil. Inst., 2001, Wilbur Hinman, Jr. Rsch. Award, 1990; fellow Jessie Ball duPont Seminar, The Cultural Politics of the Family, Nat. Humanities Ctr., 1997; Fellowship, Problems of Modernization: History and the Social Sciences, Nat. Endowment Humanities, 1976, Mellon Rsch. Fellowship, Va. Hist. Soc., 1991, 1992, Discretionary and Implementation grant for Conf.: After the Backcountry: Rural Life and Soc. in the 19th Century Valley Va., Va. Found. Humanities and Pub. Policy, 1993, Discretionary and Implementation grant for conf. After the Backcountry: Rural Life and Society in the 19th Century Valley Va., 1995, Travel fellowship, Scots-Irish Historians' Tour of No. Ireland, Brit. Coun., 1994. Mem.: Appalachian Studies Soc., Popular Culture Assn., World History Assn., Orgn. Am. Historians, So. Hist. Assn., Va. Hist. Soc. Avocations: gardening, woodworking, fly-fishing. Office: Virginia Military Institute Dept History Scott Shipp Hall Lexington VA 24450 E-mail: koonske@vmi.edu.

KOONS, LINDA, publishing executive; b. Warren, Ohio, Nov. 12, 1954; d. Louis and Anne (Zelina) Gleitsman; children: Ashley, Jeffrey. BA, Wittenberg U., Springfield, Ohio, 1976; MEd, Bowling Green State U., Huron, Ohio, 1979. Reading tchr. Bazetta Elem. Sch., Warren, Ohio, 1976-78; reading instr. Bowling Green State U., 1978-79; sr. editor Merrill Pub. Co., Columbus, Ohio, 1979-83, Silver Burdett & Ginn Co., Morristown, NJ, 1983-88, exec. editor Needham, Mass., 1988-90; editor-in-chief instructional pub. group Scholastic Inc., NYC, 1990-94, v.p., pub. early childhood divsn., 1995—97, v.p., pub. supplementary pub., 1997—2000, sr. v.p., pub. edn. group, 2000—02; dir. sch. product devel., ednl. pub. divsn. Disney Consumer Products, Inc., NYC, 1994—95; exec. v.p., pub. Haights Cross Comm., NYC, 2004—08; ind. cons., ednl. product devel., 2008—11; sr. v.p. product & digital devel. Carson-Dellosa Pub., LLC, Greensboro, NC, 2011—. Mailing: Carson Dellosa Publishing PO Box 35665 Greensboro NC 27425

KOONTZ, LAWRENCE LARKINS, JR., retired state supreme court justice; b. Roanoke, Va., Jan. 25, 1940; BS, Va. Polytech. U., 1962. Asst. commonwealth's atty., Roanoke, 1967—68; judge Va. Juvenile & Domestic Rels. Dist. Ct., 1968—76, Va. Cir. Ct. (23rd cir.), 1976—85, Ct. Appeals of Va., 1985—95; justice Va. Supreme Ct., 1995—2011, sr. justice, 2011—. Mem.: ABA. Presbyterian. Office: Va Supreme Ct PO Box 1315 Richmond VA 23218-1315 Office Phone: 540-387-6082.*

KOOP, LINDA, councilwoman; BA in Sociology, Colo. State U.; MA in Internat. Mgmt. Studies, U. Tex., Dallas. Councilwoman, Dist. 11 Dallas City Coun., 2007—, chair transp. & environ. com., mem. econ. devel. com., housing com. Bd. dirs. Dallas Area Rapid Transit

(DART), 1999—; mem exec. bd. North Ctrl. Tex. Coun. Govt.'s, chair Regional Transp. Coun., 2008—. Mem.: Nat. PTA, Tex. PTA (life), Nat. Recreation & Park Assn., Tex. Recreation & Park Soc., Dallas Zoological Soc., Dallas Arboretum & Botanical Soc., Whispering Hills Neighborhood Assn. Mailing: 1500 Marilla St Ste 5FN Dallas TX 75201-6390

KOPF, GEORGE MICHAEL, retired ophthalmologist; b. Chilton, Wis., Oct. 20, 1935; s. George and Mary (Schmid) K.; m. Sandra Mary Nolte, Dec. 29, 1962; children: Karen, Jennifer, Nancy. BS, U. Wis., 1958, MD, 1961. Diplomate Am. Bd. Ophthalmology. Intern Luther Hosp., Eau Claire, Wis., 1961-62; resident Milw. County Hosp., 1962-63, Detroit Gen. Hosp., 1965-68; ophthalmologist pvt. practice, Zanesville, Ohio, 1968—; ret., 1999. Mem. med. staff Bethesda Hosp., Zanesville; mem. med. Staff Good Samaritan Med. Ctr., Zanesville, pres., 1978, sec. bd. dirs., 1986-96. Capt. USAF, 1963-65. Fellow ACS, Am. Acad. Ophthalmology; mem. Ohio Ophthalmology Soc. (pres. 1976-77), Muskigum County Acad. Medicine (pres. 1983), Ohio State Med. Assn., Rotary. Republican. Roman Catholic. Avocations: tennis, swimming, hiking, reading, travel. Home: 10660 Glen Lakes Dr Bonita Springs FL 34135 Personal E-mail: kopfgs@comcast.net.

KOPLAN, JEFFREY POWELL, academic administrator, epidemiologist; b. Boston, Jan. 3, 1945; s. Samuel R. and Kate G. K.; m. Carol R. Bassuk, May 18, 1969; children: Adam, Kate BA, Yale Coll., 1966; postgrad., Tufts U., 1966-68; MD, Mount Sinai Sch. Medicine, NYC, 1970; M.P.H., Harvard U., 1978. Diplomate Am. Bd. Internal Medicine, Am. Bd. Preventive Medicine. Intern, resident Montefiore Hosp. and Med. Ctr., Bronx, NY, 1970-72; epidemic intelligence service officer Centers for Disease Control & Prevention, US Dept. Health & Human Services, Atlanta, 1972-74; resident Stanford U. Hosp, Calif., 1974-75; med. epidemiologist Calif. State Dept. Health, Berkeley, 1975, Caribbean Epidemiology Ctr., Port of Spain, 1975-77; med. officer Office of Program Planning Centers for Disease Control & Prevention, US Dept. Health & Human Services, Atlanta, 1978-82, asst. dir. pub. health practice, 1982-88; dir. Nat. Ctr. Chronic Disease Prevention and Health Promotion, Atlanta, 1989-94; asst. surgeon gen. US Dept. Health & Human Services, Rockville, 1989-94, dir. Centers for Disease Control & Prevention Atlanta, 1998—2002; exec. v.p., dir. Prudential Ctr. for Health Care Rsch., Atlanta, 1994-95, pres., 1995-98; v.p. for acad. health affairs, global health Emory U., Atlanta, 2002—08, dir. Emory Global Health Inst., 2002—. Contbr. articles to profl. jours. With USPHS, 1970-94. Recipient Order of Bifurcated Needle WHO, 1979; Saul Horowitz award Mt. Sinai Sch. Medicine, 1983; Commendation medal USPHS, 1984 Fellow ACP, Am. Coll. Epidemiology; mem. Assn. Tchrs. Preventive Medicine, Am. Pub. Health Assn., Soc. Med. Decision Making, Inst. Med. Office: Emory Global Health Inst Emory Univ MS 1599 001 1AH 1599 Clifton Rd NE Ste 6101 Atlanta GA 30322-4250

KOPPELL, JONATHAN, dean, political science professor; AB in Govt., Harvard U., Cambridge, Mass., 1993; PhD in Polit. Sci., U. Calif., Berkeley. Mem. Office Fed. Housing Enterprise Oversight US Dept. Housing and Urban Devel., 1993—95; Markle fellow New America Found., 1999—2000; assoc. prof. Yale U. Sch. Mgmt., New Haven, 2000—10; dir. Yale U. Millstein Ctr. Corp. Governance & Performance, 2006—09; Lattie & Elva Coor presdl. chair & dir. Sch. Pub. Affairs Ariz. State U., 2010—13, dean Coll. Pub. Programs, 2011—. Author: The Politics of Quasi-Government: Hybrid Organizations and the Dynamics of Bureaucratic Control, 2003, World Rule: Accountability, Legitimacy and the Design of Global Governance, 2010. Office: Office of Dean Ariz State University Coll Pub Programs 411 N Central Ave Phoenix AZ 85004-0685 Office Phone: 602-496-1101. Business E-Mail: koppell@asu.edu.*

KOPPLIN, RON, mining executive; BS in Civil Engring., U. Ill., Urbana-Champaign, 1989; MBA, U. Tex., San Antonio, 1999. Environ. mgr. Gaylord Container Corp., 1995—97; sales rep., sr. sales rep. Martin Marietta Materials, Inc., San Antonio, 1999—2002, gen. mgr. Black Spur Quarry and Asphalt, 2002—04, v.p., gen. mgr. Houston, 2004—08, v.p., gen. mgr. Western divsn., North Tex. Okla. dist., 2008—. Office: Martin Marietta Materials Inc Western Divsn 1825 Lakeview Dr Ste 300 Lewisville TX 75057 Office Phone: 972-350-8200.

KORB, WILLIAM BROWN, JR., retired manufacturing executive; b. Warren, Pa., Apr. 27, 1940; s. William Brown and Helen (Haslett) K.; m. Dorothy Wendell Trout, June 11, 1962; children: Karen Michel, David Wendell, Christine Leigh. BS in Indsl. Engring, Pa. State U., 1962; grad. advanced mgmt. program, Harvard U., 1979. With Reliance Electric Co., 1962—86, gen. mgr. mech. group, Mishawaka, Ind., 1977—79, operating v.p., Cleve., 1979—86; pres., CEO, bd. dirs. Gilbarco, Inc., Greensboro, NC, 1987-99, Marconi Commerce Systems, Inc., 1999—2001; ret., 2001. Bd. dirs. Cambrex Corp. Mem.: Kiawah Island Club. Home: 60 Surfsong Rd Kiawah Island SC 29455

KORCHIN, JUDITH MIRIAM, lawyer; b. Kew Gardens, NY, Apr. 28, 1949; d. Arthur Walter and Mena (Levisohn) Goldstein; m. Paul Maury Korchin, June 10, 1972; 1 son, Brian Edward. BA with high honors, U. Fla., Gainesville, 1971, JD with honors, 1974. Bar: Fla. 1974, US Ct. Appeal (2d, 5th and 11th cirs.), US Dist. Ct. (so., mid. and no. dists) Fla. Law clk. to judge U.S. Dist. Ct., 1974-76; assoc. Steel, Hector & Davis, Miami, Fla., 1976-81, ptnr., 1981-87, Holland and Knight, Miami, 1987—. Author, exec. editor U. Fla. Law Rev., 1973—74; contbr. chapters to books, articles to profl. jours. Mem. U. Fla. Law Ctr. Coun., 1980-83; pres. alumni bd. U. Fla. Law Rev., 1983; bd. dirs. Fla. Film & Rec. Inst., 1982-84; pres. Am. Jewish Com., 2009-2012, Miami-Dade, Broward, Fla., 2009. Recipient Trail Blazer award, The Women's Com. of 100, 1988; named Best of the Bar, So. Fla. Bus. Jour., 2004—06; named one of Fla. Trend's Legal Elite, 2004—13, Fla. Super Lawyers, 2006—13, Best Lawyers in Am., 2006—13, Top 100 Fla. Super Lawyers, 2007—10, 2012—13, Top 50 Fla. Women, Fla. Super Lawyers, 2006—13; named to Fla. Legal Elite Hall of Fame, Fla. Trend Mag., 2011—13. Fellow: Fla. Bar Found. (subcom. legal assistance for poor 1988—90), Am. Bar Found.; mem.: ABA (sect. alternative dispute resolution, vice chmn. 1994—95, co-chmn. fed. ct. mediation com. 1995, sect. labor and employment law, sect. litig., house of dels. 2009—10), Fla. Bar Assn. (vice chmn. jud. nominating procedures com. 1982, civil procedure rules com. 1984—89, 1993—95), Nat. Assn. Bank Women (TV panelist greater Miami chpt. 1987), Nat. Assn. Women Bus. Owners (adv. coun. 1987—88), Dade County Bar Assn. (bd. dirs. 1981—82, treas. 1982, sec. 1983, 3d v.p. 1984, 2d v.p. 1985, 1st v.p. 1986, pres. 1987), CPR Inst. Dispute Resolution (nat. panelist 1994—, exec. com. 2003—), Am. Arbitration Assn. (employment law panel, s.e. complex litig. panel 1993—, comml. law panel 1993—), Greater Miami C. of C. (com. profl. devel. 1988—90), Rabbinical Assn. Greater Miami (TV panelist Still Small Voice 1987), City Club (bd. dirs. 1988—93), Phi Kappa Phi, Phi Beta Kappa, Order of Coif. Office: Holland & Knight PO Box 015441 701 Brickell Ave Ste 3300 Miami FL 33131-2898 Office Phone: 305-789-7764. Business E-Mail: judith.korchin@hklaw.com.

KORELL, HAROLD M., energy executive; m. Patricia Korell. Degree in chem. & petroleum refining engring., Colo. Sch. Mines, Golden, 1968. Lic. profl. engr., Tex., Colo. With Mobil Oil Corp.; various positions including v.p. prodn. Tenneco Oil Co., 1973—89; exec. v.p. McCormick Resources, 1990—92; sr. v.p. ops. American Exploration Co., 1992—97; exec. v.p., COO Southwestern Energy Co., 1997—98, pres., 1998—2008, CEO, 1999—2009, chmn., 2002—09, exec. chmn., 2009—. Bd. mem. Nat. Petroleum Coun., Ind. Petroleum Assn. America, Am. Natural Gas Alliance; vice chmn. Am. Exploration and Prodn. Coun.; bd. dirs. Southwestern Energy Co., 1998—. Exec. adv. bd. U. Ark. Sam M. Walton Sch. Bus.; bd. governors Colo. Sch. Mines, mem. vis. com., dept. petroleum engring. Recipient Disting. Achievement medal, Colo. Sch. Mines, 2004, Outstanding Svc. award, U. Ark. Sam M. Walton Sch. Bus., 2006, Chief Roughneck award, US Steel Corp., 2009; named Exec. of Yr., Oil and Gas Investor mag., 2006. Mem.: Am. Gas Assn., Soc. Petroleum Engineers. Office: Southwestern Energy Co Ste 125 2350 N Sam Houston Pky E Houston TX 77032 Office Phone: 281-618-4700. Office Fax: 281-618-4820. Business E-Mail: harold_korell@swn.com.

KOREN, EDWARD FRANZ, JR., lawyer; b. Eustis, Fla., Aug. 6, 1946; s. Edward Franz Sr. and Frances (Boyd) K.; m. Louise Poole, June 19, 1970; children: Daniel Edward, Susan Louise Hines. BSBA in Acctg., U. Fla., 1971, JD with high honors, 1974. Bar: Fla. 1975, US Dist. Ct. (mid. dist. Fla.) 1977, US Supreme Ct. 1980, US Ct. Appeals (11th cir.) 1981, US Tax Ct. 1985, US Ct. Claims 1986. Instr. tax U. Fla., Gainesville, 1974-75; assoc. Holland & Knight, Lakeland, Fla., 1975-79, ptnr. Tampa, Fla., 1980—, chmn. trusts and estates dept., 1983—2004, chair pvt. wealth svcs. dept., 2004—. Adj. prof. grad. tax prog. U. Fla., Gainesville, 1996; adj. prof. grad. estate planning prog. U. Miami Law Sch., 2000-. Contbr. articles to profl. jours.; exec. editor U. Fla. Law Rev., 1973—74, lead author, editor Estate and Personal Fin. Planning (West), 1988—2013. Capt. US Army, 1971—72. Recipient Robert C. Scott Meml. award, 1991; named Gerald T. Hart Outstanding Tax Atty., 2002—03; named one of Top 100 Attys., Worth Mag., 2005—08; named to Estate Planning Hall of Fame and accredited estate planner. Fellow: Am. Bar Found., Am. Coll. Tax Counsel (bd. cert. estate planning & probate lawyer, Fla. bar bd. legal specialization and edn.); mem.: ABA (real property mem., trust estate sec. 1990—, chmn. marital deduction com. 1991—95, supervisory coun. 1995—2001, mem. exec. coun. 1995—, rep. to the Nat. Conf. Attys. and Corp. Fiduciaries 1998—, vice chmn. probate and trust divsn. 2001—03, chair, real property, probate and trust law sect. 2004—05), Am. Law Inst., Am. Judicature Soc., Hillsborough County Bar Assn., Lakeland 10th Jud. Cir., Fla. Inst. CPA, Am. Assn. Attys. and CPA, Fla. Bar Assn. (chmn., continuing legal edn. com. 1982—84, vice-chmn. bd. certification, designation and advt. 1984—88, chmn. real property, probate and trust law sect. 1988—89, chmn. tax sect. 1990—91, active various sects. and coms., legal edn. com. mem.), Am. Coll. Trust and Estates Counsel (mem. bus. planning com. 1994—, regent 1997—2003, past chmn. estate and gift tax com. 2001—04), Fla. Blue Key, Centre Club, Lakeland Yacht and Country Club, Tampa Club, Phi Delta Phi, Phi Kappa Phi, Order of Coif. Republican. Presbyterian. Office: Holland & Knight LLP PO Box 1288 100 N Tampa St Ste 4100 Tampa FL 33602-3644 Office Phone: 813-227-6655, 863-499-5314. Business E-Mail: ed.koren@hklaw.com.

KORF, BRUCE RICHARD, clinical geneticist, neurologist; b. Bklyn. AB, Cornell U., 1974, MD, 1980; PhD in Genetics and Cell Biology, Rockefeller U., 1979. Diplomate Am. Bd. Psychiatry and Neurology, 1986, Am. Bd. Pediatrics, 1988; diplomate in clin. genetics, cytogenetics and molecular genetics Am. Bd. Med. Genetics, 1984; registered, Mass. Bd. Registration in Medicine, 1983, Am. Bd. Med. Genetics, 1993. Intern in pediatrics Children's Hosp., Boston, 1980-81, jr. asst. resident in pediatrics, 1981-82, jr. asst. resident in neurology, 1982-83, sr. asst. resident in neurology, 1983-84, chief resident in neurology, 1984-85, fellow in genetics, 1982-85, asst. in neurology, 1985, asst. in medicine and genetics, dir. clin. genetics program, 1986; clin. fellow in pediatrics Harvard Med. Sch., Boston, 1980-82, clin. fellow in neurology, 1982-85, instr. neurology, 1985-86, asst. prof. neurology, 1986-93, assoc. prof. neurology, 1993, med. dir. Harvard-Partners Ctr. Genetics; dir. clin. genetics program Beth Israel Hosp., Boston, 1991; chmn. Dept Genetics U. Ala., Birmingham, Wayne H. Finley and Sara Crews Finley chmn. med. genetics. Invited lectr. in field; bd. sci. coundelor Nat. Cancer Inst., 2003-08, Nat. Human Genare Rsch. Inst., 2010-. Sect. editor genetics Current Opinion in Pediatrics, 1991; field editor Am. Jour. Med. Genetics, 1992; mem. editorial bd. Jour. Clin. Dysmorphology, 1987, Current Protocols in Human Genetics, 1992, Genetics in Medicine, Am. Jour. Human Genetics; contbr. articles and reviews to med. and sci. journals. Bd. dirs. Mass. chpt. March Dimes Birth Defects Found., 1990—92. Recipient Clin Investigator Devel. award NINCDS; Bodman scholar, 1970; Cornell Nat. scholar, 1970; Von Meyer Traveling fellow, 1983; grantee NIH, 1986-89, Muscular Dystrophy Assn., 1992—. Fellow Am. Coll. Med. Genetics (founding fellow, former v.p., pres. 2009-); mem. Am. Genetics Assn., Genetics Soc. Am., Am. Acad. Neurology (steering subcom. Continuum series 1992-93), Am. Soc. Human Genetics, Am. Acad. Pediatrics, Nat. Neurofibromatosis Found. (clin. care adv. bd. 1985, co-chmn. 1988, chmn. med. policy com. 1988, rsch. adv. bd. 1990, adv. bd. dirs. Mass. chpt. 1985, chmn. med. affairs com., 2003-; Von Recklinghausen award 1989, Pres.'s award, 1991, Courtemanche award, 1993), Assn. Professors Human and Med. Genetics (pres. 2003-05), Child Neurology Soc., Teratology Soc., Phi Beta Kappa, Phi Kappa Phi, Sigma Xi, Am. Coll. Med. Genetics (pres. elect.) Office: Genetics Dept Univ Alabama Kaul Human Genetics BldgRm 230 720 20th St S Birmingham AL 35294-0024 Office Phone: 205-934-9411. Office Fax: 205-934-9488. E-mail: bkorf@uab.edu.

KORMAN, JAMES WILLIAM, lawyer; b. Washington, Apr. 29, 1943; s. Milton D. and Bernice (Rosensweig) K.; m. Barbara Dale Lewis, June 11, 1967; 1 child, Katherine Korman Frey. AB, Coll. William & Mary, 1965; JD, George Washington U., 1968. Bar: Va. 1968, D.C. 1970, U.S. Supreme Ct. 1972, U.S. Ct. Appeals (4th cir.) 1974, U.S. Dist. Ct. (ea. dist.) Va. 1975. Assoc. Kinney, Smith and Barham, Arlington, Va., 1968-73, ptnr., 1973-78; pres. Bean, Kinney & Korman, Arlington, 1979—. Mem. Va. Bar Coun., 1983-89, 98-2004, 10th dist. grievance com., 1978-81; mem. adv. bd. Bank of Arlington, Va., 1977-78; lectr. various civil litgation topics continuing legal edn.; contbg. atty. Mathew Bender's Fed. Practice Forms, 1978; panelist Va. Conf. Nat. Assn. Bank Women, 1984; adj. prof. George Mason U. Law Sch., 1996—; neutral case evaluator, Fairax Circuit Ct., 1995-; mem. faculty Va. State Bar Profl. Course, 1998-2001; mem. bd. govs. family law sect. Va. State Bar, 2005-. Contbr. articles to profl. jours. Bd. dirs. No. Va. Jewish Cmty. Ctr., 1985-91; adv. bd. Sch. Contemporary Edn., Springfield, Va., 1985-91; Va. Commn. on Women and Minorities in the Law, 1988-92. Capt. JAG USAR, 1972—74. Recipient Meritorious Svc. award Legal Aid Bur., 1968, Adult Leadership award Boy Scouts Am., 1972; named One of 50 Top Divorce Lawyers Washingtonian Mag., 2000, 04, 09, Washington's Best Lawyers, 2004, 2007; One of Best Lawyers in Am., 1995-2010; named to Va. Super Lawyers, 2006-10, Va. Legal Elite, Va. Bus. Mag., 2007-. Fellow: Am. Bar Found., Va. Law Found., Am. Acad. Matrimonial Lawyers (Va. chpt. v.p. 1996—99, pres. 2001—03, cert. arbitrator); mem.: AAJ (Previously ATLA), ABA, Plaintiffs Bar Ltd., Va. Trial Lawyers Assn. (jud. task force 1998—, 2002), Arlington Bar Found. (bd. dirs. 1990—2008, pres. 2000—01), Arlington Bar Assn. (bd. dirs. 1977—81, pres. 1981—82, Robert J. Arthur Disting. Svc. award 2002), Va. State Bar (pro bono steering com. 1992—93, bd. govs. family law sect. 2005—09). Democrat. Avocation: collecting political buttons. Home: 2450 N Wakefield Ct Arlington VA 22207-3554 Office: Bean Kinney & Korman 2300 Wilson Blvd 7th Fl Arlington VA 22201 Office Phone: 703-525-4000. Business E-Mail: jkorman@beankinney.com.

KORNBLUM, WARREN, consumer products company executive; m. Tricia Kornblum. Attended, Boston U. Prin., owner Kornblum Internat., Toronto, Canada; pres., U.S. Ops., mng. ptnr. Bozell Worldwide; exec. v.p. Toys "R" Us, Inc., Wayne, NJ, 1999, chief mktg. officer, 1999—2004; chmn., CEO Shadow Entertainment Group; chief strategic officer Rooms To Go. Pres. Starlight Children's Found. Office: Rooms To Go 11540 Highway 92 E Seffner FL 33584 Office Phone: 813-623-5400. Office Fax: 813-620-1717.

KORONES, SHELDON BERNARR, retired pediatrician, educator; b. NYC, Apr. 26, 1924; s. Samuel Aaron and Estelle (Goldstein) K.; m. Judith Ann Kest, June 15, 1952; children: David N., Susan Gifford. BS, U. Tenn., 1944; MD, U. Tenn., Memphis, 1947. Diplomate Am. Bd. Pediatrics, Am. Bd. Neonatal/Perinatal Medicine. Intern Boston City Hosp., 1948-49; asst. resident pediat. Babies Hosp., NYC, 1950-51, 53-54; asst. in pathology Children's Med. Ctr., Boston, 1949-50; asst. clin. prof. pediat. U. Tenn., 1961-68, assoc. prof. newborn svcs. dept. pediats., 1968-72, prof. pediats., dir. newborn svcs., 1972-89, prof. ob-gyn., 1982-89, alumni disting. svc. prof. pediat. ob-gyn., 1989—2009. Project dir., prin. investigator collaborative perinatal project NIH, Bethesda, 1960-75; dir. newborn ctr. Regional Med. Ctr. Memphis, 1968-2004; perinatal adv. com. State Tenn., 1974—, chmn. subcom. standards regionalization perinatal care, 1975—, subcom. liaison, legis. funding and cmty. edn., 1979—, subcom. perinatal transp., 1979-86, gov.'s task force prevention mental retardation, 1980-83, gov.'s task force healthy children, 1983-86, subcom. follow-up, 1983-86, subcom. evaluation, 1983-86, subcom. med. home., 1983-86, task force child devel. standards dept. human svcs., 1984-86; med. svc. adv. com. March of Dimes, 1974-78, edn. adv. com., 1979-1987, exec. com. west Tenn. chpt., 1986-92; bd. examiner oral exams maternal and fetal medicine Am. Bd. Ob-Gyn., Chgo., 1975; study panel bur. med. devices diagnostic products FDA, 1976-93; prin. investigator Nat. Heart, Lung, Blood Inst., Bethesda, Md., 1976-83, Coop. Multictr. Network Neonatal Intensive Care Rsch., Bethesda, 1986-2001; profl. edn. rsch. com. Am. Lung Assn. Tenn., 1977-81; pres.-elect med. staff Regional Med. Ctr. Memphis, 1982-83, pres. 1983-84; adv. bd. Office Drug Policy, Memphis, 1991; subcom. ob-gyn. newborn svcs. TLC Family Care Healthplan, Memphis, 1994—; mem. perinatal com. devel. clin. practice guidelines TennCare, First Mental Health, Inc., 1996; spkr., cons. in field. Author: High Risk Newborn Infants: The Basis for Intensive Nursing Care, 1972, 4th edit., 1986, Spanish translation, 1979, Russian translation, 1981; co-author: Neonatal Decision Making, 1993; author, co-author: (chpts.) Synopsis of Pediatrics, 1963, 6th edit., 1984, Resuscitation of the Newborn, 3d edit., 1973, Iatrogenic Problems in Neonatal Intensive Care, 1976, Current Diagnosis, 1977, Standards and Recommendations for Hospital Care of Newborn Infants, 6th edit., 1977, Current Therapy in Obstetrics and Gynecology, 1980, 83, Assisted Ventilation of the Newborn, 1981, The Use of Computers in Perinatal Medicine, 1982, Parent-Baby Attachment in Premature Infants, 1983, Infant Stress under Intensive Care, 1985, Gynecology and Obstetrics, Vol. 2, 1985, Teratogen Update: Environmentally Induced Birth Defect Risks, 1986, Assisted Ventilation of the Neonate, 1988, 4th edit., 2003, Comprehensive Pediatrics, 1990; author: (introduction) Planning and Design for Perinatal and Pediatric Facilities, 1977; editor Ross Labs., Columbus, Ohio, 1975-82, Perinatal Press, U. Tenn., Memphis, 1976-78, Brentwood Pub. Corp., L.A., 1977-88, Am. Baby Hosp. Network Adv. Bd., 1984—, Jour. Perinatology-Neonatology, 1988—, Am. Baby Mag., 1992—; reviewer C.V. Mosby Co., 1976-77, 81, 83, J.B. Lippincott Co., 1979, Williams and Wilkins Co., 1981, Polymorph films, 1985, Pediats., 1974—, New Eng. Jour. Medicine, 1975—, Am. Jour. Ob-gyn., 1979, 92, 97, Jour. Pediats., 1997, Pediat. Nephrology, 1997-2004, Pediat. Infectious Disease Jour. 1997-2000, 2003-04, Arch. Pediat. and Adolescent Medicine, 1999, Jour. Perinatology, 2001-04, Acta Paediatrica, 2003; contbr. over 300 articles to profl. publs. Bd. dirs. Memphis Orch. Soc., 1961-70. With USPHS, 1951-53. Named Citizen of Yr. Newspaper Guild Memphis, 1974, Who's Who in Medicine, Memphis Mag., 1984-88, Top Doctors, 1996; recipient Myrtle Wreath award Hadassah, 1976, Contribn. to Perinatal Medicine commendation Commr. Pub. Health Tenn., 1978, Cmty. Svc. award Nat. Conf. Christians and Jews, 1982, City Coun. Memphis, 1982, L.M. Graves Meml. Health award Mid-South Med. Ctr. Coun., Inc., 1984, Cert. Appreciation, Gov. Lamar Alexander, 1986, Key to City Memphis, Mayor Richard Hackett, 1988, Alumni Svc. award U. Tenn. Nat. Alumni Assn., 1989, Themis award March of Dimes, 1991, Meritorious Svc. commendation State Tenn. Ho. of Reps., 1992, Person of Vision award Alliance for Blind Visually Impaired, 1994, Meritorious Svc. award Tenn. Hosp. Assn., 1995; Sheldon B. Korones Chair Neonatology U. Tenn. Coll. Medicine named in his honor, 1989, Sheldon B. Korones Newborn Ctr. named in his honor, 2004; grantee NIH, 1960-75, 1971-75, 1985-2001, Merck, Sharpe and Dohme, 1970-73, Tenn. Dept. Health, 1970—, Memphis Regional Med. Program, 1972-75, Tenn. Dept. Human Svcs., 1972—96, March of Dimes, 1973-80, Nat. Heart, Lung, Blood Inst., 1976-83, Nat. Inst. Child Health Human Devel., 1986-91, 91-96, 96—, Tenn. Dept. Children's Svcs., 1996-2001. Fellow Am. Coll. Ob-Gyn. (assoc.); mem. So. Soc. Pediat. Rsch., Am. Acad. Pediats. (com. fetus and newborn 1969-75, liaison com. perinatal health Am. Coll. Ob-Gyn. 1965-74, rep. to joint com. newborn hearing Am. Speech Hearing Assn., Am. Acad. Ophthalmology Otolaryngology 1969-75, task force on circumcision 1973-74), Tenn. chpt. Pediatrician of Yr. 1994), Tenn. Pediat. Soc., Memphis Pediat. Soc., Am. Pediat. Soc., Tenn. Perinatal Assn. (bd. dirs. 1983—), Russian Perinatologists Assn. (hon. pres. 1996), Nat. Assn. Perinatal Social Workers (hon. 1980), Sigma Xi, Alpha Omega Alpha. Office: U Tenn 853 Jefferson Ave Rm 201 Memphis TN 38103-2807 Home Phone: 901-682-3692. Business E-Mail: skorones@utmem.edu, skorones@uthsc.edu.

KORST, CHRISTOPHER A., lawyer, rental company executive; BA in Polit. Sci., Creighton U., 1981, JD, 1984. V.p., asst. gen. counsel Thorn Americas, Inc., 1992—96, v.p., bus. devel., 1996, v.p., Thorn Auto, 1996—97; COO AdvantEdge Quality Cars, 1997—99, prin., owner, 2000—01; sr. v.p., gen. counsel Rent-A-Center, Inc., Plano, Tex., 2001—08, exec. v.p., ops., 2008—. Office: Rent-A-Center Inc 5501 Headquarters Dr Plano TX 75024-3556 Office Phone: 972-801-1100. Office Fax: 972-943-0113. Business E-Mail: christopher.korst@rentacenter.com.

KORSTAD, JOHN EDWARD, biology professor; b. Woodland, Calif., July 4, 1949; s. Vernon E. and Jeanette (Beard) K.; m. Sally Diane Steffen, July 29, 1972; children: Shauna, Sarah, Joya, Janna. BA, BS, Calif. Luth. U., Thousand Oaks, 1972; MS, Calif. State U., Hayward, 1979, U. Mich., 1979, PhD, 1980. Postdoctoral fellow SINTEF, Trondheim, Norway, 1987-88; prof. biology Oral Roberts

U., Tulsa, 1980—. Asst. dir., dir. collegiate acad. Okla. Acad. Sci., 1984-89; dir. honors program Oral Roberts U., 2001—. Bd. dirs. MEND Pregnancy Crisis Ctr. and Young Life, Broken Arrow, Okla., 1991—. Fulbright fellow in aquaculture rsch., Norway, 1993-94; named Carnegie Found. Prof. of Yr. for Okla., 1996. Mem. Nat. Collegiate Honors Coun., Am. Assn. of Zool. Parks and Aquariums, (advisor marine fishes adv. com. 1991—), Am. Inst. Biol. Sci., Okla. Acad. Sci., Beta Beta Beta. Republican. Avocations: scuba diving, skiing, outdoor sports, basketball. Office: Oral Roberts U Dept Biology 7777 S Lewis Ave Tulsa OK 74171-0001 Office Phone: 918-495-6942. Business E-Mail: jkorstad@oru.edu.

KORTH, DAVID H., international space station flight director; b. Greenwich, Conn. BS in Aerospace Engring., Texas A&M U., 1990; grad. student in Electrical Engring., U. Houston. Space sta. ops. planning group Barrios Tech., Houston, 1990—98; space sta. planner NASA Johnson Space Ctr., Houston, 1998—, ops. divsn. tech. asst., Mission Ops. Directorate, 2006—, flight dir., 2007—. Support, Expeditions 1-14 NASA, ops. plan leader, Expeditions 1 and 7, acting group leader, advanced planning group, lead, Internat Space Sta. Expeditions 21 and 22 long range planning team. Achievements include first of three individuals to achieve front room certification as an Operations Plan flight controller. Office: NASA Johnson Space Ctr 2101 NASA Pkwy Houston TX 77058 Office Phone: 281-483-0123.

KORY, KAYE, state legislator; b. Chgo., Apr. 18, 1947; m. Ross; children: Matthew, Sandy, Caroline. BA in English, Western Coll. for Women. Counselor Runaway House; program analyst Fairfax County Dept. Cmty. Action; program mgr. Cmty. Agency on Aging; exec. dir. Saunders B. Moon Sr. Citizens Ctr.; mem. Mason dist. Fairfax County Sch. Bd., Va., 1999—2009; mem. Dist. 38 Va. House of Delegates, Richmond, 2010—. Vol. VISTA; active EMILY's List; mem. Sleepy Hollow Elem Sch. PTA, Glasgow Mid. Sch. PTA, Va. Dem. Women's Caucus; pres., treas. J.E.B. Stuart HS PTA; pres. Montessori Sch. No. Va.; bd. mem. Fairfax County Boys & Girls Club. Mem.: NAACP, Annandale C. of C., Va. League Conservation Voters, League of Women Voters. Democrat. Office: Va House of Dels Gen Assembly Bldg Rm 817 PO Box 406 Richmond VA 23218 also: 6505 Waterway Dr Falls Church VA 22044 Office Phone: 804-698-1038, 703-354-6024. Office Fax: 804-698-6738. Business E-Mail: delkkory@house.virginia.gov.

KOSLOW, STEPHEN HUGH, health science association administrator, pharmacologist, neuroscientist; s. Julius and Lillian Koslow; m. Diane Heisler, Aug. 18, 1962; children: Karin, James. BS, Columbia U., 1962; PhD, U. Chgo., 1967. Internat. postdoctoral fellow Swedish Med. Rsch. Coun., Karolinski Inst., 1968-69; pharmacologist, chief neurobiology unit St. Elizabeth's Hosp., Washington, 1970-77; chief biol. rsch. sect. Clin. Rsch. br. NIMH, Rockville, Md., 1975-81, chief Neurosci. Rsch. br., 1981—85, chief Basic Scis. Neurosci. Rsch., 1985—88, dep. dir. divsn. Basic Brain and Behavioral Scis., 1989—90; dir. divsn. Basic and Clin. Neurosci. Rsch. NIMH-NIH, Rockville, 1990—99; assoc. dir., dir. office neuroinformatics NIMH, Rockville, 1999—2004; dir. external rels. Allen Inst. Brain Sci., Seattle, 2005, Biomedical Consulting, 2006—; rsch. dir. Am. Found. Suicide Presentation, 2009—10; cons. U. Miami Med. Sch., 2011—. Project dir. NIHM-CRB Collaborative Program on Psychobiology of Depression-Biol. Study, 1975-85; mem. adv. bd. Tourette Syndrome Assn., Bayside, NY, 1984; chair fed. coordinating com. on the Human Brain Project, 1991—; chair neuroinformatics subgroup of Office Econ. Coop. & Devel., Megasci. Forum, Biol. Working Group, 1996-99; co-chair US/EC com. on neuroinformatics, 1998—, chair global sci. forum neuroinformatics working group, 2000-02; editl. bd. mem. Translational Psychiatry, 2011-. Mem. editl. bd. Neuropsychopharmacology, 1987-92, Critical Revs. in Neurobiol., 1991-2004, Human Brain Mapping, 1993-2004, Psychopharm. Bull., 1989-99, Neuroimage; series editor Progress in Neuroinformatics Rsch., 1996-2001, Neuroimage, 1995-2001, CNS Drug Revs., 1995-99, Biomednet, 1999-2003; editor: Databasing the Brain From Data to Knowledge, 2005, Integrative Neuroscience and Personalized Medicine, 2010; assoc. editor Jour. Integrative Neurosci. Recipient NIMH Quality Increase award, 1977-78, Health Adminstr.'s award for Meritorious Achievement, 1986, Pub. Health Svc. Spl. Recognition award, 1992, Alumni Achievement award U. Chgo. Club of Washington, 1995, two Dir.'s awards NIH, 1996, Pres. award Internat. Neural Network Soc., 2001; Swedish Med. Rsch. Coun. internat. postdoctoral fellow, 1968-69, Spl. NATO fellow, 1969. Fellow AAAS, Am. Coll. Neuropsychopharmacology, Am. Coll. Med. Informatics; mem. Am. Soc. for Neurochemistry, Am. Soc. Pharmacology and Exptl. Therapeutics, Collegium Internat. Neuro Psychopharmacologium, Soc. for Neurosci., Soc. Biol. Psychiatry. Home: 8642 Falcon Green Dr West Palm Beach FL 33412-1576 Personal E-mail: stevekoslow@gmail.com.

KOSMAS, SUZANNE M., former United States Representative from Florida, former real estate company executive; b. Washington, Feb. 25, 1944; children: Paul Jr., Michael, David, Kristen. Student, Pa. State U., George Mason U., Va.; BA, Stetson U., DeLand, Fla., 1998. Owner, broker Prestige Properties of New Smyrna Beach, Fla., 1979—2009; mem. Fla. House of Reps., Tallahassee, 1996—2004, US Congress from 24th Fla. Dist., Washington, 2009—11. Mem. Volusia County Planning/Zoning Bd., 1980—86; chair S.E. Volusia Zoning Bd., 1984, Volusia County Environ./Natural Resource Adv. Com., 1988—92; mem. Indian River Lagoon Nat. Estuary Prog., 1991, East Ctrl. Fla. Regional Planning Coun., 1992—93, Volusia County Readiness Coalition, 1999—, Volusia County Business Devel. Corp. Trustee Atlantic Ctr. for Arts, 1983—91; chair bus. intern com. Futures Inc., 1987—96; mem. adv. bd. Habitat for Humanity, 1996; mem. Volusia County Cultural Arts Adv. Bd., 1993—93; v.p. Volusia/Flagler Boys & Girls Club, 1998—; bd. dirs. United Way Volusia County, 1987—97, chair bd. dirs., 1994. Recipient Vol. of Yr., Ctr. Cmty. Involvement, 1996. Mem.: Volusia County Assn. Responsible Developers, Fla. Assn. Realtors, Nat. Assn. Realtors. Democrat. Methodist. Avocations: tennis, jogging, reading, school.

KOSTELKA, ROBERT W. (BOB), state legislator; b. Shreveport, La. m. Felicia Kostelka. Asst. dist. atty. to dist. atty. 4th Dist. Ct., 1964—71; dist. judge 4th Jud. Dist., 1983—96, 1991—92, 1997—98; mem. Dist. 35 La. State Senate, 2003—, chair senate and govtl. affairs com., interim mem. retirement com., mem. judiciary A com., revenue and fiscal affairs com. Mem.: NRA, ABA, Arthritis Found., Muscular Dystrophy Assn., Ducks Unlimited, Nat. Wildlife Fedn., Salvation Army, YMCA, Appellate Judges' Assn., Rotary Club. Republican. Presbyterian. Mailing: Dist Off PO Box 2122 Monroe LA 71207 Office: Capitol Off PO Box 94183 Baton Rouge LA 70804 Office Phone: 225-342-2040. Business E-Mail: kostelka@legis.state.la.us.

KOSTEN, THOMAS RICHARD, psychiatrist, educator; b. Bklyn., Feb. 16, 1951; s. Richard Kosten; m. Therese Kosten, Aug. 12, 1978; children: Molly, Neal. BS, Rensselaer Polytechnic Inst., Troy, NY, 1973; MD, Cornell U. Med. Coll., NYC, 1977; MA, Yale U. Sch. Medicine, New Haven, Conn., 1995. Diplomate Am. Bd. Psychiatry and Neurology, 1984, Am. Bd. Psychiatry and Neurology, Addiction Psychiatry. Intern Greenwich Hosp., Conn., 1977—78; resident Yale U. Sch. Medicine, New Haven, 1978—81, asst. to assoc. prof., psychiatry, 1983—94, assoc. dir. to dir., substance abuse treatment unit, 1984—92, dir., divsn. substance abuse, 1992—96, prof. psychiatry, 2000—06; prof. Yale Grad. Sch., 2000—06; chief of psychiatry VA Conn. Healthcare Sys., West Haven, Conn., 1996—2000, dep. chief psychiatry, 2000—; prof. psychiatry and neuroscience Baylor Coll. Medicine, Houston, 2006—. Courtesy faculty appointments Yale-New Haven Hosp., Conn., Conn. Mental Health Ctr., New Haven; rsch. dir. VA Nat. Substance Use Disorders Quality Enhancement Rsch. Initiative; congl. fellow US House Representatives, House Subcommittee on Human Resources, Washington, 1998—99; vis. rsch. prof., dept. medicine U. Minn., 1987; vis. prof., med. divsn. US Army European Command, Heidelberg, Germany, 1988; vis. prof., dept. toxicology Med. Sch. Hosp. de la Sta. Creu i Sant Pau, Barcelona, 1989, Barcelona, 1990, Barcelona, 1994; vis. prof., dept. medicine and psychiatry, Addiction Rsch. Found. U. Toronto, Canada, 1991; vis. prof. Beijing Med. U. & Chinese Nat. Inst. on Drug Dependence, 1991; disting. prof. Universidad Complutense de Madrid, Facultad de Medicina, Madrid, 1993; vis. prof., dept. psychiatry U. Athens, Greece, 1995, Greece, 1998; disting. vis. prof. North Shore U. Hosp., Einstein Med. Sch., NY, 1998; mem. of several nat. advisory and review groups; lectr. in field; presenter in field. Dep. editor to sr. dep. editor Am. Jour. on Addictions, dep. editor to editor-in chief Am. Jour. Drug and Alcohol Abuse, co-editor for Substance Abuse, Guilford Press, cons. editor Clin. Advances in the Treatment of Psychiatric Disorders, mem. editl. bd. Am. Jour. Psychiatry, Drug and Alcohol Dependence, Jour. Nervous and Mental Disease, Jour. Studies on Alcohol, Brain Pharmacology, Neuropharmacology, Sci. & Practice Perspectives; contbr. chapters to books, articles to profl. jours. Congl. fellow, u.s. ho. of rep. Ho. Subcommittee on Human Resources (Christopher Shays, Chair), Washington, 1998—99. Recipient Rsch. Scientist Develop. award, Nat. Inst. on Drug Abuse, 1987—96, Joseph Cochin award for Rsch. in Substance Abuse, Com. on Problems of Drug Dependence, Chartered Com. NAS, 1990, Nyswander award for Contributions to Rsch. in Opiate Dependence, Am. Methadone Treatment Assn., 2000, Sr. Scientist award, Nat. Inst. on Drug Abuse, 2000—; named one of New York Mag. Best Doctor, 2001—05; named to America's Top Doctors, 1st, 2nd, 3rd, 4th, 5th, 6th, 7th, 8th & 9th editions, Top Doctors, New York Metro Area, 5th, 6th, 7th, 8th & 9th editions, Castle Connolly Med. Ltd., 2001—05; NSF Fellow in Biophysics, Rensselaer Polytechnic Inst., 1972, Travel Fellowship, Com. on Problems of Drug Dependence, 1985. Fellow: Coll. on Problems of Drug Dependence (pres.-elect 2005, bd. dir., program chair, credentials com.), Am. Coll. Neuropsychopharmacology (program chair, human rsch. com., Joel Elkes Internat. award for Outstanding Contributions to Psychopharmacology 1993), Collegium Internationale Neuro-Psychopharmacologicum, Am. Acad. Addiction Psychiatry (pres. 1998—2000, founding mem., bd. dir.), Am. Psychiatric Assn. (vice chair, coun. on addictions); mem.: Inst. of Medicine. Achievements include being the founder of the divison of substance abuse at Baylor and Yale U; neroimaging research includes detecting and treating cocaine induced cerebral perfusion defects, and using functional MRI to predict pharmacotherapy outcome; medication contributions include a cocaine vaccine, immunotherapy for hallucinogens, buprenorphine for opioid dependence, disulfiram for cocaine dependence, vasodilators for cocaine induced cerbral perfusion defects, & combining medications with contingency management for opioid & cocaine dependence. Avocations: tennis, ice skating. Office: Baylor College Medicine Research 151 Bldg 110 Rm 229 Michael E DeBailey VA Med Ctr 2002 Holcombe Blvd Houston TX 77030 also: One Baylor Plaza BCM 350 Houston TX 77030 Office Fax: 713-794-7240. Business E-Mail: kosten@bcm.edu.

KOTAS, ROBERT VINCENT, pediatrician, educator; b. Buffalo, Nov. 26, 1938; s. Vincent John and Regina K.; m. Ilona Rae Fielding, Mar. 2, 1968; children: Nicole, Timothy, Robert, Rebecca. BS, Canisius Coll., 1959; MD, U. Buffalo, 1963. Diplomate: Am. Acad. Pediatrics. Research assoc. McGill U., 1969-70; intern Buffalo Children's Hosp., 1963-64; resident in pediatrics Johns Hopkins Hosp., Balt., 1964-66; asst. prof. pediatrics U. Okla. Med. Sch., 1970-72, dir. newborn services, 1970-72; dir., div. devel. physiology; career investigator W.K. Warren Med. Research Center, Tulsa, 1972-76, sci. dir., 1976-80; dir. William and Natalie Warren Med. Inst., Tulsa, 1980-83; chief pediatrician Ella Austin Health Ctr., San Antonio, 1989-95, med. dir., 1993-95; lab. dir., 1993-95; pediatrician UTHSC-SA Primary Care Cmty. Pediat., San Antonio, 1995-98, Minor Emergency Ctr., San Antonio, 1998-99; assoc. Fernando A. Guerra, MD, San Antonio, 1998-99, Lonestar Pediats., Kaufman, Tex., 1999—2002; lead staff physician Cmty. Outreach Clinic/Bluitt-Flowers, Dallas, 2003; pvt. practice, 2006—. Clin. prof. pediats. U. Okla. Med. Sch., Tulsa, 1977-99; clin. instr. pediats. U. Tex. Southwestern Med. Ctr., Dallas, 2002; assoc. prof. pediats. U. Tex. Health Sci. Ctr., San Antonio, 1983-98, dir. rsch. devel., 1993-94, also med. dir.; guest scientist Nat. Inst. Child Health and Human Devel., Bethesda, Md., 1975-77, also cons.; cons. Am. Lung Assn., others; cons. pediatrician San Antonio Ind. Sch. Dist. Contbr. articles to profl. jours. and books. Served as capt. USAF, 1966-68. Recipient continuing edn. awards AMA; Best M.D. Written Book award Am. Med. Writers Assn., 1980; Mosby scholar, 1963; grantee NIH, 1969-70, 75-79, 84-88; grantee USPHS, 1968-69, 91-95; others. Mem. Johns Hopkins Med. and Surg. Assn., So. Soc. Pediatric Rsch., Soc. Pediatric Rsch., Am. Physiol. Soc., Soc. Gynecol. Investigation, Tex. Med. Assn., Raufman County Med. Soc. Home: 604 Courageous Dr Rockwall TX 75032-5768

KOTECKI, KEVIN, beer company executive; MBA, Northwestern U., 1988. Formerly with ConAgra Foods Co., P&G; brand dir. Coors Brewing Co., Golden, Colo.; pres., COO Brach's Candy Co., 2000—02; pres., CEO Pabst Brewing Co., 2005—. Office: Pabst Brewing Co 121 Interpark Blvd Ste 300 San Antonio TX 78216-1852 Office Phone: 210-226-0231. Office Fax: 210-299-6807. Business E-Mail: kkotecki@pabst.com.

KOTOV, OLEG VALERIEVICH, cosmonaut; b. Simferopol, Oct. 27, 1965; s. Valeri Efimovich and Elena Ivanovna Kotov; m. Svetlana Nikolayevna Bunyakina; 2 children. Grad., Kirov Mil. Med. Acad., 1988. Dep. lead test doctor and lead test doctor. Gagarin Cosmonaut Tng. Ctr., 1988—96, cosmonaut candidate, 1996—98, test cosmonaut, 1998—; rep. Gagarin Cosmonaut Tng. Ctr. Johnson Space Ctr., 1999; CAPCOM Expeditions-3 & 4 in MCC-M, 2001—02, Moscow Support Group in MCC-H, 2001—02; chief CAPCOM Branch, Cosmonaut Office, 2004; flight engr., Soyuz comdr. Expedition 15 mission to Internat. Space Station; crew mem. to Internat. Space Station Expeditions 22 & 23 on Soyuz spacecraft Baikonur Cosmodrome, 2009. Rsch. cosmonaut Soyuz TM-28 Mission; flight engr. and Soyuz comdr. Expedition-15 Mission, Soyuz TMA10, 2007. Avocations: diving, computers, photography. Office: NASA Johnson Space Ctr c/o Astronaut Office/CB Houston TX 77058

KOTOWSKI, KAREN, finance company executive; BS in Mgmt., Marion Coll. With Citicorp., 1981—86; v.p., mortgage sys. Home Savings of America, 1986—93; dir., network svcs. Northern States Power, 1993—95; dir., fin. svcs. PricewaterhouseCoopers, LLP., 1996—2001; exec. v.p. US Bancorp (formerly Firstar Corp.), 2001—03; v.p., application devel. SLM Corp., 2003, sr. v.p., application devel., 2006, chief investment officer, 2008; sr. v.p., chief investment officer Sallie Mae - SLM Corp., 2006—. Bd. dirs. Sys. and Software Consortium; mem. Youth Hockey Assn., Ind., United Way, Ind. Recipient Top 100 Women in Computing award, McGraw Hill, 1996. Office: SLM Corp 12061 Bluemont Way Reston VA 20190 Office Phone: 703-810-3000. Office Fax: 703-984-5042. Business E-Mail: karen.kotowski@salliemae.com.

KOTTAS, JOHN FREDERICK, business administration educator; b. Hampton, Va., Apr. 18, 1940; s. Harry and Johnny (Edwards) K.; m. Betty Ann Hokenson, Aug. 7, 1965; children: John Bohlin, Ellen Elizabeth, Katherine Caroline, Paul Frederick. BS, Purdue U., 1962; MS, Northwestern U., 1964, PhD, 1968. Lectr. Wharton Sch., U. Pa., Phila., 1966-68; asst. prof. Sch. Bus. Adminstrn., U. N.C., Chapel Hill., 1968-73; adj. assoc. prof. Boston U. Overseas Grad. Program, Heidelberg, W. Ger., 1973-74; asso. prof. coordinator mgmt. sci. and info. systems Sch. Bus. Adminstrn., U. Mo., St. Louis, 1974-79; Zollinger prof. bus. adminstrn. Coll. William and Mary, Williamsburg, Va., 1979—. Presented three-day mgmt. seminar on Inventory Mgmt. and Control at numerous univs., U.S. and Can., 1976-78; cons. in field. Co-author: Production/Operations Management: Contemporary Policy of Managing Operating Systems, 1972, Cases and Applications in Lotus 1-2-3 (for DOS), 1995, Cases and Applications in Lotus 1-2-3 (for Windows), 1996, Cases and Applications in Microsoft EXCEL 5.0, 1996; contbr. articles to various publs. NDEA fellow, 1962-65; Walter P. Murphy fellow, 1962 Home: 109 Maxwell Pl Williamsburg VA 23185-5523 Office: Coll of William and Mary Mason Sch Bus Williamsburg VA 23187 Office Phone: 757-221-2868. Personal E-mail: jfkott@cox.net. Business E-Mail: john.kottas@mason.wm.edu.

KOTZ, NATHAN KALLISON (NICK KOTZ), news correspondent, author; b. San Antonio, Sept. 16, 1932; s. Jacob and Tibe (Kallison) K.; m. Mary Lynn Booth, Aug. 7, 1960; 1 child, Jack Mitchell. AB magna cum laude in Internat. Relations, Dartmouth Coll., 1955; student, London Sch. Econs., 1955-56. Reporter, Des Moines Register, 1958-64, Washington corr., 1964-70; also for other Cowles Publs. (newspapers); nat. corr. Washington Post, 1970-73; adj. prof. Sch. Communication, Am. U., Washington, 1978-86; sr. journalist in residence Duke U., 1983; corr. PBS Frontline, 1992. Farmer, Broad Run, Va., 1980— Free-lance writer, 1973; author: Let Them Eat Promises: The Politics of Hunger in America, 1969, Wild Blue Yonder: Money, Politics, and the B-1 Bomber, 1988, Judgment Days: Lyndon Baines Johnson, Martin Luther King, Jr., and the Laws That Changed America, 2005; co-author: The Unions, 1971, A Passion for Equality: George Wiley and the Movement, 1977. Bd. dirs. Iowa Bds. Internat. Edn., 1962-64, Suburban Md. Fair Housing, 1966-72, Black Student Fund, 1976-86—, Penn-Faulkner, 1986—; bd. dirs. Fund for Investigative Journalism, 1977-86, chmn., 1978-82. Served to 1st lt. USMCR, 1956-58. Recipient Pulitzer prize for nat. reporting, 1968; Raymond Clapper Meml. award, 1966, 68, 2d pl., 1973, Disting. Service award Sigma Delta Chi, 1966, Robert F. Kennedy Journalism award, 1968, Spl. Merit award Am. U., 1981, award for pub. svc. Nat. Mag., 1985, Adj. Faculty award Am. U., 1985, Olive Branch award NYU Ctr. War, Peace and News Media, 1989, Iowa Author award, 2005, Martin Luther King Jr. Social Justice award Dartmouth Coll., 2006, Robert F. Kennedy Meml. Book High Honor award, 2006. Mem. Nat. Press Club, Cosmos Club, Phi Beta Kappa.

KOUPLEN, STEVE, state legislator; b. Beggs, Okla. m. Anita Kouplen (dec.); children: Sean, Shanna. B in Agrl. Ed., M in Agrl. Ed., Okla. State U. Rancher; bd. mem., past pres. Okla. Farm Bureau; mem. Dist. 24 Okla. House of Representatives, 2008—. Mem.: NRA, American Hereford Assn., Okla. Cattleman's Assn., Beggs Masonic Lodge. Democrat. Office: Oklahoma House of Representatives 2300 N Lincoln Blvd Rm 546 Oklahoma City OK 73105 Address: 5910 Garfield Rd Beggs OK 74421 Office Phone: 405-557-7306. Business E-Mail: steve.kouplen@okhouse.gov.

KOURI, DONALD JACK, chemist, educator; b. Hobart, Okla., July 25, 1938; s. Eddie and Theresa LaJuan (Williams) K.; m. Shirley Ann Stewart, Apr. 9, 1965; children: Lisa Renee, David Matthew. BA, Okla. Bapt. U., 1960; MS, U. Wis., 1962, PhD, 1965. Postdoctoral fellow Joint Inst. Lab Astrophysics, U. Colo., 1965-66; asst. prof. chemistry Midwestern U., Wichita Falls, 1966-67, U. Houston, 1967-71, assoc. prof., 1971-73, prof., 1973—, Disting. Univ. prof., 1987-96, Cullen Disting. prof. chemistry, mathematics, mechanical engring. and physics, dir. Inst. for Digital Informatics and Analysis. Vis. lectr. U. Ill., 1972; vis. scientist Inst. for Strömungsforschung, Göttingen, Fed. Republic Germany, 1973-74; bd. dirs. Inst. for Digital Informatics and Analysis. Recipient U.S. Sr. Scientist award Alexander von Humboldt Found., 1973-74, Southwestern Tex. sect. award Am. Chem. Soc., 1981, Sigma Xi Rsch. award, 1995; fellow A.P. Sloan Found., 1972-74, Weizmann Inst., 1973, Inst. for Advanced Studies, Hebrew U. Jerusalem, 1978-79, Guggenheim Found., 1978-79. Fellow Am. Phys. Soc. (exec. com. mem., sec.-treas. Few Body Topical group); mem. IEEE, ASCAP, Am. Chem. Soc., Am. Assn. Physics Tchrs. Democrat. Baptist. Office: U Houston Dept Chemistry 4800 Calhoun Rd Houston TX 77204-5003 Office Phone: 713-743-3245. Business E-Mail: kouri@uh.edu.

KOVACHEVICH, ELIZABETH ANNE, federal judge; b. Canton, Ill., Dec. 14, 1936; d. Dan and Emilie (Kuchan) Kovachevich. AA, St. Petersburg JC, 1956; BBA in Fin. magna cum laude, U. Miami, 1958; JD, Stetson U., 1961, LLD (hon.), 1993. Bar: Fla. 1961, U.S. Dist. Ct. (mid. and so. dists.) Fla. 1961, U.S. Ct. Appeals (5th cir.) 1961, U.S. Supreme Ct. 1968. Rsch. and adminstrv. aide Pinellas County Legis. Del., Fla., 1961; assoc. DiVito & Speer, St. Petersburg, Fla., 1961—62; house counsel Rieck & Fleece Builders Supplies, Inc., St. Petersburg, 1962; pvt. practice atty. St. Petersburg, 1962—73; judge 6th Jud. Cir., Pinellas and Pasco Counties, Fla., 1973—82, US Dist. Ct. (mid. dist.) Fla., Tampa, 1982—96, 2002—, chief judge, 1996—2002. Chmn. St. Petersburg Profl. Legal Project-Days in Ct., 1967, Supreme Ct. Bicentennial Com. 6th Jud. Cir., 1975—76. Prodr., coord. (TV prodn.) A Race to Judgement. Bd. regents State of Fla., 1970—72; legal advisor, bd. dirs. Young Women's Residence, Inc., 1968; mem. Fla. Gov.'s Commn. on Status of Women, 1968—71; mem. Pres.'s Commn. on White House Fellowships, 1973—77; mem. def. adv. com. on Women in Svc. Dept. Def., 1973—76; Fla. publicity chmn. 18th Nat. Rep. Women's Conf., Atlanta, 1971; lifetime mem. Children's Hosp. Guild, YWCA of St. Petersburg; charter mem. Golden Notes, St. Petersburg Symphony; hon. mem. bd. of overeers Stetson U. Coll. of Law, 1986. Recipient St. Petersburg Panhellenic Appreciation award, 1964, Pinellas United Fund award in recognition of concern and meritorious effort, 1968, Disting. Alumni award, Stetson U., 1970, Woman of Yr. award, Beta Sigma Phi, 1970, 1970, Am. Legion Aux. Unit 14 Pres. award cmty. svc., 1970, Dedication to Christian Ideals award and Man of Yr. award, KC Dists. 20-21, 1972, USN Recruiting Command Appreciation award, 1975, Woman of Yr. award, Fla. Fedn. Bus. and Profl. Women, 1981, ann. Ben C. Willard Meml. award, Stetson Lawyers Assn., 1983, Alumni of Yr. award, St. Petersburg Jr. Coll., 1994, Cath. Law Person of Yr., Greater Tampa Cath. Lawyer's Guild, 1998, Disting. Svc. award, Fla. Coun. on Crime and Delinquency, 1999, J-Ben Watkins award, Stetson U. Coll. of Law, 1999, Woman of Achievement award, Delta Delta Delta, 2000, Outstanding Jurist award, Hillsborough County, 2000—01, Pub. Svc. award, William Reece Smith, Jr., 2001, Mrs. Charles Ulrick Bay award, St. Petersburg Rotary award, St. Petersburg Quarterback Club award, President's Award, Fed. Bar. Assn., 2001, Presidential Special

Recognition Award, 2002. Mem.: ABA, St. Petersburg Bar Assn. (chmn. bench and bar com., sec. 1969), Am. Judicature Soc., Pinellas County Trial Lawyers, Fla. Bar Assn., ATLA. Office: US Dist Ct Fl 17 801 N Florida Ave Tampa FL 33702-3849

KOVACIC, WILLIAM EVAN, law educator, former federal commissioner; b. Poughkeepsie, NY, Oct. 1, 1952; s. Evan Carl and Frances Katherine (Crow) K.; m. Kathryn Marie Fenton, May 18, 1985. AB with honors, Princeton U., 1974; JD, Columbia U., 1978. Bar: NY 1979. Law clk. to Hon. Roszel C. Thomsen US Dist. Ct. Md., Balt., 1978—79; atty. planning office bur. competition FTC, Washington, 1979—82, atty. adv. to commr. George W. Douglas, 1983, gen. counsel, 2001—04, commr., 2006—11, chmn., 2008—09; assoc. Bryan Cave LLP, Washington, 1983—86; prof. George Mason U. Sch. Law, Arlington, Va., 1986—99, George Washington U. Law Sch., Washington, 1999—. Mem. U.S. Senate Judiciary Subcom. on Antitrust and Monopoly, Washington, 1975—76. Contbr. legal articles to profl. jours. Harlan Fiske Stone fellow, Columbia U., 1976—78. Mem. ABA (antitrust law and pub. contract law sects.), Fed. Bar Assn. Roman Catholic. Office: George Washington U Law Sch 720 20th St NW Washington DC 20052-0001 Office Phone: 202-994-8123. Business E-Mail: wkovacic@law.gwu.edu.

KOVACS, BEATRICE, retired library studies educator; b. Seekirchen, Austria, June 2, 1945; came to U.S., 1948; d. Lorand and Helen (Magyary-Kossa) K.; m. Thomas Gordon Basler, Apr. 20, 1969 (div. 1979); m. Louis Edward Mitchum, Jan. 10, 1994. AB in English, Syracuse U., 1966; MLS, Rutgers State U., 1967; DLS, Columbia U., 1983. Libr. Nassau Acad. Medicine, Garden City, N.Y., 1967-70; cataloger, asst. acquisitions libr. Augusta (Ga.) Regional Libr., 1974-78; collection devel. libr. Med. Coll. Ga., Augusta, 1978-80; acct. specialist Readmore Publs., NYC, 1982-83; chief collection devel. U. N.Mex. Med. Ctr. Libr., Albuquerque, 1984-85; asst. prof. U. NC, Greensboro, 1985-91, assoc. prof., 1991—2007; ret., 2007. Vis. instr. Pratt Inst. Grad. Sch. Libr., Bklyn., 1982-83; adj. prof. U. N.C. Chapel Hill Sch. Info. and Libr. Sci., 1997-98. Author: Decision-Making Process for Library Collections, 1990, ALA Fingertip Guide to National Health-Information Resources, 1995; co-author: Health Sciences Librarianship, 1977, Using Science and Technology Information Resources, 1991, Lincoln County, 2012; contbr. articles to profl. jours. Bishop scholarship Med. Libr. Assn., 1966; recipient Meritorious Achievement award, NC Chpt. Spl. Librs. Assn., 2005. Business E-Mail: beamitchum@nu-z.net.

KOWALSKI, JAMES M., career military officer; b. 1957; BBA, U. Cin., 1979; M in Mgmt., Ctrl. Mich. U., 1985; M in Nat. Security and Strategic Studies, Coll. Naval Command and Staff, Naval War Coll., 1993. Commd. 2d. lt. USAF, 1979, advanced through grades to lt. gen., 2010, pilot training Laughlin AFB, Tex., 1980—81; B-52D pilot 2nd Bombardment Squadron, March AFB, Calif., 1981—82; aircraft comdr., instr. pilot and wing tactics officer 524th Bombardment Squadron, Wurtsmith AFB, Mich., 1982—86; B-1B instr. pilot and chief wing standardization and evaluation 384th Bombardment Wing, McConnell AFB, Kans., 1987—89, 96th Bomb Wing, Dyess AFB, Tex., 1989—92; chief long-range attack planning & programming USAF, Washington, 1993—94; comdr. 28th Bomb Squadron, Dyess AFB, Tex., 1994—96; chief Forces Assignment Br., Directorate of Force Structure (J-8) The Joint Staff, Washington, 1997—99; comdr. 2nd Ops. Group, Barksdale AFB, La., 1999—2000; asst. dir. aerospace ops. Air Combat Command (ACC), Langley AFB, Va., 2000—02; comdr. 28th Bomb Wing, Ellsworth AFB, SD, 2002—04, 405th Air Expeditionary Wing, SW Asia, 2002—04; dep. dir. operational plans & joint matters USAF, Washington, 2004—05; comdr. 552nd Air Control Wing, Tinker AFB, Okla., 2005—07; dep. dir. global ops. (J-39) Ops. Directorate The Joint Staff, Washington, 2007—09; comdr. (provisional) Air Force Global Strike Command (AFGSC), Bollings AFB, DC, 2009, vice comdr. Barksdale AFB, La., 2009—11, comdr., 2011—. Decorated Legion of Merit with three oak leaf clusters, Bronze Star Medal, Def. Meritorious Svc. Medal, Meritorious Svc. Medal with two oak leaf clusters, Air Medal, Aerial Achievement Medal with oak leaf cluster, Joint Svc. Commendation Medal with oak leaf cluster, Air Force Achievement Medal, Combat Readiness Medal with oak leaf cluster, Global War on Terrorism Expeditionary Medal, Global War on Terrorism Svc. Medal; Sec. of Def. Fellows Program, McDonnell Douglas Aerospace, 1996—97. Office: Air Force Global Strike Command (AFGSC) 245 Davis Ave E Room 240 Barksdale AFB LA 71110

KOZIKOWSKI, TAMI, retail executive; BS in Bus. & Acctg., U. Minn.; MBA in Mktg. & Fin., UCLA, 1987. V.p., real estate and property devel. Musicland, 1993—2001; sr. v.p., svcs. ops. Best Buy Co., Inc., sr. v.p., real estate and property mgmt., sr. v.p., retail support and ops., Geek Squad, sr. v.p., merchandising, 2001—09; chief devel. officer Advance Auto Parts, Inc., 2009—. Office: Advance Auto Parts Inc Store Ctr Support 5008 Airport Rd Roanoke VA 24012 Office Phone: 540-362-4911. Business E-Mail: tami.kozikowski@advanceautoparts.com.

KOZITKA, RICHARD EUGENE, retired consumer products company executive; b. Staples, Minn., Apr. 30, 1934; s. Michael V. and Luella H. (Drews) K.; m. Mary Elizabeth Juneau, Sept. 27, 1969; children: Michael Arthur, Laura Juneau Hensley. BA in Journalism, U. Minn., 1956. Program dir. Jr. Achievement of Chgo., 1961-63; mgr. publ./employee communications The Quaker Oats Co., Chgo., 1963-72, dir. employee and audio visual communications, 1972-78, v.p. corp. adminstrv. svcs., 1978-95. Trustee Luth. Social Svcs. Ill. Served with MIlitary Inteligence, U.S. Army, 1957-61. Mem. Westmoreland Country Club (Wilmette, Ill.), Chgo. Curling Club (Northbrook, Ill.), Univ. Club Chgo., Pelican Strand Country Club (Naples, Fla.), La Playa Beach Club (Naples). Lutheran. Home: 9790 Gulf Shore Dr Unit 205 Naples FL 34108

KOZLOWSKI, RONALD STEPHAN, retired librarian; b. Chgo., Oct. 18, 1937; s. Stephan James and Helen Marie Beck (Tancula) K.; m. Barbara Hartlein, Aug. 8, 1964; children: Ann, Keith, Ellen, Brent. BS in Edn, Ill. State U., 1961; MA in LS, Rosary Coll., 1968. Audiovisual libr. Triton Jr. Coll., River Grove, Ill., 1968-69; br. libr. Evansville (Ind.) Pub. Librs., 1969-70, asst. dir., 1971-74; head reference and acquisitions dept. Ind. State U., Evansville, 1970-71; dir. West Fla. Regional Libr., Pensacola, 1974-77, Louisville Free Pub. Libr., 1977-83, Pub. Libr. Charlotte and Mecklenburg County, NC, 1983-86; exec. dir. Cuyahoga County Pub. Libr., Cleve., 1986-89; dir. Miami-Dade Pub. Libr. Sys., Miami, Fla., 1989-1993; adminstr. Anne Arundel County Pub. Libr., Annapolis, Md., 1993—2002; ret., 2002. Del. White House Conf. on Librs.; bd. trustees State Libr. Va., 2006—. Mem. ALA, Md. Libr. Assn. Home: 5805 Gate House Dr Glen Allen VA 23059-2603 Home Phone: 804-740-0418. Personal E-mail: rskozlowski@comcast.net.

KRAJCER, ZVONIMIR, cardiologist, educator; MD, U. Zagreb. Diplomate Am. Bd. Internal Medicine, 1975, Am. Bd. Internal Medicine-cardiovasc. disease, 1977. Resident internal medicine Northwestern Med. Ctr., Chgo., 1972—84; fellow cardiovasc. disease St. Luke's Episcopal Hosp., Houston, 1975—77, co-dir. peripheral vascular disease svc. Tex. Heart Inst.; clin. prof. Baylon Coll. of Medicine. Office: Texas Heart Institute St Luke's Episcopal Hospital 6624 Fannin Ste 2780 Houston TX 77030 Office Phone: 732-235-7208. Office Fax: 732-235-6530. Business E-Mail: kostis@umdnj.edu.

KRAJEWSKI, MICHAEL, conductor; b. Detroit; m. Darcy Krajewski. Grad, Wayne State U., Detroit, U. Cinn. Coll.-Conservatory Music; student, Pierre Monteux Domaine Sch. Conductors. Music dir. Modesto Symphony Orch.; asst. condr. Detroit Symphony Orch.; music dir. Detroit Symphony Civic Orch.; resident condr. Fla. Symphony Orch.; prin. pops condr. Long Beach Symphony, 1998—, Houston Symphony Orch., 2000—, N.Mex. Symphony, 2001—, also Jacksonville Symphony, NH Music Festival Orch. Dorati fellowship condr. Detroit Symphony; artist intern Mich. Opera Theatre. Performances with Boston Pops Orch., San Francisco, St. Louis, Detroit, Balt., Atlanta, Minn., Oreg. orchestras. Office: Houston Symphony 615 Louisiana St Ste 102 Houston TX 77002

KRALLINGER, JOSEPH CHARLES, entrepreneur, consultant, writer; b. Lancaster, Pa., May 29, 1931; s. Ferdinand and Mathilde (Meyer) K.; m. Hilde Eisenhauer, Oct. 1, 1955; children— Joanne, Diane, Robert BS in Econs. cum laude, Franklin and Marshall Coll., 1953. CPA. Auditor GAO, Denver, 1953; auditor Army Audit Agy., 1953-55; ptnr. Arthur Andersen & Co., Phila., 1955-76; v.p. strategic planning and acquisitions, chief fin. officer Berwind Corp., Phila., 1976-88; cons. Palm Desert, Calif., 1988—2005. Dir., bus. advisor and investor various indsl., health care, mining, oil and gas cos., 1976—; cons. in field. Author: An Auditor's Approach to Statistical Sampling, 5 vols., 1967-72, Strategic Planning Workbook, 1989, 2d edit., 1993, How to Acquire the Perfect Business for Your Company, 1991; Planeacion Estrategica Practica, 1991; Mergers and Acquisitions: Managing the Transactions, 1997, Chinese and Spanish edits., 2000; contbr. articles to profl. jours. Bd. dirs. alumni coun. Franklin and Marshall Coll., Lancaster, 1969-75; pres., tchr. religious edn. St. Genevieve Cath. Ch., Flourtown, Pa., 1971-76; bd. dirs. Whitemarsh Twp. Citizens Coun., Plymouth Meeting, Pa., 1972-75; hon. life mem., past chmn. bd. dirs. Phila. chpt. Am. Cancer Soc. Recipient Nat. Vol. award Am. Cancer Soc., 1985, Crusade award Am. Cancer Soc., 1985, Teaching award St. Genevieve Ch., 1985, Cert. Merit Inst. Mgmt. Accts., 1998. Mem. AICPA (statis. sampling com.), Pa. Inst. CPAs, Nat. Assn. Accts. (past pres. Phila. chpt.), Planning Forum (past pres. Phila. chpt.). Avocations: golf, racquet sports, writing, reading. Home and Office: 636 McLendon Hills Dr West End NC 27376

KRAMEK, ROBERT E., board member; m. Patricia Havard; children: Tracy, Joseph, Suzanne, Nancy. Diploma Capstone Program, Nat. Def. U.; degree with highest distinction, US Naval War Coll., Newport, RI; postgrad., U. Mich., Johns Hopkins U., U. Alaska; BS in Engrng. with honors, US Coast Guard Acad., 1961; MS in Naval Architecture, Marine, Mech. & Engrng. Mgmt. Commd. ensign US Coast Guard Acad., 1961, advanced through grades to admiral, 1994; pres., COO Am. Bureau of Shipping, 1998—2006. Bd. dirs. Rowan Companies, Inc., 2007—. Recipient 2 Disting. Svc. medals U.S. Coast Guard, 2 Legion of Merit awards, Meritorious Svc. medal, 4 Commendation medals, Achievement medal, Unit Commendations award, Meritorious Unit Commendation awards, Spl. Ops. Ribbon with Silver Star, Humanitarian Svc. medal with Bronze Star, Sea Svc. Ribbon with Bronze Star. Avocation: physical fitness. Office: Rowan Companies Inc Bd Directors 2800 Post Oak Blvd Ste 5450 Houston TX 77056-6127 Office Phone: 713-621-7800. Office Fax: 713-960-7660. Business E-Mail: rkramek@rowancompanies.com.

KRAMER, PHILLIP D., oil industry executive; Contr. Plains Resources, 1983—87, treas., 1987—2001, v.p., 1988—92, v.p., CFO, 1992—97, sr. v.p., CFO, 1997—98, exec. v.p., CFO, 1998—2001, Plains All American Pipeline, LP, Houston, 1998—2008, exec. v.p., 2008—. Office: Plains All American Pipeline Ste 1600 333 Clay St Houston TX 77002

KRAMM, DEBORAH ANN, retired information technology executive; b. Pasadena, Calif., June 24, 1949; d. Donald F. and Mary (Roach) Coonan; m. Kenneth R. Kramm, Dec. 20, 1969; children: Deidre Lyn, Jonathan Russel. BA, U. Calif., Irvine, 1971; MS, Mich. Tech. U., 1981. Cert. mgmt. cons. Math. asst. NASA-Jet Propulsion Lab., Pasadena, 1967-70; libr. asst. U. Calif. Irving Libr., 1967-71; rsch. assoc. animal behavior lab. Mich. Tech. U., Houghton, 1971-80; programmer, analyst Shell Oil Co., Houston, 1981-85; corp. auditor EDP, 1985-87; team leader SLA, 1988-90, supr. resource planning adminstrn., 1990-91, adminstrv. coord. product devel. ctr.-design ctr., 1991-93, bus. analyst sr. systems analyst, 1993-96, engagement mgr., 1996-97, mgr. engagement svc., 1998-99, mgr. sales and contract support, 1999—2001; prin. cons. Shell IT Internat., 2001—03; sr. learning cons., regional svc. leader Shell Learning, 2003—08. Chmn. bd. MMARK, Houston, 1983-85. Contbr. articles to profl. jours.; designer (program application software) Shell Point-of-Sale Terminal, 1982-85. Treas. KFHS Orch., 1986-88; co-leader Boy Scouts Am., Houston, 1981-83. AAUW scholar, 1980, Calif. State scholar, 1967-71. Mem.: AAUW (pres. br. 1975—81), Inst. Mgmt. Cons., CMC (v.p., bd. dirs.), Shell Data Processors Club, Houston Bus. Forum (pres. bd. dirs.), Assn. for Women in Computing (membership bd. dirs.). Home: 2 Abercrombie Pl Conroe TX 77384

KRANC, LISA R., marketing executive; b. Brooklyn, NY; B in Am. Studies, Brandeis U., 1975; MBA in Mktg. & Fin., Columbia U., 1977. Sr. mktg. dir. Cadbury Schweppes; mgr. Clorox Co.; v.p., mktg. Giant Eagle, Inc., 1992; sr. v.p., mktg. Bruno's, Inc., 1996—97; v.p., mktg. Hannaford Bros. Co., 1997; sr. v.p., mktg. AutoZone, Inc., 2001—. Mem. AAIA; chmn., bd. dirs. Greater Memphis Arts Coun.; bd. dirs. Brandeis U. Alumni Assn. Named Aftermarket Woman of the Yr., Car Care Coun. Women's Bd., 2009. Office: AutoZone Inc 123 S Front St Memphis TN 38103 Office Phone: 901-495-6500. Office Fax: 901-495-8300. Business E-Mail: lisa.kranc@autozone.com.

KRANS, MICHELLE M., publishing executive; b. Chgo. m. Michael Krans; 1 child, Sarah. BS in Bus., Calif. State U., Northridge. With McCord Ins. Svcs., Studio City, Calif., 1985—90; dir., market devel. The Salinas Californian, 1995—98; mgr., mktg. & promotions Desert Sun, Palm Springs, Calif., 1990—95, advt. & mktg. dir., 2002—05, pres., pub., 2005—, mgr., custom pub., 1998—2002; sr. v.p., Strategy and Devel., U.S. Cmty. Pub. Gannett Co., Inc., 2008—. Recipient 4 Pres.'s Rings for outstanding work in advt. & mktg., Gannett Co. Inc., Chmn.'s Ring, 2006; named Advt. Exec. of Yr. for 2005. Office: Gannett Co Inc 7950 Jones Branch Dr Mc Lean VA 22102-3302 Office Phone: 703-854-6000. Office Fax: 703-854-2053. Business E-Mail: mkrans@gannett.com.

KRASNO, RICHARD MICHAEL, foundation executive, educator; b. Chgo., Jan. 20, 1942; s. Louis R. K. and Adeline G. (Glassman) Kaplan; children: Jeffrey Patrick, Eric Peter; m. Carin Blucher. BS, U. Ill., 1965; PhD, Stanford U., 1970; LittD (hon.), Coll. St. Rose, 1983; LLD (hon.), Sacred Heart U., 1984. Asst. prof. ednl. psychology U. Chgo., 1970-74; program advisor Brazil Ford Found., Rio de Janeiro, 1974-77, program advisor Latin Am. NYC, 1977, program advisor Mid.-East & Africa, 1978-80; deputy asst. sec. of edn. U.S. Dept. Edn., Washington, 1980-81; exec. v.p. Inst. Internat. Edn., NYC, 1981-83, pres., CEO, 1983-98; pres. Monterey (Calif.) Inst. Internat Stud, 1998-99, Kenan Charitable Trust, Chapel Hill, NC, 1999—. Commr. U.S.-Brazil Fulbright Commn., 1975-77, U.S. Nat. Commn. UNESCO, 1983; chmn. Internat. Transition Team Dept. Edn., 1979, 80; mem. U.S.-Mex. Bilateral Commn., 1980, 84; sr. Fulbright lectr., 1973-74. Contbr. articles to profl. jours. Trustee Laspau, Cambridge, Mass., 1980—82, Eisenhower Exch. Program, 2002—; chmn. Rhodes Scholars Selection Com., 2001—04; dir. U. NC Healthcare, 2004—, chmn., bd. dirs., 2009—. Nat. Defense Edn. fellow U.S. Govt., 1967-68. Mem. Coun. Fgn. Rels., Century Assn., Cosmos Club. Office: The Kenan Ctr PO Box 3858 Chapel Hill NC 27515-3858 Business E-Mail: richard_krasno@unc.edu.

KRASNOFF, ALAN P., mayor, Chesapeake, Virginia; m. Phyllis Koppelman Krasnoff; children: Matthew, Amanda. BA in Econ., Queens Coll. CUNY, Flushing, NY; MA in Urban Edn. and Counseling, Norfolk State Univ., Norfolk, VA; DC, Nat. Coll. Chiropractor. Chiropractor Krasnoff Chiropractic Ctr.; Spanish teacher Carver and Truitt Intermediate Schs., 2001; mem. City Council, Chesapeake, Va., 1990—2008; mayor City of Chesapeake, Va., 2008—. Vol. wrestling team chiropractor Deep Creak H.S., 1982—83; staff devel. consultant Chesapeake Public Sch., 2005—06. Lifetime mem. Chesapeake NAACP; vol. cross-country coach Indian River H.S., 1995—98, Oscar Smith H.S., 2002; mem., chmn. Hampton Raods Planning Dist. Commn., 1990—97, Metropolitan Planning Orgn., 1992—97; mem. Chesapeake Planning Commn., 1986—86, Va. Sch. Counseling Assn., Va. Counseling Assn., Great Bridge H.S. PTSA, Hampton Rd. Sch. Counselor Assn.; chmn. Library Bond Referendum, 1988, Rd. Bond Referendum, 1986; bd. dir. Chesapeake Juvenile Adv., 1983—85, Chesapeake Vol. in Youth Svc. Office: Office of the Mayor 1006 Cuervo Ct Chesapeake VA 23322 Address: Krasnoff Chiropractic Ctr Krasnoff for Mayor 1101 Battlefield Blvd N Chesapeake VA 23320 Office Phone: 757-382-6974, 757-547-9266. Fax: 757-547-9268. Business E-Mail: akrasnoff@cityofchesapeake.net. E-mail: alan@krasnoff08.com.*

KRASNOSTCHEKOVA, ELENA ALEXANDER, literature and language educator; b. Moscow, June 22, 1934; arrived in U.S., 1987; d. Alexander Michael Krasnostchekov and Donna Jacob Gruz; m. Sergey Michael Samoilov, Dec. 9, 1961; 1 child, Michael. M in Russian Lang. and Lit., Yaroslavl Pedagogy Inst., Russia, 1955; PhD in Russian Lit., Moscow Lenin Pedagogy Inst., 1965. Sr. rsch. assoc. USSR Book Rsch. Inst., Moscow, 1966—81; prof. Moscow Lenin Pedagogy Inst., Moscow, 1966—81; freelance writer, 1981—87; vis. asst. prof. NYU, 1988—90; from asst. prof. to prof. U. Ga., Athens, 1991—98, prof., 1998—. Author: Oblomov by I.A. Goncharov, 1970, Vsevolod Ivanov's Creative World, 1980, I.A. Goncharov: An Universe in Art, 1997, 2nd edit., 2012, Bildungsroman on the Russian Soil, 2008. Fellow Fgn. Rsch. fellow, Slavic Rsch. Ctr. Hokkaido U., 1991—92. Avocation: gardening. Home: 225 Hampton Park Dr Athens GA 30606 Office: U Ga Germanic & Slavic Studies Joseph E Brown Hall Athens GA 30602 Office Phone: 706-542-2741, 706-542-3663. Business E-Mail: krasn@uga.edu.

KRASNOW, KENNETH, real estate company executive; married; 2 children. BBA, Emory U. Various positions including exec. mng. dir. Cushman & Wakefield, NYC, 1986—2005; exec. v.p., dir., brokerage svcs. Trammell Crow Co. (subs. of CB Richard Ellis Group, Inc.), 2005—. Lectr. in field; mem. Real Estate Bd. NY, Bus. Coun. Fairfield County, Real Estate Fin. Assn. Contbr. articles to newspapers. Recipient award, Friends of Island Acad.; named one of Top 50 Leaders in Comml. Real Estate, Real Estate Weekly mag., Top 40 under 40, Real Estate NY. Office: Trammell Crow Co 2001 Ross Ave Ste 3400 Dallas TX 75201 Office Phone: 214-863-4101. Office Fax: 214-863-3138.

KRATOCHVIL, L(OUIS) GLEN, lawyer; b. Highland, Wis., Oct. 11, 1922; s. John A. and Emma (Pusch) K.; m. Evelyn Gregory, Sept. 12, 1946; 1 son, Louis Glen Jr. LLB, U. Wis., 1951; JD, U. Wis., Madison, 1951. Bar: Wis. 1951, Tex. 1952, U.S. Dist. Ct. (so. dist.) Tex. 1956, U.S. Ct. Appeals (5th cir.) 1956, U.S. Supreme Ct. 1956, U.S. Dist. Ct. (ea. dist.) Tex. 1961. Landman Shell Oil Co., Houston, 1951-52; assoc. firm Murphy & Crystal, Houston, 1953-55; asst. U.S. atty. So. Dist. Tex., 1955-57; pvt. practice Houston, 1957—99. Pres. McGregor Terr. Civic Club, Houston, 1954, Young Rep. Club U. Wis., 1950. Lt. USNR, 1941-46, PTO. Mem.: FBA, ABA, U. Wis. Alumni Assn. (pres. Houston chpt. 1972—73), Maritime Law Assn., Houston Bar Assn., Wis. Bar Assn., Tex. Bar Assn., Brazos River Club (treas. 1970—99), Lions (pres. 1955), Phi Alpha Delta (chief justice 1950). Office: Kratochvil and Powell 4600 Highway 6 N Ste 102 Houston TX 77084-2864

KRATOVIL, JANE LINDLEY, think tank associate, not-for-profit developer; b. Boston, Nov. 25, 1952; 1 child, Lindley. BA, Lynchburg Coll., 1974. Various positions US House of Representatives, Washington, 1974-77, The Pittston Co., Greenwich, Conn., 1977-79; assoc. dir. City Sports Mgmt. Inc., Washington, 1979-82; adminstrv. asst. to spl. asst. to pres. for adminstrn. The White House, Washington, 1982-85; exec. asst. to gen. and dep. gen. counsel US Dept. Treasury, Washington, 1985-88; exec. dir., sec. Eisenhower World Affairs Inst., Washington, 1988-2000; pres. Lindley & Assoc., Alexandria, Va., 2000—. Exec. dir. Home in Alexandria, 2011—12; CFO DC Jazz Festival, 2012—. Exec. dir. Eclpse Chamber Orch., 2009—11. Mem.: Eisenhower Inst. (treas. 2005—08, dir. fin. & admin. 2005—09). Office: 2230 Candlewood Dr Alexandria VA 22308-1505

KRAU, ARY, plastic surgeon; MD, NYU. Diplomate Am. Bd. Plastic Surgery. Resident gen surgery Jackson Meml. Hosp.; resident plastic surgery King's County Hosp.; fellow plastic surgery Miami Heart Inst. Fellow: Am. Coll. of Surgeons; mem.: Greater Miami Soc. of Plastic and Reconstructive Surgeons, Am. Soc. of Plastic Surgeons. Office: 1143 Kane Concourse Bay Harbour Islands Miami FL 33154 Office Phone: 305-861-6881.

KRAUS, ELIZABETH, state legislator; Mem. SD Senate Edn. Com.; vice chmn. SD Senate Health and Human Svcs. Com.; mem. SD House of Representatives, 2002—06; mem. Dist. 33 SD State Senate, 2011—. Republican. Home: 626 Wood St Dunedin FL 34698-7133 Office Phone: 605-223-9045. Office Fax: 605-721-6815. Business E-Mail: elizabeth.kraus@state.sd.us.

KRAUS, HELEN, plastic surgeon; MD, Northwestern U. Med. Sch.; grad., U. Notre Dame. Diplomate Am. Bd. of Plastic Surgery, lic. Wis., Fla. Internship gen. surgery Northwestern Meml. Hosp., Chgo., resident plastic surgery; fellow pediatric plastic sugery Children's Meml. Hosp., Chgo.; chief plastic surgery Resurrection Med. Ctr., chief surgery; attending plastic surgeon Osceola Regional Med. Ctr., St. Cloud Med. Ctr., Fla. Hosp. Named Top Doc, Connolly Castle. Mem.: Phi Beta Kappa Soc., Am. Soc. of Plastic Surgeons. Office: St Cloud Regional Medical Center 2906 17th St Saint Cloud FL 34769 Office Phone: 407-892-2135. Office Fax: 407-892-4835.

KRAUSE, JOHN R., pathologist; m. Paulette Krause, 1964. MD, U. Pitts., 1966. Diplomate in med. Pa., 1966, La., 1992, Miss., 1995. Asst. prof. pathology U. Pitts., 1970—71, 1975—81, assoc. prof. pathology, 1981—89, prof. pathology, 1989—92, Tulane U., New Orleans, 1992—; asst. prof. pathology Med. Coll. Pa., Phila.,

1973—75. Chmn. dept pathology Tulane Med. Ctr. Contbr. articles to profl. jour. Maj. Kenner Army Hosp. US Army, 1971—73, Fort Lee Va. Fellow: Am. Soc. Clin. Chemistry, La. State Pathology Soc., Am. Soc. Hematology, Soc. Hematopathology, Coll. Am. Pathologists, Am. Soc. Pathologists, Internat. Acad. Pathologists; mem.: Am. Soc. Flow Cytometry. Office: Tulane Health Sciences Ctr 1430 Tulane Ave SL79 New Orleans LA 70112 Business E-Mail: jkrause@tulane.edu.

KRAUSE, L. WILLIAM, investment company executive; b. Phila., May 20, 1942; s. Lester William and Helen Louise (Plantulli) K.; m. L. Gay Allebaugh, Aug. 5, 1967. BS, The Citadel, 1963. Gen. mgr., Gen. System divsn. Hewlett/Packard, 1967—81; CEO, pres. 3Com Corp., Santa Clara, Calif., 1981—90, chmn., 1987—93; pres., CEO Exodus Comm., Inc., 2001—02; CEO Caspian Networks, Inc., 2002—04, chmn., 2002—06; pres. LWK Ventures, 1991—. Bd. dirs. CPU Tech., Inc., Packeteer, Inc., 2001—08, TriZetto Group, Inc., 2005—08, Sybase, Inc., 1995, Brocade Comm. Systems, Inc., 2004—, CoreMark Holding Co., Inc., 2005—, Coherent, Inc., 2009, CommScope, Inc., 2011—. Mem. Am. Electronics Assn. (chmn., mem. exec. com.). Office: CommScope Inc Bd Directors 1100 CommScope Place SE Hickory NC 28602 Office Phone: 828-324-2200. Office Fax: 828-328-3400. Business E-Mail: lkrause@commscope.com.

KRAUSE, MANFRED OTTO, physicist; b. Stuttgart, Germany, Mar. 11, 1931; came to U.S., 1960, naturalized, 1970; s. Friedrich Bernhard and Friedel Ernstine K.; m. Josephine Winifred Cammer, Dec. 26, 1963; m. C. Denise Caldwell, Sept. 15, 2001. BS, Technische Universität Stuttgart, 1954, diploma in physics, 1957, PhD, 1960. Sr. physicist Wm. H. Johnston Labs., Inc., Balt., 1960-63; sr. scientist Oak Ridge Nat. Lab., 1963-95; exch. prof. U. Paris, 1975. Cons. Oak Ridge, 1995—, U. Ctrl. Fla. Contbr. articles to profl. jours., chapters to books. Recipient Alexander von Humboldt award, 1975-76. Fellow Am. Phys. Soc.; mem. AAAS, Smithsonian Instn., Audubon Soc., Nature Conservancy. Achievements include discovery of x-ray spectrometry based on photoelectric effect. Home: 125 Baltimore Dr Oak Ridge TN 37830-7837 Personal E-mail: altefritz@comcast.net.

KRAUSE, ROY G., management consultant; BS in Acctg., Ohio State U.; MBA, Ga. State U. Associated, acctg. firm KPMG Peat Warwick, LLP, 1973—80; exec. v.p HomeBanc Mortgage Corp., CFO Atlanta, 1980—95; exec. v.p., CFO SFN Group (formerly Spherion Corp.), Ft. Lauderdale, Fla., 1995—2003, COO, 2003—04, pres., 2003—, CEO, bd. dirs., 2004—. Office: SFN Group 2050 Spectrum Blvd Fort Lauderdale FL 33309 Office Phone: 954-308-7600. Office Fax: 954-308-7666. Business E-Mail: roykrause@sfngroup.com.

KRAUSNICK, E. CARL, JR., investment company executive; BBA in Banking and Managerial Fin., U. Miss. Fin. advisor Morgan Keegan & Co., Inc., Memphis, 1983, pres. Equity Capital Markets Divsn., 2001—, exec. mng. dir. Trustee Memphis Univ. Sch. Office: Morgan Keegan Morgan Keegan Tower 50 N Front St Memphis TN 38103 Office Phone: 901-524-4100. Office Fax: 901-524-4197.

KRAUSS, ALISON, country musician; b. Champaign, Ill., July 23, 1971; m. Pat Bergeson, Nov. 8, 1997 (div. 2001); 1 child, Sam Patrick. Albums (with Union Sta.) So Long So Wrong, 1997, Too Late to Cry, 1987, Two Highways, 1989, I've Got That Old Feeling, 1990, Every Time You Say Goodbye, 1992, I Know Who Holds Tomorrow, 1994 (Best Southern, Country or Bluegrass Gospel Album, Grammy Awards, 1995), Now That I've Found You, 1995, Forget About It, 1999, New Favorite, 2001, Alison Krauss and Union Sta. Live, 2002, Lonely Runs Both Ways, 2002 (Best Country Group Performance, Best Country Instrumental Performance, Best Country Album, Grammy Awards, 2006), (with Robert Plant) Raising Sand, 2007 (Album of Yr., Best Contemporary Folk Album, Grammy Awards, 2009), (with Union Station albums) Paper Airplane, 2011 (Best Bluegrass Album, Grammy Awards, 2012), songs (with Robert Plant) Gone Gone Gone (Done Moved On), 2007 (Wide Open Country Video of Yr., Country Music TV, 2008, Musical Event of Yr., Country Music Assn., 2008), Please Read the Letter, 2007 (Record of Yr., Grammy Awards, 2009), Rich Woman, 2007 (Best Pop Collaboration with Vocals, Grammy Awards, 2009), Killing the Blues, 2009 (Best Country Collaboration with Vocals, Grammy Awards, 2009); actress: (TV films) Miracle on Highway 31, 1997. Recipient Female Vocalist of Yr. award, Internat. Bluegrass Music Assn., 1990—91, 1993, 1995, Entertainer of Yr. award, 1991, 1995, Rising Video Star of Yr.-Europe award Country Music TV, 1995, Single of Yr. award, Country Music Assn, 1995, Vocal Event of Yr., 1995, Horizon award, 1995, Female Vocalist of Yr., 1995, Best New Country Artist Tour award Pollstar, 1995, Americana Artist of Yr. award Gavin, 1995, Country Artist of Yr. Rolling Stone, 1995, Grammy award Best Bluegrass Recording, 1992, Grammy award Best Country Collaboration with Vocals, 1995, Grammy award Best Female Country Vocal Performance, 1996, Bluegrass/Old-Time Music Album award, 1996, Best Female Vocalist, 1996, Grammy award Best Country Instrumental Performance, 1998, Grammy award Best Bluegrass Album, 1998, Grammy award Best Country Performance by a Duo or Group with Vocals, 1998; co-recipient with Brad Paisley, Music Video of Yr., "Whiskey Lullaby", Country Music Assoc., 2004, with Brad Paisley, Musical Event of Yr. "Whiskey Lullaby", 2004, with Brad Paisley, Video of Yr., Vocal Event of Yr., "Whiskey Lullaby", Acad. Country Music, 2005, with Robert Plant, Album of Yr. award, Americana Music Assn., 2009, with Robert Plant, Duo of Yr. award, 2009; named to Grand Ole Opry, 1993. Office: Ds Management PO Box 121499 Nashville TN 37212-1499

KRAVEKA, JACQUELINE MARIA, pediatrician, oncologist, researcher, scientist; b. Velasco, Cuba, July 29, 1966; arrived in U.S., 1971, naturalized; d. Luis R. and Glenda J. Kraveka; m. Ernesto Mario Barros, July 17, 1999; children: Alejandro Mario Barros children: Emily Marie Barros. BA, Columbia U., 1989; DO, Nova Southeastern U., 1994. Diplomate Am. Bd. Pediat., Am. Bd. Pediat. Hematology-Oncology, Nat. Bd. Osteo. Med. Examiners. Resident in pediat. Miami (Fla.) Children's Hosp., 1994—97; fellow pediat. hematology oncology Med. U. SC, Charleston, 1997—2000, asst. prof. of pediat., 2000—12, 2012—, dir., pediatric bone marrow transplant program, 2002—, interim divsn. dir., Pediatric Hematology Oncology, 2006—08; dir. Pediatric Hematology-Oncology Fellowship Program, 2006—08, Instl. Prin. Investigator for Children's Oncology Group, 2006—, Instl. Prin. Investigator for Neuroblastoma and Medulloblastoma Translational Rsch. Consortium, 2009. Study chair Children's Oncology Group, Clin. Trial for Anaplastic Large Cell Lymphoma; reviewer for various medical jours. and grant applications. Contbr. articles to profl. publs. Med. advisor SC Chpt., Make a Wish Found.; mem. med. adv. bd. Rally Found. Child Cancer Rsch. Recipient Pediatric Loan Repayment Program award, NIH, 2002—, Disting. Alumni award, Nova Southeastern U. Coll. Osteopathic Medicine, 2010; finalist Health Care Rschr., Health Care Heroes, Charleston Regional Bus. Jour., 2012; grantee Mentored Career Devel. award, NIH, 2003—; Carl Storm Under-represented Minority fellowship, 2006, Hyundai Hope Wheels grant, Hyundai Motor Am., grant, St Baldrick's Found., Rally Found. Childhood Cancer Rsch. Fellow: Am. Coll. Osteo. Pediatricians, Am. Acad. of Pediat.; mem.: AAAS, Soc. Pediat. Rsch., Am. Osteo. Assn., Am. Soc. Pediat. Hematology Oncology, Am. Soc. Hematology, Am. Soc. Clin. Oncology, Am. Assn. Cancer Rsch. (Minority Scholar award in cancer rsch. 2000, 2002), Children's Oncology Group. Roman Catholic. Office: Med University SC 135 Rutledge Ave MSC 558 Charleston SC 29425 Business E-Mail: kravekjm@musc.edu.

KRAVITCH, PHYLLIS A., federal judge; b. Savannah, Ga., Aug. 23, 1920; d. Aaron and Ella (Wiseman) K. BA, Goucher Coll., Balt., 1941, LLD (hon.), 1981; LLB, U. Pa., Phila., 1943; LLD (hon.), Emory U., Atlanta, 1998. Bar: Ga. 1943, US Dist. Ct. 1944, US Supreme Ct. 1948, US Ct. Appeals (5th cir.) 1962. Practice law, Savannah, 1944—76; judge Superior Ct., Eastern Jud. Circuit of Ga., 1977—79, US Ct. Appeals (5th cir.), Atlanta, 1979—81, US Ct. Appeals (11th cir.), 1981—96, sr. judge, 1996—. Mem. Jud. Conf. Standing Com. on Rules, 1994—2000. Trustee Inst. Continuing Legal Edn. in Ga., 1979—82; mem. Bd. Edn., Chatham County, Ga., 1949—55; mem. coun. Law Sch., Emory U., Atlanta, 1985—; mem. vis. com. Law Sch., U. Chgo., 1990—93; bd. visitors Ga. State U. Law Sch., 1994—2009; mem. regional rev. panel Truman Scholarship Found., 1993—2000; mem. vis. com. Goucher Coll., 2000—. Recipient Hannah G. Solomon award, Nat. Coun. Jewish Women, 1978, James Wilson award, U. Pa. Law Alumni Soc., 1992, Trailblazer award, Greater Atlanta Hadassah, 2000, Kathleen Kessler award, Ga. Assn. Women Lawyers, 2001, Shining Star award, Atlanta Women's Found., 2002, J. Ben Watkins award, Stetson Coll. Law, 2005, award & resolution, State Bar Ala., Fla., Ga., 2009. Fellow: Am. Bar Found.; mem.: ABA (Margaret Brent award 1991), Nat. Assn. Women Lawyers (Arabella Babb Mansfield award 1999), U. Pa. Law Soc., Am. Law Inst., Am. Judicature Soc. (Devitt award com. 1998—99), State Bar Ga., Savannah Bar Assn. (pres. 1976). Office Phone: 404-335-6300.

KRAVITZ, RUBIN, chemist; b. Framingham, Mass., Mar. 22, 1928; s. Abe and Lillian (Cohen) K. m. Geraldine Pudaim, Aug. 20, 1950 (dec.); children: Richard Alan, Steven Jay, Stuart Paul; m. Annabelle S. Durieux, July 16, 1978; 1 child, Michelle Pearl. BS, Northeastern U., 1952, D in Pharm, 1982. Analytical chemist FDA, HEW, Boston, 1956-61; analytical chemist Alcohol and Tobacco div. U.S. Treasury Dept., Boston, 1961-65; supr. phys. testing lab. plastic div. Am. Hoechst Corp., Leominster, Mass., 1967-78, rsch. chemist plastic div., 1978-83; sr. devel. engr. EPS, 1983-85; pres. Nat. Plastics Mus. Inc., 1981-85; dir., pres. T.H.E. Hypnosis Ctr., Virginia Beach, Va., 1986-89; staff pharmacist MacDonald Army Hosp., Ft. Eustis, Va., 1987-89; chief pharmacist U.S. Army Health Clin., Fort Monroe, Va.; pres., chief exec. officer Cadet Labs., Virginia Beach, 1984—; chief pharmacist U.S. Army Health Clinic, Ft. Monroe, 1989—. Del. Va. Pharm. Assn., 1988; mem. Mid-Atlantic Cholesterol Coun. Cubmaster Boy Scouts Am., Worcester, Mass., 1967-68; trustee, founding pres. Nat. Plastics Ctr. and Mus., 1985—. With USAAF, 1946-48. Recipient Hygeia Bowl award, Wyeth Ayerst, 2002. Mem. Assn. Mil. Surgeons U.S., Soc. Plastic Engrs. (newsletter editor 1969-71, treas. Pioneer Valley sect. 1972-73, v.p. 1973-74, chmn. tech. com. 1973, pres. Pioneer Valley sect. 1975-76, chmn. sect. museum 1979-85, achievement award 1981), ASTM (chmn. compression molding 1969-70, vice chmn. publicity and papers com. D-20 on plastics 1972-76, chmn. subcom. specimen preparation, chmn. sect. plastic furniture, chmn. specimen preparation 1976, chmn. task group Kravitz impact test method 1976, chmn. D 20.12 Olefin Plastics com., mem. exec. com. 1982-85), Assn. Analytical Chemists, Assn. to Advance Ethical Hypnosis, Am. Soc. Rsch. and Clin. Hypnosis, K.P. (chancellor comdr. 1963-64).

KREBS, FREDERICK JOHN, retired legal association administrator; b. Youngstown, Ohio, Dec. 18, 1949; s. Norman Frederick and Ruth Caroline (Demmel) K.; m. Cathryn Jane Stanley, Feb. 18, 1978; children: Stephen Frederick, Sarah Elizabeth. BA, Allegheny Coll., 1972; JD, Case Western Reserve U., 1975; postgrad., U. Manchester, England, 1970-71. Bar: Ohio 1975, D.C. 1976, Va. 1979. Asst. gen. counsel US Chamber of Commerce, Washington, 1975-79, mgr. dept. labor & human resources policy, 1984-91; ptnr. Stephens & Krebs, McLean, Va., 1979-84; exec. dir. The Assn. Corporate Counsel (ACC), Washington, 1991—2011. Mem. steering com. Health Policy Agenda for American People, Chgo., 1986-87; resource asst. White House Conf. Small Bus., Washington, 1986. Co-author: Associations and Lobbying Regulations, 1979. Mem. ABA, American Soc. Assn. Executives, U. Club Washington. Presbyterian. Avocations: photography, tennis.

KREBSBACH, MICHAEL J., hand surgeon; MD, U. Minn., 1985. Diplomate American Bd. Orthopaedic Surgery, 2004, American Bd. Orthopaedic Surgery-hand surgery, 2004. Intern Jackson Meml. Hosp., Miami, Fla., 1985—86, resident in orthopedic surgery, 1986—90; fellow in hand and microvascular surgery St. Vincent's Hosp., Indpls., 1990—91; hosp. affiliations include West Boca Med. Ctr., Boca Raton Cmty. Hosp. Office: Boca Raton Community Hospital 800 Meadows Rd Boca Raton FL 33486 Office Phone: 561-955-7100.*

KREEGEL, PAIGE, state legislator; b. Miami, Fla., Aug. 20, 1958; m. Erika Kim McCarthy; children: Olivia, Savannah, Christian. MD, NY Med. Coll., 1982; MBA, IMPAC U., Punta Gorda, Fla. Intern U. Tenn. Bapt. Meml., Memphis; emergency dept. physician St. Joseph's Hosp., Port Charlotte; assoc. prof. U. South Fla., Tampa, 1990; founder American-Medic; mem. Dist. 72 Fla. House of Reps., Tallahassee, 2004—, chair health care svcs. policy com., mem. agr. and natural resources policy com., criminal and civil justice appropriations com., govtl. affairs policy com., mem. health and family svcs. policy coun., select policy coun. on strategic and econ. planning. Physician Charlotte County Sheriff's Office SWAT Team. Mem.: AMA, Peace River Valley Citrus Growers Assn., Gulf Coast Citrus Growers Assn., Fla. Med. Assn., Charlotte County Cattlemen's Assn. Republican. Roman Catholic. Office: 1301 The Capitol 402 S Monroe St Tallahassee FL 32399 Home: 410 Taylor St Punta Gorda FL 33950-4849 Office Phone: 941-575-5820, 850-488-9175.

KREIDER, LEONARD EMIL, retired economics professor; b. Newton, Kans., Feb. 25, 1938; s. Leonard C. and Rachel (Weaver) K.; m. Louise Ann Pankratz, June 10, 1963; children: Brent Emil, Todd Alan, Ryan Eric. Student, Bluffton Coll., 1956-58; BA, Bethel Coll., 1960; student, Princeton U., 1960-61; MA, Ohio State U., 1962, PhD, 1968. Economist So. Ill. U., Carbondale, 1965-70; asst. prof. Beloit (Wis.) Coll., 1970—, prof., 1978—2007, chmn. dept. econ. and mgmt., 1984-89, acting v.p. acad. affairs, 1987-88, Allen Bradley prof. econ., 1991—2003. Chief of Party Devel. Assocs., Asuncion, Paraguay, 1970; economist Deere and Co., 1973, Castle and Cooke, San Francisco, 1975-76, AmCore, Rockford, Ill., 1984, Rockford Meml. Hosp., 1990-91, Stone Container, San Jose, Costa Rica, 1996, Rock Island Co., Chgo., 2003; cons. corps. and attys. Author: Development and Utilization of Managerial Talent, 1968; contbr. numerous articles, reports to profl. jours. Mem. Nat. Assn. Bus. Economists, Am. Econ. Assn., Am. Assn. Higher Edn., Soc. Internat. Devel. (pres. So. Ill. chpt. 1969), Indsl. Rels. Rsch. Assn. (elections com. 1974). Presbyterian. Home: 1548 Hawthorne Cir Harrisonburg VA 22802 Home Phone: 540-564-3688. Personal E-mail: kreidere@myvmrc.net. Business E-Mail: kreidere@beloit.edu.

KREIDLER, R. CHRIS (ROBERT C. KREIDLER), corporate financial executive; m. Karen Kreidler; 1 children. undergraduate, MBA, Rice U. With Mesa Ltd. Partnership; joined PepsiCo, Inc., 1996; sr. v.p., corp. strategy, treas. Yum! Brands, Inc., 2003—07; CFO C&S Wholesale Grocers, Inc., 2007—09; exec. v.p., CFO Sysco Corp., 2009—. Office: SYSCO Corp 1390 Enclave Pky Houston TX 77077-2099 Office Phone: 281-584-1390. Office Fax: 281-584-2721. Business E-Mail: robert.kreidler@corp.sysco.com.

KREITZER, MICHAEL N., lawyer; b. Balt., Apr. 5, 1962; s. Milton Kreitzer and Toby Greenberg; children: Kimberly, Amanda, Joshua. BS in Computer and Info. Scis. with high honors, U. Fla., 1984; JD with honors, George Washington U., 1987. Bar: Fla. 1987, U.S. Dist. Ct. (so. dist.) Fla. 1988, U.S. Dist. Ct. (mid. dist.) Fla. 2002, U.S. Dist. Ct. (no. dist.) Fla. 2005; cert. bus. litigator Fla. Bar, 2001. Assoc. atty. Fowler, White & Barnett, PA, Miami, Fla., 1987—92, ptnr., 1992—2003, Bilzin, Sunberg, Baena, Price & Axelrod, LLP, Miami, Fla., 2003—; ptnr., chmn. litigation dept., mem. exec. com. Bilzin, Sunberg et al, Miami, Fla., 2005—. Named Most Effective Lawyer, 2007; named a Top Lawyer in South Fla., 2002—, Super Lawyer, 2006—. Mem.: ABA, Dade County Bar Assn. Office: Bilzin Sunberg Baena Price 1450 Brickell Ave Ste 2300 Miami FL 33131-3456 Office Phone: 305-350-2384. Office Fax: 305-351-2224. E-mail: mkreitzer@bilzin.com.

KREMERS, MARK S., cardiac electrophysiologist; MD, Ind. U., 1979. Diplomate Am. Bd. Internal Medicine, 1982, Am. Bd. Internal Medicine-cardiovasc. disease, 1985, Am. Bd. Internal Medicine-clin. cardiovasc. electrophysiology, 2002. Resident internal medicine Univ. of Tex. Med. Ctr., 1980—82, fellow cardiovasc. disease, 1982—85; fellow cardiac electrophysiology Univ. of Penn. Med. Ctr., 1984—85; hosp. affiliation includes Presbyn. Hosp. Office: Mid Carolina Cardiology 1718 E Fourth St Ste 501 Charlotte NC 28204 Office Phone: 704-343-9800. Office Fax: 704-347-2011.

KRESA, KENT, retired manufacturing executive; b. NYC, Mar. 24, 1938; s. Helmy and Marjorie (Boutelle) K.; m. Joyce Anne McBride, Nov. 4, 1961; 1 child, Kiren BSAA, MIT, 1959, MSAA, 1961, EAA, 1966; LLD (hon.), Pepperdine U., 2003. Sr. scientist rsch. and advanced devel. divsn. AVCO, Wilmington, Mass., 1959-61; staff mem. MIT Lincoln Lab., Lexington, Mass., 1961-68; dep. dir. strategic tech. office Def. Advanced Rsch. Projects Agy., Washington, 1968-73; dir. tactical tech. office Def. Advanced Rsch. Project Agy., Washington, 1973-75; v.p., mgr. Rsch. & Tech. Ctr. Northrop Corp., Hawthorne, Calif., 1975-76, v.p., gen. mgr. Ventura divsn. Newbury Park, Calif., 1976-82, group v.p. Aircraft Group L.A., 1982-86, sr. v.p. tech. devel. and planning, 1986-87, pres., COO, 1987-90; chmn., pres., CEO Northrop Grumman Corp., L.A., 1990—2001, chmn., CEO, 2001—03, chmn. emeritus, 2003—; sr. advisor Carlyle Group, NYC, 2003—; non-exec. chmn. Avery Dennison Corp., Pasadena, Calif., 2005—10; interim chmn. General Motors Corp., Detroit, 2009. Bd. dirs. Avery Dennison Corp., 1999—2010, Fluor Corp., 2003—, Mannking Corp., 2004—, Gen. Motors Co., 2009—10. Bd. dirs. John Tracy Clinic for the Hearing-Impaired, W.M. Keck Found., Performing Arts Ctr. L.A. County Found.; bd. overseers Keck Sch. Medicine, U. So. Calif.; bd. governors, Broad Found; bd. visitors UCLA Anderson Sch. Mgmt.; mem. advisory bd., MIT Lincoln Laboratory; bd. trustees Haynes Found., Calif. Inst. Tech., 1994-, chmn., 2005-Recipient Henry Webb Salsbury award MIT, 1959, Arthur D. Flemming award, 1975, Calif. Industrialist of Yr. Calif. Mus. of Sci. and Industry and the Calif. Mus. Found., 1996, Bob Hope Disting. Citizen award Nat. Security Indsl. Assn., 1996; Sec. of Def. Meritorious Civilian Svc. medal, 1975, USN Meritorious Pub. Svc. citation, 1975, Exceptional Civilian Svc. award USAF, 1987, Howard Hughes Meml. award, Aero Club So. Calif., 2002, Laurel Citation, Aviation Week, 2002, Calif. Inst. Tech. Mgmt. Assn. Excellence in Mgmt. award, 2002, Ellis Island Medal of Honor, 2002; named a Manufacturer of the Century, Calif. Manufacturers & Tech. Assn., 2000; named one of The Top 25 Managers, Business Week, 2001, 2002 Fellow AIAA; mem. Aerospace Industries Assn. (past bd. govs.), Naval Aviation Mus. Found., Navy League U.S., Soc. Flight Test Engrs., Assn. U.S. Army, Nat. Space Club, Am. Def. Preparedness Assn., L.A. Country Club, NAE. Office: c/o Fluor Corp Bd Directors 6700 Las Colinas Blvd Irving TX 75039

KRET, ROBERT A., museum director; m. Theodora Kret; 3 children. BA in History, U. Detroit; MA in History Mus. Studies, SUNY, Oneonta. Dir., mus. Soc. for Preservation of New Antiquities, Boston; exec. dir. Ella Sharp Mus., Jackson, Miss.; dir. Leigh Yawkey Woodson Art Mus., Wausau, Wis., 1994—98, Miami U. Art Mus., Oxford, Ohio, 1998—2000, Hunter Mus. Am. Art, 2000—. Mem.: Am. Assn. Mus. (panelist, juror). Office: Hunter Mus American Art 10 Bluff View Chattanooga TN 37403 Office Phone: 423-267-0968. Office Fax: 423-267-9844.

KRETSCHMER, FRANK FREDERICK, JR., electrical engineer, researcher, consultant; b. Phila., July 31, 1930; m. Shirley J. Kretschmer; children: Frank F. III, John, Diane, Linda, Thomas. BSEE, Pa. State U., 1957; MSEE, Drexel Inst. Tech., 1961; PhD, Johns Hopkins U., 1970. Asst. devel. engr. Burroughs Corp., Paoli, Pa., 1957-58; project engr. Bendix Radio Corp., Towson, Md., 1958-64; rsch. assoc. Johns Hopkins U., Balt., 1964-70; supervisory electronics engr. Naval Rsch. Lab., Washington, 1970-90, 90—. Cons. in field. Author: Aspects of Radar Signal Processing, 1986; contbr. over 40 papers to profl. jours. and confs. With USN, 1948-52. Fellow IEEE (life). Achievements include over 20 patents in field.

KRETZSCHMAR, WILLIAM ADDISON, JR., language educator; b. Ann Arbor, Mich., Sept. 13, 1953; s. William Addison and Audrey June (Krauss) K.; m. Claudia Suzanne Miller. AB, U. Mich., 1975; MA in Medieval Studies, Yale U., 1976; PhD in English, U. Chgo., 1980. Instr. English Mundelein Coll., Chgo., 1977-82, dir. summer sch., 1979-81; asst. prof. English U. Wis., Whitewater, 1982-86, U. Ga., Athens, 1986-89, assoc. prof., 1989-95, prof., 1995—, dir. linguistics program, 1996-99, Willson prof. in humanities, 2004—. Author: Introduction to Quantitative Analysis of Linguistic Survey Data, 1996, The Linguistics of Speech, 2009; editor: Dialects in Culture (R.I. McDavid, Jr.), 1979, Handbook of the Linguistic Atlas of the Middle and South Atlantic States, 1993, Oxford Dictionary of Pronunciation for Current English, 2001; editor: Linguistic Atlas Middle and South Atlantic States, Linguistic Atlas North-Central States, 1984—; editor Jour. English Linguistics, 1983-99, Empirical Linguistic Series, 1996-99; contbr. articles to profl. jours. Mem. MLA (regional del. 1983-86), Am. Dialect Soc. (exec. com. 1999-2003, pres. 2007—09), Linguistic Soc. Am., Medieval Acad. Am., Assn. Computers Humanities (bd. dir. 1999-2003). Home: 125 Renfrew Dr Athens GA 30606-3936 Office: U Ga Dept English Athens GA 30602 Business E-Mail: kretzsch@uga.edu.

KRIBEL, ROBERT EDWARD, consultant, retired physicist, academic administrator; b. Pitts., Sept. 17, 1937; s. Joseph P. and Helen M. K.; m. Ruth Ann Gropelli; children— Robert E., Karen A., Mark P., Gary P. BS, U. Notre Dame, 1959; MS, U. Calif., San Diego, 1966, PhD in Physics, 1968. Research scientist Gen. Atomic, Inc., 1965-69; assoc. prof. physics Drake U., 1970-73; vis. assoc. prof. applied physics Cornell U., 1973-74; prof., head dept. physics James Madison

U., 1974-78, Auburn (Ala.) U., 1978-87, acting dean scis. and math., 1985-87, prof. physics, 1987-88; v.p. acad. affairs Jacksonville (Ala.) State U., 1988-92, prof. physics, 1992-93; dean natural scis. and math. Mesa State Coll., 1993-99; pres. REK Enterprises, Auburn, Ala., 1999—; chief acad. officer Air U., 2000—02. Contbr. articles to profl. jours. Served with U.S. Navy, 1959-62. Mem. Am. Inst. Physics, Sigma Xi, Phi Kappa Phi. Avocation: amateur radio. Personal E-mail: bkribel@gmail.com.

KRIEGER, ROBERT LEE, JR., government affairs, human resource management consultant, educator, writer, travel and meeting planner, political analyst, internet marketing consultant; b. Louisville, Nov. 13, 1946; s. Robert Lee and June Elise (Waters) K. BBA, U. Memphis, 1968, MBA, 1969. Cert. pers. cons., travel planner, mgmt. cons. Adminstrv. asst. to mayor City of Memphis, 1969-72; dir. devel. programs U. Memphis, 1972-74; pvt. cons. practice, Memphis, 1974—95; pres. Krieger Consulting, Memphis, 1995—. Mem. faculty U. Memphis Coll. Bus., 1984—; worldwide travel cons. and meeting planner, 1962—; keynote spkr. numerous profl. groups. Trustee, life mem. Rep. Presdl. Task Force, Washington, 1980—; mem. Rep. Nat. Adc. Com., Washington, 1972—, Rep. Regional Steering Com.; mem. US Olympic Soc., Boulder, Colo., 1968—; active Make-A-Wish, St. Jude. Recipient US Treasury award US Dept. Treasury, 1971, Nat. Presdl. Medal of Merit, Rep. Presdl. Task Force, 1984, Rep. Legion of Merit, Pres.'s award Memphis Cotton Carnival Assn., 1968-85. Mem. Data Processing Mgmt. Assn., Am. Mgmt. Assn., Soc. Profl. Journalists, Am. Film Guild, Met. Opera Guild, US Navy League, U. Memphis Alumni Assn., Mensa, Alpha Delta Sigma. Episcopalian. Avocations: writing, movies, photography, travel, internet. Personal E-mail: german711@hotmail.com.

KRISCUNAS, SUZANNE B. (SUZY KRISCUNAS), private equity firm executive; b. 1950; married. MA in French Lit., Ind. U., MBA in Fin., 1980. Credit trainee First Nat. Bank, Dallas; with First Dallas Capital Corp.; mng. dir., merchant banking group Banc One Capital Corp., Dallas; transacting ptnr. Riverside Co., Dallas, 2001—07, mng. ptnr., co-mgr. Riverside Capital Appreciation Fund, 2007—. Bd. dirs. Am. Hospice, ITEL Labs., Media Source Holdings, Sentinel Performance Solutions. Active DFW Pvt. Equity Forum, Assn. Corp. Growth, Internat. Women's Forum. Office: The Riverside Co 3131 McKinney Ave Ste 160 Dallas TX 75204 Office Phone: 214-871-9640. Office Fax: 214-871-9620.

KRISEMAN, RICHARD DAVID (RICK KRISEMAN), Mayor, St. Petersburg, Fla., former state legislator; b. Detroit, Aug. 2, 1962; s. Donald Daniel and Doris Lee (Abrahamson) K.; m. Kerry A.; children: Jordan Erin, Samuel Anthony. BS in Broadcasting, U. Fla., 1984; JD, Stetson Coll., Gulfport, Fla., 1987. Bar: US Dist. Ct. (mid. dist.) 1988, US Ct. Appeals (11th cir.) 1988. Assoc. Keane, Hayes & Reese, P.A., St. Petersburg, Fla., 1987-88, Maxwell G. Battle, Jr., P.A., Dunedin, Fla.; mem. St. Petersburg City Coun., 2000—06; mem. Dist. 53 Fla. House of Reps., Tallahassee, 2006—12, mem. econ. devel. and cmty. affairs policy coun., govt. accountability act coun., govtl. affairs policy com.; mayor City of St. Petersburg, 2014—. Mem. St. Petersburg Nuisance Abatement Bd., 1999; vice chmn. Pinellas Met. Planning Orgn., 2004—06. Editor: Paraclete, St. Petersburg, 1987—. Campaign mgr. Lars Hafner Fla. Rep. Dist. 54, St. Petersburg, 1986; vol. BOCA Ciega HS, St. Petersburg, 1985-87; coach, sponsor Gulfport Little League, 1995-97; mem. Lake Pasadena Neighborhood Assn. 1997-, Dem. Leadership Coun. Legis. Adv. Bd.; v.p. Temple Beth-El, 2000-05, bd. mem., 2000-06; founder, bd. mem. Heroes the St. Petersburg P.D., Inc., 2003—. Named One of Outstanding Young Men of Am., 1986. Mem. ABA, Trial Lawyers Am., Tau Epsilon Phi (svc. chmn. 1982, acad. chmn. 1981). Democrat. Jewish. Avocations: sports, music. Office: Office of the Mayor St Petersburg City Hall 175 5th St N Saint Petersburg FL 33701 Office Phone: 727-893-7201. Office Fax: 727-892-5365.*

KRISHNAN, KRISHNASWAMY RANGA RAMA R., psychiatry educator; b. Madras, Tamilnadu, India, Apr. 22, 1956; came to U.S., 1981; s. N. Krishnaswamy and Sulochana Krishnaswamy Reddy; m. Sripriya Chitamoor, May 21, 1987; children: Vaishnavi, Prahlad. PUC, Loyola Coll., Madras, India, 1973; MBBS, U. Madras, 1978. Chief resident Duke Med. Ctr., Durham, 1981—83, asst. prof., 1984—89, assoc. prof., 1990—95, prof., 1995—, chmn. psychiatry, 1998—. Vice dean Duke Grad. Med. Sch.- Nat. U., Singapore, 2006—. Mem.: Inst. Medicine. Office: Duke U Med Ctr Box 3950 Durham NC 27710-0001 Office Phone: 919-684-5616. Business E-Mail: krish001@mc.duke.edu.

KRISHT, ALI, neurosurgeon, educator; MD, American U. Beirut Med. Ctr., 1985. Diplomate American Bd. Neurol. Surgery, 2010. Resident in neurol. surgery Emory Univ. Hosp., 1988—94; staff dept. neurosurgery Univ. Ark. for Med. Sciences, prof. neurosurgery, vice chmn. neurosurgery; hosp. affiliation includes: St. Vincent Infirmary. Office: St Vincent Infirmary Medical Center two St Vincent Circle Little Rock AR 72205 Office Phone: 501-522-3000.*

KRISTIANSEN, MAGNE, electrical engineer, educator; b. Elverum, Norway, Apr. 14, 1932; came to U.S., 1958, naturalized, 1967; s. Martin and Ella (Sobye) K.; m. Aud Bohn, July 6, 1957; children: Sonja Bohn, Eric Bohn. BS in Elec. Engring., U. Tex., Austin, 1961, PhD (Ford Found. fellow), 1967. Registered profl. engr., Tex. Rsch. engr. U. Tex., Austin, 1964-66; faculty Tex. Tech U., Lubbock, 1966—2013, prof., 1971—2013, dir. plasma lab., 1970—80; dir. pulsed power lab. Tex. Tech. U., 1980—2001, dir. Ctr. Pulsed Power and Power Electronics, 2001—13; v.p. rsch. and engring. Enfitek, Inc., Lubbock, 1987-90; v.p. R & D Integrated Tech. Inc., Lubbock, 1990-98. Cons. def. products divsn. Varo, Inc., Garland, Tex., 1970-71; cons. Aerospace Corp., El Segundo, Calif., 1974-76, BDM Corp., Albuquerque, 1975-76, 85-87, Palisades Inst., N.Y. and NRC, 1977, Rockwell Internat., 1978, Maxwell Labs., 1979-83, LaJolla Inst., 1979, NASA, 1979, Norwegian Rsch. Coun., 1980, Sci. Applications, Inc., 1983-88, 91-92, Lawrence Livermore Nat. Lab., 1983-95, McDonnell Douglas, 1986, LTV Missiles and Electronics Group, 1987-89, NEA-Lindberg A/S, 1988, Physics Internat. Co., 1992-97, Rocket Rsch. Co., 1992, Swedish Def. Rsch. Inst., 1992-2005; Hazeltine Ocean Sys., 1995, Lockheed Martin, 1995-96, 2003, 04, Integrated Technologies, Inc., 1998-2001; collaborator Los Alamos Nat. Lab., 1974-95, others; contractor DNA, 1986-97, NASA, 1990-2001, Wright Aeronautical Labs., 1994-96. Co-author: An Introduction to Controlled Thermonuclear Fusion, 1977, Russian, Japanese, Chinese translations, 1980-81, Rotating Mirror Cameras, 1997; co-editor: Advances in Pulsed Power Technology, 1984—. Contbr. articles to profl. jours. Mem. USAF Sci. Adv. Bd., 1981-85. Served with Royal Norwegian Air Force, 1950-58. Recipient Meritorious Civilian Svc. award USAF, 1985, Excellence award Halliburton Found., 1994; grantee State of Tex., 1966-85, 88-94, NSF, 1967-87, AEC, 1968-71, Air Force Office Sci. Rsch., 1968—, Dept. Energy, 1978-79, Army Rsch. Lab., 1994-99, Strategic Missile Command, 2005-; sr. fellow sci. NATO, 1975, fellow Japan Soc. Promotion Sci., 1979. Fellow IEEE (life, Pulsed Power Conf. Peter Haas award 1987, Nuc. and Plasma Sci. Soc. Merit award 1991, Millennium medal), Am. Phys. Soc.; mem. AAAS, Russian Acad. Scis. (fgn. mem., Ural sect.), Am. Soc. Engring. Edn., Sigma Xi, Tau Beta Pi, Eta Kappa Nu, Phi Kappa Phi. Home: 3105 78th St Lubbock TX 79423-1815 Office: Tex Tech U Dept Elec/Computer Engring Lubbock TX 79409-3102 Home Phone: 806-745-1071. Business E-Mail: m.kristiansen@ttu.edu.

KRITCHEVSKY, STEPHEN BENNETT, epidemiologist, educator; b. Phila., July 15, 1960; s. David and Evelyn S. Kritchevsky; m. Nannette C. Gover, Feb. 2, 1982; children: Alexander, Samuel, Caleb. BA, U. Chgo., 1982; MSPH in epidemiology, U. NC Sch. Pub. Health, 1986, PhD in epidemiology, 1989. Asst. prof. U. Tenn., Memphis, 1989—95, assoc. prof., 1995—2001, prof. preventive medicine, 2001—03; prof. dept. internal medicine, sect. on gerontology and geriatric medicine Wake Forest U. Med. Sch., Winston-Salem, 2003—, acting dir., J. Paul Sticht Ctr. on Aging and Rehabilitation, 2003—06, dir., J. Paul Sticht Ctr. on Aging and Rehabilitation, 2006—; dir., & Claude D. Pepper Older Americans Independence Ctr. Wake Forest U. Baptist, 2006—. Reviewer for a variety of medical journals, including New England Journal of Medicine, Annals of Internal Medicine, Journal of the American Medical Association and American and European Journals of Epidemiology. Mem. Soc. for Epidemiologic Rsch., Soc. Healthcare Epidemiology, Am. Coll. Epidemiology, Gerontol. Soc. Am., Am. Soc. for Nutritional Scis. Office: Wake Forest Univ J Paul Sticht Ctr on Aging Medical Center Blvd Winston Salem NC 27157 Office Phone: 336-713-8548. Business E-Mail: skritche@wfubmc.edu.

KRIVORUCHKA, MARK WILLIAM, rental company executive; b. Nuremburg, Germany, July 2, 1954; (parents Am. citizens); s. Theodore Steven and Patty Bernice (Capar) K.; m. Terry Lynn Burnham, June 11, 1977; children: Tara MArie, Kyle William. BBA, Va. Poly. Inst. & State U., 1976, MBA, 1981. Employment rep. GTE, Bluefield, W.Va., 1977-78; various mgmt. positions McGraw-Edison, Bluefield, W.Va., 1978-1984; negotiator General Electric Co., Louisville, 1984—86, mgr., labor relations, 1986—; v.p., human resources The Pillsbury Co., 1990—96, v.p., gen. mgr., 1996—98; sr. v.p., human resources Maytag, 2002—07; pres., gen. mgr. Hoover Floorcare, 2005—07; sr. v.p., human resources and comm. Cooper Tire & Rubber Co., 2007—09; sr. v.p. RSC Equipment Rental, Inc., 2010—. Mem. Labor-Mgmt. Assn. Ky., Jaycees (treas. W.Va. chpt., 1978-84, named Keyman of Yr., 1982). Avocations: golf, reading. Home: 10803 Falkirk Rd Louisville KY 40243-1714 Office: RSC Equipment Rental Inc 200 S Lasalle St Durham NC 27705-3654 Office Phone: 919-383-8999. Office Fax: 919-382-0444. Business E-Mail: mkrivoruchka@rentalservice.com.

KROEKER, HARRALD F., food products executive; With Polaroid Corp., Procter & Gamble Co.; v.p., selling and delivery ops., v.p., ops., sr. v.p., customer initiatives Pepsi Bottling Group, Inc., sr. v.p., gen. mgr., Mid Atlantic, 2000—02, sr. v.p., gen. mgr. Mexico, 2003—04, sr. v.p., gen. mgr., West, 2004—06; sr. v.p., COO, DSD Dairy bus. Dean Foods Co., 2006—08, pres., DSD Group, 2008—. Office: Dean Foods Co 2515 McKinney Ave Ste 1200 Dallas TX 75201 Office Phone: 214-303-3400. Office Fax: 214-303-3499. Business E-Mail: hkroeker@suizafoods.com.

KROHN, ROGER, JR., metal products executive; Pres. Krohn Steel Svc. Ctr. (acquired by Metals USA), 1982—98; pres., gen. mgr. Metals USA Holdings Corp., 1998—2003, pres., Flat Rolled and Non-Ferrous Group, 2003—. Served as officer & pilot, USAF, 1975-82. Office: Metals USA Holdings Corp 2400 E Commercial Blvd Ste 905 Fort Lauderdale FL 33308-4059 Office Phone: 713-965-0990. Office Fax: 713-965-0067.

KROHN, TRACY W., energy executive; BS in Petroleum Engring., La. State U., 1978. Petroleum engr., offshore drilling supr. Mobil Oil Corp.; sr. engr. Taylor Energy; chmn., CEO Aviara Energy Corp., 1996—97; treas. W&T OffShore, Inc., 1997, pres., CEO, 1983—, chmn., 2004—. Named one of Forbes' Richest Americans, 2006. Office: W&T Offshore Inc 9 Greenway Plz Ste 300 Houston TX 77046 Office Phone: 713-626-8525. Office Fax: 713-626-8527.

KROL, GEORGE ALBERT, United States ambassador to Uzbekistan; b. 1956; s. Anthony J. Krol. BA in History magna cum laude, Harvard U.; MA in Philosophy, Politics and Economics, Oxford U. Joined US Fgn. Svc., 1982; served at US Embassy, Warsaw, New Delhi, St. Petersburg, Russia, Kiev, Ukraine, dep. chief mission, charge d'Affaires Minsk, Belarus, 1993—95, min-counselor polit. affairs Moscow, 1999—2002; spl. asst. to amb.-at-large for New Independent States US Dept. State, 1995—97, dir. Office Russian Affairs, 1997—99, US amb. to Belarus Minsk, 2003—06, dep. asst. sec. for South & Ctrl. Asian Affairs Washington, 2008—10, US amb. to Uzbekistan Tashkent, 2011—. Tchr. Nat. War Coll. Office: US Embassy 7110 Tashkent Pl Washington DC 20521

KRONENBERG, RICHARD SAMUEL, physician, administrator; b. Chgo., Aug. 7, 1938; s. Frank Paul and Ruth Ida (Zaretzsky) K.; m. Carole Marie Hurd, Oct. 11, 1963; children: Karen, Marilyn, Brenda. BA, Northwestern U., 1960, MD, 1963; MBA, LaTourneau U., Longview, Tex., 1998. Cert. internal medicine & pulmonary disease 1972. Intern Parkland Meml. Hosp., Mpls., 1967-68, resident in internal medicine, 1968; rsch. fellow Cardiovascular Rsch. Inst. U. Calif., San Francisco, 1968-70; asst. prof. medicine U. Minn., 1970-74, assoc. prof., 1974-79, prof., dir. pulmonary div., 1979-84; prof. U. Tex. Health Sci. Ctr., Houston, 1984—2002; prof. medicine, exec. v.p. for clin. affairs U. Tex. Health Ctr., Tyler, 1984—2002; sr. v.p. Mother Frances Health Sys., 2002—. Reviewer subsplty. programs in internal medicine Accreditation Coun. Grad. Med. Edn., Chgo., 1985—. Mem. editorial rev. bd. The Asbestos Monitor, Nat. Asbestos Coun. Jour., 1990-93; contbr. chpts. to books. Capt. USAF, 1965-67. Recipient Rsch. Career Devel. award NIH, 1973-78. Fellow ACP, Am. Coll. Chest Physicians; mem. Nat. Asbestos Coun. (bd. dirs. 1990-93), Asbestos Disease Assn. (pres. 1990-93), Ctrl. Soc. Clin. Rsch. Avocation: bicycling. Home: 5615 Cedar Hill Cir Tyler TX 75703-3912 Business E-Mail: kronen.r@tmfhs.org. E-mail: kronenr@tmfhs.org.

KROSKIN, PHILIP, healthcare services company executive; BArch, U. Va., 1987, M in Urban & Environ. Planning, 1991. Sr. devel. dir. Mills Corp., 1997—2002; mng. ptnr. Bos Group LLC.; sr. v.p., real estate Sunrise Sr. Living, Inc. Office: Sunrise Senior Living Inc 7900 Westpark Dr Mc Lean VA 22102 Office Phone: 703-273-7500. Office Fax: 703-744-1601.

KROTEE, LESLIE LATSHAW, special education educator; b. Boston, Jan. 26, 1943; d. Robert James and Alice Louise (Jenks) Latshaw; m. March Lee Krotee, Agu. 21, 1965; children: March Lee Jr., Robert Latshaw. BS, West Chester U., 1965; MEd, U. Minn., 1989. Phys. edn. tchr. Langley Park (Md.) Elem. Sch., 1965-67, Winchester Thurston Sch. for Girls, Pitts., 1967-69; substitute tchr. Wayzata Sch. Dist., 1985-88; rsch. asst. U. Minn., Mpls., 1988—89; spl. edn. tchr. Crest View Elem. Sch., Brooklyn Park, Minn., 1990-91, Maple Grove (Minn.) Jr. High Sch., 1991-93, Richfield Sr. HS, 1993—2000, East Cary (N.C.) Mid. Sch., 2001—, Refoy Creek Mid Sch. Cary, NC, 2001—. Rsch. asst. U. Minn., Mpls., 1988-89. Author: (rsch. project) Educational Services to Minnesota Students With Disabilities, 1990. Presbyterian. Avocations: travel, gardening. Home: 320 Whisperwood Dr Cary NC 27518-9124 Office: Reedy Creek Mid Sch Cary NC 27511 Personal E-mail: lkrotee@hotmail.com.

KROTO, SIR HAROLD WALTER (HAROLD KROTOSCHINER), chemistry researcher, educator; b. Wisbech, Cambridgeshire, Eng., Oct. 7, 1939; s. Heinz and Edith Kroto; m. Margaret Henrietta Hunter, 1963; 2 children. BSc in Chemistry, U. Sheffield, 1961, PhD, 1964; PhD (hon.), U. Stockholm, 1992; D (hon.), U. Limburg, 1993, U. Sheffield, 1995, U. Kingston, 1995. Postdoc. fellow NRC, Canada, 1964-66; rsch. scientist Bell Tel. Labs., Murray Hill, NJ, 1966-67; lectr. U. Sussex, Brighton, England, 1968-77, reader, 1977-85, prof. chemistry, 1985—2004, Royal Soc. rsch. prof., 1991—2001; Francis Eppes prof. chemistry and biochemistry Fla. State U., Tallahassee, 2004—. Mem. editl. bd. Chem. Soc. Reviews, 1990—; contbr. articles to profl. jours. Recipient Internat. prize for new materials, Am. Phys. Soc., 1992, Italgas prize for innovation in chemistry, Italy, 1992, Hewlett Packard Europhysics prize, 1994, Nobel prize for chemistry, 1996, Am. Carbon Soc. medal, 1997, John Dalton medal, European Geophysics Union, 1998, Ioannes Marcus Marci medal, 2000. Fellow: Royal Soc. Chemistry (pres. 2002—04, Longstaff medal 1993), Royal Soc. (Michael Faraday award 2001, Copley medal 2002), Royal Microscopical Soc. (hon.), Royal Soc. Edinburgh (hon.); mem.: NAS (fgn. assoc.), Finnish Acad. Scis. (fgn.), Korean Acad. Sci. & Tech. (hon. fgn.), Mexican Acad. Sci., Academia Europea (Erasmus medal). Office: Chemistry Dept Fla State U Tallahassee FL 32301 E-mail: kroto@chem.fsu.edu.

KROUSKOP, DIRK, packaging company executive; BS in Civil Engring., U. Cin., MS in Environ. Engring.; MBA, Ohio U. Environ. specialist Corp. Human and Environ. Protection Dept. Mead Corp., 1979; corp. dir. regulatory assurance and environ. mgmt. MeadWestvaco Corp., 1990, dir. safety, health, environ. global policy and strategy, v.p. safety, health, and environment. Chmn. Nat. Coun. for Air and Stream Improvement, Inc. (NCASI). Mem.: Nat. Assn. of Environ. Mgrs. Office: MeadWestvaco Corp 501 S 5th St Richmond VA 23219 Office Phone: 804-444-1000. Business E-Mail: dirk.krouskop@meadwestvaco.com.

KRSTIC, PREDRAG S., physicist; b. Belgrade, Serbia-Monteneg, Sept. 14, 1950; s. Slavko M. and Jelena Krstic; m. Vasika Pantic, Dec. 2, 1972; children: Slavko, Nina. BS in Tech. Physics, U. Belgrade, Serbia, 1975; MSc in Plasma Physics, U. Belgrade, 1979; PhD in Theoretical Physics, CUNY, NYC, 1982. Prof. Inst. Physics, Belgrade U., 1976—92; rsch. fellow U. Conn., Storrs, 1992—95, Oak Ridge Nat. Lab., Tenn., 1995—98, mem. sci. staff, 1998—2006, sr. mem. sci. staff, 2006—. Co-chair 12th SPIG Int. Conf., Sibenik, Croatia, 1984—85, CDAMP Conf., Brioni, Croatia, 1988—89; cons. IAEA, Vienna, 1988—; chair Internat. Workshop on New Directions of Advanced Computer Simulations and Experiments in Fusion-related Plasma-Surface Interactions, Oak Ridge, 2004—05; co-chair 3rd Icamdata Internat. Conf., Galtinburg, Tenn., 2002—03; mem. program com. Third Internat. Conf. on Nano-Giga Challenges in Microelectronics, Phoenix, 2006—07; adj. assoc. prof. U. Tenn., Knoxville, 2008—; mem. program com. Third Internat. Conf. on Nano-Giga Challenges in Microelectronics, Hamilton, Ontarion, Canada, 2008—; adj. lectr. U. Conn., Storrs, Conn., U. Hartford, Conn., U. New Haven. Contbr. articles to profl. jours. Fellow: Am. Phys. Soc.; mem.: AAUP, Am. Chem. Soc. Achievements include research in theoretical atomic physics, expecially in slow ion-atom-molecule collisions in fusion edge plasma; in theory of ultra-strong laser-atom interactions; in theoretical simulations of fusion plasma; the first wall surface interactions involving molecules; nano-bio-science, with particular applications in molecular electronics and DNA sequencing; patents pending for single molecule sensing by doped carbon nano-tubes; invention of 3-D quadupole aqueous nanotrap. Office: Oak Ridge Nat Lab Physics Divsn PO Box 2008 Oak Ridge TN 37831-6372 Business E-Mail: krsticp@ornl.gov.

KRUCZEK, R. PATRICK, investment company executive; BBA, U. Notre Dame; MBA, U. Tenn. CPA. Investment banker Morgan Keegan & Co., Inc., Memphis, 1993, instl. sales mgr., co-dir. syndicated dept. and COO & dir. equity rsch., chief adminstrv. officer, 2006—08, pres., COO, 2008—. Bd. dirs. RMK Advantage Income Fund Inc. Office: Morgan Keegan Morgan Keegan Tower 50 N Front St Memphis TN 38103 Office Phone: 901-524-4100. Office Fax: 901-524-4197.

KRUEGER, GERALD PETER, psychologist; b. Evanston, Ill., Apr. 3, 1944; s. Albert August and Pauline Mary (Didier) K.; m. Jessica Ann Prendergast, Aug. 26, 1967; children: Michael G., Deborah L., Kevin A. BA in Psychology, U. Dayton, 1966; MA in Exptl. and Engring. Psychology, Johns Hopkins U., 1975, PhD in Exptl. Psychology, 1977; grad., U.S. Army Command and Gen. Staff Coll., 1980, U.S. Army War Coll., 1988. Cert. profl. ergonomist Bd. Certification Profl. Ergonomics. Rschr. engring. psychology Bunker-Ramo Corp., Wright-Patterson AFB, Ohio, 1966—69; human factors rsch. psychologist U.S. Army Human Engring. Lab., Aberdeen, Md., 1969—71; R & D coord. Def. Advanced Rsch. Projects Agy., Saigon, Vietnam, 1971—72; mil. police ops. officer U.S. Army, Ft. Meade, Md., 1972, aviation psychologist Aeromed. Rsch. Lab. Ft. Rucker, Ala., 1976—80; R & D programs staff officer U.S. Army Med. R & D Command, Ft. Detrick, Md., 1980—84; dep. chief dept. behavioral biology Walter Reed Army Inst. Rsch., Washington, 1984—88; dir. biomed. applications rsch. divsn. U.S. Army Aeromed. Rsch. Lab., Ft. Rucker, 1988—90; comdr., sci. tech. dir. U.S. Army Rsch. Inst. Environ. Medicine, Natick, Mass., 1990—94; ret. col. U.S. Army, 1994; v.p. ergonomics R & D svcs. Biomechanics Corp. Am., Melville, NY, 1994—95; prin. rsch. scientist, ergonomist Star Mountain, Inc., Alexandria, Va., 1995—98; pres. Krueger Ergonomics Cons., Inc., 1998—; prin. scientist, ergonomist Wexford Group Internat., Vienna, Va., 2000—06; sr. human factors specialist TGO Brien Assoc. Inc., 2008—. Tchr. U.S. Armed Forces Inst., Saigon, 1971, Johns Hopkins U., 1974-75, U. So. Calif., 1977-80; adj. asst. prof. med.-clin. psychology Uniformed Svcs. U. Health Scis., Bethesda, Md., 1997—; mem. sci. coun. to UTEK Corp., Plant City, Fla., 1999-2010; bd. dirs. Commonwealth Biotechs., Inc., Richmond, Va., 2004-07. Book review editor Ergonomics in Design Quarterly, 1995—; assoc. editor Mil. Psychology, 1991-2003, mem. editl. bd., 2003—; guest editor jours. in field; contbr. articles to profl. jours. Recipient Richard M. Griffith Meml. award So. Soc. Philosophy and Psychology, 1978, Order of Mil. Med. merit for career contbns. Army Med. Dept., 1992, numerous mil. awards, medals and skill proficiency badges, including Legion of Merit, 1994, Bronze Star U.S. Army, 1972, Meritorious Svc. medals with 2 oak leaf clusters. Fellow APA (pres. divsn. mil. psychology 1995-96, pres. divsn. engring. psychologists 2001-02), Human Factors and Ergonomics Soc. (pres. Potomac chpt. 2003), Wash. Acad. Scis., Inst. Ergonomics & Human Factors; mem. Assn. US Army, Nat. Def. Indsl. Assn., Fedn. Assns. in Behavioral and Brain Scis. (mem. bd. dirs. 2007-10), Aerospace Med. Assn., Aerospace Human Factors Assn., Soc. for Human Performance in Extreme Environments, Army War Coll. Alumni Assn., VFW, Am. Legion. Roman Catholic. Office: Krueger Ergonomics Consultants 4105 Komes Ct Alexandria VA 22306-1252 Office Phone: 703-850-6397. E-mail: jerrykrueg@aol.com.*

KRUEGER, ROBERT CHARLES, former ambassador, congressman, senator; b. New Braunfels, Tex., Sept. 19, 1935; s. Arlon E. and Faye (Leifeste) Krueger; life ptnr. Kathleen Tobin Krueger; children: Mariana, Sarah, Christian. BA, So. Meth. U., 1957; MA, Duke U., 1958; M.Litt., Oxford U., Eng., 1961, D.Phil., 1964; D.Litt. (hon.), U. St. Thomas; D.Pub.Service (hon.), Lycoming U., 2003; DHL (hon.), Tex. Luth. U., 2006. From instr. to assoc. prof. English Duke U., 1961-72; vice provost, dean Trinity Coll. Arts and Scis., Duke U., 1972-73; chmn. bd. Comal Hosiery Mills, 1973-75; ptnr. Krueger Brangus Ranch, 1974-86; mem. 94th-95th Congresses from 21st Tex. dist., 1975-79; U.S. ambassador-at-large, coord. for Mex. affairs, 1979-81; pres. Krueger Assocs., 1981-91; Bentsen prof. govt.-bus. rels. Lyndon B. Johnson Sch., U. Tex., 1985-86; Tsanoff prof. pub. affairs Rice U., 1986-88; Disting. lectr. So. Meth. U., 1991; commr. Tex. R.R. Commn., 1991—93; U.S. senator from Tex., 1993-94; amb. to Burundi, 1994-96; amb. to Botswana, 1996—2000; spl. rep. of sec. of state So. Africa Devel. Cmty., 1998—2000; rsch. fellow Merton Coll. Oxford (Eng.) U., 2000—01; cons. on nat. and internat. bus. and fgn. affairs, 2001—. Spkr. in field; mem. chancellor's bd. advisors U. Ill. Med. Ctr.; bd. dir. ViadCorp.; vis. disting. prof. U. Tex., Austin, 2003—05, Tex. State U., San Marcos, 2002—06. Author: The Poems of Sir John Davies, 1975, From Bloodshed to Hope in Burundi, 2007; contbr. articles to profl. jours. and newspapers. Bd. dir. Cath. Charities, San Antonio, 2001—05, South Tex. Kidney Found., 2001—05; chair Rhodes Scholarship Solution Com. Tex. & Louisiana, 2005—09. Mem.: Tex. Philos. Soc. (pres. 1993), Phi Beta Kappa, Blue Key. Office: PO Box 311717 New Braunfels TX 78131-1717 Office Phone: 830-629-7347. E-mail: kruegerx@swbell.net.

KRUESI, FRANK EUGENE, lobbyist, former government executive; b. Marblehead, Mass., July 12, 1950; s. William Rogers and Lydia Abigail (Fuller) K.; m. Susan Francis Boyd, Sept. 1, 1971 (div. Jan. 1993); children: Elizabeth Ann, William Shepardson; m. Barbara Grochala, Oct. 16, 1993. BA in Econs. cum laude, Middlebury Coll., 1972; MA in Polit. Sci., U. Chgo., 1979. Lectr. polit. sci. Loyola U., Chgo., 1974, DePaul U., Chgo., 1979, Rosary Coll., Chgo., 1979; assoc. prof. pub. policy U. Chgo., 2000—; rsch. assoc. Ill. Gov.'s Commn. Individual Liberty & Personal Privacy, Chgo., 1975; cons. Ill. Gov.'s Commn. Mental Health Code, Chgo., 1975-77; exec. officer Cook County State's Atty. Office, Chgo., 1980-89; chief policy officer Office of Mayor of City of Chgo., 1989-93; asst. sec. for policy US Dept. Transp., Washington, 1993—97; pres. Chgo. Transit Authority, 1997—2007. Vis. faculty Harris Sch. Pub. Policy, U. Chgo., 2000—. Dir. affairs Wash. DC Off., Chgo., 2007- Democrat. Office Phone: 202-783-0911. Business E-Mail: kruesi@cityofchicago.org.

KRUG, JOHN CARLETON (TONY KRUG), retired academic administrator, educator, library director, consultant; b. Evansville, Ind., Nov. 27, 1951; s. John Elmer and Mary Ellen K.; m. Anna Marie Waters, July 3, 1983. BA, Ind. State U., 1972, MLS, 1973; PhD, So. Ill. U., Carbondale, 1985. Lic. to ministry Bapt. Ch. Exec. dir. Olney (Ill.) Carnegie Pub. Libr., 1973-74; assoc. dean Wabash Valley Coll., Mt. Carmel, Ill., 1974-84; mem. Com. for U.S. Depository State Plan, Springfield, Ill., 1982-84; dir. librs. Maryville Coll., St. Louis, 1984-88; dir. info. svcs. Bethany (W.Va.) Coll., 1988-97; dean libr. svcs. Carson Newman Coll., Jefferson City, Tenn., 1997—2002; dir. ctrl. libr. Appalachian Coll. Assn., Berea, Ky., 2002—07; mgr. Seymour Br., Sevier County Pub. Libr., Tenn., 2007—11; prof. Johnson U., Knoxville, Tenn., 2007—. Coord. libr. activities, Appalachian Coll. Assn., 1997-2002; sec. pro-tem Ill. Basin Coal Mining Manpower Council, Mt. Carmel, 1974-79; governing bd. exec. com. Higher Edn. Ctr. Cable TV, 1986-88; conf. speaker Kans. State U., 1982. Author: Libraries Using/Planning for Microcomputers, 1986; also computer programs. V.p. bd. dirs. Wabash Area Vocat. Enterprises, Mt. Carmel, 1978-81; bd. edn. Wabash Cmty. Unit, Mt. Carmel, 1980-83; exec. com. Cmty. Edn. and Arts Assn., Carbondale, 1983-84; visual arts adv. com. Ill. Arts Coun., Chgo., 1982-84; pastor Hopewell United Meth. Ch., Bridgeport, Ill., 1976-77; minister Terre Haute (Ind.) 1st Bapt. Ch., 1972—; elder Gateway Christian Ch., 1986-88, Woodlawn Christian Ch., 2006-; bd. dirs. Fair Haven Christian Sch., 1986-88; pres. T3-Tchrs., Tech., Tomorrow. Mem. Internat. Soc. Tech. Edn. Conservative. Home Phone: 865-621-1282. Personal E-mail: krug.tony@gmail.com.

KRUGER, LON, men's college basketball coach; b. Topeka, Aug. 19, 1952; m. Barbara Miles; children: Angie, Kevin. BS in Bus., Kans. State U., 1975; MS in Phys. Edn., Pittsburg State U., Kans., 1977. Asst. coach Pittsburg State U. Gorillas, Kans., 1976-77; grad. asst. coach Kans. State U. Wildcats, 1977-78, asst. coach, 1978-82, head coach, 1986—90, U. Tex.-Pan American Broncs, 1982-86, athletic dir., 1982-85; head coach U. Fla. Gators, 1990—96, U. Ill. Fighting Illini, 1996—2000, Atlanta Hawks, 2000—03; asst. coach NY Knicks, 2003—04; head coach U. Nev. Las Vegas Runnin' Rebels, 2004—11, U. Okla. Sooners, 2011—. Asst. coach US Pan Am. Team, 1987; head coach Big Eight Select Team, Beijing, 1987, U.S.A. Jr. World Champion Team, 1991, U.S.A. World U. Games Team, 1995; bd. dirs. Nat. Assn. Basketball Coaches, 1994—2000. Co-chairperson Alachua County's Red Ribbon Campaign, 1991-93. Named Big Eight Player of Yr., 1973, 74, Southeastern Conf. Coach of Yr., 1992, 94, Gainesville Vol. of Yr., 1995, State of Ill. Collegiate Coach of Yr., 1997; named to the Kans. Hall of Fame, 1999, Kans. State U. Hall of Fame, 2003, Topeka and Shawnee County Sports Hall of Fame, 2006. Office: University Okla Mens Basketball McClendon Ctr Intercollegiate Athletics 180 W Brooks Norman OK 73019

KRUGER, PAULA, telecommunications industry executive; b. Bklyn., July 31, 1950; d. Jean Jacques Kruger and Jo Campione; m. Lawrence C. Heller; children: Michael, Tracy, Jessica. BA in Bus. Adminstrn., C.W. Post, Brookville, NY, 1972; MBA, LI U., 1976. V.p. customer rels. Cablevision, Woodbury, NY, 1994—97; corp. v.p. customer svc. Am. Express, NYC, Citibank, NYC, v.p. devel. divsn.; v.p. consumer svcs. group Republic of Korea; v.p. teleservices Excel Comm., 1997—99, exec. v.p. customer and ind. rep. ops., 1999; gen. mgr. customer relationship mgmt. svc. line Electronic Data Systems Corp., 2002—03; exec. v.p. mass markets group Qwest Comm. Internat., Inc., Denver, 2003—08; CEO Milano Worldwide Corp., 2008—. Office: 1730 S FederalHwy Ste 379 Delray Beach FL 33483 Office Phone: 303-992-1400. Office Fax: 303-896-8515.

KRUGER, RICHARD M., oil industry executive; b. Mpls. m. Patti Kruger; 3 children. B in Mech. Engring., U. Minn., 1981; MBA, U. Houston. Joined Exxon Co. USA Exxon Corp., Houston, 1981, prodn. advisor Irving, Tex., 1994—96, tech. mgr. Ventures Houston, 1996—99; v.p. Devel. Co. ExxonMobil Corp., 1999—2001, chmn., CEO Exploration and Prodn. Malaysia Kuala Lumpur, 2001—03, v.p. Asia Pacific/Middle East Prodn. Co., 2003—05, v.p. US Prodn. Co., 2005—06, v.p., exec. v.p. Prodn. Co., 2006—. Supporter United Way Tex. Gulf Coast. Recipient Outstanding Achievement award, Inst. Tech. U. Minn., 2005. Office: Exxon Mobil Corp Hdqs 5959 Las Colinas Blvd Irving TX 75039-2298

KRUGMAN, STANLEY LIEBERT, retired science administrator, geneticist; b. St. Louis, June 8, 1932; s. Bernard and Della (Goldberg) Krugman; m. Judith Raechel Alfend, June 28, 1958; children: Mark Bernard, Jeffrey Jon. BS in Forestry, U. Mo., 1955; MF, U. Calif., Berkeley, 1956, PhD in Plant Physiology, 1961. Rsch. aide U. Calif., 1956-61, rsch. assoc., 1961-62; rsch. physiologist U.S. Forest Svc., 1962-64, project leader, 1964-71, staff geneticist Washington, 1971-80, staff dir., 1980-95; sr. for specialist, pvt. cons. World Bank Natural Resources, Washington, 1995—2000; pvt. practice, 2000—. Cons. in field. Editor: (book) Seeds of Woody Plants, 1974, Advances in Reproductive Biology, 1974, Management Biosphere Reserves, 1979, Advances in Forest Physiology, 1980. Recipient Sci. medal, USSR, 1995, Czech Republic, 1995, PRC, 1996, Poland, 1997. Fellow: AAAS, Soc. Am. Foresters (William Schlich medal 1990); mem.: Internat. Union Forestry Orgn. Jewish. Office Phone: 703-356-9145. Personal E-mail: skrugman@juno.com.

KRUJA, MIRA, concert pianist, presenter, professor, clinician; d. Pertef and Shpresa Kruja; m. Ferdinand Murati; 1 child, Ingrid Murati. DMA, Nat. U. Conservatory, 1987; MusM, Radford U., 1995; degree in Music Theory Pedagogy, U. Ky., 1999, D in Musical Arts, 2004; BM with honors, Coll. Conservatory, 1983. Nat. cert. tchr. Music Tchrs. Nat. Assn., 2005. Prof. Nat. U. Conservatory, 1987—93; piano tchr. Radford U., Va., 1993—95; music faculty U. Ky., Lexington, 1996—2005; prof. Ala. A&M U., Huntsville, 2005—. Arts coun. rep. & pub. rels. chair Huntsville Music Tchrs. Assn.; coord. MusicLink Found., Ala.; pres. Bluegrass Area Music Tchrs. Assn., Ky.; music theory chair Ky. Music Tchrs. Assn.; founding tchr. Nat. Music Cert. Program; founder Duo Armonioso. Musician: Bartok Kabalevsky Internat. Piano Competition, Nat. U. Conservatory Piano Competition; author: Art Music for the Piano Twentieth-Century Composers, Masterworks and Styles, 2009, Eterna, Piano Solo CD Album, 2004, Piano Inside Out: The Expansion of the Expressive, Technical and Sonorous Spectrum in Selected Twentieth-Century Art-Music Repertoire for the Modern Acoustic Piano, 2004, musician (pianist & adjudicator). Recipient Chancellor's Outstanding Tchg. award, UK, 1998, Internat. Innovative Electronic Diss award, NDLTD, Sydney, 2005, Tchr. Who Made A Difference Award, 2004, 2008; grant, U. Ky., 1998—2003. Master: Am. Guild Organists (mem. greater Huntsville chpt.), Music Tchrs. Nat. Assn (arts coun. rep. HMTA, pres. BAMTA, theory chair KMTA), Coll. Music Soc. (campus rep.); mem.: NEA, NEA, Nat. Guild Piano Tchrs., AMTA (composition competition chair), Am. Coll. Musicians, European Piano Tchrs. Assn., Internat. Music Coun., Nat. Fedn. Music Clubs, Huntsville Music Study Club (v.p., sub dean). Achievements include research in twentieth and twenty-first century advanced pianism and Avant-Garde piano techniques. Home: PO Box 4743 Huntsville AL 35815

KRULAK, CHARLES CHANDLER, academic administrator, retired military officer; b. Quantico, Va., Mar. 4, 1942; s. Victor Harold and Amy (Chandler) Krulak; m. Zandra Lynn Meyers, June 27, 1964; children: David Chandler, Todd Cameron. BS, U.S. Naval Acad., 1964; MS, George Washington U., 1973; advanced mil. course, Amphib. War Sch., 1968, Army Command and Gen. Staff, Coll., 1976, Nat. War Coll., 1982. Commd. 2d lt. USMC, 1964, advanced through grades to gen., 1995, retired, 1999, rifle co. comdr. Vietnam, 1965-66, 69-70, bn. comdr. Hawaii, 1983-85; mil. asst. Asst. Sec. Def. for Command, Control, Comm. and Intelligence, Washington, 1986-87; dep. dir. White House Mil. Office, Washington, 1987-89; brigade comdr. and asst. divsn. comdr. USMC, N.C., 1989-91, force svc. support group comdr. N.C., 1989-90, force svc. support comdr., brigade comdr., 1990-91; dir. pers. mgmt., pers. procurement Hdqtrs. Marine Corps, 1991-92; comdg. gen. MCCDC, Quantico, Va., 1992-94; comdr. marine forces, Pacific and comdg. gen. Fleet Marine Forces, Pacific, Camp Smith, Hawaii, 1994-95; commandant USMC, 1995-99; sr. vice chmn. MBNA America Corp., Wilmington, Del., 1999—2001; chmn., CEO MBNA Europe Bank Ltd., 2001—05; exec. vice chmn., chief adminstrv. officer MBNA Corp., 2004—05; non-exec. dir. Aston Villa F.C., Birmingham, England, 2006—; pres. Birmingham-Southern Coll., 2011—. Contbr. articles to Marine Corps Gazette. Decorated Def. Disting. Svc. Medal, Navy Disting. Svc. Medal, Silver Star, Bronze Star, Purple Heart. Avocations: running, reading. Office: Birmingham-Southern College Office of President 900 Arkadelphia Rd Birmingham AL 35254 E-mail: ckrulak@bsc.edu.

KRULL, MICHAEL, political consultant; b. Iowa, 1964; BA in Polit. Sci. & Religion and Philosophy, Luther Coll.; MA in Polit. Sci., Iowa State U. Staff asst. to Senator Chuck Grassley US Senate, Washington; Iowa field staff mem. Bush '88; with US Agy. for Internat. Devel. (USAID); exec. v.p. Corp. for Internat. Trade; dir. Midwest Agribusiness Trade Rsch. Info. Ctr.; v.p. Des Moines Chamber of Commerce; cons. Mendez England & Associates, Bethesda, Md.; prin., mng. dir. Gordon C. James Pub. Relations, Washington; nat. dir. American Solutions, 2007—11; campaign coord. Newt Gingrich 2012, 2011—12. Bd. dirs. US Coun. for Puerto Rico Statehood. Republican.

KRUSCHWITZ, WALTER HILLIS, retired physics educator; b. Edgerton, Ohio, July 20, 1920; s. Albin Gustav and Bertha Anna (Lehman) K.; m. Virginia Imogene Stone Kruschwitz, Feb. 13, 1926; children: Nancy Lynn, Sharon Leigh. BA, Taylor U., Upland, Ind., 1942; MA, Vanderbilt U., Nashville, 1948; PhD, U. Mich., Ann Arbor, 1961. Assoc. prof. physics and math. Cumberland U., Lebanon, Tenn., 1948-50; assoc. prof., prof. physics Union U., Jackson, Tenn., 1951-63; prof. physics Mobile (Ala.) Coll., 1963-67; assoc. prof. physics U. S. Fla., Tampa, 1967-90; ret., 1990. 1st lt. USAF, 1942-45. Southern Baptist. Home: 5808 NW 103rd St Oklahoma City OK 73162-6954 Personal E-mail: kruschwhk@aol.com.

KRUSE, DENNIS K., professional society administrator, retired military officer; Comdr. Carderock Divsn. Naval Surface Warfare Ctr., Bethesda, Md.; exec. dir. Am. Soc. Naval Engrs., 2006—. Spkr. in field. Ret. capt. USN. Office: Am Soc Naval Engrs 1452 Duke St Alexandria VA 22314-3458 Office Phone: 703-836-6727. Office Fax: 703-836-7491. E-mail: dkruse@navalengineers.org.

KRUSE, LAYNE E., lawyer; b. Emporia, Kans., Aug. 15, 1951; BA, Tex. A&M U., 1973; MSc, London Sch. Econs., 1974; JD, Yale U., 1977. Bar: Tex. 1978, cert.: Tex. Bd. Legal Specialization (civil trial law). Law clk. to Hon. John R. Brown U.S. Ct. Appeals (5th cir.); mem. Fulbright & Jaworski L.L.P., Houston. Past chair antitrust and bus. litigation sect. State Bar Tex. Mem.: ABA, Houston Bar Assn. Office: Fulbright & Jaworski LLP 1301 Mckinney St Ste 5100 Houston TX 77010-3031 Office Phone: 713-651-5194. E-mail: lkruse@fulbright.com.

KRYS, SHELDON JACK, retired diplomat; b. NYC, June 15, 1934; s. Martin and Anna K.; m. Doris M., May 24, 1964; children— Wendy M., Madeleine S., Susan Jennifer. N.D., U. Md., College Park, 1955; grad., Nat. War Coll., Washington, 1977; PhD (hon.), St. John Fisher Coll., 1996. Newscaster Radio Sta. KRSD, Rapid City, SD, 1955-57; dir., prodr. Radio Sta. WWDC, Washington, 1957-59; prin. Chris Sheldon Pub. Rels., Washington, 1959-61; cons. to dir. FMCS, Washington, 1961-62; ednl. and cultural affairs officer, dir. reception ctrs. Dept. State, Washington, 1962-64, mgmt. officer London, 1965-66, spl. asst. to amb., 1966-69, dir. pers. Latin Am. Washington, 1969-74, adminstrv. counselor Belgrade, 1974-76, fgn. svc. insp. Washington, 1977-79, exec. dir. Bur. Near Eastern and South Asian Affairs, 1979-83, dep. dir. mgmt. ops., 1983-84, exec. asst. to under sec. for mgmt., 1984-85; amb. to Trinidad and Tobago, 1985-88; exec. sec. Laird Commn., 1987; asst. sec. state adminstrn. and info. mgmt., 1988-89; asst. sec. state diplomatic security, 1989-92; diplomat-in-residence George Washington U., Washington, 1992-93; cons. internat. and intergovtl. affairs Fletcher, Heald & Hildreth, P.L.C., Roslyn, Va., 1994—. Co-chmn. ambassadorial seminar Dept. of State, 1992—2003. Mem. bd. George Foster Peabody Awards, 1990-95, chmn. bd. 1993-95, chmn. emeritus 1996, chmn. editl. bd. Fgn. Svc. Jour., 1994-96; bd. dirs. Sr. Living Found., 1997—; bd. dirs., v.p. Washington Inst. Fgn. Affairs, 2006—; trustee St. John Fisher Coll., 1997—2008. Recipient Meritorious Honor award, Dept. State, 1974, Disting. Honor award, 1981, Superior Honor award, 1983, Presdl. Meritorious Svc. award, 1983, Wilbur J. Carr award, 1994. Mem. Armed Forces Comm. and Electronics Assn. (bd. dirs. 1991-92), Nat. War Coll. Alumni Assn., Am. Fgn. Svc. Assn., Am. Broadcast Pioneers, Broadcast Found., City Tavern Club, Cosmos Club, Assn. Diplomatic Studies & Tng. Avocation: gardening. Office: Fletcher Heald & Hildreth PLC 1300 North 17th St 11th Fl Arlington VA 22209-3801

KRZYSZTOFOWICZ, SIR ROMAN, systems engineering and statistical science educator, consultant; b. Cieszyn, Poland, Sept. 27, 1947; came to U.S., 1974; naturalized, 1985; s. Janusz and Irena (Rogozinska) K.; m. Liana Balayan, May 27, 1995; children: Arman, Nayiri. MS with highest distinction, Cracow Tech. U., Poland, 1970; PhD, U. Ariz., 1978. Rsch. engr. Inst. for Meteorology and Water Resources, Cracow, 1970-72, head computer ctr., 1972-74; lectr. Chief Tech. Orgn., Cracow, 1973-74; asst. prof. systems engring. U. Ariz., Tucson, 1978-79; asst. prof. civil engring. MIT, Cambridge, Mass., 1979-82; assoc. prof. systems engring. U. Va., Charlottesville, Va., 1982-86, prof. systems engring., 1986—, dir. grad. program systems engring., 1984-89, assoc. dir. ctr. for risk mgmt. engring. systems, 1987-88, prof. statistics, 1995—. Vis. scientist Swiss Fed. Inst. Tech., Lausanne, 2002; lectr. George Washington U., 1982-83, NATO Advanced Study Inst., Tucson, 1985, Deauville, France, 1993, Coop. Program for Operational Meteorology, Edn. and Tng., Boulder, Colo., 1993-96; rep. NSF in coop. rsch. initiatives with Brazil and Poland, 1991; reviewer proposals NSF, 1980—, Natural Scis. and Engring. Rsch. Coun. Can., 1987—; rschr. Nat. Weather Svc., 1992, 1995; expert on flood forecasting, Commn. for Hydrology, World Meteorological Orgn., 1997-2000; mem. doctoral examination com. U. Que., 1997, 2000, U. Paris VI, 2002, École Nationale du Génie Rural des Eaux et des Forêts (ENGREF), Paris, 2004; vis. scholar Nat. Ctrs. Environ. Prediction, Camp Springs, Md., 2007-08; reviewer articles for numerous jours. Editor Jour. of Hydrology, 1996-2007; mem. editl. bd. Stochastic Hydrology and Hydraulics, 1990-98, Control and Cybernetics, 1994—, Stochastic Environ. Rsch. and Risk Assessment, 1999—10, Water Resources Monographs of the Polish Academy of Sciences, 2000—, Jour. Applied Meteorology, 2001-02; contbr. articles to profl. jours., chpts. to books, entries to Systems and Control Ency., Concise Ency. Environ. Systems, Ency. Ops. Rsch. and Mgmt. Sci., Ency. of Sci. and Tech. Recipient Prof. W. Wierzbicki award Polish Soc. Civil Engrs. and Technicians, 1970, Rsch. award NSF, 1978-99, Presdl. Young Investigator award Pres. of U.S., 1984. Mem. IEEE, Am. Statis. Assn., Soc. for Judgment and Decision Making, Internat. Inst. Forecasters, Inst. for Ops. Rsch. and the Mgmt. Scis., Am. Geophys. Union, Am. Water Resources Assn., Am. Meteorological Soc., Tau Beta Pi (Eminent Engr. award 1985). Republican. Armenian Catholic. Avocations: opera, theater, skiing, sailing, hiking, bicycling, motorcycling. Office: U Va PO Box 400747 151 Engineer's Way Charlottesville VA 22904-4747 Business E-Mail: rk@virginia.edu.

KRZYZEWSKI, MIKE (MICHAEL WILLIAM KRZYZEWSKI), men's college basketball coach; b. Chgo., Feb. 13, 1947; m. Carol Mickie Marsh; children: Debbie Savarino, Linda Frasher, Jamie Spatola. BS, US Mil. Acad., 1969. Head basketball coach US Mil. Acad. Prep Sch., Ft. Belvoir, Va., 1972—74; asst. coach Ind. U., 1974—75; head basketball coach US Mil. Acad., West Point, NY, 1975-80, Duke U. Blue Devils, Durham, NC, 1980—. Asst. coach US Men's Nat. Basketball Team, 1979, 1984, 1992, head coach, 2006—. Co-author (with Bill Brill): A Season Is a Lifetime: The Inside Story of the Duke Blue Devils and Their Championships Seasons, 1993; (with Donald T. Phillips) Leading with the Heart: Coach K's Successful Strategies for Basketball, Business and Life, 2000, 5 Point Play: Duke's Journey to the 2001 National Championship, 2001, (with Jamie Krzyzewski Spatola) Beyond Basketball: Coach K's Keywords for Success, 2006, The Gold Standard: Building a World-Class Team, 2009. Chmn. Children's Miracle Network Telethon; bd. dirs. V Found.; with Comprehensive Cancer Ctr., NABC Coaches vs. Cancer; bd. dirs. K Lab Human Performance; fundraising leader Emily Krzyzewski Ctr. Immaculate Conception Cath. Ch., Durham, NC. Served US Army, 1967—69, officer US Army, 1969—74, ret. capt. US Army, 1974. Recipient Naismith Coll. Coach of Yr. Award, 1989, 1992, 1999, Wooden award, Legends of Coaching, 2000, GTE (now Verizon) Reads with the NABC Lit. Champion award, 2000; named Met. NY Basketball Writer's Coach of Yr., 1977, Coach of Yr., Atlantic Coast Conf. (ACC), 1984, 1986, 1997, 1999, 2000, Nat. Coach of Yr., Basketball Times, 1997, CBS/Chevrolet, 1986, 2000, Sporting News, 1992, UPI, 1986, Victor awards, 2001, Sportsman of Yr., Sporting News, 1992, Sports Illus., 2011, Coach of Decade, NABC, 1990, America's Best Coach, Time/CNN, 2001, 3d Best Coach All Time, CBS show; named to Naismith Meml. Basketball Hall of Fame, 2001. Mem.: NCAA (basketball issues com.), Nat. Assn. Basketball Coaches (pres. 1998—99, Dist. Coach of Yr. 1977, 1984, 1992, 1994, 1999, 2000, Nat. Coach of Yr. 1991, 1999). Achievements include coaching the Duke University Blue Devils to the NCAA Final Four, 1986, 88, 89, 90, 91, 92, 94, 99, 2001, 04, 10; head coach of the NCAA Division I National Championship winning Duke University Blue Devils, 1991, 92, 2001, 10; one of five coaches in NCAA history to earn 3 or more national championships along with John Wooden, Adolph Rupp, Bob Knight and Jim Calhoun; second head coach in Division I NCAA men's basketball history to reach 900 career wins, 2011; becoming NCAA Division I men's basketball all-time winningest head coach (903 victories), November 15, 2011. Office: Duke University Schwartz Athletic Ctr Box 90556 Durham NC 27708-0556 Office Phone: 919-613-7505. Office Fax: 919-613-7564. Business E-Mail: gbbrown@duaa.duke.edu.

KUBIC, MICHAEL D., corporate financial executive; BA, U. Mass. CPA Tex. V.p., corp. contr. BancTec, Inc., 1993—98; v.p., fin. Kevco, Inc., 1999; joined Alliance Data Sys. Corp., 1999, sr. v.p., corp. contr.; chief acctg. officer Alliance Data Systems Corp., 2003—, interim CFO, 2009—. Office: Alliance Data Systems Corp 7500 Dallas Pkwy Ste 700 Plano TX 75024-4006 Office Phone: 972-348-5100. Office Fax: 972-348-5335.

KUBOT, LUKASZ, professional tennis player; b. Boleslawlec, Poland, May 16, 1982; s. Janusz and Dorota Kubot. Profl. tennis player ATP, 2002—. Achievements include winning Casablanca, 2009, Belgrade, 2009, Vienna, 2009, Santiago, 2010, Acapulco, 2010; mem. Polish Davis Cup Team. Office: c/o ATP Tour Inc 201 Atp Tour Blvd Ponte Vedra Beach FL 32082-3211

KUCHAR, MATT G., professional golfer; b. Winter Park, Fla., June 21, 1978; married; 2 children. Grad., Ga. Tech. U., 2000. Profl. golfer PGA Tour, 2006—. Mem. US team Ryder Cup, 2010, 2012, President's Cup, 2011, World Cup of Golf, 2011. Recipient Fred Haskins Award, 1998; named Player of Yr., ACC, 1998. Achievements include winner PGA Tour events: The Honda Classic, 2002; Turning Stone Resort Championship, 2009; Barclays, 2010; The Players Championship, 2012. Office: Group CSE 600 Galleria Pkwy Ste 1900 Atlanta GA 30339 Office Phone: 770-955-1300. Business E-Mail: clientrep@groupcse.com.

KUDLAC, JEFFREY, defense and space company executive; B, U. Calif. V.p., real estate General Dynamics Corp. Office: General Dynamics Corp 2941 Fairview Park Dr Ste 100 Falls Church VA 22042-4513 Office Phone: 703-876-3000. Office Fax: 703-876-3125. Business E-Mail: jeffrey.kudlac@gdc4s.com.

KUECHLE, SCOTT E., manufacturing executive; BBA, Univ. Wis. Eau Claire; MSIA, Carnegie Mellon Univ. Fin. mgmt. positions Goodrich Corp., Charlotte, NC, 1983—94, dir. fin. & banking, 1994—98, v.p., treas., 1998—2004, v.p., contr., 2004—05, sr. v.p., CFO, 2005—07, exec. v.p., CFO, 2007—. Office: Goodrich Corp 4 Coliseum Ctr 2730 W Tyvola Rd Charlotte NC 28217-4578

KUECHLY, LUKE AUGUST, professional football player; b. Cin., Apr. 20, 1991; s. Tom and Eileen Kuechly. Attended, Boston Coll., 2009—11. Linebacker Carolina Panthers, 2012—. Recipient Butkus award, Butkus Found., 2011, Lombardi award, Rotary Club Houston, 2011, Bronco Nagurski trophy, Football Writers Assn. America, 2011, Lott IMPACT trophy, Pacific Club IMPACT Found., 2011; named Defensive MVP, Emerald Bowl, 2009, 1st Team All-American, AP, 2009—11, 1st Team All-Atlantic Coast Conf. (ACC), 2009—11, Defensive Rookie of Yr., Atlantic Coast Conf. (ACC), 2009, Defensive Player of Yr., 2011, Defensive MVP, Kraft Fight Hunger Bowl, 2011, Athlete of Yr., Atlantic Coast Conf. (ACC), 2012, NFL Defensive Rookie of Yr., AP, 2012, NFL Defensive Player of Yr., 2013, NFL Defensive Rookie of Yr., Pro Football Weekly/Pro Football Writers Assn. (PFWA), 2012, 1st Team All-Pro, AP, 2013; named to The All-Rookie Team, Pro Football Weekly/Pro Football Writers Assn. (PFWA), 2012, The Nat. Football Conf. Pro Bowl Team, 2013. Achievements include leading the NFL in: tackles, 2012. Office: Carolina Panthers 800 S Mint St Charlotte NC 28202*

KUEHL, ALEXANDER EDWARD, physician, health facility administrator, educator, writer; b. St. John, Nfld., Can., Aug. 12, 1944; came to US, 1945; s. Frederick George and Olivia Kendall (Dwyer) K.; children: Kendall Ann Warsaw, Bruce Ongsiako. BA, Johns Hopkins U., 1966, MPH, 1976; MD, Syracuse U., 1970. Bd. cert. in Orthopaedic Surgery; bd. cert. in Emergency Medicine. Intern U. Hosp., Syracuse, 1970-71, resident, 1971-73, Johns Hopkins Hosp., 1974-78; fellow in emergency med. svc. and trauma U. Hosp., Balt., 1978-79; dir. med. affairs Md. Inst. Emergency Med. Svcs., Balt., 1979—81; v.p. med. dir. NYC Health & Hosps. Corp., 1981-89; assoc. prof. surgery and pub. health Cornell U. Med. Sch., 1985—2000; dir. emergency medicine NY Presbyn. Hosp., 1989—97; dir. Le Fleuve Inst., 2000—. Chairperson N.Y.C. Regional Coun., 1988—89, N.Y.C. Med. Adv. Com., 1981—97; med. dir. CVPH Emergency Care Ctr., 1997—2000, Noble Hosp., 2000—05; commr. pub. health St. Lawrence County, 2001—03; mem. adv. bd. WHO, 1985. Author: (textbooks) Medical Director's Handbook, 1989, Prehospital Systems and Medical Oversight, 2002. Chmn. Mayoral Transition (Health), NYC, 1993. Lt. col. USAR. Fellow ACS, Am. Coll. Emergency Dispatch (pres. 1994-99), Am. Coll. Emergency Physicians; mem. Nat. Assn. Emergency Med. Svc. Physicians (founding mem., bd. dirs. 1986-97. Stewart award 1991), Clinton County Med. Soc. (pres. 1998-2002), NYS Med. Soc. (defence bd. 2002-08), NYS Health Dept. Office Profl. Med. Conduct (bd. 2007-), Pub. Health Honor Soc. Johns Hopkins U. Home: 1705 Dunes Club Pl Fernandina Beach FL 32034-6671 Office Phone: 315-287-2056. E-mail: alexanderkuehl@msn.com.

KUEHN, KURT P., delivery service executive; BA, Yale Univ.; MBA, Univ. Miami. Mgmt. positions UPS, Atlanta, 1997—, facilities planning mgr., 1986, mgr. strategic cost dept., 1996, v.p. bus. info. analysis, v.p. investor rels., 1999—2003, sr. v.p. worldwide sales & mktg., 2004—07, CFO, 2007—. Office: UPS 55 Glendale Pky Atlanta GA 30328

KUEHNE, BENEDICT P., lawyer; b. Merced, Calif., Mar. 24, 1954; s. Ben and Jean T. K. BA cum laude, U. Miami, 1974; JD cum laude, 1977; postgrad., Fla. Atlantic U., 1979-81. Bar: Fla. 1977, D.C. 1978, U.S. Dist. Ct. (so. and mid. dists.) Fla. 1977, U.S. Dist. Ct. (so. dist.) Ala. 1983, U.S. Ct. Appeals (5th cir.) 1977, U.s. Ct. Appeals (4th cir.) 1980, U.S. Ct. Appeals (7th and 11th cir.) 1981, U.S. Ct. Appeals (9th and D.C. cirs.) 1982, U.S. Ct. Appeals (2nd cir.) 1984, U.S. Supreme Ct. 1981, Cert.fraud examiner. Asst. atty. gen. State of Fla., West Palm Beach, 1977-79; spl. asst. state atty. 15th Jud. Cir., 1978-90; sr. assoc. Bierman, Sonnett Shohat & Sale, P.A., Miami and Ft. Lauderdale, Fla., 1980-87; ptnr. Sonnet Sale & Kuehne, P.A., 1987-93, Sale & Kuehne, P.A., 1993—; spl. counsel Fla. Atty. Gen., 1995—97, Law Office Benedict P. Kuehne, P.A., 2007—; nat. counsel Gore-Lieberman Recount, 2000. Adj. instr. law U. Miami, 1987-88, Miami Dade Cmty. Coll., 1987-89; lectr. in field. Contbr. articles to profl. jours. Cmty. organizer United Way, 1987; mem. adv. bd. U. Miami Moot Ct., 1987-90; bd. dris. Dem. Forum, Fla., 1987—92, Legal Svcs. Greater Miami, Inc., 1992-98; gen. counsel Fla. Young Dems., 1986-87, pres., 1986-87; pres. Dade County Young Dems., Fla., 1982-83, bd. dirs., 1983-84; spl. counsel Biden for Pres. Campaign, 1987; dep. counsel Dade County Democratic Exec. Com., 1989-95; mem. exec. com. Alliance for Ethical Govt., 1998—2003. Named one of Outstanding Young Mem of Am., Nat. Jaycees, 1980, 82, People for Am. Way Spirit of Liberty award, 2006. Mem. Fla. Bar (bd. govs. 2004-08, exec. coun. criminal law sect., chair 1994-95, chair criminal cert. com. 1990-93, appelate cert. com. 1995—, chair, coun. section, 2000-01), Fla. Criminal Def. Attys. Assn. (chmn. brief bank com., Cert. of Merit 1984), Pub. Interest Law Bank (Award of Merit 1984), Dade County Bar Assn. (pres. 1998-99, Named One Of Criminal Justice Lawyers of Yr., 2001), Fla. Assn. Criminal Def. Lawyers (charter mem., bd. dirs., pres. 1990-91, Founder's award, 2003), Greater Miami Jewish Fedn. (atty.'s divsn.), U. Miami Iron Arrow Honor Soc., Metro-Miami Action Plant Trust (parliamentarian 1998—), Nat. Eagle Scout Assn., U. Miami Law Alumni Assn. (pres. 1992-93, Thomas Davison svc. award 1985, 98), U. Miami Gen. Alumni Assn. (bd. dirs. 1987, pres. 1995—96, Outstanding Law Alumnus award 1989, Outstanding Svc. award 1989, bd. trustees 1994—98), Coconut Grove Assn. (bd. dirs. 1982—). Home: PO Box 13620 Miami FL 33101-3620 Office: Law Office Of Kim L 1 Financial Plz Ste 2500 Fort Lauderdale FL 33394-0007 Business E-Mail: ben.kuehne@kuehnelaw.com.

KUEMPEL, JOHN, state legislator; s. Edmund and Roberta; m. Michelle Kuempel; 2 children. B, U. Tex., Austin. Salesman Commercial Metals Co., Seguin; hon. game warden Tex. Parks & Wildlife; mem. Dist. 44 Tex. House of Representatives, 2010—. Mem.: NRA, Tex. Farm Bureau, Seguin Rotary Club. Office: Room E1.208 Capitol Extension PO Box 2910 Austin TX 78768 Mailing: 523 E Donegan #102 Seguin TX 78155 Office Phone: 830-379-8732, 512-463-0602.

KUHLMANN-WILSDORF, DORIS, materials scientist, inventor, retired educator; b. Bremen, Germany, Feb. 15, 1922; 1956, naturalized, 1963; d. A. Friedrich and Elsa S. (Dreyer) K.; m. Heinz G.F. Wilsdorf, Jan. 4, 1950; children: Gabriele (dec.), Michael (dec.). BS in Physics, U. Göttingen, Germany, 1944, MS, 1946, PhD in Materials Sci., 1947; DSc in Physics-Materials Sci., U. Witwatersrand, South Africa, 1954; DSc in Physics (hon.), U. Pretoria, South Africa, 2004. Postdoctoral fellow U. Göttingen, 1947-48; postdoctoral fellow in physics U. Bristol, Eng., 1949-50; lectr. physics U. Witwatersrand, Johannesburg, 1950-56; from assoc. prof. metall. engring. to prof. U. Pa., Phila., 1957-63; prof. engring. physics U. Va., Charlottesville, 1963-66, univ. prof. applied sci., 1966—2005; prof. emeritus, 2005—. Founder, owner, Kuhlman-Wilsdorf Motors LLC; inventor in field. Editor: 4 materials sci. books; contbr. 300 articles to profl. jours. Recipient J. Shelton Horsley award Va. Acad. Sci., 1966, Americanism medal DAR, 1966, Heyn medal German Metall. Soc., 1988, Achievement award Soc. Women Engrs., 1989, Ragnar Holm Sci. Achievement award IEEE, 1991. Fellow Am. Soc. Materials Internat. (life, Edward DeMille Campbell Meml. lectr. 2002), Am. Phys. Soc.; mem. Am. Soc. Women Engrs. (life), Am. Soc. Engring. Edn. (medal for excellence 1965, 66), AIME Metall. Soc. (life), Nat. Acad. Engring. 10 patents in field. Business E-Mail: dwilsdorf@embarqmail.com.

KUHN, FREDERICK ADAIR, otolaryngologist, educator; married; 7 children. MD, Univ. of Okla., 1966. Resident Barnes Hosp. Wash. Univ., St. Louis, 1972; adj. prof. otolaryngology Univ. of NC, Univ. of Okla. Sch. of Medicine, 1974—91; dir. founder Ga. Nasal and Sinus Inst., Savannah, Ga., 1999; prof. surgery otolaryngology Med. Coll. of Ga., 1991; with sinus surgery dept. Meml. Univ. Med. Ctr., 1995. Invited lectr. Johns Hopkins, Harvard Univ., Univ.of Pa., Stanford Univ., Cleve. Clinic, Royal Coll. of Medicine, London. Maj. med. US Army, 1972—74. Recipient Cottle award, Am. Rhinologic Soc., The Golden Head Mirror award, The Am. Rhinologic Soc., The Gerald S. Gussac award, The Ga. Soc. of Otolaryngology Head and Neck Surgery; named one of the Best Doctors in America, 1994—, America's most outstanding clinicians and tchrs. Mem.: Am. Broncho-Esophagological Assn., Am. Acad.of Otolaryngology Head and Neck Surgery, Am. Rhinologic Soc. (bd. dirs., pres.). Office: Georgia Nasal and Sinus Institute 4750 Waters Ave Ste 112 Savannah GA 31404 Office Phone: 912-355-1070. Office Fax: 912-355-9773.

KUHN, NICHOLAS JOHN, mathematics professor; b. Bryn Mawr, Pa., Feb. 15, 1955; s. Harold W. and Estelle R. Kuhn; m. Beth A. Swanson; children: Michael A., Jeremy D., Emily R. BA in Math., Princeton U., NJ, 1976; MS in Math., U. Chgo., 1977, PhD in Math., 1980. Assoc. prof. math. U. Va., Charlottesville, 1986—91, prof. math., 1991—; asst. prof. math. Princeton U.; acting asst. prof. math. U. Wash., Seattle. Vis. fellow DPMMS Cambridge U., England, 1986—87, vis. prof. math., 2006; vis. prof. Math. Scis. Rsch. Inst., Berkeley, Calif., 1989; vis. prof. math. CNRS and U. Paris 13, Paris, 1994—95, U. Chgo., 2000. Contbr. scientific papers in field. Grantee Rsch. award, CNRS, 1995, SERC, 1986—87; fellow, Sloan Found., 1985—87. Fellow: Am. Math. Soc.; mem.: MAA. Office: Univ Va Kerchof Hall Dept Math Charlottesville VA 22904-4137

KUHN, WILLIS EVAN, II, lawyer, mediator; b. Indpls., July 20, 1948; s. Theodore Roosevelt and Theresa Anne (Lupinacci) K.; m. Virginia Katherine Williams, Apr. 12, 1983; children: William Franklin, Virginia Anne. BA, Vanderbilt U., 1970; JD with honors, U. Tex., 1973. Bar: Tex. 1973; cert. mediator. Assoc. Johnson & Gibbs, Dallas, 1973-75, Moore & Peterson, Dallas, 1975-80; ptnr. Baker, Smith & Mills, Dallas, 1980-85, Kuhn & Fishman, Dallas, 1985-90, Hopkins & Sutter, Dallas, 1990-93; pvt. practice Dallas, 1993—. Mem. Dallas So. Meml. Assn., 1992—. Mem. State Bar Tex., Dallas Bar Assn., Dallas Athletic Club, Order of Coif, Phi Kappa Psi. Republican. Avocations: golf, history. Office: 15851 N Dallas Pkwy #600 Dallas TX 75001-6030 Home: 6062 Jereme Trl Dallas TX 75252-5130 Office Phone: 214-642-3268.

KUKURA, RITA ANNE, pre-school educator, counselor; b. Tulsa, July 18, 1947; d. James Albert and Carmen Alberta (Parsons) Hayden; m. Joel Richard Graft, Oct. 28, 1967 (dec. Apr. 1969); m. Raymond Richard Kukura, Dec. 18, 1971 (div. 1981); children: Tiffany Carmen Noel, Austin Raymond. BS, Kent. State U., 1971; MS, Okla. State U., 1991. Cert. early childhood, nursery, elem. tchr., Okla., spl. edn. tchr. for emotionally disturbed. Tchr. kindergarten Southlyn Elem. Sch., Lyndhurst, Ohio, 1971-73; elem. tchr. Wakefield Acad., Tulsa, 1981-83, tchr. kindergarten, 1983-87; reg. early intervention coord. Okla. Dept. Edn., Tulsa, 1990-92; tchr. devel. delayed children, coord. integrated program Child Devel. Inst. Children's Med. Ctr., Tulsa, 1992-93; tchr. elem. sch. Prue Schs., 1993; early childhood tchr. Tulsa Pub. Schs., 1995—2006, counselor, 2006—. Manuscript reviewer for profl. orgns., 1989-91; mem. human rights com. Ind. Opportunities of Okla., 1995—; Oklahoma Edn. Assn. Leadership Acad., 1998; del. Okla. Edn. Assembly, 1995; grant reviewer for spl. grants State Dept. Edn., 1996; co-chair Tulsa Hispanic Resource Assn., 2007-; presenter and lectr. in field. Den leader Cub Scouts Am., Tulsa, 1984-88; com. mem. Boy Scouts Am., Tulsa, 1984-88; vol. office worker Met. Tulsa Citizen Crime Commn., 1986; adv. com. Latchkey Project, Tulsa County, 1985; ad hoc task force on day care Interagy. Coord. Coun., 1989-91; nat. rep. Tourette Syndrome Assn. to Nat. Broadcasting Assn. AERho, 1990-93; mem. resource com. Ronald McDonald House, 1990-92, vol. Tulsa area, 1991-97, STARBASE, 1993—, Drug Edn. for Youth, 1994; mem. adv. bd. Tulsa Regional Coordinating Coun. for Svcs. to Children and Youth and Families, 1991-92; planning com. symposium Magic Coun. Girl Scouts Am., 1991-93; lt. sr. mem. Tulsa Composite Squadron CAP, 1992-94; presenter numerous confs.; workshop participant Alternatives to Violence Project, 1996. Recipient Den Leader Tng. award Boy Scouts Am., 1988, State Commendation medal Air N.G., 1993. Mem. AAUW (bd. dirs. Tulsa county chpt. 1991-93, mem., 1997-2000, 2003), Nat. Assn. Early Childhood Tchr. Educators, Nat. Tourette Syndrome Assn. (state pres. 1987-92, state dir. 1992-93, hon. mem. bd. dirs. 1993, area coord., fundraiser 1988-90), Gold Star Wives Am., Tulsa Classroom Tchrs. Assn. (bldg. del. 1997-98), Okla. Edn. Assn. (leadership acad. 1998), Okla. Edn. Assn. (mem. resolution com. 1998-2000), Task Force Tulsa Pub. Schools, Kappa Delta Pi, Omicron Nu, Alpha Epsilon Rho (hon. mem. S.W. region 1990-93), Phi Delta Kappa. Roman Catholic. Avocations: piano, exercising, reading. Office Phone: 918-746-9480. Business E-Mail: kukurri@tulsaschools.org.

KUMAR, PRADEEP, physics professor, researcher; b. Allahabad, Up, India, Jan. 1, 1949; s. Kali Shankar and Shanti Devi; m. Diana Lynn Tonnessen, Oct. 30, 1987; children: Casey Alok, Vijay Alexander, Ravi Armand. PhD, U. Calif., La Jolla, 1973. Asst. prof. U. So. Calif., LA, 1977—78, U. Fla., Gainesville, 1979—83, assoc. prof., 1983—93, prof., 1993—. Guest prof. NORDITA, Copenhagen, 1978—79, HUT Helsinki, 1984. Home: 2390 NW 18th Place Gainesville FL 32605 Office: University of Florida PO Box 118440 Gainesville FL 32611-8440 Office Phone: 352-392-6690. Office Fax: 352-846-0295; Home Fax: 352-379-8781. Personal E-mail: pkumar@ufl.edu.

KUMBLE, STEVEN JAY, lawyer; b. July 3, 1933; m. Barbara Kumble (div.); children: Charles Todd, Roger Glenn; m. Peggy Basten Vandervoort (div.); m. Angela Marie Giguere. BA, Yale U., 1954; JD, Harvard U., 1959; LLD (hon.), LI U., 1990. Bar: NY 1960. Ptnr. Finley, Kumble, Wagner, Underberg, Manley & Casey, NYC, 1968-87; of counsel Summit Rovins & Feldesman, NYC, 1988-90; chmn. bd. dirs. Lincolnshire Mgmt., Inc., NYC, 1985—2004; chmn., bd. dirs. Corinthian Capital Group, LLC, 2005—. Mem. adv. bd. Inst. Civil Justice, Rand, 1999—2005; mem. dean's adv. bd. Harvard Law Sch., 2006—. Vice chmn. bd. dirs. LI U., Greenvale, NY, 1984—; chmn. 1982-94, trustee bd. Gov.'s Com. Scholastic Achievement, NYC, 1981-. 1st lt. US Army, 1955—57. Mem. Assn. of Bar of City of NY, Harvard Club, Wanumetonomy Golf Club (Newport, RI), Yale Club, Breakers Golf Club (Palm Beach), Phi Beta Kappa. Avocations: skiing, golf. Office Phone: 212-920-2300. Business E-Mail: skumble@corinthiancap.com.

KUMP, LARRY D., state legislator, political scientist, public ethics advocate; b. Chambersburg, Pa., Jan. 27, 1948; s. Willis' Theodore and Betty Ann (Steinbach) Kump; m. Carolyn Anne Daniels Kump, Dec. 3, 1976 (div. Sept. 1979); children: David Christopher, Sarah Elizabeth. Student, Hagerstown Jr. Coll., 1965—68; AA, Hagerstown CC, 1991; BS in Polit. Sci., Frostburg State U., 1970; postgrad., U. Md., 1974, Ind. U., 1980. CPA. Mediator, case mgr. Md. Correctional Profl. Staff Acad. Prison, ct. expert witness, employee tng. coord., cognitive thinking trainer, employee critical incident stress counselor; chief exec. asst. to the minority leader Pa. State Senate, 1972; labor rels. rep. Md. Classified Employees Assn., 1972—78; exec. dir. Ind. State Employees Assn., Indpls., 1978—89; pres. Palladin Assocs., 1989—; mem. Dist. 52 W.Va. House of Delegates, 2011—. Guest lectr. labor rels. Ind. U., 1981—; vol. arbitrator Better Bus. Bur., 1982—; Rep. candidate Md. House Dels., 1974; rep. vice precinct committeeman, Indpls., 1981; bd. dirs. Hoosiers Consumer Rights; mem. Marion County Exec. Com. Libertarian Party, 1982—83; leader Found. for Advancement for Idsl. Rsch. Elder Mormon Ch. Named Hon. Order Ky. Cols., 1984. Mem.: Found. Advancement Indsl. Rsch. (bd. dirs.), Am. Soc. Pub. Adminstrs. (pres. elect. Ind. chpt.), Am. Arbitration Assn. (arbitrator), Ind. Fiscal Policy Inst., Ind. Mental Health Assn. (mem. pub. policy com.), Ind. Coun. Econ. Edn., Assembly Govtl. Employees (pres. ctrl. region, nat. bd. 1978—85), Ind. State Employees Assn. (exec. dir.), Md. Classified Employees Assn. (labor rels. specialist), White River Yacht Club (bd. dirs.). Republican. Home and Office: PO Box 1131 Falling Waters WV 25419-1131 Office: WVa House of Delegates Rm 6R Bldg 1 1900 Kanawha Blvd E State Capitol Complex Charleston WV 25305 Office Phone: 304-340-3122. Business E-Mail: larry.kump@wvhouse.gov.

KUNDA, DOLORES A., advertising executive; b. 1956; BA in English Lit., Smith Coll., 1977; MBA in Mktg., Northwestern U., 1984. Exec. v.p. Leo Burnett USA, 1984—; account exec. JWT, 1986—87; account dir. Leo Burnett Mexico, 1990—92; founder, pres., CEO Lápiz Hispanic Marketing/Advertising, 1999—; pres. Leo Burnett PR, 2007—. Bd. dirs. Lenox Group Inc, 2006—09, The Finish Line, Inc., 2008—. Spkr. in field. Recipient Outstanding Achievement Award, Hispanic comm. by Hispanic mag., 2004; named Chgo. Hispanic Hero, Chgo. Fire Soccer Franchise, 2003, 2004, Woman of the Year, Chgo. Advt., 2007; named a Woman to Watch, Crain's Chgo. Bus., 2007; named one of The Top Latinas in the US, Hispanic Bus. mag., 2004, Vanidades mag., 2004. Office: Leo Burnett Puerto Rico Hato Ray Tower, Ste 2200 San Juan PR 00918 Office Phone: 312-220-5959. Office Fax: 312-220-3259. Business E-Mail: dolores.kunda@lapizusa.com.

KUNDE, GERALD RALPH, II, food service executive; b. Nuremberg, Germany, July 12, 1965; s. Gerald Ralph and Patricia Jean (Perdue) K.; m. Patria Shawn Smith, Mar. 2, 1991. BA, U. Fla., 1987; MPA, George Washington U., 1989. Spl. asst. coalitions Dole for Pres., Washington, 1987-88; legis. intern Fed. Home Loan Mortgage Corp., Washington, 1988-89; rsch. specialist Nat. Assn. Realtors, Washington, 1989-90, legis. analyst, 1990, dir. fin. instns., 1991, 1991-92; exec. v.p. Connecticut Association Realtors, Hartford, 1992—97; v.p. govt. and state affairs Grocery Manufacturers of America, 1997—2003; sr. v.p., legis. and econ. affairs Internat. Dairy Foods Assn., 2003—07; v.p., govt. rels. Darden Restaurants, Inc., 2007—. Office: Darden Restaurants Inc 1000 Darden Center Dr Orlando FL 32837-4032 Office Phone: 407-245-4000. Office Fax: 407-245-4989. Business E-Mail: ckunde@darden.com.

KUNG, PANG-JEN, materials scientist, electrical engineer; b. I-Lan, Taiwan, May 13, 1959; s. Ching-Yu and A-Se (Yu) K.; m. Tzyy-Yun Tzeng, May 18, 1986; children: Naihau, Naiwei. MSChemE, Nat. Tsing Hua U., 1983; MSEE, Auburn U., 1988; MMetE, Carnegie Mellon U., 1991, PhD in Materials Sci., 1993; MBA, U. Conn., 1998. Registered profl. engr. Jr. engr. Tatung Co., Taipei, Taiwan, 1979—80; tchg. asst. Nat. Tsing Hua U., Hsin-Chu, Taiwan, 1981—82, rsch. asst., 1982—83; assoc. scientist Indsl. Tech. Res. Inst., Hsin-Chu, 1985—86; tchg. and rsch. asst. Auburn U., Ala., 1986—89; rsch. asst. Carnegie Mellon U., Pitts., 1989—91; staff rsch. asst. Los Alamos Nat. Lab., N.Mex., 1991—92, rsch. fellow, 1993—94; sr. scientist Advanced Fuel Rsch., Inc., East Hartford, Conn., 1995—98; chmn. Pioneer Techs., Inc., West Hartford, Conn., 1996—99; cons. InfiMed, Inc., Liverpool, NY, 1998—2000; product devel. engr. JDS Uniphase, Research Triangle Park, NC, 2001—02; pres. Optotrack, Inc., Cary, NC, 2002—. Chmn. acad. affairs Tatung Inst. Tech., Taipei, 1979-80; tech. info. editor Indsl. Tech. Rsch. Inst., Hsin-Chu, 1985-86; translator tech. articles Super Tech. Books Co., Taipei, 1986; prof. Strayer U., Cary, N.C., 2004—10; campus dean Strayer U., Raleigh, NC, 2010-. Author, editor: Unit Operations in Chemical Engineering, 1986; contbr. articles to profl. jours. 2nd lt. Chinese Air Force, 1983-85. Recipient Editor's Choice award Nat. Poetry Assn., 1989, 90; Am.-Chinese Engr. scholar Am.-Chinese Assn. Engrs., 1980; Liang Ji-Duan fellow Carnegie Mellon U., 1991, Dr. S. Irving Strayer award, Strayar U., 2013. Mem. AAAS, IEEE, SPIE, NSPE, Materials Rsch. Soc., Am. Vacuum Soc. (Tech. Paper award 1992), Acad. Am. Poets, Beta Gamma Sigma. Achievements include research in diamond thin films and high Tc superconductors; superconducting quantum interference devices and biomagnetic systems; surface characterization and microstructural analysis; ferroelectric devices, giant magnetoresistive sensors, high-speed microelectronics, epitaxial heterostructures, in-process monitors, pulsed laser deposition, thermal evaporation, sputtering; pyroelectric sensor arrays, gas sensors, plasma-enhanced chemical vapor deposition, x-ray imaging materials, digital radiography and fluoroscopy, microelectromechanical systems (MEMS); optical switches and waveguides; optical communication systems; nanotechnology, microfluidics, biol. and chem. assays. Office: Optotrack Inc PO Box 1242 Cary NC 27512 Home Phone: 919-434-5006; Office Phone: 919-267-3966. Business E-Mail: ckung@optotrack.com.

KUNIHIRO, JAMES J., marketing executive; BS in Mech. Engring., MIT; MBA, Harvard U. Dir., ops. Elastomeric Technologies, Inc.; design engr. Lutron Electronics; mgr., strategy Bain & Co., Inc.; dir., strategy and bus. devel. Pepsico, 2004—05; exec. v.p., strategy and mktg. Culligan Internat., 2005—08; sr. v.p., corp. strategy mktg.

Servicemaster Co., Servicemaster Global Holdings, 2008—. Office: The ServiceMaster Co 860 Ridge Lake Blvd Memphis TN 38120 Office Phone: 901-597-1400. Business E-Mail: Jim.Kunihiro@servicemaster.com.

KUNIHOLM, BRUCE ROBELLET, academic administrator, educator; b. Washington, Oct. 4, 1942; s. Bertel Eric and Berthe Eugenie (Robellet) K.; m. Elizabeth Fairbank, June 29, 1968; children: Jonathan, Erin. AB in English, Dartmouth Coll., 1964; MA in History, Duke U., 1972, MA in Pub. Policy Sci., 1976, PhD in History, 1976. Instr. English Robert Acad./Robert Coll., Istanbul, Turkey, 1964—67; fellow Coun. Fgn. Rels./NEH US Dept. State, Washington, 1979, internat. rels. officer policy planning staff, 1979—80; from instr. to prof. Duke U., Durham, NC, 1975—87, prof. pub. policy studies and history, 1987—, chmn. dept. public policy studies, 1989—94, 2005—09, dir. Terry Sanford Inst. Pub. Policy, 1989—94, 2005—09, dean Terry Sanford Sch. Pub. Policy, 2009—13; dean emeritus, 2013—. Vis. prof. Internat. Rels. Koc U., Istanbul, Turkey, 1995-96, 2002; vice-provost for acad. and internat. affairs, Duke U., Durham, 1996—2001; dir. Ctr. for Internat. Studies, 1999—2001; guest scholar Woodrow Wilson Internat. Ctr. Scholars, 1982; cons. NEH, USMC, Dept. State, U.S. Army, United Tech. Corp.; invited lectr. numerous orgns., colls., univs., fgn. countries including U.S. Senate Fgn. Rels.Com., CIA, State Dept., Chase Manhattan Bank, Harvard U., Brown U., Dartmouth Coll., Yale U., Princeton U., France, Eng., Germany, Italy, Kuwait, Saudi Arabia, Sudan, Can., Turkey, also others. Author: Origins of the Cold War in the Near East, 1980 (Stuart L. Bernath prize 1981), The Persian Gulf and United States Policy, 1984, The Palestine Problem and United States Policy, 1986; contbr. articles to profl. jours.; contbr. chpts. books. Bd. dirs., chmn. acad. com. Found. for Ednl. Exch. between Can. and US, 2000-05; exec. com. Assn. Profl. Schs. Internat. Affairs, 2006-10; ednl. adv. bd. Govt. Accountability Office, 2005-13. Capt. USMC, 1967—71, Vietnam. Decorated Bronze Star with V device; Navy Achievement medal, Stuart Bernath prize, 1981, Disting. Tchg. award Trinity Coll., Duke U., 1989; rsch. grantee Harry S. Truman Libr., 1984, Duke U. Rsch. Coun., 1985-86, Inst. Turkish Studies, 1986-87, travel grantee Ctr. Soviet and East European Studies, 1991; Fulbright sr. rsch. fellow, Turkey, 1986-87, Woodrow Wilson Internat. Ctr. Scholars fellow Smithsonian Instn., 1986-87, sr. fellow Nobel Inst., Oslo, 1994, Harmsworth-Duke fellow Oxford U., 2014. Mem. Am. Hist. Assn., Fulbright Fellows, Coun. Fgn. Rels., Orgn. Am. Historians, Soc. Historians Am. Fgn. Rels., Mid. East Inst., Mid. East Studies Assn., Internat. Inst. Strategic Studies, Phi Beta Kappa. Democrat. Avocations: triathlons, banjo, wine. Office: Terry Sanford Sch of Pub Policy Box 90239 Durham NC 27708-0239 Office Phone: 919-613-7341. Business E-Mail: bruce.kuniholm@duke.edu.

KUNIK, MARK EDWIN, geriatric psychiatrist, educator; BA in Psychology with honors, U. Tex., 1979—82; MD, Baylor U., 1983—87; MPH, U. Tex., 2000. Diplomate Am. Bd. Psychiatry and Neurology, 1993, Am. Bd. Psychiatry and Neurology-geriatric psychiatry, 2000. Intern/resident in psychiatry Baylor Coll. of Medicine, 1987—91, asst. prof. dept. of psychiatry & behavioral sciences, 1992—99, assoc prof. dept. of medicine, 2002—, assoc. prof. Menninger dept. of psychiatry & behavioral sciences, 1999—2007, prof. Menninger dept. of psychiatry & behavioral sciences, 2007—; fellow in geriatric psychiatry western psychiatrict inst. and clinic Univ. Pitts. Sch. of Medicine, 1991—92; dir. geropsychiatry svc. Veterans Affairs Med. Ctr., 1993—99; physician investigator Houston Veterans Affairs Med. Ctr. Houston Ctr. for Quality of Care & Utilization Studies, 1999—; dir. south ctrl. spl. fellowship in advanced psychiatry Mental Illness Rsch., Edn., and Clin. Ctr. (MIRECC), 2001—, assoc. dir. rsch. tng., 2004—; assoc. dir. & chief, health svcs. delivery & orgn. Houston Ctr. for Quality of Care & Utilization Studies Michael E. DeBakey Veterans Affairs Med. Ctr., 2003—, co-chief edn. & mentoring, 2007—08; asst. prof. dept. of psychiatry Houston Health Sci. Ctr. Univ. Tex., 1993—2010, prof. dept. of psychiatry Houston Health Sci. Ctr., 2010—. Adjunct faculty clin. psychology program dept. of psychology Univ. Houston, 2007—. Recipient Dept. of Veterans Affairs award for Excellence in Mental Health Tchg., Houston VA Med. Ctr, 1999, Houston Ctr. for Quality of Care & Utilization Studies Spl. Recognition award for Leadership, Houston VA Med. Ctr., 2000, Major Contbr. award, MIRECC, 2001, South Ctrl. Mental Illness Rsch. Edn. & Clin. Ctr. Edn. award, 2004, Excellence in Rsch. award, 2010, VA Spl. Contbn. award, 2002, Fulbright & Jaworski LLP Excellence award, Baylor Coll. of Medicine, 2005; named Best Doctors in America, 1996—97, 2000—01, 2003—10, Best Doctors in Houston, 2004, Tex. Super Doctors, 2010. Office: Michael E DeBakey Veterans Affairs Medical Center 2002 Holcombe Blvd Houston TX 77030 Office Phone: 719-794-8601. Office Fax: 719-748-7359. E-mail: kunik.marke@va.gov, mkunik@bcm.edu.*

KUNKLE, DAVID M., former police chief; b. Nov. 13, 1950; BS, U. Tex., Arlington, 1976, MA, 1994. With Dallas Police Dept., 1972—82; police chief City of Grand Prairie, Tex., 1982—85, Arlington Police Dept., Tex., 1985—99, Dallas Police Dept., 2004—10; dep. city mgr. City of Arlington, 1999—2004; exec. in residence W.E. Caruth Jr. Police Inst. (CPI), U. North Tex., Dallas, 2010—. Office: WW Caruth Jr Police Institute University of North Texas 7300 Houston School Rd Dallas TX 75241

KUNTZ, EDWARD LAWRENCE, healthcare executive; b. Phila., Feb. 22, 1945; s. Samuel J. and Mary S. (Shulman) K.; m. Caroline L. Lessner, Aug. 3, 1969; m. Stuart M., David M., Beth. BA, Temple U., 1966, JD, 1969, ML, 1978. Pvt. practice, Phila., 1970-78; asst. gen. counsel ARA Svcs., Phila., 1978-79, sector counsel, 1979-84, assoc. gen. counsel, 1984-85; exec. v.p. ARA Living Ctrs., Houston, 1985-92; chmn., CEO Living Ctrs. Am., Houston, 1992-97, Vencor Inc. (now Kindred Healthcare), Louisville, 1999—2003; pres. Kindred Healthcare, Louisville, 1999—2002; chmn. of bd. Kindred Healthcare, Inc., Louisville, 2004—. Dir. Alzheimer's Assn., Houston, 1993—; advisor Woodway Fin. Group, Houston, 1994—; mem. com. Am. Health Care Assn., Washington, 1986—. Co-chmn. fundraising campaign United Way, Med. Ctr., Houston, 1993; bd. dirs. Alley Theater, 1994-97, mem. facilities com., 1994; bd. trustees, adminstrv. and pers. com. Enamu-El, 1996-97. Mem. Thyroid Soc. of Houston (bd. dirs., vice chmn. 1995—), Am. Health Care Assn. (chmn. multifacility steering com., bd. dirs., exec. com., long term financing task force 1997, former mem. numerous coms.), Alzheimer's Assn. (bd. dirs. 1992-97), Thyroid Soc. (vice chmn. bd. dirs., chmn. fund devel. 1996, chmn. bd. 1997), Anti-Defamation League (bd. dirs. 1996-97). Home: 8807 Stable Crest Blvd Houston TX 77024-7035 Office: Kindred Healthcare 680 S Fourth St Louisville KY 40202

KUNZE, OTTO ROBERT, retired agricultural engineering educator; b. Warda, Tex., May 27, 1925; s. John Paul and Hermine Amanda (Moerbe) K.; m. Alice Ruth Eifert, Aug. 5, 1951; children: Glenn, Allen, Charles, Karen. BS, Tex. A&M U., College Station, 1950; MS, Iowa State U., Ames, 1951; PhD, Mich. State U., East Lansing, 1964. Registered profl. engr., Tex. Agrl. and indsl. engr. Ctrl. Power and Light Co., San Benito, Tex., 1951-56; rsch. asst. agrl. engring. dept. Mich. State U., East Lansing, 1961-64; assoc. prof. agrl. engring. dept. Tex. A&M U., College Station, 1956-61, 64-69, prof. agrl. engring. dept., 1969-90, prof. emeritus agrl. engring. dept., 1990—. Vis. prof. Nanjing (China) Coll. Food, Grain and Oil Econs., 1993; lectr. Tsukuba U., Japan, 1993; cons. and vis. prof. Nat. Chung Hsing U. in Taichung and Nat. Taiwan U. in Taipei, Taiwan, 1994; lectr., cons. Internat. Conf. on Grain Drying in Asia, Bangkok, Thailand, 1995; engring. cons. Advanced Dryer Sys., Inc., Alachua, 1997, Farmers Rice Coop., Sacramento, 1992, Post Harvest Process and Food Engring. Ctr., G.B. Pant U., Pantnagar, India, 1985, Rice Process Engring. Ctr., Indian Inst. Tech., Kharagpur, 1975, Rice Tec, Alvin, Tex., 1996; lectr. on rice harvesting Asian Productivity Orgn., Taichung, Taiwan, 1985, 87; lectr. U. PR, Mayaguez, 1990; keynote spkr. PR sect. Am. Soc. Agrl. Engrs., Añasco, 1990; publ. coord. Rice Tech. Working Group, 1976-90. Contbr. chpts. to 7 books, over 100 articles to profl. jours. Mem. A&M Consol. Bd. Equalization, College Station, 1969-71; mem. Tex. Air Control Bd., Austin, 1979-90; mem. pediatric scholarship com. M.D. Anderson Cancer Ctr., Houston, 1990-2006. With US Army, 1944-46, ETO. Decorated 2 Bronze Stars; recipient Outstanding Svc. award Rice Tech. Working Group, 1990, Outstanding Agrl. Engring. achievement 20th Century, 2000; Faculty fellow NSF, 1961-62, Sponsor Rice Rsch. fellowship, Tex. A & M U., 2012. Fellow Am. Soc. Agrl. Engrs. (tech. dir., numerous coms.), Am. Assn. Cereal Chemists (assoc. editor), Sigma Xi (sec. 1969-70, chmn. 1970-71), Phi Kappa Phi (pub. rels. officer 1984-85). Lutheran.

KUO, MACUS TIEN, science educator, cancer researcher; arrived in Taiwan, 1978, naturalized; s. Sun-Chi and Poo-Jong Kuo; m. Yuh-Jyh Chen; 1 child, Emily. PhD in Biomed. Sci., U. Tex. Grad. Sch., Houston, 1973. Prof. M.D. Anderson Cancer Ctr., U. Tex., Houston, 1993, 1997—. Contbr. more than 120 sci. articles to profl. jours. 1st lt. Chinese Army, 1968—69, Chung-Li, Taiwan. Grantee Prin. Investigators, Nat. Cancer Inst., 1979—. Mem.: Am. Assn. Cancer Rsch. Office: Univ Texas MD Anderson Cancer Ctr 7425 Fannin Blvd Houston TX 77054

KUPER, DEBRA E., lawyer, manufacturing executive; b. 1965; m. Alberto Fornaro; children: Aaron, Luke. BA, U. Wis., 1993; JD, Marquette U., 1997. Corp. counsel, asst. sec. Tenneco Automotive, Lake Forest, Ill.; asst. gen. counsel global procurement Wal-Mart Stores Inc., Bentonville, Ark., 2005, assoc. gen. counsel; sr. corp. counsel Caterpillar Inc., Peoria, Ill., 2006—08; v.p., gen. counsel, corp. sec. AGCO Corp., Duluth, Ga., 2008—. Office: AGCO Corp 4205 River Green Parkway Duluth GA 30096 Office Phone: 770-813-9200. Office Fax: 770-813-6118.

KUPKE, KENNETH G., neonatalogist; MD, Duke U., 1984. Diplomate Am. Bd. Pediatrics, 1999, Am. Bd. Pediatrics-neonatal-perinatal medicine, 2006, cert. in clin. genetics 2006. Resident pediat. Children's Hosp., 1984—87, fellow clin. genetics, 1987—89, fellow neonatal-perinatal medicine, 1989—91; med. dir. newborn ICU Northside Hosp.; hosp. affiliations include Northside Hosp, Children's Healthcare, Atlanta. Mem.: Phi Beta Kappa. Office: Northside Hospital 1000 Johnson Ferry Rd NE Atlanta GA 30342-1611 Office Phone: 404-851-8000.

KURITA, ROSALIND, state legislator; m. George Kurita. State senator Dist. 22, Tenn., 1997—; businesswoman. Democrat. Office: 211 Deerwood Rd Clarksville TN 37043 Office Phone: 615-368-0182. Fax: 615-358-0040. E-mail: sen.rosalind.kurita@legislature.state.tn.us.

KURKUL, WEN WANG, musician, educator, administrator; b. Taipei, Taiwan, Oct. 30, 1964; arrived in U.S., 1986; d. Shih-Ming and Hsieh-Chu Wang. MusM, Ohio U., 1988; MusD, U. Mo., 1995; D in Music Edn., Ind. U., 2000; MBA, U. Md., 2009. Prof., adminstr. Sch. Music Tainan (Taiwan) Woman's Coll. Arts & Tech., 1989—92; prof. Nat. Taiwan Acad. Arts, 1989—92, Nat Sun Yat-Sen U., Kaohsiung, Taiwan, 1990-92; vis. faculty Sch. Music Ind. U., Bloomington, 1999—2000; prof. dept. music George Mason U., 2000—03, dir. music edn. dept. music Coll. Visual and Performing Arts, 2001—03, exec. dir. Orff Schulwerk Tchr. Tng. and Cert. Program, 2001—03; prof. dept. music Montgomery Coll., 2004—07, music dir., condr. symphony orch.; founder, exec. dir. Empowered to Excel program Montgomery Coll and Montgomery County Pub. Schs. Symphony Orch. Partnership Program, 2005—06. Music dir., condr. Montgomery Coll. Symphony Orch. Soloist-in-residence Nat. Chiang Kai Shek Cultural Ctr., Taipei, 1991-94; flutist Asian Composers League, Taipei, 1990-92; asst. prin. flutist Taiwan Symphony Orch., Taichung, 1984-86; founder, dir. Empowered to Excel, Montgomery Coll. and Montgomery Pub. Schs. Symphony Orch. Partnership Program, 2005-06; contbr. articles to profl. jours. Chair Aisan Bus. Initiative Reno-Sparks C. of C., 2007—; co-founder, chmn., CEO K Exec. Group LLC, 2009—. Nat. Art and Sci. Coun. scholar, Taiwan, 1989-92; Nat. Rsch. grant Ministry of Edn., Taiwan, 1989-92; named New Performing Star of Yr. Nat. Theatre and Concert Hall Planning and Mgmt. Coun., Taiwan, 1991. Mem.: APA, AAUP, Nat. Assn. Student Personnel Adminstrs., Nat. Assn. Student Affairs Profls., Internat. Soc. Philosophy Music Edn. (founding), Pub. Rels. Soc. Am., Am. Edml. Rsch. Assn., Am. Orff-Schulwerk Assn., Internat. Soc. for Music Edn. (Eng.), European Recorder Tchrs. Assn., Soc. for Rsch. in Music Edn., Music Edn. Nat. Conf., Coll. Music Soc., Nat. Flute Assn. (life), Am. Symphony Orch. League, Phi Kappa Phi, Phi Kappa Lambda. Home: 16238 Hwy 620 Ste F #225 Austin TX 78717 Personal E-mail: wen.kurkul@gmail.com.

KURLANSKY, PAUL ALAN, cardiovascular and thoracic surgeon; b. Hartford, Conn., Oct. 14, 1952; s. Philip and Roslyn (Solomon) K.; m. Helaine Schneuder, June 13, 1976; children: Aaron, Dylan. AB, Harvard U., 1975; MD, Tufts U., Boston, 1980. Diplomate Am. Bd. Surgery, Am. Bd. Thoracic Surgery. Intern Columbia U., NYC, 1980-81, residency, 1981-85, post doctoral rsch., 1985, cardiothoracic surgical residency, 1986-87; pvt. practice Miami, 1988—97; assoc. med. dir. Allied Health Group, 1998—99; dir. rsch. Miami Heart Rsch. Inst., 1999—. Presenter in field; contbr. articles to profl. jours. Recipient Disting. Recognition award, Spl. Recognition award, 1990, Honoree chmn, 1991, Outstanding Svc. in Profl. Edn., 1992, Am. Heart Assn.; named Honoree Physician award Bikkur Cholim, 1996. Fellow Am. Coll. Surgeons, Am. Coll. Chest Physicians, Am. Coll. Cardiology; mem. Soc. Thoracic Surgeons, Internat. Soc. Heart Transplantation, NY Acad. Sciences, Fla. Soc. Thoracic and Cardiovascular Surgeons, Dade County Med. Assn. Office: Miami Heart Rsch Inst 4770 Biscayne Blvd 5th Fl Miami FL 33137 Office Phone: 305-674-3154. Office Fax: 305-674-3009. E-mail: doctorwu18@aol.com.

KURTH, RONALD JAMES, retired academic administrator, military officer; b. Madison, Wis., July 1, 1931; s. Peter James and Celia (Kuehn) K.; m. Esther Charlene Schaefer, Dec. 21, 1954; children: Steven, Audrey, John, Douglas. BS, U.S. Naval Acad., 1954; MPA, Harvard U., 1961, PhD, 1970. Commd. ensign U.S. Navy, 1954, advanced through grades to rear adm., 1981; U.S. naval attache Moscow, 1975-77; comdg. officer NAS, Memphis at Millington, Tenn., 1977-79; mil. fellow Council Fgn. Relations, NYC, 1979-80; exec. asst. to dep. chief naval ops. Dept. Navy, Washington, 1980-81, dir. Pol-Mil Policy and Current Plans, 1981-83, dir. Long Range Planning Group, 1983-84; U.S. def. attache Moscow, 1985-87; pres. U.S. Naval War Coll., Newport, RI, 1987-90, Murray (Ky.) State U., 1990-94; dean acad. affairs Air War Coll., Maxwell AFB, Ala., 1994-98; pres. St. John's Northwestern Mil. Acad., Delafield, Wis., 1998—2004, pres. emeritus, 2004—. Teaching fellow Harvard U., Cambridge, Mass., 1969-70. Author: The Politics of Technological Innovation in the Navy, 1970. Former mem. nat. adv. bd. Boy Scouts Am. Decorated Def. D.S.M., Navy D.S.M., Legion of Merit with 2 gold stars, Meritorious Svc. medal with gold star. Mem. U.S. Naval Inst. (life), Naval War Coll. Found. (life), U.S. Naval Acad. Alumni, Harvard U. Alumni, Jacksonville Inst. Foreign Affairs. Episcopalian. Home: 5803 Fleet Landing Blvd Atlantic Beach FL 32233-7527 Personal E-mail: randckurth@verizon.net, randckurth@comcast.net.

KURTZ, JOSEPH EDWARD, archbishop; b. Mahanoy City, Pa., Aug. 18, 1946; s. George and Stella (Zmijewski) Kurtz. BA, St. Charles Borromeo Seminary, 1968, MDiv, 1972; MSW, Marywood Sch. Social Work, 1976. Ordained priest Diocese of Allentown, Pa., 1972, asst. dir. vocations Pa., 1973—76, diocesan dir. Cath. charities, 1988—98, diocesan coord. health affairs, 1994—98; asst. prof. Allentown Ctrl. Cath. HS, Pa., 1972; asst. pastor St. Joseph Parish, Limeport, Pa., 1972, SS. Simon & Jude Parish, Bethlehem, Pa., 1972—73; prof., counselor St. Pius X Seminary, Diocese of Scranton, Pa., 1973—76; asst. dir. Cath. Social Agency, 1976—84; exec. dir. Social Action Bureau, Diocese of Allentown, 1977—91; instr. De-Sales U. (formerly Allentown Coll. of St. Francis DeSales), Center Valley, Pa., 1978; instr. marriage and family therapy Mary Immaculate Seminary, Northampton, Pa., 1978—82; exec. dir. Cath. Social Agency and Family Life Bur., 1984—94; pastor St. Mary Parish, Catasauqua, Pa., 1988—96, Notre Dame of Bethlehem Parish, Pa., 1996—99; ordained bishop, 1999; bishop Diocese of Knoxville, Tenn., 1999—2007; archbishop Archdiocese of Louisville, 2007—. V.p. bd. dirs. Holy Family Manor, Bethlehem, Pa., 1985—99; bd. dirs. Sacred Heart Hosp., Allentown, Pa., 1988—99; personal rep. of bishop Pa. Cath. Conf., 1992—98; mem. Conception Seminary Bd. Regents, Mo., 2001—, North American Coll. Bd. Govs., 2004—; bd. mem. Catholic Relief Services, 2006—; v.p. US Conf. Catholic Bishops (USCCB), 2010—13, pres., 2013—. Mem.: Assn. Christian Denom. Leaders, Cath. Social Workers Nat. Assn. (hon.; Episcopal advisor 2007—). Roman Catholic. Office: Archdiocese of Louisville 212 E College St PO Box 1073 Louisville KY 40201 Office Phone: 502-585-3291. Office Fax: 502-585-2466.*

KURTZ, PAUL MICHAEL, retired law educator; b. Bronx, NY, Sept. 22, 1946; s. Louis and Helen (Mechanic) K. m. Carol Porter, June 6, 1971; 1 child, Benjamin. BA, Vanderbilt U., 1968, JD, 1972; LLM, Harvard U., 1974. Bar: Tenn. 1972, U.S. Ct. Appeals (6th cir.) 1973, U.S. Ct. Appeals (5th cir.) 1977, U.S. Supreme Ct. 1978. Law clk. to chief judge U.S. Ct. Appeals (6th cir.), 1972-73; instr. Boston U. Law Sch., 1973-74, Boston Coll. Law Sch., 1974-75; asst. prof. law U. Ga., Athens, 1975-78, assoc. prof., 1978-83, prof., 1983-94, assoc. dean, 1991—2013, J. Alton Hosch prof., 1994—2013. Vis. prof. U. Mo. Law Sch., 1982, Mercer Law Sch., 1984, U. Tex., 1986, Vanderbilt U., 1987; commr. on Uniform State Laws, 2001-; chair drafting com., Uniform Deployed Parents Custody and Visitation Act, 2009-12, chair drafting com., Uniform Recognition and Enforcement of Canadian Domestic Violence Protection Orders, 2013-, reporter Nat. Conf. Commrs. on Uniform State Laws, Com. on Interstate Family Support Act, Com. on Status of Children of Aided Conception, Ga. Supreme Ct. Com. on Indigent Def. Reform, 2000-03; exec. comm. Ga. Pub. Defender Stds. Coun., 2003-07; mem., 2008-09. Author: Criminal Offenses in Georgia, 1980, Family Law: Cases, Text, Problems, 1986, 5th edit., 2010; contbr. articles to profl. jours.; mem. editl. bd. Family Law Quar., 1983—. Mem. Am. Assn. Law Schs. (chmn. sect. family and juvenile law), ACLU, Am. Humane Assn. (bd. dirs. 1998-2004), Common Cause, Soc. Am. Law Tchrs., Am. Law Inst. (reporter 1995-96), Supreme Ct. Hist. Soc., Order of Coif, B'nai B'rith (Ga. state sec., pres. Athens lodge). Democrat. Avocations: reading, travel, bowling, politics. Home: 362 W Cloverhurst Ave Athens GA 30606-4212 E-mail: pmkurtz@uga.edu.

KURTZKE, JOHN FRANCIS, SR., neurologist, epidemiologist; b. Bklyn., Sept. 14, 1926; s. John Ambrose and Teresa Rose (Knipper) K.; m. Margaret Mary Nevin, June 30, 1950; children: John Francis Jr. (dec.), Catherine Kurtzke Brown, Elizabeth Kurtzke Siebert, Patricia Margaret(dec.), Joan Kurtzke Brennan, Robert, James, Christine Kurtzke Hughes. BS summa cum laude, St. John's U., NY, 1948; MD, Cornell U., Ithaca, NY, 1952; MD (hon.), U. Ferrara, Italy, 2000; med. diploma (hon.), U. degli Studi di Ferrara, Italy, 2008. Diplomate in neurology Am. Bd. Psychiatry and Neurology, 1958 (asst. examiner, then examiner and sr. examiner in neurology 1964-96, cert. appreciation 1969, 90). Intern Kings County Hosp., Bklyn., 1952—53; resident in neurology VA Hosp., Bronx, NY, 1953-56, chief neurology svc. Coatesville, Pa., 1956—63, Washington, 1963—95; chief neuroepidemiology sect. VA Med. Ctr., Washington, 1995—2002, cons. in neurology, 1995—, cons. in neuroepidemiology, 2002—; sr. cons. VA Multiple Sclerosis Ctr. Excellence East, Balt., 2004—. Mem. faculty Jefferson Med. Coll., Phila., 1958-63, asst. prof. clin. neurology, 1963; mem. faculty Georgetown Med. Sch., Washington, 1963—, prof. neurology, 1968-2000, prof. emeritus, 2000—, vice chmn. dept. neurology, 1976-95, prof. cmty. and family medicine, 1968-95; Disting. prof. neurology Uniformed Svcs., U. Health Scis., Bethesda, 1992—, USN med. student liaison officer, 1979-85; vis. prof. neurology and neuroepidemiology Temple U. Sch. Medicine, 1984-89; cons. neurology Nat. Naval Med. Ctr., Bethesda, 1966-2000, Surgeon Gen. Navy, 1970-97; mem. med. adv. bd. Nat. Multiple Sclerosis Soc., 1966-94, hon. mem., 1995—, mem. working group on design of clin. studies in multiple sclerosis, 1976-84, mem. exec. com., 1981-83, mem. task force on epidemiology, 2006—; mem. med. adv. bd. Internat. Fedn. Multiple Sclerosis Socs., 1972—, hon. mem., 1998—; mem. com. multiple sclerosis World Fedn. Neurology, 1967—, com. neuroepidemiology, 1977—; chmn. epidemiology sect. NIH Epilepsy Adv. Com., 1973-76; med. rsch. program specialist for neurology and neurobiology VA Rsch. Svc., 1977-80; chmn. work group epidemiology HEW Commn. Control of Huntington's Disease, 1976-78; mem. naval exam. bd. Naval Med. Command, 1980-83; mem. Residency Rev. Com. Neurology, 1983-88, vice chmn., 1985-86, chmn., 1987-88; chmn. US Naval Res. Med. Flag Coun., 1985-86; mem. instnl. rev. bd. Nat. Inst. Neurol. Diseases and Stroke, 1989-98; established investigator Nat. Multiple Sclerosis Soc., 1987—; mem. spl. panel Inst. Medicine, 1990; mem. oversight com. War-Related Illness and Injury Ctr., VAMC, Washington, 2002—; mem. oversight com. MS Ctrs. of Excellence, VA, 2003—; mem. Am. Com. Treatment and Rsch. in Multiple Sclerosis, L.Am. Com. on Treatment and Rsch. in Multiple Sclerosis, Consortium of Multiple Sclerosis Ctrs. Author, co-author: Epidemiology of Multiple Sclerosis, 1968, Epidemiology of Cerebrovascular Disease, 1969, Epidemiology of Neurologic and Sense Organ Disorders, 1973, Neuroepidemiology, 1998, Psychiatry/Neurology, 1998, Practice Questions. Book One, 1998, Psychiatry/Neurology, 1998, Book Two, 1998, Encyclopedia of the Neurological Disorders (Neuroepidemiology), 2003; mem. editl. bd. Neuroepidemiology, 1980—, Neurology, 1984-92, Stroke, 1986-2000, Jour. Clin. Epidemiology, 1988-2005, Jour. Neurol. Sci., 1990-96, Acta Neurologica Scandinavica, 1990-97; contbr. more than 570 articles to profl. jours., chpts. to books. Served with USN, 1944—46, rear adm. M.C. USNR, 1946—86, rear adm. USN ret., 1986—. Decorated Legion of Merit (2), Navy Commendation medal, Armed Forces Res. medal with gold hourglass, others; recipient cert. of merit, Surgeon Gen. Navy, 1969, Gold Bicennial medal, Georgetown U., 1982, Sec.'s Disting. Career award, Dept. Vets. Affairs, 1998, Dystel award for MS Rsch., NMSS, AAN, 1997, Charcot award, Internat. Fedn. MS Socs., 1999, Lifetime Achievement award, Consortium of MS Ctr., 2003, others, Kurtzke Clinician Scientist fellowship, AANF & CMSC, 2009. Fellow: ACP (life), AAAS (life), Pan Am. Med. Assn. (coun. neurology sect.), Am. Coll. Preventive Medicine, NY Acad. Sci., Am. Heart Assn. (stroke coun. 1991—2000), Am. Acad. Neurology (chmn. sect. on neuro-epidemiology 1971—75, chmn. com. nat. needs in neurology 1981—85, subcom. nat. needs in neurology 1985—86, mem. work force task force 1997, John Jay Dystel prize for mulitple sclerosis rsch. 1997), Am. Coll. Epidemiology; mem.: AMA, AAUP, European Neurol. Soc., Consortium Multiple Sclerosis Ctrs. (Lifetime Achievement award 2003), Lat. Am. Com. Treatment and Rsch. in Multiple Sclerosis, Am. Com. Treatment and Rsch. in Multiple Sclerosis, Soc. Med. Cons. to Armed Forces (com. on res. affairs 1980—83, com. on manpower 1984—98, com. on med. edn. 2001—09), Sr. Stroke Soc., Res. Officers Assn. (life), Naval Inst. (life), Fleet Res. Assn. (life), Naval Officers Assn. Am. (life), Am. Neurol. Assn. (hon.; chmn. bylaws ad hoc com. 1990—91), Danish Neurol. Soc. (hon.), French Soc. Neurology (hon.; fgn.), Assn. Nicoló Copernico (hon.), German Soc. Neurology (hon.), Assn. Mil. Surgeons (life), Naval Res. Assn. (life), Naval Order US (life), Internat. Stroke Soc., Am. Soc. Microbiology, Am. Epilepsy Soc., Assn. Rsch. in Nervous and Metal Disease, Internat. Epidemiol. Assn., Am. Epidemiol. Soc., So. Med. Assn., Navy League (life). Home: 7509 Salem Rd Falls Church VA 22043-3240 Office Phone: 703-560-6016. Office Fax: 703-560-6490. Business E-Mail: kurtzke2@aol.com.

KURTZMAN, NEIL A., medical educator; b. Bklyn., June 18, 1936; s. Louis S. and Roselie (Yegla) K.; m. Sandra Sabatini, Feb. 14, 1976; children from previous marriage: Jonathan, Laura. BA with honors, Williams Coll., 1957; MD, N.Y. Med. Coll., 1961. Intern Robert Packer Hosp., Sayre, Pa., 1961-62; resident Ohio State U. Hosp., Columbus, 1962-63; asst. chief med. services Nobel Army Hosp., Ft. McClellan, Ala., 1963-64; med. resident William Beaumont Gen. Hosp., El Paso, Tex., 1964-65, chief med. resident, 1965-66; fellow in nephrology U. Tex. Southwestern Med. Sch., Dallas, 1966-68; chief renal div. Brooke Army Med. Ctr., Ft. Sam Houston, Tex., 1969-72; prof., chief nephrology sect. U. Ill. Coll. Medicine, Chgo., 1972-84; from prof. to Grover E. Murray prof. Health Scis. Ctr. Tex. Tech U., Lubbock, Tex., 1985—2004, Grover E. Murray prof. Health Scis. Ctr., 2004—. Mem. gen. medicine B study sect. Nat. Inst. Arthritis, Metabolic and Digestive Diseases, Bethesda, Md., 1978-83; mem. merit rev. bd. VA, Washington, 1979-82, chmn., 1981-82; mem. sci. adv. bd. Nat. Kidney Found., N.Y.C., 1981-92, chmn., 1988-90, v.p., 1990-92, pres., 1992-94; prin. investigator regulation urinary acidification NIH, Bethesda, 1978—. Author: Handbook of Urinalysis and Urinary Sediment, 1974, Pathophysiology of the Kidney, 1977, Doing Nothing, 2000; also more than 300 sci. papers, more than 600 sci. presentations; editor-in-chief Seminars in Nephrology, 1981—, Am. Jour. Kidney Diseases, 1997-2002; assoc. editor Am. Jour. Nephrology; mem. editorial bd. 7 sci. jours.; referee 16 sci. jours. Faculty advisor Alpha Omega Alpha, U. Ill., 1977-84, Tex. Tech U. Health Sci. Ctr., 1985-2002. lt. col. U.S. Army, 1963-72. Decorated U.S. Army Meritorious Svc. award; recipient Pres.'s award Nat. Kidney Found., 1990, Outstanding Acad. Achievement award N.Y. Med. Coll., 1993, So. Soc. for Clin. Investigation's Founder's award, 1996, Tex. chpt. Am. Coll. Physicians Laureate award, 1996, David M. Hume award Nat. Kidney Found., 1999, Headliner award, 2003, medal IV Giovanni Alfonso Borelli Conf., 2004 Fellow AAAS; mem. Am. Physiol. Soc., Am. Soc. Clin. Investigation, Assn. Am. Physicians, Ctrl. Soc. Clin. Research, So. Soc. Clin. Investigation, Alpha Omega Alpha. Office: Dept Int Med TTUHSC 3601 4th St Lubbock TX 79430-0001 Business E-Mail: neil.kurtzman@ttuhsc.edu.

KURUGANTY, SASTRY PRATAP, electrical engineering educator; b. Masulipatam, India, Jan. 12, 1941; arrived in US, 1989, naturalized, 2008; s. Sastry A. and Lalitha (Jandhyala) K.; m. Lakshmi V. Bhagavatula, June 20, 1962; children: Saila, Padma, Saroja. B Engring., Birla Inst., Pilani, India, 1959—64; M. Engring., U. Andhra, Waltair, India, 1965—67; MSc in Engring., U. N.B., Fredericton, Can., 1971—73; PhD Elec. Engring., U. Sask., Saskatoon, Can., 1975—79. Registered profl. engr., Can. Province Manitoba. Asst. prof. Jawaharlal Nehru Tech. Inst., Hyderabad, India, 1966-71; rsch. assoc. U. N.B., Canada, 1974-75, U. Sask., 1979-80; reliability specialist Man. Hydro, Winnipeg, 1980-89; prof., chair elec. engring. dept. U. N.D., Grand Forks, 1989—96; DOE Samuel Massie chair excellence U. Turabo, PR, 1996—2000, prof. elec. engring., 2000—. Lectr. NSF USAID Summer Schs., Hyderabad, 1968; cons. Man. HVDC Rsch. Ctr., Winnipeg, 1985-88; transp. reliability task force, mem. res. requirements task force Mid Continent Area Power Pool, Mpls., 1984-89; chmn., panelist in field. Author over 40 papers in field. Rsch. fellow Can. Nat. Rsch. Coun., 1975-79, N.B., 1971-74. Mem. IEEE (sr. mem., sec.-treas. Red River Valley chpt. 1994-95, reviewer 1983—), NSPE, Am. Soc. for Engring. Edn. Achievements include research in bulk power system security assessment and reliability; HVDC transmission system reliability assessment and generation-transmission system planning using probabilistic techniques. Office: U Turabo PO Box 3030 Gurabo PR 00778-3030 Office Phone: 787-743-7979 ext. 4181. Business E-Mail: powerreleng@ieee.org. E-mail: powers124@hotmail.com.

KURVERS, TOM (THOMAS JAMES KURVERS), professional sports team executive, former professional hockey player; b. Mpls., Sept. 14, 1962; m. Heather Kurvers; children: Madison, Rose, Weston, Roman. BA in Comm., U. Minn., Duluth, 1984; MA in Sports Mgmt., U. St. Thomas, 1997. Defenseman Montreal Canadiens, 1984—86, Buffalo Sabres, 1986—87, NJ Devils, 1987—89, Toronto Maple Leafs, 1989—90, Vancouver Canucks, 1990—91, NY Islanders, 1991—94, Mighty Ducks of Anaheim, 1994; radio commentator Phoenix Coyotes, pro scout, interim asst. coach, 2004, dir. player personnel, 2005—08; asst. gen. mgr. Tampa Bay Lightning, 2008—, interim dir. hockey ops., 2010. Recipient Hobey Baker Award, 1984. Achievements include being a member of Stanely Cup Champion Montreal Canadiens, 1986. Office: Tampa Bay Lightning Hockey Club St Pete Times Forum 401 Channelside Dr Tampa FL 33602

KURZWEG, ULRICH HERMANN, engineering science educator; b. Jena, Germany, Sept. 16, 1936; came to US, 1947, naturalized, 1956; s. Hermann Herbert and Erna Herta (Michaelis) K.; m. Sophia Speth, Dec. 21, 1963; 1 dau., Tina. BS, U. Md., 1958; MA (Woodrow Wilson fellow 1958-59), Princeton U., 1959, PhD in Physics, 1961. Sr. theoretical physicist United Tech. Rsch. Labs., East Hartford, Conn., 1962-68; adj. assoc. prof. math. Hartford (Conn.) Grad. Ctr., Rensselaer Poly. Inst., 1964-68; mem. faculty U. Fla., Gainesville, 1968—, prof. mech. and aerospace engring., 1968—2004, prof. emeritus, 2004—. Contbr. numerous articles to sci. and tech. publs. Fulbright grantee, 1961-62; recipient Cert. of Recognition, NASA, 1984, award for excellence in undergrad. teaching U. Fla., 1991. Mem. AAAS. Avocations: travel, woodworking. Office: U Fla Dept Mech and Aerospace Engring Gainesville FL 32607 Business E-Mail: kurzweg@ufl.edu.

KUSHLAN, JAMES ANTHONY, scientist, science administrator, educator, conservationist, writer; b. Cleve., Oct. 11, 1947; BS in Biology and Chemistry cum laude, U. Miami, 1969, MS in Biology, 1972, PhD in Biology, 1974; DSc (hon.), Thiel Coll., Greenville, Pa., John Cabot U., Rome, Italy. Rsch. biologist U.S. Dept. of Interior, 1975-84; assoc. prof. biology Tex. A&M U., Commerce, 1984—87, prof. biology, 1987-88, dir. ctr. water resources studies, 1986-88; prof. biology U. Miss., 1988-98, chmn. dept. biology, 1988—95; dir. Patuxent Wildlife Rsch. Ctr., 1995-2001; sr. sci. advisor U.S. Geol. Survey, 2001—02; sr. rsch. assoc. Smithsonian Inst., 2001—05. Author: The Herons Handbook, 1984, Freshwater Fishes of Southern Florida, 1987, Storks, Ibises and Spoonbills of the World, 1992, Heron Conservation, 2000, Waterbird Conservation for the Americas, 2002, The Herons, 2005, Conserving Herons, A Conservation Action Plan, 2007; contbr. to Dictionary of Birds, 1985, Encyclopedia of Birds, 1985, Ecosystems of Florida, 1990, The Rivers of Florida, 1991; editor Fla. Field Naturalist, 1981-86, Colonial Waterbirds, 1985-88; mem. editl. bd. Wetlands, 1982, assoc. editor, 1993-95; author 200 papers, revs., commentaries; contbr. articles to profl. jours. Mem. United Way Planning Coun., Oxford, Miss., 1991-92; bd. dirs. Miss. Nature Conservancy, 1991-95, John Cabot U., 1990-2005, hon. trustee, 2005-, Am. Bird Conservancy, 1999-2005, N.Am. Bird Conservation Initiative US Com., 2000-2011, Waterbird Conservation for the Ams., 1996-, Hist. Miami Fla., 2010-, Everglades Found., 2011-, Fairchild Tropical Botanic Garden, 2011-, Zoological Soc. Fla., Zoo Miami, 2011-, Tropical Audubon Soc., 2005-10, Hawk Mountain Sanctuary, 2000-07, Am. Ornithologists Union, 2002-, pres., 2004-05, Biscayne Nature Ctr., 2008-12, Waterbird Soc., 1992-98, pres. 1996-98, Bahamas Environment Fund, 2009-12, pres. 2009-12, Internat. Ornithological Com., 2004-08; Friends the Everglades, 2004-12; chair North Am. Bird Conservation Alliance, 2002-05; chair Herons Specialist Group, 1985-; mem. sci bd. Station Biologique de la Tour du Valat, 1996-2006, vis. com. mem., Coll. Arts & Scis., U. Miami, 2008-; co-chair U. Miami, Coll. Arts and Scis. Momentum II Capital Campaign, 2011-. Recipient Citizen award WIOD Radio, Miami, 1980, Lindahl award Waterbird Soc., 2003; Paul Harris fellow Rotary Internat., 1989. Fellow Am. Ornithologists' Union, mem. Soc. Wetland Scientist (life), Rotary Internat. (chpt. pres. 1987-88), Sigma Xi (chpt. pres. 1983-84, finalist Indpls. prize for Wildlife Conservation 2012). Achievements include research in ornithology, wetland sciences, international wetland and biodiversity conservation, and waterbirds, recognised by Kushlan Science Institute University of Miami, Kushlan Chair for Waterbird Biology and Conservation; Fairchild Tropical Botanic Garden, Waterbird Biology Society Kushlan Research and Conservation Grants; Fairchild tropical botanic garden Kushlan bird conservation program. Office Phone: 305-365-0306. Personal E-mail: jkushlan@earthlink.net.

KUSHNER, DAVID ZAKERI, musicologist; b. Ellenville, NY, Dec. 22, 1935; s. Nathan and Rita (Forgatsh) K.; m. Rebecca Ann Stefan, Dec. 20, 1964 (div. Nov. 1979); children: Jonathan Moses (dec.), Joshua Sanford, Jeremy Avram (dec.), Jason Daniel; m. Leslie Cheryl Dack, Dec. 4, 1985. MusB, Boston U., 1957; MusM, U. Cin., 1958; PhD, U. Mich., 1967. Asst. prof. music Miss. U. For Women, Columbus, 1964—66; from assoc. prof. to prof. music Radford U., Va., 1966—69; head musicology, music history U. Fla., Gainesville, 1969—2007, prof. emeritus, 2007. Vis. prof. music Florence (Italy) Study Center, 1975; charter mem., program annotator Pro Arte Musica of Gainesville, 1970-75; host, commentator on Music from Fla., weekly radio program over WRUF-FM, 1969-75; mem. People-to-People del. Nat. Music Coun., Austria, Germany, Hungary, Poland and Czechoslovakia, 1977; lectr. Internat. Biog. Ctr., Oxford, Eng., 1997, Lisbon, Portugal, 1999; pre-concert lectr. Fla. Orch., Clearwater, Tampa, St. Petersburg, 1986-88, Internat. Congress on Arts and Comm., Nairobi, Kenya, 1990, Edinburgh, Scotland, 1994, U. Fla. Ctr. Performing Arts, 1995—2007; vis. prof. Mus. Conservatory A. Steffani, Castelfranco-Veneto, Italy, 1996, vis. prof. musicology Hebrew U., Jerusalem, 1998; adjudicator Fla. Music Tchrs. Assn., Chopin Competition; founder, dir. ann. Recitals in Schs. series 1972-; lectr., presenter, Internat. Musicological Soc., Coll. Music Soc., Soc. Am. Music, 19th Century Studies Assn., Internat. Jewish Music Conference, Hawaii Internat. Conference Arts & Humanities; lectr. Inst. Learning Ret. Oak Hammock, U. Fla. Ret. Ctr., 2007-, Sr. Ctr. Gainesville, Fla., 2013-14. Author: Ernest Bloch and His Symphonic Works, 1967, Ernest Bloch and His Music, 1973, Ernest Bloch: A Guide to Research, 1988, Ernest Bloch Companion, 2002; contbr. articles to profl. jours. & dictionaries, Am. Music, Opera Jour., Jour. Musicological Rsch., Coll. Music Symposium, Jour. Synagogue Music, Min-Ad, New Grove Dictionary of Music And Musicians, New Grove Dictionary of American Music, Encyclopedia Am. Jewish History; book reviewer: Am. Music Tchr. Mag., Conservatorio Statale di Musica A.Steffani, Castelfranco-Veneto, Italy, 1987. Mem. arts in edn. com. Arts Coun. Alachua County; pres., chmn. adv. bd. Sta. WUFT-FM, Gainesville, 1987-89; v.p. Found. for Promotion Music, 1990-91, 92-94. Javits fellowship, 1995; recipient Pro Mundi Beneficio medal, Brazilian Acad. Humanities, 1975; rsch. grantee U. Calif., Berkeley, NEH, 1986, Jaromir Weinberger Archives, Jerusalem, 1987, U. Fla., Tchg. Excellence award State of Fla., 1994-95, Professorial Excellence Program award State of Fla., 1996-97, Superior Achievement award, 1998-99; named Tchr. of Yr. Coll. Fine Arts, U. Fla., 1988-89, 2004-05, Musician of Yr., Found. for Promotion of Music, 1991-92, Internat. Educator of Yr., Coll. Fine Arts, U. Fla., 2006, Fine Arts Scholarship Enhancement Fund award, 1998-99. Mem. Am. Liszt Soc. (co-founder, bd. dirs., charter life), Coll. Music Soc. (chmn. So. chpt. 1985-87, musicology bd. dirs., charter mem.), Am. Musicological Soc. (1st chmn. So. chpt. 1971-74), Fla. Music Tchrs. Assn. (1st. pres. collegiate artist competitions 1972-73, hon. mem. com), Music Tchrs. Nat. Assn. (life, master tchr. cert. in music history and lit. 1984), Fla. State Music Tchrs. Assn., Membership Inc., Pi Kappa Lambda (charter, pres. U. Fla. chpt. 1970-76, 94-97), Phi Mu Alpha Sinfonia (life), Sigma Alpha Iota (nat. arts assoc.), 19th Century Studies Assn. (sr. adv. coun., President's award, 2014), Phi Kappa Phi, Phi Beta Delta (pres. Pi chpt. 1988-89). Democrat. Jewish. Avocations: travel, politics, reading. Home: 3518 NW 136th St Gainesville FL 32606-4764 Personal E-mail: dzk7777@gator.net.

KUSHNER, FREDERICK GARY, cardiologist, medical educator; b. NYC, May 20, 1948; s. Jack and Gloria Kushner; m. Ivy Erica Sommerstein, May 8, 1977; children: Adam Benjamin, Jared Scott. BA, Columbia U., 1970, MD, 1974. Diplomate Am. Bd. Internal Medicine. Med. intern, resident Harvard Beth Israel, Boston, 1974—76; cardiology fellow U. Pa., Phila., 1976—78, Mass. Gen. Hosp., Boston, 1978—79; clin. prof. medicine Tulane U. Sch. Medicine, New Orleans, 1993—; med. dir. Heart Clinic La., Marrero, 1995—. Chmn. credentials com. Leadership Com. of the Coun. on Clin. Cardiology of the Am. Heart Assn., Dallas, 1999—2001; com. mem. Guidelines Com. for mgmt. of ST Elevation MI of the Am. Heart Assn. and Am. Coll. of Cardiology, Washington, 2001—, mem. task force practice AHA ACCF, 2006—12; co-chmn STEMI, 2009—; mem. sci. adv. bd FDA, 2009—; mem. writting com., 2009; vice chmn. SI EMI Guidelines, 2013. Exhibitions include World Trade Ctr., New Orleans Acad. Fine Arts, others; contbr. chapters to books. Pres. The New Orleans Friends Music, 2000—03; bd. mem. Touro Cardiovascular Theragentive Synagogue, New Orleans, 2002—, Columbia Coll. Alumni Assn., NYC, 1996—; alumni coun. bd. mem. Columbia Coll. Physicians and Surgeons, NYC, 1996—. Recipient AOA Tchg. award, Tulane U., Sch. Medicine. Fellow: ACP (licentiate), Am. Heart Assn., Soc. Cardiac Angiography and Interventions (licentiate), Soc. Nuc. Cardiology (licentiate), Am. Coll. Cardiology (licentiate; v.p. La. chpt. 1990); mem.: Alpha Omega Alpha (Vol. Clin. Faculty Tchg. award 1999). Achievements include research in nuclear cardiology and perfusion scanning. Avocations: painting, sailing, travel, reading, golf. Office: Heart Clinic La Suite 613 Physicians Center North Marrero LA 70072 Personal E-mail: fred.kushner@gmail.com.

KUSHNER, MICHAEL JAMES, neurologist, consultant, educator; b. Hackensack, NJ, July 18, 1951; s. Samuel and Ruth Ellen (Paul) K.; m. Sarah Joan Warden, Aug. 14, 1976; children: Hunter Paul, Paul Macrae (dec.). BA in Physics, Yale U., 1973; MD, NYU, 1977. Diplomate Am. Bd. Psychiatry, Am. Bd. Neurology, Am. Bd. Med. Examiners; cert. Am. Bd. Electrodiagnostic Medicine, Am. Bd. Pain Medicine. Intern Parkland Meml. Hosp., U. Tex., Dallas, 1977-78; resident in neurology Neurol. Inst., Columbia-Presbyn. Med. Ctr., NYC, 1978-81; rsch. assoc. U. Pa., Phila., 1981-83, asst. prof. neurology, 1983-90; attending physician Hosp. of U. Pa., Phila., 1983-90; with Wilson (N.C.) Neurology Ctr., 1992—; clin. asst. prof. East. Carolina U. Sch. Medicine, 1997—. Dir. SPECT facility Hosp. of U. Pa., 1986-90, asst. dir. neurovascular lab., 1987-90; mem. sensory disorders and lang. study sect. NIH, Bethesda, Md., 1988-90; staff neurologist Wilson (N.C.) Orthop. Surgery Neurology Ctr.; legal medicine cons.; neurology physician advisor N.C. Blue Cross/Blue Shield; asst. prof. East Carolina U. Sch. Medicine; dir. Wilson Regional MRI Ctr. Contbr. numerous articles to profl. jours. Interviewer alumni schs. com. Yale U., Phila., 1984—. Fellow Am. Acad. Neurology, Am. Heart Assn. (stroke coun.); mem. AMA, Internat. Soc. for Blood Flow and Metabolism, N.C. Neurol. Soc. (pres. 1995-97), Yale of N.Y.C., Yale of Cen. N.C., Yale of N.C. Republican. Episcopalian. Avocations: oenology, travel, exercise, art. Home: 1110 Salem St NW Wilson NC 27893-2137 Office: Wilson Neurology Ctr PO Box 3148 Wilson NC 27895-3148 Office Phone: 252-243-9629.

KUSHNER, SIDNEY RALPH, molecular genetics and biochemistry educator; b. NYC, Dec. 14, 1943; s. Joseph B. and Dora (Cohen) K.; m. Deena Dash Kushner, June 12, 1969; children: Aaron, Ze'eva. BA, Oberlin Coll., 1965; PhD, Brandeis U., 1970. Postdoctoral fellow U. Calif., Berkeley, 1970-71, Stanford (Calif.) U. Sch. Medicine, 1971-73; from asst. prof. to prof. U. Ga., Athens, 1973—; head dept. of genetics, 1987-95; disting. rsch. prof., 2008—. Bd. dirs. Am. Type Culture Collection, Rockville, Md., 1989-93. Author book chpts.; contbr. numerous articles to profl. jours. Recipient Career Devel. award NIH, 1975-80, Lamar Dodd award. Fellow AAAS, Am. Acad. Microbiology; mem. Genetics Soc. Am., Am. Soc. Microbiology, Am. Soc. Biol. Chemists, RNA Soc. Achievements include development of a variety of techniques to improve the usefulness of E. coli as a host for genetic engineering experiments and the analysis posttranscriptional gene regulation in bacteria. Office: U Ga Dept Genetics Athens GA 30602 Office Phone: 706-542-8000. Business E-Mail: skushner@uga.edu.

KUSIN, GARY M., investment advisor; b. Texarkana, Tex., 1951; married; 4 children. BA, U. Tex., Austin; MBA, Harvard U. V.p., gen. mgr. Sanger-Harris divsn. Federated Dept. Stores; co-founder, chmn. Kusin Gurwitch Cosmetics, LLC; co-founder, pres. Babbage's Inc., Dallas, 1983—95; co-founder Laura Mercier Cosmetics, Dallas, 1995—98; pres., CEO OmniOffices, Inc., 1998—99; CEO HQ Global Workplaces, Inc., 1999—2001; pres., CEO office & print svcs. FedEx Kinko's Inc., Dallas, 2001—06; sr. advisor TPG Capital (formerly Texas Pacific Group), 2006—. Bd. dirs. Electronic Arts, Inc., 1995—, Radioshack Corp., 2004—05, PETCO, Sabre Holdings. Bd. trustees St. Mark's Sch. Tex.; chmn. Dallas Young Pres.' Orgn.; mem. Dallas Citizen's Coun. Named Entrepreneur of Yr., Inc. Mag. Mem.: Dallas C. of C. (bd. dirs.). Office: TPG Capital 301 Commerce St Ste 3300 Fort Worth TX 76102 Mailing: Electronic Arts Inc 209 Redwood Shores Pky Redwood City CA 94065 E-mail: gkusin@texpac.com.

KUSSEROW, PAUL B., insurance company executive; b. Vermont; Grad. phi beta kappa, Wesleyan U.; MA with honors, Oxford U. Sr. v.p., chief strategy officer Business-Higher Edn. Forum, ChangeNow4Health, KMG America Corp.; chmn. Healthcaredia-.Com, LLC; mng. cons. McKinsey and Co., Inc.; exec., strategic planning, new bus. devel., merger, acquisitions and mktg. capacities Reader's Digest, Nat. Geog., Colonial Williamsburg; mng. dir., chief investment officer Ziegler HealthVest Fund; sr. v.p., corp. strategy, Tenet Ventures Tenet HealthCare Corp., 1997—2004; founder, exec. advisor Broadlane, 2004—07; executive-in-residence The Adv. Bd. Co., 2004—07; mng. dir. San Ysidro Capital Ptnrs. LLC, 2004—07; mng. dir., pvt. equity, chief investment officer, healthvest fund B.C. Ziegler and Co., 2007—09; sr. v.p., chief strategy officer Humana, Inc., 2009—. Scholar Rhodes, Oxford U. Office: Humana Inc 500 W Main St Louisville KY 40202 Office Phone: 502-580-1000. Office Fax: 502-580-3677. Business E-Mail: pkusserow@humana.com.

KUSSEROW, RICHARD PHILLIP, federal agency administrator, corporate financial executive; b. San Jose, Calif., Dec. 9, 1940; s. Roger Berthold and Eve W. (Larson) K.; m. Rebecca Hatchell, Sept. 14, 1985; 1 child, Carrie Elizabeth. BA in Polit. Sci, UCLA, 1963; MA in Govt., Calif. State U., LA, 1964; postgrad., So. Meth. U., 1965, John Marshall Sch. Law, 1972, Harvard U., 1984. Cert. internal auditor, cert. govt. auditor; cert. govt. fin. mgr., cert. fraud examiner. Lectr. Calif. State U., LA, 1963, 64; case officer CIA, 1968-69; spl. agt. supr. in white collar and organized crime FBI, 1969-81; Insp. Gen., U.S. Dept. HHS, 1981-92; mem. Pres.'s Coun. on Integrity and Efficiency, 1981-92, vice chmn., 1986-89, chmn. legislation com., 1982-85, 89-92; mem. Pres.' Council on Mgmt. Improvement, 1986-89, 91-92; chair Nat. Task Force of Implementation of Chief Fin. Officers Act, 1990-91; chmn. Chief Fin. Officers Task Force, 1991; pres., CEO Strategic Mgmt. Sys., Inc., 1992—; ptnr. O.K. Real Estate, 1993—2005; pres. Govt. Mgmt. Sys., Inc., 1995—2002; pres., CEO, chmn. bd. Nat. Hotline Svcs., Inc., 1995—2006; CEO Stratesic MGI Svc. LLC, 2006—, Integrity MGI Svc., 2008—. Presdl. appointee to Nat. Adv. Commn. on Law Enforcement, 1989; mem. CFOs Coun., 1990-92, Def. Procurement Round Table, 1993-95; lectr. white collar crime, asset protection, health care, fraud and abuse, internal controls, corporate compliance programs, others; mem. Atty. Gen.'s Econ. Crime Coun., 1988-90; nat. chmn. Am. Compliance Inst., 1995. Author: Principles of Investigative Targeting, 1974, Management Principles for Asset Protection, 1995, Corporate Compliance Policies & Procedures: Guide to Assessment and Development, 2000, Compliance Training Manual, 2001, Sarbanes-Oxley: Best Practices for Private and Non Profit Health Care Entities, 2003, Compliance Office Manual Policies, 2008, Ultimate Hotline Manual, 2005, Forty-Nine Steps to Sarbonet-Oxley Compliance, 2006; contbr. articles to profl. jours. Pres. Nat. Honor Svc., 1996—. Capt. USMC, 1965-68. Recipient Sec.'s Bronze medal for good govt., 1983, Outstanding Leadership award Pres. Coun. on Mgmt. Improvement, 1988, Cert. of Svc. Appreciation, Pres. of U.S., 1989, Donald L. Scantlebury award for fin. mgmt. excellence Assn. Govt. Accts., 1992; H. Horton Rontree Disting. lectr. in health law, 1990. Mem. Assn. Fed. Investigators (nat. pres. 1984-85, chmn. awards com. 1986-87), Soc. Former FBI Agts., Assn. Govt. Accts. (nat. task force on fed. fin. mgmt. 1983-88, pres. Balt. chpt. 1987, chmn. nat. profl. devel. conf. 1989, nat. pres. 1990, nat. leadership awards Boston chpt. 1985, No. Va. chpt., Washington chpt., D.C. chpt. 1985, Nat. Assn. 1987), Am. Health Lawyers Assn., Nat. Health Care Anti-Fraud Assn. (pub. svc. award 1989), Inst.

Internal Auditors (cert.), Am. Compliance Inst. (governing bd. 1996-2001), Army-Navy Club, G Washington chpt. Song Am. Rev. (pres.). Presbyterian. Avocations: reading, travel, tennis. Office Phone: 703-535-1411. Business E-Mail: rkusserow@strategicm.com.

KUSSROW, NANCY ESTHER, educational association administrator; BA, Valparaiso U., 1952; MA, U. N.C., 1954. Exec. dir. Nat. Assn. prins. of Schs. for Girls; ret., 1996.

KUSTOFF, DAVID F., lawyer, former prosecutor; b. Memphis, Oct. 8, 1966; m. Roberta Kustoff; 1 child, Maggie. BBA, U. Memphis, 1989, JD, 1992. Bar: 1992. Ptnr. Kustoff & Strickland PLLC, Memphis; US atty. (we. dist.) Tenn. US Dept. Justice, Memphis, 2006—08. Head Bush-Cheney election effort, Tenn., 2000, 2004; chmn. Shelby County Rep. Party, Tenn. Office: Kustoff & Strickland PLLC 22 N Front St Memphis TN 38103 Office Phone: 901-544-4231. Office Fax: 901-544-4230.

KUTNER, LAWRENCE ALAN, executive director; b. NYC, Feb. 29, 1952; s. Michael and Mary (Viener) Kutner; m. Cheryl Kay Olson, Oct. 1988; 2 children. AB, Oberlin Coll., 1974; PhD in Clin. Psychology, U. Minn., 1978. Lic. consulting psychologist, Minn., NY. Psychologist Mayo Clinic, Rochester, NY, 1977—78; sci. producer Sta. WNET-TV, NYC, 1978-79; ind. producer Westport, Conn., 1979-81; producer, reporter Sta. WCCO-TV, Mpls., 1981-84; pres. Health and Sci. Comm., Inc., Mpls., 1984; psychology faculty Harvard Med. Sch., Mass. Gen. Hosp.; co-founder, co-director Harvard Med. Sch. Ctr. for Mental Health and Media. Clin. assoc. prof. U. Minn.; bd. dirs. Walk-In Counseling Ctr., Mpls.; bd. advisors Rosalynn Carter Fellowships, Mental Health Journalism Carter Ctr., Atlanta; cons. and spkr. in field. Columnist: NY Times, 1987-94 (APA Nat. Psychology award 1990), Parents mag.; co-producer TV program Project Abuse, 1984, Emmy award 1985; host KGO Radio, San Francisco; producer numerous TV programs which have received nat. and internat. awards; author: Parent and Child: Getting Through to Each Other, 1994, Pregnancy and Your Baby's First Year, 1994, Toddlers & Preschoolers, 1995, Your School-Age Child, 1996, Making Sense of Your Teenager, 1998; co-author: (with Cheryl Olson) Grand Theft Childhood: The Surprising Truth About Violent Video Games and What Parents Can Do, 2008. Psychology fellow Mayo Clinic, 1977; comm. fellow AAAS, 1976; named Dr. Dad, AP. Office: Jack Kent Cooke Found 44325 Woodridge Pky Leesburg VA 20176 Office Phone: 617-726-8471. Office Fax: 617-726-9136.

KUYKENDALL, JOHN WELLS, retired academic administrator, theology studies educator; b. Charlotte, NC, May 8, 1938; s. James Bell and Emily Jones (Frazer) K.; m. Nancy Adams Moore, July 15, 1961; children— Timothy Moore, James Frazer BA cum laude, Davidson Coll., 1959; BD cum laude, Union Sem., Richmond, Va., 1964; STM, Yale U., 1965; MA, Princeton U., 1972, PhD, 1975; DD (hon.), Hanover Coll., 1999; LHD (hon.), Wofford Coll., 1999. Ordained to ministry Presbyterian Ch., 1965. Campus minister Presbyn. Ch., Auburn, Ala., 1965-70; faculty Auburn U., 1973-84; pres. Davidson Coll., NC, 1984—97, Thatcher prof. religion, 1997—2003, pres. emeritus, 1997—, interim pres., 2010—11. Author: (with others) Presbyterians: Their History and Beliefs, 1978, Southern Enterprize: The Work of Evangelical Societies in the Antebellum South, 1982; contbr. articles to profl. jours. Recipient Algernon Sydney Sullivan award Auburn U., 1982 Mem. Am. Soc. Ch. History, Phi Beta Kappa, Omicron Delta Kappa, Phi Kappa Phi. Democrat. Office: Davidson College Office of President Box 7145 Davidson NC 28035-7145

KUZNETSOVA, SVETLANA, professional tennis player; b. St. Petersburg, Russia, June 27, 1985; d. Alexandr Kuznetsov and Galina Tsareva. Profl. tennis player WTA Tour, 2001—. Named WTA Tour Newcomer of Yr., 2002. Achievements include winning 13 career singles titles, 14 doubles titles, WTA; winning 1 career singles title, ITF; mem. Russian Fed Cup Team, 2004, 2007-2010, Russian Olympic Team, 2004, 2008; winning Fed Cup title, 2008. Office: c/o WTA Tour Corp Hdqs One Progess Plz Ste 1500 Saint Petersburg FL 33701

KVAM, PAUL, mathematics professor; BS in Math., Iowa State U., 1984; MS in Stats., U. Fla., 1986; PhD in Stats., U. Calif., Davis, 1991. Sci. staff Los Alamos Nat. Lab.; assoc. prof. ISyE, 1995—. Inst. Math. Contbr. articles to profl. jours.; assoc. editor IEEE Transactions on Reliability, 1992—2000, Technometrics, 1999—2005, Journal of the American Statistical Association, 2002—, American Statistician, 2005—. Recipient Chancellor award, Coun. Internat. Edn's Faculty, 1997, Frank Wilcoxon prize, Am. Statis. Assn & Am. Soc. Quality Control, 1997; Tchg. Fellow, Ga. Tech. Class of 1969, 1996—97. Fellow: Am. Stat. Assn. (pres., Albuquerque Chpt. 1994—95, mem. exec. com., Albuquerque Chpt. 1994—95, treas., Atlanta Chpt. 1998—2005, rep., sect. on phys. and engring. sciences 2005—08); mem.: IEEE, Inst. Ops. Rsch. and Mgmt. Sci., Inst. Math. Stats. (rep., mgmt. com. for Spring rsch. conf. 2005—08). Office: H Milton Stewart Sch Indsl And Sys Engring Ga Inst Tech 765 Ferst Dr NW Groseclose 0205 Rm 434 Atlanta GA 30332-0205 Office Phone: 404-894-6515. Office Fax: 404-894-2301. Business E-Mail: paul.kvam@isye.gatech.edu.

KWAMI, PAUL T., musical director and educator; b. Ghana; arrived in US, 1983; Student, Nat. Acad. Music, Ghana; grad., Fisk U., Nashville, 1985; student, Western Mich. U. Musical dir. Fisk U. Jubilee Singers, Nashville, 1994—; Curb-Beaman prof. and chair, music dept. Fisk U., Nashville. Achievements include under his directorship, the Fisk Jubilee Singers have received numerous awards, including induction in the Gospel Music Hall of Fame, 2000, and the National Medal of Arts, 2008. Office: Fisk U 1000 17th Ave N Nashville TN 37208 Office Phone: 615-329-8744. Office Fax: 615-329-8850. E-mail: pkwami@fiskjubileesingers.org.

KYLE, JAMES F., state legislator; b. Memphis, Tenn., Oct. 14, 1950; m. Sara Kyle; 4 children. BS in Mktg., Ark. State U., 1973; JD, U. Memphis Sch. Law, 1976. State senate mem. Dist. 28, Tenn., 1983—; chmn., majority caucus, 1987—88; dem. leader, 2004—; atty. Kyle Law Firm, Memphis. Named Legislator of Yr., Shelby County Dept. Sheriff's Assn., 1991, County Ofcls. Tenn., 1992; Henry Toll fellow, Coun. State Govt., 1986. Mem.: Am. Correctional Assn. (bd. govs.), Memphis Bar Assn., Econ. Club Memphis. Democrat. Presbyterian. Office: 309 War Memorial Bldg Nashville TN 37243-0028 also: 100 Peabody Pl Ste 1300 Memphis TN 38103 Office Phone: 615-741-4167. Office Fax: 615-253-0221. Business E-Mail: sen.jim.kyle@capitol.tn.gov.

KYLE, JOHN EMERY, retired religious organization administrator; b. San Diego, July 7, 1926; s. John E. and Agnes (McDaniel) Kyle; m. Lois Ellen Rowland, June 8, 1947; children: Arlette Marie, Jayson Duane, Marcus Justin, Darlene Patricia. BS in Agr., Oreg. State U., 1950; BDiv, Columbia Theol. Sem., 1961, MDiv, 1971; D in Ministry (hon.), Belhaven Coll., 1999. Ordained to ministry Presbyn Ch. U.S., 1961. Sr. buyer Easwest Produce Co.-Safeway Stores Inc., San Francisco, 1951-57; pastor Presbyn. Ch. in U.S., Hazard, Ky., 1961-63; adminstr. Wycliffe Bible Translators, Manila, 1964-73, coord. internat. rels., 1976—77, exec. dir. Washington, 1977-79, Mission to the World, Presbyn. Ch. in Am., Decatur, Ga., 1974-77; missions dir., v.p. Intervarsity Christian Fellowship, Madison, Wis., 1979-88; exec. dir. mission to world Presbyn. Ch. Am., Atlanta, 1988-94; sr. v.p. Evang. Fellowship Mission Agencies., Norcross, Ga., 1994—2005; ret., 2005. Co-founder Townsend Inst. Internat. Rels., 1978; dir. Student Fgn. Missions Fellow, 1978—87, World Student Mission Conv., Urbana, Ill., 1979, Urbana, 1981, Urbana, 1984, Urbana, 1987; trustee Columbia Bible Coll. and Sem., 1982—86, Overseas Missionary Fellowship, Robesonia, Pa., 1982—86, Crista Ministries Bd., 1984—88, Concerts Prayer Internat., 1988—99, Berkeley Heights, NJ, A.D. 2000 Movement, Colorado Springs, Colo., 1989—2000, Co mission, 1992—98, Christ's Coll., Taipei, Taiwan, 1992—98, World Relief Bd., 1997—2006, Culture Insights Bd., 1998—2001, Mid. East Media Bd., 1998—99; chmn. O.M. Logos Ship, 1988—91; pres. Sr. Leadership Xchange, 2006—. Editor: The Unfinished Task, 1982, Finishing the Task, 1987, Urban Missions, 1988; author: Now This Generation, 1990; co-author: Looking Forward - Voices from Church Leaders on Our Global Mission, 2002; contbr. chapters to books; co-author: Thy Kingdom Come-Aman for Such a Time As This - The Second and Third Millenium. With USNR, 1945—47, WWII, Iwo Jima. Recipient Presdl. Merit medal, Pres. of The Philiippines. Mem.: World Evang. Felloship, Assn. Ch. Missions Com., Nat. Assn. Evang., Evang. Fgn. Missions Assn. (trustee 1989—94), Concerts Prayer Internat. Presbyterian. Office: 2343A Granville Pl Monroe NC 28110 Home Phone: 704-291-7157. Business E-Mail: john-lois_kyle@wbt.org.

LAANE, JAAN, chemistry professor, physics and astronomy professor; b. Paide, Estonia, June 20, 1942; came to US, 1949. s. Robert Freidrich and Linda (Treufeldt) L.; m. Tiiu Virkhaus, Sept. 3, 1966; children: Christina J., Lisa A. BS in Chemistry, U. Ill., 1964; PhD in Chemistry, MIT, 1967; Doctorate (hon.), U. Tartu, Estonia, 2000. Asst. prof. of chemistry Tufts U., Medford, Mass., 1967-68; asst. prof. of chem. Tex. A&M U., Coll. Sta., 1968-72, assoc. prof. of chem., 1972-76, prof. of chemistry, 1976—, chmn. div. of phys. and nuc. chemistry, 1977-87, 93-94, dir. Inst. for Pacific Asia, 1987-90, assoc. dean sci., 1994-97; dep. exec. dir., sr. policy advisor Tex. A&M U./Koriyama, Coll. Sta., 1990-94; editor Jour. Molecular Structure, 1994—. Reviewer numerous profl. jour. and grant agys., 1968—; cons. indsl. and govt. orgn., 1970—; vis. prof. U. Bayreuth, Fed. Republic Germany, 1979-80; speaker Tex. A&M Faculty Senate, College Station, 1985-86; dir. NATO Advanced Rsch. Workshop, Ulm, Germany, 1992. Editor: (book) Frontiers in Molecular Spectroscopy, 2009, Structures and Dynamics of Electronic Excited States, 1999, Structures and Conformations of Non-Rigid Molecules, 1992; contbr. numerous articles to profl. jour.; lectr. numerous sci. presentations. Pres., founder College Station Assn. for Gifted and Talented, 1982-83. Recipient 13 rsch. grants Robert A. Welch Found., 1970—, 10 rsch. grants NSF, 1976-2007, US Sr. Sci. award Alex Von Humboldt Found., Fed. Republic Germany, 1979, Disting. Tchg. award Tex. A&M Assn. Former Students; elected to Estonian Acad. Sci., 1995, Lippincott award for molecular spectroscopy, 2005; Robert A. Welch Found. lectr., 1998-99. Fellow Am. Inst. Chemists, Am. Phys. Soc.; mem. Am. Chem. Soc. (sect. pres. 1977-78), Soc. for Applied Spectroscopy, Alexander von Humboldt Assn. Am. (bd. dirs. 2003-06, v.p. 2005—, pres. Tex. chpt. 2001-02, pres. 2007—), Coblentz Soc. (bd. dir., treas. 1986-89), Tex. A&M Faculty Club (pres. 1987-88), Phi Beta Delta (pres. 1990-91). Achievements include rsch. in molecular spectroscopy and vibrational potential energy functions of molecules, laser Raman spectroscopy, laser induced fluorescence spectroscopy, ft-infrared spectroscopy. Home: 1906 Comal Cir College Station TX 77840-4818 Office: Tex A&M U Chemistry Dept College Station TX 77843-3255 Office Phone: 979-845-3352. Office Fax: 979-845-3154. Personal E-mail: jaan@laane.com. Business E-Mail: laane@mail.chem.tamu.edu.

LABARDI, JILLIAN GAY, financial planner, insurance agent; b. Terre Haute, Ind., Feb. 24, 1945; d. Frank Moses and Joan (Forster) Pierson; m. Jack Alexander Labardi, June 24, 1968. Student, Am. Coll., Paris, 1963; Student, U. Madrid, 1964, Am. U., Washington, 1965, U. Florence, Italy, 1966, Ctrl. Piedmont CC, Charlotte, NC, 1984-86; student, Am. Coll., Bryn Mawr, Pa., 1982-89. CLU; ChFC, registered investment advisor. Interpreter Desesco Internat.-Export Co., Florence, Italy, 1966-67; tri-lingual sec. US Topographical Team, Livorno, Italy, 1967-68; mgr. internat. sales Whitin Internat., Charlotte, 1968-81; internat. sales cons. Concord Warehousing, NC, 1981-82; agt., fin. planner Prin. Fin. Group, Charlotte, 1982-97; assoc. Consol. Planning, 1997—2003, fin. advisor, 2003—12. Instr. Italian Ctrl. Piedmont CC, Charlotte, 1968—80; with Capital Investment Group, Charlotte, 2003—13. Vol. Internat. House, Charlotte, 1970—2008. Mem.: Soc. Fin. Svc. Profls., Women Bus. Owners (charter, treas. 1986—2000), Million Dollar Round Table (life), Italy-Am. C. of C. (bd. dirs. 2004—12), Christopher Columbus Carolinas (founder, pres., bd. dirs.). Democrat. Roman Catholic. Home: 221 Scottridge Dr Charlotte NC 28217-4045 Office: Capital Investment Group 5950 Fairview Rd Ste 500 Charlotte NC 28210 Office Phone: 704-556-0144.

LABARGA, JORGE, state supreme court justice, lawyer; b. Havana, Cuba, Oct. 21, 1952; s. Jorge and Miriam Labarga; m. Zulma Freytes, Aug. 22, 1980; children: Stephanie Marie, Caroline Ashley. BA, U. Fla., 1976, JD, 1979. Bar: Fla. 1980, U.S. Dist. Ct. (so. dist.) Fla. 1980, U.S. Ct. Appeals (5th and 11th cirs.) 1980, U.S. Supreme Ct. 1984. Asst. pub. defender Office of Pub. Defender, W. Palm Beach, Fla., 1979-82; asst. state's atty. State of Fla., W. Palm Beach, 1982-87; ptnr. Wagner Nugent Johnson Romano Roth Eriksen & Kupfer, P.A., W. Palm Beach, 1987—96; judge Fla. Cir. Ct., 1996—2009; assoc. justice Fla. Supreme Ct., Tallahassee, 2009—. Mem. ABA, Acad. Fla. Trial Lawyers, Assn. Trial Lawyers Am. Office: Fla Supreme Ct 500 S Duval St Tallahassee FL 32399-1925 Office Phone: 850-413-8371.*

LABARGE, SUZANNE B., bank executive; BA in Economics, McMaster U., 1967; MBA, Harvard U., 1971. Asst. auditor-gen., dep. supt. policy Office of Supt. Fin. Institutions Can.; exec. v.p., corp. treasury Royal Bank of Canada, 1995—85; vice chmn., chief risk officer RBC Fin. Group, 1999—2004; mem., supervisory bd. Deutsche Bank AG, 2008—. Former bd. dirs. Royal Bank of Canada; bd. dirs. Novelis, Inc., 2005—07, Coca-Cola Enterprises Inc., 2007—. Bd. govs. McMaster U., 1999-. Office: Coca Cola Enterprises Inc 2500 Windy Ridge Pky Atlanta GA 30339 Office Phone: 770-989-3000. Office Fax: 770-989-3788. Business E-Mail: suzanne.labarge@db.com.

LABBIE, ANDREW SCOTT, pediatric urologist, surgeon; b. Miami, Fla. MD, Northwestern U., Ill., 1982. Diplomate Am. Bd. Urology, lic. Fla. Intern U. Tex., Dallas, 1982—83, resident, 1983—88; fellowship Tex. Children's Hosp., Baylor U., Houston, 1988—89; staff urologist, chief dept. surgery Miami Children's Hosp., 1990—. Clin. assoc. prof. urology U. Miami Sch. Med.; bd. dirs. Miami Children's Hosp. Contbr. articles to profl. jours. Mem.: Am. Acad. Pediat. Office: Children's Hosp 3200 SW 60th Ct Ste 105 Miami FL 33155 Office Phone: 305-669-6448. Office Fax: 305-663-8464.

LABEN, NANCY JILL, consulting firm executive, lawyer; b. Boston, 1961; m. Jonathan Feiger; children: Leah, Jayce. Attended, Doshisha Univ., Japan, 1981—82; AB in Govt. & East Asian Studies, Smith Coll., 1983; JD, Columbia Law Sch., 1986. Counsel IBM Corp., 1985—89; various atty. & legal mgmt. positions Accenture LLP, 1989—2010, mng. ptnr. legal services Asia-Pacific Hong Kong, mng. dir. legal services Europe, Middle East, India & Africa London, dep. gen. counsel Chgo.; sr. v.p. legal, gen. counsel AECOM Tech. Corp., L.A., 2010—13; exec. v.p., gen. counsel Booz Allen Hamilton, McLean, Va., 2013—. Office: Booz Allen Hamilton 8283 Greensboro Dr Mc Lean VA 22102 Office Phone: 703-902-5000.*

LABENSKY, SARAH ROSS, culinary educator; b. Murray, Ky., Mar. 16, 1958; d. James Mason and Lucille Thomson Ross; m. Steven Jay Labensky, Oct. 14, 1983 (div. May 1995); m. Louis David Moline, Sept. 3, 1995 (dec. Aug. 2003) BS, Murray State U., Ky., 1980; JD, Vanderbilt U., 1983; cert., Scottsdale C.C., 1986. Atty. Hocker and Axford, Tempe, Ariz., 1983-85; cook/chef Phoenix, 1985-90; prof. Scottsdale C.C., Ariz., 1990-98; dir. Miss. U. for Women Culinary Arts Inst., Columbus, 1998—2005; editor Favorite Recipes Press, Nashville, 2005—06; restaurant owner Columbus, Miss., 2006—12; dir. food svc. East Miss. CC, Columbus, 2013—14. Author: On Cooking, 1995, 4th edit., 2006, 5th edit., 2010, Rev. edit., 2014, Webster's N.W. Dictionary of Culinary Arts, 1997, 2d edit., 2000, Applied Math for Food Service, 1998, Complete Idiot's Guide to Cooking Techniques and Science, 2002, On Baking, 2004, 2nd edit., 2009, 3rd edit., 2012, Essentials Dictionary of Culinary Arts, 2007. Named Woman Entrepreneur of Yr., Miss. U. Women, 2007. Mem.: Internat. Assn. Culinary Profls. (bd. dirs. 1999—2006, sec.-treas. 2002, v.p. 2003, pres. 2004, cert.). Office: 2331 Military Rd Columbus MS 39705 Office Phone: 662-328-4837.

LABENZ-HOUGH, MARLENE, administrator; b. St. Edward, Nebr., May 25, 1954; d. Ralph Labenz and Lorene (Laudenklos); m. Jeff Hough, Mar. 5, 1983. Assocs., Platte Coll., 1974; BS in Social Work magna cum laude, U. Nebr., 1976; MA in Clin. Psychology, Trinity U., 1980. Adminstrv. asst., mgmt. analyst II City of San Antonio Dept. Human Resources and Svcs., 1980, adminstrv. asst. II, 1980-82, casework supr., Victims of Crime Program, 1982-89, program coord., Children's Resources Divsn., 1989-90; asst. dir. Bexar County Dispute Resolution Ctr., San Antonio, 1990-92, dir., 1992—. Bd. dirs. KidShare, 1993-96, YWCA, 1990-93; mem. ADR sect. coun. State Bar Tex., 1996-99. Recipient Liberty Bell award, San Antonio Young Lawyers Assn., 2003, Recognition award, San Antonio Bar Found., 2004, Appreciation award, 2005, Recognition award for leadership. Mem.: ABA (chmn. conf. com. ADR sect. 2002), Tex. Bar Assn. (ADR sect.), Assn. Family and Conciliation Cts., Tex. Mediators Credentialing Assn., Alamo Area Mediators Assn., Tex. Dispute Resolution Ctrs. Dirs. Coun., Tex. Mediation Trainers' Roundtable, Assn. Conflict Resolution, Conflict Resolution and Peer Mediation Coun., Nat. Assn. Cmty. Mediation (founding dir.), Soc. Profls. in Dispute Resolution (co-chair S.W. region chpt. 1993, co-chair nat. conf. 1995, Profl. Dedication award 1994), Acad. Family Mediators, Tex. Assn. Mediators (chair conf. 1998, bd. dirs. 1998—2001, Heart of Tex. award 2007), Alpha Xi Delta. Home: 2518 Ashton Village Dr San Antonio TX 78248-2200

LABONTE, BOBBY, race car driver; b. Corpus Christi, Tex., May 8, 1964; m. Donna Labonte; 1 child, Robert Tyler. Profl. race car driver NASCAR, 1991—. Named winner, Coca-Cola 600, 1995, Miller 400, 1995, Goodwrench 400, 1995, NAPA 500, 1996, 1997, 1999, Primestar 500, 1998, Diehard 500, 1998, MBNA Platinum 400, 1999, Pocono 500, 1999, Pepsi 400, 1999, Pa. 500, 1999, Dura Lube/KMart 400, 2000, Internat. Race of Champions series title, 2001, Martinsville race, 2002, Atlanta race, 2003, Homestead, 2003, NASCAR Craftsman Truck Series victory, 2005. Office: Bobby Labonte Racing PO Box 607 5740 Hopewell Church Rd Trinity NC 27370-7646

LABOR, EARLE GENE, literature and language professor; b. Tuskahoma, Okla., Mar. 3, 1928; s. Earle Labor and Sylvia Kirkpatrick Steger; m. Betty Garrett, Sept. 21, 1952 (dec. Aug. 1989); children: Royce, Kirk, Kyle, Isabel; m. Gayle Johnson, May 25, 1996; 1 child, Andrea. AB, So. Meth. U., Dallas, 1949, MA, 1952; PhD, U. Wis., Madison, 1961. Instr. English So. Meth. U., Dallas, 1950-52; asst. sales mgr. Haggar Co., Dallas, 1954-55; instr. English Centenary Coll., Shreveport, La., 1955-56, asst. prof. English, 1959-62, George A. Wilson prof. Am. Lit., 1966—2009, emeritus prof. English, 2010—; tchg. asst. U. Wis., Madison, 1956-59; head dept. English, chmn. dept. Humanities Adrian (Mich.) Coll., 1962-66. Adv. bd. Jack London Found., Sonoma, Calif., 1973—. Author: Jack London, 1974, 2d edit.,94; co-author: A Handbook of Critical Approaches to Literature, 1966, 6th edit., 2010; co-editor: The Letters of Jack London, 1988, The Complete Short Stories of Jack London, 1993; editor: Viking Portable Jack London, 1994, Jack London: An American Life, 2013. Fulbright prof., Denmark, 1973-74; named Jack London Man of Yr. Jack London Found., 1975, 2011, Humanist of Yr. La. Endowment for Humanities, 1991. Mem. MLA, Coll. English Assn. (editor 1967-75, pres. 1977-79, Disting. Svc. award 1983, Lifetime Membership award 1990), Jack London Soc. (bd. dirs. 1990—), Nat. Assn. Scholars and Critics. Avocation: photography. Personal E-mail: elabor@centenary.edu.

LABUTTI, RONALD STEPHAN, orthopedist; b. Tacoma, Oct. 12, 1965; s. Ronald Justin and Judith Ann LaButti; m. Robin Michelle Ford, Sept. 2, 2001. BA in Psychology, Providence Coll., RI, 1987; DO, U. New England Coll. Osteopathic Medicine, Biddeford, Maine, 1994. Cert. Am. Osteo. Bd. of Orthop. Surgery. Intern, clin. instr., dept. internal medicine RI Hosp./Brown U., Providence, 1994—95; orthop. surgery resident Okla. State U. Coll. Osteo. Medicine, Tulsa, 1995—99, assoc. clin. prof., orthop. surgery, 2002—, asst. program dir. orthop. surgery residency program, 2003—; pediatric orthop. surgery rotation Shriners Hosp. for Children, Spokane, Wash., 1997—98; hip and knee reconstruction rotation U. Utah Med. Ctr., 1998; orthop. sports medicine rotation Detroit Med. Ctr./Hutzel Hosp., 1998; hand surgery rotation Detroit Med. Ctr./Harper Hosp., 1998; dept. orthop. surgery, lower extremity and joint reconstruction fellow Buffalo Gen. Hosp./SUNY, Buffalo, 1999—2000; pvt. practice Central States Orthop. Specialists, Inc, Tulsa, 2000—. Clin. instr. Okla. State U. Coll. Osteo. Medicine Western U. Health Scis., 1995—99; team physician Tulsa Pub. Schools, Tulsa, Okla., 1995—99, Internat. Profl. Rodeo Assn. Longhorn Rodeo, Tulsa, Okla., 1995—99, Cleve. Pub. Schools, Cleve., 1995—99, Tulsa Roughnecks Soccer Team, 1999; mem. orthop. peer review com. (rotating mem.) St. Francis Hosp., 2001—; mem. surgical morbidity and mortality com. Tulsa Regional Med. Ctr., 2000—; presenter in field; bd. trustees Okla. State Med. Assoc., 2009—11; bd. dirs. Arthritis Found. Eastern Okla. Chpt. South Ctrl. Region, 2011—; chmn. dept. orthop. St. Francis Hosp., 2013—. Contbr. articles various profl. jours. Physician for student history and phys. exams for athletic participation Cleve. Pub. Sch., Cleve., Okla., Holland Hall Sch., Tulsa, Okla., Jenks Pub. Schools, Jenks, Okla.; bd. trustees Okla. State Med. Assn., 2009—10; bd. examiner Am. Osteopathic Bd.; lifetime mem. Osteo. Founders Found., Tulsa, 2003—04, chmn., Winterset Ball" Stepping Out 2004" Charity Ball, 2004; benefactor LaButti Scholarship for Academic Excellence, Okla. State U. Coll. Osteo. Medicine, 2001—; premier sponsor Tulsa Running Club, 2003—04. Named one of Am.'s Top Physicians, Consumers' Rsch. Coun. Am., 2004—05, Leading Physicians of World, Internat. Assn. Orthop. Surgeons. Fellow: Am. Osteo. Acad. Orthop.; mem.: Tulsa Osteo. Med. Soc., Tulsa Orthop.

Soc., Tulsa Orthop. Network, Tulsa County Med. Soc., Okla. Osteo. Assn., Am. Acad. Orthop. Surgeons, Am. Osteo. Acad. Orthop. Surgery (mem. newsletter com. 2003—), Am. Osteo. Assn. (Psi Sigma Alpha 1994), Psi Sigma Alpha. Achievements include being the first orthopedic surgeon in Tulsa to offer and perform ceramic-on-ceramic total hip replacement; the first orthopedic surgeon in Oklahoma to perform computer assisted total knee replacement. Avocations: fishing, hunting, playing the guitar. Office: Ctrl States Orthop Specialists Inc William Med Bldg 6585 S Yale Ste 200 Tulsa OK 74136 Home: 1203 E 19th St Tulsa OK 74120 Home Phone: 918-592-7080; Office Phone: 918-481-2767. Office Fax: 918-481-7611. Personal E-mail: ronlabutti@cox.net.

LACHANCE, JANICE RACHEL, professional association and federal agency administrator, lawyer; b. Biddeford, Maine, June 17, 1953; d. Ralph L. and Rachel A. (Desnoyers) L. BA, Manhattanville Coll., 1974; JD, Tulane U., 1978. Bar: Maine 1978, D.C. 1982, U.S. Supreme Ct. 1999. Staff dir. subcom. on antitrust Ho. of Reps., Washington, 1982-83; adminstrv. asst. Congresswoman Katie Hall, 1983-84; asst. pres. sec. Mondale-Ferraro Campaign, Washington, 1984; press sec. Congressman Tom Daschle, 1985; ptnr. Lachance and Assocs., Washington, 1985-87; dir. communications and polit. action Am. Fedn. Govt. Employees (AFL-CIO), Washington, 1987-93; dir. policy and communications U.S. Office Pers. Mgmt., Washington, 1993-96, chief of staff, 1996-97, dep. dir., 1997, dir., 1997—2001; mgmt. consultant Analytica Inc., Alexandria, Va., 2001; exec. dir. Spl. Librs. Assn. (SLA), Washington, 2003, CEO. Vis. scholar Cornell U., 1972-73. Editor newsletter Govt. Standard, 1987-93. Mem. Delta Delta Delta, Phi Alpha Delta; fellow Nat. Acad. Pub. Admin. Democrat. Roman Catholic. Office: Spl Libraries Assn 331 South Patrick St Alexandria VA 22314 Office Phone: 703-647-4933. E-mail: janice@sla.org.

LACHS, JOHN, philosopher, educator; b. Budapest, Hungary, July 17, 1934; arrived in US, 1957; s. Julius and Magda (Brod) L.; m. Shirley Marie Mellow, June 3, 1967; children: Sheila Marie, James Richard. BA, McGill U., 1956, MA, 1957; PhD, Yale, 1961. From asst. prof. to prof. philosophy Coll. William and Mary, 1959-67; prof. philosophy Vanderbilt U., 1967—, Centennial Prof., 1993—. Chmn. faculty senate Vanderbilt U., 1990—91. Author: Marxist Philosophy: A Bibliographical Guide, 1967, The Ties of Time, 1970, Intermediate Man, 1981, Mind and Philosophers, 1987, George Santayana, 1988, The Relevance of Philosophy to Life, 1995, In Love With Life, 1998, A Community of Individuals, 2003, On Santayana, 2005, Stoic Pragmatism, 2012, (with M. Hodges) Thinking in the Ruins, 2000; editor: Animal Faith and Spiritual Life, 1967, Physical Order and Moral Liberty, 1969; co-editor: The Human Search, 1981, The Encyclopedia of American Philosophy, 2008; co-translator: Fichte, Science of Knowledge, 1970; contbr. articles to profl. jours. Past chmn. Tenn. Com. for Humanities. Recipient Award for Advancement of Scholarship Phi Beta Kappa, 1962, Harris Harbison award for disting. tchg. Danforth Found., 1967, Chancellor's cup Vanderbilt U., 1970, Madison Sarratt prize excellence undergrad. tchg., 1972, Alumni Edn. award Vanderbilt U., 1991, 2013, Grad Tchg. award, 2000, Herbert Schneider award, 1997, Tchg. Freshman award, 1999, Grad. Mentoring award, 2010. Mem. Internat. Neoplatonic Soc., American Philos. Assn., Metaphys. Soc. America (past pres.), Soc. Advancement American Philosophy (past pres.), Soc. Health and Human Values, C.S. Peirce Soc. (past pres.), William James Soc. (past pres.), Tenn. Philos. Assn., So. Soc. Philosophy and Psychology, Hasting Ctr. Episcopalian. Home: 1968 Edenbridge Way Nashville TN 37215-5809 Office: Vanderbilt University 2305 W End Ave Nashville TN 37240-1700 Office Phone: 615-322-2637.

LACKER, JEFFREY MALCOLM, bank executive, economist; b. Lexington, Ky., Sept. 27, 1955; s. William Ralph and Marion (Spears) Lacker; m. Lisa Joy Halberstadt, June 7, 1981; children: Benjamin S.H., Daniel H. BA in Econs., Franklin & Marshall Coll., Lancaster, PA, 1977; PhD in Econs., U. Wis., Madison, 1984. Rsch. assoc. Wharton Econometric Forecasting Assocs., Phila., 1977-80; instr. Wardlaw-Hartridge Sch., Plainfield, NJ, 1978-79; asst. prof. Krannert Sch. Mgmt., Purdue U., Lafayette, Ind., 1984-89; rsch. economist Fed. Res. Bank Richmond, Va., 1989-90, assoc. rsch. officer, 1991-93, rsch. officer, 1994-96, v.p., 1996-99, sr. v.p., dir. rsch., 1999—2004, pres., 2004—. Contbr. articles to profl. jours. Adv. bd. mem. Jr. Achievement Ctrl. Va.; mem. adv. coun. Maggie L. Walker Gov.'s Sch., Richmond; pres. Congregation Or Ami, Richmond, 1995—97; bd. dirs. Richmond Jewish Found., World Affairs Coun. Greater Richmond. Mem.: Richmond Assn. Bus. Economists, Am. Econ. Assn. Avocation: backpacking. Office: Fed Res Bank 701 E Byrd St Richmond VA 23219 Office Phone: 804-697-8000.*

LACKLAND, THEODORE HOWARD, lawyer; b. Chgo., Dec. 4, 1943; s. Richard and Cora Lee (Sanders) L.; m. Dorothy Ann Gerald, Jan. 2, 1970; 1 child, Jennifer Noel. BS, Loyola U., Chgo., 1965; MA, Howard U., 1967; JD, Columbia U., 1975. Bar: N.J. 1975, U.S. Dist. Ct. N.J. 1975, Ga. 1982, U.S. Tax Ct. 1983, U.S. Supreme Ct. 1979, U.S. Dist. Ct. (no. dist.) Ga. 1982, U.S. Dist. Ct. (mid. dist.) Ga. 1985, U.S. Dist. Ct. (so. dist.) Ga. 2003. Assoc. Dewey, Ballantine, Bushby, Palmer & Wood, NYC, 1975-78; asst. U.S. atty. Dist. N.J., Newark, 1978-81; ptnr. Arnall Golden & Gregory, Atlanta, 1981-93, Lackland & Assoc., Atlanta, 1993-95, Lackland & Heyward, Atlanta, 1995-2000, Lackland & Assocs., LLC, Atlanta, 2000—. Adj. prof. law Ga. State U. Law Sch., 1989-99. Assoc. editor Columbia Human Rights Law Rev., 1974-75; contbr. articles to profl. jours. Adv. dir. Atlanta Bus. Devel. Ctr., Minority Bus. Devel. Coun., Atlanta, 1983-91; mem. exec. com. Leadership Atlanta, 1986, 1990-91; bd. dirs. APEX Mus., 2002—11. Active duty US Army, 1967—71. Decorated Bronze Star with 1 oak leaf cluster, Purple Heart, Air medal. Mem.: AAJ, ABA, Atlanta Bar Assn., Ga. Bar Assn. Democrat. Roman Catholic. Home: 4400 Oak Ln Marietta GA 30062-6355 Office: Lackland & Assocs LLC 630 Village Trace NE Bldg 15 Ste C Marietta GA 30067 Office Phone: 404-522-8155. Business E-Mail: tlackland@e-lacklaw.com.

LACY, ELIZABETH BERMINGHAM, state supreme court justice; b. 1945; BA cum laude, St. Mary's Coll., Notre Dame, Ind., 1966; JD, U. Tex., 1969; LLM, U. Va., 1992. Bar: Tex. 1969, Va. 1977. Staff atty. Tex. Legis. Coun., Austin, 1969-72; atty. Office of Atty. Gen., State of Tex., Austin, 1973-76; legis. aide Va. Del. Carrington Williams, Richmond, 1976-77; dep. atty. gen. jud. affairs div. Va. Office Atty. Gen., Richmond, 1982-85; mem. Va. State Corp. Commn., Richmond, 1985-89; justice Va. Supreme Ct., Richmond, 1989—2007, sr. justice, 2007—. Office: Supreme Court of Virginia PO Box 1315 Richmond VA 02321-1315*

LACY, JOHN FORD, retired lawyer; b. Dallas, Sept. 11, 1944; s. John Alexander and Glenda Arcenia (Ford) L.; m. Cece Smith, Apr. 22, 1978. BA, Baylor U., 1965; JD, Harvard U., 1968. Bar: Tex. 1968. Atty. Akin, Gump, Strauss, Hauer & Feld, Dallas, 1968—99; ret., 1999. Co-founder, chmn., pres. rsch. coun. U. Tex. Southwestern Med. Ctr., Dallas, 1985-91; bd. dirs. Vis. Nurse Assn. Tex., 1994-2001, 1st vice chmn., 2000-01. With USAR, 1968-74. Home: 3710 Shenandoah St Dallas TX 75205-2121 Home Phone: 214-522-0026. Personal E-mail: jofola@charter.net.

LADD, BART (CHARLES), state legislator, pilot; BS in Mech. Engring., Purdue U. Pilot Delta Air Lines; mem. Ga. Ho. of Reps., Atlanta, 1990—. Mem. Ways and Means Com., Ins. Com., Banks and Banking Com. With USAF. Mem. Kiwanis. Methodist. Office: Legis Office Bldg Rm 604 Atlanta GA 30334 Home: 116 E Commons Dr Saint Simons Island GA 31522-9786

LADER, PHILIP, corporate director, lawyer, academic administrator, diplomat; b. Jackson Heights, NY, Mar. 17, 1946; BA, Duke U., 1966; MA, U. Mich., 1967, Oxford U., Eng., 1968; JD, Harvard U., 1972. Bar: Fla. 1972, DC 1973, SC 1979. Atty. Sullivan & Cromwell, NYC, 1972; law clk. to U.S. cir. judge, 1973; pres. Sea Pines Co., Hilton Head Island, SC, 1979-83, Winthrop U., Rock Hill, SC, 1983-85; exec. v.p. Sir James Goldsmith's US Holding Co., 1986-88; pres. Bus. Execs. for Nat. Security, Washington, 1990—91; pres., vice chancellor Bond U., Queensland, Australia, 1991-93; adminstr. SBA, Washington, 1994-97; mem. President's Cabinet, Washington, 1994-97; U.S. amb. to Ct. of St. James, 1997-2001; chmn. WPP plc, 2001—; sr. advisor Morgan Stanley, 2001—; ptnr. Nelson Mullins Riley & Scarborough, 2001—. Dep. dir. for mgmt. Office Mgmt. and Budget, Exec. Office Pres., 1993; dep. chief of staff White House, asst. to Pres., 1993-94; chmn. Pres.'s Coun. on Integrity and Efficiency, 1993, chmn. Pres.'s Mgmt. Coun.; chmn. policy com. Nat. Performance Rev., 1993; candidate for gov. SC, 1986; bd. dirs Marathon Oil, AES Corp, RAND Corp., Songbird Estates, Canary Wharf Plc, UC Rusal Corp.; trustee Bank Internat. Found. for Innovation, Smithsonian Mus. Am. History. Founder Renaissance Weekends; trustee Brit. Mus., 2001—06, Brit-Am. Bus. Coun., St. Paul's Cathedral Found., 2001—06, Windsor Leadership Trust, 2001—06, Found. for the 21st Century, Salzburg Global Seminar, 2001—06; chmn., Am. assoc. Royal Acad. Art., 2001—04; mem. vis. com. Harvard Law Sch., Harvard Divinity Sch., Yale Divinity Sch.; mem. internat. adv. com. Columbia U.; chmn. bd. visitors Duke U. Sanford Inst. Pub. Policy, 1999—2001; bd. dirs. ARC, 1996—97; mem. adv. bd. Prince of Wales Trust; mem. coun. Lloyd's of London, 2004—. Hon. fellow Pembroke Coll., Oxford U., London Bus. Sch., John Moores U.; hon. bencher Mid. Temple. Mem.: Chief Execs. Orgn., Coun. Fgn. Rels., Royal Soc. Arts, Mfrs. and Sci. (Benjamin Franklin medal 2001), Soc. Internat. Bus. Fellows, Rotary Internat. (Global Svc. Humanity award 2007), D.C. Met. Club, Harvard Club N.Y.C., Phi Beta Kappa. Episcopalian. Office: Liberty Ctr 151 Meeting St Ste 600 Charleston SC 29401

LADNER, TIMMY, state legislator; m. Carrie Smith. Attended, Pearl River CC, Poplarville, Miss., Miss. Realtors Inst. Small bus. owner, realtor, Miss.; mem. Dist. 93 Miss. House of Reps., Jackson, 2012—. Mem.: Nat. Assn. Realtors, Miss. Assn. Realtors, Gulf Coast Assn. Realtors. Republican. Baptist. Office: Miss House of Reps PO Box 1018 Jackson MS 39215 Business E-Mail: tladner@house.ms.gov.

LADWIG, HAROLD ALLEN, neurologist; b. Manilla, Iowa, May 11, 1922; s. Ernest and Iva Marie (Allen) L.; m. Marjorie Lois Foster, June 26, 1946; children: Stephen H., Rosemary A. BA, U. Iowa, 1942, MD, 1947. Intern St. Joseph Hosp., Sioux City, Iowa, 1947-48; pvt. practice U. Minn., 1948—50, resident, 1952—53; pvt. practice Nebr., 1954-83, NC, 1983—99; pres. Omaha Neurol. Clinic, 1972-83. Contbr. articles to profl. jours. Bd. dirs. Boys and Girls Club, Wilson, NC, 1995—, Salvation Army, Wilson, 1996-, Country Drs. Mus., Bailey, NC, 1995-2002, Mental Health Bd., Wilson, 1995-2007, Mental Health LME, 2007-10. Comdr. USNR, 1950-52. Recipient Honorable Alumnus award, Barton Coll., Wilson, NC, 2008, Physician Leadership award, Wilmed Health Care Wilson NC, 2010. Fellow ACP, Am. Acad. Neurology; mem. AMA, Am. Assn. Electrodiagnostic Medicine, Am. Soc. Electroencephalography and Neurophysiology, Wilson County Med. Soc. (sec. 1993, v.p. 1994, pres. 1995), Wilson Meml. Hosp. Found. (pres. 1993-2006), Douglas County Med. Soc. (exec. bd. 1960-63), Kiwanis (pres. Wilson chpt. 1995, Kiwanian of Yr. award 1992-93), Phi Beta Kappa, Beta Beta Beta. Methodist. Avocation: computers. Home: 1600 Canal Dr NW Wilson NC 27893-2246 Personal E-mail: hal@usa.com.

LAFFER, ARTHUR BETZ, finance company executive; b. Youngstown, Ohio, Aug. 14, 1940; s. William Gillespie Laffer; m. Traci Lynn Hickman; 6 children. BA, Yale U., 1963; MBA, Stanford U., 1965, Ph.D, 1971. Faculty mem. University of Chicago, 1967—76, assoc. prof. bus. economics, 1970—76; chief economist, Office Mgmt. & Budget Exec. Office of the Pres., Washington, 1970—72; cons. to sec. US Dept. Treasury, 1972—77; prof. fin. & bus. economics U. So. Calif., LA, 1976-84, Charles B. Thornton prof. bus. economics, 1979-84; Disting. Univ. prof. Pepperdine U., 1984—87; founder, CEO Laffer Associates, 1979—; commentator, co-host MoneyMan Report BizRadio Network, 2007—; Disting. Univ. prof. economics Mercer U., 2008—; chmn. Laffer Investments Inc. Bd. dirs. MPS Group, Inc., Rcg Fin. & Ins. Svcs., Inc. Author: Supply Side Economics: Financial Decision -Making for the 80's; co-author (with Stephen Moore & Peter Tanous): The End of Prosperity: How Higher Taxes Will Doom the Economy-If We Let It Happen, 2008; co-author: (with Stephen Moore) Return to Prosperity: How America Can Regain Its Economic Superpower Status, 2010; appeared in (documentaries) Reagan, 2011. Bd. dirs. Com. Monetary Research and Edn.; hon. bd. dirs. Los Angeles County Mus. Natural History; mem. adv. bd. Taxpayers Found. Recipient Commerce Assocs. Dean's Facility award U. So. Calif., 1979, Teaching Excellence award U. So. Calif. Assocs., 1980, John J. Knezevich Americanism award, 1979, Daniel Webster award Internat. Platform Assn., 1979, Father of Yr. award West Coast Fathers' Day Com., 1983 Republican. Achievements include the invention of the Laffer Curve. Office: Laffer Investments Inc 2909 Poston Ave Fl 2 Nashville TN 37203-1346 Office Phone: 615-320-3989. Office Fax: 615-320-3806. E-mail: jax@laffer.com.

LAFLEUR, ERIC, state legislator; b. Ville Platte; m. Julie Morein LaFleur. BA, LSU & Tulane; JD Civil Law, Tulane Law Sch. Felony prosecutor under Dist. Atty. Harry Connick, New Orleans; felony prosecutor under Richard Ieyoub La. Dept. of Justice; ptnr. Mahtook & La Fleur; mem. Dist. 28 La. State Senate, 2008—, vice chair edn. com., mem. fin. com., ins. com., judiciary B com., select com. on consumer affairs and tech. Democrat. Cath. Mailing: Capitol Office PO Box 94183 Baton Rouge LA 70804 Address: District Office PO Box 617 Ville Platte LA 70586 Office Phone: 225-342-2040, 337-363-5019. Fax: 337-363-6812.

LAFLEUR, KENNETH CHARLES, ophthalmologist; b. Lawtell, La., Aug. 22, 1941; s. Abram George and Mary Irene (Olivier) L.; m. Patricia Ione McNamara, Aug. 3, 1963; children: James Mathew, Suzanne Annette, Caroline Marie. BS, U. So. La., 1963; MD, Tulane U., 1966. Diplomate Am. Bd. Ophthalmology. Intern Hermann Hosp., Houston, 1966-67; ophthalmology resident U. Tex., 1967-70; practice medicine specializing in ophthalmology Opeloussas, La., 1972—. Clin. asst. prof. La. State U. Eye Ctr., New Orleans, 1983—. Trustee St. Landry Roman Cath. Ch., Opeloussas, 1979-99. Maj. M.C., U.S. Army, 1970-72. Fellow Am. Acad. Ophthalmology, Soc. Mil. Ophthalmologists; mem. Am. Intraocular Implant Soc., Elks, K.C. (Knight of Yr. award 1984). Democrat. Roman Catholic. Avocation: fishing. Office: 1108 Katherine Dr Opelousas LA 70570 Office Phone: 337-948-1246. Personal E-mail: klafleur@earthlink.net.

LAFUZE, WILLIAM L., lawyer; b. Washington, Feb. 21, 1946; children: Molly, Betsy, William Jr. BS in Physics, U. Tex., Austin, 1969, JD, 1973; MS in Applied Sci., So. Meth. U., 1971; postgrad., U. London, 1973. Bar: Tex. 1973, US Patent and Trademark Office, US Supreme Ct., US Ct. Appeals Fed. Cir. Rsch. scientist Ctr. for Nuclear Studies, Austin, 1966-69; instr. computer sci. U. Tex., Austin, 1968-69, 71-73; assoc. Vinson & Elkins LLP, Houston, 1973-80, ptnr., 1980—. Mem. Transition Team for Dept. Commerce, Patent and Trademark Office matters, 2000—01; mem. patent pub. adv. com. US Patent and Trademark Office, Dept. Commerce, 2002—04; mem. adv. bd. Houston Tech. Ctr. Contbr. articles to profl. jours. Fellow: Am. Intellectual Property Law Assn. (bd. dirs. 1983—94, chmn. amicus brief com. 1986—88, pres. 1992—93), Houston Bar Found., Greater Houston Partnership (life), ABA (life; intellectual property law sect. coun. 1998—, chair section of intellectual property 2004—05, chmn. 2004—), Texas Bar Found. (life); mem.: MIT Enterprise Forum of Tex. (past bd. dirs.), Licensing Executives Soc., Nat. Coun. Patent Law Associations (del. 1982—, bd. dirs. 1987—90, past pres.), US Trademark Assn. (bd. editors Trademark Reporter 1976—78), Houston Bar Assn., State Bar Tex. (intellectual property law sect. coun. 1979—83, consumer law sect. coun. 1981—88, chmn. 1984—85, computer sect. coun. 1990—97), Houston Intellectual Property Law Assn. (past pres.), Nat. Inventors Hall of Fame (bd. dirs. 1987—, pres. 1994—95). Office: Vinson & Elkins 1001 Fannin St Ste 2300 Houston TX 77002-6760 Office Phone: 713-758-2595. Business E-Mail: wlafuze@velaw.com.

LAGASSE, EMERIL, chef, restaurant owner, television show host, writer; b. Fall River, Mass., Oct. 15, 1959; s. John and Hilda Lagasse; m. Elizabeth Kief (div.); children: Jessica, Jillian; m. Tari Hohn (div.); m. Alden Lovelace, May 13, 2000; children: Emeril John Lagasse IV, Meril Lovelace. BS in Culinary Arts, Johnson & Wales U., Providence, RI, D (hon.); studied culinary arts, France. Exec. chef Commander's Palace, New Orleans, 1983—90; owner, chef Emeril's restaurant, New Orleans, 1990—, Nola restaurant, New Orleans, 1992—, Emeril's New Orleans Fish House restaurant, Las Vegas, 1995—, Delmonico Restaurant and Bar, New Orleans, 1998—, Emeril's Orlando, Orlando, Fla., 1999—, Delmonico Steakhouse restaurant, Las Vegas, 1999—, Tchoup Chop restaurant, Orlando, Fla., 2003—, Emeril's Atlanta, 2003—, Emeril's Miami Beach, 2003—11, Emeril's Gulf Coast Fish House, Gulfport, Miss., 2007—, Table 10, Las Vegas, 2008—, Emeril's Chop House, Sands Casino Resort, Bethlehem, Pa., 2009—, Lagasse's Stadium, Las Vegas, 2009—, Burgers and More by Emeril, Sands Casino Resort, Bethlehem, Pa., 2009—, Emeril's Italian Table, Sands Casino Resort, Bethlehem, Pa., 2011—, e2 Emeril's Eatery, Charlotte, NC, 2011—; host cooking show Essence of Emeril (The Food Network), 1994—, Essence of Emeril (The Fine Living Network), 2008—, Emeril Live (The Food Network), 1997—2007; food corr. Good Morning America, ABC, 1998—. Ptnr. All-Clad Metalcrafters for Emerilware, 1999—; launches Emeril's Original, gourmet food line of seasonings, salad dressing, pasta sauces and more, 2000; launches Emerilware knives with Wusthof-Trident, 2002; launches a Calif. wines line called Emerils' Classics with Fetzer Vineyards, 2002; introduces clog line called Emeril by Sanita, 2003; launches Emeril's Gourmet Meats with Sara Lee Foods, 2004; launches Emerilware Electric Appliance Collection and Emerilware Cast Iron Cookware, 2004; launches Emeril's Gourmet Produce with Pride of San Juan, 2004; ptnr. Emeril Profl. stoneware, 2005—, T-fal to develop Emerilware Fryer, Grill/Panini Maker and Steamer, 2006—; Emerilware cookware and gourmet kitchen tools brought the HSN, 2007. Author: (cookbook) Emeril's New New Orleans Cooking, 1993, Louisiana Real and Rustic, 1996, Emeril's Creole Christmas, 1997, Emeril's TV Dinners, 1998, Every Day's a Party, 1999, Prime Time Emeril: More TV Dinners from America's Favorite Chef, 2001, There's a Chef in My Soup, 2002, From Emeril's Kitchens: Favorite Receipes from Emeril's Restaurants, 2003, There's a Chef in My Family, 2004, Emeril's Potluck: Comfort Food with a Kicked-Up Attitude, 2004, Emeril's Delmonico: A New Orleans Restaurant with a Past, 2005, There's a Chef in My World, 2006, Emeril 20-40-60: Freesh Food Fast, 2009, Emeril at the Grill: A Cookbook for All Seasons, 2009, Farm to Fork: Cooking Local, Cooking Fresh, 2010, Sizzling Skillets and Other One-Pot Wonders, 2011, Emeril's Kicked-Up Sandwiches: Stacked with Flavor, 2012, Emeril's Cooking with Power: 100 Delicious Recipes Starring Your Slow Cooker, Multi Cooker, Pressure Cooker, and Deep Fryer, 2013; judge (TV series) Top Chef, 2011, host Planet Green: Emeril Green, 2008—, Emeril Live, Cooking Channel, Fresh Food Fast, Cooking Channel, 2010—, The Emeril Lagasse Show, Ion TV, 2010, Emeril's Table, Hallmark Channel, 2011—, The Originals with Emeril, Cooking Channel, 2011—, live, call-in radio program Cooking with Emeril, Martha Stewart Living Radio on SIRIUS XM, 2009—, writer with son (column) Everyday Food Mag., guest appearances Jon & Kate Plus 8, 2009, voice The Princess and the Frog, 2009, competitor Super Chef Battle, Iron Chef America, 2010, stars in comedy series Emeril, 2001. Established Emeril Lagasse Found., 2002; dedicated the Emeril Lagasse Found. Culinary Arts Studio, 2011. Recipient Esquire award for Restaurant of Yr., 1991, Food and Wine award for one of Am.'s Top 25 New Chefs, 1991, Best Chef Southeast, James Beard Found., 1991, Best Esquire award for restaurant of yr., 1993, Ivy award for restaurants and instns., 1994, Cable ACE award for Best Informational Series-Emeril Live, 1997, Salute to Excellence award, Nat. Restaurant Assn., 1998, Grand award, Wine Spectator Mag., 1999, Disting. Svc. award, Wine Spectator mag., 2005, Lifetime Achievement award, Food Network's South Beach Wine & Food Festival, 2009, of honor by the James Beard Found. for dedicated efforts to further the culinary arts in America, as well as work through the Emeril Lagasse Found., 2011; named Chef of Yr., GQ Mag., 1998, Exec. of Yr., Restaurants & Institutions mag., 2004, Restaurateur of Yr., New Orleans CityBusiness, 2007; named one of America's Top Twenty-Five New Chefs, Food & Wine, 1991, Most Intriguing People of Yr., People Mag., 1998; named to Am. Express for Fine Dining Hall of Fame, 1994, Gaming Hall of Fame, 2008, MenuMasters Hall of Fame, 2006. Achievements include being first celebrity chef to have meals and recipes developed for NASA and served in Space, 2006; restaurants have received several awards and acknowledgements; The Emeril Lagasse Foundation raises millions of dollars each year with the culinary event Carnivale du Vin. Office: Emerils Homebase LLC 829 Saint Charles Ave New Orleans LA 70130-3715*

LAGOMASINO, MARIA ELENA (MEL LAGOMASINO), investment company executive; b. Havana, Cuba, Mar. 27, 1949; B in French Lit., Manhattanville Coll., 1970; MLS, Columbia U., 1975; MBA, Fordham U., 1982. Joined Citibank, 1976, v.p., 1977—83; mgr., divsn. exec. Chase Pvt. Banking Internat., 1983—89, mgr. Western Hemisphere ops., 1989—94, mktg. exec. Ams. region, 1994—97; sr. mng. dir. Chase Manhattan Pvt. Bank, 1997—2000; chmn., CEO J.P. Morgan Pvt. Bank, NYC, 2001—05; CEO, GenSpring Family Offices, LLC (formerly Asset Management Advisors, LLC), Palm Beach Gardens, Fla., 2005—. Bd. dirs. Avon Products, 2000—, The Coca-Cola Co., 2003—06, 2008—; bd. trustees Synergos Inst.; adv. com. transformational diplomacy US Dept. State, 2006—; mem. commn. White Ho. fellowships The White House, 2006—. Bd. trustees Nat. Geographic Soc.; bd. mem. Lincoln Ctr. Theatre. Named Woman of Yr., Hispanic Bus. mag., 2007; named one of 25 Women to Watch, US Banker, 2003, 25 Most Powerful

Women in Fin., 2010; named to Hispanic Bus. Corp. Elite, 2004. Mem.: Coun. on Fgn. Rels. Office: GenSpring Family Offices LLC 3801 PGA Blvd Ste 555 Palm Beach Gardens FL 33410

LAGOW, RICHARD JAMES, chemistry professor; b. Albuquerque, Aug. 16, 1945; BA, Rice U., 1967, PhD, 1969. Instr. dept. chemistry Rice U., Houston, 1967-69; from asst. to assoc. prof. dept. chemistry MIT, Cambridge, Mass., 1969-76; assoc. prof. dept. chemistry U. Tex., Austin, 1976-80, prof. dept. chemistry, 1980-94, L.N. Vauquelin Regents prof. chemistry dept. chemistry, 1994—. Recipient Alexander von Humboldt award, 1992, award for creative work in fluorine chemistry Am. Chem. Soc., 1997; Alfred P. Sloan fellow, 1974-75. Fellow AAAS.

LAHAYE, TIMOTHY F., pastor, writer; b. Detroit, Apr. 27, 1926; s. Frank and Margaret (Palmer) LaHaye; m. Beverly LaHaye, July 5, 1947; children: Linda, Larry, Lee, Lori. BA, Bob Jones U., 1950; D in Ministry, We. Conservative Baptist Seminary, 1977; HHD (hon.), Liberty U., 1992. Pastor Shadow Mountain Com. Church, 1958—83; founder San Diego Christian Coll. (formerly Christian Heritage Coll.), 1971; co-founder Inst. Creationist Rsch., 1979, Pre-Tribulation Rsch. Ctr., 1998. Founder Coalition for Religious Freedom, Am. Coalition for Traditional Values. Author: Revelation: Illustrated and Made Plain, 1973, How to Study the Bible for Yourself, 1976, No Fear of the Storm, 1977, The Battle for the Mind, 1980, Spirit-Controlled Temperament, 1993, The Act of Marriage, 1998, The Power of the Cross, 1998, The Merciful God of Prophecy, 2002, Babylon Rising, 2003, The Secret on Ararat, 2004, The Europa Conspiracy, 2005, The Edge of Darkness, 2006; co-author (with Jerry B. Jenkins): Left Behind: A Novel of the Earth's Last Days, 1995, Tribulation Force: The Continuing Drama of Those Left Behind, 1996, Nicolae: The Rise of Antichrist, 1997, Soul Harvest: The World Takes Sides, 1998, Apollyon: The Destroyer Is Unleashed, 1999, Assassins: Assignment: Jerusalem, Target: Antichrist, 1999, The Indwelling: The Beast Takes Possession, 2000, The Mark: The Beast Rules the World, 2000, Desecration: Antichrist Takes the Throne, 2001, The Remnant: On the Brink of Armageddon, 2002, Armageddon: The Cosmic Battle of the Ages, 2003, Glorious Appearing: The End of Days, 2004, The Rising: Before They Were Left Behind, 2005, The Regime: Before They Were Left Behind, 2005, The Rapture, 2006, John's Story: the Last Eyewitness, 2006, Kingdom Come: The Final Victory, 2007, Mark's Story: The Gospel According to Peter, 2007; co-author: (with Ed Hindson) Global Warning!: Are We On the Brink of World War III?, 2007; co-host (TV series) The King Is Coming, 2001. Mem.: Coun. for Nat. Policy (pres. 1981—82, exec. com. 1984—85). Christian. Office: The Pre-Tribulation Rsch Ctr Liberty Univ 1971 University Blvd Lynchburg VA 24502 Office Phone: 434-592-3773.

LAHOWCHIC, NICHOLAS JOHN, consulting company executive; b. NYC, Apr. 11, 1947; s. Nicholas and Mary Ellen (Dunn) La H.; m. Diane Forrest; children: Tara Anne, Nicole Marie. Student, Marquette U., Milw., 1964—66; BS in Acctg., Fairleigh Dickinson U., Teaneck, NJ, 1970; MBA, Pace U., NYC, 1980; DSc, Logistic Healthcare Strategy Bd., 2011. Acct. Okonite Cable Corp., Passaic, NJ, 1966-68; cost analyst Philips Broadcast Equip. Corp., Paramus, NJ, 1968-69; from corp. acct. to mgr. Thomas J. Lipton, Inc., Englewood Cliffs, NJ, 1969—77, mgr. ops. planning, 1977—79; gen. mgr. McGraw Hill Book Co., NYC, 1979-81; dir. inventory mgmt. Nabisco Brands, Inc., Parsippany, NJ, 1981-84, 1984-85, dir. logistics planning, systems and adminstrn., 1985-87; dir. logistics Colgate-Palmolive, Inc., NYC, 1987-89, dir. customer svc. and logistics, 1989-91; v.p. corp. logistics Becton Dickinson & Co., Franklin Lakes, NJ, 1991-95; pres. Becton Dickinson Supply Chain Svcs., Franklin Lakes, NJ, 1995-97; pres., CEO Ltd. Logistics Svcs., Columbus, 1997—; exec. v.p. Ltd. Brands, Inc., 2004—07; pres. Diannic LLC, Port St. Lucie, Fla., 2007—. Bd. dirs. Express Scripts Inc., 2001-, Vitamix Inc., 2012-, Advance Arts Parts, Inc., 2006-09; bd. adv. dir. Whirlpool Co., 2007-11; cons. in field. Mem. editl. adv. bd. Supply Chain Mgmt. Rev., Med. Product Sales mag; contbr. articles to bus. publs. Trustee United Way, Greater Columbus, Ohio, 1999-2005, Columbus C. of C., 2003-06, Columbus Jazz Group, 2006-07, Compete Columbus, 2006-07. Recipient Harry Salzburg medallion award, 1997, Thinkers & Movers award, 2010. Mem. Nat. Assn. Accts., Am. Mgmt. Assn., Am. Prodn. and Inventory Control Soc. (dir. 1979-80), Nat. Coun. Phys. Distbn. Mgmt. (v.p. 1982-83), Health Industry Distbn. Assn. (bd. dirs. 1997-2001), Health Industry Mfrs. Assn., Health Industry Bar Code Coun., Grocery Mfrs. Assn. (chmn. distbn. ops. steering com.), Coun. Logistics Mgmt., Internat. Materials Mgmt. Soc. Pace U., Columbus C. of C. (bd. dirs. 2001-2005). Office: PO Box 9618 Port Saint Lucie FL 34985 Office Phone: 614-561-7100. Business E-Mail: nlahowchic@diannicltd.com.

LAING, MALCOLM BRIAN, geologist, consultant; b. Apr. 4, 1955; s. Alexander Duncan and Joan (Dawson) Laing; m. Vicki Lynne Laing; children: Megan Jené, Brian Duncan. BS in Geology, Tex. Christian U., 1978. Geologist Electro-Seise, Inc., Ft. Worth, 1978-79, Exploration Logging Co., Houston, 1979-80, Thomas-Powell Royalty Co., Ft. Worth, 1980-82, Lentex Petroleum Inc., Abilene, Tex., 1982-84; cons., 1984-90, Tex. Dept. Health, 1990-92, Tex. Water Commn., 1992-93, Tex. Natural Resource Conservation Commn., 1993—2002, Tex. Commn. on Environ. Quality, 2002—; owner Laing Aviation Svcs. Internat. cons. on Japanese and German WWII aircraft; builder, designer Ki-51 Replica Aircraft; ptnr. Laing Svcs. GP. Co-author: FW 190 D Walkaround, FW 190 AF Walkaround. Dir. Caprock chpt.; mem. Tex. Air Mus., 1995—, bd. dirs., chmn. bd., 2005—09; Cactus Air Force, 2000-04. Mem.: Llano Estacado Regional Water Planning Group, Am. Assn. Petroleum Geologists. Republican. Methodist.

LAIRD, DORIS ANNE MARLEY, retired humanities educator, musician; b. Charlotte, NC, Jan. 15, 1931; d. Eugene Harris and Coleen (Bethea) Marley; m. William Everette Laird Jr., Mar. 13, 1964; children: William Everette III, Andrew Marley, Glen Howard. MusB, Converse Coll., Spartanburg, SC, 1951; opera cert., New Eng. Conservatory, Boston, 1956; MusM, Boston U., 1956; PhD, Fla. State U., 1980. Leading soprano roles S.C. Opera Co., Columbia, 1951-53, Plymouth Rock Ctr. of Music and Art, Duxbury, Mass., 1953-56; soprano Pro Musica, Boston, 1956, New Eng. Opera Co., Boston, 1956; instr. Stratford Coll., Danville, Va., 1956-58, Sch. Music Fla. State U., Tallahassee, 1958-60, dept. humanities, 1960-68; tchr. Fla. State U., 1973-79; asst. prof. Fla. A&M U., Tallahassee, 1979-89, assoc. prof., 1990—2002; ret., 2002. Vis. scholar Cornell U., 1988; participant So. Conf. on Afro-Am. Studies, Inc. Author: Colin Morris: Modern Missionary, 1980; contbr. articles to profl. jours. Soprano Washington St. Meth. Ch., Columbia, SC, 1951-53, Copley Meth. Ch., Boston, 1953-56; soloist Trinity United Meth. Ch., Tallahassee, 1983—; mem. Saint Andrews Soc., Tallahassee, 1986—; judge Brain Bowl, Tallahassee, 1981-84; alumnae bd. Converse Coll., 2004—. Recipient NEH award, Cornell U., 1988, Disting. Alumna award, Converse Coll., 2001; named subject of article, Glamour mag., 2001, Self mag., 2003; scholar Phi Sigma Tau, 1960. Mem. AAUP, AAUW, Nat. Art Educators Assn., Tallahassee Music Tchrs. Assn., Tallahassee Music Guild, Am. Guild of Organists, DAR (mus. rep. 1984-85, registrar 2005-), Colonial Dames of 17th Century (music dir. 1984-85), Nat. Assn. Humanities Edn., U. Wyo. Women's Club, Woman's Club Tallahassee (v.p. 2004), Converse Coll. Alumni (bd. dirs. 2003—) Republican. Achievements include subject of article Self Magazine, 2004. Avocations: travel, dance, music. Home: 1125 Mercer Dr Tallahassee FL 32312-2833 Personal E-mail: dorismlaird@comcast.net.

LAIRD, JEAN ELOUISE RYDESKI (MRS. JACK E. LAIRD), author, adult education educator; b. Wakefield, Mich., Jan. 18, 1930; d. Chester A. and Agnes A. (Petranek) Rydeski; m. Jack E. Laird, June 9, 1951; children: John E., Jayne E., Joan Ann P., Jerilyn S., Jacquelyn T. Bus. Edn. degree, Duluth Bus. U., Minn., 1948; postgrad., U. Minn., 1949-50. Tchr. Oak Lawn (Ill.) H.S. Adult Evening Sch., 1964-72, St. Xavier U., Chgo., 1974—. Lectr., commencement address cir.; writer newspaper column Around The House With Jean, A Woman's Work, 1965-70, Chicagotown News column The World As I See It, 1969, hobby column Modern Maturity mag., travel column Travel/Leisure mag., beauty column Ladycom mag., Time and Money Savers column Lady's Circle mag., consumerism column Ladies' Home Jour. Author: Lost in the Department Store, 1964, Around the House Like Magic, 1968, Around the Kitchen Like Magic, 1969, How to Get the Most from Your Appliances, 1967, Hundreds of Hints for Harassed Homemakers, 1971, The Alphabet Zoo, 1972, The Plump Ballerina, 1971, The Porcupine Story Book, 1974, Fried Marbles and Other Fun Things to Do, 1975, Hundreds of Hints for Harassed Homemakers: The Homemaker's Book of Time and Money Savers, 1979, =Homemaker's Book of Energy Savers, 1981, also 427 paperback booklets; contbr. articles to mags. Mem.: Marist, Mt. Assissi Acad., St. Linus Guild, Queen of Peace Parents Clubs, Oak Lawn Bus. and Profl. Women's Club, Canterbury Writers Club Chgo. Roman Catholic. Home: 10540 Lockwood Ave Oak Lawn IL 60453-5161: Harbor Towers Yacht Club Siesta Key FL 34242

LAIRD, RICHARD JOEL, state legislator; b. Rome, Ga., June 4, 1939; s. Charles O. and Rosa Lee (Burgess) Laird; m. Peggy Laird; 1 child, Joel. Attended, U. Ala. Mem. Roanoke City Coun., Ala., 1972—76; mem. Dist. 37 Ala. House of Reps., Montgomery, 1978—; pres. Ranco Inc. Mem. Handley Ave. Ch. of God; past chmn. Roanoke United Givers Fund; past pres. Roanoke Area C. of C.; chmn., Randolph County Boy Scouts of America. Named Randolph County Man of Yr., 1979; Outstanding Legislator, 1985, 1986, 1988-90. Mem.: Ala. & Randolph County Cattlemen's Assn. and Farm Bur., Ala. Farmers Fedn., Randolph County Camp of Gideons Internat. Democrat. Office: 341 Bonner Dr Roanoke AL 36274 also: Ala House of Reps Ala State House 11 S Union St Rm 528-D Montgomery AL 36130 Office Phone: 334-863-7938, 334-863-0600, 334-863-4249, 334-242-7744. Business E-Mail: rjlsr@teleclipse.net.

LAIRD, WILLIAM EVERETTE, JR., economics professor; b. Hattiesburg, Miss., Feb. 4, 1934; s. William Everette and Mildred Alvah (Howard) L.; m. Doris Anne Marley, Mar. 13, 1964; children: William Everette III, Andrew Marley, Glen Howard. BS, Stetson U., 1956; MA, George Washington U., 1958; PhD, U. Va., 1962. Asst. prof. Fla. State U., Tallahassee, 1960-66, assoc. prof., 1966-71, prof., 1971—, chmn. dept. econs., 1974-97, SERVICE prof., 1997—2002, prof. emeritus, 2002—. Contbr. articles to profl. jours. DuPont fellow, 1959-60; recipient awards Fla. State U. Grad. Research Council, 1965, 66, Faculty Devel. awards Fla. State U., 1971 Mem. Am. Econs. Assn., So. Econ. Assn., Plantagenet Soc. Magna Charta Barons, Jamestowne Soc., St. Andrew Soc., Order of First Families of Va., Econ. Club of Fla. Methodist. Home: 1125 Mercer Dr Tallahassee FL 32312-2833 Office Phone: 850-385-2705. Business E-Mail: wlaird@fsu.edu.

LAIRD, WILLIAM R., IV, state legislator; b. Montgomery, WV, June 3, 1952; s. William R. Laird III and Clark Cook Laird; m. Michelle Laird; children: William, Paul, Amanda, Kathryn, Kara, Robert. BA, Marshall U.; MA, The American U. Sheriff Fayette County, 1989—96, 2001—08; dep. dir., asst. commr. Budget and Adminstrn. W.Va. Dept. Corrections; dir. Budget and Adminstrn. Office of the Attorney General, W.Va.; former pres., CEO Montgomery Gen. Hosp.; mem. W.Va. House of Delegates, 1996—98; mem. Dist. 11 W.Va. State Senate, 2008—, vice chair Natural Resources Com., mem. Agr. Com., Edn. Com., Enrolled Bills Com., Health and Human Resources Com., Judiciary Com. & Mil. Com. Democrat. United Methodist. Office: State Capitol Complex Rm 229W, Bldg 1 1900 Kanawha Blvd E Charleston WV 25305 Mailing: 225 Highland Ave Oak Hill WV 25901 Office Phone: 304-357-7849. E-mail: william.laird@wvsenate.gov.

LAKE, I. BEVERLY, JR., retired state supreme court chief justice; b. Raleigh, NC, 1934; s. I. Beverly, Sr. and Gertrude L.; m. Susan Deichmann Smith; children: Lynn Elizabeth, Guy, Laura Ann, I. Beverly III. Student, Mars Hill Coll., 1951; BS, Wake Forest U., 1955, JD, 1960. Bar: N.C. Pvt. practice, 1960-69, 76-85; asst. atty. gen. State of NC, 1969-74, dep. atty. gen., 1974-76; Gov.'s legis. liason, chief lobbyist, 1985; judge Superior Ct., 1985-91; assoc. justice NC Supreme Ct., 1992—2000, chief justice Raleigh, 2001—06. Chmn. bd. trustees Ridge Rd. Bapt. Ch., 1968-69; mem. N.C. Senate, 1976-80, chmn. Senate Judiciary Com.; Rep. nominee Gov. N.C., 1979-80; del. Rep. Nat. Convention, 1980; Rep. state fin. chmn., mem. ctr. com., mem. exec. com., 1980-82; N.C. eastern chmn. Reagan-Bush Campaign, 1984; bd. visitors Wake Forest U. Sch. Law, 1995—; bd. vis. Southeastern Bapt. Theol. Sem, 1998-. Military intelligence staff officer USAR, 1956—68, captain USAR, 1958—68, colonel, state staff judge advocate NC State Militia, 1989—92. Mem. AMVETS, N.C. Bar Assn., Wake County Bar Assn., Assn. Interstate Commerce Commn. Practitioners, Navy League, Am. Legion, Masons, Shriners, Phi Alpha Delta.

LAKE, KATHLEEN COOPER, lawyer; b. San Antonio, Jan. 11, 1955; d. Herschel Taliaferro and Virginia Mae (Hylton) Cooper; m. Randall Brent Lake, Apr. 9, 1977; 1 child, Ethan Taliaferro. AB in Polit. Sci. magna cum laude, Middlebury Coll., 1977; JD with high honors, U. Tex., 1980. Bar: Tex. 1980, U.S. Ct. Appeals (5th cir.) 1981, U.S. Ct. Appeals (D.C. and 3rd cirs.) 1984. Assoc. atty. Vinson & Elkins, Houston, 1980-88; ptnr. Vinson & Elkins, LLP, Houston, 1989—2012, ret. ptnr., 2013—; founding mem. Ctr. Women in Law, U. Tex. Sch. Law, 2009—. Bd. advisors, columnist Utilities, Y2K Advisor, 1998-99; vis. prof. polit. sci., Middlebury Coll., 2007, adj. prof. U. Houston Law Ctr., 2011-. Adult leader, com. mem. Sam Houston Area Coun.-Golden Arrow dist. Boy Scouts Am., 1993—, chair troop com., 1998-2001. Recipient Unit Svc. award Sam Houston Area Coun.-Golden Arrow dist. Boy Scouts Am., 1996, 98, 2005. Fellow Tex. Bar Found. (life), Houston Bar Found.; mem. ABA (vice-chair com. 1997-99), Energy Bar Assn., State Bar Tex., Coll. the State Bar Tex., Tex. Law Rev. Assn. (life), Houston Bar Assn., Middlebury Coll. Alumni Assn. (com. mem. 1980-2000, Houston com. chair 2001—, class agent 2007-), Order of Coif, Phi Beta Kappa, Phi Kappa Phi. Office: Vinson & Elkins LLP 2500 First City Tower 1001 Fannin St Houston TX 77002-6760 Office Phone: 713-758-3826. E-mail: klake@velaw.com.

LAKE, SIMEON TIMOTHY, III, federal judge; b. Chgo., July 4, 1944; BA, Tex. A&M, 1966; JD, U. Tex., 1969. Bar: Tex. 1969, U.S. Dist. Ct. (so. dist.) Tex. 1969, U.S. Ct. Appeals (5th cir.) 1969, U.S. Supreme Ct. 1976. From assoc. to ptnr. Fulbright & Jaworski, Houston, 1969-70, 72-88; judge US Dist. Ct. (so. dist.) Tex., Houston, 1988—. Past editor Houston Lawyer. Capt. U.S. Army., 1970-71. Fellow Tex. Bar Found., Houston Bar Assn., State Bar Tex., Am. Law Inst. (mem. jud. conf. com. on criminal law 1999—, chair conf. com. on criminal law 2003—). Office: US Courthouse 515 Rusk Ave Rm 9535 Houston TX 77002-2605

LALIK, JANEEN, marketing executive; BS, Ctrl. Mich. U., Mt. Pleasant. With Detroit Pistons and Palace Sports Entertainment, 1991—97; dir. MVP program ISP Sports, NC, 1997—98, asst. v.p., 1998—2005, v.p., 2005—07, sr. v.p. new bus. devel., 2007—. Bd. dirs. Nat. Assn. Collegiate Mktg. Adminstrs. Co-chair mktg. com. YMCA Northwest NC, Winston-Salem; former mem. Downtown Winston-Salem Partnership Bd., NC; mem. City/County Utility Commn., Winston-Salem, 2009—. Recipient Women Extraordinaire award, Bus. Leader Media, 2008; named one of Forty Under 40, Street & Smith's SportsBus. Jour., 2009. Office: ISP Sports 540 N Trade St Winston Salem NC 27101 Office Phone: 336-831-0700. Office Fax: 336-768-7681.

LA LIME, HELEN R. MEAGHER, ambassador; b. 1951; married; 2 children. BS, Georgetown U., 1973; MS, Nat. Def. U. Joined Fgn. Svc. US Dept. State, 1980; consul gen. US Embassy, Zurich, Switzerland, 1993; with Bur. Internat. Orgnl. Affairs US Dept. State, Washington, 1993—95; dep. chief of mission US Embassy, N'djamena, Chad, 1996—99, Rabat, Morocco, 2001—03; dir. Office Ctrl. African affairs US Dept. State, Washington, 2000—01, US amb. to Mozambique Maputo, 2003—06; consul gen. US Embassy, Cape Town, South Africa, 2006—08, dep. chief of mission Pretoria, South Africa, 2008—. Office: US Embassy 9300 Pretoria Pl Dulles VA 20189

LALLY, JOHN PATRICK, private equity investor; b. Newark, Mar. 17, 1951; s. John James and Margaret Rita L.; m. Ann Bierbower, May 2, 1987; children: John B., Mark B. BS, Boston Coll., 1973; MBA, Columbia U., NYC, 1975. Staff acct. Coopers & Lybrand, Boston, 1975-78; v.p. Goldman, Sachs & Co., NYC, 1978-86; mng. dir. Bankers Trust Co., NYC, Atlanta, 1986-90; pres. Lally Percival & Co., Atlanta, 1991-95; co-founding ptnr. Resurgens Capital Ptnrs., Atlanta, 1996—2011. Bd. dirs. Integrated Energy Svcs., Inc., Atlanta, EquipMD, Atlanta, Response Mktg. Group, LLC, Richmond, Va., Sekuworks LLC, Harrison, Ohio, adv. bd. mem. Chpt. LLC. Avocations: politics, outdoor activities, sports. Office: Premier Plz 5605 Glenridge Dr Bldg One Ste 670 Atlanta GA 30342 Office Phone: 404-475-1203. Business E-Mail: jlally@criterionpartners.com.

LAM, SIMON SIN-SING, computer science educator; b. Macau, July 31, 1947; arrived in US, 1966; s. Chak Han and Kit Ying (Tang) Lam; m. Amy Leung, Mar. 29, 1971; 1 child, Eric. BSEE with distinction, Wash. State U., Pullman, 1969; MS in Engring., UCLA, 1970, PhD in Engring., 1974. Postgraduate rsch. engr. ARPA Network Measurement Ctr., UCLA, 1971-74, postdoctoral scholar, 1974; rsch. staff mem. IBM T.J. Watson Rsch. Ctr., Yorktown Heights, NY, 1974-77; asst. prof. U. Tex., Austin, 1977-79, assoc. prof., 1979-83, prof. computer sci., 1983—, David S. Bruton Centennial prof., 1985-88, anonymously endowed prof., 1988-2001, chmn. dept. computer sci., 1992-94, regents chair computer sci., 2001—. Editor-in-chief IEEE/ACM Transactions on Networking, 1995-99; editor: Principles of Communication and Networking Protocols; contbr. articles to profl. jours. Recipient William R. Bennett prize, 2001, Software Sys. award, 2004; grantee, NSF, 1978—; Chancellor's Tchg. fellow, UCLA, 1969—73. Fellow IEEE (Leonard G. Abraham prize 1975, William R. Bennett prize 2001, W. Wallace McDowell award 2004), Assn. Computing Machinery (prog. chmn. symposium 1983, SIGCOMM award 2004, Software Sys. award 2004); mem. NAE. Avocations: skiing, travel. Office: University Tex Dept Computer Sci 1616 Guadalupe Ste 2408 Austin TX 78701 Office Phone: 512-471-9531. Office Fax: 512-471-8885. E-mail: lam@cs.utexas.edu.

LAMAR, ANN HANNAFORD, state supreme court justice; d. Leon Hannaford; m. John T. Lamar, Jr.; children: John T. III, Vance. Student, NW Miss. Jr. Coll., 1970—71; BS in Edn., Delta State U., Cleve., Miss., 1974; law degree, U. Miss., 1982. Adminstrv. asst. Gov.'s Office of Edn. and Tng., 1974—77; ct. reporter Chancery Ct., Senatobia, Miss.; atty. Senatobia, 1982—87, 1993—95; asst. dist. atty. 17th Dist., 1987—93, 1996—99, dist. atty.; cir. judge 17th Cir. Ct., Miss., 2001—07; presiding judge 17th Cir. Drug Ct., 2007; justice Miss. Supreme Ct., 2007—. Vice chair Conf. Cir. Judges, 2005—06, chair, 2006—07. Baptist. Office: Miss Supreme Ct PO Box 249 Jackson MS 39205*

LAMAR, JOHN THOMAS (TREY LAMAR), state legislator; m. Jill Anthony. Attended, U. Miss., Miss. Coll. Sch. Law, Wash. U., St. Louis. Atty., Miss.; mem. Dist. 8 Miss. House of Reps., Jackson, 2012—. Active Tate County Econ. Devel. Found.; mem. First Bapt. Ch. Senatobia, Miss. Mem.: Miss. Bar Assn., Ole Miss. M-Club, Senatobia Rotary Club. Republican. Office: Miss House of Reps PO Box 1018 Jackson MS 39215 Business E-Mail: jlamar@house.ms.gov.

LAMB, KEVIN THOMAS, lawyer; b. Quincy, Mass., Nov. 14, 1956; s. John Phillip and Kathleen Elaine (O'Brien) L. BA, Washington and Lee U., 1978, JD, 1982. Bar: Va. 1982, D.C. 1988, Mass. 1990, Fla., 2005. Law clk. to presiding justice U.S. Bankruptcy Ct. (we. dist.) Va., Lynchburg, 1982-84; atty. U.S. Dept. Justice, Los Angeles, 1984-85; assoc. Jones, Day, Reavis & Pogue, Los Angeles, 1985-86, Ballard, Spahr, Andrews & Ingersoll, Washington, 1986-89, Testa, Hurwitz & Thibeault, L.L.P., Boston, 1989-91, ptnr., 1992—2005; ptnr., shareholder Gunster, Yoakley & Stewart PA, West Palm Beach, Fla., 2005—. Mem. ABA (com. on bus. bankruptcy), Am. Bankruptcy Inst. (com. on legis.). Office: Gunster Yoakley & Stewart PA Ste 500 East 777 S Flagler Dr West Palm Beach FL 33401 Office Phone: 561-650-0656. Business E-Mail: klamb@gunster.com.

LAMB, PETER JAMES, meteorology educator, researcher, consultant; b. Nelson, New Zealand, June 21, 1947; came to U.S., 1971; s. George Swan and Dorothy Elizabeth (Smith) L.; children: Karen Deborah Lockwood, Brett Timothy. BA, U. Canterbury, Christchurch, New Zealand, 1969, MA with honors, 1971; PhD, U. Wis., 1976; DSc, U. Canterbury, 2002. Asst. lectr. U. Canterbury, 1971; rsch. asst. U. Wis., Madison, 1971-76, rsch. assoc., 1976; lectr. U. Adelaide, Australia, 1976-79; sr. scientist Ill. Water Survey, Champaign, 1979-91, sect. head, 1984-90; prof. U. Okla., Norman, 1991—, George Lynn Cross rsch. prof., 2001—. Vis. rsch. assoc. U. Miami, Fla., 1978-79; adj. prof. U. Ill., Urbana, 1983-94; W. John and Gail M. Hussey Commemorative lectr. in meteorology Pa. State U., 2003; dir. Coop. Inst. Mesoscale Meteorol. Studies, Norman, 1991—; dir. Internat. Ctr. Disaster Rsch., 1994-99; assoc. dir. Weather Ctr. Programs, Norman, 1996—06; cons. Dept. State, Dept. Energy, Agy. Internat. Devel., NOAA, NSF, World Meteorol. Orgn., Kingdom of Morocco, U. Wis., U. Adelaide, U. Witwatersrand, U. East Anglia, City U. Hong Kong, Univs. Space Rsch. Assn., Stratus Cons., Inc., EPA, 1983—; site sci. atmospheric radiation measurement program Dept. Energy, 1992—2012. Contbr. articles to profl. jours. Coach Champaign Youth Soccer Orgn., 1983-91. Grantee NSF, EPA, Dept. Energy, NOAA, AID, World Meteorol. Orgn., MacArthur Found., Ins. Inst. Property Loss Reduction, Inst. Bus. and Home Safety, The

Williams Cos., Japan Marine Sci. and Tech. Ctr., Ins. Australia Group. Fellow Am. Meteorol. Soc. (chief editor Jour. Climate 1989-95, editor Meteorol. Monographs 2009-, elected coun. mem. 2011-, elected exec. com. mem., 2012-); mem. Am. Geophysicial Union, Royal Meteorol. Soc. (Margary lectr. 1991), Sigma Xi. Achievements include research on heat transport by the Atlantic Ocean; investigations into the causes of droughts in Sahelian Africa and Morocco; study of N.Am. precipitation patterns; assessment of economic value of weather and climate information. Home: 3616 Burlington Dr Norman OK 73072-3647 Office: Univ of Oklahoma CIMMS-Nat Weather Ctr Rm 2100 120 David L Boren Blvd Norman OK 73072-7304 Office Phone: 405-325-3041. Business E-Mail: plamb@ou.edu.

LAMB, SYDNEY MACDONALD, linguistics educator; b. Denver, May 4, 1929; s. Sydney Bishop and Jean Louisa (MacDonald) L.; m. Sharon Reese Rowell, June 17, 1956 (div. 1971); children: Christina, Sarah, Nancy; m. Susan Ellen Jones, May 15, 1977. BA, Yale U., New Haven, Conn., 1951; PhD, U. Calif., Berkeley, 1958. From asst. to assoc. prof. linguistics U. Calif., Berkeley, 1958-64; from assoc. to prof. Yale U., New Haven, 1964-77; mng. ptnr. Semionics Assocs., Houston, 1977-93; prof. Rice U., Houston, 1980—. Fellow Ctr. for Advanced Study in Behavioral Scis., Stanford, Calif., 1973-74. Author: Outline of Stratificational Grammar, 1966, (with others) Sprung from Some Common Source, 1991, Pathways of the Brain: The Neurocognitive Basis of Language, 1999, Language and Reality, 2004; inventor associative computer memory, 1977, 80, 4 patents; contbr. articles to profl. jours. NSF grantee, 1959-64, 66-70; Am. Council of Learned Soc. grantee, 1973-74. Mem. Linguistic Soc. Am. (exec. com. 1966-68), Linguistics Assn. of Can. and U.S. (pres. 1983-84, chmn. bd. dirs. 1995—2009), Houston Philos. Soc. (pres. 1992-93). Avocation: music. Office: Rice U Dept Linguistics Houston TX 77251 Business E-Mail: lamb@rice.edu.

LAMB, TODD, Lieutenant Governor of Oklahoma, former state legislator, lawyer; b. Okla., Oct. 19, 1971; s. Norman and Belva M. (Clark) Lamb; m. Monica Lamb; children: Griffin, Lauren. BS, Okla. State Univ.; JD, Okla. City Univ. Spl. agt. US Secret Svc., 1998—2002; staff mem. to Senator Don Nickles US Senate; gen. counsel CLS Group, Edmond, Okla.; mem. Dist. 47 Okla. State Senate, Okla. City, 2005—11; lt. gov. State of Okla., Okla. City, 2011—. Republican. Baptist. Office: Office of the Lieutenant Governor State Capitol Room 211 Oklahoma City OK 73105 Office Phone: 405-521-5632, 405-521-2161. Office Fax: 405-522-8694. Business E-Mail: lamb@lsb.state.ok.us, lamb@oksenate.gov.*

LAMBERT, CHRISTINA, telecommunications executive; b. Panama; m. Jim Lambert; children: Bill, Christine, Monica. Attended, U. Indpls., 1983; BA in Bus. Mgmt., Ind. U.; M in Bus. Adminstrn., Ind. Wesleyan U. Joined Contel (merged with GTE in 1991), 1974; asst. v.p., process planning GTE, asst. v.p., customer care; v.p., gen. mgr., wireline svcs. PR Telephone, 1999—2003, pres., CEO, 2003—. Office: Puerto Rico Telephone Company Inc 1515 FD Roosevelt Ave Guaynabo PR 00968 Office Phone: 787-793-1818, 787-792-6262. Office Fax: 787-282-0958. Business E-Mail: clambert@prtcmail.prtc.net.

LAMBERT, DAVID L., astronomer, educator; BA in Physics, Univ. Coll., Oxford, Eng.; PhD in Astrophysics, Balliol Coll., Oxford, Eng., 1965. Rsch. fellow Calif. Inst. Tech., Pasadena, 1967—69, Mt. Wilson Palomar Observatories; faculty assoc. dept. astronomy U. Tex., Austin, 1969—70, assoc. prof., 1970—74, prof. Austin, 1974—, Isabel McCutcheon Harte Centennial prof., 1983—87, Isabel McCutcheon Harte Centennial chair, 1987—, assoc. dir. McDonald Obs., 1989—90, dir. McDonald Obs., 1990—. Guggenheim fellow, vis. Erskine fellow U. Canterbury, New Zealand, 1985. Fellow Royal Astron. Soc.; mem. Am. Astron. Soc. (Dannie Heineman Prize for Astrophysics, 1987, Henry Norris Russell Lectureship, 2007), Internat. Astron. Union. Office: University of Texas Austin Department of Astronomy RLM 15.208 Austin TX 78712 also: University of Texas Austin RLM 16.316 Austin TX 78712 also: The University of Texas McDonald Observatory 2515 Speedway Stop C1402 Austin TX 78712-1206 Office Phone: 512-471-7438, 512-471-3303. Office Fax: 512-471-6016. Business E-Mail: director@astro.as.tesa.edu. E-mail: dll@astro.as.utexas.edu.

LAMBERT, EDDIE J., state legislator; b. 1956; Rep. atty.; mem. Dist. 59 La. House of Reps., 2004—, vice chair appropriations com., house com. on homeland security, mem. natural resources and environment com., joint legis. com. on the budget, joint com. on homeland security. Republican. Address: PO Box 241 Gonzales LA 70707 Office: Capitol Off 900 N Third S, PO Box 94062 Baton Rouge LA 70804 Fax: 225-644-4395. E-mail: larep059@legis.state.la.us.

LAMBERT, JOSEPH EARL, retired state supreme court chief justice; b. Berea, Ky., May 23, 1948; s. James Wheeler and Ruth (Hilton) L.; m. Debra Hembree, June 25, 1983; children: Joseph Patrick, John Ryan. BS in Bus. and Econs., Georgetown Coll., 1970; JD, U. Louisville, 1974; PhD (hon.), Eastern Ky. U., 1999, Georgetown Coll., 1999, Northern Ky. U., 2002. Bar: Ky. 1974. Staff mem. to Senator John Sherman Cooper US Senate, Washington, 1970-71; law clk. to Hon. Rhodes Bratcher U.S. Dist. Ct., Louisville, 1974-75; ptnr. Lambert & Lambert, Mt. Vernon, Ky., 1975-87; justice Supreme Ct. Ky., Frankfort, 1987-98, chief justice, 1998—2008; chief sr. judge Ky., 2008—. Chmn. Appellate Rules Commn., 1989-91, Civil Rules Com., 1991-93, Criminal Rules Com., 1996-97, Jud. Form Retirement Commn., 1996-; Nat. Assn. Drug Ct. Professionals, 2001-, Conference of Chief Justices, 2001-03. Mem. Bd. Regents Eastern Ky. U., Richmond, 1988-92. Recipient Disting. Alumni award U. Louisville Sch. Law, 1988; named Outstanding Judge of Ky., 2000, Leadership award Nat. Assn. Drug Ct. Professionals, Ky. Public Advocate award, 2001. Fellow: Ky. Bar Foundation; mem.: ABA, Ky. Bar Assn. Republican. Baptist.

LAMBERT, LYNN, computer science professor; d. Roy and Bobbie Lambert; m. Keith Perkins, July 28, 1995; children: Ben, Kate Perkins. PhD, U. Del., Newark, 1992. Comp. sci. prof. Christopher Newport U., Va., 1992—. Office: Christopher Newport Univ 1 University Pl Newport News VA 23606

LAMBERT, MIRANDA LEIGH, musician; b. Longview, Tex., Nov. 10, 1983; d. Richard Lee and Beverly June (Hughes) Lambert; m. Blake Tollison Shelton, May 14, 2011. Solo musician, 2001—; mem. country girl group Pistol Annies, 2011—. Contestant (reality TV series) Nashville Star, 2003 (3rd-place winner); musician: (albums) Miranda Lambert, 2001, Kerosene, 2005, Crazy Ex-Girlfriend, 2007 (Album of Yr., Acad. Country Music Awards, 2008), Revolution, 2009 (Album of Yr., Acad. Country Music Awards, 2010, Album of Yr., Country Music Assn. Awards, 2010), Four the Record, 2011 (Album of Yr., Acad. Country Music Awards, 2012), Platinum, 2014, (with Pistol Annies) Hell on Heels, 2011, Hush Hush, 2013, (songs) White Liar, 2009 (Video of Yr., Acad. Country Music Awards, 2010, Female Video of Yr., CMT Music Awards, 2010), The House That Built Me, 2010 (Music Video of Yr., Song of Yr., Country Music Assn. Awards, 2010, Best Female Country Vocal Performance, Grammy Awards, 2011, Single Record of Yr., Video of Yr., Song of Yr., Acad. Country Music Awards, 2011, Female Video of Yr., CMT Music Awards, 2011), Over You, 2011 (Female Video of Yr., CMT Music Awards, 2012, Song of Yr., Country Music Assn. Awards, 2012, Song of Yr., Single Record of Yr., Acad. Country Music Awards, 2013, Performance of Yr., CMT Music Awards, 2013), Mama's Broken Heart, 2011 (Female Video of Yr., CMT Music Awards, 2013, Single Record of Yr., Acad. Country Music Awards, 2014), (song with Keith Urban) We Were Us, 2013 (Vocal Event of Yr., Acad Country Music Awards, 2014). Recipient Cover Girl Fresh Face of Country Music award, Acad. Country Music Awards, 2005; named Top New Female Vocalist, Acad. Country Music Awards, 2007, Top Female Vocalist of Yr., 2010, 2011, 2012, 2013, 2014, Female Vocalist of Yr., Country Music Assn. Awards, 2010, 2011, 2012, 2013. Office: Frontpage Publicity 1188 Ben Collier Rd Charlotte TN 37036-5900*

LAMBERT, VICKIE ANN, retired dean, nursing consultant; b. Hastings, Nebr., Oct. 28, 1943; d. Victor E. and Edna M. (Hein) Wagner; m. Clinton E. Lambert, Jr., June 30, 1974; 1 child, Alexandra. Diploma, Mary Lanning Sch. Nursing, 1964; BSN, U. Iowa, 1966; MSN, Case Western Res. U., 1973; PhD, U. Calif., San Francisco, 1981. RN, Va. Staff and head nurse U. Iowa Hosp., Iowa City, 1966—68; instr. Sch. Nursing U. Iowa, 1968—70; instr. Robert Packer Sch. Nursing, Sayre, Pa., 1970—71; instr. dept. nursing St. John's Coll., Cleve., 1973—74; asst. prof. Sch. Nursing U. Pa., Phila., 1974—78; assoc. prof., acting chair dept. nursing adminstrn. Med. Coll. Ga., Augusta, 1982-84, coord. doctoral program nursing, 1984-85, George Mason U., Fairfax, Va., 1986-88; assoc. dean Case Western Res. U., Cleve., 1989-90; dean Coll. Nursing, Ga. Regents U., Augusta, 1990—2001, emeritus dean, 2001—; prof. Yamaguchi U., Japan, 2001—03, Wuhan U., China, 2003—08, Prince Songkla U., Thailand, 2007—10, Mahidol U., 2011—12. Internat. vis. prof. Lambert and Lambert Nursing Cons., Springfield, Va., 2001—. Contbr. articles to profl. jours., chapters to books. Fellow Am. Acad. Nursing; mem. ANA, Sigma Theta Tau Methodist. Avocation: travel. Home: 7416 Spring Village Dr Apt G09 Springfield VA 22150-4927

LAMBERTH, REBECCA MCLEMORE, lawyer; b. 1960; BA summa cum laude, Vanderbilt U., 1982; JD, U. Va., 1985. Bar: Ga., US Dist. Ct. (northern dist.) Ga., US Dist. Ct. (middle dist.) Ga. Assoc. Troutman Sanders LLP, 1985—90, Alston & Bird LLP, 1990—94, ptnr., 1994—2008, Duane Morris LLP, 2008—. Named a Ga. Super Lawyer, Atlanta Mag., 2006—13. Master: Joseph Henry Lumpkin Inn of Ct.; mem.: Atlanta Bar Assn., Ga. Assn. Women Lawyers, Ga. Bar Assn., ABA. Office: Duane Morris LLP Atlantic Ctr Plz Ste 700 1075 Peachtree St NE Ste 2000 Atlanta GA 30309-3928 Office Phone: 404-253-6961. Office Fax: 404-393-5179. Business E-Mail: rmlamberth@duanemorris.com.*

LAMBORN, LEROY LESLIE, law educator; b. Marion, Ohio, May 12, 1937; s. LeRoy Leslie and Lola Fern (Grant) Lamborn. AB, Oberlin Coll., 1959; LLB, Western Res. U., 1962; LLM, Yale U., 1963; JSD, Columbia U., 1973. Bar: N.Y. 1965, Mich. 1974. Asst. prof. law U. Fla., 1965-69; prof. Wayne State U., Detroit, 1970-97, prof. emeritus, 1997—. Vis. prof. State U., Utrecht, 1981. Author: (book) Legal Ethics and Professional Responsibility, 1963; contbr. articles on victimology to profl. jours. Mem.: World Soc. Victimology (exec. com. 1982—94), Nat. Orgn. Victim Assistance (bd. dirs. 1979—88, 1990—91), Am. Law Inst. Home: 1000 N US Hwy One Unit Bermuda 402 Jupiter FL 33477-4476

LAMON, HARRY VINCENT, JR., lawyer; b. Macon, Ga., Sept. 29, 1932; s. Harry Vincent and Helen (Bewley) Lamon; m. Ada Healey Morris, June 17, 1954; children: Hollis Morris, Kathryn Gurley. BS cum laude, Davidson Coll., 1954; JD with distinction, Emory U., 1958. Bar: Ga. 1958, DC 1965. Of counsel Troutman Sanders LLP, Atlanta, 1995—. Adj. prof. law Emory U., 1960—79. Contbr. articles to profl. jours. Pension and benefits reporter adv. bd. Bur. Nat. Affairs, 1972—2003; adv. coun. employee welfare and pension benefit plans U.S. Dept. Labor, 1975—79; nat. adv. bd. Salvation Army, 1976—, chmn., 1991—93, life mem. chmns. cir., 2005—; founding trustee, pres. So. Fed. Tax Inst., Inc., 1965—, emeritus, 2000—; trustee Am. Tax Policy Inst., Inc., 1989—96, Embry-Riddle Aero. U., 1989—2001, emeritus mem., 2001—; trustee Cathedral St. Philip Endowment Fund, Atlanta, 1989—. 1st lt. US Army, 1954—56. Recipient Order of Disting. Aux. Svc., Salvation Army, 2013; named Atlanta Centennial honoree, 1990. Fellow: Am. Coll. Employee Benefits Counsel (emeritus), Internat. Acad. Estate and Trust Law, Am. Coll. Tax Counsel, Am. Coll. Trust and Estate Counsel (emeritus), Am. Bar Found. (life), Ga. Bar Found. (life), Atlanta Bar Found. (life); mem.: ABA, Emory U. Law Sch. (Disting. Alumnus award 2007), So. Employee Benefits Conf. (hon. Hazelhurst Lamon outstanding achievement award named in his honor), Atlanta Bar Assn. (life), Am. Law Inst. (life), Practicing Law Inst., Atlanta Tax Forum, Am. Judicature Soc., State Bar Ga. (chmn. sect. taxation 1969—70, vice chmn. comm. continuing lawyer competency 1982—89), Group, Inc. (hon. life), Am. Bar Retirement Assn. (bd. dirs. 1989—96, pres. 1994—95), Nat. Emory U. Law Sch. Alumni Assn. (pres. 1967), Inquiry Club, Cosmos Club (Washington), Peachtree Racket Club (pres. 1986), Capital City Club (life), Lawyers Club of Atlanta (life), Atlanta Coffee House Club, Kiwanis (hon.; pres. Atlanta 1973), Phi Beta Kappa (life fellow), Phi Delta Theta (chmn. nat. cmty. svc. day 1969—72, legal commr. 1973—76, province pres. 1976—79, Golden Legion 2001), Phi Delta Phi, Omicron Delta Kappa. Episcopalian. Personal E-mail: harrylamon@gmail.com.

LAMONICA, PAUL RAYMOND, law educator, academic administrator; b. Baton Rouge, June 10, 1944; s. Leonard and Olivia (Frank) Lamonica; m. Dianne Davis Lamonica, Aug. 23, 1971; children: Drew, Neal, Leigh. BA, La. State U., 1965; MA, 1966, JD, 1970. Bar: La. 1970. Law clk. to chief judge US Dist. Ct. (we. dist.) La., 1970—71; assoc. Hebert, Moss & Graphia, Baton Rouge, 1971; judge pro tem 19th Jud. Dist. Ct., East Baton Rouge Parish, 1979; prof. La. State U. Law Sch., Baton Rouge, 1973—86, exec. counsel to La. gov., 1983—84; US atty. for mid. dist. La., 1986—94; vice chancellor, prof. law La. State U., Baton Rouge, 1994—97; counsel La. Ho. of Reps., 1976—79, 1980—83. Fellow: Am. Bar Found.; mem.: ABA, La. Bar Assn. (bd. govs. 1979). Republican. Roman Catholic. Office: La State U 416 Lsu Law Ctr Baton Rouge LA 70803-0001

LAMONT, ALICE, accountant, financial consultant; b. Houston, July 19; d. Harold and Bessie Bliss (Knight) L. BS, Mont. State U.; MBA in Taxation, Golden Gate U., 1983. CPA; registered fin. advisor. Tchr. London Ctrl. H.S., 1974-80; acct. Signetics, Sunnyvale, Calif., 1980-82; propr. Alice Lamont Ltd., 1985—. Adj. prof. Oglethorpe U., 2009—11. Mem. High Mus. Art, 1986-89, Atlanta Bot. Garden, Atlanta History Ctr., Friend of Atlanta Opera, Jeannette Rankin Found.; Atlanta adv. bd. Nat. Osteoporosis Found., 1997-2000; mem. com. Brit. Am. Bus. Group, 1993-97, bd. dirs. Churches Home Found., trustee. Mem.: AAUW (life; mem. audit chmn. Atlanta br. 1993—95, mem. scholarship com. 1994—2000, chmn. scholarship com. 2003—05), Atlanta Tax Study Assn., Ga. Soc. CPAs (chmn. Acctg. Inst. 1995—97, mem., Estate & Fin. Planning Sect., Atlanta chpt.), Women's Commerce Club (mem. adv. bd. 1994—98), Atlanta Woman's Club (co-chair ways and means com. 1985—86, asst. treas. 1986—88, treas. 1990, 1992—94).

LAMOUREUX, GLORIA KATHLEEN, nurse, consultant, retired military officer; b. Billings, Mont., Nov. 2, 1947; d. Laurits Bungaard and Florence Esther (Nielsen) Nielsen; m. Kenneth Earl Lamoureux, Aug. 31, 1973 (div. Feb. 1979). BS, U. Wyo., 1970; MS, U. Md., 1984. Staff nurse, ob-gyn DePaul Hosp., Cheyenne, Wyo., 1970; enrolled USAF, 1970, advanced through grades to col.; staff nurse ob-gyn dept. 57th Tactical Hosp., Nellis AFB, Nev., 1970-71, USAF Hosp., Clark AB, Republic Philippines, 1971-73; charge nurse ob-gyn dept. USAF Regional Hosp., Sheppard AFB, Tex., 1973-75, staff nurse ob-gyn dept. MacDill AFB, Fla., 1976-79; charge nurse ob-gyn dept. USAF Med. Ctr., Andrews AFB, Md., 1979-80, MCH coord., 1980-82; chief nurse USAF Clinic, Eielson AFB, Alaska, 1984-86, Air Force Systems Command Hosp., Edwards AFB, Calif., 1986-90; comdr. 7275th Air Base Group Clinic, Italy, 1990-92, 42d Med. Group, Loring AFB, Maine, 1992-94; 347th Med. Group, Moody AFB, Ga., 1994-96; chief nursing svcs. divsn. Hdqrs. Air Edn. and Tng. Command, Randolph AFB, Tex., 1996-2000. Ind. cons. Customers First Cons., Universal City, 2000—05, v.p., 2000—05; sr. cons. NCI, San Antonio, 2002—10, PSI, San Antonio, 2010—11, ZCore Bus. Solutions Inc., 2011—. Mem. Assn. Women's Health, Obstetric, and Neonatal Nurses (sec.-treas. armed forces dist. 1986-88, vice-chmn. armed forces dist. 1989-91), Air Force Assn., Bus. and Profl. Women's Assn. (pub. rels. chair Prince George's County chpt. 1981-82), Bulverde Area Rep. Women (sec. 2007, v.p. 2008-, pres. 2009, legis. chmn., 2010-), San Antonio Cons. Soc., Comal County Hist. Commn. Commr., Sigma Theta Tau. Republican. Lutheran. Avocations: reading, needlecrafts, piano, photography. Home: 383 Indigo Run Bulverde TX 78163 Business E-Mail: glamoureux@gvtc.com.

LAMP, DAVID L., energy executive; BSChemE, Mich. State U. Various mgmt. positions through exec. v.p., refining and chem. ops. Koch Industries, 1980—2001; v.p., gen. mgr., Aruba refinery complex El Paso Energy Corp., 2002—04; v.p., refining ops. Holly Corp., 2004—05, exec. v.p., refining and mktg., 2005—07, pres., 2007—11; exec. v.p., COO HollyFrontier Corp., Dallas, 2011—. Office: HollyFrontier Corp Ste 1300 2828 N Harwood Dallas TX 75201 Office Phone: 214-871-3555.

LAMPEN, RICHARD JAY, executive, lawyer, investment banker; b. New Brunswick, NJ, Nov. 12, 1953; s. J. Oliver and Miriam (Walsh) L.; m. Susan Matson, June 8, 1975; children: Katharine, Caroline. BA, Johns Hopkins U., 1975; JD, Columbia U., 1978. Bar: Fla. 1978, U.S. Dist. Ct. (so. dist.) Fla. 1978. From assoc. to ptnr. Steel Hector & Davis, Miami, Fla., 1978-86, co-chmn. corp. dept., 1992-95; exec. v.p., gen. counsel New Valley Corp., Miami, Fla., 1995—2005; mng. dir. Salomon Brothers, Inc., NYC, 1986-92; exec. v.p. Vector Group Ltd., Miami, 1996—; pres., CEO Ladenburg Thalmann Financial Services, Inc., Miami, 2006—, Castle Brands, Inc., 2008—. Bd. dirs. New Valley LLC, 1995—2005, Douglas Elliman Realty, LLC, Ladenburg Thalmann Fin. Svcs. Inc., 2002—, Castle Brands Inc., 2008—, Trump Plaza Funding, Inc., Spec's Music Inc., The Internat. Bank of Miami, N.A., U.S. Can Corp., Am. Jewish Com., 2010—. Pres. Miami Children's Mus., 2000—05; chmn. Ransom-Everglades Sch., 2004—06. Mem. Fla. Bar Assn. (chmn. securities law com. 1985-86). Office: Vector Group Ltd 4400 Biscayne Blvd 10th Fl Miami FL 33137 Home Phone: 305-663-9016; Office Phone: 305-579-8000. Office Fax: 305-579-8060. Business E-Mail: rlampen@vectorgroupltd.com.

LAMPING, MARK C., professional sports team executive; b. 1958; m. Cheryl A. Lamping; children: Brian, Lauren, Timothy BS in Acctg., Rockhurst Coll., 1980; MBA, St. Louis U., 1981. Various positions including dist. sales mgr., sr. brand mgr. for new products & dir. sales ops. Anheuser-Busch, 1981—89, group dir. sports mktg., 1989—94; pres. St. Louis Cardinals, 1994—2008; CEO MetLife Stadium (The New Meadowlands Stadium Co. LLC), East Rutherford, NJ, 2008—12; pres. Jacksonville Jaguars, 2012—. Commr. Continental Basketball League, 1994. Recipient James O'Flynn award, Catholic Youth Coun. Cmty. Achievement award, 2000, Marianist Youth medal, 2001, Legacy award, Big Brothers Big Sisters St. Louis, 2001, Gateway Leadership, Internat. Leadership, 2006; named Man of Yr., Sudden Infant Death Syndrome Resources, 1998, Alumnus of Yr. award, Rockhurst U., 2000; named to The Vianney High Sch. Hall of Fame. Office: Jacksonville Jaguars One EverBank Field Dr Jacksonville FL 32202

LAMPKIN, SHEILA E., state legislator; Mem. Dist. 10 Ark. House of Reps., 2011—. Democrat. Office: District Office 350 Rabb Rd Monticello AR 71655 also: Arkansas House of Representatives State Capitol Little Rock AR 72201 Office Phone: 870-723-6449. Business E-Mail: sheila.lampkin@arkansashouse.org.

LAMY, M. REBECCA (MARY REBECCA LAMY), consultant, land developer, government official; b. Ft. Bragg, NC, Nov. 21, 1929; d. Charles Joseph and Sarah Esther (Koonce) Lamy. BA, U. N.C., Greensboro, 1952. Procurement analyst Air Force Mil. Interdept. Purchase Request Mgmt. Office, Washington, 1958-60, procurement and fiscal officer, 1960-68; budget analyst Naval Air Sys. Command, Washington, 1968-69, indsl. specialist, 1969-71, Armament Devel. and Test Ctr., Eglin AFB, Fla., 1971-74, Def. Logistics Agy., Alexandria, Va., 1974-81; logistics mgmt. specialist Strategic Sys. Project Office, Dept. Navy, Washington, 1981-82; procurement analyst Hdqrs. Dept. Army, Washington, 1982-85. Emeritus mem. Onslow Mus. Found. Bd., Richlands, NC, Onslow Meml. Hosp. Aux., Jacksonville, NC, 1985—91; mem. Eckankar Clergy, 1986. Recipient Outstanding Performance awards USAF, 1956, 65, 72, 73, Quality award Def. Logistics Agy., 1979, Outstanding Performance award, 1978, 79, Exceptional Svc. award, 1983, 84, 85, Comdr.'s award Hdqrs. Dept. Army, 1985, others. Mem. U. N.C. at Greensboro Alumni Assn. Harriet Elliott Soc., Unbroken Band, Va. Satsang Soc. (v.p., trustee 2010-13).

LAN, DONALD PAUL, JR., lawyer; b. Orange, NJ, July 19, 1952; s. Donald Paul and Hannah Paula (Resnik) L.; m. Deborah Sue Rothenberg, Aug. 20, 1978; children: Jennifer Robyn, Adam Christopher, Eric Jacob. BS in Acctg., U. R.I., 1974; JD, Rutger U., 1977; LLM in Taxation, Georgetown U., 1982. Bar: D.C. 1978, Tex. 1983, U.S. Dist. Ct. (no., so., we. and ea. dists.) Tex. 1983, U.S. Ct. Fed. Claims 1978, U.S. Tax Ct. 1977, U.S. Ct. Appeals (fed. cir.) 1978, U.S. Ct. Appeals (5th cir.) 1984, U.S. Ct. Appeals (8th cir.) 1997. Clk. to spl. trial judge U.S. Tax Ct., Washington, 1977-78; trial atty. tax div. U.S. Dept. Justice, Washington, 1978-82; assoc., ptnr. Shank, Irwin & Conant, Dallas, 1982-87; ptnr. Finley, Kumble Wagner et al, Dallas, 1987, Strasburger & Price, Dallas, 1988-96; shareholder Kroney, Mincey, Inc., Dallas, 1996—2005, Kroney Morse Lan, PC, Dallas, 2005—. Adj. prof. law So. Meth. U., 1990-2005; lectr. tax controversy and litigation, 1983—. Named one of Best Lawyers in Dallas D Mag., 2007-09, Best Bus. Lawyers, 2009, Top Personal Lawyers, 2009, Best Tax Lawyers, 2010-13, Tex. Super Lawyer, Tex. Monthly Mag., 2003-2012, Top 100 in State of Tex. & Top 100 in Dallas-Ft. Worth Region, 2010-13, named Outstanding Atty. tax div. U.S. Dept. Justice, 1980. Fellow: Am. Coll. Tax Counsel, Am. Coll. Trust and Estate Counsel; mem.: ABA (ct. procedures com. tax sect. 1987—, stds. in tax practice com. tax sect. 1992—, chmn. 2001—03), D.C. Bar Assn., Dallas Bar Assn., State Bar Tex. (chmn. ct. procedures com. tax sect.

1995—97, coun. mem. 1997—2000), Beta Gamma Sigma, Beta Alpha Psi, Phi Kappa Phi. Jewish. Avocation: sports. Office: Kroney Morse Lan PC 12221 Merit Dr Ste 825 Dallas TX 75251-2202 Office Phone: 972-386-8500. Business E-Mail: dlan@kmllaw.com.

LANCARTE, LANNY P., II, chef; Grad., Culinary Inst. Am., NYC. Mgr. Joe T. Garcia's, Fort Worth, Tex.; chef Topolobampo, Chgo., Frontera Grill, Chgo.; owner, exec. chef Lanny's Alta Cocina Mexicana, Fort Worth, Tex., 2004—. Named Forth Worth's most exciting new culinary personality, Tex. Highways; named one of Dallas' Rising Stars, StarChefs.com, 2007. Office: Lanny's Alta Cocina Mexicana 3405 W 7th St Fort Worth TX 76107

LANCASTER, CARROLL TOWNES, JR., health services executive; b. Waco, Tex., Mar. 14, 1929; s. Carroll T. and Beatrice L.; m. Catherine Virginia Frommel, May 29, 1954; children: Loren Thomas, Barbara, Beverly, John Tracy. Student, U. Tex., 1948-51, 52-53. Sales coord. Union Tank div. Butler Mfg. Co., Houston, 1954-56, sales rep. New Orleans, 1956-57, br. mgr., 1957-60; asst. to exec. v.p. Maloney-Crawford Mfg. Co., Tulsa, 1960-62; mktg. cons., sr. assoc. Market/Product Facts, Tulsa, 1962-63; market devel. asst. Norriseal Controls divsn. Dover Corp., Houston, 1963-66; area dir. Arthritis Found., Houston, 1966-69, regional dir., 1969-71; exec. dir. United Cerebral Palsy, Tex. Gulf Coast, 1971-74, Leukemia Soc. Am., Gulf Coast, 1974-76, Lancaster & Assocs., 1976—. Christian edn. tchr., 1970, supr. 1971, asst. youth football coach, Bellaire, 1967-68, 70-71; mem. Houston-Galveston Area Health Commn. Study Group, 1972-76, co-chmn. 1976; dir. essayist Tex. Low Vision Coun., 1976-79, sec.-treas., 1978-81, pres. 1981-85; pres. Bellaire Civic Action Club, 1987-88, del. Houston Interfaith Sponsoring Com., 1979-81; bd. dirs. Coun. Chs. Greater Houston, 1966-68, v.p. 1968. Active USN, 1946—48, active USNR, 1951—52. Recipient award for securing free blood for indigent Harris County Hosp. Dist., 1968. Mem. Am. Mktg. Assn., Huguenot Soc., Military Order of Stars and Bars, San Marcos Acad., Ex-Students Assn. (pres. 1982-84), SAR, Delta Sigma Phi. Episcopalian (vestryman 1975-78).

LANCASTER, JOHNATHAN M., gynecologic oncologist, educator; BSc, U. Wales, 1991, grad., 1992, MD, 1997, PhD, 2005. Diplomate Am. Bd. Ob-Gyn, Am. Bd. Ob-Gyn-gynecologic oncology. Intern gen. Univ. Wales, 1993; resident ob-gyn. dept. Addenbrooke's Hosp., 1994, Duke Univ. Med. Ctr., 2000, fellow gynecologic oncology, 2003; assoc. prof. Univ. South Fla., program leader Comprehensive Breast, program leader Gynecologic Oncology, dir. Ctr. for Women's Oncology, chair dept. women's oncology; gynecologic oncologist H. Lee Moffitt Cancer Ctr. and Rsch. Inst. Co-author: various publs. Office: H Lee Moffitt Cancer Canter and Research Institute 12902 Magnolia Dr Tampa FL 33612 Office Phone: 999-860-2778.

LANCASTER, SALLY RHODUS, retired non-profit executive, consultant; b. Gladewater, Tex., June 28, 1938; d. George Lee and Milly Marie (Meadows) Rhodus; m. Olin C. Lancaster, Jr., Dec. 23, 1960; children: Olin C. III, George Charles, Julie Meadows. BA magna cum laude, So. Meth. U., 1960, MA, 1979; PhD, Tex. A&M, Commerce, 1983. Tchr. English pub. schs., 1960-61, 78-79; exec. v.p., sr. advisor Meadows Found., Inc., Dallas, 1979-96, also trustee and dir. Trustee So. Meth. U., 1980—88, East Tex. State U., regent, 1987—93; Tex. del. White House Conf. on Tourism, 1995; dir. Inst. Nautical Archaeology, 1988—2001; dir. emeritus Meadows Found.; mem. adv. bd. Cmtys. Found. Tex., 1987—2002. Named Disting. Alumni, So. Meth. U., Tex. A&M, Commerce; recipient Ruth Lester award Tex. Hist. Commn., 1998; grant-making and evaluations coms. Jacksonville Cmty. Found., 2000-01. Mem. Plantation Ladies Assn. (pres. 2000-01), Philos. Soc. Tex., Phi Beta Kappa. Presbyterian. Personal E-mail: sallylancaster@aol.com.

LANCE, RYAN MICHAEL, oil industry executive; b. Blythville, Ark., 1962; m. Lisa Lance. BS in Petroleum Engring., Mont. Tech., Butte, 1984. Engr. ARCO, Alaska, 1984—89, ops. Bakersfield, Calif., 1989—92, supr. coalbed methane ops. Midland, Tex., 1992—94, exploration engring. mgr. Alaska, 1994—96, v.p. Western North Slope Alaska, 1998—2001; planning mgr. Vaster Resources, Houston, 1996—98; gen. mgr. Lower 48 & Can. Phillips Petroleum, Houston, 2001—03; v.p. Lower 48 ConocoPhillips, Houston, 2002—03, pres. exploration & prodn. Asia Pacific, 2003—05, pres. strategy, integration and specialty bus., 2005—06, sr. v.p. tech. & major projects, 2006—07, sr. v.p. tech., 2007, pres. exploration & prodn. Europe, Asia, Africa, Middle East, 2007—09, sr. v.p. exploration & prodn.-internat., 2009—12, chmn., CEO, 2012—. Bd. dirs. ConocoPhillips, 2012—; pres. bd. trustees Spindletop Internat. Adv. bd. mem. Mont. Tech. Found.; mem. bd. American Petroleum Inst., Ind. Petroleum Assn. America. Mem.: Soc. Petroleum Engineers. Office: ConocoPhillips PO Box 2197 Houston TX 77252*

LAND, CLAY D., federal judge; b. Shreveport, La., Mar. 24, 1960; m. Shannon Land; children: Katherine, Brooks, Clay. BBA cum laude, U. Ga., Athens, 1982, JD, 1985. Atty. to ptnr. Hatcher, Stubbs, Land, Hollis & Rothschild, Columbus, 1985—92; founder, ptnr. Buchanan & Land LLP, Columbus, 1992—2001; senator 16th dist. Ga. Gen. Assembly, 1995—2000; judge US Dist. Ct. (mid. dist.) Ga., Columbus, 2001—. Mem. Columbus City Coun., 1993-94, Ga. Future Cmtys. Commn.; past pres. Leadership Columbus; chmn. Ga. Indigent Def. Coun.; trustee Ga. Bar Found. Recipient J.R. Allen Outstanding Columbus Young Person award, 1995, H. Sol Clark Pro Bono award State Bar of Ga., 1993. Baptist. Office: PO Box 2017 Columbus GA 31902

LAND, JOHN CALHOUN, III, state legislator, lawyer; b. Manning, SC, Jan. 25, 1941; s. John Calhoun, Jr. and Anna Abbott (Weisiger) Land; m. Marie Adell Mercogliano, Oct. 23, 1965; children: John Calhoun IV, Frances Ricci, William Ceth. BS, U. SC, 1965, JD, 1968, LLD (hon.), 2007. Bar: SC 1968. Mem. Land, Parker and Welch, P.A., Manning, 1968—, SC House of Reps., 1975—76; mem. Dist. 36 SC State Senate, 1977—, Dem. majority leader, 1993—2000, Dem. minority leader, 2000—. Commr. SC Hwys. and Pub. Transpr., 1971—74; sec. Clarendon County Dem. Com., 1968—70. Named Eagle Scout, Boy Scouts Am., 1955. Mem.: ABA, SC Trial Lawyers Assn., SC Bar Assn., Claredon County Bar Assn. Democrat. Methodist. Avocations: hunting, fishing. Mailing: PO Box 138 Manning SC 29102 Office: 513 Gressette Bldg Columbia SC 29202 Home Phone: 803-435-2314; Office Phone: 803-435-8894, 803-212-6180. Business E-Mail: JCL@scsenate.org.

LAND, KENNETH CARL, sociologist, educator, demographer; b. Llano, Tex., Aug. 19, 1942; s. Otto Carl and Tillie (Lindemann) L.; m. Jacqueline Yvette Apere, Mar. 22, 1969; 1 child, Kristoffer Carl. BA, Tex. Luth. Coll., 1964; MA, U. Tex., 1966, PhD, 1969. Staff assoc. Russell Sage Found., NYC, 1969-73; lectr. Columbia U., NYC, 1970-73; assoc. prof. U. Ill., Urbana, 1973-76, prof., 1976-81; prof. sociology U. Tex., Austin, 1981-86; prof., chmn. dept. sociology Duke U., Durham, NC, 1986-97, John Franklin Crowell prof. sociology, 1990—. Co-author: Criminal Circumstance, 2003, Age-Period-Cohort Analysis: New Models, Methods, and Empirical Applications, 2013, Household and Living Arrangement Projections: The Extended Cohort-Component Method and Applications to the U.S. and China, 2014; co-editor: Social Indicator Models, 1975, Social Accounting Systems, 1981, Multidimensional Mathematical Demography, 1982, Forecasting in the Social and Natural Sciences, 1987, Handbook of Social Indicators and Quality-of-Life Research, 2012, The Well-Being of America's Children: Developing and Improving the Child and Youth Well-Being Index, 2012; contbr. articles to profl. jours. Fellow AAAS, Am. Statis. Assn., Am. Soc. Criminology, Internat. Soc. Quality Life Studies; mem. Sociol. Rsch. Assn., Am. Sociol. Assn. (Paul F. Lazarsfeld award methodology sect. 1997), Population Assn. America, Southern Sociol. Assn. (Roll of Honor award 2013). Lutheran. Office: Duke U Dept Sociology Durham NC 27708-0088 Office Phone: 919-660-5615. Business E-Mail: kland@soc.duke.edu.

LAND, RICHARD DALE, minister, religious organization administrator; b. Houston, Nov. 6, 1946; s. Leggette Sloan and Marilee (Welch) L.; m. Rebekah Ruth Van Hooser, May 29, 1971; children: Jennifer, Richard Jr., Rachel. BA magna cum laude, Princeton U., 1969; ThM, New Orleans Bapt. Theol. Sem., 1972; D.Phil., U. Oxford, Eng., 1980. Ordained to ministry So. Bapt. Conv., 1969. Pastor Vieux Carre Baptist Ch., New Orleans, 1970—72, S. Oxford Bapt. Ch., England, 1972-75; prof. theology and ch. history Criswell Coll., Dallas, 1975-76, academic dean, 1978—80, v.p. academic affairs, 1980-88; pres. ethics and religious liberty commn. So. Bapt. Conv., Nashville, 1988—. Mem. exec. com. Nat. Coalition Against Pornography, Cin., 1989—; bd. dirs. Bapt. Joint Com. Pub. Affairs, Washington, 1987-91; host For Faith & Family, 1998—, daily radio commentary 1999—; host, call-in talk show Richard Land Live, 2002—; apptd. mem. US Commn. on Internat. Religious Freedom, 2001-04, 2005—, vice chmn., 2007-08. Cons. editor Criswell Study Bible, 1979; author: The Divided States of America?, 2007. Mem. Gov.'s Task Force on Welfare Reform, Austin, Tex., 1988, Pres.'s Campaign for a Drug-Free Soc., Washington, 1991—. Recipient Disting. Alumnus award New Orleans Bapt. Theol. Sem., 1997; named one of 10 Top Church-State Experts Nat. Jour., 2004, 25 Most Influential Evangelicans in America TIME mag., 2005, 25 Most Influential Republicans Newsmax Mag., 2008. Mem. Bapt. World Alliance (spl. com. on racism 1992, gen. bd. 1993, vice chmn. Christian ethics com. 1995-2004). Office: Ethics & Religious Liberty Commn 901 Commerce St Ste 550 Nashville TN 37203-3600

LAND, SUZANNE PRIEUR, lawyer; b. Youngstown, Ohio, Oct. 26, 1964; AB in Acctg. and Econs. summa cum laude, Youngstown State U., Ohio, 1987; JD summa cum laude, Case Western Res. Sch. Law, Cleve., 1990. Bar: Ohio 1990, Ky. 2005. Atty. Greenebaum, Doll & McDonald, Covington, Ky. Adj. prof. law U. Cin. Law Sch., 1998—; bd. advs. No. Ky. C. of C. Bd. visitors Salmon P. Chase Coll. Law; bd. trustees St. Luke Cmty. Found., Redwood Rehab. Ctr., Boys & Girls Clubs Greater Cin.; corp. guild mem., steering com. mem. Dressed for Success Cin. Named one of Top 100 Attys., Worth mag., 2005—06. Mem.: ABA, Ky. State Bar Assn., Ohio State Bar Assn., Cin. Bar Assn. Office: Greenebaum Doll & McDonald 1800 RiverCenter I 50 E RiverCenter Blvd Covington KY 41011-1660 Office Phone: 513-455-7619. Office Fax: 513-762-7919. E-mail: spl@gdm.com.

LANDAU, MICHAEL B., law educator; b. Wilkes-Barre, Pa., July 3, 1953; s. Jack Landau and Florence (Rabitz) Simon. BA, Pa. State U., 1975; JD, U. Pa., 1988. Vis. prof. law Dickinson Sch. Law, Pa. State U., Carlisle; assoc. Cravath, Swaine and Moore, NYC, 1988-90, Skadden, Arps, NYC, 1990-92; assoc. prof. Coll. Law Ga. State U., Atlanta, 1992-99, prof. law, 1999—, dir. intellectual property, tech. and media law program. Vis. prof. law U. Ga. Law Sch., 1998; guest lectr. Johannes Kepler U., Linz, Austria, summer 1994, 95, 96; vis. scholar Univ. Amsterdam, 2000, U. Helsinki, Finland, 2005 Contbr. articles to law jours. on copyright, art, patent, entertainment law. Scholar, Fulbright Found., 2005. Mem. ABA, N.Y. State Bar Assn., Internat. Bar Assn., Vol. Lawyers for Arts, Am. Fedn. Musicians, Am. Intellectual Property Law Assn., Copyright Soc. U.S. Am., Phi Kappa Phi, Omicron Delta Epsilon. Democrat. Avocations: photography, jazz guitar, jazz piano. Office: Ga State U Coll Law University Pla Atlanta GA 30303 Office Phone: 404-413-9184. Business E-Mail: mlandau@gsu.edu.

LANDEN, ROBERT GERAN, retired historian, academic administrator; b. Boston, July 13, 1930; s. Harry James and Evelyn Gertrude (Geran) L.; m. Patricia Kizzia, July 19, 1958; children— Michael Geran, Robert Kizzia, Jill Arnett, Amy Patricia. AB, Coll. of William and Mary, 1952; MA, U. Mich., 1953; A.M., Princeton U., 1958, PhD (Ford Found. fellow), 1961. Asst. prof. social sci. Ball State U., Muncie, Ind., 1959-60; asst. prof. near eastern studies U. Mich., Ann Arbor, 1960-61; asst. prof. history Dartmouth, Hanover, NH, 1961-66, asst. dean of freshmen, 1963-64, assoc. prof. history, 1966-67; prof., head dept. history Va. Poly. Inst. and State U., Blacksburg, 1967-69; prof. history U. SC, Columbia, 1969-75, asso. vice provost, 1971-72, asso. provost, 1972-73, dean Coll. Social and Behavioral Scis., 1972-75; prof. history U. Tex. at Arlington, 1975-77, dean Coll. Liberal Arts, 1975-77; prof. history U. Tenn., Knoxville, 1977-86; dean Coll. Arts and Scis., 1977-85; prof. history, v.p. acad. affairs, provost U. Montevallo, 1986-88; prof. history and humanities, dir. programs in the humanities Va. Poly Inst. and State U., Blacksburg, 1988-95, prof. emeritus history and humanities, 1995—. Author: Oman Since 1856, 1967, The Emergence of the Modern Middle East, 1970, (with Abid Al-Marayati) The Middle East, Its Governments and Politics, 1972; contbr. articles to profl. jours. and book revs. to hist. publs. Served with AUS, 1953-55. Am. Coun. Learned Socs. fellow, 1965-66, Comparative Studies Ctr. Faculty fellow, 1965-66, Malone fellow, 1988. Fellow Middle East Studies Assn. of N. Am.; mem. Theta Delta Chi, Phi Kappa Phi. Roman Catholic. Home: 108 Edgewood Ln Williamsburg VA 23185-3213

LANDERS, B. LEE, consumer products company executive; BS in Indsl. Engring., Ga. State U., 1981, MBA in Fin., 1986. Various positions, IT Dept. Southern Co., 1981—99; v.p., chief info. officer Aaron's, Inc., 1999—. Office: Aaron's Inc 309 E Paces Ferry Rd NE Atlanta GA 30305-2377 Office Phone: 404-231-0011. Office Fax: 678-402-3560. Business E-Mail: lee.landers@aarons.com.

LANDES, R. STEVEN (STEVE LANDES), state legislator; b. Staunton, Va., Nov. 15, 1959; s. Robert Samuel and Elizabeth Ann Dudley Landes; m. Angela Beth Hochmeister, 1994. Media buyer, account exec. Davis & Davis Mktg. Inc., Staunton, Va., 1986; administrn. asst. to A.R. Pete Giesen Va. House of Delegates, 1988—92, mem. Dist. 25, 1996—; dist. dir. & rep. to Robert W. Goodlatte US House of Representatives, 1993—95; ins. agt. Mass. Mutual Life Ins., 1995—2000; exec. dir. NewBiz VA, 2001—06; cmty. rels. coord. DuPont Cmty. Credit Union, 2006—. Mem.: Va. Incubation Assn., United Way Greater Augusta (campaign chmn. 2004), Shonandoah Valley Tech. County, Augusta County Hist. Soc., Frontier Cult Mus. Va. (bd, trustees), Weyers Cave Ruritan Club. Republican. Presbyterian. Office: PO Box 12 Verona VA 24482 Office Phone: 540-245-5540. Office Fax: 540-248-8434. Business E-Mail: DelSLandes@house.virginia.gov.

LANDIS, EDGAR DAVID, retired business consultant; b. Myerstown, Pa., Jan. 7, 1932; s. Edgar Michael and Anna Irene (Dubble) L.; m. Patricia Ann Leininger, June 13, 1953; children: Susan, Jean. BS, Lebanon Valley Coll., 1953; MBA, U. Pa., Wharton, 1957. CPA. Acct., audit supr. Peat, Marwick, Mitchell & Co. (now KPMG), Phila., 1957-64; corp. contr., divsn. exec. v.p. Carlisle Corp., Pa., 1964-73; v.p., sr. v.p., exec. v.p. CDI Corp., Phila., 1973-97, also dir.; dir. affiliates in U.S. and Europe; dir., vice chmn., co-chmn., chmn. Allegiance Bank N.A., Bala Cynwyd, Pa., 1998—2010. Cons. to CDI Corp., Phila., 1998-2001; dir. Sabal Palm Bank, Sarasota, Fla., 2006-09. Bd. dirs. Carlisle Sch. Dist., 1967-71, YMCA, Ardmore, Pa., 1981-87, chmn., 1984-86, YMCA, Phila., 1988-97, vice chmn. 1991-97, YMCA, Sarasota, Fla., 1998—,chmn., 2008-; Capital U. Integrative Medicine, Washington, 2002-06. With U.S. Army, 1954-56, Japan. Mem. Lebanon Valley Coll. Alumni Assocs. (regional chmn. 1977-82). Republican. Methodist. Home: 988 Blvd Of The Arts 511 Sarasota FL 34236-4872

LANDOLT, ARLO UDELL, astronomer, educator; b. Highland, Ill., Sept. 29, 1935; s. Arlo Melvin and Vesta (Kraus) L.; m. Eunice Jean Casper, June 8, 1966; 1 child, Jennifer; stepchildren: Lynda, Barbara, Vicky, Debra. BA, Miami U., Oxford, Ohio, 1955; MA, Ind. U., 1960, PhD, 1963. Mem. 1st wintering-over party Internat. Geophys. Year, Amundson-Scott South Pole Sta., Antarctica, 1957; from asst. prof. physics and astronomy to Ball Family prof. emeritus physics and astronomy La. State U., 1962—2003, Ball Family prof. emeritus physics and astronomy, 2003—. Program dir. astronomy sect. NSF, 1975-76; mem. governing bd. Am. Inst. of Physics, 1985-91, 95-2004; guest investigator Kitt Peak Nat. Obs., Tucson, Cerro Tololo Inter-Am. Obs., Las Campanas Observatory, La Serena, Chile, Lowell Obs., Dyer Obs., Vanderbilt U., Goethe Link Obs., Ind. U. Rsch. grantee NSF, 1964, 66, 69, 71, 73, 75, 92—, NASA, 1965, 92, Rsch. Corp., 1964, Air Force Office Sci., 1977-87, Space Telescope Sci. Inst., 1985-90, 92; recipient George Van Biesbroeck prize, 1995, Disting. Faculty award La. State U., 1998. Fellow AAAS (sec. Sect. D 1970-78); mem. AAUP, Am. Astron. Soc. (sec. 1980-89, 95-2004), Internat. Astron. Union (sec. U.S. nat. com. 1980-89, 96-2004, v.p. commn. 25 1979-85, 2000-03, pres. commn. 25 2003-06, pres. divsn. IX 2000-03), Royal Astron. Soc. (Eng.), Astron. Soc. Pacific, Am. Assn. Variable Star Observers (councilor 2006-2012), Am. Polar Soc., Am. Philatelic Soc., The Explorer's Club, Sigma Xi, Pi Mu Epsilon. Office: La State U Dept Physics And Astro Baton Rouge LA 70803-4001 Office Phone: 225-578-6795. Business E-Mail: landolt@phys.lsu.edu.

LANDON, JAMES HENRY, retired lawyer; b. Atlanta, Oct. 24, 1945; s. Ralph Henry and Gertrude Leola (Rew) Landon. BA cum laude, Vanderbilt U., Nashville, 1967; JD cum laude, Harvard Law Sch., 1970. Bar: Ga. 1971, US Dist. Ct. (no. dist.) Ga. 1971, US Ct. Claims 1972, US Supreme Ct. 1976, US Tax Ct. 1980. Assoc. Hansell & Post, Atlanta, 1971-76, ptnr., 1976-89, Jones Day, Atlanta, 1989—2011, of counsel, 2011—12; ret., 2013. Adj. prof. Emory Law Sch., Atlanta, 1983—84; dir. TRC Staffing Svc., Inc., Atlanta, 1987—; mem. steering com. So. Pension Conf., Atlanta, 1985—88; mem. Ga. adv. coun. Genspring, 2004—08. Co-author: Transportation Politics in Atlanta, 1970; contbr. articles to profl. jours. Trustee Atlanta Hist. Soc., 1983—2006, Atlanta Bot. Garden, 1998—2004, 2006—11, Hambidge Ctr. Creative Arts & Scis., Rabun Gap, Ga., 1994—99, Cherokee Garden Libr., Atlanta, 2003—12, Atlanta Med. Heritage, Inc., Piedmont Healthcare Found.; mem. exec. com. The Bascom, 2012—; mem. cmty. adv. bd. Jr. League Atlanta, 1987—90; gen. counsel Woodruff Arts Ctr., Inc., 1993—2011, life trustee, 2011; bd. dirs. Atlanta Symphony Orch., 1981—87, 1989—92, 2011—; mem. Arts Adv. Coun. Arena Paris, 2010—. Mem.: Phi Beta Kappa, Omicron Delta Kappa. Presbyterian. Avocations: mountain climbing, hiking, gardening, calligraphy. Office Phone: 404-581-8907. Office Fax: 404-885-8330. E-mail: jhlandon@jonesday.com.

LANDON, MICHAEL DE LAVAL, retired history professor; b. St. John, NB, Can., Oct. 8, 1935; arrived in U.S., 1960; s. Arthur Henry Whittington and Elizabeth Worthington (Fair) Landon; m. Doris Lee Clay, Dec. 31, 1959 (div. May 1980); children: Clay de Laval, Letitia Elizabeth; m. Carole Marie Prather, Feb. 28, 1981. BA, Oxford U., Eng., 1958, MA, 1961, U. Wis., 1962, PhD, 1966. Asst. master Manor House Sch., Horsham, England, 1957, Dalhousie Sch., Ladybank, Scotland, 1958, Lakefield Coll. Sch., Ont., Canada, 1958—60; asst. prof. history U. Miss., Oxford, 1964—67, assoc. prof., 1967—72, prof., 1972—2000; prof. emeritus, 2000—; acting dir. libbrs. U. Miss., 1986—87, acting chair modern langs., 1996—99. Author: The Triumph of the Lawyers, 1970, The Honor and Dignity of the Profession, 1979, Erin and Britannia, 1980, The Challenge of Service, 1995, The University of Mississippi Law School--A Sesquicentennial History, 2006. Commr. City Housing Authority, Oxford, 1983—2013, chmn., 1993—2013. Am. Philos. Soc. Rsch. grantee, 1967, 1974. Fellow: Royal Hist. Soc. (Eng.); mem.: Am. Soc. Legal History (sec.-treas. 1988—97), Pi Delta Phi, Phi Alpha Theta, Eta Sigma Phi, Phi Kappa Phi. Avocation: bird feeding. Home: 219 Bramlett Blvd Oxford MS 38655-3434 Home Phone: 662-236-2373.

LANDON, ROBERT KIRKWOOD, construction executive; b. NYC, Apr. 27, 1929; s. Kirk A. and Edith (Ungar) L.; children: Chris, Kathleen Landon Staley, Kellyann Landon Spears. Attended, U. Va., 1948; BS, Ga. Inst. Tech., 1950. Joined Am. Bankers Life Assurance Co., Miami, Fla., 1952, pres., 1960—74, chmn., CEO, 1974-99; chmn., CEO Am. Bankers Ins. Group Inc., Miami, 1980-95, chmn., 1980-99; pres. Landon Corp., Dover, Del., 1971-99; charter mem. advisory bd. Florida International U., 1972-74; chmn. Orange Clothing Co., 2001—07, Innovative Surveillance Tech., 1993—2006. Bd. dirs. Lennar Corp., 1999—. Pres. Kirk A. and Dorothy P. Landon Found., 1969—, Fla. Internat. U., 2005—10. Lt. (j.g.) USN, 1950-53, trustee Barry U., bd. advisor, trustee, Fla. Internat. U. Mem. World Bus. Coun., Scabbard and Blade, Phi Gamma Delta. Republican. Congregationalist. Home: 10 Edgewater Dr Apt 16E Coral Gables FL 33133-6969 Office: Lennar Corp Bd Directors 700 NW 107th Ave Miami FL 33172 Office Phone: 305-559-4000. Office Fax: 305-228-8383. E-mail: rlandon@lennar.com.

LANDRIEU, MARY LORETTA, United States Senator from Louisiana; b. Arlington, Virginia, Nov. 23, 1955; m. E. Frank Snellings, 1988; children: Connor, Mary. BA, La. State U., 1977. Real estate agt.; mem. Dist. 90 La. House of Reps., Baton Rouge, 1980—88, vice chmn. Health & Welfare Com., 1979—88; treas. State of La., Baton Rouge, 1988—96; US Senator from La. Washington, 1997—; chair US Senate Small Bus. & Entrepreneurship Com., 2009—14, US Senate Energy & Nat. Resources Com., 2014—. Del., Democratic Nat. Conv., 1980 Author: (novels) Nine and Counting: The Women of the Senate, 2000. Volunteer Spl. Olympics, Crippled Children's Hosp. of New Orleans. Mem. LWV, Women Executives in State Govt., Fedn. Democratic Women, Delta Gamma. Democrat. Roman Catholic. Office: US Senate 703 Hart Senate Off Bldg Washington DC 20510-0001 also: Federal Bldg Rm 326 707 Florida St Baton Rouge LA 70801 Office Phone: 202-224-5824. E-mail: senator@landrieu.senate.gov.*

LANDRIEU, MITCH (MITCHELL JOSEPH LANDRIEU), Mayor, New Orleans, former Lieutenant Governor of Louisiana; b. New Orleans, Aug. 16, 1960; s. Moon and Verna Landrieu; m. Cheryl P. Quirk; children: Grace, Emily, Matthew, Benjamin, William. BA in Polit. Sci., Cath. U., Washington; JD, Loyola U. Law Sch., New Orleans, 1985. Mem. La. House of Reps., Baton Rouge, 1988—2003;

lt. gov. State of La., 2004—10; mayor City of New Orleans, 2010—. Pres. Internat. Mediation & Arbitration, Ltd.; mem. Supreme Ct. Task Force Alternative Dispute Resolution; adj. prof. Loyola U. Law Sch. Recipient Friends of the Parishes award, La. Police Jury Assn., 1988, Bus. Champion award, C. of C., 2001, 2002, Legislator of Yr. award, Alliance for Good Govt., 2002, Orleans Parish Med. Soc., 2002, Outstanding Legislator award, Victims & Citizens Against Crime, 2002. Democrat. Office: Office of the Mayor New Orleans City Hall 1300 Perdido St Rm 2E04 New Orleans LA 70112 Office Phone: 504-565-7793. Office Fax: 504-565-6423.*

LANDRY, JANE LORENZ, architect; b. San Antonio, Feb. 12, 1936; d. John Henry and Lulie Amanda (Sample) L.; m. Duane Eugene Landry, Sept. 8, 1956; children: Rachel, Claire, Ellyn, Jean. Student, U. Tex., 1952-55, Yale U., 1955-56; BArch, U. Pa., 1957. Registered arch., Tex. Project arch. O'Neil Ford & Assoc., San Antonio, 1959-65; prin. Duane Landry, Arch., San Antonio, 1965-68, Dallas, 1968-76; ptnr. Landry & Landry, Archs. & Planners, Dallas, 1976—, Meyer, Landry & Landry, Archs. & Planners, Dallas, 1977-80. Instr. San Antonio Coll., 1965. Dir. at large Interfaith Forum on Religion, Art and Architecture, 1991—; mem. Liturgical Commn. Diocese of Dallas, 1978-90. Recipient design awards Interfaith Forum on Religion, Art and Architecture, 1985, 89, 90, 97, 98, 2000, 2003, 2011. Fellow AIA (mem. hist. resources com., design awards Dallas chpt. 1970, 75, 76, 77, 80); mem. Tex. Soc. Architects (design award 1969, 81), The Liturgical Design Consultancy. Roman Catholic. Office: Landry & Landry Archs & Planners 6319 Meadow Rd Dallas TX 75230-5140 Office Phone: 214-265-8398.

LANDRY, MARY E., career military officer; b. 1956; m. Mark Landry; children: Michael, Katelyn. Grad., SUNY, Buffalo, 1978; MA in Mgmt., Webster U.; M in Marine Affairs, U. RI; PhD (hon.), Hilbert Coll., 2009. Commd. USCG, 1980, advanced through grades to rear admiral, 2007, ship inspector, 1985—89, exec. officer Marine Safety Office (MSO) Boston, commdg. officer Marine Safety Office (MSO) Providence, dir. govtl. and pub. affairs Washington, 2007—09, comdr. Eight Coast Guard Dist., comdr. Task Force 189.8 New Orleans, 2009—. Fed. on-scene coord. Deepwater Horizon Oil Spill Response US Dept. Homeland Security, 2010. Decorated Legion of Merit, Meritorious Svc. Medal, Coast Guard Commendation Medal, 9-11 Medal, Achievement Medal, Comdt.'s Letter of Commendation, Nat. Def. Svc. Medal; named Maritime Person Yr., Propeller Club of Narragansett Bay, 2006; Nat. Security Fellow, John F. Kennedy Sch. Govt., Harvard U., 2000. Office: Eighth Coast Guard District Hale Boggs Federal Bldg 500 Poydras St New Orleans LA 70130

LANDRY, NANCY R., state legislator; BA, La State U., 1985; JD, La. State Law Sch., 1990. Family law counselor; mem. Dist. 31 La. House of Reps., 2008—, mem. civil law and procedure com., natural resources and environment com. Republican. Office: State Capitol Po Box 444866 Baton Rouge LA 70804 Mailing: 109 S College Rd Lafayette LA 70503 Office Phone: 225-342-6945, 337-262-2252. Office Fax: 337-262-2254. Business E-Mail: landryn@legis.state.la.us.

LANDRY, RJ, aerospace product and parts manufacturing executive; BS in Personnel Mgmt., Nicholls State U. With FileNet Corp., Walt Disney Co., Pfizer; dir. human resources In-Flight Entertainment Group BE Aerospace, Inc., 1994—99, v.p. human resources Comml. Aircraft Products Segments, 2002—06, v.p. human resources Flight Structures, Seating Products Group, 1999—2002, v.p. human resources, 2006—. Office: BE Aerospace Inc 1400 Corporate Ctr Way Wellington FL 33414 Office Phone: 561-791-5000. Office Fax: 561-791-7900.

LANDRY, STEPHEN J., tax specialist; b. New Orleans, La. BBA in Economics, Loyola U., New Orleans. CPA. Tax ptnr. Ernst and Young LLP, 1998—2000, energy practice positions Houston, 2000—07; dir., tax, compliance and reporting Marathon Oil Corp., 2007, v.p., tax, 2008—. Mem.: AICPA. Office: Marathon Oil Corp 5555 San Felipe Rd Houston TX 77056-2723 Office Phone: 713-629-6600. Office Fax: 713-296-2952. Business E-Mail: slandry@marathonoil.com.

LANDRY, TERRY C., SR., state legislator, former protective services official; m. Sharon Landry; children: Shauna, Terry, Tory. Grad., La. State Police Acad. Detective La. State Police, sgt., dir. Gaming Enforcement Divsn., dir. Investigative Support Sect., dep. supt. patrol, dep. supt. support, chief staff, supt.; dir. security New Orleans Internat. Airport; interim chief police Southern U. and Baton Rouge CC; mem. Dist. 96 La. House of Reps., 2012—, mem. Adminstrn. of Criminal Justice Com., Agr., Forestry, Aquaculture, and Rural Devel. Com. & Transp., Highways, and Pub. Works Com. Democrat. Office: District Office 135 Northern Ave Lafayette LA 70501 E-mail: landryt@legis.la.gov.

LANDSBERG, DAVID A., publishing executive; b. Fla., 1962; m. Anoly Landsberg; children: Jessica, Natasha, Daniela. BA in Bus. Adminstrn. and Fin., U. Fla.; MBA, U. Miami. Various fin. positions including planning mgr. Miami Herald Media Co., Fla., 1984—99, CFO, 1997—99, v.p. advt., 1999—2005, gen. mgr., 2005—06, pres., pub., 2006—. Bd. dirs. United Way Miami-Dade, Goodwill Industries South Fla., Inc. Office: The Miami Herald 3511 NW 91st Ave Doral FL 33172-1216 Office Phone: 916-321-1846. Office Fax: 916-321-1964. E-mail: dlandsberg@miamiherald.com.

LANDY, BURTON AARON, lawyer; b. Chgo., Aug. 16, 1929; s. Louis J. and Clara (Ernstein) L.; m. Eleonora M. Simmel, Aug. 4, 1957; children: Michael Simmel, Alisa Anne. Student, Nat. U. Mex., 1948; BS, Northwestern U., 1950; postgrad. scholar, U. Havana, 1951; JD, U. Miami, 1952; postgrad. fellow, Inter-Am. Acad. Comparative Law, Havana, Cuba, 1955-56. Bar: Fla. 1952. Practice law in internat. field, Miami, 1955—; ptnr. firm Ammerman & Landy, 1957-63, Paul, Landy, Beiley & Harper, P.A. and predecessor firm, 1964-94, Steel Hector & Davis, 1994-97; ptnr. firm, chmn. emeritus Internat. Practice Group Akerman, Senterfitt & Eidson, P.A., 1997—; pres. ICCA Miami 2014, Inc., 2011—. Lectr. Latin Am. bus. law U. Miami Sch. Law, 1972-75; also internat. law confs. in U.S. and abroad; mem. Nat. Conf. on Fgn. Aspects of U.S. Nat. Security, Washington, 1958; mem. organizing com. Miami regional conf. Com. for Internat. Econ. Growth, 1958; mem. U.S. Dept. Commerce Regional Export Expansion Council, 1969-74, mem. Dist. Export Council, 1978—; mem. U.S. Sec. State Adv. Com. on Pvt. Internat. Law; dir. Fla. Council Internat. Devel., 1977—, chmn. 1986-87, 99; mem. U. Miami Citizens Bd., 1977—; chmn. Fla. del. S.E. U.S.-Japan Assn., 1980-82; mem. adv. com. 1st Miami Trade Fair of Ams., 1978; dir., v.p. Greater Miami Fgn. Trade Zone, Inc., 1978—; mem. organizing com., lectr. 4 Inter-Am. Aviation Law Confs.; bd. dirs. Inter-Am. Bar Legal Found., VIII FTAA Ministerial, Am. Bus. Forum; participant Aquaculture Symposium Sci. and Man in the Ams., Mexico City, Fla. Gov's Econ. Mission to Japan and Hong Kong, 1978; mem. bd. exec. advisors Law and Econs. Ctr.; mem. vis. com., internat. adv. bd. U. Miami Sch. Bus.; mem. internat. fin. council Office Comptroller of Fla.; founding chmn. Fla.-Korea Econ. Coop. Com., 1982—, Southeast U.S.-Korea Econ. Com., 1985—; chmn. Expo 500 Fla.-Columbus Soc., 1985-87; founding co-chmn. So. Fla. Roundtable-Georgetown U. Ctr. for Strategic and Internat. Studies, 1982-85; chmn. Fla. Gov.'s Conf. on World Trade, 1984—; founding gen. counsel Fla. Internat. Bankers Assn.; dir., former gen. counsel Fla. Internat. Ins. and Reins. Assn., chmn. Latin Am. Carribbean Bus. Promotion Adv. Counc. to U.S. Sec. of Commerce and Aid Adminstr; appointee Fla. Internat. Trade and Investment Coun.; mem. steering com. Summit of Ams., 1994—, co-chair post summit planning com.; strategic planning com. Mayor Miami Dade County Internat. Trade Commn.; chmn., Miami Internat. Arbitration Soc., 2008-. Contbg. editor Econs. Devel. Lawyers of the Ams., 1969-74; contbr. numerous articles to legal jours. in U.S. and fgn. countries. Chmn. City of Miami Internat. Trade and Devel. Com., 1984-86; founding chmn. Miami Internat. Arbitration Soc., 2008-; chmn. internat. task force Beacon Coun. of Dade County, Fla., 1985, dir., chmn., 1991—; bd. dirs., exec. com. Internat. Comml. Dispute Resolution Ctr., Miami Internat. Arbitration and Mediation Inst.; chmn. Comml. Dispute Resolution Ctr. Ams., Miami, 1995—; apptd. by Gov. of Fla. to Internat. Currency and Barter Commn., 1986; lectr. U. Miami Inter-Ban course L.Am. bankers; steering com. Summit of the Americas, Miami, 1994, co-chair post Summit Planning Com., 1994; co-chair mayor Miami-Dade County Strategic Planning for Internat. Trade, 1998—; co-chair strategic planning com. Mayor of Miami Dade County Internat. Trade Commn.; bd. dirs. Trade Mission Ctr. Am., 2000—, Internat. Trade Coun. Miami-Dade County, Fla., Fla. Free Trade Area Agreement, Inc.; mem. internat. adv. com. Enterprise Fla., 2000—; bd. trustee Fla. Free Trade Area of the Americas; bd. dirs. Fla. Free Trade Agreement Ams., Inc., chmn., 2006—; chmn. World Svcs. Group, 2006-07, chmn., 2006-07. With JACGC, USAF, 1952-54, Korea; to maj. Res. Recipient Pan Am. Informatica Comunicaciones Expo award, 1983, Lawyer of Americas award U. Miami, 1984, Heung-in medal (Order of Diplomatic Service), 1986, Ministerial Citation, Min. of Fgn. Affairs, 1988, Richard L. McLaughlin award Fla. Econ. Devel. Coun., 1993, Order of the Rising Sun Golden Rays with Garnet medal, Emperor of Japan, 2004; named Internat. Trader of Yr., Fla. Council Internat. Devel., 1980, Bus. Person of Yr., 1986, hon. consul gen. Republic of Korea, Miami, 1983-88, State of Fla., 99—; apptd. Hon. consul Ft. Lauderdale, Fla., 1991-98; apptd. Hon. consul gen. State of Fla., 1999—. Fellow ABA Found. (chmn. com. arrangements internat. and comparative law sect. 1964-65, com. on Inter-Am. affairs of ABA 1985-87); mem. Inter-Am. Bar Assn. (asst. sec.-gen. 1957-59, treas. 11th conf. 1959, co-chmn. jr. bar sect. 1963-65, mem council 1969—, exec. com. 1975—, pres. 1982-84, Diploma de Honor 1987, William Roy Vallance award 1989), Spanish Am. Bar Assn., Fla. Bar Assn. (vice chmn. adminstrv. law com. 1965, vice chmn. internat. and comparative law com. 1967-68, chmn. aero. law com. 1968-69), Dade County Bar Assn. (chmn. fgn. laws and lang. com. 1964-65), Internat. Ctr. Fla. (World Trade Ctr., pres. 1981-82), World Peace Through Law Ctr., Miami Com. Fgn. Rels., Inst. Ibero Am. Derecho Aero., Am. Soc. Internat. Law, Coun. Internat. Visitors, Am. Fgn. Law Assn. (pres. Miami 1958), appointed to Nat. and Internat. panels of Arbitrators of the Am. Arbitration Assn., 2003-, Bar of South Korea (hon. mem.), Greater Miami C. of C. (bd. gov. 1986—), Colombian-Am. C. of C. (bd. dirs. 1986—), Peruvian-Am. C. of C. (bd. dir.), Norwegian Am. C. of C. (bd. dir.), Phi Alpha Delta. Home: 605 Almeria Ave Coral Gables FL 33134-5602 Office: One SE Third Ave 28th Flr Miami FL 33131 Office Phone: 305-982-5690. Business E-Mail: burton.landy@akerman.com.

LANDY, RICHARD, human resources specialist; BA, MBA, Iona Coll., New Rochelle, NY. With ComEd; sr. v.p., human resources Exelon, Entergy, v.p., human resources, chief Adminstrv. officer; v.p., human resources Entergy Ops. Inc. (subs. of Entergy); pres., CEO Entergy Solutions Inc. (subs. of Entergy); chief human resource officer Energy Future Holdings Corp. (formerly TXU Corp.), exec. v.p., human resources, 2010—. Chmn. Spanish Coalition for Jobs, Chgo., Ill. Sergeant, 4th Cavalry US Army, 1967-69. Office: Energy Future Holdings Corp Energy Plz 1601 Bryan St Dallas TX 75201 Office Phone: 214-812-4600. Business E-Mail: rich.landy@energyfutureholdings.com.

LANE, ANDREW, energy executive; BS in Mech. Engring., Southern Methodist U. Prodn. engr., Gulf Oil's Pipeline Design and Permits Group Gulf Oil Corp., field engr., 1982; COO Landmark Graphics Corp., 2002, pres., CEO, 2002—03; v.p., prodn. enhancement PSL, Halliburton Energy Svcs. Group Halliburton Co., 2000—01, pres., Landmark Divsn., Halliburton Energy Svcs. Group, 2003—04, sr. v.p., global ops., Halliburton Energy Svcs. Group, 2004, exec. v.p., COO, 2004—07; pres., CEO Kellogg Brown & Root, Inc., 2004, bd. dirs., 2006—07; pres., CEO McJunkin Red Man Corp., 2008—, chmn., 2009—. Bd. dirs. Southern Methodist U. Sch. Engring. Mem.: Soc. Petroleum Engrs. Office: McJunkin Red Man Corp 835 Hillcrest Dr Charleston WV 77010 Office Phone: 304-348-5211. Office Fax: 304-348-4922. Business E-Mail: andrew.lane@mcjunkinredman.com.

LANE, ANN JUDITH, history and women's studies educator, director; b. NYC, July 27, 1931; d. Harry A. and Elizabeth (Brown) Lane; children: Leslie Patricia, Joni Alexandra. BA, Bklyn. Coll., 1952; MA, NYU, 1958; PhD, Columbia U., 1968. Mng. editor Challenge Mag., NYU, 1953-56; asst. prof. Douglass Coll., Rutgers U., New Brunswick, N.J., 1968-71; prof. John Jay Coll., SUNY, 1971-83; vis. prof. Wheaton Coll., Norton, Mass., 1981-82; prof. history, dir. women's studies Colgate U., Hamilton, N.Y., 1983-90, U. Va., Charlottesville, 1990—. Author: To Herland and Beyond, 1990, Mary Ritter Beard: A Sourcebook, 1977, 2d edit., 1988, The Brownsville Affair, 1971, Gender, Power and Sexuality: First, Do No Harm, 2006; editor: Charlotte Perkins Gilman Reader, 1980, Herland: A Lost Utopian Novel, 1979. Chair Com. on Status of Women in the Profession, Orgn. of Am. Historians, 1992-95; dir. History Tchr. Inst., N.Y. Coun. for Humanities, summer 1985; mem. historians adv. com. Nat. Women's Hall of Fame, 1986—; bd. dirs. Louis M. Rabinowitz Found., 1972-76. Recipient Va. Soc. Sci. Outstanding History scholar, 2005; fellow, Berkshire Conf. Women Historians, 1988, Ford Found., 1981—82, Nat. Endowment for Humanities, 1980—81, Lilly Endowment, Inc., 1977—79, AAUW, 1959—60. Mem. AAUP (mem. com. on women 1987—), Orgn. Am. Historians (mem. Frederick Jackson Turner prize com. 1979), Women in Hist. Profession (exec. bd., coordinating com. 1971-74). Office: Women's Studies Program Minor Hall University of Virginia Charlottesville VA 22903 Office Phone: 434-982-2962. Business E-Mail: ajl3u@virginia.edu.

LANE, JOHN RODGER, art association administrator, retired museum director; b. Evanston, Ill., Feb. 28, 1944; s. John Crandall Lane and Jeanne Marie (Rodger) L. Moritz; m. Inge-Lise Eckmann, 1992. BA, Williams Coll., 1966; MBA, U. Chgo., 1971; AM, Harvard U., 1973, PhD, 1976; DFA (hon.), San Francisco Art Inst., 1995. Asst. dir. Fogg Art Mus., Cambridge, Mass., 1974—75; exec. asst. to dir., adminstr. curatorial affairs, asst. dir. curatorial affairs Bklyn. Mus., NYC, 1975-80; dir. Carnegie Mus. Art, Pitts., 1980-86, San Francisco Mus. Modern Art, 1987-97; Eugene McDermott dir. Dallas Mus. Art, 1999—2008, dir. emeritus, 2008—; pres., CEO New Art Trust, San Francisco, 2008—. Author: Stuart Davis: Art and Art Theory, 1978; co-editor: Abstract Painting and Sculpture in America, 1927-1944, 1983, Carnegie International, 1985, Dallas Mus. Art 100 Years, 2003, Sigmar Polke: The History of Everything, Paintings, and Drawings, 1998-2003, Gerhard Richter Edits., 1965-2004, Lothar Baumgarten: Carbon, 2004, Fast Forward: Contemporary Collections for Dallas Mus. Art, 2007; exec. editor: The Making of a Modern Museum/SFMOMA, 1995. Mem. vis. com., Williams Coll. Mus. Art, 2007-; Trustee Fountain Valley Sch., Colorado Springs, 1999—2005, James Brooks Found. 2008-. Served to lt. USNR, 1966-69. Nat. Endowment Arts Mus. fellow, 1974-75 Mem. Assn. Art Mus. Dirs. (trustee 2000—02), Am. Assn. Museums. Office: Dallas Mus Art 1717 N Harwood St Dallas TX 75201-2398 Office Phone: 214-922-1304. Business E-Mail: jlane@DallasMuseumofArt.org.

LANE, KENNETH E., law educator, legal association administrator; BS, Indiana State U., 1969; MEd, U. Missouri, 1972; EdD, Tex. A&M U., 1983. Secondary administration, counseling, and teaching Plano, Tex. Sch. Dist., Hazelwood, Mo. Sch. Dist. and Ferguson-Florissant, Mo. Sch. Dist., 1969—85; asst. prof. educational leadership Southeastern Louisiana U., Hammond, La., 1985—89, prof. dept. of educational leadership & technology, 2006—, coordinator doctoral program; prof., dir. Nat. Ctr. for Excellence in Distance Learning Calif. State U., San Bernardino, 1989—2006. Exec. dir. Internat. Acad. of Educational Leaders, 1997—; presenter in field. Contbr. of articles to profl. publications. Mem.: Education Law Assn. (pres. 2013—). Address: Education Law Association 2121 Euclid Ave LL 212 Cleveland OH 44115-2214 Office: Southeastern Louisiana University TEC 1006D Hammond LA 70402 Office Phone: 985-549-3765. Office Fax: 985-549-5712. Business E-Mail: kenneth.lane@selu.edu.*

LANE, MARK, lawyer, educator, writer; b. NYC, Feb. 24, 1927; s. Harry Arnold and Elizabeth Lane; m. Patricia Ruth Erdner, 1987; children: Anne-Marie, Christina. LLB, Bklyn. Law Sch., 1951. Bar: N.Y. 1951, D.C. 1995. Mng. mem. The Lane Law Firm; pvt. practice, 1952—; founder Mid-Harlem Community Parish Narcotics Clinic, 1953, East Harlem Reform Dem. Club, 1959; prof. law Cath. U., Washington, 1975—76. Founder and dir. Citizens Commn. Inquiry; founder Wounded Knee Legal Def.-Offense Com., 1973, The Covered Wagon, Mountain Home, Idaho, 1971. Author: (books) Rush to Judgment, 1966, A Citizen's Dissent, 1968, Chicago Eye-Witness, 1969, Arcadia, 1970, Conversations with Americans, 1970, Executive Action, 1973, (with Dick Gregory) Code Name Zorro, 1977, The Strongest Poison, 1980, Plausible Denial, 1991, Murder in Memphis, 1993; prodr. films Rush to Judgment, 1967, Two Men in Dallas, 1987, 92; writer, prodr. plays Trial of James Earl Ray, 1978, Plausible Denial, 1992, Winds of Doctrine, 1994; writer, prodr. screenplays, Arcadia, 1992, Slay the Dreamer, 1992, Plausible Denial, 1993; founder publs. Citizens Quar., 1975, Helping Hand, 1971. Mem. N.Y. State Assembly, 1960-62. With AUS, 1945-47. Office: 4 Old Farm Rd Charlottesville VA 22903 Office Phone: 434-293-2349.

LANE, NEAL FRANCIS, physics professor, retired federal agency administrator; b. Oklahoma City, Aug. 22, 1938; s. Walter Patrick and Harietta (Hattie) Charlotte (Hollander) Lane; m. Joni Sue Williams, June 11, 1960; children: Christy Lynn Lane Saydjari, John Patrick. BS, U. Okla., 1960, MS, 1962, PhD, 1964, DHL (hon.), 1995; DSc (hon.), U. Ala., 1994, Mich. State U., 1995; DHL (hon.), Marymount U., Arlington, Va., 1995; DSc (hon.), Ohio State U., 1996, Washington Coll., 1998, Mt. Sinai Sch. Medicine, 1999, U. Colo., 1999, Queen's U., Belfast, No. Ireland, 2000, N.C. State U., 2001, SUNY, 2002; DHL and Sc (hon.), Ill. Inst. Tech., 2000. NSF postdoctoral fellow Queen's U., Belfast, Northern Ireland, 1964—65, Rice U., Houston, asst. prof. physics, 1966—69, assoc. prof., 1969—72, prof. physics and space physics and astronomy, 1972—84, chmn. dept. physics, 1977—82, provost, chief academic officer, 1986—93, Malcolm Gillis U. prof., 2005—; dir. divsn. physics NSF, Washington, 1979—80, dir., 1993—98; chancellor U. Colo., Colorado Springs, 1984—86; asst. to pres. for sci. and tech., dir. Office Sci. and Tech. Policy, Washington, 1998—2001; prof., Dept. Physics and Astronomy, sr. fellow James A. Baker III Inst. Pub. Policy, Rice U., 2001—. Adj. fellow Joint Inst. for Lab. Astrophysics, U. Colo., Boulder, 2001—, vis. fellow, 1965—66, 1975—76; mem. commn. on phys. sci., math. and applications NRC, 1989—93; bd. overseers Superconducting Super Collider (SSC) Univs. Rsch. Assn., 1985—93; disting. Karcher lectr. U. Okla., Norman, 1983; disting. vis. scientist U. Ky., Lexington, 1980; mem. adv. com. math. and phys. sci. NSF, 1992—93; mem. adv. bd. Kavli Inst. Theoretical Physics, U. Calif., Santa Barbara; mem. adv. com. Sci. and Tech. Adv. Group, Taiwan; mem. com. on pub. and govt. affairs Nat. Acads., mem. com. on elementary particle physics. Co-author: Quantum States of Atoms, Molecules and Solids, Understanding More Quantum Physics; contbr. articles to profl. jours. Active Cath. Commn. Intellectual and Cultural Affairs, 1991; trustee U. Corp. Atmospheric Rsch.; Houston Mus. Sci. Recipient George Brown prize for superior teaching, Rice U., 1973—74, 1976—77, Brown Coll. Tchg. award, 1972—73, Disting. Svc. award, Nat. Assn. Biology Tchrs., 1997, Pres.'s award, ASME, 1999, Support Sci. award, Coun. Sci. Soc. Pres., 2000, Pub. Svc. award, Am. Math. Soc., Am. Astron. Soc. and Am. Phys. Soc., 2001, Pub. Welfare medal, NAS, 2009; fellow Alfred P. Sloan Found., 1967—71. Fellow: AAAS (Philip Hauge Abelson award 2000, William D. Carey award 2001), Assn. for Women in Sci., Am. Acad. Arts and Sci. (mem. coun.), Am. Phys. Soc. (chmn. divsn. electron and atomic physics 1977—78, exec. com. 1981—83, councilor-at-large 1983); mem.: Am. Assn. Physics Tchrs., Am. Inst. Physics (governing bd. 1984—87), Am. Chem. Soc. (Pub. Svc. award 1999), Sigma Xi (pres.-elect 1992, pres. 1993), Phi Beta Kappa. Roman Catholic. Avocations: tennis, squash. Office: Baker Inst for Pub Policy MS-40 PO Box 1892 Houston TX 77251 Office Phone: 713-348-2925. Office Fax: 713-348-5143. E-mail: neal@rice.edu.

LANE, RICHARD ALLAN, preventive medicine physician, educator; b. Camp LeJuene, NC, Feb. 5, 1956; s. Howard Allan and Elizabeth Jane (Fischer) L.; m. Cynthia Diane Gastineau, Jan. 7, 1978; children: Tiffany Marie, Laurel Christina. BS, U. Md., 1978, MD, 1982; MPH in Tropical Medicine, Tulane U., 1986. Diplomate Am. Bd. Preventive Medicine. Intern Md. Gen. Hosp., Balt., 1982-83; squadron flight surgeon, 363rd Tactical Fighter Wing USAF, Shaw AFB, 1983-85, resident in aerospace medicine Brooks AFB, 1986-87, advanced through grades to maj., 1983-87; chief aeromed. svcs. Warner Robins Air Logistics Ctr., Robins AFB, 1987-89; staff physician, microbiology instr. Liberty U., Lynchburg, Va., 1989-91, assoc. prof. health scis., 1992—2010, dir., Health Svcs. Ctr. Med. Group, 2010—12, dir., Master in Pub. Health Program, Sch. Health Scis., 2012—; pvt. med. practitioner Light Med., 1991—2009. Cons., spkr. Liberty Godparent Home, Lynchburg, 1989—2000; mem. residency adv. bd. Meharry Med. Coll., Nashville, Tenn., 1987-89; adj. faculty health sci. Internat. Health Honduras project James Madison U., Harrisonburg, Va., 1993-2000; adj. clin. prof. nurse practitioner program Old Dominion U., 1997-2000, James Madison U., 2009-11; sentinel provider US Influenza Surveillance Network, 2004-12; mem. AstaZeneca Spkrs. Bur., 2006—09. Contbr. articles to profl. jours. Bd. dirs. Network for Women in Crisis, Lynchburg, 1990-91; exec. bd. Lynchburg chpt. ARC, 1991-93; founder Emmanuel Bapt. Ch., chpt. AWANA, Warner Robins, Ga., 1987-89; trainer Youth at the Crossraods Internat. AIDS Prevention Program, 1996—; bd. dirs. Freedom 4/24, 2009-; med. cons. World Help. Fellow Am. Coll. Preventive Medicine; mem. APHA, Gideons Internat. (camp treas. 1988-89), ACSM. Republican. Evangelical. Business E-Mail: rlane@liberty.edu.

LANE, ROBIN R., lawyer; b. Kerrville, Tex., Nov. 28, 1947; d. Rowland and Gloria (Benson) Richards; m. Stanley Lane, Aug. 22, 1971 (div.); 1 child, Joshua; m. Anthony W. Cunningham, Nov. 22, 1980 (div.); 1 child, Alexandra Cunningham. BA in Econs. with honors, U. Fla., Gainesville, 1969; MA, Aix-en-Province, France, 1968, George Wash. U., Washington, DC, 1971; JD, Stetson U., DeLand, Fla., 1978. Bar: Fla. 1979, NY 2001, DC 2002, US Ct. Appeals (11th cir.) 1981, US Supreme Ct. 1986, US Ct. Appeals (DC cir.) 1992, US Ct. Appeals (3d cir.) 1993. French instr. George Washington U., 1970; mgmt. trainee internat. banking Gulf Western Industries, NYC; internat. rsch. specialist Ryder Systems, Inc., Miami, 1973, project mgr., 1974; assoc. Wagner, Cunningham, Vaughan & McLaughlin, Tampa, Fla., 1979—85; pvt. practice law, 1985—. Guest lectr. med. jurisprudence Stetson U. Coll. Law, 1982—91; guest lectr. employment discrimation U. South Fla., Fla.; mem. exec. coun. law alumni bd. Stetson U. Coll. Law. Contbr. articles to various revs. Recipient Am. Jurisprudence award-torts, Lawyers Co-op. Fla., 1979; Scottish Rite fellow, 1968—69. Mem.: ATLA, Martindale-Hubbell Bar (register of preeminent lawyers 2003), DC Bar, NY Bar, Fla. Bar Assn., Acad. Fla. Trial Lawyers (mem. com. 1983—84), Fla. Women's Alliance, Omicron Delta Epsilon. Office: 345 Bayshore Blvd Apt 1813 Tampa FL 33606-2387 Office Phone: 917-828-5753. E-mail: RRL@RLaneLC.com.

LANE, ROGER BERT, state legislator; State rep. Dist. 167, Ga., 2005—. Republican. Mailing: 411 Legis Off Bldg Atlanta GA 30334 E-mail: rogerlane167@hotmail.com.

LANE, SHERRA HILLMAN, state legislator; b. Waynesboro, Miss., Oct. 27; m. Keith Lane; children: Michael, Angela, Steven. Atty.; mem. Dist. 86 Miss. House of Reps., 2005—. Mem.: Assn. Trial Lawyers America, Miss. Trial Lawyers Assn., Phi Kappa Phi, Phi Delta Phi, USM Alumni Assn. Democrat. Methodist. Home: PO Box 971 Waynesboro MS 39367 Home Phone: 601-735-3706; Office Phone: 601-735-5708. E-mail: slane@house.ms.gov.

LANESE, HERBERT J., retired multi-industry executive; b. 1945; BS in Bus. and Maths., Bowling Green State U., MS in Bus. Adminstrn. With engring. and prodn. mgmt. dept. GM Corp.; dir. US Chem. Ops. BF Goodrich Co.; v.p. fin. Tenneco Chems.; v.p., CFO Newport News Shipbuilding & Drydock Co., 1983-86; v.p. Tenneco, Inc. (formerly Tenneco Automotive, Inc.), 1986-89; sr. v.p. McDonnell Douglas Corp., 1989-92, exec. v.p., CFO, 1992; chmn. bd. McDonnell Douglas Fin. Corp., Long Beach, Calif., 1993, pres.; pres., CEO DynCorp Internat. Inc., Falls Church, Va., 2006—08; bd. dirs. DynCorp International, Inc., 2006—. Office: DynCorp Internat Inc 3190 Fairview Park Dr Ste 700 Falls Church VA 22042 Office Phone: 571-722-0210.

LANEY, JAMES THOMAS, former ambassador, educator; b. Wilson, Ark., Dec. 24, 1927; s. Thomas Mann and Mary (Hughey) L.; m. Berta Joan Radford, Dec. 20, 1949; children: Berta Joan Vaughan, James T., Arthur Radford, Mary Ruth Laney Reilly, Susan Elizabeth Castle. BA, Yale U., 1950, BD, 1954, PhD, 1966; DD (hon.), Fla. So. Coll., 1977, Wofford Coll., 1986, Emory U., 1994, Yonsei U., Korea, 1997, Kwansei Gakuin U., Japan, 2000; DD (hon.), Africa U., Zimbabwe, 2004; LHD (hon.), Rhodes Coll., 1979, Millsaps Coll., 1988, Austin Coll., 1990, W.Va. Wesleyan Coll., 1990, Yale U., 1993, U. S.C., 1997, Queens Coll., 1998, LaGrange Coll., 2000; LHD (hon.), Nebr. Wesleyan U., 2004; LHD (hon.), U. Richmond, 2001; HHD (hon.), Mercer U., 1980; LLD (hon.), DePauw U., 1985, U. St. Andrews, Scotland, 1994, Alaska Pacific U., 1994; LLD (hon.), Piedmont Coll., 1999; D in Internat. Affairs (hon.), Am. U., 1998. Chaplain Choate Sch., Wallingford, Conn., 1953-55; ordained to ministry Meth. Ch., 1955; asst. lectr. Yale Div. Sch., 1954-55; pastor St. Paul Meth. Ch., Cin., 1955-58; sec. student Christian movement, prof. Yonsei U., Seoul, Korea, 1959-64; asst. prof. Christian ethics Vanderbilt U. Div. Sch., 1966-69; dean Candler Sch. Theology, Emory U., 1969-77, pres. univ., 1977-93, pres. emeritus, 1993—; US amb. to Republic of Korea, 1993-97; spl. presdl. envoy, 1997—99. Vis. prof. Harvard Div. Sch., 1974. Author: The Education of the Heart, 1994; (with J.M. Gustafson) On Being Responsible, 1968, (with others) Ambassador's Memoirs, 2009; contbr. columns NY Times, Washington Post, LA Times. Fgn. Affairs pres. Nashville Cmty. Rels. Coun., 1968-69; mem. Yale Coun. Com., 1972-77; bd. dir. Fund Theol. Edn.; chmn. United Bd. Christian Higher Edn. in Asia, 1990-93, 97-2002; chmn. Fulbright Internat. Award Com., 1997-2000; bd. dir. Atlanta Symphony, 1979-91; chmn. bd. overseers com. to visit Harvard Div. Sch., 1980-85; mem. Yale U. Coun. Exec. Com., 1990-93; mem. Carnegie Endowment Nat. Commn. on Am. and the New World; mem. adv. com. Atlanta Project; chmn. so. dist. Rhodes Scholarship Com., 1980-90; bd. dir. Atlantic Coun., 1987-93. Henry Luce Found., 1990-2013, Atlanta Cmty. Found., 2008-12; mem. tercentenary steering com. Yale U., 1998-01; co-chmn. Faith & City, Atlanta, Ga.; trustee Carter Ctr., 1997-2002, Task Force Global Health, 2001-06. With AUS, 1946-48. Leadership Atlanta, 1970-71; recipient Disting. Alumnus award Yale U. Div. Sch., 1979, 93, Kellogg award for leadership in higher edn., 1983, Wilbur Cross medal Yale Grad. Sch., 1996, James Van Fleet award, Korean Soc., 1996, Kangwa medal for disting. diplomatic svc., Rep. Korea, 1997, Dept. Defense medal for disting. pub. svc., U.S. Govt., 1997, 1st Internat. Human Rights award Inst. Human Rights, Korea, 1998; D.C. Macintosh fellow Yale U., 1965-66, award ICAS Liberty, 2009, Emory U. Grad. Sch. Named in Hon., 2007, Atlanta Legend award, 2013; named Hon. Professorship Yonsei U., 2013. Mem. Soc. Values Higher Edn. (pres. 1987-91), Coun. on Fgn. Rels. (co-chair task force on Korean Peninsula 1997-2002), Pilgrim Soc., Atlanta C. of C., Commerce Club, Atlanta Rotary Club, Phi Beta Kappa, Omicron Delta Kappa, Elihu Soc. (hon). Home: 2015 Grand Prix Dr NE Atlanta GA 30345-3931 Personal E-mail: berlaney@aol.com.

LANEY, JOHN THOMAS, III, federal judge; b. Columbus, Ga., Mar. 27, 1942; s. John Thomas Jr. and Leila (Davis) L.; m. Louise Pierce, Nov. 23, 1974; children: Thomas Whitfield, Elizabeth Davis. AB, Mercer U., 1964, JD magna cum laude, 1966. Bar: Ga. 1965, U.S. Dist. Ct. (mid. dist.) Ga. 1966, U.S. Ct. Appeals (5th cir.) 1966, U.S. Ct. Mil. Appeals 1967, U.S. Ct. Appeals (11th cir.) 1981. Assoc. Swift, Pease, Davidson & Chapman, Columbus, 1970-73; ptnr. Page, Scrantom, Harris & Chapman, Columbus, 1973-86; judge mid. dist. Ga. U.S. Bankruptcy Ct., Columbus, 1986—. Co-editor-in-chief Mercer Law Rev., 1965—66; contbr. articles to profl. jours. Former pres., dir. Metro. Boys Club of Columbus. Capt. U.S. Army, 1966-70. Mem. ABA (judge adminstrv. divsn. Nat. Conf. Fed. Trial Judges), State Bar Ga. (chmn. gen. practice and trial sect. 1983-84, chmn. state disciplinary bd. 1984-85), Am. Judicature Soc., Nat. Conf. Bankruptcy Judges, Columbus Bar Assn., Inc. (pres. 1985-86), Rotary. Presbyterian. Office: US Bankruptcy Ct 1 Arsenal Pl 901 Front Ave Ste 309 Columbus GA 31901-2797 Home Phone: 706-561-7391; Office Phone: 706-596-7150. E-mail: k4bai@att.net.*

LANEY, MICHAEL L., manufacturing executive; b. LA, Sept. 10, 1945; s. Roy and Wanda Laney; m. Marti Miller, Dec. 31, 1964; children: Tynna, Kristen. BS with honors, Calif. State U., Northridge, 1967; MBA, UCLA, 1969. CPA, Calif. Sr. tax acct. Haskins-Sells, Los Angeles, 1967-69; asst. prof. acctg. Calif. State U., Northridge, 1969-72; tax prin. M. Klaiman Acctg. Corp., Beverly Hills, Calif., 1972-75; pvt. practice Beverly Hills, 1975-80; v.p., controller Ducommun, Inc., Los Angeles, 1980-87; sr. v.p., fin. and adminstrn. Monarch Mirror Door Co. Inc., Chatsworth, Calif., 1987-92; v.p. ops. feature animation Walt Disney Pictures and TV (part of The Walt Disney Co.), Glendale, Calif., 1992-93; sr. v.p. ops. Warner Bros., Glendale, Calif., 1994-96; pres. children's Wonderland, Agoura, Calif., 1996-97; CFO Dacor, Pasadena, Calif., 1997-2001; pres., CEO Cool Roof of Calif., Inc., Calabasas, 2001—; pres. M. Laney & Assocs., Portland, 2002—; CFO Energy Trust Oreg., Inc., 2004—05. Mem. Fin. Execs. Inst. (pres. Portland chpt.), Am. Inst. CPA's, Calif. Soc. CPA's; Assn. Corp. Growth., Am. Sch. Counselors Assn., Nat. Assn. Corp. Dirs. (founder, chmn. Portland chpt.), Soc. Human Resources (practioner), Assn. Psychol. Type. Office Phone: 503-946-8798. Personal E-mail: michael@mlaneyassoc.com.

LANG, ROBERTA LYNN, food products company executive, lawyer; b. South Bend, Ind., Oct. 16, 1958; d. Robert Aschielle and Charlene Theresa (Leffert) Plasschaert; m. Richard Alan Lang, Dec. 2, 1991; 1 child, Daniel Marek; 1 stepchild, Cole. BA, Ind. U., South Bend, 1987; JD, Valparaiso U., 1990. Bar: Ind. 1990, U.S. Dist. Ct. (no. and so. dists.) Ind. 1990, Ill. 1992, U.S. Dist. Ct. (no. dist.) Ill. 1992. Assoc. Krisor & Nussbaum, South Bend, 1990-91, Momkus, Ozog & McCluskey, Downers Grove, Ill., 1992-94; pvt. practice, 1994—98; v.p. legal affairs, gen. counsel Whole Foods Market, Inc., 1998—. Bd. dirs. Animal Compassion Found., 2005—, Whole Planet Found. Vol. Legal Svcs. Program No. Ind., Inc., South Bend, 1985-87. Mem. DuPage County Assn. Women Lawyers. Office: Whole Foods Market Inc 550 Bowie St Austin TX 78703

LANGBAUM, ROBERT WOODROW, language educator; s. Murray and Nettie (Moskowitz) L.; m. Francesca Levi Vidale, Nov. 5, 1950; 1 child, Donata Emily. AB, Cornell U., 1947; MA, Columbia U., 1949, PhD, 1954. Instr. English Cornell U., 1950-55, asst. prof., 1955-60; assoc. prof. U. Va., Charlottesville, 1960-63, prof. English, 1963—67, James Branch Cabell prof. English and Am. lit., 1967—99, prof. emeritus, 1999—. Vis. prof. Columbia U., summer 1960, 65-66, Harvard U., summer 1965; mem., supervising com. English Inst., 1970-71, chmn., 1972; mem., Christian Gauss Book Award Com., 1984-86; US Info. Svc. Lectr., Japan, Taiwan, Hong Kong, 1988; lectr., James Joyce, China, 1996. Author: (books) The Poetry of Experience: The Dramatic Monologue in Modern Literary Tradition, 1957 (Spanish trans. 1996); The Gayety of Vision: A Study of Isak Dinesen's Art (Danish trans. 1964), 1964; The Modern Spirit: Essays on the Continuity of Nineteenth and Twentieth Century Literature, 1970; The Mysteries of Identity: A Theme in Modern Literature, 1977; The Word From Below: Essays on Modern Literature and Culture, 1987; Thomas Hardy in Our Time, 1995; editor: The Tempest (Shakespeare), 1964; The Victorian Age: Essays in History and in Social and Literary Criticism, 1967; contbr. article to profl. jours. Served to 1st lt. US Army, 1942—46. Ford Found. fellow Center for Advanced Study, Stanford, Calif., 1961-62; Guggenheim fellow, 1969-70, Sr. fellow Nat. Endowment for Humanities, 1972-73; Am. Council Learned Socs. grantee, 1961, 75-76; fellow Clare Hall, Cambridge U., Eng., 1978; U. Va. Ctr. Advanced Study fellow, 1982; resident scholar Bellagio Study and Conf. Ctr. Rockefeller Found., Italy, 1987. Mem. MLA (del. assembly 1979-81), AAUP, PEN, Assn. Lit. Scholars and Critics, Phi Beta Kappa. Democrat. Jewish.

LANGBORT, POLLY, retired advertising executive; b. NYC; d. Julius and Nettie (Berman) L. BA, Adelphi U. Sec. Young & Rubicam, Inc., NYC, media buyer, media planner, 1960-65, planning supr., 1965-70, v.p. group supr., 1970-75, v.p. dir. planning devel., 1975-80, sr. v.p., dir. comm. planning, 1980-85, sr. v.p. direct mktg. and media services Wunderman, Worldwide div., 1985-86, exec. v.p. dir. mktg. & media services, 1986-90; assoc. pub. Lear's Mag., NYC, 1990-91; ret., 1991. Author: DMA Factbook, 1986; contbr. articles to profl. jours. Spl. gifts chairperson Am. Cancer Soc., N.Y.C., 1985-90. Recipient Bronze Life Master, 2011; named Bridge Life Master, 2009. Mem. Boca Raton Resort and Club, Boca Pointe Country Club. Avocations: classical music, outdoor activities, bridge. Home: 7614 La Corniche Cir Boca Raton FL 33433-6055 Personal E-mail: pollylang@aol.com.

LANGDON, JAMES H., JR., state legislator; m. Lena Langdon. Former chmn., bd. commr. Johnson County; tchr., ret.; state rep. Dist. 28 NC, 2005—. Republican. Baptist. Mailing: Dist Off 10176 NC 50 Hwy Angier NC 27501 Office: North Carolina House of Representatives 300 N Salisbury St Rm 417B Raleigh NC 27603-5925 Office Phone: 919-733-5849. E-mail: James.Langdon@ncleg.net.

LANGDON, JERRY J., energy executive; BS in Comm., U. Tex., 1975. Commr. Fed. Energy Regulatory Commn., 1988—93; pres. EPGT Tex. Pipeline, L.P., 1988—93; exec. v.p., chief adminstrv. officer Reliant Resources, Inc., 2003—07; chief adminstrv. & compliance officer Energy Transfer Partners, LP, 2007—. Contbr. articles to profl. jours. Active Am. Cancer Soc., M.D. Anderson Cancer Ctr.; Chmn., coordinating subcom. Nat. Petroleum Coun.; bd. dirs. North Am. Energy Stds. Bd., The Interstate Oil and Gas Compact Commn. Office: Energy Transfer Partners LP 3738 Oak Lawn Ave Dallas TX 75219 Office Phone: 214-981-0700. Office Fax: 214-981-0703. Business E-Mail: jerry.langdon@energytransfer.com.

LANGE, CARL JAMES, retired psychology professor; b. Seneca, Pa., June 1, 1925; s. Otto Carl and Rose Marie (Jetter) L.; m. Veronica Szelypecz, Jan. 14, 1950; children: David Carl, Veronica Jean. BS, Duke U., 1945; MS, U. Pitts., 1948, PhD, 1951. Lic. psychologist, Va. Project dir. Human Resources Research Office, George Washington U., 1953-60, dir. research, planning, 1960-69; asst. v.p. research George Washington U., 1969-75, v.p. adminstrn., research, prof. psychology, 1975-88, v.p. rsch., prof. psychology, 1988-89, prof. emeritus, 1989—. Cons. NSF, Ford Found.; bd. dirs. Sch. for Contemporary Edn., Nat. Lab. Higher Edn., Eric Clearinghouse for Higher Edn., Southeastern Univs. Rsch. Assn. Contbr. articles in field to profl. jours.; bd. editors: Research in Higher Education. Served with USN, 1943-45. Fellow Am. Psychol. Assn.; mem. AAAS, Sigma Xi. Home: 7 Clarendon Ct Williamsburg VA 23188-1513

LANGER, RALPH ERNEST, journalist, retired editor; b. Benton Harbor, Mich., July 30, 1937; s. Ralph L. and Mary (Skuda) L.; m. Katherine B. McGuire, June 25, 1960; children: Terri B., Tammi L. Student, Central Mich. U., 1955-57; BA in Journalism, U. Mich., 1957-59. Telegraph editor, reporter Grand Haven Daily Tribune, Mich., 1959-60; mng. editor Port Angeles Evening News, Wash., 1962-66; copy desk Detroit Free Press, 1966-68; asst. mng. editor Dayton Jour. Herald, 1968, mng. editor, 1968-75; editor Everett Herald, Wash., 1975-81; mng. editor Dallas Morning News, 1981-83, exec. editor, 1983-86, v.p., 1986-91, sr. v.p., exec. editor, 1991-96, exec. v.p., editor, 1997-98; ret., 1999; exec.-in-residence So. Meth. U., 1999—2002. Pres. Freedom of Info. Found. Tex., 1985-89; founding pres. Nat. Freedom of Info. Coalition, 1989-93, Coun. of Presidents, 1991-92. 1st lt. U.S. Army, 1960-62. Named to Journalism Hall of Fame, Ctrl. Mich. U., 2003. Mem. Am. Soc. Newspaper Editors (bd. dirs. 1997—99), Press Club Dallas (pres. 1985-86), A.P. Mng. Editors Assn. (bd. dirs. 1980—, sec. 1989, v.p. 1990, pres. 1990-91), Coun. of Pres.'s (founding pres. 1992-93), AP Mng. Editors Assn. Found. (pres. 1991-92), Scabbard and Blade, Alpha Phi Gamma, Sigma Phi Epsilon. Personal E-mail: ralphlanger@sbcglobal.net.

LANGERBEIN, HELMUT, history professor, department chairman; b. Wickede Ruhr, Nordrhein-Westfalen, Germany, June 12, 1962; permanent resident, USA, 1992; s. Heinrich and Monika Langerbein; 1 child, Ryan Whelan. PhD in History, U. Calif., Santa Cruz, 2000. Commdg. officer German Air Force Tng. Co., Mengen, Baden-Wuerthenberg, Germany, 1988—93; adj. instr. U. Calif., Santa Cruz, 1996—2003; asst. prof. history U. Tex., Brownsville, 2004—, history dept. chair, 2007—. Author: Hitler's Death Squads: The Logic of Mass Murder, 2003. Capt. German AF, 1981—93. Office: Univ Tex 80 Fort Brown Brownsville TX 78520 Office Fax: 956-882-7072. Business E-Mail: helmut.langerbein@utb.edu.

LANGUM, DAVID JOHN, law educator, historian; b. Oakland, Calif., Oct. 24, 1940; s. John Kenneth and Virginia Anne (deMattos) Langum; children: Virginia Eileen, John David, David John Jr., Audrey Leora Kari, Anna Louisa Kari. AB, Dartmouth Coll., 1962; JD, Stanford U., 1965; MA in History, San Jose State U., 1976; LLM in Legal History, U. Mich., 1981, SJD in Legal History, 1985. Bar: Calif. 1966, Mich. 1981, Ala. 2003, U.S. Supreme Ct. 1972. Rsch. clk. Calif. Ct. Appeals, San Francisco, 1965-66; assoc. Dunne, Phelps & Mills, San Francisco, 1966-68; ptnr. Christenson, Hedemark, Langum & O'Keefe, San Jose, Calif., 1968-78; adj. prof. Lincoln U. Sch. Law, 1968-78; prof. law Detroit Coll. Law, 1978-83; prof. Old Coll. Sch. Law, Reno, Nev., 1983-85, dean, 1983-84; prof. Cumberland Sch. Law Samford U., Birmingham, 1985—. Editor: Law in the West, 1985; author: Law and Community on the Mexican California Frontier, 1987 (Hurst prize, 1988); author: (with Harlan Hague) Thomas O. Larkin: A Life of Patriotism and Profit in Old California, 1990 (Caroline Bancroft prize, 1991), Crossing Over the Line: Legislating Morality and the Mann Act, 1994; author: (with Howard Walthall) From Maverick to Mainstream: Cumberland School of Law, 1847-1997, 1997, William M. Kunstler: The Most Hated Lawyer in America, 1999; author: Antonio de Mattos and the Protestant Portuguese Community in Antebellum Illinois, 2006, Quite Contrary: The Litigious Life of Mary Bennett Love, 2014; contbr. articles to profl. jours. Mem. House of Flag, pro bono litig., San Francisco, 1973-76; past pres. Victorian Preservation Assn., Santa Clara County, Calif.; bd. dirs. ACLU of Ala., 1999—2008, pres., 2000-02; founder, dir. Langum Charitable Trust; pres. Friends of Birmingham Pub. Libr., 2000-06. Recipient Superior Achievement award, Ill. State Hist. Soc., 2007. Mem.: Western History Assn. (Bolton award 1978), Hist. Soc., Am. Soc. for Legal History (bd. dirs. 1992—95). Office: Samford U Cumberland Sch Law 800 Lakeshore Dr Birmingham AL 35229-0002 Office Phone: 205-726-2424. Business E-Mail: djlangum@samford.edu.

LANGWORTHY, EVERETT WALTER, professional society administrator, natural gas exploration company executive; b. West Springfield, Mass., Aug. 17, 1918; s. Walter Carr and Lucy Anne (Laurent) L.; m. Mary Jane Mateer, Nov. 30, 1946 (dec. Oct. 1966); children: John Alan, Jo Ann Langworthy Sears, Robert Carr; m. Joan E. Scott, Feb. 27, 1982; stepchildren: Russell, Michael, Gregory BA, U. Mass., 1940; MA, George Washington U., 1964; grad., Nat. War Coll., 1964. Commd. 2d lt. U.S. Army, 1943; commd. capt. U.S. Air Force, 1947; advanced through grades to col., 1963; ret., 1972; v.p. ops. Meteor Aero Inc., Gaithersburg, Md., 1972-76; sec. contest and record bd. Nat. Aero. Assn., Washington, 1976-80, exec. v.p., 1980—. V.p. LABCO Inc., Martinsburg, W.Va., 1974—; gen. ptnr. M&E Assocs., Gaithersburg, 1976—; dir. Acad. Model Aeronautics, Reston, Va.; cons. FBI, 1992—; cons. FBI; cons., expert witness, 1995—. Contbr. articles and columns on aerospace activities to profl. publs. U.S. rep. Fedn. Aeronautique Internat., Paris, 1980—. Decorated DFC, Air medal African Campaign award, Berlin Air Life medal; recipient Paul Tissandier diploma Fedn. Aeronautique Internationale, 1987. Mem. Nat. Aviation Club (elder statesman aviation 1990), Aero Club Washington, Air Force Assn., Ret. Officers Assn., Soaring Soc. Am. (bd. dirs. 1980—), U.S. Hang Gliding Assn. (bd. dirs. 1980—), VFW. Clubs: Lakewood Country (Rockville, Md.). Republican. Avocations: golf, writing. Home: 610 Gunston Ln Wilmington NC 28405-5317 Office: Nat Aeronautic Assn 1815 Ft Myer Dr Arlington VA 22209-1805 Office Fax: 910-256-0480. Personal E-mail: ewlang@earthlink.net. Business E-Mail: elangworthy@ec.rr.com.

LANGWORTHY, ROBERT H., criminal justice educator; MS, SUNY Albany, PhD, 1983. Asst. prof. U. Ala., Birmingham, 1983—87; prof. U. Cin., 1987—97, U. Alaska, Anchorage, 1997—2007; prof. chair dept. criminal justice U. Central Fla., 2007—. Mem. Cmty. Oriented Policing Project Nat Inst. Justice, 1995—96; dir. Justice Ctr. U. Alaska, Anchorage. Author: The Structure of Police Organizations, Policing in America; contbr. articles to prof. jour. Office: U Central Florida Dept Criminal Justice Legal Studies HPA 1 Suite 311 Orlando FL 32816-1600 Office Phone: 907-786-1810. Business E-Mail: afrhl@uaa.alaska.edu.

LANHAM, BETTY BAILEY, anthropologist, educator; b. Statesville, NC, Aug. 12, 1922; d. Clyde B. and Naomi (Bailey) L. BS, U. Va., 1944, MA, 1947; PhD, Syracuse U., 1962. Mem. faculty River Falls State Tchrs. Coll., 1948-49, U. Md., 1949-50, Wakayama U., Japan, 1951-52, Randolph Macon Women's Coll., 1954-55, Oswego State Tchrs. Coll., 1956-58, Hamilton Coll., 1961-62, Ind. U., 1962-65, Western Mich. U., 1965-67, Albany Med. Coll., 1967-70, U.Guyana, 1969-70; prof. anthropology Indiana U. of Pa., 1970-88, prof. emeritus, 1988—. Contbr. articles to jours. Wenner-Gren Found. for Anthrop. Rsch. predoctoral fellow, 1951-52, AAUW predoctoral rsch. fellow, 1959-60. Mem. Am. Anthrop. Assn., Assn. for Asian Studies Democrat. Home: 2529 Willard Dr Charlottesville VA 22903-4225 Personal E-mail: blanham2529@comcast.net.

LANIER, JOHN HICKS, apparel company executive; b. Nashville, Apr. 12, 1940; s. Sartain and Claudia Gwynn (Whitson) L.; m. Jane M. Darden, Oct. 15, 1966; children: Jay, Liza, Stephen. BA, Vanderbilt U., 1962; MBA, Harvard U., 1964. Chmn. Suntrust Banks of Ga., Inc., 1981; pres. Oxford Industries, Inc., Atlanta, 1977—2003, exec. chmn., CEO, 1981—. Bd. dirs. Shaw Industries, Inc., Dalton, Ga., Crawford & Co., 1976-2010, West Point Stevens, 2001, Genuine Parts Co, 1995-, Suntrust Bank, 2003-. Trustee, Henrietta Egleston Hosp. for Children, The Westminster Schs. Vanderbilt U.; bd. dirs. Piedmont Med. Ctr., chmn. Sartain Lanier Family Found. With USAFR, 1964—65. Mem. Am. Apparel Mfrs. Assn. (past bd. dirs.). Republican. Office: Oxford Industries Inc 999 Peachtree St NE Ste 600 Atlanta GA 30309-4414 Office Fax: 404-653-1545. Business E-Mail: hlanier@oxfordinc.com.

LANIER, JOSEPH LAMAR, JR., consumer products company executive; b. Lanett, Ala., Feb. 9, 1932; s. Joseph Lamar and Lura Brown (Fowlkes) L.; m. Ann Morgan, Aug. 21, 1954; children: Joseph Lamar III, Ann M. BS, Washington and Lee U., 1954; student, Harvard Grad. Sch. Bus., 1954-55. Asst. mgr., Fairfax Mill West Point-Pepperell, Inc., 1958—62, corp. v.p., 1962-64, v.p., new product planning devel. ops., 1964—66, v.p., mfg. indsl. fabrics divsn., 1966—68, pres., indsl. fabrics div., dir., 1968—70, corp. exec. v.p., 1970—74, pres., 1974—79, pres., CEO, 1975—79, chmn. bd., chief exec. officer, dir., 1979-89; chmn. CEO Dan River Inc., Danville, Va., 1989—2006; chmn DIMON, 1999—2003. Bd. dirs. Dibrell Bros., Flowers Industries, Inc., Textile Hall Corp., Trust Co. Ga. (now Suntrust Banks), Alliance One Internat., Inc., 1995—. Trustee LaGrange Coll. Served to 1st lt. U.S. Army, 1955-57. Mem. Am. Textile Mfrs. Inst. (bd. dirs.). Office: Alliance One International Inc Bd Directors 8001 Aerial Ctr Pky Morrisville NC 27560-8417 Office Phone: 919-379-4300. Office Fax: 919-379-4346. Personal E-mail: jlanier@aointl.com.

LANIER, WILLIAM MARK (MARK LANIER), lawyer; b. Dallas, Oct. 20, 1960; m. Becky Lanier; children: Will, Gracie, Rachel, Rebecca, Sarah. BA in Biblical Languages, David Lipscomb Coll., 1981; JD, Tex. Tech. U., 1984. Bar: Tex. 1985, US Dist. Ct. (all dists. Tex.) 1985, U.S. Ct. Appeals (5th cir.) 1985, US Supreme Ct. 1985, NY 2005, cert.: Tex. Bd. Legal Specialization (personal injury trial law). With Fulbright & Jaworski, Houston, 1983—89; founder, head Litig. Counsel The Lanier Law Firm, P.C., Houston, 1990—. Actor: (films) Puncture, 2011. Named a Tex. Super Lawyer, Tex. Monthly Mag., 2003, 2004, 2005, 2006; named one of Top 40 Attys. Under the Age of 40 in US, The Nat. Law Jour., 1995, The Nation's Top Litigators, 1998, 2006, The 100 Most Influential Lawyers in America, 2006, The Decade's Most Influential Lawyers, 2010, Top 5 Personal Injury Lawyers, Tex. Lawyer Go-To-Guide, 2002, The Top 45 Lawyers Under the Age of 45, The American Lawyer mag., 2003. Mem.: ABA, Christian Trial Lawyers Assn. (founder), Am. Bd. Trial Advs., Tex. Trial Lawyers Assn., Houston Bar Assn., Com. Econ. Devel. (bd. trustees), Order of Barristers. Avocations: baking, racquetball, gardening. Office: The Lanier Law Firm, PC 6810 FM 1960 West Houston TX 77069 Office Phone: 713-659-5200. Office Fax: 713-659-2204. E-mail: wml@lanierlawfirm.com.

LANIGAN, JOHN P., JR., rail transportation executive; BS in Mgmt. Sci., USCG Acad., 1977; MBA, Baldwin-Wallace Coll., Berea, Ohio, 1989. With Schneider Nat., 1984—95, pres., transp. sector, 1995—99, COO, 1999—2000; mng. dir., COO Logistics.com, 2000—02; exec. v.p., chief mktg. officer Burlington Northern Santa Fe Corp., 2002—10, Burlington Northern Santa Fe LLC (subs. Berkshire Hathaway), 2010—. Comdr. USCG. Office: Burlington Northern Santa Fe Corp 2650 Lou Menk Dr Fort Worth TX 76131-2830 Office Phone: 817-352-1000. Office Fax: 817-352-7171. Business E-Mail: john.laniganjr@bnsf.com.

LANIGAN, SUSAN S., retired lawyer; b. May 1962; m. Greg Lanigan; children: Drew, Alex. BA in Journalism, U. Ga., 1984, JD, 1988. Reporter Oconee Enterprise; assoc. Toutman Sanders, Atlanta; in-house counsel Turner Broadcasting Sys. Inc., 1995—96; assoc. gen. counsel Zale Corp., Irving, Tex., 1996—97, sr. v.p., gen. counsel, sec., 1997—2002; v.p., gen. counsel, corp. sec. Dollar General Corp., Goodlettsville, Tenn., 2002—03, gen. counsel, corp sec., 2003, sr. v.p., gen. counsel, corp. sec., 2003—06, exec. v.p., gen. counsel, corp. sec., 2006—13.*

LANKFORD, GEORGE EMERSON, III, social sciences educator; b. Aug. 18, 1938; BA, La. State U., Baton Rouge, 1960; BD, Princeton Theol. Sem., Princeton, NJ, 1963; PhD, Ind. U., Bloomington, 1975. Instr., asst. prof. Spring Hill Coll., Mobile, Ala., 1966-71; Bradley prof. social sci. Lyon Coll., Batesville, Ark., 1976—2001, prof. emeritus, 2001—. Home and Office: 1175 Dogwood Dr Batesville AR 72501-7506 Office Phone: 870-698-1061. E-mail: glankford@sbcglobal.net.

LANKFORD, JAMES (JIM LANKFORD), United States Representative from Oklahoma; b. Dallas, Mar. 4, 1968; m. Cindy Lankford; 1 child, Hannah; 1 child, Jordan. BS in Secondary Edn., U. Tex., 1990; MDiv, Southwestern Bapt. Theol. Sem., Ft. Worth, 1994. Staff mem. Bapt. Gen. Conv. Okla., 1996—2009; dir. Falls Creek Summer Youth Camp, Davis, Okla., 1996—2009; mem. US Congress from 5th Okla. Dist., Washington, 2011—, US House Budget Com., Washington, 2011—, US House Oversight & Govt. Reform Com., Washington, 2011—, US House Transp. & Infrastructure Com., Washington, 2011—13; chmn. US House Energy, Policy, Health Care, & Entitlements Subcommittee, Washington, 2013—, US House Republican Policy Com., Washington, 2013—. Mem.: NRA, Heritage Found., Edmond Chamber of Commerce, Deer Creek Chamber of Commerce. Republican. Christian. Office: US House of Representatives 228 Cannon House Office Bldg Washington DC 20515 also: 1015 N Broadway Ave Ste 310 Oklahoma City OK 73102 Office Phone: 202-225-2132, 405-234-9900. Office Fax: 202-226-1463.*

LANKFORD, MONTY J., medical products executive; m. Shalia Lankford; 5 children. BA, Free Will Bapt. Bible Coll. Grad. Leadership Franklin, Williamson Co. Sheriff's Acad. Founder Vol. Med., Dickson, Tenn., 1986—90; med. cons.; founder, CEO TLC Med. Oxygen and Hosp. Equipment, Inc., Tenn., 1996—. Bd. mem. Tenn. Family Action Coun., Tenn. Right to Life, mem., NRA; regional fin. chmn., presdl. campaign Sen. Fred Thompson; mem., Sunday sch. tchr. Thompson Sta. Bapt. Ch. Named Rep. of Yr., Williamson County Rep. Party, 2007. Republican. Baptist. Office: TLC Med Oxygen & Hosp Equipment Inc 357 Riverside Dr Ste 120 Franklin TN 37064 Office Phone: 615-790-1556. Office Fax: 615-790-6841.

LANNES, WILLIAM JOSEPH, III, electrical engineer; b. New Orleans, Oct. 12, 1937; s. William Joseph, Jr. and Rhea Helen (Simon) Lannes; m. Patricia Ann Didier, Jan. 17, 1961; children: David Mark, Kenneth John, Jennifer Anne. BEE, Tulane U., New Orleans, 1959; MEE, US Naval Postgrad. Sch., 1966. Registered profl. engr., La. Commd. 2d lt. US Marine Corps, 1959, advanced through grades to maj., 1967, served as electronics officer, ops. officer, 1967-70; substation engr. La. Power & Light, New Orleans, 1970-71, utility engr., 1971-76, systems relay engr., 1976-77, systems substation engr., 1977-79, engring. supr. for substation, 1979-83, substation engring. mgr., 1983-86, dir. systems engring., 1986—, v.p. systems engring., 1986-88, with ctrl. engring., 1988-89; sr. v.p. Energy Supply Fossil, 1989-91; v.p. svc. and support Entergy Corp., 1991-92; assoc. dean rsch. and grad. studies Coll. Engring. U., New Orleans, 1992-97. Dir. U. New Orleans EPRI Cmty. Initiative Ctr., 1993-95; assoc. dir. Ctr. Energy Resources Mgmt., 1993-96, dir. Ctr. Energy Resources Mgmt., 1996-2002; dir. Engring. Mgmt. Program, 1995-2002, chmn. engring. mgmt. dept., 2002-06, prof. emeritus, 2006-; sr. mgmt. advisor Novaces, 2006-; instr. Delgado Jr. Coll., 1973-74; instr. elec. engring. U. New Orleans, 1979-80; lead dir. 5th Dist. Savs. Bank, 1982—2013, emeritus dir., 2013-; spkr. profl. confs. Contbr. articles to profl. jours.; others; author: The Change Cycle Handbook: How to Initiate, Implement and Institutionalize Change, 2008. Committeeman New Orleans Area Coun., Boy Scouts Am., 1972-76; vol. United Way 1975, 76, 81; treas. PTA, 1971; vol. tchr. Confraternity of Christian Doctrine, 1972; mem. bus. adv. coun. Our Lady of Holy Cross Coll., 1981-86; chmn. engring. adv. coun. U. New Orleans; bd. dirs. New Life in La.; vol. coach New Orleans Recreation Dept., 1973; mem. La. Employees Com. on Polit. Action, Tulane Univ. Engring. Coun., New Orleans Archdiocesan Pastoral Coun., 1988-91; mem. adv. bd. Bridge House, 1992-95; bd. mem. English Turn Property Owners Assn., 2010-13; dir. Sisters of St. Joseph People Program, 2014-. Decorated Bronze Star; Cross of Gallantry Republic S. Vietnam; recipient Cert. of Merit Mayor New Orleans, 1964, Disting. Svc. to Coll. of Engring. U. New Orleans, 2006, NOVACES Founders award, 2011, Appreciation award Project Mgmt. Inst., 2013-. Fellow IEEE (profl. mem. 1996, chmn. New Orleans sect. 1981-82, Outstanding Svc. award 1976, Edward Freitag award 1988, Region 3 Outstanding Engr. award 1991, Outstanding Svc. to Coll. Engring. award 2006); mem. Electric Power Rsch. Inst. (industry advisor), Edison Electric Inst. (systems and equipment com.), Soc. Power Rsch. and Implementation (chmn. 1987-94), Southeastern Electric Exch. (substation com. 1977-85), Power Engring. Soc. (Prize Paper award 1988), Sigma Xi, Eta Kappa Nu. Republican. Roman Catholic. Avocation: tai chi. Office: Coll Engring U New Orleans New Orleans LA 70148-0001 Business E-Mail: wlannes@uno.edu.

LANNIE, PAUL ANTHONY, lawyer; b. Hayti, Mo., Feb. 21, 1954; m. Donna Dean; children: Heather, Anthony. BA magna cum laude, Vanderbilt U., 1974, JD, 1978. Bar: Tex. 1978. Assoc. Johnson & Swanson, Dallas, 1978-83; exec. v.p. BusLease Inc., Dallas, 1983-87, GLI Holding Co., Dallas, 1987—91, Greyhound Lines Inc., Dallas, 1987-91; v.p., gen. counsel, sec. Baroid Corp., Houston, 1991-94; sr. v.p., gen. counsel Tejas Gas Corp., Houston, 1994—98, Coral Energy, Houston, 1995—99; pres. Coral Energy Can., 1999, Kinder Morgan Power Co., Houston, 2000—03; v.p. Apache Corp., Houston, 2003—04, sr. v.p., gen. counsel, 2004—09, exec. v.p., gen. counsel, 2009—. Bd. dirs. Dallas Indsl. Devel. Corp., 1985-87; exec. mem. Ctrl. Dallas Assn., 1990. Mem. Order Coif, Phi Beta Kappa. Office: Apache Corp Ste 100 2000 Post Oak Blvd Houston TX 77056-4400 Office Phone: 713-296-6000. Office Fax: 713-296-6480. Business E-Mail: paul.lannie@apachecorp.com.*

LANOUE, DAVID J., political science professor, department chairman; b. Central Falls, RI, June 25, 1958; s. Raymond A. and Rosalys R. Lanoue; m. Suzanne M. McGlone, July 30, 1982. BA, U. Calif., La Jolla, 1982; MA, Stony Brook U., NY, 1983, PhD, 1986. Asst. prof. Ill. State U., Normal, 1987—89; assoc. prof. U. Calif., Riverside, 1989—97; prof. Tex. Tech U., Lubbock, 1997—2001; prof., dept. chair U. Ala., Tuscaloosa, 2001—. Author: (books) From Camelot to the Teflon President, 1988; co-author: The Joint Press Conference: The History, Impact, and Prospects of American Presidential Debates, 1991. Mem.: Southwestern Polit. Sci. Assn. (v.p. 2005—06), Am. Polit. Sci. Assn.

LANTZ, PHILLIP EDWARD, security firm executive, consultant; b. Laramie, Wyo., Sept. 21, 1938; s. Everett Delmer and Elizabeth Mary (Stratton) L.; m. Paula Bogel, June 16, 1962; children: Kirk Edward, Eric William. BA in Math., U. Colo., 1960; MA in Math., U. Wyo., 1966; MS in Ops. Rsch., Johns Hopkins U., 1972. Grad. teaching asst. U. Wyo., Laramie, 1964-65; sr. engr. Applied Physics Lab. Johns Hopkins U., Silver Spring, Md., 1965-70; v.p. Ops. Rsch. Inc., Silver Spring, Md., 1970-72; dir. Tetra Tech. Inc., Arlington, Va., 1972-74; pres., chief exec. officer Systems Planning and Analysis, Inc., Alexandria, Va., 1974—, also bd. dirs. Lt. USN, 1960-64. Home: 2911 Eddington Ter Alexandria VA 22302-3503 Office: Systems Planning and Analysis Inc 2001 N Beauregard St Alexandria VA 22311-1739 Home Phone: 703-836-0866; Office Phone: 703-931-3500. Business E-Mail: plantz@spa.com.

LANZKRON, ROLF WOLFGANG, manufacturing executive; b. Hamburg, Germany, Dec. 9, 1929; arrived in US, 1951, naturalized, 1961; s. Aron Artur and Hanna (Farbstein) Lanzkron; m. Amy Virginia Yarri, Mar. 5, 1961; children: Paul Joshua, Sophie Miriam, Lisa Rachel. BS, Milw. Sch. Engring., 1953; MS, U. Wis., 1955, PhD, 1956. Registered profl. engr., Calif. Computer designer Univac Sperry Rand, St. Paul, 1956-58; guidance and control systems integrations staff Martin Marietta, Orlando, Fla., 1958-61, sys. engr. Balt., 1961-68; advanced chief command svc. module flight project divsn. NASA Manned Spacecraft Ctr., Apollo Program, Houston, 1963; graphic ops. mgr. Raytheon Co., Marlborough, Mass., 1968-82, dir. air traffic control, 1982-92, dir. air traffic control, 1992-95; pres. RWL Assocs. Cons., Gloucester, Mass., 1995—. With Israeli Army, 1948—51. Recipient Outstanding Achievement award, NASA, 1964, Spl. Svc. award, 1966, Clifford Eurto Medallion award, 1995. Mem.: IEEE, AIAA, Am. Mgmt. Assn., Am. Math. Soc., Sigma Xi. Home: 3920 N Flagler Dr Apt 403 West Palm Beach FL 33407-4434 Office Phone: 561-727-8424. Personal E-mail: rolflanz1@aol.com. Business E-Mail: rolflanz@excite.com.

LANZONE, DEBORAH VON HOFFMANN, legislative staff member; b. Montclair, NJ, Apr. 23, 1952; d. Robert Ferdinand and Anne Marie (Perdue) von Hoffmann; m. Dale Martin Lanzone, Oct. 17, 1981; 1 child, Dominic Peter. BA in Liberal Arts, Colgate U., 1974. Legis. aide Mass. Legislature, Boston, 1975; mem. advance staff Nat. Dem. Com., Washington, 1976; congrl. liaison officer Land Use Planning Commn., Washington, 1977-79, Heritage Conservation Recreation Svc., Washington, 1979-81; planner natural resources Nat. Park Svc., Washington, 1981-86; spl. asst. to dir. Fish and Wildlife Svc., Washington, 1986-88; sr. regulatory analyst Bur. Land Mgmt., Washington, 1988-89, congrl. liaison officer, 1989-91; profl. staff mem. subcommittee energy and mineral resources US House Interior and Insular Affairs, Washington, 1991—93; staff dir., subcommittee on energy and mineral resources US House Natural Resources Com., Washington, 1993—94, 2007—; Dem. profl. staff mem. US House Resources Com., Washington, 1995—2006. Del. Mass. Nat. Dem. Conv., 1976; mem. advance staff Nat. Dem. Campaign, 1976, inaugural staff Nat. Dem. Com., 1977. Episcopalian. Office: US House Natural Resources Com 1324 Longworth House Office Bldg Washington DC 20515 Office Phone: 202-225-6065, 202-225-1931. Business E-Mail: deborah.lanzone@mail.house.gov.

LAPIDES, PAUL DREW, business professor, board member; b. NYC; s. Eugene and Rosalie (Tompkins) Lapides; 1 child, John Michael. BS in Economics, Wharton Sch., U. Pa., 1975; MBA, NYU, 1980. CPA NY, Ga. Cons., sr. auditor Arthur Young, NYC, 1975—79; fin. officer Meridith Orgn., NYC, 1979—80; pres. Pauer Agy., Inc., Atlanta, 1980—86, The PRIME-PM Corp., Atlanta, 1980—86; adj. prof. real estate NYU, 1980—95; prof. mgmt. and entrepreneurship Kennesaw State University Michael J. Coles College Business, Ga., 1993—, co-founder, dir. Corp. Governance Ctr., 1995—. Mem. adv. bd. ElectroNews, Inc., Paris, 1981—85, Nat. Assn. Corp. Directors, mem. Blue Ribbon Commn. Audit Committees, 1999; bd. dirs. Sun Communities, Inc., 1993—, EasyLink Svcs. Internat. Corp., 2005—. Author: Managing Residential Real Estate, 1986, 1987, 1988, Computer Selection and Implementation for Property Managers, 1988, Real Estate Investment, 1988, Facility Management, 1995 (Disting. Author award, Internat. Facility Mgmt. Assn.); contbr. articles to profl. jours. Recipient Disting. Svc. award, Kenneshaw State U., 2000. Mem.: AICPA. Office: Kennesaw State U 1000 Chastain Rd #0404 Kennesaw GA 30144 Office Phone: 770-423-6587. Business E-Mail: plapides@kennesaw.edu.

LAPIDUS, SIDNEY, construction executive, lawyer; AB, Princeton U., 1959; LLB, Columbia U., 1962. Ptnr., mng. dir. & sr. advisor E.M. Warburg, Pincus & Co., Inc., NYC, 1967—2007. Bd. dirs. Neiman Marcus, Inc., Ingersoll Newspapers, Lee Panavision Internat., Renaissance Comm., LBS Comm., The Home Co., Knoll, Inc., 1996—, Lennar Corp., 1997—. Bd. dirs. NY U. Langone Med. Ctr., Am. Antiquarian Soc., NY Historical Soc.; chmn. Am. Jewish Historical Soc. Office: Lennar Corp Bd Directors 700 NW 107th Ave Miami FL 33172 Office Phone: 305-559-4000. Office Fax: 305-228-8383. E-mail: slapidus@lennar.com.

LAPIERRE, WAYNE R., JR., advocacy group executive; b. Schenectady, NY, Nov. 8, 1949; m. Susan LaPierre. BA in Edn., Siena Coll., Loudonville, NY, 1971; MA in Govt., Boston Coll. State liaison NRA-Inst. Legis. Action, Fairfax, Va., 1978—79, exec. dir., 1986—91; dir. state and local affairs NRA, Fairfax, Va., 1979—80, dir. fed. affairs, 1981—86, CEO, exec. v.p., chief nat. spokesperson, 1991—. Pres. Nat. Firearms Mus. Fund; bd. trustees NRA Found. Author: Guns, Crime, and Freedom, 1994, Guns, Freedom, and Terrorism, 2003, Corporate Fascism: How America's Companies Are Butting into the Private Lives of Their Employees, 2005, The Global War on Your Guns: Inside the UN Plan To Destroy the Bill of Rights, 2006, The Essential Second Amendment Guide, 2007, America Disarmed: Inside the U.N. and Obama's Scheme to Destroy the Second Amendment, 2011; co-author (with James Jay Baker): Shooting Straight: Telling the Truth About Guns in America, 2002; host (syndicated TV series) Crime Strike. Bd. dirs. American Conservative Union, American Assn. Polit. Consultants, Nat. Fish & Wildlife Found. Named one of The 50 Most Powerful People in DC, GQ mag., 2007, The 25 Most Influential Republicans, Newsmax mag., 2008, The 100 Most Influential People in the World, TIME mag., 2013. Roman Catholic. Office: NRA 11250 Waples Mill Rd Fairfax VA 22030 E-mail: wlapierre@nra.org.*

LAPOSATA, JOSEPH SAMUEL, army officer; b. Johnstown, Pa., Oct. 3, 1938; s. Joseph Thomas and Mary Marie (Coco) L.; m. Anita Louise Sabo, Aug. 12, 1961; children: Joseph S. Jr., David G., Matthew M. BS, Indiana U. Pa., 1960; MS, Cornell U., 1968; grad., Command and Gen. Staff Coll., Leavenworth, Kans., 1971, Def. Sys. Mgmt. Coll., 1974, Indsl. Coll. Armed Forces, Washington, 1980. Commd. 2d lt. US Army, 1960, advanced through grades to lt. gen., 1991; asst. chief of staff for logistics 5th Inf. Div., Ft. Polk, La., 1978-79; chief war res. div. Office Dep. Chief of Staff for Logistics, Hdqrs. Dept. Army, Washington, 1980-81; comdr. 8th Support Group, US Army So. European Task Force, Livorno, Italy, 1981-84, dep. comdr., chief of staff Vicenza, Italy, 1984; exec. to dep. chief of staff for logistics Hdqrs. Dept. Army, Washington, 1984-86; dir. plans and ops., dep. chief of staff for logistics HQDA Dept. Army, Washington, 1986—88; comdg. gen. US Army Material Command-Europe, Heidelberg, Germany, 1988-89; dep. chief of staff for logistics US Army Europe and 7th Army, Heidelberg, 1989-91; chief of staff Allied Forces So. Europe, Naples, Italy, 1991-93; Presdl. appointee as sec. Am. Battle Monuments Commn., Washington, 1994-95; ret. Apptd. NATO diplomatic post as dep. gen. mgr. and dir. logistics ops. and programs NATO Maintenance and Supply Agy., Luxembourg; ret.; lectr. in field, Fla. Inst. Tech., 2007-12; mem. bd. trustee Excelsior Coll., Albany, NY, 2007-10, adv. bd. chmn. Excelsior Coll. Campus, Washington, 2010; with Accrediting Commn. Distance Edn. & Tng. Coun. Wash., 1994-96. Established Joseph S. and Anita L. Laposata scholarship Excelsior Coll. and Ind. U., Pa.; with Quartermaster Found., distinguished sponsor. Decorated Def. DDSM, Army, DSM (2), Meritorious Svc. medal (4), Legion of Merit (3), Bronze Star (2); Air medal, Army Commendation medal (3), Navy Commendation medal, Army Parachutist, Army Parachute Rigger; knight comdr. Republic of Italy; recipient Man of Yr. award Interclub Coun., Johnstown, Pa., 1990, Disting. Alumnus award Ind. U. Pa., 1992, IUP ROTC Hall of Fame, 2013, medal for meritorious svc. Am. Battle Monuments Commn., medal for disting. svc., NATO Maint. and Supply Agy., 1999; inducted into Quartermaster Hall of Fame, 1994, Military Hall of Fame, Cambria County, Pa., 2012; Order of St. Martin; named Col. Emeritus, US Army Q.M. Rgt. Mem. Assn. US Army (pres. European dept. 1989-91, bd. trustees, 1989-91), Rotary, Phi Kappa Phi, Tau Kappa Epsilon, Mil. Officers Assoc. Am. Roman Catholic. Avocation: golf. Address: 1823 Freedom Dr Melbourne FL 32940-6875 Office Phone: 321-751-9586. Personal E-mail: jlaposata1@bellsouth.net.

LARKAM, BEVERLEY MCCOSHAM, clinical social worker, marriage and family therapist; b. Vancouver, Can., Mar. 3, 1928; arrived in U.S., 1951; d. William Howard and Marjorie Isobel (Jerome) McCosham; children: Elizabeth, Charles, Daphne, Peter, John. A Royal Conservatory of Mus., U. Toronto, Toronto, 1948; BA, U. B.C., Can., 1949; BSW, U. B.C., 1950, MSW, 1951. Bd. cert. diplomate in clin. social work; LCSW; lic. marriage and family therapist, Tex., diplomate Internat. Conf. Advanced Profl. Practice of Clin. Social Work. Psychiat. social worker Brackenridge Hosp., 1952-54; chmn. dept. sr. high. sch. Univ. Presbyn. Ch., Austin, Tex., 1952-55, mem. Christian edn. com., 1961-67, bd. dirs. developing and organizing nursery sch., 1967-70; social worker Counseling-Psychol. Svcs. Ctr., U. Tex., 1971-72; psychiat. social worker, chief supr. Adult, Children's Mental Health Human-Devel. Ctr.-South, Austin, Tex., 1972-79; pvt. practice marriage and family therapy, sex therapy and individual and group psychotherapy Austin, Tex., 1975—, Georgetown, Tex., 1979—. Field supr. Sch. Social Work U. Tex.; cons. in field. Mem. cmty. orgn. to establish classes for mentally retarded children, 1966-68, City of Austin Commn. for Women, 1978—, chmn., 1982-84, emeritus, 1985-; organizer Austin Assn. for Marriage and Family Therapy, 1980-82, bd. dirs. Tex. Assn. for Marriage and Family Therapy, 1980-82; vol. usher Austin Symphony Orch. Soc., 1973-2013, Hon. Svc. award 2013; Preservation Austin, Georgetown Heritage Soc., Women's Symphony League of Austin, Austin Art Mus., Williamson County Hist. Mus.; mem. Dean Sch. Social Work, profl. linkage com., 1993—2011; vol. family therapist Child Inc./Headstart Ranch Weekends, 1995-96. Recipient Hon. Svc. award, 2013. Mem. NASW, Am. Assn. Marriage and Family Therapy (approved supr., com. on racial, ethnic and cultural diversity 1992-95, Honored Svc. Austin chpt., 1998), Am. Group Psychotherapy Assn. (cert. group psychotherapist), Southwestern Group Psychotherapy Soc. (sr. faculty), Austin Group Psychotherapy Soc., Am. Assn. Sexuality Educators, Counselors and Therapists (cert. diplomate sex therapy), Acad. Cert. Social Workers, Register Clin. Social Workers, cert. Eye Movement Desenitization Reprocessing, Tex. Soc. for Clin. Social Work (bd. dirs. 1990—, pres. 1997-99, chmn. Austin study groups 2006—), Clin. Social Work Fedn. (fin. chmn. 1998-2000), Austin Commn. Women (honored Austin city coun. 30yr svc.), PEO Sisterhood (50 Yr. Golden Mem. award 2009), Austin Woman's Forum (pres. 1994-95, 2002-03). Presbyterian (elder, session of Univ. Presbyterian Ch. 1997—). Home and Office: 2102 Raleigh Ave Austin TX 78703-2128 also: 207 E 9th St Georgetown TX 78626-5908 Office Phone: 512-476-4182. Personal E-mail: blarkam@earthlink.net.

LARKIN, WILLIAM VINCENT, JR., corporate executive; b. NYC, July 19, 1953; s. William Vincent and Gloria Ann (Stone) L.; m. Margaret Catherine Gunn, Nov. 12, 1988; children: William Vincent III, Jeremy Stone. AB cum laude, Harvard U., 1976; MBA, Yale U., 1980. Intern White House, 1975; staff acct. Price Waterhouse & Co., NYC, 1976-78; mktg. asst. AMF Ben Hogan Co., Ft. Worth, 1980-81; asst. to pres. AMF Biol. & Diagnostic Co., Seguin, Tex., 1981-82; mktg. mgr. AMF Tuboscope, Houston, 1982-83, mgr. mill divsn., 1983-84; v.p. Tuboscope Inc., Houston, 1984-91; pres., COO Tuboscope Vetco Internat., Houston, 1991-93, pres., CEO, 1993-96; pres., COO Galtney Group, Inc., Houston, 1996-98; pres., CEO Travis

Internat., Inc., Houston, 1999—2002, The Six Stars Club, Houston, 2003—06, Corrpro Cos., Inc., Houston, 2006—09, Warren Alloy, 2009—10, Shield Air Solutions, Inc., 2010—. Trustee Groton Sch., 2000-02, Young Pres. Orgn., 1992-2004. Mem. World Pres.' Orgn., Yale Sch. Mgmt. Alumni Assn. (chmn. nominating com. 1980-82), A.D. Club (Cambridge, Mass.), Harvard Club (NYC), River Oaks Country Club, The Coronado Club. Republican. Episcopalian. Avocations: woodworking, golf, crossword puzzles. Home: 7 W Terrace Dr Houston TX 77007 Personal E-mail: grottie12@gmail.com.

LARKINS, JAMAIL, air transportation executive; A Bus. Adminstrn. in Mktg., Embry-Riddle Aero. U., 2006. Pres., CEO Larkins Enterprises, Inc., 2001—; v.p. Air Transport Group Holdings, Inc. (formerly Azure Internat., Inc.); pres. Ascension Aircraft. Nat. spokesperson, EAA Vision of Eagles Program Exptl. Aircraft Assn., 2000—03; amb., aviation and space edn. Fed. Aviation Adminstrn., 2005; spl. asst. to Pres. Nat. Bus. Aviation Assn., 2006—09; nat. spokesperson Careers in Aviation, 2002—06, chmn., 2008—. Office: Air Transport Group Holdings Inc 7453 Woodruff Way Stone Mountain GA 30087 Office Phone: 404-671-9253. Business E-Mail: jamail.larkins@atsginc.com.

LAROQUE, STEPHEN A., state legislator; b. Kinston, NC, Aug. 15, 1963; m. Susan LaRoque BSBA in Fin., East Carolina U., 1985, MBA, 1993. Mem. Econ. and Cmty. Devel.; asst. v.p., br. mgr. NC Nat. Bank/Nations Bank, 1986—92; gen. mgr., sr. loan officer Neuse River Devel. Authority, 1995—99; candidate, Dist. 10 NC House of Representatives, 2006, 2008, mem. Dist. 10, 2011—; pres. LaRoque Mgmt. Group, 1997—. Republican. Presbyn. Mailing: PO Box 1034 Kinston NC 28503 Address: North Carolina House of Representatives 300 N Salisbury St Rm 635 Raleigh NC 27603-5925 Office Phone: 252-527-3399. Business E-Mail: Stephen.LaRoque@ncleg.net.

LAROSILIERE, HARRY, mayor, Plano, Texas; b. Haiti; m. Tracy LaRosiliere; 2 children. BS in Geology, CUNY: City Coll., NYC. Owner, operator of a photography studio, 1986—94; fin. advisor Plano, Tex., 1994—; councilman Plano City Coun., 2005—11, dep. mayor pro tem, 2008—09, mayor pro tem, 2009—10; mayor City of Plano, 2013—. Active St. Luke's United Meth. Ch.; chmn. fin. com. CASA of Collin County, Tex., 1999—2000, chmn., 2000—01, mem. adv. bd., 2006—; chmn. exec. bd. Leadership Plano, 2000—01; chmn. City of Plano Cmty. Rels. Com., 2002—03; commr. Planning & Zoning Commn., 2003—05; mem. adv. bd. Jr. League Plano, 2005—06; mem. President's Coun. Tex. Health Resources of Plano, 2012—. Mem.: Plano C. of C. (vice chmn. fin. 2001—02, mem. exec. com. 2002—05), Plano Metro Rotary Club. Office: City of Plano Mayor's Office 1520 Avenue K PO Box 860358 Plano TX 75086*

LARRANAGA, JIM, men's college basketball coach; b. Bronx, NY, Oct. 2, 1949; m. Liz Larranaga; children: Jay, Jon. BA in Economics, Providence Coll., 1971. Basketball player Geronemo Basketball Club, Belgium, 1976—77, coach, 1977; asst. coach Davidson Coll. Wildcats, 1971—76; head basketball coach Am. Internat. Coll. Yellow Jackets, 1977—79; asst. coach U. Va. Cavaliers, 1979—86; head basketball coach Bowling Green State U. Falcons, 1986—97, George Mason U. Patriots, 1997—2011, U. Miami Hurricanes, Fla., 2011—. Recipient Clair Bee Coach of Yr. award, 2006; named Mid-Am. Conf. Coach of Yr., 1997, Coach of Yr., Va. Sports Info. Dirs., 1999, Richmond Times-Dispatch, 1999, Dist. 4 Coach of Yr., Nat. Assn. Basketball Coaches, 1999, Colonial Athletic Assn. Coach of Yr., 1999, 2011, Atlantic Coast Conf. Coach of Yr., 2013, Nat. Coach of Yr., AP, 2013; named to Providence Coll. Hall of Fame, 1991. Office: University Miami Mens Basketball c/o University Miami Athletics 5821 San Amaro Dr Miami FL 33146 Office Phone: 305-284-2680.

LARRICK, PAMELA MAPHIS, marketing executive; married; 3 stepchildren. BS in Advt. & Polit. Sci., West Va. U. Various positions Ogilvy & Mather Direct, 1978—92, exec. v.p., mng. dir., 1990—94, gen. mgr., 1992—94; chmn. MRM Ptnrs. (McCann customer rels. mktg.); mng. dir. MRM Worldwide (formerly McCann Direct), 1994—96, reg. dir., N.Am., exec. v.p., 1997—99, COO, 1999—2001, pres., 1999—2004, CEO, 2001—04; chmn., CEO Foot Cone & Belding Worldwide, customer rels. mktg. (FCBi), 2005—06; chief digital, direct, officer, CRM Draftfcb, 2006—07; strategic cons. Interpublic Group of Companies, Inc., 2007—08; CEO Javelin Marketing Group, 2010—. Recipient Emerson Lifetime Achievement award for Innovation in and Svc. to direct mktg., John Caples awards orgn.; named one of 25 Women Leaders of Advt. Industry, Ad Age, 1997, Global Power 100, 2002. Office: Javelin Marketing Group 7850 Belt Line Rd Irving TX 75063 Office Phone: 972-443-7000. Office Fax: 972-443-7194. Business E-Mail: pamela.larrick@javelinmarketinggroup.com.

LARSEN, MARSHALL O., manufacturing executive; b. ND; BS, U.S. Mil. Acad., West Point, 1970; MS, Purdue Univ. Op. analyst and fin. mgr. Goodrich Corp., Charlotte, NC, 1977—81, dir. of planning and analysis, dir. of product mktg., 1981—86, asst. to the pres., gen. mgr., 1986—94, v.p., 1994—95, exec. v.p., 1995—2002, pres., COO, 2002—03, pres., CEO, 2003—, chmn., 2004—. Lt. US Army, 1970—76. Office: Goodrich Corp Four Coliseum Ctr 2730 W Tyvola Rd Charlotte NC 28217-4578

LARSEN, RALPH S(TANLEY), retired pharmaceutical executive; b. Bklyn., Nov. 19, 1938; s. Andrew and Gurine (Henningsen) L.; m. Dorothy M. Zeitfuss, Aug. 19, 1961; children: Karen, Kristen, Garret. BBA, Hofstra U., 1962. Mfg. trainee, then supr. prodn. and dir. mfg. Johnson & Johnson, New Brunswick, NJ, 1962—77; v.p. ops., v.p. mktg. McNeil Consumer Products Co. div. Johnson & Johnson, Ft. Washington, Pa., 1977—81; pres. Becton Dickenson Consumer Products, Paramus, NJ, 1981—83; pres. Chicopee divsn. Johnson & Johnson, New Brunswick, NJ, 1983—85, co. group chmn., 1985—86, vice chmn., exec. com., bd. dirs., 1986—89, chmn. bd., pres., CEO, 1989—2002, bd. dirs., mem. exec. com. Bd. dirs. General Electric Co., 2002—. Trustee Robert Wood Johnson Found. Independent. Avocations: skiing, boating, art. Office: 100 Albany St Ste 200 New Brunswick NJ 08901

LARSON, BENNETT CHARLES, solid state physicist, researcher; b. Buffalo, ND, Oct. 9, 1941; s. Floyd Everet and Gladys May (Hogen) L.; m. Piola Anne Taliaferro, June 6, 1969; children: Christopher Charles, Andrea Kay BA in Physics, Concordia Coll., Moorhead, Minn., 1963; MS in Physics, U. N.D., 1965; PhD in Physics, U. Mo., 1970. Rsch. physicist, x-ray diffraction Oak Ridge Nat. Lab., Tenn., 1969—, corp. fellow materials sci. and tech. divsn. Tenn., 1969—. Contbr. numerous articles to profl. jours. Recipient Sidhu award Pitts. Diffraction Soc., 1974 Fellow Am. Phys. Soc.; mem. Am. Crystallographic Assn. (Bertram E. Warren Diffraction Physics award 1985), Materials Research Soc. Office: Oak Ridge Nat Lab Condensed Matter Scis PO Box 2008 Oak Ridge TN 37831-2008 Business E-Mail: larsonbc@ornl.gov.

LARSON, JON S., lawyer; b. Lexington, Ky., Aug. 9, 1945; 1 child, Sara. BA, U. Ky., 1966; MBA, George Wash. U., 1971; JD, U. Ky., 1973. Pub. defender Fayette County Legal Aid, 1975—84; pvt. practice atty., 1973—75, 1984—. Asst. coach Women's Softball World Series Champions; mem. Nicholasville/Jessamine County Coll. Adv. Bd.; commr. Todd County Commn.; treas. Rep. Party Fayette County, 1978—82; mem. Calvary Bapt. Ch. Officer US Army, 1966—68. Republican. Baptist. Office: 201 W Short St 404 Lexington KY 40507 Office Phone: 859-255-1001. Office Fax: 859-252-7886. Business E-Mail: larsonforcongress@gmail.com.

LARSON, KERMIT DEAN, finance educator; b. Algona, Iowa, Apr. 7, 1939; s. Loren L. and Hansena Laurena (Andersen) L.; m. Nancy Lynne Weber, June 17, 1961; children: Julie Renee, Timothy Dean, Cynthia Lynne. AA, Ft. Dodge Jr. Coll., 1960; BBA, U. Iowa, 1962, MBA, 1963; PhD, U. Colo., 1966. CPA Tex. Faculty U. Tex., Austin, 1966-94, Arthur Andersen & Co. Alumni prof. emeritus, 1994—, chmn. dept. acctg., 1971-75. Vis. assoc. prof. Tulane U., New Orleans, 1970-71; cons. sales tax audit litig., pvt. anti-trust litig., expropriation ins. arbitration. Author: (with John Wild and Barbara Chiappetta) Fundamental Accounting Principles, 1978, 18th edit., 2008, Financial Accounting, 7th edit., 1997, (with Charlene Spoede and Paul Miller) Fundamentals of Financial and Managerial Accounting, 1994; contbr. articles to profl. jours. Mem.: Beta Alpha Psi, Beta Gamma Sigma. Home: 1310 Falcon Ledge Dr Austin TX 78746-5120

LARSON, LYLE THOMAS, state legislator, commissioner; b. San Antonio, Mar. 25, 1959; BBA in Mktg., Tex. A & M. U., 1981. Salesman Nalco Chem. Co., 1981, Ethicon, 1984; owner, CEO American Consortium, 1985—; councilman Dist. 10 San Antonio City Coun., 1991—95; commr. Precinct 3 Bexar County Commissioners Ct., 1997—2008; founder San Antonio Internat. Ag Promotions, 2009—; mem. Dist. 122 Tex. House of Representatives, 2010—. Chmn. Greater San Antonio Crime Commn., 1993—95, San Antonio Met. Planning Orgn., 1998—, Alamo Area Coun. Governments, 1998—, Mil. Transformation Task Force, 2006—08; co-chmn. San Antonio Mil. Missions Task Force. Bd. mem. San Antonio Sports Found., San Antonio Golf Assn. Named a Outstanding Young San Antonian, San Antonian Jaycees, 1996. Mem.: NRA, Nat. Fedn. Ind. Bus., Coastal Conservation Assn., Alamo City Republican Women, San Antonio A&M Club, Republican Bus. Women Bexar County, Lions Club. Republican. Methodist. Avocations: fishing, golf, hunting. Office: PO Box 171148 San Antonio TX 78217 also: Bexar County Commissioner Ct 100 Dolorosa San Antonio TX 78247 also: Room E2.816 Capitol Extension PO Box 2910 Austin TX 78768 also: 14607 San Pedro Ave Ste 180 San Antonio TX 78232 Office Phone: 210-414-3536, 512-463-0646, 210-402-5402. Office Fax: 512-463-0893. Business E-Mail: llarson@co.bexar.tx.us.

LARSON, REED EUGENE, foundation administrator; b. Smith County, Kans., Sept. 27, 1922; s. George Christian and Edith Hazel (Whitney) L.; m. Marjorie Jeanne Hess, Aug. 31, 1947; children: Patricia Kay Larson Sween, Barbara Ann Larson Finnegan, Marcia Lynn Larson Craig. Student, Kans. Wesleyan U., 1940-41, Ohio State U., 1943-44; BS in E.E, Kans. State U., 1947. Design engr. Stein Labs., Atchison, Kans., 1947-48; processing engr. Coleman Co., Wichita, Kans., 1948-54; exec. v.p. Kansans for the Right to Work, Wichita, 1954-58; from exec. v.p. to chmn. exec. com. Nat. Right-to-Work Com., Washington, 1959—2013, Nat. Right-to-Work Legal Def. Found., 1968—2013. Chmn. Hallmark Bank & Trust, 1984-96; vice chmn. F&M Bank-No. Va., 1996-99. Served with AUS, 1943-46. Recipient Seldon Waldo award U.S. Jaycees, 1956; Silver Anvil award Pub. Rels. Soc. Am., 1966; James J. Kilpatrick award Internat. Platform Assn., 1980; Awarded Doctor of Laws Campbell U., 1988. Mem. Mont Pelerin Soc., Phila. Soc., Eta Kappa Nu, Tau Beta Pi. Clubs: Kansas Jaycees (pres. 1953-54), Rotary, Am. Legion. Baptist. Office: 8001 Braddock Rd Springfield VA 22160 Home: 12215 NE 128th St #439 Kirkland WA 98034 Office Phone: 703-321-9820. Business E-Mail: larson@nrtw.org.

LARUSSO, ANTHONY CARL, company executive, lecturer, consultant; b. May 5, 1949; s. Nicholas and Rose (Ruspini) LaR.; m. Marianne Elizabeth Baviello, Apr. 4, 1971; children: Anne, Tony. BA, Fordham U., 1971; MBA, NYU, 1972. Cert. mgmt. acct. Sr. project mgr. Office Mgmt. and Control NYC Dept. Human Resources, 1972-73; mgr. econ. planning Trans World Airlines, NYC, 1973-76; mgr. planning and analysis AMAX, Inc., Greenwich, Conn., 1976-81, mgr. corp. devel., 1981-84, v.p. planning and mktg. metals, 1984-86, from v.p. to pres. metal refining ops., 1986—89, pres. climax performance materials corp., 1990-93; gen. mgr. CRI-MET, White Plains, N.Y., 1994-95; pres. Elkem Metals Co., Pitts., 1995—2003; instr. Ctr. for Profl. Edn., Inc., Pa., 2003—06, AICPA, NC, 2003—. Adj. prof. mgmt. Pace U., 1975—95. Author: Management: Ready Aim Fire, 2005, Practical Financial Decision Making, 2011; author workbooks/classes and webinars in fin. and mgmt., 2006-; contbr. articles to profl. jours. Officer local homeowners assn., Pa., 1997-2003, Fla., 2010-; former chmn. local homeowners assn., Mahopac, N.Y.; asst. to chmn. ann. cookie sale Girl Scouts USA, Shrub Oak, N.Y.; coach/safety dir. Am. Youth Soccer Orgn., Yorktown, N.Y. Mem. Acad. Mgmt., Am. Mgmt. Assn., Chief Exec. Network, Inst. Mgmt. Acctg., Orgn. Devel. Inst., Strategic Mgmt. Soc., Ferroalloys Assn. (officer 1996-2003), Soc. for Advancement of Mgmt., Inc. Republican. Roman Catholic. Avocations: racquetball, swimming, fishing. Home: PO Box 7548 Naples FL 34101 E-mail: tonyclarusso@hotmail.com.

LASA-FERRER, ARMANDO, lawyer; b. 1937; BA, U. Miami, 1962; JD, Inter-Am. U. PR, 1966. Bar: P.R. Gen. counsel, sec. bd. dirs. Ricky Martin Found.; counsel, sec. bd. dirs. Banco Financiero; prof. law Inter-Am. U. PR; sr. ptnr. Lasa, Monroig & Veve, San Juan. Mem. sub-com. on universal svc. com. Assn. Competitive Providers Telecom.; mem. task force in charge of drafing the P.R. telecom. act of 1996 P.R. Ho. Reps.; prof. Interamerican U. Sch. Law, PR; mem. Gov. P.R. Task Force on Health Care Reform; gen. counsel Rep. Nat. Hispanic Assembly. Chmn. cmty. adv. bd. WMIJ and WQTO; former chair health and social planning com. City of San Juan; nat. advisor New Majority Coun., Rep. Nat. Com. Recipient Disting. Alumni Award, Inter-Am. U. PR. Mem.: ABA (bd. govs. 18th dist. 2001, sec.-elect 2002—05, sec. 2005—08, chair and mem. numerous coms.). Office: Lasa Monroig & Veve Westernbank World Plz 268 Munoz Rivera Ave Ste 1500 San Juan PR 00918 Office Phone: 787-774-0400. Office Fax: 787-774-1564. Business E-Mail: alasa@lmvpr.com. E-mail: alasa@worldnet.att.net.

LASALA, STEPHEN R., lawyer; b. NYC; B, LLD, Fordham U., NY; LLM in Taxation, NYU. Tax counsel Mobil Oil Corp., NYC, 1974, various tax positions, 1974—92; asst. treas. exploration and prodn. divsn. Mobil Corp., Fairfax, Va., 1992—96, gen. tax counsel, asst. contr., 1996—2000; assoc. gen. tax counsel ExxonMobil Corp., 2000—07, v.p., gen. tax counsel, 2007—10.

LASCHINGER, MARY A., paper company executive; b. 1960; Various sr. mgmt. positions James River Paper Corp.; with Kimberly-Clark Corp.; joined International Paper Co., 1993, various sr. mgmt. postions, sales, mktg., mfg. & supply chai, gen. mgr., indsl. papers cooling bus., 1999—2001, v.p., pulp, 2001—04, v.p., wood products, 2004—05, v.p., 2005—07, pres. Russia, 2005—09, pres., Europe, Middle East, Africa (EMEA), 2005—09, sr. v.p., 2007—10, sr. v.p., pres. xpedx distribution bus., 2010—. Bd. dirs. Kellogg Co., 2012—. Office: International Paper Co 6400 Poplar Ave Memphis TN 38197 Office Phone: 901-419-9000. Office Fax: 901-214-9682. Business E-Mail: Mary.Laschinger@ipaper.com.

LASCU, DANA-NICOLETA, marketing educator; b. Sebes, Romania, Nov. 27, 1959; d. Damian and Lucia Dora Lascu; m. Abraham Adriaan Jacobus Opstelten, Oct. 18, 1998; children: Michael Alexander Opstelten, Daniel Leonard Opstelten. PhD, U. SC, Columbia, 1991. Prof. mktg. U. Richmond, Va., 1991—, dept. chair, 1991—. Office: Univ Richmond Robins Sch 28 Westhampton Way Richmond VA 23220 Business E-Mail: dlascu@richmond.edu.

LASER, CHARLES, JR., oil company executive; b. Redford Twp., Mich., July 8, 1933; s. J.C. and Gertrude L.; m. Glenda Johnson, Sept. 27, 1972; 1 child, Susan Faye. Student, Mich. Tech. U., 1952-54, Ctrl. Mich. U., 1959-60; DD (hon.), Palm Beach Theol. Sem. Coll., 1991; LLD (hon.), Northwood U., 2000. With Retail Credit Co., 1958-60; exec. dir. Saginaw County Rep. Com., 1960-65, Rep. Com. D.C., 1967; fin. dir. San Joaquin Rep. Party, Stockton, Calif., 1968; owner Laser Advt., Bay City, Mich., 1969-75; exec. v.p. Vindell Petroleum, Inc., Midland, Mich., 1972-75, Geo Spectra Corp., Ann Arbor, Mich., 1977-86; pres. Laser Exploration Inc., Deerfield Beach, Fla.; sr. cons. Peking U. Resource Coll., 2004. Task force Domestic Violence Gov. Jeb Bush, 1999—; adv. bd. Union Bank, Boca Raton, Fla.; sr. cons. Peking U. Resource Coll., China, 2004. Chmn. Genesee County Rep. Com., 1981-82, mem. Broward County Rep. Exec. Com., 1987-88, indsl. bond screening com. Deerfield Beach, 1992; chmn. U.S. Senator Connie Mack Palm Beach County Round Table; bd. dirs. Palm Beach County Libr. Found., Shepherd Care Ministries, Hollywood, Foa., 1991—; adv. com. Tall Pines coun. Boy Scouts Am., mem. adv. bd. Gulf Stream Coun., 1980; mem. gov. prevention adv. com. Juvenile Justice Deliquency, Fla., 1988-96; mem. adv. bd. Humanitarian Soc., 1989—; bd. dirs., life mem. Large Freedoms Found., Valley Forge Broward County, Fla. chpt., 1995—; bd. govs. Northwood U., West Palm Beach, Fla., 1997; chmn. emeritus Fla. Symphonic Pops Orch., 1998; apptd. mem. Task Froce on Domestic Violence, South Fla. Gang Reduction Task Force, Brown County Sheriff's Dept. With U.S. Army, 1954-58. Decorated Knight Order of St. John of Jerusalem Knights Hospitallier. Mem. Deerfield Beach C. of C. (v.p.), World Trade Coun. (Palm Beach, Fla. chpt.), Detroit Econ. Club, Bankers Club (Boca Raton), Humanitarian Soc. (adv. bd.), Rep. Men's Club (past pres., v.p. Boca Raton chpt.), Gold Coast Venture Capital Club (Delray Beach chpt.), Palm Beach Roundtable (bd. dirs., chmn. exec. com., sec. 1994-2002), Hillsboro Cove Condominium Assn. (pres. 1994), Rotary, Elks. Home: PO Box 8604 1523 E Hillsboro Blvd Apt 131 Deerfield Beach FL 33441-4301

LASKEY, ALEXANDER, energy efficiency services company executive; b. 1976; m. Rachel Farbiarz. BA in History of Sci., Harvard U., 1999. Reporter Casper Star Tribune, 1997—98; dir. new bus. The Romann Group, 2000—01; prodr. Swing State Productions, 2003—05; campaign mgr. Nick Waugh for Supervisor, 2004, Janet Reilly for Assembly, 2005—06; rsch. analyst Fairbank, Maslin, Maullin and Associates, 2006; co-founder, pres. Opower, Arlington, Va., 2007—. Cons. Nature Conservancy, Trust for Pub. Land, League of Conservative Voters; spkr. in field. Prodr.: (films) Assisted Living. Named one of The 40 Under 40, Fortune mag., 2011; Ford Found. Grant. Office: Opower 1515 N Courthouse Rd, 8th Floor Arlington VA 22201 Office Phone: 703-778-4544. Office Fax: 703-778-4547.

LASKIN, DANIEL M., oral and maxillofacial surgeon, educator; b. Ellenville, NY, Sept. 3, 1924; s. Nathan and Flora (Kaplan) L.; m. Eve Pauline Mohel, Aug. 25, 1945; children: Jeffrey, Gary, Marla. Student, NYU, 1941—42; BS, Ind. U., 1947; MS, U. Ill., 1951; DSc (hon.), Ind. U., 2001. Diplomate Am. Bd. Oral and Maxillofacial Surgery, Am. Dental Bd. Anesthesiology. Faculty U. Ill., Chgo., 1949-84, prof. dept. oral and maxillofacial surgery, 1960-84, head dept., 1973-84, clin. prof. surgery, 1961-84, dir. temporomandibular joint and facial pain research center, 1963-84; prof., chmn. dept. oral and maxillofacial surgery Med. Coll. Va., Richmond, 1984—2002, chmn. emeritus, 2003, dir. temporomandibular joint and facial pain rsch. ctr. 1984—2002; affiliate clin. prof., dept. psychology Va. Commonwealth U.; head dept. dentistry MCV Hosp., Richmond, 1986—2002; former attending oral surgeon Edgewater, Swedish Covenant, Ill. Masonic, Skokie Valley Cmty. hosps., Chgo.; former chmn. dept. oral surgery Cook County Hosp., Chgo. Cons. oral surgery to Surgeon Gen. Navy, 1977-83; dental products panel FDA, 1988-92, cons., 1993-95; Francis J. Reichmann Lectr., 1971, Cordwainer lectr., London, 1980, Donald B. Osborn Meml. lectr., 1999. Author: Oral and Maxillofacial Surgery, Vol. I, 1980, Vol. II, 1985; contbr. articles to profl. jours.; editor-in-chief: Jour. Oral and Maxillofacial Surgery, 1972-2002; mem. editl. bd. Internat. Jour. Oral and Maxillofacial Surgery, 1978-88, Topics in Pain Mgmt., Densat, Internat. Jour. Oral and Maxillofacial Implants, Quintessence Internat., Revista Latino America Cirugia Traumatologia Maxilofacial, Va. Dental Jour., Jour. Dental Rsch.; mem. internat. editl. bd. Headache Quar.; mem. editl. bd. Greek Jour. Oral and Maxillofacial Surgery, Electronic Jour. Dentistry; assoc. editor Odontology; mem. internat. adv. bd. Asian Jour. Oral and Maxillofacial Surgery; OMFS editor Jewish Med. Jour. Nat. hon. chmn. peer campaign A.A.O.M.S. Edn. and Rsch. Found., 1990; bd. dirs. Internat. Assn. Oral and Maxillofacial Surgeons Found.; chmn. Nat. Acad. Dentistry, 1997-99; pres.-elect Nat. Acad. of Practice, 1999, pres., 2002—04. Recipient Disting. Alumni Svc. award, Ind. U., 1975, William J. Gies editl. award 1st prize, 1978—79, 1984, 1987, 1989, 1992, 1996, 2001, Simon P. Hullihen Meml. award, 1976, Arnold K. Maislen Meml. award, 1977, Thomas P. Hinman medallion, 1980, W. Harry Archer Achievement award for rsch., 1981, Heidbrink award, 1983, Disting. Alumnus award, Ind. U. Sch. Dentistry, 1984, U. Ill. Coll. Dentistry, 2003, Rene Lefort medal, 1985, Semmelweis medallion, Semmelweis Med. U., 1985, Golden Scroll award, Internat. Coll. Dentists, 1986, Internat. award, Friends Sch. Dental Med., U. Conn. Health Ctr., Donald B. Osbon award, 1991, Achievement medal, Alpha Omega, 1992, Norton M. Ross Excellence in Clin. Rsch. award, 1993, Va. Commonwealth U. Faculty award of excellence, 1994, named Zendium Lectr., 1989, Edward C. Hinds Lectr., 1990, Disting. Practitioner Nat. Acads. Practice, 1992, Hon. Diplomate Am. Soc. Osseointegration, 1992, Silver Scroll award, Internat. Coll. Dentists, 2004, Distinction medal, U. Seville, 2005, Alumni Achievement award, U. Ill., 2006; named Laskin Lectureship, U. Ill. Coll. Dentistry, 2009; fellow in dental surgery, Glasgow Royal Coll. Physicians and Surgeons (hon.), Royal Coll. Surgeons Eng. Fellow: AAAS, Am. Acad. Implant Prosthodontists (academia), Internat. Coll. Dentists (Spl. Editl. citation 1999, Silver Scroll award 2004), Am. Coll. Dentists (Lifetime Achievement award 2007), Acad. Internat. Dental Studies (hon.), Internat. Assn. Oral and Maxillofacial Surgeons (hon.; exc. com. 1980—95, pres. 1983—86, sec. gen. 1989—95, exec. dir. 1995—99, gen. chmn. 14th Internat. Conf. on Oral and Maxillofacial Surg. 1999, found. cons.); mem.: ADA (adv. com. advanced edn. in oral surgery 1968—75, cons. Coun. on Dental Edn. 1968—82, mem. Commn. on Accreditation 1975—76), Va. Soc. Oral and Maxillofacial Surgeons (Disting. Svc. award), Colo. Soc. Oral & Maxillofacial Surgeons (Lifetime Achievement award 2009), Internat. Jour. Dentistry (editl. bd. mem.), Hungarian Assn. Oral and Maxillofacial Surgeons, Odontographic Soc., William F. Harrigan Soc., Nat. Chronic Pain Outreach Assn. (adv. bd.), Am. Dental Bd. Anesthesiology (pres. 1983—92), Am. Soc.

Laser in Dentistry (hon.), Internat. Study Group for Advancement of TMJ Arthroscopy (hon.), Can. Assn. Oral and Maxillofacial Surgeons (hon.), Japanese Soc. Oral and Maxillofacial Surgeons (hon.), Scandinavian Assn. Oral and Maxillofacial Surgeons (hon.), Turkish Assn. Oral and Maxillofacial Surgeons (hon.), Phillipine Coll Oral & Maxillofacial Surgeons (hon.), Edward H. Angle Soc. Orthodontists (hon.), Internat. Piezosurgery Acad. (hon.), Brazilian Coll. Oral and Maxillofacial Surgery and Traumatology (hon.), Chilean Soc. Oral and Maxillofacial Surgery (hon.), Hellenic Assn. Oral Surgery (hon.), Sadi Fontaine Acad. (hon.), Internat. Congress Oral Implantologists (hon.), Soc. Maxillofacial and Oral Surgeons South Africa (hon.), Japanese Soc. for Temporomandibular Joint (hon.), Royal Soc. Medicine, Am. Assn. Dental Editors, Am. Soc. Exptl. Pathology, Am. Dental Soc. Anesthesiology (pres. 1976—78), Internat. Assn. Dental Rsch., Am. Assn. Oral and Maxillofacial Surgeons (editor Forum 1965—96, pres. 1976—77, editor AAOMS Today 1996—, Disting. Svc. award 1972, rsch. recognition award 1978, William J. Gies award 1979, dedication 73d ann. meeting and sci. sessions 1991), Ill. Splty. Bd. Oral Surgery, Sigma Xi, Omicron Kappa Upsilon. Rsch. and publs. on connective tissue physiology and pathology, particularly cartilage and bone metabolism, craniofacial growth, oral maxillofacial surgery, and pathology of temporomandibular joint. Office: Va Commonwealth U Dept Oral/Maxillofac Surg PO Box 980566 Richmond VA 23298-0566 Office Phone: 804-828-3547. Business E-Mail: dmlaskin@vcu.edu.

LASTE, MICHAEL H., councilman, lawyer; b. San Pablo, Calif. BA, U. Tex., Austin, 1984; JD, U. Houston, 1988. Bar: Tex. 1989. Sr. asst. city atty. Real Estate Divsn. City of Houston, Houston, 1989—95; atty. Williams, Birnberg & Andersen, LLP, Houston; councilman Dist. J Houston City Coun., 2012—. Bd. mem. Sharpstown Tax Increment Reinvestment Zone and Redevelopment Authority. Mem.: ABA, Tex. Bar Assn. Democrat. Office: City Hall Annex 900 Bagby, First Floor Houston TX 77002 Office Phone: 832-393-3015. E-mail: districtj@houstontx.gov.

LASTER, CHARLIE, state legislator; b. Shawnee, Okla., 1954; m. Kathy Laster; children: Kara, Luke. BS, Okla. State Univ., 1976; JD, Univ. Okla., 1979. Private law practice, Shawnee; mem. Dist. 17 Okla. State Senate, 2003—. Mem.: Okla. Bar Assn., Okla. State U. Alumni Assn., Shawnee C. of C. Democrat. Baptist. Avocations: hunting, tennis. Office: 2300 N Lincoln Blvd Rm 533B Oklahoma City OK 73105 Office Phone: 405-521-5539, 405-273-2910. Business E-Mail: laster@oksenate.gov.

LASTRA, ANSELMO A., computer science educator; BSEE, Ga. Inst. Tech., Atlanta; MA in Computer Sci., Duke U., Durham, NC, PhD in Computer Sci., 1988. Electronic engr. Scidata, Inc., Atlanta; project engr. Coulter Electronics, Inc., Hialeah, Fla.; rsch. asst. Duke U., 1979—85, rsch. asst. prof. computer sci., 1988—91, U. NC, Chapel Hill, 1991—97, rsch. assoc. prof., 1997—2001, assoc. prof. computer sci., 2001—06, prof., 2006—, dir. grad. studies, 2006—09, chair dept. computer sci., 2009—. Exhibitions include Virtual Monticello, New Orleans Mus. Art, 2003; assoc. editor Transactions for Visualization & Computer Graphics, 2003—07, Computer Graphics & Applications; contbr. articles to profl jours., chapters to books. Office: UNC Dept Computer Sci CB 3175 Sitterson Hall Chapel Hill NC 27599 Office Phone: 919-962-1958. E-mail: lastra@cs.unc.edu.

LATA, MIKE, chef; Exec. chef Anson, Charleston, SC, 1998; co-founder Charleston Convivium Slow Food, 2004; exec. chef Fig, Charleston. Named Best Chef: Southeast, James Beard Found., 2009. Mem.: Southern Foodways Alliance. Office: Fig 232 Meeting St Charleston SC 29401-3134 Office Phone: 843-805-5900. E-mail: mike@eatafig.com.

LATANÉ, BIBB, social psychologist; b. NYC, July 19, 1937; s. Henry Allen and Felicité Gillman (Bibb) L.; children: Julia Gillman, Claire Augusta, Henry Arbiter. BA, Yale U., 1958; PhD, U. Minn., 1963. Mem. faculty dept. social psychology Columbia U., NYC, 1962-68; prof. psychology, dir. behavioral scis. lab. Ohio State U., Columbus, 1968-82; prof. psychology, dir. Inst. Research Social Sci. U.N.C.-Chapel Hill, 1982-90. Pres. Social Sci. Confs., Inc., 1990—; founder Nags Head Confs., Sea Frolic Conf. Ctr., Ctr. Human Sci., sr. fellow, 2000—. Contbr. articles to profl. jours. Guggenheim fellow, 1974-75; James McKeen Cattell fellow, 1981-82; NSF, Office of Naval Research grantee. Mem. APA (coun. rep. 1971-75), Soc. Personality and Social Psychology (pres. 1976-79, Campbell award 1986), Midwestern Psychol. Assn. (pres. 1981-84), Acad. Mgmt., AAAS (Socio-Psychol. prize 1968, 80), Soc. Exptl. Soc. Psychology (Disting. Scientist award 1998), Am. Sociol. Assn., Animal Behavior Soc. E-mail: latane@humanscience.org.

LATHAM, JOHN K., insurance company executive; Grad., Stephen F. Austin U. Pres., CEO Colony Ins. Co., 1991—2002; pres., COO Markel Re Markel Corp., 2002—04, chief info. officer, 2004—06, sr. v.p. ops., 2006—08, pres. Southeast region, head Office Bus. Devel., 2008—10, mng. dir. regional wholesale ops., 2010—. Recipient Charles A. McAlear NAPSLO Industry Award, 2009. Office: Markel Corp 4521 Highwoods Pky Glen Allen VA 23060 Office Phone: 804-747-0136. Office Fax: 804-965-1600. Business E-Mail: jlatham@markelcorp.com.

LATHRAM, OTHNI J., state legislative agency administrator, lawyer; b. 1975; BS in Economics, Auburn U., Montgomery, Ala., 1997; JD, U. Ala., 2000. Bar: Ala. 2000, Tex. 2006. Assoc. Whatley Drake & Kallas LLC, Birmingham, Ala., 2000—05, mem., 2006—08; asst. dir. Ala. Law Inst., Tuscaloosa, 2008—. Mem.: ABA, Ala. State Bar, American Law Inst., Kiwanis Club Greater Tuscaloosa. Office: Alabama Law Institute PO Box 861425 Tuscaloosa AL 35486 Office Phone: 205-348-7411. Office Fax: 205-348-8411. E-mail: olathram@ali.state.al.us.

LATINO, JOSEPH NUNZIO, bishop; b. New Orleans, Oct. 21, 1937; BA, Notre Dame Seminary, New Orleans, 1959. Ordained priest Archdiocese of New Orleans, 1963; parochial vicar St. Francis de Sales, Houma, La., 1963—68, St. Philip the Apostle Ch., New Orleans, 1969—71, St. Angela Merici, Metairie, La., 1971—72; tchr., spiritual dir. St. John Prep. Sem., New Orleans, 1968—69; pastor St. Bernadette Parish, Houma, La., 1972—87, St. Francis de Sales, Houma, La., 1987—2003; vicar - gen. Diocese of Houma-Thibodaux, La., 1987—2003; ordained bishop, 2003; bishop Diocese of Jackson, Miss., 2003—. Roman Catholic. Office: Jackson Diocese 237 East Amite St PO Box 2248 Jackson MS 39225-2248 Office Phone: 601-969-1880. Office Fax: 601-960-8455.

LATTA, DIANA LENNOX, retired interior designer; b. Lahaina, Maui, Hawaii, Aug. 5, 1936; d. D. Stewart and Jean Marjorie (Anderson) Lennox; m. Arthur McKee Latta, Jan. 26, 1957 (dec.); children: Mary-Stewart, Marion McKee Latta de Vogel. Grad., The Bishop's Sch., La Jolla, Calif., 1954; student, U. Wash., Seattle, 1954—56. Dir. Vero Beach (Fla.) br. of Wellington Hall Ltd., Thomasville, NC, 1970—72; asst. to chief designer Rablen-West Interiors, Vero Beach, 1972—75; design and adminstrv. asst. to pres. Design Studio Archtl. & Interior Design Concepts, Inc., Vero Beach, 1975—82; owner, designer The Designery, Vero Beach, 1983—87; designer's asst. Frank J. Lincoln Interiors, Inc., Vero Beach, Locust Valley, NY, 1987—90; sr. staff designer Chancellor's Inc., Bellingham, Wash., 1992—93. Leading actress (Vero Beach Theatre Guild prodns) The Laughmaker, 1964, Oklahoma, 1966, model Holly Fashion Show, Vero Beach, 1962—69. Mem. Indian River Meml. Hosp. Women's Aux., Vero Beach, 1957—70, chmn. charity ball and gift shop, 1960, v.p., 1962—64; advisor to steering com. The Malt Shoppe After-Sch. Program, Mill Creek, 1995—97; mem. coun. Snohomish County Federated Health and Safety Network, 1999—2003; founding mem. Indian River Land Trust, Vero Beach, 1989—90; chmn. Mill Creek for Youth Com., 1994; bd. dir. and chmn. hospitality com. Vero Beach Mut. Concert Assn., 1973—76; mem. adv. bd. Indian River 4-H Horsemaster's Club, 1973—76; founding mem. McKee Jungle Gardens Preservation Soc., Inc., 1988—89, treas. bd. dir., chmn. fundraising com., pub. rels. com., 1988; bd. dir. Vero Beach Theatre Guild, 1964; mem. adv. com. Safe and Drug Free Schs. Edmonds Sch. Dist., Wash., 1996—2002; mem. key leaders bd. Cmtys. That Care Project Edmonds Sch. Dist., 2001—08. Mem.: Internat. Platform Assn., Riomar Bay Yacht Club (chmn. tennis com. 1964—66, club tennis champion 1964, 1966), Kappa Kappa Gamma (founding mem. Indian River Alumnae Club 1968—90, mem. adv. bd. U. Wash., Seattle chpt. 1997—2000, founding mem. N. Sound Alumnae Assn. 2002—08, Asheville Area Alumnae Assn. mem. 2008—). Republican. Episcopalian. Home: 509 Cokesbury Ln Asheville NC 28803

LATVALA, JACK, state legislator; b. Oxford, Miss., Nov. 3, 1951; m. Susan Richardson; children: Stephanie, Colin, Evan, Christopher. BA, Stetson U., 1973. Pres. Direct Mail Systems, Inc., Direct Response Mktg., Inc.; mem. Dist. 19 Fla. State Senate, 1994—2010, mem. Dist. 16, 2011—. Mem. edn. com., exec. bus., ethics and elections com., rules and calendar com., transp. com., ways and means com., gen. govt. subcom., chmn. natural resources com. Fla. State Senate, alternating chmn. Everglades Oversight com. 1996-98. Founding pres. North Pinellas (Fla.) Rep. Club; mem. Pinellas County Rep. Exec. Com.; active UPARC Found.; mem. Pinellas Sports Authority, 1987-93, sec., 1988-90, vice chmn., 1990-91; vice chmn., chmn. Palm Harbor Cmty. Svcs. Agy., 1985-93. Recipient Disting. Svc. award Order of DeMolay, 1971, Quality Floridian award Fla. League of Cities, Legis. award Fla. Sheriffs Assn., 1995, 96, Legis. Leadership award Fla. Restaurant Assn., 1995, Legis. Conservation award Fla. Conservation Assn., 1995, 96, Raymond B. Stewart Gavel of Authority, Fla. Assn. Sch. Adminstrs.; named Outstanding Fla. Coll. Rep., 1972, Outstanding Young Man of Am., 1983, Legislator of Yr., Eckerd Family Youth Alternatives, 1995, Freshman Legislator of Yr., Fla. Sch. Bds. Assn., Fla. Assn. Counties, South Fla. Consortium of Sch. Bds., 1995. Baptist. Avocation: fishing. Office: Fla State Senate 405 Senate Office Bldg 404 South Monroe St Tallahassee FL 32399-1100 also: Ste 102 26133 US Highway 19 N Ste 201 Clearwater FL 33763-2014 Office Phone: 727-556-6500, 850-487-5075. Business E-Mail: latvala.jack.web@flsenate.gov.

LAUBENBERG, JODIE, state legislator; b. Apr. 20, 1957; m. Bob Laubenberg; children: David, Liz. Grad., U. Tex., Austin. Mem. Parker City Coun., Tex.; mem. Dist. 89 Tex. House of Representatives, 2002—. Republican. Office: Room E2.902 Capitol Extension PO Box 2910 Austin TX 78768 Address: 206 N Murphy Rd Lufkin TX 75904 Office Phone: 972-772-8525, 512-463-0186, 972-424-6810.

LAUBER, MARK E., wholesale distribution executive; BS in Economics, U. Pa. Co-owner 24 Columbia Assoc., 47 Readington Assocs. LLC; pres., CEO Wine & Spirits Storage; ptnr., Lauber Imports Southern Wine & Spirits of America, Inc., 1981, pres., Lauber Imports. Mem., vice chmn. NJ Alcoholic Beverage Control Adv. Com., pres., v.p., NY Alliance. Office: Southern Wine & Spirits of America Inc 1600 N W 163rd St Miami FL 33169 Office Phone: 305-625-4171. Office Fax: 305-625-4720. Business E-Mail: mlauber@southernwine.com.

LAUBIES, PIERRE, food products executive; Pres., Europe, v.p. Campbell Soup Co.; pres., petcare Mars, Inc. Office: Mars Inc 6885 Elm St Mc Lean VA 22101 Office Phone: 703-821-4900. Office Fax: 703-448-9678.

LAUDER, VALARIE ANNE, retired editor; b. Detroit, Mar. 01; d. William J. and Murza Valerie (Mann) L. AA, Stephens Coll., Columbia, Mo., 1944; postgrad., Northwestern U. With Chgo. Daily News, 1944-52, columnist, 1946-52; lectr. Sch. Assembly Svc., also Redpath lectr., 1952-55; freelance writer for mags. and newspapers including New York Times, Yankee, Ford Times, Travel & Leisure, Am. Heritage, 1955—; editor-in-chief Scholastic Roto, 1962; editor U. N.C., 1975-80, lectr. Sch. Journalism, 1980—2011. Gen. sec. World Assn. for Pub. Opinion Rsch., 1988-95; nat. chmn. student writing project Ford Times, 1981-86; pub. rels. dir. Am. Dance Festival Duke U., 1982-83, lectr., instr. continuing edn. program, 1984. Contbg. editor So. Accents mag., 1982-86. Mem. nat. fundraising bd. Kennedy Ctr., 1962-63; bd. dirs. Chapel Hill Mus., Inc., 1996-98, mayor, 2009. Recipient 1st place award Nat. Fedn. Press Women, 1981, 1st place awards Ill. Women's Press Assn., 1950, 51, Town Treas. award, Chapel Hill Hist. Soc., 2008, Proclamation of Mayor, 2009. Mem. Pub. Rels. Soc. Am. (treas. NC chpt. 1982, sec. 1983, v.p. 1984, pres.-elect 1985, pres. 1986, chmn. coun. past pres., chmn. 25th Ann. event 1987, del. Nat. Assembly 1988-94, S.E. dist. officer, nat. nominating com. 1991, 1st pres.'s award 1993), Women in Comms. (v.p. matrix N.C. Triangle chpt. 1984-85), NC Pub. Rels. (mem. Hall Fame com. 1988-2006), DAR, Soc. Mayflower Desc. (bd. dirs. Ill. Soc. 1946-52), Chapel Hill Hist. Soc. (bd. dirs. 1981-85, 94-2001, chmn. pub. com. 1980-85, pres. 1996-2001, chair, calender com., 2008, editor collectible, 2009), Chapel Hill Preservation Soc. (bd. trustees 1993-96, nominating com. 1994), NC Press Club (3d v.p. 1981-83, 2d v.p. 1983-85, pres. 1985, 1st pl. awards 1981, 82, 83, 84), Univ. Women's Club (2nd v.p. 1988), The Carolina Club, The Nat. Press Club. Home Phone: 919-929-1019.

LAUDERDALE, KATHERINE SUE, lawyer; b. Wright-Patterson AFB, Ohio, May 30, 1954; d. Azo and Helen Ceola (Davis) L. BS in Polit. Sci., Ohio State U., 1975; JD, NYU, 1978. Bar: Ill. 1978, U.S. Dist. Ct. (no. dist.) Ill. 1978, Calif. 1987. Assoc. Schiff, Hardin & Waite, Chgo., 1978-82; from dir. bus. and legal affairs to sr. v.p. Sta. WTTW-TV, Chgo., 1982—2000, sr. v.p. strategic partnerships and gen. counsel, 2000—02; sr. v.p., gen. counsel PBS, Alexandria, Va., 2002—, corp. sec., 2006—. Mem. Lawyers Com. for Harold Washington, Chgo. 1983; bd. dirs. Midwest Women's Ctr., Chgo., 1985-94; active Chgo. Coun. Fgn. Rels., 1981-99, mem. fgn. affairs com., 1985-99; mem. adv. bd. Malcolm X Coll. Sch. Bus., 1996-99 Mem. ABA, Chgo. Bar Assn. (bd. dirs. TV Prodns., Inc. 1986-2002), Lawyers for Creative Arts (bd. dir. 1984-2002, v.p. 1998-2002), ACLU (bd. dirs. 1987-94), Nat. Acad. TV Arts and Scis., NYU Law Alumni Assn. Midwest (mem. exec. bd. 1982-86), The Ohio State U. Pres.'s Nat. Adv. Coun. on Pub. Affairs (Chgo. com., 1994-98), The History Makers (nat. adv. bd. 2003—), Hands on Network (nat. bd., 2005-07, sec. exec. com. 2006), Points of Light (nat. bd. 2007—). Democrat. Office: PBS 2100 Crystal Dr Arlington VA 22202 Office Phone: 703-739-5063.

LAUGHLIN, LOUIS GENE, economic analyst, consultant; b. Sept. 20, 1937; s. Eston A. and Cornelia Helen Laughlin Student, Pomona Coll., 1955-58; BA, U. Calif., Santa Barbara, 1960; postgrad., Claremont Grad. Sch., 1966-70, 85-86, Sch. Bank Mktg., U. Colo., 1974-75, Grad. Sch. Mgmt., U. Calif., Irvine, 1983. Mgr. Wheeldex-L.A. Co., 1961—62; v.p. Warner/Walker Assocs., Inc., LA, 1964—65; rep. A.C. Neilsen Co., Chgo., 1962—64; rsch. analyst Security Pacific Nat. Bank, LA, 1964—67, asst. rsch. mgr., 1967—68, asst. v.p., 1968—72, v.p., mgr. market info. and rsch. divsn., 1972—76, v.p. rsch. adminstrn., pub. affairs/rsch. dept., 1976—82, v.p. govt. rels. dept., 1982—85; dir. R & D Applied Mgmt. Sys., South Pasadena, Calif., 1986; pres. L.G. Laughlin & Assocs., Houston, 1987—. Prin. Courtyard Holdings, Houston, 1988—; pres. CEO, Mastodon Capital Corp., Houston, 1988-89, 94-98; corp. sec. Kestco Co. Inc., Laguna Beach, Calif., 1996-98; mem. Nat. Conf. on Fin. Svcs., 1982-84, mem. policy coun., 1983-84; mem. policy coun. Nat. Conf. on Competition in Banking, 1978-79, 81. Sec. econs. Town Hall of Calif., 1966. Mem. Am. Econs. Assn., Western Econs. Assn., Nat. Assn. Bus. Economists, L.A. C. of C. (food and agr. adv. com. 1981), Wildflower Green Townhomes (Houston) (dir., 2012-). Personal E-mail: unklou@sbcglobal.net.

LAUGHLIN, TERRY P. (TERRENCE P. LAUGHLIN), bank executive; b. 1955; BS in Acctg., St. Francis U., 1977; MBA in Finance, U. Pitts., 1981. Various position Mellon Bank, Pitts.; dir. corp. devel. FleetBoston Fin. Corp., 1993—2000, exec. v.p. internat. banking & corp. strategy devel., 2000—05; sr. v.p., head strategic growth opportunities Merrill Lynch & Co., Inc., NYC, 2005—09; chmn., CEO Merrill Lynch Bank & Trust Co., 2006—09; CEO OneWest Bank, 2009—10; credit mitigation strategies & secondary markets exec. Bank of America Corp., Charlotte, NC, 2010—11, legacy asset servicing exec., 2011, chief risk officer, 2011—. Bd. trustees U. Pitts. Office: Bank of America Corp 100 N Tryon St Corp Ctr Charlotte NC 28255

LAUGHTER, JOHN, air transportation executive; BS in Aerospace Engring., Ga. Inst. Tech., 1993; MBA, Emory U. Goizueta Bus. Sch., Atlanta, 2005. Various positions including gen. mgr. planning Delta Air Lines, Inc., dir. materials & planning, 2005, v.p. maintenance ops., sr. v.p. maintenance ops., 2008—. Office: Delta Air Lines Inc 1030 Delta Blvd Atlanta GA 30354-1989 Office Phone: 404-715-2600. Office Fax: 404-715-5042. Business E-Mail: john.laughter@delta.com.

LAURENT, LAWRENCE BELL, communications executive, retired journalist; b. Monroe, La., Mar. 09; s. Lewis Emeal and John Ethel (Dawkins) L.; m. Margaret F. Goodwillie, Nov. 1, 1949 (dec. May 7, 2006); children: Richard Sandford, Arthur Halliday, Margaret Funsten, Elizabeth MacLean. Student, U. Colo., 1943—44, U. Va., 1946—49; pvt. study with, Dr. W.Y. Elliott, 1954—56, Dr. Franklin Dunham, 1957—58. With Bluefield Daily Telegraph, W.Va., 1949—50, Charlottesville Daily Progress, Va., 1950—51, Washington Post, 1951—82, radio-TV editor, 1953—82, radio-TV editor emeritus, 1982—; cons. Assn. Ind. TV Stas., 1982—85, dir. comm., 1985—86, v.p. comm., 1986—91; congl. cons., 1991—; editor-in-residence Broadcast Pioneers Libr., 1985—96; adj. prof. comm. Am. U., Washington, 1963—85; chmn. editl. bd. TV Quar., 1963—74, bd. dirs. Guest prof. Syracuse U., 1965; vis. prof. U. Detroit, 1967, George Washington U., 1982-95, professorial lectr., 1996—2006; former judge Alfred I. duPont awards, Saturday Rev. Lit. TV awards, Sigma Delt Chi pub. svc. TV awards, Humanitas awards, lectr. Airlie, Va. Editor, author: (with Newton N. Minow) Equal Time, 1964; Contbr. to books, mags Trustee Human Family Edn. and Cultural Inst.; bd. dirs. Pioneers Edn. Fund, Inc., 1984-94, trustee, 1995-2002. With USNR, 1943-46 Airlie fellowship Inter-Am. Dialogue Ctr., 1972-74; recipient Front Page award, Am. Newspaper Guild, 1964, TV Acad.'s Silver Cir. award, 1988, Pres.'s medal, George Washington U., 1999; named Disting. Tchr., Am. U., 1978; named to Broadcast Pioneers' Hall of Fame, 1984; du Pont Journalism scholar U. Va., 1947-49 Mem. AAUP, NATAS (life), VFW (life), DAV (life), 593d Joint Assault Signal Co. Assn., USS Belle Grove Historic Assn., Nat. Press Club, White House Corrs. Assn., Washington Post E-Streeters, Am. Legion (life), Thomas Jefferson Soc. Alumni (U. Va.), Sigma Delta Chi, Pi Delta Epsilon, Theta Chi. Episcopalian. Home: Goodwin House Apt 558 4800 Fillmore Ave Alexandria VA 22311

LAURIA, THOMAS E., lawyer; b. 1960; BA with honors, U. Tenn., 1982, JD with honors, 1986. Bar: Tex. 1986, US Ct. Appeals (5th cir.) 1986, US Dist. Ct. (northern and southern dists.) Tex. 1986, Fla. 1995, US Dist. Ct. (southern, middle and northern dists.) Fla. 1995, US Ct. Appeals (11th cir.) 2000, US Ct. Appeals (2nd cir.) 2007. Ptnr., global practice head Fin. Restructuring and Insolvency Group White & Case LLP, Miami, Fla., NYC. Spkr. in field. Named a Dealmaker of the Yr., The American Lawyer mag., 2011. Office: White & Case LLP Southeast Financial Center 2000 S Biscayne Blvd, Suite 4900 Miami FL 33131-2352 also: 1155 Avenue of the Americas New York NY 10036-2787 Office Phone: 305-995-5282, 302-358-5744, 212-819-2637. E-mail: tlauria@whitecase.com.

LAURINO, JOSEPH PHILIP, president, chemistry professor, consultant; BS in Chemistry, Georgetown U., Washington, 1980; PhD in Chemistry, U. Va., Charlottesville, 1986; MBA, U.Tampa, Fla., 2005. Cert. clin. lab. dir. Fla., 2003. Juvenile diabetes found. postdoc. rsch. fellow Wash. U. Sch. Medicine, St. Louis, 1986—87; rsch. scientist Technicon Instruments Co., Tarrytown, NY, 1987—88; sr. rsch. scientist Hoffmann La Roche, Nutley, NJ, 1988—90; dir. clin. chemistry and toxicology Meml. Hosp. RI, Pawtucket, 1990—97; clin. asst. prof. pathology Brown U. Sch. Medicine, Providence, 1990—97; dir. sci. ops. Spectral Diagnostics, Inc., Toronto, Ontario, Canada, 1997—99; assoc. prof. chemistry U. Tampa, 1999—2005, prof. chemistry, 2005—10, assoc. dir., honors program, 2000—07, chair, chemistry, 2003—07; pres., CEO Periodic Products LLC, 2009—. Cons. GeoPharma, Largo, Fla., 2007—09. Recipient Jan K. Dargel award for Outstanding Svc., U. Tampa, 2004, Clin. Scientist of Yr., Assn. Clin. Scientists, 2004; named Young Clin. Scientist of Yr., 1993; grantee, Am. Heart Assn., RI Affiliate, 1992—94, Zambone Labs., 1992—93, Am. Coll. Clin. Pharmacy Rsch. Inst., 1993—94, Baxter Health Care, 1994, Am. Assn. Clin. Chemistry, 1994, State Fla. Dept. Edn., 2006. Fellow: Assn. Clin. Scientists (pres. 1998—99, Clin. Scientist of Yr. 2004); mem.: Am. Chem. Soc., Am. Assn. Clin. Chemistry (del. 1995—98), Alliance Northeastern Sects. Am. Assn. Clin. Chemistry (chair 1998—2000, Svc. Recognition award 2000), Beta Gamma Sigma, Sigma Xi (treas., tampa bay sect. 2005—08). Achievements include patents for chelating compound and method of use of poly and the corresponding acid; development of first immunochemical assay to measure the MB-2 isoform of creatine kinase; first three analyte simultaneous lateral flow immunoassay. Office: Periodic Products 1885 W State Rd 84 Ste 104 Fort Lauderdale FL 33315*

LAVENDER, ROBERT EUGENE, former state supreme court justice; b. Muskogee, Okla., July 19, 1926; s. Harold James and Vergene Irene (Martin) L.; m. Maxine Knight, Dec. 22, 1945; children— Linda (Mrs. Dean Courter), Robert K., Debra (Mrs. Thomas Merrill), William J. LL.B., U. Tulsa, 1953; grad., Appellate Judges Seminar, 1967, Nat. Coll. State Trial Judges, 1970. Bar: Okla.

bar 1953. With Mass. Bonding & Ins. Co., Tulsa, 1951-53, U.S. Fidelity & Guaranty Co., Tulsa, 1953-54; asst. city atty. Tulsa, 1954-55; practice, 1955-60, Claremore, Okla., 1960-65; justice Okla. Supreme Ct., 1965—2007, chief justice, 1979-80. Guest lectr. Okla. U., Oklahoma City U., Tulsa U. law schs. Republican committeeman, Rogers County, 1961-62. Served with USNR, 1944-46. Recipient Disting. Alumnus award U. Tulsa, 1993. Mem. ABA, Okla. Bar Assn., Rogers County Bar Assn., Am. Judicature Soc., Okla. Jud. Conf., Phi Alpha Delta (hon.) Methodist (adminstrv. bd.). Club: Mason (32 deg.). Home: 2910 Kerry Ln Oklahoma City OK 73120-2507

LAVERTY, RANDY, state legislator; b. Pitts., Pa., Mar. 8, 1953; m to Virginia Lee Jones; children: three. In ins. bus.; mem. Jasper Sch. Bd., 1982—87; mem. Dist. 23 Ark. House of Reps., 1995—2002; mem. Dist. 2 Ark. State Senate, 2003—. Democrat. Baptist. Mailing: PO Box 303 Jasper AR 72641 Office Phone: 870-446-5005. Office Fax: 870-446-2774.

LAVINE, ALAN, columnist, writer; b. Sharon, Pa., Feb. 17, 1948; s. Milton and Doris (Helfman) L.; m. Gail Jeanne Liberman, Dec. 20, 1991. BA, Kent State U., 1970; MA, U. Akron, 1973; MBA, Clark U., 1981. Dir. of rsch. Donoghue Orgn., Holliston, Mass., 1981-83; nat. syndicated fin. columnist North Palm Beach, Fla., 1983—; columnist Dow Jones Market Watch and other newspapers. Presenter papers in field ann. meeting AAAS, 1972, ann. meeting Mass. Psychol. Assn., Wellesley, 1978, ann. meeting APA, 1979, Nat. Symposium on Rsch. in Art, U. Ill., 1980; guest lectr. Cornell U., 1990, 91, 92, 93. Author: Diversify: Investor's Guide to Asset Allocation Strategies, 1990 (alt. selection Fortune Book Club), Your Life Insurance Options, 1993 (endorsed Inst. CFPs), Improving Your Credit and Reducing Your Debt, 1994 (endorsed Inst. CFPs), Getting Started in Mutual Funds, 1994, Diversify Your Way to Wealth, 1994 (alt. selection Fortune Book Club), 50 Ways to Mutual Fund Profits, 1995, The Complete Idiot's Guide to Making Money with Mutual Funds, 1996, Love, Marriage and Money, 1998, Rags To Riches: Motivationing Stories of Ordinary People Who Achieved Extraordinary Wealth, 2000, Short and Simple Guide to Life Insurance, 2000, More Rags to Riches: All New Stories of Ordinary People Who Achieved Extraordinary Wealth, 2002, Short and Simple Guide to Smart Investing, 2002, Rags to Retirement, 2002, Quick Step to Financial Stability, 2006; contbr. articles to profl. jours. Mem. Nat. Writers Union, Soc. Am. Bus. Editors and Writers, Inc., Authors' Guild. Office Phone: 561-630-7112. Personal E-mail: mwliblav@aol.com.

LAVINE, JAMES E., lawyer; b. Youngstown, Ohio, 1949; married; 3 children. BA, Williams Coll., Williamstown, Mass., 1971; JD, Ill. Inst. Tech. Chgo. Kect Coll. Law, 1974. Bar: Ill., Tex., cert.: Nat. Bd. Trial Advocacy and Tex. Bd. Legal Specialization (in criminal law). Asst. state atty., spl. prosecutions bur., organized crime unit Cook County, Ill., 1975—80; asst. dist. atty. Harris County, Tex., 1980—85; pvt. practice def. counsel, 1985—; joined Zimmerman, Lavine & Sampson PC, Houston, 1985, shareholder, 1986—. Faculty mem. Tex. Criminal Trial Advocacy Inst., State Bar Tex. Advanced Criminal Law Course. Contbr. articles to profl. jours. Named a Super Lawyer, Tex. Monthly mag., 2003—08, Super Lawyers Mag., 2003—13. Fellow: Tex. Bar Found. (life); mem.: Harris County Criminal Lawyers Assn. (former pres., Atty. of Yr. 2005—06), Ill. State Bar Assn., Tex. Criminal Def. Lawyers Assn. (former chmn. amicus curiae com., former dir., Presdl. award 1992, Outstanding Lawyers in the State 2005—06), Nat. Assn. Criminal Def. Lawyers (dir. 1997—2003, parliamentarian 2006—07, 2008—09, pres. 2010—11, Robert C. Heeney award 2007). Office: Zimmerman Lavine & Sampson PC 770 S Post Oak Ln Ste 620 Houston TX 77056 Office Phone: 713-552-0300. Office Fax: 713-552-0746.*

LAW, JOHN HAROLD, biochemistry educator; b. Cleve., Feb. 27, 1931; s. John and Katherine (Frampton) L.; m. Jeannette Ward Belcher, Nov. 9, 2000. BS, Case Inst. Tech., Cleve., 1953; PhD, U. Ill., 1957; D (hon.), U. Sofia, 1995, U. South Bohemia, 2004. Fellow Harvard U., Cambridge, Mass., 1957—59; instr. Northwestern U., Evanston, Ill., 1959—60; from instr. to asst. prof. biochemistry Harvard U., Cambridge, Mass., 1960—65; prof. U. Chgo., 1965—81, U. Ariz., Tucson, 1981—91, Regents prof., 1991—2001, Regents prof. emeritus, 2001—; prof. entomology U. Ga., Athens, 2007—. Gov. bd. Internat. Ctr. Insects, Nairobi, Kenya, 1980—87; chmn. dept. biochemistry U. Ariz., Tucson, 1981—86, dir. biotech. program, 1986—92, assoc. dean Coll. Agr., 1988—90; mem. bd. trustees Gordon Rsch. Conf., 1992—98, chmn., 1996; dir. Ctr. Insect Sci. U. Ariz., Tucson, 1993—98. Recipient Gregor Mendel medal Czech Acad. Sci., 1992, J.E. Purkinje medal Czech Acad. Sci., 1994, Alumni Achievement award U. Ill., 2002. Fellow AAAS, ESA (Recognition award 1999); mem. NAS, Am. Soc. Biochem. Molecular Biology (mem. coun. 1993-96), Am. Chem. Soc., Entomol. Soc. Am. Home: 201-8 Hamilton Rd Athens GA 30606-6619 Office: U Ga Dept Entomology Bio Sci 518 Athens GA 30602-2603 E-mail: jhlaw@u.arizona.edu.

LAW, THOMAS MELVIN, academic administrator; b. Bristol, Va., Sept. 23, 1925; s. Thomas Keen and Rebecca Ellen (Davis) L; m. Katherine Iris Tillar, Oct. 14, 1954; 1 child, Thomas Fenimore. BS summa cum laude, St. Paul's Coll., 1950, LHD (hon.), 1982; MA, NYU, 1953; EdD, Cornell U., 1962; LHD (hon.), Cuttington U., Liberia, 2001, SS Va. CC, 2001. Dean., prof. St. Paul's Coll., Lawrenceville, Va., 1967-69, pres., trustee, 1989—; v.p. acad. affairs Washington Tech. Inst., 1969-71; pres. Penn Valley Community Coll., Kansas City, Mo., 1971-76, Va. State U., Petersburg, 1976-82; dep. to chancellor spl. programs SUNY, Albany, 1982-86, dep. to chancellor for CC, 1986, assoc. vice chancellor contracts/purchasing, 1986-89, pres., 1989—2001; pres. emeritus St. Paul's Coll. Bd. dirs. Nat. Alumni Assn, Sch. of Human Ecology, Cornell U.; mem. Cornell U. Coun (life). Bd. dirs. Brunswick County C. of C., Lawrenceville, 1990—, Va. C. of C., Brunswick County Indsl. Devel. Authority, 1994-2002, A.L. Philpott Mfg. Extension Partnership1994-2002; life mem. NAACP; mem. commn. black mins. Union Black Episcs., Inc., by-laws com. United Negro Coll. Fund, Inc. Sgt. U.S. Army, 1942-46. Mem. Am. Assn. Higher Edn., Nat. Assn. Ind. Colls. and Univs. (com. campus concerns), Coun. Ind. Colleges in Va. (exec. com., pres.), Assn. Va. Colls. and Univs. (exec com., pres.), Am. Coun. on Edn. (com. leadership), Rotary, Phi Delta Kappa, Alpha Phi Alpha (life), Sigma Pi Phi. Address: 117 Scrimshaw Dr Chester VA 23836-1200 Personal E-mail: tlaw@saintpauls.edu.

LAWHON, JOHN, III, lawyer, retired county official; b. Denton, Tex., Dec. 14, 1934; s. John E. and Gladys (Barns) L.; m. Tommie Collins, Aug. 27, 1967; 1 son, David Collins. Student, U. N.Tex., 1951-53; BBA, JD, U. Houston, 1958. Bar: Tex. 1958; cert. specialist in estate and probate law; bd. cert. in family law. Asst. dist. and county atty., Denton County, Tex., 1958-61; dist. and county atty., 1961-77; dir. Southridge, Inc., Denton, 1962-72, Lawyers Title Agy. Denton, 1965-74; Legal adviser Denton City-County Day Nursery, 1972-80; tchr. bus. law U. North Tex. (formerly North Tex. State U.), Denton, 1969-71; mem. adv. bd. Tex. Criminal Justice Council, 1973-79; univ. atty. Tex. Woman's U., 1977-83, gen. counsel, 1983—2013, sec. bd. regents, 1987—2013, bd. dirs. found., 1988—. Bd. dirs. Denton County Welfare Coun., 1970-78, Denton Community Coun., 1978-79, 80-82; mem. Denton Forum; chmn. Denton County ARC, 1985-87, Denton County Probation Adv. Bd., 1985-92; mem. City of Denton Land Use Com., 1986-88; deacon Baptist, 1968-2005, ch. coun., 2009-11. Mem. Tex. Bar Assn., Denton Bar Assn. (pres. 1968-69, bd. dirs. 1978-81), Tex. Dist. and County Attys. Assn. (bd. dirs. 1964-66), Denton Jaycees (sec. 1961), Denton C. of C., Tex. Assn. State Univ. Attys. (pres. 1983-84, Denton County crim. justice task force 1992-93, state bar coll. fellow 1995—), K.P., Kiwanis (bd dirs 1981-86, pres 1984-85). Home: 2810 Carmel St Denton TX 76205-8310 Office: Tex Woman's U Adminstrn Tower Bldg PO Box 44 Denton TX 76202-0044 Office Phone: 940-387-4401.

LAWHON, TOMMIE COLLINS MONTGOMERY, retired humanities educator; b. Shelby County, Tex., Mar. 15; d. Marland Walker and Lillian (Tinsley) Collins; m. David Baldwin Montgomery, Mar. 31, 1962 (dec. Aug. 1964); m. John Lawhon, Aug. 27, 1967; 1 child, David Collins. BS, Baylor U., 1954; M in Home Econs. Edn., Tex. Woman's U., 1964, PhD in Child Devel. and Family Studies, 1966. Cert. tchr., Tex.; cert. family life educator. Tchr. Victoria Pub. Schs., Tex., 1954-55; stewardess, supr. Am. Airlines, Dallas/Ft. Worth, 1955-62; assoc. prof. home econs. Ea. Ky. U., Richmond, 1966-67; prof. home economics U. North Tex., Denton, 1968—2009, head divsn. child devel. and family studies, Sch. Home Econs., 1974—77, univ. tenure com., 1978—84, head program devel. and family studies, dept. counseling, devel. and higher edn., 1993-94, mem. faculty senate, 1984-90, chmn. com. on coms., 1987-88, mem. com. status on women, 1984-87, mem. faculty salary com., 1989-95, chmn., 1989-91, mem. tradition com., 1989-95, recorder, 1989-91. Bd. dirs. U. North Tex., Univ. Union, 1985-88, mem. student mentor com., 1990-00, mem. benefits com., 1994-00, vice chair, 1994-95, chair, 1997-98, mem. faculty sen. Faculty Handbook com., 1998-2004, mem. faculty sen. mentor com., 1990-2008, mem. coll. edn. greivance com., 2003-08, chair, 2003-07. Co-author: Children are Artists, 1971, Hidden Hazards for Children and Families, 1982; editor: What to Do with Children, 1974, Field Trips for Children, 1984; contbr. more than 250 papers and more than 125 profl. publs. Chmn. United Way North Tex. State U., 1980-81; chmn. crusade Am. Cancer Soc., Denton County, 1982-83; chmn. nominating com. First Bapt. Ch., Denton, 1983-84, 84-85; mem. career action adv. com. Girls Inc. of Met. Dallas, 1999, chmn., 2000-01; advisor North Tex. Student Coun. on Family Rels., 1993-2008; mem. Southmont Baptist Ch., Denton Financial Com., 2010-11. Recipient Presdl. award Tex. Coun. on Family Rels., 1979, Fessor Graham award North Tex. State U., 1980, Svc. award Am. Cancer Soc., Denton County, 1983, Outstanding Home Economists Alumni award Baylor U., 1985, Outstanding Event award, 12th Ann. State Conf., U. North Tex., 2006; named Hon. Prof. North Tex. State U., 1975, Meritorious award Nat. Coun. on Family Rels. Assn. of Couns., 2004; Disting. Svc. award Outstanding Orgn. Advisor, U. North Tex., 2005, SGA Exemplary Orgnl. award U. North Tex., 2007, Exemplary Orgn. award, UNT Student Govt. Assn.'s, 2007. Mem. Tex. Coun. on Family Rels. (pres. 1977-79, chmn. policy advisor com. 1986-88, nominating com. 1986-88, 94-96, chair 1994-96, family life edn. com. 1994-97, Moore-Bowman award 1994), Denton Assn. for Edn. Young Children (pres. 1970-72, 84-85, 85-86, v.p. 1986-87), Tex. Assn. Coll. Tchrs. (nominating com. 1988-89, 89-90, v.p. 1990-92, v.p. U. North Tex. chpt. 1987-88, pres. 1988-89, 89-90), Tex. Home Econs. Assn. (chmn. family living and child devel. nominating com. 1983-84, chmn. child devel. and family rels. sect. 1988-90, sec. rep. bd. 1989-90), Nat. Coun. Family Rels. (com. 1982-83, cert. family life's continuing edn. com. 1996-99, chair elect cert. family life continuing edn. com. 1996, chair 1997-98, cert. family life edn. focus group and regional-state coord., chair 1996-97, coord. of all student asst. annual conf., 2001-02), Nat. Assn. Early Childhood Tchr. Educators (membership com. 1995-97), North Tex. Home Econs. Inter-orgnl. Coun. (adviser 1983-85), Phi Delta Kappa (pres. local chpt. 1991-92), Alpha Iota/Phi Upsilon Omicron (advisor 1970-82, chmn. nat. com. 1984-87, nat. bd. dirs. edn. found. 1990-94, com. pubs. 1991-92, vice chair ednl. found. 1992-94), Tri D Club (v.p. Baylor U. chpt. 1953-54), Univ. Grad. Club (pres. Tex. Woman's U. chpt. 1965-66). Democrat. E-mail: tlawhon@charter.net.

LAWHORN, CARON A., gas industry executive; BS, Univ. Tulsa, 1983. CPA. Sr. mgr. KPMG LLP; CFO Emergency Med. Services Authority, Tulsa, Okla.; mgr. audit services ONEOK, Inc., Tulsa, Okla., 1998—2003, v.p. audit & risk control, 2003—04, v.p., controller, 2004—05, sr. v.p. fin. services., treas., 2005—07, sr. v.p., chief acctg. officer, 2007—, ONEOK Partners, LP, 2008—; sr. v.p., Corp. Planning and Devel. ONEOK, Inc., 2009—, ONEOK Partners, LP, 2009—. Chair adv. bd. Ronald McDonald House Charities Tulsa; treas. St. Simeon's Episcopal Home. Mem.: Am. Inst. CPAs, Inst. Internal Auditors, Okla. Bus. Ethics Consortium. Office: ONEOK Inc 100 W Fifth St Tulsa OK 74103 Office Phone: 918-588-7000. Business E-Mail: clawhorn@oneok.com.

LAWLER, DAVID C., energy executive; BS in Petroleum Engring., Colo. Sch. Mines, 1990; MBA, Tulane U., 2003. Joined Shell Exploration & Prodn. Co., 1997; various domestic engring. and ops. positions Burlington Resources, Conoco, Inc.; worked, deepwater drilling engring. and corp. bus. planning, mgr., engring. and ops. Shell Exploration & Prodn. Co.; COO, Quest Energy GP, LLC, COO Quest Resource Corp., 2007—09, pres., Quest Energy GP, LLC, pres., 2008—, CEO, Quest Energy GP, LLC, CEO, 2009—. Bd. dirs. Quest Energy GP, LLC, 2007—, Quest Resource Corp., 2008—. Office: Quest Energy Partners LP Ste 2750 210 Pk Ave Okla Tower Oklahoma City OK 73102 Office Phone: 405-600-7704. Office Fax: 405-600-7722. Business E-Mail: dlawler@qrcp.net.

LAWLER, ROBERT DOUGLAS (DOUG LAWLER), energy company executive, petroleum engineer; b. 1966; BS in Petroleum Engring., Colo. Sch. of Mines, 1988; MBA, Rice U., 2002. With Kerr-McGee Corp., 1988—2006; v.p. corporate planning Anadarko Petroleum Corp., 2008—09, v.p. ops. for southern & Appalachia region, 2009—12, v.p. for internat. ops., 2011—12, sr. v.p. for internat. & deepwater ops., 2012—13; CEO Chesapeake Energy Corp., Oklahoma City, 2013—. Bd. dirs. Chesapeake Energy Corp., 2013—. Mem.: Houston Mus. of Natural Sciences, World Affairs Coun., Soc. Petroleum Engineers. Office: Chesapeake Energy Corp 6100 N Western Ave Oklahoma City OK 73118 Office Phone: 405-848-8000.*

LAWLER-ROW, KATHLEEN ANNE, psychology professor, department chairman; b. Pitts., May 30, 1947; d. Stanley P. and Diana P. Wagner; m. James Everett Lawler, May 20, 1973 (div. Dec. 15, 1999); 1 child, Andrew James Lawler; m. Stephen Edward Row, Dec. 3, 2004. BA in Psychology, Okla. City U., 1967; MA in Child Devel., Iowa U., 1969; PhD in Psychology, U. NC, Chapel Hill, 1974. Prof. U. Tenn., Knoxville, 1975—2006; prof., chair East Carolina U., Greenville, NC, 2006—. Contbr. articles to profl. jours. Episcopal. Avocation: meditation. Office: East Carolina Univ 104 Rawl Bldg Greenville NC 27858

LAWLESS, MICHAEL RHODES, pediatrics educator; b. Baytown, Tex., Oct. 13, 1942; s. Wallace Ervin and Amy Ruth (Broussard) L.; m. E. Sandra Johnson, Aug. 27, 1967; children: Melanie Lawless York, Stephanie Lawless Setzer. BA in Zoology, U. Tex., 1964, MD, 1968. Diplomate Am. Bd. Pediat. Intern City Memphis Hosp., 1968-69; resident in pediat. U. Tex. Med. Br., Galveston, 1969-71; instr. U. Rochester (N.Y.) Sch. Medicine, 1971-72; staff pediatrician Portsmouth (Va.) Naval Hosp., 1972-74; asst. prof. pediat. Wake Forest U. Sch. Medicine, Winston-Salem, NC, 1974-80, assoc. prof. pediat., 1980-2001, prof. pediat., 2001—08, dep. assoc. dean student affairs, 1988-96, chief gen. pediat. and adolescent medicine, 1997—2005. Lt. comdr. USNR, 1972-74. Fellow U. Rochester, 1971-72. Fellow Am. Acad. Pediat. (legis. liaison 1980—); mem. Am. Profl. Soc. on Abuse of Children, N.C. Pediatric Soc. (child adv. 1974—), Coun. Med. Student Edn. in Pediat. (pres. 1998-00), Academic Pediatric Assn., Am. Bd. Pediat. (bd. dirs. 2003—08). Avocation: outdoor activities.

LAWLEY, THOMAS JOSEPH, dean, medical educator; b. Buffalo, 1947; m. Christine Lawley, 1969; children: Thomas Jr., John, Megan. Grad., Canisius Coll., 1968; MD, SUNY Sch. Medicine, Buffalo, 1972. Intern SUNY Sch. Medicine, Buffalo, 1973—74; resident Yale U. Affiliated Hosps., 1974—75; sr. investigator dermatology br. Nat. Cancer Inst. NIH; prof. and chair. dept. dermatology Emory U. Sch. Medicine, Atlanta, 1988—96, William Patterson Timmie Prof. Dermatology, 1993—, exec. assoc. dean, 1995—96, dean, 1996—; vice chair Emory U. Sys. Health Care, Atlanta, 1996—; core dir. Emory Skin Disease Rsch. Ctr., Atlanta. Pres. Emory Med. Care Found., Emory Children's Ctr.; adminstrv. coun. Assn. Am. Med. Colls. Mem.: Am. Profs. Dermatology, Soc. Investigative Dermatology, Am. Acad. Dermatology (Marion Sulzberger Award 1995), Assn. Am. Physicians, Am. Soc. Clin. Investigators. Office: Emory U Sch Medicine Woodruff Health Scis Ctr Adminstrv Bldg 1440 Clifton Rd NE Atlanta GA 30322-1053

LAWRENCE, CHARLES BERDON, exploration company executive; b. 1943; BBA, Tulane U., 1964, MBA, 1965. Founder, pres. Hollywood Marine, Inc., 1999; chmn. Kirby Corp., Houston, 1999—2010, chmn. emeritus, cons., 2010—. Bd. dirs. Pennzoil-Quaker State., Kinder Morgan Energy Ptnrs., L.P, 2009—, Kinder Morgan G.P., 2009—. Bd. trustees Tulane U., New Orleans, mem. Bus. Sch. coun.; chmn. Am. Waterways Operators, Nat. Waterways Conf., Inland Waterways Users Bd., Tex. Waterways Operators, Houston Clean Channel Assn.; active Boys and Girls Harbor, Free Ent. Edn. Ctr. Office: Kirby Corp 55 Waugh Dr Ste 1000 Houston TX 77007 Office Phone: 713-435-1000. Office Fax: 713-435-1464. Business E-Mail: charles.lawrence@kirbycorp.com.

LAWRENCE, DAVID, JR., journalist, early childhood advocate; b. NYC, Mar. 5, 1942; s. David Sr. and Nancy Wemple (Bissell) Lawrence; m. Roberta Phyllis Fleischman, Dec. 21, 1963; children: David III, Jennifer Beth, Amanda Katherine, John Benjamin, Dana Victoria. BS, U. Fla., 1963; postgrad. advanced mgmt. program, Harvard U., 1983; LHD (hon.), Siena Heights Coll., 1985; HHD (hon.), Lawrence Inst. Tech., Detroit, 1986; LHD (hon.), No. Mich. U., 1987; LD (hon.), Barry U., 1991, Fla. Meml. U., 1992, Northwood U., 1993, U. Fla., 1993, Nova Southeastern U., 1997, Colgate U., 1998, Fla. Internat. U., 2005, St. Thomas U., 2006. Reporter, news editor St. Petersburg Times, Fla., 1963—67; news editor Style/Washington Post, 1967—69; mng. editor Palm Beach Post, Fla., 1969—71, Phila. Daily News, 1971—75; exec. editor Charlotte Observer, NC, 1975—76, editor, 1976—78; exec. editor Detroit Free Press, 1978—85, pub., chmn., 1985—89, The Miami Herald, 1989—99. Edn. & comm. leadership scholar U. Miami. Founding chair The Children's Trust; mem. Fla. Children's Cabinet; chair Miami-Dade Early Learning Coalition. Recipient Nat. Human Rights award, Am. Jewish Com., 1986, First Amendment Freedoms award, Anti-Defamation League, 1988, Ida Wells Nat. award for advancement of minorities, Nat. Assn. Black Journalists and Nat. Conf. of Editl. Writers, 1988, John S. Knight Gold medal, Knight-Ridder, 1988, Silver Medallion award, NCCJ, 1992, Disting. Svc. award, Nat. Assn. Schs. Journalism and Mass Comm., 1992, Scripps Howard First Amendment award, 1993, Lifetime Achievement award, Nat. Assn. Minority Media Execs., 2002, Award of Excellence, Am. Pub. Health Assn., 2002, Lewis Hine award for Children and Youth, 2002; named Disting. Alumnus, U. Fla., 1982, Humanitarian of Yr., ARC, 2009—; named one of Miami Today Living Legends, 2013, Spirit of Father Hall of Fame Inductees, Nat. Partnership for Comm. Leadership, 2013. Mem.: Found. for Child Development (chair), Early Childhood Initiative Found. (pres.), Inter-Am. Press Assn. (pres. 1995—96), Am. Soc. Newspaper Editors (pres. 1991—92). Office: 3250 SW 3rd Ave 5th Fl Miami FL 33129 Home Phone: 305-444-8875; Office Phone: 305-646-7229. Business E-Mail: dlawrence@childreadiness.org.

LAWRENCE, MELL, architect; BArch, U. Tex., Austin, 1981. Project arch. Black Atkinson Vernooy Archs., Austin, 1983—85, Charles W. Moore, Arch., Austin, 1985—90; ptnr. Lamb and Lawrence Archs., Austin, 1987—92; founder, prin. Mell Lawrence Archs., Austin, 1992—. Prin. works include Walls Residence, Hays County, Tex., 2001 (Austin AIA Design award, 2004), Foshee Residence, Fayette County, Tex., 2002 (Austin AIA Design award, 2004), Bridle Path Addition, Austin, 2003, Travis Heights Addition, 2003, Graves Residence, 2003, Cuernvaca Pool House, 2004, Breakwater Residence, Jonestown, Tex., 2004, Red Hawk Residence, Wimberley, Tex., 2004, Boonville Hotel + Winery, Boonville, Calif., 2004, Tuttle Garage Apt., Austin, 2004, Sugar Creek Studio/Garage, West Lake Hills, 2005, Big Ranch Rd. Residence, Napa, Calif., 2005. Fellow: AIA. Office: Mell Lawrence Archs 913 W Gibson Austin TX 78704 Office Phone: 512-441-4669. Office Fax: 512-441-9125. Business E-Mail: mell@architecturalpolka.com.

LAWRENCE, TIFFANY ELIZABETH, state legislator; b. Martinsburg, WV, July 13, 1982; d. William A. and Cheryl S. BS, Shepard U.; MBA, Shenandoah U. Coordinator W. Va. Young Democrats 2nd Congressional Dist.; mem. Dist. 58 W.Va. House of Delegates, 2008—, mem. Edn. Com., Health and Human Resources Com. & Polit. Subdivisions Com. Democrat. Methodist. Office: State Capitol Complex Rm 228E, Bldg 1 Charleston WV 25305 Mailing: 19 Baltic Lane Ranson WV 25438 Office Phone: 304-340-3152. E-mail: lawrencefordelegate@hotmail.com.

LAWRENCE, WALTER, JR., surgeon, educator; b. Chgo., May 31, 1925; s. Walter and Violette May (Matthews) L.; m. Susan Grayson Shryock, June 20, 1947; children: Walter Thomas, Elizabeth, William Amos, Edward Gene. Student, Dartmouth Coll., 1943-44; PhB, U. Chgo., 1944, SB, 1945, MD with honors, 1948. Diplomate Am. Bd. Surgery (examiner 1974-78, sr. mem. 1978—). Intern Johns Hopkins, 1948-49, asst. resident, 1949-51; fellow Meml. Sloan-Kettering Cancer Ctr., 1951-52, 54-56, rsch. fellow, 1956, asst. mem., asst. attending surgeon, 1957-60, assoc. mem., assoc. attending surgeon, 1960-66; practice medicine specializing in surgery NYC, 1956-66, Richmond, Va., 1966—. Instr. surgery Cornell U., 1957-58, asst. profl. clin. surgery, 1958-63, clin. assoc. prof., 1963-66; vis. investigator Queen Victoria Hosp., East Grinstead, Eng., 1964-65; prof. surgery Med. Coll. Va., Richmond, 1966-90, prof. emeritus, 1990--, chmn. divsn. surg. oncology, 1966-90, exec. vice chmn. dept. surgery, 1966-73, acting chmn., 1973-74, Am. Cancer Soc. prof. clin. oncology, 1972-77; dir. Massey Cancer Ctr., 1974-88, dir. emeritus, 1988—; chmn. surgery test com. Nat. Bd. Med. Examiners, 1973-77; med. dir.-at-large Va. divsn. Am. Cancer Soc., 1967—, med. v.p. Am. Cancer Soc., 1975-77, pres., 1977-79, nat. del., 1972-76, mem. nat. coun. for rsch. and clin. investigation, 1974-78, mem. profl. edn. com., 1982-96, bd.

dir., 1985-98, vice chmn., chmn. M&S com., 1986-88, chmn. M&S exec. com., 1989-90, pres. elect, 1990-91, nat. pres., 1991-92, past office dir., 1993-99, hon. life mem., 1999—; bd. sci. counsellors Nat. Cancer Inst., 1978-82, chmn. surg. oncology rsch. devel. com.; mem. Nat. Cancer Adv. Bd., 1988-94; governing coun. Internat. Union Against Cancer, 1994-2002. Author: (with J.J. Terz) Cancer Management, 1977, (with J.J. Terz, J.P. Neifeld) Manual of Soft Tissue Surgery, 1983; mem. editl. bd. Va. Med., 1977-93, Jour. Surg. Oncology, 1978—, assoc. editor, 1991—, dep. editor, 2005-09; editl. bd. Jour. Cancer Edn., 1986; asst. editor Cancer, 1962-65, assoc. editor, 1991-2000, mem. editl. bd., 2000-06; contbr. articles to med. jour. Served with USNR, 1942-46, with US Army, 1952-54. Recipient Cancer Rsch. award Alfred P. Sloan Found., 1964; J. Shelton Horsley award Am. Cancer Soc., 1973; Disting. Svc. award U. Chgo., 1976; Va. Commonwealth U. Univ. Award for Excellence, 1988, Disting. Faculty award Med. Coll. Va. Alumni Assn., 1988, Va. Cultural Laureate award, 1992, OBICI award, 1992, Dean's award for Disting. Svc., 1992; named to Humera Soc. (hon.), 1992, Beckstrand Cancer Found. Cancer Fighter of Yr., 1999, Presdl. medallion Va. Commonwealth U., 2000, Lifetime Sci. Achievement award Sci. Mus. Va., 2002; Disting. Svc. Award of Richmond Acad. Medicine, 2003, Robert Irby award, MCV Found., 2009, St. George Nat. award Am. Cancer Soc., 2010. Fellow ACS, Am. Cancer Soc.(commn. on cancer 1973-85, chmn. 1979-81, St. George Nat. award 2010), NY Acad. Sci., Royal Soc. Medicine, Soc. Black Acad. Surgeons (hon.), mem. AAAS, AMA, Am. Assn. Cancer Edn., Am. Assn. Cancer Rsch., Am. Gastroenterol. Assn. (coun. on cancer 1972-76), Am. Surg. Assn., Halsted Soc. (pres. 1975), James Ewing Soc., Soc. Head and Neck Surgeons, Am. Soc. Clin. Oncology, Am. Radium Soc. (exec. coun. 1985-87), Soc. Surgery Alimentary Tract (founder), Soc. Surg. Oncology (exec. com. 1976-77, v.p. 1977-78, pres. 1979-80, chmn. exec. coun. 1980-81, Heritage honoree 2002), Soc. Univ. Surgeons, Surg. Biol. Club III (founding mem.), Transplantation Soc., Collegium Internat. Chirurgiae Digestive, Southeastern Surg. Congress, Pan Am. Med. Assn., Société Internationale de Chirurgie, Va. Surg. Soc. (v.p. 1973-74), Richmond Surg. Soc. (pres. 1986-87), Richmond Acad. Medicine (trustee 1986-87, 1st v.p. 1988, Disting. Svc. award 2003), So. Surg. Assn. (1st v.p. 1999-2000, hon. fellow, 2004), Argentine Surg. Assn. (hon.), Sigma Xi, Alpha Omega Alpha. Home: 6501 Three Chopt Rd Richmond VA 23226-3118 Office: Med Coll Va Hosps 1200 E Broad St PO Box 980011 Richmond VA 23298-0011 Business E-Mail: wlawrence@mcvh-vcu.edu.

LAWRIE, GERALD MURRAY, cardiovascular and thoracic surgeon, educator; b. Murwillumbah, N.S.W., Australia, Oct. 15, 1945; came to U.S., 1974; s. Charles Malcolm and Heather (Murray) L.; m. Susan Wagner, Dec. 28, 1978; children: Heather Cristina, Charles Murray, Elizabeth Jane. Attended, Scots Coll.; MB, BS, U. Sydney Med. Sch., Australia, 1969; MD, Baylor Coll. Medicine, 1974. Resident in gen. surgery Prince Henry/Prince of Wales Teaching Hosps., U. NSW, Sydney, 1969-72, sr. registrar in cardiothoracic surgery, 1973-74; resident in gen. surgery Royal Coll. Surgeons Eng., London, Plymouth Gen. Hosp., U.K., 1972; cardiovascular fellow Baylor Coll. Medicine, Houston, 1974-75, assoc. surgeon, dept. surgery, 1975, instr., 1975-76, asst. prof., 1976-78, assoc. prof., 1978-84, prof., 1984—97, clin. prof. surgery, 1997—, dir. thoracic surgery residency program, 1992-94; assoc. surgeon with Dr. DeBakey, 1975; attending surgeon Methodist Hosp., Houston, 1978—, Michael E. DeBakey Prof. Cardiac Surgery, 2008—, med. dir., Heart Valve Inst.; attending surgeon VA Hosp., Houston, 1980—, Ben Taub Hosp., Houston, 1975—; vice chmn. rsch., dept. surgery St. Joseph Hosp./Baylor Coll. Medicine, Houston, 1995-96; group practice Tex. Surgical Associates, 1997—; cardiothoracic surgeon Methodist DeBakey Heart & Vascular Ctr., Houston. Helped set up cardiovascular surgery programs in Saudi Arabia and Indonesia; helped set up a cardiac surgery program, Glasgow, Scotland, 1994; actively involved in the develop. of new surgical tng. facility, Methodist Inst. for Tech., Innovation and Edn. Methodist Hosp., mem. med. audit com., 1975, med. records com., 1981—82, chmn., cardiovascular patient care com., 1982—84, mem. surgical adv. com., 1983—84, mem. operating room com., 1994—95, mem. quality mgmt. com., 1997—, mem. exec. com., 1999—; mem. admissions com. Baylor Coll. Medicine, 1977—79, course curriculum com., cancer etiology, pathophysiology and prevention, 1980—91, mem. student promotions com., 1981—82, mem. curriculum com., adv. com. for pub. affairs, 1986—88, mem. grad. med. edn. com., 1992—93, mem. curriculum com., 1992—93; mem. ops. com. DeBakey Methodist Heart Ctr., 1999—; invited lectr. in field. Author of several published sci. articles and book chpts. Commonwealth Scholarship Holder, 1963-69; recipient James McRae Yeates prize for Clinical Surgery; Decorated Merit Order of Republic of Egypt, 1980; named leading adult heart surgeon in the U.S.A., Good Houskeeping Mag., 1996. Fellow Royal Coll. Surgeons (Edinburgh), Royal Australasian Coll. Surgeons, Royal Coll. Surgeons Can., Am. Coll. Cardiology (Gov.'s award 1983); mem. ACS, AMA, Am. Heart Assn. (pres. Houston chpt. 1985-86, bd. dirs. Tex. chpt. 1986-89, editl. task force, Houston Divsn. 1983-84, chmn. program com., Houston Divsn., 1984-85, Meritorious Svc. award, 1983, Vol. Recognition award, Houston, 1986), Am. Coll. Chest Physicians, South Tex. chpt. ACS, DeBakey Internat. Cardiovascular Soc., Houston Cardiology Soc. (sec./treas. 1980-81, v.p. 1981-82, pres. 1982-83), Harris County Med. Soc., Southwestern Surg. Congress, Tex. Med. Assn., Royal Soc. Medicine (assoc.), Soc. Thoracic Surgeons, Soc. for Vascular Surgery, Internat. Cardiovascular Soc. (N.Am. chpt.), Internat. Soc. for Minimally Invasive Cardiac Surgery, Am. Assn. for Thoracic Surgery, Soc. for Thoracic Surg. Edn., So. Surg. Assn., N.Am. Soc. Pacing and Electrophysiology, Soc. Med. Consultants to the Armed Forces, Houston Electrophysiological Soc. (treas. 1982-83, v.p. 1983-84, pres. 1984-85). Presbyterian. Participated in the surgical care of notable figures such as Shah of Iran, President of Turkey, the King of Belgium, and a number of royal figures; invented a technique called the American Correction; first to use a surgical robot to successfully repair a mitral valve using this advanced technique, 2007; performed heart surgery on Former First Lady Barbara Bush in 2009. Office: 6560 Fannin St Ste 1842 Houston TX 77030 Office Phone: 713-790-2089. Office Fax: 713-794-0576. Business E-Mail: glawrie@TexasSurgical.com.

LAWRIE, MIKE, information technology executive; BA in History, Ohio U.; MBA, Drexel U., Phila. Joined IBM, 1977, gen. mgr. industries for Asia-Pacific bus. ops. Tokyo, 1995—97, gen. mgr. Europe, the Mid. East and Africa, 1998—2001, sr. v.p. and group exec. worldwide sales and distbn., 2001—04; CEO Siebel Systems, Inc., San Mateo, Calif., 2004—05; ptnr. ValueAct Capital, San Francisco, 2005—06; pres., CEO Misys plc, London, 2006—12, exec. chmn. Allscripts-Misys Healthcare Solutions, Inc., 2008—10; dir., pres., CEO Computer Sciences Corp., Church Falls, Va., 2012—. Lead ind. non-exec. dir. Juniper Networks, Inc. Trustee Drexel U. Office: Computer Sciences Corporation 3170 Fairview Park Dr Falls Church VA 22042

LAWSON, GARY B., lawyer; b. NYC, Oct. 5, 1945; s. Dave and Rose Helen (Shapiro) Levy; m. Marcia Krauss, June 19, 1981. AA, Queens Coll., 1966; JD, St. Johns U., 1970; LLM in Taxation, NYU, 1974. Bar: NY, Wis. 73, Ill. 76, Ga. 83, Mass. 83, Tex. 84. Atty. Mut. Life Ins. Co., NYC, 1970—72; assoc. Hoyt, Greene, Meissner and Walsh, Milw., 1972—74, Walsh & Simon, Milw., 1974—76; ptnr. Katten, Muchin, Zavis, Pearl & Galler, Chgo., 1976—81; of counsel Haas, Holland, Lipshutz, Levison & Gilbert, Atlanta, 1981—82, Mintz, Levin, Cohn, Ferris, Glovsky & Popeo, P.C., Boston, 1982—84, Jenkens & Gilchrist, Dallas, 1987—93, Godwin & Carlton, 1987—93, Lawson & Fields P.C., 1993—2002, Lawson, Fields, McCue & Campbell P.C., Addison, Tex., 2002—03, Lawson, Fields & Calhoun P.C., 2004—05, Goodwin, Pappas, Langley & Ronquillo, LLP, Dallas, 2005—08, Strasburger Price LLP, 2008—. Instr. U. Wis.-Milw., 1975. Bd. dirs. Parental Stress Svcs., Chgo., 1980—81, Hope Found., 1989—92, Medisend Internat., 1990—98. Mem.: Boston Estate and Bus. Planning Coun., S.W. Pension Conf. (bd. dirs. 1986—89), New Eng. Employee Benefits Coun. (bd. dirs. 1983—85), ABA (tax sect.). Office: Strasburger Price LLP 901 Main St Ste 4400 Dallas TX 75202 Office Phone: 214-651-4307.

LAWSON, HUGH, federal judge; b. Hawkinsville, Ga., 1941; BA, Emory U., Atlanta, 1963, JD, 1964. Pvt. practice atty., Hawkinsville, Ga., 1965—79; judge Superior Ct. Ga., Oconee Jud. Cir., 1979—95, US Dist. Ct. (mid. dist.) Ga., Macon, 1995—2006, chief judge, 2006—08, sr. judge, 2008—. Office: PO Box 838 Macon GA 31202

LAWSON, RHEA BROWN, library director; b. SC; 1 child, Ebony. BA in Polit. Sci., Morgan State U., Balt.; M in Libr. and Info. Sci., U. Md., College Park; PhD in Libr. and Info. Studies, U. Wis., Madison. Chief Ctrl. Libr. Bklyn. Pub. Libr., NY, 1999—2003; dep. dir. Detroit Pub. Libr., Mich., 2003—05; dir. Houston Pub. Libr., Tex., 2005—. Bd. dirs. Pub. Libr. Assn.; exec. bd. mem. Black Caucus of ALA; mem. Money Smart adv. bd. Fed. Res. Bank; adv. bd. mem. Medgar Evers Coll. Ctr. Black Lit. Office: Houston Pub Libr 500 McKinney St Houston TX 77002 Office Phone: 832-393-1313. E-mail: library.director@cityofhouston.net.

LAXMINARAYANA, DAMA, geneticist, researcher, educator; b. Hyderabad, India, Apr. 20, 1953; came to U.S., 1990; s. Kishtaiah and Sathyamma; m. Dara Jayalakshmi; children: Dama Bhargavi, Dama Sriharsha, Dama Vishnupriya. BSc, Osmania U., Hyderabad, 1974, MSc, 1976, PhD, 1982. Jr. sci. asst. dept. genetics Osmania U., 1977-78, lectr. dept. zoology, 1985-90; jr. rsch. fellow Indian Dept. Atomic Energy, 1978-81, postdoctoral fellow, 1982-83, rsch. assoc., 1983-85; postdoctoral fellow dept. medicine Case Western Res. U. Sch. Medicine, Cleve., 1990-91; rsch. assoc. dept. internal medicine Wake Forest U. Sch. Medicine, Winston-Salem, N.C., 1991-94, rsch. instr., 1994-98, rsch. asst. prof., 1998—. Conf. presenter in field; editor-in-chief Clin. Medicine: Pathology, 2007-; editl. bd. mem. Clin. Medicine: Arthritis and Musculoskeletal Disorders, 2007- Contbr. articles to sci. jours., chpts. to books. Mem. AAAS, Am. Assn. Immunologists, Am. Coll. Rheumatology, Environ. Mutagen Soc. India, India Soc. Cell Biology, Soc. Geneticists and Cytologists India, N.Y. Acad. Scis. Home: 444 Lynn Ave Winston Salem NC 27104 Office: Wake Forest U Sch Medicine Dept Internal Medicine Medical Center Blvd Winston Salem NC 27157 Personal E-mail: laxmina@triad.rr.com.

LAY, NORVIE LEE, law educator; b. Cardwell, Ky., Apr. 17, 1940; s. Arlie H. and Opha (Burns) L.; 1 dau., Lea Anne. BS, U. Ky., 1960; JD, U. Louisville, 1963; LLM, U. Mich., 1964, SJD, 1967. Bar: Ky. 1963. Asst. prof. law U. Louisville, 1964-67, assoc. prof., 1967-70, prof., 1970—; asst. dean U. Louisville Sch. Law, 1971-73, assoc. dean, 1973-84, acting dean, 1981-82. Vis. prof. Southwestern U. Sch. Law, summer 1983, N.Y. Law Sch., 1983-84, Coll. of Law U. Iowa, summer 1989. Author: Tax and Estate Planning for Community Property and the Migrant Client, 1970; contbr. articles to profl. jours. Trustee St. Joseph's Infirmary, 1974-78, S.W. Jefferson Community Hosp., 1979-80, Suburban Hosp., 1981-84, Humana-Audubon Hosp., 1985-88, U. Louisville Law Sch. Alumni Found., from 1982-85; bd. dirs. Louisville Ballet, from 1982-88, Louisville Theatrical Assn., 1985-88, Louisville Art Gallery, 1984-87, Watertower Art Assn., 1986-89, Chamber Mus. Soc. of Louisville, 1985-88, Louisville Chorus, 1985-88, Ky. Contemporary Theatre, 1984, Ky. Country Day Sch., 1985-88, Ky. Arts Coun., 1991—; mem. Nat. Conf. Commrs. Uniform State Laws. Recipient Scholarship Key Delta Theta Phi, 1963, Outstanding Graduating Sr. award Omicron Delta Kappa, 1963 Fellow Am. Coll. of Trust and Estate Counsel (acad.), Am. Coll. Tax Counsel; mem. ABA, Ky. Bar Assn., Louiville Bar Assn., Am. Judicature Soc. Republican. Baptist. Office: U Louisville Sch Law Belknap Campus Louisville KY 40292-0001 Office Phone: 502-852-6374.

LAYCOCK, HAROLD DOUGLAS, law educator, writer; b. Alton, Ill., Apr. 15, 1948; s. Harold Francis and Claudia Anita (Garrette) L.; m. Teresa A. Sullivan, June 14, 1971; children: Joseph Peter, John Patrick. BA, Mich. State U., 1970; JD, U. Chgo., 1973. Bar: Ill. 1973, US Dist. Ct. (no. dist.) Ill. 1973, Tex. 1974, US Dist. Ct. (we. dist.) Tex. 1975, US Ct. Appeals (5th and 11th cirs.) 1975, US Supreme Ct. 1976, US Ct. Appeals (6th cir.) 1987, US Ct. Appeals (8th cir.) 1994, US Ct. Appeals (10th cir.) 1997, US Ct. Appeals (3rd cir.) 2003, Mich. 2007. Law clk. to judge U.S. Ct. Appeals (7th cir.), Chgo., 1973-74; pvt. practice Austin, Tex., 1974-76; asst. prof. U. Chgo., 1976-80, prof., 1980-81, U. Tex., Austin, 1981—, endowed professorships, 1983-88, assoc. dean for acad. affairs, 1985-86, endowed chair, 1988—2006, assoc. dean for rsch., 1991—2006, emeritus endowed chair, 2006—; endowed chair U. Mich., Ann Arbor, 2006—10, U. Va., Charlottesville, 2010—. Vis. prof. U. Mich., 1990; reporter com. on motion practice Ill. Jud. Conf., 1977-78, edtl. bd. mem. Ecclesiastical Law Jour., 2009- Author: Modern American Remedies, 1985, 4th. edit., 2010, Religious Liberty, The Death of the Irreparable Injury Rule, 1991; mem. bd. advisors Religious Freedom Reporter, 1990-2001 Edior: Same-Sex Marriage and Religious Liberty, 2008; contbr. articles to profl. jours. Adv. bd. Consumer Svcs. Orgn., Chgo., 1979-80; exec. bd. Ctr. for Ch./State Studies, DePaul U., Chgo., 1982-87; adv. com. on religious liberty Presbyn. Ch. U.S.A., 1983-88, advisor restatement of restitution, 1984-85, 97—; v.p. St. Francis Sch., 1990-92, bd. dirs., 1990—, pres. 1992-2001; bd. adv. J.M. Dawson Inst. Ch./State Studies, Baylor U., 1990—; judicial speech adv. com., Supreme Ct. of Tex., 2002; adv. com. jud. ethics Supreme Ct. Tex., 2004. Recipient Scribes Book award, ABA, 1991, Civil Libertarian of Yr., ACLU of Tex., 2000, Civitatis award for disting. lifetime svc., U. Tex., 2005. Fellow AAAS, Internat. Acad. for Freedom of Religion and Belief; mem. AAUP (mem. com. on status of women in acad. profession 1982-85), Am. Law Inst. (2nd. v.p., 2008-mem. coun. 2001—), Chgo. Coun. Lawyers (v.p. 1977-78), Assn. Am. Law Schs. (chmn., sec. on remedies 1983, 94), chmn., sec. on constitutional law, 2000). Home: 2197 Gray Fox Ct Ann Arbor MI 48103 Office: University Va Law Sch 580 Massie Rd Charlottesville VA 22903 Home: 1910 Carrs Hill Rd Charlottesville VA 22903 Business E-Mail: laycockd@umich.edu.

LAYDEN, SCOTT, professional sports team executive; m. Marsha Layden; children: Sarah, Hannah, Mary Frances, Emma Grace. B in Bus. Mgmt., St. Francis Coll., Loretto, Pa., 1980. Asst. coach Fairleigh Dickinson U. Knights, NJ, 1980—81, Utah Jazz, 1981—88, 2005—12, dir. player pers., 1988—92, dir. basketball ops., 1992—96, v.p., 1996—99; exec. v.p., gen. mgr. NY Knicks, 1999—2001, pres., gen.mgr., 2001—03; guest commentator NBA TV, 2004; asst. gen. mgr. San Antonio Spurs, 2012—. Named NBA Exec. of Yr., The Sporting News, 1995. Office: San Antonio Spurs 1 AT&T Center Pky San Antonio TX 78219

LAYMAN, DAVID MICHAEL, lawyer; b. Pensacola, Fla., July 28, 1955; s. James Hugh and Winifred (Smith) L. BA with high honors, U. Fla., 1977, JD with honors, 1979. Bar: Fla. 1980. Assoc. Gunster, Yoakley, Criser & Stewart, West Palm Beach, Fla., 1980-83, Wolf, Block, Schorr & Solis-Cohen, West Palm Beach, 1983-87, ptnr., 1987-88; shareholder Shapiro and Bregman P.A., 1988-91, Greenberg, Traurig, Hoffman, Lipoff, Rosen & Quentel, P.A., West Palm Beach, Fla., 1991-93, Prom, Korn & Zehmer, P.A., Jacksonville, Fla., 1993-94, Mahoney Adams & Criser, P.A., Jacksonville, Fla., 1994-96, Greenberg, Traurig, P.A., West Palm Beach, Fla., 1996—. Mem. Attys. Title Ins. Fund. Contbg. editor U. Fla. Law Rev.; contbr. articles to profl. jours. Del. Statewide Rep. Caucus, Orlando, Fla., 1986; mem. Blue Ribbon Zoning Rev. Com., West Palm Beach, 1986; bd. dirs., pres. Palm Beach County Planning Congress, 1984-89; trustee South Fla. Sci. Mus., 1994-96; bd. dirs., sec., v.p. Ronald McDonald House, Jacksonville, 1994-96, Cultural Coun. of Greater Jacksonville; bd. dirs., pres.-elect Children's Pl. at Home Safe Inc., 1996—; mem. vestry, sr. warden Holy Trinity Episcopal Ch., West Palm Beach, 2002-03, 08-10. Named one of Outstanding Young Men in Am., 1980. Mem. ABA, Fla. Bar Assn. (bd. govs. young lawyers divsn. 1989-91), Palm Beach County Bar Assn. (pres. young lawyers sect. 1987-88), Fla. Blue Key, Palm Beach County Gator Club (pres., bd. dirs. 1981-85), Omicron Delta Kappa, Sigma Chi, Phi Kappa Phi. Episcopalian. Office: 777 S Flagler Dr Ste 300E West Palm Beach FL 33401-6161 Office Phone: 561-650-7990. Business E-Mail: laymand@gtlaw.com.

LAYNE, JAMES NATHANIEL, retired vertebrate biologist; b. Chgo., May 16, 1926; s. Leslie Joy and Harriet (Hausmann) L.; m. Lois Virginia Linderoth, Aug. 26, 1950; children: Linda Carrie, Kimberly, Jamie Linderoth, Susan Nell, Rachel Pratt. BA, Cornell U., Ithaca, NY, 1950, PhD, 1954. Grad. tchg. asst. Cornell U., Ithaca, NY, 1950-54, assoc. prof. zoology, 1963-67; asst. prof. zoology Southern Ill. U., Carbondale, 1954-55; asst. prof., then assoc. prof. biology U. Fla., 1955-63; asst. curator, then assoc. curator mammals Fla. State Mus., Gainesville, 1955-63, rsch. assoc., 1963-65; Archbold curator mammals American Mus. Natural History, 1967-85; dir. rsch. and exec. dir. Archbold Biol. Sta., sr. rsch. biologist, 1985-94, sr. rsch. biologist emeritus, 1994—. Rsch. assoc. Fla. State Collection of Arthropods, American Mus. Natural History; vis. scientist primate ecology sect. Nat. Inst. Neurol. Diseases and Blindness, summers 1961-62; adj. prof. biology U. South Fla., 1968-89; adj. prof. biol. sciences Fla. Atlantic U., 1980-84; cons. ecology sect. WHO, 1969; mem. Fla. com. Rare and Endangered Plants and Animals; mem. Fla. Panther Recovery team US Dept. Interior; mem. rodent specialist group Species Survival Commn.; mem. reclamation rsch. com. Fla. Ins. Phosphate Rsch.; mem. resource planning and mgmt. com. Kissimee River. Contbr. articles and chpts. to profl. jours. and books. Hon. trustee Fla. Defenders of Environment; bd. dirs. Fla. Audubon Soc.; mem. Fla. Nongame Wildlife Adv. Council, Peace River Basin Bd., Fla. Panther Tech. Adv. Coun. Served with USAAF, 1944-46. bd., Inst. of Environ. Studies U. of South Fla. Fellow AAAS; mem. American Soc. Zoologists, American Soc. Mammalogists (pres. 1970-72, hon. mem. 1993, C. Hart Merriam award 1976), Ecol. Soc. American, Soc. for Study of Evolution, American Soc. Naturalists, Wildlife Soc., Wildlife Disease Assn., Nature Conservancy (trustee Fla. chpt.), Fla. Acad. Sciences (pres. 1984-85, medalist 1995), Orgn. Biol. Field Stas. (pres. 1986-87), Phi Beta Kappa, Sigma Xi, Phi Kappa Phi, Phi Sigma. Business E-Mail: jlayne@strato.net.

LAYTON, DONALD HARVEY, mortgage company executive, retired investment company executive; b. May 9, 1950; s. Irving and Charlotte (Bell) Layton; m. Sandra Lynn Lazo, June 1, 1974. BS in Economics, MIT, 1970, MS in Economics, 1972; MBA, Harvard U., 1974. Rsch. asst. Harvard Bus. Sch., Boston, 1974-75; various positions through sr. mng. dir. Mfrs. Hanover Trust Co., NYC, 1975-91; sr. exec. v.p. Chem. Bank, 1992—95; vice-chmn. Chem Bank, 1995, Chase Manhattan Bank, 1996—2001, J.P. Morgan Chase & Co., 2002—04; chmn. E*TRADE Financial Corp., 2007—09, CEO, 2008—09; sr. advisor, co-chair investment com. NewOak Capital LLC, NYC, 2010—12; CEO Freddie Mac (Federal Home Loan Mortgage Corp.), McLean, Va., 2012—. Bd. dirs. Assured Guaranty Ltd., 2005—12, American Internat. Group, Inc. (AIG), 2010—12, Freddie Mac (Federal Home Loan Mortgage Corp.), 2012—; sr. advisor Securities & Financial Markets Assn., 2006—08. Bd. dirs. Fgn. Policy Assn., 1998—2006; chmn. bd. dirs. Partnership for Homeless, NYC, 2005—. Baker scholar, 1974. Office: Freddie Mac 8200 Jones Branch Dr Mc Lean VA 22102 Personal E-mail: dhlaytonny@aol.com.*

LAYTON, WILLIAM GEORGE, consultant, retired human resources and import/export company executive; b. Missouri Valley, Iowa, Sept. 11, 1931; s. George Holbert and Margaret (Wilson) L.; m. Caroline R. Tiffany, June 27, 1953; children: Kathleen Layton Medl, Sara Layton Howe, Thomas William. BA, Coe Coll., 1953; MA, U. Ill., 1955. Indsl. rels. trainee Procter & Gamble Co., Cin., 1955-57, pers. specialist, 1957-62, indsl. rels. mgr. France, 1962-66, pers. mgr. European Tech. Ctr., 1966-69, pers. mgr. internat., 1969-72; v.p. human resources Food Svc. div. Heublein, Inc., Louisville, 1972-77; sr. v.p. human resources Holiday Inns, Inc., Memphis, 1977-83; pres. Layton Group, St. Petersburg, Fla., 1983—2001; sr. ptnr. Johnson-Layton Co. Mgmt. Cons., L.A. and St. Petersburg, 1985-95; pres. CompCom, Inc., 1994-97; chmn., CEO Appliances Internat., Inc., 1997—2002; cons. Transylvania County NC Econ. Devel. Dept., 2004—13; sr. mgr. Pet Protector, 2013—. Bd. dirs., pres. Jr. Achievement of Memphis, 1981-83; mem. Tenn. Jobs Tng. Coordinating Coun., 1982-88; mem. Pvt. Industry Coun. of Memphis and Shelby County, 1982-88; mem. Pres.'s Coun., Rhodes Coll., Memphis, 1983-90. Served with USAF, 1953-55. Mem.: Coun. Mgmt. Cons. (Sr. Examiner Sterling Quality award Fla. 1994), Inst. Mgmt. Cons. (cert. mgmt. cons.), Am. Mgmt. Assn. (human resources coun. 1981—83), Rotary, Phi Beta Kappa. Independent. Presbyterian.

LAZARUS, MARK, marketing executive; married; 3 children. BA, Vanderbilt U. Network buyer & planner Backer, Spielvogel & Bates, Inc.; account exec. NBC Cable, Turner Broadcasting Sales, 1990—98; exec. v.p. Turner Sports Sales, 1998—99; pres. Turner Sports, 1999—2002, Turner Entertainment Sales & Mktg., 2002—03, Turner Entertainment Group, 2003—08; pres., Media & Mktg. Svcs. Career Sports & Entertainment, 2008—. Bd. dirs. Compass Diversified Holdings, 2009—, Cincinnati Bell, Inc. Nat. trustee Boys & Girls Clubs Am. Named one of Media Mavens, Ad Age, 2000, 40 Under 40 Top Sports Execs., Sports Bus. Jour., 2000, 2001, 100 Most Powerful People in Sports, Sporting News, 2000. Mem.: Sigma Chi. Office: Career Sports & Entertainment Inc 600 Galleria Pky Ste 1900 Atlanta GA 30339 Office Phone: 770-955-1300.

LAZZARA, RALPH, cardiologist; b. Tampa, Fla., Aug. 14, 1934; s. Bennie Lazzara and Rosalie Spoto; m. Barbara Jolly; children: Ralph, Melissa, Rosalie D'Innella. BS, U. of Chgo., 1955; MD, Tulane Med. Sch., La., 1959. Lic. Am. Bd. of Internal Med, 1967, Cardiovascular

Diseases Am. Bd. of Internal Medicine, 1968. Cardiology sect. chief U. of Okla. Health Scis. Ctr., Oklahoma City, 1978—98, prof. of medicine, 1978—; med. dir. Heart Rhythm Inst., Oklahoma City, 1998—. Author: (3 medical textbooks) Cardiology Medical Textbooks; contbr. 64 med. texbook chpts., over 280 peer-rev. jour. articles to med. jours. Lt. col. US Army, 1967—70, Denver, CO. Recipient Disting. Scientist award, Heart Rhythm Soc., 1999, Regent's Prof. of Medicine, U. of Okla. Health Scis. Ctr., 2003, Disting. Alumnus award, Tulane Med. Sch., 2010. Fellow: European Soc. Cardiology, Heart Rhythm Soc. (nat. pres. 1995—96), Am. Coll. of Cardiology; mem.: AHA. Achievements include patents for System For Prevention Of Paroxysmal Supraventricular Tachycardia. Office: University Okla Health Scis Ctr Heart Rhythm Inst 1200 Everett Dr Rm 6E103 Oklahoma City OK 73104

LAZZARA, RICHARD ALLEN, federal judge; b. Tampa, Fla., 1945; BA, Loyola U. New Orleans, 1967; JD, U. Fla., 1970. Law clk. Solicitor Office Hillsborough County, Fla., 1970, asst. county solicitor, 1970—72, asst. state atty., 1973, judge, 1987; pvt. practice atty. Tampa, Fla., 1974—86; cir. judge 13th Jud. Dist. Fla., 1988—93; appellate judge 2nd Dist. Ct. Appeal, Fla., 1993—97; judge US Dist. Ct. (middle dist.) Fla., Tampa, 1997—2011, sr. judge, 2011—. Office: US Dist Ct Gibbons US Courthouse 801 N Florida Ave Tampa FL 33602 Office Phone: 813-301-5350. Office Fax: 813-301-5359.*

LE, DUY-LOAN, electrical engineer; b. Vietnam; arrived in U.S., 1975; married; 2 children. BSEE magna cum laude, U. Tex., 1982; MBA, U. Houston. With Tex. Instruments, 1982—, now sr. fellow. Contbr. articles to profl. publs. Named One of Houston's Women on the Move, Tex. Exec. Women, Nat. Technologist of Yr., Women of Color, Asian Am. Engr. of Yr.; named one of America 's Top Women in Bus.-Game Changers, Pink mag. & Forté Found., 2007; named to Women Tech. Internat. Hall of Fame, WITI. Achievements include 23 patents in field. Office: Texas Instruments MS 722 12203 SW Freeway Stafford TX 77477 Office Phone: 281-274-3714.

LEA, ANDREA, state legislator; m. Phillip Lea; children: Kevin, Andrew, Mary. BS in Emergency Adminstrn. & Mgmt., Ark. Tech. U. Mem. Dist. 68 Ark. House of Reps., 2009—. Auditor & author Ark. Law Enforcement Resource Manual; justice of the peace Pope County Quorum Ct. Mem. Russellville City Coun.; session clerk Russellville Central Presbyn. Ch.; chmn. Jail Renovation Com. Republican. Office: State Capitol Rm 350 Little Rock AR 72201 also: PO Box 1342 Russellville AR 72811 Office Phone: 501-682-6211, 501-682-7771, 479-967-4922. Business E-Mail: leaa@arkleg.state.ar.us.

LEA, LORENZO BATES, lawyer; b. St. Louis, Apr. 12, 1925; s. Lorenzo Bates and Ursula Agnes (Gibson) L.; m. Marcia Gwendolyn Wood, Mar. 21, 1953; children— Victoria, Jennifer, Christopher. BS, MIT, 1946; JD, U. Mich., 1949; grad. Advanced Mgmt. Program, Harvard U., 1964. Bar: Ill. 1950. With Amoco Corp. (formerly Standard Oil Co. Ind.), Chgo., 1949—89, asst. gen. counsel, 1963-71, assoc. gen. counsel, 1971-72, gen. counsel, 1972-78, v.p., gen. counsel, 1978-89. Trustee Village of Glenview, Ill., 1963-64, mem. Zoning Bd., 1961-63; bd. dirs. Chgo. Crime Commn., 1978—, Midwest Coun. for Internat. Econ. Policy, 1973—, Chgo. Bar Found., 1981—, Chgo. Area Found. for Legal Svcs., 1981—; bd. dirs. United Charities of Chgo., 1973—, chmn., 1985—; bd. dirs. Cmty. Found. Collier County, 1997—, Naples Bot. Garden, 2000—. Served with USNR, 1943-46. Mem. ABA, Am. Petroleum Inst., Am. Arbitration Assn. (dir. 1980—), Ill. Bar Assn., Chgo. Bar Assn., Assn. Gen. Counsel (bd. dirs. 1983-89), Order of Coif, Law Club, Econs. Club, Legal, Mid-Am. (Chgo.), Glen View, Wyndemere, Hole-In-The-Wall, Naples Yatch Club, Sigma Xi. Republican. Mem. United Ch. of Christ.

LEA, SCOTT CARTER, retired packaging company executive; b. New Orleans, Nov. 14, 1931; s. Leonard G. and Helen (Stoughton) L.; m. Marilyn Ruth Blair, Oct. 25, 1957; children: Scott, Nancy B., Mark S. BA, Amherst Coll., 1954; MBA, U. Pa., 1959. Sales and mktg. positions Riegel Paper, 1959-66, sales mgr. folding carton dept. southeastern div., 1966-67, gen. sales mgr., 1967-69, v.p. folding carton dept., 1969-71; v.p. bd. conversion div. Rexham Corp., Charlotte, NC, 1971-73, v.p. packaging group, 1973-74, pres., 1974-90; chmn. bd. Rexham Industries, Inc., 1990-92; bd. dirs. Lance Inc., Charlotte, 1994—2005, chmn. bd. dirs., 1996-99; ret., 1999. Trustee Johnson C. Smith U., Charlotte, N.C., 1977-2003, vice chmn. bd. trustees, 1998-2003; bd. dirs. Ctrl. Piedmont C.C. Found., Charlotte. With U.S. Army, 1954-57. Mem.: N.C. Zool. Soc. (bd. dirs. 1996—2002), Charlotte C. of C. (bd. dirs. 1977—78), Wild Dunes Club (Isle of Palms, S.C.), Quail Hollow Club, Carmel Country Club. Home: 3704 Stone Ct Charlotte NC 28226-7343 Office: 6135 Park South Dr Ste 510 Charlotte NC 28210

LEA, STANLEY E., artist, educator; b. Joplin, Mo., Apr. 5, 1930; s. Everett G. and Edna F. L.; m. Ruth Lowe, Aug. 19, 1951; children: Kristy Ruth, Kraig, Kelly B. B.F.A., Pitts. State U., 1953; M.F.A., U. Ark., 1961. Prof. art Sam Houston State U., Huntsville, 1961-93, Mexican Field Sch., Puebla, Mexico, 1963-65; vis. artist prof. Mus. Fine Arts, Houston, 1968, 69, 70; prof. art study abroad program London, 1977-78. Juror various art exhibits, 1970-81; workshop demonstrator, E. Tex. State U., Commerce, 1977, 10th ann. color print symposium, Tex. Tech. U., Lubbock, 1983, City of Huntsville mural, 1980; one-man shows paintings and/or prints, Valley House Gallery, Dallas, 1963, Inst. Mex. N. Am. de Rels., Mexico City, 1967, Main Place Gallery, Dallas, 1970-71, U. Tex. Med. Ctr., San Antonio, 1970, Moody Gallery, Houston, 1976, Sol Del Rio, San Antonio, 1978, 89, Adelle M. Fine Arts, Dallas, 1978, Dubose Gallery, Houston, 1980, Cultural Activities Ctr., Temple, Tex., 1982, Tex. A&M U., College Station, 1986, Mus. at E. Tex., Lufkin, 1989Cultural Ctr., Bryan, Tex., 1993, Wynne Art Ctr., Tex., 2008; numerous group shows, latest being Moody Gallery, Houston, 1975, 77, Pecan Square Gallery, Austin, Tex., 1977, Am. Painters In Paris, 1975-76, Waco Art Center, Waco, Tex., 1977, East Tex. State U., Commerce, 1977, Galveston (Tex.) Art Center, 1978, Twenty Five Nat. Printmaker, Lubbock, Tex., 1978, Beaumont (Tex.) Art Mus., 1978, Art League of Houston, 1978, Gates Gallery, Port Arthur, Tex., 1979, Ars Longa, Houston, 1974, Laguna Gloria Mus., Austin, 1979; represented in permanent collections, Library of Congress, Washington, Smithsonian Mus. Am. Art, Washington, Calif. Palace of Legion of Honor, San Francisco, Brit. Mus., London, Mus. Fine Arts, Houston, USIA, N.Y.C., N.Y. Public Library, N.Y.C., Mpls. Inst. Art, Kalamazoo Inst. Art, Boise (Idaho) Gallery of Art, Madison (Wis.) Art Center, Spiva Art Center, Joplin, Mo., Ft. Worth Art Mus., Convention Ctr., The Woodlands, Tex., Cleve. Mus., Inst. Mexicano Norteamericana de Relationes, Mexico City, also corp. and pvt. collections. (Recipient numerous awards, latest being, Southwest Graphics Invitational award 1971, Dimensions IX Exhbn. award 1974, 68th Nat. Tex. Fine Arts Exhbn. 1979), 203 competitive one-man and group exhbns. Sam Houston State U. grantee, 1970, 74, Lakeside (Mich.) Studio grantee 1972, Casa Argentina grantee, Buenos Aires, 1973, Europe, 1982. Home: 3324 Winter Way Huntsville TX 77340-8919

LEACH, KEN, retired utilities executive; b. Minden, La., Feb. 26, 1940; B, U. North Tex. Mem. sales promotion dept. Am. Petrofina; congl. aide Congressman Frank Ikard; civilian planning and devel. divsn. Dallas Police Dept.; adminstr. field ops. divsn. Ft. Worth Water Dept. Served USN, Vietnam. Democrat. Office: PO Box 264 Gainesville TX 76241

LEACH, MAURICE DERBY, JR., librarian, educator; b. Lexington, Ky., June 23, 1923; s. Maurice Derby and Sallie Eleanor (Woods) L.; m. Virginia Stuart Baskett, Mar. 16, 1953; 1 dau., Sarah Stuart. AB, U. Ky., 1945; B.L.S., U. Chgo., 1946. Bibliographer Dept. State, 1947-50; fgn. service officer Dept. State USIS, vice consul, attache Cairo and Alexandria, Beirut, 1950-59; chmn. dept. library sci. U. Ky., 1959-66; regional program officer Ford Found., Beirut, 1967-68; univ. librarian, prof. Washington and Lee U., Lexington, Va., 1968-85, prof., asst. to pres., 1985-88; library adviser Nat. Library, Egypt, Lebanon and acad. libraries in Middle East. Contbr. articles to profl. jours. Served with AUS, 1948-49. Mem. English Speaking Union (pres. Lexington br. 1970-75), Va. Libr. Assn. (pres. 1976), Assn. Preservation of Va. Activities (dir. Lexington br. 1989-91), Rockbridge Hist. Soc., SAR (v.p. 1990-93). Episcopalian. Home: 1 Courtland Cir Lexington VA 24450-1813

LEADER, CHRISTOPHER ROBERT, manufacturing executive; b. South Bend, Ind. s. Robert A. and Dorothy R. Leader; m. Linda A. Hoyt; 3 children. BS in Mech. Engring., U. Notre Dame, Ind., 1981; MBA, U. Mich. Stephen M. Ross Sch. Bus., 1991. Statis. process control analyst GM, Saginaw, Mich., 1985-87, sr. quality engr., 1987-91; prodn. mgr. Ford Motor Co., Avon Lake, Ohio, 1991-93, vehicle evaluation mgr., 1993-94; v.p. ops. Trek USA Bicycle Corp., Waterloo, Wis., 1994-96; corp. v.p. ops. Skyline Corp., Elkhart, Ind., 1997—2009; COO Hi-BeamWebDesign.com, 2009—10, Hoshizaki America, Inc., Peachtree City, Ga., 2010—. Lt. USN, 1981—85. Mailing: Hoshizaki America Inc 618 Hwy 74 S Peachtree City GA 30269

LEAHY, PAT (P. PATRICK LEAHY), geologist, former federal official; b. Troy, NY, Feb. 9, 1947; s. William P. and Shirley A. (Breen) L.; m. Catherine McGuane, July 8, 1972; children: Sarah J., W. Dennis, M. Brendan. BS, Boston Coll., 1968, MS, 1970; PhD, Rensselaer Poly. Inst., 1979. Registered profl. hydrogeologist and geologist. Hydrologist US Geol. Survey, US Dept. Interior, Dover, Del., 1974-79, asst. dist. chief Trenton, NJ, 1979-88, staff scientist Reston, Va., 1988-91, dep. asst. chief hydrologist, 1991-95, chief geologist, 1995—2006, assoc. dir. for geology, geologic discipline, 2005—06, dir., 2005—06; exec. dir. Am. Geol. Inst., Alexandria, Va., 2007—. Chair US Nat. Com. on Geology NAS, US 1999. Author: U.S. Geological Survey Professional Paper. Recipient Meritorious Svc. award, US Dept. Interior, 1996, Disting. Svc. award, Award of Excellence in Sci., Boston Coll. Alumni Assn., 1996, Khan Superior State medal, Afghanistan, 2007; named Presdl. Meritorious Exec., 2003, Presdl. Disting. Exec., 2007; Rensselaer Poly. Inst. Alumni Assn. Sci. fellow, 1995, Galey Pub. Svc. award, Am. Inst. Profl. Geologists, 2009. Fellow Geol. Soc. Am.; mem. Am. Geophys. Union, Am. Water Resources Assn., Am. Inst. Hydrology (pres. 2004), Internat. Assn. Hydrologists (pres. 1999), Am. Assn. Petroleum Geologists. Office: Am Geological Inst 4220 King St Alexandria VA 22302 Home: 2614 Checkerberry Ct Reston VA 20191

LEAK, ROBERT EDWARDS, economic development consultant; b. Charlotte, NC, Sept. 15, 1934; s. James Pickett and Cornelia (Edwards) L.; m. Martha Councill, Aug. 25, 1956; children: Robert E., James Councill. BS, Duke U., 1956; MS, U. Tenn., 1957. With Pan Am. Petroleum Co., Lafayette, La., 1957-59, Allied Securities Corp., Raleigh, NC, 1961-62, Cameron Brown Mortgage Co., Raleigh and Charlotte, 1962-64, N.C. Dept. Natural and Econ. Resources, Raleigh, 1959-61, 64-76, dir. divsn. econ. devel., until 1976; dir. S.C. State Devel. Bd., Columbia, 1976-84; pres. Rsch. Triangle Park Found., NC, 1984-88; prin. Leak-Goforth Co., LLC, Raleigh, 1988—. Mem. U.S. Dept. Commerce Small Bus. Adv. Coun., vice-chmn. Dist. Export Coun.; leader industry organized govt. approved trade and indsl. devel. missions to Can., Europe, S.Am., Australia, Far East. Bd. dirs. Raleigh YMCA, S.C. Tech. and Comprehensive Edn., N.C. Symphony Fedn., Duke Alumni Assn., Carolina Ballet; chmn. bd. dirs. Wake Tech. C.C. Found.; adv. bd. Duke Hosp.; sr. warden vestry Christ Episcopal Ch.; past pres. Internat. Econ. Devel. Coun. Mem. Nat. Assn. State Devel. Agys. (past pres.), Raleigh Rotary Club (bd. dirs., Paul Harris fellow). Episcopalian. Home: 8601 Cypress Lakes Dr 408 Raleigh NC 27615-2118 Office: 8601 Six Forks Rd Ste 400 Raleigh NC 27615 Office Phone: 919-676-5336. Personal E-mail: bobbleak@aol.com.

LEAKE, DEIRDRE, plastic surgeon; BS in Biochemistry summa cum laude, U. Tenn., 1990—94, MD, 1994—98. Diplomate Am. Bd. Otolaryngology, Am. Bd. of Facial Plastic & Reconstructive Surgery. Internship in gen. surgery Univ. of Rochester Med. Ctr., Rochester, NY, 1998—99, resident in otolaryngology head and neck surgery, 1999—2003; fellow in facial and plastic & reconstructive surgery Univ. Mich., 2003—04; fellow Am. Acad. of Facial Plastic & Reconstructive Surgery, Am. Acad. of Cosmetic Surgery. Mem.: AMA, Assn. of Women Surgeons, Skin Cancer Found., Fla. Soc. of Otolaryngology, Fla. Soc. of Facial Plastic & Reconstructive Surgery, Fla. Med. Soc., Am. Coll. of Surgeons, Am. Acad. of Otolaryngology. Office: Facial Rejuvenation Center Suite 10 1750 Tree Blvd Saint Augustine FL 32084

LEAMER, LAURENCE ALLEN, writer; b. Chgo., Oct. 30, 1941; s. Laurence Eugene and Helen Mae (Burkey) L.; m. Eliana Robitschek, Sept. 12, 1968 (div. Sept. 1980); 1 child, Daniela; m. Vesna Obradovic, Dec. 16, 1984. Diploma, U. Besancon, France, 1962; BA, Antioch Coll., 1964; M.Internat. Affairs, U. Oreg., 1968; M.J., Columbia U., 1969. Vol., tchr. Peace Corps, Nepal, 1964-66; assoc. editor Newsweek, NYC, 1969-70; dir. study on underground press 20th Century Fund, NYC, 1970-71. Author: The Paper Revolutionaries, 1972, Playing for Keeps in Washington, 1977 (Notable Book of Yr., NY Times Book Rev. 1977), Assignment, 1981, Ascent: The Spiritual and Physical Quest of Willi Unsoeld, 1982, Make-Believe: The Story of Nancy and Ronald Reagan, 1983, As Time Goes By: The Life of Ingrid Bergman, 1986, King of the Night: The Life of Johnny Carson, 1989 (N.Y. Times Bestseller list), The Kennedy Women: The Saga of an American Family, 1996 (NY Times Bestseller list), Three Chords and the Truth: Hope, Heartbreak, and Changing Fortunes in Nashville, 1997, The Kennedy Men: 1901-1963, 2001 (N.Y. Times Bestseller list), Sons of Camelot: The Fate of an American Dynasty, 2004 (N.Y. Times Bestseller list), Fantastic: The Life of Arnold Schwarzenegger, 2005, Madness Under the Royal Palms, 2009, NY Times Bestseller List, The Price of Justice: A True Story of Greed and Corruption, 2013; contbr. articles to Harper's mag., NY Times mag., New Republic, Playboy, others. Internat. fellow Columbia U., 1968-69; Pulitzer travel fellow, 1969; recipient citation Overseas Press Club, 1973. Address: Joy Harris Agy 381 Park Ave S Ste 428 New York NY 10016 Home: 2501 M St NW Apt 712 Washington DC 20037-1306

LEAMER, MARYBETH N., telecommunications industry executive; B in Pub. Rels. & Journalism, Auburn U. Various positions, including compensation analyst Cox Comm. Inc. (subs. of Cox Enterprises, Inc.), 1982—86; various positions, including corp. benefits adminstr., mgr., employee benefit plans Cox Enterprises, Inc., 1986, dir., employee benefits & compensation, v.p., human resources, 1986, sr. v.p., human resources & adminstrn., 2009—10, exec. v.p., human resources & adminstrn., 2010—. Former pres., former bd. dirs. Cystic Fibrosis Found., Ga.; bd. dirs. Metro Atlanta YMCA; mem., exec. com. Human Resources Leadership Forum; mem. Human Resources Planning Soc. Office: Cox Enterprises Inc 6205 Peachtree Dunwoody Rd Atlanta GA 30328 Office Phone: 678-645-0000. Office Fax: 678-645-1079. Business E-Mail: Marybeth.Leamer@coxinc.com.

LEARY, WILLIAM JAMES, educational association administrator, educator; b. Boston, Oct. 1, 1938; s. John Gilbert and Josephine Marie (Kelley) L.; m. Joann Linda Parodi, June 25, 1960; children: Lorraine, Lisa, Linda. S.B., Boston Coll.; M.Ed., Boston State Coll.; postgrad. (Fulbright fellow), Sophia U., Tokyo, 1967; cert. advanced study, Harvard U., 1972, Ed.D., 1973, Boston U., 1971. Tchr. pub. schs., Boston, 1960—67; chmn. dept. social studies Dorchester High Sch., Boston, 1967—68; dir. curriculum Boston Dist. Pub. Schs., 1969—72, supt. schs., 1972—75; exec. dir. Met. Planning Project, Newton, Mass., 1975—77; supt. schs. Rockville Centre, NY, 1977—82, North Babylon, NY, 1982—84, Broward County, Ft. Lauderdale, Fla., 1984—88; supt. Gloucester Pub. Schs., Mass., 1989—93; assoc. prof. dept. ednl. leadership, dept. chair U. Miss., Oxford, 1993—98, dir. PhD Program; prof. coll. edn. Lynn U., Boca Raton, Fla., 1998—2012, emeritus prof., 2013; chief Marshall Lynn U. Commencement, 2012. Assoc. prof. dept. continuing studies Boston State Coll., 1970-72; assoc. in edn. Harvard U. Grad. Sch. Edn., 1972-75; adj. prof. edn. Boston U., 1973-75, C.W. Post Ctr., L.I. U., 1979-84, Fla. Internat. U., 1984-88, Salem (Mass.) State Coll., 1990-93; prof. Suffolk U., 1977-82; TV commentator Channel 5, Boston, 1975-76; prodr. edn. programs New Eng. Cablevision, 1989-93; keynote spkr. Harvard U. Grad. Sch. Edn., 1976, NYU, 1980; faculty senate U. Miss., 1994-96, chair subcom. on athletics, 1994-95. Columnist Boston Herald, 1975-78, L.I. News, 1982-84, Gloucester Times; edn. commentator New Eng. Cablevision, 1989-93; contbr. articles to profl. jours. Edn. coord. Boston chpt. United Way, 1974, Rockville Centre United Fund, 1979-80, Broward County chpt., 1985-87; trustee Mus. Fin. Arts, Boston, 1972-77; bd. dirs. Boston Youth Symphony, 1972-77, Edn. Devel. Ctr., 1972-77, Broward Com. of 100, Boys Club Broward County, Fla., 1985-88; nat. alumni bd. Boston U., 1975—80; vis. com. Suffolk U., 1978-80; adv. bd. Harvard N.Y. Alumni Forums, 1980-84; mem. L.I. Regional Planning Bd., 1983-84, Gov.'s Task Force on Alt. Edn., Fla., 1986-88; lector, Eucharistic min. Ascension Cath. Ch., Boca Raton; bd. dirs., v.p., Mill Pond Homeowners Assn., Boca Raton, 2002-2008, 2011-, with 2d armored divsn US Army, Am. Legion; Disabled Am. vets. Decorated Royal Order of Atlantic Voyageurs, 1955; recipient Friend of Youth award Hayden Goodwill Boys' Home, 1973, Ida M. Johnston Outstanding Alumni award Boston U. Sch. Edn., 1976, Man of Yr. award Pope's Hill Assn., 1976, Jenkins Meml. award for ednl. leadership N.Y. State Coun., PTA, 1980, Ednl. Leadership award L.I. chpt. NCCJ, 1980, Broward County Med. Aux., 1984, Lifetime Achievement award Matignon H.S. Alumni, 1995, Civil Rights award NAACP Layfayette County, MS, 1996; selected as mem. Exec. Educator 100, Nat. Sch. Bd. Assn., 1987; named to Matignon H.S. Hall of Fame, 1995. Mem. ASCD (nat. commn. on supervision 1984-85), Am. Assn. Sch. Adminstrs. (del. assembly 1991-93, resolutions com. 1988-89, 93-96), Am. Hist. Assn., Horace Mann League, Assn. for Asian Studies, Nat. Coun. Social Studies (nat. urban affairs com. 1977-80), Large City Sch. Supts., Harvard Club N.Y.C., Boston Coll., Varsity Club, KC, Rotary, Harvard Club of Boston and N.Y., Harvard Club of Palm Beach, Am. Legion, DAV, Comdrs. Club, Phi Delta Kappa. Roman Catholic. Office: Lynn U Grad Sch Edn Boca Raton FL 33431 Personal E-mail: bjleary@comcast.net. Business E-Mail: wleary@lynn.edu.

LEATH, CHARLES ALEXANDER, JR., construction company executive; b. Worcester, Mass., Dec. 31, 1944; s. Charles Alexander and Eleanor (Donnelly) L.; m. Glenn Dickerson, May 23, 1970; children: Charles A. III, Martha Bruce. BS, The Citadel, 1966; BS in Engring., U. S.C., 1975, M of Engring., 1976; grad., U.S. Army Command and Staff Coll., 1985. Registered profl. engr., S.C., Tex. Chemist, agt. S.C. Law Enforcement Divsn., Columbia, 1967-73; geotechnical engr. Found. Engring., Columbia, 1975-77; sr. geotechnical engr. Geotechnical Engring. Co., Raleigh, NC, 1977-78; project mgr. Republic Contracting Corp., Columbia, 1978—79, Phillips & Jordan, Inc., Knoxville, Tenn., 1979-82, asst. regional v.p. Denton, Tex., 1982-85; chief estimator U.S. Constrn. Co., Inc., Columbia, 1985—87; pres., treas. Bridge & Hwy. Rehab. Inc., Columbia, 1987—93; project mgr. REA Constrn., Inc., Columbia, 1993—2000; pres., treas. Leath Contracting, Inc., Columbia, 2000—. 1st lt. U.S. Army, 1968-70, Vietnam, ret. col. S.C. Army N.G. Recipient Asphalt Paving award Asphalt Inst., Columbia, 1975, S.C. Pub. Works award, 1993, NAPA Sheldon B. Hayes Nat. Asphalt Paving award, 1995. Mem. ASCE, Soc. Profl. Engrs., Associated Gen. Contractors, Nat. Guard Assn. U.S. (S.C. exec. com.), Assn. of Citadel Men (steering com.), Brigadier Club (Charleston, S.C.), Tau Beta Phi. Episcopalian. Avocations: boating, hunting. Office: Leath Contracting Inc 133 Middleton Pl Prosperity SC 29127 Personal E-mail: alexleath@aol.com.

LEATHER, VICTORIA POTTS, college librarian; b. Chattanooga, June 12, 1947; d. James Elmer Potts and Ruby Lea (Bettis) Potts Wilmoth; m. Jack Edward Leather; children: Stephen, Sean. BA cum laude, U. Chattanooga, 1968; MSLS, U. Tenn., 1978. Libr. asst. East New Orleans Regional Libr., 1969-71; libr. Erlanger Nursing Sch., Chattanooga, 1971-75; chief libr. Erlanger Hosp., Chattanooga, 1975-77; dir. Eastgate Br. Libr., Chattanooga, 1977-81; dir. libr. svcs. Chattanooga State Tech. C.C., 1981-95, dean libr. svcs., 1996—. Mem. ALA, Southeastern Libr. Assn., Tenn. Libr. Assn. (past chair legis. com.), Chattanooga Area Libr. Assn. (pres. 1978-79), Tenn. Bd. Regents Media Consortium (chair 1994-95), Phi Delta Kappa. Episcopalian. Avocations: reading, needlecrafts, travel. Office Phone: 423-697-2576. Business E-Mail: vicky.leather@chattanoogastate.edu.

LEATHERBY, DENNIS, corporate financial executive; b. Overland Park, Kans., 1960; BS in Acctg. & Fin., Kans. State U. Asst. treas. Tyson Foods, Inc., 1990—94, treas., 1994—2008, v.p., 1997—98, sr. v.p., fin. Springdale, Ark., 1998—2008, interim CFO, 2004—08, exec. v.p., CFO, 2008—. Office: Tyson Foods Inc 2200 Don Tyson Pky Springdale AR 72762-6999 Office Phone: 479-290-4000. Office Fax: 479-290-4061. Business E-Mail: dennis.leatherby@tyson.com.

LEATHERMAN, HUGH KENNETH, SR., state legislator, engineering executive; b. Lincoln County, NC, Apr. 14, 1931; s. John B. and Ada Leatherman; m. Jean Helms, Nov. 11, 1978; children: Sheila Dianne, Hugh Kenneth, Karen Ann, Joyce Lynn, Amy Jean, Sarah Ada. BS in Civil Engring., NC State U., 1953. Former mng. ptnr. WyBoo Investment; engr. then sec. Florence Concrete Products Inc., SC, 1955-72, pres., 1972—93, Leacon, Inc.; mem. Quinby Town Coun., 1967—76; mem. Dist. 31 SC State Senate, 1980—, chair Fin.

Com. & Interstate Cooperation Com. Republican. Methodist. Mailing: 1817 Pineland Ave Florence SC 29501-5419 Office: 111 Gressette Bldg Columbia SC 29201 Office Phone: 803-212-6640, 843-662-0388. Business E-Mail: SFI@scsenate.org.

LEATHERMAN, STEPHEN PARKER, geologist, educator, writer; b. Charlotte, NC, Nov. 6, 1947; s. John F. and Evelyn M. (Parker) Leatherman. BS with honors, NC State U., 1970; PhD, U. Va., 1976. Asst. prof. Boston U., 1975—77; dir. rsch. unit U. Mass., Amherst, 1976—81; environ. scientist Barrier Island Task Force, Dept. Interior, Washington, 1977—78, US Geol. Survey, Reston, Va., 1980—81; asst. prof. U. Md., College Park, 1981—83, assoc. prof., 1983—91; prof. Internat. Hurricane Rsch. Ctr., Fla. Internat. U., Miami, 1991—97, dir., 1997—2009, co-dir., Lab. Coastal Rsch., 2009—. Author: Barrier Islands from the Gulf of St. Lawrence to the Gulf of Mexico, 1979, Barrier Island Migration: An Annotated Bibliography, 1985, America's Best Beaches, 1998, Dr. Beach's Survival Guide: What You Need to Know About Sharks, Rip Currents, and More Before Going in the Water, 2003; co-editor: Sea Level Rise: History and Consequences, 2000; contbr. articles to profl. jours. Served US Army, 1970—72. Mem.: AAAS, Geol. Soc. Am., Sigma Xi. Office: Fla Internat U Internat Hurricane Rsch Ctr University Park, MARC 360 11200 SW 8th St Miami FL 33199 Home: 11401 S W 87 Ave Miami FL 33176 Office Phone: 305-348-1607. Office Fax: 305-348-1761. Business E-Mail: Stephen.Leatherman@fiu.edu, leatherm@fiu.edu.

LEATHERWOOD, RICHARD L., information technology executive; BS, U. Tenn., 1962; MS, Rutgers U., 1964; PhD, Ga. Inst. Tech., 1972. V.p. Am. Freight System; vice chmn., bd. dirs. Chesapeake and Ohio Ry. Co., Cleve., 1985; pres., CEO Tex. Gas Resources Corp., 1983—85; pres., CEO, equipment group CSX Transp. Inc., Balt., 1986—91. Bd. dirs. Dominion Resources, Inc., CACI Internat. Inc. Served to 1st lt. AUS, 1964-66. Office: CSX Equipment 1 Charles Ctr 20th Fl 100 N Charles St Baltimore MD 21201-3805 also: CACI International Inc 1100 N Glebe Rd Arlington VA 22201 Office Phone: 703-841-7800. Office Fax: 703-841-7882. E-mail: rleatherwood@caci.com.

LEAVITT, DAVID ADAM, writer, English educator; b. Pitts., June 23, 1961; s. Harold Jack and Gloria (Rosenthal) L. BA, Yale U., 1983. Prof. English, MFA program in creative writing U. Fla., 2000—; faculty mem. Princeton U. Author: Family Dancing, 1984 (Nat. Book Critics Cir. award nomination 1984, PEN-Faulkner award nomination 1985), The Lost Language of Cranes, 1986 (adapted into a BBC film in 1991), Equal Affections, 1989, A Place I've Never Been, 1990, While England Sleeps, 1995, Arkansas, 1997, The Page Turner, 1998 (adapted into a film, Food of Love in 2002), Martin Bauman or a Sure Thing, 2000, The Marble Quilt, 2001, Florence, A Delicate Case, 2002, Florence, A Delicate Case, 2003, The Body of Jonah Boyd, 2004, The Man Who Knew Too Much: Alan Turing and the Invention of the Computer, 2005,The Indian Clerk, 2007, Two Hotel Francforts, 2013; co-author (with Mark Mitchell) Italian Pleasures, 1996, In Maremma: Life and a House in Southern Tuscany, 2001, revised 2011, (collections) Bloomsbury, 2003, (limited editions) Saturn Street, 1995, Crossing St. Gotthard, 2000; co-editor (with Mark Mitchell): The Penguin Book of Gay Short Fiction, 1994, Pages Passed from Hand to Hand: The Hidden Tradition of Homosexual Literature in English from 1748 to 1814, 1997, The New Penguin Book of Gay Short Stories, 2003, (with Aaron Thier) 23 Great Stories, 2013; co-screenwriter Someone's Son; founder, editor Subtropics, 2006—; contbr. to periodicals including Esquire, Harper's, New Yorker, N.Y. Times Book Rev., Washington Post, Village Voice, Vogue, Double-Take, Southern Review, Tin House, Food & Wineothers. Recipient Willets prize for fiction Yale U., 1982, O. Henry Award, 1984; Nat. Endowment for Arts grantee, 1985; vis. fgn. writer Inst. Catalan Letters, Barcelona Spain, 1989; Guggenheim fellow, 1990; named Literary Lion, NY Public Library, 1994 Mem. PEN, The Author's Guild. Office: U Florida Dept English Office Turlington 4101 PO Box 117310 Gainesville FL 32611-7310 Address: c/o Jin Auh The Wylie Agency 250 W 57th St Suite 2114 New York NY 10107 Office Phone: 352-294-2806. Office Fax: 352-392-0860. E-mail: dleavitt@english.ufl.edu.*

LEBAS, H. BERNARD, state legislator; BS in Pharmacy, Northeast La. U., Monroe, 1968. Pharmacist; mem. Dist. 38 La. House of Reps., 2008—, mem. agr., forestry, aquaculture and rural devel. com., appropriations com., health and welfare com., joint legis. com. on the budget. Democrat. Office: State Capitol PO Box 44486 Baton Rouge LA 70804 Mailing: 115 SW Railroad Ave Ville Platte LA 70586 Office Phone: 225-342-6945, 337-363-0152. Office Fax: 337-363-0179. Business E-Mail: lebasb@legis.state.la.us.

LEBDA, DOUGLAS R., bank executive; BBA, Bucknell U., 1992; attended, U. Va., 1998. Auditor, cons. PriceWaterhouse Coopers; chmn., pres. LeadingTree, LLC (acquired by IAC.InterActiveCorp in 2003), 1996, founder, CEO, 1998; pres., COO IAC/InterActiveCorp., 2005—07; CEO IAC Search & Media, Oakland, Calif., 2006—07; chmn., CEO, fin. services & real estate bus. IAC/InterActiveCorp., 2008; chmn., CEO Tree.com, 2008—. Bd. dir. Eastman Kodak Co., 2007—. Bd. dir. Bucknell U. Alumni Assn.; bd. trustee Darden Sch. Found., 2002—05; mem. Charlotte C. of C. Recipient Ernst & Young Entrepreneur of Yr. award, Coun. for Entrepreneurial Development's Trailblazer award, Inman Innovator of Yr. award; vis. scholar Shermet Scholar. Achievements include patents in field. Office: Tree.com Inc 11115 Rushmore Dr Charlotte NC 28277 Office Phone: 704-541-5351. Office Fax: 704-541-1824.

LEBLANC, EDDIE M., III, corporate financial executive; BBA, U. Southwestern La. CPA; CFA. Worked Goodyear Tire and Rubber, Celeron Corp.; sr. v.p., CFO Coho Energy; founder Interstate Natural Gas Co.; sr. v.p., CFO Range Resources Corp., 2000—03; exec. v.p., CFO Ascent Energy Co. (acquired by RAM Energy Resources), 2003—07; CFO Quest Energy GP, LLC, 2009—, Quest Resource Corp., 2009—. Office: Quest Energy Partners LP Ste 2750 210 Pk Ave Okla Tower Oklahoma City OK 73102 Office Phone: 405-600-7704. Office Fax: 405-600-7722. Business E-Mail: eleblanc@qrcp.net.

LEBLANC, HUGH LINUS, political science professor, consultant; b. Alexandria, La., Oct. 30, 1927; s. Moreland Paul and Carmen Marie (Haydel) LeB.; m. Shirley Jean Smith, Feb. 28, 1953; children: Leslie Ann, Alexander Hugh. BA, La. State U., 1948; MA, U. Tenn., 1950; PhD, U. Chgo., 1958. Asst. prof. George Washington U., Washington, 1955-58, assoc. prof., 1959-63, prof., 1964-90, prof. emeritus dept. polit. sci., 1991—, chmn. dept., 1963-65, 70-76, 82-88; v.p. Area Inc., Arlington, Va., 1961-63. Author: American Political Parties, 1982, (with D. Trudeau Allensworth) The Politics of States and Urban Communities, 1971; contbr. articles to polit. sci. jours. Served to lt. (j.g.) USNR, 1944-45, 52-55. Named Outstanding Prof. Interfraternity Council, George Washington U., 1963 Mem. Amelia Island Plantation Club (Fla.). Personal E-mail: hllssl@aol.com.

LEBLANC, ROGER MAURICE, chemistry professor; b. Trois Rivières, Que., Can., Jan. 5, 1942; s. Henri and Rita (Moreau) L.; m. Micheline D. Veillette, June 26, 1965; children: Daniel, Hughes, Marie-Jose, Nancy. BSc, U. Laval, 1964, PhD, 1968. NRC postdoctoral fellow Davy Faraday Rsch. Lab. Royal Inst. Great Britain, London, 1968-70; prof. phys. chemistry U. Que., Trois-Rivières, 1970-93, chmn. dept., 1971-75, dir. Biophysics Rsch. Group, 1978-81, chmn. Photobiophysics Rsch. Ctr., 1981-91; prof., chmn. dept. chemistry U. Miami, Coral Gables, Fla., 1994—2002. Hon. prof. Jilin U., Changchun, China, 1992. Recipient Barringer award Spectroscopy Soc. Can., 1983, Medaille du Merite U. Que. a Trois-Rivieres, 1987, Commemorative medal for 125th Anniversary of Confedn. Can., 1993, Rsch. award Soc. Cosmetic Chemists Fla. chpt., 1999, Provost's award, 2002. Fellow Chem. Inst. Can. (Noranda award 1982, John Labatt Ltd. award 1992); mem. Am. Chem. Soc. (Fla. award 2006), Assn. Canadienne Francaise pour l'Avancement des Sciences (Prix Vincent 1978), Am. Soc. Photobiology, Biophys. Soc., European Photochem. Assn., Soc. Phys. Chemistry of Serbia (hon.), Royal Sci. Sc. Belgium (corr.). Roman Catholic. Home: 713 Crandon Blvd Apt 203 Key Biscayne FL 33149-2530 Office: U Miami Dept Chemistry Cox Sci Bldg Rm 315 1301 Memorial Dr Coral Gables FL 33124-0431 Business E-Mail: rml@miami.edu.

LEBO, JEFF, men's college basketball coach; b. Enola, Pa., Oct. 5, 1966; s. Dave Lebo; m. Melissa Mills, Aug. 8, 1992; children: Addison, Mills, Creighton. BBA, U. NC, Chapel Hill, 1989. Guard San Antonio Spurs, 1989—90; asst. coach East Tenn. State U. Buccaneers, 1990—92, Vanderbilt U. Commodores, 1992—93, U. SC Gamecocks, 1993—98; head basketball coach Tenn. Tech. U. Golden Eagles, 1998—2002, U. Tenn. Chattanooga Mocs, 2002—04, Auburn U. Tigers, 2004—10, East Carolina U. Pirates, 2010—. Prodr.: (instructional video) Half-Court Trapping and Double-Teaming the Post. Named Coach of Yr., Ohio Valley Conf., 2000—02, Dist. VII Coach of Yr., Nat. Assn. Basketball Coaches, 2002, Tenn. Coach of Yr., 2002. Office: East Carolina University Basketball c/o Dept Athletics East Fifth St Greenville NC 27858 Office Phone: 252-737-4592.

LEBON, RACHEL L., musician, educator; d. Raymond Joseph and Georgette Lebon. MusB, N.Tex. State U., 1977, MusM, 1979; PhD, U. Miami, 1986. Asst. prof. Belmont Coll., Nashville, 1979—83; performer Air Force Tops in Blue, Randolph A.F.B., Tex., 1973; acad. instr. USAF, Sheppard A.F.B., Tex.; prof., coord. of jazz voice U. of Miami, Coral Gables, Fla., 1986—; vis. prof. Leeds Coll. Music, England, 2009—10; del. Women Higher Edn. People to People Ambassadorship Program, 2010. Voice specialist Profl. Voice Inst., Hallandale Beach, Fla., 1985. Author: The Professional Vocalist: A Handbook for Commerical Singers and Teachers, 1999, The Versatile Vocalist: Singing Authentically in Contrasting Styles and Idioms, 2006; singer: (CD) Voicings, Vocal Coach in Residency, Voice Coun. Mag., 2011; contbr. articles. Child adv. Guardian Ad Litem, Miami, Fla., 1990—2006; external reviewer manuscript Jour. Voice, 2012. Staff sgt USAF, 1973. Recipient Vol. of Year, Buddies of Nashville, 1983. Mem.: Internat. Assn. for Jazz Edn., Nat. Assn. Tchrs. Singing, Pi Kappa Lambda. Office Phone: 305-284-6118. Personal E-mail: rllebon@aol.com.

LEBOUITZ, MARTIN FREDERICK, diversified financial services company executive, consultant; b. Phila., May 16, 1946; s. William and Sylvia (Magen) L.; m. Helene A. Pepper, Oct. 15, 1977; children: Clarke S., Jacqueline B. BS, U.S. Air Force Acad., 1971, MA, 1972; MA Fletcher Sch. Law and Diplomacy, Tufts U., 1972. Asst. v.p. Bankers Trust Co., NYC, 1976—82; v.p. mgr. of planning Barclays Bank of N.Am., NYC, 1982—85; v.p. corp. devel. Chase Manhattan Bank, NYC, 1985—88; v.p. planning and devel. Paine Webber Group Inc., NYC, 1988—90; prin. DRI/McGraw-Hill, NYC, 1990—91; mng. dir. Fin. Svcs. Cons., NYC, 1991—95; v.p. global payments project exec. and industry issues exec. JP Morgan Chase, NYC, 1995—99; v.p. planning and devel. JP Morgan, Fin. Markets Solutions, 1999—; pres. Global Payments Strategies, Tampa, Fla., 2004—; chmn., pres. MAG Energy Techs., 2011—. Editor: (jour.) Payments Strategy and Systems. Chmn. Mag-Lev Energy, Inc., 2008-11; Capt. USAF, 1971-76. Mem. Strategic Leadership Forum (dir., chmn. program com. NY chpt.), Assn. for Corp. Growth, Am. Mgmt. Assn. (pres.), USAF Acad. Assn. of Grad. (Tampa chpt.), Harvard Club, Fletcher Sch. Club NY (chmn. sch. rels. com.), Ctr. Club, Champion Hills Country Club, Tampa Palms Country Club. Office: 4532 W Kennedy Blvd Ste 123 Tampa FL 33609 Business E-Mail: martin.lebouitz@paymentstrategies.org.

LEBOW, BENNETT S., corporate financial executive; b. Phila., 1937; BSEE, Drexel U., Phila., 1960, DSc (hon.), 1998; attended, Princeton U., NJ. Prin. DSI Systems Inc., Rockville, Md., 1961—71, B.S. LeBow Inc.; founder, chmn., CEO Brooke Group Ltd. (formerly Brooke Partners L.P.), 1980, acquired MAI Basic Four, Inc., 1985, acguired Liggett Group, 1986; chmn. Western Union Corp., Upper Saddle River, NJ, 1988, New Valley Corp.; chmn. bd. dirs. Vector Group Ltd., 2000—. Chmn. bd. dirs. Borders Group, Inc., 2010—. Served with US Army. Office: Vector Group Ltd 4400 Biscayne Blvd # 10 Miami FL 33137-3212 E-mail: blebow@vectob.com, blebow@lvbrands.com.

LECHLEITER, RICHARD A., corporate financial executive; CPA. V.p., contr. Humana, Inc., 1990—93, Galen Health Care, Inc., 1993, Columbia/HCA Healthcare Corp., 1993—95; dir., fin. Vencor, 1995, v.p., fin., corp. contr., 1995—98; v.p., fin., corp. contr., treas. Kindred Healthcare, Inc., Louisville, 1998—2002, treas., 1998—2003, CFO, 2002—, sr. v.p., 2002—05, exec. v.p., 2005—. Office: Kindred Healthcare 680 S Fourth St Louisville KY 40202 Office Phone: 502-596-7300. Office Fax: 502-596-4141. Business E-Mail: rich_lechleiter@kindredhealthcare.com.

LECLAIR, GARY DAVID, lawyer; b. NYC, Apr. 23, 1955; s. Raymond K. LeClair and Eleanor Lois (Kelly) Stevens; m. April Wells, June 18, 1977; children: Sue Collins, Laura Danielle, Eleanor Kelly. BBA, William & Mary, 1977; JD, Georgetown U., 1982. CPA, Va. CPA Price Waterhouse & Co., NYC, 1977-79; law clk. to Hon. Sam J. Ervin III U.S. Ct. Appeals (4th cir.), Morganton, N.C., 1982-83; assoc. Hunton & Williams, Richmond, Va., 1983-88; co-founder, chmn., CEO LeClairRyan, Richmond, 1988—. Instr. seminar Small Bus. Success Inst., 1989-91; bd. dirs. Office Am. Inc., Richmond, sec.; bd. dirs. Human Interface Techs., Inc., Richmond, Jefmar, Inc., Richmond, Peoples Fin. Svcs., Inc., Richmond, Investors Fidelity of Am., Inc., Fairfax, Va., Alloy Polymers, Inc., Richmond. Author: (handbook) Forming the Virginia Corporation, 1988. Dir., pres. Richmond Venture Forum, William & Mary Alumni Chpt., Richmond; dir., sec. Richmond Tech. & Enterprise Ctr., Inc., Technol. Entrepreneurship Ctr., Inc., Williamsburg, Va.; trustee, treas. William & Mary Athletic Edn. Fund, Williamsburg, Capital Area Small Bus. Devel. Ctr., Inc., Richmond. Mem. ABA (bus. law sect.), Va. Bar Assn. (bus. law sect.), Richmond Bar Assn. Avocations: hunting, jogging, reading, golf. Office: LeClairRyan Riverfront Plz E Tower 951 E Byrd St 8th Fl Richmond VA 23219 Office Phone: 804-343-4060. Office Fax: 804-783-7605. Business E-Mail: gary.leclair@leclairryan.com.

LEDBETTER, CALVIN REVILLE, JR., (CAL LEDBETTER), political science professor, legislator; b. Little Rock; s. Calvin Reville Sr. and Virginia Mae (Campbell) L.; m. Mary Brown Williams, July 26, 1953 (dec. Mar. 21, 2010); children: Grainger, Jeffrey (dec.), Snow. BA, Princeton U., 1951; LLB, U. Ark., 1954; PhD, Northwestern U., 1960. Bar: Ark., 1954. Pvt. practice, Little Rock, 1954; faculty dept. polit. sci. U. Ark., Little Rock, 1960-97, prof., 1960-97, prof. emeritus, 1997—, dean, 1978-88; cons. law enforcement program, advisor pre-law program; mem. Ark. Ho. of Reps., 1967-76; chmn. spl. legis. com., com. on legis. orgn.; vice chmn. legis. com. state agys. and govt. affairs; cons. pub. schs.; mem. Nat. Adv. Com. on Criminal Justice Goals and Standards; mem. adv. com. Nat. Inst. Law Enforcement and Criminal Justice. Dept. head. U. Ark., Little Rock, 1968-78; election night analyst for Ark. congl. and Presdl. elections ABC, 1964-84 Co-author: Politics in Arkansas: The Constitutional Experience, 1972, The Arkansas Plan: A Case Study in Public Policy, 1979, Arkansas Becomes a State, 1985, Carpenter from Conway: George W. Donaghey as Governor of Arkansas 1909-1913, 1993; contbr. 19 articles, book reviews to profl. jours., Ark Hist. Quarterly. Mem. Ark. Adv. Coun. on Pub., Elem. and Secondary Edn.; Gov.'s rep. So. Regional Growth Policies Bd.; mem. Ark. Legis. Coun.; del. Ark. Constl. Conv., 1979, v.p., 1979-80; chmn. law enforcement and criminal justice task force Nat. Legis. Conf. Former chmn. coll. and univ. sect. United Fund; del. Dem. Nat. Conv., 1968, 84; mem. exec. com. Ark. Young Dems.; bd. dirs. Health and Welfare Coun. Pulaski County; trustee Philander Smith Coll., chmn. council community advisers; sec. bd. dirs. St. Vincent's Infirmary; bd. dirs. Ark. Humanities Coun., 1989-93, v.p., 1991-93, pres. 1993-94; bd. trustees Ark. Mus. Sci. and History. Served with JAGC AUS, 1955-57. Scholarships U. Ark., Little Rock, 2002; recipient award outstanding contbn. to humanities Little Rock Arts and Humanities Commn., 1993; named Educator of Yr., Greater Little Rock Fedn. Women's Clubs, 1968. Mem. ABA, Ark. Bar Assn. (Writing Excellence award 1985-86), Pulaski County Bar Assn., Nat. Conf. State Legislators (exec. com.), Nat. Conf. Acad. Deans (pres. 1987-88), Am. Polit. Sci. Assn., So. Polit. Sci. Assn., Ark. Polit. Sci. Assn. (pres. 1980-81), Ark. Acad. Sci., Am. Acad. Polit. and Social Sci., Ark. Hist. Assn., Ark. Edn. Assn., Pulaski County Hist. Soc. (bd. dirs. 1988-90), Ark. Hist. Commn. (v.p. 1989—, pres. 1990—), Rotary (pres. West Little Rock chpt. 1987-88). Presbyterian. Achievements include endownment of a monograph press and non-traditional scholarships at the U. Arkansas at Little Rock. Home: Unit 11 3901 Cedar Hill Rd Little Rock AR 72202 Office: Univ Ark Little Rock Polit Sci Dept Little Rock AR 72204 Home Phone: 501-663-2100; Office Phone: 501-569-8766.

LEDBETTER, DAVID OSCAR, lawyer; b. Santa Rosa, Calif., Mar. 16, 1950; s. Oscar Smith Ledbetter and Nova Nell (Huckaby) Kramer; m. Judith Louise Fischer, Dec. 14, 1976; children: Hannah J., Jordan B. BA, U. Redlands, 1972; JD, Hastings Coll. Law, 1977. Bar: Calif. 1977, Va. 1987. Assoc. Moran, Urich & Evans, San Francisco, 1977-79; trial atty. land and natural resource divsn. U.S. Dept. Justice, Washington, 1979-85; assoc., counsel, ptnr. Hunton & Williams, Richmond, Va., 1985—. Bd. adv. Chem. Waste Litigation Reporter, Washington, 1983—. Co-editor: Outline RCRA/CERCLA Enforcement Issues and Holdings, 2008; contbr. articles to profl. jours. Bd. dirs. John Tyler C.C. Found., Chester, Va., 1992—. Mem. ABA, Va. State Bar Assn., Calif. Bar Assn., Environ. Law Inst., Charles City Ruritan Club. Democrat. Methodist. Avocations: gardening, fishing, hunting. Home: 16530 The Glebe Ln Charles City VA 23030-3837 Office: Hunton & Williams 951 E Byrd St Ste 200 Richmond VA 23219-4074 Office Phone: 804-788-8364. Business E-Mail: dledbetter@hunton.com.

LEDBETTER, PAUL MARK, lawyer, writer; b. San Francisco, Oct. 14, 1947; s. John Paul and Joyce (Mayo) L.; m. Jerald Ann Broyles, Sept. 18, 1971; children: Paul Mark, Sarah Broyles. BA in English, Ouachita Bapt. U., 1970; JD, U. Ark., 1973. Bar: Ark. 1974, Tenn. 1995, U.S. Dist. Ct. (ea. dist.) Ark. 1974, U.S. Ct. Appeals (8th cir.) 1974, U.S. Ct. Appeals (6th cir.) 1991, U.S. Dist. Ct. (mid. dist.) Tenn. 1995. From assoc. to ptnr. Frierson, Walker, Snellgrove & Laser, Jonesboro, Ark., 1974-82; city atty. Monette, Ark., 1979—80; regional def. counsel Sq. D. Co., 1980-82; pres. Mark Ledbetter, P.A., Jonesboro, 1982-86; ptnr. Gerber, Gerber & Agee, Memphis, 1986-89, Taylor, Halliburton, Ledbetter & Caldwell, Memphis, 1989—2002, Halliburton & Ledbetter, Memphis, 2003—. Product safety cons., sch. bus safety cons. CNN, 1997—; lectr. dept. mech. engring. U. Memphis, 1997—; lectr. dept. rehab. engring. U. Tenn., 1994—95. Author: The Hearing, 1994, The Thayer Class, 1998, The Wait, 2000; contbr. chpts. to books. Tutor Memphis Literacy Coun., 2003—; mem. forum commn. City of Jonesboro, 1978—80; co-founder St. Mark's Episcopal Day Sch., Jonesboro, Ark., 1978; mem. vestry St. Mark's Episcopal Ch., 1979. Conservation Found. grantee, 1976; Rotary Internat. grantee, Japan, 1979; named one of 50 Attys. Memphis, 2008, Mid-South Super Lawyers, 2007-; named Memphis Mag. Super Lawyer. Mem. ATLA, Am. Bd. Trial Advs. (assoc.), Tenn. Bar Assn., Ark. Bar Assn. (mem. tort reform com. 1980, ho. of dels. 1979-80), Ark. Trial Lawyers Assn. (chmn. amicus curiae com. 1980-81, gov. 1980—), Tenn. Trial Lawyers Assn., Jonesboro C. of C. (bd. dirs. 1978-80), Human Factors and Ergonomics Soc., Rotary, Blue Ribbon Selection Panel. Office: Halliburton Ledbetter 254 Court Ave 3d Fl Memphis TN 38103 Office Phone: 901-523-8153. E-mail: mark794@aol.com.*

LEDERER, ELEANOR DELAND, nephrologist, educator; b. Phila., Dec. 19, 1952; m. Paul Richard Lederer. BA, Rice U., Houston, 1974; MD, Baylor Coll. Medicine, Houston, 1978. Diplomate Am. Bd. Internal Medicine, 1981, cert. in nephrology 1984. Asst. prof. Baylor Coll. Medicine, 1984—90; prof. U. Louisville Sch. Medicine, 1991—, fellowship dir., nephrology, 2002—13, interim vice dean, rsch., 2006—08, assoc. Ombudsperson, Health Scis. Ctr., 2009, divsn. chief, nephrology and hypertension, 2010—. Interim chief, med. svcs. Robley Rex VA Med. Ctr., Louisville, 2010—12. Mem., sec.-treas., pres. Innominate Soc. Louisville, 2000. Recipient Internal Medicine Tchg. award, U. Louisville Sch. Medicine, 2003—04, 2006, 2009—10, Disting. Tchg. Prof. award, 2009, Partnership award, Nat. Kidney Found. Ky., 2009. Fellow: ACP (Ky. chpt., Internal Medicine Faculty award 2010); mem.: Am. Physiol. Soc. (Star Reviewer 2006, 2009), Am. Heart Assn., Am. Soc. Nephrology (councilor 2011—, fellowship 2005), Phi Beta Kappa Soc. Office: University Louisville Kidney Disease Program 615 S Preston St Louisville KY 40202 Office Fax: 502-852-7643. Business E-Mail: e.lederer@louisville.edu.*

LEDERMAN, CINDY S., judge; d. Donald Lee and Dolores Marie (Patton) Shellenberger; m. Robert Elliot Lederman, July 3, 1976. BA in Polit. Sci. with honors (hon.), U. Fla., 1976; JD (hon.), U. Miami, Fla., 1979; PhD in Criminal Justice (hon.), Johnson and Wales U. Bar: Fla., 1979, N.Y., 1986. County ct. judge Domestic Violence Divsn., Miami, 1992—94; circuit ct. judge Juvenile Justice Ctr., Miami, 1994—. Mem. Faculty of the Nat. Judicial Coll.; fromer pres. Nat. Assn. Women Judges; with Fla. Supreme Ct. Edn. Coun.; adv. com. mem. Nat. Ctr. Children EXposed to Violence, Yale Child Study Ctr.; mem. nat. adv. coun. Violence Against Women, 2001—06; cahir Miami Dade County Cmty. Based Care Alliance. Vice chmn. Dade County Commn. on Status of Women, 1987—; mem. Coalition Hispanic Am. Women, 1987—, Forum of North Dade, Fla. Supreme Ct. Racial and Ethic Bias Study Commn., 1989; chmn. Mediation Pilot Project Com., 1987-88; bd. dirs. Mental Health Assn. Dade County Inc., 1989. Named Outstanding Women of Yr. North Dade C. of C., 1988. Mem. ABA, Fla. Bar Assn. (vice chmn. govt. lawyer com. 1987—, chmn. grievance com. 1988), Acad. Fla. Trial Lawyers, Dade County Bar Assn. (bd. dirs. 1987—), Fla. Assn. for Women Lawyers (pres. 1986-87, pres.'s award 1986), Fla. Council of Bar Assn. Presidents, AAUW. Avocations: travel, cooking. Office: Juvenile Justice Building 3300 Nw 27th Ave Miami FL 33142

LEDFORD, JANET MARIE SMALLEY, real estate appraiser, consultant; b. Willimantic, Conn., June 1, 1951; d. Harold Eugene and Elizabeth Louise (Loehr) Smalley; m. Timothy Eugene Ledford, Jan. 23, 1988. Avocations: gardening, travel, history.

LEDING, GREG, state legislator; b. Springdale, Ark. B in Mktg., U. Ark., 2001. Web designer Fayetteville Sch. Dist.; mem. Dist. 92 Ark. House of Representatives, 2010—. Democrat. Home: 2968 N Raven Ln Fayetteville AR 72704-6613 Office Phone: 479-422-8099. Office Fax: 479-966-9201. Personal E-mail: greg@gregleding.com.

LEDSINGER, CHARLES A., JR., food service executive; b. Memphis, Jan. 1, 1950; s. Charles Albert Ledsinger Sr. and Betty L. (Clark) Heller; m. Anita Clarendon, May 11, 1974; children: Leila Grace, Katherine Elise. BA in English, U. Va., 1972; MBA in Fin., Memphis State U., 1977. Restaurant mgr. Boudreaux and Shoup Enterprises, Atlanta, 1972-74; comml. property mgr. Hoover Morris, Enterprises, Atlanta, 1974-75; fin. analyst Holiday Inns, Inc., Memphis, 1978-79, mgr. investor rels., 1980, exec. asst. to pres., 1980-83; v.p. fin. and administrn. Embassy Stes., Irving, Tex., 1983-87; v.p. project fin. Holiday Corp., Memphis, 1987-90; v.p., treas. The Promus Cos., Memphis, 1990, sr. v.p., CFO, 1990-95, Harrah's Entertainment, Inc., Memphis, 1995—97; pres., COO The St. Joe Co., 1997—98; pres., CEO Choice Hotels International, 1998—2009, non.-exec. vice chmn. of bd., 2008—. Bd. dirs. The Restaurant Co., Perkins Mgmt. Co., Inc., Friendly Ice Cream Corp., Darden Restaurants, Felcor Lodging Trust, Inc., 1997—. Mem. exec. bd. Chickasaw coun. Boy Scouts Am., 1993—; trustee St. Mary's Episcopal Sch., 1994—; bd. dirs. Memphis Devel. Found., 1992—, TBC Corp., 1996—, Sky City Ltd., Auckland, New Zealand, 1995—. Office: Darden Restaurants Inc 1000 Darden Center Dr Orlando FL 32837-4032 Office Phone: 407-245-4000. Business E-Mail: charles_ledsinger@choicehotels.com.

LEDWIG, DONALD EUGENE, election official, association executive, retired broadcast executive, military officer; s. Paul Lawrence and Rose Ledwig; m. Gail Wilcox, Jan. 30, 1965; children: Donald Eugene Jr., David W. BS, Tex. Tech U, 1959; MBA, George Washington U., 1973; disting. grad., Naval War Coll., 1977. Commd. ensign USN, 1959, advanced through grades to capt., 1980; ship's officer U.S. Pacific Fleet, 1959-65, 77-79; mem. staff Adm. H.G. Rickover, Nuclear Propulsion Program, 1966-72; dir. contract policy Naval Materiel Command, Washington, 1979-81; dep. comdr. Naval Electronic Sys. Command, Washington, 1981-84; ret., 1984; v.p., treas. Corp. for Pub. Broadcasting, Washington, 1984-86, pres., CEO, 1987-92; exec. dir. Am. Prodn. and Inventory Control Soc., Falls Church, Va., 1992-95; pres. Am. Logistics Assn., Washington, 1995-96; COO Anchor Health Assn., 1997-98; cons. Assn. Mgmt., 1998—. Chair Alexandria (Va.) Electoral Bd., 2000—, pres. CEO, Va. Electoral Bd. Assn., 2009-11. Decorated Legion of Merit; recipient Barrow Meml. award Hastings Coll. Law, 1989, award Nat. Captioning Inst., 1990, Disting. Alumnus award Tex. Tech U., 1992. Mem.: Metro Wash. Coun. Gov. Elections Com., Nat. Assn. Election Officers, Nat. Press Club, Alexandria Assn., Army-Navy Country Club, Am. Legion.

LEDYARD, ROBINS HEARD, lawyer; b. Nashville, Oct. 14, 1939; s. Quitman Robins and Alma Elizabeth (Stevenson) L.; m. Julia Bordeaux Gambill, Dec. 19, 1962; children: Stevenson Gambill, Quitman Robins II, Margaret Dabney. BA, Vanderbilt U., 1965, JD, 1966. Bar: Tenn. 1966, U.S. Supreme Ct. 1975. Atty. Nat. Life & Accident Ins. Co., Nashville, 1966-68, asst. counsel, 1968-69, assoc. counsel, 1969-70, counsel, 1970-72, assoc. gen. counsel, 1972-75, gen. counsel, 1975-80; partner Bass, Berry & Sims, 1980—. Tchr. C.L.U.s, 1967-75 Asst. editor: Vanderbilt Law Rev., 1965-66; contbr. articles to profl. jours. Active United Way, Nashville, 1967—, Heart Fund, 1970—73; vice chmn. United Diocesan Givers, 1975; bd. dirs. St. Thomas Hosp., 1990—. With USMC, 1958—61. Recipient Bennett Douglas Bell Meml. prize, 1986; named one of Best Lawyers in Am., Global Leaders for the South; Marr scholar, 1965—66. Mem. ABA, Am. Coun. Life Ins. (chmn. tax com. 1978-80), Assn. Life Ins. Counsel (chmn. tax com. 1979-80), Tenn. Bar Assn., Nashville Bar Assn., Internat. Assn. Ins. Counsel, Global Leaders for the South, Order of Coif, Phi Delta Phi, Alpha Tau Omega. Clubs: Belle Meade Country, Capitol of Nashville, KC. Democrat. Roman Catholic. Home: 1215 Chickering Rd Nashville TN 37215-4519 Office: Amsouth Ctr Ste 2700 315 Deaderick St Nashville TN 37238-3001 Office Phone: 615-742-6259. Business E-Mail: rledyard@bassberry.com.

LEE, BOK SIN See GEBHARD POWELL, JOY

LEE, CATHERINE, sculptor, painter; b. Pampa, Tex., Apr. 11, 1950; d. Paul Albert and Alice (Fleming) Porter; m. B. R. Mangham, 1967 (div. 1976); 1 child, Monk Parker; m. Sean Scully, 1977 (div. 2004). BA, San Jose State U., 1975. Asst. prof. sculpture U. Tex., San Antonio, 2000. Artist-in-residence Mpls. Coll. Art and Design, Minn. Inst. Art, 1982; vis. asst. prof. painting U. Tex., San Antonio, 1983, vis. asst. prof. sculpture, 2001; adj. asst. prof. Columbia U., N.Y.C., 1986-87. Group exhbns. include Albright-Knox Mus., Buffalo, 1987, Mus. Art, Carnegie Inst., Pitts., 1988, Am. Acad. and Inst. Arts and Letters, N.Y.C., 1988, Mus. Folkwang, Essen, Germany, 1992, Stadtische Galerie im Lenbachhaus, Munich, 1992, Neue Galerie Der Stadt Linz, Austria, 1992, Cleve. Mus. Art, 1993, Galleria Nazionale d'Arte Moderna, San Marino, Italy, 1996, The Tate Gallery, 1994, U. R.I. Art Gallery, 1996, Sonoma State U. Art Gallery, 1997, Bemis Ctr. for Contemporary Art, 1998, Städtische Gallery, Lenbachhaus, Munich, 1999, Lafayette Coll. Art Ctr., Easton, Pa., 1999, San Diego State U. Art Gallery, San Diego, 1999, Lyman-Allen Art Mus., New London, Conn., 2000, Grounds for Sculpture, The Johnson Atelier, 2002, S.W. Sch. Arts and Crafts Gallery, 2004, Irish Mus. Modern Art, Dublin, 2005, Hotel des Arts Musee, Toulon, France, 2006, Musee d'Art Moderne, St. Etienne, France, 2006. Creative Artists Pub. Svc. fellow, 1978, NEA grantee, 1989. E-mail: catherlee@aol.com.

LEE, CHARLES MCDOWELL, legislative staff member; b. Barbour County, Ala. m. Hazel Johnston; 5 children. Student, Auburn U.; BA, Troy State U., LLD (hon.), 1979. Mayor City of Clio, Ala., 1948-50; spl. agt. FBI, 1950-52; mem. Ala. Ho. Reps., 1954-62; sec. Ala. State Senate, Montgomery, 1963—. Mem. Nat. Agrl. Adv. Com. Co-author: The Role of the Senate in Alabame History, George Corley Wallace, a Legislative Legacy, 1946-86; contbr. articles to profl. jours. Trustee Troy State U., 1967, pres. pro tem. With USN, 1943-56. Named Best Debater Ala. Press Assn., One of the Oustanding Freshmen Legislators, 1955; Chales McDowell Lee Natatorium named in his honor Troy State U., 1985. Mem. Troy State Alumni Assn. (pres. 1966-67), Sigma Nu, Kappa Delta Pi. Office: Senate Chamber Alabama State House Montgomery AL 36130-4600

LEE, DAVID MORRIS, physics professor; b. Rye, NY, Jan. 20, 1931; s. Marvin and Annette (Franks) Lee; m. Dana Thorangkul, Sept. 7, 1960; children: Eric Bertel, James Marvin. AB, Harvard U., 1952; MS, U. Conn., 1955; PhD, Yale U., 1959. Instr. of physics Cornell U., Ithaca, NY, 1959—60, asst. prof. physics, 1960—63, assoc. prof. physics, 1963—69, prof. physics, 1969—99, James Gilbert White disting. prof. phys. scis., 1999—2009; prof. physics Tex. A&M U., 2009—. Vis. scientist Brookhaven Nat. Lab., Upton, NY, 1966—67; vis. prof. U. Fla., Gainesville, 1974—75, Gainesville, 1994, U. Calif., San Diego, 1988, La Jolla, 1988; vis. lectr. Peking U., Beijing, 1981; chair mcpl. Joseph Fourier U., Grenoble, France, 1994. Contbr. articles Phys. Rev. Letters, Phys. Rev., Physica and Nature. With US Army, 1952—54. Recipient Sir Francis Simon Meml. prize, Brit. Inst. Physics, 1976, Wilber Cross medal, Yale U., 1998; co-recipient Nobel prize for physics, 1996; fellow John Simon Guggenheim, Guggenheim Found., 1966—67, 1974—75, Japan Soc. Promotion of Scis., 1977. Fellow: AAAS, Am. Acad. Arts and Scis., Brit. Inst. Physics, Am. Phys. Soc. (Oliver Buckley prize 1981); mem.: Russian Acad. Sci. (fgn. mem.), Nat. Acad. Scis. Achievements include co-discovery of superfluid 3He, of the tricritical point of 3He-4He mixtures; co-observation of spin waves in spin polarized hydrogen gas. Office: Tex A&M Univ Dept Physics MPHY 572B 155 Ireland St College Station TX 77843 Office Phone: 979-458-7938. E-mail: dmlee@physics.tamu.edu.

LEE, DONALD HAN, surgeon, orthopedist; b. Huntington, W.Va., Oct. 28, 1955; s. Kwan Ho and Kay Hee Lee; m. Dawn Thomas Thomas, May 13, 1989; children: David Thomas, Dana Elizabeth, Diane Louise, Daniel Thomas, Dustin Thomas. BS, Georgetown U., 1977; MD, W.Va. Sch. Medicine, 1982. Diplomate Nat. Bd. Med. Examiners, 1983, Am. Bd. Orthop. Surgeons, 1991. Intern surgery W. Va. U. Sch. Medicine, 1982—83, George Washington U. Sch. Medicine, 1983—84, resident orthop. surgery, 1984—88; Hand fellowship Columbia Presbyn. Med. Ctr., 1988—89; assoc. prof. orthop. surgery U. Ala., Birmingham, 1989—2005; prof. orthop. surgery Vanderbilt U., Nashville, 2005—, dir. hand fellowship, 2005—. Dir. hand fellowship U. Ala., Birmingham, 1993—2005; dir. hand and upper extremity fellowship Vanderbilt U., Nashville, 2005—; bd. examiner Am. Bd. Orthop. Surgery; joint com. surgery of hand Am. Bd. Orthop. Surgeons; reviewer Jour. Bone and Joint Surgery, Clinical Orthopedics and Related Rsch., Jour. Shoulder and Elbow Surgery. Pres. parish coun., 2000—01. Rsch. grantee, Merck and Co., Biomet, Inc. Mem.: Am. Soc. Reconstructive Microsurgery, Am. Soc. Surgery of Hand, Am. Acad. Orthop. Surgeons, Assn. Bone and Joint Surgeons, Am. Orthop. Assn. Office: Vanderbilt Orthop Inst Med Ctr East South Tower Ste 3200 Nashville TN 37232-8829 E-mail: donald.h.lee@vanderbilt.edu.

LEE, DOUGLAS A., musicologist; b. Carmel, Ind., Nov. 3, 1932; s. Ralph Henley and Flossie Ellen (Chandler) Lee; m. Beverly Ruth Haskell, Sept. 2, 1961. MusB with High Distinction, DePauw U., 1954; MusM, U. Mich., 1958, PhD, 1968; postgrad., U. Md., 1985. Instr. Nat. Mus. Camp, Interlochen, Mich., 1959-62, Mt. Union Coll., Alliance, Ohio, 1959-61, chmn. keyboard instrn., 1959-61; asst. prof. music Wichita (Kans.) State U., 1964-68, assoc. prof., 1968-74, coord. Music History and Lit., 1968-71, coord. grad. studies in Music, 1969-70, chmn. dept. Musicology, 1971-74, prof. Music, 1974-86, administrv. intern, v.p. bus. affairs, 1983, spl. events coord., 1974—85; prof. musicology Vanderbilt U., Nashville, 1986—, chmn. music history and lit., advisor, 1987—98, prof. emeritus, 1998. Radio commentator Sta. KMUW-FM, 1969-76; program annotator Nashville Symphony Orch., 1988-2001; cons. U.S. Dept. Edn. Jacob Javits fellowship program, 1988, 89, United Meth. Publishing Ho., 1988, Mayfield Pub. Co., 1990, Prentice-Hall, Inc., 1993, 97. Author: The Instrumental Works of Christoph Nichelmann: The Thematic Index, 1971, Franz Benda: A Thematic Catalogue of His Works, 1984, Franz Benda: A Musician at Court, 1998, Masterworks of 20th-Century Music, 2002; editor: Christoph Nichelmann: Clavier Concertos in E Major and A Minor, 1977, Six Sonatas for Violin and Bass by Franz Benda, with Embellishments, 1981, The Sonneck Soc. Bull., 1988-90; contbg. editor: Carl Phillip Emanuel Bach: Collected Works, Accompanied Keyboard Concertos, 2005, 2009; Solo Keyboard Concertos, 2007; America in the Fifties, 2004; contbr. articles to profl. jours., chpts. to books (58). With U.S. Army, 1955-57, Japan. Rector Scholar Found., 1951-54, Pi Kappa Lambda, 1954; Rackham fellow U. Mich., 1961-63, fellow NEH, 1980, 85, Am. Philos. Soc., 1980, Kans. Arts Coun., 1985, Tenn. Arts Coun., 1988, 89, Packard Humanities Inst., Cambridge, Mass., 2002, 04, 07. Mem. Am. Musicological Soc. (program chmn. Midwest chpt. 1984, South-Ctrl. chpt. 1989, nat. coun. 1986, pres. South-Ctrl. chpt. 1990-91), Music Tchrs. Nat. Assn. (editor 1971-90), Am. Soc. Eighteenth Century Studies, Coll. Music Soc., Soc. for Am. Music (program coord. 1987-88). Roman Catholic. Avocation: photography. Office: 119 Jackson Lake Dr Franklin TN 37069 Office Phone: 615-599-2880. Business E-Mail: douglas.lee@vanderbilt.edu.

LEE, E. DENISE, councilwoman; d. John Henry and Leanora (Daniels); 1 child, Tammy Hudson. Attended, Fla. A&M U., Edward Waters Coll. Councilwoman, Dist. 8 Jacksonville City Coun., Fla., 1982—99, Fla., 2007—; mem. Fla. House of Reps., 1999—2007. Mem. Jacksonville Civil Svc. Bd.; del. Fla. Dem. Conf.; mem. Pub. Health & Safety Com. Vice chmn. intergovernmental affairs com. Fla. League of Cities, 1987—88. Democrat. Office: 117 W Duval St Ste 425 Jacksonville FL 32202 Office Phone: 904-630-1386, 904-630-1385. Business E-Mail: edlee@coj.net.

LEE, ERIC MCCAULEY, museum director, art historian; b. Clinton, NC, Feb. 23, 1966; s. Harry McCauley and Mary Thompson Lee; m. Rima Canaan, June 12, 1994; children: Edward Marshall, Graham William. BA, Yale U., 1988, MA, 1991, PhD, 1997. Rsch. asst. U.S. Senate Select Com. on Intelligence, Washington, 1989—90; acting asst. curator paintings Yale Ctr. for Brit. Art, New Haven, 1995—96; acting dir. Fred Jones Jr. Mus. Art, U. Okla., Norman, 1997—98, dir., 1998—2006, Taft Mus. Art, Cin., 2007—09, Kimbell Art Mus., Ft. Worth, 2009—. A. Bartlett Giamatti fellow, Yale U., 1990—91, Theodore Rousseau fellow, Met. Mus. of Art, N.Y., 1994. Mem.: Assn. Art Mus. Dirs. Office: Kimbell Art Mus 3333 Camp Bowie Blvd Fort Worth TX 76107-2792 Office Phone: 817-332-8451. Business E-Mail: elee@kimbellmuseum.org.

LEE, ESTHER, marketing executive; BA, Cornell U. Exec. v.p., dir., client svcs. Deutsch Inc., 1993—97; founder, ptnr. DiNoto Lee, 1997—2002; sr. v.p., global chief creative officer Coca-Cola Co., 2002—07; CEO, N.Am., pres., Global Brands Euro RSCG Worldwide, 2007—08; sr. v.p., brand mktg. & advt. AT&T Inc. (merger of SBC Communications & AT&T Corp.), 2009—. Spkr. in field. Recipient Gold and Silver Cannes Lions, Epica D'Or, FIAP gold award, FIAP silver award; named Woman to Watch, Boards' Mag., Woman of Excellence leadership honors, Asian Women in Bus., Brand Congress and NAAAP; nominee, D&Ads, Obies, Effies. Office: AT&T Inc 208 S Akard St Dallas TX 75202 Office Phone: 214-757-3520. Business E-Mail: esther.lee@att.com.

LEE, FRED C., electrical engineering educator; b. China, 1946; BSEE, Nat. Cheng Kung U., Taiwan, 1968; MSEE, Duke U., Durham, NC, 1972, PhD, 1974. Tchg. asst. Duke U., 1970-72; rsch. asst. Spacecraft Sys. Rsch. Lab., 1972-74; mem. tech. staff TRW Systems, 1974-77; asst. to assoc. prof., then prof. Va. Poly. Inst. & State U., Blacksburg, 1977-83, founder, dir. Va. Power Electronics Ctr. (VPEC), 1983—98, James S. Tucker prof., 1986-94, Lewis A. Hester engrng. chair, 1994-99, Univ. disting. prof., 1999—, dir. Ctr. Power Electronics Sys. (CPES), 1998—. Bd. dirs. Zytec Corp., 1986—97, Artesyn Technologies Inc., 1997—2004, Delta Environment & Edn. Found., 2002—, Delta Electronics, Inc., 2003—; chmn. bd. dirs. Va. Tech Intellectual Properties, 1993—2009; hon. Sun Yeen Chuan chair prof. Nat. Tsinghua U., Taiwan, 2001. Recipient Alumni award for rsch. excellence, Va. Tech, 1990, Coll. Engring. Dean's award for excellence in rsch., 1997, Arthur E. Fury award for leadership & innovation, 1998, Outstanding Alumni award, Nat. Cheng Kung U., 2004, Ernst-Blickle award, SEW-Eueodrive Found., Germany, 2005. Mem.: NAE, IEEE Power Electronics Soc. (pres. 1993—94, William E. Newell Power Electronics award 1989), Soc. Automotive Engring. (Ralph R. Teeter Edn. award 1985). Office: Virginia Tech Center Power Electronics Systems 655 Whitemore Hall Blacksburg VA 24061-0111 Business E-Mail: fclee@vt.edu.

LEE, GERALD BRUCE, federal judge; b. Washington, 1952; BA, JD, American U., 1976. Pvt. law practice Fairfax County, Va., 1976—92; judge Cir. Ct. Va. 19th Dist., 1992—98, US Dist. Ct. (ea. dist.) Va., 1998—. Office: Albert V Bryan US Courhouse 401 Courthouse Sq Alexandria VA 22314 Office Phone: 703-299-2117.

LEE, GREGORY PRICE, neuropsychology educator; b. Orange, NJ, July 3, 1952; s. John Landon and Olga (Squeo) Lee; m. Susan L. Haverstock, Oct. 3, 1988; children Stuart Haverstock Lee, Claudia Elinor Bernheim. BA in Psychology, U. No. Colo., 1975; MA in Clin. Psychology, Lone Mountain Coll., 1975; PhD in Clin. Psychology, Fla. Inst. Tech., 1980. Diplomate Am. Bd. Clin. Neuropsychology, Am. Bd. Profl. Psychology; lic. psychologist, Ga. Predoctoral intern Harlem Valley Psychiat. Ctr., White Plains, NY, 1977—78; instr. dept. psychology Coll. V.I., St. Thomas, 1981—82; rsch. assoc. Tex. Rsch. Inst. Mental Sci., Tex. Med. Ctr., Houston, 1983—84; postdoctoral fellow dept. psychology, sect. neuropsychology U. Houston, Baylor Coll. Medicine, 1983—84; postdoctoral fellow dept. neurology U. Wis. Med. Sch., Milw., 1984—86; dir. neuropsychology svc. neurosurgery and psychiatry Med. Coll. Ga., Augusta, 1986—2002, asst./assoc. prof. dept. neurosurgery, 1986—2001, prof. dept. neurology, 2001—. Dir. adult neuropsychology svc. Med. Coll. Ga.; oral examiner Am. Bd. Clin. Neuropsychology, 1989—, bd. dirs., 2004-11; cons. editor Jour. Internat. Neuropsychol. Soc., 1994-97, Archives of Clin. Neuropsychology, 2002—, clin. neuropsychologist, 2013-; mem. Med. Student Promotions Com. Med. Coll. Ga., 1989-2001, clin. rsch. I and II, Neurosci., 2001-, Brain & Behavior, others; bd. trustees Am. Bd. Profl. Psychology, 2005—2010. Author: Neuropsychology of Epilepsy and Epilepsy Surgery; co-author: Amobarbital Effects and Lateralized Brain Function: The Wada Test; contbr. numerous articles to profl. jours.; contbr. chpts. to books. Pres. Am. Bd. Profl. Psychology, 2010-2013; mem. med. adv. com. Alzheimer's Disease and Related Disorders Assn., 1986-97; bd. dirs. Red Devil, Inc., 1985-92. Grantee, Med. Coll. Ga. Found./Smith Kline Glaxo, 2003—07, Med. Coll. of Ga. Rsch. Inst., 2002—07, NIH/NINDS, 2003—10, Berlex Labs., 2002—03. Fellow APA (divsn.40, membership program com. 2000-05, chair awards com., 2000-06), Nat. Acad. Neuropsychology (chair publs. com., mem. investment com. 2001-04, program com. 2000-05); mem. Internat. Neuropsychol. Soc., Am. Acad. Neurology, Am. Epilepsy Soc., Am. Bd. Profl. Psychology (bd. trustees, pres. 2011-), Sigma Xi. Office: Med Coll Ga Dept Neurology (BA-1020) 1120 15th St Augusta GA 30912-3275 Office Phone: 706-721-3851. Business E-Mail: glee@gru.edu.

LEE, HARPER (NELLE HARPER LEE), writer; b. Monroeville, Ala., Apr. 28, 1926; d. Amasa Coleman and Frances Cunningham (Finch) Lee. Attended, Huntingdon Coll., Montgomery, Ala., U. Ala., Tuscaloosa, Oxford U.; D (hon.), U. Ala., 1990, U. Notre Dame, 2006; LHD (hon.), Spring Hill. Coll., Mobile, Ala., 1997. Reservation clk. Eastern Airlines, Brit. Overseas Airline Corp., NYC, 1950—58. Apptd. mem. Nat. Coun. Arts, 1966—72. Author: (novels) To Kill a Mockingbird, 1960 (Pulitzer prize for fiction, 1961, Brotherhood award, Nat. Conf. Christians and Jews, 1961, Ala. Libr. Assn. award, 1961, Bestsellers Paperback of Yr. award, 1962, Best Novel of Century, Libr. Jour., 1999), (essays) Love-In Other Words, 1961, Christmas to Me, 1961, When Children Discover America, 1965, Romance and High Adventure, 1985. Recipient Ala. Humanities award, Ala. Humanities Found., 2002, ATTY award, Spector Gadon & Rosen Found., Phila., 2005, LA Pub. Libr. Lit. award, 2005, Presdl. Medal of Freedom, The White House, 2007, Nat. Medal of Arts, Nat. Endowment for the Arts, 2010. Mem.: AAAL. Avocation: golf.

LEE, HWA-WEI, librarian, educator, consultant; b. Guangdong, China, Dec. 7, 1933; came to U.S., 1957, naturalized, 1962; s. Luther Kan-Chun and Mary Hsiao-Huei (Wang) L.; m. Mary F. Kratochvil, Mar. 14, 1959; children: Shirley, James, Pamela, Edward, Charles, Robert. BEd, Nat. Taiwan Normal U., 1954; MEd, U. Pitts., 1959, PhD, 1964; MLS, Carnegie Mellon U., 1961; LittD (hon.), Ohio U., 2012. Asst. libr. U. Pitts. Librs., 1959-62; head tech. svcs. Duquesne U. Libr., Pitts., 1962-65; head libr. U. Pa., Edinboro, 1965-68; dir. libr. and info. ctr. Asian Inst. Tech., Bangkok, 1968-75; assoc. dir. librs., prof. libr. adminstrn. Colo. State U., Fort Collins, 1975-78; dean librs., prof. Ohio U., Athens, 1978-99, dean emeritus, librs., 1999—; disting. vis. scholar OCLC, 2000—02; chief Asian divsn. Libr. of Congress, 2003—08. Fulbright sr. specialist, 2001; project evaluator US China Libr. Collaboration Project, 2009—12; cons. FAO, UNESCO, U.S. AID, World Bank, Internat. Devel. Rsch. Ctr., Asia Found., OCLC; del.-at-large White House Conf. Libr. and Info. Svcs., 1991. Author: Librarianship in World Perspectives, 1991, Fundraising for the 1990s: The Challenge Ahead, 1992, Modern Library Management, 1996, Knowledge Management: Theory and Practice, 2002, Collected Works of Hwa-Wei Lee, 2011; exec. editor Jour. Ednl. Media and Libr. Sci., 1982-1999; mem. editl. bd. Internat. Comm. in Libr. Automation, 1975-76, Jour. Libr. and Info. Sci., 1975-78, Libr. Acquisition: Practice and Theory, 1976-83; adv. bd. Jour. Info., Comm. and Libr. Sci., 1994—; contbr. articles to profl. jours. Recipient Disting. Svc. award Libr. Assn. of China (Taiwan), 1989; new bldg. on Ohio U. campus named in his honor: Hwa-wei Lee Libr. Annex, and 1st flr. of the main libr.: Hwa-wei Lee Ctr. for Internat. Collections, 1999, Spl. recognition, Libr. Congress, 2008. Mem. ALA (councilor 1988-92, 93-97, John Ames Humphry/Forest Press Contbn. award 1991), Acad. Libr. Assn. Ohio, Am. Soc. Info. Sci., Asian-Pacific Am. Librs. Assn. (Disting. Svc. award 1991), Internat. Fedn. Libr. Assns. and Instns. (standing com. univ. librs. and other gen. rsch. librs. 1989-93), Assn. Coll. and Rsch. Librs. Chinese-Am. Librs. Assn. (Disting. Svc. award 1983, Lifetime Achievement award, 2008), Internat. Assn. Orientalist Librs., Ohio Libr. Coun. (bd. dirs. 1991-92, Libr. of the Yr. 1987, Hall of Fame Libr. 1999), Online Computer Libr. Ctr. (users coun. 1987-91), Ohio Chinese Acad. and Profl. Assn. (founding pres. 1988-90), China Soc. Libr. Sci (hon. life). Home: 13698 W M Davis Pky W Jacksonville FL 32224 Home Phone: 904-619-8134. Personal E-mail: hwaweilee@hotmail.com. E-mail: leeh@ohio.edu.

LEE, JAMES CHING, biochemistry researcher, educator; b. Shanghai, Dec. 16, 1941; s. Winston and Annie Lee; m. Lucy Ling-york Wang; children: Genevieve Ching-wen, Amanda Ching-men. PhD, Case Western Res. U., Cleve., 1970. Prof. St. Louis U., 1976—90, U. Tex. Med. Br., Galveston, 1990—. Recipient Disting. Chair in Chemistry, R.A. Welch Found., 1990, Grad. Student Orgn. Tchg. award, U. Tex. Med. Br., 2003; fellow, AAAS, 2001. Mem.: Biophsical Soc. (coun. mem. 2002—05). Office: Univ Texas Medical Branch 301 University Galveston TX 77555-1055 Office Fax: 409-772-4298. Business E-Mail: jclee@utmb.edu.

LEE, JAN LOUISE, nursing educator; b. Grundy Center, Iowa, Oct. 30, 1953; d. Robert L. and B. Lucille (Frey) Thede; m. Henry M. Lee (div.). BSN, U. Iowa, 1975; MN, UCLA, 1980; PhD, U. So. Calif., 1988. Patient care coord. Queen of the Valley Hosp., West Covina, Calif., 1977-78; rsch. clin. nurse specialist Wadsworth VA Med. Ctr., LA, 1980-83; asst. prof. nursing U. So. Calif., LA, 1983-88, UCLA, 1988-95; dir. undergrad. and non-traditional programs U. Mich. Sch. Nursing, Ann Arbor, 1995—2003; prof., assoc. dean U. Tenn. Coll. Nursing, Knoxville, 2003—13; prof. chair nursing & health Clarke U. Dubuque Iowa, 2013—. Mem. ANCC Commn. on Cert. Contbr. articles to profl. jours. Grantee NIH, U. So. Calif., UCLA, others. Mem. Tenn. Nurses Assn., Sigma Theta Tau (past chpt. pres.). Home Phone: 865-531-1921. E-mail: jlee39@utk.edu.*

LEE, JEE YOUNG, professional golfer; b. Seoul, Republic of Korea, Dec. 2, 1985; Attended, Yong-In U., Republic of Korea. Profl. golfer Korean LPGA Tour, 2004—, LPGA Tour, 2005—. Achievements include winning LPGA Tour event: CJ Nine Bridges Classic, 2005; winning Korean LPGA Tour event: Tae Young Cup Korea Ladies Open, 2005. Avocation: cooking. Office: LPGA 1000 International Golf Dr Daytona Beach FL 32124-1092

LEE, JEROME G., lawyer; b. Chgo., Feb. 23, 1924; m. Margo B. Lee, Dec. 23, 1947; children: James A., Kenneth M. BSChemE, U. Wis., 1947; JD, NYU, 1950. Bar: N.Y. 1950, U.S. Supreme Ct. 1964. Assoc. Jeffery, Kimball, Eggleston, NYC, 1950-52, Morgan, Finnegan, Durham & Pine, NYC, 1952-59; ptnr. Morgan, Finnegan, Pine, Foley & Lee, NYC, 1959-86; sr. ptnr. Morgan & Finnegan, NYC, 1986-95, of counsel, 1995—. Lectr. in field. Author (with J. Gould): Intellectual Property Counseling and Litigation, 1988; author: USPTO Proposals to Change Rule 56 and the Related Rules Regarding a Patent Applicant's Duty of Candour, Patent World, 1992; contbr. articles to legal jours. Mem. Planning and Zoning Bd., Longboat Key, Fla., 1994—2005, chmn., 1999—2003. Fellow: Am. Bar Found.; mem.: ABA (mem. coun. intellectual property law sect., chmn. com. fed. practice and procedure, chmn. com. Ct. Appeals Fed. Cir., chmn. com. ethics and profl. responsibility, mem. stds. com., mem. fed. cir. adv. com. 1992—97), ATLA, others, N.Y. Patent, Trademark and Copyright Law Assn. (bd. dirs. 1975—80, pres. 1981), N.Y. County Bar Assn., Assn. Bar City of N.Y., N.Y. Bar Assn., Found. Creative Am. (bd. dirs.), Internat. Fedn. Indsl. Property Attys., Am. Judicature Soc., Am. Intellectual Property Law Assn. (bd. dirs. 1984—90, pres. 1991). Home: 1299 N Tamiami Trail #628 Sarasota FL 34236

LEE, JIMMIE, state legislator; b. Henry County, Ky., Mar. 27, 1937; m. Jo Nell. Owner Lee's Auto Sales; mem. Dist. 25 Ky. House of Reps., 1993—. Democrat. Baptist. Address: Elizabethtown KY Home: 901 Dogwood Drive Elizabethtown KY 42701 Office: Capitol Annex Rm 457B Frankfort KY 40601 Home Phone: 270-737-8889; Office Phone: 270-765-6222, 502-564-8100 ext 650. Fax: 270-765-2312. Business E-Mail: JOLU25@msn.com.

LEE, JOSEPH WILLIAM, sales executive; b. Florence, SC, Sept. 19, 1943; s. Warner Lou and Rosalee (Hyman) L.; m. Rita Martin, Sept. 8, 1962; children: Mark Stephen, Allison Lynette. Grad. high sch., Florence. Clk. Atlantic Coast Line R.R., Florence, 1962-69; sales rep. Durham (N.C.) & So. Rwy., 1969-74; dist. sales mgr. Westmoreland Coal Sales Co., Charlotte, NC, 1974-82, v.p. purchasing Phila., 1982-85, v.p. purchasing distbn., 1985-88, v.p. purchasing and northern sales, 1988-91, sr. v.p., 1991, pres., 1991-95; v.p. sales TECO Coal Corp., 1995. Mem., trustee So. Coals Conf., Inc., 1989—92. Mem. N.C. Coal Inst., Charlotte C. of C. Republican. Office: 11523 Glenn Abbey Way Charlotte NC 28277-2672

LEE, KENNETH STUART, neurosurgeon, educator; b. Raleigh, NC, July 23, 1955; s. Kenneth Lloyd and Myrtie Lee (Turner) L.; m. Cynthia Jane Anderson, May 23, 1981; children: Robert Alexander, Evan Anderson. BA, Wake Forest U., 1977; MD, East Carolina U., 1981. Diplomate Nat. Bd. Med. Examiners, Am. Bd. Neurol. Surgeons; med. lic. N.C., Ariz. Intern, then resident in neurosurgery Wake Forest U. Med. Ctr., Winston-Salem, N.C., 1981-88; fellow Barrow Neurol. Inst., Phoenix, 1988-89; clin. asst. prof. neurosurgery East Carolina U., Greenville, NC, 1989-93, clin. assoc. prof. neurosurgery, 1994—2001, clin. prof. neurosurgery, 2001—, adj. assoc. prof. health edn., 1997—. Assoc. editor Current Surgery, 1990—; contbr. 30 articles to profl. jours. and 6 chpts. to books. Mem. Ethicon Neurosurgical Adv. Panel, 1989-95. Bucy fellow, 1988. Fellow ACS, Am. Heart Assn. (stroke coun.); mem. AMA, N.C. Med. Soc., Am. Assn. Neurol. Surgeons, Am. Soc. Stereotactic and Functional Neurosurgery, So. Med. Assn., Congress Neurol Surgeons, N.C. Neurosurg. Soc. (sec.-treas. 1991-93, pres. 1994-95), So. Neurosurg. Soc., Leksell Gamma Knife Soc., Alpha Omega Alpha. Republican. Baptist. Achievements include research on the efficacy of certain surgical procedures, particularly carotid endarterectomy, in the prevention of strokes. Home: 792 Lexington Dr Greenville NC 27834 Office: ECU Neurosurg & Spine Ctr 2325 Stantonsburg Rd Greenville NC 27834-7534 Office Phone: 252-744-9600. Business E-Mail: leeke@ecu.edu.

LEE, KUO-HSIUNG, medicinal chemistry professor; b. Kaohsiung, Taiwan, Jan. 4, 1940; came to U.S., 1965; s. Ching-Tsung Lee and Chin-Yeh Yang; m. Lan-Huei Chen; children: Thomas Tung-Ying, Catherine Tung-Ling. BS, Kaohsiung Med. U., Taiwan, 1961; MS, Kyoto U., Japan, 1965; PhD, U. Minn., 1968. Postdoctoral scholar dept. chemistry UCLA, 1968-70; asst. prof. Sch. Pharmacy, U. N.C., Chapel Hill, 1970-74, assoc. prof., 1974-77, prof. medicinal chemistry, 1977-91, dir. natural products rsch. labs., 1983—, Kenan disting. prof. medicinal chemistry, 1992—, chair divsn. med. chem. and natural products, 1998-99. Adj. prof. Kaohsiung Med. U., 1977-10, chair prof., 2011-; chair prof., hon. dir. Chinese Med. R & D. Ctr., China Med. U. & Hosp., Taiwan, 2010-; mem. devel. therapeutics contract rev. com. Nat. Cancer Inst., NIH, 1984-88, Bio-organic and natural products chemistry study sect., 1990-94, mem. reviewers res., 1994-98; external assessor, res grants coun., Hong Kong, 1994—; cons. natural products program divsn. life scis. NSC, Taiwan, 1986-87, Food and Drug Bur., Dept. Health, Exec. Yuan of Republic of China, Taiwan, 1986-92, Genelabs, Inc., Redwood City, Calif., 1988-00, Nat. Rsch. Inst., Chinese Medicine, Taiwan, 1989—, Sphinx Pharms. Corp., Durham, N.C., 1990-94; sci. advisor Nat. Lab. Foods and Drugs, Dept. Health, Exec. Yuan of Republic of China, Taiwan, 1990—; mem. sci. adv. bd. Pharmagenesis, 1992-03; mem. acad. adv. com. planning sect. Nat. Health Rsch. Inst., Dept. Health, 1992-95, mem. recruitment and adv. com., 1996-00, mem. sci. rev. and sci. coun. com. pharm. and biotech. sect., 1996—; mem. internat. adv. com. Biotech. Rsch. Inst., Hong Kong U. Sci. and Tech., 1997—; mem. strategic adv. panel Hong Kong Jockey Club Inst. Chinese Medicine, 2002-; mem. adv. com. Inst. Plant and Microbial Biology Academia Sinica, Taiwan, 2001-, Genomic Rsch. Ctr., Academia Sinica, 2004-, Inst. Cellular and Organismic Biology Academia Sinica, 2004-, Agrl. Biotechnology Rsch. Ctr., Academia Sinica, 2007-, Inst. Biological Chem., Acad. Sinica, 2010-, Nat. Health Rsch. Insts., 2007-, Nat. Sci. Coun.'s Nat. Sci. and Tech. Program in Pharm. and Tech., Taiwan, 2002-2010, Nat. Sci. Coun.'s Genomic Medicine Res. Program, 2002-10; steering com. mem. Nat. Rsch. Program Biopharms., Nat. Sci. Coun., Taiwan, 2010-; chair sci. adv. bd. Plantaceutica, Inc., Rsch. Triangle Park, NC, 2001-04; chair com. for promotion of Chinese herbal medicine industry and tech. Ministry of Econ. Affairs, Taiwan, 2000-05; hon. advisor Chinese Medicinal Material Rsch. Ctr., Chinese U. of Hong Kong, 1999—, hon. prof. Inst. Med. Plant Devel., Chinese Acad. Med. Scis., 1999. Mem. editl. adv. bd. Abstracts of Chinese Medicines, 1986-, Oriental Healing Arts Internat. Bull., 1987-, Bot. Bull. Academia Sinica, 1988-, The Chinese Pharm. Jour., 1988-, Jour. Pharm. Sci., 1990-92, Jour. Chinese Medicine, 1990-, Internat. Jour. Oriental Medicine, 1989-, Kaohsiung Jour. Med. Sci., 1992-, Internat. Jour. Pharmacognosy, 1991-, Jour. Nat. Prod., 1994-, Jour. Asian Nat. Prod. Rsch., 1998-, Jour. Med. Chem., 1999-2003, Jour. Biomed. Sci., Current Med. Chemistry - Anticancer Agents, 2005-, Current Bioactive Compounds, 2005-. Grantee NIH, Am. Cancer Soc., U.S. Army, 1971—; recipient Soine Meml. award U. Minn., 1990, Jour. Experimental & Clin. medal, 2009-, The Nat. Products Jour. Current Med. Chem., Achievement award Genelabs, 1993, Lifu Acad. award Chinese Medicine, 1994, T.M. Tu Sci. award, 1995, Merit award Nat. Health Rsch. Insts., 1996, Editor's award Japan Oil Chem. Soc., 1997; named Hon. Prof., Shanghai Inst. Materia Medica, 1996-; recipient Outstanding Achievement award U. Minn., 1999, Achievement award Taiwanese-Am. Found. Sci. and Engring., 2003, Kitasato Microbial Chemistry medal, Japan, 2005, Norman R. Farnsworth Rsch. Achievement award, Am. Soc. Pharmacognosy, 2009, Order of the Rising Sun, Gold Rays with Neck Ribbon, Govt. Japan, 2011. Fellow AAAS, Am. Assn. Pharm. Scientists, Acad. Pharm. Sci.; mem. Am. Chem. Soc., Chem. Soc., Am. Soc. Pharmacognosy, Am. Assn. Pharm. Sci., Am. Assn. Coll. Pharm., Phytochemistry Soc. N.Am., Soc. Syn. Organic Chemistry, Am. Assn. Cancer Rsch., Academia Sinica (academician)., Am. Soc. Pharmacology. Achievements include the generation of more than 800 research articles, 100 patents, 400 invited lectures and presentations, and several thousand bioactive natural products and their synthetic derivatives or analogs as new leads for future drug design and development; elucidation of structure-activity relationships, mechanisms of action of bioactive products, herbal medicine including Chinese herbal medicine. Office: University NC Eshelman Sch Pharmacy Beard Hall 315 Chapel Hill NC 27599-7568 Office Phone: 919-962-0066. Business E-Mail: khlee@unc.edu.

LEE, MEENA, professional golfer; b. Jeon-Ju, So. Korea, Dec. 25, 1981; Graduated, Yong-In Univ. Profl. golfer Korea LPGA Tour, 2002—05, LPGA Tour, 2005—. Mem. Korean Nat. Golf Team, 2001. Recipient Rookie Yr., Korean LPGA, 2002, MVP, 2002. Achievements include winning Korea LPGA Tour events: SK EnClean Invitational, Hours Mall Invitational, Woori Stock Classic, 2002; Lakeside Open, 2003; winning LPGA Tour events: BMO Financial Group Canadian Women's Open, 2005, Fields Open in Hawaii, 2006. Office: LPGA 1000 International Golf Dr Daytona Beach FL 32124-1092

LEE, MINNIE JOYCELYN See ELDERS, JOYCELYN

LEE, PAUL W., state legislator; m. Ellen Lee; 1 child, Beth. Attended, Wallace CC, Eufaula, Ala. With magnetic tape divsn. Sony Corp.; commr. Dist. 3 City of Dothan, Ala.; salesman WDHN-TV; mem. Dist. 86 Ala. House of Representatives, 2011—. Former mem. Houston County Healthcare Authority; mem. Wiregrass United Way, Met. Planning Orgn., Ala. Mcpl. Electric Authority, Logos Bapt. Ch. Mem.: Dothan Rotary Club. Republican. Office: Ala House of Reps Rm 526-C 11 S Union St Montgomery AL 36130 Home Phone: 334-793-5232; Office Phone: 334-242-7675.

LEE, PERRY, state legislator; b. McComb, Miss., Sept. 24, 1952; m. Janella Adams Lee; children: Amanda, Lenora. With Miss. Coop. Ext. Svc.; mem. Dist. 35 Miss. State Senate, 2004—, chair forestry com., vice chair agr. com. Republican. Baptist. Home Phone: 601-847-1178; Office Phone: 601-359-3250. Fax: 601-847-7007; Office Fax: 601-359-5110. Business E-Mail: plee@senate.ms.gov.

LEE, SEON-HWA, professional golfer; b. Chonnan, Republic of Korea, Feb. 10, 1986; Profl. golfer Korea LPGA Tour, 2000—, Futures Tour, 2004—06, LPGA Tour, 2006—. Mem. Korean Team Pinx Cup, 2003. Achievements include winning Korean LPGA Tour events: McSquare Championship, 2001, HiMart Championship, 2003, Hite Championship, 2006; winning Futures Tour event: Albany FUTURES Pro Golf Classic, 2005; winner LPGA Tour events: ShopRite LPGA Classic, 2006, HSBC Women's World Match Play Championship, 2007; Ginn Tribute, P&G Beauty NW Arkansas Championship, 2008. Office: c/o Ladies Profl Golf Assn 100 Internat Golf Dr Daytona Beach FL 32124-1092

LEE, SHARON GAIL, state supreme court justice, lawyer; b. Madisonville, Tenn., Dec. 8, 1953; d. Charles James and Judith Ann (Burris) L.; children: Sarah, Laura Elizabeth. Attended, Vanderbilt Univ.; BS, Univ. Tenn., 1975, JD, 1978. Bar: Tenn. 1978. Assoc. J.D. Lee & Assocs., Madisonville, 1978-80; ptnr. Lee & Alliman Law Offices, Madisonville, 1980—90; sole practice Madisonville, 1990—2004; judge Tenn. Ct. Appeals Ea. sect., 2004—08; justice Tenn. Supreme Ct., 2008—. Atty. Town of Madisonville, 1982-88, County of Monroe, 1990-2004, City of Vonne, 1998-2004; judge City of Madisonville, 2002-2004. Co-author, Opening and Closing Arguments. Mem. ABA, Am. Judicature Soc., Nat. Assn. Women Judges, Tenn. Trial Lawyer Assn., Am. Trial Lawyers Assn., Tenn. Bar Assn., Tenn. Lawyers Assn. for Women (dir.), Ea. tenn. lawyers Assn. for Women (pres.), Knoxville Exec. Women's Assn. (sec.), Monroe County Bar Assn. Democrat. Episcopalian. Office: Ste 236 505 Main St PO Box 444 Knoxville TN 37901-0444*

LEE, STAN, state legislator; b. Sept. 26, 1961; Ptnr. Vimont & Wills PLLC; mem. Dist. 45 Ky. House of Reps., 2001—; mem. Econ. Devel. & Tourism Com., Labor & Indsl. Com., Local Govt. Com. Mem.: ABA, Fayette County Bar Assn., Ky. Bar Assn. Republican. Mailing: PO Box 2090 Lexington KY 40588 Office: Capitol Annex Rm 402 Frankfort KY 40601 Home Phone: 859-252-2202; Office Phone: 502-564-8100 673. Fax: 859-259-2957.

LEE, SUL HI, retired library administrator, dean; b. Taegu, Republic of Korea, July 13, 1936; s. Sang Moo and Won Nim L.; m. Seol Bong Ryu, Sept. 6, 1962; 1 child, Melissa Jemee. BA, Bowling Green State U., 1961; MA, U. Toledo, 1964, U. Mich., 1966. Reference libr. Toledo Pub. Libr., 1961-67; supr. info. analysts Owens-Ill., Inc., 1967-68; dir. U. Toledo Ctr. Libr. and Info. Systems, 1968-70; assoc. dir. librs. Ea. Mich. U., Ypsilanti, 1970-73, U. Rochester, NY, 1973-75; dean libr. svcs. Ind. State U., Terre Haute, 1975-78; dean univ. librs. U. Okla., Norman, 1978—2012, adj. prof. Sch. Libr. and Info. Studies, 1988—2012. Author: Library Orientation, 1972, A Challenge for Academic Libraries, 1973, Planning-Programing-Budgeting System, 1973, Library Budgeting, 1977, Emerging Trends in Library Organization, 1978, Serials Collection Development: Choices and Strategies, 1981, Reference Service: a Perspective, 1983, Library Fundraising, 1984, Issues in Acquisitions, 1984, Access to Scholarly Information, 1985, Pricing and Cost of Monographs and Serials, 1987, Acquisitions, Budgets and Materials Costs, 1988, The Impact of Rising Costs of Serials and Monographs on Library Services and Programs, 1989, Library Material Costs and Access to Information, 1990, Budgets for Acquisitions, 1991, Vendor Evaluation and Acquisitions Budgets, 1992, Collection Assessment and Acquisitions Budgets, 1993, The Role and Future of Special Collections in Research Libraries, 1993, Declining Acquisitions Budgets, 1994, Access, Ownership and Resource Sharing, 1995, Emerging Pattern of Collection Development in Expanding Resource Charing, Electronic Information and Network Environment, 1996, Economics of Digital Information: Collection, Storage and Delivery, 1997, Challenges of Collection Development: Digital Information, Internet and Print Materials, 1998, Collection Development in the Electronic Environment: Shifting Priorities, 1999; editor: Collection Management, 1996-98, Jour. Libr. Adminstrn., 1987—. Named to Okla. Higher Edn. Hall of Fame, Okla. Higher Edn. Heritage Soc., 2012. Mem. ALA (com. on accreditation 1981-83, mem. coun. 1986-90, coun. com. on coms. 1988-89), Assn. Rsch. Librs. (chair com. mgmt. rsch. librs. 1987-89, bd. dirs. 1991-94), Greater Midwestern Rsch. Librs. Consortium (chair 1994-95), U. Mich. Sch. Libr. Sci. Alumni Soc. (pres. 1983-84, mem. edtl. com. CAUSE 1995-98).

LEE, TOM STEWART, federal judge; b. 1941; m. Norma Ruth Robbins; children: Elizabeth Robbins Maron, Tom Stewart Jr. BA summa cum laude, Miss. Coll., 1963; JD cum laude, U. Miss., 1965; LLD, Miss. Coll. Ptnr. Lee & Lee, Forest, Miss., 1965—84; pros. atty. Scott County, Miss., 1968—71; judge Scott County Youth Ct., Forest, 1979—82, US Dist. Ct. (so. dist.) Miss., Jackson, 1984—96, 2003—06, chief judge, 1996—2003, sr. judge, 2006—. Asst. editor: Miss. Law Jour. Pres. Forest Pub. Sch. Bd., Scott County Heart Assn.; bd. trustees Miss. Coll. Named Alumnus of Yr., Miss. Coll.; named one of Outstanding Young Men Am. Fellow: Found. of Fed. Bar Assn. (life); mem.: 5th Cir. Jud. Coun. (CACM com. Jud. Conf., Disting. Svc. award), Fed. Judges Assn., Fed. Bar Assn., Hinds County Bar Assn., Scott County Bar Assn., Miss. Bar Assn., Ole Miss. Alumni Assn. (pres.), Am. Legion. Office: US Dist Ct 245 E Capitol St Rm 109 Jackson MS 39201-2414 Office Phone: 601-965-4963. Business E-Mail: tom_lee@mssd.uscourts.gov, lee_chambers@mssd.uscourts.gov.

LEE, WILLIAM GENTRY, lawyer; b. St. Louis, Apr. 2, 1944; s. Gentry and Wilma (Elliott) L.; m. Carter Kerr, Aug. 9, 1969; children: William Gentry Jr., Kathryn Carter. BA cum laude, Harvard U., 1966; JD, U. Okla., 1969. Bar: Okla. 1969, Tex. 1972. Assoc. Vinson & Elkins, Houston, 1973-81, ptnr., 1981—2006, of counsel, 2007—. Mem. Com. on revision of corp. laws (bus. law sect.) State Bar Tex. 1975—2000. Contbr. articles to profl. jours. Adminstrv. bd. mem. Cho-Yeh Camp and Conf. Ctr. Livingston Tex. 1990-94, mem. deacon 1st Presbyn. Ch. of Houston 1979-83, elder 1984-2009. Capt. JAGC US Army, 1969—73. Named Order of Coif U. Okla. 1969. Mem. Allegro Club, Houston Ctr. Club, River Oaks Country Club, bd. dirs. Kiwanis 1993-95, sec., 2011-12. Editor Okla. Law Rev. 1967-69. Home: 3665 Overbrook Ln Houston TX 77027-4127 Office: Vinson & Elkins LLP First City Tower 1001 Fannin St Ste 2300 Houston TX 77002-6760 Office Phone: 713-758-2180. Office Fax: 713-615-5312. E-mail: wlee@velaw.com.

LEE, WON JAY, radiologist; b. Seoul, Korea, Feb. 2, 1938; arrived in U.S., 1965; s. Kang Sei and Choon Ja (Park) L.; m. Moon Jung, Feb. 24, 1968; children: Julie, Lisa, Jennifer. MD, Yonsei U., Seoul, 1962. Diplomate Am. Bd. Radiology, Am. Bd. Nuclear Medicine. Intern Wyckoff Heights Hosp., Bklyn., 1965-66; resident in radiology N.Y. U. Med. Ctr., NYC, 1966-69; fellow, asst. radiologist L.I. Jewish Med. Ctr., New Hyde Park, 1969-71, staff radiologist, 1975-82, chief uroradiology, 1983—2001, hon. staff, 2001—; assoc. radiologist Binghamton Gen. Hosp., 1971-75. Asst. prof. SUNY, Stony Brook, 1975-86, assoc. prof. radiology, 1987-89; prof. radiology Albert Einstein Coll. Medicine, 1989-2002, prof. emeritus radiology, 2002-; clin. prof. diagnostic radiology Yonsei U. Coll. Medicine, Seoul, 1996—; cons. in field. Asst. editor: Jour. Endourology, 1987-96; assoc. editor: Jour. Korean-Am. Med. Assn., 1995-98, editor-in-chief, 1999-2000; contbr. chpts. to books and articles to profl. jours. First lt. Republic of Korea Army M.C., 1962-65. Recipient Sci. Paper award Soc. Uroradiology, 1994, Clin. award Can. Assoc. Radiologists, 1979, Disting. Svc. award Yonsei U. Col. Med. Alumni Assn., 1998. Fellow Am. Coll. Radiology, Soc. Interventional Radiology (emeritus), Soc. Abdominal Radiology (emeritus); mem. AMA, Am. Roentgen Ray Soc. (Merit award 1983), Radiol. Soc. N.Am., Korean-Am. Med. Assn. (chmn. sci. and edn. divsn. 1996), Korean Radiol. Soc. N.Am., Severance Alumni Assn. Am. (pres. 1997). Independent. Presbyn. Avocations: gardening, travel. Office: Lee Radiol Cons 6306 Adirondack Ct Gainesville VA 20155 Office Phone: 703-743-1382. Personal E-mail: wjaylee@yahoo.com.

LEEBRON, DAVID WAYNE, academic administrator, law educator; b. Phila., Feb. 12, 1955; m. Y. Ping Sun; children: Daniel, Merissa. BA, Harvard U., 1976, JD, 1979. Bar: Hawaii 1980, Pa. 1981, NY 1982. Law clk. to Judge Shirley Hufstedler US Ct. Appeals Ninth Cir., LA, 1979—80; adj. prof. UCLA Sch. Law, Los Angeles, Calif., 1980; assoc. Cleary, Gottlieb, Steen & Hamilton, NYC, 1981—83; prof., dir. Internat. Legal Studies Program NYU Sch. Law, NYC, 1983—89; prof. Columbia U. Sch. Law, NYC, 1989—2004, dean, Lucy G Moses Prof. of Law, 1996—2004; pres., prof. polit. sci. Rice U., Houston, 2004—. Vis. fellow Max Planck Inst. Fgn. and Internat. Pvt. Law, Hamburg, Germany, 1988; Jean Monnet vis. prof. law, Bielefeld, Germany, 1992—93; mem. editl. bd. Found. Press; bd. dirs. IMAX Corp. Co-editor: Human Rights, 1999. Pres. Columbia Cmty. Services. Mem.: Coun. Fgn. Rels., Assn. of the Bar of the City of NY, Am. Soc. of Internat. Law, Am. Law Inst., Am. Law Deans Assn., ABA, Am. Assn. of Law Schools. Office: Rice University Office of President 6100 Main St Houston TX 77005 E-mail: president@rice.edu.*

LEEDS, CHARLES ALAN, publishing executive; b. Mpls., Aug. 20, 1951; s. Charles Phillips and Irene (Pollard) L.; m. Karen Sue Biggs, Aug. 2, 1986; children: Charles Austin, Tyler Dixon. BA, Drake U., 1973, MPA, 1978. Mktg. coord. Register and Tribune Syndicate Inc., Des Moines, 1973-79; sales mgr. Washington Post Writers Group, Washington, 1979-89; pres. and editorial dir. LA Times Washington Post News Svc., Washington, 1989—2009, Wash. Post News Svc. Bloomberg News, 2010—. Asst. professorial lectr. George Washington U., Washington, 1986, 88. Mem. nat. adv. bd. Sch. Journalism and Mass Comm. Drake U., 1996—2001, chmn. Bus. Basics, 1999—2003. Recipient Best in Bus. award Am. Journalism Rev., 1995. Mem. Internat. Press Inst. (assoc.), Soc. Profl. Journalists, Sigma Delta Chi (dir. 2007-), Kappa Tau Alpha. Presbyterian. Avocations: golf, bicycling. Home: 4714 17th St N Arlington VA 22207-2031 Office: Washington Post News Svc Bloomberg News 1150 15th St NW Washington DC 20071-0001

LEEDS, STACY L., dean, law educator; BA, Wash. U., St. Louis; MBA, U. Tenn.; JD, U. Tulsa, Okla.; LLM, U. Wis., Madison. Law clk. Native American Rights Fund, 1996; William H. Hastie fellow U. Wis., Madison, 1998—2000; dir. No. Plains Indian Law Ctr., asst. prof. law U. ND, 2000—03; dir. Tribal Law & Govt. Ctr., prof. law U. Kans. Sch. Law, 2003—11, interim assoc. dean academic affairs, prof. law, 2010—11; dean, prof. law U. Ark. Sch. Law, Fayetteville, 2011—. Commr. US Dept. Interior Commn. on Indian Trust Adminstrn. and Reform, 2011—. Contbr. chapters to books, articles to profl. jours. Justice Cherokee Nation Supreme Ct., 2002—06; chief justice Supreme Ct. for Kickapoo Tribe; spl. judge Muscogee (Creek) Nation Dist. Ct.; assoc. judge Ct. Appeals for Turtle Mountain Band of Chippewas; citizen Cherokee Nation, Okla. Fellow, Harvard U. W.E.B. DuBois Inst., 2008—09; Fletcher fellow. Office: School of Law 1 University of Arkansas Office 166 Fayetteville AR 72701 Office Phone: 479-575-4504. Business E-Mail: sleeds@uark.edu.*

LEEPER, ROBERT (BOB) J., state legislator; b. Dec. 8, 1958; Former mayor pro tem & city commr., Paducah; state senator Dist. 2 Ky., 1991—; former chmn. Local Govt. Com.; chmn. Econ. Devel. & Labor Com.; mem. Banking & Ins., Health & Welfare Com., Licensing & Occupations Com.; state senate Ky.; former office mgr. Mem.: Paducah C. of C., World Chiropractic Alliance, Leadership Paducah Alumni Bd., Lone Oak Lions Club. Independent. Baptist. Mailing: 229 S Friendship Rd Paducah KY 42003 Office: Capitol Annex Rm 230 Frankfort KY 40601 Home Phone: 270-554-2771; Office Phone: 270-554-9637, 502-564-8100 ext 712. Office Fax: 270-554-5337. E-mail: bob.leeper@lrc.ky.gov.

LEESER, OSCAR, Mayor, El Paso, Texas; b. Chihuahua, Mex. married; 4 children. Pres., dealer operator Hyundai of El Paso, Tex.; pres. Hyundai South Ctrl. Region; mayor City of El Paso, 2013—. Mem. Nat. Dealer Coun., Nat. Parts and Svc. Com., Hyundai Advt. Com. Mem. bd. Univ. Med. Ctr. El Paso Children's Hosp. Found. Office: Mayors Office City Hall 300 N Campbell El Paso TX 79901 Office Phone: 915-212-0021. E-mail: mayor@elpasotexas.gov.

LEET, RICHARD HALE, oil industry executive; b. Maryville, Mo., Oct. 11, 1926; s. Theron Hale and Helen Eloise (Rutledge) L.; m. Phyllis Jean Combs, June 14, 1949; children: Richard Hale II, Alan Combs, Dana Ellen. BS in Chemistry, N.W. Mo. State Coll., 1948; PhD in Phys. Chemistry, Ohio State U., 1952. Rsch. chemist Standard Oil Co., Whiting, Ind., 1953-64; dir. long-range and capital planning, mktg. dept. Am. Oil Co., Chgo., 1964-68, mgr. ops. planning, mfg. dept., 1968-70, regional v.p. Atlanta, 1970-71, v.p. supply Chgo., 1971-74; v.p. planning and adminstrn. Amoco Chems. Corp., Chgo., 1974-75, v.p. mktg., 1975-77, exec. v.p., 1977-78, pres., 1978-83; dir. Amoco Corp., Chgo., 1983-91, vice chmn., 1991-92. Bd. dirs. emeritus Gt. Lakes Chem., Vulcan Materials Corp., ITW, Landauer, Inc. Former chmn. bd. mgrs. Met. YMCA, Chgo.; former pres. Boy Scouts Am.; former chmn. bd. Am. Indsl. Health Coun.; former bd. visitors Emory U., 1970-71; hon. v.p. found. bd. Ohio State U; trustee Brenau U. With USNR, 1944-46. Mem. Chem. Mfrs. Assn. (dir.), Phi Sigma Epsilon, Gamma Alpha.

LEFEBER, EDWARD JAMES, JR., internist, educator; b. Galveston, Tex., Jan. 12, 1941; s. Edward James Lefeber and Ellie Hancock Weisiger; m. Faith Linn Gabrielsen, Nov. 18, 1967; 1 child, Karin. BA cum laude, U. South, Sewanee, Tenn., 1962; MD with honors, U. Tex., Galveston, 1966. Cert. internal medicine 1976, 1997, geriatric medicine 1988, 1997, Tex. Exam. Impairment Rating Skills, 2011. Intern Georgetown U., 1966—67, resident intern med., 1969—70; chief res. William Beaumont, El Paso, 1970—71; staff, dept. internal medicine William Beaumont Army Hosp., 1970—72; pvt. practice Casa Blanca Med. Grp., Mesa, Ariz., 1972—73; staff physician VAMC, Phoenix, 1973—82, chief gen. internal medicine, dept. medicine, 1982—95; staff physician Temple VAMC, 1995—98; ret., 1973—99; attending physician Good Samaritan Phoenix VAMC Internal Medicine, 1974—95; mem., clin. staff U. Hosp. San Antonio, 1999—2011; ret. mem. UTHSC, 1999—2011; physician Tex. Workmans Compensation, 2011—13. Adj. lectr. dept. internal medicine U. Ariz. Med. Sch, 1982—95; asst. prof. internal medicine Texas A&M Med. Sch., Tex., 1996—99; clin. staff U. Physicians Grp., 1999—2010; clin. staff mem. U. Tex. Medicine, San Antonio, 2010—11; asst. prof., internal medicine UTHSCSA, 1999—2011; ret. Col. USAR, 1967—2001, gen. med. officer US Army, 1967—69, Vietnam, hosp. cmdr. US Army, 403 Combat Support Hosp., active duty US Army, 1990—91, commdg. officer, major assignment, 1988—92, Phoenix, Saudi Arabia. Decorated Bronze Star Medal US Army, Meritorious Svc. medal, Army Commendation award VALOR; named one of Top Physicians, Consumer Rsch. Coun. America, 2003—12. Fellow: Am. Coll. Physicians; mem.: ROA, MOAA, AMA, Alpha Omega Alpha. Episcopalian. Avocations: hiking, history.

LEFER, ALLAN MARK, physiologist; b. NYC, Feb. 1, 1936; s. I. Judah and Lillian G. Lefer; m. Mary E. Indoe, Aug. 23, 1959; children: Debra Lynn, David Joseph, Barry Lee and Leslie Ann (twins). BA, Adelphi Coll., 1957, Western Res. U., 1959; PhD, U. Ill., 1962. Instr. physiology, USPHS-NIH fellow Western Res. U., 1962-64; asst. prof. physiology U. Va., 1964-69, assoc. prof., 1969-71, prof., 1972-74; vis. prof. Hadassah Med. Sch., Jerusalem, 1971-72; prof., chmn. dept. physiology Jefferson Med. Coll., Thomas Jefferson U., Phila., 1974—2001, prof. emeritus, 2001—; dir. Ischemia-Shock Rsch. Inst., 1980-95. Cons. Merck & Co., Upjohn Co., Genentech Inc., Syntex, Inc., Ciba-Geigy, NIH, Nitromed, IBEX Technologies, Bristol-Myers Squibb, Cytel Corp., Wellcome Found.; vis. prof. 1985-86, Pfizer vis. prof. cardiovasc. medicine, 1995; Nat. Bd. of Med. Examiners, Step 1, 1993-95; vis. prof. U. Calif., San Diego, 1995-96. Author: Pathophysiology and Therapeutics of Myocardial Ischemia, 1977, Prostaglandins in Cardiovascular and Renal Function, 1979, Cellular and Molecular Aspects of Shock and Trauma, 1983; Leukotrienes in Cardiovascular and Pulmonary Function, 1985; mng. editor: Eicosanoids, 1988-93; editor Circulatory Shock, 1973-80; field editor Jour. of Pharmacology and Exptl. Therapeutics Cardiovasc., 1994-2000; mem. editl. bd. Critical Care Medicine, Shock, Am. Jour. Physiology, Endothelium, Cardiovasc. Pathology, Drug News and Perspectives; contbr. to World Book Ency. Sci. Yearbook, 1979, Cardiovasc. Drug Reviews, Circulation Rsch. Drugs Today; contbr. over 600 articles to profl. jours. Chmn. United Jewish Appeal of Charlottesville, Va., 1973-74; coach basketball and baseball Huntingdon Valley Athletic Assn., 1975-78. Recipient Pres. and Visitor's prize in rsch. U. Va., 1970, Disting. Alumnus award U. Ill., 1996, Disting. Svc. award Coll. Grad. Studies, Thomas Jefferson U., 1999; NSF fellow U. Ill., 1960-62. Fellow Am. Coll. Cardiology; mem. AAAS, Am. Physiol. Soc. (Carl J. Wiggers award 2003), Am. Soc. Pharmacology and Exptl. Therapeutics, Internat. Heart Rsch. Soc., Am. Heart Assn. (established investigator 1968-73, fellow circulation coun., nat. grant rev. com. 1993-95), Pa. Heart Assn. (rsch. com.), Shock Soc. (hon. life, chmn. membership com., pres. 1983-84, chmn. devel. com. 1985-89, chmn. internat. rels. com. 1993, Disting. Svc. award 1989), Internat. Fed. Shock Socs. (coun. 1994-2002, pres. 4th internat. shock congress 1996-99), Soc. Exptl. Biology and Medicine, Soc. Leukocyte Biology, Israel Soc. Physiology and Pharmacology, Phila. Physiol. Soc. (pres. 1978-79), Sierra Club, B'nai B'rith (Charlottesville chpt., v.p. 1967-68, chmn. Va. Hillel 1970-71), Sigma Xi, Oyster Reef Golf Club (golf com. 2006-11), Dolphin Head Golf Club. Democrat. Home: 57 Oyster Reef Dr Hilton Head Island SC 29926 E-mail: allefer@aol.com.

LEFFINGWELL, LEE, mayor, Austin, Texas; Degree in Mech. Engring., U. Tex. Pilot Delta Air Lines, capt.; mayor City of Austin, Tex., 2009—. Consensus appointee City of Austin Environ. Bd., chair. Officer USN, pilot USN, with USNR. Avocations: hiking, jogging. Office: Mayors Office PO Box 1088 Austin TX 78767 Office Phone: 512-974-2250. Office Fax: 512-974-2337.*

LEFKOWITZ, ROBERT JOSEPH, biomedical researcher, educator; b. NYC, Apr. 15, 1943; s. Max and Rose (Levine) Lefkowitz; m. Lynn Tilley, May 26, 1991. BA, Columbia Coll., NYC, 1962; MD, Columbia U. Coll. Physicians and Surgeons, NYC, 1966. Diplomate Am. Bd. Internal Medicine. Assoc. prof. medicine Duke U. Med. Ctr., Durham, NC, 1973—77, prof. medicine, 1977—, James B. Duke prof. medicine, 1982—, prof. biochemistry, 1985—. Established investigator American Heart Assn., 1973—76; investigator Howard Hughes Med. Inst. (HHMI), Durham, 1976—; vis. prof. NYU, 1996. Author: Receptor Binding Studies in Adrenergic Pharmacology, 1978, Receptor Regulation, 1981, Principles of Biochemistry, 1983. Recipient Young Scientist award, Passano Found., 1978, George Thorn award, Howard Hughes Med. Inst., 1979, Oppenheimer award, 1982, Gordon Wilson medal, American Clin. & Climatol. Assn., 1982, Lita Annenberg Hazen award, 1983, Outstanding Rsch. award, Internat. Soc. Health Rsch., 1985, H.B. Van Dyke award, Coll. Physicians & Surgeons Columbia U., 1986, Steven C. Beering award, Ind. U. Sch. Medicine, 1986, NC award in Sci., 1987, Internat. award, Gairdner Found., 1988, Novo Nordsk Biotechnology award, 1990, Basic Rsch. prize, 1990, Biomedical Rsch. award, Assn. American Med. Colleges, 1990, City of Medecin award, NC, 1991, The Giovani Lorenzini prize for basic biomedical rsch., 1992, Alumnus award for Disting. Achievement in Cardiovasc. Rsch., Columbia U. Coll. Physicians & Surgeons, 1992, Joseph Mather Smith prize, 1993, The Endocrine Soc. Gerald D. Aurbach Lectr. award, Inst. of Medicine NAS, 1995, J. David Gladstone Institutions Disting. Lecture award, 1996, Ciba award, Hypertension Rsch. award, 1996, Glorney-Raisbeck award in cardiology, N.Y. Acad. Medicine, 1997, Novartis/Drew award in Biomedical Rsch., 2000, F.E. Shideman-Sterling award, U. Minn., 2001, Louis & Artur Lucian award for Rsch. in Circulatory Disease, 2001, Peter Harris Disting. Scientist award, Internat. Soc. for Heart Rsch., 2001, 15th Ann. Pasarow Cardiovasc. Rsch. award, The Robert J. & Claire Pasarow Found., 2002, Bio/Tech. Winter Symposia Feodor Lynen award, Medal of Merit, Internat. Acad. Cardiovasc. Sciences, 2003, IPSEN Endocrinology prize, Found. IPSEN, Paris, 2003, Found. Lefoulon-Delalande Grand Prize for Sci. award, Inst. France, 2003, Founding Disting. Scientist award, American Heart Assn., 2003, Herbert Tabor Lecture award, American Soc. Biol. Chemistry & Molecular Biology, 2004, Shaw prize, Life Sci. & Medicine, Shaw Prize Found., 2007, Nat. Medal Sci., The White House, 2007, BBVA Frontiers of Knowledge award, 2009, Rsch. Achievement award, American Heart Assn., 2009, Disting. Lecture award, Basic Sci., Heart Failure Soc. America, 2007, Nat. Sci. medal, 2007, Rsch. Achievement award, AHA, 2009, Steven's Triennial prize, Columbia U. Coll. Physicians & Surgeons, 2009, Found. Frontiers of Knowledge award, 2010, Achievement award, SBS Soc. Biomol. Scis., 2011, Norman Weiner award, Am. Soc. Pharmacology & Exptl. Therapeutics, 2011, Kober medal, Assn. Am. Physicians, 2012; co-recipient Nobel Prize in Chemistry, Royal Swedish Acad. Sciences, 2012;, Internat. Acad. Cardiovasc. Scis., 2002. Mem.: NAS (Jessie Stevenson Kovalenko medal 2001), Inst. Medicine, American Heart Assn. Basic Rsch. Soc., American Acad. Arts & Sciences, American Fedn. Clin. Rsch. (mem. nat. coun. 1978—83, sec.-treas. 1980—83), Endocrine Soc. (Fred Conrad Koch award 2001), American Soc. Pharmacology & Exptl. Therapeutics (John J. Abel award 1978, Goodman and Gilman award 1986), Assn. American Physicians (treas. 1989—94, Francis Gilman Blake award 2001), American Soc. Clin. Investigation (counselor 1982—85, pres.-elect 1986—87, pres. 1987—88), American Soc. Biol. Chemists, Japanese Biochemical Soc. (hon.). Office: Duke U Med Ctr 467 Carl Bldg PO Box 3821 Durham NC 27710 Office Phone: 919-684-2974. Office Fax: 919-684-8875. E-mail: lefko001@receptor-biol.duke.edu.*

LEFLER, WADE HAMPTON, JR., ophthalmologist; b. Statesville, NC, Feb. 27, 1937; s. Wade Hampton and Eunice Trudye (Chilcoat) L.; m. Katherine Webb Davis, Apr. 1, 1961; children: Elizabeth Ashley Wilson, Rosemary Kirsten, Ririe. AB, U. N.C., 1959; MD, Bowman Gray Sch. Medicine, 1963. Diplomate Am. Bd. Ophthalmology. Intern N.Y. Hosp./Cornell Med. Ctr., 1963-64; resident in ophthalmology Duke U. Med. Ctr., Durham, N.C., 1966-69; practice medicine specializing in ophthalmology, Hickory, N.C., 1969—; ptnr. Graystone Eye, Ear, Nose and Throat Ctr., Hickory, 1974—; clin. assoc. prof. ophthalmology Duke Med. Ctr., 1969—. Mem. staff Catawba Meml. Hosp., Hickory, Frye Regional Med. Ctr., Hickory, Western Carolina Center, Morganton, N.C., Duke Eye Center, Durham, N.C., Oteen VA Hosp., Asheville, N.C. Trustee Catawba Meml. Hosp., 1990-94. Served to capt. M.C., U.S. Army, 1964-66. Duke U. Med. Ctr. grantee, 1968-70. Mem. AMA, N.C. Med. Soc., Catawba County Med. Soc., Med. Alumni Assn. Bowman Gray Sch. Medicine (pres. 1993, Disting. Svc. award 1995), Lake Hickory Country Club, Phi Beta Kappa, Alpha Omega Alpha. Presbyterian. Home: 1260 6th St NW Hickory NC 28601-2408 Office: PO Box 2588 Hickory NC 28603-2588 E-mail: khlefler@charter.net.

LEFTON, ROBERT A., healthcare service company executive; BA, MBA, MHA, Tulane U. Pres., CEO VistaCare, Inc. (acquired by Odyssey HealthCare, Inc.); pres., CEO and bd. dirs. Odyssey HealthCare, Inc., 2005—; regional v.p. Horizon Health Corp., 1991—95, various exec. positions, including pres., COO, 1991—98, sr. regional v.p., 1995—96, exec. v.p., ops., 1996—97; co-founder, pres. and CEO SemperCare, Inc. (acquired by Select Medical Corp.), 1999—2005; exec. v.p., ops. Horizon Health Corp., 1998—99, bd. dirs., 2003—07; bd. dirs SemperCare, Inc. (acquired by Select Med. Corp.), 2003; v.p. Select Medical Corp., 2005. Former bd. dirs. Caris Diagnostics Inc.; bd. dirs. Solis Women's Health, Pathology Ptnrs., Inc., Signature Hosp. Corp., Women's Diagnostic of Tex., Accuro Healthcare Solutions, Inc., 2008—. Office: Odyssey HealthCare Inc 717 N Harwood St Ste 1500 Dallas TX 75201 Office Phone: 214-922-9711. Office Fax: 214-922-9752. Business E-Mail: rlefton@accurohealth.com.

LEGER, WALT, III, state legislator; BA in Polit. Sci., La. State U., 2000; JD, Tulane U. Law Sch., 2003. Former orleans parish rep. La. State Bar Assn. Young Lawyers Coun.; bd./founding mem. Desire NOLA; bd. mem St. Bernard Chpt. Am. Red Cross; bd. mem. Young Leadership Coun., Am. Bar Assn., La. State Bar Assn., Fed. Bar Assn.; atty.; mem. Dist. 91 La. House of Reps., 2008—, mem. appropriations com., edn. com., judiciary com., joint legis. com. on the budget. Democrat. Cath. Office: 600 Carondelet St Ninth Fl New Orleans LA 70130 also: Capitol Office PO Box 44486 Baton Rouge LA 70804 Office Phone: 504-556-9970, 225-342-6945. Office Fax: 504-556-9972. E-mail: legerw@legis.state.la.us.

LEGG, JOHN, state legislator; b. Brooksville, Fla., Apr. 29, 1975; m. Suzanne Legg; children: Becca, Dylan, Alexa, Jack. AA, Pasco-Hernando CC, New Port Richey, Fla., 1995; BSW, U. South Fla., Tampa, 1996. Tchr., sch. adminstr.; mem. Dist. 46 Fla. House of Reps., Tallahassee, 2004—, dep. majority whip, 2006—08, chair preK-12 policy com., vice chair policy coun., mem. edn. policy coun., preK-12 appropriations com. Bd. mem. Hudson Cmty. Resource Ctr., 1996—98, Hudson SeaFest, 1998, Bayonet Point Regional Med. Ctr., 2004—; chmn. Creation Found., 1998—2000, Dayspring Acad. Edn. and Arts, 1998—2000. Recipient Faith and Family award, Christian Coalition of Fla., 2005; named FHCA Legis. of Yr., 2005. Republican. Protestant. Office: 10014 Grove Dr Port Richey FL 34668 also: 1101 The Capitol 402 S Monroe St Tallahassee FL 32399 Office Phone: 727-869-8600, 850-488-5522.

LEGG, WILLIAM JEFFERSON, lawyer; b. Enid, Okla., Aug. 20, 1925; s. Garl Paul and Mabel (Gensman) L.; m. Eva Imogene Hill, Dec. 16, 1950; children: Melissa Lou, Eva Diane, Janet Sue. Grad., Enid Bus. Coll., 1943; student, Pittsburg State U., 1944; BBA, U. Tex., Austin, 1946; JD, U. Tulsa, 1954. Bar: Okla. 1954, US Dist. Ct. (we. dist.) Okla., US Ct. Appeals (10th cir.), US Supreme Ct. With aviation sales Phillips Petroleum Co., 1946-48; atty. Marathon Oil Co., 1954-61; pvt. practice Oklahoma City, 1962—; with Andrews Davis Legg Bixler Milsten & Price, Inc. and predecessor firms, Oklahoma City, 1962—2002, pres., 1983—86, also dir., 1973-77, 80-81, 83-86, 90, sec., 1975-80, 82-83, 90; sr. counsel, 1991—2002. Adj. prof. law Oklahoma City U. Law Sch., 1975-80; lectr. Okla. U. Law Sch., 1986; dir., v.p. Woods Petroleum Corp. subs., Turkey, Australia, Brunei, 1965-82; client rep. Can., Singapore, Hong Kong, Japan, China, Switzerland, Italy, England, 1968-81; USA nat. agent of Kamera Tourism, Istanbul travel agy., 1970-; dir., gen. counsel NJR Energy Corp., Wall, NJ, 1986-91; rsch. fellow The Ctr. for Am. and Internat. Law (formerly Southwestern Legal Found.), Dallas, 1989—, CLE adv. bd., 1998—; lectr. in petroleum field. Contbr. articles to profl. jours. Legal com. Okla. Gov.'s Energy Adv. Coun., 1973, Okla. Blue Ribbon Com. on Natural Gas Well Allowables, 1983; dir. Skillpath, Inc., Kansas City, Mo., 1994—98; ordained Cmty. Christ, 1964; missionary rep. in Germany, The Netherlands, England, Can. Australia, New Zealand, Tahiti, 1971—75; trustee Am. Inst. Discussion, 1962—88, chmn., 1969—72; trustee Restoration Trails Found., 1975, Jenkins Found. Rsch., sec., 1975—81; trustee Graceland U., Lamoni, Iowa, 1986—2000, exec. com., chmn. bus. affairs com., 1988—98, investment com., 1998—2000, trustee emeritus, 2002—; trustee Met. Lib. Endowment Trust, 1986—99, treas., 1988—99, chmn. investment com., trustee emeritus, 2007—. With USN, 1943—46, lt. (j.g.) USNR, 1946—66. Mem. ABA, Okla. Bar Assn. (past com. chmn.), Oklahoma County Bar Assn. (past com. chmn.), Internat. Bar Assn., English Speaking Union US, First Families Twin Territories, Civil War Round Table, Internat. Assn. Energy Econs., Econ. Club Okla., Men's Dinner Club, Petroleum Club. Home: 3017 Brush Creek Rd Oklahoma City OK 73120-1855

LEGGETT, DONALD YATES, academic administrator; b. Windsor, NC, Oct. 31, 1935; s. Turner Carter Leggett and Ruby (Harden) Lanier; m. Nancy Lou Porter, Aug. 17, 1980; 1 stepson, Clayton Porter Johnston. BS in Phys. Edn., Social Studies, East Carolina U., 1958, MA in Edn., 1962; postgrad., N.C. State U., 1966-67. Tchr., coach Benhaven (N.C.) High Sch., 1958-59, Buies Creek (N.C.) High Sch., 1959-64; coach, tchr., Needham B. Broughton High Sch., Raleigh, NC, 1964-66, asst. prin., 1966-70; dir. alumni affairs East Carolina U., Greenville, NC, 1970-73, dir. alumni affairs and founds., 1973-79, dir. alumni rels., 1979-85, asst. to vice chancellor for instl. advancement, 1985-92, assoc. vice chancellor for alumni rels., 1992-97, acting dir. Regional Devel. Inst., 1993, spl. asst. to v. chancellor for planned giving, 1998—2003, interim assoc. vice chancellor for instnl. advancement, 2000-01, interim dir. found. and corp. rels., 2001, spl. asst. to chancellor, 2003—04, spl. asst. to the vice chancellor for univ. advancement, 2004—09; interim dir. Leo W. Jenkins Soc., 2009—; interim major gifts officer Coll. Health and Human Performance, 2012—. Driver tng. coord. Raleigh City Sch. System, 1964-66; mem. numerous coms. at East Carolina U., 1970—. Editor East Carolina U. Alumni pubs. 1979-85; contbr. articles to alumni pubs. Past mem. bd. dirs. Pitt County Boys Club, Pitt-Greenville Arts Coun. (past mem. steering com.); former bd. dirs. Ea. N.C. village of Yesteryear; former vice chmn. Pitt-Greenville Conv. and Visitors Authority. Recipient Founders award for svc. East Carolina U., 2006; named Boss of Yr. Greenville Jaycees, 1976. Mem. Coun. for Advancement and Support of Edn., East Carolina U. Pirate Club, Pitt-Greenville C. of C. (former mem.), Kiwanis Club (charter/life mem., past bd. dirs. Univ. City), Phi Kappa Phi, Phi Delta Kappa. Baptist. Avocations: wood working, gardening. Home: 113 Bells St Greenville NC 27858-8498

LEGGETT, JAMES DANIEL, bishop; b. Williamston, NC, Oct. 21, 1939; s. James S. and Hazel Louise (Wynn) Leggett; m. Clara Faye Watts, June 25, 1961; children: James Jr., Joseph Talmadge, Cynthia Faye, John David. BA, U. North Carolina at Pembroke; ThB, Holmes Coll. of the Bible; doctorate (hon.), Holmes Coll. Bible, 1988. Ordained to minstry Pentecostal Holiness Ch., 1960. Pastor Swan Quarter Pentecostal Holiness Ch., 1962-64, Pinetown Pentecostal Holiness Ch., 1962-64, Mt. Olive Pentecostal Holiness Ch., Pembroke, 1964-70, Culbreth Meml. Pentecostal Holiness Ch., Falcon, 1970-86; supr. N.C. Conf. Pentecostal Holiness Ch., 1986-89; asst. gen. supt. Internat. Pentecostal Holiness Ch., Bethany, Okla., 1989-93, gen. supt., bishop, 1997—2009, vice chmn., 1993—97. Exec. dir. Evangelism USA, 1989—97; pres. Extension Loan Fund, 1989—97; mem. exec. com. Pentecostal/Charismatic Chs. N.A.; bd. dirs. Nat. Assn. Evangs.; chmn. Pentecostal World Fellowship; mem. exec. coun. Internat. Charismatic Consultation; mem. Mission Am.; former mem. Evang. Curriculum Commn.; writer Sunday Sch. lit., instr. extension classes Holmes Coll. of the Bible, pres., SC, 2009—; writer Sunday Sch. lit., instr. extension classes Emmanuel Coll. Pres. Holmes Bible Coll., 2008—; sec. bd. trustees Holmes Coll. of the Bible, past bd. dirs. Office: Pentecostal Holiness Ch 7300 NW 39th Expy Bethany OK 73008-2340 Home: 10 Pine Hurst Greenway Greenville SC 29609 Office Phone: 405-787-7110 x 3302. Business E-Mail: jleggett@iphc.org.

LEGGETT, NANCY PORTER, administrative assistant chief legal counsel; b. Greenville, NC, Aug. 14, 1952; d. Earl Lindeburgh and Louise (Adams) Porter; m. Ted Clayton Johnston, Nov. 19, 1971 (div. Dec. 1979); 1 child, Clayton Porter; m. Donald Yates Leggett, Aug. 17, 1980. Student, East Carolina U., 1971-73, Pitt C.C., Greenville, 1975-76. Sec./coord. grad. ext. and tchr. edn. programs Divsn. Continuing Edn., East Carolina U., Greenville, 1971-80; sect. sec. ambulatory pediat. Sch. Medicine, East Carolina U., Greenville, 1981-83; adminstrv. sec. to chmn. dept. pediat. East Carolina U., Greenville, 1983-94; resource person dept. pediat. Sch. Medicine, East Carolina U., Greenville, 1984-94, exec. asst. to chmn. dept. pediat., 1994—2003, clin. adminstrv. mgr., 2003—08; asst. to adminstr. U. Health Sys. Home Care and Hospice, 2008—11, Vidant Home Health & Hospice, Greenville, NC, 2012—13; employee experience team U. Health Sys., 2010—11; asst. to pres., COO, chief adminstrv. officer U. Health Sys. East Carolina, Greenville, 2011—; employee experience team Vidant Health HealthAccess, 2011—; adminstrv. asst. to chief legal counsel Vidant Health Administration, 2013—. Traffic appeals com. East Carolina U., Greenville, 1995-96, chair benefits com., 1995-97, parking and traffic com., 1996-2002, staff forum, 1999-2000, bd. dirs. Active Greenville Mus. Art, 1980-82, Nat. Scleroderma Found., 1987-88, Hist. Hope Found., Windsor, N.C., 1990-96, Greenville Cmty. Appearance Commn., 1990-94; com. mem. N.C. Symphony, Greenville, 1988-89; steering com. Children's Miracle Network Telethon, Greenville, 1986-90; vol. Friends of Children's Hosp. Greenville, 1986-88; bd. dirs. Rose H.S. Acad. Boosters, 1994-95, mem., Svc. League Greenville, 2013-. Mem.: Greenville Country Club, Kiwanis (charter mem., bd. dirs. 1990—91).

Baptist. Avocations: gardening, reading, walking, birdwatching. Home: 113 Bells St Greenville NC 27858-8498 Office: Vidant Health Administration Greenville NC 27834

LEGLER, KEN, state legislator; m. Barbara Legler; children: Joseph, Krystina, Kathryn. Small bus. owner; pres., owner Houston Wire Works; mem. Dist. 144 Tex. House of Representatives, 2008—. Republican. Office: 1109 Fairmont Pky Pasadena TX 77504 also: Room E2.316 Capitol Extension PO Box 2910 Austin TX 78768 Office Phone: 512-463-0460. Office Fax: 512-463-0763.

LEHMANN, WILLIAM LEONARDO, electrical engineer, educator; b. Milw., Dec. 17, 1924; s. William Christian and Johanna Alma (Schrumpf) L.; m. Barbara Taylor, June 29, 1948; children: Johanna, William, Katherine, Wendy, Christianne. AB, Haverford Coll., Pa., 1944; MS, Syracuse U., NY, 1948, PhD, 1953. Registered profl. engr., Ohio. Prof. physics acting dean Air Force Inst. Tech., 1951-66; lectr. Ohio State U., 1957-60; dep. for labs. Office Asst. Sec. Air Force Research and Devel., 1966-74; dir. Air Force Office Sci. Research, 1974-78, Air Force Weapons Lab., Kirtland AFB, N.Mex., 1978-81; chief scientist Combat Devel. Experimentation Ctr. U.S. Army Sci. Support Lab, Ft. Ord, Calif., 1982-85; sr. sci. analyst N.Mex. Engring. Research Inst., 1985-93; prof. elec. engring. U. N.Mex., Albuquerque, 1988-93; sr. assoc. Ctr. for Occupational R & D, 1993—. Vis. prof. U. N.Mex., 1981-82, also adv. bd. Coll. Engring.; Past mem. Gov. N.Mex. Tech. Excellence Com.; mem. USAF Scientific Adv. Bd., 1985-92. Patentee solar orientation device. Mem. Beaver Creek (Ohio) Sch. Dist. Bd., 1965-66; trustee Lovelace Med. Found. Served with AUS, 1944-45. Recipient Air Force Exceptional Civilian Service medal with three oak leaf cluster, 1981, Ohio Engr.'s award, 1966, award Ohio Soc. Profl. Engrs., 1965 Fellow AAAS; mem. Air Force Assn. (citation honor 1978), Am. Soc. Engring. Edn., AIAA, Am. Def. Preparedness Assn., Sigma Xi, Sigma Pi Sigma, Tau Beta Pi. Lodges: Rotary. Republican. Episcopalian. Home: 700 Island Retreat Rd Port Aransas TX 78373-6012 Office: Port Aransas High Sch PO Box 0659 Port Aransas TX 78373-0659 E-mail: bblehmann@aol.com.

LEHMBERG, ROSEMARY, prosecutor; b. Taylor, Tex., Oct. 31, 1949; d. Seth Ward and RoseMary Lehmberg. BA in Natural Sci., U. Tex., 1972; JD, St. Marys U., San Antonio, 1974. Bar: Tex. 1975. Pvt. law practice, 1975-76; staff atty. through divsn. chief Office of Travis County Dist. Atty., Austin, Tex., 1976—88, dir. Family Justice Divsn., 1988—97, first asst. dist. atty., 1997—2009, dist. atty., 2009—. Mailing: Travis County Dist Atty PO Box 1748 Austin TX 78767-1748 Office: Travis County Dist Atty 509 W 11th St Austin TX 78701 Office Phone: 512-854-9400. Office Fax: 512-854-9695.

LEHRER, KENNETH EUGENE, economic consulting company executive; b. NYC, Apr. 17, 1946; s. Charles Carlton and Evelyn Estelle (Rosenfeld) L.; m. M. Newman, 1981 (div. 1988); m. Geraldine Trudy Fishman, Mar. 18, 1994. BS, NYU, 1967, MBA, 1969, MA, 1972, D in Pub. Adminstrn., 1980. Registered investment advisor; lic. real estate appraiser, real estate broker. Asst. treas. Banker's Trust Co., NYC, 1970-73; dir. devel. Coventry Devel. Corp., NYC, 1974-77; asst. v.p. Affiliated Capital Corp., Houston, 1977-80; dir. fin. Allison/Walker Interests, Houston, 1980-82; mng. dir. Lehrer Fin. and Econ. Adv. Svcs., Houston, 1982—; sr. economist Aztec Oil & Gas, Houston, 2005—, dir., 2005—. Prof. real estate fin. U. Houston Grad. Sch. Bus. Adminstrn., 1984-2002; adj. prof. econ. and fin. U. Phoenix (Houston div.) 2003—; chmn., bd. dirs. Acadia Savings and Loan Assn., Crowley, La., French Market Homestead Savs. Assn., Metairie, La., Twin City Savs. Bank, West Monroe, La., 1st Savs. La., LaPlace, 1988-89, Integrated Resource Techs., Inc., 1992-95. Pres. Cornerstone Mcpl. Utilities Dist. 1978-85; bd. dirs. Ft. Bend County Mcpl. Utility Dist #106, 1987-98, Houston Caliber Fin. Group chmn. 1994-96; Tex. Rep. Assn., Rep. Senatorial Inner Cir. (life, Medal of Freedom 1994). Mem. Am. Horse Show Assn. (life), Nat. Steeplechase and Hunt Assn. (life), U.S. Tennis Assn. (life), Am. Real Estate and Urban Econs. Assn., Am. Real Estate Soc., Nat. Assn. Bus. Economists, NYU Money Marketeers, Royal Econ. Soc., Nat. Forensic Ctr., Nat. Assn. Corp. Dirs., Am. Acad. Econ. and Fin. Experts, Internat. Coll. Real Estate Cons. Profls., Internat. Assn. Corp. Real Estate Execs., Nat. Assn. Forensic Economists, Am. Arbitration Assn., Houston Bus. Economists, Western Econ. Assn., Fin. Club N.Y.C., Real Estate Educators Assn., Am. Econ. Assn., N. Am. Econs. and Fin. Assn., So. Econ. Assn., NYU Alumni Fedn. (bd. dirs. 1974-77), Houston C. of C. (mem. govtl. rels. com.), Princeton Club (N.Y.), St. James's Club (London), Capitol Hill Club (Washington), Royal Oaks Country Club (Houston). Episcopalian. Home: 5555 Del Monte Dr Unit 802 Houston TX 77056-4117 Office: Lehrer Fin & Economic Adv Svcs 1775 Saint James Pl Ste 110 Houston TX 77056-3403 Office Phone: 713-972-7912. Business E-Mail: drken@lehecoserv.com.

LEHRMAN, IRVING, rabbi; b. Tiktin, Poland, June 15, 1911; came to U.S. 1916; s. Abraham and Rachel Minnie (Dinowitz) L.; m. Bella Goldfarb, May 21, 1935; children: David Lehrman, Rosalind Lehrman. DHL, Jewish Theol. Sem. of Am., NYC, 1948, DD, 1969; DHL, St. Thomas U., Miami, Fla., 1989; DL, Barry U., Miami, 1992; DHL, Fla. Internat. U., 1992. Ordained rabbi, 1943. Student rabbi Temple Shomrei Emunah, Montclair, N.J., 1939-43; rabbi Temple Emanu-El of Greater Miami, Miami Beach, Fla., 1943-93; founding rabbi, dean Lehrman Day Sch., 1993—. Vis. prof. Homiletics Jewish Theol. Sem. Am.; nat. pres. Synagogue Coun. Am.; chmn. United Jewish Appeal Nat. Rabbinic Cabinet; chmn. Greater Miami Combined Jewish Appeal; chmn. bd. govs. Greater Miami State of Israel Bonds; found. chmn. Jewish Nat. Fund; hon. pres. S.E. region Rabbinical Assembly of Am. Author: In the Name of God, collection of sermons, articles, 1979, L'Chaim, thoughts for Jewish living, 1985, Portraits in Charcoal, 1980. Mem. White House Commn. on Obscenity and Pornography, Aging, and Food, Nutrition and Health (co-chmn. religious task force); bd. dirs. Miami Jewish Home and Hosp. for Aged, Internat. Synagogue at JFK Airport, N.Y.C.; nat. v.p. Zionist Orgn. Am.; adv. bd. St. Thomas U., Nat. Conf. Christians and Jews; former mem. exec. com. UNESCO, Greater Miami Community Rels. Bd. Recipient silver medal NCCJ, Prime Min.'s medal State of Israel, Albert Einstein Brotherhood award Technion U., Golda Meir Leadership award State of Israel Bonds, Spirit of Excellence award Miami Herald, 1993, Pontifical medal Benemerenti Pope John Paul II, 2000, also others; Lehrman Dr. named in his honor, Miami Beach, 1986; Rabbi Irving Lehrman Park established in his honor by Miami Friends of Tel Aviv Found., Tel Aviv, 1988; Rabbi Irving & Belle Lehrman Recreation and Picnic Area established Jabotinsky Park, Shuni, Israel, 1992. Mem. Rabbinical Assn. Greater Miami (past pres.).

LEHRMANN, DEBRA H., state supreme court justice; m. Greg Lehrmann; children: Gregory Alan, Jonathan William. BA, U. Tex., 1979, JD, 1982. Atty. Law, Snakard & Gambill; lead atty., dir. Enforcement Divsn. Tarrant County Domestic Rels. Office, Tex.; judge 360th Dist. Ct., Fort Worth, Tex.; justice Supreme Ct. of Tex., 2010—. Chair drafting com. Uniform Relocation Act; commr. Nat. Conf. Commissioners on Uniform State Laws, 2005; lectr. Tex. Wesleyan U. Sch. Law. Contbr. articles to law jours. Recipient Ct. Appointed Spl. Advocates Scott Moore Award, 2005, Eva Barnes Award, 2009; named Outstanding Young Lawyer of Tarrant County, 1990. Master: Eldon B. Mahon Inn of Ct.; fellow: ABA (mem. Family Law Sect.), Tex. Bar Found.; mem.: Tarrant County Bar Assn., Tarrant County Young Lawyers Assn. (former pres.), Assn. Family and Conciliation Courts (former pres. Tex. Chap.), Phi Beta Kappa. Office: Supreme Court of Texas Supreme Court Building 201 W 14th, Room 104 Austin TX 78701 Office Phone: 512-463-1312.*

LEIBOVICH, LORI, advertising executive; With Salon.com, 1996; editor Talk, Cookie, Teen People, Babble, Whole Living; founder Indiebride.com; women's editor AOL Huffington Post Media Group. Editor: (anthology) Maybe Baby; author: (publs.) The NY Times, The Wash. Post, Harper's Bazaar, Elle, Real Simple, Slate. Office: AOL Huffington Post Media Group 22000 AOL Way Dulles VA 20166

LEIGHTON, RICHARD FREDERICK, retired dean; BA, Western Md. Coll., 1951; MD, U. Md., 1955; ScD (hon.), Med. Coll. Ohio, Toledo, 2000. Diplomate Am. Bd. Internal Medicine (Specialty Cardiovascular Disease). Intern U. Hosp., Balt., 1955—56; flight surgeon USN, 1956—58; resident Ohio State U. Hosp., 1959—61, resident, cardiology fellow, 1961—64; from asst. prof. to assoc. prof. medicine Coll. Medicine Ohio State U., 1965—74, dir. coronary care unit, 1968—69, dir. cardiac catheterization labs., 1970—74; prof. medicine, chief cardiology Med. Coll. Ohio, 1974—90, acting chmn. dept. medicine, 1988, vice chmn., 1988—90, v.p. acad. affairs, dean Sch. Medicine, 1990—95, sr. v.p. acad. affairs, dean Sch. Medicine, 1995—96, emeritus, ret., 1997; prof. medicine Mercer U. Med. Sch., 1998—; chmn. instnl. rev. bd. Meml. Health U. Med. Ctr., 1998—. Alt. mem. Biomedical Rsch. Alliance NY, IRB, 2007—; med. dir. Ctr. Heart Disease Prevention, St. Joseph's Candler Health Sys., Savannah, Ga., 2007—. Editl. bd. La Lettre du Cardiologue, 1985—; contbr. numerous articles to profl. jours. Fellow ACP, Am. Coll. Cardiology (gov. Ohio chpt. 1985-88), Am. Heart Assn (coun. circulation, epidemiology, clinical cardiology, coun. rep. Ohio 1977-80), Royal Soc. Medicine; mem. Ctrl. Soc. Clin. Rsch., U. Md. Med. Alumni Assn. (Honor award, Gold Key 2005), Societe Francaise Cardiologie (corr.), Alpha Omega Alpha. Office: Meml Health U Med Ctr Dept Internal Med Edn PO Box 23089 Savannah GA 31403-3089 Business E-Mail: leighril@memorialhealth.com. E-mail: rflfsl@bellsouth.net.

LEINOFF, ANDREW MORRIS, lawyer; b. Paterson, NJ, Mar. 28, 1950; s. Benjamin and Rhoda Leinoff; m. Ellen Judith Cohen, Aug. 19, 1973; children: Paul, Alexis, Max. BA, Ohio State U., 1971; JD, U. Miami Sch. Law, Coral Gables, Fla., 1974. Bar: Fla. 1974, US Dist. Ct. (so. dist.) Fla. 1975, US Ct. Appeals (5th cir.) 1975; cert. arbitrator American Acad. Matrimonial Lawyers. Assoc. Adams, Beeabe, Wood, Shuir & Mampson, P.A., Miami, 1974-75, Storace, Idri & Hauser, Miami, 1975-77; ptnr. Marks, Aronovitz & Leinoff, Miami, 1978-88; pvt. practice atty. Coral Gables, 1988; founding ptnr. Leinoff & Lemos, P.A., South Miami, 1988—. Guest lectr. U. Fla. Levin Coll. Law, U. Miami Sch. Law. Contbr. articles to profl. pubs. Named one of Top 100 Attorneys, Worth mag., 2005—08. Fellow: American Acad. Matrimonial Lawyers (pres. Fla. chp. 1998—99); mem.: ABA, Internat. Acad. Matrimonial Lawyers, Dade County Bar Assn., Fla. Bar, Phi Delta Phi. Office: Leinoff & Lemos PA 7301 SW 57th Ct Ste 545 South Miami FL 33143-5317 Office Phone: 305-661-1556. Office Fax: 305-665-2555. E-mail: Andy@LLPA.com.

LEINWEBER, WILLIAM F., medical association administrator; b. 1962; B, Marshall U., Huntington W.Va.; MBA in Human Resource Mgmt., Orgnl. Devel., Ohio State U., Columbus. Exec. dir., Ohio affiliate Am. Heart Assn., sr. mgmt. cons., youth market team leader, nat. ctr.; v.p. Rsch! Am., 2000—04, exec. v.p., 2004—08; exec. v.p., CEO Am. Acad. Physician Assts., Alexandria, Va., 2008—. Dir. devel. Campaign for Tobacco-Free Kids. Mem.: Profl. Assn. Healthcare Philanthropy, Assn. Fundraising Profls., Am. Soc. Assn. Execs. Office: Am Acad Physician Assts 2318 Mill Rd Ste 1300 Alexandria VA 22314-6868 Office Phone: 703-836-2272. Office Fax: 703-684-1924.

LEISNER, ANTHONY BAKER, publishing company executive; b. Evanston, Ill., Sept. 13, 1941; s. A. Paul and Ruth (Solms) L.; children: Justina, William, Sarah; m. Patricia Anne Leisner, 1996. MBA, Northwestern U., 1983; PhD, Walden U., 2005. Salesman Pitney Bowes Co., 1976-77; with Quality Books Inc., Lake Bluff, Ill., 1968—, v.p., 1972—, gen. mgr., 1979—91. Adj. faculty Lake Forest Sch. Mgmt., Ill., 1983-92, Kellogg Grad. Sch. Mgmt. Northwestern U., Evanston, Ill.; assoc. prof. internat. mktg. Schiller Internat. U., Dunedin, Fla., 1995—,faculty, Walden U. 2005-, Argosy U., 2008; faculty advisor Goddard Coll., 2007; head global strategic planning, spl. asst., CEO Dawson Group, Folkestone, Eng. pres. Watersedge Properties Inc., Tarpon Springs, Fla.; ptnr. Wikle Properties Mgmt., Palm Harbor, Fla.; bd. dirs. Highland Properties, Inc., Palm Harbor; chmn. Pinellas Workforce Bd., Pinellas County, Fla. Author: Official Guide to Country Dance Steps, 1980; contbr. articles to jours. Pres. bd. dirs. Lake Villa Pub. Libr., 1972-78; bd. dirs. No. Ill. Libr. Sys., 1973-78, St. Petersburg Coll. Found., Fla., PACE Ctr. Pinellas County, Fla.; chmn. Leepa-Rattner Mus., Libertarian Party Lake County, Ill., 1980-81, 02, Econ. Devel. Tarpon Springs, Fla.; probation officer Lake County CAP, 1981, chmn. bd. WorkNet Pinellas, 2011-12 Recipient Pres. award, Walden U., 2011. Mem.: ALA (councilor, del. pub. com. White House conf. on librs. and info. svcs.), World Future Soc., Am. Mktg. Assn., Acad. Mgmt., Ill. Libr. Assn. (Gerald L. Campbell award 1980), Tarpon Springs C. of C. (chmn. econ. devel.), World Isshin Ryu Karate Assn., Tarpon Springs Yacht Club. Home and Office: 1350 Riverside Ave Tarpon Springs FL 34689-6614 Business E-Mail: aleisner@waldenu.edu.

LEITCH, VINCENT BARRY, literary and cultural studies educator; b. Hempstead, NY, Sept. 18, 1944; s. Eugene Vincent and Lucile Jean (Amplo) L.; m. Jill Robin Berman, May 20, 1970 (div. May 1987); children: Kristin M., Rory G. BA, Hofstra U., 1966; MA, Villanova U., 1967; PhD, U. Fla., 1972; postdoc, Princeton U., 1976. Postdoctoral fellow Sch. Criticism and Theory, U. Calif., Irvine, 1978; interim asst. prof. U. Fla., Gainesville, 1972-73; from asst. prof. to prof. English Mercer U., Macon, Ga., 1973-86; prof. English and Comparative Literature Purdue U., West Lafayette, Ind., 1986—97, co-dir. English and philosophy doctoral program, 1986-93; Paul and Carol Daube Sutton chair English U. Okla., Norman, 1997—, George Lynn Cross rsch. prof. English, 2009—. Reviewer NEH, 1985—88; Moss chair of excellence U. Memphis, 1991; sr. Fulbright lectr. U. Tampere, Finland, 1979; vis. prof. U. Debrecen, Hungary, 2002, U. Mo., 2000, Fla. Atlantic U., 2003; hon. prof. Soochow U., China, 2005. Author: Deconstructive Criticism, 1983, American Literary Criticism from the 1930s to the 1980s, 1988, Cultural Criticism, Literary Theory, Poststructuralism, 1992, Postmodernism-Local Effects, Global Flows, 1996, Theory Matters, 2003, Living with Theory, 2008, American Literary Criticism Since the 1930s, 2nd edit., 2010, Literary Criticism in the 21st Century: Theory Renaissance, 2014; editor: Norton Anthology of Theory and Criticism, 2001, 2nd. edit., 2010; mem. editl. bd. Fla. State U. Press, 1983—98, South Atlantic Rev., 1985—87, Purdue U. Press, 1988—90, Modern Fiction Studies, 1992—97, Symploke, 1995—, Minn. Review, 1996—2009, Genre, 1997—, Project for Discourse and Theory U. Okla. Press, 1998—2000, South Crtl. Review, 1999—2001, Workplace: A Jour. for Acad. Labor, 2004—09, World Picture, 2007—, Works and Days, 2008—. Recipient Outstanding Acad. Book award Assn. Coll. and Rsch. Librs., 1988; Am. Philos. Soc. grantee, 1974; fellow NEH, 1980, 2005, Mellon Found., 1981, Am. Coun. Learned Socs., 1985-86, Ctr. for Humanistic Studies, Purdue U., 1989, 96, Okla. Humanities Coun., 2002 Mem. MLA (publs. com. 1990-93, assembly del. 1990-95, chair organizing com. 1995, chair ad hoc com. on governance issues 1995, mem. 1996, exec. com. lit. criticism divsn. 1994-98, exec. com. teaching as a profession divsn. 2007-12), Cultural Studies Assn., Soc. for Critical Exch. (bd. dirs. 1978-83, 2007-11), PEN Am. Ctr., Internat. Assn. for Philosophy and Lit., Am. Comparative Lit. Assn., South Ctrl. Modern Lang. Assn. Avocations: languages, contemporary painting history, wine enthusiast, blues fan. Office: U Oklahoma Dept English Norman OK 73019 Office Phone: 405-325-6218. Business E-Mail: vbleitch@ou.edu.*

LEITNER, PAUL REVERE, lawyer; b. Winnsboro, SC, Nov. 11, 1928; s. W. Walker and Irene (Lewis) L.; m. Jeannette C. Card, Mar. 16, 1985; children by previous marriage: David, Douglas, Gregory, Reid, Cheryl. AB, Duke U., Durham, NC, 1950; LLB, McKenzie Coll., 1954. Bar: Tenn. 1954; cert. civil trial specialist Nat. Bd. Trial Advocacy and Tenn. Commn. on CLE and Specialization. Pvt. practice law, Chattanooga, 1954; assoc. Leitner, Williams, Dooley & Napolitan and predecessor firms, 1952-57; ptnr. Leitner, Williams, Dooley & Napolitan and predecessor firms, 1957—. Tenn. chmn. Def. Rsch. Inst., 1978-89. Bd. dirs. Family Service Agy., 1957-63, Chattanooga Symphony and Opera Assn., 1986-89, sec., 1987-89, Prison and Prevention Ministries, 1992—, chmn. 1996-99; mem. Chattanooga-Hamilton County Community Action Bd.; mem. Juvenile Ct. Commn., Hamilton County, 1955-61, chmn., 1958-59; chmn. Citizens Com. for Better Schs.; mem. Met. Govt. Charter Commn. Served with U.S. Army, 1946-47. Named Young Man of Yr. Chattanooga Area, 1957. Fellow Am. Coll. Trial Lawyers, Tenn. Bar. Found, Chattanooga Bar Found. (founding), Am. Bar Found., Litig. Counsel America; mem. ABA, Tenn. Bar Assn., Jaycees (Chattanooga, pres. 1956-57), Chatanooga Bar Assn., Fed. Bar Assn., Fed. Def. Corp. Counsel, Internat. Assn. Def. Coun., Trial Attys. Am., Tenn. Def. Lawyers Assn. (pres. 1975-76), Am. Bd. Trial Advs. (advocate), U.S. Sixth Cir. Jud. Conf. (life), Am. Inns of Ct., Coun. Litig. Mgmt. Methodist. Home: 3926 Windward Ln Soddy Daisy TN 37379 Business E-Mail: paul.leitner@leitnerfirm.com.

LELAND, MARC ERNEST, trust company executive, consultant, lawyer; b. San Francisco, Apr. 20, 1938; s. Herbert and Sarah Betty (Robinson) L.; m. Elisabeth Gustava De Rothschild, July 7, 1970 (div. Sept. 1980); children: Natasha Hanna, Olivia Mitzi; m. Jacqueline de Botton, 1989. AB in Govt., Harvard U., Cambridge, Mass., 1959; MA in Law, St. John's Coll.-Oxford U., Eng., 1961; JD, U. Calif.-Berkeley, 1963. Ford Found. fellow Inst. Comparative Law-U., Paris, 1963-64; assoc. Cerf Robinson & Leland, San Francisco, 1964-68, ptnr., 1972-76; faculty fellow Harvard U. Law Sch., Boston, 1968-70; gen. counsel Peace Corps, Washington, 1970-71, ACTION, Washington, 1971-72; ACDA rep. Force Reduction Talks, Vienna, Austria, 1976-78; resident ptnr. Proskauer Rose Goetz & Mendelsohn, London, 1978-81; asst. sec. internat. affairs Dept. Treasury, Washington, 1981-84; pres. Marc E. Leland & Assocs., Washington, 1984—. Republican. Jewish. Home: Albion Riverside Apt B2 8 Hester Rd London SW11 4AP England

LEMAISTRE, CHARLES AUBREY, internist, epidemiologist, educator; b. Lockhart, Ala., Feb. 10, 1924; s. John Wesley and Edith (McLeod) LeM.; m. Joyce Trapp, June 3, 1952 (dec. Dec. 2003), Andreae Preyer Behlen, Jan. 29, 2005; children: Charles Frederick, William Sidney, Joyce Anne, Helen Jean; m. Andreae Preyer Behlen, Jan. 29, 2005. BA, U. Ala., 1943, LLD (hon.), 1971; MD, Cornell U., 1947; LLD (hon.), Austin Coll., 1970; DSc (hon.), U. Dallas, 1978, Southwestern U., 1981; D honoris causa, U. Guadalajara, Mex., 1989; D in Humane Letters, Stillman Coll., 2010. Intern to resident in medicine NY Hosp., 1947-49; rsch. fellow infectious diseases Cornell U. Med. Coll., 1949-51, mem. faculty, 1951-54, asst. prof. medicine, 1953-54; mem. faculty Emory U. Sch. Medicine, 1954-59, prof. preventive medicine, chmn. dept., 1957-59; prof. medicine U. Tex. Southwestern Med. Sch., 1959-78, assoc. dean, 1965-66; vice chancellor health affairs U. Tex. Sys., Austin, 1966-68, exec. vice chancellor, 1968-69, dep. chancellor, 1969-70, chancellor, 1971-78, prof. medicine, 1978-96; pres. M.D. Anderson Cancer Ctr. U. Tex., 1978—96, internist, 1978—96, prof. dept. bev. sci.-prevention, 2006—. Cons. epidemiology Communicable Disease Ctr., USPHS, 1953-69; cons. medicine VA, 1954-59; area med. cons. VA (Atlanta area), 1958-59; vis. staff physician Grady Meml. Hosp., Atlanta, 1954-59, Emory U. Hosp., 1954-59; sr. attending staff mem. Parkland Meml. Hosp., Dallas, 1959-66; med. dir. chest divsn. Woodlawn Hosp., Dallas, 1959-65; mem. Surgeon Gen.'s Adv. Com. Smoking and Health, 1963-64, AMA-Edn. Rsch. Found. com. rsch. tobacco and health, 1964-66; chmn. Gov. Tex. Com. Tb Eradication, 1963-64; cons. internal medicine Baylor U. Med. Ctr., Dallas, 1962-66, St. Paul Hosp., Dallas, 1966; cons. divsn. hosp. and med. facilities USPHS, 1966; mem. N.Y.C. Task Force on Tb, 1967; cons. Bur. Physician, HEW, 1967-70; mem. grad. med. edn. nat. adv. com. Health Resources Adminstrn., 1977-80; mem. Tex. Legislature Dept. Health, Edn. and Welfare, 1967, Tex. Legislature Com. on Organ Transplantation, 1968, Carnegie Commn. on Non-Traditional Study, 1971-73; mem. bd. commrs. Nat. Commn. on Accrediting, 1973-76; mem. joint task force on continuing competence in pharmacy Am. Pharm. Assn.-Am. Assn. Coll. in Pharmacy, 1973-74; mem. exec. com. Legis. Task Force on Cancer in Tex., 1984-86; adv. bd. 6th World Conf. on Smoking and Health. Contbr. articles to med. jours.; contbg. author: A Textbook of Medicine, 10 and 11th edits, 1963, Pharmacology in Medicine, 1958; translating author: The Tubercle Bacillus, 1955; mem. editl. bd. Am. Rev. Respiratory Diseases, 1955-58. Mem. President's Commn. White House Fellows, 1971; chmn. subcom. on diversity and pluralism Nat. Coun. on Ednl. Rsch., 1973-75; bd. dirs. Assn. Tex. Colls. and Univs., 1974-75; mem. devel. coun. United Negro Coll. Fund, 1974-78; mem. nat. adv. coun. Inst. for Svcs. to Edn., 1974-78; mem. exec. com. Assn. Am. Univs., 1975-77; mem. Project HOPE com. on Health Policy, 1977; chmn. steering com. Presbyn. Physicians for Fgn. Missions, 1960-62; mem. Ministers Cons. Clinic, Dallas, 1960-62; trustee Austin Coll., 1979-83, Stillman Coll., 1978-84; bd. dirs. Ga. Tb Assn., 1955-59; bd. dirs. Damon Runyon-Walter Winchell Cancer Fund, 1976-85, chmn. exec. com., v.p., 1978, pres., 1979-83; trustee Biol. Humanics Found., Dallas, 1973-82; chmn. health manpower com. Assn. Am. Univs., 1975-78; sec. Coun. So. Univs., Inc., 1976-78, pres., 1977-78; hon. life trustee Menninger Found.; host com. Houston Econ. Summit, 1990. Recipient Cornell Univ. Alumni of Distinction award, 1978, Disting. Alumnus award U. Alabama Sch. Medicine, 1982, Pres.' award Am. Lung Assn., 1987, Gibson D. Lewis award for Excellence in Cancer Control Tex. Cancer Coun., 1988, award of Honor Am. Soc. Hosp. Pharmacists, 1988, Svc. to Mankind award Leukemia Soc. Am. Tex. Gulf Coast chpt., 1991, People of Vision award Tex. Soc. to Prevent Blindness, 1991, Outstanding Tex. Leader award 7th Ann. John Ben Sheppard Pub. Leadership Forum, 1991; Inst. Religion's Caring Spirit Tribute, 1993, AMA Disting. Svc. award, 1995, Ala. Acad. of Honor, 1998, Disting. Svc. award NASA, 1998, Charles A. LeMaiste Clinic Bldg. U. Tex. M.D. Anderson Cancer Ctr., Houston, 1997; named Houstonian of Yr., Houston Sch. for Deaf Children, 1987, Lamar award Assn. Tex. Colls. and Univs., 2000; named to Ala. Healthcare Hall of Fame, 1999. Mem. AMA, (Disting. Svc. award 1995), NASA, NIH (chair joint adv. com. behavioral rsch. 1992), Am. Thoracic Soc. (past v.p.), So. Thoracic Soc. (past pres.), Nat. TB Assn., Tex. Med.

Assn., Ga. Med. Assn., Soc. Assn. Oncology (bd. dirs.), Am. Cancer Soc. (Tex. bd. dirs. 1977-89, med. and sci. com. 1974, chmn. study com. on tobacco and cancer 1976, pub. edn. com. 1976-87, chmn., mem. various nat. coms., v.p., pres. 1986, med. dir.-at-large 1977-89, Ted C. Mars award 1998, medal of Honor 1998, Biennial Symposium Founders award 2006), Houston C. of C. (dir. 1979-89), Philos. Soc. Tex. (pres. 1980-81), Greater Houston Partnership (bd. dirs. 1989-96), Alpha Omega Alpha. Presbyterian. Personal E-mail: clemaistre@gmail.com.

LEMANN, THOMAS BERTHELOT, lawyer; b. New Orleans, Jan. 3, 1926; s. Monte M. and Nettie E. (Hyman) L.; m. Barbara M. London, Apr. 14, 1951 (dec. 1999); children: Nicholas B., Nancy E.; m. Sheila Bosworth Bell, June 1, 2000. AB summa cum laude, Harvard U., 1949, LLB, 1952; MCL, Tulane U., 1953. Bar: La. 1953. Assoc. Monroe & Lemann, New Orleans, 1953-58, ptnr., 1958-98; of counsel Liskow & Lewis, New Orleans, 1998—. Bd. dirs. B. Lemann & Bro., Mermentau Mineral and Land Co., Avrico Inc. Contbr. articles to profl. publs. Mem. coun. La. State Law Inst., sec. trust adv. com.; chmn. Mayor's Cultural Resources Com., 1970-75; pres. Arts Coun. Greater New Orleans, 1975-80, bd. dirs.; mem. vis. com. art museums Harvard U., 1974-80; trustee Metairie Park Country Day Sch., 1956-71, pres., 1967-70, New Orleans Philharm. Symphony Soc., 1956-78, Flint-Goodridge Hosp., 1960-70, La. Civil Svc. League, pres., 1974-76, New Orleans Mus. Art, 1986-92; bd. dirs. Zemurray Found., Hever Found., Hawkins Found., Parkside Found., Azby Fund, Azby Art Fund, Greater New Orleans Found., 1996-05, Arts Coun. New Orleans, Musica da Camera. Served with AUS, 1944-46, PTO. Mem. ABA, La. Bar Assn. (bd. govs. 1977-78), New Orleans Bar Assn., Assn. Bar City N.Y., Am. Law Inst., Soc. Bartolus, New Orleans Country Club, Wyvern Club (New Orleans), Phi Beta Kappa. Jewish. Home: 6020 Garfield St New Orleans LA 70118 Office: Liskow Lewis APLC 701 Poydras St Ste 5000 New Orleans LA 70139-5099 Office Phone: 504-581-7979. Business E-Mail: tblemann@liskow.com.

LEMANSKI, LARRY FREDRICK, medical educator, academic administrator; b. Madison, Wis., June 5, 1943; s. Fredrick Everett and Marjery Ulila (Hill) L.; m. Sharon Lee Wulf, Aug. 6, 1966; children: Scott Fredrick, Jennifer Lee. BS, U. Wis., Platteville, 1966; MS, Ariz. State U., 1968, PhD, 1971. Asst. prof. U. Calif., San Francisco, 1975-77; assoc. prof. U. Wis., Madison, 1977—79, prof., 1979—83; prof. and chmn. dept. anatomy and cell biology SUNY, Syracuse, 1983—97, cell and molecular biology doctoral tng. program and consortium, 1987—97; rsch. prof. biology Syracuse U., 1988-97; assoc. v.p. for rsch., acting v.p. Tex. A&M. U., College Station, 1997—2001; prof. biomed. sci., biology and chemistry Fla. Atlantic U., 2001—07, v.p. rsch. and grad. studies, pres., CEO of FAU Rsch. Corp.; sr. v.p. Temple U., Phila., 2007—09; provost, v.p. academic affairs Tex. A & M U. Commerce, 2009—. Chmn. spl. study sect. NIH; v.p., IBM bd. gov. LA Grid, dean grad. programs Fla. Atlantic U., 2001—05; mem. bd. dirs. NIH rev. panel Roadmap Rsch. Programs, 2004—05; bd. dirs. Ctr. Human and Machine Cognition, 2004—08; founder divsn. rsch. Fla. Atlantic U.; bd. dirs. Fla. Rsch. Consortium, Fla. Space Rsch. Inst.; mem. Gov.'s Team Fla. in Germany and Switzerland, acad. exchange collaboration India, Mex. and Spain., 2005—; mem. govs. Enterprise Fla. Trade Mission to UK and other ednl. visits for rsch. collaborations, 2006—. Leader Boy Scouts Am., Jamboree nat. staff, 1989, coun. tng. chmn., 1992—94; bd. dirs. Oak Ridge Assn. Univs., 1999—2002, 2004—07, Inst. Human and Machine Cognition, gov.'s appointee, 2004—; bd. dirs. I.B.M Latin Am. Grid, 2005—07, bd. govs., 2005—07; Fla. del. Enterprise Fla. Team Trade Missions to U.K., Germany, Switzerland and Israel, 2005—07; rsch. acad. Trade Missions to China and Japan, 2007; bd. dirs. Fla.-Israeli Inst., 2006—07. Officer USAR, 1965—71. Recipient Pres'. award Rsch. SUNY HSC, 1987, Disting. Alumnus award U. Wis., Platteville, 1990, Profl. Excellence award N.Y. State/United Univ. Professions, 1990, 95, SUNY Pres.'s award for affirmative action, 1995, Outstanding Rschr. award SUNY Coll. of Medicine, 1997; NIH fellow, 1968-71, 71-73, Muscular Dystrophy fellow, 1973-75; grantee NIH, 1975—. Mem. AAAS, Am. Heart Assn. (Wis. affiliate rsch. com. 1982-83, mem. nat. review panel 2010-, Louis N. Katz Rsch. prize 1978, Outstanding Rsch. award 1982, Established Investigator award 1976-81, symposium chair Internat. Soc. Heart Rsch. Conf., Brisbane, Australia, 2004, Fla.-Puerto Rican rsch. com. 2004-06, AHA Cardiovascular Devel. Study Sect., 2010-), Electron Microscopy Soc. Am., Tex. Soc. for Biomed. Rsch. (bd. dirs. 1999-2001), Am. Assn. Anatomy, Cell Biology, and Neurobiology (chair nat. coun. 1997—), Am. Assn. Anatomists, Am. Soc. Cell Biology (congrl. liaison com.), Soc. Devel. Biology, Am. Assn. Anatomy Chmn., NY Acad. Scis., Masons (3d degree master), Sigma Xi, Beta Beta Beta, Phi Beta Delta. Avocations: gardening, fishing, boating, camping, music. Home: 2718 McCarley Dr Commerce TX 75428-3828 Office: Tex A & M University Commerce PO Box 3011 Commerce TX 75429-3011 Office Phone: 903-886-5018.

LEMASTER, ARTHUR JAMES, educator; b. San Angelo, Tex., Sept. 2, 1933; s. Arthur Brookshire and Ruth (Denham) L. BBA, U. North Tex., 1955; MA, Sul Ross State U., 1957; EdD, U. North Tex., 1962. Tchr. Odessa (Tex.) Schs., 1955-60; instr. North Tex. Ctrl. Coll., 1961-62; assoc. prof. Univ. Houston, Tex., 1962-69; editor in chief McGraw Hill Inc., NYC, 1969-74, 76-81; assoc. prof. CUNY, Baruch Coll., NYC, 1974-76; prof. Rider U., Lawrenceville, NJ, 1981—96; ret. Author: Gregg Shorthand for Colleges, Transcription, 1981, College Dictation for Transcription, Diamond Jubilee Series, 1981, Gregg Shorthand, Individual Progress Method, 1982, Gregg Dictation and Transcription, Individual Progress Method, 1983, SuperWrite Brief Course, 1990, 2d edit., 1996, Notemaking, 1990, SuperWrite Dictionary, 1990, 2d edit., 1996, SuperWrite, Vols. One and Two, 1991, 2d edit., 1996, and others; contbr. over 100 articles to profl. jours. Mem. Nat. Bus. Edn. Assn., Delta Pi Epsilon. Democrat. Home: 2801 Wycliff Apt 209 Dallas TX 75219-2699

LEMASTER, SHERRY RENEE, financial advisor, foundation administrator; b. June 25, 1953; d. John and Mary LeMaster. BAS, U. Ky., 1975; MS in Higher Edn. Adminstrn., Bryn Mawr Coll. Inst. for Women, 1984. Grant coord. Commonwealth Ky. Dept. for Natural Resources and Environ. Protection, Frankfurt, 1976—78; coord. residence hall program Murray (Ky.) State U., 1978—80; dean students Midway (Ky.) Coll., 1980—81, v.p. devel. alumnae affairs, 1981—86; dir. devel. Wilderness Road Coun. Girl Scouts U.S., Lexington, 1986—88, Coll. of Agr. and Life Sciences Va. Tech., Blacksburg, Va., 1988—94; sr. major gifts officer Sch. Medicine Wake Forest U.; sr. major gifts officer NC Bapt. Hosp., Inc., Winston-Salem, 1994—98; exec. dir. devel. and alumni affairs U. Okla. Health Sciences Ctr., Oklahoma City, 1998—2000; owner, cons. LeMaitre Fundraising and Found. Mgmt., 2001—11, Edward Jones fin. advisor, 2010—. Amb. U. Ky. Coll. Agr.; cons. US Dept. Edn., 1987—. Charter mem. planning com. Nat. Disciples Devel. Execs. Conf., 1984; chmn. Midway chpt. Am. Heart Assn., 1981; active Coun. for Advancement and Support Edn., 1981—2000, chmn. Ky. conf., 1982; active East Ky. First Quality of Life Com., 1987—88; adv. bd. mem. Easter Cantata, 2013—; adminstrv. bd. First United Meth. Ch., Lexington, 1982—84, 1987; deacon Bonhomme Presbyn. Ch., 2008—11. Recipient Young Career Woman award, Bus. and Profl. Women's Club, Frankfurt, 1981; named hon. sec. state, 1984; named to Hon. Order of Ky. Cols., 1977. Mem.: Comfort Found. (bd. chair 2007—10), Advancement Women in Higher Edn. Adminstrn. (past state planning com. Ky.), Assn. Fundraising Profls. (bd. dirs. Lexington chpt. 1986), Jr. League, PEO (amendments and recommendation com. Va. state chpt. 1990—92, corr. sec., charter mem. chpt. X Ky.), U. Ky. Alumni Assn. (life), Ninety-Nines Internat. Assn. Women Pilots (vice chmn. Ky. Bluegrass chpt. 1986—87, chmn. bd. dirs. 1987—88, dir. South Ctrl. sect. 2000—02), Rotary, Pi Beta Phi Nat. Alumnae Assn. (alumnae province pres. 1980—81, sec. bd. dirs. Ky. Beta chpt. 1982—84, pres. Va. Zeta chpt. house corp. 1991—94). Avocations: needlepoint, swimming, aviation.

LEMBERG, LOUIS, cardiologist, educator; b. Chgo., Dec. 27, 1916; s. Morris and Frances Lemberg; m. Dorothy Feinstein, 1940 (dec. 1969); children: Gerald, Laura Bott, Paula Saltzman; m. Miriam Mayer, Jan. 29, 1971. BS, U. Ill., Chgo., 1938; MD, U. Ill., 1940. Intern Mt. Sinai Hosp., Chgo., 1940-41, resident, 1945-48, asst. prof. med., 1955-58, assoc. prof. med., 1958-70; prof. clin. cardiology U. Miami (Fla.) Sch. Medicine, 1970—, dir. coronary care unit, 1965-75. Chief cardiology Mercy Hosp., 1974-79; chief staff Nat. Children's Cardiac Hosp., 1959-66; cons. cardiology VA Hosp., Miami, 1953-64; dir. cardiology Dade County Hosp., 1953-64, dir. Heart Sta. and Electrocardiography, U. Miami Jackson Meml. Med. Ctr., 1952-75, program dir. Courses in Coronary Care for Practicing Physician, 1970-2003, Courses in Coronary Care for Nurses, 1970-90; Master Approach to Cardiovascular Problems, 1972-82, Cardiology Update for Intensive Care Nurses, Am. Coll. Cardiology, 1978-92, Cardiology Update, 1987-2002. Author: Vectorcardiography, 1969, 2d edit., 1975, Electrophysiology of Pacing and Cardioversion, 1969; editor-in-chief Current Concepts in Cardiovascular Disorders, 1984-86; contbr. to med. publs. Served to maj. AUS, 1941-55, ETO. Recipient U. St. Torres (Phillippines) Luis Guerrero hon. lectr. award, 1977, Recognition award U. Miami Sch. Medicine, Lifetime Achievement award Jackson Meml. Med. Ctr. U. Miami, 1997, Key to City of Miami Beach, Fla., Nurses Pioneering Spirit award Am. Assn. Critical Care, 2000, Physicians Recognition awards AMA. Fellow ACP, Am. Coll. Cardiology (editl. bd. jour.); mem. Heart Assn. Greater Miami (pres.), Fla. Heart Assn. (pres.), Am. Heart Assn. (fellow coun. clin. cardiology). Democrat. Jewish. Achievements include pioneer in development Demand Pacemaker, 1964, a chair in cardiology established at the U. Miami Sch. of Medicine entitled The Louis Lemberg Professor of Cardiology, 1990. Home: 720 NE 69th St Apt 18 South Miami FL 33138-5738 Office: U Miami Sch Medicine Divsn Cardiology PO Box 016960 Miami FL 33101

LEMELLE, IVAN L. R., federal judge; b. Opelousas, La., 1950; BS, Xavier U., 1971; JD, Loyola U., New Orleans, 1974. Asst. dist. atty. Parish of Orleans, La., 1974-77; asst. city atty. City of New Orleans, 1977-78; asst. atty. gen. La. Dept. Justice, 1980-84; judge ad hoc City of New Orleans, 1981-83; ptnr. Douglas, Nabonne & Wilkerson; magistrate judge US Dist. Ct. (ea. dist.) La., New Orleans, 1984-98, judge, 1998—. Lectr. on bus. law Xavier U., La., 1974-75, 90-91; lectr. on evidence, criminal justice program Loyola U., 1977-78, mem. vis. com. Law Sch.; adj. prof. Loyola U. Sch. Law, 1999—. Mem. adv. bd. Tulane Med. Ctr.; bd. dirs. Amistad Rsch. Ctr., La. Ctr. for Law and civil Edn. Recipient Alumnus of Yr. award Loyola U. Sch. Law, A.P. Tureaud Civil Rights award, Dutch Morial Jud. Pacesetters award, Outstanding Mentor award for World of Work Acad. Mem. Nat. Bar Assn., Fed. Judges Assn., Fed. Bar Assn., Fed. Magistrate Judges Assn., La. Bar Assn. (pres.' com. for cmty. involvement), Martinet Soc. Bar Assn., New Orleans Bar Assn., La. Bar Found. (edn. com.). Office: US Dist Ct 500 Poydras St Rm C525 New Orleans LA 70130 Fax: 504-589-7623.

LEMMON, MARY ANN VIAL, federal judge; b. New Orleans, 1941; JD, Loyola U., New Orleans, 1964. Pvt. practice atty., Hahnville, La., 1964—75; law clk. to Hon. Harry T. Lemmon La. 4th Cir. Ct. Appeal, 1975—80, La. Supreme Ct., 1980—81; judge pro tempore La. Dist. Ct. (23rd jud. dist.), 1981—82, La. 1st Cir. Ct. Appeal, 1990; judge La. Dist. Ct. (29th jud. dist.), 1982—96, US Dist. Ct. (ea. dist.) La., New Orleans, 1996—2011, sr. judge, 2011—. Office: US Dist Ct 500 Poydras St Rm C406 New Orleans LA 70130 Office Phone: 504-589-7565.

LEMON, STANLEY M., hospital administrator; BS, Princeton U.; MD, U. Rochester Sch. Medicine and Dentistry. Cert. Am. Bd. Internal Medicine, diplomate in infectious diseases. Resident in internal medicine N.C. Meml. Hosp., Chapel Hill; postdoctoral fellow, divsn. infectious diseases University of North Carolina, Chapel Hill, 1983—89, prof. medicine, microbiology and immunology, 1989—97; Samuel Baron Disting. prof., dept. microbiology & immunology U. Tex. Med. Branch, Galveston, 1997—, prof., dept. internal medicine-infectious diseases, chmn., dept. microbiology & immunology, 1997—99, interim dean, medicine, 1999—2000, dean, medicine, 2000—04, dir., Inst. for Human Infections & Immunity, 2004—, John Sealy Disting. U. Chair, Human Infections & Immunity, 2004—. Contbr. articles to profl. jours. With U.S. Army Med. Corps, 1977—83, lt. col. USAR. Office: Inst Human Infection and Immunology Univ Tex Med Branch 301 University Blvd Galveston TX 77555-0144 Office Phone: 409-747-6500. Office Fax: 409-747-6514. E-mail: smlemon@utmb.edu.

LEMONS, DONALD W., state supreme court justice; b. Feb. 22, 1949; BA, U. Va., JD, 1976. Bar: Va. 1976. Asst. dean, asst. prof. law U. Va. Law Sch., 1976—78; pvt. law practice, 1978—95; judge Richmond Circuit Ct., 1995—98, Ct. Appeals Va., 1998—2000; justice Va. Supreme Ct., 2000—. Mem. Commn. on Family Violence Prevention, 1997—99; pres. John Marshall Inn of Ct., 2002—04; A.L. Philpott Disting. adj. prof. law U. Richmond Sch. Law, 1998—2000, John Marshall prof. judicial studies, 2005—; Disting. prof. judicial studies Washington & Lee U. Sch. Law, 2008—. Recipient William Greene award for Profl. Excellence, U. Richmond Sch. Law, 2006. Mem.: ABA, Va. Bar Assn. (mem. exec. com., judicial section 1996—99), Am. Inns of Ct. (trustee). Office: Supreme Ct Bldg 100 N Ninth St, 5th Floor Richmond VA 23219 also: PO Box 1315 Richmond VA 23218-1315 also: Washington & Lee U Sch Law 452D Sydney Lewis Hall Lexington VA 24450 E-mail: lemonsd@wlu.edu.*

LEMUNYON, JAMES M., state legislator; b. Elizabeth, NJ, Mar. 12, 1959; m. Robin Lynn Shepard; children: Mark, Heather, Kristen. BS in Physics, Math., Valparaiso U., Ind., 1981; MS in Meteorology, U. Wis., Madison, 1987. Businessman; house del. Dist. 67 Va. House of Dels., Richmond, 2010—. Mem. Holy Trinity Luth. Ch. Republican. Office: Va House of Dels Gen Assembly Bldg Rm 419 PO Box 406 Richmond VA 23218 also: 3296 Willow Glen Dr Oak Hill VA 20171-1916 Office Phone: 804-698-1067, 703-264-1432. Office Fax: 804-698-6767. Business E-Mail: deljlemunyon@house.virginia.gov.

LENARD, JOAN A., federal judge; b. Amityville, NY, 1952; AA, Rockland CC, 1972; BA, Roger Williams Coll., 1973; JD, Antioch Sch. Law, 1976. Asst. state atty. Office State Atty., 11th Jud. Cir. Fla., Dade County, 1976—78, chief consumer fraud divsn., 1978—80, chief consumer and econ. crime divsn., 1980—82; judge Dade County Ct., Fla., 1982—93; cir. judge family divsn. 11th Jud. Cir. Fla., 1993—95; judge US Dist. Ct. (so. dist.) Fla., Miami, 1995—. Office: US Dist Ct Ferguson US Courthouse 400 N Miami Ave Rm 12-1 Miami FL 33128 Office Phone: 305-523-5500.

LENDERMAN, HOMER, state legislator; Grad., Ark. State U. Tchr. Brookland High Sch., 1980—; mem. Dist. 76 Ark. House of Representatives, 2011—. Democrat. Office: 195 Country Rd 953 Brookland AR 72417 Office Phone: 870-926-7914. Business E-Mail: homer.lenderman@arkansashouse.org.

LENGYEL, ALFONZ, art history, archeology and museology educator; b. Godollo, Hungary, Oct. 21, 1921; arrived in US, 1957; s. Aurel and Margit (Furedy) Lengyel; m. Hongying Liu. Degree in mil. sci., Miskolc Law Acad. Royal Mil. Lvdovika Acad., Budapest, 1944; degree in law and polit. sci., Miskolc Law Acad., Budapest, 1948; MA, San Jose State Coll., 1959; PhD, U. Paris, 1964; LLD (hon.), London Inst. Applied Rsch., 1973. Asst. prof. San Jose State Coll., Calif., 1961-63; faculty U. Md. European Div., Paris and Heidelberg, Germany, 1963-68; intern museology Ecole du Louvre, Paris, 1965-66; prof. Wayne State U., Detroit, 1968-72, No. Ky. U., Highland Heights, 1972-77; dean, prof. Inst. Mediterranean Art and Archaeology, Cin., 1977-82; coord. art history Rosemont Coll., Pa., 1982-86; rsch. prof. art history, dir. Goebel's Print Collection, Ea. Coll., St. Davids, Pa., 1986—88; pres. Fudan Mus. Found., China, 1988—2008; dir. Sino-Americano, Sch. Archaeology, 1989—2009. Adj. curator Detroit Inst. Arts, 1968-72; cons. Paris Am. Acad., 1963—; dir. UPAO, Washington, 1983-87; adv. prof. Fudan U., Shanghai, People's Republic of China; cons. prof. Xian Jiaotong U., Xian, People's Republic of China, founder Sino-Am. Field Sch. Archaeology; mem. Sarasota County Arts Coun., Fla., 1995—. Author: Pub. Rels. for Mus., 1992, Archaeology for Museologists, 1993, Chinese Chronological History, 1993, Field Work in Archaeology, 2001, Chinese Chronological History, 2001; co-author: The Archaeology of Roman Pannonia, 1983; contbr. numerous articles to profl. jours. Bd. dirs. Hungarian-Am. Fedn., Cleve., 1983-91, exec. v.p., Ft. Lauderdale, Fla., 1991-2005; mem. Rep. Presdl. Task Force, Washington, 1982-86; mem. adv. bd. U.S. Dept. Interior Nat. Pk. Svc., 1987-91; bd. dirs. Mus. Asian Art, Sarasota, Fla., 2001-05, bd. dirs., US China Friendship Assn., 2008-; officer Cross of Honor, Hungarian Republic, 1992; bd. dirs. US-China Peoples Friendship Assn. Sarasota. Grantee Rockefeller Found., 1957, Govt. France, 1962-63, Smithsonian Instn., 1968, HEW, 1971.; S.H. Kress Found. lectureship Denison U., Ohio, 1967-68; Named Man of Yr., Am. Biog. Inst., 2006 Fellow: Internat. Acad. Sci. and Lettres, Oriental Sect. Arpad Acad. (pres. 1982—), Szechenyi Acad., Am. Assn. Swiss, German, Austrian Profs.; mem.: Internat. Coun. Mus., Renaissance Soc. Am., Coll. Art Assn. Am., Archaeol. Inst. Am., Nat. Fedn. Hungarian-Ams., Soc. Architectural Historians, NY Acad. Scis., Hungarian Acad. Scis., Mich. Acad. Scis. and Letters, Register of Profl. Archaeologists, Christopher Giest Hist. Soc., Detroit Classical Assn., Mich. Acad. Arts and Scis., Am. Assn. Mus., Manatee County Hist. Preservation Bd., Time Sifters Archaeological Assn. Sarasota Fla., 2012. Republican. Roman Catholic. Home: 4206 73d Terrace E Sarasota FL 34243 Personal E-mail: fmfsafsa@juno.com.

LENHART, CYNTHIA RAE, conservation organization executive; b. Cheverly, Md., Nov. 3, 1957; d. Donald Edward and Vesta Jean Lenhart. BS in Environ. Studies, Coll. William & Mary, 1979; MS in Environ. Sci., SUNY, Syracuse, 1983. Asst. to pres. Environ. Policy Inst., Washington, 1979-81; wildlife policy analyst Nat. Audubon Soc., Washington, 1984-90; exec. dir. Hawk Mountain Sanctuary, Kempton, Pa., 1990—2004; prin., owner Salamander, Saluda, NC, 2004—. Bd. dirs. Am. Bird Conservancy, Washington, Pa. Environ. Coun., Phila. Contbr. chpts. to Audubon Wildlife Report, 1985, 87, 88, 89. Chair Everglades Coalition, Washington, 1986-88.

LENKE, JOANNE MARIE, publishing executive; b. Chgo., Aug. 27, 1938; d. August Julian and Dorothy Anna (Gold) L. BS, Purdue U., 1960; MS, Syracuse U., 1964, PhD, 1968. Tchr. pub. schs., Evanston, Ill., 1960-63; editor Test Dept. Harcourt, Brace & World, Inc., NYC, 1967-70; rsch. psychologist Harcourt Brace Jovanovich, Inc., NYC, 1970-73, exec. editor, 1973-75; asst. dir. ednl. measurment divsn. The Psychol. Corp., NYC, 1975-83, dir. ednl. measurement and psychometrics Cleve., 1983-85, San Antonio, 1986, v.p. dir. measurement divsn., 1986-88, sr. v.p., 1988-91, exec. v.p., 1991-97, pres., 1997-99; cons., 1999—2002; assoc. v.p. Ednl. Testing Svc., 2002—06, v.p., 2006—08, cons., 2008—. Field reader U.S. Office Edn., 1972. Adv. editor Jour. Ednl. Measurement, 1974-78. NSF grantee, 1963-64. Mem. APA, Nat. Coun. Measurement in Edn., Am. Ednl. Rsch. Assn. Home: 2534 Winding VW San Antonio TX 78260-7257 Personal E-mail: jlenke@usa.net.

LENNON, FRANK THOMAS, security firm executive; b. New Brunswick, NJ; s. Frank J. and Ida Pierson (Denning) L.; m. Alice S. Suozzo, Nov. 25, 1967; 1 child, Heather Lyn. BBA in Economics, St. Anselm Coll., 1963; postgrad., U. N.H., 1966; degree in Risk Mgmt., 1976. Mgr. claims Liberty Mutual Insurance Co., Boston, 1963—69; asst. mgr. ins. Warnaco Inc., Bridgeport, Conn., 1969—72; dir. risk mgmt. Scovill Industries, Waterbury, Conn., 1972—77; joined Pittston Co., Greenwich, Conn., 1977; v.p. human resources and adminstrn. Brink's Co. (formerly Pittston Co.), 1990—2005, v.p., chief adminstrv. officer, 2005—. Chmn. Country Sch., Madison, Conn. Mem. Risk and Ins. Mgmt. Soc., Adminstrv. Soc. Office: Brink's Company 1801 Bayberry Ct Richmond VA 23226 Home: 387 W Mountain Rd Ridgefield CT 06877-2920 Office Phone: 804-289-9600. Office Fax: 804-289-9746. E-mail: frank.lennon@brinksinc.com.

LENNON, JEFFREY LYNNE, healthcare educator; m. Chona F. Lennon; 2 children. BA, The King's Coll., NY, 1976; MD, Cetec U. Sch. Medicine, Santo Domingo, Dominican Republic, 1982; MPH, U. Ala., Birmingham, 1986, MSPH, 1991, PhD in Health Edn., Health Promotion, 2001. Cert. health edn. specialist. Postdoc. assoc., dept. epidemiology Yale U. Sch. Medicine, New Haven, 1982—83; heath specialist Ambs. Internat., Dominican Republic, Philippines, 1987—89, Internat. Tech. Assistance Group, Philippines, 1991—98, 2002—06; assoc. prof. Liberty U., Va., 2008—13, prof., 2013—. Reviewer Dengue Bulletin Jour., Health Edn. & Behavior Jour., Simulation & Gaming Jour. Co-author: (book) Things Can Get Better, 2010. Vol. Eagle Scout, 1971. Recipient Mem., Delta Omega-National Pub. Health Honor Soc., Eta Sigma Gamma-National Health Edn. Hon. Mem.: Am. Assn. Health Edn., Eta Sigma Gamma-Nat. Health Edn., Health Honor Soc., Delta Omega-Nat. Pub. Presbyterian. Achievements include development of master of public health program in Silliman University. Office: Liberty University Dept Health Professions 1971 University Blvd Lynchburg VA 24502 Office Phone: 434-592-3759. Personal E-mail: jeffchona2@yahoo.com.*

LENOX, MICHAEL, business professor; BS, U. Va., Charlottesville, 1993, MS in Systems Engring., 1994; PhD in Tech. Mgmt. and Policy, MIT, 1999. Assoc. prof. environ. policy and bus. Fuqua Sch. Bus., Duke U., Durham, NC, 2002—08; Samuel L. Slover prof. bus. Darden Sch. Bus., U. Va., Charlottesville, 2008—, assoc. dean, exec. dir. The Batten Inst., faculty dir., founder Alliance for Rsch. in Corp. Sustainability. Vis. prof. Inst. Mgmt. Devel. (IMD), Lausanne, Switzerland, 2001, Harvard Bus. Sch., Cambridge, Mass., 2007, U. Coll. & Said

Bus. Sch., Oxford U., England, 2010. Contbr. articles to profl. jours. Office: Darden School of Business University of Virginia PO Box 6550 Charlottesville VA 22903 Office Phone: 434-924-3212. Office Fax: 434-924-7104. E-mail: lenoxm@darden.virginia.edu.

LENTINI, ARTHUR (ART) J., state legislator; b. Mar. 23, 1953; m. Stephany Jones. State senate, La.; asst. dist. atty. Jefferson Parish, 1978—86; atty., 1978—; mem., state rep. ctrl. com. La., 1988—92; state senator Dist. 10 La., 1996—. Mem.: La. Assn. Def. Counsel, La. Bar Assn. Republican. Christian. Address: 5520 Erlanger Rd Kenner LA 70065 Mailing: PO Box 94183 Baton Rouge LA 70804 Address: 6620 Riverside Drive, Ste 312 Metairie LA 70003 Home Phone: 504-887-7213. Fax: 504-838-9903.

LENTZ, HENRY E., JR., energy executive; b. 1945; BA, Coll. Holy Cross, 1967; MBA, U. Pa., 1973. Mng. dir., WW Energy Practice Lehman Brothers, 1993—96, mng. dir., 1993—2002, prin., Merchant Banking Group, 1996—2003, cons., 2003—04, adv. dir., 2004—08; mng. dir. Barclays Capital, 2008—09; chmn., internat. oil and gas Lazard Ltd.; chmn. Rowan Companies, Inc., 2008—; mng. dir. Lazard Frères & Co., LLC, 2009—. Vice chmn. Wasserstein Perella Group, Inc., 1988—93; bd. dirs. Peabody Energy Corp., 1998—, Carbo Ceramics, Inc., 2003—. Office: Rowan Companies Inc 2800 Post Oak Blvd Ste 5450 Houston TX 77056 Office Phone: 713-621-7800. Office Fax: 713-960-7660.

LENTZ, SAMUEL S., gynecologic oncologist, educator; BA, Wake Forest U., 1974, MD, 1978. Diplomate Am. Bd. Ob-Gyn, Am. Bd. Ob-Gyn-gynecologic oncology. Intern ob-gyn. dept. NC Baptist Hosp., 1979, resident ob-gyn. dept., 1982; fellow Mayo Clinic, 1989; prof. gynecologic oncology dept. Comprehensive Cancer Ctr.; hosp. affiliation includes Wake Forest Baptist Med. Ctr. Co-author: A Phase III Randomized Trial of Postoperative Pelvic Irradiation in Stage IB Cervical Carcinoma With Poor Prognostic Features: Follow-up of A Gynecologic Oncology Group Study, 2006, Intraperitoneal Hyperthermic Chemotherapy Using Carboplatin: A Phase I Analysis in Ovarian Carcinoma, 2007, Standardization of Pelvic Organ Prolapse on MRI, 2008, Hyperthermic Intraperitoneal Chemotherapy In Ovarian Cancer: First Report of the HYPER-O Registry, 2010, Outcomes After Cytoreductive Surgery and Hyperthermic Intraperitoneal Chemotherapy For Peritoneal Surface Dissemination From Ovarian Neoplasms, 2010, Hyperthermic Chemotherapy for Ovarian Cancer--report of the HYPERO Registry, 2010, A Phase II Study of Two Topotecan Regimens Evaluated in Recurrent Platinum-Sensitive Ovarian, Fallopian Tube or Primary Reritoneal Cancer: A Gynecologic Oncology Group Study (GOG 146Q), 2011, various publs. Office: Wake Forest Baptist Medical Center Medical Center Blvd Winston Salem NC 27157 Office Phone: 336-716-6673. Office Fax: 336-716-4334. Business E-Mail: slentz@wakehealth.edu.

LENZ, EDWARD ARNOLD, trade association administrator, lawyer; b. White Plains, NY, Sept. 28, 1942; s. Fritz and Hildegard (Bunzel) L.; m. Anna Maria Bartusiak, Mar. 21, 1987; children: Scott, Eric. BA, Bucknell U., 1964; JD, Boston Coll., 1967; LLM, NYU, 1968. Bar: N.Y. 1968, D.C. 1973, Mich. 1982. Trial atty. U.S. Dept. Justice, Washington, 1970-72; assoc. gen. counsel litigation U.S. Cost of Living Coun., Exec. Office of the Pres., Washington, 1973; assoc. Miller & Chevalier, Washington, 1973-80; counsel Health Ins. Assn. Am., Washington, 1980-82; v.p., asst. gen. counsel Kelly Svcs. Inc., Troy, Mich., 1982-89; chmn. legis. com. Am. Staffing Assn., Alexandria, Va., 1985-89, sr. v.p., gen. counsel, 1989-93, sr. v.p. legal and govt. affairs, 1993-99, sr. v.p. pub. affairs, gen. counsel, 1999—2010; sr. v.p. legal and pub. affairs, 2011—12; sr. counsel, 2013—. Author: Co-employment--Employer Liability Issues in Third-Party Staffing Arrangements, 1994, 7th edit., 2011. Capt. U.S. Army, 1968-70, Vietnam. Decorated Bronze Star. Fellow Coll. Labor and Employment Lawyers; mem. ABA, N.Y. Bar Assn., D.C. Bar Assn., Pi Sigma Alpha, Sigma Alpha Epsilon. Home: 818 S Lee St Alexandria VA 22314-4334 Office: Am Staffing Assn 277 S Washington St Ste 200 Alexandria VA 22314-3675 Office Phone: 703-253-2020.

LEO, LEONARD A., legal association administrator, lawyer; b. 1965; m. Sally Leo; children: Margaret, Anthony, Elizabeth, Thaddeus. AB, Cornell U., 1987, JD, 1989. Bar: NJ, Washington DC, US Supreme Ct., US Ct. Appeals (Federal Cir.), US Ct. Appeals (DC Cir.). Law clk. to Hon. Randall Rader US Ct. Federal Claims; law clk. to Hon. Raymond Randolph US Ct. Appeals (DC Cir.); exec. v.p. The Federalist Soc. for Law & Pub. Policy Studies, Washington. Cath. strategist Bush-Cheney campaign, 2004; commr. US Commn. for Internat. Religious Freedom (USCIRF), 2007—, chmn., 2009—. Contbr. articles to profl. jours.; co-editor: Presidential Leadership: Rating the Best and Worst in the White House, 2004. Bd. dirs. Nat. Cath. Prayer Breakfast, Youth Leadership Found., Men's Leadership Found., Cath. Action Network. Mem.: Sovereign Order of Malta. Office: The Federalist Society 1015 18th St NW Ste 425 Washington DC 20036 Office Phone: 202-822-8138. E-mail: lleo@fed-soc.org.

LEON, BENJAMIN, JR., healthcare services company executive; Pres., CEO CAC (acquired by Ramsay Group), 1977; founder Leon Med. Ctrs., Inc., 1996, CEO, chmn., 1996—2008; bd. dirs. Leon Med. Ctrs., Inc; pres. HealthSpring of Fla., Inc. Bd. dirs. Healthspring, Inc., 2007—. Office: Healthspring of Florida Inc 11501 SW 40th St 2nd Fl Miami FL 33165-3313 Office Phone: 305-642-5366.

LEON, ROBERT LEONARD, psychiatrist, educator; b. Denver, Jan. 18, 1925; s. Louis and Rae (Brown) L.; m. Willena Lee, Sept. 14, 1947; children: Alexis Kay, Mark Robert, Jeffrey Clayton, Stacy Lee. MD, U. Colo., 1948. Diplomate Am. Bd. Psychiatry and Neurology. Intern U. Mich. Hosp., Ann Arbor, 1948-49; resident in psychiatry U. Colo. Med. Ctr., Denver, 1949-52, child psychiatry fellow, 1951-52, Bur. Mental Hygiene, New Haven, Conn. Dept. Health/Student Health Svc., Yale U., 1952-53; asst. dir., acting dir. child psychiatry Greater Kansas City Mental Health Found., 1953-54; instr. psychiatry U. Kans. Sch. Medicine, Kansas City, 1956-57; asst. prof. psychiatry U. Tex. Health Sci. Ctr. at Dallas, Southwestern Med. Sch., 1957-61, assoc. prof., 1961-65, prof., 1965-67; prof., chmn. dept. psychiatry Sch. Medicine U. Tex. Health Sci. Ctr., San Antonio, 1967-95, interim chmn., 1995-96; Ashbel Smith prof. U. Tex. Health Sci. Ctr., San Antonio, 1990—2003, prof. emeritus, 2003—. Chief psychiatry U. Health Sys., Bexar County, San Antonio, 1967-96; mem. Am. Assn. Chmn. Depts. Psychiatry, 1967-96, pres., 1982-83; cons. psychiatry Audie Murphy Vet.'s Hosp., 1973—; cons. Mental Health Orgn., region IV, HEW, 1957-73; mem. Psychiat. Tng. Rev. NIMH, Rockville, Md., 1970-74; hon. cons. World Health Orgn., Geneva, 1996. Author: Psychiatric Interviewing: A Primer, 1982, 2d edit., 1989; contbr. articles to profl. jours. Sr. surgeon USPHS, 1954-57. Fellow ACP (pres. 1987-88), Am. Psychiat. Assn. (life), Am. Orthopsychiat. Assn. (life), Am. Acad. Child and Adolescent Psychiatry (life), Am. Assn. Social Psychiatry (pres. 1990-92); mem. Benjamin Rush Soc., World Assn. for Social Psychiatry. Avocation: photography. Home: 6866 Stonykirk St San Antonio TX 78240-2743 Office: U Tex Health Sci Ctr 7703 Floyd Curl Dr MS 7792 San Antonio TX 78229-3900 Home Phone: 210-696-3962; Office Phone: 210-567-5408. Business E-Mail: leon@uthscsa.edu.

LEONARD, CHARLES H. (CHUCK LEONARD), energy executive; b. 1949; Contr. Tex. Ea. Products Pipeline Co., LLC, 1988—89, v.p., 1988—90, CFO, 1989—90, sr. v.p., CFO, 1990—2005, treas., 1996—2002; CFO Eagle Global Logistics (EGL), Inc., 2006—07; exec. v.p., CFO Landmark FBO, LLC, 2008; CFO J.A.M. Distbg. Co., 2009. Bd. dirs. Delek US Holdings, Inc., 2006—. Office: Delek US Holdings Inc Bd Directors 7102 Commerce Way Brentwood TN 37027 Office Phone: 615-771-6701, 615-224-1185.

LEONARD, DAVID MORSE, lawyer; b. Akron, Ohio, Dec. 4, 1949; s. Frank O. and Barbara J. Leonard. BS in Chem. Engring., Purdue U., 1972; JD, Emory U., 1975. Bar: Ga. 1975, N.Y. 2005, U.S. Ct. Appeals (4th, 5th and 11th cirs.), U.S. Dist. Ct. (no., mid. and so. dists.) Ga., U.S. Dist. Ct. (so. dist.) Ala., U.S. Dist. Ct. (we. dist.) La.; registered atty. U.S. Patent and Trademark Office. Assoc. Montet & Smith, Atlanta, 1975-79, Hurt, Richardson, Garner, Todd & Cadenhead, Atlanta, 1979-83, ptnr., 1983-85; of counsel Locke Lord Bissell & Liddell LLP, Atlanta, 1985—87, ptnr., 1987—. Mem. panel of arbitrators Am. Arbitration Assn., 1995—, arbitrator, mediator. Mem. ABA (litigation sect., intellectual property sect., tort and ins. practice sect.), Profl. Liability Underwriting Soc., Atlanta Lawyers Club, Atlanta C. of C., Am. Arbitration Assn. (panel of arbitrators). Office: Locke Lord Bissell & Liddell LLP Ste 1900 3333 Piedmont Rd NE Ste 1200 Atlanta GA 30305-1724 Office Phone: 404-870-4676.

LEONARD, J. WAYNE, energy executive; BA in Acctg., Ball State U., 1973; MBA, Ind. U., 1987. CPA, Ind. Various positions PSI Energy, sr. v.p., CFO, 1989-94; group v.p., CFO, Cinergy, 1994-96, pres. energy commodities strategic bus. unit, 1996-98; pres. Cinergy Capital and Trading, 1996-98; pres., COO domestic bus. units, in-charge for internat. ops. Entergy Corp., New Orleans, 1998, CEO, 1999—2006, chmn., CEO, 2006—. Leader BusinessLINC, Mississippi River Delta bus.-to-bus. mentoring. Mem. AICPA. Office: Engery Corp 1340 Echelon Pkwy Ste 100 Jackson MS 39213-8210

LEONARD, JAMES, law librarian, educator; b. High Point, NC, June 27, 1954; s. Burgess Guy and Irene (Meekins) Leonard; m. Judy Ryan, Aug. 17, 1974; children: Jamie Ryan, Burgess Guy III, Sarah Ann. BA, U. NC, 1975, MSLS, 1980, JD, 1986. Bar: Ohio 1987, DC 1988, US Ct. Appeals (6th cir.) 1989, US Supreme Ct. 1990. Tech. svcs. libr. Wake Forest U. Law Libr., Winston-Salem, NC, 1981—83, acting library dir., 1984; dir. Law Libr. Ohio No. U. Pettit Coll. Law, Ada, 1986—97, dir. Legal Writing and Rsch. Program, 1986—92; prof. law, dir. Bounds Law Libr. U. Ala. Sch. Law, Tuscaloosa, 1998—. Mem.: ABA, Ohio State Bar Assn., Ohio Region Assn. Law Libraries, American Assn. Law Libraries. Democrat. Office: Bounds Law Library University of Alabama School Law Box 870383 Tuscaloosa AL 35487-0383 Office Phone: 205-348-5927. E-mail: jleonard@law.ua.edu.

LEONARD, JOSEPH B., retired air transportation executive, board member; b. 1943; BS in Aerospace Engring., Auburn U., Montgomery, Ala., 1967. Various maintenance and quality control positions American Airlines, 1969—82, asst. v.p. aircraft maintenance, 1982—84; v.p. ops. svcs. Eastern Air Lines, Inc., Miami, Fla., 1984—85, sr. v.p. ops. svcs., 1985, exec. v.p., gen. mgr. airline ops., 1985-86, pres., COO, 1986—91; exec. v.p. Northwest Airlines, 1991—93; various positions Aerospace divsn., including sr. v.p., pres. & CEO mktg., sales and svc. AlliedSignal, Inc., 1993—98; pres., CEO AirTran Holdings, Inc., Orlando, Fla., 1999—2001, CEO, 2001—07; interim CEO Walter Energy, Inc., 2010—. Bd. dirs. Walter Industries Inc., 2005—07, Mueller Water Products, Inc., 2006—, Air Can., 2008—, Walter Energy, Inc., 2009—. Mem.: Commerce Club (bd. dirs.), Wings Club (pres.). Mailing: Mueller Water Products Inc Bd directors 1200 Abernathy Rd NE Ste 1200 Atlanta GA 30328 Office: Walter Energy Inc Bd Directors 3000 Riverchase Galleria Ste 1700 Birmingham AL 35244-2378 Office Phone: 770-206-4200. Business E-Mail: jleonard@muellerwp.com.

LEONARD, JUSTIN (JUSTIN CHARLES GARRET LEONARD), professional golfer; b. Dallas, June 15, 1972; Bus. degree, U. Tex., 1994. Profl. golfer PGA, 1994—. Mem. US team Walker Cup, 1993, Presidents Cup, 1996, 98, 2003, 05, 09, Ryder Cup, 1997, 99, 2008, Dunhill Cup, 1997, World Cup, 1997. Achievements include being the only golfer in collegiate history to win 4 straight Southwest Conference titles; winning the US Amateur Championship, 1992, NCAA Championship, 1994; winning PGA Tour events: Buick Open, 1996; British Open, Kemper Open, 1997; The Players Championship, 1998; Westin Texas Open at LaCantera, 2000, 2001; WORLDCOM Classic-The Heritage of Golf, 2002; The Honda Classic, 2003; Bob Hope Chrysler Classic, 2005; FedEx St. Jude Classic, 2005; Valero Texas Open, 2007; Stanford St. Jude Championship, 2008; being a member of the Ryder Cup winning US team, 2008. Office: c/o PGA Box 109601 100 Avenue Of Champions Palm Beach Gardens FL 33418

LEONARD, MICHAEL STEVEN, industrial engineering educator; b. Salisbury, NC, Feb. 2, 1947; s. Charles Thomas and Dorothy Francis (Loflin) L.; m. Mary Elizabeth Stewart, June 21, 1969; children: Dorothy Elizabeth, Amanda Brooke, Gabrielle Francis. B in Engring., U. Fla., 1970, M in Engring., 1972, PhD, 1973. Registered profl. engr., Mo., S.C. Asst. prof. health systems rsch. ctr. Georgia Tech, Atlanta, 1973-75; asst. prof. indsl. engring. U. Mo., Columbia, 1975-79, assoc. prof. indsl. engring., 1979-82, prof. indsl. engring., 1982-90, dept. chmn. indsl. engring., 1985-90; chmn. dept. indsl. engring. Clemson (S.C.) U., 1990—95, 2001—03; sr. assoc. dean Mercer U., Sch. Engring., Ga., 2004—. Bd. dirs. Accreditation Bd. Engring. and Tech., Balt., 1999-2005. Editor Jour. Soc. for Health Systems, 1989-91; contbr. articles to profl. jours. Evaluation adv. com. Am. Blood Commn., Washington, 1977-80; bd. dirs. Am. Cancer Soc. Boone County Mo. unit, Columbia, 1978-90. Fellow: Inst. Indsl. Engrs. (nat. dir. career guidance 1987-95, v.p. acad. affairs 1995-97, bd. trustees 2006-08), ABET (adj. tng. dir., 2011-); mem.: Soc. Health Systems (bd. dirs. 1989-94, pres. elect 1991-92, pres. 1992-93), Mo. Soc. Profl. Engrs. (cen. chpt. treas. 1988-89, v.p. 1989-90). Office: Mercer Univ Sch Engring Macon GA 31207-0001 Office Phone: 478-301-2520. Business E-Mail: leonard_ms@mercer.edu.

LEONARD, TIMOTHY DWIGHT, federal judge; b. Beaver, Okla., Jan. 22, 1940; s. Dwight and Mary Evelyn Leonard; m. Nancy Louise Laughlin, July 15, 1967; children: Kirstin Dione, Ryan Timothy, Tyler Dwight. BA, U. Okla., 1962, JD, 1965; student, Mil. Naval Justice Sch., 1966. Bar: Okla. 1965, U.S. Dist. Ct. (no. and we. dists.) Okla. 1969, U.S. Ct. Appeals (10th cir.) 1969, U.S. Supreme Ct. 1970. Asst. atty. gen. State of Okla., 1968-70; mem. Okla. State Senate, 1979-88; ptnr. Blankenship, Herrold, Russell et al, Oklahoma City, 1970-71, Trippet, Leonard & Kee, Beaver, 1971-88; of counsel Huckaby, Fleming et al, Oklahoma City, 1988-89; US atty. (we. dist.) Okla. US Dept. Justice, 1988-92; judge US Dist. Ct. (we. dist.) Okla., 1992—2006, sr. judge, 2006—. Guest lectr. Oklahoma City U., 1988—89; mem. U.S. Atty. Gen.'s Adv. Com., 1990—92, chmn. office mgmt. and budget subcom., 1990—92, jud. conf. com. on fin. disclosure, 1998—2006, jud. coun. of 10th cir., 1999—2001, 10th cir. adv. coun., 2002—05; adj. prof. Okla. U. Sch. Law, 2000—05. Co-author: 4 Days, 40 Hours, 1970. Rep. Party candidate for lt. gov. of Okla., 1986; minority leader Okla. State Senate, 1985-86; White House mil. aide, Washington, 1966-67; ex officio mem. Okla. State Fair Bd., Oklahoma City, 1987-90; mem. Gov.'s Coun. on Sports and Phys. Edn., Oklahoma City, 1987-89; mem. Donna Nigh Found., Edmond, Okla., 1987-89. Lt. USN, 1965-68. Named Outstanding Legislator, Okla. Sch. Bd. Assn., 1988. Fellow ABA; mem. Okla. Bar Assn., Okla. County Bar, Phi Alpha Delta, Beta Theta Pi. Republican. Presbyterian. Avocations: golf, basketball, running, reading. Office: US Courthouse 200 NW 4th St Rm 4301 Oklahoma City OK 73102-3031 Office Phone: 405-609-5300.

LEONARD, TOMMY, JR., neonatalogist, educator; MD, Med. Coll., Ga., 1973. Diplomate Am. Bd. Pediatrics, 1979, Am. Bd. Pediatrics-neonatal-perinatal medicine, 1981. Intern pediat. Med. Coll., Ga., 1973; resident pediat. Brooke Army Med. Ctr., San Antonio, 1976—78; fellow neonatal-perinatal medicine Tripler Army Med. Ctr., Honolulu, 1978—80; assoc. prof. pediat. Baylor Coll.; med. dir nurseries Meth. Sugar Land Hosp.; hosp. affiliation includes Tex. Children's Hosp. Office: Texas Children's Hospital 6621 Fannin St Houston TX 77030-2399 Office Phone: 832-824-1000.

LEONARD, WALTER RAYMOND, retired biology professor; b. Scott County, Va., July 5, 1923; s. Homer Stanley and Minnie Eunice (Neal) L.; m. Alice Ann McCaskill, Sept. 1, 1951; children— Leslie Ann, Walter Raymond. BA, Tusculum Coll., Greeneville, Tenn., 1946; MA, Vanderbilt U., 1947, PhD, 1949. Mem. faculty Wofford Coll., Spartanburg, S.C., 1949-93, John M. Reeves prof. biology, 1954-87, William R. Kenan Jr. prof. biology, 1987-93, William R. Kenan Jr. prof. emeritus, 1993—. Instl. rev. bd. mem. Spartanburg Regional Med. Ctr., 1994-98; faculty athletic rep. NCAA. With Wofford named Village Dorm, 2012. With USAAF, 1942—43. Named to Sports Hall of Fame, Tusculum Coll., 1983; Walter Raymond Leonard scholarship created Wofford Coll., 1973; W. Ray Leonard award established Beta Beta Beta, 1993; W. Ray Leonard Retirement Fund established Former Students Wofford Coll., 1993, disting. citizen award Wofford Coll. Nat. Alumni Assn., 1999, W. Ray Leonard award, 2008. Mem. AAAS, S.C. Acad. Sci., Scabbard and Blade (hon.), Lamda Chi Alpha (named to Hall of Fame 1996), Letterman's Club (hon.), Wofford Coll. Methodist. Achievements include rsch. on cell metabolism. Home: 228 Arbours Commons Ct Spartanburg SC 29307-2938 Office: Wofford Coll N Church St Spartanburg SC 29301 Personal E-mail: wrleonard2006@yahoo.com.

LEONHARDT, FREDERICK WAYNE, lawyer; b. Daytona Beach, Fla., Oct. 26, 1949; s. Frederick Walter and Gaetane Laura Leonhardt; m. Victoria Ann Cook, Dec. 27, 1975; children: Ashley Victoria, Frederick Whitaker. BA, U. Fla., 1971, JD, 1974. Bar: Fla. 1974, N.C. 1984, D.C. 1985; cert. real estate lawyer, Fla. Gen. counsel Fla. Ho. of Reps., 1974—75; ptnr. Cobb, Cole and Bell, Daytona Beach, 1975-79; pres. Leonhardt & Upchurch, 1979-87; ptnr. Holland & Knight, Orlando, Fla., 1987-93, Gray Robinson, Orlando, Fla., 1993—. Chmn. bd. dirs. Orlando/Orange County Compact, 1989-90, Orlando/Orange County Civic Facilities Authority, 1998-2001; founder Leadership Daytona Beach; grad. Leadership Fla., chair, 2000-2001; active Leadership Ctrl. Fla., Leadership Orlando; past chmn. Ctrl. Fla. Sports Commn., bd. dirs., 1992-; bd. dirs. Enterprise Fla., Orlando/Orange County Conv. and Visitors Bur., Celebration Health Found., Ctr. for Drug Free Living, Prevent Blindness Fla., Fla. Bank Commerce; founder VCARD; past gen. campaign mgr. Volusia County United Way; mem. Gov.'s Growth Mgmt. Study Commn.; exec. com. Floridians for Better Transp., 2000—, chair, 2002, 03; treas. U. Ctrl. Fla. Found., 2000—; bd. dirs. Econ. Devel. Commn. Mid-Fla., 2001—, chmn., 2007-08; bd. dirs. Ctrl. Fla. Boy Scouts Am., 2000—, chair, 2005; bd. dirs. Ctrl. Fla. Tiger Bay Club, chair, 2006; mem. adv. bd. Ronald McDonald House; trustee U. Fla. Law Sch.; bd. dirs., Fla. Tech. Rsch. & Scholarship Bd., 2011-. Mem.: ABA (editor sect. newsletter 1991—94, chmn. state and local govt. law sect. 1997—98), James Madison Inst. (bd. dirs.), Ctrl. Fla. Partnership (bd. dirs.), Fla. Coun. of 100, Fla. C. of C. (bd. dirs. 1984—90, 1993—, chair 2004), Daytona Beach Area C. of C. (pres. 1985), Greater Orlando C. of C. (chmn. 1991—92), Orange and Volusia Counties Bar Assn., Delta Chi, Phi Alpha Delta. Office: Gray Robinson PA PO Box 3068 301 E Pine St Ste 1400 Orlando FL 32801-2731 Office Phone: 407-244-5655. Business E-Mail: fleonhardt@gray-robinson.com.

LEONHART, MICHELE MARIE, federal agency administrator; b. 1956; m. Gene Johns; children: Michael, Stephen. BS in Criminal Justice, Lakewood CC, Minn., 1978. Police officer Balt. Police Dept., Md.; spl. agt. Drug Enforcement Adminstrn. (DEA), Mpls., 1980—85, spl. agt. recruiter St. Louis, 1986—88, group supr., intelligence supr. San Diego, 1988—93, OPR (internal affairs) inspector Arlington, Va., 1993—94, asst. spl. agt. in charge of field divsn. L.A., 1995—96, sr. exec. svc. mem. spl. agt. recruitment program, 1996—97, spl. agt. in charge field divsn. San Francisco, 1997—98, L.A., 1998—2003, acting dep. adminstr. Alexandria, Va., 2003—04, dep. adminstr., 2004—07, acting adminstr., 2007—11, adminstr., 2011—. Recipient Presdl. Rank award for Meritorious Svc., The White House, 2000, 2005, Women in Fed. Law Enforcement Outstanding Fed. Law Enforcement Employee award, 2005, Law Enforcement Exploring William H. Spurgeon award, 2006; named a Disting. Exec., The White House, 2004. Office: Drug Enforcement Adminstrn (DEA) Mailstop AXS 8701 Morrissette Dr Springfield VA 22152-1080 E-mail: michele.m.leonhart@usdoj.gov.*

LEONORA, ARNOLD B., air transportation executive; Grad., Embry-Riddle Aeronautical U., 1986. Investment banker Bank of Boston, Merrill Lynch & Co., Inc.; mng. dir., Caribbean, S.Am. Regional Commuter Airlines; prin. ATG, LLC, 1989—; pres., CEO ABL Hotel Properties, Inc., 1998; pres., air svcs. divsn. River Hawk Aviation, Inc. (formerly Viva Internat. Inc.), 2003; pres., CFO, sec., treas. and prin. acctg. officer Harvard Holdings International, Inc., chmn., CEO, 2006—; treas., sec. Air Transport Group Holdings, Inc., 2008, pres., CEO, 2008—; pres. Air Transport Group, LLC, 2008—. Pres., Adv. Coun. Aeronautical U. Office: Air Transport Group Holdings Inc 7453 Woodruff Way Stone Mountain GA 30087-6137 Office Phone: 404-671-9253.

LEOPOLD, CHRISTOPHER J., state legislator; b. Apr. 22, 1968; m. Joanna Leopold; 3 children. BA, Southeastern La. U. Mem. Dist. 105 La. House of Reps., 2012—, mem. Judiciary Com., Natural Resources and Environment Com. & Transp., Highways, and Pub. Works Com. Republican. Office: District Office 1500 Woodland Highway, Suite A Belle Chasse LA 70037 Office Phone: 504-393-5649. Office Fax: 504-393-5603. E-mail: leopoldc@legis.la.gov.

LERBLANCE, RICHARD C., state legislator; m. Frances Lerblance; children: Richard Jr., John, David. AA, Ea. Okla. State Coll., 1967; BA, Ctrl State Univ., 1970; JD, Okla. City Univ., 1978. Atty.-at-law, Oil & Gas, Cattle, Race Horses; mem. Dist. 17 Okla. House of Representatives, 2002—03; mem. Dist. 7 Okla. State Senate, 2003—. Mem. Bedouin Temple, Muskogee, Okla. Mem.: Maine Anjou Assn., Okla. Cattlemen Assn., Latimer County Cattlemen Assn., Pitts. County Cattlemen Assn. (treas.), Pitts. County & Muskogee Nation Bar Assn., Okla. Bar Assn., McAlester Rotary Club, Hartshorne-Haileyville Lodge 122. Democrat. Avocations: hunting, boating, motorcycling. Office: 2300 N Lincoln Blvd Rm 535A Oklahoma City OK 73105 Mailing: PO Box 1011 Hartshorne OK 74547 Office Phone: 405-521-5604. Business E-Mail: lerblance@oksenate.gov.

LERNER, THEODORE RAPHAEL, dentist; b. Bklyn. s. Meyer and Tillie (Brimberg) L.; m. Barbara Ellen Bernstein, June 29, 1974; children by previous marriage: Andrea Holly, Evan Andrew. DDS, U. Pa., 1957. Diplomate Am. Bd. Endodontics. Dentist, endodontist pvt. practice, Bklyn., 1957-93, Forest Hills, NY, 1968-93, Boca Raton, Fla., 1992—. Fellow Internat. Coll. Dentists, Am. Coll. Dentists; mem. ADA, 2d Dist. Dental Soc. (pres. 1971), Dental Soc. State of N.Y. (pres. 1983), Fla. Dental Assn., Am. Assn. Endodontists, Diplomate Am. Bd. Endodontics Home: 7040 Lions Head Ln Boca Raton FL 33496-5931 Office: 2499 Glades Rd Ste 204 Boca Raton FL 33431-7201 Office Phone: 561-750-9004. Personal E-mail: trlray1@bellsouth.net.

LEROY, MISS JOY, model, apparel designer; b. Riverdale, Ill., Sept. 8, 1927; d. Gerald and Dorothea (Wingebach) Reasor. BS, Purdue U., 1949; LittD (hon.), World Forum Fedn., Cambridge, Mass., 2013. Model, sales rep. Jacques, Lafayette, Ind., 1950; book dept. sales rep. Loebs, 1951-52; window trimmer Marshall Field and Co., Evanston, Ill., 1952—53; sales and display rep. Emerald House, 1954-55. Model, narrator, designer J. L. Hudson Co., GM Corp., Coca Cola Co., Hoover Vacuum Co., Jam Handy Orgn., Rambler and Kelvinator divsn. Am. Motors Corp., Speedway Petroleum Corp., Ford Motor Co., auto, tractor & implement divsn., Sykes Co., Detroit, 1956—61; tour guide, model, freelance writer Christian Sci. Publ. Soc. and Monitor; spl. events coord. Prudential Ins. Co.; model Copley 7, Boston, 1962—70. Author: Puzz-its, 1986—2006. Founding angel Asolo Theatre, Sarasota, 1960; mem. Ft. Lauderdale Internat. Film Festival, 1990, Mus. of Art, 1978, Fla. Conservation Assn., Rep. Senatorial Com. Inner Cir., 1990, Rep. Nat. Hall of Honor, 1992, Congl. Com., 1990, Nat. Trust for Hist. Preservation, 1986, Fla. Trust for Hist. Preservation, 1987; one of founding friends 1000 Friends of Fla., 1991; life mem. Rep. Presdl. Task Force, 1993; mem. Grand Club Rep. Party Fla., 1996; v.p. of recognition bd. World Congress of Arts, Sci., and Comms., Washington, 2007. Recipient Rep. Presdl. Legion Honor medal, 1993, Rep. medal of Freedom and Wall of Honor, 1994, Disting. 20th Century Rep. Leader, 1994, 1998, Founder's Wall award, 1995, World Laureate of Eng., 1999, Rep. Presdl. Roundtable, 2000—10, award, Am. Order of Excellence, 2000, Order of Internat. Ambs., 2000, Presdl. Seal of Honor, 2000, Congl. medal of excellence, 2002, Rep. Senatorial Millennium Medal of Freedom, Star and Spirit, 2006, Lifetime Achievement award, World Congress of Arts, Sci. and Comm., 1998—2004, Internat. Medal of Honor, Internat. Hall of Fame, Statesman award, Da Vinci Diamond, 2004, United Cultural Convention Life Achievement award, 2004, 2006, Salute to Greatness Gold Medal, Gold Medal of Freedom, Gold Medal for USA, 2006, World Record Holder, ABI, Disting. Svc. Order & Silver Cross, 2008, Achievement and Excellence in Art decree, Internat. Biog. Assn., 2007, Pres. Cup award, World Forum Fedn. US, 2006—07, 2009, 2011, 2013, Dir. General's Leadership award, 2000 Outstanding Intellectuals of the 21st Century, 2008, Pres.'s Citation for Recognized Excellence, Gold plque, Disting. Svc. award, Orders Silver Cross, Am. Order of Merit, 2010—11, Gold medal, Olympian Achiever IBC, 2011; named Internat. Visual Artist of Yr., Ambassador Gen., ABI, Legion of Honor, Woman of Yr., 1998—2003, 2005—10, Legion of Honoor, IBC, Hon. Dir., Gen., Life Patron, Global Yr. of Excellence Gold Medal, IBA, Noble and Genius Laureate, 2005, Amb., Internat. Order Merit, 2007; named one of Top 100 Artist; named to Hallmark Hall of Fame, 2002, Order of Am. Ambassadors, World Hall of Fame, 2000, World Biog. Hall of Fame, 2014;, Order of Internat., 2010, Charter fellowship, World Forum. Master: World Acad. Letters (vice chancellor 2009—, named to Pers. Biog. Hall of Fame, IBC 2009, Internat. Peace prize, United Cultural Convention 2009, Formal Order of ABI, Magna cum Laude 2009, Am. Order of Merit, Gold medal, Order of Internat. Fellowship Peace prize 2010, US Gold medal); mem.: IBC (Internat. Pres. award 2011, named one of Top 100 Profls. 2012, 2012), Academician ABI (life, World Hall of Fame 2012, Internat. Pres. Iconic Achievement award 2012, World Congress Art Sci. & Commn. award 2013, World Hon. Doctorate of Letters and Charter fellowship), Medallian Cultural Attache World Forum, Navy League US (life; mem. pres.'s coun.), Hist. Preservation America Daughter US, Seven Seas Soc. (World Biog. Hall of Fame 2014), Eagle Soc., Am. Rivers, Ellis Island Found. (charter), The Crystal Soc. (100th Crystal 2011), Cousteau Soc., Heritage Found., USS Constn. Mus., Libr. of Congress (nat. mem.), Purdue U. Alumni Assn. (pres.'s coun.), Heralds of Nature Soc., Nat. Wildlife Fedn., Am. Queen Inaugural Soc., Stratford Shakespearean Festival of Can., Paddlewheel Steamboatin' Soc. Am., Nat. Corvette Owners Assn., Soc. Honorary Mariners, Quyana Club, Skald Club, Seabourn Club, Ducks Unltd., Internat. Gov.'s Club (continental gov.), Maupin Travelers Club, Magic Kingdom Entertainment Club, Cunard World Club, Captain's Cir., INTRAV-Pinnacle-Elite Explorer Club, Zeta Tau Alpha. Avocations: travel, art, photography. Home: 2100 S Ocean Ln Apt 2104 Fort Lauderdale FL 33316-3827

LERUP, LARS G., architecture educator, dean; Civil engring. diploma, Helsingborg Tech. Coll., Sweden, 1960; BArch, U. Calif., Berkeley, 1968; MArch in Urban Design, Harvard U., 1970. Asst. prof. architecture U. Calif., Berkeley, 1970—77, assoc. prof. architecture, 1977—87, prof. architecture, 1987—93; Harry K. and Albert K. Smith prof. and dean architecture Rice U., Houston, 1993—, dean Sch. of Architecture, 1993—. Counselor Assn. Collegiate Schs. Architecture, Western Region, 1972—73, 1976—77, 1977—78; teaching cons. CCNY Sch. of Architecture, 1974; assoc. dean, chair environ. design program U. Calif., Berkeley, 1978—79; vis. fellow Inst. Architecture and Urban Studies, NYC, 1979—81, dir. ednl. programs, 1981; Andrew Carnegie vis. prof. Cooper Union, NYC, 1980—81; vis. prof. Rice U. Sch. Architecture, Houston, 1983, Caudill vis. prof., 1987; vis. prof. Architecture Assn., London, 1985, So. Calif. Inst. Architecture, L.A. and Vico Morcote, Switzerland, 1985, L.A. and Vico Morcote, 1991—93, ednl. dir., 1990—93; vis. prof. architecture U. Grenoble, France, 1990; mem. numerous coms. U. Calif., Berkeley, So. Calif. Inst. Architecture, Rice U.; supr. grad. students; lectr., rschr., guest critic in field. Author: Building the Unfinished: Architecture and Human Action, 1977, 3rd edit., 1983, Planned Assaults: Nofamily Hous. Love/House, Texas Zero, 1987; author: (with others) Fires and Human Behavior, 1980; author: Designer's Own Homes: Private Residences of Thirty of America's Leading Interior Designers, 1984, Architecture and Body, 1988, Architect's People, 1989, Visionary San Francisco, 1990; contbr. articles to profl. jours. and catalogs; prin. works include, Folksam Ins. Co. Hdqrs., Farsta, Sweden, Ecole Maritime, La Rochelle, Bretagne, France, Cmty. Ctr., Eskilstuna, Sweden, Ch., Stora Tuna, Sweden, Bldg. Sci. Rm., U. Calif., also furniture design. Recipient citation for excellence, Progressive Architecture Awards Program, 1976, citation, Assn. Collegiate Schs. Architecture, 1986, Arnold W. Brunner Rome Prize, Am. Acad. in Rome, 2010; grantee Arthur Lehman grantee, Harvard U., 1969—70, Gulf Oil, 1969—70; scholar Regents Tuition scholar, U. Calif., 1966—67, 1967—68. Office: Rice U Sch of Architecture 6100 Main St Houston TX 77005-1892

LESAR, DAVID J., oil industry executive; b. 1954; BS, U. Wis., 1975, MBA, 1978. Ptnr. in charge of energy mfg. and retail practices Arthur Andersen & Co., Dallas, 1978—93; exec. v.p. fin. & adminstrn. Halliburton Energy Services, 1993—95; pres., CEO Brown and Root, Inc., 1996—97; exec. v.p., CFO Halliburton Co., 1995—96, pres., COO, 1997—2000, chmn., pres., CEO, 2000—. Bd. dirs. Halliburton Co., 2000—, Lyondell Chemical Co., 2000—07, Mirant Co., 2000—05. Office: Halliburton Co 5 Houston Ctr 1401 McKinney Ste 2400 Houston TX 77020

LESLIE, JOHN WILLIAM, public relations and advertising executive; b. Indpls., Nov. 22, 1923; s. John Edward and Catherine (Harris) L.; m. Joan Williams, Dec. 26, 1970; 1 dau. by previous marriage, Catherine Alexandra. Student, U.S. Naval Acad., 1943-44, George Washington U., 1949, Indsl. Coll. Armed Forces, 1956. Dep. excise adminstr., Ind., 1946-47; pvt. pub. relations bus., 1947-49; dir. pub. relations Ind. Democratic State Central Com., 1948-49, Ind. Dept. Vets. Affairs, 1949; press officer Dept. Labor, 1949-51, acting asst. dir. info., 1951-52, asst. dir., 1952-56, dep. dir., 1956-59, dir., 1959—62; dep. asst. sec. Labor and Dir. Info., 1962—81; charter mem. US Sr. Exec. Svc., 1979—; sr. assoc. Kamber Group, Washington, 1981-84, counselor, 1984-88, exec. v.p., COO, 1988-96, vice chmn., sec., 1997-98, pub. rels. cons., 1998—, also bd. dirs. Mem., dir. pub. D.C. Com. Employment Physically Handicapped, 1952-53 Author numerous articles in field. Advt. cons. Pres.'s Com. on Youth Employment, 1964-80; U.S. del Internat. Graphic Design Coun., Japan, 1973; trustee Washington chpt. Leukemia Soc. Am., 1976-82; chmn. Pub. Printers Adv. Com. on Printing and Publs, 1977-79. Served with USN and USNR, 1941-46. Recipient commendation President's Com. Employment Physically Handicapped, 1954; Disting. Service award Dept. Labor, 1962; citation outstanding service Navy Dept., 1964; Presdl. citation, 1966; Merit award Internat. Labor Press Assn., 1969; Disting. Career Service award Dept. Labor, 1973; Communications award Ga. chpt. Pub. Relations Soc. Am., 1972; Sec. Labor's Recognition award, 1974; Communicator of Yr. award Nat. Assn. Govt. Communicators, 1981 Mem. Am. Assn. Polit. Cons., Am. League Lobbyists, Nat. Press Club, English Speaking Union, Univ. Club (Winter Park, Fla.), Stag Club of Winter Park. Episcopalian. Home: 1545 Old Oaks Dr Charlottesville VA 22901-8868 E-mail: twoleslies@aol.com.

LESS, ANTHONY ALBERT, retired naval officer; b. Salem, Ohio, Aug. 31, 1937; s. Joseph Anthony and Mildred Gertrude (Bair) L.; m. Leanne Carol Kuhl, Mar. 3, 1962; children: Robyn, Pamela, Theresa, Christina. BS in Chemistry, Heidelberg Coll., 1959. Designated naval aviator. Commd. ensign USN, 1960, advanced through grades to vice adm., 1991, ret., 1994; comdg. officer USS Wichita (AOR-1), 1979-81, USS Ranger (CV-61), 1982-83; chief of staff Comdr. 7th Fleet, Yokosuka, Japan, 1983-84; dir. Polit. Mil Br. JCS, Washington, 1985-87; comdr. Carrier Group One, Pacific, 1987-88, Mid. East Force, Manama, Bahrain, 1988-89; dir. Plans and Policy Navy Staff, Washington, 1989-91; comdr. Naval Air Force Atlantic Fleet, Norfolk, Va., 1991-94; pres. Assn. Naval Aviation, Washington, 1994—95; v.p. Mil. Programs. Cons. Kaman Aerospace, Bloomfield, Conn., 1994-2003; v.p. govt. programs Kaman Aerospace, Arlington, Va., 2001-03; sr. v.p. navy programs Burdeshaw Assocs., Ltd., Bethesda, Md., 2003-07. Mem. Assn. Naval Aviation (pres. 1994), Soc. Naval Engrs. Roman Catholic. Avocations: racquetball, farming, reading. Office Phone: 703-946-4312. Personal E-mail: tonyless@aol.com.

LESSARD, RAYMOND WILLIAM, bishop emeritus; b. Grafton, ND, Dec. 21, 1930; BA, St. Paul Sem.; STL, Gregorian U., Rome, 1957, JCL, 1970. Ordained priest Diocese of Fargo, ND, 1956; mem. staff Congregation for Bishops, Roman Curia, 1964-73; ordained bishop, 1973; bishop Diocese of Savannah, Ga., 1973-95, bishop emeritus, 1973—. Adj. prof. theology St. Vincent de Paul Sem., Boynton Beach, Fla., 1995. Roman Catholic. Office: St Vincent de Paul Seminary 10701 S Military Trail Boynton Beach FL 33436-4899 Office Phone: 561-732-4424. Office Fax: 561-739-2205.

LESSTRANG, DAVID (DAVE) MATTHEW, legislative staff member; b. Ann Arbor, Mich., Feb. 22, 1963; s. Jacques Earle LesStrang and Jean Audrey Mentzer Paul; m. Elaine Marie Dalpiaz, July 31, 1993; chilcren, Matthew Jacques, Michael Joseph BA with honors, Hillsdale Coll., Mich., 1985. Editorial asst. Harbor House Pub., Inc., Boyne City, Mich., 1981-85; press sec. U.S. Congressman Jerry Lewis, Washington, 1985-95, dep. chief of staff, 1997—2002, legis. dir., 1999—2002; govt. affairs mgr. EMC Corp., 2002—05; dep. staff dir. US House Appropriations Com., 2005—. Staff asst. U.S. Congressman Carl D. Pursell, Washington, spring 1984; lectr. The Am. U.; sr. policy advisor, press sec. subcom. House Va.-HUD Appropriations, 1995-99; staff dir. Calif. Rep. Congl. Delegation, 1995-2001. Vol. Habitat for Humanity; developer House that Congress Build campaign. Mem. Alliance Francaise. Republican. Avocations: international travel, writing, investments, politics, athletics. Office: US House Appropriations Com 1016 Longworth House Office Bldg Washington DC 20510 Office Phone: 202-225-3481. Business E-Mail: david.lesstrang@mail.house.gov.

LESTER, ANDREW WILLIAM, lawyer; b. Mpls., Feb. 17, 1956; s. Richard G. and Marion Louise (Kurtz) L.; m. Barbara Regina Schmitt, Nov. 22, 1978; 1 child, Susan Erika. Student, Ludwig-Maximilians U., Munich, 1975-76; BA, Duke U., Durham, NC, 1977; MS in Fgn. Svc., Georgetown U., Washington, 1981, JD, 1981. Bar: Okla. 1981, DC 1985, Tex. 1990, US Supreme Ct. 1992, Colo. 1995. Cons. Dresser Industries, Inc., Washington, 1979-81; assoc. Conner & Winters, Tulsa, 1981-82; asst. atty. City of Enid, Okla., 1982-84; ptnr. various law firms Enid, Oklahoma City, 1984-96; ptnr. Lester, Loving & Davies PC, Edmond, 1996—. Adj. prof. Okla. City Univ. Sch. of Law; lectr. in field; US magistrate judge Western Dist. Okla., 1988-96; constl. law specialist Ctrl. and East European Law Initiative, ABA, Ukraine, Belarus and Moldova, 1993; adj. scholar Okla. Coun. Pub. Affairs. Author: Constitutional Law and Democracy, 1994; contbr. book revs. and articles to profl. jours. Intern Office of Senator Bob Dole, Washington, 1977-78; mem. transition team EEOC Office Pres.-Elect Reagan, Washington, 1980-81; chmn. law enforcement and corrections transition team, mem. budget and fin. transition team Office of Gov.-Elect Brad Henry, 2002-03; chmn. Enid Police Civil Service Commn., 1985-87; bd. dirs. Enid Habitat for Humanity, 1986-88, Booker T. Washington Cmty. Ctr., Enid, 1987-90, St. Mary's Episcopal Sch. of Edmond, 1999-2001; bd. dirs. U. Ctrl. Okla. Found., 2005—; mem. bd. advisors Oklahoma City Command Salvation Army, 2002—; mem. Martin Luther King, Jr. Holiday Commn. of Enid, 1988-91; deacon First Bapt. Ch. of Oklahoma City; bd. regents Okla. Agrl. & Mech. Colls., 2007—; trustee Eureka Coll., 2007—2010; bd. trustees Langston U., Tulsa, Oklahoma City 2009-, vice chmn. 2009-. Fellow Okla. Bar Found.; mem. Okla. Bar Assn., Colo. Bar Assn., State Bar Tex., Okla. Assn. Mcpl. Attys. (bd. dirs. 1987-91, 94-98, 2000-07, gen. counsel 1987-88, pres. 1988-90), Okla. County Bar Assn., Federalist Soc. (vice chmn. civil rights practice group 1996-2005, pres. Ctrl. Okla. chpt. 1996-99), Hist. Soc. of Tenth Jud. Cir. (bd. dirs. 2005—, pres. 2006—2007, chmn. bd. 2007-2009). Republican. Avocations: german language, cartography. Office: Lester Loving & Davis PC 1701 S Kelly Ave Edmond OK 73013-3623 Office Phone: 405-844-9900. Office Fax: 405-844-9958. Business E-Mail: alester@lldlaw.com.

LESTER, JUNE, library and information scientist, educator; b. Sandersville, Ga., Aug. 25, 1942; d. Charles DuBose and Frances Irene (Cheney) L.; 1 child, Anna Elisabeth Engle. BA, Emory U., 1963, M in Librarianship, 1971; D in Libr. Sci., Columbia U., 1987, cert. in advanced librarianship, 1982. Asst. prof., cataloger U. Tenn. Libr., Knoxville, 1971-73; libr. divsn. libr. and info. mgmt. Emory U., Atlanta, 1973-81, asst. prof. div. libr. and info. mgmt., 1976-80, assoc. prof., 1980-87; accreditation officer Am. Libr. Assn., 1987-91; assoc. dean, assoc. prof. Sch. Libr. and Info. Scis. U. North Tex., Denton, 1991—93; prof. U. Okla., Norman, 1993—2010, dir. Sch. Libr and Info. Studies, 1993—2000, prof. emerita, 2010—. UCLA sr. fellow, 1987. Mem. ALA (coun. mem. 1987), Assn. for Libr. and Info. Sci. Edn. (bd. dirs. 1985-87, 94-97, pres. 1995-96), Am. Soc. Info. Sci. and Tech. (treas., 2004-2007, bd. mem., 2004-2007), Okla. Libr. Assn., Phi Beta Kappa, Beta Phi Mu. Unitarian Universalist. Office: U Okla Sch Libr and Info Studies 401 W Brooks St Norman OK 73019-6030 Home: 1481 Leafrome Sq Decatur GA 30033 Business E-Mail: jlester@ou.edu.

LESTER, MARK CHARLES, neurosurgeon; b. Pitts., Sept. 23, 1952; AB, Cornell U., 1973; MD, U. Pitts., 1977; MBA, U. Pa., 2002. Diplomate Am. Bd. Neurol. Surgery, cert. physician exec. Intern gen. surgery U. Health Ctr. Hosps., Pitts., 1977—78, resident in neurological surgery, 1978—83; neurosurgeon Allentown, Pa., 1983—2004; chief divsn. neurol. surgery Lehigh Valley Hosp., Allentown, 1992—2001, vice-chmn. opers. dept. surgery, 1999—2004, med. dir. oper. rm., 1999—2004; clin. assoc. prof. Pa. State Coll. Medicine, Hershey, 1995—2004, Mich. State Coll. Human Medicine, Lansing, 2004—09; chief med. officer St. Mary's Mich. Med. Ctr., Saginaw, 2004—09; v.p. chief quality officer Tex. Health Presbyterian Hosp. Dallas, 2009—13, exec. v.p., zone clin. leader, 2012—. Adj. clin. asst. prof. Hahnemann U., Phila., 1988—2004; adj. prof. surgery U. North Tex. Health Scis. Ctr., 2012—, adj. prof. health mgmt. & policy, 2012—. Fellow: ACS; mem.: Am. Coll. Healthcare Execs., Am. Coll. Physician Execs., Am. Assn. Neurol. Surgeons.

LESTER, RICHARD GARRISON, radiologist, educator; b. NYC, Oct. 24, 1925; s. L. I. and Pauline (Smolan) L.; m. Marion Louise Kurtz, Jan. 17, 1949; children: Elizabeth P., Andrew W. AB, Princeton U., 1946; MD, Columbia U., 1948. Intern N.Y.C. Hosp., 1948-49; asst. resident radiology Stanford Hosp., 1950-51, 53-54; from instr. to asso. prof. radiology U. Minn., 1954-61; prof. radiology, chmn. dept. Med. Coll. Va., 1961-65, Duke Sch. Medicine, 1965-76; prof. radiology U. Tex. Med. Sch., Houston, 1976-84, chmn. dept., 1977-81; interim pres. Meharry Med. Coll., Nashville, 1981-82; dean Eastern Va. Med. Sch., Norfolk, 1984-89, prof. radiology, 1984-93, chmn. dept., 1989-91, prof. emeritus, 1993—; v.p. acad. affairs Med. Coll. of Hampton Roads (formerly Eastern Va. Med. Authority), Norfolk, 1984—89. Trustee Meharry Med. Coll., 1975—. Author: (with others) Congenital Heart Disease, 1965, Exposure of the Pregnant Patient to Diagnostic Radiations, 1985, 2d edit., 1997; also numerous articles. Mem. 1st. Bapt. Ch. Okla. City; bd. mem. Good Shepherd Ministries, Okla. City, 2010-12. Capt. USAF, 1951—53. Fellow Am. Coll. Radiology, Am. Coll. Chest Physicians; mem. Assn. Univ. Radiologists, Am. Roentgen Ray Soc., Soc. Pediatric Radiology, Radiol. Soc. N.Am. (dir. 1976—, chmn. bd. 1981, pres. 1983). Home and Office: 749 Touchmark Ct Edmond OK 73003-2164 Office Phone: 405-844-6965. Personal E-mail: rglester@aol.com.

LESTER, ROY DAVID, lawyer; b. Middletown, Ohio, Jan. 16, 1949; s. Edgel Celsus and Norma Marie (Elam) L.; children: Justin David, Benjamin, Jackson, Caroline. BS, We. Ky. U., 1970; JD, U. Ky., 1975. Bar: Ky. 1975, U.S. Tax Ct. 1979, U.S. Dist. Ct. (ea. dist.) Ky. 1976, U.S. Supreme Ct. 1979. With Stoll, Keenon, Ogden PLLC, Lexington, Ky., 1975—. Mem. YMCA (Lexington), Fayette County Bar Assn., Order of Coif, Lexington Country Club. Republican. Office: Stoll Keenon Ogden PLLC 300 West Vine St Ste 2100 Lexington KY 40507-1380 Office Phone: 859-231-3082. Business E-Mail: david.lester@skofirm.com.

LETIZIO, LISA, retail executive, human resources specialist; BS in Comm. Studies magna cum laude, U. Mass., Amherst, 1984. Intern in the human resources dept. Wang Laboratories, Lowell, Mass., 1980—84; human resources rep. Computervision, 1984—86; corp. compensation specialist Lockheed Martin, 1987—92; v.p. human resources The Timberland Co., 1992—98; exec. v.p. human resources HSN Interactive, LLC, 1998—. Vol., bd. pres. Big Brothers Big Sisters, Pinellas, Hernando and Citrus counties, Fla. Mem.: Phi Kappa Phi. Office: HSN Inc 1 HSN Dr Saint Petersburg FL 33729 Office Phone: 727-872-1000. Business E-Mail: lisa.letizio@hsn.net.

LETSOU, GEORGE VASILIOS, cardiothoracic surgeon; b. Boston, 1958; s. Vasilios George and Helen (Valacellis) L.; m. Jane Elizabeth Carter, June 1, 1985; children: Christopher George, Philip Taylor, John Carter. AB magna cum laude, Harvard U., 1979; MD, Columbia U., 1983. Diplomate Am. Bd. Surgery, Am. Bd. Thoracic Surgery. Resident in gen. surgery Yale-New Haven Hosp., 1983—88, chief resident and instr. surgery, 1987—88, clin. fellow in cardiothoracic surgery, 1988—89, Cystic Fibrosis Found. fellow cardiopulm. transplantation, 1988—89, Winchester scholar in cardiothoracic surg. rsch., 1989—90, resident in cardiothoracic surgery, 1990—91, chief resident in cardiothoracic surgery, 1991—92; attending surgeon Yale U., New Haven, 1992—95, instr. surgery, 1987-88, 91-92, asst. prof. surgery, 1992—95; attending surgeon Yale-New Haven Med. Ctr., 1992—95, Meth. Hosp., Ben Taub Hosp., Houston, 1995—; assoc. prof. surgery Baylor Coll. Medicine, Houston, 1995—99; attending surgeon Meml.-Hermann Hosp., Houston, 1998—, Tex. Heart Inst., 2009—, cardiovasc. surgery staff; assoc. prof. surgery U. Tex., Houston, 1999—2007, prof. surgery, 2007—14, Baylor Coll. Medicine, 2014—. Mem. AMA, ACS, Am. Coll. Cardiology, Am. Coll. Chest Physicians, Soc. Thoracic Surgeons, Am. Assn. Thoracic Surgery. Office: 1 Baylor Plz MS BCM390 Houston TX 77030-3411 Office Phone: 713-798-3020. Office Fax: 713-798-3122. Business E-Mail: george.letsou@bcm.edu.

LETT, ROSALIND KIMBER, library director, library and information scientist; b. Tuscaloosa, Ala., Feb. 28, 1956; d. William Lincoln and James Ella (Toney) Kimber; m. Victor Lemond Lett, June 28, 1986; children: Victor Lemond Jr., Victoria L'erin. BS in Zoology, Ala. A&M U., Normal, 1978; MLIS, Clark Atlanta U., 1983; MBA, Ga. State U., Atlanta, 2009. Info. specialists Morris Brown Coll., Atlanta, 1983-86; reference specialist Ga. State U., Atlanta, 1986; reference libr. Morehouse Sch. Medicine, Atlanta, 1986-87; med. libr. Kennestone Hosp., Marietta, Ga., 1987-90; exec. dir. Knowledge Based Info. Consultants, 1989—2009; dir. librs. Ga. Mental Health Inst., Atlanta, 1990-92; med. libr. dir. Crawford Long Hosp., Atlanta, 1992—2001; knowledge integration resources coord. Vanderbilt U. Eskind Biomed. Libr., 2002—03; CEO Info.-2-Knowledge, LLC, 2003—09, Wellness4Change, 2003—; assoc. dir. pub. services Huntsville-Madison County Pub. Libr., Huntsville, Ala., 2010—. Med. libr. cons Henry Med. Ctr., Stockbridge, Ga., Gwinnett Med. Ctr., Lawrenceville, Ga., Northside Hosp., Atlanta, 1990-92, Parkway Med. Ctr., Lithia Springs, Ga., 1995. Co-editor (rsch. sect.): Jour. Hosp. Librarianship, 2005—08. Voter registrar Dekalb County Voter Registration, 1993; info. advocate Libr.'s on the Info. Superhighway Advocacy Network; mem. NN/LM Reg. Adv. Coun., 1992-94; PTSA pres. St. Mountain High Sch., 1996-98. Named to Movers & Shakers, Libr. Jour., 2011. Mem. Med. Libr. Assn. (Leadership award 1994, chair hosp. libr. com. So. chpt. 1995-97, So. chpt. chair 1998-99, bd. dirs. 2003-06, sec. 2004-06, vital pathway chair 2006-08), Ga. Health Sci. Libr. Assn. (pres. 1993-94), Spl. Libr. Assn. (Mktg. Divsn. PR award 1995, 1996, Diversity Leader Devel. award 1996, pres. Ga. chpt. 1995-96), Southeastern Conf. Hosp. Libr. Assn. (pres. 1992-93), Atlanta Health Sci. Libr. Assn. (pres. 1990-92). Mem. AME Ch. Avocations: tennis, swimming, singing, reading, dance. Office: Huntsville-Madison County Pub Library 915 Monroe St Huntsville AL 35801 Office Phone: 256-532-5940.

LETTEN, JAMES B. (JIM LETTEN), dean, former federal prosecutor; b. New Orleans, 1953; m. JoAnn Letten; children: Erika, James. BA, U. New Orleans, 1976; JD, Tulane Law Sch., 1979. With New Orleans Dist. Attyorney's Office, 1979—82; with Organized Crime and Racketeering Strike Force US Dept. Justice, La., 1982—94, 1st asst. US atty. (eastern dist.) La. New Orleans, 1994—2005, interim US atty., 2000—05, US atty., 2005—12; asst. dean for experiential learning Tulane U. Sch. Law, New Orleans, 2013—. Advanced through ranks to comdr. USNR, 1986—2006. Recipient Atty. General's Medallion for Disting. Svc., US Dept. Justice, Atty. General's Award for Excellence in Litigation, Torch of Liberty award, Anti-Defamation League, 2010. Office: Tulane University School of Law Weinmann Hall Rm 216-B New Orleans LA 70118 Office Phone: 504-862-8840. E-mail: jletten@tulane.edu.*

LETZIG, BETTY JEAN, retired financial consultant; b. Feb. 18, 1926; d. Robert H. and Alina Violet (Mayes) L. BA, Scarritt Coll., 1950, MA, 1968. Ednl. staff The Meth. Ch. Ark., Okla., Tex., 1953-60; with Internat. Deaconess Exch. Program, London, 1961-62; staff exec. nat. divsn. United Meth. Ch., NYC, 1962-95, cons. current and deferred giving, 1995—2008. Coord. Mission Pers. Support Svcs., 1984-88; exec. sec. Deaconess Program Office, 1989-95. Contbr. articles to profl. jours. Bd. dirs. Global Health Action, Atlanta, 1974-88, Vellore Christian Med. Coll., N.Y.C., 1984-94; mem. U.S. com. Internat. Coun. Social Welfare, Washington, 1983-89; active Nat. Interfaith Coalition on Aging, Athens, Ga. and Washington, 1972—, pres., 1981-85. Mem.: LWV, AAUW, Older Women's League, Nat. Coun. Social Welfare. Avocations: travel, photography, needlecrafts. Home: 266 Merrimon Ave Asheville NC 28801

LEULIETTE, CONNIE JANE, secondary school educator; d. Audie Nelson and Sadie Laura (Gregory) Ware; m. Charles Benjamin Leuliette, Jr., Sept. 5, 1964; 1 child, Eric Wesley. BS, W.Va. U., 1963, MA, 1965. Tchr. grades 1-4 Point Mountain Elem. Sch., Webster Springs, W.Va., 1959-60; tchr. gen. sci. Webster Springs (W.Va.) High Sch., 1963-64; tchr. 2d grade Norwood Elem. Sch., Clarksburg, W.Va., 1965-66, tchr. 6th grade, 1966-67; circulation clk., librarian Clarksburg-Harrison Pub. Library, 1981-83, reference librarian, 1983-89; tchr. sci. South Harrison High Sch., Lost Creek, W.Va., 1989-90, Roosevelt-Wilson Middle Sch., Nutter Fort, W.Va., 1990-96, Washington Irving Mid. Sch., Clarksburg, W.Va., 1996—2003. Pres. Nutter Fort PTA, 1978-79; elder Presbyn. Ch. NSF grantee, 1964-65. Mem. NEA, AAUW (sec. W.Va. divsn. 1981-83, conv. chmn. 1978-80, treas. 1992-96, br. pres. 1983-85, chair W.Va. Ednl. Found. 2000-02, chair W.Va. internat. affairs 2006-10, W.Va. membership v.p.), W.Va. Sci. Tchrs. Assn., W.Va. Assn. Parliamentarians (unit sec. 1986-90, treas. 1991-94, 99-01, 1st v.p. 2005-), W.Va. Fedn. Woman's Club (chmn. edn. dept. 1982-86, continuing edn. divsn. 1990-92, cmty. improvement program 1992-94, dist. edn. dept. 1990-92, dist. treas. 1994-98, dist. 2d v.p. 1998-2000, dist. 1st v.p. 2000-02, dist. pres. elect 2002-04, North Ctrl. dist. pres. 2004-2006, chmn. conservation dept. 2006—08, pub. rels. team 2008-), Woman's Club Nutter Fort (pres. 1990-92), Alpha Delta Kappa (W.Va. chpt. v.p. 1992-94, chpt. pres. 1994-96, state historian 2000-02, state treas. 2002-2006, state chaplain 2006-08, W.Va. convention co-chair 2008-10, MM pub. rels. chair 2010-). Democrat. Presbyterian. Avocations: reading, crosswords, walking, photography, stamp collecting/philately. Home: 107 Arbutus Dr Clarksburg WV 26301-4301

LEVAN, ALAN B., investment company executive; Chmn., pres., CEO BFC Financial Corp., 1978—; chmn., CEO Woodbridge Holdings Corp., 1985—; chmn., pres. BankAtlantic Bancorp, Inc., 1987—, CEO, 1994—; chmn. Bluegreen Corp., 2002—. Bd. dirs. Benihana Inc., 2009—. Office: Woodbridge Holdings Corp 2100 W Cypress Creek Rd Fort Lauderdale FL 33309 Office Phone: 954-940-4950. Office Fax: 954-760-5415. Business E-Mail: alevan@bfcfinancial.com.

LEVAN, MARTIN DOUGLAS, chemical engineering professor; b. Chattanooga, Aug. 30, 1949; s. Martin Douglas and Charlotte Irene (McAmis) LeV.; m. Barbara Lynn Verkins, Sept. 24, 1977; children: Theodore Douglas, Gregory William. BSChemE, U. Va., 1971; PhD in Chem. Engring., U. Calif., Berkeley, 1976. Sr. research engr. Amoco Prodn. Co., Tulsa, 1976-78; asst. prof. chem. engring. U. Va., Charlottesville, 1978-83, assoc. prof., 1983—89, prof., 1989—96; Centennial prof. and chair chem. engring. Vanderbilt U., Nashville, 1997—2003, J. Lawrence Wilson prof. engring., 2004—. Cons. Amoco Prodn. Co., Tulsa, 1984—, Amoco Chems. Co., Chgo., 1986—; vis. prof. Perpignan U., France, 1994; vis. scholar U. Queensland, Australia, 2009. Contbg. author: Perry's Chemical Engineers Handbook, 1984, 97, 2008; contbr. more than 180 articles to profl. jours. and procs. Cub scout officer Boy Scouts Am., Charlottesville, 1986—; coach boys and girls soccer, Charlottesville, 1987—. Fulbright sr. scholar Coun. for Internat. Exchange of Scholars, U. Porto, Portugal, 1985-86, CNRS-LIMSI, Orsay, France, 1993-94; grantee NSF, Petroleum Research Fund of Am. Chem. Soc., Am. Inst. Chem. Engrs., others. Mem. Am. Inst Chem. Engrs. (chmn. com. on absorption and ion exchange 1985-87, chmn. symposia 1981—), Am. Chem. Soc., Alpha Chi Sigma, Phi Eta Sigma, Tau Beta Pi, Sigma Xi. Avocations: golf, art, music. Office: Vanderbilt U Dept Chem & Biomolec Engring PMB 351604 2301 Vanderbilt Pl Nashville TN 37235 Business E-Mail: m.douglas.levan@vanderbilt.edu.

LEVATO, JOSEPH ANTHONY, board member; b. Morristown, NJ, Mar. 3, 1941; s. Anthony Joseph and Julia Marie (Compoli) L.; m. Diane Claire Schlichting, Oct. 16, 1965; children: Joseph Anthony Jr., Kristin Mary, Thomas Scott. BS, U. Dayton, 1962. Various mgmt. positions U.S. Industries Inc., 1968-77, sr. v.p., corp. controller, 1977-84; sr. v.p., CFO Triangle Industries Inc., 1984—88, Trian Group, 1992—93; exec. v.p., CFO Wendy's/Arby's Group, Inc., 1993—96, bd. dirs., 1996—. Mem.: Spring Brook Country (Morristown) (pres.). Office: Wendy's Arby's Group Inc Bd Directors 1155 Perimeter Ctr W Atlanta GA 30338 Office Phone: 678-514-4100. Business E-Mail: joseph.levato@wendysarbys.com.

LEVELL, EDWARD, JR., retired jet fighter pilot, airport director, aviation consultant; b. Jacksonville, Ala., Apr. 2, 1931; m. Rosa M. (Casellas) L, Aug. 3, 1951 (dec.); children: Edward III (dec.), Ruben C., Kenneth W. (dec.), Randy C., Raymond C. (dec.), Cheryl D. Levell Rivera, Michael K. BS, Tuskegee Inst., 1953; MA in Urban Sociology, U. Northern Colo., 1972; M in Mgmt., Indsl. Coll./Air War Coll., 1974. Commd. 2d lt. USAF, 1953, advanced through grades to col., 1978, various flight tng., air ops. and command positions, 1970; comdr. cadet group, then dep. commandant cadet wing USAF Acad., 1969-73; dep. comdr., vice comdr., wing comdr. 1st spl. ops. wing USAF, 1973-77, wing comdr. 58th tactical air command tng. wing, 1977-78, col., comdr. 20th air divsn., 1978-83, ret., 1983; dep. commr. aviation City of Chgo. Dept. Aviation, 1983-89; dep. dir. aviation, fin. and adminstrn. City of New Orleans Dept. Aviation, 1989-90, dep. dir. aviation, ops. and maintenance, 1990-92, dir. aviation, 1992—99; ret., 2000. Bd. dirs. Tourist & Conv. Commn., New Orleans; trustee Dryades YMCA, New Orleans; mem. transp. com. World Trade Ctr. Decorated Legion of Merit, D.F.C. (2), Meritorious Svc. Medal (2), Air Medal (8), Air Force Commendation Medal; recipient Disting. Svc. award Jacksonville, Ala., 1974, State of Fla. Commn. Human Rels. award for spl. recognition, 1977, Air Force Assn. Spl. Citation of Merit, 1977, Disting. Svc. award City of Chgo. Dept. Aviation, 1986, 87, 88; inducted in Tuskegee Univ. Hall of Fame, 1991. Mem. Am. Assn. Airport Execs., Gulf Coast Internat. Hispanic C. of C. Home: 20540 Falcons Landing Cir #4309 Potomac Falls VA 20165 Office Phone: 703-625-1229. Personal E-mail: eddielevell@gmail.com.

LEVENSON, MARIA NIJOLE, retired medical technologist, biologist, oceanographer; b. Kaunas, Lithuania, Mar. 24, 1940; arrived in US, 1948, naturalized; d. Zigmas and Monika (Galbuogis) Sabataitis; m. Coleman Levenson, Nov. 21, 1975. BA, Annhurst Coll., 1962. Cert. technologist La. Sr. rsch. technician Case Western Res. U., Cleve., 1962-69; phys. sci. technician Nat. Oceanographic Data Ctr., Washington, 1969-70; biologist NIH, Bethesda, Md., 1970-76; nuclear medicine technologist VA Med. Ctr., New Orleans, 1977-79; paramed. examiner Hooper Industries, New Orleans, 1980-82; assoc. chemist Computer Scis. Corp., Stennis Space Ctr., Miss., 1982-83; med. technologist VA Med. Ctr., New Orleans, 1984-96. Sec. Lithuanian Cath. Youth Assn., Putnam, Conn., 1960-62, Lithuanian Club, Annhurst Coll., South Woodstock, Conn., 1960-62. Participant Freedom Movement for Baltic Independence, Slidell, La., 1990-91; counselor Life with Cancer, Slidell, 1989—; vol. docent Dauphin Island Estuarium, 1997—; v.p. ABC Homeowners Assn. 2012-2013, pres. 2013-. La. State Nursing Sch. scholar, 1989; recipient: Algebra award, German Lang. award VA Med. Ctr., Orleans; named Employee of Month VA Med. Ctr., 1990. Mem. Daus. of Lithuania, Internat. Platform Assn., Island Watch, Tenn. Assn. Family and Cmty. Edn., Coast Guard Aux. Search & Rescue (vol.). Roman Catholic. Avocations: reading, travel, cooking, flying. Home: 484 Lake Shore Dr Pikeville TN 37367 Home Phone: 423-447-8480.

LEVENSON, STANLEY RICHARD, public relations and advertising executive; b. Cin., Dec. 28, 1933; s. Irven Philip and Dorothy (Aftel) L.; m. Barbara Lind, July 23, 1962; children: Laura, Amy. BA, U. Mich., 1956; postgrad., Am. U. S.W. sales and promotion mgr. DOT Records, Hollywood, Calif., 1959-62; S.W. sales and mktg. rep. Pickwick Internat. Co., 1963-65; pres., chmn. bd. Stan Levenson Assos., Dallas, 1966-76; exec. v.p., gen. mgr. public relations div. S.W., Bozell & Jacobs, Dallas, 1976-81; pres., CEO Levenson & Levenson, Dallas, 1981-83; CEO Levenson Pub. Rels., 1984—; dir. Fidelity Nat. Bank, Dallas. Adj. prof. in pub. relations mgmt. So. Meth. U., 1987-88, mem. adv. bd. Pub. Rels. sequence studies; bd. mem. Dallas Holocast Mus. Group leader comm. task force Dallas Police Dept.; assoc. mem. Dallas Assembly; bd. dirs. Dallas Arboretum, Vis. Nurses Assn., Family Place, Dallas Coun. World Affairs, Dallas Urban League, 2001, Dallas Trees and Parks Found., Thanksgiving Found.; mem. adv. bd. Crystal Charity Ball; co-chmn. Dallas Mayor's Task Force on Mktg.; mem. exec. com., bd. dirs. Ctrl. Downtown Assn., Dallas, 1993-94; mem. Dallas Citizens Coun., 1997—; arts adminstrn. and corp. comm. adv. bd. So. Meth. U., 2000—; trustee TACA, 1980, bd. dirs., 2000; trustee Dallas Alliance, 1988; mem. exec. com. Ctrl. Dallas Assn.; state com. chmn. March of Dimes, 2002, bd. dirs. North Tex. Commn., trustee, Tex. Tree Found., pres., Dallas Ctr. Performing Arts, adv. coun. mem., U. North Tex. Coll. Music, adv. bd. mem., U. Tex. Dallas, adv.bd. mem., Arts & Humanities Divsn., With U.S. Army, 1956-58. Recipient A. Maceo Smith Cmty. Aware award for support and leadership in the African Am. Cmty., Dallas, 2005; named Father of Yr., Bridge Builder, Tex. Israel Chamber, Hall of Fame, AAF, 2011. Mem. Pub. Rels. Soc. Am. (accredited, North Tex. Teich award), Soc. Profl. Journalists, Am. Heart Assn. (bd. dir., com. chmn. 2002—), Greater Dallas Chamber (mktg. and comm. adv. coun. 2000—09), North Tex. Super Bowl XLV (super bowl host com. bd. chmn.2009-), Urban League Dallas & North Tex., Dallas Superbowl XLV Host Com., African Am. Guild Mus., Sammons Ctr. Arts Legacy Coun. Office: 717 N Harwood 20th Fl Dallas TX 75201-7484 Home: 3831 Turtle Creek Blvd # 16C Dallas TX 75219-4480 Office Phone: 214-932-6076. Business E-Mail: s.levenson@levensonbrinkerpr.com.

LEVENTIS, PHIL PETER, state legislator; b. Lexington County, SC, Nov. 3, 1945; s. Peter P. Leventis and Tina Palasis L.; m. Ellen Venable Locker, 1969; children: Gregory P., Henry C., Peter P., Christina V. Grad., U. Va., 1969. Pres. Manning Ave Free Studio, 1979—80; commr. County Airport, 1980; mgr. Dixie Beverage, Sumter, 1974—, pres.; mem. Dist. 35 SC State Senate, 1981—. Paul Harris fellowship. Mem.: America Legion, Sumter C. of C., Rotary. Democrat. Episc. Mailing: 608 Gressette Bldg PO Box 142 Columbia SC 29201 Home: 935 Andiron Dr Sumter SC 29150-6041 Home Phone: 803-469-2047; Office Phone: 803-212-6000. Business E-Mail: leventis@sumter.net.

LEVI, DAVID F., dean, former federal judge; b. 1951; BA magna cum laude, Harvard U., 1972, MA, 1973; JD, Stanford U., 1980. Bar: Calif. 1983. Law clk. to Hon. Ben C. Duniway US Ct. Appeals (9th Cir.), 1980—81; law clk. to Justice Lewis F. Powell US Supreme Ct., 1981—82; asst. US atty. (ea. dist.) Calif. US Dept. Justice, Sacramento, 1983—86, US atty., 1986-90; judge US Dist. Ct. (ea. dist.) Calif., Sacramento, 1990—2007, chief judge, 2003—07; dean Duke U. Sch. Law, Durham, NC, 2007—, prof. law, 2007—. Chmn. task force on race, religious and ethnic fairness US Ct. Appeals (9th Cir.), 1994-97, mem. jury com., 1993-95. Adv. com. on Civil Rules, 1994—2003, chair, 2000—2003; chair Standing com.on Rules Practice and Procedure, 2003-; vis. com. U. Chgo. Law Sch., 1995-98. Recipient Order of the Coif, Stanford Law Sch., 1980; fellow Am. Acad. Arts & Scis.;, 2007—. Mem. Am. Law Inst. (mem. coun. 2004-), Milton L. Schwartz Inn of Ct. (pres. 1992-95), Ninth Cir. Dist. Judges Assn., 2003-05. Office: Duke University School of Law Room 2012 210 Science Dr Box 90362 Durham NC 27708-0360 Office Phone: 919-613-7001. E-mail: levi@law.duke.edu.*

LEVIN, HERVEY PHILLIP, lawyer; b. Oct. 22, 1942; s. Julius L. and Gertrude (Cohen) L.; m. Madeleine J. Raskin, Sept. 22, 1970; children: Arianne, Nicole, David. BBA, U. Mich., 1964, MBA, 1968; JD, DePaul U., 1969. Bar: Ill. 1969, Tex. 1979, US Dist. Ct. (no. dist.) Ill. 1970, US Ct. Appeals (5th cir.) 1981, US Ct. Appeals (7th cir.) 1971, US Supreme Ct. 1972. Assoc. Potts Randall & Horn, Chgo., 1970—71; assoc., jr. ptnr. Mehlman, Ticho, Addis, Susman, Spitzer, Randall, Horn & Pyes, Chgo., 1971—75; pvt. practice Chgo., 1975—78, Dallas, 1979—. Cons. labor stds. subcom., house edn. and labor com. US Congress; cons. in workers' compensation, occupl. disease and gen. practice. Bd. dirs. Solomon Schecter Acad. Dallas, Cong. Shearith Israel, Dallas, 1981-88, Am. Jewish Congress, Dallas, 1980-85, Nat. Assn. Mortgage Planners, 1995-00. Named Ky. Col. Fellow Coll. Worker's Compensation Lawyers (pres. 2007-09), Tort Trial & Insurance Practice Sect., ABA (workers compensation com. torts and ins. practices sect., chmn. 1989-90, coun. mem. tort trial and ins. practices sect. 1995-98, 1999-05, 2008-11, ho. of dels. 1999-05, 2008-11, Am. Bar Found.; mem. Ill. Bar Assn., Tex. Bar Assn., Dallas Bar Assn., Chgo. Bar Assn. Office: 6918 Blue Mesa Dr Ste 115 Dallas TX 75252-6140 Home Phone: 972-733-0663. Office Fax: 972-733-3269. Personal E-mail: hervey@airmail.net.

LEVIN, MARK REED, radio personality, legal foundation administrator; b. Phila., Sept. 21, 1957; s. Jack Eugene and Norma (Rubin) Levin; m. Kendall Edwards, Aug. 24, 1985. BA magna cum laude, Temple U., Phila., 1977; JD, Temple U. Sch. Law, Phila., 1980. Asst. counsel Tex. Instruments, Inc., Dallas, 1980-81; adminstrv. asst. Action Agy., Washington, 1981-82; dep. asst. sec. for elem. & secondary edn. US Dept. Edn., Washington, 1982-84; assoc. dir. presdl. pers. The White House, Washington, 1984-85; dep. solicitor US Dept. Interior, Washington; chief of staff to atty. gen. US Dept. Justice, Washington; dir. legal policy Landmark Legal Found., Leesburg, Va., pres.; radio talk show host The Mark Levin Show, ABC Radio Networks, 2003—. Contributing editor National Review Online, 2009—. Author: Men in Black: How the Supreme Court is Destroying America, 2005, Rescuing Sprite: A Dog Lover's Story of Joy and Anguish, 2007, Liberty and Tyranny: A Conservative Manifesto, 2009 (Publishers Weekly bestseller), Ameritopia: The Unmaking of America, 2012, The Liberty Amendments: Restoring the American Republic, 2013; contbg. editor Nat. Review Online, 2006—07. Mem. Cheltenham Twp. Sch. Bd., Pa., 1977—80. Recipient Ronald Reagan award, American Conservative Union, 2001; named one of The 50 Highest-Earning Polit. Figures, Newsweek, 2010. Mem.: Pa. Bar Assn., Phi Beta Kappa. Republican. Jewish. Achievements include The Mark Levin Show having been rated #1 in its time slot in NY, Chgo., Detroit, Dallas - Fort Worth and Washington. Office: Landmark Legal Found 19415 Deerfield Ave Ste 312 Leesburg VA 20176 Office Phone: 703-554-6100. Office Fax: 703-554-6119. E-mail: marklevinshow@abc.com.*

LEVIN, RICHARD C., lawyer; b. Dallas, June 15, 1945; s. Paul Michael and Yetta Gail (Caplan) L.; m. Kay Robins, June 18, 1982; children: Edward C., Henry A. BA, Tulane U., 1967; JD, Georgetown U., 1970. Bar: Tex. 1975, US Supreme Ct. Law clerk Office of Hon. John C. Godbold US Ct. Appeals (5th cir.), 1970-71; assoc. Sulivan & Cromwell, NYC, 1971-74, Akin, Gump, Strauss, Hauer & Feld L.L.P., Dallas, 1974-77, ptnr., 1978—. With Dallas Mgmt. com., 1989-1995; former co-head litig. sect. Akin, Gump, Strauss, Hauer & Feld, former head antitrust sect., internat. litig. sect.; spkr. in field. Contbr. articles to profl. jours. Former mem. exec. bd. Dallas Opera; former mem. bd. govs. Dallas Symphony; corp. com. Dallas Mus. Fine Arts; former mem., v.p. bd. trustees Hist. Preservation League; former mem. Landmark Com. City Dallas, bd. trustees Arts Magnet Sch.; former mem., dep. vice chmn., mgmt. com. Arts Dist. in Dallas; former chmn. Task Force Multi-Purpose Performing Arts Hall Dallas Opera, Dallas Ballet; bd. dirs. Dallas Opera, Salzburg Music Festival. Mem. Dallas Bar Assn. (coun. mem. Antitrust, Trade Regulation sect. 1987, internat. law sect. 1990). Jewish. Avocations: classical music, art, sports. Home: 4408 Saint Johns Dr Dallas TX 75205-3825 Office: Akin Gump Strauss Hauer & Feld 1700 Pacific Ave Ste 4100 Dallas TX 75201-4624 Office Phone: 214-969-2728. Office Fax: 214-969-4343. E-mail: rlevin@akingump.com.

LEVIN, RONALD MITCHELL, geriatrician; b. Phila., July 29, 1958; s. Herbert A. and Marlene (Axelrod) L.; m. Carol Lynn Most, June 17, 1979; children: Jay Samuel, Marc Andrew, Eric Brian. BA cum laude, LaSalle U., 1980; MD with hons. in Pediats., distinction in medicine, Hahnemann U., 1984. Diplomate Am. Bd. Internal Medicine, Nat. Bd. Med. Examiners; cert. of advanced qualifications in geriatric medicine, Am. Bd. Internal Medicine, 1994, 2004. Intern, resident internal medicine Bryn Mawr Hosp., Phila., 1984-87; physician Lawndale Family Practice, Phila., 1987-88; pvt. practice Phila., 1988—95, 2001—03; clin. instr. medicine Hahnemann MCP Sch. Medicine, 1993—2003, Allegheny U. Health Scis., 1993—2003; internist Abington Meml. Hosp., 1995-2001; med. dir. U.S. Homecare, Phila., 1991-94; staff physician Salisbury Va. Med. Ctr., 2003—06, West Palm Beach VA Med. Ctr., Fla., 2006—; mem. Clin. Exec. Bd., 2009—10; chmn. Medication Use Com., 2010—; affiliated asst. prof. medicine U. Miami Miller Sch. Medicine, 2010—; mem. VISN 8 P+T Com., 2010—; clin. employee quarter 4th Quarter, VAMC, West Palm Beach, 2011. Interviewer med. sch. admissions com. Hahnemann Med. Coll. Pa. Sch. Medicine, 1995-97. Fellow ACP; mem. AMA (Physician's Recognition award 1991, 94, 97, 2000, 03, 06, 09, 12), Am. Geriatric Soc. Office: West Palm Beach VA Medical Ctr 7305 N Military Trail West Palm Beach FL 33410 Home: 10124 Cobblestone Creek Dr Boynton Beach FL 33472-4459 Home Phone: 561-752-3458; Office Phone: 561-422-8262. Personal E-mail: rmlmdfacp@aol.com.

LEVIN, VICTOR A., neurologist, oncologist, educator; b. Milw. MD, U. Wis., 1966. Diplomate Am. Bd. Psychiatry and Neurology. Intern medicine Washington U., St. Louis City Hosp., 1966—67; staff assoc. Lab. Chem. Pharmacology Nat. Cancer Inst., Bethesda, Md., 1967—69; resident neurology Mass. Gen. Hosp., Boston, 1969—72, NINDS spl. fellow dept. neurology, 1971—72; faculty Schs. Medicine and Pharmacy U. Calif., San Francisco, prof. dept. neurosurgery, pharm. chemistry and pharmacology, 1981, chief neuro-oncology svc. Brain Tumor Rsch. Ctr., 1977; prof. dept. neuro-oncology U. Tex. M.D. Anderson Cancer Ctr., Houston, 1988—, chair dept. neuro-oncology, 1988—99, dir. Brain Tumor Ctr., 1993—99. Co-founder Asilomar Conf. for Brain Tumor Rsch. and Therapy, 1975; exec. devel. program Rice U., Houston, 1990—91. Contbr. chapters to books, over 350 articles to profl. jours. Recipient medal med. faculty, Tokyo U., 1982, award in neuro-oncology, Farber Found., 1988, Heath Meml. award for cancer care, 1997. Mem.: Soc. for Neuro-Oncology (founding pres. 1995—97, Gold medal 2003), Nat. Brain Tumor Found., Am. Soc. Clin. Oncology, Am. Brain Tumor Assn., Am. Assn. Neurol. Surgeons (joint sect. on tumors), Am. Assn. for Cancer Rsch., Am. Acad. Neurology. Achievements include research in defining pharmacokinetics of anticancer drugs; development of drug and radiation combination therapies for brain tumors. Office: Victor A Levin MD Neuro Oncology Unit 431 UT MD Anderson Cancer Ctr PO Box 301402 Houston TX 77230-1402 Office Phone: 713-792-8297.

LEVIN, WARREN MAYER, family practice physician; b. Phila., Aug. 20, 1932; s. Israel and Clara Deborah (Cherim) L.; m. Marsha Ann Beinstein, Dec. 24, 1955 (div. 1975); children: Beth Ann, Julie Ruth; m. Frances Susan Teitler, Mar. 20, 1982; 1 child, Erika Alexandra. BS, Ursinus Coll., 1952; MD, Jefferson Med. Coll., 1956. Diplomate Am. Bd. Family Practice, 1973, 80, 87, 94, Am. Bd. Bariatric Medicine, 1973, Am. Bd. Environ. Medicine, 1994, Am. Bd. Chelation Therapy, 1973, Internat. Bd. Advanced Longevity Medicine, 2000, Am. Bd. Clin. Med. Toxicology, 1990; cert. homeopath, 2004. Intern US Naval Hosp., Newport, RI, 1956-57; pvt. practice SI, NY, 1959-74; founder, med. dir. Heights Holistic Health Ctr., Bklyn., 1974-79, World Health Med. Group, NYC, 1979-94; physician Physicians for Complementary Medicine, NYC, 1994-97, Comprehensive Med. Svcs., NYC, 1998—2000, Americas Med. Ctr., Ridgefield, Conn., 1998—2000; founder, med. dir. Integrative Medicine Conn., Wilton, 2001—03, with NYC office, 2001—04; physician

Issels Med. Ctr., Phoenix, 2004—05, pvt. practice, Scottsdale, Ariz., 2005—06, Vienna, Va., 2006—12, Nat. Integrative Health Assocs., 2013—. Mem. bd. examiners Am. Bd. Chelation Therapy, 1975—78, Internat. Bd. Advanced Longevity Medicine, 1998—2000. Author: (book) Beyond The Yeast Connection to The C.R.C., 2012; contbr. to books Nutrition in Pregnancy, 1981, to books Challenging Orthodoxy, 1991, to books Alternative Medicine, 1994, to books The Cholesterol Hoax, 1998, to books Whole Body Dentistry, 1999, to books Experts of Lyme Disease, 2008, book Foreword to Clinical Chemistry Nutrition. Bd. govs. Internat. Coll. Applied Nutrition, 1974-76; chmn. med. adv. bd. Survive Until a Cure, advisory coun.-Chemical Awareness Rsch. Educ. & Solutions; prin. investigator-A Study on Use of Human Growth Hormone. Lt. M.C., USNR ret. Recipient Disting. Pioneer in Alternative Medicine award Found. for Advancement of Innovative Medicine Fund, 1995, Presdl. Commendation, Am. Coll. for Advancement in Medicine, 1995. Fellow: Am. Acad. Family Pactice, Am. Coll Nutrition, Am. Acad. Environ. Medicine (bd. dirs. 2003); mem.: Nat. Autism Assn. (chmn. biomed. edn. Nova chpt.), Am. Soc. Bariatric Medicine (v.p. 1980—82), Am. Coll. Advancement Medicine (bd. dirs. 1976—80, treas. 1980). Avocations: sailing, swimming. Home: 4604 Bayard Blvd Bethesda MD 20815 Office: 5225 Wisconsin Ave Ste 401 Washington DC 20515 Office Phone: 202-237-7000. Personal E-mail: dcwmlevin@aol.com. Business E-Mail: info@warrenmlevinmd.org.

LEVINE, ALAN, health facilities company executive; BS in Health Edn. & Cmty. Health, U. Fla., Gainesville, MS in Health Sci., MBA. COO Bayonet Point/Hudson Med. Ctr., Hudson, Fla.; v.p. ops. Columbia Regional Med. Ctrs., Fla.; COO Tallahassee Cmty. Hospitals, Fla.; CEO Doctors' Meml. Hosp., Perry, Fla.; dep. chief of staff, sr. health policy advisor to Gov. Jeb Bush State of Fla., Tallahassee; CEO South Bay Hosp., Sun City Center, Fla., 2000—03; sec. Fla. Agency Health Care Adminstrn., 2004—06; pres., CEO Broward Health, Fla., 2006—08; sec. La. Dept. Health & Hospitals, Baton Rouge, 2008—10; sr. v.p. health devel. ops. & govt. rels. Health Mgmt. Associates, Inc., Naples, Fla., 2010—. Named a Up and Comer in American Healthcare, Modern Healthcare mag., 2005, Heavy Hitter in Health Care, South Fla. Bus. Jour., 2007. Office: Health Management Associates Inc 5811 Pelican Bay Blvd Ste 500 Naples FL 34108 Office Phone: 239-598-3131.

LEVINE, DANIEL BLANK, classical studies educator; b. Cin., July 22, 1953; s. Joseph and Elizabeth (Blank) L.; m. Judith Robinson, Aug. 14, 1984; children: Sarah Ruth, Amy Elizabeth. Student, Am. Sch. Classical Studies, Athens, 1974, student, 1978—79; BA in Greek and Latin magna cum laude, U. Minn., 1975; PhD in Classics, U. Cin., 1980. Seymour fellow Am. Sch. Classical Studies, 1978-79, sr. assoc. mem., 2008; asst. prof. U. Ark., 1980-84, assoc. prof., 1984-98, prof., 1998—. Dir. Summer Session Am. Sch. Classical Studies, Athens, 1987, 95, 2006; dir. study tour in Greece Vergilian Soc., 1990, Greece Univ. Ark., 2000-01, 03, 05, 07, 09; referee Classical Jour., 1984-88, Helios, 1984-88, Cornell U. Press, 1988-89, 91—, Classical Outlook, 1988-89; panelist NEH, Washington, 1986; co-dir., instr. gifted and talented HS students summer program State of Ark. Dept. Edn. Grant, 1988; mng. com. Am. Sch. Classical Studies Athens, 1991—. Contbr. articles to profl. jours. Grantee NEH 1981-84, 92; recipient Outstanding Tchr. award Mortar Bd. Sr. Honor Soc., U. Ark., 1991, Master Tchr. award Fulbright Coll., 1995. Mem. Am. Philological Assn. (Excellence in Teaching Classics award 1992), Am. Classical League, Classical Assn. Mid. West and South (Ovatio 1996, v.p. com. promotion Latin in Ark. 1980-86, 91-95, chmn. regional rep. com. for promotion Latin, Outstanding State V.P. for 1982-83), U. Ark. Teaching Acad., Golden Key, Phi Beta Kappa. Home: 904 Park Ave Fayetteville AR 72701-2027 Office: U Ark Dept World Langs, Lits and Cultures 425 Kimpel Hall Fayetteville AR 72701 Business E-Mail: dlevine@uark.edu.

LEVINE, HOWARD R., retail executive; b. 1959; With merchandising dept. Family Dollar Stores, Inc., Matthews, NC, 1981-87, v.p., gen. merchandise mgr. softlines, 1996, sr. v.p. merchandising and advt., 1996-97, pres., COO, 1997-98, CEO, 1998—2003, chmn., CEO, 2003—. Office: Family Dollar Stores PO Box 1017 Charlotte NC 28201-1017

LEVINE, JACK ANTON, lawyer; b. Monticello, NY, Dec. 23, 1946; s. Milton and Sara (Sacks) L.; m. Eileen A. Garsh, Sept. 7, 1974; children: Matthew Aaron, Dana Esther. BS with honors, SUNY, Binghamton, 1968; JD with honors, U. Fla., 1975, LLM in Taxation, 1976. Bar: Fla. 1975, U.S. Ct. Appeals (11th cir.) 1981, U.S. Tax Ct., 1982. Tax atty. legis. and regulations divsn. Office chief counsel IRS, Washington, 1977-81; assoc. Holland & Knight, Tampa, Fla., 1981-83, ptnr., 1984—. Lectr. in field. Contbr. articles to profl. jours. Mem. ABA, Fla. Bar Assn. (sect. taxation exec. coun. 1984-2003, chmn. partnership com. 1985-88, chmn. taxation regulated pub. utilities com. 1988-92, co-chmn. corps. and tax-exempt orgns. com. 1992-2001, bd. cert. in tax law 1984—). Democrat. Jewish. Avocations: golf, reading, travel. Home: 10905 Carrollwood Dr Tampa FL 33618-3903 Office: Holland & Knight Ste 4100 100 N Tampa St Tampa FL 33602-3644 Home Phone: 813-933-9877; Office Phone: 813-227-6531. E-mail: jack.levine@hklaw.com.

LEVINE, PETER, information technology executive; Attended, MIT; BS in Engring., Boston U. Software engr., Project Athena MIT; various positions, including exec. v.p., strategic & platform ops. Veritas, 1990—2001; exec. v.p. Strategic & Platform Ops., 2001—02; mng. dir. Mayfield Fund, 2002—06; CEO XenSource, Inc. (acquired by Citrix Sys., Inc), Palo Alto, Calif., 2006; joined Citrix Sys., Inc., 2007, sr. v.p., gen. mgr., Datacenter & Cloud Divsn. Office: Citrix Systems Inc 851 W Cypress Creek Rd Fort Lauderdale FL 33309 Office Phone: 954-267-3000. Office Fax: 954-267-9319. Business E-Mail: peter.levine@citrix.com.

LEVINE, RICHARD A., physician; b. Miami Beach, Fla., July 6, 1953; s. Morris Joseph and Sybil R. L.; m. Lidia Foffo; children: Mitchell, Kimberly, David. BS cum laude in zoology, U. Fla., 1975; MD, Universita di Roma, Italy, 1982. Diplomate Am. Bd. Internal Medicine, Am. Bd. Geriatric Medicine; cert. sr. aviation med. examiner FAA. Resident in internal medicine U. Va. Affiliated Hosps., Roanoke-Salem, Va., 1983-86; pvt. practice Boca Raton, Fla., 1987—; clin. asst. prof. Fla. Atlantic U. Coll. Medicine, asst. clin. prof. Lectr. in field. Dir. med. edn. com. Am. Cancer Soc., Boca Raton, 1990; local coord. 1st pilot program of Put Prevention Into Practice (partnership with ACP and Office of Disease Prevention and Health Promotion, Washington), 1994. Recipient Fla. Physician Practice Quality Improvement Recognition award, 2013; named one of Castle Connolly Best Drs., 2008—. Fellow ACP; mem. AMA, Fla. Med. Assn., Palm Beach County Med. Soc. (bd. dirs. 1994), Va. Med. Soc. Avocations: marine biology, walking, music, travel. Office: 7280 W Palmetto Park Rd Ste 205 Boca Raton FL 33433 Office Phone: 561-368-0191. Business E-Mail: drlevine@priorityconciergemd.com.

LEVINE, ROBERT JEFFREY, lawyer; b. Miami Beach, Fla., Nov. 27, 1956; s. I. Stanely and Elaine (Martz) L. BSBA magna cum laude, U. Fla., 1978; JD, George Washington U., 1981. Bar: Fla. 1981, U.S. Dist. Ct. (so. dist.) Fla. 1981, U.S. Ct. Appeals (5th and 11th cirs.) 1981, U.S. Supreme Ct. 1986; cert. civil mediator, Fla. Supreme Ct.; lic. sea capt. USCG. Assoc. Barron, Lehman & Cardenas, Miami, 1981-82; ptnr. Haves & Levine, Miami, 1982-83; pvt. practice law Miami, 1983-85; ptnr. Toland & Levine, Miami, 1985-90, Levine & Geiger, P.A., Miami, 1990-94, Levine & Ptnrs., P.A., Miami, 1994—. Mem.: ATLA, Acad. Fla. Trial Lawyers, Fla. Bar Assn. Avocations: diving, fishing, skiing, golf, tennis. Office: Levine & Ptnrs PA 1110 Brickell Ave 7th Fl Miami FL 33131-3132 E-mail: RJL@levinelawfirm.com.*

LEVINE, TONY, college football coach; b. St. Paul, Oct. 28, 1972; m. Erin Levine; children: Benjamin, Asher, Eli, Willa. B in Kinesiology, U. Minn., 1996; M in Phys. Edn., Tex. State U., San Marcos, 1999; ednl. specialist degree in adult edn., Auburn U., Ala., 2003. Wide receiver Minn. Fighting Pike, Arena Football League, 1996; asst. coach, freshman head football coach Highland Pk. HS Scots, Minn., 1996; asst. wide receivers & tight ends coach Tex. State U. Bobcats, 1997—98, asst. wide receivers & tight ends coach, co-recruiting coord., 1999; grad. asst. Auburn U. Tigers, 2000—01; spl. teams coord., tight ends coach La. Tech. U. Bulldogs, 2002; dir. football ops. U. Louisville Cardinals, 2003, spl. teams coord., outside linebackers coach, 2004—05; asst. spl. teams coach, asst. strength & conditioning coach Carolina Panthers, 2006—07; spl. teams coord., tight ends & inside receivers coach U. Houston Cougars, 2008—11, asst. head coach, 2010—11, interim head coach, 2011, head football coach, 2012—. Office: University of Houston Football Program Athletics/Alumni Ctr 3100 Cullen Blvd Houston TX 77204-6002 Office Phone: 713-743-9388. Business E-Mail: amlevine@central.uh.edu.

LEVIS, ALEXANDER HENRY, systems engineer, educator, consultant; b. Yannina, Greece, Oct. 3, 1940; came to U.S., 1959; s. Henry N. and Jeannette (Matathia) L.; m. Ilze E. Sedriks, Mar. 26, 1970 (dec. 1994); children: Livia, Philip; m. Margaret C. Miller, May 13, 2001. AB, Ripon Coll., 1963; BS, MS, MIT, 1965, ME, 1967, ScD, 1968. Asst. prof. Poly. Inst. Bklyn., 1968-73, assoc. prof., 1973-74; mgr. sys. rsch. dept. Systems Control, Inc., Palo Alto, Calif., 1973-79; sr. rsch. scientist MIT, Cambridge, 1979-90; prof. George Mason U., Fairfax, Va., 1990—, chair sys. engring. dept., 1992—95, 1996—98; chief scientist USAF, 2001—04. Mem. Air Force Sci. Adv. Bd., 1990-94, 98-2001, 04-08, Homeland Security Sci. & Tech. Adv. Com., 2008-, NASA Adv. Coun., 2008-09. Editor six books; assoc. editor IEEE Transactions on Automatic Control, 1975-77, Automatica Jour., 1980-85, Systems Engineering, 1997; contbr. articles to sci. jours. Recipient Exceptional Civilian Svc. medal Air Force, 1994, 2001, 04, Disting. Svc. Edn. award AFCEA, 1996, Meritorious Civilian Svc. award 2008. Fellow AAAS, IEEE Control Systems Soc. (v.p. 1984-85, pres. 1987, Disting. Mem. award 1987), Incose, AIAA (assoc.). Office: George Mason U ECE Dept Fairfax VA 22030 Home: 21979 Clear Creek Rd Aldie VA 20105-1735

LEVIT, HÉLOÏSE B. (GINGER LEVIT), art historian, art journalist, art dealer, consultant; b. Phila., Apr. 2, 1937; d. Elmer and Claire Frances (Schwartz) Bertman; m. Jay Joseph Levit, July 14, 1962; children: Richard Bertman, Robert Edward, Darcy Francine. BA in French Literature, U. Pa., 1959; MA in French Literature, U. Richmond, 1975; MA Art History, Va. Commonwealth U., Richmond, 1998; Cert., Alliance Française, Paris, 1991, Chambre de Commerce et d'Industrie de Paris, 1991, La Sorbonne, Paris, 1994, Istituto Lorenzo di Medici Firenze, Italy, 1996, Ecole du Louvre, 1998, Cert., 2005, U. Stranieri, Perugia, Italy. Arts broadcaster, Richmond, Va., 1976—2011; dir. Fine Arts Am., Inc., Richmond, 1982-84; tchr. Henrico County Pub. Schs., Richmond, 1984-88; mgr., dir. devel. Richmond Philharm. Orch., 1988—; fine arts and media cons. Art-I-Facts, Richmond, 1988—; french prof. Va. Commonwealth U., 2011. Author: Moments, Monuments & Monarchs, 1986 (Star award, 1986), Antique Week and Fine Art Connoisseur, Antiques and Fine Arts, 50 Plus; anchor, prodr. (syndicated radio series) Va. Arts Report, 1978—83, Va. Women, 1984, (38 Va. radio sta.) Picasso Minute, 2011. V.p. Va. Mus. Collectors Cir., Richmond, 1986-91, mem. steering com.; pres. Alliance Francaise de Richmond, Chapitre Rochambeau; mem. Va. Mus. Coun., Richmond, Richmond Symphony Orch. League, dir. pub. rels., 2000—, guest condr., 2000. Mem. Va. Press Women (v.p., 2d pl. award 2001, 02, 03, 1st pl. awards 2008, 09, 10, 12), U. Pa. Alumni Club (v.p. 1980-90, Ben Franklin award 1990), La Table Francaise (chmn. 1996—), World Affairs Coun., The Woman's Club, Young Audiences Va. (Richmond) (steering com. mem.). Avocations: antiques, classical music, travel. Home and Office: Art-I-Facts and Ginger Levit Atelier 419 Dellbrooks Pl Richmond VA 23238-5559 Office Phone: 804-398-0440, 804-740-1413. Personal E-mail: gingerlevit@comcast.net. Business E-Mail: ginger@vcu.org.

LEVIT, MAX, wholesale distribution executive; s. Joe and Dora Levit. CEO The Grocers Supply Co., Inc., pres., 1993—. Recipient Torch of Liberty award, Anti-Defamation League, 2001. Office: The Grocers Supply Co Inc 3131 E Holcombe Blvd Houston TX 77021-2199 Office Phone: 713-747-5000. Business E-Mail: mlevit@grocerssupply.com.

LEVITT, GEORGE, retired chemist; b. Newburg, NY, Feb. 19, 1925; m. Julie Zeto; children: Barbara Klein, Jeffrey, David, Gregory. BS, Duquesne U., 1950, MS, 1952; PhD, Mich. State U., 1957. Rsch. chemist Exptl. Sta. E.I. du Pont de Nemours & Co., Inc., 1956—63, rsch. chemist Stine Lab., 1963—66, rsch. chemist Exptl. Sta., 1966—68, sr. rsch. chemist, 1968—80, rsch. assoc., 1981—86. Instr, Del. Tech. and C.C., 1975—80. Pres. Ronald McDonald House of Del, 1986—87, bd. dirs., 1986—94. Recipient Internat. pesticide rsch. award, Swiss Soc. Chem. Industries, 1982, award, Chesapeake chpt. Nat. Agrl. Mktg. Assn., 1987, disting. alumni award, Duquesne U. Coll. Arts and Sci., 1988, Nat. Medal of Tech., 1993, Disting. Inventor award, Intellectual Property Owners Am., 1983. Mem.: AAAS, Internat. Union Pure & Applied Chemistry, Am. Chem. Soc. (Creative Invention award 1989, Kenneth Spencer award 1991, internat. award for rsch. in agrochems. 1998, Hero of Chem. award 1999), Sigma Xi. Achievements include research in organic syntheses, herbicides, fungicides, medicinals, pesticides; synthesis of heterocyclic compounds; characterization and identification of novel organic compounds for biological evaluation; defined and optimized chemical structure-biological activity relationships and sulfonylurea herbicides. Home: 82 Via del Corso Palm Beach Gardens FL 33418-3773 Personal E-mail: gleanr@msn.com.

LEVITT, GERALD STEVEN, retired engineering executive; b. Bronx, Mar. 21, 1944; s. Charles and Beatrice (Janet) L.; m. Natalie Lillian Hoppen; children: Mark, Roy. B in Mgmt. Engring., Rensselaer Poly. Inst., 1965; MBA, DePaul U., 1972. Registered profl. engr., Ill. Tech. rep. Worthington Air Conditioning Co., Ampere, NJ, 1965-67; indsl. sales engr. Peoples Gas Light & Coke Co., Chgo., 1967-71; planning specialist Peoples Gas Co., Chgo., 1971-72; v.p. Stone & Webster Mgmt. Cons., Inc., NYC, 1972-82; exec. v.p., chief staff officer South Jersey Gas Co., Folsom, NJ, 1982-98; v.p., CFO South Jersey Industries, Inc., Folsom, NJ, 1987-98; sr. v.p., treas., CFO, bd. dirs. Greenhorne & O'Mara, Inc., Laurel, Md., 1998—2011, chmn. bd. Md., 2010—11. Past bd. dirs. Camden County coun. Boy Scouts Am., West Collingswood, N.J., Rowan Coll. Found. Mem. Greater Atlantic City C. of C. (past bd. dirs.), N.J. State C. of C. (past bd. dirs.), Greenhorne O'Mara, Inc. (bd. dirs.). Home Phone: 863-324-3197.

LEVY, DAVID RUBEN, advertising and broadcasting executive; b. New Rochelle, NY, Apr. 6, 1962; s. Richard Paul Levy and Joan (Katz) Gerard; m. Niki Berger, May 31, 1987; children: Brett, Jake. Grad., Syracuse U., 1984. Media buyer Oakmont Advt., Syracuse, NY, 1983-84; network buyer SSC & B Worldwide, NYC, 1984-85; account exec. Cable Network Inc., NYC, 1985-86, Turner Broadcasting Sys., Inc., NYC, 1986—94, sr. v.p., internat. ad sales, 1994—97, exec. v.p., internat. ad sales, 1997—98, pres., entertainment ad sales and mktg., pres., Turner Sports, 2003—; pres., internat. advt. sales Turner Broadcasting Sys. Internat., 1998—2000, co-pres., 2000—03. Named one of 50 Most Influential People in Sports Bus., Street & Smith's SportsBus. Jour., 2007—09, The Most Influential People in the World of Sports, Bus. Week, 2007, 2008; named to CableFax 100, 2005. Office: Turner Broadcasting System Inc One CNN Ctr Atlanta GA 30303 Office Phone: 404-827-1700.

LEVY, DAVID WILLIAM, history educator; b. Chgo., May 6, 1937; s. Roy A. and Helen (Loeffler) L.; m. Lynne Ellen Hunt, Sept. 7, 1969; children: Beth Ellen, Benjamin Robert. BA, U. Ill., 1959; MA, U. Chgo., 1961; PhD, U. Wis., 1967. Instr. Ohio State U., Columbus, 1964-67; asst. prof. history U. Okla., Norman, 1967—71, assoc. prof., 1971-84, prof., 1984—, David Ross Boyd prof. Am. history, 1987—, chmn. faculty senate, 1985-86; prof. emeritus, 2006—; Maxwell Weiner vis. prof. humanities Missouri U. Scis & Tech., 2010. Author: Herbert Croly of the New Republic, 1985; co-editor: Letters of Louis D. Brandeis, 5 vols., 1971-78, Debate over Vietnam, 1991, 2d edit., 1995, University of Oklahoma: A History, 3 vols., 2004—, Mark Twain: The Divided Mind, 2010; contbr. numerous articles to scholarly, popular and legal jours. Chmn. Norman Planning Commn. Recipient Regents award for disting. teaching U. Okla., 1973, Students Assn. award for outstanding teaching, 1985; grantee NEH, 1967, 68, 69, 72-74, 84-87; fellow Rockefeller Found., 1980-81, Southwestern Bell, 1988; Danforth teaching assoc. Mem. AAUP (pres. Okla. conf. 1975-76). Home: 914 Hoover St Norman OK 73072-6153 Office: U Okla History Dept 455 W Lindsey St Norman OK 73019-2000 Business E-Mail: dwlevy@ou.edu.

LEVY, EUGENE HOWARD, planetary sciences and astrophysics educator, researcher; b. NYC, May 6, 1944; s. Isaac Philip and Anita Harriet (Gutman) L.; children: Roger P., Jonathan S., Benjamin H. AB in Physics with high honors, Rutgers U., 1966; PhD in Physics, U. Chgo., 1971. Teaching asst. dept. physics U. Chgo., 1966-69, rsch. asst. Enrico Fermi Inst., 1969-71; postdoctoral fellow dept. physics and astronomy U. Md., 1971-73; asst. prof. physics and astrophysics Bartol Rsch. Found., Franklin Inst., Swarthmore, Pa., 1973-75; asst., then assoc. prof. U. Ariz., Tucson, 1975-83, prof. planetary scis., 1983—2000, mem. faculty applied math. program, 1981—2000, head dept. planetary scis., dir. lunar and planetary lab., 1983-94, mem. theoretical astrophysics program, 1985—2000, dean coll. of sci., 1993—2000, dir. NASA-Ariz. Spacegrant Coll. Consortium Tucson, 1989—2000, prof. physics, 1996—2000; prof. physics and astronomy Rice U., Houston, 2000—, Howard R. Hughes Provost, 2000—10, Andrew Hays Buchanan prof., astrophysics, 2010—. Mem. com. on planetary and lunar exploration of space sci. bd., Nat. Acad. Scis., 1976-79, chmn., 1979-82, co-chair Space Sci. Bd. Study on Exploration Primitive Solar-System Bodies, 1978, mem. Space Sci. Bd., 1979-82, head U.S. del., co-chair Nat. Acad. Scis.-European Sci. Found. Joint Working Group on Cooperation in Planetary Exploration, 1982-84, mem. steering group com. on major directions for space sci. 1995-2015, 1984-86, chair adv. com. on internat. cooperation for Mars sample return, 1986-88; mem. Comet Halley Sci. Working Group, NASA, 1977, mem. spacelab phys. sci. rev. panel space sci. steering com., 1979, mem. rev. panel on origin plasmas in Earth's neighborhood, 1980, mem. solar system exploration com. of Adv. Coun., 1980-83, mem. Ames Rsch. Ctr. Planetary Detection Study, 1983, Solar System Exploration Mgmt. Coun., 1983-87, mem. com. on future space-sta. sci. projects, 1985, mem. Space Sta. Sci. Users' Working Group, 1985-86, Space and Earth Sci. Adv. Com., 1985-88, chair Comet Rendevous and Asteroid Flyby Rev. Panel, 1986, mem. Mars Exploration Strategy Adv. Group, 1986, Mars Rover Sample Return Sci. Working Group, 1987—; sci. cons. Rockwell Internat. Corp., 1980; mem. COSPAR Internat. Tech. Panel on Comets, 1980-82; U.S.-NASA del. to discussions on internat. cooperation investigations of Comet Halley, Padua, Italy, 1981, to U.S.-USSR Joint Working Group on Near-Earth Space, the Moon and Planets, 1981; mem. program adv. bd. Internat. Conf. on Cometary Exploration, Budapest, Hungary, 1982; mem. exec. com. univs.' space sci. working group Assn. Am. Univs., 1982-86; study panel U.S.-Soviet cooperation in space sci. U.S. Cong. Office of Tech. Assessment, 1984; chair planetary exploration panel Pacific Rim Nations Internat. Space Yr. Conf., Kona, Hawaii, 1987; mem. working group planetary systems sci. NASA, 1988—, rev. panel lunar and planetary, 1988-90, rev. panel origins solar systems programs, 1990-91; chair formation/detection group, 1993-95; mem. astronomy and astrophysics survey com., sci. opportunities panel NAS, 1989-90; mem. study panel on robotic exploration of Moon and Mars, U.S. Cong. Office Tech. Assessment, 1991; chmn. coun. of instns., bd. dirs. U.S. Space Rsch. Assn., 1991-98, vice-chmn. bd. dirs. 1993-98; NASA Origins of Solar Syss. Mgmt. Working Group (chair 1994-96), chmn. NASA Origins of Solar Syss. Planet Formation and Detection Rev. Panel, 1993-95, Am. Astron. Soc. (com. on pub. edn., 1994-95), Internat. Sci Found. Astronomy Rev. Panel, 1993-94, NASA Origins of Solar Syss. Mgmt. Ops. Working Group, 1994—, Am. Astron. Soc. Com. on Pub. Edn., 1994; chair Discovery-4 Space Flight Mission Selection Bd., NASA, 1995, mem. Keck Observatory Telescope Allocation Com., 1998-2000, mem. astronomy and astrophysics survey com. NRC/NAS Found., 1999, chair external review com. dept. of space physics and astronomy, Rice U., 1999, bd. dirs. Nat. Space Grant Alliance, 1999-2000, bd. trustees Associated Univs., Inc., 2001-; chmn. 2007-2010, NASA Planetary Protection Subcom., 2010-; mem. Space Telescope Inst. Coun., 2003-2009, NASA Adv. Coun. Sci. Com., 2010-, Nat. Task Force Physics Tchr. Preparation, 2008-2011, Com. Advancing Rsch. Sci. and Engring., Am. Acad. Arts & Scis., 2010-; mem. bd. dirs. Nat. Space Biomed. Rsch. Inst., 2004-; mem. bd. advisors Tan Tao U. Vietnam, 2009; mem. planetary protection adv. com. NASA, 2002-06, chmn. 2005-06, chair nuc. sys. initiative sci. definition team NASA, 2002, mem. jovian icy mmons tour review bd. NASA, 2002; former mem. adv. coun. sci. com., NASA, 2005-06; cons. and lectr. in field. Am. Geophys. Union (frmr), Am. Phys. Soc. (frmr), Internat. Astron. Union. Editor: Protostars and Planets III, 1993; contbr., author articles for gen. pub., adv. reports for Congl. Record, abstracts, book revs., others. Bd. dir. Nat. Space Biomed. Rsch. Inst., 2004—; bd. trustees Associated Univs., 2001, exec. com., 2001—; mem. Space Telescope Inst. Coun., 2003—; bd. advisers Tan Tao U., Ho Chi Minh City, Vietnam, 2009—. Recipient Disting. Pub. Svc. medal NASA, 1983, Alexander von Humboldt-Stiftung Sr. Scientist award Fed. Republic Germany, 1989; Disting. vis. scientist Jet Propulsion Lab., Calif. Inst. Tech., 1985-91; NASA predoctoral fellow U. Chgo., 1966-69, fellow Ctr. for Theoretical Physics, U. Md., 1971-73; rsch. grantee NASA, NSF. Mem.: AAAS, Phi Beta Kappa, Sigma Xi. Achievements include research in theoretical cosmical physics, planetary geophysics, magnetohydrodynamics, space and solar physics, magnetic field generation, physical processes associated with the formation of stars and planetary systems. Office: Rice University - Dept Physics & Astronomy MS-108 Herman Brown Hall 6100 Main St Houston TX 77005 Office Phone: 713-348-4121. Business E-Mail: ehl@rice.edu.

LEVY, JONATHAN A., real estate company executive; BS, Syracuse U., NY, 1982. Constrn. laborer Burdman Bros. Co., Youngstown, Ohio; comml. real estate lender Marine Midland Bank, Washington, 1983—87; co-founder JLB Investments, 1987—91; co-founder, mng. ptnr. Redstone Investments, 1991—. Bd. dirs. Sky Fin. Group Inc., 1999—2007, Huntington Bancshares Inc., 2007—. Bd. trustees Tampa Prep. Sch., Fla.; bd. dirs. Youngstown Symphony Soc., Youngstown Bus. Incubator. Office: Redstone Investments Ste 200 1501 W Cleveland St Tampa FL 33606 Office Phone: 813-254-6200. Office Fax: 813-254-6225. Business E-Mail: jalevy@redstoneinvestments.com.

LEVY, MAURICE, retired medical educator, researcher; b. Chgo., Aug. 15, 1933; s. Eugene and Jean Belle (Anshel) Levy; m. Loris Belle Rissman, Sept. 11, 1955 (dec. Nov. 25, 2005); children: Arden Lynn, Andrea Hilary, James Michael; m. Michele Kamet Levy, Apr. 2, 2011. BS, U. Ill., 1956, EdM, 1959; EdD, U. Ga., 1968. Asst. prof. Ga. State U., Atlanta, 1968—69; postdoc. fellow U. Southern Calif., LA, 1969—70; assoc. prof. Med. Coll. Ga., Augusta, 1970—73, prof. ednl. rsch., dir., 1976—86, prof. pediatrics, 1986—97, assoc. dean faculty devel., 1990—97, prof. emeritus, 1997—; prof., dir. Southern Ill. U. Sch. Medicine, Springfield, 1973—76. Co-founder Ga. Prevention Inst., 1981. Author: Introduction to Pediatric Cardiology, 1975; contbr. articles to profl. jours., poems to anthology. Bd. dirs. Health Info. Svcs., Virginia Beach, Va., 1982—; trustee Augusta County Day Sch., 1972—80; chmn. Med. Coll. Ga. United Fund, Augusta, 1980; bd. dirs. Am. Cancer Soc., Springfield, Ill., 1974. Recipient Outstanding Sci. Exec. award, Am. Acad. Family Practice, 1974, Gold Cert. award, Am. Acad. Pediatrics, 1973, Cert. of Merit, Am. Med. Assn., 1974; named Boss of Yr., Am. Bus. Women's Assn., 1978. Mem.: Health Scis. Commn. Assn., Am. Acad. Phys. Assts. Jewish. Home: 1 Lookout Hilton Head Island SC 29928-5265 Personal E-mail: mlevyedd@hargray.com, mlevyedd@yahoo.com.

LEVY, ROBERT EDWARD, retired management consultant; b. Cin., May 23, 1939; s. Aaron F. and Elizabeth W. (Hirsch) L.; m. Candace Ann Wolfe, June 20, 1970; children: Brian D., Jessica A. BChemE, Cornell U., 1962; PhDChemE, U. Calif., Berkeley, 1967. Various positions, including mgr. synthetic fuels devel., rsch. and engring. Exxon Co., Florham Park, NJ, 1967-80, 84-86; mgr. tech. dept. Lago Oil & Transport Co., Esso Interam. divsn. Exxon Co., Aruba, Netherlands Antilles, 1980-84; v.p., dir. tech. devel. M.W. Kellogg Co., Houston, 1987-93; v.p. govt. and regulatory affairs Energy Biosystems Corp., The Woodlands, Tex., 1993-97; mgmt. cons. Houston, 1997-99; sr. v.p. Allan F. Dow & Assocs., Houston, 1998-99, UniPure Corp., Houston, 2000—04, dir., 2001—04; pres., CEO AstroVelos, LLC, Houston, 2005—07. Cons. in field. Patentee in field. Indsl. mem. Com. for Prevention of Shoreline Pollution by Oil, Aruba, 1982—84; founder Industry Profls. for Clean Air, Houston, 2004. Mem. AIChE, Indsl. Rsch. Inst. (bd. editors 1992-95, pre-coll. edn. com. 1995-2000, chmn., 1996-97), Air Alliance Houston (bd. dirs. 2005—, pres. 2008-), Sigma Xi (pres. Kellogg chpt. 1991-92), Jung Ctr. Houston (bd. trustees, 2009-). Avocations: photography, jogging, sailing. Personal E-mail: bob@boblevy.org.

LEW, SALVADOR, radio station executive; b. Camajuani, Las Villas, Cuba, Mar. 6, 1929; s. Berko and Clara (Lewinowicz) Lew; 1 child, Esther Maria. JD magna cum laude, U. Havana, 1952. Editor Sch. Mural Newspaper, Camajuani, Cuba, 1941-43; pres. youth sect., nat. sect. Cuban People's Party, 1948-53; Lat. Am. cons. Waltes, Moore & Costanzo, Miami, 1961-72; news dir. Sta. WMIE and Sta. WQBA, Miami, 1961-70; gen. mgr., news dir. Sta. WRHC, Miami, 1973-89; host talk show, 1989—2010. Pres. adv. bd. Cuba Broadcasting, 1992—2001; dir. Office of Cuba Broadcasting, Radio & TV Marti, appointed by President Geroge W. Bush; sr. cons. Everet Clay Assocs., 1989—2001; weekly host Buenas Tardes Miami, Telemiami TV. Trustee, dir. United Way, 1985—. Recipient Lincoln Marti award, Sec. HEW, 1964, FBI award for cmty. svcs., 1983, cmty. svc. awards, various orgns. Mem.: Cuban Lawyers Assn., Exile. Jewish. Home: 2863 SW 23rd St Miami FL 33145-3309

LEWANDO, ALFRED GERARD, JR., oceanographer; b. Boston, Apr. 17, 1945; s. Alfred Gerard and Marie Helen (Coughlin) L.; m. Carol Ann Kologe, Nov. 8, 1969; children: Jennifer Ann, Christina Marie. BS in Earth Sci., State Coll. Boston, 1967; MBA, U. So. Miss., 1986, MS in Polit. Sci., 1989, MS in Pub. Rels., 1990, MEd in Adult Edn., 1991; grad., USAF Air War Coll., 2001. Lic. real estate broker and notary pub., Miss. Staff oceanographer Naval Oceanographic Office, Washington, 1967-76, head fleet support br., 1976-80, dir. tactical analysis div. Bay St. Louis, Miss., 1980-86, dir. oceanographic programs div., 1986-88; dep. asst. chief of staff for ops. Naval Oceanography Command, Stennis Space Ctr., Miss., 1988-94; asst. chief staff for command mgmt. and inspector gen. Naval Meteorology and Oceanography Command, Stennis Space Center, 1994-98; dir. ocean surveys dept. Naval Oceanographic Office, Stennis Space Ctr., 1998—; mem. policy bd. Ctr. of Higher Learning, Stennis Space Ctr., Miss., 1990—; sr. exec. fellow John F. Kennedy Sch. Govt. Harvard U., 1996; founder, pres. Navy Cares!, 1997—, HSA Gulf Coast, 1998—. Mem. adv. com. Cape Fear Jr. Coll., Wilmington, N.C., 1974—, Miss. State U. Rsch. Ctr., 1988—; mem. steering com. Summer Indsl. fellowships for Gulf Coast Tchrs., 1990—; mem. organizing com. 44th Internat. Sci. and Engring. Fair, 1993. Contbr. articles to profl. publs. Commr. City of Long Beach (Miss.) Port Authority, 1986—88; bd. dirs. United Way of South Miss., 1999—, 2000—. Sr. Exec. fellow Harvard U., 1996. Mem. Miss. Acad. Scis., Gamma Theta Upsilon. Home: 553 Mockingbird Dr Long Beach MS 39560-3134 Office: Naval Oceanographic Office Bay Saint Louis MS 39529 E-mail: aglewando@aol.com.

LEWINS, STEVEN, financial analyst, investment company executive, legislative staff member, retired military officer; b. NYC, Jan. 22, 1943; s. Bruno and Kaethe (Czhoeck) L.; m. Rayna Lee Kornreich, July 4, 1968 (div. 1991); children: Shani Nicole, Scott Asher. BA, Queens Coll., CUNY, 1964, MA in Diplomatic-Econ. History, 1966; postgrad. in pub. adminstrn., NYSCSC, SUNY, 1967; MBA, CUNY, 1972; postgrad. in info. tech., U. Va., 1979. Park ranger, historian Nat. Park Svc., Statue of Liberty, NYC, 1964-66; traffic asst. AT&T, White Plains, NY, 1966; adminstrv. intern NY State, Albany, 1966-67; asst. to commr. NY State Narcotics Addiction Control Commn., NYC, 1967—69; security analyst Value Line Investment Survey, NYC, 1969-71, assoc. rsch. dir., 1971-74, rsch. dir., directing editor, 1975-80; creator Value Line Fin. Database, NYC, 1974; v.p. Arnold Bernhard & Co., NYC, 1975-80, dir., 1976-80, mem. exec. com., 1977-80; ptnr. Ray-Lux Products, NYC, 1978-80; pres. RayLux Assocs., NYC, 1980-81, dir., 1980-86; Sr. Uerospace & transportation analyst Gruntal & Co., LLC, NYC, 1986—2009; discipline, econ., mil., espionage cons., dept. State I8 squad, brig. gen., (USSR counter intelligence) Fed. Bureau Investigation, 1986—96; chmn. Raylux Svcs., 2000—; chmn. & CEO Katiemay Co. LLC, 2010. Founder RayLux Fin. Svc., 1980; v.p. unit head investment divsn. Citibank N.A., 1981-86, v.p. Citicorp Investment Mgmt., Inc., 1986-88; v.p. transp. and aerospace investment mgmt; chancellor Capital Mgmt., 1988-92; mng. dir., rsch. dir., head of equity First Capital Advisers/F.C. Fin. Svcs., N.Y.C., 1992-93; v.p., security analysis, Investment Rsch. Gruntal & Co., Inc., 1994-00; adv. corp. disclosure com. SEC, 1977-78, ICC, 1982-92, Dept. Transp.; cons., Dept. Justice, 1982-92, 95-96, 03, Dept. State, 1986-92, Surface Transp. Bd. Legal Panel, 1996-97; advisor surface transport. bd., 1965-2000, Fed. Res. Bd., 1996-00, 2003, dept. treasury, 2003, infrastructure com. U.S. Ho. of Reps., 1997-00, Summit Bank, 1998-00; spkr. in field. Author: Fashoda Crisis of 1898, 1966, Knowing Your Common Stocks, 1979, The Social Overhaul of the USSR, 1986, Economic Reform in the U.S.S.R., 1990, USA: 21st Century World Transportation Crossroads, 1994, U.S. Needs World-Class Transportation System, 1994, Transports as Economic Indicators, 1995, The New Union Pacific, 1996, Transportation Trends into the 21st Century, 1996, The Global Terrorist Threat, 1996, The Boeing Company: Firing on All Cylinders, 1997, U.S. Transportation "Consolidations" and "Surprise," 1997, Secular Trends in Global Transportation, 1997, Katie & Stevice: The TRue Story of Love and Crack; co-author: (with Parkanskii) US-USSR Summit Agenda, 1995, (with Bogdanov and Bobrakov) US-USSR Anti-International Terrorist Protocol, 1989, Rights of Terrorists, 1990, (with Semenov) US-USSR Sub-Orbital Space Cooperation, 1990; editor: Megatrends, 1980, Witch Doctor of Wall Street, 1990; creator Global Transportation and Orbital Space Transport Investment Trust, Gruntal & Co., L.L.C., 1998-2000. Participant U.S.-USSR Emigration/Jackson Vanek, 1984-91, U.S.-USSR Pan Am.-Aeroflot Aviation Agreement, 1985, USSR Student Exch., 1985-86, U.S.-USSR Anti-Internat. Terrorism, 1985-91, U.S.-USSR Rights of Terrorists, 1985, U.S.-USSR Trans-Siberian-CSX Corp. Initiative, 1989, TRW, Inc-Energia N.P.O. Look Down Satellite Agreement, 1989-90, U.S.-USSR Sub-Orbital Space Coop. Agreement, 1989-90, U.S.-USSR Def. Conv. Projects, 1990-93, Reagan-Gorbachev Summit Preparations, 1986-88, Bush-Gorbachev Summit Preparations, 1990, U.S.-USSR AMR Corp.-Aeroflot Bilateral Discussion, 1989, U.S.-USSR Spl. Mission/Secure Info. Negotiation, 1983-92, U.S.-Japan airline bilateral negotiation, 1996, CSX Corp./CIS indsl. negotiation, 1996-97; sponsor U.S.-USSR Pace U., rsch. exch., 1990; Citicorp liaison USSR mission to UN, 1982-88, Inst. U.S. and Can., Acad. Scis. USSR, 1985-88, econs. dept. Acad. Scis. USSR, 1988; liaison Chancellor Capital Mgmt., USSR, 1988-92; overseas fact-finding visits include Saudi Arabia, Egypt, Jordan, Israel, 1979, Peoples Republic of China, Japan, Hong Kong, 1981, USSR, 1985-86, 89-90, Georgia SSR, 1985, 90, Uzbekistan SSR, 1986, Baykhal, Irkutsk, Olha, Siberia, 1989, Kazakhstan SSR, Republic of Georgia, Baykonour-Soyuz Launch Ctr., 1990, Bangkok, Thailand, 1988, Rio de Janeiro, Brazil, 1990, Athens, Greece, 1998, Constantinople, Turkey, 1998; mem. Croton-on-Hudson Narcotics Guidance Coun., 1972-75, Cortlandt Indsl. Com., 1975-77; dist. leader Dem. Party, 1979-83; founding mem. Challenger Found., 1987, Nat. Space Mus., Dallas, Tex. 1998. FBI brig. gen.'l I8 squad USAF, 1991, Peterson AFB. Recipient Commendation citations for Gulf War, 1992, Reagan-Gorbachev Summit preparartions and diplomatic achivements, 1990, USSR Supreme Soviet Red Banner election for 50th birthday anniversary award in svc. to USSR, USA for peace, 1990. Fellow Fin. Analyst Fedn.; mem. N.Y. Soc. Security Analysts (sr. security analyst, membership com., computer applications symposium, airline splinter group, motor carrier splinter group, aerospace splinter group), Bus. Economists Coun., Washington Transp. Roundtable, Assn. Computer Users, Internat. Platform Assn., N.Y. Assn. Bus. Economists, Nat. Assn. Bus. Economists, Nat. Planetary Soc., Nat. Space Soc., Nat. Air and Space Mus., Nat. Air and Space Soc. (founding mem. 1998), Tau Delta Phi (pres. 1963, 64, Undergrad. of Yr. 1963, Spl. Student Senate Recognition 1964, Coll. Distinction medal French 1964). Democrat. Office Phone: 919-285-6959. Personal E-mail: sniwelist@aol.com.

LEWIS, ALVIN EDWARD, pathology educator; b. NYC, Nov. 21, 1916; s. Herman and Libbie (Levy) L.; m. Oct. 23, 1943, (widowed 1974); children: Joan, Elizabeth; m. July, 1, 1976. BA, U. Calif., LA, 1938; MA, Stanford U., 1939, MD, 1944. Chief, pathology sect, atomic energy project UCLA, 1949-53; dir. clin. labs. Mount Zion Hosp., San Francisco, 1953-66; pathology prof. Mich. State U., East Lansing, 1966-72; pathology prof., chmn. U. S. Ala., Mobile, 1972-74; pathology prof. U. Calif., Davis, 1974-87, prof. emeritus, 1987—. Rev. com. mem. Nat. Libr. Medicine, Bethesda, Md., 1972-75, med. quality rev. com. Dist. 3, Sonoma, Calif., 1989-94. Author: Biostatistics, 1966, 1984 (2d ed.), Principles of Hematology, 1970. Lt. (j.g.) USNR, 1945-46. Fellow: Coll. Am. Pathologists; mem.: Am. Physiol. Soc. Republican. Jewish. Avocations: sailing, photography, music (recorder ensemble). Home: 26 Carriage House Way Conroe TX 77384-4527

LEWIS, CHARLES JOSEPH, journalist; b. Bozeman, Mont., July 10, 1940; s. Vern Edward James and Mary (Brooke) L.; m. Sarah Withers (div. 2002); children: Peter, Patrick, Barbara; m. Vivian Chen, July 14, 2007. BS in Humanities with Honors, Loyola U., Chgo., 1962; JD, Columbia U., 1965. Bar: Ill. 1965. Atty. McDermott, Will & Emery, Chgo., 1965-67; reporter City News Bur., Chgo., 1967-68; reporter, editor Chgo. Sun-Times, 1968-73; with AP, 1974-89, reporter, editor, Washington, 1974-78, reporter, editor, L.A., 1978-80, personnel mgr., N.Y.C., 1981-83, bur. chief, Hartford, Conn., 1980-81, bur. chief, Washington, 1984-89; bur. chief Hearst Newspapers, Washington, 1989—2009, sr. editor, 2009—. Bd. dirs. Nat. Press Found., Washington, 1985-2003, treas., 1987-88, vice chmn., 1988-90, chmn., 1990-92; dir. Reporters Com. for Freedom of the Press, 1993-98, SDX Found. Washington, 1996—; mem. adv. bd. Paul Miller Washington Reporting Fellowships, 1999-2003. Lance cpl. USMCR, 1963-67. Named to Hall of Fame, SPJ, 2006. Mem. Am. Soc. Newspaper Editors, Gridiron Club, Sigma Delta Chi (v.p. Washington chpt. 1988-89), Gridiron Club (pres. 2013). Office: Hearst Newspapers Ste 1000 700 12th Street, NW Washington DC 20005-3994 Office Phone: 202-263-6400, 202-263-6411.

LEWIS, DAVE, professional hockey coach, retired professional hockey player; b. Kindersley, Sask., Canada, July 3, 1953; m. Brenda Lewis; children: Ryan, Meagan. Defenseman NY Islanders, 1973—80, LA Kings, 1980—83, NJ Devils, 1983—86, Detroit Red Wings, 1986—88, asst. coach, 1988—97, assoc. coach, 1997—2002, head coach, 2002—05, scout, 2005—06; head coach Boston Bruins, 2006—07; asst. coach LA Kings, 2007—08, Carolina Hurricanes, 2011—. Achievements include being associate coach of Stanley Cup Champion Detroit Red Wings, 1997, 1998, 2002. Office: Carolina Hurricanes Hockey Club RBC Center 1400 Edwards Mill Rd Raleigh NC 27607

LEWIS, DAVID R., state legislator; b. Fayetteville, NC, Mar. 6, 1971; m. Michelle Lewis; 1 child, David Jr. Gen. mgr. Harnett Tactor Co. Inc., 1994—; pres. Smith Farm & Turf Distbrs., 1999—; state rep. Dist 53 NC, 2002—. Mem.: Dunn Kiwanis, Nat. Fedn. Ind. Bus. Republican. Baptist. Mailing: 1500 S Clinton Ave Dunn NC 28334 Office: North Carolina House of Representatives 300 N Salisbury St Rm 534 Raleigh NC 27603-5925 Office Phone: 919-715-3015, 910-897-8100. Business E-Mail: David.Lewis@ncleg.net.

LEWIS, DOUGLAS, retired art historian; b. Centreville, Miss., Apr. 30, 1938; s. Charles Douglas and Beatrice Fenwick (Stewart) L. BA in History; BA in History of Art, Yale U., 1960, MA, 1963, PhD, 1967; BA in Fine Arts, Clare Coll., Cambridge U., Eng., 1962, MA, 1966. Asst. in instrn. Yale U., 1962-64; asst. prof. art Bryn Mawr Coll., 1967-68; vis. lectr. U. Calif., Berkeley, spring 1970, fall 1979; adj. prof. Johns Hopkins U., 1973-77; curator sculpture and decorative arts Nat. Gallery Art, Washington, 1968—2004; dir. rsch., mus svcs. Neal Auction Co., New Orleans, 2005—. Professorial lectr. Georgetown U., 1980-93; adj. prof. U. Md., 1988-91, 93-2003; mem. art adv. coms. Mt. Holyoke Coll. Art Mus., 1978-2003, U. Va. Art Mus., 1995-2005, Lawrenceville Sch., 1988-; adv. coun. Humanities West, San Francisco, 1991-98; adv. bd. Centro Palladiano, Vicenza, Italy, 1974-, Audubon and Rosedown (La.) State Hist. Sites, Natchez Lit. and Cinema Celebration; mem. nat. citizens stamp adv. com. U.S. Postal Svc., 1979-2005, chmn., 2004-05. Author: The Late Baroque Churches of Venice, 1979, The Drawings of Andrea Palladio, 1981, rev. and enlarged edit., 2000, intro. to Renaissance Master Bronzes, 1986. Mem. Am. fellowship com. Belgian-Am. Ednl. Found., 1971—. Recipient Copley medal Nat. Portrait Gallery, 1981; Chester Dale fellow; David E. Finley fellow Nat. Gallery Art, 1964-67; Rome Prize fellow Am. Acad. Rome, 1964-66, Bruce Curatorial fellow Nat. Gallery Art, 1997-98. Mem. Coll. Art Assn. Am., Soc. Archtl. Historians, Nat. Trust Historic Preservation, Manuscript Soc. Clubs: Yale (N.Y.C.); Falcons (Cambridge U.). Episcopalian.

LEWIS, FRANK LEROY, electrical engineer, educator, researcher; b. Wuzburg, Germany, May 11, 1949; s. L. Frank and Ruth Evangeline Shirley Lewis; m. Galina Lewis; children: Christopher Shirley, Roman Ivanov. MEE, Rice U., Houston, 1971; MS in Aerospace Sys, U. West Fla., Pensacola, 1977; PhD in Elec. Engring., Ga. U. Tech., Atlanta, 1981. Cert. profl. engr., Engring. Coun., Tex., chartered engr., Engring. Coun., UK. Lt USN, 1971—81; adj. prof. Ga. Inst. Tech., 1990—; Moncrief -O'Donnel endowed prof. elec. engring. U. Tex, Arlington, 1990—; asst. prof. elec. engring. Ga. Inst. Tech., Atlanta, 1981—86, assoc. prof., 1986—90, prof., 1990. Elected guest prof. Sanghai Jiao Tong U., China; mem. editl. bd. Internat. Jour. Intelligent Control and Sys., 1995—; steering com. mem. Ctr. Internat. Control, Nat. U. Singapore, 2004; cons., Lockheed, Georgia, Marietta, 1983—87; cons., lectr. UN Umbrella Project, Warsaw, 1991; consulting prof. South China U. Tech., 2004; chartered engr. UK Engring. Coun., 2006. Contbr. articles to profl. jours.; author: Optimal Control, 1986, 1995, Optimal Estimation, 1986, Aircraft Simulation and Control, 1992, Applied Optimal Control and Estimation, 1992, Robot Control, 1992, Control of Robot Manipulators, 1993, Neural Network Control, 1999, High-Level Feedback Control Using Neurol Nets, 1999; editor: Automatica, 1999. Lt. USN, 1971—77. Recipient Terman award, Am. Soc. Engring. Edn., 1989, Best Paper award, ARRI, 1992—93, Excellence in Tchg. award, Eta Kappa Nu, 1981, Gabor award, Inst. Neurol. Network Soc., 2009; named Disting. Spkr., 10th Anniversary Ceremony Engring. Faculty, Chinese U. Hong Kong, 2001; Fullbright fellow, grant, NSF, 1982, 1986, 1988, 1990, 1992, 1994—95, 1998. Fellow: IEEE, IFAC, Sigma Xi; mem.: ASEE (F.E. Terman award, IJCNN award). Achievements include research in intelligent control, robotics, manufacturing, systems engineering. Office: Univ Tex Arlington Automation and Robotics Rsch Inst 7300 Jack Newell Blvd S Fort Worth TX 76118-7115 Home Phone: 817-277-6360.

LEWIS, GENE EVANS, retired medical equipment company executive; b. Terrell, Tex., May 17, 1928; s. John Evans and Helen Elizabeth (Patterson) L.; m. Sonya Dolishny, Jan. 21, 1950; children: Robert, Melissa. BSEE, Tex. A&M U., 1949. Sales, mktg. and engring. mgr. GE, Schenectady, Dallas, Pittsfield, Holyoke, Lynn, 1950-68, gen. mgr. various bus. Milw., 1970-77; group product mgr. Picker X-Ray, Cleve., 1968-70; pres. sci. instruments div. Am. Optical Corp., Southbridge, Mass., 1977-78, pres. internat. div., 1978-79, pres., 1979—84, Baker Instruments Corp., Allentown, Pa., 1985—88; bd. mem. Novecon Technologies, 1994—99. CEO Sterling Semicondr., Inc., 1996-2001. With Signal Corps U.S. Army, 1949. Mem.: Sea Pines Country Clubc, Calibogue Club. Home: 25 Spartina Cres Hilton Head Island SC 29928-2925 Personal E-mail: gelsl@aol.com.

LEWIS, GLADYS SHERMAN, retired university professor; b. Wynnewood, Okla., Mar. 20, 1933; d. Andrew and Minnie Elva (Halsey) Sherman; m. Wilbur Curtis Lewis, Jan. 28, 1955; children: Karen, David, Leanne, Cristen. AB, Tex. Christian U., 1956; postgrad., Southwestern Bapt. Theol. Sem., 1959-60, Escuela de Idiomas, San Jose, Costa Rica, 1960-61; MA in Creative Writing, Ctrl. State U., Okla., 1985; PhD in English, Okla. State U., 1992. Mem. nursing staff various facilities, Okla., 1953-57; instr. nursing med. missionary Bapt. Mission and Hosp., Paraguay, 1961-70; vice chmn. edn. commn. Paraguay Bapt. Conv., 1962-65; sec. bd. trustees Bapt. Hosp., Paraguay, 1962-65, 1962-65; chmn. personnel com., handbook & policy book officer Bapt. Mission in Paraguay, 1967-70; trustee Southwestern Bapt. Theol. Sem., 1974-84, chmn. student affairs com., 1976-78, vice chmn. bd., 1978-80; ptnr. Las Amigas Tours, 1978-80, writer, conf. leader, campus lectr., 1959—2013; owner, publisher Greystone Press, LLC, 1998—2008. Adj. prof. English Ctr. State U., Okla. (now U. Ctrl. Okla.),1990-91, faculty mem., asst. prof., English U. Ctrl. Okla., 1991-95, assoc. prof., 1995-2000, prof., 2000—; exec. editor New Plains Rev., 2000-08. Author: On Earth As It Is, 1983, Two Dreams and a Promise, 1984, Message, Messenger and Response, 1994, Loaves and Hyacinths, 1999, Keeping Women in Their Place, 2004, Reading Cooper, Teaching Cooper, 2006, Valley of the Shadow, 2006; editor: The Jewish Roots of Christian Monotheism, 1999, Sooner Physician's Heartbeat, 1979—82; also religious instrnl. texts in English and Spanish, 1960—75; contbr. articles to So. Bapt. and secular periodicals, chpt. to book. Active Dem. com., Evang. Women's Caucus, 1979-80; leader Girl Scouts U.S.A., 1965-75; Okla. co-chmn. Nat. Religious Com. for Equal Rights Amendment, 1977-79; tour host Meier Internat. Study League, 1978-81. Recipient Lifetime Achievement award, 2007—08, Vanderford Disting. Tchr. award, 2009, Okla. Excellence Tchg. medal, 2012, Uco Neely Tchg. award, 2012. Mem. AAUP (UCO Disting. Tchg. Mentor award, 2009, Faculty Mem. of Yr., 2009), Internat. and Am. Coll. Surgeons Women's Auxs., Okla. State, Okla. County Med Auxs., Am. Nurse Assn. Home: 2708 Portofino Pl Edmond OK 73034 Office Phone: 405-974-5607. Business E-Mail: glewis@ucok.edu.

LEWIS, GORDON GILMER, golf course architect; b. Shawnee, Okla., Sept. 7, 1950; s. Ted Eugene and Janet Garvin (Panner) Lewis; m. Karen Louise McKenzie, June 2, 1973 (div. Dec. 1981); children: Melanie Marie Lewis-Lehr, Katie McKenzie Lewis-Lehr; m. Susette Mamie London, June 11, 1988; children: London Marshall, Sarah June Victoria. B in Landscape Architecture, Kans. State U., 1974. Registered landscape arch., Ala., Kans., Fla. Golf course architect David Gill, St. Charles, Ill., 1974-75; golf course arch. Charles M. Graves Orgn., Atlanta, 1975-78, Gordon G. Lewis, Naples, Fla., 1978—. Prin. works include Meadowbrook Links, Rapid City, S.D. (Top 50 Pub. Courses in U.S.), Hulman Links at Los Creek, Terre Haute, Ind. (Top 50 Pub. Courses in U.S.), Lagoon Pk., Montgomery, Ala. (Top 75 Pub. Courses in U.S.), The Forest, Ft. Myers, Fla., The

Vines, Estero, Fla. (One of Top New Courses Golf Digest, 1986), Worthington, Bonita Springs, Fla., Tsai-Hsing, Taipei, Taiwan, others. Republican. Presbyterian. Avocation: golf. Home: 5980 Golden Oaks Ln Naples FL 34119

LEWIS, GUY M., cosmetic dentist; Grad., Baylor Coll. of Dentistry. Cosmetic dentist Houston Rocket, Rocket Powerdancers, Houston Astros, Houston Aeros; adjunct prof. Baylor Coll. of Dentistry. Co-founder Am. Acad. of Cosmetic Dentistry. Named Super Dentist, TexasMonthly Mag., Top Doc, H Texas Mag.; nominee Best Dentists in America. Fellow: Internat. Acad. for Dental Facial Esthetics; mem.: ADA, Texas Dental Assn., Am. Acad. of Cosmetic Dentistry. Office: Texas Center for Cosmetic and Implant Dentistry 4800 W Panther Creek Dr Suite 200 Spring TX 77381 Office Phone: 281-367-6465. Office Fax: 281-367-5516.

LEWIS, HUNTER, investment advisor, writer; b. Dayton, Ohio, Oct. 13, 1947; s. Welbourne Walker and Emily (Spivey) L.; m. Elizabeth Sidamon-Eristoff, July 3, 1993. AB magna cum laude, Harvard U., 1969. Asst. to office of pres. Boston Co., 1970, v.p., 1972-73; prs. Boston Co. Fin. Strategies, Inc., 1971-72; co-founder Cambridge Assocs., Inc., Boston, 1973—. Author: A Question of Values, 1990, Are The Rich Necessary?, 2007, Where Keynes Went Wrong, 2009, other books; contbr. articles to N.Y. Times, Times of London, Atlantic Monthly, Washington Post, others mags. and newspapers; author monographs on specialized fin. subjects. Mem., adv. bd. Environ. Health Sci. News; pres. Alliance Natural Health; former dir. Worldwide Fund Nature; former mem. pension fin. com. World Bank; former chmn., bd. dirs. Nat. Environ. Trust; former dir., chmn. fin. com. Groton Sch.; former chmn. adv. bd. Dumbarton Oakes affil. of Harvard U.; former chmn. Worldwatch Inst.; former treas., dir. emeritus World Wildlife Fund; former dir. Thomas Jefferson Found., Monticello, Va., Pierpont Morgan Libr., NYC, Rockefeller Bros. Fund; pres. emeritus, dir. Am. Sch. Classical Studies at Athens; chmn. bd. Inst. Edn. Foster Children. With USMC, 1969—70. Mem. Univ. Club (N.Y.C.), Knickerbocker Club (N.Y.C.), Met. Club (Washington).

LEWIS, JERRY M., psychiatrist, educator; b. Utica, NY, Aug. 18, 1924; s. Jerry M. and Margaret (Miller) L.; m. Patsy Ruth Price, Sept. 24, 1949; children: Jerry M., Cynthia Lewis-Reynolds, Nancy Minns, Tom. MD, Southwestern Med. Sch., Dallas, 1951. Diplomate Am. Bd. Psychiatry and Neurology. Staff psychiatrist Timberlawn Psychiat. Hosp., Dallas, 1957-63, chief women's svc., 1963-66, chief adolescent svcs., 1966-70, dir. profl. edn., 1970-79, psychiatrist-in-chief, 1979-88, dir. rsch., 1988-93. Dir. rsch. and tng. Timberlawn Psychiat. Rsch. Found., Dallas, 1967-88, sr. rsch. psychiatrist, 1988—; clin. prof. psychiatry, family practice and cmty. medicine Southwestern Med. Sch.; cons. in psychiatry Baylor U. Med. Ctr., Dallas. Author: No Single Thread, 1976, How's Your Family, 1978, To Be a Therapist, 1979, The Long Struggle, 1983, Swimming Upstream: Teaching Psychotherapy in a Biological Era, 1991, The Monkey-Rope, 1995, Marriage as a Search for Healing: Theory, Assessment & Therapy, 1997, (with John Gossett, Ph.D.) Disarming the Past: How an Intimate Relationship Can Heal Old Wounds, 1999, Reflections on the Good Life: A Psychotherapist Writes to His Grandchildren, 2005, Famous Marriages: What They Can Teach Us, 2006. Served with USN, 1943-45. Fellow Am. Coll. Psychiatrists (pres. 1985), Am. Psychiat. Assn., So. Psychiat. Assn. (pres. 1979); mem. Group for Advancement of Psychiatry (pres. 1987), Benjamin Rush Soc. (pres. 1994-95), AMA, Tex. Med. Assn. Office: PO Box 270789 Dallas TX 75227-0789 Office Phone: 214-275-4001.

LEWIS, JOHN ROBERT, United States Representative from Georgia; b. Troy, Ala., Feb. 21, 1940; m. Lillian Miles, 1968 (dec. Dec. 31, 2012); 1 child, John-Miles. BA in Theology, American Bapt. Theol. Sem., Nashville, 1961; BA in Religion & Philosophy, Fisk U., 1963. City councilman City of Atlanta, Atlanta, 1983—86; community affairs dir. Nat. Consumer Coop. Bank, 1980—82; mem. US Congress from 5th Ga. Dist., Washington, 1987—, US House Ways & Means Com., Congressional Black Caucus. Founder, chair Student Non-Violent Coordination Com., 1963—66; assoc. dir. Field Found., 1966—67; dir. Voter Edn. Project, 1970—77; assoc. dir. ACTION, 1977—80; bd. dirs. African Am. Inst., Friends of VISTA, Martin Luther King Jr. Ctr. for Social Change; bd. dirs Nat. Democratic Inst. for Internat. Affairs; bd. dirs. Robert F. Kennedy Meml. Co-author (with Michael D'Orso): Walking With the Wind: A Memoir of the Movement, 1998 (Robert F. Kennedy Book award, 1999); co-author: (with Brenda Jones) Across That Bridge: Life Lessons and a Vision for Change, 2012; co-author: (with Andrew Aydin & Nate Powell) March: Book One, 2013. Mem. Martin Luther King Ctr. for Social Change, African American Inst., Robert F. Kennedy Meml. Recipient Eleanor Roosevelt award for Human Rights, 1998, Pinnacle award for Lifetime Achievement, ACDelco, 1999, Martin Luther King Jr. Non-Violent Peace Prize, 1999, Raoul Wallenberg medal, U. Mich., 2000, Helen Keller Achievement award for Advocacy, American Found. for the Blind, 2001, We the People award, Nat. Constitution Ctr, 2001, John F. Kennedy Profile in Courage Award, 2001, Springarn award, NAACP, 2002, William Mott Jr. Parks Leadership award, Nat. Parks Conservation Assn., 2002, Edwin T. Dahlberg award, American Baptist Churches USA, 2003, Allies for Justice award, Nat. Lesbian and Gay Law Assn., 2004, Golden Plate award, Acad. Achievement, 2004, Dole Leadership award, Robert J. Dole Inst. Politics, U. Kans., 2007, Wiley A. Branton award, Washington Lawyers' Com., 2009, Presdl. Medal of Freedom, The White House, 2010; named one of The Most Influential Black Americans, Ebony mag., 2006—08. Mem.: Faith & Politics Inst., Americans for Democratic Action (pres. 1993—95). Democrat. Baptist. Office: US House of Representatives 343 Cannon House Office Building Washington DC 20515 also: The Equitable Bldg 100 Peachtree St NW Ste 1920 Atlanta GA 30303 Office Fax: 202-225-0351.*

LEWIS, JOSEPH, investor, real estate development company executive; b. London, 1937; married; 2 children. Founder, chmn., prin. Tavistock Group, Windermere, Fla. Owner Isleworth Golf and Country Club, Windermere, Fla., Lake Nona Golf and Country Club, Orlando, Fla.; founder Tavistock Cup, Fla., 2004—. Named one of Top 200 Collectors, ARTnews mag., 2003—12, World's Richest People, Forbes; named to Rich List, Sunday Times, London, 2007. Avocations: golf, Impressionism and modern art collection. Office: Tavistock Group Tavistock House PO Box 9000 Windermere FL 34786 E-mail: info@tavistock.com.

LEWIS, KENNETH D., retired bank executive; b. Meridian, Miss., Apr. 9, 1947; s. Vernon Kenneth and Alice Byrdine Lewis; m. Donna Lewis, 1980; 2 children. BBA in Fin., Ga. State U., 1969; Grad., Exec. Program, Stanford U. Credit analyst NC Nat. Bank, 1969—77; mgr. NCNB Internat. Banking Corp., 1977—79; sr. v.p. NCNB US dept., 1979—83; pres. NCNB Fla., 1986-88, NCNB Tex., Dallas, NC, 1988-90, Gen. Bank NationsBank, Atlanta, 1991-93, NationsBank Corp., Charlotte, NC, 1993-99; pres., COO Bank of America Corp., Charlotte, NC, 1999—2001, chmn., pres., CEO, 2001—09, pres., CEO, 2009. Bd. dirs. Health Mgmt. Assocs., Inc., Naples, Fla., 1991—2004, Bank of America Corp., 1999—2009, Lowe's Companies Inc., 2000—04, The Clearing House LLC. Bd. dirs. United Way Ctrl. Carolinas Inc., Charlotte, Homeownership Edn. & Counseling Inst.; chmn. bd. trustees Nat. Urban League; chmn., campaign dir. Arts & Sci. Coun., Charlotte, 1998; bd. dirs. Presbyn. Hosp. Found., Charlotte. Recipient Banker of Yr. award, Am. Banker mag., 2002, 2008; named Top CEO, US Banker mag., 2002; named one of The World's Most Influential People, TIME mag., 2007, The Top 25 Market Movers, US News & World Report, 2009. Mem.: Fin. Services Roundtable.

LEWIS, KEVIN PAUL, lawyer; BA, Yale U., 1983; JD, Harvard Law Sch., 1986. Bar: Tex. 1986, NY 1988. Ptnr. Vinson & Elkins, Singapore, 1995—98, Houston, 1998—. Chmn. Interfaith Care Ptnrs., Houston, 2001—03, 2008—; exec. com. mem. Asia Soc. Tex., 2004—; trustee Congregation Beth Israel, 2004—; chmn. Career & Recovery Resources, 1993—94. Recipient Best Energy Lawyers award, Euromoney, 1999, Best Project Fin. Lawyers award, 2000, 2002, 2004, 2006, Best Structured Fin. Lawyers award, 2005, Super Lawyer award, Tex. Lawyer, 2005—; named one of Best Lawyers in Am., Woodward, White, Inc., 2005—. Office: Vinson & Elkins 1001 Fannin St Ste 2300 Houston TX 77002

LEWIS, LYNWOOD W., state legislator; b. Nassawadox, Va., Nov. 26, 1961; State del. Dist. 100, Va., 2004—. Mem.: Eastern Shore CC (bd. mem.), Eastern Shore Literacy Coun. (bd. mem.), Eastern Shore United Way (bd. mem.). Democrat. Methodist. Mailing: Dist Off PO Box 760 Accomac VA 23301 Office Phone: 804-698-1000. Fax: 804-786-6310, 757-787-2456. E-mail: Del_Lewis@house.state.va.us.

LEWIS, MARY GEIGER, federal judge, lawyer; b. Columbia, SC, Dec. 18, 1958; m. A. Camden Lewis; children: Wallis, Will. BA cum laude, Clemson U., 1980; JD, U. SC, 1984. Bar: SC 1984, US Dist. Ct., SC, US Supreme Ct., US Ct. Appeals (2nd cir.), US Ct. Appeals (4th cir.), US Ct. Appeals (11th cir.). Law clk. to Hon. Owens Taylor Cobb, Jr. SC Cir. Ct. (5th cir.), 1984—85; assoc. Lewis & Babcock, LLP, Columbia, SC, 1985—87, ptnr., 1987—2012; judge US Dist. Ct. SC, Columbia, 2012—. Former commr. SC Ednl. TV. Mem.: ABA, Fed. Bar Assn., SC Assn. for Justice, SC Bar Assn., Richland County Bar Assn., Columbia Garden Club (former pres.), Order of the Coif. Office: US District Court 901 Richland St Columbia SC 29201 Office Phone: 803-765-5816. Office Fax: 803-765-5960.

LEWIS, R. FRED, state supreme court justice; b. Beckley, W.Va., Dec. 14, 1947; m. Judith Lewis, 1969; children: Elle, Lindsay. Grad. cum laude, Fla. So. Coll., 1969; JD cum laude, U. Miami, 1972; grad., U.S. Army A.G. Sch.; PhD in Public Service (hon.), Fla. So. Coll., 2000; LLD (hon.), St. Thomas U., 2002. Pvt. practice, Miami; justice Fla. Supreme Ct., 1998—, chief justice, 2006—08. Mem. Fla. Commn. on Legal Needs of Children; active in Justice Teaching Inst.; liaison Fla. Bd. of Bar Examiners, Judicial Management Council; mem. Fla. Supreme Ct. Com. on Rules of Civil Procedure, Fla. Supreme Ct. Com. on Standard Civil Jury Instructions, Fla. Supreme Ct. Code & Rules of Evidence Com. Contbr. pubs. Continuing Edn. Legal Program. Bd. dirs. Miami Children's Hosp.; inventory atty. The Fla. Bar. Recipient Friends of Justice award ABOTA, 1999, Jud. Pub. Trust and Confidence award FLREA, 2001, Citizen Yr. award, Fla., 2001, Everyday Hero award for outstanding contbn. to cmty. svc. in Fla., Justice R. Fred Lewis award U. Ctrl. Fla., 2002, Great Am. Law in Edn. award, 2005, Guardian of the Constitution award, 2006, Ed. for Democracy award, 2006, Judge Wilke Ferguson award for protector of disabled Easter Seals, 2005-06, Guardian of the Constitution Citizenship award for Law-Related Edn., Equal Opportunities in Jud. award 2007, Edn. for Justice award, 2007, Justice Thurgood Marshall award, 2007, others; named Fla. Jurist of Yr., Fla. ABOTA, 2007, Pursuit Justice award, Am. Bd. Trial Lawyers, Outstanding Citizen award, 2007, Judge mario Goderich award, Cuban Am Bar.,Gracias award, 2008, Joe Mixon award, 2007-08, Constitution Edn. award, 2009; grantee NCAA, 1969. Mem. Omicron Delta Kappa, Psi Chi, Sigma Alpha Epsilon. Address: Fla Supreme Ct 500 S Duval St Tallahassee FL 32399-6556 Office Phone: 850-488-0007. E-mail: supremecourt@mail.flcourts.org.*

LEWIS, RASHARD QUOVON, professional basketball player; b. Pineville, La., Aug. 8, 1979; Forward Seattle SuperSonics, 1998—2007, Orlando Magic, Fla., 2007—10, Washington Wizards, 2010—12, Miami Heat, 2012—. Mem. US nat. team Goodwill Games, Brisbane, Australia, 2001. Recipient Gold medal, Goodwill Games, 2001; named Player of Yr., Parade mag., 1998; named to All-USA First Team, USA Today, 1998, Western Conf. All-Star Team, NBA, 2005, Eastern Conf. All-Star Team, 2009. Achievements include member of NBA Finals championship winning Miami Heat, 2013. Office: Miami Heat 601 Biscayne Blvd Miami FL 33132*

LEWIS, RICHARD, SR., securities broker, consultant; b. Macon, Ga., Jan. 18, 1930; s. William Chapman and Florida (Zelius) L.; m. Iris Joy Clements, Sept. 10, 1949; children: Richard Jr., Linda Lee. Cert. pistol and rifle instr. State trooper Fla. Hwy. Patrol, various cities, 1951-72; pres. Gateway Shooters Supply, Inc., Jacksonville, Fla., 1973—79, Jacksonville Police Pistol Club, 1972—82, Bobcat Enterprises Inc., 1983-84; broker Global Investments Securities Inc., Miami, 1985-86, Investacorp, Inc., Miami Lakes, Fla., 1986-89. Lobbyist Fla. Assn. of State Troopers, Tallahassee, 1988-89. With U.S. Army, 1952-54, mem. Georgia Rep. Party, White County Rep. Party Recipient cert. of appreciation, State of Fla., Tallahassee, 1972; Demolay Cross of Honor, Internat. Coun., Kansas City, Mo., 1973; cert. of commendation, State of Fla., 1972, Svc. award, Masons Grand Lodge Fla. Mem. NRA (life), SAR, SCV (life), Am. Assn. State Troopers, Ret. Troopers Assn., Fla. Assn. State Troopers (legis. chmn. retirees 1987), High Meadow Landowners Assn. (pres. 2001-07), VFW., Jacksonville Pistol Club (pres. 1968-72), Marion Dunn Masons (life), Elks, Mil. Order Stars and Bars (life), Fraternal Order Police, Scottish Rite, Nobles Mystic Shrine (life, amb.-at-large), (life)Am. Legion, VFW, Republican. Methodist. Avocations: fishing, photography. Home: 461 High Meadow Trl Cleveland GA 30528-2324

LEWIS, ROBERT EDWIN, JR., pathology and immunology educator, researcher; b. Meridian, Miss., Mar. 11, 1947; s. Robert Edwin and Cecille (Ryan) Lewis. BA in Biology and Chemistry, U. Miss., 1969, MS in Microbiology, 1973, PhD in Pathology, 1976; specialty tng., Barnes Hosp., U. Miami Med. Ctr., U. Tenn. Ctr. for Health Scis., City of Memphis Hosps., St. Jude Children's Research Hosp. Instr. pathology, anesthesiology U. Miss. Med. Ctr., Jackson, 1976-77, asst. prof. pathology, 1977-84, asst. prof. anesthesiology, 1977-85, asst. dir. clin. immnuopathology lab., 1978-81, assoc. dir. tissue typing lab., 1980-84, dir. paternity testing lab., 1981—, assoc. dir. clin. immunopathology lab., 1981-84, asst. prof. nurse anesthesiology, 1981-85, assoc. prof. pathology, 1984-91, prof., 1991—, dir. clin. immunology, tissue typing lab., 1984—, mem. grad. council, 1981—, prof., 1991—. Co-author: Illus. Dictionary of Immunology, 1995, 2003, 3rd edit., 2009, Atlas of Immunology, 1999, 2d edit., 2004, 3rd edit., 2010; co-author: (with J.M. Cruse) Immunology Guidebook, 2004, Historical Atlas of Immunology, 2005; editor (with J.M. Cruse): Concepts in Immunopathology, Vols. 1-8, 1985—91; editor: The Yr. in Immunology-1984-85, 1985, The Yr. in Immunology-1986-8, 1987, The Yr. in Immunology-1988, 1989, The Yr. in Immunology-1989-90, 1990, Progress in Exptl. Tumor Rsch. Vol. 32, 1987, Contributions to Microbiology and Immunology, Vol. 8, 1986, Vol. 9, 1987, Vol. 10, 1989, Vol. 11, 1989, The Yr. in Immunopathology, 1987, Complement Profiles, Vol. 1, 1992, Historical Atlas of Immunology, 2004; sr. editor Immunologic Research, 1981—, Pathology and Immunopathology Rsch., 1982—90, Pathobiology, 1990—98, Pathology, 1990—98, Transgenics, 1993, dep. editor in chief, sr. editor Exptl. and Molecular Pathology, 1999—, series editor Concepts in Immunopathology, The Yr. in Immunology, Contributions to Microbiology and Immunology, vol. editor Progress in Exptl. Tumor Rsch, immunology editor Dorland's Illus. Med. Dictionary, 26th and 27th edits., dep. editor-in-chief Pathobiology, 1990—98; contbr. chpts. to books. Am. Cancer Soc. grantee, NIH grantee, Wilson Found. grantee, 1990-2002. Fellow Royal Soc. Health, Royal Soc. Medicine; mem. AAAS, Am. Assn. Pathologists, Am. Assn. Immunologists, Clin. Immunology Soc., Can. Soc. Immunology, Reticuloendothelial Soc., Am. Soc. Microbiology, Am. Soc. Histocompatibility and Immunogenetics (chmn. publs. com. 2000-03, bd. dirs. 2004—), Exptl. Biology and Medicine, N.Y. Acad. Scis., Miss. Acad. Scis., Sigma Xi. Office: U Miss Med Ctr Pathology Dept Dept Pathology 2500 N State St Jackson MS 39216-4500 Home Phone: 601-856-5045; Office Phone: 601-984-1562. Business E-Mail: rlewis@pathology.umsmed.edu.

LEWIS, STEPHEN E., lawyer; b. Rock Hill, SC, 1966; BS with honors, U. NC, 1988, JD with high honors, 1991. CPA NC, 1988; bar: Ga. 1991. Assoc. Troutman Sanders LLP, Atlanta, 1991—98, ptnr., 1999—, mng. ptnr., 2011—, 2011—. Mem. NC Law Rev., 1989—90. Named a Super Lawyer, Atlanta Mag., 2004, Legal Elite in corp. law, Ga. Trend Mag., 2004. Mem.: Beta Alpha Psi, Phi Beta Kappa, Order of Coif. Office: Troutman Sanders LLP Ste 5200 600 Peachtree St Atlanta GA 30308-2216 Office Phone: 404-885-3448. Office Fax: 404-962-6616. Business E-Mail: stephen.lewis@troutmansanders.com.

LEWIS, TOM E., JR., architect, architectural firm executive; m. Cynthia Lewis; 2 children. BS and BArch, MArch, Ga. Inst. Tech.; JD with honors, Fla. State U. Pvt. practice arch.; spl. asst. Adminstrn. of Fla. Gov. Bob Graham; asst. sec. Fla. Dept. Transp.; sec. Fla. Dept. Cmty. Affairs; dir., residential devel., v.p., cmty. devel. Disney Devel. Co. (later Walt Disney Imagineering), chmn., celebration cmty. devel. dist.; v.p., devel. Walt Disney World Co.; sec. Fla. Dept. Mgmt. Svcs.; spl. cons. Pennington, Moore, Wilkinson, Bell & Dunbar, P.A., Tallahassee, 2007—. Arch., mgr., mem. Air Force Design Adv. Coun. USAF. Fellow: AIA. Office: Pennington Moore Wilkinson Bell & Dunbar 215 S Monroe St 2nd Fl Tallahassee FL 32301 Office Phone: 850-222-3533. Office Fax: 850-222-2126. E-mail: tom@penningtonlaw.com.

LEWIS, TRYON D., state legislator; b. Kermit, Sept. 29, 1947; m. Trudy Lewis; children: Eleanor, Annie. Attended, Odessa Coll.; B, U. Tex., Austin; JD, Baylor U. Law Sch. Atty., 1973—85; ret. judge 161st State Dist., Tex., 1985—2006; ptnr. Atkins, Hollman, Jones, Peacock, Lewis & Lyon; mem. Dist. 81 Tex. House of Representatives, 2008—. Republican. Office: 119 W 4th St Ste 206 Odessa TX 79761 also: Room E2.508 Capitol Extension PO Box 2910 Austin TX 78768 Office Phone: 512-463-0546, 432-367-2721, 432-332-0937. Office Fax: 512-463-8067.

LEWIS, WALLACE JOE, entomologist, researcher; BS in Entomology, MS in Entomology, PhD in Entomology, Miss. State U. Rsch. entomologist USDA, Agrl. Rsch. Svc., Tifton, Ga. Contbr. articles to profl. jours. Co-recipient Wolf Found prize in Agr., Israel, 2008. Achievements include development of the first system for studying in-flight host-searching behavior of parasitoids; discovery that in response to herbivore feeding damage, plants can emit chemical distress signals that are used by parasitoids to locate and attack the herbivores. Office: Crop Protection and Mgmt Rsch Unit USDA Agrl Rsch Svc PO Box 748 Tifton GA 31793-0748 Office Fax: 229-387-2321. Business E-Mail: wjl@tifton.usda.gov.

LEWIS, WILLIAM HEADLEY, JR., manufacturing executive; b. Washington, Sept. 29, 1934; s. William Headley and Lois Maude (Bradshaw) L.; m. Susan M. Simpson, Apr. 25, 2006; children: Teresa Lynne, Bret Cameron, Charles William, Kevin Marcus. BS in Metall. Engring., Va. Poly. Inst., 1956; postgrad. Grad. Sch. Bus. Adminstrn., Emory U., 1978. Registered profl. engr., Calif. Various positions Lockheed Corp., Marietta, Ga., 1956-87, mgr. engring. tech. services, 1979-83, dir. engring. Getex divsn., 1983-86; mgr. Inspection Systems divsn. Lockheed Air Terminal, Inc., 1986-87; CEO Measurement Sys. Inc., Atlanta, 1987—2003. Chmn. Lockheed Corp. Task Force on NDE, 1980-86; mem. Com. to Study Role of Advanced Tech. in Improving Reliability and Maintainability of Future Weapon Systems, Office of Sec. of Def., 1984-85; co-founder Applied Tech. Svcs., Inc., 1967—; pres., CEO Applied Tech. Fin. Corp., Atlanta, 1983-86; mng. ptnr. Tech. Fin. Co., LLC; lectr. grad. studies and continuing edn. Union Coll., Schenectady, N.Y., 1977-82. Editor: Prevention of Structural Failures: The Role of Fracture Mechanics, Failure Analysis, and NDT, 1978; patentee detection apparatus for structural failure in aircraft. Served to 1st lt. USAF, 1957-60. Fellow: Am. Soc. for Nondestructive Testing (chmn. aerospace com. 1972—74, nat. dir. 1976—78, chmn. nat. tech. coun. 1977—78, nat. nominating com. 1982—85); mem.: NAS (mem. com. on compressive fracture 1981—83), AIAA, Am. Soc. for Metals, Brotherhood of the Knights of the Vine, Coconut Grove Sailing Club, Country Club Sapphire Valley, St. Ives Country Club (founding mem.). Home: 2843 Bayshore Dr#17B Coconut Grove FL 33133 Personal E-mail: bill@whlewis.com.

LEWIS-RAYMOND, JANE R., lawyer, gas industry executive; m. Tom Raymond; 1 child. BA in East Asian Languages, Lit., Gov. & Politics, U. Md., JD with honors. Bar: 1993. Atty. Morgan, Lewis & Bockius, Washington; legal positions through sr. mng. counsel & dir. regulatory affairs Am. Gas Assn., Washington, 1995—2005, v.p. regulatory affairs, 2005—06; v.p., gen. counsel, chief compliance officer, corp. sec. Piedmont Natural Gas Co., Inc., Charlotte, NC, 2006—. Bd. dirs. America Charlotte, Keystone Energy. Mem.: Energy Bar Assn., Audubon Soc., Phi Beta Kappa. Office: Piedmont Natural Gas 4720 Piedmont Row Dr Charlotte NC 28210 Mailing: Piedmont Natural Gas PO Box 33068 Charlotte NC 28233 Office Phone: 704-364-3120. Office Fax: 704-365-8515.

LEWY, ZACHARY, finance company executive; BA in Economics & Applied Math. with honors, Princeton U. applied and computational math., Princeton U. Mgmt. cons. Mercer Mgmt. Consulting; founding dir. 7C (acquired by Vertex Ltd.); joined Vertex Ltd., 2002, corp. devel. dir.; pres. Vertex N.Am., 2002—05; joined SLM Corp., 2005; v.p. Sallie Mae - SLM Corp., 2008—; CEO Arrow Global Ltd. (subs. of SLM Corp.), 2008—. Office: SLM Corp 12061 Bluemont Way Reston VA 20190 Office Phone: 703-810-3000. Office Fax: 703-984-5042. Business E-Mail: zachary.ewy@salliemae.com.

LEY, PETER D., corporate financial executive; BA, Dartmouth Coll.; MBA, Harvard U. Mng. dir. Bank of America Securities; CFO Commonwealth Tel. Enterprises Inc., Pa.; investment banker Dominick & Dominick, Furman Selz, Robert Fleming, Morgan Grenfell, Salomon Bros.; CFO Connexion Technologies, 2007—. Bd. dirs.

Alaska Comm. Sys. Group Inc., 2008—. Office: Connexion Technologies Ste 250 111 Corning Rd Cary NC 27518 Office Phone: 919-535-7200. Office Fax: 919-882-9338. Business E-Mail: peter.ley@cnxntech.com.

LI, TING-KAI, medical educator, researcher, former federal agency administrator; b. Nanjing, China, 1934; BA in Chemistry and Biology, Northwestern U., Ill.; MD, Harvard U., 1959; DSc (hon.), Northeastern Ohio Universities Coll. Medicine, 1998, Ind. U., 2003, Purdue U., 2003, U. So. Calif., 2010. Chief resident Peter Bent Brigham Hosp., Boston, 1965; dep. dir. biochemistry divsn. Walter Reed Army Inst. Rsch.; faculty, John B. Hickam prof. medicine & biochemistry Ind. U. Sch. Medicine, Indpls., 1971—2002, assoc. dean rsch., 1986—2000, dir. Ind. Alcohol Rsch. Ctr., 2000—02, also Disting. Prof. Medicine; dir. Nat. Inst. Alcohol Abuse & Alcoholism (NIAAA) NIH, Bethesda, 2002—08, ret., 2008; prof. Dept. Psychiatry and Behavioral Scis. Duke U. Sch. Medicine. Contbr. scientific papers numerous articles to profl. jours., chapters to books. Recipient R. Brinkley Smithers Disting. Sci. award, James B. Isaacson award for rsch. in chemical dependency diseases, Jellinek award. Fellow: UK Soc. Study of Addiction (hon.); mem.: NAS Inst. Medicine. Office: Duke University School of Medicine Box 3862 Med Ctr Durham NC 27710 also: Duke-NUS Graduate Medical School 8 College Rd 169857 Singapore Singapore Office Phone: +1 919684 2880, 919-684-2880. Office Fax: +1 919681 8400. E-mail: tk.li@duke.edu.

LI, YING SING, chemistry professor; arrived in US, 1974, naturalized, 1979; s. Mu-Sun Joseph and Tzu-Chun Maria Li; m. Jackie T. Li, May 5, 1945; children: Ming-Po Lawrence, Ming-Po Leon, Ming-Way Caroline, Ming-Yen Jason. PhD, U. Kans., Lawrence, 1967. Assoc. prof. Memphis State U., 1984—92; prof. U. Memphis, 1992—. Cons. Wuxi JC Pharm. Tech. Contbr. articles to scientific pubs. Mem.: Am. Chem. Soc., Sigma Xi, Phi Lambda Upsilon. Roman Catholic. Avocations: hiking, reading. Office: Univ Memphis 3774 Walker Ave Memphis TN 38152

LIBBY, GARY RUSSELL, museum director emeritus, writer, consultant; b. Boston, June 7, 1944; s. Charles W. and Sylvia P. Libby. BA, U. Fla., 1967, MA (NDEA fellow), 1968; MA, Tulane U., 1972. Cert. Smithsonian Inst., Mus. Mgmt. Inst. Instr. English Tulane U., 1968-71; asst. prof. Stetson U., Deland, Fla., 1972-77, vis. prof., 1977-86; dir. Mus. Arts and Scis., Daytona Beach, Fla., 1977—2001, 2004—05, dir. emeritus, 2002—. Reviewer Inst. Mus. Svcs.; panelist Mus. Assessment Program; reviewer Accreditation Commn. of Am. Assn. Mus.; cons. in field. Author: Two Centuries of Cuban Art, 1985, Cuba: A History in Art, 1997, Coast to Coast: The Contemporary Landscape in Florida, 1998, A Treasury of American Art, 2002, Reflections: Florida Landscape Painting 1865-1965, 2009, Reflections II Watercolors of Florida, 2012; editor: Archipenko: Themes and Variations, 1989, Chihuly: Form From Fire, 1994 (Southeastern Mus. Conf. award, 1994), A Century of Jewelry and Gems, 1995, Celebrating Florida, 1995; contbr. over 50 articles to profl. jours. Trustee Cuban Found.; mem. artists in edn. panel, visual arts panel, youth and children's mus. panel, sci. mus. panel Fla. Arts. Coun., 2005—07; panelist Challenge Grant Program, Cultural Instns. Program; mem. hist. mus. grants panel Fla. Divsn. History; mem. Halifax Area Advt. Authority, 1999—2008; mem. adv. bd. Daytona Beach Econ. Devel., 1999—2004; vice chmn. Mainstreet Redevel. Bd., 2004—06, 2011—13; mem., chmn. adv. bd. Environ., Cultural, Hist., and Outdoors, 2001—05, chmn., 2007—08, 2010—; mem. Cultural Coun. Volusia County, 2002—03, 2009, Daytona Beach Charter Rev.; mem. mayor's cabinet City of Daytona Beach, 2008; v.p. Hist. Pinewood, 2005—13; mem. bd. advisors Stetson U., DeLand, Fla., 2007—09, trustee, 2008—09; pres. Heritage Preservation Trust, 2008—; chmn. arts and entertainment Halifax Area Advt. Authority, 2003—13; trustee Gary R. Libby Charitable Trust, 2002—14. Recipient Bronze medal, Reflections II, 2012, Fla. Book award, 2012, Lifetime Achievement award, Fla. Art Mus. Dirs. Assn., Fla. Assn. Mus. Mem.: Cornell Fine Art Mus. (chair exhbns. com. 2013—14), Heritage Preservation Trust, Hist. Pinewood Assn., City Daytona Beach (bd. adjustments 2008—, charter rev. commn. 2014), Cuban Found. (v.p. 2006—13), Fla. Cultural and Ednl. Alliance (bd. dirs. 1995), Fla. Assn. Mus. (bd. dirs. 1992—98, sec. 1995—98), Fla. Art Mus. Dirs. Assn. (govt. liaison 1990—95, pres. 1995—97). Home and Office: 723 N Oleander Ave Daytona Beach FL 32118-3826 Business E-Mail: grlibby@cfl.rr.com.

LIBBY, WENDY B., academic administrator; m. Richard Libby; children: Glenn, Gregg. BS in Biology, Cornell U., 1972; MBA, Johnson Grad. Sch. of Mgmt. at Cornell U., 1977; PhD in Ednl. Adminstrn., U. Conn., 1994. Dir. adminstrn. pub. mgmt. program Johnson Grad. Sch. of Mgmt. at Cornell U., Ithaca, NY, 1979—80; dir. adminstrv. ops. Coll. of Architecture, Art and Planning, Ithaca, NY, 1980—84; adminstrv. mgr. Coll. Edn. Ohio State U., Columbus, 1984—85, adminstrv. assoc. Office of Fin., 1984—85; asst. dir. U. Conn. Med. Ctr. John Dempsey Hosp., Farmington, Conn., 1985—87, asst. to assoc. exec. dir., 1985—87; spl. asst. to pres. and sr. human resources officer U. Hartford, Conn., 1987—89; chief fin. and bus. officer Westbrook Coll., Portland, Maine, 1989—95; v.p. bus. affairs and CFO Furman U., Greenville, SC, 1995—2003; pres. Stephens Coll., Columbia, Mo., 2003—09, Stetson U., DeLand, Fla., 2009—. Founding bd. dirs. Tuition Plan Consortium, Caribbean Inst. Tech.; bd. dirs. Greenville Literacy Assn., Women's Coll. Coalition. Mem.: Boone County Nat. Bank Coun. Ind. Coll. (bd. mem.), Soc. Coll. and U. Planning, So. Assn. of Coll. and U. Bus. Officers, Ea. Assn. of Coll. and U. Bus. Officers (bd. dirs.), Nat. Assn. of Coll. and U. Bus. Officers. Office: Stetson Univ 421 N Woodland Blvd Deland FL 32721 Office Phone: 386-822-7250.

LIBERMAN, GAIL JEANNE, editor; b. Neptune, NJ, Feb. 26, 1951; d. Si and Dorothy (Gold) L.; m. Alan Lavine, Dec. 20, 1991. BA, Rutgers U., 1972. Youth editor AP, NYC, 1972-73; writer United Feature Syndicate, NYC, 1973; reporter, broadcast editor UPI, Phila. and Hartford, Conn., 1973-75; reporter Courier-Post, Camden, NJ, 1976-80, Bank Advt. News, North Palm Beach, Fla., 1981-82; editor Bank Rate Monitor, North Palm Beach, 1982-97. Author: Improving Your Credit and Reducing Your Debt, 1994 (endorsed Inst. CFPs), The Complete Idiot's Guide to Making Money With Mutual Funds, 1996, Love, Marriage and Money, 1998, Rags to Riches: Motivating Stories of How Ordinary People Achieved Extraordinary Wealth, 2000, Short and Simple Guide to Life Insurance, 2000, More Rags to Riches: All New Stories of How Ordinary People Achieved Extraordinary Wealth, 2002, Rags to Retirement, 2003, Quick Steps to Financial Stability, 2006; columnist: Boston Herald, 1994-2007, America Online, 1996—2008, Investor Square, 1996, Mutual Funds Interactive, 1996-2007, Quicken, 1998—2004, Palm Beach Daily News, 1998—, CNBC.com, 2000, Fasttrack mag., 2001, Pitts. Post-Gazette, 2001—10, Dow Jones Market Watch, 2006—10; contbr. articles to profl. jours. Mem. Soc. Am. Bus. Editors and Writers. Office Phone: 566-630-6098. Personal E-mail: mwliblav@aol.com.

LIBOFF, RICHARD LAWRENCE, physicist, researcher; b. NYC, Dec. 30, 1931; s. William and Sarah (Mell) L.; m. Myra Blatt, July 4, 1954; children: David, Lisa. AB, Bklyn. Coll., 1953; PhD, NYU, 1961. Asst. prof. physics NYU, 1961-63; prof. applied physics, applied math. and elec. engring. Cornell U., 1964—2005; prin. investigator Air Force Office Sci. Research, 1978-83, Army Research Office, 1984—; disting. prof. physics U. Ctrl. Fla., Orlando, 2005—. Cons. Batelle Columbus Lab. Author: Introduction to the Theory of Kinetic Equations, 1969, 1979, Russian edit., 1974, Introductory Quantum Mechanics, 1980, Korean edit., 1992, 4th edit., 2003, Waveguides, Transmission Lines and Smith Charts, 1984, Kinetic Theory: Classical, Quantum and Relativistic Descriptions, 1990, 3d edit., 2003, Primer for Point and Space Groups, 2003. Served with Chem. Corps U.S. Army, 1953-55. Recipient Founders Day cert. N.Y. U., 1961; Solvay fellow, 1972; Fulbright scholar, 1984 Fellow Am. Phys. Soc.; mem. Sigma Xi. Office: U Ctrl Fla Physics-Math Bldg Orlando FL 32816-2385

LICHLITER, WARREN EUGENE, surgeon, educator; b. Murphysboro, Ill., Jan. 24, 1952; s. Gene Estel and Dorothy Colleen (Williams) L.; m. Carol Jane Loftin, Nov. 3, 1979; children: Gary Edward, Christopher Warren, Adrienne Leigh, Abigail Meredith. BA, U. Tenn., 1974; MD, U. Tex., Galveston, 1978. Intern and resident in gen. surgery Baylor U. Med. Ctr., Dallas, 1979-83, resident in colon rectal surgery, 1983-84, mem. attending staff dept. colon rectal surgery, 1984—, assoc. dir. surg. edn., 1984—, program dir. dept. colon rectal residency, 2000—, chief dept. colon rectal surgery, 2000—; clin. asst. prof. surgery health sci. ctr. U. Tex., Dallas, 1990—. Fellow: ACS (pres. North Tex. chpt. 2007, gov.-at-large), Am. Soc. Colon Rectal Surgeons; mem.: Dallas County Med. Soc. (sec.-treas. 2001—02, pres. 2004), Dallas Soc. Surgeons, Tex. Surg. Soc., Alpha Omega Alpha. Avocations: running, bicycling, sailing, kayaking, swimming. Office: 3409 Worth St Ste 600 Dallas TX 75246-2042 Office Phone: 214-824-1730. Business E-Mail: warrenl@baylonhealth.edu.

LICHTENFELD, JAY LEONARD, internist, oncologist; b. Phila., Pa., July 23, 1946; m. Sandra Reed. Grad., U. Pa.; MD, Hahnemann U. Med. Coll. (now Drexel U. Coll. Medicine), Phila., 1971. Cert. Internal Medicine, Oncology. Intern, medicine Temple U. Hosp., Phila., 1971—72; resident, oncology John Hopkins Hosp., Balt., 1976—77, med. instr.; fellow Balt. Cancer Rsch. Ctr., 1972—75; hosp. appointment Sinai Hosp.; private practice Thomasville, Ga.; dep. chief med. officer, nat. office Am. Cancer Soc. Spkr. in field. Master: ACP; mem.: Am. Med. Assn., Alpha Omega Alpha. Office: 103 Hiding Pl Thomasville GA 31792-8829 Address: Am Cancer Soc 1599 Clifton Rd NE Atlanta GA 30329

LICHTER, ALLEN S., oncologist, medical association administrator; BS, U. Mich., 1968, MD, 1972. Intern St. Joseph Hosp., Denver; resident U. Calif., San Francisco, 1976; former dir. radiation therapy sect. radiation oncology br. Nat. Cancer Inst.; dir. breast oncology program Comprehensive Cancer Ctr., U. Mich., Ann Arbor, 1984-91, chmn. dept. radiation oncology, 1984-97, interim dean Med. Sch., 1998-99, prof. radiation oncology, 1999—2006, dean Med. sch., 1999—2006; exec. v.p., CEO Am. Soc. Clin. Oncology, Alexandria, Va., 2006—. Bd. dirs. Accreditation Coun. for Grad. Med. Edn. Assoc. editor Jour. Clin. Oncology; editl. bd. Jour. Nat. Cancer Inst., Internat. Jour. Radiation Oncology; co-editor Clinical Oncology, 1995, 2d edit., 1999. Mem.: Am. Soc. Therapeutic Radiology and Oncology (bd. dirs.), Am. Soc. Clin. Oncology (pres. 1998—99, chmn. ASCO Found. bd. dirs. 1999—2002, exec. v.p. and CEO 2006—). Achievements include research in effective breast cancer treatment. Office: Am Soc Clin Oncology 2318 Mill Rd Ste 800 Alexandria VA 22314 Office Phone: 571-483-1300.

LICHTMAN, DAVID MICHAEL, orthopedist, health facility administrator, educator, retired military officer; b. Bkyln., Jan. 14, 1942; s. Harry S. and Frances (Rubin) L.; m. Frances Lubin; children: James Matthew, Elisabeth Jill. Student, Tufts Coll., 1962; MD, SUNY, Bklyn., 1966. Diplomate Am. Bd. Orthop. Surgery. Intern U. Minn. Hosp., 1966-67, Naval Aerospace Med. Inst., Pensacola, Fla., 1967; commd. lt. USN, 1967, advanced through grades to rear adm., 1988, flight surgeon Air Wing 3, 1968-69; mem. staff orthop. svc. Nat. Naval Med. Ctr., Bethesda, Md., 1974-77, chmn. dept. orthop. surgery, head, hand surgery svc., 1984-87, dir. orthop. residency program, 1984-87, asst. chmn. dept. orthop. surgery, 1975-77, chmn. dept. orthop. surgery, head hand surgery svc., dir. orthop. residency program, 1984-87; chmn. dept. orthop. surgery and rehab. Naval Hosp., Oakland, Calif., 1977-83, dir. orthop. residency program/dir. navy hand fellowship, 1977-83, head hand and microsurgery svc., 1977-83, mem. staff orthop. surgery, sr. hand/microsurgery cons., 1988-91, commdg. officer, 1989-91; comdr. San Francisco Med. Command, Oakland, 1988-91; promoted to Rear Adm. (lower half), 1989; Rear Adm. (upper half), 1991; ret. USN, 1994; John Dunn prof. orthop. hand surgery Baylor Coll. Medicine, Houston, 1994-98; chmn. dir. orthop. residency tng. John Peter Smith Hosp., Ft. Worth, 1998—; clin. prof. orthop. Southwestern Coll. Medicine, Dallas, 1998—2005; chmn. Dept. Orthop. Surgery Health Scis. Ctr. U. North Tex., Ft. Worth, 2005—, chmn. Dept. Orthop. Surgery, 2006—, prof. Dept. Orthop. Surgery, 2006—. Cons. orthop. surgery asst. sec. def. for health affairs Dept. Def., Washington, 1988-94; specialty advisor naval surgeon gen. for orthop. surgery and hand surgery Bur. Medicine and Surgery Dept. Navy, Washington, 1983-86; prof. surgery and head divsn. orthop. surgery Uniformed Svcs. U. of Health Scis., Bethesda, 1984-94, ex-officio mem. bd. regents, 1991-94' examiner Am. Bd. Orthopaedic Surgery. Editor: The Wrist and Its Disorders, 1988, 2d edit., 1997, Hand and Wrist Sect. Current Opinion in Orthopaedics; contbr. articles to profl. jours. Mem. ACS (bd. govs. 1987-96), Am. Acad. Orthop. Surgeons, Am. Soc. Surgery of Hand (coun. 1999-2002, pres. 2005-06, AMA del. 2001-), Am. Orthop. Assn. (hon.), Mil. Surgeons U.S. (Philip Hench award 1982), Tex. Med. Assn. (del. Tarrant County 2003), Soc. Naval Flight Surgeons, Soc. Med. Consultants to the Armed Forces (coun. 1994—, pres. 2002-03), Soc. Mil. Orthop. Surgeons (bd. dirs. 1987-90), Orthopaedic RRC of the ACGME, Fedn. Ctrl. and N.Am. Hand Surgery and Therapy Soc. (pres.-elect 2007). Home: 4958 Overton Woods Ct Fort Worth TX 76109-2433 Office: John Peter Smith Hosp Dept Orthopedic Surgery 1500 S Main St Fort Worth TX 76104-4917 Office Phone: 817-920-6903. Business E-Mail: dlichtma@jpshealth.org.

LICHTSTEIN, DANIEL M., dean, internist; b. NYC, Dec. 12, 1949; s. Milton and Charlotte Louise Lichtstein; m. Shirley Ann Lichtstein, June 6, 1970; children: Jason, Michelle. MD, SUNY, Downstate Med. Ctr., Bklyn., 1974. Diplomate Am. Bd. Internal Medicine. Regional dean med, educator regional dean med. edn. U. Miami, Miller Sch. Medicine, Boca Raton, Fla., 2006—. Author: (book) Preparation for Medical Practice, 1998. Mentor Palm Beach County Schs., Palm Beach Gardens, 1994. Recipient Laureate award, ACP, 2007, William Dock Master Tchr. award, SUNY, Downstate Med. Ctr., 2009. Master ACP. Jewish. Avocations: golf, writing, travel, community mentor. Office: University Miami Sch Medicine Regional Med Camps 3651 FAU Blvd Ste 400 Boca Raton FL 33431 Office Phone: 561-447-6551.*

LICK, DALE WESLEY, educational leadership educator, mathematician; b. Marlette, Mich., Jan. 7, 1938; s. John R. and Florence M. (Baxter) L.; m. Marilyn Kay Foster, Sept. 15, 1956; children: Lynette (dec.), Kitty (dec.), Diana, Ronald. BS with honors, Mich. State U., East Lansing, 1958, MS in Math, 1959; PhD in Math, U. Calif., Riverside, 1965. Research asst. physics Mich. State U., East Lansing, 1958, teaching asst. math., 1959; instr., chmn. dept. math. Port Huron (Mich.) Jr. Coll., 1959-60; asst. to comptroller Mich. Bell Telephone Co., Detroit, 1961; instr. U. Redlands, 1961-63; teaching asst. math. U. Calif., Riverside, 1964-65; asst. prof. math. U. Tenn., Knoxville, 1965-67; postdoctoral fellow Brookhaven Nat. Lab., Upton, NY, 1967-68; assoc. prof. U. Tenn., 1968-69; assoc. prof., head dept. math. Drexel U., Phila., 1969-72; adj. assoc. prof. dept. pharmacology Med. Sch., Temple U., Phila., 1969-72; v.p. acad. affairs Russell Sage Coll., Troy, NY, 1972-74; prof. math. and computing scis. Old Dominion U., Norfolk, Va., 1974-78; also dean Old Dominion U. (Sch. Scis. and Health Professions); pres., prof. math. and computer sci. Ga. So. Coll., Statesboro, 1978-86; pres., prof. math. U. Maine, Orono, 1986-91, Fla. State U., Tallahassee, 1991-93, Univ. prof. Learning Sys. Inst. and Dept. Edn. Leadership, 1993—2008, emeritus pres., prof., 2008—. Certs. in tng. and cons., mng. orgnl. change. Author: Fundamentals of Algebra, 1970, (with C. Murphy) Whole-Faculty Study Groups: A Powerful Way to Change Schools and Enhance Learning, 1998, (with C. Mullen) New Directions in Mentoring: Creating a Culture of Synergy, 1999, (with C. Murphy) Whole-Faculty Study Groups: Creating Student-Based Professional Development, 2001, Whole-Faculty Study Groups: Creating Professional Learning Communities That Target Student Learning, 2005, (with C. Murphy) The Whole-Faculty Study Groups Fieldbook: Improving Schools and Enhancing Student Learning, 2006, (with Clauset & Murphy) Schoolwide Action Research for Professional Learning Communities, 2008; contbr. articles to profl. jours., chapters to books. Bd. dirs. Statesboro/Coll. Symphony, 1978-86, Statewide Health Coordinating Coun. Va., 1976-78, United Way of the Big Bend, 1992-98; chmn. higher edn. adv. bd. Cmty. of Christ, 1986-2004; mem. planning com. Bulloch Meml. Hosp., 1979-86; v.p., mem. Coastal Empire coun. Boy Scouts Am., 1982-86, Katalidin coun., 1986-91; bd. dirs. Health Care Ctrs. Am., Virginia Beach, Va., 1978, Ea. Va. Health Systems Agy., 1976-78; chmn., bd. dirs. Assembly Against Hunger and Malnutrition, 1977-78, pres., 1977-78; mem., high priest Cmty. of Christ. Recipient Disting. Alumni award, Mich. State U., 2006, Internat. Peace Rddar prize, United Cultural Convention, 2010; named one of 40 Alumni Who Make a Difference, U. Calif. Riverside, 1994. Mem. AAUP, AAAS, Am. Math. Soc., Math. Assn. Am., Am. Assn. Univ. Adminstrs., Am. Soc. Allied Health Professions, Am. Assn. State Colls. and Univs. (chmn. com. agr. resources and rural devel. 1981-86), Am. Assn. Higher Edn., Nat. Staff Devel. Coun., Sigma Xi, Phi Kappa Phi, Pi Mu Epsilon (governing coun. 1972-77), Beta Gamma Sigma, Pi Sigma Epsilon. Home Phone: 850-553-4080; Office Phone: 850-553-4080. Business E-Mail: dlick@lsi.fsu.edu.

LICKHALTER, MERLIN, architect, consultant; b. St. Louis, May 4, 1934; s. Frank E. and Sophia (Geller) L.; m. Harriet Braen, June 9, 1957; children: Debra, Barbara. BArch, MIT, 1957; OPM, Harvard U. Grad. Sch. Bus., Boston, 1999. Ptnr. Drake Partnership, Architects, St. Louis, 1961-77; pres. JRB Architects, Inc., St. Louis, 1977-81; sr. v.p., mng. dir. Stone, Marraccini & Patterson, St. Louis, 1981-93; sr. v.p., dir. Cannon, 1993—2002; pres. Lickhalter & Assocs. LLC, 2003—; capt. US Army Corps Engrs., 1957—67. Owner, pres. mgmt. program Harvard U. Bus. Sch., 1992; cons. Dept. Def., Washington, 1977-78; lectr. Washington U. Sch. Medicine, 1989—, co-founder, chair & pres. Arts Naples World Festival Inc., 2009-2012, chair emeritus, 2013-, vice chair, Naples Pub. Art Adv. Com., 2011-12, sr. advisor Health Facilities Planning Partners, 2010-, sr. advisor, Studiupcus Architects, 2013-, dir., Classic Chamber Concerts, 2010, chair, 2014- Prin. projects include The Mayo Clinic, Jacksonville, Fla., Washington U. Med. Ctr., St. Louis, U.S. Army Hosp., Frankfurt, Germany, Nat. AIDS Rsch. Ctr., NIH, Washington, Evanston (Ill.) Hosp., Loma Linda (Calif.) U. Med. Ctr., U. Mo. Health Scis. Ctr., Columbia, St. Louis U. Health Scis. Ctr., Children's Hosp. Rsch. Inst., New Orleans, U. Ala. Birmingham Sch. Medicine, U. Ala. Sch. Optometry. Trustee United Hebrew Congregation, St. Louis, 1980-88, 93-98, 2000-06; exec. com. bd. dir. Arts & Edn. Coun. St. Louis, 1991-2002; pres. Acad. Architecture for Health Found., 2002-06; exec. com., bd. dir. United Arts Coun. Collier County, 2003—, pres., 2007-08; vice chair, bd. mem., Pelican Bay Found., 2005-08. Recipient Renovation Design award St. Louis Producers Coun., 1976, USAF Europe Design Award, 1990. Fellow: AIA (pres. nat. acad. arch. for health 1993, bd. dir. 2003—07, exec. com.), Am. Coll. Healthcare Architects; mem.: Acad. Arch. Health Found. (pres., trustee 2000—06), Harvard Club Naples, MIT Club Southwest Fla. (dir. 2005—). Jewish. Home and Office: Lickhalter and Assocs LLC 575 Via Veneto #202 Naples FL 34108 Personal E-mail: mlickhalter@gmail.com.

LIE, BERNT AAGE, energy executive; Gen. mgr., deepwater tech. solutions Oceaneering International, Inc., Norway. Office: Oceaneering International Inc 11911 FM 529 Houston TX 77041-3011 Office Phone: 713-329-4500. Office Fax: 713-329-4951. Business E-Mail: BAaLie@oceaneering.com.

LIEBERHERR, WERNER, aerospace product and parts manufacturing executive; M in Ops. Rsch. & Indsl. Engring., Swiss Fed. Inst. of Tech., Zurich; MBA, Northwestern U. Gen. mgr. sales N.Am., Europe and Asia Alstom Power, Inc., pres., mng. dir., v.p. global program mgmt.; v.p., gen. mgr. Comml. Aircraft Products Group BE Aerospace, Inc., 2006—. Office: BE Aerospace Inc 1400 Corporate Ctr Way Wellington FL 33414 Office Phone: 561-791-5000. Office Fax: 561-791-7900.

LIEBERMAN, ROCHELLE PHYLLIS, small business owner; b. Bklyn., June 27, 1940; d. Solomon and Freda (Shapiro) Beller; m. Melvyn Lieberman, June 10, 1961; children: Eric Neil, Marc Evan. BA, Bklyn. Coll., 1961; MEd, Duke U., 1977. Tchr. Bklyn. pub. schs., 1961-64; instr. Carolina Friends, Durham, NC, 1967-70; grad. intern Duke U., Durham, 1974-75, faculty adviser, 1975-76; sales assoc. Kelly Matherly, Durham, 1978-81; pres. Shelli, Inc., Durham, 1981—. Treas. Duke Forest Assn., Durham, 1980—85; pres. Bus. Commn., 2004; mem. Predl. Bus. Commn., 2005, Nat. Rep. Congl. Com., Congl. Bus. Adv. Coun. Recipient Citizenship award, Durham Regional Assn. Realtors, 2012; named NRCC Businesswoman of Yr., Duke-Durham Campaign, 2006. Mem. LWV, Durham and Chapel Hill Bd. Realtors, Women's Council of Realtors (sec. 1980-81), Duke U. Eye Ctr. (adv. bd. mem.), Duke U. Dept. Anesthesiology (adv. bd. mem.), Kappa Delta Pi. Clubs: Duke Faculty. Jewish. Avocations: piano, walking, knitting, writing, reading. Office: Shelli Inc 1110 Woodburn Rd Durham NC 27705-5738 Home Phone: 919-493-3640; Office Phone: 919-489-8829. Personal E-mail: shelliinc@aol.com.

LIEBERMAN-CLINE, NANCY, professional sports team executive, retired professional basketball player; b. Bklyn., July 1, 1958; m. Tim Cline, 1988; 1 child, Timothy Joseph. Degree in interdisciplinary studies, Old Dominion U., Norfolk, Va., 2000. Guard Dallas Diamonds, WBL, WABA, 1980-86, Springfield Fame, USBL, 1986, LI Knights, USBL, 1987, Washington Generals, USBL, 1987-88, Athletes in Action, 1996-97, Phoenix Mercury, WNBA, 1997; head coach, gen. mgr. Detroit Shock, WNBA, 1998—2000; pres. Women's Sports Found., 1999—2000; head coach Dallas Fury, NWBL, 2004; women's basketball broadcaster ABC Sports, CBS Sports and Fox Sports; men's and women's basketball analyst ESPN; head coach Tex. Legends, NBA Devel League, 2010—11, asst. gen. mgr., 2011—. Women's basketball analyst Summer Olympic Games, 1988, 1992. Author: (autobiography) Lady Magic: The Nancy Lieberman Story, 1991; co-author: Basketball for Women; contbr. columns in newspapers. Recipient Silver medal, Summer Olympic Games, 1976, Broderick Cup, 1979, 80, Wade Trophy, 1980, 81; named Outstanding Female Athlete of Yr. Old Dominion U., 1977-80, All-Am., 1978-80, WABA MVP, 1984; named to Basketball Hall of Fame, 1996, Women's Basketball Hall of Fame, 1999. Jewish. Achievements include member of the WABA Championship winning Dallas Diamonds, 1984; becoming the first woman ever to play in a men's professional league when she joined the USBL's Springfield Fame, 1986; head coach of the National Women's Basketball League Championship winning Dallas Fury, 2004. Office: Tex Legends 2601 Avenue of the Stars Ste 300 Frisco TX 75034

LIEBMANN, GUY, state legislator; b. Shawnee, Okla., Apr. 27, 1936; s. JG Liebmann and Barbara Hoyt Liebmann; m. Judy Evans Liebmann; 3 children. BS, Univ. Okla., 1958. Profession in investments; mem. Dist. 82 Okla. House of Representatives, 2005—. Served as officer USMC, 1959—61. Republican. Methodist. Mailing: 12800 Plum Hollow Dr Oklahoma City OK 73142 Office: 2300 N Lincoln Blvd, Rm 331 Oklahoma City OK 73105 Office Phone: 405-557-7357. Fax: 405-962-7638. Business E-Mail: guyliebmann@okhouse.gov.

LIEBMANN, SEYMOUR W., construction executive, consultant; b. NYC, Nov. 1, 1928; s. Isidor W. and Etta (Waltzer) L.; m. Hinda Adam, Sept. 20, 1959; children: Peter Adam, David W. BSME, Clarkson U., 1948, US Army Engr. Sch., 1949; grad., Indsl. Coll. Armed Forces, 1963, US Army Command and Gen. Staff Coll., 1966, US Army War Coll., 1971. Registered profl. engr., NY, Mass., Ga. Area engr. constrn. divsn. E.I. DuPont de Nemours & Co., Inc., 1952-54, Savannah River Nuc. Plant, Lummus Co., Inc., 1954-56; constrn. planner, prin. mech. engr. Perini Corp., 1956-62, St. Lawrence Seaway, Mass. Turnpike Ext. & Boston Harbor Tunnel; v.p. A.R. Abrams, Inc., Atlanta, 1967-74, pres., 1974-78, also bd. dirs.; commdg. officer 185th Engr. US Army, Atlanta, 1978; under divsn. engr. South Atlantic Divsn., US Army Corps. Engrs., 1978, ret., 1988; mobilization assignment to Office of Chief Engrs. US Army, Washington, 1978—97; v.p., Boston based constructors Boston Va. Hosp., MIT & Harvard Projects. Founder Liebmann Assocs., Inc., Atlanta, 1979—; nat. adv. bd. Am. Security Coun.; steering com. Atlanta Engring. Acad. Author: Military Engineer Field Notes, 1953, Prestressing Miter Gate Diagonals, 1960; contbr. articles to publs. Active USO Coun., Atlanta, 1968—2010, v.p., 1978, exec. com., 1975-79, Nat. UN Day Com., 1975; sr. army coord., judge Sci. Fair, Atlanta Pub. Schs., 1979-88, 92-2004, 06; asst. scoutmaster Atlanta area coun. Boy Scouts Am., 1980-87, Explorer advisor, 1982-86, unit commr., 1985, commr. North Atlanta dist., 1988-90, asst. coun. commr., 1990-95, North Atlanta dist. com., 1996-1998; faculty Commrs. Coll., 1985-88, 92; alumni adv. com. Clarkson U., 1981—99, alumni bd. govs., 1983-94, Disting. Alumni Golden Knight award, 1983; exec. com., zoning chmn. neighbor planning unit "A" City of Atlanta, 1982-2006, chmn., 1988, 95-2006, vice-chmn., 1989, chmn. emeritus, 2007-; pres. West Paces/Northside Neighborhood Assn., 1991-2007; apptd. civil engr. mem. to City of Atlanta Water and Sewer Appeals Bd., 1992-, chmn., 2008-; apptd. mem. to Mayor's Bond Oversight Com. City of Atlanta, 1995-96; mem. Atlanta, Cobb County regional mil. affairs com., 2001—07; chair City of Atlanta Nancy Creek Tech. Tunnel Adv. Com., 2002-06; mem. blue ribbon panel Fulton County Juvenile Ct., 2001-04; mem. Philmont Fall Adventure Trek, 2002; apptd. mem. Mayor's Svc. Commn., 2002—04. Col. USA Ret. Corps Engrs., 1948-88, Korea, Germany, Mobilization Assignment, 1978-97., regional v.p., 2010 Decorated Legion of Merit, Meritorious Svc. medal, USAR Achievement medal with oak leaf cluster; recipient cert. achievement, Dept. Army, 1978, Bronze DeFleury medal, US Army Engr. Regiment, awarded by Chief of Engrs., US Army, for materially contbg. to the combat readiness of The Corps. during The Gulf War, 1997, USO Recognition award, 1979, Order of Arrow award, Boy Scouts Am., 1987, Scouters Key, 1988, North Atlanta Dist. Merit award, 1989, Silver Beaver award, 1991, Disting. Commr. award, 1991, Am. Inst. Plant. Engrs. award for Engring. Professionalism, 1987, Hands Across Atlanta award, 1997, Ga. Engrs. Lifetime Achievement award, 2001, Medal of Honor award, Ga. Engring. Found., 2004; named Engr. of Yr., Met. Atlanta Engrs., 1990, Ga. State Soc. Profl. Engrs., 1991. Fellow: Soc. Am. Mil. Engrs. (life; program chmn. Atlanta post 1980—81, v.p. 1982, pres. 1983, chmn. readiness com. 1986—2000, bd. dirs. 1986—, program chmn. 1988, nat. meeting, asst. regional v.p. for readiness So. region 1991—2007, life dir. Atlanta Post 1994, James Lucas Chair Atlanta Post 1994, elected nat. dir. 1994—97, program chmn. S.Ea. regional site tng. conf. 1999, Nat. award of Merit 1982—83, Atlanta Post Leadership award 1988); mem.: NRA, NSPE, ASTM, Internat. Concrete Repair Inst. (awards com. 2000), Internat. Concrete Restoration Inst. (judge awards com. 2002), Am. Arbitration Assn. (panel arbitrators 1979—2007, constrn. adv. com. 1984—2007), Engrs. Club Boston, Met. Atlanta Engrs. (chmn. Engrs. Week 2000 and 2001 awards com.), Jt. Ga. Soc. Profl. Engrs. and Am. Counsel of Engring. Cos. (chmn. state licensing com. 2002—03, bd. dirs. Buckhead chpt., state ethics com., Proclamation of Honor, Atlanta City Coun. 2006, named Outstanding Citizen award, Common Cause Ga., Atlanta 2009), Am. Concrete Inst., Army Engr. Assn. (life), US Army Hist. Found., Atlanta Area Mil. Affairs Com., Vets. of the 1st US Army Engr. Combat Bn., Atlanta Hist. Soc., Ga. Conservancy, Benyton Mackaye Trail Assn., Ga. Appalachian Trail Club, Order of Engr., Mil. Order World Wars, Atlanta C. of C. (mil. affairs com. 1999), Downtown Atlanta Kiwanis, Cobb C. of C., Def. Preparedness Assn., Nat. Def. U. Found., US Army War Coll. Alumni Assn. (life), Assn. US Army (life; v.p. exec. com. local chpt. 1998—2000), US Army War Coll. Found. (life; Alumni Assn. Disting. Alumni Selection Com. 1997—2007), Res. Officers Assn. (life), Soc. 1st US Inf. (life), Civitan, Elks, Masons (32 degree), Royal Arch Mason, Shriners, National Sojourners and Heroes of 76. Republican. Jewish. Office: Liebmann Assocs Inc 4405 Northside Pky NW Unit 2425 Atlanta GA 30327

LIENHARD, JEROME T., II, corporate financial executive; m. Sue Lienhard. B in Acctg., U. Southern Calif., M in Internat. Fin. Corp. treasury mgr. Toyota Motor Credit Corp.; sr. v.p., treas. Fed. Home Loan Mortgage Corp. (Freddie Mac); sr. exec. v.p., treas. MBNA; sr. v.p., corp. treas. SunTrust Banks, Inc., 2006—10, corp. treas., 2006—, exec. v.p., strategic fin. & adminstrn., 2010—. Trustee March of Dimes Birth Defects Found., 2007-09, Polycystic Kidney Found., 2010-. Office: SunTrust Banks Inc 303 Peachtree St NE Atlanta GA 30308 Office Phone: 404-588-7711. Office Fax: 404-332-3875. Business E-Mail: jerome.lienhard@suntrust.com.

LIENHARD, JOHN HENRY, IV, mechanical engineer, educator; b. St. Paul, Aug. 17, 1930; s. John Henry and Catherine Edith Lienhard; m. Carol Ann Bratton, June 20, 1959; children: John Henry V, Andrew Joseph. AS, Multnomah Jr. Coll., 1949; BS, Oreg. State Coll., 1951; MSME, U. Wash., 1953; PhD in Mech. Engring., U. Calif., Berkeley, 1961; DHL (hon.), U. Houston, 2002, Sacred Heart U., 2002. Assoc. prof. mech. engring. Wash. State U., Pullman, 1961-67; prof. mech. engring. dept. U. Ky., Lexington, 1967-80; prof. mech. engring. U. Houston, 1980-89, M.D. Anderson prof. mech. engring. and history, 1989—2000, prof. emeritus, 2000—. Clyde chair prof. U. Utah, Salt Lake City, 1981. Author (with C. L. Tien): Statistical Thermodynamics, 1971, 1979; author: (with J. H. Lienhard V) A Heat Transfer Textbook, 1981, 1987, 2006, 2010; author: (with E. T. Layton) History of Heat Transfer, 1988; author: The Engines of Our Ingenuity, 2000, Inventing Modern, 2003, How Invention Begins, 2006; author, host (radio) The Engines of Our Ingenuity; contbr. articles to profl. jours. Mem.: ASME (hon. Heat Transfer Meml. award, Charles Russ Richards award, Engr. Historian award 1998), Nat. Acad. Engring., Am. Soc. Engring. Edn. (Ralph Coates Roe Tchg. medal). Episcopalian. Home: 3719 Durhill St Houston TX 77025-4006 Office: U Houston Dept Mech Engring Houston TX 77204-4006 Home Phone: 713-663-7705; Office Phone: 713-743-4518. Business E-Mail: jhl@uh.edu.

LIFTON, WALTER M., psychology and education consultant; b. Bklyn., Nov. 2, 1918; s. Samuel S. and Sarah G. (Berman) L.; m. Ruth S. Knoppow, Oct. 1, 1940 (dec. Nov. 30, 2006); children: Hazel Miriam Kroesser Palmer, Robert William. BA, Bklyn. Coll., 1942; MA, NYU, 1947, PhD, 1950. Sr. vocat. appraiser Vets. Guidance Center, Hunter Coll., 1946-48; psychologist, research div. NYU, 1948-50; assoc. prof. edn., guidance and counseling U. Ill., 1950-59; dir. guidance publs. and services Sci. Research Assocs., Chgo., 1959-63; coordinator pupil personnel services Rochester City Sch. Dist., N.Y., 1964-70; initial dir., anti poverty program under pres. Johnson Rochester Monroe County, Rochester, NY, 1966—68; prof. edn. dept. counseling psychology and student devel. SUNY-Albany, 1970-82, prof. emeritus, 1982—; edn. and psychology cons., 1982—. Disting. vis. prof. Coll. Grad. Studies, W.Va., 1985-86; vis. prof., lectr. guidance and counseling 34 colls. and univs.; cons. in field Author: What Could I be?, 1960, Keys to Vocational Decisions, 1964, Working With Groups, 2d edit, 1966, Educating for Tomorrow— The Role of Media, Career Devel. and Society, 1970, Groups— Facilitating Individual Growth and Societal Change, 1972; film Just Like a Family, 1979; contbr. articles to profl. jours. Mem. White House Conf. on Children and Youth, 1969-70; cons. Title III ESEA project, Knox County, Tenn., 1967; interim dir. Action for a Better Community, Rochester, 1964-65, Center for Coop. Action in Urban Edn., 1966; apptd. to Durham NC County Youth Svcs. Bd., 1994-97. Served with AUS, 1942-46. Fellow Assn. for Specialists in Group Work (sec. 1976—, pres. 1980-81, Eminent Career award 1986); mem. Nat. Assn. Pupil Personnel Adminstrs. (pres. 1970), Nat. Vocat. Guidance Assn., Eno River Unitarian Universalist Fellowship (bd. dirs. 1998-2001), First Unitarian Soc. Albany (bd. dirs. 1989-92). Home: 3721 Virginia Ave SE Charleston WV 25304-1505 Personal E-mail: wlifton2@gamil.com.

LIGETT, WALDO BUFORD, chemist; b. Middletown, Ohio, Nov. 2, 1916; s. Waldo Buford and Mabel Louise (Berkley) L.; m. Ann Elizabeth Hartwell, Aug. 29, 1940; children: Robert A., John D., Michael T., Steven D., Daniel L. BS, Antioch Coll., Yellow Springs, Ohio, 1939; MS, Purdue U., West Lafayette, Ind., 1941, PhD, 1944, DSc (hon.), 1965; grad. in Advanced Mgmt., Harvard U., Cambridge, Mass., 1967. Chemist Eastman Kodak Co., Rochester, N.Y., 1935-38; research supr. Ethyl Corp., Detroit, 1944-51, asst. dir. chem., 1951-52, asso. dir. chem., 1952-62, dir. research and devel., 1962-63; v.p. Celanese Chem. Co., Corpus Christi, Tex., 1963-64, v.p. tech. and mfg., 1964-66; tech. dir. Celanese Corp., NYC, 1966-67, v.p., 1967-72, Franklin Inst., Phila., 1973-81; pres. Franklin Inst. Research Labs., 1975-81. Dir. Franklin-Hahnemann Inst., 1974-81 Contbr. articles to profl. jours. Mem.: Am. Chem. Soc. Achievements include patents in field. Home: 700 Carolina Meadows Apt 232 Chapel Hill NC 27517 Home Phone: 919-929-9106.

LIGHT, ALFRED ROBERT, law educator; b. Dec. 14, 1949; s. Alfred M. Jr. and Margaret Francis (Asbury) L; m. Mollie Sue Hall, May 28, 1977; children: Joseph Robert, Gregory Andrew. Student, Ga. Inst. Tech., 1967-69; BA with highest honors, Johns Hopkins U., 1971; PhD, U. N.C., 1976; JD cum laude, Harvard U., 1981. Bar: D.C. 1981, Va. 1982. Tax clk. IRS, 1967; lab technician Custom Farm Svcs. Soils Testing Lab, 1968; warehouse asst. State of Ga. Mines, Mining and Geology, 1970; clk.-typist systems mgmt. divsn., def. contract adminstrv. Def. Supply Agy., Atlanta, 1971; rsch. and teaching asst. dept. polit. sci. U. N.C., Chapel Hill, 1971-74; rsch. asst. Inst. Rsch. in Social Sci., 1975-77; program analyst Office of Sec. Def., 1974; asst. prf. polit. sci., rsch. scientist Ctr. Energy Rsch. Tex. Tech. U., Lubbock, 1977-78; rsch. asst. grad. sch. edn. Harvard U., 1978-79; assoc. Butler, Binion, Rice, Cook & Knapp, Houston, 1980, Bracewell & Patterson, Washington, 1980; Hunton & Williams, Richmond, Va., 1981-89; of counsel, 1989-93, 95-96; assoc. prof. St. Thomas U. Sch. Law, Miami, Fla., 1989-93, prof., 1993—. Interim dean, 1993-94; adj. prof. U. Miami Law, 2008, bd. advisors Toxics Law reporter, Bur. Nat. Affairs, Washington, 1987—; dir. LLM Program in Environ. Sustainability, 2010-. Contbr. articles to profl. jours. Charter mem. West Broward Cmty. Ch.; mem. First Bapt. Ch. Weston. Capt. USAR, 1971-85. Grantee NSF, Inst. Evaluation Rsch., U. Mass., Ctr. Energy Rsch., Tex. Tech. U., 1977-78, U.S. EPA, 2003-06; recipient William Anderson award Am. Polit. Sci. Assn., 1977. Mem. ABA (vice-chmn.) tort and ins. practice sect. 1988-97, nat. res. and environ. sect. 1993-95, chmn. 1995-2000, vice chair com. smart Growth & Green Bldg., 2011-13), 1st Bapt. Ch. Weston, Assn. Climate Change Officers (mem. bd. dirs. 2010-14), Leed Green Assoc., Corp. Sustainability Mgr. (cert. award 2012-), Fed. Bar. Assn., Phi Beta Kappa, Phi Eta Sigma. Republican. Home: 1042 Woodfall Ct Weston FL 33326-2832 Office: St Thomas U Sch Law 16401 NW 37th Ave Miami Gardens FL 33054-6313 E-mail: alight@stu.edu.

LIGHTNER, CANDY (CANDACE LYNNE LIGHTNER), nonprofit management consultant, advocate; b. Pasadena, Calif., May 30, 1946; d. Dykes Charles and Kathryn Josephine Doddridge; children: Serena, Travis. D (hon.), St. Francis Coll., Pa., 1984, Kutztown U., 1987, Marymount U., NYC, 1987. With various pvt. offices, 1964-70; real estate salesperson Calif., 1972-80; govt. rels. cons. Washington, 1993-94; owner Candace Lightner & Assocs., Alexandria, Va. Spkr., condr. tng. sessions various orgns. Author: Giving Sorrow Words: How to Cope With Grief and Get On With Your Life, 1990; guest nat. talk shows including Good Morning America, Today, 60 Minutes, MacNeil-Lehrer, Phil Donahue, Nightline, Turning Point. Founder, Mothers Against Drunk Driving (MADD), 1980, chmn., pres., CEO, 1980-85; mem. adv. bd. Mothers Against Sexual Abuse; bd. dirs. Air Crash Support Network; active Sacramento County Task Force on Drunk Driving, Presdl. Commn. on Drunk and Drugged Driving; bd. dirs. Nat. Commn. on Drunk Driving, 1984-86, Nat. Partnership for Drug Free Use, Nat. Hwy. Safety Adv. Com., Love is Feeding Everyone, 1988-89, others; judge Gleitsman Found.; bd. advisors Bhopal Justice Campaign. Recipient Jefferson award Am. Inst. Pub. Svc., Pres. Vol. Action award, Woman of Yr. award YWCA, Woman of Yr. award Women's Internat. Ctr., Award for Excellence Film Adv. Bd., Testimonial award Civitan Internat., 1984, Epilepsy Found award, 1984, Woman of Year award Mortar Bd. Soc., Baylor U., 1985, Anti-discriminationaward Am. Anti-descrimination Com., 1985, YWCA Woman of Year award, 1986, Commonwealth award U. Del., 1986, Black and Blue award Thomas Jefferson U. Hosp. Emergency Medicine Soc., Human Dignity award Kessler Inst. for Rehab., Woman of Distinction award Third Nat. Congress Coll. Women Student Leaders and Woman of Achievement, 1987, Disting. Leadership award World Congress of Victimology, 1987, Living Legacy award Women's Internat. Ctr., 1988, Friends of Children award Assn. Childhood Edn. Internat., 1988; Named to Good Housekeeping's Most Admired Woman's Poll, 1986; ranked in Top 25 of America's Most Influential People World Almanac & Book of Facts, 1986, one of the Original Thinkers of the Eighties, Life mag., 1990; selected by Johns Hopkins U. to participate in Anglo-Am. Successor Generation program, 1985; honored as one of Seven Who Succeeded, TIME Mag., 1985; honored by Edquire mag. as mem. America's New Leadership Class, 1985, others. Mem. Nat. Soc. Fund Raising Execs., Women in Arts, Nat. Bd. Realtors. Avocations: gardening, reading, swimming, travel. Home: 2025 Cornell Pl Port Orange FL 32128-6823 E-mail: cd_light2003@yahoo.com.

LIGI, ANTHONY V., JR., state legislator; BA in Polit. Sci., Mansfield U.; JD, Loyola U. Sch. Law, New Orleans. Atty. & real estate title ins. agt.; mem. Dist. 79 La. House of Reps., 2008—, mem. appropriations com., house and govtl. affairs com., joint legis. com. on the budget, legis. audit adv. coun. Republican. Office: 4425 Clearview Pky Ste B Metairie LA 70006 also: Capitol Office PO Box 44486 Baton Rouge LA 70804 Office Phone: 504-456-3173, 225-342-6945. Office Fax: 504-456-3175. E-mail: ligit@legis.state.la.us.

LIGON, WILLIAM T., JR., state legislator; m. Kim Lignon; 5 children. BS, Valdosta State Coll.; JD, Mercer U. Sr. ptnr. Ligon, Middleton, & Lindberg, PC; mem. Dist. 3 Ga. State Senate, 2011—. Republican. Office: 158 Scranton Connector Brunswick GA 31525 also: Ga State Senate 323B Coverdell Legis Office Bldg Atlanta GA 30334 Office Phone: 912-261-2263, 404-656-0045. Business E-Mail: william.ligon@senate.ga.gov.

LIL' BOW WOW, See MOSS, SHAD

LILLARD, MARK HILL, III, engineering consultant, retired military officer; b. Jacksonville, Fla., Sept. 1, 1943; s. Mark Hill Jr. and Cornelia Kingman (Callaway) L.; m. Marie-Jacques Le Guyader, June 3, 1972; children: Mark Hill IV, Michael Robert. BA, Bowling Green U., 1965; MS, St. Mary's U., San Antonio, 1976; MBA, Auburn U., 1977. Profl. project mgr. Commd. 2d lt. USAF, 1965, advanced through grades to brig. gen., 1991; ret., 1991; exec. v.p. Pilot Rsch. Assocs., Inc., Vienna, Va., 1991—2001, also bd. dirs.; regional v.p. RCM Technologies, Inc., Bethesda, Md., 2001—04; sr. assoc. Booz Allen Hamilton, McLean, Va., 2004; v.p. Seta Corp., McLean, 2005—06, Pennoni & Assoc., 2008—; sr. v.p. Dewberry & Davis LLC, 2006—08. Author: Simulation, 1976. Decorated Legion of Merit, Def. Superior Svc. medal, Def. Meritorious Svc. medal; Samil medal (Republic of Korea). Mem. Air Force Assn., Lions, Kiwanis, Phi Delta Theta. Republican. Avocations: tennis, golf. Home: 9516 Locust Hill Dr Great Falls VA 22066-2021 Office Phone: 703-449-6700. Personal E-mail: mlillard@earthlink.net.

LILLEY, MILI DELLA, insurance company executive, entertainment management consultant; b. Valley Forge, Pa., Aug. 29; d. Leon Hanover and Della Beaver (Jones) L. MBA, Tenn. Christian U., 1957, PhD, 1959. Various positions G & G Cons. Inc., Ft. Lauderdale, Fla., 1971-75; v.p. AMEX, Inc., Beverly Hills, Calif. and Acapulco, Mex., 1976-80; pres. The Hanover Group, Ft. Lauderdale, 1981—; personal and bus. mgr. entertainers including Ink Spots, Ft. Lauderdale, 1984—, Lanny Poffo, Ft. Lauderdale, 1990—. Dist. agt. ITT Life Ins. Corp., also other leading cos. Named to All Stars Honor Roll Nat. Ins. Sales Mag., 1989. Mem. Fla. Assn. Theatrical Agts., Fla. Guild of Talent Agts., Mgrs., Prodrs. and Orchs. Home: The Hanover Group 1861 Hickory St SE Conyers GA 30013-1647 Office Phone: 954-491-1101.

LILLISTON, ANDREW WILSON, JR., lawyer; b. Washington, Nov. 18, 1946; s. Andrew Wilson and Mary (D.) Lilliston; m. Elaine Alling Lilliston, Aug. 9, 1969; children: Jennifer Lilliston Hindman, Andrew W. III, Cortlin Alling, Kimberly Lilliston Roberts. BS in Bus., Ind. U., 1968; JD, U. Va., 1975. Bar: Ind. 1975, US Dist. Ct. (so. dist.) Ind. 1975, US Ct. Appeals (7th cir.) 1976, US Supreme Ct. 1992. Assoc. Ice Miller, Donadio & Ryan, Indpls., 1975—78; staff atty. Burger Chef Sys. Inc., Indpls., 1978—81, sr. atty., 1981—83; sr. corp. atty. Hardee's Food Sys., Inc., Rocky Mount, NC, 1983—87, asst. gen. counsel, 1987—90; spl. counsel Golden Corral Corp., Raleigh, NC, 1991—94, dep. gen. counsel, asst. sec., 1994—2013. Bd. dirs. N C Lions Inc., 2014—. Pvt. to capt. US Army, 1968—72, Vietnam. Decorated Bronze Star. Mem.: Lions (pres. Fuquay-Varina Lions club 2001—02, dist. zone chmn. 2002—03, region chmn. 2003—04, humanities/white cane chmn. 2004—05, 2nd vice dist. gov. 2009—10, 1st vice dist. gov. 2010—11, dist. govs. 2011—12, NCLI State Camp Dogwood chair 2012—13, Progressive Jack Stickley fellow 2010, Progressive Melvin Jones fellow 2005), "I" Men's Assn., Raven Soc., Beta Gamma Sigma, Kappa Delta Rho, Phi Delta Phi. Methodist. Avocations: kayaking, hiking, softball.

LILLY, EDWARD GUERRANT, JR., retired utilities executive; b. Lexington, Ky., Oct. 29, 1925; s. Edward Guerrant and Elisabeth Read (Frazer) L.; m. Nancy Estes Cobb, Nov. 25, 1961; children: Penelope Read, Edward Guerrant III, Collier Cobb (dec.), Steven Clay. BS, Davidson Coll., 1948; MBA, Wharton Sch., U. Pa., 1949. Credit analyst Citizens and So. Nat. Bank, Charleston, SC, 1949-50; asst. v.p. Wachovia Bank and Trust Co., Charlotte, 1952-55, v.p., loan adminstrv. officer Wilmington, NC, 1956-60, sr. v.p., area exec. Kinston, NC, 1961-62, Durham, NC, 1963-70, sr. v.p., mgr. trust investment svcs. dept. Winston-Salem, NC, 1970-71, also bd. dirs., 1971-88; sr. v.p., group exec. Carolina Power and Light Co., Raleigh, NC, 1971-76, sr. v.p., chief fin. officer, 1976-81, exec. v.p., chief fin. officer, 1981-90, also bd. dirs. Bd. dirs. N.C. Enterprise Corp., Gen. Tel. Co. Southeast, Colorcraft Corp., Tidewater Natural Gas Co., CSC Industries, Inc. Mem. U. N.C. bd. visitors, 1974-87; bd. dirs. 1965-1972, Rsch. Triangle Found., Rsch. Triangle Pk.; trustee Davidson Coll., 1976-88, Union Theol. Seminary; Bus. Found. NC, pres. United Fund. Lt. USNR, 1950—52, ensign USNR, 1944—46. Mem. Edison Electric Inst. (chmn. fin. group 1979) Lodges: Rotary (Raleigh). Presbyterian.

LILLY, KEVIN L., lawyer, manufacturing executive; BA, JD, U. Notre Dame. Staff atty. US Ct. Appeals (7th cir.), Chgo.; ptnr. Jamieson, Moore, Peskin & Spicer, Archer & Greiner; gen. counsel Inrange Technologies Corp. SPX Corp., Charlotte, NC, 2003, group gen. counsel tech. and industrial sys. bus., assoc. gen. counsel bus. ops., v.p., gen. counsel, sec., 2006—07, sr. v.p., sec., gen. counsel, 2007—. Office: SPX Corp 13515 Ballantyne Corporate Pl Charlotte NC 28277 Office Fax: 704-752-4400.

LILLY, THOMAS GERALD, retired lawyer; b. Belzoni, Miss., Sept. 17, 1933; s. Sale Trice and Margaret Evelyn (Butt) Lilly; m. Constance Ray Holland, Dec. 29, 1962; children: Thomas Gerald Jr., William Holland, Carolyn Ray. BBA, Tulane U., New Orleans, 1955; LLB, U. Miss., Oxford, 1960; JD, U. Miss., 1968. Bar: Miss. 1960. Assoc. firm Stovall & Price, Corinth, Miss., 1960—62; asst. U.S. atty. No. Dist. Miss., Oxford, 1962—66; assoc. Wise Carter Child & Caraway (and predecessor), Jackson, Miss., 1966—67, ptnr., 1967—94, Lilly & Wise, Jackson, 1994—2000, of counsel, 2001—03, pres., 1990—92; ret., 2003; mem., US del. Eurasia United Meth. Conf., Moscow, 2002. Del. 19th World Methodist Conf., Seoul, Republic of Korea, 2006; mem. fin. com. Oxford U. United Meth. Ch., 2011—13. With USNR, 1955—88, ret. rear adm. Supply Corps USN. Decorated Legion of Merit, Navy Commendation medal. Fellow:

Miss. Bar Found., Found. Fed. Bar Assn. (life); mem.: FBA (nat. coun. 1972—, rec. sec. 1975—76, gen. sec. 1976—77, 2d v.p. 1977—78, pres.-elect 1978—79, pres. 1979—80), Nat. Soc. Sons Am. Revolution Miss. Soc., United Way Oxford, Ms (bd. dirs. 2009—10), Nat. Lawyers Club (bd. govs. 1976—81), Ulster Geneal. and Hist. Guild, Family Rsch. Assn. Miss. (1st v.p. 2004, pres. 2005), Miss. Geneal. Soc., Democracy Devel. Inst. (bd. dirs. 1995—2003), Miss. State Bar, Salt & Light Ministry Found. (gen. sec. 2005—06, bd. dirs. 2005—07), Chester Dist. Geneal. Soc., Naval Order US, Navy Supply Corps Assn., Navy League (pres. Ctrl. Miss. coun. 1993), Naval Hist. Soc., Mil. Officers Assn. Am., Res. Officers Assn. (pres. Miss. dept. 1982—83), Assn. US Navy, Scabbard and Blade, Mil. Order World Wars, Lamar Order, Delta Sigma Pi, Sigma Nu, Phi Delta Phi (pres. Mayes Inn 1959—60), Omicron Delta Kappa. United Methodist.

LIM, DANIEL VAN, microbiology educator; b. Houston, Apr. 15, 1948; s. Don H. and Lucy (Toy) L.; m. Carol Lee, Sept. 2, 1973. BA in Biology, Rice U., 1970; PhD in Microbiology, Tex. A&M U., 1973. Postdoc. fellow Baylor Coll. Medicine, 1973-76; asst. prof. U. South Fla., Tampa, 1976-81, assoc. prof. microbiology, 1981-87, chmn. dept. biology, 1983-85, prof., 1987—, disting. univ. prof., 2006—. Pres. Micro Concepts Rsch. Corp; dir. Inst. Biomolecular Sci., 1988-93; co-dir. Ctr. Excellence, 2007-11; cons. and expert witness in field. Author: Microbiology, 1989, 98, 2003, Introduction to Microbiology, 1995. Recipient Outstanding Contbn. in Sci. and Tech. award Fla. Gov., Christopher Columbus Fellowship Found. award Homeland Security, 2004. Fellow Am. Acad. Microbiology; mem. Inter-Am. Soc. Chemotherapy (v.p. 1983-88), Am. Soc. Microbiology (pres. southeastern br. 1990-91, mem. coun. 2000—06, mem. career devel. com., 1999—2008, branch orgn. com. mem., 2008-11, Carski award com. 1983-86, Margaret Green Outstanding Tchr. award, P.R. Edwards award, Ivan Roth award). Achievements include invention of bacteriological broth. Office: University South Fla Dept Cell Biology Microbiology & Molecular Biology ISA 2015 4202 E Fowler Ave Tampa FL 33620-7115 Office Phone: 813-974-1618. Business E-Mail: lim@usf.edu.

LIM, SUNG KYU, computer scientist, educator; naturalized, USA; s. Sook Hee Lim; m. Jee Eun Lim, 2002; children: Mina, Yuna. BS in Computer Sci., UCLA, 1994, MS in Computer Sci., 1997, PhD in Computer Sci., 2000. Asst. prof. Ga. Inst. Tech., Atlanta, 2001—07, assoc. prof., 2007—. Recipient Faculty Early Career Devel. award, NSF, 2006. Office: Ga Inst Tech Sch Elec and Computer Engring 777 Atlantic Dr NW Atlanta GA 30332 Business E-Mail: limsk@ece.gatech.edu.

LIMA, MARYBETH, engineering educator; b. New Bedford, Mass., Dec. 9, 1965; d. John Joseph Lima and Kathleen Florence Rogers; life ptnr. Lynn Erin Hathaway, June 19, 1992. BS, Ohio State U., 1988, PhD, 1996. Asst. prof. La. State U., Baton Rouge, 1996—2002, assoc. prof., 2002, now prof. Dept. Biological & Agrl. Engring. and Women's & Gender Studies. Assoc. editor ASAE, St. Joseph, Mich., 1999—. Contbr. articles to profl. publs., chpts. to books. Facilitated constrn. of 6 playgrounds, Baton Rouge, 2000—04. Recipient A.W. Farrall Outstanding Young Educator award, Am. Soc. Agrl. Engrs., 2002, Ernest A. Lynton Award for Faculty Profl. Svc. & Academic Outreach, 2005, Thomas Ehrlich Faculty Award for Svc.-Learning, 2007; named La. Prof. of Yr., Carnegie Found. for Advancement of Tchg. and Coun. for Advancement and Support of Edn., 2009; grantee Cmty. U. Partnership with Old South Baton Rouge, Housing and Urban Devel., 2001—04. Fellow: Am. Inst. Med. and Biological Engring.; mem.: Biol. & Agrl. Engring., Am. Soc. Engring. Edn. (chmn. BAE divsn. 2003—04). Office: Louisiana State University 159 EB Doran Baton Rouge LA 70803 Office Phone: 225-578-1061. Office Fax: 225-578-3492. Business E-Mail: MLima@agcenter.lsu.edu.

LIMA-MAROBONA, JANICE, dermatologist, cosmetics executive; Attended, Nova Southeastern U., Fort Lauderdale, 1993. Diplomate Am. Osteo. Bd. of Dermatology. Intern Met. Gen. Hosp., Clearwater; resident Sun Coast Hosp., Largo; hosp. affiliations Miami Children's Hosp., Mercy Hosp.; dermatologist Bay Pointe Dermatology and Cosmetic Ctr. P.A. Office: Bay Pointe Dermatology and Cosmetic Center PA Ste 104 3850 Bird Rd Miami FL 33146 Office Phone: 305-669-8337. Office Fax: 305-856-4883.

LIMAYEM, MOEZ, science educator, researcher; s. Tahar and Zakia Limayem; m. Alya Chahed, July 30, 1999; children: Karim, Sara. MBA, U. Minn., Mpls., 1988, PhD, 1992. Dept. chair Laval U., Que., Canada, 1992—98, prof., City U., Hong Kong, 1998—2004, U. Lausanne, Switzerland, 2004—07, U. Ark., Fayetteville, Ark., 2007—, dept. chair. Contbr. on rsch. articles (Best Rsch. Paper award, 2003). Pres. Assn. Info. and Mgmt., Paris, 2006. Recipient 3M Best Tchr. award, Can., Hermas award for Excellence, Laval U., Tchg. Excellence award, City U. Hong Kong. Avocations: travel, walking, tennis. Office: Univ Arkansas 204 Business Bldg Fayetteville AR 72701

LIMBACHER, RANDY L., oil industry executive; b. Apr. 1, 1958; BS in Petroleum Engring., La. State U., 1980. V.p., Gulf Coast Divsn. Burlington Resources Oil & Gas Co., Houston, 1996—98, pres., CEO, Gulf Coast Divsn., 1998—2000; pres., CEO BROG GP Inc., 2000—01; sr. v.p., prod. Burlington Resources, Inc., 2001—02, exec. v.p., COO, 2002—06; exec. v.p., exploration & production Americas ConocoPhillips, Houston, 2006—07; pres., CEO Rosetts Resources, Inc., Houston, 2007—, chmn., 2010—. Bd. dirs. ConocoPhillips, 2004—07, Carbo Ceramics, Inc., 2007—, Rosetts Resources Inc., 2007—. Mem.: La. State U. Engring. Industry Adv. Bd., American Petroleum Inst., Ind. Petroleum Assoc. America, Soc. Petroleum Engineers, Houston Area Jr. Achievement. Office: Rosetta Resources Inc 1111 Bagby St Ste 1600 Houston TX 77002-2547 Office Phone: 713-335-4000. Office Fax: 713-335-4197, 713-335-4197. Business E-Mail: rlimbacher@rosettaresources.com.

LIMEHOUSE, HARRY BANCROFT, JR., real estate developer, transportation consultant; b. Charleston, SC, Dec. 3, 1938; m. Frankie Fennell, Jan. 18, 1961; children: Chip, Brien, Barry, Brad. BA in English, The Citadel, 1960, LLD (hon.), 1997, D (hon.) in Bus., 1997; D in Hospitality (hon.), Johnson & Wales U., 1995. Lic. real estate broker S.C. Mgmt. trainee Deering-Millikin, 1960-61; agt. Prudential Ins. Co., Charleston, 1962-67, mgr. W. Palm Beach, Fla., 1967-69; dir. campaign mgmt. divsn. Rep. Nat. Com., Washington, 1967-69; pres., founder Limehouse Properties, Charleston, 1970—. Bankruptcy trustee U.S. Trustee's Office, Columbia, SC, 1988—; commr., chmn. commn., exec. dir. State Transportation Infrastructure Bank Bd., 1997—. Chmn. Pub. Rys. Commn. S.C., 1989—93, 1992—93; past pres. Carolina chpt. Real Estate Securities Inst.; charter pres. Charleston chpt. Comml. Income Properties Coun.; founding pres. Palmetto State Games; chmn. So. Govs. Conf., 1992, S.C. Dept. Transp. Commn., 1994—99; cons. Ga. Dept. Transp., 2000—02; Citadel bd. visitors, 2004. Named Hotelier of the Yr., S.C. Hospitality Assn., 1994, Man of the Yr., 1996, S.F. Taxpayers Assn., Conservationist of the Yr., S.C. Wildlife Fedn., 1996—; named to, Order of the Palmetto, 1995, 1998. Mem.: Nat. Assn. Realtors, Hibernian Soc., Aircraft Owners and Pilots Assn., Downtown Athletic Club. Avocation: flying. Office: Sec Transportation 955 Park No 309 Columbia SC 29201 Office Phone: 803-737-1302. Business E-Mail: limehousehb@scdot.org.

LIMEHOUSE, HARRY BANCROFT, III, (CHIP), state legislator; b. Charleston, SC, Aug. 8, 1962; s. Harry Bancroft II Limehouse and Fennell L. Frances; m. Susan Holliday Ramsay, 1993; children: Alexander Chase, Eliza D. BS, U. SC. Mem. Dist. 110 SC House of Reps., 1994—. Recipient Legislator of Yr., Nat. Solid Waste Mgmt. Assn., 1995. Mem.: Assn. Realtors Legislature Coun., Charleston Trident Assn. Realtors, Hibernian Soc. Charleston, SC Waterfowl Assn., East Cooper Rep. Men's Club, Downtown Charleston Rep. Men's Club. Republican. Episcopal. Address: 22 Menotti St Charleston SC 29401 Mailing: 326C Blatt Bldg Columbia SC 29201 Office Phone: 803-734-2977, 843-577-6242. Fax: 803-577-0504. Business E-Mail: hbl@legis.lpitr.state.sc.us.

LIMPITLAW, JOHN DONALD, publishing executive, clergyman; b. NYC, Jan. 4, 1935; s. Robert and Olga (Lang) L.; m. Susan Elizabeth Glover, May 21, 1960; children: Alison, Amy Elizabeth. BA, Trinity Coll., Hartford, Conn., 1956; MA in Religion, Yale U., 1992. With Marine Midland Bank Trust Co. N.Y., NYC, 1956-61, Celanese Corp., NYC, 1961-63; mgr. personnel Westvaco Corp., NYC, 1963-69; v.p. Warnaco Inc., Bridgeport, Conn., 1969-77, Macmillan Inc., NYC, 1977-89; vicar Parish of Christ's Ch., Easton, Conn., 1992-97; bd. dirs. St. Mark's Day Care Ctr., Bridgeport, 1995—. Seminarian Yale Divinity Sch., New Haven, Conn., 1989-92; trustee Episcopal Investment Funds; bd. dirs. Inter-Ch. Residences, Inc., 3030 Park, Inc.; dir. Operation Hope; bd. dirs. Habitat, Easton, Conn., bd. ops., Fairfield, Conn., 1998—. Democrat. Episcopalian. Avocations: sailing, skiing. Home: 140 Whidah Way Wellfleet MA 02667-7735 also: 160 Moorings Pk Dr Naples FL 34105 Home Phone: 508-349-1190. Personal E-mail: jlimpitlaw@aol.com.

LIN, JEREMY SHUHAO, professional basketball player; b. LA, Aug. 23, 1978; s. Gie-Ming and Shirley Lin. B in Economics, Harvard U., Cambridge, Mass., 2010. Point guard Golden State Warriors, 2010—11, NY Knicks, 2011—12, Houston Rockets, 2012—. Featured in documentary Linsanity, 2013. Founder Jeremy Lin Found., Palo Alto, Calif. Named 1st Team All-Ivy League, 2009, 2010, 1st Team All-Dist. 1, Nat. Assn. Basketball Coaches, 2009, US Basketball Writers Assn., 2010; named one of The 100 Most Influential People in the World, TIME mag., 2012. Achievements include being the first Chinese-American to play in the NBA. Office: Houston Rockets 1510 Polk St Houston TX 77002

LIN, KANT, plastic surgeon, educator; b. NYC, Feb. 9, 1959; s. Samuel Pao-Hsi and Joanna Tu Lin; children: Samantha, Michelle. BA, U. Pa., 1980; MD, Mt. Sinai Sch. Medicine, 1984. Diplomate Am. Bd. Plastic Surgery. Itern Hosp. U. Pa., 1984—85, resident, 1985—91; fellow Hosp. Sick Children U. Toronto, 1991—92; asst. prof. U. Va., Charlottesville, 1992—98, assoc. prof., 1998—2006, full prof., 2007—. Author, editor: Craniofacial Surgery: Science and Surgical Technique, 2001. Named one of Am.'s Top Physicians, Consumers Rsch. Coun. Am. Fellow: ACS, Am. Assn. Plastic Surgeons, Am. Soc. Plastic Surgeons; mem.: Alpha Omega Alpha, Phi Beta Kappa. Office: Univ VA Box 800376 Charlottesville VA 22908 Home: 1105 Hilltop Rd Charlottesville VA 22903 Business E-Mail: kyl5s@virginia.edu.

LIN, MING-CHANG, physical chemistry professor, researcher; b. Hsinpu, Hsinchu, Taiwan, Oct. 24, 1936; came to U.S., 1967, naturalized, 1975; s. Fushin and Tao May (Hsu) L.; m. Juh-Huey Chern, June 26, 1965; children: Karen, Linus H., Ellena J. BSc, Taiwan Normal U., Taipei, 1959; PhD, U. Ottawa, Ont., Can., 1966. Postdoctoral rsch. fellow U. Ottawa, 1965-67; postdoctoral rsch. assoc. Cornell U., Ithaca, NY, 1967-69; rsch. chemist Naval Rsch. Lab., Washington, 1970-74, supervisory rsch. chemist, head chem. kinetics sect., 1974-82, sr. scientist for chem. kinetics, 1982-88; Robert W. Woodruff prof. phys. chemistry Emory U., Atlanta, 1988—2005, Robert W. Woodruff emeritus prof., 2005—, Woodruff sr. rsch. asst., 2005—; dir. Ctr. for Interdise Molecular Sci., 2003—, Ctr. for Green Energy Tech., 2008—; dir Nat. Chiao Tung U., Taiwan. Mem. adv. bd. Internat. Jour. Chem. Kinetics, 1990-93, Inst. Atomic and Molecular Sci., Taipei, 1991-2003, Chemistry, Inst. Physics, Taiwan, 2000-08, Nat. Ctr. for High-performance Computing, Taiwan, 2002—, Nat. Synchrotron Radiation Ctr., Taiwan, 2002-09; mem. young presdl. award com. NSF, Washington, 1990; Nat. Sci. Coun. disting. vis. prof. Nat. Chiao Tung U., Taiwan, 2002-04; Taiwan Semiconductor Mfg. Corp. disting. prof., 2005—; Taiwan Nat. Rsch. Coun. disting. vis. prof., 2005—. Contbr. over 550 articles to profl. jours. 2d lt. Taiwan ROTC, 1960-62. Recipient Civilian Meritorious award USN, 1979, Humboldt award Humboldt Found., 1982, prize in sci. tech. Taiwanese-Am. Found., 1989, The Capt. Robert Dexter Conrad award U.S. Navy, 1998; Guggenheim fellow, 1982. Mem. Am. Chem. Soc. (Hillebrand prize 1975), Combustion Inst., Materials Rsch. Soc., N.Am. Taiwanese Profs. Assn., Sigma Xi (Pure Sci. award 1976 Naval Rsch. Lab. chpt.), Academia Sinica (Taiwan). Achievements include discovery of numerous chemical lasers, use of lasers to elucidate mechanisms of combustion, propulsion and gas-surface reactions; first use of lasers to ionize nonfluorescing radicals and to probe for radicals formed in heterogeneous catalytic reactions. Business E-Mail: chemmcl@emory.edu.

LIN, STEPHEN HOUNG TZE, music educator; b. Louisville, May 20, 1953; s. Richard and Julia (Lam) L.; m. Sharon Elaine Brown, Aug. 20, 1977; children: Stephen Wang Jr, Brittany Brown Lia. B in Music Edn., Morehead State U., 1975; MEd, U. Louisville, 1980. Cert. tchr., Ky. Choral, gen. music tchr. Jefferson County Pub. Schs., 1975—; head music dept. Atherton H.S., Louisville, 1976—. Chair All Jefferson County Sr. High Chorus, Louisville, 1979; guest conductor All-Dist. Jr. H.S. Chorus, Ctrl. Ky. Music Educators Assn., Danville, 1986; mem. Ednl. Profl. Stds. Bd., Ky. 2004. Mem. So. Bapt. Theol. Sem. Oratorio Chorus, Louisville, 1975-76; deacon Broadway Bapt. Ch., Louisville, 1981-85; pres. bd. dirs. Louisville Youth Choir, 1982-83. Recipient Ashland Oil Inc. Tchr. Achievement award, 2002, Excel Tchr. award, WHAS-TV, 2003, LG, 2003, Toyota Internat. Tchr. Prog. award, 2005, Lifetime Music Mentor Achievement award, 2006; named Ky. H.S. Tchr. of Yr., 2002, Ky. Tchr. of Yr., 2002. Mem. NEA, Ky. Educators Assn., Jefferson County Tchrs. Assn., Am. Choral Dirs. Assn. (co-chair nat. conv. 1987—), Ky. Music Educators Assn. (state choral chair 1985-87), Jefferson Dist. Music Educators Assn. (dist. choral chair 1981-85, pres.-elect 1988-89), Louisville Bach Soc. Independent. Office: Atherton High Sch 3000 Dundee Rd Louisville KY 40205

LIN, YUKWENG M., engineer, educator; b. Fuzhou, Fujian, China, Oct. 30, 1923; arrived in U.S., 1954, naturalized, 1964; s. Fa Been and Chi Ying (Cheng) Lin; m. Ying-yuh June Wang, Mar. 29, 1952; children: Jane, Della, Lucia, Winifred. BS, Xiamen U., 1946; MS, Stanford U., 1955, PhD, 1957; D of Engring. (hon.), U. Waterloo, Can., 1994. Tchr. Xiamen U., China, 1946-48, Imperial Coll. Engring., Ethiopia, 1957-58; engr. Vertol Aircraft Corp., Morton, Pa., 1956-57; rsch. engr. Boeing Co., Renton, Wash., 1958-60; asst. prof. U. Ill., Urbana, 1960-62, assoc. prof., 1962-65, prof. aero. and astron. engring., 1965-83; Charles E. Schmidt Eminent scholar chair Coll. Engring., dir. Ctr. for Applied Stochastics Rsch. Fla. Atlantic U., Boca Raton, 1984—2008. Vis. prof. mech. engring. MIT, 1967-68; sr. vis. fellow Inst. Sound and Vibration Research, U. Southampton, Eng., 1976; cons. Gen. Motors Corp., Boeing Co., Gen. Dynamics Corp., TRW Corp., Brookhaven Nat. Lab. Author: Probabilistic Theory of Structural Dynamics, 1967, Probabilistic Structural Dynamics: Advanced Theory and Applications, 1995, Probabilistic Structural Dynamics, 2004; editor: Stochastic Structural Mechanics, 1987, Stochastic Approaches in Earthquake Engineering, 1987, Stochastic Structural Dynamics, 1990, Stochastic Dynamics and Reliability of Nonlinear Ocean Systems, 1994; contbr. articles to profl. jours. Recipient sr. postdoctoral fellowship, NSF, 1967—68, Alexander von Humboldt Sr. US Scientist award, 2000, J.P. Den Hartog award, ASME, 2001. Fellow: ASCE (Alfred M. Freudenthal medal 1984, Theodore von Karman medal 1998), Am. Acad. Mechs.; mem.: Am. Assn. Wind Engring., Internat. Assn. Structural Safety and Reliability (Sr. Rsch. award 1993, Spl. prize for numerous landmark contbns. 2005), Russian Acad. Engring. (fgn. mem.), Nat. Acad. Engring., Sigma Xi. Home: 2684 NW 27th Ter Boca Raton FL 33434-6001 Office: Fla Atlantic U Coll Engring Boca Raton FL 33431

LINCH, KETH, commercial real estate and partnership lawyer; children: Jonathon, Brad, Justin. BS in Acct., U. Ill., Champaign, 1983; JD, Loyola U., Chgo., 1987. CPA Ill., 1983; bar: Ga. 1989, Ill. 1987, US Dist. Ct. (no. dist.), Ga. 1989, US Ct. Appeals (11th cir.) 1989. Shareholder Greenberg Traurig, LLP, Atlanta, 2005—. Recipient Ga. Legal Elite, 2006, 2008—09; named Super Lawyer, Ga. Super Lawyers, 2004; nominee, Chambers & Ptnrs. USA Guide, 2008—10. Mem.: ABA, Urban Land Inst. Achievements include listed in Chambers & Partners USA guide. Office: Greenberg Traurig LLP 3290 Northside Pky Ste 400 Atlanta GA 30327

LINCK, KELLEY, state legislator; m. Jami Linck. BS in Bus., Ark. Tech U. Mem. Rotary Club, Ozark Mountain Region Tourism Assn., Nat. Rifle Assn., Bull Shoals Lake/White River Chamber; mgr. J.B. Hunt Transp.; mem. Dist. 86 Ark. House of Representatives, candidate, Dist. 86, 2006. Republican. Office: 13823 Hwy 14 S Yellville AR 72687-7848 Office Phone: 870-453-6149. Business E-Mail: kelley@kelleylinck.com.

LINCOLN, BLANCHE LAMBERT, lobbyist, former United States Senator from Arkansas; b. Helena, Ark., Sept. 30, 1960; m. Stephen R. Lincoln; 2 children. BS in Biology, Randolph-Macon Woman's Coll., 1982. Intern Sotheby's, NYC; sr. assoc. The Pagonis & Donnelly Group, Inc., 1989-91; mem. US Congress from 1st Ark. Dist., 1992-96; US Senator from Ark., 1999—2011; chmn. US Senate Agrl., Nutrition & Forestry Com., 2009—11; spl. policy adv. Alston & Bird LLP, Washington, 2011—13; founder Lincoln Policy Group, 2013—. Bd. dirs. Entergy Corp., 2011—. Author (with Catherine Whitney): Nine and Counting: The Women of the Senate, 2000. Bd. dirs. Ark. Delta Coun., U. Ark. Med. Sci. Found.; mem. Lower Miss. Delta Develop. Coun., American Red Cross. Recipient Congressional Leadership award, Nat. Telephone Coop. Assn., 2001, Humanitarian of Yr., Ark. Rice Depot, 2002, Humanitarian award, Alzheimer's Assn., 2003, Nat. Energy Leadership award, Nat. Bio-Diesel Bd., 2003, Legislator of Yr. award, Biotechnology Industry Orgn., 2005; named Woman of Yr., Nat. Sportfishing Assn., 1996; named an Outstanding Young American, Jr. Chamber of Commerce, 1999. Democrat. Episcopalian.*

LINCOLN MICHEL, KAREN, publishing executive; b. 1958; BS in Industrial Tech., U. Wis.-Stout, 1981; MA in Journalism, Marquette U., Milw., 1989. Co-owner Indian Country Comm., 1987—2005; reporter La Crosse Tribune, Wis., 1989—92; religion writer, metro staff reporter The Dallas Morning Star, 1992—96; freelance writer, 1997—2005; state bur. chief Green Bay Press-Gazette, Madison, Wis., 2005—08, asst. mng. editor, 2008—12; dir. nat. sales, v.p./gen. mgr. Comcast Spotlight Comcast Cable, 2003—08; owner, pres. Lincoln Media & Consulting Services, Inc., 2008—12; pres., publisher, exec. editor The Daily Advertiser, Lafayette, 2012—, The Daily World, Opelousas, 2012—. Pres. UNITY: Journalists of Color, 2007—09; bd. mem. Wisconsin Ctr. for Investigative Journalism, American Indian Sci. & Engring. Soc. Publishing, Inc.; mem. Gannett Leadership & Diversity Coun. Tribal mem. Ho-Chunk Nation. Mem.: Atlanta Interactive Mktg. Assn. (AIMA), Women in Interactive Mktg. (WIIM), Atlanta Web Executives Round Table (AWERT), Native American Journalists Assn. (pres. 1994—96, v.p. Woodland chpt., Wassaja award). Office: The Daily Advertiser PO Box 5310 Lafayette LA 70502

LIND, THOMAS OTTO, barge transportation company executive; b. New Orleans, Apr. 24, 1937; s. Henry Carl Lind and Elinor (Rooney) Messersmith; m. Eugenia Niehaus, June 8, 1963; children: Elinor Ashley, Elizabeth Kelly. BSME, Tulane U., 1959, LLB, 1965. Cert. mech. engr., 1959. Assoc. Jones, Walker, Waechter, Poitevent, Carrere and Denegre, New Orleans, 1965-66; v.p., sec., counsel Ingram Corp., New Orleans, 1966-84; v.p. Gulf Fleet Marine Corp., New Orleans, 1984-85; v.p., regulatory counsel, sec. and asst. treas. New Orleans Pub. Svc., Inc. and La. Power and Light Co., 1985-92; regional counsel for La. Entergy Svcs., Inc., 1993-94; risk mgr. Canal Barge Co., Inc., New Orleans, 1994-97, sec., 1995—, gen. counsel, 1997—; bd. dirs. Isidore Nowman Sch. Alumni Assn., 2011—12. Trustee Metairie Park Country Day Sch., 1991-95; mem. bd. govs. Trinity Sch., New Orleans, 1982-85; vestryman Trinity Ch., New Orleans, 1987-91; active Family of Cmty. and Utility Supporters, New Orleans, 1987-94; bd. dirs. Greater New Orleans (La.) Coun. Navy League U.S., 2004—. Lt. (j.g.) USN, 1959-62; comdr. USNR, 1962-79. Mem. ABA (ho. of dels. 1996-97), Fed. Energy Bar Assn. (bd. dirs. New Orleans chpt. 1988-92, pres. 1992), La. Bar Assn. (bd. dirs. corp. law sect. 1973-75), La. Assn. Waterway Operators and Shipyards (bd. dirs. 1999—, sec. 2007-09, chair 2009-2011), New Orleans Bar Assn. (bd. dir. 1989-97, 2d v.p. 1989-90, sec. 1992-93, 1st v.p. 1993-94, pres.-elect 1994-95, pres. 1995-96, bd. dirs. New Orleans Pro Bono project 1994-96), New Orleans Bar Found. (bd. dirs. 2008-13), Assn. Corp. Counsel (bd. dirs. La. chpt. 2006—, v.p. 2009-11, pres. 2012-13), La. Orgn. Jud. Excellence (bd. dirs., sec. 1998-2000, v.p. 2000—08), Jud. Excellence Found. (bd. dirs., 2000-), New Orleans Lawn Tennis Club (pres. 1986-88), New Orleans Bar Found. (bd. dirs. 2008-). Republican. Episcopalian. Avocation: tennis. Home: 5423 Perrier New Orleans LA 70115-3130 Office: Canal Barge Co Inc 835 Union St Ste 300 New Orleans LA 70112-1469 Home Phone: 504-895-3893; Office Phone: 504-584-1531. Office Fax: 504-584-1529. Business E-Mail: tlind@canalbarge.com.

LINDBLOM, ERIC, medical products executive; BS in Acctg., The Coll. of NJ, 1982; MBA in Fin., Montclair State U., 1990. Auditor Deloitte & Touche, 1986—89; internal auditor Hoffmann-La Roche, 1989—2001, dir., fin., mfg. svcs., 1991—2001; contr., divisonal, ops. Laboratory Corp. of America Holdings, 2001—07, sr. v.p. investor rels., 2007—09, sr. v.p. investor & media rels., 2009—. Office: Laboratory Corp of America Holdings 358 S Main St Burlington NC 27215 Office Phone: 336-229-1127. Office Fax: 336-513-4510. Business E-Mail: eric_lindblom@labcorp.com.

LINDGREN, CARL EDWIN, educationist, genealogist, historian, photographer; b. Coeburn, Va., Nov. 20, 1949; s. Carl and Ruby (Corder) L. AA in Edn. with honors, N.W. Jr. Coll., 1970; BA in Edn., U. Miss., 1972, MEd, 1977, EdS, 1993; DEd, U. South Africa, 1999. FCP, Coll. of Preceptors, London, 1993. Coord. dept. edn. Delta Hills Edn. Assn., 1976-79; lectr. photography U. Miss., 1979-81; instr. health edn. Batesville Job Corps Ctr. U.S. Dept. Labor, 1980-82; pres., dir. Inst. Ednl. and Hist. Rsch., London, Courtland, Miss., 1981—2000; prof., mil. and medieval history Am. Mil. U. Former sec. gen. His Majesty King Kigeli V of Rwanda; chancellor Imperial Order Dragon of Annam, Crown Prince Bao Long. Contbr. over 200 articles to profl. jours. and mags.; author 10 books; mem. several adv., rev. and editl. bds. including London Inst. Sci. Tech., Ednl. Forum, Introductions, others; one-man shows and exhbns. U.S., Eng. and India. Lay assoc. the Priesthood, Handmaids of the Precious Blood, Cor Jesu Monastery; mem. Internet Franciscan Fraternity, Italy, Confraternity of the Most Holy Rosary (Dominican 15th Century); oblate novice Order of St. Benedict, v.p. Decorated Grand Cross Order of St. Ignatius of Antioch (Vatican), Noble Compania de Ballesteros Hijosdalgo de San Felipe y Santiago; named professed brother Real Irmandade de São Miguel da Ala, professed venerable brother Royal Brotherhood of the Most Holy Miracle of Eucharistic Shrine of Santarém, grand cross Imperial Order of Star of Honor of Ethiopian Empire, knight comdr. with star. The Equestrian Order of Holy Sepulchre of Jerusalem, grand cross Order of St. Michael of the Wing, Knight Comdr., Order of Vila Vicosa, knight comdr. cross Order of Civic and Cultural Merit, Brazil, grand cross Imperial Order of the Dragon of Arman, grand cross Order of the Lion, Rwanda, grand crosses of merit of Democrat Republic of Congo and Ivory Coast, Red Cross; recipient Acad. Achievement award, 1970; EDPA fellow, 1973, Robert A. Taft fellow, 1977; Hon. Life fellow (Jnana Ratna) World Jnana Sadhak Soc., Calcutta, 1978, Cert. of Excellence and Svc. Associateship award India Internat. Photog. Coun., New Delhi, 1991, Mahatma Gandhi Meml. award, 1994, Brotherhood of Blessed Gerard. Fellow: Royal Soc. Arts, Royal Asiatic Soc., Coll. Tchrs. London, World Acad. Art and Sci., Royal Anthrop. Inst.; mem.: Royal Soc. South Africa, Academia Portuguesa de Ex Libris (academician), Hist. Geneal. Soc. Moscow (hon.), Medieval Acad. Am., Asiatic Soc. Calcutta (affiliate), Phi Alpha Theta, Phi Delta Kappa, Kappa Delta Pi, Phi Theta Kappa, KC, Wash. Acad. Sci. Republican. Home: Avalon Woods 10431 Highway 51 Courtland MS 38620-9425 Office: 10431 Highway 51 Courtland MS 38620-9425 Personal E-mail: celindgren@panola.com.

LINDQUIST, JUDITH DOWDLE, lawyer; b. Elmhurst, Ill., Sept. 30, 1949; d. John Axel and Ethel Linea (Johnson) Lindquist; m. John Anthony Dowdle, June 26, 1970; children: John Erick, Andrew Ryden, Lindsay Julia, Claire Linea. BS, U. Ill., 1971; JD, U. Chgo., 1974. Cert. math. tchr. Ill.; bar: Minn. 1974. Atty., rschr. Ill. Legis. Investigating Commn., Chgo., 1972; atty., shareholder Fredrikson & Byron Law Firm, Mpls., 1974—84; of counsel Gray, Plant, Mooty, Mooty & Bennett, Mpls., 1985—88; atty. Hewitt Associates; corp. sec., gen. counsel HE Butt Grocery Co., San Antonio. Mem. Tex. Tax Reform Commn.; bd. dir. Tex. Taxpayers & Rsch. Assn.; mem. employee benefits adv. bd. Jour. of Taxation. Bd. dir., v.p. Southside Family Nurturing Ctr., Mpls., 1978—85; past trustee Minn. Pub. Employees Retirement Assn. Mem.: ABA (com. on continuing profl. edn., adv. group on pensions, tax sect.), Minn. Bar Assn. (chairperson employee benefits sect. 1983—84), Am. Law Inst. (mem. continuing edn. adv. group), Phi Kappa Phi, Phi Beta Kappa, Order of the Coif. Office: HE Butt Grocery Co 646 S Main Ave San Antonio TX 78204 Office Phone: 210-938-8357.

LINDQUIST, STEFANIE A., dean, political science professor; B, Ursinus Coll., Collegeville, Pa.; JD, Temple U., Phila., 1988; PhD in polit. sci., U. SC, 1996. Clk. to Hon. Anthony J. Scirica US Ct. Appeals (3rd cir.), Philadelphia; atty. Latham and Watkins, Washington; rsch. assoc. Fed. Jud. Ctr., Washington; faculty mem. Sch. Pub. and Internat. Affairs, U. Ga., Athens, 1996—2003, assoc. prof., 2003—04, dean, Arch prof. internat. affairs, 2013—; assoc. prof. polit. sci. and law Vanderbilt U., Nashville; positions up to Charles Alan Wright chair in Fed. Cts., assoc. dean external affairs U. Tex. Sch. Law, Austin, 2008—13. Co-dir. Lilly Tchg. Fellows Program U. Ga.; panel mem. Law and Social Sciences Divsn. NSF. Mem. editl. bd.: profl. jours. Rev. Pub. Pers. Adminstrn., 2004—, Jour. of Politics, 2010—; co-author: (books) Judging on a Collegial Court: Influences on Appellate Court Decision Making, 2006; co-author: (with Frank Cross) Measuring Judicial Activism, 2009. Mem.: American Polit. Sci. Assn. (chair law and cts. sect. 2008—09, program chair ann. meeting of law and cts. sect. 2008, Best Conf. Paper Award 2011). Office: School of Public and International Affairs Univ Georgia 201 Candler Hall Athens GA 30602 Office Phone: 706-542-2059. E-mail: sl@uga.edu.

LINDSAY, JOHN W., oil industry executive; BS in Petroleum Engring., U. Tulsa, 1986. Various positions through ops. mgr., Mid-Continent region, divsn. mgr., U.S. land ops. Helmerich & Payne Inc., drilling engr., 1987—97; v.p., U.S. land ops. Helmerich & Payne Internat. Drilling Co., 1997—2006; exec. v.p., U.S. & internat. ops. Helmerich & Payne, Inc., 2006—. Bd. dirs. TerraVici Drilling Solutions, Inc.; chmn. Internat. Assn. Drilling Contractors, 2008; mem. U. Tulsa Petroleum Engring. Adv. Bd. Office: Helmerich & Payne Inc 1437 S Boulder Ave Ste 1400 Tulsa OK 74119 Office Phone: 918-742-5531. Office Fax: 918-742-0237.

LINDSAY, RONALD THOMAS, lawyer; b. Charlotte, NC, 1950; BSChem, NC. State U., 1972; JD, U. NC, 1975. Bar: N.C. 1975. Law clerk, Eastern dist. US Dist. Judge, NC, 1976; assoc. Beaman, Kellum, Mills & Kafer, 1977; ptnr. Bell, Seltzer, Park & Gibson, 1978-86; v.p., gen. coun. & sec. Collins Aikman Corp., Charlotte, NC, 1988—99, sr. v.p., gen. coun. & sec., 1999—2002, sr. v.p., law, 2003; v.p. through exec. v.p., gen. counsel, sec. Bowater, Inc., Greenville, SC, 2004—09; sr. v.p., gen. counsel SCANA Corp., Cayce, SC, 2009—. Office: SCANA Corp 100 SCANA Pky Cayce SC 29033 Office Phone: 803-217-9000. Office Fax: 803-217-8119. Business E-Mail: rlindsay@scana.com.

LINDSAY, SAM A., federal judge; b. San Antonio, 1951; BA, St. Mary's U., 1974; JD, U. Tex., 1977. Staff atty. Tex. Aeronautics Commn., 1977—79; head fed. litig. sect. Dallas City Atty.'s Office, 1979—86, chief litig. divsn., exec. asst. city atty., 1986—90, first asst. city atty., 1990—91, acting city atty., 1991, city atty., 1992—98; judge US Dist. Ct. (no. dist.) Tex., Dallas, 1998—. Office: US Dist Ct 1100 Commerce St Rm 1544 Dallas TX 75242-1003 Office Phone: 214-753-2365.

LINDSEY, EDWARD, state legislator; b. Buckhead, Ga. m. Elizabeth Lindsey; 3 children. BA in History, Davidson Coll., 1981; JD, Ga. Law Sch., 1984. Founding ptnr. Goodman McGuffey Lindsey & Johnson LLP; mem. Dist. 54 Ga. House of Reps., Atlanta, 2005—. Republican. Office: 3340 Peachtree Rd Atlanta GA 30326 also: Ga House of Reps 415 State Capitol Atlanta GA 30334 Office Phone: 404-264-1500, 404-656-5024. Business E-Mail: edward.lindsey@house.ga.gov.

LINDSEY, JENNIFER H., pediatrician; MD, U. Va. Diplomate Am. Bd. Pediatrics, Am. Bd. Pediatrics-pediatric cardiology. Pediatric tng. Univ. NC, Chapel Hill, Univ. Va., fellow in pediatric cardiology; pvt. practice Child Cardiology Assocs., Va. Named to Hall of Fame, Nat. Coll. Athletes. Fellow: Am. Coll. of Cardiology (pediat. sect.), Am. Acad. of Pediatrics; mem.: Am. Acad. of Pediatrics (cardiology sect.). Office: Child Cardiology Associates 8316 Arlington Blvd Ste 500 Fairfax VA 22031 Office Phone: 703-876-8410.

LINDSEY, JOHN H., former insurance agency executive; b. Waxahachie, Tex., July 28, 1922; s. Harry E. and Marie (Smith) L.; m. Sara Houstoun, Aug. 30, 1946; children: Edwin (dec.), David C. BA, Tex. A&M U., 1944. Cons. Lindsey Ins. Agy., Houston, 1953—2002. Past bd. regents Texas A&M U. Sys. Former v.p. Houston Mus. Fine Arts; former pres. Alley Theatre; former bd. dirs. South Tex. Coll. Law, Tex. A&M Rsch. Found., College Station; bd. dirs. George Bush Presdl. Libr. Found.; pres. Tex. A&M U. Alumni, 1964; former vice chmn. bd. visitors U.S. Mil. Acad.; former mem. bd. visitors Tex. A&M at Galveston. 1st lt. US Army, WWII. Recipient Disting. Alumni award Tex. A&M U. Home: 4718 Hallmark Dr Apt 557 Houston TX 77056-3916

LINDSEY, JONATHAN ASMEL, retired academic administrator, academic librarian; b. Bulloch County, Ga., June 9, 1937; s. Joel Wesley and Ethel Iora (Stickland) L.; m. Edythe Annette Loewer, Apr. 3, 1965; children: Julianna Elizabeth, Jonathan Edward. AB, George Washington U., 1961; BD, So. Bapt. Sem., Louisville, 1964; PhD, So. Bapt. Sem., 1968; MSLS, U. Ala., 1975. Assoc. prof., libr. Judson Coll., Marion, Ala., 1967-77; assoc. dean, libr. Meredith Coll., Raleigh, NC, 1977-83; libr. Baylor U., Waco, Tex., 1983-89, dir. found. devel., 1989-95, dir. donor info. and recognition, 1995-2001, asst. v.p. donor and info. svcs., 2001—07. Author librarianship and profl. fund raising, 1988—. Author: (monographs) Free To Be, 1975, Change and Challenge, 1978, Professional Ethics and Librarians, 1985, Performance Evaluation: A Management Basic, 1986; editor: N.C. Libraries (H.W. Wilson award 1981), 1979-83, contbr. articles and book revs. to profl. publs. Mem. Waco Peace Alliance, PTA. Mem. ALA, Assn. Profl. Rschrs. in Advancement, Assn. Fundraising Profls., Coun. for Advancement and Support of Edn., Tex. Libr. Assn. Home: 8265 Mosswood Dr Waco TX 76712-2407

LINDSEY, LAWRENCE BENJAMIN (LARRY LINDSEY), economist, former federal official; b. Peekskill, NY, July 18, 1954; s. Merritt Hunt and Helen Ruth (Hissam) Lindsey; m. Susan Ann McGrath, Aug. 28, 1982; 1 adopted child, Thomas children: Troy, Emily. AB magna cum laude, Bowdoin Coll., Brunswick, Maine, 1976, LLD (hon.), 1993; MA, Harvard U., 1981, PhD, 1985. Sr. tax policy economist Coun. Econ. Advisers, Exec. Office of the Pres., Washington, 1981—84; from asst. prof. to assoc. prof. Harvard U., Cambridge, Mass., 1984—90; faculty rsch. fellow Nat. Bur. Econ. Rsch., Mass., 1984—89; from assoc. dir. to spl. asst. to Pres. for policy devel. The White House, Washington, 1989—91; bd. govs. Fed. Res. Sys., 1991—97; Arthur F. Burns scholar in economics American Enterprise Inst., 1997—2001; mng. dir. Econ. Strategies, Inc., 1997—2001; asst. to Pres. for econ. policy The White House, Washington, 2001—02, dir. Nat. Econ. Coun., 2001—02; pres., CEO The Lindsey Group, Fairfax, Va., 2003—. Chmn. Neighborhood Reinvestment Corp., 1993—97; chief econ. adv. George W. Bush campaign, 1999—2000; vis. scholar Am. Enterprise Inst. Author: The Growth Experiment: How the New Tax Policy is Transforming the U.S. Economy, 1990, Economic Puppetmasters: Lessons From the Halls of Power, 1999; co-author (with Marc Sumerlin): What a President Should Know... but Most Learn Too Late, 2008; contbr. articles to profl. jours. Recipient Outstanding Doctoral Dissertation award, Nat. Tax Assn., 1985, Walter Wriston award, Manhattan Inst., 1988, Disting. Pub. Svc. award, Boston Bar Assn., 1994; fellow Citicorp Wriston Fellow for Econ. Rsch., Manhattan Inst. Office: The Lindsey Group 11320 Random Hills Rd Ste 650 Fairfax VA 22030-7480

LINDSEY, RICHARD J., state legislator; b. June 30, 1956; m. Johna Lindsey, 1983; children: Rich, Anna. BS, Jacksonville State U., Ala. Mem. Dist. 39 Ala. House of Reps., Montgomery, 1983—; mgr. Lindsey Brothers, Inc. Bd. dirs. Farmers & Merchants Bank. Mem. Ebenezer United Meth. Ch. Recipient Lifetime Legis. Leadership award, Coun. Leaders in Ala. Schs.; named Legislator of Yr., Ala. Rural Electric Cooperatives, State Rep. of Yr., Ala. Assn. Conservation Districts. Mem. Centre Rotary, Cherokee County Extension Coun., Forneg Masonic Lodge, Ebenezer Men's Club, Cherokee County C. of C., Southeastern Cotton Ginners Assn. (pres.), Howells Cemetery Assn. (pres.). Democrat. Methodist. Office: 14160 County Rd 22 Centre AL 35960 also: Ala House of Reps Ala State House 11 S Union St Rm 514 Montgomery AL 36130 Office Phone: 256-475-6438, 334-242-7713.

LINDSEY, STEVE, gas industry executive; married; 2 children. B in Mech. Engring., Ga. Inst. Tech. Mng. dir., mktg., new bus. & marketer svcs. Atlanta Gas Light Co., mng. dir., field ops., mgr., engring. and new constrn. supr., distribution engr., comml. and indsl. rep.; joined AGL Resources, Inc., 1989, v.p., ops., 2005—; v.p., gen. mgr. Chattanooga Gas, 2005—. Mem., Govtl. Affairs Coun. Atlanta Com. for Progress (ACP); bd. dirs. Atlanta Union Mission, Liveable Cmty. Coalition; mem. Rotary Club Chattanooga, Tenn. Gas Assn. Office: AGL Resources Inc 10 Peachtree Pl NE Atlanta GA 30309 Office Phone: 404-584-4000. Office Fax: 404-584-3714. Business E-Mail: SLindsey@aglresources.com.

LINDSEY, STEVEN W., astronaut, military officer; b. Arcadia, Calif., Aug. 24, 1960; s. Arden L. and Lois Lindsey; m. Diane Renee Trujillo; 3 children. BS in Engring. Scis., USAF Acad., Colo. Springs, Colo., 1982; MS in Aeronautical Engring., USAF Inst. Tech., Wright Field, Dayton, Ohio, 1990. Commd. 2d lt. USAF, Colo. Springs, 1982, advanced through grades to lt. col., student pilot Reese AFB, Tex., 1982—83; pilot USAF 12th Reconnaissance Squadron, Bergstrom AFB, Tex., 1984—87; grad. student USAF Inst. Tech., Wright AFB, Dayton, Ohio, 1987; test pilot student USAF Test Pilot Sch., Edwards AFB, Calif., 1989—90; test pilot USAF, Eglin AFB, Fla., 1990—93; grad. student USAF Air Command and Staff Coll., Maxwell AFB, Ala., 1993—94; team leader integrated product USAF, Eglin AFB, Fla., 1994—95; astronaut NASA Johnson Space Flight Ctr., Houston, 1996—; ret. USAF, 2006. Dep. Shuttle Ops.; co-chmn. Space Shuttle Cockpit Coun.; chief Internat. Space Station Ops.; pilot STS-87, 1997, STS-95, 1998; mission comdr. STS-104, 2001, STS-121 Discovery, a return-to-flight test mission and assembly flight to the Internat. Space Station, 2006; comdr. STS-133-Final Flight of Discovery, 2011. Recipient Leithen-Tittle award, USAF Test Pilot Sch. Class 89A, 1989, 3 Space Flight medals, NASA, Disting. Flying Cross, Legion of Merit, Def. Superior Svc. medal, Def. Meritorious Svc. medal, NASA Outstanding Leadership medal, NASA Exceptional Svc. medal, Air Force Meritorious Svc. medal, Air Force Commendation medal, Air Force Achievement medal, Aerial Achievement medal; named Disting. Grad. Undergrad. Pilot Tng., USAF, 1983. Mem.: Soc. Exptl. Test Pilots, USAF Acad. Assn. Grads., Assn. Space Explorers. Achievements include 4500 flying hours using 50 different types of aircraft; 3 space flights, mission commander on 1, 896 hours in space. Avocations: camping, skiing, scuba diving, windsurfing, mountain and dirt biking, reading. Office: Astronaut Office/CB Johnson Space Ctr Houston TX 77058

LINDSEY, UVALDE, state legislator; m. Jo Lindsey; 8 children. BSBA in Bus., U. Ark. Mem. Dist. 88 Ark. House of Reps., 2009—. Mem. Harrison City Coun., 1972—82, former chmn. Budget Com. With USAR. Democrat. Office: State Capitol Rm 350 Little Rock AR 72201 also: 2257 E Gentle Oaks Ln Fayetteville AR 72703 Office Phone: 501-682-6211, 501-682-7771, 479-582-2100. Business E-Mail: uvalde.lindsey@gmail.com.

LINDSTROM, ERIC EVERETT, ophthalmologist; b. Helena, Mont., Nov. 28, 1936; s. Everett Harry and Nan Augusta (Johnson) L.; m. Nancy Jo Alexander, July 24, 1960; children: Laura Ann, Eric Everett. BS, Wheaton Coll., 1958; MD, U. Md., 1963; MPH, Harvard U., 1966. Diplomate Am. Bd. Preventive Medicine, Am. Bd. Ophthalmology. Intern Madigan Army Med. Ctr., Tacoma, 1963-64; resident in aerospace medicine Sch. Aerospace Medicine, Brooks AFB, Tex., 1966-68; resident in ophthalmology Brooke Army Med. Ctr., Ft. Sam Houston, Tex., 1972-75; surgeon 12th combat aviation group U.S. Army, Vietnam, 1968-69; chief profl. svcs. and aviation medicine Beach Army Hosp., Ft. Wolters, Tex., 1969-72; asst. chief ophthalmology clinic Madigan Army Med. Ctr., Tacoma, 1975-76; with Lindstrom Eye Clinic, 1987—; med. dir. Palo Pinto County (Tex.) Mental Health Clinic, 1970-72; ret. Cons. Tex. State Rehab. Com., 1971-72; chmn. bd. trustees South Ctrl. Regional Med. Ctr., 1982-2001; sr. aviation med. examiner, FAA; flight surgeon Miss. Air N.G. (ret.). Deacon First Bapt. Ch., Laurel, Miss., 1978—; bd. dirs. Laurel Salvation Army, Good Shepherd Clin., Laurel, William Carey U., Hattiesburg, Miss. Decorated Bronze Star, Air medal with 2 oak leaf clusters, Meritorious Svc. medal. Fellow ACS, Am. Coll. Physician Execs., Am. Coll. Preventive Medicine, Aerospace Med. Assn. (assoc.), Am. Acad. Ophthalmology; mem. AMA, Am. Acad. Cataract and Refractive Surgery, New Orleans Acad. Ophthalmology, Miss. Med. Assn. (pres.), South Miss. Med. Soc., So. Med. Assn. (pres.), Flying Physicians Assn., Soc. Mil. Ophthalmologists, Soc. USAF and US Army Flight Surgeons, Alliance Air N.G. Flight Surgeons, Mil. Officers Assn. Am., Aircraft Owners and Pilots Assn., Kiwanis, Nu Sigma Nu. Home: 809 Cherry Ln Laurel MS 39440-1651 Office: Lindstrom Eye Clinic PO Box 407 Laurel MS 39441-0407 Office Phone: 601-426-9454. Business E-Mail: drelindstrom@gmail.com.

LINEHAN, SCOTT THOMAS, professional football coach; b. Sunnyside, Wash., Sept. 17, 1963; s. William and Margaret Linehan; m. Kristen Linehan; children: Matthew, Michael, Marcus. BA, U. Idaho, 1987. Wide receivers coach U. Idaho Vandals, 1989—91, offensive coord., quarterbacks coach, 1992—94; quarterbacks coach U. Nev. Las Vegas Rebels, 1991—92; wide receivers coach U. Wash. Huskies, 1994—96, offensive coord., 1996—98; offensive coord., quarterbacks coach U. Louisville Cardinals, 1999—2001, Minn. Vikings, 2002—05; offensive coord. Miami Dolphins, 2005—06, Detroit Lions, 2009—13; head coach St. Louis Rams, 2006—08; passing game coord. Dallas Cowboys, 2014—. Office: Dallas Cowboys 1 Cowboys Pky Irving TX 75063*

LINEN, JONATHAN S., diversified financial services company executive; Joined American Express Co., 1969; pres., CEO, dir. mktg. group and travelers cheque group Am. Express Co. Travel Related Svcs., 1988-90; pres., CEO Shearson Lehman Bros., 1990—92; pres., COO Am. Express Travel Related Svcs., 1992—93; vice chmn. American Express Co., NYC, 1993—2005, adv. to chmn., 2006—, mem. Global Leadership Team. Bd. dir. Yum! Brands Inc., Bausch & Lomb, Intercontinental Hotels Group. Mailing: Yum! Brands Bd Directors 1900 Col Sanders Lane Louisville KY 40213

LINER, DAVID B., lawyer; b. 1955; m. Lori Liner; children: Michael, Daniel. BA, U. Mich., 1976; JD, Wayne State U., Detroit, 1980. Mem. legal dept. Masco Corp., 1980—97; v.p., gen. counsel MascoTech, Inc. (now Metaldyne Corp.), 1997—2001; atty., mem. corp. fin. group, head automotive industry practice team and China practice Dykema Gossett, PLLC, Mich., 2001—05; v.p., gen. counsel, sec. Roper Industries, Inc., 2005—. Office: Roper Industries Inc Ste 200 6901 Professional Pky E Sarasota FL 34240 Office Phone: 941-556-2601. Office Fax: 941-556-2670.

LINGAMFELTER, L. SCOTT, state legislator; b. NYC, Mar. 27, 1951; m Shelley Elizabeth Glick; children: Amy, John, Paul. BA in History, Va. Mil. Inst., Lexington, 1973; MA in Govt. and Fgn. Affairs, U. Va., 1981. Career officer, ret. col. US Army, 1973—2001; mil. asst. to the dir., operational test and evaluation Office of Sec. Def.; mem. Dist. 31 Va. House of Delegates, Richmond, 2001—. Mem Christ Our Lord Ch., Lake Ridge, Va. Decorated Bronze Star, Legion of Merit, Def. Superior Svc. medal, Def. Meritorious Svc. medals, Joint Svc. Commendation medal, Army Commendation medal, Nat. Def. Svc. medal, SW Asia Svc. medal, Kuwait Liberation medal, Saudi-Kuwaiti Liberation medal, UN Svc. medal; named Citizen of Yr., Va. Family Found., 2000. Mem.: Soc. 1st Divsn., America Legion, VFW, Assn. US Army, William C. of C., Lake Ridge Rotary. Republican. Episcopalian. Office: 5420 Lomax Way Woodbridge VA 22193 also: Capitol Office Gen Assembly Rm 403 PO Box 406 Richmond VA 23218 Office Phone: 703-580-1294, 703-590-7090, 804-698-1031. Office Fax: 804-698-6731. Business E-Mail: DelSLingamfelter@house.virginia.gov.

LINGINFELTER, HENRY P. (HANK), gas distribution company executive; B in Indsl. Mgmt., Ga. Tech; MBA, Ga. State U. Pres. Va. Natural Gas AGL Resources, Inc., 2000—07, pres. Elizabethtown Gas, 2004—07, pres. Elkton Gas, 2004—07, sr. v.p., Mid Atlantic ops., 2004—07, exec. v.p., utility ops. & chmn, CEO utility subs., 2007—. Recipient Paul A Askew Cmty. Svc. Award. Mem.: Leadership Atlanta Class, Leadership Coun. Am. Gas Assn., The Nature Conservancy, Southern Gas Assn., Ctrl. Atlanta Progress. Office: AGL Resources Inc Ten Peachtree Place Atlanta GA 30309 Office Phone: 404-584-4000. Office Fax: 404-584-3945. Personal E-mail: HLinginfelter@aglresources.com.

LINK, SCOTT J., lawyer; b. Kankakee, Ill., Oct. 16, 1961; BS with honors, Ea. Ill. U., 1983; JD magna cum laude, No. Ill. U., 1986. Bar: Fla. 1986, US Dist. Ct. (no., so., middle dist. Fla.), US Ct. Appeals (11th cir.). Ptnr. Gunster Yoakley & Stewart, 1986—96; founding ptnr., bus. & securities litig. Ackerman Link & Sartory P.A., West Palm Beach, Fla., 1996—. Mem. NASD Nat. Arbitration & Mediation Com. Recipient Legal Elite, 2006—11; named Fla. Super Lawyers, 2006, 2008—09, 2011; named one of Fla. Legal Elite, Fla. Trend mag., 2004, 2005, Best Lawyers in America, 2003—06, 2011; named to Top Lawyers List, South Fla. Legal Guide mag., 2003, 2004, 2005, 2006. Mem.: ABA, Fla. Bar, Palm Beach County Bar Assn. Office: Suite 1250 222 Lakeview Ave West Palm Beach FL 33401 Office Phone: 561-838-4100. Office Fax: 561-838-5305. Business E-Mail: slink@alslaw.com.

LINKER, RAYMOND OTHO, JR., lawyer; b. Charlotte, NC, Jan. 18, 1946; s. Raymond Otho Sr. and Frances (Baucom) L.; m. Nola Grady Jenning, June 24, 1969; 1 child, John Raymond. BS in Chem.

Engring., N.C. State U., 1968; JD, Georgetown U., 1972. Bar: N.C. 1972, U.S. Dist. Ct. (we. dist.) N.C. 1972, U.S. Patent Trademark Office 1972. From assoc. to ptnr. Bell, Seltzer, Park & Gibson, Charlotte, 1972—; ptnr., intellectual property, chem.,pharmaceutical patents practice group Alston & Bird LLP, Charlotte. Mem. N.C. Bar Assn., Am. Intellectual Property Assn., Carolinas Patent, Trademark and Copyright Law Assn. (past pres.). Presbyterian. Office: Alston & Bird LLP Ste 4000 Bank of Am Plaza 101 S Tryon St Charlotte NC 28280 Office Phone: 704-444-1010. E-mail: rlinker@alston.com.

LINKOUS, WILLIAM JOSEPH, JR., lawyer; b. Roanoke, Va., July 17, 1929; s. William Joseph and Mary Virginia (Lester) L.; m. Anita Marie Stedronsky, Oct. 15, 1960; children: William Joseph III, Brian Keith BA, Roanoke Coll., Salem, Va., 1951; MA in Econs., U. Va., 1954, JD, 1956. Bar: Va. 1956, Ga. 1957. Assoc. Powell, Goldstein, Frazer & Murphy, Atlanta, 1956-62, ptnr., 1962—79, 1985—2008, mng. ptnr. Atlanta, 1979-85; of counsel Bryan Cave LLP, Atlanta, 2009—. Trustee Holy Innocents Episcopal Sch., Atlanta, 1974-80, Roanoke Coll., 1980-95, emeritus 1995—. Fellow Am. Coll. Trust and Estate Counsel, Am. Bar Found.; mem. State Bar Ga. (past chmn. fiduciary sect., chmn. Ga. trust code revision com. 1988-91, 2003-08, chmn. Ga. probate code revision com. 1991-97, chmn. Ga. guardianship code revision com.1997-2003), Va. State Bar, Am. Law Inst., Atlanta Estate Planning Coun. (pres. 1983-84). Avocation: tennis. Office: Bryan Cave LLP One Atlantic Ctr Fourteenth Fl 1201 West Peachtree St NW Atlanta GA 30309-3488 Office Phone: 404-572-6610. Business E-Mail: william.linkous@bryancave.com.

LINNEHAN, RICHARD M., astronaut, veterinarian; b. Lowell, Mass., Sept. 19, 1957; BS in Animal Scis. with minor in Microbiology, U. New Hampshire, Durham, 1980; DVM, Ohio State U. Coll. Vet. Medicine, Columbus, 1985; DSc (hon.), U. New Hampshire, 2002, Suffolk U., 2002. Veterinarian Pvt. Practice, 1985—86; intern in Zoo animal medicine and comparative pathology Balt. Zoo and Johns Hopkins U., 1987—89; commd. Capt. U.S. Army Vet. Corps., 1989; chief clin. vet., Naval Ocean Systems Ctr. USN Marine Mammal Program, San Diego, 1989—92; astronaut NASA Johnson Space Ctr., Houston, 1992—. Flight software verification, Shuttle Avionics Integration Lab. (SAIL); assigned to astronaut Office Mission Develop. Br, working on payload develop. and mission develop. flight support for future Space Shuttle missions; mission specialist, Life Scis. and Microgravity Spacelab mission STS-78 Mission (Columbia), 1996; payload comdr. STS-90, Neurolab Mission (Columbia), 1998; mem. of 4-man EVA crew STS-109/HST Servicing Mission 3B (Columbia), 2002; crew mem., mission to deliver the Japanese Logistics Module and the Canadian Spl. Purpose Dexterous Manipulator to the Internat. Space Station (ISS) STS-123 Mission (Endeavour), 2008; faculty mem. N.C. State U. Coll. Vet. Medicine, Raleigh-Durham, NC, 1998—; bd. dirs. Tulane/Xavier Astrobiology Ctr., New Orleans, 1998—, Channel Islands Marine and Wildlife Inst., Santa Barbara, Calif. Recipient NASA Space Flight medals, 1996, 1998, 2002, NASA Outstanding Leadership medal, 1999, Navy Group Achievement award, Navy Commendation medal, Alumni award, Ohio State U. Coll. Vet. Medicine, Disting. Alumni award, Ohio State U., 1997, 2002, U. New Hampshire Disting. and Outstanding Alumni awards. Mem.: Assn. Space Explorers, Internat. Assn. Acquatic Animal Medicine, Am. Assn. Zoo Veterinarians, Am. Vet. Med. Assn. (president's award), Explorers Club. Achievements include 3 space flights, 43 days in space including 3 space walks. Avocations: sports, natural history, oudoor activities. Office: Astronauts Office/CB Johnson Space Ctr Houston TX 77058

LINQUIST, ROGER D., telecommunications industry executive; children: Corey A., Todd C. Founder PageMart Wireless, 1989, chmn., CEO, 1989—93, chmn., 1993—94; co-founder MetroPCS Comm., Dallas, 1994, chmn., pres., CEO, 1994—2011, chmn., CEO, 2011—. Founding dir. Cellular Telecommunications & Internet Assn. Mailing: MetroPCS Comm PO Box 601119 Dallas TX 75360

LINSZ, MARK DOUGLAS, diversified financial services company executive; b. May 23, 1964; Joined Chgo. Rsch. & Trading Group (CRT), 1987, CRT purchased by NationsBank; head market risk NationsBank-CRT (now Bank of America); Asia market risk mgr. Bank of America Corp., Hong Kong, 1998, mgr. global corp. & investment banking compliance group, chief compliance officer, chief risk officer Europe, Middle East & Africa (EMEA) and Asia, global market risks mgmt. exec., corp. treas., 2009—. Bd. dirs. BlackRock Inc., 2009—. Office: Bank of America Corp Hdqs 100 N Tryon St Charlotte NC 28255 Business E-Mail: mark.linsz@bankofamerica.com.

LINTON, DAVID J., aerospace and defense manufacturing executive; BS in Mech. Engring., U. Wis., Madison; MBA, Rockford Coll. V.p., gen. mgr., Electric Sys. Hamilton Sundstrand Corp., 1998—2001; CEO Cordiem, Inc., 2001—02; v.p., program mgmt. Raytheon Network Centric Sys., 2003—04; pres. Curtiss-Wright Flow Control Corp., 2004—; v.p. Curtiss-Wright Corp., 2004—, co-COO, 2008—. Bd. dirs. Cordiem LLC, Jet-A.com. Bd. dirs. Fairfax Symphony Orchestra, Valve Mfrs. Assn. Office: Curtiss Wright Flow Control Co 2941 Fairview Pk Dr Ste 850 Falls Church VA 22042 Office Phone: 973-597-4700. Office Fax: 703-286-2000.

LINZEY, DONALD WAYNE, biologist, educator, researcher; b. Balt., Md., Sept. 4, 1939; s. Charles Herbert and Dorothy Katherine Linzey; m. Juanita Bird Linzey, May 18, 1985; m. Alicia Terry Vogt, June 2, 1963 (div. Oct. 19, 1982); children: David Wayne, Thomas Alan. BA, Western Md. Coll. (now McDaniel Coll.), Westminster, Md., 1961; MS, Cornell U., Ithaca, NY, 1963, PhD, 1966. Instr. biology Cornell U., Ithaca, 1966—67; assoc. prof. biology U. South Ala., Mobile, 1967—77; instr., rsch. assoc. Va. Tech., Blacksburg, 1977—82, instr., 2012—, adj. instr., 2013—; prof. biology Wytheville CC, Va., 1989—. Chmn. Va. Cougar Investigation, Blacksburg, 1978—; rsch. assoc. Va. Mus. Natural History, Martinsville, 1988—90; dir. Blue Ridge Highlands Regional Sci. Fair, Dublin, 1992—; chmn. mammal taxonomic working group All Taxa Biodiversity Inventory, Gt. Smoky Mountains Nat. Pk., Gatlinburg, Tenn., 1996—; lectr. Wilderness Wildlife Week, Pigeon Forge, Tenn., 1996—; rsch. assoc. Bermuda Zool. Soc., Flatts, Hamilton, Bermuda, 1997—; cons. in field. Author: Mammals of Great Smoky Mountains National Park, 1971, 1995, Alabama Wildlife, Vols. 1 and 2, 1972—73, Snakes of Alabama, 1979, Snakes of Virginia, 1981;; rev. edit., 1995, The Mammals of Virginia, 1998, Vertebrate Biology, 2001, 2nd edit, 2012, A Natural History Guide To Great Smoky Mountains National Park, 2008; editor: Endangered and Threatened Plants and Animals of Virginia, 1979. Mem. bd. dirs. Montgomery County Humane Soc., 2009—; active Ea. Cougar Found., North Springs, W.Va., 2000—07, Va. Mus. Natural History, Martinsville, 1988—90. Recipient Outstanding Faculty award, Commonwealth of Va. State Coun. of Higher Edn., 1996, C.C. Leadership Program award, Nat. Orgn. for Staff and Orgnl. Devel. Austin, Tex., 1996, 1998, 2001, Chancellor's Professorship award, Va. CC Sys., 1998, Disting. Svc. award, Wytheville CC, 1998, Disting. Alumni award, McDaniel Coll. (formerly Western Md. Coll.), 2003, 2010, Alumni Cmty. Svc. award, 2010, 2014, Thomas Jefferson medal, Va. Mus. Natural History., 2014; named Va. Prof. of Yr., Carnegie Found. for the Advancement Sci., 1999—2000. Mem.: Human Soc. Montomery County (bd. dir.), Discover Life In America (bd. dir.), Yellowstone Assn. for Natural Sci., History, and Edn. (assoc.), Va. Natural History Soc. (assoc.), Va. Herpetological Soc. (assoc.), Gt. Smoky Mountains Assn. (assoc.), Friends of the Gt. Smoky Mountains (assoc.), Human Anatomy and Physiology Soc. (assoc.), Nature Conservancy (assoc.), Am. Soc. Mammalogists (life), Sigma Xi. Democrat. Methodist. Avocations: travel, hiking, wildlife observation, collecting mechanical banks. Home: 1418 Nellies Cave Rd Blacksburg VA 24060 Office: Wytheville Cmty Coll 1000 E Main St Wytheville VA 24382 Office Phone: 450-231-2290. Office Fax: 276-223-4826. Business E-Mail: dlinzey@wcc.vccs.edu, dlinzey@vt.edu.

LIPINSKI, JOHN J. (JACK), oil industry executive; BChemE, Stevens Inst. Tech.; JD, Rutgers Univ. Mgmt. positions Texaco; mgmt. positions through v.p. refining Coastal Corp., 1985—2001; exec. v.p. refining & chemicals El Paso Corp., 2001—02; ptnr., mng. dir. Prudentia Energy, 2004; pres., CEO Coffeyville Resources, 2005—06, CVR Energy, Inc., Sugar Land, Tex., 2006—07, chmn., pres., CEO, 2007—; CEO CVR Partners LP. Office: CVR Energy Ste 500 2277 Plaza Dr Sugar Land TX 77479

LIPNICK, ROBERT LOUIS, chemist, toxicologist, consultant; b. Balt., Sept. 9, 1941; s. David Aaron and Dorothy (Moss) L.; m. Anne Ruth Goldberg, June 11, 1967; children: Deborah Lipnick Silverman, David Henry. BS in Chemistry, U. Md., Coll. Pk., 1963; PhD in Organic Chemistry, Brandeis U., 1969. Postdoctoral fellow dept. chemistry U. Minn., Mpls., 1968-72; rsch. assoc. Sloan-Kettering Inst. Cancer Rsch., Rye, NY, 1974-79; leader, structure activity group US EPA, Washington, 1980—85, sr. chemist, 1985—2008; com. sci. fellow US Dept. of State, Washington, 1993—94. Vis. lectr. various African univs., 1973-74, 125th anniversary of Pharmacological Inst. U. Marburg, Germany, 1992; Crafoord Found. vis. scientist Pharm. Inst., U. Lund, Sweden, summer 1989; Umweltbundesamt vis. scientist Borstel Rsch. Inst., Fed. Republic of Germany, summer 1986; co-organizer EPA workshop on structural properties determining mechanisms of toxic action, 1988; invited lectr. on quantitative structure-activity relationships in environ. chemistry and toxicology Commn. of European Communities, Ispra, Italy, 1990; invited feature lectr. Duke U. Med. Ctr. Libr., 2004; invited sci. specialist, 1992; mem. internat. sci. com. 4th Internat. Workshop on Quantitative Structure-Activity Relationships Environ. Toxicology, Netherlands, 1990, 5th, Duluth, Minn., 1991; invited speaker Rekker Symposium, Netherlands, 1993; organizer Am. Chem. Soc. Symposium, San Francisco, 2006, SETAC Nat. Meeting, New Orleans, 2009; mem. EPA Agy.-wide Risk Assessment Forum project on guidance and tools for modeling metals bioaccumulation, 2005-08. Author: (with others) Probing Bioactive Mechanisms, 1989, Comprehensive Medicinal Chemistry, 1990, SETAC Special Symposium (New Orleans), From Molecular Structure to Properties and Toxicology, In Honor of Dr. Bob Lipnick, 2010; editor: C.E. Overton's Studies of Narcosis, 1991; mem. editorial bd. Xenobiotica, Quantitative Structure Activity Relationships; co-editor Persistent Bioaccumulative and Toxic Chemicals, 2000, Chemicals in the Environment: Fate, Transport, and Remediation, 2002; assoc. editor Spl. Publs., Soc. Environ. Toxicology and Chemistry; manuscript reviewer; contbr. 72 sci. pubs., articles to profl. jours., chapters to books. Bd. dirs., v.p. Friends of Marshlands, Rye, 1977-79; bd. dirs. Dowden Terr. Recreation Assn., Alexandria, Va., 1984-85; mem. publs. com. Wood Libr.-Mus. of Anesthesiology, 1993—94; mem. validation and tech. transfer com. Johns Hopkins U. Ctr. for Alternatives to Animal Testing; mem. Interagency Regulatory Alternatives Group; US rep. sound mgmt. chem. group working group, Trilateral CEC 2004-07. Mem. Am. Chem. Soc. (mem. environ. chem. divsn. exec. com.), Soc. Environ. Toxicology and Chemistry (charter), QSAR Soc., Phi Kappa Phi Hon. Frat. Jewish. Home: 5308 Pender Ct Alexandria VA 22304-1937 Office Phone: 703-864-6082. Personal E-mail: rllipnick@verizon.net.

LIPOFF, NORMAN HAROLD, lawyer; b. NYC, Dec. 9, 1936; s. Benjamin and Anna (Lippow) L.; m. Nancy B. Bressler, June 12, 1960; children: Ann, Elise. BSBA in Acctg., U. Fla., 1958, JD with honors, 1961; LLM in Taxation, NYU, 1962. Bar: Fla. 1961. With Carlton, Fields, Ward, Emmanuel, Smith & Cutler, Tampa, Fla., 1962-70; ptnr. to of counsel Greenberg Traurig (formerly Greenberg, Traurig, Hoffman, Lipoff, Rosen & Quentel), Miami, Fla., 1970—. Pres. Greater Miami Jewish Fedn., 1982-84; nat. chmn. United Israel Appeal, 1990-94; chmn. Endowment Fund Devel. Coun. of Jewish Fedns., 1980-85; nat. vice-chmn. United Jewish Appeal, 1978-98; bd. govs. Tel-Aviv U.; bd. govs., exec. com. Jewish Agy. for Israel, 1984-96; vice-chmn. Fla. Philharmonic Orch. Governing Coun., 1998-2001; pres. Jewish Telegraphic Agy., 2001-03, chmn., 2003-05. Recipient Pres. Leadership award Greater Miami Jewish Fedn., 1972, Pres. award Tel Aviv U., 1982, Brotherhood award NCCJ, 1988. Mem. ABA (tax sect.), Fla. Bar Assn. (chmn. tax sect. 1972, Outstanding Tax Lawyer in Fla. award 1989), U. Fla. Norman H. Lipoff Hall Hillel Jewish Student Ctr. Democrat. Home: Three Grove Isle Dr 1009 Coconut Grove FL 33133 Office: Greenberg Traurig 333 SE 2nd Ave Ste 4400 Miami FL 33131 Home Phone: 305-856-9718; Office Phone: 305-579-0503. Office Fax: 305-961-5503. Business E-Mail: lipoffn@gtlaw.com.

LIPPMAN, IRVIN M., museum director; b. 1948; BFA, U. Denver; MA in Art History, U. Tex., Austin. Staff lectr. Nat. Gallery Art, Washington, 1977—82; chief of pub. affairs Amon Carter Mus., Ft. Worth, 1983—88, asst. dir., 1988—94; exec. dir. Columbus Mus. Art, Columbus, Ohio, 1994—2002; pres., exec. dir. Mus. Art, Ft. Lauderdale, Fla., 2003—. Mem.: Assn. Art Mus. Dirs. Office: Mus Art Ft Lauderdale 1 E Las Olas Blvd Fort Lauderdale FL 33301 Office Phone: 954-525-5500. Office Fax: 954-524-6011.

LIPPMAN, MARC ESTES, oncologist, educator, medical researcher; b. Bklyn., Jan. 15, 1945; BA magna cum laude, Cornell U., 1964; MD, Yale U., 1968. Intern Osler med. svc. Johns Hopkins Hosp., Balt., 1968-69, asst. resident, oncology, 1969-70; clin. assoc. leukemia svc. Nat. Cancer Inst., NIH, Washington, 1970-71, clin. assoc. lab. biochemistry, 1971-73, sr. investigator med. br., 1974-88, head med. breast cancer sect., 1976-88; clin. prof. medicine and pharmacology Uniformed Svcs. U. Health Scis., 1978-88; dir. Vincent T. Lombardi Cancer Rsch. Ctr. Georgetown U., Washington, 1988—2001, prof. medicine and oncology, 1988—2001, also chair, dept. oncology, chief, divsn. hematology/oncology; John G. Searle prof. and chair, dept. internal medicine U. Mich. Health Sys., 2001—07; Kathleen & Stanley Glaser prof., chmn., dept. medicine Leonard M. Miller Sch. Medicine, U. Miami, 2007—. Mem. merit rev. bd. oncology Vet. Adminstrn. Med. Rsch. Svc., 1977-81, endocrine treatment com. Nat. Surg. Adjuvant Breast Project, 1977-86; cons. dept. pharmacology George Washington Sch. Medicine, 1978-89; co-chmn. Gordon Rsch. Conf. on Hormone Action, 1984, chmn., 1985; treas. Internat. Congress Hormones & Cancer, 1984—; mem. med. adv. bd. Nat. Alliance Breast Cancer Orgn., 1986—; mem. stage III monitoring com. Nat. Surg. Adjuvant Project Breast & Bowel Cancers, 1987-89; bd. trustees Am. Cancer Soc., Washington, 1989-92; mem. sci. adv. bd. Coordinated Coun. Cancer Rsch., 1989—; hon. dir. Y-ME, Nat. Orgn. Breast Cancer Info. & Support, 1990—; Woodward vis. prof., mem. Sloan-Kettering, 1990; Sidney Sachs Meml. lectr. Case Western Reserve, 1985, D.R. Edwards lectr. Tenovus Inst., Wales, 1985, Gosse lectr. Dalhousie U., Halifax, N.S., 1987, Transatlantic lectr. Brit. Endocrine Socs., 1989, Barofsky lectr. Howard U., 1990, Rose Kushner Meml. lectr. Long Beach Meml. Med. Ctr., 1990, Constance Wood Meml. lectr. Hammersmith Hosp., Eng., 1991; adj. prof. internal medicine, U. Mich. Med. Sch., Ann Arbor, Mich., 2007-; mem. clin. adv. bd., Raven Biotechnologies, Inc.; mem. scientific adv. bd., Seattle Genetics, 2000-, Perseus-Soros Fund; bd. dir. Ascenta Therapeutics; co-founder Oncologix (sold to Aronex), Peregrine Biotechnology (sold to Techniclone); invited spkr. in field. Contbr. articles to profl. jours., chapters to books. Endocrinology fellow Yale Med. Sch., 1973-74; recipient Mallinckrodt award Clin. Radioassay Soc., 1978, D.R. Edwards medal Tenovus Inst., 1985, Transatlantic medal Brit. Endocrine Socs., 1989, Tiffany award of Distinction, Komen Found., 1989, Brinker Internat. prize for Basic Rsch. in Breast Cancer. Fellow ACP, Am. Fedn. Clin. Rsch.(Clin. Investigator prize), Am. Soc. Cell Biology, Am. Assn. Cancer Rsch. (program com. 1986, Richard and Hinda Rosenthal Found. award, 1994), Am. Soc. Clin. Oncology (program com. 1987-89, chmn. local organizing com. 1989-90), Endocrine Soc. (pub. affairs com. 1980-81, Edward B. Astwood Lecture award, 1991), Metastasis Rsch. Soc.; mem. Assn. Am. Physicians, Am. Soc. Clin. Investigators (program com. 1988), Am. Soc. Biol. Chemists, Alpha Omega Alpha. Achievements include research in growth regulation of cancer, breast cancer, cancer endocrinology, growth factor receptors. Office: U Miami Dept Medicine Room 1001 MSTL 1430 NW 11th Ave Miami FL 33101 Office Phone: 305-243-9120. Business E-Mail: mlippman@med.miami.edu.

LIPPMAN, SCOTT MICHAEL, oncologist, educator; b. Columbia, SC, Apr. 2, 1955; s. Melvyn and Nanette (Gwirtzman) Lippman; m. Mary Elizabeth Marsh, Feb. 27, 1987; children: Kyle Andrew, Elizabeth Pauline. BS in Biol. Sci., magna cum laude, U. Calif., Irvine, 1977; MD, Johns Hopkins U. Sch. Medicine, Balt., 1981. Diplomate Am. Bd. Internal Medicine, cert. in Hematology, Med. Oncology, lic. Calif., Ariz., Tex. Intern in internal medicine Johns Hopkins Hosp., 1981—82; resident internal medicine Harbor-UCLA Med. Ctr., 1982—84; resident hematology Stanford U. Sch. Medicine, Calif., 1984—85; fellow med. oncology U. Ariz. Cancer Ctr., Tucson, 1985—87; clin. dir., faculty mem. cancer prevention/control prog. U. Ariz., 1987-88; asst. prof. medicine U. Tex. M.D. Anderson Cancer Ctr. & Grad. Sch. Biomed. Scis., Houston, 1988-92, assoc. prof. medicine, 1992-96, clinic chief head & neck medical oncology, 1994—96, prof. medicine, chair dept. clin. cancer prevention, 1996—. Mem. Am. Fedn. Clin. Rsch., 1982, Gulf Coast Hematology Soc., 1989, Am. Assn. Cancer Edn., 1989—99, Am. Soc. Preventive Oncology, 1989—99; chmn. chemoprevention subcom. Radiation Therapy Oncology Group, Phila., 1990—98; mem. numerous spl. rev. coms./panels Nat. Cancer Inst., Bethesda, Md., 1991—; vis. prof. U. Calif. Cancer Ctr., Irvine, 1991, Cancer Therapy & Rsch. Ctr., San Antonio, 1993, Orlando Cancer Ctr., Fla., 1993, Vancouver Cancer Ctr., Canada, 1997; cons. FDA, 1999. Assoc. editor Cancer Prevention Internat., 1993—95, Jour. of Nat. Cancer Inst., 1994—, Cancer Epidemiology Biomarkers & Prevention, 1998—, Clin. Cancer Rsch., 1999—, mem. editl. bd. Investigational New Drugs, 1995—97, 1997—, Jour. Cancer Edn., 1996—, Jour. Oncology: Index & Reviews, 1996—2000, Jour. Cellular Biochemistry, 1997—99, Cancer Therapeutics, 1997—99, Breast Cancer, 1998—, Internat. Jour. Oncology, 2002—, Head & Neck, 2003—, Oral Oncology, 2005—; contbr. articles to profl. jours., chapters to books. Recipient Tchg. award, Am. Acad. Family Physicians, 1987, Career Development award, Am. Cancer Soc., 1989—92, Sci. Writers award, 1990, 1994, Faculty Achievement award for cancer prevention, U. Tex., 1998; grantee NIH, 1980. Fellow: ACP, Internat. Acad. Oral Oncology (founding fellow), Am. Coll. Nutrition; mem.: AMA (cons. divsn. drugs/toxicology 1994), Internat. Assn. for Study of Lung Cancer, Soc. Head & Neck Surgeons (membership com. 1994), Am. Soc. Hematology, Am. Assn. Cancer Rsch. (prog. com. 1993—2002, awards com. 2000—03, pubs. com. 2002—07), Am. Soc. Clin. Oncology (cancer prevention/control com. 1993—96, edn. com. 2000—03, mem. Breast Cancer Risk Reduction Update Panel 2005—, Travel award 1985), Am. Chem. Soc., Harris County Med. Soc., Tex. Med. Assn. Avocation: tennis. Office: U Tex MD Anderson Cancer Ct Cancer Prevention Bldg CPB6 3468 1155 Pressler Houston TX 77030-4009 Office Phone: 713-745-3672. Office Fax: 713-794-4679. Business E-Mail: slippman@mdanderson.org.

LIPSCOMB, OSCAR HUGH, archbishop emeritus; b. Mobile, Ala., Sept. 21, 1931; s. Oscar Hugh and Margaret (Saunders) Lipscomb. STL, Gregorian U., Rome, 1957; PhD, Cath. U. Am., 1963. Ordained priest Diocese of Mobile-Birmingham, Ala., 1956, vice chancellor, 1963—66, chancellor, 1966—80; asst. pastor Mobile, 1959—65; tchr. McGill Inst., Mobile, 1959—62; pastor St. Patrick Parish, Mobile, 1966—71; lectr. history Spring Hill Coll., Mobile, 1971—72; asst. pastor St. Matthew Parish, Mobile, 1971—79, Cathedral Immaculate Conception, Mobile, 1979—80; adminstr. sede vacante Archdiocese of Mobile, 1980, archbishop, 1980—2008, archbishop emeritus, 2008—; ordained bishop, 1980. Pres. Cath. Housing Mobile, Mobile Senate Priests, 1978—80; chmn. com. on doctrine Nat. Conf. Cath. Bishops, 1988—91. Contbr. articles to profl. jours. Chmn. NCCB Com. on Ecumenical and Interreligious Affairs, 1993—96, Cath. Common Ground Initiative, 1996—, chmn. com. on the liturgy, 1999—2002; mem. Mixed Internat. Commn. for Theol. Dialogue Between the Cath. Ch. and the Orthodox Ch., 1999—, Vox Clara commn. Congregation for Divine Worship, Rome, 2002—; Chmn. bd. dirs. Mobile Mus., 1966—88, Ala. Dept. Archives and History, 1979—, chmn., 1999—; chmn. bd. dirs. Cath. U. Am., Washington, 1983—98, Spring Hill Coll., Mobile, 1982—; chmn. bd. govs. N.Am. Coll., Rome, 1982—85. Mem.: Am. Cath. Hist. Assn., Ala. Hist. Assn., So. Hist. Assn. (pres. 1971—72, exec. com. 1981—88), Hist. Mobile Preservation Soc., Lions. Roman Catholic. Address: 400 Government St PO Box 1966 Mobile AL 36633-1966

LIPTON, JOHN M., state representative; b. Warren, AR, Feb. 26, 1936; m. Jenelle Neal; c.: Robin, Stacey, Michael BS, U. Arkansas, Monticello. Congressman Ark. General Assembly, dist. 90, Little Rock, 1969—93; speaker of the house Ark. General Assembly, Little Rock, 1991. Co-chrm., Joint Performance Rev. Com., mem., House Insurance and Commerce Com., House Public Health Com., Welfare and Labor Com., Joint Budget Com.; mem., Science, Energy and Environmental Resources Com., Nat. Conf. of State Legislature's Assembly, Fiscal Affairs and Governmental Operations Com., AR Commn. Interstate Cooperation; chrm., AR Quality Management Bd., co-chrm, Correction Resources Study Commn., mem., Special Com. on the State Police, Depart. of Correction, Game and Fish Commn.; co-chrm., AR Adv. Coun. for Vocat.-Tech. Edn., mem., Nat. Adv. Coun. on Vocat. Edn. Mem. Bradley County Chamber of Commerce, Brady County Industrial Development Corp. Baptist. Office: Ark House of Representatives State Capitol Little Rock AR 72201-1088

LISCHER, CHARLES D., beverage company executive; Various positions Deloitte & Touche, 1999, ptnr., 2004; CFO, European Group Coca-Cola Enterprises, Inc., 2005, v.p., contr., prin. acctg. officer, 2005—07, v.p., fin., European Group, 2007—. Office: Coca Cola Enterprises Inc 2500 Windy Ridge Pky Atlanta GA 30339 Office Phone: 770-989-3000. Office Fax: 770-989-3790. Business E-Mail: clischer@na.cokecce.com.

LISENBY, TERRY S., manufacturing executive; BS, U. NC, 1976. Mgr. fin. acctg. Nucor Corp., Charlotte, NC, 1985—91, v.p., corp. contr., 1991-2000, exec. v.p., treas., CFO, 2000—. Office: Nucor Corp 1915 Rexford Rd Charlotte NC 28211 Office Phone: 704-366-7000. Office Fax: 704-362-4208.

LIST, ERICSON JOHN, environmental engineering science educator, consultant; b. Whakatane, New Zealand, Mar. 27, 1939; came to U.S., 1962; s. Ericson Bayliss and Freda Helen (Sunkel) L.; m. Olive Amoore, Feb. 3, 1962; children: Brooke Meredith, Antonia Michael. B.E. with honors, U. Auckland, New Zealand, 1961, B.Sc., M.E., U. Auckland, New Zealand, 1962; PhD, Calif. Inst. Tech., 1965. Registered profl. engr., Calif., Nev. Sr. lectr. U. Auckland, 1966-69; asst. prof. Calif. Inst. Tech., Pasadena, 1969-72, assoc. prof., 1972-78, prof. environ. engring. sci., 1978-97, exec. officer, 1980-85, prof. emeritus, 1997; with Flow Sci. Inc., Pasadena, 1997—. Bd. dirs. Environ. Def. Scis., Pasadena; bd. chmn., prin., cons. Flow Sci. Inc., Pasadena, 1983-. Author: (with Hugo B. Fischer et al), Mixing in Inland and Coastal Waters, 1979, (with W. Rodi) Turbulent Jets and Plumes, 1982, (with Roscoe Moss Co.) Handbook of Ground Water Development, 1990. Mem. Blue Ribbon Commn. City of Pasadena, 1976-78. Recipient Spl. Creativity award NSF, 1982 Fellow ASCE (life, editor Jour. Hydraulic Engring. 1984-89, Athenaeum (Pasadena) (chmn. wine com. 1981-83). Office: Flow Sci Inc 723 E Green St Pasadena CA 91101-2111 Home: 169 Broomfields Rd RD1 Howick 2571 New Zealand Office Phone: 626-233-6014. Business E-Mail: ejlist@flowscience.com.

LISTER, GEORGE, pediatrician; b. Miami, May 8, 1947; BA in Psych., Religious Studies, Brown U., Providence, 1969; MD, Yale U. Sch. Medicine, New Haven, 1973. Diplomate Am. Bd. Pediat., Nat. Bd. Med. Examiners, cert. Pediat. Cardiology, Neonatal-Perinatal Med., Pediat. Critical Care Med. Resident pediat. med. Yale U. Sch. Medicine, 1973—75; fellowship pediat. cardiology and neonatology U. Calif. Cardiovasc. Rssc. Inst., San Francisco, 1975—78; asst. to full prof. pediat. and anesthesiology Yale U. Sch. Medicine, 1978—2003; Robert L. Moore chair pediat. and prof. pediat. Southwestern Med. Sch., Dallas, 2003—. Sect. chief pediat. critical care medicine, dir. pediat. ICU Yale U. Sch. Medicine, 1978—2003; former editor-in-chief Pediat. Rsch.; sr. editor Rudolph's Pediat.; editor Rudolph's Pediat. Online. Contbr. articles to profl. jours. Recipient Established Investigator award, Am. Heart Assn., 1985; named one of Best Doctors Am., 1992;, Fulbright fellowship, 1990. Mem.: Inducted to Ist. Medicine (IOM), Acad. of Medicine, Engring. & Sci. Tex., Am. Bd. Pediat. (chair bd. dirs. 2004), Soc. Pediat. Rsch. (pres. 1993, Maureen Andrew Mentor award 2004), Internat. Pediat. Rsch. Found., Am. Pediat. Soc. (pres. 2008—09), Am. Acad. Pediat. (Disting. Career award, sect. on critical care 1999). Office: UT Southwestern Med Ctr 5323 Harry Hines Blvd Dallas TX 75390-9063 Office Phone: 214-648-3563. Business E-Mail: george.lister@utsouthwestern.edu.

LISTON, THOMAS J., insurance company executive; BS in acctg., U. Ky., 1983. CPA. Acct., ptnr. Coopers & Lybrand (now PriceWaterhouseCoopers), 1983—94; dir., Devel. Humana, Inc., 1995—97, v.p., Corp. Devel., 1997—2000, sr. v.p., Strategy and Corporate Devel., head ptnr., Humana Venture, 2000—08, sr. v.p., senior products, 2008—. Mem. AICPA, Corp. Strategy Bd., Ky. Soc. of CPAs, Nat. Assn. of Corp. Dirs. Office: Humana Inc 500 W Main St Louisville KY 40202 Office Phone: 502-580-1000. Office Fax: 502-580-3677. Business E-Mail: tliston@humana.com.

LITKE, DONALD PAUL, acquisition executive, retired military officer; b. Denver, Nov. 7, 1934; s. Walter Monroe and Alice Vivian (Fowler) L.; m. Myrna Kay McDonald, July 1, 1956; children—Bradley, Susan, Lisa BS in Econs., Colo. A&M U., 1956; MS in Internat. Affairs, George Washington U., 1966. Ops. and staff positions U.S. Air Force, 1956-79; vice comdr. Oklahoma City Air Logistics Ctr., 1979-81; dep. dir. logistics and security assistance U.S. European Command, Stuttgart, Germany, 1981-83; comdr. U.S. Logistics Group, Ankara, Turkey, 1983-85; dep. dir. Def. Logistics Agy., Alexandria, Va., 1985-86; pres. Bus. Devel. Internat., Alexandria and Niceville, Fla., 1986—2004. Contbr. articles to profl. jours. Mem. Air Force Assn. (Middle Mgr. of Yr. 1970, award of excellence 1977), Alpha Tau Omega Methodist. Avocations: auto restoration, racquetball. Home and Office: 2422 Edgewater Dr Niceville FL 32578-2305

LITOFF, ROBERT, accountant; b. New Haven, Conn., June 19, 1945; children: Dorothy, Naomi. BA in Psychology, U. Conn., 1969. Social worker; buyer; acct. Mem.: Am. Family Assn. Republican. Office: 7026 Forest Crest North San Antonio TX 78240 Business E-Mail: wxyztruth@yahoo.com.

LITTEL, JOHN E., lawyer; BA in Philosophy & Polit. Sci., U. Scranton; JD, Catholic U. Bar: Pa. Regional office mgr. for U.S. Senator H. John Heinz III; dep. dir., counsel, citizenship project Heritage Found.; assoc. dean Regent U.; dir., intergovernmental affairs, The White House's Office of Nat. Drug Control Policy; dep. sec., health, human resources Commonwealth of Va.; joined Amerigroup Corp., 2001, exec. v.p., external rels. Assoc. prof., law, govt. Regent U. Former bd. dirs Va. Family Violence Prevention Agy.; former bd. dirs. Family and Children's Trust Fund. Mem.: Pa. Bar. Office: Amerigroup Corp 4425 Corporation Ln Virginia Beach VA 23462 Office Phone: 757-490-6900. Business E-Mail: jlittel@amerigroupcorp.com.

LITTLE, CAROLINE H., trade association administrator; BA in English, Wesleyan U., Middletown, Conn., 1981; JD with honors, NYU Sch. Law, 1986. Assoc. Arnold & Porter, Washington; dep. gen. counsel Applied Graphics Technologies/Applied Printing Technologies, 1993—97, US News & World Report, The Atlantic Monthly & Fast Co., 1997; gen. counsel Washingtonpost.Newsweek Interactive (WPNI), 1997—98, v.p. adminstrn., gen. counsel, 1998—99, sr. v.p. bus. affairs, gen. counsel, 1999—2000, COO, 2004—08, pub., CEO, 2004—08; CEO North America Guardian News & Media Ltd., 2008—11; pres., CEO Newspaper Assn. America, 2011—. Bd. dirs. Internet Advt. Bur., 2005—08, Citybizlist, 2011—, American Press Inst.; mem. pub. adv. coun. Google Inc., 2007—08. Bd. trustees Grinnell Coll., Iowa, 1996—; mem. journalism adv. com. Knight Found.; bd. dirs. Posse Found. Named to Digital Hall of Fame, MinOnline.com, 2008. Mem.: DC Bar, Online Pub. Assn. (chair 2006—08), Phi Beta Kappa. Office: NAA 4401 Wilson Blvd Ste 900 Arlington VA 22203 Office Fax: 703-469-2995.

LITTLE, CHRISTOPHER MARK, retired publishing executive; b. Tazewell, Va., Mar. 11, 1941; s. Haskin Vincent and Janet Koe (Kessinger) L.; m. Virginia Elizabeth Silver, Dec. 27, 1963 (div. Oct. 1988); children: Timothy Mark, Margaret Elizabeth; m. Elizabeth Foster Anderson, Oct. 15, 1988. BA, Yale U., 1963; LLB, U. Tex., 1966. Bar: D.C. 1966. Assoc. Covington & Burling, Washington, 1966-68, 70-75; adminstrv. asst. to Rep. Bob Eckhardt, US House of Representatives, Washington, 1968-70; asst. gen. counsel EPA, Washington, 1975-76; v.p., counsel The Washington Post, 1976-80; pres., pub. The Herald, Everett, Wash., 1980-84; sr. v.p. adminstrn. Newsweek, Inc., NYC, 1984-86, pres., 1986-89, Cowles Mags., Inc., Harrisburg, Pa., 1989-92; v.p., pub. Meredith Corp., Des Moines, 1992-94, pres. mag. group, 1995—2000. Internat. bd. trustees American Field Svc., N.Y.C., 1989-95, chmn., 1992-95. Mem. Mag. Publications America, Wakonda Club, Des Moines Club. Episcopalian. Avocations: landscape architecture, 18th century american history, classical music.

LITTLE, PETER D., anthropology professor; PhD, Ind. U., Bloomington, 1983. Prof. anthropology, chair U. Ky., Lexington, 1994—2007; prof. anthropology Emory U., Atlanta, 2008—. Author: (book) Somalia: Economy with State (Book award, Choice Academic, 2004); contbr. chapters to books, articles to profl. jours. Advisor Oxfam-USA, Boston, 1987—91, Fulbright Scholar Program, Coun. Internat. Exch. Scholars, DC, 1996—98. Recipient Amaury Talbot Book prize, Royal Anthrop. Inst., 2003, Kirwan Rsch. prize, U. Ky., 2006; grantee Rsch. and Writing grant, Catherine and John T. McArthur Found., 2000—02; Guggenheim fellowship, John and Simon Guggenheim Found., 2007—08. Fellow: Am. Anthrop. Assn.

LITTLE, THOMAS M., public relations executive; b. Columbus, Ohio, Dec. 21, 1935; s. John William and Eulalia Josephine (Mayer) L.; m. Susan Mulford, Sept. 29, 1959; children: Carin Andrea, Debora Mayer, Sharon Mulford, Patricia Anne. BS in Journalism, Northwestern U., 1958; postgrad., Bradley U., 1958. Account supr. Philip Lesly Co., Chgo., 1962—65; v.p., account supr. Burson-Marsteller, NYC, 1966—76; v.p. Foote Cone & Belding, Inc., NYC, 1977-78; pres. FCB Pub. Rels., NYC, 1978-81, Bus. Orgn., Inc. divsn. Carl Byoir & Assocs., NYC, 1982, Tracy-Locke/BBDO Pub. Rels., Dallas, 1983-85; exec. v.p., gen. mgr. Manning, Selvage & Lee, NYC, 1986; pres. T.J. Ross & Assocs., NYC, 1986-87; pres., gen. mgr. Golin/Harris Communication, NYC, 1987-91; pub. rels. cons., 1992—. Bd. dirs. Damon Runyon-Walter Winchell Cancer Fund, NYC Lt. (j.g.) USN, 1959-62. Mem. Am. Mktg. Assn., Pub. Rels. Soc. Am. (SC and Ga. chpts.), Publicity Club NYC, Sea Pines Country Club (Hilton Head Island), Lotos Club (NYC), Sigma Alpha Epsilon. Roman Catholic. Home: 5333 Myrtlewood Sarasota FL 34235-4615 Personal E-mail: littlevthh@aol.com.

LITTLE, WM. A. (WILLIAM ALFRED LITTLE), language educator, researcher, musicologist; b. Boston, July 28, 1929; s. Wm. A. and Myrle A. (Holmes) L. BA, Tufts U., 1951; LTCL, Trinity Coll., London, 1952; MA, Harvard U., 1953; PhD, U Mich., 1961. Asst. prof. Williams Coll., Williamstown, Mass., 1957-63; assoc. prof., chair Tufts U., Medford, Mass., 1963-66; chair U. Va., Charlottesville, 1966-72, prof., 1966—96, prof. German and music emeritus, 1996—. Vis. prof. musicology U. Rochester, N.Y., 1996 Author: G.A. Bürger, 1974, Mendelssohn & the Organ, 2010 (John Ogasapian Book award, Organ Hist. Soc., 2010); editor: Mendelssohn-Complete Organ Works, 5 vols., 1987-90, The German Quarterly, 1970-78; contbr. articles to profl. jours. Cpl. U.S. Army, 1953-55. Sesquicentennial fellow U. Va., 1972-73, 78-79, 88-89. Mem. MLA (chair comp. lit. 1970-72), Am. Assn. Tchrs. German (nat. exec. coun. 1968-78), Am. Guild Organists (registrar Mass. chpt. 1949-53, dean Charlottesville chpt. 1977-78, 2010-12, registrar, archivist Ctrl. Fla. chpt. 1995-99, nat. com. profl. edn. 1990-2002), Am. Mus. Soc., Orgn. Hist. Soc., Am. Bach Soc., Neue Bachgesellschaft (Leipzig). Home: 245 Terrell Rd West Charlottesville VA 22901 Personal E-mail: wal@virginia.edu.

LITTLEPAGE, GLENN E., social psychology educator; b. Dallas, Nov. 21, 1946; s. Gordon Ray and Mary Lucille Littlepage; 1 child from previous marriage, Nick; m. Anna Littlepage, June 1, 1986; 1 child, Morgan A. Jones. BS, U. N.Mex., 1969; MS, Kans. State U., 1971, PhD, 1974. Rsch. psychologist U.S. Army Retraining Brigade, Ft. Riley, Kans., 1971—73; prof. psychology dept. Mid. Tenn. State U., Murfreesboro, 1973—. Cons. editor Jour. Personality and Social Psychology, 2000-2001; assoc. editor Group Dynamics, 2007—, Small Group Rsch., 2011-. Contbr. articles to profl. jours. Fellow Soc. Exptl. Social Psychology; mem. Interdisciplinary Network for Group Rsch., Soc. for Indsl. and Orgnl. Psychology. Avocations: bass fishing, woodworking, stained glass, motorcycling. Office: Mid Tenn State U Box 534 Murfreesboro TN 37132 Business E-Mail: glittlepage@mtsu.edu.*

LITTLETON, ISAAC THOMAS, III, retired library director; b. Hartsville, Tenn., Jan. 28, 1921; s. Isaac Thomas Jr. and Bessie (Lowe) L.; m. Dorothy Etta Young, Aug. 12, 1949; children: Sally Lowe Littleton Phillips, Thomas Young, Elizabeth Ann BA, U. N.C., 1943; MA, U. Tenn., Knoxville, 1950; MSLS, U. Ill., Champaign-Urbana, 1951, PhD, 1968. Circulation librarian, asst. librarian U. NC, Chapel Hill, 1951—58; asst. dir. then dir. librs. NC State U., Raleigh, 1959—87, emeritus dir. librs., 1987—. Mem. NC Libr. Networking Steering Com., Raleigh, 1982-85; bd. dirs. Southeastern Libr. Network, Atlanta, 1973-74, 83-86, chmn., 1985-86; chmn. Assn. Southeastern Rsch. Librs., 1969-71; mem. com. Gov.'s Conf. on Libr. and Info. Svcs., 1990. Author: The Literature of Agricultural Economics, 1969, State Systems of Higher Education and Libraries, 1977, D.H. Hill Library: An Informal History, 1993; editor: NC Union List of Scientific Serials, 1967. Bd. dirs., treas. Theater in Park, Raleigh, 1982-85, Friends of Wake County Pub. Librs.; sec. NC State U. Friends of Libr., Raleigh, 1964-87, bd. dirs., 1990-94, life mem. 1988; pres. Friends of NC Libr. for Blind and Physically Handicapped, 1989-93, bd. dirs. 1993-94; v.p. Wake County UN Assn., 1994-95, sec., 1999-2000, pres., 2001-04. Lt. (j.g.) USN, 1943-46, PTO. Council on Library Resources fellow, Washington, 1975-76 Mem. Southeastern Libr. Assn. (exec. bd. 1974-78), NC Libr. Assn. (exec. bd. 1969-71, hon. life), Torch Club (pres. Raleigh 1974-75), Raleigh Golden K Kiwanis Club (pres. 2001-02). Mem. Community United Ch. of Christ. Avocations: theater, reading. Home: 4813 Brookhaven Dr Raleigh NC 27612-5706 Business E-Mail: littletons@bellsouth.net. E-mail: littletons@mindspring.com.

LITTLETON, NAN ELIZABETH FELDKAMP, psychologist, mental health educator; b. Covington, Ky., Oct. 23, 1942; AAS, No. Ky. U., Highland Heights, 1976, BS, 1978; MACE, Morehead State U., Ky., 1981; MA, U. Cin., 1986, PhD in Psychology, 1995. Emeritus prof. No. Ky. U., Highland Heights, 1976—2011, dir. counseling and human svcs. program, 1989—2011. Officer, pres. Holly Hill Children's Home, Cold Spring, Ky., 1980-86; cons. Attituding Healing Ctr., Cin., 1990-94; treas. ADO Nat. Honor Soc., 2003-10. Treas., editor So. Orgn. Human Svcs. Edn. Link, 1997-2002. Bd. dir. Coun. Stds. in Human Svc. Edn., Chgo., 1990-98—, Cancer Family Care, Cin., 1992-96, Sr. Svcs. Northern Ky., 2005-08. Mem. APA, Am. Psychol. Soc., Nat. Orgn. Human Svc. Edn., Am. Coun. Assn., So. Orgn. Human Svc. Edn. (state rep. 1991-2007, treas., 1999-2002), Nat. Women's Studies Assn., Alpha Delta Omega (treas. 2003-10). Home: 333 W 17th St Covington KY 41014-1007 Business E-Mail: littleton@nku.edu.

LITTMAN, EARL, advertising and public relations executive; b. Jan. 29, 1927; s. David and Cele Littman; m. Natalie Carol Jacobson, Dec. 21, 1948; children: Erica Humphrey, Bonnie Likover, Michael L. Littman. BS, NYU, 1948. With George N. Khan, NYC, 1948-50, Jones & Brown, Pitts., 1950-52; chmn., CEO Goodwin, Dannenbaum, Littman & Wingfield Inc., Houston, 1952-92; pres. The Advertizing Firm, Inc., 1992, Two Nerds and a Suit, Inc., 1994; chmn., CEO Point of Product Broadcasting Co. Founder, inventor new wireless advt. in-store P.O.P. Broadcasting Co. Inc., 2003—. Bd. dir. Ctr. Am. History, U. Tex., mem. Chancellor's Coun.; chmn. Anti-Defamation League, Tex., 1984; bd. dir. Am. Heart Assn., Houston, Glassell Sch, Houston chpt. World Pres. Orgn.; active End Hunger Network, Houston, 1984; active NCCJ; founder, exec. dir. Drugs Kill Prevention/Edn. Program, 1997; exec. dir. Drugs Kill, founder, Back Our Vets, 2012. With USN, 1944-45. Recipient Silver medal Am. Advt. Fedn., 1989, Outstanding Vol. award Savvy, 1990, Anti-Defamation League Popkin award, 1990, End Hunger Network award, 1992; Am. Heart Assn. honoree, 1988, John McMahon award Am. Heart Assn., 1996; Heritage award Am. Women in Radio and TV, 1992, Cmty. Champion award Tex. Commn. Alcohol and Drug Abuse, 2000; named Mktg. Man of Yr., Am. Mktg. Assn., 1999; named to Advt. Hall of Fame, 2008, Southwest Advt. Hall of Fame, 2009. Mem.: Black-Our-Vets (founder), Am. Advt. Agy. Assn. (gov. Houston chpt. 1990, Paul Dudley White award 1991), Marathon Assn., Winedale Hist. Assn. (former pres.), Houston Advt. Fedn. (Living Legend award 1993, Heritage award), Affiliated Advt. Agys. Internat. (pres. 1979—80). Office Phone: 713-621-7678. E-mail: earl@popbroadcasting.com.

LITTMAN, MARLYN KEMPER, information scientist, educator; b. Mar. 26, 1943; d. Louis and Augusta (Jacobs) Janofsky; m. Bennett I. Kemper, Aug. 1, 1965 (dec. June 1987); children: Alex Randall, Gari Hament, Jason Myles; m. Lewis Littman, Apr. 22, 1990. BA, Finch Coll., 1964; MA in Anthropology, Temple U., 1970; MA in Info. Sci., U. South Fla., 1983; PhD in Info. Sci., Nova Southeastern U., 1986. Dir. Hist. Broward County Preservation Bd., Hollywood, Fla., 1979—87; automated systems libr. Broward County Main Libr., Ft. Lauderdale, Fla., 1984—86; prof. info. sci. Nova U., Ft. Lauderdale, Fla., 1987—94, dir. info. sci. doctoral program, 1987—94; prof. info. sci. Nova Southeastern U., Ft. Lauderdale, Fla., 1995—. Weekly columnist Ft. Lauderdale News, 1975—79; contbg. editor Hyper Nexus-Jour. Hypermedia and Multimedia Studies, 1996—2000; assoc. editor Jour. On-Line Learning, 1997—2002. Author: A Comprehensive Documented History of the City of Pompano Beach, 1982, A Comprehensive History of Dania, 1983, A Comprehensive History of Hallandale, 1984, A Comprehensive History of Deerfield Beach, 1985, A Comprehensive History of Plantation, 1986, A Comprehensive History of Davie, 1987, Networking: Choosing a LAN Path to Interconnection, 1987, Building Broadband Networks, 2002; author: (with others) Mosaics of Meaning, New Ways of Learning, 1996; contbr. articles to profl. jours., chapters to books. Pub. info. officer Broward County Hist. Commn., 1975—79; vice chmn. Broward County Adv. Bd., 1987—92; bd. dirs. Ctrl. Agy. Jewish Edn., 1992—94. Recipient Judge L. Clayton Nance award, 1977, Broward County Hist. Commn. award, 1979. Mem.: IEEE, Assn. Computing Machinery, Info. Resources Mgmt. Assn. Internat., Phi Kappa Phi, Beta Phi Mu, Upsilon Pi Epsilon. Home: 2845 NE 35th St Fort Lauderdale FL 33306-2007 Office: Nova Southeastern U Grad Sch Computer and Info Sci 3301 College Ave Fort Lauderdale FL 33314 Office Phone: 954-262-2078. Business E-Mail: marlyn@nova.edu.

LIU, DONALD, mechanical engineer; BS, U.S. Merchant Marine Acad.; BS in Naval Architecture, MS in Naval Architecture, Mass. Inst. Tech.; PhD in Mech. Engring., U. Arizona. Chief rsch. engr. Am. Bur. of Shipping (ABS), asst. v.p., v.p. rsch. and devel. divsn., sr. v.p. tech. svcs. group, sr. v.p. tech, exec. v.p., chief tech. officer, bd. dirs. Recipient Gibbs Brothers medal, US Nati. Acad. of Sci. (NAS), David W. Taylor medal, Soc. of Naval Architects and Marine Engrs. (SNAME), 2004. Mem.: NAE. Office: ABS 16855 Northchase Drive Houston TX 77060 Office Phone: 281-877-5800.

LIUKIN, NASTIA, former Olympic gymnast; b. Moscow, Oct. 30, 1989; d. Valeri and Anna (Kotchneva) Liukin. Attended, So. Meth. U., Dallas, 2008. Mem. Olympic team USA Gymnastics, Beijing, 2008. Appeared in (films) Stick It, 2006. Recipient 1st Pl., balance beam, Am. Cup, 2005, 1st Pl., individual all-around, 2006, 2008, 1st Pl., uneven bars, balance beam, World Championships, 2005, 1st Pl., team competition, balance beam, 2007, 1st Pl., all-around, uneven bars, balance beam, US Classic, 2005, 1st Pl., balance beam, 2006, 1st Pl., individual all-around, uneven bars, balance beam, Visa Championships, 2005, 2006, 1st Pl., uneven bars, 2007, 1st Pl., team competition, Pan Am. Games, 2007, Gold medal, individual all-around; Silver medal, team competition, balance beam, uneven bars; Bronze medal, floor exercise, Beijing Olympic Games, 2008; named Gymnast of Yr., Internat. Gymnastics Hall of Fame, 2005, Sportswoman of Yr., Women's Sports Found., 2008; nominee World Top 10 Athletes award, US Sport's Acad. Athlete of Yr. award. Achievements include tying the record for most gymnastics medals won by an American in a single Olympic Games (5), 2008. Avocations: swimming, reading, shopping. Office: World Olympic Gymnastics Acad 1937 W Parker Rd Plano TX 75023 Office Phone: 972-985-9292. Office Fax: 972-964-8209.

LIVANOS, ALEXIS C., aerospace transportation executive; B in Mech. Engring., Calif. Inst. Tech., M in Engring. Sci., PhD in Engring. Sci. & Physics. Exec. v.p. ops. Loral Space & Comm.; various mgmt. positions TRW Inc., dep. gen. mgr., Electronic Sys. & Tech. Divsn., 2000—03; exec. v.p., ops. Boeing Satellite Sys., 2003; v.p., gen. mgr., sys. devel. and tech., Space Sensors Divsn. Northrop Grumman Corp., 2003—05, pres., space tech. sector, 2005—09, corp. v.p., chief tech. officer, 2009—. Bd. councilors U. So. Calif. Viterbi Sch. Engring.; bd. dirs. Nat. Def. Indsl. Assn., Space Found; fellow Calif. Coun. on Sci. & Tech.; mem. visiting com. on sci. & tech. UCLA. Recipient Caltech Disting. Alumni Award, Internat. Von Karman Wings Award, Aerospace Hist. Soc., IS exec. Leadership Award, UCLA Anderson Sch. of Mgmt. Fellow: AIAA (assoc.); mem.: IEEE, Armed Forces Comm. & Elec. Assn., Nat. Acad. Engring. Office: Northrop Grumman Corp 2980 Fairview Park Dr Falls Church VA 22042-4511 Office Phone: 310-553-6262. Office Fax: 310-553-2076. Business E-Mail: alexis.livanos@ngc.com.

LIVINGSTONE, JOHN LESLIE, accountant, economist, management consultant, educator; b. Johannesburg, Aug. 29, 1932; m. Trudy Dorothy Zweig, Aug. 7, 1977; children: Roger Miles, Adrienne Jill, Graham Ross, Robert Edward. B of Commerce, U. Witwatersrand, South Africa, 1956; MBA, Stanford U., 1963, PhD, 1966. CPA, N.Y., Tex.; cert. in bus. valuation. Budget dir. Edgars Stores Ltd., South Africa, 1958-61; asso. prof. Ohio State U., Columbus, 1966-69, Arthur Young Disting. prof., 1970-73; Fuller E. Callaway prof. Ga. Inst. Tech., Atlanta, 1973-78, mem. exec. bd., 1976-78; ptnr. Coopers & Lybrand, NYC, 1978-81; prin., v.p. Mgmt. Analysis Center, Inc., Cambridge, Mass., 1975-90; prof., chmn. div. acctg. and law Babson Coll., 1985-89, adj. prof., 1990-99; ret., 1999. Cons. FPC, SEC, HEW, also maj. corps.; MBA program dir. and prof. UMUC. Author: Accounting for Changing Prices: Replacement Cost and General Price Level Adjustments, 1976, Management Planning and Control, 1987, The Portable MBA: Finance and Accounting, 4th edit., 2009, Finance Made Easy, 3rd edit., 2012, The Economics of Energy, 2008, Economics Made Easy, 3rd edit., 2012, Ethics Made Easy, 2nd Edit., 2011, Common Sense, 2010, Guide to Bus. Valuation, 2007, What Government Should and Should Not Do, 2008, Golf Made Easy, 2008, The Economics of Public Choice, 2010; assoc. editor: Decision

Scis., 1973-78; mem. editl. bd. The Acctg. Rev., 1969-72, 76-78, Acctg., Orgns. and Socs., 1975-78, Jour. Acctg. and Pub. Policy, 1983-95; contbr. numerous articles to profl. jours.

LLEWELLYN, RALPH ALVIN, physics professor; b. Detroit, June 27, 1933; s. Ralph A. and Mary (Green) L.; m. Laura Diane Alsop, June 12, 1955; children: Mark Jeffrey, Rita Annette, Lisa Suzanne, Eric Matthew. BS in Chem. Engring. with high honors, Rose-Hulman Inst. Tech., 1955; PhD in Physics, Purdue U., 1962. Mem. faculty Rose-Hulman Inst. Tech., Terre Haute, Ind., 1961-70, assoc. prof. physics, 1964-68, prof., 1968-70, chmn. dept. physics, 1969-70; prof., chmn. dept. Ind. State U., Terre Haute, 1970-72, 74-80; dean Coll. of Arts and Scis. U. Ctrl. Fla., Orlando, 1980-84, prof., 1980—, chmn. dept. physics, 2003—06, prof. emeritus. Exec. sec. Energy Bd., staff officer environmental Studies Bd. NAS/NRC, Washington, 1972-74; vis. prof. Rensselaer Poly. Inst., Troy, N.Y., 1964; cons. Commn. on Coll. Physics, 1987-89, NSF, 1965-66; mem. Ind. Lt. Gov.'s Sci. Adv. Coun., 1974-80; adv. bd. Ind. Gov.'s Energy Extension Svc., Fla. Solar Energy Ctr., policy coun. Fla. Inst. Govt., Fla. Radon Adv. Coun., 1988-96; mem. environ. adv. com. Fla. Inst. Phosphate Rsch.; mem. grievance com. Fla. Bar, nat. adv. coun. Nat. Commn. on Higher Edn. Issues, 1982. Author: (with others) Physics 3E, 1991, Elementary Modern Physics, 1992, Modern Physics 3E, 1999, Modern Physics 4E, 2003, Modern Physics 5E, 2008; contbr. articles to profl. jours.; producer instructional films and TV. Trustee Merom (Ind.) Inst. Recipient Tchg. Incentive award Fla. State Univ. Sys., 1994, 97; NSF Coop. fellow, 1959-60, Am. Coun. Edn. Acad. Adminstrn. Internship Program fellow. Fellow Ind. Acad. Sci. (chmn. physics divsn. 1969-70, Spkr. of Yr. award 1975, pres.-elect 1980); mem. AAAS, AAUP, Am. Phys. Soc., Am. Assn. Physics Tchrs. (pres. Ind.), N.Y. Acad. Scis., Fla. Acad. Scis. (endowment com.), Internat. Oceanographic Found., Ind. Acad. Sci., Sigma Xi, Tau Beta Pi. Home: 1463 Palomino Way Oviedo FL 32765-9304 Office: U Cen Fla Dept Physics Orlando FL 32816-0001 Business E-Mail: ral@physics.ucf.edu.

LLOYD, ANNE H., corporate financial executive; BSBA, U. NC, Chapel Hill, 1983. CPA. Sr. mgr. Ernst & Young, LLP; v.p., contr. Martin Marietta Materials Inc., 1998—99, chief acctg. officer, 1999—2005, sr. v.p., 2005—09; CFO Martin Marietta Materials, Inc., 2005—, treas., 2006—, exec. v.p., 2009—. Bd. dirs. Terra Nitrogen Co., LP, 2009—. Mem. Blue Ribbon Panel Transp. Experts, SAFETEA-LU Reauthorization Com.; bd. dirs., mem., fin., audit com. NC C. of C. Mem.: Nat. Stone Sand Gravel Assn. (treas., mem., exec. com., bd. dirs.). Office: Martin Marietta Materials Inc 2710 Wycliff Rd Raleigh NC 27607 Office Phone: 919-781-4550. Office Fax: 919-783-4535.

LLOYD, CECIL RHODES, pediatric dentist; b. Corpus Christi, Tex., Aug. 18, 1930; s. Cecil Rhodes Hilbun and Cidney W. (Linxwiler) Lloyd; m. Donna Mae Thomas, Dec. 31, 1955 (div. 1973); children: James Michael, Leigh Ann, Lisa Kendall; m. Glenda Sue Williams, Dec. 31, 1979; children: Lauren Cecily, Sutton Rhodes. Student, La. State U., 1949, La. Tech. Inst., 1950, Centenary Coll., 1952-54; DDS, Loyola U., New Orleans, 1958. Pvt. practice pediatric dentistry, Shreveport, La., 1958—. Cons. in pediatric dentistry Barksdale AFB, La., 1970—; mem. staff and surg. com. Christus Schumpert Hosp., Shreveport. Chmn. Cen. YMCA, Shreveport, 1974, met. bd., 1969, Ind. Bowl Football Classic, Shreveport, 1984, 85, Fellowship Christian Athletes, 1986; bd. dirs. Riverside Hosp., Bossier, La., 1982-84; pres.-elect Sports Found., 1989, pres., 1990; founder Sports Mus. of Champions, Shreveport-Bossier; interim mem. Shreveport City Coun., 1990. With USMC, 1950-52. Named Southwestern Handball Hall of Fame, 1996. NW La. Dental Assn., La. Dental Assn., ADA, Am. Acad. Pediatric Dentistry, La. Bd. Dentistry (pres., 1969-70, 77-78, 83-84), Ark.-La.-Tex. Dental Congress (chmn. 1979-80). Republican. Baptist. Avocation: golf. Office: 9402 Stonebriar Cir Shreveport LA 71115-3724

LLOYD, REGINALD IVAN, state agency administrator, former prosecutor; b. Camden, SC, Feb. 16, 1967; m. Melissa Lloyd; 1 child, Will. Student, U. Miami, 1985—86; BA, Winthrop Coll., 1989; JD, U. SC Sch. Law, 1993. Atty. Nexsen, Pruit, Jacobs, & Pollard, 1993—95; with Office Atty. Gen. State of SC, 1995—98; chief counsel, dir. rsch. to jud. com. SC Ho. Reps., 1998—2000; atty. Nelson, Mullins, Riley & Scarborough, Willoughby & Hoefer; judge-at large SC Cir. Ct. Seat No. 9, 2003—06; US atty. Dist. SC US Dept. Justice, Columbia, 2006—08; dir. SC Law Enforcement Divsn. (SLED), Columbia, 2008—. Recipient Compleat Lawyer award, U. SC Sch. Law. Achievements include being the first African American to become the US Attorney of South Carolina. Office: SC Law Enforcement Divsn (SLED) PO Box 21398 Columbia SC 29221 Office Phone: 803-896-7001.

LLOYD, ROBERT A., corporate financial executive; BBA, Tex. Tech. Univ., 1983. CPA. CPA positions Ernst & Young LLP, 1983—88; v.p., contr. Intellicall Inc., 1988—92; CFO ActionFax Internat., 1993—95; contr. GameStop Corp. & predecessor companies, 1996—2000; v.p. fin. GameStop Corp., Grapevine, Tex., 2000—05, sr. v.p., chief acctg. officer, 2005—10, exec. v.p., CFO, 2010—. Office: GameStop Corp 625 Westport Pkwy Grapevine TX 76051 Office Phone: 817-424-2000.

LOBB, WILLIAM ATKINSON, financial services executive; b. Arlington, Pa., Apr. 21, 1951; s. Anthony William and Annamarie (Hilpert) L.; m. Maureen Veronique O'Hagan, July 7, 1977; children: William Atkinson III, Anthony Hagan. BS, Georgetown U., 1977. Account exec. Johnston Lemon, Washington, 1977-78; sr. account exec. Merrill Lynch, Alexandria, Va., 1979-83; asst. v.p. E.F. Hutton, Washington, 1983-85; mng. dir., ptnr.-in-charge Oppenheimer, Inc., Atlanta, 1985—2011, mng. dir. investments, 2012—. Bd. dirs. Atlanta Charity Clays Mem. Nat. Securities Traders Assn., Ga. Securities Assn., Univ. Club, Burge Plantation Hunt Club, Piedmont Driving Club, Nairn Golf Club (Scotland), City of Atlanta (lic. review bd.), Waterville Golf Links(Ireland), Worshipful Co. Gunmakers (London). Avocation: squash. Office: Oppenheimer Inc 7000 Central Pky Ste 1515 Atlanta GA 30328 Office Phone: 404-262-5355. Business E-Mail: will.lobb@opco.com.

LOBER, IRENE MOSS, educational consultant; b. NYC, Aug. 1, 1927; d. David and Beckie Moss; m. Solomon William Lober, Oct. 25, 1947; children: Clifford Warren, Richard Wayne, Lori Ann. BS in Edn., CCNY, 1948; MA, George Washington U., 1967; EdD, Va. Poly. Inst. and State U., 1974. Registered sch. bus. adminstr. Formerly tchr., libr.; prin. staff devel. Fairfax County Pub. Schs., Va., 1965—77; supt. University City (Mo.) Pub. Schs., 1977—81, Danbury (Conn.) Pub. Schs., 1981—85; prof. SUNY, New Paltz, 1985—98, chmn. dept. ednl. adminstrn., 1990—98, dir. EdD program, 1993—98, coord. distance learning programs, 1995—98, cons. ednl. adminstrn., 1998—. Guest lectr. Washington U., George Washington U., Va. Poly. Inst. and State U., U. Va., Fordham U., C.W. Post Coll., L.I. U.; mem. bus. adv. coun. Datahr, Inc., 1982—85; pres. N.Y. State Coun. for Advancement of Depts. of Ednl. Adminstrn., 1994; cons. in field; founding incorporator Sci. Horizons, Inc., Danbury, 1984—85, COMPUtourney, Inc., 1990—98; designated disting. expert and peer reviewer Asst. Sec. Edn. Chester Finn, 1987—89; spkr./presenter various internat., nat. and state confs. and convs.; book reviewer Tchrs. Coll. Press, Columbia U., 2004. Author: Promoting Your School, 1993; contbr. articles to profl. jours.; book reviewer: Teacher's Coll. Press, 2004. Mem. legal and govt. studies group Nat. Inst. Edn. Dept. HEW; nat. adv. bd. U. Wis. R & D Ctr., 1978—80; chairperson Mo. Instml. TV Coun., 1981; lay adv. bd. St. Louis Met. Med. Soc., 1980—81; bd. advisors St. Joseph's Inst. Deaf, 1980—81; apptd. supt. in residence Western Conn. State U., 1984; divsn. chairperson United Way Campaign, 1982—86; mem. bd. edn. Poughkeepsie City Sch. Dist., 1993—96; mem. instl. rev. bd. M.D. Anderson Cancer Ctr., Orlando, 2002—04; pres. Lake Mary chpt. AARP, 2001—03; pres. Rishona-Chavaret group, Orlando chpt. Hadassah, 2005—08, co-pres., 2004—05; bd. dirs. Temple Israel, Longwood, Fla., 2005—, v.p. edn., 2006—08, adminstrv. v.p., 2005—07; pres. Temple Israel Sisterhood, Longwood, 2007—, bd. dirs.; pres. adv. cabinet Greater St. Louis coun. Girl Scouts U.S., 1980—81, bd. dirs. Southwestern Conn. Coun., 1981—85; bd. dirs. Fairfield coun. Boy Scouts Am.; bd. dirs. Danbury region Jr. Achievement, 1981—86, Regional Hospice, Danbury, 1984—86, Danbury Coun. Am. Heart Assn., 1985—86; exec. bd., trustee United Way No. Fairfield County; trustee, bd. dirs. United Way, Danbury, 1982—85; bd. dirs. TRIAD Seminole County, Fla., 2001—04, Meals on Wheels Inc. Seminole County, Fla., 2000—04. Recipient Townsend Harris medal, CCNY Alumni Assn., Nat. Leadership award, Hadassah, 2005;, IDEA fellow, Ford Found. grantee, 1977—78. Mem.: NEA, ASCD, Muirfield Village Civic Assn., Authors League, Authors Guild, Nat. Assn. Secondary Sch. Prins. (chair profs. secondary sch. adminstrn. com.), Assn. Sch. Bus. Ofcls. Internat. (nat. chmn. maintenance and ops. rsch. com. 1985—89), N.Y. State Assn. Sch. Bus. Ofcls., N.Y. State Coun. Sch. Supts., Ednl. Rsch. Svc., Sch. Adminstrs. Assn. N.Y. State, Am. Assn. Sch. Adminstrs. (nat. chmn. higher edn. com. 1987—89, chmn. membership svcs. com. 1995—96), Pi Lambda Theta (publs. adv. bd. 1981—84), Phi Kappa Phi, Phi Delta Kappa (pres. New Paltz chpt. 1991—93). Home Phone: 407-537-6777. Personal E-mail: irenelober@gmail.com.

LOCHNER, JAMES VICTOR (JIM LOCHNER), food products executive; b. 1952; BS in Animal Sci., MS in Animal Sci., U. Wis. Exec. v.p., then pres. mfg. fresh meats IBP, Inc., Dakota Dunes, SD, 1998—2001; group v.p. fresh meats Tyson Foods Inc., Springdale, Ark., 2001—05, sr. group v.p. margin optimization, 2005—07, sr. group v.p. fresh meats, 2007—09, COO, 2009—. Office: Tyson Foods Inc PO Box 2020 Springdale AR 72765-2020

LOCHRIDGE, LLOYD PAMPELL, JR., lawyer; b. Austin, Tex., Feb. 3, 1918; s. Lloyd Pampell and Franklyn (Blocker) Lochridge; m. Frances Potter, Jan. 23, 1943; children: Anne, Georgia, Lloyd P. III, Patton G., Hope N., Frances P. AB, Princeton U., 1938; LLB, Harvard U., 1941. Bar: DC 1942, Tex. 1945, U.S. Ct. Appeals (5th cir.), U.S. Supreme Ct. Assoc. Law Office Vernon Hill, Mission, Tex., 1945-46; ptnr. Hill & Lochridge, Mission, 1946-49, Hill, Lochridge & King, Mission, 1949-59, McGinnis, Lochridge & Kilgore, Austin, 1959—. Mem. adv. bd. Salvation Army, Austin, 1962—; trustee Austin Lyric Opera, 1986—; mem. vestry Ch. Good Shepherd, Austin, 1968—73. Comdr. USNR, 1941—46, ETO. Mem.: ABA (bd. govs. 1989—92), Hidalgo County Bar Assn. (pres. 1954—55), Travis County Bar Assn. (pres. 1970—71), State Bar Tex. (pres. 1974—75). Episcopalian. Avocations: tennis, squash, sailing. Office: McGinnis Lochridge and Kilgore 600 Congress Ave Ste 2100 Austin TX 78701-2499 Office Phone: 512-495-6002. Business E-Mail: llochridge@mcginnislaw.com.

LOCHRIDGE, PATTON G., lawyer; b. McAllen, Tex., Dec. 30, 1949; s. Lloyd and Frances (Potter) L.; m. Candy Lundgren, June 28, 1975; children: Eleanor, Patton, Joe, Lloyd. BA, U. Tex., 1972, JD, 1976. Bar: Tex. 1976, Okla. 2005, US Dist. Ct. (no., so., ea. and we. dists.) Tex., US Ct. Appeals (5th cir.), US Supreme Ct. Law clk. to Hon. Joseph T. Sneed US Ct. Appeals (9th cir.), San Francisco, 1976-77; assoc. to ptnr., comml. litig. McGinnis Lochridge & Kilgore LLP, Austin, Tex., 1977—, mng. ptnr., 2000—10. Chmn. com. ct. adminstrn. US Dist Ct. we. dist. Tex., 1986—97, chmn. admissions com., 1995—97. Trustee Salvation Army, Austin, St. Andrews Episc. Sch. Austin. Fellow: Am. Coll. Trial Lawyers; mem.: ABA, Am. Bd. Trial Advocates, Travis County Bar Assn., Phi Delta Phi, Order of the Coif. Avocations: rugby, skiing, ranching. Office: McGinnis Lochridge & Kilgore 600 Congress Ave Ste 2100 Austin TX 78701 Office Phone: 512-495-6044. Office Fax: 512-505-6344. Business E-Mail: plochridge@mcginnislaw.com.

LOCIGNO, PAUL ROBERT, retired public relations executive; b. Cleve., Sept. 17, 1948; s. Paul Robert and Anna Mae (Zingale) L.; m. Ki Cho Rim; children: Paul III, Tammy, Robert. AA, Cuyahoga C.C., Parma, Ohio, 1974; BA, Case We. Res. U., 1976; postgrad., Cleve. State U., 1977—78. Part-time faculty Cuyahoga C.C., 1979—83; vice-chmn. Presdl. Inaugural Labor Com., Washington, 1980—81; vice-chmn. labor com. Presdl. Inaugural Com., Washington, 1984—85; legis. agt. Internat. Brotherhood of Teamsters, Washington, 1977—90, dir. govt. internat. affairs, 1983—89, dir. Asian/Pacific br. Taipei, Taiwan, 1985—88; spl. rep. of chmn. Hill & Knowlton Pub. Affairs Worldwide, Washington, 1989—92; founding ptnr. Capitoline Internat., Inc., 1992—96; pres., founding ptnr. Rollins Internat. Ltd., Alexandria, Va., 1997—2004; CEO Ganeden Biotech Inc., San Diego, 2004—07; pres. Locigno Internat. Inc., 2004—. Mem. budget com., Prince William County, 2002, 05. Mem. Pres.'s Export Coun., 1988-89; mem. Asia adv. com. Bicentennial of U.S. Constitution, 1990; bd. govs. Am. League for Exports and Security Assistance, 1989; mem. Nat. Commn. for Employment Policy, Washington, 1981-86; mem. zoning ordinance rev. com. Prince William County, Va., budget com., 2001, 04. With USMC, 1068—1970. Mem.: Marine Corps. Assn. Home: 8610 Liberty Trail Unit 301 Manassas VA 20110-2117 Home Phone: 703-369-1759. Personal E-mail: locigno@comcast.net.

LOCKE, ELIZABETH HUGHES, retired foundation administrator; b. Norfolk, Va., June 30, 1939; d. George Morris and Sallie Epps (Moss) Hughes; m. John Rae Locke, Jr., Sept. 13, 1958 (div. 1981); children: John Rae III, Sallie Curtis. BA magna cum laude, Duke U., 1964, PhD, 1972; MA, U. N.C., 1966; DHum (hon.), Furman U., 2004. Instr. English U. N.C., Chapel Hill, 1970-72; dir. univ. pubs. Duke U., Durham, NC, 1973-79; corp. contbns. officer Bethlehem Steel Corp., Pa., 1979-82; dir. edn. divsn. & comm. Duke Endowment, Charlotte, NC, 1982-96, exec. dir., 1996-97, pres., 1997—2004; ret., 2004. Vis. prof. English Duke U., 1972—73. Editor: Duke Encounters, 1977, prospectus for Change: American Private Higher Education, 1985, (mag) Issues, 1985-96. Pres. Angier B. Duke Meml., Inc., 1997-2005, Duke Endowment, 1997-2005, Nanaline H. Duke Fund, 1997-2005, Doris Duke Trust, 1998, Jr. League, Durham, 1976, Hist. Preservation Soc., Durham, 1977, Charlotte Area Donors Forum; past pres. Comm. Philanthropy, Washington, Sch. of Arts, Charlotte; mem. legis. com. Coun. on Founds., 1997-, Washington, 1995; trustee Southeastern Coun. of Founds., 1997—, Wing Haven Found.; commr. So. Assn. Colls. & Schs., 1998—; bd. vis. Davidson Coll., Charlotte Country Day Sch., Duke U., Johnson C. Smith U.; trustee Winghaven Found. Recipient Leadership award Charlotte C. of C., 1984; Danforth fellow, 1972. Mem. Nat. Task Force, English Speaking Union, The Most Venerable Order of St. John of Jerusalem (commander), Colonial Dames Am., Charlotte City Club (bd. govs.), Bd. Regents, Gunston Hall, Phi Beta Kappa. Democrat. Episcopalian. Office: 100 N Tryon St Ste 3500 Charlotte NC 28202-4001 Personal E-mail: betsL@earthlink.net.

LOCKE, JULIE, medical insurance company executive; MBA, U. Va. Mgr., Network Program Anthem Blue Cross and Blue Shield, dir., Medicaid Program, regional v.p., Commonwealth bus.; sr. auditor Marriott Corp., Wash., DC; mgmt. assoc. Mobil Corp., Fairfax, Va.; CEO, health plans, Mid Atlantic Region Amerigroup Corp., 2007—. Office: Amerigroup Corp 4425 Corporation Ln Virginia Beach VA 23462 Office Phone: 757-490-6900. Office Fax: 757-518-3600. Business E-Mail: jlocke@amerigroupcorp.com.

LOCKE, MAMIE E., state legislator; b. Brandon, Miss., Mar. 19, 1954; d. Ennis and Amanda Mcmahon Locke. Mem. Hampton City Coun., 1996—98; vice mayor Hampton, Va., 1998—2000; mayor, 2000—04; dean Sch. Liberal Arts & Edn. U. Hampton; state senator Dist. 2 Va., 2004—. Recipient Lindback Disting. award, 1990, Pathfinder award, Gamma Iota Chpt. Alpha Phi Alpha, Outstanding Pres. award, Mid-Atlantic Region, Alpha Kappa Alpha, Outstanding Woman Govt., Peninsula Women's Forum, Outstanding Pub. award, Conf. Minority Pub. Adminstrs., Martin Luther King Cmty. Svcs. award, Old Dominion U.; named Meritorious Cmty. Svcs. & Ewcelence Acad. leadership, Gamma Iota chpt Delta Sigma Theta. Mem.: Black & Multi-Racial Polit. America NY U., Yvette Alex-Assenoh and Lawrence Hanks, Gender & Politics Post Civil RIghts Era, Women Transforming Polit., Implications Constitution African American Women, Women Civil Rights Movemen, Vicki L Crawford, Fannie Lou Hamer and the Miss. Freedom Dem. Party, Downtown Hampton Child Devel. Ctr., Links Inc., Va. Law Found, Transitions, Regional Dir. Region 3 Nat Black Caucus Local Elected Office (bd. dir.), Women Munic Govt. (bd. dir.), Coun. Acad. Deans, America Coun. Edn., Southern Polit Sci Assn. (com. status woman), America Polit. Sci Assn. (former coun. mem. 1993, bd dir. 1994—99, program com. mem.), Nat. Conf. Black Polit. Scientists (former pres., former nat. polit. sci. rev. editor bd.). Democrat. Home: PO Box 9048 Hampton VA 23670-0048 Office Phone: 757-825-5880. E-mail: district02@sov.state.va.us.

LOCKE, ROBERT JOHN, academic administrator; EdD in Edn. Adminstrn., George Washington U., 1988. Resident dir., Internat. Living Ctr. Cornell U., 1975—77, assoc. dir., Internat. Student and Scholar Svcs., 1979—89; asst. dir. Internat. Student Advising Office, George Washington U., 1977—79; dir. U. NC, Chapel Hill, 1989—. Editor: (NAFSA Field Svc. Working Paper) Internat. Living Centers: The State of the Art. Peace corps vol., Kampala, Uganda, 1972, Mara Inst. Tech., Shah Alam, Malaysia, 1972—74; del. leader People to People Internat. Edn. Del. China, 2006. Grant, Phi Delta Kappa, George Washington U. chpt. Mem.: NAFSA: Assn. Internat. Educators (pres. 2005, Strategic Task Force Internat. Student Access US Edn., chair coun. adv., Fgn. Students and Scholars, Com. Immigration Policy and Practice, Baltic East Ctrl. European Assistance Awards Program Com., Korean Student Assistance Awards Program Selection Com., exec. com. bd. dirs. 2004—06). Office: Internat Student & Scholar Svcs UNC CB#5240 2004 FedEx Global Ed Ctr Chapel Hill NC 27599-5240 Office Phone: 919-962-5661. Office Fax: 919-962-4282.

LOCKE, STANLEY P., electronics executive; B in Acctg., Drake U.; MS in Bus., Columbia U. CPA. Mgmt. positions fin. & corp. develop. CFO, Coffee & Tea Divsn. Sara Lee Corp., 1985—2003; mng. dir. Concord Group, 2003—04; v.p., contr. Thomas & Betts Corp., 2004—08, v.p., bus. devel. & strategic planning, 2008—. Office: Thomas & Betts Corp 8155 T&B Blvd Memphis TN 38125 Office Phone: 901-252-8000. Office Fax: 901-680-5112. Business E-Mail: stanley.locke@tnb.com.

LOCKEY, RICHARD FUNK, allergist, immunologist, educator; b. Lancaster, Pa., Jan. 15, 1940; s. Stephen Daniel and Anna (Funk) L.; m. Carol Lee Madill, July 3, 1982; children: Brian Christopher, Keith Edward. BS, Haverford Coll., 1961; MD, Temple U., 1965; MS, U. Mich., 1972. Diplomate Am. Bd. Internal Medicine, Am. Bd. Allergy and Immunology. Intern Temple U. Med. Sch., Phila., 1965-66; asst. resident internal medicine Univ. Hosp. U. Mich., Ann Arbor, 1966-67, resident, 1966-68, fellow in allergy and immunology, 1969-70; asst. prof. medicine U. South Fla. Coll. Medicine, Tampa, 1973-77, assoc. prof. medicine, 1977-83, asst. dir. divsn. allergy and immunology, 1979-82, dir. allergy and immunology, 1982—, prof. medicine, 1983—, prof. pediat., 1983—, prof. pub. health, 1987—; asst. chief sect. allergy and immunology VA Hosp., Tampa, 1973-82, chief sect. allergy and immunology, 1983—, Joy McCann Culverhouse endowed chair allergy and immunology, 1997. Mem. allergenic adv. com. FDA, 1985-89. Editor: Allergy and Clinical Immunology, 1980, World Allergy Orgn. website, 2005—; co-editor: (with S.C. Bukantz) Fundamentals of Immunology and Allergy, 1987, (with S.C. Bukantz) Principles of Immunology and Allergy, 1987, JAMA Primer on Allergic and Immunologic Diseases, 1987, (with S. C. Bukantz) Allergen Immunotherapy, 1991, (with M. Levine) Monograph on Insect Allergy, 1995, (with S. Bukantz) Allergens and Allergen Immunotherapy, 1999, (with D. Ledford) Immunotherapy: A Practical Review and Guide, 2000, (with S. Kemp) Diagnostic Testing of Allergic Disease, 2000, (with S. Bukantz) Allergens and Allergen Immunotherapy Allergic Diseases, 4th edit., 2004, (with M. Levine) Insect Allergy, 4th edit., 2004; mem. editl. bd. Jour. on Allergy and Immunology, 1999-04; contbr. more than 500 articles to profl. jours. and chpts. to books; author monographs. Hon. chmn. R.I. chpt. Asthma and Allergy Found., 2004. Served as maj. USAF, 1971-73. Rrecipient Alumni Achievement award Temple U. Sch. of Medicine Alumni Assn., 1990, Outstanding Leadership in Chpt. Devel. and Patient Support, Nat. Asthma and Allergy Found. of Am. award, 1992, Cert. of Appreciation Fla. Med. Assn., 1992, medalist Fla. Acad. Scis., 2000, Disting. Svc. award Univ. S. Fla., 2001, Alumni award McCaskey HS, 2007; Named Outstanding Med. Specialist, Town and Country Mag., 1989, Claude P. Brown Meml. lectr. Assn. Clin. Scientists, ADA, 1981, Disting. Visitor Ann. Meeting of Coll. of Medicine, Republic of Costa Rica, 1979, spl. mem. Internat. Sci. Bd. Pharmacia Allergy Rsch. Found., 1992—. Fellow ACP, AAAS, AMA, Am. Coll. Chest Physicians, Am. Acad. Allergy and Immunology (chmn. com. on insects 1978-81, chmn. undergrad. and grad. edn. com. 1982-88, com. on occupl. lung disease 1982—, chmn. com. on standardization of allergenic extracts 1983-86, exec. com. mem. at large 1986-88, historian 1988-89, sec. 1989-90, treas. 1990-91, pres.-elect 1991-92, pres. 1992-93, Am. Bd. Allergy and Immunology (bd. dirs. 1993-98), World Allergy Orgn. (bd. dirs. 1997—, editor web page, 2004, treas. 2006—, pres. elect, 2008-09), Soc. Allergy and Immunology of Cordoba, Argentina (hon.), John M. Sheldon U. of Mich. Allergy Soc. (councilor 1977-80, pres. 1980-82), Fla. Allergy and Immunology Soc. (sec.-treas. 1979-80, pres. 1981-82, Disting. Svc. award 2002), Southeastern Allergy Assn., Hillsborough County Med. Assn., Joint Coun. Allergy and Immunology, Clin. Immunology Soc., Fla. Thoracic Soc., Univ. Club, Tampa Yacht Club. Avocations: antique cut glass, antique tools, hunting, fishing. Home: 2708 W Marlin Ave Tampa FL 33611 Office: U So Fla VA Hosp 13000 Bruce B Downs Blvd 111D Tampa FL 33612 Office Phone: 813-972-7631.

LOCKHART, DENNIS P., bank executive; b. Bakersfield, Calif., Feb. 1, 1947; BA in Polit. Sci. and Econs., Stanford U., Calif., 1968; MA in Internat. Econs. and Am. Fgn. Policy, Johns Hopkins U. Sch. Adv. Internat. Studies, Balt., 1971. Head, infrastructure project financing Citicorp/Citibank (now Citigroup), Saudi Arabia, tng. dir. Greece, COO, comml. and consumer banking joint venture Iran, sr. corp. officer, southeast office, 1978—86, head, Latin-Am. debt-to-equity swap investment prog., 1987—88; pres. Heller Internat. Grp., 1988—2001; mng. ptnr. Zephyr Mgmt., L.P., NY, 2001—03; adj. prof. Nitze Sch. Adv. Internat. Studies, Johns Hopkins U., 2001; faculty Walsh Sch. Fgn. Svc., Georgetown U., 2003—; pres., CEO Fed. Res. Bank Atlanta, 2007—. Mem. adv. coun. Export-Import Bank; mem. bd. dirs. CapitalSource Inc., Tri-Valley Corp., Greenfield Holdings Credit Ltd., Bunge Corp., Brazil; chmn. Small Enterprise Assistance Funds. Lt. USMC, 1968—74. Mem.: Emerging Markets Pvt. Equity Assn. (mem. adv. com.). Office: Fed Res Bank Atlanta 1000 Peachtree St NE Atlanta GA 30309-4470 Office Phone: 404-498-8500.*

LOCKHEAD, GREGORY ROGER, retired psychology professor; b. Boston, Aug. 8, 1931; s. John Roger and Ester Mae (Bixby) L.; m. Jeanne Marie Hutchinson, June 9, 1957; children: Diane, Elaine, John. BS, Tufts U., 1958; PhD, Johns Hopkins, 1965. Psychologist rsch. staff IBM Research, Yorktown Heights, NY, 1958-61; rsch. assoc., instr. Johns Hopkins U., Balt., 1961-65; asst. prof. psychology Duke U., Durham, NC, 1965-68, assoc. prof., 1968-71, prof., 1971-2001, chmn. dept. exptl. psychology, 1991-97, prof. dept. psychol. and brain scis., 2001—06; prof. emeritus, 2006—. Scholar Stanford U.; rsch. assoc. U. Calif., Berkeley, 1971-72; fellow Wolfson Coll., Oxford (Eng.) U., 1980-81; scholar Fla. Atlantic U., 1981; cons. in human engring. Cons. editor: Perception and Psychophysics, 1972-92; contbr. articles to profl. jours., co-author, editor chpts. in books. With USN, 1951-55. NSF grantee, 1966-69, 79-84, USPHS grantee, 1963-69, 70-79, Air Force Office Sci. Rsch., 1983-91. Fellow APA, Am. Psychol. Soc., Soc. Exptl. Psychologists; mem. Psychonomic Soc., Internat. Soc. Psychophysics, Sigma Xi, Phi Beta Kappa (hon.). Home: 37 Gardenia Ct Durham NC 27705 Business E-Mail: greg@psych.duke.edu.

LOCKWOOD-BENET, MILDRED M., language educator; b. Mo., Dec. 24, 1962; d. William Lockwood and Ilia Irma Benet; m. Juan Fernandez-Gonzalez, Feb. 13, 1988; children: Camila, Guillermo, Marilia. BA in Elem. Edn., Boston Coll., 1984; M, Columbia U., 1987; EdD, U. P.R., 2003. Prof. English U. P.R., Guaynabo, PR, 1988—. Cons. Coll Bd., PR, Santillana Docentes, PR, First Hosp. Corp. Health Svcs., PR. Mem.: TESOL, Am. Ednl. Rsch. Assn. Avocations: reading, pilates, sewing. Home: S-21 California St Urb Mallorca Guaynabo PR 00969 Office: Univ PR Coll Gen Studies English Dept PO Box 23323 San Juan PR 00931 Office Phone: 787-764-0000 2186. Business E-Mail: mlockwood@uprrp.edu.

LODDER, ROBERT A., science educator; PhD, Ind. U., 1988. Prof. U. of Ky., Lexington, Ky., 1988—; v.p. MAReNIR Technologies, Houston, Tex., 2002—03. P.s. adv. com. U.S. FDA, Washington, 2002—. Contbr. articles to profl. jours.; patentee in field. Recipient 100 award R & D mag., 1988, Tomas Hirschfeld award Pitts. Conf., 1988; 1st prize IBM Supercomputing Competition, 1990, NSF New Young Investigator award 1992, Paper award ASAE, 1993, Buchi NIR award, 2001, Orville N. Green award, 2005; Technicon near-infrared analysis rsch. fellow, 1987. Mem. AAAS, ASTM, Coun. for Near-Infrared Spectroscopy (del.-at-large to nat. bd. dirs.), Am. Chem. Soc., Am. Assn. Pharm. Scientists, Am. Pharm. Assn., Ky. Acad. Sci. Achievements include patents for 5553610. Home: 192 Timberlane Ct Nicholasville KY 40356-9779 Office: Univ of Kentucky A123 ASTeCC Bldg Lexington KY 40506-0286 Business E-Mail: l0dder@uky.edu.

LODHI, M. A.K., physicist, educator; b. Agra, UP, India, Sept. 17, 1933; came to U.S., 1963; s. Abdulhakeem Khan and Hasina Lodhi; m. Shanaz Akhtar Hashmi, Aug. 27, 1965 (dec. Jan. 1973); children: Asra, Saima; m. Khalida Bano Farooqui, June 14, 1973; 1 child, Sundus A. PhD, U. London, 1963. Prof. Tex. Tech U., Lubbock, 1963—. Cons. in field. Editor: Superheavy Element, 1979; contbr. 200 articles to profl. jours. Grantee NSF, 1978, 85, SAAR Found., 1988. Mem. Am. Phys. Soc. Muslim. Achievements include research in nuclear and particle physis nuclear systematics, nuclear re4actor design, quark-gluon plasma, space science, orbital debris, space radiationh, space power generation, Hadron quark hybrid model, new and renewable energy sources, devices and distribution. Office: Texas Tech U Dept Physics MS 1051 Lubbock TX 79409 Office Phone: 806-742-3778. Business E-Mail: a.lodhi@ttu.edu.

LODZINSKI, FRANK A., oil and gas industry executive; BSBA in Acctg. & Fin., Wayne State U. CPA. With Arthur Andersen LLP; founder Energy Resource Assocs., Inc., 1984—92; pres. Hampton Resources Corp., 1992—95; cons. Bellwether Exploration Co., 1995—96; pres., founder Cliffwood Oil & Gas Corp., 1996; pres., CEO Texoil Inc., 1997—2001, AROC Inc., 2001; founder Southern Bay Energy, LLC, 2005, pres., 2005; pres., CEO GeoResources, Inc., 2007—. Bd. dirs. Hampton Resources Corp., 1992—95; former bd. dirs. Cliffwood Oil & Gas Corp., 1996; bd. dirs. GeoResources Inc., 2007—. Office: GeoResources Inc Southern Bay Energy 110 Cypress Station Dr, Ste 220 Houston TX 77090 Office Phone: 281-537-9920. Office Fax: 281-537-8324. Business E-Mail: flodzinski@georesourcesinc.com.

LOEB, BEN FOHL, JR., retired law educator; b. Nashville, May 15, 1932; s. Ben Fohl and Frances (Paysinger) L.; m. Anne Nelson, Sept. 23, 1961 (div. 1982); children: Charles Nelson, William Nelson. BA, Vanderbilt U., 1955, JD, 1960. Bar: Tenn. 1960, NC 1975, US Supreme Ct. 1966. Law clk. Office of Sec. of Navy, 1959; assoc. Crownover, Branstetter & Folk, Nashville, 1960-64; asst. dir. Inst. Govt. U. N.C., Chapel Hill, 1964—2004, prof. pub. law and govt. Sch. Govt., 1972—2004, prof. emeritus, 2004—. Counsel to N.C. legis. coms. on motor vehicle law and transp., Raleigh, 1973-83; cons. on alcohol beverage control, 1985-89; cons. on wildlife, natural and scenic areas, 1989-93; mem. U. N.C. Faculty Coun., 1994-97. Author: Traffic Law and Highway Safety, 1970, Alcohol Beverage Control Law, 1971, Motor Vehicle Law, 1975, Legal Aspects of Dental Practice, 1977, Eminent Domain Procedure, 1984, Punishments for Crimes and Motor Vehicle Offenses, 1999; assoc. editor Vanderbilt Law Rev., 1959-60. 1st lt. US Army, 1955—57. Mem. ABA, Tenn. Bar Assn., Phi Beta Kappa, Phi Delta Phi, Pi Kappa Alpha (chpt. pres. 1954-55), Carolina Club (Chapel Hill). Democrat. Baptist. Home: 108 Bayview Dr Chapel Hill NC 27516-9232 Personal E-mail: benloeb@bellsouth.net.

LOEB, MICHEL, food products executive; MS in Mgmt., U. Belgium, Belgium, 1972. Sales & mktg. mgr., pet food & dairy products, sr. brand mgr., chocolate products Nestlè, Belgium; sr. mktg. & mgmt. positions S.C. Johnson & Son, Inc., 1988—2003; pres., Chiquita Fresh Group, Europe Chiquita Brands Internat Inc., 2004—07; pres., Europe and Middle East Chiquita Brands International, Inc., 2007—. Office: Chiquita Brands International Inc 550 S Caldwell St Ste 1010 Charlotte NC 28202-2681 Office Phone: 513-784-8000. Office Fax: 513-784-8030. Business E-Mail: mloeb@chiquita.com.

LOEFFLER, NANCY B., volunteer, board member; m. Tom Loeffler; 3 children. Bd. dirs. SW Airlines Co., 2003—. Bd. dirs. Blanton Mus. Fine Art; bd. regents Nat. Cowgirl Mus., St. Mary's U.; mem., capitol adv. com. Tex. Lutheran U.; bd. Visitors U. Texas M.D. Anderson Cancer Ctr.; v.p. Residence Found. Recipient Trefoil award, Girl Scouts of San Antonio Area, 2006. Office: SW Airlines Co 2702 Love Field Drive Dallas TX 75235 Office Phone: 214-792-5015. Office Fax: 214-792-4000. Business E-Mail: Loeffler.Nancy@southwest.com.

LOEHLIN, JOHN CLINTON, psychologist, educator; b. Ferozepore, India, Jan. 13, 1926; s. Clinton Herbert and Eunice (Cleland) L.; m. Marjorie Leafdale, Jan. 2, 1962; children: Jennifer Ann, James Norris. AB, Harvard U., 1947; PhD, U. Calif., Berkeley, 1957. With rsch. dept. McCann-Erickson, Inc., Cleve., 1947-49; instr. to asst. prof. psychology U. Nebr., Lincoln, 1957-64; faculty U. Tex., Austin, 1964—69, prof. psychology and computer scis., 1969-92, prof. emeritus, 1992—. Author: Computer Models of Personality, 1968, Latent Variable Models, 1987, Genes and Environment in Personality Development, 1992; co-author: Race Differences in Intelligence, 1975, Heredity, Environment and Personality, 1976, Introduction to Theories of Personality, 1985. With USNR, 1945-47, 51-53. Fellow Ctr. Advanced Study Behavioral Scis., 1971-72. Fellow Psychol. Soc. (assoc.); mem. Behavior Genetics Assn., Soc. Multivariate Exptl. Psychology. Home: 304 Almarion Dr Austin TX 78746-5644 Office: U Tex Dept Psychology 1 U Station A8000 Austin TX 78712-0187 Home Phone: 512-732-0092; Office Phone: 512-475-7008. E-mail: loehlin@psy.utexas.edu.

LOEWE, BARBARA, speech educator, theater educator, humanities educator; d. Oscar U. and Lillian (Freund) L. BS in Education, Speech, Theater, Fla. So. Coll., 1960; MA in Theater, Western Res. U., 1961; postgrad., U. Denver, Fla. State U., 1965. Tchr. Manatee County Schs., Bradenton, Fla., 1960-63; instr. SUNY, Brockport, 1965; asst. prof. Bloomsburg (Pa.) State Coll., 1965-68; prof. Hillsborough CC, Tampa, 1969—2003. Guest lectr., counselor, Min. Universal Ch. of Master, Santa Clara, Calif., 1979—; real estate investor, Tampa, 1970—. Bd. dirs. Meadowood Condominium Assn., Tampa, 1979-85, pres., 1979-85; bd. dirs. Hillsborough C.C. chpt. Fla. United Svcs., 1988, Stageworks Theatre, 1989-90, Mary Walker Apts. of Tampa Jewish Fedn., 1995—. Recipient B'nai Brith award, Fla. So. Coll., 1958. Mem. Fla. Comms. Assn. (exec. sec., treas. 1986-90), SE Regional Minister's Assn. Universal Ch. of Master (treas. 1994-95, chair 1995-98), Mensa (mem. exec. com. Tampa Bay chpt. 1987—). Jewish. Home: 12401 N 22nd St Apt C111 Tampa FL 33612 Personal E-mail: bloewe@juno.com.

LOEWY, ROBERT GUSTAV, aerospace executive, engineering educator; b. Phila., Feb. 12, 1926; s. Samuel N. and Esther (Silverstein) L.; m. Lila Myrna Spinner, Jan. 16, 1955; children: David G., Esther Elizabeth, Joanne Victoria, Raymond Matthew. B in Aero. Engring., Rensselaer Poly. Inst., 1947; MS, MIT, 1948; PhD, U. Pa., 1962. Sr. vibrations engr. Martin Co., Balt., 1948-49; assoc. rsch. engr. Cornell Aero. Lab., Buffalo, 1949-52, prin. engr., 1953-55; staff stress engr. Piasecki Helicopter Co., Morton, Pa., 1952-53; chief dynamics engr., then chief tech. engr. Vertol divsn. Boeing Co., Essington, Pa., 1955-62; from assoc. prof. to prof. mech. and aerospace scis. U. Rochester, 1962-73, dean Coll. Engring. and Applied Sci., 1967—73; dir. Space Sci. Ctr., 1966—71; v.p., provost Rensselaer Poly. Inst., Troy, NY, 1973—78, inst. prof., 1978-93; dir. Rotorcraft Tech. Ctr., 1982-93; chmn. sch. aerospace engring. Ga. Inst. Tech., 1993—2009, Wm. R.T. Oakes prof., 2000—09, prof. aerospace engring., 1993—. Chief scientist USAF, 1965-66; cons. govt. and industry, 1959—; mem. aircraft panel Pres.'s Sci. Adv. Coun., 1968-72; mem. Air Force Sci. Adv. Bd., 1966-75, 1978-85, vice chmn., 1971, chmn., 1972-75, chmn. aero. systems div. adv. group, 1978-84; mem. Post Office Rsch. and Engring. Adv. Coun., 1966-68; mem. rsch. and tech. adv. com. on aeros. NASA, 1970-71, mem. rsch. and tech. adv. coun., 1976-77, chmn. aero. adv. com., 1978-83; mem. aerospace engring. bd. NRC, 1972-78, 1988-93, mem. bd. on army sci. and tech., 1986-90; mem. naval studies bd. NAS, 1979-82; chmn. tech. adv. com. FAA, 1976-77; bd. dirs. Vertical Flight Found. Contbr. articles to profl. jours. Served with USNR, 1944-46. Recipient NASA Disting. Pub. Svc. award, 1983; Gotshall-Powell scholar, 1946; named to Alumni Hall of Fame, Rensselaer Poly. Inst., 2009; USAF Exceptional Civilian Svc. awards, 1966, 75, 85, Spirit of St. Louis medal ASME, 1996, Guggenheim medal, 2007. Fellow AAAS; hon. fellow AIAA (Lawrence Sperry award 1958, Dryden lectr. 1999), Am. Helicopter Soc. (pres. 2002-03, tech. dir. 1963-64, chmn. bd. 2003-04, Nikolsky lectr. 1984); mem. Am. Soc. Engring. Edn., Nat. Acad. Engring., Sigma Xi, Sigma Gamma Tau, Tau Beta Pi. Achievements include research on unsteady rotor aerodynamics first showing it to be fundamentally different from fixed wing. Office: Ga Inst Tech Sch Aerospace Engring Atlanta GA 30332-0001 Home: 3420 Wood Valley Rd NW Atlanta GA 30327-1518 Office Phone: 404-894-3002.

LOFTIN, RICHARD BOWEN, academic administrator; b. Hearne, Tex., June 29, 1949; s. Richard and Dorothy Mae (Weems) L.; m. Karin Christiane Juhn Cibula, Nov. 23, 1972; children: Elisabeth Christiane, Benjamin Bowen. BS in Physics, Tex. A&M U., 1970; MA in Physics, Rice U., 1973, PhD in Physics, 1975. Asst. physics prof. Tex. A&M U., Galveston, 1975-76; asst. prof. U. Houston, 1976-80, assoc. prof., 1980-88, prof. physics, 1988—2000, prof. computer sci., 1994—2000; faculty assoc. software tech. br. NASA Johnson Space Ctr., 1986—2000; exec. dir. Va. Modeling, Analysis, and Simulation Ctr., prof. elect. and computer engring., prof. computer sci.; prof. electrical & computer engring., prof. computer sci. Old Dominion U., 2000—05, dir. simulation programs, 2000—05; v.p., CEO Tex. A&M U., Galveston, Tex., 2005—, prof. maritime systems engring., 2005—, interim pres. College Station, Tex., 2009—. Cons. McDonnell Douglas Space Systems Co., 1990-92, LinCom, 1992-93. Contbr. articles to Innovative Applications of Artificial Intelligence, Machine Mediated Learning, ASCE Monograph, Internat. Advances in Nondestructive Testing, Jour. of Applied Physics and numerous others. Mem. bd. Ministerial Edn. Wis. Luth. Synod, 1990—, dist. coord. parish edn. south cen. dist., 1981-91. Recipient Space Act award NASA, 1992, Pub. Svc. medal NASA, 1993, Invention of the Yr. award, 1995, Award for Excellence in Teaching & Svc. U.Houston Downtown, Am. Assn. Artificial Intelligence award Mem. AIAA (vice chmn. com. on stds. for space automation and robotics 1990-93, tech. com. on artificial intelligence 1992-2002), IEEE (computer soc. tech. com. visualization and graphics 2002-), Am. Assn. Artificial Intelligence, Am. Assn. Physics Tchrs., Am. Phys. Soc., Assn. for Computing Machinery. Achievements include co-design of architecture for intelligent computer-aided training systems; patent in computer software. Office: Tex A&M University Office of President 1246 TAMU College Station TX 77843-1246 Office Phone: 979-845-2217. Office Fax: 979-845-5027. E-mail: president@tamu.edu.*

LOFTIS, DWIGHT A., state legislator; b. Greenville, SC, Feb. 4, 1943; s. Stephen A. and Stella M. Loftis; m. Sandra Elaine Jones, 1963; children: Kerry Lants, Kevin Douglas, Alison. AA, North Greenville Coll., 1966. Mem. Dist. 19 SC House of Reps., 1996—; mem. Edn. Com., Pub. Works Com., Invitations & Mem. Resolutions Com. Mem.: Crime Stoppers Greenville (former pres., mem. bd. dir.). Republican. Address: 540 Sulphur Springs Rd Greenville SC 29617 Mailing: 522C Blatt Bldg Columbia SC 29201 Office Phone: 803-734-3101, 864-246-7917. Business E-Mail: dal@legis.lpitr.state.sc.us.

LOGAN, ANA RIVAS, state legislator; b. Nicaragua, May 16, 1961; children: Alexandra, Nicole, Mario. B in Computer Sci., Fla. Internat. U.; M in Computer Sci., Nova Southeastern U. Educator; mem. sch. bd. Miami-Dade County Pub. Schools, Fla., 2006—10; mem. Dist. 114 Fla. House of Representatives, 2011—. Republican. Office: 11010 N Kendall Dr #102-A Miami FL 33176-1205 also: Fla House of Reps 1301 The Capitol 402 S Monroe St Tallahassee FL 32399-1300 Office Phone: 305-275-1912, 850-488-2831.

LOGAN, DON, retired communications executive; b. Mobile, Ala., Feb. 2, 1944; m. Sandra Logan; children: Jeff, Stan. BA in Math., magna cum laude, Auburn U., Ala., 1966, D (hon.), 1997; MS in Math., Clemson U., SC, 1968, D (hon.), U. Ala., Birmingham. Mgr. Southern Progress Corp., 1970—78, pres. Oxmoor House divsn., 1978—84, exec. v.p., 1984—85, chmn. CEO, 1985—92; pres., COO Time Inc., NYC, 1992—94, chmn., CEO, 1994—97; chmn. media & comm. group AOL Time Warner, NYC, 2002—05; owner Birmingham Barons, 2005—. Bd. dirs. Time Warner Cable Inc., 2003—, non-exec. chmn., 2006—09. Trustee Samford U., Birmingham; bd. dirs. Auburn U. Found., Civil Rights Inst., Birmingham, Ala. Assn. Ind. Coll.'s & U.'s. Recipient Henry Johnson Fisher award, Mag. Pubs. of America, 2001, Lifetime Achievement award, Auburn Alumni Assn., 2005; named to The Ala. Acad. of Honor, 2003, The U. Ala. Coll. Comm. & Info. Sciences Hall of Fame, 2004, The Advt. Hall of Fame, American Advt. Fedn., 2009. Avocation: fly fishing.

LOGAN, KATHRYN VANCE, research engineer; b. Atlanta, June 12, 1946; d. Charles Monroe Vance, Sr. and Lucille (James) Evitt; m. William Stephen Logan, Sr. Sept. 9, 1967; children: Stephanie Anne, William Stephen Jr. B Ceramic Engring., Ga. Inst. Tech., 1970, MS in Ceramic Engring., 1980, PhD in Civil Engring., 1992. Lic. profl. engr., Ga. Student rsch. asst., cons. Ga. Tech. Rsch. Inst., Atlanta, 1965—68, rsch. engr. I, 1970—76, rsch. engr. II, 1976—85, head thermite processing, 1985-93, head ceramics br., 1985—90, sr. rsch. engr., 1985—93, lab. dir., MSTL/GTRL, 1990-92; interim asst. v.p. Office Interdisciplinary Programs Ga. Inst. Tech., Atlanta, 1992-94, prin. rsch. engr., assoc. dir. rsch. Sch. Materials Sci. and Engring., 1994-95, mem., Ctr. for Computational Mechanics, 1992—94, spl. asst. to Vice Provost, 1996—97, assoc. dir. for rsch. Sch. Materials Sci. & Engring., 1994—95, dir. rsch. Sch. Materials Sci. and Engring., 1995—96, prin. rsch. engr., 1993—2001, prin. rsch. engr. emerita, 2001—; materials engr. IPA, 1998—2000; dir., Nat. Inst. Aerospace Ctr. for Multifunctional Aerospace Materials Va. Tech., 2004—10, Samuel P. Langley Prof., 2004—10, adj. prof., 2010—. Pres., bd. dirs. Powder Technologies, Inc., Roswell, Ga., 1989-; exec. com. Bd. on Army Sci. and Tech. Nat. Rsch. Coun., 1997-2002; IPA, vis. prof., US Army Corps of Engrs., US Army Rsch. Office, 2000-01; external adv. bd., Clemson U., 2005-; invited presenter in field. Contbr. articles to engring. jours.; peer reviewer for several journals and organizations. Instr. ARC, Ga., 1980-82. Recipient Frederick Greaves Walker award, 2007; named Outstanding Grad. Student Ga. Inst. Tech., Soc. Women Engineers, 1980, Ga. Tech. Rsch. Inst. Outstanding Performance in Program Develop., 1989. Fellow Am. Ceramic Soc. (sec. 1992, vice chair engring. ceramics divsn. 1992, vice chair, 1993, chair, 1994, mem. programs and meetings com., 1995-99, counselor, 1995-97, ann. meeting chair, 1996-97, rules chair engring. ceramics divsn., 1998-2000, bd. dirs. 2000-05, v.p. programs, meeting and exposition 1998-99, pres.-elect 2002-03, pres. 2003-04, engring. ceramics divsn. James I. Mueller Lecture, 1999), Nat. Inst. Ceramic Engrs. (sec./treas. 1996-97, v.p. 1997-98, pres.-elect 1998-99, pres. 1999-2000, past pres. 2000-01, mem. exec. com. 1996-2002); mem. NSPE, Keramos, Materials Rsch. Soc., Am. Assn. of Engring. Socs. (gov. bd. dirs. 2000-02, vice chair 2001-02), Internat. Acad. of Ceramics, Sigma Xi (Monie A. Ferst award for Excellence in Undergraduate Rsch., 1970), Alpha Xi Delta, Gamma Beta Phi. Episcopalian. Achievements include patents in field. Avocations: gardening, jewelry making, sewing. Office: National Inst of Aerospace 100 Exploration Way Rm 214 Hampton VA 23666 also: Va Tech Dept Materials Sci & Engring Coll Engring 213 Holden Hall Blacksburg VA 24061 Office Phone: 757-325-6820. Office Fax: 757-325-6754. Business E-Mail: kvlogan@vt.edu.

LOGAN, SHARON BROOKS, lawyer; b. Nov. 19, 1945; d. Blake Elmer and Esther N. (Statum) Brooks; children: John W. III, Troy Blake. BS Econs., U. Md., 1967, MBA Mktg., 1969; JD, U. Fla., 1979. Bar: Fla. 1979. Prin. Raymond Wilson, Esq., Ormond Beach, Fla., 1980; atty. Landis, Graham & French, Daytona Beach, Fla., 1981, Watson & Assocs., Daytona Beach, 1982—84, Sharon B. Logan, PA, Ormond Beach, 1984—. Legal adv. to paralegal program Daytona Beach CC, 1984—. Sponsor Ea. Surfing Assn., Daytona Beach, 1983—, Nat. Scholastic Surfing Assn., 1987—; bd. dir. Ctr. for Visually Impaired, 1991—. Recipient Citizenship award, Rotary Club, 1962—63; fellow Woodrow Wilson, U. Md., 1967. Mem.: Oceanside CC, Daytona Beach Area Bd. Realtors, Volusia County Estate Planning Coun., Fla. Supreme Ct. Hist. Soc., Volusia County Real Property Coun., Inc. (sec. 1987—88, bd. dirs., v.p. 1988—89, pres. 1989—90, sec. 1990—91, 1991—97, pres. 1997—98, 1998—), Volusia County Bar Assn. (bd. dir.), Fla. Bar Assn. (cert. real estate atty. 1996, real property and probate sect.), Oceanside Country Club, Daytona Beach Ski & Travel Club, Ducks Unlimited, Mus. Arts and Scis., Gator Club, Md. Club, Beech Mountain Country Club, Halifax River Yacht Club, Dunn-Blount Inn of Cts., Univ. Club, Moose Lodge, Sigma Alpha Epsilon, Delta Delta Delta (Scholarship award 1964), Omicron Delta Epsilon, Phi Kappa Phi, Alpha Lamba Delta, Beta Gamma Sigma. Democrat. Episcopalian. Avocations: interior decorating, cooking, sewing, aerobics. Office: Sharon B Logan PA 180 Vining Ct PO Box 4258 Ormond Beach FL 32175-4258 Office Phone: 386-673-5787. Business E-Mail: loganlaw@sharonloganpa.com.

LOGSDON, DANIEL, political organization administrator; V.p. state & local govt. affairs Windstream Communications, 2005—10; dep. chief of staff Office of Ky. Gov. Beshear, 2009—; chmn. Ky. State Dem. Party, 2010—. Democrat. Office: Ky State Democratic Party PO Box 694 Frankfort KY 40602*

LOGUE, JUDITH FELTON, psychoanalyst, educator; b. Phila., Aug. 21, 1942; d. Martin and Laura (Goldman) Kirshenbaum; m. Stephen Felton, Feb. 8, 1966 (div. Aug. 1989); 1 child, Jane Jennifer; m. A. Douglas Logue, Feb. 14, 1990. AB in Govt., Wheaton Coll., Mass., 1963; MSW, Rutgers U., 1966, PhD, 1983; grad., NY Ctr. Psychoanalytic Tng., 1978. Diplomate Am. Bd. Psychotherapy, Am. Bd. Forensic Medicine, Am. Bd. Examiners Clin. Social Worker, Am. Bd. Forensic Examiners, Am. Bd. Psychol. Specialties, cert. profl. coach, mentor coach. Clin. social worker VA, Newark, 1967; psychotherapist Santa Barbara (Calif.) Mental Health Svcs., 1967-69; supr. Santa Barbara Counselling Ctr., 1967-69; pvt. practice psychoanalysis, 1969—; pres. Goldilox Co. Inc., 1997—, Shairing Co., 2001—. Psychoanalyst, therapist Fifth Ave. Ctr. for Psychotherapy, NYC, 1969-72; instr. Marymount Manhattan Coll., 1971; psychotherapy supr. clin. dept. psychiatry Rutgers Med. Sch., New Brunswick, NJ, 1972-75, tchg. asst. Grad. Sch. Social Work, 1974-76; vis. lectr. Bryn Mawr Coll. Sch. Social Work and Social Rsch., 1980;

faculty NY Ctr. for Psychoanalytic Tng., 1980—, NJ Inst. Psychoanalysis and Psychotherapy, 1982—; adv. bd. Am. Bd. Forensic Social Workers, 1999—, chair adv. bd., 2000; pres. Goldilox Co., Inc., 1997, ShAIRing, Inc., 2000; faculty So. NJ Psychoanalytic Inst., Brigantine, 2004—, bd. dirs. Mem. editl. bd. jour Current Issues in Psychoanalytic Practice, 1983-93; contbr. articles to profl. jours. Bd. dirs. N.Y. Ctr. for Psychoanalytic Tng., Inst. for Psychoanalysis and Psychotherapy N.J. Faculty, 1982—. Recipient Disting. Faculty award Atlantic County Psychoanalytic Soc., 1987; NIMH fellow, 1965. Fellow N.J. Soc. for Clin. Social Work; mem. AAUP, NASW, APA (pres. divsn. 39 2003-04, bd. dirs. 2005—, com. psychoanalytic psychotherapists, bd. dirs. divsn. 39 2006—), Nat. Assn. for Advancement of Psychoanalysis, Acad. Cert. Social Workers, Soc. for Psychoanalytic Tng. (bd. dirs. 1983-90, dir. social sci. program 1983-86), Am. Coll. Forensic Examiners Internat. (mem. editl. bd. jours. 1999—, Outstanding Svc. award 2000), Internat. Coach Fedn.; mem. APA (pres. div. 39 sec. III, 2003-04), Am. Psychoanalytic Assn. (psychotherapy task force, psychoanalysis and undergrad. edn. task force, com. on psychotherapist assocs. 2003—13, com. status women and girls, 2013-), Am. Coll. Forensic Social Workers (chair 2000-01), Women in Aviation Internat, 99's Internat. Orgn. Women Pilots, Nat. Bus. Aviation Assn, Rutgers U. Alumni Assn. (bd. dirs. 2003-05), So. NJ Psychoanalytic Inst. (faculty mem. 2004-06, bd. dirs. 2004-06). Home: 18604 Tranquility Base Ln Port Saint Lucie FL 34987-3236 Home Phone: 609-915-9155; Office Phone: 609-921-0828. Personal E-mail: judith@judithlogue.com.

LOGUE, WILLIAM J., delivery service executive; Various ops. mgmt. positions FedEx Express, 1989—95, v.p. nat. hub ops. Memphis hub, 1995—99, sr. v.p. air-ground freight svcs., 1999—2004, sr. v.p. ops., 2004—06, exec. v.p. ops. and system support, 2006—08, exec. v.p. and COO, 2008—09; pres. FedEx Freight Corp., 2009—10, pres. and CEO, 2010—. Office: FedEx Corporation 942 South Shady grove Rd Memphis TN 38120 Office Phone: 901-818-7500.

LOHMANN, GEORGE YOUNG, JR., neurosurgeon, health facility administrator, artist; b. Scranton, Pa., Aug. 9, 1947; s. George Young Lohmann and Elizabeth (Nichols) Frantzen; m. Joette Calabrese, May 15, 1973 (div. 1981); m. Rosemary Ei-Ling Ma, Sept. 24, 1988 (div. 1998); 1 child, Norelle Christa Victoria. AB in Chemistry with honors, Hobart Coll., 1968; MD, SUNY, Buffalo, 1972. Diplomate Am. Bd. Neurol. Surgeons, Am. Acad. Pain Specialists, Am. Bd. Forensic Medicine, Am. Acad. Disability Analysts. Resident gen. surgery Wesley Meml. Hosp., Chgo., 1972-73; asst. med. dir. West Side Orgn., Chgo., 1973-74; emergency physician St. James Hosp., Chicago Heights, Ill., 1973-74; from jr. resident to chief resident neurosurgery Georgetown U. Hosp., Washington, 1975-79; chief resident neurosurgery Washington Vets. Hosp., 1978; pvt. practice Baton Rouge, 1979-81, 81-84; dir. dept. neurosurgery Brookdale Hosp. Med. Ctr., Bklyn., 1984-93; pres. Bklyn. Neurosurg. Svcs., Inc., 1985—; pvt. practice Midland, Tex., 1994-96; founding pres. Dragongate Adoption Cons., Inc., 1999—; CEO Doc Mktg. LLC, 2008—; founder Lohmann Found., DOC Devel. ME Midland LLC, Midland European Way LLC, Midland Double Daves. Mem. Med. Dir. Com., Risk Mgmt. Com., Exec. Quality Assurance Com., 1987-93; mem. Med. Bd. Com., 1985-93, Exec. Bd. Com., 1984-93, Pain Mgmt. Com., 1988-91; regional dir. Tex. Physicians Resource Coun., 1996-97. Editl. bd. Computerized Radiology, 1975—85, assoc. editor, 1975—85; contbr. articles to profl. jours.; actor: (in amatur theatre). Mem. adv. bd. Ctr. Latin Affairs, Baton Rouge, 1982-84; mem. Senatorial Inner Cir., 1988, mem. presdl. roundtable, 1991; mem. Presdl. Roundtable, 1992; trustee Christian Victory Ctr., Hempstead, N.Y., 1986-88; vol. Appalachian Project, 1970; mem. transition team for Pres. Ronald Reagan, 1980-81. Named to Compton-Connolly Guide to Best Physicians in the N.Y. Met. Area, Best Surgeons America, 2007-10, Guide to America's Top Surgeons-Neurol. Surgery, Consumer's Rsch. Coun. America, 2007-09; selected by peers as one of Best Doctors in America Ctrl. Region, 1996-97. Fellow ACS, Am. Coll. Pain Mgmt., Am. Coll. Forensic Examiners, Am. Coll. Disability Analysts, Lohman Found. (dir.); mem. AMA, Am. Assn. Neurol. Surgeons (sect. intensive care), Christian Med. and Dental Soc., Am. Assn. Neurologic Surgeons, N.Y. State Neurosurg. Soc., N.Y. Soc. Neurosurgery, Congress Neurologic Surgeons (spine sect., sect. on trauma, sect. on intensive care), Tex. State Med. Soc., So. Med. Soc. Presdl. Roundtable (presdl. transition team 1980-81), NRA (life), West Tex. Cigar Soc., Physicians Resource Coun. (Tex. regional dir.), Cmty. Resource Coun. troubled Youth West Tex., Mission Bd. China, 2005; Argentier Honoraire Confrerie de la Chaine des Rotisseurs, Bailli Foundateur de Midland-Confrerie de la Chaine des Rotisseurs, Midland Confrerie de la Chaine des Rotisseurs (Bailli Honoraire), Chaine des Rotisseurs (comdr.), Consul de L'Ordre Mondial des Gourmets Degustateurs, Brilliat-Savarin Soc., Shanhai Tiffin Club, Donyin Sister City Assn., Midland Arts Assn., Midland C. of C., Midland-Odessa Symphony and Choral Soc. Achievements include patents in field. Avocations: skiing, painting, poetry, music, cooking.

LOHR, JACOB ANDREW, pediatrician, educator; b. Lexington, NC, Aug. 15, 1940; s. Dermot and Blanche (Grimes) L.; m. Elizabeth Waite, June 19, 1967 (div. 1978); m. Lura Galloway, Nov. 27, 1993; children: Jason Merrill, Lara Jane Parker (dec.), Jonathan Waite, Elizabeth Brice. AB, U. N.C., 1962, MD, 1967. Diplomate Am. Bd. Pediats. Chief resident dept. pediat. U. Va., Charlottesville, 1969-70, prof., 1984-90, divsn. chief, assoc. chair, 1976-90; prof. dept. pediat. U. NC, Chapel Hill, 1990—, divsn. chief, assoc. chair, 1990—98, vice chair dept. pediat., 1998—2000, disting. prof. pediat., 2006—; pediatrician-in-chief NC Children's Hosp., Chapel Hill, 1999—2000, sr. clinician, 2000—02; exec. dir. Gov.'s Inst. Alcohol and Substance Abuse, 1998—2007. Cons. to task force on urinary tract infections Am. Acad. Pediats., 1992-99, WHO Com. on Hospitalized Children at Risk, Geneva, 1999-2000; McLemore Birdsong disting. prof. U.Va., 1984-90. Editor: Pediatric Outpatient Proceedings, 1992, Guidelines for Nurse Practitioners, 1994, 5th edit., 1999, Essence of Pediatrics, 2000; med. editor Am. Bd. pediats., 1996—; contbr. articles to profl. jours. Bd. dirs. Head Start, Charlottesville, 1973-76, Ronald McDonald House, 1980-82, Orange County Ptnrship. for young Children, Chapel Hill, 1994-96; trustee Bowman Fund, U. Va., 1972—. Lt. comdr. USN, 1970-72. Recipient H. Fleming Fuller award, U. NC Healthcare Sys. Fellow Am. Acad. Pediats.; mem. Am. Soc. for Microbiology, Ambulatory Pediat. Assn., Pediat. Infectious Disease Soc., Infectious Disease Soc. Lutheran. Avocations: golf, boating. Office: U NC Dept Pediat 231 Mac Nider Chapel Hill NC 27517-6208 Office Phone: 919-966-2504. Office Fax: 919-966-3852. Business E-Mail: jacob_lohr@med.unc.edu.

LOHR, MATTHEW J., state agency administrator, former state legislator; b. Harrisonburg, Va., Aug. 28, 1971; m. Andrea Sue Lynch; children: Caroline Belle, Carson Jacob. Grad. in agrl. edn., Va. Polytechnic Inst. and State U., Blacksburg. Poultry, beef & crop farmer, Va.; mem. Rockingham County Sch. Bd., Va., 2002—05; mem. Dist. 26 Va. House of Delegates, Va., 2006—10; mem. Edn. Com., Counties, Cities & Towns Com., Agr. Chesapeake & Natural Resources Com.; commr. Va. Dept. Agr. & Consumer Services, Richmond, 2010—. Mem. Harrisonburg Baptist Church. Recipient Nat. Excellence award, America Farm Bur., 2003, Environ. award, Va. Poultry Fedn., 2005. Mem.: Rockingham County Planning Commn. (chmn.), Broadway Timberville Ruritan (former pres.), Rockingham County Farm Bur. (former pres.), Nat. FFA (former v.p.). Republican. Office: Va Dept Agr & Consumer Services 102 Governor St Richmond VA 23218 Office Phone: 804-786-3501. Office Fax: 804-371-2945.

LOLLAR, JOHN HENRY, III, oil company executive; b. Cleve., Nov. 30, 1938; s. John H. Jr. and May Ruth (Jerauld) L.; m. Carolyn Carroll Garrett, Mar. 30, 1961; children: Carolyn, Kristen. BS in Geology, U. Okla., 1960; MBA, U. Houston, 1965. Pres. Pend Oreille Oil and Gas, Houston, 1978-82, BS&B Engring., Houston, 1981-82; exec. v.p. Gulf Resources and Chem., Houston, 1982; pres., COO Transco Exploration and Prodn. Co., Houston, 1982—92; chmn., pres. and CEO Cabot Oil & Gas Corp., 1992—95; mng. ptnr. Newgulf Exploration, LP, 1996—. Bd. dirs. Vulcan Energy Corp., Plains Resources, 1995—2002, Lufkin Industries, Inc., 1997—, Plains Exploration & Prodn. Co., 2002—. Chmn. bd. Houston Mus. Natural Sci., Houston, 1987—. Served to 1st lt. USMC, 1960-65. Mem. Am. Assn. Petroleum Geologists, Am. Petroleum Inst., Ind. Petroleum Assn. of Am. Office: Transco Exploration and Prodn Co 2800 Post Oak Blvd PO Box 1396 Houston TX 77251 also: Newgulf Exploration L P 2040 N Loop W Houston TX 77018 Office Phone: 713-812-7300. Business E-Mail: jlollar@pxp.com.

LOLLAR, RON, state legislator; b. Jackson, Tenn., Aug. 13, 1948; Former mem. Shelby County Sch. Bd.; mem. Agr. Com., Edn. Com.; rep. Tenn. Legislature Network, bd. mem., 2001—02, 2005, chair-elect., 2005, chair, 2006; state rep. Dist. 99 Tenn., 2007—. Decorated Navy Commendation medal W/V, Combat Action ribbon Navy Unit Citation; recipient Vietnamese Cross of Gallantry award, Good Conduct medal, Meritorious Unit Citation, Vietnamese Svc. medal, Vietnamese Campaign medal. Mem.: Future Farmers America (pres.), Arlington Kiwanis Club, Memphis Jaycees. Republican. Baptist. Office: 7559 Olivia Hill Dr Bartlett TN 38133 also: 214 War Memorial Bldg Nashville TN 37243-0199 Office Phone: 615-741-7084. E-mail: rep.ron.lollar@capitol.tn.gov.

LOMAN, MARY LAVERNE, retired mathematics professor; b. Stratford, Okla., June 10, 1928; d. Thomas D. and Mary Ellen (Goodwin) Glass; m. Coy E. Loman, Dec. 23, 1944; 1 child, Sandra Leigh Loman Easton. BS, U. Okla., 1956, MA, 1957, PhD, 1961. Grad. asst., then instr. U. Okla., Norman, 1956-61; asst. prof. math. U. Ctrl. Okla., Edmond, 1961-62, assoc. prof., 1962-66, prof., 1966-93, prof. emeritus, 1993—. NSF fellow, 1965-67. Mem. Math. Assn. Am., Nat. Coun. Tchrs. Math., Okla. Coun. Tchrs. Math. (v.p. 1972-76), Higher Edn Alumni Coun. Okla., VFW Aux., Delta Kappa Gamma. Home: 2201 Tall Oaks Trl Edmond OK 73025-2325

LOMBARDI, JOHN V., academic administrator, historian; b. LA, Aug. 19, 1942; s. John and Janice P. Lombardi; m. Cathryn Lee; children: John Lee, Mary Ann. BA, Pomona Coll., 1963; MA, Columbia U., 1964, PhD, 1968. Prof. contratado Escuela de Historia, Universidad Central de Venezuela, Caracas, 1967; lectr. history Ind. U. S.E., Jeffersonville, 1967-68, asst. prof., 1968-69; vis. asst. prof. Ind. U., Bloomington, 1968-69, from asst. prof. history to dean, 1969—85, dean Coll. Arts and Scis., 1985—87; prof. history Johns Hopkins U., 1987-89, provost, vp. for acad. affairs, 1987-89; pres. U. Fla., Gainesville, 1989-99, prof. history, dir. The Ctr., 1999; prof. history, chancellor U. Mass., Amherst, Mass., 2002—07; pres. La. State U. Sys., 2007—. Author: (with others) Venezuelan History: A Comprehensive Working Bibliography, 1977, People and Places in Colonial Venezuela, 1976, Venezuela: Search for Order, Dream of Progress, 1982, The Top American Research Universities, 2000-; Mem. editorial bd.: (with others) UCLA Statis. Abstracts Latin Am, 1977—; contbr. (with others) articles to profl. jours. Fulbright-Hayes research fellow, 1965-66 Mem. Am. Hist. Assn., Latin Am. Studies Assn., Pan Am. Inst. Geography and History, Academia Nacional de la Historia (corr. mem.) Office: Louisiana State University System 3810 W Lakeshore Dr Baton Rouge LA 70808

LOMBARDO, JOSEPH T., aerospace transportation executive; B in Sociology, San Diego State U., 1971; MBA, Long Beach State U., Calif., 1984. With Douglas Aircraft, 1975, various leadership roles in prodn. and material control, planning and mfg., gen. mgr. prodn. for twin-jets; v.p. co-prodn. Gulfstream Aerospace Corp. (subs. of General Dynamics), 1996—98, sr. v.p., 1998—2001, COO, 2001—07, pres., 2007—; v.p. General Dynamics, 2001—07, exec. v.p. aerospace, pres., 2007—. Recipient Silver Knight award, Nat. Mgmt. Assn. Office: Gulfstream Aerospace Gen Dynamics 500 Gulfstream Rd Savannah GA 31408 Office Phone: 912-965-3000. Office Fax: 912-965-3775.

LOMONOSOFF, JAMES MARC, marketing professional; b. Van Nuys, Calif., Apr. 29, 1951; s. Boris Marc and Eileen Fairfax (Thomson) Lomonosoff; m. Elisabeth Maas, June 12, 1982; children: Marc Frederik, James Forrest. BA in Econs., Colgate U., 1973; MBA in Gen. Mgmt., U. Va., 1975. With Saatchi and Saatchi Advt., NYC, 1975-93, v.p., account supr., 1975-85, sr. v.p., mgmt. supr., 1986-87, exec. v.p., mgmt. dir., 1987-93, pres. Collateral Plus divsn., 1987-90; CEO, pres. Saatchi & Saatchi Specialized Comm., 1991-92; account dir. VDB/Compton B.V., Amsterdam, Netherlands, 1980-83; acct. dir. Saatchi and Saatchi Compton S.A., Madrid, 1983-84; regional acct. dir. Saatchi and Saatchi Compton Worldwide, London, 1984-86; mng. dir., CEO BSB/Saatchi and Saatchi, Prague, 1992-93; v.p. internat. mktg. Walt Disney Attractions Inc., Lake Buena Vista, Fla., 1994-98, v.p. internat. mktg. and sales L.Am. Coral Gables, Fla., 1999; sr. v.p. mktg. Celebrity Cruises Inc., Miami, Fla., 1999—2001; pres. Lomonosoff Ptnrs., Inc., Miami, Fla., 2001—. Mem.: LB2 Group Ltd. (CEO 2006—), Beta Theta Pi. Republican. Home: 4211 Monserrate St Coral Gables FL 33146-1207 Office Phone: 305-666-7019. Personal E-mail: jamesmlomonosoff@netscape.net.

LONDON, J. PHILLIP (JACK LONDON), information technology executive; b. Oklahoma City, Apr. 30, 1937; s. Harry Riles and Laura Evalyn (Phillips) L.; children: J. Phillip Jr., Laura McLain. BSc, U.S. Naval Acad., 1959; MSc, U.S. Naval Postgrad. Sch., 1967; D in Bus. Adminstrn., George Washington U., 1971. Commd. ensign USN, 1959, advanced through grades to capt., resigned, 1971; program mgr. Challenger Research Inc., 1971-72; mgr. CACI International, Inc., Arlington, Va., 1972-76, v.p., 1976-77, sr. v.p., 1977-79, exec. v.p., 1979-82, pres. operating div., 1982-84, pres., chief exec. officer, 1984-90, chmn., pres., CEO, 1990—2007, exec. chmn., 2007—. Recipient Alumni of Yr. award George Washington U. Sch. Govt. & Bus. Adminstrn., Washington, 1987, High Tech Entrepreneur award KPMG Peat Marwick, 1995. Mem. George Town Club (Washington), Cosmos Club (Washington). Episcopalian. Office: CACI Internat Inc 1100 N Glebe Rd Ste 200 Arlington VA 22201-4797

LONDON, MIKE, college football coach; b. West Point, NY, Oct. 9, 1960; m. Regina London; children: Michael Jr., Brandon, Kristen, Ticynn, Korben, Jaicyn, Madicyn. B in Sociology, U. Richmond, Va., 1983; degree in law enforcement, Richmond Police Acad., Va., 1984. Defensive back Dallas Cowboys, 1983; detective, street crimes unit City of Richmond, Va., 1985—87; outside linebackers coach U. Richmond Spiders, 1988—89, outside linebackers coach, recruiting coord., 1994—96, head football coach, 2008—09; defensive line coach Coll. William & Mary Tribe, 1990—93, Boston Coll. Eagles, 1997—2000; defensive line coach, recruiting coord. U. Va. Cavaliers, 2001—04, defensive coord., 2006—07, head football coach, 2009—; defensive line coach Houston Texans, 2005. Named Football Championship Subdivision Nat. Coach of Yr., Am. Football Coaches Assn., 2008, Schutt Sports/Am. Football Monthly mag., 2008, Male Coach of Yr., Black Coaches Assn., 2008, State Coach of Yr., Va. Coll. Sports Info. Dirs., 2008, Peninsula Sports Club, 2008, Atlantic Coast Conf. Coach of Yr., 2011. Achievements include head coach of NCAA Football Championship Subdivision National Championship winning University of Richmond Spiders, 2008. Office: University Va Football McCue Ctr PO Box 400837 Charlottesville VA 22904 Office Phone: 434-982-5900. Business E-Mail: fbheadcoach@virginia.edu.

LONEY, MARY ROSE, former airport administrator, aviation industry consultant; b. Ohio, 1952; B in Sociology and Philosophy, U. Pitts., 1973; MPA, U. Nev., Las Vegas, 1983. Ticket sales staff Grand Canyon Airlines, 1973—75; mgr. Lucky's Grocery Stores, 1976—78; planning svcs. mgr. McCarran Internat. Airport, Las Vegas, Nev., 1979-84; asst. aviation dir. Albuquerque Internat. Airport, 1984-86; asst. dir. aviation San Jose (Calif.) Internat. Airport, 1986-89; first dep. commr. aviation Chgo. Airport Sys., 1989-92; dep. exec. dir. fin. and adminstrn. Dallas/Ft. Worth Internat. Airport, 1992-93; dir. aviation Phila. Internat. Airport, 1993-96; commr. aviation Chgo. Airport Sys., 1996—99; pres. Travelways, Inc., NJ, 1999—2000; pres., CEO The Loney Group, Satellite Beach, Fla., 2000—. Bd. dirs. Chgo. Tourism and Visitors Bur., 1993—2000, Phila. Conv. and Visitors Bur., 1993—2000, Chgo.-Gary Airport Authority, 1996—2000; bd. mem. Chgo. Econ. Devel. Commn., 1996—2000. Trustee St. Joseph's U., Phila., 1994—97; bd. dirs. Chgo. Pub. Art Commn., 1996—2000. Named Santa Clara County Woman of Achievement, 1988, Woman of Yr., Phila. Customs Brokers and Freight Forwarders Assn., 1994, one of State Pa. Honor Roll of Women, 1996; recipient YWCA's Tribute to Women in Industry award, 1989, Bus. Woman of Yr. award Great Valley Regional C. of C., 1994, Transp. award March of Dimes, 1995. Mem. FAA (appointed rsch. engring. and devel. adv. com.), Am. Assn. Airport Execs. (accredited airport exec., nat. bd. dirs. 1995-97, chmns. award 1994), St. Joseph's U. (bd. trustees). Home: 121 Desoto Pkwy Satellite Beach FL 32937-3328

LONG, CHARLES FARRELL, insurance company executive; b. Charlottesville, Va., Nov. 19, 1933; s. Cicel Early and Ruth Elizabeth (Shifflett) L.; m. Ann Tilley, May 28, 1960; children: C. Farrell, Linda. CLU; chartered fin. analyst. Founder, pres. Casualty Underwriters, Inc., Charlottesville, 1959-72, Group Underwriters, Inc., Charlottesville, 1959—. Mem. Assay Commn. of U.S., 1975; bd. dirs. Am. Heart Assn.; mem. U. Va. Student Aid Found. With USN, 1954-58. Mem. Am. Soc. CLUs, Ctrl. Va. CLUs Assn. (dir.), Va. Press Assn., Inland Press Assn. Chgo., Million Dollar Round Table. Creator Queen's medal for Queen Elizabeth, 1976. Home: 1400 W Leigh Dr Charlottesville VA 22901-7719 Office: Madison Park Charlottesville VA 22903

LONG, DEBORAH, state legislator; b. Chapel Hill, NC, Nov. 27, 1955; d. Don and Sue N. Adair; m. Jim Long, 1981; stepchildren: Leta, Phil. BA, U. NC, at Greensboro, 1976; OD, Southern Coll. Optometry, 1980. Pres. Fort Mill Lions Club, 1998, SC Optometric Assn., 2004; mem. SC Bd. of Examiners in Optometry, 2006—; mem. Dist. 45 SC House of Reps., SC, 2008—. Republican. Presbyn. Office: Dist/Home Office 1115 John Short Rd Fort Mill SC 29707 also: Capitol Office 414A Blatt Bldg Columbia SC 29201 Home Phone: 803-547-5215; Office Phone: 803-547-5547, 803-212-6874. E-mail: deborahlong@schouse.org.

LONG, DEBORAH JOYCE, lawyer; b. Oct. 26, 1953; d. Thomas C. and Margaret N. (Falks) Long; m. William Daniel Sockwell, May 26, 1979; 1 child, Daniel Long Sockwell. BA, Auburn U., 1975; JD, U. Ala., 1980. Bar: Ala. 1980, US Ct. Appeals (5th cir.) 1980, US Ct. Appeals (11th cir.) 1981, US Dist. Ct. (no. dist.) Ala. 1981. Law clk. U.S. Ct. Appeals for 5th Cir., Montgomery, Ala., 1980-81; assoc. Cabaniss, Johnston, Gardner, Dumas & O'Neal, Birmingham, Ala., 1981-84, Maynard, Cooper & Gale, P.C., Birmingham, 1984—94; exec. v.p., gen. counsel Protective Life Corp., Birmingham, Ala., 1994—. Recipient Cert. of Appreciation, Ala. Bar Assn., Montgomery. Mem. Farrah Soc., Ala. State Bar (bd. bar examiners 1987-92, bd. editors 1991-94), Birmingham Bar Assn. (bd. editors 1989-90), Assn. Life Ins. Counsel (pres. 2005) Office: Protective Life Corp 2801 Highway 280 S Birmingham AL 35223-2488

LONG, EDWARD ARLO, management consultant, retired manufacturing executive; b. Detroit, May 5, 1927; s. Arlo Russell and Florence Viola (Magown) L.; m. Lorraine Ruth Nordin, May 21, 1947; children: Karin Louise Long Schelke, Marian Elizabeth Long Benton. BS, Wayne State U., 1956, MBA, 1964. Mfg. mgr. Ex-Cell-O Corp., Detroit, 1950-68; v.p. mktg. Colonial Broach & Machine, Warren, Mich., 1968-70; group v.p. Blue Bird Body Co., Fort Valley, Ga., 1970-75; pres. tool equipment div. Chgo. Pneumatic Tool, Franklin, Pa., 1975-77; group v.p. Joy Mfg. Co., Pine Bluff, Ark., 1977-87; v.p., gen. mgr. Wheeling Machine Products Co./Cooper Industries, Pine Bluff, 1987-94; ret., 1994. Dir. Security Nat. Bank, Wheeling, W.Va.; elected score Counselor to Am.'s Small Bus., 2007. Bd. dirs. Franklin Hosp., 1976-76, pine bluff zoning and planning commn.,2008 Oglebay Inst., Wheeling, 1981-83, Ohio Valley Hosp. Trust, Wheeling, 1982-83, Ark. Ind. Colls., 1984, Jefferson County Indsl. Found., 1985; pres. Pine Bluff Fifty for the Future, 1985, Pine Bluff Symphony Orch., 1987, Leadership Pine Bluff, 1990; apptd. zoning commr., Pine Bluff, 1995, re-apptd, 2008. Served with USCG, 1945-46. Scholar Nat. Office Mgmt. Assn., 1952, Beta Gamma, Detroit, 1953 Mem. AIME, Am. Petroleum Inst., Duquesne (Pitts.) Club, Rotary, Alpha Kappa Psi, Psi Chi, Sigma Iota Epsilon. Democrat. Roman Catholic. Home and Office: 7409 S Laurel St Pine Bluff AR 71603-8121

LONG, EUGENE THOMAS, III, philosophy educator, academic administrator; b. Richmond, Va., Mar. 16, 1935; s. Eugene Thomas and Emily Joyce (Barker) L.; m. Carolyn Macleod, June 25, 1960; children: Scott, Kathryn. BA, Randolph-Macon Coll., 1957; BD, Duke U., 1960; PhD, U. Glasgow, Scotland, 1964. Asst. prof. philosophy Randolph-Macon Coll., 1964-67, assoc. prof., 1967-70, U. S.C., Columbia, 1970-73, prof., 1973—2002, prof. emeritus, 2002—, chmn. dept., 1972-87. Musician Columbia Cmty. Concert Band, pres., 2012—. Musician Gene Dykes Jazz Orch., 2010-, Blythewood Jazz Orch. Bd., 2012-; author: Jaspers and Bultmann, 1968, Existence, Being and God, 1985, Twentieth Century Western Philosophy of Religion, 1900-2000, 2000; contbr., editor: God, Secularization & History, 1974, Experience, Reason and God, 1980, Prospects for Natural Theology, 1992, God, Reason and Religions, 1995; editor: Handbook of Contemporary Philosophy of Religion, 1995—; editor-in-chief Internat. Jour. for Philosophy of Religion, 1990—2011; assoc. editor Internat. Jour. Philosophy of Religion, 1975-90, So. Jour. Philosophy, 1978-83; contbr., co-editor: God and Temporality, 1984, Being and Truth, 1986, Ethics of Belief: Essays in Tribute to DZ Phillips, 2008; mem. editl. bd. The Works of William James, 1974-88, Correspondence of William James, 1988—; editor, contbr. Issues in Contemporary Philosophy of Religion, 2001, Self and Others: Essays in Continental Philosophy of Religion, 2007; contbr. articles to profl. jours. Mem. S.C. Com. for Humanities, 1980-85; mem. adv. bd. The Franklin J. Matchette Found., 1992—. Recipient Rsch. award NEH, 1968, Duke U./U. N.C. Coop. Program in Humanities, 1968-69. Mem.

Soc. Philosophy in Religion (pres. 1980-81), Metaphys. Soc. Am. (sec. treas. 1977-81, exec. coun. 1991-94, v.p./pres.-elect 1996-97, pres. 1997-98), So. Soc. Philosophy and Psychology (exec. coun. 1976-79), Am. Philos. Assn. (sec. treas. eastern divsn. 1985-94). Office: U SC Dept Philosophy Columbia SC 29208-0001 Office Phone: 803-777-4166. Business E-Mail: longq@mailbox.sc.edu, longq@mindspring.com.

LONG, GERALD, state legislator; b. Winnfield, La., July 9, 1944; m. Rose Long; 3 children. BS, Northwestern State U., 1966. Former pres. Kiwanis Club; Deacon bd. First Bapt. Ch., Natchitoches; bd. dirs. Kiwanis Club Natchitoches; agent State Farm Ins., 1979—99; min. Fellowship Christian Athletes, 1999—2007; mem. Dist. 31 La. State Senate, 2008—, vice chair ins. com., mem. agr., forestry, aquaculture and rural devel. com., edn. com., fin. com., select com. on homeland security, joint legis. com. on the budget. Republican. So. Bapt. Mailing: Capitol Office PO Box 94183 Baton Rouge LA 70804 Address: District Office PO Box 151 Winnfield LA 71483 Office Phone: 225-342-2040, 318-628-5799. Office Fax: 318-628-6120. E-mail: longg@legis.state.la.us.

LONG, LELAND TIMOTHY, retired geophysics educator, seismologist; b. Auburn, NY, Sept. 6, 1940; s. Walter K. and Carmalita Rose Long; m. Sarah Alice Blackard, Mar. 1970; children: Sarah Alice, Katherine Rose, Amy Virginia. BS in Geology, U. Rochester, 1962; MS in Geophysics, N.Mex. Inst. Mining and Tech., 1964; PhD in Geophysics, Oreg. State U., 1968. Registered profl. geologist, Ga. From asst. to assoc. prof. Sch. Earth and Atmosphere Scis. Ga. Inst. Tech., Atlanta, 1968-81, prof., 1981—2005, ret., 2005. Cons. in seismology, near-surface seismic imaging, seismic road vibrations, blast vibrations and gravity data analysis. Contbr. articles to profl. jours. on topics of seismology and near surface geophysics; author, Acquisition and Analysis of Terrestrial Gravity Data Mem. BentTree Found., 2010—11; bd. dir. BentTree Cmty., Inc., 2012—14. Recipient award, Jesuit Seismology Assn., 2006. Business E-Mail: tim.long@eas.gatech.edu, timlong@tds.net.

LONG, LETITIA A., federal agency administrator; b. 1959; m. John Skibinski; 3 children. BS, Va. Polytechnic Inst. and State U., 1982; MS in Elec. Engring., Cath. U. of Am. Project engr. David Taylor Rsch. Ctr. USN, Annapolis, Md., 1978; mgr. Intelligence Rsch. and Devel. Programs Office of Naval Intelligence (ONI), Washington, 1988, dir. requirements, plans, policy and programs, dir. resource mgmt., 1994, dep. dir. naval intelligence, 2000—03; dep. dir. info. sys. and svcs. Def. Intelligence Agency (DIA), Washington, 1996, chief info. officer, dep. under sec. def. for policy, requirements and resources, 2004—06, dep. dir., 2006—10; assoc. exec. dir. intelligence cmty. affairs Dir. Ctrl. Intelligence (DCI), Langley, Va., 1997, exec. dir. intelligence cmty. affairs, 1998—2000; dir. Nat. Geospatial-Intelligence Agy. US Dept. Def., Bethesda, Md., 2010—. Recipient Nat. Intelligence Disting. Svc. Medal. Office: National Geospatial-Intelligence Agency 7500 Geoint Dr Springfield VA 22150-7500*

LONG, OLIVER WESLEY (WES LONG), state legislator, lawyer; b. Guntersville, Ala., Aug. 13, 1977; m. Jordan Long; 2 children. BS in Fin., U. Ala., Tuscaloosa; JD, U. Mo., Kansas City, MBA in Entrepreneurship. Lic. realtor Ala. Mng. ptnr. Long, Flanagan and McDonald, 2004—; mem. Dist 27 Ala. House of Representatives, 2011—. Mem. Guntersville First United Meth. Ch. Mem.: ABA, Marshall County Hotel and Restaurant Assn., Guntersville C. of C. (bd. dirs.), Marshall County Renters Assn. (bd. dirs.), Guntersville Rotary Club. Republican. Office: Long Flanagan and McDonald 3446 Hwy 69 S Guntersville AL 35976 also: Ala House of Reps Rm 524-D 11 S Union St Montgomery AL 36130 also: 412-A Gunter Ave Guntersville AL 35976 Office Phone: 256-582-2940, 334-242-7511, 256-582-0619. Business E-Mail: weslong@mclo.org.

LONG, RALPH, III, state legislator; b. Atlanta, Ga., Nov. 19; m. Erica Morris Long; 1 child, Ralph. BFA in Interior Design, Art Inst., Atlanta. Owner Ralph Abbott Realty & Mindsweat Properties; mem. Dist. #61 Ga. House of Reps., Ga., 2008—. Democrat. Office: Capitol Office 612-F Coverdell Legislative Office Bldg Atlanta GA 30334 also: District Office PO Box 11372 Atlanta GA 30310 Office Phone: 404-656-0325. E-mail: ralph.long@house.ga.gov.

LONG, RALPH STEWART, clinical psychologist; b. Pitts., Feb. 23, 1926; s. Ralph S. and Virginia (Hawk) L.; m. Vera Lazorchak, June 16, 1951; children: Karen Virginia, Brian Reed, Lauri Michelle. BS, Lock Haven U., 1950; MEd, Pa. State U., 1951; PhD, Washington U., St. Louis, 1965. Lic. psychologist, Tex. Commd. 2d lt. med. svc. corp USAF, 1951, clin. psychologist to chief clin. psychology svcs. hosp. Sampson AFB, NY, 1951—55; chief psychology svc. hosp. Warren AFB, Wyo., 1955—57; Inst. Tech. scholar, Wash. U. USAF, St. Louis, 1957—61, chief psychology dept. med. ctr. Andrews AFB, DC, 1961—62, dir. psychol. svcs. Scott AFB, Ill., 1962—65, dir. psychol. svcs. regional med. ctr. Sheppard AFB, Tex., 1965—67, dir. psychol. svcs. hosp. Wiesbaden, Germany, 1967—70, dir. psychol. svcs. regional med. ctr. Sheppard AFB, Tex., 1970—71, advanced through grades to lt. col., 1968; ret., 1971; dir. psychol. svcs. Cmty. Ctr. Mental Health, Mental Retardation, Wichita Falls, Tex., 1971-72; psychol. cons. Family Counseling Ctr., Wichita Falls, 1972-74; dir. psychol. svcs. Nueces County Mental Health-Mental Retardation Cmty. Ctr., 1974-77; dir. Corpus Christi Counseling Ctr./Physicians-Surgeons Hosp., Tex., 1977-79, Psychol. Cons., Corpus Christi, 1979-82; exec. dir. Personal Dynamics Inst., Corpus Christi, 1982—2005, dir., 1988—2005, emeritus, 2005—. Instr. dept. psychology McKendree Coll., Lebanon, Ill., 1962-63; instr. So. Ill. U., 1962-64; adj. prof. human rels. Webster U., Webster Groves, Mo., 1976-79, 88-93; adj. prof. psychology Del Mar Coll., Corpus Christi, 1977-83, adj. prof. bus. adminstrn., 1991-93; cons. Tex. Dept. Corrections, 1988-90; bd. dir. Ctr. Creative Living; cons., trainer Crisis Svc., 1980-2005; profl. adv. bd. North Tex. Regional Coun. Alcoholism, 1971-74, Mental Health Assn. Coastal Bend, 1974-83, Wichita Mental Health Assn., 1965-67, 70-74; adj. prof. Embry-Riddle U., Corpus Christi, 1991-93; clin. dir. Shoreline Chem. Dependency Treatment Ctr., 1989-92; consulting psychologist Nueces County Juvenile Justice Ctr., Corpus Christi, 1992-2005, Warm Springs Rehab. Ctr., Corpus Christi, 1992-2005, MCC Managed Behavioral Care, Inc., Eden Prairie, Minn., 1992—2005, Champus Provider, 1972-2005; presenter in field. Active Tex. chpt. ARC; founding mem. Nat. Campaign for Tolerance; charter sponsor Air Force Meml. Found., Statue of Liberty-Ellis Island Found.; mem. Nat. Com. to Preserve Social Security and Medicine; charter mem. Citizens Against Govt. Waste. With USN, 1944—51, Pacific Theater WWII. Named Am. Man Sci., 1962. Fellow: Soc. Air Force Clin. Psychologists; mem.: DAV, APA, VFW (life), Air Force Meml. Found. (charter sponsor), Military Officers Assn. of Am., Anti-Defamation League, Prescribing Psychologists Register, Nat. Air and Space Soc. (founding), US Naval Inst., Air Force Assn. (life), Nat. Register Health Svc. Providers in Psychology, Tex. Assn. Mental Health, Tex. Assn. Mental Health (exec. com. 1980—83), Libr. of Congress (charter), Am. Inst. Hypnosis, U.S. Navy Meml. (charter mem.), Nat. D-Day Mus. (charter), Mil. Officers Assn. Am., Am. Air Mus. in Britain (charter), US Holocaust Meml. Mus. (charter), Am. Assn. Ret. Persons, Ret. Officers Assn., Am. Mil. Soc., Common Cause, Citizens Against Govt. Waste (charter), WWII Meml. Soc. (charter), Earth Justice Legal Def. Fund., Nat. Arbor Day Found., United Srs. Assn., Theosophical Soc. Am., Nat. Wildlife Fedn., Nat. Mus. Am. Indian (charter), F.D. Roosevelt Meml. (founding), Nat. Trust Hist. Preservation, National Audubon Soc., Smithsonian, Sierra Club, Shriners, Masons, Am. Legion, Sigma Xi (life). Avocations: painting, writing, travel, camping, fishing.

LONG, ROBERT RADCLIFFE, fluid mechanics engineer, educator; b. Glen Ridge, NJ, Oct. 24, 1919; s. Clarence D. and Gertrude (Cooper) L.; m. Cristina Nersing, 1962; children: John Radcliffe, Robert William. AB in Econs, Princeton, 1941; MS in Meteorology, U. Chgo., 1949, PhD, 1950. Meteorologist U.S. Weather Bur., Paris, France, 1946-47; asst. prof. Johns Hopkins U., Balt., 1951-56, assoc. prof., 1956-59, prof. fluid mechanics, 1959-88, prof. emeritus, 1988—, dir. hydrodynamics lab., 1951-88. Assoc. dept. aero. and mech. engring. Ariz. State U. Author: Mechanics of Solids and Fluids, 1960, Engineering Science Mechanics, 1964; contbr. articles to profl. jours. Home: 3989 Myrtle St Sarasota FL 34235-5157 Personal E-mail: rrlong4@comcast.net.

LONG, RUSSELL CHARLES, retired academic administrator; b. Alpine, Tex., Oct. 9, 1942; s. Roy Joel and Lovis Lorene (Graham) L.; m. Elaine Gresham, May 8, 1964 (div. Jan. 1986); 1 child, Mark Roy; m. Natrelle Hedrick, Mar. 28, 1986. BS, Sul Ross State U., Alpine, 1965; MA, N.Mex. State U., 1967; PhD, Tex. A&M U., 1977. Assoc. prof. Schreiner Coll., Kerrville, Tex., 1967-69; instr. Tarleton State U., Stephenville, Tex., 1969-72, asst. prof., 1972-77, assoc. prof., 1977-85, prof., 1985-92, asst. v.p. acad. adminstrn., 1987-90, chair dept. English and Lang., 1990-92; provost and v.p. acad. adminstrn. West Tex. A&M U., Canyon, 1992-94, interim pres., 1994-95, pres., 1995—2005; pres. emeritus, 2005—. Office: West Texas A&M Univ Wt Sta 2501 4th Ave Canyon TX 79016-0001 Business E-Mail: rlong@mail.wtamu.edu.

LONG, THAD GLADDEN, lawyer; b. Dothan, Ala., Mar. 9, 1938; s. Lindon Alexander and Della Gladys (Pilcher) L.; m. Carolyn Frances Wilson, Aug. 13, 1966; children: Louisa Frances Stockman, Wilson Alexander. AB, Columbia U., 1960; JD, U. Va., 1963. Bar: Ala. 1963, U.S. Dist. Ct. (no. dist., so. dist., mid. dist.) Ala., U.S. Ct. Appeals (11th cir., 5th cir.), U.S. Supreme Ct. Assoc. atty. Bradley Arant Boult Cummings LLP, Birmingham, Ala., 1963—70, ptnr., 1970—2011. Adj. prof. U. Ala., Tuscaloosa, 1988—2002, Samford U., Birmingham, Cumberland Law Sch., 1999—2002. Co-author: Unfair Competition Under Alabama Law, 1990, Protecting Intellectual Property, 1990; mem. editl. bd. The Trademark Reporter, 1994-2007; contbr. articles to profl. jours. Chmn. Columbia U. Secondary Schs. Com. Ala. Area, 1975—, pres., chmn., Greater Birmingham Arts Alliance, 1977-79; trustee, pres. Birmingham Music Club, 2000-03; trustee Oscar Wells Trust for Mus. Art, Birmingham, 1983—, Canterbury Meth. Found., 1993-2002, sec., 1993—; chmn. Entrepreneurship Inst. Birmingham, 1989; vice chmn., trustee Soc of the Revolution Found., Ala., 1994-2002; pres. Birmingham-Jefferson Hist. Soc., 1995-97; trustee Birmingham Music Club Endowment, 1995—, Birmingham-Jefferson History Mus., 2004-06; mem. Birmingham Com. Fgn. Rels. Recipient Spl. Svc. award, Ala. Assn. for Retarded Children; named one of Ala. Super Lawyers, Best Lawyers in America. Fellow: Ala. Law Found.; mem.: Soc. Revolution, U.S. Patent Bar, Internat. Trademark Assn., Am. Law Inst., Ala. Law Inst., Birmingham Legal Aid Soc., Ala. Bar Assn. (chmn., founder bus. torts and antitrust sect.), Biotechnology Assn. of Ala., Inc. (sec. 1998—2001), St. Andrew's Soc. of Middle South, S.R., U. Va. Law Alumni (chmn. Birmingham chpt. 1984—89), Soc. Colonial Wars (gov. Ala. chpt., deputy Gov. General of General Soc.), Gen. Soc. S.R. (gen. solicitor 1994—2000), Order of the Coif, Omicron Delta Kappa. Republican. Methodist. Avocations: travel, writing, ping pong/table tennis. Office Phone: 205-870-0171. Business E-Mail: thadlong@aol.com.

LONG, TRACY L., manufacturing executive; BS in Mktg., Pitts. State U., 1987; BBA in Acctg., U. of Ozarks, Clarksville, Ark., 1993. Sec. tax dept. Baldor Electric Co., Ft. Smith, Ark., 1988—91, gen. accountant, 1991—92, treasury analyst, 1992—97, sr. treasury & fin. analyst, 1997—2001, mgr. treasury & investor devel., 2001—03, treas., asst. sec., 2003—06, v.p. investor rels., 2006—. Office: Baldor Electric Co 5711 RS Boreham Jr St PO Box 2400 Fort Smith AR 72901 Office Phone: 479-646-4711. Office Fax: 479-648-5792. Business E-Mail: tlong@baldor.com.

LONGORIA, EVAN MICHAEL, professional baseball player; b. Downey, Calif., Oct. 7, 1985; Attended, Rio Hondo CC, Whittier, Calif., Calif. State U., Long Beach. Infielder Tampa Bay Rays, 2008—. Mem. US nat. team World Baseball Classic, 2009. Recipient Gold Glove award, Maj. League Baseball, 2009, 2010, Silver Slugger award, 2009; named Rookie of Yr., The Sporting News, 2008, Am. League Outstanding Rookie, Maj. League Baseball Players Assn., 2008, Am. League Rookie of Yr., Maj. League Baseball, 2008; named to Am. League All-Star Team, 2008—10. Office: Tampa Bay Rays 1 Tropicana Dr Saint Petersburg FL 33705

LONGWITZ, WILLIAM, state legislator; b. Meridian, Miss., Nov. 30, 1972; m. Leigh Cox; children: Sophie, June. B, Georgetown U., Washington; JD, U. Miss. Law Sch. Atty.; mem. Dist. 25 Miss. House of Reps., Jackson, 2012—. Mem.: NRA, Miss. Bar Assn., American Legis. Exch. Coun., Madison County Bus. League, Madison County Rep. Party, Madison County Tea Party, Madison-Ridgeland Rotary. Republican. Episcopalian. Office: Miss State Senate PO Box 1018 Jackson MS 39215 Business E-Mail: wlongwitz@senate.ms.gov.

LOOMIS, MICKEY, professional sports team executive; b. 1956; m. Melanie Loomis; children: Alex, Katherine. BS in Acctg., U. Oreg., Eugene, 1979; MA in Sports Adminstrn., Wichita State U., Kans. With Seattle Seahawks, 1983—98, v.p. fin., 1990—92, exec. v.p., 1992—98; dir. football adminstrn. New Orleans Saints, 2000—02, exec. v.p., gen. mgr., 2002—; gen. mgr. New Orleans VooDoo, Arena Football League. Named NFL Exec. of Yr., Pro Football Weekly, Pro Football Writers America, 2006, George Young NFL Exec. of Yr., The Sporting News, 2007. Office: New Orleans Saints 5800 Airline Dr Metairie LA 70003 Office Phone: 504-733-0255.

LOONEY, WILLIAM R., III, career military officer; b. Norman, Okla., Mar. 5, 1949; BS, USAF Acad., 1972; student, Squadron Officer Sch., 1977; M in Mgmt., Ctrl. Mich. U., 1979; student, Armed Forces Staff Coll., 1983, Nat. War Coll., 1990, Exec. Warfare Course, 1993, Joint Flag Officer Warfighting Course, 1997, Joint Force Air Component Comdr. Course, 1997, Undergraduate Space & Missile Training Staff Course, 1998, Nat. & Internat. Security Seminar, 1999. Commd. 2d lt. USAF, 1972, advanced through grades to gen., 2005, AC-130 gunship pilot Ubon Royal Thai AFB, Thailand, 1973-74; instr. pilot 50th Flying Tng. Squadron, Columbus AFB, Miss., 1975-78; air staff tng. program Directorate of Pers. Plans, The Pentagon, Washington, 1978-79; instr. pilot, flight comdr. and asst. ops. officer 94th Tactical Fighter Squadron, Langley AFB, Va., 1980-83; aide-de-camp to dep. comdr. in chief U.S. European Command, Stuttgart, West Germany, 1983-85; chief of wing plans 36th Tactical Fighter Wing, Bitburg AB, West Germany, 1985-86; ops. officer to comdr. 22nd Tactical Fighter Squadron, Bitburg AB, 1986-89; conventional negotiations br. chief Directorate of Strategic Plans and Policy, The Pentagon, Washington, 1990-92; vice comdr. Air Forces Iceland, Keflavik Naval Air Sta., Iceland, 1992-93; comdr. 33rd Fighter Wing, Eglin AFB, Fla., 1993-95, 1st Fighter Wing, Langley AFB, Va., 1995-96; comdt. Armed Forces Staff Coll., Norfolk, Va., 1996—98; comdr. Space Warfare Ctr., Schriever AFB, Colo., 1998-99; dir. ops. USAF, Peterson AFB, Colo., 1999—2000; comdr. 14th Air Force & Component Comdr. US Space Command, Vandenberg AFB, Calif., 2000—02; comdr. Aero. Systems Ctr. Air Force Material Command (AFMC), Hanscom AFB, Mass., 2002—03, Wright Patterson AFB, Ohio, 2003—05; comdr. Air Edn. & Training Command (AETC), Randolph AFB, Tex., 2005—. Decorated DSM with oak leaf cluster, Def. Superior Svc. medal, Def. Meritorious Svc. medal with oak leaf cluster, Legion of Merit with oak leaf cluster, Air medal, Aerial Achievement medal, Air Force Commendation medal with oak leaf cluster, Air Force Achievement medal, Combat Readiness medal with oak leaf cluster, Global War on Terrorism medal with oak leaf cluster, Humanitarian Svc. medal, Air and Space Campaign medal. Office: Air Edn & Training Command 12FTW/PA Randolph AFB TX 78150

LOOSER, WILLIAM GREGORY, lawyer; b. Houston, July 24, 1969; BA, JD, Baylor U., 1991. Bar: Tex. 1994, U.S. Dist. Ct. Tex. (No. dist.) 1995, U.S. Dist. Ct. Tex. (So. dist.) 1996. Atty. Bracewell & Guiliani, LLP; chief adminstrv. officer Pride International, Inc., asst. gen. counsel, 1999—2003, v.p., 2003—05, gen. counsel, sec., 2003—, sr. v.p., 2005—. Mem.: ABA, Am. Corp. Counsel Assn., Internat. Assn. Def. Counsel, Houston Young Lawyers Assn. (co-chair profl. devel. com. 1997), State Bar Tex., Houston Bar Assn., Nat. Order Barristers, Phi Delta Phi. Office: Pride International Inc 5847 San Felipe St Ste 3300 Houston TX 77057 Office Phone: 713-789-1400. Office Fax: 713-789-1430. Business E-Mail: glooser@prde.com.

LOPDRUP, KIM AXEL, food service executive; b. Galveston, Tex., May 20, 1958; s. Kjeld Emil and Gunild (Poulsen) Lopdrup; m. Kathleen Bosworth, Aug. 29, 1987 (dec. Sept. 29, 1999); m. Lillian Cathryne Foedisch, Sept. 23, 2000. BBA, Coll. William & Mary, Williamsburg, Va., 1980; MBA with distinction, Harvard U., 1984. Brand asst. Procter & Gamble Co., Cin., 1980-81, asst. brand mgr. Frostproof, Fla., 1981-82, Cin., 1984-85; product mgr. Dunkin' Donuts, Inc., Randolph, Mass., 1985-86, dir. advt. & sales promotion, 1986-89, dir. advt., sales promotion & market rsch., 1989-90, v.p. advt. & sales promotion, 1991, v.p. internat. mktg., 1991-93; v.p. mktg. & planning Allied Domecq Quick Svc. Restaurants Internat., 1993-94, sr. v.p. mktg. & planning, 1994-96, new concept officer, 1996—97, CEO, 1998—2001, acting pres. TOGOS, 1997—98; acting pres. Togo's, 1997—98; exec. v.p., COO N.Am. ops. Burger King Corp., Miami, Fla., 2001—02; exec. v.p. mktg. Red Lobster divsn. Darden Restaurants, Inc., Orlando, Fla., 2003—04, sr. v.p. Darden, pres. Red Lobster, 2004—. Bd. dirs. Hiram Walker & Sons Ltd, 1994—98, Rubio's Restaurants, Inc., 1997—2001, 31 Ice Cream Ltd., 1999—2001, Wawa Inc., 2006—, Boys & Girls Clubs Ctrl. Fla., 2004—. Vol. Boys & Girls Clubs Ctrl., Fla., 2004—, Sr. Governance Com. Summit Ch., 2010—. Mem.: US Chess Fedn., Phi Eta Sigma, Delta Sigma Rho, Beta Gamma Sigma. Republican. Avocations: running, chess, investing. Mailing: Darden Inc PO Box 695011 Orlando FL 32869-5011 Business E-Mail: klopdrup@darden.com.

LOPER, ROBERT MICHAEL, otolaryngologist; BS in Chemistry and Biology, U. Miss., 1972, MD, 1977. Diplomate American Bd. Otolaryngology, 1983, lic. Fla., 1986. Intern Naval Regional Med. Ctr., San Diego, 1977—78, resident otolaryngology, 1979—83; gen. practice USN, 1978—79; physician North Fla. Surgeons; hosp. affiliations include St. Vincent's Med. Ctr., Bapt. Hosp., Wolfson Children's Hosp. Avocations: fishing, scuba diving. Office: North Florida Surgeons 11945 San Jose Blvd Ste 300 Jacksonville FL 32223-1627 Office Phone: 904-396-1725. Office Fax: 904-396-4893.*

LOPEZ, ALFONSO H., state legislator; b. Williamsport, Pa., July 28, 1970; m. Sarah Mitte Zevin; 1 child, Aaron Rafael. BA, Vassar Coll., 1992; JD, Tulane U., 1995. Mem. Dist. 49 Va. House of Delegates, 2012—, mem. Militia Police and Pub. Safety Com. & Sci. and Tech. Com. Bd. mem. Northern Va. Region Inst. Polit. Leadership. Democrat. Office: General Assembly Building PO Box 406 Richmond VA 23218 also: PO Box 40366 Arlington VA 22204 Office Phone: 804-698-1049. Office Fax: 804-698-6749. E-mail: DelALopez@House.virginia.gov.

LOPEZ, DAVID TIBURCIO, lawyer, arbitrator, mediator, educator; b. Laredo, Tex., July 17, 1939; s. Tiburcio and Dora (Davila) L.; m. Romelia G. Guerra, Nov. 20, 1965; 1 child, Vianei López Braun. Student, Laredo Jr. Coll., 1956-58; BJ, U. Tex., 1962; JD summa cum laude, South Tex. Coll. Law, 1971. Bar: Tex. 1971, US Dist. Ct. (so. dist.) Tex. 1972, US Ct. Appeals (5th cir.) 1973, US Dist. Ct. (we. dist.) Tex. 1975, US Ct. Claims 1975, US Ct. Appeals (fed. cir.) 1975, US Supreme Ct. 1976, US Dist. Ct. (ea. dist.) Tex. 1978, US Dist. Ct. N.Mex. 2000, US Ct. Appeals (11th cir.) 1981, US Ct. Appeals (9th cir.) 1984; cert. internat. com. arbitrator panelist Internat. Ctr. Dispute Resolution; mediator tng. Atty.-Mediator Inst. Reporter Laredo Times, 1958-59, Corpus Christi Caller-Times, Tex., 1962-64; state capitol corr. Long News Svc., Austin, Tex., 1964-65; publs. dir. Interam. Regional Orgn. of Workers, Mexico City, 1965-67; nat. field rep. AFL-CIO, Washington, 1967-71, publs. dir. Tex. chpt. Austin, 1971-72; pvt. practice Houston, 1971—. Adj. prof. U. Houston, 1972-74, Thurgood Marshall Sch. Law, Houston, 1975-76; mem. adv. bd. Inst. Transnat. Arbitration; charter mem. Resolution Forum Inc.; mem. adv. bd. Frank Evans Ctr. for Conflict Resolution; mem. panel of neutrals, Internat. Ctr. Dispute Resolution, Am. Arbitration Assn. Mem. bd. edn. Houston Ind. Sch. Dist., 1972—75; bd. dirs. Pacifica Found., NYC, 1970—72, Houston CC, 1972—75, FM Radio Sta., 2000—02. With US Army. Recipient Outstanding Trial Lawyer award, Tex. Bar Found., 2007. Fellow: Chartered Inst. Arbitrators (London); mem.: FBA, ABA (steering group Internat. Comml. Dispute Resolution), Internat. Ctr. Dispute Resolution (mediator & arbitrator), Indsl. Rels. Rsch. Assn., Am. Judicature Soc., World Assn. Lawyers (chair internat. lab. sect.), Hispanic Bar Assn., US-Mex. Bar Assn., Inter-Pacific Bar Assn., Mex.-Am. Bar Assn., Bar of US Fed. Cir., Interam. Bar Assn., Internat. Bar Assn., Houston Bar Assn., Tex. Bar Assn. (bd. editors bar jour.), Phi Alpha Delta, Sigma Delta Chi. Democrat. Roman Catholic. Home: 28 Farnham Ct Houston TX 77024 Office: 3900 Montrose Blvd Houston TX 77006-4959 Office Phone: 713-523-3900. Business E-Mail: dtlopez@lopezlawfirm.com.

LOPEZ, JOHN C., meat processing company executive; b. Glendale, Ariz. m. Patricia Lopez; children: John Patrick, Dave, Kathy Thorley, Kristy Berdin, Ken McWilliams. Student, No. Ariz. U. Various positions, banking; operator McDonald's restaurant franchises, 1978—92; various positions, purchased controlling interest Normac Foods, 1992; CEO Lopez Foods, Inc., 1992—2004, chmn., 1992—. Bd. mem. Latino Cmty. Devel. Agy., Oklahoma City, 1997—; mem. nat. adv. bd. Hispanic Am. Committment to Ednl. Resources. Office: Lopez Foods Inc 6016 NW 120th Ct Oklahoma City OK 73162 Office Phone: 405-603-7500. Office Fax: 405-603-6009. Business E-Mail: jlopez@lopezfoods.com.

LÓPEZ, LORRAINE M., writer, literature and language professor; b. LA; BA, Calif. State U., Northridge, 1989; MA, PhD in English, U. Ga., 1997. Tchg. asst. dept. English U. Ga., 1996—2000; asst. prof. dept. humanities Brenau U., Gainesville, Ga., 2000—02; assoc. prof. dept. English Vanderbilt U., Nashville, 2002—. Author: (novels) Call Me Henri, 2006 (Paterson prize for young adult lit., 2007), The Gifted Gabaldón Sisters, 2008, (short story collections) Soy la Avon Lady and Other Stories, 2002 (Miguel Marmol prize for fiction, Curbstone Press, 2002, Latino Book award for short stories, Latino Lit. Hall of Fame, 2003, Ind. Publishers Book award for multicultural fiction, 2003), Homicide Survivors Picnic and Other Stories, 2009; contbr. numerous short stories and works of poetry to profl. publs.; editor: An Angle of Vision: Women Writers and Their Poor and Working-Class Roots, 2009. Recipient Best of Mag. Poetry award, Stillpoint Mag., 1994, Virginia R. Walter prize, Acad. Am. Poets, 1997, Mellon Faculty Devel. award, Vanderbilt U. Coll. Arts & Scis., 2007, Ernest A. Jones award for best faculty advisor, 2007; grantee Walter E. Dakin fellowship, Sewanee Writers' Conf., 2002. Office: Vanderbilt U Dept English Benson Hall 425 2301 Vanderbilt Pl Nashville TN 37235 Office Phone: 615-322-2328. Business E-Mail: lorraine.lopez@vanderbilt.edu.

LOPEZ, LOURDES, performing company executive, choreographer; b. Havana, Cuba, 1958; came to U.S., 1959; Studied with, Alexander Nigodoff and Martha Mahr, Miami, Perry Brunson; attended, Sch. of Am. Ballet, NYC. Mem. corps de ballet N.Y.C. Ballet, 1974-80, soloist, 1980-84, prin., 1984—2007; founder Morphoses, N.Y.C., 2007—; artistic dir. Miami City Ballet, Miami, Fla., 2012—. Culture reporter WNBC, N.Y.C.; admin Ballet Academy East, N.Y.C.; exec. dir. George Balanchine Found, N.Y.C., 2002. Created roles in Peter Martins' Sonate di Scarlatti and Rejouissance; other repertory includes: La Sonnambula, Divertimento No. 15, Serenade, Stars and Stripes, Apollo, Kammermusik No. 2, Firebird, The Four Seasons, The Goldberg Variations, Moves, Violin Concerto, Concerto Barocco, Theme and Variations, N.Y.C. Ballet's Balanchine Celebration, 1993, Cortège Hongrois, others; appeared in PBS series Dance in Am. Founder Cuban Artists Fund. Address: Morphoses 800 5th Ave Ste 18B New York NY 10065 Mailing: c/o Miami City Ballet 2200 Liberty Ave Miami Beach FL 33139

LOPEZ, RAYNALDO T., councilman; m. Evelyn Lopez; 4 children. Dir. Signature Client Group AT&T; councilman, Dist. 6 San Antonio City Coun., 2009—. Elected mem. Northside IDS Bd. Trustees, 1990. Named to AT&T's Leaders Coun. & Circle of Excellence, Harlandale ISD Hall of Fame. Avocations: golf, sailing, skiing. Office: 7042 Alamo Downs Pkwy Ste 500 San Antonio TX 78238 also: City Hall PO Box 839966 San Antonio TX 78283 Office Phone: 210-679-6506. E-mail: district6@sanantonio.gov.

LÓPEZ-CANTERA, CARLOS, Lieutenant Governor of Florida, former state legislator; b. Madrid, Dec. 29, 1973; m. Renee López-Cantera; children: Sabrina, Sofia. AA, Miami-Dade CC, Fla., 1994; BA, U. Miami, Fla., 1996. Comml. real estate cons. Pan American Cons., Inc., 1999—; mem. Dist. 113 Fla. House of Reps., Tallahassee, 2004—12, majority whip, 2008—10, majority leader, 2010—12; property appraisor Miami-Dade County, 2013—14; lt. gov. State of Fla., 2014—. Mem. Miami-Dade Living Wage Adv. Bd., 2000—02, Miami-Dade County Planning Adv. Bd., 2002—04; chmn. Miami-Dade Legislative Delegation, 2011—12. Mem.: Hispanic American Bus. Assn., Greater Miami Realtors Assn., Delta Sigma Pi. Republican. Roman Catholic. Office: Lieutenant Governor The State Capitol Tallahassee FL 32399 Office Phone: 850-488-4711. Office Fax: 850-921-6114.*

LOPINTO, JOSEPH P., III, state legislator; m. Lauren Vuljoin. BA in Criminal Justice, Loyola U.; JD, Loyola U. Sch. Law. Dep. narcotics detective Jefferson Parish Sheriff's Office, 1997—2004; owner/atty. Lopino Law Firm LLC, 2005—; mem. Dist. 80 La. House of Reps., 2008—, mem. adminstrn. of criminal justice com., commerce com. Republican. Office: 4532 West Napoleon Ave Ste 104 Metairie LA 70001 also: Capitol Office PO Box 44486 Baton Rouge LA 70804 Office Phone: 504-456-3806, 225-342-6945. Office Fax: 504-456-3808. E-mail: lopintoj@legis.state.la.us.

LOPREATO, JOSEPH, evolutionary sociologist, writer; b. Stefanaconi, Italy, July 13, 1928; arrived in US, 1947; s. Frank and Marianna (Pavone) L.; m. Carolyn H. Prestopino, July 18, 1954; (div. 1971); children: Gregory F., Marisa S. Schmidt; m. Sally A. Cook, Aug. 24, 1972 (div. 1978). BA in Sociology and Anthropology, U. Conn., Storrs, 1956; MA in Sociology, Yale U., New Haven, Conn., 1957, PhD in Sociology, 1960. Asst. prof. sociology U. Mass., Amherst, 1960-62; vis. lectr. U. Rome, 1962-64; assoc. prof. U. Conn., Storrs, 1964-66; prof. sociology U. Tex., Austin, 1968-98, chmn. dept. sociology, 1969-72. Vis. prof. U. Catania, Italy, 1974, U. Calabria, Italy, 1980; lectr.in various European U.; steering com. Council European Studies, Columbia U., 1977-80; chmn. sociology com. Council for Internat. Exchange Scholars, 1977-79; mem. Internat. Com. Mezzogiorno, 1986-88; Calabria Internat. Com., 1988-90. Author: Italian Made Simple, 1959, Vilfredo Pareto, 1965, Peasants No More, 1967, Italian Americans, 1970, Class, Conflict and Mobility, 1972, Social Stratification, 1974, The Sociology of Vilfredo Pareto, 1975, La Stratificazione Sociale negli Stati Uniti, 1945-1975, 1977, Human Nature and Biocultural Evolution, 1984, Evoluzione e Natura Umana, 1990, Mai Più Contadini, 1990, Crisis in Sociology: The Need for Darwin, 1999; contbr. articles to profl. jours. Mem. Nat. Italian-Am. Com. for U.S.A. Bicentennial; mem. exec. com. Congress Italian Politics, 1977-80. Served to cpl. U.S. Army, 1952-54. Fulbright faculty research fellow, 1962-64, 73-74; Social Sci. Research Council faculty research fellow, 1963-64; NSF faculty research fellow, 1965-68; U. Tex. Austin research fellow, 1973-74, spring 1985, spring 1993; Guido Dorso award for U.S.A., Italy, 1992. Mem.: AAAS (behavioral sci. rsch. prize com. 1992—94), Internat. Soc. Human Ethology, Evolution and Behavior Soc., Internat. Sociol. Assn. Catholic-Episcopalian. Home: 421 Monarch Trail Georgetown TX 78633 Office Phone: 512-943-4429. Business E-Mail: lopreato@utexas.edu.

LOPUS, THOMAS ALBERT, petroleum engineer; b. Union City, Pa., May 4, 1958; s. Ralph Thomas and Rita Mary (Dahlkemper) L.; m. Donna M. Schmitt, June 27, 1981; children: Daniel, David, Katlyn, Ryan. BS in Petroleum & Natural Gas Engring., Pa. State U., 1980. Registered profl. engr., Tex. Prodn. engr. Tenneco, Oklahoma City, 1980-82, coord. coll. recruiting Houston, 1982-84, sr. prodn. engr., 1984-88; area engr. Fina, Houston, 1988-90, mgr. drilling and prodn. Midland, Tex., 1992-93, mgr. divsn. prodn. Oklahoma City, 1990-92, gen. mgr. Houston, 1993—; sr. mgmt. positions Equitable Resources, Inc., 2002—05; sr. v.p. ops. Linn Energy, LLC, 2006—08; exec. v.p. Appalachia Quest Resource Corp., 2008—09; mem. dir. Marcellus Shale Com., 2008—10; Appalachian bus. mgr. Cohort Energy, 2010—. Chmn. March of Dimes, Midland, 1992-93; dist. sales chmn. Boy Scouts Am., Houston, 1994-96., leadership positions Ind. Petroleum Assn. of America, Am. Petroleum Inst., United Way. Named Mentor of Yr., Inroads, 1986. Mem. Soc. Petroleum Engrs. (social dir. Oklahoma City chpt. 1980-82, benefits com. Midland chpt. 1992-93). Office: Cohort Energy 15508 Wright Brothers Dr Addison TX 75001 Office Phone: 972-233-8191. Office Fax: 972-991-0704.

LORBERBAUM, JEFFREY S., textiles executive; With Aladdin Mills, Inc., Calhoun, Ga., 1976-86, v.p. ops., 1986-94; pres., CEO Mohawk Industries, Inc., Calhoun, Ga., 1994—2004, chmn., pres., CEO, 2004—09, chmn., CEO, 2009—. Office: Mohawk Industries Inc 160 S Indsl Blvd Calhoun GA 30701

LORCH, GEORGE A., corporate board member, retired manufacturing executive; b. Glenridge, NJ, 1941; BS, Va. Poly. Inst. & State U., 1963. Joined Armstrong World Industries, Inc., 1963, v.p. mktg. E&B Divsn., 1974-76, mktg. mgr., 1976-78, gen. sales mgr., 1978-83, group v.p. carpet ops., 1983—88, exec. v.p., 1988—93, pres., CEO, 1993—2000, chmn., 1994—2000; CEO Armstrong Holdings, Inc., 2000, chmn. emeritus, 2000—; chmn. Pfizer, Inc., 2010—11. Bd. dirs. Armstrong World Industries, Inc., 1988—2000, HSBC Financial Corp., 1994—, Pfizer, Inc., 2000—, Williams Companies, Inc., 2001—11, Autoliv Inc., 2003—.

LORD, EVELYN MARLIN, mayor; b. Melrose, Mass., Dec. 8, 1926; d. John Joseph and Mary Janette (Nourse) Marlin; m. Samuel Smith Lord Jr., Feb. 28, 1948 (dec. 2011); children: Steven Arthur, Jonathan Peter, Nathaniel Edward (dec.), Victoria Marlin, William Kenneth. BA, Boston U., 1948; MA, U. Del., 1956; JD, U. Louisville, 1969. Bar: Ky. 1969, U.S. Supreme Ct. 1973. Exec. dir. Block Blight Inc., Wilmington, Del., 1956—60; mem. Del. Senate, Dover, 1960—62; administrv. asst. county judge Jefferson County, Louisville, 1968—71; corr. No. Ireland News Jour. Co., Wilmington, 1972—74; legal adminstr. Orgain, Bell & Tucker, Beaumont, Tex., 1978—83; v.p. Tex. Commerce Bank, Beaumont, 1983—84; councilman City of Beaumont, 1980—82, mayor pro tem, 1982—84, mayor, 1990—94, 2002—05; spokesperson Dauphin Cancer Ctr. Bapt. Hosp., 2006—11, Altus Health Care Mgmt., 2012—. Tourism chmn. U.S. Conf. Mayors, 1994, adv. bd., chmn. arts, culture and recreation, 1992—94; sr. counselor Ky. Bar, 2002—; adv. bd. US Conf. Mayors, 1992—94, 2002—05. Pres. United Way, 1994, 1997; adv. bd. Boy Scouts Am., Three Rivers, 1978—84, 1989—94, exec. bd., 2000—05, 2007—; life mem. Girl Scouts U.S.A., pres. Kentuckiana coun., 1966—70, governing bd. San Jacinto coun., 2006—07; trustee Lamar U. Found., 1999—2003; adv. coun. mem. Gladdy City Boomtown Mus., 2011—; pres. Tex. Energy Mus., 1995—96; lifetime trustee United Way, Beaumont; mem. Salvation Army, Beaumont, Tex., 2006—09, adv. bd. sec., 2007—09; adv. bd. Found. S.E. Tex., 2010—; bd. dirs. Evelyn M. Lord Teen Ct., 1993—, Found. S.E. Tex., 1990—2010, Lincoln Inst., 1994—2001, Beaumont Pub. Schs. Found., 1993—99, 2011—12, pres., 2012; bd. dirs. Ptnrs. for Children, 1990—2009, Child Protective Svcs., adv. bd., 2009—, pres., 1990—91; chmn. Spindletop 2001 Com. Recipient Silver Beaver award, Boy Scouts Am., Beaumont, 1979, Disting. Alumni award, Boston U., 1983, Disting. Leadership award, Nat. Assn. Leadership Orgns., Indpls., 1991, Labor-Mgmt. Pub. Sector award, 1991, Cmty. Builder award, Grand Masonic Lodge of Tex., 1991, 2003, Disting. Grad. award, Leadership Beaumont, 1993, Rotary Svc. Above Self award, 1994, Excellency award, Tex. State Hist. Commn., 2001, Athena award, Beaumont C of C, 2003, Mrs. S.E. Tex. award, Dogwood Festival, 2004, Regional Leadership award, S.E. Tex. Regional Planning Commn., 2005, Thanks Badge, Girl Scouts San Jacinto Coun., 2009, Cliff Dochterman award, Scouting Rotarians, Evelyn M. Lord Humanitarian of Yr. award, Baptist Hosp. Southeast Texas; named Citizen of Yr., Sales and Mktg. Assn., 1990, Beaumont Man of the Yr., 1993, Woman with Heart, Am. Heart Assn., 2000, Free Ent. Person of the Yr., Assn. Bldg. Contrs., 2000, Newsmaker of the Yr., Press Club Jefferson County, 2001, Hurricane Evelyn, ARC, 2001, Disting. Law Alumni, U. Louisville, 2002, Woman of Yr., Quota Club Internat., 2002. Mem.: DAR, LWV (Del. state pres. 1960—62, bd. dirs. Tex. 1978—80), Bus. and Profl. Women Assn. (Woman of Yr. 1983), Colonial Dames (Citizenship award 2004), Symphony Soc. S.E. Tex. (hon.; bd. dirs. 1990—98, 2002—), Soc. Mayflower Descs., Rotary, 100 Club (pres. 1995—97). Avocations: writing, reading, genealogy. Home: 7080 Calder Ave H-1 Beaumont TX 77706-6086 Personal E-mail: evelynlord@aol.com.

LORD, JACQUELINE WARD, retired accountant, photographer, artist; b. Andalusia, Ala., May 16, 1936; d. Marron J. and Minnie V. (Owen) Ward; m. Curtis Gaynor, Nov. 23, 1968. Student, U. Ala., Montgomery, 1966, Auburn U., Ala., 1977, Huntingdon Coll., Montgomery, 1980, Troy State U., Ala., 1980; BA in Bus. Adminstrn., Dallas Bapt. U., 1985. News photographer corr. News photographer corr., Ala., 1954—59, Sta. WSFA-TV, Montgomery, 1954—60; acct. & bus. mgr. Reihardt Motors, Inc., Montgomery, 1962—69; office mgr. & acct. Ctrl. Ala. Supply, Montgomery, 1969—71; pres. Foxy Lady Apparel, Inc., Montgomery, 1973—76; acct. Chambers Constrn. Co., Montgomery, 1972—75, Rushton, Stakely, Johnston & Garrett, Montgomery, 1975—81; acctg. supr. Arthur Andersen & Co., Dallas, 1981—82; staff acct. Burgess Co., CPAs, Dallas, 1983; owner Lord & Assocs. Acctg. Svc., Dallas, 1983—2001; tax acct. John Hasse, CPA, Dallas, 1984—86, Dallas Bapt. Assn., 1986—2006, ret., 2006. Vol. election law commr. Sec. State of Ala. Don Siegelman, Montgomery, 1979—80; active mem. Montgomery Art Guild, 1964—65, Ala. Art League, 1964—65, 1963—65, Montgomery Choral Soc., 1965. Recipient Outstanding Achievement Bus. Mgmt. award, Am. Motors, 1968. Mem.: Nat. Assn. Ch. Bus. Adminstrn., Soroptimists Internat. (pres. elect Montgomery chpt. 1975—76, area day chmn. 1978), Am. Soc. Women Accts. (del. ann. meeting 1975—78, pres. Montgomery chpt. 1976—77). Home: 3806 Heatherbrook Pl Dothan AL 36303

LORD, JEROME EDMUND, education administrator, writer; b. Waterbury, Conn., Dec. 24, 1935; s. James Andrew and Mary Frances (Hayes) L.; m. Eleanor Louise de Peverel. Fitz Warim. Collins, Apr. 22, 1967; children: Hayes Alexander FitzWarin, Stavely Hampston deHodnet, Savile Collins de Montenay, Dorian Warfield d'Amours, Wallis Jennings dePantulf Lord-Hart. BA, Georgetown U., 1957; MA, Boston Coll., 1962, Columbia U., 1963, PhD, 1969; diploma (hon.), U. Madrid, 1962. Tchr. The Taft Sch. Peekskill Mil. Acad., 1957—60; editor, lang. recs. supr. Allyn and Bacon Inc., Boston, 1961—62; adminstrv. assoc. internat. programs and services Tchrs. Coll. Columbia U., NYC, 1963—65, assoc. in higher edn., 1965—66; asst. prof. edn., exec. asst. to dean acad. devel. CUNY, 1965—67, assoc. prof. edn., exec. asst. to vice chancellor exec. office, 1967—69; dir. rsch. Ford and Carnegie Study of Fed. Politics of Edn. Brookings Instn., Washington, 1969—70; program officer Nat. Ctr. for Ednl. Tech., US Dept. Edn., Washington, 1971—73; sr. assoc. Nat. Inst. Edn., Washington, 1973—86, Office Ednl. Rsch. and Improvement, Washington, 1986—2002, Inst. Edn. Scis., Dept. Edn., Washington, 2002—06. Pres. Jerome Lord Enterprises, Inc., Palm Beach, Fla.; advisor to vol. edn. policy group Office Dir. Def. Edn., US Dept. Def., 1975-76; chmn. Fed. Interagy. Panel for Rsch. on Adulthood; pub. Humble Pie Pub., Palm Beach, Fla.; cons. and lectr. in field. Playwright: Teresa, 1971, The Election, 1972, Audition!, 1973, Decent Exposure, 1979, Amazing Grace, 1987, Heads You Win, 1991, Making Believe, 1996, My One and Only, 1997, All About Me, 2014-; author: Perfectly Proper, 1993-, Teacher Training Abroad: New Realities, 1993, Adult Literacy Programs: Guidelines for Effectiveness, 1995-, Alternative Schools and Programs for Violent and Disruptive Students, 2004, Letters To Minerva from a Mind Unraveling, 2011, The Greatest French Food Book in The World, 2012, A Mind Unraveled: More Letters to Minerva, 2014, So You're Getting Engaged, 2014, Moments in My Gorgeous Life, 2014; contbr. articles to profl. mags. and jours. Trustee St. John's Child Devel. Ctr., Washington, 1978-83; mem. nat. bd. sponsors Protestant and Orthodox Ctr., NY World's Fair, 1964; mem. adv. bd. NYC Urban Corps, 1965-69, others; mem. coun. of friends Folger Shakespeare Libr.; sponsor Nat. Symphony Orch.; mem., donor reception rooms Dept. State, bd. trustee Opportunity Inc. West, Palm Beach, Fla., 2009-, patron Henry Morrison Flagler Mus., Palm Beach, Fla., French Heritage Soc., NY, Palm Beach, adv. coun. Palm Beach Theater Guild. Named Coakley scholar, 1953-57, M.T. Runyan scholar, 1967-68; fellow W.T. Kellogg Found., 1968-69, Rinehart Found., 1970-71, others; recipient Pillow Lee Outstanding Leadership award, St. John's Cmty. Svcs., Washington, DC, Va., Tenn., Pa., 2012. Mem. Nat. Soc. Aesthetic and Competitive Garglers Am. (founder, grand-garglemaster pro-tem 2005), Soc. Friends St. George's and Desc. Knights of Garter, Acad. Am. Poets, Pilgrims of the US, World Affairs Coun., BlackTie Soc. (Palm Beach, Fla.)The Lansdowne Club (London), Met. Club (Wash., DC), Kappa Delta Pi, Phi Delta Pi, Eta Sigma Phi. Atheist. Avocations: historic preservation, music, art history, architecture, antiques, genealogy, history, jewelry. Office: Humble Pie Publ Box 2802 Palm Beach FL 33480 Home: 2520 NE 1st Ct Apt 307 Boynton Beach FL 33435-2075 Personal E-mail: jeromeelord@gmail.com.

LORD OF CURSONS, See RAWL, ARTHUR

LOREN, DONALD PATRICK, national security business executive, small business leader, former administration and federal official, retired military officer; b. NYC, Mar. 17, 1952; s. Nicholas A. and Helen T. (Carrado) L.; m. Maureen M. Lynch, Jan. 12, 1991. BS in Ops. Analysis, U.S. Naval Acad., 1974; MS in Edn., Old Dominion U., 1983; postgrad., Harvard U., 1993-94, MIT, 1994-95. Commd. ens. USN, 1974, advanced through grades to rear adm., combat sys. officer, Destroyer Squadron Thirty-One, 1978; ops. officer USS Peterson, 1979-80; ops. and readiness officer Destroyer Squadron Two Staff, 1981-82; asst. chief of staff for comms. Cruiser Destroyer Group Eight Staff, 1983-85; exec. officer USS John Hancock, 1985-86; flag sec. to comdr. in chief U.S. Naval Forces, Europe, 1986-88; NATO policy officer Strategic Plans and Policy Directory, Joint Staff, 1989-91; comdg. officer USS Elrod FFG-55, 1991-93; doctrine devel. officer Naval Doctrine Command, 1993; fed. exec. fellow Ctr. for Internat. Affairs Harvard U., Cambridge, Mass., 1993-94; profl. staff mem. Ind. Commn. on Roles and Missions of Armed Forces, 1993-94; comdr. Destroyer Squadron Twenty-eight, Norfolk, Va., 1995-97; dep. dir. strategy and policy divsn. Office the the Chief of Naval Ops., 1997-98; exec. asst. to comdr. in chief U.S. Naval Forces Europe, 1998—2001; and comdr. in chief Allied Forces So. Europe, 1998—2001; exec. asst., prin. advisor to operational comdr. NATO Combat Forces, 1999—2001; dep. dir. surface ships Office of the Chief of Naval Ops., 2001—03; dep. dir. politico-mil. affairs Europe, NATO,Russia and Africa, The Joint Staff, 2003—05; dep. dir. ops. support Nat. Counterterrorism Ctr., Washington, 2006—07; dep. asst. sec. def. homeland security integration Dept. Def., Washington, 2007—09; spl. asst. nat. security Tauri Group; appointed Va. Gov Military Advisory Council; pres. Old Dominion Strategies LLC - SDVOSB, CEO. Governance fellow Nat. Assn. Corp. Dirs.; fellow MIT, Seminar XXI, fgn. politics, internat. rels. and the nat. interest, 1994-95; fellow nat. security studies Maxwell Sch., Syracuse U., 2003; fellow NATO Def. Coll., Rome, 2004; fellow sr. execs. in nat. and internat. security program Harvard U. JFK Sch. Govt., 2004, Northwestern U. Kellogg Sch. Mgmt., 2006, U. Md. Sch. Pub. Policy, 2006, sr. defense advisor, Homeland Defense and Security Bus. Coun.; bd. chmn. Nat. Assoc. Uniformed Svcs.; mem, Homeland Security Intelligence Coun., 2010-, trustee US Nat. Meml.; adj. lectr., sr. fellow Joint Forces Staff Coll., prof. mil. sci. Old Dominion U. Author: Shape Up! A Shipboard Program for Physical Fitness, 1981; contbr. articles to profl. publs. Decorated Def. Superior Svc. medal, Bronze star, Order Merit Italian Republic, Conspicuous Svc. Star and Cross N.Y. State; recipient Sec. Def. medal for Outstanding Public Serv., Legion of Merit. Mem. Phi Kappa Phi, Sigma Iota Epsilon. Avocations: jogging, weight training, classical music, ballet, opera. Office: 6504 John Thomas Dr Alexandria VA 22315 Office Phone: 571-214-4084.

LORENZ, TED R., lawyer; m. Lesley Howe Lorenz. BA, U. Tex., Austin; JD, U. Houston, 2000. Bar: Tex. Trial atty., Dallas; founding ptnr. Lorenz & Lorenz, L.L.P., Austin, Tex., 2001—. Named a Rising Star, Tex. Super Lawyers mag., 2006. Mem.: Assn. Trial Lawyers of Am., Capital Area Trial Lawyers Assn., Austin Bar Assn. Office: Ste 401 1705 S Capital of Texas Hwy Austin TX 78746-6562 Office Phone: 512-477-7333. E-mail: TedLorenz@AustinAccidentAttorney.com.

LORIA, JEFFREY H., professional sports team executive; b. NYC; 3 children. Grad. in art history, Yale U., New Haven, Conn., 1962; MBA, Columbia U., NYC. Head of artwork collection Sears Roebuck, 1962—65; founder, internat. art dealer Jeffrey H. Loria & Co., NYC, 1965—; owner Oklahoma City 89ers, 1989-93; chmn., CEO Montreal Expos, 1999—2002; owner Miami Marlins (formerly Fla. Marlins), 2002—, World Series Champions, 2003—. Author: Collecting Original Art, What's It All About Charlie Brown. Former bd. dirs. Art Dealers Assn. Am. Named Triple A Exec. of Yr., Am. Assn., 1992. Office: Miami Marlins 501 Marlins Way Miami FL 33125

LORING, HARRIS E., III, financial services executive; BBA, Bryant Coll., North Smithfield, RI; MS in Taxation, Bentley Coll., Waltham, Mass. CPA. Dir. tax Stone & Webster, Inc.; mng. dir. tax Svc. Corp. Internat., 2000—04, asst. treas., 2004—06; v.p., treas. Service Corp. International, 2006—. Office: Service Corporation International 1929 Allen Pky Houston TX 77019 Office Phone: 713-522-5141. Office Fax: 713-525-5586.

LORUSSO, NICK, state legislator; BA, U. New Orleans, 1988; JD, La. State U., 1992. Atty.; mem. Dist. 94 La. House of Reps., 2007—09, 2010—, vice chair civil law and procedure com., mem. adminstrn. of criminal justice com., judiciary com., spl. com. on mil. and vets. affairs. Lt. col., dep. staff judge advocate USAR, 2009—10. Republican. Office: 4431 Canal St Ste B New Orleans LA 70119 Office Phone: 504-483-4711. Office Fax: 504-483-4713. E-mail: larep094@legis.state.la.us.

LOTT, HAMILTON, JR., manufacturing executive; Design engr. Vulcraft, Florence, SC, 1975, engring. mgr. St. Joe, Ind., 1982—86, sales mgr., 1987, gen. mgr. Grapeland, Tex., 1987—93, Florence, 1993—99; v.p. Nucor Corp., Charlotte, NC, 1988—99, exec. v.p., 1999—. Office: Nucor Corp 1915 Rexford Rd Charlotte NC 28211 Office Phone: 704-366-7000. Office Fax: 704-362-4208.

LOTT, HANK, state legislator; m. Melinda Cooksey. Attended, U. So. Miss., Hattiesburg. Bldg. supply co. owner; mem. Dist. 101 Miss. House of Reps., Jackson. Active Sumrall Devel. Found., Miss. Mem.: Hattiesburg Homebuilders Assn., Forrest Lamar Forestry Assn., Sumrall Lion's Club. Republican. Baptist. Office: Miss House of Reps PO Box 1018 Jackson MS 39215 Home Phone: 601-758-4265. Business E-Mail: hlott@house.ms.gov.

LOTT, MICHAEL A., state legislator; b. Hattiesburg, Miss., Apr. 25, 1956; m. Eleanor Anderson. State rep. Dist. 104, Miss., 2000—; mem. County Affairs Com., Constrn. Com., Edn. Com., Juvenile Justice Com., Labor Com. Mem.: Petal C. of C. Republican. Baptist. Mailing: 6925 US Highway 49 Hattiesburg MS 39402-9162 Office Phone: 601-408-2598, 601-359-2430. E-mail: mlott@mail.house.state.ms.us.

LOTT, WAYNE THOMAS, systems engineer; b. Pitts., Mar. 20, 1959; s. Wayne Thomas Lott Sr. and Patricia Julia (Malanowski) Lott Martin; m. Diane Mary Phillips, Sept. 11, 1982; children: Sarah Marie, Justin Thomas. AS in Computer Sci., C.C. Allegheny County, Pitts., 1984; BSBA in Info. Sys., Robert Morris U., 1986; MS in Mgmt. Info. Sys., Am. U., 1997. Intern, programmer Thrift Drug Co., Pitts., 1986; contract programmer Comsource Tech. Svcs., Pitts., 1986-87; programmer Tippins Inc., Pitts., 1987; initial designer tng. AT&T, Herndon, Va., 1988, tech. tester, 1988-89, sys. analyst, 1989-92; sys. engr. AT&T Bell Labs., Herndon, 1992-94, AT&T, Herndon, 1995-97, tech. mgr. ordering software devel., 1998-2000; dist. mgr. ordering software devel. IBM Global Svcs., 2000—03; IT cons., delivery mgr. Anteon Internat. Corp., 2004, program mgr. II; sr. sys. analyst Sallie Mae Inc., 2005—06; program mgr. AEM Corp., Chantilly, Va., 2007. Mem. IEEE, Upsilon Pi Epsilon. Roman Catholic. Home and Office: 12779 Misty Creek Ln Fairfax VA 22033-1728 E-mail: Lott_Wayne@hotmail.com.

LOUDERMILK, BARRY DEAN, state legislator; b. Ga., Dec. 22; BA in Occupl. Edn. and Info. Systems Tech., Wayland Bapt. U., Plainview, Tex. Co-owner, pres. Innovative Network Systems, Inc., Cartersville, Ga., 1995—; mem. Dist. 14 Ga. House of Reps., 2005—11; mem. Dist. 52 Ga. State Senate, 2011—. Chmn. Bartow County Rep. Party, 2000—04. Served with USAF, 1984—92, Tex., Hawaii, Alaska, lt. col. Civil Air Patrol. Named State of Ga. Legis. of Yr., Civil Air Patrol, 2006, Nat. Legis. of Yr., 2006, Pub. Servant of Yr., Advocates for Children, 2006; named one of 50 Most Influential Georgians, James Mag., 2008. Republican. Office: PO Box 465 Cassville GA 30123 also: Ga State Senate 323 A Coverdell Legis Office Bldg Atlanta GA 30334 also: Innovative Network Systems Inc 654 Joe Frank Harris Parkway PO Box 968 Cartersville GA 30120 Office Phone: 678-721-5612, 404-656-0034. Business E-Mail: barry@barryloudermilk.com.

LOUDERMILK, JOEY M., lawyer, insurance company executive; b. Warner Robins AFB, Ga., Apr. 4, 1953; m. Ramona Loudermilk; children: Matt, Justin, Jenny, Joanna, John Mark, Jackson. BS cum laude, Ga. State U., 1975; JD, U. Ga., 1978. Bar: Ga. 1978, US Dist. Ct. (mid. and no. dists. Ga.) 1978, US Ct. Appeals (11th cir.) 1981. Assoc. Moore & Worthington, Columbus, Ga., 1981—83; dir. legal dept. AFLAC, Inc., Columbus, Ga., 1983—2000, dir. govt. rels., 1988—2000, sr. v.p., corp. counsel, 1989—91, sr. v.p., gen. counsel, 1991—2000, exec. v.p. legal & govt. affairs, gen. counsel, 2000—, corp. sec. Bd. dirs. Ga. Pub. Policy Found. Pres. Rotary Club, Columbus, Ga.; elder Edgewood Bapt. Ch.; bd. dirs. Ga. State U. Law Sch., Columbus Regional Med. Found., Ga. Humanities Coun., Ga. Mil. Affairs Coordinating Com. Mem.: Am. Soc. Corp. Secs., Am. Corp. Counsel Assn., State Bar Ga. Office: AFLAC Inc 1932 Wynnton Rd Columbus GA 31999 Office Phone: 706-323-3431.*

LOUDERMILK, R. CHARLES, rental company executive; b. Atlanta, July 12, 1927; m. Marilyn McQueen; children: Lisa, Robert C. Jr., Linda. BS in Commerce, U. NC, Chapel Hill, 1950. Founder, chmn. Aaron's Inc. (formerly Aaron Rents, Inc.), Atlanta, 1955—, pres., CEO, 1962—97, CEO, 1997—2008. Chmn. bd. Buckhead Coalition; bd. dirs. The Buckhead-Chattahoochee Bancorp., Inc., Buckhead Bus. Assn. Mem. bd. visitors U. NC, U. NC Sch. Bus.; sr. trustee Archbold Hosp. Found.; bd. dirs. Piedmont Hosp. Found.; steering com. Shepherd Spinal Ctr.; co-chmn. Andrew Young's Mayoral Campaign, Atlanta, 1981, 85; bd. dirs., chmn. bd. Metro Atlanta Rapid Transit Authority. Served with USN. Mem. Nat. Rental Svc. Assn. (pres. 1962-63, Man of Yr. award 1979), Atlanta C. of C. (bd. dirs.), Piedmont Driving Club, Capital City Club, Commerce Club, Buckhead Club, Rotary. Office: Aaron's Inc 309 E Paces Ferry Rd NE Atlanta GA 30305

LOUGHRIDGE, JOHN HALSTED, JR., lawyer; b. Chestnut Hill, Pa., Oct. 30, 1945; s. John Halsted Sr. and Martha Margaret (Boyd) L.; m. Amy Claire Booe, Aug. 3, 1980 (div. Apr. 1995); 1 child, Emily Halsted. BA, Davidson Coll., 1967; JD, Wake Forest U., 1970. Bar: N.C. 1970, US Middle Dist. Ct. NC 1970, U.S. Ct. Mil. Appeals 1986, U.S. Supreme Ct. 2002. Divsn. head, v.p., counsel Wachovia Mortgage Co., Winston-Salem, N.C., 1971-79; sr. v.p., counsel Wachovia Corp. and Bank, Charlotte and Winston-Salem, NC, 1980—2007, mng. coun., 2001—07; trustee J. T. Bacon Trust, 2007—; mng. ptnr. JWJC Assocs., Winston-Salem, NC, 2008—, mng. counsel, 2001—07. UCC Article 5 drafting com. NC Gen. Statues Commn., 1999; dir. NC Mil. Support Corp., Greensboro, 2008—11. Founding sponsor Nat. Mus. U.S. Army, 2005; mem. cabinet, chair profl. divsn. United Way Forsyth County, 1994; mem. Rep. Nat. Com., 1986—, Rep. Presdl. Taskforce, 2004, Reagan Congrl. Commn., 2006, 2007; NC del. Rep. Candidates Conv., 2007, Nat. Rep. Congl. Com., 2004—; del. to NC Rep. Party State Conv., 2008—; mem. GOP Attys. Com. Help Am. Vote Act, 2004, 2008, 2012, Presdl. Bus. Commn., 2005—08; leader Rep. Presdl. Victory Team, 2004; exec. com. & ctrl. com. mem., audit com. chair Forsyth County Rep. Party, 2009—; mem. cmty. adv. bd. US Army Winston-Salem Recruiting Command, 2013—. Col. JAGC USAR, 1970—2000. Recipient Ronald Reagan Rep. Gold Medal award, 2004, 2005, Congl. Medal of Distinction, Nat. Rep. Congl. Com., 2006, 2008, Pres. Vol. Svc. award, 2006—12, Congrl. Order of Merit, Nat. Rep. Congrl. Com., 2005—06, 2007, 2008; named Businessman Yr., 2005, 2006; named to Presdl. Commn., 2008. Mem.: ABA (bus. law sect. 1970—, internat. law and practice sect. 1999—2002, real estate financing subcom. 2006—, comml. fin. com. 2006—, adv. panel 2006—, bus. law com. mem. 2008—, consumer fin. svcs. com. 2009—, pvt. equity and venture capital com. 2009—, mem. com. on bus. and corp. litig. 2011—, mem. subcom. on alt. dispute resolution 2011—, Housing Fin. Subcom. 2011—), Dept. Def. Office of Employer Support Guard and Res. (NC Com. area chair 2005, exec. com. mem. 2005—, ombudsman, mediator 2006—, dir. mil. outreach 2006—, nat. outreach sub-com. mem. 2008—), NC Bar Found. (CLE program planner 2000, 2001, 2007), Mortgage Bankers Assn. Am. (legal issues com. 1982—92, fin. affiliates com. 1988—92), Assn. Corp. Counsel (bd. dirs. and v.p. NC chpt. 1988—98, 2001—04, fin. svcs. com. 2006—), Forsyth County Bar Assn., NC Coll. Advocacy, NC State Bar (bar examination candidate interviewer 2001, 2002), NC Bar Assn. (real property sect. 1971—, bus. law sect. 1971—, internat. law sect. 1984—2013, fin. instns. com. 1985—, governing coun. real property sect. 1988—91, corp. counsel sect. 1989—, real property curriculum com. 1990—93, governing coun. corp. coun. sect. 1992—98, treas. 1999—2000, bus. law curriculum com. 1999—2001, corp. coun. sect. sec. 2000—01, sect. vice chair 2001—02, chmn. 2002—03, nominating com. bd. govs. and officers 2003—05, sect. vice chair 2006—07), Res. Officers Assn. (chpt. pres. 1996—97, sec. 1997—, named to Nat. Brigade Vols. 2005, Leadership award 2005), Davidson Coll. (bd. dirs. Alumni Assn. 2001—03, Fideles Soc., Alumni Svc. award 2007), Rotary Club (Paul Harris fellow), Forsyth Country Club, Twin City Club (sec. 1990—97, gov. 1994—2005, pres. 1997—2001), Union League Phila., Phi Delta Theta, Phi Delta Phi. Republican. Presbyterian. Avocations: golf, tennis. Home: 615 Arbor Rd Winston Salem NC 27104 Office: JWJC Assocs 615 Arbor Rd Winston Salem NC 27104 Office Phone: 336-723-5002. Business E-Mail: jhloughridge@gmail.com.

LOUGHRY, ALLEN H., II, state supreme court justice; b. Elkins, W.Va., 1970; m. Kelly Loughry; 1 child, Justus. BS in journalism, W.Va. U.; SJD, American U., LLM in law and govt.; LLM in criminology and criminal justice, U. London; JD, Capital U. Personal asst. Tucker County Pros. Atty., 1988, 1989; spl. asst. to Rep. Harley O. Staggers Jr. US House of Representatives; direct aide to Gov. Gaston Caperton State of W.Va.; sr. asst. atty. gen. W.Va. Atty. General's Office, 1997—2003; assoc. justice W.Va. Supreme Ct., Charleston, 2013—. Tchr. polit. sci. U. Charleston, 2010. Author: (books) Don't Buy Another Vote, I Won't Pay for a Landslide, 2006. Office: West Virginia Supreme Ct CapitolComplex Bldg 1 Rm 308 Charleston WV 25305 Office Phone: 304-558-2605. E-mail: Allen.Loughry@courtswv.gov.

LOUIS, WILLIAM ROGER, historian; b. Detroit, May 8, 1936; s. Henry Edward and Bena May (Flood) L.; m. Dagmar Cecilia Friedrich; children: Antony Andrew, Catherine Ann. BA, U. Okla., 1959; MA, Harvard U., 1960; DPhil, Oxford U., 1962, DLitt, 1979; DLitt (hon.), Westminster Coll., 1998. Asst. prof., then assoc. prof. history Yale U., 1962-70; prof. history U. Tex., Austin, 1970-85, dir. Brit. Studies, 1975—, Kerr chair English history and culture, 1985—, disting. teaching prof., 1998—. Royal Soc. Lit. Benson Supernumerary fellow St. Antony's Coll., U. Oxford, Eng., 1986-96, hon. fellow, 1996—; fellow Brit. Acad., 1993—; Chichele lectr. All Souls Coll., U. Oxford, Eng., 1990, 2002, 03, 06, 10; Disting. lectr. London Sch. Econs., 1992; Cust lectr. Nottingham U., 1995; Elie Kedourie Meml. lectr. Brit. Acad., 1996; Churchill Meml. lectr., 1998; history faculty lectr. U. Oxford, Eng., 2001; disting. vis. prof. Am. U. in Cairo, 2001; Kalb lectr. Rice U., 2001; Fusco lectr. U. Conn., 2001, Costa lectr. U. Ohio, 2002; dir. summer seminars NEH, 1985, 88, 90, 91, 96, 2000; dir. Mellon Decolonization Summer Seminars, 2006-; Antonius lectr. Oxford U., 2002, Leonard Stein lectr., Oxford U., 2005; Strelitz lectr., Tel Aviv, 2008; Hinckley lectr. U. Utah, 2008, founding dir. Nat. History Ctr., 2001-13, US State Dept. Hist. Adv. Com., 2002-08; scholars coun., Libr. Congress; co-dir. Wash. History Seminar, 2010-. Author: Ruanda-Urundi, 1963, Germany's Lost Colonies, 1967, (with Jean Stengers) The Congo Reform Movement, 1968, British Strategy in the Far East, 1919-1939, 1971, Imperialism at Bay, 1977 (History Book Club), British Empire in the Middle East, 1984 (George Louis Beer prize Am. Hist. Assn. and Tex. Inst. Letters award), In The Name of the God Go! Leo Amery and the British Empire in the Age of Churchill, 1992; editor British Documents on the End of the Empire, 1988—; editor-in-chief Oxford History of the British Empire, 1992—; editor: (with P. Gifford) Britain and Germany in Africa, 1967, France and Britain in Africa, 1971, The Origins of the Second World War: A.J.P. Taylor and His Critics, 1972, National Security and International Trusteeship in the Pacific, 1972, Imperialism: The Robinson and Gallagher Controversy, 1976, (with William S. Livingston) Australia, New Zealand and the Pacific Islands Since the First World War, 1979, (with P. Gifford) The Transfer of Power in Africa, 1982, (with R. Stookey) End of the Palestine Mandate, 1986, (with H. Bull) The Special Relationship: Anglo-American Relations Since 1245, 1986, (with P. Gifford) Decolonization and African Independence, 1988, (with James Bill) Musaddiq, Iranian Nationalism and Oil, 1988, (with Roger Owen) Suez 1956: The Crisis and Its Consequences, 1989, (with Robert A. Fernea) The Iraqi Revolution of 1958, 1991, (with Robert Blake) Churchill, 1993, Adventures with Britannia, 1995, More Adventures with Britannia, 1998, Still More Adventures with Britannia, 2003, Yet More Adventures with Britannia, 2005, Burnt Orange Britannia, 2006, Penultimate Adventures with Britannia, 2007, Ultimate Adventures With Britannia, 2009, Resurgent Adventures with Britannia, 2011, Ends of British Imperialism, 2006, (with Michael Howard) The Oxford History of the Twentieth Century, 1998, (with Judith Brown) The Oxford History of the British Empire: The Twentieth Century, 1999, (with Ronald Hyam) The Conservative Government and the End of Empire, 1957-64, 2000, Festschrift: The Statecraft of British Imperialism: Essays in Honor of William Roger Louis, 1999, (with Roger Owen) A Revolutionary Year: The Middle East in 1958, 2002, (with Avi Shlaim) The 1967 Arab-Israeli War, 2012. Trustee Brit. Empire Mus., Bristol, England, 2005—13. Decorated comdr. Brit. Empire; Woodrow Wilson fellow Harvard U., 1959-60, Marshall scholar Oxford U., 1960-62, NEH fellow, Am. Inst. Indian Studies fellow, Guggenheim fellow, vis. fellow All Souls Coll., U. Oxford, Balliol Coll., Oxford U., overseas fellow Churchill Coll., U. Cambridge, Eng.; guest scholar Brookings Instn.; disting. visitor hist. dept. Peking U., Beijing, 1999, Prof. of Yr., U. Tex., 2009, Kluge Chair Libr. Congress, 2010. Fellow Royal Hist. Soc., Woodrow Wilson Internat. Ctr. (sr. scholar 2012-); mem. Am. Acad. Arts and Scis., Am. Hist. Assn. (pres. 2001), Coun. on Fgn. Rels. (N.Y.C.), Tex. Inst. Letters, Reform Club (London), Century (N.Y.C.), Met. Club (Washington). Democrat. Office: University Texas Humanities Rsch Ctr Dept History Austin TX 78712

LOUPASSI, G. MANOLI, state legislator; b. Richmond, June 8, 1967; m. Rebecca Hyde Stewart; children: Doxey, Stewart, Manoli. BA, Washington & Lee U., 1989; JD, U. Richmond, 1992. Atty. Va. Law and Govt. Affairs, P.C.; asst. commonwealth atty. City of Richmond, County of Hanover; mem. Dist. 68 Va. House of Delegates, 2009—. Mem. Richmond City Council, 2000—06; vice mayor Richmond, 2005—06. Bd. mem. Elk Hill Farm, Richmond Holocaust Museum, Scottish Rite Childhood Language Ctr. Republican. Mailing: 6002A West Broad St Richmond VA 23230 Office: General Assembly Bldg PO Box 406 Richmond VA 23218 Office Phone: 804-440-6222, 804-440-6223. Fax: 804-698-6768. E-mail: DelMLoupassi@house.virginia.gov.

LOURIE, JOEL B., state legislator; b. Columbia, SC, Sept. 24, 1962; m. Rebecca Lourie; 2 children. BA, U. SC, 1984. Stockbroker E. F. Hutton and Co., Prudential Bache, 1985—87; founder, pres. Ice Cream Products, Inc., 1990—99; pres. Lourie's Dept. Store, Inc., 1999—; mem. Dist. 78 SC House of Reps., 1999—2005; mem. Dist. 22 SC State Senate, 2005—; founder & pres. ICP, Inc., 1990—. Mem.: Leadership Columbia & U. SC Alumni Assn., Midland Boys & Girls Club (corp. bd. mem.). Democrat. Jewish. Mailing: PO Box 6212 Columbia SC 29260 Office: 601 Gressette Bldg Columbia SC 29201 Home Phone: 803-787-5802; Office Phone: 803-779-0939, 803-212-6116. Business E-Mail: jbl@legis.lpitr.state.sc.us. E-mail: JBL@scsenate.org.

LOVE, DENNIS M., consumer products company executive; b. Aug. 15, 1955; BS, Princeton U, Princeton, NJ; MBA, Harvard U, Chestnut Hill, Mass. CEO, pres. Printpack, Inc., Atlanta, 1987—. Bd. dirs. Caraustar Inc., AGL Resources Inc., 1999—. Office: Printpack Inc 2800 Overlook Pky NE Atlanta GA 30339 Office Phone: 404-460-7000. Business E-Mail: dlove@printpack.com.

LOVE, FREDRICK J., state legislator; m. ShaRhonda Love. BA in Polit. Sci. & Legal Studies, Govs. Sch., 1999; MPA, U. Ark., Little Rock, 2004; PhD in Pub. Health, U. Ark. Coord., Child and Adult Svcs. Ark. Foodbank Network; chmn. Legislative Task Force for Poverty and Econ. Devel. Individual Security Com., Little Rock Racial and Cultural Diversity Commn. Edn. Com.; mem. Prince Hall Masons; chmn. Pulaski County Youth Svcs. Adv. Bd. Fundraising Com.; mem. St. Paul United Methodist Ch., Youth Mentor, Pulaski County Democratic Com., 1998; mem. Dist. 35 Ark. House of Representatives, 2011—. Democrat. Office: PO Box 4963 Little Rock AR 72214 Office Phone: 501-612-3939. Personal E-mail: fred@fredricklove2010.com.

LOVE, JAY, state legislator; m. Cheri Love; children: Rachel, Addison, Rebecca, Caroline. BBA, Auburn U., Montgomery, Ala. Owner Subway Sandwich Shops, 1992—2006; mem. Dist. 74 Ala. House of Reps., 2002—. Mem. First Bapt. Ch., Montgomery. Named one of Top 40 Under 40, Montgomery C. of C., 2001. Republican. Baptist. Office: PO Box 3221 Montgomery AL 36109 also: 1020 Monticell Ct Ste 205 Montgomery AL 36117 also: Ala House of Reps Ala State House 11 S Union St Rm 527-A Montgomery AL 36130 Office Phone: 334-356-7827, 334-224-0822, 334-242-7716. Business E-Mail: jlove32376@aol.com.

LOVE, JIM, councilman; b. Washington, 1963; m. Robin Lynn Carter; children: Jimmy, Jason, Jonathan. Grad., Auburn U.; MA in Bus. Adminstrn., Webster U., 1982. Jet flight instr. NAS Chase Field; comdr. NAS Cecil Field, NAS Jacksonville; owner State Farm Ins. Agy.; councilman Dist. 14 Jacksonville City Coun., 2011—. Capt. USNR. Office: Jacksonville City Council 117 W Duval St Jacksonville FL 32202 Office Phone: 904-630-1390. E-mail: JimLove@coj.net.

LOVE, SCOTT ANTHONY, lawyer; b. Houston, Dec. 30, 1969; BA in Hist. with honors, U. Houston, 1993, JD, 1997. Bar: Tex. 1997, Pa. 2008, US Dist. Ct. (so. dist. Tex.) 1998, US Dist. Ct. (ea., we., and no. dists. Tex.) 1999. Law clk. Abraham, Watkins, Nichols & Friend, Houston, 1995-97; assoc. Duckett, Bouligny & Collins, L.L.P., El Campo, Tex., 1997-99, Wojciechowski & Assocs., P.C., Houston, 1999—2001, Fleming & Assocs., L.L.P., Houston, 2001—09; ptnr. Clark, Burnett, Love & Lee GP. Lectr. in field. Named Top Prof. on Fast Track, H Tex. Mag., 2006—09, Top Lawyer for People, Tex. Mag., 2008—09; named a Rising Star, Tex. Super Lawyers mag., 2006, 2008—09. Mem. Assn. Trial Lawyers Am., Tex. Young Lawyers Assn., Tex. Trial Lawyers Assn., Houston Young Lawyers Assn., Houston Bar Assn., Houston Trial Lawyers Assn. Office: Clark Burnett Love & Lee GP 440 Louisiand St Ste 1600 Houston TX 77002 Office Phone: 713-621-7944, 713-757-1400. Office Fax: 713-621-9638. Business E-Mail: slove@triallawfirm.com.

LOVE, SHIRLEY DEAN, state legislator; b. Oak Hill, W.Va., May 15, 1933; s. Earl Clinton and Winona Hall Love; m. Eunice Audrey Painter, 1952; children: James Chappell IV, Crystal Lynn, Brian Stephen. Former committeeman & chmn. Fayette County Dem. Exec. Com., W.Va.; former mem. & chmn. Housing Devel. Fund, W.Va.; former mem. Cable Advisor Bd., W.Va.; former vice chmn. Transpn. Com.; dir. Fayette County Civil Defense, 1969—73; del. Dem. Nat. Conv., 1972, 1976, 1980, 1984; former chmn. Fayette County Dem. Com.; sec. Fayette County Dem. Conv., 1972, 1976, 1980, 1984; mem. State Dem. Exec. Com., W.Va.; vice chmn. Nat. Resources Com.; news dir. Woay TV, 1966—68, sales mgr., 1968—73, sports dir., 1974—76, broadcasting, sales, mktg.; state senator Dist. 11 W.Va., 1994—. Recipient Skeet Champion award, Fayette County Sportsman Assn., 1966—67, 1969—72; named Outstanding Young Man of Yr., Jr. C of C., 1970. Mem.: Nat. Rifle Assn., RAM, Oak Hill Merchants Assn., Civitan, Fayette Plateau Gun-Sportsman Club, Mason, Beni Kedem Temple Shrine. Democrat. Protestant. Address: PO Box 1173 Oak Hill WV 25901 Office Phone: 304-469-3361.

LOVE, TOM, retail executive; Attended, U. Okla., St. John's U., Saint Cloud, MN. Chmn., CEO Love's Travel Stops & Country Stores, Inc. Mem. the National Petroleum Council, St. Gregory's U.; exec. bd. Society of Independent Gasoline Marketers of America; former chmn. Oklahoma Transportation Commission, pres., nat. oil jobbers coun., 1968-69, bd. dirs., nat. oil jobbers coun., 1970-71, v.p., nat. oil jobbers coun., 1971. With USMC. Recipient Corporation of the Year, Sales and Marketing Executives International., 1991, Hall of Honor, Oklahoma Commerce and Industry, 1998, Distinguished Marketer award, Sigma, 2002. Office: Love's Travel Stops & Country Stores 10601 N Pennsylvania Ave Oklahoma City OK 73120 Office Phone: 405-751-9000. Office Fax: 405-749-9110. Business E-Mail: toml@loves.com.

LOVEL, GENE ARTIE, economics professor; b. Carnegie, Okla., Mar. 19, 1946; s. Artie Boyd and Martha Marie Lovel. BA in Economics, Okla. State U., Stillwater, 1968; MA in Economics, U. Chgo., 1974. Lectr. economics So. Ill. U., Edwardsville, 1974—78; asst. prof. economics Benedictine Coll., Atchison, Kans., 1978—81; assoc. dir. Kans. Energy Office, Topeka, 1981—82; prof. economics Pikeville Coll., Ky., 1982—; eligibility chair Mid-South Conf., Pikeville, 2000—. Office: Pikeville Coll 147 Sycamore St Pikeville KY 41501 Office Fax: 606-218-5225.

LOVELAND, EUGENE FRANKLIN, retired gas industry executive; b. Anderson, Ind., Sept. 11, 1920; s. Irving Eugene and Clare (Macfarlane) L.; m. Joan King, Aug. 4, 1944; children: Jeffrey, David C. and Peter F. (twins), Mark, Laurie E. BA, Wesleyan U., Middletown, Conn. With Shell Oil Co., 1946-80, v.p. central mktg. region, 1968-71, v.p. oil products Houston, 1972-80; pres. Transworld Oil USA, Inc. (formerly T.W. Oil Inc.), Houston, 1981—; chmn., chief exec. officer T.W. Oil Inc., 1983-89, ret., 1989. Bd. dirs. Transworld Oil Ltd., Bermuda. Bd. dirs. Lyric Theatre, Houston, Am. Dance Cos.; chmn. Houston Ballet Found., Combined Arts Corp., Campaign, Houston, Greater Houston Skating Coun., vice chmn. Better Bus. Bur., Houston; hon. counsul gen. Republic of Malta in Tex.; dir. Cultural Arts Coun. Houston, 1989-93; chmn. Greater Houston Ice Skating Coun., 1989—; mem. exec. com. Houston Internat. Festival, 1992; chmn. devel. commn. Fay Sch., 1992. With USNR, 1943-45. Decorated D.F.C., Air medal (2); recipient Disting. Alumnus award Wesleyan U., 1993, Nat. Order of Merit, Country of Malta, 2003. Mem. Mil. and Hospitaller Order St. Lazarus Jerusalem.

LOVELAND, L. JOSEPH, JR., lawyer; b. Richmond, Va., July 27, 1951; BA with highest honors, U. NC, 1973; JD cum laude, Harvard U., 1976. Bar: Ga. 1976, Tex. 1994. Ptnr. King & Spalding. Contbr. articles to profl. jours. Named Best Lawyers Am., one of Ga's. Top 100 Super Lawyers, Am's. Leading Bus. Lawyers, by Chambers USA, 2006. Mem. ABA, State Bar Ga., State Bar Tex., Atlanta Bar Assn., Houston Bar Assn., Phi Beta Kappa, fellow Am. Coll. Trial Lawyers. Office: King & Spalding 1180 Peachtree St NE Atlanta GA 30309 Office Phone: 404-572-4783. Office Fax: 404-572-5100. Business E-Mail: jloveland@kslaw.com.

LOVELESS, PATTY (PATTY RAMEY), country music singer; b. Pikeville, Ky., Jan. 4, 1957; m. Terry Lovelace (div.); m. Emory Gordy, Jr., Feb. 1989. Recording artist MCA, 1985-93, Sony Music, 1993—. Albums: Patty Loveless, 1987, If My Heart Had Windows, 1988, Honky Tonk Angel, 1988 (gold), On Down the Line, 1990, Up Against My Heart, 1991, Only What I Feel, 1993, Greatest Hits, 1993, When Fallen Angels Fly, 1994, The Trouble With the Truth, Sings

Songs of Love, 1996, Long Stretch of Lonesome, 1997, Classics, 1999, Strong Heart, 2000, 20th Century masters: The Millenium Collection, 2000, Mountain Soul, 2001, Bluegrass & White Snow, 2002, On Your Way Home, 2003, Dreamin' My Dreams, 2005, Sleepless Nights, 2008, 16 Biggest Hits, 2007, Mountain Soul II, 2009 (Best Bluegrass Album, Grammy Awards, 2011); # 1 hit singles Timber, I'm Falling in Love, Chains. Named Favorite New Country Artist by Am. Music Awards, 1989, Album of Yr. Country Music Awards, 1995, Top Female Vocalist Acad. Country Music, 1996, Female Vocalist of Yr. Country Music awards, 1996, Vocal Event of Yr., Country Music awards, 1993, 98, 99; recipient TNN Music City News Country Award, Female Artist, 1990, Country Music Awards' Album of the Yr.; co-recipient Grammy award for Best Country Collaboration with Vocals, 1998; inductee Grand Ole Opry, 1988. Office: c/o Saguaro Road Records 8280 Willow Oak Corporate Dr, Suite 84 Fairfax VA 22031 Office Phone: 703-663-4604.

LOVELL, LARRY D. (BUDDY LOVELL), state legislator; Mem. Dist. 56 Ark. House of Reps., 2007—. Served Ark. Nat. Guard. Democrat. Methodist. Address: 201 W Riverside Dr Marked Tree AR 72365 Office Phone: 870-358-4104. Office Fax: 870-358-2835. Business E-Mail: lovellb@arkleg.state.ar.us.

LOVERDE, PAUL STEPHEN, bishop; b. Framingham, Mass., Sept. 3, 1940; Degree, St. Thomas Sem., Bloomfield, Conn., 1960; BA summa cum laude, St. Bernard Sem., Rochester, NY; STL, Gregorian U., Rome, Italy, 1966; JCL, Cath. U., Washington, DC, 1982. Ordained priest Diocese of Norwich, Conn., 1965, dir. campus ministry, 1973-79, chmn. bd. vicars for priests, 1975-79; asst. pastor St. Sebastian Ch., Middletown, Conn., 1966-69; chaplain Wesleyan U., Middletown, Conn., 1966-68, Conn. Coll., New London, Conn., 1970-79; chaplain, religion instr., chmn. religious studies dept. St. Bernard Girls' Sch., New London, Conn., 1969-72; religion instr., chmn. religious studies dept. St. Bernard HS, Montville, Conn., 1972-73; assoc. defender of the Bond Diocesan Tribunal of Norwich, 1970-81; campus min. Eastern Conn. State Coll., Willimantic, Conn., 1973-76; mem. bd. of dirs. Conn. Catholic Conf., 1973-78; vicar for priests Wyndham Co., 1974-75; vice-officialis Diocesan Tribunal, 1981-88; priests' rep. Diocesan Pastoral Coun., 1984-88, vice-chmn., 1984-87; mem. Coll. of Consulters, 1985-90; reg. rep. US Cath. Bishop's Nat. Adv. Coun., 1986-90; ordained bishop, 1988; aux. bishop Diocese of Hartford, 1988—94; bishop Diocese of Ogdensburg, NY, 1994—99, Diocese of Arlington, Arlington, Va., 1999—. Mem. continuing edn. for clergy com. Diocese of Norwich, 1967-71, rep. task force on race & ministry with minorities, 1970; mem. Clergy Assn. of Middletown, 1966-69; bd. dirs. Conn. Project Equality, 1968-73; vocation promoter Middletown area, 1968-69; mem. Senate of Priests of Norwich Diocese, 1971-75 (v.p. 1971-72, pres. 1972-75); v.p. Church Vocations Task Group, 1973-79; temp. admin. Holy Trinity Ch., Pomfret, Conn., 1981, St. Catherine of Siena Ch., Preston, Conn., 1982, 85-86. Contributor of articles to The Priest, Pastoral Life, and Today's Parish. 1st Hon. Brother, Altruism House, New London, CT, 1970. Roman Catholic. Office: Diocese of Arlington Chancery Office 200 N Glebe Rd Ste 914 Arlington VA 22203-3728 Office Phone: 703-841-2511. Office Fax: 703-524-5028.

LOVETT, MELENDY EWING, electronics executive; b. 1958; BS in Mgmt. & Mgmt. Info. Systems, Tex. A&M U., College Station, 1979; MS in Acctg., U. Tex. Sch. Mgmt., Dallas, 1982. CPA. Bus. analyst Republic Bank of Dallas, 1979—81; acctg. supervisor & land adminstrn. analyst ARCO Oil & Gas, 1981—85; sr. mgr. Coopers & Lybrand, 1985—93; mgr. info. technology consulting Texas Instruments, Inc., 1993—95, mgr. HR ops. & info. technology, 1995—98, v.p., mgr. total compensation & HR services, 1998—2004, sr. v.p., pres. ednl. teaching Dallas, 2004—. Bd. dirs. Trinity Industries, Inc., 2012—. Named to Hall of Fame, Women in Tech. Internat., 2005. Office: Texas Instruments Inc PO Box 660199 Dallas TX 75266-0199 Office Phone: 972-995-2011. Office Fax: 972-995-4360.

LOVINGER, ANDREW JOSEPH, polymer scientist; b. Athens, Greece, May 15, 1948; s. Joseph and Berta (Gross) L.; m. Eleanor Saul, Feb. 29, 1976; children: Michael Joseph, Daniel Abraham. BSChemE and Applied Chemistry, Columbia U., 1970, MSChemE and Applied Chemistry, 1971, ScDChemE and Applied Chemistry, 1977. Mem. tech. staff Bell Labs. Lucent Tech. (formerly AT&T Bell Labs.), Murray Hill, NJ, 1977—85, disting. mem. tech. staff, 1985—2001, head polymer chemistry rsch. dept., 1985-94; dir. polymers program divsn. materials rsch. NSF, Arlington, Va., 1995—. Adj. assoc. prof. dept. chem. engring. Columbia U., N.Y.C., 1980-83; lectr. in field. Assoc. editor Macromolecules, 1988—; contbr. over 160 articles to profl. publs., chpts. to books. Recipient Frazer Price award U. Mass., 1993. Fellow AAAS, Am. Phys. Soc. (Dillon medal 1985, Polymer Physics prize 2003); mem. NAE, Am. Chem. Soc. (Applied Polymer Sci. award 2010), Materials Rsch. Soc. Achievements include research on structures and properties of polymeric materials, morphology and phase transitions, ferroelectric polymers, high-performance polymers, silicon-based polymers, organic and polymeric thin-film transistors.

LOVOI, JOHN V., investment company executive; BSChemE, Tex. A&M U., 1984; MBA, U. Tex., 1988. Sr. fin. exec. Baker Hughes; energy investment banker Credit Suisse First Boston; oilfield svcs. & equipment rsch. analyst Morgan Stanley, 1995—2000, global oil & gas investment banking positions, 2000—02; mng. ptnr. JVL Advisors LLC, 2002; founder JVL Ptnrs., prin.; mng. ptnr. Belridge Energy Advisors. Bd. dirs. Evergreen Energy, Inc., 2003—08, Baseline Oil & Gas Corp., 2008—09, Cal Dive Internat., Inc., Helix Energy Solutions, Inc., 2003—, KFX Inc., 2003—, Dril-Quip, Inc., 2005—. Office: Helix Energy Solutions Group Inc Bd Directors 400 N Sam Houston Pky ESte 400 Houston TX 77060 Office Phone: 281-618-0400. Office Fax: 281-618-0501.

LOWDER, ROBERT E., bank executive; BS, Auburn Univ., 1966. Chmn., CEO Colonial Banc Group, Inc., Montgomery, Ala., 1990—. Trustee Auburn Univ. Office: Colonial Banc Group Inc PO Box 1108 Montgomery AL 36101-1108

LOWE, GREGG A., electronics executive; b. Cleve. BSEE, Rose Hulman Inst. Tech., Terre Haute, Ind., 1984; grad. from Stanford Exec. Program, Stanford U., Calif. Field sales Texas Instruments, Inc., 1984—89, dir. European automotive sales teams (led teams in Germany, Italy, Eng. and Spain), 1989—94, mgr. microcontroller orgn., 1994—98, mgr. ASIC orgn., 1998—2001, mgr. high speed comm. and controls, High Performance Analog Unit Dallas, 2001, sr. v.p., mgr. High Performance Analog bus. unit, 2001—06, sr. v.p., mgr. total analog bus. unit, 2006—. Office: Tex Instruments Inc PO Box 660199 Dallas TX 75266-0199 Office Phone: 972-995-2011. Office Fax: 972-995-4360.

LOWE, JOHN B., JR., retail executive; m. Mary Lowe; 6 children. Degree in Engring. magna cum laude, Rice U. CEO TDIndustries, 1980—2005, chmn., 1980—, Zale Corp., 2007—. Mem. bd. dirs. Drew Industries Inc., Zale Corp., 2004—. Pres. bd. trustees, Dallas Ind. Sch. Dist. Office: Zale Corp 901 W Walnut Hill Ln Irving TX 75038-1003 Office Phone: 972-580-4000. Office Fax: 972-580-5547.

LOWE, JOHN E., oil industry executive, accountant; b. Oskaloosa, Iowa, Jan. 22, 1959; BS, Pitts. State U., Kans., 1981. Dir. fin. Phillips Petroleum Co., Houston, 1993—97, supply chain mgr. for refining, mktg. & transport., 1997—99, mgr., strategic growth projects, 1999, v.p. planning & strategic growth, 1999—2000, sr. v.p. planning & strategic trans., 2000—01, sr. v.p. planning & devel., 2001—02; exec. v.p. planning & strategic trans. ConocoPhillips Co., 2002—06, exec. v.p. comml., 2006—07, exec. v.p. exploration & prodn., 2007—08, asst. to CEO, 2008—09. Bd. dirs. ChervonPhillips Chem. Co., Duke Energy Field Svcs., Houston Mus. Natural Sci., DCP Midstream Ptnrs. Office: ConocoPhillips Co 600 N Dairy Ashford Rd PO Box 2197 Houston TX 77079 Office Phone: 281-293-1000. Office Fax: 281-293-1440.

LOWE, JOHN STANLEY, law educator; b. Marion, Ohio, May 11, 1941; s. John Floyd and Florence (Andrews) L.; m. Jacquelyn Taft, Jan. 15, 1968; children: Sarah Staley, John Taft. BA, Denison U., 1963; LLB, Harvard U., 1966. Bar: Ohio 1966, Okla. 1980, U.S. Supreme Ct. 1972, Tex. 1989. Adminstrv. officer Govt. of Malawi, Limbe, 1966-69; assoc. Emens, Hurd, Kegler & Ritter, Columbus, Ohio, 1970-75; asst. and assoc. prof. law U. Toledo, 1975—78; prof. law U. Tulsa, 1978-87, Southern Meth. U., 1987—. Vis. prof. U. Tex., 1983, U. Sydney, 2009-; disting. vis. prof. natural resources law U. Denver, 1987; disting. vis. prof. U. N.Mex., 1996; vis. lectr. U. Dundee, Scotland, 2001-; sr. fellow U. Melbourne, Australia, 2006-, internat. legal advisor, US Dept. Commerce, 2006-; fulbright scholar U. Alberta 2008. Author: Oil and Gas Law in a Nutshell, 1983, 6th edit., 2014, Hemingway on Oil and Gas Law, 3rd edit., 2004; editor: Cases and Materials on Oil and Gas Law, 1986, 6th edit., 2012; editor Internat. Petroleum Transactions, 1993, 3rd edit., 2010, others. Pres., trustee Rocky Mtn. Mineral Law Found., 2003-04. Mem. ABA (chair natural resources, energy and environ. law sect. 1992-93), Ctr. Am. and Internat. Law (former vice chair, mem. exec. com. adv. bd. Energy Law Inst. 1998-04), Am. Arbitration Assn., CPR Inst. Dispute Resolution, Internat. Chamber of Commerce Arbitration Panel. Episcopalian. Avocation: sailing. Office: So Meth U 3315 Daniel Ave Dallas TX 75275-0116 Home: 12014 Lueders Ln Dallas TX 75230-2373 Office Phone: 214-768-2595. Business E-Mail: jlowe@smu.edu.

LOWE, KENNETH W., broadcast executive; BA in Radio, TV & Motion Pictures, U. NC, Chapel Hill. With Southern Broadcasting, 1969, Harte-Hanks Broadcasting, 1970—80; founder Home & Garden TV (HGTV), 1994; gen. mgr., Radio Properties E.W. Scripps Co., 1980—88, v.p., programming, promotion, mktg., 1988—94, pres., CEO, 2000—08, COO, bd. dirs., 2000; CEO Scripps Networks Interactive, Inc., 1994—2000, chmn., pres., CEO Knoxville, Tenn., 2008—. Bd. dir. Greater Cincinnati Chamber of Commerce; chmn. Cincinnati USA Partnership; bd. dirs. Cin. Ctr. City Devel. Corp.; trustee Fine Arts Fund; bd. of advisors U.N.C. Dept. of Communication; bd. dirs. Nat. Cable & Telecom. Assn., Paley Ctr. for Media, U. Cin. Coll. Medicine, Cin. Bus. Com.; active Comml. Club; vice chmn. Cin. Mus. Ctr. Mailing: Scripps Network Interactive Inc 9721 Sherrill Blvd Knoxville TN 37932 Office Phone: 865-694-2700. Office Fax: 865-985-7778. Business E-Mail: klowe@scrippsnetworks.com.

LOWE, LYLE JUSTIN, lawyer; b. Oklahoma City, Feb. 22, 1973; s. Lyle Don and Cheri Lyn Lowe. BA, BS in Criminal Justice, Oklahoma City U., 1995, JD, 2000. Atty. Dellvomo & Crow, Oklahoma City; owner, atty. Justin Lowe P.C., Oklahoma City. Mem.: ABA, ATLA, Okla. Bar Assn., Okla. Trail Lawyers Assn. Office: 3133 NW 63 Oklahoma City OK 73116

LOWE, MIRA, media consultant, educator, former editor-in-chief; b. 1963; m. Herbert Lowe. BA in TV and Radio, Bklyn. Coll., 1984; MS in Journalism, Columbia U., NYC, 1988. Copy editor The Register, Shrewsbury, NJ, 1988—89; news editor, asst. news editor, asst. editor Newsday, Melville, NY, 1989—2005, assoc. editor recruitment, 2005—07, LI life editor, 2006—07; asst. mng. editor Jet mag. Johnson Pub. Co., Chgo., 2007—08, asst. mng. editor Ebony, 2007—09, mng. editor Jet, 2008—09, editor-in-chief, 2009—11; prin. Aim High Media, 2009—. Lectr. Northwestern U. Medill Sch. Journalism, 2011—, Loyola U. Sch. Comm., Chgo., 2011—. Mem.: Assn. Women Journalists Chgo. Home: 4809 Trolley Ct SE Smyrna GA 30080-7095

LOWE, PHILLIP D., state legislator; b. Thomasville, Ga., Dec. 16, 1958; s. Don and Naoma L. Lowe; m. Sonya Cox; children: Kristen, Hunter, Drake. BS, Med. U. SC, 1982. Former bd. mem. Dept. Natural Resources, SC; founding bd. mem. Florence Nat. Bank, 1998; mem. State Waterfowl Focus Group, 2001—04; mem. Dist. 60 SC House of Reps., 2007—; mem. Agr. Com., Natural Resources & Environ. Affairs Com.; adj. bd. Florence-Darlington Tech. Coll. Recipient Sportsmanship award, Wildlife Action, 1988, Wildlife Disting. Svc. award, 1995. Mem.: Flyway Found (founding pres. 2005—), Farm Bur., Florence Bd. Realtors, Nat. Rifle Assn., SC Sporting Protection League, SC Wildlife Assn. (sponsor), SC Physical Therapy Assn., America Physical Therapy Assn., Santee Cooper Wildlife & Fisheries Coalition, Wild Turkey Fedn., Ducks Unlimited, Blue Water Fishing Club. Republican. Address: 507 W Cheves St Florence SC 29501 Home: 3215 Lakeshore Dr Florence SC 29501 Office: 327A Blatt Building Columbia SC 29201 Home Phone: 843-622-0011; Office Phone: 843-662-1234, 803-734-2975. Business E-Mail: LoweP@schouse.org.

LOWE, RICHARD C., lawyer; grad., JD, U. Tenn. Ptnr. King & Ballow, Nashville; outside labor counsel, dir. Young Broadcasting Inc., NYC, dir. Mem.: Nat. Inst. Trial Advocacy, Tenn. Bar Assn., Ohio Bar Assn. Office: Young Broadcasting Inc 441 Murfreesboro Pike Nashville TN 37210-2842 Office Phone: 615-726-5420. E-mail: rlowe@kingballow.com.

LOWE, ROBERT CHARLES, lawyer; b. New Orleans, July 3, 1949; s. Carl Randall and Antonia (Morgan) L.; m. Theresa Louise Acree, Feb. 4, 1978; 1 child, Nicholas Strafford. BA, U. New Orleans, 1971; JD, La. State U., 1975. Bar: La. 1975, U.S. Dist. Ct. (ea. dist.) La. 1975, U.S. Ct. Appeals (5th cir.) 1980, U.S. Dist. Ct. (we. dist.) La. 1978, U.S. Supreme Ct. 1982. Assoc. Sessions, Fishman, Rosenson, Boisfontaine, and Nathan, New Orleans, 1975—80, ptnr., 1980—87, Lowe, Stein, Hoffman, Allweiss and Hauver, New Orleans, 1987—. Author: Louisiana Divorce, West Pub. Co., 1984, Thomson Reuters updated annualy; mem. La. Law Rev., 1974-75; contbr. articles to profl. jours. Mem. reserve USMC, 1971—77. Named New Orleans Family Law Lawyer of Yr., Best Lawyers in Am., 2014; named one of Listed in Top Fifty La. SuperLawyers, 2007, 2014, Top Fifty La. Super Lawyers, 2008; named to Listed in Best Lawyers in America, 1983—, La. State U. Law Ctr. Hall of Fame, 1987. Mem. ABA, La. State Bar Assn. (chmn. family law sect. 1984-85), New Orleans Bar Assn. (chmn. family law sect. 1991-92), La. State Law Inst., La. Assn. Justice (chmn. family law sect. 2006-07), Order of Coif, Phi Kappa Phi. Republican. Home: 9625 Garden Oak Ln New Orleans LA 70123-2005 Office: 701 Poydras St Ste 3600 New Orleans LA 70139-7735 Office Phone: 504-581-2450. Personal E-mail: b.lowe@lowestein.com.

LOWENBERG, MICHAEL J., lawyer; BBA in Engring. Route to Bus., U. Tex., Austin, 1995; JD, South Tex. Coll. Law, Houston, 1997. Bar: Tex., US Dist. Ct. (so. and no. dists.) Tex., US Ct. Appeals (5th cir.), US Supreme Ct. Assoc. O'Quinn Law Firm, Houston, 1998—. Mem.: ATLA, Am. Inns Ct., Tex. Trial Lawyers Assn., Houston Trial Lawyers Assn., Houston Young Lawyers Assn., Houston Bar Assn. Office: O'Quinn Law Firm 440 Louisiana St Ste 2300 Houston TX 77002 Office Phone: 713-223-1000. Office Fax: 713-222-6903.

LOWENSTEIN, RALPH LYNN, university dean emeritus; b. Danville, Va., Mar. 8, 1930; s. Henry and Rachel (Berman) L.; m. Bronia Grace Levenson, Feb. 6, 1955; children: Joan, Henry. BA, Columbia U., 1951, MS in Journalism, 1952; PhD in Journalism, U. Mo., 1967. Reporter Danville Register, Va., 1952, El Paso Times, 1954-57; asst. prof. journalism U. Tex. at El Paso, 1956-62, assoc. prof., 1962-65; publs. editor Freedom of Info. Ctr., Columbia, Mo., 1965-67; vis. prof., head journalistic studies Tel Aviv U., 1967-68; assoc. prof. Sch. Journalism, U. Mo., Columbia, 1968-70, prof., 1970-76, chmn. news-editorial dept., 1975-76; press critic CBS Morning News, 1975-76; dean Coll. Journalism and Communications, U. Fla., Gainesville, 1976-94. Bd. dirs. Aliyah Bet & Machal Archives U. Fla. Librs. Author: Bring My Sons from Far, 1966, Pragmatic Fund-Raising, 1997; author: (with John C. Merrill) Media, Messages and Men, 2d edit., 1979, Macromedia, 1990; editor (with Paul Fisher): Race and the News Media, 1967. Dir. Mus. Am. and Can. Vols., Israel's War of Independence, 2004-. Served with Israeli Army, 1948; AUS, 1952-54. Recipient Disting. Svc. award, Columbia Journalism Alumni, 1957, 30th Anniversary award, State of Israel, 1978, Freedom Forum Journalism Adminstr. of Yr. award, 1994; named to Fla. Freedom of Info. Hall of Fame, 1997. Mem.: Soc. Profl. Journalists (Rsch. in Journalism award 1971), Assn. Edn. in Journalism and Mass Comm. (pres. 1990—91). Home: 1705 NW 22nd Dr Gainesville FL 32605-3953 Office Phone: 352-392-6525. Business E-Mail: rlowenstein@jou.ufl.edu.

LOWER, ROBERT CASSEL, lawyer, educator; b. Oak Park, Ill., Jan. 8, 1947; s. Paul Elton and Doris Thatcher (Heaton) L.; m. Jean Louise Lower, Aug. 24, 1968 (dec. Aug. 1985); children: David Elton, Andrew Bennett, James Philip Thatcher; m. Cheryl Bray, July 26, 1986. AB magna cum laude with highest honors, Harvard U., 1969, JD, 1972. Bar: Ga. 1972. Assoc. Alston & Bird, Atlanta, 1972-78; ptnr., e-commerce, healthcare, privacy area Alston & Bird LLP, Atlanta, 1978—. Adj. prof. Emory U., 1978-85, 92. Contbr. articles to profl. jours. Co-founder, pres. Ga. Lawyers for the Arts, Inc., 1975—79; chmn. Fulton County (Ga.) Arts Coun., 1979—87; trustee Woodruff Arts Ctr., 1988—95, Piedmont Coll., Ga. Found. Ind. Colls. Mem. Ga. Bar Assn., Atlanta Bar Assn., Midtown Bus. Assn. (bd. dirs. 1988-90), Author's Ct. Harvard Club (Ga.), Phi Beta Kappa. Presbyterian. Avocations: music, bonsai, backpacking. Office: Alston & Bird LLP 1 Atlantic Ctr 1201 W Peachtree St NW Atlanta GA 30309-3400 Office Phone: 404-881-7455. Business E-Mail: bob.lower@alston.com.

LOWERY, CHARLES DOUGLAS, historian, dean, educator; b. Greenville, Ala., May 8, 1937; s. Reuben F. and Frances Louise (Jordan) L.; m. Sara Bradford, June 24, 1961; children: Thomas Bradford, Douglas Trenton, Charles Daniel. BA, Huntingdon Coll., 1959; MA, Fla. State U., 1961; PhD, U. Va., 1966. Asst. prof. history Ball State U., Muncie, Ind., 1964-66; from asst. prof. to prof. Miss. State U., Starkville, 1966—99, head dept. history, 1985—99, asst. dean Coll. Arts and Scis., 1971-74, assoc. dean, 1974-81, dir. Inst. for Humanities, 1981-85. Author: James Barbour: The Biography of A Jeffersonian Republican, 1984, (with others) America: The Middle Period, 1973, Encyclopedia of African-American Civil Rights: From Emancipation to the Present, 1992, The Greenwood Encyclopedia of African-American Civil Rights, 2004; contbr. articles to profl. jours. Mem. Miss. Com. for Humanities, Jackson, 1986-88; vice chmn. Miss. Humanities Coun., Jackson, 1988-89; active Habitat for Humanity. Grantee NEH, 1980, 81, 84, Miss. Humanities Coun., 1983, 84, 88. Mem. Orgn. Am. Historians, Soc. Historians of Early Am. Rep., So. Hist. Soc., Miss. Hist. Soc. (com. chmn. 1989-90). Democrat. Presbyterian. Avocations: camping, travel, fishing, historical preservation, woodworking. Home: 609 Sherwood Rd Starkville MS 39759-4009 Office: Miss State U Dept History Drawer H Mississippi State MS 39762 Personal E-mail: charsue36@excite.com.

LOWERY, LEE LEON, JR., civil engineer; b. Corpus Christi, Tex., Dec. 26, 1938; s. Lee Leon and Blanche Lowery; children: Kelli Lane, Christianne Lindsey. BSCE, Tex. A&M U., 1960, ME, 1961, PhD, 1965. Prof. dept. civil engring. Tex. A&M U., 1960; rsch. engr. Tex. A&M Rsch. Found., 1962—. Pres. Tex. Measurements, Inc., College Station, 1965—; dir. Braver Corp. Recipient Faculty Disting. Achievement Tchg. award, Tex. A&M U., 1979, Zachry Tchg. award, 1989, 1991, award of merit, Tex. A&M Honor Soc., 1991; fellow, NDEA, 1960—63. Mem. ASCE, NSPE, Tex. Soc. Profl. Engrs., Sigma Xi, Phi Kappa Phi, Tau Beta Pi. Baptist. Achievements include patents in field. Office: Tex A&M U Dept Civil Engring College Station TX 77843-3136

LOWMAN, ROBERT PAUL, photographer, small business owner, retired academic administrator; b. Lynwood, Calif., Jan. 23, 1947; s. Hubert Alden and Martha Guynn (Howard) L.; m. Kathleen Marie Drew, June 25, 1972; children: Sarah Guynn, Amy Katherine. AB, U. So. Calif., 1967; MA, Claremont U., 1969, PhD, 1973. Asst. prof. U. Wis., Milw., 1972-76; adminstrv. officer APA, Washington, 1976-81; asst. dean Kans. State U., Manhattan, 1981-86, assoc. dean grad. sch., 1986-90, assoc. vice provost, 1990-91; dir. rsch. svcs. U. NC, Chapel Hill, 1991—2002, adj. assoc. prof., psychology, 1991—2006, rsch. prof., psychology, 2006—14, assoc. vice chancellor, rsch., 1994—96, 2001—14, assoc. vice provost, rsch., 1996-2001; owner Lowman Pub. Co., 2006—. Author: All 21 California Missions, 2005 (two edits., English and Spanish), The Spanish Missions of California, 2011; editor: APA's Guide to Rsch. Support, 1981; contbr. over 30 articles to profl. jours. Pres. Chapel Hill Rotary Club, 2008—09. Recipient numerous grants. Mem. AAAS, Soc. Psychologists in Mgmt. (newsletter editor 1994-96, bd. dirs. 1996-01, pres. 2000), Nat. Coun. U. Rsch. Adminstrs. (mag. co-editor 2006-08, profl. devel. com. 2006-08, bd. dirs. 2009-10), NC Assn. Biomed. Rsch. (bd. dirs. 2010-2014), Phi Beta Kappa (exec. sec. Alpha NC chpt. 2005-2014), Phi Kappa Phi, Phi Eta Sigma, Psi Chi. Democrat. Methodist. Home and Office: Lowman Publishing Co 104 Chesley Ln Chapel Hill NC 27514-1459 Business E-Mail: lowman_r@bellsouth.net.

LOWMAN, SARA ALLISON, library director; b. Iowa City, Dec. 26, 1961; d. George Willard and Eileen Audrey Sudenga; m. Christopher Jon Lowman; children: Abigail, Kathryn. BA, Carleton Coll., 1984; MLS, U. Iowa, 1985. Sci. and engring. reference libr. Rice U., Houston, 1985—90, head reference dept., 1990—95, asst. univ. libr. pub. svcs., 1995—98, assoc. univ. libr., 1998—2000, dir. Fondren Libr., 2001—, vice provost, univ. libr., 2007—. Mem.: ALA (multiple coms. 1985—2001), Jr. League Houston, Beta Phi Mu. Presbyterian. Avocations: travel, aerobics, gardening. Office: Fondren Library MS 44 Rice University PO Box 1892 Houston TX 77251-1892 Office Phone: 713-348-2457. Business E-Mail: lowman@rice.edu.

LOWREY, BILL, oil industry executive; Grad., Baylor Law Sch., 1977. Atty. Tex. Ct. of Civil Appeals; joined Shell Oil Co. (subs. of Royal Dutch Shell plc), 1980, assoc. gen. counsel, Trading/Gas & Power, sr. v.p., gen. counsel & corp. sec., 2007—. Mem.: ABA, State Bar of Tex. Mailing: Shell Oil Co PO Box 2463 Houston TX 77252 Office Phone: 713-241-6161. Business E-Mail: BillLowrey@shell.com.

LOWRIE, JEAN ELIZABETH, librarian, educator; b. Northville, Oct. 11, 1918; d. A. Sydney and Edith (Roos) L. AB, Keuka Coll., 1940, LLD (hon.), 1973; B.L.S., Western Res. U., 1941, PhD, 1959; MA, Western Mich. U., 1956. Childrens librarian Toledo Pub. Library, 1941-44; librarian Elementary Sch., Oak Ridge, Tenn., 1944-51; exchange tchr., libr. Nottingham, England, 1948—49; campus sch. librarian Western Mich. U., Kalamazoo, 1951-56; asso. prof. Western Mich. U. (Sch. Librarianship), 1958-61, prof., 1962-83, dir. sch., 1963-81. Mem. faculty summer U. Ky., 1951, U. Calif., Berkeley, Calif., 1958; chmn. Internat. Steering Com. for Devel. Sch. Librs.; del. meetings World Conf. Orgns. Tchg. Profn., Paris, 1964, Vancouver, 1967, Dublin, 1998, Abidjan, 1969, Sydney, 1970; pres. Internat. Assn. Sch. Librarianship, 1971—77, exec. sec., 1978—96; mem. exec. bd. Internat. Fedn. Libr. Assns. and Instns.; pres. Jensen Beach Friends of Libr., 1997—2005; chair Martin County Libr. Br. Coun., 1998—2004. Author: Elementary School Libraries, rev. edit., 1970, School Libraries: International Developments, 1972, 2d edit., 1991, also articles.; adviser: filmstrip Using the Library, 1962. Pres. Friends of Hoke Libr., Jensen Beach, 1998—2005; mem. Br. Coun., Martin County Libr. Sys., 1996—2003. Recipient Dutton-Macrae award ALA, 1957, Profl. Achievement award Keuka Coll. Alumni, 1963 Mem. ALA (pres. 1973-74), Mich. Library Assn., Assn. Libr. & Info. Sci. Educators, Am. Assn. Sch. Librarians (dir., past pres., 1st President's award 1978), Fla. Libr. Assn., Altrusa Club (Kalamazoo), Delta Kappa Gamma, Beta Phi Mu. Home: 1235 NE Oceanview Cir Jensen Beach FL 34957-3715

LOWRY, ALAIRE HOWARD, psychologist; b. Phila., June 4, 1943; d. Lorn Lambier and Etha Johannaber Howard; m. Thomas Wells Lowry, Apr. 20, 1963; children: Michael Andrew, Thomas Ethan. BA in Music with high honors, So. Meth. U., Dallas, 1965; MusM in Conducting, U. Tex., Austin, 1969, Dr.Mus.Arts, 1972, PhD in Psychology, 1988. Diplomate in group psychology Am. Bd. Profl. Psychology, cert. modern group leadership Ctr. Group Studies, NYC, 2005; lic. psychologist Tex., 1990. Harpist Dallas Symphony Orch., 1962—65, 1967; tchr. 2d grade St. Mary's Cathedral Sch., Austin, 1965—66; tchr. Ursuline Acad., Dallas, 1966—67; tchg. asst. U. Tex., Austin, 1967—72; instr. Southwestern U., Georgetown, Tex., 1972—73; from asst. to assoc. prof. U. Tex., Austin, 1973—82; psychologist in pvt. practice Austin, 1988—. Asst. scoutmaster, Philmont Trek leader Boy Scouts Am., Austin, 1988—90; chair Psy-Pac, Tex., 1993—94; adminstrv. bd. chair Univ. United. Meth. Ch., Austin, 2001—03; v.p. bd. dirs. Capital Area Mental Health Ctr., Austin, 1992—94; bd. dirs. Am. Group Psychotherapy Found., 2000—01. Fellow: Am. Bd. Profl. Psychology (bd. dirs. 2008—11), Am. Group Psychotherapy Assn. (ann. meeting mktg. chair 2006); mem.: Am. Acad. Group Psychology (bd. dirs. 2008—11), Southwestern Group Psychotherapy Soc. (sec., inst. chair, tng. chair, newsletter editor, mem. chair), Austin Mental Health Ind. Practice Assn. (sec. bd. dirs. 1996—97), Tex. Psychol. Assn. (bd. trustees 1998—2001), Phi Beta Kappa. Democrat. Methodist. Avocations: travel, reading, photography, hiking, skiing, knitting. Office: 8140 N Mopac Bldg 2 Ste 200 Austin TX 78759 Office Phone: 512-346-2332. Business E-Mail: dr_lowry@mac.com.

LU, MI, computer engineer, educator; b. Chongqing, Sichuan, China, July 22, 1949; d. Chong Pu Lu and Shu Sheng Fan. MS, Rice U., Houston, 1984, PhD, 1987. Registered profl. engr. From asst. prof. to assoc. prof. Tex. A&M U., Coll. Sta., 1987-98, prof., 1998—. Conf. chmn. Internat. Conf. Computer Sci. and Informatics, 2000, 02, 03. Author: (book) Arithmetic and Logic in Computer Systems; assoc. editor Jour. Computing and Info., 1995-97, Info. Sci., 1996-97, 2002-03, Computer Sci. and Engring., 2011-; contbr. articles to profl. jours. Mem. Computer Soc. of IEEE (sr.). Office: Tex A&M U Dept Elec Co Engring College Station TX 77843 Office Phone: 979-845-3749. Business E-Mail: mlu@ece.tamu.edu.

LUBBOCK, MILDRED MARCELLE (MIDGE LUBBOCK), former small business owner; b. Cleburne, Tex., Apr. 9, 1920; d. Richard Talmadge and Nell Bouregarde (Boykin) Hardin; m. Wilson Neibuhr Munz; children: Pamela Ann Sanders, Timothy Ray Munz, Phyllis Gail Glasscock; m. Charles William Lubbock, Aug. 12, 1990. Grad. high sch. and bus. sch., Houston. Asst. photographer Robinson Portraits, Houston; clk.-typist U.S. Naval Lighter-Than-Air Base, Houma, La., U.S. Naval Air Sta., Norfolk, Va.; sales distbr. Nina Ross Cosmetiques, Brenham, Tex., Midge's Health Food Store, Brenham, 1992-95. Contbr. poetry to various anthologies; judge: yr. book cover San Jacinto Dist. High Fedn. Bd. Mem. libr. bd. Fortnightly Club, Brenham, 1970—, pres. arts dept., TFWC, GFWC; pres. Brenham Fine Arts League, 1985, Joy Bible Class, FBC. Recipient Golden Poet award, 1987-90, medal of honor World of Poetry, 1990, Outstanding Acheivement in Poetry award Internat. Soc. Poetry; Vol. Woman of Yr., Fortnightly Club, 2004, 05, Judge of Yr., State Bd., 2008-. Mem. UDC (pres.), Am. Legion Aux. (pres.), Fortnight Club (reporter, 2008-) Baptist. Avocations: painting, travel, poetry, reading. Home: 1501 E Stone St Brenham TX 77833-5050

LUBER, THOMAS J(ULIAN), lawyer; b. Louisville, Feb. 16, 1949; s. John J. and Martha E. (Cotton) L.; m. Dorothy Ann Carter, Dec. 19, 1975; children: Katharine Ann, Allison Julia. BS in Acctg., U. Louisville, 1972, JD with honors, 1976; LLM in Taxation, NYU, 1977. Bar: Ky. 1976. Agt. IRS, Louisville, 1972-73; assoc. Fahey & Gray, Louisville, 1977-79; from assoc. to ptnr. Wyatt, Tarrant & Combs and predecessor firms, Louisville, 1979—, chmn. tax sect., 1983—. Lectr. U. Louisville, 1978-80; speaker in field; bd. advisors Jour. Multistate Taxation. Contbr. articles to profl. jours. Bd. dirs. Univ. Pediatrics Found., Louisville, Univ. Ob-gyn. Found., Louisville, Assumption High Sch., Louisville. With USAF, 1967-69. Mem. ABA, Ky. Bar Assn. (chmn. tax sect. 1983-84), Louisville Bar Assn., Ky. Inst. Fed. Taxation (mem. planning com. 1981—, chmn. 1984—), Jefferson Club, Big Spring Country Club. Democrat. Roman Catholic. Avocations: hiking, working out. Office: Wyatt Tarrant & Combs PNC Plz 500 W Jefferson St Ste 2800 Louisville KY 40202-2898 Business E-Mail: tluber@wyattfirm.com.

LUBIN, MICHAEL FREDERICK, physician, educator; b. Phila., Mar. 20, 1947; BA, Johns Hopkins U., 1969, MD, 1973. Resident Emory U. Affiliated Hosp., Atlanta, 1973-76; asst. prof. medicine Emory U. Sch. Medicine, Atlanta, 1976-82, assoc. prof. medicine, 1982—2001, dir. div. gen. medicine, 1989-95; dir. preoperative clinic Grady Hosp., Atlanta, 1995—; chmn. housestaff evaluation com. dept. medicine Emory U. Sch. Medicine, 1985—2001, dir. geriatrics assessment clinic, 1998—, prof. medicine, 2001—; vis. prof. U. Tokyo, 2008. Chmn. univ. adv. coun. tchg. Emory U., 2004—08. Editor: Medical Management of the Surgical Patient, 1982, 4th edit., 2006, Med. Rounds, 1988—90; mem. editl. bd. I-M: Internal Medicine, 1992—95; contbr. to Med. Knowledge Self Assessment Program X, 1994. Chmn. univ. adv. coun. on tchg. Emory U.; mem. alumni coun. Johns Hopkins U., 1995—2001; mem. Cmty. Supporters of Atlanta Symphony Orch., 1996—98, bd. dirs., 1996—97. Scholar Hartford scholar in Geriatrics, UCLA, 1984—85, Ctr. for Medicare & Medicaid Svcs. Health Policy scholar, 2003. Fellow: ACP, Phi Beta Kappa (bd. dirs. Met. Atlanta chpt. 1996—2000, v.p. 2000—05, bd. dirs. 2005—, nat. nominating com. mem. 2010—); mem.: Soc. Gen. Internal Medicine (edn. com. 2003—), Am. Geriat. Soc., Alpha Omega Alpha, Fellows of Phi Beta Kappa (bd. dirs. 2002—), Phi Lambda Upsilon. Office: Emory U Sch Medicine 49 Jesse Hill Jr Dr Atlanta GA 30303 Office Phone: 404-778-1607.

LUBLINSKI, MICHAEL, lawyer; b. Eskilstuna, Sweden, Sept. 11, 1951; came to U.S., 1956; s. Walter and Dora L. BA magna cum laude, CCNY, 1972; JD, Georgetown U., 1975. Bar: N.Y. 1976, Calif. 1980, D.C. 2001, Ct. Internat. Trade 1981, U.S. Dist. Ct. (cen. dist.) Calif. 1981, U.S. Dist. Ct. (so. dist.) N.Y. 1981, U.S. Ct. Appeals (D.C. cir.) 1982. Atty. U.S. Customs Service, Washington, 1975-79, U.S. Dept. Commerce, Washington, 1980; assoc. Mori & Ota, LA, 1980-84, Kelley Drye & Warren LLP, LA, 1984-85, ptnr., mem. intellectual property practice group, 1986—2003. Panel moderator Calif. continuing edn. of bar Competitive Bus. Practices Inst., L.A. and San Francisco, 1984. Mem. ABA, Calif. Bar Assn., Los Angeles County Bar Assn., NY State Bar Assn., DC Bar Assn., Phi Beta Kappa. Avocations: travel, movies. E-mail: mlublinski@bellnet.ca.

LUCÀ-MORETTI, MAURIZIO, research scientist, nutritionist; b. Rome, June 2, 1945; came to U.S., 1995; s. Giuseppe and Elena (Moretti) L.; m. Anna Grandi, Jan. 2, 1974; 1 child, Elena. BS, Ministry of Edn., Caracas, Venezuela, 1969; PhD in Allied Health Scis., Pacific Western U., 1990, DSc in Human Nutrition, 1990; MD (hon.), Universidad Santo Tomas, La Paz, Bolivia, 1994; MPH (hon.), Inst. Superiore di Studi Sanitari, Rome, 1995. Rschr. Inst. Italiano di Terapia Fisica e Medicina Interna, Rome, 1974-76, sr. rschr., 1976-78, dir. rsch., 1978-80, Caracas, Venezuela, 1980-88; dir. human nutrition rsch. program and AIDS rsch. program InterAm. Med. and Health Assn., Boca Raton, Fla., 1989—, pres., 1989—; gen. sec. World Acad. Medicine, 1992—; prof. emeritus Pacific Western U., New Orleans, 1992; dir. rsch. Internat. Nutrition Rsch. Ctr., 1995—. Invited prof. Univ. di Chiete, Italy, 1991, Univ. de Asuncion, Paraguay, 1992, Univ. di Roma, Rome, 1995; hon. prof. Univ. de Granada, Spain, 1994, Univ. Nacional Pedro Enrique Ureña, Santo Domingo, Dominican Rep., 1994, Inst. Superiore di Studi Sanitari, 1996, Univ. Catolica Santo Domingo, Dominican Rep., 1996, St. Thomas U., Miami, 1998. Recipient medal Univ. Asuncion, Paraguay, 1992, medal Univ. Granada, Spain, 1993; decorated Cruz de Alfonso X el Sabio, Spani, 1997. Fellow NAS (Dominican Rep.), Royal Nat. Acad. Medicine Spain, Royal Acad. Scis. Spain, Royal Acad. Medicine Salamanca, Royal Acad. Medicine Granada, Royal Acad. Medicine Valencia, Royal Acad. Medicine of Zaragoza, Nat. Acad. Medicine Bolivia, Nat. Acad. Medicine Ecuador, Nat. Acad. Medicine Paraguay, Nat. Acad. Medicine Dominican Rep., Acad. Medicine Maracaibo, Reial Acad. Medicina Catalunya. Achievements: discovery of the Master Amino Pattern (MAP); discovery of the Dietary Protein Engring. (DPE); also patents in nutritional amino acids formulations with extremely high human Net Nitrogen Utilization (NNU). Home: 3025 Saint James Dr Boca Raton FL 33434-3370 Office: Internat Nutrition Rsch Ctr 7900 Los Pinos Cir Coral Gables FL 33143 Office Phone: 305-740-7480. E-mail: inrc@msn.com.

LUCAS, AUBREY KEITH, retired university president; b. State Line, Miss., July 12, 1934; s. Keith Caldwell and Audelle Margaret (Robertson) L.; m. Ella Frances Ginn, Dec. 18, 1955; children: Margaret Frances, Keith Godbold (dec.), Martha Carol Pittman, Alan Douglas, Mark Christopher. BS, U. So. Miss., 1955, MA, 1956; PhD, Fla. State U., 1966; DHL, Miss. Coll., 1997. Instr. Hinds Jr. Coll., Raymond, Miss., 1956-57; pres. Delta State U., Cleveland, Miss., 1971-75; asst. dir. reading clinic U. So. Miss., Hattiesburg, 1955-56, dir. admissions, 1957-61, registrar, 1963-69, dean Grad. Sch., 1969-71, pres., 1975-96, pres. emeritus and prof. higher edn., 1997—; interim commr. higher edn. Miss., 2008—09. Author: The Mississippi Legislature and Mississippi Public Higher Education, 1890-1960; contbg. author: A History of Mississippi, 1973. State chmn. Am. Cancer Soc., 1978; campaign chmn. Forrest United Way, 1979, So. U. Conf., 1995-96; mem. Commn. on Nat. Devel. Postsecondary Edn., 97th Congress; pres. Miss. Econ. Coun., 1982-83; bd. dir. Africa U., 1997-, treas., 1999-2006; bd. dir. Miss. Assn. Coll., 1979-80, pres., 1979-80; bd. dir. Miss. Inst. Tech. Devel., 1984-96, Miss. Arts Commn., 1977-87,chmn., 1983-85; bd. dir.Pine Burr Area coun. Boy Scouts Am., 1990-2003; exec. bd. Commn. on Colls. So. Assn. Colls. and Schs., 1990-93; bd. visitors Air U., 1990-94, chmn., 1991-92; bd. dir. Salvation Army, chmn., 2000-02; gen. bd. Global Ministries, United Meth. Ch., 1984-92, gen. bd. higher edn. and ministry, 1992-2000, investment com., 2002—; lay leader Miss. Meth. Conf., 1980-88, 2004—08. Mem. Hattiesburg C. of C., Miss. Forestry Assn., Newcomen Soc. N.Am., Am. Assn. State Colls. and Univs. (bd. dirs. 1982-86, chmn. 1984-85), Am. Coun. Edn. (bd. dirs. 1984-86), Miss. Inst. Arts and Letters (pres. 1999-2000), Miss. Assn. Coll. (pres. 1979-80), Miss. Hist. Soc. (pres. 2011-), Hattiesburg Cmty. Found., Hattiesburg Conv. Ctr. Commn., Lauren Rogers Mus. Art (bd. trustees, chmn. 2001-04), Red Red Rose Club, Sigma Phi Epsilon, Omicron Delta Kappa, Phi Kappa Phi, Pi Gamma Mu, Pi Tau Chi, Kappa Delta Pi, Phi Delta Kappa, Kappa Pi. Home: 3200 Jamestown Rd Hattiesburg MS 39402-2333 Office: U So Miss 118 College Dr # 5164 Hattiesburg MS 39406-0001 Office Phone: 601-266-4351. Business E-Mail: aubrey.lucas@usm.edu.

LUCAS, CONRAD G., II, political organization administrator; b. Huntington, W.Va. B, D, Vanderbilt U.; M, Harvard U.; law degree, Tulane U.; cert. in internat. law, Sorbonne, Paris. Aide to Rep. Shelley Capito US House of Representatives; policy analyst New Orleans; atty.; asst. counsel W.Va. Rep. Party, 2009—10, gen. counsel, 2010—12, chmn., 2012—; pres. Lucas Holdings LLC. Adj. prof. Mountain State U. Chmn. W.Va. Young Republicans, 2011—12; Victory Dir. for W.Va. Rep. Nat. Com., 2010; del. Rep. Nat. Conv., 2012. Recipient Cmty. Svc. Award, Gov. of W.Va. Republican. Office: West Virginia Republican Party PO Box 2711 Charleston WV 25330

LUCAS, FRANK D., United States Representative from Oklahoma; b. Cheyenne, Okla., Jan. 6, 1960; m. Lynda L. Bradshaw, 1988; 3 children. BS in Agrl. Economics, Okla. State U., 1982. Mem. Okla. House of Reps., 1989-94, US Congress from 6th Okla. Dist., Washington, 1994—2003, US Congress from 3rd Okla. Dist., Washington, 2003—; chmn. US House Agrl Com., Washington, 2011—. Recipient Wheat Champion award, Nat. Assn. Wheat Growers, Friend of the Farm Bur. award, Am. Farm Bur. Fedn., Staff of Life award, Okla. Wheat Commn., Guardian of Small Bus. award, Nat. Fedn. Ind. Bus., Champion of Small Bus. award, Small Bus. Survival Com.; named a Congl. Conservation Champion, 2001, Property Rights Champion, League of Property Voters, 2002. Mem.: Okla. Cattlemen's Assn., Okla. Farmer's Union, Okla. Farm Bur. Republican. Baptist. Office: US House of Representatives 2311 Rayburn House Office Bldg Washington DC 20515 also: 720 South Husband Ste 7 Stillwater OK 74075 Office Phone: 202-225-5565, 405-624-6407. Office Fax: 405-624-6467.*

LUCAS, JAMES H., state legislator; b. Columbia, SC, Aug. 11, 1957; BA, U. SC, 1975, MPA, 1981, JD, 1987. Atty. Darlington County, SC, 1990—94; city judge City of Hartsville, 1995—96; ptnr. Lucas, Auman & Warr, 1994—; mem. Dist. 65 SC House of Reps., 1999—. Republican. Mailing: 505D Blatt Bldg Columbia SC 29201 Office: 113 Lyndale Dr Hartsville SC 29550 Home Phone: 843-383-9421; Office Phone: 803-734-2701. E-mail: jl@legis.lpitr.state.sc.us.

LUCAS, L. LOUISE, state legislator; b. Portsmouth, Va., Jan. 22, 1944; 3 children. Former mem. Hampton Rds. Planning Dist. Cmty., Portsmouth Group Housing-Condominuim Study Com.; former adminstrn. v.p. Nat Women's Polit. Caucus Va.; coun. woman Portsmouth, Va., 1984—92; vice chairwoman Pub. Safety Policy Com., 1991; chairwoman Human Devel. Policy Com., 1991; govt. mem. 4th Congressional Dist.; mem. Va. Munic League, State Pub. Rec. Advisor Coun., Cts. of Justice, Edn. & Health, Local Govt. & Rehab. & Social Svc. Com.; apprentice shipfitter Norfolk Naval Shipyard, 1967—71, shipfitter, 1971—75, eng. draftsman, Design Divsn., 1975—76, naval architect technician, 1976—79; program mgr., comdr in chief United States Atlantic Fleet, 1979—81; mgr., supr. Conversion & Repair, 1981—85; interim exec. dir. Southeastern Tidewater Opportunity Project Inc., 1985—86, exec. dir., 1986—92; bd. mem. Va. Assn. Black Elected Officials, 1984—; mem. Southern Legislature Conf., 1992—; state senator, Dist. 18 Va., 1992—; vice chairwoman Orgn. & Devel., Va. Democratic Party, 1992—; asst. prof., fed liaiso Dept. Acad. Affairs, Norfolk State U., 1994—. Recipient Jr. Cmty. Svc. award, SCLC, Va. State Unit, 1992, Serwa Achievement award, Va. Commonwealth Chpt., 1992, Woman of Achievement, Tidewater Chpt., 1992, Outstanding Svc. Legislature Performance award, NAACP, Suffolk Br., 1992, Excellence award, Finer Womanhood of Am., 1993; named Disting. Alumni Citation of Yr., Nat. Assn. Equal Opportunity Higher Edn., 1987, Woman of Yr., Black Women's Health Network, Maryview Med. Ctr., 1991, Alumnae of Yr., Student Advisor Com., Norfolk State U., Sch. Tech., 1992. Mem.: Nat. Polit. Congressional Black Women, Norfolk State U. Alumni Assn., Va. Cmty. Action Re Entry Sys., Inc. (bd. mem.), Va. Assn. Cmty. Action Agys., Nat. Coun. Christians & Jews, United Civic League Portsmouth, Cent Civic Forum, Kiwanis, NAACP (life), Crusade Va. Voters, Nat Order Women Legislator, Delta Sigma Theta Sorority, Inc (Golden Anniversary Cmty. Svc. aeard 1993, Proj Cherish award 1994), Alpha Beta Sigma (First Black Citizen of Portsmouth award 1992), Zeta Pi Beta (Woman of Yr. 1985). Democrat. African Methodist Episcopal. Mailing: PO Box 700 Portsmouth VA 23705-0700 E-mail: district18@sov.state.va.us.

LUCAS, LAUREN SUDEALL, lawyer; BA, Yale U., New Haven, 1999; JD, Harvard U., Mass., 2005. Law clk. to the Honorable Stephen Reinhardt US Ct. Appeals 9th Cir.; law clk. to the Honorable John Paul Stevens US Supreme Ct.; staff atty. Southern Ctr. Human Rights, 2007—. Adj. faculty mem. Ga. State U. Coll. Law. Recipient Stuart Eizenstat Young Lawyer award, Anti-Defamation League, 2010; named one of 10 On the Rise, ALM Daily Report, 2010, Minority 40 Under 40, The Nat. Law Jour., 2011; Soros Justice fellow, Open Soc. Inst., 2007. Office: Southern Center Human Rights 83 Poplar St NW Atlanta GA 30303 Office Phone: 404-688-1202. Office Fax: 404-688-9440.

LUCAS, MARVIN W., state legislator; Former state rep. Dist. 17, NC; former mayor Spring Lake; state rep. Dist. 42 NC, 2003—. Mem. Pub. Utilities com., Wildlife Resources com., Ethics com., Local Govt. II com., Appropriations com.; vice chmn. Alcoholic Beverage Control com., Appropriations Subcom. on Edn. com.; chmn. Edn. com. Democrat. Office: NC House of Reps 300 N Salisbury St Rm 417A Raleigh NC 27603-5925 Office Phone: 919-733-5775. E-mail: Marvin.Lucas@ncleg.net.

LUCAS, WILLIAM RAY, aerospace scientist, consultant; b. Newbern, Tenn., Mar. 1, 1922; married 1948; 3 children. BS, Memphis State U., 1943; MS, Vanderbilt U., 1950, PhD in Chem. Metallurgy, 1952; L.H.D. (hon.), Mobile Coll., 1977; D.Sc. (hon.), Southeastern Inst. Tech., 1980, U. Ala., Huntsville, 1981. Instr. chemistry Memphis State U., 1946-48; chemist guided missile devel. div. Redstone Arsenal, 1952-54, chief chem. sect., 1954-55; chief engr. material sect. Army Ballistic Missile Agy., 1955-56, chief engr. material br., 1956-60; with Marshall Space Flight Center, NASA, 1960—, chief engring. materials br., 1960-63, material div., 1963-66, dir. propulsion and vehicle engring. lab., 1966-68, dir. program devel., 1968-71, dep. dir., 1971-74, dir., 1974-86; pvt. practice aerospace cons. Hunstville, Ala., 1986—2002; ret. Served as lt. USNR, 1943-46. Recipient Exceptional Sci. Achievement medal NASA, 1964, 2 Exceptional Service medals, 1969, Disting. Service medal, 1972, Disting. Service award, 1981, 86; Presdl. rank Disting. Exec., 1980; Roger W. Jones award for outstanding exec. leadership Am. U., 1981; Space award for outstanding contbns. in field of space VFW, 1983; Disting. Alumni award Memphis State U., 1984; Aubrey D. Green award Lions Club Ala., 1986; named one of Tenn. Outstanding Scientists and Engrs., Tenn. Tech. Found., 1986; named to Ala. Engring. Hall of Fame, 1990, Von Brown Space Flight Trophy Nat. Space Club, Huntsville, 2009. Fellow Am. Soc. Metals, Am. Astronautical Soc. (Space Flight award 1982), AIAA (Oberth award 1965, Holger N. Toftoy award 1976, Elmer A. Sperry group award 1986); mem. Nat. Acad. Engring., Am. Chem. Soc., Sigma Xi, Tau Beta Pi. Achievements include research in materials engring. metallurgy, inorganic chemistry, environ. effects on materials, especially space environ. effects.

LUCCI, JOSEPH A., III, gynecologic oncologist, educator, obstetrician, gynecologist; Grad., St. Edwards U., Austin; MD, U. Tex., Houston. Diplomate Am. Bd. Ob-Gyn, Am. Bd. Ob-Gyn-gynecologic oncology, lic. Fla. Intern Christus St. Joseph Hosp., 1985, resident Houston, 1988; fellow Univ. Calif., Irvine, 1992; prof. clin. ob-gyn. dept. Univ. Miami, dir. gynecologic oncology divsn., co-leader Gynecologic Oncology Site Disease Group Sylvester Comprehensive Cancer Ctr.; hosp. affiliations include Univ. Miami Hosp., Univ. Miami Hosp. and Clinic, Univ. Tex. Med. Br. Gal; program dir. Jackson Meml. Hosp. Named Recognized Dr., HealthGrades. Mem.: ACOG, ACS, AAAS, Western Assn. of Gynecologic Oncologists, Tex. Med. Assn., Tex. Assn. of Obstetricians and Gynecologists, Soc. Gynecologic Oncologists, Am. Soc. of Clin. Oncology, Am. Assn. for Cancer Rsch. Office: Jackson Memorial Hospital Holtz Center Rm 3062 1611 NW 12th Ave Miami FL 33136 Office Phone: 305-243-2233. Office Fax: 305-243-4938.

LUCCOCK, THOMAS NELSON, auditor, director; s. Randolph Napthali and Jewel Norene (Nelson) Luccock; m. Catherine Marcella Orr, Aug. 2, 1986. At, Southwestern U., Georgetown, Tex., 1966—67; BS, U. Okla., Norman, 1970; MBA, U. Tex., Austin, 1972; grad. Exec. Mgmt. Program, Ind. U., Bloomington, 1983. CPA Tex., 1975, Okla., 1978, Mich., 2000, cert. internal auditor, 2000. Staff acct. Arthur Andersen LLP, Dallas, 1973—75; mgr. auditing Cities Svc. Co., Tulsa, 1976—83; corp. mgr. internal audit Occidental Petroleum Corp., 1983—99; dir. internal audit Mich. State U., East Lansing, 2000—. Bd. Inst. Internal Auditors, Okla., 1983—99, pres. Tulsa chpt., 1988—89, bd., Lansing, Mich., 2000—06, pres. Lansing chpt., 2003—04; bd. mem. U. Okla., Norman, 1995—, chmn. acctg. adv. bd., 2002—05. Established Catherine and Thomas Luccock Libr. Endowment U. Okla.; mem. Tulsa Opera Bd., Okla., 1989—90; bd.

mem. Bizzell Libr. U. Okla, Norman, 1999—; chmn. bd. Am. Heart Assn., Tulsa, 2001—02, revenue generation com. mem. Heartland affiliate St. Louis, 2002—06; established Jewel Luccock Piano scholarships, Randolph Luccock Petroleum Engring. scholarships, Thomas Luccock Audit Scholarships, Mich. State U., 2007, Thomas Luccock Acctg. Study Abroad Endowment U. Okla., 2010, Thomas and Catherine Luccock French Horn Endowments Mich. State, 2013. Capt. USAR, 1971—79. Recipient Paragon award, Leadership Tulsa, 2002, Established Thomas & Catherine Luccock Libr. award of Excellence, 2007, Outstanding Profl. Contbns. award, Assn. Coll. and U. Auditors, 2013. Mem.: AICPA, IIA, Phi Beta Kappa. Avocations: golf, art, travel. Home: 7216 E 65th Pl Tulsa OK 74133 Office: Mich State University Olds Hall 408 W Cir Dr Rm 309 East Lansing MI 48824 Home Phone: 918-495-1046; Office Phone: 517-355-5036.

LUCE, EDWARD ANDREW, plastic surgeon; b. Syracuse, NY, Mar. 5, 1940; s. Edward Andrew and Constance Faith (Jones) L.; m. Rebecca Sue Wall (div.); children: Darcie, Michael, Caitlin. BS, U. Dayton, 1961; MD, U. Ky., 1965. Diplomate Am. Bd. Surgery, Am. Bd. Plastic Surgery (chmn. 1990-91). Resident in surgery Barnes Hosp., St. Louis, 1965-71; resident in plastic surgery Johns Hopkins Hosp., Balt., 1971-73, asst. prof. plastic surgery, 1973-75; assoc. prof. plastic surgery U. Ky., Lexington, 1975-87, prof. plastic surgery, 1987-95, chief plastic surgery, 1975-95, VA Hosp., 1975-95; Kiehn-DesPrez prof. surgery Case Western Reserve U., Cleve., 1995—2004; chief plastic surgery U. Hosps. of Cleve., 1995—2004, VA Hosp., Cleve., 1995—2004; prof. plastic surgery U. Tenn., Memphis, 2004—; pvt. practice Plastic Surgery Group of Memphis, 2004—. Attending plastic surgeon St. Joseph Hosp., Lexington, 1975-95, Good Samaritan Hosp., Lexington, 1978-95, Humana Hosp., Lexington, 1982-95; Kiehn-DesPrez Prof. and Chief of Plastic Surgery, Case Western Reserve U. and Univ. Hosps. of Cleveland; pres. Assn. Acad. Chmn. of Plastic Surgery, 1989-90, Am. Soc. Maxillofacial Surgeons (pres. 1990-91), Southeastern Soc. Plastic and Reconstructive Surgeons (pres. 1992-93) Pres. U. Ky. Med. Alumni Assn., 1977-78; pres. John Hoopes Plastic Surgery Found., 1993. Recipient Clinician of Yr., Am. Assn. Plastic Surgeons, 1990, Prejidential citation Am. Soc. Head and Neck Surgeons, 2000, Dist. Svc. award Am. Soc. Plastic Surgeons, 2000 Mem. Plastic Surgery Ednl. Found. (pres. 1993-94), Am Coll. Surgeons, Am. Surg. Assn., So. Surg. Assn., Am. Assn. Plastic Surgeons (pres. 2000-2001), Am. Soc. Plastic and Reconstructive Surgeons (pres. 2001-2002), Soc. Head and Neck Surgeons. Avocations: clinical photography, military history of small, obscure wars, collecting old and rare medical books. Home Phone: 901-374-9184; Office Phone: 901-761-9030. Personal E-mail: edluce@yahoo.com.

LUCE, RICHARD, library director; BA in Polit. Sci., Univ. San Diego; MPA, San Diego State Univ.; MS in Libr. Info. Sci., Univ. S. Fla. Asst. dir. Boulder Pub. Libr., Colo.; network dir. Irving Libr. Network, Boulder, Colo., 1985—88; exec. dir. SE Fla. Libr. Info. Network, 1988—91; rsch. libr. dir. Los Alamos Nat. Lab., N.Mex., 1991—2006; vice provost, dir. libr. Emory U., Atlanta, 2006—12; prof., dean univ. libraries, Peggy V. Helmerich chair, assoc. v.p. rsch. U. Okla., Norman, 2012—. Mem. exec. bd. Nat. Info. Standards Orgn., 1998—2004, Coalition Networked Info., Digital Libr. Fedn.; sr. advisor Max Planck Soc. Ctr. for Info. Mgmt., 2000—06; co-founder Open Archives Initiative; mem. Nat. Acad. Com. on Assuring the Integrity of rsch. Data in an Era of e-Sci.; faculty mem. Frye Leadership Inst., coun. on Libr. and Info Resources, EDUCAUSE. Recipient Fellows' Leadership prize, Los Alamos Nat. Lab., 2005. Office: University of Oklahoma Libraries 401 W Brooks St Norman OK 73019 Office Phone: 405-325-2611. Office Fax: 405-325-7550. Business E-Mail: rluce@ou.edu.

LUCE, WILLARD RAY, historian, director; b. Blanding, Utah, Mar. 2, 1942; s. Willard Ray and Celia Geneva (Larsen) Luce; m. Mary Kay Rogers, Feb. 9, 1968; children: Mary Katurah Wheeler, David Ray, Rachel Ann Pena, Amy Rebecca Cisneros, Thomas Jay. BS, Brigham Young U., Provo, Utah, 1966, MA, 1968; PhD, U. Va., Charlottesville, 1978. Historian Nat. Register Hist. Places Nat. Pk. Svc., Washington, 1974—79; hist. preservation officer Ohio Hist. Soc., Columbus, Ohio, 1980—95; mgr. Hist. Preservation Divsn. Ga. Dept. Natural Resources, Atlanta, 1996—99, dir. Hist. Preservation Divsn., 1999—2009, Missionary Ch. Jesus Christ of LDS, 2011—12. Guide Nauvoo Restoration, Ill., 1966; adj. instr. Hist. Preservation Program Ga. State U., Atlanta, 1998—. Author: Cohens v Virginai (1821) The Supreme Court and State Rights, a Reevaluation of Influences and Impacts, 1990; co-author: National Register Bulletin #22, Guidelines for Evaluating and Nominating Properties that Have Achieved Significance within the Last Fifty Years., Orson Squire Fowler, in Master Builders, A Guide to Famous American Architects (National Trust for Historic Preservation), 1985; contbr. articles to profl. jours. Mem. Cambell Task Force Orgn. of Preservation Movement, Washington, 1995—96; mem. adv. com. Ga. Cities Found., Atlanta, 2001—09; mem. adv. coun. hist. preservation Washington, 1994—95; mem. gov.'s commn. Ga. History and Hist. Tourism, Atlanta, 2001—02; mem. Ga. Capitol Commn., Atlanta, 1999—2009. Recipient Spl. Commendation award, Nat. Pk. Svc., 1996. Mem.: Nat. Conf. State Hist. Preservation Officers (pres. 1994—95), Ga. Trust Hist. Preservation (assoc.; hon. trustee 1999—2009), Phi Eta Sigma, Phi Alpha Theta, Blue Key, Phi Kappa Phi. Mem. Lds Ch. Avocations: travel, birdwatching, photography. Home: 2902 Cheshire Dr Marietta GA 30062-4553 Personal E-mail: luce7@bellsouth.net.

LUCHT, JOHN CHARLES, management consultant, writer; b. Reedsburg, Wis., June 1, 1933; s. Carl H. and Ruth A. (Shultis) L.; m. Catherine Ann Seyler, Dec. 11, 1965 (div. 1982). BS, U. Wis., 1955, LLB, 1960. News dir. Sta. WISC-AM/FM, Madison, Wis., 1952-55; merchandising dir. The Bartell Group (radio and TV stas.), Milw., 1955-56; instr. U. Wis. Law Sch., 1959-60; TV contracts exec., account exec. J. Walter Thompson Co., NYC, 1960-64; product mgr., new products supr., dir. new product mktg. Bristol-Myers Co., NYC, 1964-69; dir. mktg. W.A. Sheaffer Pen Co., Ft. Madison, Iowa, 1969-70; gen. mgr. Tetley Tea div. Squibb Beech-Nut Inc., NYC, 1970-71; v.p. Heidrick & Struggles, NYC, 1971-77; pres. The John Lucht Consultancy, Inc., NYC, 1977—, The Viceroy Press Inc., 1987—, RiteSite.com, 1998—. Lectr. in field. Author: Rites of Passage at $100,000 to $1 Million Plus, The Insiders's Guide to Executive Job-Changing, Executive Job-Changing Workbook, Insights for the Journey—Navigating to Thrive, Enjoy and Prosper in Senior Management. Mem. Soc. Am. Bus. Editors and Writers, Internat. Assn. Corp. and Profl. Recruiters, State Bar Wis., Assn. Exec. Search Cons., Overseas Press Club, Met. Club, Can. Club, Phi Beta Kappa, Phi Eta Sigma, Phi Kappa Phi, Phi Delta Phi, Sigma Alpha Epsilon. Office: PNC Bank Plz 301 Fayetteville St Ste #3106 Raleigh NC 27601

LUCIO, EDDIE, III, state legislator; b. Brownsville, Tex., Dec. 19, 1978; s. Eddie and Herminia Cerda Lucio; m. Jamie Barrera; 1 child, Olivia Rose. BBA, U. Tex., Austin; JD, U. Tex. Sch. Law. Atty., Tex.; mem. Dist. 38 Tex. House of Representatives, 2006—. Democrat. Office: Room E2. 518 Capitol Extension PO Box 2910 Austin TX 78768 Mailing: 1906 E Tyler Ave Ste F-2 Harlingen TX 78550 Office Phone: 956-361-2795, 512-463-0606, 956-365-4458.

LUCIO, EDUARDO, JR., state legislator; b. Brownsville, Tex., Jan. 20, 1946; s. Eduardo Lucio; m. Herminia C. Lucio; children: Lynda Anne, Eduardo III. BS in Edn., U. Tex. Pan Am. Jr. HS tchr., coach, 1966—70; treas. Cameron County, Tex., 1971—78, commr., 1979—82; tchr., coach Porter HS, Tex., 1983—84; pres. Rio Shelters, Inc.; advertising exec.; mem. Dist. 39 Tex. House of Representatives, 1986—90; mem. Dist. 27 Tex. State Senate, 1991—. Recipient Govt. Advisor award, US Hispanic C. of C., 1993, John A Traeger award, Tex. Pub. Employees Assn., 1994, Friend of Family award, Tip of Texas Family Outreach, 1996, and several others; named South Tex. Tort Reformer of Yr., Tex. Civil Justice League, 1991, State Senator of Yr., Combined Law Enforcement Assns. Tex., 1993. Mem.: Jaycees, County Treas. Tex. (estate pres. 1978), Nat. Assn. County Treas. & Fin. Office (mem. bd. dir. 1977), West Brownsville Lions (former pres.). Democrat. Roman Catholic. Office: 7 N Park Plz Brownsville TX 78521 also: PO Box 12068 Capitol Station Austin TX 78711 also: 500 S Kansas Weslaco TX 78596 Office Phone: 956-548-0227, 512-463-0127, 956-968-9927.

LUCKE, JAMES T., textiles executive; Mem. legal dept. Johnson Controls, Inc., 1992—99, gen. counsel battery divsn., 1997—99; sr. v.p., sec., gen. counsel Spectrum Brands, Inc., 1999—2007; v.p., asst. sec., gen. counsel Mohawk Industries, Inc., Calhoun, Ga., 2007—. Office: Mohawk Industries, Inc PO Box 12069 160 S Industrial Blvd Calhoun GA 30701

LUCKOVICH, MICHAEL EDWARD, cartoonist; b. Seattle, Jan. 28, 1960; BS in Polit. Sci., U. Wash., 1982. Cartoonist Greenville News, Greenville, SC, 1984; editl. cartoonist New Orleans Times-Picayune, 1984—89, Atlanta Jour.-Constitution, 1989—. Cartoonist (books) Lots of Luckovich, 1996, Four More Wars, 2006, illustrator Take Them at Their Words: Startling Quotations from the G. O. P., Their Friends and a Few Others, 1994-2004, 2004. Recipient Overseas Press Club award, 1989, 1994, Nat. Headliner award, 1991, Robert F. Kennedy award, 1994, Pulitzer prize for editl. cartooning, 1995, 2006, Thomas Nast award, Overseas Press Club, 2006, Reuben award, Nat. Cartoonist Soc., 2006, Nat. Journalism award for Editl. Cartooning, Scripps Howard Found., 2008; nominee Pulitzer prize, 1986. Office: Atlanta Journal-Constitution 223 Perimeter Center Pkwy NE Atlanta GA 30346-1301

LUCY, DENNIS DURWOOD, JR., neurologist, educator; b. Little Rock, July 3, 1934; s. Dennis Durwood and Ann Louise (Besiegel) L.; m. Patricia Wilch, Nov. 26, 1958; children: Stephen H., Vincent A., Denise D., David D. BS, MD, U. Ark., 1959. Diplomate: Am. Bd. Psychiatry and Neurology. Intern U. Ark. Med. Scis., 1959-60, resident in internal medicine, 1960-62, resident in psychiatry, 1962-63; resident in neurology U. Iowa Hosp., 1963-64, 65-66; from instr., acting head dept. neurology to prof. U. Ark., 1964—74, prof., 1974—; chmn. Coun. Departmental Chmn., 1980—81; chief of staff Univ. Hosp., 1973—76; chmn. acad. senate U. Ark. for Med. Scis., 2002—03. Bd. dirs. Ark. chpt. Multiple Sclerosis Soc., 1965-78; mem. Ark. Council Devel. Disabilities, 1971-74; bd. dirs. Ark. chpt. Epilepsy Soc., 1972-76; bd. dirs. Holy Souls Cath. Sch., 1974-77, pres. bd., 1976-77. Recipient Golden Apple award U. Ark., 1968-69 Mem. Am. Acad. Neurology, Alpha Omega Alpha. Roman Catholic. Home: 17 Robinwood Dr Little Rock AR 72227-2241 Office: 4301 W Markham St Little Rock AR 72205-7101 Office Phone: 501-686-5135.

LUDACRIS, (CHRISTOPHER BRIAN BRIDGES), musician, actor; b. Champaign, Ill., Sept. 11, 1977; s. Wayne Brian Bridges and Roberta Shields; 1 child, Karma. Attended, Ga. State U., 1998—99. CEO Disturbing Tha Peace Records; DJ, radio personality Hot 97.5-FM, Atlanta. Musician: (albums) Incognegro, 1999, Back for the First Time, 2000, Word of Mouf, 2001, Chicken-N-Beer, 2003, Red Light District, 2004, Disturbing tha Peace, 2006, Release Therapy, 2006 (Grammy award for Best Rap Album, 2007), Theater of the Mind, 2008, Battle of the Sexes, 2010, Ludaversal, 2013, (with Disturbing Tha Peace) Golden Grain, 2002, Disturbing tha Peace, 2005, (songs) Money Maker, 2006 (Grammy award for Best Rap Song, 2007); actor: (films) The Wash, 2001, 2 Fast 2 Furios, 2003, Crash, 2004, Hustle and Flow, 2005, Fred Claus, 2007, RocknRolla, 2008, Max Payne, 2008, Ball Don't Lie, 2008, Gamer, 2009, Fast Five, 2011, New Year's Eve, 2011, The Fast and the Furious 6, 2013; (TV series) Chappelle's Show, 2004, Saturday Night Live, 2005; composer: (films) The Fast and the Furious, 2001, Rush Hour 2, 2001, How High, 2001. Co-founder, chmn., CEO The Ludacris Found., Atlanta, 2001. Recipient Rap Song of the Year, Billboard Awards, 2005, Outstanding Performance by a Cast in a Motion Picture, Screen Actors Guild, 2006; co-recipient Best Rap/Sung Collaboration award for Yeah, Grammy Awards, 2005, (with Mary J. Blige) Best Collaboration for Runaway Love, Black Entertainment TV (BET) Awards, 2007. Office: The Ludacris Foundation PO Box 768511 Roswell GA 30076

LUDLUM, ALIA MOSES, federal judge; b. Eagle Pass, Tex., 1962; BBA, Tex. Woman's U., 1983; JD, U. Tex., 1986. Atty. Travis County Atty.'s Office, Tex., 1986—90; asst. US atty., chief of Del Rio Office US Atty.'s Office (we. dist.) Tex., 1990—97; part-time mediator Tex., 1997—2000; part-time magistrate judge US Dist. Ct. (we. dist.) Tex., 1997—2000, magistrate judge, 2000—02, judge Del Rio, 2002—. Office: US Dist Ct 111 East Broadway Del Rio TX 78840 Office Phone: 830-703-2038. Office Fax: 830-703-2159.

LUEBKE, PAUL, state legislator; b. Chgo. m. Carol Luebke; 2 children. Assoc. prof. UNC; state rep. Dist. 23 NC, 1991—2002; state rep. Dist. 30, 2003—. Mem. Energy and Energy Efficiency com., Environ. and Natural Resources com.; vice chmn. Election Law and Campaign Fin. Reform com., Rules, Calendar and Ops. of the House com.; sr. chmn. Fin. com. Democrat. Office: NC House of Reps 300 N Salisbury St Rm 513 Raleigh NC 27603-5925 Office Phone: 919-733-7663. E-mail: Paul.Luebke@ncleg.net.

LUEPNITZ, ROY ROBERT, psychologist, consultant; b. Ft. McClellan, Ala., June 3, 1955; s. Carl A. and Helen Elizabeth (Brown) L.; m. Mary Kinloch Bush, Dec. 18, 1981; children: Mary, George, Noel. BA cum laude, Southwestern U., 1979; MS in Counseling Psychology, U. So. Miss., 1981; PhD in Counseling Psychology, Tex. A & M U., 1985. Fellow Am. Bd. Forensic Examiners; cert. health svc. provider in psychology; cert. travel agt. Internat. Airlines Travel Agt. Network; registered treatment provider of sex offenders; bd. cert. forensic examiner; lic. marital and family therapist; lic. psychologist. Intern, vol. Austin (Tex.) State Hosp., 1978-79; counselor Univ. Counseling Psychology Clinic, Hattiesburg, Miss., 1980; master level psychologist Pine Belt Mental Health Ctr., Hattiesburg, 1981, Tex. Rehab. Commn., Bryan, 1981-82; grad. tchr. Tex. A & M Univ., College Station, 1982-83; psychologist Brazos Valley MHMR Authority, Bryan, 1983-84, mental health dir., 1984-86; pvt. practice psychologist College Station, 1987—. Chmn. bd. for sex abuse Am. Bd. Forensic Psychol. Spltys; cons. Dept. Human Svcs., Bryan, 1987—, Brazos Valley MHRA, Bryan, 1987—, St. Joseph's Hosp., Bryan, The Med. Ctr., College Station, 1991—, Brazos Valley Physicians Orgn., 1997—, various chs., schs., govt. agys.; ptnr. Noel's World of Travel. Sec. Miss. APGA, 1979-81; active sex offender's assessment/treatment program. Mem. Assn. Treatment of Sexual Abuses, Am. Assn. Christian Counselors, Nat. Register Health Svc. Providers in Psychology, Tex. Psychol. Assn., Nat. Criminal Justice Assn., Tex. Asn. Treatment of Sexual Abusers (pres. 2005—). Republican. Methodist. Avocations: teaching sunday school, travel cruises, fine dining. Home: 1200 Noel Ct College Station TX 77845-8756 Office: Brazos Valley Christian Counseling 4444 Carter Creek Pkwy Ste 204 Bryan TX 77802 Home Phone: 929-693-7248; Office Phone: 979-260-6700. Personal E-mail: drroy63@yahoo.com.

LUHNOW, JEFF, professional sports team executive; b. Mexico; BS in Economics and Engring., U. Pa., Phila.; MBA, Northwestern U., Evanston, Ill. Engr. Gore Fabrics; mgmt. cons. McKinsey & Co.; gen. mgr., v.p. PetScore.com; co-founder, pres. Archetype Solutions Inc.; various positions including v.p. baseball devel., scouting dir., farm dir., dir. L.Am. ops. and v.p. amateur scouting & player devel. St. Louis Cardinals, 2003—11; gen. mgr. Houston Astros, 2011—. Office: Houston Astros 501 Crawford St Houston TX 77002

LUIGS, CHARLES RUSSELL, retired gas and oil drilling industry executive; b. Evansville, Ind., Apr. 4, 1933; s. Charles Anthony and Agnes A. (Russell) L.; m. Mary M. McClaine, Sept. 7, 1957; children: Charles Edwin, James Russell, Carol Lynn, Susan Nadine, Michael Alan. BS in Petroleum Engring., U. Tex., 1957; student, St. Edwards U., 1951-52. With U.S., Industries, various locations, 1957-76, v.p., 1969-71, exec. v.p., 1971-74, pres., 1974-76; dir. U.S. Industries, 1971-76; pres., chief exec. officer, dir. Global Marine, Inc., 1977-98, chmn. bd., 1982-99; ret., 1999. Mem. NSPE. Office: Global Santa Fe Corp 4 Greenway Plz Houston TX 77046-0400

LUING, GARY ALAN, financial management educator; b. Collins, Iowa, Apr. 24, 1937; s. Dwight Orn and Marjorie Mae (Clemons) L.; m. Sherry Lea Gates, Dec. 19, 1954; 1 child, Heather Sherry-Anne. BS cum laude, Stetson U., 1960; MA, U. Ill., 1961; Dr. Adminstrn. (hon.), Canadian Sch. Mgmt. CPA. Auditor Arthur Andersen & Co., Chgo., 1963; prof. Fla. Atlantic U., Boca Raton, 1965—, dean Sch. Bus., 1970-87. Cons. U.S. Treasury; expert witness on valuing closely held corps., 1972—; lectr., U.S., various fgn. countries; dir. Fla. Liquid Assets, Templeton Trust Co., Stewart Pvt. Found., 1999—; mem. faculty Internat. Assn. Fin. Planners. Editor Fla. C.P.A., 1974; assoc. editor Intellect, 1975-79; tax editor Quick Print, 1988—; contbr. articles to profl. jours. Chmn. Palm Beach County Transp. Com., 1972-75; treas. Ridge Audubon Soc., 1997-98. Served to 1st lt. U.S. Army, 1961-63, XVIII Airborne Corps. Cash control officer 82nd Airborne Divsn. Recipient Disting. Svc., Fla. Accountants Assn., 1991, Alumni Assn. award for Outstanding Svcs., Fla. Atlantic Univ., 1997. Hon. fellow Internat. Soc. Preventive Medicine, Canadian Sch. Mgmt.; mem. AICPA, Am. Acctg. Assn., Acctg. Rsch. Assn., Beta Gamma Sigma, Beta Alpha Psi, Phi Beta Phi (pres. 1974), Phi Kappa Phi. Baptist. Home: 2612 Lake Front Dr Lake Wales FL 33898-7206 Home Phone: 863-696-4804. Personal E-mail: luing@msn.com.

LUJAN, MANUEL, JR., think-tank executive, former United States Secretary of the Interior; b. San Idlefonso, N.Mex., May 12, 1928; s. Manuel and Lorenzita (Romero) L.; m. Jean Kay Couchman, Nov. 18, 1948; children: Terra Kay Everett, James Manuel, Barbara Frae, Robert Jeffrey. BA, Coll. Santa Fe, 1950; postgrad., St. Mary's Coll., Calif., 1946-47. Engaged in ins. bus., Santa Fe and Albuquerque, 1948; mem. US Congress from 1st N.Mex. Dist., 1969-89; sec. US Dept. Interior, Washington, 1989-93; founder, chmn. Hispanic Alliance for Progress Ins., Washington, 2004—. Recipient Medal of Honor, Condecoracion de la Order de Francisco Morazen, 1991. Mem.: St. Michael's Coll. Alumni Assn., KC, Elks. Republican. Office: Hispanic Allience For Progress 480 Liberty St Liberty Hill TX 78642

LUKACS, FRANK C., manufacturing executive; BS in Indsl. Engring., Gen. Motors Inst., MS in Mfg. Mgmt. Various mgmt. positions Case Corp., Australia; v.p., ops, Europe Dresser Inc.; sales engr., plant mgr. Gen. Motors OEM Supply side; mfg. supr., sr. indusl. engr. Gen. Motors; sr. v.p., mfg. technologies, quality Agco Corp., Duluth, Ga., 2003; sr. v.p mfg. AGCO Corp., Duluth, Ga., 2003—. Mem.: Soc. Automotive Engrs., Am. Soc. Quality. Office: Agco Corp 4205 River Green Pky Duluth GA 30096 Office Phone: 770-813-9200. Office Fax: 770-813-6118.

LUKE, JOHN ANDERSON, JR., paper, packaging and chemical company executive; b. Nov. 24, 1948; s. John Anderson Luke Sr. and Joy (Carter) Luke; m. Kathleen Allen, June 30, 1984; children: Lindsay Allen, Elizabeth Carter, John A. III. BA, Lawrence U., 1971; MBA, U. Pa., 1979. Unit sales mgr. Procter & Gamble Co., 1974—77; corp. assoc. Westvaco Corp., NYC, 1979—81, sr. fin. analyst, 1981—82, asst. treas., 1982, treas., 1983—86, v.p., treas., 1986, sr. v.p. mktg., internat. and Brazilian subsidiary, 1987—90, exec. v.p., 1990—92, pres., 1992—2002, chmn., 1996—2002; CEO Westvaco Corp. (now MeadWestvaco Corp.), Stamford, Conn., 1992—; chmn. MeadWestvaco Corp., Stamford, Conn., 2002—. Dir. FM Global, The Timken Co.; trustee Am. Enterprise Inst. for Pub. Policy Rsch.; chmn. Am. Forest Found., Nat. Assn. Mfr.; vice chmn. Sustainable Forestry Bd.; bd. dirs. Bank of N.Y., The Tinker Found., Ams. Soc., Bank of N.Y.; bd. trustees Lawrence U.; mem. President's Export Coun. Bd. govs. NCASI; dir. United Negro Coll. Fund. Officer USAF, 1971—74, S.E. Asia, Vietnam conflict. Mem.: Am. Forest and Paper Assn. (dir., exec. com.), The Commonwealth Club, The Links, Univ. Club. Office: Meadwest Vaco 501 S 5th St Richmond VA 23219-0501

LUKEHART, CHARLES MARTIN, chemistry professor; b. DuBois, Pa., Dec. 21, 1946; s. David Blair and Grace Dorothy L.; m. Marilyn Orleana McKinney, Aug. 4, 1973; children: Mark, Brian, Laura. BS in Chemistry, Pa. State U., 1968; PhD in Inorganic Chemistry, MIT, 1972. Postdoctoral assoc. Tex. A&M U., College Station, 1972-73; asst. prof. chemistry Vanderbilt U., Nashville, 1973-77, assoc. prof. chemistry, 1977-82, prof., 1982—. Author: Fundamental Transition Metal Organometallic Chemistry, 1985. Rsch. fellow Alfred P. Sloan Found., 1979-81. Mem. Am. Chem. Soc. (chmn. Nashville sect. 1979, 92), Materials Rsch. Soc. Office: Vanderbilt U Dept Chemistry VU Station B 351822 Nashville TN 37235 Office Phone: 615-322-2935. Business E-Mail: charles.m.lukehart@vanderbilt.edu.

LUKER, JAMES CHARLES, state legislator, lawyer, former mayor; b. Little Rock, Ark., Feb. 4, 1942; m to Myra; children: three. LLB, Univ. Ark. Bar: Ark. 1966. Mayor & city atty., Wynne, Ark.; mem. Dist. 90 Ark. House of Reps., 1995—2000; mem. Dist. 17 Ark. State Senate, 2003—. Democrat. Presbyterian. Mailing: PO Box 216 Wynne AR 72396 Office Phone: 501-238-8588. Office Fax: 501-238-7680. Business E-Mail: lukerj@arkleg.state.ar.us.

LUMB, ROBIN, councilman; m. Joanna Lumb. Councilman-at-large Group 5 Jacksonville City Coun., Fla., 2011—. Bd. dirs. Riverside-Avondale Prevention, 2010, chmn. Pub. Safety Com. Mem. Duval County Exec. Com., 2004—; vice chmn. Republican Party of Duval County; pres., chmn. bd. Jacksonville Jr. C. of C.; bd. govs. Jacksonville Regional C. of C.; bd. mem. Clara White Mission, Suicide

Prevention Ctr.; civic roundtable mem. Jacksonville Jaycees Cmty. Found. Republican. Office: Jacksonville City Council 117 W Duval St Jacksonville FL 32202 Office Phone: 904-630-1387. E-mail: rlumb@coj.net.

LUMPKIN, THOMAS RILEY, retired physician; b. Tuskegee, Ala., Jan. 4, 1926; s. William Clifford and Harriet Graham (Riley) L.; m. Jean D. Perry, June 10, 1955; children: Leah, Ry, Mary Lyman, Cliff BS, U. Ala., 1949; MD, Med. Coll. Ala., 1958. Diplomate Am. Bd. Family Physicians. Pvt. practice, Tuskegee, Ala., 1959—65, Enterprise, Ala., 1965—74; asst. prof. Coll. Cmty. Health Scis., Tuscaloosa, Ala., 1974—77; assoc. prof. U. Ala., Tuscaloosa, 1977—81, prof. family medicine, 1981—91, prof. emeritus, 1991—93; interim dean Coll. Cmty. Health Scis. Capstone Med. Ctr., Tuscaloosa, 1979—80. Councilman City of Tuskegee, 1962-64; active Leadership Ala. Class III, 1992-93; bd. dirs. free med. care for under and non-insured Good Samaritan Clinic, 1999; chmn. bd. trustees Tuscaloosa Dist. Meth. Bd, 2003-07. With USAAC, 1946, inf., sgt. 1st class AUS, 1951-52 Recipient Martha Myers Role Model award, U. Ala. Med. Alumni Assoc., 2011. Mem.: Ala. Acad. Family Physicians (pres. 1968-69), Med. Assn. State of Ala. (pres. 1990-91), Rotary Internat. (pres. Enterprise Club 1968-69, pres. Tuscaloosa 1993-94, dist. gov. 1997-98, vice chmn. world cmty. svc., 2004-06, One of 23 Worldwide Polio Plus award 2003, Disting. Svc. award 2004-05), U. Ala. Sch. Med. Alumni Assn. (pres. 2001-03), Rotary (Dist. 6860 Outstanding Svc. award 2005, Found. Dist. Svc. award 2004-05), Pillar West Ala. Cmty. (Disting. Svc. award 2009), Kappa Alpha, Alpha Omega Alpha Methodist. Avocations: travel, hunting, reading. Home: 2 Ridgeland Tuscaloosa AL 35406-1607 Business E-Mail: snakedoc.lumpkin@gmail.com.

LUNDBERG, JON CLARK, state legislator, public relations executive, former newscaster, reporter; b. Royal Oak, Mich., June 26, 1961; m. Lisa Lundberg; 2 children. BS in Mass Communications, U. Southern Colo., 1983. Dir. Sta. KTSC-TV, Pueblo, Colo., 1982-83; account exec. Sta. KCBN/KRNO, Reno, 1983; news anchor Sta. KRDO-TV, Colorado Springs, Colo., 1984-85; news anchor, reporter Sta. KVMT-FM, Vail, Colo., 1985, Sta. KSPN-TV, Aspen, Colo., 1985, Sta. KSNW-TV, Wichita, Kans., 1985-87; news anchor, mng. editor Sta. WCYB-TV, Bristol, Tenn., 1988-94; pres., CEO The Corporate Image, Inc., Bristol, Tenn., 1994—; mem. Dist. 1 Tenn. House Reps., 2007—, fl. leader. Capt. USNR. Recipient 1st place award Colo. Broadcasters Assn., 1985, Sports Program award Kans. Assn. Broadcasters, 1987, 2nd pl. award Tenn. Assn. Broadcasters, 1989. Mem. Soc. Profl. Journalists, Pub. Rels. Soc. of Am. (award of excellence). Republican. Methodist. Mailing: 212 Skyline Dr Bristol TN 37620-4141 Office: 205 War Memorial Bldg Nashville TN 37243-0104 Office Phone: 615-741-7623. Office Fax: 615-253-0272. Business E-Mail: rep.jon.lundberg@capitol.tb.gov.

LUNDBLAD, ROGER LAUREN, biotechnology consultant; b. San Francisco, Oct. 31, 1939; s. Lauren Alfred and Doris Ruth (Peterson) L.; m. Susan Hawly Taylor, Oct. 15, 1966 (div. 1985); children: Christina Susan, Cynthia Karin. BSc, Pacific Luth. U., 1961; PhD, U. Wash., 1965. Rsch. assoc. U. Wash., Seattle, 1965-66, Rockefeller U., NYC, 1966-68; asst. prof. U. NC, Chapel Hill, 1968-71, assoc. prof., 1971-77, prof. pathology and biochemistry, 1977-91, adj. prof., 1991—; dir. sci. tech. devel. Baxter-Hyland/Immuno, Duarte, Calif., 1991-99; biotech. cons., 2000—. Vis. scientist Hyland divsn. Baxter Healthcare, Glendale, Calif., 1988-89. Author: Applications of Solution Protein Chemistry to Biotechnology, 2009, Chemical Reagents for Protein Modification, 1984, 2d edit., 1990, 3d edit., 2004, 4th edit., 2014, The Evolution of Protein Chemistry to Proteomics, 2005, Compendium for Biochemistry and Molecular Biology, 2007, Applications of Solutions Protein Chemistry to Biotechnology, 2009, Approaches to the Conformational Analysis of Biopharmaceuticals, 2010, Development and Application of Biomarkers, 2010, Clinical Modification & Biological Polymers, 2011, Biotechnology of Plasma Protein, 2012; editor: Chemistry and Biology of Thrombin, 1977, Chemistry and Biology of Heparin, 1980, Techniques in Protein Modification, 1994; editor-in-chief: Biotechnology and Applied Biochemistry, 1996-2003, Internet Jour. Genomics and Proteonics, 2005-10; contbr. articles to profl. jours. Mem. Am. Soc. Biochem. Molecular Biology. Office: PO Box 16695 Chapel Hill NC 27516-6695 Personal E-mail: lundbladr@bellsouth.net. Business E-Mail: roger@lundbladbiotech.com.

LUNDEBERG, PHILIP KARL BORAAS, curator, historian; b. Mpls., June 14, 1923; s. Olav Knutson and Vivian Juliet (Boraas) L.; m. Eleanore Lillian Berntson, July 18, 1953; 1 son, Karl Fredrik. BA summa cum laude, Duke U., 1944, MA, 1947; PhD, Harvard U., 1954. Asst. to historian U.S. Naval Ops. in World War II, Navy Dept., 1950-53; asst. prof. history St. Olaf Coll., 1953-55, U.S. Naval Acad., 1955-59; assoc. curator naval history Nat. Mus. History and Tech., Smithsonian Instn., 1959-61, curator of naval history, 1961-84, curator emeritus, 1984—. V.p. Am. Mil. Inst., 1968-71, pres., 1971-73; chmn. Internat. Congress Maritime Mus., 1972-75; v.p. US Commn. on Mil. History, 1975-79, pres., 1980-83; sec. Internat. Com. Mus. Security, 1975-79; pres. Coun. Am. Maritime Museums, 1976-78. Author: The Continental Gunboat Philadelphia, 1966, 2d edit., 1995, Samuel Colt's Submarine Battery, 1974, American Anti-submarine Operations in the Atlantic, 1943-1945, 1997; co-author: Sea Power: A Naval History, 1960, 81; contbg. author: Guide to the Sources of U.S. Military History, 1975, 93, Seafaring and Society, 1987, To Die Gallantly, 1994, The Battle of the Atlantic, 1939-1945, 1994; editor: Bibliographie de L'Histoire des Grandes Routes Maritimes: États-Unis d'Amèrique, 1970; exhibits: Armed Forces of U.S., 1961-2004, By Sea and by Land, 1981, The Continental Gondola, Phila., 1963-. With USNR, 1943-83, 89, comdr. USNR ret., 1992. Decorated Bronze Star, Purple Heart; recipient Bronze medal Internat. Commn. Mil. History, 1975; Austin fellow Harvard U., 1949. Fellow Am. Mil. Inst. (Moncado prize 1964); mem. Coun. Am. Maritime Mus. (hon.), N.Am. Soc. for Oceanic History (K. Jack Bauer award 1998), Naval Hist. Found. (life), Internat. Congress Maritime Mus. (life). Home: 1107 Croton Dr Alexandria VA 22308-2009 Office Phone: 202-633-3924.

LUNDEEN, WILLIAM BRUCE, radiologist; b. Minn., 1928; s. Harry William and Alice Mary (Gessner) L.; 1 child, Letitia Marshall. BS, U. Richmond, 1951; MD, Med. Coll. Va., 1955. Diplomate Am. Bd. Radiology. Intern U. Minn. Hosps., 1955-56, resident, fellow, 1957-61; resident Med. Coll. VA Hosps., 1957-58; fellow radiation oncology U. Minn., 1960—61; assoc. clin. prof. radiation oncology Med. Coll. Va., 1961—; dir. radiation oncology Va. Hosp. Ctr., Arlington, 1975—. Gov.'s ad hoc com. self-referral med. practice Va. State Legis., Richmond, 1991-93; bd. health sys. H.S.A. No. Va., 1980-84. Staff sgt. USAAF, 1946—48, air weather svc. Fellow AMA, Am. Coll. Radiology; mem. Am. Soc. Therapeutic Radiology & Oncology, Med. Soc. Va., Arlington Med. Soc. (bd. dirs. 1979-83), Air Weather Assn., Annapolis Yacht Club, Alpha Omega Alpha. Republican. Episcopalian. Home: PO Box 971 Falls Church VA 22040-0971 Personal E-mail: blragtime@aol.com.

LUNDERGAN GRIMES, ALISON, state official; b. Maysville, Ky., Nov. 23, 1978; d. Jerry Lundergan; m. Andrew Grimes. BA in Polit. Sci., Rhodes Coll., Memphis, 2001; JD, American U. Washington Coll. Law, Washington. Legislative & public policy fellow Nat. Kidney Found., Washington; assoc. Stoll Keenon Ogden PLLC, Lexington, 2004—11; sec. of state State of Ky., Frankfort, 2011—. Precinct officer 75th Legis. Dist., Ky.; mem. rules com. Democratic Nat. Com., 2008. Vol. Salvation Army, Cardinal Hill Rehab. Hosp.; bd. dirs. God's Pantry Food Bank. Mem.: Fayette County Bar Assn. Women's Lawyers' Assn. (pres. 2009—11, Outstanding Young Lawyer award 2010). Democrat. Roman Catholic. Office: Office of the Secretary of State The Capitol Bldg 700 Capital Ave Ste 152 Frankfort KY 40601 Office Phone: 502-564-3490. Office Fax: 502-564-5687.*

LUNDQUIST, CHARLES ARTHUR, academic administrator; b. Webster, SD, Mar. 26, 1928; s. Arthur Reynald and Olive Esther (Parks) L.; m. Patricia Jean Richardson, Nov. 28, 1951; children: Clara Lee, Dawn Elizabeth, Frances Johanna, Eric Arthur, Gary Lars. BS, S.D. State U., 1949, DSc, 1979; PhD, U. Kans., 1953. Asst. prof. engrng. rsch. Pa. State U., 1953-54; sect. chief U.S. Army Ballistic Missile Agy., Huntsville, Ala., 1956-60; br. chief NASA-Marshall Space Flight Ctr., Huntsville, 1960-62; dir. Space Scis. Lab., 1973-81; asst. dir. sci. Smithsonian Astrophys. Obs., Cambridge, Mass., 1962-73; assoc. Harvard Coll. Obs., 1962-73; dir. rsch. U. Ala., Huntsville, 1982-90, assoc. v.p. for rsch., 1990-96, dir. consortium for materials devel. in space, 1985-98, dir. interactive projects office, 1999—. Editor: (with G. Veis) Smithsonian Institution Standard Earth, 1966, The Physics and Astronomy of Space Science, 1966, Skylab's Astronomy and Space Sciences, 1979. With US Army, 1954—56. Recipient Exceptional Sci. Achievement medal NASA, 1971, Hermann Oberth award AIAA, 1978. Mem. AAAS, Am. Geophys. Union, Am. Astron. Soc., Am. Phys. Soc., Nat. Speleological Soc. Home: 214 Jones Valley Dr SW Huntsville AL 35802-1724 Office: U Ala Research Inst Rm E-37 Huntsville AL 35899-0001 Office Phone: 256-824-2684. Business E-Mail: lundquc@uah.edu. E-mail: lundquist5@comcast.net.

LUNDY, VICTOR ALFRED, architect, educator; b. NYC, Feb. 1, 1923; s. Alfred Henry and Rachel Lundy; m. Shirley Corwin, 1947 (div. 1959); children: Christopher Mark, Jennifer Alison; m. Anstis Manton Burwell, Sept. 19, 1960; 1 child, Nicholas Burwell. BArch, Harvard U., 1947, MArch, 1948. Registered architect, Tex., N.Y., Calif. Pvt. practice architecture, Sarasota, Fla., 1951-59, NYC, 1960-75; prin. Victor A. Lundy & Assocs., Inc., Houston, 1976-84; design. prin., v.p. HKS Inc., Dallas, 1984-90. Vis. prof. Grad. Sch. Design, Harvard U., Sch. Architecture, Yale U., Columbia U., U. Calif., Berkeley, Calif. Poly. State U. San Luis Obispo, U. Houston, U. Rome, others; U.S. specialist-architect in U.S.I.A. exhibit, USSR, 1965. Responsible for design St. Paul's Luth. Ch., Sarasota, 1959, new sanctuary, 1970, 1st Unitarian Ch. of Fairfield County, Westport, Conn., 1961, 1st Unitarian Congl. Soc., Hartford, Conn., 1964, Ch. of Resurrection, East Harlem Protestant Parish, N.Y.C., 1966, exhbn. bldg. and exhibit for AEC in S.Am. (Buenos Aires, Rio de Janeiro, Bogota, Santiago), 1967 (Silver medal for exhbn. Archtl. League N.Y. 1965), recreation shelters for Nat. Mus. History and tech., Smithsonian Instn., Washington, 1967, U.S. States Tax Ct. bldg. and pla., Washington, 1976, U.S. Embassy, Colombo, Sri Lanka, for Office of Fgn. Bldgs., Dept. State, 1983 (U.S. Presdl. Design Awards Program 1988, Fed. Design Achievement award), Austin Centre-Omni Hotel, Austin, Tex., 1984, One Congress Pla., Austin, Tex., 1984, Walnut Glen Tower, Dallas, 1985, Mack Ctr. II, Tampa, Fla., 1990, Greyhound Corp. Ctr., Phoenix, 1991, GTE Telephone Ops. World Hdqrs., Irving, Tex., 1991, Tex. A&M Found Hdqs., 1999, others; archtl. work represented in Berlin Internat. Archtl. Exposition, 1957, Sao Paulo Internat. Biennial Exposition, 1957, 5th Congress Union Internat. Des Architectes, Moscow, 1958, Expo '70 Exhbn., Osaka, Japan, 1970, travelling exhbn. of architecture in S.Am. Sgt. inf. U.S. Army, 1943-46, ETO. Decorated Purple Heart; recipient Gold medal award Buenos Aires Sesquicentennial Internat. Exhbn., 1960, Gold medal award Buenos Aires Sesquicentennial Internt.Exhbn., 1960; Silver medal Archtl. League N.Y., 1965; Charles Hayden Meml. Scholastic scholar, 1939-43, Edward H. Kendall scholar Harvard U., 1947-48, Rotch travelling scholar Boston Soc. Architects, 1948-50; travelling fellow Harvard U., 1948-50; Dept. State grantee, 1965. Fellow AIA. Avocations: painting, sculpture. Home: 701 Mulberry Ln Bellaire TX 77401-3805

LUNTZ, FRANK I., political consultant, strategist, pollster; b. Feb. 23, 1962; BA with honors in History & Polit. Sci., U. Pa., 1984; D Politics, Oxford U., 1987. Pres. Frank I. Luntz & Associates, Washington, Luntz Weber Rsch. & Strategic Services, Inc., Washington; founder, chmn. emeritus Luntz, Maslansky Strategic Rsch., Alexandria, Va. Adj. asst. prof. U. Pa., 1989-1996; tchr. Grad. Sch. Polit. Mgmt. George Washington U. Author: Candidates, Consultants and Campaigns: The Style and Substance of American Electioneering, 1988, Words that Work: It's Not What You Say, It's What People Hear, 2006, What Americans Really Want...Really: The Truth About Our Hopes, Dreams and Fears, 2007, Win: The Key Principles to Take Your Business from Ordinary to Extraordinary, 2011; contbg. author: Media Technology and the Vote: A Source Book, 1988; guest on Nightline, Crossfire, Inside Politics, McNeil Lehrer, The Today Show, Hardball, others; cons. to The West Wing. Fellow Harvard U. Inst. Politics, 1993, Thouron fellow, U. Pa.; named one of The 50 Rising Stars, Campaigns and Elections, Four Top Rsch. Minds, Bus. Week, 1992, 25 Most Influential Republicans, Newsmax Mag., 2008, The 50 Highest-Earning Polit. Figures, Newsweek, 2010; recipient Crystal Ball award, Washington Post, 1992. Republican. Achievements include development of Instant Response focus group technique. Office: Luntz Global LLC 1800 Diagonal Rd Ste 600 Alexandria VA 22314 Office Phone: 571-299-2050.*

LUO, JIAN, engineering educator, researcher; s. Guangwu Luo and Qiaoling Wang; m. Qiong Jiang, Feb. 14, 2002; children: Annie W. children: Kevin J. BEng in Materials Sci. and Engring. with honors, Tsinghua U., Beijing, 1994; BEng in Electronics and Computer Tech., Tsinghua U., Beijing, China, 1994; MS in Materials Sci. and Engring., MIT, Cambridge, Mass., 1999; PhD in Ceramics, MIT, Cambridge, 2001. Mem. tech. staff Lucent Technologies, Inc. Bell Lab. & OFS Fitel/Furukawa Electric Co., Norcross, Ga., 2001—03; summer faculty rschr. Oak Ridge Nat. Lab., Tenn., 2005; asst. prof. Clemson U., SC, 2003—09, assoc. prof., 2009—12; prof. UC San Diego, Calif., 2013—. Recipient CAREER award, Nat. Sci. Found., 2005, Ralph E. Powe Jr. Faculty Enhancement award, Oak Ridge Associated Universities, 2005, Faculty Excellence award, Clemson U. Bd. Trustees, 2006, 2007, Young Investigator award, Air Force Office Scientific Rsch., 2007. Mem.: Minerals, Metals and Materials Soc., Am. Ceramic Soc., Materials Rsch. Soc., Sigma Xi. Office: UCSD MC 0448 La Jolla CA 92093-0448

LUONGO, ROBERTO, professional hockey player; b. Montreal, Quebec, Canada, Apr. 4, 1979; s. Antonio and Pasqualina Luongo; m. Gina Cerbone; children: Gabriella, Gianni Antonio. Goaltender NY Islanders, 1999—2000, Florida Panthers, 2000—06, 2014—, Vancouver Canucks, 2006—14, capt., 2008—10. Mem. Team Canada, World Championships, 2003, 2004, Team Canada, World Cup of Hockey, 2004, Team Canada, Olympic Games, Torino, Italy, 2006, Vancouver, 2010, Sochi, Russia, 2014. Recipient Mark Messier Leadership Award, 2007, Scotiabank/NHL Fan Fav Award, 2009; co-recipient William M. Jennings Trophy, NHL, 2011; named to NHL All-Star Game, 2004, 2007, 2008, 2009, Second All-Star Team, NHL, 2007. Achievements include being a member of gold medal winning Canadian World Championships Team, 2003, 2004; being a member of World Cup Champion Team Canada, 2004; setting NHL record for saves in a single season (2,303), 2004; being a member of gold medal winning Canadian Hockey Team, Vancouver Olympics, 2010, Sochi Olympics, 2014. Office: c/o Florida Panthers 1 Panther Pkwy Sunrise FL 33323*

LUPSKI, JAMES R., medical geneticist, educator; b. Hicksville, NY, Feb. 22, 1957; BA, NYU, 1979, PhD, 1984; MD, NYU Sch. Medicine, 1985. Diplomate Am. Bd. Pediat., Am. Bd. Med. Genetics, cert. in molecular genetics and clin. molecular genetics. Intern med. genetics Tex. Children's Hosp./Baylor Coll. Medicine, Houston, 1986—87, resident pediat., 1987—89, fellow med. genetics, 1989—91; attending physician Tex. Children's Hosp., 1989—; prof. dept. molecular and human genetics Baylor Coll. Medicine, 1995—, Cullen endowed chair molecular genetics. Attending physician Ben Taub Gen. Hosp., Houston, 1989—. Contbr. articles to profl. jours. Fellow: AAAS; mem.: AMA, Harris County Hosp. Soc., Tex. Med. Assn., Am. Fedn. Med. Rsch., Am. Acad. Pediat., Am. Soc. Microbiology, Am. Soc. Human Genetics (Curt Stern award 2002), Genetics Soc. America, Soc. Pediatric Rsch., Inst. Medicine, Am. Soc. Clin. Investigation, Am. Neurol. Inst. Office: Baylor Coll Medicine Dept Molecular & Human Genetics One Baylor Plz MS BCM225 Houston TX 77030 Office Phone: 713-798-6530. Office Fax: 713-798-5073. E-mail: jlupski@bcm.edu.

LURASCHI, WILLIAM R., utilities executive, lawyer; BS in Fin., U. Conn.; JD, Rutgers U. Assoc. Chadbourne & Parke LLP; gen. counsel AES Corp., Arlington, Va., 1994—, sec., 1996—2002, v.p., 1998—2002, sr. v.p., 2002—03, exec. v.p., 2003—. Office: The Aes Corp 4300 Wilson Blvd 11th Fl Arlington VA 22203-4168 Office Phone: 703-522-1315. Office Fax: 703-528-4510.

LUSAS, EDMUND WILLIAM, food processing research executive; b. Woodbury, Conn., Nov. 25, 1931; s. Anton Frank and Damicele Nellie (Kasputis) L.; m. Jeannine Marie Muller, Feb. 2, 1957; children: Daniel, Ann, Paul. BS, U. Conn., 1954; MS, Iowa State U., 1955; PhD, U. Wis., 1958; MBA, U. Chgo., 1972. Project leader Quaker Oats Rsch. Labs., Barrington, Ill., 1958-61, mgr. canned pet foods rsch., 1961-67, mgr. sci. svcs., 1972-77; assoc. dir. Food Protein R&D Ctr., Tex. A&M U., College Station, 1977-78, dir., 1978-93, head fats, oils and extrusion programs, 1993-97; pres. Ed Lusas, Problem Sovlers, Inc., Bryan, Tex., 1997—. Author more than 175 publs.; editor Jour. Am. Oil Chem. Soc., 1980-88; patentee in field. Fund raiser YMCA, Crystal Lake, Ill., 1970-77, chmn. fin. com., 1977. Recipient F.N. Peters rsch. award Quaker Oats Co., 1968; Gen. Foods rsch. fellow, 1956, 57. Fellow. Am. Oil Chemists Soc.; Mem. Inst. Food Technologists, Am. Chem. Soc., Am. Assn. Cereal Chemists, Sigma Xi, Phi Tau Sigma. Home and Office: 3604 Old Oaks Dr Bryan TX 77802-4743 E-mail: edlusaspsi@cs.com.

LUSK, GLENNA RAE KNIGHT, librarian; b. Aug. 16, 1935; d. Otis Harvey and Lou Zelle Knight; m. Bruce 2d Edwin Lusk, Nov. 28, 1970; m. John Earle Uhler, May 26, 1956; children: Anne Knight, Camille Allana. BS, La. State U., 1956, MS, 1963. Asst. libr. Iberville Parish Libr., Plaquemine, La., 1956—57, 1962—68; tchr. Iberville Parish Pub. Schs., Plaquemine, 1957—59, Plaquemines Parish Pub. Schs., Buras, La., 1959—61; dir. Iberville Parish Libr., Plaquemine, 1969—89. Chmn. La. State Bd. Libr. Examiners, 1979—89; pres. Camille Navarre Gallery, Ltd., Zachary, La., 1989—94. Author (with John E. Uhler Jr.): Cajun Country Cookin', 1966, Rochester Clarke Bibliography of Louisiana Cookery, 1966, Royal Recipes from the Cajun Country, 1969, Iberville Parish, 1970. Mem. Iberville Parish Econ. Devel. Coun., Plaquemine, 1970—71; sec. Iberville Parish Bicentennial Commn., 1973—; mem. La. Bicentennial Commn., 1974; bd. dirs. McHugh House Mus., 1991—92. Named Outstanding Young Woman Plaquemine, La. Jr. C. of C., 1970. Mem.: Capital Area Libr. (chmn. com. 1972—74), Riverland Libr. Assn. (sec. 1973—74), La. Libr. Assn. (sect. chmn. 1967—68). Republican. Episcopalian. Home: 13291 Legacy Ct Baton Rouge LA 70816-7936

LUSKIN, BRANDON J., hand surgeon; MD, SUNY, 1990. Diplomate American Bd. Orthopaedic Surgery-hand surgery, 2003, American Bd. Orthopaedic Surgery, 2009. Resident in orthopedic surgery Long Island Jewish Med. Ctr., New Hyde Park, NY, 1991—95; fellow in hand surgery Hand Ctr. Western NY, Buffalo, 1995—96; hosp. affiliation includes Delray Med. Ctr. Office: Delray Medical Center 5352 Linton Blvd Delray Beach FL 33484 Office Phone: 561-498-4440. Office Fax: 561-495-3103.*

LUSS, DAN, chemical engineering professor; b. Tel Aviv, May 5, 1938; came to U.S., 1963, naturalized, 1973; s. Manfred and Gertrude (Weinstein) L.; m. Amalia Rubin, Sept. 4, 1966; children: Noya, Limor. BS, Technion Inst. Tech., Haifa, Israel, 1960, MSc, 1963; PhD, U. Minn., 1966. Registered profl. engr., Tex. Asst. prof. chem. engring. U. Minn., Mpls., 1966-67, U. Houston, 1967-69, assoc. prof., 1969-72, prof., 1972—, chmn. dept., 1975-95, 99-00; assoc. dir. Tex. Ctr. for Superconductivity, 1988-92. Cons. to several chem. cos. Editor: Revs. in Chem. Engring.; mem. editorial bd. Sci. and Engring, Catalysis Rev. Fellow Am. Inst. Chem. Engrs. (Allan P. Colburn award 1973, Profl. Progress award 1979, Wilhelm award 1986, Founders award 2005, chmn. awards com., former mem. editl. bd. jour., former dir.), Am. Chem. Soc. (Honor Scroll award Indsl. Engring. Chemistry div. 1967); mem. NAE, Am. Soc. Engring. Edn. (Curtis McGraw award 1977 3M-Chem. Engring. Lectureship award 1985, Amnundson Award, Int. Symp. Chem. React. Eng. 2010). Home: 115 Stablewood Ct Houston TX 77024 Office: U Houston Dept Chem Engring Houston TX 77204-4004 Office Phone: 713-743-4305. Business E-Mail: oluss@uh.edu.

LUTER, JOSEPH WILLIAMSON, III, food products executive; b. Smithfield, Va., 1940; married. BBA, Wake Forest Coll., 1962. Pres. Smithfield Packing Co., Arlington, Va., 1964—69, Bryce Mountain Resort Inc., 1969—75; Joined Smithfield Foods, Inc., 1975, pres., 1975—86, CEO, 1975—2006, chmn., 1977—, cons., 2006—. Bd. dirs. Smithfield Foods Inc., 1975—; lectr. Harvard Bus. Sch., Darden Grad. Sch. Bus., Univ. Va.; mem. exec. com. American Meat Inst. Trustee Wake Forest Univ. Office: Smithfield Foods Inc 200 Commerce St Smithfield VA 23430-1204

LUTHEY, GRAYDON DEAN, JR., lawyer, educator; b. Topeka, Sept. 18, 1955; s. Graydon Dean Sr. and S. Anne (Murphy) L.; m. Deborah Denise McCullough, May 26, 1979; children: Sarah Elizabeth, Katherine Alexandra. BA in Letters with highest honors, U. Okla., 1976, JD, 1979. Bar: Okla. 1979, U.S. Ct. Appeals (10th cir.) 1979, U.S. Dist. Ct. (no., we. and ea. dists.) Okla. 1980, U.S. Supreme Ct. 1982. Assoc. Jones, Givens, Gotcher, Bogan & Hilborne, Tulsa, 1979-84, ptnr., 1984-92, also bd. dirs.; ptnr. Hall, Estill, Hardwick, Gable, Golden & Nelson, Tulsa, 1992—, also bd. dirs. Adj. assoc. prof. U. Tulsa, 1985-87, adj. prof., 1987—; vis. fellow in theology Keble Coll., Oxford U., Eng., 1976; presiding judge Okla. Temporary Ct. Appeals, 1993-94; mem. Okla. Supreme Ct. Rules Com., 1992-94. Bd. dirs. Tulsa Ballet, 1987-2000; chmn. Tulsa Pub. facilties Authority, 1990-93; trustee Episcopal Theol. Sem. of S.W., 1991-99, exec.

com., 1992-99; vice chmn. Univ. Hosps. Authority, 1993-94, chmn. 1994-98, sec., 1998-99; chancellor Episcopal Diocese Okla., 1986-99; mem. bd. visitors U. Okla. Coll. Arts and Scis., 1997—; mem. State of Okla. Futures Auth., 1998-2002, chmn., 1999-2002; mem. adv. bd. U. Okla. Tulsa, 2003-. Master Am. Inns of Ct. (pres. 2007); fellow Am. Bar Found. (life, chmn. Okla. chpt. 2003-06, mem. nat. fellows rsch. adv. com.); mem. ABA, Okla. Bar Assn. (chmn. continuing legal edn. com. 1989-91), Tulsa County Bar Assn. (bd. dirs. 1983-89, Disting. Svc. award 1988), Am. Law Inst., Fellow, Litigation cousel Am., Summit Club, So. Hills Country Club, Beta Theta Pi, Phi Beta Kappa, Omicron Delta Kappa. Office: Hall Estill Hardwick Gable Golden & Nelson 320 S Boston Ave Ste 400 Tulsa OK 74103-3704 Office Phone: 918-594-0437. Business E-Mail: dluthey@hallestill.com.

LUTZ, JACOB A., III, (JAKE LUTZ), lawyer; b. Radford, Va., 1956; BS in Fin. with distinction, Va. Polytechnic Inst. State U., 1978; JD, Coll. William and Mary, 1981. Bar: Va. 1982, Tenn. 1987. Atty. FDIC, Washington, 1981—84, sr. regional atty. Atlanta, 1984—87; assoc. Borod & Huggins, Memphis, 1987—90; ptnr., chair fin. instns. Troutman Sanders LLP, Richmond, 1990—, chair bus. dept., 1994—99, mng. ptnr., 1999—2003. Mem. bd. visitors Va. Tech., 2000—08, vice rector, 2004—06, rector, 2006—08; chair Va. Bioinformatics Inst. Policy Bd., 2002—06, mem. bd. dirs., 2006—08; exec. com. Va. Tech. Found., 2006—08; bd. dirs., regional co-chair & chair Banking Proctic Group Terralex Law Firm Network, 2005—; bd. dirs. Banking Law Ctr., U. NC Sch. Law, 2009—; mem., bd. dir. First Presbyn. Ch., elder Richmond. Fellow: Va. Law Found.; mem.: ABA (life fellow), Va. Bar Found., State Coun. Higher Edn. Va., Tenn. Bar Assn., Va. Bar Assn. Office Phone: 804-697-1490. Office Fax: 804-698-6014. Business E-Mail: jake.lutz@troutmansanders.com.

LUTZ, THEODORE COMPTON, retired publishing executive; m. Willa Lutz; 2 children. Grad., Carleton Coll., Minn., 1967; MPA, Syracuse U., 1968. Dep. undersecretary budget and program rev. US Dept. Transp., 1973—76, adminstr. Urban Mass Transp. Adminstrn., 1979—81; gen. mgr. Washington Metropolitan Area Transit Authority, 1976—79; with The Washington Post, Washington, 1981—2006, v.p. circulation, bus. mgr., 1986—2000, v.p., bus. mgr., 2000—03, v.p. comm., 2003—06; trustee Imogene Elrod Wilden Meml. Seed Capital Fund Falls Church Housing Corp.; trustee Philip L. Graham Fund, Washington. Cmty. advisor Jr. League Northern Va.; trustee Eugene and Agnes E. Meyer Found., 1983—95, chair, 1993—95; mem. governing bd. Fairfax-Falls Church Cmty. Partnership to Prevent and End Homelessness; bd. dirs. Green Door, Washington. Named Washingtonian of Yr., Washingtonian mag., 1978. Office: Philip L Graham Fund c/o Washington Post Co 1150 Fifteenth St NW Washington DC 20071

LUXBACHER, ROBERTA, oil industry executive; married; 2 children. BS in Chem. Engring., U. Pitts. Joined Exxon Corp., 1978, with US downstream mktg. and supply divsns., mktg. mgr. natural gas, 1995—98, v.p. US natural gas, 1998—99; v.p. Americas Gas Mktg. Co. ExxonMobil Corp., 1999, dir. Europe Gas and Power Mktg., ExxonMobil Internat. Ltd., 2002—07, gen. mgr. corp. planning, 2007—. Mem. bd. visitors U. Pitts. Sch. Engring., mem. Mascaro Sustainability Initiative adv. bd.; mem. Natural Gas Coun. Mem.: Natural Gas Supply Assn. (ExxonMobil bd. mem. 2000—02, sec., treas., chmn. 2001—02). Office: Exxon Mobil Corp Hdqs 5959 Las Colinas Blvd Irving TX 75039-2298

LUXENBERG, MALCOLM NEUWAHL, ophthalmologist, educator; b. Philipsburg, Pa., July 29, 1935; s. Maurice and Henrietta (Neuwahl) L.; m. Sandra Diane Rosen, June 16, 1957; children: Steven Neuwahl, Cathy Ann. Student, Tulane U., 1953-56; MD, U. Miami, Fla., 1960. Diplomate: Am. Bd. Ophthalmology. Intern Cin. Gen. Hosp., 1960-61; resident in neurology U. Vt. Affiliated Hosps., Burlington, 1961-63; resident in ophthalmology Bascom Palmer Eye Inst., U. Miami-Jackson Meml. Hosp., Miami, Fla., 1963-66; asst. prof. ophthalmology Coll. Medicine, U. Iowa, Iowa City, 1968-70; chief ophthalmology service VA Hosp., Iowa City, 1968-70; practice medicine specializing in ophthalmology West Palm Beach, Fla., 1970-72; clin. asst. prof. ophthalmology Bascom Palmer Eye Inst., Sch. Medicine, U. Miami, 1971-72; prof., chmn. dept. ophthalmology Med. Coll. Ga., Augusta, 1972-2000, prof. emeritus, 2000—. Cons. ophthalmology VA Hosp., Augusta, 1972-2011; sr. surgeon USPHS, 1966-68; mem. Residency Review Com. Ophthalmology, 1987-92, Am. Bd. Ophthalmology, 1987-94. Mem. editl. bd.: Archives of Ophthalmology, 1986-94. Recipient Outstanding Civilian Service Medal Dept. of Army, 1986. Mem. AMA, Am. Acad. Ophthalmology (hon. award 1986), Am. Ophthalmol. Soc., Assn. Univ. Profs. in Ophthalmology (pres. 1982-83), Ga. Soc. Ophthalmology, Med. Assn. Ga., Richmond County Med. Soc. Office: Med Coll Ga Dept Ophthalmology Augusta GA 30912

LYKOS, PATRICIA R., prosecutor, former judge; m. William A. Allen. BS, Univ. Houston; JD, So. Tex. Coll. Law. Bar: Tex. 1971. Police officer, Houston; atty. pvt. practice; judge Harris County Criminal Ct., Houston, 1980—81, 180th State Criminal Dist. Ct., Houston, 1981; chief judge Harris County Criminal Ct., Houston, dir. spl. projects, dir. judicial & legal issues; dist. atty. Harris County, Houston, 2009—. Adj. prof. So. Tex. Coll. Law; instr. Nat. Judicial Coll., Tex. Ctr. for the Judiciary; mem. Tex. Gov. Coun. on Sex Offender Treatment, 2002—10. Tex. State Coord. Do the Write Thing Challenge. Fellow: Houston Bar Found., Am. Bar. Found.; mem.: Am. Inns of Ct., Garland R. Walker chapter (bd. mem.), Houston Bar Assn. (bd. mem. criminal law & procedure sect.), Nat. Dist. Atty. Assn. (dir. at large), Retired, Senior and Former Judges of Tex. (past. pres.). Republican. Greek Orthodox. Office: Harris County Dist Atty Office Ste 600 1201 Franklin St Houston TX 77002-1923 Office Phone: 713-755-5800.

LYLE, JAMES ARTHUR, real estate broker; b. Charlottesville, Va., Mar. 9, 1945; s. James Aaron and Sallie (Tuthill) Lyle; m. Yolanda Zarina Ramirez, Nov. 28, 2002; children: Cory Jackson, Mariel Karissa, Iliana Marissa, Martha Jessica, Ariana Zarina. BS in Indsl. Mgmt., Ga. Inst. Tech., Atlanta, 1968. Cert. comml. investment mem. Mktg. rep. IBM, Atlanta, 1970-71; investment cons. La Salle Ptnrs., El Paso, Tex., 1971-76; owner James Arthur Lyle and Assocs., El Paso, 1976—. Bd. dirs. Hueco Mountain Estates, Inc., pres., 1983—. Vice chmn. El Paso City Plan Commn., 1978-82, chmn., 1997-2003; vice-chmn. Internat. Airport Bd., 1982; adv. bd. El Paso Bikeway, 1986-88; active El Paso County Planning Commn., 1986-98; bd. dirs. NCCJ, 1978-82, Southwestern Gen. Hosp., 1979-83, El Paso Econ. Devel. Bd., 1980-82; bd. dir. Am. Heart Assn., 1989-93; mem. Leadership El Paso, 1981-82 1st lt. US Army, 1968-70. Bus. Assoc. of Yr. award, Am. Bus. Womens Assn., 1984, SW Challenge Series Champion, 1991-09, Ironman World Triathlon Championship, 1992, N.Mex. State Triathlon champion, 1999, Tuscon Triathlon Series Champion, 2001, Tex. Sr. Games Triathlon Champion, 2002, Border Grand Prix Series Champion, 2002, El Paso Sr. Games Hall of Fame, 2000, El Paso Athletic Hall of Fame, 2005, Guiness World Record for Most Triathlons Completed, 2007. Mem. SAR (dist. v.p., Bronze Good Citizenship medal 1996, Cert. Disting. Svc.), Nat. Assn. Realtors, Realtors Nat. Mktg. Inst., Nat. Assn. Indsl. and Office Parks, Tex. Property Exchangors (Best Exch. 1979), Tex. Assn. Realtors, Tex. Real Estate Polit. Action Com. (life), El Paso Bd. Realtors (bd. dirs. 1975-88, cert. comml. investment mem. 1975—, El Paso-West Tex. cert. comml. investment mem., pres., sec.-treas. 1975—, comml.-investment real estate coun. 1971—), El Paso Indsl. Devel. Bd., El Paso Investment Exch. Svc., Sons Confederate Vets, Sunturians (life), Half Fast Track Club (v.p. multisports), USA Triathlon (bd. dirs. 1995-2001), Team El Paso, Delta Sigma Pi, Sigma Alpha Epsilon. Republican. Episcopalian. Avocations: running, swimming, bicycling. Home: 811 Rim Rd El Paso TX 79902 Office: 720 Arizona Ave El Paso TX 79902-4402

LYLES, KENNETH W., geriatrician, educator; MD, Va. Commonwealth U., 1974. Diplomate Am. Bd. Internal Medicine, 1977, Am. Bd. Internal Medicine-endocrinology, 1979, Am. Bd. Internal Medicine-geriatric medicine, 2000. Resident internal medicine Med. Coll. Va., 1975—77; fellow in endocrinology, diabetes & metabolism Duke Univ. Med. Ctr., 1977—79; fellow in geriatric medicine Duke Univ. / VA Med. Ctr., 1979—81; hosp. affiliation includes: Durham Veterans Affairs Med. Ctr.; prof. medicine Duke Univ. Sch. of Medicine, vice chair clin. rsch. dept. of medicine, dir. departmental site based rsch. unit. Office: Duke University Medical Center 5213 S Alston Ave Durham NC 27713 Office Phone: 919-620-4555.

LYLES, LESTER LAWRENCE, corporate board member, retired military officer; b. Apr. 20, 1946; m. Mina M. Lyles; children: Rene, Phillip, Leslie, Lauren. BSME, Howard U., Washington, 1968; MS in Mech. and Nuc. Engring., N.Mex. State U., 1969; Grad., Def. Systems Mgmt. Coll., Ft. Belvoir, Va., 1980, Armed Forces Staff Coll., Norfolk, Va., 1981, Nat. War Coll., Ft. Lesley J. McNair, Washington, DC, 1985, Nat. & Internat. Security Mgmt.Course, Harvard U., Cambridge, Mass., 1991; LLD (hon.), N.Mex. State U., 2003. Commd. 2d. lt. USAF, 1968, advanced through grades to gen., 1999, ret., 2003; propulsion & structures engineer Standard Space Launch Vehicles Program, LA Air Force Station, Calif., 1969—71; propulsion engineer Headquarters Aeronautical Systems Divsn., Wright-Patterson AFB, Ohio, 1971—74; program element monitor for the short-range attack missile USAF, Washington, 1974—75, exec. officer to dep. chief of staff for rsch. & devel., 1975—78; spl. asst. & aide-de-camp to comdr. Headquarters AFSC, Andrews AFB, Md., 1978—80; chief avionics divsn. F-16 Systems Program Office Headquarters Aeronautical Systems Divsn., Wright-Patterson AFB, Ohio, 1981, dep. dir. for spl. & advanced projects, F-16 Systems Program Office, 1981—84; dir. tactical aircraft systems Headquarters AFSC, Andrews AFB, Md., 1985—87; dir. medium-launch vehicles program office space systems divsn. USAF, L.A., 1987—88, asst. dep. comdr. for launch systems Space Systems Divsn., 1988—89, asst. dep. chief of staff for requirements Andrews AFB, Md., 1989—92; vice comdr. Ogden ALC, Hill AFB, Utah, 1992—94; comdr. Space & Missile Systems Ctr., L.A., 1994—96; dir. ballistic missile def. org. USAF, 1996—99, vice chief of staff Washington, 1999—2000; comdr. Air Force Material Command (AFMC), Wright-Patterson AFB, Ohio, 2000—03; mem. President's Fgn. Intelligence Advisory Bd., 2009—13, Def. Sci. Bd., 2009—. Bd. dirs. Gen. Dynamics Corp., 2003—, MTC Technologies, Inc., 2003—, United Services Automobile Assn., 2004—, KBR, Inc., 2007—, Precision Castparts Corp., 2008—, Edn. Mgmt. Corp. (EDMC), 2013—. Bd. dirs. Battelle Meml. Inst., 2006—; vice chmn., sec. Wolftrap Found. Performing Arts, 2010—. Decorated Disting. Svc. medal, Def. Disting. Svc. medal, Def. Superior Svc. medal, Legion of Merit with oak leaf cluster, Meritorious Svc. medal with two oak leaf clusters, Air Force Commendation medal; recipient Roy Wilkins Renown Svc. award, NAACP, 1994, Sociedad de Ingenieros award, N.Mex. State U., 1999, Hiram Hadley Founder's award of excellence, 1999, Gen. Bernard A. Schriever award, Air Force Assn., 2000, Black Engr. of Yr. award for lifetime achievement, Nat. Soc. Black Engineers, 2003, Thomas D. White award, USAF Acad., 2011; named Astronautics Engr. of Yr., Nat. Space Club, 1990; named one of The 100 Most Influential African-Americans in America, Ebony Mag.; named to The Air & Space Mus. Hall of Laureates, 2002. Mem.: NAE.*

LYMAN, GARY HERBERT, epidemiologist, cancer researcher, educator; b. Buffalo, Feb. 24, 1946; s. Leonard Samuel and Beatrice Louise Lyman; children: Stephen Leonard, Christopher Henry. BA, SUNY, Buffalo, 1968, MD, 1972; MPH, Harvard U., 1982. Diplomate Am. Bd. Internal Medicine, Am. Bd. Oncology and Hematology. Resident in medicine U. NC, Chapel Hill, 1972-74; fellow in oncology Roswell Park Meml. Inst., Buffalo, 1974-77; rsch. instr. medicine SUNY Med. Sch., Buffalo, 1974-77; mem. faculty U. South Fla. Coll. Medicine, Tampa, 1977-2000, assoc. prof. medicine, 1980-86, prof. medicine, 1986-2000, dir. divsn. med. oncology, 1979-93, chief medicine H. Lee Moffitt Cancer and Rsch. Inst., 1985—93, prof. epidemiology and biostats., 1988-2000; Thomas Ordway prof. medicine divsn. hematology and oncology Albany (NY) Med. Coll., Union U., 2000—02, dir. Cancer Ctr., 2000—02; prof. biometry and stats. SUNY Sch. Pub. Health, 2000—02; prof. medicine, dept. medicine U. Rochester (NY) Sch. Medicine and Dentistry, 2002—07, Duke U., 2007—14, dir., 2002—07; dir. comparative effectness and outcomes rsch. Duke Comprehensive Cancer, Seattle, 2007—14; sr. fellow Duke Ctr. Clin. Health Policy Rsch., Seattle, 2007—14; bd. dirs. Am. Soc. Clin. Oncology, 2012—; prof. medicine, pub. health, pharmacy U. Wash., Seattle; mem. Fred Hutchinson Cancer Rsch. Ctr., 2014—; dir. Hutchinson Inst. Cancer Outcomes Rsch., 2014—. Vis. prof. med. stats. London Sch. Hygiene and Tropical Medicine, 1997—98; editor-in-chief Cancer Investigation, 2006—. Editor: Geriatric Oncology, 1998, Comprehensive Geriatric Oncology, 1997, 2d edit., 2004, Breast Cancer: Transitional Therapeutic Strategies, 2007, Cancer Supportive Care-Advances in Therapeutic Stragies, 2009, Hematopoietic Growth Factors, 2011; contbr. chpts. to books, nearly 500 articles to profl. jours. Spl. fellow Leukemia Soc. Am., 1976-77; postdoctoral fellow biostats. Harvard U., 1981-82; spl. clin. rellow Roswell Park Meml. Inst., 1975-76, Statesman award Am. Soc. Clin. Oncology, 2010. Fellow ACP, Am. Coll. Preventive Medicine, Am. Coll. Clin. Pharmacology, Royal Coll. Physicians (Edinburgh); mem. Am. Soc. Clin. Oncology (statesman, mem. bd. dirs. 2012-). Achievements include research in cancer clinical trials, biostatistics, epidemiology and clinical decision analysis. Office: Hutchinson Inst Cancer Outcomes Research PO Box 19024 M3-B232 Seattle WA 98109 Home: 120 Westlake Ave N Apt 509 Seattle WA 98109 Office Phone: 206-667-6670. Business E-Mail: glyman@fhctc.org.

LYNCH, CHRISTOPHER S., mortgage company executive, retired accounting executive; With KPMG LLP, 1979—2007, ptnr., lead & audit signing San Francisco; ind. cons., 2007—; non-exec. chmn. Freddie Mac (Federal Home Loan Mortgage Corp.), McLean, Va., 2011—. Bd. dirs. Freddie Mac (Federal Home Loan Mortgage Corp.), 2008—, American Internat. Group, Inc. (AIG), 2009—. Office: Freddie Mac Bd Directors 8200 Jones Branch Dr Mc Lean VA 22102 Office Phone: 703-903-2000. Office Fax: 703-903-4045. Business E-Mail: christopher_lynch@freddiemac.com.*

LYNCH, GARY G., lawyer, bank executive; b. Middletown, NY, July 25, 1950; BA, Syracuse U., 1972; JD, Duke U., 1975. Atty. Securities & Exchange Commn. (SEC), 1976—89, dir., enforcement divsn., 1985—89; ptnr. Davis Polk & Wardwell, NYC, 1989—2001; gen. counsel Credit Suisse First Boston, NYC, 2001, vice chmn. rsch. and legal, 2002—05; chief legal officer, mem. mgmt. com. Morgan Stanley, NYC, 2005—10, vice chmn. London, 2009—11; global head legal, compliance & regulatory rels. Bank of America, Charlotte, NC, 2011—. Named Phi Beta Kappa. Mem.: DC Bar Assn., NY State Bar Assn. Office: Bank of America Corp Ctr 100 N Tryon St Charlotte NC 28255*

LYNCH, JOHN BROWN, plastic surgeon, educator; b. Akron, Ohio, Feb. 5, 1929; s. John A. and Eloise Lynch; m. Mary Joyce Burrus, Dec. 1, 1994; children: John Brown, Margaret Frances Lynch Callihan. Student, Vanderbilt U., Nashville, Tenn., 1949; MD, U. Tenn., Memphis, 1952. Diplomate Am. Bd. Plastic Surgery. Rotating intern John Gaston Hosp., Memphis, 1953—54; resident gen. surgery U. Tex. Med. Br., Galveston, 1956—59, resident plastic surgery, 1959—62, instr., 1962, asst. prof. surgery, 1962—67, assoc. prof., 1967—72, prof., 1972—73; prof., plastic surgery, chmn. dept. plastic surgery Vanderbilt U. Med. Ctr., 1973—. Co-editor (with S.R. Lewis): Symposium on the Treatment of Burns, 1973; contbr. articles to porfl. jours. Capt. USAF, 1954—56. Fellow: ACS; mem.: AMA, Am. Surg. Assn., Southern Surg. Assn., Am. Soc. Maxillofacial Surgeons, Nashville Surg. Soc., Jr. Soc., H. William Scott, Southeastern Surg. Soc., Southeastern Soc. Plastic Surgeons, Tenn. Soc. Plastic Surgeons, Nashville Acad. Medicine, Tenn. Med. Assn., Southern Med. Assn. (pres.-elect 1983—84), Am. Cancer Soc. (pres. Galveston County, Tex., Chpt. 1968), Pan Am. Med. Assn., Internat. Burn Assn., Soc. Head and Neck Surgeons, Am. Burn Assn., Am. Cleft Palate Assn., Plastic Surgery Rsch. Coun., Am. Assn. Plastic Surgeons, Am. Soc. Plastic and Reconstructive Surgeons (pres. 1983—84), Singleton Surg. Soc. (pres. 1982—83), Sigma Xi. Home: 5810 Hillsboro Pike Nashville TN 37215-4602 Office: Vanderbilt Hospital Nashville TN 37232-0001 Personal E-mail: jblynchsr@bellsouth.net.

LYNCH, JOHN CHRISTOPHER, lawyer; b. Jacksonville, Fla., July 11, 1962; s. John Irving and Beverly Anne Beale Lynch; m. Anna Maria Szaz, Apr. 16, 1988; children: Flannery Elizabeth, Riley Davis. BA with honors, U. Va., Charlottesville, 1984; JD cum laude, Harvard U., Cambridge, Mass., 1988. Bar: NC 1993, Calif. 1988. Assoc. Wilson Sonsini Goodrich & Rosati, Palo Alto, Calif., 1988—92; ptnr. Wyrick Robbins Yates & Ponton LLP, Raleigh, NC, 1992—. Charter mem. The Indus Entrepreneurs, Research Triangle Park, NC, 2006—; bd. mem. Coun. for Entrepreneurial Devel., Durham, NC, 2002—. Democrat. Avocations: mountaineering, skiing, soccer. Office: Wyrick Robbins Yates & Ponton LLP Ste 300 4101 Lake Boone Trail Raleigh NC 27607 Business E-Mail: clynch@wyrick.com.

LYNCH, JOHN F., lawyer; BSChemE, Rensselaer Poly. Inst., 1960; JD, Fordham U., 1964. Bar: DC, Fla., NY, Tex., Wash., registered: US Ct. Appeals, Fed. Cir., US Patent & Trademark Office, US Supreme Ct. Engr. Hercules Power Co.; atty. Monsanto Company; atty. & patent agent Union Carbide Corp.; ptnr. & mem. exec. com. Howrey Simon Arnold & White LLP, Houston. Author: Patent Litig.: Procedure & Tactics; contbr. articles to profl. jours. Named one of top 20 patent lawyers, Euromoney Legal Media Group's Best of the Best: 2000 Ed., 100 most influential lawyers in Am., Nat. Law Jour., 2000. Mem.: ABA, Wash. State Bar Assn., Tex. Bar Assn., Licensing Exec. Soc., Houston Bar Found., Houston Bar Assn., Fed. Cir. Bar Assn., Am. Intellectual Property Law Assn. Office: Howrey LLP 1111 Louisiana 25th Fl Houston TX 77002-5230 Home Phone: 360-437-7605. Office Fax: 713-787-1440. Business E-Mail: lynchj@howrey.com.

LYNCH, JOHN THOMAS, retired science administrator, physicist; b. Washington, Mar. 21, 1938; s. John Thomas and Mary Ellen (Kaye) L.; m. Leslie Gray, June 22, 1959 (div. June 1972); children: John Thomas III, Michael Gray; m. Carol Rollins, July 5, 1980. BS in Physics, Va. Poly. Inst., 1963; MS in Physics, U. Wis., 1965, PhD, 1972. Lab. technician Nat. Bur. Standards, Washington, 1957-60; rsch. scientist U. Wis., Madison, 1965-78; staff Los Alamos (N.Mex.) Nat. Labs., 1978-81; program scientist NASA Hdqs., Washington, 1981-85; program dir. aeronomy and astrophysics Polar programs NSF, Washington, 1985-2000; ret., 2000. Contbr. articles to sci. jours. Recipient Antarctic svc. medal USN, 1986; named Disting. Alumni fellow dept. physics U. Wis., Madison, 2003; a mountain in Antarctica is named in his honor. Avocations: music, sailing. Personal E-mail: jlynch137@comcast.net.

LYNCH, PHILIP J., beverages manufacturing company executive; BA in Polit. Sci., U. Ky., Lexington, 1975. Press sec., mayor, Louisville, 1981—89; v.p., dir., corp. comm. Brown-Forman Corp., 1989—. Mem. Louisville Regional Airport Authority Bd. Dir., 2003—, chmn., 2009—. Democrat. Office: Brown Forman Corp 850 Dixie Hwy Louisville KY 40210 Office Phone: 502-585-1100. Office Fax: 502-774-6633. Business E-Mail: phil_lynch@b-f.com.

LYNCH, ROBERT NUGENT, bishop; b. Charleston, W.Va., May 27, 1941; BA, Pontifical Coll. Josephinum, Worthington, Ohio, 1963; MDiv, Pope John XXIII Nat. Sem., Weston, Mass., 1978. Ordained priest Archdiocese of Miami, Fla., 1978; assoc. pastor St. James parish, North Miami, Fla.; rector, pres. St. John Vianney Coll. Sem., Miami; pastor St. Mark parish, Ft. Lauderdale, Fla.; ordained bishop, 1996; bishop Diocese of St. Petersburg, Fla., 1996—; apostolic adminstr. Diocese of Palm Beach, 1998-99. Roman Catholic. Office: PO Box 402000 Saint Petersburg FL 33743-0200 Office Phone: 727-344-1611. Office Fax: 727-345-3086.

LYNN, BARBARA MICHELE, judge, federal judge; b. Binghamton, NY, Sept. 19, 1952; d. Stanley Donald and Nelda Ruth (Brounstein) Golden; m. Michael Paige Lynn, Aug. 12, 1973; children: Tara Paige, Whitney Reed. BA with distinction, U. Va., 1973; JD summa cum laude, So. Meth. U., 1976. Bar: U.S. Dist. Ct. (no. dist.) Tex. 1976, U.S. Ct. Appeals (5th and 11th cirs.) 1981, U.S. Dist. Ct. (we. dist.) Tex. 1983, U.S. Dist. Ct. (ea. dist.) Tex. 1986, U.S. Dist. Ct. (so. dist.) Tex. 1991, U.S. Supreme Ct. 1987. Assoc. Carrington, Coleman, Sloman & Blumenthal, Dallas, 1976-83, ptnr., 1983-99; judge US Dist. Ct. (no. dist.) Tex., Dallas, 1999—. Instr. Nat. Inst. Trial Advocacy, 1979—. Master Higginbotham Inn of Ct.; fellow Am. Coll. Am. Coll. Trial Lawyers; mem. ABA (chmn. comml. litigation 1989-91, dir. of divs. 1992-93, coun. litigation sect. 1993-96, sect. chair 1998-99), Am. Bar Found., Dallas Assn. Young Lawyers, Dallas Bar Assn. (bd. dirs. 1985-88), Tex. Bar Found., Dallas Bar Found. Office: US Dist Ct 1100 Commerce St Rm 1572 Dallas TX 75242-1495

LYNN, EVELYN JOAN, state legislator; b. NY, Feb. 2, 1930; d. Leo A. and Helen (Shep) Hoes; children: Karen Jans, Robert Grimm. BA in Psychology, Queens Coll., NYC, 1950; MA English and Edn., Stetson U., 1969; EdD, U. Fla., 1979. Cons. for bus., edn. and govt., 1979—; commr. City of Ormond Beach, Fla., 1991—94; mem. Fla. House of Reps., Tallahassee, 1994—2002; mem. Dist. 7 Fla. State Senate, Tallahassee, 2002—, chair higher edn. appropriations com., mem. commerce com., higher edn. com., mil. affairs and domestic security com., rules com., policy and steering com. on ways and means. Bd. dirs. Edn. Commn. States; mem. So. Regional Edn. Bd. Mem. Commn. State Women Govt. (dir. edn.). Republican. Office:

536 N Halifax Ave Ste 101 Daytona Beach FL 32118 also: 416 Senate Office Bldg 404 South Monroe St Tallahassee FL 32399-1100 Office Phone: 386-238-3180, 850-487-0160. Business E-Mail: lynn.evelyn.web@FLsenate.gov.

LYNN, LARRY (VERNE LAURISTON LYNN), engineering executive; b. Seattle, Sept. 5, 1930; s. Eldin Verne and Irma (Tuell) Lynn; m. Emily Jean Badger, Oct. 4, 1952 (div. 1988); m. Shirley Marie Pieczynski, Sept. 27, 1988. BS in Physics, Tufts U., 1951. Assoc. divsn. head, mem. steering com. Lincoln Lab. M.I.T., Lexington, Mass., 1953-79; dir. defensive systems Office of the Undersecretary of Defense, Washington, 1979-81; dep. dir. Adv. Rsch. Project Agy., Washington, 1981-85; v.p., COO Atlantic Aerospace Electronics, Greenbelt, Md., 1985-93; dep. under sec. defense Office Sec. Defense, Washington, 1993-95, dir. def. adv. rsch. project agy., 1995-98; pres., owner, cons. Larry Lynn Assocs., Williamsburg, Va., 1998—. Mem. Def. Sci. Bd. Contbr. articles to profl. jours. Lt. JG USNR, 1951-53. Fellow: IEEE (life); mem.: NAE. Home and Office: 124 The Green Williamsburg VA 23185 Personal E-mail: larry.lynn1@cox.net.

LYNN, LAURENCE EDWIN, JR., academic administrator, educator; b. Long Beach, Calif., June 10, 1937; s. Laurence Edwin and Marjorie Louise (Hart) L.; m. Patricia Ramsey Lynn; 1 dau., Katherine Bell; children from previous marriage— Stephen Louis, Daniel Laurence, Diana Jane, Julia Suzanne. AB, U. Calif., 1959; PhD (Ford Found. fellow), Yale, 1966; MA with honors, Harvard U., 1975. Dir., dep. asst. sec. def. (OASD/SA) Dept. Def., Washington, 1965-69; asst. for program analysis NSC, Washington, 1969-70; assoc. prof. bus. Grad. Sch. Bus., Stanford (Calif.) U., 1970-71, vis. prof. pub. policy, 1982-83; asst. sec. planning and evaluation HEW, Washington, 1971-73; asst. sec. program devel. and budget U.S. Dept. Interior, Washington, 1973-74; sr. fellow Brookings Instn., 1974-75; prof. pub. policy John Fitzgerald Kennedy Sch. Govt. Harvard U., Cambridge, Mass., 1975-83; dean Sch. Social Service Adminstrn. U. Chgo., 1983-88, prof., sch. of social svc. adminstrn. and Harris grad. sch. pub. policy studies, 1983—2002, dir. Ctr. for Urban Rsch. and Policy Studies, 1986—2002; dir. Mgmt. Inst., 1992-99; Sydney Stein, Jr. prof., 1997—2002; emeritus prof., 2002—; George H.W. Bush chair and prof. Bush Sch. Govt. and Pub. Svc., Tex A&M U., 2002—07; prof., public mgmt. U. Manchester, Manchester Bus. Sch., England, 2007—11; Sid Richardson rsch. prof. Lyndow B. Johnson Sch. Pub. Affairs U. Tex., Austin, 2008—14. Author: Designing Public Policy, 1980, The State and Human Services, 1980, Managing the Public's Business, 1981, Managing Public Policy, 1987, Public Management as Art, Science and Profession, 1996, Teaching and Learning with Cases: A Guidebook, 1999, Public Management: Old and New, 2006; co-author: The President as Policymaker, 1981, Improving Governance: A New Logic for Empirical Research, 2001, Madison's Managers: Public Administration and the Constitution, 2006, Public Management: A Three Dimensional Approach, 2008; contbr. articles to profl. jours. Bd. dirs. Chgo. Met. Planning Coun., 1984-89, Leadership Greater Chgo., 1989-92; mem. coun. of scholars Libr. of Congress, 1989-93. 1st lt. AUS, 1963-65. Recipient Sec. Def. Meritorious Civilian Svc. medal, Presdl. Cert. of Disting. Achievment, Vernon prize, best book award Acad. Mgmt., 1996; Charles Levine Lectr. award, 2012. Fellow Nat. Acad. Public Adminstrn.; mem. Am. Soc. for Pub. Adminstn. (Dwight Waldo award 2006, Paul Van Riper award, 2007), U. Calif. Alumni Assn., Coun. on Fgn. Rels., Assn. Pub. Policy Analysis and Mgmt. (past pres.), Pub. Mgmt. Rsch. Assn. (H. George Frederickson award 2005), Am. Polit. Sci. Assn. (Gaus award, 2007), Phi Beta Kappa. Office: 6820 Cypress Point N Unit #28 Austin TX 78746 Personal E-mail: llynnjr@gmail.com.

LYNN, LORETTA WEBB, singer; b. Butcher Hollow, Ky., Apr. 14, 1935; d. Ted and Clara (Butcher) Webb; m. Oliver V. Lynn, Jr., Jan. 10, 1948 (dec. 1996); children: Betty Sue Lynn Markworth (dec.), Jack Benny (dec.), Clara Lynn Lyell, Ernest Ray, Peggy, Patsy. Student pub. schs. Sec.-treas. Loretta Lynn Enterprises; v.p. United Talent, Inc.; hon. chmn. bd. Loretta Lynn Western Stores. Country vocalist with MCA records, 1961— (numerous gold albums); albums: Loretta Lynn Sings, 1963, Before I'm Over You, 1964, Songs from My Heart, 1965, Hymns, 1965, Blue Kentucky Girl, 1965, (with Ernest Tubb) Mr. & Mrs. Used to Be, 1965, I Like Em' Country, 1966, You Aint Woman Enough, 1966, Don't Come Home a Drinkin', 1967, Ernest Tubb & Loretta Lynn Singin' Again, 1967, Singin' With Feelin', 1967, Fist City, 1968, Who Says God id Dead!, 1968, Your Squaw is on the Warpath, 1969, (with Ernest Tubb) If We Put Our Heads Together, 1969, Woman of the World / To Make a Man, 1969, Wings Upon Your Horns, 1970, Loretta Lynn Writes 'em & Sings 'em, 1970, Coal Miner's Daughter, 1970, I Wanna Be Free, 1971, (with Conway Twitty) We Only Make Believe, 1971, You're Lookin' At Country, 1971, (with Conway Twitty) Lead Me On, 1972, One's on the Way, 1972, Here I Am Again, 1972, Entertainer of the Year - Loretta, 1973, (with Conway Twitty) Louisiana Woman, Mississippi Man, 1973, Love is the Foundation, 1973, They Don't Make 'em Like My Daddy, 1974, (with Conway Twitty) Country Partners, 1974, Back to the Country, 1975, (with Conway Twitty) Feelin's, 1975, Home, 1975, When the Tingle Becomes a Chill, 1976, (with Conway Twitty) United Talent, 1976, Somebody, Somewhere, 1976, I Remember Patsy, 1977, (with Conway Twitty) Dynamic Duo, 1977, Out of My Head and Back in Bed, 1978, (with Conway Twitty) Honky Tonk Heroes, 1978, We've Come a Long Way Baby, 1979, (with Conway Twitty) Diamond Duet, 1979, Loretta, 1980, Lookin' Good, 1980, (with Conway Twitty) Two's a Party, 1981, I Lie, 1981, Making Love from Memory, 1982, Lyin', Cheatin', Woman Chasin', Honky Tonkin', Whiskey Drinkin' You, 1983, Just a Woman, 1985, Who Was That Stranger, 1988, (with Conway Twitty) Making Believe, 1989, The Country Music Hall of Fame, 1991, Greatest Hits Live, 1992, Country's Favorite Daughter (reissue), 1993, (with Dolly Parton and Tammy Wynette) Honky Tonk Angels, 1993, Making More Memories, 1994, All Time Gospel Favorites, 1997, Still Country, 2000, Van Lear Rose, 2004; author: Coal Miner's Daughter, 1976, Still Woman Enough, 2002, You're Cookin' It Country, 2004, Honky Tonk Girl: My Life in Lyrics, 2012; appearance (TV film) Loretta Lynn: The Seasons of My Life, 1992, Big Dreams and Broken Hears: The Dottie West Story, 1995; discs include (boxed set) Honky Tonk Girl: The Loretta Lynn Collection, 1994, (MCA special products) Hymns, 1995, Christmas Without Daddy, 1995, On Tour #1, 1996, On Tour #2, 1996, 20th Century Masters: The Millenium Collection, 1999, Still Woman Enough, 2000. Hon. rep. United Giver's Fund, 1971. Named Country Music Assn. Female Vocalist of Year 1967, 1972, 1973, Entertainer of Year, 1972, Top Duet of 1972, 1973, 1974, 1975, Entertainer of Decade, Acad. Country Music 1980; recipient Grammy award 1971, American Music award 1978, Johnny Cash Visionary award, Country Music Television Music award, 2005, Pioneer award, Acad. County Music, 1995, Kennedy Ctr. Honors. John F. Kennedy Ctr. for the Performing Arts, 2003, Grammy Lifetime Achievement, 2010, Presdl. Medal of Freedom, The White House, 2013; inducted into Country Music Hall of Fame, 1988, Songwriter's Hall of Fame, 2008; first country female vocalist to record certified Gold album. Office: c/o Loretta Lynn Ranch 44 Hurricane Mills Rd Hurricane Mills TN 37078*

LYON, JOHN, information technology executive; V.p., dir., corp. fin. Perot Systems Corp. Office: Perot Systems Corp 2300 W Plano Pky Plano TX 75075 Office Phone: 877-737-6973. Office Fax: 877-577-6791. Business E-Mail: john.lyon@ps.net.

LYON, WILFORD CHARLES, JR., insurance executive; b. Blackfoot, Idaho, June 1, 1935; s. Wilford Charles and Nellie Anna (Estenson) L.; m. Eleanor Perkins, Aug. 23, 1957; children: Katherine Ann, Wilford Charles III. BS, Ga. Inst. Tech., 1958; MA in Actuarial Sci., Ga. State Coll., 1962. Asst. v.p. Ind. Life and Accident Ins. Co., Jacksonville, Fla., 1963-69, asst. v.p., dir. methods and planning dept., 1969-70, v.p., home office coord., 1970-79, pres., chief adminstrv. officer, 1979-84, chmn. bd., CEO, 1984-96; ret., 1996. Exec. compensation com., audit com. Fla. Bank, Inc., 1997-2004; trustee, exec. com. Edward Waters Coll., Jacksonville, 1983-96, chmn., bd. visitors, 1993-96, 2001-02. Pres. Jacksonville Jaycees, 1966; trustee Gator Bowl Assn., Jacksonville, 1981—, pres., 1981, mem. fin. com. and selection com.; pres. Jacksonville C. of C., 1984; trustee Cmty. TV, Inc., Jacksonville, 1980-93, chmn., 1991-92, exec. com., 2001-02; trustee Univ. Hosp., Jacksonville, Inc., 1985-86; bd. trustees Jacksonville Cmty. Found., 1999-2008; bd. dirs. YMCA Fla.'s First Coast, 1985-2007, sec., 1986, vice-chmn., 1987, chmn., 1988, chmn. devel. com. 2006-08; chmn. 1991 Nat. Vol. Week, Vol. Jacksonville, Inc.; pres. bd. Cypress Village, Inc., 1998-99; bd. dirs. Bolles Sch., 2001-07; trustee Gooding Found., 2002—; deacon, elder, clk., trustee Presbyn. Ch. Recipient Disting Svc. award Jacksonville Jaycees, 1972, Jack Donnell award Outstanding Businessman of Yr., 1983, Dick Hutchinson award Sertoma Club South Jacksonville, 1972, Svc. to Mankind award, 1972, Boss of Yr. award Profl. Secs. Internat., 1972-73, Victory Crusade award Fla. Cancer Soc., 1969, Ins. Industry Cmty. Svc. award Jacksonville Assn. Life Underwriters, 1986, C.G. Snead Meml. award Jacksonville Assn. of Life Underwriters, 1991, Top Mgmt. award Sales and Mktg. Execs. of Jacksonville, 1990, Clanzel T. Brown award Jacksonville Urban League, 1991, Svc. to Youth award YMCA of Fla.'s First Coast, 1991, Humanitarian award NCCJ, 1994; named to Gator Bowl Hall of Fame, 2010. Mem. Life Insurers Conf. (exec. com. 1981-91, chmn. membership com. 1981-86, sec. 1984-85, vice chmn. 1985-86, chmn. 1986-87), Am. Coun. Life Ins. (Fla. state v.p. 1981-96, bd. dirs. 1987-88, bd. dirs. Polit. Action Com. 1988-94), Southeastern Actuaries Club, Rotary Club Jacksonville (pres. Mandarin club 1977-78, Paul Harris fellow, dist. gov. 697 1985-86), Masons (33d degree), York Rite, Scottish Rite Bodies, Shriners (potentate Morocco Temple 1973, emeritus rep., investment com. 2005-09), Epping Forest Yacht Club (past commdr.). Republican. Home: 4035 Alhambra Dr W Jacksonville FL 32207

LYONS, AL(PHA) L., museum director, retired manufacturing executive; b. Memphis; BBA in Acctg., U. Memphis. Pres. Bodine Co., Collierville, Tenn., 1995—2007, ret., 2007; interim dir. Brooks Mus. Art, Memphis, 2008—. V.p. bd. trustees Brooks Mus. Art; bd. dirs. Ballet Memphis, Memphis in May, RivertArtsFest, Collierville C. of C. Office: Brooks Mus Art Overton Pk 1934 Popular Ave Memphis TN 38104 Office Phone: 901-544-6200. Office Fax: 901-725-4071.

LYONS, BRUCE MARTIN, lawyer; b. New Rochelle, NY, Sept. 22, 1942; s. Mildred Goodavitch; m. Madeline Lyons, Nov. 29, 1971 (div. 1981); m. Marcia Mae Lyons, June 8, 1983; children: Scott, Marc. BA, U. Miami, 1964, JD, 1967. Bar: Fla. 1967, US Dist. Ct. (so. dist. Fla.) 1967, US Fed. Ct. 1969, US Ct. Appeals (5th cir.) 1972, US Supreme Ct. 1976, US Ct. Appeals (11th cir.) 1981, Colo. 1993. Asst. county solicitor Broward County, 1967—71; mcpl. judge City of Coconut Creek, 1969—72; assoc. mcpl. judge City of Lauderdale Lakes, 1972—73; pres. Lyons & Sanders Chartered, Ft. Lauderdale, Fla.; instr. Cardozo Sch. ITAP Program, 2006—09. Adv. Nat. Criminal Justice Student Trial Advocacy Competition, 1990-91; trial practice instr. Nat. Coll. Criminal Def., Macon, Ga., 1991; mem. Broward County Narcotics Guidance Coun., 1971; master of the bench, Stephen R. Booher Inn of Ct.; spkr. in field. Contbr. articles to profl. jours. Dir. The Starting Place, Hollywood, Fla.; mem. Youth Leadership of Broward County, Juvenile Delinquency and Gang Prevention Coun., Narcotics Guidance Coun. of Broward County. Mem. ABA (criminal justice coun. 1992-93, 95, vice-chmn. CLE 1996-97, chmn.-elect criminal justice sect. 1998, chmn. 1999-2000, chmn. def. function com. 1989-92), NACDL (pres. 1986-87, dir. 1976-81, sec. 1982-83, 2nd v.p. 1984-85, pres. 1986-87, Robert C. Heeney award 1997), Broward County Criminal Def. Attys. Assn. (pres. 1988-89), Fla. Bar Assn. (mem. criminal rules com. 1988-89, exec. coun. criminal law sect. 1994), Broward County Bar Assn. (chmn. criminal law sect. 1976-77), Acad. Fla. Trial Lawyers (criminal law sect. chmn. 1974-76), Fed. Bar Assn., Fla. Assn. Criminal Def. Lawyers (dir. 1988-95), Am. Acad. Forensics Sci., Phi Delta Phi. Office: Lyons & Sanders Chartered 1301 E Broward Blvd Ste 220 Fort Lauderdale FL 33301-2111 Office Phone: 305-467-8700. Office Fax: 954-763-4856. E-mail: brucelyons@aol.com.

LYONS, CHAMP, JR., retired state supreme court justice; b. Boston, Dec. 6, 1940; m. Emily Lee Oswalt, 1967; children— Emily Olive, Champ III. AB, Harvard U., 1962; LL.B., U. Ala., 1965. Bar: Ala. 1965, U.S. Supreme Ct. 1973; registered mediator, Ala. Ctr. Dispute Resolutions. Law clk. U.S. Dist. Ct., Mobile, Ala., 1965-67; assoc. Capell, Howard, Knabe & Cobbs, Montgomery, Ala., 1967-70, ptnr., 1970-76, Helmsing, Lyons, Sims & Leach, Mobile, 1976-98; legal advisor Hon. Fob James, Jr. Gov. State Ala., 1998; assoc. justice Supreme Ct. Ala., Montgomery, 1998—2011; supernumerary supreme ct. justice Ala. Ctr. Dispute Resolutions. Mem. adv. commn. on civil procedure Ala. Supreme Ct., 1971-98, chmn., 1985-98. Author: Alabama Practice, 1973, 3d edit., 1996; contbr. articles to law jours. Mem. ABA, Ala. Bar Assn., Mobile Bar Assn. (pres. 1991), Am. Law Inst., Ala. Law Inst., Farrah Law Soc., Harvard U. Alumni Assn. (S.E. regional dir. 1988-91, v.p.-at-large 1992-94, 1st v.p. 1994-95, pres. 1995-96). Office Phone: 334-462-6262.

LYONS, GERALD, corporate financial executive; m. Claire Lyons; 7 children. BS in Fin., Clemson U., 1981; MBA, Cleve. State U., 2002. Group contr. Cooper Industries Ltd., 1989—98; plant contr. Moen, Inc., 1998—2002, global group contr., 2002—06, plant mgr., 2006—07; v.p., corp. contr. ScanSource, Inc., 2007—. Office: ScanSource Inc 6 Logue Ct Greenville SC 29615 Office Phone: 864-288-2432. Office Fax: 864-288-1165. Personal E-mail: glyons3@gmail.com.

LYONS, JOHN DAVID, literature and language professor; b. Springfield, Mass., Oct. 14, 1946; AB, Brown U., 1967; MA, Yale U., 1968, PhD, 1972. Asst. prof. French, Italian and comparative lit. Dartmouth Coll., Hanover, NH, 1972-78, assoc. prof., 1978-82, prof., 1982-87, chmn. comparative lit. program, 1981-84, chmn., prof. dept. French and Italian, 1987; dir. Am. Univ. Ctr. for Film and Critical Studies, Paris, 1984-85; prof. French U. Va., Charlottesville, 1987-92, Commonwealth prof. French, 1993—, chmn. dept., 1989—92, 1998—99, 2005—08. Vis. prof. U. Paris III, 2005. Author: A Theatre of Disguise, 1978, The Listening Voice, 1982, Examplum, 1989, The Tragedy of Origins, 1996, Kingdom of Disorder, 1999, Before Imagination, 2005, French Literature: A Very Short Introduction, 2010; co-editor: Mimesis: Mirror to Method, 1982, Dialectic of Discovery, 1983, Critical Tales, 1993; editor: Art, Architecture, Text: The Late Renaissance, 1985; assoc. editor Continuum, 1987—93, editor Academe, 1994—97, mem. editl. adv. bd. Philosophy and Literature, 1992—2002, French Forum; co-editor: Chance Literature and Culture, 2009. Recipient Robert Fish award for teaching Dartmouth Coll., 1978, Outstanding Tchr. award U. Va., 1996, Chevalier Legion d'Honneur, 2007; Woodrow Wilson fellow, 1967, ACLS study fellow, 1978, NEH fellow, 1985-89, 92-93, ACLS contemplative practice fellow, 2002, J.S. Guggenheim fellow, 2002-03, Ctr. for Advanced Studies U. Va. fellow, 1987-89. Mem.: N.Am. Soc. for Seventeenth-Century French Lit. (pres. 2002).

LYTLE, MICHAEL ALLEN, forensic criminologist, consultant; b. Salina, Kans., Oct. 22, 1946; s. Milton Earl and Geraldine Faye (Young) L.; div.; 1 child, Eric Alexander. BA, Ind. U., 1973; grad. cert., Sam Houston State U., Huntsville, Tex., 1977; MEd, Tex. A&M U., 1978; postgrad., 1978-80; student, Nat. Def. U., 1988; grad. cert., U. Calif., Riverside, 2007. Substitute high sch. tchr., Butler Cty., KS, 1969; instr. criminal justice Cleve. State C.C., Tenn., 1974-77; adj. instr. criminal justice U. Tenn., Chattanooga, 1975-76; tchg. asst. Tex. A&M U. Sys., 1977-80, intern adminstrv. asst. Office Vice Chancellor Legal Affairs and Gen. Counsel, 1980, staff assoc. Office Chancellor, 1980-81, asst. to chancellor, 1981-83, asst. dir. govt. rels., 1983-84, spl. asst. to chancellor for fed. rels., 1984-87; dir. rsch. devel. and spl. asst. to v.p. for rsch. and grad. studies Syracuse U., NY, 1987, exec. dir. govt. rels. NY, 1987-89, sr. rsch. assoc. tech. and info. policy prog. Maxwell Sch. Citizenship and Pub. Affairs NY, 1987-92, dir. fed. rels. NY, 1989-92, adj. prof. internatl. bus. studies NY, 1990-92; prin. and sr. couns. The Erik Alexander Group, 1992-93; exec. dir. instl. devel. U. Tex., Brownsville, 1993-95, sr. lectr. criminal justice, 1995-97; rsch. fellow Office Undersec. Def., 1997; sr. rsch. assoc. Sci. Applications Internat. Corp., 1997-99; adj. prof., criminal justice Marymount U. and Luth. Colls. Wash. Consortiums, 1999—2005; dep. mgr. tech. svcs. divsn. Sci. Applications Internat. Corp., 2000—06; asst. prof. criminal justice U. Tex., Brownsville, 2006—08, coord., Forensic Investigation Program, 2008—. Rep. Coun. on Fed. Rels., Assn. Am. Univs.; instl. rep. Rsch. Univs. Network; exec. dir. Tex. Com. for Employer Support of the Guard and Res., 1982-86; mem. U.S. Mexico Com. Philanthropy and the Border, 1994-95, militarily critical techs. adv. com. U.S. Internat. Bus. Studies, Tex. A&M Univ., 1986-87; res. asst. army attache to Rep. of Ireland, 1986-87; mem. exec. com. N.E. Parallel Architectures Ctr.; mem. Sec. of Army's adv. panel in ROTC affairs, 1988-92; cons. Nat. Inst. Justice, 2000—, Office of Victims of Crime, 2002—. Mem. editl. bd., Jour. Tech. Transfer, 1987-95, contbr. articles to profl. jours. Served with USAR, Vietnam and Bosnia. Decorated Legion of Merit, Bronze Star, Purple Heart, Meritorious Svc. medal with 2 oak leaf clusters, Joint Svc. Commendation medal, Army Commendation medal with 4 oak leaf clusters; recipient Disting. Alumni award Sam Houston State U., 2003. Fellow Inter-Univ. Seminar Armed Forces and Soc. Am. Coll. Forensic Examiners (life); mem. AAAS (bd. advs. nat. security and sci. comm. proj. mem. awd. sel. panel. sci. freedom and responsibilty), Nat. Assn. State Univs. and Land-Grant Colls. (vet. affairs and nat. svc. com.), Am. Soc. for Pub. Adminstrn. (exec. com. sect., past chair on Nat. Security and Def. Analysis), Atlantic Counc. U.S. (councilor), Forensic Sci. Soc., Acad. Criminal Justice Scis., Internat. Assn. for the Study of Organized Crime, Internat. Assn. Chief's Police, mem., US Attorney's Law Enforcement Coordinating Com., southern dist., Tex., 1995-97. Mem. Army and Navy Club, Capitol Hill Club, Sigma Xi, Phi Delta Kappa, Alpha Phi Sigma, Lambda Alpha Epsilon, Zeta Beta Tau, Am. Criminal Justice Assn.(life), Internat. Assn. Cities of Police(life) Republican. Episcopalian. Address: 206 Parkview Cir Harlingen TX 78550 Personal E-mail: malytle@aol.com.

LYTTON, ROBERT LEONARD, civil engineer, educator; b. Port Arthur, Tex., Oct. 23, 1937; s. Robert Odell and Nora Mae (Verrett) Lytton; m. Eleanor Marilyn Anderson, Sept. 9, 1961; children: Lynn Elizabeth, Robert Douglas, John Kirby. BSCE, U. Tex., 1960, MSCE, 1961, PhD, 1967. Registered profl. engr., Tex., La., land surveyor, La., diplomate of geotech. engrng., Am. Acad. Geo Profls., 2009. Cowhand Slaughter Ranch, Douglas, Ariz., 1963; assoc. Dannenbaum and Assocs., Cons. Engrs., Houston, 1963—65; U.S. NSF fellow U. Tex., Austin, 1965—67, asst. prof., 1967—68; NSF fellow Australian Commonwealth Sci. & Indsl. Rsch. Orgn., Melbourne, Australia, 1969—70; assoc. prof. Tex. A&M U., College Station, 1971—76, prof., 1976—90, Wiley chair prof., 1990—95, dir. ctr. for infrastructure engrng., 1995—, Benson chair prof., 1995—; divsn. head Tex. Transp. Inst., College Station, 1982—91, head infrastructure and transp. divsn. civil engrng. dept., 1993—95. Bd. dir. MLA Labs., Inc., Austin, Lyric Tech., LLC, Houston; v.p., bd. dir. Electronic Pavement and Infrastructure Charting, Inc., MLAW Cons., Inc., Austin, Geostructural Tool Kit, Inc.; prin. investigator strategic hwy. rsch. program A005 rsch. project, 1990—93; keynote spkr. 5th Internat. Conf. Rsch. Inst. Labs. Materials Testing, Limoges, France, 2004; keynote lectr. 7th Internat. Conf. Rsch. Inst. Labs. Materials Testing Delft, Netherlands, 2012. Active St. Vincent de Paul Soc., Houston, 1963—65, Redemptorist Lay Mission Soc., Melbourne, Australia, 1969—70. Capt. US Army, 1961—63. Recipient SAR medal of Honor, St. Mary's U., 1957, Disting. Mil. Grad. award, 1960, Hamilton Watch award, Coll. Engrng., U. Tex. Austin, 1960, Everite Bursary award, Coun. Sci. and Indsl. Rsch., South Africa, 1984, Disting. Achievement award, Tex. A&M U. Assn. Former Students, 1996, Zachry Sr. Rschr. award, Tex. Transp. Inst., 1996, Birdwell Endowed Tchg. award, 2006—07, Lifetime Achievement award, Geo Shanghai Internat. Conf., 2010, Excellence in Tchg. award, Tex. A & M U., Coll. Engrng., 2013; named Soc. Am. Mil. Engrs. Outstanding Sr. Cadet, U. Tex., 1959, Trendsetter, Pub. Works Mag., 2005, Academy of Distinguished Alumni, U. Tex. Austin Civil Archit. & Environ. Engrng. Dept., 2010. Fellow: ASCE (John B. Hawley award Tex. sect. 1966, Geo Inst. Transp. and Devel. Inst. Carl L. Monismith lectr. 2013), Post-Tensioning Inst. (adv. bd., Named Legend of Post-Tensioning 2005); mem.: NSPE, Internat. Congresso De Ingenieria Civil Queretaro, Mex. (invited lectr. 2011), Acad. Geo-Profls., Am. Acad. Geo Profls., Am. Soc. Civil Engrs. (elected diplomate geotech. engrng. 2009), Constrn. Users Round Table (Constrn. Innovation Forum NOVA award 2006), Found. Performance Assn. Houston (hon. life mem.), Internat. Soc. Asphalt Pavements, Tex. Soc. Profl. Engrs., Assn. Asphalt Paving Technologists, Internat. Soc. Soil Mechanics and Geotechnical Engrng. (US rep. tech. com. TC-6 1987—, keynote address 7th internat. conf. expansive soils 1992, keynote address 1st internat. conf. unsaturated soils 1995, keynote address 1st pan american conf. unsaturated Soils Cartagen 2013), Transp. Rsch. Bd. (chmn. com. A2L06 1987—93, disting. lectr. 2000), Sigma Xi, Phi Kappa Phi, Tau Beta Pi, Chi Epsilon, Phi Kappa Delta. Roman Catholic. Achievements include patents for sys. identification, analysis of subsurface radar signals. Office: Tex A&M U 503A CE Tex Transp Inst Bldg College Station TX 77843-3136 Personal E-mail: rllytton@mail.com.

MA (XUEZHENG), MARY, investment company executive; married; 1 child. BA, Capital Normal U., Beijing, 1976. Bureaucrat, Chinese Academy of Sciences' Internat. Corp. bureau China State Coun., 1978—90; joined Lenovo Group, 1990, sr. v.p. Beijing & Purchase NY, 1997—2007, CFO, 2000—07, non-exec. vice-chmn., 2007; ptnr., mng. dir. TPG Capital, LP, Hong Kong & Beijing, 2007—. Bd. dirs. SOHU.com; bd. dir. Lenovo Group, 1997—2007. Named Best CFO, Finance Asia; named one of most powerful women,

Forbes mag., 2005, 50 Most Powerful Women in Global Bus., Fortune mag., 2005, 50 Women to Watch, Wall St. Jour., 2006. Office: TPG Capital LP Ste 3300 301 Commerce St Fort Worth TX 76102 Office Phone: 817-871-4000. Office Fax: 817-871-4010.

MABE, KATHERINE, insurance company executive; MBA, Ohio State U., 2001—03, attended, Northwestern U. Sr. v.p., chief mktg. officer Nationwide Ins., 2004—06, pres. western ops., 2006—08; pres. Titan Ins. Co., 2008—10; CEO Victoria Ins. Co., 2008—10; pres., CEO The Economical Ins. Group, 2010—11; pres. Allstate Protection Central/West Regions Allstate, 2011—. Trustee Columbus Mus. of Art, 2007—09. Mem.: Alumni of The Ohio State Univ., YWCA Bd. Columbus Art Mus. Bd., Women Presidents Orgn. (WPO). Office: Allstate 2775 Sanders Rd Northbrook IL 60062 also: Allstate Insurance Co 1819 Electric Rd S W Roanoke VA 24018 Office Phone: 847-402-5000.

MABRY, DONALD JOSEPH, retired academic administrator, history professor; b. Atlanta, Apr. 21, 1941; s. Jerry Leon and Eunice Leigh (Harris) M.; m. Susan Strong Johnston, July 28, 1962 (div. Oct. 1986); children: Scott, Mark; m. Paula Ann Crockett, Dec. 18, 1992. BA, Kenyon Coll., Gambier, Ohio, 1963; MEd, Bowling Green State U., 1964; PhD, Syracuse U., 1970. Instr. St. Johns River CC, Palatka, Fla., 1964—67; rsch. asst. fin. aid Syracuse U., NY, 1967—68, teaching fellow in history, 1968—69, Maxwell fellow, 1969—70, vis. lectr. dept. history, 1969—70; asst. to chancellor U. Kans., Lawrence, 1978—79; from. asst. prof. to prof. dept. history Miss. State U., Mississippi State, 1970—, asst. to pres., 1979—81, assoc. dean for budget and rsch., 1991—2001; now dir., assoc. dean Biol. Physical Sciences Rsch. Inst., Mississippi State, Miss.; ret. Sr. fellow, Ctr. for Internat. Security and Strategic Studies Miss. State U., 1981—91. Author: Mexico's Accion Nacional, 1973, The Mexican University and the State, 1982, (with others) Neighbors--Mexico and the United States, 1981; editor: The Latin American Narcotics Trade and U.S. National Security, 1989, Colonial Latin America, 2002, World's First Beach, 2010; contbr. articles to profl. jours. Mem. Am. Coun. on Edn. (exec. com. Coun. of Fellows 1980-83), South Ea. Coun. on Latin Am. Studies, Hist. Text Archive (founding editor) Avocation: computer telecommunications. Home: 206 Hiwassee Dr Starkville MS 39759-2105 Home Phone: 662-323-6852; Office Phone: 662-325-3604.

MABRY, JOSEPH M.(MIKE), JR., consumer products company executive; B math, Univ. No. Ala.; MBA, Okla. City Univ. Mgmt. positions through v.p. global services Wal-Mart, 1991—2003; sr. v.p. distbn. Lowe's Companies, Inc., Mooresville, NC, 2003—04, exec. v.p. logistics & distbn., 2004—. Office: Lowe's Companies 1000 Lowe's Blvd Mooresville NC 28117

MACADAM, STEPHEN E., wholesale distribution executive; BS, Univ. Ky.; MS, Boston Coll.; MBA, Harvard Univ. Cons. positions through prin. McKinsey & Co., Charlotte, NC, 1988—98; sr. v.p. containerboard & packaging Georgia-Pacific Corp., 1998—2000, exec. v.p. pulp & paperboard, 2000—01; pres., CEO Consolidated Container Co., 2001—05; CEO BlueLinx Holdings, Atlanta, 2005—08; pres., CEO and dir. EnPro Industries, Charlotte, NC, 2008—. Bd. dirs. Georgia Gulf Corp., 2009—. Office: EnPro Industries 5605 Carnegie Blvd Charlotte NC 28209-4674 Office Phone: 704-731-1500. Office Fax: 704-731-1511. Business E-Mail: stephen.macadam@enproindustries.com.

MACAVOY, THOMAS COLEMAN, manufacturing executive, educator; b. Jamaica, NY, Apr. 24, 1928; s. Joseph V. and Edna M. Mac A.; m. Margaret M. Walsh, Dec. 27, 1952; children: Moira Mac Avoy, Ellen Mac Avoy Jennings, Christopher, Neil. BS in Chemistry, Queens Coll., 1950; MS in Chemistry, St. John's U., 1952, DSc (hon.), 1973; PhD in Chemistry, U. Cin., 1952. Chemist, Charles Pfizer & Co., Bklyn., 1957-60; mgr. electronics rsch. Corning Glass Works, NY, 1960-64, dir. phys. rsch., 1964-66, v.p. electronic products divsn., 1966-69, v.p. tech. products divsn., 1969-71, pres., 1971-83, vice-chmn., 1983-87; prof. mgmt. grad. sch. U. Va., 1988—. Patentee in field; contbr. articles to tech. jours. Trustee Corning Mus. Glass; past pres. Boy Scouts Am. With USN, 1946; with USAF, 1952-53. Recipient Silver Antelope award Boy Scouts Am., 1976, Silver Beaver award, 1975, Silver Buffalo award, 1982, Bronze Wolf award, 1988. Roman Catholic. Personal E-mail: tmacavoy@aol.com.

MACDONALD, ALLAN H., physics professor; b. Antigonish, Nova Scotia, Can., Dec. 1, 1951; Grad., St. Francis Xavier U., 1973; PhD, U. Toronto, 1978. Rsch. assoc. Nat. Rsch. Coun., Canada, 1978—80, asst. rsch. officer, 1980—82, assoc. rsch. officer; prof. physics Ind. U., 1987—92, disting. prof. physics, 1992—2000; Sid. W. Richardson Found. regents chair U. Tex., Austin, 2000—. Organizer and com. mem. to numerous conferences and symposiums. Contbr. articles to numerous profl. jours. Recipient Herzberg medal, Can. Assn. Physicists, 1987. Fellow: Am. Phys. Soc. (mem. Buckley prize com. 1993, chmn. Buckley prize com. 1994, mem. exec. com., DCMP 1995—99); mem.: NAS. Office: Dept Physics University Texas Austin TX 78712 Office Phone: 512-232-9113. Office Fax: 512-471-9637. Business E-Mail: macd@physics.utexas.edu.

MACDONALD, BRIAN PATRICK, oil industry executive; b. 1965; BS, Mount Allison U., 1987; MBA in Finance, McGill U., 1989. Treas. GM Canada GM Canada, 1998—2000; dep. CFO Izuzu Moters Ltd.; head mergers and acquisitions orgn. and global treasury group Dell, Inc., corporate v.p., treas., CFO comml. bus. unit, 2008—09; sr. v.p., CFO Sunoco, Inc., Phila., 2009—12, chmn., pres., CEO, 2012; pres. & CEO ETP Holdco Corp., 2012—. Bd. dirs. SunCoke Energy, Inc., 2010—12, Sunoco, Inc., 2012, Phila. Energy Solutions, 2012—. Office: ETP Holdco Corporation 3738 Oak Lawn Ave Dallas TX 75219*

MACDONALD, JAMES ROSS, physicist, researcher; b. Savannah, Ga., Feb. 27, 1923; s. John Elwood and Antonina Jones (Hansell) Macdonald; m. Margaret Milward Taylor, Aug. 3, 1946; children: Antonina Hansell, James Ross IV, William Taylor. BA, Williams Coll., 1944; SB, MIT, 1944, SM, 1947; PhD, Oxford U., Eng., 1950, DSc, 1967. Staff Digital Computer Lab., MIT, 1946-47; physicist Armour Rsch. Found., Chgo., 1950-52; assoc. physicist Argonne Nat. Lab., 1952-53; with Tex. Instruments Inc., Dallas, 1953-74, v.p. corp. rsch. and engring., 1968-73, v.p. corp. R & D, 1973-74; cons., 1974—; dir. Simmonds Precision Products Inc., 1979-83; William Rand Kenan Jr. prof. physics U. N.C., Chapel Hill, 1974-91, prof. emeritus, 1991—. Adj. prof. biophysics U. Tex. Med. Sch., Dallas, 1954—74; mem. solid state scis. panel NRC, 1965—73; mem. adv. com. sci. edn. NSF, 1971—73; mem. vis. com. physics MIT, 1971—74; mem. external adv. com. Engring. Exptl. Sta. Ga. Inst. Tech., 1976—79. Editor, co-author: Impedance Spectroscopy-Theory, Experiment, and Applications, 2005, 2d edit., 2005; mem. editl. bd. Jour. Applied Physics, 1984—86; contbr. articles to profl. jours. Bd. dirs. League Ednl. Advancement Dallas, 1965—70; mem. Dallas Radio Commn., 1967—71; mem. sci. adv. coun. Callier Hearing and Speech Ctr., Dallas, 1974—78; mem. adv. com. Weber Rsch. Inst., 1985—90. Rhodes scholar, Oxford U., 1948—50. Fellow: AAAS, IEEE (editor Transactions Profl. Group Audio 1961—66, editor Transactions Audio and Electroacoustics 1966—73, award 1962, 1974, Edison Gold medal 1986), Am. Phys. Soc. (mem. com. edn. 1973—75, mem. com. applicaitons physics 1975—78, George E. Pake prize 1985); mem.: NAS (chmn. numerical data adv. bd. 1970—74, mem. com. motor vehicle emissions 1971—74, chmn. com. motor vehicle emissions 1973—74, mem. com. satellite power sys. 1979—81, mem. com. sci., engring., and pub. policy 1981—83, mem. commn. phys. scis., math. and applications 1985—88, mem. report rev. com. 1990—97), NAE (mem. coun. 1971—74, mem. exec. com. assembly engring. 1975—78), Audio Engring. Soc., Electrochemical Soc., Am. Inst. Physics (mem. governing bd. 1975—78), Sigma Xi, Phi Beta Kappa, Tau Beta Pi. Achievements include patents in field. Office: U NC Dept Physics and Astronomy Chapel Hill NC 27517-7549 Business E-Mail: macd@email.unc.edu.

MACDONALD, ROBERT RIGG, JR., retired museum director; b. Pitts., May 11, 1942; s. Robert Rigg and Ruth (Johnson) M.; m. Catherine Ronan, Nov. 27, 1965; children: Matthew, Robert, Catherine. BA, U. Notre Dame, 1964, MA, 1965, U. Pa., 1970. Asst. curator Smithsonian Instn., Washington, 1965; curator Mercer Mus., Doylestown, Pa., 1966-70; dir. New Haven Colony Hist. Soc., 1970-74, La. State Mus., New Orleans, 1974-85; dir., CEO Mus. of City of N.Y., 1985—2002; ret., 2002. Adj. prof. mus. studies NYU, 1989—; adj. prof. pub. adminstrn. Coll. Charleston, 2006—; mem. Commn. Mus. for a New Century; vice-chmn. SC Aquarium, 2007-; bd. dirs. Internat. African Am. Mus.; mem. adv. bd. Riley Inst., Coll. Charleston, 2004-; vice chair Internat. Coms. Mus. of City, Internat. Coun. Mus., 2005-; vis. scholar Coll. Charleston, 2011-; mem. Gullah Geechee Cultural Heritage Found. Bd. Editor: Editor: New Haven Colony Furniture, 1973, Louisiana Images 1880-1920, 1975, Louisiana Black Heritage, 1977 Louisiana Portraitures, 1979, Louisiana Legal Heritage, 1981, The Sun King: Louis XIV and the New World, On Being Homeless, A Community of Many Worlds: Arab American New Society, 2002, City Museum & City Development, 2008; organizer (children's art, photographs) The Day Our World Changed: Children's Art of 9/11, The City Resilient: Photographs by Joel Meyerowitz. Decorated chevalier de l'Ordre des Arts et des Lettres (France), cruz de Caballero de la Order de Isabel La Catolica (Spain); assoc. fellow Berkeley Coll., Yale U., 1978; Hagley fellow U. Del., 1970-71; Univ. scholar U. Notre Dame, 1964-65; named to Centennial Honor Roll Am. Assn. Museums, 2006; vis. scholar Charleston Coll., 2011-. Mem.: Mus. City N.Y. (dir. emeritus 2002—), Am. Assn. Mus. (pres. 1985—88, chmn. ethics task force 1988—91, Disting. Svc. award 2003), Am. Assn. State and Local History (coun.), Century Assn. Roman Catholic. Home: 602 Island Walk East Mount Pleasant SC 29464 Office Phone: 843-670-7440. Personal E-mail: robertrm2@gmail.com.

MACDOUGALL, WILLIAM LOWELL, magazine editor; b. Des Moines, July 24, 1931; s. David Gregory and Elizabeth Jeanette (Dugan) MacD. AB, Willamette U., Salem, Oreg., 1952; M.J. in Journalism (Pulitzer scholar 1953-54), Columbia U., 1953. Reporter Washington Star, 1958-62; corr. Los Angeles Times, 1962-63; asso. editor, then London corr. U.S. News & World Report, 1964-68, asst. mng. editor Washington, 1978-86; mng. editor Artsreview mag. NEA, 1987; pres. Mid-Atlantic Media Co., Arlington, Va., 1989—. Author: American Revolutionary: A Biography of General Alexander McDougall, 1977. Served with USAF, 1954-57. Recipient George Washington medal Freedoms Found., 1978, citation U.S. Bicentennial Commn., 1976 Methodist. Office: Mid-Atlantic Media Co 5000 37th St N Arlington VA 22207-1823

MACESICH, GEORGE, economics professor; b. Cleve., May 27, 1927; m. Susana Sonja Svorkovich, Feb. 16, 1955; children: Maja, Milena, George M.P. AA, George Washington U., 1951, BA, 1953, MA, 1954; PhD, U. Chgo., 1958. Tchg. and rsch. positions while completing graduate study, 1953—58; rsch. economist U.S. C. of C., Washington, 1958—59; asst. prof. Econs. Fla. State U., Tallahassee, 1959—61, assoc. prof. Econs., 1961—63, prof. economics Tallhassee, 1963—2008, prof. emeritus economics, 2008—; prof. econs. U. Belgrade, Serbia and Montenegro, 1972—. Cons. U.S. Dept. Commerce, 1961-65; vis. economist Nat. Bank Yugoslavia, 1965; founding dir. Ctr. for Yugoslav-Am. Studies, Rsch. and Exchanges, Fla. State U., 1961—, Inst. Comparative Policy Studies Rsch. and Exchanges, 1992—; cons. Jour. Polit. Economy, U. Chgo., 1968-81, Coun. Grad. Schs. in U.S., Washington, 1971-82, Jour. Money, Credit and Banking, 1977-89. Author, co-author, editor 41 books including The International Monetary Economy and the Third World, 1981, Politics of Monetarism: Its Historical and Institutional Development, 1984, Monetary Reform and Cooperation Theory, 1989, Money and Democracy, 1990, (with D. Dimitrijevic) The Money Supply Process: A Comparative Analysis, 1990, World Debt and Stability, 1990, Reform and Market Democracy, 1991, Yugoslavia in the Age of Democracy: Essays on Economic and Political Reform, 1992, Monetary Policy and Politics: RulesVersus Discretion, 1992, Successor States and Cooperation Theory, 1994, Monetary Reform in Former Socialist Countries, 1995, Integration and Stabilization: A Monetary View, 1995, Transformation and Emerging Markets, 1996, The U.S. in a Changing Global Economy: Policy Implications and Issues, 1997, World Economy at the Cross Roads, 1997, Money, Systems and Growth, 1998, Political Economy of Money: The Emerging Fiat Monetary Regime, 1999, Issues in Money and Banking, 2000, Money and Monetary Regimes, 2002; mem. editl. bd. So. Econ. Jour., 1961-63, 72-76, Foreign Trade and Cycles, 1970-76; contbr. over 120 articles to profl. jours. Bd. dirs. Coun. Econ. Devel., Tallahassee, 1961-63, Nikola Tesla Meml. Soc., 1980-81; mem. U.S.-Yugoslav Econ. Coun., 1987—, Inst. for Internat. Edn. Screening Com., 1984-87. With U.S. Navy 1944-53 Recipient Ford Found. fellowship, 1959-60, Fulbright fellowship, 1965, Order of Yugoslav Star with Gold Wreath, Yugoslav Govt., 1983, award of Merit, U. Zagreb, 1989 Mem. Am. Acad. Polit. and Social Sci., Am. Econ. Assn., Am. Fgn. Svc. Assn., Am. Statis. Assn., So. Econ. Assn., U.S. Naval Inst., Pi Gamma Mu. Office: Inst Comparative Policy and Dept Economics Fla State U Tallahassee FL 32306 Address: 6492 Crabtree Ln Brecksville OH 44141 Home: 6492 Crabtree Ln Brecksville OH 44141-1736 Home Phone: 850-576-1658, 440-838-0443; Office Phone: 850-644-5001.

MACEWAN, BONNIE, librarian, dean; b. Memphis, Sept. 10, 1950; m. Thomas Manig. BA, Whitter Coll., 1972; M, U. Denver, 1978. Humanities libr. Ctl. Mo. State Coll., Warrensburg, 1978—84; art, archaeology and music libr. U. Mo., Columbia, 1984—91; asst. dean scholarly comm. Pa. State U., University Park, 1991—98, dean collections and scholarly comm., co-dir. digital scholarly pub., 1998—2005; dean librs. Auburn U., Ala., 2005—. Mem.: ALA (vice chair, chair-elect collection mgmt. and develop. sect. 2001—02). Office: Auburn U Librs 231 Mell St Auburn University AL 36849 Office Phone: 334-844-1715. E-mail: macewbj@auburn.edu.

MACGILLIVRAY, ROBIN G., telecommunications industry executive; BA in Journalism Magna Cum Laude, U. of Southern Calif, MA in Telecom. Mgmt.; completed Stanford Exec. Program, Stanford U., 1997. Sr. v.p., regional and local markets AT&T Inc. (merger of SBC Communications & AT&T Corp.), sr. v.p., strategic process improvement, joined, 1979, various positions in engring., ops., fin., human resources, mktg., customer svc. and sales, 1979—2010, sr. v.p., bus. comm. svcs., 2010—. Bd. dirs. Simpson Mfg. Co., Inc. Pres. Girl Scouts of Northern Calif. Office: AT&T Inc 208 S Akard St Dallas TX 75202-2233 Office Phone: 210-821-4105. Business E-Mail: robin.macgillivray@att.com.

MACHEN, JAMES BERNARD (BERNIE MACHEN), academic administrator; m. Chris; children: Maggie, Michael, Lee. DDS, St. Louis U., 1968; MS, U. Iowa, 1972, PhD in Edn. Psychology, 1974. Prof., assoc. dean U. N.C., 1983-89; pres. Am. Assn. Dental Schs., 1987; dean U. Mich. Sch. Dentistry, 1989-95; provost, exec. v.p. acad. affairs U. Mich., 1995-97; pres. U. Utah, 1998—2003, U. Fla., Gainesville, 2004—. Mem. Inst. Medicine Com. in Future Dental Edn. Nat. Acad. Scis., 1993-95. Office: University of Florida Office of President 226 Tigert Hall PO Box 113150 Gainesville FL 32611-3150 Office Phone: 352-392-1311. Fax: 352-392-9506. E-mail: president@ufl.edu.*

MACHOVEC, FRANK J., psychologist; b. Balt., May 16, 1930; s. James Joseph and Theresa Anna MacH.; m. Evelyn Mary Stultz, May 5, 1951; 1 child, Frank. BA, U. Md., 1964; MA, Loyola U., Balt., 1965; PhD, Fielding Inst., 1979. Diplomate Am. Bd. Psychol. Hypnosis, Am. Bd. Med. Psychotherapy; lic. clin. psychologist. Psychologist Victoria Hosp., Winnipeg, Man., Canada, 1975—76, Alta. Mental Health, Lethbridge, Canada, 1976—78, Alaska Psychol. Inst., Anchorage, 1978—80, State Hosp. South, Blackfoot, Idaho, 1979-81; dir. psychol. svcs. South Va. Mental Health Inst., Danville, 1981-86; dir. quality assurance Va. Dept. Mental Health, 1986-90; supr. psychology Va. Juvenile Corrections, 1991-95, ret., 1995. Prof. Piedmont Va. Com. Coll.; instr. Jefferson Inst. Author: Hypnosis Complications, 1986, Expert Witness Survival Manual, 1987, Humor Theories, History, 1988, Interview and Interrogation, 1989, Cults and Personality, 1989, Becoming Street Smart, 1994, Spiritual Intelligence, 2002, Light from the East, 2005, Private Investigative and Security Science, 2006, Divine Spark, 2007, Buddha, Tao, Zen, 2007, Lead and Manage, 2007, Whats Funny, Psychology of Humor, 2008, Cults and Terrorism, Zen Classics, 2009. With USMC, 1950—52. Avocations: writing, travel, teaching.

MACK, CARL B., engineering executive; b. Jackson, Miss. m. Jamiyo Mack; children: Joshua, Jonathan. BS in Mech. Engring., Miss. State U., 1986. Engr. METRO-King County, Seattle; exec. dir. Nat. Soc. Black Engineers, 2005—. Named to Power 150, Ebony mag., 2008; Disting. Engring. Fellow, Miss. State U., 2006. Mem.: NAACP (pres. Seattle King County Br. 2003—04). Office: Nat Soc Black Engineers 205 Daingerfield Rd Alexandria VA 22314

MACK, DAVID, III, state legislator; b. Charleston, SC, Dec. 13; s. David James and Dorothy P. Mack; m. Sheryl Ann Shaw, 1996; children: David IV, Daniel, Brandon. BS, Howard U., Washington, 1975. Mem. Dist. 109 SC House of Reps., 1997—. Mem.: NAACP, Urban League, African-Am. Jewish Coalition, African Am. Network. Democrat. Methodist. Address: 4340 Evanston Blvd North Charleston SC 29418 Mailing: 328D Blatt Bldg Columbia SC 29201 Home Phone: 843-760-0198; Office Phone: 803-734-3192, 843-225-4869. Business E-Mail: djm@legis.lpitr.state.sc.us.

MACK, SHERMAN Q., state legislator, lawyer; BA in Historical Studies, Southeastern La. U., 1995; JD, Southern U., 1999. Law clk. to Judge Brenda Bedsole Ricks and Judge Wayne Ray Chutz 21st Judicial Dist. Ct., La.; pvt. practice The Mack Law Firm, Albany, La., 2000—; mem. Dist. 95 La. House of Reps., 2012—, mem. Adminstrn. of Criminal Justice Com., Judiciary Com. & Transp., Highways, and Pub. Works Com. Republican. Office: District Office PO Box 1450 Livingston LA 70754 E-mail: macks@legis.la.gov.

MACKAY, TRUDY FRANCES CHARLENE, genetics professor; b. Moncton, NB, Can., Sept. 10, 1952; d. Charles Edward Mackay and Jean McGregor Somerville; m. Robert Rene Henri Anholt, July 10, 1990. BSc, Dalhousie U., Halifax, NS, Can., 1974; MSc, Dalhousie U., 1976; PhD, U. Edinburgh, Scotland, 1979. Lectr. U. Edinburgh, 1980—87; assoc. prof. genetics NC State U., Raleigh, 1987—93, prof. genetics, 1993—96, William Neal Reynolds prof. genetics, 1996—, Disting. Univ. prof. genetics, 2006—, assoc. faculty dept. entomology, 2008—. Adj. faculty U. NC, Chapel Hill, 2007—. Recipient medal, Genetics Soc. Am., 2004; fellow AAAS, 2003, Am. Acad. Arts and Scis., 2005, Royal Soc., 2006. Fellow: Am. Acad. Arts and Sciences, AAAS; mem.: NAS, NY Acad. Sciences, Royal Soc. Office: NC State U Dept Genetics Box 7614 Raleigh NC 27695 E-mail: trudy_mackay@ncsu.edu.

MACKEN, JODI, real estate company executive; d. Lillian Macken; 1 child, Alexandra. Grad., Gold Coast Sch. Real Estate, Miami, 1988. Assoc. dir. Macken Realty, Inc., Macken Realty Comml., Macken Realty Signature Properties, Aventura, Fla., 1989—. Named a Power Woman in Real Estate, Miami SunPost, 2004, 2005. Office: Macken Realty Inc 17071 W Dixie Hwy North Miami Beach FL 33160-3773 Office Phone: 305-933-3800. Office Fax: 305-933-3128. Business E-Mail: jmacken@mackenrealty.com.

MACKENZIE, MORI C., retail executive; Regional dir., Stores Ltd., Inc., 1976—87; v.p., Stores Pk. Ln., 1987—91; with Conston Corp., 1991—92; v.p., Stores United Retail Group, 1992—94; v.p., Store Devel. Goody's Family Clothing, 1994; v.p., Store Ops. Canadians Corp., 1995; dir., Stores Chico's FAS, Inc., 1995—99, v.p., Stores, 1999—2001, sr. v.p., Stores, 2001—04, exec. v.p., chief stores officer, 2004—. Office: Chico's FAS Inc 11215 Metro Pky Fort Myers FL 33966 Office Phone: 239-277-6200. Office Fax: 239-274-4018. Business E-Mail: mori.mackenzie@chicos.com.

MACKEY, JOHN P., food products executive; s. Bill and Margaret Mackey; m. Deborah Morin. Student, Trinity Coll., San Antonio, Tex., U. of Texas, Austin. Owner Safer Way Natural Foods, Austin, 1978—80; co-founder, chmn. Whole Foods Market, Inc., Austin, 1978—2009, pres., 2001—04, CEO, 1980—2010, co-CEO, 2010—. Named Overall Nat. Entrepreneur of Yr., Ernst & Young, 2003. Achievements include hiking entire Applachian Trail (2168 miles), 2002. Avocations: yoga, meditation, scuba diving. Office: Whole Foods Market Inc 550 Bowie St Austin TX 78703-4677

MACKEY, STEVEN R., lawyer; b. Enid, Okla., Nov. 10, 1950; s. Emil R. and Ruby M.; children: Jason, Paige. BS in Bus., Okla. State U., 1972; JD, Notre Dame U., 1976. Bar: Okla. 1976, Tex. 1990. Assoc. Fellers, Snider et al, Okla. City, 1976-77, Sneed, Long et al, Tulsa, Okla., 1980-81; assoc. gen. counsel Weeks Petroleum, Westport, Conn., 1981-83; lawyer pvt. practice, Tulsa, 1983-84; regional atty. Kaiser Aluminum, Tulsa, 1984-85; v.p., gen. counsel, sec. Helmerich & Payne, Inc., Tulsa, 1986—. Bd. dirs. Tulsa chpt. Am. Heart Assn., 1996-99. Capt. U.S. Army, 1977-80. Fellow Tulsa County Bar Found. (pres. 2000-01); mem. Tulsa County Bar Assn. (pres. elect 1998-99, pres. 1999—, Pres. award 1992-93, Disting. Pres. award 1993-94, Golden Rule award 1995). Republican. Methodist. Avocations: judo (2d degree black belt), reading, running. Office: Helmerich & Payne Inc 1579 E 21st St Ste 748 Tulsa OK 74114-1336

MACK-HARVIN, DIONNE L., library director; b. SC, June 18, 1972; BA in History and African-Am., SUNY, Brockport; MA in Africana Studies, SUNY, Albany, 1995, MLS in Info. Sci., 1996. Libr. Queens Coll., NY, 1996; libr. Crown Heights Libr. Bklyn. Pub. Libr., NY, 1996, asst. branch libr. NY, branch mgr. NY, regional libr. NY, dir. Ctrl. Libr. NY, chief of staff NY, 2005—06, interim dir. NY, 2006—07, exec. dir. NY, 2007—10; owner DMHarvin Consulting, 2010—11; dir. libraries El Paso Pub. Libr., 2011—. Office: El Paso Pub Library 501 N Oregon El Paso TX 79901 Office Phone: 915-543-5406.

MACKOWIAK, MATTHEW, lobbyist, former legislative staff member; b. Cin., Sept. 13, 1979; BS in Comm. Studies, U. Tex., Austin, 2003. Confidential asst., border & transp. security US Dept. Homeland Security, 2003—04; Linn County mgr. Republican Nat. Com. Victory '04/Iowa GOP, 2004; presdl. advance rep., 2005; press sec. to Senator Conrad Burns US Senate, Washington, 2005—07, press sec. to Senator Kay Bailey Hutchison, 2007—09; assoc. Burson Marsteller, 2007; founder, pres. Potomac Strategy Group, LLC, Washington, 2009—. Mem. Big Brothers/Big Sisters, Washington, 2006—, St. John-Neumann Roman Catholic Ch., 1999—. Recipient Meritorious Svc. award, Dept. Homeland Security, 2004; named Outstanding New Man, Tex. Cowboys, 2001, Frat. Pres. of the Yr., Interfraternity Coun., 2003. Mem.: DC Tex. Execs. (pres.-elect 2006), Tex. State Soc., Heritage Found. Young Pres.'s Club, Capitol Hill Club, Delta Chi. Republican. Roman Catholic. Home: 800 Brazos St Unit 1109 Austin TX 78701-2552 Office Phone: 202-737-2630. Office Fax: 319-856-7380. E-mail: matt@potomacstrategygroup.com.

MACKWELL, STEPHEN JOSEPH, geophysicist, educator; b. Christchurch, New Zealand, June 5, 1956; arrived in U.S., 1984; s. Alan Gordon Mackwell and Mary Veronica (Carter) Francis; m. Kathleen Garland, March 27, 2004. BSc in Physics and Math., U. Canterbury, Christchurch, New Zealand, 1978, MSc in Physics, 1979; diploma of edn., Christchurch Tchrs. Coll., New Zealand, 1979; PhD in Geophysics, Australian Nat. U., Canberra, 1985. Postdoctoral assoc. Cornell U., Ithaca, NY, 1984—86, rsch. fellow, 1984—87; asst. prof. Pa. State U., University Park, 1987—92, assoc. prof., 1992—98; prof. exptl. geophysics Bayerisches Geoinst., Germany, 1998—2000, dir., 2000—02, Lunar and Planetary Inst., Houston, 2002—. Program dir. for geophysics, divsn. of earth sci., NSF, Washington, 1993-94, expert cons., 1995; panelist proposal rev. NASA, Houston, 1994-95; expert rev. Geoscis. Rsch. program, Dept. Energy, 1993; mem. rev. panel Planetary Geology and Geophysics program, NASA, 1994-96, 2002-, group chief, 1996-98, 2004, panel chief, 2005—. Assoc. editor Jour. Geophys. Rsch. - Solid Earth, 1992—97, mem. editl. bd. Physics of the Earth and Planetary Interiors, 1992—98, Tectonophysics, 2002; editor: (Solid Earth) Geophys. Rsch. Letters, 2000—01; editor-in-chief Geophys. Rsch. Letters, 2002—05; contbr. articles to profl. jours. Recipient Stipendiat der Alexander von Humboldt-Stiftung, Bayreuth, Germany, 1996; grantee, NSF, 1988—98, NASA, 1993—98. Fellow: Mineral. Soc. Am.; mem.: AAAS, Am. Geophys. Union (mem. meetings program com. 1988—91, mem. mineral acquisition and distbn. subcom. 1989—90, mem. phys. properties of Earth materials com., tectonophysics section 1989—91, mem. mineral physics com. 1990—92, mem. 75th anniversary com. 1992—94, mem. meetings com. 1992—96, mem. mineral and rock physics com. 2000—03, mineral physics editor for EOS trans. 1990—92, editor-in-chief, frontiers in mineral physics 1988). Office: Lunar & Planetary Inst USRA Ctr Advanced Space Studies 3600 Bay Area Blvd Houston TX 77058 Office Phone: 281-486-2128. Business E-Mail: mackwell@lpi.usra.edu.

MACLEAN, JOHN, professional hockey coach, retired professional hockey player; b. Oshawa, Ont., Canada, Nov. 20, 1964; m. Adrienne MacLean; children: John Carter, Kyle Christopher. Right wing NJ Devils, 1983—97, San Jose Sharks, 1997—98, NY Rangers, 1998—2000, Dallas Stars, 2000—02; asst. coach NJ Devils, 2002—09, head coach, 2010, Lowell Devils, 2009—10; asst. coach Carolina Hurricanes, 2011—. Named to NHL All-Star Game, 1989, 1991. Achievements include being a member of Stanley Cup Champion New Jersey Devils, 1995; holding the New Jersey Devils franchise record for most points with 701, 1997-2009. Office: Carolina Hurricanes Hockey Club RBC Center 1400 Edwards Mill Rd Raleigh NC 27607

MACLEAN, JOHN RONALD, lawyer; b. Pueblo, Colo., Jan. 19, 1938; s. John Ronald and Mary Victoria (Curlin) MacL.; m. Carol Jean Turner, Aug. 18, 1962; children— Leslie Carol, John Ronald. Student, U. Okla., 1956; BS, U.S. Mil. Acad., 1961; JD, Vanderbilt U., 1967. Bar: Tex. 1967; cert. in personal injury trial law Tex. Bd. Legal Splzn. Practicing atty. Turner & MacLean, Cleburne, Tex., 1967-68; county atty. Johnson County, Tex., 1968-76; dist. atty. 18th Jud. Dist. Tex., 1976-84; dist. judge 249th Jud. Dist. Tex., 1984-91; pvt. practice MacLean & Boulware, 1992—. Pres. Johnson County United Fund, 1976 With US Army, 1961—64. Fellow Tex. Bar Found.; mem. Tex. Bar Assn., Johnson County Bar Assn. (pres. 1969), Am. Bd. Trial Advocates (past nat. dir.), Vanderbilt U. Law Sch. Bar Assn. (past pres.), Elks. Democrat. Methodist. Home: 1216 W Westhill Dr Cleburne TX 76033-6021 Office: 11 N Main St Cleburne TX 76033-5543 Office Phone: 817-645-3700.

MACLEOD, DONALD MARTIN, corporate executive; b. NYC, May 21, 1929; s. John and Annie Campbell (Martin) MacL.; m. Beverly Ann Thomson, Feb. 16, 1952 (div. Nov. 18, 1979); children: James Donald, Terry Ann; m. Harriet Elaine Hoff, Feb. 17, 1989 (dec. Mar. 1993). BS in Mech. Engring., Rensselaer Poly. Inst., 1951. Engr. IBM Corp., Endicott & Kingston, N.Y., 1951-54; supr. quality control Ronson Corp., East Stroudsburg, Pa., 1954-55; pres. Manco Specialties, Apalachin, N.Y., 1955-58; engring. supr. Link Aviation, Binghamton, N.Y., 1958-59; sales mgr. Universal Instruments Corp., Binghamton, 1959-61; mktg. mgr. Xerox Corp., Rochester, N.Y., 1961-71; pres. Industry Search Inc., Rochester, 1971-83; gen. mgr. Consler Sci. Design, Inc., Tampa, Fla., 1983-88; pres. Industry Tech, Oldsmar, Fla., 1989—2005, Industry Imports, Inc., Palm Harbor, Fla., 2005—07, Fire Tech., Palm Harbor; ret., 2011. Home: 110 Lesley Ln Oldsmar FL 34677-2090

MAC MAHON, THOMAS P., pharmaceutical executive; b. 1946; BS in Mktg., St. Peter's Coll. NJ, 1968; MBA in Mktg., Fairleigh Dickinson U., 1972. Joined as mktg. rsch. analyst Roche Biomedical Labs., 1969; v.p., pub. affairs and planning Hoffmann-La Roche, Inc., 1982—83, v.p., gen. mgr. diagnostics sys. unit, 1983—86, sr. v.p., 1993—97; pres. Roche Diagnostics Group, 1988—96, mem. exec. com., 1988—96; with HLR (Hoffman-La Roche) Holdings Inc., 1988—95; vice-chmn. Laboratory Corp. of America Holdings, 1995—96, chmn., 1996—2009, pres., CEO, 1997—2006; chmn. Pharmerica Corp., 2007—. Bd. dirs. Roche Diagnostics Group, 1988—96, Lab. Corp. of America Holdings, 2009—, Golden Pond Health Care, Inc., Express Scripts, Inc., 2001—. Named to The Pinnacle (highest award), Fairleigh Dickinson U., 2001. Mem.: Am. Clin. Lab. Assn. (chmn.). Office: PharMerica Corp 1901 Campus Pl Louisville KY 40299 Office Phone: 502-627-7000. Business E-Mail: tmacmahon@pharmerica.com.

MACMANUS, SUSAN ANN, political science professor, researcher; b. Tampa, Fla., Aug. 22, 1947; d. Harold Cameron and Elizabeth (Riegler) MacM. BA cum laude, Fla. State U., 1968, PhD, 1975; MA, U. Mich., 1969. Instr. Valencia C.C., Orlando, Fla., 1969-73; rsch. asst. Fla. State U., 1973-75; asst. prof. U. Houston, 1975-79, assoc. prof., 1979-85, dir. MPA program, 1983-85; rsch. assoc. Ctr. Pub. Policy, 1982-85; prof., dir. PhD progam Cleve. State U., 1985-87; prof. pub. adminstrn. and polit. sci. U. South Fla., Tampa, 1987—, chair dept. govt. and internat. affairs, 1987-93, disting. univ. prof., 1999. Vis. prof. U. Okla., Norman, 1981—; field rsch. assoc. Brookings Inst., Washington, 1977—82, Princeton (N.J.) U., 1979—, Cleve. State U., 1982—83, Westat, Inc., Washington, 1983—; summer field rsch. assoc. Columbia U., NYC, 1979, Nat. Acad. Pub. Adminstrn., Washington, 1980. Author: Revenue Patterns in U.S. Cities and Suburbs: A Comparative Analysis, 1978, Reapportionment and Representation in Florida: A Historical Collection, 1991, Doing Business with Government: Federal, State, Local and Foreign Government Purchasing Practices for Every Business and Public Institution, 1992, Federal Aid to Houston, 1993, Young v. Old: Generational Combat in the 21st Century, 1996, Targeting Senior Voters, 2000; co-author (with others): Governing A Changing America, 1984; co-author: (with Francis T. Borkowski) Visions for the Future: Creating New Institutional Relationships Among Academia, Business, Government, and Community, 1989; co-author: (with Elizabeth R. MacManus) Citrus, Sawmills, Critters & Crackers: Life in Early Lutz and Central Pasco County, 1998, The Lutz Depot, 2000; editor: Mapping Florida's Political Landscape: The Changing Art and Politics of Reapportionment and Redistricting, 2002; co-editor (with Thomas R. Dye): Politics in States and Communities, 11th edit., 2003; co-editor: (with Dano Moreno and Kevin Hill) Florida's Politics: Ten Media Markets, One Powerful State, 2004; writer: manuals in field, mem. editl. bd.: various jours; contbr. articles to profl. jours., chapters to books. Bd. dirs. Houston Area Women's Ctr., 1977, past pres., v.p. fin., treas.; mem. LWV, Gov.'s Coun. Econ. Advisers, 1988-90, Harris County (Tex.) Women's Polit. Caucus, Houston; bd. dirs. USF Rsch. Found., Inc.; chair Fla. Elections Commn., 1999-2003; mem. Fla. Gov.'s Coun. Econ. Advisers, 2000—. Recipient U. Houston Coll. Social Scis. Tchg. Excellence award, 1977, Herbert J. Simon award for best article in 3d vol., Internat. Jour. Pub. Adminstrn., 1981, Theodore & Venette Askounes-Ashford Disting Scholar award U. South Fla., 1991, Disting. Rsch. Scholar award, 1991, Tchg. Excellence award, 1999; Ford Found. fellow, 1967-68; grantee Valencia C. C. Faculty, 1972, U. Houston, 1976-77, 79, 83; Fulbright Rsch. scholar, Korea, 1989; Choice mag. award, 1996; named Disting. Univ. Prof., 1999; rsch. fellow Fla. Inst. of Govt., 2000—. Mem. Am. Polit. Sci. Assn. (program com. 1983-84, chair sect. intergovtl. rels., award 1989, mem. exec. coun. 1994—, pres.-elect sec. urban politics 1994-95, pres. sect. urban politics 1995-96), So. Polit. Sci. Assn. (v.p. 1990-91, pres.-elect 1992-93, pres. 1993-94, V.O. key award com. 1983-84, best paper on women and politics 1988, Diane Blair award 2001), Midwest Polit. Sci. Assn., Western Polit. Sci. Assn., Southwestern Polit. Sci. Assn. (local arrangements com. 1982-83, profession com. 1977-80), ASPA (nominating com. Houston chpt. 1983, bd. mem. Suncoast chpt., pres.-elect 1991, Lilly award 1992), Policy Studies Orgn. (mem. editl. bd. jour. 1981—, exec. coun. 1983-85), Women's Caucus Polit. Sci. (portfolio pre-decision rev. com. 1982-83, projects and programs com. 1981, fin.-budget com. 1980-81), Fla. Polit. Sci. Assn. (pres. 1997-98, Manning Dauer Disting. Fla. Polit. Sci. award 2001), Acad. Polit. Sci., Mcpl. Fin. Officers Assn., Phi Kappa Phi (Artist/Scholar award U. South Fla. 1997), Phi Beta Kappa, Pi Sigma Alpha (mem. exec. coun. 1994-96, pres. 2000-02), Pi Alpha Alpha.(hon., leader, Fla., 2010 Methodist. Home: 2506 Collier Pky Land O Lakes FL 34639-5228 Office: U South Fla Dept Polit Sci Tampa FL 33620 E-mail: samacmanus@aol.com.

MAC NAUGHTON, DUNCAN, retail executive; b. 1962; BA in Economics, U. Wis. Various positions in sales mgmt. & planning, sales strategy, brand & product devel., trade planning and strategic food mktg. & bus. planning Kraft Foods, Inc., 1985—98; group v.p. grocery merchandising and own brand HE Butt Grocery Co., 1998—2003, group v.p. merchandising, 2003—04; sr. v.p. merchandising Albertson's, Inc., 2004—05, exec. v.p. merchandising and mktg., 2005—06, Supervalu, Inc., 2006—09; chief merchandising officer Wal-Mart Can., 2009—10; exec. v.p. merchandising Wal-mart Stores USA, 2010—11, chief merchandising officer, 2011—. Dir. Nat. Assn. Chain Drug Stores. Bd. dirs. Big Brothers and Big Sisters SW Idaho. Office: Walmart 702 SW 8th St Bentonville AR 72716-8611

MACOMBER, DEBBIE, writer; b. Yakima, Wash., Oct. 22, 1948; m. Wayne Macomber; 4 children. Author: (novels) Starlight, 1983, Girl Like Janet, 1984, Undercover Dreamer, 1984, Thanksgiving Prayer, 1984, That Wintry Feeling, 1984, Gift of Christmas, 1984, Heartsong, 1984, Borrowed Dreams: Alaska, 1985, Love Thy Neighbor, 1985, Adam's Image, 1985, Promise Me Forever, 1985, Laughter in the Rain, 1985, The Trouble with Caasi, 1985, A Friend or Two, 1985, Christmas Masquerade, 1985, Let It Snow, 1986, The Matchmakers, 1986, Reflections of Yesterday, 1986, Shadow Chasing, 1986, Yesterday's Hero, 1986, White Lace and Promises, 1986, Jury of His Peers, 1986, Yesterday Once More, 1986, Friends and Then Some, 1986, All Things Considered, 1987, Love by Degree, 1987, Sugar and Spice, 1987, Mail-Order Bride, 1987, No Competition, 1987, Love 'N' Marriage, 1987, Husband Required, 1987, Any Sunday, 1988, The Playboy and the Widow, 1988, Denim and Diamonds, 1989, Yours and Mine, 1989, Almost an Angel, 1989, For All My Tomorrows, 1989, Country Bride, 1990, Fallen Angel, 1990, A Little Bit Country, 1990, Rainy Day Kisses, 1990, The Courtship of Carol Sommars, 1990, First Comes Marriage, 1991, Here Comes Trouble, 1991, Stolen Kisses, 1991, Father's Day, 1991, The Forgetful Bride, 1991, My Hero, 1992, The Man You'll Marry, 1992, Lone Star Lovin', 1993, Ready for Romance, 1993, Morning Comes Softly, 1993 (Waldenbooks Best-selling Non-Series Debut Romance, Colo. Romance Writers Keeper award, 1996), One Night, 1994, This Matter of Marriage, 1997, Three Brides, No Groom, 1997, Montana, 1998, Can This Be Christmas?, 1998, Thursdays at Eight, 2001 (Named one Amazon.com's Top 10 Women's Fiction titles, 2001), Between Friends, 2002, The Christmas Basket, 2002 (Romance Writers of America RITA award), Changing Habits, 2003, The Snow Bride, 2003, When Christmas Comes, 2004, There's Something About Christmas, 2005, The Perfect Christmas, 2009;: (novels) Hannah's List, 2010, Call Me Mrs. Miracle, 2010, Learning to Love, 2011, Trading Christmas, 2011, Glad Tidings, 2012, Starry Night, 2013, (Legendary Lovers series) Cindy and the Prince, 1987, Some Kind of Wonderful, 1988, Almost Paradise, 1988, (Navy series) Navy Wife, 1988, Navy Blues, 1989, Navy Brat, 1991, Navy Woman, 1991, Navy Baby, 1991, Navy Husband, 2005, (The Manning Sisters) The Cowboy's Lady, 1990, The Sheriff Takes a Wife, 1990, (Those Manning Men) Marriage of Inconvenience, 1992, Stand-In Wife, 1992, Bride on the Loose, 1992, (Orchard Valley series) Valerie, 1992, Stephanie, 1992, Norah, 1993, (From This Day Forward series) Groom Wanted, 1993, Bride Wanted, 1993, Marriage Wanted, 1993, (Midnight Sons series) Marriage Risk, 1995, Brides for Brothers, 1995, Daddy's Little Helper, 1995, Because of the Baby, 1996, Falling For Him, 1996, Ending In Marriage, 1996, (Rose Harbor Series) The Inn at Rose Harbor, 2012, Rose Harbor in Bloom, 2013, Lost and Found in Cedar Grove, 2013, (Blossom Street series) The Shop on Blossom Street, 2004, A Good Yarn, 2005, Susannah's Garde, 2006, Back on Bloom Street, 2007, Twenty Wishes, 2007, Summer on Blossom Street, 2009;: (novels) Hannah's List, 2010, A Turn in the Road, 2011, Starting Now, 2013, Blossom Street Brides, 2014, (Cedar Cove Series) 16 Lighthouse Road, 2001, 204 Rosewood Lane, 2002, 311 Pelican Court, 2003, 44 Cranberry Point, 2004 (Quill award for romance, 2005), 50 Harbor Street, 2005, 6 Rainier Drive, 2006, 74 Seaside Avenue, 2007 (#1 NY Times bestseller), 8 Sandpiper Way, 2008 (#1 Publishers Weekly bestseller), A Cedar Cove Christmas, 2008, (Cedar Cove series) 92 Pacific Boulevard, 2009, 1022 Evergreen Place, 2010, 1105 Yakima Street, 2011, 1225 Christmas Tree Lane, 2011, (Dakota series) Dakota Born, 2000, Dakota Home, 2000, Always Dakota, 2001, Buffalo Valley, 2001, (Heart of Texas series) Lonesome Cowboy, 1998, Texas Two-Step, 1998, Caroline's Child, 1998, Dr. Texas, 1998, Nell's Cowboy, 1998, Lone Star Baby, 1998, Promise, Texas, 1999, Return to Promise, 2000, (Deliverance Company series) Someday Soon, 1995, Sooner or Later, 1996, Moon Over Water (The Sooner the Better-Reissued/Retitled), 1999, (Angelic Intervention series) A Season of Angels, 1993, The Trouble With Angels, 1994 (Waldenbooks Trend Book award), Touched by Angels, 1995, Mrs. Miracle, 1996, Shirley, Goodness & Mercy, 1999, Those Christmas Angels, 2003, Where Angels Go, 2007, Angels at the Table, 2012, numerous stories in anthologies and novellas, (nonfiction) Knit Along with Debbie Macomber, 2005, Knit Together, 2007, The Knitting Diaries, 2011, (cookbook) Debbie Macomber's Christmas Cookbook, 2011, (Inspirational) Once Upon a Time: Discovering Our Forever After Story, 2013. Recipient Regional Svc. award, Romance Writers America, 1989, Nora Roberts Lifetime Achievement award, 2010, Career Achievement award, Romantic Times, 1993, Woman of Distinction award, Soroptimist Internat., 1997; named a Tenn. Colonel for Humanitarian Svc., Gov. State of Tenn., 1994, Favorite Top 10 Author, Affaire de Coeur Mag., 1995. Avocation: knitting. Mailing: c/o Nancy Berland Pub Rels Inc 2816 NW 57th St Ste 101 Oklahoma City OK 73132*

MACRIS, JACK ACHILLES, surgeon; b. Highland Park, Mich., Nov. 3, 1924; MD, U. Mich., 1950. Diplomate Am. Bd. Surgery. Intern Grace Hosp., Detroit, 1950-51; resident in surgery U. Mich. Hosp., 1951-52, 1952-55, fellowship in surgery, 1955; hosp. staff mem. St. Anthonys Hosp., St. Petersburg, Fla. Fellow ACS (past pres. Fla. chpt.); mem. Fla. Med. Assn. (past pres.), Frederick A. Coller Surg. Soc. (past pres.), Fla. Surg. Soc. (past pres.). Home: # 822 555 5th Ave NE Saint Petersburg FL 33701

MADDEN, DAVID, author; b. Knoxville, Tenn., July 25, 1933; s. James Helvy and Emile (Merritt) M.; m. Roberta Margaret Young, Sept. 6, 1956; 1 son, Blake Dana. BS, U. Tenn., 1957; MA, San Francisco State Coll., 1958; postgrad., Yale Drama Sch., 1959-60. Faculty Appalachian State Tchrs. Coll., Boone, NC, 1957-58, Centre Coll., Danville, Ky., 1960-62, U. Louisville, 1962-64, Kenyon Coll., Gambier, O., 1964-66, Ohio U., Athens, 1966-68; writer-in-residence La. State U., Baton Rouge, 1968-92, dir. creative writing program, 1992-94, dir. U.S. Civil War Ctr., 1992-99, Robert Penn Warren prof. creative writing, 2007—09, emeritus prof., 2009—. Alumni prof. La. State U., 1994. Author: (novels) Cassandra Singing, 1969, Bijou, 1974, The Suicide's Wife, 1978, Pleasure Dome, 1979, On the Big Wind, 1980, Sharpshooter: A Novel of the Civil War, 1996, Abucted By Circumstance, 2010, (stories) The Shadow Knows (Nat. Coun. on Arts selection), 1970, The New Orleans of Possibilities (lit. criticism) Wright Morris, 1964, Poetic Image in Six Genres, 1969, James M. Cain, 1970, A Primer of the Novel, 1980, Writers' Revisions, 1981, Cain's Craft, 1985, Revising Fiction, 1988, Rediscoveries II, 1988; asst. editor: The Kenyon Rev., 1964-66; editor: Remembering James Agee, 1974; co-editor: (with P. Bach) Classics of Civil War Fiction, 1991, Beyond the Battlefield, 2000, The Legacy of Robert Penn Warren, 2000, Thomas Wolfe's Civil War, 2004, Losses of the Sultana, 2004, Touching the Web of Southern Novelists, 2006, Primer of the Novel, 2006. Served with AUS, 1953-55. Recipient Rockefeller grant in fiction, 1969; John Golden fellow in playwriting, 1959; recipient Robert Penn Warren award for excellence in fiction. Mem. Authors League, Associated Writing Programs (bd. dirs.). Democrat. Home Phone: 828-669-2757. Personal E-mail: david@davidmadden.net.

MADDEN, DOUGLAS M., chemicals executive; b. Chgo., Ill. BSBA, U. Ill. Operational and distrbn. mgmt. Johnson & Johnson, Warner-Lambert; mgr., corp. distrbn. American Hoechst Corp., 1984; pres. Acetate, 2006—09, AT Plastics Inc. (now Celanese Corp.), 2006—09, The Emulsions & PVOH, 2006—09, Celanese Acetate Ltd., 2003—06; v.p., fin., global procurement, and bus. support, Hoechst Celanese Life Sciences Group Celanese Corp., v.p., fin., global procurement, and bus. support, Celanese Fibers and Celanese Chemicals businesses, v.p., gen. mgr., acrylates bus., head, global supply chain, Celanese Chemicals, 2000—03, exec. v.p., 2006—, COO, 2009—. Office: Celanese Corp 1601 W LBJ Freeway Dallas TX 75234 Office Phone: 972-443-4000. Office Fax: 972-443-8555. Business E-Mail: Douglas.Madden@celanese.com.

MADDEN, JERRY AGNEW, state legislator; b. Council Bluffs, Iowa, Feb. 20, 1943; s. Jerry Agnew and Lucille Swanson Madden; m. Barbara Diane Szumachowski, 1965; children: Jerry Anthony, Stephanie Ann, Kristina Allison. BS in Engring., US Mil. Acad., West Point, NY; MS in Mgmt. and Adminstrn. Sciences, U. Tex., Dallas, 1979. Engr. Tex. Instruments, Dallas, 1971—82; chmn. precinct 48 Richardson Rep. Com., 1974—84; pres. Collin County Sch. Bd., 1974—77; mem. Collin County Hosp. Bd., 1980—82, pres., 1982—83; prodn. mgr. Teledyne Geotech., Garland, Tex., 1982—85, mfg. mgr., 1985—91; bus. owner, 1991—94; chmn. Collins County Rep. Com., 1984—; mem. Dist. 67 Tex. House of Representatives, 1992—; founder, ret. ins. acctg. exec. Jerry Madden Ins., 2000—08. Mem.: Soc. Mfg. Engrs., Am. Legion, Collin County Rep. Club. Republican. Protestant. Office: PO Box 940844 Plano TX 75074 also: Room CAP GW.11 Capitol PO Box 2910 Austin TX 78768 Home Phone: 512-463-0544; Office Phone: 972-424-2235.

MADDEN, WALES HENDRIX, JR., retired lawyer; b. Amarillo, Tex., Sept. 1, 1927; s. Wales Hendrix and Kathryn (Nash) Madden; m. Alma Faye Cowden, Nov. 8, 1952; children: Wales Hendrix III, Straughn. BA, U. Tex., 1950, LLB, 1952. Bar: Tex. 1952. Pvt. practice, Amarillo. Mem. Tex. Constl. Revision Commn., 1973. Mem. Tex. Coll. and Univ. Sys. Coord. Bd., 1964—69, Amarillo Area Found., Cal Farley's Boys Ranch, Pres.'s Export Coun., 1981, Select Com. Higher Edn., 1985, 1987; chmn. SWST regional panel Pres.'s Commn. White Ho. Fellowships, 1989—90; chmn. Tex. Water Devel. Bd., 2002; mem. Gov.'s Com. Ad Valorem Taxes, 1996; bd. regents Amarillo Coll., 1958—59, U. Tex., 1959—65; trustee Trinity U., San Antonio; chmn. bd. Internat. Food and Agrl. Devel., 1990—94. USNR, 1945—46, Pacific. Named Outstanding Man of Amarillo, 1972, Disting. Alumnus, U. Tex., 1979, U. Tex. Law Sch., 1986. Mem.: ABA, State Jr. Bar Tex. (pres. 1956), State Bar Tex. (Outstanding 50 Year Lawyer award 2003), Amarillo Bar Assn. (pres. 1956), Friar Soc., Amarillo C. of C. (pres. 1968), Tex. Philos. Soc., Sigma Alpha, Phi Eta Sigma, Phi Delta Theta, Phi Alpha Delta. Presbyterian. Avocations: mountain climbing, hiking. Home and Office: PO Box 15288 Amarillo TX 79105-5288

MADDIN, ROBERT, metallurgist, educator; b. Hartford, Conn., Oct. 20, 1918; s. Isadore I. and Mae (Jacobs) Levine; married, July 8, 1945; children: Leslie, Jill. BS in Metall. Engring., Purdue U., 1942; DEng., Yale U., 1948. Registered profl. engr., Pa. Asst., assoc. prof. Johns Hopkins U., Balt., 1949-55; prof. U. Pa., phila., 1955-73, univ. prof., 1973-83; vis. prof. Harvard U., Cambridge, Mass., 1983-87, curator, 1987—; vis. prof. Oxford (Eng.) U., 1970, vis. fellow Wolfson Coll., 1987. Vis. prof. U. Birmingham, Eng., 1953-54; vis. scholar Hebrew U., Jerusalem, 1976; hon. prof. Beijing Sci. and Engring. U., 1986; hon. mem. Japan Metals, hon. prof. Dali U., 2006. Editor-in-chief Met., Sci., and Engring, 1965-82; contbr. more than 150 publs. to profl. jours. 1st Lt. USAF, 1942-45. Disting. Sr. Sci. fellow A. von Humboldt Found., Germany, 1989-90, Disting. Alumnus Purdue U., 1974; recipient Pomerance award Archaeol. Inst. Am., 1994, medal of merit U. Pa., Merit medal, DBM, 2008. Fellow Am. Soc. Metals, TMS. Avocation: history early metallurgy. Personal E-mail: bobmaddin@gmail.com.

MADDON, JOE (JOSEPH JOHN MADDON), professional baseball manager; b. Hazleton, Pa., Sept. 19, 1954; m. Jaye Sousoures, Nov. 8, 2008; children from previous marriage: Sarah, Joey. BS in Economics, Lafayette Coll., Easton, Pa., 1976; LittD (hon.), Lafayette Coll., 2010. Mgr. Idaho Falls Minor League Baseball, 1981, Salem Minor League Baseball, Peoria Minor League Baseball, Midland Minor League Baseball, 1985—86; coord. Calif. Angels Arizona Instrnl. League, 1984—93; roving hitting instructor Calif. Angels, 1987—93, dir. player develop., 1994, bullpen coach, 1994, first base coach, 1995, bench coach, 1996, interim mgr., 1996, 1999, bench coach, 2000—05; mgr. Tampa Bay Devil Rays, 2005—. Named American League Mgr. of Yr., The Sporting News, 2008, Baseball Writers' Assn. America, 2008, 2011. Office: Tampa Bay Devil Rays One Tropicana Dr Saint Petersburg FL 33705

MADDOX, ALVA HUGH, retired state supreme court justice; b. Andalusia, Ala., Apr. 17, 1930; s. Christopher Columbus and Audie Lodella Maddox; m. Virginia Roberts, June 14, 1958; children: Robert Hugh, Jane Maddox, Hoesel. AB in Journalism, U. Ala., Tuscaloosa, 1952, JD, 1957. Bar: Ala. 1957. Law clk. to Judge Aubrey Cates, Ala. Ct. Appeals, Montgomery, 1957-58; field examiner Chief Atty.'s Office, VA, Montgomery, 1958-59; law clk. to Judge Frank M. Johnson, U.S. Dist. Ct., Montgomery, 1959-61; pvt. practice Montgomery, 1961-65; cir. judge, spl. cir. judge Montgomery Cir. Ct., 1963, asst. dist. atty., 1964; legal advisor to govs. including George C. Wallace, Lurleen B. Wallace, Albert P. Brewer, State of Ala., Montgomery, 1965-69; assoc. justice Supreme Ct. Ala., Montgomery, 1969-2001; ret., 2001. Author: Billy Boll Weevil: A Pest Becomes A Hero, 1976, Alabama Rules of Criminal Procedure, 1991, supplements, 1992—. Founder youth jud. program YMCA, Montgomery, 1978, also mem. metro. bd. dir. 2d lt. USAF, 1952-54, col. USAF Res. ret. Recipient Man of Yr. award YMCA, 1988, Disting. Program Svc. award, 1989, Srs. of Achievement award Montgomery Coun. on Aging, 1999, Sherman Christensen award Am. Inns Ct., 2008. Mem.: ABA, Am. Inns of Ct. (former trustee), Hugh Maddox Inn of Ct. Montgomery (charter, founding mem.), Christian Legal Soc., Inst. Jud. Adminstrn., Ala. Bar Assn. (Jud. award of merit 1997), Order of Samaritan/U. Ala. Law Sch., Kiwanis. Baptist. Office: 3137 Hathaway Pl Montgomery AL 36111-1707 Home Phone: 334-264-8732; Office Phone: 334-264-0505.

MADDOX, BILLY, state legislator; b. Apr. 26; m. Meredith Moody; 1 child, Jake. Attended, Gordon Coll., U. Ga.; JD, John Marshall Law Sch. Atty.; mem. Dist. #127 Ga. House of Reps., Ga., 2008—. Republican. Bapt. Office: Capitol Office 504 Coverdell Legislative Office Bldg Atlanta GA 30334 also: District Office 440 Whitfield Walk Zebulon GA 30295 Office Phone: 404-656-0109. E-mail: billy.maddox@house.ga.gov.

MADDOX, SCOTT E., gas industry executive; 2 children. BBA, U. Houston. Mgr., info. sys. Apache Corp.; v.p., trading, sys., N.Am. Duke Energy; various mgmt. positions Panhandle Energy; v.p., info. sys., tech. Sequent Energy Management, LP, 2003—. Sec., treas. Houston Ear Rsch. Found., 1996-. Office: Sequent Energy Management LP Two Allen Ctr 1200 Smith St Houston TX 77002 Office Phone: 832-397-1700. Office Fax: 832-397-1722. Business E-Mail: smaddox@sequentenergy.com.

MADDOX, TONY, broadcast executive; Various positions including reporter, news prodr. and news editor BBC, editor news and current affairs South West Eng. Plymouth, head news and current affairs Belfast, Northern Ireland; mng. editor Europe, Mid. East and Africa CNN Internat., 1998—2000, v.p., 2000, sr. v.p. Europe, Mid. East and Africa London, sr. v.p. internat. newsgathering Atlanta, 2003—07, exec. v.p., mng. dir., 2007—. Office: CNN Internat One CNN Ctr Atlanta GA 30348*

MADDOX, VICTOR B., lawyer; b. Louisville, 1956; BBA summa cum laude, Ohio U., Athens, 1978; JD cum laude, Ind. U., Bloomington, 1981. Bar: Ky. 1981, US Dist. Ct. (ea., we. dists.) Ky., US Dist. Ct. (so. dist.) Ind., US Ct. Appeals (6th, 9th, fed. cirs.), US Ct. Fed. Claims, US Supreme Ct. Assoc. Ind. Law Jour., 1979—80, Brown, Todd & Heyburn, 1981—84, 1987, ptnr., 1988—95; trial atty., comml. litig. br. US Dept. Justice, 1984—85; counsel to the com. on the jud. and legis. aide to Mitch McConnell US Senate, Washington, 1985—86; founding ptnr. Fultz Maddox Hovious & Dickens PLC, Louisville, 1995—. Bd. dirs. Legal Services Corp., Washington, 2010—. Apptd. mem. Ky. Registry Election Fin., 1994. Avocation: bicycling. Office: Fultz Maddox Hovious & Dickens PLC 2700 National City Tower Louisville KY 40202-3116 Office Phone: 502-588-2025. Office Fax: 502-588-2020. Business E-Mail: vmaddox@fmhd.com.

MADDREY, WILLIS CROCKER, medical educator, internist, academic administrator, consultant, researcher; b. Roanoke Rapids, NC, Mar. 29, 1939; s. Milner Crocker and Sara Jean (Willis) M.; m. Ann Marie Matt; children: Jeffrey, Gregory, Thomas. BS, Wake Forest U., 1960; MD, Johns Hopkins U., 1964. Diplomate: Am. Bd. Internal Medicine. Intern Osler Med. Service Johns Hopkins Hosp., Balt., 1964-65, asst. resident, 1965-66, 68-69, chief resident, 1969-70; fellow in liver disease Yale U., 1970-71; asst. prof. medicine Johns Hopkins U., Balt., 1971-75, assoc. prof., 1975-79, prof., 1980—82, asst. dean Sch. Medicine, 1975-79, assoc. dir. dept. medicine, 1979-82; prof., chmn. dept. medicine Jefferson Med. Coll., Phila., 1982-90; v.p. clin. affairs U. Tex. Southwestern Med. Ctr., Dallas, 1990-93, exec. v.p. clin. affairs, 1993—2010, pres. asst., 2010—. Assoc. editor: Medicine, 1972-82, Hepatology, 1988-95, mem. editl. bd., 1981-84, 86-87, Gastroenterology, 1982-87, Am. Jour. Medicine, 1978-88; contbr. articles to profl. jours. Bd. dirs. Am. Liver Found., 1978-81, Dallas County Med. Soc., 1996-98; trustee Magee Rehab. Hosp., Phila., 1982-87. With USPHS, 1966-68. Mem. ACP (bd. regents 1986-92, pres. 92-93), Am. Soc. Clin. Investigation, Am. Gastroenterol. Assn., Am. Assn. Study Liver Disease (pres. 1981). Republican. Office: U Tex Southwestern Med Ctr 5323 Harry Hines Blvd Dallas TX 75390-8570 Office Phone: 214-648-2024.

MADDUX, GREG (GREGORY ALAN MADDUX), professional sports team executive, retired professional baseball player; b. San Angelo, Tex., Apr. 14, 1966; m. Kathy Maddux; children: Amanda Paige, Chase Alan. Grad., H.S., Las Vegas. Pitcher Chgo. Cubs, 1986—92, 2004—06, asst. to the gen. mgr., 2010—11; pitcher Atlanta Braves, 1993—2003, LA Dodgers, 2006, 2008, San Diego Padres, 2007—08; ret. Maj. League Baseball, 2008; spl. asst. to the gen. mgr. Tex. Rangers, 2012—. Co-founder Maddux Found., 1993—. Recipient Gold Glove award, 1990—2002, 2004—08, Cy Young award, Baseball Writers' Assn. America, 1992—95, William J. Slocum award, Baseball Writers' Assn. America, NY Chpt., 2009; named Nat. League Pitcher of Yr., The Sporting News, 1992—95, Nat. League Outstanding Pitcher, Maj. League Baseball Players Assn., 1994, 1995, 1998; named to Nat. League All-Star Team, Maj. League Baseball, 1988, 1992, 1994—98, 2000, All-Time Rawlings Gold Glove Team, 2007. Achievements include leading the National League in: starts, 1990-93, 2000, 03, 05; innings, 1991-95; wins, 1992, 94, 95; ERA, 1993-95, 98; complete games, 1993-95; shutouts, 1994, 95, 98, 2000, 01; being the first pitcher in Major League Baseball history to win the Cy Young award for four consecutive years, 1992-95; being a member of the World Series Championship winning Atlanta Braves, 1995; becoming 13th pitcher in MLB history to throw 3,000 strikeouts, 2005; holding the all-time record for Gold Glove awards with 18. Office: Texas Rangers 1000 Ballpark Way Arlington TX 76011

MADEWELL, JOHN EDWARD, radiologist; Student, Ctrl. State Coll., Oklahoma City, 1960-69; MD, U. Okla., 1969. Intern Madigen Gen. Hosp., Tacoma, 1969-70; resident in diagnostic radiology Walter Reed Med. Ctr., Washington, 1970-73; fellow in radiol. pathology Armed Forces Inst. Pathology, Washington, 1973-74; radiologist Pa. State Geisinger Health Sys.; prof., chmn. dept. radiology Milton S. Hershey Med. Ctr./Pa. State U., 1987—2000; exec. dir. Univ. Physicians/Pa. State U., Hershey, 1996-97, MDACC, 2000—. Mem. Am. Coll. Radiology, Am. Roentgen Ray Soc., Assn. Univ. Radiologists, Internat. Skeletal Soc., Radiologic Soc. N.Am.

MADHAVAN, SUNDARESWARAN SURESH, pharmacy educator; b. Kalyan, India, Apr. 4, 1959; MBA, Symbiosis Inst. Mgmt., 1982; PhD, Purdue U., 1988. Prof., chair, pharm. sys. and policy W.Va. U. Sch. Pharmacy, 1988—; co-dir. WV IDeA-CTR Grant. Prin. investigator and dir. WV Collaborative Health Outcomes Rsch. Therapies and Svcs. Ctr., 2006; editl. bd. mem. Jour. Am. Pharmacists Assn. Recipient Nat. award, Coun. State Govt., award, W.Va. U. Health Scis. Ctr., Acad. Excellence Tchg. and Learning, Excellence Rsch. award, W.Va. U. Sch. Pharmacy Bd. Advisors; grant, Agy. Healthcare Rsch. and Quality, W.Va. CoHORTS Ctr., NIH. Fellow: Am. Assn. Colls. Pharmacy, Am. Pharmacists Assn.; mem.: Acad. Pharm. Rsch. and Scis., Agy. Healthcare Rsch. and Quality (HCQER study sect. mem.), Internat. Soc. Pharmacoeconomics and Outcomes Rsch. Achievements include research in health services research and health policy, with particular emphasis on improving access to and quality of health and preventive care services. Avocations: woodworking, travel, reading, sports. Office: 1129 HSCN Medical Center Dr Morgantown WV 26506-9510 Office Phone: 304-293-1652. Office Fax: 304-293-2529. Business E-Mail: smadhavan@hsc.wvu.edu.*

MADIGAN, JOSEPH EDWARD, financial executive, director, consultant; b. Bklyn., June 26, 1932; s. James Peter and Mary (Goldman) M.; m. Catherine Cashman, July 26, 1980; children: Kerri Ann, Kimberly Ann Madigan, Elizabeth Ann Laginess. BBA cum laude, Baruch Coll., CUNY, 1958; MBA, NYU, 1963. Adminstrv. asst. Assoc. Metals & Minerals Corp., 1961-63; fin. analyst, fgn. exch. trader, corp. portfolio trader AMAX, Inc., 1963—65; mgr. corp. portfolio, dir. cash mgmt., asst. treas. TWA, Inc., 1965-68; treas. Borden, Inc., 1968-76, v.p., treas., 1976-80; exec. v.p., chief fin. officer, dir. Wendy's Internat., Inc., Dublin, Ohio, 1980-87; mem. IATA Cuurrency Sub Com., IATA India Working Group. Gen. ptnr. Horton Emergency Vehicles Co., 1987—98; pres. Madigan Assocs., 1987—99. Chmn. bd. Lexford Residential Properties, 1997-99. Yeoman 1st Class USN, 1951—55. Mem.: Fin. Execs. Internat., Baruch Coll. CUNY Alumni Assn. (Alumnus of Yr. award), NYU Alumni Assn., Imperial Golf Club, Allendale Country Club, Beta Gamma Sigma. Republican. Roman Catholic. Home and Office: 5555 Heron Point Dr Unit 2102 Naples FL 34108

MADISON, SUE WOOD, state legislator; b. Okinawa, Japan, Feb. 10, 1948; m to Bernard L Madison; children: Blair & Eva. BA, La. State Univ., 1970, MS, 1977. Real estate investor, property mgr. Madison Rental Property, 1980—; Justice of the Peace Washington County Quorum Ct., Ark., 1990—94, Dist. 9, Ark., 1994; mem. Dist. 8 Ark. House of Reps., 1995—2000; mem. Dist. 7 Ark. State Senate, 2003—. Mem. Fayetteville Planning Commn., 1984—88, Fayetteville C. of C., 1994—2002; bd. mem. Terra Genesis Housing. Mem. Friends of Fayetteville Pub. Lib., Friends for Fayetteville; v.p. Nat. Conf. for Cmty. & Justice, 1997—99. Mem.: Am. Assn. Univ. Women (v.p.), League of Women Voters, Washington County Master Gardeners, Fayetteville Garden Club. Democrat. Presbyn. Office: 573 Rock Cliff Rd Fayetteville AR 72701 Office Phone: 479-442-2997. Business E-Mail: madisons@arkleg.state.ar.us.

MADISON, THOMAS F., investment company executive; b. Mpls., Feb. 25, 1936; s. Earl E. and Bernice E. (O'Brien) M.; m. Marilyn L. Johnson, June 22, 1956; children— Mike T., Mary A., Mark R. BS, U. Minn., 1959. Joined Northwestern Bell Tel. Co., 1954, bd. dirs., exec. v.p., 1983-85, pres., CEO, 1985; joined US West Comm., 1987, exec. v.p., pres.; vice chmn. Minn. Mut. Life Ins. Co., 1992—94; pres., CEO MLM Ptnrs., Mpls., 1993—; chmn. Communication Holdings, Inc., 1994—99. Bd. dirs. First Bank Sys., Valmont Industries, Inc., 1987—2010, Del. Group of Funds, 1993—, Digital River, Inc., 1996—, Rimage Corp., 2001—, CenterPoint Energy, Inc., 2003—. Bd. dirs. Creighton U., Omaha, Guthrie Theater, Mpls., Minn. Orch., Mpls., Coll. St. Thomas, Mpls. Served with USNG, 1953-54 Mem.: Omaha, Omaha Country; Minikahda, Minn. Alumni, Mpls. Athletic (Mpls.). Roman Catholic. Avocations: golfing; hunting; skiing; fishing. Home: 134 S 122nd St Omaha NE 68154-2243 Office: MLM Partners 2212 Shenandoah Ave Charlotte NC 28205-6024 also: CenterPoint Energy Bd Directors 1111 Louisiana St Houston TX 77002 Office Phone: 704-358-9593. Business E-Mail: thomas.madison@centerpointenergy.com.

MADORE, MARSHA M., wholesale distribution executive; BA in English, Furman U., Greenville, SC; MEd, U. SC. Cert. sr. profl. human resources. With TV station, Greenville; dir. anti-litter campaign Hawaii; mgr. tng. Greenville Tech; mgr. tech. tng. Lockheed Martin, Greenville; v.p. human resources ScanSource, Inc., 2006—. Mem. Nat. Assn. of Wholesaler Distbrs. Office: ScanSource Inc 6 Logue Ct Greenville SC 29615 Office Phone: 864-288-2432. Office Fax: 864-288-1165.

MADORY, JAMES RICHARD, hospital administrator, retired military officer; b. Staten Island, NY, June 11, 1940; s. Eugene and Agnes (Gerner) M.; m. Karen James Clifford, Sept. 26, 1964; children: James E., Lynn Anne, Scott J., Elizabeth Anne, Joseph M. (dec.). BS, Syracuse U., 1964; MHA, Med. Coll. Va., 1971. Enlisted USAF, 1958; x-ray technician Keesler Area Med. Ctr., Biloxi, Miss., 1959-62; commd. 2d lt. USAF, 1964, advanced through grades to maj., 1979—; x-ray technician Keesler Area Med. Ctr., Biloxi, Miss., 1959-62; adminstr. Charleston (S.C.) Clinic, 1971-74, Beale Hosp., Calif., 1974-77; assoc. adminstr. Shaw Regional Hosp., S.C., 1977-79; ret. USAF, 1979; asst. adminstr. Raleigh Gen. Hosp., Beckley, W.Va., 1979-81; adminstr., dir., sec. bd. Chesterfield Gen. Hosp., Cheraw, S.C., 1981-87; pres., CEO Grand Strand Hosp., Myrtle Beach, S.C., 1987-95, trustee, 1987-95; elected vice chairman Horry County Planning Commn., 1996-98; cons. Healthcare Adminstrn., 1995—. Adv. bd. Cheraw Nursing Home, 1984-85. Contbr. articles to profl. jours. Chmn. bd. W.Va. Kidney Found., Charleston, 1980-81; chmn. youth bd. S.C. TB and Respiratory Disease Assn., Charleston, 1972-73; county chmn. Easter Seal Soc., Chesterfield County, S.C., 1984-85; campaign crusade chmn. Am. Cancer Soc., Chesterfield County, 1985-86; chmn. dist. advancement com. Boy Scouts Am., 1987-90; bd. dirs. Horry County United Way, 1989-95, Horry County Access Care, 1989-91; trustee Cheraw Acad., 1982-85, Grand Strand Gen. Hosp., 1987-94, Coastal Acad., 1988-90; commr. Horry County Planning Commn., 1995-97, vice chmn., 1996-97; mem. Myrtle Beach AFB Redevel. Authority, 1997—; chmn. Horry County Boys & Girls Clubs Am., 1998-99, bd. dirs., 1998-2000; apptd. Myrtle Beach Air Base Redevel. Authority, 1998, Waccamaw Regional Workforce Investment Bd., 1998-01, vice-chmn., 1998—01; vice-chmn. Horry County Republican Party, 1998-99; S.C. fin. steering com.; campaign chmn. McCain 2000 for Pres., 1999-2000, Harry County. volunteer med. missionary Haiti Hosp. Lumieer, 2002, mem. Parish Coun., St. Mary Help Christians RC Ch., Auban, SC, 2007-. Decorated Bronze Star, Vietnamese Cross of Gallantry, Vietnamese Medal of Honor; named to S.C. Order of Palmetto Gov. David Beasley, 1995. Fellow Am. Coll. Hosp. Adminstrs., Am. Coll. Health Care Execs; mem. S.C. Hosp. Assn. (com on legislation 1984-86, trustee 1989-94), Am. Acad. Healthcare Adminstrs., Cheraw C. of C. (bd. dirs. 1982-83), Rotary (pres. 1984-85). Republican. Roman Catholic. Home and Office: 341 Implement Dr Aiken SC 29803-6293 E-mail: jmadory@yahoo.com.

MADRID, OLGA HILDA GONZALEZ, retired elementary school educator; b. San Antonio, May 4, 1928; d. Victor A. and Elvira Ardilla Gonzalez; m. Sam Madrid, Jr., June 29, 1952; children: Ninette Marie, Samuel James. Student, U. Mex., San Antonio, St. Mary's U.; BA, Our Lady of Lake U., 1956, MEd, 1963. Cert. bilingual tchr., adminstr., Tex. Sec. Lanier HS San Antonio Ind. Sch. Dist., San Antonio, 1945-52; tchr. Collins Garden Elem. Sch., Storm Elem. Sch., San Antonio Ind. Sch. Dist., 1963-92; tutor Dayton, Ohio, 1952-54. Bd. dir., sch. rep. San Antonio Tchr. Coun., 1970-90; chair various coms. Collins Garden Elem., 1970-92. Elected dep. precinct, senatorial and state Dem. Conv., San Antonio, 1968—; apptd. commr. Keep San Antonio Beautiful, 1985; life mem., past pres. San Antonio YWCA; bd. dir. Luth. Gen. Hosp., Nat. Conf. Christians and Jews, Cath. Family and Children's Svc., St. Luke's Luth. Hosp.; nat. bd. dir. YWCA, 1985-96, also mem. exec. com.; mem. edn. commn. Holy Rosary Parish, 1994—; mem. bus. assoc. com. Our Lady of the Lake U., 1995—; co-founder UTSA Madrid Scholarship. Recipient Outstanding Our Lady Lake Alumni award Our Lady Lake U., 1975, Guadalupana medal San Antonio Cath. Archdiocese, 1975, Yellow Rose Tex. citation Gov. Briscoe, 1977; Olga H. Madrid Ctr. named in her honor, YWCA San Antonio and San Antonio City Coun., 1983, Salute to Quality Edn. Honoree, Kappa Gamma, 1993; Lo Mejor De Lo Nuestro honoree San Antonio Light, 1991, honoree San Antonio Women's History Month Coalition, 1996; named Our Lady of Lake Outstanding Alumna, 1999, one of five women honored for promoting literacy and cultural heritage with a sch. wall mural titled "Mis Palabras, Mi Poder", 2002, named one of ten Women of Decades, YWCA Centennial Celebration, 2010, San Madrid scholarship. Avocations: reading, gardening. Home: 2726 Benrus Blvd San Antonio TX 78228-2319

MADSEN, CLIFFORD KIMBALL, music educator, therapist; b. Price, Utah, May 3, 1937; s. Charles Henry Sr. and Lenora (Kimball) M.; m. Mary Marakis, Aug. 17, 1956; children: Sitka, Cort, Katia. BA, Brigham Young U., 1959, MA, 1960; PhD, Fla. State U., 1963. Instrumental music Carbon County Schs., Helper, Utah, 1955-57; Robert O. Lawton disting. prof. music Fla. State U., Tallahassee, 1961—. Mem. editl. bds. Psychology of Music, 1989-96, Jour. of Rsch. in Music Edn., 1970-76, 2000-06, Jour. of Music Therapy, 1974—2000, Coun. for Rsch. in Music, 1991—2011; author: (books) Experimental Research in Music, 1970, Teaching/Discipline, 1970, Contemporary Music Education, 1978, Applications of Research in Music Behavior, 1987. Juv. Ct. Counselor, Leon County, Tallahassee, 1963-73, sr. citizens adv., 1984-91. Recipient Sr. Rschr. award Music Educators Nat. Conf., 1988; named to Nat. Assn. Music Edn. Hall of Fame, 2002. Mem. AAAS, APA, Music Educators Rsch. Coun. (chmn. nat. conf. 1982-84), Am. Music Therapy Assn.(chmn. rsch. com. 1976—2011, award of merit 1988, Lifetime Achievement award 2006), Am. Ednl. Rsch. Assn., Internat. Soc. Music Edn., Coll. Music Soc. Democrat. Office: Fla State U Ctr for Music Rsch Tallahassee FL 32306-1180 Office Phone: 850-644-3554. Business E-Mail: cmadsen@fsu.edu.

MAEHARA, PAULETTE V., fundraising executive; b. Happy, Tex., 1949; married; 2 children. BA, U. Hawaii. Cert. Fund Raising Exec. (CFRE), Assn. Exec. (CAE). Exec. U. Hawaii Found., March of Dimes Birth Defects Found., Hawaii Chap.; v.p. devel. Project HOPE; exec. American Red Cross; CEO Epilepsy Found.; pres., CEO Assn. of Fundraising Professionals (AFP). Exec. com. Internat. Bur. for Epilepsy, Internat. Svc. Agencies, chair membership com.; bd. dirs. Nat. Health Coun.; mem. Assn. Com. of 100, US C. of C. Recipient Best Direct Mail Program award, Direct Mktg. Assn. of Am., 1994. Mem.: Am. Soc. of Assn. Execs. (bd. dirs. 2000—02, vice chair exec. bd. dirs. 2001, sec., treas. 2003, past chair Exec. Mgmt. Coun., bd. chair 2005—). Office: Assn Fundraising Professionals (AFP) 4300 Wilson Blvd Ste 300 Arlington VA 22203 Office Phone: 703-684-0410. Office Fax: 703-684-0540.

MAFFUCCI, DAVID G., manufacturing executive; b. Stamford, Conn., 1950; Degree, Sacred Heart U., 1972. Cert. CPA. Asst. contr. Bowater, Inc., 1977, v.p., treas., CFO Greenville, SC, 1995—2002; exec. v.p., pres., Newsprint Divsn. Bowater Inc., 2005—06; exec. v.p., CFO Xerium Technologies, Inc., 2009—10. Bd. dirs. Martin Marietta Materials Inc., Xerium Technologies, Inc., 2008—10. Office: Martin Marietta Materials Inc Bd Directors 2710 Wycliff Rd Raleigh NC 27607-3033 Office Phone: 919-781-4550. Office Fax: 919-783-4695. E-mail: david.maffucci@martinmarietta.com.

MAGADAN, DAVID JOSEPH, professional baseball coach, retired professional baseball player; b. Tampa, Fla., Sept. 30, 1962; m. Monique Magadan; children: Jordan, Christian, Peyton. Attended, U. Ala., Tuscaloosa. 1st baseman, 3d baseman NY Mets, NYC, 1986—92, Fla. Marlins, Miami, 1993, 1994; 1st baseman, 3d baseman, designated hitter Seattle Mariners, 1993; 1st baseman, 3d baseman Houston Astros, 1995; 1st baseman, 3d baseman, designated hitter Oakland Athletics, Calif., 1997—99, San Diego Padres, 1999—2001, minor league batting instr., 2002, batting coach, 2003—06, Boston Red Sox, 2006—12, Tex. Rangers, 2013—. Drafted Boston Red Sox, declined, 1980. Chmn. No Small Affair-South. Recipient Payson award for humanitarian svc., N.Y. chpt. Baseball Writers' Assn. Am., Golden Spikes award, USA Baseball, 1983; named Coll. Player of Yr., Baseball Am., 1983, All-Southeast

Conf., 1983. Achievements include leading U. Ala. to championship game 1983 Coll. World Series, 1983; leading NCAA divsn. 1 with .525 batting average, 1983. Office: Texas Rangers 1000 Ballpark Way # 400 Arlington TX 76011

MAGDOVITZ, LAWRENCE MAYNARD, real estate company executive, lawyer; b. Clarksdale, Miss., Aug. 21, 1937; s. Harry David and Lenabel (May) M.; m. Kerin Coffey, June 25, 1972 (dec. Apr. 1994); children: Beth, Larry. BA, Vanderbilt U., 1959, JD, 1961. Bar: Tenn. 1961, Miss. 1961, Ky. 1962. Trust officer First Nat. Bank, Mayfield, Ky., 1961-62; practice law Clarksdale, 1962—; br. office Cordova, Tenn.; realtor Valley Realty Co., Clarksdale, 1962—, Magdovitz Agy., Inc., Clarksdale, 1972—, First, Inc., Clarksdale, 1973—. Mem. Miss. State Bar Assn., Ky. State Bar Assn., Tenn. State Bar Assn., Memphis Bar Assn., Clarksdale Bd. Realtors. Lodges: B'nai Brith (pres. Clarksdale br. 1979-82), Elks. Republican. Jewish. Office: 222 Issaquena Clarksdale MS 38614-4206 Office Phone: 662-627-6250. Office Fax: 662-624-4821. Business E-Mail: lawrence@magdovitz.com.

MAGEE, KATHLEEN S., foundation executive; b. NJ; m. William Preston Magee, Jr.; 5 children. BSN, Coll. Misericordia, Pa.; MEd, U. Md.; MSW, Norfolk State U. Nurse, social worker; co-founder (with William P. Magee, Jr.) Operation Smile, 1982, pres., bd. dir. Featured guest Montel Williams, guest appearances Dateline NBC, CBS Sunday Morning, 48 Hours, NBC Nightly News. Bd. gov. World of Children; adv. bd. World Healing Inst.; founder, organizer World Journey of Hope, 1999. Recipient Conrad N. Hilton Humanitarian prize, 1996, Servants of Peace award, 1997, Golden Plate award, Am. Acad. Achievement, 1999, Kellogg's Hannah Neil World of Children award, 1999, Lifetime Volunteer Achievement award, Operation Smile, 2005; co-recipient Common Wealth Disting. Svc. award, 2001; named one of America's Best Leaders, US News & World Report, 2009; named to Med. Mission Hall of Fame, 2004. Office: Operation Smile 6453 Tidewater Dr Norfolk VA 23509

MAGEE, WILLIAM PRESTON, JR., plastic surgeon; b. NJ; m. Kathleen S. Magee; 5 children. BS, Mt. St. Mary's Coll., Maryland; DDS, U. Md.; MD, George Washington U. Resident gen. surgery U. Va. Med. Sch.; resident plastic surgery Ea. Va. Grad. Sch. Medicine; pvt. practice Norfolk, Va.; co-founder (with Kathleen S. Magee) Operation Smile, 1982, CEO; co-dir. Inst. Craniofacial and Plastic Surgery Children's Hosp. of King's Daughters, chmn. Plastic Surgery Dept.; assoc. prof. plastic surgery Ea. Va. Med. Sch. Contbr. chapters to books, articles to med. jours.; guest appearances NBC Nightly News, Dateline NBC, Fox News, Leeza, The Rosie O'Donnell Show, Hour of Power, 48 Hours, CBS Sunday Morning, Touched by an Angel. Bd. dirs. Operation Smile; founder, organizer World Journey of Hope, 1999; bd. dirs. talksurgery.com. Recipient Conrad N. Hilton Humanitarian prize, 1996, Servants of Peace award, 1997, Golden Plate award, Am. Acad. Achievement, 1999, Frank Annunzio award, Christopher Columbus Fellowship Found., 2002; co-recipient Common Wealth award disting. svc., 2001; named one of America's Best Leaders, US News & World Report, 2009; named to Med. Mission Hall of Fame, 2003. Mem.: Am. Soc. Plastic Surgeons (Disting. Svc. award 1998), Va. Soc. Plastic and Reconstructive Surgeons (pres. 1991—93), AMA (Pride in the Profession award 2000). Office: Operation Smile 3641 Faculty Blvd Virginia Beach VA 23453-8000

MAGGART, DEBRA YOUNG, state legislator; b. Nashville, Tenn., Oct. 11, 1960; 1 child. Mem. Dist. 45 Tenn. House of Reps., 2005—. Recipient Sumner County Rep. Party Chmn.'s award, 2000, 2002; named Western Ky. U. Outstanding Greek Advisor. Mem.: Gallatin C. of C., Mid. Tenn. Home Builders, Nat. Fed. of Independence Bus., Dandridge Trust (bd. mem.), Tenn. Anglican Coun., Henersonvile C. of C. (v. chmn.), Tenn. Right of Life, Sumner County Chpt., St. Joseph of Arimathea Episc. Ch., Sumner County Rep. Women's Club, Hendersonville Rotary Club (chmn.). Republican. Episcopalian. Office: 112 La Bar Dr Hendersonville TN 37075 also: 203 War Memorial Bldg Nashville TN 37243-0145 Office Phone: 615-741-3893. Office Fax: 615-253-0350. Business E-Mail: rep.debra.maggart@capitol.tn.gov.

MAGGIO, THERESA GRIFFIN (TERRI MAGGIO), librarian; b. Shreveport, La., May 27, 1952; d. James Henry and Annie Laurie (Rosenblath) Griffin; m. Edward James Maggio, July 2, 1977; 1 child, Kelli Suzanne. BS in Social Studies Edn., La. State U., 1975, MLS, 1980; PhD in Libr. and Info. Studies, Fla. State U., 1988. Cert. Pub. Libr. Adminstr., 2008. Libr. La. State Libr., Baton Rouge, 1980—82; med. libr. Lallie Kemp Hosp., Independence, La., 1982—85; med. libr. cons. 7th Ward Hosp., Hammond, La., 1984—86; reference libr. Roddenbery Meml. Libr., 1988—89; dep. dir., pub. svc. libr. SW Ga. Regional Libr., Bainbridge, 1989—2005; collection devel. libr. State Libr. Fla., 2006, Jackson Correctional Inst., 2006—07; dir. Assumption Parish Libr., Napoleonville, La., 2007—. Recipient Baker and Taylor Grassroots award, 1980, Outstanding Reference Work award, 2000; named La. Libr. Assn. scholar, 1979; Title IIB fellow, 1985—86. Mem.: ALA. Democrat. Roman Catholic. Avocation: horse racing. Office: Assumption Parish Libr 293 Napoleon Ave Napoleonville LA 70390 Home Phone: 985-387-3156; Office Phone: 985-369-7070. Office Fax: 985-369-6019. Personal E-mail: terimaggio@hotmail.com. Business E-Mail: tmaggio@state.lib.la.us.

MAGIDSON, KENNETH, federal prosecutor; b. NYC, 1948; BA, U. Md., 1973; JD, South Tex. Coll. Law, 1976. Law clk. Glassman, Hittner, and Cezeaux, Houston, 1975—76; atty. US Customs Svc., Washington, 1976—77; asst. dist. atty. Harris County Dist. Atty.'s Office, Houston, 1977—83, chief felony prosecutor 177th Dist. Ct., 1981—83, dist. atty., 2008; asst. US atty. (southern dist.) Tex. US Dept. Justice, 1983—2011; regional coord. SW Region Organized Crime Drug Enforcement Task Force (OCDETF), 1987—2011, chief Narcotics Sect., 1987—89, dir. Exec. Office, Criminal Divsn., 1996—97; US atty. (southern dist.) Tex. US Dept. Justice, 2011—. Office: Office of US Attorney Southern District of Texas PO Box 61129 Houston TX 77208 Office Phone: 713-567-9000. Office Fax: 713-718-3300. E-mail: usatxs.atty@usdoj.gov.*

MAGILL, KENT B., lawyer; b. Kansas City, Mo., Dec. 2, 1952; m. Teresa A. Magill. BS, Kans. State U., 1975; JD, U. Iowa, 1977. Bar: Mo. 1977, Kans. 1987, US Dist. Ct. Dist. Kans. Assoc. Shughart, Thomson & Kilroy, Kansas City, Mo., 1977—80, atty., 1980—89; assoc. gen. counsel, v.p. The Marley Co., Mission Woods, Kans., 1989—92; v.p., gen. counsel & sec. Layne Christensen Co., Mission Woods, Kans., 1992—2000; assoc. gen. counsel Hostess Brands, Inc. (formerly Interstate Bakeries Corp.), 2000—02, v.p., 2002—05, gen. counsel, sec., 2002—, exec. v.p., 2005—. Office: Hostess Brands Inc 6031 Connection Dr Irving TX 75039 Office Phone: 972-532-4500. Office Fax: 972-892-7694. Business E-Mail: kent.magill@hostessbrands.com.

MAGILL, SAMUEL HAYS, academic administrator, consultant; b. Decatur, Ga., July 19, 1928; s. Orrin Rankin and Ellen Howe (Bell) M.; children: Samuel Hays Jr., Katherine Magill Walters, Suzanne Magill Weintraub; m. Eunice M. Brock. AB, U. N.C., 1950; BD, Yale U., 1953; PhD, Duke U., 1962; LHD (hon.), Stockton State Coll., 1990; EdD (hon.), Monmouth U., 2005. Ordained to ministry Congl. Christian Ch., 1953; gen. sec. Davidson Coll. YMCA, 1953-55; dir. student activities U. N.C., Chapel Hill, 1955-58, asst. dean student affairs, 1958-59; chaplain Dickinson Coll., 1962-63, asst. prof. religion, 1962-66, asso. prof. religion, 1966-68, dean coll., 1963-68; pres. Council Protestant Colls. and Univs., Washington, 1968-70; exec. asso., chief office acad. affairs Assn. Am. Colls., 1971-76; pres. Simon's Rock Early Coll., Great Barrington, Mass., 1976-79, Monmouth U., West Long Branch, NJ, 1980-93, pres. emeritus, 1993—; higher edn. cons., 1993-98; assoc. dir. gift planning U. N.C., 1999—2004, major gifts officer, 2004—06; vice chair Coker Hills Democratic Precinct, 2008—09; bd. dirs. Chapal Hill Carrboro YMCA, 2009—11. Adj. prof. Duke U., 1996. Trustee Jersey Shore Med. Ctr., 1985-93; bd. overseers N.J. Gov.'s Schs., 1986-93; bd. dirs., pres. Falconbridge Homeowners Assn., 2003-06; bd. trustees, Chapel Hill Preservation Soc., 2007-2009; bd. dirs. Chapel Hill Carrboro YMCA, 2009-. Guerney Harris Kearns fellow in religion, 1960-61; Danforth Found. spl. grad. fellow, 1959-61. Fellow Soc. Values in Higher Edn. (dir. 1969-81); mem. Am. Assembly Collegiate Sch. Bus. (accreditation task force 1989-90), NCAA (pres.'s commn. 1990-93), Am. Coun. Edn. (commn. leadership devel. 1982-85, commn. on minority affairs 1986-89), Harvard Inst. Ednl. Mgmt., Assn. Ind. Colls. and Univs. N.J. (dir. 1980-93, exec. com. 1983-93, chair 1987-89), Order of Golden Fleece U. N.C., Fearrington Dem. Club (co-chair 1997-98), Delta Psi. Home: 319 Burlage Cir Chapel Hill NC 27514 Personal E-mail: sambomag@gmail.com.

MAGNUS, SANDRA H., astronaut; b. Belleville, Ill., Oct. 30, 1964; BS in Physics, U. Mo., Rolla, 1986, MS in Elec. Engring., 1990; PhD, Ga. Inst. Tech., 1996. Stealth engr. McDonnell Douglas Aircraft Co., 1986—91; fellow Inst. Tech. Ga., 1991—96; astronaut NASA Johnson Space Ctr., Houston, 1996—. Worked in Astronaut office payloads/habitability br. NASA, 1997—98; Russian Crusader for hardware testing and operational products develop., 1998; served as CAPCOM for Internat. Space Station, 2000; crew mem. STS-112 Atlantis Mission, 2002; flight engr., NASA sci. officer STS-126 Endeavour Mission, 2008; mission specialist STS-135-Atlantis-The Final Space Shuttle Mission, 2011. Recipient NASA Space Flight medal, 2002. Mem.: AAAS. Avocations: reading, soccer, travel, water-skiing. Office: Astronaut Office Johnson Space Ctr Houston TX 77058

MAGRILL, JOE RICHARD, JR., religious organization administrator, minister; b. Marshall, Tex., Aug. 7, 1946; s. Joe Richard and Mary Belle (Chadwick) M. BA summa cum laude, East Tex. State U., 1967; MDiv, Princeton Theol. Sem., 1970, MTh, 1972; MLS, Rutgers U., 1971. Ordained to ministry Cumberland Presbyn. Ch., 1970. Stated supply min. Newsome (Tex.) Cumberland Presbyn. Ch., 1966-67; Christian edn. asst. United Presbyn. Ch., Carlstadt, NJ, 1967-70; order libr. Princeton (N.J.) Theol. Sem., 1969-72; head libr., prof. Memphis Theol. Sem., 1972-79; pastor Brookhaven Cumberland Presbyn. Ch., Nashville, 1987-89; asst. to stated clk. Gen. Assembly Office, Cumberland Presbyn. Ch., Memphis, 1979-83, supr. ctrl. acctg. div., 1980-87, editor The Cumberland Presbyn., 1984-87, chief exec. bd. stewardship, 1989—2007, mem. Gen. Assembly Coun., 1993—2007, chief exec. Cumberland Presbyn. Investment Loan Program, Inc., 1999—2007, cons., 2007—09. Mem. Trinity Presbytery of Cumberland Presbyn. Ch., 1970—; sec.-treas. Hist. Found. Cumberland Presbyn. Ch., Memphis, 1974—2009; bd. dirs. Hist. Found. Presbyn. Ch. U.S., Montreat, N.C., 1980-83, mem. Harrison County Historical Commn., 2009-; sec. Harrison County Hist. Commn., 2013-. Editor: In the Valley of the Cauca, 1981, One Family Under God, 1982, Family of Faith, 1998, Jerusalem Cumberland Presbyterian Church, 2013. Recipient achievement award Hist. Found. Cumberland Presbyn. Ch., 1980; scholar Phi Alpha Theta, 1967, Am. Theol. Libr. Assn., 1970. Democrat. Presbyterian. Avocations: computers, historical research. Home Phone: 903-928-0981. Business E-Mail: richardmargrill@att.net.

MAGUIRE, CHARLOTTE EDWARDS, retired pediatrician; b. Richmond, Ind., Sept. 1, 1918; d. Joel Blaine and Lydia (Betscher) Edwards; m. Raymer Francis Maguire, Sept. 1, 1948 (dec.); children: Barbara, Thomas Clair II (dec.). Student, Stetson U., 1936—38, U. Wichita, 1938—39; BS, Memphis Tchrs. Coll., 1940; MD, U. Ark., 1944; LHD (hon.), Fla. State U., 2002. Intern, resident Orange Meml. Hosp., Orlando, Fla., 1944—46, med. staff., 1944—69, instr. nurses, 1947—57; resident Bellevue Hosp. and Med. Ctr., NYU, NYC, 1954—55; staff mem. Fla. Santarium and Hosp., Orlando, 1946—56, Holiday House and Hosp., Orlando, 1950—62; mem. courtesy and cons. staff West Orange Meml. Hosp., Winter Garden, Fla., 1952—67; active staff, chief dept. pediat. Mercy Hosp., Orlando, 1965—68; med. dir. childrens med. svcs., asst. sec. Fla. Dept. Health and Rehab. Svcs., 1969—71, med. dir. med. svcs. and basic care, 1975—84; med. exec. dir., med. svcs. divsn. worker's compensation Fla. Dept. Labor, Tallahassee, 1984—87; chief of staff physicians and dentists Ctrl. Fla. divsn. Children's Home Soc. Fla., 1947—56; dir. Orlando Child Health Clinic, 1949—58; pvt. practice Orlando, 1946—68; asst. regional dir. HEW, 1970—72; ret., 1987. Asst. dir. health and sci. affairs Dept. Health Edn. & Welfare, Atlanta, 1971-72, Washington, 1972-75; pediat. cons. Fla. Crippled Children's Commn., 1952-70, dir., 1968-70; med. dir. Office Med. Svcs. and Basic Care, sr. physician Office of Asst. Sec. Ops., Fla. Dept. Health and Rehab. Svcs.; clin. prof. dept. pediat. U. Fla. Coll. Medicine, Gainesville, 1980-87; mem. Fla. Drug Utilization Rev., 1983-87; real estate salesperson Investors Realty, 1982-2003; bd. dirs. Stavros Econ. Ctr. Fla. State U., Tallahassee; pres.'s coun. Fla. State U., U. Fla., Gainesville; Charlotte Edwards Maguire eminent scholar chair and scholarships for qualified students, 1999. Mem. profl. adv. com. Fla. Ctr. for Clin. Svcs. at U. Fla., 1952-60; del. to Mid-century White House Conf. on Children and Youth, 1950; U.S. del from Nat. Soc. for Crippled Children to World Congress for Welfare of Cripples, Inc., London, 1957; pres. of corp. Eccleston-Callahan Hosp. for Colored Crippled Children, 1956-58; sec. Fla. chpt. Nat. Doctor's Com. for Improved Med. Svcs., 1951-52; med. adv. com. Gateway Sch. for Mentally Retarded, 1959-62; bd. dirs. Forest Park Sch. for Spl. Edn. Crippled Children, 1949-54, mem. med. adv. com., 1955-68, chmn., 1957-68; mem. Fla. Adv. Coun. for Mentally Retarded, 1965-70; dir. ctrl. Fla. poison control Orange Meml. Hosp.; mem. orgn. com., chmn. com. for admissions and selection policies Camp Challenge; participant 12th session Fed. Exec. Inst., 1971; del. White House Conf. on Aging, 1980; dir. Stavros Econ. Ctr. Fla. State U.; trustee Fla. State U. Found., 1998—, mem. campaign com. Charlotte Edwards Maguire Eminent Scholarship named in her honor Fla. State U., Charlotte Edwards Maguire MLS Med. Libr., Fla. State U. Coll. Medicine named in her honor, 2005; named Outstanding Woman in Our Cmty. AAUW, Tallahassee, 2002; recipient David M. Solomon Disting. Pub. Svc. award Am. Geriatric Soc., 2005, Torch award Fla. State U., 2005. Mem. AMA (life), Nat. Rehab. Assn., Am. Congress Phys. Medicine and Rehab., Fla. Soc. Crippled Children and Adults, Ctrl. Fla. Soc. Crippled Children and Adults (dir. 1949-58, pres. 1956-57), Am. Assn. Cleft Palate, Fla. Soc. Crippled Children (trustee 1951-57, v.p. 1956-57, profl. adv. com. 1957-68), Mental Health Assn. Orange County (charter mem.; pres. 1949-50, dir. 1947-52, chmn. exec. com. 1950-52, dir. 1963-65), Fla. Orange County Heart Assn., Am. Med. Women's Assn., Am. Acad. Med. Dirs., Fla. Med. Assn. (life, chmn. com. on mental retardation), Orange County Med. Assn., Orange Med. Soc. (life), Fla. Pediat. Soc. (pres. 1952-53), Fla. Cleft Palate Assn. (counselor-at-large, sec.), Nat. Inst. Geneal. Rsch., Nat. Geneal. Soc., Assn. Profl. Genealogists, Tallahassee Geneal. Soc., Fla. State U. Found. Inc. (bd. dirs. Stavoris Ctr. for Econ. Edn.), Capital City Tiger Bay Club, Fla. Econs. Club, Francis Eppes Soc. Fla. State U., Econ. Club Fla., Governors Club. Home: 4158 Covenant Ln Tallahassee FL 32308-5765

MAGUIRE, MARTIE (MARTHA ELENOR ERWIN MAGUIRE), musician; b. York, Pa., Oct. 12, 1969; d. Paul and Barbara Erwin; m. Ted Seidel, June 17, 1995 (div. 1999); 1 stepchild, Carter Seidel; m. Gareth MaGuire, Aug. 10, 2001; children: Eva Ruth, Kathleen Emilie, Harper Rose. Student, So. Meth. U. Performer Blue Night Express, 1984—89; musician and vocalist Dixie Chicks, 1989—, Court Yard Hounds, 2010—. Musician: (albums) (with The Dixie Chicks) Thank Heavens for Dale Evans, 1990, Little Ol' Cowgirl, 1992, Shouldn't a Told You That, 1993, Wide Open Spaces, 1998 (Album of Yr., Acad. Country Music, 1998, Best Country Album, Grammy Awards, 1998, Best Country Artist Clip of Yr., Billboard Awards, 1998, Maximum Vision Clif of Yr., Billboard Awards, 1998, Best Selling Album, Can. Country Music Award, 1999, Song of Yr. (Country), WB Radio Music Awards, 1999, Album of Yr., Acad. Country Music, 1999), Fly, 1999 (Best Country Album, Grammy Awards, 1999, Best Selling Album, Can. Country Music Awards, 2000, Internat. Album, British Country Music Awards, 2000, Country Album of Yr., Billboard Awards, 2000, Album of Yr., Acad. Country Music, 2000, Album of Yr., CMA, 2000), Home, 2002 (Favorite Country Album, Am. Music Awards, 2002, Best Recording Package, Grammy Awards, 2002, Best Country Album, Grammy Awards, 2002), Top of the World Tour: Live, 2003 (Best Country Group Vocal Performance, Grammy Awards, 2005), Taking the Long Way, 2006 (Album of Yr. and Best Country Album, Grammy Awards, 2007), (with Court Yard Hounds) Court Yard Hounds, 2010, (songs) Not Ready to Make Nice, 2006 (Record of Yr., Song of Yr., Best Performance by a Duo or Group with Vocal, Grammy Awards, 2007); performer: (documentary) Dixie Chicks: Shut Up and Sing, 2006. Recipient Horizon award, CMA, 1998, others; named Top New Country Artist, Billboard, 1998, Most Significant New Country Act, Country Monitor, 1998, Group of Yr., CMA, 1998, Top Vocal Group, Acad. Country Music, 1998, Internat. Rising Star, British Country Music Awards, 1999, Country Artist of Yr., Rolling Stone, 1999, Artist of Yr. (Country), WB Radio Music Awards, 1999, Favorite New Artist (Country), AMA, 1999, Vocal Group of Yr., CMA, 1999, Country Artist of Yr., Billboard, 1999, 2000, Vocal Group of Yr., CMA, 2000, Entertainer of Yr., 2000, ACM, 2000, 2001, Vocal Group of Yr., 2001, Favorite Musical Group or Band, People's Choice Awards, 2001, Favorite Country Band, Am. Music Award, 2002, Vocal Group of Yr., Country Music Assn. Award, 2002, Country Duo/Group of Yr., Billboard, 2002; named one of 100 Most Influential People, Time Mag., 2006.

MAGURNO, RICHARD PETER, lawyer; b. Suffern, NY, June 29, 1943; s. Eugene and Rose (Foresta) M. BS, Georgetown U., 1964; MS, U. Wis., 1965; JD, Fordham U., 1968. Bar: N.Y. 1970, Fla. 1982, U.S. Supreme Ct. 1974, U.S. Ct. Appeals (2d, 5th, 11th cirs.) 1976, U.S. Dist. Ct. (so. and ea. dists.) N.Y. 1979. Atty. Eastern Air Lines, NYC, 1970-73, sr. atty., 1973-76, gen. atty., 1976-79, dir. legal Miami, Fla., 1980, v.p. legal, asst. sec., 1980-84, gen. counsel, sr. v.p. legal, sec., 1984-88; ptnr. Lord Day & Lord, Barrett Smith, 1989-94; gen. counsel, sr. v.p. legal Trans World Airlines, St. Louis, 1994-98; aviation cons., 1998-2000; gen. counsel, sr. v.p., sec. AirTran Airways, Inc., 2000—11. Author: Romantic Suffern, 1773-1973, 1973. Served in Peace Corps, 1968-69. Mem. ABA, Fla. Bar Assn. Democrat. Roman Catholic.

MAHADEVAN, KUMAR, marine life administrator, researcher; b. Madras, Tamilnadu, India, Sept. 29, 1948; came to U.S., 1971; s. Sockalingam Ponnusamy and Pankajam (Nadar) M.; m. Linda Claire Goggin, Sept. 27, 1980; children: Andrew, Alexander, Chad, Vijayan. BS, Madras U., 1967; MS, Annamalai U., Chidambaram, India, 1971; PhD, Fla. State U., 1977. Instr. Chingleput (India) Med. Coll., 1967-68, Lakshman's Coll., Madras, 1968-69; rsch. asst. Fla. State U., Tallahassee, 1971-75; staff scientist Conservation Cons., Inc., Palmetto, Fla., 1975-78; sr. scientist Mote Marine Lab., Sarasota, Fla., 1978-79, dir. divsn., 1979—86, interim co-dir., 1984; pres. Mote Marine Found., Sarasota, Fla., 1986—; trustee Mote Sci. Found., Sarasota, Fla., 1999—. Mem. Coun. on Ocean Affairs, Washington, 1989-91, steering com. Gulf of Mex. Program, Atlanta, 1988-96; mem. South Atlantic and Gulf States Coastal Protection Commn., 1990-93; vice chmn. NOAA Marine Rsch. Bd., Gulf of Mex., 1992-96. Contbr. articles to profl. jours. Mem. sch. adv. bd., Sarasota, 1988-89; mem. tech. adv. bd. Myakka River, Sarasota, 1987-90; legis. liason Parents Assn. of Sarasota Schs., 1988-89; bd. dirs. Jason Found. for Edn., 1991-2004, Health Care Sarasota, 1997-98; vice chmn. Fla. Ocean Alliance, 2000—; mem. Fla. Gov.'s Ocean Com., 1997-98; mem. adv. bd. Harte Inst. for Gulf of Mex. Studies, 2001—; active Sarasota Cmty. Video Archives Hall of Fame, 2005. Nat. Merit scholar Univ. Grants Commn., India, 1969-71. Fellow Explorers Club (nat.); mem. N.Am. Benthological Soc., Oceanographic Soc., World Aquaculture Soc., Deep Sea Biol. Soc. (hon.), Fla. Acad. Scis. (councillor 1975), So. Assn. Marine Labs (pres. 1990, exec. bd. 1986-91, treas. 1995—), Assn. Marine Labs Caribbean (pres. 1987-88, exec. bd. 1984—), Nat. Assn. Marine Labs. (pres. 1994-95), Sci. and Environ. Coun. Sarasota (chmn. 2003-06, Fla. Coastal Ocean Observing Systems Rsch. Consortium (chmn. 2006-07), Greater Sarasota C. of C. (dir. 2005—), Sarasota Rotary Club, Nat. Marine Sanctuary Found. (dir., 2007—), Sarasota Convention & Visitor's Bur. (dir. 2008-), Nat. Aquarium (dir. 2010-), Arts Coun. Sarasota (dir. 2010-), Sigma Xi. Republican. Avocations: racquetball, fishing, gardening. Office: Mote Marine Lab 1600 Ken Thompson Pky Sarasota FL 34236-1096 Home Phone: 941-346-9338.

MAHAFFEE, JOSEPH W., management consultant; BSEE, Clemson U.; MSEE, Johns Hopkins U. Officer-in-charge, Partnership Program Johns Hopkins University; info. security engr., client svc. officer Nat. Security Agency; joined Booz Allen Hamilton Holding Corp., 1981, v.p., 1998—2007, sr. v.p., 2008—10, exec. v.p., 2010—. Bd. dirs. AFCEA Ctrl. Md. Chapter; pres., Exec. Steering Com., chmn., Nat. Security Scholarship Program Coll. Fund of Md. Office: Booz Allen Hamilton Holding Corp 8283 Greensboro Dr Mc Lean VA 22102 Office Phone: 703-902-5000. Office Fax: 703-902-3333. Business E-Mail: mahaffee_joseph@boozallen.com.

MAHAFFY, DENISE, retail executive; Dir. advt. Dillard's, Inc., 2000, v.p. advt. & product devel., 2005—. Named to Nat. Retail Advt. & Mktg. Assn. Hall of Fame, 1993. Office: Dillard's Inc 1600 Cantrell Rd Little Rock AR 72201 Office Phone: 501-376-5200. Office Fax: 501-399-7831. E-mail: dmahaffy@dillards.com.

MAHAJAN, ARVIND, finance educator; b. Delhi, India, Nov. 24, 1951; arrived in U.S., 1974; s. Vedavrata and Shakuntala Mahajan; m. Vanita Mahajan, Jan. 16, 1983; children: Aseem K., Sia S. B of Commerce in Acctg. and Fin., U. Delhi, 1972; MBA in Fin., U. Scranton, 1975; PhD in Fin., Ga. State U., 1980. Fin. officer Raisina Press, Delhi, 1972—74; instr., rsch. asst. Ga. State U., Atlanta, 1976—79; sr. cons. Mfrs. Hanover Trust Co., NYC, 1987—88; asst.

prof. fin. Tex. A&M U., College Station, 1980—86, assoc. prof., 1986—92, prof., 1992—94, Lamar Savings prof. fin., 1994—, regents prof., 2010—; dir. Aggies Wall St Program; assoc. dir. acad. programs Ctr. Internat. Bus. Studies and CIBER Tex. A&M U., College Station, 1990—99; dir. MSF Program, CFA Inst. Ptnr. Program. Vis. prof. Group Ecole Superieure de Commerce, Rennes, France, 2000, Johannes Kepler U., Linz, Austria, 1992—99, Group Ecole Superieure de Commerce, Dijon, France, 1991, Indian Inst. Tech., New Delhi, 2003—; faculty mem. Acad. Future Internat. Leaders, 1998—2000. Contbr. articles to rsch. jours. and confs. Pres. Coalition Support Pub. Schs., College Station, 2003. Avocations: travel, reading, music. Office: Tex A&M U Mays Bus Sch College Station TX 77843

MAHAN, CLARENCE, federal agency administrator, writer; b. Dayton, Ohio, Jan. 1, 1939; s. Clarence Mahan and Elsie (Crouch) Diltz; m. Suky Mahan, May 27, 1962; children: Sean M., Christiane Elizabeth. BA, U. Md., 1963; MA, Am. U., 1968; MBA, Syracuse U., 1969. Dep. comptroller U.S. Army, Japan, 1974-76; dep. chief program and budget Defense Commn. Agy., Arlington, Va., 1976; aide Asst. Sec. Army, Washington, 1976-77; chief operating appropriations Dept. AF, Washington, 1979-80; dir. fin. and acctg. Dept. Energy, Washington, 1980-81, dep. comptroller, 1981-82; dir. fiscal and contracts mgmt. EPA, Washington, 1982-83, dep. comptroller, 1983-85, dir. Rsch. Program Mgmt. Office, 1985-95. Instr., lectr. in field. Author: Classic Irises and the Men and Women Who Created Them, 2007; contbr. articles to profl. jours. and hort. mags. With U.S. Army, 1959-62, Korea. Mem. Am. Iris Soc. (bd. dirs., 2d v.p. 1991-95, 1st. v.p. 1995-98, pres. 1998-2001), Hist. Iris Preservation Soc. (pres. 1991-93), Soc. Japanese Irises (pres. 1989-92), Reblooming Iris Soc. (bd. dirs. 1986-94, pres. 2002-05). Democrat. Home and Office: 7311 Churchill Rd Mc Lean VA 22101-2001 Business E-Mail: cemahan@aol.com.

MAHAN, HUNTER, professional golfer; b. Orange, May 17, 1982; Student, Okla. State U., Stillwater. Mem. PGA Tour, 2003—. Mem. US Team Presidents Cup, 2007, 2009, 2011, Ryder Cup, 2008, 2010. Recipient Jack Nicklaus award, 2003, Fred Haskins award, 2003; co-recipient Ben Hogan award, 2003. Achievements include winning PGA Tour events: Travelers Championship, 2007; Waste Management Phoenix Open, World Golf Championships-Bridgestone Invitational Turning Stone Resort Championship, 2010; World Golf Championships-Accenture Match Play Championship, 2012, Shell Houston Open, 2012; being a member of the Ryder Cup winning US team, 2008. Office: c/o PGA Tour 112 PGA TOUR Blvd Ponte Vedra Beach FL 32082

MAHANY, KEVIN J., retail executive; BBA in Mgmt., Southwest Tex. State U. Ops. mgr. Dayton-Hudson, Southland Corp., Dillard Dept. Stores Inc., 1979—81, 7-Eleven Stores, 1981—88; joined Susser Holdings Corp. (formerly Southland Corp.), 1989; ops. mgr. Target Stores, 1989; v.p., merchandising & category mgmt. Susser Holdings Corp. (formerly Southguard Corp.), 2009—. Office: Susser Holdings Corp 4525 Ayers St Corpus Christi TX 78415-1401 Office Phone: 361-884-2463. Office Fax: 361-884-2494. Personal E-mail: kmahany@susser.com.

MAHER, DAVID WILLARD, Internet company executive; b. Chgo., Aug. 14, 1934; s. Chauncey Carter and Martha (Peppers) M.; m. Jill Waid Armagnac, Dec. 20, 1954; children: Philip Armagnac, Julia Armagnac. BA, Harvard, 1955, LLB, 1959. Bar: NY 1960, Ill. 1961, Wis. 1996, US Patent Office 1961. Pvt. practice, Boston, NYC, 1958-60; assoc. Kirkland & Ellis, and predecessor firm, 1960-65, ptnr., 1966-78, Reuben & Proctor, 1978-86, Isham, Lincoln and Beale, 1986-88, Sonnenschein, Nath & Rosenthal, Chgo., 1988—2003; ret., 2003; chmn. bd. dirs. Publ. Interest Registry, 2003—04, sr. v.p law and policy, 2004—. Dir. BBB Chgo. and No. Ill., 2004—; lectr. DePaul U. Sch. Law, 1973—79, Loyola U. Law Sch., Chgo., 1980—84. Contbr. articles to profl. jours. Vis. com. U. Chgo. Div. Sch., 1986—. 2nd lt. USAF, 1955—56. Recipient Torch of Integrity award, Better Bus. Bureau, Chgo. and N. Ill., Inc. Fellow Am. Bar Found. (life); mem. ABA, Am. Law Inst., Wis. State Bar, Chgo. Bar Assn., Chgo. Lit. Club. Roman Catholic. Home: 501 N Clinton St Apt 1503 Chicago IL 60654-8886 Office: Pub Interest Registry 1775 Wiehle Ave Ste 100 Reston VA 20190 Office Phone: 312-876-8055. Business E-Mail: dmaher@pir.org.

MAHESH, VIRENDRA BHUSHAN, endocrinologist; b. India, Apr. 25, 1932; came to U.S., 1958, naturalized, 1968; s. Narinjan Prasad and Sobhagyawati; m. Sushila Kumari Aggarwal, June 29, 1955; children: Anita Rani, Vinit Kumar. BSc with honors, Patna U., India, 1951; MSc in Chemistry, Delhi U., India, 1953, PhD, 1955; DPhil in Biol. Sci, Oxford U., 1958. James Hudson Brown Meml. fellow Yale U., 1958-59; asst. rsch. prof. endocrinology Med. Coll. Ga., Augusta, 1959-63, assoc. rsch. prof., 1963-66, prof., 1966-70, Regents prof., 1970-86, Robert B. Greenblatt prof., 1979-99, chmn. endocrinology, 1972-86, chmn., Regents prof. physiology and endocrinology, 1986-99, chmn. physiology and endocrinology, 1986-99, regents prof., chmn. emeritus physiology and endocrinology, 1999—, Robert B. Greenblatt prof. emeritus endocrinology, 1999—. Dir. Ctr. for Population Studies, 1971-99; mem. reproductive biology study sect. NIH, 1977-81, mem. human embryology and devel. study sect. NIH, 1982-86, 90-93, chmn., 1991-93. Contbr. articles to profl. jours., chpts. to books; editor: The Pituitary, a Current Review, Functional Correlates of Hormone Receptors in Reproduction, Recent Advances in Fertility Research, Hirsuitism and Virilism, Regulation of Ovarian and Testicular Function, Excitatory Amino Acids: Their Role in Neuroendocrine Function; mem. editl. bd. Steroids, 1963—, Jour. of Clin. Endocrinology and Metabolism, 1976-81, Jour. Steroid Biochemistry and Molecular Biology, 1991—, Assisted Reproductive Tech./Andrology, 1993-98, Endocrinology, 1999-2003; mem. adv. bd. Maturitas, 1977-81; editor-in-chief Biology of Reprodn., 1999-2004, cons. editor, 2004-09. Recipient Rubin award Am. Soc. Study Sterility, 1962, Billings Silver medal, 1965, Best Tchr. award freshman class Sch. Medicine, Med. Coll. Ga., 1969, Outstanding Faculty award Sch. Medicine, 1992, Outstanding Faculty award Sch. Grad. Studies, 1981, 94, Disting. Tchg. award, 1988, Excellence in Rsch. award Grad. Faculty Assembly, 1987-91, 93-95, Disting. Scientist award Assn. Scientist Indian Origin in Am., 1989, Lifetime Achievement award Sch. Medicine, 1997, Lifetime Achievement award Med.Coll. Ga. Rsch. Inst., 2006; rsch. grantee NIH, 1960-2000. Mem. Fedn. Am. Soc. Exptl. Biology (bd. dirs. 2004-07, 2008-12), AAUP, Chem. Soc. (Eng.), Soc. Biochem. and Molecular Biol., Soc. Neurosci., Endocrine Soc., Soc. for Gynecologic Investigation, Internat. Soc. Neuroendocrinology, Soc. for Study Reproduction (Carl G. Hartman award 1996, Disting. Svc. award 2005), Am. Physiol. Soc. (chmn. endocrinology and metabolism sect. 2004-06), Internat. Soc. Reproductive Medicine (pres. 1980-82), Soc. Exptl. Biology and Medicine, Am. Fertility Soc., Am. Assn. Lab. Animal Sci., NY Acad. Scis., Sigma Xi. Business E-Mail: vmahesh@gru.edu.

MAHON, ARTHUR J., lawyer; b. NYC, Jan. 13, 1934; s. Arthur Logan and Mary Agnes (Craine); m. Myra E. Murphy, Aug. 10, 1957 (dec. Jan. 29, 2011); children: Maura, Madonna, Arthur, Nancy. BA, Manhattan Coll., 1955; JD, NYU, 1958. Bar: NY, Fla., DC. Adj. prof. law NYU Sch. of Law, NYC, 1964-78; ptnr. Mudge, Rose, Guthrie, Alexander & Ferdon, NYC, 1970-94; counsel Donovan Leisure Newton & Irvine, NYC, 1994-98, McDermott, Will & Emery, 1998—2007. Trustee Manhattan Coll., NYC, 1988-03, Adrian and Jesse Archbold Charitable Trust, NYC, 1976-, NY Presbyn. Hosp., NYC, 1994—, Alvin Ailey Am. Dance Theatre, 1998—2012; mem. joint bd. NY Hosp.-Cornell Med. Ctr., NYC, 1990-98; com. on trust and estate gift plans Rockefeller U., NYC, 1984—; bd. dirs. United Way Internat., 1988-94, Alexandria, Va., chmn. planned giving and endowments com. Archdiocese, NYC, 1982-97, pres. Royal Soc. Medicine Edn., 1980-94; bd. overseers Cornell Med. Coll., NYC, 1986—, chmn., 1992-95, vice chmn., 1990-91, 96-; dir. Am. Skin Assn., NYC, 1989-00; pres., dir. Cath. Communal Fund, Archdiocese of NY, 1997—, chmn. 2012-, trustee Inner City Scholarship Fund, 1998—. Served to capt. USAF, 1958-60. Root-Tilden scholar NYU Law Sch. Mem. NY State Bar Assn., Bar Assn. City of NY, Fla. Bar Assn., DC Bar Assn. Home: 4333 N Ocean Blvd Gulf Stream FL 33483 Personal E-mail: arthurjmahon@gmail.com.

MAHONEY, GEORGE LEFEVRE, lawyer; b. Washington, Mar. 28, 1952; s. George Francis Xavier and Elaine (LeFevre) M.; m. Lucinda Stuart, July 11, 1986. BA, U. Va., 1974, JD, 1978. Bar: N.Y. 1979, U.S. Dist. Ct. (so. and ea. dists), N.Y. 1979, U.S. Ct. Appeals (5th cir.), 1980, U.S. Ct. Appeals (2d cir.) 1981, U.S. Ct. Appeals (D.C. cir.) 1991. Assoc. Satterlee & Stephens, NYC, 1978-82; asst. gen. counsel Dow Jones & Co., Inc., NYC and Princeton, N.J., 1982—93; corp. sec., gen. counsel Media General, Inc., Richmond, Va., 1993—, v.p., 2006—.

MAHONEY, GEORGE R., JR., lawyer; b. Oct. 18, 1942; m. Linda L. Mahoney. AB, Ohio Wesleyan U.; LLB, Duke U. Gen. counsel Family Dollar Stores Inc., 1976—2005, v.p., sec., 1977—2005, sr. v.p., 1984—91; bd. dirs. Family Dollar Stores, Inc., 1987—; exec. v.p. Family Dollar Stores Inc., 1991—2005. Office: Family Dollar Stores Inc 10401 Monroe Rd Matthews NC 28105 Office Phone: 704-847-6961. Office Fax: 704-847-0189.

MAHONEY, MARY, hotel executive; b. Orlando, Fla., Dec. 20, 1959; Various positions Days Inn of Am., Inc., 1980—90; founder Targa Internat., Inc, 1990—94; dir. preferred vendor mktg. Cendant Corp., dir. market devel., 1994—96, v.p. mktg., Howard Johnson, 1996-98, pres., CEO, Howard Johnson Internat. Inc., 1998—2003, sr. v.p., member relations and customer support, Fairfield Resorts, 2003—. Adv. bd. William F. Harrah Coll. Hotel Admin., UNLV. Mem. state bd. Junior Achievement, NJ; bd. dirs. Nat. Academy's Found. Travel & Tourism. Named Most Powerful Women in Travel Travel Agt. mag., 1997, 98, 99, Next Generation of Hot New Marketers list Brandweek. Mem.: Am Hotel & Lodging Assoc. Coun. Inns & Suites (audit com., fin. com.), Hospitality Industry Hall of Honor. Office: Fairfield Resorts 8669 Commodity Cir Orlando FL 32819

MAHONEY, PAUL G., dean, law educator; b. St. Louis, 1959; m. Julia Mahoney; 2 children. BS, MIT, 1981; JD, Yale Law Sch., 1984. Bar: NY 1987. Law clk. to Hon. Ralph K. Winter Jr. US Ct. Appeals (2nd Cir.), New Haven, 1984—85; law clk to Hon. Thurgood Marshall US Supreme Ct., Washington, 1985—86; assoc. Sullivan & Cromwell LLP, NYC, 1986—90; assoc. prof. U. Va. Sch. Law, Charlottesville, 1990—95, prof., 1995—, Albert C. BeVier rsch. prof., 1996, acad. assoc. dean, 1999—2004, Brokaw prof. corp. law, Arnold H. Leon prof. law, David & Mary Harrison Disting. prof. law, dean, 2008—. Vis. prof. U. Chgo. Law Sch., U. Southern Calif. Law Sch., U. Toronto Faculty of Law; assoc. editor Jour. Economic Perspectives, 2004—07. Associate editor Journal of Economic Perspectives, 2004—07. Recipient All-Univ. Tchr. Award, U. Va., 1997, Traynor award, U. Va. Law Sch. Fellow: American Acad. Arts & Sciences; mem.: American Law & Economics Assn. (dir. 2002—04). Office: University of Virginia School of Law 580 Massie Rd WB319 Charlottesville VA 22903-1789 Office Phone: 434-924-7343. E-mail: pmahoney@virginia.edu.*

MAHURIN, STEVE, retail executive; BA in Industry, U. Northern Iowa, 1985. Sr. v.p., merchandising decor & merchandising hardlines Home Depot, Inc., v.p., merchandising, 1989—2002; v.p., merchandising & mktg. PGA Tour Superstore, 2002—04; sr. v.p. & CMO True Value Co. (formerly TruServ Corp.), 2004—08; exec. v.p., merchandising Office Depot, Inc., 2008—. Office: Office Depot Inc 6600 N Military Trail Boca Raton FL 33496 Office Phone: 561-438-2199. Office Fax: 561-438-4001. Business E-Mail: steve.mahurin@officedepot.com.

MAIDIQUE, MODESTO ALEX, engineering educator, former academic administrator; b. Havana, Cuba, Mar. 20, 1940; s. Modesto Maidique and Hilda Rodriguez; m. Nancy; children: Ana Teresa, Mark Alex. BS, MIT, 1962, MS, 1964, PhD, 1970. Pres., CEO Genome Therapeutics Corp. (formerly known as Collaborative Rsch., Inc.); instr. MIT, Boston, 1976-79; v.p., gen. mgr. Analog Devices Semiconductor, Boston, 1970-76; asst. prof. Harvard University, Boston, 1976-81; assoc. prof. Stanford University, Palo Alto, Calif., 1981-84; sr. ptnr. Hambrecht and Quist Venture Ptnrs., Palo Alto, Calif., 1981-86; co-founder, dir. U. Miami Innovation and Entepreneurship Inst., 1984-86; dir.,Ctr. for Leadership Florida International U., Miami, pres., 1986—2009, faculty mem. Coll. of Bus. Adminstrn., 2009—, prof., Mgmt., 2009—. Bd dirs. Nat. Semiconductor Corp., 1993; bd. dirs. Carnival Corp., 1994—, Carnival plc, 2003—. Mem. Pres.'s Edn. Policy Adv. Com.; chmn. Beacon Coun., 1992-93. Recipient Citizenship award HEW, 1973, Teaching award Stanford U., 1983 Mem. IEEE, Assn. Cuban Engrs. Republican. Roman Catholic. Office: Florida International University 11200 SW 8th St Miami FL 33199 Office Phone: 305-348-2000. Office Fax: 305-348-6476. E-mail: maidique@fiu.edu.

MAIER, ROBERT HENRY, retired real estate executive; b. Greenville, Tex., Nov. 19, 1932; s. William Lokey and Charlsie Lorraine (Nation) M.; m. Ruth Jean Chapman, Mar. 1, 1968; children: Alice, Joy Kupp. BA, So. Meth. U., 1964. Pers. dir. Atlantic Richfield Co., Dallas, 1954-69; v.p. adminstrn. ETMF Freight System, Dallas, 1969-78; chief pers. officer Varo, Inc., Garland, Tex., 1978-80; corp. v.p. adminstrn. Comml. Metals Co., Dallas, 1980-88; pres., COO The Staubach Co., Dallas, 1988-93; pres., CEO, bd. dirs. Cornerstone Mgmt. Co., 1993-96; pres., CEO ProblemSolvers, Inc., 1996—2004.

MAIN, EDNA DEWEY (JUNE MAIN), emeritus education professor; b. Hyannis, Mass., Sept. 1, 1940; d. Seth Bradford and Edna Wilhelmina (Wright) Dewey; m. Donald John Main, Sept. 9, 1961 (div. Dec. 1989); children: Alison Teresa Main Ronzon, Susan Christine Main Leddy, Steven Donald Main. Degree in merchandising, Tobe-Coburn Sch., NYC, 1960; BA in Edn., U. North Fla., Jacksonville, 1974, MA in Edn., 1979, M in Adminstrn. and Supervision, 1983; PhD in Curriculum and Instrn., U. Fla., Gainsville, 1990. Tchr. Holiday Hill Elem. Sch., Jacksonville, Fla., 1974-86; instr. summer sci. inst., 1984—92; prof. edn. Jacksonville U., 1992—, dir. masters program in integrated learning and ednl. tech., emeritus prof., 2010—. Instr. U. Fla., 1987—90, U. North Fla., 1990—92; cons. Assn. Internat. Schs. Africa, 1994—97. Co-author: (book) Developing Critical Thinking Through Science, Book II, 2001; author: Developing Critical Thinking Through Science, Book I, 2005. Tchr. rep., chpt. leader White Ho. Young Astronaut Program, 1984—85; team leader NSF Shells Elem. Sci. Project. Recipient Innovative Excellence in Tchg., Learning and Tech. award, Internat. Coll. Conf., 1999, Outstanding Alumni award, U. North Fla., 1999, Eve award for Edn., 2001, Apple Disting. Educator award, 2003—; named Fla. Prof. of the Yr., Carnegie Found., 2002, Prof. of Yr., Jacksonville U., 2003. Mem.: Internat. Soc. Tech. Edn., Soc. Info. Tech. and Tchr. Edn., ASCD, NSTA (Sci. Tchrs. Achievement Recognition award 1983), Am. Assn. for Advancement Scis., Kappa Delta Pi, Phi Delta Kappa, Phi Kappa Phi. Personal E-mail: main750@bellsouth.net.

MAIN, JAMES ALLEN, state supreme court justice; m. Gale Main; children: Jay, Saxon, Ashley. BS in Pharmacy, Auburn U.; JD, U. Ala. Pvt. practice, Anniston, Ala., 1972, Montgomery, Ala., 1989; legal advisor to gov. State of Ala., sr. counsel to gov., dir. fin., 2004—09; judge Ala. Ct. Criminal Appeals, 2009—11; assoc. justice Supreme Ct. Ala., 2011—. City atty. City of Anniston, Ala., City of Oxford, Ala.; judge City of Lineville, Ala. Recipient Parke Davis Leadership Award, Bowl of Hygeia, Disting. Alumnus Award, Auburn U. Sch. Pharmacy, Pres.'s Award, American Soc. Pharmacy and Law. Fellow: Ala. Law Found.; mem.: American Pharmacists Assn., Ala. Bar Assn. Office: Alabama Supreme Court 300 Dexter Ave Montgomery AL 36104 Office Phone: 334-229-0700.*

MAIN, JOSEPH A., federal agency administrator; b. Waynesgurg, Pa., 1948; Grad., Nat. Mine Health & Safety Acad., Beckley, W.Va. Coal mine worker, 1967—2004; asst. to internat. pres. United Mine Workers of America (UMWA), 1974—76, safety inspector, adminstrv. asst. and dep. dir. safety divsn., 1976—82, adminstr. UMWA Occupl. Health & Safety Dept., 1982—2004, ret.; mine safety cons.; asst. sec. for mine safety & health (MSHA), US Dept. Labor, Washington, 2009—. Office: MSHA 1100 Wilson Blvd 21st Fl Arlington VA 22209 Office Phone: 202-693-9414.*

MAIN, TIMOTHY L., electronics company executive; b. 1957; BS, Mich. State U.; M in Internat. Mgmt., Am. Grad. Sch. Internat. Mgmt. Comml. lending officer internat. divsn. Nat. Bank Detroit; mgr. prodn. control Jabil Circuit, Inc., St. Petersburg, Fla., 1987, ops. mgr., 1987-89, project mgr., 1989-91, v.p. bus. devel., 1991, sr. v.p. bus. devel., pres., 1999—, CEO, 2000—. Bd. dirs. Jabil Circuit Inc., 1999—. Office: Jabil Cir 10560 9th St N Saint Petersburg FL 33716

MAINELLA, FRAN (FRANCES P. MAINELLA), educator, former federal agency administrator; b. Groton, Conn., 1947; BS cum laude, U. Conn.; MS cum laude in Counseling, Ctrl. Conn. State Coll.; PhD in Pub. Svc. (hon.), Ctrl. Conn. State U., 2002. H.S. phys. edn. tchr. Vernon Pub. Sch., Rockville, Conn., 1969—77; asst. ctr. dir. Tallahassee Parks and Recreation Dept., 1977—78; dir. recreation Town of Lake Park, Fla., 1978—83; exec. dir. Fla. Recreation and Park Assn., Tallahassee, 1983—89; dir. divsn. Recreation and Parks Fla. Dept. Environ. Protection, Tallahassee, 1989—2001; dir. Nat. Park Svc. US Dept. Interior, Washington, 2001—06; vis. scholar Clemson U., SC, 2006—. Spkr. in field. Contbr. numerous articles to profl. publs. Co-chair Com. for Preservation of the White House, mem. adv. coun. on hist. preservation; bd. trustees John F. Kennedy Ctr. for Performing Arts; liaison White House Hist. Soc.; sec., treas. Nat. Park Found.; mem. Am. Folklife Bd.; past pres. Nat. Assn. State Park Dirs.; past bd. mem. Am. Acad. Park and Recreation Adminstr.; past mem. Fla. Commn. Ttourism; past officio bd. mem. Fla. Recreation and Park Assn.; past mem. Gov.'s Mansion adv. com.; past bd. mem. Fla. Gov.'s Coun. on Phys. Fitness and Sports; past sec., bd. dirs. Spl. Olympics; past pres. Tallahassee Soc. Assn. Execs.; past chair United Way Drive for Tallahassee Soc. Assn. Execs.; past bd. dirs. Tallahassee Leon County Convention and Visitors Bur.; bd. dirs. Ford's Theatre Soc., Wolf Trap Found. for Performing Arts. Recipient Disting. Svc. award, Nat. Assn. Recreation Resource Planners, 1996, Woman of Distinction award, Girl Scout Coun. of Apalachee Bend, 1998, Pugsley medal, Am. Acad. Park and Recreation Adminstrn., 1998, Disting. Svc. award, Nat. Assn. State Park Dirs., 1999, Senator Bob Williams award, State of Fla., 2001, Sheldon Coleman Outdoors award, 2002, Walter T. Cox Pub. Svc. Achievement award, Clemson U., 2002. Mem.: Nat. Recreation and Park Assn. (congress planning com. 1984, 1987, past chair coun. exec. dirs., pres. 1997—, Harold D. Meyer Profl. award 2000). E-mail: fmainella@clemson.edu.

MAINIERI, PAUL, college baseball coach; b. Morgantown, W.Va., Aug. 29, 1957; s. Demie Mainieri; m. Karen Fejes; children: Nicholas, Alexandra, Samantha, Thomas. Attended, La. State U., Miami-Dade CC, U. New Orleans; BS in Phys. Edn., Fla. Internat. U., Miami, 1980; MS in Sports Adminstrn., St. Thomas U., Miami, Fla., 1982. Asst. baseball, football coach Columbus HS, Miami, 1979—82; head baseball coach St. Thomas U. Bobcats, 1983—88; athletic dir. St. Thomas U., 1985—88; head baseball coach USAF Acad. Falcons, 1989—94, U. Notre Dame Fighting Irish, 1995—2006, La. State U. Fighting Tigers, 2007—. Chmn. divsn. I baseball coaches Am. Baseball Coaches Assn., mem. exec. com.; mem. divsn. I baseball issues com. NCAA, mem. academic enhancement working group. Named Coach of Yr., Sunshine State Conf., 1984, CBI Nat. Coach of Yr., 1999, Big East/Midwest Coach of Yr., 2001, Mideast Region Coach of Yr., 2002, Am. Baseball Coaches Assn., 2006, South Region Coach of Yr., 2009, Nat. Coach of Yr., 2009, Baseball America, Collegiate Baseball, 2009, Coach of Yr., Southeastern Conf., 2009. Achievements include head baseball coach of College World Series NCAA national championship winning Louisiana State University Fighting Tigers, 2009. Office: La State Univ Baseball Athletics Dept PO Box 25095 Baton Rouge LA 70894-5095 Office Phone: 225-578-4148. Business E-Mail: paulmainieri@lsu.edu.

MAIRE, BARBARA JEAN, volunteer; b. Chgo., Feb. 23, 1932; d. Eldee W. and Emilie (Gadecki) Sayre; m. L. Thomas Maire, July 25, 1953. Student, Art Inst., Chgo., 1946-50. Officer mgr., asst. sec., cost acct. Buchen Advt., Inc., Chgo., 1952-72; with pub. rels. dept. Sebring (Fla.) Internat. Raceway, 1986—. Bd. mem. Sebring Internat. Raceway Adv. Coun., 1986—; bd. dirs. Lake Briarwood Homeowners Assn., Arlington Heights, Ill., 1976-80; active Citizens for Utility Rate Equity, Sebring, 1989-92, SE div. Adminstr. Race Control, Sports Car Club Am., 1989-96; coord. Highlands County, Fla. Lakewatch, 1991-99; mem. code enforcement bd. City of Sebring, 1993-2003. Mem. Fla. Steinmetz Alumni Assn., Sports Car Club Am. (bd. govs. 1985-92, chmn. race ofcl. licensing 1986-91, Race Ofcl. of Yr. 1988), MG Car Club Am. (officer 1962-67, Mem. of Yr. 1966), Am. Model Yachting Assn. (exec. sec. 1977-87), Sebring Country Club. Democrat. Home and Office: 190 Lake Drive Blvd Sebring FL 33875-5021 Home Phone: 863-385-8529; Office Phone: 863-655-1442. Personal E-mail: tbmaire@earthlink.net.

MAIRONE, REBECCA, mortgage company executive; BS in Chem. Engring., Drexel U., Phila., Pa.; MBA, Villanova U., Phila., Pa. With indsl. chem and mfg. industry; with various positions Cendant Mortgage, Countrywide Home Loans; mgr. ctrl. sales mortgage orgn. JP Morgan Chase; default servicing exec. home loans Bank of America, nat. mortgage outreach exec., 2011—. Mem. global diversity and inclusion coun. Bank of America; exec. sponsor Leadership Edn. Advocacy and Devel. Active LA Juvenile Diabetes Found. Office: Bank of America 100 N Tyron St Charlotte NC 28255 Office Phone: 704-386-5972.

MAIWURM, JAMES JOHN, lawyer; b. Wooster, Ohio, Dec. 5, 1948; s. James Frederick and Virginia Anne (Jones) M.; m. Wendy S. Leeper, July 31, 1971; children: James G., Michelle K. BA, Coll. Wooster, 1971; JD, U. Mich., 1974. Bar: Ohio 1974, D.C. 1986, Md. 1987, N.Y., 1987. Ptnr. Squire, Sanders & Dempsey, Cleve. and Washington, 1974-90; ptnr., group head Crowell & Moring, Wash, 1990-98; ptnr. Squire, Sanders & Dempsey, Washington, 1998-99; chmn., CEO Kaiser Group Internat., Inc., Fairfax, Va., 1999-2000; mng. ptnr. Squire, Sanders & Dempsey LLP, Washington, 2001—03, firmwide mng. ptnr., 2003—09, chmn., global CEO, 2009—. Contbr. articles to profl. jours. Mem. ABA, DC Bar Assn., Leadership Washington, The Tower Club (bd. govs. 2003-10). Office: Squire Sanders LLP 1200 19th St NW Washington DC 20036 Office Phone: 202-626-6669. Business E-Mail: james.maiwurm@squiresanders.com.

MAIZE, JOHN CHRISTOPHER, dermatologist, educator; b. Elizabeth, NJ, July 23, 1943; s. Donald Adam and Caroline Marie (Costanzo) Maize; m. Janice Lee Bentley, May 21, 1966; children: Sandra Kristine Tolly, John C. Jr., Jennifer Lee. MD, U. Mich., 1968. Cert. Am. Bd. Dermatology. Intern U. Mich., Ann Arbor, 1968—69, residency in dermatology, 1968—72; asst. prof. dermatology SUNY, Buffalo, 1972—77, assoc. prof., 1977—80, Med. U. SC, Charleston, 1980—83, prof., 1983—89, prof., chmn. dept. dermatology, 1989—2003, clin. prof., 2003—. Author: Pigmented Lesions of the Skin, 1987, Cutaneous Pathology, 1998; editor-in-chief Am. Jour. Dermatology, 1986—90. Fellow: Am. Soc. Dermapathology (pres. 1995), Am. Acad. Dermatology; mem.: Am. Bd. Dermatology (dir. 1990—99, pres. 1999), S.C. Dermatol. Assn. (pres. 2001), S.C. Med. Assn., Internat. Soc. Dermatopathology (sec. 1987—89, pres. 1989—91), Am. Dermatol. Assn. Roman Catholic. Avocations: fishing, golf, travel. Office: 266 W Coleman Blvd Unit 101 Mount Pleasant SC 29464 Home Phone: 843-881-1007; Office Phone: 843-388-6911. E-mail: jmaizesr@ameripath.com.

MAJETTE, DENISE, former congresswoman, real estate broker; b. Bklyn., May 18, 1955; d. Voyd and Olivia Majette; m. Rogers Mitchell Majette; 2 children. BA, Yale U., 1976; JD, Duke U., 1979. Atty. Legal Aid Soc. Winston-Salem, NC, 1981—83; law asst. Ga. Ct. Appeals, 1984—89; ptnr. Jenkins Nelson & Welch, 1989—92; spl. asst. atty. gen. State of Ga., 1991—92; adminstrv. law juste Ga. State Bd. Workers' Compensation, 1992; judge State Ct. of DeKalb County, 1993—2002; congresswoman 4th Dist. Ga. US House of Representatives, 2003—05; broker Chapman Realty, Brunswick, Ga., 2008—. Grad. Leadership DeKalb, 1992; mem. Kidney Caucus; former com. mem. Miller Grove PTA; past mem. vestry Episcopal Ch. of Holy Cross; former pres. DeKalb Lawyers Assn.; mem. Childcare Com. YMCA, Decatur; mem. adv. bd. Jr. League DeKalb County; mem. Congl. Black Caucus, Congl. Caucus on India and Indian Ams.; mem. steward bd. Antioch AME Ch. Recipient Judge's Cmty. Recognition award, Black Law Students' Assn., Ga. State U. Coll. Law, 2001, You Go Girl award, Ga. Assn. Black Women Attys., 2003. Democrat. Office: 123 Benedict Rd Brunswick GA 31520 Office Phone: 912-280-0088.

MAJEWSKI, THEODORE EUGENE, chemist; b. Boonton, NJ, July 5, 1925; s. Witold Charles and Felixa (Tkacz) M.; m. Cynthia Ann Davis, Sept. 26, 1953; children: Andrea, Theodore, Steven, Felicia, Cynthia, Melissa. BA, Syracuse U., 1951; MS, U. Del., 1953, PhD, 1960. Chemist Dow Chem. Co., Midland, Mich., 1957—69; rsch. chemist Philip Morris USA, Richmond, Va., 1969—92; ret., 1992. Cons. Herald Pharmacal, Richmond, 1979-81. Contbr. articles to profl. jours.; patentee in field. Bd. dirs. Boy Scouts Am., Richmond, 1957-91. With USN, 1943-46, PTO. Recipient Silver Beaver award Boy Scouts Am., 1980. Mem. Am. Chem. Soc., AAAS, Alpha Ci Sigma. Avocations: travel, fishing, reading, camping. Home: PO Box 8117 Duck NC 27949-8117 Personal E-mail: tmaje32613@aol.com.

MAJHAIL, RUBY, healthcare company executive; Sr. mgr. Plante & Moran; CFO Physician's Group of Ariz., Inc.; v.p. fin. Sun Health Corp., 1997—2006; CFO Biltmore Surgery Ctr., 2006—07, Tempe St. Luke's, 2006—08, St. Luke's Behavioral Health Ctr., 2006—08, St. Luke's Med. Ctr., 2006—08; CFO Ariz. and Nev. markets IASIS Healthcare Corp., 2007—. Office: IASIS Healthcare Corp Bldg E 117 Seaboard Ln Franklin TN 37067 Office Phone: 615-844-2747. Office Fax: 615-846-3006.

MAJID, DEWAN SYED ABDUL, physiologist, educator; b. Sylhet, Bangladesh, Apr. 10, 1954; s. Dewan Syed Abdul Matin and Zohurun Nessa; m. Nina R. Tarafder; children: D. S. Adnan, D. S. Safwan. MBBS, Chittagong U., Sylhet, 1977; PhD, Leeds U., Eng., 1989. Prof. physiology Tulane U. Sch. Medicine, New Orleans, 1990—. Fellow: Am. Soc. Nephrology, Am. Heart Assn.; mem.: Am. Physiol. Soc. Achievements include research in role of nitric oxide, superoxide and inflammation in hypertension. Office: Tulane University Sch Medicine 1430 Tulane Ave New Orleans LA 70112 Home: 4441 Rue Saint Martin Kenner LA 70065 Office Fax: 504-988-2675. Business E-Mail: majid@tulane.edu.*

MAJORS, CHARLES H., bank executive; BA in History, Auburn U., Ala., 1967; JD, U. Va. Sch. Law, 1970. Atty., asst. dean U. Va., 1970—72; ptnr., pres. Clement & Wheatley PC, 1972—92; prin. atty. Am. Nat. Bank and Trust Co., 1977—92, pres., 1993; pres., CEO American National Bank and Trust Co., 1994—. Bd. dirs. Am. Nat. Bank and Trust Co., 1981—, Danville Regional Health Sys. Chmn. bd. dirs. Va. Econ. Devel. Partnership, 2005—09. Office: American National Bankshares Inc 628 Main St Danville VA 24541 Office Phone: 434-773-2219. Office Fax: 434-792-1582. Business E-Mail: majorsc@amnb.com.

MAKAR, SCOTT D., lawyer; m. Nancy Hogshead-Makar; children: Aaron, Clare, Millicent. BS in Math., Economics, Mercer U., Macon, Ga., 1980; MA in Economics, U. Fla., Gainesville, 1982, JD with honors, 1987, PhD in Fin., 1993. Law clk. antitrust divsn. US Dept. Justice, Washington, 1985; law clk. Holland & Knight LLP, Tampa, Fla., 1986, capital ptnr. Tallahassee, Jacksonville, Fla., 1989—2001, law clk. Tallahassee, 1987; law clk. to Hon. Thomas A. Clark US Ct. Appeals (11th Cir.), Atlanta; chief of appellate divsn. City of Jacksonville Office of Gen. Counsel, 2001—07; solicitor gen. Office of Atty. Gen., Fla., 2007—. Adj. and vis. prof. bus. law U. Fla.; law instr. Fla Coastal Sch. Law, U. North Fla., Jacksonville U., Fla. State U. Coll. Law. Former mem. Gov. Jeb Bush's Task Force on Capital Cases, Fla.; apptd. mem. standard jury instructions com., chmn. Fla. Supreme Ct.; grad. Leadership Jacksonville, 1999. Named one of Fla. Trends Legal Elites, 2004, 2005. Mem.: American Law Inst. (mem. bd. dirs. ALI-ABA com. on continuing legal edn.), The Fla. Bar (founding mem. appellate and advocacy practice sect.), Jacksonville Bar Assn. (founding mem. appellate practice sect.), Fla. Blue Key. Office: State of Fla Office of Atty Gen 400 S Monroe St The Capitol PL-01 Tallahassee FL 32399-1050 Office Phone: 850-414-3300.

MAKI, MARK A., corporate financial executive; Prin. fin. officer Enbridge Energy Management, LLC, Enbridge Energy Co., Inc., chief acct., 1997—99; contr. Enbridge Pipelines Inc., 1999—2001, Enbridge Energy Co., Inc., 2001—02, Enbridge Energy Management, LLC, 2001—02, v.p., fin., 2002—, Enbridge Energy Co., Inc., 2002—, Enbridge Energy Partners, LP, 2002—. Office: Enbridge Energy Partners LP 1100 Louisiana St Ste 3300 Houston TX 77002 Office Phone: 713-821-2000. Office Fax: 713-821-2232. Business E-Mail: Mark.Maki@enbridge.com.

MAKOUS, WALTER LEON, visual scientist, educator; s. Lawrence and Ruth Lorraine (Luehring) Makous; m. Marilyn Ann Carlson, Feb. 2, 1958 (div. 1973); children: Ann, James, Matthew; m. Joyce Brown Menconi, 1974 (div. 1981); m. Barbara Anne Duggins, Apr. 29, 1982 (dec. 2010); m. Robbie Nell Shanklin, Oct. 17, 2010. BS, U. Wis., 1958; MSc, Brown U., Providence, 1961, PhD, 1964. Mem. staff IBM, Yorktown Heights, NY, 1963-66; asst. prof. psychology U. Wash., 1966-69, lectr. in physiology and biophysics, 1966-69, assoc. prof. psychology, 1969-74, prof. psychology, 1974-79; prof. psychology, ophthalmology and visual sci. U. Rochester, 1979-95, prof. brain and cognitive sci., ophthalmology & visual sci., 1995—2012, emeritus prof. brain and cognitive sci., & visual sci., 2012—, dir., Ctr. Visual Sci., 1979-90, chmn., Ctr. SYMP, 1981—82; adj. prof. psychology U. Ala., Birmingham, 2012—. NW rep., charter mem. steering com. West Coast Regional Consortium Univs in Neuroscis., 1976—79; mem coun on energy saving through more efficient lighting NAS-NRC, 1978—79, night vision coun, 1985—86; sensory processes panelist NSF, Washington, 1977—82, mem. adv. com. applied sci and rsch. applicaitons policy, 1978—81; rev. com. mem. Presidential Young Investigator Award Program, 1984; vis scientist IBM Rsch., 1970—71. Editor (consult ed): Sensory Processes, 1977—79, Jour of the Optical Soc Am, 1982—86; contbr. articles to profl jours. With USNR, 1953—55. Grantee, Nat Eye Inst, 1969—2006, NSF, 1959—62, 1981—82. Fellow: AAAS, Optical Soc. Am. (ed vision and color 1982—86, mem coord vision and physiological optics comt 1983—89, coord vision and med optics comt 1983—89, publs comt 1985—89, chmn fellows and hon mems comt 1986, feature ed applied vision 1989—90); mem.: Am Nat Standards Inst/Human Factor & Ergonomics Soc-100 (rev comt 1992—2006, chmn. visual displays 2002—06, 2011—12), Assn. Rsch. in Vision and Ophthalmology (chmn sect psycho-physics 1977). Home: 623 Flag Cir Birmingham AL 35226 Office Phone: 585-260-8953. Business E-Mail: walt@cvs.rochester.edu.

MAKRINOS, STEPHEN T., information technology executive; m. Demetra Mavroidis. BS, CUNY; MS in Physics, Bklyn. Coll.; MBA, Monmouth U. Rschr. Hdqs. Comm. Electronics Command (HQ CECOM), Ft. Monmouth, NJ, asst. dir. digital integration lab., asst. to dir. for battlefield digitization, asst. to dir. Advanced Sys. Directorate; chief scientist info. dominance sys. group CACI International, Inc., Arlington, Va., 2000—. Recipient Medal of Merit, AFCEA Internat., 2009. Office: CACI International Inc 1100 N Glebe Rd Arlington VA 22201 Office Phone: 703-841-7800. Office Fax: 703-841-7882. Business E-Mail: smakrinos@caci.com.

MAKSI, GREGORY EARL, retired engineering educator; b. Wilkes-Barre, Pa., May 9, 1939; s. Stephen Cedric and Laura Victoria (Pytell) M.; children: Sabrina, Jared, Joshua. BSME, Ga. Inst. Tech., 1961, MS in Indsl. Mgmt., 1964; PhD in Edn. Adminstrn., U. Miss., 1983. Registered profl. engr., Tenn. Mech. engr. Ellicott Machine Corp., Balt., 1961-62; project engr. Celanese Corp., Rock Hill, SC, 1964-67; assoc. prof. State Tech. Inst., Memphis, 1967-71, prof., 1971—2007, program chmn. of indsl. engring., 1973-90, chmn. dept. mech. engring./indsl. engring., 1990—2000; athletics coach S.W. Tenn. CC, 1972—85, chair dept. engring. technologies Memphis, 2001—07, prof. emeritus, 2007—11. Cons. Tenn. Ednl. Alliance, Nashville, 1994, U. Ark., Millington, Tenn., 1988, instr., 1988—2005; curriclum coord. Memphis City H.S., 1993; quality-productivity adv., 1990; CAD/CAM cons., 1995. Hon. sheriff Shelby County Sheriff's Office, 1991; hon. state legis. Tenn. Ho. Reps., Nashville, 1992. Named Disting. Engr. Memphis Engrs. Coun., 1986, Outstanding Tech. Tchr. Am. Tech. Edn. Assn., 1998, Leadership Excellence award Nat. Inst. of Staff and Orgnl. Devel., 1997. Mem. Soc. Mfg. Engrs. (Outstanding Engr. 1998), Inst. of Indsl. Engrs., World Future Soc., Tenn. Profl. Engrs. Soc., Epsilon Pi Tau. Avocations: photography, tennis, racquetball, fishing.

MALAVE, ANDRES, pharmacologist, educator; b. San Juan, Puerto Rico, Nov. 18, 1949; s. Andres Malave, Adela Nevarez; m. Lillian Arce, July 28, 1972; children: Jose A., Jaime E., Josue I., Jessica M. BS in Pharmacy, U. P.R., 1972; MS, Purdue U., 1981, PhD, 1983. Registered pharmacist P.R. Instr. U. P.R., San Juan, 1975—78, asst. prof., 1984—87, assoc. prof., 1988—91; prof., chmn. Nova Southeastern U., Ft. Lauderdale, Fla., 1992—2001, assoc. dean, 2001—04, dean Coll. Pharmacy, 2004—. CEO Malave Consulting Svcs., Inc., Ft. Lauderdale, 2001—04; dean coll. pharmacy U. P.R., 1987—91. Recipient Bristol Meyers/Squibb Faculty Devel. award, 1991—92; scholar, Fulbright, 2001. Mem.: Am. Assn. Pharm. Scientist, Peruvian Acad. of Pharmacy, N.Y. Acad. Sci., Soc. Neurosci., Am. Assn. Coll. Pharmacy. Achievements include development of simple non-radioactive assay for estimating protein kinase C and protein phosphatase-1. Avocations: sports, racquetball, basketball, music, guitar. Home: 224 La Costa Way Weston FL 33326 Office Phone: 954-262-1304. E-mail: amalave@nova.edu, copdean@nova.edu.

MALDONADO, CARLOS MANUEL, surgeon; b. Barcelona, Sept. 25, 1938; came to U.S., 1964. MD, U. Barcelona, 1964. Diplomate Am. Bd. Surgery. Intern Columbia Hosp., Milw., 1964—65; resident gen. surgery Marquette Affiliate Hosps., Milw., 1966—68; fellow thoracic cardiac surgery Newark Beth Israel Med. Ctr., 1969—70, resident gen. surgery, 1972—75. Mem. staff Martin Meml. Hosp., Stuart, Fla., Martin Meml. Hosp. South, Ft. Salerno, Fla., 1975—, chief surgery, 1983-85, chmn. quality coun., 1994— Fellow ACS; mem. AMA, Fla. Med. Assn., Internat. Soc. Cardiovasc. Surgery, Southeastern Surg. Congress, Martin County Med. Soc. (pres. 1999) Republican. Roman Catholic. Home: 2392 SE Ocean Blvd Stuart FL 34996-4230 Office Phone: 772-286-0050. Business E-Mail: carlosmmaldonado@bellsouth.net.

MALECHA, MARVIN JOHN, architect, academic administrator; b. Lonsdale, Minn., June 26, 1949; s. George and Barbara Malecha; m. Cynthia Marie Miller, Aug. 8, 1970; children: Peter, Michelle. Student, St. Thomas Coll.; BArch, U. Minn.; MArch, Harvard U. Registered architect, Calif. Designer Wallace and Mundt Architects, Edina, Minn., 1969-73, Hugh Stubbins and Assocs., Cambridge, Mass., 1973-76; instr. Cambridge Urban Awareness Program, 1973-76, Boston Archtl. Ctr., 1974-76; asst. chmn., asst. prof. dept. arch. Coll. Environ. Design Calif. State Poly. U., Pomona, 1976-77, chmn., assoc. prof., 1979-82, prof., dean Coll. Environ. Design, 1982-94; dean Coll. Design N.C. State U., 1994—. Chmn. Univ. Fall Conf. com. Calif. State Poly. U., 1984; mem. steering com. Architects for Social Responsibility; mem. bd. advisors Tchrs. cert. program City Bldg. Edn. Program, planning com. So. Calif. Assn. Govts.; vis. critic UCLA, 1985, U., Minn., 1981-83, 87, U. So. Calif., 1980-87, Calif. Poly. State U., San Luis Obispo, 1979-87, Clemson U., 1988, Columbia U., 1993, U. Tenn., 1994, U. Md., 1995, Miss. State U., 1995, U. Wis., Milw., 1996, Roger Williams U., 1997; lectr. to schs. and archtl. assns.; cons. in architecture and research, Claremont, Calif., 1976—; master juror Nat. Council Archtl. Registration Bds.; mem. edn. equity com. Calif. State U. System, 1985-86; pres. Calif. Coun. Archtl. Edn., 1986-88; mem. accreditation vis. team for collegiate programs in landscape architecture, 1988—; bd. dirs. Nat. Archtl. Accreditation Bd.; campus architect cons. U. Calif., Riverside, 1990-94. Author: The Learning Organization and the Evolution of Practice Academy Concepts, Reconfiguration in the Study and Practice of Architecture, Form of Performance, The Fabric of Architecture, The Pomona Method; co-sgner, author internat. protocol for internat. exch. in arch. edn.; contbr. articles to profl. jours. Mem. Art and Liturgy com. Our Lady Assumption Ch., Claremont, Calif., 1982-94; mem. bldg. and real estate com. Archdiocese of Raleigh; bd. dirs. United Arts Raleigh, City Gallery Raleigh, 1995—; nat bd. dirs. Am. Inst. Architects; master juror workgroup, bd. dirs. Downtown Raleigh Alliance; pres. elect AIA, 2008-. Recipient Ellerbe Archtl. award, 1972, Hon. Mention Mass. Housing Dept., 1976, Topaz medallion for excellence in archtl. edn., 2003, Prize for Creative Integration of Practice and Edn. in the Acad., Nat. Coun. Archtl. Registration, 2002, Jackson Rigney award, NCSU, 2006, Date prize, Cal-Pol, Pomona, 2007, Haecker Leadership award, 2008, William R June dale prize, 2008; Rotch scholar, 1980. Fellow AIA (bd. dirs. L.A. chpt. 1982-83, chmn. state and nat. awards coms. 1983-85, chmn. Monterey design conf. com., Henry Adams award 1973, mem. steering com. archs. in edn. com. 1991, chair archs. in edn. com. 1994-95, adv. bd. ArchVoices, presdl. citation L.A. chpt. 1987, mem. Calif. coun. 1994, nat. bd. dirs. 2005, Excellence in Arch. Edn. award), European Assn. for Arch. Educators (hon.), Soc. Am. Registered Archs., Assn. Collegiate Schs. Arch. (v.p. 1988-89, chair ann. meeting, pres. 1988-89, adminstrs. conf. Wash. 1985, Disting. Prof. 2002), Calif. Coun. Archtl. Edn. (pres. 1988-89), Golden Key (hon. mem. N.C. chpt.), Sigma X. Office: NC State U Coll Design PO Box 7701 Raleigh NC 27695-0001 Office Phone: 919-515-8300. E-mail: marvin_malecha@ncsu.edu.

MALECKY, ROBERT A., manufacturing executive; b. Berwyn, Ill., Apr. 21, 1963; s. Walter M. and Marie Lousie (Mulhall) M.; m. Linda Ann Lange, Aug. 19, 1989; children: Bryan Robert, Nathan Patrick. BS, Pa. State U., 1985, MBA, 1988. Field engr. Dowell Schlumberger, Jackson, Mich., 1985—86; drilling engr. Tenneco, Lafayette, La., 1987—88; sr. bus. analyst Buckeye Pipeline Co., Allentown, Pa., 1989—91, mgr., Mktg., 1991—94, mgr., Corp. Devel., 1994—; v.p., Mktg. Buckeye GP Holdings, LP, 2000—09, v.p., Customer Svcs., 2010—. Home: 107 Tweed Way Harleysville PA 19438-3073 Office: Buckeye GP Holdings LP One Greenway Plz Houston TX 77046 Office Phone: 832-615-8600. E-mail: rmalecky@buckeye.com.

MALEK, FREDERIC VINCENT, finance company executive; b. Oak Park, Ill., Dec. 22, 1936; s. Fred W. and Martha (Smickilas) M.; m. Marlene A. McArthur, Aug. 5, 1961; children: Fred W., Michelle A. BS, U.S. Mil. Acad., 1959; MBA, Harvard U., 1964; D of Humanities (hon.), St. Leo Coll., St. Petersburg, Fla., 1970. Assoc. McKinsey & Co., Inc., LA, 1964-67; chmn. exec. com. Triangle Corp., Columbia, SC, 1967-69; dep. under sec. HEW, Washington, 1969-70; spl. asst. to Pres. U.S., Washington, 1970-73; dep. dir. U.S. Office of Mgmt. and Budget, Washington, 1973-75; with Marriott Corp., Washington, 1975-88, sr. v.p., 1975-77, exec. v.p., 1978-88; pres. Marriott Hotels and Resorts, 1981-88, Northwest Airlines, Mpls., 1989-90, vice chmn., 1990-91, also bd. dirs.; campaign mgr. Bush-Quayle '92, 1991-92; co-chmn. CB Richard Ellis Group, Inc., 1989-96; chmn. Lodging Opportunities Fund, 1991—, Thayer Hotel Investors, 1994—, Thayer Lodging Group, 1992. Chmn. 1996 Rep. Presdl. Trust, 1995-96; bd. dirs. DuPont Fabros Tech., CBRE; dir. with rank of amb., 1990 Econ. Summit, 1989—; adj. prof. U. S.C., 1986-89; lectr. Kennedy Sch. Govt., Harvard U., 1976. bd. dirs. Automatic Data Processing, Inc., 1978-2009 Mem. Pres.'s Commn. on White House Fellows, 1971-75, White House Domestic Coun., 1974-75, Pres.'s Commn. on Pers. Interchange, 1974-76; dep. dir. com. for Re-election of Pres., 1972; Pres.'s Commn. on Pvt. Sector Initiatives, 1982-85, dir. conv. Bush for Pres., 1988; mem. Nat. Coun. on Surface Transp. Rsch., 1993-95; nat. adv. bd. Nat. Ctr. Econ. Edn. of Children, 1980-82; mem. Pres.'s Coun. on Phys. Fitness and Sports, 1986-91; bd. visitors US Mil. Acad., West Point; co-chmn., McCain Campaign, 2008. Named Bus. Statesman of Yr. Harvard Bus. Sch. Club Washington, 2000, Citizen of Yr. Boy Scouts Am. Nat. Capitol Coun., 2000, Am. Friends of Czech Republic Civil Soc. Vision award, Woodrow Wilson award for corp. citizenship, 2004; named to Washington Bus. Hall of Fame, 2005; bd. trustees, Bush Libr. Found., Churchil Ctr. Leadership award, Named to Horatio Alger Soc., Named West Points Disting. Grad, 2014. Mem. Am.-Israel Friendship League (bd. trustees 1991—), Aspen Inst. (bd. trustees 1996—), Am. Friends Czech Republic (chmn. 2007-), Am. Action Forum(founder chmn.), Am. Action Network(founder), Rep. Govs. Assn.(fin. chmn.) Episcopalian. Avocations: bicycling, hiking. Home Phone: 703-522-6848. Business E-Mail: fmalek@thayercapital.com.

MALEK, MARLENE ANNE, foundation administrator; d. William and Yolanda (Stella) McArthur; m. Frederic Malek; children: Frederic William, Michelle A. Olson. Degree in Nursing, Marymount U. Pres. Friends Cancer Rsch., Washington, 2000—. Vice chmn. bd. dirs. Marymount U., Arlington, Va.; Internat. Com. J.F. Kennedy Ctr. Performing Arts, bd. dirs., Fords Theatre; bd. dirs. Nat. Mus. Women in Arts, Vital Voices Global Partnership, MD Anderson Cancer Ctr., Houston; bd. overseers Duke U. Cancer Ctr.; mem. Nat. Dialogue Cancer; bd. dirs. Va. Mus. Fine Arts. Avocations: cross country skiing, bicycling, hiking.

MALHOTRA, NARESH KUMAR, marketing educator; arrived in US, 1975, naturalized; s. Har Narian and Satya (Kakar) M.; m. Veena Bahl, Aug. 13, 1980; children: Ruth Veena, Paul Naresh. BTech with honors, Indian Inst. Tech., Bombay, 1971; MBA, I.I.M., Ahmedabad, India, 1973; MS, SUNY, Buffalo, 1978, PhD, 1979. Cert. Implementer of Enterprise Resource Planning 2001. Mgmt. cons. ASCI, Hyderabad, India, 1971-73; asst. prof. Ga. Tech. Inst., Atlanta, 1979—, assoc. prof. mgmt., coord. mktg., 1982-87, 89—, prof., 1988, Regents' prof., 1992—2009, sr. fellow, 2012—; Nanyang prof., sr. fellow NTU, 2009—12; mktg. legend, 2010. Organizer several nat. and internat. mktg. mgmt. confs. Author: Marketing Research: An Applied Orientation (N.Am., European, Internat., Australia and New Zealand, Indian, Spanish, Portuguese, Chinese, Russian, French, Japanese, Bahasa Indonesia and Hungarian edits.), Basic Marketing Research: Integration of Social Media, Essentials of Marketing Research: A Hands-On Orientation; founding editor Review of Mktg. Rsch.; contbr. articles to profl. jours. Founder, pres. Global Evangelistic Ministries Inc. Recipient Outstanding Mktg. Educator, Acad. of Mktg. Sci., 2005; named one of Best Prof. in Mktg. Mgmt., Asia's Best B-Sch. Awards, 2011. Fellow Acad. Mktg. Sci. (disting., program chmn. 1984-85, 85-86, v.p. programs 1988-90, chmn. bd. 1990-92, pres. 1994-96, chmn. found. 1996-98, Top Rschr., Jour. Mktg. Rsch., Jour. Acad. Mktg. Sci., Jour. Healthcare Mktg., Internat. Mktg. Rev.), Decision Scis. Inst. (track chmn. 1984-86); mem. Am. Mktg. Assn. (track chmn. 1983-84). Republican. Baptist. Achievements include selection as a marketing legend, globally top ranked a Cop researcher based on seven independent publication rankings. Avocations: reading, writing, outdoor activities. Home: 1956 Lenox Rd NE Atlanta GA 30306-3035 Office: Ga Tech Scheller Coll Business 800 West Peachtree Atlanta GA 30308-1149 Business E-Mail: naresh.malhotra@scheller.gatech.edu.

MALIN, ROBERT ABERNETHY, retired investment company executive; b. Mt. Vernon, NY, Dec. 13, 1931; s. Patrick Murphy and Caroline Cooper (Biddle) M.; m. Gail Lassiter, Nov. 5, 1960; children: Alison Campbell, Robert Lassiter. AB, Dartmouth Coll., 1953, MBA, 1954. Asst. to comptr. Biddle Purchasing Co., NYC, 1958-59; with Blyth & Co., Inc., NYC, 1960-71, v.p., 1965-71, dir., 1968-71, sr. v.p., mem. exec. com., 1971-72; sr. v.p. corp. fin. Reynolds Securities Inc., NYC, 1972-74, dir., 1973-74; mng. dir. First Boston Corp., NYC, 1974-90; gen. ptnr. Tiedemann Investment Group, NYC, 1991-96; mng. dir. SeaBridge Investment Advisors, Summit, NJ, 1997—2006; ret., 2006. Mem. adv. coun. Fin. Acctg. Stds. Bd., 1973-78. Served as lt. (j.g.) USNR, 1954-57. Mem.: Securities Industry Assn. (acctg. com.), Investment Bankers Assn. Am., The Moorings Club, Morris County Club, Beacon Hill Club. Republican. E-mail: malinroberta@gmail.com.

MALINOWSKI, DARIUSZ PIOTR, horticulturist, educator; s. Ryszard Wojciech Malinowski and Gabriela Maria Malinowska. Degree in Horticulture, Warsaw Agrl. U., Poland, 1989; PhD in Natural Scis., Swiss Fed. Inst. Tech., Zurich, Switzerland, 1995. Assoc. prof. Tex. A&M U., College Station, 2001—. Mem.: Am. Forage and Grasslands Coun. (assoc. Emerging Scientist award 1998, Merit award 2006), Am. Soc. Agronomy (assoc.). Achievements include research in discovery of chemical modifications in the rhizosphere of grasses infected with shoot-located Neotyphodium spp. fungal endophytes. Office: Texas Agrilife Research Stn 11708 Hwy 70W Vernon TX 76385 Business E-Mail: d-malinowski@tamu.edu.

MALKI, HEIDAR A., dean; arrived in US, 1979; s. Karim A. and Rokhsareh A. Malki; m. Layla F. Niaki, June 12, 1962; 1 child, Armeen. PhD, U. Wis., Milw., 1990. Prof. U. of Houston, 1991—2005, assoc. dean, 2004—. Adviser Mind and Vision Computing, Houston, 1992—2000. Author: (textbook) Control Systems Technology (Best Paper award, 1998). Recipient Rsch. in Outstanding Faculty award; named Alumnus of Yr., 2005. Mem.: IEEE, Am. Soc. Engring. Edn. (zone chair 1997—98, Best Paper award). Office: U Houston 4800 Calhoun Rd Houston TX 77204-4020 Office Fax: 713-743-4032. Business E-Mail: malki@uh.edu.

MALLET, ALEXIS, JR., construction company executive; b. New Iberia, La., Nov. 9, 1951; s. Alexis Sr. and Adelia Maria (Comeaux) M.; m. Brenda King (div.); children: Lorphy, Devlin, Casey, Reagan; m. Sarah Elizabeth Roach, Oct. 24, 1987 (div.); children: Thomas Wilson, Alexis III, Joseph Taylor. BA, U. S.W. La., 1975. Bookkeeper A & A Home Supplies, New Iberia, 1969-71; sales staff Voorhies Supply Co., New Iberia, 1972-74; CEO Royal Constrn. Co., New Iberia, 1974—. Bd. dirs. 1st Gen. Enterprises, Ft. Lauderdale, Fla.; CEO First Gen. Svcs., South La., 1990; legal constrn. cons. in field. Prodr. (album) Fourth Hour, 1982. Cert. restorer Nat. Inst. Disaster Restoration; past v.p., bd. dirs. Iberia Bldg. Assn. Recipient Sales Achievement award Southern Structures, La., 1987, Superior Performance award Southern Structures, 1984, Facility award U.S. Tennis Assn., 1982. Mem. Inst. Inspection Cleaning and Restoration, Assn. Specialists in Cleaning and Restoration (cert. fire restoration specialist), Nat. Inst. Disaster Repair (Phoenix award for innovation in reconstruction 1999, Chrysalis Design Build award 1999). Republican. Roman Catholic. Avocations: fishing, hunting, golf. Office: 103 Bradbury Xing Lafayette LA 70508-6640 Office Phone: 337-988-3556.

MALLETT, EDWARD A., lawyer; Grad., Dartmouth Coll.; JD, U. Tex. Bar: Tex. Ptnr. Mallett & Saper, LLP, Houston. Lectr. U. Houston Sch. Law, Nat. Criminal Defense Coll. Contbr. articles to profl. jours. Office: Mallett Saper Berg LLP 600 Travis St Ste 1900 Houston TX 77002 Office Phone: 713-236-1900. E-mail: edward@mgscounsel.com.

MALLIA, MARIANNE, medical writer; b. Davenport, Iowa, Feb. 14, 1948; d. Norman Bramblett and Mary Jane (Hilkemeyer) Hagar; 1 child from previous marriage, Lindsay Sharyn. BA in English, U. Iowa, 1970. Cert. tchr., editor in life sci. Tchr. tech. writing Houston Ind. Sch. Dist., 1970—76; med. writer Tex. Heart Inst., Houston, 1976—; editl. cons. Tex. Heart Inst. Jour., Houston, 1977—87, head sci. publ., 1986—, sr. med. writer, 1994—. Instr. Sch. Allied Health Sci. and Sch. Pub. Health U. Tex., 1990—94. Editor: Techniques in Cardiac Surgery, 1984; editor: (with Denton A. Cooley) Surg. Treatment of Aortic Aneurysms, 1985; editor: (essays) Reflections and Observation, Denton A. Cooley, MD, 1985; author: (handbook) Heart Owner's Handbook, 1995; bd. editors: Life Sci., 2002. Fellow: Am. Med. Writers Assn. (core curriculum cert. 1984, instr. 1985—, advanced curriculum cert. 1989, honor roll workshop leader 1992—, bd. dir., exec. com. 1996—2005, pres. 2002—03, writer advanced core curriculum, Award Tchg. Excellence 1998, Golden Apple award 1998, Swanberg Disting. Svc. award 2010); mem.: Women in Comm. (Matrix award 1996—2000), Coun. Biology Editors, Pi Beta Phi. Avocation: classic cars. Office: Tex Heart Inst PO Box 20345 Houston TX 77225-0345 Office Phone: 832-355-6776. Business E-Mail: mmallia@heart.thi.tmc.edu.

MALLORY, SANDRA MOSS, legal administrator; b. Atlanta, Dec. 24, 1945; d. Harold Melvin and Velma Aileen (Norton) H.; m. Marshall L. Moss, May 1, 1965 (dec. Aug. 2000); children: Tara Celise, Justin Hughes; m. Tom Mallory, March 21, 2004. Student, West Ga. Coll., 1964-65, Ga. State U. Legal sec. Smith, Cohen, Ringel, Kohler & Martin, Atlanta, 1965-78; real estate sales Century 21-Phoenix, College Park, Ga., 1978-80; office mgr./pers. dir. Smith, Cohen, Ringel, Kohler & Martin, Atlanta, 1980-85; exec. dir. Smith, Gambrell & Russell LLP, Atlanta, 1985—. Bd. dirs., sec. North Clayton Athletic Assn., Riverdale, Ga., 1981-83; sec. E.W. Oliver PTA, Riverdale, 1981; exec. com. E.W. Oliver and N. Clayton Jr. PTA, Riverdale, 1980, 81, 82; den leader Cub Scouts, Pack 959, Riverdale, 1984; pres. Women's Coun., 1st Christian Ch. Tyrone, 2000-02; pres., bd. mem. Hope of Africa, 2005-06; fundraising com. mem. Run for Justice benefitting Atlanta Legal Aid. Mem. Assn. Legal Adminstrs. (sec. Atlanta chpt. 1988, v.p., pres. 1990-91, nat. conf. com. mem. 1991-92, regional meetings officer 1993-94). Avocation: painting. Home: 405 Pendleton Trail Tyrone GA 30290 Office: Smith Gambrell & Russell LLP 1230 Peachtree St NE Ste 3100 Atlanta GA 30309-3592 Office Phone: 404-815-3504. Business E-Mail: smallory@sgrlaw.com.

MALLORY CARAWAY, BARBARA, state legislator; b. Clarksville, Tex. m. Dwaine Caraway. BA in Telecomm., Theatre, Tex. So. U., Houston. Former instr. Nova Charter Sch., Dallas; mem. Dallas City Coun., 1993—2001; founder Dallas Youth Commn., Tenn. Ct. Sys., Barbara Mallory Caraway & Assocs., 2000, Showcase Group LLC, 2004; mem. Dist. 100 Tex. House of Representatives, 2007—. Mem.: Nat. Found. of Women Legislators, Nat. Conf. of State Legislators, North Ctrl. Tex. Coun. Govt. (bd. dirs.), Nat. Assn. Black Elected Offcls., Nat. League Cities, Tex. Mcpl. League, Cedar Crest Neighborhood Assn. Democrat. Office: 2908 E 11th St Ste B Dallas TX 75203 also: Room E2.420 Capitol Extension PO Box 2910 Austin TX 78768 Address: PO Box 764171 Dallas TX 75376 Office Phone: 214-941-4619, 512-463-0664.

MALLOY, GERALD, state legislator; b. Chesterfield County, Oct. 26, 1961; s. John and Geraldine Malloy; m. Davita McFarland, July 8, 1989; children: Donovan, Jonthan, Jordan, Morgan. BS, U. SC, 1984, JD, 1988. Chmn. Pub. Defenders Bd. Downtown Devel. Bd.; mem. SC Supreme Ct. Com. Lawyers Conduct, 1996—; mem. Dist. 29 SC State Senate, 2002—. Mem.: SC Bar Assn., SC Trial Lawyer Assn., Nat. Football Assn., Nat. Basketball Assn., Lions Club. Democrat. Mailing: 1216 Salen Rd Hartsville SC 29550 Office: 512 Gressette Bldg Columbia SC 29201 Home Phone: 843-332-5533; Office Phone: 843-339-3000, 803-212-6148. E-mail: malloyg@scstatehouse.net.

MALLUCHE, HARTMUT HORST, nephrologist, medical educator; b. Jan. 1, 1943; arrived in U.S., 1975, naturalized, 1985; s. Harald E. and Renate (Muenzberg) M.; children: Nadine, Danielle, Tiffany. Abitur, Albertus Magnus Coll., Koenigstein, Germany, 1963; postgrad., Phillips U., Marburg/Lahn, Fed. Republic Germany, 1963—65, U. Innsbruck, Austria, 1965—66, U. Vienna, 1966; MD, J.W. Goethe U., Frankfurt, Fed. Republic Germany, 1969. Diplomate German Bd. Internal Medicine. Intern County Hosp., Aichach, Germany, 1969—70; resident in internal medicine, fellow in nephrology Cen. Internal Medicine, Univ. Hosp., Frankfurt Am Main, Germany, 1970—75; asst. prof. medicine U. So. Calif., Calif., 1975—78, assoc. prof., 1978—81; prof., dir. divsn. nephrology, bone and mineral metabolism U. Ky. Med. Ctr., Lexington, 1981—. Cons. NIH, FDA; mem. Va. Merit Rev. Bd. Nephrology; program dir. Gen. Clin. Rsch. Ctr. Author: (monograph) Atlas of Mineralized Bone Histology, 1986; editor-in-chief Clinical Nephrology; contbr. articles to profl. jours. and books. Grantee, NIH, 1982—, Shriner's Hosp. for Crippled Children. Fellow: ACP; mem.: AAAS, Internat. Soc. Bone Morphometry (founder), Internat. Soc. Nephrology, Am. Fedn. Clin. Rsch., European Dialysis and Transplantation Assns., Am. Soc. Physiol. endocrinology, Am. Soc. Bone and Mineral Rsch., Am. Soc. Clin. Investigation, Am. Soc. Nephrology. Office Phone: 859-323-5049 221.

MALONE, BENNETT, state legislator; b. Carthage, Miss., Jan. 6, 1944; m. Teresa Dolan; children: Ricky Bennett, Gina Marie, Brittany Nicole, Krystal Yvonne. Mem. Dist. 45 Miss. House of Reps., 1980—; automobile & tractor dealer; cattle rancher. Named one of Mississippi's Outstanding Young Businessmen, 1974—75. Mem.: Leake Cattlemen's Assn. (former pres.), Miss. Cattlemen's Assn., Mason. Democrat. Baptist. Mailing: PO Box 528 Carthage MS 39051-0528 Office Phone: 601-267-0201, 601-395-3367. Business E-Mail: bmalone@house.ms.gov.

MALONE, CHARLES R., circuit court judge; b. Tuscaloosa, Ala., 1954; m. Terri Avery; 2 children. BS in Commerce & Bus. Adminstrn., U. Ala., Tuscaloosa, 1976; JD, Samford U. Cumberland Sch. Law, Birmingham, Ala., 1981. Bar: Ala. Pvt. practice atty., Tuscaloosa, 1981—2000; cir. judge Sixth Jud. Cir., 2000—11, Tuscaloosa, Ala., 2013—, presiding judge, 2003, 2010; chief of staff to Gov. Robert Bentley Office of Gov., Ala., 2011; chief justice Supreme Ct. of Ala., 2011—13. Adj. prof. U. Ala. Sch. Law, U. Ala. Sch. Commerce and Bus.; guest lectr. Ala. Peace Officers Standards and Tng. Commn. Law Enforcement Acad. Coach YMCA Little League, Ala.; deacon, adult Sunday sch. tchr., trustee First Bapt. Ch., Tuscaloosa; dir. First Bapt. Ch. Found.; former mem. vol. steering com. West Ala. Easter Seals Rehab. Ctr. Mem.: Tuscaloosa County Bar Assn. (former pres.). Office: 6th Judicial Circuit Tuscaloosa County Courthouse 714 Greensboro Ave Tuscaloosa AL 35401 Office Phone: 205-349-3870 ext. 270.

MALONE, CLAUDINE BERKELEY, management consultant; b. Louisville, May 9, 1936; d. Claude McDowell and Mary Katharine (Smith) Malone. BA, Wellesley Coll., 1963; MBA, Harvard U., 1972. CPA Md. Sys. engr. IBM Corp., Washington, 1964; sr. sys. analyst Crane Co., Chgo., 1966; contr., mgr. data processing Raleigh Stores, Washington, 1967—70; asst. prof. Harvard U., 1972—72, assoc. prof., 1977—81; pres., CEO Fin. & Mgmt. Consulting Inc., McLean, Va., 1981—. Vis. prof. Georgetown U., 1982—84, U. Va., 1984—87; dir. Scott Paper Co., Houghton Mifflin Co., Campbell Soup Co., Boston Co., Dart Group Inc., Hasbro Inc., 1994—, Novell Inc., 2003—, Apollo Investment Corp., 2007—. Trustee Penn Mut. Life Ins. Co. Chmn. Bus. for Reagan-Bush Com. Mass., 1980, Wellesley Coll., 1982—. Recipient Candace award, 1982. Mem.: Washington Wellesley Club, Wellesley Coll. Alumnae Assn., UN Assn., Assn. Women CPA's. Episcopalian.

MALONE, DAVID ROY, public fund consultant retired educational association administrator, director; b. Beebe, Ark., Nov. 4, 1943; s. James Roy and Ila Mae (Griffin) M.; m. Judith Kaye Huff, June 20, 1965 (div. Feb. 1990); m. Deborah W. Thomas, Jan. 23, 2004; 1 child, Michael David. BSBA, U. Ark., 1965, JD, 1969, MBA, 1982. Bar: Ark. 1969, US Dist. Ct. (we. dist.) Ark. 1969, US Tax Ct. 1972, US Ct. Appeals (8th cir.) 1972, US Supreme Ct. 1972. Pvt. practice, Fayetteville, Ark., 1969-72; atty. City of Fayetteville, 1969-72; asst. prof. bus. U. Ark., Fayetteville, 1972-76, asst. dean law, 1976-91; mem. Ark. Ho. of Reps., 1980-84, Ark. Senate, 1984—2002; exec. dir. U. Ark. Found., 1991—2002, Ark. Tchr. Ret. Sys., 2003—06; ret., 2006; pub. fund cons. Berstein, Litowitz, & Grossman LLP, NYC, ret. Chair Senate edn. com., 1997-2002, co-chair legis. coun., 1999-2000; bd. dirs. Bank of Elkins, 1976-98, S.W. Edn. Devel. Lab., Austin, Tex., 1988-94; legal adv. coun. So. Regional Edn. Bd., Atlanta, 1991-2002. Contbr. articles to profl. jours.; bd. dirs. Ark. Law Rev., 1978-92; contbg. author U. Ark. Press, 1989. Mayor City of Fayetteville, 1979-80; mem. Jud. Article Task Force, Little Rock, 1989-91; chair Motor Voter task force, 1994-95; bd. dirs. Music Festival Ark., 1989-91, Washington County Hist. Soc., 1993-96, 2008-09; bd. dirs. Walton Arts Ctr. Found., 1994-2000, chmn., 1994-98; chmn. bd. dirs. Washington County Law Libr., 1970-84; chmn. Ark. Tuition Trust Authority, 1997-99; v.p., fin. Washington County Hist. Soc., 2010-, State Lib Bd., 2009-; Blue Ribbon Com. State Hwys., 2010. Recipient Svc. award, Ark. Mcpl. League, 1980, Disting. Svc. award, U. Ark., 1988, Lucas Svc. award, Ark. Alumni Assn., 1998, award, Walton Coll. Bus., U. Ark., 2004. Mem. Ark. Bar Assn. (ho. of dels. 1977-81, award of merit 1980, exec. 1981-82, Outstanding Lawyer-Citizen award 1990), Washington County Bar Assn., Ark. Inst. Continuing Legal Edn. (bd. dirs. 1979-88), Fayetteville C. of C. (bd. dirs. 1984-89), Ark. Genealogy Soc. (bd. dirs. 1990-92). Democrat. Methodist. Avocations: genealogy, stamp collecting/philately. Home: 3411 Sassafras Hill Rd Fayetteville AR 72703 Mailing: PO Box 1366 Fayetteville AR 72702-1366 Personal E-mail: davidr_malone@yahoo.com.

MALONE, MAX TATUM, state legislator; b. Mar. 3, 1953; m. Elizabeth Anderson. Geologist, 1981—86; pres. Malone Oil & Gas Exploration Inc., 1987—; state senator Dist. 37 La., 1996—. Mem.: Am. Assn. Petroleum Geologists, Shreveport Geol. Soc. Republican. Methodist. Mailing: 610 Marshall St Ste 722 Shreveport LA 71101 Fax: 318-676-5733.

MALONE, MELVIN J., lawyer; BS Fin., U. Tenn., Knoxville, 1985—85; JD, U. Tenn. Coll. Law, 1989. Bar: Tenn., US Dist. Ct. (ea., we., mid. dists.) Tenn., US Ct. Appeals (6th cir.). Law clk. US Dist. Ct. (we. dist.) Tenn., 1989—90, US Ct. Appeals (6th cir.), 1990—91; assoc. Baker, Donelson, Bearman & Caldwell, Knoxville, Tenn., 1991—95; dep. legal counsel to Don Sundquist Office of Gov., Tenn., 1995—96; dir. Tenn. Regulatory Auth., 1996—2002; ptnr. Miller & Martin PLLC, Nashville, chmn. of firm, 2009—. Contbr. articles to profl. jours. Vol. Gov. Children's Cabinet Initiative, 2006—; bd. advisors U. Tenn. Coll. Law Speakers Series, 1997—; bd. dirs. Youth Life Learning Ctr., chmn., 2003—08, Tenn. Title VI Compliance Commn., 2002—04; commr. emeritus Nat. Assn. Regulatory Utility Commissioners, 2002—; bd. dirs. 100 Black Men Mid. Tenn., 2003—, Internat. Leadership Devel. Inst., 2004—06, Bridges Acad., 2006—09; bd. trustees Tenn. State U. Found., 2007—, chmn., 2011—. Fellow: Tenn. Bar Found., Nashville Bar Found.; mem.: ABA, Tenn. Bar Assn., Nashville Bar Assn., Knoxville Bar Assn., Napier-Lobby Bar Assn. Office: Miller & Martin PLLC One Nashville Pl Ste 1200 150 Fourth Ave N Nashville TN 37219 Office Phone: 615-744-8572. Office Fax: 615-256-8197. Business E-Mail: mmalone@millermartin.com.

MALONE, STEPHANIE, state legislator; b. Rogers, Ark., Mar. 23, 1978; BA in Journalism, U. Ark., 2000. Dir. media buying Advertising Plus dba e-magination.com, 2006—; mem. Dist. 64 Ark. House of Reps., 2009—. Comm. chmn. Jr. League Fort Smith, 2004—; bd. dirs. Abilities Unlimited Fort Smith, Inc., 2008—. Republican. Southern Baptist. Office: State Capitol Rm 350 Little Rock AR 72201 also: 2105 South O St Fort Smith AR 72901 Office Phone: 501-682-6211, 501-682-7771, 479-629-1023. Business E-Mail: malones@arkleg.state.ar.us.

MALONE, W. PERCY, state legislator; b. Rosedale, Miss., Aug. 23, 1942; m to Donna Sanders; children: Amy, Emily. Pharm. degree, Univ. Miss., 1965. Owner & pres. W.P. Malone Inc.; mem. Dist. 36 Ark. House of Reps., 1995—2000; mem. Dist. 26 Ark. State Senate, 2001—, former majority leader. Pres. Ark. Bus. Edn. Alliance, Arkadelphia C. of C., Clark County Indsl. Coun. Ark. Vol. of Year, Ark. Indsl. Develop. Coun., 1989. Democrat. Baptist. Office: 518 Clay Arkadelphia AR 71923 also: Ark Senate State Capitol, Rm 320 Little Rock AR 72201 Office Phone: 870-246-4141. Office Fax: 870-246-6616. Business E-Mail: pmalone@arkleg.state.ar.us.

MALONEY, JAMES EDWARD, lawyer; b. Hackensack, NJ, Apr. 28, 1951; s. Edward James Maloney and Kathleen Elizabeth (Lamont) Leaf. BA cum laude (hon.), Yale U., 1972; JD, Harvard U., 1975. Bar: Tex. 1975, ABA, US Dist. Ct. (no., so., ea. and we. dists.) Tex., US Ct. of Appeals (2nd, 3rd, 5th, 9th and DC cirs.), US Supreme Ct. Assoc. Baker & Botts, Houston, 1975-82, ptnr., 1982—. Bd. dirs. Fotofest, Inc., Houston Ctr. for Photography. Contbr. articles to profl. jours. Trustee Woodberry Forest (Va.) Sch., 1991-97, Museum Fine Arts, Houston. Recipient Best Lawyers in Am., 2001—11, Tex. Super Lawyers, Tex. Monthly & Law & Politics, 2001—11, award, Chambers USA, 2008—10; named to Def. Hot List, Nat. Law Journal's, 2006. Mem. ABA, Tex. Bar Assn., Tex. Bar Found., Houston Bar Assn., Houston Bar Found., Yale Club Houston Republican. Episcopalian. Office: Baker & Botts One Shell Plz 910 La Houston TX 77002-4592 Office Phone: 713-229-1234. Business E-Mail: james.maloney@bakerbotts.com.

MALONEY, MARILYN C., lawyer; b. New Orleans, Nov. 24, 1950; BA, La. State U., 1972, JD, 1975. Bar: La. 1975, Tex. 2005, U.S. Dist. Ct. (ea. dist.) La. Ptnr. Liskow & Lewis, New Orleans, 1975—, Houston, 2005—. Contbr. articles to profl. jours. Fellow: Am. Coll. Comml. Fin. lawyers, Am. Coll. Real Estate Lawyers; mem.: La. State Law Inst. (chair emeritus), Order of Coif, Omicron Delta Kappa. Office: Liskow & Lewis Ste 1800 1001 Fannen First City Twr Houston TX 77002 Office Phone: 713-651-2938. Business E-Mail: mcmaloney@liskow.com.

MALONEY, ROBERT B., federal judge; b. 1933; BBA, So. Meth. U., 1956, postgrad., 1960. Asst. dist. atty. County of Dallas, 1961-62; ptnr. Watts, Stallings & Maloney, 1962-65, Maloney, Miller & McDowell, 1966-75, Maloney & McDowell, 1976-78, Maloney & Hardcastle, 1979-80, Maloney & Maloney, 1981-84; assoc. judge Tex. Ct. Appeals (5th cir.), Tex., 1983-85; judge US Dist. Ct. (no. dist.) Tex., Dallas, 1985—2000, sr. judge, 2000—. State rep., Austin, Tex., 1973-82. Mem. Tex. Bar Assn. Office: US Dist Ct 1100 Commerce St Rm 13e15 Dallas TX 75242-1495

MALPOCHER, RAYMOND V., manufacturing executive; BS in Mech. Engring., Rochester Inst. Tech.; MS in Applied Math., U. Rochester, MBA. Held sr. exec. positions Eagle Industries, 1981—95, Danaher Corp., 1995—98; group pres., Marine/Indsl. divsn. Teleflex Corp., 1998—2002; pres., CEO Telex Comm., 2003—06. Bd. dirs. Anchor Glass Container Corp., Tech. Rsch. Corp., 2007—. Office: Technology Research Corp 5250 140th Ave N Clearwater FL 33760 Office Phone: 727-812-0659. Office Fax: 727-535-4828. Business E-Mail: rmalpocher@trci.net.

MALVEAUX, SUZANNE, news correspondent; BA, Harvard U., Cambridge, Mass.; MA in Journalism, Columbia U., NYC. Prodr. documentaries, Egypt, Kenya; reporter FXT-TV, New Eng. Cable News, Boston, 1991—94; gen. assignment reporter WRC-TV, Washington; corr. NBC News, Chgo., Washington; White House corr. Cable News Network (CNN), Washington, 2002—. Recipient Emmy award, 1996; named Nat. Black MBA's Communicator of Yr., 2004; named one of America's Most Powerful Players Under 40, Black Enterprise mag., Outstanding Women in Marketing & Comm., Ebony mag.; named to Power 150, 2008. Achievements include breaking coverage of top news stories including the Sept. 11, 2001, terrorist attacks in Pennsylvania and the Pentagon, the Kosovo and Afghanistan wars from the Pentagon, Clinton's impeachment trial, retirement of Supreme Court Justice Sandra Day O'Connor and others. Office: 1 CNN Ctr Atlanta GA 30303 Office Phone: 404-827-1700. Office Fax: 404-827-1099.

MALZAHN, DAN, construction executive; V.p. bus. planning NVR, Inc., dir. corp. comm. Office: NVR Inc Ste 500 Plz America Tower I 11700 Plz America Dr Reston VA 20190 Office Phone: 703-956-4204. Office Fax: 703-956-4750. Business E-Mail: Dan.Malzahnir@nvrinc.com.

MALZAHN, GUS (ARTHUR GUSTAV MALZAHN), college football coach; b. Irving, Tex., Oct. 28, 1965; m. Kristi Otwell; children: Kylie, Kenzie. Attended, U. Ark., Fayetteville; BA in Phys. Edn., Henderson State U., Arkadelphia, Ark., 1990. Defensive coord. Hughes HS Blue Devils, Ark., 1991, head football coach, 1992—95, Shiloh Christian HS Saints, Ark., 1996—2000, Springdale HS Bulldogs, Ark., 2001—05; offensive coord., wide receivers coach U. Ark. Razorbacks, 2006; asst. head coach, co-offensive coord., quarterbacks coach U. Tulsa Golden Hurricane, Okla., 2007—08; offensive coord., quarterbacks coach Auburn U. Tigers, 2009—11, head football coach, 2013—, Ark. State U. Red Wolves, 2012. Recipient Frank Broyles award, Rotary Club Little Rock, 2010, Eddie Robinson Coach of Yr. award, Football Writers Assn. America, 2013, Paul "Bear" Bryant award, Nat. Sportscasters & Sportswriters Assn., 2013; named Southeastern Conf. Coach of Yr., 2013, Home Depot Nat. Coach of Yr., ESPN, ABC Sports, 2013, Sporting News Coach of Yr., 2013, AP Coach of Yr., 2013. Office: Auburn University Football Program c/o Athletics Department PO Box 351 Auburn AL 36831-0351 Office Phone: 334-844-9890.*

MAMPRE, VIRGINIA ELIZABETH, communications executive; b. Chgo., Sept. 12, 1949; d. Albert Leon and Virginia S. (Joboul) M. BA with honors, U. Iowa, 1971; Masters degree, Ind. U., 1972; spl. cert., Harvard U., 1981, Purdue U., 1999. Cert. tchr. Harris Intern WTTW-TV Sta., Chgo., 1972, asst. dir., 1972-73; prod. and dir. WSIU/WUSI-TV Sta., Carbondale, Ill., 1973-74; instr. So. Ill. U., Carbondale, 1972-77; prog. and prod. mgr. WSIU/WUSI-TV, Carbondale, 1974-77; prog. dir. KUHT-TV Sta., Houston, 1977-83; pres. Victory Media, Inc., Houston, 1984-89, Mampre Media Internat., Houston, 1984—. Cons. Corp. Pub. Broadcasting, Washington, 1981—83; bd. dirs. TVPC; program bd. Ea. Ednl. Network; spkr., presenter in field Europe, Asia, Australia, S. Am.; owner Meetings and Incentive Travel, 1983—. Contbg. author/editor to mags. including Focus, 1989, News & Views, 1987-88, In the Black, 1984-93, Festivals; creator: (report card campaign) Multi-media, U.S., 1985—; exec. prodr. TV spls., pub. affairs and info., 1977-83 (awards 1978-91). Pres. Child Abuse Prevention Coun., Houston, 1984—97; chmn. exhbns. Mayor's 1st Hearing, Children and Youth, Houston, 1985—88; rep. Houston 2nd World Conf. on Mayors, Japan, 1989; bd. govs. Houston Read Commn., pres., 1995—2001, chair adv. bd., 1993—2001; mem. nat. faculty Ctr. Children's Issues, 1995—97; pres. Episcopal Ch. Women, 2002—, 2006; pres. bd. dirs. Houston Fin. Coun., 1983—; bd. dirs. Child Abuse Prevention Network, 1990—97; chmn. bd. dirs., gala chair Crime Stoppers Houston, 1984—99; founder, bd. dirs. Friends of WSIU-TV, 1974—77; chmn. St. Kevork/ACYO Nat. Sports Fair, St. John the Divine, 1990; mem. exec. bd. Nat. Com. To Prevent Child Abuse, 1990—97; pres., bd. dirs. Fedn. Houston Profl. Women Found., 1996; bd. dirs. Humanities Tex., 1998—, Tex. Coun. Humanities, Operation Rainbow, 1997—, pres. bd. gala chair; bd. dirs. Kellogg Fellows Leadership Alliance; adv. bd. Southwest Area Media Project. Fellow W.K. Kellogg Found., Battle Creek, Mich., 1987-90; recipient award for Excellence Pres. Pvt. Sector, White House, Washington, 1987, Ohio State U., Columbus, 1983, Feddersen award for excellence in Pub. TV Ind. U., Bloomington, 1981, Heritage award Child Abuse Prevention Coun., 1990, Dona J. Stone Founders award Nat. Assn. for Prevention of Child Abuse, 1990; named among Outstanding Women Vols. for community, civic and profl. contbns., Fedn. Houston Profl. Women, 1989; honoree Woman on Move, 1997. Mem.: Houston Culinary Guild (pres. 2006—), Internat. Festivals Events. Assn. (officer 1994—2003, sec. 1994—, bd. dirs. 1995—2002, creator Mampre Media Internat. Leadership Devel.), Profls. in Culinary Arts (pres. 2002—04, bd. dirs.), TV Program Conf. (sec. bd. 1990—), Ctr. Bus. Women's Devel., Nat. Assn. Programming TV Execs., Nat. Assn. Ednl. Broadcasters (presenter nat. conv. 1975—76), Houston Fed. Profl. Women (del. 1986—93, chmn. 1994—, pres.), Am. Women in Radio and TV (bd. dirs. 1985—, nat. v.p. 1986—90, award 1987, pres. Houston chpt. 1990), Kellogg Fellows Leadership Alliance (bd. trustees), Dau. of the King, Christ in the Arts (chair), Dephians, Tex. Lyceum (v.p., bd. dirs. 1990—96). Republican. Episcopalian. Avocations: photography, swimming, sailing, languages, travel. Office: Mampre Media Internat 5123 Del Monte Dr Houston TX 77056-4391 Office Phone: 713-960-9849. Personal E-mail: mampremedi@aol.com.

MAN, DANIEL, plastic surgeon; married; 3 children. MD, Tel Aviv U., 1973. Lic. Maine, 1976, Del., 1976, Ky., 1978, Fla., 1981, diplomate in Plastic and Reconstructive Surgery Am. Bd. Plastic Surgery, 1981. Intern in gen. surgery Tel Hashomer Hosp., Ramat Gan, Israel, 1972—73; resident in gen. surgery Montefiore Hosp., Bronx, NY, 1974—76; resident in surgery Wilmington Gen. Hosp., Del., 1976—78; resident in plastic and reconstructive surgery U. Louisville, 1978—80; pvt. practice Boca Raton, Fla., 1981—. Presenter in field; profl. interviewed various mags., newspapers, and TV programs. Author: The Art of Man: Faces of Plastic Surgery, 1998, The New Art of Man: Faces of Plastic Surgery, 2002, Man at Work: A Photographic of Plastic Surgery and Art, 2010; contbr. books, anthologies, and profl. jours. in field. Recipient Humanitarian of Yr. award, Palm Beach County Victim Svcs., 2001, Letter of Recognition for Humanitarian Contbns., Fla. State Senator M. Mandy Dawson, 2001, Fla. State Senator Tom Rossin, 2001, US Congressman Robert Wexler, 2001, US Senator Bill Nelson, 2001, US Senator Bob Graham, 2001, Gov. Jeb Bush, Fla., 2001, US Atty. Gen. Nat. Crime Victim Rights Week Svc. award, 2009; named Dr. Man Day in his honor, Boca Raton, Fla., 2001; Hand fellowship, U. Louisville, 1978—80, Microvascular fellowship, 1980. Fellow: Am. Soc. Laser Surgery and Medicine; mem.: AMA, Y-ME Fla. (founding bd. mem. 1982—87, med. advisor 1982—87), Lipolysis Soc. N.Am., Broward County Soc. Plastic Surgeons, Palm Beach County Soc. Plastic Surgeons, Palm Beach County Med. Soc., Am. Soc. Aesthetic Plastic Surgery, Am. Soc. Plastic Surgeons. Office: 851 Meadows Rd Ste 222 Boca Raton FL 33486 Office Phone: 561-395-5508.

MANCHIN, JOSEPH, III, (JOE MANCHIN), United States Senator from West Virginia, former Governor of West Virginia; b. Farmington, W. Va., Aug. 24, 1947; s. John and Mary Manchin; m. Gayle Conelly, 1967; children: Heather, Joseph IV, Brooke. BS in Bus. & Economics, W.Va. U., 1970. Cert. pilot. Operator Manchin's Carpet Center, Marion County, W.Va., 1970; mem. W.Va. House of Delegates, 1982—86, W.Va. State Senate, 1986—92; sec. of state State of W.Va., Charleston, 2001—05, gov., 2005—10; US Senator from W.Va. Washington, 2010—; mem. US Senate Armed Services Com., Washington, 2010—, US Senate Energy & Natural Resources Com., Washington, 2010—, US Senate Select Com. on Aging, Washington, 2010—; co-host "No Labels Radio: A Town Hall with America" Sirius XM Radio, 2013—. Mem.: NRA. Democrat. Catholic. Office: US Senate 306 Hart Senate Office Bldg Washington DC 20510 also: 300 Virginia St E Ste 2630 Charleston WV 25301 Office Phone: 888-438-2731, 202-224-3954, 304-342-5855. Office Fax: 202-228-0002, 304-343-7144.*

MANCINI, ERNEST ANTHONY, geologist, educator, researcher; b. Reading, Pa., Feb. 27, 1947; s. Ernest and Marian K. (Filbert) M.; m. Marilyn E. Lee, Dec. 27, 1969; children: Lisa L., Lauren N. BS, Albright Coll., 1969; MS, So. Ill. U., 1972; PhD, Tex. A&M U., 1974. Petroleum exploration geologist Cities Svc. Oil Co., Denver, 1974-76; asst. prof. geology U. Ala., Tuscaloosa, 1976-79, assoc. prof., 1979-84, prof., 1984—2010, disting. rsch. prof., 2005—09, prof. emeritus, 2010—; rsch. prof., geology & geophysics Tex. A&M U., 2010—12, adj. prof., geology & geophysics, 2012—. State geologist, oil and gas supr. State Ala., Tuscaloosa, 1982-96; regional dir. Ea. Gulf Region of the Petroleum Tech. Transfer Coun., 1995-2007; founding dir. Ctr. Sedimentary Basin Studies, U. Ala., 1998-2009; interim chair, Dept. Geol. Scis. U. Ala., 2008-09; founding dir. Berg-Hughes Ctr. For Petroleum and Sedimentary Sys. Tex. A&M U., 2010-12. Contbr. articles to profl. jours. Recipient award Nat. Coun. Citation Albright Coll., 1983, Pratt-Haas Disting. Lectr. award Am. Assn. Petroleum Geologists, 1987-88, Blackman Moody Outstanding Prof. award, U. Ala., 2007, Burnum Disting. Faculty award U. Ala., 2009, Founder's award, 2010. Fellow: Geol. Soc. Am. (past chmn. S.E. sect.); mem.: Am. Assn. Petroleum Geologists (hon., A.I. Levorsen petroleum geology Meml. award Gulf Coast Assn., geol. socs. sect. 1980, chair rsch. com. 2001-04, assoc. editor, 2003-04, editor, 2004-07, Disting. Educator award 2000), Assn. Am. State Geologists (hon., past pres., Disting. Svc. award 2010), Am. Geol. Inst. (past pres., Ian Campbell medal 2004), Am. Geol. Inst. Found. (past trustee), Nat. Assn. State Univs. and Land-Grant Colls. (past chair, mineral and energy resources sect. mem. bd. natural resources), Soc. Econ. Paleontologists and Mineralogists Gulf Coast sect. (hon., past pres., Doris Curtis medal, 2013), Paleontol. Soc. (past pres. southeast sect.), Ala. Geol. Soc. (past pres.), Gulf Coast Assn. Geol. Scis. (hon., Outstanding Educator award 1998, Don Boyd medal, 2011), Sigma Xi (past chpt. pres.), Phi Kappa Phi (past chpt. pres.), Phi Sigma. Presbyterian. Office: U Ala Dept Geol Scis PO Box 870338 Tuscaloosa AL 35487-0338 Home: 15271 Four Winds Loop Northport AL 35475-3325 Business E-Mail: emancini@geo.ua.edu.

MANCINI, LISA A., rail transportation executive; B in Math., U. Va; M in City & Regional Planning, Harvard U. Exec. positions Southeastern Pa. Transp. Authority, San Francisco Mcpl. Transp. Authority; COO San Francisco Mcpl. Rlwy.; v.p., strategic infrastructure initiatives CSX Transp., Inc. (subs. CSX Corp.); joined CSX Corp., 2003, v.p., labor resl., v.p., strategic infrastructure initiatives, 2007—09, sr. v.p., human resources, labor rels., 2009—. Office: CSX Corp Inc 15th Fl 500 Water St Jacksonville FL 32202 Office Phone: 904-359-3200. Office Fax: 904-633-3450. Business E-Mail: lisa_mancini@csx.com.

MANCUSO, ANTHONY A, diagnostic radiologist; MD, U. Miami, 1973. Diplomate Am. Bd. Radiology-diagnostic radiology, 1978. Resident diagnostic radiology UCLA Med. Ctr., 1974—77, fellow neuroradiology, 1977—78; prof. radiology Coll. of Medicine Univ. of Fla.; hosp. affiliations include Shands at the Univ. of Fla. Office: University of Florida Shands Hospital Radiology Department 1600 SW Archer Rd Gainesville FL 32610 Office Phone: 352-265-0296.

MANDEL, HERBERT MAURICE, retired civil engineer; b. Port Chester, NY, May 11, 1924; s. Arthur William and Rose (Schmeiser) M.; m. Charlotte Feldman, Aug. 22, 1954; children: Rosanne Mandel Levine, Elliott D., Arthur M. BSCE, Va. Poly. Inst., 1948; M Engring., Yale U., 1949. Registered profl. engr., N.Y., Conn., Fla., Md., Mich., Minn., Ohio, Pa., Va., W.Va. Structural engr. Madigan Hyland Co., LI, NY, 1949—50; mem. Parsons, Brinckerhoff, Quade & Douglas, Inc., 1950—86; v.p. GAI Cons., Inc., Monroeville, Pa., 1986—2004, prin. staff cons., 1993—2004, sr. staff cons., 2004—. Resident engr., Chgo., 1961, Atlanta, 1962, project. mgr., N.Y.C., 1963-70, Honolulu, 1970-74, v.p., 1974, sr. v.p., Pitts., 1977-86; mem. faculty Yale U., 1948-49; adj. faculty Bklyn. Poly. Inst., 1956-64, U. Pitts., 1986; gen. chmn. 6th Internat. Bridge Conf., Pitts., 1989. Prin. works include (prin.-in-charge) Williamstown-Marietta Bridge, W.Va.-Ohio, Dunbar Bridge, W.Va., I-64 Bridge over Big Sandy River, W.Va.-Ky., Davis Creek Bridge, Charleston, W.Va., Tygart R. Bridge, W.Va., Easley Bridge, Bluefield, W.Va., Fayette Sta. Bridge, Fayetteville, W.Va., Mon Valley Expwy., W.Va., King Coal Hwy, W.Va., Romney Bridge, W.Va., (project mgr.) Newport Bridge, Narragansett Bay, R.I., (designer/project engr.) Hackensack River Bridge, N.J., Housatanic River Bridge, Conn., Arthur Kill Vertical Lift R.R. Bridge, S.I., N.Y., 62d St. Bridge, Pitts., Savannah River Cantilever Bridge, Ga., I-84 Bridges, Danbury, Conn., (structural rehab. designer) Avondale Bridge, N.J, Lincoln Bridge, N.J., B&O R.R. Bridge, Vincennes, Ind., Hawk St. Viaduct, Albany, N.Y., Congress Ave. Bridge, Austin, Tex., Ohio St. Bridge, Buffalo, Panhandle Bridge, Pitts.; project dir. design and constrn. Pitts. Light Rail Transit Sys., 1977-84; designer Elizabeth R. Tunnel, Norfolk, Va., 1950. Served to 1st lt. U.S. Army, 1943-46, 50-52, ETO. Fellow ASCE, Soc. Am. Mil. Engrs.; mem. NSPE, Engrs. Soc. We. Pa. (exec. com. Internat. Bridge Conf. 1986—, gen. chmn. 1988-89), Am. Rlwy. Engring. and Maintenance of Way Assn. (steel structures specifications com. 1974—), Profl. Engrs. in Pvt. Practice (bd. govs. 1994-96, profl. devel. coun. 1995-97), Pa. Profl. Engrs. in Pvt. Practice (state vice-chmn. 1992-94, chmn. 1994-96), Pa. Soc. Profl. Engrs. (dir. Pitts. chpt. 1995-98), Internat. Assn. Bridge and Structural Engring., Assn. for Bridge Constrn. and Design, Engrs. Club Pitts., Tau Beta Pi, Chi Epsilon, Omicron Delta Kappa, Phi Kappa Phi, Pi Delta Epsilon, Scabbard and Blade. Jewish. Home: 1149 Hillsboro Mile Hillsboro Beach FL 33062 also: 5715 Beacon St Apt 104 Pittsburgh PA 15217-2079 Home Phone: 412-561-4881. Personal E-mail: hmmcfm@aol.com.

MANDELL, GERALD LEE, internist, educator; b. NYC, Aug. 20, 1936; s. Herman and Sylvia (Keller) M.; m. Judith Rensin Mandell, Dec. 22, 1960; children: James, Pamela, Scott. BA, Cornell U., 1958; MD, Cornell U., NYC, 1962. Diplomate Am. Bd. Internal Medicine. Intern, resident NY Hosp. Cornell Med. Ctr., NYC, 1965-67; instr. Med. Coll., Cornell U., NYC, 1968-69; asst. prof. U. Va., Charlottesville, 1969-71, assoc. prof., 1972-75, prof., 1976—, Owen R. Cheatham prof. sci., 1981—, chief infectious diseases, 1970—2002. Editor: Principles and Practice of Infectious Diseases, 1979, 6th edit., 2005. Lt. comdr. USPHS, 1963-65. Recipient MERIT award NIH, 1986; named Outstanding Alumnus, Cornell Med. Coll, 2002. Master ACP; fellow AAAS, Infectious Diseases Soc. Am. (pres. 1994, Maxwell Finland award 2000), Nat. Inst. Allergy and Infectious Diseases (adv. coun.), Inst. Medicine; mem. Assn. Am. Physicians, Am. Soc. Clin. Investigation (emeritus prof. 2006—), Phi Beta Kappa, Alpha Omega Alpha, Coun. Am. Climatology Soc. (pres. elect 2009). Avocations: photography, tropical fish, sculling.

MANDY, STEPHEN HOWARD, dermatologist, educator; b. Balt., Jan. 6, 1943; s. Arthur Jennings and Sylvia Bliss Mandy; 1 child, Ashley Jacqueline. BA, George Washington U., 1962, MD, 1966. Cert. dermatology Am. Bd. Dermatology, 1972. Intern U. Fla., Gainesville, 1966—67; resident ob-gyn. Sinai Hosp., Balt., 1967—68; resident dermatology Johns Hopkins, Balt., 1968—69, U. Miami, Fla., 1969—71; pvt. practice South Miami, 1973—91, Aspen, Colo., 1991—2003, South Miami Beach, Fla., 2003—; chmn. bd. and founder DVM Pharm., 1976—92; clin. prof. dermatology U. Miami, Fla., 1982—; chmn. bd. Sirius Pharm., 2005—. Chmn. bd. Dermatologics For Vet. Medicine, Miami, 1976—92; pres. Am. Soc. for Dermatologic Surgery, Rolling Meadows, Ill., 2000—01; bd. dirs. Am. Acad. Dermatology, Evanston, Ill., 2012—. Contbr. articles to profl. jours. Maj. USAF, 1971—73. Jewish. Avocations: skiing, travel, photography. Office: South Beach Dermatology 555 Washington Ave Ste 210 Miami Beach FL 33139 Office Phone: 305-672-1233. Office Fax: 305-673-6422.

MANETTA, RICHARD L., chemicals executive, lawyer; b. 1945; BA, U. Mich.; JD, Wayne State U. Legal advisor Detroit City Coun., 1973—74; chief supervising asst./corp. counsel City of Detroit Law Dept., 1974—78; asst. gen. counsel for automotive safety and product litigation Ford Motor Co., 1989—94, asst. gen. counsel for discovery, 1994—99, assoc. gen. counsel for litigation, 1999—2000, dep. gen. counsel, dir. regulatory compliance, 2000—01; corp. v.p., gen. counsel The Dow Chem. Co., Midland, Mich., 2001—04, corp. v.p., spl. counsel to pres., 2004—05. Spkr. in field. Recipient Pres. award, Nat. Bar Assn., 2001, award, Wolverine Bar Assn., 2001, Access to Justice award, State of Mich., 2003. Fellow: Mich. State Bar Found. (life); mem.: ABA, Mich. Gen. Counsel Assn., Mich. State Bar. Home: 216 Audubon Blvd Naples FL 34110-4400

MANGUM, DAVID, data processing executive; Mgmt. positions Dun & Bradstreet Corp., XcelleNet Inc.; v.p. fin. and adminstrn. managed sys. divsn. Sterling Commerce Inc.; sr. v.p., fin. and acctg. CheckFree Corp.(acquired by Fiserv Inc.), 1999, exec. v.p., CFO, 2007, Global Payments, Inc., 2008—. Recipient CFOs Office: Global Payments Inc 10 Glenlake Pkwy NE N Tower Atlanta GA 30328 Office Phone: 770-829-8000. Office Fax: 770-829-8224. Business E-Mail: dmangum@checkfree.com.

MANGUM, MYLLE H., consumer products company executive; b. Thomas, Ga., 1948; BA, Emory U., 1970. Worked General Electric Co.; pres. BellSouth Internat., 1985—86; dir., corp. planning and devel. BellSouth Corp., 1986—92; exec. v.p., Strategic Mgmt. Holiday Inn Worldwide, 1992—97; pres., Global Payment Sys., sr. v.p., Expense Mgmt. and Strategic Planning Carlson Wagonlit Travel, Inc, 1997—99; CEO MMS Incentives, Inc, 1999—2002, True Mktg. Svcs., LLC, 2002—03, IBT Enterprises, LLC (formerly International Banking Technologies), 2003—. Bd. dirs. Collective Brands Inc., 1997—, Haverty Furniture Companies, Inc., 1999—, Barnes Group Inc., 2002—, Emageon, Inc., 2004—09, Matria Healthcare, Inc., 2006—, Express, Inc., 2010—. Former pres. Com. of 200, mem.; bd. trustee Piedmont Coll. Named Woman of the Year in Tech., WIT, 2004; named Top 25 Entrepreneurs in Atlanta, Catalyst's Magazine, 2007. Mem.: Soc. Internat. Bus. Fellows, Committee of 200 (former pres.). Office: IBT Enterprises LLC Ste 300 1770 Indian Trail Norcross GA 30093 Office Phone: 770-381-2023. Office Fax: 770-381-2123. Business E-Mail: mylle.mangum@ibtenterprises.com.

MANION, MARK D., rail transportation executive; Joined Norfolk Southern Corp., Va., 1975, v.p. transportation services and mechanical Va., sr. v.p. transportation ops. Va., 2003—04, exec. v.p. ops. Va., 2004—09, exec. v.p., COO Va., 2009—. Office: Norfolk Southern Corp Three Commercial Pl Norfolk VA 23510-2191 Office Phone: 757-629-2680. Office Fax: 757-629-2361.

MANKA, ROGER, wire and cable manufacturing company executive; BS in Mktg., U. Ill., Chgo. V.p., worldwide sales 3Com Corp., US Robotics; group v.p., worldwide sales CommScope, Inc. Office: CommScope Inc 1100 CommScope Pl SE Hickory NC 28603 Office Phone: 828-324-2200. Office Fax: 828-328-3400. Business E-Mail: rmanka@commscope.com.

MANKEL, FRANCIS XAVIER, retired principal, priest; b. Knoxville, Tenn., Nov. 8, 1935; s. George Whitehead Sr. and Willia Frances (Duncan) M. BA, St. Ambrose U., Davenport, Iowa, 1957; STB, St. Mary's Sem. and U., Balt., 1959, STL, 1961; MEd, Loyola Coll., Balt., 1965. Ordained priest, Roman Cath. Ch., 1961. Assoc. pastor St. John Ch., Memphis, 1961, Our Lady of Fatima Ch., Alcoa, Tenn., 1961—62, Holy Ghost Ch., Knoxville, 1962-67; tchr. Knoxville Cath. H.S., 1961—67, prin., 1967-79; pastor Sacred Heart Ch., Lawrenceburg, Tenn., 1979-84, St. John Neumann Ch., Knoxville, 1984-87, Sacred Heart Cathedral, Knoxville, 1987-97, Holy Ghost Ch., Knoxville, 1997—. Chancellor Cath. Diocese Knoxville, 1988-96, vicar gen., 1988-98, 1999-2007, 2009-; reverend monsignor, 2006, Knights of the Equestrian Order of the Holy Sepulchre Jerusalem, 2012, supt. Cath. Schs., Diocese of Knoxville, 1989-92. Bd. dirs. Knoxville area chpt. ARC, 1986—2005; sch. bd. Knoxville Cath. HS, 1967—79, 1984—85, 1987—; com. mem. Sacred Heart Cathedral Sch., Knoxville, 1987—97, St. Joseph Sch., Knoxville, 1997—. Mem. Knoxville Ministerial Assn. Home and Office: 111 Hinton Ave Knoxville TN 37917-6418 Office Phone: 865-522-2205. Personal E-mail: hgchurch@bellsouth.net.

MANKOFF, RONALD MORTON, retired lawyer; b. Gettysburg, SD, Oct. 13, 1931; s. Harry B. and Sarah (Frank) M.; m. Joy Faith Shechtman, Nov. 3, 1959; children: Jeffrey Walker, Douglas Frank. BSL, U. Minn., JD, 1954; LLM in Taxation, NYU, 1959. Bar: Minn. 1954, Tex. 1959. With Leonard, Street & Deinard, Mpls., 1957-58; research analyst Inst. Jud. Adminstrn., NYC, 1958-59; assoc. Lyne, Blanchette, Smith & Shelton, Dallas, 1959-60; ptnr. Durant and Mankoff, Dallas, 1960-85; pres. Brice & Mankoff P.C., Dallas, 1985-89, Mankoff, Hill, Held & Metzger, L.L.P., Dallas, 1989-95; chmn., gen. counsel RAC Fin. Group, Inc., 1994—96. Lectr. law So. Meth. U., 1974-77; speaker in field. Contbr. articles to profl. jours. Mem. Dallas Mcpl. Libr., 1973—75, Mayor's Task Force on Child Care, 1984; chmn. bd. Dallas chpt. Am. Cancer Soc., 1976—77, bd. dirs. Tex. divsn., 1981—94; chmn. Dallas Crusade, 1974—75, bd. dirs., mem. exec. com., 1963—88; mem. exec. com. Nat. Pooled Income Fund, Coun. Jewish Welfare Fedns. and Funds, 1975—77; adv. dir. Dallas Cmty. Chest Trust Fund, 1976—78; chmn. Found. Dallas Jewish Fedn., 1976—77; pres. Temple Emanu-el Dallas, 1977—79; bd. dirs. Jewish Fedn. Greater Dallas, 1977—79, 1999—2002, with centennial com., 2010—12; bd. dirs. Dallas Civic Opera, 1981—83, World Union Progressive Judaism, 1981—90; mem. S.W. regional liaison com. IRS, 1980—83; mem. exec. com. Union Am. Hebrew Congregations, 1979—89, trustee, 1979—97, chmn. nat. coll. com., 1983—87, vice chmn. bd. dirs., 1984—88, vice chmn. devel. commn., 1997—99; sec. Dallas Assembly, 1979—84; mem. exec. com. Jewish Cmty Rels. Coun., 1982—83, Com. for Qualified Judiciary, 1982—2010; sec. Child Care Partnership, 1984—86, bd. dirs., 1986—88, Dallas Women's Found., 1985—89, mem. adv. coun., 1989—, chair adv. coun., 1997—99; bd. dirs. Am. Jewish Com., 1982—88, pres. Dallas chpt., 1986—90; bd. dirs. Tex. coun. Girl Scouts U.S., 1982—85; bd. dirs. Goodwill Industries of Greater Dallas, 1979—83, Title One Home Improvement Lender's Assn., 1994—96; bd. govs. Dallas Symphony Assn., 1988—92, 1998—; chmn. Temple Emanu El Found., 1988—95, chair capital campaign, 2011—; bd. dirs. Dallas Inst. Humanities and Culture, 1998—2005, mem. adv. com., 2005—; bd. dirs. Ctr. for Interreligious Understanding, 2001—05, Cardio-Pulmonary Rsch. Inst., 2002—08, Jane's Due Process, Inc., 2002—07, Cmty. Home for Adults Found., 2001—12, Am. Film Inst., Dallas, 2007—10; adv. bd. Rockridge Inst., 2006—08; bd. mem. ATT Performing Art Ctr., 2011—, Dallas Theater Ctr., 2011—. Lt. (j.g.) USN, 1954—57. Mem. ABA, State Bar Tex., Dallas Bar Assn., Honors Golf Club (bd. dirs. 1967-73), LaJolla Country Club, Crescent Club, Park Cities Club, Zeta Beta Tau, Delta Sigma Rho. Democrat. Jewish. Home: 22 Lakeside Pk Dallas TX 75225 also: 8510 El Paseo Grande La Jolla CA 92037 Personal E-mail: ron@mankoff.com.

MANLY, ROBERT W., IV, food products executive; Grad., Stanford U., Calif.; MBA, Harvard Bus. Sch. Asst. to pres. IBP, Inc., 1981—86; exec. v.p. Smithfield Foods, Inc., 1986—96; pres., COO Smithfield Packing, 1994—95; pres. Premium Std. Farms, 1996—2006; exec. v.p. Smithfield Foods, Inc., 2006—, interim CFO, 2007—08, exec. v.p., CFO, 2008—. Office: Smithfield Foods Inc 200 Commerce St Smithfield VA 23430 Office Phone: 757-365-3000.

MANN, PAUL, research scientist; BA, Oberlin Coll., 1978; PhD, SUNY, Albany, 1983. Univ. fellow SUNY, Albany, 1978—81, grad. rsch. asst., 1981—82, grad. tchg. asst., 1982—83; rsch. assoc. Inst. For Geophysics, Univ. Tex., Austin, 1983—91, rsch. scientist, 1991—99, sr. rsch. scientist, 1999—. Invited spkr. in field. Contbr. several articles to profl. jours.; assoc. editor Geological Society of America Bulletin, 2000—. Recipient Joseph C. Walker Excellence award, Univ. Tex., Jackson Sch. Geosciences, 2006, Outstanding Rsch. award, 2008; Orgn. of Am. States fellow, Dominican Republic, 1983—84, French Acad. Sciences fellow, Univ. Nice, France, 1999—2000, Leiv Eiriksson Fellow, Norwegian Rsch. Coun., 2008. Fellow: Geological Soc. Am.; mem.: Am. Assn. Petroleum Geologists (Top 10 poster award (Jiang et al.), Annual Convention, San Antonio,

Tex. 2008, Top 10 poster award (Contreras et al.), Annual Convention, San Antonio, Tex. 2008), Am. Geophysical Union, Phi Beta Kappa. Office: Inst for Geophysics Univ Texas Austin Office 3.110F 1000 Burnet Road Bldg 196 (ROC) Austin TX 78758-4445 Office Phone: 512-471-0472. Office Fax: 512-471-0348. Business E-Mail: paulm@ig.utexas.edu.

MANN, STEPHEN ASHBY, financial consultant; b. Richmond, Va., Feb. 20, 1947; s. Milton Ashby and Rebecca (George) Mann; m. Patricia Ann Kofron, Aug. 25, 1982; 1 child, Michael Joseph Ashby stepchildren: Christine Ford, Tracy Kofron. BS in Gen. Bus., Va. Poly. Inst. and State U., 1970. Cert. sr. advisor, CLU. Supr. mfg. Brown & Williamson Tobacco Corp., Petersburg, Va., 1970—72; pres. Cumberland Woodyard, Va., 1972—79; mgr. Ragland Woodyards, Goochland, Va., 1980—81; advt. mgr., reporter Gazette Newspapers, Goochland, 1982—85; fin. counselor, ins. and fin. planner Peoples Security Ins. Co., Mechanicsville, Va., 1986—98, Monumental Life Ins. Co., Mechanicsville, Va., 1999—2003; v.p. Roberts-Funai Ins. Agy., Richmond, 2003—. Pres. Millquarter Property Owners Assn., Powhatan, Va., 1987, v.p., 2006—10. Named to All-Star Honor Roll, Ins. Sales Mag., 1989—90; Life Underwriters Tng. Coun. fellow. Fellow: Life Underwriters Tng. Coun.; mem.: SCV (lt. comdr. Powhatan 1980—82, inspector gen. state divsn 1981, nat. adc 1982—83, comdr.), All Harley Drag Racing Assn. (Racer of Yr. Award 1996, nat. ranked # 4 st. eliminator 1996—97, nat. ranked #2 super sport 1999, ranked #6 in East, 13th Nat. 2002, ranked #1 in East, 7th Nat. 2003), Richmond Assn. Ins. and Fin. Advisors (bd. dirs. 1989—92), Assn. Health Ins. Agts., Soc. Fin. Svc. Profls., Nat. Assn. Ins. and Fin. Advisors (Nat. Quality Award 1986, Nat. Sales Achievement Award 1986, Nat. Health Inst. Award 1986), Sons of South Motorcycle Club (founder & pres. 1993—2005), Masons (master 1990, Samis Grotto treas. 1991—93, master 1994, 16th dist. blood coord. 1995—96, chaplain Powhatan Lodge # 295 1995—2010, life mem. Royal Arch), Golden Key Soc (com. mem. 1991—96). Republican. Baptist. Avocations: organ, history, motorcycling, piano. Home: 1433 E Overlook Dr Powhatan VA 23139 Office: Roberts & Funai Ins Agy Richmond VA 23236

MANNING, DANNY (DANIEL RICARDO MANNING), men's college basketball coach, retired professional basketball player; b. Hattiesburg, Miss., May 17, 1966; s. Ed and Darnelle; m. Julie Manning; children: Taylor, Evan. B in Comm., U. Kans., Lawrence, 1988. Forward LA Clippers, 1988-93, Atlanta Hawks, 1993-94, Phoenix Suns, 1994-99, Milw. Bucks, 1999—2000, Utah Jazz, 2000—01, Dallas Mavericks, 2001—02, Detroit Pistons, 2002—03; ret. NBA, 2003; dir. student athlete devel., team mgr. U. Kansas Jayhawks, 2003—07, asst. coach, 2007—12; head basketball coach U. Tulsa Golden Hurricane, Okla., 2012—13, Wake Forest U. Demon Deacons, Winston-Salem, NC, 2014—. Recipient Bronze medal US Olympic Basketball Team, 1988, Sixth Man of Yr. award NBA, 1998; named Player of Yr. Big Eight Conf., 1986-88, Most Outstanding Player NCAA Final Four, 1988, Naismith award, 1988, Wooden award, 1988; named to Sporting News NCAA All-Am. First Team, 1987, 88, Western Conf. All-Star Team NBA, 1993, 1994. Achievements include member of the NCAA Division I Final Four championship winning University of Kansas Jayhawks, 1988; being the first overall pick in the NBA Draft, 1988. Office: Wake Forest U Demon Deacons PO Box 7506 Winston Salem NC 27109*

MANNING, GEORGE TAYLOR, lawyer; b. June 27, 1948; s. Howard M.; children: Nell, Taylor; m. Catherine Zick, Apr. 9, 1999. BA, U. NC, 1970; JD, Columbia U., 1973. Bar: NY 1974, DC 1982, GA 2001. Assoc. Chadbourne, Parke & Whiteside, NYC, 1973-78, ptnr. NYC and Washington, 1982-85; asst. US Atty. So. Dist., NYC, 1978-82; ptnr. Jones, Day, Reavis & Pogue, Washington, 1985—99; ptnr.-in-charge Atlanta office Jones Day, 2000—07, ptnr.-in-charge Dallas office, 2008—. Office: Jones Day 2727 N Harwood St Dallas TX 75201 Office Phone: 214-969-3676. Office Fax: 214-969-5100. Business E-Mail: gtmanning@jonesday.com.

MANNING, JUDITH HUBERT, state legislator, real estate company executive; b. Ga., Oct. 24, 1942; children: Hank, Elizabeth. Postgrad., Vienna U., Austria, 1963-64; BS in Edn., U. Ga., 1964. Tchr. soc. studies Coll. Pk. H.S., Fulton County, Ga., 1966-67, McEachern Middle Sch., Cobb County, Ga., 1967-69; real estate agent, broker Hubert Realty Co., 1982—91; past real estate agent, broker, co-owner Manning Properties, Marietta, Ga., 1991—; mem. Dist. 32 Ga. House of Reps., Atlanta, 1997—. Mem. Retirement Com., Natural Resources Com., Banks and Banking Com.; active Women Leaders Summit, 1995, 96; mem. edn. task force Am. Legis. Exch. Coun. Del. 7th dist. Rep. Party Convention; past adv. pres. ARC; mem. Atlanta Regional Commn., Cobb Emergency Aid, Cobb Youth Leadership; mem. Girls, Inc., past chair, bd.dirs.; bd. dirs. Jubilee Fine Arts Fesival, OpenGate, Gateway Vis. and Info. Ctr., Dept. Family and Children Svcs.; past bd. dirs. Cobb Symposium, Vol. Atlanta; publicity chair, past bd. dirs. YMCA; vol. Kennestone Hosp.; vol. task force, exec. mem. United Way; 1st pres. Vol. Cobb-Marietta; vice-chmn. Friends of the Park; historian, past bd. dirs. Ptnrs. Fund; participant Women Leaders Summit, 1995-96. W. Wyman Pilcher Jr. Meml. scholar; recipient Leadership Cobb Class of 1984-85, Leadership Ga. Class of 89-90, Disting. Leadership award Nat. Assn. Cmty. Leadership, 1989, Phoenix award Cobb County Bd. Realtors, 1996. Mem. Nat. Assn. Realtors, Cobb-Marietta Jr. League, Hon. Comdrs. Assn., The Walker Sch. Parents Assn., Assn. Metro Atlanta DFCS (co-vice chmn.). Republican. Office: Dist 32 480 Davis Carnes Ln NW Marietta GA 30064-4716 also: 401-E State Capitol Atlanta GA 30334 Office Phone: 404-656-7857. Business E-Mail: judy.manning@house.ga.gov.

MANNINO, J(OSEPH) ROBERT, retired medical educator; b. Altoona, Pa., May 6, 1941; s. Joseph Robert and Helen La Rue (Menza) M.; m. Rosemary Kathleen McGrath, Apr. 8, 1978; 1 child, Angela Christine. BS, Juniata Coll., 1963; MA, East Carolina U., 1965; PhD, Colo. State U., 1974; DO, Kansas City Coll. Osteo. Med., 1971. Diplomate Am. Osteo. Bd. Family Practice. Intern Rocky Mountain Hosp., Denver, 1971-72; physician pvt. practice, Denver, 1972-77; dir. med. edn.nt Kansas City Coll. Osteo. Medicine, 1977-80; prof. family medicine Ohio U. Coll. Osteo. Medicine, Athens, 1981-94, Nova Southeastern U., Coll. Osteo. Medicine, North Miami Beach, Fla., 1994—2000. Teaching asst. physiology East Carolina U., 1965; coord. rsch. Phila. Coll. Osteo. Medicine, 1966-67; asst. dir. med. edn. Rocky Mountain Hosp., Denver, 1972-73, dir. med. edn., 1975-77, bd. trustees, 1975-77; dir. gen. practice residency Drs. Hosp., Columbus, 1980-94; dir. med. edn. & program dir. family practice residency North Broward Hosp. Dist., Ft. Lauderdale, Fla., 1994-96; clin. assoc. Cleveland Clinic, Ft. Lauderdale, 1996-2000; regional med. dir., Wexfold Health Sources, Ft. Lauderdale, Fla., 2002—2003; cons. in field. Contbr. articles to profl. jours. Rsch. fellow Colo. State U., 1968-69. Fellow Am. Coll. Osteo. Family Practice, Am. Soc. Colposcopy & Cervical Pathology, Am. Soc. Laser Medicine & Surgery; mem. Am. Osteo. Assn., Am. Coll. Cyrosurgery, N.Y. Acad. Scis., Fla. Soc. Osteo. Medicine, Fla. State Soc. Am. Coll. Osteo. Family Physicians, Broward County Acad. Fla. Soc. Osteo. Medicine, Endocrine Soc., Chi Beta Phi. Republican. Roman Catholic. Avocation: restoring antique cars.

MANSBACH, CHARLES, gastroenterologist, researcher; b. Norfolk, Va., Aug. 21, 1937; m. May Lynn Mansbach; children: Samuel Ross, Jonathan children: Harry. BA, Yale U., New Haven, 1963; MD, NYU, NYC, 1963. Lic. internal medicine Am. Bd. of Internal Medicine, gastroenterology Am. Bd. of Internal Medicine. Assoc. prof. of medicine Duke U. Med. Ctr., Durham, NC, 1970—86; prof. of medicine and physiology U. of Tenn., Memphis, 1986—. Lt. cdr. USNR, 1968—70. Recipient Merit Rev. grant, VA, 1971—2006; NIH rsch. grantee, 1975—. Achievements include research in Identified the pre-chylomicron transport vesicle. Office: University Tenn Rm H210 956 Court Ave Memphis TN 38163 Office Phone: 901-448-5813. Business E-Mail: cmansbach@uthsc.edu.

MANSFIELD, ERIC LEMOINE, state legislator; b. La. m. Donna Mansfield; children: Thomas Mansfield, Erica Mansfield. Attended, Howard U, Morehouse Sch. Medicine; attended Surgical & Otolaryngology Residency, Tulane U.; M in Health Policy, U. NC, Chapel Hill. Mem. Am. Acad. of Otolaryngology Head and Neck Surgery; bd. dirs. Cape Fear Regional Bureau for Cmty. Action; original donor EE Smith Giving Cir.; co-founder, bd. pres. Father's Found.; min., Young Adults Lewis Chapel Baptist Ch.; mem. Nat. Med. Assn., Old North State Med. Soc.; primary sponsor Partnership for Children's Evening with the Stars; bd. dirs. Fayetteville Arts Coun., 2005—08, Fayetteville State U. Found., 2005—08, Fayetteville Mus. of Art, 2007—08; mem. Dist. 21 NC State Senate, 2011—. Battalion med. officer US Army. Democrat. Office: NC Senate 16 W Jones St Room 1119 Raleigh NC 27601-2808 Home: 2866 Skye Dr Fayetteville NC 28303-5922 Office Phone: 919-733-9349, 910-368-6395. Business E-Mail: Eric.Mansfield@ncleg.net.

MANSFIELD, NORMAN CONNIE, bookkeeper; b. Rayle, Ga., Apr. 27, 1916; s. Boykin Carswell and Cleo (Norman) M.; m. Ila Ruth Poss, Jan. 3, 1943; children: Jonathan Norman, Jerry Carswell. Cert., U. Ga. Notary Pub., Ga. Mgr. Railway Express Agy., Washington, Ga., 1943-78; semi-retired bookkeeper Russell Transfer Co. Inc., Washington, 1979—. Mgr. Rwy. Express. Exec. bd. mem. Ga. Carolina Coun.; deacon First Baptist Ch., Washington; cubscout master, Washington, Ga., 1962. With USNG. Recipient Baseball and Little League award Coca Cola Co., Washington, Ga., 1951, 68, Woodmen of World award Life Ins. Soc., Augusta, Ga., 1978; named Boy Scout of Yr., Ga. Carolina Coun., Thomson, 1956. Mem. Masons (Shriner, worship master 1984), Order of Eastern Star (worthy patron), Woodman of the World (pres.), Lions (pres.), Washington (Ga.) Country Club, Ida Cason Callaway Found., Ga. Sheriffs Assn. Office: The News-Reporter 116 W Robert Toombs Ave Washington GA 30673-1664 Home: 1027 Sunset Rd Canon GA 30520-3755

MANSON, CONNIE JEANE, librarian; b. Seattle, Mar. 28, 1950; d. Richard A. and E. Elaine (Hereth) Manson. BA in English Lit., cum laude, U. Wash., 1972, M in Librarianship, with distinction, 1974. Reference libr. Mont. State Libr., Helena, 1974-75; libr. mgr. Wyo. Dept. Econ. Planning, Cheyenne, 1975-77; sr. geology/earth libr. Wash. Divsn. Natural Resources, Olympia, 1978—2004; now spl. projects libr. GeoRef Am. Geological Inst. Contbr. articles to profl. jours.; published more than one hundred bibliographies on the geology, mineral resources, urban planning, and natural hazards of the state, several volumes of Index to Geologic and Geophysical Mapping of Washington. Mem.: Western Assn. Map Librs., Assn. Engring. Geologists, Geosci. Info. Soc. (newsletter co-editor 1986—2007, v.p., pres. 1997—99, Meritorious Svc. award 1993, Mary B. Ansari Disting. Svc. award 2008). Office: Am Geological Inst 4220 King St Alexandria VA 22302

MANSUKANI, SHARAD, healthcare service company executive; Fellowship, quality mgmt. and managed care Wharton Sch Bus.; residency, fellowship, ophthalmology, Sch. Medicine University of Pennsylvania; chief strategic officer NationsHealth, Inc.; faculty Temple U. Schs. Medicine, University of Pennsylvania; sr. advisor Tex. Pacific Group; sr. v.p., chief med. officer Health Partners, 1999—2003; sr. advisor Medicare and Medicaid Svcs., 2003—05; exec. v.p., chief strategy officer HealthSpring, Inc., 2008—. Bd. dirs. Surg. Care Affiliates, Moksha8 Pharmaceuticals, Inc., Aerie Pharmaceuticals, Inc., Matrix Labs. Ltd., IASIS Healthcare, LLC, Health-Spring, Inc., 2007—. Office: HealthSpring Inc Ste 501 9009 Carothers Pkwy Franklin TN 37067 Office Phone: 615-291-7000. Office Fax: 615-401-4566.

MANTELL, MURRAY I., engineering educator; b. NYC, Sept. 6, 1917; s. John and Anna Mantell; m. Rose T. Plansky, Apr. 29, 1944; children: Melodie, Andrea, Tobi, John. B in Mech. Engring., U. Fla., 1940; MS in Civil Engring., So. Calif. U., 1945; PhD, U. Tex., 1952. Registered profl. engr., Fla. Pres. Mantell Constrn. Co., Miami, Fla., 1940—41, 1946; consulting engr. R. Belsham, Miami, Fla., 1941; naval arch. Charleston (S.C.) Navy Yard, 1941—43, Terminal Island Naval Shipyard, Long Beach, Calif., 1943—45; prof., dept. chmn. emeritus U. Miami, Coral Gables, Fla., 1946—. Chmn. Parks Planning Com., Miami Beach, Fla., 1950; vis. prof. U. Sheffield, England, 1965—66; mem. Fire Prevention and Safety Bd., Dade County, Fla., 1968; chmn. Adv. Panel on Planning and Zoning, Coral Gables, 1970; vice chmn. U.S. Dept. Agrl., County Farm Svc. Agy. Com., 2005—. Author: Ethics & Professionalism in Engineering, 1964, Strength of Materials, 1968, Handbook for Living, 1992, Ethics Problem Solving and Discourse on Living, 2010; co-author: Orientation in Engineering, 1955, Structural Analysis, 1962, Engineering Properties and Construction Applications of Phosphogypsum, 1990. State sport chmn. Amateur Athletic Union, Fla., 1949; pres. Tigertail Civic Assn., Coconut Grove, Fla., 1960—62; v.p. Pine Ridge Civic Assn., Miami, 1966. Recipient Commendation for Engring. Achievement, Brit. Admiralty, 1942; named Engr. of Yr., Fla. Engring. Soc., 1961. Fellow: NSPE (life; chpt. v.p.), ASCE (life; chpt. pres.), Am. Soc. for Engring. Edn. (life; sect. pres., award for excellence in tchg. Western Electric Fund 1969). Home: 5900 SW 84 Ave Miami FL 33143 Office: Dept Civil Engring Univ Miami Coral Gables FL 33124

MANTLE, RAYMOND ALLAN, lawyer; m. Judith Ann LaGrange, Nov. 26, 1967; children: Amanda Lee, Rachel Ann, Leah Amy. BSBA summa cum laude, BA summa cum laude, Kent State U., 1961; LLB cum laude, NYU, 1964. Bar: N.Y. 1964, Fla. 2005, U.S. Supreme Ct. Asst. counsel Gov. Nelson A. Rockefeller, NYC, 1964-65; assoc. Paul Weiss Rifkind Wharton & Garrison, 1967-69; mem. Varet & Fink P.C. (formerly Milgrim Thomajan & Lee, P.C.), NYC, 1969-95; ptnr. Piper & Marbury L.L.P., NYC, 1995-98; mem. Reitler Brown & Rosenblatt LLC (formerly Brock Silverstein, LLC), 1998—2003, counsel, 2004—06. Lectr. in computer law field. Contbr. author: Doing Business in China and Intellectual Property China, 1990—. Capt. US Army, 1965—67. Mem.: Fla. Bar, N.Y. State Bar Assn. (co-chmn. ann. meeting seminar on intellectual property 2000—05, exec. com. intellectual property sect. 2003—14, co-chair intellectual property sect. internat. com. 2004—05). Republican. Methodist. Office: 808 Third St Suite C Neptune Beach FL 32266 Office Phone: 904-635-6242. Business E-Mail: rmantle@rmantlelaw.com.

MANUELLA, FRANK, retired art and design educator; b. NYC; BFA, Cooper Union U., 1963; M in Comm. Design, Pratt Inst., 1982. Pres. Manuella & Assocs., NYC, 1963-82; prof. art & design U. Tex., Edinburg, 1982—2008, prof., 2006—08, prof. emeritus, 2008. Asst. prof. design Pratt Inst., N.Y.C., 1975-82; adv. bd. U. Tex. Press, 1982—, coun. mem., 1989-92, officer Phi Kappa Phi, 1990-92, faculty senator, 1986-93. Solo exhbns. include U. Tex. Gallery, 1991, 92, Reynosa, Mex., 1993, McAllen Internat. Mus., 1994, del Prado, Found., Edinburg, Tex., 1996; Artist, Other, Design NYC 9/11 Meml., 2003, One Man Show, Internat. Mus. Art Sci. McAllen, Tex., 2006. Recipient gov.'s award for acad. excellence, State of Tex., 1989, Master Prof. award U. Tex.; Fulbright grantee, 1993.

MANYPENNY, MIKE, II, state legislator; b. East Liverpool, OH, Aug. 1, 1959; s. Michael and Lois Hulme. BS in Agr. & Forestry, W.Va. U., 1986. Owner Blue Ridge Landscaping and environ. svcs., 1979—87; mgr. Prime Landscaping, 1986—90, Central Coast Landscape, 1990—94; dir. Global Impact, Inc., 1999—2008, ops. mgr., 2003—08; mem. Dist. 42 W. Va. House of Delegates, 2008—, mem. Agr. Com., Govt. Orgn. Com., Health and Human Resources Com. & Natural Resources Com. Democrat. Methodist. Office: State Capitol Complex Rm 217E, Bldg 1 Charleston WV 25305 Mailing: Route 3, Box 202 Grafton WV 26354 Office Phone: 304-340-3193, 304-677-3079. E-mail: mmany@mail.wvnet.edu.

MANZIEL, JOHNNY (JOHNATHAN PAUL MANZIEL), student athlete; b. Tyler, Tex., Dec. 6, 1992; s. Paul and Michelle Manziel. Student in Bus., Tex. A&M U., College Station, 2011—. Quarterback Tex. A&M U. Aggies, 2012—. Recipient Davey O'Brien award, Davey O'Brien Found., 2012, Heisman Meml. Trophy award, The Heisman Trust, 2012, Manning award, Sugar Bowl Com., 2012; named First Team All-Conf., Freshman of Yr. & Offensive Player of Yr., Southeastern Conf., 2012, Male Athlete of Yr., 2013, Sporting News Player of Yr., 2012, First Team All-American, AP, 2012, Coll. Football Player of Yr., 2012. Achievements include first freshman in NCAA history to win the Heisman Memorial Trophy Award, 2012. Office: Texas A&M University Football Program c/o Athletic Department PO Box 30017 College Station TX 77842-3017*

MAPLES, MICHAEL DAVID, career military officer; b. Bonham, Tex., 1949; m. Lynn; children: Meredith, Katherine, Elizabeth. Graduate, US Mil. Acad., 1971; MA in Organizational Behavior, Pacific Lutheran U. Commd. 2d. lt. US Army, 1971, advanced through grades to lt. gen., 2005; stationed at Ft. Lewis, Wash., Republic of Korea; tng. mgmt. officer Ft. Sam Houston, Tex.; various assignments Desert Shield/Desert Storm; sr. military aide to sec. US Army; comdr. Babenhausen, Hungary; dep. chief staff ops. US Army Europe, Tazar, Hungary, asst. chief of staff G3, V Corps Heidelberg, Germany; asst. divsn. comdr. (support) 1st Armored Divsn. US Army Europe & Seventh Army, Germany; dir. mil. support, Office Dep. Chief of Staff for Ops. & Plans US Army, dir. ops., readiness & mobilization, Office Dep. Chief of Staff for Ops. & Plans Washington, 2000—01; commdg. gen. US Army Field Artillery Ctr., Ft. Sill, Okla., 2001—03; vice dir. mgmt. The Joint Staff US Dept. Def., Washington, 2003—05; dir. Def. Intelligence Agy., Washington, 2005—09. Decorated Legion of Merit with oak leaf cluster, Bronze Star medal, Def. Superior Svc. award with oak leaf cluster, Meritorious Svc. medal with three oak leaf clusters, Army Commendation medal with oak leaf cluster, Army Achievement medal, French Croix du Guerre with silver star.

MARA, SHAUN, food products executive; b. 1964; Grad., Bentley U., 1986. Auditor KPMG, 1986—91; mgr. financial reporting Staples, Inc., 1991—93; finance roles Gillette Co., 1993—2002, v.p. fin., 2002, William Wrigley Jr. Co., 2002—06, v.p., controller, 2006—08; sr. v.p. fin. Wm. Wrigley Jr. Co., 2008—10; sr. v.p. fin., chief acctg. officer Dean Foods Co., Dallas, 2010, CFO, 2010—. Office: Dean Foods Company 2711 N Haskell Ave, Suite 3400 Dallas TX 75204 Office Phone: 214-303-3400.

MARACH, OLIVER, professional tennis player; b. Graz, Austria, July 16, 1980; s. Hans-Karl and Hildegard Marach; m. Jessie Marach, July 4, 2009. Profl. tennis player ATP, 1998—. Achievements include winning Bucharest, 2007, Acapulco, 2008, 2010, Casablanca, 2009, Belgrade, 2009, Vienna, 2009, Santiago, 2010, Munich, 2010. Office: c/o ATP Tour Inc 201 Atp Tour Blvd Ponte Vedra Beach FL 32082-3211

MARATHE, SHRIRAM S., nephrologist; MD, India, 1973. Diplomate American Bd. Internal Medicine, 2000, American Bd. Internal Medicine-nephrology, 2000. Resident in internal medicine Edward Hines Jr. VA Hosp., Ill., 1976—78; fellow in nephrology USPHS Hosp., San Francisco, 1979—80; physician Flagler Hosp.; pvt. practice Med. Specialists of St. Augustine. Office: Medical Specialists of St Augustine 665 State Road 207 Ste 102 Saint Augustine FL 32084-5939 Office Phone: 904-824-5158.*

MARBUT, ROBERT GORDON, communications executive; b. Athens, Ga., Apr. 11, 1935; s. Robert Smith and Laura Gordon (Powers) M.; m. Margo Susan Spitz, Sept. 24, 1989; children: Robert Gordon, Laura Dodd, Michael Powers, Marcy Lizbeth. B Indsl. Engring., Ga. Inst. Tech., 1957; MBA with distinction, Harvard U., 1963. Registered profl. engr., Calif. Instr. Armstrong Coll., 1951; engr. Esso Standard Oil Co., Baton Rouge, 1957; corp. dir., engring. & plans Copley Press, La Jolla, Calif., 1963-70; instr. Calif. State U., 1964, Woodbury Coll., 1964; v.p. Harte-Hanks Newspapers, Inc., 1970-71; pres., CEO Harte-Hanks Comm., Inc., 1971-91, bd. dirs., 1971-91, vice chmn., 1991; founder Argyle Comm., Inc., 1992, chmn., CEO, 1992—; founder, CEO & bd. dirs. Argyle TV Holding, Inc., San Antonio, 1993-95; co-founder, chmn. & CEO Argyle TV, Inc., 1994-97; chmn., co-CEO Hearst-Argyle TV, Inc., 1997-2000, chmn., 2001—02; co-mng. ptnr. Argyle Global, LP, 2001; founder, chmn. & CEO SectecGLOBAL, Inc., 2002. Bd. dirs. Hearst-Argyle TV, Inc., Tupperware Brands Corp., Bus. Execs. Nat. Security, Valero Energy Corp., Newspaper Advt. Bur., 1974—88; bd. adv. U. Ga. Henry W. Grady Sch. Journalism, 1975—83; bd. dirs. AP, 1979—87; mem. U. Tex. Centennial commn., 1981—83; founding mem. Am. Bus. Conf., 1981—89; pres., adv. coun. U. Tex. Coll. Comm., 1982—83; bd. dirs. Up With People, 1983—2001; vice chmn. AP, 1987—88; chmn. Newspaper Advt. Bur., 1988—90; bd. adv. Ga. Tech., 1978—81, 1998—. Author: (with Healy, Henderson and others) Creative Collective Bargaining, 1965. Coordinating chmn. San Antonio Target 90 commn., 1983-84; campaign chmn. United Way, San Antonio, 1985, chmn. bd. trustees 1988-89; vice chmn. Tex. select com. on Tax Equity, 1987-89; mem select com. Tex. Revenues, 1991-92; mem. Tex. World Trade Coun., 1986-87. Capt. USAF, 1958-61. Salzburg Inst. Am. Studies sr. fellow, 1997—; recipient Isaiah Thomas award Rochester Inst. Tech., 1980, EXCEL award in comm., 1987, People of Vision award, 1991; selected to Acad. Disting. Engring. Alumni Ga. Tech., 1995. Mem. Am. Newspaper Publs. Assn. (chmn. task group on future, chmn. telecomm. com. 1974-81, bd. dirs. 1976-84, chmn. future task group), So. Newspaper Pubs. Assn. (pres. 1979-80, dir. 1975-81, treas. 1977), Am. Newspaper Pubs. Assn. Found. (trustee 1976-79), Tex. Daily Newspaper Assn. (pres. 1979, Tex. Newspaper Leader of Yr., 1981), N.Y. Met. Club, Doubles, San Antonio Country Club, Argyle Club, Greater San Antonio C. of C., Delta Tau Delta (Alumni Achievement award 2000), Omicron Delta Kappa, Phi Eta Sigma. Office: Tupperware Brands Corp Bd Directors 14901 S Orange Blossom Trail Orlando FL 32837 Office Phone: 407-826-5050. Office Fax: 407-826-8268. Business E-Mail: robertmarbut@tupperware.com.

MARCET, JORGE E., colon and rectal surgeon, educator; MD, Cornell U., 1985. Diplomate Am. Bd. Surgery, 2001, Am. Bd. Colon and Rectal Surgery, 2003. Intern St. Luke's/Roosevelt Hosp. Ctr., NY, resident in surgery, 1986—90, fellow in colon and rectal surgery, 1990—91, NY Presbyn. Hosp./Columbia Univ. Med. Ctr., 1986—90; hosp. affiliation includes Tampa Gen. Hosp.; assoc. prof. surgery coll. medicine Univ. South Fla., Tampa. Co-author: Colon and Rectal Obstruction; co-author: (with A. Durkin) Anal Cancer; co-author: (with R. Karl) Local Excision for Rectal Tumors, 2003; co-author: Devastating Complications after brachytherapy in the treatment of prostate adenocarcinoma, 2004, Failure of Medicare Health Maintenance Organizations to Control the Cost of Colon Resections in Elderly Patients, 2004, Flat and polypoid adenocarcinomas of the colorectum: a comparative histomorphologic analysis of 47 cases, 2004. Office: University of South Florida 1 Tampa General Cir Ste F-145 Tampa FL 33606 Office Phone: 813-844-4545. Business E-Mail: jmarcet@hsc.usf.edu.

MARCH, BOYD LEE, dean, political science professor, researcher; b. Macon, Mo., Apr. 11, 1958; s. Virgil Boyd and Ruby Marceine March; m. Debra Lynn Branson, Apr. 21, 1984; children: William, Benjamin. BA, Truman State U., Kirksville, Mo., 1980, MA, 1983; PhD, U. Mo., Columbia, 1993. Asst. city mgr. City of Kirksville, 1983—84; city mgr. City of Marceline, Mo., 1984—85; asst. exec. dir. Mo. Local Govt. Retirement, Jefferson City, 1985—86; city adminstr. City of Willow Springs, Mo., 1986—87; adj. instr. Buena Vista Coll., Creston, Iowa, 1987—88; John H. Harland prof. polit. sci. Young Harris Coll., Ga., 1993—. Dir. Vietnam Vets. Oral History Project, Young Harris, 2001—; dean Divsn. Social & Behavioral Sci., 2007—. Author: If You Ain't Cav, 2005. Moderator candidate forum LWV, Hiawassee, Ga., 1993—; spkr. vets. support, 1995—. Recipient Faculty Mem. of Yr., Young Harris Coll., 2010, Vulcan Tchg. award, Vulcan Techs., 2005; named Faculty Mem. of Yr., Young Harris Coll., 1994, 1995, 1997, 2000, 2005, 2006, 2007, 2008. Methodist. Office: Young Harris Coll PO Box 456 Young Harris GA 30582 Office Phone: 706-379-5143. Office Fax: 706-379-4314. Business E-Mail: leem@yhc.edu.

MARCH, KEVIN P., electronics executive; BS in Econs., U. Pitts., 1983, MBA, 1984. Various positions including dir. fin., contr. semiconductor units Texas Instruments, Inc., Dallas, 1984—97, v.p. fin. planning, mgr. global ops., 1997—2002, contr., 2002—03, sr. v.p., CFO, 2003—. Mem. Fin. Exec. Internat., Conf. Bd.'s Coun. Fin. Exec. Office: Tex Instruments Inc PO Box 660199 Dallas TX 75266-0199 Office Phone: 972-995-2011. Office Fax: 972-995-4360.

MARCHANT, KENNY EWELL, United States Representative from Texas; b. Bonham, Tex, Feb. 23, 1951; m. Donna Marchant; children: Luke, Matthew, Kenny, Dallas. BA, So. Nazarene U., Bethany, Okla., 1974, DHL (hon.), 1999; attended, Nazarene Theol. Sem., Kansas City, Mo. Councilman Carrollton City Coun., Tex., 1980—84, mayor, city of Carrollton, 1984—87; mem. Tex. House of Reps., Austin, 1987—2004, chair House Rep. Caucus, 1999—2003; mem. US Congress from 24th Tex. dist., 2005—. Named Citizen of Yr., Metrocrest C. of C., Legislator of Yr., Tex. Mcpl. League, Top Pro-Family Legislator of Yr., Am. Family Assn.; named a Top Ten Legislator, Tex. Monthly mag. Republican. Nazarene. Office: US House of Representatives 1110 Longworth House Office Bldg Washington DC 20515 also: 9901 E Valley Ranch Pkwy Ste 3035 Irving TX 75063 Office Phone: 202-225-6605.*

MARCHASE, RICHARD BANFIELD, cell biologist, educator, research administrator; b. Sayre, Pa., Mar. 12, 1948; s. Nicholas and Vivian H. (Banfield) M.; m. Gail C. Andrews, Sept. 2, 2006; children: Nicholas Darrow, Allison Elizabeth. BS in Engring., Cornell U., 1970; PhD in Biophysics, Johns Hopkins U., 1976; postgrad., Duke U., 1978. Muscular Dystrophy Assn. postdoctoral fellow divsn. neurology Duke U. Med. Ctr., 1976-77, USPHS postdoctoral fellow dept. anatomy, 1977-78, asst. prof. anatomy, 1978-86; assoc. prof. cell biology U. Ala.-Birmingham, 1986—90, prof., 1990—, chmn., 1992—2000, sr. assoc. dean biomed. rsch., 2000—06, v.p. rsch. and econ. devel., 2004—. Contbr. chpts. to books, articles to profl. jours. Recipient Hamilton Watch award Cornell U., 1970, award Juvenile Diabetes Found., 1995-2002; Grad. fellow NSF, 1970-73, Danforth Found. grad. fellow, 1973-76; Nanaline H. Duke scholar, 1982-85; grantee USPHS 1979-, NSF, Presdl. Young Investigator grant, 1982-87. Mem. AAAS, Am. Soc. Cell Biology, Am. Soc. Zoology, Assn. of Anatomy, Cell Biology, and Neurobiology Chairpersons (pres. 1995-96), Am. Assn. Anatomists, Fed. Am. Soc. Exptl. Biology (bd. dirs. 2000— v.p. sci. policy, 2005, pres.-elect 2007), Sigma Xi. Office: U Ala Birmingham 720 AB Birmingham AL 35294-0001 Home: 4012 Lenox Rd Birmingham AL 35213 Office Phone: 205-934-1294. Business E-Mail: marchase@uab.edu.

MARCHETTI, ROBERT A., aerospace product and parts manufacturing executive; BBA, U. Bridgeport; M, Fairleigh Dickenson U. With Carlisle Corp., Copperweld Corp.; with Component Repair Division GE Aircraft Engines, 1986—89; pres. AWA Inc., 1989—90; corp. v.p. mktg., pres. Tri-Remanufacturing, COO Accessory Overhaul Divsn. UNC, Inc., 1990—97; sr. v.p., COO Fairchild Corp., 1997—2001; v.p. Machined Products BE Aerospace, Inc., 2001—02, v.p., gen. mgr. Consumables Mgmt., 2002—. Office: BE Aerospace Inc 1400 Corporate Ctr Way Wellington FL 33414 Office Phone: 561-791-5000. Office Fax: 561-791-7900.

MARCHIOLI, NELSON JEROME, restaurant chain executive; b. 1949; BA in Comm., U. Ctrl. Fla. With General Mills Restaurant Group, 1972—86; mgr. trainee Red Lobster, v.p.; exec. v.p. internat. ops. Burger King Corp., sr. v.p. worldwide supply, 1995—96; exec. v.p., COO Bruegger's Corp., 1996—97; pres. El Pollo Loco, Inc., 1997—2001; pres., CEO Denny's Corp. (formerly Advantica Restaurant Group, Inc.), 2001—. Former dir. FRD Acquisition Co. (FDR). Office: Denny's Corp 203 E Main St Spartanburg SC 29319-9966

MARCHIONINI, GARY JOSEPH, information science educator; b. Altoona, Pa., Sept. 12, 1949; s. Arthur and Claudia (Serventi) M.; m. Suzanne Bernhardt, July 10, 1970; children: Brian, Deanna. BA, Western Mich. U., 1971; MEd, Wayne State U., 1974, PhD, 1981. Tchr. math. East Detroit (Mich.) Pub. Schs., 1971-78; inservice specialist, rschr. Wayne State U., Detroit, 1978-82, asst. prof. inst. tech., 1982-83; asst. prof. info. sci. U. Md., College Park, 1983-90, assoc. prof. info. sci., 1990-95, prof. info. sci., 1995-98; Boshamer prof. info. sci. U. N.C., Chapel Hill, 1998—. Expert NSF, Washington, 1989-90; adj. prof. George Washington U., Washington, 1992. Author: Information Seeking in Electronic Environments, 1995; editor-in-chief: Transactions on Information Systems, 2002-2008; editor: Morgan Claypool Synthesis Series on Information Concepts, Retrieval & Services; contbr. articles to profl. jours. Grantee: NSF, 1987-90, Harvard U., Annenberg Corp. Pub. Broadcasting, 1988-93, Coun. on Libr. Resources, 1990-91, Nat. Libr. Medicine, 1992, NASA, 1993-94. Mem. Assn. for Computing Machinery, Am. Soc. for Info. Sci. (Rsch. award 1997), Am. Ednl. Rsch. Assn., Assn. for Advancement Computers in Edn., Am. Soc. Info. Sci. & Tech. (pres., 2009-). Office: U NC 203 Maning Hill Chapel Hill NC 27599-0001

MARCOM, PAUL KELLY, oncologist; MD, Baylor Coll. Medicine, Tex., 1989. Resident, medicine Duke U. Med. Ctr, 1989—92, resident, hematology and oncology, 1992—95, post-doctoral fellow, 1995—97, with med. oncology dept., 1997—. Contbr. several articles to profl. jours. Office: Duke U Med Ctr Box 3395 Med Ctr DUMC 3147 Durham NC 27710 Office Phone: 919-684-3877. Office Fax: 919-681-0874.

MARCOTTE, EDWARD MICHAEL, biochemist, researcher; b. Gainesville, Fla., Dec. 13, 1967; s. Ronald Edward and Clara Mae Marcotte. BS in Microbiology, U. Tex., Austin, 1990, PhD in Biochemistry, 1995. Postdoctoral rschr. U. Tex., Austin, 1995-96, UCLA, 1996, Hollaender Disting. Postdoctoral Fellow, 2000; prof. biochemistry U. Tex., Austin. Contbr. articles to profl. jours. Nat. Merit Scholar, 1990; NSF Grad. fellow, 1990-95; David and Lucile Packard Fellowship in Sci. and Engring., 2002-2007; recipient Outstanding Dissertation award U. Tex., 1996, Edith and Peter O'Donnell award in Sci., 2008. Mem. AAAS, Am. Crystallography Assn. (Pauling Prize). Achievements include determination of atomic structure, mechanism and evolution of the anti-fungal protein chitosanase. Office: Dept Chemistry & Biochemistry University of Texas Austin 1 University Station A5300 MBB 3.210 Austin TX 78712-0165 Office Phone: 512-471-5435. Business E-Mail: marcotte@icmb.utexas.edu.

MARCOTTE, MICHAEL STEVEN, municipal official; b. New Orleans, Jan. 17, 1951; s. Steven Stephen and Gloria Catherine (DeValcourt) Marcotte; m. Mary Jane Kilgore, May 28, 1972; children: Matthew David, Margaret Katherine. BA, M of Environ. Engring., Rice U., 1973. Cert. profl engr, Tex, Colo. Engr., sr. engr., mgr. Turner, Collie & Braden, Inc., Houston, 1973—82; chief maintenance engr. water divsn. City of Houston, 1982—83, mng. engr. water divsn., 1984—85, asst. to dir. Pub. Works dept., 1985—87, exec. asst. to dir. Pub. Works dept., 1987—88, acting dir. dept. planning and devel., 1988—89; dir. Dallas Water Utilities, 1989—95; dir. econ. devel. City of Dallas, 1995—97; chief engr. D.C. Water & Sewer Authority, 1997—2004; dir. pub. works City Houston, 2004—. Fellow: ASCE; mem.: Houston Galveston Area Coun., Am. Acad. Water Resource Engrs., Am Acad Environ Engrs (trustee), Tex Water Conservation Asn (bd dirs), Water Environ Fedn (life), Am Water Works Assn. (life; trustee Rsch. Found.). Presbyterian. Avocation: high school and college sports official. Home: 204 Travis St Apt 2D Houston TX 77002-1775 Office: City Houston 611 Walker 25th Fl Houston TX 77002 Home Phone: 713-226-8029; Office Phone: 832-395-2450. Personal E-mail: marcottem@prodigy.net.

MARCUM, JAMES A., retail executive; BS in Economics, Southern Conn. State U., 1980. CPA. Treas. Melville Corp., sr. v.p., CFO Marshall's Inc.; vice chmn., CFO Stage Stores, Inc.; exec. v.p., COO Lids, Inc.; exec. v.p., CFO Hollywood Entertainment Corp., 2001—03; operating ptnr./exec. Tri-Artisan Capital Ptnrs., LLC, 2004—08; chmn., CEO Ultimate Electronics, Inc., 2005—06; chmn., chief strategic officer Enabl-u Technologies Corp., 2007—08; vice chmn. Circuit City Stores, Inc., 2008—09, interim pres., CEO, 2008—09; pres., CEO Central Parking Corp., Nashville, 2010—. Bd. dirs. Enabl-u Technologies Corp., 2007—, Iconix Brand Group, Inc, 2007—, Circuit City Stores, Inc., 2008—09. Office: Central Parking Corp 2401 21st Ave S Nashville TN 37212 Office Phone: 615-297-4255.

MARCUS, BERNARD, lawyer, arbitrator, mediator; b. Wilkes-Barre, Pa., Mar. 10, 1924; m. Frances Frank; children: Kate, Aaron, Charles, Mary. Student, U. Pa., 1941-43, Carnegie-Mellon U., 1943-44; LL.B., Harvard U., 1948; postgrad., Loyola U. of South, New Orleans, 1958. Bar: D.C. 1949, La. 1958. Atty. legis. reference service Library of Congress, 1949-50; acting counsel small bus. com. Ho. of Reps., 1950; atty. NLRB, Washington, Cin., Buffalo and New Orleans, 1950-57; assoc. Deutsch, Kerrigan & Stiles, New Orleans, 1957-58, ptnr., 1958-95, mng. ptnr., 1985-89, emeritus ptnr., 1995—2004; of counsel Lehmann, Norman & Marcus, New Orleans, 2004—. Cons. Dept. State, 1965-69; labor arbitrator Am. Arbitration Assn., 1960-; arbitrator Fed. Med. and Conciliation Svc., 1960-. Author: Congress and the Monopoly Problem, 1950; contbr. to casebooks. Pres. New Orleans Jewish Cmty. Ctr., 1973-75; active Nat. Jewish Welfare Bd., 1974-83; bd. dirs. New Orleans Jewish Welfare Fedn., Jewish Family and Children's Service, New Orleans, Communal Hebrew Sch.; v.p. New Orleans Home for Jewish Aged, 1978-80, Florence Heller Rsch. Found. With U.S Army, 1943-46. Mem. ABA, Fed. Bar Assn., La. Bar Assn., New Orleans Bar Assn. (exec. com. 1971-74), D.C. Bar Assn., Nat. Acad. Arbitrators. Home: 630 Burdette St New Orleans LA 70118-3937 Office: Texaco Bldg Ste 2050 400 Poydras St New Orleans LA 70130 Home Phone: 504-866-2929; Office Phone: 504-680-6045. Business E-Mail: bmarcus@lnmlaw.com.

MARCUS, PAUL, law educator; b. NYC, Dec. 8, 1946; s. Edward and Lillian (Rubin) M.; m. Rebecca Nimmer, Dec. 22, 1968; children: Emily, Beth, Daniel. AB, UCLA, 1968, JD, 1971. Bar: Calif. 1971, U.S. Dist. Ct. (cen. dist.) Calif. 1972, U.S. Ct. Appeals (D.C. cir.) 1972, U.S. Ct. Appeals (7th cir.) 1976. Law clk. U.S. Ct. Appeals (D.C. cir.), 1971-72; assoc. Loeb & Loeb, LA, 1972-74; prof. law U. Ill., Urbana, 1974-83; dean Coll. Law U. Ariz., Tucson, 1983-88, prof., 1988-92; Haynes prof. law Coll. William and Mary, Williamsburg, Va., 1992—, Kelly prof. tchg. excellence, 1992—, interim dean, 1993-94, 97-98. Reporter, cons. Fed. Jud. Ctr. Commn., Nat. Com. on the Right to Counsel, 2004-07. Author: The Entrapment Defense, 1989, 4th edit., 2009, The Prosecution and Defense of Criminal Conspiracy, 1978, 6th edit., 2007, Gilbert Law Summary, 1982, 8th edit., 2004, Criminal Law: Cases and Materials, 1982, 6th edit., 2007, Criminal Procedure in Practice, 2001, 2d edit., 2003. Office: Coll William & Mary Law Sch PO Box 8795 Williamsburg VA 23187-8795 Home Phone: 757-253-0431; Office Phone: 757-221-3900. Business E-Mail: pxmarc@wm.edu.

MARCUS, ROBERT R., lawyer; b. Boston, Aug. 6, 1968; BA cum laude, Hamilton Coll., Clinton, NY, 1990; JD with honors, Duke U., Durham, NC, 1993. Bar: NC 1993, US Dist. Ct. (mid. dist.) NC 1993, US Dist. Ct. (ea. dist.) NC 1994, US Ct. Appeals (4th cir.) 1997, US Dist. Ct. (we. dist.) NC 2003, US Ct. Appeals (8th cir.) 2007. Ptnr., chair mgmt. com. Smith Moore Leatherwood, LLP, Charlotte, NC. Named a NC Super Lawyer, Law & Politics Mag., 2006—11; named an Impact Law Leader, Charlotte Bus. Leader Mag., 2008. Mem.: ABA, Litig. Counsel America, Fedn. Def. & Corp. Counsel, Def. Rsch. Inst., NC Assn. Def. Attorneys, NC Bar Assn. Office: Smith Moore Leatherwood LLP 525 N Tryon St Ste 1400 Charlotte NC 28202 Office Phone: 704-384-2630. Office Fax: 704-384-2910. E-mail: rob.marcus@smithmoorelaw.com.

MARCUS, STANLEY, federal judge; b. NYC, 1946; BA, CUNY, 1967; JD, Harvard U., 1971. Law clerk Hon. John Bartels, US Dist. Ct. (ea. dist.), NY; assoc. Botein, Hays, Sklar & Herzberg, NYC, 1974-75; asst. atty. US Dist. Ct. (ea. dist.)NY, 1975-78; spl. atty., dep. chief U.S. organized crime sect. Detroit Strike Force, 1978-79, chief U.S. organized crime sect., 1980-82; US atty. So. Dist. of Fla., Miami, 1982-85; judge US Dist. Ct. (so. dist.) Fla., Miami, 1985-97, US Ct. Appeals (11th cir.), 1997—. Mem. Fed. Bar Assn., Fla. Bar Assn, NY Bar Assn. Mem. US Army, 1968—74. Office: US Ct of Appeals 11th Cir 99 NE 4th St Rm 1262 Miami FL 33132-2185

MARCUSE, ADRIAN GREGORY, academic administrator; b. NYC, Mar. 25, 1922; s. Maxwell Frederick and Mildred Ann (Hitter) M.; m. Janet Constance Radlo, Oct. 28, 1945 (dec. Mar. 22, 1980); children: Nancy Ruth Marcuse Marshall, Sally Ann Marcuse Crawford, Elizabeth Susan Marcuse Martin; m. Betty Jane Lieberman Rossman, Jan. 11, 1985; 1 stepchild, Amy Beth Rossman Schurtz. BS, MIT, 1942, MS, 1946; LLD (hon.), LIM Coll., 1992. Registered profl. engr. N.Y., Fla. Rsch. assoc. MIT, Cambridge, Mass., 1945-46; rsch. scientist United Aircraft Co., E. Hartford, Conn., 1946-47; application engr. Westinghouse Electric Corp., Boston, NYC, 1947-60; consulting engr. pvt. practice, NYC, 1955-62; v.p. mktg. and sales Corrosion Control Corp., NYC, 1960-62; sales and merchandising mgr. B. Altman & Co., NYC, 1962; v.p., COO LIM Coll., NYC, 1962—72, pres., CEO, 1972—2002, pres. emeritus, counsel to pres., 2002—; trustee Lab. Inst. of Merchandising, 1972—. Pres. LIM Fashion Edn. Found., N.Y.C., 1978—; chmn. Assn. Regionally Accredited Prvt. Colls. and Univs., Washington, 1990-93. Charter commr. City of Glen Cove, N.Y., 1964, chmn. bd. engrs., 1964-68, mem. planning bd., 1980-87; past treas. Community Concert Assn., Glen Cove; past trustee and budget chmn. North Country Reform Temple, Glen Cove; past mem. YMCA Fund-Raising Coun., Glen Cove; ranger, vol. JD McArthur Beach State Pk, Fla.; v.p., bd. dirs. Gov.'s Pointe Condominium, 2005-07. 1st lt. USAAF, 1942-45, PTO. Mem.: Assn. Proprietary Colls. (pres. 1975—76), Sigma Beta Delta, Sigma Xi. Republican. Avocations: sailing, bicycling, travel, theater. Office: LIM Coll 12 E 53rd St Fl 2 New York NY 10022-5268 Home: 356 Golfview Rd #306 North Palm Beach FL 33408 Home Phone: 561-776-7420. Business E-Mail: amarcuse@limcollege.edu.

MARCY, KEVIN MICHAEL, film producer, lawyer; BS, U. Nev., Reno, 1974—78; JD, U. So. Calif., LA, 1978—81. Bar: Calif. 1981, DC 2006. Atty. Kinsella, Boesch, Fujikawa & Towle, LA, 1981—83; assoc. prodr. Paramount Pictures, LA, 1983—87, 1995; asst. to Dan Aykroyd Applied Action Rsch., LA, 1987—95, prodr., 2003—, Snake River Productions, Malibu, Calif., 1996—2003; assoc. prodr. Miramax Films, LA, 2003. V.p., guest rels. Ho. of Blues, LA, 1994; cons. Hitplay Media, LA, 2000. Prodr.: (films) The Testimony Of Taliesin Jones, 2000, (short film) Mr. Bill Goes To Law School; assoc. prodr. (films) The Naked Gun, 1988, The Coneheads, 1993, Scary Movie 3, 2003. Mem.: Ho. of Blues Found. (life), Dan Aykroyd Biker Gang (life), Phi Kappa Phi (life), Beta Gamma Sigma (life), Phi Alpa Delta (life), Delta Sigma Pi (life).

MARENGI, JOSEPH ALEXANDER, private equity firm executive, board member; b. Lynn, Mass., June 9, 1953; s. Joseph and Anna Maria (Fatello) Marengi. BS in Pub. Adminstrn., U. Mass., Boston, 1977; MS in Sys. Mgmt., U. So. Calif., 1983. Ops. mfg. sys. analyst General Electric Co., Lynn, 1972—74, supr., 1974—77; mgr. ops. sys. Westinghouse Electric Corp., Sunnyvale, Calif., 1981—84; sys. sales exec. Stanley Vidmar, Sunnyvale, 1984; dir. channels Excelan Inc.; v.p. Eastern region Novell Inc., 1989, exec. v.p. worldwide sales & field ops., 1991—96, pres., COO, 1996—97; sr. v.p. relationship group Dell, Inc., Round Rock, Tex., 1997, sr. v.p. Americas, 1997—2007; venture ptnr. Austin Ventures, Tex., 2007—. Chmn. bd. dirs. Portivity, Inc., 1997—; bd. dirs. Hovnanian Enterprises, Inc., 2006—, Augmentix Corp., 2007—, Quantum Corp., 2007—, Entorian Technologies, Inc., 2007—, chmn. bd. dirs., 2008—. Lt. comdr. USCG/USCGR, 1978—81. Mem.: Nat. Greyhound Assn., Tech. Comm. Assn., Res. Officers Assn., Soc. Mfg. Engrs. Roman Catholic. Office: Austin Ventures 300 W 6th St Ste 2300 Austin TX 78701 Mailing: Hovnanian Enterprises Inc Bd Directors 110 W Front St Red Bank NJ 07701 Office Phone: 732-747-7800. Office Fax: 732-747-6835. E-mail: jmarengi@khov.com.

MARES, MICHAEL ALLEN, ecologist, educator, museum association administrator; b. Albuquerque, Mar. 11, 1945; s. Ernesto Gustavo and Rebecca Gabriela (Devine) M.; m. Lynn Ann Brusin, Aug. 27, 1966; children: Gabriel Andres, Daniel Alejandro. BS in Biology, U. N.Mex., 1967; MD, Ft. Hays Kans. State U., 1969; PhD, U. Tex.-Austin, 1973. From asst. to assoc. prof. U. Pitts., 1973-81; assoc. prof., curator mammals U. Okla., Norman, 1981-83; dir. Okla. Mus. Nat. Hist., 1983—2003; assoc. prof. zoology U. Okla., 1983-85, prof., 1985—2003, presdl. prof., 2003—. Adj. prof. U. Nacional de Cordoba, Argentina, 1971-72, U. Nacional de Tucuman, Argentin, 1972, vis. prof., 1974; vis. scientist U. Ariz., Tucson, 1980-81; cons. Argentine Nat. Sci. Found., Inst. Arid Zone Rsch., Mendoza, 1983, World Wildlife Fund, Brazil, 1986; mem. Coun. Internat. Exch. Scholars, Am. Republics Bd., Fulbright Commn., 1983-86, 88-91; bd. dirs. Coun. Internat. Exch. of Scholars, 1988-91; NUS cons., Venezuela, 1980-81; sci. cons. interim working group White House Biodiversity, Ecology, and Ecosystems, 1992-94; apptd. adv. bd. Ctr. Biol. Diversity, Dept. Interior; mem. Commn. on Future of Smithsonian Instns., 1993-96, Smithsonian Coun., 2000—. Contbr. articles to profl. jours. NSF grantee, 1974-79, 82-93, 99-2000; Nat. Fulbright Rsch. fellow, 1976; Nat. Geo. Soc. grantee, 1992-95, 99; rsch. fellow Chicano Coun. on Higher Edn., 1978, Ford Found. Minority Rsch., 1980-81; recipient Brazilian Nat. Acad. Sci. Rsch. award, 1975-78. Mem. AAAS (Western Hemispheric coop. com. 1989-93), Am. Soc. Mammalogists (1st. v.p. 1990-94, C. Hart Merriam award 2000), Am. Ecol. Soc., Interam. Assn. Advancement Sci., Am. Inst. Biol. Sci., Am. Soc. Naturalists, Soc. Study of Evolution, Southwestern Assn. Naturalists (Donald W. Tinkle rsch. excellence award), Paleontol. Soc., Natural Sci. Collections Alliance (pres), Sigma Xi, Phi Kappa Phi, Beta Beta Beta. Office: U Okla Hist and Dept Zoology 2401 Chautauqua Ave Norman OK 73072 Home: 505 Bethany Oaks Dr Norman OK 73071-2171 Office Phone: 405-325-9007. Office Fax: 405-325-7699.

MARGER, EDWIN, lawyer; b. NYC, Mar. 18, 1928; s. William and Fannie (Cohen) M.; m. Kaye Sanderson, Oct. 1, 1951; children: Shari Ann, Diane Elaine, Sandy Ben; m. L. Suzanne Smyth, July 5, 1968; 1 child, George Phinney; m. Mary Susan Hamel, May 6, 1987; 1 child, Charleston Faye. BA, U. Miami, 1951, JD, 1953. Bar: Fla. 1953, Ga. 1971, D.C. 1978. Pvt. practice, Miami Beach, Fla., 1953—67, Atlanta, 1971—90, Jasper, Ga., 1990—. Gen. counsel Physicians Nat. Risk Retention Group, 1988-91, Physicians Reliance Assn., 1988-91, Physicians Nat. Legal Def. Corp., 1988-91; spl. asst. atty. gen. Fla., 1960-61; atty., agt. Republic of Haiti, 1962-67, City of Port-au-Prince for Transp. and Housing, 1962, Dominican Republic for Trade and Industry, 1964-65; of counsel Richard Burns, Miami, 1967—. Contbr. articles to profl. jours. Tchr. Nat. Inst. Trial Advocacy; mem. Miami Beach Social Svc. Commn., 1957; chmn. Fulton County Aviation Adv. Com., 1980—; chmn. Pickens County Airport Adv. Com., 2004-06; trustee Forensic Scis. Found., 1984-88, v.p., 1986-88; lt. col., a.d.c. Gov. Ga., 1971-74, 80-84; col., a.d.c. Gov. La., 1977-87; Khan Bahador and mem. exiled King of Afghanistan Privy Coun., 1980—. With USAAF, 1946-47, with, USAF, 1950-1978. Fellow Am. Acad. Forensic Scis. (chmn. jurisprudence sect. 1977-78, sec. 1976-77, bd. dirs. 1978-79, exec. com. 1983-86); mem. Fla. Bar Assn. (aerospace com. 1971-83, bd. govs. 1983-87, 90-94, exec. com. 1993-94), State Bar Ga. (chmn. sect. environ. law 1974-75, aviation law sect. 1978, bd. govs. 1999-2005, stds. of the profession com.), Ga. Trial Lawyers Assn., Nat. Assn. Criminal Def. Lawyers, Ga. Assn. Criminal Def. Lawyers, Am. Judicature Soc., Am. Arbitration Assn. (commn. panel 1978), Inter-Am. Bar Assn. (sr.), World Assn. Lawyers (founding), Lawyer-Pilots Bar Assn. (founding, v.p. 1959-62), VFW, Am. Legion,

Rotary, Lions, Navy League, U.S. Naval Inst., Advocates Club, Lawyers Club Atlanta, Martindale Hubbell Peer Rev. Rating AV. Office: 44 N Main St Jasper GA 30143-1501 Office Phone: 706-253-3060. Personal E-mail: wanda@edmarger.com.

MARGO, DONALD RUPERT, II, state legislator, insurance company executive; b. Feb. 3, 1952; s. Donald Rupert and Sammy (Sloneker) M.; m. Adair Wakefield, Aug. 21, 1976; children: William Wakefield, Donald Rupert III. B in History and Economics, Vanderbilt U., Nashville. Rep. John Hancock Mut. Life Ins. Co., Nashville, 1974-77; v.p. John D. Williams Co., El Paso, 1977-81, pres., 1981-2000, chmn., CEO, 2000—; mem. Dist. 78 Tex. House of Representatives, 2011—. Bd. dirs. El Paso Symphony Orch. Assn., 1978-81, Pvt. Industry Coun., 192-84, Jr. Achievement, 1982-87, pres. 1986-87; mem. Leadership El Paso Alumni, City-County Bd. Health, 1986-89; vice chmn. El Paso Empowerment Zone Corp., 2000, chmn. 2001; officer Greater EP Cafe; chmn. Bus. Adv. Coun., U. Tex. El Paso Bus. Sch., 2000-02. Mem. Greater El Paso C. of C., Internat. Bd. YPO, Young Pres.' Orgn., Fellowship Christian Athletes, Assn. US Army, Sunturians, Sunturica Alumni, Rotary (dir. El Paso 1982-84). Republican. Baptist. Office: John D Williams Co PO Box 981021 El Paso TX 79998-1021 also: Room E1.316 Capitol Extension PO Box 2910 Austin TX 78768 Address: 6006 North Mesa Ste 503 El Paso TX 79912 Office Phone: 512-463-0728, 915-875-0150. Office Fax: 512-463-0397.

MARGOLIN, ANN, councilwoman, insurance company executive; b. Newark, Aug. 27, 1952; d. Morris and Edith (Zimring) Epstein; m. Fred Harold Margolin, Sept. 4, 1977; children: Richard, Jane. BS, Northwestern U., 1974, MA in Comm., 1974; MBA in Fin., Columbia U., 1977. Founder & ptnr. Intercon Gen. Ins. Agy.; trainee Std. Oil Ohio, Cleve., 1977—78; owner Intercon Gen. Agy., Dallas, 1978—82, Margolin Properties, Dallas, 1982—; councilwoman, Dist. 13 Dallas City Coun., 2009—. Mem. Dallas City Planning Commn., Dallas Pk. and Recreation Bd., Parkland Hosp. Bd. Mem.: North Dallas C. of C., Exec. Women of Dallas. Republican. Jewish. Home: 10515 Lennox Ln Dallas TX 75229-5415

MARGOLIS, DAVID MICHAEL, medical educator; b. New Haven, Aug. 23, 1959; AB, Harvard Coll., Cambridge, Mass., 1981; MD, Tufts U. Sch. Medicine, Boston, 1985. Asst. prof. medicine, microbiology & immunology U. Md. Sch. Medicine and Inst. Human Virology, Balt., 1994—99; prof. medicine, microbiology & immunology U. Tex. Southwestern Med. Ctr., Dallas, 1999—2005; prof. medicine, microbiology & immunology, epidemiology U. NC, Chapel Hill, 2005—. Mem. AIDS Rsch. Adv. Com., DAIDS, NIH, Bethesda, 2004—08. Fellow: ACP, Infectious Diseases Soc. Am.; mem.: Am. Soc. Clin. Investigation. Achievements include research in demonstration of the role of HDACs in HIV latency. Office: Univ NC Sch Medicine 3302 Michael Hooker Res Ctr CB #7435 Chapel Hill NC 27599-7435

MARGOLIS, GWEN, state legislator; b. Phila., Oct. 4, 1934; d. Joseph and Rose Liedman; children: Edward, Ira, Karen, Robin. Grad., Temple U. Mem. Fla. House of Reps., 1975—80, Fla. State Senate, 1981—92, 2003—08, pres., 1990-92, mem. Dist. 35, 2011—; mem. dist. 4 Metro-Dade County Commn., Fla., 1994—2002, chairperson Fla., commr. dist. 4 Fla.; realtor, appraiser. Bd. dirs. Holocaust Documentation Ctr. Fla., 1997—, bd. dirs. New Theater, 2009, Jewish Mus. LA, 2009. Recipient Econ. Devel. award Fla. C. of C., 1992, Legislator of Yr. award Fla. C. of C., 1992, Good Govt. award Dade League of Cities, 1992, Fla. Motion Picture and TV award, 1992, Glass Ceiling award Fla. Fedn. Bus. and Profl. Women, 1992. Named to Fla. Womens Hall of Fame, 2009, Women of Valor Greater Miami Jewish Fedn. Mem.: Miami Bd. Realtors. Democrat. Jewish. Office: Ste 600 3050 Biscayne Blvd Miami FL 33137 also: Fla State Senate 414 Senate Office Bldg 404 S Monroe St Tallahassee FL 32399-1100 Office Phone: 305-571-5777, 850-487-5121. Business E-Mail: margolis.gwen.web@flsenate.gov.

MARGULIES, MARTIN Z., real estate developer, philanthropist; b. Feb. 1938; Owner Martin Z. Margulies Sculpture Park, Miami, Fla., 1994—, Margulies Collection at the Warehouse, Miami, Fla., 1999—. Bd. dirs. Arts for Learning (A4L), Miami; co-founder Overtown Youth Ctr., Miami, 2003—. Named one of Top 200 Collectors, ARTNews Mag., 2004—12. Avocation: art collection. Home: 445 Grand Bay Dr Key Biscayne FL 33149-1905

MARGULIS, HEIDI S., insurance company executive; BA in Internat. Studies, U. Louisville, 1974. Licensure analyst Humana, Inc., 1985—95, v.p., govt. affairs, 1995—2000, sr. v.p., govt. affairs, 2000—. Mem. fed. adv. com. to streamline regulations to ensure quality health care svcs., 2002; mem. com., Medicare edn. HFCA. Mem.: Women's Polit. Forum (bd. dirs.), Bus. and Profl. Women (pres. 1978—79), Bus. Roundtable, Health Care Leadership Coun., Am. Assn. Health Plans (policy, legis., advocacy and strategic planning coms.). Office: Humana Inc 500 W Main St Louisville KY 40202 Office Phone: 502-580-1000. Office Fax: 502-580-3639. Business E-Mail: hmargulis@humana.com.

MARIAM, YITBAREK H., chemistry professor; BA in Chemistry with high honors, Rutgers U., Newark, NJ, 1974; PhD, Rutgers U., 1977. Prof. chemistry Clark Atlanta U., 1979—. Disting. Scholar, UNCF, 1985—86. Mem.: Am. Chem. Soc.

MARIENTHAL, GEORGE, telecommunications industry executive; b. Kansas City, Mo., Nov. 15, 1938; s. George and Sadie (James) M.; children: Shawn Ann Capon, Patrick James, Shannon Lee Van Winter. BS, U.S. Naval Acad., 1962; MS, Stanford U., 1963; MBA, Am. U., 1974. Sr. rsch. assoc. Logistics Mgmt. Inst., Washington, 1967-71; dir. regional ops. EPA, 1971-75, dir. water policy, 1984-85; dep. asst. sec. def. Dept. Def., Washington, 1975-81; v.p. Survival Tech., Inc., Bethesda, Md., 1981-84; dep. asst. sec. agr. Dept. Agr., Washington, 1985-86; dep. adv. programs Titan Systems, Inc., 1986-87; mgr. mktg. Computer Scis. Corp., Falls Church, Va., 1987-89; v.p. Verizon Business, Vienna, 1989—2007; pres. RTB Sys., Naples, Fla., 2007—. Bd. dirs. Home Security Title Ins. Co. Served with USAF, 1962-67. Mem.: Nat. Def. Indsl. Assn., Internat. Telephone Pioneers Assn., Armed Forces Comms. and Electronics Assn., Masons. Republican. Episcopalian. Home: PO Box 9983 Naples FL 34101-1983 Office Phone: 301-807-6350.

MARIN, PEDRO, state legislator; State rep. Dist. 66, Ga., 2003—04; state rep. Dist. 96 Ga., 2004—; mem. Econ. Devel. & Tourism Coms., Indsl. Rels. Coms., Legislature & Congressional Reapportionment Coms.; sec. Interstate Coop. Com.; program mgr. Gwinnett Housing Resource Ptnrs. Democrat. Mailing: 2625 Ridge Brook Trail Duluth GA 30096 Office: 611 Legis Office Bldg Atlanta GA 30334 Office Phone: 678-291-0305. E-mail: marinstatehouse@aol.com.

MARINELLI, ROD, professional football coach; b. Rosemead, Calif., July 13, 1949; m. Barbara Marinelli; children: Chris, Gina. Attended, U. Utah, 1968, Calif. Lutheran, 1970—72. Asst. coach Rosemead HS, Calif., 1973—75; defensive line coach Utah St. U. Aggies, 1976—81, offensive line/spl. teams coach, 1982; defensive line coach U. Calif. Golden Bears, 1983—91; asst. coach, defensive line coach Ariz. State U. Sundevils, 1993—95; defensive line coach U. So. Calif. Trojans, 1995—96, Tampa Bay Bucaneers, 1996—2006; head coach Detroit Lions, 2006—08; defensive line coach, asst. head coach Chgo. Bears, 2009—10, defensive coord./asst. head coach, 2010—12; defensive line coach Dallas Cowboys, 2013, defensive coord., 2014—. Served in US Army, 1969, Vietnam. Recipient All-American honors, NAIA, 1972. Achievements include being a member of Super Bowl XXXVII winning Tampa Bay Buccaneers, 2003. Office: Dallas Cowboys 1 Cowboys Pky Irving TX 75063*

MARINESCU, DAN CRISTIAN, computer sciences educator, consultant; b. Craiova, Dolj, Romania, Mar. 4, 1942; s. Nicolae and Aurelia Marinescu; m. Gabriela Magdalena Sezon; 1 child, Andrei. PhD in EECS, Polytechnic Inst., Bucharest, Romania, 1972—75. Prof. computer sci. Purdue U., West Lafayette, Ind., 1984—2001, U. Ctrl. Florida, Orlando, 2001—02; sr. rschr. GSI, Darmstadt, Fla., Germany, 1980—84, Inst. Atomic Physics, Bucharest, Romania, 1965—79; assoc. prof. Polytechnic Inst., Bucharest, 1970—79. Vis. prof. INRIA Rocquencourt, Paris, 2000—00, Paris, 1999—99, IBM Rsch., Yorktown Heights, NY, 1985—85, Intel Supercomputer Sys., Portland, 1992—92. Author: Internet-Based Workflow Management, 2002; contbr. articles to profl. jours., 1987. Recipient Grand Challenge, National Science Foundation, 1995-2002, Virtual Lab for Computational Biology, Nat. Sci. Found., 2001—, Workflow Management, 2001—, 3D Reconstruction of Viruses, 2000—. Greek Orthodox. Avocations: skiing, photography, travel. Home: 14449 Dover Forest Dr Orlando FL 32828 Office: Computer Sci Dept UCF 4000 Central Florida Blvd Orlando FL 32816 Personal E-mail: danc.marinescu@gmail.com.

MARINI, ROBERT CHARLES, environmental engineering executive; b. Quincy, Mass., Sept. 29, 1931; s. Larry and Millie (Cirillo) M.; m. Myrna Lydia Pellegrini, June 26, 1955 (dec. June 1994); children: Debra, Robert Charles, Larry; m. B. Anne Jones, May 27, 1995. BSCE (hon.), Northeastern U., 1954, doctorate (hon.), 1997; SMSE, Harvard U., 1955, postgrad. in advanced mgmt., 1985. Registered profl. engr., Mass. Jr. engr. Camp Dresser & McKee Inc., Boston, 1955-56, project engr., 1958-64, assoc., 1964-67, ptnr., sr. v.p., 1967-77, pres. environ. engring. div., 1977-82, exec. v.p., 1982-84, pres., 1984-90, CEO, 1989-98, chmn. bd. dirs., 1998—99, vice chmn. bd. dirs., 1999-2001, chmn. emeritus, 2001—09. Mem. civil engring. adv. com. Worcester (Mass.) Poly. Inst., 1985-90, U. Mass., 1986-90, U. Tex., Austin, 1989-91, chmn., 1991-92, mem. engring. found. adv. coun., 1991-98; trustee South Shore Savs. Bank, 1990—2008, audit com., 2001-08. Contbr. articles to profl. jours. Dir. nat. coun. Northeastern U., Boston, 1983-2004, mem. corp. bd., 1983-2004, bd. overseers, 1985-89, trustee, 1989-2004; chmn. Leadership Phase Century II Fund, 1989-91, chmn. devel. com., 1991-98, vice chmn. bd. trustees, 1997-2004, vice chmn. emeritus, 2004-; bd. dirs. Mass. Bus. Round Table, 1991-99, vice chmn., 1995-97, chmn., 1997-99, Plimoth Plantation, 2005-09. Recipient Disting. Eagle Scout award Boy Scouts Am., 1986, Mass. Patriots award Old Colony Coun., 1998, W. Erwin Story award, 1991, Outstanding Civil Engring. Alumni award Northeastern U., 1992, Outstanding Alumni award, 1993; named Man of Yr., Don Orione, 1999. Mem ASCE (hon., disting. mem., Opal award 2003), fellow NAE, Boston Soc. Civil Engrs. (hon.); mem. Am. Pub. Works Assn. (Man of Yr. award New Eng. chpt. 1981), Am. Water Works Assn., Mass. Soc. Profl. Engrs. (Young Engr. of Yr. award 1966), Am. Acad. Environ. Engrs. (diplomate, trustee at large 1989-92, v.p. 1992-93, pres.-elect 1993-94, pres. 1994-95, Stanley E. Kappe award 1992, Gordon Maskew Fair award, 2005), Water Environment Fedn. (hon., N.E. chpt., Founders award 1999), Internat. Assn. Water Pollution Rsch. and Control, Engring. Soc. New Eng. (New Eng. award 1994), Greater Boston C. of C. (bd. dirs. 1997-99), Water Environ. Rsch. Found. (bd. dirs. 1998-2001), Tau Beta Pi, Phi Kappa Phi. Roman Catholic. Home: P O Box 1070 Boca Grande FL 33921 Home Phone: 941-964-2089; Office Phone: 617-452-6000. Business E-Mail: marinirc@comcast.net.

MARINI-MIR, LUIS A., insurance company executive; DMD, U. Puerto Rico. CERT. Pediatric Dentistry, U. Puerto Rico; CERT. Pediatric Dentistry, Sch. of Dentistry. CEO Triple-C Mgmt. Corp. (subs. Triple-s Mgmt. Corp.); with Triple-S Management Corp., 1975—2000, dental dir., 1998—99; pres., commonwealth puerto rico health bus. Triple-C, Inc. (subs. of Triple-S Management Corp.), 1999—. Former dean U. Puerto Rico, 1993-97. Office: Triple-S Management Corp 1441 FD Roosevelt Ave San Juan PR 00920 Office Phone: 787-749-4949.

MARINIS, THOMAS PAUL, JR., lawyer; b. Jacksonville, Tex., May 31, 1943; s. Thomas Paul and Betty Sue (Garner) M.; m. Lucinda Cruse, June 25, 1969; children: Courtney, Kathryn, Megan. BA, Yale U., 1965; LLB, U. Tex., 1968. Bar: Tex. 1968. Assoc. Vinson & Elkins, Houston, 1969-76, ptnr., 1977—2012, ofcounsel, 2013—. Bd. dirs. Phoenix House of Tex., Inc. Fellow Tex. Bar Found.; mem. ABA (sec. taxation sect. 1986-87), Houston Country Club, Houston Ctr. Club, Coronado Club. E-mail: tmarinis@velaw.com.

MARINO, DAN (DANIEL CONSTANTINO MARINO JR.), sportscaster, retired professional football player; b. Pitts., Sept. 15, 1961; s. Daniel and Veronica Marino; m. Claire Veazey, Jan. 30, 1985; adopted children: Niki Lin, Lia children: Daniel Charles, Michael Joseph, Joseph Donald, Alexandra Claire. BA in Comm., U. Pitts., 1983. Quarterback Miami Dolphins, 1983—99; co-host Inside the NFL, HBO, 2000—08; analyst, The NFL Today CBS Sports, 2002—13. Actor: (films) Ace Ventura: Pet Detective, 1994; co-author (with David Hyde): Dan Marino: My Life in Football, 2005. Founder Dan Marino Found., 1991—, Dan Marino Ctr., 1998—. Recipient Bert Bell Most Valuable Player award, Maxwell Club, 1984, NFL MVP award, AP, 1984, NFL Comeback Player of Yr., 1994, Walter Payton Man of Yr. award, 1998; named The All-American Team, The Sporting News, 1981, NFL Rookie of Yr., 1983, NFL All-Pro, 1984—86; named to The American Football Conf. Pro Bowl Team, 1983—87, 1991—92, 1994—95, The Coll. Football Hall of Fame, 2003, The Pro Football Hall of Fame, 2005. Achievements include leading the NFL in: pass attempts, 1984, 1986, 1988, 1992, 1997; pass completions, 1984-86, 1988, 1992, 1997; passing yards, 1984-86, 1988, 1992; passing touchdowns, 1984-86, passer rating, 1984. Office: Dan Marino Found 400 N Andrews Ave Fort Lauderdale FL 33301-3257*

MARINO, EUGENE LOUIS, publishing executive, director; b. NYC, Jan. 7, 1929; s. Salvatore A. and Florence M. (Casabona) M.; m. Patricia Ryan, Mar. 11, 1948; children: Jeanette, Anthony, John, Eugene III. Student, Columbia U., 1945-48. Credit mgr. Sears, Roebuck Inc., LI, NY, 1951-60; gen. credit mgr. Davison-Paxon div. R.H. Macy, Inc., Atlanta, 1960-63, Grand-Way div. Grand Union Co., NYC, 1963-66; v.p., gen. credit mgr. Consumer Products div. Singer Co., NYC, 1966-75, Grolier, Inc., Danbury, Conn., 1975-90; ret. Officer, v.p., gen. credit mgr., dir. numerous subsidiaries. Recipient Quarter Century cert. Internat. Consumer Credit Assn., 1981. Mem. Mchts. Rsch. Coun., Internat. Consumer Credit Assn., Nat. Assn. Credit Mgmt., Alpha Sigma Phi. Home: 14332 Sundial Pl Lakewood Ranch FL 34202-5887 Personal E-mail: elmarino1@verizon.net.

MARINO, WILLIAM FRANCIS, telecommunications industry executive, consultant; b. Phila., Dec. 28, 1948; s. William F. and Edith Ellen (Dougherty) M.; m. Mary Ellen Klems, Sept. 29, 1979; children: Kiersten Leigh, Meghan Lyn. Student, Ohio State U., 1967; BS in Fin. and Acctg., Widener U., 1970. Sr. acctg., fin. positions U.S. Steel Corp., Pitts., 1970-83; v.p. U.S. Steel Credit Corp., Pitts., 1983-85; dir. fin. programs CIS Corp., Syracuse, N.Y., 1985, v.p. instl. sales, 1986; pres. CIS Credit Corp., Syracuse, N.Y., 1987, v.p. fin., 1988; v.p., chmn. reorganization com. Continental Info. Systems Corp., Syracuse, N.Y., 1989; v.p. fin., CFO ITEC Corp., Lake Bluff, Ill., 1990-91, pres., CEO, 1991—, Global Telecom Svcs. Corp., 2000—. Advisor, cons. Chong & Assocs., N.Y.C., 1989. Advisor Hiawatha coun. Boy Scouts Am., Syracuse, 1987; dir. Cystic Fibrosis Found., Syracuse, 1987-88. Recipient Century award Boy Scouts Am., Syracuse, 1988. Mem. Am. Assn. Equipment Lessors, Am. Mgmt. Assn., Fin. Execs. Inst., Aircraft, Owners & Pilots Assn. Republican. Avocations: flying, cross country skiing. Home: 8763 Muirfield Dr Naples FL 34109-4352 Office: Global Telecom Svcs Corp 8763 Muirfield Dr Naples FL 34109-4352 Personal E-mail: billmarino@comcast.net.

MARION, ELAINE D., corporate financial executive; BS in Acctg., George Mason U., 1995. Gen. mgr. Bristow Devel. Corp.; contr. ePlus, Inc., 1998—2004, v.p., acctg., 2004—08, CFO, 2008—. Office: ePlus Inc 13595 Dulles Technology Dr Herndon VA 20171-3413 Office Phone: 703-984-8400. Office Fax: 703-984-8600. Business E-Mail: emarion@eplus.com.

MARION, SHAWN, professional basketball player; b. Waukegan, Ill., May 7, 1978; Student, Vincennes U., Ind., UNLV. Forward Phoenix Suns, 1999—2008, Miami Heat, Fla., 2008—09, Toronto Raptors, 2009, Dallas Mavericks, 2009—. Mem., Team USA Goodwill Games, Brisbane, Australia, 2001, World Championships, Indpls., 2002; mem. US Olympic Basketball Team, Athens, Greece, 2004. Recipient Gold medal, Goodwill Games, 2001, Bronze medal, men's basketball, Athens Olympic Games, 2004; named to All-Rookie Second Team, NBA, 2000, Western Conf. All-Star Team, 2003, 2005, 2007. Achievements include member of the NBA Finals Championship winning Dallas Mavericks, 2011. Office: Dallas Mavericks 2909 Taylor St Dallas TX 75226

MARIOTTO, MARCO JEROME, dean, psychology educator, researcher; b. Ill., Oct. 21, 1946; s. Marco Anibele and Sally (Hughes) M.; m. Danita Irene Czyzewski, May 4, 1985; children: Ana-Sofia Antonia, Marco Luca. BS, U. Ill., 1968, PhD, 1974. Diplomate Am. Bd. Sexology, Am. Bd. Forensic Examiners; lic. psychologist; cert. sex therapist, cert. health svcs. provider. Asst. rsch. dir. Adolf Meyer Ctr. Rsch. Units, Decatur, Ill., 1972-74; psychologist U.S. Army Acad. Health Scis., San Antonio, 1974; asst. prof. Purdue U., West Lafayette, Ind., 1975-79; assoc. prof. U. Houston, 1979-90, supervisory psychologist, 1979—, prof., 1990—, dept. chmn., 1994—99, founding dean grad. and profl. studies, 1999—; co-dir. Abramson Ctr. For Future of Health, 2007—. Cons. NIMH, Bethesda, Md., 1977—, NSF, Washington, 1980-84, Nat. Inst. Drug Abuse, Bethesda, 1986-89; adj. prof. U. Tex. Health Scis., Houston, 1980—. Contbr. chpts. to books and articles to profl. jours.; also rsch. monographs and tech. reports. Forensic cons. Harris County Dist. Atty.'s Office, Houston, 1988—, ABA, 1989—; founding mem. Gulf Coast Consortium on Mental Health, Houston and Galveston, Tex., 1989. Officer US Army, 1968—74. Named one of top 35 Young Scientist Profls. Jour. Cons. and Clin. Psychology, 1988; David Ross fellow Purdue U., 1977. Mem. APA, Am. Psychol. Soc.; mem. AAAS, Midwestern Psychol. Assn. (local rep. 1979—), Sigma Xi. Achievements include co-devel. of TSBC/SRIC planned access infosystem for rsch. and svc. for patients in residential treatment settings; rsch. in observational measurement in mental health, schizophrenia, chronic mental patients. Office: University Houston Psychology Dept 126 Heyne Bldg Houston TX 77204-5022 Home Phone: 713-748-2783. Business E-Mail: mmariotto@uh.edu.

MARIS, STEPHEN S., lawyer, educator; b. Dallas, Dec. 19, 1949; children: Shane, Kara. BS, Stephen F. Austin State, Nacogdoches, Tex., 1971; JD, So. Meth. U., Dallas, 1975. Bar: US Dist. Ct. (no. dist.) Tex. 1975, US Dist. Ct. (ea. dist.) Tex. 1986, US Dist. Ct. (so. dist.) Tex. 1992, US Ct. Appeals (5th cir.) 1980, US Ct. Appeals (11th cir.) 1981, US Supreme Ct. Tex. 1975. Assoc. Passman & Jones, Dallas, 1975-80, ptnr., 1980-87, Fulbright & Jaworski, Dallas, 1987-97, Jenkens & Gilchrist, Dallas, 1997—2007, Hunton & Williams, 2007. Prof. So. Ill. U., 1979-80, So. Meth. U., Dallas, 1980—; mem. faculty Nat. Inst. Trial Advocacy, 1980—. Editor: Southwest Law Journal, 1973-75. Mem. ABA, State Bar Tex., Dallas Bar Assn., Barristers, Order Coif, Phi Delta Phi. Office: Hunton & Williams 1445 Ross Ave Ste 3700 Dallas TX 75202-2785 Office Phone: 214-468-3352. Business E-Mail: smaris@hunton.com.

MARK, HANS MICHAEL, physicist, former federal agency administrator; b. Mannheim, Germany, June 17, 1929; arrived in U.S., 1940, naturalized, 1945; s. Herman Francis and Maria (Schramek) M.; m. Marion G. Thorpe, Jan. 28, 1951; children: Jane H., Rufus J. AB in Physics, U. Calif., Berkeley, 1951; PhD, MIT, 1954; ScD (hon.), Fla. Inst. Tech., 1978; DEng (hon.), Poly. U. NY, 1982, Milw. Sch. Engring., 1991; LHD (hon.), St. Edward's U., 1993; ScD (hon.), Royal Mil. Coll. Sci., UK, 2004; DEng (hon.), Tri-State U., 2005. Rsch. assoc. MIT, Cambridge, 1954-55, asst. prof., 1958-60; rsch. physicist Lawrence Radiation Lab. U. Calif., Livermore, 1955-58, 60-69, exptl. physics divsn. leader, 1960-64, assoc. prof. nuc. engring. Berkeley, 1960-66, prof., 1966-69, chmn. dept. nuc. engring., 1964-69, lectr. dept. applied sci. Davis, 1969-73; cons. prof. engring. Stanford (Calif.) U., 1973-84; dir. NASA-Ames Rsch. Ctr., 1969-77; undersec. Air Force, dir. Nat. Reconnaissance Office USAF, Washington, 1977-79, sec. Air Force, 1979-81; dep. adminstr. NASA, Washington, 1981-84; chancellor U. Tex. Sys., Austin, 1984-92; prof. aerospace engring. and engring. mechanics U. Tex., Austin, 1988—; dir. defense rsch. and engring. Dept. Def., Washington, 1998-2001. Mem. Pres.'s Adv. Group Sci. and Tech., 1975-76; bd. dirs. Astronautics Corp. Am.; trustee Poly. U., 1984—. Author: (with N.T. Olson) Experiments in Modern Physics, 1966; (with E. Teller and J.S. Foster, Jr.) Power and Security, 1976; (with A. Levine) The Management of Research Institutions, 1983, The Space Station-A Personal Journey, 1987, (with Victor G. Szebehely) Adventures in Celestial Mechanics, 1998; also numerous articles; editor: (with S. Fernbach) Properties of Matter Under Unusual Conditions, 1969; (with Lowell Wood) Energy in Physics, War and Peace, 1988. Recipient Disting. Svc. medal NASA, 1972, 77, medal for exceptional engring. achievement, 1984, Exceptional Civilian Svc. award USAF, 1979, Disting. Pub. Svc. medal, Dept. Def., 1981, 2001, Sec.'s Gold medal Dept. Energy, 2001. Fellow AIAA (hon., Von Karman lectr. astronautics 1992), Am. Phys. Soc.; mem. NAE, Am. Nuc. Soc., Am. Geophys. Union, Coun. Fgn. Rels., Cosmos Club. Achievements include research on nuclear energy levels, nuclear reactions, applications, nuclear energy for practical purposes, atomic flourescence yields, measurement X-rays above atmosphere, spacecraft and experimental aircraft design. Office: U Tex Dept Aerospace Engring/Engr Austin TX 78712 Home Phone: 512-477-2753; Office Phone: 512-471-5077. Business E-Mail: hmark@mail.utexas.edu.

MARKEY, JAMES KEVIN, lawyer; b. Springfield, Ill., July 15, 1956; s. James Owen and Marjorie Jean (Diesness) M.; m. Allison Markey; children: Lauren, Katherine. BBA with highest honors, U. Notre Dame, 1977; JD cum laude, U. Mich., 1980; MBA, U. Chgo., 1987; LLM in Taxation, DePaul U., 1993. CPA Ill.; bar: Ill. 1980. Assoc. Chapman & Cutler, Chgo., 1980-81; atty. Quaker Oats Co., Chgo., 1981-84; corp. counsel Baxter Healthcare Corp., Deerfield, Ill., 1984-90; v.p. law and other positions Motorola, Inc., Schaumburg, Ill., 1990-2000; v.p., chief counsel-securities and internat. Kellogg Co., Battle Creek, Mich., 2000—06; v.p., sec., gen. counsel MAG Industrial Automation Sys., LLC, Sterling Heights, Mich., 2006—08; sr. v.p. & sr. corp. counsel Affiliated Computer Svcs. Inc. Xerox Corp., 2008—. Mem. ABA, Beta Alpha Psi, Beta Gamma Sigma. Avocations: racquetball, running, bridge. Home: 8101 Greensboro Dr Plano TX 75025-2588 Office: 2828 N Haskell Plano TX 75024 Business E-Mail: jim.markey@att.net.

MARKIDES, KYRIAKOS SOCRATES, gerontology educator; b. Nicosia, Cyprus, Mar. 21, 1948; arrived in U.S., 1968; s. Socrates and Persoulla Markides; m. Angela Lera, June 12, 2004. BA, Bowling Green State U., 1972; MA, La. State U., 1973, PhD, 1976. Asst. prof. U. Tex. Health Sci. Ctr., San Antonio, 1976—82, assoc. prof., 1982—87; prof. U. Tex. Med. Br., Galveston, 1987—, Annie and John Gnitzinger Endowed prof., 1999—. Author (with others): Older Mexican Americans, 1983, Aging and Ethnicity, 1987, Retirement in Industrialized Societies, 1987, Aging and Health, 1989, Aging, Stress and Health, 1989, Minorities, Aging and Health, 1997, Encyclopedia of Health and Aging, 2007; mem. edit. bd. The Gerontologist Jour., 1980—, founding editor Jour. of Aging and Health, 1989—; author: Aging and Longevity in The Mexican Origin Population. Recipient Disting. Mentorship award, Gerontol. Soc., 2006, Disting. Prof. award, UCLA, Pearmain prize, Edward Royal Inst. Aging, U. Southern Calif., 2010; grantee Rsch. grantee, Nat. Inst. Aging, 1980—, Hogg Found., 1984—, Rockefeller Found. Fellow: Am. Coll. Epidemiology, Gerontol. Soc. Am.; mem.: APHA, Population Assn. Am., Am. Sociol. Assn. Office: Univ Tex Med Branch Galveston TX 77550 Office Phone: 409-772-2551. E-mail: kmarkide@utmb.edu.

MARKOFF, BRAD STEVEN, lawyer; b. NYC, July 29, 1957; s. Daniel and Geri (Skitol) M.; m. Danna Kay Schmidt, May 17, 1980; children: Andrew David, Paul Steven, Samuel Joseph. AB, Duke U., 1979; JD, Washington U., St. Louis, 1982. Bar: Mo. 1982, U.S. Tax Ct. 1984, N.C. 1985. Assoc. Stolar Partnership, St. Louis, 1982-84; assoc., ptnr. Moore & Van Allen, Raleigh, NC, 1984-92; ptnr. Smith Helms Mulliss & Moore, Raleigh, NC, 1992-97, Alston & Bird LLP, Raleigh, NC, 1997—2005, ptnr. in charge Research Triangle Park, NC, 1997—2005, DLA Piper Rudnick Gray Cary US LLP, Raleigh, NC, 2005—; co-chair nat. REIT practice, mng. ptnr. Raleigh office. Bd. dirs. Coun. for Entrepreneurial Devel., Research Triangle Park, NC; spl. coun. apptd. by NC Gov. NC. R.R. Study Group, 1992-93; practice group head Alston & Bird's NC Bus. Practice, 1997—2005. Contbr. articles to profl. jours. Mem. ABA, Nat. Assn. Bond Lawyers, Nat. Assn. Real Estate Investment Trusts (mem. bd. advisors), Asian Pub. Real Estate Assn. (mem. bd. govs.), Mo. Bar Assn., N.C. Bar Assn. Avocations: golf, skiing. Home Phone: 919-787-5021.

MARKOPOULOS, JODY A., information technology executive; BS in Engring., Clarkson U., 1993. Gen. mgr., quality General Electric Energy, gen. mgr., sourcing, 2003—07, v.p. sourcing, 2007—; pres., CEO, General Electric Intelligent Platforms General Electric Home and Bus. Solutions, 2011—. Office: General Electric Co c/o Intelligent Platforms 4200 Wildwood Pkwy Atlanta GA 30339 Business E-Mail: jody.markopoulos@ps.ge.com.

MARKOS, CHRIS, retired real estate company executive; b. Cleve., Nov. 25, 1926; s. George and Bessie (Papathatou) Markos; m. Alice Zaharopoulos, Dec. 11, 1949 (dec.); children: Marilyn Martin, Irene Matthews, Betsy Feierabend; m. Marilyn Gardanier, Nov. 8, 2002; children: Kathleen Mitchell, Patricia Hickle. BA, Case Western Res. U., Cleve., 1960; LLB, LaSalle Ext. U. Law Sch., Chgo., 1964. Cert. gen. real estate appraiser Ohio. Pres. Brooklyn Realty Co., Cleve., 1953—63; vice-pres. Herbert Laronge Inc., Cleve., 1963-76; v.p. Calabrese, Racek and Markos Inc., Cleve., 1976-83, Herbert Laronge Inc., Cleve., 1983-87, pres., 1987-88; v.p. Cragin Lang, Inc., Cleve., 1989-91; sr. cons. Grubb & Ellis, Cleve., 1991-93; sr. v.p. Realty One Appraisal Divsn., Independence, Ohio, 1993-98. Pres. Alcrimar Inc., 1989—98. Co-author: Ohio Supplement to Modern Real Estate Practice, 5th-7th edits.; cons. editor, co-author: Modern Real Estate Practice in Ohio, 1st-3rd edits. Bd. dirs. Meyers U., Cleve., 1984-97; instr. Real Estate Law, Real Estate Principals and Practices, Real Estate Brokerage, 1961-79, Cleve. State U., Cuyahoga and Lorain CC, Western Reserve U. divsn general studies; guest lectr. Kent State U. With US Army, 1945—46. Mem. Am. Soc. Appraisers (sr., pres. Akron Cleve. Chpt. 1973, state dir. 1976), Cleve. Area Bd. Realtors (hon. life mem., pres. 1974, Realtor of Yr. award 1976). Republican. Greek Orthodox. Home: Corinthian Condominium 936 Intracoastal Dr Apt 6-H Fort Lauderdale FL 33304 Personal E-mail: alcrimar@bellsouth.net.

MARKS, BRUCE, performing company executive, choreographer; b. NYC, Jan. 23, 1937; s. Albert and Helen (Kosersky) M.; m. Toni Pihl Petersen, Jan. 27, 1966 (dec. May 1985); children: Erik Antony, Adam Christopher, Kenneth Rikard. Student, Brandeis U., 1954—55, Juilliard Sch., 1955—56; DFA, D, Northeastern U., 1997. Prof. U. Utah, 1981, 1984—86; artistic dir. Boston Ballet Co., 1985—97, artistic dir. emeritus, 1998—; artistic dir. Orlando Ballet, 2006—. Mem. dance adv. panel Nat. Endowment for Arts, 1979, chmn. internat. selection com., 1979, chmn. dance adv. panel, 1981, mem. nat. adv. bd. on arts and edn., 1989; bd. dirs., mem. exec. com., Dance/USA 1989, 92—, chmn., 1990-92, chmn. govt. affairs, 1992—; mem. U.S.-USSR Commn. on Dance and Theatre Studies, Am. Coun. Learned Socs./IREX; mem. jury Internat. Moscow Internat. Ballet Competition, 1989; mem. arts in edn. adv. coun. Harvard U., 1997; chmn. 3d Japan Internat. Ballet and Modern Dance competition, 1999; jury mem. Prague Internat. Ballet Competition, 2001; jury Shangh Internat. Ballet Competition, 2007; jury Seol Internat. Ballet Modern Dance Competition; artistic advisor Ft. Worth/Dallas Ballet, 2000-01; tchr. 1st Seoul (Korea) Internat. Dance Competition, 2004. Prin. dancer Met. Opera, 1956-61, Am. Ballet Theatre, 1961-72, Royal Swedish Ballet, 1963, Festival Ballet, London, 1965, Royal Danish Ballet, 1971-76; artistic dir. Ballet West, Salt Lake City, 1976-85; choreographer Eliot Feld Ballet Co., 1970, Royal Danish Ballet, 1971-76, Netherlands Dance Theatre, 1974, Ballet West, 1976-85; artistic fellow Aspen Inst. for Humanistic Studies, 1979—. Bd. dirs. Am. Arts Alliance, 1983-85, Am. Coun. for Arts, 1985—, Dance U.S.A., 1988-94, chmn., 1990-92; chmn. U.S.A. Internat. Ballet Competition, Jackson, Micc., 1990—, vice chair jury Helsinki, Finland, 1991, judge Helsinki Ballet Competition 1995; mem. nat. adv. bd. on arts and edn. NEA, 1989-91; mem. internat. jury 1st and 2d Japan Internat. Ballet Competition, Nagoya, Japan, 1993, 96, 2005, Am. jury for Prix de Lausanne, 1994, 98; mem. Brandeis Creative Arts Awards Commn., 1993, chmn. Brandeis Creative Arts Awards Dance, 1994; chair Grants to Dance Cos. panel NEA, 1993, overview panel, 1994; chmn. 3d Japan Internat. Ballet Competition, Nagoya, 1999; artistic advisor Ft. Worth/Dallas Ballet, 2000-2001; mem. Princess Grace Awards panel, 2005. Recipient Disting. Svc. award for artistic prodn. Nat. Govs. Assn., 1994, Capezio award Balletmakers, Inc., 1995, Dance Mag. award, 1997, Honors award Dance/USA, 1998, Proscenium award, Boston, 2001, Juilliard medal Svc. to Arts, 2005

MARKS, DANIEL J., janitorial services company executive; BBA in Mgmt. Info. Sys., U. Iowa. Software engr. General Dynamics; sr. v.p., chief info. officer American Home Shield Corp., 1994—2007, Servicemaster Co., Servicemaster Global Holdings, 2007—. Office: The ServiceMaster Co 860 Ridge Lake Blvd Memphis TN 38120 Office Phone: 901-597-1400. Office Fax: 630-663-2001. Business E-Mail: dmarks@corporate.servicemaster.com.

MARKS, JOHN R., III, mayor, Tallahassee, Florida, lawyer; m. Jane Marks; 1 child, John IV. BS, Fla. State U. Sch. Bus., 1969; JD, Fla. State U. College Law, 1972. Adminstrv. law judge Fla. Pub. Svc. Commn., served on, 1979, chmn.; regulatory atty. Katz, Kutter, et al., P.A., 1987, Knowles, Marks & Randolph, P.A., 1997; mng. ptnr. Adorno & Yoss, LLP; adj. prof. Fla. State U. Coll. Law; faculty mem. Nat. Assoc. Regulatory Utility Cmmrs. Utility Rate Sch.; mayor City of Tallahassee, 2003—. Bd. adv. U.S. Conf. Mayors; vice-chair Transp. & Comm. Com.; mem. Cmty. & Econ. Devel. Com., Nat. League Cities; pres. Fla. League Mayors, 2005—07; v.p. Fla. League Cities, pres. Judge adv. USAF. Named Super Lawyer, Fla. Super Lawyer Mag. Mem.: ABA, Am. Law Assn., Tallahassee Barristers Assn., Fla. Bar Assn., National Bar Assn., Omega Psi Phi Fraternity, Inc. Democrat. Office: City Hall Office of the Mayor 300 S Adams St Tallahassee FL 32301 Office Phone: 850-891-2000. Business E-Mail: john.marks@talgov.com.*

MARKS, MIKE A., corporate financial executive; m. Leigh Ann Marks; 3 children. B in Fin., U. Tenn. Sr. mgr., internal audit HCA, Inc., 1996—2000, contr., Eastern Group, 2000—03, CFO, two hosp. system Ocala, Fla., 2003—04, CFO, West Fla. Divsn., 2004—08, CFO, Eastern Group. Mem. Healthcare Fin. Mgmt. Assn., Fla. Low Income Pool Panel Mem.: AICPAs. Office: HCA Inc One Park Plz Nashville TN 37203 Office Phone: 615-344-9551. Office Fax: 615-344-2266. Business E-Mail: mike.marks@hcahealthcare.com.

MARKS, ROBERTA BARBARA, artist, educator; b. Savannah, Ga. d. Philip W. and Eleanore (Margolis) Dilner; children: Jeffery Allen, Steven Craig. BFA, U. Miami, Coral Gables, Fla., 1980; MFA, U. South Fla., Tampa, 1981. Juror Miami Lakes Art Festival, Fla., 1975, Ybor Square Art Festival, Tampa, 1980, Riverside Avondale Preservation Art Festival, Jacksonville, Fla., 1981; instr., lectr. multi-media, lectr., vis. artist U. Miami Lowe Art Mus., Fla., Armory Art Ctr., Palm Beach, Valparaiso U., Ind., Rochester Inst. Tech. Am. Sch. Crafts, NY, Galerie de Koull, Murten, Switzerland, Santa Fe CC, Gainesville, Brookfield Craft Ctr., Conn., Fla. Keys CC, U. Wis., Milw., Parson Sch. Design, Key West CC, Fla., 1991, Am. Embassy, Bern, Switzerland, 1993, Numerous Art Schs., U. South Fla., 1998—2005, Custom House Mus., Armory Art Ctr., Palm Beach, Fla., 2002, Key West, Fla., 2003, Galerie Jonas, Neuchatel, Switzerland, 2003, Chgo. Anderson Ranch Art Sch., Colo., 2004. One-man shows include Brevard Community Coll., Melbourne, Fla., 1982, Cocoa, Fla., 1982, Coventry Galleries, Ltd., Tampa, 1983, Barbara Gillman Gallery, Miami, 1984, 1987, Tennessee Williams Fine Arts Ctr., Key West, 1985, Garth Clark Gallery, NYC, 1985, Fred Gros Gallery, Key West, 1985, Key West Art and Historical Soc. East Martello Mus. and Gallery, 1985, U. Miami New Gallery, Fla., 1987, Katie Gingrass Gallery, Milw., 1987, Zimmerman Saturn Gallery, Nashville, 1987, Bern, Zurich Switzerland, 1988, Galerie Alte Krone, Altstadt, Biel, Switzerland, 1990, Helander Gallery, NYC, 1990, Gump's Gallery, San Francisco, 1990, Helander Gallery, NYC, 1991, LeMieux Gallery, New Orleans, 1991, Helander Gallery, Palm Beach, 1992, Galerie Etc., Bern, 1992, Galerie Bel Arte, Lengnau, Switzerland, 1992, Galerie Vinelz, Switzerland, 1994, Galerie Quattro, Zurich, 1994, Lucky Street Gallery, Key West, 1994—2005, Barbara Gillman Gallery, Miami, 1994—2005, exhibited in group shows at Netsky Gallery, Miami, 1982, The Craftsman's Gallery, Scarsdale, NY, 1982, Garth Clark Gallery, LA, 1983, Nelson-Atkins Mus. Art, Kansas City, Mo., 1983, Am. Craft Mus., NYC, 1984, Joanne Lyon Gallery, Aspen, Colo., 1984, N. Miami Mus. and Art Ctr., 1985, Key West Art and Hist. Soc. East Martello Mus. and Gallery, 1985, Garth Clark Gallery, NYC and LA, 1985, Artforms Gallery, Louisville, 1986, 24X24, Ruth Siegel Ltd., NYC, 1987, The Pvt. Collection Women Artists, Ohio, 1987, East Martello Mus., Key West, 1990, 1990, Philharmonic Ctr. for Arts, Naples, Fla., 1993, Ctr. for Arts, Vero Beach, Fla., 1993, Helander Gallery, Palm Beach, 1993, Gingrass Gallery, Milw., 1993, Represented in permanent collections Mint Mus., Charlotte, NC, N.Mex Mus. Fine Arts, Sante Fe, Smithsonian Instn., Renwick Gallery, Rochester Inst. Tech. Fine Arts Dept., U. Utah Mus., U. South Fla. Fine Arts Dept., Galerie du Manoir, La Chaux-de-Fonds, Switzerland, Valencia CC, Okum Gallery, Victoria and Albert Mus., London, IBM, Jacksonville, Fla., AT&T, NYC, Lucky St. Gallery, Key West, Custom Ho. Mus., Key West, U. South Fla., Galerie Jonas, Neuchatel, Lucky St. Gallery, one-man shows include Mary Woerner Gallery, Palm Beach, Fla., 2006, 2008, Miami Internat. U. Art and Design, Fla., 2007, Lemieux Gallery, New Orleans, La., 2008, Galerie Jonas, Neuchatel, Switzerland, 2008, CourtHouse Gallery, Stuart, Fla., 2010, Represented in permanent collections Mint Mus., Charlotte, NMex. Mus. Fine Arts, Sante Fe. Recipient Numerous awards; Regional Visual Artist fellowship, Miami, 1990. Mem.: Internat. Sculpture Ctr., Artists Equity Assn., World Craft Coun.

MARKS, TERRANCE M. (TERRY MARKS), food products executive; BA, U. Southern Calif. Account mgr. Coca-Cola Enterprises, Inc., 1987—89, LA sales ctr. mgr., 1989—94, v.p., gen. mgr. New Eng. divsn., 1994—99, CFO, v.p. Ea. N.Am. group, 1999—2003, v.p., chief rev. officer N.Am. group, 2003—05, sr. v.p. to exec. v.p. & pres. N.Am. group, 2005—08; pres., CEO The Pantry Inc., 2009—11, Hooters of America, LLC, 2011—. Office: Hooters of America LLC 1815 The Exchange SE Atlanta GA 30339

MARKUS, ROBERT MICHAEL, retired journalist; b. Chgo., Jan. 30, 1934; s. David White and Anna (Tonkonogy) M.; m. Leslie Winnifred Ator, Aug. 25, 1962; children— Catherine Mary, Patricia Anne, Michael Hughes. B.J., U. Mo., 1955. Gen. assignment reporter Moline (Ill.) Dispatch, 1955-59; successively copy editor, sports columnist, feature writer, baseball writer, coll. sports writer, hockey writer Chgo. Tribune, 1959-96, ret., 1996. Mem. Northbrook (Ill.) Caucus, 1967. Served with U.S. Army, 1956-58. Recipient Nat. Headliner award as best columnist, 1973; named Ill. Sports Writer of Year, 1970, 71, 72 Mem. Football Writers Assn. Am., Baseball Writers Assn. Am., Am. Auto Racing Writers and Broadcasters Assn. Home: 8404 Caldbeck Dr Raleigh NC 27615-2500 Personal E-mail: bobmarkus34@gmail.com.

MARKWOOD, STEPHEN ERNEST, educator, consultant, college president; b. Glasgow, Ky., Nov. 26, 1942; s. Chester Ray and Mary (Tandy) Markwood; m. Susan Hendee, Dec. 26, 1965; children: Christopher, M., Kathryn M. BS in Edn., Bowling Green U., 1964, MA in Edn., 1968; EdD, Pa. State U., 1983; degree (hon.), Eastern U., 2007, PhD (hon.), 2009. Asst. dean student life Waynesburg Coll., Pa., 1968—70; assoc. dean students Dickinson Coll., Carlisle, Pa., 1970—77; dean student devel. Rio Grande Coll., Ohio, 1977—80; v.p. Marietta Coll., Ohio, 1980—82, provost Ottawa U., 1992—95; pres. Alderson-Broaddus Coll., 1995—2008; cons. Academic Vice Chair W.Va. Ind. Colls., 2000—03; chair Appalachian Coll. Assn., 2003—05; hon. doctorate Eastern U., 2007. Contbr. articles to prof. jours. Served to capt. US Army, 1964—66. Recipient Disting. Leadership, Pa. State U., 2005, Edn. Leadership award, 2007. Mem.: Philip/Barboul C. of C. (dir.), W.Va. Intercoll. Assn. (chair 2002—04), Ottawa C. of C. (treas.), Ohio Assn. Student Personnel Adminstrs, Marietta C. of C., Ohio C. of C. (, Am. Coll. Personnel Assn. (mem. com. 1983—87), Ohio Coll. Personnel Assn. (pres. 1983—84, outstanding leadership award 1984, 1987), Am. Coll. Personnel Assn. (commn. 1983—84), Nat. Assn. Student Personnel Adminstrs., Kiwanis ((BD. dir.). Avocations: golf, running. Office: 12 Raindrop Ln Bluffton SC 29909 Office Phone: 843-304-6502, 843-705-0960. Business E-Mail: markwoodse@ab.edu.

MARLATT, BRYCE, state legislator; m. Tatum Marlatt; children: Kade, Kole, Kloey. Degree in Agrl.-Bus., Northwestern Okla. State U. Oil & gas services/real estate; former staff to Senator Jim Inhofe & Congressman Frank Lucas; mem. Dist. 27 Okla. State Senate, 2008—. Republican. Office: 2300 N Lincoln Blvd Rm 427 Oklahoma City OK 73105 also: PO Box 647 Woodward OK 73802 Office Phone: 405-521-5626. Business E-Mail: marlatt@oksenate.gov.

MARLEY, BRIAN THOMAS, retail executive; b. Asheboro, NC, Apr. 29, 1957; s. Edison Earl and Irma Patricia (Krewson) M.; m. Mary Anna Jackson; 1 child, Brian Thomas Jr. BS, U. NC, 1980. CPA, N.C. Chmn. Belk Nat. Bank; staff acct. KMG Main Hurdman, Charlotte, NC, 1980—83; sr. acct. Peat Marwick Main and Co., Charlotte, 1983—86, audit mgr., 1986; ptnr. KPMG LLP, 1993—2000; exec. v.p., CFO Belk, Inc., 2000—. Bd. dirs. Apex Analytix, Inc. Mem. acctg. adv. com. Cen. Piedmont Community Coll., Charlotte, 1986—; merit badge counselor Boy Scouts Am., Charlotte, 1985—; mem. membership com. Charlotte Uptown YMCA, 1988—. Mem. Am. Inst. CPA's, N.C. Assn. CPA's, Constrn. Fin. Mgmt. Assn. (bd. dirs. Charlotte chpt. 1987—). Office: Belk Inc 2801 W Tyvola Rd Charlotte NC 28217-4500 Office Phone: 704-357-1000. Office Fax: 704-357-1876. Business E-Mail: brian_marley@belk.com.

MARLOWE, EDWARD, retired pharmaceutical executive; b. NYC, May 5, 1935; children: Shari Marlowe Kasten, Steven Richard. BS, Columbia U., 1956, MS, 1958; PhD, U. Md.-Balt., 1962. Rsch. assoc. Merck, Sharp & Dohme Rsch. Lab., West Point, Pa., 1962—64; sr. scientist Ortho Pharm. Corp. div. Johnson & Johnson, Raritan, NJ, 1964—67; dir. R&D Whitehall Labs. div. Am. Home Products Corp., Hammonton, NJ, 1967—72; v.p. R&D Plough Products divsn. Schering-Plough Corp., Memphis, 1972—81; v.p. R&D, consumer products group Warner-Lambert Co., Morris Plains, NJ, 1981—83, pres. consumer products div. R&D, 1983—91, v.p., 1984—91, v.p. parent Co.; v.p. R&D Clairol Inc., Stamford, Conn., 1992—97; sr. v.p. Bristol-Myers Squibb World Wide Beauty Care, 1997—2000; pres., CEO NFG Stuff Inc., Short Hills, NJ, 2001—. Contbr. articles to profl. publs. Chmn. bd. Papermill Playhouse, Millburn, NJ, 2000—03. Recipient award Skin Cancer Found., 1979; Pfizer fellow, 1958; Robert Lincoln McNeil fellow, 1961 Mem. Am. Pharm. Assn., Acad. Pharm. Soc., Soc. Cosmetic Chemists, Indsl. Rsch. Inst., Cosmetic Toiletry & Fragrance Assn. (sci. adv. exec. com. 1998-2000), Non-Prescription Drug Mfrs. Assn. (sci. affairs com. 1976-91, policy planning subcom. 1977-91, bd. dirs. 1981-83), N.Y. Acad. Sci., Sigma Xi, Rho Chi. Home: 7548 Bella Verde Way Delray Beach FL 33446-4408 Home Phone: 561-638-4435; Office Phone: 561-638-8499. Personal E-mail: marlowegg@aol.com.

MARMONTI, DAVID A., information technology executive; B in Bus. Adminstrn. & Mktg., U. Mo., St. Louis. Various sr. positions in sales and mktg. AT&T Inc. (merger of SBC Communications & AT&T Corp.); joined Dell, Inc., 1998, v.p., gen. mgr., Pub. Bus. Group, Mid-Markets and Preferred Corp. Accounts segments, v.p., gen. mgr., Home and Small Bus. divsn., EMEA region, v.p., mktg. & e-bus., US Consumer Segment, dir., gen. mgr., US Asset Recovery Bus., sr. v.p., pres., Europe, Mid. East and Africa, 2007—. Office: Dell Inc 1 Dell Way Round Rock TX 78682-2222 Office Phone: 512-338-4400. Office Fax: 512-283-6161. Business E-Mail: david.marmonti@dell.com.

MARNEY, SAMUEL ROWE, JR., retired allergist, immunologist, educator; b. Bristol, Va., Feb. 15, 1934; m. Elizabeth Ann Bingham, Oct. 1, 1966; children: Samuel Rowe III, Annis Morison. BA in Chemistry, U. Va., 1955, MD, 1960. Diplomate Am. Bd. Internal Medicine, Am. Bd. Allergy and Immunology; cert. in Diagnostic Lab. Immunology, 1988. Staff physician VA Hosp., Nashville, 1968—69, clin. assoc., 1969—71, clin. investigator, 1971—74, staff physician, infectious disease and allergy cons., 1974—; asst. prof. medicine Med. Ctr. Vanderbilt U., Nashville, 1971—76, assoc. prof., 1976—2008, dir. allergy and immunology, 1974—2008. Vis. investigator Scripps Clinic and Rsch. Found., La Jolla, Calif., 1973-74. Capt. USAF, 1962—64, Korea. Fellow ACP, Am. Acad. Allergy and Immunology, Am. Coll. Allergy and Immunology; mem. Southeastern Allergy Assn. (pres. 1986-87, Hal M. Davison Meml. award, 1981, 99), Tenn. Soc. Allergy and Immunology. Home: 4340 Sneed Rd Nashville TN 37215-3242 Personal E-mail: smarney@att.net.

MARON, DAVID JOEL, cardiologist, educator; b. Nov. 1, 1954; Undergraduate degree, Stanford Univ.; MD, U. Southern Calif. Sch. Medicine, 1981. Cert. Internal Medicine, Cardiovascular Disease. Intern, internal medicine UCLA Med. Ctr., 1981—82, resident, medicine, 1982—84; fellow, cardiology Stanford U., 1989—91; staff mem. St. John's Hosp., Santa Monica, 1991—93, Santa Monica Hosp., 1991—93, Vanderbilt Univ. Hosp., Nashville, 1993; clin. instr. Stanford U., 1984—89, UCLA, 1992—93; asst. prof. medicine Vanderbilt Univ. Med. Ctr., Nashville, 1993—2002, assoc. prof. medicine, 2002—10; med. dir. Dayani Ctr. for Health Promotion, prof. medicine, 2010—. Co-founder Cardiovascular Services of Am. Contbr. articles to profl. jours. Office: Vanderbilt University Med Ctr 1215 21st Ave S 5th Fl MCE Nashville TN 37232

MARONEY, JAMES FRANCIS, III, lawyer, energy executive; b. Houston, Mar. 24, 1951; s. James Francis and Ellen B. (Cuenod) Maroney; m. Maureen K. O'Sullivan, May 14, 1983; 1 child, Molly. BA cum laude, U. Tex., Austin, 1973; JD, U. Tex., 1976. Assoc. Ray A. Morrison Assocs., 1977; legal mgr. AMF Tuboscope, Inc., 1978—82; gen. counsel Koomey, Inc., 1982—85; pvt. law practice Seguin, Tex., 1985—87; assoc. gen. counsel, chief ligit. TransAm. Natural Gas Corp., 1987—89; v.p., gen. counsel, sec. Tuboscope, Inc., 1989—2000, Varco Internat., Inc., 2000—05; counsel Nat. Oilwell Varco Inc., 2005; v.p., gen. counsel, sec. Complete Production Services, Inc., 2005—. Mem.: ABA, Tex. Bar Assn., Houston Bar Assn. Roman Catholic. Office: Complete Production Services Inc 1001 Louisiana St Houston TX 77002-5089 Office Phone: 281-372-2300. Office Fax: 281-372-2301. Business E-Mail: jmaroney@varco.com, jmaroney@completeproduction.com.

MARONI, DONNA FAROLINO, retired biologist; b. Buffalo, Feb. 27, 1938; d. Enrico Victor and Eleanor (Redlinska) Farolino; m. Gustavo Primo Maroni, Dec. 16, 1974. BS, U. Wis., 1960, PhD, 1969. Project assoc. U. Wis., Madison, 1960-63, 68-74; Alexander von Humboldt fellow Inst. Genetics U. Cologne, Fed. Republic Germany, 1974-75; Hargitt fellow Duke U., Durham, NC, 1975-76, rsch. assoc., 1976-83, rsch. assoc. prof., 1983-87; sr. program specialist N.C. Biotech. Ctr., Research Triangle Park, 1987-88, dir. sci. programs div., 1988-92, v.p. for sci. programs, 1992-94, ret., 1995. Mem. adv. com. MICROMED at Bowman Gray Sch. Medicine, Winston-Salem, NC, 1988—94; mem. sci. adv. bd. NC Biosci. Fund, LLC, 1998—99, Minority Sci. Improvement Alliance for Instrn. and Rsch. in Biotech, Ala. A&M U., Normal, 1990—91. Contbr. articles to profl. jours. Grantee NSF, 1977-79, NIH, 1979-82, 79-83, 82-87. Mem. Genetics Soc. Am., N.C. Acad. Sci., Inc. (bd. dirs. 1983-86), Sigma Xi (mem. exec. com. Duke U. chpt. 1989-90). Achievements include research in electron microscopy, evolution of chromosomes, chromosome structure, evolution of mitosis, and mitosis and fungal phylogeny. Home: 355 Carolina Meadows Villa Chapel Hill NC 27517 Personal E-mail: maroni.donna@gmail.com.

MAROSKY, KURT, hotel executive; Grad., Fachhochschule fur Technik und Wirtschaft Berlin, 1982. Regional engr. ctrl., Europe Hilton Worldwide, Inc., 2002—, chief engr. Office: Hilton Worldwide Inc 7930 Jones Branch Dr Ste 1100 Mc Lean VA 22102 Office Phone: 703-883-1000. Business E-Mail: kurt.marosky@hilton.com.

MARPLE, STANLEY LAWRENCE, JR., electrical engineer, educator and researcher; s. Stanley and Geraldine Marple; m. Suzanne Marple, Aug. 30, 1974; children: Darci Papoulias, Rebecca Sanne, Matthew. B, Rice U., Houston, 1969, M, 1970; PhD in Engring., Stanford U., Palo Alto, Calif., 1976. Staff engr. Argo Sys., Inc., Sunnyvale, Calif., 1972—78; sr. staff engr. Advent Sys., Inc., Mountain View, Calif., 1978—79, TASC, Mc Lean, Va., 1980—82; sr. devel. engr. Schlumberger Well Svcs., Houston, 1983—85; mgr., devel. engr. Martin Marietta Aero & Naval Sys., Balt., 1986—88; chief scientist Orincon Corp., San Diego, 1989—93, 1996—2002, Acuson Corp., Mountain View, Calif., 1993—96; prof. Sch. Elec. Engring. & Computer Sci. Oreg. State U., Corvallis, 2003—09; chief scientist Sensors and Electromagnetic Applications Lab. Ga. Tech. Rsch. Inst., Atlanta, 2009—12, Signal Rsch., Depoe Bay, Oreg., 2013—. Author: (textbook) Digital Spectral Analysis (fellow, 1989). Capt. US Army, 1972—79, San Jose, Calif. Fellow: IEEE (adcom mem. 1985—88, Sr. Paper award 1983). Baptist. Achievements include patents for ultrasound beamforming techniques. Avocations: stamp collecting/philately, hiking, writing. Business E-Mail: l.marple@ieee.org.

MARQUÉS GONZALEZ, AMINDA, newspaper editor; BA in Journalism, U. Fla., 1986. Reporter Miami Herald, Fla., 1986—95, editor city, state & Neighbors sect. news ops., 1995—2000, dep. metro editor., 2000—02, assoc. editor multimedia, 2007, exec. features editor, Sunday editor, 2007—09, sr. editor news, 2009—10, exec. editor, 2010—; Miami bur. chief People Mag., 2002—07. Office: The Miami Herald 3511 NW 91st Ave Doral FL 33172-1216

MARQUEZ, MARISA, state legislator; b. Houston, Tex., Sept. 27, 1978; d. Ricardo and Gloria (Flores). BBA in Fin. & Bus. Economics, U. Notre Dame, Ind., 2000, ThM, 2004. Americorps vol. ACCION-Tex., 2000—01; grants admin. El Paso Empowerment Zone Corp., 2001—02; cmty. rels. mgr. Tex. Cmty. Care; mem. Dist. 77 Tex. House of Representatives, 2008—. Seasonal theology tchr. Tepeyac Inst. Democrat. Office: Room E2.414 Capitol Extension PO Box 2910 Austin TX 78768 also: 310 N Mesa St Ste 906 El Paso TX 79901-1329 Office Phone: 512-463-0638, 915-532-2755. Office Fax: 512-463-8908.

MARRA, KENNETH A., federal judge; b. Queens, NY, 1951; BA, SUNY, Stony Brook, 1973; JD, Stetson U., 1977. Atty. US Dept. Justice, 1977—80; pvt. practice atty. Washington, 1980—83, Fla., 1984—96; cir. judge 15th Jud. Cir. Ct. Fla., 1996—2002; judge US Dist. Ct. (so. dist.) Fla., West Palm Beach, 2002—. Office: US Dist Ct Rogers Fed Bldg and US Courthouse 701 Clematis St Rm 316 West Palm Beach FL 33401 Office Phone: 561-514-3760.

MARRERO, BEVERLY, state legislator; b. Memphis, Jan. 23, 1939; 3 children. Former cons. retail real estate; state rep. Dist. 89 Tenn., 2004—07; mem. Rules Com., Dem. Nat. Conv., Tenn., 1976, Health & Human Resources Com., 2004—07, Children & Family Affairs Com., 2004—07, Domestic Rels. Subcom., 2004—07, Judiciary Com., 2007—, Govt. Ops. Com., 2004—07, v. chairwoman, 2007—; house rep. Tenn.; state senator, Dist. 30 Tenn., 2007—. Mem.: Evergreen Hist. Dist. Assn., Memphis Brooks Mus. of Art, Memphis Zoological Coun., Vollintine Evergreen Cmty. Assn. Democrat. Episcopalian. Office: 243 Hawthorne St Memphis TN 38112 also: 312 War Memorial Bldg Nashville TN 37243-0030 Office Phone: 615-741-9128. Office Fax: 615-253-0291. Business E-Mail: sen.beverly.marrero@capitol.tn.gov.

MARRETT, CORA B., federal official, science educator; b. Richmond, Va., June 15, 1942; d. Horace Sterling and Colra Ann (Boswell) Bagley; m. Louis Everand Marrett, Dec. 24, 1968. BA, Va. Union U., 1963; MS, U. Wis., 1965, PhD, 1968. Asst. prof. U. NC, Chapel Hill, 1968-69; from asst. to assoc. prof. Western Mich. U., Kalamazoo, 1969-73; from assoc. prof. to full prof. U. Wis., Madison, 1973-97; asst. dir. for social, behavioral, & econ. sciences NSF, Arlington, Va., 1992-96; provost, vice chancellor for acad. affairs U. Mass., Amherst, 1997—2001; sr. v.p. for acad. affairs U. Wis. System, 2001—07; asst. dir. for edn. & human resources NSF, Arlington, Va., 2007—09, acting dep. dir., 2009—11, acting dir., 2010, dep. dir., 2011—, acting dir., 2013—14. Mem. sci. adv. panel US Army, Washington, 1976—77; mem. Naval Rsch. Adv. Com., Washington, 1978—81, Pres. Commn. on the Accident at Three Mile Island, 1979; bd. govs. Argonne Nat. Lab., Ill., 1983—90, Ill., 1996—99. Editor: Research in Race and Ethnic Relations, 1988, Gender and Classroom Interaction, 1990. Resident fellow, NAS, 1973—74, fellow, Ctr. for Advanced Study in Behavioral Scis., 1976—77. Mem.: ASA, AAAS, Phi Kappa Phi. Avocations: reading, travel, film appreciation. Office: National Science Foundation Suite 1205N 4201 Wilson Blvd Arlington VA 22230 Office Phone: 703-292-8001. Office Fax: 703-292-9232. E-mail: cmarrett@nsf.gov.*

MARS, FORREST E., JR., candy company executive; s. Forrest Mars Sr.; m. Virginia Cretella, Oct. 20, 1955 (div. Jan. 1990); children: Victoria B., Valerie A., Pamela D., Marijke E. BA, Yale U., 1953, BS. Chmn. bd. dirs., former CEO Mars Inc., Mc Lean, Va. Named one of World's Richest People, Forbes Mag., 1999—, Forbes 400: Richest Americans, 1999—. Office: Mars Inc 6885 Elm St Mc Lean VA 22101-3810

MARS, JACQUELINE BADGER, candy company executive; b. Oct. 10, 1939; d. Forrest Edward and Audrey (Ruth) Mars; m. David Badger, 1961 (div. 1984); children: Alexandra, Stephen, Christa; m. Harold Vogel, 1986 (div. 1994). BS in Anthropology, Bryn Mawr Coll., Pa., 1961. Co-owner Mars, Inc., McLean, Va., 1973—, corp. v.p., 1990—. Trustee Bryn Mawr Coll.; bd. trustee mem.-at-large Washington Nat. Opera. Named one of Forbes 400: Richest Americans, 1999—, The World's Richest People, Forbes Mag., 2000—. Office: Mars Inc 6885 Elm St Mc Lean VA 22101*

MARS, JOHN FRANKLYN, candy company executive; b. 1935; m. Adrienne Mars; 2 children. BA, Yale U., 1957, BS. Chmn. Kal Kan Foods Inc.; co-pres. Mars Inc., 1973—, CEO, 2000—, chmn. Named one of World's Richest People, Forbes Mag, 1999—, Forbes 400: Richest Americans, 1999—. Office: Mars Inc 6885 Elm St Mc Lean VA 22101

MARSDEN, DAVID W., state legislator; b. Alexandria, Va., Apr. 5, 1948; m. Julia-Anna Thompson; children: Nathan, Stuart, Connor. Attended, Randolph-Macon Coll., Ashland, Va. Dir. state and local programs Devel. Services Group, Inc.; house del. Dist. 41 Va. House of Dels., 2006—09, mem. ct. of justice com., mem. transp. com., 2006—09; senator Dist. 37 Senate of Va., 2009—. Recipient Commn.'s award, Cardinal Basketball Assn., 1998, Svc. to Youth award, YMCA, 2007. Master: Va. Juvenile Justice Assn. (former pres., Adminstr. of Year 1997, Robert H. Sutton Humanitarian award 2006); mem.: Northern Va. Literacy Coun. (adv. bd.), Enterprize Sch. (bd. dir., former pres.), Va. Coun. Juvenile Detention (former pres.), West-Lynch Found. (former pres.). Democrat. Methodist. Office: PO Box 10889 Burke VA 22009 also: Senate of Va Rm 307 PO Box 396 Richmond VA 23218 Office Phone: 703-323-4733, 804-698-7537. Office Fax: 804-698-7651. Business E-Mail: district37@senate.virginia.gov.

MARSH, DEL C., state legislator; b. Wheeling, W.Va., Sept. 2, 1956; m. Ginger; children: Justin, Christine. Grad., Auburn U., Ala. Owner Indsl. Plating Co., Inc.; mem. Dist. 12 Ala. State Senate, Montgomery, 1999—; dir. Colonial Bank, Southern States Bank. Mem. Greater Anniston Bus. & Profl. Assn. Republican. Episcopalian. Office: PO Drawer 2365 Anniston AL 36202 also: Ala State Senate Ala State House 11 S Union St Rm 735 Montgomery AL 36130 Office Phone: 256-237-8647, 334-242-7877.

MARSH, HENRY L., III, state legislator; b. Richmond, Va. m. Diane Harris Marsh. Former mayor, Richmond, Va.; state senator, Dist. 16 Va., 1992—; mem. Richmond Renaissance Exec. Com., Va., Cts. of Justice, Local Govt., Rehab. & Social Svc. & Transp. Com. Recipient Humanitarian award, Met. Bus. League, 1992; named one of Citizen of Yr., Astoria Beneficial Club, 1966; grantee, Nat. Conf. Christians & Jews, 1994. Democrat. Methodist. Mailing: Senate of Va PO Box 396 Richmond VA 23218 also: Dist Off 600 E Broad St, Ste 402 Richmond VA 23219-1800 Fax: 804-648-2116. E-mail: district16@sov.state.va.us.

MARSH, JOSEPH VIRGIL, investment advisor, analyst, broker, consultant, research scientist; b. Winston-Salem, NC, Apr. 28, 1952; s. Gilliam Hughes and Dovie Elizabeth (Watson) Marsh. Student, Surry CC, 1970-72, US Govt. Schs., Md., SC, Washington, 1972-74; BSEE, U. Md., 1976; diploma, NY Inst. Fin., 1978, NYU, 1978, MBA, 1980. Cert. comml. real estate broker NC. With Joint Armed Svcs. Tech. Liaison, Washington, 1974-75; cons. US Govt., 1975-76; corr., cons. individuals, bus. on tech. matters Ararat, NC, 1977—. Registered advisor SEC, 1981—2000. Contbr. scientific papers. Active U.S. Presdl. Task Force, 1981—2000; founder Marsh Found., 1989; tech. liaison NASA, 1992. Recipient Presdl. medal of merit, Pres. of US, 1988, 1990. Mem.: VFW (hon.), Coun. Civilian Tech. Advisers, Internat. Assn. Sci. Devel., Ind. Cons. Assn., Internat. Entrepreneurs Assn., Armed Forces Assn. Independent. Achievements include development of energy from lightning bolt which has captured and stored. Office: Hwy 2019/2026 Ararat NC 27007-0178 Office Phone: 336-374-4405.

MARSH, KEVIN B., energy executive; b. Atlanta; married; 2 children. CPA. Acct. Deloitte & Touche, Columbia, SC; group mgr. tech. acctg. SC Electric & Gas Co., 1984—89, v.p., contr., CFO, 1996—98, former v.p. corp. planning, pres., 2006—11; former v.p. fin., treas., contr. SCANA Corp., Columbia, SC, v.p., CFO, 1996—98, sr. v.p., CFO, 1998—2001, pres. COO PSNC Energy, 2001—03, pres., COO, 2011, chmn., CEO, 2011—. Past bd. dirs. Palmetto Place Children's Emergency Shelter; bd. dirs. Bus. Devel. Corp. of S.C. Mem.: AICPA. Methodist. Office: SCANA Corp 220 Operation Way Cayce SC 29033-3701

MARSH, PAMELA COTHRAN, federal prosecutor; b. Atlanta, 1965; BS in Fgn. Svc., magna cum laude, Georgetown U., 1991; JD cum laude, Georgetown U. Law Ctr., 1995. Bar: Fla. 1995, US Dist. Ct. (no., so. and mid. dist.) Fla., US Ct. Appeals (3rd and 11th cir.), US Supreme Ct. Law clk. Arnold & Porter LLP, Washington, 1992—93; rsch. asst. Georgetown U. Law Ctr., 1993—94; assoc. Miller & Chevalier, Washington, 1994; law clk. Jenner & Block LLP, Washington, 1994—95, assoc., 1995; law clk. to judge Jane R. Roth US Ct. Appeals (3rd cir.), Phila., 1995—96; assoc. Annis, Mitchell, Cockey, Edwards & Roehn, Tampa, Fla., 1996—97, Akerman Senterfitt, Tallahassee, 1997—99, of counsel, 2006—10; asst. US atty. (middle dist.) Fla. US Dept. Justice, Tampa, 1999—2006, US atty. (northern dist.) Fla. Tallahassee, 2010—. Office: US Attorneys Office 111 N Adams St 4th Fl Tallahassee FL 32301 Office Phone: 850-942-8430.*

MARSH, PAT, state legislator; b. Fayetteville, Tenn., Jan. 6, 1949; m. Mary Marsh; children: Rob, John. BS in Bus./Transp., U. Tenn. Owner Big G Express; mem. Dist. 62 Tenn. House of Reps., 2009—. Republican. Office: 110 War Memorial Bldg 301 6th Ave N Nashville TN 37243 Office Phone: 615-741-6824. Office Fax: 615-253-0344. Business E-Mail: rep.pat.marsh@capitol.tn.gov.

MARSH, WILLIAM ANDREW, III, lawyer; b. Durham, NC, Mar. 6, 1958; s. William Andrew Jr. and Bernice (Sawyer) M.; m. Sonja Denalli, July 20, 1991; 1 child, William Andrew IV. BA, Hampton Inst., 1979; JD, U. N.C., 1982. Bar: DC 1983, NC 1984, admitted to practice: US Dist. Ct. (DC) 1987, US Ct. Appeals (4th Cir.) 1995, US Supreme Ct. 1998. Assoc. Marsh & Banks, Durham, 1982-83, 85-86; asst. legal counsel Gov. of N.C., Raleigh, 1983-85; assoc. Hyatt Legal Svcs., Washington, 1987; asst. corp. counsel Govt. of D.C., 1987-92; gen. ptnr. Marsh & Marsh, Durham, 1993—. Interim dir. Land Loss Prevention, Durham, 1985. Mem. ABA, N.C. Assn. Black Lawyers, N.C. Bar Assn., D.C. Bar Assn., Durham County Bar Assn. (bd. dirs. 1994—), Kappa Alpha Psi. Democrat. African Methodist Episcopalian. Office: AME Church 120 E Parrish St Ste 310 Durham NC 27701-3346 Office Phone: 919-688-2374. Office Fax: 919-688-2376.

MARSHAK, ALAN HOWARD, electrical engineer, educator; b. Miami Beach, Fla., Mar. 21, 1938; s. Jerome and Yetta (Feiner) M.; children: Jerry Brian; m. Joan Grode Milner, May 25, 1997. BSeEE, U. Miami, 1960; MS, La. State U., 1962; PhD, U. Ariz., 1969. Asst. prof. elec. engring. La. State U., Baton Rouge, 1969-73, assoc. prof., 1973-78, prof., 1978—2002, chmn. dept. elec. and computer engring., 1983—2002, prof. emeritus, 2002—. Vis. prof. Electron Device Rsch. Ctr., U. Fla., Gainesville, 1979-80; tech. reviewer NSF, 1976—, panelist, 1993-96; panelist NRC, 1993, 2001, 04; mem. Southeastern Ctr. Elec. Engring. Edn., 1984-2002, life mem., 2002—, chmn., CEO, 1992-2001, trustee, 1994—; spkr. profl. confs. Tech. referee various jours. including Solid-State Electronics, Jour. Applied Physics; editor: Device and Process Modeling, IEEE Trans. Electron Devices, 1991-2001; author: (with D. J. Hamilton and F. A. Lindholm) Principles and Applications of Semiconductor Device Modeling, 1971, Basic Experiments in Electronics: A Laboratory Manual, 1978, also 56 jour. articles and conf. proceedings. NSF grad. trainee, 1967-69; grantee, 1970, 73, 75, 78; named F.H. Coughlin/CLECO prof. of elec. engring., La. State U., 1993, Valued Svc. & Contribution Cert. award, Electron Devices Soc., IEEE, 2001, Disting. Svc. award, Southeastern Assoc. Elec. Engring. Dept. Heads, 2001. Fellow IEEE (life); mem. Electron Devices Soc., Sigma Xi, Eta Kappa Nu. Achievements include contributions to the physics and analysis of devices with nonuniform band structure. Home: 113 Clipper Cove Lafayette LA 70508-7023

MARSHALL, ALAN GEORGE, chemistry and biochemistry educator; b. Bluffton, Ohio, May 26, 1944; s. Herbert Boyer Marshall and Cecil (Mogil) Rosser; m. Marilyn Gard, June 13, 1965; children: Gwendolyn Scott, Brian George. BA in Chemistry with honors, Northwestern U., 1965; PhD in Phys. Chemistry, Stanford U., 1970. Instr. II U. B.C., Vancouver, Can., 1969-71, asst. prof., 1971-76, assoc. prof., 1976-80; prof. chemistry and biochemistry, dir. Chem. Instrument Ctr. Ohio State U., Columbus, 1980—93; prof. chemistry and biochemistry Fla. State U., Tallahassee, 1993—, disting. rsch. prof., 1999, Kasha prof., 2000—06, Robert O. Lawton prof., 2006—. Dir. Ion Cyclotron Resonance Program Nat. High Magnetic Field Lab., 1993—. Author: Biophysical Chemistry, 1978, Fourier Transforms in NMR, Optical and Mass Spectroscopy, 1990; editor: Nat. High Magnetic Field Lab. ICR/ION Trap newsletter, 1986—97, Rapid Comm. in Mass Spectrometry, 1998—2005; mem. editl. bd. Rapid Comm. in Mass Spectrometry, 2005—; mem. editl. adv. bd.: Analytical Chemistry, 1990—92, mem. editl. bd.: Internat. Jour. Mass Ion Procs., 1987—, Mass Spectrometry Rev., 1994—, Jour. Magnetic Resonance, 1996—2000, Chemometrics and Intelligent Lab. Systems, 1986—89, Ency. of Mass Spectrometry, 2000—, mem. internat. editl adv. bd.: ACS Ency. of Chem. Instrumentation, 1992—95; mem. internat. editl adv. bd. Ann. Review Analytical Chemistry, 2009—13; contbr. 578 articles to profl. jours. Recipient Disting. Scholar award, Ohio State U., 1988, award in analytical chemistry, Ea. Analytical Symposium, 1991, Maurice F. Hasler award, Spectroscopy Soc. Pitts., 1997, Two-Yr. Creativity award, NSF, 1997, gold medal, N.Y. Soc. Applied Spectroscopy, 1998, Pitts. Spectroscopy award, Spectroscopy Soc. Pitts., 2002, New Frontiers Hydrocarbons award, 2009, Analytical Chemistry award, Soc. Analytical Chemists Pitts., 2012, ABRF award, Assn. Biomolecular Rsch. Facilities, 2012; grad. fellow, NSF, 1965—69, Alfred P. Sloan rsch. fellow, 1976. Fellow: AAAS, Am. Inst. Chemists (Chem. Pioneer award 2007), Soc. Applied Spectroscopy, Am. Chem. Soc. (Cin. sect. 2008, Akron Sect. award 1988, award in chem. instrumentation 1990, Frank H. Field and Joe L. Franklin award in mass spectrometry 1995, award in analytical chemistry 2002, Herty medal (Ga. sect.) 2003, Fla. sect. award 2003, So. Chemist award (Memphis sect.) 2004, Ralph Helen Oesper award 2008, William H. Nichols medal 2012), Am. Phys. Soc.; mem.: Am. Acad. Arts & Scis., Soc. Applied Spectroscopy (hon.; chmn. local sect. 1990—93), Eni (New Frontiers in Hydrocarbons award 2009), Eastern Analytical Symphony (award Mass Spectrometry 2009), Am. Soc. Mass Spectroscopy (mem. jour. editl. bd. 1987—89, bd. dirs. 1991—93, mem. jour. editl. bd. 1999—2004, bd. dirs. 2003—, pres. 2004—06, Disting. Contbn. award 1999), Internat. Mass Spectrum Soc. (Thomson medal 2000). Achievements include invention of Fourier transform ion cyclotron resonance mass spectrometry. Office: Fla State U Nat High Magnetic Field Lab 1800 E Paul Dirac Dr Tallahassee FL 32310-4005 Office Phone: 850-644-0529. Business E-Mail: marshall@magnet.fsu.edu.

MARSHALL, ALLEN WRIGHT, III, communications executive, financial consultant; b. Griffin, Ga., Dec. 4, 1941; s. Allen Wright and Evelyn Louise (Halliburton) Marshall; m. Monica Hodgins McKellar; 1 child, Allen Wright IV. BA in Journalism, U. Ga., 1964; diploma, Elkins Inst. Radio, Atlanta, 1964; postgrad., Ga. State U., 1968, MBA, 1988; cert., Coll. Fin. Planning, Denver, 1991. 1st class radio telephone lic. FCC; cert. fin. planner. Pres. Sta. WKEU-AM-FM, Griffin, 1954-86; co-founder, v.p. Griffin Cable TV, 1971-74; co-founder, pres. Custom Svcs. Inc. (now Marshall Plans Inc.), Griffin, 1974—; co-founder, v.p. Cobbwells Marshall Inc., Griffin, 1982-87, Page One, Griffin, 1983-87; co-founder, pres. Toolware Inc., Griffin, 1993-97; co-founder, sec./treas. Magnolia Broadcasting Inc., laGrange, Ga., 1993-95; founder, mng. mem. Spalding Speculators LLC, Griffin, 1995—, Carpediem Ventures, LLC, Griffin, 2005—, Renaissance Griffin LLC, 2006. With Madame's Fine Dining LLC, Griffin, 2008—09; bd. dirs. Face Internat. Corp., Norfolk, Va.; spkr. in field. Author radio progrms, editorials (Ga. AP award 1969-84); also articles. Bd. dirs. Goals for Griffin and Spalding Counties INc., 1981-92, pres. 1991; mem. adv. com. Griffin Vocat.-Tech. Sch., 1982-87; bd. dirs. Jr. Achievement, Griffin, 1977-87; chmn. Griffin-Spalding Indsl. Authority, 1984; mem. Gov.'s Adv. Com. on Area Planning and Devel. Commns., 1971-72, Downtown Devel. Authority, 2009; bd. dirs. McIntosh Trail Area Planning and Devel. Commn., Ga., 1971-73; founding trustee, vice chair, treas. St. George's Episc. Sch., 1995-2001; chair, Main St. Adv. Bd., 2008-09; treas., trustee Nat. Episc. Radio/TV Found., 1986-93. Sgt. U.S. Army, 1966-68. Named Man of Yr., Exch. Club of Griffin, 1984. Mem. Ga. Assn. Broadcasters 9bd. dirs. 1970-74, Radio Sta. of Yr. 1977), Griffin Area C. of C. (bd. dirs. 1980, chmn. indsl. com. 1980, 81), C.C. (charter mem. 1966), Rotary (pres. 1976-77). Avocations: photography, architecture. Home and Office: 34 Peppertree Ct Marietta GA 30068

MARSHALL, BYRD F., JR., lawyer; b. Miami, Fla., Aug. 19, 1953; Attended, So. Meth. U., Dallas, 1971—73; BS in Acctg. and Fin., Fla. State U., Tallahassee, 1975, MBA, 1978, JD with high honors, 1978. Bar: Fla. 1979, US Dist. Ct. (mid. dist.) Fla. 1982. Pvt. practice atty., Jacksonville, Tampa, Fla.; shareholder GrayRobinson PA (formerly Gray, Harris and Robinson PA), Orlando, pres., mng. dir., 1992—. Mem. adv. bd. Mng. Ptnr. Forum. Bd. dirs. Give Kids the World. Named Top Mng. Ptnr., Fla. Trend, 2005—07; named a Best Lawyer, Orlando Mag., 2009, 2010; named one of Best Lawyers in America, 2006—11. Mem.: ABA, Fla. Bar Assn., Orange County Bar Assn., Beta Alpha Psi, Beta Gamma Sigma, Order of Coif. Office: Gray-Robinson PA 301 E Pine St Ste 1400 PO Box 3068 Orlando FL 32801 Office Phone: 407-843-8880. Office Fax: 407-244-5690. Business E-Mail: biff.marshall@gray-robinson.com.

MARSHALL, DANIEL W., III, state legislator; b. Danville, Va., Jan. 20, 1952; s. Webster and Elizabeth Marshall; m. D. Kaye Hardy; 1 child, Jessica Elizbeth Marshall Younginer. Joined as ready mix truck driver Marshall Concrete Products, W.Va., 1971, pres., 1990—; councilman Danville City Coun., 2000—01; mem. Dist. 14 Va. House of Delegates, 2002—. Mem. Dan River Region Vision Com., Pittsylvania Econ. Devel. Orgn., 1996—2000. Mem.: Va. Masonry Coun. (former chmn.), Va. Concrete Masonry Assn. (former chmn.), Nat. Concrete Masonry Assn. (former chmn.), Pittsylvania C. of C. (former pres.), West Main Bapt. Ch. Republican. Baptist. Office: PO Box 439 Danville VA 24543 also: Capitol Office Gen Assembly Bldg Rm 809 PO Box 406 Richmond VA 23218 Office Phone: 434-797-5861, 804-698-1014. Office Fax: 434-797-2642, 804-698-6714. Business E-Mail: DelDMarshall@house.virginia.gov.

MARSHALL, DENZIL PRICE, JR., federal judge; b. Memphis, Jan. 20, 1963; BA, Ark. State U., 1985; MSc, London Sch. Econs. & Polit. Sci., 1987; JD, Harvard U., 1989. Pvt. practice atty., Jonesboro, Ark., 1989, 1991—2006; law clk. to Judge Richard S. Arnold US Ct. Appeals (8th cir.), 1989—91; assoc. judge Ark. Ct. Appeals, Little Rock, 2007—10; judge US Dist Ct. (ea. dist.) Ark., Little Rock, 2010—. Adj. faculty Webster U., St. Louis, 1990; adj. faculty dept. polit. sci. U. Ark., Little Rock, 1990—91, 2001, 2008—10. Office: US Dist Ct Ea Dist Ark 500 W Capitol Ave Little Rock AR 72201 Office Phone: 501-604-5351.

MARSHALL, ELAINE FOLK, state official; b. Lineboro, Md., Nov. 18, 1945; d. Donald and Pauline Folk; m. Solomon Marshall (dec.); m. Bill Holdford (dec.). BS in Textiles and Clothing, U. Md., 1968; JD, Campbell U. Norman Adrian Wiggins Sch. Law, Buies Creek, NC, 1981, LLD (hon.), 2008; D (hon.), Meredith Coll., 2004, Lees McRae Coll., 2004. Bar: NC, US Dist. Ct. (eastern & middle dist.) NC, US Ct. Appeals (4th cir.), US Supreme Ct. Camping dir. Md. 4-H Found., 1964—66; tchr. Lenoir County Sch. Sys., NC, 1969—70; instr. Lenoir Cmty. Coll./Johnston Tech. Cmty. Coll., Lenoir County/Smithfield, NC, 1970—77; assoc. Law Office Edgar R. Bain, Lillington, NC, 1981-84; ptnr. Bain & Marshall, Lillington, 1985-92, Marshall & Marshall, Lillington, 1993—97; mem. Dist. 15 NC State Senate, 1993—94; sec. of state State of NC, Raleigh, 1997—. Trial judge/appellate judge for law students Campbell U., 1982—, adj. faculty trial advocacy program, 1982—84; legal advisor Bus. & Profl. Women, NC, 1982—90; mem. NC Cts. Commn., 1993—94; bd. dirs. Nat. Assn. Secretaries of State, 1998—2001, Nat. Electronic Commerce Coordinating Coun., 2000—03, mem., 2005—, v.p., 2006, pres., 2007. Bd. trustees Meredith Coll., Raleigh, NC, 1998—2002; bd. dirs. Harnett County United Way, 1987—96, NC 4-H Devel. Fund, Inc., 1990—, NC Justice Acad. Found., 1994—96, NC Ctr. Pub. Policy Rsch., 1994—2000, NC Inst. Polit. Leadership, 1997—, L.Am. Resource Ctr., 2003—. Recipient Richter Moore Public Svc. award, NC Polit. Sci. Assn., 1997, Leadership in Tech. award, NC Electronics & Info. Tech. Assn., 1998, James Earl Carter Outstanding Alumni award, Young Democrats America, 2001, Lifetime Achievement award, NC 4-H Found., 2003, Triangle Bus. Jour., 2006; named Harnett County 4-H Alumni of Yr., 1989, Public Citizen of Yr., Nat. Assn. Social Workers (NC chpt.), 1994; named a Disting. Citizen, NC Coun. Women, 1997. Mem.: ABA, American Acad. Trial Lawyers (Spl. Achievement award 2001), NC Assn. Women Attorneys (legis. chmn. 1995, Gwyneth B. Davis award 1996, Disting. Attorney award 2004), NC Acad. Trial Lawyers, NC Bar Assn. (com. on women in profession 1999—), NC State Bar, Delta Theta Phi. Democrat. Office: Office of the Secretary of State PO Box 29622 Raleigh NC 27626 Office Phone: 919-807-2005. Office Fax: 910-807-2010. Business E-Mail: emarshall@sosnc.com.*

MARSHALL, ELIZABETH LIBBY, landscape architect; d. Hamilton West Marshall, Jr. and Mary Barno Marshall; BA, Princeton U., 1981; M in Landscape Arch., Fla. Internat. U., 1998. Policy analyst N.J. Legislature, 1981; field devel. dir. The Rouse Co., 1984; devel. mgr. Disney Devel. Co., Orlando, Fla., 1988; devel. dir. Norton Mus. Art, West Palm Beach, Fla., 1995; state orgn. dir. Jeb Bush for Gov., Tallahassee, 1996; project mgr., apprentice Morgan Wheelock Inc., West Palm Beach, 1999—2001; cons. Elizabeth Libby Marshall, West Palm Beach, 2001—02; pres. Elizabeth Marshall-Libby, MLA, West Palm Beach, 2002—. Pres. coun. Nat. Pub. Radio, Washington, 2001—; gov. apptd. Bd. Landscape Arch., Tallahassee, 2002—, Town Palm Beach Landmarks and Preservation Commn.; bd. dirs. Habitat for Humanity, West Palm Beach, New Horizon Svc. Dogs, Orlando. Sponsor Nantucket Conservation Found.; mem. curriculum com. Fla. A&M U. Grad. Sch. Arch.; active US VA Task Force Health and Rehab. Gardens; apptd. mem. City West Palm Beach Art in Pub. Places Commn.; mayor Art in Pub. Places Commn., 2006—. Recipient, ADDY, 1987, Comml. Project of 1989, Architecture Record, 1989; Fairchild Tropical Gardens: Off Site Collection Grad. scholar, 1997. Mem.: Am. Soc. Landscape Arch. (cert.), Sigma Alpha Lambda, Phi Kappa Phi. Episcopalian. Avocations: travel, theater. Office: 225 Southern Blvd Ste 100 West Palm Beach FL 33405 Office Phone: 561-833-2268. Business E-Mail: libby@landplandesign.com.*

MARSHALL, FRANCIS JOSEPH, aerospace engineer; b. NYC, Sept. 5, 1923; s. Francis Joseph and Mary Gertrude (Leary) M.; m. Joan Eager, June 14, 1952; children— Peter, Colin, Stephen, Dana. BS in Mech. Engring, CCNY, 1948; MS, Rensselaer Poly. Inst., 1950; Dr. Eng. Sci., N.Y. U., 1955. Engr. Western Union Co., NYC, 1948, Gen. Electric Co., Schenectady, 1948-50; engr. Wright-Aero Corp., Woodridge, NJ, 1950-52; group leader Lab. for Applied Scis., U. Chgo., 1955-60; instr. Ill. Inst. Tech., 1957-59; prof. Sch. Aeros. and Astronautics, Purdue U., West Lafayette, Ind., 1960—90. Engr. U.S. Naval Underseas Warfare Center, Pasadena, Calif., 1966-68; faculty fellow NASA-Langley, 1969-70; vis. prof. Inst. Tech. Mara-Midwest Univs. Consortium for Internat. Activities, Malayasia, 1989. Contbr. articles to profl. jours. Served with U.S. Army, 1943-46. Decorated Combat Inf. badge.; Rsch. grantee NASA, 1970-76; Fulbright scholar, Turkey, 1988-89. Asso. fellow AIAA; mem. Am. Soc. Engring. Edn., AAUP. Office: Sch Aeros and Astronautics Purdue U West Lafayette IN 47907

MARSHALL, GAILEN DAUGHERTY, JR., allergist, educator; b. Houston, Sept. 9, 1950; s. Gailen D. and Evelyn C. (Gresham) M.; m. Elizabeth M. Marek, Nov. 5, 1978; children: Sarah Elizabeth, Jonathan David, Rebecca Marie. BS, U. Houston, 1972; MS, Tex. A&M U., 1975; PhD, U. Tex., 1979, MD, 1984. Rsch. sci. U. Tex., Galveston, 1981-84; rsch. fellow U. Iowa, Iowa City, 1985-86; lab. dir. Biotherapeutics Inc., Memphis, 1986-88; chief med. resident Bapt. Meml. Hosp., Memphis, 1988-89; assoc. dir. Rsch. for Health Inc., Houston, 1989-90; dir. divsn. allergy and immunology U. Tex., Houston, 1990—2004, clin. asst. prof. medicine, 1990-91, asst. prof. medicine, 1991—98, assoc. prof. medicine and pathology, 1998—2003, prof., 2003—04; vice chair medicine, dir. divsn. clin. immunology and allergy U. Miss. Med. Ctr., Jackson, Miss., 2004—, prof. medicine and pediatrics. Mem. sci. adv. com. Carrington Labs., Dallas, 1992-94; mem. Merck Rhinitis Adv. Bd., 2002-05, Genentech/Novartis Adv. Bd., 2003—. Mem. editl. bd. Molecular Biotherapy, 1992-93, Cancer Biotherapy, 1994-96, Allergy Procs., 1994-2003, Annals Allergy, Asthma and Immunology, 1995-99, Jour. Interferon Cytokin Rsch., 1999-2005, Clin. Immunology, 2001-05, Jour. Clin. Immunology, 2002-05, Cellular Molecular Allergy, 2003-05; editor-in-chief Annals of Allergy, Asthma and Immunology, 2006—; contbr. articles to profl. jours. Judge Greater Houston Sci. Fair, 1992—; adv. bd. Merck Rhinitis, 2002-04, Grenentech Worch's, 2003-05. Fellow ACP, Am. Coll. Allergy and Immunology, Am. Acad. Allergy-Immunology (chair com.); mem. Tex. Allergy-Immunology Soc. (chair com., bd. dirs. 1999-2002), Greater Houston Allergy Soc. Republican. Baptists. Avocations: classical music, fishing. Office: U Miss Med Ctr 2500 N State St Jackson MS 39216 Home Phone: 601-899-1793; Office Phone: 601-815-5527. Business E-Mail: gmarshall@medicine.umsmed.edu.

MARSHALL, HEMAN ALEXANDER, III, lawyer; b. Roanoke, Va., Feb. 15, 1950; s. Heman Alexander Jr. and Jeanne (Martin) M.; children: Alexander Tevis, Claiborne Henebry, Courtney Littlepaige; m. Judith Skaff, July 6, 1996. BA, U. Va., 1972, JD, 1975. Bar: Va. Assoc. Woods, Rogers, Muse, Walker & Thornton, Roanoke, Va., 1975-80, ptnr., 1981-85, Woods, Rogers & Hazlegrove, P.L.C., Roanoke, Va., 1985-93, prin., 1994—, pres., 1995—2001, chmn., 1997—2002. Contbr. articles to profl. jours. Bd. dirs. Binaba Found., 2003—06, Nat. Conf. Cmty. and Justice, Roanoke, 2000—04, Art Mus. Western Va., 2000—04. Fellow Va. Law Found., Am. Bar Found.; mem. ABA, Va. State Bar (chmn. health law sect. 1988-89, antitrust law sect. 1989-90), Va. Bar Assn. (chmn. health law sect. 1991-92, bd. govs. 2000-04, chmn. law practice mgmt. divsn. 2002-04), Health Law Sect. Governing Coun. 2007-, Roanoke Bar Assn., Am. Health Lawyers Assn. Home: 6629 Cotton Hill Rd Roanoke VA 24018-6915 Office: Woods Rogers PLC 10 S Jefferson St Ste 1400 Roanoke VA 24011-1331 Office Phone: 540-983-7654. Business E-Mail: marshall@woodsrogers.com.

MARSHALL, JAMES ARTHUR, chemistry professor; b. Oshkosh, Wis., Aug. 7, 1935; s. Claude Wendal and Alice (Rodat) M.; m. Elizabeth Binder, Aug. 3, 1983; children: Amy Sue, Andrew Robert, Samantha Leigh. BS, U. Wis., 1957; PhD, U. Mich., 1960; postdoctoral rsch., Stanford U., 1962. Mem. faculty Northwestern U., 1962-80, prof. chemistry, 1968-80; faculty, prof. chemistry U. S.C., 1980-95, Guy Lipscomb prof., 1984-95; prof. associaté Univ. Paris, 1991; prof. associaté U. Jos Fourier, Grenoble, 1994; faculty, Thomas Jefferson prof. chemistry U. Va., 1995—. Cons. to industry; mem. com. phys. scis. NRC, 1969; mem. U.S.-Brazil grad. edn. in chemistry study group, 1971—; lectr. Am. Swiss Found., 1972; Mobay lectr., 1981; Merck-Frosst lectr., 1989, 90; Monsanto lectr., 1989; FACS lectr., 1990, 94; mem. NIH Study Sect. on Fertility and Human Welfare, 1972-75; chmn. U.S.-Japan Conf. on Organic Synthesis, 1973; mem. medicinal chemistry study sect. USPHS, 1977-81; mem. adv. com. chemistry NSF, 1981-84; mem. devel. therapeutics rev. com. USPHS; chmn. Gordon Rsch. Conf. on Stereochemistry, 1990. Author papers in field; mem. editl. bd. Organic Reactions, 1970-77, adv. bd., 1977—; editl. bd. Jour. Organic Chemistry, 1972-76, assoc. editor, 1993—; editor Synthetic Communications, 1972-93. Named Depth Charger of Yr., 1978; Alfred P. Sloan fellow, 1967-68 Fellow AAAS, ACS (lectr. 1989), Japan Soc. Promotion of Sci.; mem. Am. Chem. Soc. (mem. exec. com. organic divsn. 1978—, chmn. organic divsn. 1992, Ernest Guenther award 1979, Russell award 1985, Stone award Piedmont sect. 1986, com. on nomenclature 1979—, Govs. award 1991, Arthur C. Cope Scholar award, 2007), Chem. Soc. (London), Brazilian Acad. Scis. (corr.). Office: Univ Va Dept Chem McCormick Rd PO Box 400319 Charlottesville VA 22904-4319 Office Phone: 434-924-7997. Office Fax: 434-924-3710. Business E-Mail: jam5x@virginia.edu.

MARSHALL, JOHN CROOK, internal medicine educator, researcher; b. Blackburn, Lancashire, Eng., Feb. 28, 1941; came to US, 1976; s. Albert Acey and Marion Miller (Crook) M.; m. Marilyn Dallas Parry, Sept. 20, 1969; children: Samantha Jane, Susannah Crook. BS, Victoria U., Manchester, Eng., 1962, MB, ChB, 1965, MD, 1973. Diplomate Am. Bd. Internal Medicine, Am. Bd. Endocrinology and Metabolism. Intern Manchester Royal Infirmary, 1965-66; resident Brompton Hosp., Nat. Heart Hosp., Nat Hosp. Queen Sq., London, 1966-69, Hammersmith Hosp., London, 1966-69, rsch. fellow, 1969-72; lectr. U. Birmingham, Eng., 1972-76; assoc. prof. internal medicine U. Mich., Ann Arbor, 1976-79, prof., 1979-91, chief endocrinology and metabolism, 1987-91; prof. U. Va., Charlottesville, 1991—, dir. Ctr. for Rsch. in Reprod., 1996—. Sci. counselor NIH, Bethesda, Md., 1983-84. Editor: Endocrinology Jour., 1979-84, Endocrinology Text, 1990—; contbr. articles to profl. jour. Grantee NIH, 1977-. Fellow ACP, Royal Coll. Physicians, Royal Soc. Medicine; mem. Ctrl. Soc. for Clin. Rsch. (coun. 1983—), Assn. Am. Physicians, Am. Soc. for Clin. Investigation, Am. Clin. and Climatological Soc. Anglican. Avocations: vintage racing cars, golf. Office: U Va Sch Medicine Dept Internal Medicine Charlottesville VA 22908-0001 Personal E-mail: jcrookm@aol.com. Business E-Mail: jcm9h@virginia.edu.

MARSHALL, JOHN L., III, accounting and finance staffing executive; b. 1934; Grad., Brown U., 1957. Various positions Marshall Contractors, Inc., Rumford, RI, 1957—63, pres., treas., 1963; pres. Special Counsel, Inc., Acctg. Principals, Inc. Bd. dirs. MPS Group, Inc. Office: Accounting Principals Inc 10201 Centurion Pkwy N Ste 400 Jacksonville FL 32256-4101 Office Phone: 904-360-2400. Office Fax: 904-360-2394. Business E-Mail: john.marshall@accountingprincipals.com.

MARSHALL, JOHN STEVEN, artist, educator, museum administrator; b. Oct. 20, 1957; Spl. studies, U. of the South, 1979-80; AA, Motlow State Community Coll., Tullahoma, Tenn., 1981; BFA, Middle Tenn. State U., 1983; MFA, U. N.C., Greensboro, 1985. Art instr. Meridian Cmty. Coll.; curator Meridian Cmty. Coll. Art Gallery; registrar, curatorial asst. Weatherspoon Art Gallery, U. N.C., Greensboro, 1983-85, asst. curator, lectr., 1985, acting curator, 1986; instr./curator Meridian C.C., 1986—; dir. Meridian Mus. Art, 1986-89; represented by Artworks Gallery, Laurel, Miss., Sylvia Schmidt Gallery, New Orleans, Miss.; co-owner Horne-Marshall Gallery, Meridian. Lectr. art various Tenn. and Miss. orgns.; curator, jury mem. various exhbns. One-man shows include Meridian Mus. Art, 1989, 2008, Miss. State U., 1990, 92, Miss. U. for Women, 1990, Tusculum Coll., 1992, Gen. Art Gallery, Miss., 1993, Coleman Art Ctr., Ala., 1995, Meridian C.C., 1995, Lauderdale Cmty. Gallery, 1995, Meridian Underground Gallery, 1996, Arts in the Park, 1996, Eula Bass Lewis Gallery, Miss., 1996, Dauphin Way Gallery, Mobile, Ala., 1997, Horne-Marshall Gallery, Meridian, 1997, Sylvia Schmidt Gallery, New Orleans, 1997, Casteel Gallery, Meridian, Miss., 1997, Bi-State Comp. Meridian Museum of Art, 1998, East Central Cmty. Coll., Meridian Mus. Art, 2008; 2-person show Winfield Gallery, 1991; exhibited in group shows Elliot U. Ctr. Gallery, Brentwood and Nashville, 1984, Weatherspoon Art Gallery, Greensboro, 1985, 86, Waterworks Gallery, Winston-Salem, N.C., 1985, Meridian Mus. Art, 1987, 89, Casteel Art Gallery, Meridian, 1987, U. So. Miss., 1988, Greenville Art Gallery, 1988, Space-One-Eleven Gallery, 1990, Birmingham-So. Coll., 1990, Winfield Gallery, 1991, Marie Hall Gallery, Jackson, Miss., 1998, East Ctrl. CC, 2008, Miller Art Gallery, 2008; represented in pvt. collections. Mem. Meridian Mus. Art, Meridian Coun. for the Arts. Named Arts Educator of the Yr., Meridian, Miss., 1996; recipient Lamplighter Ednl. Excellence award, 1996. Mem.: Miss. Teachers Assn. Avocations: sailing, guitar, scuba diving. Office: Meridian Community Coll 910 Highway 19 N Meridian MS 39307-5890 Business E-Mail: jmarshal@mcc.cc.ms.us.

MARSHALL, JOHN TREUTLEN, lawyer, educator; b. Macon, Ga., Nov. 1, 1934; s. Hubert and Gladys (Lucas) Marshall; m. Katrine White, May 1, 1959; children: Allison, Rebecca, Paul, Mary Anne. BA, Vanderbilt U., 1956; LLB, Yale U., 1962. Bar: Ga. 1962, US Dist. Ct. (no., mid. and so. dists.) Ga. 1962, US Ct. Appeals (5th cir.) 1962, US Supreme Ct. 1978, US Ct. Appeals (11th cir.) 1982. Of counsel Bryan Cave LLP, Atlanta, 1962—. Chmn. bd. visitors Ga. State U. Law Sch., 2005—10; chmn. No. Dist. Ga. Bar Coun., 1989, Ga. State Bar Commn. Continuing Lawyer Competency, 1991—93, Ga. State Commn. Stds. Profession, 1996—; bd. dirs. Ga. Eye Bank, Inc., 2007—13, Atlanta Bar Found. Bd. editor Yale Law Jour. Trustee Ga. Inst. Continuing Legal Edn., 1983—90; bd. dirs. Atlanta Legal Aid, 1972—73. Capt. USMC, 1959—62. Recipient S. Phillip Heiner award, Atlanta Vol. Lawyers Assn., 1992, A. Gus Cleveland award, Ga. Commn. Continuing Legal Edn., Tradition of Excellence award, State Bar Ga., 1995, Disting. Svc. award, Ga. State Bar, 2006, Professionalism award, Am. Inns of Ct. (11th Jud. Cir.), 2005, Ben F. Johnson, Jr. award for Pub. Svc., 2007. Fellow: Ga. Bar Found., Atlanta Bar Found., Am. Acad. Appellate Lawyers, Am. Coll. Trial Lawyers (state chmn. 1985—86); mem.: ABA (ho. of dels. 1976—86, Harrison Tweed award 1986), Ga. Inst. Trial Advocacy (chmn. 1982—83), Atlanta Bar Assn. (pres. 1974—75, Charles E. Watkins Jr. award 1988, Leadership award 1996), Atlanta Bar Found. (bd. dirs.), State Bar Ga. (chmn. stds. profession com., Disting. Svc. award 2005, Lifetime Achievement award Anti Defimation League 2009), Am. Arbitration Assn. Office: Bryan Cave LLP One Atlantic Ctr Fl 14 1201 W Peachtree St NW Atlanta GA 30309-3488 Office Phone: 404-572-6615. Business E-Mail: jmarshall@pogolaw.com.

MARSHALL, MCALISTER C., II, security firm executive, lawyer; BA, Hampden-Sidney Coll., Va., 1992; JD, U. Va. Sch. Law, 1995. Assoc. Hunton & Williams, 1996—2000; asst. gen. counsel Brink's Co. (formerly Pittston Co.), 2000—06, dir. corp. governance and compliance, 2004—06, v.p., gen. counsel, corp. sec., 2008—; v.p., gen. counsel, sec. Tredegar Corp., 2006—08. Office: The Brink's Company PO Box 18100 Richmond VA 23226-8100 Office Phone: 804-289-9600. Office Fax: 804-289-9770. Business E-Mail: mmarshall@brinkscompany.com.

MARSHALL, MICKEY, metal products executive; Grad., U. So. Miss., Hattiesburg. Various mgmt. positions in sales, purchasing & ops. Jeffreys Steel Co., 1984—97; v.p. plates & shapes SE Metals USA Holdings Corp., 2000—08, pres. plates & shapes group, SE, 2009—. Office: Metals USA Holdings Corp 2400 E Commercial Blvd Ste 905 Fort Lauderdale FL 33308-4059 Office Phone: 713-965-0990. Office Fax: 713-965-0067.

MARSHALL, ROBERT G., state legislator; b. May 3, 1944; s. James and Betty Marshall; m. Catherine Ann Fonseca; children: Teresa, Christopher, Mary, Joey, Tommy. BA in History, Belmont Abbey Coll., NC, 1969; MA in Humanities, Calif. State U., 1991. Staff mem. Exec. Office of Pres., 1973; legis. asst. US House of Reps., US Senate, 1973-79; dir. Congl. info. Am. Life League, Inc., 1980—; mem. Dist. 13 Va. House of Delegates, 1992—. Mem. Prince William C. of C., Greater Manassas C. of C., KC. Office: PO Box 421 Manassas VA 20108-0421 Office Phone: 703-853-4213. Business E-Mail: DelBMarshall@house.virginia.gov.

MARSTON, CHRISTOPHER M., consulting firm executive, former federal agency administrator; b. Grosse Pointe, Mich., 1974; m. Michelle Marston; 1 child, Abby. AB in Govt., cum laude, Dartmouth Coll., Hanover, NH, 1996; JD cum laude, Georgetown U. Law Ctr., DC, 2003. Congressional intern to staff mem. US House Govt. Reform & Oversight Com., 1996—97; asst. to Rep. Rob Portman US House of Representatives, 1998, sys. analyst Office of Parliamentarian, 1998—2001; chief of staff Office Nat. Drug Policy (ONDP), 2001—04; dir. Ohio state/fed. rels. to Gov. Bob Taft State of Ohio, DC, 2004—06; White House liaison US Dept. Interior, 2006—07; dep. asst. sec. for mgmt. US Dept. Edn., 2007—08, asst. sec. for mgmt., 2008—09; founder, prin. Election CFO, LLC, Alexandria, Va., 2009—. Past pres. Alexandria Vol. Bur.; chmn. Alexandria Rep. City Com. Recipient Gov.'s award, Va. Rep. Party, 2007. Republican. Office: Election CFO LLC PO Box 26141 Alexandria VA 22313 Office Phone: 571-482-7690. Office Fax: 703-997-2549. E-mail: Chris@ElectionCFO.com.

MARSTON, EDGAR JEAN, III, lawyer; b. Houston, July 5, 1939; s. Edgar Jr. and Jean (White) M.; m. Graeme Meyers, June 21, 1961; children: Christopher Graham, Jonathan Andrew. BA, Brown U., 1961; JD, U. Tex., 1964. Bar: Tex. 1964. Law clk. to presiding justice Supreme Ct. Tex., Austin, 1964-65; assoc. Baker & Botts, Houston, 1965-71; ptnr. Bracewell & Patterson, L.L.P., Houston, 1971-89, 96—, of counsel, 1990-96; exec. v.p., gen. counsel Southdown, Inc., Houston, 1987-95, also bd. dirs. Mem. ABA, Tex. Bar Assn., Tex. Bar Found., Houston Bar Assn., Houston Country Club, Coronado Club. Episcopalian. Avocations: hunting, fishing, stamp collecting/philately, reading. Office: Bracewell & Giuliani LLP 711 Louisiana St Ste 2300 Houston TX 77002-2770 Office Phone: 713-221-1315. E-mail: edgar.marston@bgllp.com.

MARTA, DAWN RENEÉ, clinical psychologist; b. Ottawa, Ill., Sept. 10, 1963; d. Bruce Roger Rooks and Marsha Ann (Meade) Monroe; m. David Lee LeBeau (div. Oct. 1987); 1 child, Nicholas Scott LeBeau; m. Scott Kennedy Echols (dec. Feb. 1996); m. Anthony John Marta, Dec. 21, 2001 (div. Jan. 2012); m. Lou A. Nelson, June 2012. Student, Fla. C.C., Jacksonville, 1990—93; AA in Medicine, Ctrl. Fla. C.C., Ocala, Fla., 1994; student, Santa Fe C.C., Gainesville, 1994; BA in Philosophy with high honors, U. Fla., 1997; MDiv in Theology, Duke U., 2000; postgrad., George Fox U., 2000; D in Psychology, Argosy U., 2004. Cert. personal trainer Am. Coun. Exercise. Membership dir. Duval County Med. Soc., Jacksonville, Fla., 1987—93; emergency rm. admissions rep. Munroe Regional Med. Ctr., Ocala, Fla., 1993—94; admissions rep. Shands Hosp. U. Fla., Gainesville, 1994; adminstr. Covenant Presbyn. Ch., Gainesville, 1994—95; chaplain Duke U. Med. Ctr., Durham, NC, 1998—2000; personal trainer Ottawa, Elgin, 2000—04; resident Meridian Behavioral Health Svcs., 2004—05; clin. psychologist, owner, operator Ctr. Human Flourishing, Murphy, 2005—. Usher First United Meth. Ch., Chgo., 2002, Elgin, 2003—04, trustee edn. com., 2003—04. Mem.: Nat. Alliance Profl. Psychology Providers, Potters Touch. Avocations: bodybuilding, hiking, kayaking, travel. Office: 225 Valley River Ave Ste F Murphy NC 28906 Office Phone: 828-321-9900.

MARTELLO, WAN LING, retail executive; b. Philippines; MBA in Mgmt. Info. Sys., U. Minn. CPA. Diverse fin. roles Krafts; corp. contr. Borden Foods; US pres. NCH Mktg. Svcs.; sr. v.p., CFO and strategy Wal-Mart Stores, Inc., exec. v.p. global e-Commerce, 2010—. Bd. dirs. Com. of 100. Recipient Asian Women In Bus. Leadership award, 2008. Mem.: Museum of Chinese in Am. (trustee), The Chgo. Network, Internat. Women's Forum. Office: Wal-Mart Stores, Incorporated 702 SW 8th St Bentonville AR 72716 Office Phone: 479-273-4000. Office Fax: 479-273-4053.

MARTENS, DAVID A., metal products executive; With Singer Steel, Inc., 1978—87; various positions Uni-Steel, Inc., 1987—92, exec. v.p., 1992—97, pres., 1997—99; v.p. plates and shapes, South-ctrl. region Metals USA Holdings Corp., 1999—2005, pres. plates and shapes group West, 2005—. Office: Metals USA Holdings Corp Ste 1100 2400 E Commercial Blvd Ste 905 Fort Lauderdale FL 33308-4059 Office Phone: 713-965-0990. Office Fax: 713-965-0067.

MARTIN, ALICE HOWZE, former prosecutor, executive recruiter; b. Memphis, Apr. 25, 1956; married; 3 children. BSN, Vanderbilt U., 1978; JD, U. Miss., 1981. Bar: Tenn. 1981, Miss. 1981, Ala. 1989. Asst. US atty. US Attys. Office, Memphis, 1983-89; ptnr. Harris Harris & Martin, Florence, Ala., 1992—94; dist. mcpl. judge City of Florence, Ala., 1993—97; judge Cir. Ct. State of Ala., 1997—99; US atty. (no. dist.) Ala. US Dept. Justice, 2001—09; sr. ptnr. Wheless Assoc., 2009—. Avocations: travel, skeet shooting. Office: 1740 Oxmoor Rd Ste A Birmingham AL 35209

MARTIN, BENJAMIN GAUFMAN, ophthalmologist; b. Louisville, Aug. 18, 1937; s. Benjamin and Catherine L. Martin; m. Caroline Sue Martin, May 25, 1975; children: Benjamin, Lori, Tamara, Farrell, Steven, David. BME, U. Louisville, 1954, M. Engring., 1973; MD, U. So. Calif., 1964; BA in Philosophy, Fraser Coast U., 2013. Design engr. Philco/Ford, Palo Alto, Calif., 1957-60; rsch. engr. N.Am./Rockwell, Inglewood, Calif., 1961-63; intern Wright-Patterson Med. Ctr., Dayton, Ohio, 1964-65; ophthalmology resident Wilford Hall Med. Ctr., San Antonio, 1968-71; commd. USAF, 1963, advanced through grades to col., ret., 1980; CEO Cape Coral (Fla.) Eye Ctr., 1980—. With USN, 1954-57. Decorated Legion of Merit, DFC, Bronze Star, Air medal. Mem.: DFC Soc., Daedalions, Elks, Shriners, Masons. Republican. Lutheran. Office: Cape Coral Eye Ctr 4120 Del Prado Blvd S Cape Coral FL 33904-7165 Home Phone: 239-481-8071; Office Phone: 239-542-2020.

MARTIN, BEVERLY BALDWIN, federal judge; b. Macon, Ga., 1955; BA, Stetson U., Deland, Fla., 1976; JD, U. Ga., 1981. Bar: Ga. 1981. Assoc. Martin, Snow, Grant & Napier, Macon, Ga., 1981-84; trial and appellate ct. litigator, sr. asst. atty. gen. and dir. bus. and profl. regulation divsn. Office of Atty. Gen. State of Ga., Macon, 1984-94; asst. U.S. atty. (mid. dist. Ga.) US Dept. Justice, Macon, 1994-98, US atty., 1998-2000; judge US Dist. Ct. (no. dist.) Ga., Atlanta, 2000—10, US Ct. Appeals (11th Cir.), 2010—. Mem. Ga. Bar Assn., Macon Bar Assn., Am. Judicature Soc., Ga. Assn. Women Lawyers, Lawyers Club of Atlanta. Office: US Courthouse 56 Forsyth St NW Atlanta GA 30303

MARTIN, BOE WILLIS, lawyer; b. Texarkana, Ark., Oct. 6, 1940; s. E.H. and Dorothy Annette (Willis) M.; m. Carol J. Edwards, June 12, 1965; children: Stephanie Diane, Scott Andrew. BA, Tex. A&M U., 1962; LLB, U. Tex., 1964; LLM, George Washington U., 1970. Bar: (Tex.) 1964. Law clk. Tex. Supreme Ct., 1966-67; assoc. Snakard, Brown & Gambill, Ft. Worth, 1967-69, assoc., ptnr., 1971-72; asst. counsel US Senate Labor and Pub. Welfare Com., 1969; legal asst. U.S. Senator Ralph W. Yarborough, 1969-71; assoc., ptnr. Stalcup & Johnson, Dallas, 1972-77; assoc. ptnr. Coke & Coke, Dallas, 1977-80; ptnr., shareholder Johnson & Gibbs, Dallas, 1981—95, Bell, Nunnally & Martin, Dallas, 1996—2011. Vis. prof. law So. Meth. U. Sch. Law, 1972-73, 75, 88-89, 95, 99-2000, 2002-2011, U. Tex. Sch. Law, 1977, 79, U. Houston Law Ctr., 2005. Contbr. articles to profl. jours. Staff Carter-Mondale Campaign, 1976, 80; cons. to v.p. of US, 1977-80; cons. Mondale for Pres. Campaign, 1983-84, Dukakis for Pres. Campaign, 1988; dep. coord. of visit of Pres. Mikhail Gorbachev to State of Minn., 1990. Capt. US Army, 1964-69. Mem. ABA, Tex. Bar Assn., Dallas Bar Assn. Democrat. Episcopalian. Home: 4055 Sweetwater Dr College Station TX 77845-9650

MARTIN, CAROL JACQUELYN, artist, educator; b. Ft. Worth, Tex., Oct. 6, 1943; d. John Warren and Dorothy Lorene (Coffman) Edwards; m. Boe Willis Martin, Oct. 6, 1940; children: Stephanie Diane, Scott Andrew. BA summa cum laude, U. North Tex., 1965; MA, U. Tex., El Paso, 1967; attended, Art Students League NY, 2007. Tchr. English Edgemere Elem. Sch., El Paso, 1965—66; tchr. Fulmore Jr. H.S., Austin, Tex., 1966—67, Monnig Jr. H.S., Ft. Worth, 1967—68, Paschal H.S., Ft. Worth, 1968—69; instr. English Tarrant County Jr. Coll., Ft. Worth, 1968—69, 1971—72, Eastfield C.C., Dallas, 1981, Richland C.C. Dist., 1982; instr. art Meml. Student Ctr. UPlus Tex. A&M U., 2002—03; instr. art Brenham Fine Arts League, 2006, 2009, 2011, 2014, Brazos Valley Fine Arts League, 2011—12, Galerie Pavilion, Wichita Falls, Tex., 2008; guest lectr. art Tex. A & M Forsyth Gallery, 2010. Artist Vt. Studio Ctr., 1998; press sec. Senator Gaylord Nelson, Washington, 1969—71. Editor The Avesta Mag., 1964-65; various group art exhbns., Solo Artist Exhbn. Galerie Pavilion, 2008. Mem. Nat. Mus. Women in Arts. Mem. Lone Star Art Guild (sec. 2006-07, bd. mem. 2007-08), Brazos Valley Art League, Brenham Fine Arts League, Mortar Board, Alpha Chi, Sigma Tau Delta, Kappa Delta Pi, Delta Gamma. Democrat. Episcopalian. Avocations: travel, photography, painting. Address: 4055 Sweetwater Dr College Station TX 77845-9650

MARTIN, CHARLES NEIL, JR., surgical hospital company executive; b. Florence, Ala., Dec. 11, 1942; s. Charles Neil Sr. and Hazel Lucy (Hawkins) M. BS, So. Coll., Chattanooga, 1964. Adminstr. El Reposo Nursing Home, Florence, 1964-66, Parkwood Convalescent Ctr., Chattanooga, 1966-67; project dir. Tenn. Hosp. Assn., Nashville, 1967-68, asst. dir., 1968-69; v.p. Gen. Care Corp., Nashville, 1969-76, exec. v.p., 1976-79, pres. & COO, 1979-80; sr. v.p. HCA, Inc., Nashville, 1980-85, exec. v.p., 1985-87, also bd. dirs.; pres., chief oper. officer HealthTrust, Inc., Nashville, 1987—92; chmn., pres., CEO OrNda HealthCorp., 1992—97; chmn., CEO Vanguard Health Sys., Inc., Nashville, 1997—. Bd. dirs. Equicor, Nashville, 1986—. Bd. dirs. Cystic Fibrosis Found., Nashville, 1987. Office: Vanguard Healthcare Systems Inc Ste 100 20 Burton Hills Blvd Nashville TN 37215 Office Phone: 615-665-6000. Office Fax: 615-665-6099. Business E-Mail: c.martin@vanguard.com.

MARTIN, CUONZO LAMAR, men's college basketball coach; b. St. Louis, Sept. 23, 1971; m. Roberta Martin; children: Joshua, Chase, Addison. B in Restaurant, Hotel, Instl. and Tourism Mgmt., Purdue U., West Lafayette, Ind., 2000. Forward Vancouver Grizzlies, 1995—96, Milw. Bucks, 1996—97, Grand Rapids Mackers, 1996—97, Grand Rapids Hoops, 1997—99, Feliz Scandone, Avellino, Italy, 1997; asst. coach West Lafayette HS, 1999—2000, Purdue U. Boilermakers, 2000—07, assoc. head coach, 2007—08; head coach Mo. State U. Bears, 2008—11, U. Tenn. Volunteers, 2011—. Named Mo. Valley Conf. Coach of Yr., 2011. Office: University Tenn Mens Basketball Thompson-Boling Arena 1600 Phillip Fulmer Way Knoxville TN 37996

MARTIN, DANIEL C., surgeon, gynecologist, educator; b. St. Louis, Apr. 7, 1946; s. Dan Allen and Ruth Keel (Fields) M.; m. Glenn Ann Blakemore, July 7, 1970; children: Josh, Adam. BS in Physics, Emory U., Atlanta, 1968, MD, 1972. Diplomate Am. Bd. Ob-Gyn. Rsch. asst. physics and radiology Emory U., Atlanta, 1968-69; intern, resident, fellow, instr. The Johns Hopkins Med. Instns., Balt., 1972-77; from asst. prof. to clin. asst. prof. U. Tenn., Memphis, 1977-90, clin. assoc. prof., 1990—2005, clin. prof., 2005—06, prof., 2006—; divsnl. dir. vascular gynecology U. Tenn., Health Sci. Ctr., 2010—, divsnl. dir. reproductive endocrinology, 2012—, faculty senate, 2010—; surgeon Reproductive Surgery, P.C., Memphis, 1977—2006, UT Med. Group, Memphis, 2006—. Gynecologist, reproductive surgeon Bapt. Meml. Hosp., 1977—; Axel Munthe presenter, Naples, Italy, 1992; guest spkr.Annual Japanese Endometrosis Symposium, Osaka, 1994, 2004; dir. gynecologic laser and endoscopy workshops, 1982-93. Editor: (textbooks) Lasers in Endoscopy, 1990, Laparoscopic Appearance of Endometriosis, 1990, Manual of Endoscopy, 1990, Atlas of Endometriosis, 1993, Endoscopic Management of Gynecologic Disease, 1996. Picker Found. fellow Emory U., 1969; Tex. Assn. Ob-Gyn. hon. fellow, 1989; recipient Bridges trophy for athletics Emory U., 1968, Codman surg. award, 1982, 83, Video award Am. Fertility Soc., 1992, Physician Recognition awrd Endometriosis Assn., 1995, APGO Tchg. award, 2010; named one of Best Drs. Am. Woodward and White Inc., 1992, 94, 96, 98, 00, 02, 04, 06, 08, 10, 12; Hon. mem. Australian Gynecol. Endoscopy Soc., 1993, named to Sports Hall of Fame, Emory Coll., 2002; named one of Memphis Mag. Top Drs., 2010-2013. Mem. ACOG (sect. chair jr. fellows Md.), Tenn. Med. Assn., Memphis and Shelby County Med. Soc. (comm. com.), Am. Nat. Std. Inst. (subcom. on laser safety in med. facility), Am. Assn. Gynecol. Laparoscopists (pres. 1990-91, Videoendoscopy award 1993), Gynecologic Surgery Soc. (pres. 1994-96, chmn. bd. 1996-98), Australian Gynecol. Endoscopy Soc. (hon.), Argentinian Ob-Gyn. Soc. (hon.), Alpha Omega Alpha. Office Phone: 901-866-8220.

MARTIN, DAVID ALAN, lawyer, law educator; b. Indpls., July 23, 1948; s. C. Wendell and Elizabeth Bowman (Meeker) M.; m. Cynthia Jo Lorman, June 13, 1970; children: Amy Lynn, Jeffrey David. BA, DePauw U., 1970; JD, Yale U., 1975. Bar: D.C. Law clk. to Hon. J. Skelly Wright U.S. Ct. Appeals (D.C. cir.), 1975—76; law clk. to Hon. Lewis F. Powell U.S. Supreme Ct., Washington, 1976—77; assoc. Rogovin, Stern & Huge, Washington, 1977—78; spl. asst. bur. human rights & humanitarian affairs US Dept. State, Washington, 1978—80; from asst. prof. to assoc. prof. U. Va. Sch. Law, Charlottesville, 1980—86, prof., 1986—91, Henry L. & Grace Doherty prof. law, 1991—2003, F. Palmer Weber Rsch. prof. civil liberties and human rights, 1992—95, F. Palmer Weber Rsch. prof. civil liberties & human rights, 2000—03, Warner-Booker disting. prof. internat. law, 2003—, Class of 1963 rsch. prof., 2004—07; gen. counsel US Immigration & Naturalization Svc. (INS), US Dept. Justice, Washington, 1995—98; prin. dep. gen. counsel US Dept. Homeland Security, Washington, 2009—10, acting gen. counsel, 2009. Cons. Adminstrv. Conf. US, Washington, 1988-89, 91-92, US Dept. Justice, 1993-95, US Dept. State, 2003-04 Author: Forced Migration: Law and Policy, 2007, Immigration: Process and Policy, 1985, 6th edit., 2008, Asylum Case Law Sourcebook, 1994, 7th edit., 2007, The Endless Quest: Helping America's Farm Workers, 1994, The United States Refugee Admissions Program: Reforms for a New Era of Refugee Resettlement, 2005; editor: The New Asylum Seekers, 1988, Immigration Admissions, 1998, Immigration Controls, 1998, Rights and Duties of Dual Nationals: Evolution and Prospects, 2002, Immigration Stories, 2005; bd. editors American Jour. Internat. Law, 2004—; contbr. articles to profl. jours. Nat. governing bd. Common Cause, Washington, 1972-75; elder Westminster Presbyn. Ch., Charlottesville, 1982-84, 89-92; bd. dirs. Internat. Rescue Com., 2000-03. German Marshall Fund Rsch. fellow, Geneva, 1984-85. Mem. American Soc. Internat. Law (v.p. 2003-05, Book award 1986), Internat. Law Assn. Democrat. Office: University Va Sch Law 580 Massie Rd Charlottesville VA 22903-1738 Office Phone: 434-924-3144. Business E-Mail: dam3r@virginia.edu.

MARTIN, DAVID HUBERT, internist, epidemiologist, educator; b. Detroit, Mar. 24, 1943; s. Hubert Cillis and Mable Anita (Stewart) M.; m. Jane Ellen Schlichtemeier, Nov. 22, 1970; children: Jennifer, Jason. BA with distinction, U. Kans., 1965; MD cum laude, Harvard Coll., 1969. Diplomate Nat. Bd. Med. Examiners, Am. Bd. Internal Medicine, Infectious Disease Subspecialty Bd. Am. Bd. Internal Medicine. Intern Bronx (N.Y.) Mcpl. Hosp. Ctr., 1969-70; staff assoc. Nat. Inst. Allergy and Infectious Diseases, Mid. Am. Rsch. Unit, NIH, Panama Canal Zone, 1970-73; med. resident U. Wash. Affiliated Hosps., 1973-75; sr. fellow in infectious diseases U. Wash., 1976-78; chief resident in medicine USPHS Hosp., Seattle, 1975-76, staff internal medicine clinic, 1975, attending physician internal medicine, 1976-78, staff dept. internal medicine New Orleans, 1979-81; staff Hotel Dieu Hosp., New Orleans, 1982-94; clin. asst. prof. medicine La. State U. Med. Sch., New Orleans, 1979-81, asst. prof. medicine divsn. infectious diseases, 1981-82, assoc. prof. medicine divsn. infectious diseases, 1982-88, assoc. prof. microbiology, 1986-88, prof. internal medicine and microbiology, 1988, asst. chief sect. infectious diseases, 1988-89, chief sect. infectious diseases, 1990—, Harry E. Dascomb M.D. prof. of medicine, 1990—. Instr. dept. medicine U. Wash. Sch. Medicine, Seattle, 1975-78, acting asst. prof. medicine, 1978-79; chmn. infection control com., chmn. instnl. rev. bd. human rsch. com., chmn. antibiotic utilization com., sec. rsch. and editl. com., sec. animal welfare com. USPHS Hosp., New Orleans, 1979-81, dep. chief clin. rsch. dept., 1979-81, chmn. credentials com., 1980-81; mem. infection control com. Hotel Dieu Hosp., New Orleans, 1983-84, chmn. pharmacy and therapeutics com., 1988-94, mem. infection control com., 1990-94; vis. physician Charity Hosp. (now Med. Ctr. of La. at New Orleans), New Orleans, 1982—, chmn. antiobiotics com., 1982—, dir. infection control program, 1993—, chmn. infection control com., 1993—, vice chmn. pharmacy and therapeutics com., 1995—; chmn. comprehensive medicine head search com. La. State U. Med. Sch., 1989-90, dept. medicine faculty promotion com., 1988—, AIDS policy com., 1992; adv. bd. La. State Labs., 1993—, State La. Pub. Health Lab. Adv. Com., 1994—, U.S. Pub. Health Region 6 Infertility Prevention Adv. Com., 1995—; mem. nat. STD treatment guidelines com. Ctrs. Disease Control, 1993, 98, nat. Chlamydia and gonorrheadiagnosis guidelines com., 1997—; dir. La. STD/HIV rsch. ctr., 2001-04, Gulf South STI/TM Collaborative Rsch. Ctr., 2004—. Peer reviewer various jours. including Sexually Transmitted Diseases, The Jour. of Infectious Diseases, The Am. Jour. of the Med. Scis., Archives of Internal Medicine, Clin. Infectious Diseases, New Eng. Jour. Medicine, Annals Internal Medicine, Jour. AMA; contbr. chpts. to books and articles to profl. jours. Dir. La. STD/HIV Rsch. Ctr., 2002—. With USPHS, 1970-82. Fellow ACP (La. chpt. program chmn. 1994-95), Infectious Diseases Soc. Am.; mem. Internat. Soc. for Sexually Transmitted Disease Rsch. (bd. dirs. 1991-99, chmn. 1995 meeting organizing com., pres. 1993-95, sec.-treas. 1999—), Am. Fedn. for Clin. Rsch., Am. Sexually Transmitted Diseases Assn. (v.p. 1992-94, pres. 1994-96), Am. Soc. for Microbiology, European Soc. for Clin. Microbiology and Infectious Diseases, So. Soc. for Clin. Investigation, La./Miss. Infectious Diseases Soc. (bd. dirs., sci. program chmn. 1993, pres. 1997-99), Phi Beta Kappa. Achievements include research in the effect of sexually transmitted microorganisms on pregnancy outcome, antibiotic treatment of sexually transmitted diseases and in particular C. trachomatis, epidemiology of C. trachomatis in normal populations, chancroid and other genital ulcer diseases; establishment of first chlamydia laboratory in the Gulf South. Office: La State U Med Sch 1542 Tulane Ave New Orleans LA 70112-2825 Office Phone: 504-568-5031.

MARTIN, DAVID W., corporate financial executive; BS in Acctg., Christian Brothers U. Audit ptnr. Arthur Anderson, LLP, Grant Thornton, LLP, 2003—05; fin. contr. Terminix (acquired by The ServiceMaster Co.), 2005—06, v.p., 2005—07, CFO, 2006—07; sr. v.p., corp. contr. Servicemaster Co., Servicemaster Global Holdings, 2007—. Office: The ServiceMaster Co 860 Ridge Lake Blvd Memphis TN 38120 Office Phone: 901-597-1400. Office Fax: 630-663-2001. Business E-Mail: David.Martin@servicemaster.com.

MARTIN, DEAN FREDERICK, retired chemistry professor; b. Woodburn, Iowa, Apr. 6, 1933; s. Herman A. and Frances M. (Rausis) M.; m. Barbara Bursa, Dec. 22, 1956; children: Diane, Bruce, John, Paul, Brian, Eric. BA, Grinnell Coll., 1955; PhD, Pa. State U., 1958. NSF postdoctoral fellow Univ. Coll., London, 1958—59; instr. inorganic chemistry U. Ill., Champaign-Urbana, 1959—61, asst. prof., 1961—64; assoc. prof. chemistry U. South Fla., Tampa, 1964—69, prof., 1969—, Disting. Svc. prof. chemistry, 1992—2006, prof. emeritus, 2006—. Vis. prof. physiology and pharmacology Duke, 1970-71 Author: (with Barbara B. Martin) Coordination Compounds, 1964, (with Therald Moeller) Laboratory Chemistry, 1965, Marine Chemistry, 2 vols, 1968, 70; editor (with George M. Padilla) Marine Pharmacognosy, 1973; editor Fla. Scientist, 1984—2010. Recipient Alumni award Grinnell Coll., 1971; USPHS rsch. career award, 1969-74; named Disting. Svc. prof., 1992—, Disting. U. Prof. Emeritus, 2006-. Fellow AAAS; mem. Am. Chem. Soc., Royal Soc. Chemistry (London), Aquatic Plant Mgmt. Soc., Alpha Chi Sigma, Phi Beta Kappa, Sigma Xi. Roman Catholic. Avocation: woodworking. Home: 3402 Valencia Rd Tampa FL 33618-3950 Office: U South Fla Dept Chemistry CHE 205 4202 E Fowler Ave Tampa FL 33620-5205 Office Phone: 813-974-2374. Business E-Mail: dfmartin@usf.edu.

MARTIN, EDWARD CURTIS, JR., landscape architect, educator; b. Albany, Ga., Aug. 21, 1928; s. Edward Curtis and Mildred Lee (Tyler) M.; m. Roberta Inman Parker, Mar. 18, 1967; children: Edward Curtis III, Andrew Parker. BFA, U. Ga., 1950, M of Landscape Architecture, 1969. Landscape arch. Norman C. Butts Landscape Contractor, Atlanta, 1950, M.T. Brooks Office of Landscape Architecture, Birmingham, Ala., 1950—55; Univ. campus landscape arch., horticulture dept. educator rschr. Miss. State U., 1956-70, prof. landscape architecture, 1970-92, Disting. prof., 1988, prof. emeritus, 1993—; lectr. in fields. Originator, chmn., lectr. Edward C. Martin Jr. Landscape Design Symposium, 1957-2005; guest lectr. U. San Luis Potosi, Mex., 1990, U. Mex. Sch. Architecture, Mexico City, 1991, La. State U., 1990-92, 94, 96, Biendenharn Found., Monroe, La., 1991, Longue Vue Found., New Orleans, 1991; prof. Miss. State U., 1992-93; guest instr. in field; originator, lectr. Garden Design Workshops, Miss. State U., 1988-2001; host numerous flower and garden shows and tours abroad; So. hist. gardens lectr. Miss. U. for Women, 1997-2000, Delta Queen, MS Queen, Am. Queen Steamboats, Memphis, Tenn., 1993-95; photog. landscape archtl. rsch. study: Europe, 1958, 66, 74, 85, S.Am., 1960, Israel, 1993, 95, Greece, Turkey, 1998; vis. prof. La. State U., 1990-94, 97; instr. landscape design Bot. Gardens, Huntsville, Ala., 1996; instr. ecology tour Copper Canyon, Mex., 1994; spkr. and lectr. in field. Author: Landscape Plants in Design, A Photographic Guide, 1983; co-author: Home Landscapes, Planting Design and Management, 1994; invited to participate in Attingham Summer Program in Hist. Preservation (English country houses and gardens) Eng., 1985; author/photographer of 80-captioned slide series, one on Home Landscapes, another on Urban Landscape Design for use by Nat. Coun. State Garden Clubs, Inc., 1994; guest spkr. 53rd Ann. Landscape Design Symposium, Miss. State U., 2008. Mem. Miss. State Bd. Landscape Archs. for Profl. Registration, 1973-74; mem. Starkville Park and Recreation Bd., Miss., 1973-79; civic beautification com. Black Mountain, NC, 2002—; bd. visitors Warren Wilson Coll., Asheville, NC, 2002—; Mont. Presbyn. Conf. Ctr., Montreat NC, 2004-, elder Trinity Presbyn. Ch., Starkville, Miss., Warren Wilson Presbyn. Ch. and Coll. Chapel, Asheville; garden tour guide Biltmore Estate, Asheville, 2003—11, Edward C. Martin Jr. vol. Recipient Silver Seal award Nat. Coun. State Garden Clubs 1969, honoree 1995, Helent S. Hull Lit. award Nat. Coun. State Gordon Club, 1996; Paul Harris fellow Rotary Internat., 1998; reception area (lobby) of Miss. State U. Dept. Landscape Architecture donated in his honor by Garden Clubs Miss. Inc., 2003, Edward C. Martin award, Garden Clubs, Mass., 2008, Disting. Alumni medal, U. Ga. Coll. Environ. & Design, 2012. Fellow Am. Soc. Landscape Archs. (chmn. edn. com. 1960-61, pres. Miss. sect. S.W. chpt. 1975, chmn. S.W. chpt. ann. awards com. 1976, trustee Miss. chpt. 1977-81, nominated Jot Carpenter Tchg. medal Miss. chpt. 2006, Landscape Heritage award Fraser Found. Calif. 1986); mem. Nat. Coun. State Garden Clubs (chmn. landscape design 1993-97, Appreciation cert. 2005), Garden Clubs Miss. (bd. dirs. 1958-2005, Silver Trophy 1961, Spl. Silver award 1980, Gold trophy 1993, Appreciation citation 2005), Am. Soc. Landscape Archs. (spkr., spring conf. NC chpt., Asheville, 2009). Presbyterian. Avocations: photography, gardening, writing. Home: 200 Tabernacle Rd Apt 239 K Black Mountain NC 28711-2640 Personal E-mail: edonthemountain@gmail.com.

MARTIN, E.X., III, lawyer; b. Dallas, Sept. 9, 1946; BA, Univ. Okla., 1969; JD, So. Meth. Univ., Dallas, 1972. Bar: Tex. 1972, US Dist. Ct. (no. dist.) Tex. 1977, US Dist. Ct. (no. dist.) Calif. 1980. Felony prosecutor Dallas County Dist. Atty. Office, 1972—76; pvt. practice, fed., state criminal cases Dallas, 1976—. Recipient Nat. Assn. Criminal Def. Lawyers President's Commendation, 1992, Tex. Criminal Def. Lawyers Presidential award, 1992. Mem.: Calif. Attys. for Criminal Justice, Cyberspace Bar Assn. (founder, pres. 1995—), Dallas County Criminal Bar Assn. (past dir.), Tex. Criminal Def. Lawyers Assn., Nat. Assn. Criminal Def. Lawyers, State Bar Tex., Dallas Bar Assn., Phi Alpha Delta. Achievements include being first atty. in Tex. to successfully use computer-generated crime scene animation in a criminal case trial. Office: 8828 Greenville Ave Dallas TX 75243 Office Phone: 214-343-7400. Office Fax: 214-343-4755. Business E-Mail: exmartin@airmail.net.*

MARTIN, FLOYD W., art educator; b. Gainesville, Ga., June 30, 1951; s. Raymond J. and Lois Jean Martin; m. Rebecca Jane Edge, Nov. 30, 1985; 1 child, Mary Rebecca. BA cum laude, Carleton Coll., Northfield, Minn., 1973; MA, U. Iowa, Iowa City, 1975; PhD, U. Ill., Urbana Champaign, 1982. Lectr. U. Ill., Urbana Champaign, 1981—82; prof. art history U. Ark., Little Rock, 1982—, chair dept. art, 1994—95, 2005. Inaugural prof. UA Clinton Sch. of Pub. Svc., Little Rock, 2003—06; bd. dirs. Southeastern Coll. Art Conf., 1986—89, 2001—07, editor, 1991—98, 2007, 1st v.p., 2008—11, pres., 2011—. Flutist: U. Ark. Little Rock Cmty. Orch. Vestry mem. Christ Episcopal Ch., Little Rock, 2000—03, 2007—10; bd. dirs. Friends of KLRE-KUAR Pub. Radio, Little Rock, 1990—96. Recipient Sir George Trevelyan scholarship, Attingham Trust Summer Sch., 1982, AHAS! Spl. award of Distinction, Little Rock Arts and Humanities Promotion Commn., 1996, Exemplary Achievement award, Southeastern Coll. Art Conf., 1999, Pres. award for Svc. in the Arts, 2005; fellow U. Fellowship in Art and Design, U. Ill., 1978-81, Nat. Endowment for the Humanities, 1985; scholar, Victorian Soc. Am., 1980. Mem.: Victorian Soc. in Am., Midwest Art History Assn., Coll. Art Assn., Southeastern Coll. Art Conf., Phi Kappa Phi (pres. U. Ark. Little Rock chpt. 1985—86). Episcopalian. Avocations: opera, gardening. Office: Univ Ark 2801 S University Ave Little Rock AR 72204-1099

MARTIN, FRANK (FRANCISCO J. MARTIN), men's college basketball coach; b. Miami, Fla., Mar. 23, 1966; m. Anya Martin; children: Brandon, Amalia, Christian. B in Phys. Edn., Fla. Internat. U., Miami, 1993. Asst. varsity coach, head jr. varsity coach Miami Sr. HS, Fla., 1985—93, head coach, 1995—99, North Miami Sr. HS, 1993—95, Booker T. Washington HS, 1999—2000; asst. coach Northeastern U. Huskies, Boston, 2000—04, recruiting coord., 2002—04; asst. coach U. Cin. Bearcats, 2004—06, Kans. State U. Wildcats, Manhattan, 2006—07, head coach, 2007—12, U. SC Gamecocks, Columbia, 2012—. Named Coach of Yr., Big 12 Conf., 2010, Dist. VIII Coach of Yr., Nat. Assn. Basketball Coaches, 2010. Office: University South Carolina Basketball Program Rex Enright Athletic Ctr 1300 Rosewood Dr Columbia SC 29208 Office Phone: 803-777-4197.

MARTIN, GARY L., corporate financial executive; BBA, U. Okla.; grad. in Advanced Mgmt. Program, Harvard Bus. Sch. CPA. Pres., CEO Whitmore Mfg. Co., 1979—2007; CFO, v.p., sec., treas. Capital SW Corp., 1972, pres., chmn. Former bd. dirs. Alamo Group Inc., All Components, Inc., Discovery Alliance, LLC., Heelys, Inc., Humac Co., Lifemark Group, The RectorSeal Corp., The Whitmore Mfg. Co. Office: Capital Southwest Corp 12900 Preston Rd Ste 700 Dallas TX 75230 Office Phone: 972-233-8242, 972-233-7362.

MARTIN, GARY WAYNE, lawyer; b. Cin., Feb. 14, 1946; s. Elmer DeForrest and Nellie May (Hughes) M.; m. Debra Lynn Goldsmith, June 25, 1982; children: Christopher, Jeremy, Joie, Casey. BA, Wilmington Coll., 1967; JD, U. Cin., 1974. Bar: Fla. 1974. With Fowler White Boggs, Tampa, Fla., 1974—. Lt. USNR, 1967-73. Mem. Harbour Island Athletic Club. Republican. Presbyterian. Avocation: tennis. Office: Fowler White Boggs 501 E Kennedy Blvd Ste 1700 Tampa FL 33602-5240 Home Phone: 813-287-0079; Office Phone: 813-228-7411. Business E-Mail: gmartin@fowlerwhite.com.

MARTIN, GRACE BURKETT, psychologist; b. Sumter, SC, Aug. 27, 1939; d. John Hazel and Grace Thomasine (Briggs) Burkett; m. H. Russell Jr. Martin, Oct. 9, 1957; children: H. Russell, Carolyne, Melinda. BA magna cum laude, Armstrong State Coll., 1976; MS, Fla. State U., 1979, PhD, 1980. Lic. psychologist. Hist. preservationist, 1962—; dir. Christian Edn. St. Thomas Parish, Savannah, Ga., 1970—74; prof. psychology Armstrong State Coll., Savannah, 1980—2001, prof. emeritus, 2002—, dept. head psychology, dir. gen. studies degree program, head. divsn. social and behavioral scis.; interim dean arts and scis.; pres. Orgn. Cons.; lectr.; radio and TV appearances; author, collaborator nat. and cross-nat. studies of women and work; cons. editor Jour. Supplementary Abstract Svc., 1980—81. Bd. dirs. Coastal Empire YMCA, 1972—75; mem. Savannah Symphony Soc.; mem. commn. mission Episcopal Diocese Ga., 1972—74, mem. liturg. commn., 1972—74, lic. lay reader; pres. Operation Return, 1972—76. Named Mrs. Ga., 1962. Mem.: Ga. Edni. Research Assn., Commerce Club Savannah (charter mem.), Ga. Assn. Women Deans and Adminstrators, Nat. Assn. Women Deans & Administrators, Am. Mgmt. Assn., Soc. Indsl. Organizational Psychology, Southeastern Psychol. Assn., Am. Psychol. Soc. (charter mem.), Am. Psychol. Assn. Home: 50 Shipwatch Rd Savannah GA 31410-2950 Personal E-mail: martingrace@comcast.net.

MARTIN, GRIER, state legislator; m. Louise Martin; 1 child. BA, Davidson Coll., 1991; JD, UNC Sch. Law, 1995; LLM, Judge Advocate General's Sch., 2004. Atty. pvt. practice, 1995—; mem. Dist. 34 NC House of Reps., 2009—. With USAR, 1991—. Democrat. Presbyterian. Office: North Carolina House of Representatives 16 W Jones St Rm 1219 Raleigh NC 27601-1096 Office Phone: 919-733-5758. Business E-Mail: Grier.Martin@ncleg.net.

MARTIN, HARRY CORPENING, lawyer, retired state supreme court justice; b. Lenoir, NC, Jan. 13, 1920; s. Hal C. and Johnsie Harshaw (Nelson) M.; m. Nancy Robiou Dallam, Apr. 16, 1955; children: John, Matthew, Mary. AB, U. N.C., 1942; LLB, Harvard U., 1948; LLM, U. Va., 1982. Bar: N.C. 1948. Pvt. practice, Asheville, NC, 1948-62; judge NC Superior Ct., Asheville, 1962-78, NC Ct. Appeals, Raleigh, 1978-82; justice NC Supreme Ct., 1982-92; ptnr. Martin & Martin, Attys., Hillsborough, 1992—99. Adj. prof. U. N.C. Law Sch., 1983-92, Duke U., 1990-91, Dan K. Moore disting. vis. prof., U. N.C. Law Sch., 1992-94; sr. conf. atty. U.S. Ct. Appeals for 4th Cir., 1994-99; chief justice Supreme Ct. ea. bd. of Cherokee Indians, 2000-2007, ret. With U.S. Army, 1942-45, South Pacific. Mem. U.S. Supreme Ct. Hist. Soc., N.C. Supreme Ct. Hist. Soc. (pres.). Democrat. Episcopalian. Home: 1 Hilltop Rd Asheville NC 28803-3017 Office: Martin Law Firm Asheville NC 28803 Office Phone: 828-274-4633. Personal E-mail: judgemartin@bellsouth.net.

MARTIN, HOWARD W., JR., lawyer; b. Norfolk, Va., Mar. 10, 1942; BS in Bus. Adminstrn., Washington & Lee U., 1964; LLB, U. Va., 1967. Sr. ptnr. Crenshaw Ware & Martin PLC, Norfolk, Va., mng. ptnr. Mem. Norfolk Divsn. Bd. Hampton Roads C. of C., 2001—05; adminstrv. bd. mem. Ghent United Methodist Church, Norfolk, Va., 1978—, chmn., 1984—86; bd. dirs. Tidewater YMCA, 1978—84. Line officer USN, navy lawyer Judge Advocate General's Corp. USN. Mem.: Va. Law Found. (bd. mem. 1990—97, sec. 1993—94, pres. 1995—96, fellow 1997—), Norfolk & Portsmouth Bar Assn. (treas. 1994—96, pres. 1997), Va. Bar Assn. (exec. com. mem. 1987—90, sec. 1989—90), Va. State Bar (coun. mem. 2000—09, exec. com. mem. 2003—09, pres. 2007—08), ABA. Office: Crenshaw Ware & Martin PLC One Commercial Pl 1200 Bank of America Ctr Norfolk VA 23510-2111 Office Phone: 757-623-3000. Office Fax: 757-623-5735. E-mail: hmartin@cwm-law.com.

MARTIN, JAMES KIRBY, historian, educator; b. Akron, Ohio, May 26, 1943; s. Paul Elmo and Dorothy Marie (Garrett) M.; m. Karen Wierwille, Aug. 7, 1965; children: Darcy Elizabeth, Sarah Marie, Joelle Kathryn Garrett. BA summa cum laude, Hiram Coll., 1965; MA, U. Wis., 1967, PhD, 1969. Asst. prof. history Rutgers U., New Brunswick, NJ, 1969-73, assoc. prof., 1973-79, prof., 1979-80, asst. provost, 1972-74, v.p. acad. affairs, 1977-79; vis. prof. Rutgers Ctr. of Alcohol Studies, 1978-88; prof. history U. Houston, 1980-97, disting. univ. prof., 1997—, chmn. dept., 1980-83; vis. prof. history Rice U., Houston, 1992. Chmn. bd. sponsors Papers of Thomas Edison Project, 1977-80; founding ptnr. PastQuest Rsch. Svcs., 1999. Author: Men in Rebellion, 1973, In the Course of Human Events, 1979, (with M.E. Lender) A Respectable Army: The Military Origins of the Republic, 1982, 2d edit., 2006, (contemporary mil. reading list), Drinking in America: A History, 1982, rev. edit. 1987, (with others) America and Its Peoples, 1989, 5th edit. 2004, concise edit. 1995, Benedict Arnold: Revolutionary Hero, 1997 (Homer D. Babbidge, Jr. award), audio edit., 2001,(with J.T. Glatthaar) Forgotten Allies: Oneida Indians and the American Revolution, 2006; editor: Interpreting Colonial America, 1973, 2d edit. 1978, The Human Dimensions of Nation Making, 1976, (with K. Stubaus) The American Revolution, Whose Revolution?, 1977, 81, (with M.E. Lender) Citizen-Soldier: The Revolutionary War Journal of Joseph Bloomfield, 1982 (R.P. McCormick prize), Ordinary Courage: The Revolutionary War Adventures of Joseph Plumb Martin, 1993, 2d edit., 1999, 3rd edit., 2008; mem. editl. bd. Papers of William Livingston Project, 1973-80, Houston Rev., 1981-2003, N.J. History, 1986—, Conversations with the Past Series, 1993-95; gen. editor Am. Social Experience Series, 1983-2002; advisory editor, Critical Historical Encounters Series, Oxford U., 2007-. Recipient N.J. Soc. of the Cin. prize for Disting. Achievement in Am. History, 1995, Hiram Coll. Alumni Achievement award, 1996. Mem. Tex. Assn. for Advancement History (bd. dirs. 1981-93, v.p. 1986-90), Inst. for Internat. Bus. Analysis (adv. coun. 1982-86), Am. Hist. Assn. (Beveridge-Dunning prize com. 1990-93), Orgn. Am. Historians, So. Hist. Assn., Soc. Historians Early Am. Republic (adv. coun. 1985-88), Soc. for Mil. History, Phi Beta Kappa, Phi Kappa Phi, Pi Gamma Mu, Omicron Delta Kappa, Phi Alpha Theta. Office: U Houston Dept History 524 Arnold Hall Houston TX 77204-3003

MARTIN, JAMES LARENCE, dentist, educator; b. Dubuque, Iowa, Sept. 3, 1940; s. James Larence and Ada Virginia (Boone) M.; m. Willie Mae Walker, Jan. 23, 1941; children: Linda Gail, James Larence III, John Lance. BS, Loras Coll., Dubuque, 1959, LittD, 1982; MS, Tenn. State U., 1960; DDS, Meharry Med. Coll., 1966; MPH, U. Mich., 1975. Dental dir. children and youth Meharry Med. Coll., Nashville, 1967-72, acting dir. children and youth program, 1972-73, dir. primary dental svcs., 1973-75, coord. dental component Ctr. for Health Care Rsch., 1975-77, prof., 1981—; owner Martin Dental, Nashville, 1980—. Dental cons. Medically Dedicated, Washington, 1992—; pres. faculty senate Meharry Med. Coll., 1989-93, mem. pres.'s exec. mgmt. team, 1989-93, dir. divsn. dental public health 1999—, chmn. dept. dental pub. health, 1999—. Contbr. articles to profl. jours., chpts. to books. Bd. regents Loras Coll., 1997—. Recipient Meritorious Svc. award Acad. Oral Medicine, 1977. Mem. ADA, Am. Pub. Health Assn. (med. com.), Am. Assn. Pub. Health Dentistry, Nat. Assn. Cmty. Health Ctrs., Am. Acad. Goil Foil Operators, Soc. of the Upper 10th, Nashville Area C. of C., Beta Kappa Chi, Phi Sigma. Achievements include discovery of leukoedema in childrem. Avocations: reading, swimming, photography. Home: 3515 Geneva Cir Nashville TN 37209-2524 Office: 908 34th Ave N Nashville TN 37209-2502 Personal E-mail: jmarti3817@aol.com.

MARTIN, JAMES RUSSELL, lawyer; b. Columbus, Ohio, June 24, 1947; s. Robert Wells and Gwendolyn (Collins) M.; m. Susan Virginia Jarman, Aug. 4, 1973; children: James Russell Jr., Elizabeth Collins. BA in History, Denison U., Granville, Ohio, 1969; JD, U. Denver, 1972. Bar: Colo. 1972, U.S. Dist. Ct. Colo. 1972. Assoc. Brundage & Yates, Denver, 1973; asst. atty. gen. State of Colo., Denver, 1974-76; assoc. Thomas & Esperti PC, 1976—78; v.p. Butterwick Enterprises Ltd., Denver, 1978-81, pres., 1981-83; ptnr. Baker & Hostetler LLP, Denver, 1985—2004; sr. v.p., gen. counsel, clerk Bluegreen Corp., Boca Raton, Fla., 2004—. Mem.: ABA, Authorized House Coun., Fla., Assn. Corp. Counsel, Denver Bar Assn., Colo. Bar Assn., Am. Resort Devel. Assn. Avocations: skiing, tennis, bicycling. Office: Bluegreen Corp 4960 Conference Way N Ste 100 Boca Raton FL 33431 Business E-Mail: jim.martin@bluegreencorp.com.

MARTIN, JENNY BETH, political organization worker, consultant; Attended, Reinhardt Coll., Waleska, Ga., U. Ga. Terry Coll. Bus. Co-owner Computer Health Spa, Woodstock, Ga., 2008—; state coord. Ga. Tea Party Patriots, 2009—; co-founder, co-coord. Atlanta Tea Party, 2009—; co-founder, nat. coord. Tea Party Patriots, 2009—. Nat. co-coord. 912 March on DC Tea Party Movement, 2009—; dir. political ops. Smart Girl Politics orgn. (smartgirlpolitics.ning.com). Writer (weblog) JenuineJen.com. Named one of The 100 Most Influential People in the World, TIME mag., 2010. Republican. Office: Atlanta Tea Party LLC 809 Roxholly Ln Buford GA 30518-8519 E-mail: jennybethm@gmail.com.

MARTIN, JERRY E. (GERALD E. MARTIN), lawyer, former federal prosecutor; b. Murfreesboro, Tenn., Mar. 10, 1974; Attended, Univ. Coll. Galway, Ireland; BA cum laude, Dartmouth Coll., Hanover, NH, 1996; JD, Stanford Law Sch., Calif., 1999. Adminstrv. aide Democratic Leadership Coun., Washington, 1996; law clk. Legal Aid of East Tenn., Knoxville, 1997; law clk. Office Atty. Gen. State of Tenn., Nashville, 1998; assoc. Wyatt, Tarrant & Combs LLP, Nashville, 1998, assoc. litig. dept., 1999—2000; legislative analyst to Rep. Robert Clement US House of Representatives, Washington, 1998; rschr. Cornerstone Rsch., Menlo Park, Calif., 1999; assoc. litig. dept. Bass, Berry & Sims PLC, Nashville, 2000—03; assoc. Barrett, Johnston & Parsley, Nashville, 2003—07, ptnr., 2007—10; US atty. (middle dist.) Tenn. US Dept. Justice, 2010—13; of counsel Robbins Geller Rudman & Dowd LLP, 2013—. Investor Creative Restaurant Group, LLC, Nashville, 2002—06. Finance dir. Jim Cooper's Congressional Campaign, Tenn., 2002; bd. dirs. Autism Soc. Middle Tenn. Mem.: ABA, Nashville Bar Assn., Tenn. Bar Assn. Office: Robbins Geller Rudman & Dowd LLP 217 Second Ave North Nashville TN 37201 Office Phone: 800-449-4900. Office Fax: 615-252-3798. E-mail: jmartin@rgrdlaw.com.*

MARTIN, JOHN CHARLES, judge; b. Durham, NC, Nov. 9, 1943; s. Chester Barton and Mary Blackwell (Pridgen) Martin; m. Margaret Rand; children: Lauren M. Smith, Sarah M. Morgan, Susan M. Prince stepchildren: Louise Short, Carl (Trip) Short. BA, Wake Forest U., 1965, JD, 1967; postgrad., Nat. Judicial Coll., Reno, 1979; cert. justice execs. program, U. NC, 1982. Bar: NC 1967, US Dist. Ct. (mid. dist.) NC 1967, US Dist. Ct. (ea. dist.) NC 1972, US Dist. Ct. (we. dist.) NC 1975, US Ct. Appeals (4th cir.) 1976, US Supreme Ct. 2002. Assoc. Haywood, Denny & Miller, Durham, N.C., 1969-72, ptnr., 1973-77; resident judge Superior Ct. 14th Jud. Dist. N.C., Durham, 1977-84; judge N.C. Ct. Appeals, Raleigh, 1985—88, 1993—2004, chief judge, 2004—; ptnr. Maxwell & Hutson, P.A., Durham, 1988-92; arbitrator U.S. Dist. Ct. (mid. dist.) N.C., 1988-92. Study com. rules of evidence and comparative negligence NC Legis. Rsch. Commn., 1980; mem. NC Pattern Jury Instrn. drafting com., 1978-84, NC Trial Judge's Bench Book Drafting Com., 1984-87, NC News Media-Adminstrn. of Justice Coun., 1987, state/fed. Jud. Coun. NC, 1985-87, chmn., 1987; bd. visitors Wake Forest U. Sch. Law, 1986—; mem. alumni coun. Wake Forest U., 1993-96, 2001—04; mem. NC Jud. Coun., 2004-; mem. NC State Jud. Edn. Study Com., 2000-2003, NC Jud. Coll. Adv. Coun., 2004-; chmn. NC Jud. Stds. Commn., 2001-2014; exec. com. mem. Chief Justice's Commn. Professionalism, 2004-. Mem. Durham City Coun., 1975—77, chair pub. works com.; panel of arbitrators Duke U. Pvt. Adjudication Ctr., 1988—92; mem. parent adv. bd. Chatham Hall Sch., 2003—05; mem. parent coun. Wake Forest U., 2006—09; bd. dirs. Appalachian State U. Parents Assn., 1997—2001. With Mil. Police Corps USAR, 1967—69. Recipient Disting. Svc. award Durham Jaycees, 1976. Mem.: ABA, Appellate Judges Conf., Coun. of Chief Judges State Ct. Appeals (mem. edn. com. 2008, mem. fin. com. 2009-, mem. exec. com., 2010-, sec.-treas., 2012, pres.-elect, 2013, pres. 2013-14), Am. Judicature Soc., NC Bar Assn. (chmn. adminstrn. of justice study com. 1990-92, bench, bar and law sch. com. 1987-91, jud. campaign oversight com. 1990, Lit. Sect. Coun. 1991-94, conv. planning com. 1995-98, adminstrn. justice task force 1996-98, appellate rules study com. 1999-2001, strategic planning/emerging trends com. 2002-04, endowment com. 2004—, v.p. 1997-98, John J. Parker award, 2013), Durham County Bar Assn. (bd. dirs. 1991-92), Wake County Bar Assn., 10th Jud. Dist. Bar Assn., NC Jud. Conf. (v.p. 1999-00), Phi Delta Phi. Democrat. Episcopalian. Office: PO Box 888 Raleigh NC 27602-0888 Office Phone: 919-831-3700. Business E-Mail: jmartin@coa.nccourts.org.

MARTIN, JOHN K., broadcast executive; b. 1968; married; 1 child. BS in Economics, U. Pa. Wharton Sch. Bus., 1989; MBA in Financial & Orgnl. Behavior, Columbia U., 1994. CPA Ernst & Young LLP, NY; mgr., SEC financial reporting Time Warner, Inc., 1993, dir., Financial Special Projects, dir., Office of Pres., v.p. investor rels., 1999—2000; dir., Equity Rsch. Grp. ABN AMRO Securities LLC, 2000—02; sr. v.p. investor rels. Time Warner, Inc., 2002—05, exec. v.p., CFO, 2007—10, exec. v.p., CFO, chief adminstrv. officer, 2011—14; exec. v.p., CFO Time Warner Cable, 2005—07; CEO Turner Broadcasting System, Inc., 2014—. Client adv. bd. Thomson Fin. Services; mem. Conf. Bd. Global Coun. of Investor Rels. Executives. Named Next Generation analyst for cable TV industy, Institutional Investor, 2001; named one of The 40 Executives Under 40, Multichannel News, 2006. Mem.: Mus. TV & Radio, Nat. Investor Rels. Inst. Office: Turner Broadcasting System Inc One CNN Ctr Atlanta GA 30303*

MARTIN, LARRY A., state legislator; b. Greenville, SC, June 20, 1957; s. Edgar M. and Lois B. Martin; m. Susan Evatt, 1983; children: Caroline Elizabeth, Larry Anthony Jr., Anna Leigh. Dir. safety Alice Mfg. Co., 1981—; mem. Dist. 2 SC State Senate, 1993—, chair Rules Com., mem. Banking and Ins. Com., Edn. Com., Gen. Com. & Judiciary Com. Recipient SC 4-H Alumni award, 1983. Mem.: Partnership Area & Career Edn., 4-H Found., United Way, Rocky BoHom Camp of Blind. Republican. Baptist. Mailing: PO Box 247 Pickens SC 29671 Office: 311 Gressette Bldg PO Box 142 Columbia SC 29201 Home Phone: 864-878-6105; Office Phone: 864-306-2126, 803-212-6340. Fax: 864-859-6328. E-mail: lam@legis.lpitr.state.sc.us.

MARTIN, LINDA GAYE, demographer, economist; b. Paris, Ark., Dec. 17, 1947; d. Leslie Paul and Margie La Verne (Thomas) Martin. BA in Math., Harvard U., 1970; MPA, Princeton U., 1972, PhD in Econs., 1978; DHL (hon.), Marlboro Coll., 2002; D in Pub. Policy (hon.), Rand Grad. Sch., 2006. Dir. mgmt. info. sr. ctrs. bur. purchased social svcs. for adults City of N.Y., 1972—74; rsch. assoc., rsch. dir. U.S. Ho. of Reps. Select Com. on Population, Washington, 1977—79; rsch. assoc. East-West Population Inst., Honolulu, 1979—89, asst. dir., 1982—84; asst. prof. econs. U. Hawaii, Honolulu, 1979—81, assoc. prof., 1981—89, prof., 1989; dir. com. on population Nat. Acad. Scis., Washington, 1989—93; dir. domestic rsch. divsn., v.p. RAND, Santa Monica, Calif., 1993—95, v.p. for rsch. devel., 1995—99, sr. fellow, 2007—; pres. Population Coun., NYC, 1999—2004; scholar in residence Inst. Medicine, 2004—07; adj. prof., Bloomberg Sch. Pub. Health Johns Hopkins U., 2007—. Neurosci. behavior and sociology of aging rev. com. Nat. Inst. on Aging, Bethesda, 1991—95; chair panel on aging in developing countries NAS, Washington, 1987, com. on population, 1993—99, panel on internat. aging data, 1999—2001; peer rev. oversight group NIH, 1998—2004. Editor: The ASEAN Success Story, 1987; co-editor: Demographic Change in Sub-Saharan Africa, 1993, The Demography of Aging, 1994, Racial and Ethnic Differences in the Health of Older Americans, 1997; contbr. articles to profl. jours. Mem. adv. coun. Woodrow Wilson Sch. Pub. and Internat. Affairs, Princeton U., NJ, 2000—08. Recipient Fulbright Faculty Rsch. award, Coun. for Internat. Exch. of Scholars, 1988. Fellow: Am. Assn. Advancement Sci.; mem.: AAAS (adv. coun. 2003—06, chair social, econ. and polit. scis. sect. 2007—08), Population Assn. Am. (bd. dir. 1991—93), Internat. Union for Sci. Study Population, Gerontol. Soc. Am. Democrat. Home: 3419 Mansfield Rd Falls Church VA 22041 Office: RAND Corp 1200 S Hayes St Arlington VA 22202

MARTIN, MARK D., state supreme court justice; b. Apr. 29, 1963; s. M. Dean and Ann Martin. Student, U. Dayton; BS summa cum laude, We. Carolina U., 1985; JD (hon.), U. NC, 1988; grad., Nat. Jud. Coll., 1993; LLM, U. Va., 1998. Bar: NC, US Dist. Ct. (ea. and mid. dists.) NC, US Ct. Appeals (4th cir.), US Supreme Ct. Law clk. to Hon. Clyde H. Hamilton US Dist. Ct., Columbia, SC, 1988-90; pvt. practice McNair Law Firm, Raleigh, NC, 1990-91; legal counsel to gov. Office of Gov., Raleigh, NC, 1991-92; superior ct. judge Jud. Dist. 3A, Greenville, NC, 1992-94; judge NC Ct. Appeals, 1994-99; assoc. justice Supreme Ct. NC, Raleigh, 1999—2006, sr. assoc. justice, 2006—. Mem. legis. and law reform com. Conf. Superior Ct. Judges; sec. NC Jud. Conf., co-chair legis. liaison com.; adj. prof. law U. NC, Chapel Hill; adj. faculty NC Ctrl. U. Sch. Law; sr. lecturing fellow Duke U. Law Sch.; chair Chief Justice's Commn. Future NC Bus. Ct. Editor-in-chief: Jour Internat. Law and Comml. Regulation. Office coord. United Way Ann. Combined Campaign, 1991, 1992; mem. master plan adv. com. N.C. Dept. Correction, 1992; mem. N.C. Coun. Women, 1992. Recipient Order Long Leaf Pine, Disting. Alumnus award, Western Carolina U., Svc. award, City of Raleigh Cmty. Svc. Dept., Book award, Sci. Methods for Lawyers; Lloyd C. Balfour fellow, N.C. Inst. Polit. Leadership fellow, Coun. State Govt. Toll fellow. Mem.: ABA (editl. bd. Judges' Jour., coalition justice com., commn. state ct. funding, John Marshall award rev. com., nominating com., com. to develop nat. issues forum programs on Am. jury, coalition for justice rep., com. to develop nat. issues forum programs on separation of powers, adv. commn. World Justice Project, program chair jud. divsn., edn. chair appellate judges conf., exec. com., Appellate Judges Conf., sec. Appellate Judges Conf., co-chair presidential commn. on fair and impartial ct., vice chair, chair elect. Appellate Judges Conf., chair Justice Ctr. Coordinating Coun., chair bd. elections), Am. Law Inst., Am. Judicature Soc. (nat. adv. coun. mem.), Appellate Judges Ednl. Inst. (chair, program planning com., bd. dirs.), Mortar Bd., Wake County Bar Assn. (bd. dirs., continuing legal edn. presenter), Assn. NC Women Attys., NC Assn. Black Lawyers, NC Bar Assn. (strategic planning emerging trends com., litig. sect. coun., v.p., multidisciplinary practice task force, minorities profession com., program com. 2004 Brown v. Bd. Edn. 50th anniversary), Carolina Law Alumni Assn. (bd. dirs.), U. NC Law Davis Soc., Rotary, Internat. Hon. Soc., Beta Gamma Sigma, Delta Sigma Phi (scholar), Phi Alpha Delta, Omicron Delta Epsilon, Pi Gamma Mu, Phi Kappa Phi, Alpha Lambda Delta. Office: NC Supreme Ct PO Box 2170 Raleigh NC 27602-2170 Office Phone: 919-831-5712. Business E-Mail: maj@sc.state.nc.us, mmartin@sc.state.nc.us.*

MARTIN, MARK RUSSELL, state official, former state legislator; b. Kansas City, Kans., Feb. 18, 1968; m. Sharon Martin; children: Rachel, Joshua, Rebekah. BSME, Univ. Ark., Fayetteville, 1998. Pres. PsyberSimula, 1998—2002; v.p. rsch. & tech. Engring. Inst. Inc., 2002—06; pres. MS Engring. Inc., 2008—11; mem. Dist. 87 Ark. House of Reps., Little Rock, 2005—11; sec. of state State of Ark., 2011—. Mem.: American Soc. Mech. Engineers, Ark. Soc. Mech. Engineers (vice-chmn.), Internat. Soc. Biomechanics, Nat. Soc. Profl. Engineers (bd. dir. 2002—03). Republican. Baptist. Office: Office of the Secretary of State 256 State Capitol Building Little Rock AR 72201 Office Phone: 501-682-1010. Office Fax: 501-682-3510. E-mail: sos@sos.arkansas.gov.*

MARTIN, NORMAN MARSHALL, computer science educator; b. Chgo., Jan. 16, 1924; s. Harry Eugene and Fay Cohen; m. Emilia Regina van Deene, Aug. 16, 1950; children: Gabrielle Block, Gwenwyn (Wendy) Janett. Student, Central YMCA Coll., 1940—42; MA, U. Chgo., 1947; postgrad., U. Amsterdam, Netherlands, 1949-50; PhD, U. Calif. at Los Angeles, 1952. Instr. philosophy U. Ill. at Urbana, 1950-51, UCLA, 1952-53; research asso. Willow Run Research Center, U. Mich., 1953-55; mem. tech. staff Space Tech. Labs., El Segundo, Calif., 1955-61, head logic techniques group, 1957-61; staff logician, dir. Logicon, Inc., Torrance, Calif., 1961—65, treas. LA, 1962-65; assoc. prof. philosophy U. Tex. at Austin, 1965-68, assoc. prof. computer sci., 1966-68, prof. philosophy and computer sci., 1968-74, prof. philosophy, computer sci. and elec. and computer engring., 1974-90, prof. emeritus, 1990—, assoc. chmn. computer sci., 1975-78. Lectr. engring. UCLA, 1956-65; cons. Logicon, Inc., 1965-71. Author: Systems of Logic, 1989, Closure Spaces and Logic, 1996. Served with F.A. & ICD AUS, 1943-45. Decorated Purple Heart., Croix du combattant Volontaire; Fulbright grantee Netherlands, 1949 Mem. Am. Math Soc., Am. Philos. Assn., Assn. Symbolic Logic, Assn. Computing Machinery, Sigma Xi. Democrat. Unitarian Universalist. Home: 4200 Jackson Ave 5026 Austin TX 78731 E-mail: martin@cs.utexas.edu.

MARTIN, PETER ROBERT, psychiatrist, pharmacologist; b. Budapest, Hungary, Sept. 6, 1949; arrived in US, 1980, naturalized, 1987; s. Nicholas M. and Eva (Horvat) M.; m. Barbara Bradford, Dec. 23, 1985; 1 child, Alexander Bradford. BSc with honors, McGill U., Montreal, Que., Can., 1971, MD, CM, 1975; MSc, U. Toronto, Ont., Can., 1978. Diplomate Am. Bd. Psychiatry and Neurology, Psychiatry, Addiction Psychiatry. Resident in internal medicine U. Toronto, 1975-76, resident in psychiatry, 1978-80; fellow clin. pharmacology Addiction Rsch. Found., Toronto, 1976-78; chief sect. clin. sci. Nat. Inst. on Alcohol Abuse & Alcoholism, Bethesda, 1983-86; assoc. prof. Vanderbilt U. Sch. Medicine, Nashville, 1986-92, prof., 1992—, dir. divsn. addiction psychiatry, 1986—2013, dir. addiction ctr., 1994—; dir. Vanderbilt Inst. for Coffee Studies, 1999—. Vis. scientist Lab. of Clin. Sci., NIMH, Bethesda, Md., 1980-83; investigator John F. Kennedy Ctr. for Rsch. on Human Devel., Nashville, 1993—. Fellow Royal Coll. Physicians (Can.), Am. Psychiat. Assn. (disting.), Am. Acad. Addiction Psychiatry (disting.); mem. AAAS, Rsch. Soc. on Alcoholism, Internat. Soc. Biomed. Rsch. in Alcoholism, Internat. Network History of Neuropsychopharmacology (mem. operating com.). Avocations: reading, writing, exercise, sports. Office: Vanderbilt Psychiat Hosp Ste 3068 1601 23rd Ave South Nashville TN 37212 Office Phone: 615-322-0387.

MARTIN, R. BRAD, bank executive; b. Nov. 5, 1951; BA, U. Memphis, 1976; MBA, Vanderbilt U., 1980. Chmn. RBM Venture Co.; mem. Dist. 94 Tenn. House of Representatives, 1973—82; chmn. Saks Inc., 1987—2007, CEO, 1989—2006. Bd. dirs. Lululemon Athletica Inc.; bd. dir. First Tenn. Corp., Harrah's Entertainment, Pilot Corp.; bd. dirs. First Horizon Nat. Corp., 1994—, Ruby Tuesday, Inc., 2008—, Dillard's, Inc., 2008—. Achievements include being youngest person elected to Tenn. Gen. Assembly. Office: Dillards Inc Bd Directors 1600 Cantrell Rd Little Rock AR 72201 also: RBM Venture Co 5810 Shelby Oaks Dr Memphis TN 38134-7315 Office Phone: 865-379-5700, 901-372-4300. Office Fax: 865-379-5004. Business E-Mail: rmartin@rubytuesday.com.

MARTIN, ROBERT SIDNEY, librarian, educator; b. Houston, Aug. 13, 1949; s. Sidney A. and Elizabeth Ann Martin. BA, Rice U., 1971; MLS, U. N. Tex., 1979; PhD, U. N.C., 1988; LHD (hon.), Dominican U., 2006. Libr. assoc. U. Tex., Austin, 1972-76, libr. Arlington, 1977-80; debt claims adjustor US Gen. Acctg. Office, Washington, 1977; instr. Sch. Libr. and Info. Sci. U. Wis., Madison, 1984; assoc. dean Librs. La. State U., Baton Rouge, 1985-95; dir., libr. Tex. State Libr. and Archives Commn., Austin, 1995—99; prof., interim dir. Sch. Library and Info. Studies, Texas Women's U., 1999—2001, Lillian Bradshaw endowed chair, 2005—; dir. The Inst. Mus. & Library Services, Washington, 2001—05. Co-author: Contours of Discovery, 1982, Maps of Texas and the Southwest, 1513-1900, 1984 (Kate Broock Bates award 1985); editor: Scholarly Communication in an Electronic Environment: Issues for Research, 1993, Carnegie Denied: Communities Rejecting Carnegie Library Construction Grants, 1993; mem. editl. bd. Am. Archivist, 1994-01, Libr. Quar., 1995-01, Libraries and Culture, 1999-01, Libraries and the Cultural Record, 2005-, Encyclopedia of Library and Information Sciences, 2005-. Exec. bd. Urban Libraries Coun., 2006—; bd. dirs. Inst. Learning Innovation, 2006—; mem. Nat. Coun. Humanities, 2006—, US Nat. Commn. UNESCO, 2004—, exec. com., 2005—. Recipient Presdl. Citizens medal, 2008. Fellow Soc. Am. Archivists; mem. ALA (councilor 1998-01), Nat. Assn. Govt. Archivists and Records Adminstrs. (mem. exec. bd. 1996—), Tex. Map Soc. (v.p. 1996-00), Book Club Tex. (v.p. 1996-00). Avocations: hiking, photography, music.

MARTIN, ROGER JOHN, computer scientist; b. Ft. Atkinson, Iowa, Sept. 11, 1947; s. Raymond Charles and Linda R. (Kuennen) M.; m. Jane Degnan, Nov. 21, 1970; children: John, Kathryn, Susan, Jacquelyn. BS in Computer Sci., Iowa State U., 1969, MS in Computer Sci., 1971. Computer specialist Naval Ship R & D Ctr., Bethesda, Md., 1971-76; supervisory sys. analyst Exec. Office of Pres., Washington, 1976-82; computer scientist, mgr. software engring. group Inst. Computer Scis. and Tech., Nat. Inst. Stds. and Tech., Washington, 1982-92, chief sys. and software tech. divsn., 1993-95, mgr. software methods, 1995-96; mgr. stds. strategy. Sun Microsys., Palo Alto, Calif., 1996—2002; dir. stds. AOL, LLC, Dulles, Va., 2002—10. Program co-chmn. Conf. on Software Maintenance, 1985, gen. mgr., 1987; gen. chmn. Computer Stds. Conf., 1988. Soccer coach Montgomery Country Recreation Dept., Rockville, Md., 1979-83; treas., del. Mill Creek Towne Elem. Sch. PTA, Rockville, 1981-84, pres., 1986-87; Magruder clustr PTA coord., 1984-856; leader Cub Scouts Am., Rockville, 1983-84, asst. troop scoutmaster, 1984-92. Recipient award for tech. excellence Interagy. Com. on Info. Resources Mgmt., 1989, Fed. Computer Week 100 award, 1992, cert. of recognition Nat. Bur. Stds., 1983, bronze medal Dept. Commerce, 1984, silver medal, 1989, Hans Karlsson award IEEE, 1995, Standards Medallion, 1992. Mem. Assn. for Computing Machinery, IEEE Computer Soc. (chmn. working group on test methods for POSIX 1986-93, tech. com. on conformance testing 1989-94, mem. tech. com. on operating sys. project mgmt. com. 1991-93, cert. of recognition 1987, Meritorious Svc. award 1991, Stds. medal 1992).

MARTIN, SANDRA J. (SANDY MARTIN), corporate financial executive; BBA in Acctg., U. Tex., Arlington; MBA, Tex. Christian U. CPA. Sr. auditor Touche Ross; dir., fin., reporting & investments, dir., fin. planning & analysis Pier 1 Imports, various positions, 1992—2006; v.p., investor rels. Sally Beauty Holdings, 2006—08; corp. contr., chief acctg. Officer Entech Solar, Inc., CFO, 2009—. Office: Entech Solar Inc Ste 100 641 Industrial Blvd Grapevine TX 76051-3915 Office Phone: 817-379-0100. Office Fax: 817-379-0300. Business E-Mail: smartin@entechsolar.com.

MARTIN, SCOTT, state legislator; b. Tulsa, Okla., Dec. 28, 1971; s. Lavaughn and Phyllis (Penland) Martin; m. Angela Berglan; children: Luke, Blake. BS in Polit. Sci., Univ. Okla., 1995. Bank officer; projects dir. City of Noble, Okla., 1995—99, pub works dir., 1999; asst to city mgr. City of Norman, Okla., 1999—2006; mem. Dist. 46 Okla. House of Representatives, 2007—. Mem.: Newcastle C. of C., Noble C. of C., Norman C. of C., Norman Bus. Assn., U. Okla. Alumni Assn., Nat. Rifle Assn. (life). Republican. Baptist. Address: 2916 Stonebridge Ct Norman OK 73071-1704 Office: 2100 N Lincoln Blvd Rm 335 Oklahoma City OK 73105 Home Phone: 405-701-8811; Office Phone: 405-557-7329. E-mail: scott.martin@okhouse.gov.

MARTIN, SHANE, state legislator; b. Spartanburg, SC, Dec. 31, 1971; s. Shellie and Cheryl Martin; m. Amy M. Martin, June 7, 1997; children: Ashlyn, Aidan. BS, Clemson U., 1994, MS, 1999. Bd. mem. Spartanburg Co. Sch. Dist. Six, 2005; mem. Amer. Soc. of Mech. Engrs., 1994—; mem. Dist. 13 SC State Senate, 2008—. Republican. Bapt. Mailing: 2741 Glenn Springs Rd Spartanburg SC 29302 Office: Capitol Office 501 Gressette Bldg Columbia SC 29201 Home Phone: 864-597-1619; Office Phone: 864-585-4933, 803-212-6100. E-mail: shanemartin@scsenate.org.

MARTIN, STACEY, public accountant; d. Orval Calvin and Adella Aloise (Morgan) M.; m. Bryan Keith Ellis, Jan. 31, 1987 (div.); children: Martin Harrison, Morgan Houston Ellis. BA in Bus. Adminstrn., Austin Coll., 1973; MBA in Acctg., So. Meth. U., 1974. CPA, 1982. Jr. acct. MacIver & Bell, CPA's, Dallas, 1974-76; staff acct. Steak & Ale Restaurants, Inc., Dallas, 1975-76; internal auditor Columbia Gen. Corp., Dallas, 1976-80; tax specialist MARC, Inc., Dallas, 1981—2003; owner Curves Dallas Northwest, 2004—08; sr. acct. Point Group, Dallas, 2006—11; tax mgr. Encompass Home Health, 2011—. Owner Sallie's Baby, Infant & Toddler Knitwear, 1988—, Wooly Reds, 2012-. Mem. Greenland Hills Neighborhood Assn., Dallas, 1983-94, Dallas Heritage Soc., 1987, Dallas Arboretum Soc., 1987; treas. MacArthur HS, PTA BD., Irving, Tex., 2009-11, treas. Jack E. Sinocey Acad., PTSA, 2012-14 Mem. AICPA, PTA (life), Tex. Soc. CPA's, DAR (treas. White Oak chpt. 1988—), United Daus. of the Confederacy (treas. Gen. Richard Gano chpt. 2002—), Daus. Republic of Tex. (treas. Peter James Bailey chpt. 1993—), Irving Heritage Soc., (bd. mem., 2012-), Irving Elks Lodge, Austin Coll. Alumni Bd. Republican. Methodist. Office: Encompass Home Health 6688 N Central Expy Ste 1300 Dallas TX 75206

MARTIN, STEPHEN F., chemist, educator, researcher; BS, U. N.Mex., 1968; PhD, Princeton U., 1972. Alexander von Humboldt stipendiat Inst. fur Organische Chemie U. Munich, 1972-73; NIH postdoctoral fellow MIT, 1973-74; M. June and J. Virgil Waggoner Regents Chair in chemistry, prof. U. Tex., Austin. Contbr. articles to profl. jours. Recipient Rsch. Career Devel. award NIH, 1980-85, Arthur C. Cope Scholar award Am. Chem. Soc., 1996, Alexander von Humboldt Sr. Scientist award, 1995-97, Japan Soc. for Promotion of Sci. award, 2001, Wyeth Rsch. award, 2003. Fellow: AAAS. Office: Chem & Biochem Dept Univ Texas 1 University Sta A5300 Austin TX 78712-1095 Office Phone: 512-471-3915. Office Fax: 512-471-4180. Business E-Mail: sfmartin@mail.utexas.edu.

MARTIN, STEPHEN HOLIDAY, state legislator; b. Chesterfield County, Va., June 15, 1956; m. Sharon Christine Wiley; children: Stephen Chad, Nathan Tyler. Ins. cons. Martin Fin. Svc.; chmn. Am. Legis. Exch. Coun.; state del. Dist. 27 Va., 1988—94; former mem. Gen. Laws Com., Health, Welfare & Inst. Com., Mining & Mineral Resources Com.; state senator Dist. 11 Va., 1994—; mem. Chesterfield Emergency Planning Commn., Nat. Edn. & Health Task Forces, Gen. Laws Com., Edn. & Health Com., Local Govt. & Privileges Com., Elections Com. Recipient Nat. Sales Achievement award, 1985—86, Nat Quality award, Nat. Assn. Life Underwriters, 1985; named Legislator of Yr., Coun. Affordable Health Ins., 1993, Am. Legislature Exch. Coun. Empowerment, 1994; fellow, Life Underwriting Tng. Coun. Mem.: Chesterfield Alternatives Inc. (former sec., pres. & bd. chmn.), Chesterfield Bus. Coun., Nat. Assn. Security Dealers, Richmond Assn. Life Underwriters. Republican. Baptist. Mailing: PO Box 36147 Richmond VA 23235-8003 Office: Dist Off PO Box 700 Chesterfield VA 23832 Fax: 804-674-7241. Business E-Mail: district11@sov.state.va.us. E-mail: martindistrict@comcast.net.

MARTIN, STEVE, state legislator; m. Barbara Martin; 3 children. Mem. Dist 10 Okla. House of Representatives, 2005—. Republican. Office: Oklahoma House of Representatives 2300 N Lincoln Blvd Rm 330 Oklahoma City OK 73105 Mailing: 2458 Country Road 3102 Bartlesville OK 74003 Office Phone: 405-557-7402. E-mail: stevemartin@okhouse.gov.

MARTIN, STEVEN J., corporate financial executive; BA in Acctg., U. Memphis, 1981. Sr. v.p., corp., comptr. Promus; audit ptnr. Arthur Anderson, LLP, 1985—99; sr. v.p., CFO TruGreen Companies, 2000—03, TruGreen LawnCare, 2003—07, Servicemaster Co., Servicemaster Global Holdings, 2007—. Office: The ServiceMaster Co 860 Ridge Lake Blvd Memphis TN 38120 Office Phone: 901-597-1400. Office Fax: 630-663-2001. Business E-Mail: Steve.Martin@servicemaster.com.

MARTIN, THOMAS LYLE, JR., academic administrator; b. Memphis, Sept. 26, 1921; s. Thomas Lyle and Malvina (Rucks) M.; m. Helene Hartley, June 12, 1943 (dec. Sept. 1983); children: Michele Marie, Thomas Lyle; m. Mildred L. Moore, June 5, 1984. B.E.E., Rensselaer Poly. Inst., 1942, M.E.E., 1948, D.Eng., 1967; PhD, Stanford U., 1951; DSc (hon.), So. Meth. U., 2004. Prof. elec. engring. U. N.Mex., 1948-53; prof. engring. U. Ariz., 1953-63, dean engring., 1958-63, U. Fla., Gainesville, 1963-66, So. Meth. U., Dallas, 1966-74; pres. Ill. Inst. Tech., Chgo., 1974-87, pres. emeritus. Capt. Signal Corps AUS, 1943-46. Mem. ASEE Hall of Fame. Fellow IEEE; mem. Nat. Acad. Engring. Achievements include being one of the founders of Dallas-Ft. Worth Internat. Airport. Home and Office: PO Box 167845 Irving TX 75016-7845

MARTIN, THOMAS RHODES, communications executive, writer, educator; b. Memphis, July 10, 1953; s. Otis Knox and Joe Anne Coggin Martin; m. Wanda C. Benderman, Dec. 1, 1984; children: Seth Knox, Cyrus Rhodes. BA, Vanderbilt U., Tenn., 1975. Sales communication writer Schering and Plough Corp., Memphis, 1976-78; media devel. specialist, Fed. Express Corp., Memphis, 1978-81, sr. media devel. specialist, 1981-82, mgr. of mgmt. comm., 1982-84, mng. dir. employee comm., 1984-92, mng. dir. pub. rels., 1992-95, v.p. corp. comm., 1995-96; v.p. corp. rels., ITT Industries, White Plains, NY, 1996-99, sr. v.p., dir. corp. rels., 1999—2007; sr. counselor Pulse Point Group, LA, 2007—; chair Adv. Coun. Dept. Comm., Coll. of Charleston, SC. Exec.-in-residence Dept. Comm. Coll. Charleston, 2007—. Contbg. editor Memphis mag., 1984—94, contbr. PR Week mag.; contbr. articles to profl. jours. Bd. dirs. Big Bros. and Big Sisters, Memphis, 1983—87, Memphis Oral Sch. for the Deaf, 1985—91, Leadership Memphis, 1986—87, 1992—96, Pub. Rels. Soc. Am. Found, 1999—2001; trustee Inst. for Pub. Rels., 1999—; bd. govs. Josephson Inst. Ethics. Recipient Journalism award, Sigma Delta Phi, 1983, Mobius Advt. award, 1998, NY ADDY Award, 2001; named to PR News Hall of Fame, 2006. Mem.: Arthur W. Page Soc. (bd. dirs. 2001—, pres. 2004—05), Pub. Rels. Soc. Am. (Silver Anvil award 1995, Bronze Anvil award 1996), Internat. Assn. Bus. Communicators, The Wisemen. Avocations: writing, backpacking, sailing, skiing, bicycling. Office: Coll Charleston Dept Comm 66 George St Charleston SC 29424 also: Pulse Point Group Ste 2000 8491 Sunset Blvd Los Angeles CA 90069 Office Phone: 843-953-6383. E-mail: tom@pulsepointgroup.com, martintr@cofc.edu.

MARTIN, VICKI JOAN, biology professor, assistant dean; BS, U. N.C., Charlotte, 1970—74; MS, Wake Forest U., NC, 1974—76, PhD, 1977—80. Postdoctoral fellow U. Alta., Edmonton, Canada, 1980—81; asst. prof. U. Louisville, Ky., 1981—83; asst. to assoc. prof. U. Notre Dame, Ind., 1983—99; prof. biology Appalachian State U., Boone, NC, 1999—2012, chair, dept. biology, 1999—2004; prof. biology NC State U., Raleigh, 2012—, asst. dir. academic programs Coll. Agr. & Life Scis., 2012—13, asst. dean academic affairs Coll. Scis., 2013—. Dir., optical lab. U. Notre Dame, Notre Dame, 1983—99, dir. grad. studies, dept. biology, 1990—92; cons. Earth and Sky NPR, 1999—; invited vis. scholar James Cook U., Australia. Contbr. chapters to books, articles to profl. jours. and pubs. Recipient Career Advancement award, NSF, 1987—90, Frank O'Malley Undergraduate Tchg. award, U. Notre Dame, 1995—96, 100 Scholar's Rsch. award, Appalachian State U., 2004, Leading Scientist of World award, 2005, Excellence award; named to Registry of Outstanding Profl. Mem.: NSF (program dir., divsn. biol. infrastructure 2010—12), Am. Micros. Soc. (pres. 2009—11), Nat. Coun. on Undergraduate Rsch. (elected councilor 2005—, pres. biology divsn.). Achievements include research in demonstration of visual pigments in primitive eyes of invertebrates. Office: Academic Affairs Coll Scis NC State University 116 Cox Hall Box 8201 Raleigh NC 27695

MARTIN, W. TERRY, librarian; b. Tuscaloosa, Ala., Sept. 5, 1948; s. W. Harry and Eleanor (Ambrose) M.; m. Carol Prewitt, May 25, 1973; 1 child, W. Brian. AB in History and Religion, Samford U., 1970, MA in Baptist History, 1977; MLS, U. Ala., 1973. Libr. tech. svcs. Samford U., Birmingham, Ala., 1973-79; circulation and tech. svcs. libr. Southeastern Bapt. Theol. Sem., Wake Forest, N.C., 1979-85; dir. libr. svcs. Georgetown (Ky.) Coll., 1985-93; dir. libr., assoc. prof. libr. svcs. to prof. La. Coll., Pineville, 1993—, chair, SACS review com., 2008—09, faculty sec., Omicron Delta Kappa Circle, 2002—. On-site and off-site peer evaluator for commn. on colls. Southern Assn. Colls. & Sch. Contbr. articles to profl. jours. Served with Ala. Army Nat. Gaurd, 1970—77. Mem. So. Bapt. Libr. Assn. (pres. 1990-91), Am. Libr. Assn., Assn. Christian Libr., Assn. Baptist Libr. & Archivists, La. Libr. Assn. Baptist. Avocations: camping, travel, genealogy, local history. Office: LA Coll Lib 1140 Coll Dr Pineville LA 71359-0001

MARTIN, WILLIAM C., social studies educator, writer; b. San Antonio, Dec. 31, 1937; s. Lowell Curtis and Joe Bailey (Brite) M.; m. Patricia Dale Summerlin, Dec. 31, 1957; children: Rex Martin, Jeff Martin, Elisabeth Dale Martin Thomas. BA, Abilene Christian U., 1958, MA, 1960; BD, Harvard Divinity Sch., 1963; PhD, Harvard U., 1969. Instr. history Dana Hall Sch., Wellesley, Mass., 1965-68; instr. sociology Rice U., Houston, 1968-69, asst. prof. sociology, 1969-73, assoc. prof. sociology, 1973-79, prof. sociology, 1979—, Chavanne prof. religion and pub. policy, 1996—, emeritus, 2005—, master Sid W. Richardson Coll., 1976-81, chair dept. sociology, 1983—86, 1989—94, 2003—04. Cons., spkr. in field. Author: These Were God's People, 1966, Christians in Conflict, 1972, A Prophet With Honor: Billy Graham Story, 1991 (Christianity Today's Critic's Choice award 1992), My Prostate and Me: Dealing With Prostate Cancer, 1994, With God on our Side: The Rise of the Religious Right in America, 1996; contbg. editor Tex. Monthly (Nat. Headliner award 1982); contbr. articles to profl. jours. and pop mags.; radio and TV appearances. Dir. House of the Carpenter, Inc., inner-city youth program, Boston, 1963-66, pres. and bd. dirs. non-profit housing corp.; bd. dirs. Fellowship Racial and Econ. Equality, 1970-71; mem. exec. com. Houston Coun. Human Rels. Sr. scholar James A. Baker III Inst. Pub. Policy, 1996-2005; Chavenne Sr. fellow for religion and pub. policy; grantee Am. Coun. Learned Socs. and Am. Philos. Soc., 1974; recipient Nicholas Salgo Outstanding Tchr. award Rice U., 1971, 93, Brown Coll. award for Tchg. in the Humanities Rice U., 1974, 76, George R. Brown Award for Superior Tchg., alumni Rice U., 1974, 76-77, 84, for Excellence in Tchg., 1975, 82, Life Honor award, 1985. Mem. Am. Sociol. Assn., Soc. Scientific Study Religion, Religious Rsch. Assn., Tex. Inst. Letters (J. Frank Dobie/Paisano fellowship 1980). Democrat. Avocation: bicycling. Home: 2929 Buffalo Speedway 312 Houston TX 77098 Office: Rice U Baker Inst MS40 6100 Main St Houston TX 77005-1892 Home Phone: 713-599-0369; Office Phone: 713-348-3481. Business E-Mail: wcm@rice.edu.

MARTIN, WILLIAM ROYALL, JR., retired technical society administrator; b. Raleigh, NC, Sept. 3, 1926; s. William Royall and Edith Ruth (Crocker) M.; m. Betty Anne Rader, June 14, 1952; children: Sallie Rader Martin Busby, Amy Kemp Martin Lewis. AB, U. N.C., 1948, MBA, 1964; BS, N.C. State U., 1952. Chemist Stamford (Conn.) rsch. labs. Am. Cyanamid Co., 1952—54; chemist Dan River Mills, Danville, Va., 1954—56, Union Carbide Corp., South Charleston, W.Va., 1956—59; rsch. assoc. Sch. Textiles N.C. State U., 1959—63; tech. dir. Am. Assn. Textile Chemists and Colorists, Research Triangle Park, NC, 1963—73, exec. dir., 1974—96. Adj. asst. prof. Coll. Textiles, N.C. State U., 1966-88, adj. assoc. prof., 1989-97; del. Internat. Standards Orgn., Pan Am. Standards Commn. With USNR, 1944—46. Fellow Am. Inst. Chemists, Soc. Dyers and Colourists, Textile Inst.; mem. Am. Chem. Soc., Coun. Engring. and Sci. Soc. Execs. (past pres. 1992-93), Fiber Soc., Am. Assn. Textile Chemists and Colorists (hon.), Masons, Rotary, Phi Kappa Phi, Phi Gamma Delta. Methodist. Home and Office: 224 Briarcliff Ln Cary NC 27511-3901 Personal E-mail: wrbrm1952@gmail.com.

MARTINE, CATHY, telecommunications industry executive; BA in Econ., Coll. Mt. St. Vincent; MS, MIT; MBA, NYU Stern Sch. Branch mgr. AT&T Bus. Svcs., NYC; hired into mgmt. tng. prog. and had assignments in Network Ops., Fin., and Mktg. AT&T Inc. (merger of SBC Communications & AT&T Corp.), led consumer long distance svcs., v.p., internat. traffic mgmt., gen. mgr., internat. consumer long distance bus., 1994—97, mktg. v.p., consumer svcs., 1997—99, pres., internat. carrier svcs., 1999, sr. v.p., Voice over Internet Protocol (VoIP), 2003, sr. v.p., Internet Telephony, Consumer Mktg. and Sales Morristown, NJ, 2004—07, pres., CEO, AT&T Midwest, 2007, exec. v.p., small bus. solutions & alt. channels. Bd. dirs. MIT Sloan Sch. Bd. of Gov., 1998—2001, US Telecommunications Tng. Inst., Washington, 1998—2001, Jersey Battered Women's Shelter, Brooklyn Acad. of Music, NYC, After School Matters, 2007—; mem. fin. com. Brooklyn Acad. of Music; bd. advisors Rutgers Sch. Bus.; co-lead Women of AT&T org. Sloan Fellow, 1993. Office: AT&T Inc 175 E Houston St San Antonio TX 78205 Office Phone: 210-821-4105. Office Fax: 314-331-9896. Business E-Mail: cmm@att.com.

MARTINEAU, ROBERT JOHN, retired law educator; b. Oconto, Wis., May 18, 1934; s. Francis Joseph and Gertrude (Schauer) Martineau; m. Constance Ann Zimmerman, Dec. 21, 1957; children: Robert John, Renee, Anne, Jeanne. BS, Coll. Holy Cross, 1956; JD, U. Chgo., 1959. Bar: Md. 1960, U.S. Supreme Ct. 1964, Iowa 1969, Wis. 1974. Law clk. to chief judge Md. Ct. Appeals, 1959-60; pvt. practice Md., 1960-68; asst. atty. gen. Md., 1964-65; assoc. prof. U. Iowa, 1968-71; prof., 1971-72; cir. exec. U.S. Ct. Appeals (8th cir.), Mo., 1972-74; exec. officer Wis. Supreme Ct., 1974-78; prof. U. Dayton, Ohio, 1978-80; prof. law U. Cin., 1980-88, disting. rsch. prof., 1988-93, emeritus, 1994—, assoc. dean, 1980—83, acting dean, 1985—86. Cons. Inst. Jud. Adminstrn., 1970—72, Fed. Jud. Ctr., 1978, Nat. Ctr. State Cts., 1978—79, 1987, Inst. Jud. Adminstrn., 1987—88, UN Devel. Program, Bhutan, 1999; spl. prof. U. Birmingham, England, 1987. Author: Wisconsin Appellate Practice, 1978, Judicial Reform in Wisconsin, in Court Reform in Seven States, 1980, Modern Appellate Practice-Federal and State Civil Appeals, 1983, Fundamentals of Modern Appellate Advocacy, 1985, Cases and Materials on Appellate Practice and Procedure, 1987; author: (with others) 2d edit., 2005; author: Appellate Justice in England and the United States: A Comparative Analysis, 1990, Drafting Legislation and Rules in Plain English, 1991; author: (with M. Salerno) Legal, Legislative, and Rule Drafting in Plain English, 2005; author: (with R. Martineau, Jr.) Plain English for Drafting Statutes and Rules, 2012. Reporter Wis. Supreme Ct. Com. Discipline Attys., 1975—77, Wis. Jud. Coun. Com. Appellate Practice and Procedure, 1976—78, Com. Contempt and Extraordinary Remedies, 1979—80; sec. Md. Constl.

Conv. Commn., 1965—67, Md. Constl. Conv., 1967—68, Wis. Supreme Ct. Com. Study State Bar, 1975—77; mem. Iowa Mcpl. Laws Study Com., 1970—71, Wis. Legis. Coun. Com. Ct. Reorganization, 1977, Ohio Supreme Ct. Adv. Com. Rules, 1988—91; mem., reporter ABA Appellate Judges Conf. Com. Appellate Skills Tng., 1984—85, Com. Appellate Skills Tng., 1984—85; co-chair Com. Appellate Practice, 1986—88. Mem.: Am. Jud. Soc. (bd. dirs. 1966—68), Md. Bar Assn. (reporter com. jud. selection 1962—64, v.p. 1967), Assn. Am. Law Schs. (ho. reps. 1982—87). Democrat. Roman Catholic. Home Phone: 941-488-0455; Office Phone: 941-488-0455. Personal E-mail: r.j.martineau@gmail.com.

MARTINEZ, ARMANDO, state legislator; b. Jan. 6, 1976; s. Alfredo and Esmeralda Martinez; m. Jessica Martinez; children: Kuentin, Kristian, Javin. BS, U. Tex.-Pan Am. Lic. in paramedicine Tex. State Tech. Coll. EMT, paramedic, firefighter City of Weslaco, 1998—2001; critical care flight paramedic Valley Aircare, 2000—; health instr., coord. Tex. Dept. Health; mem. Dist. 39 Tex. House of Representatives, 2004—. Mem.: Dem. Caucus, NALEO, MALC, Weslaco Firefighters Assn., Lions Club. Democrat. Roman Catholic. Office: 800 W Railroad St Rm H-111 Weslaco TX 78596 also: Room EXT E2.312 Capitol Extension PO Box 2910 Austin TX 78768 Office Phone: 956-447-9473, 512-463-0530.

MARTINEZ, ARTHUR C., broadcast executive; b. NYC, Sept. 25, 1939; s. Arthur F. and Agnes (Caulfield) M.; m. Elizabeth Rusch, July 30, 1966; children: Lauren, Gregory. BSME, Polytech. U., 1960; MBA, Harvard U., 1965; LLD (hon.), U. Notre Dame, 1997. Dir., Planning International Paper Co., NYC, 1967—69; asst. to pres. Talley Industries, Mesa, Ariz., 1969—70; dir., Fin. RCA Corp., NYC, 1970—73, v.p., 1973—80; sr. v.p., CFO Saks Fifth Ave. Inc., NYC, 1980—84, exec. v.p., 1984—87, vice chmn., 1990—92; sr. v.p., group chief exec. Batus Inc., Louisville, 1987—90; chmn., CEO Sears Mdse. Group, Chgo., 1992—95; chmn., pres., CEO Sears, Roebuck and Co., 1995—2000; interim chmn., CEO International Flavors & Fragrances, Inc., NYC, 2006; chmn. supervisory bd. ABN AMRO Holdings N.V., 2006—09; chmn. HSN, Inc., 2008—. Bd. dirs. Saks Fifth Ave., Inc., 1990-92, PepsiCo, Inc., 1999-2012, Internat. Flavors & Fragrances Inc., 2000-, Liz Claiborne, Inc., 2001-12, Fifth & Pacific Companies, Inc. (formerly Liz Claiborne Inc.), 2012-, IAC/InterActiveCorp., 2005-, Martha Stewart Living Omimedia, Inc., 2001-04, American Internat. Group, Inc. (AIG), 2009-; bd. dirs. Fed. Res. Bank Chgo., 1996-2002, chmn., 2000-01. Bd. dirs. Defenders of Wildlife, 1992—, Nat. Urban League; chmn. bd. trustees Polytech. U., 1990—; trustee Art Inst., Orch. Assn. Chgo. Symphony Orch., Greenwich Hosp.; bd. dirs. Northestern Meml. Hosp., Chgo. 1st lt. US Army, 1961—63. Named CEO of Yr., Financial World Mag., 1996; recipient T.C. & Elizabeth Clarke medallion Sch. of Bus., Coll. William & Mary, 1997, Olin Sch. Bus. Excellence in Bus. award, Washington U., St. Louis, 1997. Mem. Nat. Retail Fedn. (chmn. bd. dirs.). Avocations: tennis, golf, gardening. Office: HSN Inc Bd Directors 1 HSN Dr Saint Petersburg FL 33729-0001

MARTINEZ, GEORGE, bank executive; BA in Bus. Adminstrn. & Economics, Rice U., 1963. Chmn. Sterling Bancshares, Inc, 2001—04; co-founder Allegiance Bank Texas, 1974, CEO, 1980—2001, 2007—; sr. ptnr. Chrysalis Partners, LLC, pres., 1999—. Bd. dirs. NCI Bldg Sys., Inc., 2003—. Mem., coun. of overseers, Jesse H. Jones Grad. Sch. of Mgmt. Rice U.; bd. dirs. Greater Houston Partnership; chmn. Ctr. for Houston's Future. Recipient Ethical Leadership in Action award, U. St. Thomas Ctr. for Bus. Ethics, Exemplary Leader award, Houston Gulf Coast Chapter of the Am. Leadership Forum. Office: Allegiance Bank Texas 5410 Bellaire Blvd Bellaire TX 77401 Office Phone: 713-432-1935.

MARTINEZ, JOSE E., federal judge; b. Santo Domingo, Dominican Republic, 1941; BBA, U. Miami, 1962, JD, 1965. Legal officer USN, 1965—68; pvt. practice law clk., 1965; asst. US atty. US Atty.'s Office (so. dist.) Fla., 1968—70; pvt. practice atty. Fla., 1970—2002; regional dir. Office Drug Abuse Law Enforcement US Dept. Justice, 1972—74; judge US Dist. Ct. (so. dist.) Fla., Miami, 2002—. Mem. USNR, 1964—93. Office: US Dist Ct Ferguson US Courthouse 400 N Miami Ave Rm 10-2 Miami FL 33128 Office Phone: 305-523-5590.

MARTINEZ, LOUIS E., corporate financial executive; BS in Acctg., Bentley Coll. Dir., fin., contr. Aegis Comm. Group, 1996—2000; corp. contr. Cotelligent Inc., 2000—03, Airgate PCS Inc., 2003—05; asst. corp. contr. Exide Technologies, 2005, v.p., chief acctg. officer, corp. contr., 2008—. Office: Exide Technologies 13000 Deerfield Pky Milton GA 30004 Office Phone: 678-566-9000. Office Fax: 678-566-9188. Business E-Mail: lou.martinez@exide.com.

MARTINEZ, MELQUIADES R. (MELQUIADES RAFAEL MARTINEZ), bank executive, lawyer; b. Sagua La Grande, Cuba, Oct. 23, 1946; arrived in US, 1962, naturalized, 1971; s. Melquiades C. and Gladys V. (Ruiz) M.; m. Kathryn Tindal, June 13, 1970; children: Lauren Elizabeth, John Melquiades, Andrew Tindal. AA, Orlando Jr. Coll., 1967; BA in Internat. Affairs, Fla. State U., 1969, JD, 1973. Bar: Fla. 1973, US Dist. Ct. (mid. dist.) Fla. 1973, US Supreme Ct. 1979, US Dist. Ct. (so. dist.) Fla. 1986; cert. Nat. Bd. Trial Advocacy. Civil trial atty., ptnr. Martinez, Dalton, Dellecker and Wilson, Orlando, Fla., 1973-85; ptnr. Martinez, Dalton, Dellecker, Wilson and King, 1985-98; chmn. Orange County, Fla., 1998-2001, mayor Fla.; sec. US Dept. Housing & Urban Devel. (HUD), Washington, 2001—04; mem. Florida State Senate, 2005—09, US Senate Armed Svcs. Com., 2005—09, US Senate Banking Housing & Urban Affairs Com., 2005—09, US Senate Commerce, Sci. & Transp. Com., 2005—09, US Senate Spl. Com. on Aging, 2005—09, US Senate Fng. Rels., 2005—09; gen. chmn. Rep. Nat. Com., 2007; ptnr. DLA Piper, Orlando, Fla., 2009—10; chmn., Fla., Mexico, Ctrl. America, Caribbean Region JPMorgan Chase & Co., Orlando, Fla., 2010—. Bd. dirs. Progress Energy, Inc., 2010—. Co-author (with Ed Breslin): A Sense of Belonging: From Castro's Cuba to the US Senate, One Man's Pursuit of the American Dream, 2008. Bd. dirs. Orlando Utilities Commn., Cath. Social Svcs. Orlando, 1978-86; founder, chmn. Mayor's Hispanic Adv. Com., Orlando, 1981-82; chmn. bd. commrs. Orlando Housing Authority, 1983-86., mem., Fla. Utilities Commn., 1994-1997, pres., 1995-1997 Named one of The 25 Most Influential Hispanics, TIME mag., 2005 Mem. Fla. Bar (bd. govs. young lawyers sect. 1980-81), Acad. Fla. Trial Lawyers (dir. 1981-85, treas. 1986-87, pres. 1988-89), 9th Jud. Cir. (jud. nomination commn. 1986), Congressional Hispanic Leadership Inst. Republican. Roman Catholic. Office: JPMorgan Chase & Co 270 Park Ave New York NY 10017-2070 Office Phone: 212-270-6000. Office Fax: 212-270-1648. Business E-Mail: melquiades.martinez@pgnmail.com.

MARTINEZ, NELDA, mayor, Corpus Christi, Texas; d. Roosevelt and Maria Consuelo Martinez. BA in Govt., U. Tex., Austin. Founder, pres. First American Closing Office, Inc., Nueces Title, Adlen Enterprises, Inc.; at-large mem. Corpus Christi City Coun., 2007—12; mayor City of Corpus Christi, Tex., 2012—. Mem. Bd. Plumbing Examiners, 1-69 Com.; vol. Lozano-Shaw Spl. Emphasis Sch., Clowns Who Care Driscoll Hosp.; bd. mem., chair KEDT Pub. TV; bd. dirs. Foster Angels South Tex., Palmer Drug Abuse Program, Corpus Christi Internat. Airport; mem. fin. coun. Diocese of Corpus Christi; treas. Del Mar Coll. Bond Election; chair mktg. & comm. task force Corpus Christi Cmty. Cultural Plan; forum mod. & organizer League of Women Voters; trustee Christus Spohn Health Sys. Found. Recipient Y Women in Careers award, Corp./Bus. Mgmt., YWCA, 2000, Vol. Ctr. Sweetheart of Yr. award, 2003; named Outstanding Businesswoman of Yr., Coastal Bend Area GI Forum, Women's Chpt., 1999; named to Del Mar Coll. Wall of Honor, 2001. Mem.: NAACP (life). Office: Corpus Christi Mayor's Office 1201 Leopard St PO Box 9277 Corpus Christi TX 78469-9277 Office Phone: 361-826-3103. Business E-Mail: neldam@cctexas.com.*

MARTINEZ, PHILIP RAY, federal judge; b. El Paso, Tex., 1957; BA, U. Tex., El Paso, 1979; JD, Harvard U., 1982. Pvt. practice atty., El Paso, 1982—90; judge County Ct. at Law #1, El Paso County, 1991—94, 327th Jud. Dist. Ct., Tex., 1991—2002, US Dist. Ct. (we. dist.) Tex., El Paso, 2002—. Office: US Dist Ct 525 Magoffin Ave El Paso TX 79901 Office Phone: 915-534-6736. Office Fax: 915-534-6715.

MARTINEZ, RAFAEL E. (RALPH E. MARTINEZ), lawyer, former federal commissioner; b. Sangua La Grande, Cuba, Apr. 26, 1950; s. Gladys V. Ruiz and Melquiades C. Martinez; m. Rebecca Martinez; children: Rebecca, Will, Maggie. BS, U. Fla., 1973; JD, Fla. State U., 1976. Cert.: Fla. Supreme Ct. 1977, U.S. Supreme Ct. 1981. Public delegate United Nations 57th General Assembly, 2003; part-time commr. US Foreign Claims Settlement Commn., US Dept. Justice, Wash., DC, 2008—10; mng. partner McEwan, Martinez, & Dukes, P.A. Mem. Ninth Cir. Judicial Nominating Commn., 1990—94, commn. chair, 1993—94; bd. dirs. health law section Fla. Bar, 1992—97; judicial nominating commn. Fifth District Ct. Appeals, 1995—99; mem. American Bd. Trial Advocates Central Fla. Chapter, 1996—, pres., 2004—; products liability com. Internat. Assn. Defense Counsel, 1996—; mem. Pharmaceutical Medical Device & Biotechnology Com., 1996—; judicial relations com. chmn. Orange Co. Bar Assn., 1997—98, professionalism com. chmn., 1999—2000; chair Medical Defense Com., 2000—01; IADC trial acad. faculty Stanford U., 2004. Fellow: American Bar. Found. Republican. Office: McEwan Martinez & Dukes PA 108 E Central Blvd Orlando FL 32801 Office Phone: 407-423-8571 126. Business E-Mail: rmartinez@mmdorl.com.*

MARTINEZ, RAUL L., public relations executive; b. Santiago, Oriente, Cuba, Mar. 6, 1949; arrived in US, 1960; s. Chin and Aida Martinez; m. Angela Callava, Jan. 10, 1970; children: Aida, Raul Jr. AA, Miami Dade Coll.; BS in Criminal Justice, Fla. Internat. U., Miami, 1977. Pub., founder Spanish lang. newspaper El Sol de Hialeah, Fla., 1969—; pres. Martex Realty, Inc., 1975—91; council mem. City of Hialeah, 1977-81, mayor, 1981—90, 1993—2005; pres. Martinez & Fernandez Pub. Rels., Miami Lakes, 2005—. Chmn. Fla. Hispanic Commn., 1976—83; mem. Fla. State Commn. Hispanic Affairs, 1979—82, Gov.'s Commn. Statewide Prosecution Function, 1984—85, Fla. State Comprehensive Plan Com., 1985—87; mem. Roundtable on Defense & Fgn. Policy Dem. Policy Commn., 1985—86; chmn. Dade County Council Mayors, So. Fla. Employment & Tng. Consortium, Hialeah Dade Devel. Inc. Hon. adv. Miami Dade Cmty. Coll., Hialeah Ctr. Fedn. Hispanic Students; bd. advs. Barry U., Miami Shores; mem. cmty. devel. com. United Way Dade County. Recipient Legion of Honor award, 1977, Citizen Involvement award, Crime Commn. Greater Miami, 1977, Over the Top award, Hialeah-Miami Springs YMCA, 1979, Orden del Merito de Duarte Sanchez y Mella award, President of Dominican Republic, 2003; named Pub. Adminstr. of Yr., South Fla. chpt. Am. Soc. Pub. Adminstrn., 1984. Mem.: Dade County Assn. Chiefs of Police, Fla. League Cities (past pres., Lifetime Achievement award 2006), Nat. League Cities (bd. dirs.), Dade County C. of C., Hialeah Latin C. of C., Kiwanis. Democrat. Catholic. Office: Martinez & Fernandez Public Relation 11900 Biscayne Blvd Ste 630 North Miami FL 33181-2734 Office Phone: 305-558-6555. Office Fax: 305-820-9906.

MARTINEZ, ROMAN, IV, retired diversified financial services company executive, board member; b. Santiago, Cuba, Dec. 29, 1947; arrived in US, 1960, naturalized, 1971; s. Roman and Virginia (Gomez) Martinez; m. Helena Hackley, Dec. 20, 1974; children: Roman, Helena Catalina. BS, Boston Coll., 1969; MBA, U. Pa., 1971. Assoc. Kuhn, Loeb & Co., NYC, 1971-73, v.p., 1974-77; corp. v.p. Lehman Bros. (formerly Lehman Bros., Kuhn, Loeb, Inc./Shearson Lehman Bros., Inc.), NYC, 1977, mng. dir., 1978—2003, ret., 2003. Bd. dirs. Alliant Techsystems Inc., 2004—, CIGNA Corp., 2005—, Bacardi Ltd., 2008—. Trustee NY-Presbyn. Hosp. Republican. Roman Catholic. Office Phone: 212-634-1190. Business E-Mail: roman@rmiv.com.

MARTINEZ, TINO, professional baseball coach, retired professional baseball player; b. Tampa, Fla., Dec. 7, 1967; m. Marie Prado, 1991; children: Olivia, Tino Jr., Victoria. First baseman Seattle Mariners, 1988-95, NY Yankees, 1996—2001, 2005, St. Louis Cardinals, 2002—03, Tampa Bay Devil Rays, 2004; spl. instr., spl. asst. to gen. mgr. NY Yankees, 2008—12; batting coach Miami Marlins, 2012—. Recipient Pride of The Yankees Award, 2007; named to Am. League All-Star game, 1995, 1997. Achievements include being a member of World Series Champions New York Yankees, 1996, 1998, 1999, 2000. Office: Miami Marlins 501 Marlins Way Miami FL 33125*

MARTINEZ, TONY, mayor, Brownsville, Texas; m. Carla Saenz; children: T.J., Trey, Andy, Melissa. JD, St. Mary's U. Pvt. practice atty. Martinez y Barrera; mayor City of Brownsville, Tex., 2011—. Founder, benefactor Guadalupe Regional Mid. Sch.; pres. St. Joseph's Acad.; bd. dirs. Tex. Southmost Coll. Found., Our Lady of Perpetual Help Nursing Home. Office: Brownsville City Hall Office of the Mayor PO Box 911 Brownsville TX 78522 Office Phone: 956-546-7159. Office Fax: 956-544-0602. E-mail: mayormartinez@cob.us.*

MARTINEZ-FISCHER, TREY, state legislator; m. Elizabeth Martinez-Fischer; children: Francesca Maria, Camilla Marie. BA in Polit. Sci., U. Tex., San Antonio; MPA, Baruch Coll.; JD, U Tex. Sch. Law. Atty., San Antonio; mem. Dist. 116 Tex. House of Representatives, 2000—. Recipient of several awards and honors; Nat. Urban fellow. Democrat. Office: 1910 Fredericksburg Rd San Antonio TX 78201 also: Room 4S.04 Capitol PO Box 2910 Austin TX 78768 Office Phone: 210-727-7200, 512-463-0616.

MARTINEZ-FRAGA, PEDRO J., lawyer; b. Havana, Cuba, Sept. 9, 1960; BA with high honors, St. John's Coll., 1984; JD, Columbia U., 1987. Bar: Fla. 1988, DC 1988, US Dist. Ct. (so., mid. districts) Fla. 1988, US Ct. Appeals (11th cir.) 1989, US Dist. Ct. (Colo. dist.) 1991, US Supreme Ct. 1999. Adj. prof. law U. Miami, 2002—04; mem. com. Fla. Bar Rules of Civil Procedure, 1990—97, Fla. Bar Rules of Judicial Adminstrn., 1996—97; chair com. Fla. Bar Code & Rules of Evidence, 1996; mem. ad hoc com. on rules and procedures US Dist. Ct., So. Dist. Fla. Author, editor Florida Civil Procedure, 2000, 2001, (chapters to books); contbr. articles to profl. journals. Dir. Cuban-Am. Endowment for Arts; bd. dirs. Miami Lighthouse for Blind, New World Sch. Arts; bd. mem. bd. visitors and governors St. John's Coll. Recipient Harlan Fiske Stone scholarship, 1987; named 2001 Lawyer of the Americas, U. Miami Inter-Am. Law Review; named one of Top Lawyers in So. Fla., So. Fla. Legal Guide, 2001—05, Fla. Legal Elite, Fla. Trend Mag., 2004—05, Top Lawyers in Fla., Fla. Monthly Mag., 2004, Best Lawyers in Am., 2005—07; named to, Am. Law Inst., 1999, Best of the Bar, So. Fla. Bus. Jour., 2003—05. Fellow: Am. Bar Found.; mem.: Hispanic Bar Assn., Am. Trial Lawyers Assn., Cuban-Am. Bar Assn., Dade County Bar Assn. (chair internat. law com. 2001—02, chair fed. ct. com. 1996), Internat. Bar Assn. Office: Greenberg Traurig LLP 1221 Brickell Ave Miami FL 33131 Office Fax: 305-579-0717. Business E-Mail: martinezp@gtlaw.com.

MARTINEZ-LOPEZ, JORGE IGNACIO, internist, educator, cardiologist, consultant; b. Santurce, PR, Oct. 5, 1926; s. Jorge Martinez-Rivera and Dolores (Lopez) Martinez; m. Mona Hagan, June 12, 1950 (div. 1982); children: Jorge Alan, Anthony James, Ricardo, Matthew Joseph; m. Glenda Gayle Tomlinson, Mar. 4, 1983. MD, La. State U., 1950. Diplomate Am. Bd. Internal Medicine, Am. Bd. Cardiovascular Diseases. Intern Arecibo Dist. Hosp., PR, 1950-51; resident in internal medicine La. State U. Medicine Svc., Charity Hosp. La., New Orleans, 1954-57; trainee in cardiology, instr. dept. medicine La. State U. Med. Ctr., 1957-59, asst. prof., 1960-63, assoc. prof., 1963-70, prof., 1970-86, prof. emeritus, 1986—; clin. prof. dept. internal medicine Tex. Tech. U. Health Scis. Ctr., Lubbock, 1988; prof. dept. internal medicine Tex. Tech. U. Health Sci. Ctr., El Paso, 1988—; mem. staff R. E. Thomason Gen. Hosp., U. Med. Ctr., El Paso. Cardiologist Heart Sta., Charity Hosp. La., 1960-75, dir. dept. cardiology, 1975-86, vis. physician, 1957-64, sr. vis. physician, 1964-86; cardiologist Hotel Dieu, New Orleans, 1961-86, dir. cardiology dept., 1970-75; dir. cardiac work evaluation unit Delgado Rehab. Ctr., New Orleans, 1967-86; cons. cardiology Edward F. Hebert Meml. Hosp., USN, Gretna, La., 1977-78; bd. govs. Orleans Parish Med. Soc., 1974-76; v.p. New Orleans Acad. Internal Medicine, 1969-70, pres., 1970-71. Contbr. more than 300 articles to profl. jour. Col. U.S. Army, 1951-53, 86-88, res. 1953-88, ret. Scholar Govt. P.R., 1947-50. Fellow Am. Coll. Cardiology, Am. Coll. Chest Physicians, Am. Coll. Physicians, Am. Heart Assn., Coun. Clin. Cardiology; mem. Am. Heart Assn. (fellow Coun. Clin. Cardiology, La. bd. dir. 1965-86, v.p. 1972-73, pres.-elect 1973-74, pres. 1974-75, El Paso div. pres.-elect 1989-90, pres. 1990-91, bd. dir. 1989—), Assn. Army Cardiology, La. State Med. Soc., Res. Officers Assn. (La. dept. surgeon 1963-69, 74-75, pres. Chpt. 19, 1963-69), Mil. Officers Assn. Am. Avocations: photography, music, painting. Office: Tex Tech U Health Science Ctr Paul L Foster Sch Medicine 4800 Alberta Ave El Paso TX 79905-2709

MARTINEZ-MALDONADO, MANUEL, academic administrator, medical and science educator; b. Yauco, PR, Aug. 25, 1937; s. Manuel and Josefa Maldonado (Josefa Maldonado) Martinez; m. Nivia Elena Rivera, Dec. 18, 1959; children: Manuel, David, Ricardo, Pablo. BS, U. PR, 1957; MD, Temple U., 1961. Diplomate Am. Bd. Internal Medicine, Am. Bd. Nephrology. Intern St. Charles Hosp., Toledo, 1961—62; resident VA Hosp., San Juan, 1962—65, chief resident, 1964—65, chief med. svcs., 1973—90, co-dir. renal metabolic lab., 1973—90; instr. U. Tex. Southwestern Med. Sch., Dallas, 1967—68; from asst. prof. to prof. medicine, co-dir. renal sect. Baylor Coll. Medicine, Houston, 1968—73; prof. medicine U. PR Sch. Medicine, 1973—90, prof. physiology, 1974—90; prof. medicine U. Caribbean, Bayamon, PR, 1980—90; prof., vice chmn. dept. medicine Emory U. Sch. Medicine, 1990—98; chief med. svcs. and clin. affairs Atlanta VA Med. Ctr., 1990—98; v.p. for rsch., prof. medicine Oreg. Health Scis. U., Portland, 1998—99, v.p. rsch., 1999—2000; pres., dean, prof. medicine and physiology Ponce Sch. Medicine, 2000—06; prof. medicine, pharmacology, toxicology U. Louisville, 2007—, exec. v.p. rsch., 2007—. Assoc. mem. nephrology com. Am. Bd. Internal Medicine, 1982—86; nat. adv. bd. gen. medicine B study sect. Nat. Inst. Arthritis, Metabolism and Digestive Diseases NIH; bd. sci. counselors, sci. advisors com. Nat. Heart, Lung and Blood Inst., NIH. Author: La Voz Sostenida, 1984, Palm Beach Blues, 1986, Por Amor al Arte, 1989, Hotel Maria, 1989, Isla Verde, 1999, Novela de Mediodia, 2003; film critic: El Reportero, 1983—86, El Mundo, 1987—90, editor/co-editor: in field, mem. editl. bd.: U. P.R. Press; editor: Am. Jour. of Med. Scis., 1994—98, Am. Jour. Kidney Disease, 1997—2002; contbr. over 200 articles to profl. jours. Com. mem. 500th Anniversary of Discovery Am., PR, 1987—92; pres. bd. trustees Inst. Puerto Rican Culture and Performing Arts Ctr., 2001—05; trustee Corp. Musical Arts, 2001—05, Inst. Puerto Rican Lit., 2001—05; chair culture and recreation panel PR 2025; health com. Popular Dem. Com., PR, 1982—84; bd. dirs. Alliance for PR, Inc., bd. sec., 2004—06. Recipient Lederle Internat. award, Lederle Corp., 1966—67, Macy Faculty Scholar award, The Josiah Macy Jr. Found., 1979—80, Grand Mobil prize medicine, Mobil Oil Corp., 1981, Disting. Alumnus award, Temple Med. Sch., 1988, Presdl. award, Nat. Kidney Found., 1988, Donald W. Seldin award, 1994, Disting. Physician award, PR Hosps. Assn., 1988, Orden del Cafetal award, Municipality of Yauco, 1989, Abelardo Díaz Alfaro award, Medicine & Humanites Acad. of Family Medicine, 2002, Svc. Exec. award, PR Mfrs. Assn., 2005, Svc. Exec. of Yr. award, PR Mfrs. Assn. (So. region), 2006; named one of Outstanding Young Men, PR C. of C., 1976. Master: ACP; fellow: AAAS, Am. Heart Assn. (hypertension rsch. coun.), Coun. for High Blood Pressure Rsch.; mem.: Am. Acad. Arts and Scis. (hon. fgn.), Nat. Kidney Found. (chmn. pub. policy com. 1992—94, chmn. sci. adv. com. 1987—91, Pub. Svc. medal, Donald W. Seldin award), Consortium Southeastern Hypertension Ctrs. (bd. dirs.), Assn. Am. Physicians, Inter-Am. Soc. Hypertension Assn. (bd. govs., chmn. 8th Sci. Congress 1989, U.S. Pharmacopeial Conv. Cardio Renal Drugs com. 1990—96), L.Am. Soc. Nephrology (v.p. 1987—91, pres.-elect 1991—94, pres. 1994—96, Miatello award 1999), Am. Soc. for Clin. Investigation, So. Soc. Clin. Investigation (sec.-treas. 1983—85, pres. 1985—86, Founders medal 1990), Am. Soc. Nephrology (legis. liaison com., chmn. audit com. 1988), Inst. Medicine of NAS (com. on human rights 1987—92), Alpha Omega Alpha. Roman Catholic. Achievements include research in kidney physiology and pathophysiology, treatment of clinical disturbances of blood composition, clinical use of diuretics, mechanisms of the devel. of hypertension. Avocations: theater, art, music, poetry, films. Office: U Louisville Rm 200 Jouett Hall 2310 S Third St Louisville KY 40292 Office Phone: 502-852-8373. Business E-Mail: m0mart10@louisville.edu.

MARTINEZ TORRES, RAFAEL L., territorial supreme court justice; b. Humacao, PR, Feb. 14, 1959; s. Luis Martinez and Aurea Torres; m. Sandra S. Cruz Rodriguez. BA magna cum laude, Univ. PR, JD cum laude, 1983. Legal adv. PR Supreme Ct.; atty. Cestero Marchand & Quintero Rivera; atty. litigation div. Fiddler, Gonzalez & Rodriquez; exec. dir. Govt. Commn. PR House Reps., 1993—95; judge PR Cir. Ct. Appeals, 1995—2009; assoc. justice PR Supreme Ct., 2009—. Mailing: Rama Judicial de Puerto Rico PO Box 9022392 San Juan PR 00902-2392*

MARTINEZ TUCKER, SARA (SARA ALICIA TUCKER), educational initiative administrator, former federal agency administrator; b. Laredo, Tex., 1955; m. Greg Tucker. BA in Journalism, U. Tex., Austin, 1976, MBA with high honors, 1979; D (hon.), Boston Coll., U. Md., U. Notre Dame, 2001. Reporter San Antonio Express-News; various positions through regional v.p. AT&T Inc. (merger of SBC Communications & AT&T Corp.), 1981—97; pres., CEO Hispanic Scholarship Fund (HSF), San Francisco, 1997—2006; under sec. US

Dept. Edn., Washington, 2006—08; pres., CEO The Nat. Math & Sci. Initiative (NMSI), Dallas, 2013—. Bd. dirs. American Electric Power, 2009—, Xerox Corp., 2011—, Sprint Corp., 2013—; mem. Commn. on Future of Edn. US Dept. Edn., 2005. Bd. trustees U. Notre Dame, 2009—; mem. external advisory council Wal-Mart Stores Inc. Recipient Disting. Alumnus award, U. Tex., 2005; named Hispanic of the Year, Hispanic mag., 2000; named one of The 80 Elite Hispanic Women, Hispanic Bus. mag., 2003, The 25 Most Influential Hispanics, TIME mag., 2005. Democrat. Office: The National Math & Science Initiative (NMSI) 8350 North Central Expressway Ste M2200 Dallas TX 75206 Office Phone: 214-346-1200.

MARTINOVICH, ROBERT F., gas industry executive; b. Bartlesville, Okla. m. Mary Millen; 2 children. Grad. in Advanced Mgmt. Program, Harvard Bus. Sch.; BSChemE, U. Notre Dame, South Bend, Ind., 1980. Resin devel. engr. Phillips Petroleum Co., Bartlesville, Okla., 1980, various engrng., sales and mktg. positions; bus. devel. mgr. GPM Gas Corp. (subs. Phillips Petroleum Co.), 1994—96, mktg. svcs. mgr., 1993—94, v.p., Okla. region, 1996—99, sr. v.p., 1999; sr. v.p., permian basin assets DCP Midstream, LLC, 2000—02, sr. v.p., mid continent and Rocky Mountains assets, 2002—07, group v.p., environment, health and safety, ops. and tech. svcs.; sr. mgmt. positions ONEOK, Inc., 2007—09, sr. v.p., COO, 2009—11, sr. v.p., treas., CFO, 2011—. Pres. Gas Processors Assn., 2004-06. Office: ONEOK Inc 100 W Fifth St Tulsa OK 74103 Office Phone: 918-588-7000. Office Fax: 918-588-7960. Business E-Mail: robert.martinovich@oneok.com.

MARTINS, ALEX, professional sports team executive; b. Kearny, NJ; m. Julia Martins; children: Sophia, Gabrielle. BSBA, Villanova U., 1986; MBA, U. Ctrl. Fla. Asst. pub. rels. dept. Phila. 76ers, 1986—88; asst. sports info. dir. Georgetown U., 1988—89; dir. publicity/media rels. Orlando Magic, 1989—96, sr. dir. comm., 1996—98, exec. v.p. mktg. and franchise rels., 2005—06, COO, 2006—10, pres., 2010—11, CEO, 2011—; sr. v.p. mktg. and branding New Orleans Hornets; v.p. comm. and pub. affairs Cleve. Browns; v.p. sports ventures Tavistock Grp., 2003—05. Former chmn. bd. Magic Action Team Cmty. Fund (now Orlando Magic Youth Fund). Office: Orlando Magic 400 W Church St # 250 Orlando FL 32801-2515

MARTINSON, JACOB CHRISTIAN, JR., academic administrator; b. Menomonie, Wis., Apr. 15, 1933; s. Jacob Christian and Matilda Kate (Wisner) M.; m. Elizabeth Smathers, Apr. 29, 1962; children—Elizabeth Anne, Kirsten Kate. BA, Huntingdon Coll., Ala., 1954, LLD (hon.), 1993; MDiv, Duke U., 1957; DDiv, Vanderbilt U., 1972; grad., Inst. Ednl. Mgmt., Harvard U., 1981. Ordained elder United Methodist Ch. Minister Trinity United Meth. Ch., Lighthouse Point, Fla., 1960-67; sr. minister First United Meth. Ch., Winter Park, Fla., 1967-71; supervising instr. Vanderbilt U. Div. Sch., Nashville, 1971-72; pres. Andrew Coll., Cuthbert, Ga., 1972-76, Brevard Coll., NC, 1976-85, High Point (N.C.) U., 1985—2005, hon. chancellor, 2005—; interim pres. Garrett-Evang. Theol. Sem., Evanston, Ill., 2006. Chmn. bd. dirs. 1st Union Nat. Bank, High Point, 1989; lectr. St. Mary's Theol. Soc., U. St. Andrews, Scotland. Chmn. N.C. Friends of Higher Edn., 1986; mem. W.I.H. and Lula E. Pitts Found., Atlanta, 1972-76. Recipient Hickman Preaching award Duke U. Div. Sch.; Glen Slough scholar Vanderbilt U., 1971; hon. fellow Westminster Coll., Oxford, Eng., 1994; Rotary Paul Harris fellow. Mem. Brevard C. of C. (pres. 1979), High Point C. of C. (chmn. 1992), Piedmont Ind. Coll. Assn. (chmn. 1991-93), Carolinas Intercollegiate Athletic Conf. (pres. 1991-93), Phi Theta Kappa. Methodist. Avocation: mountain hiking. Home: 556 Crum Dr Lake Junaluska NC 28745 Office Phone: 828-456-5457. Personal E-mail: jmartinson@bellsouth.net.

MARTINSON, RITA R., state legislator; b. Gloster, Miss., Sept. 11, 1937; d. Denson Mack Randall and LeDoux R. Beulah; m. William Kelly Sr. Martinson, 1958; children: Vampran Virginia, McKie Karen, William K. Jr., Allen R. Mem. Dist. 58 Miss. House of Reps., 1992—; v.p. Garden Ctr.; mem. Green Oak Nursery, Inc., 1960—. Mem.: Madison County Friends Lib., Madison & Ridgeland C. of C., Madison-Ridgeland Acad. (sch. bd. 1980—86), Madison County C. of C. (amb. 1987—90), Official Miss. Women's Club (pres. 1996—97), Ridgeland-Northpark Lions Club (v.p. dir. 1988—90), S Madison County Rep. Womans Club. Republican. Catholic. Address: 1472 Hwy 51 Madison MS 39110 Mailing: PO Box 1018 Jackson MS 39215-1018 Office Phone: 601-359-2438. Fax: 601-853-6629. Business E-Mail: rmartinson@house.ms.gov.

MARTINUZZI, LEO SERGIO, JR., banker; b. Newton, Mass., Aug. 1, 1928; s. Leo Sergio and Jessica (Stewart) Martinuzzi; m. Helen Renfrew Gibson, Oct. 26, 1957 (dec. Oct. 1996); children: John James, Georgiana Gibson, Samuel Stewart; m. Sandra Stetson, Nov. 18, 2004. BA, Harvard U., 1950; B.Litt., Oxford U., 1952. With Chase Manhattan Bank, NYC, 1956-81, asst. treas., 1960, asst. v.p. Japanese brs., 1961-64, v.p. Japanese brs., 1964-68, marketing exec. internat. staff, 1968-72, sr. v.p., 1971-81; corporate devel. officer Chase Manhattan Corp., 1972-75, group exec. info. services, 1975-81; chmn. Chase Econometric Assocs. Inc., 1975-80; sr. v.p. strategic planning Squibb Corp., NY, 1981-87, cons., 1988-91. Chmn. Strategic Dimensions, Inc., 1990—; adj. prof. econs. Edison CC, 1992—96. Lt. (j.g.) USNR, 1952—56. Home: 867 17th Ave Naples FL 34102 Personal E-mail: jmartinuzzi@yahoo.com.

MARTIN-VACHON, ANNE, retail executive; b. 1962; B in Commerce, Finance & Mktg., Université du Québec à Trois-Riviéres, 1983; MBA in Mktg. & Internat. Bus., McGill U., 1985. Various positions including v.p., global beauty, gen. mgr., cosmetics & innovation Procter & Gamble Co., 1985—2006; chief mktg. officer Bath & Body Works, LLC, 2006—08; pres., CEO Lise Watier Cosmetiques Inc., 2008—10; exec. v.p., chief mktg. officer Nordstrom, Inc., Seattle, 2010—12; chief merchandising officer HSN, Inc., St. Petersburg, Fla., 2012—. Office: HSN Inc 1 Hsn Dr Saint Petersburg FL 33729 Office Phone: 727-872-1000.

MARTINY, DANIEL, state legislator; m. Nina McCarthy; children: Ryan, Jeffrey, Steven. Former coach Soccer & Baseball, La. Freniere Pk. & Bertolino Playground; asst. parish atty., 1978—94; mem. Dist. 79 La. House of Reps., 1995—2007, vice chmn. environment com., 1995—2007, mem. enrollment com., 1995—2007; mem. Dist. 10 La. State Senate, 2008—, chair judiciary B com., mem. commerce, consumer protection and internat. affairs com., labor and indsl. affairs com. Named Disting. Svc. award, Morality Media; named to Medallion of Order St. Louis, Archbishop Schulte. Mem.: Jefferson Bar Assn., La. Assn., Fed. Assn., Chateau Estates Lakefront Civic Assn., St. Elizabeth Ann Seton Home & Sch. Assn., New Orleans Saints Sixty-five Roses Found. Republican. Address: 622 Carmenere Dr Kenner LA 70065 Mailing: Dist Off 131 Airline Hwy Ste 201 Metairie LA 70001 Home Phone: 504-464-9045. Fax: 504-864-5409. E-mail: martinyd@legis.state.la.us.

MARTIRE, FRANK R., diversified financial services company executive; B in Economics, Sacred Heart U., Fairfield, Conn.; M in Fin., U. New Haven, Conn. Mgmt. positions Nat. Sharedata Corp.; mgmt. positions through chmn., CEO Citicorp Info. Resources, Stamford, Conn., 1983—91; pres., COO, Fin. Instn. Sys. and Svcs. Group Fiserv, Inc., 1991—2001; pres., COO Call Solutions, 2001—03; pres. fin., services group Metavante Corp., 2003, pres., CEO, 2003—09; chmn. Metavante Technologies; pres., CEO Fidelity National Information Services, Inc., 2009—. Bd. dirs. Fidelity Nat. Info. Svcs. Inc. Bd. dirs. Children's Hosp. and Health System Found., Greater Milwaukee Com., Metropolitan Milwaukee Assn. of Commerce; mem., Bus. Adv. Coun. Sheldon B. Lubar Sch. of Bus. Named one of 2007 Innovators, Bank Tech. News. Office: Fidelity National Information Services Inc 601 Riverside Ave Jacksonville FL 32204 Office Phone: 904-854-5000. Office Fax: 904-357-1105. Business E-Mail: Frank.Martire@fnis.com.

MARTORE, GRACIA C., publishing company executive; b. Mass., 1951; m. Joseph Martore; 2 children. BA in History & Polit. Sci., Wellesley Coll., 1973. Asst. treas. Gannett Co., Inc., McLean, Va., 1985—93, v.p. treasury services, 1993—95, v.p. investor rels., 1996—98, v.p. investor rels., treas., 1998—2001, sr. v.p. finance, treas., 2001—03, sr. v.p., CFO, 2003—06, exec. v.p., CFO, 2006—10, pres., COO, CFO, 2010, pres., COO, 2010—11, pres., CEO, 2011—. Bd. dirs. Gannett Co., Inc., 2011—, MeadWestvaco Corp., 2012—; mem. advisory bd. Florence Crittendon. Named CFO of Yr., Va. Bus., 2006; named one of The Best CFO's in America, Institutional Investor, 2004, 2005, 2006, Washington's 100 Most Powerful Women, The Washingtonian mag., 2011, The 50 Most Powerful Women in Bus., Fortune mag., 2012—13. Office: Gannett Co Inc 7950 Jones Branch Dr Mc Lean VA 22107-0910*

MARUPUDI, SAMBASIVA RAO, surgeon, educator; b. Chintalapudi, India, July 1, 1952; arrived in US, 1976; s. Venkateswarlu and Nagendramma (Gaddipati) M.; m. Usha Nandipati, Mar. 25, 1976; children: Neena, Neelima. MB, BS, Guntur Med. Coll., India, 1974. Diplomate Am. Bd. Surgery, Am. Bd. Colon and Rectal Surgery. Rotating internship St. Clare's Hosp., Schenectady, NY, 1976-77; resident in gen. surgery St. Agnes Hosp., Balt., 1977-78, Franklin Sq. Hosp., Balt., 1978-82; fellow in colon and rectal surgery U. Tex. Health Scis. Ctr., Houston, 1982-83; pvt. practice Amarillo, Tex., 1983—. Clin. asst. prof. dept. surgery Tex. Tech. U. Health Scis. Ctr., Amarillo, 1984—. Fellow ACS, Am. Soc. Colon and Rectal Surgeons, Internat. Coll. Surgeons; mem. AMA, Tex. Med. Assn., Potter-Randall County Med. Soc. (past pres.), Tex. Soc. Colon and Rectal Surgeons (past pres.). Republican. Hindu. Office: 800 Quail Creek Dr # 103 Amarillo TX 79124-1634 Home: 8800 Blackhawk Rd Amarillo TX 79119 Office Phone: 806-358-7911. Personal E-mail: smarupudi@aol.com, drmarupudi@hotmail.com.

MARVEL, KEVIN BOYD, professional society administrator, astronomer; b. Colorado Springs, Colo., Sept. 29, 1967; s. Kenneth Barry and June Anne (Neaves) M. BS in Astronomy and Physics, U. Ariz., Tucson, 1990; MS in Astronomy, N.Mex. State U., Las Cruces, 1994; PhD in Astronomy, N.Mex. State U., 1996. Summer rsch. asst. Nat. Radio Astronomy Obs., Socorro, N.Mex., 1988, predoctoral rschr., 1994—96; summer rsch. asst. Commonwealth Sci. and Industry Orgn. - Divsn. Radio Physics, Sydney, 1989; postdoctoral scholar Owens Valley Radio Obs. Calif. Inst. Tech., 1996—98; assoc. exec. officer policy programs Am. Astron. Soc., Washington, 1998—2001, dep. exec. officer, 2002—06, exec. officer, 2006—. Contbr. articles to sci. jours. Recipient Undergraduate Rsch. grant U. Ariz., Tucson, 1988, 89. Mem. AAAS, Am. Assn. Variable Star Observers, Am. Astron. Soc., Am. Geophys. Union, Astron. Soc. of Pacific, Sigma Xi, Internat. Dark Sky Assn., Nat. Radio Astronomy Obs., Commonwealth Sci. and Indsl. Rsch. Orgn. Office: Am Astron Soc 2000 Florida Ave NW Ste 400 Washington DC 20009 Office Phone: 202-328-2010. Office Fax: 202-234-2560. E-mail: marvel@aas.org.

MARVIN, CHARLES ARTHUR, law educator; b. July 14, 1942; s. Burton Wright and Margaret Fiske (Medlar) Marvin; m. Elizabeth Maureen Woodrow, July 4, 1970 (div. July 1987); children: Colin, Kristin; m. Elizabeth Dale Wilson, Mar. 20, 1999. BA, U. Kans., Lawrence, 1964; postgrad., U. Toulouse, France, 1964-65; JD, U. Chgo., 1968, M of Comparative Law, 1970. Bar: Ill. 1969. Legal intern EEC, Brussels, 1970; lectr. law U. Kent, Canterbury, England, 1970-71; asst. prof. law Laval U., Quebec City, Que., Canada, 1971-73; legal adv. Constnl., internat. and adminstrv. law sect. Can. Dept. Justice, Ottawa, Ont., 1973-76, dir. Adminstrv. Law Reform Project, 1983-85; assoc. prof. law U. Man., Winnipeg, Canada, 1976-77; dir. adminstrv. law project Law Reform Commn., Ottawa, 1977-80; prof. law Villanova U., Pa., 1980-83, Ga. State U., 1985—2012, assoc. dean, 1987-89. Legal advisor on adminstrv. code revision Govt. of Kazakhstan, 1993; law faculty devel. adviser, Bulgaria, 1993; dir. internat. human rights law summer program Regent U. Sch. Law., 1998; USIS lectr., Ivory Coast, 1998; Fulbright prof. Riga Grad. Sch. Law, Latvia, 2000—03; vis. prof. law Vytautas Magnus U., Lithuania, 2004—06, Riga Grad. Sch. Law, 2013. Fulbright scholar, U. Toulouse, 1964—65, Summerfield scholar, U. Kans., 1961—64, Ford Found. Comparative Law fellow, 1968—70. Fellow: Am. Bar Found. (life); mem.: ABA, Internat. Law Assn., Internat. Bar Assn., Am. Soc. Internat. Law, Chgo. Bar Assn., Ill. Bar Assn., Phi Beta Kappa, Phi Delta Phi, Phi Beta Delta, Omicron Delta Kappa. Office Phone: 404-835-2590.

MARX, GARY DEAN, educational consultant, futurist, think-tank executive; b. Manchester, SD, Nov. 28, 1938; s. Harvey Frederick and Lucille (Stemple) Marx; m. Judy Rae Marx, June 18, 1961; children: John Fredrick, Daniel Winston. BA, U. S.D., 1960. Cert. Pub. Rels. Soc. Am., Nat. Sch. Pub. Rels. Assn., Am. Soc. Assn. Execs. Newscaster, announcer, dir. KSOO radio and TV sta., Sioux Falls, SD, 1958-61; newscaster, announcer WOW radio and TV sta., Omaha, 1961-71; dir. comms. Westside Cmty. Schs., Omaha, 1971-77; exec. dir. comms. Jefferson County Pub. Schs., Denver, 1977-79; sr. assoc. exec. Am. Assn. Sch. Adminstrs., Arlington, Va., 1979-96, exec. dir. Leadership for Learning Found., 1996-98; pres. Ctr. for Pub. Outreach, Inc., Vienna, Va., 1998—. Sr. rsch. fellow Health, Energy and Productivity in Sch. project, Bethesda, Md., 2000-02; pub. rels. cons. Nat. Sch. Pub. Rels. Assn., Rockville, Md., 1972—; v.p., owner Sta. KOAK Radio, Red Oak, Iowa, 1977-82; v.p. Comms. Devel. Inc., Denver, 1974-76; evaluator CIVITAS Internat. Exch. Program, Calabasas, Calif., 2000—11; cons., internat. spkr. on six continents, 80 countries. Author: Radio...Your Publics are Listening, 1976; Radio-...Get the Message, 1977; Excellence in Our Schools...Making it Happen, 1984; Public Relations for Administrators, 1984, 88; Working with the News Media, 1993; Preparing Students for the 21st Century, 1996, 99; The Future of Cmty., 1999; Preparing Schools and School Systems for the 21st Century, 1999; Ten Trends...Educating Children for a Profoundly Different Future, 2000, Future Focused Leadership...Preparing Schools, Students and Communities for Tomorrow's Realities, 2006, Sixteen Trends...Their Profound Impact on Our Future, 2006, 2011, Twenty-One Trends for the 21st Century: Out of the Trenches...Into the Future, 2014; contbr. articles to profl. jours. Founder, chmn. Keystone Cmty. Task Force, Omaha, 1970-77; mem. Omaha Parks and Recreation Bd., City of Omaha, 1975-77; mem. urban growth policy bd., 1976; mem. nat. edn. adv. com. for restoration Statue of Liberty-Ellis Island Found. NYC, 1984-86, Nat. Press Club, 1984-98, Omaha Press Club, 1962-2013; founder Nat. Supr. of Yr. program, 1987; mem. Horace Mann League, 1985-, bd. dirs. 2005—; mem. exec. com. edn. Commn. for Bicentennial of the US Constitution, Washington, 1986-92,; bd. dir. Campaign New Priorities, Washington, 1992-93, US Coalition Edn. for All, 1993-1997, Manchester Monument Adv. Coun., SD, 2006-07, bd. dirs., Laura Ingalls Wilder Meml. Soc., 2007—13, Harvey Dunn Soc. SD, 2009-, founder Coalition for America's Children, Washington, 1992-98; mem. steering com. Libr. of Congress, Ctr. for the Book, Washington, 1992-99, Goals 2000 Arts Edn. Partnership NEA, Washington, 1993-98; steering com. mem. Civitas Internat., Brussels, Belgium, 1996—, Fulbright Scholars, selection com., 1998-; mem. design arts program steering com. NEA, Washington, 1993-94; mem. grants selection com. Alliance for Arts Edn., John F. Kennedy Ctr. for the Performing Arts, Washington, 1993-96, announcer emcee presdl. scholars program, 1994-2009, selection com. advisor Nat. Tchr. of Yr. Program, Washington, 1979-99; mem. steering com., mem. selection com., judge Disney Salute to the Am. Tchr., Burbank, Calif., 1993-97; Emmy awards judge NATAS, NYC, 1995-97; mem. adv. bd. NBC The More You Know campaign, NYC, 1992-98; mem. nat. adv. bd. PBS, 1990-98; judge USA Today All USA Acad. Team, Arlington, Va., 1995-2000, judge Nat. History Day, 2002-; mem. Apple Fed. Scholars Selection Com., Va., 2012-; internat. cons., spkr., Ctr. Civic Edn., Calabasas, Calif., 1996—, USIA, US Dept. State, Washington, 1996—; mem. steering com., facilitator Nat. Ctr. Energy Mgmt. and Bldg. Techs., 2004—09, twelve-mem. alternative futures panel Washington Metro Area in 2025, Washington Post, 2007-08, Harvard U. Think Tank Global Edn., 2011, Future Learning, 2012. Recipient Radio Advertising Bureau Commercial award, 1967, Pres. award, Nat. Sch. Pub. Relations Assn., 1999, Disting. Svc. award, Am. Assn. Sch. Administrs., 2000. Mem. Nat. Sch. Pub. Rels. Assn. (numerous coms. 1971—, accredited, Pres.'s award 1999), Pub. Rels. Soc. Am. (accredited), Am. Soc. Assn. Exec. (cert. 1979-), Edn. Writers Assn. (bd. dir. 1983-86), Am. Assn. Sch. Adminstrs. (Disting. Svc. award 2000), World Future Soc. (profl. mem.), ASCD, Horace Mann League (bd. dirs. 2005-, v.p. 2012-, pres. 2014, Ambs. award 2009-11), Am. Fedn. TV and Radio Artists, AFTRA-SAG. Avocations: folk art, travel, reading, writing, photography. Office: Ctr for Pub Outreach 1831 Toyon Way Vienna VA 22182-3355 Office Phone: 703-938-8725. Personal E-mail: gmarxcpo@aol.com.

MARZIAN, MARY LOU, state legislator; b. Sept. 16, 1954; Registered nurse & transplant coord.; mem. Dist. 34 Ky. House of Reps., 1994—; mem. Appropriations & Revenue Com., Edn. Com., Health & Welfare Com., State Govt. Com. Mem.: Ky. Nurses Assn., Met. Louisville Women's Polit. Caucus, Jefferson County Nat. Orgn. Women (former pres.), Older Women's League. Democrat. Catholic. Address: 2007 Tyler Dr Louisville KY 40205 Home: 2007 Tyler Lane Louisville KY 40205 Home Phone: 502-451-5032; Office Phone: 502-564-8100 643. Business E-Mail: maryloumarzian@lrc.state.ky.us.

MAS, JOSÉ RAMON, construction executive; BBA, MBA, U. Miami. Exec. v.p., vice chmn. Burnup & Sims Inc., 2001; joined MasTec, Inc., 1992, head comm. group, 1999—2001, vice chmn., exec. v.p. bus. develop., 2001—07, pres., CEO, 2007—. Former bd. dirs. Neff Corp., 1995, Neff Rental LLC (subs. Neff Corp.), 1997. Bd. dirs. Mas Family Found., Miami, Fla. Named one of America's 15 Most Powerful CEOs 40 and Under, Forbes mag., 2010, America's 20 Most Powerful CEOs 40 and Under, 2012. Office: MasTec, Inc 12th Fl 800 S Douglas Rd Coral Gables FL 33134 Office Phone: 305-599-1800. Office Fax: 305-406-1960. Business E-Mail: jmas@mastec.com.

MASELLI, JOHN ANTHONY, food products executive; b. NYC, Feb. 18, 1928; s. Anthony and Livia M.; m. Brigitta Degenkolb, Dec. 26, 1948; children: Elisa, John A. Jr. BS in Chemistry, CCNY, 1947; MS in Chemistry, Fordham U., 1949, PhD in Chemistry, 1952. Dir. research and devel. Standard Brands, Stamford, Conn., 1952-64; mgr. product devel. M&M/Mars, Hackettstown, NJ, 1964-67; pres. OZ Food Corp., Chgo., 1967-79; v.p. tech. Nabisco Brands, East Hanover, NJ, 1979-85; v.p. corp. research and devel. RJR Nabisco, Winston-Salem, NC, 1985-87; sr. v.p. tech. Planters LifeSavers Co., Winston-Salem, 1987-91, cons., 1991—2006. Bd. dirs. Cultor Food Scis. (Finland), NC Biotech. Ctr., Sci-Works, Winston Salem, Winston Salem Symphony. Patentee in field. Bd. dirs. Chgo. Boy's Club, 1975-79, YMCA, Wilton, Conn, 1980-84. Mem. AAAS, ACS, Inst. Food Tech., Am. Soc. Bakery Engrs., Indsl. Biotechnology Assn., Indsl. Research Inst. Republican. Avocations: sailing, photography, music. Home: 529 Knob View Pl Winston Salem NC 27104-5107

MASK, BARRY, state legislator; b. Alexander City, Ala., July 25, 1959; s. Bob and Brenda; m. Jill Mask. BS in Pub. Adminstrn., Auburn U., Ala. Position in govtl. affairs Ala. State Employees Assn., Ala. Assn. Realtors, Bus. Coun. Ala., Ala. Industry & Manufacturers Assn.; positions with archtl. & engrng. firm including project mgr., Montgomery Riverfront master plan, 1999—; mem. Dist. 31 Ala. House of Reps., 2006—. Co-founder Shug Jordan/Dean Katherine Cater Lukemia Fund; co-founder, chmn. Joe Sewell Award, 2005. Mem. Elmore County Econ. Devel. Authority (co-founder, vice chmn.), Leadership Elmore County, Ctrl. Elmore Water & Sewer Authority (former chmn.), Elmore County Auburn Club (past pres.), Auburn Alumni Assn. (life), Nat. Coun. Phi Kappa Tau Fraternity, Elmore County Cmty. Found. (bd. dirs.), Lion's Club Wetumpka, Redland Cmty. Assn. Republican. Office: 41 Brookland Ct Wetumpka AL 36093 also: Ala House of Reps Ala State House 11 S Union St Rm 527-C Montgomery AL 36130 Office Phone: 334-242-7732. Business E-Mail: barry.mask@alhouse.org.

MASON, ELLSWORTH GOODWIN, retired librarian; b. Waterbury, Conn., Aug. 25, 1917; s. Frederick William and Kathryn Loretta (Watkins) Mason; m. Rose Ellen Maloy, May 13, 1951 (div. Oct. 1961); children: Kay Iris Morice, Joyce Iris Lande; m. Joan Lou Shinew, Aug. 16, 1964; 1 child, Sean David. BA, Yale U., 1938, MA, 1942, PhD, 1948; LHD, Hofstra U., 1973; diploma, Inst. Children's Lit., 1996. Cert. Christian Writer's Guild. Reference asst. Yale Library, 1938-42; export license officer Bd. Econ. Warfare, 1942-43; instr. English Williams Coll., 1948-50; instr. humanities Marlboro (Vt.) Coll., 1951-52; serials libr. U. Wyo. Libr., 1952-54; reference libr. Colo. Coll. Libr., Colorado Springs, 1954-58; lectr., libr. Colo. Coll., 1958-63; prof., dir. libr. svcs. Hofstra U., Hempstead, NY, 1963-72; prof., dir. U. Colo. Librs., Boulder, 1972-76; freelance writer children's lit., 1995—. Libr. cons., 1958—; vis. lectr. Northwestern U., 1961, Colo. Coll., 1965, Syracuse U., 1965—68, Elmira Coll., 1966, Columbia U., 1966—68, Lincoln U., 1969, U. BC, Canada, 1969, U. Toronto, 1970, U. Tulsa, 1971, 1976, U. Rutgers, 1971, U. Ill., 1972, Colgate U., 1972, Simmons Coll., 1972, U. Oreg., 1973, Hofstra U., 1974, U. N.C., 1976, U. Ala., 1976, Ball State U., 1977, U. Lethbridge, Canada, 1977, U. Ariz., 1981, Ariz. State U., 1981, Victoria U., New Zealand, 1983, U. Canterbury, New Zealand, 1983, U. Nev., Las Vegas, 1992, Remember Pearl Harbor Assn., 1993, 1994; rsch. assoc. U. Calif., Berkeley, 1965; adj. prof. U. Ill., Urbana, 1968; pres. Mason Assocs., Ltd., 1977—; libr. value engr., 1992—. Author (with Walter and Jean Shine): A MacDonald Potpourri, 1988, The University of Colorado Library and Its Makers, 1876-1972, 1994; editor (with Stanislaus Joyce): The Early Joyce, 1955; editor Xerox U.M. edit., 1964, Norwood: Norwood Editions, 1977, Philadelphia (R. West), 1978, editor with Richard Ellmann The Critical Writings of James Joyce, 1959, 2d edit., 1989, editor Colorado College Studies, 1959—62, Critical Commentary on a Portrait of the Artist as a Young Man, 1966, The Bookover's Bounty, 1977—82; translator: Recollections of James Joyce (S. Joyce), 1950, Essais de J. Joyce, 1966, Escritos Criticos de James Joyce, Portuguese edit., 1967, Spanish edit., 1973, 1975, James Joyce's Ulysses and Vico's Cycle, 1973, Krittische Schriften v. James Joyce, 1975, Mason on Library Buildings, 1980; editor, compiler: Focus on Robert Graves, 1972—88, adv. editor: Focus on Robert Graves and His Contemporaries, 1988—; mem. editl. bd. Serial Slants, 1957—59, Choice, 1962—65, Coll. and Rsch. Librs., 1969—72, Serials Libr., 1977—98; contbr. articles to 120 profl. jours. Mem. chancellor's coun. U. Tex., Austin, 1982—; exec. bd. U. Ky. Libr. Assocs., 1991—94, Concerned Christians in Ky., 1993—98, Littlefield Soc. U. Tex., Austin, 2004—. With USN, 1943—46. Recipient Harry Bailly Spkr.'s award, Assn. Colls. Midwest, 1975; named Ky. Col., 1993; grantee, Am. Coun. Learned Socs., Edn. Facilities Labs., Hofstra U., U. Colo.; fellow, Coun. Libr. Resources, 1969—70. Mem.: ALA (councilor-at-large 1961—65), Am. Christian Writers, Nat. Assn. Scholars, James Joyce Found. (chmn. sect. translation from Joyce 2d Internat. James Joyce Symposium 1969), Inst. Vico Studies, New Zealand Royal Forest and Bird Protection Soc., Conf. Editors Learned Jours., Alcuin Soc. Vancouver, Pvt. Librs. Assn., New Zealand Libr. Assn., Libr. Assn. (London), Bibliog. Soc. Am., Colo. Libr. Assn. (pres. so. dist. 1960—61), Black Am.'s PAC, Colo. Book Collectors (founder, pres. 1975—86), Ghost Town Club, Caxton Club, Archons of Colophon, Sigma Kappa Alpha (pres. 1969—70), Alpha Sigma Lambda. Home: 736 Providence Rd Lexington KY 40502-2267 also: 39 Discovery Dr Whitby New Zealand

MASON, FRANK HENRY, III, automotive and rental company executive; b. Paris, Tenn., Nov. 16, 1936; s. Frank H. and Dorothy (Carter) M.; children: Robert C., William C. B of Elec. Engring., Vanderbilt U., 1958; MS in Indsl. Mgmt., MIT, 1965. With Ford Motor Co., 1965-71; asst. controller Ford Brazil, Sao Paulo, 1971-74; mgr. overseas fin. dept. Ford Motor Co., Dearborn, Mich., 1974-76, asst. controller engine divsn., 1976-78, mgr. facilities and mgmt. svcs., 1978-81; controller Ford Motor Credit Co., Dearborn, Mich., 1981-87; dir. fin. Ford Fin. Svcs. Group, Dearborn, Mich., 1987-89; exec. v.p., chief fin. officer U.S. Leasing, Internat., San Francisco, 1989-92; retired, 1992. Lt. USN, 1958-63.

MASON, PHILLIP HOWARD, aircraft company executive, retired military officer; b. Cash, Va., Mar. 13, 1932; s. Phillip Howard and Mary Armisted (Hogg) M.; m. Frances Murray Gallogly, Mar. 3, 1962 (dec. 1995); children: Mary Catherine, Patrick Howard, Susan Frances, Sheryl Ann; m. Barbara Martin, Sept. 23, 2006. BS in BA, magna cum laude, St. Benedicts, 1966; MBA, Shippensburg State Coll., 1976; postgrad., U.S. Army Command and Gen. Staff Coll., 1965-66, U.S. Army War Coll., 1975-76. Enlisted in U.S. Army, 1948, advanced through grades to brig. gen., 1980, bn. comdr. 1st Bn., 1st ADA Ger., 1971-73, sec. gen. staff 32d Army Air Def. Command, 1974, systems coordinator ODCSRDA, Dept Army Washington, 1975; project mgr. AD Command and Control Redstone Arsenal, Ala., 1976-78; comdr. 11th ADA Bde CMPR Fort Bliss, Tex., 1978-79; project mgr. STINGER Redstone Arsenal, 1979-83; dir. combat support system ODCSRDA, Dept. Army Washington; ret. U.S. Army, 1983; v.p. bus. devel. Sanders Assocs., Nashua, N.H., 1984-90; project mgr. Hughes Aircraft Co., 1990—; ret., 1998. Decorated Disting. Svc. medal, Legion of Merit with oak leaf cluster, Bronze star, Meritorious Svc. medal with two oak leaf clusters, Joint Svcs. Commendation medal, Army Commendation medal. Home: 3514 Gulf Blvd Saint Petersburg Beach FL 33706 Office Phone: 978-725-8044. Personal E-mail: phmason@verizon.net.

MASON, THOMAS EDWARD, physicist, science administrator; b. Halifax, Nova Scotia, Canada, Aug. 9, 1964; s. Clive Steventon and Elizabeth Joyce Mason; m. Jennifer Mary MacGillivray, Nov. 1, 1991; children: William I.M., Simon A.M. BSc, Dalhousie U., Halifax, 1986; PhD, McMaster U., Hamilton, Ont., 1990. Fellow AT&T Bell Lab., Murray Hill, NJ, 1990—91; sr. scientist Risoe Nat. Lab., Roskilde, Denmark, 1991—93; asst. prof. physics U. Toronto, 1993—98, assoc. prof. physics, 1998; dir. SNS exptl. facilities divsn. Oak Ridge Nat. Lab., Tenn., 1998—2001, assoc. lab. dir. spallation neutron source, 2001—06, assoc. lab. dir. neutron scis., 2006—07, lab. dir., 2007—. Assoc. quantum materials program Can. Inst. Advanced Rsch., Toronto, 1993—; spkr. in field. Contbr. to numerous profl. jours.; mem. exec. editl. bd.: Jour. Physics: Condensed Matter, 2003—. Chmn. Oak Ridge Pub. Sch. Edn. Found., Tenn., 2004. Named one of 100 Canadians to Watch, MacLeans Mag., 1997, Tenn.'s 40 under 40, Tenn. Bus. Mag., 2004; named to Alumni Gallery, MacMaster U., 2003; Can fellow, Natural Sci. and Engring. Rsch. Coun., 1986—90, 1990—91, Alfred P. Sloan Rsch. fellow, 1997—99. Fellow: AAAS, Inst. of Physics; mem.: Am. Phys. Soc. Office: Oak Ridge National Lab PO Box 2008 Oak Ridge TN 37831 Office Fax: 865-241-2967. E-mail: masont@ornl.gov.

MASON, THOMAS P., lawyer; BA with high distinction, U. Nebr., 1978; JD with honors, U. Tex., 1981. Bar: Tex. 1981. Ptnr. Andrews & Kurth, Houston; sr. energy and securities ptnr. Vinson & Elkins, Houston, 2001—07; sec., gen. counsel Energy Transfer Partners, LP, Dallas, 2007—08, v.p., sec., gen. counsel, 2008—. Office: Energy Transfer Group Ptnrs LLP 3738 Oak Lawn Ave Dallas TX 75219 Office Phone: 214-981-0700. Business E-Mail: tom.mason@energytransfer.com.

MASON, WILLIAM GRAY, pediatric radiologist; MD, U. Fla., 1975. Diplomate Am. Bd. Radiology-diagnostic radiology, 1979, Am. Bd. Radiology-pediatric radiology, 2005. Resident pediatrics Univ. of Minn., Minneapolis, 1975—76, resident diagnostic radiology, 1976—79; fellow pediatric radiology Children's Hosp. Med. Ctr., Boston, 1979—80; hosp. affiliations include Bapt. Hosp., Bapt. Hosp. - Pensacola (Bapt. Med. Ctr.). Office: Nemours Childrens Clinic 807 Nira St Jacksonville FL 32207-8426

MASSA, CONRAD HARRY, retired religious studies educator; b. Bklyn., Oct. 27, 1927; s. Harry Frederick and Josephine W. (Lepold) M.; m. Anna W. Rossi, Aug. 19, 1951; children: Stephen Mark, Barbara Ann. AB with honors, Columbia U., 1951; M.Div., Princeton Theol. Sem., 1954, PhD, 1960; HHD, Lafayette Coll., 1987. Ordained to ministry Presbyn. Ch., 1954. Pastor Elmwood Presbyn. Ch., East Orange, NJ, 1954-57; asst. prof. homiletics Princeton Theol. Sem., 1957-61; sr. pastor Old First Ch., Newark, 1961-66, Third Presbyn. Ch., Rochester, NY, 1966-78; dean acad. affairs Princeton Theol. Sem., 1978-94, dean emeritus, 1994—, Charlotte W. Newcombe prof., 1978-95, Charlotte W. Newcombe prof. emeritus, 1995—. 1st moderator Synod of the Northeast, United Presbyn. Ch.; vis. prof. St. Bernard's Roman Cath. Sem., Rochester, 1968-70; keynote speaker 11th ann. conf. Inst. Theology, Yonsei U., Seoul, Republic of Korea, 1991, pres. Marion County Audubon Soc. Author articles and book revs. Trustee Lafayette Coll., Easton, Pa., 1982-93. Served with U.S. Army, 1946-47. Mem. Acad. Homiletics, Am. Acad. Religion, Internat. John Bunyan Soc. Home: 9583 SW 90th St Ocala FL 34481-7495 E-mail: chm1@sprynet.com.

MASSAD, STEPHEN ALBERT, lawyer; b. Wewoka, Okla., Dec. 20, 1950; s. Alexander Hamilton and Delores Jean (Razook) Massad; children: Caroline, Sarah, Margaret. AB, Princeton U., 1972; JD, Harvard U., 1975. Bar: Tex. 1975. Assoc. Baker Botts LLP, Houston, 1975-82, ptnr., 1983—, corporate dept. chair, 1994—2002, mem. exec. com., 1995—2001. Office: Baker Botts LLP 3000 One Shell Plz 910 Louisiana St Houston TX 77002 Office Phone: 713-229-1475. Business E-Mail: stephen.massad@bakerbotts.com.

MASSANELLI, CLIFTON TIMOTHY, US marshal; b. 1957; BA in Criminal Justice, U. Ark., 1980. Patrolman Pine Bluff Police Dept., Ark., 1981—82, detective Ark., 1982—83; dep. US marshal US Marshals Svc., US Dept. Justice, 1983, chief dep. US marshal, 2006—10, US marshal (ea. dist.) Ark., 2010—. Office: US Marshals Service US Courthouse 600 W Capitol Ave, Rm A328 Little Rock AR 72201 Office Phone: 201-324-6256.

MASSANELLI, STEPHEN C., retail executive; BBA in Mktg., U. Ark., Little Rock, 1990. Various fin. roles NationsBank of Tex.; prin. Treadstone Partners, LLC, Dallas, 1993—97; sr. v.p., treas. Zale Corp., 1997—2004, sr. v.p., real estate, 2004—07, sr. v.p., fin., 2007—08, sr.v.p., shared svcs., loss prevention and security, 2008—09, sr. v.p., info. tech., real estate, 2009—. Bd. dirs. AMRESCO, 1990—93, Treadstone Partners, LLC, Dallas, 1993—97. Office: Zale Corp 901 W Walnut Hill Ln Irving TX 75038-1003 Office Phone: 972-580-4000. Office Fax: 972-580-5523.

MASSARO, ANTHONY A., retired metal products executive; b. 1945; BSChemE, U. Pitts., 1967. Various positions, including gen. mgr., Indsl. Control divsns., group pres. Westinghouse, 1967—93, pres., Environ. Sys. Group, exec. v.p., Industries and Environ. Group, 1967—93; pres. Lincoln Internat., Lincoln Europe, 1993—96; COO Lincoln Electric Holdings, Inc., 1996, CEO, pres., 1996—2004, chmn., 1997—2004; non-exec. chmn. Comml. Metals Co., 2012—. Former bd. dirs. Gardner Denver Thomas, Inc., Merc. Bankshares Corp.; bd. dirs. MAPI Inc., Thomas Industries, Inc., 1997—, Cleveland-Cliffs Inc., 1999—, Comml. Metals Co., 1999—, PNC Fin. Svcs. Group, Inc., 2002—. Former bd. dirs. Cleve. Tomorrow, Mfrs. Alliance for Productivity and Innovation, US-Korea Bus. Coun., Cleve. Coun. on World Affairs; trustee Gilmour Acad., Cleve., Ohio, John Carroll U. Office: Commercial Metals Co Bd Directors 6565 N MacArthur Blvd Ste 800 Irving TX 75039 Office Phone: 214-689-4300. Office Fax: 214-689-5886. Business E-Mail: Anthony.Massaro@cmc.com.

MASSENGILL, STEVE, state legislator; m. Dina Whiteside. With Big M Transportation; mem. Dist. 13 Miss. House of Reps., Jackson, 2012—. Mem.: Pott's Camp Booster Club, Ebenezer Men's Club (pres.). Republican. Methodist. Office: Miss House of Reps PO Box 1018 Jackson MS 39215 Business E-Mail: smassengill@house.ms.gov.

MASSERANG, DEVERL, wholesale distribution executive; BS in Indsl. Engring., Tex. Tech U., 1983. V.p., logistics, N.Am. Product Supply Chiquita Brands International, Inc., 2003—. Office: Chiquita Brands International Inc 550 S Caldwell St Ste 1010 Charlotte NC 28202-2681 Office Phone: 513-784-8000. Office Fax: 513-784-8030. Business E-Mail: dmasserang@chiquita.com.

MASSEY, A. SHANE, state legislator; b. Greenville, Tenn., June 28, 1975; s. Gary M. and Linda S. Massey; m. Blair Lee Ballard, Jan. 31, 2004. BA, Clemson U., 1997; JD, U. SC, 2000. Mem. Dist. 25 SC State Senate, 2008—, mem. Corrections and Penology Com., Edn. Com., Judiciary Com., Labor, Commerce and Industry Com. & Rules Com. Republican. Bapt. Mailing: PO Box 551 Edgefield SC 29824 Office: Capitol Office 608 Gressette Bldg Columbia SC 29201 Office Phone: 803-649-6200, 803-480-0419, 803-212-6000. E-mail: shanemassey@scsenate.org.

MASSEY, CHARLES KNOX, JR., advertising agency executive; b. Durham, NC, Jan. 16, 1936; s. Charles Knox and Louise (Southerl) M.; m. Mary Ann Keith, Aug. 27, 1960; children: Elizabeth, Knox, Louise. BS in Bus. Adminstrn, U. N.C., Chapel Hill, 1959. Account exec. Tucker Wayne & Co., advt. agy., Atlanta, 1964-78, pres., 1978-88, Tucker Wayne/Luckie & Co., Atlanta, 1988-95; chmn., CEO West Wayne, Inc., Atlanta, 1996—2000; mng. gen. ptnr. Keith Massey Family Investments LLLP, 2000—. Trustee The Lovett Sch., Atlanta. Mem. Piedmont Driving Club (pres. 1990-92), Highlands (N.C.) Country Club, Univ. Club (N.Y.C.). Episcopalian. Home: 67 Brighton Rd NE Atlanta GA 30309-1518 Office: PO Box 77388 Atlanta GA 30357

MASSEY, CHRIS, state legislator; b. Greenville, Miss., Sept. 13, 1971; m. Cathy Herron; children: Katie, Dalton, Morgan. Attended, Northwest CC. Homebuilder, Miss.; mem. Dist. 1 Miss. State Senate, Jackson, 2012—. Active Habitat for Humanity Desoto; mem. Desoto Econ. Coun. Mem.: Home Builder's Assn. North Miss., Nat. Home Builder's Assn. Republican. Office: Miss State Senate PO Box 1018 Jackson MS 39215 Business E-Mail: cmassey@senate.ms.gov.

MASSEY, JAMES EARL, retired clergyman, educator; b. Ferndale, Mich., Jan. 4, 1930; s. George Wilson and Elizabeth (Shelton) M.; m. Gwendolyn Inez Kilpatrick, Aug. 4, 1951. Student, U. Detroit, 1949-50, 55-57; BTh, BRE, Detroit Bible Coll., 1961; AM, Oberlin Grad Sch. Theology, 1964; postgrad., U. Mich., 1967-69; DD, Asbury Theol. Sem., 1972, Ashland Theol. Sem., 1991, Huntington Coll., 1994; HumD, Tuskegee U., 1995; DD, Warner Pacific Coll., 1995; LittD, Anderson U., 1995; DD, Wash. and Jefferson Coll., 1997, North Park Theol. Sem., 1999. Ordained to ministry Ch. of God, 1951. Assoc. min. Ch. of God, Detroit, 1951-53; sr. pastor Met. Ch. of God, Detroit, 1954-76, pastor-at-large, 1976; spkr. Christian Brotherhood Hour, 1977-82; prin. Jamaica Sch. Theology, Kingston, 1963-66; campus min. Anderson Coll., Ind., 1969-77, asst. prof. religious studies Ind., 1969-75, assoc. prof. Ind., 1975-80, prof. N.T. and homiletics Ind., 1981-84; dean of chapel and univ., prof. religion and society Tuskegee U., Ala., 1984-89; dean, prof. preaching and bibl. studies Anderson Sch. Theology, 1989-95, dean emeritus, prof. at large, 1995—; dean emeritus Tuskegee U. Chapel, 1998—; ret., 1998. Chmn. Comm. on Higher Edn. in the Ch. of God, 1968-71; vice chmn. bd. publs. Ch. of God, 1968-78; dir. Warner Press, Inc.; rsch. scholar Christianity Today Inst. Author: When Thou Prayest, 1960, The Worshipping Church, 1961, Raymond S. Jackson, A Portrait, 1967, The Soul Under Seige, 1970, The Church of God and the Negro, 1971, The Hidden Disciplines, 1972, The Responsible Pulpit, 1973, Temples of the Spirit, 1974, The Sermon in Perspective, 1976, Concerning Christian Unity, 1979; gen. editor: Christian Brotherhood Hour Study Bible, 1979, Designing the Sermon, 1980; co-editor: Interpreting God's Word for Today, 1982; editor: Educating for Service, 1984, The Spiritual Disciplines, 1985, The Bridge Between, 1988, Preaching From Hebrews, 1992, The Burdensome Joy of Preaching, 1996, Sundays at The Tuskegee Chapel, 1999, Aspects of My Pilgrimage: An Autobiography, 2002, Remembering William L. Dawson, 2004; co-editor: African Americans and the Church of God, 2005, Stewards of the Story, 2005, Our Sufficiency is of God: Essays on Preaching in Honor of Gardner C. Taylor, 2010, The Pastoral Letters & Philemon, 2012; mem. editl. bd. The Christian Scholar's Rev. Leadership mag.; mem. editl. bd., contbg. editor Vol I New Interpreter's Bible, 1990—; contbg. editor Preaching mag.; sr. editor Christianity Today mag. Mem. Corp. Inter-Vrsity Christian Fellowship; bd. dirs. World Vision. Served with AUS, 1951-53. Mem. Nat. Assn. Coll. and Univ. Chaplains, Nat. Com. Black Churchmen, Nat. Negro Evang. Assn. (bd. dirs. 1969-86). Office: 367 Beverly Rd Greensboro AL 36744-6034*

MASSEY, RICHARD N., finance company executive, lawyer; JD with honors, U. Ark. Ptnr. Kutak Rock, 1998—2000; mng. dir. Stephens, Inc., 2000—06; chief strategy officer, gen. counsel, exec. v.p., & corp. sec. Alltel Corp., 2005—09; founding ptnr. West Rock Capital Partners, LLC, Little Rock, 2009—. Bd. dirs. Fidelity Nat. Info. Svcs., Inc., Fidelity Nat. Fin., Inc. Office: West Rock Capital Partners LLC 900 S Shackleford Rd Little Rock AR 72211-3817 Office Phone: 501-320-4860. Business E-Mail: richard.massey@fisglobal.com.

MASSEY, THOMAS BENJAMIN, retired university president; b. Charlotte, NC, Sept. 5, 1926; s. William Everard and Sarah (Corley) M.; m. Bylee Hunnicutt Massey, July 10, 1968; children: Pamela Ann, Caroline Forest. AB, Duke U., 1948; MS, N.C. State U., 1953; PhD, Cambridge U., 1968. Assoc. dean students Ga. Inst. Tech., Atlanta, 1950-58; lectr. U. Md. Univ. Coll., 1960-66, dir. London, 1966—69, dir. Toyko, 1969-71, dir. Heidelberg (Fed. Republic of Germany), 1971-76, vice chancellor, 1976-78, chancellor, 1978-88, pres., 1988-98, pres. emeritus, 1998—. Served with USN, 1943-46. Mem. APA, Internat. Confs. on Improving Learning and Tchg. at the Univ. (chair 1975—). Personal E-mail: benmassey@mac.com.

MASSEY, WILLIAM WALTER, JR., sales executive; b. Lawrenceburg, Tenn., Sept. 21, 1928; s. William Walter and Bess Ann (Brian) M.; m. Virginia Claire Smith, Aug. 16, 1952; children: William Walter III, Laura Ann, Lynn Smith, Lisa Claire. BBA, U. Miami, Fla., 1949; BFA, U. Fla., 1969. Co-owner Massey Motors, Inc., Jacksonville, Fla., 1950—; v.p., dir. Atlantic Discount Co. Inc., Jacksonville, 1954-64; pres. Owners Surety Corp., Jacksonville, 1959—, General Svcs. Corp., Jacksonville, 1960-69, Owners Guaranty Life, Phoenix, 1960-64, Securities Guaranty Life, Phoenix, 1961-64, Fla. Properties, Inc., Jacksonville, 1961-66, Chi-Cha, Inc., Jacksonville, 1965-70, Univ. Square Properties, Jacksonville, 1969-80; v.p., sec./treas. Spring Forest Properties, Cashiers, NC, 1978—2001. V.p., bd. dir. Southside Country Day School, Jacksonville, 1963-68; bd. dirs. Southside Atlantic Bank, Jacksonville, 1965-93. Exhibited in group shows at Internat., N.Y., 1970, Ball State U., 1972; author Massey Genealogy, 2000. Lt. USAF, 1950-1952. Mem. Ponte Vedra Club, River Club, Epping Forest Club, Deerwood Club, Sigma Chi. Methodist. Avocations: music, painting, writing. Personal E-mail: billmasseyii@prodigy.net.

MASSIE, JAMES P., III, state legislator; b. Norfolk, Va., May 3, 1958; m. Elizabeth Wallis; children: James P. IV, William P., Rebecca Q., John H. BA in Economics, U. Va., 1980. Pvt. equity investor; mem. Dist. 72 Va. House of Delegates, 2009—. Republican. Presbyterian. Office: PO Box 29598 Richmond VA 23242 also: General Assembly Bldg PO Box 406 Richmond VA 23218 Office Phone: 804-377-0100, 804-698-1072. Fax: 804-698-6772. E-mail: DelJMassie@house.virginia.gov.

MASSIE, THOMAS HAROLD, United States Representative from Kentucky, farmer; b. Huntington, W.Va., Jan. 13, 1971; m. Rhonda Massie; 4 children. BS in Electrical Engring., MS in Electrical Engring., MIT. Co-founder, chmn., chief technology officer SensAble Technologies, Inc. (formerly SensAble Devices Inc.), 1993—2003; judge-exec. Lewis County, Ky., 2011—12; mem. US Congress from 4th Ky. Dist., Washington, 2013—, US House Oversight & Govt. Reform Com., 2013—, US House Sci., Space & Technology Com., 2013—, US House Transp. & Infrastructure Com., 2013—. Recipient Lemelson-MIT Student prize, 1995. Republican. Office: US House of Representatives 314 Cannon House Office Bldg Washington DC 20515 also: 1405 Greenup Ave Ste 236 Ashland KY 41101 Office Phone: 202-225-3465, 606-324-9898. Office Fax: 202-225-0003, 606-325-9866.*

MASSIMINO, ROLAND V. (ROLLIE MASSIMINO), men's college basketball coach; b. Hillside, NJ, Nov. 13, 1934; s. Salvatore and Grace (Alberti) M.; m. Mary Jane Reid, Aug. 13, 1958; children: Thomas, Lee Ann, Michele, R.C., Andrew Degree in Bus., U. Vt., 1956; M.P.E., Rutgers U., 1959; guidance cert., Tufts U., 1969. Asst. basketball coach Cranford HS Cougars, NJ, 1956-59; head basketball coach Hillside HS Comets, NJ, 1959-63, Lexington HS Minutemen, Mass., 1963-69, SUNY-Stony Brook Seawolves, 1969-71; asst. basketball coach U. Pa. Quakers, 1971-73; head basketball coach Villanova U. Wildcats, Pa., 1973-92, U. Nev. Las Vegas Runnin' Rebels, 1992—94, Cleve. State U. Vikings, 1996—2003; dir. basketball ops., head basketball coach Northwood U. Seahawks, Fla., 2005—. Named Phila. Big 5 Coach of Yr., 1976, 1978, 1982, 1983, 1985, Ea. Athletic Assn. Coach of Yr., 1977, Ea. 8 Conf. Coach of Yr., 1979, 1980, Widmer Cup Ea. Coach of Yr., 1982, Big East Conf. Coach of Yr., 1982, Ea. Basketball Ea. Coach of Yr., 1985, Nat. Coach of Yr., MacGregor Sporting Goods, Playboy mag., 1985, NAIA Divsn. II Coach of Yr., Nat. Assn. Basketball Coaches, 2011; named to Stony Brook Athletic Hall of Fame, 1991, Big 5 Hall of Fame, 2010. Mem.: Nat. Assn. Basketball Coaches. Achievements include head coach of NCAA Final Four national championship winning University of Villanova Wildcats, 1985. Office: Northwood University Mens Basketball c/o Athletics Dept 2600 N Military Trail West Palm Beach FL 33409 Office Phone: 561-681-7987.

MASSIN, EDWARD KRAUSS, physician; b. Houston, 1939; MD, Washington U., St. Louis, 1965; BA, Rice U., 1961. Intern Barnes Hosp., St. Louis, 1965-66, resident, 1966-67; with St. Lukes Episcopal. Hosp., Houston. Clin. prof. Baylor Coll. Medicine. Cardiology fellow U. Colo. Med. Ctr., 1969-71. Fellow Am. Coll. Cardiology Office: Cardiology Cons Houston 6624 Fannin St Ste 2310 Houston TX 77030-2335 Office Phone: 713-796-2668.

MASSINGALE, LYNN, healthcare staffing company executive; MD, U. Tenn. Ctr. for Health Sciences. Cert. Am. Bd. Emergency Medicine. Co-founder, pres., CEO Southeastern Emergency Physicians (predecessor to Team Health), 1980—94; med. dir., divsn. emergency med. services Tenn. Dept. Health, 1989—93; CEO Health Financial Corp., Team Fin., LLC, Team Health, Inc., 1994—; pres. Team Health Holdings, Inc., 2004, exec. chmn., 2008—. Various capacities involving emergency care Knoxville Acad. Medicine, Am. Heart Assn. (East Tenn. Divsn.); exec. chmn., chmn. nominating com. Team Health Holdings, Inc., bd. mem., 1999; exec. chmn., mem. nominating com. Health Fin. Corp. Named one of Modern Healthcare/Modern Physician's 50 Most Powerful Physician Executives, 2006, 2007. Mem.: Am. Coll. Healthcare Executives, Emergency Dept. Practice Mgmt. Assn. (former chmn.). Office: Team Health Holdings Inc 265 Brookview Town Centre Way Ste 400 Knoxville TN 37919

MASSMAN, RICHARD ALLAN, lawyer; b. Beaumont, Tex., Aug. 19, 1943; s. Irwin Massman and Sylvia (Schmidt) Schwartz; m. Barbara Elaine Kessler; children: Jason Todd, Karen Faye. BS cum laude, U. Pa., 1965; JD cum laude, Harvard U., 1968. Bar: Tex. 1968; cert. in taxation, Tex. Bd. Legal Specialization. Assoc. Coke & Coke, Dallas, 1968-70, Johnson & Wortley, P.C. (formerly Johnson & Gibbs,

P.C.), Dallas, 1970-71, ptnr., 1971-88, shareholder, 1988-94; of counsel Johnson & Wortley P.C., Dallas, 1994-95; sr. v.p., gen. counsel Hunt Consolidated, Inc., Dallas, 1994—2009, gen. counsel emeritus, 2009—. Lectr. So. Meth. U., Dallas, 1973; trustee Am. Beacon Funds, 2004—, chmn., 2008—; bd. dirs. Retina Found. Southwest, 2004—. Chmn. Dallas Civil Svc. Bd., 1983; trustee Greenhill Sch., Dallas, 1985-92, vice chmn., 1990-92; trustee Dallas Opera, 1999—; chmn. Dallas Opera Found., 2007-2011; bd. dirs. Presbyn. Hosp. Found., 2007-2013, exec. bd. Dallas Symphony, 2011-, treas. 2012-; chmn. Temple Emanu-El Found., 2006-10. Recipient Jurisprudence award Anti-Defamation League, 2000, Best Gen. Counsel award Dallas Bus. Jour., 2006. Mem. Am. Coll. Tax Coun., Tex. State Bar (chmn., sec. taxation 1983-84), Dallas Bar Assn. (chmn., sec. taxation 1978), Trophy Club, Bent Tree Country Club, Beaver Creek Club.

MASTEJ, J. MICHAEL, retired hospital administrator; b. Detroit, Mar. 19, 1949; s. Joseph Albert and Bertha A. (Toleikis) Mastej; m. Laura Thtatcher Wright, Dec. 28, 1975 (div. 1983); 1 child; m. Lucy Shafer Mastej, July 28, 1984. BBA in Acctg., U. Notre Dame, 1971. Group dir., dir., devel. Universal Health Svcs., Inc.; medicare and medicaid auditor Mich. Blue Cross; asst. contr. Emma L. Bixby Hosp., Adrian, Mich., 1973—75; CEO, acute care hosps. Humana, Inc., reimbursement specialist, 1975—77; exec. dir. Humana Hosp., Ft. Walton Beach, Fla., 1981; assoc. exec. dir. Llano Estacado Med. Ctr., Hobbs, N.Mex., 1977—78, The Wellington Hosp., 1978—79; exec. dir. Garden State Cmty. Hosp., Marlton, NJ, 1979—81; bd. advisor Okaloosa County Emergency Med., 1984; v.p., acquisitions Health Management Associates, Inc., 2001—05, CEO, Collier Regional Med. Ctr. Naples, Fla., 2005—07. V.p. Okaloosa Symphony; bd. dirs. Okaloosa chpt. Am. Heart Assn. Recipient Humana Mgmt. Club award, Louisville, 1981—82; named King of Hearts, Am. Heart Assn., Okaloosa County, 1985. Mem.: Greater Ft. Walton Beach C. of C. (v.p. 1985), Am. Coll. Hosp. Adminstrs., Rotary (program chmn. 1985). Republican. Episcopalian. Avocations: sailing, skiing, golf.

MASTERS, ANNE, library director; With Pioneer Libr. System, Okla. Recipient Outstanding Alumni award, U. Okla. Sch. Libr. and Info. Studies, 2007. Mem.: Continuing Libr. Edn. and Networking Exchange Round Table (pres. 2006—07), Pub. Libr. Assn. (mem. trainer cadre), Urban Libraries Coun. (exec. leadership inst. sponsor, Joey Rodger Leadership award 2005), Okla. Libr. Assn. (Disting. Svc. award, Meritorious Svc. award, named Okla. Libr. Legend 2007), Norman Sooner Rotary. Office: Pioneer Libr System 225 N Webster Norman OK 73069 Office Phone: 405-701-2642. Office Fax: 405-701-2649. Business E-Mail: amsters@pls.lib.ok.us.

MASTERS, CLAUDE BIVIN, lawyer; b. Cleburne, Tex., July 25, 1930; s. Claude Pinkney and Ola Mae (Rollins) M.; m. Jenita Whites, June 1, 1949 (div.); children: C. Thomas, Cl Danette Masters McClanahan, Teresa Masters Leck; m. Cynthia McCormack, Nov. 4, 1983 (div.). BS, U. Houston, 1953, JD, 1969, LLM, 1985. Bar: Tex. 1969, U.S. Dist. Ct. (so. dist.) Tex. 1972, U.S. Dist. Ct. (we. dist.) Tex. 1972, U.S. Ct. Appeals (5th cir.) 1971, U.S. Ct. Appeals (11th cir.) 1983, U.S. Supreme Ct. 1978. Ptnr. Martin & Masters, Houston, 1971-73; v.p., gen. counsel Summit Ins. Co. N.Y., NYC, 1973-75; sr. atty. Ashland Oil Co., Ky., 1975-78; v.p. Houston Oil and Minerals Co., 1978-84, assoc.; risk mgmt. cons. Masters & Assocs., Houston, 1975—. Adj. prof. law U. Houston, 1984—. Dir.-gen. Tex. Safety Assn., Austin, 1959, mng. atty., 1999-2009. Served with U.S. Army, 1946-47. Named Outstanding Speaker, Southwest Ins. Info. Svc., Dallas, 1961-62. Fellow Tex. Bar Found. (life), Houston Bar Found. (life), Atty.-Mediators Assn. (Houston chpt., sec.); mem. Jaycees (bd. dirs. Tulsa 1962; named Outstanding Mem. Tex. 1960), Am. Corp. Counsel (Houston chpt., pres., treas.) Phi Delta Phi. Republican. Mem. Ch. of Christ. Home: 314 College St Cleburne TX 76033 Office: 5444 Westheimer Rd Ste 1775 Houston TX 77056-5325 Office Phone: 713-598-8797.

MASTERS, JOHN CHRISTOPHER, psychologist, educator; b. Terre Haute, Ind., Oct. 25, 1941; s. Robert William and Lillian Virginia (Decker) M.; m. Mary Jayne Capps, June 6, 1970; children—Blair Christopher, Kyle Alexander. AB, Harvard Coll., 1963; PhD, Stanford U., 1967. Asst. prof. Ariz. State U., Tempe, 1968-69; from asst. prof. to prof. U. Minn., Mpls., 1969-79; assoc. dir. Inst. Child Devel., 1974-79; Luce prof. pub. policy and the family, prof. psychology Vanderbilt U., Nashville, 1979-87, interim chair dept. psychology, 1986-88; pres. Profl. Mgmt. Group, Inc., 1991—; dir. Master Ventures, 1989—, Master Travel, 1989—. Assoc. editor: Child Development, 1973-76, Behavior Therapy: Techniques and Empirical Findings, 1974, 79, 88; editor: Psychol. Bull., 1987-89. Home: 4923 Old Oakleaf Dr Sarasota FL 34233-3947 Office Phone: 800-767-6162.

MASTERSON, KENNETH RHODES, lawyer, board member; b. Kennett, Mo., Feb. 22, 1944; s. H. Byron and Mary (Rhodes) M.; children— Michael K., Elizabeth Megel, Grace Megel BA, Westminster Coll., 1966; JD, Vanderbilt U., 1970. Bar: Mo. 1970, Tenn. 1976. Ptnr. Thomason, Crawford & Hendrix, Memphis, 1976-79; v.p., legal Federal Express Corp., 1980—81, sr. v.p., 1981—96, exec. v.p., gen. counsel & sec., 1996—98; exec. v.p., gen. counsel and sec. FedEx Corp., 1998—2005. Bd. dirs. Accredo Health, Inc., Thomas & Betts Corp., 1995—. Mem. ABA, Mo. Bar Assn., Am. Corp. Counsel Assn. Home: 8679 Classic Dr Memphis TN 38125-8824 Office: Thomas & Betts Corp Bd Directors 8155 T&B Blvd Memphis TN 38125 Office Phone: 901-252-8000. Office Fax: 901-252-1354. Business E-Mail: kenneth.masterson@tnb.com.

MASTERSON, KLEBER SANLIN, JR., physicist; b. San Diego, Sept. 26, 1932; s. Kleber Sandlin and Charlotte Elizabeth (Parker) M.; m. Sara Ann Cooper, Dec. 21, 1957; children: Thomas Marshall, John Cooper. BS in Engring., US Naval Acad., Annapolis, 1954; MS in Physics, US Naval Postgrad. Sch., Monterey, Calif., 1961; PhD in Physics, U. Calif., San Diego, 1963; grad. in advanced mgmt. program, Harvard Bus. Sch., 1982. Commd. ensign USN, 1954, advanced through grades to rear adm., 1979, comdg. officer USS Preble Pearl Harbor, Hawaii, 1969-71, mgr. antiship missile def. project Washington, 1974-77, exec. asst. to sec. of Navy, 1977-79, asst. dep. comdr. Naval Sea Systems Command, 1979-81, chief Studies, Analyses and Gaming Agy., 1981-82, ret., 1982; prin. Booz, Allen and Hamilton, Inc., Arlington, Va., 1982-87, v.p. and ptnr., 1987-92; sr. v.p. Sci. Applications Internat. Corp., 1992—96; pres. The Riverside Group, Ltd., 1994—2005; ret. Bd. control, editl. bd. US Naval Inst., Annapolis, Md., 1971-82, chmn. editl. bd. 1974-82; bd. dirs. Mil. Ops. Rsch. Soc., 1984-90, pres., 1988-89; mem. divsn. rev. com. TSA divsn. Los Alamos Nat. Lab., 1996-2001, chmn. 1998-2001; asst. professorial lectr. Bus. Adminstrn., George Washington U., Washington, 1966-69. Editor: Book of Navy Songs, 1954; contbr. articles on plasma and theoretical nuclear physics, computer science, radars, ops. rsch. to profl. publs. Active Historic Alexandria Resources Commn., 1998—2008, vice-chmn. 2001-02, chmn., 2002-04, Old Town Citizens Assn., 1975-1987, pres. 1985-1887. Ret. rear admiral USN. Decorated Defense Superior Svc. medal, Legion of Merit with 2 gold stars, Navy Commendation medal with combat V and 2 gold stars. Mem.: Am. Phys. Soc., US Naval Acad. Alumni Assn. (pres. Washington chpt. 1989-90), US Naval Acad. Found. (trustee 1991—2010, trustee emeritus 2010-), Soc. of Cin. (chmn. edn. com. 1997-2001, asst. sec. gen. 2001-04, editor Cin. Fourteen 2001-04, treas. gen. 2004-07, v.p. gen. 2007-10, pres. gen. 2010-13), Mass. Soc. of Cin. (mem. standing com., v.p. 1999-2001, pres. 2001-04), Sigma Xi. Achievements include development of NELIAC computer program and strategic simulation methodology. Home and Office: 101 Pommander Walk Alexandria VA 22314-3844 Home Phone: 703-548-4464; Office Phone: 703-548-6183. Personal E-mail: skidmasterson@cs.com.

MASTRACCHIO, RICHARD A. (RICK), astronaut; b. Waterbury, Conn., Feb. 11, 1960; s. Ralph and Georgiana Mastracchio (Stepmother), Helen Cooke; m. Candace L. Stolfi; 3 children. BSEE and Computer Sci., U. Conn., 1982; MSEE, Rensselaer Poly. Inst., 1987; MS in Phys. Sci., U. Houston, Clear Lake, Tex., 1991. Engr. sys. design group Hamilton Std., Conn., 1982—87; with Rockwell Shuttle Ops. Co., Houston, 1987—90; engr. flight crew ops. directorate NASA, Houston, 1990—93, ascent/entry guidance and procedures officer in mission control, 1993—96; astronaut NASA, Johnson Space Ctr., Houston, 1996—. Mission specialist STS-106 Mission (Atlantis), 2000, STS-118 Mission (Endeavour) to Internat. Space Station, 2007, STS-131 Mission (Discovery), 2010, Expedition 38/39, 2013. Mem.: IEEE. Achievements include 12 day mission aboard space shuttle Atlantis in Sept. 2000 to prepare International Space Station for arrival of first permanent crew; over 283 hours in space; performed rare Christmas Eve spacewalk outside the International Space Station in 2013; only the second Christmas Eve speacewalk in NASA history. Avocations: flying, baseball, basketball, swimming, woodworking. Office: Astronaut Office NASA Johnson Space Ctr Houston TX 77058*

MASTREAN, MICHELE, rail transportation executive; Attended, Tex. A&M U., 1993. V.p., human resources total compensation Halliburton Co., 1994—2008; v.p., compensation & benefits CSX Corp., 2008—. Office: CSX Corp 15th Fl 500 Water St Jacksonville FL 32202 Office Phone: 904-359-3200. Office Fax: 904-633-3450. Business E-Mail: michele_mastrean@csx.com.

MASUD, FAISAL, cardiologist; b. Pakistan, Jan. 21, 1965; MBBS, Rawalpindi Med. Coll., 1988. Assoc. prof. clin. anesthesiology, Weil Cornell Med. Coll. Meth. Hosp., Meth. DeBakey Heart & Vascular Ctr., 1997, vice chair qulality & patient safety, med. dir., CVICU, 1997—. Recipient Fulbright & Jaworski Faculty Excellence award, Baylor Coll. Medicine. Fellow: Am. Coll. Chest Physician; mem.: Acad. Disting. Educators, Assn. Profl. Infection Control & Epidemiology (named Hero in Infection Prevention 2010), Soc. Cardiovasc. Anesthesiologists, Soc. Critical Care Medicine (Alan I Fields award, Tex. chpt. 2010). Avocations: basketball, cricket. Office: 6565 Fannin St B452 Houston TX 77030 Business E-Mail: fmasud@tmhs.org.*

MASYS, DANIEL RICHARD, medical educator, department chairman; b. Columbus, Ohio, Mar. 6, 1949; s. Paul John and Jane Marie (Mollenauer) M.; m. Linda Suzanne Bross, June 2, 1974; 1 child, Christopher. AB in Biochemistry, Princeton U., 1971; MD, Ohio State U., 1974. Diplomate Am. Bd. Internal Medicine. Staff hematologist, oncologist U.S. Naval Hosp., San Diego, 1980-84; chief ICRDB br. NIH, Bethesda, Md., 1984-86; dir. Lister Hill Nat. Ctr. Nat. Libr. Medicine, Bethesda, Md., 1986-94; dir. biomed. informatics, prof. Sch. Medicine U. Calif., San Diego, 1994—2004; prof., chair dept. biomedical informatics Vanderbilt U., 2005—. Assoc. editor Acad. Medicine jour., 1988-91, Jour. Am. Med. Informatics, Assn., 1994-2004. Mem. high performance computing White House Office of Sci., Washington, 1991-94; rep. Fed. Networking Coun., Washington, 1991-94. Capt. USPHS, 1984-94; NASA Adv. Aerospace Medicine, 2004-. Fellow: ACP, Am. Coll. Med. Informatics (exec. com. 1989—92, pres. 2006—); mem.: Nat. Acad. Scis., Inst. Medicine, Am. Med. Informatics Assn. (bd. dirs. 1992—95, assoc. editor jour. 1993—2004, Pres.'s award 1992), Alpha Omega Alpha. Office: Vanderbilt Univ 416 EBL 2209 Garland Ave Nashville TN 37232-8340

MATALIN, MARY JOE, political consultant, editor; b. Chgo., Aug. 19, 1953; d. Steven and Eileen Matalin; m. Artie Arnold (div.); m. James Carville, Nov. 25, 1993; 2 children. BA in Political Sci., Western Ill. U.; student, Hofstra Law Sch., Hempstead, NY. Voter contact dir. Reagan-Bush re-election campaign, 1984; chief staff to co-chmn. RNC, 1985; Midwest regional political dir. primary elections Bush-Quayle election campaign, 1988, dir. nat. victory '88 gen. election, 1988; polit. dir. George Bush's 1992 re-election campaign; co-host Equal Time, CNBC, 1993—96; host The Mary Matalin Show, CBS Talk Radio Network, 1996—98; co-host Crossfire, 1999—2001; asst. to Pres. & counselor to v.p. The White House, 2001—02; chief editor Threshold Editions (Simon & Schuster), 2005—. Author: All's Fair: Love, War and Running for President, 1992, Letters to My Daughters, 2004; appearances include (TV series) K-Street, (documentaries) Boogie Man: The Lee Atwater Story. Named one of 25 Most Influential Republicans, Newsmax Mag., 2008, The 50 Highest-Earning Polit. Figures, Newsweek, 2010. Republican. Office: The Office of Mary Matalin 424 S Wash St Lower Level Alexandria VA 22314 Office Phone: 703-739-6006. E-mail: mary@matalin.info.*

MATCHAR, DAVID B., physician, researcher; b. Balt., Sept. 29, 1955; s. Joseph Charles and Evelyn M.; m. Barbara Fran Goldfinger, May 4, 1980; children: Emily Ruth, Benjamin Jacob, Daniel William. MD, U. Md., 1980. Diplomate Am. Bd. Internal Medicine. Prof. medicine Duke U. Med. Ctr., Durham, NC, 1985—, dir. Duke Ctr. Clin. Health Policy Rsch., 1985—; dir., program health svcs. rsch. Duke Nat. U. Singapore Grad. Med. Sch., 2008—. Fellow ACP, Soc. Gen. Internal Medicine (pres. so. sect. 1988), Am. Heart Assn., Soc. for Med. Decision Making (editl. bd., chair 1993 ann. meeting, trustee), Am. Acad. Neurology, Svoke Coun. Office: Duke Ctr Clin Health Policy Rsch 2400 Pratt St # 311 Durham NC 27705-3976 Office Phone: 919-286-3399. Business E-Mail: david-matchar@duke-nus.edu.sg.

MATECKI, PAUL L., lawyer; b. 1955; BA in Economics, Grinnell Coll., 1978; JD, St. Louis U., 1981. Bar: Mo. 1981, Fla. 1987. Corp. counsel Raymond James Financial, Inc., St. Petersburg, Fla., 1989—97, sr. v.p., 1989—, dir., compliance, 2004, gen. counsel, 2004—, corp. sec., 2006—. Mem.: ABA, Assn. Corp. Counsel West Fla. Chpt. Office: Raymond James Financial Inc 880 Carillon Pky Saint Petersburg FL 33716 Office Phone: 727-567-1000. Office Fax: 727-567-8915. Business E-Mail: paul.matecki@raymondjames.com.

MATHENY, ADAM PENCE, JR., child psychologist, educator, consultant, researcher; b. Stanford, Ky., Sept. 6, 1932; s. Adam Pence and Dorotha (Steele) Matheny; m. Ute I. Debus, July 10, 1962 (div.); m. Mary P. Tolbert, June 24, 1967 (div.); children: Laura Steele, Jason Gaverick. BS, Columbia U., 1958; PhD, Vanderbilt U., 1962. Sr. human factors engr. Martin Aerospace divsn., Balt., 1962—63; instr. Johns Hopkins U. Med. Sch., Balt., 1963—65; staff fellow Nat. Inst. Child Health and Human Devel., 1965—67; from asst. prof. to prof. pediat. U. Louisville Med. Sch., 1967—75; assoc. dir. to dir. Louisville Twin Study, 1986—. Mem. rev. panel NIH, 1991—95. Co-author: Genetics and Counseling in Medical Practice, 1969; contbr. articles to profl. jours. With USN, 1951—55. Recipient Outstanding Rsch. medal, U. Louisville. Fellow: APA, Am. Psychol. Soc., Am. Assn. Applied and Preventive Psychology, Internat. Soc. Twin Studies; mem.: AAAS, Internat. Soc. Infant Study, Internat. Soc. Behavior Devel., Behavior Genetics Assn., Soc. Rsch. Child Devel., Sigma Xi, Phi Beta Kappa. Office Phone: 502-634-0050. Business E-Mail: apmathol@louisville.edu. E-mail: adammatheny9@gmail.com.

MATHENY, DRUE (DRUE DILLARD CORBUSIER), retail executive; b. 1946; d. William T. and Alexa Dillard. Joined Dillard's, Inc., 1968, bd. dirs., 1994—, exec. v.p., 1998—, dir. regional merchandising, Ft. Worth divsn. Office: Dillards Inc 1600 Cantrell Rd Little Rock AR 72201 Office Phone: 501-376-5200. Office Fax: 501-399-7831. E-mail: drue.corbusier@dillards.com.

MATHENY, JUDD, state legislator; b. Apr. 9, 1970; m. Christy Matheny; children: Abigail, Aulden. Mem. Dist. 47 Tenn. House of Reps., 2003—; mem. Commerce & State & Local Com.; chmn. Coffee Co Rep. Party; security, pvt. investigator; police officer. Master: Masons; mem.: NRA, Tullahoma Bus. & Profl. Women, Tenn. Farm Bur., Manchester & McMinnville C. of C., Tullahoma Rotary Club, Quail Unlimted, Nat. Wild Turkey Fedn., Davidson Counter Crime Stoppers. Republican. Office: 205 War Memorial Bldg Nashville TN 37243-0147 also: 113 Crestwood Dr Tullahoma TN 37388 Office Phone: 615-741-7448. Office Fax: 615-253-0226. Business E-Mail: rep.judd.matheny@capitol.tn.gov.

MATHENY, RUTH ANN, editor; b. Fargo, ND, Jan. 17, 1918; d. Jasper Gordon and Mary Elizabeth (Carey) Wheelock; m. Charles Edward Matheny, Oct. 24, 1960. BE, Mankato State Coll., 1938; MA, U. Minn., 1955; postgrad., Universidad Autonoma de Guadalajara, Mex., 1956, Georgetown U., 1960. Tchr., U.S. and S.Am., 1938-61; assoc. editor Charles E. Merrill Pub. Co., Columbus, Ohio, 1963-66; tchr. Confraternity Christian Doctrine, Washington Court House, Ohio, 1969-70; assoc. editor Jr. Cath. Messenger, Dayton, Ohio, 1966-68; editor Witness Intermediate, Dayton, 1968-70; editor in chief, assoc. pub. Today's Cath. Tchr., Dayton, 1970—2002, editor-in-chief emeritus, 2002—; editor in chief Catechist, Dayton, 1976-89, Ednl. Dealer, Dayton, 1976-80; v.p. Peter Li, Inc., Dayton, 1980—. Editl. collaborator: Dimensions of Personality series, 1969—; co-author: At Ease in the Classroom; author: Why a Catholic School?, Scripture Stories for Today: Why Religious Education?; freelance writer, 1943—2011. Bd. dirs. Friends Ormond Beach Libr. Mem.: 3d Order St. Francis (eucharistic min. 1990—2006), Nat. Coun. Cath. Women. Home: 26 Reynolds Ave Ormond Beach FL 32174-7043 Office: Peter Li Ednl Group 2621 Dryden Rd Ste 300 Dayton OH 45439 Personal E-mail: chilermat@aol.com.

MATHER, STEPHANIE JUNE, lawyer; b. Kansas City, Mo., Dec. 5, 1952; d. Edward Wayne and H. June (Kunkel) M.; m. Miles Christopher Zimmerman, Sept. 23, 1988. BA magna cum laude, Okla. City U., 1975, JD with honors, 1980. Lawyer Pierce, Couch, Hendrickson, Johnston & Baysinger, Okla. City, Okla., 1980—88, Manchester, Hiltgen & Healy, P.C., Okla. City, 1989—90; sr. staff counsel Nat. Am. Ins. Co., Chandler, Okla., 1990—98; atty. Ctr. for Edn. Law, Oklahoma City, 1998—2012, v.p., shareholder, 2003—12; atty., dir. Okla. State Sch. Bds. Assn., 2012—. Asst. v.p. Lagere & Walkingstick Ins. Agy., Inc., Chandler, Okla., 1993-98. Co-chair Lincoln County Dem. Party, 1991-92, 95-97; v.p. Lincoln County Dem. Women, 1992-95, pres., 1995-97; bd. dirs. Lincoln County Partnership for Children, 1994—, Gateway to Prevention and Recovery, 1996-97; election precinct official Lincoln County, 2011-. Mem.: Lincoln County Profl. Women, Okla. State Sch. Bds. Assn. (coun. sch. attys. 1998—, bd. dirs. 2002—05, pres. 2005—06), Nat. Sch. Bds. Assn. (coun. sch. attys. 1998—), Lincoln County Bar Assn. (libr. bd. 1990—), Okla. Bar Assn. (editor, bd. editors 1992—99), Alpha Phi (treas. Ctrl. Okla. Alumnae 1997—99, Outstanding Okla. City Alumnae 2005, Panhellenic Woman of Yr. Oklahoma City 2005). Democrat. Avocations: reading, genealogy, ranching, cooking. Home: PO Box 39 Agra OK 74824 Office Phone: 405-528-2800. Business E-Mail: stephaniem@ossba.org.*

MATHERNE, G. PAUL, medical educator; b. Lafayette, La., Oct. 30, 1958; s. Gaynell Paul and Marie Annette Matherne; m. Linda Ann Binko, June 21, 1980; children: Gregory James, Benjamin Thomas, Stephanie Leigh, Nicholas Scott. MD, Tex. A&M U., College Sta., 1982. Pediatric resident U. Okla., 1982—85. Pediatric cardiology fellow U. Iowa, 1985—88; prof. pediat. U. Va., Charlottesville, 1988—, dept. chair, 1988—, divsn. head, 2003—. Fellow: Am. Coll. Cardiology, Am. Heart Assn. (chair congenital cardiac defects sect.); mem.: Cardiovasc. Disease of Young Coun. (vice chair), Soc. Pediat. Radiology, Am. Pediat. Soc., Am. Acad. Pediat. Office: Univ Va Dept Pediat Charlottesville VA 22908 Home: 4255 Redwood Ln Earlysville VA 22936-2847 Business E-Mail: gpm2y@virginia.edu.

MATHEU, FEDERICO MANUEL, university chancellor; b. Humacao, PR, Mar. 17, 1941; s. Federico Matheu-Baez and Matilde Delgado-Vazquez; m. Myrna Delgado-Miranda, May 30, 1963; children: Federico Antonio, Rosa Myrna, Alfredo Javier, David Reinaldo. BS in Chem. Engring, U. P.R., 1962; PhD in Phys. Chemistry, U. Pitts., 1971. Chem. engr. Commonwealth Oil Refining Co., 1962-63; mem. adminstrv. staff and faculty U. P.R., 1963-78, dir. Humacao Coll., 1976-78; chancellor San German campus Inter Am. U. P.R., 1978-91; exec. dir., gen. coun. on edn. Commonwealth of P.R., Hato Rey, 1991-96; chancellor U. Metropolitana-Ana G. Méndez U. System, 1996—. Cons. in field. Author papers, reports in field. Named Disting. Educator P.R. Jaycees, 1974 Mem. Colegio de Quimicos P.R., Am. Chem. Soc., Sci. Tchrs. Assn. P.R. (pres. 1975-76), P.R. Acad. Arts and Scis., Phi Delta Kappa, Phi Tau Sigma. Home: Parque de Villa Caperra No 17 Zuania St Guaynabo PR 00966 Office: UMET PO Box 21150 San Juan PR 00928-1150 Office Phone: 787-766-1743. Business E-Mail: um_fmatheu@suagm.edu.

MATHEWS, SHARON WALKER, performing company executive, secondary school educator; b. Shreveport, La., Feb. 1, 1947; d. Arthur Delmar and Nona (Frye) Walker; m. John William (Bill) Mathews, Aug. 14, 1971; children: Rebecca, Elizabeth, Anna. BS, La. State U., 1969, MS, 1971. Cert. Am. Ballet Theatre Tchr. Tng. Curriculum, 2009. Dance grad. asst. La. State U., Baton Rouge, 1969-71, choreographer, 1975-76; 6th grade tchr. East Baton Rouge Parish, 1971-72, health phys. edn. tchr., 1972-74; dance instr. Magnet High Sch., Baton Rouge, 1975—; artistic dir. Baton Rouge Ballet Theatre, 1975—; dance dir. Dancers' Workshop, Baton Rouge, 1971—; choreographer Baton Rouge Opera, 1989-94, Univ. H.S. Musical Theatre, 1998—; choreographer Baton Rouge Gilbert and Sullivan Soc. summer musical La. State U., 2000, 2001; choreographer Baton Rouge Little Theater, 2000, 2002. Author: East Baton Rouge Parish Dance Curriculum. Mem. La. Supts. Task Force Arts in Edn., 1999—2001, La. Content Stds. Com. Dance, 2001, East Baton Rouge Parish Curriculum Com. Dance, 1997, La. Arts Consortium, 2000—, La. Arts Content Stds. Com., 2002—, La. Arts Content Revision Com., 2002—03. Recipient Stream award for Artistic Excellence, S.W. Regional Ballet Assn., 1991, Mayor's Pres.'s award for Excellence in the Arts, 1999, Creative Ticket award for excellence in the arts, Kennedy Ctr., 2005, John W. Barton Sr. Excellence in Nonprofit Mgmt. award, Baton Rouge Area Found., Standford Financial award, 2007; named Dance Educator of the Yr., La. Alliance Health, Phys. Edn., Recreation and Dance; named to Univ. HS Hall of Distinction,

2003, Baton Rouge Magnet HS Hall of Fame, 2003. Mem.: SW Regional Dance Am. (parlimentian 2007—), La. Assn. Health, Phys. Edn., Recreation and Dance (dance chairperson 1995), Southwestern Regional Ballet Assn. (bd. dirs. 1981—, treas., exec. bd. dirs. 1989—92). Republican. Baptist. Office: Baton Rouge Ballet Theater 10745 Linkwood Ct Baton Rouge LA 70810 Office Phone: 225-767-5814.

MATHEWS, TOMAS GOODWIN, broadcast executive; b. Haverhill, Mass., May 28, 1960; s. Harry Thomas and Janet Vivian (Normand); m. Lori Ann Kusmierek, June 30, 1990. BS, Trinity Coll., Hartford, Conn., 1982; MBA, U. Mich., 1984. Sr. human resources rep. Data Gen., Westboro, Mass., 1984-87; human resources mgr. Shearson Lehman Bros., NYC, 1987-90; dir., compensation and benefits International Data Group, Inc., Framingham, Mass., 1990-93, v.p., human resources, 1993; exec. v.p., human resources Time Warner Cable, Inc. Active Big Bros./Big Sisters, Hartford, 1978-82, ConnPirg, Hartford, 1980-82. Mem. Am. Compensation Assn. (cert. compensation prof. 1989), Soc. for Human Resource Mgmt., New England Internat. Pers. Forum (bd. dirs.), Met. Wine Group. Episcopalian. Avocations: athletics, wine collecting, music. Home: 1008 Seminole Dr Waxhaw NC 28173-6594 Office: Time Warner Cable Inc 60 Columbus Cir New York NY 10023 Office Phone: 212-364-8200. Office Fax: 203-328-0604. Business E-Mail: tomas.mathews@timewarnercable.com.

MATHEWSON, CHRISTOPHER COLVILLE, engineer, geologist, educator; b. Plainfield, NJ, Aug. 12, 1941; s. George Anderson and Elsa Rae (Shrimpton) M.; m. Janet Marie Olmsted, Nov. 2, 1968; children: Heather Alexis, Glenn George Anderson. BSCE, Case Inst. Tech., 1963; MS in Geol. Engring., U. Ariz., 1965, PhD in Geol. Engring., 1971. Registered profl. engr., Tex., Ariz.; profl. geologist Tex., Oreg., Alaska. Officer, lt. Nat. Ocean Survey, 1965-71; prof. Tex. A&M U., College Station, 1981—2011, regents prof., 2005—11; sr. prof., 2011—12; reagents prof. emeritus, 2011—; sr. tng. specialist Tex. Engring. Ext. Svc., 2012—. Mem. coun. examiners Assn. State Bds. Geology, 1994-, cons., speaker in field. Author: Engineering Geology, 1981 (C.P. Holdredge award); contbr. articles to profl. publs. Chmn. College Station Planning and Zoning Commn., 1973—81; trustee Geol. Soc. Am. Found., 2001—03. Fellow Geol. Soc. Am. (chmn. engring. geology divsn. 1986-87, Meritorious Svc. award 1991), Soc. Am. Mil. Engrs., Assn. Engring. Geologists (editor bull. 1981-88, pres. 1988-89, C.P. Holdredge award 1981, F.T. Johnston Svc. award 1995, Karl & Ruth Terzaghi Outstanding Mentor award 2008, exec. dir. 1998-2002), Am. Geol. Inst. (pres. 1991-92), Nat. Coal Coun., Internat. Assn. Engring. Geologists (chmn. U.S. nat. com. 1995-98), Tex. Bd. Profl. Geoscientists Gov. Perry(appointed mem., 2012-, profl. mem.). Achievements include Christopher C. Mathewson Scholarship established in his honor, 2011. Office: Tex A&M U Dept Geology And Geophysics College Station TX 77843-3115 Office Phone: 979-845-2488. E-mail: mathewson@geo.tamu.edu.

MATHIESON, ROBERT WILLIAM (BOBBY MATHIESON), federal marshal, former state legislator; b. NYC, June 16, 1956; m. Terry Rookus; children: Robert W. Jr., Daniel J. Graduated, St. Leo U., Fla., 1988. Police officer Va. Beach Police Dept., 1975—2002; mem. Dist. 21 Va. House of Delegates, 2009—10; US marshal (eastern dist.) Va. US Marshals Svc., US Dept. Justice, 2011—. Recipient Beacon of Light Award, The Lighthouse Center, 2007. Democrat. Roman Catholic. Office: US Marshals Service 401 Courthouse Sq Alexandria VA 22314 Office Phone: 703-837-5500.

MATHIS, LUSTER DOYLE, academic administrator, political scientist, educator; b. Gainesville, Ga., May 5, 1936; s. Luster and Fay Selena (Wingo) M.; m. Rheba Burch, June 5, 1958; children—Douglas James, Deborah Jane. AB, Berry Coll., 1958; MA, U. Ga., 1958, PhD (Univ. Alumni Found. fellow), 1966. Asst. prof. polit. sci. Brenau Coll., Gainesville, 1960-61; asso. prof. Calif. Baptist Coll., 1961-62, Belmont Coll., Nashville, 1962-64; asso. prof., head dept. polit. sci. W.Ga. Coll., Carrollton, 1965-68, prof., 1969-75, head dept., 1969-71, chmn. div. grad. studies, 1970-73; assoc. dean, 1972-75; research asso., asst. editor Papers of Thomas Jefferson Princeton U., 1968-69; v.p., dean of coll. Berry Coll., Mt. Berry, Ga., 1975-93, v.p. acad. affairs, 1993-99, provost, 1999-2000, coll. historian, prof. govt., 2000—03. Cons. Citizens Com. on Ga. Gen. Assembly. Co-author: Courts as Political Instruments, 1970. Mem. Ga. Democratic Charter Commn., 1974-75; mem. consumer adv. com. Floyd Med. Center, 1978-80. Fellow, Nat. Hist. Publs. Commn., 1968—69. Mem. Am. Assn. Higher Edn., Am. Conf. Acad. Deans, Ga. Polit. Sci. Assn. (pres. 1968-69). Democrat. Baptist.

MATLOCK, JACK FOUST, JR., diplomat; b. Greensboro, NC, Oct. 1, 1929; s. Jack Foust and Nellie (McSwain) M.; m. Rebecca Burrum, Sept. 2, 1949; children: James, Hugh, Nell, David, Joseph. AB summa cum laude, Duke U., 1950; MA, Columbia U., 1952; cert., Russian Inst., 1952; LLD (hon.), Greensboro Coll., 1989, Albright Coll., 1992, Conn. Coll., 1993; LLD (hon.), Latvian Acad. Scis., 2002. Instr. Dartmouth, 1953-56; fgn. service officer Dept. State, 1956-91; assigned Washington, 1956-58, Am. Embassy, Vienna, 1958-60; Am. consul. gen. Munich, 1960-61; assigned Am. Embassy, Moscow, 1961-63, Accra, Ghana, 1963-66, Am. Consulate, Zanzibar, 1967-69, Am. Embassy, Dar es Salaam, Tanzania, 1969-70, Sr. Seminar in Fgn. Policy, Dept. State, 1970-71; country dir. for USSR State Dept., 1971-74; minister-counselor, dep. chief mission Am. Embassy, Moscow, 1974-78; diplomat-in-residence Vanderbilt U., Nashville, 1978-79; dep. dir. Fgn. Service Inst., Washington, 1979-80; chargé d'affaires ad interim Am. Embassy, Moscow, 1981; ambassador to Czechoslovakia, 1981-83; spl. asst. to pres., sr. dir. European and Soviet Affairs Nat. Security Council, 1983-87; U.S. ambassador to the Soviet Union, Moscow, 1987-91; sr. rsch. fellow Columbia U., NYC, 1991-93, Kathryn and Shelby Collum Davis prof. Practice Internat. Diplomacy, 1993-96; George F. Kennan prof. Inst. for Advanced Study, Princeton, NJ, 1996-2001; John L. Weinberg/Goldman Sachs and Co. vis. prof. pub. and internat. affairs Princeton U., 2001—02; Sol Linowitz prof. internat. rels. Hamilton Coll., 2006, 2009; Cyrus Vance prof. internat. rels. Mt. Holyoke Coll., 2007—. Adj. prof. Columbia U., 2007—. Author: Autopsy on an Empire: The American Ambassador's Account of the Collapse of the Soviet Union, 1995, Reagan and Gorbachev: How the Cold War Ended, 2004, Superpower illusionsion How Myths & False Ideologies Led America Astray and How to Return to Reality, 2010; compiler, editor: Index to J.V. Stalin's Works, 2d edit., 1971. Mem. Am. Acad. Diplomacy, Coun. on Fgn. Rels., Century Assn. N.Y., Am. Philos. Soc. Home: 32 Wagoner Hill Rd Fayetteville TN 37334 Office Phone: 609-252-1953. Business E-Mail: matlock@ias.edu.

MATLOCK, JIMMY C., state legislator; b. Loudon, Tenn., Feb. 5, 1959; 3 children. State rep. Dist. 21, 2007—; mem. State Com., Local Com., Transp. Com. Republican. Office: 190 Matlock Rd Lenoir City TN 37771 also: 219 War Memorial Bldg Nashville TN 37243-0121 Office Phone: 615-741-3736. Business E-Mail: rep.jimmy.matlock@capitol.tn.gov.

MATSDORF, TYLER R., consulting firm executive, former legislative staff member; b. 1981; Dep. press sec. to Senator Max Baucus, US Senate, Washington, 2006—09, press sec., comm. dir., 2009—10; press sec. US Senate Finance Com., Washington, 2009; comm. dir. to Senator Richard Blumenthal US Senate, Washington, 2010—11; sr. adv. war room dir. American Bridge 21st Century, Washington, 2011—13; lobbyist The Messina Group, Washington, 2013—; campaigns & comm. dir. Senate Majority Polit. Action Com. (PAC), Washington, 2013—. Democrat.

MATSUI, HIDEFUMI, insurance company executive; b. Japan; Grad., Tokyo U., 1968. Sys. planner, mfg. processes Kawasaki Steel Corp.; joined AFLAC Inc, Japan, 1974, asst. v.p., 1981—85, v.p., 1985—87, sr. v.p., 1987—90, dir., mktg., 1990—92, exec. v.p., 1992—95, pres., 1995—2002; chmn. AFLAC, Inc., Japan, 2003—. Office: AFLAC Inc 1932 Wynnton Rd Columbus GA 31999 Office Phone: 706-323-3431. Office Fax: 706-324-6330. Business E-Mail: hmatsui@aflac.com.

MATTAUCH, ROBERT JOSEPH, retired electrical engineering educator, retired dean; b. Rochester, Pa., May 30, 1940; s. Henry Paul and Anna Marie (Mlinarcik) M.; m. Frances Sabo, Dec. 29, 1962; children: Lori Ann, Thomas J. BS, Carnegie Inst. Tech., Pitts., 1962; MEE, N.C. State U., Raleigh, 1963, PhD, 1967. Asst. prof. elec. engring. U. Va., Charlottesville, 1966-70, assoc. prof. elec. engring., 1970-76, prof. elec. engring., 1976-83, Wilson prof. elec. engring., 1983-86, Standard Oil Co. prof. sci. and tech., 1986-89, chmn. dept. elect. engring., 1987-95, BP Am. prof. sci. and tech., 1989-95; Commonwealth prof., founding chair dept. elec. engring. Va. Commonwealth U., Richmond, 1995-99, dean engring., Commonwealth prof., 1999—2006, dean emeritus, Commonwealth prof., 2006—. Cons. The Rochester Corp., Culpepper, Va., 1983—88, Milltech Corp., Deerfield, Mass., 1985. Patentee: infrared detector; solid state switching capacitor; thin wire pointing method, whiskerless Schottky diode, controlled in-situ etch back growth technique. Bd. dirs. U. Va. Patent Found., 1989-95, Greater Richmond Tech. Coun., 2001—, Va. Bioscis. Devel. Ctr., 2000—06, Richmond Symphony Orch., 2003-10, mem. Ellen Shew de Parades Breast Cancer Fedn., 2013- Recipient Excellence in Instruction of Engring. Students award Western Electric, 1980, Greater Richmond Tech. Coun. Leadership award, 2006; named one of Top Ten Talents of 1990 Wash. Tech. Fellow IEEE (Centennial medal 1984); mem. Eta Kappa Nu (recipient Oustanding Prof. in Elec. Engring. 1975), Sigma Xi, Tau Beta Pi, Sigma Pi Sigma, Phi Kappa Phi. Office: Va Commonwealth U PO Box 843072 Richmond VA 23284-3072 Business E-Mail: robert.mattauch@gmail.com.

MATTESON, KARLA J., medical geneticist, educator, former health science association administrator; BS in Chemistry, Beloit Coll., Wis., 1969; MS in Chemistry, Marquette U., 1976; PhD, Med. Coll. Wis., 1981. Postdoctoral fellow Baylor Coll. Medicine, Houston, 1981—83; former asst. dir. U. Tenn Devel. and Genetic Ctr., Knoxville; assoc. prof. med. genetics and pathology U. Tenn., Knoxville, 1986—, dir. biochem. and molecular genetics lab., 1986—; bd. dirs. Am. Bd. Med. Genetics, 1998—2001, exec. dir., 2001—09. Fellow: Am. Coll. Med. Genetics; mem.: AAAS, Soc. for Inborn Metabolic Disorders. Office: U Tenn Grad Sch Medicine Ste 435 1930 Alcoa Hwy Knoxville TN 37920-1514

MATTHEWS, BRUCE RANKIN, professional football coach, retired professional football player; b. Raleigh, NC, Aug. 8, 1961; m. Carrie Matthews; children: Steven, Kevin, Marilyn, Jake, Michael, Luke, Gweneth. BS in Indsl. Engring., U. So. Calif., 1983. Offensive lineman Houston Oilers, 1983-96, Tenn. Oilers (formerly Houston Oilers), 1996-97, Tenn. Titans, 1997—2001, offensive line coach, 2011—; ret. NFL, 2001; vol. coach Elkins HS, Missouri City, Tex.; offensive asst. Houston Texans, 2009—10. Named 1st Team All-Pro, AP, 1988—90, 1992, 1998—2000; named to Am. Football Conf. Pro Bowl Team, NFL, 1988—2001, NFL All-Decade Team, 1990s, Tenn. Titans Hall of Fame, 2002, Pro Football Hall of Fame, 2007. Achievements include setting the all-time NFL record for: consecutive Pro Bowl selections (14); games started (292); games played by a non-kicker (296); seasons played by an offensive lineman (19). Office: Tennessee Titans One Titans Way Nashville TN 37228-1404

MATTHEWS, DANE DIKEMAN, urban planner; b. Memphis, Dec. 19, 1950; d. Neil Jude and Virginia Ann (Turnbull) Dikeman; m. John Wesley Matthews, Dec. 28, 1971. BA with distinction, U. Okla., 1972, M of Regional and City Planning, 1974. Planner Hudgins, Thompson & Ball, Inc., Tulsa, 1975-76; econ. devel. planner Tulsa Metro. Area Planning Commn., 1976-77; planner II Tulsa Met. Area Planning Commn., 1977-80; prin. regional planner Indian Nations Coun. Govts., Tulsa, 1980—2004; asst. mgr. Land Devel. Svcs. Inc., 2004—. Project dir. Kendall-Whittier Neighborhood Master Plan, 1992. Bd. dirs., chair house com. Arts and Humanities Coun., Tulsa, 1991—96, 2000—03; divsn. chair Tulsa Area United Way, 1988—96; mem. adv. coun. Mobile Outreach and Crisis Svcs., 1995—2002, co-chair, 2000—02; chmn. Tulsa County Long Term Care Authority, 1999—2000, 2002—03, 2008—; bd. dirs. Met. Tulsa Urban League, 1993—95, Parkside Cmty. Mental Health Ctr., Tulsa, 1986—2000, Tulsa County Long Term Care Authority, 1995—2003, 2007—. Recipient Spl. Recognition award, Downtown Tulsa Unltd., 1988. Mem. Am. Inst. Cert. Planners (cert.), Am. Planning Assn. (Okla. chpt. pres. 1988-89, Master Plan award 1992, Outstanding Profl. Planner 1991), Phi Beta Kappa. Democrat. Episcopalian. Avocations: cooking, reading, raising dogs. Office: INCOG 2 W 2nd St Ste 800 Tulsa OK 74103-3116 Office Phone: 918-579-9471. Fax: (918) 583-1024. E-mail: dmatthews@incog.org.

MATTHEWS, JOHN WESLEY, state legislator; b. Bowman County, SC, Apr. 21, 1940; s. John Wesley and Victoria Williams Matthews; m. Geraldine Hill, 1961; children: Michael Andre, Stephanie Renata, John III, Brian DeReef. Attended, Lincoln Elec. Inst., 1972. Mem. Dist. 94 SC House of Reps., 1975—84; chmn. Legislature Black Caucus, SC; pres. Bowman Dem. Precinct, SC; instr. agr. Cainboy HS, 1967—70, Roberts HS, 1970—73; exec. committeeman N. Bowman Precinct; mem. Dist. 39 SC State Senate, 1985—; mem. Agr. & Natural Resources Com., Banking & Ins., Com., Edn., Fin., Invitations & Rules Com.; instr. Elem. Sch. Prin & Farmer. Democrat. Methodist. Mailing: PO Box 142 Columbia SC 29202 Office: 613 Gressette Bldg Columbia SC 29201 Home Phone: 803-829-2383; Office Phone: 803-212-6056. E-mail: JWM@scsenate.org.

MATTHEWS, KATHLEEN SHIVE, biochemistry educator; b. Austin, Tex., Aug. 30, 1945; d. William and Gwyn Shive; m. Randall Matthews. BS in Chemistry, U. Tex., 1966; PhD in Biochemistry, U. Calif., Berkeley, 1970. Post doctoral fellow Stanford (Calif.) U., 1970-72; mem. faculty Rice U., Houston, 1972—, chair dept., 1987-95, Wiess prof., 1989-96, Stewart Meml. prof., 1996—, dean natural scis., 1998—2008. Mem. BBCB study sect. NIH, Bethesda, Md., 1980-84, 86-88, BRSG adv. com., 1992-94; mem. adv. com. on rsch. programs Tex. Higher Edn. Coord. Bd., Austin, 1987-92; mem. undergrad. edn. initiative rev. panel Howard Hughes Rsch. Inst., Bethesda, 1991, mem. rsch. resources rev. panel, 1995, mem. predoctoral fellowships rev. panel, 2001, trustee S.W. Rsch. Inst., 2003-08, mem. adv. bd. Vinson & Elkins Women's Initiative, 2000-06. Mem. editl. bd. Jour. Biol. Chemistry, 1988-93, assoc. editor, 1994-99; contbr. more than 165 reviewed papers. Fellow AAAS; mem. Am. Soc. Biochemistry and Molecular Biology (nominating com. 1993-94, 96-97, fin. com. 2001-2002), Protein Soc., Biophys. Soc. (pub. affairs com. 2002-05), Am. Chem. Soc., Phi Beta Kappa. Office: Rice Univ Dept Biochem Cell Biology PO Box 1892 6100 Main St MS140 Houston TX 77005-1892 Office Phone: 713-348-4871. Business E-Mail: ksm@rice.edu.

MATTHEWS, STEVE ALLEN, lawyer; b. Columbia, SC, Oct. 11, 1955; s. Philip Garland and Vernecia Neely (Wilson) M.; m. Caroline Elizabeth FitzSimons, Sept. 26, 1987; children: Philip Garland II, Nathalie FitzSimons, Caroline Salley. BA in History, U. S.C., 1977; JD, Yale U., 1980. Bar: S.C. 1980, D.C. 1982. Assoc. Boyd, Knowlton, Tate & Finlay, Columbia, 1980—81, Dewey, Ballantine, Bushby, Palmer & Wood, Washington, 1981—85; spl. counsel to asst. atty. gen. Civil Rights Divsn. U.S. Dept. Justice, Washington, 1985—86, dep. asst. atty. gen. for jud. selection, Office of Legal Policy, 1986—88; exec. asst. to U.S. Atty. Gen., 1988; mem. Haynsworth Sinkler Boyd, PA, Columbia, 1988—, mng. ptnr., 2001—08; nominated by pres. Bush 4th Cir. Ct. of Apeals, 2007. Sec. Landmark Legal Found., 2003—07; chair Gov.'s Edn. Reform Coun., SC, 2005—06. Mem. Federalist Soc., Nat. Assn. Bond Lawyers (bd. dirs. 1995-96), Am. Coll. Bond Counsel (bd. dirs. 1995-99), Collegiate Network, Inc. (chmn. bd. dirs.), 1995-2007, Am. Intellectual Property Law Assn., SC Ind. Colls. and Univs. (bd. dirs.), 2004-07, Phila. Soc., St. Andrews Soc. Columbia, Jr. Achievement (bd. dirs.), 2004-07, SC Govs. Sch. Sci. Maths. Found.(bd. dirs. 2009-). Office: Haynsworth Sinkler Boyd PA 1201 Main St Fl 22 Columbia SC 29201-3226 Office Phone: 803-779-3080. Business E-Mail: smatthews@hsblawfirm.com.

MATTICE, HARRY SANDLIN, JR., federal judge; b. Chattanooga, Tenn., Mar. 10, 1954; s. Harry Sandlin Sr. and Kathryn (McCoy) M.; m. Janet Lynn LeVan, Jan 4, 1975; children: Harry Sandlin III, Bryan Christopher, Kevin LeVan. BS, U. Tenn., Chattanooga, 1976; JD, U. Tenn., 1981. Bar: Tenn. 1981, US Dist. Ct. (ea. dist.) Tenn. 1981, US Ct. Appeals (6th cir.) 1984, US Tax Ct. 1984, US Claims Ct. 1984, US Dist. Ct. (we. dist.) Tenn. 1989. Staff acct. Deloitte, Haskins & Sells, Chattanooga, 1976-78; from assoc. to ptnr. Miller & Martin, Chattanooga, 1981—2000; shareholder Baker, Donelson, Bearman & Caldwell, Chattanooga, 2000—01; U.S. atty. (ea. dist.) Tenn. US Dept. Justice, 2001—05; judge US Dist. Ct. (ea. dist.) Tenn., Chattanooga, 2005—. Pres. Chattanooga Tax Practitioners, 1987-88; sr. counsel U.S. Senate Com. on Govtl. Affairs, Spl. Investigation, 1997. Asst. to pres. Chattanooga Goodwill Industries, 1988-92; chmn. Hamilton County Rep. Party, 1993-95. Mem. Order of Coif, Rotary Club Chattanooga, Tenn., Phi Kappa Phi. Republican. Episcopalian. Home: 609 Marr Dr Signal Mountain TN 37377-2280 Office: US Dist Ct Rm 104 900 Georgia Ave Chattanooga TN 37402

MATTOX, JOHNNY LYNN, biologist, educator; b. Corinth, Miss., Apr. 13, 1951; s. Oliver Lee Mattox Jr. and Margaret Joyce Mills; m. Glenda Jean Eaton, Aug. 11, 1973; children: Jason Lynn, Jenny Amanda, Julia Elizabeth. AA, NE Miss. C.C., Booneville, 1971; BA Edn., U. Miss., Jackson, 1973, MCS, 1974, PhD, 1979. Tchr. sci. Kossuth HS., Miss., 1973—74; instr. sci. Itawamba CC, Fulton, Miss., 1975—80; instr. Biology NE Miss. CC, Booneville, 1981—2005; HEADWAE faculty rep. Blue Mountain Coll., Miss., 2008—09, assoc. prof. Biology, 2005—10, prof. biology, 2010—. Adj. asst. prof. Miss. U. Women, Columbus, 1984—2000, U. Miss., University, 1991—93, 1996—, U. Tenn. Martin, Selmer, 2000—; prof. biology; chair dept. math. and natural scis. Blue Mountain Coll., 2007—; vice chair, sci. edn. div. Miss. Acad. Scis. Chmn. Sci. Edn. divsn. Miss. Acad. Sci., 1980—81, vice chmn. sci. edn. divsn., 2008—09; deacon Union Bapt. Ch., Kossuth, 1963—, treas., 1963—, organist, 1963—. Named Outstanding Coll. Sci. Tchr., MS Sci. Tchrs. Assn., 2008. Mem.: NSTA, SAR (Booneville chpt.), Assn. Southeastern Biologists, Miss. Acad. Scis., Miss. Sci. Tchrs. Assn. (Outstanding Coll. Sci. Tchr. award 2008—09, Disting. Sci. Tchr. 2013), Nat. Assn. Biology Tchrs., Alcorn County Hist. Soc. (pres. 1982—83), Kossuth Hist. Soc. (pres. 1996—98), Kappa Delta Pi, Phi Theta Kappa (advisor 1979—2005, Regional Alumnus of Yr. award 2011, Outstanding Alumnus MS/LS Region award 2011), Phi Kappa Phi. Baptist. Office Phone: 662-685-4771 ext. 164. Business E-Mail: jmattox@bmc.edu.*

MATTOX, SHARON M., lawyer; b. Wichita Falls, Tex., Oct. 4, 1952; BA, Emporia State U., 1974; JD, U. Tex., 1974, PhD, 1978. Ptnr. Vinson & Elkins LLP, Houston, environ. law sect. Fellow: Tex. Bar Found. Office: Vinson & Elkins LLP First City Tower 1001 Fannin St, Ste 2300 Houston TX 77002 Office Phone: 713-758-4598. E-mail: smattox@velaw.com.

MATTRAN, DONALD ALBERT, management consultant, educator; b. Chgo., July 8, 1934; s. George Charles and Lucille Alice (Boule) M.; m. Betty Elena Flores, July 18, 1953 (div. Mar. 1988); children: Donald, Julie, Kimberly, Guy, Christy; m. Rose Lynn Castellano, May, 1988. B.Mus., U. Mich., 1957, M.Mus., 1960. Tchr. Van Buren Schs., Belleville, Mich., 1957-61; asst. prof. U. N.H., Durham, 1961-65, Boston U., 1965-66; assoc. prof. Hartt Sch. Music, West Hartford, Conn., 1966-82, dean, 1971-80; dir. Syracuse U. Sch. Music, NY, 1982-83; dean Sch. Fine and Performing Arts Montclair State Coll, Upper Montclair, NJ, 1983-87; pres. The Mattran Group Inc., 1987—. Cons. Music div. Kaman Corp., Bloomfield, Conn.; cons., evaluator Nat. Assn. Schs. of Music and Joint Commn. Theater and Dance Accreditation; guest condr. Hartford Symphony Orch., Hartt Opera Theatre, All-State Festivals, 1976-83, Soc. New Music, Syracuse, N.J. Sch. Arts Orch., 1985-87. Co-author: (with Mary Rasmussen) A Teacher's Guide to the Literature of Woodwind Instruments, 1966; condr.: rec. Concerto for Cello and Jazz Band, 1972. Chmn. adv. com. Prodigy Inc., Syracuse, 1982-86; trustee Conn. Opera Assn., 1977-80; bd. advs. Watkinson Sch. Creative Arts Program, Hartford, 1977-80; mem. humanities adv. com. N.J. Dept. Higher Edn., 1984—; mem. multi-disciplinary panel N.J. State Council on Arts, 1985-87; mem. adv. com. on auditions Met. Opera Nat. Council, 1984-87; mem. adv. com. Frank and Lydia Bergen Found., 1986-87; grants panelist, Sarasota County Arts Coun., 2005-2008; bd. mem. WUSF Ptnrs., 2006-2009; pres. Condo on the Bay Tower 1 Assn., 2007-2008; v.p. Condo on the Bay Mgmt. Corp., 2007-2008. Mem. Nat. Assn. Schs. Music (exec. bd., sec. 1978-81). Avocations: yachting, auto racing. Home: Apt 204 888 Boulevard Of The Arts Sarasota FL 34236-4827 Office: 1343 Main St Ste 600 Sarasota FL 34236-5630 Home Phone: 941-952-0639; Office Phone: 941-365-5151. Business E-Mail: dmattran@mattrangroup.com.

MATULICH, SERGE, accounting educator, writer; b. Split, Croatia, June 8, 1933; came to U.S., 1946; s. Daniel M. and Josephine (Schuster) Raseta; m. Margarete Manderscheid, Dec. 7, 1957; children: Alexander Matulich, Erika Matulich. BS in Acctg. with honors, Calif. State U., Sacramento, 1964; PhD in Bus., U. Calif., Berkeley, 1971. CPA, Fla.; cert. cost analyst. Grad. asst. U. Calif., Davis, 1964-65; asst. prof. Calif. State U., Hayward, 1966-67; assoc. in acctg. U. Calif., Berkeley, 1968-71, vis. asst. prof., 1974-75; asst. prof. Sch. Bus. Ind. U., 1971-76; assoc. prof. acctg. Sch. Bus. Tex. Christian U., 1976-84; vis. prof. U. North Tex., spring 1983; prof. Crummer Grad. Sch. Bus. Rollins Coll., Winter Park, Fla., 1984—2001, prof. emeritus, 2002—. Bd. dirs. Marconi Med. Ctr., Inc., Sacramento, 1967-71, Bazeghi Corp., Oakland, Calif., 1968-71,

Crescent Gen. Corp., 1969-71 (also v.p.), Fin. Floorplans, Inc., Ft. Worth, 1980-2003, Way To Go, Inc., Orlando, Fla., 1988-2000, Unicorn Rsch. Corp., Orlando, 1989—, Global Ptnrs. Corp., Orlando, 1994-2000 (also sec.). Author number of fin. acctg., mgmt. acct., cost acctg. textbooks, study guides; contbr. many articles to profl. jours. With U.S. Army, 1956-58. Recipient U. Pitts. BEFEE grant, 1993, 94, Ernst & Ernst Acctg. Achievement award, 1967, EMBA Outstanding Prof. award Class of 1986, 88, Delta Sigma Pi Scholarship key, 1964; Fulbright fellowship, 1999; Fulbright Alumni Initiatives Awards program grant, 2000-02. Mem. AICPA, Am. Acctg. Assn., World Future Soc., Fulbright Assn. (founding mem., treas. mid-Fla. chpt. 2002--), Beta Alpha Psi, Beta Gamma Sigma. Avocations: classical music, travel. Home: 4621 N Landmark Dr Orlando FL 32817-1235 Office: Crummer Grad Sch Bus Rollins Coll 1000 Holt Ave Winter Park FL 32789-4499 Home Phone: 407-657-4974. Personal E-mail: serge@unicorn.us.com. Business E-Mail: serge@rollins.edu.

MATUS, KRISTI ANN, insurance company executive; B, U. Wis., Oshkosh. Product devel. actuary Thrivent Fin. Bank, Wis., Medicare supplement actuary, product mgr. Wis., exec. v.p., COO Wis.; Joined USAA (United Svcs. Automobile Assn.), San Antonio, 2002, v.p. products and regulatory mgmt. Life Ins. Co., pres. Life Ins. Co., 2004—08, CFO, 2008—. Bd. dirs. Am. Coun. Life Insurers. Fellow: Soc. Actuaries; mem.: Am. Acad. Actuaries. Office: USAA 9800 Fredericksburg Rd San Antonio TX 78288 Office Phone: 210-498-8222.

MATZ, DEBORAH (DEBBIE MATZ), federal agency administrator; b. 1950; m. Marshall Matz; children: Hayley, Peter. BS, Cornell U., 1971; MA in Legis. Affairs, George Washington U. Cmty. devel. rep. US Dept. Housing & Urban Devel. (HUD), 1971—73; legis. asst. to Rep. Peter Peyser US House of Representatives; dir. Office Tech. Assessment, U.S. Congress; economist Joint Econ. Com.; chief of staff adminstrs. Farm Svc. Agy and Farmers Home USDA, dep. asst. sec. for adminstrn., 1997—2001; exec. officer Liaison Office N.Am. Food and Agrl. Orgn., UN, 2001—02; mem. Nat. Credit Union Adminstrn. (NCUA), Alexandria, 2002—05, chmn., 2009—; exec. v.p., COO Andrews Fed. Credit Union, Suitland, Md., 2006—08. Office: Nat Credit Union Adminstrn 1775 Duke St Alexandria VA 22314-3428 Office Fax: 703-518-6319.

MATZ, JAMES RICHARD, municipal official; BA with honors, U. Tex., 1961; postgrad., Mexico city Coll., 1961-62. Mktg. exec. Fluor Corp.; mem. diplomatic corps Dept. of State; commr. City of Harlingen, Tex., Cameron County. Mem. Pres.'s Exec. Interchange Program, Bank of Am.; mayor Palm Valley, Tex. Contbr. articles to profl. jours. Founder Harlingen Proud; founder, chmn. Valley Proud Environ. Coun., 1990; mem. citizen's exec. adv. coun. Rio Grande State Mental Health and Retardation Ctr.; bd. dirs. Harlingen, South Padre Island, San Benito Emergency Med. Svcs.; chmn. Tex. Reg. Cmty. Devel. Grant Rev. Com.; mem. Met. Planning Orgn., Cameron County; mem. exploration com. World Birding Ctr.; bd. dirs. Tex. Urban Forestry Coun.; mem. Tex. Energy Coord. Coun., Govt. Adv. Com. to U.S. Rep. to N.Am. Commn. for Environ. Coop.; past vice chmn. legis. policy com. on utility regulation and environment Tex. Mcpl. League; past chmn. City of Harlingen Utility Rate Rev. Bd., pub. works com. Harlingen Capital Improvement Adv. Bd.; past. bd. dirs. Rio Grande basin Sustainable Devel. Initiative, Border Trade Alliance, Area Health Edn. Ctr. South Tex., Keep Tex. Beautiful; former commr. Cameron County; past exec. com. Rio Grande Valley Emergency Mgmt. Coord. Coun., numerous others. Recipient Dist. Svc. award Rotary Found., 1990, Svc. Above Self award Harlingen Rotary, 1991, Tex. Urban Forestry Individual Accomplishment award, 1992, Harlingen Proud, Chairman's award, 1992, Outstanding Dist. Gov., Keep Tex. Beautiful, 1995, Leadership award, 1995, Pres.'s Nat. Svc. award, 1995, Outstanding tex. Urban Forester award, 1996, State of Tex. Senate Resolution #989, 1995, Joint Resolution of Appreciation, San Benito City Commn. and San Benito Area C. of C., 1997, Tex. Environ. Excellence award Tex. Commn. Environ. Quality, 2004, Gulf Guardian award, 2004, Tex. Gov.'s Lonestar Cmty. Svc. award, 2005, Lone Star Land Steward award Tex. Parks and Wildlife Dept., 2006, Frederick Law Olmsted award Nat. Arbor Day Found., 2006, One Nation award Valley Morning Star Newspaper. Mem. Harlingen Area C. of C. (past dir.), Assn. for Local Control of Utility Rates (past officer, dir.). Office: 900 Palm Valley Dr W Harlingen TX 78552

MAU, CHRISTINE, consumer products company executive; BS in Comm. and Design, U. Wis., Green Bay, 1987. Cert. Eiseman Ctr. Color Info. & Training 2004. Prin. MauHaus Inc., Neenah, Wis., 1989—2006; mgr. packaging graphics Kimberly-Clark Corp., 2001—06, assoc. dir. packaging graphics, 2006—09, brand design dir., 2009—. Named a Woman to Watch, Advt. Age, 2010. Mem.: Am. Inst. Graphic Arts. Office: Kimberly Clark Corp Hdqs PO Box 619100 Dallas TX 75261 Office Phone: 972-281-1200. Office Fax: 972-281-1435.

MAUCH, LOY, state legislator; Mem. Dist. 26 Ark. House of Representatives, 2011—. Republican. Baptist. Office: 593 Fendley Rd Bismarck AR 71929 Office Phone: 501-865-3132. Business E-Mail: loy.mauch@arkansashouse.org.

MAULDIN, JEAN ANN, pharmaceutical executive; b. Ft. Chaffee, Ark., Oct. 12, 1957; d. Lawrence Ray and Antoinette Marie (Tusa) Mitchell; 1 child, Michele L. Carter. BBA in Acctg., U. Ctrl. Ark., 1979, MBA, 1985. V.p., CFO TAMKO Bldg. Products, Inc.; cost acct. FMC Automotive Svc. Divsn., Conway, Ark., 1979—82, mgr., cost acctg., 1982—85, with, divsnl. fin. analyst, 1985, plant contr., 1985—86, divsn. contr., 1986—88; mgr., cost acctg. Columbian Chems. Co., 1988—90, dir., field acctg., 1990—92, contr., Northern Am., 1992—93, corp. contr., 1993—94; v.p., CFO Accuride Corp., Henderson, Ky., 1995—97; exec. v.p., CFO English China Clays, Roswell, Ga., 1997—98; v.p. Phelps Dodge Industries, 1998—99, pres., 1999, Phelps Dodge Wire and Cable (divsn. of Phelps Dodge Corp.); joined Merial Ltd., 2002, CFO, Merial Inc. Bd. dirs. Baldor Electric Co., 2006—11. Recipient Young Career Woman award Bus. and Profl. Women, 1986. Mem. Inst. Mgmt. Accts. (cert., v.p. adminstrn. 1993-94). Republican. Roman Catholic. Avocations: art, antiques, doll collecting. Office: Merial Inc 3239 Satellite Blvd Duluth GA 30096-4640 Office Phone: 678-638-3000. Office Fax: 678-638-3901. Business E-Mail: jean.mauldin@merial.com.

MAULDIN, JOHN INGLIS, public defender; b. Atlanta, Nov. 6, 1947; s. Earle and Isabel (Inglis) M.; m. Cynthia Ann Balchin, Apr. 15, 1967 (div. Dec. 1985); children: Tracy Rutherford, Abigail Inglis; m. Linda W. Farmer, Nov. 7, 1998. BA, Wofford Coll., 1970; JD, Emory U., 1973. Bar: S.C. 1974, U.S. Ct. Appeals (4th cir.) 1974, U.S. Dist. Ct. S.C. 1975, U.S. Supreme Ct. 1978. Asst. pub. def. Defender Corp. Greenville County, S.C., 1974-76; ptnr. Mauldin & Allison, Greenville, 1977-92; pub. defender Greenville County, SC, 1992—2008, 13th judicial cir. pub. defender SC, 2008—. Chair S.C. Commn. on Indigent Def., 1993-96. Bd. dirs. Speech Hearing and Learning Ctr., Greenville, 1977-90, pres., 1982; bd. dirs. Def. Corp. Greenville County, 1979-92, Save Our Sons, 1995-2006, Palmetto Innocence Project, 2002—, NAMI Greenville, 2005-2014. Named SC Atty. Yr. ACLU, SC, 1986. Master: Haynsworth/Perry Inn Ct.; mem.: SC Pub. Defender Assn. (bd. dirs. 1992—2006, SC Atty. of Yr. 2006), SC Assn. Criminal Def. Lawyers (bd. dirs. 1997—99), SC Trial Lawyers Assn., Nat. Legal Aid and Defender Assn. (defender policy group 1999—2007, bd. dirs. 2002—07, 2011—), Nat. Assn. Criminal Def. Attys., Rotary, Sigma Delta Psi. Democrat. Methodist. Office: PO Box 10264fs Greenville SC 29603 Office Phone: 864-467-8522.

MAULER, MICHAEL K., retail executive; B in Tech. Mgmt., St. Leo U., 1987. Dir., distbn., mfg. svcs. Baxter Corp, 1988—94; v.p., worldwide ops. Fisher Scientific, 1998—2000; v.p., supply chain Electronics Boutique, 2001—05; sr. v.p., supply chain and internat. support GameStop Corp., 2005—10, exec. v.p., internat., 2010—. Office: GameStop Corp 625 Westport Pky Grapevine TX 76051 Office Phone: 817-424-2000. Office Fax: 817-424-2002.

MAUNDER, ADDISON BRUCE, agronomic research company executive; b. Holdrege, Nebr., May 13, 1934; s. Addison Haynes and Marie Sophia (Luebs) M.; m. Katherina Marlene Blum, Sept. 8, 1978; children: Lynda Diane, Christopher Allen. B.Sc., U. Nebr., 1956; M.Sc., Purdue U., 1958, PhD, 1960; DSc (hon.), U. Nebr., 1991; DAgr (hon.), Purdue U., 2003. With DeKalb AgResearch, Inc., Lubbock, Tex., 1960-96, sorghum breeder, 1960-61, dir. sorghum research, 1961-76, v.p. sorghum research, 1976-78, v.p. rsch., 1978-82; v.p. DeKalb-Pfizer Genetics, DeKalb, Ill., 1982-89; v.p. agronomic research DeKalb Plant Genetics, DeKalb, Ill., 1989-91; sr. v.p. DeKalb Genetics Corp., DeKalb, Ill., 1991-96; rsch. advisor Nat. Grain Sorghum Prodrs. Assn., 1997—; with Lubbock Water Adv. Commn., 2008—. Bd. dirs. Diversity Mag., Washington, 1984-95; adj. prof. Tex. Tech. U., 1992—; pres. Nat. Grain Sorghum Prodrs. Found., 2004—, pres., Crop Sci. Soc. America, 1995-96. Contbr. articles to profl. jours., chapters to books. Mem. deans adv. com. Tex. Tech. U., Lubbock, 1983-86; chmn. external rev. INTSORMIL of U.S. AID, Lincoln, Nebr., 1980-2001; bd. dirs. Tex. Tech. U. Rsch. Found., 1986-92; mem. Nat. Plant Genetic Resources Bd., 1991-92, Nat. Plant Variety Protection Bd., 1991-94; mem. World Food Prize Com., 1997-2003. Recipient Gerald Thomas award Tex. Tech. U., 1974, Prodn. award Grain Sorghum Producers Assn., 1985, Genetics and Plant Breeding award for Industry, 1987, Indsl. Agronomy award, 1988, Purdue Disting. Alumni award, 1997, Monsanto Crop Sci. Disting. Career award, 2000, Pres.'s Disting Svc. award Am. Seed Trade Assn., 2001; Henry Beachell Disting Alumni award, U. Nebraska, 2007. Fellow AAAS, Am. Soc. Agronomy (bd. dirs. 1991-92), Crop Sci. Soc. Am. (bd. dirs. 1991-92, pres. 1995-96); mem. Am. Seed Trade Assn., Sigma Xi, Alpha Zeta. Republican. Achievements include development of plant products (150 hybrids) emphasizing yield, improved drought and insect resistance as well as nutritional quality. Office Phone: 806-749-3478. Personal E-mail: texasgreenbug@aol.com.

MAUPIN, ELIZABETH THATCHER, theater critic; b. Cleve., Oct. 21, 1951; d. Addison and Margaret (Thatcher) M.; m. Jay Yellen, Dec. 29, 1995. BA in English, Wellesley Coll., Mass., 1973; M in Journalism, U. Calif., Berkeley, 1976. Editorial asst. Houghton Mifflin Co., Boston, 1973-74; reporter, movie critic Times-Standard, Eureka, Calif., 1976-78; theater and movie critic Chronicle-Telegram, Elyria, Ohio, 1978-79; movie critic Ledger-Star, Norfolk, Va., 1979-82; feature writer Va.-Pilot and Ledger-Star, Norfolk, 1982-83; sr. theater critic Orlando (Fla.) Sentinel, 1983—. Fellow Nat. Arts Journalism program Columbia U., 1995-96. Fellow Nat. Critics Inst.; mem. Am. Theatre Critics Assn. (exec. com. 1993-99, 05-06, chair 1996-99). Office: Orlando Sentinel 633 N Orange Ave Orlando FL 32801-1349

MAUPIN, JOHN E., JR., hospital administrator; b. LA, Oct. 28, 1946; m. Eilene; three children. Diploma, San Jose State Coll.; DDS, Meharry Med. Coll., 1972; MBA, Loyola Coll., Balt., 1979; DSc (hon.), Morehouse Sch. Medicine, 1995; LLD (hon.), Va. Union U., 1996. Chmn. LifePoint Hosps.; CEO Southside Healthcare, Inc., Atlanta; dentistry resident Provident Hosp., Balt., 1973; dentist, capt. & lt. col. U.S. Army Dental Corps/Walter Reed Med. Ctr., Washington, 1974-97; various health/dental positions including dep. commr. Balt. City Health Dept., 1981-87; pres. Meharry Med. Coll., Nashville, 1994—2006; exec. v.p. Morehouse Sch. Medicine, Atlanta, pres., 2006. Mem. adv. groups Nat. Com. on Fgn. Med. Edn. and Accreditation, Bd. of Scientific Counselors, Nat. Ctr. for Infectious Diseases, Managed Care Task Force; bd. dirs. Monarch Dental Corp., Am. Gen. Series Portfolio Co., U.S. Life Mut. Funds, HealthSouth Corp. Exec. coun. Boy Scouts of Mid. Tenn.; bd. dirs. Nashville Cmty. Found., BellSouth Sr. Classic at Opryland; former chair bd. dirs. United Way of Mid. Tenn.; former mem. bd. govs. Nashville Area C. of C. Recipient A.B. Cooper award North Ga. Dental Soc., 1994, Dentist of Yr. award, 1991, Mayor's Citation for outstanding pub. svc., Balt., 1987, others. Mem. Nat. Dental Assn. (past pres.), Nat. Med. Assn., Ga. State Med. Assn., Nat. Assn. Cmty. Health Ctrs., Nat. Assn. Health Care Execs., others. Office: LifePoint Hospitals Inc 103 Powell Ct Ste 200 Brentwood TN 37027 Office Phone: 614-372-8500. E-mail: john.maupin@lpnt.net.

MAURER, VIRGINIA GALLAHER, law educator; b. Shawnee, Okla., Nov. 7, 1946; d. Paul Clark Gallaher and Virginia Ruth (Watson) Abernathy; m. Ralph Gerald Maurer, July 31, 1971(dec. May12, 2006); children: Ralph Emmett, William Edward. BA, Northwestern U., 1968; MA, Stanford U., 1969, JD, 1975. Bar: Iowa 1976. Tchr. social studies San Mateo H.S. Dist., Calif., 1969—71; spl. asst. to pres. U. Iowa, Iowa City, 1976—80, adj. asst. prof. law, 1979—80; affiliate asst. prof. law U. Fla., Gainesville, 1981, asst. prof. bus. law, 1980—85, assoc. prof., 1985—93, prof., 1993—, Huber Hurst prof., 1997—2011, Darden Restaurant prof., 2011—. Dir. Poe Bus. Ethics Ctr., 1998—, interim dir. MBA program U. Fla., 1987, chair dept. mgmt., 1994-2003; vis. scholar Wolfson Coll., Cambridge, 1994; vis. prof. SDA Bocconi U., Milan, 1994-96, Helsinki Sch. Econs. and Bus., 1998, U. Catania, Sicily, 1999, 2002-11, U. Mich., 2008; cons. Gov.'s Com. on Iowa 2000, Iowa City, 1976-77, Fla. Banker's Assn., Gainesville, 1982, various law firms, 1995—; exec. mem. Wall St. Jour. Exec. Task Force for Women in the Economy, 2012. Contbr. articles to profl. jours.; jr. editor Am. Bus. Law Jour., 1989-90, mng. editor, 1990-91, editor-in-chief, 1992-94 Bd. dirs. Gainesville Chamber Orch., 1990-93; fundraising com. Pro Arte Musica, Gainesville, 1980-84; sr. warden, vestry Holy Trinity Episc. Ch., 1991-93, 99-2004, 2014-, jr. warden, 2000-02, 2007-2013, vestry clk, 2013-; bd. dirs. Holy Trinity Found., Gainesville, 1991-93, 2010-, vice chair, 2012-; com. charter and canon law Episc. Diocese Fla., 1994-96; bd. dirs. Samaritan Ctrs. of North Ctrl. Fla., Inc., 1995-97, Early Childhood Learning Coalition Alachua County, Fla., 2007-09. Recipient Kay Duffy Award for Extraordinary Serv., Acad. Legal Studies in Bus., 2010; named Fla. Blue Key Disting. Faculty mem., 2004, Woman of Distinction, Alachua County, 2005. Fellow Soc. Advanced Legal Studies (UK); mem. ABA, AAUW, Acad. Legal Studies in Bus. (ho. of dels. 1989-90, exec. com. 1992, 98—2010, sec.-treas. 1998-99, v.p. 1999-2000, pres-elect 2000-01, pres. 2001-02, exec. com. 2002-10), Southeastern Bus. Law Assn. (proc. editor 1984-87, treas. 1985-86, v.p. 1986-87, pres.-elect 1987-88, pres. 1988-89), Iowa Bar Assn., LWV, U. Fla. Athletic Assn. (bd. dirs. 2004-, v.p. chmn. fin. com. 1982-88), Gainesville Womens' Forum (bd. dirs. 1988-91), Fla. Women' Network (bd. dirs. 1995-99), Univ. Woman's Club (Gainesville, Fla.), Rotary (bd. dirs. 1989-91, dist. scholarship com. 1997-99, regional scholarship com. 2000, chair 2001), Ctr. Applied Psychological Type, Gainesville, Fla.(bd. dir. 2008-),Beta Gamma Sigma, Kappa Alpha Theta, Delta Sigma Pi. Home: 2210 NW 6th Pl Gainesville FL 32603-1409 Office: U Fla Grad Sch Bus Gainesville FL 32611 Office Phone: 352-392-1048.

MAURIN, JAMES E., real estate executive; Grad. in Aerospace Engring., La. State U., 1970; MBA, Tulane U., 1972. Acct. Ernst and Ernst, New Orleans; mng. ptnr. Maurin-Ogden Properties, Covington, La., 1975—; chmn. Stirling Properties, Covington, La., 1975—2012. Mem. bus. sch. coun. Tulane U., La. State U.; bd. dirs., chmn. Ochsner Found. Hosp. Bd. Mem.: LSU Flogship Coalition (founding mem. exec. com.), Nat. World War Two Mus. (bd. trustee), Northshore Arena Found. (bd. dirs., past bd. chair), LSU Tiger Athletic Found. (past chmn., exec. com., bd. mem., chmn. constrn. com.), Northshore Cmty. Found. (past chmn. mem. exec. com.), Blueprint La. (chmn. 2011—12, founding trustee), Internat. Coun. Shopping Ctrs. (chmn. 2004—05), World Pres.'s Orgn. (chmn. La. chpt. 2005), Urban Land Inst. (chmn. La. dist. coun. 2002—04). Office: Stirling Properties 109 Northpark Blvd Ste 310 Covington LA 70433-5005 Office Phone: 985-898-2022. Business E-Mail: jmau@stirlingprop.com.

MAUSKOPF, SEYMOUR HAROLD, history professor; b. Cleve., Nov. 11, 1938; s. Philip and Dora (Trompeter) M.; m. Josephine Mary Album, Aug. 9, 1964; children: Deborah, Philip, Alice. AB, Cornell U., 1960; PhD, Princeton U., 1966. Instr. history Duke U., Durham, NC, 1964-66, asst. prof., 1966-72, assoc. prof., 1972-80, prof., 1980—, dir. program in sci. tech. and human values, 1979-84, dir. Focus Interdisciplinary programs, 1995—2003; resident dir. U. Mich.-U. Wis.-Duke U. Program, Florence, Italy, 2008. Founder, first chmn. Forum for History Chem. Scis., 2011—13. Author: Crystals and Compounds, Molecular Structure and Composition in Nineteenth Century French Science, 1976, (with M.R. McVaugh) The Elusive Science; Origins of Experimental Physical Research, 1915-1940, 1980; editor: The Reception of Unconventional Science by the Scientific Community, 1979, Chemical Sciences in the Modern World, 1993; co-editor (with Matthew D. Eddy and William R. Newman) Chemical Knowledge in the Early Modern World, History of Science Society, Osiris, vol. 29. Recipient Dexter award for outstanding achievement in history of chemistry, 1998, award Sci. and Religion Course Program, Ctr. Theology and the Natural Scis., 2002, Alumni Disting. Undergraduate Tchg. award Duke U., 2006; NSF postdoctoral fellow, 1971-72, Charles Price fellow Chem. Heritage Found., 2000; NSF grantee, 1974, 92-93; Am. Philos. Soc. travel grantee, 1979; Nat. Endowment for Humanities summer stipend, 1982; Edelstein internat. fellow in history chem. scis. and tech. Beckman Ctr. U. Pa. and Hebrew Univ., Jerusalem, 1988-89. Mem. History Sci. Soc. (exec. com. treas. 1979-83, coun. 1993-95). Jewish. Office Phone: 919-684-2581.

MAVROS, GEORGE S., hospital administrator, director; b. Adelaide, Australia, Oct. 14, 1957; came to U.S., 1970; s. Sotirios George and Angeliki (Korogiannis) M.; m. Renee Ann Cuddeback, June 24, 1979. BA in Microbiology, U. South Fla., 1979, MS in Microbiology, 1987; MBA, Nova U., 1991; PhD in Health Sci. Mgmt., LaSalle U., 1995. Cert. lab. dir. Nat. Certifying Agy. for Clin. Lab. Pers.; diplomate Am. Coll. Health Care Execs. Med. technologist Jackson Meml. Hosp., Dade City, Fla., 1979-81; microbiology supr. HCA Bayonet Point-Hudson Med. Ctr., Hudson, Fla., 1981-82, dir. labs., 1982-88; lab. mgr., adminstrv. and tech. dir. Citrus Meml. Hosp., Inverness, Fla., 1988—2005, dir. profl. svcs., 2005—. Lab. cons. HCA Oak Hill Hosp., Spring Hill, Fla., 1983-84; cons. lab. info. systems Citation Computer Systems, St. Louis, 1983—, Hosp. Corp. of Am., Nashville, 1986; instr. Microbiology Pasco Hernando Com. Coll., New Port Richey, Fla., 1986-88, Inst. Biolog. Scis. Cen. Fla. Community Coll., Lecanto, 1989—; bd. dirs. Gulf Coast chpt. Clin. Lab. Mgrs. Assn., Tampa, Fla., 1987, pres., 1987-89. Parish pres. Greek Orthodox Ch. of West Cen., Inverness, Fla.; chmn. Bayonet Point Hosp. Good Govt. Group, Hudson, 1986-88. Mem. APHA, Am. Mgmt. Assn., Am. Soc. Microbiology, Am. Soc. Clin. Pathologists (cert. in lab. mgmt.), Am. Soc. Med. Technologists (cert.), Fla. Soc. Med. Technologists, Clin. Lab. Mgmt. Assn. (pres. Gulf Coast chpt. 1988-90), Am. Assn. Clin. Chemists, Am. Acad. Microbiology (cert.), Fla. State Bd. Clin. Lab. Pers. (chmn. 1994). Clubs: Greek Orthodox Youth Am. (Clearwater, Fla.). Lodges: Order of DeMolay, Sons of Pericles (sec.). Democrat. Home: 6 Byrsonima Ct W Homosassa FL 34446-4610 Office: Citrus Meml Hosp 502 W Highland Blvd Inverness FL 34452-4754 Personal E-mail: gmavros@tampabay.rr.com. Business E-Mail: gmavros@citrusmh.org.

MAX, ERNEST, surgeon; b. Vienna, Mar. 3, 1936; m. Silvia Neger, Mar. 18, 1964; children: Yvette Rosa, Oliver Fredrick. MD, U. Chile, 1961. Diplomate Am. Bd. Surgery, Am. Bd. Colon and Rectal Surgeons, Am. Bd. Laser Surgery. Intern Hosp. San Borja, Santiago, Chile, 1960-61, resident, 1962-63; fellow in gen. surgery, colon and rectal surgery Lahey Clinic Found., Boston, 1969-70; resident Sinai Hosp., Balt., 1971-72, The Western Pa. Hosp., Pitts., 1972-74; resident in colon and rectal surgery Hermann Hosp., Houston, 1974-75, staff, 1975—, Park Plz. Hosp., 1975—, Meml. Hosp. Southwest, 1975—, Meml. NW Hosp., 1975—, Diagnostic Ctr. Hosp., 1975—, The Methodist Hosp., 1976—, Meml. City Hosp., 1976—, Houston NW Med. Ctr., 1976—, St. Luke's Episcopal Hosp., 1981—, Cypress Fairbanks, 1983—; chief of staff Meml. Hosp., 1983; staff HCA Med. Ctr., 1986—; CEO Colon and Rectal Clinic PA, 1989—. Clin. assoc. prof. surgery Baylor Coll. Medicine; clin. instr. surgery U. Tex. Med. Sch., Houston. Author: (with others) Current Diagnosis, 1971. Recipient Walter A. Fansler Travel Edn. award Am. Soc. Colon and Rectal Surgeons, 1974, Harriet Cunningham award Tex. Med. Assn., 1988, Best of the Best award Tex. Med. Assc., 1989; The Purdue Fredrick fellow Am. Soc. Colon and Rectal Surgeons, 1974. Mem. Am. Coll. Surgeons, Tex. Med. Soc., Harris County Med. Soc., Tex. Soc. Colon and Rectal Surgeons (pres. 1982-83), Am. Soc. Laser Medicine and Surgery, Internat. Soc. Univ. Colon and Rectal Surgeons, Lahey Clinic Alumni Assn., Am. Soc. Colon and Rectal Surgeons, Tex. Gulf Coast Colon and Rectal Surgical Soc. (sec. treas. 1992—), Colombian Soc. Colo-Proctology (hon. mem.). Office: Colon & Rectal Clinic PA 6550 Fannin St Ste 2307 Houston TX 77030-2723 Office Phone: 713-790-9250. Business E-Mail: emax@crchouston.com.

MAXWELL, CHARLES DARRYL, investment company executive; BS in Acctg., Harding U. CPA. Joined Ernst & Young LLP, 1976, sr. mgr., 1984—86; sr. v.p. Morgan Keegan & Co., Inc., Memphis, 1995—97, mng. dir., 1998, asst. sec., treas., sec., treas., CFO, 2006—. Bd. dirs. RMK Advantage Income Fund Inc. Office: Morgan Keegan Morgan Keegan Tower 50 N Front St Memphis TN 38103 Office Phone: 901-524-4100. Office Fax: 901-524-4197.

MAXWELL, HOWARD R., state legislator; b. Jan. 23, 1949; m. Linda Maxwell; children: Jason, Angela. Former state rep. Dist. 27, Ga.; former state rep. Dist. 17 Ga., 2004—; mem. Retirement Coms., State Insts. & Property Coms., Transportation Coms.; ins. agt. Republican. Mailing: # 412 Legis Office Bldg Atlanta GA 30334 Home: 716 Graham Rd Dallas GA 30132 Business E-Mail: hmaxwell@legis.state.ga.us.

MAXWELL, PHILLIP L., retail executive; V.p., home video info. sys. Walt Disney Co.; group mgr., applications Frito-Lay; dir., route mgmt. sys. Coca-Cola Enterprises, Inc.; v.p., chief info. officer, info. sys., eBusiness Strategy, N. Am. Nissan Motor Acceptance Corp., chief info. officer, dir., mgmt. info. sys., 1993—2000; sr. v.p., chief info. officer Neiman Marcus Group, Inc., 2000—, Neiman Marcus, Inc., 2005—. Office: Neiman Marcus Inc 1618 Main St Dallas TX 75201 Office Phone: 214-743-7600. Business E-Mail: phillip.maxwell@neimanmarcus.com.

MAXWELL, RICHARD ANTHONY, retail executive; b. NYC, Apr. 1, 1933; s. Arthur William and Mary Ellen (Winestock) M.; m. Jacqueline Ann Creamer, Oct. 27, 1962. Student, NYU, 1957-58, Acad. Advanced Traffic, 1959. Import ops. mgr. Associated Merchandising Corp., NYC, 1950-52, 56-65; v.p. Associated Dry Goods Corp., NYC, 1965-86, sr. v.p. mktg., 1980-82, exec. v.p. mktg., 1982-86; pres. A.D.G. Export Mktg., Florence, Italy, 1982-86, Associated Dry Goods Ltd., Hong Kong, 1983-86, Inter Textyle Corp., 1987-89; with Matol Botanical Internat. Ltd.; exec. v.p. Matol World Corp., Montreal, Que., Canada, 1992-94; dir. Matol Botannical New Zealand, 1994-96; v.p. internat. ops. L'Aprina Internat. Inc., 1994-96; chief internat. officer Camelot Concept Co., Montreal, 1995-96; CFO Showcase Prodns., Phoenix, 1996; exec. v.p. Harmony House Internat., Phoenix, 1996-97, IGW Trust, Phoenix, 1997-99, Pre-Paid Legal Svcs., Inc., 1999—; pres. Team 39, Inc., Dunedin, Fla., 2000-2001; dir. Presley Promotions Inc., Memphis, 2001—02; pres., COO Home Farms Techs. Inc., Brandon, Man., Canada, 2002—08; COO Fire Block Internat. Halifax M. S. Can., 2010—11; chief logistics officer Zeroignition Inc., Barbados, BWI, 2011. Mem. industry sector adv. com. Dept. Commerce, 1984-93; mem. shippers adv. com. Nat. Maritime Coun. Served with USAF, 1952-56. Recipient Silver medal for contbns. to trade expansion, Republic of China, 1980; appt. to rank of comdr. in Order of Merit in recognition of improvement of trade between Italy and U.S., Republic of Italy, 1985. Mem. Am. Assn. Exporters and Importers (past pres., dir.), Shippers Conf. Greater N.Y. (past pres., dir.), Nat. Retail Mchts. Assn. (vice chmn. fgn. trade com.), Nat. Com. Internat. Trade Documentation (past vice chmn. gen. bus. com.), Transp. Assn. Am., Italy-Am. C. of C. (past pres., dir.), Am. Soc. of Italian Legion of Merit (dir.). Home: 2408 Stag Run Blvd Clearwater FL 33765-1832 Office Phone: 727-791-8885.

MAXWELL, RICHARD CALLENDER, retired lawyer, educator; b. Mpls., Oct. 7, 1919; s. Bertram Wayburn and Blossom (Callender) M.; m. Frances Lida McKay, Jan 27, 1942; children: Richard Callender, John McKay. BSL, U. Minn., 1941, LLB, 1947; LLD (hon.), Calif. Western U., 1983; LLD, Southwestern U., 1993. Assoc. prof. U. ND, 1947-49, U. Tex., 1949-51, prof., 1951-53; counsel Amerada Petroleum Corp., 1952-53; prof. UCLA, 1953-81; dean UCLA Sch. Law, 1959-69, Connell prof., 1979-81, Connell prof. emeritus, 1981—; Chadwick prof. Duke U. Sch. Law, 1981-89, Chadwick prof. emeritus, 1989—. Vis. prof. Columbia U., 1955; vis. Alumni prof. U. Minn., 1970-71; Fulbright lectr. Queen's U., No. Ireland, 1970; vis. Ford Found. prof. U. Singapore, 1971; Thompson prof. U. Colo., 1982; vis. prof. Hastings Coll. Law, 1976, Duke U., 1979-80, U. Tex., 1985; pres. Minn. Law Rev., 1946; chmn. Coun. Legal Edn. Opportunity, 1971-72; pres. Assn. Am. Law Schs., 1972; chmn. adv. com. law Fulbright Program, 1971-74, chmn. adv. com. U.K., 1974-77; mem. com. on gas prodn. opportunities NRC, 1977-78; mem. law sch. editl. and adv. bd. West Pub. Co., 1971-94. Author: (with S. A. Riesenfeld) Cases and Materials on Modern Social Legislation, 1950, (with H.R. Williams and C.J. Meyers) Cases on Oil and Gas Law, 1956, 8th edit., (with Patrick H. Martin, Bruce M. Kramer), 2007, (with S.A. Riesenfeld) California Cases on Security Transactions, 1957, 4th edit. (with S.A. Riesenfeld, J.R. Hetland, W.D. Warren), 1991; West Coast editor Oil and Gas Reporter, 1953-. Mem. LA Employee Rels. Bd., 1971-74; bd. dirs. Constl. Rights Found., 1963-81; trustee Calif. Western U., 1979-81; bd. visitors Duke U. Sch. Law, 1973-79, chmn. bd. Pvt. Adjudication Ctr., 1984-89; bd. visitors Southwestern U. Sch. Law, 1981-90. Served to lt. comdr. USNR, 1941-46. Recipient Clyde O. Martz Tchg. award Rocky Mountain Mineral Law Found., 1994, Disting. Tchg. award, UCLA, 1977, Duke Law Sch., 1986, UCLA medal, 1982. Mem. ABA (com. on youth edn. for citizenship 1975-79, spl. com. on pub. understanding about the law 1979-84), Order of Coif. (nat. exec. com. 1980-86). Office: Duke U Sch Law Durham NC 27708-0362 Personal E-mail: rcmaxwell@mindspring.com.

MAXWELL, TERRY, food service executive; b. 1958; m. Cindy Maxwell; 7 children. Degree in bus. adminstrn., Trevecca Nazarene U., Nashville. Various mgmt. positions in restaurant and retail ops. including gen. mgr. at several stores Cracker Barrel Old Country Store, Inc., 1980—94, regional dir., 1994—97, regional v.p., 1997—2003, sr. v.p. ops., 2003—06, sr. v.p. retail, 2006—. Office: Cracker Barrel Old Country Store Inc 305 Hartmann Dr Lebanon TN 37087 Office Phone: 865-522-8232.

MAY, CECIL RICHARD, JR., academic administrator; b. Memphis, June 13, 1932; BA in Biblical Langs. magna cum laude, Harding U., MA in New Testament, MTh; LLD (hon.), Freed-Hardeman U., 1984. Min., Holly Springs, Miss., 1954-57, Ripley, Miss., 1957-59, Pine Bluff Ch., Ctrl. Acad. Ch., Miss., 1959-60; dist. scout exec. Yocona Area Coun. Boy Scouts Am., Oxford, Miss., 1959-60; min. Ashland, Miss., 1961, Fulton, Miss., 1962-67, Eastside Campus Ch., Portland, Oreg., 1967-69; Bible tchr. Columbia Christian Coll., Portland, 1967-69; min. Vicksburg, Miss., 1969-76; dean Internat. Bible Coll., Florence, Ala., 1977-80; pres. Magnolia Bible Coll., Kosciusko, Miss., 1980-97; dean bibl. studies Faulkner U., Montgomery, Ala., 1998—; dean emeritus, author in residence. Lectr. in field. Author: Finally Brethren, (book) Bible Questions Answered by Pillar; editor: Preacher Talk; assoc. editor: Magnolia Messenger; contbr. articles to profl. jours., columns in newspapers. Elder Vicksburg Ch., Miss., 1971-76, South Huntington St. Ch., Kosciusko, 1981-97, U. Ch., Montgomery, 2003-; active mem. Boy Scouts America, 1954-76; com. chair Kosciusko-Attala County C. of C., 1992; bd. dirs. Am. Cancer Soc., 1971-74, fin. campaign chmn., 1971; bd. dirs. Miss. Econ. Coun., 1985-86, 89-92, area vice-chmn., 1991-92; chmn. Attala County Med. Study Task Force, 1991-92; mem. Evang. Theol. Soc. Recipient Disting. Christian Svc. award, Harding U., 2003, Tower of Strength award, Cloverdale Ctr. Family Strengths, Faulkner U., Montgomery, Ala., 2009. Mem.: Evangelical Theol. Soc. Achievements include Classroom Building at Magnolia Bible College named Cecil May Jr. Classroom Building, 1997. Office: Faulkner Univ 5345 Atlanta Hwy Montgomery AL 36109-3390 Office Phone: 334-386-7155. Business E-Mail: cmay@faulkner.edu.

MAY, DONALD ROBERT LEE, ophthalmologist, educator, academic administrator; b. Spring Valley, Ill., Nov. 26, 1945; BS in Liberal Arts and Scis. with high honors and distinction, U. Ill., 1968, MD, 1972. Diplomate Am. Bd. Ophthalmology, Nat. Bd. Med. Examiners. Rsch. fellow dept. ophthalmology U. Ill. Eye and Ear Infirmary, Chgo., 1971—72; intern Northwestern U. Sch. Medicine Meml. Hosps., Chgo., 1972—73; resident in ophthalmology U. Ill. Eye and Ear Infirmary, Chgo., 1973—76, instr. dept. ophthalmology, 1974—77, attending surgeon dept. ophthalmology, 1976—77, fellow in diabetic retinopathy study, diabetic retinopathy vitrectomy study, and retina and vitreous surgery, 1976—77; founder, dir. retina svc., dept. ophthalmology Wilford Hall USAF Med. Ctr., San Antonio, 1977—79; asst. prof. ophthalmology, founder, dir. Retina/Vitreous/Ocular Trauma Svc. U. Calif. Davis Sch. Medicine, Calif., 1979—81; assoc. prof., dir. retina, vitreous and ocular trauma svc. U. Calif. Sch. Medicine, Davis, 1981—84; prof. ophthalmology Tulane U. Sch. Medicine, New Orleans, 1984—89, dir. med. student edn. dept. ophthalmology, 1985—89, dir. ophthalmology Charity Hosp., 1985—89; prof. Tex. Tech U. Health Scis. Ctr., Lubbock, Tex., 1989—2001, chmn. dept. ophthalmology and visual scis., 1989—94, prof. dept. health orgn. mgmt., 1993—2001, assoc. dean Sch. Medicine, 1994—96; del. 19th Congaessional Dist. to Repulican Nat. Convention, Tex. Co-investigator in the intraocular gentamicin prophylaxis study Govt. Erskine Hosp., Madurai, India, 1975, Dept. Ophthalmology, Audie Murphy VA Hosp., San Antonio, 1977—79, Martinez VA Hosp., Calif., 1979—84, VA Hosp., New Orleans, 1984—89, VA Med. Ctr., Big Spring, Tex., 1989—93, 1996—2001, VA Ctr., Lubbock, Tex., 1989—92, Lubbock, 1996—2001; vis. prof., Germany, 1984, Switzerland, 1987; pres. US Eye Injury Registry, 1994—96; founder, med. dir. Tex. Eye Injury Registry, 1991—2001; cons. in field; co-owner Fullanime Cos., Lubbock, Tex., Selenium Ltd. Concert Lighting Internat., Compliance Svcs. Group Internat.; ptnr. Concert Lighting Internat.; with Brit. Parliament & Royal Family, Et al. Contbg. editor: Outcome/Fragmatome Newsletter, 1978—81; assoc. editor: Vitreorentinal Surgery and Tech., 1989—98, mem. editl. bd.: Jour. Eye Trauma, 1996—2001; contbr. articles to profl. jours.; appeared in numerous TV and radio programs. Com. mem. Sch. Medicine U. Calif., Davis, Tulane U. Sch. Medicine, New Orleans, Sch. Medicine Tex. Tech. U. Health Scis. Ctr.; bd. dirs. Lubbock Internat. Cultural Ctr., Inc., 1997—, pres. bd. dirs., 2005—07; planning com., chmn. medicine and history com., liaison Vatican Mus. Exhbn. Found., 2001—02; bd. trustees Nat. Exhibits Assn. Mus., Post, Tex., 2007—; Tex. del. 19th Congl. Dist. to Rep. Nat. Convention, 2008. Maj. USAF, 1973—80. Decorated Air Force Commendation medal. Mem.: AMA, ACS, Mil. Officers Assn. of Am., Mil. Officers Assn. Am. (bd. dirs. Greater Lubbuck chpt. 2007—), Ill. Farm Bur., Ill. Agrl. Assn., Am. Farm Bur. Fedn., Soc. Med. Cons. Armed Forces, Vitreous Soc. (charter), Retina Soc., Schepens Internat. Soc., Tex. Tech. Rsch. Found. (bd. dirs. 1993—96), Tex. Ophthal. Assn. (chair edn. com. 1990—93, coun. 1990—93, nominating com. 1991—93), So. Retina Study Group, Tex. Med. Assn. (com. continuing edn. 1993—96, bd. dirs. TEXPAC 2000—02), So. Med. Assn. (vice-chmn. sec. ophthalmology 1995—96, chmn. sec. ophthalmology 1996—97), Christian Med. Assn., Assn. Rsch. Vision and Ophthalmology (pub. rels. com. 1997—2000), Am. Acad. Ophthalmology (bylaws and rules com. 1990—95, com. internat. ophthalmology 1991—95), Lubbock C. of C., Am. Legion, Sigma Xi (sec. Tex. Tech. chpt. 1990—91, v.p., pres.-elect 1999—2000, pres. 2000—01). Republican. Lutheran. Avocations: travel, photography, bicycling, hiking. Office: PO Box 1678 Lubbock TX 79408-1678

MAY, GENNY (GENEVIEVE LYNN MAY), US marshal; BS in Zoology, So. La. U.; MPA, La. State U.; M in Criminal Justice, So. U., Baton Rouge; grad., FBI Nat. Acad. With Jefferson Parish Sheriff's Office, La.; state trooper La. State Police Dept., 1978—2010, comdr. Gaming Enforcement Divsn., Operational Devel. Sect., dep. supt. Bur. of Investigations and Support; US marshal (ea. dist.) La. US Marshals Svc., US Dept. Justice, 2010—. Adj. prof. Southeastern La. U., 2005, Baton Rouge CC, 2006. Master chief intelligence specialist USNR, 1986—2009. Office: US Marshals Service US Courthouse 500 Camp St, Rm C-600 New Orleans LA 70130 Office Phone: 504-589-6079.

MAY, JOE T., state legislator; b. Broadway, Va., June 8, 1937; m. Roberta Compton Downs; children: S. Elizabeth, Elaine. BSEE, Va. Polytechnic Inst. and State U., Blacksburg. Various positions in the tech. field; founder & owner EIT, Sterling, Danville, Va., 1977—; mem. Dist. 33 Va. House of Delegates, 1994—. Judge, group leader No. Va. Regional Sci. Fair; judge Loudoun County Sci. & History Fairs; umpire Battlefield Little League; bd. mem. No. Va. 4-H Edn. Ctr. Served with US Army. Mem.: Radtech Internat., Loudoun C. of C., Airplane & Pilots Assn., Va. Soc. Profl. Engineers, Sons Confederate Vet. (treas.). Republican. Episcopalian. Office: PO Box 2146 Leesburg VA 20177 also: Capitol Office 504 Gen Assembly Bldg PO Box 406 Richmond VA 23218 Office Phone: 703-777-1191, 703-777-6059, 804-698-1033, 804-698-6733. Business E-Mail: deljmay@house.virginia.gov.

MAY, JOHN S., pediatric otolaryngologist, educator; BS, High Point U., 1977; MD, Wake Forest U., 1982. Diplomate American Bd. Otolaryngology, 1989. Resident surgery NC Bapt. Hosp., Winston-Salem, 1982—84, intern surgery, 1983, resident otolaryngology, 1984—88; fellow skull base surgery Univ. Zurich Hosp., Switzerland, 1988—90; assoc. prof. otolaryngology pediat. Wake Forest Univ.; physician Wake Forest Bapt. Med. Ctr. Co-author articles to profl. publs. Mem.: AMA, ACS, American Neurotological Soc., American Laryngol. Rhinol. and Otol. Soc.- Triological Soc., American Acad. of Otolaryngology Head and Neck Surgery. Office: Wake Forest Baptist Medical Center Medical Center Blvd Winston Salem NC 27157 Office Phone: 336-716-3895. Office Fax: 336-716-9440. E-mail: jsmay@wakehealth.edu.

MAY, KENNETH AUSTIN, former consumer products company executive; b. Memphis, Nov. 14, 1960; s. Forrest Sherman and Elizabeth (Austin) M. Degree in real estate, Memphis State U., 1983; MBA, U. Tenn., 1994. Supr. United Parcel Svc., Memphis, 1979-82; sr. mgr. Federal Express Corp., Memphis, 1982-90, mng. dir. Miami, 1990-96, v.p. Memphis, 1996—2004; exec. v.p., CEO FedEx Kinko's Inc., Dallas, 2004—06, pres., CEO, 2006—08. Trustee March of Dimes Birth Defects Found., White Plains, NY. Republican. Baptist. Avocations: water-skiing, skiing, basketball, golf, fishing. Home: 5139 Palomar Ln Dallas TX 75229-6407

MAY, MICHAEL C., mortgage company executive; BS, Old Dominion U. CPA; cert. internal auditor. Internal auditor Student Loan Mktg. Corp.; various exec. positions, including v.p., loan prospector, v.p., structured fin. Freddie Mac (Fed. Home Loan Mortgage Corp.), 1983—98, sr. v.p., customer services and control, 1998—2002, sr. v.p., single family ops., 2002—03, sr. v.p., mortgage, ops. and funding, 2003—05, sr. v.p., ops., 2005, sr. v.p., multifamily, 2005—10, exec. v.p. multifamily, 2010—. Office: Federal Home Loan Mortgage Corp 8200 Jones Branch Dr Mc Lean VA 22102-3110 Office Fax: 703-903-4045. Business E-Mail: mike_may@freddiemac.com.

MAY, PHILIP ALAN, sociologist, educator; b. Bethesda, Md., Nov. 6, 1947; s. Everette Lee and Marie (Lee) M.; m. Doreen Ann Garcia, Sept. 5, 1972; children: Katrina Ruth, Marie Ann. BA in Sociology, Catawba Coll., 1969; MA in Sociology, Wake Forest U., 1971; PhD in Sociology, U. Mont., 1976. NIMH predoctoral fellow U. Mont., Missoula, 1973-76; dir. health stats. and rsch. Navajo Health Authority, Window Rock, Ariz., 1976-78; from asst. prof. to prof. U. N.Mex., Albuquerque, 1978—89, prof., 1989—2011, emeritus prof., 2011—, from dir. Ctr. on Alcoholism, Substance abuse and Addictions to sr. rsch. scientist Albuquerque, 1990—2000, sr. rsch. scientist Ctr. on Alcoholism, Substance abuse and Addictions, 2000—, assoc. dir. Ctr. on Alcoholism, Substance abuse and Addictions, 2002—04, interim dir. Ctr. on Alcoholism, Substance abuse and Addictions, 2004; rsch. prof. U. NC, Nutrition Rsch. Inst., Sch. Pub. Health, 2011—. Fetal alcohol syndrome study com. Inst. Medicine of NAS, 1994-96; dir. Nat. Indian Fetal Alcohol Syndrome Prevention Program, Albuquerque, 1979-85; adv. bd. Nat. Orgn. on Fetal Alcohol Syndrome, Washington, 1990—; rsch. assoc. Nat. Ctr. for Am. Indian and Alaska Native Mental Health Rsch., 1986—; mem. U.S. Surgeon Gens. Task Force on Drunk Driving, 1988-89; prin. investigator fetal alcohol syndrome epidemiology rsch. in South Africa, 1997—; com. on pathophysiology and prevention of adolescent and adult suicide Inst. Medicine of NRC, NAS, 2000-02, mem. bd. visitors, Catawba Coll., 2010-; cons. in field. Contbr. chpts. to books, articles to profl. jours. V.p. Bd. Edn., Laguna Pueblo, N.Mex., 1998—2002, pres., 2002—08; mem. N.Mex. Indian Edn. Adv. Coun., 2006—10, N.Mex. Gov.'s Commn. on Compulsive Gambling, 2006—11; bd. mem. Laguna Pueblo Edn. Found., 2009—10. Lt. (s.g.) USPHS, 1970—73. Recipient Spl. Recognition award U.S. Indian Health Svc., 1992, award Navajo Tribe and U.S. Indian Health Svc., 1992, Human Rights Promotion award UN Assn., 1994, Program award for Contbns. to Mental Health of Am. Indians, U.S. Indian Health Svc., 1996, O.B. Michael Outstanding Alumnus award Catawba Coll., 2000, Wayne S. Fenton award, NIMH, 2007, Hon. award U. N.Mex., 56th Annual Rsch. Lectr. award, U. NM, 2011, Excellence award Nat. Org. on Fetal Alcohol Syndrome, 2011, Starfish award, U. BC, 2013 Mem. APHA, Am. Assn. Suicidology, Population Ref. Bur., Coll. on Problems of Drug Dependence, Rsch. Soc. Alcoholism. Methodist. Home: 6835 US Hwy 601 Salisbury NC 28147 Office: University NC Nutrition Research Inst 500 Laureate Way Kannapolis NC 28081 Office Phone: 505-925-2307, 704-250-5002. Business E-Mail: pmay@unm.edu.

MAY, ROBERT M., retired obstetrician, gynecologist, educator; b. Camberg, Germany, Feb. 17, 1926; came to U.S., 1940; s. Herman and Flora May; m. Anita S. Wynne, Sept. 6, 1953; children: Harvey, Ann, Julie. MD, La. State U., 1948. Diplomate Am. Bd. Ob-Gyn. Intern Touro Infirmary, New Orleans, 1948-49, resident in ob-gyn., 1949-53; practice medicine specializing in gynecology Birmingham, Ala., 1954-97; mem. staff Bapt. Med. Ctr., pres. med. staff, 1985-86, chmn. dept. ob-gyn., 1980-86; assoc. clin. prof. ob-gyn. U. Ala., Birmingham, 1975-97. Served to capt. USAFR, 1950-52. Mem. Ala. Med. Soc., Am. Soc. Study Infertility, Am. Coll. Ob-Gyn.

MAY, RONALD ALAN, lawyer; b. Waterloo, Iowa, Sept. 8, 1928; s. John W. and Elsie (Finlayson) M.; m. Naomi Gray, Aug. 18, 1950 (div. Feb. 1974); children: Sarah, Jonathan, Andrew, Rachel; m. Susan East Gray, May 9, 1975. BA, U. Iowa, 1950; LL.B., Vanderbilt U., 1953. Bar: Ark. 1953. Atty. Daggett & Daggett, Marianna, 1953-57, Wright, Lindsey & Jennings LLP, Little Rock, 1957-84, sr. ptnr., 1984-96; of counsel Wright, Lindsey & Jennings, LLP, 1996—. Editor: Automated Law Research, 1972, Sense and Systems in Automated Law Research, 1975; contbg. editor Fifty State Construction Lien and Bond Law, 1992, Fifty State Public Construction Contracting, 1996; assoc. editor Jour. Irreproducible Results. Pres. Spl. Com. on Pub. Edn., Ark. Assn. for Mental Health, Friends of Library, Central Ark. Radiation Therapy Inst.; chmn. Ark. Cancer Research Ctr., 1990-92; bd. dirs. Nat. Assn. for Mental Health, Ark. State Hosp., Gaines House, State Bd. Architects; bd. dirs. State Bd. Bar Examiners, chmn. 1987-88, Ark. ethics com., 1991-93; trustee Mus. Sci. and Natural History, Little Rock, chmn., 1973; mem. profl. adv. bd. sch. architecture U. Ark., 1990-96, mem. profl. adv. bd. sch. urban studies and design, 1993—; mem. instl. rev. bd. U. Ark. for Med. Scis., 2000—. Served with AUS, 1946-47. Mem. ABA (chmn. sci. and tech. sect. 1975-76), Ark., Pulaski County Bar Assns., Internat. Assn. Def. Counsel, Am. Inns of Ct. (Master of the Bench), Assn. for Computing Machinery, Order of Coif, Phi Beta Kappa. Episcopalian. Home: 821 Ash St Little Rock AR 72205-2051 Office: Wright Lindsey & Jennings LLP 200 W Capitol Ave Ste 2300 Little Rock AR 72201-3699 Office Phone: 501-371-0808. Business E-Mail: rmay@wlj.com.

MAY, STERLING RANDOLPH, biology professor, department chairman; b. Muskogee, Okla., Dec. 27, 1946; s. William Sterling and Mary Catherine (Griffith) May. BA with honors, U. Kans., 1968; MS, U. Mich., 1969, PhD, 1977; M in Bus., Johns Hopkins U., 1995, MBA, 2000. Coord. Skin Bank St. Agnes Med. Ctr., Phila., 1977-79, assoc. dir. Burn Rsch., 1980, dir. Burn Rsch., 1981-83; dir. Southeastern Burn Rsch. Inst., Augusta, Ga., 1983-87; v.p. LifeCell Corp., The Woodlands, Tex., 1987-91; chief oper. officer ARC Nat. Hdqs., Arlington, Va., 1991-2000; pres. Health Care Rsch., Arlington, 2000—04; assoc. prof. biology and genetics, chmn. dept. math. and sci. Brenau U., Gainsville, Ga., 2004—09; prof. biology and genetics, Richard & Phyllis Leet disting. chair, biol. sci., dir. Anna Thomas Biosci. Ctr., 2009—. Rsch. asst. prof. Hahnemann U. Sch. Medicine, Phila., 1979-82, rsch. assoc. prof., 1983; assoc. clin. prof. Med. Coll. Ga., 1984-87; adj. prof. U. Tex. Med. Sch., Houston, 1987-91. Editor: Care of the Burn Wound, 1985; author 84 published articles in biomed. lit., 1974—; mem. editorial bd. Jour. Burn Care and Rehab., 1982-90, Burns, 1985-92, Cryobiology, 1987-93. Mem. Soc. for Cryobiology (pres. 1989-91, chmn. 23d ann. meeting, 1986), Am. Burn Assn. (chmn. rsch. com. 1998-2000), Internat. Soc. For Burn Injuries (mem. gen. coun. 1982-90), Am. Assn. Tissue Banks (sec. 1991-93, v.p. 1993-95, pres. 1995-97, bd. govs. 1989-93), Sigma Xi, Phi Kappa Phi (chartered mem., founding mem. Brenau U. chpt.). Avocations: antique furniture, music. Office: Dept Math and Sci Brenau Univ 500 Washington St NE Gainesville GA 30501 Home Phone: 770-536-9171; Office Phone: 770-534-6278. Business E-Mail: rmay@brenau.edu.

MAYBERRY, ANDY, state legislator; b. Pine Bluff, Ark., Sept. 21, 1970; m. Julie Mayberry; children: Ellie Jo Mayberry, Katie Mayberry, Zoe Mayberry. BA, Henderson State U., 1992. Owner Spirit Publs., Inc., The East Ender; prodn. coord., Comm. TCBY Enterprises, 1993—94; fundraising co-ord. Alltel's United Way Campaign, 1996; comm. assoc. Baptist Health, 1996—98; mgr., Corp. Comm. Alltell Corp., 1994—96, 1998—; mem., Mktg. Comm. Team Am. Cancer Soc., 1997—99, pub. chmn., Pulaski County Relay for Life, 1998; chmn. Maple Creek Farms Property Owners Assn., 1999—; mem. Dist. 2 US House of Representatives, 2006; mem. Dist. 51 Ark. State House of Representatives, 2000, mem. Dist. 27, 2011—. Republican. Baptist. Office: 3022 E Woodson Lateral Rd Hensley AR 72065 Office Phone: 501-888-3522. Business E-Mail: andymayberry@windstream.net.

MAYBERRY, WILLIAM EUGENE, retired foundation administrator, board member; b. Cookeville, Tenn., Aug. 22, 1929; s. Henry Eugene and Beatrice Lucille (Maynard) M.; m. Jane G. Foster, Dec. 29, 1953; children: Ann Graves, Paul Foster. Student, Tenn. Tech. U., 1949; MD, U. Tenn., 1953; MS in Medicine, U. Minn., 1959; D.H.L. (hon.), Jacksonville U., 1983. Diplomate Am. Bd. Internal Medicine. Intern U.S. Naval Hosp., 1953-54; resident Mayo Grad. Sch. Medicine, Rochester, Minn., 1956-59; mem., staff New Eng. Med. Ctr., 1959-60, Nat. Inst. Arthritis and Metabolic Diseases, 1962-64; cons., internal medicine, endocrine rsch. and lab. medicine, chmn. dept. lab. medicine Mayo Clinic, Rochester, 1971-75, bd. govs., 1971-87, prof., lab. medicine, 1971, vice chmn., 1974-75, chmn., CEO, 1976-87, prof., medicine, 1983-92; chmn., CEO, pres. Mayo Found., Rochester, 1993. Asst. in medicine Tufts U. Med. Sch., 1959-60; mem. faculty Mayo Grad. Sch. Medicine and Mayo Med. Sch., 1960-92; trustee

Mayo Found., 1971-87, vice chmn., 1974-85, pres. 1986-87, chmn. bd. devel. 1988—; trustee Minn. Mut. Life Ins., 1983-92; bd. dirs. George A. Hormel & Co., 1986-92. Mem. editorial bd. (Jour. of Clin. Endocrinology and Metabolism), 1971-73; contbr. articles to profl. jours. Trustee Mpls. Soc. Fine Arts, 1983-91, Cumberland U., 1984-86, Twin Cities Pub. TV, Inc., 1991-92, trustee, 1991-92; bd. overseers Mpls. Coll. Art and Design, 1983-86, U. Minn. Sch. Mgmt., 1985-88; bd. dirs. Greater Rochester Area Univ. Ctr., 1986-87, Minn. Acad. Excellence Found., 1986-87, U.S. West-Minn. Exec. Bd., 1988-92; rep. Congl. Dist. 1 State of Minn. Compensation Council, 1986; chmn. Presdl. Commn. on Human Immunodeficiency Virus Epidemic, 1987. Recipient Disting. Alumni award Tenn. Technol. U., 1976, chair of excellence in bus. adminstrn. named in his honor, 1989; recipient Outstanding Alumni award U. Tenn., 1982, Med. Exec. Award Am. Coll. Med. Group Adminstrs., 1986; rsch. fellow NIH, 1959-60, Am. Cancer Soc., 1962-64; NIH research grantee, 1965-71 Fellow ACP; mem. Inst. Medicine of NAS, Am. Thyroid Assn., Am. Clin. and Climatological Soc., Endocrine Soc., Soc. Med. Administrs., Am. Acad. Med. Dirs., Am. Coll. Physician Execs. (bd. regents 1983, vice chmn. 1985-86), Sigma Xi. Clubs: Mpls. Club, Rochester Golf & Country, The Club at Pelican Bay (Naples, Fla.). Home: 734 Big Canoe Jasper GA 30143-5115 Office: Health Management Associates Inc Bd Directors 5811 Pelican Bay Blvd Ste 500 Naples FL 34108 Office Phone: 239-598-3131. Office Fax: 239-913-2715. Business E-Mail: wmayberry@healthmanagement.com.

MAYDEN, BARBARA MENDEL, lawyer; b. Chattanooga, Sept. 18, 1951; d. Eugene Lester Mendel and Blanche (Krugman) Rosenberg; m. Martin Ted Mayden, Sept. 14, 1986. AB, Ind. U., 1973; JD, U. Ga., 1976. Bar: Ga. 1976, N.Y. 1980. Assoc. King & Spalding, Atlanta, 1976-79, Willkie Farr & Gallagher, NYC, 1980, Morgan Lewis & Bockius, NYC, 1980-82, White & Case, NYC, 1982-89; spl. counsel Skadden, Arps, Slate, Meagher & Flom, NYC, 1989-95; mem. Bass, Berry & Sims PLC, Nashville, 1996—2006; lectr. Vanderbilt U. Sch. Law, Nashville, 1995-97; mem. Young Mayden, LLC, 2008—. Mem. editl. bd.: mag. Business Law Today; editor: Business Lawyer; chair sect. bus. law:, 2004—05. Mem. bd. visitors U. Ga. Sch. Law, Athens, 1986—89; mem. Leadership Nashville, 1999—2000; mem. adv. bd. Women's Fund of the Cmty. Found. of Mid. Tenn., 2001—; co-pres. Nashville sect. Nat. Coun. Jewish Women, 2007—; 1st v.p. West End Synagogue, 2007—; bd. dirs. YWCA, 2001—07, Jewish Cmty. Ctr., 2001—02. Fellow Am. Bar Found. (life); mem. ABA (chair young lawyers divsn. 1985-86, ho. of dels. 1986—2004, 2006-, commn. on women 1987-91, commn. opportunities for minorities in profession 1986-87, select com. of the house 1989-91, chmn. assembly resolutions com. 1990-91, membership com. of the house 1991-92, bd. govs. 1991-94, 2001-, chair com. on rules and calendar 1996-98, chair bd. govs. ops. com., exec. com. 1993-94, task force long range fin. planning 1993-94, com. scope correlation of work 1998-2003, chair 2001-02, sec. bus. law sect. 2001-02, vice-chair 2002-03, chair-elect 2003-04, chair 2004—05), Nat. Assn. Bond Lawyers (bd. dirs. 1985-86), Bond Attys.' Workshop (chmn. 1986), N.Y. State Bar Assn. (ho. of dels. 1993-95), Assn. Bar City N.Y. (internat. human rights com. 1986-89, 2d century com. 1986-90, com. women in the profession, 1989-92), N.Y. County Lawyers Assn. (com. spl. projects, chair com. rels with other bars), Am. Law Inst., Tenn. Bar Assn. (com. chair), Am. Bar Ins. Plans Cons., Inc. (bd. dirs., treas.). Democrat. Jewish. Home: 4414 Herbert Pl Nashville TN 37215-4544 Office Phone: 615-742-6208. Business E-Mail: bmayden@bassberry.com.

MAYER, JOHN, musician; b. Bridgeport, Conn., Oct. 16, 1977; s. Richard and Margaret. Student, Berklee Coll. Music, Boston. Musician: (albums) Inside Wants Out, 1999, Room for Squares, 2001, Any Given Thursday, 2003, Heavier Things, 2003, As/is, 2004, Continuum, 2006 (Best Pop Vocal Album, Grammy Awards, 2007), Where the Light Is, 2008, Battle Studies, 2009, Born and Raised, 2012, Paradise Valley, 2013; musician: (with John Mayer Trio) Try! John Mayer Trio Live In Concert, 2005; musician: (songs) Your Body is a Wonderland (Grammy award for Best Male Pop Vocal Performance, 2002), Daughters (Grammy award for Song of Yr., 2005), Waiting on the World to Change (Grammy award for Best Male Pop Vocal Performance, 2007), Say (Grammy award for Best Male Pop Vocal Performance, 2009), Gravity (Grammy award for Best Solo Rock Vocal Performance, 2009); composer: (films) Serendipity, 2001, Vanilla Sky, 2001, How to Deal, 2003, Win a Date with Tad Hamilton!, 2004; exec. prodr.: (TV series) John Mayer Has a TV Show, 2004; monthly columnist Esquire mag., 2004—. Named one of The World's Most Influential People, TIME mag., 2007. Office: Creative Artists Agency c/o Scott Clayton 3310 West End Ave 5th Fl Nashville TN 37203*

MAYER, JOHN D., management consultant; Grad. in Statistics, Ops. Rsch. & Bus., Stanford U., LI U.; undergraduate in Engring., US Mil. Acad.; grad. in Sr. Exec. Program, Harvard U. Cons. Electronic Industries Assn.; dep. asst. dir., Capitol Hill Congl. Budget Office; dir., strategic planning and program devel. CNA Corp.; joined Booz Allen Hamilton Holding Corp., 1997, exec. v.p., 2009—. Mem., corp. adv. bd., Darden Sch.of Bus. U. Va.; bd. dirs. Washington Edn. and Tennis Found.; chmn. Homeland Security and Def. Bus. Coun. Office: Booz Allen Hamilton Holding Corp 8283 Greensboro Dr Mc Lean VA 22101 Office Phone: 703-902-5000. Office Fax: 703-902-3333. Business E-Mail: mayer_john@bah.com.

MAYER, SUSAN MARTIN, art educator; b. Atlanta, Oct. 25, 1931; d. Paul McKeen and Ione (Garrett) Martin; m. Arthur James Mayer, Aug. 9, 1953; 1 child, Melinda Marilyn. Student, Am. U., 1949-50; BA, U. N.C., Greensboro, 1953; postgrad., U. Del., 1956-58; MA, Ariz. State U., 1966. Artist-in-residence Armed Forces Staff Coll., Norfolk, Va., 1968-69; mem. art faculty U. Tex., Austin, 1971—2003; ret., 2002. Co-editor: Museum Education: History, Theory and Practice, 1989; author various mus. publs.; contbr. articles to profl. jours. Recipient award Austin Ind. Sch. Bd., 1985. Mem. Nat. Art Edn. Assn. (bd. dirs. 1983-87, award 1987, 91), Tex. Art Edn. Assn. (mus. edn. chair 1982-83, Mus. Educator of Yr. 1986), Tex. Assn. Mus. (mus. edn. chair), Austin Visual Arts Assn., Am. Assn. Mus. Business E-Mail: susanm@mail.utexas.edu.

MAYES, WENDELL WISE, JR., former broadcasting company executive; b. San Antonio, Mar. 2, 1924; s. Wendell Wise and Dorothy Lydia (Evans) M.; m. Mary Jane King, May 11, 1946; children: Cathey, Sarah, Wendell Wise, III. Student, Schreiner Inst., 1941-42, U. Tex., 1942, Daniel Baker Coll., 1946; BS, Tex. Tech. Coll., 1949; BA summa cum laude, St. Edward's U., 2002, MLA, 2005, MBA, 2006; PhD, Walden U., 2013. Program dir., sta. mgr. Sta. KBWD, Brownwood, Tex., 1949-57; mgr. Sta. KCRS, Midland, Tex., 1957-63, pres., 1965-84, chmn., 1984-96; pres. Sta. KNOW, Austin, Tex., 1970-81, Stas. KVIC and KAMG, Victoria, Tex., 1970-84, chmn., 1984-98, Sta. KCRS-FM, Midland, 1984-96; pres. Sta. KCSW, San Marcos, 1976-81; sec.-treas. Sta. KSNY-AM-FM, Snyder, 1952-94; mem. bd. mgrs. Sta. KLBJ/KHHT-AM-FM, Austin, 1991-97. Bd. advisors Patton Med. Devices, 2006—08; lectr. Coll. Comm., U. Tex., Austin, 1978—81. Chmn. bd. Am. Diabetes Assn., 1974—77; mem. Nat. Diabetes Adv. Bd., 1977—84; v.p. Internat. Diabetes Fedn., 1980—88, pres.-elect, 1988—91, pres., 1991—94, hon. pres., 1997—; pres. Tex. Broadcast Edn. Found., 1973—76, dir., 2002—; mem. Tex. Diabetes Coun., 1983—86, chmn., 1983—86, exec. dir., 1999; bd. regents Tex. Tech U., 1985—91, chmn., 1987—88; bd. dirs., treas. Writer's League Tex., 2005—08. With USNR, 1943—46. Recipient Addison B. Scoville award, Am. Diabetes Assn., 1977, first Wendell Mayes Jr. award, 1986, Josiah K. Lilly award, 1991, Harold Rifkin award, 1994, Masaji Takeda medal, Kobe, Japan Colloquium Med. Sci., 1994, Lifetime Learning award, St. Edward's U., 2013; named Disting. Alumnus, Tex. Tech U., 1981, Disting. Engr., 1985, Disting. Alumnus, Schreiner U., 2006, St. Edward's U., MLA Program, 2010; named to Tex. Tech. Mass Comm. Hall of Fame, 1978, Hall of Fame Tex. affiliate, Am. Diabetes Assn., 1994, Tex. Radio Hall of Fame, 2002. Mem. Tex. Assn. Broadcasters (pres. 1964, named Pioneer Broadcaster of Year 1978), Nat. Assn. Broadcasters (dir. 1969-72), Am. Council on Edn. in Journalism (dir. 1977-80), Broadcast Edn. Assn. (dir. 1973-77), AP Broadcasters (bd. dirs. 1988-91), Tex. Tech. Elec. Engring. Acad. Episcopalian (vestryman 1966-69, 86-88; sr. warden 1988). Home: 2834 Montebello Rd Apt 1 Austin TX 78746-6820 Office: 1907 N Lamar Blvd 200 Austin TX 78705-4992

MAYFIELD, DEBBIE, state legislator; b. Pensacola, Fla., Dec. 2, 1956; m. Stan Mayfield (dec.); children: Evan, Samuel, Coleman. Mem. Dist. 80 Fla. House of Reps., 2008—, vice chair agr. and natural resources policy com., mem. gen. govt. policy coun., govtl. affairs policy com., natural resources appropriations com. Mem. Indian River County Econ. Devel. Coun., Vero Beach Fin. Com., Indian River County C. of C. Mem.: Treasure Coast Builders Assn., Nat. Mortgage Brokers Assn., Indian River County Bd. Realtors, Fla. Mortgage Brokers Assn., Indian River County United Way (former funds distribution chmn.), Rep. Women Aware, Rep. Exec. Com., Jr. League Indian River County (former v.p. fin.). Republican. Baptist. Office: House Office Bldg 402 S Monroe St Rm 317 Tallahassee FL 32399-1300 also: 1053 20th Pl Vero Beach FL 32960-5359 Office Phone: 850-488-0952, 772-778-5077. Business E-Mail: debbie.mayfield@myfloridahouse.gov.

MAYFIELD, DONNA, state legislator; b. July 18, 1955; Legal stenographer US Attorney's Office, Lexington, Ky., 1973—75; adminstrv. officer US Marshals Svc., Lexington, 1975—2001; custodian of records Clark County Sheriff's Office, Winchester, Ky., 2007—; mem. Dist. 73 Ky. House of Reps., Frankfort, 2011—. Mem. Calvary Christian Ch., Ky. Republican. Office: Ky House of Reps Annex Rm 405F 702 Capitol Ave Frankfort KY 40601 Office Phone: 502-564-8100 ext. 630.

MAYFIELD, MAX (BRITT MAYFIELD), meteorologist; b. Okla. City, Sept. 19, 1948; m. Linda C. Mayfield; 3 children. BS in Math., U. Okla., 1970; MS in Meterology, Fla. St. U., 1987. With NOAA/Nat. Weather Svc., Miami, 1972—2007, hurricane forecaster, 1988—90, sr. forecaster, 1990—98, dep. dir. Nat. Hurricane Ctr., 1998—2000, acting dir., 2000, dir., 2000—07; hurricane specialist WPLG-TV Local 10, Miami, 2007—. Chmn. regional assn. IV hurricane com. World Meterological Orgn.; chmn. office of fed. coord. Meteorology Working Group on Hurricanes; spkr. in field. Contbr. articles to profl. jours. Recipient Francis W. Reichelderfer award, Am. Meterological Soc., 1996, Outstanding Achievement award, Nat. Hurricane Ctr., 2000, Richard Hagemeyer award, Interdepartmental Hurricane Conf., 2004, Emmy award, 2004, Presdl. Rank award for Meritorious Svc., 2005, NOAA Bronze medal, US Dept. Commerce. Mem.: Nat. Weather Assn., Am. Meteorological Soc. Office: WPLG-TV 3900 Biscayne Blvd Miami FL 33137

MAYHALL, CLIFFORD WESLEY, lawyer; b. Birmingham, Ala., Aug. 23, 1972; s. Clyde Wesley and Pamela Hayes Mayhall. BA in Govt. and English, Coll. William and Mary, Williamsburg, Va., 1994; MA in Polit. Sci., U. Fla., Gainesville, 1996; JD, Fla. State U., Tallahassee, 2000. Bar: Fla. 2000, US Dist Ct. (no. dist.) Fla. 2002, US Dist. Ct. (so. dist.) Fla. 2002, US Dist. Ct. (mid. dist.) Fla. 2005, US Ct. Appeals (11th cir.) 2005, US Supreme Ct. 2005. Rsch. asst. Reubin Askew Inst., Gainesville, 1994—96; staff aide US Senator Bob Graham, Tallahassee, 1995; rsch. specialist Legis. Com. on Intergovtl. Rels., Tallahassee, 1996—98; jud. clk. Sr. US Dist. Judge Maurice Paul, Gainesville, 2000—01; atty. Katz, Kutter, Alderman & Bryant, PA, Tallahassee, 2001—04, Akerman Senterfitt, Tallahassee, 2004—08; regulatory counsel Home Shopping Network, St. Petersburg, 2008—10; sr. atty. Universal Parks & Resorts, Orlando, 2010—. Legis. editor Fla. State U. Law Rev., 2000. Sec., past pres. Tree House Children's Shelter, Tallahassee, 2001—08; mem. rector search com. St. John's Episcopal Ch., Tallahassee, 2006—08; bd. dirs. So. Shakespeare Festival, Tallahassee, 1998—2002. Mem.: FBA, ABA, Fla. Bar, Emerge Tallahassee, Emerge Fla., Capital Tiger Bay Club, Order of Coif. Office: Universal Parks & Resorts 1000 Universal Studios Plz Orlando FL 32819 Office Phone: 407-224-6390. Office Fax: 407-224-7704. Personal E-mail: cwmayhall@yahoo.com. Business E-Mail: cliff.mayhall@universalorlando.com.

MAYHEW, KENNETH EDWIN, JR., retired transportation executive; b. Shelby, NC, Sept. 27, 1934; s. Kenneth Edwin and Evelyn Lee (Dellinger) M.; m. Frances Elaine Craft, Apr. 7, 1957 (dec. 2005); m. Darlene Burgess Randall, Jan. 7, 2006; 1 dau., Catherine Lynn Prince. AB, Duke U., 1956. CPA NC. Sr. auditor Arthur Andersen & Co., Atlanta, 1956-58, 60-63; controller Trendline, Inc., Hickory, NC, 1963-66; with Carolina Freight Corp., Cherryville, 1966-93, treas., 1969-74; v.p. Carolina Freight Carriers Corp., Cherryville, 1971-72, exec. v.p., 1972-85, pres., COO, 1985-89, dir., 1968-93, chmn., pres., CEO, 1989-93; ret., 1993. Pres., dir. Robo Auto Wash Shelby Inc., 1967-73, Robo Auto Wash Cherryville, Inc., 1968-73; dir. Cherryville Nat. Bank. Mem. Bus. Adv. Bd., Fuqua Sch. Bus., Duke U.; bd. dirs., vice-chmn. Gaston Meml. Hosp.; trustee Pfeiffer U. With AUS, 1958-60. Mem. AICPA, Am. Trucking Assn. (dir., v.p.), N.C. Trucking Assn. (dir., chmn.), Gaston County C. of C. (v.p. pub. affairs), Lions Club (pres. Cherryville 1972-73), Phi Beta Kappa, Omicron Delta Kappa, Phi Eta Sigma. Methodist. Home: 507 Spring St Cherryville NC 28021-3540

MAYMAN, TODD A., publishing executive, lawyer; BA, Swarthmore Coll.; JD, Boston Univ. Bar: DC 1988. Assoc. Arent, Fox, Kintner, Plotkin & Kahn, Washington, 1988—93; asst. gen. counsel through assoc. gen. counsel & sec. Gannett Co., McLean, Va., 1993—2009; sr. v.p., sec., gen. counsel Gannett Co., Inc., McLean, Va., 2009—. Office: Gannett Co 7950 Jones Branch Dr Mc Lean VA 22107-0910

MAYNARD, CHARLES DOUGLAS, radiologist; b. Atlantic City, Sept. 11, 1934; m. Mary Anne Satterwhite; children: Charles D., Deanne, David. BS, Wake Forest U., 1955, MD, 1959. Diplomate Am. Bd. Radiology (trustee 1987-99, sec.-treas., v.p. 1992-94, pres. 1994-96, guest examiner). Intern U.S. Army Hosp., Honolulu, 1959—60; resident N.C. Baptist Hosp., 1963—66; dir. Nuclear Medicine Lab., 1966—77; asst. dean admissions Bowman Gray Sch. Medicine, 1966—71, asso. dean student affairs, 1971—75, prof. radiology, chmn. dept., 1977—2000. Mem. Am. Bd. Med. Specialists; acting dean Wake Forest U. Sch. Medicine, 2001—02. Author: Clinical Nuclear Medicine, 1969; mem. editl. bd.: Yearbook of Diagnostic Radiology, Contemporary Diagnostic Radiology. Mem. Leadership Winston-Salem, Triad Leadership Network; bd. dirs. Downtown Devel. Corp., 1995—2000, Winston-Salem Bus., Inc., 1995—99, Forsyth Tech. CC, 1997—2005, pres., 2004—05; bd. dirs. Va. Tech. Coll. Engring., 2002—06, Wake Forest U. Health Scis., 2003—. Mem.: AMA, Greater Winston-Salem C. of C. (bd. dirs.), Acad. Radiology Rsch. (pres. 1999—2001), Soc. Chairmen Radiology Depts. (past pres.), Assn. Univ. Radiologists, Radiol. Soc. N.Am. Rsch. and Edn. Found. (chmn. bd. 1999), Radiol. Soc. N.Am. (pres. 1999—2000), Am. Coll. Radiology (past bd. chancellors, past chmn. commn. on nuc. medicine), Soc. Nuc. Medicine (past pres.). Office: Wake Forest U Sch Medicine Dept Radiology Medical Center Blvd Winston Salem NC 27157-1088

MAYO, BRAD, state legislator; m. Kathleen Elliott. Attended, U. Miss. Investment advisor; mem. Dist. 12 Miss. House of Reps., Jackson, 2012—. Mem. Tommy Tosh Meml. Scholarship Com.; mem. adv. com. Oxford-Lafayette Sch. Applied Tech. Mem.: NRA, U. Miss. Alumni Assn., Rotary Club. Republican. Episcopalian. Office: Miss House of Reps PO Box 1018 Jackson MS 39215 Business E-Mail: bmayo@house.ms.gov.

MAYO, CLYDE CALVIN, psychologist, educator; b. Robstown, Tex., Feb. 2, 1940; s. Clyde Culberson and Velma (Oxford) Mayo; m. Jeanne Lynn McCain, Aug. 24, 1963; children: Brady Scott, Amber Camille. BA, Rice U., Houston, 1961; BS, U. Houston, 1964, PhD, 1972; MS, Trinity U., 1966. Lic. psychologist Tex., La. Mgmt. engr. LWFW, Inc., Houston, 1966-72, sr. cons., 1972-78, prin., 1978-81; ptnr. Mayo, Thompson, Bigby, Houston, 1981-83; founder Mgmt. and Pers. Systems, Houston, 1983—; mgmt. coach Rice U. MBA Students, 2009—. Counselor Interface Counseling Ctr., Houston, 1976—79; dir. Mental Health HMO Group, 1985—87; instr. St. Thomas U., Houston, 1979—90, U. Houston Downtown Sch., 1972, 2002—06, U. Houston, Clear Lake, 1983—88, U. Houston-Ctrl. Campus, 1984—; dir. mgmt. devel. insts. U. Houston Woodlands and West Houston, 1986—91; adj. prof. U. Houston, 1991—; mem. 50th reunion com. Rice U., 2011. Author: LWFW Annual Survey of Manufacturers, 1966—81, Bi/Polar Inventory of Strengths, 1978. Coach, mgr. Meyerland Little League, 1974—78, So. Belles Softball, 1979—80, S.W. Colt Baseball, 1982—83, Friends of Fondren Libr. Rice U., 1988—; charter mem. Holocaust Mus. Mem.: Rice U. Hist. Soc., Houston Area Indsl. Orgnl. Psychologists (bd. dirs. 1989—92, orgnl. renewal com. 2010—, bd. dirs. 2011—), Am. Psychol. Soc., Tex. Psychol. Assn., Houston Psychol. Assn. (membership dir. 1978, sec. 1984, bd. dirs. 2010—), Tex. Indsl. Orgnl. Psychologists (founder, bd. dirs. 1995—, pres. 1999—2002), Soc. Indsl. Orgn. Psychologists, Found. Contemporary Theology (bd. dirs. 2005—, chair youth recruitment com. 2006—), Romeo, Meyerland Club (bd. dirs. 1988—92, pres. 1991), Forum Club. Home: 8723 Ferris Dr Houston TX 77096-1409 Office: Mgmt and Personnel Systems 4545 Bissonnet St Bellaire TX 77401-3121 Office Phone: 713-667-9251. Personal E-mail: mpsmayo@aol.com.

MAYO, LOUIS ALLEN, policy management counseling company executive; b. Durham, NC, Nov. 27, 1928; s. Louis Allen and Amy Earl (Overton) M.; m. Emma Jean Minshew, Oct. 31, 1953 (div.); children: Louis Allen III, Robert Lawrence, Carolyn Jean; m. Myrna Ann Smith, Feb. 16, 1980 (div.). Student, Calif. State Poly. Coll., 1948—50; BA in Criminology, Calif. State Coll., Fresno, 1952; MA in Pub. Adminstrn., Am. U., 1960, PhD in Pub. Adminstrn., 1983; postgrad., U. So. Calif., 1960—62. Spl. agt. U.S. Secret Svc., Treasury Dept., LA, 1956-58, 60-63, White House, Washington, 1958-60, 63-66; program mgr. law enforcement Office Law Enforcement Assistance, Justice Dept., 1967-68; acting chief Rsch. Ctr., rsch. program mgr. Nat. Inst. Law Enforcement and Criminal Justice, 1968-74; alternate assoc. mem. Fed. Coun. on Sci. and Tech., White House, 1973-74; dir. tng. and testing divsn. Nat. Inst. Justice, 1975—87; pres. Mayo, Mayo & Assocs., Alexandria, Va., 1987—. Lectr. criminology Armed Forces Inst. Tech., 1954-55; professorial lectr. Am. U., 1974-82; adj. prof. August Vollmer U., 1990-95. 2d lt. to 1st lt. USAF, 1952-56. Mem. Police Assn. Coll. Edn. (exec. dir., founder), Internat. Assn. Chiefs of Police, ASPA (nat. chmn. sect. on criminal justice adminstrn. 1975-76), Acad. Criminal Justice Scis., Police Exec. Rsch. Forum, Soc. Police Futurists Internat., Pi Sigma Alpha. Methodist. Home: 63 Lake Forest Dr Mineral VA 23117 Office Phone: 540-894-8781. Personal E-mail: loumayo@police-association.org, drloumayo@yahoo.com.

MAYO, RAHN, state legislator; b. Nov. 11; s. Whitman Mayo. Former advt. sales exec.; former mentor Big Bros. Big Sisters; former participant Youth Vibe; former mem. United Way of Met. Atlanta; former mem. sect. 8 program Atlanta Housing Authority Landlord Advisory Bd.; amb. Am. Heart Assn.; vice chmn. Henry County Legis. Del.; bd. chmn. Cedar Grove High Sch. Career Tech. Acad. Program; v.p. Brook Glen Neighborhood Assn.; bd. mem. Arthink DeKalb; mem. Dist. #91 Ga. House of Reps., Ga. Democrat. Office: Capitol Office 511 Coverdell Legislative Office Bldg Atlanta GA 30334 also: District Office PO Box 360549 Decatur GA 30036 Office Phone: 404-656-6372. Fax: 404-591-8693. E-mail: rahn.mayo@house.ga.gov.

MAYO, SUSANN C., retail executive; Attended, Fordham U. V.p., off mall logistics Sears, Roebuck & Co., various positions, 1973—2001; v.p., logistics and distbn. The Bombay Co., 2001—05; sr. v.p., supply chain Zale Corp., 2005—. Office: Zale Corp 901 W Walnut Hill Ln Irving TX 75038-1003 Office Phone: 972-580-4000. Office Fax: 972-580-5523.

MAYOR, HEATHER DONALD, molecular biology educator; b. Melbourne, Victoria, Australia, July 6, 1930; d. Joseph A. L. and Elizabeth Emily (Boyd) Donald; m. Richard Blair Mayor, May 28, 1956; children: Diana Boyd (Mrs. Russell Hawkins), Philip Hastings. BS, U. Melbourne, Australia, 1949; MS, U. Melbourne, 1951, DSc, 1970; PhD, U. London, 1954. Electron microscopist Nat. Inst. for Med. Research, London, 1952-55; postdoctoral fellow Walter and Eliza Hall Inst., Melbourne, 1955-56; post doctoral fellow Harvard U. Med. Sch., Boston, 1956-60; from asst. prof. to prof. Baylor Coll. Medicine, Houston, 1960—, prof., 1970-96, prof. emeritus, 1996—. Cons. AEC, Washington, 1971—, Nat. Cancer Inst., Bethesda, Md., 1975—, U. Tex. Med. Sch., Houston, 1975—. Contbr. articles and papers to profl. jours.; artist, coordinator Life Shapes, Contemporary Arts Mus. Houston, Tex. art exhbn., 1974. Recipient Disting. award Ctr. for Interaction Man-Sci.-Soc., Houston, 1973, Sir Hiram Maxim award, 1990; named Scientist of Yr., Ency. Britannica, 1992; scholar in residence Rockefeller Inst. and Found., Bellagio, Italy, 1983. Mem. Am. Assn. Immunologists, Biophysical Soc. (program chmn.), Am. Soc. for Cell Biology (program chmn.), Houstonian Club, Houston Harpsichord Soc. (bd. dirs.). Anglican. Avocations: piano, harpsichord. Home: 19 Pine Briar Cir Houston TX 77056-1113 Personal E-mail: hdmayor@aol.com. Business E-Mail: hmayor@bcm.tmc.edu, heatherdm@aol.com.

MAYOR, RANDY E., corporate financial executive; Grad., U. Okla.; BBA, U. Ctrl. Ark. CPA. Various positions First Nat. Bank (subs. First Comml.), Conway, 1988—98, sr. v.p., fin. officer, 1992—98; CFO, bd. dirs. Centennial Bank (subs. of Home BancShares, Inc.), 1998—; exec. v.p. through prin. acctg. officer Home BancShares, Inc.,

1998—2004, CFO, bd. dirs., 2004—, treas., 2009—. Mailing: Home BancShares Inc 719 Harkrider St Ste 100 Conway AR 72032 Office Phone: 501-328-4770. Office Fax: 501-328-4679. Business E-Mail: rmayor@homebancshares.com.

MAYORAL, FLOR A., dermatologist; MD, U. Fla., Gainesville. Diplomate Am. Bd. Dermatology. Resident Univ. of Miami, assoc. clin. prof. dept. of dermatology; leader Flor A. Mayoral M.D. Dermatology Group. Mem.: Dade County Med. Assn., Am. Acad. of Dermatology, AMA, Miami Dermatol. Soc. Mailing: Flor A. Mayoral MD Dermatology Group Ste 314 Plz San Remo 6705 Red Rd Miami FL 33143 Office Phone: 305-665-6166. Office Fax: 305-662-4649.

MAYORAS, DONALD EUGENE, corporate executive, writer, consultant, educator; s. Andrew John and Katherine Ann (Shelato) M.; m. JoAnna Marie Kacmer, June 9, 1962; children: D. Tyler, Stacie J. BS in Edn., Purdue U., 1962; postgrad., Northwestern U., 1968-71; MBA, So. Ill. U., 1977. Regional mgr. Pacific Intermountain Express, Akron, Ohio, 1972-74; v.p. United Van Lines, Fenton, Mo., 1974-78; pres. Bekins Van Lines, LA, 1978-83; pres., CEO Sun Carriers, Inc., Phila, 1983—91, chmn. bd. dirs., 1991—92; chmn., CEO Truckload Holding, Inc., Chester, NY, 1995—2004; Cloverleaf Transp. Inc., Chester, 1997—2004; founder MDC Svcs. Inc., Gallatin, Tenn., Fishkill, NY, Lebanon, 2004—. Spkr., cons. in logistics, transp., distribution field. Contbr. to profl. rsch. publs. Trustee Ross Ade Found., West Lafayette, Ind., 1962—. Capt. Transp. Corps. US Army, 1962—68. Decorated Bronze Star Vietnam. Mem. Am. Trucking Assn. (v.p. 1983—, trustee Found. 1983-91), Nat. Spkrs. Assn., Nat. Coun. Logistics, Nat. Pvt. Truck Coun., Purdue U. Alumni Assn., Nat. Def. Transp. Assn., Aronomink Golf Club, Orange County Golf Club, Club Fairvue Plantation, Delta Nu Alpha, Omicron Delta Kappa (Purdue), Beta Gamma Sigma (SIU-Edwardsville) Republican. Roman Catholic. Avocations: golf, antiques, classic automobiles. Business E-Mail: demayoras@aol.com.

MAYPOLE, JOHN FLOYD, real estate company executive; b. Chgo., May 17, 1939; s. John James and Althea Floyd M.; m. Anne White, 1961; children: Cynthia, John, Kimberly. BA in Econs, Yale U., 1961. With Arthur Andersen & Co., 1961-62, 65-66; mgr. corp. acctg. Interpace Corp., 1966, asst. treas., 1967-68, treas., 1968-70, treas., controller, 1970-73, v.p. fin., 1973-77, sr. v.p., 1977-80, exec. v.p., 1980-81, pres., 1981-83; pres., chief operating officer Clevepak Corp., 1983—; mng. ptnr. Peach State Real Estate Holding Co., Toccoa, Ga., 1984—. Bd. dirs. Knoll, Inc., Mass. Mut. Fin. Group, Nat. Captioning Inst., Inc. Bd. adjustment Borough of Mountain Lakes, N.J., 1971-81, chmn., 1980-81. Served with USMC, 1962-65. Mem. Yale Club, Ivy League Club (Sarasota), Rockaway River Country Club, Laurel Oak Country Club. Republican. Office: PO Box 1223 Toccoa GA 30577-1421

MAYS, GREGORY, retail executive, publishing executive; CEO Simon Worldwide Inc.; various fin. positions Fisher Foods, Ohio; cons. RFS, leverage buy-out firm; CFO Food 4 Less Modesto (Calif.), Inc. and Cala Foods, Inc., 1988-89; CFO, pres. and CEO Almac's, New Eng. grocery chain subs. The Yucaipa Cos., 1989-92; exec. v.p. fin. adminstrn., CFO, Food 4 Less Supermarkets, 1992-95; exec. v.p. fin. and adminstrn. Ralphs Grocery Co., Compton, Calif., 1995; mgmt. cons. pvt. practice, 2000—06; chmn., CEO Wild Oats (acquired by Whole Foods), 2006—07; CEO Source Interlink Companies Inc., Bonita Springs, Fla., 2008—10; chmn. Source Interlink Companies, Inc., Bonita Springs, Fla., 2008—. Bd. dirs. Simon Worldwide Inc., Pathmark Stores, Inc., 2005—07, Source Interlink Companies Inc., 2005—, Great Atlantic & Pacific Tea Co., Inc., 2007—. Office: Source Interlink Companies Inc 27500 Riverview Ctr Blvd Bonita Springs FL 34134 Office Phone: 239-949-4450. Office Fax: 239-949-7623. Business E-Mail: gmays@sourceinterlink.com.

MAYS, JANICE ANN, legislative staff member, lawyer; b. Waycross, Ga., Nov. 21, 1951; d. William H. and Jean (Bagley) M. BA cum laude, Wesleyan Coll., Macon, Ga., 1973; JD, U. Ga. Sch. Law, Atlanta, 1975; MLT in Taxation, Georgetown U., Washington, 1981. Bar: Ga. 1976. Tax counsel subcommittee on select revenue measures US House Ways and Means Com., Washington, 1975—87, chief tax counsel, staff dir. subcommittee on select revenue measures, 1987—92, staff dir., chief counsel, 1993—95; Dem. staff dir., chief counsel US House Com. on Ways and Means, 1995—. Recipient Disting. Achievement in Profession Alumnae award, Wesleyan Coll., 1998; named one of The Fabulous 50, Roll Call, 2009. Mem. Tax Coalition (past chair). Avocation: collecting chintzware teapots and vintage jewelry. Office: Ways & Means Com 1102 Longworth Office Bldg Washington DC 20515-0001 Office Phone: 202-225-3625. Business E-Mail: janice.mays@mail.house.gov.

MAYS, L(ESTER) LOWRY, broadcast executive; b. Houston, July 24, 1935; s. Lester T. and Virginia (Lowry) M.; m. Peggy Pitman, July 29, 1959; children: Kathryn Mays Johnson, Linda Mays McCaul, Mark P., Randall T. BS in Petroleum Engring., Tex. A&M U., 1959; MBA, Harvard U., 1962. Gen. ptnr. LLM Ptnrs. Ltd.; comml. recorder San Antonio; with Sta. KTTU-TV, Tucson, Sta. KOKI/KTFO-TV, Tulsa, Sta. WMPI/WJTC-TV, Mobile and Pensacola, Okla., Sta. WAWS-TV, Jacksonville, Fla., Sta. KSAS-TV, Wichita, Kans., Sta. KLRT/KASN-TV, Little Rock, Sta. WFTC-TV, Mpls., Sta. WFTC-TV, WLMT/WMTU-TV, Memphis, Sta. WXXA, Albany, Sta. WQUE-AM-FM, New Orleans, Okla. News Network, Oklahoma City, Va. News Network, Stas. KJYO and KTOK, Oklahoma City, Sta. KEBC, Oklahoma City, Sta. WELI, New Haven, Sta. WKCI-WAVZ, New Haven, Sta. KPEZ, Austin, Tex., Stas. KHYS, KALO, KBXX, KMJQ, KPRC, KSEV and KYOK, Houston and Point Arthur, Tex., KMOD & KAKC, Tulsa, KTAM & KORA, Bryan and College Station, Tex., WHAS & WAMZ, Louisville; with radio and TV broadcasting WOAI, KQXT, and KAJA, San Antonio; sr. v.p., corp. fin. Russ & Co., 1962—72; founder, pres., COO and exec. v.p. CC Media Holdings, Inc., 1972—97, CEO, 1997—2004, chmn., 1997—2008; with Clear Channel Sports, Des Moines; founder Clear Channel Ind. (Pty) Ltd.; chmn., CEO and founder Clear Channel Comm. Inc., San Antonio, 1975—2004; chmn. Clear Channel Comm., Inc., 1997—; CEO Clear Channel Outdoor Holdings, Inc., 2004, chmn., 2005; pres. Clear Channel Metroplex Inc.; chmn., CEO AMFM Oper. Inc. (formerly Capstar Comm. Inc.). Past chmn. bd. CBS Radio Affiliates Bd., bd. dirs., CCE Spinco, Inc., 2005-, U. Tex. Investment Mgmt. Co., Clear Channel Outdoor Holdings, Inc., 1997, AMFM Oper. Inc., CC Media Holdings Inc., 1972, Live Nation, Inc., 2005-2010, NBC Internet Inc., 1999, Xoom.com Inc., 1999, USLD Comm. Corp., 1997. Bd. dirs., trustee Tex. Rsch. Pk.; bd. dirs., mem. exec. com. United Way, Harvard Bus. Sch.; chmn. United Way San Antonio and Bexar County, 1995, Nat. Assn.of Broadcasters, 1996, Benefactor of the Mays Sch. of Bus.,; regent emeritus Tex. A&M U. Sys.; trustee Tex. Rsch. and Tech. Found.; mem. deve. bd. U. Tex. Health Sci. Ctr.; adv. dir. Permanent Univ. Fund Tex. Recipient Alumni award, Tex. A&M U., Internat. Citizen Year award, San Antonio World Affairs Coun., 1997, Nat. Radio award, Nat. Assn. of Broadcasters. Mem. Nat. Assn. Broadcasters (past chmn. joint bd.), Greater San Antonio C. of C. (past chmn.), Rotary. Office: AMFM Inc 1845 Woodall Rogers Freeway Dallas TX 75201 Office Phone: 214-922-8700. Office Fax: 214-922-8701. Business E-Mail: lmays@clearchannel.com.

MAYS, SAMUEL H., JR., federal judge; b. Memphis, 1948; BA, Amherst Coll., 1970; JD, Yale U., 1973. Pvt. practice atty., Tenn., 1973—95, Tenn., 2000—02; legal counsel to gov. State of Tenn., 1995—97, dep. to gov., chief of staff, 1997—2000; judge US Dist. Ct. (we. dist.) Tenn., Memphis, 2002—. Office: US Dist Ct Fed Bldg 167 N Main St Rm 1111 Memphis TN 38103 Office Phone: 901-495-1200. Office Fax: 901-495-1250.

MAZANEC, GEORGE L., natural gas company executive; b. Chgo., May 30, 1936; s. Charles and Catherine (Traczyk) M.; m. Elsa Weiffenbach, Oct. 1, 1960; children: Robert A., John C. AB in Economics, DePauw U., 1958; MBA, Harvard U., 1960. Sr. v.p. Tex. Eastern Corp.; pres. TETCO; various positions Internorth Inc., 1964-82; exec. v.p., CFO Tex. Gas Resources Corp., Owensboro, Ky., 1982—85; CFO, v.p. fin. Duquesne Light Co., 1985—87; exec. v.p. PanEnergy Corp., Houston, 1991—93, group v.p., 1989—91, vice chmn., 1989—96; COO Duke Energy Corp., 1997—2000. Bd. dirs. TEPPCO Ltd., 1992—97, Northern Border Pipeline Co. Partnership, 1993—98, Associated Electric and Gas Ins. Svcs. Ltd., 1995—, Nat. Fuel Gas Co., 1996—2012, Westcoast Energy Inc., 1998—2002, Northern Trust Bank of Tex., 1998—2007, Dynegy Inc., 2004—10. Mem. Am. Gas Assn. (bd. dirs.), Houston Mus. of Natural Sci. (bd. dirs.), Houston Grand Opera (bd. dirs.), Ramada Club, Houston Country Club, Old Baldy Club.

MAZZEI, MIKE, state legislator; m. Noel Mazzei; children: Carissa, Caleb, Jackson, Maria, Mykaela. BA in Govt. and Politics, George Mason Univ. Founder, pres. The Financial Coach, Inc.; bd. dirs. The Salvation Army; mem. Dist. 25 Okla. State Senate, 2004—. Fin. chmn. Northeast Oklahoma Festival; mem. Asbury United Methodist Church. Mem.: Restore Hope Ministries (bd.mem.). Republican. Office: 2300 N Lincoln Blvd Rm 424 Oklahoma City OK 73105 Mailing: PMB 394 6528 E 101st Ste D-1 Tulsa OK 74133 Address: 1375 E 71st St Tulsa OK 74136 Office Phone: 405-521-5675. Business E-Mail: mazzei@oksenate.gov.

MCABEE, THOMAS ALLEN, psychologist; b. Spartanburg, SC, Mar. 31, 1949; s. Thomas Walker and Doris Lee (Gillespie) McA. Student, Ga. Inst. Tech., 1967-69; BA, Furman U., 1971; MA, U. SC, 1975, PhD, 1979. Clin. counselor Adolescent Inpatient Svc. William S. Hall Psychiat. Inst., Columbia, SC, 1971-73; counselor children's therapeutic camp Columbia Area Mental Health Ctr., 1974; co-dir. cmty. problems survey Eau Claire Cmty. Project, Columbia, 1975; asst. aging svcs. planner Ctrl. Midlands Regional Planning Coun., Columbia, 1976; instr. U. SC, 1976; NSF intern SC State Legislature, 1978; rsch. dir. SC Legis. Gov.'s Com. Mental Health and Mental Retardation, Columbia, 1979-80; co-dir. Children's TV project "Feelings Just Are" Columbia Area Mental Health Ctr., 1980-89; psychologist SC Dept. Mental Retardation, 1982-93, SC Dept. Disabilities and Spl. Needs, 1993—2003, SC Vocat. Rehab. Dept., 2004—. Cons. SC Protection and Advocacy System for Handicapped Citizens, 1980, 81, SC Dept. Mental Health, 1981; mem. deinstitutionalization task force SC Developmental Disabilities Coun., 1979-80; mem. subcom. State Commr.'s Ad Hoc Com. to Study and Develop Work/Lodge System for SC, SC Dept. Mental Health, 1979-80; mem. Media Task Force of Gov.'s Adv. Com. on Early Childhood Devel. and Edn., 1980-81; chmn. primary prevention public media com. SC Dept. Mental Health, 1979-81; adj. faculty U. SC, Spartanburg, 2003; treas. Direct Client Svcs. Divsn. SC Vocat. Rehab. Assn., 2006-08; chmn. Workforce Readiness Com., Spartanburg Human Resources Assn., 2008-2009; pres. Victor Mill Cmty. Assn., 2009-10. Recipient Palmetto Pictures Photography award, 1977; NIMH fellow, 1976-77. Mem. APA, SC Psychol. Assn., Zoning Appeals Bd., City of Greer, SC Psychol. Assn. Home: 310 Snow St Greer SC 29651-4006 Office Phone: 864-249-8030. Business E-Mail: tmcabee@scvrd.state.sc.us.

MCADAMS, JOHN POPE, lawyer; b. Phila., June 5, 1949; s. Eugene P. and Mary (Miller) McA.; m. Anne Christina Connelly, Sept. 5, 1970; children: Emily Lane, Anne Connelly. BA, U. NC, 1971; JD, Wake Forest U., 1976. Bar: Fla. 1976, NC 1976, US Dist. Ct. (mid. dist.) Fla. 1977. Assoc. Carlton Fields, Tampa, Fla., 1976-82, ptnr., 1982—2007, of counsel, 2007—. Contbg. editor: The Developing Labor Law, 1983, Employee Duty of Loyalty, 1995; contbr. articles to profl. jours. Pres. Hillsborough Cmty. Mental Health Ctr., Tampa, 1983; trustee City of Temple Terrace Pension Plan, Fla., 1985-89; pres. Hyde Park Preservation, Inc., Tampa, 1993; bd. dir., pres. Child Abuse Coun., Inc., Tampa Lighthouse Blind. Mem. ABA, ABA Equal Rights & Responsibilities Com., Fla. Bar Assn. (exec. coun. labor sect. 1987-89). Democrat. Episcopalian. Home: 820 S Delaware Ave Tampa FL 33606-2915 Office: Carlton Fields PO Box 3239 Tampa FL 33601-3239 Office Phone: 813-223-7000, 813-229-4320. Business E-Mail: jmcadams@carltonfields.com.

MCADOO, BOB (ROBERT ALLEN MCADOO JR.), professional basketball coach, retired professional basketball player; b. Greensboro, NC, Sept. 25, 1951; m. Patrizia McAdoo; children: Robert III, Rita, Ross, Russell, Rasheeda, Ryan. Grad., U. NC, Chapel Hill, 1973. Ctr., forward Buffalo Braves, 1972—76, NY Knickerbockers, 1976—79, Boston Celtics, 1979, Detroit Pistons, 1979—81, LA Lakers, 1981—85, Phila. 76ers, 1985—86, Olimpia Milano, Italy, 1986—90, Filanto Forli, Italy, 1990—92, Teamsystem Fabriano, Italy, 1992—93; asst. coach Miami Heat, 1995—. Mem. US nat. team Pan Am. Games, 1971. Tech. advisor: The Air Up There, 1993. Participant NBA Legends Tour, South Africa, 1993, Basketball Without Boarders, China, 2009. Named Rookie of the Yr., NBA, 1973, NBA Most Valuable Player, 1975; named one of 50 Most Influential Personalities in European Club Basketball, 2008; named to NBA All-Star Team, 1974—78, Naismith Meml. Basketball Hall of Fame, 2000. Achievements include leading the NBA in: field goal percentage, 1973-74; scoring, 1973-1976; total rebounds, minutes, 1974-75; free throw attempts, 1974-76; field goal attempts, free throws, 1975-76; member of NBA Finals championship winning Los Angeles Lakers, 1982. Office: Miami Heat 601 Biscayne Blvd Miami FL 33132

MCADORY, LAWRENCE, state legislator, retired principal; b. Bessemer, Ala., June 21, 1929; s. Tommie and Annie Mae (Cowan) McAdory; m. Marjorie Turner, June 6, 1958; children: Vicki M. Britton, Virgil, Vernon. AA, Ala. State U., BSc, 1958, MSc, 1961. Science tchr., attendance supr. Bessemer Bd. Edn., Ala., 1958-89, prin., 1989-94, ret., 1994; mem. Ala. House of Reps., Montgomery, Ala., 1994-98, mem. Dist. 56, 2009—; founder McAdory Vault Co. Bd. dirs. Jefferson County Transit Authority, Birmingham, 1988-92; founder Project Chance Learning Ctr., 1997. Mem. Jefferson County Dem. Conf., Ala., 1990-97, Jefferson County Coalition, 1990-97; pres. Bessemer Voters League, 1992-2000; chmn. Scholarship and Building Project; deacon Jerusalem Bapt. Ch., Bessemer. Served with US Armed Forces. Recipient Ednl. Leadership award Miles Coll., Birmingham, Ala., 1973, Silver Beaver Boy Scouts of Am., 1974, Cmty. Svc. award Les Vingt Amies Club, Bessemer, 1986, Svc. award Bessemer Voters League, 1994, Trailblazers Merit award, 2000; named Newsmaker of Yr., Birmingham News, 1996. Mem. NEA (life), NAACP, Ala. Edn. Assn., Nat. Assn. Secondary Sch. Prins., Ala. State Alumni (pres. Bessemer chpt. 2000), Ala. Ret. Teachers Assn., Alpha Phi Alpha. Democrat. Baptist. Avocations: photography, reading, fishing, gardening, travel. Office: Ala House of Reps Rm 539-C 11 S Union St Montgomery AL 36130 Office Phone: 334-242-7595.

MCAFFREY, AL, state legislator; b. Okla. 3 children. Funeral dir.; mem. Dist. 88 Okla. House of Representatives, 2007—. Democrat. Address: 2315 N Hudson Ave Oklahoma City OK 73103 Office: Oklahoma House of Representatives 2300 N Lincoln Blvd Room 544 Oklahoma City OK 73105 Home Phone: 405-521-9100; Office Phone: 405-587-7396. E-mail: al.mcaffrey@okhouse.gov.

MCALEENAN, DONALD FRANCIS, lawyer, construction executive; BS, Georgetown U.; JD, NYU. Asst. gen. counsel AT&E Corp.; dep. gen. counsel Fibreboard Corp., 1992—97, v.p., 1996—97; chief legal officer, sec. Builders FirstSource, Inc., sr. v.p., gen. counsel & co-founder Dallas, 1998—. Office: Builders FirstSource Inc 2001 Bryan St Ste 1600 Dallas TX 75201 Office Phone: 214-880-3500. Office Fax: 214-880-3599. Business E-Mail: don.mcaleenan@buildersfirstsource.com.

MCALISTER, HAROLD ALISTER, astronomer; b. Chattanooga, July 1, 1949; s. Harold Joy and Edna (Robbins) McA.; m. Susan Paulette Johnson, Aug. 5, 1972; 1 child, Merritt Ellen. BA in Physics, U. Tenn., Chattanooga, 1971; MA in Astronomy, U. Va., 1974, PhD in Astronomy, 1975. Grad. rsch. asst. dept. astronomy U. Va., Charlottesville, 1971-75; rsch. assoc. Kitt Peak Nat. Obs., Tucson, 1975-77; asst. prof. dept. physics and astronomy Ga. State U., Atlanta, 1977-82, assoc. prof., 1982-87, prof., 1987—98, founder, dir. Ctr. High Angular Resolution Astronomy, 1987—, regents' prof., 1998—; dir., CEO Mt. Wilson Inst., Pasadena, Calif., 2003—. Contbr. articles to profl. jours. Capt. US Army, 1971-78. Prin. investigator numerous grants NSF, AFOSR, NASA. Mem. Am. Astron. Soc., Astron. Soc. Pacific (Maria & Eric Muhlmann award 2007), Internat. Astron. Union (pres. Commn. 26 1988-91). Office: Ga State U Ctr for High Angular Resolution Atlanta GA 30303

MCALLISTER, DEUCE (DULYMUS JENOD MCALLISTER), small business owner, retired professional football player; b. Lena, Miss., Dec. 27, 1978; s. Carl and Cornelia McAllister. Attended, U. Miss., 2000—01. Running back New Orleans Saints, 2001—09; owner Deuce McAllister Nissan, Jackson, Miss. Founder Catch 22 Found., 2003—. Recipient Conerly Trophy, 1999; named to Nat. Football Conf. Pro Bowl Team, NFL, 2002, 2003. Office: Deuce McAllister Nissan 5 Old River Pl Ste 107 Jackson MS 39202-3449

MC ALLISTER, GERALD NICHOLAS, retired bishop, minister; b. San Antonio, Feb. 23, 1923; s. Walter Williams and Leonora Elizabeth (Alexander) McA.; m. Helen Earle Black, Oct. 2, 1953; children— Michael Lee, David Alexander, Stephen Williams, Elizabeth. Student, U. Tex., 1939-42, Va. Theol. Sem., 1948-51, DD (hon.), 1977. Ordained to ministry Episcopal Ch. as deacon, 1953, as priest, 1954. Rancher, 1946-48; deacon, priest Ch. of Epiphany, Raymondville, Ch. of Incarnation, Corpus Christi, St. Francis Ch., Victoria, Tex., 1951-63; 1st canon Diocese of West Tex., 1963-70; rector St. David's Ch., San Antonio, 1970-76; consecreated Episcopal bishop of Okla., Oklahoma City, 1977-89, ret., 1989; bishop-in-residence Episcopal Theol. Sem., Austin, Tex., 1990-93. Trustee Episcopal Theol. Sem. of S.W., 1961-2000, adv. bd., 1974—; mem. Case Commn. Bd. for Theol. Edn., 1981-82; pres. Tex. Council Chs., 1966-68, Okla. Conf. Chs., 1980-83; bd. dirs. Presiding Bishop's Fund for World Relief, 1972-77, Ch. Hist. Soc., 1976—; chmn. Nat. and World Mission Program Group, 1973-76; mem. Structure of Ch. Standing Commn., 1979, mem. standing com. on Stewardship/Devel., 1979-85; founder Chaplaincy Program, Bexar County Jail, 1968; mem. governing bd. nat. council Ch. of Christ, 1982-85; chmn. standing commn. on stewardship Episcopal Ch., 1983-85; v.p., trustee The Episc., Episc. Theol. Sem. of Southwest, 1987-93, chmn. bd. trustees, 1993-97. Author: What We Learned from What You Said, 1973, This Fragile Earth Our Island Home, 1980. Bd. dirs. Econ. Opportunity Devel. Corp., San Antonio, 1968-69; mem. exec. com. United Way, 1968-70, vice-chmn., 1970. With U.S. Mcht. Marines, 1942; to 1st lt. USAAF, 1942-45. Recipient Agudas Achim Brotherhood award, 1968. Mem.: Alumni Coun. Va. Theol. Sem. Episcopalian. Home: 311 W Nottingham Dr Apt 130 San Antonio TX 78209-1826

MCALLISTER, VANCE MICHAEL, United States Representative from Louisiana, entrepreneur; b. Oak Grove, La., Jan. 7, 1974; s. Gene and Kathy McAllister; m. Kelly Duncan, Aug. 9, 1997; 1 adopted child, Anna Claire children: Emilie Katherine, Duncan Michael, Vance Michael, Eva Grave. Attended, U. Northeast La. Co-owner Contractors LLC, 2005—, Mc's Group LLC, 2008—; owner McAllister Properties, 2008—; co-owner Tex. Coastal Entergy, 2010—, Batteries & Bulbs, 2012—; owner McAllister Promotions, LLC, 2013—; with Mustang Engring., 1997—2013; mem. US Congress from 6th La. Dist., Washington, 2013—, US House Agrl. Com., 2013—, US House Natural Resources Com., 2013—. Served in US Army, 1992—94 La. Nat. Guard. Republican. Southern Baptist. Office: US House of Representatives 316 Cannon House Office Bldg Washington DC 20515 Office Phone: 202-225-8490.*

MCALLISTER, WILLIAM HOWARD, III, newspaper reporter, columnist, public affairs consultant; b. Durham, NC, Nov. 6, 1941; s. William Howard, Jr. and Dorothy Fisk (Tillett) McA.; m. Rena Catherine Farrell, June 13, 1965; children: William Howard IV, Christopher F., Jonathan T., Benjamin J. BA in Polit. Sci, U. NC, Chapel Hill, 1964, MA in Journalism, 1966. Cecil Prince research asst. U. NC, 1965; reporter The Virginian-Pilot, Norfolk, 1964-67; reporter, city editor Virginian-Pilot, 1972-75; reporter Wall St. Jour., San Francisco, 1968-72, Washington Post, 1975-78, Va. editor, 1978-86, nat. reporter, 1986-99, columnist stamp and coin sect., 1987-99, lobbying columnist, 1997-99; Washington bur. chief Denver Post and MediaNews Newspapers, 1999—2003; Washington corr. Linn's Stamp News, 1997—. TV cons. Ford Found., 1969-72; cons. The Newseum, Arlington, Va., 2003-06. Capt. USNR, 1966—93, commdr. Naval Res. Pub. Affairs Units, Va., commdr. NR Pub. Affairs Ctr. Det 106, Norfolk. Decorated Navy Commendation medal, Meritorous Svc. medal, Gold Star; recipient Lidman prize for philatelic writing, 1990. Mem. Kappa Tau Alpha. Presbyterian. Home and Office: 10121 Ratcliffe Manor Dr Fairfax VA 22030-2427 Business E-Mail: whmcallister@verizon.net.

MCALPIN, KIRK MARTIN, lawyer; b. Newark, Sept. 14, 1923; s. Aaron Champion and Margaret (Martin) McAlpin; m. Sarah Frances Morgan, Dec. 14, 1951 (dec.); children: Kirk Martin Jr., Philip Morgan, Margaret Champion Margeson. LLB, U. Ga., 1948; postgrad., Columbia U., 1949. Bar: Ga. 1949. Asst. solicitor gen. Ea. Jud. Cir. Ct. Ga., 1951; assoc. Bouhan, Lawrence, Williams, Levy & McAlpin, Savannah, Ga., 1952-53, ptnr., 1954-63; sr. ptnr. King & Spalding, Atlanta, 1963-86; pvt. practice Savannah, 1987—97, Atlanta, 1998—. Chmn. Inst. Continuing Legal Edn., 1980-81, Inst. Continuing Jud. Edn. in Ga., 1981-84, Jud. Council Ga., 1979-82. Pres. Atlanta Legal Aid Soc., 1971. Fellow Am. Bar Found., Am. Law Inst., Am. Coll. Trial Lawyers, Internat. Acad. Trial Lawyers, Internat. Soc. Barristers; mem. ABA (Jr. Bar Conf. chmn. 1958-59, chmn. gen. practice sect. 1972-73, chmn. sr. lawyers div. 1986-87, ho. of dels. 1960-90, state del. 1970-90, bd. govs. 1973-76), State Bar Ga. Assn. (chmn. Young Lawyers 1953-54, bd. govs. 1953-63, pres. 1979-80), Atlanta Bar Assn., Savannah Bar Assn. (v.p. 1960-61), Nat. Conf. Bar Pres. (exec. com. 1981-83), Ga. Def. Lawyers Assn., Am. Judicature Soc., Assn. R.R. Trial Counsel, Soc. of Cin., Sons Colonial Wars, St.

Andrews Soc., Capital City Club, Piedmont Driving Club, Oglethorpe Club, Phi Delta Phi, Sigma Alpha Epsilon. Episcopalian. Home and Office: 479 E Paces Ferry Rd NE Apt 522 Atlanta GA 30305 Office Phone: 404-467-8307. Personal E-mail: kmcasratty@mindspring.com.

MCALPIN, TERI, electronics executive; BBA, Ga. State U., Atlanta. CPA. Contr. Amtico Internat., v.p. strategy and bus. planning, CFO, World Micro Inc., 2011—. Office: World Micro Incorporated 205 Hembree Park Drive Suite 105 Roswell GA 30076 Office Phone: 770-698-1900. Office Fax: 770-698-1901.

MCANALLY, MAC (LYMAN CORBITT MCANALLY JR.), musician; b. Red Bay, Ala., July 1, 1959; Mem. Jimmy Buffett's Coral Reefer Band; session artist and songwriter for numerous musicians. Musician: (albums) Mac McAnally, 1977, Finish Lines, 1978, Cuttin' Corners, 1980, Nothin' But the Trugh, 1989, Simple Life, 1990, Live and Learn, 1992, Knots, 1994, Word of Mouth, 1999, No Problem Here, 1999, Semi-True Stories, 2004, Down by the River, 2009, Live: In Muscle Shoals, 2011; composer: (songs) I Need You Tonight, It's a Crazy World, It's My Job, Old Flame, When the Coast is Clear, Crime of Passion, Back Where I Come From, It's a Precious Thing, The Trouble With Diamonds, Junk Cars. Named Musician of Yr., Country Music Assn. awards, 2008, 2009, 2010, 2011, 2012, 2013; named to Nashville Songwriters Hall of Fame, 2007, Ala. Music Hall of Fame, 2010. Office: TKO Artist Management 2303 21st Ave S Nashville TN 37212-4947*

MCANDREW, MARK S., insurance company executive; Pres. Globe Life & Accident Insurance Co., 1991—2005, CEO, 1999—2005; pres. United American Insurance Co., 1991—2004, CEO, 1999—2004; pres., CEO Am. Income Life Ins. Co., 1999—2003; joined Torchmark Corp., McKinney, Tex., 1980, bd. dirs., 1998—, exec. v.p., 1999—2003, chmn. ins. ops., 2003—05, CEO, 2005—06, 2006—12, chmn., 2006—12. Office: Torchmark Corp 3700 S Stonebridge Dr PO Box 8080 Mc Kinney TX 75070-8080

MCANNALLY, ROBERT SIDNEY, energy company executive, lawyer; b. Decatur, Ala., Sept. 30, 1963; s. Robert C. and Donna (Yates) McA.; m. April Southard, June 22, 1985; children: Mary Catherine, Parker. BS, Auburn U., 1985; JD, U. Ala., 1990. Bar: Ala. 1990, Tenn. 1993, U.S. Dist. Ct. (no. dist.) Ala. 1993, U.S. Dist. Ct. (so. dist.) Ala. 1990. Assoc. Lyons Pipes & Cook, Mobile, Ala., 1990-92, Lange, Simpson, Robinson & Somerville, Huntsville, Ala., 1993-94; policy advisor to the gov. State of Ala., Montgomery, Ala., 1994; asst. commr. Ala. Dept. Human Resources, Montgomery, 1994; ptnr. Cauthen, Cauthen & McAnnally, Decatur, 1994; head Govtl. and Regulatory Affairs practice group Maynard, Cooper & Gale, P.C; v.p., External Affairs Energen Corp., 2009—. Guest lectr. Windeshiem Hogesch., Swolle, Netherlands, 1994. Contbr. articles to profl. jours. Bd. dirs. A-Plus Edn. Reform Found., Montgomery, 1993—; reporter Gov.'s Sch. Violence Task Force, Montgomery, 1994; chair Criminal Justice Adv. Commn., Montgomery, 1994. Mem. Ala. Bar Assn., Ala. Def. Lawyers, Newcomen Soc. Kiwanis. Methodist. Office: Energen Corp 605 Richard Arrington Jr Blvd N Birmingham AL 35203-2707 Office Phone: 205-326-2700. Business E-Mail: sid.mcannally@energen.com.

MCARDLE, JANINE J., energy executive; b. 1960; B in Chem. Engring., U. Nebr.; MBA, U. Houston. Ptnr. Hesse Gas, 1991—93; various exec. and mgmt. positions, including v.p., trading, v.p., mergers and acquisitions Aquila Energy Mktg., 1993—2001; mng. dir. Aquila Europe Ltd., 2001—02; v.p., oil & gas mktg. Apache Corp., Houston, 2002—10, sr. v.p. monetization, 2010—. Bd. dirs. IntercontinentalExchange, Inc., 2000—02. Bd. dirs. Palmer Drug Abuse Program. Office: Apache Corp 2000 Post Oak Blvd Ste 100 Houston TX 77056-4400 Office Phone: 713-296-6000. Office Fax: 713-296-6496. Business E-Mail: janine.mcardle@apachecorp.com.

MCARTHUR, GARY L., telecommunications industry executive; B in Acctg., U. Utah; MBA, Harvard U. CPA 1985. Variuos fin. and acctg. positions Deloitte & Touche, Cellcom Corp.; investment banker Lehman Brothers, Inc.; dir., mergers and acquisitions Nextel Comm., Inc., 1993—95, exec. dir., Mexico, 1995—96; CFO 3D/EYE, Inc., 1996—97; dir., corp. devel. Harris Corp., 1997—2000, v.p., corp. devel., 2001—05, v.p., fin., treas., 2005—06, v.p., 2006, CFO, 2006—, sr. v.p., 2008—; v.p., CFO Harris Info. Tech. Svcs., Inc. (subs. Harris Corp.). Mem.: AICPA. Office: Harris Corp 1025 W NASA Blvd Melbourne FL 32919-0001 Office Phone: 321-727-9100. Office Fax: 321-674-4740. Business E-Mail: Gary.McArthur@harris.com.

MCARTHUR, JOHN R., utilities executive, lawyer; b. Rock Hill, SC, Jan. 5, 1956; BA cum laude, Davidson Coll., 1977; JD with honors, Univ. So. Carolina, 1981. Bar: NC 1982. Law clk. Judge Sam. J. Ervin III, US Ct. Appeals, 4th cir., 1981—82; assoc. to ptnr. Hunton & Williams, Raleigh, NC, 1982—92; chief counsel NC Atty. Gen. Office, NC, 1993—97; sr. advisor NC Gov., Mike Easley, NC, 1998—2001; v.p., pub. affairs Progress Energy, Inc., Raleigh, NC, 2001—02, sr. v.p., corp. rels., 2002—, gen. counsel, corp. sec., 2004—08, exec. v.p. admin. & corp. rels., corp. sec., gen. counsel, 2008—11; exec. v.p. regulated utilities Duke Energy, 2011—. Editor Law Rev. U.S.C.; law clerk Hon. Sam J. Ervin III US Ct. Appeals Fourth Cir. Mem.: NC Bar Assn., Order of the Coif, Wig & Robe. Office: Duke Energy Corporation 550 Tryon St Charlotte NC 28202 Office Phone: 919-546-4070. Business E-Mail: john.mcarthur@pgnmail.com.

MCATEE, DAVID RAY, lawyer; b. Rosebud, Tex., Nov. 20, 1941; s. Lee Ray and Florine (Davis) McAtee; m. Carole Kay Pendergraft, Jan. 28, 1967; children: David Ray, Kristin Carole. BBA with honors, Baylor U., 1964; JD, U. Tex., 1967. Bar: Tex. 1967, US Dist. Ct. (no. dist.) Tex. 1968, US Dist. Ct. (so. dist.) Tex. 1994, US Dist. Ct. (ea. dist.) Tex. 1996, US Ct. Appeals (5th cir.) 1969, US Ct. Appeals (11th cir.) 1981, US Tax Ct. 1993. Law clk. to Hon. Jack Pope Tex. Supreme Ct., Austin, 1967—68; ptnr. Thompson & Knight, Dallas, 1968—90, Gibson, Dunn & Crutcher, Dallas, 1990—95, Akin Gump Strauss Hauer & Feld LLP, Dallas, 1995. Mem. City of Dallas Plan Commn., 1979—83, vice chmn., 1981—83; chmn. City of Dallas Thoroughfare Com., 1979—81; mem. City of Dallas Citizens Safety Adv. Com., Goals for Dallas Com.; founder, bd. dirs. No. Hills. Neighborhood Assn., 1974—76; pres., bd. dirs. Montessori Sch. of Park Cities, 1975—76; chmn. bd. dirs. Dallas Area Rapid Transit, 1992; bd. dirs. Friends of the Katy Trail, 2005—06. Mem.: Tex. Bar Found. (trustee 2005—), ABA (antitrust sect.), Tex. Bar Assn. (legal ethics com. 1975—81), Dallas Bar Assn., U. Tex. Law Alumni Assn. (exec. com. 2003—08). Democrat. Methodist. Office: Akin Gump Strauss Hauer & Feld LLP 1700 Pacific Ave Ste 4100 Dallas TX 75201-4624 Office Phone: 214-969-2736. Office Fax: 214-969-4343. Business E-Mail: dmcatee@akingump.com.

MCAULIFFE, TERRY (TERENCE RICHARD MCAULIFFE), Governor of Virginia, former political organization administrator; b. Syracuse, NY, Feb. 9, 1957; s. Jack and Millie McAuliffe; m. Dorothy Swann, 1988; children: Dori, Jack, Mary, Sally, Peter. BA in Polit. Sci., Cath. U. America, 1979; JD, Georgetown U. Law Ctr., 1984. Finance chmn. Dick Gephardt for President Campaign Com., 1988; amb., commr. gen. Korean Internat. Exposition, 1993; chmn. Democratic Bus. Coun., 1993; finance chmn. Democratic Nat. Com. (DNC), 1994, Bill Clinton/Al Gore Re-election Campaign, 1996; co-chair Presdl. Inaugural Com., 1997; chmn. Democratic Nat. Conv., L.A., 2000, Democratic Nat. Com. (DNC), 2001—05; founder, chmn. GreenTech Automotive, 2010—13; gov. Commonwealth of Va., Richmond, 2014—. Chmn. 53rd Presdl. Inauguration Com., White House Millenium Celebration. Author: What A Party: My Life Among Democrats: Presidents, Candidates, Donors, Activists, Alligators, and Other Wild Animals, 2007. Named one of The 50 Politicos to Watch, Politico, 2010. Democrat. Roman Catholic. Office: State Capitol 3rd Fl Richmond VA 23219 Office Phone: 202-783-1769. Office Fax: 202-783-7687.*

MCBEE, MARY LOUISE, state legislator, academic administrator; b. Strawberry Plains, Tenn., June 15, 1924; d. John Wallace and Nina Aileen (Umbarger) McB. BS, East Tenn. State U., 1946; MA, Columbia U., 1951; PhD, Ohio State U., 1961. Tchr. East Tenn. State U., Johnson City, 1947-51; asst. dean of women, 1952-56, 57-60; dean of women, 1961-63, U. Ga., Athens, 1963-67; world campus afloat adminstr., 1966-67; assoc. dean of students, 1967-72; dean of students, 1972-74; asst. v.p. acad. affairs, 1974-76; assoc. v.p. acad. affairs, 1976-86; v.p. acad. affairs, 1986-88; ret., 1988; state rep. Clarke County Ga. Gen. Assembly, 1991—2004. Author: College Responsibility for Values, 1980; co-author: The American Woman: Who Will She Be?, 1974, Essays, 1979, 2d edit. 1981. Bd. dirs. Salvation Army, Athens, 1978—, United Way, Athens. Fulbright scholar, The Netherlands, 1956-57. Mem. Athens C. of C. (bd. dirs.). Democrat. Methodist. Avocations: gardening, tennis, hiking. Home: 145 Pine Valley Pl Athens GA 30606-4031 Personal E-mail: louisemcbee@charter.com.

MCBRAYER, TONY, state legislator; b. Tifton, Nov. 19; m. Diane McBrayer; children: Shane, Ryan. Attended, Abraham Baldwin Agr. Coll.; B in Acctg., Valdosta State Coll., Ga. Owner, operator TMM Enterprises, Inc., 1989—; mem. Dist. 153 Ga. House of Representatives, 2011—. Mem.: Ga. Food Industry Assn. Republican. Office: Georgia House of Reps 411 Coverdell Legis Office Bldg Atlanta GA 30334 Home: 91 Springhill Church Rd Tifton GA 31793-6843 Office Phone: 404-656-0126. Business E-Mail: tony.mcbrayer@house.ga.gov.

MCBRIDE, MARTINA, singer; b. Medicine Lodge, Kans., July 29, 1966; d. Daryl and Jeanne (Clark) Schiff; m. John McBride, May 15, 1988; children: Delaney Katherine, Emma Justine, Ava Rose Kathleen. Vocalist Schiffters, 1975-86, assorted bands, Wichita, Kans.; backup singer Garth Brooks, 1992—93. Singer: (albums) The Time Has Come, 1992, The Way That I Am, 1993, Wild Angels, 1995, Evolution, 1997, Martina McBride Christmas, 1998, Emotion, 1999, White Christmas, 1999, Greatest Hits, 2001, Martina, 2003, Timeless, 2005, Waking Up Laughing, 2007, Martina McBride: Live In Concert, 2008, Shine, 2009, Eleven, 2011, The Classic Christmas Album, 2013, Everlasting, 2014, (albums with various artists) Girls Night Out, 1999. Recipient Breakthrough Artist Video for "My Baby Loves Me", Music Row Ind. Summit Award, 1994, Music Video Yr. for "Independence Day", Country Music Assn. Awards, 1994, Best Video Yr. for "Independence Day", Gt. Brit. Music Awards, 1994, Video Yr. for "Independence Day", Nashville Music Awards, 1995, TNN Music City News Award, 1995, Gold Clio for Country Music Video Yr. for "Independence Day", Clio Awards, 1995, Best Southern Gospel, Country Gospel or Bluegrass Gospel for "Amazing Grace - A Country Salute To Gospel", Grammy Awards, 1995, Country Album Yr. for "Wild Angels", Nashville Music Awards, 1996, Video Yr. for "Safe In The Arms of Love", 1996, Female Video Yr. for "Blessed", CMT Flameworthy Awards, 2002, Female Video Yr. for "Concrete Angel", CMT Flameworthy Award, 2003, Top Female Vocalist, Acad. Country Music, 2002, Acad. Country Music award, 2003, 2004, Female Vocalist Yr., Country Music Assn. Award, 2002, Female Vocalist Yr. award, Country Music Assn., 2003, 2004, Country Female Artist Yr., Billboard Music Award, 2002, Best Female Artist, Country Radio Music Awards, 1996, Favorite Female Artist, Country, Am. Music Awards, 2003, Favorite Female Artist, Country Weekly, 2003; nominee Best Country Song for "Independence Day", Grammy, 1994, Video Yr. for "Independence Day", Acad. Country Music, 1994, Best Country Collaboration with Vocals for "Own My Own" with Reba McEntire, Linda Davis, and Trisha Yearwood, Grammy, 1995, Vocal Event Yr. for "On My Own" with Reba McEntire, Linda Davis, and Trisha Yearwood., Country Music Assn., 1996, Album Yr. for "Wild Angels", 1996, Best Country Female Vocal Performance for "Safe In The Arms of Love", Grammy, 1995, Vocal Event Yr. for "Still Holding On" with Clint Black, Country Music Assn., 1997, Best Country Collaboration with Vocals for "Still Holding You" with Clint Black, Grammy, 1997, Video Yr. for "A Broken Wing", Country Music Assn., 1998, Single Yr. for "A Broken Wing", 1998, Acad. Country Music, 1999, Song Yr. for "A Broken Wing", 1999, Video Yr. for "A Broken Wing", 1999, Best Country Female Vocal Performance for "I Love You", Grammy, 1999, Single Yr. for "Blessed", Country Music Assn., 2002, Best Female Country Vocal Performance for "Blessed", Grammy, 2002, Video Yr. for "Concrete Angel", Country Music Assn., 2003, Top Female Vocalist, Acad. Country Music, 1993, 1998, 2000, 2001, Horizon award, Country Music Assn., 1994, Female Vocalist Yr., 1996, 1998, 1999, 2001, Am. Music Awards, 2003. Office: RCA Records 1400 18th Ave S Nashville TN 37212-2809*

MCBRIDE, SANDRA TEAGUE, psychiatric nurse; b. Corinth, Miss., Sept. 13, 1958; d. Clarence R. and Alice (Ingram) T. AAS, Shelby State Community Coll., 1983; BSN, U. North Ala., 1987; MSN, Union U., 2001. RN, Miss., Tenn. Nurse supr. Alcorn County Care, Inc., Corinth, Miss., 1985-87; staff nurse Bolivar (Tenn.) Cmty. Hosp., 1988-90; shift supr. Tenn. Dept. of Corrections, West Tenn. High Security Facility, Ripley, 1990-91; staff nurse U.S. Med. Ctr. for Fed. Prisoners, Springfield, Mo., 1991-92, Western Mental Health Inst., Bolivar, 1992—.

MCBRIDE, WILLIAM J., healthcare company executive; Various positions, including v.p., contr., Life and Healthcare Group INA Corp.; pres., CEO. v.p., fin., Affiliated Bus. Group CIGNA Healthplans, Inc.; pres., COO, co-founder Value Health, Inc., 1987—95. Former bd. dirs. Value Health, Inc.; bd. dirs. Internet Health Care Group, Women's Health USA, Inc., Amerigroup Corp., 1995—, Evolution Benefits, Inc., 2003—, Magellan Health Svcs., Inc., 2004—. Office: Amerigroup Corp 4425 Corporation Ln Virginia Beach VA 23462 Office Phone: 757-490-6900.

MCBRYDE, JOHN HENRY, federal judge; b. Jackson, Oct. 9, 1931; m. Betty Vinson; children: Rebecca, Jennifer, John Blake. BS in Commerce, Tex. Christian U., 1953; LLB, U. Tex., 1956. Bar: Tex. 1956, U.S. Ct. Appeals (5th cir.) 1958, U.S. Dist. Ct. (no. dist.) 1958, U.S. Dist. Ct. (ea. dist.) 1989, U.S. Supreme Ct. 1972. Assoc. Cantey, Hanger, Johnson, Scarborough & Gooch, Ft. Worth, 1956-62; ptnr. Cantey & Hanger and predecessor firm, Ft. Worth, 1962-69, McBryde, Bennett and predecessor firms, Ft. Worth, 1969-90; judge US Dist. Ct. (no. dist.) Tex., Ft. Worth, 1990—. Fellow Am. Bar Found. (life), Tex. Bar Found. (life), Am. Coll. Trial Lawyers. Office: US Dist Ct US Courthouse 501 W 10th St Ste 401 Fort Worth TX 76102-3642

MCBRYDE, NEILL GREGORY, lawyer; b. Durham, NC, Jan. 11, 1944; s. Angus M. and Priscilla (Gregory) McBryde; m. Margaret McPherson, Aug. 1, 1970; children: Margaret Courtauld McBryde Young, Neill Gregory Jr. AB cum laude, Davidson Coll., 1966; JD with high honors, U. N.C., Sch. Law, 1969. Bar: N.C. 1969., Ga. 1972. Assoc. King & Spalding, Atlanta, 1971-76; ptnr. Fleming, Robinson, Bradshaw & Hinson, Charlotte, NC, 1977-81, Helms, Mulliss & Johnston, Charlotte, 1981-86, Smith Helms Mulliss & Moore, Charlotte, 1986-90, Moore & Van Allen PLLC, Charlotte, 1990—. Lectr. in field; condr. workshops in field; chair, bd. dirs. Crossroads Corp. Affordable Housing & Cmty. Devel. Inc., 2008-; dir. Residential & Support Svcs. Inc., 2008-. Author, editor: First Union National Bank of North Carolina Will Book, 1986; contbr. articles to profl. jours. Elder and Deacon Myers Park Presbyn. Ch., Charlotte, 1980-86, 92-95, 2001-04, 05-08; bd. dirs., sec. Presbyn. Home for Aged, Charlotte, 1978-82; trustee Charlotte Latin Schs., Inc., 1980-86, 87-93; past chmn., past trustee Mint Mus. Charlotte. Fellow Am. Coll. Trust and Estate Counsel (past mem. bd. regents, past pres.), Am. Coll. Tax Counsel; mem. ABA, Ga. Bar Assn., NC Bar Assn. (probate and fiduciary law sect.), So. Fed. Tax Inst. (trustee 1999—2011, pres. 2005-06), Order of Coif, Phi Beta Kappa, Omicron Delta Kappa. Avocations: tennis, golf, fishing. Office: Moore & Van Allen PLLC Bank of Am Corp Ctr 100 N Tryon St Fl 47 Charlotte NC 28202-4003 Office Phone: 704-331-1094.

MCBURNEY, CHARLES WALKER, JR., state representative, lawyer; b. Orlando, Fla., June 6, 1957; s. Charles Walker McBurney and Jeane (Brown) Chappell; children: Katherine Turpin, Madeline. BA, U. Fla., 1979, JD, 1982. Bar: Fla. 1982, US Dist. Ct. (mid. dist.) Fla. 1983, US Ct. Appeals (11th cir.) 1984. Assoc. Mathews, Osborne, McNatt, Gobelman & Cobb, Jacksonville, Fla., 1982-84; asst. state's atty. State's Atty.'s Office, Jacksonville, 1984-90, civil atty., 1987-88, sr. trial atty., 1988-90; dir. Serious or Habitual Juvenile Offender Program, 1986; ptnr. Fischette, Owen, Held & McBurney, Jacksonville, 1990—2004; pvt. practice Law Office Charles W. McBurney Jr., Jacksonville, 2004—; mem. Dist. 16 Fla. House of Reps., Tallahassee, 2007—, chair, justice appropriations sub-com., mem. jud. com., mem. edn., legis. budget commn.; com. mem. appreciation com. Mem. adv. coun. Mandarin Oaks Elem. Sch., vice chmn., 2003—04, chmn., 2004—06; mem. Mayor's Bicentennial Constnl. Commn., 1989—91; chmn. com. congl. campaigns Jacksonville, 1982, 1984, 1988; deacon South Jacksonville Presbyn. Ch., 2003—; bd. dirs. Civic Round Table, 1988—92, treas., 1988—89, pres., 1989—90; dir. Internat. Devel. Commn. for Jacksonville, 1993—2003, treas., 1995—97; chmn. S.E. Citizens Planning Adv. Com., 2005—07; bd. dirs. Am. Heart Assn. N.E. Fla., 1990—92. Mem.: Comml. Law League (So. region exec. coun. 1998—, treas. 2000—), Jacksonville Bankruptcy Bar Assn. (bd. dirs. 1999—2004, treas. 2003—04), Jacksonville Bar Assn. (chmn. bankruptcy sect. 1998—2000, 2002—03), Duval County Rep. Party (treas. 2002—07), Jacksonville Hist. Soc., James Madison Inst., Summit Civitan (judge adv. 1991—93, 2001—02), Jacksonville Jaycees (pres. 1986, Jaycee of yr. 1984, Businessperson of Yr. 2006), Fla. Jaycees (legal counsel 1987—88, Most Outstanding Local Pres. award 1987), Jacksonville C. of C. (bd. govs. 1987, govtl. affairs com. 1998—2007), First Coast Tiger Bay Forum (bd. dirs. 2001—07, Leadership award 2004, Statesman award 2012), Southside Bus. Men's Club (v.p. 2003—04, parliamentarian 2006—07), Bull Snort Club (pres. 1995—96, chmn. bd. 1996—99, pres. 1999—2000), Masons, N.E. Fla. Phi Beta Kappa Alumni Assn. (v.p. 1998—2000, 2003—04). Republican. Presbyterian. Office: 76 S Laura St Ste 590 Jacksonville FL 32202 also: 214 House Office Bldg 402 S Monroe St Tallahassee FL 32399-1300 Business E-Mail: cmcburney@mcburneylaw.net.

MCBURNEY, ELIZABETH INNES, dermatologist, physician, educator; b. Lake Charles, La., Dec. 24, 1944; d. Theodore John and Martha (Caldwell) Innes; divorced, 1980; children: Leanne Marie, Susan Eleanor. BS, U. Southwestern La., 1965; MD, La. State U., 1969. Diplomate Am. Bd. Internal Medicine, Am. Bd. Dermatology. Intern Pensacola (Fla.) Edn. Program, 1969-70; resident in internal medicine Boston U. and Carney Hosps., 1970-72; resident in dermatology Charity Hosp., New Orleans, 1972-74; staff physician Ochsner Hosp., New Orleans, 1974-80; assoc. head of dermatology Ochsner Clinic, New Orleans, 1974-80; clin. asst. prof. La. Health Scis., New Orleans, 1976-79, clin. assoc. prof., 1979-90, clin. prof., 1990—; clin. asst. prof. Tulane Health Scis., New Orleans, 1976-88, clin. assoc. prof., 1988-91, clin. prof., 1991—. Courtesy staff Northshore Regional Med. Ctr., Slidell, La., 1985—; staff Slidell Meml. Hosp., 1988—, chmn. CME courses, 1988—, pres.-elect med. staff, 2000-01, pres., 2001—02; regional dir. Mycosis Fungoides Study Group, Balt., 1974-94. Contbr. articles to profl. jours. Bd. dirs. Slidell Art Coun., 1988—, Camp Fire, New Orleans, 1979-83, Cancer Assn. New Orleans, 1978-83; juror Art in Pub. Places, Slidell, 1989; councilman St. Tammany Art Coun., 2003-06, with Dermatology fdn. Exec. Comm., 2008- Recipient Disting. Woman Physician award AMA, 1999, Thomas Pearson edn. meml. award, 2004. Fellow ACP; mem. Am. Soc. Dermatologic Surgery (treas. 1991-94, bd. dirs. 1988-91, pres. elect 1995-96, pres. 1996-97), Women's Dermatol. Soc. (pres. 2006—07, Samuel Stegman award 2000, Pub. Svc. award, 2001), Am. Acad. Dermatology (bd. dirs. 1994-98), Am. Bd. Laser Medicine and Surgery (bd. dirs. 1991-96), La. Dermatologic Soc. (pres. 1989-90), Am. Dermatologic Soc. (pres. 2007-08), St. Tammany Med. Soc. (pres. 1988), Phi Kappa Phi, Alpha Omega Alpha. Avocations: reading, gardening, fine art, music, films. Office: 1051 Gause Blvd Ste 460 Slidell LA 70458-2985 Office Phone: 985-649-5880.

MCCABE, BROOKS FLEMING, JR., state legislator; b. Charleston, W.Va., Jan. 19, 1949; s. Brooks F. Sr. and Jane (Mason) McC.; m. Barbara Given McCabe; 1 child, Katherine Jane. BS, U. Vt., 1975, MEd, 1972; EdD, W.Va. U., 1975. Asst. to dir. Gov.'s Office Fed. and State Rels. Gov.'s Office Fed. and State Rels., Charleston, 1975-77; comml. real estate salesperson Home Finders, Inc., Charleston, 1979-80; sr. mng. dir. McCabe Hanley LP, Charleston, 1980—2005, brokerage mgr., 2005—; mem. Dist. 17 W.Va. State Senate, Charleston, 1998—, vice chair Fin. Com., mem. Banking and Insurance Com., Econ. Devel. Com., Govt. Orgn. Com., Natural Resources Com. & Pensions Com. Bd. dirs. Charleston Renaissance Corp., 1995-02; pres., bd. dirs. Silver Creek Properties, Inc., Slaty Fork, W.Va., 1988-92. Pres. Cmty. Coun. of Kanawha Valley, Charleston, 1987-89; campaign chmn. United Way of Kanawha Valley, Charleston, 1988; trustee U. Vt., Burlington, 1976-82, The Gow Sch., South Wales, NY, 1988-97, W.Va. Wesleyan Coll., Buchanon, 2000-02; bd. dirs. Greater Kanawha Valley Found., 1988-91, Charleston Area Med. Ctr. Found., 1992-98, W.Va. State Coll. Found., Inc., 1994-98; bd. trustee Nature Conservancy, W.Va., 2009-. Named Vol. of the Yr., United Way of Kanawha Valley, 1986-87. Mem. Am. Inst. Cert. Planners, W.Va. Planning Assn., Kanawha Valley Bd. Realtors, W.Va. Assn. Realtors, Urban Land Inst., Nat. Trust Hist. Preservation, W.Va. Roundtable. Democrat. Episcopalian. Avocations: reading, history, gardening. Office: W Va Comml Real Estate 107 Capitol St Charleston WV 25301-2609 also: WVa State Senate 1900 Kanawha Blvd E Rm

441M Bldg 1 Charleston WV 25305-0009 Office Phone: 304-347-7500, 304-357-7990. Business E-Mail: brooks.mccabe@wvsenate.gov, bmccabe@wv-commercial.com.

MCCABE, JOSEPH, JR., corporate financial executive; B in Mgmt., St. John's U., MBA in Quantitative Analysis, MBA in Acctg. With NY Telecom.; internat. v.p., contr., Bus. Comm. Sys. AT&T Inc. (merger of SBC Communications & AT&T Corp.), v.p., CFO strategy and new svcs. innovation divsn., 1996—99, exec. v.p., CFO Redmond, Wash., 1999—. Office: AT&T Wireless 5565 Glenridge Connector Atlanta GA 30342 Office Phone: 404-236-7895.

MCCABE, ROBERT HOWARD, college president; b. Dec. 23, 1928; s. Joseph A. and Kathryn (Greer) McC.; m. Arva Moore Parks, June 1992. BEd, U. Miami, 1952, LLD (hon.), 1992; MS, Appalachian State U., Boone, NC, 1959; PhD, U. Tex., 1963; LLD (hon.), Barry U., 1986, Fla. Internat. U., 1990. Asst. to pres. Miami Dade C. of C., Fla., 1963-65, v.p. Fla., 1965-67, exec. v.p. Fla., 1967—80, pres. Fla., 1980—95, Essex County Coll., Newark, 1967-69; sr. fellow League for Innovation in the C.C., 1995—; Disting. fellow Edn. Commn. of the States, 2000—; exec. dir. Nat. Alliance Cmty. & Tech. Colls., 2004—. Exec. com. So. Regional Edn. Bd., Atlanta, 1981-83; trustee Coll. Bd., chmn., 1988-90; vice chair The Miami Coalition for a Drug-Free Cmty., 1989-94, chair, 1991—; dir. The Bridge Partnership, 2002-, exec. dir. Nat. Alliance Cmty. Tech. Coll., 2005-. Author: Man and Environment, 1971, No One to Waste, 2000, Yes We Can, 2002, several monographs; editor: Jour. Environ. Edn.; cons. editor Change Mag., 1980—; contbr. articles to profl. jours. Bd. dirs. Nat. Ctr. Pub. Policy and Higher Edn., 1998—. Recipient Disting. Svc. award Fla. Congl. Del., 1983, Spirit of Excellence award The Miami Herald, 1988, Harold W. McGraw Jr. prize in Edn., 1991, The Coll. Bd. medal, 1995; named Outstanding Grad., Coll. Edn., U. Tex., 1982, named one of the 18 Most Effective Chief Exec. Officers in Am. Higher Edn. Bowling Green U., 1988; Disting. Svc. award Dade County, Fla., 1983; Kellogg fellow, 1962-63, MacArthur sr. fellow John D. and Catherine T. MacArthur Found., 1992. Fellow League for Innovation in the C.C. (sr. fellow, dir. exec. com. 1985—, Disting. Svc. award 1995); mem. Am. Assn. C.C. (bd. dirs. 1991—, Disting Svc. award 1995), Am. Assn. Higher Edn. (dir. on Higher Edn. Issues, Higher Edn. Consortium), Am. Coun. Edn. (dir. 1973-75), Am. Assn. for Environ. Edn. (pres. 1970-73), Am. Coun. on Edn. (bd. dirs. 1983-85, 92—), Southeast Fla. Edn. Consortium (chmn. bd. 1981-83). Episcopalian. Home: 1601 S Miami Ave Miami FL 33129-1103 Office Phone: 305-854-4428. Personal E-mail: rmccabe@bellsouth.net.

MCCAFFREE, MARY ANNE WIGHT, pediatrician, neonatal-perinatal specialist, educator; b. Guatemala City, Dec. 9, 1945; m. Robert McCaffree; 2 children. MD, U. Okla. Coll. Medicine, 1971. Diplomate American Bd. Pediat., cert. in neonatal-perinatal medicine. Intern pediat. Bethesda Nat. Naval Med. Ctr., Md., 1971—72; resident neonatal perinatal Medicine Children's Hosp. Nat. Med. Ctr., Washington, 1972—74, fellow, 1973—75; prof. pediat. U. Okla. Health Sciences Ctr.; co-dir., Infantile Apnea Diagnostic Ctr. Children's Hosp. Okla. Named Physician of Yr., U. Okla. Coll Medicine, 1996, Alumnus of Yr., 2006. Mem.: AMA (mem. Commn. on Unity 1998—2000, bd. trustees 2008—, past chair Coun. Sci. & Pub. Health, mem. pediat. sect. coun.), Okla. State Med. Assn. (pres. 1998—99, Ed. L. Calhoon MD Leadership in Medicine award 2005, Women in Medicine award 2007), American Acad. Pediat. (Abraham Jacobi award 2005). Office: U Okla Childrens Physicians PO Box 26307 Oklahoma City OK 73126

MCCAFFREY, BARRY RICHARD, consulting firm executive, retired military officer; b. Taunton, Mass., Nov. 17, 1942; s. William Joseph and Mary Veronica (Curtin) McC.; m. Jill Ann Faulkner, June 8, 1964; children: Sean, Tara, Amy. BS, U.S. Mil. Acad., 1964; MA, Am. U., 1971; postgrad., Command and Gen. Staff Coll., Ft. Leavenworth, Kans., 1976, Army War Coll., Carlisle Barracks, Pa., 1982. Commd. 2d lt. U.S. Army, 1964, advanced through grades to gen., 1994; ret., 1996; co.-comdr. 7th Cavalry Divsn., Vietnam, 1968-69; assoc. prof. dept. social sci. US Mil. Acad., West Point, NY, 1972-75; from chief ops. br. to comdr. 2d battalion 3d Inf. Divsn., Germany, 1976-81; from chief staff to comdr. 3d brigade 9th Inf. Divsn., Ft. Lewis, Wash., 1982-86, comdr. 3d brigade, 1984-86; asst. comdt. US Army Inf. Sch., Ft. Benning, Ga., 1986-88; dep. U.S. mil. rep. NATO, Brussels, 1988-89; div. comdr. 24th Inf. Divsn., Ft. Stewart, Ga., 1990-92; asst. to Chmn. Joint Chiefs of Staff US Dept. Def., Washington, 1992-93, dir. strategic plans and policy directory, The Joint Staff, 1993-94; comdr. US So. Commd. (USSOUTHCOM), Quarry Heights, Panama, 1994-96; dir. Office Nat. Drug Control Policy (ONDCP), Washington, 1996—2001; pres. B.R. McCaffrey Associates, LLC, Alexandria, Va., 2001—; mil. analyst NBC News. Bradley Disting. prof. nat. security studies US Mil. Acad., 2001—05, adj. prof. internat. affairs, 2005—; bd. dirs. HNTB Corp., 2008—, DynCorp Internat., CRC Health Corp/, McNeil Technologies, The Wornick Co. Contbr. articles to mil. publs. Bd. advisors Nat. Infantry Found.; sr. exec. assoc. Army Aviation Assn. America; chmn. advisory bd. Vietnam Veterans Meml. Edn. Center. Decorated: D.S.C. with oak leaf cluster (2), D.M.S. with oak leaf cluster, Silver Star with oak leaf cluster, Def. Superior Svc. medal, Purple Heart with two oak leaf clusters; recipient: Health & Human Services Lifetime Achievement award for Extraordinary Achievement in the Field of Substance Abuse Prevention, 2004, Superior Honor award for Strategic Arms Limitation Talks, US Dept. State, CIA Great Seal Medallion, US Coast Guard Disting. Pub. Svc. award, NAACP Roy Wilkins Renown Svc. award, Norman E. Zinberg award, Harvard Med. Sch., Fed. Law Enforcement Found. Nat. Svc. award, Lifetime Achievement award, The Cmty. Anti-Drug Coalitions of America, Golden Eagle award, The Soc. Am. Mil. Engineers, 2007, W. Stuart Symington award, Air Force Assn., 2008; named one of The 500 Most Influential People in Am. Fgn. Policy, World Affairs Councils Am., 2004; named to The US Army Ranger Hall of Fame, 2007 Mem. NAACP, Assn. of U.S. Army, Coun. of Fgn. Rels., Inter-Am. Dialogue, Legion of Valor of U.S., CSIS US-Mexico Bilateral Coun.; prin. Coun. Excellence in Govt. Democrat. Avocations: hunting, reading. Office: BR McCaffrey Associates LLC 211 N Union St Ste 100 Alexandria VA 22314-2643

MCCAFFREY, EDMUND F., abbot emeritus; b. Savannah, Ga., Jan. 9, 1933; AB, Belmont Abbey, 1955, STB, 1959; MA, Cath. U. of Am., 1963, PhD, 1969. Ordained priest Order of Saint Benedict, 1959; abbot Territorial Abbey of Belmont-Mary Help of Christians, NC, 1970—75, abbot emeritus, 1975—; founder polit. sci. dept. Belmont Abbey Coll., NC. Priest, retreat master, lectr. Diocese of Charleston, SC; past pres. Eternal Life, Bardstown, Ky., 2013. Recipient Pro Fidelitate et Virtute award, Inst. on Religious Life, Chgo., 2003. Mem.: Equestrian Order of Holy Sepulcher (knight comdr.), KC (fourth degree). Roman Catholic. Office: PO Box 70548 Myrtle Beach SC 29572-0028 Office Phone: 843-213-0528.

MCCAFFREY, JUDITH C., otolaryngologist, educator; MD, Loyola U., 1991. Diplomate American Bd. Otolaryngology, 1997. Intern surgery Mayo Clinic Grad. Sch. of Medicine, Rochester, Minn., 1992, resident otorhinolaryngology, 1992—96; fellow head and neck surgery Univ. of Cin., 1996—98; dir. thyroid disease mgmt. group; co-dir. videostroboscopy; asst. prof. otolaryngology Univ. of South Fla. Coll. of Medicine; with dept. of head and neck oncology, exptl. therapeutics; physician, assoc. mem. Moffitt Cancer Ctr. Co-author articles to profl. publs. Office: H Lee Moffitt Cancer Center and Research Institute 12902 Magnolia Dr Tampa FL 33612 Office Phone: 813-745-8363.*

MCCAFFREY, THOMAS P., corporate financial executive; CPA Fla., Colo., Calif. Various positions, including audit ptnr. Coleman & Grant LLP, 1976—89; audit dir. Deloitte & Touche LLP, 1989—93; corp. sr. v.p. adminstrn., CFO BE Aerospace, Inc., 1993—. Mem.: AICPA, Fla. Inst. CPAs, Calif. Soc. CPAs. Office: BE Aerospace Inc 1400 Corporate Ctr Way Wellington FL 33414 Office Phone: 561-791-5000. Office Fax: 561-791-7900.

MCCAIN, BETTY LANDON RAY, retired political party and state official; b. Feb. 23, 1931; d. Horace Truman and Mary Howell (Perrett) Ray; m. John Lewis McCain, Nov. 19, 1955; children: Paul Pressly III, Mary Eloise. Student, St. Mary's Jr. Coll., Raleigh, NC, 1948—50; AB in Music, U. N.C., Chapel Hill, 1952, LLD (hon.), 1998; MA, Columbia U., NYC, 1953; LittD (hon.), U. N.C., Wilmington, 1997; LLD (hon.), Wake Forest U., Winston-Salem, NC, 1999, Barton Coll., Wilson, NC, 1999; DHL (hon.), U. NC, Greensboro, 2007. Courier, European tour guide Ednl. Travel Assocs., Plainfield, NJ, 1952-54; asst. dir. YWCA, U. N.C., Chapel Hill, 1953-55; chmn. N.C. Dem. Exec. Com., 1976-79; mem. Dem. Nat. Com., 1971-72, 76-79, 80-85, chmn. sustaining fund NC, 1981, 88-91, mem. com. on presdl. nominations (Hunt Commn.), 1981-82, mem. rules com., 1982-85, mem. cabinet Gov. James B. Hunt, Jr., 1993-2001, sec. dept. cultural resources, 1993-2001; mem. State Dem. Exec. Com., 1971—99, 2001—. Mem. Winograd Commn., 1977-78; pres. Dem. Women of N.C., 1971-72, dist. dir., 1969-72; pres. Wilson County Dem. Women, 1966-67; precinct chmn., 1972-76; del. Dem. Nat. Conv., 1972, 88; mem. Dem. Mid-Term Confs., 1974, 78, mem. jud. coun. Dem. Nat. Com., 1985-89; dir. Carolina Tel. & Tel. Co. (now Century Link), 1981-97 (1st woman); bd. trustees U. N.C.-TV, 2002—, vice chmn., 2006—, chair, 2008-; interim chair McCain Internet Empowerment Project, 2001—, founding bd. dirs. mem. NC Women's Forum. Contbg. editor: History of N.C. Med. Soc. Treas. Wilson on the Move, 1990—92, mem., 2007—, Coun. on State Goals and Policy, 1970—72, Gov.'s Task Force on Child Advocacy, 1975—78; chmn. Wilson-Greene Morehead scholarship com., 1986—89; mem. career and personal counseling svc. adv. bd. St. Andrews Coll.; charter mem. Wilson Edn. Devel. Coun.; active Arts Coun. of Wilson, Inc.; pres. Wilson County Mental Health Assn., bd. dirs., legis. chmn.; bd. govs. U. N.C., 1975—81, 1985—93, pers. and tenure com., 1985—91, chmn. budget and fin. com., 1991—93; bd. regents Barium Springs Home for Children, chair Founds. com. Capital Campaign, 2003—; bd. dirs. N.C. Mus. History Assocs., 1982—83, pres., 1982—83, membership chair, 1987—88; co-chmn. Com. to Elect Jim Hunt Gov., 1976, 1980, co-chmn. senatorial campaign, 1984; mem. N.C. Adv. Budget Com. (1st woman), 1981—85; chmn. State Employees Combined Campaign N.C., 1993; found. chair Peace Coll., 2008—10, bd. visitors, Wake Forest U. Sch. Law, 1980—83, U. N.C., Chapel Hill; co-chmn. fund dr. Wilson Cmty. Theater; v.p. Wilson County Hist. Assn., 2004—; chmn. devel. com., bd. visitors Lineberger Comprehensive Cancer Ctr., 2006—, vice chmn. bd. visitors, 2007—, chmn., 2009—; chmn. centennial Am. Lung Assn., NC, hon. chmn. hist. observance centennial N.C., 2006—07; Sunday sch. tchr. 1st Presbyn. Ch., Wilson, 1970—71, 1986—88, 1990—92, mem. chancel choir, 1985—, deacon, 1986—92, chmn. fin. com., 1990—91, chair, 1992—93, Pastor Nominating Com., 2008; elder 1st Presbyn. Ch., 1992—98, 2006—09; N.C. state bd. dirs. Am. Lung Assn., state bd. dirs., 1985—88; bd. dirs. Roanoke Island Commn.; mem. battleship commn. USS/NC, 1993—2001; bd. dirs. Wilson Rose Garden, 2002—. Recipient state awards N.C. Heart Assn., 1967, Easter Seal Soc., 1967, Cmty. Svc. award Wilson Downtown Bus. Assocs., 1977, award N.C. Jaycettes, 1979, 85, Women in Govt. award N.C. and U.S. Jaycettes, 1985, Alumni Disting. Svc. award U. N.C., Chapel Hill, 1993, Flora Mac Donald Scottish Heritage award, 1995, Carpathian award N.C. Equity, 1995, Pinnacle award, 1997, 1st winner Holderness-Weaver award U. N.C., Greensboro, 1999, Citizen of Yr. award Wilson C. of C., 2001, Ruth Coltrane Cannon award for hist. preservation Preservation N.C., 2000, N.C. State U. Sch. of Design award, 2000, The North Caroliniana award, 2006; named to Order of Old Well and Valkyries, U. N.C., 1952, Disting. Woman award, NC Gov.'s Conf. Woman, 2010; named Dem. Woman of Yr., N.C., 1976, Internat. Founders award Eta State Delta Kappa Gamma Soc., 2005, Morrison award Roanoke Island Hist. Assn., NC award, 2009, Order of Long Leaf Gov. Robert Scott & Gopv. Jim Hunt; named Outstanding Wilson Citizen of Yr., Wilson Red Cross, 2004. Mem.: DAR, UDC (former historian John W. Dunham chpt.), UNC-TV (chair, bd. trustees 2009—), Peace Coll. Found. (chair 2009—10), Carolinas Ctr. Med. Excellence (bd. dir. 2008—), Rotary Internat. (Paul Harris fellow 2003), N.C. Inst. Medicine (bd. dirs. 1993—2005), N.C. Sch. Arts (trustee 1993—2001), N.C. Equity (bd. dirs.), N.C. Soc. Internal Medicine Aux. (pres.), N.C. Symphony (trustee 1993—2001, 2002—05), Info. Resources Mgmt. Commn. N.C. (bd. dirs. 1993—2001), N.C. Agy. Pub. Telecom. (bd. dirs. 1993—2001, 2009), N.C. Found. for Nursing (bd. dirs. 1989—92), St. Mary's Alumni Assn. (regional v.p., Disting. Alumna 2005), U. N.C. Chapel Hill Alumni Assn. (chmn. 2001—02, bd dir.), Nat. Soc. Colonial Dames Am. NC (sec. local com., program co-chmn.), AMA Alliance (dir., nat. vol. health svcs. chmn., aux. liaison rep. AMA Coun. on Mental Health, aux. rep. Counsel on Vol. Health Orgns.), N.C. Art Soc., N.C. Lit. and Hist. Assn., Wilson Sertoma Club (Svc. to Mankind award 2006), The Book Club (past pres.), Little Book Club, Wilson Country Club, Pi Beta Phi. Home: 1134 Woodland Dr NW Wilson NC 27893-2122 Home Phone: 252-243-4248. Home Fax: 252-243-4248. Personal E-mail: bmccain5@nc.rr.com.

MCCALEB, GARY DAY, university official; b. Anson, Tex., Nov. 2, 1941; s. Victor Earl and Vivian (Day) McC.; m. Sylvia Ravanelli, June 5, 1964; children: Cara Lee Cranford, Bryan Day. BA, Abilene Christian Coll., 1964; MBA, Tex. A&M U., 1975, PhD, 1979. Asst. dir. alumni rels. Abilene (Tex.) Christian U., 1964-65, dir. alumni rels., 1965-69, dir. coll. rels., 1969-73, asst. acad. dean, 1978-80, v.p. pub. rels., 1980-83, v.p., dean campus life, 1983-91, v.p., 1991—, exec. dir. Ctr. for Bldg. Cmty., 1999—; asst. dir. devel. Tex. A&M U., Bryan, 1973-75. Leader internat. travel and goodwill groups; U.S. rep. to world exec. com. Internat. Union Local Authorities, 1996-99. Author: Community, The Gift of Community. Coun. mem. City of Abilene, 1985-90, mayor, 1990-99; bd. dirs. Taylor County Am. Cancer Soc., 1972-73; mem. adv. bd. United Way of Abilene, 1979-83, dir. pub. svc. divsn., 1987, chmn. consortium on drug and alcohol abuse, 1989; bd. dirs. Civic Abilene, Inc., 1981-83; treas. Abilene Task Force on Drug and Alcohol Abuse, 1984-86; active March of Dimes; mem. Tex. Sci. and Tech. Coun., 1997-2000. Recipient Polit. Courage award John Ben Shepperd Pub. Leadership Forum, Austin, Tex., 1993, Tex. Urban Leadersip award U. Tex.-Arlington Sch. Urban and Pub. Affairs, 1995. Mem. Nat. League Cities (nat. steering com. on fin., adminstrn. and intergovtl. rels. 1989-90, adv. bd. 1994, bd. dirs. 1992-94), U.S. Conf. Mayors, Internat. Mcpl. Consortium (chmn. 1994-95), Tex. Mcpl. League (legis. policy com. Houston 1986, resolutions com. Dallas 1988, v.p. region 6 1988-89, bd. dirs. 1989-90, pres. 1992), Abilene C. of C. (aviation com. 1981, 94). Republican. Mem. Ch. of Christ. Avocations: art, baseball, jogging. Office: Abilene Christian Univ PO Box 29136 Abilene TX 79699-0001 E-mail: mccalebg@acu.edu.

MCCALL, BRIAN, former state legislator; b. Oct. 27, 1958; B, M, So. Meth. U., Dallas; vis. post-grad. student, Oxford U., England; PhD, U. Tex., Dallas. Operator Snow Hill Farm; pres. Westminster Capitol Corp.; advisor Quest Network Bus. Solutions; mem. Dist. 66 Tex. House of Reps., 1991—2011. Republican. Office: 2301 W Plano Pky Ste 108 Plano TX 75075 Office Phone: 972-881-0890, 512-463-0594.

MCCALL, CHARLES BARNARD, retired health facility administrator; b. Memphis, Nov. 2, 1928; s. John W. and Lizette (Kimbrough) McCall; m. Carolyn Jean Rosselot, June 9, 1951 (dec. Feb. 2002); children: Linda, Kim, Betsy, Cathy; m. Ernestine Mann, Jan. 5, 2004. BA, Vanderbilt U., 1950, MD, 1953. Diplomate Am. Bd. Internal Medicine, Am. Bd. Pulmonary Diseases. Intern Vanderbilt U. Hosp., Nashville, 1953-54; clin. assoc., sr. asst. surgeon USPHS, Nat. Cancer Inst., NIH, 1954-56; sr. asst. resident in medicine U. Ala. Hosp., 1956-57, chief resident, 1958-59; fellow chest diseases Nat. Acad. Scis.-NRC, 1957-58; instr. U. Ala. Med. Sch., 1958-59; from asst. prof. to assoc. prof. medicine U. Tenn. Med. Sch., 1959-69, chief pulmonary diseases, 1964-69; mem. faculty U. Tex. Sys., Galveston, 1969-75, prof. med. br., 1971-73; assoc. prof. medicine Health Sci. Ctr., Southwestern Med. Sch., Dallas, 1973-75, also assoc. dean clin. programs, 1973-75; dir. Office Grants Mgmt. and Devel., 1973-75; dean, prof. medicine U. Tenn. Coll. Medicine, 1975-77, Oral Roberts U. Sch. Medicine, Tulsa, 1977-78; interim assoc. dean U. Okla. Tulsa Med. Coll., 1978-79; clin. prof. medicine U. Colo. Med. Sch., Denver, 1979-80; prof. medicine, assoc. dean U. Okla. Med. Sch., 1980-82; exec. dean and dean U. Okla. Coll. Medicine, 1982-85; v.p. patient affairs, prof. medicine U. Tex. M. D. Anderson Cancer Ctr., 1985-94; chief of staff VA Med. Ctr., Oklahoma City, 1980-82; ret., 2004. Exec. dir. Worldwide Healthcare Svcs., Inc., Waco, Tex., 1998—2002; clinic dir. Claremore Family Medicine, 2002—04, cons., 2002; bd. dirs. Amigos Internacionales, Inc. Contbr. articles to med. jours. Fellow: ACP, Am. Coll. Chest Physicians; mem.: AMA, Am. Fedn. Clin. Rsch., So. Thoracic Soc. (pres. 1968—69), Am. Thoracic Soc., Sigma Xi, Alpha Omega Alpha. Baptist. Home: 10920 East 83rd Pl Tulsa OK 74133 Personal E-mail: cbmroadsri@cox.net.

MCCALL, JOHN CLARK, JR., interior designer, writer, theatre organist; b. Vidalia, Ga., Sept. 6, 1949; s. John Clark McCall and Carolyn Elizabeth Kay. BA, Ga. State U., 1972, MPA, 1980. Cert. personal property appraiser GPPA, 2009. Program coord. dept. music Ga. State U., Atlanta, 1972-73, adminstrn. supr. dept. music, 1973-78, asst. to dir. office acad. assistance Coll. Arts and Scis., 1978-81; dir. Ctr. for Career Devel. Winthrop U., Rock Hill, S.C., 1981-83, dir., founder Office Campus Planning and Design, 1983-85, asst. prof. interior design, 1985-89; pres. John Clark McCall, Jr. Design Cons., Inc., Rock Hill, S.C., Hahira, Valdosta, Moultrie, Ga., 1983—. Acting chair dept. interior design Winthrop U., Rock Hill, 1985-86. Author: (foreword) Frank McCall: A Complete Designer in the Class Tradition, 1985, (book) Tales of a Southern Palazzo, 2011, (monograph) Atlanta Fox Album: Mecca on Peachtree Street, 1975; contbr.: The Alabama Theatre: Showplace of the South, 2002; designer interiors for residential and non-residential projects; Artist: (cd recordings) A Paramount Idea, 2003, A Capital Idea, 2006, Alabama Album, 2008, Clap Yo' Hands, 2011, McCall Takes Davidson, 2012, Your Packard Hit Parade, Vol. II, 2012, Your Packard Hit Parade, Vol. III, 2014. Dir. Friends of Albany (Ga.) Theatre, 1998-99; bd. trustees Valdosta (Ga.) Symphony Orch.; vol. Save the Atlanta Fox, 1974-80; project dir. Rylander Theatre Moller Pipe Organ Donation, Americus, Ga., 1998-99; co-prodr. Atlanta Fabulous Fox Organ Weekend. Mem. Am. Soc. Interior Designers (allied mem., D. Brahms H. Presv. award, 1985, Pres.'s award, 1987), Am. Theatre Organ Soc. (Atlanta chpt., Lifetime Achievement award), Theatre Hist. Soc., Found. for Interior Design Edn. Rsch. (bd. visitors), Packard Club, Theatre Organ Club (Britain)(life), Lancastrian Organ Trust. Episcopalian. Avocations: watercolor painting, European porcelain. Office: John Clark McCall Jr Design Cons 2117 N Troup St Valdosta GA 31602 Office Phone: 229-560-7540.

MCCALL, JOHN PATRICK, college president, educator; b. Yonkers, NY, July 17, 1927; s. Ambrose V. and Vera E. (Rush) McC.; m. Mary-Berenice Morris, June 15, 1957; children: Claire, Anne, Ambrose, Peter. AB, Coll. of Holy Cross, 1949; MA, Princeton U., 1952, PhD, 1955; DHL, Knox Coll., Galesburg, Ill., 1993. Instr. Georgetown U., 1955-57, asst. prof. English, 1957-62, assoc. prof., 1962-66; prof. U. Cin., 1966-82, head dept. English, 1970-76, sr. v.p., provost, 1976-82; pres. Knox Coll., 1982-93, pres. emeritus and prof. emeritus English, 1993—; vol. Peace Corps, Turkmenistan, 1993-95. Vis. prof. Turkmen State U., 1994-95; vice chmn. Gov.'s Task Force on Rural Ill., 1986; pres. Associated Colls. Ill., 1986-88; chmn. Associated Colls. of M.W., 1991-92; mem. edn. com. Ill. Bd. Higher Edn., 1985, 90; mem. rural libr. panel, State of Ill., 1992. Author: Chaucer Among the Gods: the Poetics of Classical Myth, 1979, Medieval Exegesis: Some Documents for the Literary Critic, 1960; contbr. articles to profl. jours.; research in medieval lit. and Chaucer's poetry. Exec.-in-residence Xavier U. La., 1997—. With Signal Corps, U.S. Army, 1952-54. Am. Coun. Learned Socs. fellow, 1962-63; John Simon Guggenheim Meml. Found. fellow, 1975; Fulbright grantee, 1962; vis. scholar Binghamton U., 2013- Mem. Medieval Acad. Am. MLA, AAUP, Order of St. Louis, Archdiocese of New Orleans. Democrat. Roman Catholic. Home: 1750 St Charles Ave #317 New Orleans LA 70130 Office Phone: 504-520-6795. Business E-Mail: jmccall@xula.edu.

MCCALL, TOM, state legislator; m. Jane McCall. Former state rep. Dist. 90, Ga.; house rep. Ga.; state rep. Dist. 78, 2003—04; state rep. Dist. 30, 2004—; mem. Transp. Com., Agr. & Consumer Affairs Com., Legislature & Congressional Reaapportionment Com., Natural Resources Com., Environ Com.; farmer. Democrat. Address: 2835 Washington Hwy Elberton GA 30635 Mailing: State Capitol 607 Legis Off Bldg Atlanta GA 30334 Office Phone: 706-283-5436, 404-656-0287. E-mail: tmccall@legis.state.ga.us.

MCCALLA, JON PHIPPS, federal judge; b. Memphis, Feb. 16, 1947; m. Mary R. McCalla; children: Marjorie Katherine, Elisabeth Clair. BS in Agrl. Econs., U. Tenn., 1969; JD, Vanderbilt U., 1974. Law clk. to Hon. Bailey Brown US Dist. Ct. (we. dist.) Tenn., 1974-75, judge Memphis, 1992—2008, chief judge, 2008—; assoc. Armstrong, Allen, Braden, Goodman, McBride & Prewitt, 1975-80; ptnr. Armstrong, Allen, Prewitt, Gentry, Johnson & Holmes, 1980-87, Heiskell, Donelson, Bearman, Adams, Williams & Kirsch, 1987-92. Active Ctrl. Gardens Area Neighborhood Assn., 1979-84; church deacon pers. com., Sunday Sch. tchr., 1987-90; bd. dirs. Idlewild Friends of Music. 2nd lt., then 1st lt. U.S. Army, 1969-71. Decorated Bronze Star. Mem. Fed. Bar Assn., Tenn. Bar Assn., Memphis Bar Assn., 6th Cir. Jud. Conf. Presbyterian. Office: US Dist Ct 167 N Main St Ste 1157 Memphis TN 38103

MCCALLIE, JOANNE P., women's college basketball coach; b. Monterey, Calif. m. John McCallie; children: Madeline, John (Jack) Wyatt. BA in Polit. Sci., Northwestern U., 1987; MBA, Auburn U., 1990. Asst. basketball coach Auburn U. Tigers, 1988—92; head women's basketball coach U. Maine Black Bears, 1992—2000, Mich. State U. Spartans, 2001—07, Duke U. Blue Devils, 2007—. Color commentator Detroit Shock, WNBA, 2003—05; head coach US nat. under-21 team FIBA Americas Championships, Mexico City, 2006. Hon. chair Women Working Wonders, 2001—04, Memory Walk, 2001—04, Haven House, 2001—05, MSU/Mid-Mich. Children's Initiative, 2003—05; bd. dirs. Gov. Coun. on Phys. Fitness, 2003—05, Jackson Nat. Life, 2004—05. Named North Atlantic Conf. Coach of Yr., 1995, 1996, America East Conf. Coach of Yr., 1999, Big 10 Conf. Coach of Yr., 2005, Coach of Yr., Basketball Coach Assn. Mich., 2005, Nat. Coach. of Yr., AP, 2005, Atlantic Coast Conf. Coach of Yr., 2012, 2013; named to Maine Sports Legends Hall of Fame, 2005. Mem.: Women's Basketball Coaches Assn. (Big 10 Conf. chair 2003—04, bd. dirs. 2011—12). Office: Duke Athletics 118 Cameron Indoor Stadium Durham NC 27708

MCCALLISTER, MIKE (MICHAEL B. MCCALLISTER), insurance company executive; b. Indpls., May 27, 1952; m. Charlene Gray, 1985; children: Megan, Ryan. BA in Acctg., La. Tech. U., 1974; MBA, Pepperdine U., 1983. Financial specialist Humana, Inc., Louisville, 1974—75, exec. dir. finance Cmty. Hosp. Springhill, La., 1975; exec. dir. Humana Hospitals, Huntington and West Anaheim, Calif., 1978—85, Humana Hosp. West Hills, Canoga Park, Calif., 1985—88; pres. Humana Hosp. Phoenix, 1988—89; v.p. Humana Health Care Plans, Phoenix, 1989—92, San Antonio, 1992—96, pres. divsn. 1 with responsibility for Tex., Fla. and P.R., 1996—97; sr. v.p. health sys. mgmt. Humana, Inc., Louisville, 1997—99, sr. v.p., Office Chmn., 1999—2000, pres., CEO, 2000—10, chmn., CEO, 2010—12, chmn., 2012—. Bd. dirs. Humana Inc., 2000—, Nat. City Corp., 2008, Fifth Third Bancorp, 2011—, AT&T Inc., 2013—, Zoetis Inc., 2013—. Bd. mem. Bellarmine U. Recipient Tower Medallian Award, La. Tech., 2003. Mem.: Am. Assn. Health Plans (bd. dirs.). Office: Humana Inc 500 W Main St Ste 300 Louisville KY 40202-4268*

MC CALLUM, CHARLES ALEXANDER, academic administrator; b. North Adams, Mass., Nov. 1, 1925; s. Charles Alexander and Mabel Helen (Cassidy) McC.; m. Alice Rebecca Lasseter, Dec. 17, 1955; children: Scott Alan, Charles Alexander III, Philip Warren, Christopher Jay. Student, Dartmouth Coll., 1943-44, Wesleyan U., Middletown, Conn., 1946-47; DMD, Tufts U., 1951; MD, Med. Coll. Ala., 1957; DSc (hon.), U. Ala., 1975, Georgetown U., 1982, Tufts U., 1988, Chulalongkorn U., Thailand, 1993, U. Medicine and Dentistry, NJ, 1993. Diplomate Am. Bd. Oral Surgery (pres. 1970). Intern oral surgery Univ. Hosp., Birmingham, Ala., 1951-52, resident oral surgery, 1952-54, intern medicine, 1957-58; mem. faculty U. Ala. Sch. Dentistry, 1956-96, prof., chmn. dept. oral surgery, 1959-65, dean sch., 1962-77; prof., dept. surgery U. Ala. Sch. of Medicine, 1965-96; v.p. for health affairs, dir. U. Ala. Med. Center, Birmingham, 1977-87; pres. U. Ala., Birmingham, 1987-93, chief sect. oral surgery Sch. Dentistry, 1958-65, 68-69; prof., 1959-93; disting. prof., 1992-2000; disting. prof. emeritus, dean emeritus, 2000—. Mem. nat. adv. dental rsch. coun. NIH, 1968-72; mem. Joint Commn. on Accreditation of Hosps., 1980-91, vice chmn., 1985, chmn., 1986-88. Fellow Am. Coll. Dentists, Internat. Coll. Dentists; mem. ADA (council on dental edn. 1970-76), Am. Assn. Dental Schs. (pres. 1969), Ala. Acad. of Honor, AMA, Am. Soc. Oral Surgeons (trustee 1972-73, pres. 1975-76), Southeastern Soc. Oral Surgeons (pres. 1970), Inst. of Medicine of Nat. Acad. of Scis., Assn. Acad. Health Ctrs. (chmn. bd. dirs. 1984-85), Omicron Kappa Upsilon, Phi Beta Pi. Home: 2328 Garland Dr Birmingham AL 35216-3002 Home Phone: 205-822-8445. Personal E-mail: cmccallum@charter.net.

MCCAMPBELL, ARTIS (A.J. MCCAMPBELL), state legislator; m. Diana England; children: Erica D. Hargrove, Joy. BA in Polit. Sci., U. Ala., 1976. Patrolman City of Tuscaloosa, Ala., 1975—77, investigator, 1977—79; juvenile probation officer Greene County, Ala., 1979—85; investigator 17th Jud. Cir. Dist. Atty's Office, 1985—90; ins. salesman State Farm Ins., 1990—; mem. Dist. 71 Ala. House of Reps., Montgomery, 2006—. Democrat. Office: PO Box 487 Demopolis AL 36732 also: Ala House of Reps Ala State House 11 S Union St 539-C Montgomery AL 36130 Office Phone: 334-295-5634, 334-242-7747.

MCCAMPBELL, ROBERT GARNER, lawyer, former prosecutor; b. Oklahoma City, Nov. 23, 1957; s. Stanley Reid and Joan Fontane (Garner) McC. BA in History with honors, Vanderbilt U., 1980; JD, Yale U., 1983. Bar: Okla. 1983. Assoc. Crowe & Dunlevy, Oklahoma City, 1983-87, dir., 1994—2001, 2005—; asst. US atty. (we. dist.) Okla. US Dept. Justice, 1987-94, chief fin. fraud unit (we. dist.) Okla., 1990-94, Us atty. (we. dist.) Okla., 2001—05. Dir. Ctr. for Advancement of Sci. and Tech., 1995, chmn., 1999—2001; chmn. sub-com. sentencing Atty. Gen., 2004—05. Fellow: Am. Coll. Trial Lawyers; mem. ABA, Nat. Assn. Former U.S. Attys., Phi Beta Kappa. Republican. Episcopalian. Office: Crowe & Dunlevy 20 N Broadway Ste 1800 Oklahoma City OK 73102 Office Phone: 405-235-7700. Business E-Mail: mccampbr@crowedunlevy.com.

MCCANLESS, ROSS WILLIAM, lawyer, manufacturing executive; b. 1957; BS in Acctg., U. NC, 1979; JD cum laude, Wake Forest U., 1982. CPA. Pvt. practice, 1982—89; various positions, vice chmn. Delhaize Am., Inc., 1989—2003, Food Lion LLC, 1989—2003, founder, legal & tax dept., 1989—95, sr. v.p., chief adminstrv. officer, 1995—99, pres., CEO, 1999—2002; sr. v.p., gen. counsel & sec. Lowe's Companies, Inc., Mooresville, NC, 2003—06. Former bd. dirs. Delhaize Group; bd. dirs. Kewaunee Sci. Corp., 2010—. Mem.: Am. Corp. Counsel Assn., Rowan County Bar Assn., Am. Bar Assn., N.C. State Bar Assn. Office: Kewaunee Scientific Corp Bd Directors 2700 W Front St Statesville NC 28677-2927 Office Phone: 704-873-7202. Office Fax: 704-873-1275. Business E-Mail: rossmccanless@kewaunee.com.

MCCARDELL, JOHN MALCOLM, JR., academic administrator, history professor; b. Frederick, Md., June 17, 1949; s. John Malcolm and Susan (Lane) McCardell; m. Bonnie Greenwald, Dec. 30, 1976; children: John Malcolm III, James Benjamin Lee. AB, Washington and Lee U., 1971, LittD (hon.), 1997; PhD, Harvard U., 1976; LHD (hon.), St. Michael's Coll., 2004. From asst. prof. history to prof. Middlebury Coll., Vt., 1976—87, prof. history, 1987—2010, dean facuty, 1988—89, provost, v.p academic affairs, 1989—91, acting pres., 1991—92, pres., 1992—2004, pres. emeritus, 2004—; sr. rsch fellow U. SC, Columbia, 1980—81, 1996; pres. & vice chancellor Univ. of the South, Sewanee, Tenn., 2010—. Bd. dirs. Nat. Bank Middlebury, Comm. fin. Svcs. Group; vice chmn. bd. trustees Episc. H.S., 2004—. Author: The Idea of a Southern Nation, 1979 (Allan Nevins award, 1977); editor: A Master's Due, 1985. Sr. warden St. Stephen's Episcopal Ch., Middlebury, Vt.; bd. trustees Am. Civil War Ctr., Tredegar, Va. Sgt. USAR, 1971—77. Recipient Algernon Sydney Sullivan prize, Washington and Lee U., 1971, Charles Eliot medal, Eliot House Harvard U., 1976; fellow, NEH, 1980, Am. Philosophical Soc., 1979. Mem.: Vt. Hist. Soc., S.C. History Soc., So. Hist. Assn., Orgn. Am. Historians, Am. Hist. Assn., Lambda Chi Alpha, Phi Beta Kappa, Omicron Delta Kappa. Office: The University of the South Office of Vice Chancellor 735 University Ave Sewanee TN 37383 Office Phone: 931-598-1000. Office Fax: 931-598-1145.*

MCCARTER, THOMAS NESBITT, III, investment company executive, consultant; b. NYC, Dec. 16, 1929; s. Thomas N. Jr. and Suzanne M. (Pierson) McCarter. Student, Princeton U., 1948-51. Chartered investment counselor. Sales exec. Mack Trucks, Inc., NYC, 1952—59; ptnr. Kelly, McCarter, D-Arcy Investment Counsel, NYC, 1959—62; v.p., sec., dir. D-Arcy McCarter & Chew, NYC, 1962—66; v.p., dir. Trainer, Wortham & Co., Inc., NYC, 1967—71, exec. v.p., 1971—75; chmn. bd., dir. Island Security Bank Ltd., 1976—78; pres. Knottingham Ltd., NYC, 1976—84; gen. ptnr. W.P. Miles Timber Properties, New Orleans, 1974—; exec. v.p., dir. Yorke McCarter Owen & Bartles, Inc., NYC, 1985—89. Cons. Laidlaw Holdings, Inc., 1990—92; pres. Mentor Mgmt. Group, Inc., NYC, 1986—90; chmn. bd. dirs. Ramapo Land Co., Sloatsburg, NY, 1990—, Stillrock Mgmt., Inc., NYC, 1992—96, Pendragon Tech., 1996—98; past dir. Anker Coal Group Inc., Haber Inc., Hyseq, Inc., Nuvelo, Inc.; bd. advisors Knowledge Delivery Sys. Inc.; vice chair Runnymede Capital Mgmt., 1997—2002; adv. dir. Runnymede Capital Mgmt., Inc.; bd. dirs. Inst. Scientific Investment and Governance KCK Tokyo, So. Union Co. Chmn. bd. trustees Christodora Found., Inc., NYC, 1970-93; charter trustee Dalton Sch., NYC, 1969-76, v.p., 1972-76; pres., trustee Civil War Libr. and Mus., Phila., 1985-92; chmn. bd. trustees ASPCA, 1984-95; chmn. loyal Legion Found., NYC; trustee Children's Aid Soc. NYC, 1973-94, Joffrey Ballet, Found. for Am. Dance, 1973-77; pres., trustee NYC Marble Cemetery Assn., 1990-2002; mem. Nat. Com. for Preservation of US Treasury Bldg., 1988-92; trustee Nat. Symphony Orch., Washington, 1990-94; chmn. Gibraltar Am. Coun., 1998-2002; bd. assocs. Whitehead Inst., Cambridge, Mass., 2000—09; adv. bd. mem. Venture Capital Fund America, 2010. Mem. Loyal Legion US (comdr. NY State 1964-66, nat. comdr. in chief 1977-81), Brook Club, Links Club, River Club, St. Nicholas Soc., Pilgrims of US (NYC), Meadow Club (Southampton, NY), Ivy Club (Princeton, NJ), Moorings Club (Vero Beach, Fla.), Everglades Club (Palm Beach, Fla.). Republican. Office: PO Box 2380 Palm Beach FL 33480

MCCARTHY, BRIAN NELSON, Real Estate professional; b. Detroit, May 24, 1945; s. Andrew Nelson and Ruth Elizabeth (Hill) McC.; children: Amanda Lang, Kelly Elizabeth, Meghan Virginia, Connor Michael; m. Valerie Lojewski, 1997. BS in Engring. Sci., Oakland U., 1966; MBA, Harvard U., 1972; grad., Sarasota Sheriff's Office Civilian Law Enforcement Acad., 2012. Lic. real estate broker Fla., cert. cmty. assn. mgr. Fla. Engr. Gen. Motors Corp., Pontiac, Mich., 1965-67; co-owner Sound Wave Systems, Costa Mesa, Calif., 1971-78; CFO, controller A&W Gershenson Co., Farmington, Mich., 1972-75; pres. Devel. Group, Inc., Southfield, Mich., 1975—81; CEO Brichard & Co., San Francisco, 1982-87; pres. Watermark Corp., Sausalito, Calif., 1987—92, Indian Wells Water Co., Inc., Sausalito, 1993—2000; dir. Co-Investor Group, Sonoma, Calif., 2000—01; chmn., pres. Southfork Devel. Group, El Dorado Hills, Calif., 2002—07; CEO Watermark Property Group, Balt., 2008—10, Starboard Tack LLC, Sarasota, Fla., 2009—. Mem. Humane Soc., Golden Retriever Rescue. Ret. USNR, former dir. Navy Supply Corps. Assn. Recipient Navy Achievement medal, Navy Commendation medal with gold star, Joint Commendation medal, Navy Meritorious Svc. medal with 2 gold stars, Joint Meritorious Svc. medal with oak leaf cluster, Longboat Key C. of C. Small Bus. award, 2012, others. Mem. Navy Supply Corps Assn. (bd. dirs. 1987-96), Trusted Profls. Sarasota (v.p.), Mil. Officers Assn. America (Sarasota chpt.), Navy League US Sarasota-Manatee Coun., Longboat Key C. of C., Siesta Key c. of C., Venice C. of C. Republican. Avocations: racquetball, squash, tennis, kayaking, sailing. Mailing: Starboard Tack LLC 8499 S Tamiami Trail Ste 203 Sarasota FL 34238 Office Phone: 941-806-6880. Office Fax: 888-662-9140. Personal E-mail: bnmccarthy@gmail.com.

MCCARTHY, CATHERINE J., food service executive; Regional v.p. retail ops. Cracker Barrel Old Country Store, Inc. Office: Cracker Barrel Old Country Store Inc 305 Hartmann Dr Lebanon TN 37088-0787 Office Phone: 615-444-5533. Office Fax: 615-443-9476.

MCCARTHY, JOHN EDWARD, bishop emeritus; b. Houston, June 21, 1930; s. George Gaskell and Grace Veronica (O'Brien) McCarthy. Attended, St. Mary's Sem., Houston, 1949-56; MA, St. Thomas U., Houston, 1979. Ordained priest Archdiocese of Galveston-Houston, 1956; served various Houston Cath. parishes; exec. dir. Nat. Bishops Com. for Spanish speaking, 1966-68; asst. dir. Social Action Office, US Cath. Conf., 1967-69; exec. dir. Tex. Cath. Conf., Houston, 1973-79; ordained bishop, 1979; aux. bishop Diocese of Galveston-Houston, 1979—85; bishop Diocese of Austin, Tex., 1986—2001, bishop emeritus, 2001—. Bd. dirs. Nat. Center for Urban Ethnic Affairs, Mexican-American Cultural Ctr., Sisters of Charity of the Incarnate Word, Houston, 1981-, St. Thomas U., Houston, 1980—. Mem. Cath. Conf. for Urban Ministry. Democrat. Roman Catholic. Office: Chancery PO Box 13327 Austin TX 78711-3327

MCCARTY, DORAN CHESTER, religious organization administrator; b. Bolivar, Mo., Feb. 3, 1931; s. Bartie Lee and Donta Marian (Russell) McC.; m. Gloria Jean Laffoon, June 14, 1952 (dec.); children: Gaye, Risë, Marletta, Leslie; m. Catherine Hearne McCarty, Dec. 30, 2007. AA, Southwest Bapt. Coll., 1950; AB, William Jewell Coll., 1952; BD, So. Bapt. Theol. Sem, 1956, PhD, 1963. Pastor 1st Bapt. Ch., Switz City, Ind., 1956-62, Pleasant Hill, Mo., 1962-65, Susquehanna Bapt. Ch., Independence, Mo., 1965-67; prof. Midwestern Bapt. Theol. Sem., Kansas City, Mo., 1967-81, Golden Gate Bapt. Theol. Sem., Mill Valley, Calif., 1981-87; coord. Northeastern Bapt. Sch. Ministry, NYC, 1987-94; exec. dir. Sem. Ext., Nashville, 1988-94. Cons. Bapt. Home Mission Bd., 1981—; assoc. dean So. Bapt. Theol. Sem., Louisville, 1989; pres. McCarty Svcs., St. Augustine; dir. doctrate program Hong Kong Bapt. Theol. Sem., 2007. Author: Rightly Dividing the Word, 1973, Teilhard de Chardin, 1976, The Supervision of Ministry Students, 1978, The Supervision of Mission Personnel, 1983, The Inner Heart of Ministry, 1985, Working With People, 1987, Leading the Small Church, 1991, Supervision: Developing and Directing People on Mission, 1994, Making the Most of Your Time, 1996, Making the Most of Conflict, 1997, Making the Most of Change, 1998, Making the Most of Empowerment, 1999, Making the Most of Coping, 2000, Making the Most of Pastoral Leadership, 2002, Hallowed Be Thy Name, 2002; editor: Key Resources, 5 vols., Broadman Leadership Series, 16 vols., The Practice of Ministry: A Sourcebook, 1995. Preaching min. Hammock Cmty. Ch., Palm Coast, Fla.; dir. dr. ministry program Hong Kong Bapt. Theol. Sem.; asst. to coord. Coop. Bapt. Fellowship Fla. Recipient Life Service award Southwest Bapt. U., Bolivar, 1973, William Jewell Coll. Achievement citation, 1987. Mem. Assn. for Theol. Field Edn. (chairperson 1979-81), Inst. Theol. Reflection (exec. dir. 1978-86), Fellowship In Service Guidance Dirs. (pres. 1986-87, Lewis Newman award 1988). Home: 116 Village Del Lago Ln Saint Augustine FL 32080 E-mail: doranmccarty@bellsouth.net.

MCCARTY, RICHARD CHARLES, psychology professor, provost; b. Portsmouth, Va., July 12, 1947; s. Constantine Ambrose and Helen Marie (Householder) McC.; m. Sheila Adair Miltier, July 15, 1965; children: Christopher Charles, Lorraine Marie, Ryan Lester, Patrick James. BS in Biology, Old Dominion U., 1970, MS in Zoology, 1972; PhD in Pathobiology, Johns Hopkins U., 1976. Rsch. assoc. NIMH, Bethesda, Md., 1976-78; asst. prof. U. Va., Charlottesville, 1978-84, assoc. prof., 1984-88, prof., 1988-2001, chair psychology, 1990-98, chair Coun. of Grad. Depts. Psychology, 1996-97; exec. dir. sci. directorate APA, Washington, 1998-2001; dean arts and sci. Vanderbilt U., Nashville, 2001—08, provost, 2008—. Mem. editl. bd. Behavioral and Neural Biology, 1985—90, Physiology and Behavior, 1989—2007, editor-in-chief Stress, 1995—99; editor: Am. Psychologist, 2000—01. Lt. comdr. USPHS, 1976—78. Recipient Rsch. Scientist Devel. award, NIMH, 1985—90; sr. fellow, Nat. Heart Lung Blood Inst., NIH, 1984—85. Fellow AAAS, APA, Assn. Psychol. Sci. Roman Catholic. Office: Office of the Provost Vanderbilt Univ 205 Kirkland Hall Nashville TN 37240 Business E-Mail: richard.mccarty@vanderbilt.edu.

MCCASLIN, RICHARD BRYAN, history educator; b. Atlanta, Feb. 21, 1961; s. Jerry L. and Ann Elizabeth (Sharman) McCaslin; m. Jana Dawn Maryovich, Apr. 5, 1979; 1 child, Christina Michele. BA, Delta State U., 1982; MA, La. State U., 1983; PhD, U. Tex., 1988. Tchg. asst. La. State U., 1982-83, grad. asst. La. Bus. Rev., 1983; tchg. asst. U. Tex., Austin, 1983-87, rsch. assoc., 1984-87; rsch. asst. prof. U. Tenn., Knoxville, 1988-90; asst. prof. High Point U., 1990-94, assoc. prof., 1994-2000, prof., 2000—04; assoc. prof. U. N. Tex., Denton, 2004—07, prof., 2007—, chair dept. history, 2008—. Instr. Pellissippi State CC, 1988—89, Roane State CC, 1989; adj. prof. Corpus Christi State U., Tex., 1989, Hawaii Pacific U., 2003—; lectr. E. Tenn. Hist. Soc., 1990; rsch. cons. Tex. Senate, 1986—89, Nat. Pk. Svc., 1989—90, Tex. State Hist. Assn., 2000—; assoc. historian Futurepast: History Co., Spokane, Wash., 1987—89. Author: Andrew Johnson: A Bibliography, 1992, Portraits of Conflict: A Photographic History of South Carolina in the Civil War, 1994, Tainted Breeze: The Great Hanging at Gainesville, Texas, October 1862, 1994 (Tullis prize Tex. State Hist. Assn., commendation Am. Assn. State and Local History), Remembered Be Thy Blessings: High Point University - The College Years, 1924-1991, 1995, Portraits of Conflict: A Photographic History of North Carolina in the Civil War, 1997, Lee in the Shadow of Washington, 2001 (Slatten award Va. Hist. Soc., Laney prize Austin Civil War Roundtable), The Last Stronghold: The Fort Fisher Campaign, 2003, Portraits of Conflict: A Photographic History of Tennessee in the Civil War, 2007 (Freeman award, MOSB), At the Heart of Texas: One Hundred Years of the Texas State Historical Association, 2007 (award Merit Tex. Philosophical Soc.), Fighting Stock: John S. "Rip" Ford of Texas, 2011 (Pate award Fort Worth Civil War Round Table, Bates award Tex. State Hist. Assn.); co-author (with Earnest F. Gloyna): Commitment to Excellence: One Hundred Years of Engineering Education at the University of Texas at Austin, 1986; columnist: Greensboro News and Record, 1993—94; referee Southwestern Hist. Quar., La. State U. Press, U. Nebr. Press, US Car Press, Tex. A&M U. Press, U. N. Tex. Press, Tex. State Hist. Assn., U. Okla. Press; co-editor: Papers of Andrew Johnson, U. Tenn., 1988—90, This Corner of Canaan, 2012; editor: A Soldier's Letter to Charming Nellie, 2008; contbr. numerous articles to profl. publs. Recipient McWhiney award, Dallas Civil War Roundtable, 2009, Jefferson Davis Gold medal, UDC, 2000; Dissertation fellow, U. Tex., 1987—88, Clara H. Driscoll fellow, Daus. Republic of Tex., 1985—87, James H. and Minnie M. Edmonds Ednl. Found. scholar, 1983—85, Colonial Dames Am. grad. scholar, 1987. Fellow: Tex. State Hist. Assn. (presenter); mem.: Soc. Mil. History (presenter, regional dir.), Am. Hist. Assn., E. Tex. Hist. Soc. (presenter), Soc. Civil War Historians (presenter), So. Hist. Assn. (presenter,). Episcopalian. Home: 601 Ticonderoga Dr Denton TX 76205 Office: University North Tex 1155 Union Circle 310650 Denton TX 76203-5017 Office Phone: 940-565-4207. Business E-Mail: mccaslin@unt.edu.

MCCAUL, MICHAEL THOMAS, United States Representative from Texas; b. Dallas, Jan. 14, 1962; m. Linda Mays; children: Caroline, Jewell, Lauren, Michael, Avery. BS, Trinity U., San Antonio, 1984; JD, St. Mary's U., San Antonio, 1987; attended, Harvard U. John F. Kennedy Sch. Govt. Dep. atty. gen. State of Tex., Austin, Tex., 1987—90, spl. asst. atty. gen., 1999—2000, dep. atty. gen., 2000—02, chief Terrorism & Nat. Security sect., 2002; fed. prosecutor, pub. integrity sect. US Dept. Justice, Washington, 1990—99; mem. US Congress from 10th Tex. Dist., 2005—, US House Ethics Com. (formerly House Standards of Official Conduct Com.); chmn. US House Homeland Security Com., 2013—. Vice chmn. US-Mex. Inter-Parliamentary Group, 2005. Republican. Roman Catholic. Office: US House of Representatives 131 Cannon House Office Bldg Washington DC 20515 also: 5929 Balcones Dr Ste 30 Austin TX 78731 Office Phone: 202-225-2401.*

MCCAULEY, STEPHEN R, medical educator; PhD, U. Houston, 1997. Assoc. prof. Baylor Coll. Medicine, Houston, 1997—. Office: Baylor Coll Medicine 6550 Fannin St Ste 1801 Houston TX 77030 Office Fax: 713-798-8573. Business E-Mail: mccauley@bcm.edu.*

MCCAWLEY, AUSTIN, psychiatrist, educator; b. Greenock, Scotland, Jan. 17, 1925; arrived in U.S., 1954; s. Austin and Anna Theresa (McBride) McC.; m. Gloria Klein, Feb. 15, 1958; children: Joseph, Tessa. MBCHB, U. Glasgow, 1948. Diplomate Am. Bd. Psychiatry and Neurology; DPM Royal Coll. London. Intern Glasgow Royal Infirmary, Scotland, 1948; resident Inst. Living, Harford, Conn., 1954-57, clin. dir., 1960-66; med. dir. Westchester br. St. Vincent's Hosp., NYC, 1966-72; dir. psychiatry St. Francis Hosp., Hartford, 1972-88; prof. psychiatry U. Conn. Med. Sch., Farmington, 1983-93; pvt. practice, West Hartford, Conn., 1988—2000. Dir. psychiatry Kaiser Permanente of Conn., 1996-99. Author: A Comb for a Bald Man: A Psychiatrist's Experience, 2009, The Mind of an Arsonist, 2011; co-author: The Physician, 1983; contbr. articles to profl. jours. Chmn. Bd. Mental Health, State of Conn., 1981-84, Search Com. for Commr. Mental Health, Conn., 1981; mem. Gov.'s Spl. Task Force on Mental health Policy, Conn., 1982. With RAF, 1948-50. Fellow: Conn. Psychiat. Soc. (pres. 1978—79), Am. Coll. Psychiatry (charter fellow, founder, Disting. Life fellow), Am. Psychiat. Assn. Democrat. Roman Catholic. Avocation: music. Home and Office: 6020 Piney Grove Way Gainesville VA 20155-6670 Office Phone: 571-248-0277. Business E-Mail: amccawley@olviasart.com.

MCCAY, JOHN, III, minister; b. Gulfport, Miss., July 8, 1975; AA, Miss. Gulf Coast CC, 1995; BA in Polit. Sci., U. So. Miss., 1997; MDiv, Memphis Theol. Sem., 2000. Chaplain Miss. Air Nat. Guard; min. Winborn Chapel, 2000—02, Shipman United Meth. Ch., 2000—02, Gateway United Meth. Ch., 2002—04, Trinity United Meth. Ch., 2004—. Mem. Rep. Nat. Com. Mem.: NRA, Nat. Wildlife Turkey Found., Nat. Eagle Scout Assn., Nat. Fraternal Order of Police, Kiwanis Internat. Republican. Office: PO Box 7696 Gulfport MS 39506

MCCHESNEY, ROBERT MICHAEL, SR., retired academic administrator; s. J.D. and Helen Grace (Russell) McC.; m. Laraine Freestone Freeman, Aug. 28, 1965; children: Robert M. Jr., Todd Patrick, Jennifer Laraine Turner, Grant Russell, Brent Steven. BA, U. La., Lafayette, 1964; MA, U. Va., 1967, PhD, 1969. Asst. instr. U. Va., Charlottesville, 1967-68; chmn. dept. polit. sci. U. Ctrl. Ark., Conway, 1971-76, dean coll. scis. and humanities, 1976-82, v.p. for acad. affairs, 1982-89, disting. prof., 1989-90; provost U. Montevallo, Ala.,

1990-92, pres., 1992—2006, emeritus pres., 2006—. V.p. Survey Rsch., Inc., Conway, 1989-92; spl. cons. U. Ark. System, Little Rock, 1989. Mem. Carmichael Found., Conway, 1975-79; exec. bd. Quapaw coun. Boy Scouts Am., Little Rock, 1982-88; Greater Ala. Area Coun., 1995-2006; chair Ala. Coun. Univ. Pres., 1994-96, Ala. Higher Edn. Partnership, Pres. Adv. Coun., 1999-2001. Capt. med. svcs. US Army, 1969—71. Grantee, State Justice Inst./Adminstrv. Office of Cts., Ark., 1989. Mem. Ala. Coun. Univ. and Coll. Pres. (chmn. 1993-95, vice chmn. 2005-06), So. Com. Colls. and Schs. (exec. coun. 1996-99), Birmingham C. of C. (met. devel. bd. mem.), Montevall C. of C., Rotary (pres. Conway Club 1987-88, Paul Harris fellow 1986), Phi Beta Kappa, Phi Kappa Phi, Alpha Chi, Golden Key, Phi Alpha Theta, Phi Eta Sigma, Blue Key. Mem. Lds Ch. Avocations: hunting, fishing, golf. Home: 402 Norwick Cir Alabaster AL 35007 Personal E-mail: rmcchesney@gmail.com.

MCCHRYSTAL, STANLEY ALLEN, consulting firm executive, retired military officer; b. Ft. Leavenworth, Kans., Aug. 14, 1954; s. Herbert J. and Mary Gardner (Bright) McChrystal; m. Annie McChrystal, 1977; 1 child, Sam. BS, US Mil. Acad., 1976; MA in Nat. Security & Strategic Studies, US Navel War Coll.; MS in Internat. Rels., Salve Regina U.; Student, Spl. Forces Officer Course, Spl. Forces Sch., Ft. Bragg, NC, 1978—79, Infantry Officer Advanced Course, Ft. Benning, GA, 1980—81, Command & Staff Course, US Naval War Coll., Newport, RI, 1989—90. Advanced through grades to gen. US Army, 2009; weapons platoon leader C Co., 1st Bn., 504th Parachute Inf. Regiment, 82nd Airborne Divsn, Ft. Bragg, NC, 1976—78; rifle platoon leader C Co., 1st Bn., 504th Parachute Inf. Regiment, 82nd Airborne Divsn., Ft. Bragg, NC, 1978, exec. officer, 1978—79; comdr., Detachment A, A Co. 7th Spl. Forces Group, Ft. Bragg, NC, 1979—80; S-2/S-3 (intelligence, ops.) UN Command Support Group-Joint Security Area, Republic of Korea, 1981—82; training officer Directorate Plans & Training, Headquarters Command, Ft. Stewart, Ga., 1982; comdr. A Co. 3rd Bn., 19th Infantry, 24th Infantry Divsn. (Mechanized), Ft. Stewart, Ga., 1982—84, S-3 (ops.), 1984—85; liaison officer 3rd Bn., 75th Ranger Regiment, Ft. Benning, Ga., 1985—86, 1987—88, comdr. A Co., 1986—87, S-3 (ops.), 1988—89; Army spl. ops. action officer (J-3) Joint Spl. Ops. Command (JSOC), Ft. Bragg, NC, 1990—93; comdr. 2d Bn., 504th Parachute Infantry Regiment, 82d Airborne Divsn., Ft. Bragg, NC, 1993—94, 2d Bn., 75th Ranger Regiment, Ft. Lewis, Wash., 1994—96; sr. svc. coll. fellow John F. Kennedy Sch. Govt., Harvard U., Cambridge, Mass., 1996—97; comdr. 75th Ranger Regiment, Ft. Benning, Ga., 1997—99; mil. fellow Coun. on Fgn. Rels., NYC, 1999—2000; asst. divsn. comdr. (ops.) 82d Airborne Divsn., Ft. Bragg, NC, 2000—01; also comdr. Combined Joint Task Force-Kuwait, Camp Doha, 2000—01; chief staff XVIII Airborne Corps and Fort Bragg, Ft. Bragg, NC, 2001—02; also chief of staff Combined Joint Task Force-180, OPERATION ENDURING FREEDOM, Afghanistan, 2001—02; vice dir. ops. (J-3) The Joint Staff, US Dept. Def., Washington, 2002—03, dir., 2008—09; commdg. gen. Joint Spl. Ops. Command (JSOC), Ft. Bragg, NC, 2003—06; comdr. Joint Spl. Ops. Command (JSOC) and Joint Spl. Ops. Command Forward, US Spl. Ops. Command (USSOCOM), Ft. Bragg, NC, 2006—08, US Forces Afghanistan (USFOR-A), Kabul, 2009—10; comdr., Internat. Security Assistance Force (ISAF) NATO, Kabul, 2009—10; sr. fellow, Jackson Inst. for Global Affairs Yale U., New Haven, 2010—; chmn. advisory bd. Joining Forces, 2011—; co-founder, ptnr. McChrystal Group LLC, Alexandria, Va., 2011—; adv. Ctr. for New American Security, 2011—; chmn. Siemens Govt. Technologies Inc., 2011—. Bd. dirs. JetBlue Airways Corp., 2010—, Navistar Internat. Corp., 2011—; mem. mil. & veterans affairs advisory council JP Morgan Chase & Co., 2011—; mem. strategic advisory bd. Knowledge Internat. LLC, 2011—. Author: My Share of the Task: A Memoir, 2013. Bd. dirs. Yellow Ribbon Fund, 2010—. Decorated Disting. Svc. medal, Def. Disting. Svc. medal, Def. Superior Svc. medal with oak leaf cluster, Legion of Merit with 2 Oak Leaf Clusters, Bronze star, Meritorious Svc, medal with 3 oak leaf clusters, Army Commendation medal, Army Achievement medal, Expert Infantryman Badge, Master Parachutist Badge, Ranger Tab, Spl. Forces Tab, Joint Chiefs of Staff Identification Badge; named one of The 100 Most Influential People in the World, TIME mag., 2010. Office: McChrystal Group LLC 333 N Fairfax St Ste 100 Alexandria VA 22314 Office Phone: 571-312-8637.

MCCLAIN, EDWARD B. (E.B. MCCLAIN), former state senator; b. Jefferson County, Ala., Apr. 29, 1940; m. Eloise Saunders; children: Edward, Jr, Kevin, Kim, April. BS, Miles Coll., Fairfield, Ala. Chief chemist Koppers Co., Inc., 1963—; safety & environ. engr.; rep., dist. 57 Ala. House of Reps., Montgomery, 1987—94; senator, dist. 19 Ala. State Senate, Montgomery, 1995—2009. Mem. Brighton Parent-Teacher Assn., Mason, Bessemer Voter's League, Ala. Dem. Conf., Jefferson County Citizens Coalition. Democrat. Baptist.

MCCLAIN, KATRINA, retired professional basketball player; b. Charleston, SC; children: Malachi, Emmanuel, Genesis. B, U. Ga., Athens, 1987. Profl. basketball player Kyoto Petroleum, Japan, 1989—91, Sidis Ancona, Italy, 1992, Valencia, Spain, 1993—95, Galatasaray, Turkey, 1995—96, Atlanta Glory, American Basketball League. Mem. US nat. team FIBA World Championships, Moscow, 1986, Malaysia, 1990, Sydney, 1994, Summer Olympic Games, Seoul, 1988, Barcelona, 1992, Atlanta, 1996. Founder The Katrina McClain Found. Recipient Gold medal, FIBA World Championships, 1986, 1990, Bronze medal, 1994, Gold medal, women's basketball, Summer Olympic Games, 1988, 1996, Bronze medal, women's basketball, 1992; named Nat. Player of Yr., Women's Basketball Coaches Assn., 1987, Female Athlete of Yr., USA Basketball, 1988, 1992; named to Women's Basketball Hall of Fame, 2006, Naismith Meml. Basketball Hall of Fame, 2012. Office: The Katrina McClain Foundation PO Box 40893 Charleston SC 29416*

MCCLAIN, PAULA DENICE, political scientist, educator; b. Louisville, Jan. 3, 1950; d. Robert Landis and Mabel (Molock) McC.; stepdau. of Annette Williams McClain; m. Paul C. Jacobson, Jan. 30, 1988; children: Kristina L., Jessica A. BA, Howard U., Washington, 1972; MA, Howard U., 1974, PhD, 1977; postgrad., U. Pa., 1981—82. Asst. prof. dept. polit. sci. U. Wis., Milw., 1977-82; assoc. prof. and prof. pub. affairs Ariz. State U., Tempe, 1982-91; prof. govt. and fgn. affairs U. Va., Charlottesville, 1991-2000, chair govt. and fgn. affairs, 1994-97; prof. dept. polit. sci. Duke U., Durham, NC, 2000—. Co-author: Can We All Get Along? Racial and Ethnic Minorities in American Politics, 1995, 4th edit. 2006, 5th 2010, American Goverment in Black and White, 2010, Race, Place and Risk: Black Homicide in Urban America, 1990; editor: Minority Group Influence, 1993; co-editor: Urban Minority Administrators, 1988. Mem. Nat. Conf. Black Polit. Scientists (pres. 1989-90), Am. Polit. Sci. Assn. (exec. coun. 1985-87, v.p. 1993-94), So. Polit. Sci. Assn. (exec. coun. 1992-95, v.p. 2002-03, pres. elect 2004, pres. 2005), Internat. Polit. Sci. Assn. (exec. com. 1997-2003, v.p. 1997-2003), Midwest Polit. Sci. Assn. (v.p. 2002-04). Office: Duke U Dept Polit Sci Perkins Libr PO Box 90204 Durham NC 27708-0204 Office Phone: 919-660-4303. E-mail: pmcclain@duke.edu.

MCCLAIN, TIM S., lawyer; b. 1948; m. Lynn Hollyfield; children: Scott, Brendan. Grad., U.S. Naval Acad., 1970; JD, Calif. We. Sch. Law, San Diego, 1978. Bar: Calif., DC, US Supreme Ct. Commd. Navy JAG Corps USN, ret., 1990, mil. def. counsel Navy Legal Svc. Office San Diego, head claims officer Navy Legal Svc. Office, head legal assistance officer Navy Legal Svc. Office, staff judge adv. for the commanding officer Naval Air Station Miramar, 1981—83, dept. head, instr. Naval Justice Sch. Newport, RI, 1981—86, gen. court-martial mil. judge Navy-Marine Trial Judiciary, S.W., 1986—90; with litigation law firm, San Diego, 1990—96; joined internat. mgmt. cons. firm, dir. opers., 1996—99; pvt. practice Principi and McClain, La Jolla, Calif., 1999—2001; gen. counsel US Dept. Vets. Affairs, Washington, 2001—06, acting asst. sec. for human resources & adminstrn., 2004; mem. Womble Carlyle Sandridge & Rice PLLC, Washington, 2007—; CFO, chief procurement exec., agency environ. exec. Vets. Affairs, 2005; pres., CEO Humana, Inc., 2009—. Office: Humana Inc 500 W Main St Louisville KY 40202 Office Phone: 502-580-1000. Office Fax: 502-580-3639. Business E-Mail: tmcclain@humana.com.

MCCLAMMY, THAD C., state legislator; b. Monroe County, Ala., Oct. 22, 1942; s. Thad C. and Ukla Maye McClammy; m. Patricia Larkin; children: Patrice, Christopher. Attended, Tuskegee Inst., 1959—60; BA, Alabama State U., 1966, Auburn U., Montgomery, MS in Vocat. and Adult Edn.; LLD (hon.), Selma U., Ala. Real estate officer, Montgomery, Ala., 1967—69; self employed real estate broker & developer, 1970—73; classification officer State of Ala., 1973—74; instr. Trenholm State Tech. Coll., 1974—, pres., 1981—95; mem. Dist. 76 Ala. House of Reps., Montgomery, 1995—. Nat. fin. sec. Tots & Teens, Inc.; mem. Ala. Dem. Conf., Montgomery Dem. Conf. Mem.: NEA, Southern Placement Coun, Ala. Edn. Assn., Montgomery Dem. Club, Montgomery Lion's Club, Iota Lambda Sigma, Omega Psi Phi. Democrat. Baptist. Office: 858 W South Blvd Montgomery AL 36105 also: Ala House of Reps Ala State House 11 S Union St Rm 525-D Montgomery AL 36130 Office Phone: 334-284-1769, 334-242-7780. Business E-Mail: thadmcclammy@bellsouth.net.

MCCLANAHAN, DAVID M., energy executive; B in Math., U. Tex.; MBA, U. Houston. Various exec. capacities Reliant Energy, Inc., 1986—; pres., COO electric utility divsn. Reliant Energy HL&P, 1997—99; pres., COO delivery group Reliant Energy, Inc., 1999—2000, vice-chmn., 2000—02; pres., CEO, dir. CenterPoint Energy, Inc., Houston, 2002—. Chmn. bd. dirs. ERCOT; bd. dirs. Edison Electric Inst., Am. Gas Assn., Interstate Natural Gas Assn. Am. Chmn. bd. Univ. St. Thomas. Office: CenterPoint Energy PO Box 4567 Houston TX 77210-4567

MCCLANAHAN, ELIZABETH A., state supreme court justice; m. Byrum Geisler; 2 children. Grad. in govt. and sociology, Coll. William & Mary, Williamsburg, Va., 1981; law degree, U. Dayton, Ohio, 1984. Ptnr. Penn, Stuart and Eskridge, Abingdon, Va.; chief dep. atty. gen. Va. Atty. General's Office; judge Va. Ct. Appeals, 2003—11; assoc. justice Va. Supreme Ct., Richmond, 2011—. Vice rector bd. visitors Coll. William & Mary. Recipient Tribute to Women Award for Vol. Cmty. Svc., YMCA, Alumni Award, Va. 4-H Found. Office: Virginia Supreme Ct PO Box 1315 100 N Ninth St Richmond VA 23219-1315

MCCLANAHAN, LELAND, university director; b. Hammond, Ind., Mar. 14, 1931; s. Alonzo Leland and Eva (Hermanson) McC.; m. Lavaughn Adell Meyrer, June 5, 1954; children: Lindel, Loren. Diploma, Ctrl. Bible Coll., Springfield, Mo., 1954; BA, Southwestern Coll., Chula Vista, Calif., 1973; MA, Fla. State Christian Coll., Kissimee, Fla., 1964; PhBB, Nat. Postgrad. Bible Acad., 1969; ThD, Fla. State Christian Coll., Kissimee, Fla., 1970; PhD, Faith Bible Coll. and Sem., Ft. Lauderdale, Fla. and Marina, Lagos, Nigeria, 1969; MA, Bapt. Christian U., Shreveport, La., 1988; PhD, Freedom U., 1989; ThD, Bapt. Christian U., Shreveport, La., 1989, DLitt (hon.), 1990, PsyD, 1981; PhD, Hawaii U., 1995; DEd, Bapt. Christian U., Shreveport, La., 1992, D in Bus. Adminstrn., 1993; DD (hon.), Internat. Evangelism Crusades, 1969, Trinity Union Coll., 1991; LLD, La. Bapt. U., 1994; StD, PhD, Trinity Internat. U., 1994; HHD (hon.), La. Bapt. U., 1995; LittD (hon.), Cambridge Theol. Sem., 1995; PhD, LittD, PsyD, DBA, LLD, EdD, U. Hawaii, 1995; LittD (hon.), Messianic Coll. Rabbinical Studies; MA, Am. Bible Coll. & Sem., 1998; MDiv, Chapel Christian U., 1991; PhD in Bibl. Health, Chapel Christian U., Merritt Island, Fla., 2006, PhD in Bibl. Health, 2008, PhD in Bibl. Sci., 2011; PhD, Midwestern U., 1998; D in Min., Am. Bible Coll. and Sem., 1999; PhD, Gulf Coast Coll. and Seminary, 2005; MBD; D in Bibl. Medicine, Chapel Christian U., 2011. Diplomate Nat. Bd. Christian Clin. Therapists; ordained pastor, Christian Ch., 1950. Founder, pastor Evangel Temple, Griffith, Ind., 1954-73, Abundant Life Temple, Cocoa, Fla., 1974-77; mgr. ins. divsn. United Agys., Cocoa, Fla., 1979-81; assoc. pastor Merritt Assembly of God, Merritt Island, Fla., 1982-85, Palm Chapel, Merritt Island, 1987-89, 1990-93; founder Hawaii U., Merritt Island Offices, Merritt Island, Fla., 1990-97; chancellor Hawaii U. Merritt Island Offices, 1995-97; dir. Fla. Hawaii U. Schs., 1994-97; dir., founder Chapel Christian U., Merritt Island, Fla., 1990—; founder People's Ch. Internat., Inc., 2000—. Founder, dir. Griffith Youth Ctr., 1960-70, Todd Nursery Sch., Griffith, 1971-73; founder, chancellor Ind. Bible Coll., Griffith, 1971-73; dir. Chapel Counseling Ctr., Merritt Island, 1990-94; nat. accreditation com. Hawaii U.; founder, pres. Brevard Humanity Ctr., Inc., 2002; founder Mini Job Link, 2002, Adult Edn., 2003, pres. commn., 2008, Nat. Senatorial Com., 2008. Author: Is Divine Healing For Today? 1989, 2013, Truths From the Book of St. John, 1991, An Outline of the Revelation, 1993, Numbers in the Bible, 1994, An Outline of the Acts of the Apostle, 1995, An Outline of the Book of Proverbs, 2000, How to Feel Better and Live Longer, 2006, An Outline of the Book of Isaiah, An Outline of the Book of Psalms, 2010-2011, An Outline of the Book of Propet Isaiah, 2011; author 144 coll. courses and books. Recipient Disting. Svc. award US Jaycees, 1966, Govs.'s Points of Light award, Fla., 2003, Congl. Order of Merit award, 2004, 06, 07; named Hon. Lt. Col., Gov. Guy Hunt, 1988, Archbishop, Hierarchical Christ Ch., 2000, Rep. Presdl. Honor Roll, 2005, Nat. Congl. Com., 2005, Humanitarian the Yr. Conscious Living Partnership, 2007, Presdl. Commn. Art award, 2008. Fellow Am. Biog. Inst. (life); mem. Internat. Platform Assn., Order of Internat. Fellowship (life), Am. Inst. Clin. Psychotherapists, Am. Assn. christian Counselors, Nat. Christian Counseling Assn. (assoc., lic.), Internat. Assn. Pastoral Psychologists (lic.), Order of St. John, Knight of Malta (comdr. 1990), Angel Soc. Republican. Avocations: reading, walking, watching sports, watching television adventures, weightlifting. Office: Chapel Christian Univ 870 Australian St Merritt Island FL 32953-4676 Office Phone: 321-633-7008, 321-338-2537. Office Fax: 321-338-2537. Personal E-mail: mcclanahanleland15@yahoo.com.

MCCLANE, ROBERT SANFORD, entrepreneur, bank executive; b. Kenedy, Tex., May 5, 1939; s. Norris Robert and Ella Addie (Stockton) McC.; m. Sue Nitschke, Mar. 31, 1968; children: Len Stokes McClane Brown, Norris Robert. BS in Bus. Adminstrn., Trinity U., San Antonio, 1961. With Ford Motor Co., Detroit, 1961-62; with Frost Nat. Bank, San Antonio, 1962-97; exec. v.p. Cullen/Frost Bankers, Inc., 1976—85, pres., 1985-97, dir., 1985—2010, Benefit Planners, Inc., 1997-2001; advisor, dir. Ellison Grandchildren Trust, 1996—2009; pres., owner McClane Ptnrs., LLC, 1997—; dir., vice chmn. Tobin Internat., 1998—2003. Bd. dirs. Frost Nat. Bank, San Antonio, 1987-2010, Princeton eCom., 1999-2006, CCI Telecom, Inc., 2004-06, CareNet, 2005—. Crusade chmn. Bexar County chpt. Am. Cancer Soc., 1974; bd. dirs. Bexar County ARC, 1969-72; sr. warden St. Luke's Episopal Ch., San Antonio, 1980; trustee Alamo Pub. Telecomms. Coun., San Antonio, 1981-88; chmn. San Antonio Econ. Devel. Found., 1987-89, exec. com. 1985-91; bd. trustees Trinity U., 1990—, chmn., 2001-04 Mem. Greater San Antonio C. of C. (chmn. leadership San Antonio 1975-76, bd. dirs. exec. com. 1994-97, chmn. 1996), Trinity U. Alumni Assn. (pres. 1968-69, disting. alumnus 1987), Free Trade Alliance San Antonio (bd. dirs., 1997—, chmn. 1998-2000), Southwest Rsch. Inst. (trustee 1997—), San Antonio German Club, Order Alamo, Tex. Cavaliers, Argyle Club, Club Giraud, Plaza Club (bd. dirs. 1973-92). Episcopalian. Office Phone: 210-220-5353.

MCCLARD, JACK EDWARD, lawyer; b. Lafayette, La., May 13, 1946; s. Lee Franklin and Mercedes Cecile (Landry) McClard; m. Marilyn Kay O'Gorman, June 3, 1972; 1 child, Lauren Minton. BA in History, Rice U., 1968; JD, U. Tex., 1974. Bar: Va. 1974, U.S. Dist. Ct. (ea. and we. dists.) Va. 1974, U.S. Ct. Appeals (4th cir.) 1978, DC 1981, U.S. Dist. Ct. DC 1981, U.S. Ct. Appeals (DC cir.) 1981, N.Y. 1985, U.S. Dist. Ct. (so. and ea. dists.) N.Y. 1985, U.S. Ct. Appeals (5th cir.) 1993, Tex. 1996, U.S. Dist. Ct. (ea. dist.) Tex. 1998, U.S. Ct. Appeals (7th cir.) 2001. Assoc. Hunton & Williams, Richmond, Va., 1974-81, ptnr., 1981—2006, sr. counsel, 2006—. Contbr. articles to profl. jours., chapters to books. Served to lt. (j.g.) USN, 1968—71. Mem.: Lewis F. Powell, Jr. Inns Ct. (exec. com. 2003—07), 5th Cir. Bar, Richmond Bar Assn. Democrat. Episcopalian. Avocations: bridge, gardening, wine. Home: 100 Trowbridge Rd Richmond VA 23238 Office: Hunton and Williams Riverfront Plz E Tower 951 E Byrd St Richmond VA 23219-4074 Home Phone: 804-740-0898; Office Phone: 804-788-8490. Business E-Mail: jmcclard@hunton.com.

MCCLELLAN, JENNIFER L., state legislator; b. Petersburg, Va., Dec. 28, 1972; State del. Dist. 71, Va., 2006—; mem. Edn. Com., Commerce & Labor Com., 2006—; house del. Va. Recipient Servant Leadership award, Leadership Metro Richmond, 2005. Mem.: Delta Sigma Theta, Sorensen Ins. Polit. Leadership (statewide vice chair bd.), Fan Dist. Assn., Va. State Bar (past chair, corp. counsel sect., past pres. young lawyer conf.), Va. Alliance of Boys & Girls Clubs. Democrat. Presbyterian. Office: PO Box 406 Richmond VA 23218 Home Phone: 804-340-2629; Office Phone: 804-698-1171. Business E-Mail: DelJMcClellan@house.state.va.us.

MCCLELLAN, SCOTT, consulting company executive, former White House press secretary; b. Austin, Tex., Feb. 14, 1968; s. Barr McClellan and Carole Keeton Strayhorn; m. Jill Martinez, Nov. 2003. BA, U. Tex., Austin, 1991. Campaign mgr., Carole Keeton Strayhorn Tex. Comptroller, 1998; dep. comm. dir. to Gov. State of Tex., 1999—2000; traveling press sec. Bush-Cheney Presdl. Campaign, 2000; dep. press sec. The White House, Washington, DC, 2001—03, asst. to Pres., press sec., 2003—06; sr. v.p., corp. & govt. affairs HHB, Inc., Washington, 2007—. Mem., Internat. Advisory Coun. APCO Worldwide, 2008—. Author: What Happened: Inside the Bush White House and What's Wrong with Washington, 2008. Recipient Outstanding Young Tex. Ex Award, 2005. Independent. Office: HHB Inc 816 Connecticut Ave 5th Fl Washington DC 20006 Home Phone: 202-783-3232.

MCCLELLAND, CHARLES A., JR., police chief; b. Center, Tex. 2 children. BS in Criminology, U. Houston, MA in Sociology; grad., FBI Nat. Acad. Joined Houston Police Dept., Tex., 1977, patrol officer Tex., 1977, asst. chief of police Tex., 1998, exec. asst. chief of police Tex., head Investigative Ops. Command Tex., acting chief Tex., police chief Tex., 2010—. Office: Houston Police Department 1200 Travis St Houston TX 77002 Office Phone: 713-308-3200.

MCCLELLAND, JAMES RAY, lawyer; b. Eunice, La., June 21, 1946; s. Rufus Ray and Homer Florene (Nunn) McClelland; m. Sandra Faye Tate, Feb. 6, 1971; children: Joseph Ray, Jeffrey Ross. BS, La. State U., 1969, MBA, 1971, JD, 1975. Bar: La. 1975, US Ct. Appeals (5th cir.) 1976, US Dist. Ct. (ea. dist.) La. 1976, US Dist. Ct. (we. dist.) La. 1976, US Dist. Ct. (mid. dist.) La. 1994. Assoc. Aycock, Horne & Coleman, Franklin, La., 1975—78, ptnr., 1978—. Bd. dirs. Bayou Bouillon Corp., Cotten Land Corp. Exec. com. Dem. Party; del. La. Dem. Party, 1982, 1984; Exec. com. St. Mary Parish, 1980—88. Mem.: St. Mary Parish Bar Assn. (pres. 1978—79), La. State Bar Assn. (ho. of dels. 1982—95, law reform com. 1984—86, bd. govs. 1995—2002, ho. of dels. 1998—99, sec. 2003—05), Rotary (pres. 1981—82), Order of Coif. Home: PO Box 268 Franklin LA 70538-0268 Office: PO Box 592 Franklin LA 70538-0592 Office Phone: 337-828-1880.

MCCLELLAND, ROBERT NELSON, surgeon, educator; b. Gilmer, Tex., Nov. 20, 1929; s. Robert Hilton and Verna Louise (Nelson) McC.; m. Connie Logan, May 5, 1958; children: Robert Christopher, Alison, Julie. BA, U. Tex., Austin, 1952; MD, U. Tex., Galveston, 1954. Diplomate Am. Bd. Surgery. Rotating intern U. Kans. Med. center, 1954-55; resident in gen. surgery Parkland Hosp., Dallas, 1957-59, 60-62; instr. surgery Southwestern Med. Sch., U. Tex., Dallas, 1962-63, asst. prof., 1963-67, asso. prof., 1967-71, prof., 1971—, Alvin Baldwin prof. surgery, 1977—. Examiner Nat. Bd. Med. Examiners Editor Audio Jour. Rev. Gen. Surgery, 1971-82, Selected Readings in Gen. Surgery, 1974—2005; contbr. numerous articles to profl. jours., chpts. to books. Served to capt. M.C. USAF, 1955-57. Fellow ACS (mem. grad. edn. com.); mem. AMA, Am. Surg. Assn., Western Surg. Assn., Soc. Surgery of Alimentary Tract, Am. Gastroent. Assn., Southwestern Surg. Soc., So. Surg. Assn., Dallas Soc. Gen. Surgeons (pres. 1987-88), Tex. Surg. Soc., Tex. Med. Assn., Dallas County Med. Soc., Soc. Internatale de Chiurgie (bd. dirs. Am. chpt.), Phi Beta Kappa, Alpha Omega Alpha. Republican. Methodist. Office: 5323 Harry Hines Blvd Dallas TX 75390-7208 Business E-Mail: surgprof@aol.com.

MCCLENDON, JIM, state legislator; b. Mobile, Ala., Jan. 10, 1943; m. Ellen Tate; children: Lara, Molly. BS, Birmingham So. Coll., 1965; OD, U. Houston, 1967. Pvt. practice optometrist, 1971—2002; asst. prof. optometry U. Ala. Birmingham, 1971—78; mem. Dist. 50 Ala. House of Reps., Montgomery, 2002—. Founding dir. Davis Lake Fire Dept.; mem. First United Meth. Ch., Springville. Served with Med. Svc. Corp USN, 1968—71, Vietnam. Republican. Methodist. Office: 361 Jones Rd Springville AL 35146 Mailing: Ala House of Reps Ala State House 11 S Union St Rm 527-C Montgomery AL 36130 Office Phone: 334-242-7749.

MCCLENDON, RUTH JONES, state legislator; m. Denver McClendon; 4 children. B, Tex. So. U., Houston, LHD (hon.), 2010; MA, Webster U., St. Louis; PhD (hon.), Guadalupe Coll. Theol. Sem.; A (hon.), St. Philip's Coll. Unit. dir. Bexar County juvenile probation dept. Juvenile Justice System, Tex.; city councilwoman, mayor pro tempore San Antonio, 1993—96; founder Cmty. Crime Prevention Network, Inc.; pres., CEO RJMcClendon and Co.; former chairwoman City Planning Comm., San Antonio, Greater San Antonio Crime Prevention Commn.; former mem. Tex. Dem. Exec. Com.; mem. Dist. 120 Tex. House of Representatives, 1996—. Mem. bd. dirs. Crimestoppers, Carver Cmty. Culture Ctr., Children's Mus.,

Bexar County Housing Fin. Corp. & Cellular Patrol. Recipient Women Who Make A Difference award, Internat. Women's Forum Global Conf., and several others; named to San Antonio Women's Hall Fame. Mem.: Nat. Coalition 100 Black Women (founder, former pres.). Democrat. Roman Catholic. Office: 403 South WW White Rd San Antonio TX 78219 also: Room CAP 3S.02 Capitol PO Box 2910 Austin TX 78768 Office Phone: 210-225-2107, 512-463-0708.

MC CLENDON, WILLIAM HUTCHINSON, III, retired lawyer; b. New Orleans, Feb. 19, 1933; s. William H. and Eleanor (Eaton) McC.; m. Eugenia Mills Slaughter, Feb. 6, 1960; children: William Hutchinson, IV, Virginia Morris, Eleanor Eaton, Bryan Slaughter. BA, Tulane U., 1956, LLB, 1958. Bar: La. 1958, US Supreme Ct. 1964. Atty. Humble Oil & Refining Co., 1958-60; with firm Taylor, Porter, Brooks & Phillips, Baton Rouge, 1960—, ptnr., 1966-2001, mem. exec. com., 1987-2001; mediator, assoc. Mediation Arbitration Profl. Sys., Inc., 1999—2001. Instr. comml. law and negotiable instruments Am. Inst. Banking, 1963-74; lectr. movable Property La. Bar Assn. Bridging the Gap Inst., 1965; lectr. La. State U. LAw Sch. and Real Estate Seminar chmn., 1972, 74, 76, 80, 82, 85, 87, 95, La. Soc. of Profl. Surveying, 1989, La. Soc. CPA's, 1991, Banking Seminar, 1995; adj. prof. La. State U. Legal Negotiation, 1983—, U. Tenn., 2003-2008, Western Carolina U., 2003-10; mem. faculty Profl. Edn. Group, Inc. Author: Deal Makers: Negotiating More Effectively Using Timeless Values, 2011, Professionalism Seminar, La. State Legislature, 2013; Contbr. articles to legal jour. Bd. dir. Cancer Soc. Baton Rouge, 1968-71; trustee Episcopal HS, 1976-78; mem. Dean's council Tulane U. Law Sch., 1984-88. Served to capt. AUS. Recipient Preservation award Found. for Hist. La., 1997 Mem. ABA, Am. Judicature Soc., La. Bar Assn. (chmn. sect. trust estates, probate and immovable property law 1969-70, Meml. award article 1987), Baton Rouge Bar Assn. (chmn. title standards com. 1968-69), Tulane Alumni Assn. Greater Baton Rouge (pres. 1968-69), Baton Rouge Green (bd. dir. 1991-93), Hilltop Aboretum (bd. dir. 1993-95), La. Civil Svc. League (pres. 1992-94), La. Tulane Law Alumni (treas., 2d v.p. 1964-65), Baton Rouge Assembly (treas. 1983, ball chmn. 1997, chmn. 1999), Toastmasters (pres. 1970), Pickwick Club, Rotary (bd. dir. Baton Rouge club 1972), Kappa Alpha, Baton Rouge Symphony (bd. dir. 2001-02). Republican. Episcopalian (vestry, sr. warden 1975, 81, 84, diocesan standing com. 1985-89). Mailing: 5844 Creekside Ave Saint Francisville LA 70775

MCCLINTON, DONALD GEORGE, retired diversified holding company executive; b. Pitts., June 30, 1933; s. Donald K. and Ethel M. McC.; m. Jane Ann Knoebel, Apr. 12, 1958; children: Catherine, D. Scott. BS, Miami U., Oxford, Ohio, 1955. Audit mgr. Arthur Andersen & Co., Cleve., 1955-62; mgr. accounting E. Ohio Gas Co., Cleve., 1962-66; exec. v.p. Nat. Industries, Inc., Louisville, 1966-79; pres. Yellow Cab Co., Louisville, 1979-94; owner, chmn. bd. Interlock Industries, Inc., 1982-94; pres. Skylight Thoroughbred Tng. Ctr., Inc., 1994—2002. Bd. dirs. Almost Framily, 1996—, Clifton Ctr., MidAm. Bancorp, 1980—2002; trustee Jewish Hosp. Health Care Systems, Inc., 1983—2004, 2006—12. Mem. Louisville-Jefferson County Bicentennial Commn., 1976-77; mem. coun., treas. Old Kentucky Home. coun. Boy Scouts Am., 1976-94; mem. Citizens at Large Jefferson County Budget Com., 1978-84; bd. overseers Bellarmine Coll., 1978-84; bd. dirs. Ky. Derby Festival, 1978—, Jewish Hosp., Louisville, 1978-83; trustee Spalding U., 1985-91. Mem.: Fin. Execs. Inst.

MCCLINTON, JAMES LEROY, city administrator; b. Longview, Wash., Oct. 14, 1949; s. James Delmer and Norma Jean (Ammons) McC.; m. Carmen Lassaphine Amador, Nov. 7, 1983; children: James Andrew, Ian Tyler, Kevin Riley. AA, SUNY, Albany, 1973; BA, Upper Iowa U., 1974; MA, Calif. State U., Carson, 1984; PhD, Calif. Coast U., 1985. Cert. mgr. Inst. Cert. Profl. Mgrs. With USCG, 1967-89, commd. officer, 1981-83, advanced through grades to comdr., 1987, ret., 1989; bur. mgr. adminstrv. svcs. Charleston (S.C.) County Sheriff's Office, 1989—2003; chief dep. clk. of ct. Berkeley County, SC, 2003—; dir. fin. and planning IT Dept. Coll. Charleston, 2007—. Spkr. pro tem S.C. Criminal Justice Acad., Columbia, 1989—; mem. auditor selection com. Charleston County Govt., 1989—, computer users action com., 1989—; mem. various coms. County Govt. and Sheriff's Office, Charleston, 1989—; chief dep. clerk of ct. Berkeley County, S.C., 2003-, dir. fin. and planning, Info. and Tech. Coll. Charleston, 2007-. Editor: (newsletter) The Badge, 1989—; author: Pawprints in Heaven, —; contbr. articles to profl. jours. and mags.; newspaper columnist. Mem. Charleston Police Pipes and Drums, 1994—; grad. Leadership S.C., 1993, Leadership Charleston, 1997. With USCG, 1989, Vietnam. Recipient Achievement award Nat. Assn. Counties, Washington, 1993, 96, Golden Pen award The Post and Courier Newspaper, Charleston, 1996. Mem. ASPA, SC Law Enforcement Officers Assn., Rotary Internat. (bd. dirs. North Charleston), Nat. Assn. Count Mgrs., SC Assn. Countywide Elected Execs., SC Assn. Clerks of Ct. Republican. Avocations: bagpipes, writing. Office Phone: 843-953-3989. Personal E-mail: ag4nm@comcast.net. Business E-Mail: mcclintonj@cofc.edu.

MCCLOUD, MELODY T., obstetrician, gynecologist, surgeon, media consultant, health care strategist; BA, Boston U., 1977, MD, 1981. Intern Emory U. Affiliated Hosps., Atlanta, 1981-82, resident in ob-gyn., 1982-85; pres., founder, med. dir. Atlanta Women's Health Care, Coll. Women's, 1985—; founder McCloud Renaissance LLC, 2008—; health expert Tom Joyner Morning Show, 2010—; intern Emory U. Bd. Visitors; staff physician Emory U. Hosp. Midtown. Bd. dirs. Vis. Nurses Health Sys., Atlanta; spkr. Nat. Dental Assn.-Atlanta Bus. League, 1995, Speaking of Women's Health, Universal Sisters, Nat. Coalition 100 Black Women, Congl. Black Caucus-Women, others; cons. health WXIA-TV, Atlanta, 1995, 99; owner McCloud Renaissance, LLC, pres., med. editor Nat. Orgn. African-Am. Women Author: Medical Bloopers!! Amusing, Amazing Stories, 1994, The Health Diary for Women, 1999, Blessed Health, 2003, Melodies of the Heart, 2004, Living Well, Despite Catching Hell, 2010; med. advisor Body and Soul, 1994; author: First Do No Harm, 2013. Med. support group Com. Olympic Games, Atlanta, 1996; blogger, Psychology Today 1992, health care heroes physician, Atlanta Bus. Chronicle, 2012 Inductee Leadership Atlanta, YWCA Acad. for Women Achievers; named Bus. Woman of Yr. Am. Bus. Women's Assn., Atlanta's Top 100 Black Women of Influence Atlanta Bus. League, 2008; recipient Cmty. Health Svc. award Black Pages, Health-care Heroes Physician award, Atlanta Bus. Chronicle, 2012, Most Influential Doctor in Atlanta, Black Health Mag., 2012. Mem. Med. Assn. Ga., Ga. Ob-Gyn Soc., Med. Assn. Atlanta, Atlanta Med. Assn., Soc. Laparoendoscopic Surgeons. Baptist. Avocations: tennis, bowling, water sports, theater, travel. Office: Melody T McCloud MD PO Box 344 Roswell GA 30077-0344 Business E-Mail: mtm@DrMcCloud.com.

MCCLOUD, SHELBY L., wholesale distribution executive; V.p., warehouse ops. ScanSource, Inc. Office: ScanSource Inc 6 Logue Ct Greenville SC 29615 Office Phone: 864-288-2432. Office Fax: 864-288-1165.

MCCLUNG, PHIL ORAN, psychology professor; s. Basil McClung Jesse and Virginia Pearl McClung; m. Mary Denise McClung, Sept. 14, 1979; children: Dustin Chad, Donovan Shane. BA in Psychology, W.Va. U., Morgantown, 1970, MS in Indsl. Rels., 1974, EdD, 1993. Cert. counselor NBCC, 1984, lic. practical counselor W.Va. Bd. Examiners Counseling, 1988. Dir. W.Va. U., 1970—90, prof., 1970—2007. Cons. W.Va. U. Mgmt. Inst., Parkersburg, 1975—2007; adj. prof. Marshall U. Grad. Sch., Charleston, W.Va., 2000—03. Author: (books) Desulfurization Technology, 1975, Potential Waste Products from Coal, 1975. Bd. mem. Sharpe Hosp., Weston, W.Va., 2000—07, W.Va. Alliance Mentally Ill, Charleston, 2000—07, Transitional Living Facility, Weston, 2007. Recipient Outstanding Staff Support Person award, W.Va. UP Student Body, 1976—77, 1980, W.Va. Prof. of Yr. award, Nat. Merit Found., 2007, Prof. of Yr. award, W.Va. UP Student Body, 2006; named APA Small Coll. Prof. of Yr., 2010, CASE W.Va. Prof. of Yr., 2011, Bennie McDonough Outstanding Prof., 2012; finalist W.Va. Prof. of Yr. award, Nat. Merit Found., 2006. Mem.: W.Va. Career Counseling Assn. (assoc.; pres. 1979—80), W.Va. Alliance Mentally Ill (assoc.; dir. 2000—07). Democrat-Npl. Achievements include development of an environmental psychology program. Avocations: tennis, volleyball, golf, badminton, table tennis. Home: 136 Whispering Pines Rd Davisville WV 26142 Office: WVa Univ 300 Campus Dr Parkersburg WV 26104 Office Phone: 304-424-8268. Office Fax: 304-424-8315; Home Fax: 304-424-8315. Personal E-mail: philwvup@gmail.com. Business E-Mail: phil.mcclung@mail.wvu.edu.

MCCLURE, CHARLES RICHARD, retired school system administrator; b. Morgantown, W.Va., Apr. 8, 1935; s. C.W. and Alta M. (Cale) McClure; m. Shirley Pat Tallman McClure, July 11, 1964; children: Marilyn, Scott, Mary, Marlin. BA, W.Va. U., 1957, MA, 1960. Tchr. Preston County Schs., W.Va., 1957—60, supr., pers. dir. fed. programs, 1960—67; program coord. North Ctrl. W.Va., Dept. Edn., 1967—73; adminstrv. asst. Harrison County Schs., Clarksburg, W.Va., 1974, supt., 1974—98; ret., 1998. Mem. exec. bd. Harrison County United Way. Contbr. scientific papers. With 197th tank W.Va. Nat. Guard, 1953—56, with 249th army band, 1956—67. Mem.: Clarksburg C. of C. (edn. com.), W.Va. Assn. Supervision & Curriculum Devel., W.Va. Sch. Bd. Assn., W.Va. U. Alumni Assn., W.Va. Assn. Sch. Adminstrs., Nat. Assn. Supervision & Curriculum Devel., Nat. Sch. Bd. Assn., Am. Assn. Sch. Adminstrs. (Svc. award 1979), Shriners, Masons, Kingwood Rotary, Clarksburg Elks Club, W.Va. Univ. Emeritus Club, Clarksburg Lions, Phi Mu Alpha Sinfonia, Phi Delta Kappa. Home: 402 James St Bridgeport WV 26330-1336

MCCLURE, CHARLES ROBERT, library and information science educator, consultant; b. Syracuse, NY, May 24, 1949; s. Robert C. and Doris C. (Gordon) McC.; m. Victoria A. Jones, Dec. 30, 1971; 1 child, Gwendolyn A. BA in Spanish, Okla. State U., 1971, MA in History, 1972; MLS, U. Okla., 1973; PhD in Info. Studies, Rutgers U., 1977. Head govt.-history dept. U. Tex. Libr., El Paso, 1972-73; instr. Sch. Libr. and Info. Scis., Rutgers U., New Brunswick, NJ, 1974-76; prof. Sch. Libr. and Info. Scis., U. Okla., Norman, 1977-86, Sch. Info. Studies, Syracuse U., 1986—94, disting. prof., 1994—99; pres. Info. Mgmt. Cons. Svcs. Inc., 1986—; Francis Eppes prof. info. studies Coll. Info., Fla. State U., Tallahassee, 1999—, dir. Info. Use Mgmt. and Policy Inst. Cons. US Govt. Printing Office, Washington, 1989-90, US Congress Office Tech. Assessment, Washington, 1990-91; assoc. Rsch. Librs., NC State Libr., Am. Libr. Assn., 2005, Cornell U. Libr., 2007. Author: Federal Information Policies in the 1980s, 1988 (Best Book of Yr. Am. Soc. Info. Sci.), Public Access to Government Information, 1989, Stats. and Performance Measures for Pub. Librs., Evaluating Networked Svcs., 2002, Librs. Connect Cmtys., 2007, Pub. Libr. Svc. Roles, 2008. Named Disting. Rschr. Nat. Commn. Librs. and Info. Sci., 1993, Disting. Prof. Syracuse U., 1996, Francis Eppes Prof. Fla. State U., 1999 Mem. ALA (cons. 1986-), Am. Soc. for Info. Sci., Assn. Libr. and Info. Sci. Educators. Office: Coll Info Fla State U Louis Shores Bldg Rm 226 Tallahassee FL 32306-2100 Office Fax: 850-644-9763.

MCCLURE, DANIEL M., lawyer; b. Enid, Okla., Feb. 5, 1952; s. Larry M. and Marie Dolores (Sarver) McC.; m. Judy Lynn Pinson, Jan. 3, 1976; children: Andrew Mead, Mark William, Kathleen Claire. BA with highest hons., U. Okla., 1974; JD cum laude, Harvard U., 1978. Bar: Tex. 1978, Okla., 2005, Colo., 2006, U.S. Dist. Ct. (so. dist., ea. dist., no. dist. we dist.) Tex. 1979, U.S. Ct. Appeals (5th cir., 10th cir., 11th cir.) 1981, U.S. Supreme Ct., 2003. Assoc. Fulbright & Jaworski, LLP, Houston, 1978-86, ptnr., 1986—. Vice chair exec. com. Inst. Energy Law. Fellow Tex. Bar Found.; mem. ABA, Nat. Health Lawyers Assn., Nat. Assn. R.R. Trial Counsel, Tex. Bar Assn.(cert. civil trial law), Houston Bar Assn., Am. Inns of Ct., Harvard Law Sch. Assn. Avocations: tennis, bicycling. Home: 2 Long Timbers Ln Houston TX 77024-5445 Office: Fulbright & Jaworski LLP 1301 McKinney St Houston TX 77010-3031 Office Phone: 713-651-5151. E-mail: dmcclure@fulbright.com.

MCCLURE, ROGER JOHN, lawyer; b. Cleve., Nov. 22, 1943; s. Theron R. and Colene (Irwin) McClure. BA, Ohio State U., 1965, JD cum laude, 1972; MA, Northwestern U., 1966. Bar: Va. 1973, Md. 1973, U.S. Ct. Appeals (D.C. cir.) 1974, U.S. Supreme Ct. 1978, Ohio, U.S. Ct. Appeals (4th, 5th & 10th cirs.). Asst. atty. gen. State of Ohio, Columbus, 1972; trial atty. FTC, Washington, 1972-76; sr. assoc. Law Offices of A.D. Berkeley, Washington, 1976-81; pvt. practice Alexandria, Va., 1981—; pres. Wash. Wealth Counsellors, McLean, 1987—; del. Va. Gen. Assembly, 1992—2002, co-chmn. militia and police com., 1998—2002; dean Bus. Coll. Nat. Network Estate Planning Attys., 2003—. Adj. prof. Acad. Multidisciplinary Practice Mich. State U., Lansing, 2001—; host talk show Sta. WRC Radio, 1987—93, 1999—2001, Sta. WPGC, 1993—94. Co-author: (book) Winning the Syndication Game, 1988, Advanced Estate Planning in Virginia, 2001, Virginia Elder Law, 1988, Asset Protection in Virginia, 1999, Estate and Wealth Strategies Planning, 2000, Choice of Entity in Virginia, 2000, Business Succession and Sale of Businesses, 2003, (book) Family Limited Partnerships and LLCS, 2005; contbg. reviewer; contbr. articles to profl. jours. Mem. No. Va. Transp. Commn., 2001, commr.; adv. bd. dirs. No. Va. Cmty. Found., 1995—. With US Army, 1967—69. Decorated Bronze Star; fellow Masters, Espertis Peterson Inst., 1996—. Mem.: Dulles Area Transp. Assn. (bd. dirs.), Nat. Network Estate Planning Attys., No. Va. Apt. Assn. (bd. dirs. 1988—92, 1st v.p. 1987—88, pres. 1988—89), D.C. Bar Assn. (real estate steering com. 1982—84, chmn. antitrust divsn. 1975—76), Wolf Trap Found. (adv. coun.). Avocation: sailing. Office: NNEPA 1355 Beverly Rd Ste 225 Mc Lean VA 22101 Mailing: 1355 Beverly Rd Ste 225 Mc Lean VA 22101 E-mail: rmcclure@ix.netcom.com.

MCCLURE, TERI PLUMMER, lawyer, delivery service executive; b. Kansas City, Dec. 31, 1963; m. Roderick McClure; 2 children. BS, BA, Washington U., 1985; JD, Emory U., 1988. Bar: Ga. 1988. Employment counsel United Parcel Service of America, Inc. (UPS), 1995—98, coord. labor and practice group, 1998—2003, mgr. ctrl. Fla. dist., 2003—05, gen. counsel, sr. v.p. legal, compliance & pub. affairs, corp. sec., mgmt. com. mem., 2005—. Bd. dirs. Jr. Achievement Ga., Anne E. Casey Found., UPS Found., Ctr. for Working Families. Mem.: Nat. Employment Law Counsel (mem. coord. com.), State Bar Ga. (mem. labor and employment law sect.), Am. Corp. Counsel Assn., Atlanta Bar Assn. Office: United Parcel Svc Inc 55 Glenlake Pkwy NE Atlanta GA 30328*

MCCLURKIN, MARY SUE, state legislator; b. Feb. 14, 1947; m. Van McClurkin; children: Burt, Ben, Daniel. BS, Huntingdon Coll., Montgomery, Ala.; MA, Auburn U., Ala. Owner McClurkin Enterprises; mem. Dist. 43 Ala. House of Reps., 1998—. Mem. Briarwood Presbyn. Ch.; bd. dirs. Bus. Coun. Ala., Women in Govt. Mem.: Ala. Propane Gas Assn., Columbia Rotary Club. Republican. Presbyterian. Office: 1134 County Services Dr Pelham AL 35124 also: Ala House of Reps Ala State House 11 S Union St Rm 517-D Montgomery AL 36130 Office Phone: 205-620-6610, 334-242-7682. Office Fax: 205-620-6611.

MCCLUSKEY, MARY T., health insurance company executive; grad., MD, St. Louis U. Urgent care physician; residency in internal medicine Jewish Hosp., U. Wash.; internist, med. dir. Bridgeton Health Ctr.; v.p., med. affairs Medpartners Med. Mgmt., Tampa; various sr. med. positions, including nat. med. dir., head, clin. cost mgmt. Aetna, Inc., 1999—2007, sr. regional med. dir., SE region, chief med. officer, NE region, 1999—2007; exec. v.p., chief med. officer Amerigroup Corp., 2007—. Office: Amerigroup Corp 1330 Amerigroup Way Virginia Beach VA 23464 Office Phone: 757-490-6900. Office Fax: 757-518-3600. Business E-Mail: mmccluskey@amerigroupcorp.com.

MCCOLGAN, ELLYN A., former diversified financial services company executive; b. Jersey City, Jan. 16, 1954; BA in Psychology & Social Studies Edn., Montclair State Coll., NJ, 1975; MBA, Harvard U., 1983; LLD (hon.), Babson Coll., 2005. With Shearson Lehman Bros., NYC, 1983, Bank of New Eng., Fidelity Investments, 1990—2007; pres. Fidelity Investments Tax-Exempt Svcs. Co., 1996—2000, Fidelity Investments Instl. Retirement Group, 2000—01, Fidelity Fin. Intermediary Svcs., 2001—02, Fidelity Brokerage Co., 2002—07; pres., distbn. & ops. Fidelity Investments, 2007; pres., COO, Global Wealth Mgmt. Grp. Morgan Stanley, 2008—10. Co-chmn. Securities Industry & Fin. Markets Assn., 2006—07; bd. dirs. Primerica, Inc., 2010—. Trustee Mus. Fine Arts, Boston. Named one of 50 Most Powerful Women in Bus., Fortune mag., 2006—07. Office: Primerica Inc Bd Directors 3120 Breckinridge Blvd Duluth GA 30099 Office Phone: 770-381-1000. Office Fax: 770-564-6110. Business E-Mail: ellyn.mccolgan@primerica.com.

MCCOLL, HUGH LEON, JR., investment company executive, retired bank executive; b. Bennettsville, SC, June 18, 1935; s. Hugh Leon and Frances Pratt (Carroll) McColl; m. Jane Bratton Spratt, Oct. 3, 1959; children: Hugh Leon III, John Spratt, Jane Bratton. BS in Bus. Adminstrn, U. N.C., 1957. Trainee NCNB Nat. Bank, Charlotte, 1959-61, officer, 1961-65, v.p., 1965-68, sr. v.p., 1968, div. exec., 1969, exec. v.p., 1970-73, vice chmn. bd., 1973-74, pres., 1974-83; chmn., pres., CEO Bank of America Corp., Charlotte, NC, 1983—2001, chmn. emeritus, 2001—; co-founder, chmn. The McColl Group LLC, Charlotte, NC, 2001—; founder, chmn. Falfurrias Capital Partners, Charlotte, NC, 2006—. Bd. dir. Sonoco Products Inc., Hartsville, SC. Trustee Heineman Found., Charlotte, 1976—, Queens Coll., Charlotte; bd. visitors Grad. Sch. Bus. U. N.C. at Chapel Hill; chmn. Charlotte Uptown Devel. Corp., 1978-81, 85. 1st lt. USMCR, 1957-59. Named to SC Bus. Hall of Fame, 1999. Mem. Bankers Roundtable (mem. trialateral commn.), Am. Bankers Assn., N.C. Bankers Assn. (pres. 1974). Democrat. Presbyterian. Office: McColl Partners 100 N Tryon St 54th Fl Charlotte NC 28202

MCCOLLAM, MARION ANDRUS, consulting firm executive, educator; b. New Orleans, Feb. 8, 1931; d. Gerald Louis and Lucile Gordon (Isacks) Andrus; m. Andrew McCollam, Jr., Jan. 29, 1955 (div. 1978); children: Andrew III, Gerald Andrus, Marion Cage. BS in Engring., Tulane U., 1952; M. Urban and Reg. Planning, U. New Orleans, 1978. Human affairs coord. Office of the Mayor, City of New Orleans, 1978, arts coord., 1978-80; dir. planning, prin. cons. Duncan Plaza Design Project, New Orleans, 1978-80; dir. planning Downtown Devel. Dist., New Orleans, 1980-81; pres. Andrus and Roberts Inc., Phoenix, New Orleans, 1980-84; exec. dir. Arts Coun. New Orleans, 1981-90, Cultural Arts Coun. of Houston and Harris County, 1991-98; pres. McCollam Cons., LLC, 1998—. Adj. instr. Goucher Coll. Master's Program in Arts Adminstrn., 1999—2004, mem. nat. adv. com., 2004—; mem. nat. adv. bd. Tulane U., 2005—12; vice chair Newcomb Art Gallery, 2009—12; cons. in field. Mem. nat. adv. com. Working Capital Fund, Mpls., 1995-99, Nat. Arts Stabilization, Balt., 1998—; adv. panel design Nat. Endowment for the Arts, Washington, 1995, adv. and chair local arts agencies, 1992-94; bd. dirs., sr. fellow Am. Leadership Forum, Houston, 1994-97; mem. cmty. assessment com. United Way of Tex. Gulf Coast, 1995-99; bd. dirs. Urban League of New Orleans, 1984-89; pres. Jr. League of New Orleans, 1969-70. Recipient Arts Adminstr. of Yr. award Arts Mgmt. Inst./Nat. News Svc., 1987, Award for Sustained Mgmt. Excellence, Greater New Orleans Found., 1989. Mem. Am. Inst. Cert. Planners, 1978-, AIA (hon.), Am. Leadership Forum (mem. curriculum com. 2006-12, mem. collaboration pub. edn. com. 2012-), U.S. Urban Arts Fedn. (pres. 1988), Am. for Arts (formerly Nat. Assembly of Local Arts Agencies) (vice chmn. bd. dirs. 1988-94, Chairman's award 1992), Phi Kappa Phi Honor. Soc. Avocations: music, art, reading, travel, photography. Office: 1914 Bissonnet St Houston TX 77005-1645*

MCCOLLOUGH, NEWTON CLARK, III, orthopaedic surgeon; b. Butler, Pa., July 17, 1934; s. Newton C. and Margaret Elizabeth (Mattocks) McC.; m. Mary Eva Semanski, Feb. 22, 1968; children: Peter Scott, Amy Marie. BA, Duke U., 1956; MD, U. Pa., 1959. Diplomate: Am. Bd. Orthopaedic Surgery. Intern Jackson Meml. Hosp., Miami, Fla., 1959-60, resident in orthopaedic surgery, 1960-64; dir. orthopaedic resident edn. Orange Meml. Hosp., Orlando, Fla., 1965-66; asst. prof. orthopaedics and rehab. U. Miami Sch. Medicine, 1968-72, assoc. prof., 1972-76, prof., vice chmn. dept., 1976-78, prof., chmn. dept., 1978-86; dir. rehab. Jackson Meml. Hosp., Miami, 1972-82, chief orthopedics and rehab., 1978-86; dir. med. affairs Internat. Shriners Hosps. Children, Tampa, Fla., 1986-2001, 2001—, mem. med. adv. bd., 2001—09, dir. med. affairs emeritus, 2001—, med. adv. bd. mem., 2001—10. Dir. Am. Bd. for Certification in Prosthetics/Orthotics, 1974-77; mem. Health Planning Council So. Fla. Task Force on Long Term Patient Care, 1974-77; asst. med. dir. Div. of Children's Med. Services, State of Fla., 1975-86; chmn. Statewide Com. for Spinal Cord Injury, 1976-78 Trustee Jour. Bone and Joint Surgery, 1992-98, vice chmn., 1996-98; contbr. articles to med. jours. Served to lt. comdr. M.C. USNR, 1966-68. Decorated Legion of Merit. Mem. ACS, AMA, Am. Acad. Orthopaedic Surgeons (bd. dirs. 1978-79, 87-92, 2d v.p. 1987-88, 1st v.p. 1988-89, pres. 1989-90), Am. Burn Assn. (Disting. Achievement award 2001), Fla. Orthopaedic Soc. (mem. exec. com. 1978-79), Miami Orthopaedic Soc. (v.p. 1978-79), Am. Acad. Orthotists and Prosthetists (hon.), Fla. Med. Soc. Hillsborough County Med. Assn., Am. Congress Rehab. Medicine, Nat. Rehab. Assn., Scoliosos Rsch. Soc., Internat. Soc. Prosthetics and Orthotics, Am. Orthopaedic Assn., Orthopaedic Rsch. and Edn. Found. (trustee 1991-97, sec. 1995-97), Internat. Soc. Prosthetics and Orthotics (dir. 1980-83), Assn. Children's Prosthetic and Orthotic Clinics (pres. 1983-84), Rehab. Engring. Soc. N.Am. (dir. 1980-83), Am. Spinal Injury Assn., Internat. Med. Soc. Paraplegia, Pediatric Orthopaedic Soc. (dir. 1983-84, pres. 1984-85, Disting. Achievement award 2000), 20th Century Orthopaedic Assn. (treas.

1984-89), Am. Acad. Pediatrics, Phi Beta Kappa, Alpha Omega. Republican. Lutheran. Office: 5524 Simonton St Bradenton FL 34203 Office Phone: 941-962-2839. Personal E-mail: newt3md@gmail.com.

MCCOLLOUGH, W. ALAN, retired board member; Gen. mgr., corp. ops. Circuit City Stores Inc., Richmond, Va., 1988, asst. v.p., 1989-91, pres., ctrl. operating divsn., 1991-95, sr. v.p., merchandising, 1995-97, COO, 1997—2000, pres., 1997—2005, chmn., CEO, 2000—06. Bd. dirs. V.F. Corp., 2000—. Office: V F Corp Bd Directors 105 Corporate Ctr Blvd Greensboron NC 27408 Office Phone: 336-424-6000. Business E-Mail: w_mcCollough@vfc.com.

MCCOLLUM, JOHN MORRIS, tenor; b. Coalinga, Calif., Feb. 21, 1922; s. Fay James and Ingabord Telette (Mason) McC.; m. Mary Margaret Wilson, Jan. 23, 1944; children: Kristi Elizabeth, Timothy James. Student, Coalinga Coll., 1939—40; BA in Journalism, U. Calif., Berkeley, 1947; student, Am. Theatre Wing, 1951—53. Reporter, city editor Coalinga Record, 1947-50; editor agrl. news U. Calif. Coll. Agr., 1950-51. Prof. music and chmn. voice faculty U. Mich.; dir. U. Mich. div. Nat. Music Camp; faculty Aspen Music Festival and School, 1963-76 Concert and opera singer, 1951—, soloist, Fifth Ave. Presbyn. Ch., NYC, 1953-56, debut, Town Hall, NYC, 1952, with, Boston Symphony Orchestra, Tanglewood, Mass., 1952, engagements with Symphony Orchestras in, N.Y.C., Chgo., Phila., San Francisco, Cleve., Washington, St. Louis, Detroit, New Orleans, Toronto, London, Mexico; with opera companies of, Boston, Washington, Toronto, Ft. Worth, Central City, Colo., NBC-TV, music festivals and oratorio societies, European debut, Festival of Two Worlds, Spoleto, Italy, summer 1958, Santa Fe Opera Co., leading tenor, NYC Opera Co., performing mem., Music Assos. of Aspen. (Recipient award Atwater Kent Auditions 1950, Am. Theatre Wing award 1952). Mem. Rep. Ctrl. Com., Fresno County, Calif., 1950; pres. Ann Arbor Civic Theatre, 1987-88; mem. Sarasota County Rep. exec. com.; mem., bd. dirs. Sarasota Concert Assn.; bd. dirs. Univ. Mich. Alumni Club. Served with U.S. Navy, 1942-49. Mem. U. Calif. Alumni Assn., Nat. Assn. Tchrs. Singing, Am. Acad. Tchrs. Singing, Alpha Tau Omega, Sigma Delta Chi, Pi Kappa Lambda. Episcopalian (lay reader). Clubs: Rotary (pres. 1977, Paul Harris fellow), Ann Arbor Golf and Outing (pres. 1979), The Meadows Country Club (Sarasota, Fla.). Home: 3380 W Chelmsford Ct Sarasota FL 34235-0947

MCCOLLUM, MARK A., corporate financial executive; BBA, Baylor U., Waco, Tex. CPA Tex. Assoc. Arthur Andersen, 1980—91, audit & bus. adv. ptnr., 1991—94; v.p., fin. analysis & planning, corp. controller Tenneco, Inc. (formerly Tenneco Automotive, Inc.), v.p., corp. devel.; sr. v.p., CFO Tenneco Automotive, 1999—2003; dir. KBR, Inc., 2006—07; sr. v.p., chief acctg. officer Halliburton Co., 2003—07, exec. v.p., CFO, 2008—. Bd. dirs. Exterran Holdings, Inc., 2009—. Bd. dirs. Exterran Partners; bd. trustees Found. for the Retarded, Star of Hope Mission, Houston. Mem.: Fin. Execs. Internat., Inst. Mgmt. Accountants, Tex. Soc. CPA's, Am. Inst. CPA's. Office: Halliburton Co 3000 N Sam Houston Pky E Houston TX 77032 Office Phone: 281-575-3000. Business E-Mail: mark.mccollum@halliburton.com.

MCCOLLUM, RANDALL HAMPTON, investigation service company executive; b. Houston, Dec. 13, 1944; s. Herbert Hampton and Verna (Duke) McC.; m. Gretchen McCollum (div. Dec. 1975); m. Nancy Dennis McCollum, Nov. 24, 1979; children: Derek, Kyle, Tyler. BS, Lamar U., 1968, MEd, 1969. Area sales mgr. Xerox Corp., Houston, 1970—80; regional mgr. O.C. Tanner Co., Houston, 1979—82; exec. v.p. Texas Arai, Inc., Houston, 1982—84; pres., CEO Hampton Energy Corp., San Antonio, 1984—88; v.p., corp. divsn. Tiffany & Co., NYC, 1987—94, Neiman Marcus, 1994—97; sr. v.p., Strategic Alliances Administaff Inc., 1997—2010; nat. sales mgr. Stewart Business Information, 2010—. Bd. dirs. Camelot Found., San Antonio, 1988-89; advisor San Antonio Airport Bd., 1988-89. Mem. Dominion County Club Golf Assn. (bd. dirs. 1987-89), Kingwood Country Club. Office: Stewart Business Information 1980 Post Oak Blvd Ste 800 Houston TX 77056 Home: 13426 Vista Del Rey San Antonio TX 78216-2233 Office Phone: 800-783-9278. E-mail: randalmccollum@stewart.com.

MCCOMAS, DANIEL F., state legislator; m. Betty McComas. Bus. exec.; state rep. Dist. 13 NC, 1995—2002; state rep. Dist. 19 NC, 2003—. Mem. Environ. and Natural Resources com., Fin. Instns. com., Health com., Marine Resources and Aquaculture com., Pub. Utilities com.; vice chmn. Fin. com., Transp. com. Republican. Address: PO Box 2274 Wilmington NC 28402 Office: NC House of Reps 300 N Salisbury St Rm 506 Raleigh NC 27603-5925 Office Phone: 919-733-5786, 910-343-8372. E-mail: Danny.McComas@ncleg.net.

MCCOMAS, DAVID JOHN, science administrator, space physicist; b. Milw., May 22, 1958; s. Harrold James and Hazelyn McC.; m. Richelle Wolff, May 30, 1981; children: Random A., Koan I., Orion G. BS in Physics, MIT, Cambridge, 1980; MS in Geophysics and Space Physics, UCLA, 1985, PhD in Geophysics and Space Physics, 1986. Mem. staff Los Alamos Nat. Lab., N.Mex., 1980-91, sect. leader space plasma and planetary physics N.Mex., 1991-92, group leader for space and atmospheric scis. N.Mex., 1992-98, founding dir. Ctr. for Space Sci. and Exploration, NASA program N.Mex., 1998—2000; exec. dir. space sci. and engring. divsn. S.W. Rsch. Inst., San Antonio, 2000—03, sr. exec. dir., 2003—09, asst. v.p., 2009—. Strategic planning com. earth and space scis. divsn. Los Alamos Nat. Lab, 1986; advanced composition explorer phase A study team NASA, 1988-89, space physics data system steering com., 1990-91, inner magnetosphere imaging study team, 1991-94, prin. investigator Interstellar Boundary Explorer, Ulysses Solar Wind Observations Over the Poles of the Sun Experiment, Two Wide-Angle Imaging Neutral-Atom Spectrometers, Explorer Mission-of-Opportunity, Solar Wind Electron Proton Alpha Monitor (instrument on the Advanced Composition Explorer, co-investigator Medium Energy Neutral Atom instrument on IMAGE Midsized Discovery Mission, plasma instrument for Cassini mission to Saturn, GENESIS Discovery mission, ISTP Polar Spacecraft's Thermal Ion Dynamics Experiment, Cluster plasma electron instrument, team New Millennium Plasma Experiment for Planetary Exploration, Space Sci. Adv. Com., chmn. Sun-Earth Connections Adv. Subcom., Solar Probe Sci. and Tech. Definition Team, NASA, 2004-05; com. solar-terrestrial rsch. Nat. Rsch. Coun., 1991-94, com. space sci. tech. planning Aeronautics and Space Engring. Bd./space studies bd., 1992, task group rsch. prioritization future space sci. space studies bd., 1994—; former prin. investigator series of 10 magnetospheric plasma analyzer instruments at geosynchronous orbit Dept. Energy; com. mem., panelist Nat. Acad. Sci.'s Nat. Rsch. Coun., U. Calif., State of N.Mex., others; adj. prof. dept. physics and astronomy U. Tex., San Antonio. Assoc. editor Jour. Geophys. Rsch.-Space Physics, 1993-94; contbr. articles to profl. jours. Grad. fellow Inst. Geophysics and Planetary Physics, 1983-84. Fellow AAAS, Am. Geophys. Union (James B. Macelwane award 1993). Achievements include patents in field. Office: SW Rsch Inst PO Drawer 28510 San Antonio TX 78228-0510

MCCOMBS, BILLY JOE (RED MCCOMBS), automotive executive, former professional sports team executive; m. Charlene McCombs; 3 daughters. Founder Red McCombs Automotive Group, San Antonio, McCombs Partners; co-founder Clear Channel Comm., Inc.; former owner, chmn. San Antonio Spurs; owner, chmn. Denver Nuggets, 1982—86; owner, chmn., pres. Minn. Vikings, Eden Prairie, 1998—2005. Film appearances: The Longest Yard, 2005. Chmn. bd. trustees Southwestern U.; former chmn. United Way of San Antonio, HemisFair World's Fair '68, U. Tex. M.D. Anderson Cancer Ctr., Houston. Named to Bus. Hall of Fame; named one of Forbes 400: Richest Americans, 2006-. Mem. San Antonio C. of C. (former chmn.), Nat. Ford Dealers, U. Tex. Longhorn Club. Office: McCombs Partners 755 E Mulberry St Ste 600 San Antonio TX 78212-3860 Office Phone: 210-821-6523.

MCCONNELL, BRIGHT, III, orthopaedic surgeon; b. Augusta, Ga., Mar. 3, 1953; s. Bright McConnell, Jr. and Elizabeth Custer McConnell; m. Pam Hollings, Oct. 14, 1978; children: Elizabeth Anne, Bright McConnell, IV, Ian Deryck. BS, Davidson Coll., NC, 1971—75; MD, Med. Coll. Ga., Augusta, 1975—79. Lic. orthopaedic surgeon Am. Bd. Orthopaedic Surgery, 1987, cert. clin. densitometrist Internat. Soc. Clin. Densitometry, 2001. Residency in orthopaedic surgery U. Fla., 1984; fellowship in sports medicine Kerlan-Jobe Orthopaedic Clinic & Nat. Athletic Health Inst., 1985; orthopaedic surgeon, ptnr. Orthopaedic Specialists of Charleston, SC, 1985—2002; CEO Prevecare, Charleston, 2002—05; pvt. practice Daniel Island, SC, 2005—. Bd. dir. Internat. Ctr. Birds of Prey, Awendaw, SC, 2000—. Named to Best Doctors in Am., 2006. Fellow: Am. Acad. Orthopaedic Surgery; mem.: Charleston County Med. Soc., Am. Orthopaedic Soc. Sports Medicine, Aircraft Owners & Pilots Assn. Avocations: aerobatics, fishing, flying. Home: 8863 Hwy 17N Mc Clellanville SC 29458 Office: 900 Island Park Dr Ste 105 Charleston SC 29492 Office Fax: 843-284-5201. Personal E-mail: makaira1@aol.com. Business E-Mail: drbrightmcconnell@yahoo.com, pmcconnell@charlestonsportsmed.com.

MCCONNELL, CHARLES DEWITT, academic administrator, former federal agency administrator; b. Steubenville, Ohio, 1955; BS in Chemical Engring., Carnegie-Mellon U., 1977; MBA in Finance, Cleve. State U., 1985. Various positions including global v.p. Praxair, Inc. (formerly Union Carbide), 1977—2009; v.p. carbon mgmt. Battelle Energy Technology, Columbus, Ohio, 2009—11; COO Office Fossil Energy, US Dept. Energy, 2011—12, asst. sec. for fossil energy, 2012—13; exec. dir. Energy and Environment Initiative Rice U., Houston, 2013—. Office: Energy & Environment Initiative Rice U 315A Allen Ctr 6100 Main St MS 603 Houston TX 77005 E-mail: charles.d.mcconnell@rice.edu.*

MCCONNELL, EDWARD BOSWORTH, legal association administrator, lawyer; b. Greenwich, Conn., Apr. 3, 1920; s. Raymond Arnott and Anna Bell (Lee) McC.; m. Jeanne M. Rotton (dec. 1984); children: Annalee, Marilyn, Edward (dec. 1994), Barbara, William; m. Florence M. Leonard, (dec. 1991); stepchildren: Susan L. Little, William R. Leonard, Molly M. Leonard. AB, U. Nebr., 1941, LLB, 1947; MBA with distinction, Harvard U., 1943. Bar: Nebr. 1947, NJ 1950. Mem. faculty Rutgers U. Sch. Bus. Adminstrn., Newark, 1947-53; assoc. firm Toner, Speakman and Crowley, Newark, 1949-50; adminstrv. asst. and law sec. to Chief Justice of NJ, 1950-53; adminstrv. dir. Cts. of NJ, Trenton, 1953-73; also standing master Supreme Ct., 1953-73; pres. Nat. Center for State Cts., Williamsburg, 1973-90, bd. dirs., 1980-90, pres. emeritus, 1990—, cons. on ct. mgmt., 1990—92. Mem. US Dept. Justice Coun. on Role of Cts. in Am. Soc., 1978-83; mem. adv. com. Dispute Resolution Policy Study, Social Sci. Rsch. Inst., U. So. Calif., 1975-79, Civil Litigation Rsch. Project, U. Wis. and U. So. Calif., 1979-83, nat. judge edn. program to promote equality for men and women in the cts., 1980-92; mem. Nat. Inst. Criminal Justice Task Force, Urban Consortium, 1979-83; participant Access To Justice Colloquium, European Univ. Inst., Florence, Italy, 1979; nat. adv. coun. Ctr. Adminstrn. Justice, Wayne State U., 1973-77; nat. project com. State Jud. Info. Sys. Project SEARCH Group, 1973-76; lectr. Inst. of Local and State Govt. Wharton Sch. U. Pa., 1955-65, Appellate Judges Seminar, Inst. Jud. Adminstrn., NYU, 1962-75; vis. expert UN Asia and Far East Inst., Tokyo, 1971; mem. Cts. Task Force Nat. Adv. Commn. Criminal Justice Standards and Goals, 1971-73; nat. adv. com. DC Ct. Mgmt. Project, 1966-70; trustee Inst. Ct. Mgmt., 1969-73, 84-86; chmn. Nat. Conf. Ct. Adminstrv. Officers, 1956; mem. nat. task force on gender bias in cts. Nat. Assn. Women Judge's 1985-90; mem. adv. bd. Nat. Ctr. for Citizen Participation in Adminstrn. of Justice, 1984-90; mem. Nat. Commn. Trial Ct. Performance Standards, 1991-95. Mem. adv. com. on article III Commn. on the Bicentennial of the Constitution, 1989-91; adv. com. Judicary Leadership Coun., 1990-95. Maj. C.E., AUS, 1943-46, European Theater, 1944-46. Decorated Bronze Star medal; recipient Warren E. Burger award for greatest contbn. to improvement of ct. adminstrn. Inst. for Ct. Mgmt., 1975, Herbert Lincoln Harley award for efficient adminstrn. justice Am. Judicature Soc., 1973, Glenn R. Winters award for outstanding service in jud. adminstrn. Am. Judges Assn., 1974, Tom C. Clark award for outstanding contbns. to field of ct. adminstrn. Nat. Conf. Met. Cts., 1983, Award of Merit Nat. Assn. Ct. Mgmt., 1987, Spl. award, Nat. Assn. Women Judges, 1989, Paul C. Reardon award for disting. svc. Nat. Ctr. for State Cts., 1991, Alumni Achievement award U. Nebr., 1991, Robert B. Yegge award ABA Jud. Divsn. Lawyers Conf., 1997. Fellow Nat. Acad. Pub. Adminstrn. (mem. panel on evaluation budget decentralization project of fed. cts. 1989-91, chmn. panel long range planning in fed. cts. 1991-92, mem. panel for study of fed. trial ct. adminstrv. structure 1995-96); mem. ABA (fellow-at-large, coun. mem. 1960-66, 71-80, house of dels., 1977-80, chmn. com. on oversight and goals 1975-76, chmn. com. on jud. compensation jud. adminstrn. div. 1984-89, chmn. jud. adminstrn. div. 1976-77, sect. of litigation task force on excess litigiousness in Am. 1986-88, task force on reduction of litigation cost and delay, jud. adminstrn. dir. 1984-94, chmn. 1991-94, mem. long range planning com. 1989-94), N.J. Bar Assn., Nebr. Bar Assn., Fellows of Am. Bar Found. (life), Warren E. Burger Soc., Kingsmill (Va.) Golf Club, Kingsmill Tennis Club (pres. 2001), Kingsmill Yacht Club, Order of Coif (hon.), Delta Upsilon, Sigma Delta Phi, Phi Delta Phi. Office Phone: 757-220-3012. Personal E-mail: ebm80@aol.com.

MCCONNELL, GLENN FANT, Lieutenant Governor of South Carolina, former state legislator; b. Charleston, SC, Dec. 11, 1947; s. Samuel Winfield and Evelyn McDaniel McConnell. BS, Coll. of Charleston, 1969; JD, U. South Carolina, 1972; LHD (hon.), U. Charleston, 1999, Medical U. of South Carolina, 2005; LLD (hon.), Citadel, 2000; HD (hon.), Francis Marion U., 2001. Staff atty. Neighborhood Legal Assistance Program; labor management relations specialist Charleston Naval Shipyard; atty. Riesen Law Firm, 1976—85, Glenn McConnell, 1987—97; ptnr. Tillman & McConnell, 1985—87; pres. CSA Galleries Inc., 1990—2009; mem. Dist 41 South Carolina State Senate, 1981, pres. pro tempore, 2001—12; lt. gov. State of South Carolina, Columbia, 2012—. Recipient C Norwood Hastie award, 1969, Bingham Oratorical Medal, 1969, Area Governor of Year, 1972, Alumnus of Year, 1976, 1977, 1995, Outstanding Achievement award, South Carolina Republican Party, 1980. Mem.: ABA, Charleston County Bar Assn., South Carolina Bar Assn., Fort Sumter Camp, Sons of Confederate Veterans, Scottish Soc. of Charleston, Nat Ritual & Insignia, America Legislature Exchange Coun., Marion Lt. Artillery, Assn. for the Preservation of Civil War Sites, Exchange Club of Charleston. Republican. Episcopal. Avocations: jet skiing, snow skiing. Mailing: 27 Bainbridge Dr Charleston SC 29407 Office: Office of the Lieutenant Governor PO Box 142 Columbia SC 29201 Office Phone: 803-212-6340, 803-734-2080. Office Fax: 803-734-2082.*

MCCONNELL, JOHN MICHAEL, retired management consultant; Vice admiral USN; dir. to pres. Bill Clinton Nat. Security Agy.; dir. to pres. George H.W. Bush Nat. Security Agy; bd. dirs. Nat. Intelligence Agy., 2007—09; officer Booz Allen Hamilton Holding Corp., 1996—2007, sr. v.p., 2009, exec. v.p., 2009—. Office: Booz Allen Hamilton Holding Corp 8283 Greensboro Dr Mc Lean VA 22102 Office Phone: 703-902-5000. Office Fax: 703-902-3333. Business E-Mail: mcconnell_john@bah.com.

MCCONNELL, JOYCE E., dean, law educator; BA, Evergreen State Coll., 1979; JD, Anitoch Sch. Law, 1982; LLM, Georgetown U., 1990. Tchg. fellow Ctr. for Applied Legal Studies, Georgetown U. Law Ctr.; assoc. prof. CUNY Sch. Law; faculty mem. W.Va. U. Coll. Law, Morgantown, 1995—, assoc. dean academic affairs, William J. Maier, Jr. dean, Thomas R. Goodwin prof. law, 2008—. Vis. prof. U. Md. Sch. Law; v.p. W.Va. Land Trust. Fellow: American Bar Found.; mem.: Assn. American Law Schs. (chair-elect Sect. on Natural Resources). Office: West Virginia University College of Law Room 100E PO Box 6130 Morgantown WV 26507-6130 Office Phone: 304-293-6502. Office Fax: 304-293-8102. E-mail: joyce.mcconnell@mail.wvu.edu.*

MCCONNELL, MICHAEL ARTHUR, lawyer; b. Ft. Worth, Jan. 15, 1947; BA, Loyola U., New Orleans, 1969; JD, U. Tex., 1975. Bar: Tex. 1976, U.S. Dist. Ct. (no. dist.) Tex. 1976, U.S. Dist. Ct. (ea. dist.) Tex. 1981, U.S. Dist. Ct. (we. dist.) Tex. 1982, U.S. Dist. Ct. (so. dist.) Tex. 1989, U.S. Ct. Appeals (5th cir.) Tex. 1980, U.S. Ct. Appeals (10th cir.) 1987. Briefing atty. U.S. Dist. Ct. Hon. Eldon B. Mahon, Ft. Worth, 1976-77; assoc. atty. Cantey, Hanger, Gooch, Munn and Collins, Ft. Worth, 1977-81, ptnr., 1981-83; judge no. dist. U.S. Bankruptcy Ct., Ft. Worth, 1983-86; ptnr. Jackson Walker LLP, Ft. Worth, 1988—95, McConnell & Assocs., Ft. Worth, 1995—2000, Winstead Sechrest & Miniak P.C., Ft. Worth, 2000—06, Kelly Hart & Hallman LLP, Ft. Worth, 2006—. Trustee Am. Inns of Ct. Nat. Found. Sgt. USAF, 1969—73. Fellow: Am. Coll. Bankruptcy; mem.: Am. Law Inst. Office: Kelly Hart & Hallman LLP 201 Main St Ste 2500 Fort Worth TX 76102 Office Phone: 817-332-2500. Business E-Mail: michael.mcconnell@khh.com.

MCCONNELL, MITCH (ADDISON MITCHELL MCCONNELL), United States Senator from Kentucky, lawyer; b. Tuscumbia, Ala., Feb. 20, 1942; s. Addison Mitchell and Julia (Shockley) McC.; m. Elaine Lan Chao, Feb. 6, 1993; children: Eleanor Hayes, Claire Redmon, Marion Porter. BA with honors, U. Louisville, 1964; JD, U. Ky., 1967. Bar: Ky. 1967. Chief legislative asst. to Senator Marlow Cook US Senate, Washington, 1968-70; pvt. law practice Louisville, 1970-74; dep. asst. atty. gen. US Dept. Justice, Washington, 1974-75; judge Jefferson County, Louisville, 1978-85; US Senator from Ky., 1985—; asst. majority leader (majority whip) US Senate, 2002—07, minority leader, 2007—. Chmn. Jefferson County Republican Com., 1973-74; co-chmn. Nat. Child Tragedies Coalition, 1981; chmn., founder Ky. Task Force on Exploited and Missing Children, 1982; mem. Pres.'s Partnership on Child Safety. Recipient commendation, Nat. Trust on Hist. Preservation in US, 1982, Conservationist of Yr. award, League Ky. Sportsmen, 1983, cert. of appreciation, American Correctional Assn., 1985, Golden Plow award, American Farm Bur. Fedn., 1996, Freedom award, Nat. Coun. Union Burma, 1999, Sam Rainsy Pary Freedom award, 2002, Ky. Warbler Migratory Songbird Conservation award, US Fish & Wildlife Svc., Ky. Dept. Fish and Wildlife Resources, 2002, Defender of Freedom award, James Madison Ctr. Freedom Speech, 2002, Disting. Svc. award, American Farm Bur., 2002; named one of The 50 Most Powerful People in DC, GQ mag., 2007. Mem. Ky. Assn. County Judge Executives (pres. 1982), Nat. Inst. Justice (adv. bd. 1982-84) Republican. Baptist. Avocations: fly-fishing, cooking. Office: US Senate 317 Russell Senate Office Bldg Washington DC 20510-0001 also: Gene Snyder US Courthouse Rm 630 601 West Broadway Louisville KY 40202-2228 Office Phone: 202-224-2541, 502-582-6304. Office Fax: 202-224-2499, 502-582-5326.*

MCCOOK, RICHARD PAUL, automotive parts manufacturing executive, grocery chain financial executive; b. Miami, Fla., Mar. 15, 1953; s. Leon Ennis and Ruth Erminor (Davenport) McC.; m. Anne Thackerson, Mar. 22, 1975; children: Ryan Wesley, Kelly Lauren. BS in Acctg., Fla. State U., 1975, M in Accountancy, 1976. CPA, Fla. Sr. audit mgr. Peat, Marwick, Mitchell & Co., Jacksonville, Fla., 1976-84; fin. v.p., CFO Winn-Dixie Stores, Inc., 1984, sr. v.p., CFO, 1984—2004; exec. v.p., CFO Raytech, 2005—06, US Oncology, 2006—08, Gen. Parts Internat., Inc., 2010—. Participant Leadership Jacksonville, 1986-87. Mem. Am. Inst. CPA's, Fla. Inst. CPA's, Fin. Execs. Inst. Clubs: River (Jacksonville). Democrat. Methodist. Avocations: hunting, fishing, tennis. Office: General Parts International Inc 2635 E Millbrook Rd Ste B Raleigh NC 27604 Office Phone: 919-573-3000. Office Fax: 919-790-9867. Business E-Mail: rick.mccook@usoncology.com.

MCCORD, CLINTON D., JR., oculoplastic surgeon; b. Dec. 10, 1935; married; 2 children. BA, Emory U., Ga., 1957; MD, Emory Sch. Medicine, 1961; MS in Physiology, Emory U., Ga., 1963. Cert. Am. Bd. Ophthalmology, diplomate Am. Acad. Ophthalmology, lic. Ga. Resident, ophthalmology Emory U., Ga., 1963—66; Heed fellowship, oculoplastic Manhattan Eye and Ear Hosp., 1966—67; mem. USAF Keesler AFB (Biloxi, Miss.) & Andrews AFB (Washington, DC), 1967—69; private practice Atlanta, 1969—79; chief of staff Metropolitan Eye and Ear Hosp., 1974; prof., ophthalmology Emory U. Sch. Medicine, Ga., 1979—80, assoc. clin. prof., plastic surgery Ga., 2002—; private practice Paces Plastic Surgery, Atlanta, 1980—; clin. prof., ophthalmology Emory U., 1980—2002. Invited spkr. in field; vis. professorship at nat. universities and institutions. Contbr. chapters to books, several articles to profl. jours.; co-author: (textbooks) Optical Techniques, 1971; author: Oculoplastic Surgery, 1981, Oculoplastic Surgery, 2nd edit., 1987, Oculoplastic Surgery, 3rd edit., 1994, Eyelid Surgery, Standard and Advanced, 1996; co-author: Color Atlas of Cosmetic Oculofacial Surgery, 2004. Med. missions Interplast Mission Nicaragua (Managua)-Oculoplastica Jornada, 2003, Tanzanian Project (Moshi, Tanzania) Surgical Lectures-Surgical Demonstrations, Kilimanjari Christian Med. Ctr., 2007. Recipient Montague Boyd award, Best Physician Book award, Piedmont Hosp., Atlanta, Oculoplastic Surgery-2nd edit., 1988, Best Clin. Paper of the Yr.-Midfacial Rejuvenative Surgery, Am. Soc. Aesthetic Surgery, NYC, 1997; co-recipient Best Resident's Paper (with Hisham Seify)-Quantitating Ptosis Surgery, 2007; named one of Best Doctors in US, 1979, 1981, The Doctor's Doctors, Atlanta Mag., 1988, Top Docs, Atlanta's most trusted specialists, 2005, Outstanding Med. Specialists in the US, Town and Country Mag., 1989, Best Doctors in America, 1992, Best 200 Ophthalmologist in America, Ophthalmology Times, 1996; named to Guide to the 1,500 Best Doctors in America, Town and Country Mag., 1984, America's Top Doctors, Castle Connolly Med. Inc, 2004, NY Times Beauty Supplement Edit., Best Three Cosmetic Eyelid Surgeons in US, 2005. Fellow: ACS (program chmn. 1975); mem.: Med. Assn. Atlanta, Med. Assn. Ga., Internat. Orbital Soc., Am. Acad. Ophthalmology (Edni. Honor award 1980), Atlanta Ophthal. Soc. (pres. 1978), Ga. Soc. Ophthalmology (program chmn. 1978, coun. mem. 1983—87), Am. Soc. Ocularists (program chmn. 1978), Am. Soc. Ophthalmic Plastic Surgery and Reconstructive Surgery (program chmn. 1982, pres. 1989, chmn. adv. bd. 1990, mem. adv. bd. 1991—99, with Am. Acad. Ophthalmology, Wendell Hughes Lecture Coun. 1995—2000, Lester Jones Surgical Anatomy award, Best Clin. Presentation of Anatomy 1984), Byron Smith Study Club. Avocations: hiking, mountaineering. Office: Paces Plastic Surgery 1411 Grayson Pt Buckhead GA 30625-2237 Office Phone: 404-351-0051. Office Fax: 404-351-0632.

MCCORKINDALE, DOUGLAS HAMILTON, publishing executive; b. NYC, June 14, 1939; s. William Douglas and Kathleen (Miles) McC.; m. Nancy Walsh, Dec. 24, 1991; children by previous marriage: Laura Ann, Heather Jean. BA, Columbia U., 1961, LLB cum laude (Harlan Fiske Stone scholar), 1964. Bar: N.Y. 1964. Assoc. Thacher Proffitt & Wood, NYC, 1964-70, ptnr., 1970-71; gen. counsel, sec. Gannett Co., Inc., Arlington, Va., 1971-72, v.p., gen. counsel, sec., 1972-77, sr. v.p. fin. and law, 1977-79, sr. v.p., chief fin. officer, 1979-83, pres. diversified media div., 1980-83, exec. v.p., 1983, vice chmn., 1985—2001, CFO, 1985—97, chief adminstrv. officer, 1986—97, pres., 1997—2005, CEO, 2000—05, chmn., 2005—06. Bd. dirs. Lockheed Martin Corp. Mem. Pine Valley Golf Club, Mid Ocean Club, Burning Tree Club. Office: Gannett Co Inc 7950 Jones Branch Dr Mc Lean VA 22102

MCCORMACK, RICHARD THOMAS FOX, former ambassador; b. Bradford, Pa., Mar. 6, 1941; s. C.H. and Ruth N. (Fox) McC.; m. Karen L. Hagstrom, Oct. 18, 1980; children: Charlotte Louise, Justin Randall, Elizabeth Caroline. BA, Georgetown U., 1963; PhD, U. Fribourg, Switzerland, 1966. With Peace Corps, 1966-67; sr. staff mem. Pres.' Adv. Council on Exec. Orgn., White House, Washington, 1969-71; with Am. Enterprise Inst., 1975-77; dep. asst. sec. for internat. econ. affairs US Dept. Treasury, 1974; mem. staff U.S. Senate, 1979-81; asst. sec. state for econ. and bus. affairs U.S. Dept. State, Washington, 1982-85, US amb. to OAS, 1985-89, under sec. for econ. affairs, 1989-91; sr. advisor Ctr. Strategic Internat. Studies, Washington, 2004—06, 2012—; exec. vice chmn. Bank of America Merrill Lynch, NYC, 2006—12. Candidate in primary elections for U.S. Congress, 1972, 74; cons. Office Telecommunications Policy, 1971, Coun. on Internat. Econ. Policy, 1972, Office Spl. Trade Rep., 1975, Exec. Office of the Pres., White House, Washington; guest scholar Woodrow Wilson Ctr. Smithsonian Instn., Washington, 1991-92; bus. advisor Am. companies, cons. U.S. Govt. on Internat. Econ. Affairs, 1992-2005. Author: Asians in Kenya, 1971, The Twilight War, 1979, Microeconomic Reforms for Israel, 1991, Managing Japan's Financial Crisis, 1992, Vulnerabilities in the Global Economy: Looking Forward in War Time, 2005, The Politics and Economics of the Global Financial Crisis, 2012, Conversation with Ambassador Richard McConners, 2013 Recipient Superior Honor award Dept. State, 1987, Sec. of State's Disting. Svc. award, 1991; decorated Legion of Honor (France). Mem. Econ. Club NY, Coun. Am. Ambs., Coun. Fgn. Rels. Republican.

MCCORMACK, ROBERT CORNELIUS, consumer products company executive; b. NYC, Nov. 7, 1939; m. Mary Lester, Dec. 14, 1963; children: Robert Cornelius Jr., Walter, Scott. BA, U. N.C., 1962; MBA, U. Chgo., 1968. V.p. Dillon Read & Co. Inc., 1968—81; mng. dir. Morgan Stanley, 1981—87; dep. asst sec., def. prodn. support U.S. Dept. Def., 1987—88, dep. under sec., def. indsl. and internat. programs, 1988—89, acting dep. under sec., def. acquisition, 1989—90, asst. sec., Navy fin. mgmt. Washington, 1990—93; founding ptnr. Trident Capital LP, Chgo., 1993—2004. Bd. dirs. MeadWestvaco Corp., 2002—. Served to lt. USNR, 1963-66. Office: MeadWestvaco Corp Bd directors 501 S 5th St Richmond VA 23219-0501 Office Phone: 804-327-5200.

MCCORMICK, AILEEN, healthcare company executive; Grad., Montclair State U., NJ, 1977; MBA in Fin., U. St. Thomas, Houston, 1984. Cons.; with Tex. Med. Mgmt.; dir., Prucare of Houston Prudential Health Care, 1984—97; exec. v.p., Houston health plan AmeriHealth, 1997—2000; CEO, Houston health plan Amerigroup Corp., 2002—06, CEO, Southwestern region, 2007—. Office: Amerigroup Corp 4425 Corporation Ln Virginia Beach VA 23462 Office Phone: 757-490-6900. Office Fax: 757-222-2330. Business E-Mail: amccorm@amerigroupcorp.com.

MCCORMICK, DARRELL G., state legislator; 2 children. BA, Appalachian State U. Owner Real Estate Firm; former owner Commercial Herb Farm; former project mgr. Piedmont Facilities; mem. Dist. 92 NC House of Reps., 2009—. Republican. Office: North Carolina House of Representatives 16 W Jones St Rm 2119 Raleigh NC 27601-1096 Address: 1325 Ivy Ave Bldg 2 Winston Salem NC 27105 Office Phone: 919-733-5654, 336-631-5778. Business E-Mail: Darrell.McCormick@ncleg.net.

MCCORMICK, GERALD, state legislator; b. Feb. 22, 1962; married; 2 children. State rep. Dist. 26, Tenn., 2005—. Mem.: VFW, Farm Bur., America Legion, US Army Vet. 1st Gulf War, Chattanooga Jaycees (former bd. mem.), Blood Assurance (bd. dir.), Hamilton County Rep. Party (former v. chmn., former fin. chmn.), Pachyderm Club (former pres.), Harrison Ruritan. Republican. Methodist. Mailing: PO Box 4741 Chattanooga TN 37405 Office: 117 War Memorial Bldg Nashville TN 37243-0126 Office Phone: 615-741-2548. Office Fax: 615-253-0305. Business E-Mail: rep.gerald.mccormick@capitol.tn.gov.

MCCORMICK, J. PHILIP, natural gas company executive; b. San Antonio, Feb. 21, 1942; s. Eugene Hay and Beulah (Barber) McC.; m. Jo Ann Wendland, July 17, 1965; children: J. Philip Jr., Scott Daniel. BBA, Tex. A&I U., 1964, MS in Bus. and Econs., 1965. CPA, Tex. Sr. acct. Price Waterhouse, Houston, 1965-70; mgr. KMG Main Hurdman, Houston, NYC, 1970-73, ptnr. El Paso, Houston, 1973-83, mng. ptnr. Houston, 1983-85, mng. ptnr. So. region, 1985-87; mng. ptnr. KPMG Peat Marwick, Austin, Tex., 1987-91; sr. v.p. transmission and office of pres. Lone Star Gas Co., Dallas, 1994-95, sr. v.p. fin., 1991-93; sr. v.p., CFO Enserch Exploration, Dallas, 1995—97; exec. v.p., CFO Highwaymaster Comm., Inc., 1997—98; sr. mgmt. positions, Lone Star Gas Divsn. Enserch Corp., 1991—95. Mem. State of Tex. Natural Gas Reliability Coun., 1993-95.; mem. bd. dirs. The Dallas Opera, KMG Main Hurdman, 1973-91, KPMG Peat Marwick, 1973-91, Renaissance Growth and Income Fund III, Advanced Neuromodulation Sys. Inc., 2003-05, QEGP, 2006-, Quest Energy Ptnrs., L.P., 2008-, RENN Global Entrepreneurs Fund, Inc. Mem. Bd. dirs. Austin Symphony, 1988-92, Tex. Bus. Hall of Fame, Houston, 1990-94, Tex. A&I Found., 1989— (chmn. 1992—); fin. coun. Seton Hosp., Austin, 1990-91; search com. bus. sch. dean Tex. A&I U., 1990, Tex. A&I alumni assn. (pres. 1977-78, nat. chmn. ann. alumni fund drive 1978-80), chmn. industry adv. coun. to dean, 1968-69; sec. bbd. regents Univ. System South Tex., Corpus Christi, 1988-89; steering com. St. Edward's U., Austin, 1990-91; founding dir. Escape Ctr. for Prevention Child Abuse, Houston, 1980-89; dir. Exch. Club Child Abuse Prevention Ctr., Dallas, 1993—, others. Named Disting. Alumnus Tex. A&I U., 1991, one of Outstanding Young Men Am., 1971. Mem. Am. Gas Assn. (fin. and adminstrv. sect., acctg. adv. coun. 1991—, mng. com., corp. planning com. 1991-93), AICPA, Tex. Soc. CPAs, Tower Club Dallas, Petroleum Club Houston, Houston Club, Headliners Club Austin, Delta Sigma Pi (life). Office: Quest Energy Partners LP Ste 2750 210 Park Ave Oklahoma City OK 73102 Office Phone: 405-600-7704.

MCCORMICK, JOHN HOYLE, lawyer; b. Pensacola, Fla., July 30, 1933; s. Clyde Hoyle and Orrie Brooks (Frink) McC.; m. Patricia McCall, Dec. 27, 1974. BS, U. Fla., 1955; JD, Stetson U., 1958. Bar: Fla. 1958. County atty., 1973—. Hamilton County; atty. Hamilton County Devel. Authority, 1970-91; bd. dirs. 1st Fed. Savs. Bank Fla.; bd. dirs., v.p., atty. Hamilton County Bank. Mayor City of White Springs, Fla., 1959; pres. Hamilton County C. of C., Jasper, 1961. Mem.: Masons, Phi Delta Phi. Democrat. Methodist. Avocations: gardening, motorhome camping, college football. Home: 403 2nd Ave NW Jasper FL 32052-6687 Office: 215 2nd St NE Jasper FL 32052-6616 Address: PO Drawer O Jasper FL 32052-0695 Office Phone: 386-792-2395.

MCCORMICK, ROBERT JUNIOR, former federal agency administrator; b. Boone, Iowa, Aug. 1929; s. Ivyl Robert and Darlene Adel (Bowes) McC.; m. Shirley May Zerbe, Dec. 24, 1950; children: Elaine McCormick Newland, Kathleen, Michael, Tara McCormick Wieting, Tammy McCormick Kirby. Grad., Flying Sch., Williams Field, Ariz., 1951, Parachute Jump Sch., 1964, Armed Forces Staff Coll., Norfolk, Va., 1966, Def. Systems Mgmt. Coll., Ft. Belvoir, Va., 1975; BS in Mech. Engring., Tex. Tech. U., 1963; cert., Harvard U. Def. Studies Program, 1984. Served as enlisted man USAF, 1948—51, commd. 2d lt., 1951, advanced through grades to col., 1971, pilot U.S., Japan, Europe, Vietnam, fighter pilot Korean War, 1951—52; exec. officer to Gen. George Brown 7th Air Force, Saigon, Vietnam, 1969—70; mil. asst. to asst. sec. of Air Force for research and devel. USAF, Washington, 1970—74, ret., 1975; exec. officer NASA, Washington, 1976—80; adminstrv. asst. to sec. of Air Force USAF, Washington, 1980—94; mem. U.S. Sr. Exec. Service, 1979—94; pres. McG, Ltd., Fairfax, Va. Mem. Pres.'s transition team Dept. of Def., 2001. Decorated Air Force Legion of Merit, Bronze star, Air medal, Meritorious Svc. medal, Air Force Exceptional Civilian Svc. medal, NASA Exceptional Svc. medal, 1980; recipient Presdl. Meritorious Rank, 1989, Disting. Civilian Svc. medal Dept. Def., 1994, Commendation medal State of Calif., 2001. Mem. ASME, DAV, Air Force Assn., Nat. Def. Indsl. Assn., Order of Daedalians, St. Andrews Soc. Washington, Mil. Order of Carabao, Chevaliers du Testevin. Clubs: Army-Navy Country (Fairfax, Va.). Personal E-mail: mcgltd1@aol.com.

MCCORMICK, WALTER BERNARD, JR., telecommunications industry executive; b. Kans. City, Mo., Feb. 8, 1954; s. Walter Bernard and Dorothy Ann (Power) M.; m. Mary Lou Edlefsen, Jan. 3, 1987; children: Walter Patrick, Megan Boutin. Student, Georgetown U., 1975; BJ, U. Mo., 1976, JD in Law, 1979. Bar: Mo. 1979, D.C. 1980. Assoc. Leighton, Conklin, Lemov & Jacobs, Washington, 1980-81, Pepper, Hamilton & Scheetz, Washington, 1981-82; legis. asst. US Senate, Washington, 1982-84; gen. counsel US Senate Com. Commerce, Sci. and Transp., Washington, 1985-87, minority chief counsel, staff dir., 1988-92; gen. counsel US Dept. Transp., Washington, 1992-93; ptnr. Bryan Cave LLP, Washington, 1993—98; pres., CEO Am. Trucking Assns., 1998—2001, US Telecom Assn., 2001—. Author: Search of the Newsroom: The Battle for a Reporter's Privilege Moves to New Ground, 44 Missouri Law Review 297, 1979. Mem. US Nat. Security Telecom. Adv. Com., 2005—10, US Adv. Com. Internat. Comm. and Info. Policy, 2005—10; trustee Rockhurst U., Kans. City, 2005—14; bd. dir. Good Shepherd Housing & Family Svcs., Alexandria, Va., 2008—. Mem. Capitol Hill Club, Washington, City Club, Washington, Belle Haven Country Club, Alexandria. Roman Catholic. Office: US Telecom Assn 607 14th St NW Ste 400 Washington DC 20005 Office Phone: 202-326-7244. Office Fax: 202-326-7333.

MCCOUGHTRY, ANGEL, professional basketball player; b. Balt., Sept. 10, 1986; B in Comm., U. Louisville, 2009. Forward Atlanta Dream, WNBA, 2009—. Mem. US nat. team Pan American Games, Brazil, 2007, FIBA World Championship, Czech Republic, 2010, Summer Olympic Games, London, 2012. Recipient Gold medal, women's basketball, Pan American Games, 2007, Summer Olympic Games, 2012, Gold medal, FIBA World Championship, 2010; named Big East Conf. Player of Yr., 2007, Big East Conf. Defensive Player of Yr., 2009, 1st Team All-American, AP, US Basketball Writers Assn., 2009, WNBA Rookie of Yr., 2009, 1st Team All-Defense, WNBA, 2010, 2011, 1st Team All-WNBA, 2011; named to WNBA All-Rookie Team, 2009, Ea. Conf. All-Star Team, WNBA, 2011. Achievements include being the number one pick in the WNBA Draft, 2009. Office: Atlanta Dream 225 Peachtree St NE Ste 2400 Atlanta GA 30303*

MCCOWAN, OTIS BLAKELY, mathematics professor; b. Monterey, Tenn., June 17, 1934; s. Burton and Martha Catherine (Phipps) McC. BS, Tenn. Tech. U., 1959; MA, La. State U., 1966; PhD, Vanderbilt U., 1975. Mathematician Missile Devel. Ctr., Holloman AFB, N.Mex., 1962-63; math. tchr. Rhea Ctrl. H.S., Dayton, Tenn., 1963-65; math. instr. Kilgore (Tex.) Coll., 1966-67; asst. prof. math. Belmont U., Nashville, 1967-72, assoc. prof. math., 1972-75, prof. math., 1975—2004, Chaney disting. prof., 1981, prof. emeritus, 2004—. With U.S. Army, 1959-62. Named Outsting Young Educator in Rhea County, Dayton C. of C., 1964. Mem. Nat. Coun. Tchrs. Math., Math. Assn. Am., Kappa Delta Pi, Kappa Mu Epsilon, Pi Mu Epsilon, Omicron Delta Kappa, Alpha Chi (Region III v.p. 1980-82, pres. 1982-84, nat. v.p. 1991-93). Democrat. Baptist. Avocations: travel, gardening, reading, attending concerts and theatre. Office: Belmont Univ Dept Math and Computer Sci Nashville TN 37212 Home: 210 E Hoyt Ave Monterey TN 38574 Business E-Mail: mccowano@mail.belmont.edu.

MCCOY, DUSTAN ELWOOD, manufacturing executive, lawyer; b. Ashland, Ky., July 16, 1949; s. Elwood and Mary Anna (Mullins) McC.; m. Rebecca Lancashire, Feb. 28, 1970; children: Dustan Chad, Drew Christopher. BA, Eastern Ky. U., 1971; JD, No. Ky. U., 1978. Bar: Ky. 1978. Atty. Ashland Oil Inc., Ky., 1973-83, sr. atty. Ky., 1983-85, gen. atty. Ky., 1985, assoc. gen. counsel Ky.; sr. v.p., gen. counsel, corp. sec., exec. v.p. Witco Corp.; v.p., gen. counsel Brunswick Corp., 1999—2000, pres. Brunswick boat group, 2000—05, chmn., CEO, 2005—. Bd. dirs. La.-Pacific Corp. Local bd. mem. U.S. SSS, 1987; mem. law bd. visitors No. Ky. U. Mem. ABA, Ky. Bar Assn. Avocations: jogging, hunting, fishing. Office: Brunswick Corp 1 N Field Ct Lake Forest IL 60045-4811 Office Phone: 847-735-4700. Office Fax: 847-735-4765.

MCCOY, JOSEPH G., oil industry executive; V.p. global products supply and trading Chevron Corp., 2001—05, v.p. trading capability, 2005—07; sr. v.p. supply and optimization Tesoro Corp., San Antonio, 2008—. Office: Tesoro Corp 19100 Ridgewood Pkwy San Antonio TX 78259-1828 Office Phone: 210-828-8484.

MCCOY, MICHAEL D., lawyer; b. Joliet, Ill., Apr. 8, 1950; BSEE with honors, U. Ill., 1972; JD with honors, Chgo.-Kent Coll. Law, 1975. Bar: Ill. 1975, NC 1983, US Patent and Trademark Office. Ptnr. and coord. intellectual property law practice Alston & Bird LLP, Charlotte, NC. Mem. panel patent dispute arbitrators Am. Arbitration Assn. Contbr. articles to profl. jours. Named one of Best Lawyers in Am., 2005—. Mem.: ABA, Licensing Exec. Soc. Office: Alston & Bird LLP Bank of Am Plz Ste 4000 101 S Tryon St Charlotte NC 28280-4000 Office Phone: 704-444-1011. Office Fax: 704-444-1111. Business E-Mail: mike.mccoy@alston.com.

MCCOY, PETER M., JR., state legislator; b. Charleston, Aug. 20, 1978; s. Peter Michael McCoy Sr; m. Jennifer Blanchard McCoy. BA in History & Religion, Hampden-Sydney Coll., 2001; JD, Regent U., 2005. Lic., SC State Cts.; Lic., SC Fed. Dist. Ct.; Lic., Fourth Cir. Ct. of Appeals. With Barton and Burwell Fishing Supplies, Carlock, Copeland & Stair, LLP; mem. Ducks Unlimited, Friends of McLeod Plantation; criminal prosecutor Ninth Circuit Solicitor; mem. NRA, Save the Morris Island Lighthouse, SC Saltwater Sportfishing Assn.; pathologist Veterans Adminstrv. Hosp., Charleston, SC; v.p., treas., sec. Charleston Lawyers Club, 2010—; mem. Dist. 115 SC House of Representatives, 2011—. Mem.: Charleston County Bar Assn., SC Bar Assn., Criminal Law Bar Assn. Republican. Avocations: tennis, fishing, hunting. Office: South Carolina House of Representatives District 115 326A Blatt Bldg Columbia SC 29201 Address: PO Box 13826 Charleston SC 29422 Office Phone: 803-212-6872.

MCCOY, R. WESLEY, biology educator; b. Augusta, Ga., Sept. 20, 1954; s. Roger and Frances (Amick) McC.; m. Deborah Stringer, June 16, 1984. BS in Biology, Ga. State U., 1975; MEd in Sci. Edn., U. Ga., 1977; PhD, Ga. State U. Tchr. North Cobb High Sch., Kennesaw, Ga., 1978-83, sci. dept. chmn., 1987—, tchr., Biology, Genetics, and Astronomy; edn. specialist NASA, Kennedy Space Ctr. (Fla.), 1983-87; tchr. Ga. Govs. Honors Program, Dahlonega, 1981-82. Adj. asst. prof. Okla. State U., Stillwater, 1983-87; mem. NSF DNA literacy program, Cold Spring Harbor Lab, NOAA Nat. Undersea Rsch. Program Marine Biology Workshop; del. leader People to People Youth Sci. Exch. to Soviet Union; Fulbright tchr. exch. to U.K.; vice-chair, Ga. Citizens for Integrity in Sci. Edn. Christa McAuliffe fellow, 1992, SCI-MAT fellow, NSF, 1992, Ga. Sci. Tchr. of Yr., GTE G.I.F.T. fellow, 1993, Tandy scholar 1994; recipient Presdl. Award for Excellence in Sci. and Math. Teaching, 1996, Outstanding Biology Tchr. for Ga., Evolution-Education award, Found. for the Furure, 2003, 2006 AAAS Award for Scientific Freedom and Responsibility, 2007. Mem. NSTA, Vice Pres. Presbyn. Assn. for Sci., Tech. and Christian Faith, Ga. Sci. Tchrs. Assn., Fulbright Assn., Phi Delta Kappa. Presbyterian. Office: North Cobb High Sch 3400 Old Highway 41 Kennesaw GA 30144-1072

MCCOY, SUE, retired surgeon, biochemist, bioethicist; b. Charlottesville, Va., Nov. 14, 1935; d. Hulburt Christopher and Evelyn (Savage) McC. AB, Radcliffe Coll., 1957; PhD, Johns Hopkins U., 1964; MD, U. Va., 1980, postgrad., 2001—. Fellow in physiol. chemistry Johns Hopkins U., Balt., 1964-67; asst. prof. chemistry U. South Fla., Tampa, 1967-69; asst. prof. orthopedics U. Va., Charlottesville, 1969-73, asst. prof. surgery, 1973-78; resident in surgery Hosp. U. Pa., Phila., 1980-83; resident in surgery Cooper Hosp. Rutgers U. Med. Sch., Camden, N.J., 1983-85, asst. prof. surgery, 1985-86, East Tenn. State U., Johnson City, 1986-91, assoc. prof., 1991-2000, prof., 2000—01; ret., 2001. Fellow: ACS; mem.: Assn. for Women Surgeons, Southeastern Surg. Congress, Shock Soc., Assn. for Acad. Surgery, Royal Soc. Chemistry, N.Y. Acad. Sci., Am. Chem. Soc., Sigma Xi. Achievements include research in hemorrhagic shock, aging, oxygen transport. Home: 8658 Batesville Rd Afton VA 22920

MCCOY, WESLEY LAWRENCE, musician, educator, conductor; b. Memphis, Jan. 27, 1935; s. Harlan Eftin and Gladys (Coggin) McC.; m. Carolyn June Noble, Aug. 26, 1960; children: Jill Laurene McCoy Kurtz, Scott Edward. B of Music Edn., La. State U., 1957, PhD, 1970; M of Music Edn., U. Louisville, 1958; M of Sacred Music, So. Bapt. Theol. Sem., 1960. Min. of music Beechmont Bapt. Ch., Louisville, 1959-62; also instr. music So. Bapt. Theol. Sem., Louisville; asst. prof. music, dir. bands Carson Newman Coll., Jefferson City, Tenn., 1962-67; asst. prof. music U. S.C., Columbia, 1969-72; assoc. prof. music U. Ark., Little Rock, 1972-77, prof., 1977-80, asst. dean for pub. svc. Coll. Fine Arts, 1978-79; condr. Wind Ensemble, River City Cmty. Band, 1972-80, Oklahoma City Youth Symphony, 1985—87; chmn. dept. music Phillips U., Enid, Okla., 1980-82, chmn. fine arts divsn., 1982-84; music tchr. Bishop Sullivan H.S., 2003—04; supr. Baton Rouge Recreation Dept., 2004—; asst. conductor Baton Rouge Concert Band, 2008—10. Choral dir. 1st United Meth. Ch., Edmond, Okla., 1983-2000; owner WJ Travel, Oklahoma City, 1985-2002; choir dir. 1st United Meth. Ch., Hammond, La., 2004-. French horn player, Knoxville (Tenn.) Symphony Orch., 1962-67, Columbia Philharm. Orch., 1969-72, Ark. Symphony Orch., 1972-80, Enid-Phillips Symphony, 1980-84; contbr. to Ch. Musician, 1974-76, 85-86. Co-chmn. Jefferson County (Tenn.) Com. for Goldwater for Pres., 1962; mem. Pulaski County (Ark.) Rep. Com., 1977-81; mem. Oklahoma County Rep. exec. Com., 1995-97; pres. Ctrl. Okla. La. State U. Alumni, 1997-98. Mem. SC Music Educators Assn. (pres. coll. divsn. 1971-73), Ark. Music Edn. Assn. (chmn. rsch. 1975-80), Phi Mu Alpha, Pi Kappa Lambda, Phi Delta Kappa, Alpha Tau Omega, Music Club Baton Rouge (treas. 2008-). Republican. Baptist. Home and Office: 8548 Kaylynn Ave Baton Rouge LA 70810 Personal E-mail: wesleymccoy@yahoo.com.

MCCRACKEN, EUGENE LUKE, lawyer; b. Savannah, Ga., Aug. 9, 1932; s. John and Estelle (Powers) McCracken; m. Helen Kelly Morekis, May 9, 1964. AA, Armstrong State Coll., 1952; BA, Mercer U., Macon, Ga., 1954; LLB, U. Ga., Athens, 1957. Bar: Ga. 1958, US Dist. Ct. (so. dist.) Ga. 1959, US Ct. Appeals (11th cir.) 1961, US Supreme Ct. 1978. Assoc. Brannen, Clark & Hester, Savannah, 1958—64; sole practice Savannah, 1964—; asst. dist. atty. Chatham County, Ga., 1963—64. Asst. city atty. City of Savannah, 1970—74; judge pro tem Juvenile Ct. Chatham County, 1974—80. Mem. Chatham County Zoning Bd. Appeals, 1967—70; bd. dirs. United Way Savannah, 1973—74; chmn. Chatham County Reps., 1985—87; chmn. 1st congl. dist. Ga. Rep. Party, 1987—89. Recipient Named Savannah's Outstanding Young Man of Yr., Jaycees, 1966, Sword of Hope award, Am. Cancer Soc., 1968. Mem.: St. Andrews Soc. Savannah, Hibernian Soc. Savannah (pres. 2004—05), Armstrong State Coll. Alumni Assn. (pres. 1973, 1983), Savannah (Ga.) Bar Assn., State Bar of Ga. Roman Catholic. Home: 16 Brightwater Dr Savannah GA 31410-3301 Office: 223 W York St Savannah GA 31401-3636 Home Phone: 912-897-2373. Business E-Mail: eugenemccracken@aol.com.

MCCRADY, JAMES DAVID, veterinarian, educator; b. Beaumont, Tex., June 26, 1930; s. James Homer and Lucyle (Ward) McCrady; m. Mary Elizabeth McDougald, Sept. 8, 1951; children: David, Diane, Darla. BS, Tex. A&M U., 1952, DVM, 1958; PhD, Baylor U., 1965. From instr. to asst. prof. Tex. A&M U., 1958- 62, mem. faculty, 1964—, prof., head dept. vet. physiology and pharmacology, 1966-90, prof., dir. spl. programs, 1990—95, prof. emeritus, 1995—; dir. animal rsch., instr. Baylor U. Coll. Medicine, 1962-64. Dir. Russian-Am. Tng. Partnership, 1995—; adj. prof. Baylor Coll. Medicine, M.D.

Anderson Hosp., Tumor Inst. With USAF, 1952—54. Mem.: AVMA, Am. Physiol. Soc., Tex. Acad. Sci., Sigma Xi, Phi Zeta, Phi Kappa Phi. Achievements include research in comparative cardiovascular and respiratory physiology. Office: Tex A&M U College Station TX 77843-0001 Home: 10244 Dyess Rd College Station TX 77845-3012 Office Phone: 979-845-7261. Business E-Mail: jd-mccrady@tamu.edu.

MCCRARY, CHARLES D., utilities executive; b. 1951; BS in Mech. Engring., Auburn U., Ala.; JD, Birmingham Sch. Law. Asst. project planning engr. Ala. Power Southern Co., 1973, various exec. positions Ala. Power and Southern Nuc., chief prodn. officer, exec. v.p. external affairs Ala. Power, 1994—98, pres. Southern Co. Generation and Energy Mktg., 1998—2001, v.p., 1998—2001, pres., COO Ala. Power, 2001, pres., CEO Ala. Power, 2001—, exec. v.p., 2002—. Bd. dirs. Amsouth Bancorporation, 2001—, Protective Life Corp., 2005—, Mercedes-Benz US Internat., Inc. Office: Southern Co 30 Ivan Allen Jr Blvd NW Atlanta GA 30308 Office Phone: 404-506-5000.

MCCRARY, WALLS, state legislator; m. Emma Woodward McCrary; children: Jay, Bill. BS in Bus. Adminstrn., U. Ark., Fayetteville. Former owner McCrary's Clothing Store; former treas. City of Lonoke, Ark.; mem. Dist. 15 Ark. House of Reps., 2009—. Bd. mem. Lonoke First State Bank, Lonoke Indsl. Devel. Commn.; chmn. Bayou Met. Drainage Dist. Bd.; treas. Lonoke County Mus., Lonoke Ministerial Alliance; mem. Lonoke Area C. of C., former charter pres.; former mem., pres. & sec. Lonoke Sch. Bd.; former pres. Lonoke County Libr. Bd.; elder & trustee Lonoke First Presbyn. Ch. Recipient Outstanding Cmty. Svc. award, Lonoke Area C. of C.; named Retailer of Yr., Grocers & Retail Merchants Assn., 1996, Educator of Yr., Lonoke Area C. of C. Mem.: Ark. Farm Bur., Lonoke Cemetery Assn. (treas.). Democrat. Office: State Capitol Rm 350 Little Rock AR 72201 also: 319 W Academy St Lonoke AR 72086 Office Phone: 501-682-6211, 501-682-7771, 501-676-2317. Business E-Mail: ewmccrary@sbcglobal.net.

MCCRAY, NIKKI KESANGAME, women's college basketball coach, former professional basketball player; b. Collierville, Tenn., Dec. 17, 1971; BA in Sports Mktg. and Edn., U. Tenn., 1995. Basketball player USA Women's Nat. Team, 1996; guard Washington Mystics WNBA, 1998—2001, Ind. Fever WNBA, 2003, Phoenix Mercury WNBA, 2004, San Antonio Silver Stars WNBA, 2005, Chgo. Sky WNBA, 2006; asst. coach Western Ky. U. Hilltoppers, 2006—08, U. SC Gamecocks, 2008—. Recipient Gold Medalist, Atlanta Olympic Games, 1996, Sydney Olympic Games, 2000; named to Women's Basketball Hall of Fame, 2011. Achievements include a park named in her honor in hometown of Colliersville, Tenn. Avocation: singing. Office: U SC c/o Dept Athletics Roost Bldg B 1322 Heyward St Columbia SC 29208

MCCREA, MARSHALL S., III, energy executive; Joined Energy Transfer Partners, LP, Dallas, 1997, sr. v.p. bus. devel. and prodr. svcs., 1997, sr. v.p. comml. devel., 2004, pres. midstream ops., 2005—08, pres., COO, 2008—. Office: Energy Transfer Company 3738 Oak Lawn Ave Dallas TX 75219-4333 Office Phone: 214-981-0700. Office Fax: 214-981-0703.

MCCREARY, FRANK E., III, retired lawyer; b. Santa Monica, Calif., Mar. 25, 1943; s. Frank Elijah and Irma (Holland) McC.; m. Jacqueline Moehlman, Feb. 15, 1969; children: Jennifer Claire, Frank Ward. BA, Cornell U., 1965; LLB with honors, U. Tex., 1968. Bar: Tex. 1968. Ptnr. Vinson & Elkins, Houston, 1970—2006. Trustee United Way Tex. Gulf Coast, Houston, 1988-90; bd. dir. Vol. Ctr., Houston, 1987-99. Capt. US Army, 1968-70, Vietnam. Mem. Nat. Assn. Bond Lawyers, Tex. Law Rev. Assn., Houston Bar Found. Office: Vinson & Elkins Ste 2500 First City Tower 1001 Fannin St Houston TX 77002-6760 Office Phone: 713-758-2440. Office Fax: 713-615-5256. E-mail: fmccreary@velaw.com.

MC CREARY, JAMES FRANKLIN, lawyer, mediator; b. Farmington, Mo., June 15, 1942; s. Frank J. and Bernice E. (Dugal) McCreary; m. Martha Jean Tucker, June 30, 1962; children: James Franklin, III, Jason Tucker, Josh Adam. BSBA, U. Evansville, 1964; JD, Nashville Law Sch., 1969; MBA, Vanderbilt U., 1980. Bar: Tenn. 1969, rule 31 listed mediator: Tenn. With Old Nat. Bank, Evansville, Ind., 1960-64; with First Am. Corp., Nashville, 1972-80, exec. v.p., corp. sec., gen. counsel, 1974-80; with First Am. Nat. Bank Nashville (N.A.), 1964-72, 80-86, exec. v.p., 1980-86; ptnr. Borod & Huggins Attys., Memphis, 1986-87, Gerrish McCreary Smith PC, Memphis, 1988, of counsel, 1988—92, dir., 1993—. Pres. Met. Fed. Bank, 1988-91; vis. prof. bus. law David Lipscomb U., 1975-77; instr. law and banking Am. Inst. Banking, 1969-75. Recipient Mid South Superlawyer award, 2006—; named one of Best Lawyers in America, 2005—, Best Lawyers in Nashville. Mem. Am. Arbitration Assn., Beta Gamma Sigma Mem. Ch. of Christ. Office: Gerrish McCreary Smith PC 700 Colonial Rd Memphis TN 38117 E-mail: fmccreary@gerrish.com.

MCCREERY, SCOTT COOKE (SCOTTY MCCREERY), singer; b. Garner, NC, Oct. 9, 1993; s. Michael and Judy (Cooke) McCreery. Winner Season 10 American Idol, 2011. Singer: (albums) Clear as Day, 2011, Christmas with Scotty McCreery, 2012, See You Tonight, 2013, (songs) I Love You This Big, 2011, The Trouble with Girls, 2011 (USA Weekend Breakthrough Video of Yr., CMT Music Awards, 2012). Named Artist of Yr.: New Artist, Am. Country Awards, 2011, Best New Artist, Acad. Country Music Awards, 2012. Home: 2813 Azalea Pl Nashville TN 37204-3117*

MCCRORY, PAT (PATRICK LLOYD MCCRORY), Governor of North Carolina, consulting firm executive, former mayor; b. Columbus, Oct. 17, 1956; m. Ann Gordon McCrory. BA in Polit. Sci. & Edn., Catawba Coll., 1978, DLitt (hon.), 2001. Various positions Duke Energy Corp., NC, 1978—2007; at-large rep. Charlotte City Coun., NC, 1989—95; mayor pro tempore City of Charlotte, 1993-95, mayor, 1995—2009; ptnr. McCrory & Co., Charlotte, 2009—; sr. dir. strategic initiatives Moore & Van Allen PLLC, Charlotte, 2010—12; gov. State of NC, Raleigh, 2013—. Mem. Homeland Security Advisory Bd., 2003—06; bd. dirs. Tree.com, Keewaunee Scientific Corp. Co-chmn. Charlotte's Fighting Back Commn.; mem. Children Svcs. Network; hon. chmn. Cystic Fibrosis Found., Arthritis Found., Charlotte Bond Campaign, ARC Pers. Recruitment Com.; HS basketball ofcl.; founder Uptown Crime Prevention Coun., Mayor's Mentoring Alliance, 1995; mem. adv. coun. President's Homeland Security; pres. Republican Mayors and Local Ofcls.; bd. dir. US Conf. of Mayors, chair, Hosing and Cmty. Develop. Com.; chair NC Metropolitan Coalition; hon. chair Charlotte chpts., Alzheimer Found., Cystic Fibrosis Found., Arthritis Found.; bd. trustees Catwaba Coll. Recipient Governor's Outstanding Local Ofcl. award, 2001. Mem.: Mayor's Mentoring Alliance (founder 1995), Republican Mayors and Local Ofcls. Orgn. (pres.), U.S. Conf. Mayors. Republican. Office: Office of the Governor 20301 Mail Service Ctr Raleigh NC 27699 Office Phone: 919-733-5811. Office Fax: 919-733-2120.*

MCCRUMMEN, RONALD L., food products executive; Various positions Ernst & Young LLP, 1986—93, sr. mgr., 1993—98, ptnr., 1998—2004; sr. v.p., chief acctg. officer Dean Foods Co., 2004—. Office: Dean Foods Co 2515 McKinney Ave Ste 1200 Dallas TX 75201 Office Phone: 214-303-3400. Office Fax: 214-303-3499. Business E-Mail: ronald_mccrummen@deanfoods.com.

MCCUISTION, PEG OREM, retired health facility administrator; b. Houston, July 28, 1930; d. William Darby and Dorothy Mildred (Beckett) Orem; m. Palmer Day McCuistion, Sept. 4, 1949 (div. 1960); 1 child, Leeanne E. BBA, Southwest Tex. State, 1963; MBA, George Washington U., 1968; EdD, Wayne State U., 1989. Patient care adminstr. Holy Cross Hosp., Silver Spring, Md., 1968-79; exec. dir. Hospice of S.E. Mich., Southfield, 1979-86, Hospice Austin, Tex., 1987-94; CEO EMBI, Inc., Arlington, Tex., 1994—98; gen. mgr. Hospice Home Care, San Antonio, 2001—04, ret., 2004. Bd. dirs. Cmty. Home for the Elderly, Austin, 1989-92. Fellow Am. Coll. Health Care Execs. (membership com.); mem. Internat. Hospice Inst. (assoc.), Nat. Hospice Orgn. (chair standards and accreditation com.), Tex. Hospice Orgn. (pres. 1993-94), exec. com., standards and ethics com., edn. com., chair legis. com.), Mich. Hospice Orgn. (chair edn. com., bd. dirs.).

MCCUISTION, ROBERT WILEY, hospital administrator, management consultant, lawyer; b. Wilson, Ark., June 15, 1927; s. Ed Talmadge and Ruth Wiley (Bassett) McC.; m. Martha Virginia Golden, June 11, 1949 (dec. Nov. 1991); children: Beth, Dan, Jed.; m. Sudola M. Getz, Feb. 12, 1994. AB in History, Hendrix Coll., Conway, Ark., 1949; JD, U. Ark., 1952. Bar: Ark. 1952, U.S. Dist. Ct. (we. dist.) Ark. 1953. Practice in, Dermott, Ark., 1952-57; dep. pros. atty. 10th Jud. Dist. Ark., 1952-57; bus. mgr. St. Mary's Hosp., Dermott, 1953-56, asst. adminstr., 1956-57; adminstr. Stuttgart (Ark.) Meml. Hosp., 1957-60, Forrest Meml. Hosp., Forrest City, Ark., 1960-68; assoc. adminstr. St. Edward Mercy Hosp., Ft. Smith, Ark., 1968-70; pres. Meml. Med Center, Corpus Christi, Tex., 1970-79; adminstr. Methodist Hosp., Mitchell, SD, 1979-85, cons., 1985-86; mgmt. cons., owner Creative Leadership Concepts, Arlington, Tex., 1985—; adminstr. Cen. United Meth. Ch., Fayetteville, 1986-91. Sec. Ark. Hosp. Adminstrs. Forum, 1958-59, pres., 1959-60; pres. Ark. Hosp. Assn., 1964-65, Areawide Health Planning, 1970; pres. Ark. Conf. Cath. Hosps., 1970; chmn. Twin City Hosp. Coun. West Ark., 1968; v.p. Ark. Assn. Mental Health, 1966-70. Feature writer, make up editor, editor Wiesbaden Post, Germany, 1946—47; editor: Air Force Publ. Div. chmn. Forrest City United Cmty. Svcs., 1961, Corpus Christi United Way Cmty. Svcs., 1972, DeSoto coun. Boy Scouts Am., Explorer advisor, 1954-57; vice-chmn., sec. ofcl. bd. Meth. Ch., 1957, lay del. S.D. ann. conf., 1980-85, cert. lay spkr., 1960—, Stephen minister, 1995-; trustee Midwest Hosp. Conf., Kansas City, Mo., 1964-1966. With USAAF, World War II. Recipient Eminent Leadership award DeSoto Area council Boy Scouts Am., 1956 Mem. Am. Assn. Hosp. Accts. (pres. Ark. chpt. 1957), S.D. Hosp. Assn. (dist. chmn. 1980-81), Am. Coll. Health Execs. (life), Rotary (pres. Forrest City 1964-65, Internat. Order of St. Luke (grief counselor, Stephen min.). Home and Office: 2401 St Gregory St Arlington TX 76013 Home Phone: 817-275-8378. Personal E-mail: sudobobm@tx.rr.net.

MCCULLOUGH, DAVID LEGARDE, urologist; b. Chattanooga, 1938; MD, Bowman Gray, 1964. Intern U. Hosps. Case Western Res. U., Cleve., 1964-65, resident in surgery, 1965-66; fellow urology Baylor U. Coll. Medicine, Houston, 1968-69; resident in urology Mass. Gen. Hosp., Boston, 1969-72; chief urologist N.C. Bapt. Hosp., Winston-Salem, 1983—; prof., former chmn. urology Wake Forest U. Coll. Medicine, Winston-Salem. Past pres. Am. Bd. Urology. Mem. ACS, AMA, Am. Urol. Assn. (past pres. southeastern sect., past pres., bd. dirs., chair for edn.), Am. Assn. Genitourinary Surgeons (past pres.), Clin. Soc. Urol. Surgeons, Halsted Soc. Office Phone: 336-217-9242. Business E-Mail: dmcullough@allianceurology.com.

MCCULLOUGH, LAURENCE BERNARD, medical educator, consultant; b. Phila., Aug. 2, 1947; s. Henry Joseph and Marie J. (Burns) McC.; m. Linda Jean Quintanilla, May 14, 1977. AB, Williams Coll., 1969; PhD, U. Tex., 1975. Postdoctoral fellow Hastings Ctr., Hastings-on-Hudson, N.Y., 1975-76; Asst. prof. med. humanities and philosophy Tex. A&M U., College Station, 1976-79; from asst. prof. to prof. cmty. and family medicine Georgetown U., Washington, 1979-88; prof. medicine and med. ethics Baylor Coll. Medicine, Houston, 1988—, Dalton Tomlin chair med. ethics & health policy, 2008—. Adj. prof. ethics in ob-gyn. and pub. health Weill Med. Coll., Cornell U., N.Y.C., 1988—. Co-author: Ethics in Obstetrics & Gynecology, 1994, Medical Ethics, 1984, Spanish transl., 1987, Japanese transl., 1992; author: Leibniz on Individuals and Individuation, 1996, John Gregory and the Invention of Professional Medical Ethics and the Profession of Medicine, 1998; co-editor: Surgical Ethics, 1998, The Cambridge World History Med. Ethics, 2009. Recipient Barbara and Corbin J. Robertson Presdl. award, Bayor Coll. Medicine, 2013, Baylor Pediatric award, 2014. Office Phone: 713-798-3505. Business E-Mail: laurence.mccullough@bcm.edu.

MCCULLOUGH, MARK, state legislator; BS in General Agriculture, Okla. State Univ., 1989, MS in Technology Edn., 1992; JD, Univ. Tulsa, 1998. Asst. atty. gen., Ill., 1998—2000; dep. prosecutor Marion County, 2001—03; sales rep. Eli Lilly & Co., 2003—06; atty. Sapulpa, Okla., 2006—; mem. Dist. 30 Okla. House of Representatives, 2007—. Mem.: Okla. Bar Assn., Creek County Bar Assn., Sapulpa Kiwanis. Republican. Address: 4125 Dogwood Pl Sapulpa OK 74066 Office: Oklahoma House of Representatives 2300 N Lincoln Blvd Rm 435-A Oklahoma City OK 73105 Home Phone: 918-227-1282; Office Phone: 405-557-7414. Business E-Mail: mark.mccullough@okhouse.gov.

MCCULLOUGH, RALPH CLAYTON, II, law educator; b. Daytona Beach, Fla., Mar. 28, 1941; s. Ralph C. and Doris (Johnson) McCullough; m. Elizabeth Grier Henderson, Apr. 5, 1986; children: Melissa Wells, Clayton Baldwin. BA, Erskine Coll., 1962; JD, Tulane U., 1965; LLD (hon.), Charleston Sch. Law, 2013. Bar: La. 1965, SC 1974. Assoc. Baldwin, Haspel, Maloney, Rainold and Meyer, New Orleans, 1965-68; from asst. prof. law to prof. U. SC, Columbia, 1968—2002, disting. prof., 2002—03; founder, prof. Charleston Sch. Law, 2005—. Asst. dean U. SC Sch. Law 1970-75, Disting. prof. law, 2001, Disting. prof. law emeritus, 2003—; of counsel Finkel & Altman, 1978-; adj. prof. medicine Med. U. SC, 1984-, adj. prof. pathology, 1985—, mem. bd. vis.; mem. adv. com. rules and procedures US Ct. Appeals (4th cir.), 2001—, chair, 2006-08. Author: (with J.L. Underwood) The Civil Trial Manual, 1974, 7th supplement, 1987, The Civil Trial Manual II, 1984, 87, (with Myers and Felix) New Directions in Legal Education, 1970, (with Finkel) S.C. Torts II, 1986, III, 1990, IV, 1995; co-reporter S.C. Criminal Code, 1977, S.C. Study Sentencing, 1977. Mem. bd. visitors Med. U. SC, 2006—08. Mem. ATLA, ABA, La. Bar Assn., SC Bar (sec. 1975-76, exec. dir. 1972-76, award of service 1978), New Orleans Bar Assn., Am. Law Inst. (life), Am. Coll. Trial Lawyers, Southeastern Assn. Am. Law Schs. (pres.), SC Trial Lawyers Assn. (bd. govs. 1984-88, Algernon Sydney Sullivan award, 2012), Carolina Yacht Club, Phi Alpha Delta. Republican. Presbyterian. Home: PO Box 939 Charleston SC 29402 Office: 414 King St Charleston SC 29402 Office Phone: 843-723-3521. Personal E-mail: ralphcmccullough@gmail.com.

MCCURDY, LAYTON, medical educator; b. Florence, SC, Aug. 20, 1935; m. Gwendolyn A. McCurdy, 1958; children: Robert Jr., David Barclay. BS, U. NC, 1956; MD, Med. U. SC, 1960. Resident in psychiatry NC Meml. Hosp., Chapel Hill, 1961—64; with psychiatry tng. br. NIMH, Bethesda, Md., 1964—66; asst. prof. dept. psychiatry Sch. Medicine Emory U., Atlanta, 1966—68; prof., chmn. dept. psychiatry and behavioral scis. Med. U. SC, 1968—82, v.p. med. affairs, dean, 1990—2001, dean emeritus, disting. prof., 2001—; prof. psychiatry Sch. Medicine U. Pa., Phila., 1982—90; psychiatrist-in-chief Inst. of Pa. Hosp., Phila., 1982—90. Vis. colleague Inst. Psychiatry, U. London, 1974—75; nat. adv. mental health coun. NIMH, 1980—83; apptd. Pa. Adv. Com. for Mental Health and Mental Retardation, 1984—87. Recipient Disting. Alumnus award, Med. U. SC, 1988, Earl B. Higgins Diversity Achievement award, 1999, Disting. Alumnus award, George C. Ham. Soc., 1990, Humanatati award, La Soc. Francaise, 2002. Fellow: Am. Coll. Psychiatrists (pres. 1993—94, Bowis award 1997); mem.: Am. Bd. Psychiatry and Neurology (pres. 1993), Assn. Academic Psychiatry (pres. 1970—71), SC Commn. on Higher Edn. (chmn. 2005—), Royal Coll. Psychiatrists (UK), Am. Psychiat. Assn. (joint commn. pub. affairs 1981—84, chmn. com. on diagnosis and assessment 1988—94), Cosmos Club. Office: Med Univ SC Inst Psychiatry PO Box 250861 Charleston SC 29425 Home Phone: 843-723-1186; Office Phone: 843-792-2084. Business E-Mail: mccurdy@musc.edu.

MCCURLEY, ROBERT LEE, JR., lawyer, educator; b. Gadsden, Ala., Sept. 7, 1941; s. Robert Lee and Nellie Ruth McC.; m. Barbara; 1 child, Allison Leah. BS, U. Ala., 1963, JD, 1966. Bar: Ala. 1966, D.C. 1973, U.S. Ct. Mil. Appeals 1966, U.S. Supreme Ct. 1970, U.S. Ct. Appeals (5th cir.) 1972, U.S. Ct. Appeals (11th cir.) 1973, U.S. Ct. Appeals (fed. cir.) 1981. Asst. to dir. Fed. Savs. & Loan Ins. Corp., Washington, 1966-67; partner firm Rains, Rains, McCurley & Wilson, Gadsden, Ala., 1967-75; city judge Southside, Ala., 1970-75; dir. Ala. Law Inst., 1975—; assoc. dir. U. Ala. Center Public Law and Service, 1981-82; asst. dean Sch. Law U. Ala., 1978-81. Panelist White House Conf. on Volunteerism; pres. Gadsden Jaycees, 1972; mem. White House Fifty States Project; adj. prof. Ala. Sch. Law, 1975-2006, Cumberland Sch. Law, 2005-07. Editor: Divorce, Alimony and Child Support Custody, 4th edit., 2005, Land Laws of Alabama, 9th edit. rev., 2007, The Legislative Process, 10th edit., 2010, Alabama Law Office Practice Deskbook, 11th edit., 2010, Federally Mandated State Legislation, 1990, Alabama Legislation, Cases and Statutes, 7th edit., 2010, Alabama Election Handbook, 15th edit., 2011. Pres. Gadsden Boys Club, 1971, Kiwanis Internat. Found., 1998—2000; mem. Nat. Dem. Charter Commn., 1974. Recipient Svc. award, Ala. Bar Commr., 2004, Gewin award, Ala. State Bar, 2000, Bar Commnrs. award, 2004, Roger Sayers Disting. Svc. award, U. Ala., 2005; Henry Toll fellow, Coun. State Govt., 1992. Fellow ABA, Ala. Bar Assn., mem. Am. Law Inst. (life), Order of Coif, Scribes, Farrah Law Soc., Commn. Uniform State Laws, Kiwanis (pres. Tuscaloosa club 1976, gov. Ala. dist. 1984, 91-92) Kiwanis Internat. Found. (pres., v.p. 1998-2000), Indian Hills County Club, Univ. Club. Presbyterian. Office Phone: 205-348-7411.

MCCUTCHEON, MAC, state legislator; b. Madison County, Ala. m. Debbie McCutcheon; 2 children. AS in Criminal Justice, Calhoun CC, Decatur, Ala.; BS in Criminal Justice Adminstrn., Trinity U., San Antonio. Police officer, police trainer, major crimes investigator, hostage negotiator, probation officer Huntsville Police Dept., City of Huntsville Mcpl. Ct. Sys.; mem. Dist. 25 Ala. House of Reps., Montgomery, 2006—. Mem. Coll. Pk. Church of God. Mem. Am. Legion, Fraternal Order Police, Ala. Peace Officers, North Ala. Emmaus Cmty., Madison C. of C., Tenn. Valley Smallmouth Bass Club. Republican. Office: 100 St Clair Huntsville AL 35801 also: Ala House of Reps Ala State House 11 S Union st Rm 524-B Montgomery AL 36130 Office Phone: 256-539-5441, 334-242-7705. Business E-Mail: macmccutcheon@knology.net.

MCCUTCHEON, STEVEN CLIFTON, ecological and environmental engineer, hydrologist; b. Decatur, Ala., Oct. 29, 1952; s. Bernard Clifton and Rosa May (Askenburg) McC.; m. Sherry Lynn Sharp; children: Michael Ian, Alexander Tavis. BS, Auburn U., 1975; MS, Vanderbilt U., 1977, PhD, 1979. EIT Ala., 1975, diplomate, Am. Acad. Water Resources Engrs., 2005, registered civil and environ. engr., La., 1982, profl. engr., Miss., 2007. Hydrologist US Geol. Survey, Bay St. Louis, Miss., 1977-86; sr. environ. engr. US EPA, Athens, Ga., 1986—. Instr., asst. Vanderbilt U, 1977-79; adj. asst. prof. Tulane U., New Orleans, 1984-85; cons., expert witness in field, 1985—; panel mem. Nat. Rsch. Coun., Washington, 1989-92; adj. prof. forestry, mem. faculty engring., affiliate ecology U. Ga., Athens, 1989—; asst. prof. Clemson U., SC, 1990-97; program evaluator Accreditation Bd. Engring. & Tech., 1992—; sci. oversight panel, Interagency Fla. Bay Sci. Program, 1996-; MS com. Fla. Internat. U. Dept. Civil Engring., 1998; reader U. Roorkee, India, 2001-02; prof. U. Parma, Italy, 2004; U. Miss. PhD com., 2004-06; reader U. Ctrl. Queensland, Australia, 2005-06; temp mem. grad. faculty U. Ala., Tuscaloosa, 2005-08; assoc. editl. & mem. editl. bd. Ecol. Studies, Hazards & Solution, 1999-. Author: Water Quality Modeling, vol. 1, 1989, Water Quality, Handbook of Hydrology, 1993; editor and author (with others): Manual for Performing Estuarine Waste Load Allocations, 1990, Hydrodynamics and Transport for Water Quality Modeling, 1999, editor and author: Phytoremediation, 2003; editor Jour. Environ. Engring., 1992—94, mem. editl. bd. Ecol. Engring., 1995—, Hazardous Toxic and Radioactive Waste Mgmt., 1996—97, Internat. Jour. Phytoremediation, 2000—, mem. editl. bd., adv. bd. (book series) Science, Education, Innovations, 2004—, co-editor Environ. Sci. and Pollution Rsch., 2003—05, assoc. editor, 2005—06, assoc. subject editor, 2006—07, advisor, 2008—; contbr. chapters to books, articles to profl. jours. Mem. Zoning Commn., St. Tammany Parish, La., 1984-85; vice=chmn. Planning Adv. Bd., St. Tammany Parish, 1985; asst. den leader Cub Scouts Am., Athens, pack 83, 1991-92, pack 96, 1998-99, den leader, 1999-2001; mem. Am. Inst. Architects Recon. Team, Sri Lanka, 2005; originator Hurricane Relief Fund Am. Soc. Civil Engrs. Found., 2005-07. Recipient medal and plaque, Korea Soc. Water Pollution Rsch. and Control, Seoul, 1986, Engr. of Yr. award in EPA, NSPE, 1992, Engr. of Yr. in Govt. award, Ga. Engr. Week Com., 2004, Performance award, EPA, 1986—99, Spl. Svc. award, 1990, 1991, Superior Accomplishment Recognition award, 2009; co-recipient EPA Sci. Achievement award in waste mgmt., Air and Waste Mgmt. Assn., 1995, EPA Sci. Achievement award in Chemistry, Am. Chem. Soc., 1997, Sci. and Tech. Achievement award, EPA, 1999, 2006, Bronze medal, 2001, 2002; grantee Tewkesbury fellowship, U. Melbourne, Australia, 2004. Mem.: ASCE (br. pres. 1983—84, sect. dir. 1984—85, 1995—2001, sect. v.p. 2001—03, sect. pres.-elect 2003—04, rep. Dist. 14 coun. 2003—04, sect. pres. 2004—05, nat. dir. Dist. 14, Region 5 2004—07, exec. com. 2006—07, chair bd. govs. region 5 2006—07, Young Civil Engr. of Yr. award 1984, Richard R. Torrens award 1994, Environ. Engring. Divsn. Service award 1995, Govt. Civil Engr. of Yr. award 2004, Outstanding Membership Chair 2004, Louisiana Sect. Svc. award 2006, Ga. Civil Engrs. award 2008, Founder award 2010), Internat. Soc. Phytotechnologies (charter, chair awards com.), Am. Acad. Water Resources Engrs. (elected founding diplomate 2005), Water Environ. Fedn., Internat. Assn. Hydrologic Scis., Internat. Water Assn., Internat. Soc. Environ. Ethics (charter), Am. Geophys. Union, Am. Ecol. Engring. Soc. (chair com. registration and certification 2001—04, v.p., pres.-elect 2004—05, pres. 2005—06, past pres. 2006—07, charter),

Phi Theta Kappa, Phi Kappa Phi, Sigma Xi (chpt. sec. 1982—84, membership com. 1984—85). Achievements include pioneering research in phytoremediation and ecological engring. to clean up federal facilities and response to Exxon Valdez oil spill. Avocations: travel, reading, history. Home: 147 Spalding Ct Athens GA 30605-3716 Office: US EPA 960 College Station Rd Athens GA 30605 Home Phone: 706-543-6972; Office Phone: 706-355-8235. Personal E-mail: EnvironHyd@aol.com. Business E-Mail: mccutcheon.steven@epa.gov.

MCDANIEL, A. STEPHEN, lawyer; b. Memphis, Nov. 13, 1946; BBA, U. Memphis, 1968, JD, 1973. Bar: Tenn. 1973, Mo. 1975, cert.: Tenn. Commn. Continuing Legal Edn. and Specialization (estate planning specialist). Estate and gift tax atty. US Treasury Dept., 1973—75; positions up to mng. ptnr. Williams, McDaniel, Wolfe & Womack, P.C., Memphis, 1975—. Instr. estate planning and estate & gift tax U. Memphis Sch. Law, 1990—2000. Contbr. articles to profl. jours. Named one of Top 100 Attys., Worth mag., 2006—08. Fellow: Am. Coll. Trust and Estate Counsel; mem.: Tenn. Bar Assn., Memphis Bar Assn. Office: Williams McDaniel Wolfe & Womack 5521 Murray Ave Memphis TN 38119 Office Phone: 901-767-8200. E-mail: sMcDaniel@wmww.com.

MCDANIEL, CHRIS, state legislator; b. Laurel, Miss., June 21, 1971; m. Jill Tullos; 1 child, Cambridge. Attended, Jones County Jr. coll., William Carey U.; JD, U. Miss. sch. of Law. Atty.; ptnr. Hortman, Harlow, Martindale, Bassi, Robinson & McDaniel; mem. Dist. 42 Miss. State Senate, 2008—. Republican. Baptist. Home: 506 South Court Ellisville MS 39437 Office: PO Box 1018 Jackson MS 39215 Office Phone: 601-477-2291, 601-649-8611, 601-359-4090. Fax: 601-649-6062. E-mail: cmcdaniel@senate.ms.gov.

MCDANIEL, CONNIE D., consumer products company executive; B in Acctg., Ga. State U. CPA. With Ernst & Young LLP; dir., fin. reporting Coca-Cola Co., divsn. fin. mgr., Southeast and West Asia Divsn., divsn. fin. mgr. Germany, contr., 1999—2007, v.p., global fin. transformation, 2007—, v.p., chief of intenal audit, 2009—. Office: The Coca Cola Co 1 Coca Cola Plz Atlanta GA 30313-2499 Office Phone: 404-676-2121. Business E-Mail: cmcdaniel@na.ko.com.

MCDANIEL, DAVID HENRY, physician; b. Clarksburg, W.Va., May 12, 1952; s. Hubert Harold and Ada Virginia (Henry) McD.; m. Sheila Marie Travis, Sept. 17, 1994. BS in Chemistry cum laude, W.Va. U., Morgantown, 1974, MD, 1978. Diplomate Am. Bd. Dermatology, 1983. Emergency physician Monongalia Gen. Hosp., Morgantown, 1979—82; dir. McDaniel Lasu & Cosmestic Ctr., Va. Beach, 1982—; asst. prof., clin. dermatology Eastern Va. Med. Sch., Norfolk, 1991—, asst. prof., clin. plastic surgery, 1992—2010; command cons., dept. plastic surgery Naval Med. Ctr., Portsmouth, Va., 1994—2005; dir., rsch. and innovation Light BioSci. LLC, 2002—09. Adj. asst. prof., dept. biol. scis. Old Dominion U., 2001-; pres. The Ctr. for Disfigurement, Virginia Beach, 1993-, McDaniel Inst. Anti Aging Rsch., Va. Beach, 1995-; co-dir. Skin Color Rsch. Inst. Hampton U., 2008-; adj. prof., sch. sci., 2008-. Contbr. numerous articles to sci. jours. Named one of Best Drs. in America, 1994—2013. Fellow Am. Acad. Dermatology, Am. Soc. Laser Medicine and Surgery, Am. Soc. Dermatologic Surgery (com. practice mktg. and pub. rels. 1993-96, chair 1996); mem. Tidewater Dermatology Soc. (pres. 1987-88), Space Dermatology Found. (founding), Va. Space Bus. Roundtable (charter), Phi Lambda Upsilon. Avocations: nature and wildlife photography, bicycling, gardening, hiking, church and charitable activities. Office: Laser & Cosmetic Ctr 125 Market St Virginia Beach VA 23462 Office Phone: 757-437-8900. Business E-Mail: info@drmcdaniel.com.

MCDANIEL, DIXIE N., insurance company executive; V.p., home svc. adminstrn. Am. Nat. Ins. Co., 2007; v.p., career sales & svc. divsn. adminstrn. American National Insurance Co., 2007—. Office: American National Insurance Co One Moody Plz Galveston TX 77550-7999 Office Phone: 409-763-4661. Office Fax: 409-766-2912. Business E-Mail: Dixie.McDaniel@anico.com.

MCDANIEL, DUSTIN, state attorney general; b. Fayetteville, Ark., Apr. 29, 1972; m. Amanda Miller (div. 2007); 1 child, Emma Grace. BA in Pub. Adminstrn., U. Ark., Fayetteville, 1994; JD, U. Ark. Law Sch., 1998. Patrol officer Jonesboro Police Dept., Ark., 1994—96; legal counsel Craighead County Dem. Ctrl. Com.; ptnr. McDaniel & Wells, Jonesboro; mem. Dist. 75 Ark. House of Reps., Little Rock, 2005—06; atty. gen. State of Ark., Little Rock, 2007—. Named Outstanding State Legislator, Ark. Mcpl. League; named one of 10 Best Legislators, Ark. Dem. Gazette, 2005. Mem.: Craighead County Bar Assn., Ark. Trial Lawyers Assn. (bd. governors), Ark. Bar Assn. (chmn. civil litig. sect. 2002—03, chmn. Consumer Law Handbook com., Golden Gavel award, Disting. Svc. award). Democrat. Office: Office of the Attorney General 323 Center St Ste 200 Little Rock AR 72201-2610 Office Phone: 800-482-8982, 501-682-2007.*

MCDANIEL, JARREL DAVE, retired lawyer; b. Clovis, N.Mex., Oct. 17, 1930; s. Raymond Lee and Blanch McD.; m. Anne Louise McAllister; children: Jarrel Dave Jr., Julia Anne. AA, Riverside Coll., 1951; BA, U. Tex., 1956, LLB, 1957. Bar: Tex. 1957. Assoc. Vinson & Elkins, Houston, 1957-69, ptnr., 1969-96; of counsel Sheinfeld, Maley & Kay, Houston, 1997-2001; sr. counsel Akin Gump Strauss Hauer & Feld LLP, Houston, 2001—06; counsel King & Spalding, LLP, Houston, 2007—11. Author, lectr. in field. Served with USAF, 1950-54. Mem.: State Bar Tex., Am. Coll. Bankruptcy, Houston Club. Roman Catholic. Home: 1217 Potomac Dr Houston TX 77057-1919

MCDANIEL, JEANNIE, state legislator; b. Dec. 10, 1948; m. Joseph McDaniel; 4 children. Associate degree, Tulsa Cmty. Coll.; BA, Univ. Okla. Coordinator Tulsa Mayor's Office for Neighborhoods; staff Citizens Crime Commn., 1981—91; former mem. Tulsa Pub. Works Dept.; mem. Southern Regional Edn. Board's Legislative Adv. Council, Interagency Coordinating Coun. for Early Childhood Intervention; mem. Dist 78 Okla. House of Representatives, 2005—. Democrat. Mailing: 1416 S Marion Ave Tulsa OK 74112 Office: 2300 N Lincoln Blvd Rm 508 Oklahoma City OK 73105 Office Phone: 405-557-7334. E-mail: jeanniemcdaniel@okhouse.gov.

MCDANIEL, MICHAEL K., wholesale distribution executive, human resources specialist; b. Durham, NC, 1949; Grad., U. NC, Chapel Hill, 1972. Dir. human resources & orgnl. devel. City of Wilson, NC, 1978—95; dir. human resources Standard Comml. Corp., 1996—97, v.p. human resources, 1997—2004, sr. v.p. human resources, 2004—05, Alliance One International, Inc., 2005—. Office: Alliance One International Inc 8001 Aerial Ctr Pky Morrisville NC 27560-2009 Office Phone: 919-379-4300. Office Fax: 919-379-4346.

MCDANIEL, RANDY, state legislator; b. Alva, Okla., Aug. 8, 1967; m. Julie M. Elizabeth; children: Grace, John Thomas. BA, Univ. Okla.; MPhil, Cambridge Univ., England; postgraduate studies, Georgetown Univ. Inst. Bus. & Govt. Affairs. Trust officer City Bank & Trust, 1992—95, investment officer, 1992—95; first v.p. investments dept. Wachovia Securities; mem. Dist. 83 Okla. House of Representatives, 2007—. Field artillery officer, engr. officer Okla. Nat. Guard, 1988—99. Mem.: Am. Red Cross. Republican. Address: 1104 Fenwick Pl Oklahoma City OK 73116 Office: 2300 N Lincoln Blvd Rm 302-B Oklahoma City OK 73105 Office Phone: 405-557-7409. E-mail: randy.mcdaniel@okhouse.gov.

MCDANIEL, STEVE K., state legislator; b. Wildersville, Tenn., Oct. 20, 1951; m. Phyllis Taylor; 1 child, Andrea. House rep., Tenn.; city mgr. Parkers Crossroads, 1981—88; pres. Henderson County C. of C., 1987—88; state rep. Dist. 72 Tenn., 1989—; minority leader; mem. Health & Human Resources Com., Fin. Com., Ways & Means Com., Calendar, Rules & Ethics Com., Select Com. on Rules, TennCare Oversight Com.; restaurateur, pres. & gen. mgr. Cotton Patch Inc. Recipient Jefferson Davis award, UDC, 1983, Robert E. Lee award, SCV, 1987; named Tenn. Restaurateur of Yr., 1985. Mem.: Tourism Assn. SW Tenn. (chmn. 1984—85), Henderson County Hist. Soc. (pres. 1976—77), Jackson Area C. of C., Carroll County C. of C., West Tenn. Hist. Soc., Tenn. Restaurant Assn. (pres. 1983—84, bd. dir.), Nat. Restaurant Assn., Henderson County Possum Club. Republican. Office: 97 Battleground Dr Wildersville TN 38388 also: 115 War Memorial Bldg Nashville TN 37243-0172 Office Phone: 731-968-7883, 615-741-0750. Office Fax: 731-968-8069, 615-253-0214. Business E-Mail: rep.steve.mcdaniel@capitol.tn.gov.

MCDAVID, GEORGE EUGENE (GENE), retired newspaper executive; b. McComb, Miss., June 30, 1930; s. O. C. and Inez S. McDavid; m. Betty Ernestine Tinsley, Sept. 24, 1949; children: Carol, Martha Gene Newman. BBA cum laude, U. Houston, 1965. Owner, pub. Wilk Amite Record, Gloster, Miss., 1949-58; with Houston Chronicle, 1958—, prodn. mgr., 1967-74, v.p. ops., 1974-85, v.p., gen. mgr., 1985-90, pres., 1990-98, ret., 1998. Mem. adv. bd. Am. Press Inst.; past pres., bd. dirs. S.W. Wch. Printing Mgmt. Chmn. Greater Houston chpt. ARC, 1st vice-chmn.; pres.'s counsel Houston Bapt. U; vice-chmn. Sam Houston Boy Scouts Am., United Negro Coll. Fund, Asia Soc. Goodwill Industries, YMCA; chmn. Houston Forum, Houston region Am. Cancer Soc., bd. regents, 1997—; spl. deacon Second Bapt. Ch., Houston.; bd. dirs. Nat. Conf. Christians and Jews; nat. bd. govs. Greater Houston chpt. ARC; bd. dirs. Greater Houston Partnership; bd. dirs., pres. Houston Symphony; bd. dirs., v.p. Books of the World; vice-chmn. devel. bd. U. Houston, chair bd. regents, 2003; sec. U. Houston Found., bd. dirs. Recipient Franklin award, U. Houston, 1961, Disting. Alumnus award, 1990, 1997, Taggart award, Tex. Newspaper, 1992, Man of Yr. award, NCCJ, 1993, named Outstanding Ex-Citizen Gloster, 1973, Houston Father of Yr., 1996, named to Miss. Jour. Hall of Fame, 2002. Mem.: So. Newspaper Pubs. Assn. (pres.), Am. Newspaper Pubs. Assn. (chmn. tech. com.), Pine Forest Country Club, Houston C. of C. (Houston Citizen's Cmty. Svc. award 1993, named Houston Cultural Leader of Yr. 1998), Tex. Daily Newspaper Assn. (pres.), Crown Colony Country Club, Beta Gamma Sigma, Phi Kappa Phi. Address: 403 Hunters Park Ln Houston TX 77024-5438 Personal E-mail: exegem@hotmail.com.

MCDAVID, WILLIAM HENRY, lawyer, mortgage company executive; b. NYC, May 10, 1946; m. Sylvia Noin, Dec. 21, 1984; children: Andrew, Madeline, William, Flora. AB, Columbia Coll., NYC, 1968; JD, Yale Law Sch., 1972. Assoc. Debevoise & Plimpton LLP, NYC, 1972-81; asst. gen. counsel Bankers Trust Co., NYC, 1981-83, assoc. gen. counsel, 1983-84, v.p., 1984-85, v.p., counsel, 1986-88; gen. counsel J.P. Morgan & Co., NYC, 1988—2000, J.P. Morgan Chase & Co., NYC, 2000—03, co-gen. counsel, 2004—06; exec. v.p., gen. counsel, corporate sec. Freddie Mac (Fed. Home Loan Mortgage Co.), McLean, Va., 2012—. Office: Freddie Mac (Federal Home Loan Mortgage Co 8200 Jones Branch Dr Mc Lean VA 22102*

MCDERMID, MARGARET E. (LYN MCDERMID), information technology executive; b. 1948; BBA, Mary Baldwin Coll., 1995; MBA, U. Richmond, 2000. With Stone & Webster Engring. Corp.; joined Va. Power, 1982, various positions, engring. & constrn. dept., 1982—86, dir., adminstrv. svcs., 1986—98; v.p., info. tech. Dominion Resources, Inc., 1998—2000, sr. v.p., info. tech., 2001—12; chief info officer Dominion Va. Power, 2001—12; chief info. officer (CIO) Fed. Reserve Bank Richmond, 2013—. Mem. apptd. by Gov. Gilmore CIO Adv. Bd., 2000; bd. dirs. Fed. Res. Bank, Richmond, 2007—. Chair bd. trustees Mary Baldwin Coll.; chair bd. dirs. RichTech. Recipient Exec. Women in Bus. Achievement award, 2008; named one of The 100 Premier IT Leaders, Computerworld, 2004, The YWCA's Outstanding women, 2010. Achievements include first woman to enter the Apprentice Program at Newport News Shipyard where she completed the Patternmaker's program. Office: Federal Reserve Bank Richmond 701 E Byrd St Richmond VA 23219 Office Phone: 804-697-8000.

MCDEVITT, JOHN, delivery service executive; b. Upper Darby, Pa., Aug. 15, 1958; m. Lori McDevitt; children: Kelly, Tara, Shannon, John. BS in Polit. Sci., Rutgers U., 1980; grad., U. Mich., 1999. Part-time loader UPS, Edison, NJ, 1976—77, part-time supr. Bound Brook, 1977—80, package car driver, 1980—81, supr., 1981—84, mgr. Parsippany, 1984—87, divsn. mgr. Meadowlands, 1987—92, dist. mgr. East Long Island, NY, 1992—94, West Long Island, 1994—96, v.p. corp. compliance Atlanta, 1996—98, mgr. corp. labor rels., 1998—99, v.p. air ops., 1999—2003, sr. v.p. strategic integration, 2003—05, sr. v.p. global transp. services & labor rels., 2005—. Office: UPS 55 Glenlake Kwy NE Atlanta GA 30328

MCDEVITT, JOHN, retail executive; BA in Economics, Siena Coll., 1986; MBA in Bus. Mgmt., U. Ga., 1991. With fin. Pentagon Fed. Credit Union, 1996; v.p., fin. HSN, Inc., v.p., advanced svcs. Office: HSN Inc 1 HSN Dr Saint Petersburg FL 33729 Office Phone: 727-872-1000. Business E-Mail: John.mcdevitt@hsn.net.

MCDEVITT, LARRY S., lawyer; b. Asheville, NC, June 2, 1942; AB, Univ. NC, 1964, JD, 1968. Bar: NC 1968, US Supreme Ct. 1973. Ptnr. Van Winkle, Buck, Wall, Starnes and Davis, PA, Asheville, NC. Mayor, city councilman, Asheville, NC, 1981—85. Fellow: Am. Coll. Trial Lawyers, Am. Bar Found.; mem.: NC State Del., UNL Law Alumni (pres.), Internat. Soc. Barbaristers, Am. Judicature Soc., NC Assn. Def. Attys., NC Bar Assn. (pres. 1989—90, 1989—90), ABA (bd. govs. 2003—09). Office: Van Winkle Buck Wall Starnes 11 North Market St PO Box 7376 Asheville NC 28802-7376 Office Phone: 828-258-2991. Office Fax: 828-255-0255. Business E-Mail: lmcdevitt@vwlawfirm.com.

MCDEVITT, SHEILA MARIE, retired lawyer, energy executive, business consultant; b. St. Petersburg, Fla., Jan. 15, 1947; d. Frank Davis and Marie (Barfield) McD. AA, St. Petersburg Jr. Coll., 1966; BA in Govt., Fla. State U., 1968, JD, 1978. Bar: Fla. 1978. Rsch. asst. Fla. Legis. Reference Bur., Tallahassee, 1968-69; adminstr., research assoc. Constitution Revision Commn. Ga. Gen. Assembly, Atlanta, 1969-70; adminstrv. asst., analyst Fla. State Sen., Tallahassee, Tampa, 1970-79; assoc. McClain, Walkley & Stuart, P.A., Tampa, Seminole, Fla., 1979-81; govtl. affairs counsel Tampa Electric Co., 1981-82, corp. counsel, 1982-86; sr. corp. counsel TECO Energy, Inc., Tampa, 1986-89, asst. v.p., 1989-92, v.p., asst. gen. counsel, 1992-99, corp. compliance officer, 1993-99, v.p., gen. counsel Tampa, 1999—2001, sr. v.p., gen. counsel, chief legal officer, 2001—. Mem. Worker's Compensation adv. coun. Fla. Dept. Labor, Tallahassee, 1984-86; trustee St. Leo U., 1999—, vice chair, 2001-2005, chair 2005-; mem. bd. visitors Fla. State U. Coll. Law, 1996—, chmn., 2003-2005; mem. bd. advisors The Centre for Women, 1998—, Met. Ministries, 1996-99; mem. ethics adv. bd. U. Tampa Ctr. for Ethics, 1997-99; mem. jud. nominating commn. 13th Jud. Cir., 2001-2003; mem. Fla. bd. govs. State Univ. sys., 2003, vice chair, 2006-. Mem. Fla. Rep. Exec. Com., Tallahassee, 1974-75, Hillsborough County Rep. Exec. Com., 1974-75, Fed. Jud. Adv. Commn., 1989-93, Fla. Humanities Coun., 2000-2004, WW Women's Leadership, 2004—; bd. dirs. Vol. Ctr. Hillsborough County, Tampa, 1984-85, Hillsborough County Easter Seal Soc., 1994-95, Fla. Aquarium, 1999-2000, Lowry Park Zoo Soc., 1999-2004, chmn., trustee, 1986-94, also legal advisor; mem. transition team for Fla. Gov. Bob Martinez, 1986-87; trustee St. Leo U., 1999, vice chair, 2001-05, chair, 2005-07; trustee Fla. Orch., 2004—. Recipient Spl. Contbn. award for pioneering efforts in bus. ethics, U. Tex. Ctr. for Ethics, 2007; named Alumni of Yr., Fla. State U. Coll. Law, 2006. Mem ABA, Fla. Bar (vice chmn., then chmn. energy law com. 1984-87, jud. nominating procedures com. 1986-91, jud. adminstrn. selection and tenure com. 1991-93), Hillsborough Bar Found. (trustee 2002-), Hillsborough County Bar Assn. (chmn. law week com. 1990, corp. counsel com. 1986-87, internat. law com. 1994-95, Corp. Counsel of Yr. award 2003), Am. Corp. Counsel Assn. (bd. dirs. Ctrl. Fla. chpt. 1986-87), Hillsborough County Bar Found., Tampa Club, Tiger Bay Club, Tampa Yacht and Country Club. Roman Catholic. Avocations: bicycling, reading. Office: TECO Energy Inc PO Box 111 702 N Franklin St Fl 5 Tampa FL 33602-4440

MCDONALD, ALDEN J., JR., bank executive; m. Rhesa Ortique; 3 children. Grad., La. State U. Sch. Banking, Columbia U. Positions up to v.p. consumer lending Internat. City Bank, New Orleans, 1966—72; pres., CEO Liberty Bank & Trust, Baton Rouge, 1972—. Bd. dirs. FannieMae, Minority Alliance Capital, Ernest N. Morial Convention Ctr., Port Authority New Orleans, Stewart Enterprises, Inc.; mem. adv. bd. Entergy New Orleans; chmn. New Orleans C. of C. Mem. adv. coun. So. U., New Orleans; mem. fin. coun. Archdiocese New Orleans; chmn. Lindy Boggs Med. Ctr.; bd. mem. Tulane U. Sch. Medicine; mem. bd. trustees Loyola U.; bd. mem. United Negro Coll. Fund; mem. 100 Black Men Metro New Orleans; mem. met. area com. Com. for Better New Orleans. Recipient Loving Cup, Times-Picayune, 2001, A.G. Gaston Lifetime Achievement award, Black Enterprise, 2005, Whitney Young award, Urban League Greater New Orleans, Civil Rights award, Nat. Dental Assn., Minority Suppliers award, J.C. Penney; named to Bus. Hall of Fame, Jr. Achievement. Mem.: La. Bankers Assn., Nat. Bankers Assn. (R.R. Wright Presdl. award), Am. Bankers Assn. Office: Liberty Bank & Trust P O Box 60131 New Orleans LA 70160-0131 Office Phone: 504-240-5200. Office Fax: 504-240-5166. Business E-Mail: amcdonald@libertybank.net.

MCDONALD, BERNARD ROBERT, retired federal agency administrator; b. Kansas City, Nov. 17, 1940; s. Bernard Luther and Mabel McD.; m. Jean Graves, June 7, 1963 (div. 1996); children: Aaron Michael, Elizabeth Kathleen; m. Joann Huffaker, Aug. 2, 1997. BA in Math., Park Coll., Parkville, Mo., 1962; MA in Math. and Physics, Kans. State U., 1964; PhD in Math., Mich. State U., East Lansing, 1968. Prof. dept. math. U. Okla., Norman, 1968—83, chmn. dept. math., 1981—83; program dir. div. math. scis. NSF, Washington, 1983—86, program dir. spl. projects, 1986—88, dep. dir. div. math. scis., 1988—2004; ret., 2004. Author: R-linear Endomorphism, 1983, Geometric Algebra, 1976, Finite Rings, 1974, Ring Theory III, 1980. Recipient Meritorious Svc. award, NSF, 1995, Disting. Svc. award, 1999. Mem. AAAS, Am. Math. Soc., Math. Assn. Am., Soc. Ind. and Applied Math., Assn. Women Math., Sigma Xi. Home: 5016 35th St N Arlington VA 22207-2816 Personal E-mail: math1940@aol.com.

MCDONALD, JOHN WARLICK, diplomat; b. Coblenz, Germany, Feb. 18, 1922; s. John Warlick and Ethel Mae (Raynor) McD.; m. Barbara Jane Stewart, Oct. 23, 1943 (div.); children: Marilyn Ruth, James Stewart, Kathleen Ethel, Laura Ellen; m. Christel Meyer, Oct. 24, 1970. AB, U. Ill., 1943, JD, 1946; PhD (hon.), Mt. Mercy Coll., 1989, Teikyo Marycrest U., 1991, Salisbury State U., 1993; JD (hon.), St. John's U., 2007. Bar: Ill. 1946, U.S. Supreme Ct. 1951. With legal div. Office Mil Govt., Berlin, 1947; asst. dist. atty. U.S. Mil. Govt. Cts., Frankfort, Germany, 1947-50; with Allied High Commn., Bonn, Germany, 1950-52; U.S. mission to NATO and OEEC, Paris, 1952-54; fgn. affairs officer Dept. State, Washington, 1954-55; exec. sec. to dir. ICA, Washington, 1955-59; U.S. econ. coord. for CENTO affairs Ankara, Turkey, 1959-63; chief econ. and comml. sect. Am. Embassy, Cairo, 1963-66; student Nat. War Coll., Washington, 1966-67; dep. dir. office econ. and social affairs Bur. Internat. Orgn. Affairs, Dept. State, 1967-68, dir., 1968-71; coord. UN Multilateral Devel. Programs, Dept. State, 1971-74, acting dep. asst. sec. econ. and social affairs, 1971, 73; dep. dir. gen. ILO, Geneva, 1974-78; pres. INTELSAT Conf. Privileges and Immunities, 1978; U.S. coord. Tech. Coop. among Developing Countries, 1978; rep. with rank of amb. to UN Conf., 1978—83. Sec. gen. 27th Colombo Plan Ministerial Meeting, 1978; U.S. coord. UN Decade on Drinking Water and Sanitation, 1979; U.S. coord., amb. Third World Conf. on Indsl. Devel., 1979, World Assembly on Aging, 1980-82; chmn. fed. inter-agy. com. Internat. Yr. of Disabled Persons, 1980-81; U.S. rep. Internat. Youth Yr., 1981-83; coord. multilateral affairs Ctr. Study of Fgn. Affairs, 1983-87; profl. lectr. in law George Washington U. Nat. Law Ctr., 1987-88, lectr. in conflict resolution, multilateral diplomacy and art of negotiation; pres. Iowa Peace Inst., Grinnell, 1988-92; prof. polit. sci. Grinnell Coll., 1989-92; Disting. vis. prof. George Mason U., Fairfax, Va., 1992-93; chmn., CEO Inst. for Multi-Track Diplomacy, Wash, DC, Arlington, Va, 1992—; mem. Fgn. Affairs Res. Corps., 1993—; adj. prof. Union Inst., 1993-94, 97-98; adj. prof. conflict resolution, 1998-01, 05-06, George Mason U., 2008-09. Author: The North-South Dialogue and the UN, 1982, How to Be a Delegate, 1984, 2nd edit., 1994, Conflict Peacebuilding: Stories & Lessons, 2008; co-editor: International Negotiation, 1985, Perspectives on Negotiation, 1986, Conflict Resolution: Track Two Diplomacy, 1987, 2nd edit., 1995, U.S. Soviet Summitry, 1987, US Bases Overseas: Negotiations with Spain, Greece and The Philippines, 1990, Multi-Track Diplomacy, 1991, 2nd edit., 1993, 3rd edit., 1996, Chinese edit., 2006, Defining A U.S. Negotiating Style, 1996, The Shifting grounds of conflict and Peacebuilding, 2008, paperback, 2009, Conflict Resolution & Peacebuilding-The Role of NGO's in Historical Reconciliation & Twintorial Issue,2009; contbr. articles on aging, terrorism, water and conflict resolution; featured in exhibit Va. Hist. Soc., 2006, The Role of NGOs in Historical Re Peacebuilding,2009 Bd. dirs. Global Water, 1982-, chair, 1982—, Touchstone Theatre, 1982-88, World Com.-UN Decade of Disabled Persons, 1983-1992, Countdown 2001, 1987-93, People-to-People Com. on Disability, 1987—2003, Am. Impact Found., 1987-89, chmn. bd., 1988-89; dir. Am. Assn. Internat. Aging, 1983—2003, chmn., 1983—2003; v.p. nat. capital area UN Assn., 1993-98, mem., 1978—. Recipient Superior Honor award, State Dept., 1972, Presdl. Meritorious Svc. award, State Dept., 1984, Peace Builders award Search for Common Ground Internat., 2005, Alumni Achievement award U. Ill. Sch. Liberal Arts and Sci., 2004, Alumni of Yr. award U. Ill., 2006, Peace Maker award, Assn. Conflict Resolution, 2009, Lifetime Achievement award, People to People Internat., 2010, John W. McDonald Ann. award, U. Mass., Boston, 2011; named Patriot of Yr., Kansas City, 1987; nominee Nobel Peace prize, 1994. Mem. ABA, Am. Fgn. Svc. Assn., U.S. Assn. for Club of Rome (chair 2002-05), People to People Internat. (bd. trustees 2003-12), Soc. Profls. in Dispute Resolution, Consortium of Peace Rsch., Edn. and

Devel., Cosmos Club, Delta Kappa Epsilon, Phi Delta Phi. Office: IMTD 1901 North Fort Myer Drive Ste 405 Arlington VA 22209 Office Phone: 703-528-3863. Business E-Mail: jmcdonald@imtd.org.

MCDONALD, MARTIN, oil industry executive; Attended, Fraserburgh Acad., 1976, The Robert Gordon U., 1981, Harvard Bus. Sch., 2009. V.p., gen. mgr., ROV, Africa, Mid. East & Caspian Sea Oceaneering International, Inc. Office: Oceaneering International Inc 11911 FM 529 Houston TX 77041 Office Phone: 713-329-4500. Office Fax: 713-329-4951. Business E-Mail: MMcdon@oceaneering.com.

MCDONALD, MICHAEL RAY (MIKE), state legislator; b. Nashville, Tenn., Feb. 21, 1949; m. Mila Ezell McDonald; children: Amy, Lance. Former mem. advisor com. Farm Credit Svc.; former mem. Exec. Com., Sumner County Democratic Party, Tenn.; asst dir. debate U. Ill, Urbana, 1970—71; grad. tchg. asst., 1970—72; asst. prof. speech & theatre Austin Peay State U., Clarksville, Tenn., 1972—77, dir. debate & forensics, 1972—77; asst. prof. comm. Vol. State CC, Gallatin, Tenn., 1978—86; sec., exec. com. mem. Sumner County Dem. Party, 1983—87; prof. comm., 1986—2002; color commentator Portland High Sch., WQKR-AM, 1991—2001; chmn. rural rds. 100th, 101st & 102nd Gen. Assembly; mem. United Way, 1988; campaign coord. VSCC, 1989; state rep. Dist. 44 Tenn., 1995—; majority whip 100th, 101st & 102nd Tenn. Gen. Assembly; vice chmn. House Conservation & Environment Com., 103rd Gen. Assembly; chmn. rural rds. Subcom. House Transp. Com.; mem. comms. Com. Mem.: Sumner County Farm Bureau, Sumner County Hist. Soc., Bledsoe's Lick Hist. Soc., Tenn. State Employees Assn., White House C. of C., Gallatin (Portland, Westmoreland), Tenn. Farm Bureau, Sumner County Mus. Assn. Democrat. Church Of Christ. Office: 1695 A B Wade Rd Portland TN 37148 also: 37 Legislative Plz Nashville TN 37243-0144 Office Phone: 615-741-1980, 615-888-3081. Office Fax: 615-741-4322. Business E-Mail: rep.michael.mcdonald@capitol.tn.gov.

MCDONALD, PATRICK L., electronics executive; b. 1953; BS in Bus. & Acctg., Ind. U., Bloomington, 1975. Various positions in fin., ops. and product mktg. including v.p. in the internat. and svcs. divsns. Sq. D (now Groupe Schneider), 1979—2001; pres. Delta Consolidated Industries Danaher Corp., 2001—03; gen. sales mgr. Walt Disney Co., 2005—06; gen. mgr. elec. power products bus. Powell Industries, Inc., Houston, 2006—07, COO, 2007—08, pres., 2007—, CEO, bd. dirs., 2008—. Office: Powell Industries Inc 8550 Mosley Dr Houston TX 77075 Office Phone: 713-944-6900. Office Fax: 713-947-4435. Business E-Mail: Patrick.McDonald@powellind.com.

MCDONALD, PETER J., publishing executive; V.p., gen. mgr. Nat. Tel. Directory Co., various positions, sales trainee NJ; vice chmn. CMGI Inc., RH Donnelley (now Dex One Corp.), pres., CEO, dontech pub., pres., CEO, ameritech pub. yellow Pages bus., various positions NY, exec. v.p., gen mgr., donnelly Info. pub., 1987—93, pres., CEO, SBC Directory Ops., 1999—2000, pres. COO, 2004; CEO SuperMedia, LLC, 2010—. Vice chmn. Yellow Pages Publishers Assn. Office: SuperMedia LLC 2200 W Airfield Dr Dallas TX 75261 Office Phone: 972-453-7000. Office Fax: 972-453-3969. Business E-Mail: peter.mcdonald@supermedia.com.

MCDONALD, REBECCA ANN, natural gas company executive; b. Phoenix, June 14, 1952; d. William Robert and Regenia Lucille (Hall) Kennedy; m. John Edward McDonald Sr., May 26, 1977; 1 child, John Edward Jr. BS in Edn., Stephen F. Austin State U., 1973. Project procurement mgr., buyer Fluor Engrs. and Constructors, Houston, 1974-79; pvt. practice cons. Houston, 1979-81; devel. mgr. Panhandle Ea. Pipeline, Houston, 1981-82, mgr. customer rels., 1982-84, mgr. sales, 1984-85; mgr. gas sales Panhandle Trading Co., Houston, 1985-88, v.p., gen. mgr., 1988-90; v.p. Strategic Planning Tenneco Gas Co., 1990—; pres. Houston Mus. of Natural Sci., 2001—04; pres., gas and power BHP Billiton, 2004—07; CEO Laurus Energy Inc., 2008. Cert. power trainer Situation Mgmt. Systems, Plymouth, Mass., 1981—. Pres. bd. trustees The Chinquapin Sch., Highlands, Tex., 1986—; mem. Houston Jr. Forum, 1986—. Mem. Natural Gas Men of Houston (bd. dirs. Houston chpt.), Am. Soc. Tng. & Devel. (membership chair 1975-76, Most Valuable Mem. award 1976), Am. Bus. Women (hon. nom. bd.). Episcopalian. Office: Tenneco Gas Co 1010 Milam St Houston TX 77002-5312 also: Granite Construction Inc Bd Directors 585 W Beach St Watsonville CA 95076 Office Phone: 831-724-1011. Office Fax: 831-722-9657. Business E-Mail: rebecca.mcdonald@graniteconstruction.com.

MCDONALD, TIMOTHY F., marketing executive; Grad., Princeton U.; MBA, U. Penn. Sr. corp. mktg. and bus. devel. positions UnitedHealth Group, Inc.; sr. mktg. exec. Value Health; sr. v.p., Strategic Market Initiatives Amerigroup Corp., 2009—. Office: Amerigroup Corp Ste 100 4425 Corporation Ln Virginia Beach VA 23462 Office Phone: 757-490-6900. Office Fax: 757-518-3600. Business E-Mail: tmcdona@amerigroupcorp.com.

MCDONALD, WILLIAM E., retired telecommunications industry executive; Pres. NC Divsn. Ctrl. Tel. Co.; pres., CEO Ea. Region Sprint/United Tel., 1988—93; pres., CEO Mid-Atlantic Ops. Sprint Corp., 1993—97, sr. v.p. customer svc. ops., 1997—2000. Bd. dirs. Ctrl. Tel. Co., Martin Marietta Materials, Inc., 1996—, chair Nominating and Corp. Governance Com., mem. Exec. Com. & Mgmt. Devel. and Compensation Com. Office: Martin Marietta Materials Inc Bd Directors 2710 Wycliff Rd Raleigh NC 27607-3033 Office Phone: 919-781-4550. Office Fax: 919-783-4695.

MCDONNELL, BOB (ROBERT FRANCIS MCDONNELL), former Governor of Virginia, former state attorney general; b. Phila., June 15, 1954; s. John Francis and Emma (Meiller) McDonnell; m. Maureen Patricia Gardner; children: Jeanine, Cailin, Rachel, Robert, Sean. BBA in Mgmt., U. Notre Dame, Ind., 1976; MBA, Boston U., 1980; MA, JD, Regent U. Sch. Law, Virginia Beach, 1989. Various positions American Hosp. Supply Corp., 1981—85; policy intern Republican Policy Com., 1988; law clk. Office Commonwealth's Atty., Chesapeake, Va., 1989, asst. Commonwealth atty. Virginia Beach, 1990—91; mem. Dist. 84 Va. House of Delegates, 1992—2006, co-chair com. on Chesapeake & Tributaries, 2000—01, mem. rules com., 2000—05, asst. majority leader, 2002—06, chair courts of justice com., 2003; ptnr. Huff, Poole & Mahoney, P.C., Virginia Beach, 1992—2006; atty. gen. Commonwealth of Va., Richmond, 2006—09, gov., 2010—14. Chmn. Republican Governors Assn., 2011—12. Served in US Army, 1976—81 USAR, 1981—97. Named Legislator of Yr., Network Victims of Crime, 1996, Family Found., 1998, 2001, Nat. Legislator of Yr., Nat. Child Support Enforcement Assn., 1998, Legislator of Yr., Va Sheriff's Assn., 2005. Republican. Roman Catholic.*

MCDONOUGH, WILLIAM ANDREWS, architect, former dean; b. Tokyo, Feb. 20, 1951; s. James Edwin and Sara (Andrews) McDonough; m. Elizabeth Demetriades, May 30, 1981. BA magna cum laude, Dartmouth Coll.; MArch, Yale U.; AB, Dartmouth Coll., 1973; postgrad. in Art Studies, Yale U., 1973—76, MArch, 1976. Registered architect, NY. Photographer Kilkenny Design Workshop, Ireland, 1974; architect, builder William A. McDonough, Cork, 1974—77; architect Davis, Brody & Assocs., NYC, 1977—81; prin. Mad River Hydro, Warren, Vt., 1981—, McDonough, Rainey Architects, NYC, 1981—85, McDonough Nouri Rainey & Assocs., Inc., 1985—. Cons. Inst. for Indsl. Rsch. and Stds., Dublin, 1975—77; founder Solar Energy Soc. Ireland, Dublin, 1976, McDonough Braungart Design Chemistry, 1995—; dir. North Wind Power Co., Inc., Moretown, Vt., 1982, Am. Residential Architecture Found., NYC, 1983—; founding ptnr. William McDonough & Ptnrs.; dean sch. architecture U. Va., Charlottesville, 1994—99. Author (with Michael Braungart): Hannover Principles: Design for Sustainability, 1992; author: Cradle to Cradle: Remaking the Way We Make Things, 0202. Recipient Presdl. award for Sustainable Devel., 1996, Design of Yr. award, Bus. Wk. & Archtl. Record mags., 1997, Presdl. Green Chemistry award, 2003, Nat. Design award, 2004; named one of 50 Who Matter Now, CNNMoney.com Bus. 2.0, 2006. Mem.: AIA, Yale Club NYC. Office: William McDonough & Ptnrs 700 E Jefferson St Charlottesville VA 22902

MCDOUGLE, RYAN T., state legislator; b. Richmond, Va., Nov. 9, 1971; Pvt. practice atty. McDougle Law Firm, PC; state del. Va., 2002—06; state senator Dist. 4, 2006—; chmn. Joint Subcom. on Appellate Ct. Candidates. Mem.: Senate Cts. of Justice Com., Senate Agr. Conservation & Natural Resources Com., Senate Transp. Com., Va. Coun. on Indians, Va. Criminal Justice Conf., Atty. Gen.'s Youth Internet Safety Task Force, Senate Rehabilitation & Social Svcs. Com., AF&AM Lodge 344, Va. Supreme Ct. Com. on Dist. Cts., Va. Code Commn., Va. Crime Commn. Joint Legislature Task Force on Computer Crimes, Nat. Conf. of State Legislators Justice Info. Sharing Advisor Group, Hanover Ruritan. Republican. Baptist. Mailing: Dist Off PO Box 187 Mechanicsville VA 23111 Office: Gen Assembly Bldg PO Box 396 Richmond VA 23218 Office Phone: 804-730-1026. Office Fax: 804-730-1051. Business E-Mail: district04@sov.state.va.us.

MCDOWELL, DAVID LYNN, mechanical engineering educator; b. Red Oak, Iowa, Dec. 20, 1956; s. Leland Lee and Wilma McDowell; m. Kathryn M. McDowell, May 26, 1979; children: Matthew Todd, Andrew Joel, James Neal. BSME, U. Nebr., Lincoln, 1979; PhDME, U. Ill., Champaign, 1983. Asst. prof. mech. engring. Ga. Inst. Tech., Atlanta, 1983-87, assoc. prof., 1987-92, prof., 1992—, regents prof., 1996—, Carter N. Paden Jr. Disting. chair in metals processing, 1998—. Dir. Mech. Properties Rsch. Lab., 1992—; presenter in field. Mem. editl. bd. Internat. Jour. Plasticity, Fatigue and Fracture of Engring. Material Structure, Internat. Jour. Damage Mechs., Jour. Multiscale Computational Engring., Mechanics Advanced Materials and Structures; co-editor, Internat. Jour. Fatigue; contbr. over 300 articles to profl. jours. and confs. Recipient Alfred Noble prize ASCE, 1986, Ralph R. Teetor award Soc. Automotive Engrs., Outstanding Young Faculty award Dow Chem. Soc., 1990, Presdl. Young Investigator award NSF, 1986. Fellow ASME (Henry Hess award 1988, Nadai award 1997, editor Jour. Engring. Material Tech. 1997-2002), ASM Internat., Soc. Engring. Sci.; mem. ASTM (ann. fatigue lectr., 2002), Materials Rsch. Soc., TMS, Am. Acad. Mechanics, Am. Soc. for Engring. Edn., Soc. Engring. Sci. (v.p. 2001, pres. 2002), Khan Internat. (Medal Plasticity, 2008). Office: Ga Inst Tech GWW Sch Mech Engring Atlanta GA 30332-0405

MCDOWELL, JOHN HENRY, JR., lawyer; b. Las Cruces, N.Mex., June 1, 1957; s. John H. and Jacqueline (O'Sullivan) McD.; 1 child, Michal Jillian. BA in Econs., Stanford U., 1979; JD, U. Va., 1982. Bar: Tex. 1983, US Dist. Ct. (no. dist. Tex.) 1983, US Dist. Ct. (ea. dist. Tex.) 1985, US Dist. Ct. (we. dist. Tex.) 1987, US Dist. Ct. (so. dist. Tex.) 1995. Ptnr. Hughes & Luce, LLP, Dallas. Spkr. in field. Named one of Best Lawyers in Dallas, D Mag., 2005. Fellow: Dallas Bar Found., Tex. Bar Found., Dallas Assn. Young Lawyers Found. (life; chair fellows prog. 2004); mem.: Am. Intellectual Property Law Assn. (antitrust com.), Dallas Assn. Young Lawyers (pres. 1991), Tex. State Bar Assn. (long range planning com. 1990—91), Tex. Young Lawyers Assn. (bd. dir. 1991—93, Award of Achievement 1990), Dallas Bar Assn. (bd. dir. 1990—91), ABA (antitrust com. litig. sect., litig. and antitrust sect. Award of Achievement 1990). Office: Hughes & Luce LLP 1717 Main St Ste 2800 Dallas TX 75201 also: 5 Nonesuch RD Dallas TX 75214-3432 Office Phone: 214-939-5413. Office Fax: 214-939-5849. E-mail: john.mcdowell@hughesluce.com.

MCDUFFIE, HARVEY THOMAS, JR., construction executive; b. Hamlet, NC, Sept. 3, 1949; s. Harvey Thomas and Peggy (Baggette) McD.; m. Judi Elizabeth Scott, Oct. 23, 1969; 1 child, Aimee Katherine. BA, U. NC, 1978. Registered architect, N.C., Va., D.C., Md., N.Y., Pa., Colo. Designer Austin-Faulk Assocs., Southern Pines, 1968-70, Newman Bower Architects, Charlotte, N.C., 1970-73, Clark Tribble Harris & Li, Charlotte, 1973-75, pres., 1979; mgr. interior constrn. Cousins Properties, 1975-76; designer Omni Architects, Charlotte, 1976-79; group v.p. Jacobs Engineering Group, Inc. Recipient R.P. Beagley award Sandhills Coll., 1968. Mem. AIA, Real Estate Group, Nat. Assn. Indsl. Office Parks (NOVA chpt. bd. dirs. 1988), Soc. Mktg. Profl. Services (program chairman Washington 1986-87, bd. dirs. 1987—). Clubs: Washington Golf and Country, City of Washington, McLean Racquet and Health. Home: 6634 Madison Mclean Dr Mc Lean VA 22101-2901 Office: Jacobs Engineering Group Inc 1111 S Arroyo Pky Pasadena CA 91105 Office Phone: 626-578-3500. Office Fax: 626-568-7144. Business E-Mail: harvey.mcduffie@jacobs.com.

MCEACHERN, JOSEPH A., state legislator; b. Dillon, SC, Apr. 10; s. Lawrence and Gilbertine McEachern; m. Penny Smith, June 21; children: Joseph II, Aaron. Attended, Furman U., Columbia Internat. U. Real estate broker; mem. Dist. 77 SC House of Reps., SC, 2008—, mem. Agr., Natural Resources and Environ. Affairs Com. Democrat. Bapt. Mailing: PO Box 3751 Columbia SC 29230 Office: PO Box 192 Columbia SC 29202 also: Capitol Office 330A Blatt Bldg Columbia SC 29201 Home Phone: 803-786-8304; Office Phone: 803-735-1808, 803-576-2060, 803-212-6875. Office Fax: 803-576-2136. E-mail: mceachernj@rcgov.us, joemceachern@schouse.org.

MCEACHIN, ASTON DONALD, state legislator; b. Nuremburg, Germany, Oct. 10, 1961; m. E Colette Wallace; children: Meagan, Brianna, Alexandra. Atty.; state del. Dist. 74 Va., 1996—2002, Va., 2006—07; former mem. Mil. & Police Coms.; state senator Dist. 9 Va., 2008—; mem. Privileges & Elections Com., Cts. Justice Coms., Agr., Labor & Commerce Coms. Recipient Recognition award, Family Found, 1998, award, Alpha Kappa Alpha Education Advance Found., 1998. Mem.: Family & Children's Svc. (bd. dir.), Va. & Old Dominion Bar Assns. Democrat. Baptist. Office: Law Off Ste 100 5905 W Broad St Richmond VA 23230 Home Phone: 804-262-7377. Business E-Mail: DelDMcEachin@house.state.va.us.

MC ELHANEY, JOHN HESS, lawyer; b. Milw., Apr. 16, 1934; s. Lewis Keck and Sara Jane (Hess) McE.; m. Jacquelyn Masur, Aug. 4, 1962; children— Scott, Victoria. BBA, So. Meth. U., 1956, JD, 1958. Bar: Tex. bar 1958. Pvt. practice law, Dallas, 1958—; pntr. Locke, Liddell & Sapp, L.L.C., Dallas, 1976—. Lectr. law So. Meth. U., 1967-76 Contbr. articles to legal jours. Trustee St. Mark's Sch. Tex., 1980-86. Fellow Am. Coll. Trial Lawyers; mem. Am. Bd. Trial Advs., ABA, Tex. Bar Assn., So. Meth. U. Law Alumni Assn. (pres. 1972-73, dir. 1970-73), Town and Gown Club (pres. 1981-82). Presbyterian. Office: Locke Liddell & Sapp 2200 Ross Ave Ste 2200 Dallas TX 75201-6776 Home: 4906 Stanford Ave Dallas TX 75209-3122 Home Phone: 214-363-7700.

MCELRAFT, PAT, state legislator; Tech. sales rep.-Microbiology Products Co.; real estate broker; state rep. Dist. 13 NC, 2007—. Republican. Mailing: PO Box 4477 Emerald Isle NC 28954 Office: North Carolina House of Representatives 300 N Salisbury St Room 637 Raleigh NC 27603-5925 Office Phone: 919-733-6275. Business E-Mail: Pat.McElraft@ncleg.net.

MCELREATH, VICKI W. See WILSON-MCELREATH, VICKI

MCELROY, JACK, editor; m. Debra McElroy; 3 children. B in English & Journalism, U. Ariz.; M in Mgmt., U. N.Mex. Mng. editor The Albuquerque Tribune; reporter Douglas (Ariz.) Daily Dispatch, 1976; assoc. mng. editor, mng. editor Rocky Mountain News, editor, asst. mng. editor, dep. mng. editor, mng. editor, spl. projects editor, 1991, gen. mgr., combined internet ops., 1999; gen. mgr., combined Internet ops. Boulder's Daily Camera, 1999; editor Knoxville News Sentinel, 2011—. Office: The Knoxville News Sentinel 2332 News Sentinel Dr Knoxville TN 37921-5766 Office Phone: 865-523-3131. Office Fax: 865-673-3492. Business E-Mail: mcelroyj@scripps.com.

MCELVEEN, JOSEPH JAMES, JR., journalist, writer, newscaster, educator; b. Sanford, Fla., Feb. 23, 1939; s. Joseph James Sr. and Genevieve (Stoll) McE.; m. Mary Louise Young, Aug. 18, 1979; 1 child, Ryan Leighton. BA, Furman U., 1961; MA, U. S.C., 1968. Newsman WSAV Radio-TV, Savannah, Ga., 1950, 1959; editor, pub. West Ashley News, Charleston, SC, 1951-57; reporter, photographer Charleston Post, 1955-57; tchr. English and journalism St. Andrew's Parish High Sch., Charleston, 1961-65; dir. info., prof. journalism Columbia Coll., SC, 1965-68; prof. journalism U. S.C., Columbia, 1968-79; sr. pub. affairs specialist FCC, Washington, 1979-81; dir. pub. affairs adminstrn. Nat. Cable TV Assn., Washington, 1981-87; dir. internal communications Corp. for Pub. Broadcasting, Washington, 1987-92, dir. program adminstrn., 1992-96, sr. program officer, 1996-99; media/comms. cons. Vienna, Va., 1999—; tchr. English, Fairfax County Pub. Schs., Vienna, Va., 2002—. Ombudsman, columnist Alexandria Gazette, Va., 1981—88; pres. McElveen Seminars, Vienna, 2000—. Author: Introduction to Creative Writing, 1963, Modern Communications, 1964; contbr. chpt. to Dictionary of Literary Biography (Mencken), 1986, Words, Words, Words: A Journalist's Memoir, 1997, Effective Writing and Editing, 2000, 1940s: Decade on the Threshold, 2000. Mem. Orgn. of News Ombudsmen, Soc. Profl. Journalists, Mencken Soc. Episcopalian. Avocations: photography, reading. Office: 1807 Hursley Ct Vienna VA 22182-2105 Home Phone: 703-281-4237. Personal E-mail: jjmcelveen@aol.com.

MCELVEEN-HUNTER, BONNIE, international relief organization executive; b. SC, Jan. 1945; m. Bynum Merritt Hunter, Sr.; 1 child, Bynum Merritt Hunter Jr. Grad., Stephens Coll., Columbia, Mo., 1972; LHD (hon.), NC State U., 2006; LLD (hon.), Pepperdine U., Graziadio Sch. Bus. and Mgmt., 2008. Founder, pres., CEO, owner Pace Mag. (now Pace Comm.), Greensboro, NC, 1973—; US amb. to Finland Dept. of State, Helsinki, 2001—03; nat. chair Am. Red Cross, Washington, 2004—. Chmn. Alexis de Tocqueville Soc., United Way Greater Greensboro, NC; bd. mem. United Way Am., chair nat. women's leadership giving campaign; chair Women in Philanthropy Summit, Washington; internat. bd. mem. Habitat for Humanity; bd. mem. Internat. Women Build Habitat for Humanity, Habitat for Humanity First Ladies Build; founder $1 Billion dollar Women's Leadership Initiative. Recipient Dr. Carl--Christian Rosenbröijer award, Woman Entrepreneur of the Yr. award, Nat. Found. for Women Legislatures, Nat. Athena award for bus. and civic contbn., US C. of C., Trailblazer of the Yr. award, Women Leaders Forum, Outstanding Bus. Leader award, Northwood U., Nat. Alexis de Tocqueville Soc. award, United Way, 2004, Ellis Island Medal of Honor, 2005, Appeal Conscience award Pub. Svc. award, 2006; named Comdr. Grand Cross Order of Lion, Pres. of Finland; named to Jr. Achievement Bus. Hall of Fame, 2004. Achievements include being the first woman to be selected as Chairman to the American Red Cross in it's 126-year history. Office: American Red Cross National Headquarters 2025 E St NW Washington DC 20006 also: Pace Comm 1301 Carolina St Greensboro NC 27401 Office Phone: 202-737-8300.

MCENTEE, GERALD W. (GERRY MCENTEE), retired labor union administrator; b. Phila., Jan. 11, 1935; m. Barbara McEntee; 4 children. B in Economics, LaSalle U., Phila., 1956; student, Temple U., Phila.; grad. trade union prog., Harvard U. Labor leader American Federation of State, County and Municipal Employees (AFSCME), Pa., 1957, exec. dir. Dist. Coun. 13 Harrisburg, Pa., 1973, internat. v.p., mem. exec. bd., 1974, internat. pres. Washington, 1981—2012. V.p., mem. exec. coun., chair polit. edn. com. AFL-CIO; co-founder, chmn. Econ. Policy Inst., Washington; mem. Presdl. Adv. Commn. Quality & Consumer Protection in Health Care Industry, 1997. Contbg. writer Huffington Post. Recipient Hubert H. Humphrey award, Leadership Conf. on Civil Rights, 2004.

MCENTIRE, REBA NELL, musician, actress; b. McAlester, Okla., Mar. 28, 1955; d. Clark Vincent and Jacqueline (Smith) McE.; m. Charlie Battles June 21, 1976 (div. 1987); m. Narvel Blackstock, June 3, 1989; 1 child, Shelby Steven McEntire Blackstock; 3 stepchildren. Student elem. edn., music, Southeastern State U., Durant, Okla., 1976. Rec. artist Mercury Records, 1978-83, MCA Records, 1984—2008, Valory Music Co., 2008—. Albums: Reba McEntire, 1977, Out of a Dream, 1979, Feel the Fire, 1980, Heart to Heart, 1981, Unlimited, 1982, Behind the Scene, 1983, Just a Little Love, 1984, My Kind of Country, 1984, Have I Got a Deal for You, 1985, The Best of Reba McEntire, 1985, Reba Nell McEntire, 1986, Whoever's in New England, 1986, What Am I Gonna Do About You, 1987, Greatest Hits, 1987, Merry Christmas To You, 1987, The Last One To Know, 1988, Reba, 1988, Sweet 16, 1989, Rumor Has It, 1990, Reba Live, 1989, For My Broken Heart, 1991, Forever in Your Eyes, 1992, It's Your Call, 1992, Greatest Hits Vol. 2, 1993, Read My Mind, 1994, Oklahoma Girl, 1994, Starting Over, 1995, What If It's You, 1996, If You See Him, 1998, Forever Reba, 1998, Moments and Memories: The Best of Reba, 1998, Star Profile, 1999, So Good Together, 1999, The Secret of Giving: A Christmas Collection, 1999, I'll Be, 2000, Greatest Hits Vol. III: I'm a Survivor, 2001, Room to Breathe, 2003, The Christmas Collection: The Best of Reba, 2003, Reba #1's, 2005, The Best of Reba McEntire, 2007, Reba Duets, 2007, 50 Greatest Hits, 2008, Love Revival, 2008, Keep On Loving You, 2009, All the Women I Am, 2010; author: (with Tom Carter) Reba: My Story, 1995, Comfort from a Country Quilt, 2000; actress: (stage) Annie Get Your Gun, 2001 South Pacific, 2006, (films) Tremors, 1990, The Little Rascals, 1994, North, 1994, One Night at McCool's, 2001, (voice) The Fox & the Hound 2, 2006, (voice) Charlotte's Web, 2006, (TV films) The Gambler Returns: The Luck of the Draw, 1991, The Man From Left Field, 1993, Is There Life Out There?, 1994, Buffalo Girls, 1995, Forever Love, 1998, Secret of Giving, 1999, (TV series) Malibu Country, 2012-13, (TV appearances) Country Gold, 1982, Bob Hope Winterfest Christmas Show, 1987, (video) Wrestlemania VIII, 1992, Evening Shade, 1993, Frasier, 1994, The Roseanne Show, 1998, (voice) Hercules, 1998, One Life to Live, Working Class, 2011;

actress, prodr.: (TV series) Reba, 2001-07 (Favorite Female Performer in a New TV Series, People's Choice Awards, 2002); (host) Acad. Country Music awards, 2004-12. Spokesperson Middle Tenn. United Way, 1988, Nat. and State 4-H Alumni, Bob Hope's Hope for a Drug Free Am.; Nat. spokesperson Am. Lung Assn., 1990-91. Recipient numerous awards in Country music including Disting. Alumni award Southeastern State U., Female Vocalist award Country Music Assn., 1984, 85, 86, 87, Grammy award for Best Country Vocal Performance, 1987, Grammy award, Best Country Vocal Collaboration for "Does He Love You" with Linda Davis, 1994, Entertainer of Yr. award Country Radio Awards, 1994, Female Vocalist award, 1994; named Entertainer of Yr., Country Music Assn., 1986, Female Vocalist of Yr. Acad. Country Music, 1984, 85, 86, 87, 92, Top Female Vocalist, 1984, 85, 86, 87, 1991, 94, Internat. Artist Achievement award, 2004, Am. Music award Favorite Female Country Artist, 1988, 90, 91, 92, 93, 94, 98, 2004, Am. Music award, 1989, 90, 91, 92, Favorite Country Album, 1991, 1993, 1995, Favorite Female Musical Performer, People's Choice Awards, 1992, 1993, Favorite Female Country Performer, 1992, 1994, 1995, TNN Viewer's Choice Awards, 1993, Favorite Female Country Artist, Billboard, 1994, Favorite Country Album award Am. Music Awards, 1995, Favorite Female Country Vocalist, 1995, Favorite Female Artist-Country, 2004, Favorite Female Vocalist award People's Choice Awards, 1995, Top Female Vocalist of Yr. award Acad. Country Music, 1995, Entertainer of Yr. award, 1995, Home Depot Humanitarian award, 2002, Leading Lady award, 2003, Special award for Most Female Vocalist Wins, 2005, Favorite Female Vocalist award TNN Viewer's Choice Awards, 1995, Star on the Walk of Fame, 1999; named to Country Music Hall of Fame, 2011. Mem. Country Music Assn., Acad. County Music, Nat. Acad. Rec. Arts and Scis., Grand Ol' Opry, AFTRA, Nashville Songwriters Assn. Inc. Avocations: golf, horse racing, raising horses. Office: c/o Starstruck Entertainment 40 Music Square West Nashville TN 37203*

MCEVOY, M. KEVIN, energy executive; Undergraduate in Biology & Geology, Brown U., 1972; MBA in Marine Resources Mgmt., Tex. A&M U., 1979. Joined Oceaneering International, Inc., 1984, variou sr. mgmt. postions, v.p., 1990—98, sr. v.p., 1998—2006, exec. v.p., 2006—10, exec. v.p., COO, 2010—11, pres., CEO, 2011—. Office: Oceaneering International Inc 11911 FM 529 Houston TX 77041 Office Phone: 713-329-4500. Office Fax: 713-329-4951. Business E-Mail: mmcevoy@oceaneering.com.

MCFADDEN, DENNIS, psychologist, educator; b. Oakland, Calif., Oct. 2, 1940; s. Samuel John and Evelyn (Dinnerson) McF.; m. Nancy L. Wilson, Dec. 28, 1960; children: Tracie Ann, Devin James. BA, Sacramento State Coll., 1962; PhD, Ind U., 1967. Asst. prof. U. Tex., Austin, 1967-72, assoc. prof., 1972-77, prof., 1977—, Piper prof., 1987, Ashbel Smith prof., 1998—2011, prof. emeritus, 2011—. Contbr. articles to profl. jours. Recipient Jacob K. Javits Neurosci. Investigator award, NIH, 1984-89, Claude Pepper award of Excellence, 1989-91; NIH grantee. Fellow AAAS, Acoustical Soc. Am., Am. Psychol. Soc.; mem. Assn. for Rsch. in Otolarynology, Com. Hearing, Bioacoustics and Biomechanics (NAS-NRC com. on hearing, bioacoustics and biomechanics), Soc. Neurosci., Soc. for Behavioral Neuroendocrinology, Internat. Acad. for Sex Rsch., Orgn. for Study of Sex Differences. Avocations: jogging, bicycling, birdwatching, travel. Office: U Tex Dept Psychology 1 University Station Seay Bldg A 8000 Austin TX 78712-0187 Business E-Mail: mcfadden@psy.utexas.edu.

MCFADDEN, FRANK HAMPTON, lawyer, former judge; b. Oxford, Miss., Nov. 20, 1925; s. John Angus and Ruby (Roy) McF.; m. Jane Porter Nabers, Sept. 30, 1960; children— Frank Hampton, Angus Nabers, Jane Porter. BA, U. Miss., 1950; LL.B., Yale U., 1955. Bar: N.Y. 1956, Ala. 1959. Assoc. firm Lord, Day & Lord, NYC, 1955-58, Bradley, Arant, Rose & White, Birmingham, Ala., 1958-63, partner, 1963-69; judge U.S. Dist. Ct. No. Dist. Ala., Birmingham, 1969-73, chief judge, 1973-81; sr. v.p., gen. counsel Blount, Inc., Montgomery, Ala., 1982-91, exec. v.p. adminstrn. and govt. affairs, 1991, exec. v.p. legal affairs, 1991-93, exec. v.p., gen. counsel, 1993-95; mem. Capell & Howard, P.C., Montgomery, 1995—. Chmn. Blount Energy Resource Corp., Montgomery, 1983-88. Mem. jud. panel CPR Inst. for Dispute Resolution, 1985—. Served from ensign to lt. USNR, 1944-49, 51-53. Fellow Am. Coll. Constrn. Lawyers; mem. Am. Corp. Counsel Assn. (bd. dirs. 1984-93, chmn. 1989). Office: Capell & Howard PC 150 S Perry St Montgomery AL 36104-4227 Home Phone: 334-241-3700; Office Phone: 334-241-8041. Business E-Mail: fhm@chlaw.com.

MC FADDEN, JOSEPH MICHAEL, historian, educator; b. Joliet, Ill., Feb. 12, 1932; s. Francis Joseph and Lucille (Adler) McF.; m. Norma Cardwell, Oct. 11, 1958; children: Timothy Joseph, Mary Colleen, Jonathan Andrew. BA, Lewis Coll., 1954; MA, U. Chgo., 1961; PhD, No. Ill. U., 1968. Tchr. history Joliet Cath. High Sch., 1957-60; mem. faculty history dept. Lewis Coll., Lockport, Ill., 1960-70, asso. prof., 1967-70, v.p. acad. affairs, 1968-70; prof. history, dean sch. Nat. and Social Sci., Kearney (Nebr.) State Coll., 1970-74; prof. history, dean Sch. Social and Behavioral Scis., Slippery Rock (Pa.) State Coll., 1974-77; pres. No. State Coll., Aberdeen, SD, 1977-82, U. S.D., Vermillion, 1982-88, U. St. Thomas, Houston, 1988-97, pres. emeritus, prof. history, 1997—2007. Served with USNR, 1954-56. Roman Catholic. Office Phone: 713-942-5905. Business E-Mail: mcfadden@stthon.edu.

MCFALL, JOHN, performing company executive; b. Kansas City, Mo. Studies with Tatiana Dokoudovska, Conservatory of Music; student, San Francisco Ballet Sch., 1964-65. Formerly with San Francisco Ballet, prin. dancer, 1969; artistic dir. BalletMet, Columbus, Ohio, 1986-94; artistic dir., CEO Atlanta Ballet Co., 1994—. Choreographer Nat. Ballet Can., Am. Ballet Theatre, Dance Theatre Harlem, San Francisco, Hubbard St. Dance Co., Atlanta Ballet, for other artists, including Mikhail Baryshnikov and Cynthia Gregory. Choreographer Commd. 2 world premieres for 1996 Olympic Arts Festival; repertory includes: The Nutcracker; Peter Pan; Prisma; Precipice; The Great Attractor; Requim and this too shall pass; The Great Gatsby; Sleeping Beauty; Stella; Jupiter; Swan Lake; Cinderella; Giselle; Firebird. Ford Found. scholar, San Francisco Ballet Sch., 1964, Nat. Endowment for Arts fellow, 1978, 1980, 1985. Office: Atlanta Ballet 1695 Marietta Blvd NW Atlanta GA 30318-3644 E-mail: jmcfall@atlantaballet.com.

MCFARLAND, DEBORAH S., alderman, nurse; b. Panama City, Fla., Dec. 30, 1952; m. Paul McFarland; children: Angie, Janis, Theresa. RN, Baptist Sch. Nursing. Practical nurse, psychiatric technician nurse Youth Home Inc., Charter Hosp., Bridgeway Hospital Pool, 1991—94; RN Bridgeway Hosp. 1989-1991, 1989—91; contract nurse Little Rock, 1990—. Alderman Guy City Coun., 2005—; sec. Green Party of Faulkner County, 2008—. Mem.: Guy Assn. for Improvement of Neighborhood. Green Party. Baptist. Office: 335 Banister Rd Greenbrier AR 72058 Office Phone: 501-581-0070.

MCFARLAND, JOSEPH, retail executive; Joined Home Depot, Inc., 1993, various store positions, including dept. supvr., asst. store mgr., dist. mgr. Atlanta, Hawaii, store mgr., dist. mgr. LA, store mgr. Orange County, elec. sales assoc. Calif., dist. mgr., 1999—2003, regional v.p. NJ, 2003—07, NY, 2003—07, pres., Western Divsn., 2007—. Gulf war veteran USMC. Office: The Home Depot Inc 2455 Paces Ferry Rd NW Atlanta GA 30339 Office Phone: 770-433-8211. Office Fax: 770-384-2356.

MCFARLAND, KATRINA (KATHARINA G. MCFARLAND), federal agency administrator; b. 1959; BS in Metallurgy, Queen's U., Can., 1985. Lic. profl. engr.; DAWIA level III cert. in program mgmt., PMP cert. Gen. engr. US Marine Corps, 1986—90, acquisition responsibilities with the Marine Corps Sys. Command and dir. battle mgmt. and air def., 1992—2005; procurement head electronics Dept. Nat. Def., Ottawa, Ont., Canada, 1990—92; dir. acquisition Missile Def. Agency, 2006—10; pres. Def. Acquisition U., Ft. Belvoir, Va., 2010—; asst. sec. for acquisition US Dept. Def., Washington, 2011—. Contbr. articles to profl. jours. Recipient Meritorious Civilian Svc. medal, US Dept. Def., Commendation Meritorious Civilian Svc. medal, Dept. of Navy, US Marine Corps. Office: Defense Acquisition University 9820 Belvoir Rd Fort Belvoir VA 22060 Office Phone: 703-805-3360.*

MCFARLAND, MAC A., energy executive; 2 children. B in Environ. Engring., Va. Tech; MBA, U. Del. Lic. profl. engring., Del. Sr. v.p., mergers, acquisitions and divestitures Exelon Corp., v.p., wholesale mktg. and trading divsn.; exec. v.p., mergers and acquisition and strategy Energy Future Holdings Corp. (formerly TXU Corp.); chief comml. officer, exec. v.p. Luminant (subs. of Energy Future Holdings Corp.), 2008—. Recipient Bertuch Fellow, U. Del. Office: Energy Future Holdings Corp Energy Plz 1601 Bryan St Dallas TX 75201 Office Phone: 214-812-4600. Business E-Mail: mac.mcfarland@luminant.com.

MCFARLAND, TERRY LYNN, retired construction company executive; b. Knoxville, Tenn., July 8, 1947; s. Jacob E. and Virginia Kay (Allen) McF.; m. Hazel C. Davis, Nov. 1, 1975. Student, Ind. U., 1969-70, Wickes U., 1977-79. Prodn. control staff R.R. Donnelley & Sons, Warsaw, Ind., 1965-68; insp. Bendix Corp., South Bend, Ind., 1968-69; mgr. Wickes Bldgs. divsn. Wickes Corp., Argos, Inc., 1970-71, Crawfordsville, Ind., 1971—73, Macon, Ga., 1973-76, dist. mgr. Midwest, 1976-78, regional mgr., 1978-80; v.p., gen. mgr. Douglass Bldg. divsn. Stanley Smith & Sons, Columbia, S.C., 1980-81; ter. mgr. Butler Mfg. Co., Kansas City, Mo., 1981-84, southeastern area mgr., 1984-89; dist. mgr. Varco-Pruden Bldgs. divsn. United Dominion Industries, Memphis, 1989-96; dist. sales mgr. Nucor Bldg. Sys. divsn. Nucor Corp., Charlotte, N.C., 1996-98, Ga. ACI Bldg. Sys., Inc., 1998-99; S.E. area sales mgr. Ga. divsn. Nationwide Homes, Inc., 2000—03; ret., 2003. Served with U.S. Army, 1966-68, Korea. Mem. NRA, VFW, Am. Legion, Moose, Masons (Scottish Rite), Shriners. Home: 1665 Wesleyan Dr Apt 714 Macon GA 31210-0810

MCFARLANE, NANCY, mayor, Raleigh, North Carolina; b. Washington; d. Ralph and Jean Pletcher; m. Ron McFarlane; 3 children. BS in Pharmacy, Va. Commonwealth U., Richmond. Drug-store pharmacist; pharmacist Raleigh Cmty. Hosp., NC; owner MedPro Rx, Inc., Raleigh, 2002—; mem. Dist. A Raleigh City Coun., 2007—11; mayor City of Raleigh, 2011—. Coach, program coord. Odyssey of Mond; mem. NC Conservation Coun., Sierra Club, Sanderson Area Adv. Coun., Lead Mine Elem. Sch. PTA; North area v.p. Wake County PTA Coun.; v.p. Durant Mid. Sch. PTA; bd. dirs. Pharmacy Found. of NC at U. NC-Chapel Hill; pres. Ligon Arts Boosters, Greystone Homeowners Assn., 2003—07. Office: MedPro Rx Inc 140 Northway Ct Raleigh NC 27615-4916 also: Office of the Mayor City of Raleigh 222 W Hargett St Raleigh NC 27601 Office Phone: 919-996-3050.*

MCFARLANE, ROBERT CARL (BUD), energy company executive, former national security advisor; b. Washington, July 12, 1937; s. William doddridge and Alma (Carl) McFarlane; m. Jonda Louise Riley, 1959; children: Lauren, Scott, Melissa. BS in Elec. Engring., US Naval Acad., 1959; MS in Strategic Studies magna cum laude, Inst. des Hautes Etudes, Geneva, 1967. Commd. 2d lt. USMC, 1959, advanced through ranks to lt. col., 1975, ret., 1979; White House fellow, exec. asst. Pres.'s Coun. Legis. Affairs, 1971—72; mil. asst. to sec. US Dept. State, 1973—75, counselor, 1981—82; exec. asst. to asst. to Pres. for nat. security affairs NSC, 1975—76, spl. asst. to Pres., 1976—77, dep. asst. to the Pres. for nat. security affairs, 1982—83, asst. to Pres. for nat. security affairs, 1983—85; rsch. fellow Nat. Def. U., Washington, 1977—78; mem. profl. staff US Senate Armed Services Com., 1979—81; presdl. envoy to Middle East The White House, 1983; counselor Ctr. for Strategic & Internat. Studies, 1987—89; founder Global Energy Investors; founder, prin. Energy & Comm. Solution, LLC; bd. dirs. Vadium Tech, Inc., 2002—. Author: At Sea Where We Belong, 1971, The Political Potential of Parity, 1979; co-author: Crisis Revolution, 1979 (Alfred Thayer Mahan award for Lit. Achievement). Decorated Disting. Svc. Medal, Disting. Svc. award Sec. State, Disting. Pub. Svc. medal Sec. Navy, Meritorious Svc. medal, Commendation medal with Combat "V" USN, Army Commendation medal US Army, Bronze Star medal with Combat "V"; named Man of Yr., Am.-Swiss Found., 1985. Presbyterian. Office: ECS Group LLC 2300 Clarendon Blvd, Ste 306 Arlington VA 22201 Office Phone: 703-522-8211. Office Fax: 703-522-7506.

MCFARLIN, DIANE HOOTEN, publisher; b. Lake Wales, Fla., July 10, 1954; d. Ruffie Denton Hooten and Anna Loraine (Peeples) Huff; m. Henry Briggs McFarlin, Aug. 28, 1976 (div. 1993). BS, U. Fla., 1976. Reporter Sarasota (Fla.) Jour., 1976-77, asst. news editor, 1977-78, city editor, 1978-82; asst. mng. editor Sarasota (Fla.) Herald Tribune, 1983-84, mng. editor, 1985-87; exec. editor Gainesville (Fla.) Sun, 1987-90; from exec. editor to assoc. publ. Sarasota Herald-Tribune, 1990-99, publ., 1999—. Adv. bd. U. Fla. Coll. Journalism and Comm., 1987—; Pulitzer juror Columbia U., 1995-96, 2001-02, 2007-08. Mem. accrediting coun. Edn. in Journalism and Mass Comms., 1994-96. Recipient Alumna of Distinction award U. Fla., 1999. Mem. Am. Soc. Newspaper Editors (com. chair 1992, 94, 96, 2000, bd. dirs. 1994—, treas., sec., v.p. 2001, pres. 2002), Fla. Soc. Newspaper Editors (sec.-treas. 1993, v.p. 1994, pres. 1995), Southern Newspaper Pub. Assn. (bd. dirs. 2009-), Fla. Press Assn. (bd. dirs. 2009-), Cmty. Found. Sarasota County (bd. dirs. 2000-, vice chair 2010-). Office: Sarasota Herald-Tribune PO Box 1719 Sarasota FL 34230-1719: 1741 Main St Sarasota FL 34236-7824

MCFEE, ARTHUR STORER, physician; b. Portland, Maine, May 1, 1932; s. Arthur Stewart and Helen Knight (Dresser) McF.; m. Iris Goeschel, May 13, 1967. BA cum laude, Harvard U., Cambridge, Mass., 1953, MD, 1957; MS, U. Minn., Mpls., 1966, PhD, 1967. Diplomate: Am. Bd. Surgery. Intern U. Minn. Hosp., 1957-58, resident in surgery, 1958-65; asst. prof. surgery U. Tex. Med. Sch., San Antonio, 1967-70, asso. prof., 1970-74, prof., 1974-2001, ret., 2001, prof. emeritus, 2001—. With U. Health Sys., Bexar-County, 1968-; spl. cons. on emergency med. care text to AAOS. Contbr. articles to profl. jours. Served with USNR, 1965-67. Fellow ACS; mem. AMA, Am. Assn. History of Medicine, Assn. Acad. Surgery, Tex. Med. Assn., Bexar County Med. Soc., Tex. Surg. Soc., Western Surg. Assn., San Antonio Surg. Soc., Soc. Surgery Alimentary Tract, So. Med. Assn., N.Y. Acad. Scis., Royal Soc. Medicine, So. Surg. Assn., Internat. Surg. Soc., Halsted Soc., J. Bradley Aust Surg. Soc., Am. Surg. Assn. Home: 131 Brittany Dr San Antonio TX 78212-1721 Office: MC 7842 7703 Floyd Curl Dr San Antonio TX 78229-3900 Office Phone: 210-567-5730, 210-567-5726. Business E-Mail: mcfee@uthscsa.edu.

MCGAHA, VERNIE, state legislator; b. Columbia, Ky., Sept. 13, 1947; m. Connie McGaha; children: Brian, Susan. BS, Campbellsville U., 1969; MA, Western Ky. U., 1973. Prin. Union Chapel Elementary, 1986—88, Russell County Middle Sch., 1988—96; mem. appropriations and revenue com. Ky. Senate, Frankfort, mem. econ. devel. and tourism com., mem. agr. and natural resources com., mem. edn. com., energy com., labor and industry com.; mem. dist. 15 Ky. State Senate, Frankfort, 1996—. Band dir. Russell County H.S., 1969-86; prin. Union Chapel Elem. Sch., 1986-88, Russell County Mid. Sch, 1988-96. Republican. Baptist. Office: Office Ky State Senate 4787 W Highway 76 Russell Springs KY 42642-9670 also: Ky State Senate 15th Dist Office 702 Capitol Ave Rm 209 Frankfort KY 40601-3448

MCGANN, JEROME JOHN, language educator; b. NYC, July 22, 1937; s. John Joseph and Marie Violet (Lecouffe) McG.; m. Anne Patricia Lanni, July 26, 1938; children: Geoffrey, Christopher, Jennifer. BS, Le Moyne Coll., 1959; MA, Syracuse U., 1962; PhD, Yale U., 1966; LHD (hon.), U. Chgo., 1966, LHD (hon.), 1996, U. Athens, 2009. From asst. prof. to prof. U. Chgo., 1966-75; prof. Johns Hopkins U., Balt., 1975-80; Dreyfuss prof. humanities Calif. Inst. Tech., Pasadena, 1980-86; John Stewart Bryan univ. prof. U. Va., Charlottesville, 1987—. Author: Swinburne: An Experiment in Criticism, 1972 (Melville Cane award 1972), The Romantic Ideology, 1983, The Beauty of Inflections, 1985, Social Values and Poetic Acts, 1987, Towards a Literature of Knowledge, 1989, The Textual Condition, 1991, Black Riders: The Visible Language of Modernism, 1993; editor: The New Oxford Book of Romantic Period Verse, 1993, Poetics of Sensibility: A Revolution in Literary Style, 1996, Byron: Complete Poetical Works, 7 vols., 1980-93, Dante Gabriel Rossetti and the Game That Must Be Lost, 2000, The Complete Writings and Pictures of Dante Gabriel Rosetti: A Hypermedia Research Archive, 2000—, Radiant Textuality, Literature after the World Wide Web, 2001, Byron and Romanticism, 2002, D.G. Rossetti. Collected Poetry and Prose, 2003, Swinburne, Selected Poetry and Prose, 2004, The Scholar's Art: Literary Studies in a Managed World, 2006, The Point Is To Change It, Literature in the Continuing Present, 2007; author Are the Humanities Inconsequent?, Byron's Manfred, Black Riders: And Other Lines, 2009, The Shape of Things to Come: Online Humanities Scholarship, 2010; The Invention Tree, 2012; editor 27 scholarly books and 5 poetry books. Steering com. and adv. com., Digital Pub. Libr. America Recipient Mellon Achievement award, 2003, Richard Lyman award, 2002, James Russell Lowell award, 2002; Fulbright fellow, Fels Found. fellow, Eng., 1965-66; Melville Cane award, 1973; Wilbur Cross medal, 1994; etty Found. Rsch. award, 1999-2002 Guggenheim fellow, Eng., 1970-71, 74-75; NEH fellow, Eng. and Europe, 1975-76, 87-88, 2003—05. Fellow: Am. Acad. Arts and Scis.; mem.: MLA. Address: English Department Bryan Hall U VA Charlottesville VA 22903 Office Phone: 434-924-4064. Business E-Mail: jjm2f@virginia.edu.

MCGAREY, JENNIFER CAMPBELL, aerospace defense company executive; b. 1963; m. Tim McGarey; children: Kelly, Emily. BBA, Coll. William and Mary, 1985; JD, U. Va. Law Sch., 1990. CPA. V.p., dep. gen. counsel, sec. US Airways, Inc., 1992—2004; v.p., corp. sec. MCI Corp., 2004—06; v.p. human resources, asst. gen. counsel, chief compliance officer RCN Corp., gen. counsel, sec., 2006—11; corp. v.p., sec. Northrup Grumman Corp., L.A., 2011—. Bd. dirs. Wash. Met. Area Corp. Counsel Assn. Mem.: ABA, DC Bar Assn., Md. Bar Assn., Va. Bar Assn., American Soc. Corp. Secretaries and Governance Professionals. Office: Northrop Grumman 2980 Fairview Park Dr Falls Church VA 22042-4511 Office Phone: 310-553-6262.

MCGARVEY, JOHN T., lawyer; b. Cynthiana, Ky., July 26, 1947; BA, U. Ky., Lexington, 1970; JD, U. Ky. Coll. Law, 1973. Bar: Ky. 1973, US Dist. Ct. (ea. and we. dists.) Ky., US Ct. Appeals (6th and 11th cirs.), US Supreme Ct. Asst. law dir. City of Louisville, 1978—79; city atty. City of Anchorage, Ky., 1987—; shareholder, chair exec. com. Morgan & Pottinger, P.S.C., Louisville. Spl. justice Ky. Supreme Ct., 1990; adj. prof. U. Ky. Coll. Law, 2002—. Co-editor: Banking & Comml. Litigation Newsletter, 1991—93; contbg. author (numerous edits.) Civil Procedure Before Trial, election commentator Ky. Ednl. TV, 1979—2007; contbr. articles to profl. jours. Trustee, sec. Anchorage Fire Protection Dist., 1982—89; mem. adv. bd. Jefferson County EMS, Louisville, 1986—87; pres. alumni bd. U. Ky. Coll. Law, 1998—2006; chair Greater Louisville, Inc. Energy Policy Task Force, 2008—; mem. Ky. Study Commn. Uniform Comml. Code, Conf. Consumer Fin. Law. Mem.: ABA, Nat. Coun. Commrs. Uniform State Laws, American Law Inst., Louisville Bar. Assn., Ky. Law Assn. Office: Morgan & Pottinger PSC 601 W Main St Louisville KY 40202 Office Phone: 502-589-2780. Office Fax: 502-589-3498.

MCGEE, HENRY ALEXANDER, JR., academic administrator; s. Henry Alexander and Arrie Mae (Mallory) McG.; m. Betty Rose Herndon, July 29, 1951; children: Henry Alexander, Charles Nelson, Kathy Nan. BChemE, Ga. Inst. Tech., 1951, PhD, 1955; postgrad., U. Wis., 1955-56. Rsch. scientist Army Rocket and Guided Missile Agy. and NASA, Huntsville, Ala., 1956-59; from assoc. prof. to prof. chem. engring. Ga. Inst. Tech., Atlanta, 1959-71; prof. Va. Poly. Inst. and State U., Blacksburg, 1971-94, head dept. chem. engring., 1971-82; assoc. provost for engring. Va. Commonwealth U., Richmond, 1994-95, founding dean engring., 1995-99, founding dean emeritus, prof. chem. engring., 1999—; asst. to dean engring. and mfg. techs. J. Sargeant Reynolds C.C., 2006—09. Vis. prof. Calif. Inst. Tech., 1984; dir. chem. and transport sys. div. NSF, Washington, 1990-93; cons. in field. Author: Molecular Engineering, 1991; editorial adv. bd.: Chemical Abstracts; contbr. numerous articles to profl. publs. Bd. dirs. Greater Richmond Tech. Coun., Math. Sci. Innovation Ctr., 1995-2012; deacon, tchr. River Rd. Ch., 1995-. Recipient Cmty. Svc. award Richmond Joint Engrs. Coun., 2000, Leadership award Greater Richmond Tech. Coun., 2002; Rsch. grantee NSF, NASA, Air Force Office Sci. Rsch.; named one of five Outstanding Young Men of Yr. Atlanta, 1964, Acad. Disting. Engring. Alumni, Ga. Tech., 1994; Danforth assoc.; named to Hall of Fame, Ga. Tech., 2006. Fellow AIChE (chmn. nat. program com., mem. editl. bd. jour), AAAS (chmn. sect. on engring. 1985-86); mem. Am. Chem. Soc.; mem. Sigma Xi. Republican. Baptist. Home: 6 River Court Ln Richmond VA 23238-5581 Office Phone: 804-754-1412. Business E-Mail: hmcgee@vcu.edu.

MCGEE, HUMPHREY GLENN, retired architect; b. June 26, 1937; s. James Gladney and Elizabeth Adams (Williams) McG. BArch, Clemson U., 1960. Designer Clark, McCall & Leach, Hartsville-Kingstree, S.C., 1961; designer prodn. A. G. Odell & Assocs., Charlotte, N.C., 1962; chief designer Clark, McCall & Leach, Hartsville-Kingstree, 1963; sr. designer LBC & W, Inc., Columbia, SC, 1965—76, sr. v.p. client svcs. and design, 1976; pres. CEDA, Inc., Columbia, S.C., 1976-86; pres., treas. McGee-Howle & Assocs., Vero Beach, Fla., 1986—2002; pvt. practice Indian River Shores, Fla., 2002—05, Chattanooga, 2002—05; ret., 2005. Pub.: Who's Who in Interior Design, 1993-95; cited in 100 Designer's Favorite Rooms,

1993, 94, 95. With USAR, 1961-67. Mem. AIA, Nat. Soc. Interior Designers (award 1972), Am. Soc. Interior Designers (chmn. S.C. chpt. com. on Found. Interior Design Edn. and Rsch. 1976). Personal E-mail: hglennmcgee@comcast.net.

MC GEE, JOHN FRAMPTON, communications company executive; b. Charleston, SC, Jan. 9, 1923; s. Hall Thomas and Gertrude (Frampton) McG.; m. Ruth Bouknight Smedley, June 19, 1971; children: Beverly C. McGee Kinder, Catharine F. McGee Mebane, Charles V. Smedley. BS in Bus. and Polit. Sci., Davidson Coll., 1943. With Charleston Post-News and Courier, 1946-62; asst. gen. mgr. State-Rcords Newspapers, Columbia, S.C., 1962-64, gen. mgr., pres., co-pub., 1964-69; gen. exec. Knight Newspaper, Inc., Miami, Fla., 1969-70; pres., assoc. pub. Charleston (W.Va.) Daily Mail, 1970-87, pub., 1987-90; gen. ptnr. McGee Enterprises, Charleston, 1987—. Pres. Clay Comms., Inc. parent co Charleston Daily Mail, Raleigh Register, Post-Herald, Beckley, W.V.a, Enquirer-Jour., Monroe, NC, Shelby (NC) Daily Star, Sta. WWAY-TV, NC, others; bd. dirs., exec. com. AP, NYC; bd. dirs. Thomson Newspapers, Inc., NYC and Toronto, United Nat. Bank, Charleston, W.Va.; adv. bd. Sch. Journalism, W.Va. U.; vis. prof. Grad. Sch. Journalism, U. Nairobi, Kenya, 1992, 93, Harare Zimbabwe, 1993-94; vis. lectr. media matters USIS Wind Hook Namibia, 1994; print media counselor, Namibia and Botswana, 1995. Vice chmn. Charleston Area Med. Ctr., U. Charleston; chmn. bd. visitors, trustee Davidson (NC) Coll.; co-chmn. McGee Found.; bd. dirs. Coun. for Cmty. and Economic Devel. W.Va.; gen. exec. bd Presbyn. Ch. U.S.A., 1974-76; active SC Commn. for Higher Edn., 1966-69, Capt. inf. U.S. Army, 1943-45. Decorated Purple Heart with oak leaf cluster, Bronze Star with three oak lead clusters, Combat Inf. badge, Croix de Guerre with palm (France and Belgium); recipient Presdl. Merit citation Knight Found., 1995. Fellow Internat. Press Inst. (bd. dirs. Am. com., mem. UNESCO commn. for free press during South African elections 1994); mem. So. Newspaper Pubs. Assn. (bd. dirs. 1967-69, W.Va. Press Assn. (pres. 1977-78, New Eng. Soc. S.C., Cosmos Club (Charleston), Edgewood Country Club of W.Va. Office: McGee Enterprises Bank One Ctr Ste 312 Charleston WV 25301 E-mail: jfm@citynet.net.

MCGEE, KEVIN, state legislator; b. Mar. 21, 1970; m. Teri Dawn Milner. BS, U. Miss. Bus. owner; mem. Dist. 59 Miss. House of Reps., 2008—, mem. edn. com., investigate state offices com., pub. utilities com., select com. on utility cost recovery, tourism com., univs. and colls. com. Republican. Methodist. Office: PO Box 1018 Jackson MS 39215 Home: 400 S Lamar Blvd Ste D Oxford MS 38655-4002 Home Phone: 601-829-9701; Office Phone: 601-939-4910. E-mail: kmcgee@house.ms.gov.

MCGEE, LINDA MACE, judge, lawyer; b. Marion, NC, Mar. 20, 1949; d. Cecil Adam and Norma Jean (Hogan) Mace; m. B. Gary McGee, Dec. 19, 1970; children: Scott Adam, Jeffrey Sean. BA, U. N.C., 1971, JD, 1973. Bar: N.C. 1973. Exec. dir. N.C. Acad. Trial Lawyers, Raleigh, 1973-78; assoc. Finger, Watson & di Santi, Boone, NC, 1978-80; ptnr. Finger, Watson, di Santi & McGee, Boone, 1980-89, di Santi, Watson & McGee, Boone, 1989-95; judge N.C. Ct. of Appeals, 1995—. Mem. trustee panel U.S. Bankruptcy Ct., Greensboro, N.C., 1980-82; bd. dirs. Legal Services of N.C., Raleigh, 1980-84; mem. N.C. Bd. Law Examiners, 1986-93. Vice-chairperson Watauga County Coun. on Status of Women, Boone, 1979-82; trustee Caldwell C.C. and Tech. Inst., Hudson, N.C., 1980-89; mem. exec. bd. N.C. Assn. C.C. Trustees, 1983-85; trustee Caldwell C.C., 1981-89; mem. Pub. Edn. Commn., 2000—. Mem. ABA, AAUW, LWV, ABA Found., Am. Law Inst., N.C. Assn. Women Attys. (charter, treas. 1980-84, chair jud. divsn. 1997, Gwyneth B. Davis award 1997, Outstanding Judge of Yr. award 1999), N.C. Bar Assn. (bd. govs. 1983-86, co-chair lawyers in schs. com., Pro Bono Svc. award, 1992), N.C. Acad. Trial Lawyers (bd. govs. 1993-95), N.C. State Bar, Boone C. of C. (bd. dirs. 1982-85), N.C. Bus. and Profl. Womens Clubs (chair polit. action com. 1982-83, Young Career Woman 1980), Boone Bus. and Profl. Women's Club (Woman of Yr. 1980), NC Women's Forum, NC Supreme Ct. Hist. Soc. (bd. mem.). Democrat. Presbyterian. Home: PO Box 508 Corolla NC 27927 Office: PO Box 888 Raleigh NC 27602-0888

MCGEE, RICHARD K., energy executive; b. Houston, 1961; m. Kris McGee; 4 children. BA in Econ., Polit. Sci. & Managerial Studies, Rice U., 1983; JD, U. Tex., Austin, 1986. Ptnr. Vinson & Elkins LLP, 1986—98; sr. v.p., gen. counsel energy svcs. divsn. Duke Energy, Charlotte, NC, 1999—2001, pres., CEO, Internat. Divsn., 2001—09; v.p., legal & bus. devel., sec. PAA Natural Gas Storage, L.P., 2010—; v.p. Plains All American Pipeline, LP, 2009—. Bd. dirs., exec. com. Houston Ballet Found., Houston, Coun. of Overseers, Jones Grad. Sch. Mgmt., Rice U., M.D. Anderson Cancer Prevention Ctr. Advance Team. Office: Plains All American Pipeline LP 333 Clay St Ste 1600 Houston TX 77002 Office Phone: 713-646-4100. Office Fax: 713-646-4572. Business E-Mail: rmcgee@paalp.com.

MCGEE, WILLIAM C., state legislator; Former state rep. Dist. 93, NC; state rep. Dist. 75 NC, 2003—. Mem. Fin. com., Commerce, Small Bus. and Entrepreneurship com., Mental Health com., Transp. com.; vice chmn. Pensions and Retirement com.; chmn. House Select Com. on Homeowners Assns. With NC Army Nat. Guard, 1958—64. Republican. Mailing: Dist Off PO Box 5 Clemmons NC 27012 Office: North Carolina House of Representatives 300 N Salisbury St Rm 634 Raleigh NC 27603-5925 Office Phone: 336-766-4481, 919-733-5747. E-mail: William.McGee@ncleg.net.

MCGEE, WILLIAM HOWARD JOHN, retired library director; b. Rochester, NY, May 15, 1942; s. William Peter and Cecilia Matilda (Kuhn) McG.; m. Sheila Anne Drumm, Sept. 4, 1965; children: Kathleen Moira, Margaret Frances. BA with honors, U. Toronto, Ont., Can., 1965; MEd, U. Toronto, 1973; MLS, U. Western Ont., London, 1980. Tchr. Mimico (Ont.) High Sch., 1966-67; tchr., libr. Applewood Secondary Sch., Mississauga, Ont., 1967-71; libr. Crestwood Secondary Sch., Peterborough, Ont., 1971-74; libr. cons. Cayman Islands Edn. Dept., Grand Cayman, B.W.I., 1975-79; adminstrv. asst. Lake Erie Regional Libr., London, Ont., 1980-83; chief libr. Ft. Erie (Ont.) Pub. Libr., 1983-86; asst. dir. McAllen (Tex.) Pub. Libr., 1986-89; coord. Hidalgo County Libr. System, McAllen, 1989—2001; libr. br. mgr. Lark Cmty. Ctr. Library, McAllen, 2001—08. Cons. Grand Ct. Libr., Grand Cayman, 1974-79; mem. Tex. State Libr. Task Force, Austin, Tex., 1991-93; adv. coun. Libr. Svcs. Tech. Act, Austin, 1993—. Editor InTraLogue jour., 1980-83; assoc. editor Can. Jour. Info. Sci., 1980. Bd. dirs. C-ME-CU Credit Union, 1994-99, chmn., 1999. Mem. ALA, Ont. Libr. Assn., Tex. Libr. Assn. (chmn. dist. 4 1994-95, 96-97, intellectual freedom com. 1995-96, profl. rights, responsibilities, and recruitment, 1996—, centennial celebration com. 2000—), Bibliothecaires Francophones Internat. Roman Catholic. Avocations: gourmet cooking, music, travel, reading. Office: Lark Community Center P R PO Box 220 Mcallen TX 78505-0220 Personal E-mail: liam_mcgee@hotmail.com.

MCGEORGE, DON W., retired retail executive; b. 1954; Joined The Kroger Co., Cin., 1977, sr. v.p., 1997—2000, pres., Tex. Divsn., pres. Mich. mktg. area, 1993—96, pres. Columbus mktg. area, 1996—97, v.p., 1997—2000, exec. v.p., 2000—03, pres., COO, 2003—09, spl. adv. to CEO, 2009. Bd. dirs. The Kroger Co., 2003—09.

MCGERVEY, TERESA ANN, technical information specialist; b. Pitts., Sept. 27, 1964; d. Walter James and Janet Sarah (Donehue) McG. BS in Geology, Calif. U. Pa., 1986, MS in Earth Sci., 1988; MLS, Cath. U. Am., 1998. Phys. sci. technician U.S. Geol. Survey, Reston, Va., 1989-90; editor, indexer Am. Geol. Inst., Alexandria, Va., 1990-91; cartographer Def. Mapping Agy., Reston, 1991-93; tech. info. specialist Nat. Tech. Info. Svc., Springfield, Va., 1993-2000, Dept. of Def., Arlington, Va., 2000—04, FBI, Washington, 2004—06, Joint Staff, Arlington, 2006—07, Def. Contract Mgmt. Agy., Alexandria, 2007—08, Naval Rsch. Lab., Washington, 2008—11, Nat. Def. U., 2011—. Intern dept. mineral scis. Smithsonian Instn., 1985—86. Mem.: ALA, Geosci. Info. Soc. Office: 500 Fifth Ave Ft McNair Washington DC 20319

MCGETTRICK, MARK F., energy executive; V.p., customer svc. and mktg. Dominion; sr. v.p., customer svc. & metering Dominion Resources, Inc., 2000—01, sr. v.p., chief adminstrv. officer, 2002, exec., v.p., CFO, 2009—; pres., CEO Dominion Generation, 2003—06, pres., COO, 2006—09. Bd. dirs. Nuc. Energy Inst. Office: Dominion Resources Inc PO Box 26532 120 Tredegar St Richmond VA 23219 Office Phone: 804-819-2000. Office Fax: 804-819-2233. Business E-Mail: mark.mcgettrick@dom.com.

MCGHEE, CARLA RENEE, women's college basketball coach, retired professional basketball player; b. Peoria, Ill., Mar. 6, 1968; B in Sports Mgmt. with honors, U. Tenn., 1990. Forward Germany, France, Turkey, South Korea, Spain, Italy and Greece, Atlanta Glory, 1996—99, Orlando Miracle, 1999—2002; asst. coach Temple U. Owls, 2003—04, Auburn U. Tigers, 2004—06; amb., cons. Atlanta Dream, 2007; asst. coach U SC Gamecocks, 2008—. Mem. USA Women's Nat. Team, 1996. Recipient Gold medal, Olympic Games, Atlanta, 1996. Achievements include being a member of two Tennessee Lady Volunteers NCAA Women's National Basketball Championship teams, 1987, 1989. Office: U SC c/o Dept Athletics Roost Bldg B 1322 Heyward St Columbia SC 29208

MCGIFFERT, MICHAEL, retired historian; b. Chgo., Oct. 5, 1928; s. Arthur Cushman and Elisabeth (Eliot) McG.; m. Genevieve White Mischel, Aug. 13, 1960 (dec. Mar. 15, 2007); m. Elizabeth Eastman, June 19, 1949 (div. 1960). BA, Harvard Coll., 1949; B.D., Yale U., 1952, PhD, 1958; postgrad., Union Theol. Sem., NYC, 1949-50. Instr. history Colgate U., Hamilton, NY, 1954-55, 56-60, U. Md., College Park, 1955-56; asst. prof. history U. Denver, 1960-64, assoc. prof., 1964-69, prof. history, 1969-74; editor William and Mary Quar., Inst. Early Am. History and Culture, prof. history, Coll. William and Mary, Williamsburg, Va., 1972-97; ret. Author: The Higher Learning in Colorado, 1964; editor: The Character of Americans, 1964 (rev. edit.), 1969, Puritanism and the American Experience, 1969, (with Robert A. Skotheim) American Social Thought, 1972, God's Plot: The Paradoxes of Puritan Piety, 1972, God's Plot: Puritan Spirituality in Thomas Shepard's Cambridge, 1994. Faculty rsch. grantee U. Denver, 1970, Coll. William and Mary, 1981-82, 89; rsch. fellow NEH, 1977-78. Mem. Am. Hist. Assn., Orgn. Am. Historians, Confr. of Hist. Jours. (pres.1987-89), Am. Antiquarian Soc., Mass. Hist. Soc. Home: 102 Old Glory Ct Williamsburg VA 23185-4914 Personal E-mail: mcgiff@widomaker.com.

MCGILL, HENRY COLEMAN, JR., pathologist, educator, researcher; b. Nashville, Oct. 1, 1921; s. Henry Coleman and Thursa (Lowry) McG.; m. Cloace Laurite Ferguson, Sept. 12, 1945; children: Margaret Ann, Laurilynn, Elizabeth Gail. BA, Vanderbilt U., 1943, MD, 1946. Intern Vanderbilt Hosp., Nashville, 1946-47; asst. prof. pathology La. State U. Med. Ctr., New Orleans, 1950-55, assoc. prof., 1955-61, prof., chmn. dept., 1961-66; prof. pathology U. Tex. Health Sci. Ctr., San Antonio, 1966-92, chmn. dept., 1966-72; sci. dir. S.W. Found. for Biomed. Rsch., San Antonio, 1978-92, sr. scientist, 1992-96, sr. scientist emeritus, 1996—. Contbr. articles to med. jours. Capt. M.C., U.S. Army, 1948-50. Mem. Phi Beta Kappa, Sigma Xi, Alpha Omega Alpha. Home: 4102 Fawnridge Dr San Antonio TX 78229-4212 Office: PO Box 760549 San Antonio TX 78245-0549 Business E-Mail: hmcgill@txbiomed.org.

MCGILL, JOHN YANCEY, state legislator, real estate broker, homebuilder; b. Kingstree, SC, Sept. 18, 1951; s. Frank H. and Peggy (Tomlinson) McG.; m. Pamela Jean Fennell, May 18, 1974; children: Lisa, John, Maggie. Attened, The Citadel, Francis Marion Coll. Mem. Dist. 32 SC State Senate, 1989—, chair Subcommittee on Natural Resources. Mem. agr. and natural resources com., fin. com., fish, game and forestry com., invitations com., rules com., transp. com. Chmn., deacon Kingstree 1st Bapt. Ch., 1987-88; past pres. Kingstreee Jaycees; mem. Kingstree Town Coun., 1976-79, mayor pro tem, 1978-79, mayor, 1984-88; bd. dirs. Waccamaw Regional Planning and Devel. Coun.; past chmn. Waccamaw Indsl. Revolving Loan Commn.; former mem. S.C. Dem. Com. Exec. Com.; mem. select com. Edn. Improvement Act; mem. Am. Legis. Exch. Coun.; bd. visitors Med. U. S.C., 1990-91. Named Legislator of Yr., S.C. Assn. Counties, 1993. Mem. Kingstree C. of C. (past pres.). Democrat. Office: 508 Gressette Bldg Columbia SC 29202 Mailing: 601 Longstreet St Kingstree SC 29556 Home Phone: 803-779-7790; Office Phone: 843-355-7217. E-mail: jym@scsenate.org.

MCGILL, SHADRACK, state legislator; b. Jackson County, Ala., Nov. 6, 1975; s. Dwight and Nita McGill; m. Heather Baugh Shadrack; 6 children. Attended, North Ala. CC. Owner Hydraulic Seals & Svc., Scottsboro, Ala.; mem. Dist. 8 Ala. State Senate, 2011—. Republican. Avocations: basketball, baseball. Office: Alabama State Senate State House Rm 731 11 S Union St Montgomery AL 36130 Office Phone: 334-242-7858. E-mail: shadrack.mcgill@alsenate.gov.

MC GIMSEY, CHARLES ROBERT, III, anthropologist; b. Dallas, June 18, 1925; s. Charles Robert, Jr. and Ellen Randolph (Parks) McG.; m. Mary Elizabeth Conger, Dec. 20, 1949; children— Charles Robert, Brian Keith, Mark Douglass. Student, Vanderbilt U., 1942-43, U. of South, 1943-44; BA, U. N.Mex., 1949; MA, Harvard U., 1954, PhD, 1958. Instr. U. Ark., Fayetteville, 1957, asst. prof., 1958-62, assoc. prof., 1962-67, prof. anthropology, 1967-90, prof. emeritus, 1990—, chmn. dept., 1969-72; asst. curator U. Ark. Mus., 1957-59, dir., 1959-83, Ark. Archeol. Survey, 1967-90, dir. emeritus, 1990—. Cons. archeology U.S. GAO, 1979-87, U.S.-Internat. Com. on Monuments and Sites; Rep. to Internat. Com. on Archeol. Heritage Mgmt., 1988-95. Author: (with G.R. Willey) Monagrillo Culture of Panama, 1954, Mariana Mesa, 1980, Indians of Arkansas, 1969, Public Archeology, 1972, Archeology and Archeological Resources, 1973, (with H.A. Davis) The Management of Archeological Resources, 1977, CRM on CRM, 2004; assoc. editor Am. Antiquity, 1972-80; Co-editor (with H. A. Davis) Southeastern Museums Conf., 1964-73; Contbr. articles to profl. jours. Mem. Ark. Rev. Com., Historic Preservation Program, 1968-76; collaborator Nat. Park Service, 1971-74, adviser, 1974-77; mem. Com. on Recovery Archeol. Remains, 1971-78; mem. adv. bd. dirs. Red River Mus., 1975-76; mem. adv. bd. Am. Indian Archeol. Inst., 1975-80, Ark. Natural and Cultural Heritage Dept., 1976-90. Served to lt. (j.g.) USNR, 1943-47. Recipient Cert. Recognition State of Ark., 1990; rsch. grantee Am. Philos. Soc., Am. Acad. Arts and Scis., Andean Rsch. Inst., Nat. Park Service, NSF, Smithsonian Instn., Wenner-Gren Found.; rsch. fellow dept. archaeology U. Cambridge, 1985-86, assoc. mem. Darwin Coll., 1985— Fellow: Am. Anthrop. Assn.; mem.: Archeol. Inst. Am. (Conservation and Heritage Mgmt. award 2006), Register Profl. Arch., Am. Assn. State and Local History (award of merit 1985), Am. Assn. Mus., Soc. Profl. Archeologists (bd. dirs. 1976—79, pres. 1983—84, founder, emeritus, life, Seiberling 1989, presidential recognition award 1997), Am. Soc. Conserv. Archeology (founding, outstanding contrib. 1980), Southeastern Mus. Conf. (coun. 1962—71, editor 1964—77), Ark. Archeol. Soc. (editor 1960—83, Preservationist 1989), Soc. Am. Archeology (exec. comm. 1971—73, v.p., pres. 1973—75, pres. 1974—75, Distinguished Serv. 1975, excellence in cultural resource mgt. 1995), Register of Profl. Archeologists (Disting. Svc. award 2005). Office: Ark Archeol Survey 2475 N Hatch Ave Fayetteville AR 72704-5590 Home: 1923 E Joyce Blvd PO Box 125 Fayetteville AR 72703-3104

MCGINNIS, CHARLES IRVING, civil engineer; b. Kansas City, Mo., Jan. 31, 1928; s. Paul Sherman and Sidney (Bacon) McG.; m. Shirley Ann Meyer, Nov. 5, 1955; children: Gail B., Ann K., James P. BS, Tex. A & M Coll., 1949, M.Engring., 1950; grad., Army Engr. Sch., 1955, Command and Gen. Staff Coll., 1959, Armed Forces Staff Coll., 1962, Army War Coll., 1969. Registered profl. engr., Tex., Mo. Enlisted as pvt. U.S. Army, 1945, advanced through grades to maj. gen., 1976; area engr. Ethiopia and Somalia, 1962-65; dist. engr. St. Paul, 1969-71; dir. engring. and constrn. bur. Panama Canal Co., 1971-72, v.p., 1972-74; lt. gov. C.Z., 1972-74; div. engr. southwestern div. C.E., Dallas, 1974-77; dir. civil works Office Chief of Engrs. U.S. Army, Washington, 1977-79; civil engr., 1979—; exec. v.p. Fru-con Corp.; pres. Fruco Engrs., Inc., 1983-87; assoc. dir. Constrn. Industry Inst. U. Tex., Austin, 1987-93, sr. lectr. civil engring. dept., 1992-97; vice chmn. chem. weapons stockpile com. NRC, 2000—04. Vis. com. dept. civil engring. MIT, 1978-81; mem. Mississippi River Commn., 1975-77, Bd. Engrs. for Rivers and Harbors, 1975-77; chmn. water policy task force NSPE, 1979-81. Chmn. Combined Fed. Campaign coordinating com., C.Z., 1972-74; pres. C.Z. coun. Boy Scouts Am., 1973-74, exec. bd. St. Louis area coun., 1983-87, Capitol Area coun., 1987-90, Stonewall Jackson Area coun., 1999-2006; com. mgmt. Balboa YMCA, 1973-74; trustee C.Z. United Way, 1972-74, bd. mem. Gt. Hills Residents Assn. Austin, Tex., 1997-98, pres. Peacock Hill Svc. Co., Charlottesville, Va., 2005-07, vice chair Patriots Colony Resident's Assn., Williamsburg, Va., 2009-11 Decorated D.S.M., Legion of Merit with oak leaf cluster, Joint Svcs. Commendation medal, U.S. Army Commendation with oak leaf cluster, Chuong My medal 1st class Vietnam; named Disting. Grad. Civil Engring. Dept., Tex. A&M U., 2002. Fellow ASCE, Soc. Am. Mil. Engrs. (past pres. Twin Cities post and Panama post); mem. Assn. U.S. Army, Mil. Order of the World Wars, Mil. Officers Assn. America, Nat. Acad. Constrn. (charter), Tau Beta Pi, Chi Epsilon.

MC GINTY, JOHN MILTON, architect, consultant; b. Houston, Apr. 24, 1935; s. Milton Bowles and Ruth Louise (Dreaper) McG.; m. Juanita Jones, May 4, 1957; children: Christopher Harold, Jacqueline Ruth McGinty Carlson. BS, Rice U., 1957; M.F.A., Princeton U., 1961. With archtl. firm Barnes, Landes & Goodman, Austin, Tex., 1957-58, Ingram & Harris, Beaumont, Tex., 1958-59; prin. McGinty Partnership, Architects, Inc., Houston, 1961-89, City Assos., Inc., 1979-91, Bovay-McGinty, Inc., engrs. & architects, Houston, 1989-91; founder, pres. Am. Constrn. Investigations Inc., Houston, 1991-2000, McGinty Archtl. Consultants, LLP, Houston, 2001—. Instr. archtl. design U. Houston, 1965-67; White House fellow, asst. to Sec. of Interior, 1967-68; vis. prof. architecture Rice U., 1969-70 Named Disting. Alumnus Rice U., 1986. Fellow AIA (mem. U.S. delegation to USSR 1972, pres. Houston chpt. 1973, nat. pres. 1977) Office Phone: 713-868-7021. Personal E-mail: jmginty@arch.com.

MCGLADE, PETER GERARD, airline executive; b. Newry, Northern Ireland, Aug. 30, 1953; came to U.S., 1954; s. Peter and Josephine (Smyth) McG.; m. Nancy Carol O'Brien, July 23, 1976; children: Sean Peter, Erin Rose, Ryan Patrick. BS in Mgmt., Purdue U., 1975. Prodn. supr. L.D. Sehrieber Cheese Co., Green Bay, Wis., 1975-76; with Northwest Orient Airlines, Mpls., 1976-80; mgr. planning Air Cal, Orange County, Calif., 1980-82; mgr. market planning Pacific Southwest Airlines, San Diego, 1982-83; market planner, ramp agt., ticket agt., station svc. mgr., reservations control analyst, mgr. revenue mgmt. Southwest Airlines Co., Dallas, 1983-86, dir. scheduling, 1986; v.p., network planning Southwest Airlines Co. Roman Catholic. Home: 2913 Redwood Dr Carrollton TX 75007-4840 Office: Southwest Airlines Co 2702 Love Field Dr Dallas TX 75235-1600 Office Phone: 214-792-4000. Office Fax: 214-792-5015. Business E-Mail: pmcglade@southwest.com.

MCGLAMRY, MAX REGINALD, retired lawyer; b. Wilcox County, Ga., Sept. 12, 1928; s. Edgar Lee and Allie Bea (Faircloth) McGlamry; m. Jean Louise Hilyer, Dec. 28, 1950; children: Sharon Kay McGlamry Christopher, Michael Lee. BS, Auburn U., 1948; LLB cum laude, Mercer U., 1952, JD cum laude, 1970. Bar: Ga. 1953, U.S. Dist. Ct. (mid. dist.) Ga. 1954, U.S. Ct. Appeals (5th cir.) 1964, U.S. Supreme Ct. 1972, U.S. Ct. Appeals (11th cir.) 1981, U.S. Ct. Appeals (4th cir.) 1985, U.S. Dist. Ct. (no. dist.) Calif. 1988, U.S. Dist. Ct. (no. dist.) Ga. 1989. Pvt. practice, Columbus, Ga., 1953-64; from ptnr. to officer Swift, Pease, Davidson & Chapman (name changed to Page, Scrantom, Harris, McGlamry, & Chapman, P.C.), Columbus, 1964-85; ptnr. Pope, Kellogg, McGlamry, Kilpatrick & Morrison, Columbus, 1985-90, Pope, McGlamry, Kilpatrick & Morrison, LLP, Columbus, 1990-2000; pres. Max R. McGlamry, P.C., Columbus, 2000—04. Exec. com. Muscogee County Dem. Orgn., Columbus, 1956-60; bd. dirs. Columbus Jr. C. of C. Ens. USN, 1948—49, Ens. USNR, 1949—59. Fellow, Am. Coll. Trust & Estate Counsel, 1973, Lawyers Found. Ga., 1983. Mem. ABA, State Bar Ga. (emeritus), Ga. Trial Lawyers Assn., Ga. Sr. Golfers Assn., Valley Sr.'s Golf Assn. (pres. 2003), Urban League of Greater Columbus, Inc., Columbus Lawyers Club (pres. 1964-65), Lions (Columbus chpt. pres. 1967-68), Green Island Country Club, Phi Kappa Phi, Alpha Epsilon Delta, Phi Alpha Delta, Pi Kappa Alpha. Democrat. Methodist. Avocations: golf, fishing. Home: 6941 Wethersfield Rd Columbus GA 31904-3317

MCGLONE, MICHAEL ANTHONY, lawyer; b. New Orleans, Jan. 6, 1951; s. James Godfrey and Dorothy (Barta) McG.; m. Suzanne Blanchard, Nov. 27, 1976; children: Kevin, Kathleen, Meghan. BBA cum laude, Loyola U., New Orleans, 1972, JD, 1975. Bar: La. 1975, U.S. Dist. Ct. (ea. dist.) La. 1975, U.S. Ct. Appeals (5th and 11 cirs.) 1975, U.S. Dist. Ct. (we. dist.) La. 1978, U.S. Dist. Ct. (mid. dist.) La. 1979, U.S. Supreme Ct. 1981. Law clk. to Hon. Herbert W. Christenberry U.S. Dist. Ct., New Orleans, 1975-76; ptnr. Kean Miller, 1976—. Fellow Am. Coll. Trial Lawyers; mem. ABA, FBA (bd. dirs. New Orleans chpt. 1986—, pres. 1995-96), La. Bar Assn., Southeastern Admiralty Law Inst., New Orleans Bar Assn., Maritime Law Assn., St. Thomas More Inn of Ct. (master barrister), Alpha Sigma Nu, Beta Gamma Sigma. Democrat. Roman Catholic. Home: 4708 N Turnbull Dr Metairie LA 70002-1447 Office: Kean Miller 601 Poydras St New Orleans LA 70130-6029 Office Phone: 504-585-3059. Business E-Mail: mike.mcglone@keanmiller.com.

MCGLOTHLIN, JAMES W., wholesale distribution executive; b. 1940; B, William & Mary Coll.; Law degree, William & Mary. Bar: Va. 1964. CEO United Co., Big Rock, Va., 1970—; dir. Birmingham

Steel Corp., CSX, 1989—. Bd. dirs. King Pharmaceuticals, Summit Fund, Massey Energy, Basset Furniture Industries Inc., Va. Bus. Higher Edn. Coun. Named one of Top 200 Collectors, ARTnews Mag., 2006—08. Office: United Coal Co 110 Sprint Dr Blountville TN 37617-5455

MC GLYNN, SEAN PATRICK, physical chemist, educator; b. Dungloe, Ireland, Mar. 8, 1931; arrived in U.S., 1952, naturalized, 1957; s. Daniel and Catherine (Brennan) Mc Glynn; m. Helen Magdalena Salacz-von Dohnanyi, Apr. 11, 1955 (div.); children: Sean Ernst, Daniel Julian, Brian Charles, Sheila Ann, Alan Patrick; m. Maureen G. Potts, Oct. 23, 1985; children: Shane Joseph, Brennan John, Colin Michael. BS, Nat. U. Ireland, 1951, MS, 1952; PhD, Fla. State U., 1956. Fellow Fla. State U., 1956, U. Wash., 1956-57; mem. faculty La. State U., 1957—, prof. chemistry, 1964—, Boyd prof. chemistry, 1967—, dean Grad. Sch., 1981-82, vice chancellor rsch., 1981-91. Assoc. prof. biophysics Yale U., 1961; Humboldt prof. physics U. Bonn, Germany, 1979—80; cons. to pvt. cos. Author (with others): (book) Molecular Spectroscopy of the Triplet State, 1969, Introduction to Applied Quantum Chemistry, 1971, Photophysics and Photochemistry in the Vacuum Ultraviolet, 1985, The Geometry of Genetics, 1988; editor: Wiley-Interscience Monographs in Chem. Physics; contbr. articles to profl. jours., chapters to books. Recipient award, Baton Rouge Coun. Engring. and Sci. Socs., 1962—63, Sr. Scientist award, Alexander von Humboldt Found., 1979, Disting. Rsch. medal, U. Bologna, Italy, 1979; fellow, Rsch. Corp., 1960—63; Sloan fellow, 1964—68. Mem.: AAAS, Am. Phys. Soc., Am. Chem. Soc. (S.W. Regional award 1967, Fla. sect. award 1970, Coates award 1977). Achievements include research in molecular electronic spectroscopy; electronic structure; energy transfer; molecular genetics; bioenergetics; mathematical biology; optoaccoustics; optogalvanics. Home: 12048 Pecan Grove Ct Baton Rouge LA 70810-4835 Office Phone: 225-578-3392. Business E-Mail: chspm@lsu.edu. E-mail: maureenpotts@cox.net.

MCGOVERN, JAY, aeronautical engineer, consultant; b. Sanford, Fla., Mar. 28, 1961; m. Carolyn McGovern; 2 children. BS in Marine Engring., US Naval Acad., 1983; MS in Aeronautical Engring., US Naval Postgrad. Sch. Registered profl. engr., Fla.; lic. gen. contractor Fla. Officer, pilot USN, 1983—96, officer, 2004—05; engr. Carpco, Inc., 1996—98, Hubbard Construction Co., Winter Park, Fla., 1998—99, McGovern Grp., Jacksonville, Fla., 1999—2002, engring. cons., 2008—; engr. US Dept. Navy, 2006—08. Chmn. Riverside Avondale Devel. Orgn., Inc., 1997—98, Riverside Avondale Preservation, 1999—2001; rehab. dir. Housing Partnership N.E. Fla., Jacksonville, 2002—04. Democrat. Roman Catholic. Achievements include patents for a process & apparatus used in plastics recycling. Office: PO Box 41103 Jacksonville FL 32203 Office Phone: 904-626-9618.

MCGOVERN, JOHN FRANCIS, investment company executive; b. Port Chester, NY, June 4, 1946; s. Charles William and Jeanette Mary (Farrell) McG.; m. Gertrude Anne Mills, June 21, 1969; children: Robert Francis, Sarah Mills BS in Economics, Fordham U., 1968. Joined Chase Manhattan Bank, 1971, asst. treas., 1973-74, 2d v.p., 1974-76, v.p., 1976-80, v.p., div. treas., forest products, 1980-81; v.p., project fin Georgia-Pacific Corp., Portland, Oreg., 1981-83, v.p., 1983—99, exec. v.p., fin., CFO, 1995—99; founder, ptnr. Aurora Capital, LLC, 1999. Bd. dirs. fibermarket.com, Atlanta, 2000-01. Fund raiser Am. Heart Assn., Atlanta, 1985—; adviser Atlanta Ballet, 1985. Served with U.S. Army, 1968-70 Mem. Fin. Execs. Inst. Clubs: Atlanta Country. Republican. Roman Catholic. Avocations: golf, tennis, skiing, jogging. Office: Aurora Capital LLC 17 Park Ave New York NY 10016 Office Phone: 917-834-7206. Business E-Mail: john.mcgovern@collectivebrands.com.

MCGRADY, CHUCK, state legislator; JD, Mercer U., 1978. Commr. Dist. 5 Henderson County; trustee Sierra Club Found., 1998—2000; nat. pres. Sierra Club, 1998—2000; sr. corp. counsel Contel Corp., 1984—92; exec. dir. NC Youth Camp Assn., 2010—; mem. Dist. 117 NC House of Representatives, 2011—. Republican. Office: PO Box 723 Hendersonville NC 28793 Address: North Carolina House of Representatives 300 N Salisbury St 418A Raleigh NC 27603-5925 Office Phone: 828-697-4808, 919-733-5956, 828-692-3696. Office Fax: 828-692-9855. Business E-Mail: cmcgrady@hendersoncountync.org, Chuck.McGrady@ncleg.net.

MCGRATH, JAMES EDWARD, chemistry professor; b. Easton, NY, July 11, 1934; s. Thomas Augustine and Marguerite Monica (Hiland) McG.; m. Marlene Mary Potter, May 9, 1959; children: Colleen McGrath Kraft, Patricia McGrath Hoover, Matthew, Barbara, Elizabeth McGrath Throckmorton, Joseph. BS in Chemistry, St. Bernadine of Siena Coll., 1956; MS in Chemistry, U. Akron, 1964, PhD in Polymer Sci., 1967. Rsch. chemist rsch. divsn. Rayonier, Inc., Whippany, N.J., 1956-59, Goodyear Tire & Rubber Co., Akron, Ohio, 1959-65; mem. staff Inst. Polymer Sci., U. Akron, 1965-67; sr. rsch. chemist Union Carbide Corp., Bound Brook, N.J., 1967-69, project scientist, 1969-72, rsch. scientist, 1972-74, rsch. scientist, group leader, 1974-75; asst. prof. chemistry Va. Poly. Inst. and State U., Blacksburg, 1975-76, assoc. prof. chemistry, 1976-79, prof. chemistry, 1980-87, dir. Materials Inst., 1987-89, 96—, prof. dept. chem., co-dir. polymer materials and interface lab., 1979—, Ethyl prof. polymer chemistry, 1986—, dir. Ctr. for Polymer Adhesives and Composites, 1989—, Univ. disting. prof., 1996—. Bd. dirs. ChemFab Inc., N.H.; mem. fire safety report com. NAS/NRC; mem. external adv. com. High Performance Polymers and Ceramics Ctr., Clark Atlanta U. Author, editor: Polyimides: Materials, Chemistry and Characterization, 1989; co-author (with Noshay): Block Copolymers: Overview and Critical Survey, 1977; mem. editl. bd. Jour. Polymer Sci., 1987—, Polymer, 1990—, High Performance Polymeric Polymers, 1990—; adv. bd. Jour. Polymer Sci., 1989—, Advances in Polymeric Sci. Capt. U.S. Army, 1957. Recipient H.F. Mark award Polymer divsn. Am. Chem. Soc., 1996, Polymer Chemistry award, Am. Chem. Soc., 2008; named Va. Scientist of Yr., 1997; named to SPE Plastics Hall of Fame, 1997. Mem. NAS (mem. nat. materials bd. 1992-95), NAE, Soc. Plastics Engrs. (Internat. Rsch. award 1987, Outstanding Achievement award 1992). Republican. Roman Catholic. Avocations: music, tennis, travel. Office: Va Poly Inst and State U Materials Inst 2108 Hahn Hall Blacksburg VA 24061-0344

MCGRAW, GARY, computer scientist, writer; m. Amy Barley; children: Jack, Eli. BA in Philosophy, U. Va.; PhD in Computer Sci. and Cognitive Sci., Ind. U. Chief technology officer Cigital, Inc. (formerly Reliable Software Technologies), Dulles, Va., also bd. dir. Co-founder, software security group Cigital, Inc., 1999—; cons. with major software producers and consumers on software and application security; prin. investigator on grants from Air Force Research Labs, DARPA, Nat. Sci. Found., and NIST's Advanced Technology Program; mem. adv. bd. Authentica, Counterpane, Fortify Software, Indigo Security, Cenzic, Finjan, Netcertainty, Tovaris; advises computer sci. dept. U. Davis. Co-author (with Ed Felten): Java Security: Hostile Applets, Holes, and Antidotes, 1996; co-author: (with Jeffrey Voas) Software Fault Injection: Inoculating Programs Against Errors, 1997; co-author: (with Ed Felten) Securing Java: Getting Down to Business with Mobile Code, 1999; co-author: (with John Viega) Building Secure Software: How To Avoid Security Problem the Right Way, 2001; co-author: Exploiting Software, 2004; author: Exploiting Online Games, 2007, monthly Silver Bullet Security Podcast, IEEE Security & Privacy mag.; written over 60 peer-reviewed tech. publs.; contbr. articles to popular trade publs.; quoted in nat. press articles. Mem.: IEEE Computer Soc. (mem. bd. gov.). Avocation: musician. Office: Cigital Inc 21351 Ridgetop Cir Ste 400 Dulles VA 20166-6503 Office Phone: 703-404-9293. Office Fax: 703-404-9295. Business E-Mail: gem@cigital.com.

MCGRAW, TIM, musician, actor; b. Delhi, La., May 1, 1967; s. Tug McGraw; m. Faith Hill, Oct. 6, 1996; children: Gracie Katherine, Maggie Elizabeth, Audrey Caroline. Musician: (albums) Tim McGraw, 1993, Not a Moment Too Soon, 1994 (triple-platinum, Album of Yr., Acad. County Music Awards, 1994), All I Want, 1995, Everywhere, 1997 (Album of Yr., Country Music Assn. Awards, 1998), A Place in the Sun, 1999 (Album of Yr., Country Music Assn. Awards, 1999), Tim McGraw Greatest Hits, 2000, Set the Circus Down, 2001 (Best Country Album, Am. Music Awards, 2002), Tim McGraw and the Dancehall Doctors, 2002, Live Like You Were Dying, 2004 (Most Inspiring Video of Yr., Country Music Television Music award, 2005, Single Record of Yr., Acad. Country Music Awards, 2005, Favorite Country Album, Am. Music Awards, 2005), Tim McGraw Reflected Greatest Hits Vol. 2, 2006 (Favorite Country Album, Am. Music Awards, 2006), Let it Go, 2007, Greatest Hits: Limited Edition, 2008, Collector's Edition, 2008, Greatest Hits Vol. 3, 2008, Limited Edition: Greatest Hits: Volumes 1, 2 & 3, 2008, Southern Voice, 2009, Number One Hits, 2010, Emotional Traffic, 2012, Two Lanes of Freedom, 2013, (songs) It's Your Love, 1997 (Single of Yr., Song of Yr., Acad. Country Music Awards, 1998), Grown Men, 2001 (Single of Yr., Radio Music Assn., 2001), (with Faith Hill) Let's Make Love, 2001 (Grammy award for Vocal Collaboration, 2001); singer Live Like You Were Dying, 2004 (Single of Yr., Song of Yr., Country Music Assn. Awards, 2004, Song of Yr., Acad. Country Music Awards, 2005); musician (with Tracy Lawrence and Kenny Chesney) Find Out Who Your Friends Are, 2007 (Musical Event of Yr., Country Music Assn. Awards, 2007, Vocal Event of Yr., Acad. Country Music Awards, 2008), (with Kenny Chesney) Feel Like a Rock Star, 2012 (Musical Event of Yr., Country Music Assn. Awards, 2012), (with Taylor Swift and Keith Urban) Highway Don't Care, 2013 (Musical Event of Yr., Music Video of Yr., Country Music Assn. Awards, 2013, Video of Yr., Acad. Country Music Awards, 2014); actor: (films) Black Cloud, 2004, Friday Night Lights, 2004, Flicka, 2006, Four Christmases, 2008, The Blind Side, 2009, Country Strong, 2010, Dirty Girl, 2011, (TV appearances) The Jeff Foxworthy Show, 1997. Recipient Favorite New Artist, Am. Music Awards, 1995, Favorite Male Country Artist, 2002, 2001, 2003, 2005, 2007, Top Male Vocalist, Acad. Country Music, 1994, 1999, 1998, Vocal Event of Yr., 1997, 1998, Country Music Assn., 1997, Male Vocalist of Yr., 1999, 2000, Entertainer of Yr., 2001, Male Artist of Yr., TNN/Music City News, 1999, Favorite Male Artist, Blockbuster Award, 2001, Country Male Artist, Radio Music Awards, 2003, Favorite Male Musical Performer, People's Choice Awards, 2004, Favorite Male Performer, 2006, Best Country Collaboration With Vocals (with Faith Hill), 2006; named Favorite Country Music Icom, People's Choice Awards, 2014. Office: Red Light Management 124 12th Ave Suite 600 Nashville TN 37203*

MCGRUDER, LARRY, history professor; b. Rocky Mount, Ga., June 13, 1958; m. Linda Wilkins-McGruder; 1 child, Stephen Alden. EdB, Ft. Valley State U., 1980; MA in History, Miami U., Ohio, 1981, PhD, 1984. Tchg. fellow Miami U., Oxford, Ohio, 1982—84; prof. history Abraham Baldwin Agrl. Coll., Tifton, Ga., 1984—. Mem. chancellor search com. U. Sys. Ga., Atlanta, 1993—94; mem. fund raising com. Friends United for Edn., Tifton, Ga., 1994—95; chairperson Goizueta Found. Scholarship Selection Com., Tifton, 2003—04; mem. several sub-committees Habitat for Humanity, Tifton, 1990—94; chair incentive grants com. Tift County Found. Ednl. Excellence, Tifton, 1996—2005; chair sub-committee Reading Capital of the World, Tifton, 2002—05. Recipient Alumnus of Yr. award, Ft. Valley State U., 1985, Tchg. Excellence award, Phi Theta Kappa, 1993, W. Bruce Donaldson Faculty award, Abraham Baldwin Coll., 2000; named one of Outstanding Young Men of Am., Outstanding Young Americans, 1985—86; fellow, Miami U. Dept. History, 1982—84. Mem.: Alpha Kappa Mu, Phi Alpha Theta. Avocations: researching local history, hiking, travel. Office: Abraham Baldwin Agricultural Coll 2802 Moore Hwy Tifton GA 31793 Business E-Mail: lmcgruder@abac.edu.

MCGUFFEY, CARROLL WADE, JR., lawyer; b. Decatur, Ga., Dec. 1, 1951; s. Carroll Wade and Dorothy (Landers) McG.; m. Virginia Elizabeth Miller, Aug. 12, 1972; children: Carroll Wade, III, Michelle Elizabeth, Jennifer Lanier. BBA, U. Ga., 1973, JD cum laude, 1976. Bar: Ga. 1976, Fla. 1977, U.S. Dist. Ct. (mid. dist.) Ga. 1976, U.S. Supreme Ct. 1980. Capt. Chief Claims Tort Litigation Div. USAF, Eglin AFB, Fla., 1976-80; assoc., ptnr. Savell and Williams, Atlanta, 1980-90; mng. ptnr., CEO Goodman McGuffey Aust & Lindsey LLP, Atlanta, 1990—2003; CEO Goodman McGuffey Lindsey & Johnson, LLP, Atlanta, Orlando, Savannah, Charlotte, 2003—. Mem. adv. coun. Ga. State Bd. Workers' Compensation, 2005—; lectr. in field. Editor: Employers Guide to Workers Compensation in Georgia, Employee Leasing: An Employer's Guide. Ward capt. Athens Mayoral Campaign (Ga.), 1975; adminstr., co-chair, adjudication com., Southern Assn. Workers' Compensation, 2012-; commr., dir. Stone Mountain Dixie Youth Baseball, 1982-87; cubmaster Boy Scouts Am., 1986-88, scoutmaster, 1988-90, troop chmn., 1991-92, dist. chmn., 1993-95; mgr., coach Murphy Candler Girls Softball Assn., 1996-2003; mem. Citizen Dunwoody Cts. Task Force, 2008; chair jud. qualification com. City of Dunwoody, 2008, mem., bd. ethics, 2009-, vice chmn. Recipient Dist. Award of Merit, Boy Scouts Am., 1995, named Super Lawyer, Atlanta Mag. Mem. ABA, Fla. Bar Assn., Atlanta Bar Assn. (workers compensation seminar chmn. 1993, 97, fundraising chmn. Kid's Chance Found. Race, 1992, workers compensation section, bd. dirs. 1994-01, sec.-treas. 1997, chair-elect 1998, chair 1999), Ga. Def. Lawyers Assn. (trial acad. instr. 1987), Def. Rsch. Inst., Ind. Ins. Agts. of Ga. (hon. life, young agents com.), Ga. Mental Health Assn. (bd. dirs. 1987). Clubs: Athens Boat (dir. 1982-90), Lawyers (Atlanta), UGA Pres. Club. Methodist. Office Phone: 404-264-1500. Business E-Mail: wmcguffey@gmlj.com.*

MCGUIRE, ROBERT C., retired federal judge; b. 1935; AB, Dartmouth Coll., 1957; JD, Boston Coll., 1960. Bar: Mass. 1960, Tex. 1961. Assoc. Turner, White, Dallas, 1961-64, Ungerman, Hill, Angrist & Dolginoff, 1965-78; probate judge Dallas County, 1979-80; ptnr. Skibell & McGuire, 1981-83; judge U.S. Bankruptcy Ct., Dallas, 1983—2002, chief judge, 1985—2002. Mem.: John C. Ford Am. Inn of Ct. (pres. 2000—01), Dallas Bar Assn., Tex. Bar Assn., Nat. Conf. Bankruptcy Judges. Home: 4729 Alta Vista Ln Dallas TX 75229-2923

MCGUIRE, SANDRA LYNN, nursing educator; b. Jan. 28, 1947; d. Donald Armstrong and Mary Lue (Harvey) Johnson; m. Joseph L. McGuire, Mar. 6, 1976; children: Matthew, Kelly, Kerry. BSN, U. Mich., 1969, MPH, 1973, EdD, 1988, MSN, 1997. Staff nurse Univ. Hosp., Ann Arbor, Mich., 1969; pub. health nurse Wayne County Health Dept., Eloise, Mich., 1969—72; instr. Madonna Coll., Livonia, Mich., 1973; pub. health coord. Plymouth Ctr. for Human devel., Northville, Mich., 1974—75; asst. prof. cmty. health nursing U. Mich., Ann Arbor, 1975—83; asst. prof. U. Tenn., Knoxville, 1983—88, assoc. prof., 1990—2007, prof., 2007—09, coord. gerontol. nurse practitioners program, 1998—2006, chair MSN program Coll. Nursing, coord. gerontology, 2008—09, emeritus prof., 2009; asst. dean, prof. Lincoln Meml. U. Sch. Nursing, 2009—. Dir. Kids Are Tomorrow's Srs. Program, 1988—; resource person Gov.'s Com. Unification of Mental Health Svcs. in Mich.; spkr. profl. assns. and workshops; mem. Coun. Accreditation Nurse Anesthesia Ednl. Programs, 2007—10. Author (with S. Clemen-Stone and D. Eigsti): Comprehensive Community Health Nursing, 1981, Comprehensive Community Health Nursing, 5th edit., 1998, Comprehensive Community Health Nursing, 6th edit., 2002; author: Growing Up and Growing Older: Annotated Bibliography of Early Children's Literature, 2013. Bd. dirs. Ctr. Understanding Aging, 1987-93, v.p., 1995; bd. dirs. Mich. chpt. ARC, 1980-83, Knoxville chpt., 1984-85; founder Knoxville Intergenerational Network, 1989; mem. nat. policy coun. AARP, 2006-12. Recipient John W. Runyan, Jr. Cmty. Health Nursing award U. Tenn. Memphis, 2002, Outstanding Svc. award U. Tenn. Knoxville Libr. Friends, 2004; USPHS fellow, 1972-73, Robert Woodruff fellow Emory U., 1996-97, Hewlett Innovative Tech. fellow U. Tenn., Knoxville, 1999-00, Profl. Devel. awardee U. Tenn. Knoxville, 1996-97, 99-2000 Mem. ANA, Southern Gerontol. Soc., Tenn. Nurses Assn., Assn. Gerontology Higher Edn. (mem. k12 com., 2008-, mem. book awards suBcom., 2008-13, fellow 2013), Nat. Gerontol. Nursing Assn., Mich. Pub. Health Assn. (chmn. mental health sect. 1976, dir., co-chmn. residential svcs. com. 1976-79, chmn. health svcs. 1979-82), Nat. Assn. Retarded Citizens, Mich. Assn. Retarded Citizens, Nat. Coun. on Aging, Ctr. for Understanding Aging (v.p. 1994-95), Plymouth, Assn. Retarded Citizens (chmn. residential svcs. com. 1975-77), Tenn. Assn. Retarded Citizens, Knox County Assn. Retarded Citizens, Sr. Citizens Home Assistance Svcs. (bd. mem. 2009-), Sigma Theta Tau, Pi Lambda Theta, Phi Kappa Phi; fellow Assn. Gerontology Higher Edn. Home: 11008 Crosswind Dr Knoxville TN 37934 Office: Cumberland Gap Pky Harrogate TN 37752 Office Phone: 800-325-0900. Business E-Mail: sandra.mcguire@lmunet.edu.

MCGUIRE, WILLIAM DENNIS, healthcare consultant, corporate director; b. Glen Ridge, NJ, Sept. 24, 1943; s. John William and Kathleen Mary (Sexton) McG.; m. Nancy Katherine Hoyne, Aug. 13, 1966; children: Kathleen Anne, Colleen Dempsey. BA, U. Notre Dame, 1965; M.H.A., U. Mich., 1968. Asst. adminstr. U. Wis. Hosps., Madison, 1971-74; adminstr. Children's Med. Ctr., Dayton, Ohio, 1974-79; COO Mercy Cath. Med. Ctr., Phila., 1979-80; CEO Wills Eye Hosp., Phila., 1980-85; pres., CEO Mercy Health Care Sys., Scranton, Pa., 1985-89, Mt. Carmel Health, Columbus, Ohio, 1989-92, Incarnate Word Health Svcs., San Antonio, 1992-95, Cath. Med. Ctrs. of Bklyn. and Queens, NYC, 1996—2000, Kaleida Health, Buffalo, 2002—06; pvt. practice San Antonio, 2000—02; dir. HBCS, Wilmington, 2005—, Chair., 2010—; dir. CTG, Buffalo, 2008—, Ziegler, 2010—, chair, 2013—. Asst. clin. prof. U. Wis., 1971—74, instr., 1972—73; asst. clin. prof. Wright State U. Sch. Medicine, Dayton, Ohio, 1978—79; asst. prof. Ohio State U., 1990—92; adj. faculty dept health care Trinity U., 1992—95, Harvard Bus. Sch. Club, 2003—06; allied health techs. adv. com. Sinclair CC, 1974—79; mem. Dayton Pub. Schs. Lay Adv. Com. on Vocat. Edn., 1974—79; pres. Dayton Area Young Adminstrs. Group, 1977. Trustee Cath. Social Svcs., 1976—79, pres., 1978—79; trustee Cmty. Blood Ctr., 1977—79; pres. elect Greater Dayton Area Hosp. Assn., 1979; mem. Wilkes Coll. Health Administrn. Adv. Com., 1988—89; bd. dirs. Coop. Purchasing Corp., 1974—79, Coll. Misericordia Health Care Task Force, 1988—89, Covenant Health Sys., 1992—2003, chmn. fin. com., 2001—03, Fletcher Allen Health Care, 2002—03; Consol. Cath. Risk Retention Group, 1992—95; consol. Cath. Charities, 1996—2000, Primary Care Devel. Corp., 1997—2000, Buffalo Niagara Partnership, 2002—06, D'Youville Coll., 2004—06, Hosp. Billing & Collection Svc. Ltd., 2004—, chmn., 2010—; with Computer Task Group, 2008—; consol. The Ziegler Co., 2010—; bd. govs. League Vol. Hosps., 1996—2000, sec., 1997—2000; bd. govs. Fidelis Care NY, 1996—2000, Queensbrook Ins. Ltd., 1996—2000, vice chmn., 1996—97, chmn., 1997—2000; active Health Policy Forum, United Hosp. Fund, United Way, ARC. Fellow Am. Coll. Healthcare Execs. (life), NY Acad. Medicine, Royal Soc. Medicine; mem. Acad. for Cath. Health Care Leadership, Mercy Leadership Group. (nat. commn. Cath. health care ministry), Maj. Cath. Health Alliance (sec. 1990-95, chmn. 1997-99), Health Care Fin. Mgmt. Assn. (advanced mem.), Am. Assn. Univ. Profs. Ophthalmology, Am. Soc. Law and Medicine, Am. Hosp. Assn., Am. Assn. Eye and Ear Hosps. (pres.-elect 1984-85), Health Mgmt. Edn. Assn. (pres. 1987-88, 2008-), Hosp. Assn. NY State (bd. dirs. 1998-2000, 02-05), Greater NY Hosp. Assn. (bd. govs. 1997-2000, 02-06), Tex. Hosp. Assn., We. NY Hosp. Assn. (bd. dirs. 2002-05), Ohio Hosp. Assn., Hosp. Assn. Pa., Wis. Hosp. Assn., Cath. Health Assn., Am. Pub. Health Assn., Pa. Pub. Health Assn., Del. Valley Hosp. Council, Pa. Emergency Health Svcs. Coun., Del. County Emergency Health Svcs. Coun., Nat. Union Hosp. and Health Care Employees (plan trustee), Pa. Hosps. Ins. Co. Adv. Coun., 1988-89. C. of C., U. Notre Dame Alumni Assn., U. Mich. Alumni Assn., Pres.'s Soc., U. Wis. Med. Sch. Alumni Assn., Wills Eye Soc., Sorin Soc., Badin Guild, Notre Dame Club (pres. 1971, v.p. 1983-84), Dominion Country Club. Conservative. Roman Catholic. Office: 6 Clubhouse Green San Antonio TX 78257 Home: 395 Blueberry Point Ln Barton VT 05822 Personal E-mail: billmcg@together.net.

MCGUIRT, WILLIAM FRANKLIN, county sheriff; b. Monroe, NC, June 10, 1946; s. Robert Hall and Lucille (Price) McGuirt; m. Jenny Lee Ratliff McGuirt, June 12, 1976; children: William Sean, Jonathan Hall. AS, Wingate Coll., 1967, B in Gen. Studies, 1984. Sheriff's lt. Union County, NC, 1970—79, sheriff mem., 1979—2002; bd. dirs. United Way, Charlotte, NC, 1981—, Contact Counseling Svc., Charlotte, 1985—, Union County Arts Coun., Monroe, 1983—; mem. exec. com. Union County Democrats, 1972—78; owner McGuirt Advertising; state rep. Dist. 69 NC, 2011—. With NC Nat. Guard, 1966—72. Named Young Law Enforcement Officer of Yr., Monroe Jaycees, 1980, Wingate Jaycees, 1981. Mem.: NC Sheriff's Assn. (2d. v.p. 1986—), Nat. Sheriff's Assn., Masons, Rotary (Monroe-Union) (bd. dirs. 1983—84). Avocation: photography. Office: PO Box 613 Wingate NC 28174 Address: North Carolina House of Representatives 16 W Jones St Room 1015 Raleigh NC 27601-1096 Office Phone: 919-715-3007, 704-233-4618. Business E-Mail: frank.McGuirt@ncleg.net.

MCHALE, KEVIN EDWARD, professional basketball coach, retired professional basketball player; b. Hibbing, Minn., Dec. 19, 1957; m. Lynn McHale; children: Kristyn, Michael, Joseph, Alexandra (dec.), Thomas. Student, U. Minn., 1976—80. Player Boston Celtics, 1980—93; spl. asst. Minn. Timberwolves, 1993—94, asst. gen. mgr., 1994—95, v.p. basketball ops., 1995—2008, interim head coach, 2005, head coach, 2008—09; studio analyst NBA TV, Turner Sports, 2009—11; head coach Houston Rockets, 2011—. Recipient NBA Sixth Man of Yr. award, 1984, 85; named to NBA All-Rookie First Team, 1981, NBA All-Defensive Second Team, 1983, 89, 90, NBA All-Defensive First Team, 1986-88, All-NBA First Team, 1987, NBA All-Star Team, 1984, 86-91, Basketball Hall of Fame, 1999, Nat. HS Sports Hall of Fame, 2000; named one of Top 50 Players in first 50 years of NBA, 1995; named Top Player in U. Minn. History.

Achievements include member of the NBA Championship winning Boston Celtics, 1981, 84, 86; leading the NBA in: field goal percentage, 1987, 88. Office: Houston Rockets 1510 Polk St Houston TX 77002

MC HARGUE, CARL JACK, lab administrator, educator; b. Ky., Jan. 30, 1926; s. John David and Virginia (Thomas) McH.; m. Edith Trovillion, Aug. 28, 1948; children: Anne Odell McHargue Diegel, Carol Virginia Hornberger, Margaret Katherine McHargue; m. Betty Ford, Sept. 30, 1960. BS in Metall. Engring., U. Ky., 1949, MS, 1951, PhD, 1953. Instr. U. Ky., Lexington, 1949-53; with Oak Ridge Nat. Lab., 1953-90, sect. head, 1960-80, program mgr. for materials scis., 1961-88, sr. rsch. staff, 1980-90; prof. materials sci. and engring. U. Tenn., Knoxville, 1991—, dir., Ctr. Materials Processing, 1991—2012, rsch. prof., 2013—. Vis. prof. U. Newcastle upon Tyne, Eng., 1987; adj. prof. Vanderbilt U., 1988—; bd. dirs. Accreditation Bd. for Engring. and Tech., 1998—; bd. dirs. The Minerals, Metals and Materials Soc. Contbr. numerous articles in field to profl. jours. With inf. US Army, 1944—46. Recipient Disting. Svc. award The Minerals, Metals and Materials Soc., 2001, medal Radiation Effects in Insulators, 2005, Ferris award U. Tenn. Coll. Engring., 2010; named to Engring. Hall of Distinction, U. Ky., 1995; fellow Minerals, Metals and Materials Soc., ASM Internat., ABET Inc. Fellow: Metall. Soc. AIME, Am. Soc. for Metals, Accreditation Bd. Engring. Tech.; mem.: Materials Rsch. Soc., Optimist Internat. (life), Sigma Xi, Tau Beta Pi. Republican. Presbyterian. Avocations: photography, travel. Home: 7201 Sheffield Dr Knoxville TN 37909-2414 Office: University Tenn 420 Ferris Hall Knoxville TN 37996-2200 Office Phone: 865-974-0881. Business E-Mail: crl@utk.edu.

MCHENRY, PATRICK TIMOTHY, United States Representative from North Carolina; b. Mecklenburg, NC, Oct. 22, 1975; Attended, NC State U.; BA in Hist., Belmont Abbey Coll., 1999. Exec. DCI/New Media, Inc., Washington; owner & broker McHenry Real Estate, Gastonia, NC; spl. asst. to Sec. Elaine L. Chao US Dept. Labor, Washington, 2000; mem. NC State Ho. Reps., 2003—05, US Congress from 10th NC dist., 2005—. Mem. fin svcs. com. US Congress, 2005—, mem. budget com., mem. oversight and govt. reform com., vice chmn. fin. for exec. com. Nat. Rep. Congl. Com., dep. Rep. whip. Bd. dirs. United Success by Six Youth Prog. Recipient Spirit of Enterprise award, US C. of C.; named a Small Bus. Champion, Small Bus. and Entrepreneurship Coun., Hero of the Taxpayer, Ams. for Tax Reform, Protector of Property Rights, Property Rights Alliance; named one of The Politics 40 Under 40, TIME Mag., 2010. Mem.: Gaston C. of C., NRA, Gastonia Rotary Club. Republican. Roman Catholic. Office: US House of Representatives 2334 Rayburn House Office Bldg Washington DC 20515 Office Phone: 202-225-2576. Office Fax: 202-225-0316.*

MCHUGH, THOMAS EDWARD, lawyer, former state supreme court justice; b. Charleston, W.Va., Mar. 26, 1936; s. Paul and Melba McHugh; m. Judith McHugh, Mar. 14, 1959; children: Karen, Cindy, James, John. AB, W.Va. U., 1958, LLB, 1964. Bar: W.Va. 1964. Pvt. practice law, Charleston, 1964-66, 69-74; law clk. to presiding judge Harlan Calhoun W.Va. Supreme Ct. of Appeals, 1966-68; chief judge Cir. Ct. (13th cir.) W.Va., Charleston, 1974-80; justice W.Va. Supreme Ct. of Appeals, Charleston, 1980-97, 2008—12, chief justice, 1984, 88, 92; atty, mediation practice Allen Guthrie McHugh & Thomas, PLLC, Charleston, 1997—2003, of counsel, 2003, Bowles Rice, Charleston, 2013—. Served to 1st lt. U.S. Army, 1958-61. Mem. W.Va. Jud. Assn., W.Va. Bar Assn., Order of the Coif. Democrat. Roman Catholic. Office: Bowles Rice 600 Quarrier St Charleston WV 25301 Office Phone: 304-347-2133. Office Fax: 304-347-1746.

MCHUGH, WILLIAM, healthcare company executive; CEO, Health Care Plans, Fla. Amerigroup Corp. Office: Amerigroup Corp 4425 Corporation Ln Virginia Beach VA 23462 Office Phone: 757-490-6900. Office Fax: 757-518-3600. Business E-Mail: wmchugh@amerigroupcorp.com.

MCILVRIED, MAC D., landscape company executive; B in Criminal Justice, Pa. State U., 1986. V.p., gen. mgr. Pepsi Bottling Group, 1993—2007; v.p., ops., East Div. ServiceMaster Co., 2008—09, acting pres., TruGreen LandCare, 2010—. Maj. USMC, 1986-07. Office: ServiceMaster Co 860 Ridge Lake Blvd Memphis TN 38120 Office Phone: 901-597-1400. Office Fax: 630-663-2001. Business E-Mail: mac.mcilvried@servicemaster.com.

MCINERNEY, THOMAS J., insurance company executive; b. May 5, 1956; BA in Economics with honors, Colgate U., 1978; MBA, Dartmouth Coll., 1982. Ins. underwriter to various mgmt. positions Aetna, Inc., Hartford, Conn., 1978-95, v.p. strategy, 1995-96; sr. v.p. for sales and nat. accounts Aetna U.S. Healthcare, 1996-97, strategic planning profl., 1997-98; pres. Aetna Financial Services, Hartford, Conn., 1997—2000; CEO, US Worksite Financial Services after ING's acquisition of Aetna Financial Services ING Group, 2000—01, CEO, US financial services, 2001—06, chmn., CEO ING Insurance Americas, 2006—09, COO, mem. Groep's management bd. for insurance, 2009—10; sr. adv. Boston Consulting Group Inc., 2011—13; pres., CEO Genworth Financial, Inc., 2013—. Bd. dirs. Genworth Financial, Inc., 2013—. Bd. dirs. Nat. Conf. Community and Justice; mem. MBA advisory bd. Dartmouth Coll. Tuck Sch. Bus. Mem.: Metro Atlanta C. of C., Financial Services Roundtable, American Coun. Life Insurers. Office: Genworth Financial Inc 6620 W Broad St Richmond VA 23230

MCINNIS, JEFF, chef; Grad., Johnson & Wales U., Charleston, SC. Sous chef Atlanticville Restaurant, Asolare, St. John, VI, Azie, San Francisco, Five Star Orient Express; garde manger chef Ritz-Carlton South Beach, 2004—06; chef de cuisine The DiLido Beach Club, Miami, 2006—. Named one of Fla.'s Rising Stars, StarChefs.com, 2008. Office: The DiLido Beach Club 1 Lincoln Rd Miami Beach FL 33139

MCINTIRE, LARRY VERN, biomedical engineering educator; b. St. Paul, June 28, 1943; s. James Lawrence and Lenore Vineal (Converse) McI.; m. Suzanne G. Eskin, June 27, 1997. BChemE, MS, Cornell U., 1966; MA, Princeton U., 1968, PhD, 1970. Registered profl. engr., Tex. Asst. prof. Rice U., Houston, 1970-74, assoc. prof., 1974-78, prof. chem. engring., 1978—2003, E.D. Butcher prof., 1983—2003, chmn. dept., 1981-91, chmn. Bioscis. and Bioengring. Inst., 1991—2003, chmn. rsch. coun., 1988-91, dir. biomed. engring. lab., 1980—99, chmn. dept. biomed. engring., 1997—2003; Wallace Coulter prof. Ga. Tech., 2003—. Adj. prof. medicine Baylor Coll. Medicine, Houston, 1982—2007, U. Tex. Med. Sch., Houston, 1982—2007, M.D. Anderson Cancer Ctr., 2001-08; Emory U. Sch. Medicine, 2003-, chmn. blood/materials working group NIH, Bethesda, Md., 1982-85; surgery and bioengring. study sect. NIH, 1984-88, 99-2003; com. bioprocessing NRC, 1991-94; chmn. rheology subcom. Internat. Coun. Thrombosis and Hemostasis, 1985-89; engring. directorate adv. coun. NSF, 2002-05; chmn. Coulter dept. biomed. engring. Gal Tech., 2003-. Editor-in-chief: Annals of Biomed. Engring., 2002—; contbr. over 278 articles to profl. jours. Recipient Merit award NIH, 1989; NSF fellow Cornell U., Princeton U., 1965-69, NATO-NSF postdoctoral fellow Imperial Coll., London, 1976-77. Fellow AAAS, Am. Inst. Med. Biol. Engring. (sec., treas. 1993-96, pres. 1997-98), AICHE (officer local sect. 1980-81, 86, Food Pharm. and Bioengring. divsn. award 1992, divsn. chair 1998), Biomed. Engring. Soc. (bd. dirs. 1992-97, pres. 1995-96, Disting. lectr. 1992, Presdl. award, 2004); fellow Am. Heart Assn.; mem. N.Am. Soc. Biorheology (v.p. 1992-94, pres. 1994-96), N.Y. Acad. Scis., Faculty Club Rice U. (bd. dirs., chmn. 1982-84), Sigma Xi (nat. lectr. 1993-96), Nat. Acad. Engring. (editor-in-chief Annals Biomed. Engring., 2002-). Presbyterian. Avocations: tennis, squash, classical music, hiking. Office: Ga Tech Dept Biomed Engring Atlanta GA 30332-0535 Office Phone: 404-894-5057. Office Fax: 404-385-5028. Business E-Mail: larry.mcintire@bme.gatech.edu.

MCINTOSH, DENNIS KEITH, veterinarian, consultant; b. Glen Ridge, NJ, June 12, 1941; s. Sheldon Weeks and Enid Nicholson (Casey) McIntosh; children: Kevin, Jamie. BS in Animal Sci., Tex. A&M U., College Station, 1963, BS in Vet. Sci., 1967, DVM, 1968. Asst. county agrl. agt., Cleburne, Tex., 1963—65; owner, operator Park North Animal Hosp., San Antonio, 1970—75, El Dorado Animal Hosp., San Antonio, 1973—. Founding mem. and vet. liaison Tex. Assn. Animal Technicians (now TARVT), 1976-81; chmn., founding mem. vet. tech. adv. coun. Palo Alto Coll., 1995—, tchr. Animal Health Tech., San Antonio Coll., 1985-95; tchr. ethics for vet. students Tex. A&M U. Coll. Vet. Medicine, 1990-; pres., mgr. Bexar County Emergency Animal Clinic, Inc., 1978-81; cons. vet. practice mgmt., mktg., client rels.; spkr. for vet. meetings, assns.; co-host Ask the Vet, Adopt a Pet, Sta. KENS-TV, 1980-93; vet. mem. Tex. Bd. Health, 1984-89, chmn. disease control com., pers. com.; mem. environ. health, hosps. com. Team capt. Alamo Roundup Club and Pres.' Club of San Antonio C. of C., 1970-75; mem. Guadalupe County Youth Fair Bd., 1978-80. Contbg. author: Mosby's Review Questions and Answers for Veterinary Boards, 1998, Chicken Soup for the Pet Lover's Soul, 1998, Chicken Soup for the Soul: Loving Our Cats, 2008; contbr. articles to profl. jours. With Vet. Corps, USAF, 1968-70. Recipient Alumnus award Guadalupe County 4-H Club, 1979, Outstanding Svc. award San Antonio Coll., 1986-87, Lynn Anderson Outstanding Svc. award San Antonio chpt. Delta Soc., 1990, Outstanding Bus. Ptnrs. award N.E. Ind. Sch. Dist., 1995-96. Mem.: AVMA, Tex. Vet. Med. Assn. (pres., chmn. bd. dirs.), Tex. Acad. Vet. Practice (charter mem., pres.), San Antonio C. of C. (life), Tex. County Agrl. Agts. Assn. (4th v.p. 1964), Am. Legion Post 245, Delta Soc. (first pres.and founding mem. San Antonio chpt. 1989-90), Alpha Zeta. Office: 13039 Nacogdoches Rd San Antonio TX 78217-1960 Office Phone: 210-656-1444.

MC INTOSH, JAMES EUGENE, JR., interior designer; b. Dadeville, Ala., Nov. 13, 1938; s. James Eugene and Jessie (Latimer) McI. B.Interior Design, Auburn U., Ala., 1961. Designer contract div. Rich's Dept. Store, Atlanta, 1961-64; assoc. William Trapnell & Assocs., Atlanta, 1964-70; dir. Interior Concepts, Inc., Atlanta, 1970-72; dir. design comml. design div. Rich's Dept. Store, 1972-80; v.p. Comml. Interior Designs, Inc., 1980-82; exec. staff Rollins Inc., 1982—; pres. Gene Mc Intosh & Assocs., 1985—. Fellow Am. Soc. Interior Designers (Presdl. citation 1974); mem. Nat. Trust Hist. Preservation, Ala. Hist. Soc., High Mus. Art Home and Office: 325 W Ponce de Leon #202 Decatur GA 30030 Personal E-mail: cmeneg@earthlink.net.

MCINTYRE, CONNIE, gas industry executive; BBA, Ga. Coll.; MBA, Brenau U. Region mgr., Northeast Ga. Atlanta Gas Light (subs. of AGL Resources Inc.); joined AGL Resources, Inc., 1977, dir., customer care ctr., mgmt. position, info. sys., mgmt. position, process improvements, v.p., customer experience, 2007—. Bd. dirs. YWCA Atlanta, Am. Cancer Soc., Greater North Fulton C. of C. Office: AGL Resources Inc 10 Peachtree Pl NE Atlanta GA 30309 Office Phone: 404-584-4000. Office Fax: 404-584-3714. Business E-Mail: Cmclntyre@aglresources.com.

MCINTYRE, JOHN ARMIN, physics professor; b. Seattle, June 2, 1920; s. Harry John and Florence (Armin) McI.; m. Madeleine Forsman, June 15, 1947; 1 son, John Forsman. BS, U. Wash., 1943; MA, Princeton U., 1948, PhD, 1950. Mem. faculty elec. engring. Carnegie Inst. Tech., Pitts., 1943; radio engr. Westinghouse Elec. Co., Balt., 1944; research asso. Stanford, 1950-57; mem. faculty Yale, 1957-63, assoc. prof., 1960-63; prof. physics Tex. A&M U., College Station, 1963-95, emeritus prof., 1995—; asso. dir. Cyclotron Inst., 1965-70. Mem. council Oak Ridge Asso. Univs., 1964-71 Contbr. articles to profl. jours. Fellow Am. Phys. Soc., Am. Sci. Affiliation (exec. council 1968-73); mem. AAAS. Presbyterian. Achievements include research and publs. on scintillation counters for gamma ray spectroscopy; determination of nuclear charge distbns. by electron scattering; study of nuclear structure by neutron transfer reactions; devel. variable energy gamma ray beams, gamma ray cameras. Home: 9807 Brandywine Cir Austin TX 78750-2803 E-mail: jmcintyre@physics.tamu.edu.

MCINTYRE, MIKE (DOUGLAS CARMICHAEL MCINTYRE II), United States Representative from North Carolina; b. Lumberton, NC, Aug. 6, 1956; s. Douglas Carmichael and Thelma Riley (Hedgpeth) McIntyre; m. Lola Denise Strickland, June 26, 1982; children: Joshua Carmichael, Stephen Christopher. BA, U. NC, 1978, JD, 1981. Bar: NC 1981, US Dist. Ct. (ea. dist.) NC 1984, US Dist. Ct. (mid. dist.) NC 1985., US Ct. Appeals (4th cir.) 1987, US Supreme Ct., 1987. Assoc. Law Office Bruce Huggins, Lumberton, 1981-82, McLean, Stacy, Henry & McLean, Lumberton, 1982-86; ptnr. Price & McIntyre PA, Lumberton, 1987-89; prin. McIntyre Law Firm, PA, Lumberton, 1989-96; mem. US Congress from 7th NC dist., 1997—. Mem. law-focused edn. adv. com. NC Dept. Pub. Instrn., 1986-87; mem. US Ho. Com. on Agr., 1997—, Armed Svcs. Com., 1997—; co-chmn. Coalition Task Force on Edn., 1997-98, Congrl. Task Force on Promotion of Fatherhood, Rural Health Care Coalition, 1999-2002, Dem. Task Force on Children, 1999-2000, Coalition Task Force on Bus. and Tech., Spl. Forces Caucus, 2002—; chmn. U.S. H. Agr. Subcom. on Splty. Crops, Rural Devel. and Fgn. Agr.; mem. Pres.'s Summit on Am.'s Future, 1997. Del. Dem. Nat. Conv., NYC, 1980, NC Dems., Raleigh, 1974—; pres. Robeson County Young Dems., Lumberton, 1982; sec.-treas. 7th Congl. Dist. Young Dems., NC, 1983, chmn., 1984; 2nd vice chmn. 7th Congl. Dist. Dems. So. NC, 1986-89, 1st vice chmn., 1989; mem. state adv. bd. North Carolinians Against Drug and Alcohol Abuse, Raleigh, 1984-85; chmn. Morehead Scholarship Selection Com., Robeson County, 1985-94; deacon, elder, clk. of session Presbyn. Ch.; active Boy Scouts Am., Lumberton, 1983; mem. NC Commn. on Children and Youth, 1987-89, NC Commn. on the Family, 1989-91; mem. Young Life Lumberton com., 1987-89; chmn. Robeson County US Constn. Bicentennial com., 1986-87; mem. lawyers' adv. com. to NC Commn. on Bicentennial of US Constn., 1986-89; bd. dirs. Robeson County Grp. Home, Lumberton, 1984-87, Lumberton Econ. Advancement for Downtown, Inc., 1987-90, pres., 1988-89, 89-90; chmn. legis. affairs com. C. of C., 1991, 92, 93, bd. dirs., 1992-94; mem. NC Mus. Hist. Assocs., 1987-89; mem. regional selection com. Gov.'s Award for Excellence in Tchg. Social Studies, 1991. Morehead Found. scholar, 1974-78; named one of Outstanding Young Men in Am., 1981, 84-85, 88; Outstanding Young Dem. Robeson County Young Dems., 1984-85; one of State's Outstanding Young Dems. Young Dems. NC, 1984-85; recipient Algernon Sydney Sullivan award U. NC, 1978, Outstanding Young North Carolinian award NC Jaycees, 1988, Outstanding Young North Carolinians, Heart Robeson Jaycees, 1988, Nat. Bicentennial Leadership award for Individual Achievement Coun. for Advancement of Citizenship and Ctr. for Civic Edn., Washington, 1987, Gov.'s Outstanding Vol. Svc. award, 1989, Thomas Jefferson award Food Distbrs. Internat., 1998, 2002, Guardian of Small Bus. award, Nat. Fedn. Ind. Bus., 1997-99, Nat. Rural Health Legis. award, 1999, 2003, Outstanding Health Svc. award Cmty. Ptnrs. Health Net, 2000, Spirit of Enterprise award, US C. of C., 1997-98, Super Hero award Nat. Assn. Cmty. Health Ctrs., 2001-05, Internat. Pub. Policy award Internat. Assn. Pers. Employment, 2002, Law Enforcement award, NC Narcotics Officers Assn., 2002, Quality Pub. Svc./Pub. Edn. and Health Care award Am. Fedn. Tchrs., 2001, Charles Dick Medal of Merit Nat. Guard Assn., 2000, Disting. Svc. to Agr. award Robeson County Crop Promotion Assn., 2001, Congrl. Partnership award Nat. Assn. Devel. Orgns., 2002, 2004-05, Nat. Leadership award, 2006, Admiral's Cir. award Nat. Marine Mfrs. Assn., 2004, MVP award Sr. Citizens League, 2004, True Blue Pro-Family award, Family Rsch. Coun., 2006, 07, Disting. Christian Statesman award, 2006, Nat. Lagislator Tr. award, Svc. Agency Employees Assn., 2007, Nat. Assn. County Veterans Svc. Officers, 2008; named to Legis. Honor Roll So. Econ. Devel. Coun., 1997, 2001-06, Beach Preservationist of Yr., Oak Island Preservation Soc., 2005; Nat. Sports Ethics fellow, Positive Coaching Alliance, 2008. Mem. ABA (exec. com. citizenship edn. com. 1985-87, nat. cmty. law week com. 1982-83), Internat. Platform Assn., NC Bar Assn. (chmn. youth edn. and constn. bicentennial com. 1986-87, youth edn. com., exec. coun. young lawyers divsn. 1986-87), Robeson County Bar Assn. (founder, chmn. citizenship edn. com. 1982-94, law day com.), 16th Jud. Dist. Bar Assn., NC Acad. Trial Lawyers, NC Coll. Advocacy, Christian Legal Soc. (state adv. bd. 1986-90, state pres. 1987), Lumberton C. of C. (bd. dirs. 1992-94), Mil. Officers' Assn. (hon. life), Order of Old Well, Lumberton Rotary Club (bd. dirs. 1995-96), Phi Beta Kappa, Phi Eta Sigma. Democrat. Avocations: tennis, skiing, softball, dance, bible study. Office: US House of Representatives 2428 Rayburn House Office Bldg Washington DC 20515 Office Phone: 202-225-2731. Office Fax: 202-225-5773. E-mail: congmcintyre@mail.house.gov.*

MCINTYRE, PETER MASTIN, physicist, researcher; b. Clewiston, Fla., Sept. 26, 1947; s. Peter Mastin and Ruby Eugenia (Richaud) McI.; m. Rebecca Biek, June 29, 1968; children: Peter B., Colin H., Jana M., Robert J. AB with honors, U. Chgo., 1967, MS, 1968, PhD, 1973. Asst. prof. Harvard U., Cambridge, Mass., 1975-80; group leader Fermilab, Batavia, Ill., 1978-80; assoc. prof. Tex. A&M U., College Station, 1980-84, prof. physics, 1985—, assoc. dean Coll. of Sci., 1990-92; pres. Accelerator Tech. Corp., Bryan, Tex., 1988—. Dir. Tex. Accelerator Ctr., The Woodlands, 1991—93. Recipient IR-100 award, Indsl. Rch. Mag., 1980; fellow, Sloan Found., 1976—78. Fellow: Am. Phys. Soc. (pres. Tex. sect. 1990—91); mem.: AAAS. Achievements include proton-antiproton colliding beams; E-beam assisted removal of mercury and sub-micron carbon particles from power plant exhausts; electronic pasteurization system for destroying organic contaminants in water; 16 tesla superconducting magnets for future hadron colliders; silicon microdevices for DNA sequencing; structured cable using high-temperature superconductors for practical coils; flux-coupled isochronous cyclotron driver for thorium-cycle nuclear fission power; Visual Physics, a new laboratory/problem solving curriculum for first-year college physics; spectroscopy solenoids to 30 Tesla; polyhedral superconducting country for linac colliders and free-electron lasers; modular emergency sea wall to protect city blocks from hurricane sea surge; patents for continuous unitized tunneling system, gigatron high power microwave amplifier; accelerator-driven subcritied fission in a molten-salt core as basis for green nuclear fission power; textured powder wire technology for Bi-2212 superconducting wire. Office: Tex A&M U Dept Physics College Station TX 77843-0001

MCKANE, DAVID BENNETT, business executive; b. Salem, Mass., July 10, 1945; s. Vernon Wilson and Barbara Inez (Bennett) McK.; m. Wilson Lineburgh Baldwin, Apr. 16, 1977; adopted daughters, Taylor A., Lee and Paige Baldwin. BA, Dartmouth Coll., 1967; MBA, Amos Tuck Sch., 1969. Product mgr. Church & Dwight Co. Inc. (Arm and Hammer Products), NYC, 1969-72; v.p. NTA Inc. NYC, Nanuet, NY, 1972-75; v.p., exec. asst. to chmn. Schick Inc., Westport, Conn., 1975-77, sr. v.p., 1977-79, COO, exec. v.p., 1979-84, treas., 1980-84; chmn., CEO A.I. Friedman, Inc., NYC, 1985-87; chmn. McKane Robbins & Co. Inc., NYC and Westport, 1986-96; mng. gen. ptnr. Riverland and Indian Sun, L.C., Westport, 1996—. Bd. dirs. Oakhurst Dairy, Portland, Maine, Impax Corp., Westport, Sprout Foods, Inc., NYC, Aponia Labs.,Inc., Greenwich,Ct. Bd. trustees Greens Farms (Conn.) Acad., 1991—; bd. overseers Tuck Sch. Bus., Dartmouth Coll., Hanover, NH, 2008-. Mem. New Eng. Soc. in City N.Y., Mass. Mayflower Soc., Union Club (N.Y.C.), Country Club Fairfield, John's Island Club (Vero Beach, Fla.), RedStick Golf Club (Vero Beach, Fla.), Tucker's Point Club (Bermuda). Episcopalian. Home: 180 Orchid Way Vero Beach FL 32963-3321

MCKAY, LAMAR, oil industry executive; b. 1958; m. Nancy McKay. BS in Petroleum Engring., summa cum laude, Miss. State U.; MBA, Ind. U. Reservoir engr. Amoco Production Co., 1980, various comml. and oper. roles in US, then gen. mgr. Arkoma Basin, 1993—97, bus. unit leader Gulf of Mexico, 1997, (merger with Brit. Petroleum), 1998; head strategy/planning, worldwide exploration & prodn. BP Plc, London, 1999—2000, Ctrl. North Sea bus. unit leader Aberdeen, Scotland, 2000, chief of staff worldwide exploration/prodn. London, chief of staff to dep. group chief exec., 2002—03, group v.p. Russia & Kazakhstan upstream/downstream bus. London, 2003—07, sr. group v.p. Houston, 2007—08, exec. v.p. spl. projects, 2008—09, pres., CEO Gulf Coast Restoration unit, 2010—; exec. v.p., COO BP America, 2007—08, chmn., pres., 2009—. Bd. dirs. TNK-BP Ltd, 2004—07, vice chmn. remuneration/compensation com.; former mem. adv. coun. Russian Fedn. Fgn. Investors; bd. mem. US-Russia Bus. Coun. Office: BP America Inc 501 Westlake Pk Blvd Houston TX 77079

MCKAY, PATRICIA A., accounting firm executive; BBA, Fla. Atlantic U., 1978. CPA. V.p. fin., contr. Dole Food Co., 1993—96; various positions including sr. v.p. fin. AutoNation Inc., 1997—2003; exec. v.p., CFO Restoration Hardware, Inc., 2003—05, Office Depot, Inc., Delray Beach, Fla., 2005—08; ptnr. Templeton & Co. LLP, Miami, 2009—. Mem. Fla. Atlantic U. Found. Bd., 2009—. Named one of The 100 Most Influential People in Finance, Treasury and Risk mag., 2007; named to The Fla. Atlantic U. Nat. Alumni Assn. Hall of Fame, 2006. Office: Templeton & Co LLC Cypress Financial Center 301 E Las Olas Blvd Ste 800 Fort Lauderdale FL 33301-2254 Office Phone: 954-333-0001. Office Fax: 954-938-2444. E-mail: pmckay@templetonco.com.

MCKAY, RICHARD JAMES, professional sports team executive; b. Eugene, Oreg., Mar. 16, 1959; s. John H. and Nancy Jean (Hunter) McK.; m. Terrin Lea Few, May 19, 1984; children: K. Hunter, John Crosby. BA, Princeton U., 1981; JD, Stetson Coll. Law, St. Petersburg, Fla., 1984. Bar: Fla. 1984, U.S. Dist. Ct. (mid. dist.) Fla. 1984. Law clk. to Hon. William Terrell Hodges U.S. Dist. Ct. (middle dist. Fla.), Tampa, 1984-86; ptnr. Hill, Ward & Henderson, Tampa, Fla., 1986-92; gen. mgr. Tampa Bay Bucaneers, 1993—2003, Atlanta

Falcons, 2003—07, pres., 2003—. Adj. prof. Stetson Coll. Law, St. Petersburg, 1989-92; co-chmn. NFL Competition Com., 1994—. Office: Atlanta Falcons 4400 Falcon Pkwy Flowery Branch GA 30542

MCKEAN, THOMAS WAYNE, retired dentist, military officer; b. Adams County, Ind., May 18, 1928; s. Gorman F. and Elmira B. (Staley) McK.; m. Marilyn Kimberlin, Aug. 9, 1952; children: Thomas Wayne, Randall K., Dana K. D.D.S., Ind. U., 1953; grad., Naval Dental Sch., 1963. Diplomate: Am. Bd. Oral Surgery. Commd. ensign Dental Corps USN, 1949—53, advanced through grades to rear adm., 1980; stationed at Naval Tng. Ctr., Great Lakes, Ill., 1953; dental officer U.S.S. Randall, 1953-56; head dental svc., asst. dental officer U.S. Naval Acad./Naval Hosp., Annapolis, Md., 1956-59; dental officer FASRON III; asst. dental officer U.S. Naval Sta., Bermuda, 1959-63; postgrad. student Naval Dental Sch., Bethesda, Md., 1963-64; resident oral and maxillofacial surgery Naval Hosp., Great Lakes, Ill., 1964-66; dental officer U.S.S. America, 1966-68; chief oral surgery Naval Hosp., Orlando, Fla., 1968-70; dir. oral surgery and gen. practice residency tng. programs Naval Regional Med. Ctr., Great Lakes, 1970-74, chmn. dept. dentistry, 1970-74; cons., lectr. U.S. Army, Fort Sheridan, Ill., 1970-74; dir. oral surgery and gen. practice residency tng. programs Naval Regional Med. Ctr., Oakland, Calif., 1974-78, chmn., dept. dentistry, 1974-78; lectr. oral surgery Letterman Army Med. Ctr., San Francisco, 1974-78; clin. lectr. dept. oral surgery U. of Pacific Sch. Dentistry, San Francisco, 1974-78; comdg. officer Naval Regional Dental Ctr., Pensacola, Fla., 1978-80; lectr. oral surgery Pensacola (Fla.) Jr. Coll., 1978-80; cons., lectr. Dwight D. Eisenhower Army Regional Med. Ctr., Augusta, Ga., 1978-80; insp. gen. dental Bur. Medicine and Surgery, Dept. of Navy, Washington, 1980-81; comdg. officer Naval Regional Dental Ctr., San Diego, 1981-82; insp. gen. Naval Med. Command, Washington, 1983-85; ret., 1985—2008. Contbr. articles to profl. jours. Chmn. bd. trustees UMC, Winter Park, 1992, mem. bd. adminstrs. 1995-98; bd. dirs. Circle of Friends Fla. Hosp. Found., 1989-91, Fla. Hosp. Found., 1991—, chmn. bd., 1995-96; bd. dirs., Fla. Hosp. Found., 1991-, chmn., Ctrl. Fla. Veterans, Inc., 2007-, bd. trustees 2008-; chmn. Fla. Hosp. Shares (Internat. Med. Missions), 1994—2010; mem. Fla. Hosp. Cmty. Benefits subcom., 1996-, Leadership Coun. FUMC Winter Pk., 2007-09. Decorated Humanitarian Service medal, Legion of Merit with Gold Star, Meritorious Service medal, Nat. Def. Service medal with star, Vietnam Service medal, Republic of Vietnam Campaign medal with device, others; recipient Alumnus of Yr. award Ind. U. Sch.of Dentistry Alumnus Assn., 1988, Ret6irement award, SHARES, 2010 Fellow Am. Dental Soc. of Anesthesiology, Internat. Coll. Dentists, Am. Coll. Dentists, Internat. Assn. Oral Surgeons; mem. Am. Assn. Oral and Maxillofacial Surgeons, ADA, Western Soc. Oral Surgeons, Assn. Mil. Surgeons U.S. (medal), Fla. Soc. Oral Surgeons, Delta Sigma Delta, Sigma Chi (Significant Sig award 1983). Home: 557 Village Pl Longwood FL 32779 Home Phone: 407-644-9672. Personal E-mail: tmckean3@cfl.rr.com.

MCKECHNIE, JOHN CHARLES, gastroenterologist, educator; b. Louisville, Feb. 1, 1935; s. Albert Hay and Edna Scott (Johnson) McKechnie; children: Steven Keith, Kevin Stuart. BA, U. Louisville, 1955; MD, Baylor Coll. Medicine, Houston, 1959. Diplomate Am. Bd. Internal Medicine, Am. Bd. Gastroenterology. Intern Jefferson Davis Hosp., Houston, 1959—60; resident internal medicine Baylor Affiliated Program, Houston, 1960—61, 1965—66; gen. practice medicine Benham, Ky., 1964; practice medicine specializing in gastroenterology Houston, 1966—; clin. instr. Baylor Coll. Medicine, Houston, 1966—69, asst. prof., 1969—72, assoc. prof., 1972—77, prof., 1977—. Mem. staff Meth. Hosp., assoc. dir. internal medicine program; cons. Ben Taub Hosp., St. Luke's Episcopal Hosp.; clin. prof. Weill Cornell Med. Coll., NYC. Contbr. articles to profl. jours. Capt. USMC, 1962—64. Fellow: ACP, Am. Coll. Gastroenterology (gov. Tex. chpt. 1979—80, trustee 1981—84); mem.: AMA, Houston Gastroent. Soc. (pres. 1983), Tex. Soc. Gastrointestinal Endoscopy, Am. Soc. Gastrointestinal Endoscopy, Digestive Disease Found., Am. Gastroent. Assn., Tex. Med. Assn., So. Med. Assn., Alpha Omega Alpha. Republican. Presbyterian. Office: Th-Meth Hosp 6560 Fannin St Ste 1630 Houston TX 77030-2734 Office Phone: 713-797-0916.

MCKEE, ELLSWORTH R., food products executive; BA in Bus. and Econs., So. Adventist U., 1954; postgrad., Andrews U., 1987. Shipping/receiving clk. Jack's Cookie Co., Charlotte, NC, 1949-50; various positions McKee Foods, Collegedale, 1951-54, v.p. prodn. and fin., 1954-62, exec. v.p., treas., 1962-71, pres., CEO, 1971-96, also bd. dirs., 1954—, chmn. bd. dirs., 1997—. Bd. dirs. So. Adventist U., Collegedale, Andrews U., Berrien Springs, Mich., 1976—2000. Recipient Pvt. Sector Initiative Commendation, Pres. Ronald Reagan, 1988. Office: McKee Foods PO Box 750 Collegedale TN 37315-0750

MCKEE, FRANCIS JOHN, medical association consultant, lawyer; b. Bklyn., Aug. 31, 1943; s. Francis Joseph and Catherine (Giles) McK.; m. Antoinette Mary Sancis; children: Lisa Ann, Francis Dominic, Michael Christopher, Thomas Joseph. AB, Stonehill Coll., 1965; JD, St. John's U., 1970. Bar: N.Y. 1971. Assoc. Samuel Weinberg, Esquire, Bklyn., 1970-71, Finch & Finch, Esquire, Long Island City, NY, 1971-72; staff atty. Med. Soc. of State of NY, Lake Success, NY, 1972-77; of counsel Suffolk County Med. Soc., Hauppauge, NY, 1977—81; exec. dir. Suffolk Physicians Rev. Orgn., East Islip, NY, 1977-81, Medical Soc. Oneida, Herkimer, Madison, and Chenango, 1981—84, Central NY Acad. Med., 1981—84; prin. Francis J. McKee Assocs., Clinton, NY, 1984—2001; exec. dir. NY State Soc. Surgeons, Inc., Clinton, NY, 1981-2000, NY State Soc. Orthopaedic Surgeons, Inc., Clinton, NY, 1981—2000, Upstate NY chpt. ACS, Inc., Clinton, NY, 1981-2000, NY State Ophthalmol. Soc., 1984-92, NY State Soc. Obstetricians and Gynecologists, 1985-2001, Orthopac of NY, 1986-2000, Nat. Com. for the Preservation Orthopaedic Practice, New Hartford, NY, 1989-2000, L.I. Ophthalmol. Soc., 1994-2000. Mgr. Thomas J. McKee and Assocs., LLC, 2005-10; exec. v.p. Thomas J. McKee and Assocs., Inc., 2011-; mgr. Michael C. Mckee and Assoc., 2009-10; exec. v.p. Michael C. Mckee and Assoc., Inc., 2011-. With U.S. Army, 1966-68. Mem.: NY State Bar Assn., Am. Legion, Taberna Country Club, Elks (presiding justice, subordinate order 2007—11). Republican. Roman Catholic. Home and Office: 908 Taberna Cir New Bern NC 28562 E-mail: frank4mets@embarqmail.com.

MCKEE, PATRICK ALLEN, physician; b. Tulsa, Apr. 30, 1937; s. Charles and Estelle Marie McK. Student, U. Tulsa, 1955-58; MD, U. Okla., 1962. Intern, resident Duke Hosp., Durham, NC, 1962—63, 1963—64; rsch. fellow cell biology Duke U. Med. Ctr., 1963—64; chief resident U. Okla. Med. Center, Oklahoma City, 1967-68; clin. assoc. Framingham Heart Program, NIH, Framingham, MA, 1965-67; assoc. medicine dept. medicine Duke U. Med. Center, 1969-70, clin. investigator, 1970-71, asst. prof. medicine, 1970-72, asst. prof. biochemistry, 1971-85, assoc. prof. medicine, 1972-75, prof. medicine, 1975—, dir. outpatient clinic, 1975-85, chief div. gen. medicine, 1976-85; chmn. dept. medicine U. Okla., Health Sci. Ctr., 1985-95; Laureate chair in molecular medicine and prof. medicine, sci. dir. W.K. Warren Medical Rsch. Ctr. U. Okla., 1995—; investigator Howard Hughes Med. Inst., Duke U. Med. Ctr., 1977—85. Cons. thrombosis research Nat. Heart and Lung Inst., 1970-71; mem. hematology study sect. NIH, 1973-77, NASA Aerospace Medicine Occupl. Health Adv. Subcom., 1995-2000. Contbr. numerous articles to profl. jours. Trustee Okla. Sch. Math. and Sci., 1986-90; vice chmn. Okla. Ctr. for Advancement Sci. and Tech., 1987-91. Recipient McGovern Lectr. & medal Am. Osler Soc., 2009, Hall of Fame, U. Tulsa, 2012; NIH grantee U. Okla. Med. Center, 1968-69, 2003-07; NIH grantee Duke U. Med. Center, 1972-85, 2003-07. Mem. US Pharmacop (coun. experts, 1995-), Hematology and Blood Products Com. (chair, coun. experts, 2005-, dir. devel. Laureate Inst., 1998-2008); fellow Am. Heart Assn., ACP; Assn. Am. Physicians, Am. Soc. Clin. Investigation, So. Soc. Clin. Investigation, Cen. Soc. Clin. Investigation, Am. Fedn. Medical Research, Internat. Soc. Thrombosis and Haemostasis, Am. Soc. Hematology, Am. Soc. Biochem. Molecular Biol., Am. Clin. and Climatol. Soc., Am. Soc. Internal Medicine, Sword and Key, Alpha Omega Alpha, Phi Eta Sigma, Sigma Xi. Roman Catholic. Office: University Okla Health Scis Ctr PO Box 26901 Oklahoma City OK 73126-0901

MCKEE, THOMAS MILES, state legislator; b. Cynthiana, Ky., Mar. 13, 1941; s. William Miles and Anna Myers (Ross) McKee; m. Sue Lloyd Kelsey, 1963; children: Katie, Jim. BA, Centre Coll., Danville, Ky. Former farmer; bd. dir. Harrison Meml. Hosp., 1976—96; magistrate Harrison County, 1978—96; bd. dir. Nat. Bank Cynthiana, 1981—96; adv. bd. mem. Fifth Third Bank, Cynthiana, 1993—; mem. Dist. 78 Ky. House of Reps., 1997—. Named Farmer of Yr., Cynthia Harrison County C. of C., 1973. Mem.: Ky. Farm Bur., Harrison Cunty Beef Cattle Assn., Nat. & Ky. Cattlemen's Assn., America Angus Assn., Harrison County Farm Bur. (former pres.). Democrat. Presbyterian. Office: Capitol Annex Rm 351B 702 Capitol Ave Frankfort KY 40601 Office Phone: 502-564-8100 ext. 667. Business E-Mail: tom.mckee@lrc.state.ky.us.

MCKEE, TIMOTHY CARLTON, retired taxation educator; b. South Bend, Ind., Mar. 9, 1944; s. Glenn Richard and Laura Louise (Niven) McK.; m. Linda Sykes Mizelle, Oct. 13, 1984; children: Brandon Richard. BS in Bus. Econs., Ind. U., 1970, MBA in Fin., 1973, JD, 1979; LLM in Taxation, DePaul U., 1980. Bar: Ill. 1980, U.S. Dist. Ct. (no. dist.) Ill. 1980; CPA, Va.; cert. govt. fin. mgr. Procedures analyst Assocs. Corp., South Bend, 1969-71; asst. dir. fin. Ind. U., Bloomington, 1971-79; sr. tax mgr. Peat Marwick Mitchell & Co., Chgo., Norfolk, Va., 1979-84; corp. counsel K & K Toys, Norfolk, 1984; assoc. prof. acctg. Old Dominion U., Norfolk, 1985-98, chmn. dept., 1994-95, chmn. acctg., fin. and law dept., 1995, univ. prof. dept. acctg., 1998—2012. Computer coord. Peat, Marwick, Mitchell & Co., 1982-84; micro computer cons. Old Dominion U., 1985-91. Contbr. articles to profl. jours. Active Friends of Music, Bloomington, 1978, Art Inst., Chgo., 1981; loan exec. United Way, Chgo., 1981; telethon chmn. Va. Orch. Group, Norfolk, 1983. Mem. Assn. Govt. Accts., Am. Acctg. Assn., Am. Assn. Atty. CPAs, Inc., Am. Tax Assn., Fin. Execs. Inst. (pres. 1995-96), Hampton Rds. Tax Forum, Inst. Internal Auditors, Beta Alpha Psi, Beta Gamma Sigma. Home: 322 Greens Edge Dr Chesapeake VA 23322-8078

MCKEEL, SETH, state legislator; b. Lakeland, Fla., June 5, 1975; s. Seth Douglas McKeel and Ellen (Tucker); m. Kimberley McKeel, Oct. 26, 2002; children: Seth D. III, Caroline. BA in Polit. Sci., U. Fla., 1997. Intern Publix Supermarkets, Lakeland, Fla., 1995—97; pub. rels. cons. Rodda Constrn., Inc.; v.p. Lakeland Properties & Mgmt., Inc., 1997—99; real estate manager Heritage Equities, Inc., Lakeland, Fla.; mem. Dist. 63 Fla. House of Reps., 2006—, chair state univs. and pvt. colls. policy com., vice chair state univs. and pvt. colls. appropriations com., mem. edn. policy coun., energy and utilities policy com., select policy coun. on strategic and econ. planning. Mem. Lakeland City Commn., 2000—05. Bd. mem. McKeel Acad. Tech. Charter Schools, 1997—, chmn., 2000—04; bd. mem. Volunteers in Svc. to the Elderly, 1999—2008, Imperial Symphony Orch., v.p., 2003, pres., 2005—06; chmn. Young Patriots Found., 2001—. Mem.: Kiawanis Club of Lakeland. Republican. Methodist. Office: 250 E Highland Dr Lakeland FL 33813-1725 also: 1102 The Capitol 402 S Monroe St Tallahassee FL 32399-1300 Office Phone: 863-647-4896, 850-488-9890.

MCKEEL, SHERYL WILSON, pharmacist; b. Nashville, Apr. 6, 1957; d. Robert Lewis and Norma Anne (Cox) Wilson; m. Vaughn Allen McKeel, Apr. 22, 2000. BS in Biology, David Lipscomb U., 1979; BS in Pharmacy, Auburn U., 1985. Lic. pharmacist, Tenn. Student extern/intern East Alabama Med. Ctr., Opelika, Ala., 1982-86; staff pharmacist Metro Nashville Gen. Hosp., 1987-95, PharmaThera, Inc., Nashville, 1995-99, Mid. Tenn. Mental Health Inst., Nashville, 1999-2000, Kmart, 2009, Maxim Staffing Solutions, 2010—11. Flutist Nashville Cmty. Concert Band, 1973-97; presch. tchr. Donelson Ch. of Christ, 1988—; active Lipscomb U. Cmty. Chorus, 1998—2008 Mem. Am. Pharm. Assn., Am. Soc. Health Sys. Pharmacists, Am. Soc. Parenteral and Enteral Nutrition, Tenn. Soc. Health Sys. Pharmacists, Nashville Area Pharmacists Assn. Democrat. Avocations: art, music, reading, cooking, sewing. Home: 1439 McGavock Pike Nashville TN 37216-3231 Home Phone: 615-228-7285. Personal E-mail: sheryl.mckeel@hotmail.com.

MC KEEN, CHESTER M., JR., retired manufacturing executive; b. Shelby, Ohio, Mar. 18, 1923; s. Chester Mancil and Nettie Augusta (Fox) McKeen; m. Alma Virginia Pierce, Mar. 1946 (dec. Feb. 1998); children: David Richard(dec.), Karin, Thomas Kevin; m. Sally Ann Werst, Nov. 1999; 1 stepchild, Stephen Harry Werst. BS in Mil. Sci., U. Md., 1962; MBA, Babson Coll., Wellesley, Mass., 1962. Advanced through grades to maj. gen. U.S. Army, 1942-77; dir. logistics Bell Helicopter Internat., Tehran, Iran, 1977-79; v.p. procurement Bell Helicopter Textron, Ft. Worth, 1979-82, v.p. materiel, 1982-89; pres. Logistics Svcs. Internat., Arlington, Tex., 1990—2002; chmn., CEO ISES Inc., 1991—2002; ret., 2002. Decorated D.S.M., Legion of Merit (3), Commendation medal (3); named to U.S. Army Ordnance Hall of Fame. Mem. Nat. Def. Indsl. Assn., Assn. U.S. Army, Ridglea Country Club, Rotary, Masons (33 degree), Shriners, Sojourners, Sigma Pi. Home: 2501 Museum Way Apt 702 Fort Worth TX 76107

MCKELDIN, WILLIAM EVANS, management consultant; b. Richmond, Va., Aug. 14, 1927; s. Robert A.W. and Mary E. (Burk) McK.; children: William Evans, Roberts Evans; m. Phyllis Shellhase, Jan. 23, 1982. BSBA, Temple U., 1951, postgrad., 1951—53, U. Pitts., 1953—54. Various mgmt. positions Westinghouse Corp., Pitts., 1950-62, Farrel Corp., Rochester, NY, 1963-66, Gen. Signal Corp., Norwalk, Conn., and Watertown, N.Y., 1966-71, Copperweld Steel Co., Warren, Ohio, 1971-75, Tenn. Forging Steel, Knoxville, 1975-77, Val Bradley Assocs., West Chester, Pa., 1977-79; pres., owner McKeldin Assocs., West Chester, 1979-95; founder, co-owner McKeldin Group, Bala Cynwyd, Pa., 1995—. Contbr. articles to profl. jours. Bd. dirs. United Fund, YMCA, ARC, Rochester Inst. Tech., Jefferson C.C., Kent State U. With USAAF, 1945—47. Mem. Inst. Mgmt. Cons., Am. Soc. Safety Engrs., Am. Soc. Personnel Adminstrn., C. of C. (bd. dirs.), Masons, Rotary. Republican. Presbyterian. Office: The McKeldin Group 24 Timber Ln Hilton Head Island SC 29926-1002 Office Phone: 843-837-6565. Personal E-mail: mckeldin@webtv.net.

MCKENNEY, RICHARD P., insurance company executive; BS in Mech. Engring. summa cum laude, Tufts U. Mfg. mgmt. program General Electric Co., 1991; various positions in fin. and ops. GE Fin. Assurance Holdings Inc.; sr. v.p., CFO Genworth Fin. Inc, 2004; exec. v.p. Sun Life Fin. Inc., 2006, CFO, 2007; exec. v.p., CFO Unum Group, 2009—. Office: Unum Group 1 Fountain Sq Chattanooga TN 37402 Office Phone: 423-294-1011. Business E-Mail: Rmckenney@unum.com.

MCKENZIE, R. ANDY, mayor; b. Wheeling, W.Va., Aug. 16, 1970; son of Ronald A McKenzie & Karen D M; married to Carrie A Martin; children: R. Austin, Levi, Quinn. Grad., West Liberty State Coll., 1989—92; MBA, West Va. U. Cert. CRPS, AAMS. Mgr. Doc Williams Country, 1988—92; pres., CEO Doc Williams Internat. Inc., 1992—; W. Va. State Senator, Dist. 1, W. Va. State Senate, 1996—2008, minority whip, mem. Confirmations, Energy, Indust & Mining, Enrolled Bills, Judiciary, Labor & Transportation Committees. Grad Leadership Wheeling, 91; Entrepreneur of Year, Small Bus Admin, 96. Wheeling Area Chamber of Commerce (exed board, currently); Wheeling Conv & Visitors Bureau (board director, currently). Republican. Protestant. Mailing: 1900 Kanawha Blvd E Charleston WV 25305 Office: Office of the Mayor City County Bldg 1500 Chapline St Wheeling WV 26003 Office Phone: 304-234-3617.

MCKENZIE, TRACEY, sociology professor; BA in English & Social Sciences, U. N. Tex., MS in Sociology, PhD in Sociology, U. N. Tex. Prof. Sociology Collin County Cmty. Coll., chmn. Learning Communities Prog. Mem. Student Leadership Acad. Collin County Cmty. Coll. Recipient Outstanding Cmty. Colleges Prof. of Yr., Carnegie Found. for Advancement of Teaching & the Coun. for the Advancement & Support of Edn., 2009. Office: Collin County Cmty Coll Preston Ridge Campus 9700 Wade Blvd Rm F169 Frisco TX 75035 Office Phone: 972-377-1662. Business E-Mail: tmckenzie@ccccd.edu.

MCKENZIE, VASHTI MURPHY, bishop; m. Stan McKenzie; 3 children. Grad., U. Md., Coll. Park; MDiv, Howard U.; D in Ministry, United Theol. Sem., Dayton, Ohio; D (hon.), Howard U., Wilberforce U., Morgan State U., Goucher Coll. Radio program dir.; city desk reporter; staff writer; corp. v.p. programming; pastor Payne Meml. AME Ch., Balt.; chief pastor 18th Episcopal Dist. (Lesotho, Swaziland, Botswana, Mozambique) AME, 2000—04, presiding bishop 13th Episcopal Dist. (Tenn. and Commonwealth Ky.), 2000—, pres. Coun. Bishops. Founding pres., organizer Collective Banking Group Balt.; organizer Ch. Health Coalition; pres. AME Ministerial Alliance. Author: Not without a Struggle, Strength in the Struggle, Journey to the Well. Named one of 15 Greatest African Am. Female Preachers, Ebony mag.; named to Honor Roll of Great Am. Preachers, 1993, 1997, Power 150, 2008. Mem.: NAACP (life), Delta Sigma Theta Sorority, Inc. (nat. chaplain). Achievements include first woman ever to be elected to Bishop and Titular Head of AME. Office: AME 500-8th Ave S Nashville TN 37203 Office Phone: 615-242-6814. Business E-Mail: 13th_episcopal@bellsouth.net.

MCKEON, JOHN C., publishing executive; BA in Polit. Sci., NYU, MBA. V.p. mktg. Times Mirror Nat. Mktg.; various advt. and mktg. positions Newsday, Melville, NY, 1986—98, retail advt. mgr., 1991—92, advt. dir., 1992—94, v.p. advt., 1994—98, sr. v.p. advt., chief innovation officer, 1998, exec. v.p., gen. mgr., 2004—05; sr. v.p. advt. L.A. Times, 1998—2001; sr. v.p., gen. mgr. South Fla. Sun-Sentinel, 2001—04; sr. v.p. mktg. Knight-Ridder Newspapers, 2005—06; pres. LA paper group MediaNews Group, 2006—07; pres., pub. The Dallas Morning News, 2007—12, San Antonio Express-News, 2012—. Office: San Antonio Express-News 301 Avenue E San Antonio TX 78205*

MCKEOWN, MICK, aerospace and defense manufacturing executive; Grad., Nat. War Coll., Wash., DC; BA in Bus. Adminstrn., U. Wash.; BS in in Math. & Sci., U. Ore. Dep. & acting chmn. Dept. Internat. Studies; dir., Legislative Affairs LTV Corp.; chief senate affairs Northrop Grumman; dir., Heath & Clinical Affairs U. Calif. Academic Med. System; dir., Legislative Affairs Vought Aircraft Co.; v.p., ops. Vought Aircraft Holdings, Inc., Wash., 2001—. Bd. trustees Air Force Aid Soc., 2004-. Sr. mil. officer USAF. Office: Vought Aircraft Industries Inc Tower 1 201 E John Carpenter Freeway Ste 900 Irving TX 75062 Office Phone: 972-946-2011. Business E-Mail: mick_mckeown@voughtaircraft.com.

MCKERNS, CHARLES JOSEPH, lawyer; b. Shenandoah, Pa., July 17, 1935; s. Charles Francis and Bridgett Ann (Barrett) McK.; m. Helen Patricia Nott, Feb. 13, 1960; children: Charles J. Jr., Michael H., Patricia B. BS, Georgetown U., 1957, JD, 1960. Bar: DC 1960, US Ct. Appeals (DC cir.) 1961, US Supreme Ct. 1971, Va. 1992. Law clk. to assoc. judge US Ct. Appeals (DC cir), Washington, 1960—61; assoc. Dow, Lohnes & Albertson, Washington, 1961—65, ptnr., 1965—91, of counsel, 1991—95; ptnr. McKerns and McKerns, Heathsville, Va., 1991-96, of counsel, 1996—98. 1st lt. US Army, 1957—59. Mem. ABA, University Club (Washington), Belle Haven Country Club (Alexandria, Va.), Indian Creek Yacht and Country Club (Kilmarnock, Va.). Republican. Roman Catholic. Avocations: hiking, reading, swimming. Office: McKerns Law Office PO Box 220 Heathsville VA 22473-0220 also: Dow Lohnes & Albertson 1200 New Hampshire Ave NW Washington DC 20036-6802 Home: 132 Lancaster Dr Apt 112 Irvington VA 22480-9741 Office Phone: 804-580-8225. Personal E-mail: cmckerns@yahoo.com.

MC KETTA, JOHN J., JR., chemical engineering professor; b. Wyano, Pa., Oct. 17, 1915; s. John J. and Mary (Gelet) McK.; m. Helen Elisabeth Smith, Oct. 17, 1943; children: Charles William, John J. III, Robert Andrew, Mary Anne. BS, Tri-State Coll., Angola, Ind., 1937; BSE., U. Mich., 1943, MS, 1944, PhD, 1946; D.Eng. (hon.), Tri-State Coll., 1965, Drexel U., 1977; Sc.D., U. Toledo, 1973. Diplomate: registered profl. engr., Tex., Mich. Group leader tech. dept. Wyandotte Chem. Corp., Mich., 1937-40, asst. supt. caustic soda div., 1940-41; teaching fellow U. Mich., 1942-44, instr. chem. engring., 1944-45; faculty U. Tex., Austin, 1946—, successively asst. prof. chem. engring., assoc. prof., then prof. chem. engring., 1951-52, 54—, E.P. Schoch prof. chem. engring., 1970-81, Joe C. Walter chair, 1981-94, prof. emeritus, 1994—. Asst. dir. Tex. petroleum research com., 1951-52, 54-56, chmn. chem. engring. dept., mem. bd. regents, Tri State Univ, 56-, disting. service in trusteeship, 2002, 1950-52, 55-63, dean Coll. Engring., 1963-69; exec. vice chancellor acad. affairs U. Tex. System, 1969-70; editorial dir. Petroleum Refiner, 1952-54; pres. Chemoil Cons., Inc., 1957-73; chmn. Tex. AEC, So. Interstate Nuclear Bd., 1963-70; mem. Tex. Radiation Adv. Bd., 1978-84; chmn. Nat. Energy Policy Com., 1970-72, Nat. Air Quality Control Com., 1972-85; mem. adv. bd. Carnegie-Mellon Inst. Research, 1978-84; pres. Reagans's rep. on U.S. Acid Precipitation Task Force, 1982-88; apptd. mem. Nuclear Waste Tech. Rev. Bd., 1992-97. Author: series Advances in Petroleum Chemistry and Refining (10 vols.); Chmn. editorial com.: series Petroleum Refiner; mem. adv. bd.: series Internat. Chem. Engring. mag; exec. editor: series Ency. of Chem. Processing and Design (68 vols.). Recipient Bronze plaque Am. Inst. Chem. Engrs., 1952, Charles Schwab award Am. Steel Inst., 1973, Lamme award as outstanding U.S. educator, 1976, Joe J. King Profl. Engring. Achievement award U. Tex., 1976, Gen. Dynamics Teaching Excellence award, 1979, Triple E award for contbns. to nat. issues on energy, environment and econs. Nat. Environ. Devel. Assn., 1976, Boris Pregal Sci. and Tech. award NAS, 1978, Internat. Chem. Engring. award, Italy, 1984, Pres. Herbert Hoover award for advancing well-being of humanity and developing richer and more enduring civilization Joint Engring. Socs., 1989, Centennial award exceptional contbn. Am. Soc. Engring. Edn., 1993; named Disting. Alumnus U. Mich Coll. Engring., 1953, Tri-State Coll., 1956; fellow Allied Chem. & Dye, 1945-46; named Disting. fellow Carnegie-Mellon U., 1978; Chem. Engring. Dept. at U. Tex. named The John J. McKetta Ctr. for Excellence in Chem. Engring. Edn. in his honor, 1995, Chem. Engring. Dept. at Tri State U. named The Dr. John J. McKetta Chem. Engring. Dept. in his honor, 1998. Mem. Am. Chem. Soc. (chmn. Central Tex. sect. 1950), Am. Inst. Chem. Engrs. (chmn. nat. membership com. 1955, regional exec. com., nat. dir., nat. v.p. 1961, pres. 1962, service to soc. award 1975), Am. Soc. Engring. Edn., Chem. Markets Research Assn., Am. Gas Assn. (adv. bd. chems. from gas 1954), Houston C. of C. (chmn. refining div. 1954, vice chmn. research and statistics com. 1954), Engrs. Joint Council (dir.), Engrs. Joint Countil Profl. Devel. (dir. 1963-85), Nat. Acad. Engring., Sigma Xi, Chi Epsilon, Alpha Psi Omega, Tau Omega, Phi Lambda Upsilon, Phi Kappa Phi, Iota Alpha, Omega Chi Epsilon, Tau Beta Pi, Omicron Delta Kappa. Home: 4100 Jackson Ave Apt 229 Austin TX 78731-6070 Office Phone: 512-451-1501, 512-471-5227. Business E-Mail: mcketta@mail.utexas.edu, mcketta@mail.edu.

MCKETTA, JOHN J., III, lawyer; b. Austin, Tex., May 5, 1948; s. John J. and Helen Elisabeth (Smith) McK.; m. Sallie Martin Sharp, Aug. 6, 1977; children: Elisabeth, Mary Elliott, Sarah, John. BA, Harvard U., 1969; JD, U. Tex., Austin, 1977. Bar: Tex. 1977, D.C. 1978, U.S. Ct. Appeals (D.C. cir.) 1978, U.S. Dist. Ct. D.C. 1978, U.S. Dist. Ct. (we. dist.) Tex. 1982, U.S. Ct. Appeals (5th cir.) 1982. Assoc. Covington & Burling, Washington, 1977-82, Graves, Dougherty, Hearon & Moody, Austin, Tex., 1982-84, ptnr., 1984—, pres., 1998—2008. Fellow: Am. Coll. Trial Lawyers; mem.: Internat. Acad. Trial Lawyers, Am. Law Inst. (coun. 1998—). Democrat. Episcopalian. Office: PO Box 98 Austin TX 78767-0098 Business E-Mail: mmcketta@gdhm.com.

MCKIBBIN, WILLIAM ALEX, artist; b. Phila., May 7, 1940; s. William A. and Jane Harrison (Pippin) McK.; m. Dorothy K. McKibbin, Jan. 26, 1963; children: Erin P., William Alex IV. Student, Barnes Found., Merion, Pa., 1958-59, 60-61; BFA, Temple U., Phila., 1963; MFA, The Claremont Grad. Sch., 1965; postgrad., U. Hartford, Conn., 1967-68. Instr. Mt. Pleasant Jr. HS, Del., 1965-66, U. Hartford Coll. Basic Studies, 1966-68; instr. evening divsn. Cen. Conn. State Coll., 1967-68; instr. Aegean Sch. Fine Arts, Paros, Greece, summers 1967-68; asst. prof. Western Coll., 1968-74, acting chair, 1968, 69, 70-71; instr. Cin. Art Acad., 1972-74; asst. prof. Miami U., Oxford, Ohio, 1974-77, assoc. prof., 1977-84, full prof., 1984—. Juried various exhbns. throughout US One-man shows at Evansville (Ind.) Mus. Arts and Scis., Main Artist Gallery, 1985, Museum of the Maya Culture, Chetumal, Q.R., Mex., 2002, Casa de la Cultura de Cancun, Mex., 2001, Carrollton Cultural Art Ctr., Ga., 2006, Cultural Arts Coun. Douglasville, Douglas County, Ga., 2006, Rome Gal Carrollton Ga., 2008, Met. Structures One Ill Ctr. Chgo., 1983, Rippon Coll., Harwood Gal Ripon WI74; exhibited in over 200 exhbns. including group shows at East Carolina U., Greenville, NC, 1981, Second Crossing Gallery, Valley City, ND, 1981, 93, Okla. Art Ctr., Oklahoma City, 1981-82, U. ND, Grand Forks, 1982, 85, Art Chgo. Internat. Art Expo, 1982-90, Trenton (NJ) State Coll., 1983, Fort Hays (Kans.) State U., 1984, 88, Owensboro (Ky.) Mus. Fine Arts, 1984, Middletown (Ohio) Fine Arts Ctr., 1985, Cameron U., 1986, Springfield (Mo.) Art Mus., 1978, 2009, La Fond Galleries, Inc., Pitts., 1994, numerous others; represented by Zaks Gallery, Chgo., The Art Exch., Columbus, Boody Fine Arts, Inc., St. Louis, Nancy Mulle Assocs., Cleve., Steinway Gallery, Chapel, NC, Yvonne Rapp Gallery, Louisville, Orbe Gallery, Cancun, Mex., Gallery Henoch, NYC; 27 pub. collections include Pomona Coll., Claremont, Calif., Thomas More Coll., Ft. Mitchell, Ky., The Springfield Mus., 88-90, 94, 2007-10, Ind. U. East, Richmond, Evansville (Ind.) Mus. Art and Sci., Art Ctr., Inc., South Bend, Ind., Cin. Art Mus., Grinnell (Iowa) Coll., Ft. Hays State U., Hays, Kans., Des Moines Art Ctr., Charles H. MacNider Mus., Mason City, Iowa, Ohio State U., Columbus, Clark State U., Springfield, Ohio, U. NC, Chapel Hill, Ohio State U. Law Sch., So. Alleghenies Mus. of Art, Loretto, Pa., Blanden Meml. Art Mus., Ft. Dodge, Iowa, Ark. Arts Ctr., Little Rock, Taos Art Mus., Taos, N.Mex., Casa de la Cultura de Cancun, Mex., Fitton Ctr. for Creative Arts, Hamilton, Ohio; pvt. collections, 70 corporate collections; reprodns. of work appear in (books) Watercolor Bold and Free, 1980, Figure Drawing, 5th edit., 2000, The Watercolor Solution Book, 1988, Splash I, 1990, The Art of Responsive Drawing, 1992, Splash II, 1993, Watercolor Step-By-Step, 1993, Watercolor School, 1993, Collins' Artist's Manual, 1995, Splash IV, 1995, The Encyclopedia of Watercolour Landscape Techniques, 1996, Painting Shapes and Edges, 1996, North Light Illustrated Book of Watercolor Techniques, Splash VIII, 2004; (mags.) Artist's Mag., The Bull., Jiangsu Pictorial, China, Watercolor Magic, Tropo a la una, Cancun, Mex., Internat. Artist, 2000, Vibrant Watercolours, 2006; work included as cover art on CDs Music for Winds, The Miami Wind Quintet, Vol. 1, 1995, Vol. 2, 1996, Watercolor Handbook: A Comprehensive Guide To The Art of Watercolor, 2004. Recipient Cert. of Merit Tyler Sch. of Art Temple U., Gen. Alumni Assn., 1991, Art of Tchg. citation, 2004, 10, First State Bank award for watercolor Vechten-Lineberry, Taos Art Mus., 19 cash and purchase awards from various orgns. Home: 199 Berkley Dr Villa Rica GA 30180-2400

MCKILLIP, DOUG, state legislator; b. Dec. 20; m. Mary McKillip; children: Jackson, William, John. State rep. Dist. 115, Ga., 2007—; mem. Natural Resources and Environ. Com., 2007—, Industrial Relations and Intragovernmental Coord. Com., 2007—; former atty. Winburn, Lewis And Barrow; founding ptnr. Lancaster & Mckillip Pc. Democrat. Presbyterian. Home: 1200 Tanglebrook Dr Athens GA 30606-5775 Home Phone: 706-546-6279; Office Phone: 706-613-1900. Fax: 706-613-1906. E-mail: dcmckillip@aol.com.

MCKIM, RUTH ANN, financial planner; b. Keokuk, Iowa, Nov. 26, 1932; d. Carl Edward and Ruby Irene (Martin) McKim; m. William James Ashbrook, Aug. 15, 1959 (div. 1974); children: Leslie, Diane. BS, U. Louisville, 1955, MS in Cmty. Devel., 1977. Dir. art therapy Ky. Bapt. Hosp., Louisville, 1955—56; co-dir. art therapy Norton-Children's Hosps. Inc., 1956—57; dir. art therapy NKC Hosps., 1957—59; rschr. Bd. Aldermen, 1976; pub. rels. staff Dept. Consumer Affairs, 1976—78, realtor assoc., 1979—86; fin. planner Nat. Life Vt., 1986—. Tutor Ky. Assn. Specific Perceptual-Motor Disability, Louisville, 1970—74. Author: Banking Survey, 1977. Arts festival com., 1975—77; coord. Louisville Food Day, 1978; vol. and art donor PBS, 1985—88; voter registration canvasser, 1976, 1978, 1982; active Rep. Nat. Com., Rep. Presdl. Task Force, Nat. Rep. Senatorial Com., Nat. Rep. Congl. Com. Com.; sec., treas. St. Francis in the Fields Espicopal Ch., Louisville, 1975—76. Recipient Rep. Presdl. Legion of Merit medal, Order of Merit; scholar Allen R. Hite Art Inst., 1952—54; Bd. Realtors scholar, 1979—. Mem.: Inst. Community Devel. Assn., Ky. Artists and Craftsmen, Louisville Craftsmans Guild (life), U. Louisville Alumni Assn. Republican. Episcopalian. Avocation: oil and acrylic painting. Home: No 43 410 Mockingbird Valley Rd Louisville KY 40207-1318

MCKINLAY, THOMAS, energy executive; B in Chem. Engring., Strathclyde U., Glasgow, Scotland. Joined Murphy Oil USA, Inc., 2008, Murphy Oil Corp., 1991; supply dir., UK refining and mktg. Murphy Oil Corp, 2007—08; gen. mgr., supply & transp. Murphy Oil Corp., 2008—09, v.p., US mfg., supply and transp., US refining and mktg., 2009—11, exec. v.p. worldwide downstream ops., 2011—. Office: Murphy Oil Corp 200 Peach St El Dorado AR 71730 Office Phone: 870-862-6411. Office Fax: 870-864-6373. Business E-Mail: thomas_mckinlay@murphyoilcorp.com.

MCKINLEY, DAVID B., United States Representative from West Virginia; b. Wheeling, W.Va., May 28, 1947; m. Mary McKinley. BS in Engring., Purdue U., West Lafayette, Ind., 1969. Founder, prin. McKinley & Associates, Wheeling, 1981—; mem. Dist. 3 W.Va. House of Delegates, 1981—94; mem. US Congress from 1st W.Va. Dist., 2011—, US House Energy & Commerce Com., 2011—. Chmn. W.Va. Rep. Party, 1992—96. Named one of The 50 Most Influential People in W.Va., W.Va. Exec. Mag. Mem.: Nat. Soc. Profl. Engineers. Republican. Episcopalian. Office: US House of Representatives 412 Cannon House Office Bldg Washington DC 20515 Office Phone: 202-225-4172. Office Fax: 202-225-7564.*

MCKINLEY, JOHN, investment company executive; Grad. in Sci. & Fin., U. Pa., 1979. Advisor ObectVideo, Found. Capital, Xoopit, Nuconomy, Powerset; ptnr. Ernst & Young LLP, 1982—95; sr. v.p., chief tech. officer & chief info. officer GE Capital Corp., 1995—98; sr. v.p., head, global tech. & svcs. Merrill Lynch & Co., Inc., 1998, exec. v.p., chief tech. officer, 1998—2003; chief tech. strategist AOL, chief tech. officer, pres., AOL Technologies Dulles, Va., 2003—04, pres., digital svcs. bus., 2004—07, interim chief tech. officer, 2006—07; advisor Xoopit, 2007—09; founder Great Falls Ventures, 2007; co-founder LaunchBox Digital, 2007—; founder, CEO OurParents, Inc., 2009. Bd. dirs. Powerset, 2007—08; former bd. dirs. MessageLabs, 2008; bd. dirs. Equifax Inc., 2008—, SEC Watch, Inc., 2009—. Office: LaunchBox Digital 1740 N St NW Washington DC 20036 also: Equifax Inc Bd Directors 1550 Peachtree St NW Atlanta GA 30309 Office Phone: 404-885-8000. Office Fax: 404-885-8988. Business E-Mail: john@launchboxdigital.com.

MCKINLEY, JOSEPH H., JR., federal judge; b. Owensboro, Ky., 1954; BS, U. Ky., 1976; JD, U. Louisville, 1979. Pvt. practice atty., Owensboro, Ky., 1979—91; commr. Ky. Oil and Gas Conservation Commn., 1982—90; asst. county atty. Daviess County, Ky., 1985—87; hearing officer Natural Resources and Environ. Protection Cabinet, 1990—91; judge divsn. I Daviess County Cir. Ct., 1992—95; judge US Dist. Ct. (we. dist.) Ky., Owensboro, 1995—. Office: US Dist Ct 423 Frederica St Rm 206 Owensboro KY 42301-3013 Office Phone: 270-689-4430. Office Fax: 270-689-4445.

MCKINNEY, CYNTHIA ANN, former United States Representative from Georgia; b. Atlanta, Ga., Mar. 17, 1955; d. Billy and Leola McKinney; 1 child, Coy Grandison. BA in internat. rels., U. So. Calif., 1978; MA, Tufts U. Fletcher Sch. Law & Diplomacy; postgrad., Ga. State U., U. Wis. Former instr. Clark Atlanta U., Atlanta Met. Coll.; mem. Ga. House of Reps., 1988-92, US Congress from 4th Ga. dist., 1993—2003, 2005—07. Mem. HIV Health Services Planning Coun., Atlanta, 1991—92; Frank H.T. Rhodes vis. prof. Cornell U., Ithaca, NY, 2003—04. US presdl. candidate Green Party, 2008. Recipient Edgar Wayburn award, Sierra Club, 1998, Outstanding Contribution award, Nat. Orgn. Sierra Leonians in N Am., 2000; named a Diplomatic fellow, Spellman Coll., 1984; named one of Most Influential Black Americans, Ebony mag., 2006. Mem.: Progressive Caucus, Congl. Black Caucus, Agrl. Com., Sierra Club, Nat. Coun. Negro Women, Metro Atlanta, NAACP. Green Party. Roman Catholic. Achievements include the first African American woman elected to Congress from Georgia. Office: Hon Cynthia McKinney 5656 Hunters Chase Dr Lithonia GA 30038-1644 Office Phone: 202-225-1605. Office Fax: 202-226-0691.

MCKINNEY, DONALD LEE, magazine editor; b. Evanston, Ill., July 12, 1923; s. Guy Doane and Cora Redfield (Brenton) McK.; m. Mary Frances Joyce, Dec. 14, 1958; children— Jennifer Joyce, Douglas Guy. AB, U. N.C., 1948. Salesman textbooks John Wiley & Sons, NYC, 1949-52; freelance writer mostly comic books with some short articles and fiction, 1952-54; asst. mng. editor True mag., NYC, 1955-62; editor articles Saturday Evening Post, 1962-69; spl. features editor N.Y. Daily News, 1969-70; mng. editor McCalls mag., NYC, 1969-86; Gonzales prof. journalism U. S.C., Beaufort, 1986-90, prof. emeritus, 1990—. Author: Magazine Writing That Sells, 1994; reporter, book reviewer. Served with USNR, 1943-46. Democrat. Home: 1512 Springmoor Cir Raleigh NC 27615

MCKINNEY, JAMES CLAYTON, electronics executive, electrical engineer; b. Charleston, W.Va., June 3, 1940; s. George Clayton and Leona (Adams) McK. BSE.E., W.Va. Inst. Tech., 1963. Mem. staff Sta. WMON, Montgomery, W.Va., 1961-63; stringer AP, Charleston, W.Va., 1961-63; with FCC, Washington, 1963-87, chief ops. br., 1969-73, chief monitoring div., 1973, chief enforcement div., 1974, dep. chief Field Ops. Bur., 1974-80, chief Field Ops. Bur., 1980-81, chief Pvt. Radio Bur., 1981-83, chief Mass Media Bur., 1983-87; dep. asst. to Pres., dir. White House Mil. Office Washington, 1987-89; chmn. Advanced TV Systems Com., Washington, 1989-96; CEO Model HDTV Sta. Project, Inc., 1996-97. Chmn. U.S. del. UN Conf. on Radio, Geneva, 1986.; mem. U.S. Dels., Geneva, 1978-79, Can., 1984, Italy, 1985, Mexico, 1986, S.Am., 1986, Fed. Republic Germany, 1990; mem. presdl. dels., NATO, UN, Mexico, USSR, Can., Eng., Finland, Econ. Summit, 1987-88; U.S. Spokesman High Definition TV Conf., Geneva, 1989. Author: (with Eliot Maxwell) Future of Electronic Information Handling at the FCC— Blue Print for the 80's, 1980; (with G.A. Fehlner) Direct Broadcast Satellites in the United States, 1985; New Look at AM Radio, 1986, HDTV Approaches the End Game, 1991. Vice chmn. Montreux Medal Award Com., 1990-95; chmn. High Definition TV World Conf., 1990-93; chmn. strategic planning group for Internat. Consultative Com. for Radio, Dept. State, 1990-91; bd. dirs. Bowler Found., 1990-95, PICA Found., Inc., 1996-97; CEO & bd.dirs. HDTV Sta. Project, Inc., 1996-97; bd.dirs. Deercreek Country Club Owners Assn., 2005-08, treas. Assn. Glenmoor Inc., 2011-. Recipient Outstanding Fed. Exec. award FCC, 1979, 80, 82, 83, 85, 86; Presdl. Rank award for disting. exec. svc., 1985, Gold medal for disting. fed. svc., 1987, TV Engring. Achievement award, 1992, NAB award of honor, 1996, Broadcast Pioneers' Disting. Svc. award, 1996; W.Va. Broadcasters Disting. West Virginian, 1997. Fellow Radio Club Am., Soc. Broadcast Engrs. (sr.), Broadcast Pioneers, Soc. Motion Picture and TV Engrs. (presdl. proclamation 1991); mem. Fed. Exec. Assn., Cosmos Club Washington. Episcopalian. Home: 700 Berkshire Ter Saint Augustine FL 32092-3100 Personal E-mail: jimmckin@comcast.net.

MCKINNON, MARK DAVID, consulting firm executive; b. 1955; m. Annie McKinnon; children: Brita, Kendall. Attended, U. Tex. Austin. Democratic campaign cons., Tex.; media advisor Gov. Ann Richards, Tex., 1990, Pres. George W. Bush, 2000, 2004; founder, pres. Maverick Media, 2004—; vice chmn. Pub. Strategies, Inc., Austin, 2004—; founding mem. hotsoup.com, 2006; media advisor Senator John McCain's Presdl. Campaign, Arlington, Va., 2006—08. Lectr. Harvard U. JFK Sch. Govt.; adj. prof. pub. affairs U. Tex. Austin LBJ Sch. Pub. Affairs, 2007. Former songwriter: Kris Kristofferson. Bd. mem. Lance Armstrong Found. Recipient More than 30 Pollie and Tellie awards. Republican. Office: Public Strategies Inc 98 San Jacinto Blvd Ste 1200 Austin TX 78701 Office Phone: 512-474-8848. Office Fax: 512-474-0120.

MCKINNON, STUART J., ophthalmologist, educator; MD, La. State U. Sch. Medicine, New Orleans, 1990; PhD in Physical Chemistry, U. New Orleans, 1990. Diplomate Am. Bd. Ophthalmology, lic. La., Md., Tex., NC. Resident ophthalmology La. State U. Eye Ctr., 1991—95; glaucoma fellow Wilmer Ophthal. Inst., Johns Hopkins U. Sch. Medicine, Balt., 1995—96; prof. ophthalmology U. Tex. Health Sci. Ctr., San Antonio; assoc. prof. dept. ophthalmology & dept. neurobiology Duke U. Med. Ctr., Durham, NC, 2009—. Mem. editl. bd. Jour. Ocular Pharmacology & Therapeutics; contbr. articles to profl. jours. Com. mem. Am. Health Assistance Found. Mem.: Southern Med. Assn., Am. Glaucoma Soc., Am. Acad. Ophthalmology. Office: Duke U Med Ctr Box 3802 Durham NC 27710 Office Phone: 919-681-3937. Office Fax: 919-681-8267. Business E-Mail: stuart.mckinnon@duke.edu.

MCKISSICK, FLOYD B., JR., state legislator; BA in Geography, Clark U.; MA in Regional Planning, UNC, Chapel Hill; MPA, Harvard U.; JD, Duke U. Sch. Law. Former atty. Faison, Brown & Broug, Dickstein, Shapiro & Morin; ptnr. McKissick & McKissick, 1990—; mem. Dist. 20 NC State Senate, 2007—. Democrat. Office: NC Senate 300 N Salisbury St Rm 520 Raleigh NC 27603-5925 Address: 4011 University Dr Durham NC 27707 Office Phone: 919-733-4599, 919-490-5373. Business E-Mail: Floyd.McKissick@ncleg.net.

MCKNIGHT, JOSEPH WEBB, lawyer, educator, historian; b. San Angelo, Tex., Feb. 17, 1925; s. John Banning and Helen Katherine (Webb) McK.; m. Julia Ann Dyer, July 20, 1957 (dec. Jan. 1972); children: John Banton, Joseph Adair; m. Mildred Katherine Virginia Payne, Aug. 9, 1975 BA, U. Tex., Austin, 1947, Oxford U., Eng., 1949, BCL, 1950, MA, 1954; LLM, Columbia U., NYC, 1959. Bar: Tex. 1951, U.S. Ct. Appeals (5th cir.) 1982. Assoc. Cravath, Swaine & Moore, NYC, 1951-55; asst. prof. So. Meth. U., Dallas, 1955-57, assoc. prof., 1957-63, prof. law, 1963—, acad. dean, 1977-80, Larry and Jane Harlan faculty fellow, 1991—. Vis. prof. various univs. Gen. editor Creditors' Rights in Texas, 1963; author: (with William A. Reppy, Jr.) Texas Matrimonial Property Law, 1983, 11th edit. 2007-08, Texas Marital Property Law, 1967-2009, 2010; contbr. articles to profl. jours. Pres., Tex. Old Missions and Forts Restoration Assn., 1977-79, 99-2001; bd. dirs. San Jacinto Mus. History Assn., 1976-99; exec. coun. Tex. State Hist. Assn., 1988-91, fellow, 2004; bd. trustees Tex. Supreme Ct. His. Soc., 1990-; dir. History of Tex. Supreme Ct. History Project, 1998-. Lt. USNR, 1942-47 Rhodes scholar, 1947-50; James Kent fellow Columbia Law Sch., 1958-59; Academico, Acad. Mexicana de Derecho Internat., 1988, Hall of Legends, State Bar of Texas Fam. Law Sec., 1997. Fellow, Soc. for Advanced Legal Studies (London), 1998; mem. ABA, State Bar Tex., Dallas Bar Assn., Tex. Bar Found. (v.p. 1959), Nat. Legal Aid and Defenders Assn. (bd. dirs. 1963-66), Selden Soc., Am. Soc. Legal History (v.p. 1967-68, bd. dirs. 1967-75), Inst. Texan Cultures (exec. bd. 1990-95), Oxford and Cambridge Club (London), Sigma Chi. Democrat. Episcopalian. Office: So Meth U Law Sch 3315 Daniel Ave Dallas TX 75275-0116 Home Phone: 214-361-0894; Office Phone: 214-768-2591, 214-768-3851. Business E-Mail: jmcknigh@smu.edu.

MCKONE, TIMOTHY P., lobbyist, telecommunications industry executive; b. Phoenix; m. Joey McKone; children: Ally, Sam, Jack. Dir. govt. affairs Ind. Ins. Agents of America; joined Southwestern Bell, 1993; lobbyist, ptnr. Davis, Manafort & Freedman, Inc., Arlington, Va., 1998—99; lobbyist, sr. v.p. congl. affairs SBC Comm., Inc., 1999—2005; lobbyist, exec. v.p. fed. rels. AT&T Svcs., Inc., 2005—. Dir. congl. rels. presdl. campaign Bob Dole Rep. Nat. Conv., San Diego, 1996. Named one of Best in the Bus., The Hill, 2007. Republican. Office: AT&T Corp Hdqs 175 E Houston San Antonio TX 78205 Business E-Mail: timothy.mckone@att.com.

MCKOON, JOSHUA, state legislator; b. Columbus, Ga., Feb. 25; BA in Polit. Sci. & Comm., Furman U.; JD, U. Ala. Atty. Page, Scrantom, Sprouse, Tucker & Ford, PC, Columbus, Ga., McKoon & Associates; mem. Dist. 29 Ga. State Senate, 2011—. Recipient Man of Yr. award, Ga. Young Rep. Fedn. Mem.: Ala. State Bar, State Bar of Ga. Republican. Office: PO Box 2565 Columbus GA 31902 also: Ga State Senate 319A Coverdell Legis Office Bldg Atlanta GA 30334 Office Phone: 706-442-9130, 404-463-3931. Business E-Mail: jrm2016@yahoo.com.

MCLAIN, ROBERT S., JR., wholesale distribution executive; Grad., U. SC, 1982. Dir. mktg. Gates/FA Distbg. Inc., 1993—95; pres. Transition Mktg., Inc., 1995—97; v.p. mktg. ScanSource, Inc., 1997—2003, v.p. mktg. & bus. devel., 2003—. Office: ScanSource Inc 6 Logue Ct Greenville SC 29615 Office Phone: 864-288-2432. Office Fax: 864-288-1165.

MCLANE, DRAYTON, JR., former professional sports team executive; m. Elizabeth McLane; 2 children. M, Mich. State U., East Lansing, 1959. Grocery store distributor; vice chmn. Wal-Mart, Benton, Ark.; owner, chmn., CEO Houston Astros, 1993—2011. Active Boy Scouts America; deacon First Bapt. Ch. Temple, Tex. Named one of Forbes 400: Richest Americans, 2009. Office: McLane Co Inc PO Box 6115 Temple TX 76503-6115

MCLAREN, BRIAN D., advocate, writer; b. 1956; m. Grace McLaren; 4 children. BA in English, U. Md., Coll. Park, 1978, MA in English, 1981; DD (hon.), Carey Theol. Sem., Vancouver, Can., 2004. English tchr., 1978—86; founding pastor Cedar Ridge Cmty. Ch., 1986—2006; theologian-in-residence Life in the Trinity Ministry, Dallas, 2012—. Lectr. in field. Author: (novels) The Church on the Other Side, 1998, Finding Faith, 1999, A New Kind of Christian, 2001 (Merit award, Christianity Today, 2002), More Ready Than You Realize: Evangelism as Dance in the Postmodern Matrix, 2002, A Is for Abductive, 2002; co-author Adventures in Missing the Point, 2003, Church in Emerging Culture: Five Perspectives, 2003; author The Story We Find Ourselves In, 2003, A Generous Orthodoxy, 2004, The Last Word and the Word After That, 2005, The Secret Message of Jesus: Uncovering the Truth that Could Change Everything, 2006, Everything Must Change, 2007, Finding Our Way Again, 2008, A New Kind of Christianity, 2010, Naked Spirituality: A Life With God in 12 Simple Words, 2011; contbr. articles to profl. jours including Leadership, Sojourners, Worship Leader, and Conversations. Founding mem. Red Letter Christians; former bd. mem. Internat. Teams, Chgo., Mars Hill Grad. Sch., Seattle, Off the Map; bd. chair Sojourners/Call to Renewal; bd. dirs. Orientacion Cristiana, Emergent Village. Named one of 25 Most Influential Evangelicals, TIME mag., 2005. Evangelical. Avocations: fishing, art, ecology, hiking, kayaking, song writing, camping, literature. Office: Life in the Trinity Ministry PO Box 742405 Dallas TX 75374-2405

MCLAUGHLIN, BETHLEE, retail executive; Grad., Regis Coll., 1990. V.p. quality assurance & product info HSN, Inc., sr. v.p. customer care. Office: 1 HSN Dr Saint Petersburg FL 33729-0001 Office Phone: 727-872-1000. Office Fax: 727-872-6615. Business E-Mail: bethlee.mclaughlin@hsn.net.

MCLAWHORN, MARIAN NELSON, state legislator; b. Kinston, NC, Feb. 23, 1943; m. Richard McLawhorn. Former media coord.; commr. Town Grifton, 1993—97, mayor, 1997—98; state rep. Dist. 9 NC, 1999—; house majority whip, 2003—04. Recipient Libr. Champion award, Pub. Libr. Dirs, 2000, East Carolina U. Edn. Hall Fame, 2004, Libr. Champion award, Pub. Libr. Dirs, 2005, Outstanding Friend, 2005, Sch. Social Work, East Carolina; named to NC Bus & Prof. Career Woman Yr, 1999. Mem.: Greenville/Pitt County C. of C., Women's Forum, LWV, NC Ctr. Pub. Policy Rsch. Democrat. Methodist. Office: North Carolina House of Representatives 16 W Jones St Rm 1217 Raleigh NC 27601-1096 Office Phone: 919-733-5757. E-mail: Marian.McLawhorn@ncleg.net.

MCLEAN, JAMES, state legislator; m. Katie Mclean; 1 child, Evan. BS in Polit. Sci., U. Ozarks. Funeral dir. Roller-Crouch Funeral Home; mem. Dist. 72 Ark. House of Reps., 2009—. Mem.: Batesville Jaycees (former pres., v.p.). Democrat. Meth. Office: State Capitol Rm 350 Little Rock AR 72201 Home: PO Box 2001 Batesville AR 72503-2001 Office Phone: 501-682-6211, 501-682-7771, 870-613-0617. Business E-Mail: vote.james.mclean@gmail.com.

MCLEMORE, JAMES, bank executive; b. Macon, Ga. m. Ellen McLemore; 4 children. BS in Acctg., U. Fla. CPA; CFA. Sec. Americorp, Inc.; v.p., treas. Bank Corp. of Ga., 1990—97; staff acct. Securities and Exch. Commn., 1997—98; sr. v.p., CFO IBERIABANK Corp., Lafayette, La., 1998—2000; exec. v.p., CFO Ind. Bankers Bank, 2000—02; sr. v.p., chief acctg. officer Security Bank of Bibb County; exec. v.p., CFO Security Bank Corp., Macon, Ga., 2002—09, sr. v.p., fin. affairs, 2002; exec. v.p., CFO Security Bank of Bibb County (subs. Security Bank Corp.). 2002—09; chief acctg. officer Security Bank Corp.; sr. exec. v.p., CFO MidSouth Bank, N.A. (subs. of MidSouth Bancorp, Inc.), 2009—, MidSouth Bancorp, Inc., 2009—. Mailing: MidSouth Bancorp Inc 102 Versailles Blvd Lafayette LA 70501 Office Phone: 337-237-8343. Office Fax: 337-267-4434. Business E-Mail: jmclemore@midsouthbank.com.

MCLENNAN, BARBARA NANCY, writer, historic site interpreter, tax specialist; b. NYC, Mar. 25, 1940; d. Sol and Gertrude (Rochkind) Miller; m. Kenneth McLennan, Aug. 14, 1962; children: Gordon, Laura. BA magna cum laude, CCNY, 1961; MS, U. Wis., 1962, PhD, 1965; JD, Georgetown U., 1983. Bar: DC 1983, U.S. Ct. Internat. Trade 1988, U.S. Ct. Appeals (DC cir.) 1988, U.S. Supreme Ct. 1988, Va. 1991; cert. accredited valuation analyst Nat. Assn. Cert. Valuation Analysts, 2004. From asst. prof. to assoc. prof. Temple U., Phila., 1965—78; budget analyst Com. Budget, U.S. Ho. of Reps., Washington, 1978—81; legis. asst. fin. and budget Senator Dan Quayle, Washington, 1981—84; internat. tax specialist IRS U.S. Dept. Treasury, Washington, 1984—89; dep. asst. sec. trade, info. and analysis U.S. Dept. Commerce, Washington, 1989—91; prin., atty.-at-law Bitonti and Wilhelm, PC., McLean, Va., 1991—93; staff v.p. govt.-legal affairs consumer electronics group Electronic Industries Assn., Washington, 1993—94, staff v.p. tech. policy, consumer electronics group, 1994—95; v.p. Van Scoyoc Assocs., Washington, 1995—96; cons. on tax related issues in U.S., former Soviet Union, and West Bank and Gaza McLean, Va., 1996—. Adj. prof. Coll. William and Mary, 2005—; sr. polit. scientist SRI-Internat., Arlington, Va., 1971—74; vis. prof. Am. Coll., Paris, 1975—76; cons. UNESCO, Paris, 1977—78. Author: (book) Comparative Political Systems, 1975, 1980, Reagan's Mandate, 2009, The Wealth of Jamestown, 2013; contbr. articles to profl. jours. Docent Jamestown Settlement Pk., 2005—, Hist. Jamestown Archaearium, 2014; mem. Asian Adv. Bd. to the Governor of Virginia, 2014—; mem. parents adv. coun. Randolph-Macon Coll., Ashland, Va., 1989—92. Fellow NDEA, 1962—65. Mem.: Chesapeake Bay Writers (bd. mem. 2014). Avocations: tennis, golf. Home: 1620 Harbor Rd Williamsburg VA 23185 Personal E-mail: barb.mcl@cox.net.

MCLEOD, ALEXANDER CANADAY, physician; b. Fayetteville, NC, Jan. 14, 1935; s. Walter Guy and Vida (Canaday) McLeod; m. Dorothy Venning Woods, Aug. 21, 1965; children: Alexander Woods, Dorothy Seward. Akat., Städische Akad. Tönkunst, 1955; AB, Princeton U., 1956; postgrad., Johns Hopkins U., 1959-60; MD, Duke U., 1960; MBA, Vanderbilt U., 1988. Diplomate Am. Bd. Internal Medicine, Nat. Bd. Med. Examiners. Intern, asst. resident N.Y. Hosp.-Cornell Med. Ctr., NYC, 1960-62; resident in medicine and neurology, fellow Vanderbilt U. Hosp., Nashville, 1964-67; pvt. practice internal medicine Nashville, 1967-98; clin. prof. med. adminstrn. Vanderbilt U., Nashville, 1999—2002, clin. prof. medicine, 1999—2002, clin. prof. medicine emeritus, 2002—, adj. prof. mgmt. Owen Grad. Sch. Mgmt., 1995—2002, faculty coord. health care mgmt. Owen Grad. Sch. Mgmt., 1996-2000. Bd. dirs. Nat. Security Alliance, Inc., 1990—2000; cons. internal medicine student health svc. Vanderbilt U., Nashville, 1991—96, cons. health ins., 1997—99. Presenter papers to various orgns.; contbr. numerous articles to med. jours. Trustee Friends of Heard Libr. Vanderbilt U., Nashville, 1998; past trustee, past chmn. Dunvegan Found.; bd. dirs. Nashville Symphony, 1988—91, Symphony Hall subcom., 2002; bd. dirs. Skye Terrier Found., 1998—2000; bd. dirs. music ensemble, bd. mem. Belle Meade Baroque, 2008—09; former fellow Hugenot Soc. Gt. Britain and Ireland, Soc. Antiquaries Scotland; former mem. St. Andrew's Soc. NC, Nassav Club, Sloane Club, Farmington Country Club, Princeton Club NY, Grolier Club; mem. KeyBoard Blair Sch. Music, Vanderbilt, 2011—; bd. mem. Middle Tenn. Partnership Internal Medicine, 2011—13; past music com. mem. Westminster Presbyn. Ch., 1989—91, liturgy com. mem.; past vestryman, jr. warden St. George's Episc. Ch., music. com. mem., 2009—. With USNR, 1962—64. Recipient Physicians Achievement award, AMA, 1971, 1974, 1977, 1981, 1984, 1987, 1990, 1993, 1996, 1999; fellow Summer fellow in neurology, USPHS, 1957—58, Mid. Tenn. Heart Assn., 1966—67. Fellow: ACP; mem.: Nashville Acad. Medicine, Tenn. Med. Assn., Am. Coll. Physician Execs., Soc. Scottish Armigers (life), World War II Study Group, Gaelic Soc. of Inverness, Associated Clan MacLeod Socs. (pres. 1998—2006, past co-chmn. Alasdair Crotach com., past exec. v.p.), Clan MacLeod Soc. (life; past pres.), Scottish Soc. Mid. Tenn. (life), Heraldry Soc. Scotland, Coun. Scottish Clan Assns., Inc. (former trustee), Belle Meade Country Club, Tower Club Princeton, Princeton Club Nashville (past pres., treas. and trustee), Univ. Club Nashville, Skye Terrier Club Am. Independent. Episcopalian. Avocations: reading, music, writing. Home: 203 Evelyn Ave Nashville TN 37205-3307 Office: PO Box 50451 Nashville TN 37205-0451 Office Phone: 615-383-1276. Personal E-mail: acmcl@aol.com.

MCLEOD, CHANSE L., lawyer; b. Dallas, 1965; BBA with honors in Fin., U. Tex., Austin, 1988; JD, Houston U., 1991. Bar: Tex. 1991. Ptnr., Real Estate Andrews Kurth LLP, Houston. Assoc. editor Houston Law Rev., 1989—91. Mem.: Houston Bar Found., Tex. Bar Found., Houston Bar Assn., Houston Young Lawyers Assn., State Bar Tex., Tex. Young Lawyers Assn., ABA, Phi Delta Phi. Office: Andrews Kurth LLP 600 Travis St Ste 4200 Houston TX 77002-3090 Office Fax: 713-238-7257, 713-220-4020. Business E-Mail: cmcleod@andrewskurth.com.

MCLEOD, DOUG, state legislator; m. Michele R. Fontenelle; children: Lauren, Ryan. Attended, Miss. Gulf Coast CC, Hinds CC, Raymond, Miss. Owner McLeod's Tire and Automotive Co., Lucedale, Miss.; mem. Dist. 107 Miss. House of Reps., Jackson, 2012—. Bd. dirs. George County Econ. Devel. Found. Mem.: Miss. Farm Bur. Republican. Presbyterian. Office: Miss House of Reps PO Box 1018 Jackson MS 39215

MCLEOD, E. DOUGLAS, real estate developer, lawyer; b. Galveston, Tex., Aug. 6, 1941; s. Vaughan Watkins McLeod and Dorothy (Milroy) Burton; m. Sarah Jackson Helms, Mar. 20, 1965 (div. 1979); children: Chanse, Alexandra, Lindsey; m. Joan Margaret Williams, Dec. 26, 1979; 1 child, Joanie stepchildren: Meg, Libbie. BBA, U. North Tex., 1965; postgrad., So. Meth. U., 1965-66; JD, South Tex. Coll. Law, 1990; LLM, U. Houston, 1993. Bar: Tex., U.S. Dist. Ct. (so. dist.) Tex.; lic. real estate broker. Pres., owner McLeod Properties & co., Galveston, 1967—; tchr. Galveston Ind. Sch. Dist., 1967-69, pres., trustee, 1969—73; banker W. L. Moody & Co., Galveston, 1969-72; developer, broker McLeod Properties/Builders, Galveston, 1972-82; developer Moody Found., Galveston, 1982—. Bd. dirs. Am. Nat. Ins. Co., Galveston, Nat. Western Life Ins. Co., Austin, Anrem Corp., Galveston, Colonel Inc., Galveston, Moody Gardens Inc., Galveston, chmn., 1984—. Mem. editl. bd.: Currents Internat. Trade Law Jour., 1992—. Mayor pro-tem, mem. city coun. City of Galveston, 1973—76; state legislator Tex. Ho. Reps., Austin, 1976—83; bd. visitors South Tex. Coll. Law, 1990—96, bd. dirs., 2000—09; mem. adv. bd. U. Houston, 1986—95; bd. dirs. STCL, Ronald McDonald House, 1986—93, Trinity Episcopal Sch., 1990—96, Galveston Econ. Devel. Partnership, 1998—2002; vestryman, sr. warden, chancellor Episc. Ch. With USMC, 1961—67. Mem.: ABA, Am. Judicature Soc., Galveston County Bar Assn., Tex. Bar Assn., Marine Corps League. Avocations: physical fitness advocate, legal history collector. Home: 53 Cedar Lawn Cir Galveston TX 77551-4631 Office: The Moody Found 2302 Post Office St Ste 704 Galveston TX 77550-1994 Office Phone: 409-797-1521. Business E-Mail: dmcleod@moodyf.org.

MCLEOD, JOHN EDMOND, history professor; b. Toronto, Mar. 5, 1963; s. Wallace Edmond McLeod and Elizabeth Marion McLeod (nee Staples); m. Mary Frances Hora, June 15, 1991. BA, U. Toronto, 1985, MA, 1986, PhD, 1993. Tchg. asst., then lectr., dept. history U. Toronto, 1987—95; asst. prof. history U. Louisville, 1995—2001, assoc. prof., 2001—08, prof., 2008—, chair dept. history, 2004—09, mem. faculty senate, 2011—; hon. rajvanshi genealogist Rajkumar Coll. Rajkot, India, 2001. Bd. dirs. Can. Royal Heritage Trust, Toronto, Canada, 2003—, English-Speaking Union of the US (Ky. Br.), Louisville, 2004—06. Author: (history books) Sovereignty, Power, Control, The History of India; co-author (with Kenneth X. Robbins): African Elites in India; contbr. articles to profl. jours. Commd. Ky. Col., 2012; mem., US dels. to Bangladesh, India, Pakistan, Islamic Life in US & Religion & Soc. Exch. Programs US State Dept., 2004—09. Recipient Pres.s Award for Outstanding Scholarship, Rsch., and Creative Activity, U. of Louisville, 2003, Outstanding Scholarship, Rsch. and Creative Activity Award in the Social Sci., Coll. of Arts and Sci., U. of Louisville, 2002—03, Queen Elizabeth II Diamond Jubilee medal, Can., 2012; fellow, Royal Asiatic Soc. Gt. Britain and Ireland, 2006; Postdoctoral fellow, Shastri Indo-Canadian Inst., 1993—94, Sr. Short-term Rsch. fellow, Am. Inst. of Indian Studies, 2004. Mem.: Ancient Heraldic and Chivalcic Order of Albion, Flagon & Trencher, United Empire Loyalists Assn. Can., Soc. Colonial Wars, Assn. for Asian Studies. Office: ULouisville Dept History Louisville KY 40292 Office Fax: 502-852-0770. E-mail: john.mcleod@louisville.edu.

MCLEOD, SUZANNE M., drilling company executive; Grad., Tex. A&M U., 1987. US investor rels. Petroleum Geo-Services ASA; mgr. investor rels. Cheniere Energy, Inc.; dir. investor rels. Rowan Companies, Inc., Houston, 2008—. Office: Rowan Companies Inc 2800 Post Oak Blvd Ste 5450 Houston TX 77056-6127 Office Phone: 713-621-7800. Office Fax: 713-960-7660. Business E-Mail: smcleod@rowancompanies.com.

MCLEOD, WALTON JAMES, III, state legislator, lawyer; b. Walterboro, SC, June 30, 1937; s. Walton James Jr. and Rhoda Lane (Brown) M.; m. Julie Edwina Hamiter, Feb. 15, 1969; 1 child, Walton James IV. BA, Yale U., 1959; LLB, U. S.C., 1964; postgrad., Pub. Health Sch. U. Minn., 1972. Bar: SC 1964, US Supreme Ct. 1974. Law clk. to Chief Judge Clement Haynsworth US Ct. Appeals (4th cir.), Richmond, Va., 1964-65; assoc. Pope and Schumpert, Newberry, SC, 1965-67; asst. US Atty. Columbia, SC, 1967-68; gen. counsel SC Dept. Health & Environ. Ctrl., Columbia, 1968-94, spl. counsel, 1994-96; dep. SC atty. gen. Columbia, 1987-88. Magistrate Newberry County, Little Mountain, SC, 1973—81; mcpl. judge Town of Little Mountain, 1981—83, mayor, 1983—89, 1993—96; mem. Dist. 40 SC House of Reps., 1996—. Author: Legal Perspectives of Environmental Health, 1973; co-author: Environmental Quality Law, 1975, Hospital Franchising Law and Regulation, 1979. Pres. Newberry (SC) Jaycees, 1967; bd. dirs. SC Housing Fin. & Devel. Authority, Columbia, 1977-96, Newberry County Coun. Aging, 2001—, Newberry Coll. Found., 2005—, SC Alzheimers Assn., 2007-, Southestern Inst. Woman Politics, 2007-2012, SC Humanities Coun., 2008-, SC Legis. Audit Coun., 2008-, SC State House Comt., 2010-; chair Ctrl. Midlands Coun. Govts., Columbia, 1981-82, 2001-03; trustee SC State Mus., Columbia, 1981-85. Lt. (j.g.) USN, 1959-61, served to Capt. USNR, 1961-92, ret. Recipient Outstanding Jaycee award Newberry Jaycees, 1967, Howell Excellence award Naval Res. Law Program, Washington, 1991, Outstanding Legislator award Gift of Life Trust Fund, 1999, Legislative Appreciation award SC Assn. Conservation Dists., 2006, Outstanding Svc. award SC Am. Legion, 2006; named Outstanding Freshman Rep. of Yr. Carolina Hist. Found. Soc., Inc., 1997, Legis. of Yr. award, SC Human Svc. Providence Assn., 2008-. Fellow SC Bar Found.; mem. SC Magistrates Assn. (pres. 1976-77, Disting. Jud. Svc. award 1975, 77), Judge Advs. Assn. (nat. pres. 1991-92), SC Res. Officers Assn. (state pres. 1981-82, Res. Officer of Yr. 1998), SC Soc. (pres. 1990-93). Democrat. Luth. Avocations: reading, physical fitness. Home: 308 Pomaria St Little Mountain SC 29075-9003 Office: SC House of Reps PO Box 11867 Columbia SC 29211-1867 also: 422B Blatt Bldg Columbia SC 29201 Home Phone: 803-945-7461; Office Phone: 803-345-1538, 803-734-3276. Fax: 803-345-0770. Business E-Mail: waltmcleod@aol.com.

MCMAHAN, HOWARD CLEVELAND, physician; MD, Medical Coll. of Georgia, Augusta, 1980. Intern family medicine Medical Ctr., Columbus, 1980—81, residency, 1981—83; practiced medicine Family Practice Associates of Washington, Ga., 1983—84, Adel, Ga., 1984—90; private practice Irwin Family Medicine, Ocilla, Ga., 1990—. Actively practicing with Irwin County Hosp., Osceola Nursing Home, Palemon Gaskins Nursing Home, Irwin County Detention Ctr.; key leader Patient Centered Med. Home, Ga. Lay leader, delegate to the annual conference Ocilla United Methodist Church. Mem.: American Acad. of Family Physicians (alternate delegate), Georgia Acad. of Family Physicians (past pres., Georgia Physician of the Year award 2012). Office: Irwin Family Medicine 361 Cargile Rd Ocilla GA 31774 Office Phone: 229-468-9903. Office Fax: 229-468-5417.

MCMAHON, CATHERINE DRISCOLL, lawyer; b. Mineola, NY, Apr. 28, 1950; d. Matthew Joseph and Elizabeth (Driscoll) McM.; m. Gregory Arthur McGrath, Sept. 10, 1977 (div. 1991); children: Elizabeth Driscoll, Kerry Margaret, Michael Riley. BA, Simmons Coll., 1972; JD, Boston Coll., 1975; postgrad., Suffolk U., 1972-73; LLM, NYU, 1980. Bar: NY 1976, DC 1979, US Supreme Ct. 1980, US Tax Ct. 1991. Tax atty. asst. Exxon Corp., NYC, 1975-76, asst. tax atty., 1976-77, sr. tax atty., 1979-81; tax atty. Exxon Internat. Co., NYC, 1977-79; sr. tax counsel Florham Park, NJ, 1990-92, Exxon Co. USA, Houston, 1992—98, Exxon Coal and Minerals Co., Houston, 1998—2002, Exxon Mobil Corp., 2003—. Tax mgr. Exxon Rsch. & Engring. Co., Florham Park, 1981-90. Bd. dirs. S.E. Morris chpt. ARC, Madison, NJ, 1983. Recipient TWIN award YMCA, Plainfield/Westfield, NJ, 1983. Mem. ABA, NY State Bar Assn., DC Bar Assn. Roman Catholic. Office: Exxon Mobil Corp 800 Bell St Houston TX 77002-7497 Business E-Mail: catherine.d.mcmahon@exxonmobil.com.

MCMAHON, JOHN J., JR., manufacturing executive, lawyer; Undergraduate, Birmingham-Southern Coll.; JD, U. Ala. Pres., sec., treas. & chmn. McWane, Inc., Birmingham, Ala.; CEO Clow Corp., Birmingham, Ala.; chmn. Ligon Industries, LLC. Bd. dirs. ProAssurance Corp., Nat. Bank of Commerce, Cooper/T. Smith Corp., UAB Health Sys., Protective Life Corp., 1987—. Bd. trustees U. of Ala., Birmingham-Southern Coll. Office: Ligon Industries LLC 5th Fl 1927 First Ave N Birmingham AL 35203 Office Phone: 205-322-3302. Office Fax: 205-322-3188. Business E-Mail: jmcmahon@ligonindustries.com.

MCMANUS, DAVID, oil and gas company executive; Grad. in Civil Engring., Heriott-Watt U., Edinburgh, Scotland. With Fluor, Shell, LASMO plc, Ultramar; pres. ARCO Europe, 1994—2000; exec. v.p. Eastern Hemisphere BG Group plc, 2000—04; v.p. internat. ops. Pioneer Natural Resources Co., 2005—07, exec. v.p. internat. ops., 2007—. Bd. dirs. Cape PLC, 2004—, chmn., 2006—08. Office: Pioneer Natural Resources Co Ste 200 5205 N O Connor Blvd Irving TX 75039 Office Phone: 972-444-9001. Office Fax: 972-402-7023.

MCMANUS, STEPHEN, state legislator; b. Oct. 16, 1951; 2 children. State rep. Dist. 96, Tenn., 2007—; regional bus. commentator Fox News. Mem.: Shelby County Rep. Party (fin. chair exec. com.). Republican. Roman Cath. Office: 405 Riveredge Dr Cordova TN 38018 also: 107 War Memorial Bldg Nashville TN 37243-0196 Office Phone: 615-741-1920. Office Fax: 615-253-0232. Business E-Mail: rep.steve.mcmanus@capitol.tn.gov.

MCMANUS, WILLIAM PAUL, police chief; married; 3 children. BA, Villanova U.; MS, Johns Hopkins U.; grad., FBI Nat. Inst. and Nat. Acad. Police officer Met. Police Dept., Washington, asst. police chief, 1998—2001; police chief City of Dayton, Ohio, 2001—03, City of Mpls., 2004—06; chief police San Antonio Police Dept., 2006—. Office: San Antonio Police Department 214 W Nueva San Antonio TX 78207-4585 Office Phone: 210-207-7360. Office Fax: 210-207-4377.

MCMASTER, BELLE MILLER, religious organization administrator; b. Atlanta, May 24, 1932; d. Patrick Dwight and Lila (Bonner) Miller; m. George R. McMaster, June 19, 1953; children: Lisa McMaster Stork, George Neel, Patrick Miller. BA, Agnes Scott Coll., 1953; MA, U. Louisville, 1970, PhD, 1974. Assoc. corp. witness Presbyn. Ch. USA, Atlanta, 1974-77, dir. corp. witness, 1977-81, dir. div. corp. and social mission, 1981-87, dir. social justice and peacemaking unit Louisville, 1987-93; acting dir. program women in theology and ministry Candler Sch. Theology Emory U., 1993-96, dir. advanced studies Candler Sch. Theology, 1995—2003. Vice-moderator chs. commn. internat. affairs World Coun. Chs., 1984-91, mem. justice, peace and creation commn., 1991-99; chair commn. internat. affairs Nat. Coun. Chs., NYC, 1986-89, v.p., 1990-95, exec. bd., 1986-2003, chair ch. world svc. and witness unit com., 1989-1995; chair fin. com. Ch. World Svc. and Witness Unit Com., NC, 1997-99, bd. dirs., 1989-2003., chair Ch. World Serira, 1995-2000 Author: Witnessing to the Kingdom, 1982, book columnist "What I Have Been Reading" in Church and Society Magazine, 1993-2001; contbr. articles to profl. jours. Pres. League of Women Voters, Greenville, S.C., 1963-64; bd. dirs. Interfaith Housing, Atlanta, 1975-81. Danforth fellow, 1969-74. Mem.: MLA, Soc. for Values in Higher Edn., Acad. Am. Religion, Phi Beta Kappa. Presbyterian. Business E-Mail: bmcmast@emory.edu.

MCMECHAN, GEORGE, science educator; b. Vancouver, BC, Can., Aug. 21, 1947; BASc, U. BC, Vancouver, Can., 1970; MS, U. Toronto, 1971; BS, U. Victoria, Can., 1983. Registered profl. engr., B.C. Prof. geosci. U. Tex. at Dallas, Richardson, 1983—, dir. Ctr. for Lithospheric Studies, 1985—. Rsch. scientist Pacific Geosci. Ctr., Sidney, BC, 1972—82. Contbr. articles to profl. jours. Mem.: Seismol. Soc. Am., Am. Geophys. Union, Soc. Exploration Geophysicists (hon. Virgil Kauffman Gold medal 1997, Maurice Ewing medal 2012). Avocations: physical fitness, movies. Office: University Tex Dallas 800 W Campbell Rd ROC21 Richardson TX 75080 Business E-Mail: mcmec@utdallas.edu.

MCMILLAN, CHARLES WILLIAM, consulting company executive; b. Ft. Collins, Colo., Feb. 9, 1926; s. Charles and Margaret (Jennings) McM.; m. Jardell Hollier, Feb. 12, 1951; children: Brett W., Kurt C., Scott P. BS, Colo. State U., 1948. Asst. 4-H agt., Denver, 1948; county agrl. agt. LaJara, Colo., 1949-50, Julesburg, 1950-53; faculty Colo. State U., 1954; div. head, agrl. research dept. Swift & Co., Chgo., 1954-59; exec. v.p. Am. Nat. Cattlemen's Assn., 1959-77; v.p. Nat. Cattlemen's Assn., 1977-81; asst. sec. for mktg. and inspection services USDA, Washington, 1981-85; pres. McMillan and Farrell Assocs., Inc., Washington, 1985-94, C.W. McMillan Co., Alexandria, Va., 1994—. Served to lt. (j.g.) USNR, World War II. Mem. Sigma Alpha Epsilon. Home: 4003 Pine Brook Rd Alexandria VA 22310-2144

MCMILLAN, STEPHEN A., state legislator; b. Mobile, Ala, July 6, 1941; s. John Murphy and Madie (Troutman) McMillan; m. Gayle McMillan; children: Scott, Jason. BA, Auburn U., Ala., 1964. Owner McMillan & Associates; mem. Dist. 95 Ala. House of Reps., Montgomery, 1980—. Served with USAR. Mem. Ala. Assn. Realtors (pres., 1981), Nat. Assn. Realtors, Baldwin County Bd. Realtors, Bay Minette Rotary Club, Ala. & Baldwin County Wildlife Fedn., Bay Minette, Cent Baldwin, South Baldwin & Ala. Gulf Coast Area C. of C. Republican. Presbyterian. Office: PO Box 776 Bay Minette AL 36507 also: PO Box 337 Bay Minette AL 36507 also: Ala House of Reps Ala State House 11 S Union St Rm 532 Montgomery AL 36130 Office Phone: 251-937-6048, 251-943-5061 ext. 2240, 334-242-7723. Business E-Mail: bclegislators@co.baldwin.al.us.

MCMILLON, DOUG (CARL DOUGLAS MCMILLON), retail executive; b. Jonesboro, Ark., 1966; m. Shelley McMillon; children: Blake, Spencer. BA in Bus. Adminstrn., U. Ark., 1989; MBA in

Finance, U. Tulsa, 1991. Buyer trainee in sporting goods Wal-Mart Stores, Inc., 1984, rejoined company, 1991, sr. v.p., gen. merchandise mgr., 1999—2002, exec. v.p., 2005—09, pres., CEO, 2014—, Wal-Mart International, 2009—14; exec. v.p. merchandising & replenishment Sam's Club Divsn., 2002—05, pres., CEO, 2005—09. Bd. dirs. Wal-Mart Stores, Inc., 2013—. Bd. advisors Nat. Coun. La Raza; mem. exec. bd. Ctr. Retailing Excellence, U. Ark.; dir. emeritus The Sunshine Sch., Bentonville, Ark. Office: Wal-Mart Stores Inc 702 SW Eighth St Bentonville AR 72716*

MCMULLEN, DONALD A., JR., bank executive; BS, MBA, U. Pitts. CFA. Pres. Am. Capital Mgmt. Rsch.; pres., adminstrn. Van Kampen/Am. Capital Mgmt. Cos., 1994; head, capital mgmt. group Wachovia Corp. (now Wells Fargo & Co.), 1995—99, exec. v.p., 1999, vice chmn., 1999—2001, sr. exec. v.p. Charlotte, NC, 2001—. Office: Wachovia Corp 100 N Main St Winston Salem NC 27150 Office Phone: 336-770-5000. Office Fax: 336-732-2281. Business E-Mail: donald.mcmullen@wachovia.com.

MCMULLEN, GREERSON G., lawyer; Various positions, including gen. counsel, attesting sec., GE Power Control Technologies, sr. v.p., gen. counsel, N.Am. GE Co., 1996—2004; exec. v.p., gen. counsel, sec. Global Signal, 2004—05; sr. v.p., gen. counsel, sec., exec. v.p., gen. counsel, sec. CNL Hotels & Resorts, 2005—07; sr. v.p., gen. counsel Servicemaster Co., Servicemaster Global Holdings, 2007—. Office: The ServiceMaster Co 860 Ridge Lake Blvd Memphis TN 38120 Office Phone: 901-597-1400. Office Fax: 630-663-2001. Business E-Mail: greerson.mcmullen@servicemaster.com.

MCMULLEN, RYAN D., former state legislator; b. Cordell, Okla., Apr. 5, 1979; s. Tommy and Beverly Wall, David and Iva McMullen; m. Danya McMullen. BS in Agrl. Economics, Okla. State U., 2002. Farmer/ rancher; former chmn. Washita Co. Dem. Party; dir. El Reno C of C & Devel. Corp.; radio broadcaster & engr. KTJS/KTIJ, Hobart; vice pres. Burns Flat - Dill City Ednl. Found.; mem. Dist. 55 Okla. House of Reps., 2008—09; state dir. rural develop. USDA, 2009—. Democrat. Office: 2300 N Lincoln Blvd Rm 505 Oklahoma City OK 73105 also: PO Box 525 Burns Flat OK 73624 Office Phone: 405-557-7312. Business E-Mail: ryanmcmullen@okhouse.gov.

MCMULLIN, RUTH RONEY, retired publishing executive; b. NYC, Feb. 9, 1942; d. Richard Thomas and Virginia (Goodwin) Roney; m. Thomas Ryan McMullin, Apr. 27, 1968; 1 child, David Patrick. BA, Conn. Coll., 1963; M Pub. and Pvt. Mgmt., Yale U., 1979. Market rschr. Aviation Week Mag., McGraw-Hill Co., NYC, 1962-64; assoc. editor, bus. mgr. Doubleday & Co., NYC, 1964-66; mgr. Natural History Press, 1967-70; v.p., treas. Weston (Conn.) Woods, Inc., 1970-71; staff assoc. GE, Fairfield, Conn., 1979-82; mng. fin. analyst GECC Transp., Stamford, Conn., 1982—84; credit analyst corp. fin. dept. GECC, Stamford, Conn., 1984-85; sr. v.p. GECC Capital Markets Group, Inc., NYC, 1985-87; exec. v.p., COO, CEO, John Wiley & Sons, NYC, 1987—90, pres., CEO; CEO Harvard Bus. Sch. Pub. Corp., Boston, 1991-94; mem. chmn.'s com., acting CEO UNR Industries Inc., Chgo., 1991-92, also bd. dirs.; mgmt. fellow, vis. prof. Sch. Mgmt. Yale U., New Haven, 1994-95; chairperson trustees Eagle-Picher Personal Injury Settlement Trust, 1996—2014; chairperson Claims Procesing Facility, Inc., 1998—2014. Bd. dirs. Bausch & Lomb, Rochester, NY, 1987-2007; vis. prof. Sch. Mgmt., Yale U., New Haven, 1994-95; bd. dirs. John Wiley & Sons, Inc., NYC, 86-90, Fleet Fin. Group, Boston, 91-96, Rohn Industries/UNR Chgo., 90-96, Middlesex Mutual Assurance Co., Middletown, 90-98. Mem. dean's adv. bd. Sch. Mgmt. Yale U., 1985—92, 2014—; bd. dirs. Yale U. Alumni fund, 1986—92, Math. Scis. Edn. Bd., 1990—93; bd. dirs., treas. Mighty Eighth Air Force Heritage Mus., 2000—; chmn. Mighty Eighth Found., 2003—; trustee Yale U. Press, 1988—99; bd. dirs. Savannah Symphony, 1999—2003, The Landings Club, 2002—04, Landings Co., 2011—13. Mem. N.Y. Yacht Club, Yale Club, Landings Club. Avocations: sailing, skiing, travel, tennis. Home: 8 Breckenridge Ln Savannah GA 31411-1701 Personal E-mail: rrmcmullin@aya.yale.edu. Business E-Mail: ruthmcmullin@mac.com.

MCMUNN, WILLIAM H., real estate company executive; BA in Econ., Rollins Coll., MBA in Bus. & Fin. Licensed real estate broker, cert. bldg. contractor. Pres. Indigo Devel. Inc., 1990; exec. officer Consolidated-Tomoka Land Co., 2000, chmn., 2008—09, pres., 2000—, CEO, 2001—. Bd. dirs. Consol.-Tomoka Land Co., 1999—. Past chmn. Assn. Fla. Cmty. Developers. Mailing: Consolidated-Tomoka Land Co PO Box 10809 Daytona Beach FL 32120-0809 Office: Consol-Tomoka Land Co Ste 100 1530 Cornerstone Blvd Daytona Beach FL 32117 Office Phone: 386-274-2202. Office Fax: 386-274-1223. Business E-Mail: wmcmunn@consolidatedtomoka.com.

MCMURRAY, JAMIE, race car driver; b. Joplin, Mo., June 3, 1976; Race car driver Brewco Motorsports, Central, Ky., Roush Racing, 2006—. 1st pl. UAW-GM 500 Lowe's Motor Speedway, 2002; 1st pl. Pepsi 400 Daytona Internat. Speedway, 2007, 1st pl. Daytona 500, 2010; 1st pl. Amp Energy 500 Talladega Superspeedway, 2009; 1st pl. Brickyard 400 Indpls. Motor Speedway, 2010; 1st pl. Bank of America 500 Charlotte Motor Speedway, 2010. Film appearances: Talladega Nights: The Ballad of Ricky Bobby, 2006. Fundraiser Autism Soc. America; founder Jamie McMurray Found. Named NASCAR Winston Cup Rookie of Yr., 2003, Rookie of Yr., The Sporting News, 2003. Office: Chip Ganassi Racing 8500 Westmoreland Dr Concord NC 28027

MCMURRY, JAMES FINLEY, JR., endocrinologist, researcher; b. Sentinel, Okla., Aug. 25, 1940; s. James Finley and Anna Jo McMurry; m. Rebecca L. Lomax, May 21, 1987. MD, U. Okla., 1965. Diplomate Am. Bd. Internal Medicine. Chief, med. services USAF Hosp., Dover, Del., 1969—71; endocrinologist Scott and White Clinic, Temple, Tex., 1972—81; assoc prof., internal medicine Tex. A & M U., Temple, 1979—81; asst prof. internal medicine U. Ky., Lexington, 1981—84, Georgetown U., Washington, 1984—87; pvt. practice Rockville, Md., 1984—2009; with Nova Med. Group. Editor: Jefferson, Callender and the SALLY Story, 2000; co-author: Anatomy of a Scandal: Thomas Jefferson and the SALLY Story, 2002, John Lomax of Fauquier County. Capt. USAF, 1969—71. Fellow: ACP; mem.: Montgomery County Med. Assn., Md. (com. chmn. 1987—89), Am. Diabetes Assn. (pres. South Tex. chpt. 1980—81, pres. DC chpt. 1986—87, chmn. Ky. affiliate 1983—84), Endocrine Soc. Independent. Avocations: history, photography, gardening. Office: Martinsburg Va Med Ctr 510 Butler Ave Martinsburg WV 25401*

MCMURTRIE, M. TODD, automotive executive; Pres., gen. mgr. NAPA Memphis Genuine Parts Co., regional v.p. Southeast distbn., v.p. Atlantic divsn., US Automotive parts group. Office: Genuine Parts Co 2999 Cir 75 Pky Atlanta GA 30339 Office Phone: 770-953-1700. Office Fax: 770-956-2211. Business E-Mail: m_mcmurtrie@genpt.com.

MCMURTRY, NANCEY M., finance company executive; Joined International Assets Holding Corp., 1988, dir., Internat. Trading, asst. sec., chief compliance officer, Internat.Trading, 2007—08, v.p., corp. sec., 2007—. Office: International Assets Holding Corp 329 N Park Ave Ste 350 Winter Park FL 32789-7407 Office Phone: 407-741-5300. Office Fax: 407-740-0808. Business E-Mail: nmcmurtry@intlassets.com.

MCNABB, DUNCAN JAMES, retired military officer; b. Shaw AFB, SC, Aug. 8, 1952; BS, USAF Acad., 1974; MS in Internat. Rels., U. Southern Calif., LA, 1984. Commd. 2d lt. USAF, 1974, advanced through grades to gen., 2005; instr. navigator 14th Mil. Airlift Wing Squadron, Norton AFB, Calif., 1978-79, instr., pilot, chief pilot, 1980-83; gen.'s aide Air Force Inspection and Safety Ctr., Norton AFB, 1983-84; chief plan integration br. Hdqrs. Mil. Airlift Command, Scott AFB, Ill., 1984-86; aide to the comdr. in chief U.S. Transp. Command and Mil. Airlift Command, Scott AFB, 1986-88; chief pilot to ops. officer 17th Mil. Airlift Squadron, Charleston AFB, S.C., 1988-90; comdr. 41st Mil. Airlift Squadron, Charleston AFB, 1990-92; dep. group comdr. 437th Ops. Group, Charleston AFB, 1992; chief Logistics Readiness Ctr. the Joint Staff, Logistics, the Pentagon, Washington, 1993-95; comdr. 89th Ops. Group, Andrews AFB, Md., 1995-96, 62nd Airlift Wing, McChord AFB, Wash., 1996-97, Tanker Airlife Control Ctr., Hdqrs. Air Mobility Command, Scott AFB, 1997—99; dep. dir. programs, Office of Dep. Chief of Staff for Plans & Programs USAF, Washington, 1999, dir. programs, 1999—2002, dep. chief of staff plan & programs, 2002—04; dir. logistics (J-4) The Joint Staff, US Dept. Def., Washington, 2004—05; comdr. Air Mobility Command (AMC, Scott AFB, Ill., 2005—07; vice chief of staff USAF, Washington, 2007—08; comdr. US Transp. Command (USTRANSCOM), Scott AFB, Ill., 2008—11. Decorated Def. Superior Svc. medal, Def. Meritorious Svc. medal, Meritorious Svc. medal with oak leaf cluster, Joint Svc. Commendation medal, Air Force Commendation medal with oak leaf cluster, Air Force achievement medal, Combat Readiness medal with oak leaf cluster, Nat. Def. Svc. medal, Legion of Merit with oak leaf cluster, Armed Forces Expeditionary medal, Southwest Asia Svc. medal with two bronze stars, Humanitarian Svc. medal, Kuwait Liberation medal (Kingdom of Saudi Arabia), Kuwait Liberation medal (Kingdom of Kuwait); recipient Orville Wright award Order of Daedalians.

MCNAIR, CARL HERBERT, JR., military officer, aeronautical engineer; b. Pensacola, Fla., Sept. 22, 1933; s. Carl Herbert and Hallie Rebecca (Edwards) McN.; m. Jo Ann Wilson, Oct. 26, 1957; children: Cynthia Leigh, Carl Herbert III, Courtney Ann. BS, U.S. Mil. Acad., 1955; B.Aero. Engring., Ga. Inst. Tech., 1963, MS in Aero. Engring., 1963; MS in Pub. Adminstrn., Shippinsburg State Coll., 1971. Commd. 2d lt. U.S. Army, 1955, advanced through grades to maj. gen., 1987; comdr. troop brigade U.S. Army Aviation Ctr., Fort Rucker, Ala., 1974-75; dep. for aviation to asst. sec. of Army Office Sec. of Army, U.S. Army, Washington, 1975-77, exec. to dep. chief of staff for research, devel. and acquisition, 1977-78; dep. dir. requirements and aviation officer Office of Dep. Chief of Staff for Ops. and Plans, 1978-79; dep. comdg. gen. U.S. Army Aviation Ctr., Fort Rucker, Ala., 1979-80, comdg. gen., 1980-83; dep. chief of staff combat devels. U.S. Army Tng. and Doctrine Command, Fort Monroe, Va., 1983-84, chief of staff, 1985-87; ret. U.S. Army, 1987; v.p. Burdeshaw Assocs., Ltd., Bethesda, Md., 1988-90; pres. Dyncorp Support Svcs. Div., Reston, Va., 1990-94, Dyncorp Enterprise Mgmt., Reston, 1994-99; corp. v.p. Dyncorp, Reston, 1994-99. Spl. asst. to CEO, Dyncorp, 1999-2003, Govt. Rels. CSC, 2003-; bd. dirs., chmn. audit com. Air Methods Corp., Englewood, Colo., 1995—; mem. strategic adv. bd. A&T Systems, Inc., Silver Spring, Md., 2002—2006; mem. bd. advisors H&K Strategic Bus. Solutions, LLC, McLean, Va., 2002-05; chmn. bd. Dynport Vaccine Co., Frederick, Md., 1997-2004, chr. bd. Geonex Martel, Inc., Clearwater, Fla., 2000-01; sr. advisor Altus Assoc., McLean, 2006—2008; mem. bd. advisors, KihoMac, Alexandria, Va, 2010-; mem. bd. advisors, CPS Prof. Servs. LLC, Fairfax, Va., 2011-. Contbr. articles to profl. jours. Pres. Uniformed Svcs. Benefit Assn., Kansas City, Mo., 1980-82, (life) Assn. of U.S. Army, Washington, 1988-92, Washington chpt., exec. v.p. 2 region 1992-96, pres. 2 region 1996-98, coun. of trustees, chmn. fin. com., audit com., 1997-2005; v.p. Ala.-Fla. coun. Boy Scouts Am., Dothan, Ala., 1979-83; mem. nat. bd. dirs. Mil. Cmty. Youth Ministries, 1988-93; pres. West Point Soc., Washington, 1992-95; mem. bd. dirs. Army Aviation Mus. Found.; mem. West Point Fund Com.; trustee U.S. Mil. Acad., 1992-2002, U.S. Mil. Acad. Assn. Grads.; lay leader Aldersgate United Meth. Ch., 2001-04; bd. dirs. Army Hist. Found., 1999—; bd. dirs. Civil Engring. Inst., George Mason U., 2004—2010. Decorated D.S.M. with oak leaf cluster, Legion of Merit with two leaf clusters, D.F.C. with three oak leaf clusters, Bronze Star medal with V devices with oak leaf cluster, Air medal with V devices and 51 oak leaf clusters, Disting. Service medal State of Ala.; named Disting. Grad. Sch. Aerospace Engring. Ga. Inst. Tech., Sigma Gamma Tau, 1963; recipient Silver Beaver Achievement Boy Scouts Am., 1981; recipient Crosses of Military Svc., Korean Conflict, Vietnam, Jeff Davis award United Daus. of the Confederacy, 1987, 88; numerous fgn. awards Korea, Vietnam, Republic of China, Legion of Honor, France; elected to Army Aviation Hall of Fame, 2004. Mem.: Fairfax County C. of C. (bd. dirs.), Nat. Def. Indsl. Assn. (pres. Washington chpt. 1998, bd. dirs. Washington chpt.), Am. Def. Preparedness Assn. (bd.dirs. Washington chpt. 1993—97, sec. 1994—95, 2d v.p. 1995—97, 1st v.p. 1997—98), Assn. U.S. Army (mil. advisor 1979—87, pres.), Army Aviation Assn. Am. (life; v.p. 1979—83, 1985—87, 1990—93, sr. v.p. 1997—99, pres. 1999—2001, pres. scholarship found. 2005—, Order of St. Michael Gold award 2002), Navy League, Order of Daedalians (life), Air Force Assn., Am. Helicopter Soc., Mil. Officers Assn. (life), Masons. Methodist. Home: 7871 Rolling Woods Ct Apt 407 Springfield VA 22152-3615 Office: Air Methods Corp 7301 S Peoria St Englewood CO 80112

MCNAIR, JOHN WILLIAM, JR., civil engineer; b. Asheville, NC, June 17, 1926; s. John William and Annie (Woody) McN.; m. June Clemens Kratz; childrn: Jeffry, Marsha, Cathy. BS in Forestry, Pa. State U., 1950; BSCE, Va. Poly Inst. State U., 1955; postgrad., U. Va., 1957—2004. Registered profl. engr., Va., Md., W.Va., Pa., NY, Ky. Forester U.S. Forest Svc., Flagstaff, Ariz., 1950, U.S. Gypsum Co., Altavista, Va., 1951; mem. engring. faculty U. Va., Charlottesville, 1955—58; prin. John McNair & Assocs., Waynesboro, Va., 1958—; owner Brucheum Group, Waynesboro, 1983—; chmn., CEO Info. Systems Support, Inc., Waynesboro, 1998—2007. With Va. Bd. Architects, Profl. Engrs. and Land Surveyors, 1969-79, v.p., 1977-78, pres., 1978-79. Author numerous engring. and land mgmt. study reports. Mem. Waynesboro City Coun., 1968-72, vice mayor, 1970-72; chmn. Waynesboro Indsl. Devel. Authority, 1984-2000. Capt. AUS, 1944-46, 51-53, France, Okinawa. Recipient Disting. Svc. cert. Va. Soc. Profl. Engrs., 1971. Fellow ASCE; mem. Am. Acad. Environ. Engrs. (bd. cert. environ. engr.), Rotary, Rappahannock River Yacht Club (founding mem.). Republican. Presbyterian. Home Phone: 540-949-6261; Office Phone: 540-942-1161. Business E-Mail: jmcnair@ntelos.net.

MCNAIR, ROBERT C., professional sports team executive, energy executive, entrepreneur; b. Tampa, Fla. m. Janice McNair. BS, U. SC, Columbia, 1958, LHD (hon.), 1999. Chmn. Cypress Telecom. Corp., US Telesys, Inc.; founder, CEO Cogen Techs. Energy Group, Houston; chmn. The McNair Group; chmn., CEO Palmetto Partners, Ltd., RCM Fin. Services LP; founder Houston NFL Holdings, 1998; chmn., CEO Houston Texans, 1999—. Owner, thoroughbred horse farm Stonerside Stable, Ky.; bd. dirs. Fed. Res. Bank, Dallas, Houston, Mosher, Inc.; chmn. emeritus The Tex. Bowl; chmn. investment com. NFL, mem. audit, fin., stadium and expansion committees; spkr. in field. Chmn. bd. trustees McNair Found., Free Enterprise Inst.; pres. Houston Grand Opera Assn.; bd. trustees Baylor Coll. Medicine, Houston, Sigma Chi Found., Mus. Fine Arts, Greater Houston Partnership, Greater Houston Convention Ctr. and Visitors Bur.; bd. govs. Rice U.; founder Cotswold Project, Houston; elder Meml. Dr. Presbyn. Ch., Houston. Recipient Torch of Liberty award, ADL, Outstanding Bus. Leader award, Northwood U., Herman W. Lay Meml. award, Assn. Pvt. Enterprise Edn., Disting. Am. award, Nat. Football Found. Houston Chpt., Disting. Citizen award, Rotary Club Houston, Sam Houston Area Coun. of Boy Scouts America, City Builder award, South Main Ctr. Assn., Trailblazer award, Houston Advt. Fedn., Denton A. Cooley Leadership award, Tex. Heart Inst., Nat. Patriotism, Responsible Citizenship and Cmty. Involvement award, Freedoms Found. at Valley Forge, Pres. & Mrs. George H.W. Bush Cmty. Impact award, Fellowship Christian Athletes; named Entrepreneur of Decade, Houston Tech. Ctr., 2009; named one of Forbes 400: Richest Americans, 2006—; named to Tex. Bus. Hall of Fame. Office: Houston Texans Two Reliant Pk Houston TX 77054

MCNALLY, JAMES RANDY, III, state legislator; b. Dedham, Mass., Jan. 30, 1944; s. James Randy and Margaret McKinna McNally; m. Janice Rebecca Buck, 1967; children: Melissa Kathleen, Margaret Diane. Former rep. fl. leader; house rep. Tenn.; state rep. Dist. 33 Tenn.; state senate Tenn.; bd. dir., cmty. svc. except citizens, 1974—78; treas. Anderson County Rep. Com., Tenn., 1975—78; panel mem. Tenn. Law Enforcement Planning Commn., 1976; campaign chmn., citizens for brock Oak Ridge, 1976; vice chmn. 3rd Dist. young rep., 1977; bd. mem. Elder Citizens Adv. Coun., 1977—, Am. Red Cross, 1978—80; pres. Am. Cancer Soc. Anderson County, 1978—79; pharmacist Meth. Med. Ctr., Oak Ridge, Tenn., 1978—; sec. House-Senate Rep. Joint Caucus, 1979; adv. com. mem. Martin Marietta Energy Sys. Environment, 1985—93; state senator Dist. 5 Tenn., 1987—; chmn., calender com.; chmn., edn. com.; mem. Rules, Gen. Welfare, Health & Human Resources & Tenncare Oversight Coms. Recipient Outstanding Legislator award, Mothers Against Drunk Driving, Tenn., Bird Dog award, Common Cause, 1994, Disting. Svc. award, Am. Coun. Alcohol Problems, 1994, U. Tenn. Coll. Pharmacy, 1996, Vocat. Svc. award, Oak Ridge Rotary Club, 2001, Appreciation award, 2002, Jr. Leagues award, C. of C., Tenn., 2002—03, Svc. award, Sweetwater Fire Dept., 2003, Edn. Persuits award, Internat. Assn. Adminstrv. Profl., 2003, Legislature award, Tenn. Sch. Bds. Assn., 2004, Outstanding Legislature Leadership award, 2005, Outstanding State Senator award, County Ofcl. Assn., 2006; named Young Man of Yr., 1977, Legislator of Yr., Nat. Retail Lumbermen's Assn., 1990, Man of Yr., Sertoma, 1991, Legislator of Yr., Tenn. Devel. Dist. Assn., 1997, Tenn. Men's Health Network, 2004, 2005, Mothers Against Drunk Driving, Tenn.; grantee, Tenn. Dept. Revenue Work to Create Excise Tax on Controlled Substances, 2005; Paul Harris fellow, Rotary Internat., 1996. Mem.: Nat. Conf. State Legislature, Anderson County Pharm. Soc., Tenn. Pharm. Assn., Big Bros & Big Sisters (bd. mem. 1980—), Girls Club, Rotary Club. Republican. Catholic. Office: 307 War Memorial Bldg Nashville TN 37243-0205 also: 94 Royal Troon Cir Oak Ridge TN 37830 Office Phone: 615-741-6806. Office Fax: 615-253-0285. Business E-Mail: sen.randy.mcnally@capitol.tn.gov.

MCNALLY, THOMAS F., library director; BSEd, Kent State U., 1973; MLS, U. Wash., 1978. Classroom tchr., Cleve., 1973—76; reference libr. and selector undergraduate libr. Ohio State U., 1978—83, head circulation, 1985—88; coord. grad. bibliog. instrn. U. Mich., 1983—85; asst. libr. pub. svcs. Loyola U., Chgo., 1988—91; univ. libr. pub. svcs. U. SC, 1991—2003, dir. Thomas Cooper Libr., 2003—07, interim dean libraries, 2007—09, dean libraries, 2009—. Author: (publs.) Battle of the Library Superstars: Professional Media Production Techniques in Library User Education, 1983, Planning for Security in Libraries, 1987, Security in Libraries, 1988, The End of my Summer Vacation, 2005, My New Year's Resolution, 2006. Mem.: ALA, Assn. Coll. and Rsch. Libraries (program planning com. biliog. instrn. sec. 1982—85, chairperson program planning com. biliog. instrn. sec. 1984—85, profl. edn. com. 1987—89, continuing edn. course adv. com. 1989—92, program planning com. univ. libraries sec. 1994—96), Libr. Adminstrn. and Mgmt. Assn., Partnership Among South Carolina Libraries (PASCAL). Office: University of South Carolina 1322 Greene St Columbia SC 29208 Office Phone: 803-777-6212. Office Fax: 803-777-4661. Business E-Mail: Tom@mailbox.sc.edu.

MCNAMARA, A. J., federal judge; b. New Orleans, 1936; BS, La. State U., 1959; JD, Loyola U., New Orleans, 1968. Bailiff, law clk. US Dist. Ct., New Orleans, 1966-68, sole practice, 1968-72; ptnr. Monton, Roy, Carmouche, Hailey, Bivens & McNamara, New Orleans, 1972-76, Hailey, McNamara, McNamara & Hall, 1978-82; judge US Dist. Ct. (ea. dist.) La., New Orleans, 1982—99, chief judge, 1999—2001, sr. judge, 2001—. Mem. La. Ho. of Reps., 1976-80. Office: US Dist Ct 500 Poydras St Rm C107A New Orleans LA 70130

MCNAMARA, JOHN J(OSEPH), advertising executive, writer; b. Yonkers, NY, Mar. 7, 1934; m. Patricia A. Widmann, Sept. 14, 1963; children: Mary, John. BS, Yale U., 1956; MBA, NYU, 1963. Pres. Young & Rubicam Inc., from 1982; later pres. McCann Erickson Worldwide, ret., 1990. Cons. in field. Author: Advertising Agency Management, 1989; columnist: Gulf Stream mags. Pres. Pelham United Way, NY; chmn. Pelham Manor Planning Bd.; trustee Village of Pelham Manor, mayor, 1989—90; pres. Boys and Girls Club, Indian River County, Fla.; pres., bd. dirs. John's Island Property Owners Assn. Mem.: John's Island Club (bd. dirs.), Winged Foot Club, Pelham Country Club (pres.). Office: 6001 N A1A PMB 8204 Vero Beach FL 32963

MCNAUGHT, CLARK, retail executive; Attended, U. Tex., Austin, 1982; MBA in Mgmt. & Strategic Planning, U. St. Thomas, 1991. With Foley's, Sanger-Harris; divisinal mdse. mgr., Men's Divsn. J.C. Penney Corp., Inc., 1996—2008, divisional v.p., Men's Divsn., 2001—08, sr. v.p., gen. mdse. mgr., Children's Divsn., 2008—. Office: J C Penney Corp Inc 6501 Legacy Dr Plano TX 75024 Office Phone: 972-431-1000. Office Fax: 972-431-4898. Business E-Mail: cmcna3@jcpenney.com.

MCNEAL, SHAY, advertising executive; b. Sturgis, Ky., Nov. 5, 1946; d. John H'Earl Evans and Mary Ellen Baird; 1 child, Richard McNeal (dec. 1972); 1 child, Hethur; m. Gordon K. Smith, Oct. 24, 1975 (div. 1982); 1 child, Paris. Student, DeKalb Coll. Asst. dir. Savannah St. Mission, Atlanta, 1968-70; spl. project asst. Lovable Co., Atlanta, 1970-71; assoc. buyer Montgomery Ward/Knit Div., NYC, 1971-73; nat. fashion dir. Dan River Mills, NYC; mktg. dir. Macy's SE div., Atlanta, 1974-78; pres. Smith McNeal Advt., 1978-86; sr. v.p., gen. mgr. William Cook Advt., Atlanta, 1986-89; pres. Preemptive Ltd., Beverly Hills, Calif., 1989-91, Georgetown Prodns., Washington, 1991—. Key cons. Jack Watson for Gov., Atlanta and Savannah; mem. faculty, jurist Portfolio Ctr., Atlanta, 1988-89; media cons. anti David Duke campaign Dem. Party, Washington. Bd. dirs.

Travelers Aid, Atlanta, 1982-84; vol. ARC, Atlanta, 1978—, various advt. clubs nationwide; appointed by the gov. to Ga. Film Commn., 1989; media cons. Anti-David Duke Campaign for Dem. Party, Washington. Named one of the Top Advt. Women in the S.E. AdWeek, Atlanta, 1987. Mem. Am. Assn. Advt. Agys., Exec. Womens Assn., Atlanta Advt. Club, Ansley Golf Club Atlanta. Democrat. Avocation: horseback riding. Office: Aspen Dale 3175 Aspen Dale Ln Delaplane VA 20144

MCNEALEY, ERNEST, college president; m. Earnestine Green; children: Ernest II, David. BS, Ala. State U.; MAT, Ind. U.; PhD, Ohio State U. V.p. acad. affairs undergrad. acad. affairs Claflin (S.C.) U.; assoc. provost, dean of undergrad. acad. affairs SUNY, Stony Brook; pres. Stillman Coll., Tuscaloosa, Ala., 1997—. Office: Stillman Coll PO Box 1430 Tuscaloosa AL 35403-1430 E-mail: emcnealey@stillman.edu.

MCNEILL, THOMAS RAY, lawyer; b. Pitts., June 2, 1952; s. Thomas William McNeill and Mary (Shiveley) Hiss; m. Patsy Lynch, June 25, 1977; children: Elizabeth, Kathleen, Thomas. BSBA, U. Fla., Gainesville, 1974; JD, Emory U., 1977. Bar: Ga. 1977, US Dist. Ct. (no. dist.) Ga. 1977. Assoc. Powell Goldstein LLP, Atlanta, 1977-84, ptnr., 1984—2008, mgr. corp. dept., 1993-95, bd. ptnrs., 1998—2004, leader Bus. Transactions Group, 2005—08, mng. ptnr., 2008; ptnr. Bryan Cave, 2009—, Atlanta mng. ptnr., mem. mgmt. com., 2009—11. Bd. dirs. Metro Atlanta C. of C., 2009—, Boys and Girls Clubs of Metro Atlanta, 2010—, chmn., 2014—; ann. campaign co-chair Atlanta Legal Aid Soc., 2013. Mem.: ABA (mem. com. on corp. laws 2007-12), Ga. Bar Assn. (exec. com. bus. law sect., 2001-10, chmn. 2008), Emory U. Alumni Assn. (pres. exec. com. 1988-89, Law Sch. coun. 1990-2000, 2003—10, chmn. 2005-07), Soc. of Internat. Bus. Fellows, Beta Gamma Sigma. Office: Bryan Cave One Atlantic Ctr 14th Fl 1201 W Peachtree St NW 14th Fl Atlanta GA 30309-3488 Office Phone: 404-572-6681. Office Fax: 404-420-0681. Business E-Mail: tom.mcneill@bryancave.com.

MCNEW, BENNIE BANKS, retired finance educator; b. Greenbrier, Ark., Nov. 12, 1931; s. Roland H. and Stella (Avery) McNew; m. Bonnie Lou Stone, Mar. 31, 1956; children: Bonnie Banks, Mary Kathleen, William Michael. BS, Ark. State Tchrs. Coll., 1953; MBA, U. Ark., 1954; PhD, U. Tex., 1961. Asst. nat. bank examiner, 1954-56; indsl. specialist Indsl. Rsch. and Ext. Ctr. U. Ark., 1956-59; lectr. finance U. Tex., 1959-61; prof. banking U. Miss., University, 1961-65, dean Sch. Bus. Adminstrn., 1965-79; dean Sch. Bus. Mid. Tenn. State U., Murfreesboro, 1980-88; prof. econs. and fin. U. Ctrl. Ark., Conway, 1988-98; ret., 1998. Asst. dir., v.p. Grad. Sch. Banking La. State U., 1966—97. Author (with Charles L. Prather): (book) Fraud Control for Commercial Banks, 1962; co-author: Money and Banking Casebook, 1966, The Bankers Handbook, 1966, A History of Mississippi, 1973. Pres. Faulkner County Singing Conv., Ark., 2002—04. With US Army, 1950—51. Recipient Appreciation awards, Faulkner County and Arkansas State Singing Conventions, 2013, McNew Lectureship endowed, U. Ctrl. Ark., 2013; named Disting. Undergraduate Alumnus, Sch. Bus. Adminstrn., U. Ctrl. Ark., 2002. Mem.: Lions (pres. Oxford, Miss. 1964—65, Edward Dalstrom Disting. Svc. award 2002, Melvin Jones fellow 2003). Home: 12 Bainbridge Dr Conway AR 72034-7217

MCNICHOLS, GERALD ROBERT, consulting company executive; b. Cleve., Nov. 21, 1943; s. Charles Wellington and June Beatrice (Kalal) McN.; m. Paula Kay Austin, Dec. 26, 1964; children: G. Robert Jr., Katherine Lynn Loftis, Melissa Sue Cardon. BS with honors, Case Western Res. U., 1965; MS, U. Pa., 1966; ScD, George Washington U., 1976. Cert. cost estimator/analyst. Sr. ops. analyst Office of Sec., Dept. of Def., Washington, 1970-76; v.p. GenTech, Inc., Bethesda, Md., 1976-77, J. Watson Noah, Inc., Falls Church, Va., 1977-78; pres., chief exec. officer Mgmt. Cons. and Rsch., Inc., McLean, Va., 1978-99; sr. v.p. GRC Internat. (acquired Mgmt. Cons. and Rsch., Inc.), 1999-2000, also bd. dirs.; CEO McNichols & McNichols, Inc., Middleburg, Va., 2000—. Pres. McNichols Family Found., 2000—; bd. dir. Ordia Solution Inc., Aframe Digital Inc., Wide area Sys., Inc.; mem. bd. advisors The Baldwin Group; vice chmn. com. arts Kennedy Ctr., Wash., 2005—08, also bd. dirs. Co-author: Operations Research for Decision Making, 1975; contbg. author: Software Reliability, 1986, Software System Design Methods, 1986, Electronic Systems Effectiveness and Life Cycle Costing, 1983; editor Cost Analysis, 1984; contbr. articles to profl. jours. Pres. Rondelay Civic Assn., Fairfax Sta., Va., 1985-87; bd. dirs. Kennedy Ctr. Cir., 1995-2000; vice chmn. Washington Com. on the Arts, 2006-08; bd. dirs.VSA Arts, 2007-, Columbia Lighthouse for Blind, 2008-, Capt. USAF, 1967-70; USAF Reserve 1970-82. Recipient Meritorious Achievement award, Case Western Res U., 1995, Engr. Alumni Achievement award, George Washington U., 1989. Mem. Assn. for Corp. Growth; Potomac Officers Club; Inst. Cost Analysis (pres. 1985-88), Internat. Soc. Parametric Analysts (bd. dirs. 1982-84, Frieman Lifetime Achievement award 1990), Ops. Rsch. Soc. American (chmn. mil. applications sect.), Assn. for Small Rsch., Engring., and Tech. Svcs. Cos. (pres.), Mil. Ops. Rsch. Soc. (sec., treas. 1986-87, v.p. adminstrn. 1987-88, bd. dirs. 1985-88, 92-96), Soc. Cost Estimating and Analysis (bd. dirs. 1990-93, Lifetime Achievement award 2000), Century Club George Mason U. (bd. dirs. 1997-2000). Home: 23349 Parsons Rd Middleburg VA 20117-2817 Business E-Mail: drmcnichols@mcnichols.org.

MCNICOL, DAVID LEON, retired federal official, researcher; b. South Gate, Calif., May 18, 1944; s. Charles D. and Mary W. (Heisel) McN.; m. Lore Anne Long, Mar. 25, 1967; children: Katharine Anne, Elizabeth Mary. BA magna cum laude, Harvard U., 1966; MS, MIT, 1968, PhD, 1973. Asst. prof. econs. U. Pa., Phila., 1971-75; sr. staff economist Pres.'s Coun. of Econ. Advisors, Washington, 1976; vis. assoc. prof. econs. Calif. Inst. Tech., Pasadena, 1976-77; sr. economist Office of the Sec., U.S. Dept. of Treasury, Washington, 1977-79; dir. Office of Econ. Analysis U.S. Dept. Energy, Washington, 1980-81, dep. asst. adminstr. Office of Applied Analysis, 1981-82; dir. Econ. Analysis and Resource Planning Divsn. Office of Sec. of Def., Office of Program Analysis and Evaluation, Washington, 1982-88, dep. asst. sec., dep. dir., 1988—2002, chmn. cost analysis improvement group, 1988—2002; sr. fellow, mem. rsch. staff, dir., cost analysis and rsch. divsn. Inst. for Def. Analyses, Alexandria, Va., 2002—. Author over 20 publs. on commodity markets, regulatory econs., energy issues and econ. aspects of the U.S. def. program. Recipient Spl. Svc. award Dept. Energy, 1981, Presdl. Rank award U.S. Govt., 1988, 93, 96, 2001, Disting./Meritorious Civilian Svc. medal Dept. Def., 1988, 91, 93, 96, 97, 2001, 2002. Home: 6901 Pineway University Park MD 20782-1163 Office: Inst for Defense Analyses 4850 Mark Center Dr Alexandria VA 22311-1882 Office Phone: 703-573-4668. Business E-Mail: dmcnicol@ida.org.*

MCNIEL, SKYE, state legislator; Mem. Dist. 29 Okla. House of Representatives, 2007—. Republican. Address: 36970 W Hwy 6 Bristow OK 74010 Office: Oklahoma House of Representatives 2300 N Lincoln Blvd Rm 433-B Oklahoma City OK 73105 Office Phone: 405-557-7353. E-mail: skye.mcniel@okhouse.gov.

MCNULTY, CARRELL STEWART, JR., retired manufacturing executive, architect; b. Newark, Dec. 4, 1924; s. Carrell Stewart and Marjorie (Yaegerlehner) McN.; m. Barbara Brokaw, June 21, 1952 (dec. Oct. 31, 2003), m. Miitie Brown, May 27, 2005; children: Peter Carrell, Susan Abigail. Student, Emory U., 1941-43, U. NC, 1943-44; BArch, Columbia U., 1950, MS in Urban Planning, 1963. Registered arch., Conn., NY, NJ, 1978. Assoc. SMS Architects, Stamford, Conn., 1950-58, gen. ptnr., 1958-73; pvt. practice architecture Weston, Conn., 1973-76; pres. CMW Co., Weston, 1975-77, NB Products, Inc., Horsham, Pa., 1976-94, NB Instruments, Inc., Horsham, 1979-93, Environ. Svcs. and Products, Inc., Horsham, 1994-96; ret. Mem. Conn. Soc. Architects, 1963-73, sec., 1964-67, pres., 1969-70. Chair S.W. Regional Planning Agy., Norwalk, Conn., 1967-71; mem. Gov.'s Com. on Environment, New Haven, 1970, chair Gov.'s Task Force on Housing, Norwalk, 1972; bd. dirs., sec. Habitat for Humanity of Greater Bucks, Doylestown, Pa., 1990-97; pres. Ctrl. Bucks Crossroads, 1995-96; WWII vol., USU, 1942-46. Lt. (j.g.) USNR, 1942-46; PTO. Recipient citation Am. Assn. Sch. Adminstrs., 1960, 6th Biennial Design award HUD, 1973; grantee HUD, Housing Rsch., 1970. Fellow AIA (mem. urban design com. 1963-73, chmn. 1971); mem. Bucks County Choral Soc., Mid-Fla. Master Choir, Ocala Art Group (editor), Sigma Nu. Democrat. Mem. United Ch. of Christ (deacon 1965-71, elder 1989-92). United Ch. Of Christ. Avocations: choral music, computers, painting. Home: 400 E Howry Ave Apt 627 Deland FL 32724-5436 Personal E-mail: llerracm@gmail.com.

MCNULTY, JAMES A., pharmaceutical executive; BA in Acctg., U. South Fla. CPA. Treas., corp. sec. Accentia Biopharmaceuticals, Inc.; founder, prin. McNulty & Co.; founder, prin.founder, prin. McNulty Garcia & Ortiz; co-founder Pender McNulty & Newkirk, 1971—97; CFO Star Science, Inc., 1998—2000, Hopkins Capital Group, LLC, 2000; CFO, COO Am. Prescription Providers, Inc., 2000—02; CFO Biovest Internat., Inc., 2007; part time sec., treas., CFO BioDelivery Sciences International, Inc., 2000—08, sec., treas., CFO, 2008—. Co-author (Published): Bus. Golf. Mem.: Fla. Insts. of CPA's., Am. Insts. of CPA's. Office: BioDelivery Sciences International Inc 801 Corporate Ctr Dr Ste 210 Raleigh NC 27607 Office Phone: 919-582-9050. Office Fax: 919-582-9051. Business E-Mail: jmcnulty@bdsinternational.com.

MCNULTY, JOHN PETTY, internist, consultant; b. New Orleans, Dec. 13, 1927; s. John Perkins and Edith Petty McNulty; m. Margaret Lillian DeMouy, Apr. 5, 1952; children: John Michael, Marcia Ann, Kevin Arthur, Brian Robert, Susan Margaret. BS in Pharmacy, Loyola U., New Orleans, 1946; MD, Tulane U., New Orleans, 1951. Lic. internist Am. Accreditation Grad. Med. Edn., 1961, in palliative medicine Am. Acad. Hospice & Palliative Medicine, 2001. Assoc. clin. prof. medicine Tulane U. Sch. Medicine, 1967—90; hospice med. dir. Hospice St. Tammany, Covington, La., 1999—; pres. Palliative Care Inst. SE La., Covington, La., 2002—, La. Palliative Care Consortium, Covington, 2006—; assoc. clin. prof. medicine La. State U. Health Sci. Ctr., New Orleans, 2004—07. Cons. chronic pain& palliative care St. Tammany Parish Hosp., Covington, 1999—. Contbr. articles to profl. jours. End-of-life edn. found. Palliative Care Inst. SE La., 2002—07. Capt. US Army, 1955—57, Ft. Lewis, Wash. Recipient Jensen Holliday award, Mary Bird Perkins Cancer Ctr., 2006, Heart of Hospice Svc. award, La.-Miss. Hospice & Palliative Care Orgn., 2006; fellow Fellow, Am. Acad. of Hospice & Palliative Medicine, 2007. Fellow: ACP; mem.: Commanderie de Bordeaux, Alpha Omega Alpha. Avocations: baseball, classical music, travel. Home: 752 N Columbia St Covington LA 70433 Office: Palliative Care Inst SE LA 4410 Hwy 22 Mandeville LA 70471 Office Fax: 985-871-5977; Home Fax: 985-892-7891. Personal E-mail: jackmcn12@bellsouth.net. Business E-Mail: jmcnult@stph.org.

MCPARLAND, JEFFREY J., energy executive; Various engring. and fin. positions with power generation & engring. and constrn. companies; sr. v.p., CFO, treas. PG&E Gas Transmission, 1999—2000; sr. v.p. fin. Dynegy, Inc., 2000—02; energy industry cons., 2003; sec. Targa Resources, Inc., 2004, exec. v.p., CFO, 2004—10; pres. fin. and adminstrn. Targa Resources Investments, Inc., 2010—. Office: Targa Resources Inc 1000 Louisiana Ste 4300 Houston TX 77002 Office Phone: 713-584-1000. Office Fax: 713-584-1100.

MCPEAK, JERRY, state legislator; b. Checotah, Okla., 1946; Tchr. Be a Champ Camps; produce show cattle; mem. Dist. 13 Okla. House of Representatives, 2004—. Mem.: Nat. Livestock Coaches Assn. (pres.). Democrat. Mailing: 2300 N Lincoln Blvd Rm 503 Oklahoma City OK 73105 Office: PO Box 63 Warner OK 74469 Office Phone: 405-557-7302. Business E-Mail: jerrymcpeak@okhouse.gov.

MCPHEE, GEORGE, former professional sports team executive; b. Guelph, Ont., Canada, July 2, 1958; BA in Bus., Bowling Green State U., 1982; JD, Rutgers U., 1992. Foward Guelph Platers, 1978, Bowling Green State U., 1978—82, NY Rangers, 1982, NJ Devils; v.p., dir. hockey ops. Vancouver Canucks, 1992—97, alt. gov., 1992—; gen. mgr., v.p Washington Capitals, 1997—2014. Recipient Hobey Baker Meml. award, 1982.*

MCPHERSON, ALICE RUTH, ophthalmologist, educator; b. Regina, Sask., Can., June 30, 1926; came to U.S., 1938, naturalized, 1958; d. Gordon and Viola (Hoover) McP. BS, U. Wis., 1948, MD, 1951, DSc (hon.), 1997. Diplomate Am. Bd. Ophthalmology. Intern Santa Barbara (Calif.) Cottage Hosp., 1951-52; resident anesthesiology Hartford (Conn.) Hosp., 1952; resident ophthalmology Chgo. Eye, Ear, Nose and Throat Hosp., 1953, U. Wis. Hosps., 1953-55; ophthalmologist Davis and Duehr Eye Clinic, Madison, Wis., 1956-57; clin. instr. U. Wis., 1956-57; fellow retina svc. Mass. Eye and Ear Infirmary, 1957-58; ophthalmologist Scott and White Clinic, Temple, Tex., 1958-60; practice medicine specializing in ophthalmology and retinal diseases Houston, 1960—; pres. Retina Rsch. Found., Houston, 1969—. Staff Meth., St. Luke's, Tex. Children's Hosps., Harris County Hosp. Dist., Houston; clin. asst. prof. Baylor Coll. Medicine, Houston, 1959-61, asst. prof. ophthalmology, 1961-69, clin. assoc. prof., 1969-75, clin. prof., 1975-98, prof., 1998—; cons. retinal diseases VA Hosp., Houston, 1960—, Ben Taub Hosp., Houston, 1960—; mem. adv. com. for active staff appt. sect. ophthalmology Meth. Hosp., 1986-91, mem equipment com., 1993-95, mem. grievance panel, 1997; vol. clin. faculty appts. and promotions com., 1993; bd. dirs. Highlights of Ophthalmology; v.p. N.Am. Highlights of Ophthalmology Internat. Editor: New and Controversial Aspects of Retinal Detachment, 1968, New and Controversial Aspects of Vitreoretinal Surgery, 1977, Retinopathy of Prematurity: Current Concepts and Controversies, 1986. Amb. Houston Ballet, mem. Houston Ballet Found.; mem. pres.'s coun. Houston Grand Opera; condrs. cir. Houston Symphony, mem. Houston Symphony Soc.; mem. campaign for 80s Baylor Coll. Medicine; mem. Assn. for Cmty. TV, BBB, Physicians' Benevolent Fund, South Tex. Diabetes Assn. Inc., Jr. League Houston; bd. dirs. U. Wis. Found., Madison; mem. Bd. Internat. Coun. Ophthalmology Found., 2008, external adv. bd. mem. U. Wis. Eye Rsch. Inst., 2010. Recipient Award of appreciation KT Eye Found., 1978, Woodlands Medal for Outstanding Contbn. to the Econ. Devel. of Cmty., 1988, spl. recognition award Assn. for Rsch. in Vision in Ophthalmology, Crystal award Recognizing Generous Support-Ptnrs. with an Eye for Vision Found. Am. Acad. Ophthalmology, 2000, Benjamin Boyd Humanitarian award Pan Am. Assn. Ophthalmology, 2001, Philip Corboy Meml. award Disting. Svc. Ophthalmology, 2002, Women of Vision Houston Delta Gamma Found., 2002, Cir. of Vision Mem. at Gold Level, Am. Acad. of Ophthalmology, 2011, Disting. Alumni Profl. Achievement award Harvard Med. Sch., 2012, Dedication of the McPherson Eye Rsch. Inst., U. Wisc., 2012, Book Dedication-Clinical Atlas of Procedures in Ophthalmic and Oculofacial Surgery, Dr. Daniel M. Albert & Dr. Mark J. Llucaelli, Establishment of McPherson Eye Research Inst. Lectureship, Dr. Jean Bennett, Inaugural Lecturer, 2013, Honored Guest, Pan-Am. Congress of Ophthalmology, 2013; Alice R. Mc Pherson Lab. for Retina Rsch. dedicated Baylor Ctr. for Biotech., 1988; Alice R. Mc Pherson Day proclaimed in her honor Mayor of City of Houston, Mar. 12, 1988. Fellow: ACS (credentials and Tex. credentials com., com. on applications), Am. Acad. Ophthalmology (2nd v.p. 1979, vice chmn. program devel. found. bd. trustees 1993—, nominating com. subspecialty/specialized sect. of coun. 2001, com. for pub. and profl. rels., bd. dirs. opthalmology ednl. trust fund found., laureate award selection com., mem. coun. representing PAAO, hon. found. bd. dirs., cir. vision mem. 2011, honor award 1956, sr. honor award 1986, guest of honor 1998 meeting); mem.: AMA, Internat. Coun. Ophthal. Found. (bd. dirs. 2006—), Highlights Ophthal. Internat., Schepens Internat. Soc. (sec. 1986—93, v.p. 1993—95, pres. 1995—97), U. Wis. Ophthal. Alumni Assn. (founding pres. 1990—93, founded Alice R. McPherson lectureship 1994), Assn. Rsch. Surgeons, Pan Am. Assn. Ophthalmology Found., Tex. Ophthal. Assn., So. Med. Soc., Rsch. to Prevent Blindness, Pan Am. Assn. Opthalmology (v.p. 1991—92, pres. elect 1992—95, AJO lectr. 1993, pres. 1995—97, pres. found. 1997, bd. dirs., membership com., Benjamin Boyd Humanitarian award 2001), Macula Soc. (credentialing com. 1992), Internat. Soc. Eye Rsch. (credentials com. 1992), Houston Ophthal. Soc. (pres. 1990—91, credentials com.), Harris County Med. Soc., Am. Bd. Laser Surgery, Am. Soc. Contemporary Ophthalmology (Charles Schepens Hon. award), Internat. Coll. Ocular Surgeons (vice regent 1991), Retina Soc. (v.p. 1976—77, pres. 1978—79, credentials com.), Am. Med. Women's Assn., Internat. Coll. Surgeons (vice regent 1991—), Tex. Med. Assn., Vitreous Soc., Jules Gonin Club. Achievements include research in vision and ophthalmology. Office: 1977 Butler Blvd Houston TX 77030 Office Phone: 713-798-3276.

MCPHERSON, ROBERT C., III, metal products executive; Cash mgmt. adminstr. Calif. Steel Industries, Inc., 1989—92, asst. treas., 1992—96, treas., contr., 1996—2003; sr. v.p. bus. devel. Metals USA, Inc., 2003—04, pres. Bldg. Products Group, 2004—05; sr. v.p., CFO Flag Intermediate Holdings Corp.; sr. v.p. Metals USA, Inc., 2003—, CFO, 2005—; sr. v.p., CFO Metals USA Holdings Corp., 2006—. Office: Metals USA Holdings Corp 2400 E Commercial Blvd Ste 905 Fort Lauderdale FL 33308-4059 Office Phone: 713-965-0990. Office Fax: 713-965-0067.

MCPHERSON, WILLIAM JOSEPH (JOE), state legislator; b. Dec. 18, 1950; m. Karen Saucier. State senator Dist. 29, La., 1984—; advisor counselor Alex Vo-Tech. Inst.; businessman. Mem.: Chem. Dependency Coun. (bd. dir.), Indsl. Devel. Bd., C. of C., Rapides Wildlife Assn. (pres.), La. Wildlife Fed. (exec. com. mem.), Exchange Club. Democrat. Baptist. Address: 2000 Mason Rue Woodworth LA 71485 Mailing: PO Box 4623 Pineville LA 71361 Address: 880 Robinson Bridge Rd Woodworth LA 71485

MCQUAID, JANET, lawyer; BS in Chem. Engring., U. Pitts., 1978; MBA, Houston Bapt. U., 1989; JD, U. Tex., Austin, 1992. Bar: Tex., Colo. Engr. Exxon Co. USA, Houston, 1978—89; assoc. atty. Fulbright & Jaworski LLP, Austin, 1992—2000, ptnr., 2001—07, Smith-Robertson LLP, 2008; sr. counsel El Paso Corp., 2008—. Sec., treas. Paramount & State Theatres, Austin, 2006—08; prog. chair Air & Waste Mgmt. Assn., 2004—06; vol. Therapy Pet Pals Tex. Mem.: Coll. State Bar Tex. (assoc.). Office Fax: 713-445-8804. Business E-Mail: janet.mcguaid@elpaso.com.

MCQUIGG, MICHÈLE B., state legislator; b. Bay Shore, NY, Sept. 2, 1947; m. F. Clancy McQuigg; children: Heather Lukes, Katie Schneider. Mem. Cts. Justice, Cts. Counties, Cts. Cities & Towns; house del. Va.; state del. Dist. 51 Va., 1998—; mem. Labor & Commerce & Gen. Laws Com., 2001—. Mem.: PTA (Va.) (life), Prince William County Regional County C. of C., Ladies Aux. VFW No. 1503, Friends Libr., ACTS, Clean Cmty. Coun., Lake Ridge Occoquan Coles Civic Assn. Republican. Episcopal. Mailing: Gen Assembly Bldg Off 418 PO Box 406 Richmond VA 23218 Address: 1415 Admiral Dr Woodbridge VA 22192 Office: Dist Off PO Box 6 Occoquan VA 22125 Fax: 703-551-4924. E-mail: michele@mcquigg.com, del_McQuigg@House.state.va.us.

MCQUINN, DELORES L., state legislator; b. Henrico County, Va., Nov. 26, 1954; m. Jonathan McQuinn; children: James E. Minor III, Daytriel J. Attended, Va. Commonwealth U., Va. Union U. Mem. Richmond City Council, 1999—2009; mem. Dist. 70 Va. House of Delegates, 2009—. Democrat. Baptist. Office: General Assembly Bldg PO Box 406 Richmond VA 23218 Office Phone: 804-698-1070. Fax: 804-698-6770. E-mail: DelDMcQuinn@house.virginia.gov.

MCRAE, WILLIAM FRANK, bank executive; BA in Fin., Ga. Southern U.; grad., Stonier Nat. Grad. Sch. Banking. V.p., br. mgr. Commercial Bank & Trust, LaGrange, Ga., 1980—85, sr. v.p., 1985—90, exec. v.p., chief credit officer, 1990—2009, pres., CEO, 2009—. Chmn. Troup County Parks & Recreation Commn.; past chmn. LaGrange/Troup County C. of C.; past pres. LaGrange Cancer Soc., LaGrange Heart Assn.; mem. ch. coun. First United Meth. Ch. Office: Commercial Bank & Trust Main Office 200 N Greenwood St Lagrange GA 30240

MCRAITH, JOHN JEREMIAH, bishop; b. Hutchinson, Minn., Dec. 6, 1934; s. Arthur Luke and Marie (Hanley) McR. BA, Loras Coll., Dubuque, Iowa, 1956. Ordained priest Diocese of New Ulm, Minn., 1960; assoc. pastor St. Mary's Ch., Sleepy Eye, Minn., 1960—64, 1968—71; pastor St. Michael's Ch., Milroy, Minn., 1964—67, St. Leo's Ch., St. Leo, Minn., 1967—68; dir. Nat. Cath. Rural Life, Des Moines, 1971—78; vicar gen. Diocese of New Ulm, Minn., 1978—82; ordained bishop, 1982; bishop Diocese of Owensboro, Ky., 1982—2009, bishop emeritus, 2009—. Roman Catholic. Home: 501 W 5th St Owensboro KY 42301-0765 Office: 600 Locust St Owensboro KY 42301-2130 Office Phone: 270-683-1545 ext 339.

MCRAVEN, WILLIAM HARRY (BILL MCRAVEN), career military officer; b. Nov. 6, 1955; BA in Journalism, U. Tex., 1976; MA, Naval Postgraduate Sch. Commd. 2d. lt. USN, 1976, advanced through grades to admiral, 2011; commodore Naval Spl. Warfare Group 1; comdr. SEAL Team 3; task unit comdr. Desert Storm and Desert Shield; squadron comdr. Naval Spl. Warfare Devel. Group; SEAL platoon comdr. Underwater Demolition Team 21/SEAL Team 4; assessment dir. Spl. Ops. Resources and Requirements Directorate US Spl. Ops. Command; staff Chief of Naval Ops., Washington; chief staff officer Naval Spl. Warfare Group 1; training officer Naval Spl. Warfare Command; intelligence officer Naval Spl. Warfare Unit 1; dep. commdg. gen. ops. Joint Spl. Ops. Command (JSOC), Fort Bragg, NC, comdr., 2008—11, Spl. Ops. Command Europe (SOCEUR), 2006—08; dir. NATO Spl. Ops. Forces Coordination Centre

(NSCC), 2006—08; comdr. US Spl. Ops. Command (USSOCOM), 2011—. With Office of Combating Terrorism Nat. Security Coun. (NSC), Washington. Author: Spec Ops: Case Studies in Special Operations Warfare Theory and Practice, 1996. Decorated Def. Superior Svc. Medal, Legion of Merit, Bronze Star. Office: US Special Operations Command 7701 Tampa Point Blvd MacDill AFB Tampa FL 33621*

MCREE, SANDRA KAY, healthcare executive; b. Lawrenceburg, Tenn., Jan. 18, 1956; d. Floyd and Marvenell (Forsythe) Burgess; m. Harold Glen McKee, Feb. 8, 1974; children: Sharon, Leslie, Glynda. Student, Ind. U. Acct. supr. Giles County Hosp., Pulaski, Tenn., 1975-79, bus. office mgr., 1979-84; adminstrv. asst. Hillside Hosp., Pulaski, 1984-86; dir. bus. sys. Cmty. Health Sys., Inc., Brentwood, Tenn., 1986-94, asst. v.p. revenues and receivables, 1994-95; ops. v.p. Columbia Healthcare Corp., Nashville, 1995—97; divsn. pres. Columbia HCA Healthcare Corp., Nashville, 1997—98; v.p., ops. Province Healthcare Corp., 1998—99, regional v.p., 1999—2001; pres., COO IASIS Healthcare LLC, 2003—10, vice chmn., 2010—. Mem. monitor adv. team Health Care Mgmt. Systems, Nashville, 1989-90; chair Columbia Patient Acctg. Svcs. Mem. Healthcare Fin. Mgmt. Assn. (matrix and com. mem. 1986—, Follmer award 1991, Muncie Gold award 1997, Cert. Mgr. Patient Acctg. 1992, Tenn. chpt. 2d v.p. 1994-95). Avocations: literature, swimming, pta and related activities, travel. Office: IASIS Healthcare LLC 117 Seaboard Ln Bldg E Franklin TN 37067 Office Phone: 615-844-2747. Office Fax: 615-846-3006. Business E-Mail: sandra_mcree@iasishealthcare.com.

MCREYNOLDS, JOHN W., clinical geneticist, educator; MD, U. Okla., Norman, 1972. Lic. Fla., 1980, diplomate Am. Bd. Pediatrics, 1978, cert. Am. Bd. Med. Genetics-clin. genetics, 1982, Am. Bd. Med. Genetics-clin. biochemical genetics, 1982. Intern Naval Hosp., 1973; resident pediat. Nat. Naval Med. Ctr., 1973—75; fellow genetics and metabolism New Haven Hosp., 1975—77; asst. clin. prof. pediat. Univ. Fla.; hosp. affiliation includes Orlando Regional Med. Ctr., Fla. Hosp., Arnold Palmer Hosp. Mailing: c/o Nemours Children S Clinic 1717 S Orange Ave Ste 100 Orlando FL 32806 Office Phone: 407-650-7245.

MCSHANE, MICHAEL M., corporate financial executive; BBA in Acctg., U. Tex., Austin. CPA. Various fin. mgmt. positions, including corp. contr., regional contr., Far East Ops. Reed Tool Co.; v.p., fin. BJ Svcs. Co., 1987—90, sr. v.p., fin., CFO, bd. dirs., 1990—2002; pres., CEO, bd. dirs. Grant Prideco, Inc., Houston, 2002—08, chmn., 2003—08. Bd. dirs. Globalogix, 2007—, Complete Prodn. Svcs., Inc., 2007—, Spectra Energy Corp, 2008—, Triton LLC, 2009—. Office: Complete Production Services Inc 1001 Louisiana St Houston TX 77002-5089 Office Phone: 281-372-2300. Office Fax: 281-372-2301. Business E-Mail: mmcshane@completeproduction.com.

MCSLARROW, KYLE E., broadcast executive, former federal agency administrator; b. Va., 1960; m. Alison H. McSlarrow. BA, Cornell U., 1982; JD, U. Va., 1985. Asst. to gen. counsel Dept. Army, US Dept. Def., 1985—89; assoc. Hunton & Williams LLP, Washington, 1989—95; dep. chief of staff, chief counsel to majority leaders Bob Dole and Trent Lott US Senate, 1995—97, chief of staff to Senator Paul Coverdell, 1997—2000; nat. chmn. Quayle 2000 Presdl. Campaign, 1998—2000; v.p. polit. & govt. affairs, lead Washington office Grassroots.com, 2000—01; chief of staff to sec. Spencer Abraham US Dept. Energy, Washington, 2001—02, dep. sec., 2002—05; pres., CEO Nat. Cable & Telecom. Assn. (NCTA), Washington, 2005—11; pres. Comcast/NBC Universal, Washington, 2011—. Co.-chmn. US-Russia Energy Working Group, 2002—05; mem. Arlington County, Va. Planning Commn., Nat. Security Telecommunications Advisory Com., 2007. Republican. Office: c/o Comcast/NBC Universal 1 Comcast Ctr Philadelphia PA 19103

MCSPADDEN, JODY SODD, lawyer; b. Corsicana, Tex., Feb. 21, 1975; BS, Tex. A&M U., 1998; JD, Baylor U. Law Sch., 2002. Bar: Tex. 2002. Ptnr. Dawson, Sodd, Ellis & Hudge LLP, Corsicana, Tex. Named a Rising Star, Tex. Super Lawyers mag., 2005—07. Office: Dawson & Sodd PC 121 N Main St PO Box 837 Corsicana TX 75151 Office Phone: 903-872-8181. E-mail: jody@dawsonsodd.com.

MCSWAIN, BYRDIE ENGLE, laboratory scientist, immunohematologist; b. Ethel, Ark., Oct. 13, 1939; d. James Marvin and Katherine Engle (Martin) McSwain. BS, U. Ark., 1968; BS in Med. Tech., U. Ark. Sch. Medicine, 1969; MS, U. Ctrl. Ark., 1973; Specialist in Blood Banking, U. Ark. Med. Scis., 1976. Cert. in regulatory affairs (RAPS). Supr. blood bank Univ. Ark. Med. Scis., Little Rock, clin. instr.; dir. tech. svcs., dir. product mgmt. ARC Blood Svcs., dir. transplantation svcs., dir. regulatory affairs, South Ctrl. area dir. tech. and regulatory svcs., acting area dir. quality assurance. Contbr. 13 articles to profl. jours. Grad. scholar Am. Soc. Med. Tech.; recipient Omicron Sigma award, Am. Soc. for Med. Tech., Outstanding Svc. award, Disting. Alumni award U. Ark. for Med. Scis. Mem. Ark. Soc. Clin. Lab. Scientists (Med. Technologist of Yr.), Am. Assn. Blood Banks, South Ctrl. Assn. Blood Banks (pres., author, editor), Am. Soc. Clin. Lab. Scientists, Clin. Lab. Mgmt. Assn. (pres. Ark. chpt.), Am. Soc. Clin. Pathologists, Regulatory Affairs Profl. Soc., Am. Soc. Quality Assurance, Phi Beta Kappa.

MCSWEEN, HARRY YOUNGER, JR., geology educator; b. Charlotte, NC, Sept. 29, 1945; s. Harry Younger and Frances (Williams) McS.; m. Susan Prescott, May 27, 1972; 1 child, Lindsay Allison. BS in Chemistry, Citadel, 1967; MS in Geology, U. Ga., 1969; PhD in Geology, Harvard U., 1977. Asst. prof. geology U. Tenn., Knoxville, 1977-82, assoc. prof., 1982-87, prof. to Disting. Prof. of Science, Chancellor's Prof., 1987—, head dept. earth & planetary sciences, interim Dean, Coll. of Arts & Sciences, 2011. Mem. sci. team for Mars Pathfinder and Mars Global Surveyor spacecraft missions. Author: Meteorites and Their Parent Planets, 1987, Stardust to Planets, 1993, Fanfare for Earth, 1997. Capt. USAF, 1969-74. Recipient Nininger award Ariz. State U., 1977, Antarctica Svc. medal NSF, 1982, Bradley prize Geol. Soc. Wash., 1985, J. Lawrence Smith medal, NAS, 2012. Fellow Meteoritical Soc. (pres. 1995-96, chair planetary divsn., councilor, Leonard medal), Geol. Soc. Washington (divsn. chair 1992-93), Mineral. Soc. America (nat. lectr. 1990-91), American Geophys. Union; mem. American Acad. of Arts and Sciences Achievements include research on meteorites, particularly those from Mars. Office: University of Tennessee Dept Earth and Planetary Sciences 1412 Circle Dr Knoxville TN 37996-1410 Office Phone: 865-974-9805. Business E-Mail: mcsween@utk.edu.

MC SWINEY, JAMES WILMER, retired pulp and paper manufacturing company executive; b. McEwen, Tenn., Nov. 13, 1915; s. James S. and Delia (Conroy) McS.; m. Jewel Bellar, 1940; children: Charles Ronald, Margaret Ann. Grad., Harvard Advanced Mgmt. Program, 1954. Lab. technician, shipping clk. Nashville div. The Mead Corp., 1934-39; asst. office mgr. Harriman div., 1939; plant mgr. Rockport, Ind., 1940; asst. office mgr. Kingsport (Tenn.) div.), 1941-44; exec. asst. to pres. Dayton, Ohio, 1954-57; v.p. devel., 1957-59; adminstrv v.p. Harriman div. (Kingsport (Tenn.) div.), 1959; group v.p., gen. mgr. Mead Bd. div., 1961-63, exec. v.p. corp., 1963-67, pres., chief exec. officer, 1968-71, chmn. bd., chief exec. officer, 1971-78, chmn. bd., 1978-82; ret., 1982. Acct., office mgr., asst. sec.-treas. Brunswick Pulp & Paper Co., Ga., 1944-45; bd. dirs. Ultra-Met, Gosiger, Inc., Sea Island Co. Trustee Com. for Econ. Devel. Aviation cadet USAAF, 1942-44. Home: PO Box 30604 401 Ocean Rd Sea Island GA 31561 Home Phone: 912-638-5262; Office Phone: 912-638-5262. E-mail: mcswineyj@bellsouth.net.

MCTEER, ROBERT D., JR., former academic administrator, bank executive; b. Oct. 1942; married; 2 children. BBA in Economics, U. GA, 1963, PhD in Economics, 1971. With Fed. Reserve Bank Richmond, 1968—91; sr. v.p. Baltimore branch Fed. Reserve Bank of Richmond, 1980—91; pres., CEO Fed. Res. Bank Dallas, Tex., 1991—2004; chancellor Texas A&M U. System, College Station, Tex., 2004—06; Disting. fellow Nat. Ctr. for Policy Analysis (NCPA), 2007—. Adj. prof. U. Richmond, Va. Commonwealth U., Johns Hopkins U.; bd. dirs. Nat. Coun on Econ. Edn.; bd. overseers U. Ga. Terry Coll. Bus. Office: National Center for Policy Analysis 12770 Coit Rd Ste 800 Dallas TX 75251 Office Phone: 972-386-6272. Office Fax: 972-386-0924.

MCTIER, CHARLES HARVEY, former foundation administrator; b. Columbus, Ga., Jan. 28, 1939; s. Roy and Julia (Harvey) McT.; m. Margaret Lucy Ruyl, Aug. 23, 1962; children: Margaret Marie, Charles Harvey Jr. BBA, Emory U., 1961. Administrv. asst. hosp. Emory U., Atlanta, 1961-63, bus. mgr., dept. psychiat. Sch. Med., 1963-66, assoc. dir., personnel, 1966-69, asst. to pres., bd. trustees, 1969-71; sec. Robert W. Woodruff Found., Joseph B. Whitehead Found., Lettie Pate Evans Found., Inc., Lettie Pate Whitehead Found., Inc., Atlanta, 1971-77, sec., treas., 1977-87, v.p., sec., treas., 1987-88, pres., 1988—2006, Ichauway Inc. Chmn. Atlanta Founds. Forum, 1985-86; trustee Southeastern Coun. Founds., Atlanta, 1985-92, chmn. membership com., 1986-89, chmn. program com., 1989, chmn. bd. trustees, 1989-90; vice chmn. Coun. on Founds., Washington, 1995-97, program com., 1985-87, nominating com., 1987-88, chmn. audit and fin. com., 1990-95, chmn. mgmt. com., 1996-97; chmn. bd. trustees Found. Ctr. N.Y.C., 1994-2000, fin. and audit com., 1991-2000, exec. com., 1992-93, chmn. nominating com.; former pub. mem. Joint Commn. on Accreditation of Health Care Orgns., 1994-2003; dir. SunTrust Bank of Ga., SunTrust Bank Atlanta, 1995—, Coca-Cola FEMSA.; bd. dirs. AGL Resources, 2006- Trustee, North Ga. United Meth. Found., 1985—; trustee, treas. Meth. Found. Ret. Mins., 1980; chmn. new ch. devel. com. North Ga. United Meth. Conf., 1980-85; mem. bd. vis. Emory U., 1985-87. Mem. Assn. Emory Alumni (bd. govs. 1987-91), Pres.'s Cir. of NAS/Inst. of Medicine, Commerce Club (bd. dirs.), Peachtree Golf Club, Piedmont Driving Club. Avocations: golf, travel. Mailing: AGL Resources Bd Directors P O Box 4569 Atlanta GA 30302-4569 Office Phone: 404-584-4000. Personal E-mail: pmctier@bellsouth.net.

MCVEY, HENRY HANNA, III, retired lawyer; b. Richmond, Va., Aug. 12, 1935; s. Henry Hanna Jr. and Eva Lawson (Jennings) McVey; m. Reba Jean Robinson, Dec. 12, 1964; children: Margaret Anne McVey Singleton, Lewis Lawson, Ian Douglas. BS, BA magna cum laude, Hampden-Sydney Coll., Va., 1957, LLD (hon.), 2008; LLB, U. Va., Charlottesville, 1960. Bar: Va. 1960, U.S. Dist. Ct. (ea. dist.) Va. 1960, U.S. Ct. Appeals (4th cir.) 1965, U.S. Supreme Ct. 1970, cert.: Hampden Sydney Coll. (honary doc. law) 2008. Assoc. Battle, Neal, Harris, Minor & Williams, Richmond, 1960-66; ptnr. McGuireWoods LLP and predecessor firms, Richmond, 1966—99; ret., 1999. Mem. adv. group under Civil Justice Reform Act of 1990 U.S. Dist. Ct. (ea. dist.) Va. Trustee Hampden-Sydney Coll., 1989—94, 1995—2001, vice chair, 2001—03, chair bd. trustees, 2003—08; mem. Commn. on Archtl. Rev. City of Richmond, 1985—95; mem. Planning Commn. Gloucester County, 2001—, vice chmn., 2006; bd. dirs. Richmond Symphony, 1977—86, 1987—99, v.p., 1979—81, exec. v.p., 1981—83, pres., 1983—85, chmn. bd. dirs., 1985—87, pres. Symphony Coun., 1999—2001; bd. dirs. Carpenter Ctr. for Performing Arts, 1982—89, Rosewell Found., 1999—2004, pres., 2001—02, v.p., 2002—03. Recipient Algernon Sydney Sullivan medallion for svc. to coll., Hampden Sydney Coll., 2001, Alumni Citation for loyal Svc., Hampden-Sydney Coll., 2002, Excellence in Civil Litigation award, Va. Assn. Defense Attys., 2006. Fellow: Am. Bar Found., Am. Coll. Trial Lawyers; mem.: Va. Bar Assn., Va. Assn. Def. Attys. (v.p. 1981—83, treas. 1983—84, pres.-elect 1984—85, pres. 1985—86). Presbyterian. Home: PO Box 8 Ware Neck VA 23178 Home Phone: 804-694-0992. Personal E-mail: hmcvey@cox.net.

MCWATERS, JEFFREY L., state legislator, retired healthcare executive; b. Paducah, Ky. m. Cynthia Lamb McWaters; 2 children. B in Acctg., U. Ky., 1978. With Ernst and Young, Nashville, 1978—79, Hosp. Affiliates, 1979—93; founder, pres., CEO Options Mental Health (now Value Options), 1990—94; founder, chmn., CEO AMERIGROUP Corp., Virginia Beach, Va., 1994—2007, chmn., 2007—08; senator Dist. 8 Senate of Va., 2010—. Bd. dirs. Am. Assn. Health Plans, Man in the Mirror; mem. adv. bd. Monarch Bank, Envest Entrepreneurial Investments. Chmn. Amerigroup Found., 2000—. Named Entrepreneur of Yr., Ernst and Young, 1999; named to Hall of Fame, Gatton Coll. Bus. and Econs., U. Ky., 2003. Office: Senate of Va Rm 310 PO Box 396 Richmond VA 23218 also: 1207 Laskin Rd Virginia Beach VA 23451 Office Phone: 804-698-7508, 757-965-3700. Office Fax: 804-698-7651. Business E-Mail: district08@senate.virginia.gov.

MCWATTERS, DENISE C., lawyer; BS in Psychology, Southern Meth. U., MA in Psychology, 1981; JD summa cum laude, Univ. Tex., Austin, 1984. Bar: Tex. 1984. Counsel Citigroup, N.A.; atty., pvt. practice, 2002—05; gen. counsel The Beck Group, 2005—07; dep. gen. counsel Holly Corp., 2007, v.p., gen. counsel & sec., 2008—11, Holly Logistic Svcs., LLC, 2008—11, Holly Refining & Marketing Co., 2008—11, HollyFrontier Corp., Dallas, 2011—. Mem.: ABA, State Bar Tex., Dallas Bar Assn. Office: HollyFrontier Corp Ste 1300 2828 N Harwood Dallas TX 75201 Office Phone: 214-871-3555.

MCWETHY, PATRICIA JOAN, educational association administrator; b. Chgo., Feb. 27, 1946; d. Frank E. and Emma (Kuehne) McW.; m. H. Frank Eden; children: Kristin Beth, Justin Nicholas. BA, Northwestern U., 1968; MA, U. Minn., 1970; MBA, George Washington U., 1981. Geog. analyst CIA, McLean, Va., 1970-71; rsch. asst. NSF, Washington, 1972-74, spl. asst. to dir., 1975, assoc. program dir. human geography and regional sci. program, 1976-79; exec. dir. Assn. Am. Geographers, Washington, 1979-84, Nat. Assn. Biology Tchrs., Reston, Va., 1984-95, Nat. Sci. Edn. Leadership Assn., Arlington, Va., 1995-97; edn. dir. Nat. Alliance for Mentally Ill, Arlington, 1998-99. Prin. investigator grant on biotech. equipment ednl. resource partnership NSF, 1989-93, NSF funded internat. symposium on Basic Biol. Concepts: What Should the World's Children Know?, 1992-94; co-prin. investigator NSF grant, 1995-97; mem. chmn.'s adv. com. Nat. Com. Sci. Stds. and Assessment, 1992-95; mem. Commn. for Biology Edn., Internat. Union Biol. Sci., 1988-97; mem. exec. com. Alliance for Environ. Edn., 1987-90, chmn. program com., 1990; condr. seminars in field; lectr. in field. Author monograph and papers in field; editor handbook. NSF grantee, 1989-93, 95-97; NSF fellow, 1968-69; recipient Outstanding Performance award, NSF, 1973. Mem. Phi Beta Kappa.

MCWHORTER, HOBART AMORY, JR., lawyer; b. Birmingham, Ala., Dec. 24, 1931; s. Hobart Amory and Marjorie (Westgate) McW.; remarried Feb. 1, 1997; children: Margaret G., Marjorie W. BA, Yale U., 1953; LLB, U. Va., 1958. Bar: Ala. 1958. Ptnr. Bradley Arant Rose & White, Birmingham, 1958—. 1st lt. U.S. Army, 1953-55. Fellow Am. Coll. Trial Lawyers; mem. Internat. Assn. Ins. Counsel, Nat. Assn. r.R. Counsel. Republican. Presbyterian. Office: Bradley Arant Boult Cummings LLP One Federal Pl 1819 Fifth Ave N Birmingham AL 35203-2104 Office Phone: 205-521-8241. Business E-Mail: hmcwhorter@bradleyarant.com.

MCWILLIAMS, JOHN LAWRENCE, III, lawyer; b. Phila., Dec. 21, 1943; s. John Lawrence Jr. and Elizabeth Dolores (Chevalier) McW.; m. Paula Ann Root, July 19, 1969 (dec.); children: John Lawrence, IV, Robert Root, Anne Elizabeth, David Stanford, Peter Farrell; m. Kathleen Nolan Pradella, Apr. 3, 1993. BS, St. Joseph's U., 1965; JD, Seton Hall U., 1969. Bar: NJ 1969, NY 1975, US Supreme Ct. 1975, Fla. 1977. Trial atty., regional office SEC, NYC, 1969-72; assoc. Mudge Rose Guthrie & Alexander, NYC, 1972-77; mem. Freeman, Richardson, Watson & Kelly, P.A., Jacksonville, Fla., 1977-89, chmn., pres., 1984-89; ptnr. Squire, Sanders & Dempsey, Jacksonville, 1989-98, Livermore, Freeman & McWilliams, P.A., Jacksonville, 1998—. Trustee Mcpl. Svc. Dist. Ponte Vedra Beach, 1981-85, chmn. bd. trustees, 1984-85; treas. Ponte Vedra Cmty. Assn., 1980-82; mem. Leadership Jacksonville, 1981, steering com., 1982; dir. Jacksonville Country Day Sch., 1985-87; pres. Jacksonville Beaches Ponte Vedra Unit Am. Cancer Soc., 1988-90; bd. dirs. Sawgrass Property Owners Assn., Inc., 2000-02. Fellow Am. Coll. Bond Counsel (bd. dir. 2007-); mem. Nat. Assn. Bond Lawyers, The Fla. Bar, Jacksonville C. of C., Jacksonville Cmty. Coun. Inc., Univ. Club, Ponte Vedra Club, Sawgrass Club, River Club. Republican. Roman Catholic. Home: 3040 Timberlake Pt Ponte Vedra Beach FL 32082-3726 Office: Livermore Freeman & McWilliams PA 320 N First St Ste 603 Jacksonville Beach FL 32250 Home Phone: 904-285-2499; Office Phone: 904-399-0500. Personal E-mail: jmcwilliams3@gmail.com. Business E-Mail: jmcwilliams@lfmlaw.net.

MCWILLIAMS, MIKE C., lawyer; b. Dallas, Nov. 10, 1948; s. Earl Dewitt and Mary Louise (Campbell) McWilliams; m. Sally Swatzell, Sept. 1, 1973; children: Michael, Matthew. BBA in Fin., U. Tex., 1969, JD, 1973. Bar: Tex. 1973. Assoc. Elliott, Meer, Vetter, Denton & Bates, Dallas, 1973-78; ptnr. Denton & Generis, Dallas, 1978-80, Moore & Peterson, P.C., Dallas, 1980-89, Winstead PC, Dallas, 1989—. Editor: Texas International Law Journal, 1972—73. Mem.: Dallas Bar Assn., Tex. State Bar Assn., Beta Gamma Sigma, Phi Delta Phi. Office: Winstead PC 500 Winstead Bldg 2728 N Harwood St Dallas TX 75201 Business E-Mail: mmcwilliams@winstead.com.

MEACHAM, JON (JONATHAN ELLIS MEACHAM), publishing executive, journalist, writer; b. Chattanooga, May 20, 1969; m. Margaret Keith Smythe; 2 children. BA in English Lit., summa cum laude, U. of South, Sewanee, Tenn., 1991; LHD (hon.), Yale U. Berkley Div. Sch., 2005, Loyola Coll., Md., 2007. Journalist Chattanooga Times, 1991—93; editor The Washington Monthly, 1993—95; writer Newsweek mag., NYC, 1995, nat. affairs editor, 1995—98, mng. editor, 1998—2006, editor-in-chief, 2006—10; exec. v.p., exec. editor Random House Publishing Group, NYC, 2011—. Co-host Need to Know PBS-TV, 2010—11; contributing editor Time Mag., Washington Monthly; editor-at-large WNET; written essays and reviews for The New York Times, New York Times Book Review, Washington Post and Los Angeles Times Book Review; commentator on politics, history, and religion in America. Editor: Voices in Our Blood: America's Best on the Civil Rights Movement, 2001; author: Franklin and Winston: An Intimate Portrait of an Epic Friendship, 2003 (Emery Reves award, Churchill Centre, 2005, William H. Colby Military Writers' Symposium's Book of Yr., 2005, L.A. Times Book of Yr., 2005), American Gospel: God, the Founding Fathers, and the Making of a Nation, 2006, American Lion: Andrew Jackson in the White House, 2008 (Pulitzer prize for Biography, 2009), Thomas Jefferson: The Art of Power, 2012; editor: American Homer: Reflections on Shelby Foote and His Classic The Civil War: A Narrative, 2011. Bd. regents U. of South; mem. leadership coun. Harvard Divinity Sch.; communicant St. Thomas Ch. Fifth Ave., NYC; vestryman Trinity Ch. Wall St., NYC. Recipient Hubert H. Humphrey First Amendment Freedoms prize, Anti-Defamation League, 2007; named one of The 50 Highest-Earning Polit. Figures, Newsweek mag., 2010. Mem.: Coun. Fgn. Rels., Soc. American Historians. Episcopalian. Address: c/o Barbara Fillon Random House Publishing Group 1745 Broadway New York NY 10019

MEACHUM, DANIEL RAY, lawyer; b. Badin, NC, 1955; BA in Polit. Sci. cum laude, NC Ctrl. U., 1977; JD cum laude, Howard U. Sch. Law, Wash. DC, 1981; LLM in Internat. Comparative Law, U. Brussels, 1985. Bar: Pa. Supreme Ct. 1984, Ga. Superior Ct. 2002, US Dist. Ct. (ea. dist.) Pa, US Ct. Appeals (3rd Cir.). Atty. US Atty. Office (so. dist.) NY, Phila.; gen. counsel NY, Atlanta; counsel power brokers Herman J. Russel, Jesse Hill, and Felker Ward, Atlanta; founder Daniel R. Meachum & Assocs. LLC, Atlanta; ptnr., gen. counsel Le Jardin, Atlanta. Recipient Pres. Nat. Citizenship award; Fulbright fellow. Mem.: US Dept. Justice Hon. Program. Achievements include successfully trying 122 out of 126 major jury trials and arbitrations. Office: Daniel R Meachum & Assocs LLC 101 Marietta St NW Ste 2400 Atlanta GA 30303-2782 Office Phone: 770-988-9600. Office Fax: 770-988-9690. Business E-Mail: dmeachum@dmeachumlaw.com.

MEADE, ANDREA D., wholesale distribution executive; B, Georgetown U.; MBA, Harvard U. Assoc., Fin. Instns. Group J.P. Morgan & Co.; sr. assoc. Green, Manning & Bunch, Ltd.; dir., strategic devel. ScanSource, Inc., 2000—02, exec. v.p., corp. ops., 2002—07, exec. v.p., corp. devel., 2007—. Office: ScanSource Inc 6 Logue Ct Greenville SC 29615 Office Phone: 864-288-2432. Office Fax: 864-288-1165.

MEADORS, ALLEN COATS, academic administrator, educator; b. Van Buren, Ark., May 17, 1947; s. Hal Barron and Allene Coats (Means) Meadors. AA, Saddleback Coll., 1981; BBA, U. Ctrl. Arki., 1969; MBA, U. No. Colo., 1974; MPA, U. Kans., 1975; MA in Psychology, Webster U., 1979, MA in Health Svcs. Mgmt., 1980; PhD in Adminstrn., So. Ill. U., 1981. Assoc. adminstr. Forbes Hosp., Topeka, 1971-73; asst. dir. health svcs. devel. Blue Cross Blue Shield of Kans., Topeka, 1973-76; asst. dir. Kansas City Health Dept., Mo., 1976-77; program dir., asst. prof. So. Ill. U., Carbondale, 1977—82, Webster U., St. Louis, 1979—82; mem. faculty Calif. State U., Long Beach, 1977-81; assoc. prof., dir. divsn. health adminstrn. U. Tex., Galveston, 1982-84; exec. dir. N.W. Ark. Radiation Therapy Inst., Springdale, 1984-87; mem. grad. faculty Sch. Bus. Adminstrn. U. Ark., Fayetteville, 1984-87; prof., chmn. dept. health adminstrn. U. Okla., Oklahoma City, 1987-90, dean Coll. Pub. Health, 1989—90; dean Coll. Health, Social and Pub. Svcs. Ea. Wash. U., Cheney, 1990—94; chancellor U. NC, Penbroke, 1994—99, Pembroke, 1999—2009; pres. U. Ctrl. Ark., 2009—. Cons. Surgeon Gen. Office and Air Force Sys.; bd. dirs. Lumbar Guartoner Bank, Southeastern Regional Med. Ctr. Contbr. articles to profl. jours. Command bd. dirs. Blair County Hall of Fame, Blair County Hist. Soc., Martin Luther

King Hosp., Health Care Svcs. Adv. Bd.; bd. dirs., exec. com. Altoona Symphony Orch.; bd. dirs. Home Health Agy., NC Retirement Fund, Southwestern Regional Med. Ctr. With Med. Svc. Corps USAF, 1969—73. Fellow: Am. Coll. Healthcare Execs.; mem.: Am. Hosp. Assn., C. of C. (v.p.). Office: U Ctrl Ark / Office of Pres Wingo Hall RM 207G 201 Donaghey Ave Conway AR 72035

MEADORS, MARYNELL, professional basketball coach; B in Health, Phys. Edn. and Recreation, Mid. Tenn. State U., 1965, M in Physiology of Exercise, 1966. Head coach Tenn. Tech. U. Golden Eagles, 1970-86, Fla. State U. Seminoles, 1986-96; head coach, gen. mgr., dir. player and staff pers. Charlotte Sting, 1997-99; dir. scouting Miami Sol, 1999; asst. coach U. Pitts. Panthers, 2003—05, Washington Mystics, 2005—07; head coach, gen. mgr. Atlanta Dream, 2007—. Named Ohio Valley Conf. Coach of Yr., 1978, 83, Metro Conf. Coach of Yr., 1990, Conf. Co-Coach of Yr., 1991; named to Tenn. Tech. Hall of Fame, 1992, Ohio Valley Conf. Hall of Fame, 1992. Office: Atlanta Dream 83 Walton St NW Ste 500 Atlanta GA 30303

MEADOWS, JOHN, state legislator; b. Calhoun, Ga., Aug. 1944; Mayor, Calhoun, 1986—98; v.p. Starr-Mathens Agy., Inc., 1991—, Life & Health; state rep. Dist. 5 Ga., 2004—. Republican. Baptist. Mailing: Legis Off Bldg Atlanta GA 30334

MEADOWS, MARK RANDALL, United States Representative from North Carolina, real estate developer; b. Verdun, France, July 28, 1959; m. Debbie Meadows; children: Blake, Haley. BS in Bus. Mgmt., U. South Fla., 1981. Dir. customer rels. & public safety Tampa Electric, 1983—86; owner sandwich shop, 1986—90; owner Highland Properties, 1990—; chmn. Macon County Republican Party, 2002; mem. US Congress from 11th NC Dist., 2013—, US House Fgn. Affairs Com., 2013—, US House Oversight & Govt. Com., 2013—, US House Transp. & Infrastructure Com., 2013—. Republican. Evangelical Christian. Office: US House of Representatives 1516 Longworth House Office Bldg Washington DC 20515 also: 2345 Morganton Blvd Lenoir NC 28645 Office Phone: 202-225-6401, 828-426-8701. Office Fax: 202-225-6422.*

MEAGHER, LAURA CATHERINE, lawyer, apparel executive; b. 1960; BA in English & Polit Sci. cum laude, Washington U., St. Louis, Mo., 1982; JD magma cum laude, Case Western Res. U., Cleveland, Ohio, 1989. Bar: OH 1989, NC 2005. Assoc. Benesch, Friedlander, Coplan & Aronoff LLP, Cleveland, Ohio, 1989—99; sec., gen. counsel Allen Telecom, Inc., 1999—2003; asst. gen. counsel VF Corp., Greensboro, NC, 2004—08, v.p., dep. gen. counsel, 2008—12, v.p., gen. counsel, sec., 2012—. Office: VF Corp 105 Corporate Ctr Blvd Greensboro NC 27408 Office Phone: 336-424-6145. Office Fax: 336-424-7631. E-mail: laura_meagher@vfc.com.

MEANS, ANTHONY ROSS, pharmacology educator; PhD, U. Tex., 1967. Nanaline H. Duke prof., chmn. pharmacology & cancer biology, dep. dir. comprehensive cancer inst. Duke U. Med. Ctr., Durham, NC. Contbr. articles to profl. publs. Fellow AAAS, Am. Acad. Arts and Sci.; mem. Endocrine Soc. (pres. 2004-05, Fred Conrad Koch award 1998), Am. Soc. Pharmacology and Exptl. Therapeutics (Goodman and Gilman award 2006). Office: Duke U Med Ctr PO Box 3813 Durham NC 27710-0001 E-mail: means001@mc.duke.edu.

MEANS, ROBERT TAYLOR, JR., hematologist, educator, researcher; b. Midland, Tex., July 14, 1957; s. Robert Taylor and Anna Therese (Cassidy) M.; m. Stacey W. McKenzie, May 23, 1992; children: Anna, Robert III, Patrick. BA in Biochemistry, Rice U., Houston, 1979; MD, Vanderbilt U., Nashville, 1983. Diplomate Am. Bd. Internal Medicine; cert. in hematology. Resident Baylor Coll. Medicine, Houston, 1983-86; fellow in hematology Vanderbilt U., Nashville, 1986-88, instr. medicine, 1988-90, asst. prof. medicine, 1990-92; assoc. investigator VA Med. Ctr., 1988-91, asst. chief hematology/oncology Cin., 1992-98, chief hematology/oncology Charleston, SC, 1998—2004, prof. internal medicine, 2004—, chief med. svc. Lexington, Ky., 2004—06; assoc. prof. med. U. Cin., 1992-98; prof. med., head hematology, assoc. divsn. chief Med. U. SC, 1998-2000, dir. divsn. hematology-oncology, 2000—04; prof. internal medicine U. Ky., 2004—14, assoc. rsch. chair internal medicine, 2004—07, interim assoc. dean, 2004—06, sr. assoc. chair, 2007—11, exec. vice dean, 2011—12, exec. dean, 2012—14; dean Quillen Coll. Med., E Tenn State U., 2012—; prof. internat. med., 2012—; pres. Med. Edn. Assistance Corp., 2012—. Interim dir. Markey Cancer Ctr., 2006—09, assoc. dean vets. affairs, 2011—12. Editor (assoc.) Jour. Investigative Medicine; mem. editl. bd. Internat. Jour. Hematology, Hematology, Am. Jour. Med. Sci., Winthrobe's Clinical Hematology, 12th & 13th edit.; contbr. chpts. to books, articles to profl. jours. Recipient Career Devel. award Dept. Veterans Affairs., 1988, Henry Christian award Am. Fedn. Clin. Rsch., 1991, Chief Resident's Faculty of Yr. award, U. Ky., 2006. Fellow Am. Coll. Physicians; mem. Am. Soc. Hematology, Internat. Soc. Exptl. Hematology, Am. Fed. Med. Rsch. (v.p. mtgs., programs, 1998-2002), Southern Soc. Clin. Investigation (councillor, 2005-2010, exec. adv. com. 2010-11, pres. elect. 2011-12, pres. 2012-13), Phi Beta Kappa. Achievements include being first to report response of anemia of chronic disease to erythropoietin; first description of erythropoietin receptor in polycythemia. Home: 3 Straw Flower Pl Johnson City TN 37604 Office: Quillen Coll Med PO Box 70694 C200 Stanton Gerbal Hall Johnson City TN 37614-1710 Home Phone: 423-328-7632; Office Phone: 423-439-6315, 859-323-6582. Business E-Mail: meansr@etsu.edu.

MEANS, TERRY ROBERT, federal judge; b. Roswell, N.Mex., July 3, 1948; s. Lewis Prude and Doris Emaree (Hightower) M.; m. JoAnn Huffman Harris, June 2, 1973; children: Robert, MaryAnn, Emily. BA, So. Meth. U., 1971, JD, 1974. Bar: Tex. 1974, U.S. Dist. Ct. (no. dist.) Tex. 1976, U.S. Ct. Appeals (5th cir.) 1978, U.S. Dist. Ct. (we. dist., ea. dist.) Tex. 1991. Ptnr. Means & Means, Corsicana, Tex., 1974-88; Presdl. elector, 1980; justice 10th Ct. Appeals, Waco, Tex., 1989-90; judge US Dist. Ct. (no. dist.) Tex., Ft. Worth, 1991—. Chmn. Navarro County Rep. Party, Corsicana, 1976-88; pres. YMCA, Corsicana, 1984, Ft. Worth Youth Soccer Assn., 1996-97. Recipient Disting. Alumni award for jud. svc. So. Meth. U., 2006. Mem. State Bar Tex., Tarrant County Bar Assn. (Silver Gavel award 2006). Baptist. Avocations: coaching soccer, racquetball. Office: 201 US Courthouse 501 W 10th St Fort Worth TX 76102-3637

MEARS, CASEY, race car driver; b. Bakersfield, Calif., Mar. 12, 1978; s. Roger Mears. Profl. race car driver, NASCAR Hendrick Motorsports, 2002—08, Richard Childress Racing, 2008—. 1st pl. Coca-Cola 600 Charlotte Motor Speedway, 2007. Office: c/o NASCAR 1801 Internat Speedway Blvd Daytona Beach FL 32115

MEARS, WALTER ROBERT, retired journalist; b. Lynn, Mass., Jan. 11, 1935; s. Edward Lewis and Edythe Emily (Campbell) M.; m. Sally Danton, Dec. 28, 1956 (dec. Dec. 1962); children: Pamela (dec.), Walter Robert Jr. (dec.); m. Joyce Marie Lund, Aug. 4, 1963 (div. 1983); children: Stephanie Joy, Susan Marie; m. Carroll Ann Rambo, Mar. 1, 1986 (div. 1995); m. Frances R. Richardson, July 5, 1997. BA, Middlebury Coll., 1956, LittD (hon.), 1977. Newsman AP, Boston, 1956, corr. Montpelier, Vt., 1956-60, state house corr. Boston, 1960-61, newsman Washington, 1961-69, chief polit. writer, 1969-72, asst. chief Washington bur., 1973-74, spl. corr., 1975, chief, 1977-83, v.p., 1978-2001, exec. editor, 1984-88, v.p., columnist, 1989-2001. Author: (with John Chancellor) The News Business, 1983, The New News Business, 1995, Deadlines Past, 2003, Kennedy Bros., 2009. Trustee Middlebury Coll., 1980-84. Recipient ann. award AP Mng. Editors Assn., 1973; Pulitzer prize for Nat. Reporting, 1977. Mem.: Govs. Club, Burning Tree Club, Gridiron Club, Delta Kappa Epsilon, Phi Beta Kappa. E-mail: wmears@nc.rr.com.

MEATH, JAMES V., lawyer; b. Norfolk, Va., May 26, 1948; BA, Old Dominion U., 1971; MUA, Va. Polytechnic Inst. and State U., 1974; JD, U. Richmond, 1979. Bar: Va. 1979, D.C. 1985. Atty. Williams Mullen, Richmond, Va., chmn. labor and employment sect., 1984—2004, vice chmn. bd. dirs., 1994—2011, regional head Richmond, Charlottesville, chmn. of firm, 2011—. Adj. prof. labor law U. Richmond, mem. bd. associates, 1998—2010. Co-editor: Virginia Employment Law Letter, 1990—2002; contbr. articles to profl. jours. Bd. dirs. Richmond Soc. Prevention of Cruelty to Animals; bd. trustees The Valentine Richmond History Ctr., 2007—, Va. Commonwealth U. Sch. Bus., 2007—. Named Number One Employment Defendant Atty in Va., Chambers USA; named one of Legal Elite, Va. Bus. Mag.; fellow, Coll. Labor and Employment Lawyers. Mem.: ABA (mem. developing labor law com., mem. alternate dispute com.), Am. Arbitration Assn. (large complex case panel arbitrator, comml. panel arbitrator, employment panel arbitrator), D.C. Bar Assn., Va. Bar Assn. (chmn. labor rels. and employment sect. 1995—97, mem. exec. com. 2002—, chmn., bd. govs. 2003, pres.-elect 2004, pres. 2005). Office: Williams Mullen Williams Mullen Ctr 200 S 10th St Richmond VA 23219 Office Phone: 804-420-6412. Office Fax: 804-420-6507. Business E-Mail: jmeath@williamsmullen.com.

MEBANE, WILLIAM DEBERNIERE, newspaper publisher; b. Durham, NC, Jan. 14, 1949; s. John Gilmer and Harriet deBerniere (Elmore) M.; m. Catharine Frampton McGee, May 30, 1970; children— William deBerniere, Harriet Bacot, Jane Bacot, Catharine Frampton, John McGee, Beverly Canby BA, U. N.C., 1971, cert. in exec. program, 1981. V.p. Greenville News-Piedmont, S.C., 1976-82, bus. mgr. S.C., 1976-78, gen. mgr. S.C., 1978-81, co-pub. S.C., 1981-84, pres. S.C., 1982—, pub. S.C., 1984-92, 97-99; v.p. Multimedia Newspaper Co., Greenville, 1984-92, pres., 1989-95; v.p. Multimedia Inc., 1989-95; sr. group pres., newspaper divsn. Gannett Co. Inc., Gannett newspaper operating com., 1995-99; pres. Crescent Pub. LLC, 1999—. Commr. SC Mental Retardation Commn., 1983-89, vice chmn., 1988; past pres. Greenville Symphony Assn.; campaign chmn. United Way Greenville County, 1984, v.p. resource devel., 1985, v.p. mktg. and comms., 1986, 1st v.p., 1987, pres., 1988; treas. Goodwill Industries Upper SC, 1980-81; past pres. Greenville Assn. Retarded Children; mem. First Amendment Congress Bd., 1987-88, NC Soc. Cin., Corp. Coalition Infant Mortality, 1988; bd. dirs. Greenville Hosp. System, 1993-99, chmn. 1999, bd. dirs. Greenville Health Corp., 2008; communicant Christ Episcopal Ch., vestry, 2003-05. Mem. AP (com. 1985—, nominating com. 1991—, chmn. 1992-95), Am. Newspaper Pubs. Assn. (com. 1982—), So. Newspaper Pubs. Assn. (treas. 1990, chmn. com. 1983-84, pres. 1992, chmn. 1993, found. treas. 1996-99), Urban League of Upstate (chair 2006), So. Govs. Assn., SC Press Assn. (treas. 1984-85, v.p. dailies 1986, pres. 1987), Young Pres.'s Orgn., Huguenot Soc., Anglican Compass Rose Soc., Telecom. Commn. Anglican Commmunion, Greenville C. of C. (bd. dirs., v.p. 1981-82, bd. dirs. 1987-88), Poinsett Club, Delta Kappa Epsilon. Avocation: outdoor activities. Home: 119 Crescent Ave Greenville SC 29605-2812 Office: Crescent Pub LLC 109 Laurens Rd Ste 4-C Greenville SC 29607-1860 Office Phone: 864-250-4446. Business E-Mail: bmebane@crescentsc.com.

MECKE, WILLIAM MOYN, public relations consultant; b. Detroit, May 7, 1957; s. Theodore Hart McCalla Jr. and Mary Eleanor (Flaherty) M.; m. Katherine E. Bauer-Mecke. BA, Georgetown U., 1979; MA, Am. U., 1982; postgrad., Oxford U., 1982, U. N.C., 1982-85. Asst. dir. Found. Study Presdl. and Congrl. Terms, Washington, 1979-82; acct. exec. Hill and Knowlton, Inc., Chgo., 1985-86; tchr. The Bolles Sch., Jacksonville, Fla., 1986-88, St. Andrew's Sch., Savannah, 1988-91, Joseph Walker Sch., Marietta, Ga., 1991-92; polit. cons. various Democratic candidates, 1992-95; tech. writer Total Sys. Svcs. Inc., Columbus, Ga., 1995; dir. mktg. Habitat for Humanity Internat., Americus, Ga., 1995-2000, media svcs. mgr., 2000-2001; chief pub. rels. officer Ga. Regional Transp. Authority, 2001—12, bus. devel. dir., 2012—13; pub. rels. cons., 2013—. Co-author, editor: Presidential and Congressional Term Limitation: The Issue That Stays Alive, 1981. Asst. dir. Found. Study Presd. and Congl. Terms, Washington, 1979-82. Mem. Assn. Strategic Planning. Office Phone: 404-402-1874. Business E-Mail: wmecke@bellsouth.net.

MEDIETA, CONSTANTINO, plastic surgeon; Attended, Santa Clara U., 1981—82; BS in Psychology, Creighton U., 1985—89, MD, 1985—89. Diplomate Am. Bd. of Plastic Surgery, lic. Fla., 1994, Ga., 1998. Internship gen. surgery Maricopa County Hosp., Phoenix, resident, chief resident; resident plastic & reconstructive surgery Univ. Miami / Jackson Meml. Hosp., 1995—97; fellow The Royal Coll. of Surgeon, Edinburgh, 1994—94, Harvard Med. Sch., 1998—98, Am. Coll. of Surgeons; med. dir. Adams Air Ambulance, 1996—97; flight surgeon, 1996—97. With LA Olympics, 1984; med. volunteer Am. Cancer Soc., 1987, 1991, 1993; support instr. Advance Trauma Life, 1991—95. Mem.: AMA, Am. Soc. of Plastic Surgeons, Am. Soc. for Aesthetic Plastic Surgery, Dr. D. Ralph Millard, Jr. Soc., Dade County Med. Assn. Office: Constantino G Mendieta MD FACS 2310 & 2320 South Dixie Hwy Miami FL 33133 Office Phone: 305-860-0717. Office Fax: 305-860-0760.

MEDINA, CRIS, councilman; m. Jacqueline Medina; children: CJ, Joaquin. AA in Govt., Palo Alto Coll.; AA in Air Transp., Cmty. Coll. of Air Force; BA in Polit. Sci., U. Tex., San Antonio. Owner, CEO Diligent Mechanical; councilman Dist. 7 San Antonio City Coun., 2011—. Bd. mem. Voz de Mujer Inc.; mentor Big Brothers Big Sisters of South Tex. Staff sgt. USAFR. Mem.: Woodlawn Lake Cmty. Assn., French Creek Village Homeowners Assn. (past pres.). Office: City Hall PO Box 839966 San Antonio TX 78283 also: 4414 Centerview Dr, Suite 160 San Antonio TX 78228 Office Phone: 210-207-0870, 210-207-7044.

MEDINA, DAVID L., councilman; Attended, Palo Alto Coll. Construction project mgr., San Antonio; councilman, Dist. 5 San Antonio City Coun., 2009—. Bd. mem., v.p., pres. Palm Heights Neighborhood Assn. Avocations: running, basketball. Office: 1410 Guadalupe, Ste 109 San Antonio TX 78207 also: City Hall PO Box 839966 San Antonio TX 78283 Office Phone: 210-212-2275, 210-207-7043.

MEDINA, DAVID M., lawyer, former state supreme court justice; b. Galveston Island, Tex., 1958; m. Francisca Medina. BS, Southwest Tex. State U., 1980; JD, S. Tex. Coll. of Law, 1989. Joined Cooper Industries Inc., Houston, 1987—89, litigation counsel, 1989; judge 157th State Dist. Ct., Tex., 1990—99; assoc. gen. counsel Cooper Industries Inc., Houston, 2000—04; gen. counsel Gov. Rick Perry, Tex., 2004—05; justice Tex. Supreme Ct., 2005—13; atty. Brent Coon & Associates., Houston, 2013—. Former adjunct prof. S. Tex. Coll. of Law. Former bd. mem. Habitat for Humanity, Houston Metro; bd. mem. Spring Klein Baseball Assn. Mem.: ABA, Mexican Am. Bar Assn., Assn. for Advancement of Mexican Am., Houston Bar Assn. Office: Brent Coon & Associates 300 Fannin Ste 200 Houston TX 77002

MEDINA, MANUEL D., information technology services company executive; BS in Acctg., Fla. Atlantic U., 1974. CPA. Worked Pricewaterhouse Coopers LLP; mng. ptnr. Communication Investors Group; founder Terremark Worldwide, Inc., 1980, chmn., pres., CEO, 1982—. Former bd. dirs. ITFlorida. Office: Terremark Worldwide Inc Ste 2900 2 S Biscayne Blvd One Biscayne Tower Miami FL 33131 Office Phone: 305-856-3200. Office Fax: 305-856-8190. Business E-Mail: manuel.medina@napoftheamericas.net.

MEDLEY, WILLIAM FRANCIS, bishop; b. Marion County, Ky., Sept. 17, 1952; s. James Werner and Dorothy C. (Hayden) Medley. BA in philosophy & psychology, Bellarmine Univ.; MDiv, St. Meinrad Sch. Theology. Social worker Ky. Dept. Human Resources, 1974—78; ordained priest Archdiocese of Louisville, Ky., 1982; assoc. pastor St. Pius X parish, Louisville, 1982—85; chaplain Assumption High Sch., Louisville, 1982—85; assoc. pastor Cathedral of the Assumption, Louisville, 1985—88; adminstr. St. Benedict, St. Charles Borromeo, Holy Cross parishes, Louisville, 1988—89; dir. Office of Clergy Personnel Archdiocese of Louisville, 1989—90; pastor St. Martin de Porres parish, Louisville, 1990—93, St. Joseph Proto-Cathedral, Bardstown, Ky., 1993—2005; adminstr. St. Monica parish, Bardstown; pastor Mother of Good Counsel parish, Louisville, 2005—07, Transfiguration of Our Lord parish, Goshen, Ky., 2007—08, St. Bernadette parish, Louisville, 2008—09; ordained bishop, 2010; bishop Diocese of Owensboro, Ky., 2009—. Mem. Archdiocese of Louisville Coll. of Consultors, Priests' Coun., Planning Commn., Priests' Health Panel, Priests' Personnel Bd. Mem. Nelson County Human Rights Commn., Bardstown / Nelson County Ministerial Assn. Roman Catholic. Office: Diocese of Owensboro PO Box 364 600 Locust St Owensboro KY 42301 Office Phone: 270-683-1545. Office Fax: 270-683-6883.

MEDOWS, RHONDA M., healthcare company executive, former public health service officer; married; 3 children. BS, Cornell Univ.; MD, Morehouse Sch. Med., Atlanta. Cert. family medicine. Residency Univ. Hosp., Stony Brook, NY; physician Kaiser Permanente, Atlanta, 1989—93; private practice Mayo Clinic, Jacksonville, Fla., 1993—2000; med. dir. Blue Cross Blue Shield Fla., Jacksonville, 2000—01; sec. Fla. Agy. Health Care Adminstrn., 2001—04; chief med. officer Centers for Medicare & Medicaid Svc. Region IV, Atlanta, 2004—05; commr. Ga. Dept. Cmty. Health, Atlanta, 2005—10; chief med. officer, exec. v.p. Pub. & Senior Markets UnitedHealthcare, 2010—. Instr. Univ. Fla., Fla. State Univ. Mem.: Am. Acad. Family Physicians, Nat. Med. Assn., Am. Coll. Physician Executives, Fla. Med. Assn., Fla. Acad. Family physicians, Nat. Assn. Managed Care Physicians. Office: UnitedHealthcare Suite 300 3720 Davinci Ct Norcross GA 30092

MEDRANO, PAULINE, councilwoman, language educator; b. Dallas, Nov. 16, 1955; BA, U. Tex., Arlington, 1976. Dist. dir. Texas Dept Agr., Austin, 1988—91; dist. sales supr. GTECH Corp., 1992—95, dist. sales mgr., 1995—2003; ESL instr. Adult Basic Edn. Dept. Dallas Ind. Sch. Dist., 2003—; councilwoman, Dist. 2 Dallas City Coun., 2005—, chair transp. & environ. com., Trinity River Corridor Project, mem. housing com., quality of life & govt. svcs. com., dep. mayor pro tem, 2009—; vice chair US Census Bur.'s 2010 Census Adv. Com. Bd. dirs. Friends of Esperanza Hope Medrano Elem. Sch., Dallas; tutor Walnut Hill Elem. Sch., Dallas; translation svcs. to patients Parkland Meml. Hosp., Dallas. Vol. Dallas Summit Youth Volleyball; past bd. dirs. Dallas County Hist. Commn., Maple Ave. Econ. Devel. Corp. Mem.: Mex.-Am. Bus. & Profl. Club (Young Career Woman award 1983). Democrat. Office: Dallas City Hall 1500 Marilla St Rm 5FN Dallas TX 75201 Office Phone: 214-670-4048. Office Fax: 214-670-5117. Business E-Mail: pmedrano@mail.ci.dallas.tx.us.

MEDVECKY, ROBERT STEPHEN, lawyer; b. Bridgeport, Conn., Feb. 12, 1931; s. Stephen and Elizabeth (Petro) M.; m. Ellen R. Munt, Nov. 11, 1966; children— Allison L., Beth A., Craig R. AB, Dartmouth, 1952; JD, Harvard, 1955. Bar: Ill. bar 1955, Conn. bar 1958, D.C. bar 1972, Fla. bar 1989. Asso. firm Lord, Bissell & Brook, Chgo., 1955-57; gen. atty. So. New Eng. Telephone Co., New Haven, 1957-71; v.p., gen. counsel, sec. Amtrak, Washington, 1971-75; partner firm Lord, Bissell & Brook, Washington, 1975-78, Reid & Priest, NYC, 1978-87. Clubs: Harvard (N.Y.C.), Fiddlesticks Country (Ft. Meyers, Fla.), Saphire Valley Country (Cashlers, N.C.). Office: 15491 Kilbirnie Dr Fort Myers FL 33912-2424 Home (Summer): 457 Round Hill Rd Sapphire NC 28774 Personal E-mail: bmedvecky@yahoo.com.

MEDVINSKY, NATHALIA, library director; b. Kiev, Ukraine, Aug. 1, 1961; arrived in U.S., 2003; d. Vladimir Kroutoy and Ioanna Tabachnikov; m. Boris Dregalo (div.); m. Felix Medvinsky, Jan. 24, 2003. BLS, Kiev Inst. Culture, 1982; MLS, Sch. Libr. Info. and Archives, Jerusalem, Israel, 2001. Chief librarian Conservatory and HS of Jerusalem Acad. Music and Dance, 1992—2002; libr. dir. Fla. Nat. Coll., Hialeah, 2004—. Mem.: ALA, Fla. Libr. Assn. Home: 20336 NE 10th Court Rd N Miami FL 33179-2522 Office: Fla Nat Coll 4425 W 20th Ave Hialeah FL 33012

MEEHAN, WILLIAM A., air transportation executive; Pres., COO Continental Micronesia, Inc. Continental Airlines, Inc., Guam, 1998—2002, v.p. Cleve. hub, 2002—03, v.p. Houston hub, 2003—04, sr. v.p. airports svcs. Houston, 2004—. Office: Continental Airlines Inc PO Box 4607 Houston TX 77210 Office Phone: 713-324-5000. Office Fax: 713-324-2637.

MEEK, JERRY (GERALD FRANCIS MEEK), lawyer, former political organization administrator; b. Fort Worth, Tex., 1971; m. Patricia Ann Cotham. BA magna cum laude, Duke U., 1992, JD, 1997; MA in Govt., U. Notre Dame, 1995. Congl. page for Rep. Charlie Rose US Congress, 1989; assoc. med. malpractice Law Offices of Wade Byrd, Fayetteville, NC, 1998—99, 2000—08; ptnr. Simpson and Meek, PC, Dallas, 1999—2000, Poyner Spruill LLP, Raleigh & Charlotte, 2008—. Del. Dem. Nat. Conv., 1988. Del. Dem. Nat. Conv., 1988; chmn. Cumberland County Dem. Party, 1997; first vice chair NC Dem. Party, 2003—05, chair, 2005—09. Mem.: Am. Assn. Suicidology. Democrat. Office: Poyner Spruill LLP 301 Fayetteville St Ste 1900 Raleigh NC 27601 also: 301 S College St Ste 2300 Charlotte NC 28202 Office Phone: 910-323-2555, 919-783-6400, 704-342-5250. Office Fax: 910-323-9694, 919-783-1075, 704-342-5264.

MEEKER, CHARLES C., lawyer, former mayor; b. Washington, July 27, 1950; BA, Yale U., 1972; JD, Columbia U., 1975. Bar: NC 1975, DC 1984. Atty. Parker, Poe, Adams & Bernstein, Raleigh, NC, ptnr.; mem. Raleigh City Coun., 1985—89, 1991—95; mayor City of Raleigh, 2001—11. Mem. editorial bd.: Columbia Law Rev., 1974-75. Mem. DC Bar, Mayors Against Illegal Guns Coalition. Named one of Best Lawyers in America in Admin. Law, Woodward/White, 2007—.

Democrat. Office: Parker Poe et al Wells Fargo Capitol Ctr 150 Fayetteville St Ste 1400 Raleigh NC 27601 Office Phone: 919-890-4168. Office Fax: 919-835-4552. Business E-Mail: charlesmeeker@parkerpoe.com.

MEEKS, DAVID M., state legislator; b. Trenton, Mich. m. Naomi Meeks, Feb. 14, 2009. B in Pastoral Ministries. Mem. Bible Baptist Ch.; project mgr., customer svc. agent Blue Cross & Blue Shield of Fla., 2003; mem. Dist. 46 Ark. House of Representatives, 2011—. Served US Army, 1990-95; served US Army, South Korea, 1991. Baptist. Office: 2625 Donaghey Ave #108 PMB 301 Conway AR 72032 Office Phone: 501-277-9340. Business E-Mail: david.meeks@arkansashouse.org.

MEEKS, REGINALD K., state legislator; b. Louisville, Mar. 21, 1954; s. Florian and Eloise (Kline) M.; divorced Apr. 1979; 1 child, Nilaja. BA, Wabash Coll., 1976; JD, U. Iowa, 1979; PhD, pending, U. Louisville. Legal staff Louisville Legal Svcs., 1981-82; assoc. law Christian & Bynum, Louisville, 1982-84, Bleidt Barnett & Shanks, Louisville, 1984-88; career planner Jefferson County Bd. Edn., Louisville, 1988-90; adj. prof. McKendree College; assoc. dir. admissionsminority recruitment U. Louisville, 1990—; dir. of external Progs. U. of Louisville Coll. of Arts & Sciences; instr. U. of Louisville and McKendree Coll.; mem. Dist. 42 Ky. House of Reps., 2000—. Alderman City of Louisville 1982, Nat. Conf. of State Legislatures, Nat. Black Caucus of State Legislators, Kentucky Assn. of Blacks in higher edn. Mem. Nat. Black Caucus Local Elected Ofcls., Washington, 1982—, dist. dir., 1988-89; chmn. Ky. African-Am. Mus. Devel. Com., Louisville, 1988—; sec., bd. dirs. Seven Counties Svcs., Inc., Louisville, 1984-87; exec. bd. mem. NAACP, Louisville, 1989-90; trustee Farm & Wilderness Camps, Inc., Plymouth, Vt. 1988, Kentucky Native Am. Heritage Com., bd. mem. Kentucky Native Am. Arts & cultural Cntr., Lewis & Clark Bicentennial Commn., Kentucky Polar Bear Club, Kentucky Sportsmen's Caucus mem. Named as One of Fifty Future Leaders of Am., Ebony Mag., 1986, one of Outstanding Young Men of Am., Louisville Mag., 1987—, one of People to Watch, Louisville Mag., 1989, Who's Who Among Emerging Leaders In Am., Who's Who Among Black Am., Who's Who in South, Y.M.C.A. Adult Achiever award. Mem. Nat. Bar Assn., Ky. Mcpl. League, Nat. League of Cities (rep.), Cntr. for Policy Alternatives Fellow, adv. bd Cntr. for Policy Alternatives, Leadership Kentucky, Charter Class mem., bd. of dirs. Kentucky Long-Range Policy Rsch.,hon. mem. Sunshine Srs., Hon. Order of Kentucky Colonels, Nat. Assn. of Black Scuba Divers, found. mem. Kentucky Assn. of Black Scuba Divers. Democrat. Protestant. Avocations: travel, writing, martial arts, camping. also: City Hall Bd Aldermen Louisville KY 40292-0001 Office: Dist 42 Kentucky Capitol Annex Rm 329 C Frankfort KY 40601 also: Annex Rm 329C 702 Capitol Ave Frankfort KY 40601 Office Phone: 502-564-8100 ext. 653, 502-564-8100 653. Personal E-mail: srmeeks42@aol.com. Business E-Mail: reginald.meeks@lrc.ky.gov.

MEEKS, STEPHEN A., state legislator; b. Trenton, Mich., Oct. 30, 1970; AS in Telecom. Engring., Fla. Cmty. Coll., 1997; AA, 1999. Pres. Northeast Fla. Astron. Soc., 1989—2006; instr. Fla. Cmty. Coll., 1997—2003; tchr. Baymeadows Baptist Day School, 2001—03; mgr. Am. Multi Cinema, 2003—06; sound technician Faith Bapt. Ch., 2006—; technician The Computer Works, 2006—; mem. Dist. 47 Ark. House of Representatives, 2011—. Served with USAR, 1987-93. Republican. Office: 552 Hwy 225 E Greenbrier AR 72058 Office Phone: 501-205-3272. Business E-Mail: stephen.meeks@arkansashouse.org.

MEGGS, WILLIAM JOEL, toxicologist, allergist, emergency physician, educator, author; b. Newberry, SC, May 30, 1942; s. Wallace Nat and Elizabeth (Pruitt) M.; m. Susan Nancy Spring, June 11, 1966 (div. June 1998); m. Susan Krause Martin, Apr. 21, 2001; children: Jason Nathaniel, Benjamin Maffey, Thomas Clute. BS, Clemson U., 1964; PhD, Syracuse U., 1969; MD, U. Miami, 1979. Diplomate Am. Bd. Internal Medicine, Am. Bd. Allergy and Immunology, Am. Bd. Emergency Medicine, Am. Bd. Med. Toxicology. Resident in internal medicine Rochester (N.Y.) Gen. Hosp., 1979-82; staff fellow in allergy and clin. immunology Nat. Inst. Allergy and Infectious Diseases, Bethesda, Md., 1982-85; asst. dir. med. edn. emergency dept. Washington Hosp. Ctr., 1985-88; from asst. prof. allergy, immunology to sr. vice chmn. Sch. Medicine E. Carolina U., Greenville, NC, 1988—2004, sr. vice chmn. Sch. Medicine, 2004—; chmn., dir. emergency dept. Lenoir Meml. Hosp., Kinston, NC, 1990-91. Mem. Emergency Svcs. Com. Lenoir Meml. Hosp., Kinston, 1988-92; mem workshop on immune testing, Agy. for Toxic Substances and Diseases Registry, 1992, workshop on equity in environ. health, U.S. EPA, 1992, workshop on multiple chem. sensitivity syndrome, NRC, 1991; mem. rsch. adv. com. on Gulf War illnesses Dept. VA, 2002-; fellow med. toxicology NYU, 1992-96. Co-author: The Inflammation Cure, 2003; co-editor: Health and Safety in Agriculture, 1997; contbr. numerous articles and abstracts to profl. jours. Vol. physician Indigent Clinic E. Carolina U., Pitt County Med. Soc., 1988—, Pitt County Shelter, 1989—; advanced cardiac life support instr. E. Carolina U. Sch. of Medicine, 1988-2000, advanced trauma life support instr., 1991-2002; mem. Pitt County Traffic Injury Prevention Program, 1989-92; bd. dirs. Rachael Carson Coun., 1988—; mem. adv. bd. Pamplico Tar River Found., 1990—. Named Woodrow Wilson Hon. fellow, 1964, NSF post-doctoral fellow, 1969; grantee N.C. United Way, 1988-89, Greer Labs., 1989-90, Am. Lung Assn. N.C., 1992-93, rsch. award Am. Coll. Med. Toxicology Fellow Am. Coll. Emergency Physicians, Am. Coll. Med. Toxicology; mem. AMA, Am. Acad. Allergy and Immuniology, Am. Acad. Clin. Toxicology, Pitt County Med. Soc., N.C. State Med. Soc., Soc. for Acad. Emergency Medicine, N.C. Thoracic Soc. (physicians' sect.). Achievements include creator of the biological homing theory of the origins of life. Office: E Carolina U Sch Medicine Dept Emergency Medicine Rm 3ED311 600 Moye Blvd Greenville NC 27858-4300 Office Phone: 252-744-2954. Business E-Mail: meggsw@ecu.edu.

MEGILL, ALLAN, historian; b. Regina, Sask., Apr. 20, 1947; arrived in US, 1980; s. Ralph Peter and Jean Tudhope (Dickson) M.; div.; children: Jason Robert, Jessica Susan, Jonathan David; m. Rita Felski; 1 child, Maria Megill Felski. BA, U. Sask., 1969; MA, U. Toronto, 1970; PhD, Columbia U., 1975. From instr. to prof. history U. Iowa, Iowa City, 1974—90; prof. history U. Va., Charlottesville, 1990—. Rsch. fellow in history of ideas Australian Nat. U., Canberra, 1977—79, temp. lectr. modern European studies, 1979; vis. prof. Sch. Advanced Studies in Social Scis., Paris, 1997. Author: Prophets of Extremity, 1985, Karl Marx: The Burden of Reason, 2002, Historical Knowledge, Historical Error: A Contemporary Guide to Practice, 2007, (Russian edn.) Istoricheskaya epistemologia, 2007, Karl Marx: Bremya Razuma, 2010; editor: Rethinking Objectivity, 1994; co-editor: The Rhetoric of the Human Sciences, 1987; cons. editor Jour. of History of Ideas, 1986—89, mem. editl. bd., 1990—, v.p., 2004—05, pres., 2005—; mem. editl. bd.: U. Press of Va., 1991—94, Rethinking History, 1996—; contbr. articles to profl. jours. Chmn. Page-Barbour and Richard Lectures com. U. Va., 1994-96. Mem.: Internat. Commn. for the History and Theory of Historiography, Internat. Soc. for Intellectual History, Am. Hist. Assn. Office: Univ Va Corcoran Dept History PO Box 400180 Charlottesville VA 22904 Office Phone: 434-924-6414. Business E-Mail: megill@virginia.edu.

MEHTA, EILEEN ROSE, lawyer; b. Colver, Pa., Apr. 1, 1953; d. Richard Glenn and Helen (Wahna) Ball; m. Abdul Rashid Mehta, Aug. 31, 1973. Student, Miami U., 1971-73; BA with distinction, Fla. Internat. U., 1974; JD cum laude, U. Miami, 1977. Bar: Fla. 1977, US Dist. Ct. (so. dist.) Fla. 1977, US Ct. Appeals (11th cir.) 1981. Law clk. to presiding judge US Dist. Ct. (so. dist.) Fla., Miami, 1977-79; asst. atty. County of Dade, Miami, 1979-89; shareholder Fine Jacobson Schwartz Nash Block & England, Miami, Fla., 1989-94; ptnr. Eckert Seamans Cherin & Mellott, Miami, 1994-98, Bilzin Sumberg Baena Price & Axelrod, Miami, 1998—. Lectr. in field. Miami U. scholar, 1971-73. Mem. Fla. Bar Assn., Dade County Bar Assn. Office: Bilzin Sumberg Baena Price & Axelrod 1450 Brickell Ave Ste 2300 Miami FL 33131 Office Phone: 305-350-2380. Business E-Mail: emehta@bilzin.com.

MEHTA, JAWAHAR LAL, cardiologist; b. India, Aug. 10, 1946; arrived in US, 1970; s. Mohan L. and Ishwar D. (Valecha) M.; m. Paulette Smedresman, Oct. 20, 1977; children: Asha, Jason. MD, GN Med. Coll. U. Amritsar, 1968; PhD, Uppsala U., Sweden. Diplomate Am. Bd. Internal Medicine, Am. Bd. Cardiovascular Diseases. Intern N.Y. Med. Coll., Valhalla, NY, 1970, resident in pediat., 1971; resident in internal medicine Mt. Sinai-Beth Israel Hosp., NYC, 1971-73; fellow in cardiology SUNY, NY, 1973-75; from asst. prof. to prof. medicine & physiology U. Fla. Coll. Medicine, Gainesville, 1976-2000; dir. molecular cardiology, Stebbins chair in cardiology U. Ark. Med. Sci., Little Rock, 2000—. Rsch. fellow, instr. in medicine U. Minn., Mpls., 1975—76; staff physician VA Med. Ctr., Gainesville, 1976—2000, clin. investigator, 1980—85; dir. cardiology svcs. Ctrl. Ark. Vets. Healthcare Sys., 2000—. Fellow: ACP, Am. Heart Assn., Am. Coll. Cardiology; mem.: Assn. Univ. Cardiologists, Assn. Am. Physicians, Am. Soc. Clin. Investigation. Office: U Ark for Med Scis Slot 532 Little Rock AR 72205-7199 Personal E-mail: arheartdoc@gmail.com. Business E-Mail: mehtajl@uams.edu.

MEHTA, KIRAN H., lawyer; AB magna cum laude, Cornell U., 1978; JD cum laude, Harvard U., 1981. Bar: NC 1983, US Dist. Ct. all NC Districts, US Ct. Appeals 4th Cir. Law clk. Chief Judge Frank A. Kaufman, US Dist. Ct. (Md. Dist.), 1982—82; ptnr. Kennedy Covington (merged with K&L Gates LLP), Charlotte, NC; ptnr., litigation practice K&L Gates LLP, Charlotte, NC, 2008—. Contbr. articles to profl. jours., chapters to books. Dean, solid & hazardous waste Charlotte C. of C. Environ. Sch., 1991—94, chmn. hazardous waste/superfund com., 1992—94; dir. Cmty. Sch. Arts, 1997—; mem. supt. council Charlotte-Mecklenburg Sch. Sys., 1999. Mem.: ABA, NC Bar Assn., Mecklenburg County Bar Assn., Harvard Law Sch. Assn. NC (pres. 1996—), Phi Beta Kappa. Office: K&L Gates LLP Hearst Tower 47th Fl 214 N Tryon St Charlotte NC 28202 Office Phone: 704-331-7437. Office Fax: 704-353-3137. Business E-Mail: kiran.mehta@klgates.com.

MEIER, KENNETH JOHN, political scientist; b. Aberdeen, SD, Mar. 3, 1950; s. John and Elizabeth (Malsam) M.; m. Diane Jones Meier, Dec. 31, 1972. BA, U. S.D., 1972; PhD, Syracuse U., 1975. Prof. polit. sci. Rice U., Houston, 1975-78, U. Okla., 1978-85, U. Wis., Madison, 1985-89, Milw., 1989-97; Charles Puryear prof. liberal arts Tex. A&M U., College Station, 1998—2005, Sara Lindsey prof. govt., 2001—04, Charles Gregory chair in liberal arts, 2006—. Fellow com. for hispanic pub. policy issues Inter Univ. Program Social Sci. Rsch. Coun., 1991-92; dir. Ctr. for Presdl. Studies, Policy and Governance, 2001-02, dir., Project Equity Rep. Gov., 2004-. Author: Race, Class and Education, 1989, The Politics of Hispanic Education, 1991, Politics and the Bureaucracy, 1993, The Politics of Sin, 1994, The Case Against School Choice, 1995, Regulation and Consumer Protection, 1995, Applied Statistics for Public Administration, 1997, What Works: A New Approach to Program and Policy Analysis, 2000, The Politics of Fertility Control, 2001, Politics, Policy and Organizations, 2003, Bureaucracy in a Democratic State, 2006, Public Service Performance, Latino Politics, 2007, Pub. Management, 2011; editor Am. Jour. Polit. Sci., 1994-98; assoc. editor Jour. Pub. Adminstrn. Rsch. and Theory, 2000-08, editor-in-chief, 2011-. Recipient Clarence A. Kulp award, 1990, Gustavus Myers award, 1991, 93, Herbert Kaufman award, 1992, 2002, 11 Herbert A. Simon award, 1999, award Acad. Mgmt., 2000, disting. rsch. award, Nat. Assn. Schs. Pub. Affairs and Adminstrn./ASPA, 2003; Big XII Faculty fellow, 2003. Fellow: Nat. Acad. Pub. Adminstrn. (Charles Levine award 2005, William Mosher award 2005), Advanced Inst. Mgmt. (Joseph Wholey award 2004, Dwight Waldo award ASPA 2010); mem.: APHA, MW Polit. Sci. Assn. (pres.-elect 2004—05, pres. 2005—06), Nat. Pub. Mgmt. Rsch. Assn. (pres. 2003—05, H George Fed. award 2011), SW Polit. Sci. Assn. (pres.-elect 1998—99, pres. 1999—2000), Am. Polit. Sci. Assn. (Latino Mentor award 2005, John Gaus award 2006, Women's Caucus Mentor award 2008, Career Achievement award). Office: Tex A&M U Dept Polit Sci TAMUS 4348 College Station TX 77843-0001 Office Phone: 979-845-4232. Business E-Mail: kmeier@polisci.tamu.edu.

MEINDL, JAMES DONALD, electrical engineering educator, academic administrator; b. Pitts., Apr. 20, 1933; s. Louis M. and Elizabeth F. (Steinhauser) Meindl; m. Frederica Ziegler, May 21, 1961; children: Peter James, Candace Ann. BS, Carnegie Mellon U., 1955, MS, 1956, PhD, 1958. Engr. Autonetics Co., Downey, Calif., 1957, Westinghouse Co., Pitts., 1958-59; head sect. microelectronics US Army Electronics Command, Ft. Monmouth, NJ, 1959-62, chief br. semiconductors and microelectronics, 1962-65, dir. divsn. integrated electronics, 1965-67; assoc. prof. elec. engring. Stanford University, 1967-70, prof., 1970-84, John M. Fluke prof. elec. engring., 1984-86, assoc. dean rsch., 1984-86, dir. integrated circuits lab., 1969-84; co-founder Telesensory Systems Inc., 1971-84; dir. Electronics Labs. Stanford University, 1972-86, dir. Ctr. Integrated Systems, 1981-86; v.p. acad. affairs, provost Rensselaer Polytechnic Institute, Troy, NY, 1986-88, prof. sci. and engring., 1986-93, sr. v.p. acad. affairs, provost, 1988-93; Joseph M. Pettit Chair prof. microelectronics Ga. Inst. Tech., Atlanta, 1993—, dir. Microelectronics Rsch. Ctr., 1997—. Cons. to govt., industry. Author: Micropower Circuits, 1969; editor: Brief Lessons in High Technology, 1989; patentee integrated cir. field; contbr. numerous articles to profl. publs. Served to 1st lt. AUS, 1959-61. Recipient Arthur S. Flemming Commn. award Washington Jr. C. of C., 1967; J.J. Ebers award IEEE Electron Devices Soc., 1980, Univ. Rsch. award Semiconductor Industries Assn., 1999. Fellow IEEE (Solid State Circuits Coun. editor jour. 1966-71, Internat. Outstanding Paper ann. awards 1970, 75-78, Beatrice K. Winner award Internat. conf. 1988, solid State Circuits medal 1989, Edn. medal 1990, Third Millenium medal 2000, Medal of Honor 2006), AAAS, Am. Acad. Arts and Scis.; mem. AAUP, NAE, Am. Soc. Engr. Edn. (Benjamin Garver Lamme medal 1991), Electrochemical Soc., Biomedical Engring. Soc. (co-editor Annals of Biomedical Engring. 1976-80), Sigma Xi, Tau Beta Pi, Eta Kappa Nu, Phi Kappa Phi. Office: Ga Inst Tech Microelectronics Rsch Ctr 791 Atlantic Dr Atlanta GA 30332-0001 Home: 1521 Jacksons Ridge Rd Greensboro GA 30642-5210 E-mail: james.meindl@mirc.gatech.edu.

MEIROVITCH, LEONARD, engineering educator, educator; b. Maxut, Romania, Nov. 28, 1928; came to U.S., 1956, naturalized, 1964; s. Carol and Adelle (Schoenfeld) M.; m. Jo Anne Reifer, Oct. 15, 1960. BSc summa cum laude, Technion-Israel Inst. Tech., 1953; MS in Engring., UCLA, 1957, PhD, 1960. Structural engr. Water Planning for Israel, Tel Aviv, 1953—55, asst. sect. head, 1955—56; asst. rsch. engr., asso. in engring. UCLA, 1956—60; staff engr. IBM, Endicott, NY, 1960—62; assoc. prof. Ariz. State U., 1962—66; prof. U. Cin., 1967—71, Va. Poly. Inst. and State U., Blacksburg, 1971—79, Reynolds Metals prof., 1979—83, Univ. disting. prof., 1983—98, Univ. disting. prof. emeritus, 1998—. Cons. Goodyear Aerospace, Phoenix, 1962-63; cons. C.S. Draper Labs., Cambridge, Mass., 1976-78, Naval Research Lab., Washington, 1977-79, Intelsat, Washington, 1980-82 Author: Analytical Methods in Vibrations, 1967, Methods of Analytical Dynamics, 1970, Elements of Vibration Analysis, 1975, 2d edit., 1986, Computational Methods in Structural Dynamics, 1980, Introduction to Dynamics and Control, 1985, Dynamics and Control of Structures, 1990, Principles and Techniques of Vibrations, 1997, Fundamentals of Vibrations, 2001, also articles; assoc. editor Jour. Spacecraft and Rockets, 1971-76, Jour. Optimization Theory and Applications, 1984—2010; mem. internat. editorial bd. Jour. European Mechanics, 1977-93. Served with Israeli Army, 1948-49. Recipient Alumni award for rsch. excellence Va. Poly. Inst. and State U., 1981, Japan Soc. Mech. Engrs. medal, 1989, Alexander von Humboldt Sr. Rsch. award Germany, 1991, Den Hartog award ASME, 1999; Am. Soc. Engring. Edn.-NASA fellow, 1964; NAS sr. rsch. assoc. Langley Rsch. Ctr., Hampton, Va., 1966-67. Fellow AIAA (Structures, Structural Dynamics and Materials award 1983, Pendray Aerospace Lit. award 1984, Mechanics and Control of Flight award 1987); mem. Sigma Xi, Tau Beta Pi. Home: 1505 Highland Cir Blacksburg VA 24060-5668 Home Phone: 540-951-2901. Business E-Mail: lmeirovi@vt.edu.

MEISELS, GERHARD GEORGE, academic administrator, chemist, educator; b. Vienna, May 11, 1931; came to U.S., 1951, naturalized, 1961; s. Leo and Adele Josefa Maria (Seehofer) M.; m. Sylvia Claire Knopsnider, June 28, 1958; 1 dau., Laura Germaine. Student, U. Vienna, 1949-51, 52-53; MS, U. Notre Dame, Ind., 1952, PhD, 1956. Postdoctoral rsch. assoc. U. Notre Dame, 1955-56; chemist Gulf Oil Corp., Pitts., 1956-59; part-time instr. Carnegie Inst. Tech., Pitts., 1956-58; chemist nuclear divsn. Union Carbide Corp., Tuxedo, NY, 1959-63, asst. group leader, 1964-65; assoc. prof. U. Houston, 1965-70, prof., 1970-75, dept. chmn., 1973-75; prof., chmn. dept. chemistry U. Nebr., Lincoln, 1975-81, dean Coll. Arts and Scis., 1981-88; provost, COO U. South Fla., Tampa, 1988-94; dir. Coalition Sci. Literacy, 1994—, Suncoast Area Ctr. for Ednl. Enhancement (SACEE), 1996-99. Editor (spl. issue) Jour. Radiation Physics and Chemistry, 1980; contbr. writings in field to profl. publs. Sec., pres. Ramsey (N.J.) Jr. C. of C., 1959-64; chmn. Fla. Coalition for Improving Math. and Sci. Edn., 1998—2010, interim exec. dir., 1998-2008 Fulbright fellow, Smith-Mundt fellow, 1951-52; sr. fellow Sci. Rsch. Coun., Eng., 1976. Mem. Am. Chem. Soc. (com. chmn.), Am. Soc. for Mass Spectrometry (charter, com. chmn., v.p. 1984-86, pres. 1986-88, bd. dirs. 1988-90), Fla. Acad. Scis., AAAS, Am. Phys. Soc., Coun. Sci. Soc. Pres. (exec. bd. 1989-92, chmn. elect 1990, chmn. 1991, chmn. com. on sci. priorities), Nat. Alliance State Sci. and Math. Coalitions (bd. dirs. 1999—, v.p., 2007—), Coun. for Chem. Rsch. (bd. dirs. 1982-85), Conformation Judges Assn. Fla. (pres. 1996—2004), West Highland White Terrier Club America (bd. dirs., 2008-12), Fla. Higher Edn. Consortium Math. and Sci. (ctrl. steering com. 1995—, chmn. 1998-2000), Houston Kennel Club (bd. dirs. 1968-70), Cornhusker Kennel Club (pres., bd. dirs., del. to Am. Kennel Club 1976-88), St. Petersburg Dog Fanciers Assn. (sec. 1996-98, 2000-04, del. to Am. Kennel Club 1998—, pres. 2012-), Lakeland-Winter Haven K.C. (pres. 2006-09), Fla. Stem Coun., Sigma Xi, Triangle Coalition Scis. & Technol. Edn. (bd. dirs. 2011-). Home: PO Box 1347 Thonotosassa FL 33592-1347 Office: U South Fla 4202 E Fowler Ave/CHE 205 Tampa FL 33620 Office Phone: 813-974-7135. Business E-Mail: meisels@usf.edu.

MEISENHEIMER, FRED E., gas industry company executive; BS, Stephen F. Austin State U.; MBA, Southern Methodist U. Contr. Vartec Telecom Inc.; Audit mgr. Deloitte & Touche LLP, 1970—79; gen. auditor Oryx Energy Corp., 1988—99; asst. contr. Oryx Energy Corp. (formerly Sun Exploration & Prodn. Co.), 1979—99; v.p., contr. Atmos Energy Corp., 2000—09, interim CFO, 2009, sr. v.p., CFO, 2009—. Office: Atmos Energy Corp 1800 Three Lincoln Centre Dallas TX 75240 Office Phone: 972-934-9227. Office Fax: 972-855-3040.

MELANCON, GLENN, history professor; b. Heidelberg, Germany, Jan. 24, 1966; s. Yves and Anna Mae Melancon; m. Jackie Melancon; children: Christopher, Alexandre. BA in History, U. Southwestern La., 1989, BA in Philosophy, 1989, MA in History, 1991; PhD in History, La. State U., 1994. Instr. history and world religions Acad. Sacred Heart, 1994—95; asst. prof. Southeastern Okla. State U., 1995—2000, assoc. prof., 2000—05, prof., 2005—. Mem. faculty transfer curriculum com.: history Okla. State Regents for Higher Edn., 1995—2005; reviewer social studies curriculum review com. Okla. Commn. Tchr. Preparation, 1998—; com. chair policies and issues Grayson Dem. Party, 2004—05. Cubmaster Cub Scout Pack 9, 1998—2002, com. chair, 2002—05, charter rep., 2005—; mem. adult edn. team St. Mary's Cath. Ch., instr. rite of Christian initiation of adults, 2004—. Mem.: Southwestern Hist. Assn. (pres. 2003—04), Southwestern Social Studies Assn. (sec. 2006—). Democrat. Cath. Office: PO Box 1861 Sherman TX 75091

MELANÇON, TUCKER LEE, federal judge; b. Bryan, Tex., 1946; BS, La. State U., 1968; JD, Tulane U., 1973. Atty. Knoll & Knoll, 1973-75; pvt. practice Marksville, La., 1975-83; prin. Melancon & Rabalais, Marksville, 1984-94; judge US Dist. Ct. (we. dist.) La., Lafayette, 1994—2009, sr. judge, 2009—. Mem. adv. bd. Catalyst Old River Hydroelectric Partnership, Vidalia, La., 1989-92, La. Workers Compensation, 1990-91; mem. com. Study Backlog in Cts. of Appeal, 1st and 3d Cirs., 1991; bd. dirs. Catalyst Vidalia Corp., N.Y.C., 1993-94. Mem. Am. Judicature Soc., Am. Inns of Ct., La. State Bar Assn., Bar Assn. 5th Fed. Cir. Office: US Dist Ct 800 Lafayette St Ste 4700 Lafayette LA 70501-6879

MELCHER, DAVID F., defense industry executive, retired military officer; b. Allentown, Pa., May 20, 1954; s. Donald Frederick and Gloria Melcher. BSc, U.S. Mil. Acad., West Point, 1976; MBA, Harvard U., 1983; MPA, Shippensburg U., 1996. Registered profl. engr., N.H. Commd. 2d. lt. US Army, 1976, advanced through grades to brig. gen., various staff positions, 1976—92, bn. comdr. Fort Wainwright, Ark., 1992—94, regimental tactical officer US Mil. Acad. West Point, NY, 1994—95, brigade comdr. 1st Cavalry Divsn. Fort Hood, Tex., 1996—98, comdr. gen. Corps Engineers SW divsn. Dallas; dep. chief staff programs US Dept. Def., The Pentagon, 1998—99, dep. dir., 1999—2000; v.p., strategy & bus. devel. ITT Def. & Info. Solutions, 2008, pres., 2008—11; sr. v.p. ITT Corp., 2010—11; pres., CEO ITT Exelis, 2011—. Contbr. articles to profl. jours. Mem. sch. bd. Fairbanks North Star Borough, Fairbanks, Alaska, 1993—94; bd. trustees Nat. Def. Industry Assn., 2009—;

cons. Army Sci. Bd., 2010—. Fellow, Commn. White House Fellowships, 1987—88. Mem.: Army Engr. Assn., Assn. U.S. Army, Soc. Am. Military Engrs. Office: ITT Exelis 1650 Tysons Blvd Ste 1700 Mc Lean VA 22102

MELE, STEPHEN E., human resources specialist; BSBA, Fairleigh Dickinson U. Dir., human resource Schlumberger; dir., human resources Clearstream; group head, human resources ops. Std. Chartered Bank; v.p., human resources Prudential Internat.; chief people officer, chief tech. officer Mercer Human Resources Consulting; v.p., chief human resources officer Watson Wyatt Worldwide, Inc., 2007—. Office: Watson Wyatt Worldwide Inc 901 N Glebe Rd Arlington VA 22203 Office Phone: 703-258-8000. Office Fax: 703-258-7593. Business E-Mail: Stephen.Mele@watsonwyatt.com.

MELLEN, FRANCIS JOSEPH, JR., lawyer; b. Williamsport, Pa., Dec. 19, 1945; s. Francis Joseph and Mary Emma (Oberst) M.; m. Mary Wilder Davison, Aug. 2, 1975 (div. 1987); m. Beverly Joan Glascock, Sept. 2, 2000; children: Elizabeth, Catherine, Robert, Christine. BA, U. Ky., 1967, MA, 1971; JD, Harvard U., 1973. Bar: NY 1974, Ky. 1975, US Dist. Ct. NY 1974, US Dist. Ct. (ea. dist.) Ky. 1977, US Dist. Ct. (we. dist.) Ky. 1978, US Ct. Appeals (2d cir.) 1975, US Ct. Appeals (6th cir.) 1982, US Supreme Ct. 2005. Assoc. atty. Rogers & Wells (now Clifford Chance), NYC, 1973-75, Wyatt, Grafton & Sloss, Louisville, 1975-80; ptnr. Wyatt, Tarrant & Combs, Louisville, 1980—. Co-author: Kentucky Mineral Law, 1986, Kentucky Forms and Transactions, 1991; contbr. articles to profl. jours. Spl. study com. Uniform Comml. Code, Ky. Legis. Rsch. Commn., Frankfort, 1984-91; bd. dirs. Leadership Louisville Found., 1995-02, counsel, 1996-98, 2000-02; bd. dirs. Stage One: The Louisville Children's Theatre, 1995-01, v.p., 1997-98, pres., 1998-00; bd. dirs. Louisville-Jefferson County A.W.A.R.E. Coalition, 1994-98; bd. trustees Cherokee Gardens, 2005—09. chair, 2007-08, Lt. (j.g.) USNR, 1967-69. Lt. USNR, 1967—69. Mem. ABA, Am. Arbitration Assn. (panel), Nat. Arbitration Forum (panel), Ky. Bar Assn. (ho. of dels. 1986-92, ethics com. 2004—, arbitration panel 2005—), Louisville Bar Assn. (chmn. com. profl. responsibility 1992-94), Jefferson Club, Filson Club, Am. Mensa, Hon. Order Ky. Cols. Republican. Home: 2944 Lexington Rd Louisville KY 40206-2934 Office: Wyatt Tarrant & Combs LLP 2800 PNC Plz Louisville KY 40202 Home Phone: 502-893-9254; Office Phone: 502-562-7290. Business E-Mail: fmellen@wyattfirm.com.

MELLMAN, MICHAEL J., endocrinologist; MD, U. Mich., 1987. Diplomate American Bd. Internal Medicine-endocrinology, diabetes and metabolism, 2003. Resident internal medicine North Shore Univ. Hosp., NYC, 1988—90; fellow endocrinology, diabetes and metabolism Albert Einstein Coll. of Medicine, Bronx, NY, 1990—92; physician Delray Med. Ctr., Delray Beach, Fla., Bethesda Meml. Hosp., Boynton Beach, Fla.; pvt. practice Boynton Beach Endocrinology, P.A., Fla. Office: Boynton Beach Endocrinology PA Ste 5 11135 Jog Rd Boynton Beach FL 33437 Office Phone: 561-374-8969. Office Fax: 561-374-8929.*

MELLON, WILLIAM DANIEL, communications executive; b. Darby, Pa., June 22, 1951; s. William and Eleanor M.; m. Nikki Dersin, July 15, 1978; children: William D. III, Logan, Megan. BA in Broadcast Journalism, St. Louis U., 1972, MA in Pub. Rels. and Advt., 1974. Various positions, regional dir., pub. rels. Boeing Comml. Airplane Co., 1978—85; dir., corp. comm. Raytheon Beech Aircraft Corp., Wichita, Kans., 1985—87; dir., news and info. Rockwell Internat., Seal Beach, Calif., 1987—92, dir., pub. rels., 1992—94, dir., internat. comm. and pub. affairs Arlington, Va., 1994—97, v.p., pub. rels., 1997—2008; sr. v.p., corp. comm. Amerigroup Corp., 2008—. Capt. USAF, 1973-78; Lt. Col. USAFR, 1978-95. Mem. Aerospace Industries Assn. (mem. comm. coun.), Pub. Rels. Soc. Am., Internat. Assn. Bus. Communicators, Internat. Pub. Rels. Dirs. Roundtable, Coun. Communication Mgmt., Nat. Investor Rels. Inst., Am. Mktg. Assn., Global Pub. Affairs Inst. (bd. dirs.), Nat. Press Club, Mfrs. Alliance (pub. affairs coun.). Office: Amerigroup Corp 4425 Corporation Ln Virginia Beach VA 23462 Office Phone: 757-490-6900. Office Fax: 757-222-2330.

MELLOTT, JOHN C., management consultant, former publishing executive; Grad., Case Western Reserve U., 1979. CPA. Contr. Atlanta Jour.-Constitution, 1987—91, v.p. & gen. mgr., 1992—2000, pub., 2004—09; treas. Cox Enterprises, 1991—92, v.p. bus. devel. & planning, 2000—02; pres. Dent Wizard Internat., 2002—04; advisor Bain & Co., Atlanta, 2009—. Bd. trustees Dian Fossey Gorilla Fund Internat., Inc., Ga. State U.; chmn. Atlanta Zoo; vice chmn. United Way Atlanta; mem. exec. com. Atlanta C. of C.; bd. dirs. Commerce Club Atlanta. Office: Bain & Co Inc 3280 Peachtree Rd NE Ste 2400 Atlanta GA 30305 Office Phone: 404-869-2727. Office Fax: 404-869-2222.

MELOY, MATT, gas industry executive; BA in Fin., U. Tex., Austin. Mem. structured finance group Royal Bank of Scotland; dir. corp. devel. Targa Resources, Inc., 2006, v.p. fin. & treas. Targa Resources GP, v.p. fin. & treas., 2008—. Office: Targa Resources, Inc 1000 Louisiana St Ste 4300 Houston TX 77002 Office Phone: 713-584-1000. Office Fax: 713-584-1100. Business E-Mail: MMeloy@targaresources.com.

MELSHEIMER, MEL P(OWELL), venture capitalist; b. LA, July 9, 1939; s. Oscar Merrill M.; m. Sara Sturdevant, Sept. 1, 1962; children: Heidi, Erich, Douglas. AB, Occidental Coll., 1961; MBA, U. So. Calif., 1965. With United Calif. Bank, Los Angeles, 1962-66; sr. fin. analyst Ford Motor Co., Newport Beach, Calif., 1966-67; v.p., chief fin. officer Pepsi Cola Co. Pepsico, Inc., Purchase, NY, 1968-75; exec. v.p., chief operating officer AZL Resources, Inc., 1975-84; chmn. bd., CEO PHX Pacific, Inc., 1984-89; pres., CEO MPM Capital Corp., 1987-89; exec. v.p. Finevest Foods, Inc., Greenwich, Conn., 1989-92; pres., CEO Land-O-Sun Dairies Inc., 1991-92, Atlanta Dairies, Inc., 1991-92; exec. v.p., sec., COO Dairy Holdings, Inc., Johnson City, Tenn., 1992-94; exec. v.p., COO, CFO Sonex Internat. Corp., Brewster, NY, 1994; pres., CEO M.P. Melsheimer & Co., Ridgefield, Conn., 1994-97; pres. NFX, 1995-96; pres., COO, CFO Harris & Harris Group, Inc., NYC, 1997—2004; pres. Linkhorn Capital Advisors, Inc., 2005—; chmn. bd. Patriot Capital Funding Inc., 2006—09. Served with U.S. Army, 1961-62. Home: 1418 N Woodhouse Rd Virginia Beach VA 23454 E-mail: melmelsheimer@msn.com.

MELTON, DARRIO TRAMEN, state legislator; m. Christi Melton; 1 child. BS, U. Ala., Birmingham, 2001; MDiv, Emory U., Atlanta, 2004. Grad. Selma-Dallas County Leadership. Constituent svc. rep. to Arthur Davis US House of Representatives, 2004—; mem. Dist. 67 Ala. House of RepS., 2011—. Adj. instr. Wallace CC of Selma. Assoc. pastor, ch. adminstr. Tabernacle of Praise Ch.; bd. dirs. Voices Ala. Children. Democrat. Office: PO Box 346 Selma AL 36702 also: Ala House of Reps Rm 525-C 11 S Union St Montgomery AL 36130 Office Phone: 334-242-7540.

MELTON, HAROLD D., state supreme court justice; b. Washington; BA, Auburn U.; JD, U. Ga., 1991. Former atty. Ga. Dept. of Law, former section leader, consumer interests div.; former exec. counsel Gov. Perdue; justice Ga. Supreme Ct., 2005—. Former volunteer leader Young Life Ministries. Dir. teen ministry Southwest Christian Fellowship Church; bd. mem. Atlanta Youth Academies. Office: Ga Supreme Ct Ste 300 244 Washington St SW Atlanta GA 30334 Office Phone: 404-656-3470. Office Fax: 404-656-2253.*

MELTON, HOWELL WEBSTER, SR., federal judge; b. Atlanta, Dec. 15, 1923; s. Holmes and Alma (Combee) M.; m. Margaret Catherine Wolfe, Mar. 4, 1950; children— Howell Webster, Carol Anne. JD, U. Fla., 1948. Bar: Fla. 1948. With Upchurch, Melton & Upchurch, St. Augustine, 1948-61; judge 7th Jud. Cir. Fla., St. Augustine, 1961-77, US Dist. Ct. (mid. dist.) Fla., Jacksonville, 1977-91, sr. judge, 1991—. Past chmn. Fla. Conf. Cir. Judges, 1974; past chmn. coun. bar pres.'s Fla. Bar. Trustee Flagler Coll., St. Augustine. Served with U.S. Army, 1943-46. Recipient Disting. Service award St. Augustine Jaycees, 1953 Mem. ABA, St. Johns County Bar Assn., Jacksonville Bar Assn., Fed. Bar Assn., Fla. Blue Key, Officers Club, Masons, Phi Delta Theta, Phi Delta Phi. Methodist. Office: US Dist Ct 300 N Hogan St Ste 11-300 Jacksonville FL 32202 Office Phone: 904-549-1940.

MELTON, WAYNE CHARLES, real estate executive; b. Oak Ridge, Tenn., Aug. 30, 1954; s. Charles Estel and Una Faye (Hull) M.; m. Maria Piedad. AB in European Intellectual History, U. Ga., 1975; MBA in Real Estate, Shepperton U., 2001, PhD in Real Estate Fin., 2003. Cert. Five Star Inst., 2011. Mgr. Household Internat., Athens, Ga., 1975—85; asst. mgr. Athens and Hickory, NC, Doraville, Ga., 1975—76; pres., CEO Impact Realty-Melton & Assocs. Inc., Athens, 1987—. Cons. Ga. Furniture, Charlotte Realty, NC, 1987—, US Fed. Res. Bank, Atlanta, Ga. Trustee Mu, Inc., Page, Ga. Ho. of Reps., 1968; chmn. Madison County Reps., 1973-74; mem. Congl. Bus. Coun., 2002. Recipient Ronald Reagan award, Rep. Congl. Com., 2004; named Cir. of Achievement, 2009. Mem. AAAR (GR dir., 2004-10, Good Neighbor award 2005), NAR, Ga. Cattlemen's Assn., Madison County Cattlemen's Assn., Ga. Assn. Realtors (Fla. & Ga. Charolais growers dir. 2005-, dir. 2006-, Good Neighbor award 2005, Cir. Distinction award, 2009) Phoenix Club, Pres. Club, Ga. Charlois Assoc., Zeta Beta Tau, Athens Area Assn. Realtors (dir.), Riverbend Ranch Consumer, Ga. (CEO, pres.), Ministerio La Cosecha (dir.), Nat. Ga. Cattlemans Assn., Madison County, Charolais Cattle Assoc. Ga., Fla., Assn. Hispanic Real Estate Profl., 2011. Office: Impact Realty Melton & Assoc Inc 855 Sunset Dr Ste 11 Athens GA 30606-7718 Office Phone: 706-549-1799. Personal E-mail: waynemelton@hotmail.com.

MELTSNER, JIM, lobbyist; V.p. legis. affairs Northrop Grumman. Named one of Washington's Top Lobbyists, The Hill, 2010. Office: Northrup Grumman Corp Govt Rels 1000 Wilson Blvd Arlington VA 22209-2278 Office Phone: 703-875-8400.

MELTZER, BRAD, writer; b. Apr. 1, 1970; m. Cori Flam; 2 children. Grad., U. Michigan, Columbia Law Sch. Author: (novels) The Tenth Justice, 1998, Dead Even, 1999, The First Counsel, 2001, The Millionaires, 2002, Zero Game, 2004, The Book of Fate, 2006, The Book of Lies, 2008 (#1 Publishers Weekly bestseller), The Inner Circle, 2011 (#1 Publishers Weekly bestseller), The Fifth Assassin, 2013, (nonfiction) Heroes for My Son, 2010, Heroes for My Daughter, 2012; co-creator (TV series) Jack & Bobby, 2004—05; author: (comic books) Green Arrow, 2003, Identity Crisis, 2005, Justice League of America, 2006. Achievements include participation in a work group along with the CIA, FBI, various psychologists, and Department of Homeland Security intelligence staff to brainstorm new ways that terrorists might attack the US.

MELVIN, BILLY ALFRED, clergyman; b. Macon, Ga., Nov. 25, 1929; s. Daniel Henry and Leola Dale (Seidell) Melvin; m. Marcia Darlene Eby, Oct. 26, 1952; children: Deborah Ruth, Daniel Henry II. Student, Free Will Baptist Bible Coll., Nashville, 1947—49; BA, Taylor U., Upland, Ind., 1951, LLD (hon.), 1984; postgrad., Asbury Theol. Sem., Wilmore, Ky., 1951—53; BD, Union Theol. Sem., Richmond, Va., 1956; DD, Azusa Coll., Calif., 1968, Huntington Coll., 1995. Ordained to ministry Free Will Baptist Ch., 1951; pastor First Free Will Baptist Chs., Newport, Tenn., 1951—53, Richmond, Va., 1953—57, Bethany Ch., Norfolk, 1957—59. Exec. sec. Nat. Assn. Free Will Baptists, 1959—67; exec. dir. Nat. assn. Evangelicals, 1967—95. Baptist. E-mail: bam1929@verizon.net.

MELVIN, CHARLES EDWARD, JR., lawyer; b. Greensboro, NC, July 13, 1929; s. Charles Edward and Mary Ruth (Plunkett) M.; m. Jacklyn McDaniel, Mar. 1, 1958; 1 child, Dana W. BS, U. N.C., 1951, JD with honors, 1956. Bar: N.C. 1956. Of counsel Smith Moore Leatherwood LLP, Greensboro, 1958—. Capt. U.S. Army, 1952-54. Mem. N.C. Bar Assn. (chmn. real property sect. 1981), Am. Coll. Real Estate Lawyers, Greensboro C. of C. (pres. 1978). Office: Smith Moore Leatherwood LLP PO Box 21927 Greensboro NC 27420-1927 Office Phone: 336-378-5204. Business E-Mail: charlie.melvin@smithmoorelaw.com.

MELVIN, LELAND D., astronaut; b. Lynchburg, Va., Feb. 15, 1964; s. Deems and Grace Melvin. BS in Chemistry, U. Richmond, 1986; MS in Materials Sci. Engring., U. Va., 1991. Rschr. fiber optic sensors group, nondestructive evaluation scis. br. Langley Rsch. Ctr., NASA, Va., 1989—94, head vehicle health monitoring team, 1994—98; astronaut, mission specialist candidate Johnson Space Ctr. NASA, Houston, 1998—. Co-mgr., Educator Astronaut Program NASA; crew mem. Atlantis STS-122 mission to deliver the European Space Agency's Columbus Lab. to the Internat. Space Station, 2008; mission specialist STS-129 Atlantis Mission, 2009. Recipient Key to City of Lynchburg, Va., Inventions Disclosure award for Lead Insensitive Fiber Optic Phase Locked Loop Sensor; named Acad. All Am., NCAA Divsn. I; named to U. Richmond Athletic Hall of Fame. Mem.: Soc. for Exptl. Mechanics, Am. Chemical Soc., Nat. Technical Assn. (Hampton Roads chpt. sec. 1993). Achievements include being chosen by the Detroit Lions in the 11th round of the 1986 NFL college draft; participation in Toronto Argonauts and Dallas Cowboys football training camps. Avocations: piano, reading, music, bicycling, tennis, photography, snowboarding. Office: Astronaut Office/CB NASA Johnson Space Ctr Houston TX 77058

MELZER, JURGEN, professional tennis player; b. Vienna, May 22, 1981; s. Rudolf and Michaela. Profl. tennis player ATP, 1999—. Achievements include winning (doubles) St. Petersburg, 2005, Newport, 2006, Casablanca, 2006, Hertogenbosch, 2008, Tokyo, 2009, New Haven, 2009, Wimbledon, 2010, Zagreb, 2010; (singles) Bucharest, 2006, Vienna, 2009. Avocations: soccer, golf, movies. Office: c/o ATP Tour Inc 201 Atp Tour Blvd Ponte Vedra Beach FL 32082-3211

MENA, DANIEL, lawyer; Cert. in Spanish History, U. Salamanca, 1991; BA, Fla. Internat. U., 1992; JD, U. Pa., 1995. Bar: US Dist. Ct. (so. dist.) Fla. 1996, US Dist. Ct. (mid. dist.) Fla. 1997, US Dist. Ct. (no. dist.) Fla. 1998, US Ct. Appeals (11th cir.) 1995, US Supreme Ct. 1999, Fla. 1995. Assoc. atty. Baker & McKenzie, Miami, Fla., 1993—94; intern civil litig. US Atty.'s Office, Phila., 1994—95; assoc. atty. Gunster, Yoakley & Stewart, Miami, 1995—98; ptnr. Holland & Knight LLP, Miami, 1998—2007, Avila Rodriguez Hernandez Mena & Ferri, 2007—. Mem. civil procedure rules com. Fla. Bar, Tallahassee, 2004—10. Contbr. articles to profl. jours. Mem. legal bd. Amigos Together For Kids, Miami, Fla., 2003. Recipient State's Legal Leaders, Fla. Trend's Fla. Legal Elite, 2012, Fla. Super Lawyers, 2007—14; named Selected Up & Comer, South Fla. Legal Guide, 2002, Best Lawyers in America, 2010—14, Top Lawyers, South Fla. Legal Guide, 2002, 2007, 2009—14; named one of State's Legal Leaders, Fla. Trend's Fla. Legal Elite, 2006—08. Mem.: ABA, Cuban Am. Bar Assn., Hispanic Nat. Bar Assn., Dade County Bar Assn. (com. internat. litig.). Independent. Avocations: travel, scuba diving, fishing, boating. Office: Avila RodrijuezHernandez mena and Ferri LLP 2525 Ponce De Leon Blvd Ste 1225 Coral Gables FL 33134 Office Phone: 305-779-3575. Business E-Mail: dmena@arhmf.com.

MENAKER, MICHAEL, biology professor; b. Vienna, May 19, 1934; came to U.S., 1934; s. William and Esther (Astin) M.; m. Shirley Ann Lasch, June 4, 1955(dec. 2004); children: Ellen Margaret, Nicholas; m. Kazuko Watanabe, Oct. 8, 2010. BA in Biology, Swarthmore Coll., 1955; PhD in Biology, Princeton U., 1960; PhD in Math. and Natural Sci. (hon.), U. Groningen, Netherlands, 2009. Asst. instr. Princeton (N.J.) U., 1955-57; postdoctoral fellow Harvard U., Cambridge, Mass., 1960-62; asst. prof. zoology U. Tex.-Austin, 1962-68, assoc. prof., 1968-72, prof., 1972-79; prof. biology U. Oreg., Eugene, 1979-86, dir. interdisciplinary program for neuroscis., 1979-81, dir. Inst. Neurosci., 1981-85; Commonwealth prof. biology U. Va., Charlottesville, 1987—, chmn. dept., 1987-93; dir. Howard Hughes Undergrad. Rsch. Program in Biol. Sci., Charlottesville, 1989-94; core investigator Sci. and Tech. Ctr. in Biol. Timing U. Va., Charlottesville, 1991—. Benjamin Meaker vis. prof. U. Bristol, Eng., 1986. Assoc. editor Behavioral Neurosci., Jour. Biol. Rhythms; contbr. articles to profl. jours. Recipient Lifetime Achievement award Am. Soc. for Photobiology, 2002, Life Achievement in Sci. award Va.'s Outstanding Scientists and Industrialists, 2003, Peter C. Farrell prize Sleep Medicine, 2007, Disting. Scientist award U. Va., 2009; NSF fellow, 1958-59, 60-62; NIH fellow, 1960-62; Guggenheim Found. fellow, 1971-72, ASCHOFF HONMA prize, Biol. Rhythm Rsch., 2009. Fellow AAAS, Am. Acad. Arts and Scis., Japan Soc. Promotion of Scis. (sr.); mem. Soc. Neuroscis., Am. Physiol. Soc., Soc. Rsch. Biol. Rhythms. Avocations: literature, music, sailing. Office: University Va Dept Biology PLSB 408PO Box 400328 Charlottesville VA 22904-4328 Office Phone: 434-982-5767. Business E-Mail: mm7e@virginia.edu.

MENCH, JOHN WILLIAM, retail executive, electrical engineer; b. NYC, Feb. 27, 1943; s. John William and Edna (Ilgen) M.; m. Rose Irene Miller, Aug. 12, 1962 (dec. Jan. 1997); 1 child, William Ilgen; m. Ann Ward Frentress, Mar. 7, 1998. BSEE, U. S.C., 1969; MBA, Ohio U., 1983; PhD, Calif. Coast U., 1994. Registered profl. engr., Ohio, Ga.; cert. in heating, ventilating and air conditioning; accredited profl. Leadership in Energy and Environ. Design, 2006. Elec. engr. Uniroyal, Shelbyville, Tenn., 1969-74; facility engr. Kroger, Nashville, 1974-77, asst. mgr. facility engring. Atlanta, 1977-79, Kroger mktg. area mgr. facility engring. Columbus, Ohio, 1979-85; divsn. mgr. facility engring., v.p. Safeway Stores, Inc., Oakland, Calif., 1985-86; v.p. constrn., engring. Big V Supermarkets, Inc., Florida, NY, 1986-95; pres. Mench & Assocs. Inc., 1994-98. Assoc. prof. Pa. Coll. Tech., 1996-99; sr. lectr. Southern Poly. State U., 1999—; prof. Am. Contr. Exch., 1999-2003. Author: (tech. manuals) Comments on Commercial Refrigeration, 1998, Comments on Commercial Air Conditioning, 1998, Plan Review, 1995, others, (textbook) Finance for Construction Management 8th edit., 2009. Trustee Meth. Ch., 1987—93; bd. dirs. Goshen Day Care Ctr., 1988—95, Elec. Distbn. Systems, 1993—94; past v.p. Tri State V.W. Assn.; exec. adv. bd. Ohio U. Coll. Bus. Adminstrn., 1992—97, life mem.; v.p. Prime Time Group, 2003—05, pres., 2006. Recipient Outstanding Faculty award, Southern Poly. State U., 2007, 2010; named Ga. Engr. of Yr. in Edn., Ga. Profl. Engring. Soc., 2007, Engr. of Yr., Southern Poly. State U., 2006. Mem. ASHRAE, IEEE (life; sr. mem.), Assn. Energy Engrs. (sr.). Republican. Methodist. Business E-Mail: jmench@spsu.edu.

MENDELS, JOSEPH, psychiatrist, educator; b. Cape Town, South Africa, Oct. 29, 1937; came to U.S., 1964; s. Max and Lily (Turecki) M.; m. Ora Kark, Jan. 22, 1960; children: Gilla Avril, Charles Alan, David Ralph. MB, BChir, U. Cape Town, 1960; MD, U. Witwatersrand, Johannesburg, South Africa, 1965. Asst. prof., assoc. prof. psychiatry and pharmacology U. Pa., Phila., 1967-73; prof. U. Pa. and VA Hosp., Phila., 1973-80; med. dir. Fairmount Inst., Phila., 1980-81; hon. prof. psychiatry and human behavior Thomas Jefferson Med. Ctr., 1985—; med. dir. Med. Inst., Phila., 1981-95, Therapeutics PC, Phila., 1981-98. Cons., lectr. in field. Author, editor: Concepts of Depression, 1971, Biological Psychiatry, 1973, Psychobiology of Affective Disorders, 1981; contbr. over 200 articles to med. jours. Fellow Internat. Coll. Neuropsychopharmacology, Am. Coll. Neuropsychopharmacology. Home: 655 Longboot Club Rd #12A Longboat Key FL 34228 Personal E-mail: jos737@mac.com.

MENDELSOHN, JOHN, oncologist, hematologist, educator, medical researcher; b. Cin., Aug. 31, 1936; s. Joe and Sarah (Feibel) M.; m. Anne Charles, June 23, 1962; children: John Andrew, Jeffrey Charles, Eric Robert. BA in BioChemical Sciences, Harvard U., 1958, MD, 1963. Diplomate Am. Bd. Internal Medicine, Am. Bd. Hematology, Am. Bd. Med. Oncology. Intern, resident Peter Bent Brigham Hosp., Boston, 1963-65, 67-68; fellow in hematology Washington U. Sch. Medicine, St. Louis, 1968-70; asst. prof. to prof. medicine U. Calif., San Diego, 1970-85, Am. Cancer Soc. prof. clin. oncology La Jolla, 1982-85, dir. Cancer Ctr., 1977-85; prof. medicine, vice-chmn. Cornell U. Med. Coll., NYC, 1985-96; Winthrop Rockefeller chmn. dept. medical oncology, co-head, molecular pharmacology and therapeutics program Meml. Sloan Kettering Cancer Ctr., NYC, 1985-96; pres., prof. medicine U. Tex. M.D. Anderson Cancer Ctr., Houston, 1996—2011, co-dir. Sheikh Khalifa Bin Zayed Al Nahyan Inst. for Personalized Cancer Therapy, 2011—; vice chmn. BioHouston, 2001—. Bd. sci. counselors Nat. Cancer Inst., 1986—90, 1996—2001; cons., mem. sci. adv. bd. Progenics Pharms.; founder, 1st dir. U. Calif. San Diego Cancer Ctr.; mem. Nat. Dialogue on Cancer, 1999, Team on Cancer Rsch., 2001, U. Calif. San Diego External Adv. Com., 2000, Gov.'s Biotech. Panel, Ctr. for Houston's Future; mem. external adv. bd. John Hopkins Oncology Ctr., 1993—; faculty U. Tex. Graduate Sch. Biomedical Sciences. Editor-in-chief: (textbook) The Molecular Basis of Cancer; mem. editl. bd. Growth Factors, Jour. Biol. Response Modifiers, Expert Rev. Anticancer Therapy; editor-in-chief Clin. Cancer Rsch.; founding editor Clin. Cancer Rsch.; contbr. articles to profl. jours. Mem. Gov.'s Cancer Coun., Calif., 1981—85; bd. dirs. Am. Cancer Soc., San Diego, 1981—85, Houston Grand Opera, BioHouston, Ctr. for Houston's Future, Houston Forum; bd. dirs., mem. healthcare task force Greater Houston Partnership, 1997; bd. dirs., mem. exec. com. Houston Tech. Ctr., 1998—, nat. cancer policy bd., 1999—; mem. bd. overseers Harvard Med. Sch.; trustee Houston Grand Opera. Recipient Bourgine award for excellence in cancer rch., Svc. d'Oncologie Med. Pitie-Saltpetriere, 1997, Jill Rose award for oustanding breast cancer rsch., Breast Cancer Rsch. Found., 1999, Gold medal of Paris, 1997, Cancer Rsch. award, Bristol-Myers Squibb, 1997, Joseph H. Burchenal Clin. Rsch. award, Am. Assn. for Cancer Rsch., 1999, Simon Shubitz prize, Univ. Chgo., 2002, David A. Karnofsky award, Am. Soc. of Clin. Oncology, 2002, Freedom to Discover Achievement award in Cancer, Bristol-Myers Squibb, 2004; named Headliner of Yr. in Medicine, San

Diego, 1985; Fulbright scholar, U. Glasgow, Scotland, 1958—59. Mem.: ACP, AAAS (electorate nominating com. sect. on med. scis. 2001), Am. Clin. and Climatol. Assn., Harvard Overseers' Com., Royal Netherlands Acad. Arts and Scis., Inst. Medicine U.S. NAS, Century Assn., Am. Soc. Hematology, Am. Assn. Cancer Rsch. (4th Joseph H. Burchenal award 1999), Am. Soc. Clin. Oncology (lectr., David A. Karnofsky award 2002), Am. Soc. Clin. Investigation, Assn. Am. Physicians, Phi Beta Kappa. Achievements include rsch. in establishing inhibition of tumor growth by antibodies against growth factor receptors. Office: University of Texas MD Anderson Cancer Center 1515 Holcombe Blvd # 91 Houston TX 77030-4009 E-mail: jmendelsohn@mdanderson.org.

MENDELSOHN, LOUIS BENJAMIN, financial analyst; b. Providence, Mar. 26, 1948; s. Alvin Harold and Frances (Leitner) M.; m. Illyce Deborah Greenspan, Aug. 29, 1976; children: Lane Jeffrey, Ean Graham, Forrest Lee. BS, Carnegie Mellon U., 1969; MSW, SUNY, Buffalo, 1973; MBA with hons., Boston U., 1977. Rsch. asst. Mass. Gen. Hosp., Boston, 1969-71; regional health planner Comprehensive Health Planning Coun., Buffalo, 1973-74; adminstv. resident New Eng. Hosp., Boston, 1976; mgmt. specialist Humana Hosp. Bennett, Ft. Lauderdale, Fla., 1977-78; asst. exec. dir. Humana Women's Hosp., Tampa, Fla., 1978-80; pres., CEO Market Techs. Corp., Wesley Chapel, Fla., 1979—, CEO, 2004—, Predictive Techs. Group LLC, Wesley Chapel, 2004—. Author: Trend Forecasting with Techinal Analysis: Unleashing the Hidden Power of Intermarket Analysis to Beat the Market, 2000, Forex Trading Using Intermarket Analysis, 2006, Trend Forecasting with Intermarket Analysis: Predicting Global Markets with Technical Analysis, 2008, Trend Forecasting with Intermarket Analysis, 2nd edit., 2013; contbg. rschr.: The Encyclopedia of Technical Market Indicators, 1988; contbg. author: High Performance Futures Trading, 1990, Virtual Trading, 1995, Artificial Intelligence in the Capital Markets, 1995, Trade Your Way to Financial Freedom, 1999, Trading Chicago Style, 1999, SFO Personal Investor Series: Forex Trading, 2009; contbg. writer Tech. Analysis of Stocks and Commodities Mag.; editor newsletter Neural-Financial News, 1991; developer investment software ProfitTaker, 1979—, VantagePoint, 1988—. Recipient Louis B. Mendelsohn Entrepreneur award Hope HS, Providence; USPHS fellow, 1975-77. Mem. Market Technicians Assn., Colleague Internat. Fedn. of Tech. Analysts, Beta Gamma Sigma. Achievements include pioneering strategy back-testing and optimization in technical analysis software for personal computers, 1983; introduction of first commercial strategy testing trading software in financial industry for personal computers and first intermarket analysis software in financial industry for personal computers; patents in fiels. Office: Mkt Techs LLC 5807 Old Pasco Rd Wesley Chapel FL 33544-5108 Office Phone: 813-973-0496. E-mail: ww@tradertech.com.

MENDELSOHN, STUART, lawyer, municipal official; b. Jersey City, Aug. 8, 1952; s. Norman and Florence M.; m. Laura Dick, May 30, 1987; children: Michelle, Sarah. BS in Ocean Engring., Fla. Inst. Tech., 1974, MS in Environ. Engring., 1975; JD, George Mason U., 1984. Bar: Va. 1986, US Ct. Appeals (4th cir.) 1986, DC 1988. Project mgr. Naval Facilities Engring. Command, Washington, 1975-80; divsn. mgr. Analysis & Tech., Inc., Arlington, Va., 1980-87; mng. prin. Mendelsohn & Ishee, P.C., Fairfax, Va., 1987-99; supr. Fairfax County Bd. Suprs., Mclean, Va., 1996—2003; of counsel Piper Rudnick LLP, 1999—2004; ptnr. Holland & Knight, Mclean, Va., 2004—, exec. ptnr., Tyson Corner, Va. Office, 2011—; bd. mem. Tyson Partnership, 2011—, exec. com. mem., 2011—, sec., 2012—; mem. bd. dirs. George Mason U., 2012—; co-chair Fairlox County Bipartison Election Commn., 2013; mem. Tysons Commn. Transporation Tax Dist. Adv. Com., 2013—. Bd. suprs. Fairfax County, 1996—2003; No. Va. Planning Dist. Commn., 1996—2003; coord. coun. Transportation, 1997-2002; chmn. Fairfax county task force Tree Preservation, 1997—2003; active Boy Scouts Am., Patowomack Dist., 1996, 97; mem., vice chair sch. bd. Fairfax County, 1993-95; Sunday sch. tchr. Andrew Chapel United Meth. Ch., 1994-2001, adminstrv. bd. 1997-2000, staff-parish rels. com. 1995-97, cert. lay spkr., 2001-03; cmty. roundtable on edn. WJLA-TV, 1992-93; mem. Mclean Bible Church. Recipient Gold Medal award Spl. Olympics, Va., 1985, Spirit of Spl. Olympics award, 1987, Mem. Fairfax County C. of C. (chmn. 2009-10, bd. dirs. 1991—, exec. com. 1992-95, 2003-, dir. 1994-95, com. co-chair 1991-93, edn. com. 1987—, legis. affairs com. 1988—, edn. subcom. 1991—, congressional affairs com. 1988—), Herndon C. of C., McLean C. of C., Elem. Sch. PTA, Fairfax Bar Assn., Kiwanis (lt. gov. 1983-84, gov. 1991-92, charter pres. Fair Oaks club 1988, pres. McLean Club 1980-81), Jill's House (bd. dirs. 2004-10), McLean Bible Ch. Republican. Evangelical. Avocation: golf. Office: Holland & Knight LLP 1600 Tysons Blvd Ste 700 Tysons Corner Mc Lean VA 22102 Office Phone: 703-720-8071. Business E-Mail: stuart.mendelsohn@hklaw.com.

MENDELSON, LAURANS ADAM, manufacturing executive; b. NYC, July 7, 1938; s. Samuel and Blanche (Lederer) M.; m. Arlene Hope Lobel, Sept. 18, 1962; children: Eric Arthur, Victor Howard. BA, Columbia Coll., 1960; MBA, Columbia U., 1961. CPA, N.Y., Fla. Chmn., CEO HEICO Corp., Hollywood, Fla., 1990—, pres., 1991—. Prin. dir. HEICO Corp., mem. bd. govs., Aerospace Industries Assn.; mem. exec. com. bd. trustees Mt. Sinai Med. Ctr., Miami Beach, Fla. Emeritus trustee Columbia U., NY; past chmn. bd. trustees Mt. Sinai Med. Ctr., mem. Executive Com., Miami Beach; guest lectr. Exec. Forum MBA Program Fla. Atlantic U. Coll. Bus. Recipient Ernst & Young Entrepreneur of Yr. award, 1999, John Jay award, Columbia Coll., NYC. Mem. AICPA, Fla. Inst. CPAs, Greater Miami C. of C. (trustee), Aerospace Industries Assn. (bd. govs.). Jewish. Office: HEICO Corp 825 Brickell Bay Dr Ste 1644 Miami FL 33131 Office Phone: 305-374-1745. Office Fax: 305-374-6742. Business E-Mail: lmendelson@heico.com.

MENDELSON, RICHARD DONALD, former communications company executive; b. NYC, Dec. 2, 1933; s. George and Martha (Goodman) M.; m. Marilyn Miller, July 28, 1956; children: Sandra, Kenneth. BS, Wharton Sch. U. Pa., 1955; JD, NYU, 1959. Bar: N.Y., 1960; CPA, N.Y. Asst. atty. gen. N.Y. State Dept. Law, NYC, 1959-70; v.p., treas. Petry TV, NYC, 1971-75; v.p., dir. corp. devel. Katz Communications, Inc., NYC, 1975-77, sr. v.p. ops., 1977-79, sr. v.p., chief fin. officer, 1979-81, exec. v.p., chief operating officer, 1981-82, pres., chief oper. officer, 1982-89; free-lance writer, 1989—. Mem. Employee Stock Ownership Assn. Am. (pres. 1987-88, bd. dirs.), Ballen Isles Country Club (Palm Beach Gardens, Fla.l bd. dirs. 2000-06, pres. 2006). Home and Office: 71 Saint George Pl Palm Beach Gardens FL 33418-4024 Personal E-mail: themeri@aol.com.

MENDELSON, ROBERT ALLEN, polymer scientist, rheologist; b. Cleve., 1930; s. Julius and Theodora Anne M.; m. Lura Lauzon, 1971 (dec. 1999); children: John A. Blackstone, Marie L. Taylor. BS in Indsl. Chemistry, Case Inst. Tech., 1952, PhD in Phys. Chemistry, 1956. From sr. rsch. chemist to sci. fellow rsch. dept. Monsanto Co., Texas City, Tex., 1956-71, sci. fellow Springfield, Mass., 1972-89, sr. sci. fellow, 1989-91; rheology focus area leader Baytown (Tex.) Polymers Ctr. Exxon Chem., 1991-94, rheology prin. investigator, 1995-99; ret., 1999; cons., rheology, IP, 2000—02. Mem. com. for pub. policy Am. Inst. Physics, 1985-89; collaborator Univ. Rsch. Programs, Cornell U., 1989-91. Mem. editl. bd. Journal of Rheology, 1986-99; contbr. chpts. to books and articles to profl. jours.; patentee in field. Mem. AAAS, Soc. Rheology (pres. 1989-91, v.p. 1987-89, sec. 1974-78), Am. Chem. Soc. (Arthur Doolittle award div. organic coatings and plastics 1982). Home: 5001 Woodway Dr Unit 1803 Houston TX 77056-1701

MÉNDEZ, CARLOS (DON CARLOS MÉNDEZ MARTÍNEZ), political organization administrator, mayor; b. Aguadilla, PR; s. Don Pablo Méndez and Dona Rosita Martinez. Attended, U. Washington. Mayor, Aguadilla City, 1996—; chmn. Rep. Party of PR, 2007—. Pres. Fedn. of Mayors of PR, 2003—04. Republican. Office: Office of the Mayor Aguadilla PR 00605 Office Phone: 787-793-8084.*

MENDOZA, WILLIAM A., physics professor; b. NYC; s. Mario Mendoza and Macie Virginia Thrift; married. BSc in Psychology, Valdosta State U., Georgia; MSc in Rehab. Svcs., Fla. State U., Tallahassee, BSc in Physics, MSc in Physics, Fla. State U., Tallahassee, PhD in Physics, 1998. Adj. prof. Fla. State U., 1998; vis. prof. Jacksonville U., Fla., 1998—2000, asst. prof., 2000—06; tech. analyst Dept. State, Washington, 2006—07; prof., physics Fla. State Coll., Jacksonville, 2007—. Mem.: IEEE, United Faculty Fla., Mars Soc., Am. Chem. Soc., Am. Assn. Physics Tchrs., Am. Assn. Adv. Sci., Am. Phys. Soc., Nat. Space Soc., Planetary Soc., Sigma Xi. Office: Atom Sci Consulting PO Box 50906 Jacksonville Beach FL 32240 Business E-Mail: atom@sigmaxi.net, atom@ieee.org.*

MENEAR, CRAIG, retail executive; b. Flint, Mich. m. Dawn Menear; children: Courtney, Danielle. BA in Bus., Mich. State U., 1979. With IKEA Wholesale, Inc., Builders Emporium, Grace Home Ctrs., Montgomery Ward; divsn. mdse. mgr. Home Depot, Inc., Atlanta, merchandising v.p. S.W. divsn., merchandising v.p. hardware, sr. v.p. merchandising, 2003—07, exec. v.p. merchandising, 2007—. Office: Home Depot Inc 2455 Paces Ferry Rd NW Atlanta GA 30339-4024

MENEFEE, SAMUEL PYEATT, lawyer, academic; b. Denver, June 8, 1950; s. George Hardiman and Martha Elizabeth (Pyeatt) M.; m. Mary W., April 21, 2000; 1 child: Mary Elizabeth. BA in Anthropology and Scholar of Ho. summa cum laude, Yale U., 1972; diploma in Social Anthropology, Oxford U., Eng., 1973, BLitt, 1975; JD, Harvard U., 1981; LLM in Oceans, U. Va., 1982, SJD, 1993; MPhil in Internat. Rels., U. Cambridge, Eng., 1995. Bar: Ga. 1981, US Ct. Appeals (11th cir.) 1982, Va. 1983, La. 1983, US Ct. Mil. Appeals 1983, US Ct. Internat. Trade 1983, US Ct. Claims 1983, US Ct. Appeals (10th cir.) 1983, US Ct. Appeals (fed., 1st, 3d, 4th, 5th, 6th, 7th, 8th and 9th cirs.) 1984, DC 1985, Nebr. 1985, Fla. 1985, US Supreme Ct. 1985, US Ct. Appeals (DC cir.) 1986, Maine 1986, Pa. 1986. Assoc. Phelps, Dunbar, Marks, Claverie & Sims, New Orleans, 1983-85; of counsel Barham & Churchill PC, New Orleans, 1985-88; sr. assoc. Ctr. for Nat. Security Law U. Va. Sch. Law, 1985—, fellow Ctr. for Oceans Law and Policy, 1982-83, sr. fellow, 1985-89, Maury fellow, 1989—, adv. bd., 1997—. Vis. lectr. U. Cape Town, 1987; vis. asst. prof. U. Mo., Kansas City, 1990; law clk. Hon. Pasco M. Bowman US Ct. Appeals (8th cir.), 1994-95; vis. prof. Regent U., 1996-97, scholar-at-large, 1997—2003, prof., 1998—2003; adv. Am. Maritime Forum/Mariners' Mus., 1997-99; lectr. various nat. and internat. orgns.; mem. ICC Consultative Task Force on Comml. Crime, 1996—. Author: Wives for Sale: An Ethnographic Study of British Popular Divorce, 1981, Contemporary Piracy and International Law, 1995, Trends in Maritime Violence, 1996; co-editor: Materials on Ocean Law, 1982; nat. editor: Assn. Rsch. on Peasant Diaries, 1996-; mem. editl. bd. Internat. Jour. Marine and Costal Law, 1997-2003; contbr. numerous articles to profl. jours. Recipient Katharine Briggs prize Folklore Soc., 1992; Bates traveling fellow Yale U., 1971, Rhodes scholar, 1972; Cosmos fellow Sch. Scottish Studies U. Edinburgh, 1991-92, IMB fellow, ICC Internat. Maritime Bur., 1991—, Piracy Reporting Ctr. fellow, Kuala Lampur, 1993—, Huntington fellow The Mariners Mus., 1997. Fellow Royal Anthrop. Inst., Am. Anthrop. Assn., Royal Asiatic Soc., Royal Soc. Antiquaries Ireland, Soc. Antiquaries Scotland, Royal Geog. Soc., Soc. Antiquaries; mem. ABA (vice-chmn. marine resources com. 1987-90, chmn. law of sea com. subcom. naval warfare, maritime terrorism and piracy 1989—, mem. law of sea com. steering com. 1996—99, mem. working group on terrorism), Southeastern Admiralty Law Inst. (com. mem.), Maritime Law Assn. (proctor, com. mem., chmn. subcom. law of sea 1988-91, vice chmn. com. internat. law of sea 1991—99, chmn. com. internat. law of sea 1999-2003, chair working group piracy 1992—2003, UNESCO study group 1998—), Marine Tech. Soc. (co-chmn./chmn. marine security com. 1991—2004), Selden Soc., Am. Soc. Internat. Law, Internat. Law Assn. (com. mem., rapporteur Am. br. com. EEZ 1988-90, rapporteur Am. br. com. Maritime Neutrality 1992, observer UN conv. on law of sea meeting of states parties 1996, chmn./co-chmn. Am. br. com. on law of sea 1996—2001, rapporteur joint internat. working group on uniformity of law of piracy 1998—2001), Com. Maritime Internat., Am. Soc. Indsl. Security (com. mem.), US Naval Inst., USN League, Folklore Soc., Royal Celtic Soc., Internat. Studies Assn., Royal Scottish Geog. Soc., Royal African Soc., Egypt Exploration Soc., Arctic Inst. N.Am., Internat. Studies Assn., Am. Hist. Soc., Soc. for History of Discoveries, Soc. Nautical Rsch., Internat. Assn. Rsch. on Peasant Diaries, Christian Aid Mission, Nat. Eagle Scout Assn., Raven Soc., Jefferson Soc., Fence Club, Mory's Assn., Elizabethan Club, Yale Polit. Union, Leander Club, Cambridge Union, United Oxford and Cambridge Univ. Club, Yale Club NYC, Paul Morphy Chess Club, Pendennis Club, Round Table Club New Orleans, Phi Beta Kappa, Omicron Delta Kappa. Republican. Avocations: anthropology, archaeology, crew, hiking. Office: PO Box 5291 Charlottesville VA 22905-2591 also: U Va Ctr Nat Sec Law 580 Massie Rd Charlottesville VA 22903-1738 Office Phone: 434-924-7441. Business E-Mail: colp@virginia.edu.

MENENDEZ, JAMES N., information technology executive; With Nat. Computer Security Ctr., U.S. Govt.; v.p., global security solutions Computer Sciences Corp., dir., comml. security solutions, North America, 2008, v.p., gen. mgr., global security solutions, N.Am. pub. sector, 2008—. Office: Computer Sciences Corp 3170 Fairview Park Dr Falls Church VA 22042 Office Phone: 703-876-1000. Business E-Mail: james.menendez@csc.com.

MENENDEZ, JORGE, plastic surgeon; Grad., Southwestern Med. Sch., Dallas. Lic. Tex., Conn., cert. NY. Gen. surgery tng. Parkland Meml. Hosp., Dallas; tng. plastic surgery Mt. Sinai Med. Ctr., NYC; asthetic & craniofacial surgery externship Paris; fellowship in asthetic & craniofacial surgery Internat. Asthetic & Craniofacial Inst., Dallas; asst. attending surgeon plastic surgery dept. Manhattan Eye, Ear and Throat Hosp.; cons. to skincare companies. Mem. Interplast Inc. Office: The Aesthetic Plastic Surgery Center Ste 210 7744 Broadway San Antonio TX 78209 Office Phone: 210-829-7411. Office Fax: 210-829-7899.

MENENDEZ, JOSE, state legislator; b. Mar. 11, 1969; m. Cehlia Nicole Newman, Sept. 1996; children: Dominic Michael, Victoria Elise, Austin Maxwell. Grad. in Bus. Adminstrn. and Latin Am. Studies, So. Meth. U., Dallas. Zoning commissioner, Dist. 6 then vice-chair zoning commission, San Antonio, 1994—97; city councilman, Dist. 6, 1997—2001; nat. dir. Stewart Title Co.; mem. Dist. 124 Tex. House of Representatives, 2000—. Democrat. Office: 7121 US Hwy 90 W Ste 240 San Antonio TX 78227 also: Room EXT E1.420 Capitol Extension PO Box 2910 Austin TX 78768 Office Phone: 210-673-3579, 512-463-0634.

MENÉNDEZ CAMBÓ, PATRICIA, lawyer; b. NYC, June 7, 1966; BBA, U. Miami, 1986; JD, U. Pa., 1989. Bar: Fla. 1991, DC 1993. Atty. Greenberg Traurig, LLP, Miami, 1994—2000, shareholder, chair global practice group, 2002—, mem. exec. com.; chief US legal counsel Telefónica S.A., 2000—02. Bd. mem. Coun. of Americas, U. Pa. Sch. Law; adv. bd. mem. Inst. Internat. and Comparative Law; mem. Coun. Fgn. Rels.; spkr. in field. Contbr. articles to profl. jours. Trustee Nat. Alliance for Autism Rsch. Named one of The Top Up and Comers in So. Fla., So. Fla. Legal Guide, 2004, The Top 40 Lawyers Under 40, Nat. Law Jour., 2005, 100 Most Influential Lawyers in America, 2006, 50 Most Influential Women Lawyers in America, 2007, 50 Most Influential Minority Lawyers in America, 2008. Mem.: ABA (mem. Internat. Law Sect.), Internat. Bar Assn. Office: Greenberg Traurig LLP 333 Avenue of Americas 333 SE 2nd Ave Miami FL 33131 Office Phone: 305-579-0766. Office Fax: 305-579-5766. Business E-Mail: pmc@gtlaw.com.

MENG, RU-LING, research scientist; children: Meng Huang, He Huang. BA, Ctrl. So. U. of Tech. Mining and Metallurgy Coll., Hunan, China, 1958. Instr. Ctr. So. U. Tech. (Mining and Metallurgy Coll.), Hunan, China, 1958—59; rsch. asst. Acad. Sci., Inst. of Mining and Metallurgy, Beijing, 1959—73; rsch. assoc. Chinese Acad. Sci., Inst. Physics, Beijing, 1973—79, U. Houston, Dept. Physics, 1979—81, 1984—; vis. scholar U. Konstanz, Dept. Physics, Germany, 1981; rsch. assoc. Acad. Sci., Inst. Physics, Beijing, 1982—84; sr. rsch. scientist Tex. Ctr. for Superconductivity at the U. of Houston, Dept. of Physics, 1987—. Sr. cons. Chan-Sha Rsch. Inst. of Mining and Metallurgy, China, 1992. Recipient ranked 25th out of the 1000 most cited physicists, Inst. for Sci. Info., 1981—97, Hon. professorship, Zhong-Shan U. (Sun Yat-Sen U.), 1992, Ctr. So. U. of Tech., 1992, Beijing Polytechnic U., 1998; named one of the most worlds most cited authors, Inst. for Sci. Info. Current Contents, 2000. Mem.: Chinese Assn. of Professionals in Sci. and Tech. (founder/1st pres.), Materials Rsch. Soc., Phi Beta Delta Internat. Assn. Achievements include discovery of high temperature superconducting Y-Ba-Cu-O system; first to succeed in fabricating texturing Y-Ba-Cu-O bar, obtained first record trapped field of 8T at 4.2k by 20 mmx6 mm YBCO discs, first to grow C60 (or carbon 60) single crystal with no defect; development of and the patent for processing techniques for highest transition superconducting temperature Hg-Ba-Ca-Cu-O and co-developed the first Hg-1212 film; first to succeed in fabricating Hg-1223 tape; first to succeed in fabricating Bi-sr-ca-cu-o on a low cost ni metal substrate. Office: Texas Ctr for Superconductivity U of Houston High Pressure Low Temperature Lab Houston TX 77204 E-mail: rmeng@uh.edu.

MENIUS, ESPIE FLYNN, JR., electrical engineer; b. New Bern, NC, Mar. 5, 1923; s. Espie Flynn and Sudie Grey (Lyerly) M.; adopted children: James Benfield, Ruben Hughes, James Sechler, Steve Walden. BEE, N.C. State U., 1947; MBA, U. S.C., 1973. Registered profl. engr., N.C., S.C., Tenn., Ga., Fla. With Carolina Power & Light Co., 1947-63, asst. to dist. mgr. Raleigh, Henderson, NC, 1947-50, Sumter, SC, 1947-50, elec. engr. Asheville, Southern Pines and Dunn, NC, 1950-52, dist. engr. Hartsville, SC, 1952-63; sr. elec. engr. Sonoco Products Co., 1963-74, engring. group leader, 1974-89, sr. profl. engr., 1989-91; profl. cons. and elec. engr., 1991—. Instr. Florence-Darlington Tech. Ednl. Ctr. Author: Adoption of Older Children; contbr. articles to profl. jours. Active Hartsville Vol. Fire Dept., 1958-94; Fire dept. and Law Enforcement Chaplain 1985—; Eagle Scout Boy Scouts Am., 1938, scout troop leader New Bern, 1940-41, Raleigh, 1941-47, Henderson, 1948-49, Sumter, 1949-50, Asheville, N.C., 1950, Southern Pines, N.C., 1951-52, Hartsville, 1952-64; bd. mgrs. Nazareth Children's Home, Rockwell, N.C., 1980—2011; chmn. bd. examiners City of Hartsville, 1980-90; advocate Thornwell Children's Home, Clinton, S.C., 1990-98; bd. dir. Darlington (S.C.) County Youth Home, 1992-98; active Hartsville Leadership Coun., 1993-2000; deacon, elder, trustee, tchr. men's Bible class First Presbyn. Ch., Hartsville. Served with US Army, 1943-46. Recipient Citzenship award S.C. State Firemen's Assn., 1993; named Hartsville Citizen of Yr., Rotary, 1960; named to S.C. Fire Fighters Hall of Fame, 1995. Mem. IEEE, AAAS, VFW, Nat. Assn. Engrs., Am. Legion, Knight of St. Patrick, Scabbard and Blade, Eta Kappa Nu, Pine Burr, Phi Eta Sigma, Theta Tau, Beta Gamma Sigma. Presbyn. Home and Office: 423 W Richardson Cir Hartsville SC 29550-5437 Office Phone: 843-332-8502.

MENSCHER, BARNET GARY, steel company executive; b. Laurelton, NY, Sept. 5, 1940; s. Samuel and Louise (Zaimont) M.; m. Diane Elaine Gachman, June 12, 1966; children: Melissa Denise, Corey Lane, Scott Jay. Student, Centenary Coll., 1958-59; BBA, U. Tex., 1963. Vice pres. mktg. Ella Gant Mfg., Shreveport, La., 1964-66; warehouse mgr., dir. material control Gachman Steel Co., Fort Worth, 1966-68, gen. mgr. Houston, 1968-70; v.p. sales Gachman Metal Co., Houston, 1971-76; pres. Menko Steel Service, Inc., Houston, 1979—; CEO NEXTLEVEL, Houston, 1998—. Investment cons. D & L Enterprises, 1966—. Mem. solicitation com. United Fund, 1969-76; mem. Nat. Alliance of Businessmen Jobs Program, 1969—. Served with AUS, 1963-65. Mem. Tex. Assn. Steel Importers, Purchasing Agts. Assn. Houston, Credit Assn. Houston, Am. Mgmt. Assn., Assn. Steel Distbrs., Nat. Assn. Elevator Contractors, Phi Sigma Delta, Alpha Phi Omega. Home: Apt 1002 3388 Sage Rd Houston TX 77056 Home Phone: 713-464-8700. Personal E-mail: bdmenscher@gmail.com.

MENTZ, HENRY A., III, plastic surgeon; b. New Orleans, Apr. 9, 1958; s. Henry A. Jr. and Ann (Lamantia) M.; m. Paula Comiskey, May 20, 1989; children: Henry A. IV, James August. BS, La. State U., 1980, MD, 1984. Diplomate Am. Bd. Facial Plastic and Reconstructive Surgery, Am. Bd. Otolaryngology, Am. Bd. Plastic Surgery. Intern otolaryngology Tulane U., New Orleans, 1984-89; resident plastic surgery St. Joseph's Hosp., Houston, 1989-91; founder, ptnr. Aesthetic Ctr. for Plastic Surgeons, Houston, 1991—. Clin. assoc. prof. Baylor U., Houston, 1992—, St. Joseph U., Houston, 1992—; chief surgery Sharpstown Gen. Hosp., Houston, 1994—, chief plastic surgery, 1994—; pres., Houston Soc. of Plastic Surgeons, 2000-01. Fellow ACS, Internat. Coll. Surgeons, Am. Acad. Otolaryngology; mem. Am. Soc. Plastic and Reconstructive Surgeons, Am. Soc. Plastic Surgeons, Am. Soc. Aesthetic Plastic Surgeons, Internat. Soc Aesthetic Plastic Surgeons, Am. Acad. Otolaryngology Head and Neck Surg, AMA, Tex. Medical Assn., Houston Soc. Plastic Surgeons, Harris County Medical Soc. Republican. Episcopalian. Office: Aesthetic Ctr for Plastic Surgery Ste 300 Kimberly Profl Bldg 12727 Kimberley Houston TX 77024

MEO, MARK, engineering educator; b. Marblehead, Mass., June 20, 1948; s. Dominic and Mary Meo; m. Patti S. Meo, May 7, 1983; 1 child, Alexander M. BA, Northeastern U., Boston, 1971; MS, La. State U., Baton Rouge, 1974; PhD, U. Calif., Davis, 1983. Postdoc. fellow Woods Hole Oceanog. Instn., Mass., 1983—85, rsch. fellow, 1985—, dir., 1995—2000; sci. and pub. policy prof., dept. civil engring., environ. sci. U. Okla., Norman, 1985—. Contbr. article to academic jour., Tulsa Turnaround: From Disaster to Sustainability. Mem.: AAAS (assoc.). Office: Univ of Oklahoma 100 E Boyd St Norman OK 73019 Business E-Mail: mmeo@ou.edu.

MEPHAM, TOM, aerospace and defense manufacturing company executive; b. Palatine, Ill. BS in Mech. Engring., U. Iowa, MBA. Mktg. mgr. Honeywell Internat., Inc.; tech. dir. Rockwell Collins, Inc.; joined Goodrich Corp., 1997, v.p., gen. mgr., regional, bus. & mil., pres., aircraft interior products, 2006—. Office: Goodrich Corp Four Coliseum Ctr22730 W Tyvola Rd Charlotte NC 28217-4578 Office Phone: 704-423-7000. Office Fax: 704-423-7002. Business E-Mail: tom.mepham@goodrich.com.

MERCER, MELVIN RAY, electrical engineer, educator; b. Lubbock, Tex., Sept. 5, 1946; s. Dixie Melvin and Ollie Faye (Sheppard) M.; m. Sharry Billene Cannon, Sept. 9, 1967; children: Rebecca Raylene, Elizabeth Anne. BSEE, Tex. Tech U., 1968; MSEE, Stanford U., 1971; PhD in Elec. Engring., U. Tex., 1980. Registered profl. engr., Tex. Rsch. and devel. engr. GTE Sylvania, Mountain View, Calif., 1968-73; mem. tech. staff Hewlett-Packard Labs., Palo Alto, Calif., 1973-77; lectr. U. Tex., San Antonio, 1977-80; mem. tech. staff Bell Labs., Murray Hill, N.J., 1980-83; asst. prof. elec. and computer engring. U. Tex., Austin, 1983-87, assoc. prof., 1987-91, prof., 1991—95; prof. computer engring. dept. elec. engring. Tex. A&M U., College Station, 1995—2005, computer engring. chair elec. engring., 1995—2005, prof. emeritus, 2005—; tech. cons. & owner Mercer & Assocs., 2005—. Lectr. Kilgore (Tex.) Jr. Coll., 1977; cons. Rothe Devel. Co., San Antonio, 1979, Lockheed Missiles and Space Co., Austin, 1983, IBM, Austin, 1984, 88-90, Harris Semicondr., Dallas, 1983-86, 99-2000, State of Tex., Austin, 1984-85, CBS, N.Y.C., 1985-86, Teltech Resource Network, Mpls., 1986-93, Motorola Semicondr., Austin, 1987-88, 91, 99, TSSI, Beaverton, Oreg., 1988-94, MCC, Austin, 1989, Cimflex Teknowledge, Pitts., 1989-90, Rockwell, Newport Bch., Calif., 1991, 95, Integra-Test, L.I., N.Y., 1993, Teradyne, 1993-94, Sematech, 1994, AT&T, Oklahoma City, 1995-97, Sanke & Luck, Houston, 1997-98, Taylor & Dunham, 1995, 97, 99-2000, Fulbright & Jaworski, 1997, 99-2002, Hale & Dorr, 2001, 03, Akin, Gump, Strauss, Haner & Feld, 2000, Harris Corp, Melbourne, Fla., 1999-2002, Sigma Tel, Austin, 1999-2000, others; advisor NSF, Washington, 1987-88, mem. engring. initiation awards evaluation panel, 1987, 1993; mem. program com. 1st MCC-Univ. Rsch. Symposium, 1987; lectr. in field; expert witness; cons. Contbr. articles to profl. jours.; patentee in field. Recipient Presdl. Young Investigator award NSF, 1986, rsch. award Office Naval Rsch., 1986-95, Advanced Projects Rsch. Adminstrn., 1992-95; Werner W. Dornberger Centennial tchg. fellow U. Tex., 1984-90, Engring. Found. endowed faculty fellow, 1990-91, Temple Found. endowed prof. engring., 1991-95; grantee Univ. Rsch. Inst., 1983, Bur. Engring. Rsch., 1984, AT&T Info. Sys., 1985-88, Microelectronics and Computer Tech. Corp., 1985-90, Internat. Test Found., 1986-89, Semicondr. Rsch. Corp., 1989-95, 2000—, IBM, 1989-92, 2001—, Tex. Advanced Tech. Program, 1990-92, 98-2000, 02—, Motorola, 1991-98. Fellow IEEE (editor Design and Test of Computers mag. 1985-88, mem. program com. design for testability workshop Vail, Colo. 1989-95); mem. Computer Soc. of IEEE (vice chmn. Ctrl. Tex. chpt. 1983-85, chmn. 1985-86), Internat. Test Conf. (program com. 1986-89, program vice chmn. 1988, program chmn. 1989, steering com. 1988-93, mktg. vice chmn. 1990, planning chmn. 1992-93, best paper award 1982, hon. mention 1988), Internat. Conf. on CAD (program com. 1987), Design Automation Conf. (best paper award 1991, best paper award Very Large Scale Integrated Cir. Test Symposium 1999), Austin C. of C. (recruitment resource 1983-87), Tau Beta Pi, Eta Kappa Nu, Phi Kappa Phi, Phi Eta Sigma. Avocations: racquetball, swimming, scuba. Office: Tex A&M U Dept Elec Engring 214 Zachry Bldg College Station TX 77843-3259 Home: 3515 B Longmire Dr Ste B #333 College Station TX 77845 Business E-Mail: ray@rmercer.com.

MERCURIO, RENARD MICHAEL, real estate company executive; b. NYC, June 22, 1947; s. Pasquale J. and Ann F. Mercurio; m. Abbie Gonzalez, June 29, 1968; children— Kristin, Allison. BA, Queens Coll., NYC, 1968; MBA, U. Rochester, 1969. CPA, N.Y.; lic. real estate broker, Calif. Sr. accountant Peat, Marwick & Mitchell, NYC, 1969-73; mgr. Gulf & Western Industries, Inc., NYC, 1973-78; v.p., treas. Famous Players Ltd., Toronto, Ont., Canada, 1978-81; exec. v.p. Famous Players Realty Ltd., Toronto, 1981-84; pres. Design Twenty-Seven Ltd., Toronto, 1984—; v.p. Renric Holdings, Ltd., 1987—; CFO Schickedanz Real Estate, Palm Beach Gardens, Fla., 1999—2003. Mem. AICPA, NY State Soc. CPAs. Personal E-mail: amercu6@aol.com.

MEREDITH, MICHAEL LEE, state legislator; b. Apr. 25, 1985; BS in Bus. Mgmt., Western Ky. U., Bowling Green, 2007. Mktg. officer Bank of Edmonson County, 2001—; mem. Dist. 19 Ky. House of Reps., Frankfort, 2011—. Mem. Brownsville Missionary Bapt. Ch.; bd. dirs. LifeSkills, Inc., Edmonson County Tourism Commn. Republican. Baptist. Office: Kentucky House of Reps Annex Rm 413A 702 Capitol Ave Frankfort KY 40601 Office Phone: 502-561-8100 ext. 719.

MEREDITH, THOMAS J., investment company executive; b. 1950; m. Lynn Maureen Mullen; 4 children. BA in Polit. Sci., St. Francis Coll., Loretto, Pa., 1972; JD, Duquesne U. Law, 1975; LLM in Taxation, Georgetown U., 1977; PhD (hon.), St. Francis, Duquesne U. Bus. Sch. Bar: Calif., DC, Pa. Dir. tax rsch. and planning Castle & Cooke, Inc.; sr. tax cons. Arthur Young & Co.; co-founder, gen. mgr. Amdahl Capital Corp., 1979—89; v.p., treas. Sun Microsystems, Inc., 1989—92; sr. v.p., CFO Dell Computer Corp., Round Rock, Tex., 1992—2000, sr. v.p., bus. devel & strategy, 2000—01; mng. dir. Dell Ventures, 2000—01; co-founder, gen. ptnr. Meritage Capital, L.P., 1998—; CEO MFI Capital, LLC; acting CFO Motorola, Inc., Schaumburg, Ill., 2007—08. Bd. dir. Freemarkets, Inc., Divine, Inc., VoxPath Networks, Tipping Point, 2001—, Motive, Inc., 2003—, Motorola, Inc., 2005—; adj. prof., McCombs Sch. Business Univ. Texas; adv. bd. Wharton Sch., U. Pa., U. Tex., adj. prof., McCombs Sch. Bus. Chair, pres. Meredith Private Found., 1998—; founding investor & chair Austin Idea Network. Mem.: Fin. Execs. Inst. Office: MFI Capital LLC 248 Addie Roy Rd Austin TX 78746

MEREDITH, WESLEY, state legislator; b. Tupelo, Miss., Dec. 22, 1963; m. Angela Meredith. Mem. Internat. Soc. of Arborists, March of Dimes, Cape Fear Bot. Gardens, Cape Fear Kiwanas; founder, owner Cardinal Landscaping; Councilman Fayetteville City Coun., 2005—; mem. Dist. 19 NC State Senate, 2011—. Sergeant US Army. Republican. Address: PO Box 26210 Fayetteville NC 28314 Office: NC Senate 16 W Jones St Room 2106 Raleigh NC 27601-2808 Office Phone: 910-433-1990, 919-733-5776, 910-867-9595. Business E-Mail: Wesley.Meredith@ncleg.net.

MERGLER, H. KENT, investment counselor; b. Cin., July 1, 1940; s. Wilton Henry and Mildred Amelia (Pulliam) M.; m. Judith Anne Metzger, Aug. 17, 1963; children: Stephen Kent, Timothy Alan, Kristin Lee. BBA with honors, U. Cin., 1963, MBA, 1964. CFA, C.I.C. Portfolio mgr. Scudder, Stevens & Clark, Cin., 1964-68, exec. v.p. Chgo., 1970-73; v.p. Gibralter Rsch. & Mgmt., Ft. Lauderdale, Fla., 1968-70; ptnr. Stein Roe & Farnham, Ft. Lauderdale, 1973-84; ptnr., pres., dir., prin., mem. exec. com. Stein Roe & Farnham, Inc., Chgo., 1984-91; pres. Stein Roe Investment Trust, 1988—91; mng. ptnr., chief investment officer Loomis, Sayles & Co., L.P., Palm Beach Gardens, Fla., 1992-2000; pres. Northstar Capital Mgmt., Inc., 2000—04, chmn., 2005—12. Arbitrator Nat. Assn. Security Dealers, Inc., 1976-82. Chmn. adminstrv. bd. Christ United Meth. Ch., Ft. Lauderdale, 1981—83; mem. fin. com. Kenilworth Union Ch., 1989—92; elder, chmn. fin. com. First Presbyn. Ch., Stuart, 2001—04, 2006—09; chmn. Presbytery of Tropical Fla.-Coral Gables Fund, 2006—11; chmn. investment com. Cmty. Found. Broward, 1992—2001, 2006—09, bd. dirs., chmn. investment com., 1994—2001; mem. Martin County Econ. Coun., 1992—2000; bd. dirs. Pine Crest Prep. Sch., 1982—84, bd. advisors, 1984—87; corp. adv. bd. U. Cin. Coll. Bus. Adminstrn., 1991—94; bd. dirs. Hibiscus House Children's Found., 1993—99, 2001—07, chmn. investment, endowment com., 1994—99, 2001—12. Mem. Fin. Analysts Soc. So. Fla. (bd. dirs. 1974-78, pres. 1975), Bond Club Ft. Lauderdale (bd. dirs. 1978-82), Yorktown University (bd. trustees, 2006-2012), Cullasaja Club (Highlands, N.C.), Mariner Sands Golf Club, Beta Gamma Sigma, Beta Theta Pi (found. bd. dirs. 2008-). Republican. Presbyterian. Home: 6306 SE Oakmont Pl Stuart FL 34997

MERKEL MORAN, CHRISTA ILSE, investor, linguist, educator; b. Leipzig, Saxony, Germany, Jan. 5, 1946; arrived in US, 1968; d. Erich Harry and Ilse Dora (Waehnert) Merkel; m. William Joseph Moran, May 5, 1967 (dec. Mar. 4, 1979); children: Leslie Paige, Linda Christa. BA, U. Tuebingen, 1968; postgrad., U. Alaska, 1968—69. German linguistics. Clk. Anchorage Westward Hotel, 1969—71; sales mgr. Windsor Park Hotel, Washington, 1971—75; linguist, instr. Def. Lang. Inst., Dept. Def., Washington, 1975—79; investor in real estate, sports cars Atlanta, 1979—. Real estate agt., Northside Realty Co., Atlanta, 1992—. Author: Die Millie Miglia, 1969; Der Nuerburgring, 1975; German Culture, 1977. Chairperson for a United Germany Com., Washington, Atlanta, Leipzig chpt.; fundraiser UNICEF. Named Sportswriter of Yr., ADAC of Germany, 1977. Democrat. Home: PO Box 34165 Pensacola FL 32507-4165 Office: KeyConcept Realty 13880 Perdido Key Dr Pensacola FL 32507 Home Phone: 850-261-0700; Office Phone: 850-492-0025. Personal E-mail: christamoran@bellsouth.net.

MERRELL, RONALD CLIFTON, surgeon, educator; b. Birmingham, Ala., June 17, 1946; s. Greene Lawrence and Florence (Jones) M.; m. Marsha Karen Cox, Dec. 24, 1966; children: Alexandria, Alison, R. Clifton. BS in Chemistry, U. Ala., 1967, MD, 1970. Diplomate Am. Bd. Surgery. Resident and fellow in surgery Wash. U., St. Louis, 1970-77; asst. prof. surgery Stanford U., Calif., 1979-84; assoc. prof. surgery U. Tex. Med. Sch., Houston, 1984-88, prof. surgery, 1988—93, M.D. Anderson Cancer Ctr., Houston, 1988—93; assoc. dean clin. affairs U. Tex. Med. Sch., Houston, 1988-92, vice dean, 1992-93; Lampman prof. surgery, chmn. dept. surgery Yale U., 1993—99; Stuart McGuire prof. surgery, chmn. dept. surgery Va. Commonwealth U., Richmond, 1999—2003, prof. surgery, 2003—10, emeritus prof. surgery, 2010—; dir. Med. Informatics Tech. Applications Consortium, 1997—2008. Editor-in-chief Telemedicine and e-Health. Contbr. chapters to books, articles to profl. jours. Maj. US Army, 1977—79. Recipient Basil O'Connor award March of Dimes, 1979, Rsch. Career Devel. award NIH, 1979-84, Henry J. Kaiser award Stanford U., 1982, 83, John P. McGovern Outstanding Tchr. award U. Tex. Med. Sch., 1988, Dean's Teaching Excellence award, 1983-89, Pub. Svc. medal NASA, 1998, 2005, 06, Disting. medal as Friend of Democritus, U. Thrace, Greece, 1998, Lifetime Achievement award Internat. Soc. Telemedicine and e-Health, 2013; grantee NASA, Dept. Def., Internat. Coop. medal, Russian Space Agy., 2005. Fellow: ACS, Am. Telemedicine Assn., Soc. Univ. Surgeons; mem.: Am. Surg. Assn., Am. Assn. Endocrine Surgery, Alpha Omega Alpha. Democrat. Episcopalian. Achievements include research in telemedicine and in the transplantation of islets of Langerhans. Home: PO Box 165 Mentone AL 35984

MERRICK, AARON S.G., energy executive; B in Acctg., Bob Jones U. With KPMG Peat Marwick, 1984—90; asst. dir., gas flow mgmt. T-NETIX, Inc., 1991—94, v.p., 1995—2000; owner Aaron Merrick Computer Consulting, 2002; pres. Merrick Applied Consulting, Inc., 2005—06; dir., info. tech. Apache Corp., 2006—09, v.p., info. tech., 2009—. Office: Apache Corp 2000 Post Oak Blvd Ste 100 Houston TX 77056-4400 Office Phone: 713-296-6000. Office Fax: 713-296-6496. Business E-Mail: aaron.merrick@usa.apachecorp.com.

MERRICKS, DONALD W., state legislator; b. Danville, Va., Jan. 13, 1952; m. Patti Faye Cassada; children: Lori Allison, Donald W. II. BS in Bus., Averett Coll., 1974, MBA, 1991. Pres./owner J. W. Squire Co., Inc.; mem. Dist. 16 Va. House of Delegates, 2009—. Pres. Danville Host Lions; mem. Danville-Pittsylvania County United Way, Mount Hermon Vol. Fire Dept. Republican. Baptist. Office: 2276 Franklin Tpk Danville VA 24540 also: General Assembly Bldg PO Box 406 Richmond VA 23218 Office Phone: 434-836-3370, 804-698-1016. E-mail: DelDMerricks@house.virginia.gov.

MERRIFIELD, JEFFREY S., engineering company executive, former commissioner; b. Antrim, NH, 1963; m. Diana M. Merrifield; 3 children. BA magna cum laude, Tufts U., 1985; JD, Georgetown U.Law Ctr., 1992. Bar: NH, DC. Legis. asst. to Senator Gordon Humphrey US Senate, Washington, 1987—90, legis. asst. to Senator Robert Smith, 1990—92; assoc. McKenna & Cuneo LLP, Washington, 1992—95; majority coun. & staff dir. Senate Subcommittee on Superfund, Waste Control and Risk Assessment, Washington, 1995—98; commr. US Nuclear Regulatory Commn., Rockville, 1998—2007; sr. v.p. Power Group The Shaw Group Inc., Charlotte, NC, 2007—; dir. Am. Ecology, 2007—. Mem.: DC Bar Assn., NH State Bar Assn. Achievements include appointed by president Clinton and reappointed by president Bush for two terms as an NRC Commission. Office: The Shaw Group Inc 128 S Tryon St Charlotte NC 28202 Office Phone: 704-378-5227.

MERRILL, ALLAN P., construction executive; BS in Economics, U. Pa. Mng. dir., co-head global resources group Dillon Read & Co., 1987—2000, UBS, 1987—2000; pres. Homebuilder.com, 2000—01; exec. v.p., corp. develop. & strategy Move Inc., 2001—07; exec. v.p., CFO Beazer Homes USA, Inc., Atlanta, 2007—. Bd. mem. Homebuilding Cmty. Found.; mem. policy adv. bd. Joint Ctr. Housing Studies Harvard Univ. Office: Beazer Homes USA Inc 1000 Abernathy Rd NE Ste 260 Atlanta GA 30328-5648 Office Phone: 770-829-3700. Office Fax: 770-481-2808. Business E-Mail: AMerrill@beazer.com.

MERRILL, JAMES H., state legislator; b. Pensacola, Fla., Jan. 15, 1967; s. James H. and Annette McGregor Merrill; m. Noel Marie Gaillard Merrill; children: Delaney Marie, Haley McGregor. BA, U. SC, 1989, MPA, 1992. Press sec. to rep. Floyd Spence US House of Representatives, 1989—92, dist. adminstr. to rep. Mark Sanford, 1994; polit. dir. SC Rep. Party, 1992—98; mem. Dist. 99 SC House of Reps., 2000—, majority leader, 2004. Pub. rels. cons., owner Geechie Comm., 1994—. Mem.: SC Policy Coun., U. SC Alumni Assn., Daniel Island Neighborhood Assn. Republican. Roman Catholic. Office: 308D Blatt Bldg Columbia SC 29201 Mailing: 2401 Daniel Island Dr Daniel Island SC 29492 Home Phone: 843-849-7306; Office Phone: 803-734-3072, 843-884-9108. E-mail: JM1@schouse.org.

MERRILL, JOHN H., state legislator; b. Wedowee, Ala., Nov. 12, 1963; s. Horace and Mary Merrill; m. Cindy Benford; children: Brooks, Allie Grace. BA in History & Polit. Sci., U. Ala., 1990. Govtl. affairs intern C. of C. West Ala., 1987—88, dir. bus. devel., 1993—94; nat. account exec. Randall Pub. Co., 1988—90; asst. dir. The Tuscaloosa County Indsl. Authority, 1990—93; dir. cmty. rels. and cmty. edn. Tuscaloosa County Bd. of Edn., 1994—; mem. Dist. 62 Ala. House of Representatives, 2011—. Bd. advisors Tuscaloosa Solid Waste Disposal Authority, 1990—91; chmn. The Children's Trust Fund Ala. Dept. Child Abuse and Neglect Prevention, 2010—. Mem. Tuscaloosa County Schs. Drug Free Schs. Adv. Coun., 1991—94, Tuscaloosa County Schs. Vocat. Adv. Coun., 1993—94, Tuscaloosa County Schs. Audit Edn. Adv. Coun., 1995—2002, State Rep. Exec. Com.; deacon Cavalry Bapt. Ch. Mem.: Nat. Sch. Pub. Rels. Assn. (SE v.p. 2009—), Ala. Sch. Communicator's Assn. (pres. 2000—01, 2009—10), Tuscaloosa County Edn. Assn., Nat. Cmty. Edn. Assn., Ala. Cmty. Edn. Assn. Republican. Baptist. Office: PO Box 2117 Tuscaloosa AL 35403 also: Ala House of Reps Rm 205-B 11 S Union St Montgomery AL 36130 Office Phone: 334-242-7554. Business E-Mail: john@tuscaloosagop.org.

MERRILL, JOSEPH MELTON, medical educator; b. Andalusia, Ala., Dec. 8, 1923; s. Walter C. and Mary T. (McLaney) M.; m. Gudrun Wallgren, Sept. 15, 1960; children: Maria, Caroline. MD, Harvard Med. Sch., 1948. Diplomate Am. Bd. Internal Medicine. With VA Med. Ctr., Nashville, 1960-64; chief Gen. Clin. Rsch. Ctrs. NIH, Bethesda, 1964-67; dean sci. affairs Baylor Coll. Medicine, Houston, 1967-77, prof., 1967—. Capt. USAF, 1951-53.

MERRITT, GILBERT STROUD, federal judge; b. Nashville, Tenn., Jan. 17, 1936; s. Gilbert Stroud and Angie Fields (Cantrell) M.; m. Louise Clark Fort, July 10, 1964 (dec.); children: Stroud, Louise Clark, Eli. BA, Yale U., 1957; LLB, Vanderbilt U., 1960; LLM, Harvard U., 1962. Bar: Tenn. 1960. Asst. dean Vanderbilt U. Law Sch., 1960-61, lectr., 1963-69, 71-75, assoc. prof. law, 1969-70; assoc. Boult Hunt Cummings & Conners, Nashville, 1962-63, adj. prof., 2003—; asst. metro. atty. City of Nashville, 1963-66; US Dist. atty. for (mid. dist.) Tenn., 1966-69; ptnr. Gullett, Steele, Sanford, Robinson & Merritt, Nashville, 1970-77; judge US Ct. Appeals (6th cir.), Nashville, 1977-2001, chief judge, 1989—96, sr. judge., 2001—; chmn. exec. com. US Judicial Conf., 1993—96; chmn. internat judicial rel. com. US Judiciary, 1993—95. Exec. sec. Tenn. Code Commn., 1977. Mng. editor: Vanderbilt Law Rev, 1959-60; contbr. articles to law jours. Del. Tenn. Constl. Conv., 1965; chmn. bd. trustees Vanderbilt Inst. Pub. Policy Studies. Mem. ABA, Fed. Bar Assn., Tenn. Bar Assn., Nashville Bar Assn., Vanderbilt Law Alumni Assn. (pres. 1979-80), Am. Law Inst., Order of Coif. Episcopalian. Office: US Ct Appeals Customs House 701 Broadway Ste 303 Nashville TN 37203-3967

MERRYDAY, STEVEN DOUGLAS, federal judge; b. Palatka, Fla., 1950; BA, U. Fla., 1972, JD, 1975. With Holland & Knight, Tampa, 1975-83; ptnr. Glenn, Rasmussen, Fogarty, Merryday & Russo, Tampa, 1983-91; judge US Dist. Ct. (mid. dist.) Fla., Tampa, 1992—. Mem. Fed. Bar Assn., The Fla. Bar, Hillsborough County Bar Assn. Office: US Courthouse 801 N Florida Ave Tampa FL 33602-3849

MERSINI-HOUGHTON, LAURA, physicist, educator; d. Nexhat and Stela Mersini; m. Jeffrey Houghton, Feb. 2, 2003. MSc in Physics, U. Md., 1997; PhD, U. Wis., Milw., 2000. Cert. theoretical physics U. Wis., Milw. Physics Dept., 2000. Rsch. fellow Scuola Normale Superiore, Pisa, Italy, 2000—02; postdoctoral fellow Syracuse U., Physics Dept., NY, 2002—03; vis. prof. Perimeter Inst. Theoretical Physics, Waterloo, Ontario, Canada, 2003—04; asst. prof. physics U. NC, Chapel Hill, 2004—. Contbr. articles to profl. jours. Fellow, Fulbright Found., 1994. Achievements include research in addressing fundamental problems of cosmology and modern physics by means of a new field and direction, string cosmology. Connecting and testing models and the new field to astrophysical observables. Office: U NC Dept Physics and Astronomy Phillips Hall UNC-Chapel Hill Chapel Hill NC 27599 Office Fax: 919-962-0480. Business E-Mail: mersini@physics.unc.edu.

MERSON, MICHAEL HOWARD, public health physician, epidemiologist, educator; b. NYC, June 7, 1945; s. Leo and Paula Enid (Katz) M.; 1 child: Jonathan. BA, Amherst Coll., 1966; MD, SUNY, Bklyn., 1970. Commd. officer USPHS, 1972, advanced through grades to capt.; chief enteric disease br. Ctrs. for Disease Control, Atlanta, 1974-75; chief epidemiologist Cholera Rsch. Lab., Dacca, Bangladesh, 1977-78; dir. diarrheal diseases control program WHO, Geneva, 1978-90, dir. global program on AIDS, 1990-95; prof., dean pub. health Sch. Medicine Yale U., New Haven, 1995—2004, Anna M.R. Lauder prof. pub. health; prof., dir. Duke U. Global Health Inst., 2006—. Trustee, bd. dirs. Internat. Ctr. for Diarrheal Diseases, Dacca, 1985-90. Recipient Arthur Fleming award U.S. Jaycees, 1975. Mem. Royal Soc. Tropical Medicine and Hygiene, Internat. Epidemiol. Assn., Am. Soc. for Epidemiology, Soc. Scholars. Office: Duke U Box 90519 Global Health Inst Durham NC 27708 Office Phone: 919-681-7760. E-mail: michael.merson@duke.edu.

MERZ, KENNETH M., JR., chemistry professor; b. Niagara Falls, NY, Jan. 24, 1959; s. Kenneth M. and Dorothea L. Merz; m. Deborah S. Johnston, Feb. 26, 1958; children: Charles K., Margaux R. BS, Wash. Coll., Chestertown, Md., 1981; PhD, U. Tex. Austin, 1985. Prof. chemistry Pa. State U., University Park, 1989—2005, U. Fla., Gainesville, 2005—08. Sr. dir. Pharamcopeia, Inc., Princeton, NJ, 1998—2001. Contbr. scientific papers to profl. publs. Grantee, NIH, 1989—2008, NSF, 1989—2008, ONR, 1989—95, DOE, 1997—98. Fellow: AAAS. Independent. Avocations: travel, reading, bicycling. Office: Univ Florida Dept Chemistry Gainesville FL 32611 Business E-Mail: merz@qtp.ufl.edu.

MERZBACHER, EUGEN, retired physics professor; b. Berlin, Apr. 9, 1921; came to U.S., 1947, naturalized, 1953; s. Siegfried and Lilli (Wilmersdoerffer) M.; m. Ann Townsend Reid, July 11, 1952; children: Celia, Charles, Matthew, Mary (dec.). Licentiate, U. Istanbul, 1943; AM, Harvard U., 1948, PhD, 1950; DSc (hon.), U. N.C., Chapel Hill, 1993. HS tchr., Ankara, Turkey, 1943—47; mem. Inst. Advanced Study, Princeton, NJ, 1950—51; vis. asst. prof. Duke U., Durham, NC, 1951—52; from mem. faculty to Kenan prof. physics U. N.C., Chapel Hill, 1952—91, Kenan prof. emeritus, 1991—; ret., 1991. Vis. prof. U. Wash., 1967-68, U. Edinburgh, Scotland, 1986; Arnold Bernhard vis. prof. physics Williams Coll., 1993; chair Internat. Conf. on Physics of Electronic and Atomic Collisions, 1987-89; sr. advisor APS, 1998-99. Author: Quantum Mechanics, 3d edit., 1998; also articles. NSF Sci. Faculty fellow U. Copenhagen, Denmark, 1959-60; recipient Thomas Jefferson award U. N.C., 1972; Humboldt sr. scientist award U. Frankfurt, Germany, 1976-77. Fellow AAAS, Am. Phys. Soc. (pres. 1990; Frances E. Slack award south-eastern sect., 2009); mem. Am. Assn. Physics Tchrs. (Oersted medal 1992), Sigma Xi. Achievements include research on applications of quantum mechanics to study atoms and nuclei. Home: 750 Weaver Dairy Rd #119 Chapel Hill NC 27514-1439 Home Phone: 919-918-3675. Personal E-mail: merzie@mindspring.com.

MESLAY, OLIVIER, museum director, curator; b. Rabat, Maroc, Dec. 4, 1956; s. Jacques and Hélène (Mis) M.; m. Laure Jacquin de Margerie, Aug. 14, 1989; children: Mélanie, Cyprien, Gabriel. BA, The Sorbonne, Paris, 1981, MA, 1982, Ecole du Louvre, 1983; grad., Inst. Nat. Patrimoine, 1993. Documentaliste Galerie Bailly, Paris, 1984-91; curator British, American and Spanish paintings Musée du Louvre, Paris, 1993—2006, chief curator Louvre Lens, 2006—09; sr. curator European and American art, Barbara Thomas Lemmon curator European art Dallas Mus. Art, 2009—, interim dir., 2011, assoc. dir. curatorial affairs, 2012—. Prof. Ecole du Louvre, 1997—2006. Contbr. articles to profl. jours.; author numerous exhibition catalogues. Lt. French Army, 1976-77. Recipient Chevalier des Arts et Lettres, 2009; fellow Clark Art Inst., Williamstown, Mass., 2000—01. Office: Dallas Art Museum 1717 North Harwood Dallas TX 75201 Office Phone: 214-922-1810. Business E-Mail: Omeslay@dallasmuseumfart.org.*

MESSICK, ANDREW, sports association executive; BA in Econs. and Psych., U. Calif., Davis; MBA, Yale Sch. Mgmt. With McKinsey & Co., Chgo. and Amsterdam; various bus. devel., mktg. and gen. mgmt. positions Sara Lee Corp.; sr. v.p. internat. NBA; exec. v.p. mktg. and internat. AEG, 2007, pres., 2007—11; CEO World Triathlon Corp., 2011—. Office: World Triathlon Corp 2701 N Rocky Point Dr Ste 1250 Tampa FL 33607 Office Phone: 813-868-5940. Office Fax: 813-868-5930.

MESSIER, LUC J., oil industry executive; BS in Civil Engring., U. Sherbrooke; studied at, McGill U., INSEAD. Engring., project mgmt. and mng. dir. Bouygues Construction and Pomerlau; COO Technip USA, 2003, pres., CEO Technip Offshore Inc., pres., CEO, 2005—07; sr. v.p. project devel. ConocoPhillips, Houston, 2007. Spkr. in field. Bd. trustees AWTY Internat. Sch. Office: ConocoPhillips PO Box 2197 Houston TX 77252-2197

MESSMER, DONALD JOSEPH, business management educator, marketing consultant; b. St. Louis, July 30, 1936; s. Edgar Louis and Lucille Louise (Straub) Messmer; m. Charlotte Jean Fox; 1 child, Angeline Charlotte. BSBA with honors, Washington U., St. Louis, 1969, PhD, 1974. Asst. mgr. M.A. Bell Co., St. Louis, 1956-61; dist. sales exec. U. S. Gypsum Co., St. Louis, 1962-65; br. sales exec. Victor Comptometer Corp., St. Louis, 1965-68; pres. The Wessex Group, Ltd., Williamsburg, 1979—; asst. prof. Coll. William and Mary, Williamsburg, Va., 1973-76, assoc. prof., 1976-81, prof., 1981—2006, J.S. Mack prof., 1982—2006, J.S. Mack prof. emeritus, 2006—. Bd. dirs. Williamsburg Winery, Ltd., 2005—07, chmn. bd. dirs., 2005—07; co-founder, mem. adv. com. Coll. William and Mary Exec. Ptnrs. Editor (assoc ed): Decision Scis Jour, 1985—88; contbr. articles to profl jours. Bd. dirs., treas. Cmty. Action Agy., Williamsburg, 1984—91, United Way Greater Williamsburg, 1985—91, pres., 1989; founder Cmty. Svcs. Coalition, pres., chmn., 1992—98, bd. dirs., 2008—; owner Hist. Triangle Cmty. Svcs. Bldg. Recipient Pres.'s cmty. svc. award, Coll. William and Mary, 1999. Mem.: Greater Williamsburg Chamber and Tourism Alliance's (chmn. ednl. liaison com. 2008—10), Southeastern Decision Scis Inst (pres 1985—86), Am Mkt Asn (Dissertation award 1974), Decision Scis Inst (mkt coord 1985—86), Rotary (bd. dirs. 1990—92, program chair 2003, bd. dirs. 2003—07, pres. 2004), Beta Gamma Sigma, Alpha Mu Alpha. Republican. Avocations: fishing, golf. Home Phone: 757-229-0764; Office Phone: 757-253-5606. Personal E-mail: don.messmer@cox.net. Business E-Mail: don.messmer@wessexgroup.com.

METCALF, JOHN STEVENSON, surgical pathologist, dermatopathologist; s. Isaac Stevens Halstead and Margaret Schnabel Metcalf; m. Marilyn Sadler Metcalf; 1 child, Christian Halstead. BS in Biology, Wofford Coll., Spartanburg, SC, 1970; MD, Med. U. SC, Charleston, 1974. Diplomate in dermatopathology Am. Bd. Pathology and Dermatology, 1983, in anatomic pathology Am. Bd. Pathology, 1977, Am. Bd. Pathology, 2008, Am. Bd. Pathology, 2014. Asst. prof. pathology Med. U. SC, 1978—86, assoc. prof. pathology and dermatology, 1986—95, prof. pathology and dermatology, 1995—. Fellow: Am. Soc. Dermatopathology, Internat. Soc. Dermatopathology, Am. Soc. Clin. Pathology, Coll. Am. Pathologists. Independent. Avocations: photography, motorcycling, scuba diving. Office: MUSC Dept Pathology and Lab Med 165 Ashley Ave Charleston SC 29425 Business E-Mail: metcalfj@musc.edu.

METTETAL, NOLAN, state legislator; b. Baton Rouge, Nov. 19, 1945; m. Kay Ford; children: Cary, Kimberly. Attended, NW Miss. CC; BS in Pharmacy, U. Miss. Pharmacist; mem. Dist. 10 Miss. State Senate, 1996—2011, Miss. House of Reps, 2012—. Mem.: NW CC Alumni Assn., U. Miss. Alumni Assn., Miss. Pharmacy Assn. Republican. Methodist. Office: Miss House of Reps PO Box 1018 Jackson MS 39215 Business E-Mail: nmettetal@house.ms.gov.

METZ, LARRY EDWARD, state legislator, lawyer; b. Abington, Pa., Mar. 20, 1955; s. Harry Franz and Joan (Nye) Metz; m. Mariko Tomisato, Mar. 26, 1980; children: Maria Jo, Christina Jill. BA, U. Fla., 1976; JD with high honors, Fla. State U., 1983. Bar: Fla. 1983, U.S. Dist. Ct. (so., mid. and no. dists.) Fla. 1984, U.S. Ct. Appeals (11th cir.) 1984, U.S. Supreme Ct. 1987. Assoc. Fleming, O'Bryan & Fleming, Ft. Lauderdale, Fla., 1983-86; atty. Westinghouse Electric Corp., Coral Springs, Fla., 1986—88; pvt. practice Ft. Lauderdale, 1988-91, Coral Springs, 1991—93; assoc. Herzfeld & Rubin, Miami, Fla., 1992—96, ptnr. Ft. Lauderdale, 1996—99; assoc. Unger, Swartwood, Latham & Indest PA, Orlando, Fla., 1999—2000; ptnr. The Unger Law Group PL, Orlando, 2000—06; pvt. practice Mertz Law Firm PA, Eustis, Fla., 2007—; mem. Dist. 25 Fla. House of Reps., 2010—. Cert. cir. ct. mediator Fla. Supreme Ct., 2006—. Mem. Lake County Sch. Bd., 2004—10; chmn. Sch. Bd., 2006—08; mem. Lake County Zoning Bd., 2005—10, Lake-Sumter Met. Planning Orgn., 2008—10; mem. bd. dir. Four Corners Charter Sch., Davenport, Fla., 2004—10; alt. mem. bd. dir. Fla. Sch. Bds. Assn., 2006—08, mem., 2008—10; chmn. Legislative Com., Fla. Sch. Bds. Assn., 2008—09; Rep. nominee U.S. Ho. Reps. 19th dist. Fla., 1992; area leader, sign co-chmn., spkr. George Bush for Pres. Broward County (Fla.) Victory Com., 1988; pres. Broward County Regional Rep. Club, 1991, 1995; mem. exec. com. Broward County Reps., 1988—91, 1993—96, Lake County Reps., 1999—; Rep. candidate Fla. Ho. Reps., 2004; mem. Cmty. Ch. Howey-in-the-Hills, Fla., 1999—2003, chmn. stewardship and fin. com. Fla., 2000—02; mem. Fla. Guardian Ad Litem Program, 1991—97. Capt. USMC, 1976—82. Recipient Outstanding Mem. of the Yr. award, Broward Lawyers Care, 1989, 1990, Fla. Guardian Ad Litem Program 5 Yr. Svc. award, 1996, Disting. Svc. Award, Marine Corps League, N Lake Detachment, Fl., 2002, Cmty. Svce. Award for Leadership, Lake County, Fla., 2008. Mem.: ABA, Order of Coif, Lake County Bar Assn., Marine Corps League (judge adv. North Lake detachment, Fla. 2000—03, trustee 2003—06, color guard 2000—). Republican. Presbyterian. Office: 15930 US Hwy 441 Ste B Eustis FL 32726-6552 also: 301 West Ward Ave Eustis FL 32726-4033 also: Capitol Office 1101 The Capitol 402 South Monroe St Tallahassee FL 32399-0348 Office Phone: 352-483-3900, 352-742-6275, 850-488-0348. Business E-Mail: larry@metzlawyer.com.

METZ, THOMAS FREDERIC, retired military officer; b. Elkin, NC, Sept. 21, 1948; m. Pamela Redmond; children: Elizabeth, Cade, Patrick. BS, U.S. Mil. Acad., 1971; M in Mech. Engring., N.C. State U., 1980; grad., Command and Gen. Staff Coll., Army War Coll. Registered profl. engr., Va. Enlisted U.S. Army, 1966, commd. 2nd lt. inf., 1971, advanced through grades to lt. gen., 2002, various positions, 1972-76, aide-de-camp for Comdr., Readiness Region VI Ft. Knox, Ky., 1976, comdr. C Co., 4th Bn., 54th Inf., 194th Armor Brigade, 1977-78; asst. prof. mech. engring. dept. U.S. Mil. Acad., West Point, N.Y., 1981-84; S-3/XO 3d Bn., 7th Inf., S-3 197th Separate Inf. Brigade Ft. Benning, Ga.; divsn. chief Inf. Sch. Combat Devel. Directorate, 1984-87; comdr. 4th Bn., 15th Inf., 194th Armor Brigade Ft. Knox, 1987-89; G-3, 2d Inf. Divsn. Republic of Korea, 1990-92; comdr. 2d Brigade, 1st Inf. Divsn., 1992-94; chief of staff Ft. Riley, 1994-95; dir. exptl. force coordination cell, 4th Inf. Divsn. U.S. Army, Fort Hood, 1995-97; asst. divsn. comdr. for support 4th Inf. Divsn., 1997-98; dep. dir. Joint Warfighting Capability Assessment, J-8 The Joint Staff, Washington, 1998-2000, vice dir., force structure, resources, & assessment (J-8), 2000—01; comdr., 24th Infantry Divsn. (Mechanized) US Army, Fort Riley, Kans., 2001—03; chief of staff US Centl. Command, Operation Enduring Freedom, 2002—03; comdr., III US Corps US Army, Fort Hood, Tex., 2003—06; comdr. Multi-Nat. Corps. Iraq, Baghdad, 2004—05; dep. commdg. gen., chief of staff US Army Training & Doctrine Command (TRADOC), Ft. Monroe, Va., 2006—07; dir. Joint IED Defeat Orgn. (JIEDDO), Washington, 2007—09. Decorated Legion of Merit with two oak leaf clusters, Bronze Star medal, Meritorious Svc. medal with three oak leaf clusters, Army Commendation medal with two oak leaf clusters, Good Conduct medal.

METZNER, DAVID MARK, plastic and reconstructive surgeon; b. Cleve., Jan. 16, 1939; children: Damon Hires, Rowan Aliya von Zanthier. AB, U. Mich., 1960; MD, Case Western Res. U., 1964. Diplomate Am. Bd. Otolaryngology, Am. Bd. Plastic Surgery, Nat. Bd. Med. Examiners; lic. MD, Ohio, Calif., Mass., La. Internship Mt. Sinai Hosp., Cleve., 1964-65, residency in gen. surgery, 1965-66; residency in otolaryngology Harvard Med. Sch., Boston, 1966-69; chief of otolaryngology The Cambridge (Mass.) Hosp., 1971-74; residency in plastic and reconstructive surgery La. State U., New Orleans, 1975-76; active staff Lakeside Hosp., Metairie, La., 1977—2007, Highland Pk. Hosp., Covington, La., 1997—2007, Prytania Surgery Ctr., New Orleans, 1986—2007; pvt. plastic surgery New Orleans & Covington, 1977—2007; plastic surgeon Vermont Ctr. Plastic Surgery Dermatology. Active, courtest staff So. Bapt. Hosp., New Orleans, 1977—; courtesy staff St. Tammany Parish Hosp., Covington, 1977—; clin. instr. Harvard Med. Sch., 1971-75; vis. prof. Nassau County, N.Y. Med. Ctr., 1988, Med. Coll. Wis., 1992; vis. lectr. U. Calif. San Diego, 1991; clin. asst. prof. La. State U., 1994-2007; lectr. in field. Recipient AMA Physician's Recognition award, 1981, 84, 87, 90, Appreciation award North Am. Med./Dental Assn.; named one of Top Plastic Surgeons, New Orleans Mag. Mem. Am. Soc. Plastic and Reconstructive Surgeons, Inc., The Am. Soc. for Aesthetic Plastic Surgery (Walter Scott Brown award, 1989), Southeastern Soc. Plastic and Reconstructive Surgeons, Inc., Am. Acad. Facial Plastic and Reconstructive Surgery, Inc., Am. Acad. Otolaryngology-Head and Neck Surgery, Inc., La. Soc. Plastic and Reconstructive Surgeons (pres.), The Double Boarded Soc. (pres.), Southeastern Soc. Plastic and Reconstructive Surgeons, La. Soc. Plastic and Reconstructive Surgeons, La. State Med. Soc., Orleans Parish Med. Soc., Harvard Club La. (pres.). Avocations: art, sculpting, jewelry. Office: 106 Park Pl Ste 115 Covington LA 70433

MEYER, BRUCE C., wholesale distribution executive; BA in Economics & Bus. Adminstrn., Furman U., Greenville, SC, 1979. Various positions of increased responsibility in sales including global segment dir. electronic mfg. KEMET Electronics Corp., 1980—2006, v.p. sales-Americas, 2006—07, v.p. mktg.-direct customers, 2007; v.p. merchandising Catalyst Telecom (subs.) ScanSource, Inc., 2009—. Office: Catalyst Telecom 6 Logue Court Greenville SC 29615 Office Phone: 864-627-1951. Office Fax: 864-675-1537.

MEYER, DAVID DOUGLAS, dean, law educator; b. Grinnell, Iowa, Nov. 4, 1961; s. Richard DeWitt and Nancy Meyer; m. Amy Gajda, Apr. 29, 1986; children: Michael, Matthew. BA with highest honors, U. Mich., 1984, JD magna cum laude, 1990. Bar: Mich. 1992, Ill. 1995, US Ct. Appeals (7th cir.) 1995. Spl. asst. to Senator Charles McC. Mathias, Jr. US Senate, Washington, 1984—87; law clk. to Judge Harry T. Edwards US Ct. Appeals (DC cir.), Washington, 1990—91; law clk. to Justice Byron R. White US Supreme Ct., Washington, 1992—93; assoc. Sidley & Austin, Washington, 1991—92, Chgo., 1994—96; asst. prof. law U. Ill., Champaign, 1996—2000, assoc. prof. law, 2000—02, prof. law, 2002—10, Mildred Van Voorhis Jones faculty scholar, 2005—07, assoc. dean academic affairs, 2009—10; dean, Mitchell Franklin prof. law Tulane U. Law Sch., New Orleans, 2010—. Legal advisor to Judge Howard M. Holtzmann Iran-US Claims Tribunal, The Hague, Netherlands, 1993—94; prof. Bar-Bri, Chgo., 1998—2006; vis. prof. George Washington U. Law Sch., Washington, 2002, Bklyn. Law Sch., NY, 2008; lectr. in field. Editor-in-chief Mich. Law Rev., Ann Arbor, 1989—90; contbr. articles to law jours. Recipient Henry M. Bates Award, Abram W. Sempliner Meml. Award, Simpson & Moran Award; Mildred Van Voorhis Jones scholar, 2005—07. Mem.: ABA, American Law Inst. Office: Tulane University Law School John Giffen Weinmann Hall 6329 Freret St New Orleans LA 70118 Office Phone: 504-865-5937. Office Fax: 504-862-8746. E-mail: meyer@tulane.edu.*

MEYER, ELLEN L., academic administrator; BA and MS Geo Wash U. V.p. mktg. dean continuing studies, dir. extension program and summer sch. Mpls. Coll. Art and Design; dir. continuing edn. and spl. programs RI Sch. Design; pres. Atlanta Coll. Art, 1992—2007, Watkins College of Art, Design & Film, Nashville, 2008—. Mem.: Nat. Black Arts Festival (bd. dirs.), Metro Atlanta Arts Fund (adv. bd. mem.). Office: Watkins College of Art, Design & Film 2298 Rosa L Parks Blvd Nashville TN 37228

MEYER, FREDERICK RAY, retired manufacturing executive, board member; b. Highland Park, Ill., Dec. 30, 1927; s. Raymond Thorne and Marian Catherine (Anderson) Meyer; m. Barbara Spreuer, Oct. 24, 1963; children: Cheryl L., Amy Sue, Bradley A. BS, Purdue U., 1949; MBA, Harvard, 1958. Registered profl. engr. Treas. Aladdin Industries, Nashville, 1958-67; pres. Crescent Dallas divsn. Tyler Corp., 1967-68, v.p. Tyler corp. staff, 1968-70, sr. v.p., 1970-77, exec. v.p., 1977-83, pres., COO, 1983—86; chmn. Aladdin Industries LLC, 1985—2005, pres., CEO, 1987—94, 1995—99. Bd. dirs. SWS Group, Inc., 1991—, Palm Harbor Homes Inc., 1994—, Westwood Holdings Group Inc., 2001—10, Oaks Bank & Trust Co. Served with US Army, 1953—55. Office: Palm Harbor Homes Inc 15301 Spectrum Dr Ste 500 Addison TX 75001-6425 Office Phone: 972-991-2422. Office Fax: 972-991-5949. Business E-Mail: mfrederick@palmharbor.com.

MEYER, J. HORST, physics professor; b. Berlin, Mar. 1, 1926; arrived in US, 1957; BS, U. Geneva, 1949; PhD in physics, U. Zurich, 1953. Fellow Swiss Assn. Rsch. Physics and Math. Studies, Oxford, Eng., 1953-55; Nuffield fellow Clarendon Lab. U. Oxford, 1955-57; lectr., rsch. assoc. dept. engring. and applied physics Harvard U., Cambridge, Mass., 1957-59; from asst. prof. to prof. Duke U., Durham, NC, 1959-84, Fritz London prof. physics, 1984—2004, Fritz London prof. physics emeritus, 2004—. Vis. prof. Technische Hochschule, Federal Republic of Germany, 1965, Tokyo U., 1980, 81, 83; traveling fellow Japanese Soc. for Promotion Sci., 1971, vis. scientist, 1979; guest scientist Inst. Laue-Langevin, France, 1974, 75; Yamada Found. fellow, Japan, 1986; guest scientist USSR Acad. Sci., 1988; guest prof. Toyota Inst. Tech., Nagoya, Japan, Oct. 1998; chmn. Gordon Conf. on Solid H2, 1990; western chmn. conf. quantum crystals, Almaty, Kazakhstan, 1995. Editor Jour. Low Temperature Physics, 1992—, mem. editorial bd., 1988-92; contbr. articles to profl. jours. Alfred P. Sloan fellow, 1961-65. Fellow Am. Phys. Soc. (Jesse Beams prize, 1982, Fritz London prize 1993). Achievements include exptl. rsch. on the properties of liquid and solid helium, critical phenomena in fluids, solid hydrogen and deuterium, magnetic insulators, phase transitions, convection in supercritical helium. Office: Duke U Dept Physics PO Box 90305 Durham NC 27708-0305 Office Phone: 919-660-2520, 919-660-2522. Business E-Mail: hm@phy.duke.edu.

MEYER, PHILIP EDWARD, journalism educator; b. Deshler, Nebr., Oct. 27, 1930; s. Elmer Edward and Hilda Grace (Morrison) M.; m. Sue Quail, Aug. 5, 1956; children: Caroline, Katherine, Melissa, Sarah. BS, Kans. State U., 1952; MA, U. N.C., 1963. Asst. state editor Topeka (Kans.) Daily Capital, 1954-56; reporter Miami (Fla.) Herald, 1958-62; Washington corr. Akron Beacon Jour., 1962-66; nat. corr. Knight-Ridder, Inc., Washington, 1967-78, dir. news research Miami, 1978-81; William Rand Kenan Jr. prof. journalism U. N.C., Chapel Hill, 1981-93; Knight prof., 1993—2008; prof. emeritus, 2008—. Author: Precision Journalism, 1973 (Sigma Delta Chi Disting. Service award 1974), The Newspaper Survival Book, 1985, Ethical Journalism, 1987, The New Precision Journalism, 1991, The Vanishing Newspaper, 2004; co-author: To Keep the Republic, 1975; co-editor: Evaluating Public Journalism, 1998; editor: Letters From The Editor, 2007. Project dir. Russell Sage Found., N.Y.C., 1969-70. Served with USNR, 1952-54. Recipient Disting. Contbns. to Journalism award Nat. Press Found., 1994, Disting. Contbns. to Media and Media Studies award Freedom Forum Media Studies Ctr., 1995, award of merit Newspaper Assn. Am. Rsch. Fedn., 1996; Nieman fellow Harvard U., 1966-67, fellow Freedom Forum Ctr. for Media Studies, 1985. Fellow Soc. Prof. Journalists, mem. Am. Assn. for Pub. Opinion Rsch. (pres. 1989-90, award exceptionally disting. achievement 2000), World Assn. for Pub. Opinion Rsch. (pres. 1994-95), Assn. for Edn. in Journalism and Mass Comm. (mem. USA Today bd. contbrs. 1998—), Nat. Press Club (Washington), NC Journalism (Hall of Fame). Democrat. Episcopalian. Avocation: photography. Business E-Mail: philip_meyer@unc.edu.

MEYER, RICHARD W., retired university librarian; b. St. Louis, Jan. 22, 1943; s. Norman K. Meyer and Melba R. Reisel; m. Clare A. Siesennop, Apr. 12, 1944; children: Sharyn C. Moore, Karyn A. BS in Chemistry, U. Mo., 1967; BA in Libr. Sci., U. Mo., Columbia, 1967; MS in Libr. Sci., U. Ill., Champaign, 1970; MA in Econs., Clemson U., SC, 1986. Asst. libr. E.I. duPont de Nemours, Aiken, SC, 1967—69; asst. dir. libr. U. Tex. at Dallas, Richardson, 1970—76; dir. libr. tech services Ind. State U., Terre Haute, Ind., 1976—79; assoc. dir. libraries Clemson U., 1979—91; dir. libr. Trinity U., San Antonio, 1991—2000; dean, dir. libraries Ga. Inst. Tech., Atlanta, 2000—08. Cons. Harris Corp., Melbourne, Fla., 1985—86, Chemists Club, NYC, 1991—92, Mackenzie U., Sao Paulo, Brazil, 1998—99, Mercer U., 2001, Westminster Coll., 2003, Winona St. U., 2004. Contbr. articles to profl. jours. Field svc. rev. team mem. United Way of San Antonio, 1998—2000; Solinet Bd., 2004—07. Recipient G.K. Saur Best Article award, Coll. and Rsch. Libraries, 1999; grantee, Andrew W. Mellon Found., 1995—2000; Blackwell scholarship, Coll. and Rsch. Libraries, 2002. Mem.: So. Assn. Colls. and Schs. (mem. reaffirmation rev. teams 1999—2002), ALA. Conservative. Personal E-mail: rwmeyer@charter.net.

MEYERROSE, DALE WILLIAM, information technology company executive, retired military officer; b. 1953; BS in Economics, USAF Acad., 1975; Grad, Squadron Officer Sch., Maxwell AFB, 1977; MBA, U. Utah, 1978; Grad., Nat. War Coll., Ft. Lesley J. McNair, 1992, Sr. Info. Warfare Applications Course, Maxwell AFB, 2000, Program for Nat. & Internat. Security, JFK Sch. Govt., Harvard U., 2001, Joint Flag Officer Warfighting Course, Maxwell AFB, 2003, USN Exec. Bus. Course, U. Calif-Berkeley, 2005. Commd. 2d lt. USAF, 1975, advanced through grades to major gen., 2002, ret., 2005; maintenance officer 4th Combat Comms. Group, Altus AFB, Okla., 1976-77; aide-de-camp, asst. exec. officer to the comdr. European Comms. Divsn., Kapuan Air Sta., West Germany, 1977-79; aide-de-camp to the comdr. Air Force Comms. Command, Scott AFB, Ill., 1979-80; chief of maintenance 1974th Comms. Group, Scott AFB, 1980-82; mem., air staff tng. program officer Sec. of the Air Pers. Coun., The Pentagon, Washington, 1982-83; various assignments USAF, Washington, 1983-85, chief future concepts, dep. chief of staff, 1990-91; comdr. 2048th Comms. Squadron, Carswell AFB, 1985-87; comms. support officer Nat. Mil. Command Ctr. the Joint Staff, The Pentagon, Washington, 1987-90; comdr. 3rd Combat Comms. Group, Tinker AFB, Okla., 1992-94; dir. comms. Operation Southern Watch, Riyadh, Saudi Arabia, 1993; dir. communications & info. USAF in Europe, Ramstein AB, Germany, 1994-96; dir. communication & info. Air Combat Command, Langley AFB, Va., 1996—2000; dir. command control systems, chief info officer N. Am. Aerospace Def. Command (NORAD) & US Space Command (USSPACECOM), Peterson AFB, Colo., 2000—02; dir. comm. & info., chief info. officer US Space Command (USSPACECOM), Peterson AFB, Colo., 2002—05; dir. architecture & integration, chief info. officer US No. Command (USNORTHCOM), Peterson AFB, Colo., 2002—05; assoc. dir., chief info. officer Office Nat. Intelligence, Washington, 2006—09; v.p., gen. mgr. cyberspace solutions Harris Corp., 2009—. Adj. prof. Sch. Info. Studies, Syracuse U., 2009—. Decorated Disting. Svc. medal, Def. Superior Svc. medal, Legion of Merit with oak leaf cluster, Def. Meritorious Svc. medal woth oak leaf cluster, Meritorious Svc. medal with silver oak leaf cluster, Air Force Commendation medal, Joint Svc. Commendation medal, Air Force Achievement medal, Combar Readiness medal, Nat. Def. Svc. medal with two bronze stars, Southwest Asia Svc. medal with bronze star, Kuwait Liberation medal; Recipient Outstanding Young AFCEAN awars, Armed Forces Comm. & Electronics Assn., 1987, Medal of Merit, 1992; Named Internat. AFCEAN of the Yr., 1999, "Top 100" Info. Tech. Profl., Fed. Computer Weekly, 2005, named one of Premier 100 IT Leaders, Computerworld, 2007. Office: Harris Corp 1025 W NASA Blvd Melbourne FL 32919 E-mail: dale.meyerrose@gmail.com.

MEYERS, ARCHIE L., JR., risk management consultant; Various mgmt. positions Crawford & Co., Atlanta, 1959, br. mgr., 1976, pres., claims svc. bus. unit, 1995-98, pres., CEO, 1998, chair, CEO, 1999—. Office: Crawford & Co 5620 Glenridge Dr NE PO Box 5047 Atlanta GA 30302

MEYERS, CAROLYN WINSTEAD, academic administrator, mechanical engineer, educator; b. Hampton, Va., May 11, 1946; d. John Selner and Eva Carroll (Tonsler) Winstead; divorced; m. James E. Cofield, Jr.; children: Timothy C. III, Leslie C., Lisa A.; m. Timothy C. Meyers, Jr. BSME, Howard U., 1968; MSME, Ga. Inst. Tech., 1979, PhD in Metallurgy, 1984. Steam generator analyst Machinery Apparatus Operation div. Machinery Apparatus Ops. div. GE, Schenectady, 1968; systems analyst Info. Svcs. div. Info. Svcs. div. GE, Bethesda, Md., 1969; instr. Atlanta U. Ctr. Corp., 1972-77; instr. mech. engring. Ga. Inst. Tech., Atlanta, 1979-84, asst. prof., 1984-90, assoc. prof., 1990-96; dir. SUCCEED Coalition Ctr. for Profl. Success, 1992-93; assoc. dean rsch. Coll. Engring. Ga. Inst. Tech., Atlanta, 1993-96; dean Coll. Engring. NC A&T State U., Greensboro, 1996, prof. mech. engring., 1996—2006, vice chancellor acad. affairs, 2000—06, provost, 2001—06; pres. Norfolk State U., Va., 2006—10, Jackson State U., 2011—. Summer faculty fellow USAF Materials Lab., Wright-Patterson AFB, Ohio, 1988; program officer NSF, 1996-99. Contbr. articles to profl. jours. Chmn. waste volume reduction subcom. Atlanta Mayor's Commn. on Solid Waste Disposal, 1989-92; trustee Westminster Schs., Atlanta, 1989-93; program dir. divsn. undergrad edn. NSF, 1997-99, divsn. human resources devel., Arlington, V., 1999—; bd. dirs. Piedmont Triad Coun. Internat. Visitors, N.C. Sch. Sci. and Math. 2000-, Moses Cone Health Sys., 2003-, United Way Greater Greensboro, 2002-03, Rsch. Triangle Inst., MentorNet; chair, bd. dirs. Nat. Inst. Aerospace, 2003—. Recipient Faculty award for women NSF, 1991, Disting. Alumni award Atlanta-Howard U. Alumni Assn., 1992; named Black Engr. of Yr. in Higher Edn. U.S. Black Engr. Mag. and Coun. Engring Deans, 1990; Pres. Young Investigator grantee NSF, 1988; inducted to Acad. of Disting. Engring. Alumni Ga. Tech. U., 1996; honored alumna in edn. on Charter Day Howard U., 1997. Fellow ASME (Engr. of Yr. 1990); mem. AIME, SAE (Ralph Teetor Ednl. award 1986), Am. Soc. Engr. Edn. (v.p. pub. affairs 2001-2003), Foundry Ednl. Found. (key prof. 1985-95), Soc. Women Engrs. (state pres. Atlanta sect. 1987-90), Am. Foundrymen's Soc. (sponsor student sect. 1987-95, aluminum divsn. sci. merit award 1994), Soc. Black Engrs. (Golden Torch award 2002, Emerald honors Women in Sci and Tech. 2003), Links (pres. Atlanta chpt. 1987-89), Jack and Jill Am., The Girl Friends, Golden Key, Sigma Xi, Tau Beta Pi, Phi Kappa Phi, Alpha Kappa Alpha, Beta Gamma Sigma. Roman Catholic. Office: Jackson State University Office President / Administration Tower 1400 John R Lynch St Jackson MS 39217-0280 E-mail: president@nsu.edu.

MEYERS, ERIC MARK, religion educator; b. Norwich, Conn., June 5, 1940; s. Karl D. and Shirlee M. (Meyer) M.; m. Carol Lyons, June 25, 1964; children: Julie Kaete, Dina Elisa. AB, Dartmouth Coll., 1962; MA, Brandeis U., 1964; PhD, Harvard U., 1969. Lerner prof. religion, archeol., bibl. study, ancient hist. Duke U., Durham, NC, 1969—, dir. grad. program in religion, 1979—86, 2001—06; dir. Annenberg Inst., Phila., 1991-92, Ctr. Jewish Studies, 1972—90, 2000—. Pres. Am. Schs. Oriental Rsch., Boston, 1990—96, 2006—08; commentator on biblical archaeology; dir. 8 digs Israel, Italy, 1970—2000; co-dir. NEH seminar Duke U., 2004; dir. Jewish St. Program, 1972—90, 2002—; vis. prof. Jewish Theol. Sem., Williams Coll., Free U. Berlin, Goethe U. Frankfurt, Germany. Author: 12 books; co-author: The Cambridge Companion to the Bible, 1997, 2008; editor (in chief): The Oxford Encyclopedia of Archaeology in the Near East, 5 vols., 1997; contbr. articles more than 400 to profl. jours.; frequent guest (TV series) A&E channel, Discovery channel; frequent guest: History Channel. Recipient Richard J. Scheuer medal, Am. Schs. Oriental Res., 2007, Lifetime Achievement award, Upper Coll, Regional Coun., 2009. Jewish. Avocations: singing (baritone), golf, the arts, travel. Home: 3202 Waterbury Dr Durham NC 27707-2416 Office: Duke U 118 Gray Bldg PO Box 90964 Bldg Durham NC 27708-0964 Office Phone: 919-660-3517. Business E-Mail: emc@duke.edu.

MEYERS, JAMES FRANK, electronics engineer; b. Binghamton, NY, Sept. 9, 1946; s. Edwin Fox and Louise (Okrepkie) M. BEE, U. Louisville, 1969, ME, 1972; postgrad., George Washington U. Instr. elec. engring. lab. U. Louisville, 1968-69; engring. coop. technician Langley Research Ctr., NASA, Hampton, Va., 1966-69, aerospace technologist, 1969—2006; disting. rsch. assoc. Langley Rsch. Ctr., NASA, Hampton, Va., 2006—08; sr. electronics engr. AS&M, Hampton, 2008—. Contbr. articles to profl. jours. Mem. IEEE (sect. chmn. 1975), Turnberry Two Owners Assn. (pres., dir. 1979-82), Sports Car Club Am. (div. rallye exec. 1982-86), Eta Kappa Nu, Tau Beta Pi, Sigma Tau. Achievements include patents in field. Office: NASA Langley Rsch Ctr Mail Stop 493 Hampton VA 23681-0001 Business E-Mail: James.F.Meyers@nasa.gov.

MEYERS, TEDSON JAY, lawyer; b. Bayonne, NJ, May 6, 1928; s. Irving and Norma Miriam (Anson) M.; m. Patricia Elizabeth Sullivan, Apr. 10, 1965 (div. Apr. 1978); children: Mary, John, Katherine; m. Lynn Scholz, Aug. 6, 1978 (div. Oct. 1992); m. Arden Schell, Dec. 27, 2000. Student, Ohio State U.; BA, NYU, 1949, MA, 1950; JD, Harvard U., 1953. Bar: DC 1953, NY 1957, US Supreme Ct. 1971. Asst. counsel Office Gen. Counsel, Dept. Navy, Washington, 1955-56; assoc. Liebman, Eulau & Robinson, NYC, 1956-58; staff counsel for govt. regulations ABC, NYC, 1958-61; adminstrv. asst. to chmn. FCC, Washington, 1961-62; asst. to dir., dir. overseas ednl. TV projects Peace Corps, Washington, 1962-68; pvt. practice Washington, 1968-70; ptnr. Sullivan Beauregard Meyers & Clarkson, Washington, 1970-74, Peabody Lambert & Meyers, Washington, 1974—84, Reid & Priest, Washington, 1984-96, Coudert Brothers, Washington, 1996—2003. Adj. prof. comm. San Diego State U., 1993—; founding pres. Harvard Legis. Rsch. Bur., 1952—53; mem. White House Task Force on Ednl. TV Overseas, 1966—68; trustee Global Legal Info. Network Found., 2001—; mem. adv. panel internat. telecomm. law US State Dept., 1987—; bd. govs. Internat. Coun. Computer Comm., 1986—, pres., 2000—02; bd. dirs. Cyber Century Forum; chmn. ABA Standing Com. Law Libr. Congress, 2002—12, spl. advisor, 2012—; bd. dirs. Arthur C. Clarke Foundation, 1983—, chmn., 2000—; mem. Strategic Adv. Coun., Arthur C. Clarke Ctr. Human Imagination, U. Calif., San Diego, 2013—, Nat. Policy Coun. AARP, 2012—, Exec. Coun., AARP, Ala., 2011—; vice chair Citizens Adv. Com., Eastern Shore Met. Planning Orgn., Baldwin County, Ala., 2013—; mem. Adv. Coun., Ala. Coastal Foundation, 2014—. Contbr. conf. papers and articles to profl. publs. Mem. City Coun. Washington, 1972-75; bd. govs. Met. Washington Coun. Govts., 1973-75; chmn. Bicycle Fedn. of Am., 1977-2008, bd. dirs. 2009-, U.S. Coun. for World Comm. Yr. 83, 1982-84; dir. The Arthur C. Clarke Found. of the US Inc., 1987—, chmn., 2003—; bd. dirs. Friends of Law Libr. Congress, 2001-. Lt. USMC, 1953-55, Korea. Recipient Sec. of Army Pub. Svc. medal; rsch. fellow Carnegie Found., 1949. Fellow: Am. Bar Found.; mem.: ABA (sect. sci. and tech. 1982—85, coun. mem. sect. sci. and tech. 1983—87, chmn. standing com. law libr. congress 2000, co-founder and chmn. internat. telecomm. com.), Internat. Telecomm. Acad. Russia (hon. academician 2002—), Cosmos Club Found. (trustee, chmn. 1985—88, 1990—), Cosmos Club (pres. 1988—90), Alpha Epsilon Pi. Avocations: bicycling, motorcycling, computers, sculling, music. Office Phone: 202-236-0200. Personal E-mail: tmeyers@tedson.com.

MEYER VON BREMEN, MICHAEL S., state legislator; b. Aug. 19, 1957; m. Peggy Hicks Meyer Von Bremen; children: Meg, Welsley. State senator Dist. 12, Ga., 1999—2008; sec. Ethics Com., 1999—; ptnr. Cannon, Meyer Von Bremen & Goss, 1999—; mem. Agr., Appropriations Judiciary & Pub. Safety Coms.; state senate Ga.; mem. Chancel Choir, Porterfield Meml. United Methodist Ch. Mem.: Dougherty Circuit Bar Assn. (former pres.), America & Ga. Bar Assns., Albany Sertoma Club. Democrat. Methodist. Office: PO Box 72065 Albany GA 31700 Mailing: 121 B State Capitol Atlanta GA 30334 Business E-Mail: mmeyer@legis.state.ga.us.

MEZA, LUIS ALBERTO, internist, researcher; s. Luis Alberto and Susana Cartes Meza; m. Teresa I. Ibarra, Sept. 3, 1966; children: Luis A. Jr., Monica Meza Hernandez, Leticia Ann Canizaro, Lisa Cristina Harrell. MD, U. Nat. Asuncion, Paraguay, 1966. Diplomate Am. Bd. Internal Medicine, Am. Bd. Oncology, Am. Bd. Hematology. Intern Mercy Hosp., Des Moines, 1970—71; resident in internal medicine La. State U., New Orleans, 1971—74; fellow Ochsner Found. Hosp., New Orleans, 1974—76; assoc. prof. medicine La. State U., Lafayette, 1976—; physician SW Oncology, Lafayette, 1979—. Chief med. staff Southpark Hosp., Youngsville, La., 2005—06. Capt. Paraguay Nat. Army, 1964—69. Fellow: ACP, Internat. Soc. Hematology; mem.: Am. Soc. Hematology, So. Assn. for Oncology, La. State Med. Soc., So. Med. Assn., Am. Soc. of Clin. Oncology, Lafayette Parish Med. Soc. Roman Catholic. Achievements include research in growth factor support in treating side effects related to chemotherapy. Avocations: travel, golf, photography. Office: Cancer Ctr Acadiana Rsch dept 1211 Coolige Blvd Ste 100 Lafayette LA 70503 Office Phone: 337-289-8400. Office Fax: 337-235-4272. Personal E-mail: lamezamd@aol.com.*

MIAH, ABDUL MALEK, electrical engineer, educator; b. Dhaka, Bangladesh, Feb. 14, 1948; arrived in U.S., 1985; s. Abdur Rahim Miah and Monjuman Begum; m. Meherunnesa Begum, Dec. 11, 1972; children: Tanveer Ahmed, Rudia Begum. BSEE, Bangladesh U. Engring. & Tech., 1969, MSEE, 1981; PhD in Elec. Engring., Wayne State U., 1992. Asst. works mgr. Bangladesh Ordnance Factories, Ghazipur, 1972—76; asst. prof. Bangladesh U. Engring. and Tech., Dhaka, 1976—82; elec. engr. SWS Engring., Inc., Birmingham, Mich., 1989; asst. prof. S.C. State U., Orangeburg, 1990—95, assoc. prof., 1995—2003, prof., 2003—. Mem.: IEEE. Avocations: reading, travel.

MICA, JOHN L., United States Representative from Florida; b. Binghamton, NY, Jan. 27, 1943; s. John and Adeline (Resciniti) Mica; m. Patricia Szymanek, 1972; children: D'anne, Clark. AA, Miami-Dade C.C., 1965; BA, U. Fla., 1967. Pres. MK Devel. Inc., 1976—92; mem. Fla. House of Reps., 1976—80; chief of staff to Senator Paula Hawkins US Senate, Washington, 1981—85; mng. gen. ptnr MD Cellular Comm., 1987—92; mem. US Congress from 7th Fla. Dist., Washington, 1993—; chmn. US House Subcommittee on Civil Svc., 1995—99, US House Subcommittee on Aviation, 2001—06; ranking mem. US House Transp. & Infrastructure Com., 2007—11, chmn., 2011—12. Exec. dir. Local Govt. Study Commn. Palm Beach/Orange County, 1970—72; co-chair Speaker's Task Force Drug-Free America, 1998—, US Capitol Preservation Commn., 1998—. Mem. bd. vis. US Coast Guard; bd. trusstees Kennedy Ctr. Recipient Outstanding Svc. award, Fla. Conservative Union, Fla. Cancer Soc. Mem.: Fla. Jaycees (Good Govt. award 1973), Winter Park Jaycees (Good Govt. award 1972), Tiger Bay Club, Kiwanis, Delta Chi. Republican. Episcopalian. Office: US House of Representatives 2187 Rayburn House Office Bldg Washington DC 20515 also: PO Box 756 Winter Park FL 32790-0756 Office Phone: 202-225-4035.*

MICALI, JAMES M., lawyer; b. 1947; m. Lisa Micali; children: Peter Micali, Christopher Micali. BA with honors, Lake Forest Coll., 1969; JD, Boston Coll., 1973. Bar: Mass. & RI 1973, SC 1990. Gen. counsel, sec. Michelin N.Am., Inc., 1985—90, exec. v.p., legal and fin., 1990—96; chmn., pres. Michelin N.Am., Inc., Greenville, 1996—2008; mem., exec. coun. Michelin Group, 2001—09; sr. advisor Azalea Capital, LLC, Greenville; of counsel Ogletree Deakins, LLC, Greenville, 2008—. Bd. dirs. Ritchie Bros. Auctioneers, Inc., Am.Tire Distributors Holdings, Inc., Sonoco Products Co., 2003—, Lafarge N.Am., 2004—, SCANA Corp., 2008—. Chmn. SC Mfrs. Alliance, SC C. of C., Rubber Manufacturers' Assn., 2001-; mem. Union League Club of NY, Palmetto Bus. Forum, SC. Recipient Outstanding Scholar Athlete award. Office: Ogletree Deakins LLC 300 N Main St The Ogletree Bldg Greenville SC 29601 Office Phone: 864-271-1300. Office Fax: 864-235-8806. Business E-Mail: james.micali@ogletreedeakins.com.

MICEK, SANDRA CORDOVA, publishing executive; BS, Syracuse U.; MBA, U. Pennsylvania. Mgr. Turner Broadcasting Sales, Accenture; with Yahoo! Personals; head mktg dept. Nokia; v.p. NBC Universal; sr. v.p. mktg. USA Today, 2011—. Office: USA Today 7950 Jones Branch Drive Mc Lean VA 22108-0605 Office Phone: 800-872-0001.

MICHA, DAVID ALLAN, chemistry and physics professor; came to U.S., 1966, naturalized, 1974; s. Simon David and Catalina (Cohen) M.; m. Rebecca Stefan, 1991; children: Michael F., Anna K. MS, U. Cuyo, Bariloche, Argentina, 1962; DSc, U. Uppsala, Sweden, 1966. Rsch. assoc. Theoretical Chemistry Inst. U. Wis., Madison, 1966-67; asst. rsch. physicist Inst. Pure and Applied Sci. U. Calif., La Jolla, 1967-69; assoc. prof. chemistry and physics U. Fla., Gainesville, 1969-74, prof., 1974—, dir. Ctr. Chem. Physics, 1982-91, head phys. chem. divsn., 1999—2004; co-organizer Pan Am. Workshop Theor. & Comp. Molecular & Materials Sci., 1993—2007, Sanibel Internat. Symposia, 1984—. Vis. prof. U. Gothenburg, Sweden, 1970, Harvard U., 1972, 90, 98, 2000, 01, Max-Planck Inst., Göttingen, Germany, 1976, 96, Imperial Coll., London, 1977, U. Calif., Santa Barbara, 1982, U. Colo. and Weizmann Inst., Israel, 1983, U. Buenos Aires, 1988, 95, Supercomputer Inst., Fla. State U., 1991, Ecole Normale Superieure, Paris 2004, 05, 07, 10, Inst. Math. Applications, U. Minn., 2009; mem. adv. panel div. advanced sci. computing NSF, 1990-92, Max-Planck Inst. Astrophysik, Munich, Germany, 1996, 97. Mem. editl. bd. Internat. Jour. Quantum Chemistry, 1979-88, Few-Body Systems, 1985—; editor Finite Systems and Multiparticle Dynamics, 1990-2005, 2 symposium procs., 6 workshop books; contbr. several book chpts., numerous articles to sci. jours. Recipient U.S. Sr. Scientist award A. Von Humboldt Found., 1976, Sr. Faculty Rsch. award Sigma Xi, 1985; Alfred P. Sloan Found. fellow, 1971-74; Nat. Bur. Standards JILA fellow, 1983, Mentors award, Dreyfus Found., 2009; grantee, NSF, 1971-. Fellow Am. Phys. Soc. (vice chmn. topical group on few body sys. and multi-particle dynamics 1986-88, chmn. 1988-89); mem. Am. Chem. Soc. Office: U Fla 2318 New Physics Bldg Gainesville FL 32611-8435

MICHAELIS, LYNN OTTO, forest products industry executive; b. Salt Lake City, Mar. 6, 1944; s. Otto Walter and Ella (Gsang) M.; m. Carla Rose-Thompson, Sept. 23, 1967; 1 child, Jenine K. BA in Math. with honors, U. Utah, 1966; MA in Economics, Wash. State U., 1971, PhD in Economics, 1975. Rsch. engr. Boeing Co., Seattle, 1966-69; instr. U. Mont., Missoula, 1972-73; v.p., mktg. and econ. rsch. Weyerhaeuser Co., Tacoma, econ. analyst, 1973-78, bus. mgr., particleboard, 1978-82, chief economist, 1982-91; regular contbr., N.Am. Housing and Macroeconomic Forecasts and Analysis RISI, Inc., chief economist, v.p., mktg. and econ. rsch., 2009—; pres. Strategic Economic Analysis, LLC, 2010—. Adj. prof. dept. forestry U. Wash., 1992—; mem. coun. econ. advisors Gov. Wash. State, Olympia, 1982—. Assoc. dir. St. Francis Hosp., Federal Way, Wash., 1985—; bd. dirs. Seattle Econ. Devel. Coun., 1984-92. NSF fellow Wis. State U., 1969-71. Mem. Nat. Assn. Bus. Economists (pres., bd. dirs. 1983-92), Am. Econ. Assn., N.W. Regional Economists (bd. dirs.), Beta Gamma Sigma. Avocations: racquetball, fishing, skiing. Home: 2832 SW 171st St Seattle WA 98166-3268 Office: RISI Inc 7915 Jones Branch Dr Ste 3200 Mc Lean VA 22102 Office Phone: 703-790-5827. Office Fax: 703-790-5825. Business E-Mail: lmichaelis@risi.com.

MICHAELS, JENNIFER EMMONS, engineering educator; b. Nashville, Oct. 29, 1955; d. Arthur Stoddard and Billie McMurry Emmons; m. Thomas Ellsworth Michaels, Jan. 27, 1981. BEE, Ga. Inst. Tech., Atlanta, 1976; MS, Cornell U., Ithaca, NY, 1982, PhD, 1984. Co-owner and v.p. JTM Sys. & Consulting Inc., Ithaca, 1980—88; mgr. software devel. Parametrics Inc., Ithaca, 1988—94, mgr. sys. devel. Waltham, Mass., 1994—2002; assoc. prof. Ga. Inst. Tech., 2002—11, prof., 2011—. Contbr. articles to profl. jours. Recipient Coun. Outstanding Young Engring. Alumni award, Ga. Inst. Tech., 1995. Mem.: IEEE, Acoustical Soc. America, Am. Soc. Nondestructive Testing. Achievements include patents for ultrasonic inspection and deployment apparatus, ultrasonic signal processing system including a flaw gate. Office: Ga Inst Tech Sch Electrical & Computer Engineering Atlanta GA 30332-0250*

MICHAELS, PAUL S., food products executive; Pres. Masterfoods USA; Americas regional pres. Mars, Inc., global pres. Office: Mars Inc 6885 Elm St Mc Lean VA 22101 Office Phone: 703-821-4900.

MICHALAK, SARAH C., university librarian; BA in English, Univ. Calif. Riverside, 1969; MLS, UCLA, 1970. Head bio-agrl. dept. U. Calif., Riverside; various libr. positions U. Wash., Seattle; dir. J. Willard Marriot Libr. U. Utah, Salt Lake City, 1995—2004; univ. libr. and assoc. provost for univ. libraries U. NC, Chapel Hill, 2004—. Bd. dirs. Ctr. Rsch. Libraries. Mem. editl. bd.: Jour. Libr. Adminstrn., Coll. and Rsch. Libraries. Mem.: Scholarly Pub. and Academic Resources Coalition (steering com.), Libr. Adminstrn. and Mgmt. Assn., Assn. Rsch. Libr. (ex-officio mem. bd. dirs.). Office: Walter Royal Davis Library CB 3900 208 Raleigh St University NC Chapel Hill NC 27514-8890 Office Phone: 919-962-1301. E-mail: smichala@email.unc.edu.

MICHALSON, GORDON E., JR., academic administrator; BA magna cum laude, Yale U., 1970; RelM in Philosophy of Religion/Theology, Claremont Sch. Theology, 1972; PhD in Philosophy of Religion, Princeton U., 1976. Tchg. asst. Princeton U., 1974—75; from instr. to asst. prof. Dept. Religion Davidson Coll., 1975—79; from asst. prof. to prof. Oberlin Coll., 1977—92, dept. chair, 1989—92; dean, warden New Coll., U. So. Fla., 1992—97, prof. humanities, 1992—; acting pres. New Coll. of Fla., Sarasota, 2001, pres., 2001—. Bd. trustees Leroy Collins Inst. Pub. Policy, 2004. Author: Kant and the Problem of God, 1999; contbr. articles to profl. jours. Mem.: Am. Theol. Soc. Office: New Coll of Fla 5800 Bay Shore Rd Sarasota FL 34243-2109 Office Phone: 941-487-4100.

MICHAUX, HENRY (MICKEY) M., JR., state legislator; b. Durham, NC, Sept. 4, 1930; s. Henry M. Michaux and Isadore Coates M.; m. June Michaux; 1 child, Jocelyn Winston. Asst. dist. atty, Durham, NC, 1969—72; state rep. NC, 1972—77; del. Dem. nat. conv., 1976; US atty. Mid Dist. NC, 1977—81; state rep. Dist. 23 NC, 1985—2002; exec. vice rep. Union Ins. Realty Co., Durham, NC, 1955—, Glenview Mem. Pk., 1955—, Washington Ter. Apt. Inc., Raleigh, 1956—; real estate appraiser Durham, 1964—; state rep. Dist. 31 NC, 2003—. Recipient Pub. Affairs award, Nat. Assn. Real Estate Brokers, 1972, Svc. award, America Fedn. State & Mcpl. Employees, 1972, 1977. Mem.: America Judicature Soc., Nat. Bar Assn., Nat Assn. Real Estate Brokers (mem. gen. coun. 1976—), NAACP, Durham Com.Affairs of Black People. Democrat. Meth. Address: PO Box 2152 Durham NC 27702-2152 Office: NC House of Reps 16 W Jones St Rm 1220 Raleigh NC 27601-1096 Office Phone: 919-715-2528. Business E-Mail: Mickey.Michaux@ncleg.net.

MICHEL, ARTURO G., lawyer; b. Kankakee, Ill. m. Renee Michel; 3 children. BA in Econ., Northwestern Univ., Ill., 1981; JD, Univ. Mich., 1986. Assoc. to ptnr. Bracewell & Patterson LLP, Houston, 1986—2004; city atty. Legal Dept., Houston, 2004—10; ptnr. Thompson & Horton, LLP, Houston, 2010—. Staff Mexican Am. Legal Def. & Ednl. Fund, San Antonio, 1981—82. Bd. directors Family Svc. Greater Houston, Houston Vol. Lawyers Program Inc. Mem.: Hispanic Bar Assoc. (former pres.). Office: Thompson & Horton LLP Phoenix Tower Ste 2000 3200 SW Freeway Houston TX 77027 Office Phone: 713-554-6766. E-mail: amichel@thompsonhorton.com.

MICHEL, DANIEL JOHN, communications educator, writer, photographer, artist; b. New Orleans, June 18, 1949; s. Nolan Joseph and Evelyn Marie (Breaux) M. Diploma, Sta. WKG-TV, 1986; BA in Mktg. Mgmt., Kensington U., 1989; cert. diploma photography, Media West, 1990; cert., Art Instrn. Schs. Inc., 1991, Brit.-Am. Sch. of Writing, 1991. Instr. English East Baton Rouge Sch. Bd., 1982-84; instr. broadcast prodn. Sta. WKG-TV, Baton Rouge, 1986—; freelance writer Baton Rouge, 1987—; technician, photographer Evangeline Downs Race Track. Announcer Nat. Sports Festival, Baton Rouge, 1985. Writer song lyrics including I've Sat So Long, Now I Became Lonely, stage plays, works in Libr. of Congress, 1982—. Camera dir. La. Pub. Broadcasting Fund Raising, Baton Rouge, 1986—; instr. TV broadcasting, 1996-2005. Recipient award, Motion Industry Picture, 2013. Roman Catholic. Office Phone: 337-356-9009.

MICHELINI, MATTHEW R., investment company executive; BS in Math., Princeton U. Mem. Mergers & Acquisitions Group Lazard Frères & Co., LLC, 2004—06; prin. Apollo Investment Corp., NYC, 2006—. Bd. dirs. Noranda Aluminum Holding Corp., 2007—, Metals USA Holdings Corp., 2008—. Office: Apollo Investment Corp 9 W 57th St New York NY 10019 also: Metals USA Holdings Corp One Riverway Ste 1100 Houston TX 77056 Office Phone: 713-965-0990. Office Fax: 713-965-0067.

MICHELSON, MICHAEL W., investment company executive, lawyer; m. Ellen Michelson; 2 children. AB cum laude, Harvard Coll., 1973; JD cum laude, Harvard Law Sch., 1976. With Latham & Watkins, LA, 1976—81; joined Kohlberg Kravis Roberts & Co., Menlo Park, 1981, gen. ptnr., 1987—, co-head, North Am. pvt. equity bus., head, healthcare industry; chmn. Alliance Imaging Inc., Owens Ill. Inc. Bd. dirs. Promus Hotel Corp., New South Holdings Inc., Accellent Inc., AutoZone Inc., Union Tex. Petroleum Holdings Inc., 1985—, Owens Ill. Inc., 1987—2005, Doubletree Corp., 1996—, Amphenol Corp., 1997, Alliance Imaging Inc., 1999, KinderCare Learning Centers Inc., 1999—, Jazz Pharmaceuticals Inc., Biomet, Inc., HCA Inc. Office: HCA Inc One Park Plz Nashville TN 37203 Office Phone: 615-344-9551. Office Fax: 615-344-2266. Business E-Mail: michm@kkr.com.

MICHENER, JAMES LLOYD, medical educator; b. Dec. 19, 1952; m. Gwendolyn Curtis Murphy; children: Rebecca Liane, Joshua Kieran. BA, Oberlin Coll., Ohio, 1974; MD, Harvard Med. Sch., 1978. Diplomate Am. Bd. Family Practice. Resident in family medicine Duke U. Med. Ctr., Durham, NC, 1978-81, Kellogg fellow, 1981-82, prof. dept. cmty. and family medicine, 1994—, chmn. dept. cmty. and family medicine, 1994—; dir. Duke Ctr. Cmty. Rsch., 2006—. V.p. Durham Health Care, Inc., 1985-86; project reviewer Ctrs. Disease Control and Prevention, 2002-; vis. prof. work group pub. health and med. edn. Ctrs. Disease Control, Atlanta, 2005. Co-author: Nutrition in Practice, 1990, 2d edit., 1992; contbr. numerous articles to med. pubs. including Academic Medicine, The Jour. of Family Practice, Medical Care, others; mem. editl. bd. Rx Nutrition, 1989-91; presenter in field. Bd. dirs. N.C. Med. Soc. Found., 1995—2004; STFM rep. resource com. on nutrition edn. Am. Acad. Family Practice Found., 1987-91. Grantee The Fullerton Found., Inc., The Josiah Macy, Jr. Found., U.S. Dept. Health and Human Svcs., Kate B. Reynolds Charitable Trust, N.C. Health and Wellness Trust. Mem. AMA, NIH (co chair com. engagement com., NCRR, 2007-, Fogarty/Ellison fellowship selection com. 2005-), Assn. Am. Med. Colls. (exec. com. 2005-06, exec. coun. 2001-07, bd. dirs. 2008-), Assn. Tchrs. Preventive Medicine (chmn. coun. acad. units 2002-, pres. 2008-), Am. Acad. Family Physicians Found., N.C. Acad. Family Physicians, Assn. Dept. Family Medicine (bd. dir. 1997—, sec. 1998—2005), Coun. Acad. Socs. (adminstrn. bd. 2000-07, chair 2005-06), World Orgn. Nat. Colls., Acads. and Academic Assn. Gen. Practitioners and Family Physicians, Am. Austrian Founds. Internat. Health Forum (mem. steering com.), Nat. Patient Safety Found. (bd. govs. 2009). Home: 4011 Duck Pond Trail Chapel Hill NC 27514-9758 Office: Duke U Med Ctr PO Box 2914 Durham NC 27710-0001 Business E-Mail: miche001@mc.duke.edu.

MICKELSON, PHIL (PHILIP ALFRED MICKELSON JR.), professional golfer; b. San Diego, June 16, 1970; s. Philip and Mary Mickelson; m. Amy McBride, Nov. 19, 1996; children: Amanda Brynn, Sophia Isabel, Evan Samuel. BS in Psychology, Ariz. State U., Tempe, 1992. Profl. golfer PGA, 1992—. Mem. US team Presidents Cup, 1994, 1996, 1998, 2000, 2003, 2005, 2007, 2009, 2011, Ryder Cup, 1995, 1997, 1999, 2002, 2004, 2006, 2008, 2010, 2012. Co-author (with Donald T. Phillips): One Magical Sunday (But Winning Isn't Everything), 2005; appeared in (TV series) Entourage, 2008. Founder The Phil and Amy Mickelson Charitable Fund. Recipient Fred Haskins award, 1990, 91, 92, Jack Nicklaus award, 1990, 91, 92; won NCAA Championships, 1989, 90, 92; 1st team All-American with Sun Devils; Espy Award for Best Male Golfer, Best Championship Performance, ESPN, 2004; named one of The 100 Most Powerful Celebrities, Forbes.com, 2008, The 100 Most Influential People in the World, TIME mag., 2010; named Player of Yr. Golf mag., 2013 Achievements include 1st left-hander to win US Amateur, 1990; 1st player in PGA history to win same tournament as amateur and profesional (No. Telecom Open); winner PGA Tour events: Northern Telecom Open, 1991, 1995; Buick Invitational, 1991, 2000, 2001; The International, 1993; Mercedes Championship, 1994, 1998; Nortel Open, Phoenix Open, GTE Byron Nelson Golf Championship, NEC World Series of Golf, 1996; Bay Hill Invitational, Sprint International, 1997; AT&T Pebble Beach National Pro-Am, 1998, 2005, 2007, 2012; Bell South Classic, 2000, 2005, 2006; MasterCard Colonial, 2000; THE TOUR Championship, 2000, 2009; Canon Greater, 2001; Canon Greater Hartford Open, 2002; Bob Hope Chrysler Classic, 2002, 2004; FBR Open, 2005; THE PLAYERS Championship, Deutsche Bank Championship, 2007; Northern Trust Open, 2008, 2009; Crowne Plaza Invitational, 2008; Shell Houston Open, 2011; winner Major Championships: The Masters, 2004, 2006, 2010; PGA Championship, 2005; Open Championship (British Open), 2013; member of the President's Cup winning US national team: 1994, 1996, 2000, 2005, 2007, 2009; member of the Ryder Cup winning US national team: 1999, 2008; winner World Golf Championship events: CA Championship, HSBC Champions, 2009. Avocation: flying. Office: c/o PGA Box 109601 100 Avenue Of Champions Palm Beach Gardens FL 33418*

MICKENS, RONALD ELBERT, mathematician, physics professor; b. Petersburg, Va., Feb. 7, 1943; s. Joseph Persival and Daisy (Brown) M.; m. Maria Kelker, Aug. 13, 1977; children James Williamson, Leah Maria. BA, Fisk U., 1964; PhD, Vanderbilt U., 1968. NSF postdoctoral fellow MIT, Cambridge, 1968-70, vis. prof., 1973-74; prof. physics Fisk U., Nashville, Tenn., 1970-81, Clark Atlanta U., 1982—, Callaway prof., 1986. Vis. prof. Morehouse Coll., Atlanta, 1979-80, Joint Inst. for Lab. Astrophysics, Boulder, Colo., 1981-82; cons. adv. bd. NSF, Nat. Urban Coalition, Nat. Rsch. Coun., Am. Inst. Physics and a variety of univs. and nat. labs. Author: Nonlinear Oscillations, 1981, Difference Equations, 1987, Difference Equations: Theory and Applications, 1990, Nonstandard Finite Difference Models of Differential Equations, 1994, Oscillations in Planar Dynamical Systems, 1996; editor: Mathematics and Science, 1990, Applications of Nonstandard Finite Difference Schemes, 2000, Edward Bouchet: The First African American Doctorate, 2002, Mathematical Methods for the Natural and Engineering Sciences, 2004; editor: Advances in the Applications of Nonstandard Finite Difference Schemes, 2005; co-editor: Mathematical Studies on Human Disease Dynamics, 2006, Truely Nonlinear Oscillator; contbr. numerous rev. articles, abstracts and gen. articles to publs. Fellow Woodrow Wilson Found., Danforth Found., UNCF, Joint Inst. for Lab. Astrophysics; grantee ARO, NSF, DOE, NASA, NIH, 1968—. Fellow Am. Phys. Soc. (con., adv. bd.), Nat. Soc. Black Physicists; mem. AAAS, European Phys. Soc., Soc. Indsl. and Applied Math., Am. Math. Soc. Achievements include construction of new finite-difference schemes for numerical solution of differential equations; new perturbation techniques for nonlinear difference and differential equations; construction of global methods for nonlinear oscillatory systems; investigation of properties of rate constants for third-order chemical react; mathematical modeling in the biosciences; history of African American scientists. Office: Clark Atlanta U Physics Dept Atlanta GA 30314 Home Phone: 404-696-0739; Office Phone: 404-880-6923. Business E-Mail: rmickens@cau.edu.

MICKIEWICZ, ELLEN PROPPER, political and social science educator; b. Hartford, Conn. d. George K. and Rebecca (Adler) Propper; m. Denis Mickiewicz; 1 son, Cyril. BA, Wellesley Coll., MA, Yale U., PhD, 1965. Lectr. dept. polit. sci. Yale U., 1965-67; asst. prof. dept. polit. sci. Mich. State U., East Lansing, 1967-69, assoc. prof., 1969-73, prof., 1973-80; prof. dept. polit. sci. Emory U., Atlanta, 1980-88, dean Grad. Sch. Arts and Scis., 1980-85, Alben W. Barkley prof. polit. sci., 1988-93; James R. Shepley prof. pub. policy, prof. polit. sci. Duke U., Durham, N.C., 1994—, dir. DeWitt Wallace Ctr. for Comm. and Journalism Terry Sanford Inst. Pub. Policy, 1994—2008. Vis. prof. Kathryn W. Davis Chair Wellesley Coll., 1978; vis. com. dept. Slavic lang. and lit. Harvard U., 1978-85, vice chmn. vis. com. Russian Rsch. Ctr., Harvard U., 1986-92; mem. subcom. on comms. and society Am. Coun. Learned Socs./Soviet Acad. Scis., 1986-90; mem. com. on internat. security studies, Am. Acad. Arts and Scis., 1988-90; fellow The Carter Ctr., 1985—, dir. Commn. on Radio and TV Policy, 1991-2012; mem. area adv. com. for Ea. Europe and USSR, Coun. for Internat. Exch. Of Scholars, 1987-90; mem. acad. adv. coun. The Kennan Inst. for Advanced Russian Studies, 1989-93; mem. bd. overseers Internat. Press Ctr., Moscow, 1995; senior fellow, Coun. Fgn. Rels., Mem. adv. Bd., Inst. Study New Media and Soc., New Econ. Sch. U., Moscow. Author: Soviet Political Schools, 1967, Media and the Russian Public, 1981, Split Signals: Television and Politics in the Soviet Union, 1988 (Electronic Book of Yr. award Nat. Assn. Broadcasters and Broadcast Edn. Assn. 1988); co-author: Television and Elections, 1992, Television/Radio News and Minorities, 1994, Changing Channels: Television and the Struggle for Power in Russia, 1997, revised and expanded edit., 1999, Television, Power, and the Russian Public, 2008; editor: Soviet Union Jour., 1980-90; co-editor: International Security and Arms Control, 1986, The Soviet Calculus of Nuclear War, 1986; editor, contbr.: Handbook of Soviet Social Science Data, 1973; mem. editl. bd. Jour. Politics, 1985-88, Harvard Internat. Jour. Press/Politics, 1995—, Polit. Comms., 1996—, Polit. Comm., 1995—2008. Founder, 1st chmn. bd. dirs. Opera Guild of Greater Lansing, Inc., 1972-74. Recipient Outstanding Svc. to Promote Dem. Media in Russia award Journalists Union of Russia, 1994; Ford Found. Fgn. Area Tng. fellow, 1962-65, Guggenheim fellow, 1973-74; Sigma Xi grantee, 1972-74, John and Mary R. Markle Found. grantee, 1984-88, 94-96, 95—, Ford Found. grantee, 1985, 88-91, 92—, Rockefeller Found. grantee, 1985-87, W. Alton Jones Found. grantee, 1987-88, Eurasia Found. grantee, 1993-94, Carnegie Corp. of N.Y. grantee, 1996—. Mem. Am. Assn. for Advancement Slavic Studies (bd. dirs. 1978-81, mem. awards com., mem. endowment com. 1984-86, pres. 1987-88), Am. Polit. Sci. Assn.,Internat. Studies Assn. (v.p. N.Am. 1983-84), Dante Soc. Am., So. Conf. Slavic Studies (exec. com. 1983-84), Counc. Fgn. Rels. Office: Duke U Sanford Sch Pub Policy PO Box 90241 Durham NC 27708-0241

MICKLE, STEPHAN P., federal judge; b. NYC, 1944; BA, U. Fla., Gainesville, 1965, MEd, 1966; JD, U. Fla. Coll. Law, Gainesville, 1970. Atty. Office Legal Services US Office Equal Opportunity, Washington, 1970; pvt. practice atty. Ft. Lauderdale, Fla., 1971, Gainesville, Fla., 1972—79; adj. prof. U. Fla. Coll. Law, 1971; spl. asst. pub. defender 8th Jud. Cir. Ct. Fla., 1974, cir. judge, 1984—92; judge Alachua County Ct., Fla., 1979—84; appellate judge Fla. 1st Dist. Ct. Appeals, 1993—98; judge US Dist. Ct. (northern dist.) Fla., Gainesville, Fla., 1998—2011, chief judge, 2009—11, sr. judge, 2011—. Office: US Dist Ct US Courthouse 401 SE First Ave Gainesville FL 32601 Office Phone: 352-380-2742.

MIDDLEBROOKS, DONALD M., federal judge; b. Orlando, Fla., Dec. 31, 1946; BSBA, U. Fla., 1968, JD with honors, 1972. Bar: Fla. 1972. Pvt. practice atty., Orlando, 1973—74, West Palm Beach, Fla., 1977—97; gen. counsel, govtl. asst. for Gov. Reubin Askew Fla., 1974—77; judge US Dist. Ct. (so. dist.) Fla., West Palm Beach, 1997—. Adj. faculty Fla. Internat. U. 1980-81. Exec. editor: U. Fla. Law Review, 1971-72. Mem. ABA, Dade County Bar Assn, Palm Beach Bar Assn., The Fla. Bar (chmn. comm. for children 1989-91), Phi Delta Phi. Office: US Dist Ct Rogers Fed Bldg and US Courthouse 701 Clematis St Rm 257 West Palm Beach FL 33401 Office Phone: 561-514-3720.

MIDDLEDITCH, LEIGH BENJAMIN, JR., lawyer, educator; b. Detroit, Sept. 30, 1929; s. Leigh Benjamin and Hope Tiffin (Noble) M.; m. Betty Lou Givens, June 27, 1953; children: Leigh III, Katherine Middleditch McDonald, Andrew B. BA, U. Va., 1951, LLB, 1957. Bar: Va. 1957. Assoc. James H. Michael, Jr., Charlottesville, Va., 1957-59; ptnr. Battle, Neal, Harris, Minor & Williams, Charlottesville, 1959-68; legal adviser U. Va., Charlottesville, 1968-72; ptnr. McGuire, Woods, Battle & Boothe (now McGuire Woods LLP), Charlottesville, 1972-99, of counsel, 2000—; v.p. McGuire Woods Cons. LLC, Charlottesville, 2001—. Lectr. Grad. Bus. Sch., U. Va., Charlottesville, 1958-90, lectr. Law Sch., 1970-90. Co-author: Virginia Civil Procedure, 1978, 2d edition, 1992; contbr. articles to profl. jours. Chmn. U. Va. Health Svcs. Found., 1988-97; bd. mgrs. U. Va. Alumni, 1994-2001, pres., 2000-01; bd. dirs., chmn. Va. Health Care Found., 1997-98; trustee Claude Moore Found., 1991—; bd. visitors U. Va., 1990-94; trustee Thomas Jefferson Meml. Found., Monticello, 1994-2002, Montpelier Found., 2010-; counsel mem. U. Va. Miller Ctr. for Study of Presidency, 2000-. Fellow Am. Bar Found., Va. Bar Found.; mem. ABA (bd. govs. 1999-2002), Va. State Bar (coun., chmn. bd. govs. various sects.), Charlottesville-Albemarle Bar Assn. (pres. 1979-80), U. Va. Law Sch. Alumni Assn. (pres. 1979-81), U.S. C. of C. (bd. dirs. 1998—2004), Va. C. of C. (pres. 1988-90), Omicron Delta Kappa. Episcopalian. Office: McGuire Woods LLP PO Box 1288 Charlottesville VA 22902-1288 Office Phone: 434-977-2543. E-mail: lmiddleditch@mcguirewoods.com.

MIDDLETON, AMERICA CHUCK, state legislator; b. Natchez, Miss., Dec. 10, 1959; Mem. Dist. 85 Miss. House of Reps., 1996—, chair enrolled bills com.; owner Surface Tech. Mem.: Friends Progress (founder, pres.). Democrat. Church Of Christ. Mailing: PO Box 685 Port Gibson MS 39150 Office Phone: 601-786-0258, 601-437-8502. Business E-Mail: amiddleton@mail.house.state.ms.us.

MIDDLETON, CHRISTOPHER, Germanic languages and literature educator; b. Truro, Cornwall, Eng., June 10, 1926; arrived in US, 1966; s. Hubert Stanley and Dorothy May (Miller) M. BA, U. Oxford, Eng., 1951, DPhil, 1954. Lectr. King's Coll., London, 1955-65; prof. Germanic langs. and lit. U. Tex., Austin, 1966-98. Author: Selected Writings, 1989, Andalusian Poems, 1993, The Balcony Tree, 1992, Intimate Chronicles, 1996, Twenty Tropes for Doctor Dark, 2000, The Word Pavilion and Selected Poems, 2001, Of the Mortal Fire, 2003, Jackdaw Jiving: Essays on Poetry and Translation, 1998, In the Mirror of the Eighth King, 1999, Faint Harps and Silver Voices-Selected Translations, 2000, Crypto-Topographia: Stories of Secret Places, 2002, Palavers and A Nocturnal Journal, 2004, The Anti-Basilisk, 2005, The Tenor on Horseback, 2007, Collected Poems, 2008, Depictions of Blaff, 2010, Poems, 2006-10 Recipient trans. prize Schlegel-Tieck/Govt. Fed. Republic Germany, 1985, Anglo-Swiss Cultural Rels. prize Max Geilinger Stiftung, Zurich, Switzerland, 1987; Guggenheim Found. poetry fellow, 1974-75, NEH poetry fellow, 1980. Mem. Akademie der Künste Berlin. Office: U Tex Dept Of Germanic Langs Austin TX 78712

MIDDLETON, HERMAN DAVID, SR., retired theater educator; b. Sanford, Fla., Mar. 24, 1925; s. Arthur Herman and Ruby Elmerry (Hart) Middleton; m. Amelia Mary Eggart, Dec. 1, 1945; children: Herman David, Kathleen Hart. BS, Columbia U., 1948, MA, 1949; PhD, U. Fla., 1964; postgrad., N.Y. U., 1950, Northwestern U., 1951. Instr., dir. drama and speech Maryville (Tenn.) Coll., 1949-50; instr., designer, tech. dir. theatre U. Del., 1951-55; asst. prof., head dept. drama U. N.C., Greensboro, 1956-59, assoc. prof., head dept. drama and speech, 1959-65, prof., head dept., 1965-74, prof., 1974-79, Excellence Fund prof. dept. communication and theatre, 1979-90, prof. emeritus, 1990. Stage mgr. Unto thee Hills Cherokee Hist. Assn., 1953—56; designer Chucky Jack Gt. Smokey Mountains Hist. Soc., Gatlinburg, Tenn., 1956, designer, dir., 1957; comm. cons. NC Nat. Bank, 1968, Jefferson Std. Life Ins. Co., Greensboro, NC, 1969, Gilbarco, Inc., Greensboro, 1969—70, Greensboro, 1973. Drama critic, columnist: Wilmington Sunday Star, 1952, theater editor: Players Mag., 1959—61, theater columnist: Sunday edits. Greensboro Daily News, 1959—62; contbr. articles to profl. jours. Mem. NC Arts Coun. Commn., 1964—66, Guilford County Bi-Centennial Celebration Commn., 1969—70; pres. Shanks Village Players, Orangeburg, NYC, 1947—48, Univ. Drama Group, Newark, Del., 1954—55; bd. dirs. Broadway Theatre League Greensboro, 1958—60, Greensboro Cmty. Arts Coun., 1964—67, 1969—72, Greensboro Cmty. Theatre, 1983—86, Carolina Theatre commn., 1990—93; organizer-cons. Market Players, W. Market St. United Meth. Ch., 1979—82. With USN, 1943—46. Recipient O. Henry award, Greensboro C. of C., 1966, Gold medallion, Amoco Oil Co., 1973, Suzanne M. Davis award, Southeastern Theatre Conf., 1975, Marian A. Smith Disting. Career award, NC Theatre Conf., 1990. Mem.: Assn. Theater Higher Edn., NC Theater Conf. (co-organizer 1971, bd. dirs. 1984—92, pres. 1987—88), NC Drama and Speech Assn. (pres. 1966—67), Carolina Dramatic Assn. (bd. dirs. 1958—59), Southeastern Theatre Conf. (bd. dirs. 1963—68, 1987—92, pres. 1965, pres. pro tem 1966), Nat. Collegiate Players, Speech Communication Assn. Am., Assn. Theatre Higher Edn. (founding mem. 1986—87), Am. Coll. Theatre Festival (regional festival dir. 1973, 1980, regional dir., mem. nat. com. 1978—80), Am. Theatre Assn. (chmn. bd. nominations 1971—72), Am. Nat. Theatre and Acad. (organizer, exec. v.p. Piedmont chpt. 1957—60), Alpha Psi Omega, Theta Alpha Phi, Phi Kappa Phi, Phi Delta Kappa. Democrat. Methodist. Home: 203 Village Ln Unit A Greensboro NC 27409-2517 Personal E-mail: hmiddleton@triad.rr.com.

MIDELFORT, HANS CHRISTIAN ERIK, retired history professor; b. Eau Claire, Wis., Apr. 17, 1942; s. Peter Albert and Gerd (Gjems) M.; m. Corelyn Forsyth Senn, June 16, 1965 (div. Dec. 1981); children: Katarina, Kristian; m. Cassandra Clemons Hughes, May 25, 1985 (div. April 1996); 1 child, Lucy; m. Anne L. McKeithen, June 22, 1996. BA, Yale U., 1964, MPhil, 1967, PhD, 1970. Instr. Stanford U., Calif., 1968-70; asst. prof. U. Va., Charlottesville, 1970-72, assoc. prof., 1972-87, prof., 1987—2009, Charles Julian Bishko prof. history, 1996—2009. Vis. prof. Harvard U., Cambridge, Mass., 1985, U. Stuttgart, Germany, 1988, U. Bern, Switzerland, 1988, Wolfson Coll., Oxford U., 2002, Yale U., 2003; prin. Brown Coll., U. Va., 1996-2001; Dwight Terry lectr. Yale U., 2003; vis. fellow All Souls Coll., Oxford U., 2005, Am. Acad. Berlin, 2011. Author: Witch Hunting in Southwestern Germany, 1972 (Gustave Arlt prize 1972), Mad Princes of Renaissance Germany, 1994 (Roland H. Bainton prize 16th Century Studies Conf. 1995), A History of Madness in 16th Century Germany, 1999 (Ralph Waldo Emerson prize, Phi Beta Kappa, 1999, Roland H. Bainton prize 16th Century Studies Conf. 2000), Exorcism and Enlightenment, 2005; editor: Johann Weyer, On Witchcraft, 1998; co-editor: Europe, 1450-1789. Encyclopedia of the Early Modern World, 2003; translator: Imperial Cities and the Reformation (Bernd Moeller), 1972, Revolution of 1525 (Peter Bickle), 1981, Shaman of Oberstdorf (Wolfgang Behringer), 1998, Witchcraft and the Papacy (Rainer Decker), 2008, Ideas and Cultural Margins in Early Modern Germany, 2009, Witchcraft, Madness, Society, and Religion in Early Modern Germany. A Ship of Fools, 2013. Mem. Soc. Reformation Rsch. (pres. 1992-93). Business E-Mail: hem7e@virginia.edu.

MIDKIFF, CHARLES FRANKLIN, lawyer; b. Charleston, SC, Mar. 27, 1947; s. Leslie S. and Virginia M. (DeBord) Midkiff; m. Sue A. Samuelson Midkiff; 1 child, Alyssa Boyd. BS, Old Dominion U., 1968; JD, Coll. William & Mary, 1970. Bar: Va. 1970, DC Ct. Appeals 1975. Mem. law firm Christian, Barton, Epps, Brent & Chappell, Richmond, Va., 1987, ptnr., 1978—87; prin. Midkiff & Assocs. PC, 1987—; panelist energy issues ABA, Washington, 1979; prin. spkr. ann. meeting Va. Soc. CPA's, 1986, Accts. & Auditors Roundtable, 1988. Editor-in-chief Coll. William & Mary Law Rev., 1969—70. Gen. counsel campaign com. Atty. Gen. Gerald Baliles Va., 1981; v.p., bd. dirs. Big Bros. Richmond Inc., 1974—78; bd. dirs. Old Dominion U. Rsch. Found., 1989—. Served to 1st lt. US Army, 1970—71. Mem.: ABA (chmn. young lawyers divsn. com. assoc. lawyers 1981, vice chmn. natural gas transp. com. natural resources sect. 1986—), Am. Judicature Soc., Va. Assn. Def. Attys., Richmond Bar Assn., Va. State Bar (bd. govs. adminstrv. law sect. 1981—85, chmn. 1984), Va. Bar Assn. (chmn. young lawyers sect. 1980), Bull and Bear (Richmond). Episcopalian.

MIDLER, BETTE, singer, actress; b. Honolulu, Dec. 1, 1945; m. Martin von Haselberg, 1984; 1 child, Sophie. Student, U. Hawaii. Singer: (albums) The Divine Miss M, 1972, Bette Midler, 1973, Broken Blossom, 1977, Live at Last, 1977, Thighs and Whispers, 1979, Songs for the New Depression, 1979, No Frills, 1984, Mud Will Be Flung Tonight, 1985, Some People's Lives, 1990, Bette of Roses, 1995, Bathhouse Betty, 1998, Bette, 2000, Bette Midler Sings The Rosemary Clooney Songbook, 2003, Bette Midler Sings the Peggy Lee Songbook, 2005, Cool Yule, 2006, (soundtracks) The Rose, 1979, Divine Madness, 1980, Beaches, 1989; actress: (plays) Salvation, 1970, Tommy, Seattle Opera Co., 1971; (Broadway plays) Fiddler on the Roof, 1964—72, Bette Midler (special concert), 1973, Bette Midler's Clams on the Half Shell Revue, 1975, Bette! Divine Madness, 1979—80, I'll Eat You Last: A Chat with Sue Mengers, 2013; (films) Hawaii, 1966, The Rose, 1979, Jinxed, 1982, Down and Out in Beverly Hills, 1986, Ruthless People, 1986, Outrageous Fortune, 1987, (voice) Oliver and Company, 1988, Big Business, 1988, Beaches, 1988, Stella, 1990, Scenes From a Mall, 1991, For the Boys, 1991, Hocus Pocus, 1993, Get Shorty, 1995, The First Wives Club, 1996, That Old Feeling, 1997, Get Bruce, 1999, Isn't She Great, 1999, Drowning Mona, 2000, The Stepford Wives, 2004, Then She Found Me, 2007, The Women, 2008, (voice) Cats & Dogs: The Revenge of Kitty Galore, 2010, Parental Guidance, 2012; appeared in cable TV (HBO) prodn. Bette Midler's Mondo Beyondo, 1988, TV appearances Gypsy, 1993 (Golden Globe award for Best Actress in a Mini-Series or Movie Made for Television, 1994), Kathy Griffin: My Life on the D-List, 2009; performer: (concert films) Divine Madness, 1980, (Las Vegas show) Bette Midler: The Showgirl Must Go On, 2008—10; exec. prodr., composer (TV show) Bette, 2000, exec. prodr. Some of My Best Friends, 2001, (films) Divine Secret of the Ya-Ya Sisterhood, 2002; co-prodr.: (Broadway plays) Priscilla: Queen of the Desert, 2011—; author: A View From A Broad, 1981, The Saga of Baby Divine, 1984. Founder NY Restoration Project, 1999—. Recipient After Dark Ruby award, 1973, Grammy award for Best New Artist, 1974, Grammy award for Best Female Pop Performance, 1981, Grammy award for Record of teh Yr., 1990, spl. Tony award, 1973, Emmy award for NBC Spl., Ol' Red Hair is Back, 1978, 2 Golden Globe awards for The Rose, 1979, Golden Globe award for The Boys, 1991, Emmy award The Tonight Show appearance, 1992, Star, Hollywood Walk of Fame, 1986, Sammy Cahn Lifetime Achievement award, Songwriters Hall of Fame, 2012. Home: 700 12th Ave S Unit 201 Nashville TN 37203-3329

MIELE, ANGELO, engineering educator, researcher, consultant, author; b. Formia, Italy, Aug. 21, 1922; arrived in U.S., 1952, naturalized, 1985; s. Salvatore and Elena (Marino) Miele. DCivil Engring., U. Rome, Italy, 1944, DAero. Engring., 1946; DSc (hon.), Inst. Tech., Technion, Israel, 1992. Asst. prof. Poly. Inst. Bklyn., 1952-55; assoc. prof. Purdue U., 1955—58, prof., 1958—59; dir. astrodynamics Boeing Sci. Rsch. Labs., 1959-64; prof. aerospace scis., math. scis. Rice U., Houston, 1964-88, Foyt Family prof. engring., 1988-93, Foyt prof. emeritus engring., aerospace scis., math. scis., 1993—, rsch. prof., 2001—. Cons. Douglas Aircraft Co., 1956—58, U.S. Aviation Underwriters, 1987, Boeing Comml. Airplane Co., 1989, European Space Tech. Engring. Ctr., 2002; cons. Allison divsn. GM

Corp., 1956—58; Breakwell Meml. lectureship Internat. Astron. Fedn., 1994; Gaspare Santangelo Meml. lectureship Italian Assn. of Aeronautics and Astronautics, 2001. Author: Flight Mechanics, 1962; editor: Theory of Optimum Aerodynamic Shapes, 1965, Applied Mathematics in Aerospace Science and Engineering, 1994, Advanced Design Problems in Aerospace Engineering, 2003; editor-in chief Jour. Optimization Theory and Applications, 1966—, assoc. editor Jour. Astronautical Scis., 1964—93, Applied Math. and Computation, 1975—, series editor Math. Concepts and Methods in Sci. and Engring., 1975—, Optimal Control Applications and Methods, 1979—, mem. editl. bd. RAIRO-Ops. Rsch., 1990—, mem. adv. bd. AIAA Edn. Series, 1991—98; contbr. articles to profl. jours. Pres. Italy in Am. Assn., 1966—68. Decorated knight comdr. Order Merit Italy; recipient Levy medal, Franklin Inst. of Phila., 1974, Brouwer award, AAS, 1980, Schuck award, Am. Automatic Control Coun., 1988, Latina prize, 2002, Flight Mechanics award, AIAA, 1982, Pendray Aerospace Lit. award, 1982, Cicerone City of Formis prize, 2010. Fellow: Am. Astronautical Soc., AIAA (hon. Pendray Aerospace Lit. award 1982, Mechs. and Control of Flight award 1982); mem.: Tex. Acad. Engring., Scis. and Medicine, Nat. Acad. Engring. of Argentina (corr.), Internat. Acad. Astronautics, Acad. Scis. Turin (corr.), Russian Acad. Scis. (fgn.), NAE. Achievements include aerospace engring., windshear problems, hypervelocity flight, interplanetary flight, math. programming, optimal control theory and computing methods. Home: 3106 Kettering Dr Houston TX 77027-5504 Office: Rice Univ MS-322 Aero-Astronautics Group 6100 Main St Houston TX 77005-1827 Office Phone: 713-348-4907. Business E-Mail: miele@rice.edu.

MIELKE, WAYNE J., financial services company executive; Attended, Mich. State U. Accredited in pub. rels. Account supr. Casey Comm. Mgmt.; v.p., corp. comm. Comerica Bank, Comerica, Inc. Mem. adv. bd. Pub. Rels. Student Soc. America James S. Measell Chpt. Mem.: Pub. Rels. Soc. America (past pres. Detroit chpt., Hefty Disting. Svc. award 2006). Office: Comerica Inc Comerica Bank Tower 1717 Main St Dallas TX 75201 Office Phone: 214-462-4831. Business E-Mail: wjmielke@comerica.com.

MIERS, HARRIET ELLAN, lawyer, former federal official; b. Dallas, Aug. 10, 1945; BS in Math., So. Meth. U., 1967, JD, 1970; LLD (hon.), Pepperdine U. Sch. of Law. Bar: Tex. 1970. Law clk. to Hon. Joe E. Estes US Dist. Ct. (northern dist.) Tex., 1970—72; assoc. Locke Purnell Rain Harrell (formerly Locke, Purnell, Boren, Laney & Neely PC), Dallas, 1972—78, shareholder, 1978—98, pres., 1996—99; co-mng. ptnr. Locke Liddell & Sapp LLP, Dallas, 1999—2001; staff sec. The White House, Washington, 2001—03, asst. to Pres., 2001—05, dep. chief of staff for policy, 2003—05, gen. counsel to Pres., 2005—07; ptnr. Locke Lord Bissell & Liddell LLP, Dallas, 2007—. Nominee for assoc. justice US Supreme Ct., 2005; chair Tex. Lottery Commn., 1995—2000; at-large mem. Dallas City Coun., 1989—91. Recipient Justinian award for cmty. svc., Dallas Lawyers Auxiliary, 1992, Human Rels. award, American Jewish Com., 1992, Merrill Hartman award, Legal Services North Tex., 1996, Jurisprudence award, Anti-Defamation League, 1996, Louise B. Raggio award, Dallas Women's Lawyers Assn., 1996, Women of Excellence award, Women's Enterprise Mag., 1997, Robert C. Storey award for disting. achievement, So. Meth. U., 2005, Sandra Day O'Connor award, Tex. Ctr. Legal Ethics & Professionalism, 2005, Agy. Seal Medal, CIA, 2007, Edmund J. Randolph award, US Dept. Justice, 2007, YWCA Centennial award, 2008; named Woman of Yr., Today's Dallas Woman, 1997; named an Outstanding Young Lawyer, Dallas Assn. Young Lawyers, 1979; named one of 100 Most Powerful Attorneys, The Nat. Law Jour., 1997, 50 Most Influential Women Lawyers in America, 1998, 100 Most Influential Lawyers in America, 2000, Best Women Lawyers in Dallas, D Mag., 2010. Fellow: Dallas Bar Found., Tex. Bar Found. (life), American Bar Found. (life); mem.: ABA, Dallas Bar Assn. (pres. 1985—90), State Bar Tex. (bd. dirs. 1986—89, pres. 1992—93, Women in Law sect. Sarah T. Hughes award 1993). Republican. Office: Locke Lord Bissell & Liddell LLP 2200 Ross Ave Ste 2200 Dallas TX 75201-6776 also: Locke Lord Bissell & Liddell LLP 100 Congress Ave Ste 300 Austin TX 78701 Office Phone: 214-740-8450, 202-220-6925. Office Fax: 214-740-8800, 512-305-4800. E-mail: hmiers@lockelord.com.

MIGDOL, MARVIN JACOB, public relations and marketing executive, consultant; b. Rochester, NY, Jan. 11, 1937; s. Frank and Dorothy (Krieger) M.; m. Frances Scheiner, June 13, 1959 (div. June 1970); children: Helene Ellen, Steven Gary, Larry Jay; m. Grace Miron, Dec. 26 1970 (div. Aug. 1986); children: Michael Alan, Susan Renee, Honi Faith; m. Roni Habel, June 30, 1991 (div. Dec. 1992); m. Fay Herschberg, Dec. 27, 2003. BA in Sociology, U. Buffalo, 1959; postgrad., U. Miami, 1959-60; MS in Communications, Boston U., 1961. Dir. pub. rels. United Fund, Reading, Pa., 1961-63, Rensselaer Poly. Inst., Troy, NY, 1963-64, Touro Infirmary, New Orleans, 1964, Hamot Hosp., Erie, Pa., 1964-65, United Jewish Fedn., Buffalo, 1965-68; pres. Marvin J. Migdol Inc., Dallas, 1968—. Instr. Boston U., 1962—, Pa. State U., 1962—, U. Tex., 1962—, Collin County C.C., Plano, 1990-91. Author: Public Relations Handbook, 1963, Comics as a Public Relations Tool in Communications, 1971, The Migdol Manual, 1972, Success in the 1990's, 1987, Greater Virility: Overcoming Impotence, 1993; contbr. numerous articles to profl. jours. Reporter Rep. Nat. Conv., Dallas, 1964; asst. dist. commr. Boy Scouts Am., Dallas, 1980-85; exec. bd. dirs. EPCOT Resorts, Lake Buena Vista, Fla., 1992—; v.p. Am. Jewish Congress, S.W. Region, 2001-05; v.p. Am. Friends of Magen David Adoin, 2004-07; commencement U. Phoenix, Dallas, 2005. Recipient Pub. Rels. award Coun. Jewish Welfare Funds & Fedn., N.Y.C., 1967, Nat. Bus. League, West Palm Beach, Fla., 1968, Merit award Big Brothers & Sisters, Dallas, Tex., 1987, Major League Volleyball award San Jose, Calif., 1987.; named Entrepreneur of the Yr. Venture Mag., Dallas, Tex., 1987 Mem. U.S. Profl. Mktg. Assn. (pres. 1990—), Am. Assn. Indsl. Editors (bd. dirs. 1967-70), Am. Coll. Pub. Rels. Assn. (bd. dirs. 1964-66), Inst. for Info. and Comm. (bd. dirs. 1971—), Dallas Belles (dir. mktg. and pub. rels. 1987—), Jewish Nat. Fund (area dir.), Dallas Bridge Assn. (chmn. publicity, Tex. Star award, 2009), Dallas C. of C. (mem. econ. and internat. coun.), U. Buffalo Alumni Assn. We. Pa. and Tex. (expert witness, 1972-, Cert. Recognition Outstanding Dedicated Svc., 2007), 1964-65, Temple Shalom (vice chmn. bldg. fund 1971-72, mem. Brotherhood bd. 1985-86), Jewish Cmty. Ctr., Am. Contract Bridge League (chmn. pub. rels. 1983—, award Memphis chpt. 1983-87), Alpha Epsilon Pi (gov., 1970-79), Phi Delta Phi, (v.p. 1959-60, treas. 1960—). Jewish. Avocations: writer, lecturer. Home: 18715 Gibbons Dr Dallas TX 75287-4045 Office Phone: 972-978-5487, 972-248-9667. Personal E-mail: fmmigdol@gmail.com.

MIGHELL, KENNETH JOHN, lawyer; b. Schenectady, NY, Mar. 17, 1931; s. Richard Henry and Ruth Aline (Simon) M.; m. Julia Anne Carstarphen, Aug. 24, 1961; children: Thomas Lowry, Elizabeth Anne. BBA, U. Tex., 1952, JD, 1957. Bar: Tex. 1957. Assoc. Scurry, Scurry, Pace & Wood, Dallas, 1957-61; asst. U.S. Atty. Justice Dept., Dallas, 1961-77; 1st asst. No. Dist. Tex., 1972-77; U.S. Atty. No. Dist., Tex., 1977-81; ptnr. Cowles & Thompson, Dallas, 1981-96, of counsel, 1996—. Chmn. bd. mgmt. Downtown Dallas YMCA, 1974-76; pres. Dallas Area Am. Lung Assn., 1985-87; bd. dirs. YMCA Met. Dallas, 1987—; chmn. adv. bd. Southwestern Law Enforcement Inst., 1994-98; mem. Ctr. Am. & Internat. Law, CLE adv. com. 1999-2003. With USN, 1952-54; capt. USNR, 1954-78. Mem.: FBA, Nat. Assn. Former U.S. Attys. (pres. 1995), State Bar Tex. (bd. dirs. 1994—95), Dallas Bar Found. (trustee 1994—2001, vice chmn. 1999—2000, chmn. 2001—02), Dallas Bar Assn. (bd. dirs. 1984—89, chmn. 1989, v.p. 1990—91, pres. 1993). Democrat. Methodist. Office: Cowles & Thompson 901 Main St Ste 3900 Dallas TX 75202-3793 E-mail: kmighell@cowlesthompson.com.

MIGLIARO, MARCO WILLIAM, electrical engineer; b. NYC, Mar. 29, 1948; s. Marco Salvatore and Anna (Dalton) M.; children: Kristen Marie, Meredith Anne, Marie Angela, Marco Thomas; m. Jasoda Badlu, Nov. 19, 1988. BEE, Pratt Inst., 1969; postgrad., N.J. Inst. Tech., 1970-72. Registered profl. engr., N.Y., N.J., Pa., Mass., Fla. Engr. Am. Electric Power, NYC, 1969-78; staff engr. Gibbs & Hill, Inc., NYC, 1978-81; sr. cons. engr. Ebasco Svcs., Inc., NYC, 1981-88; tech. mgr. ABB Impell Corp., Melville, NY, 1988-90; sr. staff specialist for nuc. engring. Fla. Power & Light, Juno Beach, 1990-96, chief elec./I&C engr., 1996—2003; pres. ESA Cons. Engrs., PA, Jupiter, Fla., 2003—; pres., CEO IEEE Industry Stds. and Tech. Orgn., 2003—. Developer seminar on stationary batteries, 1987. Contbg. author: Handbook of Power Calculations, 1984, 99, Standard Handbook for Electrical Engineers, 1999, 2006; also articles. Recipient Meritorious Svc. award Am. Nat. Standards Inst., 1994. Fellow IEEE (pres. 2001—, stds. assn. bd. govs. 1998—, bd. dirs. 1990-92, 2001, fin. com. 1990-92, dir. stds. 1990-91, mem. exec. com. 1992, v.p. stds. activities, 1992, 2001, Stds. medal 1986, Stds. Bd. Disting. Svc. award 1993, Charles Proteus Steinmetz award 1996, Third Millennium medal 2000); mem. IEEE Power Engring. Soc. (Disting. Svc. award 1988, 92), Industry Standards and Tech. Orgn. (bd. dirs. 2000—, chmn. 2000-03). Avocations: fishing, travel, music. Home: PO Box 9253 Jupiter FL 33468-9253 Office: ESA Cons Engrs PA PO Box 9251 Jupiter FL 33468-9251 Home Phone: 561-624-4743; Office Phone: 561-691-1946. Business E-Mail: marco@esaconsulting.com.

MIGUEL, RAFAEL, anesthesiologist; b. Havana, Cuba; MD, U. Cadiz. Diplomate Am. Bd. Anesthesiology-pain medicine, 2007, Am. Bd. Anesthesiology, 2009. Resident anesthesiology Tulane Univ. Med. Ctr., 1982—84; prof. anesthesiology Univ. of S. Fla. Coll. of Medicine. Mem.: Fla. Soc. of Anesthesiologist (pres.). Office: H. Lee Moffitt Cancer Center & Research Institute 12902 Magnolia Drive Tampa FL 33612 Office Phone: 888-663-3488.

MIHAL, SANDRA POWELL, research scientist; b. Balt., Dec. 15, 1941; d. Sanford William and Mary Louise (Barry) Powell; m. James George Anderson, June 15, 1963; children: Robin Marie, James Brian, Melissa Lee, Derek Clair; m. Charles Turner Barber, Apr. 18, 1978; stepchildren: Gretchen Jayco, Katrina Hope; m. Ladislaw Paul Mihal, May 25, 1991; stepchildren: Alexander Paul, Suzie May, Natasha Elizabeth, Rudy Darius. BA, Mt. St. Agnes Coll., 1963; MA, N.Mex. State U., 1970, Purdue U., 1975; EdD, Vanderbilt U., 1990; postdoc in Info. Assuarance, U. Md., 2009. Cert. tchr., Md., info. assurance UMUC, 2009. Tchr. Ridgely-Dulaney Jr. H.S., Towson, Md., 1964; grad. asst. N.Mex. State U., Las Cruces, 1967—69; acad. advisor, instr. polit. sci. Purdue U., West Lafayette, Ind., 1974—78; prof., acad. sys. analyst U. So. Ind., Evansville, 1978—82; assoc. prof., chair dept. computer info. sys. Henderson (Ky.) C.C., 1982—88; prof. computer tech., divsn. chair Anne Arundel C.C., Arnold, Md., 1988—91; sys. analyst immigration and naturalization svc. Dept. of Justice, Washington, 1991—92, sr. rsch. sys. analyst immigration and naturalization svc. Glynco, Ga., 1995—; dep. program mgr. distributed learning Fed. Law Enforcement Training Ctr., Homeland Security, Glynco, Ga., 2002—. Bd. dirs. Ind. Polit. Sci. Assn., Muncie, 1984-88, Internat. Studies Assn.-Midwest, Chgo., 86-88; pres. Ky. Acad. Computer Users' Group, Lexington, 1985-86; telecom. adv. bd. C.C. Sys., Annapolis, Md., 1990-91; computer sys. network analyst CLARC Svcs., Pt. Charlotte, Fla., 92-95; adj. prof. history and polit. sci. Edison C.C., Punta Gorda, Fla., 1993-95; spkr. in fied Author: Learning By Doing BASIC, 1983, Computers Learning By Doing, 1984; contbr. articles to profl. jours Block coord. several neighborhood assns.; computer adv. bd. Henderson County Sch., 1982-88; chmn. Newburgh (Ind.) Youth Orgn., 78-86; judge Sci. Fair, Annapolis, 1988-90; nomination bd. Ky. Higher Edn. Assn., 1989-91; mem. Charlotte Chorale, Port Charlotte, 1992-94, Peace River Power Squadron, Port Charlotte, 1994-96. Coast Guard Aux., 1995-97. Fellow, Sloan Found., 1973—75, U. Ky., 1984, Ky. Col., 2003; scholar, Md. State Tchr. Bd. Edn., 1960—63. Mem, Soc. Applied Learning Tech., Assn. Computing Machinery (v.p. 85—), Am. Legion, Pi Gamma Mu. Democrat. Mem. Ch. Of Christ. Avocations: sailing, singing, swimming, cooking, music. Home: 112 Oak Ridge Rd Brunswick GA 31523-9741 Office Phone: 912-262-2509. Personal E-mail: sandramihal@bellsouth.net. Business E-Mail: sandy.mihal@dhs.gov.

MIHM, JOHN CLIFFORD, chemical engineer; b. Austin, Tex., July 28, 1942; s. Clifford Henry and Adeline (Cleary) M.; m. Janet Eleanor Skales, May 29, 1964; 1 child, Mary Lynn AA, Frank Phillips Coll., 1962; BSChemE, Tex. Tech. U., 1964. Registered profl. engr., Tex., Okla. With Phillips Petroleum Co., 1964—2003, v.p. corp. engring. Bartlesville, Okla., 1987-92, v.p. R & D, 1992-93, sr. v.p. corp. tech., 1993-99, sr. v.p. tech. and project devel., 1999—2002; engr. mgr. E & P Phillips Petroleum Co., Stavanger, Norway, 1977-82; chmn. bd. Far East Energy Corp., 2005—07, vice chair. high nitrogen natural gas, 2006—. Mem. adv. bd. Tex. Tech U., Lubbock, 1985—, pres. deans coun., 1996-98. Bd. dirs. Boy Scouts Am., Bartlesville, 1986—, area III pres., 1998-2002, area 8 pres., 2008-10, Southern region bd. dirs., 1998—. Named Disting. Engr., Tex. Tech. U., 1984; named to Okla. State U. Coll. of Engring. Arch. and Tech. Hall of Fame, 1999. Fellow ASME (ind. adv. bd. 1989-2002, found. bd. dirs. 2000—); mem. NSPE (mem. adv. bd. 1994-2002), AIChE (ECC divsn., bd. dirs. 1989-93, chmn. 1992-93), Okla. Soc. Profl. Engrs. (Outstanding Engr. in Mgmt. award 1991), Soc. Petroleum Engrs. (bd. dir., 2004-08, Disting. Mem. 2000), Okla. Engring. Found. (bd. dirs., pres. 1993-97), Nat. Acad. Constrn. (pres. 2008). Republican. Roman Catholic. Home: 5413 Braemar Dr Frisco TX 75034 Home Phone: 214-705-7207; Office Phone: 972-658-8583. E-mail: jcmihmr66@aol.com.

MIKALSON, JON DENNIS, classics educator; b. Milw., Aug. 1, 1943; s. John Martin and Evelyn Kathryn (Heuser) M.; m. Mary Helen Villemonte, Aug. 28, 1966; children: Melissa, Jacquelyn. BA, U. Wis., 1965; postgrad., Am. Sch. Classical Studies, Athens, Greece, 1968-69; PhD, Harvard U., 1970. Asst. prof. classics U. Va., Charlottesville, 1970-75, assoc. prof., 1975-84, prof., 1984—, William R. Kenan Jr. prof. classics, 1999—, chmn. dept. classics, 1978-90. Dir. Echols Scholar Program, 1997-2000; vis. scholar Corpus Christi Coll., Cambridge, Eng., 1977-78; mem. Inst. for Advanced Study, Princeton, N.J., 1984-85; Whitehead prof. Am. Sch. Classical Studies, 1995-96. Author: The Sacred and Civil Calendar of the Athenian Year, 1975, Athenian Popular Religion, 1983, Honor Thy Gods: Popular Religion in Greek Tragedy, 1991, Religion in Hellenistic Athens, 1998, Herodotus and Religion in the Persian Wars, 2003, Ancient Greek Religion, 2004, Greek Popular Religion in Greek Philosophy, 2010; contbr. articles to profl. and scholarly jours. James Rignall Wheeler fellow Am. Sch. Classical Studies, 1968-69, NEH fellow, 1977-78, Herodotus fellow Inst. for Advanced Study, 1984-85. Mem. Am. Philol. Assn., Am. Sch. Classical Studies, Archeol. Inst. of Am., Classical Assn. of Middle West and South (pres. so. sect. 1988-90), Classical Assn. of Va., Phi Beta Kappa, Phi Eta Sigma, Phi Kappa Phi, Omicron Delta Kappa. Clubs: Lions. Home: PO Box 664 Crozet VA 22932-0664 Office: U Va Dept Classics PO Box 400788 B002 Cocke Hall Charlottesville VA 22904-4788 Home Phone: 434-823-2163; Office Phone: 434-823-2163, 434-924-3008. Business E-Mail: jdm9x@virginia.edu.

MIKLIUS, AUDREY B., endocrinologist, educator; BS in Biol. Sciences, Stanford U., 1983; MD, U. Hawaii, 1988. Diplomate American Bd. Internal Medicine-endocrinology, diabetes and metabolism, 2004, lic. Tex., 1997. Resident internal medicine Massachusetts Gen. Hosp., Boston, 1988—91; fellow endocrinology Mass. Gen. Hosp., Boston, 1991—93, rsch. fellow endocrinology, 1992—93; rsch. fellow medicine Harvard Univ., Cambridge, Mass., 1991—93; med. dir., women's health svcs., divsn. endocrinology St. Elizabeth's Med. Ctr., Boston, 1993—96; asst. prof. medicine Tufts Univ., Boston, 1993—96; asst. prof. internal medicine, divsn. endocrinology Univ. Tex. Southwestern Med. Ctr., Dallas, 1996—98; clin. endocrinologist Endocrine Asscs. of Dallas, P.A., 1998—; hosp. affiliations include Med. City Dallas Hosp., Tex. Health Presbyn. Hosp. Dallas, Baylor Richardson Med. Ctr., Tex., Baylor Regional Med. Ctr., Plano, Tex., Tex. Health Presbyn. Hosp., Plano. Recipient Upjohn Achievement award, 1988, Janet M. Glasgow Meml. award, American Med. Women's Assn., 1988. Fellow: American Coll. of Endocrinology. Office: Endocrine Associates of Dallas PA Ste 100N 10260 N Central Expy Dallas TX 75231 Office Phone: 214-363-5535.*

MIKUEN, SCOTT THEODORE, lawyer; b. 1961; m. Monica Mikuen; children: Brett, Sean, Megan. BA in Polit. Sci. with high honors, Colgate U., 1984; JD, Harvard Law Sch., 1987. Bar: Fla., NY. Atty. Meltzer, Lippe, Goldstein & Breitstone, Mineola, NY, Breed, Abbott & Morgan, NY; various positions in legal dept., through v.p., counsel, corporate & comml. divsn. legal affairs & financial counsel Harris Corp., Melbourne, Fla., 1996—2004, v.p., assoc. gen. counsel & sec., 2004—10, v.p., sec. gen. counsel, 2010—. Bd. mem. Melbourne Airport Authority; dir. Club Esteem. Mem.: ABA, Fla. Bar Assn., NY State Bar Assn., American Soc. Corporate Sec. & Governance Professionals, Assn. Corporate Counsel. Office: Harris Corp 1025 W NASA Blvd Melbourne FL 32919 Office Phone: 321-727-9100. Office Fax: 321-674-4740. Business E-Mail: Scott.Mikuen@harris.com.

MIKULAK, ROBERT PETER, federal official; b. St. Paul, Minn., Oct. 5, 1942; s. Peter H. and Inez H. (Haugen) M.; m. Gunnel Margareta Porelius, July 30, 1977; children: Lena, Anna. BS in Chemistry, Hamline U., 1964; PhD in Chemistry, MIT, 1969. Rsch. fellow Max Planck Inst. for Biophys. Chemistry, Göttingen, Germany, 1969-70; rsch. fellow polit. sci. MIT, Cambridge, 1970; asst. prof. chemistry and polit. sci. Hamline U., St. Paul, 1970-71; phys. sci. officer US Arms Control and Disarmament Agy., Washington, 1971-87; sr. scientist U.S. Arms Control and Disarmament Agy., Washington, 1987-92; spl. negotiator-chem. weapons US Arms Control & Disarmament Agy., Washington, 1987-92, chief chemical & biological policy divsn., 1996-99; alternate US rep. Chem. Weapons Convention, The Hague, Netherlands, 1993—; dir. Office Chemical & Biological Weapons Conventions US Dept. State, Washington, 1999—2010, US rep. to Org. for the Prohibition of Chemical Weapons (OPCW), 2010—. Sr. negotiator U.S.-Russia, 1989, 90, Chem. Weapons Convention, 1992. Co-author: Stereochemistry, 1976; contbr. articles to profl. jours. Predoctoral fellowship NSF, 1964-68, postdoctoral fellowship, 1969-70. Mem. AAAS (Hilliard Roderick prize in arms control 1992), American Chem. Soc., Sr. Execs. Assn., Sr. Exec. Svc. Avocations: reading, investments, gardening, travel. Office: US Dept State 2201 C St NW Washington DC 20520-0001 Home: 215 N Highland St Arlington VA 22201-1232 E-mail: mikulakrp@t.state.gov, bobmik1@yahoo.com.*

MILAM, JOHN DANIEL, pathologist, educator; b. Kilgore, Tex., May 22, 1933; s. Ott G. and Effie (White) Milam; m. Carol Jones, Aug. 1, 1959; children: Kay, Beth, John Daniel, Julie. BS, La. State U., 1955, MS, 1957, MD, 1960. Attending pathologist St. Luke's Episcopal Hosp., Houston, 1967—89, chief of staff, 1981—83; emeritus Tex. Children's Hosp., Houston, 2000—; adj. prof. lab. medicine M.D. Anderson Cancer Ctr., U. Tex., Houston, 1990—2001; prof. pathology and lab. medicine U. Tex. Med. Sch., Houston, 1989—2001, prof. emeritus, 2001—; active med. staff Hermann Hosp., Houston, 1988—, med. dir. lab. svcs., 1990—95; chief pathology Lyndon B. Johnson Gen. Hosp., Houston, 1995—2001. Trustee Am. Bd. Pathology, 1985—96, pres., 1995, life trustee, 1996—; cons. in field. Contbr. articles and abstracts to profl. jours., chapters to books. Bd. dirs. Greater Houston area chpt. ARC, 1978—. Recipient Disting. Physician award, Hermann Hosp., 1996. Mem.: Coll. Am. Pathologist (bd. govs., vice spkr. house of dels. 2005—), Houston Soc. Clin. Pathologists (pres. 1975, Harlan J. Spjut award 2003), Am. Soc. Clin. Pathologists (Commn. on Continuing Edn. Disting. Svc. award 1993, Israel Davidsohn Disting. Svc. award 2001), Tex. Soc. Pathologists (pres. 1978, George T. Caldwell award 1981), Am. Assn. Blood Banks (pres. 1984, Disting. Svc. award 1988). Republican. Baptist. Home: 11927 Arbordale Ln Houston TX 77024-5001 Office: U Tex Houston Med Sch Rm 2-022 Dept Pathology 6431 Fannin St Houston TX 77030-1501 Office Phone: 713-500-5336. Business E-Mail: john.d.milam@uth.tmc.edu.

MILDENHALL, JONATHAN, beverage company executive; b. 1967; Student, Manchester Poly.; grad. Advanced Mgmt. Programme, Harvard Bus. Sch., 2005. Grad. trainee McCann-Erickson, 1990—93; with Bartle Bogle Hegarty, 1993—96; account dir. Smirnoff worldwide Lowe Howard-Spink, 1996—97, bd. dirs., 1997; head account mgmt. HHCL & Ptnrs., 2000—02; joint mng. dir. TBWA\LONDON, 2002—03, mng. dir., 2003—05; strategy dir., Mother Coca-Cola Co., London, 2005—06, v.p., global mktg. strategy & creative comm., 2007, creative dir. Co-chair ethnic diversity com. IPA, coun. steering mem. Fellow: British Am. Project. Office: Coca-Cola Co PO Box 1734 Atlanta GA 30301 Office Phone: 404-676-2121. Office Fax: 404-676-6792.

MILES, AMY E., film company executive; m. Dan Miles; children: Connor, Nick. With PricewaterhouseCoopers, LLC, 1989—98; sr. mgr. Deloitte & Touche, 1998—99; sr. v.p., fin. Regal Cinemas, Inc. (subs. Regal Entertainment Group), 1999—2000, exec. v.p., treas., CFO, 2000—02, Regal Entertainment Group, 2002—09, CEO, bd. dirs., 2009—. Named one of The 100 Most Powerful Women in Entertainment, Hollywood Reporter, 2012—13. Office: Regal Entertainment Group 7132 Regal Ln Knoxville TN 37918*

MILES, BORRIS L., state legislator; b. Sunnyside, Tex., Oct. 23, 1965; married; children: Justus, Faith. BS in Criminal Justice, Sam Houston State U., Huntsville, Tex. Police officer; founder Borris L. Miles Ins., Houston; mem. Dist. 146 Tex. House of Representatives, 2006—08, 2011—. Founder Sickle Cell Rsch. Endowment, North Forest Scholarship Endowment; mem. State Tex. Auto Theft Prevention Bd.; active Across the Track PAC. Recipient Leadership award, Farmers Ins., 1999, Super Achievers award, YMCA, 2003, Pinnacle award, Houston Citizen C. of C., 2005, and several other honors. Mem.: Urban League (bd. mem.), 100 Black Men Houston (founder),

Houston Sickle Cell Assn. (former bd. mem.), United Negro Coll. Fund (former bd. mem.), Alpha Phi Alpha (life). Democrat. Baptist. Office: Room E2.506 Capitol Extension PO Box 2910 Austin TX 78768 Address: 2656 South Loop West Ste 265 Houston TX 77054 Office Phone: 512-463-0518, 713-665-8322. Office Fax: 512-463-0941.

MILES, BRIAN JOHN, urologist; b. Belfast, No. Ireland, Nov. 8, 1946; s. William Livingston and Kathleen (Jamison) M.; m. Renee' Gig DeBlaise, Sept. 15, 1990. BS, Mich. State U., 1967; MS in Engring., U. Mich., 1968, MD, 1974. Diplomate Am. Bd. Urology. Surg. intern Georgetown U., Washington, 1974-75; resident in urology Walter Reed Army Med. Ctr., Washington, 1978-82; instr. dept. urology Army Med. Ctr., Tacoma, 1982-84; instr. dept. surgery U. Wash., Seattle, 1982-84; staff physician dept surgery Henry Ford Hosp., Detroit, 1984-91; assoc. prof. U. Mich., Ann Arbor, 1984-93; dir. resident edn. Henry Ford Hosp., Detroit, 1987-93, dir. urologic oncology, 1988—91; assoc. prof. Scott Dept. Urology, Houston, 1993-2000, prof., 2000—08, disting. Cullen chair in Urology, 2003—08; chief of urology VA Med. Ctr., Houston, 1993-98, St. Luke's Episcopal Hosp., Houston, 1993—; med. dir. Tex. Cancer Inst., 1999—2008; assoc. dir. for clin. affairs Baylor Comprehensive Cancer Ctr., Houston, 2006—08; clin. prof. urology, 2008—. Assoc. editor: Comprehensive Textbook of Genitourinary Oncology, 1995. Lt. col M.C., U.S. Army, 1975-84. Mem. ACS, Am. Urologic Assn. (Prostate Cancer Outcomes Analysis Grant 1995, 96), Soc. Urologic Oncology, Soc. Univ. Urologists, Internat. Soc. Urology. Avocations: history, sports, reading. Home: 4008 Driscoll St Houston TX 77098-3508 Office Phone: 713-441-8110. Business E-Mail: bmiles@drbrianmiles.com.

MILES, DAVID W., personal care industry executive; CPA. Various positions Ernst & Young LLP; dir., fin. reporting ResCare, Inc., 1998, v.p., contr., 2001—06, CFO, 2005—. Office: Res-Care Inc 9901 Linn Station Rd Louisville KY 40223 Office Phone: 502-394-2100. Office Fax: 502-394-2206. Business E-Mail: dmiles@rescare.com.

MILES, JOHN BENJAMIN, lawyer; b. Greensboro, NC, Oct. 19, 1930; s. John Richard and Lois (Wilson) Miles; m. Daphne Rees, June 25, 1960; children: Lois Rose, John Benjamin Jr. BA, Guilford Coll., 1952; LLB, Wake Forest U., 1955. Bar: NC 1955, US Dist. Ct. (mid. dist.) NC 1959. Pvt. practice law, Greensboro, 1958—61, 1969—2008; mcpl. judge City of Greensboro, 1961—68. With US Army, 1955—58. Mem.: NC Bar, Phi Delta Phi. Republican. Presbyterian. Home: 5045 Harvest Rd Mc Leansville NC 27301-9702

MILES, JOHN CARLEN, II, dental company executive; b. Portland, Maine, Feb. 22, 1942; s. John Carlen and Dorothy Clare (Hanson) M.; m. Anna Maria Chico, Sept. 10, 1977; children—Karen, Shirley, Lawrence, Suzanne BSI.E., Lehigh U., 1964; MBA, NYU, 1971. Mfg. mgr. Permacel div. Johnson & Johnson, New Brunswick, N.J., 1964-71; prodn. planning mgr. Coty div. Pfizer, Inc., Sanford, N.C., 1971-73; v.p.-gen. mgr. FDI Inc., Edison, N.J., 1973-78; sr. v.p., gen. mgr. Rhone-Poulenc, Inc., Monmouth Junction, N.J., 1978-85; v.p., gen. mgr. York divsn. Dentsply Internat. Inc., York, Pa., 1985—86, dir. European ops., 1986—88, pres., COO, 1991—95; chmn., CEO DENTSPLY International, Inc., York, Pa., 1996—. Bd. dirs. Respironics Inc. Bd. dirs. Nat. Found. Dentistry for the Handicapped. Recipient Claude V. Swank award Johnson & Johnson, 1967 Mem.: Am. Dental Trade Assn. (bd. dirs.), Bonita Bay Country Club (Fla.), Country Club of York. Republican. Presbyterian. Avocations: golf, boating, reading. Office: Dentsply Internat Inc 570 W College Ave York PA 17404-3880 Home: 27810 Riverwalk Way Bonita Springs FL 34134-1675

MILES, LAVEDA ANN, advertising executive; b. Greenville, SC, Nov. 21, 1945; d. Grady Lewis and Edna Sylvia (Mahaffey) Bruce; m. Charles Thomas Miles, Nov. 10, 1974; 1 child, Joshua Bruce. A in Bus. Adminstrn., North Greenville Jr. Coll. Traffic mgr. WFBV-TV, Greenville, 1968-74; pub. svc. dir., traffic mgr. WTCG-TV, Atlanta, 1974-75; traffic mgr. Henderson Advt. Co., Greenville, 1975-77, broadcast coord., 1977-79, dir. broadcast bus., 1979-82, v.p., dir. broadcast bus., 1982-89, bus. mgr. creative dept., 1989-91, dir. creative svcs., 1991-93, sr. v.p., 1994-96, v.p., dir. creative svcs., 2000—06; creative svcs. mgr. The Bounce Agy., 2006—; owner Altamont Mktg., 1996-99. Mem. Leadership S.C., 1994-95; bd. dirs. Boys Home of the South, 2003—. Named one of 100 Best and Brightest Women, Ad Age and Advt. Women of N.Y., 1988. Mem. Advt. Fedn. Greenville (sec. 1979-81), Greenville Ad Club (sec. 1999-2000, pres. 2000—02, Silver medal award 2003). Republican. Baptist. Home: PO BOX 924 Greenville SC 29602-0924 Office Phone: 864-271-8340. E-mail: laveda.miles@thebounceagency.com.

MILES, LELAND WEBER, retired academic administrator; b. Balt., Jan. 18, 1924; s. Leland Weber and Marie (Fitzpatrick) M.; m. Mary Virginia Geyer, July 9, 1947; children: Christine Marie, Gregory Lynn. AB cum laude, Juniata Coll., 1946; MA, U. N.C., 1947, PhD, 1949; postgrad., Duke U., 1949; DLitt (hon.), Juniata Coll., 1969; LHD (hon.), Rosary Hill Coll., 1970; LLD (hon.), Far East U., 1979; DHC (hon.), U. Guadalajara, Mex., 1984; Order of Merit, Alfred U., 1986. Assoc. prof. English Hanover Coll., 1949-50, prof., chmn. English dept., 1950-60; assoc. prof., asst. to head English dept. U. Cin., 1960-63, prof., 1963-64, founder humanities reading program for engrs., 1961; dean Coll. Arts and Scis., U. Bridgeport, Conn., 1964-67; pres. U. Bridgeport, 1974-87; founder U. Bridgeport Sch. Law, 1977; pres. emeritus U. Bridgeport, 1987—; pres. Alfred U., 1967-74. Bd. dirs. United Illuminating, 1978-94, chmn. audit com., 1992-94, Grolier, 1984-88, Wright Managed Investment Funds, 1988-04, Internat. Peace Acad., 1982-90; Danforth scholar Union Theol. Sem., 1956; Lilly fellow Sch. Letters Ind. U., 1959; Am. Council Learned Socs. fellow Harvard, 1963-64; Sr. Fulbright Research scholar Kings Coll. U. London, 1964, vis. scholar, 1972; seminar leader, deans and presidents insts. Am. Council on Edn., 1973-79; chmn. bd. Acad. Collective Bargaining Info. Service, Washington, 1977-79; producer, moderator Casing the Classics CBS Sta. WHAS-TV, Louisville, 1958-61; moderator Aspen (Colo.) Inst. for Humanistic Studies, 1969-70; lectr. Keedick Lecture Bur., N.Y.C., 1956-83; vis. prof. New Coll., Sarasota, Fla., 1989. Author: John Colet and the Platonic Tradition, 1961; editor: St. Thomas More's Dialogue of Comfort Against Tribulation, 1965, Where Do You Stand On Linquistics?, 1964, revised, 1968; sr. editor: (with Stephen Graubard and later Stephen B. Baxter) Studies in British History and Culture, 1965-79, Provoking Thought: What Colleges Should Do For Students, 2001, The Hijacking of Jesus, 2012; contbg. editor Nat. Forum, 1983-91; contbr. articles to learned jours., chpts. in books. Mem. Eagle Scout, 1939; trustee Western NY Nuc. Rsch. Ctr., 1967-73; chmn. bd. Coll. Ctr. Finger Lakes, 1968-71; vice-chmn. bd. Empire State Found., 1969-71, chmn., 1971-73; mem. New Eng. Bd. Higher Edn., 1985-87, Ambs. Roundtable World Affairs Forum, 1986-92, Fuld Found./Nat. League Nursing Adv. Coun. on Accreditation, 1986-88; chmn. Ettinger scholarship com. Ednl. Found. Am., 1987-93; bd. dirs. Conn. Grand Opera, 1978-89, Bridgeport Bus. Coun., 1982-88; bd. dirs. Save the Children, 1988-95, chmn. adv. coun., 1990-95; adviser Asolo Theater-Fla. State U. Conservatory Actors Tng., 2004-. 1st lt. USAAF, 1944-45; capt. USAFR. Decorated DFC with oak leaf cluster, Crown Decoration of Honor 3rd Order Iran, 1978; chevalier l'Ordre des Palmes Académique (France), 1984; recipient Rosa and Samuel Sachs prize Cin. Inst. Fine Arts, 1961, Cultural medal Republic of China, 1983, Disting. Svc. award Greater Bridgeport Bar Assn., 1986, Outstanding Civilian Svc. medal Dept. Army, 1988; Miles scholars Alfred U., 1995—. Fellow Royal Soc. Arts, Manufactures and Commerce (life); mem. Renaissance Soc. Am., English Speaking Union (bd. dirs. Greenwich, Conn. chpt. 1998-04), UN Assn. (bd. dirs. Sarasota Manatee chpt., coord. young profl. for internat. coop. 2005-08), Internat. Assn. Univ. Pres. (pres. 1981-84, pres. emeritus 1984—, chief UN mission 1988-97, World Peace award 1987, chmn. UN commn. on arms control edn. 1991-96, mem. coun. sr. advisers 1992—), Knights of Malta (order of the Orthodox Knights Hospitaller of St. John of Jerusalem, Russian Orthodox br.), Mil. Officers Assn. Sarasota, West Coast Symphony Assn., Sarasota Opera Guild, Univ. Club (NYC), Phi Delta Kappa. Episcopalian. Home (Summer): 87 Field Point Dr Fairfield CT 06824-6329 Home (Winter): The Fountains 3240 Lake Point Blvd #319 Sarasota FL 34231 Personal E-mail: lelandwmiles@yahoo.com.

MILES, LES (LESLIE EDWIN MILES), college football coach; b. Elyria, Ohio, Nov. 10, 1953; m. Kathy Miles; children: Kathryn, Leslie Matthew, Benjamin, Macy Grace. BS in Economics, U. Mich., Ann Arbor, 1976. Grad. asst. U. Mich., 1980—81, asst. coach, 1987—94, U. Colo., 1982—86; offensive coord. Okla. State U., Stillwater, 1995—97, head coach, 2001—04, La. State U., Baton Rouge, 2005—; tight ends coach Dallas Cowboys, 1998—2000. Active Spl. Olympics; event host Children's Miracle Network; active celebrity waiter event Baton Rouge Children's Advocacy Ctr.; active Mary Bird Perkins Cancer Ann. Fundraiser. Named Big 12 Conf. Coach of Yr., 2002, Southeastern Conf. Coach of Yr., 2011, Home Depot Coach of Yr., ESPN, ABC Sports, 2011, Coach of Yr., AP, 2011, Liberty Mutual Coach of Yr., 2012. Achievements include coaching La. State U. to the 2007 BCS Nat. Championship. Office: LSU Athletic Dept Football PO Box 25095 Baton Rouge LA 70894 Office Phone: 225-578-1151. Business E-Mail: lem042@lsu.edu.

MILES, MIKE, school system administrator; m. Karen Miles; children: Nicholas, Madeleine, Anthony. Grad., UD Mil. Acad., West Point, NY, 1978; student in Slavic languages, U. Calif., Berkeley, U. Leningrad, Russia; grad., Columbia U., NYC, 1989. Ranger Bn. officer, Inf. Rifle Co. comdr. US Army; Soviet desk officer US State Dept., fgn. svc. officer Warsaw, spl. asst. to the amb. Moscow; former tchr. prin. & asst. supt.; supt. Harrison Sch. Dist., Colorado Springs, Colo., 2006—12, Dallas Ind. Sch. Dist., 2012—. Recipient Meritorious Svc. medal, US State Dept., 1994; Mellon fellow, Nat. Sci. Found. Grad. scholar. Office: Dallas Independent School District 3700 Ross Ave Dallas TX 75204*

MILES, TOM, state legislator; Attended, Miss. State U. Small bus. owner; mem. Dist. 75 Miss. House of Reps., Jackson, 2012—. Active Scott County Dive Team, Habitat for Humanity, Relay for Life; mem. Forrest Bapt. Ch. Mem.: NRA (life), Morton and Forest C. of C., Miss. State U. Alumni Assn., Forest Lion's Club, Forest Rotary Club. Democrat. Baptist. Office: Miss House of Reps PO Box 1018 Jackson MS 39215 Business E-Mail: tmiles@house.ms.gov.

MILES-LAGRANGE, VICKI, federal judge; b. Oklahoma City, Okla., Sept. 30, 1953; d. Charles and Mary (Greenard) Miles. BA, Vassar Coll., 1974; LLB, Howard U., 1977; cert., U. Ghana, West Africa; DHL (hon.), Oklahoma City U., 1995. Legis. aide Spkr. House Rep. Carl Albert, 1974-76; law clerk Judge Woodrow Seals U.S. Dist. Ct. (so. dist.), Tex., 1977-79; fellow, atty. criminal divsn. U.S. Dept. Justice, Washington, 1979-83; asst. dist. atty. Dist. Atty.'s Office, Oklahoma County, 1983-86; pvt. practice Oklahoma City, 1986-93; mem. Okla. Senate (Dist. 48), 1987-93; U.S. atty. U.S. Dept. Justice, Oklahoma City, 1993-94; judge US Dist. Ct. (we. dist.) Okla, Oklahoma City, 1994—2008, chief judge, 2008—. Bd. trustees Vassar Coll. Mem. ABA, Nat. Bar Assn., Okla. Bar Assn., Am. Inns Ct. Democrat. Baptist. Office: US Dist Judge US Courthouse 200 NW 4th St Ste 5011 Oklahoma City OK 73102-3031

MILFORD, MURRAY HUDSON, retired soil science educator; b. Honey Grove, Tex., Sept. 29, 1934; s. Murray Lane and Vivian Ione (Hudson) M.; m. Marsha Ann Rasmussen, July 21, 1961; children: Rebecca Ione, Murray Daniel. BS in Agronomy, Tex. A&M, 1955, MS in Agronomy, 1959; PhD in Soil Science, U. Wis., 1962. Rsch. assoc. Cornell U., Ithaca, NY, 1962-63, asst. prof., 1963-68, assoc. prof., 1968, Tex. A&M U., College Station, 1968-74, prof., 1974-2001; ret., 2001. Author: (lab. manual) Soils and Soil Science-Lab. Exercises, 1970. 1st lt. USAR, 1955-57. Recipient so. region award for excellence in coll. and univ. tchg. in food and agrl. scis. Nat. Assn. State Univs. and Land Grant Colls., Higher Edn. Program, USDA, 1995. Fellow: AAAS, Am. Soc. Agronomy (pres. Tex. chpt. 1982-83, Resident Edn. award 1978), Soil Sci. Soc. Am. (Edn. award 1988); mem.: Kiwanis Club. Democrat. Presbyterian. Avocations: gardening, stamp collecting/philately. Home: 3606 Tanglewood Dr Bryan TX 77802-3320

MILINAZZO, ALAN W., medical products executive; B cum laude, Boston Coll., 1981. Mktg. profl. Am. Hosp. Supply; various sales and mktg. positions including v.p. mktg. SCIMED Europe Boston Scientific Corp., 1988—2000; gen. mgr. internat. Neoforma, Inc., 2000; group pres. cardiology and vascular Northpoint Domain, Inc., 2000—01; v.p. North Am. field ops. Aspect Med. Sys., 2001; v.p., gen. mgr. coronary and peripheral businesses Medtronic, Inc., 2002—05, v.p. vascular bus., 2002—05; COO Orthofix International N.V., 2005—06, pres., CEO, bd. dirs., 2006—. Former bd. dirs. Percardia, Inc. Office: Orthofix International NV 1720 Bray Ctrl Dr Mc Kinney TX 75069 Office Phone: 469-742-2500. Business E-Mail: alanmilinazzo@orthofix.com.

MILLAR, FRAN, state legislator; b. New London, Conn., Dec. 9, 1949; BS in Economics, West Va. Wesleyan Coll. Ins. broker Wells Fargo Ins. Services; mem. Dist. 59 Ga. House of Reps., 1999—2003, mem. Dist. 52, 2003—04, mem. Dist. 79, 2004—11; mem. Dist. 40 Ga. State Senate, 2011—. Bd. dirs. Dunwoody Homeowners Assn. Recipient Advocacy award, Heart of Gold Ann. Awards Celebration, 2010. Republican. Office: Dist Address PO Box 88096 Atlanta GA 30356 also: Ga State Senate 319B Coverdell Legis Office Bldg Atlanta GA 30334 Office Phone: 404-923-3607, 404-463-2260. Business E-Mail: fran.millar@senate.ga.gov.

MILLAR, JOHN DONALD, physician, occupational & environmental health services consultant, musician; b. Newport News, Va., Feb. 27, 1934; s. John and Dorothea Virginia (Smith) M.; m. Joan M. Phillips, Aug. 17, 1957; children: John Stuart, Alison Gordon, Virginia Taylor. BS, U. Richmond, 1956; MD, Med. Coll. Va., 1959; DTPH, London Sch. Hygiene and Tropical Medicine, 1966; D of Pub. Svc. (hon.), Greenville Coll., Ill., 1994. Cert. specialist in Gen. Preventive Medicine 1969. Intern U. Utah Affiliated Hosps., Salt Lake City, 1959-60, asst. resident in medicine, 1960-61; chief Epidemic Intelligence Svc., Ctr. for Disease Control, USPHS, HEW, Atlanta, 1961-63, dep. chief surveillance sect. epidemiology br., 1962-63, chief smallpox unit, 1963-65, dir. smallpox eradication program, 1966-70, dir. Bur. State Svcs., 1970-78, asst. dir. Ctr. for Disease Control for Pub. Health Practice, 1979-80; dir. Nat. Ctr. Environ. Health, Atlanta, 1980-81, Nat. Inst. for Occupation Safety and Health, Atlanta, 1981-93, chmn. exec. com. Nat. Toxicology Program, 1989-93; pres. Don Millar & Assocs., Inc., Atlanta, 1993—. Adj. prof. occupl. and environ. health Sch. Pub. Health Emory U., Atlanta, 1988-98; cons. on smallpox, smallpox eradication, immunization programs and occupl. and environ. health WHO; mem. WHO expert adv. panel on occupl. health; bd. dirs. Farm Safety 4 Just Kids, 1993-98; tech. adv. bd. Ctr. Protect Workers' Rights, 1993; disting. fellow, vice chmn. Pub. Health Policy Adv. Bd., Inc., Washington, 1998-2007; mem. bd. dirs. Coll. Pub. Health, U. Ga., 2007-08, mem. Dean's Practice Com., 2008-; mem. string bass sect. DeKalb Symphony Orch., 1982-06, Gainesville (Ga.) Symphony Orch., 2000-04, N.E. Ga. Mountain Chamber Orch., 2001-05, Truett-Macconnell Coll. Wind Symphony, 2002-10, Toccoa Falls Coll. Orch., 2005—, Toccoa Symphony Orch., 2005—11, Piedmont Coll. diameber Orchestra, 2011-. Mem. editl. bd. Am. Jour. Indsl. Medicine, 1985-05, Am. Jour. Occupl. Psychology, 1993-00, Am. Jour. Preventive Medicine, 1993-00; contbr. articles to profl. jours. Recipient Surgeon Gen's. Commendation medal, 1965, Okeke prize London Sch. Hygiene and Tropical Medicine, 1966, Presdl. award for mgmt. improvement, 1972, W.C. Gorgas medal Assn. Mil. Surgeons U.S., 1987, Lucas lectr. Faculty Occupational Medicine Royal Coll. Physicians, London, 1987, Outstanding Med. Alumnus award Med. Coll. Va., 1988; also recipient Equal Employment Opportunity award, 1975, Medal of Excellence, 1977, Joseph W. Mountin lectr. award, 1986, Alexander D. Langmuir MD Meml. lectr. award, 2001, all from Ctrs. for Disease Control, Disting. Svc. medal USPHS, 1983, 88, Exemplary Svc. medal Surgeon Gen. U.S., 1988, Giants in Occupational Medicine lectr. U. Utah, 1989, William S. Knudsen award Am. Coll. Occupational Medicine, 1991, presdl. citation APA, 1991, William Steiger Meml. award Am. Conf. Govtl. Indsl. Hygienists, 1993, Health Watch award for outstanding contbns. toward improving health of minority populations, 1992, Award of Merit Minerva Edn. Inst., 1993, Alumni Disting. Svc. award U. Richmond, 1993, Jeff Lee Mem. Lectr. Am. Indusl. Hygiene Assoc. San Diego, Calif., 2002; named to Order Bifurcated Needle, World Health Orgn., 1978, Faculty Occupational Medicine, Royal Coll. Physicians, London, 1990; elected Safety and Health Hall of Fame Internat., Nat. Safety Coun., 1997. Mem. Am. Indsl. Hygiene Assn. (hon.), Am. Coll. Occupl. and Environ. Medicine, Am. Epidemiol. Soc., Collegium Ramazzini, Am. Assn. Pub. Health Physicians., Assn. Mil. Surgeons U.S., Pub. Health Svc. Commissioned Officers Assn., Alpha Omega Alpha.

MILLAY, ROGER FOSTER, accountant; b. Montreal, Que., Can., Sept. 24, 1957; came to U.S., 1962; s. Clifford Clarence and Elizabeth Pearl (McLeod) M.; m. Robin Anne Scott, June 27, 1981; children: Kristin Anne, Kelsey Lynn. BA in English Lit., U. Va., 1979; MS in Acctg., Georgetown U., 1980. CPA Conn. Audit mgr. ARthur Young & Co., Stamford, Conn., 1980-85; asst. v.p. Citibank, N.A., NYC, 1985-87; mgr. corp. fin. practices GE Capital Corp., Stamford, 1987-90, mgr. bus. analysis, 1990-91, CFO, 1991-93, General Electric Capital, Mexico City, 1993—; v.p., CFO Watson Wyatt Worldwide, Inc., 2008—. Tutor Literacy Vols., Stamford, 1985. Mem. AICPA, Conn. Soc. CPAs. Avocations: golf, skiing, reading. Home: Monte Everest 510 Lomas de Chapultepec Mexico City 11000 Mexico Office: Watson Wyatt Worldwide Inc 901 N Glebe Rd Arlington VA 22203 Office Phone: 703-258-8000. Office Fax: 703-258-8585. Business E-Mail: Roger.Millay@gecapital.com.

MILLBERG, JOHN C., lawyer; b. New London, Conn., Jan. 4, 1956; s. Melvin Roy and Dorothy (Van Zandt) M.; m. Lori Bruce, Oct. 18, 1981; children: Kathryn Faye, Rebecca Ann, Melvin Roy III. BA, Bowling Green State U., 1977; JD, Wake Forest U., 1980. Bar: Tex. 1980, NC 1986, SC 2000, US Dist. Ct. (so. dist.) Tex. 1981, US Ct. Appeals (5th and 11th cirs.) 1981, US Dist. Ct. (ea., mid. and we. dists.) NC 1986, US Ct. Appeals (4th cir.) 1986, US Dist. Ct. SC 2002. Assoc. Crain Caton James & Womble, Houston, 1981—85; assoc., dir. Maupin, Taylor, Ellis & Adams, Raleigh, NC, 1985—94; mng. ptnr. Millberg, Gordon & Stewart, PLLC, Raleigh, NC, 1994—. Mem. bar candidate com. NC Bd. Law Examiners, 1988-90. Scholar Wake Forest U. Sch. Law, 1977-80. Mem. NC Assn. Def. Attys. (exec. com., v.p. southeastern region), Nat. Assn. R.R. Trial Counsel. Office: Millberg Gordon & Stewart PLLC S 104 1101 Haynes St Raleigh NC 27604-1455

MILLER, BARRY RIXMANN, lawyer; b. Tempe, Ariz., Feb. 8, 1945; s. Ray E. and Dorothy (Rixmann) Miller; m. Patricia A. Cunningham, Aug. 10, 1968; children: Christy, Brandy Ann. BS with honors, U. Ill., 1967, JD with honors, 1970. Bar: Ill. 1970, Tex. 1972, US Tax Ct. 1972. Mem. firm Andrews & Kurth, Houston, 1972—79, ptnr., 1979, mgmt. com., 1990—92; ptnr., co-head tax law sect. Vinson & Elkins, LLP, 2003—05; treas. Askew PTO, 1980. Contbr. articles to profl. jours. Served to 1st lt. US Army, 1970—72. Decorated Army Commendation medal US Army; recipient Bronze Tablet, U. Ill., 1967; James scholar, 1963. Mem.: ABA (sect. on taxation), Tex. Bar Assn., Phi Alpha Mu, Beta Alpha Psi, Order of Coif, Sigma Chi. Republican. Office: Vinson & Elkins LLP First City Tower 1001 Fannin St, Ste 2300 Houston TX 77002 Office Phone: 713-758-4438. Business E-Mail: brmiller@velaw.com.

MILLER, BRIAN A., lawyer, electric power industry executive; BA, Boston Coll.; JD, Univ. Conn. Counsel Chadbourne & Parke LLP; v.p., dep. gen counsel, corp. sec. AES Corp., 2001—05, exec. v.p., gen. counsel & corp. sec., 2005—. Office: AES Corporation 11th Fl 4300 Wilson Blvd Arlington VA 22203*

MILLER, BRIAN STACY, federal judge; b. Pine Bluff, Ark., 1967; AA, Phillips CC of U. Ark., 1990; BS, U. Ctrl. Ark., 1992; JD, Vanderbilt U., 1995. Bar: Tenn. 1995, Ark. 1996. Assoc. atty. Martin, Tate, Morrow, & Marston PC, 1995—2006; city atty. City of Helena, Ark., 1999—2005; dep. prosecuting atty. Phillips County, Ark., 2000—06; judge Ark. Ct. Appeals, 2007, US Dist. Ct. (ea. dist.) Ark., Little Rock, 2008—. Served with USNR, 1984, 1989-92, served with USN, 1985—89. Mem.: ABA, Memphis Bar Assn. (pub. coun. 1997), Phillips County Bar Assn., Tenn. Bar Assn., Ark. Bar Assn., Nat. Bar Assn. Office: US Dist Ct Ea Dist Ark 500 W Capitol Ave Little Rock AR 72201 Office Phone: 501-604-5351.

MILLER, BUTCH, state legislator; b. Nov. 24; m. Teresa Miller; 3 children. BS in Biology, North Ga. Coll. & State U., Dahlonega. Automobile dealer Milton Martin Honda, Gainesville, Ga.; mem. Dist. 49 Ga. State Senate, Atlanta, 2010—. Bd. dirs. North Ga. Honda Dealers, former pres.; mem. adv. bd. America Honda Motor Co. Nat. Dealers. Active Meals on Wheels, Relay for Life, Eagle Ranch, Hall County YMCA, Edmondson-Telford Ctr. Children, NE Ga. Med. Ctr. Found., United Way; deacon, Sunday sch. tchr. Lakewood Bapt. Ch.; former mem. bd. dirs. Challenged Child and Friends, Hall County Parks and Leisure, Field of Dreams, Greater Hall C. of C.; bd. dirs. Ga. Bapt. Children's Home. Mem.: Nat. Automobile Dealers Assn. (chmn. Group 20), Ga. Automobile Dealers Assn. (chmn. bd. dirs.). Republican. Office: 2420 Brown Bridge Rd Gainesville GA 30504 also: Ga State Senate 325B Coverdell Legis Office Bldg Atlanta GA 30334 Office Phone: 678-989-5301, 404-656-6578.

MILLER, CHARLES, state legislator; b. Aug. 2, 1939; Bd. trustee Pleasure Ridge Pk. Vol. Fire Dept., Columbia Hosp.; mem. Dist. 28 Ky. House of Reps., 1998—. Named one of Outstanding Prin. of Yr., Dist. 15 PTA, 1987—88, 1990—91, 1994—95; named to Hall of Fame, Dist. 15, 1994. Mem.: Leadership Louisville, Area 1 Coun. C of C (pres. 1993—95). Democrat. Baptist. Mailing: 3608 Gateview Circle Louisville KY 40272 Office: Capitol Annex Rm 451C Frankfort KY 40601 Home Phone: 502-937-7788; Office Phone: 502-564-8100 ext 631. Business E-Mail: charlie.miller@lrc.ky.gov.

MILLER, CHARLES T., prosecutor; b. Winslow, Wash., June 27, 1948; s. Charles Wilbur and Pharoeba H. (Good) M.; m. Rebecca Louise Campbell, Aug. 17, 1974; chidren: Angela Dawn, Emily Grace, Kathryn Louise. BS in Criminal Justice, W.Va. State Coll., 1973; JD, W.Va. U., 1977. Bar: W.Va. 1977, U.S. Ct. Appeals (4th cir.) 1977. Asst. prosecuting atty., Kanawha County, W.Va., 1977-82; assoc., ptnr. E. F. Thaxton Attys., Charleston, 1982-84; 1st asst. US atty. (so. dist.) W.Va. US Dept. Justice, Charleston, 1984—, interim US atty., 1991—92, 1993, 2001, 2006—10. With USN, 1966-69, Vietnam; maj. W.Va. Army Nat. Guard; lt. col. W.Va. Air Nat. Guard. Decorated Navy Achievement medal, Rep. of Vietnam Svc. medal, Rep. of Vietnam Campaign ribbon, Rep. of Vietnam Cross of Gallantry, Combat Action ribbon, Presdl. Unit citation. Presbyterian. Avocation: carpentry. Office: US Atty's Office PO Box 1713 Charleston WV 25326

MILLER, CHERYL DEANN, sportscaster, former professional basketball player and coach; b. Riverside, Calif., Jan. 3, 1964; BA in Broadcast Journalism, U. So. Calif., 1985. Basketball player Jr. Nat. Team, 1981, U.S. Nat. Team, 1982, U.S. Olympics, 1984; commentator ABC Sports; head coach women's basketball U. So. Calif., 1993-94; NBA analyst and reporter Turner Sports, Atlanta, 1995—; gen. mgr., head coach Phoenix Mercury, 1997—2000. Player JC Penney All-Am. Team Five, U. So. Calif. Women's Basketball Team, World Championship Team, 1983. Recipient Sports Illustrated Player of Yr., 1986, Naismith Player of Yr. award, Kodak All-Am. award, more than 1,140 trophies and 125 plaques including Nat. Sports Festival, 1981, Pan Am. Games, 1983, FIBA World Championship, Goodwill Games, gold medal 1984 Olympic Games; elected to Naismith Basketball Hall of Fame, 1995. Achievements include being the first female analyst to call a nationally televised NBA game, 1996. Office: Turner Sports 1 CNN Ctr 100 International Blvd Atlanta GA 30348

MILLER, CHRISTINE MARIE, sales, marketing and public relations executive; b. Williamsport, Pa., Dec. 7, 1950; d. Frederick James and Mary (Wurster) M.; m. Robert M. Ancell, Mar. 30, 1985. BA, U. Kans., Lawrence, 1972; MA, Northwestern U., Evanston, Ill., 1978, PhD, 1982. Pub. rels. asst. Bedford County Commr., Pa., 1972—73; tchg. asst. Northwestern U., Evanston, Ill., 1977—80; asst. prof. U. Ala., Tuscaloosa, 1980—82, Loyola U., New Orleans, 1982—85; vis. prof. Ind. U. Sch. Journalism, Bloomington, 1985—86; dir. mktg. Nat. Inst. Fitness & Sport, Indpls., 1986—88; mgmt. assoc. cmty. and media rels. Subaru-Isuzu Automotive, Inc., Lafayette, Ind., 1988—91; dir. pub. rels. Giddings & Lewis, Fond Du Lac, Wis., 1991—93; v.p. comm. and enrollment mgmt. Milton Hershey Sch., Pa., 1993—94, dir. adminstrn., 1994—95; account mgr. Verizon Bus., Vienna, Va., 1995—2007, Terremark Fed., 2007—08; strategic comm. analyst Navy Warfare Devel. Command, 2008—10; customer acct. mgr. Computer Sci. Corp., 2011—. Program dir. Nat. Entrepreneurship Acad., Bloomington, 1986—88. Co-author: The Biographical Dictionary of World War II General and Flag Officers, 1996; contbr. articles to profl. jours. Bd. dirs. Indpls. Entrepreneurship Acad., 1988-91, Area IV Agy., Greater Lafayette Mus. Art, 1989-91. With USN, 1973-77, capt. USNR, 1977—. Mem. Armed Forces Comm. Electronics Assn., Pub. Rels. Soc. Am., Naval Order of the U.S. (nat. pub. affairs com.), U.S. Naval Pub. Affairs Alumnae Assn. (bd. dirs.), Naval Res. Assn., Res. Officers Assn. Presbyterian. Avocations: cooking, swimming, reading, travel, bicycling. Home: 1515 Runnymede Rd Norfolk VA 23505 Personal E-mail: drchrismiller@yahoo.com.

MILLER, CLAYTON, chef; b. Sewickley, Pa., 1971; Degree in Hotel and Restaurant Mgmt., Widener U., Phila.; degree, Pa. Inst. Culinary Arts, Pitts., 1995. Chef de commis Ritz-Carlton Co., Atlanta; entremetier The Dining Room, chef de partie, garde manger, poissonier; stage Daniel, NYC; chef de partie, garde manger and meat The French Laundry, Yountville, Calif.; exec. chef Norman's, Grande Lakes, Fla., 2003, Trummer's on Main, Clifton, Va. Named one of America's Best New Chefs, Food & Wine Mag., 2010. Office: Trummers on Main 7134 Main St Clifton VA 20124 Office Phone: 703-266-1623.

MILLER, D. DOUGLAS, cardiologist, educator; MD, McGill U., 1978. Resident internal medicine Montreal Gen. Hosp., Que., Canada, 1979—81; resident cardiovasc. disease Montreal Heart Inst., Que., Canada, 1981—82; fellow cardiovasc. disease Emory Univ. Med. Ctr., Atlanta, 1982—84; fellow nuclear cardiology Mass. Gen. Hosp.-Harvard, Boston, 1984—86; hosp. affiliation includes MCG Health, Augusta; prof. medicine Med. Coll. of Ga. Office: MCG Health System 1003 Chafee Ave Augusta GA 30912 Office Phone: 706-721-2426.

MILLER, DAVID L., lawyer; b. Bklyn., Nov. 4, 1954; BA with distinction, George Washington U., 1976; JD magna cum laude, U. Mich., 1979. Bar: DC 1979, Va. 1986. Ptnr. Real Estate practice, former mem. bd. dir., former chmn. Legal Opinion com. Pillsbury Winthrop Shaw Pittman, McLean, Va. Former bd. mem. Appleseed Found.; bd. mem. Langley Sch., McLean, Va. Mem.: ABA (former chmn. com. on legal opinions in real estate transactions), Am. Coll. Real Estate Lawyers (former chmn. com. on legal opinions), Urban Land Inst., Nat. Assn. Industrial & Office Properties, Va. State Bar Assn., DC Bar Assn. (former vice chmn. steering com. real estate, housing & land use sec.), Phi Beta Kappa, Order of the Coif. Office: Pillsbury Winthrop Shaw Pittman 1650 Tysons Blvd Mc Lean VA 22102-4859 Office Phone: 703-770-7925. Office Fax: 702-770-7901. Business E-Mail: david.miller@pillsburylaw.com.

MILLER, DENNIS EDWARD, health medical executive; b. Detroit, Dec. 21, 1951; m. Deborah Ann Keith, Feb. 12, 1977. BS, Austin Peay State U., 1973; MBA, U. South Fla., 1981. CPA. Chief exec. officer Hosp. Corp. of Am., Bennettsville, SC, 1976-84; div. v.p. Westworld Community Healthcare, Waco, Tex., 1984-86; group v.p. Nat. Healthcare, Inc., Dothan, Ala., 1986-87; COO Healthcare Connections, Brentwood, Tenn., 1988; cons. VHA Physician Svcs., Inc., Dallas, 1988-90; asst. adminstr., CFO Clarksville (Tenn.) Meml. Hosp., 1990; Franklin, Tenn., 1990; sr. v.p., COO Eastside Ventures, Inc., Birmingham, Ala., 1990-93; sr. v.p. Ea. Health System, Inc., Birmingham, 1993—2002; CEO Williamson Med. Ctr., Franklin, 2002—. Chmn. Minority Leadership Task Force, Ea. Health System, Inc., 1994-95. Sec. Ala. Health Svcs. Bd.; mem. Literacy Coun. Ala., Ala. Hosp. Assn. State Legis. Com., future directions com.; chmn. Birmingham Regional Healthcare Exec. Forum; chmn. friends of scouting campaign Boy Scouts Am., 1996; mem. Franklin Land Use Steering Com. subcom., Leadership Franklin, 2002, Franklin Tomorrow, Williamson 25, 2004, 05, Franklin Bus. Leadership Coun., 2006, Hosp. Alliance Tenn., 2006, Tenn. Hosp. Ass., 2006; chmn. Healthcare Exec. Forum Mid. Tenn., 2006; mem. coun. Boy Scouts Mid. Tenn., 2006; mem. archives and mus. com. Williamson County, 2006; adv. com. mem. Tenn. Pub. Health Emergency, 2006-08., with Hosp. Alliance TN Exec. Com., 2011, MIddleton Coun., BSA, 2011 Recipient ACHE Svc. award, Miiddle TN, 2008; named one of Top 25 Hop. Operators, 2009—11. Fellow Am. Coll. Healthcare Execs. (chmn diplomate credentials com., pres. mid. Tenn. chpt. 2006, Ala. Regent's award for exec. excellence 1995), Hosp. Fin. Mgmt. Assn. (Follmer Bronze Merit award for outstanding svc.); mem. AICPA, Tenn. Soc. CPAs, Ala. Soc. CPAs (chmn. state legis. com.), Ala. Hosp. Assn. (future directions com.), Birmingham C. of C. (chmn. memberhsip com.), Birmingham East Rotary Club (pres., chmn. membership com.), Leadership Franklin Class 2003, Franklin Noon Rotary Club, Mensa, Shriners, Masons, Birmingham Touchdown Club, Sigma Chi. Avocations: hunting, fishing, gardening, antiques. Office: Williamson Med Ctr 2021 Carothers Rd Franklin TN 37067 Home Phone: 615-599-0325; Office Phone: 615-435-5151.

MILLER, DONALD EUGENE, lawyer; b. Providence, Mar. 20, 1947; s. Meyer Samuel and Beatrice (Wattman) M.; m. Deborah Neary Miller, Mar. 14, 1987. BA, Boston U., 1968; JD, U. Pa., 1972. Law clk. Assoc. Justice Alfred H. Joslin Supreme Ct., Providence, 1972-73; prin., lawyer Temkin, Merolla & Zurier, Providence, 1973-81, Temkin & Miller, Ltd., Providence, 1981-91; exec. v.p., gen. counsel, cro, corp. sec. The Fairchild Corp., McLean, Va., 1991—. Author: (treatise) Buying and Selling a Small Business, 1987. Mem. RI Bar, Mass. Bar, DC Bar. Avocation: Shetland Sheepdog breeding and exhibiting. Home: 10704 Riverwood Dr Potomac MD 20854-1332 Office: The Fairchild Corp 8130 Boone Blvd Ste 260 Vienna VA 22182

MILLER, DOUG, state legislator; m. Anne Miller; children: Douglas II, Amanda. BS in Law Enforcement, Tex. State U., 1976. Cert. ins. counselor, profl. ins. agent; lic. real estate broker. Ins. industry profl., 1978—; pres. Miller & Miller Ins. Agnecy; former mayor City of Braunfels; mem. Dist. 73 Tex. House of Representatives, 2008—. Bd. dirs. First State Bank, New Braunfels. Recipient of several awards and honors. Republican. Office: Room E1.314 Capitol Extension PO Box 2910 Austin TX 78768 also: 400 W San Antonio St New Braunfels TX 78130-7902 Office Phone: 830-625-1313, 512-463-0325.

MILLER, EMILIE F., former state senator, consultant; b. Chgo., Aug. 11, 1936; d. Bruno C. and Etta M. (Senese) Feiza; m. Dean E. Miller (dec.); children: Desireé M., Edward C. BSBA, Drake U., 1958. Asst. buyer Jordan Marsh Co., Boston, 1958-60, Carson, Pirie, Scott & Co., Chgo., 1960-62; dept. mgr., asst. buyer Woodward & Lothrop, Washington, 1962-64; state labor coord. Robb Davis Daliles Joint Campaign; legis. aide Senator Adelard Brandt, Va., 1980-83; fin. dir. Saslaw for Congress, 1984; legis. cons. Va. Fedn. Bus. Profl. Women, 1986-87, 98-00; senator Va. Gen. Assembly, Richmond, 1988-92; cons. apptd. by Gov. Wilder to bd. dirs. Innovative Tech. Authority, 1992-94, Ctr. for Innovative Tech., 1992-94; sr. mgr. Thompson, Cobb, Bazilio & Assocs., 1999—2006; bd. visitors Mt. Vernon, 2009—13; with Govt. Kaine; charter mem. Inagural Com., 1977; spkr. Internat. Womens Conf. St. Peterburg, Russia, 1995. Bus. tng. seminars, Moscow, Nizhny Novgorod, Russia, 1993, Novgorod, St. Petersburg, 1995; cons. in field. Guest editl. writer No. Va. Sun, 1981; host, prodr. weekly TV program, Channel 61. Active State Ctrl. Com. Dem. Party Va., Richmond, 1974—2005, steering com., 2000-05, chair 11th congrl. dist., 2001-05; mem. Fairfax County Dem. Com., 1968—, chair, 1976-80, 98-2000, Presdl. Inaugural Com., 1977, 1992 Dem. Nat. Platform Com., Va., Dem. Adv. Com. Robb-Spong Commn., 1978-79; founder, chair Va. Assoc. Dem. County and City Chmn., 1976-80; chmn. Fairfax County Dem. Com., 1976-80, 1998-2000; security supr. 1980 Dem. Nat. Conv.; v.p. Va. Fedn. Dem. Women, 1992-94; bd. dirs. Stop Child Abuse Now, 1988, Ctr. Innovative Tech., 1992-94, Ct. Apptd. Spl. Advs., 1993-96; nat. alumni bd. J.A. Achievement, BRAVO adv. com. for the first Gov.'s Awards for Arts in Va., 1979-80; lay tchr. St. Ambrose Cath. Ch., 1963-80; del. to White House Conf. on Children, 1970; chair Va. Coalition for Mentally Disabled, 1992-94; com. of 100, Va. Opera bd. dirs., 1994-99, guest lect., Osher Inst. GMU, 2006; bd. dirs. Social Action Linking Together; chair Women for Warner, 2009. Recipient Disting. Grad. award Jr. Achievement, 1973, Woman of Achievement award Fairfax (Va.) Bd. Suprs. and Fairfax County Commn. for Women, 1982, Cmty. Svc. award Friends of Victims Assistance Network, 1988, Founders award Fairfax County Coun. of Arts, 1989, Mental Health Assn. of Northern Va. Warren Stambaugh award, 1991, Ann. Svc. award Va. Assn. for Marriage and Family Therapy, 1991, Psychology Soc. of Washington Cmty. Svc. award, 1993, pacesetter award So. Women in Pub. Leadership Conf., 1996. Mem. NOW, Nat. Mus. Women in the Arts, Va. Assn. Female Execs. (adv. bd., bd. dirs., v.p. 1992-99), Va. Assn. Cmty. Svc. Bds. (chmn. 1980-82), North Va. Assn. Cmty. Bds. (chmn. 1978-79, 95-98), Fairfax County Coun. Arts (v.p. 1980—2008, mem. exec. com. internat. children's festival, Founders award 1989), Fairfax County C. of C. (legis. com.), Greater Merrifield Bus. and Profl. Assn., Mental Health Assn. No.Va. (bd. dirs.), Ctrl. Fairfax C. of C., Falls Church C. of C., Bus. and Profl. Women's Fedn. Va., Mantua Citizens Assn. (exec. bd.), Bus. and Profl. Women's Club (pres. Falls Church chpt. 1994-96, 2007—09, Woman of Yr. award 1990), Women's Nat. Dem. Club (past v.p., bd. govs., com. of 100, 1976-), Va. Assn. Female Execs. (bd. dirs. 1992-99), Phi Gamma Nu, Emil Verban Soc. Democrat. Roman Catholic. Avocations: tennis, art, baseball. Home: 8701 Duvall St Fairfax VA 22031-2711 Office Phone: 703-560-0291. Personal E-mail: emiliemiller1@cox.net.

MILLER, EUGENE, business educator, consultant; b. Chgo., Oct. 6, 1925; s. Harry and Fannie (Prosterman) M.; m. Edith Sutker, Sept. 23, 1951 (div. Sept. 1965); children: Ross, Scott, June; m. Thelma Gottlieb, Dec. 22, 1965; stepchildren: Paul Gottlieb, Alan Gottlieb. BS, Ga. Inst. Tech., 1945; AB magna cum laude, Bethany Coll., 1947, LLD, 1969; diploma, Oxford U., Eng., 1947; MS in Journalism, Columbia U., 1948; MBA, NYU, 1959; postgrad., Pace U., 1973—. Reporter, then city editor Greensboro (N.C.) Daily News, 1948-52; S.W. bur. chief Bus. Week mag., Houston, 1952-54, assoc. mng. editor NYC, 1954-60; dir. pub. affairs and communications McGraw-Hill, Inc., 1960-63, v.p., 1963-68; sr. v.p. pub. rels. and investor rels., exec. com. N.Y. Stock Exch., NYC, 1968-73; sr. v.p. CNA Fin. Corp., Chgo., 1973-75; chmn. Eugene Miller & Assos., Glencoe, Ill., 1975; v.p. USG Corp., Chgo., 1977-82, sr. v.p., 1982-85, mem. mgmt. com., 1982-91, exec. v.p., CFO, 1985-87, elected vice chmn., CFO, 1987-91, mem. exec. com., also bd. dirs.; prof., exec.-in-residence Coll. Bus. Fla. Atlantic U., Boca Raton, 1991—, sr. advisor, 2014; chmn., CEO Ideon Group, Inc., Jacksonville, Fla., 1996. Campaign speechwriter Pres. Dwight Eisenhower, 1956; adj. prof. mgmt. NYU, 1963-65; prof. bus. adminstrn. Fordham U., 1969-75; prof. fin., chmn. dept. Northeastern Ill. U., 1975-78; lectr. to bus. and ednl. groups; bd. dirs. MRFI, Inc., Chgo., 1990-, bd. dirs., mem. adv. bd. dirs. Nationwide Acceptance Corp., Chgo.; cons. to sec. Dept. Commerce, 1961-66; editor-in-residence U. Oreg., 1992; exec.-in-residence U. Ill., 1991, U. Wis., 1991, U. Toronto, 1992; exec.-in-residence, POHL fellow U. Wyo., 1992; mem. adv. bd. CFO mag., 1991-99; bd. dirs. The Strive Group, Chgo., 2000-12; cons. Arthur Andersen & Co., Chgo., 1992-97; arbitrator NYSE, 2002—, NASD, 2005-. Author: Your Future in Securities, 1974, Barron's Guide to Graduate Business Schools, 1977, 15th edit., 2007; contbg. editor: Public Relations Handbook, 1988, Boardroom Reports, 1986—; writer syndicated bus. column., Newsday Syndicate, 1964-86; mem. editl. bd. IRQ mag., 1997-. Trustee Bethany Coll., 1970-2012; mem. alumni bd. Columbia U. Sch. Journalism. Comdr. USNR, World War II, ret. Recipient outstanding achievement award Bethany Coll., 1963, 50th anniversary award Sch. Journalism Columbia U., also honors award, 1963, Sch. Journalism Ohio U., 1964, disting. svc. award in investment edn. Nat. Assn. Investment Clubs, 1980, Roalman award Nat. Investor Rels. Inst., 1987; honored with Eugene Miller Bd. Rm. Bethany Coll., 1999, Eugene Miller Bd. Rm. Coll. Bus. Fla. Atlantic U., 2007, disting. alumni award Navy Supply Corps. Found., 2010 Fellow Pub. Rels. Soc. Am.; mem. Soc. Am. Bus. Editors and Writers (founder, Pres.'s award 2003, 2013), Fin. Execs. Inst., St. Andrew's Country Club, Sigma Delta Chi, Alpha Sigma Phi. Home: 7351 Ballantrae Ct Boca Raton FL 33496-1423 Office: Fla Atlantic U Coll Business 777 Glades Rd Boca Raton FL 33431-6424 Personal E-mail: gene160@aol.com.

MILLER, FORREST E., telecommunications industry executive; BS in acctg., Univ. So. Calif.; MBA, Stanford Univ. CPA. Acct. Coopers & Lybrand; sr. assoc. Marakon Assoc.; mgmt. positions through pres. Pacific Bell directory Pacific Telesis, 1984—97; pres., CEO SBC directory ops. SBC Comm., 1997—99, pres., CEO SNET, 1999, pres., CEO Southwestern Bell, group pres. corp. planning, group pres. external affairs & planning, 2004; group pres. AT&T Comm. Corp. AT&T Inc. (merger of SBC Comm. with AT&T Corp.), San Antonio, 2005—06; group pres. strategic initiatives & HR AT&T Inc. (merger of SBC Communications & AT&T Corp.), San Antonio, 2006—07, group pres. corp. strategy & develop., 2007—. Office: AT&T Inc 175 E Houston San Antonio TX 78205

MILLER, GARY EVAN, psychiatrist, mental health services professional; b. Cleve., Aug. 19, 1935; s. Henry M. and Mollie (Price) M.; m. Karen Ann Marie Barrett, Sept. 16, 1972; children: Anna Charis, Rebecca Elizabeth. MD, U. Tex., Galveston, 1960. Diplomate in psychiatry, addiction psychiatry, and geriatric psychiatry Am. Bd. Psychiatry and Neurology. Intern Montefiore Hosp., NYC, 1960-61; resident in psychiatry U. Hosp. Cleve., 1961-62, Austin State Hosp., Tex., 1963-65; dep. commr. mental health services Dept. Mental Health and Mental Retardation, Tex., 1967-70; dir. Rio Grande State Ctr. for Mental Health and Mental Retardation, Dept. Mental Health, Harlingen, Tex., 1966-67; asst. commr., dir. Rochester regional office State Dept. Mental Hygiene, NY, 1970-72; clin. asst. prof. psychiatry U. Rochester Sch. Medicine and Dentistry, 1970-72; asst. clin. prof. psychiatry SUNY, Buffalo, 1970-72; cons. mental health Ga. Dept. Human Resources, Atlanta, 1972, dir. div. mental health, 1972-74; clin. prof. psychiatry Emory U. Sch. Medicine, Atlanta, 1972-74; vice chmn. Ga. State Planning and Adv. Coun. for Devel. Disabilities Services and Constrn., 1972-73; cons. mental health services orgn. and adminstrn., 1974-76; dir. mental health and devel. services State of NH Concord, 1976-82; commr. Tex. Dept. Mental Health and Mental Retardation Austin, 1982-88; clin. prof. psychiatry U. Tex. Health Sci. Ctr., Houston, adj. assoc. prof. psychiatry San Antonio, 1984-95; dir. profl. svcs. HCA Gulf Pines Hosp., Houston, 1988-94, chief of staff, 1993; clin. dir. adult psychiatry Cypress Creek Hosp., Houston, 1994-2000, med. dir., 2000—03, pres. med. staff, 1996; assoc. clin. psychiatry Post Oak Psychiatry Assoc., Houston, 1988-90; pres. Alternative Svc. Network, Houston, 1990—; chief of staff Kingwood (Tex.) Pines Hosp., 2003—04, dir. Psychiatric Svcs., 2004—08, med. dir., 2008—11. Dir. state alcoholism program in South Tex. region, 1966—67; dir. state alcoholism program in Ga., 1972—74; mem. faculty U. SC Sch. Alcohol and Drug Studies, 1975; mem. quality assurance com. Aetna US Healthcare Pharmacy, 1999—2001. Contbr. articles to profl. jours. Served as capt. M.C., US Army, 1962-63. Recipient Cert. Recognition, Ga. Psychol. Assn., 1973, Resolution Commendation, Assn. Retarded Citizens Tex., 1990, Helen Farabee Cmty. Leadership award, Mental Health Assn. Greater Houston, 1993, Pres.'s award, 1990, Elected Top Docs Houston, H Tex. Mag., 2004. Fellow Am. Psychiat. Assn. (disting. life; cert. in adminstrv. psychiatry, com. on psychiat. adminstrn. and mgmt. 1999-2002); mem. AMA, Am. Soc. Clin. Psychopharmacology (cert.), Am. Soc. Addiction Medicine (cert. alcoholism and other drug dependencies), Am. Acad. Addiction Psychiatry, NH Psychiat. Soc. (pres. 1981-82), Nat. Assn. State Mental Health Program Dir. (bd. dir. 1984-88, sec. 1986-88), NH Med. Soc., Am. Acad. Psychiatry and the Law, Am. Assn. Psychiat. Adminstr. (pres. Tex. chpt. 1986), Tex. Med. Assn., Tex. Soc. Psychiat. Physicians (chair socioecons. com. 2006-10), Profl. Practices Mgmt. Com. (vice chair, 2010-), Mental Health Assn. Greater Houston (bd. dir. 1989-95, v.p. advocacy 1990-95, adv. coun. 1999—), Alpha Omega Alpha. Home: 5314 Westminister Ct Houston TX 77069-3338 Office: 17115 Red Oak Dr Ste 119 Houston TX 77090-2607 Office Phone: 281-440-6899. Personal E-mail: gemhou@yahoo.com.

MILLER, GERALDINE (TINCY MILLER), real estate company executive, educational association administrator; m. Vance Miller; 4 children. BS, Southern Meth. U.; MS in Reading, Tex. A&M U. Vice chmn. Henry S. Miller Cos., 1994—. Tchr., reading lab. Tex. Scottish Rite HOsp. for Crippled Children, Highland Park Presbyn. Hillier Sch. for Dyslexia; bd. dirs. Literacy Instrn. for Tex. Mem. Tex. State Bd. Edn., 1988—, pres., 2003—; chair fund-raising events United Cerebral Palsy Assn., Dallas Opera, Dallas Symphony Orch., TACA, Crystal Charity Ball; active I Have A Dream Found., Nat. Orton-Dyslexia Soc., Boy's and Girl's Club Greater Dallas, Dallas County Heritage Soc. Recipient Hall of State award for civic involvement, Dallas Hist. Soc., 1995, Tom Landry award of excellence in volunteerism, 1999. Mem.: Acad. Lang. Therapist Assn., Internat. Reading Assn., Kappa Delta Pi, Phi Delta Kappa. Republican. Office: Henry S Miller Companies 1100 Providence Tower W 5001 Spring Valley Rd Dallas TX 75244 Office Phone: 972-419-4000. Office Fax: 972-419-4099. Business E-Mail: gmiller@henrysmiller.com.

MILLER, GRAY HAMPTON, federal judge; b. Houston, Dec. 9, 1948; Student, US Merchant Marine Acad.; BA, U. Houston, 1974, JD, 1978. Bar: Tex. 1978. Assoc. Fulbright & Jaworski LLP, Houston, 1978—86, head admiralty dept, 1996—2004, ptnr., 1986—2004, sr. ptnr., 2004—06; judge US Dist. Ct. (so. dist.) Tex., Houston, 2006—. Mem. ABA, Maritime Law Assn. U.S., State Bar Tex., Houston Bar Assn., Southeastern Admiralty Law Inst. (bd. dirs. 1989-91), Order of Barons. Office: US Dist Ct 515 Rusk Ave Houston TX 77002

MILLER, GREGORY A., state legislator; BA in Polit. Sci., La. State U., 1985, JD, 1988. Pvt. practice atty., La.; mem. Dist. 56 La. House of Reps., 2012—. Republican. Office: La House of Reps 900 N 3rd St PO Box 94062 Baton Rouge LA 70804 Business E-Mail: millerg@legis.la.gov.

MILLER, GREGORY R., retired prosecutor; BA, Drew U.; JD, Ohio No. U. Chief asst. US atty. (no. dist.) Fla. US Dept. Justice, Tallahassee, US atty. (no. dist.) Fla., 1993-98, asst. US atty. (no. dist.) Fla., 2000—02; US atty (no. dist.) Fla. US Dept Justice, Tallahassee, 2002—08; assoc. Fowler, White, Gillen, Boggs, Villareal and Banker, PA, Tallahassee, 1998-2000; ptnr. Beggs & Lane, RLLP, Tallahassee, 2008—. Office: 215 S Monroe St Ste 710 Tallahassee FL 32301 Office Phone: 850-391-0001. Business E-Mail: grm@beggslane.com.

MILLER, JACKSON H., state legislator; b. Washington, Apr. 30, 1967; m. Suzanne Miller; children: Jackson Jr., Nathaniel. BS in Urban Planning, Va. Commonwealth U., Richmond, 1990. Realtor, Va.; councilman Manassas City Coun., Va., 2004—06; mem. Dist. 50 Va. House of Delegates, 2006—. Active Va. Citizen's Def. League; mem. Grace United Meth. Ch. Capt. USAR, 1989—99. Recipient Excellence in Tng. award, Northern Va. Criminal Justice Acad., 1991. Mem.: Prince William County Assn. Realtors (Million Dollar Club 2001, 2002, Top Prodr. 2003—05), Prince William County C. of C., Greater Manassas C. of C., Prince William County Police Assn. (former pres. 2002—03), Fraternal Order Police, Battlefield Lodge. Republican. Methodist. Office: PO Box 10072 Manassas VA 20108 Office Phone: 703-244-6172. E-mail: DelJMiller@house.virginia.gov.

MILLER, JANEL HOWELL, psychologist; b. Boone, NC, May 18, 1947; d. John Estle and Grace Louise (Hemberger) Howell; m. C. Rick Miller, Nov. 24, 1968; children: Kimberly, Brian, Audrey, Rachel. BA, DePauw U., 1969; postgrad., Rice U., 1969; MA, U. Houston, 1972; PhD, Tex. A&M U., 1979. Lic. clin. psychologist, sch. psychologist Tex. Assoc. sch. psychologist Houston Ind. Sch. Dist., 1971-74; rsch. psychologist VA Hosp., Houston, 1972; assoc. sch. psychologist Clear Creek (Tex.) Ind. Sch. Dist., 1974-76; instr. psychology, counseling psychology intern Tex. A&M U., 1976-77; clin. psychology intern VA Hosp., Houston, 1977-78; coord. psychol. svcs. Clear Creek Ind. Sch. Dist., 1978-81, assoc. dir. psychol. svcs., 1981-82; pvt. practice Houston, 1982—. Faculty U. Houston-Clear Lake, 1984—; adolescent suicide cons., 1984—; mem. DePaww U. Alumni Bd. Dirs., 2008-. DePauw U. Alumni scholar, 1965-69; NIMH fellow U. Houston, 1970-71. Mem. APA, Am. Assn. Marriage and Family Therapists, Soc. for Personality Assessment, Am. Coll. Forensic Examiners, Internat. Rorschach Soc., Tex. Psychol. Assn., Tex. Assn. Marriage and Family Therapists, Houston Psychol. Assn. (media rep. 1984-85), Houston Assn. Marriage and Family Therapists. Home: 806 Walbrook Dr Houston TX 77062-4030 Office: 16854 Royal Crest Dr Houston TX 77058-2529 Office Phone: 281-461-4098. Business E-Mail: shrinkskate@sbcglobal.net.

MILLER, JEFF, United States Representative from Florida; b. St. Petersburg, Fla., June 27, 1959; m. Vicki Griswold; children: Scott, Clint. BA in Journalism, U. Fla., 1984. Exec. asst. to commr. agriculture Doyle Conner, Tallahassee, 1984—88; mem. Fla. House of Reps., 1998—2001, US Congress from 1st Fla. Dist., 2001—; chmn. US House Veterans Affairs Com., 2011—. Mem. Environ. Land Mgmt. Study Commn., 1992; vice-chair Santa Rosa County Planning Bd., 1996—98; chmn. Escambia County Legis. Del., 1999—2000; mem. Rep. Study Com., TEAM Santa Rosa Econ. Devel. Coun. Mem. Elizabeth Chapel United Meth. Ch., Chumuckla; bd. dirs. West Fla. Hosp., Fla. FFA Found., Gulf Coast Coun. Boy Scouts America, Santa Rose County United Way; adv. bd. mem. Milton Pregnancy Resource Ctr. Mem.: Fla. Hist. Soc., Kiwanis Club Milton. Republican. Methodist. Office: US House of Representatives 336 Cannon House Office Bldg Washington DC 20515*

MILLER, JO CAROLYN DENDY, family and marriage counselor, educator; b. Gorman, Tex., Sept. 16, 1942; d. Leonard Lee and Vera Vertie (Robison) Dendy; m. Douglas Terry Barnes, June 1, 1963 (div. June 1975); children: Douglas Alan, Bradley Jason; m. Walton Sansom Miller, Sept. 19, 1982. BA, Tarleton State U., Stephenville, Tex., 1964; MEd, U. North Tex., Denton, 1977; PhD, Tex. Woman's U., Denton, 1993. Tchr. Mineral Wells H.S., Tex., 1964-65, Weatherford Mid. Sch., Tex., 1969-74; counselor, instr. psychology Tarrant County Jr. Coll., Hurst, Tex., 1977-82; pvt. practice Dallas, 1982—. Author: (with Velma Baker, Jeannene Ward) Becoming: A Human Relations Workbook, 1981. Mem. ACA, Tex. State Bd. Examiners Profl. Counselors, Tex. State Bd. Marriage and Family Therapists, Tex. Counseling Assn., North Ctrl. Tex. Counseling Assn., Dallas Symphony Orch. League, Nat. Coun. Family Rels., Tex. Mental Health Counselors Assn., Internat. Assn. for Marriage and Family Counselors. Methodist. Office: 8222 Douglas Ave Ste 777 Dallas TX 75225-5938 Office Phone: 214-691-0400. Personal E-mail: jcdmphd@sbcglobal.net.

MILLER, JOHN C., state legislator; b. Bryn Mawr, Pa., Dec. 9, 1947; married; 2 children. BS, ED, Northern Ill. U. News anchor WVEC TV, 1990—96; v.p. univ. rels. Christopher Newport U., 1996—2001, assoc. dir. Va. Electronic Commerce Technology Ctr.; mem. Dist. 1 Va. State Senate, 2008—. Democrat. Office: PO Box 6113 Newport News VA 23606 also: Senate of Virginia PO Box 396 Richmond VA 23218 Office Phone: 757-595-1100, 804-698-7501. Fax: 804-698-7651. E-mail: district01@senate.virginia.gov.

MILLER, JOSEPH (BUZZ), lobbyist, nuclear energy industry executive; BSChemE, Auburn U., Montgomery, Ala., 1983. Various positions in oil/gas svcs. and utilities svcs. sectors, Houston; engr. chemistry/environ. support sect. nuc. generation Ala. Power (subs.) Southern Co., 1986, various assignments at Ala. Power and Southern Nuc. Oper. Co., 1987—93, fed. affairs mgr. Washington, 1993—98, asst. to CEO Atlanta, 1998—99, v.p. govt. rels. Washington, 1999—2006, sr. v.p. nuc. devel., 2006—, pres. (subs.) Southern Nuc. Devel., LLC, 2006—. Acting v.p. legis. affairs Nuc. Energy Inst., Washington, 1996—97. Office: Southern Co Hdqs 30 Ivan Allen Jr Blvd NW Atlanta GA 30308 Office Phone: 404-506-5000.

MILLER, LARRY J., state legislator; b. Mar. 11, 1954; 1 child, Nekayla. State rep. Dist. 88, Tenn., 1995—; fireman. Mem.: NAACP, Memphis Fire Fighters Local 1784, Pioneers Black Fire Fighters. Democrat. Office: 550 Techno Ln Apt 803 Memphis TN 38105 also: 20 Legislative Plz Nashville TN 37243-0188 Office Phone: 615-741-4453, 901-272-7884. Office Fax: 615-741-7535. Business E-Mail: rep.larry.miller@capitol.tn.gov.

MILLER, MARGERY, psychologist, educator, consultant, speech pathology/audiology and mental health services professional, university administrator, professor, academic administrator, coach; m. Donald F. Moores; children: Kip Lee, Tige Justice. BA, Elmira Coll., 1971; MA, NYU, 1972; EdS, MS, SUNY, Albany, 1975; MA, Towson State U., 1987; PhD, Georgetown U., 1991. Lic. speech pathologist Md., psychologist Md., diplomate sch. neuropsychologist, sch. neuropsychologist; cert. tchr. nursery-6th grades, spl. edn. NY, nationally cert. sch. psychologist. Speech and lang. pathologist Mental Retardation Inst. Flower and Fifth Ave. Hosp., NYC, 1971—72; cmty. speech/lang. pathologist, dir. speech and hearing svc. NY State Dept. Mental Hygiene, Troy, 1972—74; instr. comm. disorders dept. Coll. St. Rose, Albany, NY, 1975—77; clin. supr. U. Md., College Park, 1978; speech/lang. pathologist Md. Sch. for Deaf, Frederick, 1978—84; auditory devel. specialist Per Diem Sch. Psychologist, Montgomery County Pub. Schs., Rockville, Md., 1984—87; coord. Family Life program Nat. Acad. Gallaudet U., Washington, 1987—88, interim dir., 1988—89; dir. Counseling and Devel. Ctr. N.W. Campus, Washington, 1989—93; prof. psychology, coord. psychology internship program, dir. undergrad. psychology program Gallaudet U., Washington, 1993—2007, dean enrollment mgmt., 2007—11; lic. practicing psychologist Bethesda, Md., 1998—; higher ed. cons., life exec. coach, writer, 2011—; rsch. fellow New Leadership Alliance Student Learning & Accountability, Washington, 2011—13. Instr. sign-lang. program Frederick CC; dance instr. for deaf adolescents; diagnostic cons. psychology and speech pathology; presenter at confs.; profl. coaching, Md., Fla., 2002—; rsch. fellow New Leadership Alliance Student Learning and Accountability, Washington, 2011—13. Author: It's O.K. to be Angry, 1976; co-author: Cognition, Education and Deafness: Directions for Research and Instruction, 1985, Deaf People Around the World: Educational and Cultural Perspectives, 2009; mem. editl. rev. com. Gov.'s Devel. Disabilities Coun., Md., editl. bd. mem. Am. Anns. Deaf; contbr. articles to profl. jours. Vol., choreographer Miss Deaf Am. Pageant, 1984. Office Edn. Children's Bur. fellow, 1971. Mem.: APA, Montgomery County Md. Mental Health Assn., Am. Assn. Higher Edn., Nat. Assn. Sch. Psychologists, Nat. Assn. Deaf, Am. Speech, Lang. and Hearing Assn. (cert. clin. competence in speech/lang. pathology). Personal E-mail: margeryrose@aol.com.

MILLER, MARILYN LEA, library and information scientist, educator; AA, Graceland Coll., 1950; BS in English, U. Kans., 1952; AMLS, U. Mich., 1959, PhD of Librarianship and Higher Edn., 1976. Bldg.-level sch. libr. Wellsville HS, Kans., 1952-54; tchr.-libr. Arthur Capper Jr. HS, Topeka, 1954-56; head libr. Topeka HS, Topeka, 1956-62; sch. libr. cons. State of Kans. Dept. of Pub. Instrn., 1962-67; from asst. to assoc. prof. Sch. Librarianship Western Mich. U., Kalamazoo, 1967-77; assoc. prof. libr. sci. U. NC, Chapel Hill, 1977-87, prof., chair dept. libr. and info. studies Greensboro, 1987-95, prof. emeritus, 1996—. Vis. faculty Kans. State Tchrs., Emporia, 1960, 63, 64, 66, U. Minn., Mpls., 1971, U. Manitoba, Winnipeg, Can., 1971; vis. prof. Appalachian State U., Boone, NC, 1987; adv. bd. sch. libr. media program Nat. Ctr. for Ednl. Stats., 1989, user rev. panel, 1990; chair assoc. dean search com. Sch. Edn., 1988, coord. Piedmont young writers conf., 1989-94, 97-99, chair race and gender com., 1990-93, SACS planning and evaluation com., 1990-91, learning resources ctr. adv. com., 1991-93; hearing panel for honor code U. NC Greensboro, 1988-91, assn. women faculty and administrv. staff, 1987-95, faculty coun., 1987-95, chair, 1994-95, univ. libr. com., 1987-88, com. faculty devel. in race and gender scholarship, 1990-92; lectr. and cons. in field. Editor: Pioneers and Leaders in Library Service to Youth, 2003; mem. editl. bd. The Emergency Librarian, 1981-97, Collection Building: Studies in the Development and Effective Use of Library Resources, 1978-96; contbr. chpt. to books, articles to profl. jour. Children's libr. specialists to visit Russian sch. and pub. libr., book publs., Moscow, Leningrad, Tashkent, 1979; hon. del. White House Conf. on Libr. and Info. Svcs., Washington, 1991; head del. Romanian Summer Inst. on Librarianship in U.S., 1991; citizen amb. People to People Internat. Program, People's Republic of China, 1992, Russian and Poland, 1992, Russia, 1994, Barcelona, 1995; exec. bd. dirs. Friends of Greensboro Pub. Libr., 1996-99, chair Booklovers' Shop adv. com., 1996-2002, v.p., 2003-05, pres. 2005—07, past pres., 2007-09; chair Citizens Materials Adv. com., 1999-; chair Citizens Strategic Long Range Planning com., 1994-95, 2001-03, chair, 2003, 06, Sch. Pub. Libr. Com., 2002-09, chair, 2003-07; pub. libr. trustee, 2005-, NC State Libr. Commn., 2006-. Recipient Freedom Found. medal, 1962, Disting. Svc. to Sch. Librs. award Kans. Assn. Sch. Librs., 1982, Disting. Svc. award Graceland Coll., 1992, Disting. Alumnus award Sch. Libr. and Info. Studies, U. Mich., 1988, Contribution to Libr. Info. Sci. award Assn. Libr. Info. Sci., 1999; Delta Kappa Gamma scholar, 1972. Mem.: ALA (awards com. 1971—72, chair Chgo. conf. resolutions 1972, chair 1973—75, resolutions com. 1976—78, adv. com. Nat. Ctr. Ednl. Stats. 1984, standing com. libr. edn. 1987—91, yearbook adv. com. 1988—90, chair 1989—90, pres. 1992—93, exec. dir. 1994, chair rsch. com., chair search com., Disting. Svc. award Am. Assn. Sch. Librs. 1993), Friends of N.C. Pub. Librs. (bd. dirs. 2000—04), So. Assn. Colls. and Schs. (accreditation team 1988), Southeastern Libr. Assn. (chair libr. educators sect. 1990—92), N.C. Assn. Sch. Librs. (Disting. Svc. award 2004), Assn. Libr Svc. to Children (bd. dirs. 1976—81, pres. 1979—80, rsch. com. 1982—85, chair 1984—85, Disting. Svc. award 2005), Assn. Ednl. Comms. and Tech., Am. Assn. Sch. Librs. (nominating com. 1980, pub. com. 1981—82, chair search com. exec. dir. 1985, v.p., pres.-elect 1985—86, pres. 1986—87, coord. coms. nat. stds. vision and implementation 1995—98), N.C. Libr. Assn. (life; edn. libr. com. 1978—80, 1982—86, bd. dirs. 1987—99, exec. bd. status women roundtable 1989—2003, chmn.-elect 1995—97, chmn. 1997—99, commn. on status of sch. librs. 1999—2000). Home: 6100 W Friendly Ave Greensboro NC 27410-4085 Personal E-mail: mmiller127@trial.rr.com.

MILLER, MERRILL ANTHONY, JR., energy executive; b. Burlington, Iowa, July 4, 1950; s. Merrill Anthony Sr. and Florence Mae (Douglas) M.; m. Diana Sue Wagner, June 17, 1972; 1 child, Paul. BS in Engring., U.S. Mil. Acad., 1972; MBA, Harvard U., 1980. Team mgr. Procter & Gamble Co., Mehoopany, Pa., 1977-78; asst. to pres. Helmerick & Payne, Tulsa, 1980-82, v.p. and gen. mgr. no. div. Okla. City, 1982; Joined National Oilwell Varco, Inc., Houston, 1996, pres., 2000—, COO, 2000—05, CEO, 2001—, chmn., 2002—. Bd. dirs. Internat. Computer Exchange, Inc., Boulder, Colo. Mem. Internat. Assn. Drilling Contractors (bd. dirs. 1985—, chmn. midcontinent chpt. 1986-87). Roman Catholic. Avocations: sports, reading. Office: National Oilwell Varco 10000 Richmond Ave Houston TX 77042-4200

MILLER, MORRIS HENRY, lawyer; b. Thomasville, Ga., June 14, 1954; s. Gibbes Ulmer and Marianne (Morris) M.; m. Anita Carol Payne, Mar. 23, 1985; children: Morris Payne, Rose Elizabeth, David Gibbes, Paul Louis Henry, John Henry. BS in Acctg. summa cum laude, Fla. State U., 1976; JD, U. Va., 1979. Bar: Fla. 1979. Assoc. Holland & Knight, Tampa, Fla., 1979-84, ptnr. Tallahassee, 1985, chmn. health law practice, 1989—2001, knowledge mgmt. ptnr., 2001—04, CLE ptnr., 2004—05. Of counsel Seminole Boosters, Inc., 2006—. Dist. fin. chmn. Gulf Ridge coun. Boy Scouts Am., 1988-89, mem. pack com., cubmaster Pack 23, Suwannee River Area coun., 1995-98, scoutmaster Troop 182, 1997-99, scoutmaster Troop 10, 2000-01, asst. scoutmaster, 2002-06, scoutmaster Troop 50, 2006—, dist. nominating com., exec. bd., 2005-; mem. Leadership Tampa, 1986, Leadership Tampa Bay, 1989; bd. dirs. John G. Riley House Mus. Ctr. for African-Am. History and Culture, 1998-99, Tallahassee YMCA, 1994-2002, chmn. long range planning com., 1997; founder, chmn. Tampa Bus. Com. for Arts, Inc., 1988-89; elder Presbyn. Ch. Mem. Fla. Bar (chmn., vice chmn. computer law com. 1983-89, Fla. corp. law revision com. 1986-89, health and bus. law sects.) Office: Holland & Knight 315 S Calhoun St Ste 600 Tallahassee FL 32301-1897 Home Phone: 850-668-4193; Office Phone: 850-425-5655. Business E-Mail: morris.miller@hklaw.com.

MILLER, NORMAN RICHARD, lawyer; b. Oak Ridge, Tenn., Apr. 4, 1948; s. Francis J. and Sylvia R. Miller; children: Russell, Adam, Jordan. BA with distinction, Northwestern U., 1970; JD, Harvard U., 1973. Bar: Tex. Law clk. to Judge Latham Castle U.S. Ct. Appeals (7th cir.), Chgo., 1973-74; ptnr. Akin, Gump, Strauss, Hauer & Feld, Dallas, 1980-90, Kirkpatrick & Lockhart LLP, Dallas, 1995, Patton Boggs LLP, Dallas. Trustee Temple Shalom. Hon. Woodrow Wilson fellow. Mem. ABA (task force securities law opinions, com. fed. regulation securities, com. negotiated acquisitions), State Bar Tex. (securities com.), Dallas Bar Assn.; fellow Tex. Bus. Law Found., Phi Beta Kappa. Office: Patton Boggs LLP 2000 Mckinney Ave Ste 1700 Dallas TX 75201-2095 Office Phone: 214-758-6630. Office Fax: 214-758-1550. E-mail: nmiller@pattonboggs.com.

MILLER, PAMELA GUNDERSEN, retired mayor; b. Cambridge, Mass., Sept. 7, 1938; d. Sven M. and Harriet Adams Gundersen; m. Ralph E. Miller, July 7, 1962; children: Alexander, Erik, Karen. AB magna cum laude, Smith Coll., 1960. Feature writer Congl. Quar., Washington, 1962-65; dir. cable TV franchising Storer Broadcasting Co., Louisville, Lexington, Ky., 1978—80; mem. 4th dist. Lexington Fayette County Urban Coun., 1973-77; councilwoman-at-large, 1982-93; vice mayor, 1984-86, 89-93; mayor, 1993—2003. Dep. commr. Ky. Dept. Local Govt., Frankfort, 1980-81; pres. Pam Miller, Inc., 1984-94, Cmty. Ventures Corp., 1985-95. Mem. Fayette County Bd. Health, 1975—77, Downtown Devel. Commn., 1975—77; bd. dirs. YMCA, Lexington, 1975—77, 1985—90, Fund for the Arts, 1984—93, Coun. of Arts, 1978—80, Sister Cities, 1978—80; chmn. Prichard Com. for Acad. Excellence, 2004—09; treas. Planned Parenthood, 2003—08, Fayette Edn. Found., 2005—07; pres. Lexington Opera Soc., 2007—09; vice chair Ky. Coun. Post Secondary Edn., 2008—, chair, 2012—; alt. del. Dem. Nat. Com., 1976; bd. dirs. Lexington Opera Soc., 2003—11; chair Fund for Arts Campaign, 2003—04. Named woman of achievement YWCA, 1984, outstanding Woman of Blue Grass AAUW, 1984. Mem. LWV (dir. 1970-73), Profl. Women's Forum. Home: 140 Cherokee Park Lexington KY 40503-1304

MILLER, PATRICIA A., music educator, opera and concert artist; b. Washington, June 16; d. Robert Lee and Bernice (Echols) Miller. MusB, Boston U.; MusM, New Eng. Conservatory; artist's diploma, Accademia di Santa Cecilia, Rome; postdoctoral diploma, Mozarteum, Salzburg. Artist Thea Dispeker Artist's Mgmt., Inc., NYC, 1981—95; assoc. prof. music, artist-in-residence U. Mo., Columbia, 1983—85; prof. music, dir. vocal studies, artist-in-residence George Mason U., Fairfax, Va., 1991—, dir. Vocal Inst. Seoul, Republic of Korea, 2005—, artistic dir. Vocal Inst., 2009; prof. voice Oberlin Coll. Conservatory, Oberlin, Ohio, 2000—01; voice faculty Amalfi Coast Internat. Music Festival, 2008—. Dir. vocal studies George Mason U., 1995—, prodr. opera theater, 2000—, dir. Inst. Vocal Arts, 2004—08; lectr. Smithsonian, Wash., DC, 2000—02; artist faculty Amalfi Coast Music Festival, Italy, 2008—; artistic bd. dirs. Amadeus Concerts, Great Falls, Va., 2006—11; pvt. practice vocal studio, Va.; govs. Nat. Assn. Tchrs. Singing Va., 2011—; guest artist voice faculty Amalfi Coast Music Festival, Italy, 2009—; dir. Internat. Vocal Inst. EWHA Womens U., Seoul, Republic of Korea, 2010—11; mem. Nat. Assn. Tchrs. Singing Bd. Va. State Chamber, 2012—, Nat. Philharmonic Orchestra Strathmore Music Ctr., 2012; nat. govs. Nat. Assn. Treas. Singing Va. State Chpt., 2012—, bd. dirs., 2012—; soloist U. NC Chapel Hill, 2012; gen. dir. GMU Opera, 2010—12. Performer: (Operas) ERCOLE Amante, 1986, Carmen, 1981, 1985, Porgy & Bess, 1996, Basel, Lyon, San Francisco, NYC, Bogota, Munich, Frankfort, Verona, Ge, Tokyo, Melbourne, Paris (Chatelet), Rome, Berlin; concert/recital artist Kennedy Ctr., Washington, 2000, Kiev, 2002, Austrian Embassy, 2003, Salzburg, Austria, 2004, Kaynon Concert Hall, Seoul, Korea, 2005; performer (soloist): Schloss Leopololskron Great Hall, 2004, 2006, Lincoln Ctr.'s Alice Tully Hall, Kiev Philharmonic Orch., 2004, New Strathmore Music Ctr., 2005, Nat. Philharmonic Orch. and Chorus, 2005, 2011—12, Moscow State U., 2006, Pushkin Mus. and Concert Hall, 2006, Schloss Leopoldskron, 2006, Internat. Conf. on Edn., Health, Culture, Pub. Opinion, 2006; guest artist Philharmonic Hall, TULA, Moscow, 2007, guest artist vocal master class clinician Weimar Cons. Germany, 2012, artist faculty Amalfi Coast Music Festival Internat. Italy, 2009—12, Shandung U. Sch. Music China, 2011. Mem. opera panel Nat. Endowment Arts, 2003—04, 2006; mem. panel Va. Commn. for the Arts, 2004—05. Recipient Shining Star Cmty Svc. award, Nat. Urban League, Sojourner Truth Leadership award, George Mason U., 2004, Disting. U. Prof., 2007—, Outstanding Voice Tchr. award, Northern Va. Opera Guild, 2010—11, Outstanding Prof. Voice, Northern Va. Opera Guild, Excellence Tchg. award, Lambda Sigma Honor Soc., 2011, Opera Panel Nat. Endowment Art award, 2010, 2012; grantee, Am. Embassy, 2002; Fulbright scholar, Rome. Mem.: NEA (opera panel mem. 2012), Elass Lists Sch. Weimac Germany (guest artists master 2012), Nat. Philharmonic Orchestra (mello Saprano soloist), Fulbright Assn. (bd. dirs. Nat. Capitol area), Nat. Assn. Tchrs. Singing Va. State (gov. 2012—, state bd. dirs., gov., bd. dirs.), Phi Kappa Phi (Inducted Hon. award 2012), Phi Beta Delta (Epsilon Delta Chpt. mem. 2012), Sigma Alpha Iota (Alumni Artistry Leadership award 2004, Outstanding Artist award 2004). Methodist. Avocations: travel, walking, swimming, cooking. Office: George Mason Univ Dept Music MSN-3E3 4400 University Dr Fairfax VA 22030-4444 Office Phone: 703-993-1382. Personal E-mail: labellavoce1@aol.com. Business E-Mail: pmilleb@gmu.edu.

MILLER, PEGGY GORDON ELLIOTT, retired academic administrator; b. Matewan, W.Va., May 27, 1937; d. Herbert Hunt and Mary Ann (Renfro) Gordon; m. Robert Lawrence Miller, Nov. 23, 2001; stepchildren: Rohn J., Robert K.;children from previous marriage: Scott Vandling Elliott III, Anne Gordon Elliott. BA, Transylvania Coll., 1959; MA, Northwestern U., 1964; EdD, Ind. U., 1975; DHL (hon.), Transylvania U., 1993; degree (hon.), Chungnam Nat. U., Korea, 2000; D in Pub. Svc., SD State U., 2006. Tchr. Horace Mann H.S., Gary, Ind., 1959-64; instr. English Am. Inst. Banking, Gary, 1969-70, Ind. U. N.W., Gary, 1965-69, lectr. Edn., 1973-74, asst. prof. edn., 1975-78, assoc. prof., 1978-80, supr. secondary student tchg., 1973-74, dir. student tchg., 1975-77, dir. Office Field Experiences, 1977-78, dir. profl. devel., 1978-80, spl. asst. to chancellor, 1981-83, asst. to chancellor, 1983-84, acting chancellor, 1983-84, chancellor, 1984-92; pres. U. Akron, Ohio, 1992-96, SD State U., 1998—2006, pres. emeritus, 2006—; interim dean Grad Sch. Tex. Tech. U., 2010—; v.p. Tex. Tech., 2012—14. Sr. fellow Nat. Ctr. for Higher Edn., 1996-97; vis. prof. U. Ark., 1979-80, U. Alaska, 1982; bd. dirs. Lubrizol Corp., A. Schulman Corp., Commn. on Women in Higher Edn., SD Mus. Art, Akron Tomorrow, Ohio Aerospace Consortium, Ohio Super Computer Com., Brookings C. of C.; holder VA Harrington disting. chair in edn., 1994-96, Charles G. Herbrich chair in leadership mgmt., 1996—; chmn. Growth partnership Rsch. Pk. Author: (with C. Smith) Reading Activities for Middle and Secondary Schools: A Handbook for Teachers, 1979, Reading Instruction for Secondary Schools, 1986, How to Improve Your Scores on Reading Competency Tests, 1981, (with C. Smith and G. Ingersoll) Trends in Educational Materials: Traditionals and the New Technologies, 1983, The Urban Campus: Educating a New Majority for a New Century, 1994, also numerous articles. Bd. dirs. Am. Humanics Meth. Hosp., N.W. Ind. Forum, N.W. Ind. Symphony, S.D. Art Mus., Boys Club N.W. Ind., Akron Symphony, NBD Bank, John S. Knight Conv. Ctr., Inventure Pl., Akron Roundtable, Cleve. Com. Higher Edn., 4-H Found., S.D. Art Mus., S.D. Value. Recipient Authority Disting. Alumni award, Northwestern U., UA Hon. Alumni award, 1994, Dist. Alumni award, Ind. U., 2004, Disting. Hon. Alumni, S.D. State U.; numerous grants; Am. Council on Edn. fellow in acad. adminstrn. Ind. U., Bloomington, 1980-81, Thomas Hart Benton Medallion, 1988 Mem. Assn. Tchr. Educators (nat. pres. 1984-85, Disting. Mem. 1990), Ind. Assn. Tchr. Educators (past pres.), North Ctrl. Assn. (mem. commn. at large), Am. Assn. State Colls. and Univs. (acting v.p. divsn. acad. and internat. programs 1997, bd. dirs., treas., chmn. global priorities commn.), Am. Coun. Edn. (bd. dirs., exec. com.), Leadership Devel. Coun. ACE, Office Women Higher Edn. (mem. emerita of exec. bd), Am. Humanics (bd. dirs.), Ohio Inter Univ. Coun. (chairperson), Internat. Reading Assn., SD Women's Exec. Leadership

Coalition, Akron Urban League (bd. dirs.), P.E.O., Cosmos Club, Phi Delta Kappa (Outstanding Young Educator award), Delta Kappa Gamma (Leadership/Mgmt. fellow 1980), Pi Lambda Theta, Pi Kappa Phi, Chi Omega. Episcopalian. Avocation: music. Home: 4836 Sweet Meadow Cir Sarasota FL 34238 Office Phone: 605-691-7391. Business E-Mail: peggy.miller@sdstate.edu.

MILLER, R. TERRY, lawyer; b. San Jose, Calif., Feb. 28, 1947; BA, U. Calif., Berkeley, 1968; JD, Southern Meth U., 1971. Bar: Tex. 1971. Sr. ptnr. Fulbright & Jaworski LLP, Dallas; ptnr., co-chair real estate and fin. practice group, mem. mgmt. com. Akin Gump Strauss Hauer & Feld LLP, Dallas. Mem. ABA, State Bar Tex., Dallas Bar Assn., Phi Alpha Delta. Office: Akin Gump Strauss Hauer & Feld LLP Ste 4100 1700 Pacific Ave Dallas TX 75201-4624 Office Phone: 214-969-4237. Office Fax: 214-969-4343. Business E-Mail: tmiller@akingump.com.

MILLER, REGINALD WAYNE (REGGIE MILLER), sportscaster, retired professional basketball player; b. Riverside, Calif., Aug. 24, 1965; Student, UCLA. Profl. basketball player Ind. Pacers, 1987—2005; NBA analyst Turner Sports, 2005—; founder, exec. prodr. Boom Baby Prodns., 2006—. Mem. Dream Team I, 1994, Dream Team II, 1996. Recipient Walter J. Kennedy Cmty. Svc. award, 2003—04; named to Ea. Conf. NBA All-Star Team, NBA, 1990, 1995, 1996, 1998, 2000, Naismith Meml. Basketball Hall of Fame, 2012. Achievements include setting the NBA Playoffs record for most three-point field goals in one quarter (5), 1994; co-holder of NBA Playoffs record for most three point field goals in one half (6), 1994, 95; being first Pacers player to surpass 15,000 career points. Office: Turner Sports 1 CNN Ctr 100 International Blvd Atlanta GA 30348

MILLER, RICHARD JACKSON (RICK MILLER), lawyer; b. Milw., July 17, 1946; s. Wayne D. and Margarite M. (Von Sitany) Miller; m. Irene Nikki Tsacoyeanes, May 28, 1972; children: Nicole Elizabeth, Andrew James, Katherine M., Penelope Constance. BA, U. N.C., 1968; JD, U. Va., 1971. Bar: NY 1973, US Dist. Ct. (so. dist.) NY 1975, US Ct. Appeals (2nd cir.) 1975, Fla. 1988, Ill., 2012. Assoc. Brown and Wood, NYC, 1971-78, Wood and Dawson, NYC, 1978-82; ptnr. Alexander and Green, NYC, 1982-86, Mudge, Rose, Guthrie, Alexander & Ferdon, West Palm Beach, Fla., 1986-95, Edwards Wildman Palmer LLP, West Palm Beach, Fla., 1995—. Contbr. articles to jours., chpts. to books; co-author: State and Local Govt. Debt Financing. Chmn. Fin. Com., Palm Beach County Sch. Dist., 2000—; co-founder Katie Miller Young Adult Cancer Conf. Des Moines U. Coll. Osteopathic Medicine. Capt. lt. USAR, 1971—79. Recipient award, Miami-Dade, Broward and Palm Beach Daily Bus. Rev.; named Top Dealmaker of Yr., Pub. Sector, 2007. Mem. Fla. Bar Assn., NY State Bar Assn., Ill. State Bar Assn., Univ. Club, NYC. Episcopalian. Avocations: golf, tennis, swimming, gardening. Office: Edwards Wildman Palmer LLP 525 Okeechobee Blvd Ste 1600 West Palm Beach FL 33401 Office Phone: 561-820-0274. Business E-Mail: rmiller@edwardswildman.com.*

MILLER, RICHARD JOSEPH, retired lawyer; b. San Diego, Jan. 20, 1941; s. Daniel Preston and June (Beissel) M.; divorced, 1972; 1 child, Shelli Renee; m. Paula Anne English, May 29, 1982. BA, U. Tex., Arlington, 1970; M of Pub. Adminstrn., So. Meth. U., Dallas, 1974; JD, Baylor U., 1983. Bar: U.S. Dist. Ct. (we. dist.) Tex. 1988. Officer, supr. Dallas Police Dept., 1963-75; program coord. Tex. Organized Crime Prevention Council, Austin, 1975-76; chief of police Killeen (Tex.) Police Dept., 1976-79; tng. cons. Tex. Commn. on Law Enforcement Officer Standards and Edn., Austin, 1979-80; chief of police Denton (Tex.) Police Dept., 1980; sole practice Killeen, 1983-88; ptnr. Kleff, Lewis, Miller & Assocs., Killeen, 1989; pvt. practice Killeen, Tex., 1989-92; elected county atty. Bell County (Tex.), Bell County, 1993—2012. Author: The Train Robbing Bunch, 1981, Texas Firemen's and Policemen's Civil Service Law, 1987, Bounty Hunter, 1988, Bloody Bill Longley, 1996, Sam Bass & Gang, 1999, Bloody Bell County, 2011, Texas Ranger: John B. Jones and the Frontier Battalion, 1874-1881, 2012, Rube Burrow, Desperado, 2014. Vice chmn. Leon Valley dist. Boy Scouts Am., 1987-88; bd. dirs. Killeen Crimestoppers, Inc., 1986-91, Killeen Literacy Coun., 1987-90; mem. Bell County Hist. Commn., 1988-91. With U.S. Army, 1958-61. Served with 82nd Airborne Divsn US Army, 1958—61. Fellow Tex. Bar Found.; mem. Tex. Dist. and County Attys. Assn., Wild West History Assn. (bd. dirs. 2008). Avocations: old west research, jogging, cartooning. Home: 1917 Sutton Pl Trl Harker Heights TX 76548-6043

MILLER, ROBERT, retired military officer; b. Charleston, SC, Aug. 28, 1974; m. Shane Miller, 1997; 1 child. Attended, Coll. Charleston; BA in Criminal Justice, U. SC; M Justice Adminstrn., Norwich U. Sch. Grad. Studies, 2008. Grad. Marine Corps Close Combat Instrs. Course, 1995, 2nd Spl. Ops. Tng. Group Scout Skier Package, 1996, Corporals Leadership Course, 1996, Marine Corps Close Combat Instr. Tng. Course, 1997, Inf. Squad Leaders Course, 1997, Tactical Recovery Aircraft Personnel Course, 2002, Expeditionary Warfare Sch. Seminar, 2006. Enlisted USMC, 1995, advanced through grades to capt., 2005; basic infantryman 2nd Bn. 8th Marines, 2D Marine Divsn.; mem. Bn. Landing Team 2/8, 24th Marine Expeditionary Unit deployed to Mediterranean, Operation Decisive Endeavor, 1996—98; bn. planning officer, bn. comdr. U. SC Naval Res. Officers Tng. Corps, 1998; inf. rifle platoon comdr. for 1st Platoon, inf. platoon comdr., weapons platoon comdr., fire support team leader Charlie Co., 1st Bn. 8th Marines, 2D Marine Divsn., Camp Lejeune, NC; deployed aboard USS Iwo Jima, Bn. Landing Team 1/8, 26th Marine Expeditionary Unit, Operation Iraqi Freedom, Operation Sheltering Sky, 2003; deployed with Bn. Combat Team 1/8 Operation Iraqi Freedom II, Operation Phantom Fury; series comdr. for Charlie Co. Marine Corps Recruit Depot, Parris Island, SC, 2005—06, comdr. Company A, First Recruit Training Battalion, 2006—07, hdqs. co. comdr., ops. officer for 1st Recruit Tng. Bn., 2007; ret., 2007. Decorated Navy and Marine Corps Commendation medal with Combat Distinguishing Device, Navy and Marine Corps Achievement medal, Combat Action Ribbon, Navy Unit Commendation, Good Conduct medal (X2), Nat. Def. medal (X2), Armed Forces Expeditionary medal, Iraqi Campaign medal, Global War on Terrorism Expeditionary medal, Global War on Terrorism Svc. medal, Armed Forces Svc. medal, Humanitarian Svc. medal, Sea Svc. Deployment Ribbon (X3), Marine Corps Drill Instr. Ribbon, NATO medal. Democrat. Office: 219 Scotts St Beaufort SC 29902 Office Phone: 843-522-6841. Business E-Mail: info@robmillerforcongress.com.

MILLER, ROBERT HAROLD, medical association administrator, otolaryngologist, educator; b. Columbia, Mo., July 2, 1947; s. Harold Oswald and Ruth Nadine (Ballew) M.; m. Nancy Eaves, Aug. 19, 2007; children: Morgan Guillory, Reed Thurston. BS in Biology, Tulane U., 1969, MD, 1973, MBA, 1996. Diplomate Am. Bd. Otolaryngology. Resident otolaryngology, head/neck surgery UCLA, 1978; from asst. prof. to assoc. prof. otolaryngology-head and neck surgery Baylor Coll. Medicine, Houston, 1978—87; prof., chmn. otolaryngology-head and neck surgery Tulane Sch. Medicine, New Orleans, 1987—98, vice-chancellor for clin. affairs, 1997—99; dean U. Nev. Sch. Medicine, 1999—2001, prof., 1999—2002; prof. otolaryngology-head and neck surgery Tulane Sch. Medicine, New Orleans, 2002—03; exec. dir. Am. Bd. Otolaryngology, Houston, 2004—. Bd. dirs. Am. Bd. Otolaryngology; chief of staff Tulane Hosp., 1995-96; vis. prof. otolaryngology Baylor Coll. Medicine, Houston, Tex., 2004—. Mem. editl. bd. Archives of Otolaryngology, 1986-05, Head & Neck Surgery, 1987-03, Laryngoscope, 1996-, ENToday, chmn., 2006-. Named Outstanding Young Man, Houston C. of C., 1980; Robert Wood Johnson Health Policy fellow, 1996-97. Fellow ACS, Am. Soc. Head & Neck Surgery, Am. Acad. Oto-Head & Neck Surgery (Disting. Svc. award 1994, Honor award 1991), Triological Soc. (exec. sec. 1992-97, treas. 1997-2004). Avocations: tennis, computers. Home: 2616 Wroxton Rd Houston TX 77005 Office: Am Bd Otolaryngology 5615 Kirby Dr 600 Houston TX 77005 Office Phone: 713-850-0399. Business E-Mail: rmiller@aboto.org.

MILLER, SID, state legislator; m. Debra Miller; 2 children. AA, Cisco Jr. Coll., Tex.; BS in Vocat. Agrl. Edn., Tarleton State U., Stephenville, Tex., 1978. Former sch. tchr.; small businessman; mem. Dist. 59 Tex. House of Reps., 2000—. Recipient of several awards and honors. Republican. Office: 6407 S US Hwy 377 Eastland TX 76448 also: Room CAP GN.11 Capitol PO Box 2910 Austin TX 78768 Office Phone: 254-968-3535, 512-463-0628. Office Fax: 254-968-6903.

MILLER, STEVEN L., oil industry executive; b. Kansas City, Mo., Oct. 23, 1945; s. Irvin Earl and Betty Jane (Scharbach) M.; m. Sheila Margaret Porn, July 7, 1945; children: Steven Louis Jr., Ashley Margaret. BSChemE, U. Ill., 1967. Various engring. assignments Shell Oil Co., Houston, 1966-73; spl. assignment SIPM-Shell Internat., The Hague, The Netherlands, 1973-74; various mgmt. positions Shell Oil Co., Houston, Norco, La., 1974-92, Shell Internat. Petroleum Co., London, 1992-96; mng. dir. Royal Dutch/Shell Group Cos., London, 1996-99; chmn., pres., CEO Shell Oil Co., Houston, 1999—2002; chmn., pres. SLM Discovery Ventures, 2002—; chmn. RRI Energy, Inc. (now GenOn Energy, Inc.), Houston, 2009—10; chmn., pres. SLM Discovery Ventures. Bd. dirs. Genon Energy, Houston, Tex., Applied Materials Inc., Santa Clara, Calif., Am. Petroleum Inst., Washington, Coun. of the Ams., N.Y.C.; bd. advisors James A. Baker Inst. Pub. Policy, Houston, 1999—. Bd. dirs. Greater Houston Partnership, 1999, World Golf Found., St. Augustine, Fla., 1999; trustee United Way Tex.-Gulf Coast, Houston, 1999, George C. Marshall Found. Mem. Nat. Petroleum Coun., Bus. Roundtable, Gov.'s Bus. Coun. Presbyterian. Avocations: golf, american history, antiques. Mailing: Genon Energy Bd Directors 1000 Main St Houston TX 77002

MILLER, STUART A., construction executive; s. Leonard and Sue Miller. Grad., Harvard U.; JD, U. Miami, 1982. V.p. Lennar Corp., Miami, Fla., 1988—97, bd. dirs., 1990—, pres., Homebuilding Divsn., 1991—97, pres., prin., Real Estate & Mgmt. Divsn., 1995—97, pres. Miami, Fla., 1997—2011, CEO, 1997—; chmn. Riley Property Holdings, LLC (formerly LNR Property Corp.), 1997—2005. Bd. dirs. Union Bank, Fla. Bd. advisor, Joint Ctr. Housing Studies Policy Harvard U. Named one of 50 Most Generous Philanthropists, BusinessWeek, 2005. Office: Lennar Corp 700 NW 107th Ave Ste 400 Miami FL 33172-3154 Office Phone: 305-559-4000. Office Fax: 304-228-8383. E-mail: smiller@lennar.com.

MILLER, TERI L., corporate financial executive; Dir. strategic analysis ions.com; v.p., treas. Spherion Corp., dir. strategic analysis, v.p. fin. and acctg. Office: Spherion Corp 2050 Spectrum Blvd Fort Lauderdale FL 33309 Office Phone: 954-308-7600. Office Fax: 954-308-7666. Business E-Mail: terilmiller@spherion.com.

MILLER, TYSON, environmental advocate; b. San Diego, 1973; BA in Environ. Studies, UCLA. Dir. enviorn. edn. prog. LA County Secondary Schs.; founder, dir. Recycled Products Coop., 1997—2001, Green Press Initiative, 2001—. Dir.: (documentaries, about enviorn. edn. progs.) Generation Earth. Office: Green Press Initiative 68 Morningside Dr Ste 1 Asheville NC 28806

MILLER, W. GREG, pathologist, educator; BS, Santa Clara U., Calif., 1969; PhD, U. Ariz., Tucson, 1973. Diplomate in clin. chemistry Am. Bd. Clin. Chemistry, 1976. Postdoctoral fellow Ohio State U., Columbus, 1973—75; prof. pathology Va. Commonwealth U., Richmond, Va., 1977—. Contbr. chapters to books, articles to profl. jours. and monographs. Recipient Excellence in Consensus Mgmt. award, Clin. and Lab. Standards Inst., 2007. Fellow: Nat. Acad. Clin. Biochemistry; mem.: Clin. Chemistry Jour. (assoc. editor 2008), Am. Assn. Clin. Chemistry (bd. dirs. 2008—, Joseph Roe award 1997, Miriam Reiner award 2006, Outstanding Contributions to Clin. Chemistry award 2007, Presdl. Citation award 2007), Clin. and Lab. Standards Inst. (treas. 2006—). Office: Va Commonwealth Univ 403 N 13th St Rm 501 Richmond VA 23298-0286 Business E-Mail: gmiller@vcu.edu.

MILLER, W. THADDEUS, energy executive; BS, US Merchant Marine Acad.; JD, St. John's Sch. Law. Atty., NYC; v.p. Goldman Sachs & Co., 1994—99; exec. v.p., chief legal officer Orion Power Holdings, Inc., 1999—2002; cons. Tex. Pacific Group, 2002—04; exec. v.p., chief legal officer Tex. Genco LLC, 2004—06; exec. v.p., chief legal officer, sec. Calpine Corp., 2008—. Officer USCG. Office: Calpine Corp Ste 1000 717 Texas Ave Houston TX 77002

MILLER, WILBUR RANDOLPH, academic administrator; b. Elsberry, Mo., Nov. 12, 1932; s. Charles Clifton and Pauline Jean (Dryden) M. Student, SE Mo. U., 1951-53; BEd, U. Mo., 1954, MEd, 1955, EdD, 1960. Cert. secondary tchr., Mo. Tchr. indsl. arts Hazelwood Sch. Dist., St. Louis, 1955-56, U. Lab. Sch., Columbia, Mo., 1956-60; indsl. tchr. educator Purdue U., West Lafayette, Ind., 1960-63; asst. prof. U. Mo., Columbia, 1963-67, assoc. prof. and chmn. dept. coll. edn., 1967-76, prof. and assoc. dean coll. edn., 1976-86, dean coll. edn., 1986-91, prof., dean emeritus, 1992; cons. Rep. of Turkey, 1993, 94; assoc. v.p. devel. Auburn U., Ala., 1996—2007; ret., 2007. Chmn. adv. coun. Fed. Rsch. Ctr. in Vocat. Edn., Ohio State U., Columbus, 1981-84; internat. edn. cons. 1992—; edn. adv. bd. DeVry Inc., Oakwood Terrace, Ill., 1986—; mem. pvt. post-sec. tech. sch. accreditation commn. Accrediting Commn. Career Schs. and Colls. Tech., 1994-98. Author: Teaching Children Through Construction Activities, 1985, Instructors and Their Jobs, 1998, 4th edit., 2009, The Golf Primer, 1991, Handbook for College Teaching, 2d edit., 2003; editor: (series) Basic Industrial Arts, 1978; contbr. more than 40 articles to profl. jours. Pres., bd. dirs. Lenoir Inc., Columbia, 1977-84; mem. Woodhaven Sch. Bd., Columbia, 1982-83. With USNR, 1955-63. Recipient U. Mo. Faculty/Alumni award, 1985. Mem. Nat. Assn. Indsl. Tchr. Educators (pres., officer 1965-74), Am. Indsl. Arts Assn. (v.p. 1980), Mo. Vocat. Assn. (pres. 1974-75), Mo. Assn. Colls. for Tchr. Edn. (pres. 1987-90), Am. Vocat. Assn. (Outstanding Svc. award 1979), U. Mo. Faculty Club (officer 1977-82), Kiwanis. Mem. Christian Ch. (Disciples Of Christ). Avocations: golf, travel, home maintenance. Office: PO Box 2683 Auburn AL 36831-2683 Office Phone: 334-332-7125.

MILLETTE, LEROY F., JR., state supreme court justice; b. Pa. m. M. Elizabeth O'Brien Millette; children: Lauren Elizabeth, LeRoy F. III. Degree in Economics, Coll. William and Mary, JD, 1974. Assoc. prof. Northern Va. Cmty. Coll., 1976—; asst. commonwealth atty. Prince William County; sole practitioner Compton, Latimer, Compton & Compton; judge Va. 31st Jud. Cir., 1993—98, chief judge, 1998—2000, 2006; judge Va. Ct. of Appeals, 2007—09; justice Va. Supreme Ct., 2009—. Office: Va Supreme Ct PO Box 1315 Richmond VA 23219-1315 Office Phone: 804-786-2251.*

MILLICAN, MIKE, state legislator; b. Dec. 5, 1950; m. Debbie Millican; 1 child. BA, Athens State U. Cmty. coll. instr.; mem. Dist. 17 Ala. House of Reps., Montgomery, 1990—. Mem. Hamilton C. of C., Adult Edn. Adv. Coun., First Bapt. Ch., Hamilton, Ala.; bd. dirs. Marion County Red Cross, Winston-Marion Cmty. Action Assn.; mem. adv. bd. Marion County Extension Svc. Mem.: Marion County Cattleman's Assn., Hamilton Kiwanis Club, Masonic Lodge. Democrat. Baptist. Office: Ala House of Reps Ala State House 11 S Union St Rm 628-F Montgomery AL 35130 Office Phone: 334-242-7768. Office Fax: 334-353-3350. Business E-Mail: mike.millican@alhouse.gov.

MILLIGAN, PETER J., corporate financial executive; BBA in acctg., Hofstra Univ., 1989; MBA in econ. & fin., NYU, 2006. Acct. Arthur Andersen, Price Waterhouse; v.p. fin., investor rels. AT&T Corp., 2005—06; dir. investor rels. ITT Corp., White Plains, NY, 2006—08, v.p., contr. electronic systems, 2008—10, CFO def. & info. systems, 2010—11; sr. v.p., CFO ITT Exelis, Inc., McLean, Va., 2011—. Office: ITT Exelis Inc 1650 Tysons Blvd Ste 1700 Mc Lean VA 22102

MILLIKAN, LARRY EDWARD, dermatologist; b. Sterling, Ill., May 12, 1936; s. Daniel Franklin and Harriet Adeline (Parmenter) M.; m. Jeanine Dorothy Johnson, Aug. 27, 1960; children: Marshall, Rebecca. BA, Monmouth Coll., 1958; MD, U. Mo., 1962. Intern Great Lakes Naval Hosp., Ill., 1962-63; housestaff in tng. U. Mich., Ann Arbor, 1967-69, chief resident, 1969-70; asst. prof. dermatology U. Mo., Columbia, 1970-74, assoc. prof., 1974-81; chmn. dept. dermatology Tulane U., New Orleans, 1981—, chair/prof. emeritus, 2006—. Cons. physician Charity Hosp., New Orleans, Tulane U. Hosp., New Orleans, Riley Hosp., Anderson Hosp., Rush Hosp., all Meridian, Miss.; mem. bd. trustees Sulzberger Inst. for Dermatological Edn., 1995-99; chmn. cont. med. edn. com. La. State Med. Soc., 1994-97. Assoc. editor Internat. Jour. Dermatology, 1980-99, Clinics in Dermatology, 1999—; mem. editl. bd. Current Concepts in Skin Disorders, Am. Jour. Med. Scis.; mem. editl. bd. Clinics in Dermatology, 1985—, assoc. editor, 1999—; contbr. articles to med. jours. Bd. dirs. Women's Dermatol. Assn., 1994-99. With USN, 1960-67. Recipient Andres Bello awrd Govt. of Venezuela, 1989, citation of merit Sch. Medicine, U. Mo., 1993, Faculty Alumnus award U. Mo., 1997; named Disting. Alumnus, Monmouth Coll., 1990; Nat. Cancer Inst. grantee, 1976-84. Fellow ACP; mem. AAAS, AMA, Am. Acad. Dermatology (bd. dirs. 1986-90), Am. Dermatol. Assn., Am. Dermatol. Soc. for Allergy and Immunology (pres., bd. dirs.), Soc. for Investigative Dermatology (past pres. South sect.), So. Med. Assn. (vice chmn. dermatology sect. 1984, chmn. 1994), Coll. Physicians Phila., Assn. Profs. Dermatology (bd. dirs. 1984-86), Orleans Parish Med. Soc., La. Med. Soc., Pan Am. Med. Assn., Internat. Soc. Dermatology (dep. sec. gen. 1989-99), Mo. Allergy Assn. (past pres.), Am. Coll. Cryosurgery, Assn. Acad. Dermatol. Surgeons, Internat. Soc. Dermatol. Surgery, Internat. Acad. Cosmetic Dermatology (sec. gen. 1996-), Dermatol. Found. Leaders Soc. (state chmn. 1993-97). Office: Tulane Univ Sch Medicine Dept of Dermatology 1430 Tulane Ave TB36 New Orleans LA 70112-2699

MILLMAN, RICHARD GEORGE, architect, educator; b. St. Johns, Mich., Feb. 12, 1925; s. Harold Fildew and Elizabeth Hill (Van Deusen) M.; m. Mary Louise Manley, June 17, 1950; childen: John Richard, Ruth Barbara. BArch, U. Mich., 1951, MArch, 1962. Registered arch., Mich., Ohio, Ala. Job capt. Smith Hinchman & Grylls, Detroit, 1951-52; designer assoc. Eliot Robinson, AIA, Birmingham, Mich., 1952-55; designer Eero Saarinen Assocs., Bloomfield Hills, Mich., 1955-56; assoc. Chas. W. Lane Assocs. Inc., Ann Arbor, Mich., 1956-59; prin. Kainlauri, MacMullan, Millman, Ann Arbor, 1959-62; assoc. prof. Ohio U., Athens, 1962-68; prof. Auburn (Ala.) U., 1968—, head architecture dept., 1968-73, 84-85, head indsl. design dept., 1988-89. Prof. Mid. East Tech. U., Ankara, Turkey, 1966-67, King Faisal U., Dammam, Saudi Arabia, 1979-81. One man shows include Dhahran Art Group, Saudi Arabia, 1981, Peet Gallery, Auburn U., 1983, 91, Heritage Hall Mus., Talladega, Ala., 1998; author: Washtenaw Community College, 1962, Auburn U. Tour Guide, 1990. With U.S. Army, 1943-46, ETO, PTO. Decorated Bronze Star; recipient Cert. of Honor Ala. Hist. Commn., 1977; Alumni scholar U. Mich., 1961; Fulbright lectr. Exch. Com., Mid. East Tech. U., 1966. Mem. AIA (treas. Ala. coun. 1969, v.p. 1970, pres. 1972, emeritus 1990, Auburn chpt. pres. 1970, emeritus), Nat. Coun. Archtl. Registration Bd. (cert.), Auburn Arts Assn., Ga. Watercolor Soc. (signature mem.), Watercolor Soc. Ala. (signature mem.; pres. 2003), So. Watercolor Soc. (signature mem.). Avocations: painting, photography. Home: 736 Brenda Ave Auburn AL 36830-6038 Office Phone: 334-887-6428. E-mail: millmmm@charter.net.

MILLS, FRED H., JR., state legislator; BS in Pharmacy, U. La., Monroe. Pharmacist; owner Mills Cashway Pharmacy; pres./CEO Farmers-Merchants Bank; mem. Dist. 46 La. House of Reps., 2008—11, mem. agr., forestry, aquaculture and rural devel. com., civil law and procedure com., health and welfare com.; mem. Dist. 22 La. State Senate, 2011—. Democrat. Mailing: 1010 Martin St Parks LA 70582 Office: State Capitol PO Box 94183 Baton Rouge LA 70804 Office Phone: 225-342-2040. E-mail: millsf@legis.state.la.us.

MILLS, GREY, state legislator; m. Jennifer Mills; 3 children. BS in Edn. & Social Sci., Appalachian State U., Boone, NC, 1990; JD, Regent U. Sch. Law, 1994. Former tchr. Central Piedmont Cmty. Coll., Richmond Cmty. Coll., South Iredell High Sch.; former asst. dist. atty.; cofounder Mills & Levine, 1998—; mem. Dist. 95 NC House of Reps., 2009—. Republican. Baptist. Office: North Carolina House of Representatives 16 W Jones St Rm 2221 Raleigh NC 27601-1096 Home: 156 Brick Kiln Way Mooresville NC 28117 Office Phone: 919-733-5741. Business E-Mail: Grey.Mills@ncleg.net.

MILLS, HUGH MILTON, JR., retired college president; b. Albany, Ga., Oct. 24, 1922; s. Hugh Milton Mills Sr. and Johnie Lamar West; m. Evelyn Heath, Oct. 6, 1944 (dec. Aug. 1994); children: Hugh Milton III, Ralph West, Rebecca Ann; m. Patsy Faulkner Howell, May 30, 1998 (dec. May 29, 2009). AA, N. Ga. Coll., 1943; BS in Edn., U. Ga., 1945, MEd, 1947, EdD, 1956; LLD (hon.), Brenau Coll., 1983. Cert. profl. tchr., Ga. Tchr., coach Rockmart (Ga.) H.S., 1945-47, Albany (Ga.) H.S., 1947-48; from instr. to asst. prof. U. Ga., Athens, 1948-51, from asst. prof. to assoc. prof., 1953-65; supervising prin. Rockmart Pub. Schs., 1951-53; pres. Gainesville (Ga.) Jr. Coll., 1965-84; interim pres. Brenau Coll., Gainesville, 1985; pres. emeritus Gainesville Coll., 1985—. Cons. Ga. Dept. Vocat. Rehab., Atlanta, 1955-65. With USAAC, 1942-43. Named Ga. Man of the Yr. Conservation Dist. Ga., 1986. Mem. Phi Beta Kappa, Phi Kappa Phi, Kappa Delta Pi, Phi Delta Kappa. Baptist. Avocation: woodworking. Office: Gainesville Coll PO Box 1358 Gainesville GA 30503

MILLS, JON, dean emeritus, law educator; b. Miami, Fla., July 24, 1947; s. Herb J. and Marguerite (Sweat) M.; m. Beth Bechard; children: Marguerite St. Amand, Elizabeth Buchanan Mills. BA in

Economics, Stetson U., 1969, LLD (hon.), 1986; JD with honors, U. Fla., 1972. Bar: U.S. Ct Appeals (11th Cir.). Jud. clerk 2nd Dist. Ct. Appeals, Fla., 1972; spl. asst. State Atty. Rolling vs. State, 1990; ptnr. McGalliard, Mills, DeMontomollin, Smith, Monaco & Sieg, 1980—86, Consel, Boies, Schiller & Flexner LLP, 2008—; mem. Fla. Ho. of Reps., 1978-88, majority leader, 1985—86, speaker, 1987-88; mem. faculty U. Fla., Gainesville, 1973—80; prof. law U. Fla., Coll. Law, Gainesville, 1995—, founding dir., Ctr. for Governmental Responsibility, 1973—80, 1988—, dir., Ctr. for Governmental Responsibility, 2003—, interim dean, 1999—2001, dean, 2001—03, dean emeritus, 2003—. Mem. Fla. Constitution Revision Commn., 1987—88, Commn. on the Future of the South, State Comprehensive Plan Com., 1985, Fla. Motion Picture, TV, and Recording Industry Bd.; adv. coun., bd. dir. State Legis. Leaders Found.; chair Fla. Coun. on Far East R&D; chair com. privacy and ct. records Fla. Supreme Ct., 2003—05; spkr. in field. Author: Privacy: The Lost Right, 2008; co-author: Voting Rights and Democracy: The Law and Politics Districting, 1996; prodr., moderator, Florida Forum, 1989; exec. prodr., moderator, Sunshine Showdown, 1991; co-editor, moderator, Common Ground, 1995 (recipient 1998 Suncoast Regional Emmy award for Common Ground TV program "Whose Water Is It Anyway?"; contbr. articles to profl. jours. Del., Dem. Nat. Convention, 1984; chair, State Dem. Convention, 1987; founding chmn., Fla. Chpt. Dem. Leadership Coun., 1987; pres., Fla. Chpt. Dem. Leadership Coun., 1993-; mem. Coun. Internat. Administrative Units, Office of Internat. Studies and Programs, Governor's Growth Mgmt. Adv. Com., 1993, U. Fla. Found. Investment Com., 1998-2002; founding pres. bd. dirs., So. Legal Coun., Fla. Arts Celebration; former mem. exec. com. Fla. Dem. Party; chair, U. Fla. President's External Rels. Com.; trustee, Fla. Nature Conservancy Bd., 1988-; bd. dir. U. Fla. Ctr. for Performing Arts, Everglades Found., 1996-, Internat. Computer and Automated Rsch. 1st lt. USAR. Decorated Order of Coif; recipient Allen Morris award, 1979-80, 1985-86, Outstanding Legis. award Fla. Health Care Assn., 1982, Legis. award, Fla. Audubon Soc., 1983, Sierra Club Fla. Chpt., 1983, 1984, Fla. C.ofC. Legis. award for Leadership in Quality of Life Legislation, 1984, Dept. Health and Human Services Commissioner's award for Outstanding Leadership Services in Preventation of Child Abuse and Neglect, 1985, League of Women Voters Outstanding Elected Official, 1985, Nature Conservancy Pub. Svc. award, 1986, President's 1997 Conservationist of Yr. award, Fla. Audubon Soc., 1998, Spl. Recognition award, Fla. Assn. Countries for outstanding work as a mem. of the Constitution Revision Commn., 1998, Conservation Civic Leader of Yr., Fla. Wildlife Fedn., 1998, Bd. Regents Disting. Cmty. Svc. award, 1998; named Rep. of Yr. Assn. Retarded Citizens Fla., 1981, Most Effective Mem. of the House, 1985, 1986, Gainesville Sun 1998 Person of Yr. for Govt., 1998, Most Valuable Mem., Fla. Constitutional Revision Commn., 1998. Fellow Am. Bar Found.; mem. ABA (adv. com. World Justice Project, 2007-), Fla. Bar Assn., Fla. Supreme Ct. Hist. Soc., Pi Kappa Alpha, Fla. Blue Key, Fla. Supreme Ct. Professionalism Commn. Methodist. Avocations: flying, scuba diving, skiing, photography, Karate. Home: 2727 NW 58th Blvd Gainesville FL 32606-8516 Office: U Fla Coll Law 230 Bruton-Geer Hall Gainesville FL 32611 also: PO Box 117625 Gainesville FL 32611 Office Phone: 352-273-0835. Office Fax: 352-392-1457.

MILLS, LINDA ANNE, aerospace transportation executive; b. 1949; BS in Mathematics, Santa Clara U., 1971; MS in Computer Sci., U. Ill., 1973. Mgmt. positions in missions systems sector Northrop Grumman Corp., 1979—2003, v.p., mission assurance & six sigma, mission sys. sector, 2003—05, v.p., ops. & processes, info. tech. sector, 2005—07, pres., Civilian Agencies Bus. Group, IT sector, 2007—08, corporate v.p., pres., info. systems, 2008—12, corporate v.p. ops., 2013—. Recipient CEO Leadership Award, 2000, 2001, 2005, Disting Alumni award, Ill. Coll. Engring., 2010; named one of The Women Worth Watching, Diversity Journal, 2007, The 100 Most Powerful Women in DC, Washingtonian mag., 2009, The 50 Most Powerful Women in Bus., Fortune mag., 2013. Office: Norththrop Grumman Corp 2980 Fairview Pk Dr Falls Church VA 22042 Office Phone: 703-280-2900.*

MILLS, MICHAEL PAUL, federal judge; b. Charleston, SC, Aug. 25, 1956; s. Paul H. and Shirley (Dulaney) M.; m. Mona (Robinson), Aug. 2, 1976; children: Alysson, Chip, Rebekah, Penn. AA, Itawamba CC, Fulton, Miss., 1976; BA, U. Miss., 1978, JD, 1980; LLM, U. Va., 2001. Bar: Miss., 1980; U.S. Ct. Appeals (Fed. Cir.), 1986; U.S. Ct. Appeals (5th cir.), 1980; U.S. Supreme Ct., 1990. Pvt. practice, Miss., 1980-95; legis. Miss. Ho. of Reps., Jackson, Miss., 1983-95; mem. Nat. Conf. Commr. on Uniform State Laws, 1993—; justice Miss. Supreme Ct., Jackson, Miss., 1995—2001; judge US Dist. Ct. (no. dist.) Miss., Oxford, 2001—07, chief judge, 2007—. Adj. prof. law U. Miss. Office: Fed Bldg Rm 335 911 Jackson Ave Oxford MS 38655 Office Phone: 662-234-1538. Office Fax: 662-234-1447.

MILLS, MIKE, musician; b. Orange County, Calif., Dec. 17, 1958; s. Frank and Adora; 1 child, Julian. Student, U. Ga. Bass guitarist R.E.M., 1980—. Rec. albums include Chronic Town, 1982, Murmur, 1983 (Rolling Stone Album of Yr. 1983), Reckoning, 1984, Fables of the Reconstruction, 1985, Life's Rich Pageant, 1986, Dead Letter Office, 1987, Document, 1987, Eponymous, 1988, Green, 1988, Out of Time, 1991 (Group Grammy award, Best Alternative Music Performance, 1992), Automatic for the People, 1993 (4 Grammy nominations), Monster, 1994, Murmur, 1995, New Adventures in Hi-Fi, 1996, Up, 1998, Reveal, 2001, Around the Sun, 2004, Live, 2007, Accelerate, 2008, Collapse into Now, 2011, Part Lies, Part Heart, Part Truth, Part Garbage 1982-2011, 2011; songs include The One I Love, Orange Crush (MTV Video Music award for Best Post Modern Video, 1990), Losing My Religion, 1991 (6 MTV Video Music Awards, 1991, 2 Grammy awards: Best Group Pop Vocal Performance, Best Short Form Music Video, 1992), Everybody Hurts, 1992 (4 MTV Video Music Awards, 1994), Man on the Moon, The Great Beyond, Imitation of Life, It's the End of the World As We Know It; appeared on Robbie Robertson's album, Storyville, 1991, Backbeat soundtrack, 1994, Man on the Moon soundtrack, 1999. Recipient Top Modern Rock Artist, Top World Album awards, Billboard Music Awards, 1991, 3 Grammy awards for Best Group Pop Vocal Performance, Best Alternative Music Performance, and Best Short Form Music Video, 1992, Best Internat. Group, Brit Awards, 1992, 1993, Patrick Lippert award, Rock the Vote, 1994, Video Vanguard award, MTV Video Music Awards, 1995; named to Rock & Roll Hall of Fame, with R.E.M., 2007. Office: REM PO Box 8032 Athens GA 30603-8032

MILLS, OLAN, II, photography company executive; b. 1930; married. Grad., Princeton U., 1952. With Olan Mills, Inc., Chattanooga, 1955—, now chmn. Office: Olan Mills Inc Gen Offices 4325 Amnicola Hwy Chattanooga TN 37406-1014

MILLS, STEPHEN, performing company executive; Prin. dancer Ballet Austin, 1987—88, choreographer, 1988—92, resident choreographer, 1992—99, assoc. artistic dir., 1999—2000, artistic dir., 2000—. Instr. Internat. Theatrical Inst., Cyprus; master tchr. Booker T. Washington H.S. for the Performing Arts, Va. Sch. of the Arts, New Orleans Ctr. for Creative Arts, Stephens Coll., Point Park Coll.; guest faculty Jabob's Pillow, Goucher Coll. Choreographed works have been shown at Ballet Builders at Lincoln Ctr., 1998, Rencontres Chorégraphiques Internat. des Seine-Saint-Denis, Paris, Cuballet, Havana, The Dayton Ballet, The Sarasota (Fla.) Ballet, Ballet Pacifica, Dallas Black Dance Theatre, Dance Kaleidoscope, Ontario Ballet Theatre, Toronto, Icelandic Ballet Co., Reykjavik; performing mem. Harkness Ballet, Am. Dance Machine, Cin. Ballet, Indpls. Ballet Theatre, Balanchine Repertoire; Collaborations with Asleep at the Wheel, Shawn Colvin Recipient Humanitarian award, Austin Anti-Defamation League, 2006. Mem.: Dance/USA (bd. trustees). Office: Ballet Austin 501 W 3rd St Austin TX 78701-3807

MILLS, TERRY, state legislator; b. Oct. 12, 1950; m. Patty Lee; 3 children. BBA, Western Ky. U., Bowling Green, 1973. Ret. US Social Security Adminstrn., Ky., 2007; mem. Dist. 24 Ky. House of Reps., 2010—. Mem. St. Augustine Cath. Ch., former chmn. parish coun. Mem.: Lebanon Lions Club, Disabled Am. Veterans. Democrat. Roman Catholic. Mailing: 695 McElroy Pike Lebanon KY 40033 Office: Ky Legislature Annex Rm 329B 702 Capitol Ave Frankfort KY 40601 Office Phone: 502-564-8100 ext. 684. Business E-Mail: terry.mills@lrc.ky.gov.

MILLS, WILLIAM HAROLD, JR., construction executive; b. St. Petersburg, Fla., July 24, 1939; s. William Harold and Caroline (Bonfoey) M.; m. Sylvia Ludwig, Jan. 4, 1962 (div. 1975); children—William Harold III, Robert Michael, Leslie Anne; m. Kimberly Keyes, May 4, 1985 (div. 1988); m. Gigi Alice Schmidt, Aug. 1, 1990. Grad., Woodberry Forest Sch., 1954-57; BS in Civil Engring., U. Fla., 1961. Cert. Class A gen. contractor, Fla. V.P. bus. devel. Mills & Jones Constrn., St. Petersburg, Fla., 1964-68; v.p. Wellington Corp., Atlanta, 1968-71; exec. v.p. Mills & Jones Constrn., St. Petersburg, Fla., 1971-79; pres., chmn. Federal Constrn. Co., St. Petersburg, 1979-88, vice chmn., 1988—; pres., chair Univ. Housing Svcs., Inc., St. Petersburg. Mem. adv. com. St Petersburg Port, 1993—. Pres. St. Petersburg Progress, Inc., 1986-87; active mem. Suncoasters, St. Petersburg, 1974—, St. Anthony's Devel. Found., St. Petersburg, 1983-86; past chmn. Pinellas Marine Inst., St. Petersburg, Blue Ribbon Zoning Com., City of St. Petersburg; mem. Tony Janus Award Com.; former mem. Pinellas County Constrn. Licensing Bd., Tampa Bay Aviation Adv. Com., United Fund Pinellas County; former mem. U. South Fla. Campus Adv. Bd. Served with USPHS, 1962-64. Named Hon. Royal Navy Liaison officer Her Majesty's Royal Navy, 1984. Mem. ASCE, NSPE, Am. Mgmt. Assn., Mensa, St. Petersburg Area C. of C. (bd. govs. 1983-85), Fla. Sports Adv. Coun., Order of Salvador/Salvador Dali Mus., St. Petersburg Yacht Club, Dragon Club, Les Ambassadeurs Club (London), Annabel's Club (London), Useppa Island Club (past bd. govs.), Sigma Alpha Epsilon, U.S. Croquet Assn., Univ. Fla. Pres.'s Coun. (life). Republican. Episcopalian. Home: 1260 Brightwaters Blvd NE Saint Petersburg FL 33704-3728 E-mail: wmillsjr@uhsi.com.

MILLS, WILLIAM HAYES, lawyer; b. Gordo, Ala., Mar. 30, 1931; s. Early S. and Bama (Cameron) M. LLB, U. Ala., 1956. Bar: Ala. 1956. Pvt. practice, Birmingham, Ala.; ptnr. Rogers, Howard, Redden & Mills, 1961—79, Redden, Mills & Clark, 1979—, Redden, Mills, Clark & Shaw, 2013—. Arbitrator Fed. Mediation and Conciliation Svc., Am. Arbitration Assn. Served with AUS, 1948-50, 50-51. Mem. ABA, Ala. Bar Assn., Birmingham Bar Assn. Baptist. Home: 2105 Williamsburg Way Birmingham AL 35223-1740 Office: Redden Mills & Clark 940 Financial Ctr Birmingham AL 35203 Home Phone: 205-870-4139; Office Phone: 205-322-0457. Business E-Mail: whm@rmclaw.com.

MILNE, EDWARD LAWRENCE, biomedical engineer; came to U.S., 1985; s. Roderick Francis and Mary Angela (Massiah) M.; children: Marc Aaron, Adam Daniel. BSc, Dalhousie U., 1971. Rsch. asst. Tech. U. N.S., Halifax, Canada, 1973-76; technologist Dalhousie U., Halifax, 1976-85; tech. dir. Max Biedermann Inst. Mt. Sinai Med. Ctr., Miami Beach, Fla., 1986—. Contbr. articles to profl. jours. Avocations: computers, reading, fresh water fishing, gardening. Office: Mt Sinai Med Ctr 4300 Alton Rd Miami Beach FL 33140-2800 Office Phone: 305-674-2790. Business E-Mail: tmilne@msmc.com.

MILNER, CLYDE A., II, historian; b. Durham, NC, Oct. 19, 1948; s. Charles Fremont and Eloyse (Sargent) M.; m. Carol Ann O'Connor, Aug. 14, 1977; children: Catherine Carol, Charles Clyde. AB, U. N.C., 1971; MA, Yale U., 1973, MPhil, 1974, PhD, 1979. Admissions counselor Guilford Coll., Greensboro, NC, 1968-70; acting instr. Yale U., New Haven, 1974-75; research fellow McNickle Ctr., Chgo., 1975-76; instr. Utah State U., Logan, 1976-79, asst. prof., 1979-82, assoc. prof., 1982-88, prof., 1988—2002; dir. Mountain West Ctr. for Regional Studies, 1997-2000; dir. PhD program in heritage studies Ark. State U., 2002—, prof., 2002—. Reader of manuscripts History Book Club, Inc., 1986—; exec. dir. Am. Studies program Utah State U., 1997-2000, vis. prof. Yale U., 2006-07, sr. rsch. fellow Beinecke Libr., 2006-07. Author: With Good Intentions, 1982; co-author As Big as The West: The Pioneer Life of Granville Stuart, 2009; editor: Major Problems in the History of the American West, 1989, co-editor 2d edit., 1997; editor: A New Significance: Re-envisioning the History of the American West, 1996; assoc. editor The Western Hist. Quar., 1984-87, co-editor, 1987-89, editor, 1990-97, exec. editor, 1998-2002; co-editor: Churchmen and the Western Indians, 1985, Trails: Toward a New Western History, 1991, Oxford History of the American West, 1994 (Western Heritage award for non-fiction Nat. Cowboy Hall of Fame 1994, Caughey Western History Assn. award for best book on history of Am. West 1995). Recipient Paladen Writing award The Montana Mag. Western History, 1987, Faculty Svc. award Associated Students Utah State U., 1987, Outstanding Social Science Researcher award Utah State U., 1983, (with Carol A. O'Connor) Charles Redd prize Utah Acad. Scis.,(with Carol O'Connor) Arts and Letters, 1996, Outstanding Rschr Coll. & Humanities Social Scis, Ark. State U., 2008; fellowship fund established in his honor Western Hist. Quar. Utah State U., 2002, Grad. Editl. Assistantship in his honor with Anne M. Butler, 2004, Lifetime award Western History Assn., 2012, Kiwanian of Yr. Kiwanis Club, Jonesboro, Ark., 2013. Mem. Western History Assn., Orgn. Am. Historians (Disting. lectr. 2004—, adv. bd. newsletter 2005—09), Phi Alpha Theta, Phi Beta Kappa. Mem. Soc. Of Friends. Home: 1306 E Country Club Terr Jonesboro AR 72401-4325 Office: Ark State U Heritage Studies PhD Program PO Box 69 State University AR 72467 Office Phone: 870-972-3509. Business E-Mail: cmilner@astate.edu.

MILNER, ROSS, surgeon, educator; b. Phila., Apr. 18, 1968; s. Martin Sheldon and Janie Lynn Milner; m. Dara Leigh Jacobsohn, Aug. 10, 1996; children: Jake Michael, Callie Grace. BA in Biology, U. Pa., Phila., 1990; MD, U. Pa., 1994. Resident in surgery U. Pa., 1994—2001, fellow in vascular surgery, 2001—02; Marco Polo fellow Utrecht, Netherlands, 2002—03; asst. prof. surgeon Emory U. Sch. Medicine, Atlanta, 2003—. Grantee Wallace Coulter award, Ga. Inst. Tech., 2007. Office: Emory Univ Sch Medicine 1364 Clifton Rd NE Ste H-122 Atlanta GA 30322 Office Fax: 404-727-3316. Business E-Mail: ross.milner@emoryhealthcare.org.

MILSAP, RONNIE, singer; b. Robinsville, NC, Jan. 16, 1943; s. James Lee and Grace (Calhoun) Milsap; m. Frances Joyce Reeves, Oct. 30, 1965; 1 child, Ronald Todd. AA, Young-Harris Jr. Coll., 1964. Singer: (albums) Where My Heart Is, 1973, Pure Love, 1974, A Legend in My Time, 1975 (Country Music Assn. award for Album of Yr., 1975), Ronnie Milsap Live, 1976 (Country Music Assn. award for Album of Yr., 1977), It Was Almost Like a Song, 1977 (Country Music Assn. award for Album of Yr., 1978), Only One Love in My Life, 1978, Milsap Magic, 1980, Out Where the Bright Lights Are Glowing, 1981, There's No Gettin' Over Me, 1981 (Grammy award for Best Male Country Vocal Performance, 1982), Country Keyed Up, 1985, Lost in the Fifties Tonight, 1986 (Grammy award for Best Male Country Vocal Performance, 1986), Believe It, Christmas with Ronnie Milsap, 1986, (with Kenny Rogers) Make No Mistake She's Mine, 1987 (Grammy award for Best Country Collaboration with Vocals, 1988), Heart and Soul, Stranger Things Have Happened, 1989, Back to the Grindstone, 1991, Greatest Hits Vol. 3, 1992, True Believer, 1993, The Ultimate Ronnie Milsap, 1994, The Essential Ronnie Milsap, 1995, Super Hits, Ronnie Milsap Sings His Best, 1996, 40 #1 Hits, #1 Hits Collection, 2000, Just for a Thrill, 2004, My Life, 2006, Playlist: The Very Best of Ronnie Milsap, 2008, Then Sings My Soul, 2009, Country Again, 2011, Summer Number Seventeen, 2014, (songs) I'm a Stand by My Woman Man, 1976 (Grammy award for Best Male Vocal Country Performance, 1977). Recipient Pioneer award, Acad. Country Music Awards, 2002; named Male Vocalist of Yr., Country Music Assn. Awards, 1974, 1976, 1977, Entertainer of Yr., 1977, Top Male Vocalist, Acad. Country Music Awards, 2002, Instrumentalist of Yr., 1988; named to Grand Ole Opry, 1976, Country Music Hall of Fame, 2014. Mem.: Nat. Acad. Rec. Arts and Scis. (Country Male Vocalist of Year 1974, 1976), Country Music Assn. (Male Vocalist of Yr. 1974, Album of Yr. 1975, Male Vocalist of Yr. 1976, 1977, Entertainer of Yr. 1977, Album of Yr. 1977, 1978). Office: care RCA Records 1540 Broadway New York NY 10036-4039*

MILSTEN, ROBERT B., lawyer; b. Tulsa, Nov. 6, 1932; s. Travis I. and Regina (Jankowsky) M.; m. Jane Herskowitz, June 24, 1956; children: Stuart Paul, Leslie M. Thornton. BS, Ind. U., 1954; LL.B., U. Okla., 1956; postgrad., So. Meth. U., 1959. Bar: Okla. 1956, U.S. Ct. of Appeals 1956, U.S. Tax Ct 1956. Practiced in, Oklahoma City, 1962—; govt. atty. Office Chief Counsel, IRS, 1958-62; atty. Fuller, Smith, Mosburg & Davis, 1962-63; sr. counsel Andrews, Davis, Legg, Bixler, Milsten & Price, Inc., 1964—2008, mem. firm, 1966—, dir., 1977-82, 96-98; ret., 2008. Mem. S.W. region IRS/Bar Liaison Com., 1994-97; docent, Nat. Cowboy Western Heritage Mus. Past pres., trustee Temple B'nai Israel. Served as lt., JAGC USAF, 1956-58. Mem. ABA (com. civil and criminal tax penalties sect. taxation 1962—98), Okla. Bar Assn., Fed. Bar Assn. (2d v.p. local chpt. 1976), Econ. Club Okla., Gaillardia Country Club, Men's Dinner Club, Phi Delta Phi (treas. 1955-56)

MILTON, KIMBALL ALAN, physics professor; b. La Grande, Oreg., Nov. 29, 1944; s. Fletcher Robert and Ethel Lorene Milton; m. Margarita Banos-Milton; children: Ysabel Alice Giraldo, Madeleine Diane Keevy, Camille Kathryn Jimenez. BS, U. Wash., Seattle, 1967; AM, Harvard U., Cambridge, Mass., 1968, PhD, 1971. Asst. and assoc. rsch. physicist UCLA, 1971—79; vis. assoc. prof. Ohio State U., Columbus, 1979—81; assoc. prof. Okla. State U., Stillwater, 1981—84, prof., 1984—86, U. Okla., Norman, 1986—2007, George Lynn Cross rsch. prof., 2007—. Sr. vis. fellow Imperial Coll., London, 1995; mem. adv. bd. Jour. Physics A, 2003—; E.T. Jaynes vis. prof. Wash. U., St. Louis, 2005—06; editl. bd. resource letters Am. Jour. Physics, 2008—11; Simons fellow U. Pierre et Marie Curie, Paris, 2013—. Author: (textbook) Classical Electrodynamics, Electromagnectic Radiation, Climbing the Mountain, The Casimir Effect; contbr. articles to sci. publs. Spkr., issues of sci. and soc. to civic, religious and ednl. groups. Recipient Regents award, U. Okla., 1991, Outstanding Referee award, Am. Phys. Soc., 2008; named Assoc. Disting. Lectr., U. Okla., 1988; fellow, Inst. Physics, UK, 2004. Mem.: Royal Norwegian Soc. Letters and Sci. (elected foreign mem. 2011), AAAS, Am. Phys. Soc., Sigma Xi. Achievements include research in nature of the quantum vacuum with applications to cosmology and nanotechnology. Office: Homer L Dodge Dept Physics and Astr University Okla Norman OK 73019-2061 Office Fax: 405-325-7557. Business E-Mail: milton@nhn.ou.edu.*

MILUNAS, J. ROBERT, health care organization executive; b. Aug. 7, 1947; s. Joseph John M.; m. Glenetta Graham; children: Amy, Ryan, Anna Kate. BS, Tulane U., 1969; postgrad., Samford U., 1973; MBA, Ga. State U., 1977. Mgr. internal and govt. reporting, corp. contr.'s staff Arvin Industries Inc., Columbus, Ind., 1977-80; mgr. consol. acctg., corp. contr.'s staff Mattel Inc., Hawthorne, Calif., 1980-82; asst. contr. Times Mirror Cable TV Inc., Irvine, Calif., 1982-83; Western Divsn. contr. SCA, Santa Ana, Calif., 1983-84; v.p., corp. contr. Tchrs. Mgmt. Investment Corp., Newport Beach, Calif., 1984-86; v.p., CFO Beech St. Inc., Irvine, 1987-89; v.p. fin. and adminstrn. ConsumerHealth Inc., Newport Beach, Calif., 1989-93; pres. Aegis Consulting Svcs., Dana Point, Calif., 1993—. 1st lt. U.S. Army Transp. Corps., 1969-71. Decorated Bronze Star. Roman Catholic. Office Phone: 404-321-4232. Personal E-mail: bob@milunas.com.

MIMS, SAM C., V, state legislator; b. McComb, Miss., Apr. 2, 1972; m. Amy Legg Mims. Mem. Dist. 97 Miss. House of Reps., 2004—, mem. conservation and water resources com., judiciary B com., judiciary en banc com., juvenile justice com., oil, gas and other minerals com. Mem.: Pike County Arts Coun., McComb Rotary Club. Republican. Methodist. Address: 605 Lakeshore Dr Mccomb MS 39648 Home Phone: 601-684-0281; Office Phone: 601-359-2430. Business E-Mail: smims@house.ms.gov.

MIMS, WILLIAM CLEVELAND (BILL MIMS), state supreme court justice; b. Harrisonburg, Va., June 20, 1957; s. David Lathan and Lurleen Shirley (Stovall) M.; m. Jane Ellen Rehme, Dec. 20, 1980; children: Katherine Grace, Emily Anne, Sarah Joy. AB, Coll. of William & Mary, 1979; JD, George Washington U., 1984; LLM, Georgetown U., 1986. Bar: Va. Legis. asst. Congressman Paul Trible, Washington, 1981-82; dep. legis. dir. Senator Paul Trible, Washington, 1983-85; chief of staff Congressman Frank Wolf, Washington, 1986-87; atty. Hazel & Thomas, P.C., Leesburg, Va., 1987-91, Worcester, Mims & Atwill, P.C., 1993—2002, Mims, Atwill & Leigh, P.C., Leesburg, 2002—05; mem. Dist. 32 Va. House of Delegates, 1992-98; mem. Dist. 33 Va. State Senate, 1998—2006; chief dep. atty. gen. State of Va., 2006—09, atty. gen., 2009—10; justice Va. State Supreme Ct., 2010—. Adj. prof. law George Mason U., 2002-05; mem. Va. Housing Commn., 1994-2005, chmn. 2000-03; mem. Va. Code Commn., 2000, 05, chmn., 2003. Active Nat. Eagle Scout Assn., 1992—. Mem. Va. Bar Assn. (Boyd-Graves Conf., bd. govs.). Republican. Presbyterian. Office: Supreme Ct Virginia PO Box 1315 100 N Ninth St Richmond VA 23219-1315*

MINAJ, NICKI (ONIKA TANYA MARAJ), rap artist; b. St. James, Port of Spain, Trinidad and Tobago, Dec. 8, 1984; d. Robert and Carol Maraj. Signed with Young Money Entertainment, 2009. Singer: (albums) Pink Friday, 2010 (Favorite Rap/Hip-Hop Album, American Music Awards, 2011), Pink Friday: Roman Reloaded, 2012 (Favorite Rap/Hip-Hop Album, American Music Awards, 2012, Top Rap Album, Billboard Music Awards, 2013), The Pink Print, 2014, (songs) Super Bass, 2011 (Top Streaming Song-Video, Billboard Music Awards, 2012), Starships, 2012 (Best Female Video, MTV Video Music Awards, 2012); judge American Idol, 2013; actress: (films) Ice Age: Continental Drift (voice), The Other Woman, 2014. Recipient

Best Hip-Hop Video for the song Super Bass, MTV Music award, 2011; named Female Artist of Yr., Underground Music Awards, 2008, Best New Artist, Black Entertainment TV (BET) Awards, 2010, Best Female Hip-Hop Artist, 2010, 2011, 2012, Breakthrough Artist of Yr., Nat. Assn. Recording Merchandisers, 2011, Favorite Rap/Hip-Hop Artist, American Music Awards, 2011, 2012, Favorite Hip-Hop Artist, People's Choice Awards, 2013, Top Rap Artist, Billboard Music Awards, 2013, Top Streaming Artist, 2013; named to MTV's Ann. Hottest MC List, 2010. Office: The Blueprint Group 555 Washington Ave Suite 240 Miami Beach FL 33139-6607*

MINALDI, PATRICIA HEAD, federal judge; b. Somerville, Mass., 1959; BA, Wesleyan U., 1980; JD, Tulane U., New Orleans, 1983. Asst. dist. atty. Orleans Parish, La., 1983—86, Calcasieu Parish, La., 1986—96; judge 14th Jud. Dist. Ct., La., 1996—2003, US Dist. Ct. (we. dist.) La., Lake Charles, 2003—. Office: US Dist Ct Edward F Hunter Jr US Courthouse 611 Broad St Ste 328 Lake Charles LA 70601 Office Phone: 337-437-3880.

MINARD, JOSEPH M., state legislator; b. Clarksburg, W.Va., Jan. 5, 1932; m. Mary Contento; children: Michele, Marisa, Marcia, Michael, Maria, Samuel. BS, W.Va. U. Mem. Dist. 30 W.Va. House of Delegates, 1983—88; mem. Dist. 12 W.Va. State Senate, 1990—94, 1999—, chair Banking and Insurance Com., mem. Agr. Com., Confirmations Com., Energy, Industry and Mining Com., Govt. Orgn. Com. & Judiciary Com. Mem.: Moose, W.Va. Restaurant Assn., W.Va. Alumni Assn., Columbian, Sierra, Rotary, Lions Club. Democrat. Catholic. Mailing: 510 Haymond Hwy Clarksburg WV 26301 E-mail: joe.minard@wvsenate.gov.

MINARDI, CHRISTINA, retail executive; b. Patterson, NJ; Various positions, asst. store team leader, store team leader Whole Foods Market, Inc., v.p., ops., Northeast Region, 2005, pres., Northeast Region, 2005—. Office: Whole Foods Market Inc 550 Bowie St Austin TX 78703 Office Phone: 512-477-4455. Office Fax: 512-482-7000. Business E-Mail: christina.minardi@wholefoods.com.

MINCHEW, JOHN RANDALL, state legislator, lawyer; b. Washington, July 31, 1957; s. John Randall and Lucile Elizabeth (Shaw) Minchew; m. Teresa Hatterick; 1 child, Jack. AB, Duke U., 1980; JD, Washington & Lee U., 1984; diploma in Theology, Va. Theol. Seminary, 2010. Bar: Va. 1984, U.S. Dist. Ct. (ea. dist.) Va. 1985, U.S. Ct. Appeals (4th cir.) 1985, U.S. Supreme Ct. 1997. Judicial clk. Supreme Ct. Va., 1984—85; mng. shareholder Loudoun Office Walsh Colucci Lubeley Emrich & Walsh PC, Leesburg, Va., 1998—; mem. Dist. 10 Va. House of Delegates, 2012—. V.p., dir. devel. The Minchew Corp., Fairfax, Va., 1985—; chmn. Loudon County Econ. Devel. Commn., 1996-98. Mng. editor: Washington & Lee Law Rev., 1984. Pro bono caseworker Legal Aid Soc. Roanoke Valley, Lexington, Va., 1982-84; chmn. London County Republican Party, 2002-06. Mem. ABA, Va. State Bar (mem. Commn. on Unauthorized Practice of Law 1994-98), Loudoun Bar Assn. (pres. 1995-96), Phi Delta Phi. Republican. Avocations: scuba diving, aviation, rugby. Office: Walsh Colucci Lubeley Emrich & Walsh PC One East Market St, Third Floor Leesburg VA 20176-3014 also: General Assembly Building PO Box 406 Richmond VA 23218 Office Phone: 804-698-1010. Office Fax: 804-698-6710. E-mail: jrminchew@ldn.thelandlawyers.com, DelRMinchew@house.virginia.gov.

MINER, CAROL SPALDING, academic administrator; b. Louisville, Jan. 6, 1950; d. Wallace H. and Martha (Ratterree) Spalding; m. John Miner, Oct. 1, 1971. BA in Internat. Studies, U. Louisville, 1971; MA Human Resource Mgmt., Pepperdine U., 1976; postgrad., Harvard U., 1987. Coord. Fla. Jr. Coll., Jacksonville, Fla., 1975-77; assoc. dir. Jacksonville Community Coun., Inc., Fla., 1977-81; dir. of continuing edn. Fla. Community Coll. at Jacksonville, 1981-86, dean of Open Campus, 1985-87, pres., Open Campus, 1987—. Chmn. Mayor's Commn. on Status of Women, 1992; bd. dirs. 1st Performance Bank. Writer: jour. of women's art, Kalliope, 1989; interviewer, TV Series, 1985—. Bd. dirs. Leadership Jacksonville, 1985-88, 93—, Jacksonville Transp. Authority, 1993; chmn. State Pub. Affairs Com., 1984; TV host LWV, 1983-89; pres. Tree Hill, Jacksonville, 1984; v.p. Jacksonville Women's Network, EVE award, 1987; judge Fla. Time-Union EVE awards, 1991—. Recipient EVE award, Fla. Times Union, Jacksonville, 1987, Orgn. Environ. award Mimi & Lee Adams, Jacksonville, 1987 Women in Power award Nat. Coun. Jewish Women, Fla., 1991; named Excellence for Interaty. Coop., Fla. Community Edn. Found., 1987, Region IV Person of Yr., Nat. Coun. on Continuing Edn. and Community Svcs., 1992. Mem. Fla. Assn. of Community Coll., Am. Soc. for Training & Devel., Leadership Fla., Jr. League (v.p. 1985), Aspen Inst. Humanistic Studies, San Marco Preservation Assn.; chmn. Women's Pub. Leadership Consortium. Avocation: travel. Home: 1968 Largo Pl Jacksonville FL 32207-3921 Office: Fla Community Coll Office of the Campus Pres 101 W State St Jacksonville FL 32202-3099

MINICUCCI, ROBERT A., investment company executive; b. Waterbury, Conn., May 7, 1952; s. Arnold A. and Mary (Garafola) M.; children: Robert A. Jr., Alexandra H. BA, Amherst Coll., Mass., 1975; MBA, Harvard U., 1979. CPA. Staff acct. Price Waterhouse, Boston, 1975-77; assoc. Lehman Bros., NYC, 1979-82, v.p., 1982-85, sr. v.p., 1985-88, mng. dir., 1988-91; sr. v.p., treas. American Express Co., 1991-92; CFO First Data Corp., NYC, 1992-93; gen. ptnr. Welsh, Carson, Anderson & Stowe, NYC, 1993—; chmn. Alliance Data Systems. Bd. dirs. Amdocs Ltd. Inc., Attachmate Corp., Global Knowledge Network Inc., BancTec, Inc., Alliance Data Systems, Inc., Ruesch Internat., Inc., Electronic Evidence Discovery, Inc Home: 159 Long Neck Point Rd Darien CT 06820 Office: Welsh Carson Anderson Stowe 320 Park Ave Ste 2500 New York NY 10022-6815 also: Alliance Data 7500 Dallas Pkwy Ste 700 Plano TX 75024

MINISSALE, JOE, corporate financial executive; CFO Hill Regional Hospital, Hillsboro, Tex., 1998—2006, Titus Regional Med. Ctr., Mt. Pleasant, Tex., 2004—06; CFO, v.p., fin. Rockwall Hosps., Inc., Richardson, Tex., 2006—08; CFO, Tex. and La. markets IASIS Healthcare Corp., 2008—. Office: IASIS Healthcare Corp 117 Seaboard Ln Bldg E Franklin TN 37067 Office Phone: 615-844-2747. Office Fax: 615-846-3006.

MINOR, GEORGE GILMER, III, drug and hospital supply company executive; b. 1940; married. BA, Va. Mil. Inst., 1963; MBA, U. Va., 1966. With Owens & Minor, Inc., Richmond, Va., 1963—, mgr. sales Acme Candy Co. div., 1966-68, mgr. retail mktg., 1968-73, div. mgr. wholesale drug br., 1973-77, v.p., 1977-80, exec. v.p., 1980-81, pres., 1981—99, CEO, 1984—2005, chmn., 1994—. Bd. dir. SunTrust Banks Inc. Bd. dir. Va. Biotechnology Rsch. Park Authority, Richmond Renaissance; v.p. bd. vis. Va. Mil. Inst.; chmn. bd. trustees Va. Health Care Found.; mem. adv. bd. Univ. Va. Sch. Nursing. Named Va. Industrialist of the Year, 2001; named to Greater Richmond Bus. Hall of Fame, 2003. Office: Owens & Minor Inc 9120 Lockwood Blvd Mechanicsville VA 23116

MINOR, JOSEPH EDWARD, civil engineer, educator; b. Corpus Christi, Tex., June 2, 1938; s. William Smoot Jr. and Irene (Schiller) M.; m. Treva Ann Edmiston, Sept. 3, 1960; children: Joseph Edward Jr., Sharon Diane. BSCE, Tex. A&M U., 1959, M of Engring., 1960; PhD, Tex. Tech U., 1974. Registered profl. engr., Tex., Mo., Fla. Sr. rsch. engr. Southwest Research Inst., San Antonio, 1962-69; P. Whitfield Horn prof. Tex. Tech U., Lubbock, 1969-88; emeritus prof., 2008; Thomas Reese prof., chmn. dept. civil engring. Mo. U. Sci. and Tech., Rolla, 1988-93; rsch. prof. U. Mo., Rolla, 1993—2000. Pres. Insulating Glass Cert. Council, N.Y., 1986-89; vis. prof. Tex. A&M U., Kingsville, 2003-; bd. dirs. Tex. Windstorm Ins. Assn., 2010-12. Contbr. articles to profl. jours. Served with USAR; with USA Corps Engrs., 1960-62. Recipient Disting. Engr. award Tex. Tech U., 1989, Disting. Svc. award Nat. Hurricane Conf., 1999; Nat. Def. fellow, 1959-60; Sr. Fulbright scholar, 1978. Fellow ASCE (pres. Tex. sect. 1984-85, award of honor 2003); mem. NSPE, Tex. Soc. Profl. Engrs. (Engr. of Yr. Nueces chpt. 2006). Presbyterian. Avocation: fishing. Office: Joseph E Minor PE Consulting Engineer PO Box 603 Rockport TX 78381-0603 E-mail: josephminor@sbcglobal.net.

MINTER, DAVID LEE, English literature educator; b. Midland, Tex., Mar. 20, 1935; s. Kenneth Cruse and Frances (Hennessy) M.; m. Cynthia Caroline Sewell, Dec. 22, 1957; children: Christopher Sewell, Frances Elizabeth. BA, N. Tex. State U., 1957, MA, 1959; BD, Yale U., 1961, PhD, 1965. Univ. lectr. Hamburg (W. Ger.) U., 1965-66; lectr. Yale U., 1966-67; asst. prof. Rice U., Houston, 1967-69, assoc. prof., 1969-74, prof., 1974-80; prof. English Emory U., Atlanta, 1981-89, Asa G. Candler prof. Am. lit., 1989-90, dean Coll. Arts and Scis., 1981-90, v.p. arts and scis., 1984-90; Libbie Shearn Moody prof. English Rice U., Houston, 1990-99, interim vice provost, univ. libr., 1995-96, interim provost, 1999-2000, Bruce and Elizabeth Dunlevie prof. English, 1999—2002. Author: The Interpreted Design as a Structural Principle in American Prose, 1969, William Faulkner: His Life and Work, 1980, 82, 91, 97, French edit., 1984, Korean edito., 1999, A Cultural History of the American Novel: Henry James to William Faulkner, 1994, 96, Faulkner's Questioning Narratives: Fiction of the Major Phase, 2001, 04; editor: Twentieth-Century Interpretations of Light in August, 1969, The Norton Critical Edit. of The Sound and the Fury, 1987, 93; co-editor: The Harper American Literature, 1986, 93, 96, 97, The Columbia Literary History of the United States, 1987 (Italian edit. 1990, Chinese edit. 1994, Japanese edit. 1997); also articles and revs. Fulbright Travel fellow, 1966; Nat. Endowment for Humanities fellow, 1969-70; Am. Council Learned Socs. grantee, 1975; Fred Harris Daniels fellow, 1980 Mem. MLA, Am. Lit. Group, Am. Studies Assn., Phi Beta Kappa. Methodist. Home: 2145 Swift Houston TX 77030-1215 E-mail: dcmint@rice.edu.

MINTON, JERRY DAVIS, retired banker, lawyer; b. Ft. Worth, Aug. 13, 1928; s. Robert Bruch and Anna Elizabeth (Davis) M.; m. Martha Drew Fields, Nov. 28, 1975; children: Marianne, Martha, John Morgan. BBA, U. Tex., Austin, 1949, JD, 1960; grad. cert., Nat. Trust Sch., Northwestern U., 1960. Of counsel Michener, Larimore, Swindle, Whitaker, Flowers et al., 1991—96; adv. dir. Kanaly Trust Co., Houston, 1992-2000. Vice chmn. 1st Nat. Bank Ft. Worth, 1982-84; chmn., CEO 1st City Nat. Bank Ft. Worth, 1986-91. Pilot USAF, 1951-55, pilot Tex. Air N.G., 1955-57; capt. USAFR Ret. Decorated D.F.C., Air medal with 3 oak leaf clusters. Mem. Air Force Assn., State Bar Tex., Tarrant County Bar Assn., Soc. Descs. of Washington's Army at Valley Forge, SAR, Mil. Order of Stars & bars, Mil. Order World Wars, D.F.C. Soc., Order Quiet Birdmen, Order of Daedalians, River Crest Country Club, Sigma Iota Epsilon, Phi Delta Phi. Episcopalian. Home: 5404 El Dorado Dr Fort Worth TX 76107-3236

MINTON, JOHN DEAN, JR., state supreme court chief justice; b. Ky., Mar. 19, 1952; 2 children. BA in English & History, Western Ky. U., 1974; JD, U. Ky. Coll. of Law, 1977. Assoc. Cole, Harned & Broderick, 1977—88; ptnr. Cole, Broderick, Minton, Moore & Thornton, Ky., 1988—91, Cole, Minton & Moore, Ky., 1991—92; judge Divsn. 2 Warren County Cir. Ct., Ky., 1992—2003; chief administrative judge Green River Region Judicial Circuits, Ky., 1996—2003; judge Second Appellate Dist. Ky. Ct. of Appeals, 2003—06; justice Ky. Supreme Ct., 2006—, chief justice, 2008—. Leader Ky. Conf. of United Methodist Church, 1996—2004. Mem.: Ky. Bar Assn. (Outstanding Judge award 2003). Office: Ky Supreme Ct 231 Capitol Bldg 700 Capital Ave Frankfort KY 40601 Office Phone: 270-746-7867. E-mail: johnminton@kycourts.net.*

MINTZ, ALBERT, lawyer; b. New Orleans, Oct. 19, 1929; s. Morris and Goldie (Goldblum) M.; m. Linda Barnett, Dec. 19, 1954; children— John Morris, Margaret Anne Easthope. BBA, Tulane U., 1948, JD, 1951. Bar: La. 1951; cert. tax specialist, estate and adminstrn. specialist. Since practiced in, New Orleans; former ptnr. Montgomery, Barnett, Brown, Read, Hammond & Mintz, Hurwitz-Mintz Realty Cos., New Orleans. Bd. dirs. Strauss Distbrs., Avrico, Inc. Mem. editl. bd. Tulane Law Rev. Adv. bd. Law Sch. Tulane U.; chmn., dir. adv. bd. Tulane Summer Lyric Theater; former bd. dirs. Tulane Ctr. Stage Talent and Shakespearean Theatre; bd. dirs. Jewish Cmty. Ctr., New Orleans, 1965-72, Jewish Fedn., 1968-, Home for Jewish Aged, 1968-71, Jewish Family Svc., New Orleans, 1968-72; trustee, bd. mgrs. Touro Infirmary Hosp. and Found.; trustee Jewish Endowment Found.; charter mem. La. Hist. Assn.; bd. trustees, mem. Temple Sinai. Recipient Judah Touro Society Award, 1999, Tulane Outstanding Alumnus award, Class of 1951, 2001, Outstanding Vol. award Tulane U., 2003, Role Model award Young Leadership Com., 2004, Young Profl. Excellence and LAdership award, 2005. Mem. ABA, La. Bar Assn. (lectr., publ. on corp., tax, real estate law), New Orleans Bar Assn. (exec. com. 1971-74), Am. Law Inst., U.S. Hist. Assn., New Orleans C. of C. (chmn. com. civic affairs and state legis. 1968-69), Tulane Emeritus Club (chmn. exec. com., pres. 2004), Phi Delta Phi, Omicron Delta Kappa, Zeta Beta Tau. Jewish. Home and Office: 1915 State St New Orleans LA 70118-6251 Home Phone: 504-899-0756; Office Phone: 504-899-2104. Business E-Mail: amintz@amintzlaw.com.

MINTZ, DANIEL HARVEY, endocrinologist, educator, academic administrator; b. NYC, Sept. 16, 1930; s. Jacob A. and Fanny Mintz; m. Dawn E. Hynes, Jan. 15, 1961 (dec.); children: David, Denise, Debra; m. Marge Kleiman, Nov. 30, 1996. BS cum laude, St. Bonaventure Coll., 1951; MD, N.Y. Med. Coll., 1956. Diplomate Am. Bd. Internal Medicine. Intern Henry Ford Hosp., Detroit, 1956-57; resident Georgetown med. div. D.C. Gen. Hosp., Washington, 1957-59, Georgetown U. Hosp., Washington, 1958-59; fellow medicine Nat. Inst. Arthritis and Metabolic Diseases, 1959-60, Am. Diabetes Assn., 1960-61; practice medicine, specializing in diabetes and endocrinology U. Miami. (Fla.) Sch. Medicine, prof. medicine, 1969—2011, Mary Lou Held prof. medicine, 1981-96, chief div. endocrinology and metabolism, dept. medicine, 1969-80, Sci. dir. Diabetes Rsch. Inst., 1980-96, sci. dir. emeritus, 1996—; asst. prof. medicine Georgetown U. Sch. Medicine, 1963-64; assoc. prof. medicine U. Pitts. Sch. Medicine, 1964-69; chief svc. Georgetown U. Med. div. D.C. Gen. Hosp., Washington, 1963-64; chief medicine Magee-Women's Hosp., Pitts., 1964-69, emeritus prof. medicine, 2011—. Guest prof. U. Geneva, 1976—77. Contbr. articles to profl. jours. Fellow: ACP; mem.: Am. Assn. Physicians, So. Soc. Clin. Investigation, Ctrl. Soc. Clin. Investigation, Am. Soc. Clin. Investigation, Am. Fedn. Clin. Rsch., Am. Diabetes Assn., Endocrine Soc. Office: U Miami Diabetes Rsch Inst PO Box 016960 R-77 Miami FL 33101-6960

MINTZ, NORMAN NELSON, investment banker, educator, retired academic administrator; b. NYC, Sept. 18, 1934; s. Alexander and Rebecca (Nelson) M.; m. Marcia Lynn Belford, Aug. 27, 1960; children: Geoffrey Belford, Douglas Nelson. AB, Bucknell U., Lewisburg, Pa., 1955; PhD, NYU, NYC, 1966. Asst. gen. mgr. Ross Products Inc., NYC, 1957-59; media analyst Benton & Bowles Inc., NYC, 1960; asst. prof. fin. Syracuse (N.Y.) U., 1965-69; asst. prof. econs. Columbia U., NYC, 1968-72, assoc. dean Grad. Sch. Arts and Scis., 1972-77, dep. provost, 1977-80, acting provost, 1978-79, sr. v.p., 1980-82, exec. v.p. for acad. affairs, 1982-89, exec. v.p., ret., 1990—; mng. dir. Loeb Ptnrs. Corp., 1990—2013. Economist U.S.-P.R. Commn. on Status of P.R., 1965-66; bd. dirs. Loeb Holding Corp., 1990-2013, Loeb Ptnrs. Corp., 1990-2013, Intersections, Inc., Ultramercial, LLC. Author: Monetary Union and Economic Integration, 1970; contbr. articles to profl. jours. Dir. Conf. on Jewish Social Studies, 1975—94, N.Y.C. Coun. on Econ. Edn., 1993—. 1st lt. Signal Corps. US Army, 1955—57. Earhart Found. fellow, 1963-65. Mem. Phi Beta Kappa, Omicron Delta Epsilon. Business E-Mail: num1@columbia.edu.

MINTZ-HITTNER, HELEN ANN, physician, researcher; b. Houston, Aug. 12, 1944; d. Bert and Jeanette (Haydis) Mintz; m. David Hittner, Sept. 8, 1968 (div. May 11, 1989); children: Miriam Annette Hittner Tondera, Susan Michelle Hittner, George Jacob Hittner. BA, Rice U., 1965; MD, Baylor Coll. Medicine, 1969. Lic. Tex. Bd. of Med. Examiners, 1969. Intern pediat. Baylor Affiliated Hosps., Houston, 1969—70, resident ophthalmology, 1970—73; fellow pediat. ophthalmology Tex. Children's Hosp., Houston, 1973—74; pediat. ophthalmologist Houston, 1974—95; Alfred W. Lasher III prof. pediat. ophthalmology U. Tex. Health Sci. Ctr. Houston Med. Sch., 1995—. Prin. investigator clin. trial Bevacizumab Eliminates the Angiogenic Threat of Retinopathy of Prematurity (BEAT-ROP). Author: several rsch. reports and jour. articles. Fellow: Am. Acad. Ophthalmology (Honor award 1986, Sr. Honor award 2005); mem.: N.Y. Acad. Med., N.Y. Acad. Sci., Ciba Found., Soc. Heed Fellows (life), Assn. Rsch. in Vision and Ophthalmology, Am. Assn. Pediat. Ophthalmology and Strabismus, Phi Beta Kappa (life), Alpha Omega Alpha (life). Independent. Jewish. Achievements include discovery of Primary etiology of retinopathy of prematurity; research in Genetic linkage of aniridia to chromosome 11p13 (PAX6); Genetic identification of anterior segment dysgenesis on chromosomes 10q25 (PITX3), 1p32 (FOXE3), 20p11.2 (VSX1); Genetic linkage of Exudative Vitreo Retinopathy AR to chromosome 7q31.31 (TSPAN12). Home: 1500 A California St Houston TX 77006-2605 Office: University Tex Health Sci Ctr Houston Med Sch 6400 Fannin St #1800 Houston TX 77030 Office Phone: 713-559-5277. Business E-Mail: helen.a.mintz-hittner@uth.tmc.edu.

MIRACLE, ROCKY REED, electric power industry executive; b. Terrell, Tex., Feb. 18, 1953; s. Haskell Laney and Jean (Reed) M.; m. Sarah Ann Caughran; children: Ross, Paul. BBA, U. Tex., Austin, 1975; MBA, East Tex. State U., 1978; MA, U. Tex., Dallas, 1982. With Tex. Utilities Co. Sys., Dallas, 1975-90; dir. devel. bus. Cen. and South West Corp., Mexico, 1993-95, asst. treas. Dallas, 1990-93, sr. case mgr. regulatory, 1995; dir. bus. ops. support Am. Electric Power Co., Inc.; dir. mergers and acquisitions and comml. ops. AEP; with CSW Energy; v.p. corp. planning El Paso Electric Co., sr. v.p. corp. planning and devel., 2009—. Bd. dirs. East Tex. State U. Found., Commerce, 1992—. Lt. USNR, 1987—. Serves U.S. Navy Res. Mem. Navy Supply Corps Assn., Omicron Delta Epsilon. Office: El Paso Electric Co Stanton Tower 100 N Stanton El Paso TX 79901 Office Phone: 915-543-5711. Office Fax: 915-543-2299. Business E-Mail: rmiracle@epelectric.com.

MIRANDA, CARLOS SA, food products company executive; b. Fall River, Mass., Nov. 16, 1929; s. Carlos Sa and Annette (Pratt) M.; m. Natalie Cardoso, Jan. 5, 1949; children: Carla, Lucy, John. BS in Mech. Engring., Marquette U., 1956. With internat. divsn. Kellogg Co., Battle Creek, Mich., 1964—65; gen. mgr. Kellogg Co. Brazil, 1965—80; v.p. Kellogg Internat., Battle Creek, 1980—89; gen. mgr. Kellogg's Spain, 1983—84; country dir. internat. exec. svc. corps. Costa Rica, 1990—91; mediator Fla. County Cts., 1994—2008. Recipient Pero Vaz Caminha award, Brazil, 1976; conferred title Comdr. of Legion of Honor of Marshal Rondon, Brazil, 1971. Mem. ASME. Independent. Roman Catholic. Home: 7333 Scotland Way Apt 1407 Sarasota FL 34238

MIRANDA-RODRIGUEZ, CESAR R., attorney general; b. PR; BBA in Mgmt. & Acctg., U. PR, Rio Piedras; JD, Rutgers U. V.p; Puerto Rico Telephone Co.; prof., assoc. dean, dir. Sch. Legal Assistance U. PR; chief of staff to Sila Maria Calderon Govt. of PR, 2001—04, atty. gen. San Juan, 2014—. Democrat. Office: Attorney General PO Box 902192 San Juan PR 00902 Office Phone: 787-721-2900.*

MIRNYI, MAX, professional tennis player; b. Minsk, July 6, 1977; s. Nikolai and Tatiana; m. Xenia Mirnyi, July 10, 2004; 1 child, Melashka. Profl. tennis player ATP, 1996—. AIDS amb. UN, Belarus, 2002—; mem. Belarusian nat. team Summer Olympic Games, London, 2012. Recipient State Hon. Title, Belarus pres., 2001, Orden Otechestva, 2004, Gold medal, mixed doubles, Summer Olympic Games, 2012. Mem.: Belarus Tennis Fedn. (pres. 2004—). Achievements include winner 1 career singles title, 45 career doubles titles, 4 career mixed doubles title, ATP; winner Grand Slam mixed doubles titles: Wimbledon, 1998; US Open 1998, 2007, 2013. Avocation: guitar. Office: c/o ATP 201 ATP Tour Blvd Ponte Vedra Beach FL 32082*

MIRT, MICHAEL G., healthcare company executive; BS in Health Care Adminstrn., Wichita State U., Kans.; MS in Health Care Adminstrn., Wichita State W., Kans. Regional pres. Cigna Healthcare, 1999—2003; pvt. cons. in the healthcare industry, 2004—05; exec. v.p., COO AmeriChoice, 2005—07; pres., COO HealthSpring, Inc., 2008—10, pres., 2010—. Office: HealthSpring Inc Ste 501 9009 Carothers Pkwy Franklin TN 37067 Office Phone: 615-291-7000. Office Fax: 615-401-4566.

MISCHLER, HARLAND LOUIS, investment company executive; b. Troy, Ohio; m. Jean O'Connor; children: Marilyn West, Thomas O'Connor. BS, MBA, Ohio State U. CPA, Ohio. Mgr. DeLoitte & Touche, Cin., 1959-66; mgr. internat. fin., v.p., controller, treas. Hobart Corp., Troy, Ohio, 1966-81; v.p. fin. Bausch & Lomb Inc., Rochester, N.Y., 1981-84; vice chmn., exec. v.p. fin. Applied Research Labs., Rochester, 1984-87; CEO, COO HLM Capital Resources Inc., Boca Raton, Fla., 1987—. Bd. dirs., exec. v.p., fin. officer, Gradco Systems Inc., Las Vegas, Nev., 1990—. Past pres., bd. dirs. Troy C. of C., Stouder Meml. Hosp., Miami County Hosp. Assn.; mem. Ohio State adv. coun. Served to maj. USAF. Mem. Fin. Execs. Inst. (pres. Dayton chpt. 1981), Am. Inst. CPA's, Alpha Kappa Psi, Sigma Alpha Epsilon. Lodges: Rotary. Republican. Episcopalian. Home: 17037 Brookwood Dr Boca Raton FL 33496-5930 Home Phone: 561-432-6316; Office Phone: 561-479-2450.

MISIEK, DALE JOSEPH, oral and maxillofacial surgeon; b. Hartford, Conn., Dec. 10, 1952; s. Joseph John and Jadwiga Magdelena (Wojtowicz) M.; m. Patricia Ann Munson, June 28, 1975; children:

Matthew Bryan, Stacey Lynne, Michael Stephen. BA magna cum laude, U. Conn., 1974, DMD, 1978; cert. advanced tng. oral and maxillofacial surgery, La. State U., 1982. Diplomate Am. Bd. Oral and Maxillofacial Surgery. Resident oral surgery Charity Hosp. La., New Orleans, 1978—82; asst. prof. dept. oral and maxillofacial surgery Sch. Dentistry La. State U., New Orleans, 1984—87, assoc. prof. Sch. Dentistry, 1987—94, prof. dept. oral and maxillofacial surgery Sch. Dentistry, 1994—98, also mem. various coms. Sch. Dentistry; practice dentistry specializing in oral surgery New Orleans, 1982—84; pvt. practice Charlotte, NC, 1998—. Mem. staff Univ. Hosp., New Orleans, 1982-; cons. Presbyn. Med. Ctr., Charlotte, 1998—, Univ. Hosp., Charlotte, 1998—, Northeast Med. Ctr., Concord, 1999—; lectr. in field. Contbr. articles and abstracts to profl. jours. Recipient C.V. Mosby Book award. Fellow Am. Assn. Oral and Maxillofacial Surgeons (mem. spl. com. for devel. stds. and criteria for care 1986, spl. com. on oral and maxillofacial surgery self-assessment program 1990), Am. Coll. Oral and Maxillofacial Surgeons; mem. ADA (cons. commn. on dental accreditation 1986-2000), Am. Bd. Oral and Maxillofacial Surgery (adv. com. 1990-95, regional advisor Dist. III 1996-99), Am. Acad. Cosmetic Surgery, La. Soc. Oral and Maxillofacial Surgeons (anesthesia com. 1983-85, advanced cardiac life support com. 1986-88, sec./treas. 1991-95, v.p. 1996—), Internat. Assn. Oral and Maxillofacial Surgery, Acad. Osseointegration, Charlotte Dental Soc., 2d Dist. Dental Soc., N.C. Dental Soc., N.C. Soc. Oral and Mexillofacial Surgeons, Phi Beta Kappa, Phi Kappa Phi, Omicron Kappa Upsilon. Republican. Roman Catholic. Avocations: baseball, weightlifting, fishing. Office: 8738 University City Blvd Charlotte NC 28213-3558 Home Phone: 704-825-4363; Office Phone: 704-547-0837. Personal E-mail: drdjm1@aol.com.

MISRA, RAGHUNATH PRASAD, physician, educator; b. Kolkata, West. Bengal, India, Feb. 1, 1928; came to U.S., 1964; s. Guru Prasad and Anandi M.; m. Therese Rettenmund, Sept. 13, 1963; children: Sima, Joya, Maya, Tara. BSc honors, Calcutta U., 1948; MBBS, Med. Coll., Calcutta, 1953; PhD, McGill U., Montreal, Que., 1965. Diplomate Am. Bd. Anat. and Clin. Pathology. Asst. prof., dir. kidney lab. U. Louisville Sch. Medicine, 1964—68; assoc. investigator and dir. kidney lab Mt. Sinai Hosp., Cleve., 1968—73; asst. prof. Case We. Res. Med. Sch., Cleve., 1973—76; asst. prof., dir. kidney lab. Sch. Medicine La. State U., Shreveport, 1976—80, assoc. prof. Sch. Medicine, 1980—86, prof. Sch. Medicine, 1986—98, emeritus prof. Sch. Medicine, 1998—. Cons. VA Med. Ctr., Shreveport, 1977-98, EA Conway Meml. Hosp., Monroe, La., 1980-98; clin. prof. ophthalmology & dir. Ocular Pathology Sch. Medicine La. State U., Shreveport, 1988— Author: Atlas of Skin Biopsy, 1983 Pres. India Assn. of Shreveport, 1979, 81 Tallisman fellow Mt. Sinai Hosp., 1970-73. Fellow Am. Coll. Pathologists, Am. Soc. Clin. Pathologists, Am. Coll. Internat. Physicians, U. Calcutta Med. Alumni Assn. Am. (pres. 1992-93), Sigma Xi (pres. 1987-89) Democrat. Hindu. Avocations: photography, travel. Office: La State U Health Scis Ctr 1501 Kings Hwy Shreveport LA 71103-4228 Office Phone: 318-675-5012. Business E-Mail: rmisra@lsuhsc.edu.

MISTRETTA, PAUL L., insurance company executive; B in Mgmt. Sci., Kean U., Union, 1979. Sr. v.p., COO First Colony Life Ins. (Known as Genworth Fin. Co.); exec. v.p. Am. Gen. Life Ins. Companies (Known as AIG Co.), Am. Internat. Life Assurance Co., NY; with, exec. roundtable CSC; mem. Deloitte Ops. Exec. Forum; COO, ING ins. U.S. ING Group, 2005—. Mem. Info. Sys. coms.; bd. dirs. Ins. Marketplace Stds. Assn.; fellow Life Mgmt. Inst. Mem.: Life Office Mgmt. Assn. (assoc.). Office: ING North America Insurance Corp 5780 Powers Ferry Rd NW Atlanta GA 30327 Office Phone: 770-980-5100. Office Fax: 770-980-3301. Business E-Mail: paul.mistretta@us.ing.com.

MITCH, WILLIAM EVANS, nephrologist; b. Birmingham, Ala., July 22, 1941; s. William Evans and Mary Elizabeth (Ackerman) Mitch; m. Frances Alexandra Fisher, Aug. 21, 1965; children: Eleanor Baylor, William Armistead. BA, Harvard Coll., Cambridge, Mass., 1963; MD, Harvard Med. Sch., 1967. Cert. internal medicine and nephrology Am. Bd. Internal Medicine. Intern Brigham & Women's Hosp., Boston, 1967-68, resident, 1968-69, 1973—74, Johns Hopkins Hosp., Balt., 1972-73; clin. assoc. NIH, Bethesda, Md., 1969-72; from asst. prof. to assoc. prof. dept. pharmacology Johns Hopkins U., Balt., 1974-78; assoc. prof. medicine Harvard Med. Sch., Boston, 1978-87; prof. Emory U. Sch. Medicine, Atlanta, 1987—2002; disting. prof. U. Tex., Galveston, 2002—04; prof. Baylor Coll. Medicine, Houston, 2004—. Mem. study sect. NIH, 1988—92, mem. nat. adv. com., Nat. Inst. Diabetes, Digestive and Kidney Diseases, 2007—. Editor: The Progressive Nature of Renal Disease, 1986, 2d edit., 1992, Nutrition and the Kidney, 1988, 6th edit., 2010. Pres. region II Nat. Kidney Found., 1990—92, chmn. sci. adv. bd., 1996—98; chmn. exec. coun. kidney Am. Heart Assn. Recipient John Peters award, Am. Soc. Nephrology; grantee, NIH, 1979—, Merit award, 2004—. Mem.: Internat. Soc. Nephrology (treas. 1997—2003), Am. Soc. Nephrology (pres. 2004), Am. Clin. and Climatol. Assn., Assn. Am. Physicians, Am. Soc. Clin. Investigation. Office: Baylor Coll Nephrology Divsn MS Alkek N-520 1 Baylor Plz Houston TX 77030 Office Phone: 713-798-8350. Business E-Mail: mitch@bcm.edu.

MITCHELL, BILLY P., retired arbitrator; b. Fairmont, NC, Apr. 5, 1930; s. Julius Pender Mitchell and Dolibel Mitchell Caudell; m. Jerry Stevenson Mitchell (div.); children: Sharon Lynne Huggins, Steven Lee, Amy Elizabeth Harrison; m. Rebecca Burroughs, Apr. 2, 1983. AB, Duke U., 1953. Exec. v.p. Gainesville (Fla.) Area C. of C., 1961—70, Greater Macon (Ga.) C. of C., 1970—80; pres. Metro Jackson (Miss.) C. of C., 1980—82; mgr. chamber rels. U.S. C. of C., Washington, 1982—95; pres. Arlington Mediation Svc., Henderson-ville, NC, 1994—. Bd. dirs. Carolina Forum, Hendersonville, 2002—. Aviation cadet USAF, 1953—55. Mem.: N.C. Bar Assn. (dispute resolution sect.), N.C. Assn. Profl. Family Mediators (pres. 2002). Republican. Lutheran. Home Phone: 828-890-5461. Personal E-mail: bmitch@bellsouth.net.

MITCHELL, BURLEY BAYARD, JR., lawyer; b. Oxford, NC, Dec. 15, 1940; s. Burley Bayard and Dorothy Ford (Champion) M.; m. Mary Lou Willett, Aug. 3, 1962; children: David Bayard (dec.), Catherine Morris. BA with honors, N.C. State U., 1966, DHL (hon.), 1995; JD, U. N.C., 1969; LLD (hon.), Campbell U., 1998. Bar: N.C. 1969, U.S. Ct. Appeals (4th cir.) 1970, U.S. Ct. Appeals (3d cir.) 2002, U.S. Supreme Ct. 1972. Asst. atty. gen. State of N.C., Raleigh, 1969-72, dist. atty., 1973-77, judge Ct. Appeals, 1977-79, sec. crime control, 1979-82; justice Supreme Ct. N.C., Raleigh, 1982-94; chief justice Supreme Ct. of N.C., Raleigh, 1995-99; ptnr. Womble Carlyle Sandridge and Rice, Raleigh, 1999—. Served with USN, 1958-62, Asia. Recipient N.C. Nat. Guard Citizen Commendation award, 1982 Mem. ABA, VFW, N.C. Bar Assn., Mensa, Am. Legion, Phi Beta Kappa. Democrat. Methodist. Home: 4301 City of Oaks Wynd Raleigh NC 27612-5316 Office: Wacovia Capital Ctr 150 Fayetteville St Mall Ste 2100 PO Box 831 Raleigh NC 27602-0831 Office Phone: 919-755-8166.

MITCHELL, GARY EARL, physicist, researcher; b. July 5, 1935; s. Earl Raymond and Delma Kathlene (Lockard) Mitchell; m. Carolyn Fey Stutz, Aug. 4, 1957; children: Scott Frederick, Karen Lee(dec.). BS, U. Louisville, 1956; MA, Duke U., 1958; PhD, Fla. State U., 1962. Rsch. assoc. Columbia U., NYC, 1962—64, asst. prof., 1964—68; assoc. prof. NC State U., Raleigh, 1968—74, prof. physics, 1974—, assoc. head physics dept., 1982—97; assoc. dir. Triangle Univs. Nuc. Lab., 1992—2009. Sr. scientist Alexander von Humboldt Found., Bonn, Germany, 1975, Bonn, 1997. Contbr. numerous articles to sci. publs. Recipient Alumni Disting. Prof. award, NC State U. Fellow: Am. Phys. Soc. (Jesse Beams award 1997, Mentorship award 2010); mem.: numerous sci. assns. Avocation: history. Home: 2913 Harriman Rd Durham NC 27705-5423 Office: NC State U Dept Physics PO Box 8202 Raleigh NC 27695-0001 Office Phone: 919-660-2638. Business E-Mail: mitchell@tunl.duke.edu, gary_mitchell@ncsu.edu.

MITCHELL, GEORGE ERNEST, JR., zoology educator; b. Duoro, N.Mex., June 7, 1930; s. George Ernest and Alma Thyrza (Hatley) M.; m. Billie Carolyn McMahan, Mar. 14, 1952; children: Leslie Dianne, Karen Leigh, Cynthia Faye. BS, U. Mo., 1951, MS, 1954; PhD, U. Ill., 1956. Asst. prof. animal sci. U. Ill., 1956-60; assoc. prof. U. Ky., Lexington, 1960-67, prof., 1967-98, prof. emeritus, 1998—, dir. grad. studies in animal scis., 1964-96, coord. beef cattle and sheep, 1974-90. Contbr. articles to profl. jours. Served with USAF, 1951-53. Fulbright research scholar New Zealand, 1973-74; Rsch. scholar Japan Soc. for Promotion of Sci., Japan, 1989 Mem. Am. Soc. Animal Sci. (sec. 1969-70, v.p. 1970-71, pres. So. sect. 1971-72, rsch. fellow 1989, Disting. Svc. award 1994), Am. Dairy Sci. Assn., Am. Inst. Nutrition, AAAS, Council for Agrl. Sci. and Tech., Sigma Xi, Alpha Zeta, Gamma Sigma Delta, Omicron Delta Kappa. Democrat. Methodist. Home: 690 Hill N Dale Rd Lexington KY 40503-2164 Office: U Ky 809 W P Garrigus Bldg Lexington KY 40546-0001 Personal E-mail: gmitchel@earthlink.net.

MITCHELL, HAROLD, state legislator; b. Spartanburg, June 6, 1965; s. Harold and Margaret Duckett Mitchell; m. Wanda Dawkins; children: David Benjamin, Elizabeth Ann. Exec. dir. ReGenesis; mem. Dist. 31 SC House of Reps., 2005—, second vice chair Interstate Cooperation Com., mem. Edn. and Pub. Works Com. Mem.: Dominion Cmty. Ch., Spartanburg C. of C. (govtl. bd. mem.). Democrat. Address: PO Box 3046 Spartanburg SC 29304-3046 Office: 414C Blatt Building Columbia SC 29201 Home: 505 North St Spartanburg SC 29304 Home Phone: 864-621-0881; Office Phone: 864-583-2712. E-mail: MITCHELLH@schouse.org.

MITCHELL, JAMES KENNETH, civil engineer, educator; b. Manchester, NH, Apr. 19, 1930; s. Richard N. and Henrietta (Moench) M.; m. Virginia D. Williams, Nov. 24, 1951; children: Richard A., Laura K., James W., Donald M., David L.; m. Holly R. Taylor, May 19, 2007. BCE, Rensselaer Poly. Inst., 1951; MS, MIT, 1953, DSc, 1956. Mem. faculty U. Calif., Berkeley, 1958-93, prof. civil engring., 1968-89, chmn. dept., 1979-84, Edward G. and John R. Cahill prof. civil engring., 1989-92, Edward G. and John R. Cahill prof. civil engring. emeritus, 1993—; Via prof. civil engring. Va. Poly. Inst. and State U., Blacksburg, 1994-99, Univ. Disting. prof., 1996-99, Univ. Disting. prof. emeritus, 1999—. Geotech. cons., 1960—. Author: Fundamentals of Soil Behavior, 1976, 3d edit., 2005; contbr. articles to profl. jours. Asst. scoutmaster Boy Scouts Am., 1975-82; mem. Moraga Environ. Rev. Com., Calif., 1978-80. Served to 1st lt. AUS, 1956-58. Recipient Exceptional Sci. Achievement medal NASA, 1973, Berkeley citation, 1993, Chief of Engrs. Outstanding Svc. award US Army Corps Engrs., 1999, Rensselaer Alumni Assn. Fellows award, 2006, Dept. of Army Outstanding Civilian Svc. medal, 2007, Davies Medal for Engring. Achievement Rensselaer Poly. Inst., 2010. Mem. ASCE (hon., Huber prize 1965, Disting. Middlebrooks award 1962, 70, 73, 01, Norman medal 1972, 95, Terzaghi lectr. 1984, Terzaghi award 1985, H. Bolton Seed medal 2004, Outstanding Projects and Leaders award in edn., 2006, pres. San Francisco sect. 1986-87), NAS, Nat. Acad. Engring. (vice chair civil engring. sect. 2001-03, chair 2003-05), Am. Soc. Engring. Edn. (We. Electric Fund award 1979), NRC (geotech. bd. chmn. 1990-94, bd. on infrastructure and constrn. environ. 1994-96, transp. rsch. bd. exec. com. 1983-87, mem. water sci. and tech. bd. 2005—08), Internat. Soc. Soil Mechanics and Geotech. Engring. (v.p. N.Am. 1989-94, Kevin Nash Gold medal 2001), Earthquake Engring. Rsch. Inst., Japanese Geotech. Soc. (internat. hon. mem.), Brit. Geotech. Soc. (Rankine lectr. 1991), Sigma Xi, Tau Beta Pi. Office: Va Tech Dept Civil Engring Blacksburg VA 24061-0105 Office Phone: 540-231-7351. Business E-Mail: jkm@vt.edu.

MITCHELL, JERRY, investigative reporter; b. Texarkana, Tex., 1959; BA in Comm., Harding U., Ark., 1982; MA in Journalism, Ohio State U., Columbus, 1997. Bur. reporter Clarion-Ledger, Jackson, Miss., 1986—89, investigative reporter, 1989—. Author: The Preacher & the Klansman, 1998; cons. (documentaries) Killed by the Klan, 1999. Recipient Heywood Broun award for disting. journalism, 1999, Outstanding Alumnus award, Harding U., 1999, Nat. Assn. Black Journalists award, 1999, Sidney Hillman Found. newspaper award, 1999, Sigma Delta Chi award for pub. svc. in journalism, Soc. Profl. Journalists, 1999, 2 Best of Gannett awards, 1999, Silver Em award, U. Miss. Dept. Journalism, 2000, Outstanding Achievement award of Excellence, Gannett Co., 2002, John Chancellor award for Excellence in Journalism, Columbia U., 2005, Pres.'s medal, CUNY Queen's Coll., 2005, Vernon Jarrett award, NC Agrl. & Tech. State U. Inst. Advanced Journalism Studies, 2006, Tom Renner medal for outstanding crime reporting, Investigative Reporters & Editors, 2006, George Polk award for Justice Reporting, 2006, George Polk award for State Reporting, 2007; named a MacArthur Fellow, John T. & Catherine MacArthur Found., 2009; finalist Pulitzer Prize, 2006. Achievements include investigative reporting leading to the prosecution and conviction of white supremacists who had committed murders in the 1960s; including the murders of civil rights activists in Mississippi and the 1963 bombing of a church in Birmingham that killed four girls. Office: Clarion-Ledger PO Box 40 Jackson MS 39205 Office Phone: 601-961-7064. Office Fax: 601-961-7211. E-mail: jmitchell@clarionledger.com.

MITCHELL, JOHN CHARLES, marketing professional; b. Bedford, Ind., May 25, 1947; s. John Lewis and Mary Ellen (Rowe) M.; m. Marie Elizabeth Bruland, Aug. 21, 1971; 1 child, Allison Anne. BA in Econs., Va. Mil. Inst., 1969; MBA, JD, Ind. U., 1975. Bar: Ind., 1975, Fed. Cts., 1975. Brand mgr. Procter and Gamble Co., Cin., 1975-82; group product mgr. RJR/Del Monte, San Francisco, 1982-84; dir. mktg. RJR/Nabisco, Parsippany, NJ, 1984-87, v.p. mktg., 1987-88, v.p., gen. mgr., 1988-90, pres. sales and logistics co., 1991-94, pres. Planters, Lifesavers co. Winston-Salem, NC, 1994-96; pres. bus. printer divsn. Lexmark Internat., Inc., Lexington, Ky., 1997-99; founder Collaborative Leaders, Inc., Chapel Hill, NC, 2001—. 1st lt. US Army, 1969-71. Inductee Va. Mil. Inst. Sports Hall of Fame, 1981. Republican. Methodist. Avocations: golf, skiing. E-mail: jandmmitchell@nc.rr.com.

MITCHELL, JONATHAN, lawyer, law educator; BA summa cum laude, Wheaton Coll., Ill., 1998; JD with high honors, U. Chgo., 2001. Bar: Pa. 2003, DC 2006, US Supreme Ct. 2008, Tex. 2010, US Ct. Appeals (5th cir.) 2010. Law clk. to Hon. Michael Luttig US Ct. Appeals (4th cir.), 2001—02; law clk. to Hon. Antonin Scalia US Supreme Ct., 2002—03; atty.-advisor, office of legal counsel US Dept Justice, 2003—05; vis. rschr. Georgetown U. Law Ctr; vis. asst. prof. U. Chgo. Law Sch., 2006—08; asst. prof. law George Mason U., 2008—; solicitor gen. Office of Atty. Gen., Tex., 2011—. Contbr. articles to profl. jours. Mem.: Order of Coif. Office: W 14th St Austin TX 78701 Office Phone: 512-936-1695. Office Fax: 512-474-2697. Business E-Mail: jonathan.mitchell@oag.state.tex.us.

MITCHELL, JOSEPH, state legislator; b. Mobile, Ala., May 28, 1948; s. J. Christopher and Julia (Craig) Mitchell; m. Janetta Whitt-Mitchell. BA, Morehouse Coll., Atlanta, 1969; MA, U. Southern Ala., 1979; PhD, Tex. A&M U., 1983. Founder Ala. Am. Rsch. and Edn. Associates, Inc.; mem. Dist. 103 Ala. House of Reps., Montgomery, 1994—. Steward Met. African Meth. Episc. Ch. Democrat. African Methodist Episcopalian. Avocation: jazz. Office: 465 Dexter Ave Mobile AL 36604 also: Ala House of Reps Ala State House 11 S Union St Rm 517-A Montgomery AL 36130 Office Phone: 251-473-5020, 334-242-7735. Business E-Mail: house3@alhouse.org.

MITCHELL, KENNETH DAVID, physiologist, educator; b. Musselburgh, Scotland, Mar. 5, 1959; children: Elaine J., Fraser K., Keith J. BSc with upper 2d class honors, U. Edinburgh, Scotland, 1981, PhD in Physiology, 1986. Physiology tutor Univ. Med. Sch., Edinburgh, 1981-84; rsch. assoc. dept. physiology and biophysics Nephrology Rsch. and Tng. Ctr. U. Ala., Birmingham, 1984-86, postdoctoral rsch. fellow, 1986-87, rsch. instr., 1987-88, scientist I, 1987-88; asst. prof. dept. physiology Tulane U. Sch. Medicine, New Orleans, 1988-95, assoc. prof., 1995—. Contbr. articles to profl. jours. Fellow Am. Heart Assn. (fellow Coun. High Blood Pressure Rsch. 1993—, Established Investigator award 1995-2000), Am. Soc. Nephrology; mem. Am. Physiol. Soc., Internat. Soc. Nephrology. Office: Tulane U Sch Medicine Dept Physiology SL39 1430 Tulane Ave New Orleans LA 70112-2699 Office Phone: 504-988-2593. Business E-Mail: kdmitch@tulane.edu.

MITCHELL, KEVIN J., energy executive; V.p. fin., adminstrn. ConocoPhillips Alaska Inc.; gen. mgr. fin., strategy and planning, exploration & prodn. ConocoPhillips, v.p. exploration, prodn., strategy, adminstrn., tech. svcs., 2009—. Office: ConocoPhillips 600 N Dairy Ashford Houston TX 77079 Office Phone: 281-293-1000. Business E-Mail: kmitchell@conocophillips.com.

MITCHELL, MADELEINE ENID, retired nutritionist; b. Jamaica, West Indies, Dec. 14, 1941; came to U.S., 1963, naturalized, 1974. d. William Keith and Doris Christine (Levey) M. BSc in Home Economics, McGill U., Montreal, Que., Can., 1963; MS in Nutrition, Cornell U., Ithaca, NY, 1965, PhD in Nutrition, 1968. Asst. prof. Wash. State U., Pullman, 1969-77, assoc. prof., 1978—2004, acting. chmn. home econs. rsch. ctr., 1981-83; ret., 2004. Nutrition scientist U.S. Dept. Agr., Washington, 1980-81. Author: Jamaican Ancestry: How to Find Out More, 2009. Episcopalian. Avocations: genealogy, music. Personal E-mail: mitchelm@pullman.com.

MITCHELL, MALONE, III, oil industry executive, venture capitalist; married. BS, Okla. State Univ., 1983. Founder Riata Energy (formerly SandRidge Energy), 1984, ops. mgr., 1984—89, CEO & chmn., 1989—2006; founder Riata Mgmt. LLC, 2005, Longfellow Energy LP, 2006; chmn. & bd. mem. TransAtlantic Petroleum Corp. Bd. mem. ImmunoBiosciences, Inc. Named one of Forbes 400: Richest Americans, 2009. Office: 4801 Gaillardia Pkwy Ste 225 Oklahoma City OK 73142 Office Phone: 405-286-6324. Office Fax: 406-286-6399.

MITCHELL, MOZELLA GORDON, professor, scholar, writer; b. Starkville, Miss., Aug. 14, 1936; d. John Thomas and Odena Mae (Graham) Gordon; m. Edrick R. Woodson, Mar. 20, 1951 (div. 1974); children: Cynthia LaVern, Marcia Delores Woodson Miller. AB, LeMoyne Coll., 1959; MA in English, U. Mich., 1963; MA in Religious Studies, Colgate-Rochester Divinity Sch., 1973; PhD, Emory U., 1980. Instr. in English and Speech Alcorn A&M Coll., Lorman, Miss., 1960-61; instr. English, chmn. dept. Owen Jr. Coll., Memphis, 1961-65; asst. prof. English and religion Norfolk State Coll. U. Norfolk, Va., 1965—81; assoc. prof. U. South Fla., Tampa, 1981—93, prof., 1993—, chair, religious studies dept., 2005—11, prof. emeritus, 2014; pastor Mount Sinai AME Zion Ch., 1982—89; presiding elder Tampa dist. AME Zion Ch., 1988—; pastor, founder Love of Christ AME Zion Tabernacle, Branden, 1993—; candidate for bishop AME Zion Ch., 2003—04, presiding Elder, 1998—2004. Vis. assoc. prof. Hood Theol. Sem., Salisbury, N.C., 1979-80, St. Louis U., 1992-93; vis. asst. lectr. U. Rochester, N.Y., 1972-73; co-dir. Ghent VISTA Project, Norfolk, 1969-71; cons. Black Women and Ministry Interdenominational Theol. Ctr; lectr. Fla. Humanities Coun., 1994-95; Meml. lectr. Mordecai Johnson Inst., Colgate Rochester Div. Sch., 1997; Ruben Speaks Meml. lectr. Hood Theol. Sem., 2009. Author: Spiritual Dynamics of Howard Thurman's Theology, 1985, Howard Thurman and the Quest for Freedom, Proc. 2d Ann. Howard Thurman Convocation (Peter Lang), 1992, African American Religious History in Tampa Bay, 1992;, New Africa in America: The Blending of African and American Religious and Social Traditions Among Black People in Meridian, Mississippi and Surrounding Counties (Peter Lang), 1994, Crucial Issues in Caribbean Religions (Peter Lang), 2006, Crucial Issues in Caribbean Religion, 2006; editor: Martin Luther King Meml. Series in Religion, Culture and Social Devel.; editorial bd. Cornucopia Reprint Series; contr. articles and essays in field. Mem. Tampa-Hillsborough County Human Rels. Coun., 1987—; founder Women at the Well, Inc.; del. 7th assembly World Coun. Chs., Canberra, Australia, 1991, 17th World Meth. Coun., Rio de Janiero, 1996; del. 18th World Meth. Coun., Brighton, England, 2001; mem. connectional coun. A.M.E. Zion Ch., Charlotte, 1984—, staff writer Sunday sch. lit., 1981—, mem. jud. coun., candidate for bishop, 2002—04; pres. Fla. Coun. Chs., Orlando, Fla., 1988—90, pres.-elect, 1998—, pres. exec. bd., 2000. Recipient ecumenical leadership citation Fla. Coun. Chs., 1990, Inaugural lectr. award Geddes Hanson Black Cultural Ctr. Princeton Theol. Sem., 1993; fellow Nat. Doctoral Fund, 1978-80; grantee NEH, 1981, Fla. Endowment for Humanities, 1990—, U. South Fla. Rsch. Coun., 1990—. Mem. Coll. Theology Soc., Am. Acad. Religion, Soc. for the Study of Black Religion (pres. 1992-96), Joint Ctr. for Polit. Studies, Black Women in Ch. and Soc., Alpha Kappa Alpha. Phi Kappa Phi. Democrat. Methodist. Avocations: piano, poetry, tennis, bicycling, Scrabble. Office: Univ South Florida Religious Studies Dept CPR 107 Tampa FL 33620 Office Phone: 813-974-1852. Personal E-mail: mozellam@aol.com. Business E-Mail: mitchellm@usf.edu.

MITCHELL, NORMA TAYLOR, history professor; b. Norfolk, Va., Nov. 14, 1936; d. Orville Carson Sr. and Emma (Heal) Taylor; m. Frank Joseph Mitchell, Sept. 5, 1959; 1 child, Anne Mitchell Whisnant. BA in History, Coll. William and Mary, 1958; MA, Duke U., 1962, PhD, 1967. Assoc. prof. history Troy (Ala.) State U. (now Troy U.), 1970—84, prof. history, 1984—99, prof. emerita, 1999—. Part-time instr. history and polit. sci. Union Coll., Barbourville, Ky., 1962-64; part-time dean women Ctrl. Meth. U. (formerly Ctrl. Meth. Coll.), Fayette, Mo., 1968-70; gen. commn. on archives and history United Meth. Ch., 1972-80, chair women's history project, 1977-80; vice chair nat. planning com. Bicentennial of Methodism in Am., 1979-80; lectr., presenter in field. Contbr. chpts. in books; author articles and revs. Lay leader United Meth. Ch., local, state and nat. levels, 1960—, including bd. dirs. AL-WFL United Meth. Bd.

Pastoral Care and Counseling, 1984-92, bd. dirs. AL-W.FL United Meth. Children's Homes, 1989-99; del. Southeastern Jurisdictional Conf., 1980; AL-W.FL United Meth. Women conf. officer, 1976-80; Ala.-West Fla. conf. chair Commn. on Status and Role of Women, 1976-80; bd. dirs. Scarritt-Bennett Ctr., 2003—10, bd. dirs. Wesley fellowship, Duhe U., 2010- Recipient awards and honors; So. Fellowships Fund grantee, 1958-61; Cokesbury Tchg. fellow, 1964-65, Alice Lee award, United Methodist Ch., 2013 Mem. AAUP, NEA, NOW, AAUW (v.p. for membership Troy br. 1995-99, honoree Edn. Found. 1998-99), Ala. Edn. Assn., Am. Hist. Assn., So. Hist. Assn. (membership com. 1992), So. Assn. Women Historians, Ala. Assn. Historians, Ala. Hist. Assn., North Ala. United Meth. Hist. Soc., Bread for the World, Amnesty Internat., Humane Soc. U.S., Phi Beta Kappa, Phi Kappa Phi, Phi Alpha Theta, Omicron Delta Kappa. Democrat. Home: 7 Vandora Pl Durham NC 27705-5481 Office: Troy U Dept History Bibb Graves Hall 305 Troy AL 36082-0001 Office Phone: 919-402-0984. E-mail: normatmitchell@gmail.com.

MITCHELL, PAULA RAE, nursing educator, dean; b. Independence, Mo., Jan. 10, 1951; d. Millard Henry and E. Lorene (Denton) Gates; m. Ralph William Mitchell, May 24, 1975. BS in Nursing, Graceland U., Lamoni, Iowa, 1973; MS in Nursing, U. Tex., 1976; EdD in Ednl. Adminstrn., N.Mex. State U., 1996. RN, Tex., Mo. Instr. nursing El Paso C.C., Tex., 1979-85, dir. nursing Tex., 1985—2003, acting divsn. chmn. health occupations Tex., 1985-86, divsn. dean Tex., 1998-99, dean health occupations Tex., 1999-2000, curriculum facilitator Tex., 1984—85, dean health occupations, math and sci., campus dean Rio Grande, 2000—08, dean health career tech. edn. Math and sci. campus dean Rio Grade, 2008—. Ob-gyn. nurse practitioner Planned Parenthood, El Paso, 1981-86, med. com., 1986-98; cons. in field, army med. dept. officer Acad. Health Scis.Ft. Author: (with Grippando) Nursing Perspectives and Issues, 1989, 93; contbr. articles to profl. jours. Founder, bd. dirs. Health-CREST, El Paso, 1981—85; mem. pub. edn. com. Am. Cancer Soc., El Paso, 1983—84, mem. profl. activities com., 1992—93; mem. El-Paso City-County Bd. Health, 1989—91; mem. Govt. Applications Rev. Com. Rio Grande Coun. Govts., 1989—91; mem. collaborative coun. El Paso Magnet H.S. for Health Care Professions, 1992—94; co-chair health and human svcs. task force Unite El Paso Health, 1996—98, mem. steering com., 1999—2000; co-chair health taskforce El Paso Cmty. Legis. Agenda, 1997—99; mem. adv. com. Ctr. for Border Health Rsch., Paso del Norte Health Found., 1998—2004; mem. Leadership El Paso, 1999; mem. health profl. shortage task force Greater El Paso C. of C., 2001—, mem. health care coun., 2002—; mem. star adv. com. Canutillo Tex. Ind. Sch. Dist., 2003—05; mem. El Paso County Civil Svc. Commn., 2006—10, chair, 2009—10; coord. West Tex. Med. Res. Corps, 2006—; vice chair El Paso VOAD, 2011—13, chair, 2013—; bd. dirs. Border Health Inst., El Paso, 2001—08, sec.-treas., 2003—08; mem. cmty. adv. bd. Victory Warriors Drill and Dance Acad., El Paso, 2001—11; mem. governing bd. Mesa Hills Specialty Hosp., 2002—09. Capt. US Army, 1972—78, capt. USAR, 1978—98, ret. USAR, 1998. Decorated Army Commendation medal, Meritorious Svc. medal; named to Women's Hall Fame, El Paso Commn., 1999; named Outstanding Alumni, N.Mex. State U. Dept. Edn. Mgmt. and Devel., 2002-03; recipient Unite El Paso Legacy award 1997, Merit and Svc. cert. Victory Warriors Drill and Dance Acad., 2003, Outstanding Cmty. Svc. award, 2003, Appreciation and Cmty. Responsibility cert., 2005, Appreciation cert., 2006. Mem. Nat. League Nursing (resolutions com. Assocs. Degree coun. 1987-89, accreditation site visitor, AD coun. 1990—2010, Tex. edn. com. 1991-92, Tex. 3d v.p. 1992-93, Tex. 1st v.p. 1997-99, nominating com. 1999-2000), Am. Soc. Psychoprophylaxis Obstetrics (cert. childbirth educator 1978), Nurses Assn. Am. Coll. Ob-Gyn. (cert. in ambulatory women's healthcare, 1983-, chpt. coord. 1979-83, nat. program rev. com. 1984-86, corr. 1987-89), Advanced Nurse Practitioner Group El Paso (coord. 1980-83, legis. com. 1984), Am. Phys. Therapist Assn. (commn. on accreditation, site visitor for phys. therapist asst. programs 1991-), Orgn. Assoc. Degree Nursing (Tex. membership chmn. 1985-89, chmn. goals com. 1989-2004, nat. bylaws com. 1990-95), Am. Vocat. Assn., Am. Assn. Women Cmty. and Jr. Colls., Tex. Orgn. Nurse Execs., Nat. Coun. Workforce Edn. (articulation task force 1986-89, program standards task force 1991-93), Nat. Coun. Instrnl. Adminstrs., Tex. Soc. Allied Health Profls. (sec. 2004-2007, elect pres. 2007-08, pres. 2008-09, past pres. 2009-10; Disting. Svc. award, 2013), Tex. Nurses Assn. (pres. elect dist. one 2002-03, pres. 2003-05, past pres. 2005-06, bd. mem., 2008-09, nomination com. mem. 2009-11), Am. Soc. Allied Health Profls. (edn. com. 1993-96), El Paso C. of C. (healthcare coun. 2001-05), El Paso Commn. for Women (treas. 2007—), Am. Legion, Mil. Order World Wars (El Paso chpt. staff officer 2007-08, jr. vice comdr., 2008-10, sr. vice comdr., 2010-12, El Paso chpt. comdr.2012-, chair Phoenician Award Com. 2009-, Dept. Rio Grande jr. vice comdr., 2010-11, sr. vice comdr., dept. Rio Grande 2010-12,comdr., Dept. Rio Grade, 2012-, Merit award, 2008, Silver Patrick Henry, 2009, Otstanding Chpt. Companion, 2010, Outstanding Svc. medal, 2011), Sigma Theta Tau, Phi Kappa Phi. Mem. Christian Ch. (Disciples Of Christ). Home: 4616 Cupid Dr El Paso TX 79924-1726 Office: El Paso C C PO Box 20500 El Paso TX 79998-0500 Office Phone: 915-831-4030. Business E-Mail: pmitche8@epcc.edu.

MITCHELL, STEPHEN MILTON, investor and company executive; b. Atlanta, Oct. 23, 1943; s. Judge Stephenson and Elizabeth Ruth (Morgan) M.; m. Carolyn Docia Goss, June 29, 1968; children: William Stephenson, Scott Milton, Gregory Stephen. B of Indsl. Engring. with honors, Ga. Inst. Tech., 1965, MS in Indsl. Engring., 1966. Registered profl. engr., Ga. Sr. engr. Lochkeed-Ga. Corp., Marietta, 1966-70; mgr. material control Snapper Power Equipment, McDonough, Ga., 1970-73; pres. Atlanta Processing Co., Conley, Ga., 1973-86; sr. v.p., gen. mgr. Norcom, Inc., Norcross, Ga., 1986-93; chmn., CEO Atlanta Processing B, Inc., Tucker, Ga., 1993-94; CEO Internat. Processing Corp., Atlanta, 1994, Sertec Corp., Atlanta, 1995—, also bd. dirs. Bd. dirs. Atlanta Processing Co., Conley, Ga., Norcom, Inc., Norcross, APB Inc., Tucker, Ga., IPC, Atlanta; mem. exec. com., chmn., bd. dirs. Clairmont Oaks, Inc., 1988—. Bd. dirs., treas. Common Cause, Ga., 1989—; active First Bapt. Ch. of Decatur, Ga., 1968—, chmn. bd. deacons, 1993, 95. Named to Georgia Tech Acad. Disting. Engring. Alumni. Mem. Young Presidents Orgn., World Presidents Orgn., Ga. Tech. Alumni Assn. (trustee 1981-87). Republican. Home: 5268 Browning Way SW Lilburn GA 30047-7029 Office: Sertec Corp 2100 Powers Ferry Rd NW Ste 200 Atlanta GA 30339-5014

MITCHELL, TEDDY LEE, physician; b. Columbia, La., Feb. 24, 1962; s. Oliver Clayton nad Mary Elizabeth (Johnston) M.; m. Janet Luisa Tornelli, Apr. 9, 1988; children: Mary Katherine, Oliver Charles, Christopher Tornelli. BS in Biology, Stephen F. Austin State U., 1983; MD, U. Tex. Med. Br., 1987. Diplomate Am. Bd. Internal Medicine, Cert. of Added Qualification-Sports Medicine. Intern U. Tex. Med. Br., Galveston, 1987-88, resident, 1988-90, 90-91; med. dir. wellness program Cooper Aerobics Ctr., Dallas, 1991—2006, pres., med. dir., 2006—, pres. & CEO, 2008—. Mem. Rep. Sen. Inner Cir., Washington, 1993, Heritage Found., Washington, 1993. Capt. U.S. Army Res. Med. Corps, 1988-96. Fellow ACP (cert. Merit 1990), Am. Coll. Sports Medicine; mem. AMA, Tex. Med. Assn., Dallas County Med. Soc. Methodist. Avocations: exercise, travel, music. Home: 3224 Lovers Ln Dallas TX 75225-7626

MITCHELL, WILFRID BEDE, librarian, library association executive; b. Bloomington, Ind., Nov. 5, 1953; s. W. Bede and Barbara Plumb Mitchell; m. Carrie N. Cornejo, May 30, 1992. BA in Philosophy, U. Mich., 1975, MLS, 1977; EdD, Mont. State U., 1989. Circulation and reserve libr. Mont. State U., Bozeman, 1978-85; head circulation libr. U. N.C., Greensboro, 1985-90; assoc. univ. libr. Appalachian State U., Boone, N.C., 1990-99; dean libr. Ga. So. U., Statesboro, 1999—. Contbr. articles to profl. jours. Mem. ALA, Assn. Coll. and Rsch. Librs. (chair acad. status com. 1995-96, chair instnl. priorities and faculty rewards task force, 1996-98, bd. dirs. 2002-06, chair, liaisons coordinating com., 2010-11), Libr. Adminstrn. Mgmt. Assn. (chair publs. and bibliography com. sys. and svcs. sect. 1997-98, strategic planning implementation com. 2001-03, pres.-elect, 2006-07, pres. 2007-08, past pres. 2008-09), Ga. Libr. Assn. (chmn. academic libr. divsn. 2001-02, chmn. adminstrv. svcs. com. 2003), Southeastern Libr. Assn. (chmn. legis com. 2005-06), Friends Ga. Librs., (pres. 2009-11). Office: Ga So U Henderson Libr PO Box 8074 Statesboro GA 30460-8074 Office Phone: 912-478-5115. Office Fax: 912-478-0093. Business E-Mail: wbmitch@georgiasouthern.edu.

MITCHELL, WILLIAM, state legislator; b. Savannah, Ga. m. Shawn Mitchell; 1 child, Maya. Sec. Legislature & Congressional Reapportionment Com.; coun. mem. Stone Mountain, Ga., 1995—2002; mem. Health & Ecology Com., State Planning & Cmty. Affairs Com.; mayor pro tem Stone Mountain; sr. dir. South Fulton Med. Ctr., 1998—2002; state rep. Dist. 61 Ga., 2004—; pres. Billy Mitchell & Assocs. Mem.: East Point Bus. Assn. (pres. 2002), DeKalb Mcpl. Assn. (pres. 1998), Airport C. of C. (pres. 2001—02), South Fulton Rotary Club (pres. 2001—02). Democrat. Methodist. Mailing: PO Box 55 Stone Mountain GA 30086 Office: 409 Legis Office Bldg Atlanta GA 30334 Office Phone: 770-498-0055. Office Fax: 770-498-5055. E-mail: electbilly@aol.com, mitchell@legis.state.ga.us.

MITCHELL, WILLIAM JOHN, mathematics educator; b. Mpls., Dec. 30, 1943; s. John Edwards and Jane (Cavert) M.; m. Jean Ann Larson, Oct. 1, 1988. Student, Carleton Coll., 1961-63; BA, U. Wis., 1965; PhD, U. Calif., Berkeley, 1970. Lectr. U. Chgo., 1970-72; asst. prof. Rockefeller U., NYC, 1972-77; from assoc. prof. to prof. Pa. State U., State College, 1979-89; prof. U. Fla., Gainesville, 1989—. Office: U Fla Dept Math Gainesville FL 32611

MITCHELL, WILLIAM MARVIN, pathology educator; b. Atlanta, Mar. 3, 1935; s. William Joseph and Marvin Eugenia (Peavy) M.; m. Shirley Ann Crowell, Dec. 22, 1959; children: Alexander James, Keith Townsend, Derek Loren. BA, Vanderbilt U., 1957, MD, 1960; PhD, Johns Hopkins U., 1966. Diplomate Am. Bd. Pathology. Asst. prof. microbiology and medicine Vanderbilt U., Nashville, 1966-70, assoc. prof. pathology, 1970-78, prof., 1978—. Med. dir. Specialized Assays, Nashville, 1981-91; med. dir. Vanderbilt Pathology Lab. Svcs., 1994—2010; med. dir. Home Health Care Am., 1998—2013; planning dir. Vanderbilt Cancer Rsch. and Treatment Ctr., 1971-72; founder ActivBiotics, Inc., Boston, Genocyte, Inc., Nashville; cons. NIH, DuPont Co., Smith Kline, others. Patentee in field; contbr. articles to profl. jours. Bd. dirs. St. Augustine's Chapel, Nashville, 1981-86, Hemispherx Biopharma, Inc., Phila., 1998—, Chronix Biomedical, Inc., 2006-, San Jose Calif., Rokeby Assoc., 2009-12, pres., 2011-12; judge Regional Sci. and Engring. Fair, Nashville, 1985, 88; judge Internat. Sci. Engring. Fair, Nashville, 1992, Birmingham, 1994. Eleanor Roosevelt Internat. Cancer fellow Internat. Union Against Cancer, 1976-77; grantee NIH. Mem. AAAS, Am. Soc. Investigative Pathology, Am. Chem. Soc., Am. Soc. Biol. Chemistry & Mol. Biol., Am. Soc. Microbiology, Internat. Acad. Pathology, Am. Soc. Interferon Rsch., Am. AIDS Soc., Sigma Xi. Episcopalian. Avocations: skiing, crafts, music. Home Phone: 615-297-6308; Office Phone: 615-322-3238. Business E-Mail: bill.mitchell@vanderbilt.edu.

MITCHEM, CHERYL E., accounting educator; b. South Bend, Ind., June 24, 1947; d. Roy Francis and Marcella Evelyn (Chryst) Drake; m. Allen Pershing Mitchem, Jr., Nov. 28, 1969; children: Michael, Marlo, Megan, Melissa. BA, Tex. Christian U., 1969; MBA, San Diego State U., 1980; PhD, Va. Commonwealth U., 1990. CPA, Va.; cert. mgmt. acct. Vis. prof. acctg. Coll. William and Mary, Williamsburg, Va., 1986-88; adj. prof. acctg. Va. Commonwealth U., Richmond, 1988-89; asst. prof. acctg. Christopher Newport U., Newport News, 1989-91; asst. prof. Va. State U., Petersburg, 1991—98, chair acctg., 1993—2003, assoc. prof., 1998—, acting asst. dean Sch. Bus., 2004—10, asst. dean, Sch. Bus., 2010—. Contbr. articles to profl. jours. Mem. AICPA, Am. Acctg. Assn., Inst. Mgmt. Accts, USCPA, Va. Soc. CPAs. Mem. Christian Ch. (Disciples Of Christ). Avocations: travel, reading.

MITROVGENIS, JAMES WILLIAM, JR., retired journalist; b. McAlester, Okla. s. James William Sr. and Kula Mitrovgenis; m. Brigitte Dunnebier. Student, U. Okla., 1968-72. Reporter McAlester Daily Dem., 1973—76; news editor Muskogee Phoenix, Okla., 1976—81; night copy editor The Oklahoman, Oklahoma City, 1981—86, night news editor, 1986—91, copy editor, 1991—2008. Mem. NRA, AP Okla. News Execs. (bd. dirs. 1987-89, 1st pl. page one layout award 1987, 2d pl. gen. excellence award 1987, 3d pl. page one layout award 1987, 2d pl. gen. excellence award 1986). Greek Orthodox. Achievements include first editor at the Oklahoman to digitally manipulate a photograph for publication in the 1980s. Avocations: travel, photography, stock market.

MIXSON, MICKEY (H. LAMAR MIXSON), lawyer; b. Atlanta, Apr. 12, 1949; BA in English, magna cum laude, Washington & Lee U., Lexington, Va., 1970; JD cum laude, Harvard Law Sch., 1974. Bar: Ga. 1974, US Dist. Ct. (no. and mid. dists.) Va., US Ct. Appeals (3d, 4th, 5th and 11th cirs.), US Supreme Ct. Ptnr. Bondurant Mixson & Elmore LLP, Atlanta. Contbr. articles to profl. jours. Pres. Atlanta chpt., bd. dirs., mem. exec. com. Internat. Network Boutique Law Firms; bd. dirs., past pres. Ga. Lawyers for Arts. Named one of Leading Plaintiffs' Lawyers in America, Lawdragon 500, 2007, America's Premiere Lawyers, Law Bus. Insiders, 2009, The Nation's Top Litigators, The Nat. Law Journal, 2009, Top 100 Ga. SuperLawyers, Atlanta Mag., 2010, 2011. Fellow: American Coll. Trial Lawyers; mem.: ABA, State Bar Ga., American Bar Found., Atlanta Bar Assn., Lawyers Club Atlanta. Office: Bondurant Mixson & Elmore LLP 1201 W Peachtree NW Ste 3900 Atlanta GA 30309 Office Phone: 404-881-4171. Office Fax: 404-881-4111. E-mail: mixson@bmelaw.com.

MIYAGAWA, ICHIRO, physicist; b. Hiratsuka, Kanagawa, Japan, Mar. 5, 1922; s. Shigejiro and Tsuma (Itoh) M.; m. Mitsuko Yamada, Feb. 10, 1950; children: Shigeru, Haruyo, Mari. BS, Nagoya U., Japan, 1945; DSc, U. Tokyo, 1954. Asst. prof. U. Tokyo, 1959-62; vis. asst. prof. Duke U., Durham, NC, 1963-65; asst. prof. physics U. Ala., Tuscaloosa, 1965-66, assoc. prof., 1966-70, prof., 1970-80, Univ. Research prof. physics, 1980-92, prof. emeritus, 1992—. Contbr. articles to profl. jours. Recipient Samuel Ullman award, 1998; USPHS grantee; EPA grantee; NIH grantee. Fellow Am. Phys. Soc.; mem., AAAS, Sigma Xi. Home: 6434 Misty Ridge Dr Birmingham AL 35235-

MIYAZATO, AI, professional golfer; b. Okinawa, Japan, June 19, 1985; Profl. golfer LPGA Japan Tour, 2004—, LPGA Tour, 2006—. Achievements include winning LPGA of Japan Tour events: Miyagi TV Cup Dunlop Ladies Open, 2003; Daikin Orchid Ladies, Suntory Ladies Open, APiTA Circle K Sunkus Ladies, Masters GC Ladies, Daio Paper Elleair Ladies Open, 2004; Vernal Ladies, New Catapillar Mitsubishi Ladies, Hisako Higuchi IDC Otsuka Kagu Ladies, Daio Paper Elleair Ladies Open, 2005; Miyagi TV Cup Dunlop Ladies Open, 2006; Sankyo Ladies Open, 2009; winning LPGA of Japan major championships: Janpan's Women's Open Golf Championship, 2005; JLPGA Championship Konica Minolta Cup, 2006; winning LPGA Tour events: Evian Masters, 2009; Honda PTT LPGA Thailand, HSBC Women's Champions, Tres Marias Championship, Shop Rite LPGA Classic, Safeway Classic, 2010. Office: LPGA 100 International Golf Dr Daytona Beach FL 32124-1092

MIZE, JOE HENRY, industrial engineer, educator; b. Colorado City, Tex., June 14, 1934; s. Kelly Marcus and Birtie (Adams) M.; m. Betty Bentley, Mar. 16, 1966; 1 dau., Kelly Jean. BS in Indsl. Engring, Tex. Tech. Coll., 1958; MS (Research Found. grantee) in Indsl. Engring, Purdue U., 1963, PhD, 1964. Registered profl. engr., Ala., Okla. Indsl. engr. White Sands Missile Range, N.Mex., 1958-61; grad. research asst. Purdue U., Lafayette, Ind., 1961-64; asso. prof. engring. Auburn (Ala.) U., 1964-69; dir. Auburn (Ala.) U. (Computer Center), 1965-66; prof. engring. Ariz. State U., Tempe, 1969-72; prof., head Sch. Indsl. Engring. and Mgmt. Okla. State U., Stillwater, 1972-80, dir. Univ. Ctr. for Energy Research, 1980-83, Regents prof., 1982-94; v.p. Hong Kong U. of Sci. and Tech., 1994-98; prof., v.p. Hong Kong U. Sci. & Tech., 1994-98; rsch. affiliate engring. sys. divsn. MIT, 1998—. Cons. to Air War Coll., 1968-69, U.S. Army, Ops. Analysis Standby Unit, U. N.C., 1965-69, various mfg. firms, 1964—; program adv. Office of Mgmt. and Budget, Exec. Office of the President, Washington, 1974-79; adv. to NSF, 1974-94, Nat. Center for Productivity and Quality of Work Life, 1973-78; chmn. tech. adv. council So. Growth Policies Bd., 1975-77; accrediting visitor Engrs. Council for Profl. Devel., 1973-80 Author: (with J.G. Cox) Essentials of Simulation (translated into Japanese 1970), 1968, Prosim V.: Instructor's Manual, 1971, Student's Manual, 1971, (with C.R. White and George H. Brooks) Operations Planning and Control, 1971, (with J.L. Kuester) Optimization Techniques with Fortran, 1973, (with W.C. Turner and K.E. Case) Introduction to Industrial and Systems Engineering, 3d edit., 1993 (named Book of Yr., Am. Inst. Indsl. Engrs. 1979), Guide to Systems Integration, 1991; contrbr. articles to profl. jours., more. Recipient Disting. Engring. Alumnus award Purdue U., 1978 Mem. Am. Inst. Indsl. Engrs. (exec. v.p. 1978-80, pres. 1981-82, H.G. Maynard Innovative Achievement award 1977, Gilbreth Indsl. Engring. award 1990), Am. Soc. for Engring. Edn. (sec. govt. rels. com. 1975-76), Nat. Soc. Profl. Engrs., Okla. Soc. Profl. Engrs. (Outstanding Engring. Achievement award 1977, Outstanding Engr. in Okla. 1981), Inst. Mgmt. Scis., Coun. Indsl. Engring. Acad. Dept. Heads (chmn. 1975-76), NAE, Nat. Rsch. Coun., Sigma Xi, Tau Beta Pi, Alpha Pi Mu. Office: Oklahoma State U Dept Indsl Engring Stillwater OK 74078-0001

MIZUGUCHI, NANA N., plastic surgeon; BA, UCLA, 1986—91; MD, Tulane U., 1992—96. Diplomate American Bd. Surgery, 2001, Am. Bd. Plastic Surgery, 2005. Fellow plastic surgery, divsn. plastic and reconstructive surgery Univ. of NC, 2001—03; intern dept. surgery Univ. of Louisville, Ky., 1996—97, resident dept. surgery Ky., 1997—2001, chief resident dept. surgery Ky., 2000—01, asst. prof., dept. surgery Ky., 2003—06, dir., microsurgery program Ky., 2005—06, dir., student tchg. program Ky., 2005—06, clin. faculty, dept. surgery Ky., 2006—, hosp. affiliations include, Jewish Hosp., Norton Hosp., Dupont Surgery Ctr., Calobrace Plastic Surgery Ctr. Recipient Conf. Attendance award, Univ. of Louisville, 2001, Better Care award, Norton Hosp., 2004; fellow Acad. of Surgeons, 2006. Mem.: Facial Action Coding System, Hirum C. Polk Surg. Soc., Am. Soc. of Plastic Surgeons, Ky. Soc. of Plastic Surgeons. Office: Calobrace Plastic Surgery Center 2341 Lime Kiln Lane Louisville KY 40207 Office Phone: 502-899-9979.

MIZUGUCHI, TETSUYA, video game designer; b. Hokkaido, Japan, May 22, 1965; Grad., Nihon U. With Sega, 1990—2003; founder, chief creative officer Q Entertainment, Japan, 2004—. With AM Annex, 1996. Developed with team Sega Touring Car Championships, Sega Rally Championship, creator, Sonic Jam, 1997, Space Channel 5, 1999, Shenmue, 1999, D-2, 1999, Rez, 2001, Rez: Part 2, 2002, Meteos, Lumines; prodr.: Quest Beat Label; maintains web blog 1UP.com. Office: Q Entertainment 2345 Clark Ave Albany GA 31705 Office Phone: 229-251-6972.

MJOR, IVAR ANDREAS, dental educator; b. Norderhov, Norway, Sept. 18, 1933; came to U.S., 1992; s. Peter Sigvart and Thora (Elnaes) M.; m. Birgit E. Gron, Dec. 26, 1959; children: Per I., Siri E., Thor A. BDS, U. St. Andrews, Dundee, Scotland, 1957; MS in Dentistry, U. Ala., 1960, MS in Anatomy, 1961, D in Odontology, 1967, U. Umeå, Sweden, 1983, U. Turku, 1986, U. Copenhagen, Greece, 1991, U. Lund, 1993; LLD, U. Dundee, 1987; D Dentistry, U. Athens, Greece, 1995. Postdoctoral fellow U. Ala., Birmingham, 1959-61; rsch. assoc. Norwegian Inst. Dental Rsch., Oslo, 1961-67; assoc. prof. U. Oslo, 1968-70, prof., 1970-73; dir. NIOM Scandinavian Inst. Dental Materials, Oslo, 1973-93; prof., eminent scholar U. Fla., Gainesville, 1993—. Author, co-editor: Histology of the Human Tooth, 1973, Human Oral Embryology and Histology, 1986, Modern Concepts in Operative Dentistry, 1988; author, editor: Reaction Patterns in Human Teeth, 1983, Dental Materials: Biological Properties and Clinical Evaluation, 1985; editor-in-chief Acta Odontologica Scandinavica, 1977-81; sect. editor Quintessence Internat., 1989—. Lt. Dental Corps Norwegian armed forces, 1957-59. Mem. ADA (hon.), FDI World Dental Fedn. (mem. coun. 1992—, chmn. commn. 1992—), Acad. Operative Dentistry, Internat. Assn. for Dental Rsch. (pres. 1988, sci. award 1987), Finnish Dental Assn. (hon.), Danish Dental Assn. (hon.), Accademia Italians de Conservativa (hon.). Avocations: tennis, hiking. Office: U Fla Coll Dentistry 1600 SW Archer Rd Gainesville FL 32610-3001

MLADICK, RICHARD ANTHONY, plastic surgeon; b. Melrose Park, Ill., May 28, 1934; s. Edward Anthony and Gladys Jane (Castens) M.; m. Elly Dalgas Jensen, Aug. 13, 1966; children: Kristen, Richard. BA, Northwestern U., 1955, MD, 1959. Diplomate Am. Bd. Plastic Surgery, Am. Bd. Surgery. Intern Cook County Hosp., 1959—60, resident in gen. surgery, 1960—64; resident in plastic and reconstructive surgery Duke U. Med. Ctr., 1965—68; asst. prof. plastic surgery Duke U. Med. Sch., Durham, N.C., 1968-69; prof. plastic surgery Eastern Va. Med. Sch., Norfolk, 1969-75; dir. Ctr. for Cosmetic Plastic Surgery, Virginia Beach, Va., 1975—. Guest editor: Clinics in Plastic Surgery, 1989; contbr. articles, chpts. to profl. publs. Bd. dirs. Va. Orchestral Assn., Virginia Beach; mem. Orgn. Pub. Safety. Fellow Am. Coll. Surgeons; Mem. AMA, Am. Assn. Plastic Surgeons, Am. Soc. Aesthetic Plastic Surgery, Lipoplasty Soc. N.Am. (bd. dirs., past pres.), Med. Soc. Va., Seaboard Med. Assn., Am. Soc. Plastic and Reconstructive Surgeons, Va. Soc. Plastic and Reconstructive Plastic Surgeons (pres. 1973-74), Southeastern Soc. Plastic Surgeons, So. Med. Assn., Va. Beach Med. Soc. Virginia Beach Rotary Club. Presbyterian. Avocations: running, tennis, gardening, biking. Office Phone: 757-481-5151.

MO, LUKE WEI, physicist, researcher; b. Shangtung, China, June 3, 1934; s. Si-leng and Shu-feng (Lo) M.; m. Doris Chang, Dec. 31, 1960; children: Curtis L., Alice. BSEE, Nat. Taiwan U., 1955; MS in Physics, Nat. Tsinghua U., 1959; PhD, Columbia U., 1963. Rsch. assoc. Columbia U., NYC, 1963—64; rsch. physicist Stanford Linear Accelerator, Calif., 1965—69; asst. prof. physics U. Chgo., 1969—76; prof. physics Va. Poly. Inst. and State U., Blacksburg, 1976—. Contbr. articles to profl. jours. Served with Taiwan Air Force, 1955-56. Recipient Alumni Research Excellence award Va. Poly. Inst. and State U., 1980, Guggenheim fellow, 1981. Fellow Am. Phys. Soc. Office: Va Poly Inst Dept Physics Blacksburg VA 24061-0435 Mailing: 1387 Camininto Diadema La Jolla CA 92037 Office Phone: 858-699-0162. Business E-Mail: lmo@vt.edu.

MOAG, RODNEY FRANK, language educator, country and bluegrass singer, musician, record producer; b. Warsaw, NY, Oct. 15, 1936; s. Hugh Alexander and Imogene (Hodges) Moag; m. Rachel Ann Foley, Feb. 9, 1964 (div. Aug. 1974); children: Robin Gray, Hugh Daniel, Jeffrey Lee. BS, Syracuse U., 1961; MA, U. Wis., 1966, PhD, 1973. Instr., asst. prof. U. Mo., Columbia, 1968—74, dir. college preparatory program for visually impaired, 1974; vis. Fulbright prof. U. S. Pacific, Suva, Fiji, 1975-78; vis. assoc. prof. U. Mich., Ann Arbor, 1978-80, adj. prof., 1981, vis. assoc. prof., 1982; sr. lectr. U. Tex., Austin, 1981, 83-90, assoc. prof., 1990—2004, prof. emeritus, 2004—. Author: (reference grammar) Fiji Hindi, 1977, Malayalam, 1986, singer (country music artist) 6 albums. Mng. dir. Amateur Radio Repeaters Washtenaw, 1984—86; pres. Mich. Repeater Coun., 1985—88; vol. programmer KO-OP, 1995—. Mem.: Austin Repeater Orgn., Tex. VHF FM Soc., Ctrl. Tex. Bluegrass Assn., Austin Amateur Radio Club (v.p. 1993—94). Avocations: amateur radio, music. Home: 6909 Miranda Dr Austin TX 78752-3119 Office Phone: 512-467-6825. Personal E-mail: rodmoag@texas.net.

MOAK, ROBERT WARREN (BOBBY), state legislator; b. Chgo., June 13, 1958; s. Alvin Monette and Peggie Nixon Moak; m. Gerre Lanier Cumbaa; children: Drew, Sykes. Asst. pers. dir. See Land Drilling, 1980—81, pers. dir., 1981—82; mem. Dist. 53 Miss. House of Reps., 1984—. Toll fellow, CSG & U. Kentucky. Mem.: America & Miss. Bar Assn., U. Miss. Alumni Assn., Moose, Ole Miss. Alumni Assn., SW JC Alumni Assn., Pub. Rels.Socc., Miss. Hunting Dog Assn., Moak's Creek Landowners Assn. Democrat. Baptist. Address: 402 Monticello St Bogue Chitto MS 39629 Mailing: PO Box 242 Bogue Chitto MS 39629 Office Phone: 601-359-2860. Office Fax: 601-734-2563. Business E-Mail: bmoak@house.ms.gov. E-mail: bmoak@locnet.net.

MOAKE, JAMES, healthcare company executive; CFO Grant Regional Health Ctr., Inc., Wis., 1994—98; asst. CFO Biloxi Regional Med. Ctr., Miss., 1998—99; CFO Cmty. Hosp. Lancaster, Pa., 1999—2000, Province Healthcare Corp., 2000—02; ops. contr. IASIS Healthcare Corp., 2002—03; CFO Tex. and Fla. markets Iasis Healthcare LLC, 2003—05; v.p., CFO ops. IASIS Healthcare, LLC, 2005—. Office: Iasis Healthcare LLC Bldg E 117 Seaboard Ln Franklin TN 37067 Office Phone: 615-844-2747. Office Fax: 615-846-3006.

MOBLEY, ANNIE W., state legislator; Ret. chief court counselor; state rep. Dist. 5 NC, 2007—. Democrat. Office: North Carolina House of Representatives 300 N Salisbury St Rm 501 Raleigh NC 27603-5925 Home Phone: 252-332-5463; Office Phone: 919-733-5780. E-mail: Annie.Mobley@ncleg.net.

MOBLEY, BARBARA JEAN, former state legislator, lawyer; b. Dec. 1, 1947; m. James L. Savage, Jr. BS, Savannah State Coll.; MSW, U. Ill.; JD, So. Meth. U. Atty.; mem. Ga. Ho. of Reps. from 69th Dist., 1992—2002; mem. higher edn. com., chair ethics com. Ga. Ho. of Reps., mem. pub. safety com., mem. judiciary com., 1999; mem. Ga. Ho. of Reps. from 58th Dist., 2003—05. Flemming fellow. Mem.: Delta Sigma Theta. Democrat. Baptist. Home: 3009 Miriam Ct Decatur GA 30032

MOBLEY, EMILY RUTH, library director, educator, retired dean; b. Valdosta, Ga., Oct. 1, 1942; d. Emmett and Ruth (Johnson) M. AB in Edn., U. Mich., 1964, AM in Libr. Sci., 1967, postgrad., 1973-76. Tchr. Ecorse (Mich.) Pub. Schs., 1964-65; adminstrv. trainee Chrysler Corp., Highland Park, Mich., 1965-66, engring. libr., 1966-69; libr. II Wayne State U., Detroit, 1969-72, libr. III, 1972-75; staff asst. GM Rsch. Labs. Libr., Warren, Mich., 1976-78, supr. reader svcs., 1978-81; libr. dir. GMI Engring. & Mgmt. Inst., Flint, Mich., 1982-86; assoc. dir. for pub. svcs. & collection devel., assoc. prof. libr. sci. Purdue U. Librs., West Lafayette, Ind., 1986-89, acting dir. librs., assoc. prof. libr. sci., 1989, dean librs., prof. libr. sci., 1989—2004; Esther Ellis Norton Disting. Prof. Libr. Sci. Purdue U., West Lafayette, Ind., 1997—2008. Adj. lectr. U. Mich. Sch. Libr. Sci., Ann Arbor, 1974-75, 83-86; grants reader Libr. of Mich., 1980-81; project dir. Mideastern Mich. Region Libr. Cooperation, 1984-86; cons. Libr. Coop. of Macomb, 1985-86, Clark-Atlanta U., 1990-91; search com. for new dir. of libr. Smithsonian Instn., 1988; mem. GM Pub. Affairs Subcom. on Introducing Minorities to Engring.; presenter in field. Author: Special Libraries at Work, 1984; mem. editl. bd. Reference Svcs. Rev., 1989-2004, Infomanage, 1993-97. Corp. vis. com. for librs. MIT, 1990-2004, Carnegie-Mellon U., 1998—; mem. Ind. Statewide Libr. Automation Task Force, 1989-90; state tech. strategy subcom. on info. tech. and telecomms. Ind. Corp. for Sci. & Tech., 1989; nat. adv. com. Libr. of Congress, 1988; trustee Libr. of Mich., 1983-86, v.p., 1986, long range plan com., 1979-82, task force on document access and delivery, 1977-79; info. project mem. Rep. Nat. Conv., 1980; bd. dirs. Small Farms Assn., Southfield, Mich., Lafayette Symphony Orch., YWCA. Recipient Bausch & Lomb award, 1960, Cert. for Outstanding Performance in Acad. Achievement State of Mich. Ho. of Reps., 1976, Spl. Tribute for Outstanding Contbns. Libr. of Mich. Bd. Trustees, 1986, Disting. Alumnus award U. Mich. Sch. Info. & Libr. Studies, 1989; U. Mich. Regents Alumni scholar, 1960-64; CIC doctoral fellow in libr. sci., 1973-76. Mem. ALA (com. on accreditation, subcom. to rev. 1972, standards for accreditation 1988-89, OLOS minority internship com. 1988-89, nominating com. 1992-93, mem. coun. resolutions com. 1993-97), Assn. Coll. & Rsch. Librs. (task force on libr. sch. curriculum 1988-89, com. on profl. edn. 1990-92), Libr. Adminstrn. & Mgmt. Assn., Assn. Rsch. Librs. (bd. dirs. 1990-93), Spl. Librs. Assn. (pres. 1987-88, fellow 1991, com. mem.), Alpha Kappa Alpha, Phi Kappa Phi, Sigma Xi, Iron Key. Home: 10010 Lost Hollow Ln Missouri City TX 77459 Business E-Mail: ermo@umich.edu.

MOBLEY, STACEY J., retired chemical company executive, lawyer; b. Chester, Pa., Nov. 19, 1945; s. James Otis and Retha B. (Hollis) M.; m. Joan Thompson, Aug. 28, 1970; children: Michele. BS in Pharmacy, Howard U., 1968, JD, 1971. Bar: Pa. 1972, D.C. 1979, U.S. Supreme Ct. 1979; registered pharmacist. Sr. v.p., chief admin. officer, gen. counsel DuPont Co., Wilmington, Del., 1972—83, dir. fed. affairs Washington, 1983—86, v.p. fed. affairs, 1986—92, sr. v.p. comm. in external affairs Wilmington, Del., 1992—99, chief adminstrv. officer, gen. counsel, 1999—2008, sr. v.p., 2001—08. Bd. dirs. Wilmington Trust Co. State chmn. Del. United Way campaign, 1998; chair Del. Strategic Econ. Coun., 2001. Recipient LexisNexis Corp.egal Times Disting. Legal Svc. award, Alumni award for disting. postgrad. achievement in law, Howard U., 2002, Gerald Kandler Award, Am. Civil Liberties Union of Del, 2006, Award for Excellence in Corp. Practice, Assn. of Corp. Counsel, 2006, Lifetime Achievement award, The Am. Lawyer mag., 2008; named one of America's Top Black Lawyers, Black Enterprise mag., 100 Most Influential Lawyers, Nat. Law Jour., 2006. Mem. Wilmington Club, Carlton Club. Avocations: tennis, golf.

MOCK, FRANK MACKENZIE, lawyer; b. South Bend, Ind., May 17, 1944; s. Frank Carlton and Julia (Baughmann) M.; m. Virginia Johns, Dec. 31, 1974 (div. Feb. 1991); children: Shannon, John, Bridget; m. Christine Mall, June 1995; 1 child, Mackenzie Ann. BA, Duke U., 1966, JD, 1969. Bar: Fla. 1969. Assoc. Mahoney, Adams, Criser, Jacksonville, Fla., 1969-74, ptnr., 1977-92; gen. counsel Builders Investment Group, Valley Forge, Pa., 1974-77; ptnr. Baker & Hostetler, Orlando, Fla., 1992—2006, Ruden McClosky, Orlando, Fla., 2006—08. Mem. ABA, Am. Coll. Mortgage Lawyers, Duval County Bar Assn., Orange County Bar Assn., Dade County Bar Assn., Palm Beach County Bar Assn., Turnaround Mgmt. Assn., Retirement Housing Coun. Fla. Republican. Episcopalian. Avocations: hiking, fishing, reading. Home: 2147 Santa Antilles Rd Orlando FL 32806-1533 Home Phone: 407-894-6402; Office Phone: 407-418-6211. Business E-Mail: frank.mock@lowndes-law.com.

MOCKETT, ALFRED T., marketing company executive; b. Lancashire, Eng., 1949; Grad., U. London, 1971, Caes Run U., UK, 1976. Joined Memorex Telex Corp., Tulsa, 1977, v.p. fin., sr. v.p. world trade, exec. v.p. sales and svc., pres. US sales and svc., mng. dir., 1988—91; mng. dir. spl. bus. divsn. Brit. Telecomm. PLC, 1991—92, mng. dir. bus. comm. divsn., 1992—94, pres., CEO BT Worldwide, 1994—2000, CEO, 2000—01; chmn., CEO CGI Technologies and Solutions, Inc. (formerly American Mgmt. Systems, Inc.), 2001—06, Motive, Inc., 2006—08, Corinthian Capital, LLC, 2008—10; CEO Dex One Corp. (formerly R.H. Donnelley Corp.), 2010—. Vice chmn. Wolftrap Found. for Arts; trustee Com. Econ. Devel. Office: Dex One Corp 1001 Winstead Dr Cary NC 27513

MODDELMOG, HALA, fast food chain executive; b. Ga., Jan. 3, 1956; BA in English, Ga. Southern U., 1979; MA in Journalism & Mass Comm., U. Ga. Pres. Church's Chicken, 1995—2004; founder Catalytic Ventures, 2004—; pres., CEO Susan G. Komen for the Cure, Dallas, 2006—09; pres. Arby's Restaurant Group, Inc., Atlanta, 2010—. Bd. dirs. Fiesta Brands, Inc., 2006—08, HyperActive Technologies, 2006—07, AMN Healthcare Services, Inc., 2008—, Amerigroup Corp., 2009—. Bd. trustees Ga. Southern U. Found., 2005—08, Clark Atlanta U., 2004—06. Recipient Rising Star award, Restaurant Hospitality, Pacesetter award, Roundtable for Women in Food Svc., Woman of Achievement award, YMCA Greater Atlanta, 2003, Disting. Alumnus award, American Assn. State College & Universities (AASCU), 2009. Mem.: Internat. Franchise Assn. (Bonny LeVine award). Office: Arby's Restaurant Group Inc 1155 Perimeter Center West 12th Fl Atlanta GA 30338

MODELL, JEROME HERBERT, anesthesiologist, educator; b. St. Paul, Sept. 9, 1932; s. William and Frieda (Singer) M.; m. Shirley Graves, Nov. 25, 1977; children— Charles, Jack, Julie. BA, U. Minn., 1954, BS, MD, U. Minn., 1957; DSc (hon.), U. Fla., 2004. Intern U.S. Naval Hosp., St. Albans, NY, 1957-58, resident, 1958-60; practice medicine specializing in anesthesiology Gainesville, Fla., 1969—; attending staff U.S. Naval Hosp., St. Albans, 1960-61, chief anesthesiology Pensacola, Fla., 1961-63; asso. prof. dept. anesthesiology U. Miami (Fla.) Sch. Medicine, 1963-69; prof., chmn. dept. anesthesiology U. Fla. Coll. Medicine, Gainesville, 1969-92, sr. assoc. dean clin. affairs, 1990-95, exec. assoc. dean, 1996-97, interim dean, 1997; assoc. v.p. U. Fla. Health Sci. Ctr. Affiliations, 1992-96, courtasy prof. psychiatry, 2010—. Assoc. v.p. U. Fla. Health Sci., 1998-2000, emeritus prof. 2000—, courtesy prof. large animal scis., 1999—. Author: The Pathophysiology and Treatment of Drowning and Near-Drowning, 1971, (with others) Introduction to Life Support, 1973; also numerous scientific articles. Served to lt. comdr. USN, 1957-63. Recipient Rsch. Career Devel. award, NIH, 1967—69, Lifetime Achievement award, Am. Soc. Critical Care Anesthesiologists, 1991. Mem. AMA, AAAS, Assn. U. Anesthetists, Am. Soc. Anesthesiologists (Disting. Svc. award, 2005), N.Y. Acad. Scis., Am. Coll. Chest Physicians. Home: PO Box 14347 Gainesville FL 32604-2347 Office: U Fla Coll Medicine PO Box 100254 Gainesville FL 32610-0254 Office Phone: 352-265-8076. Business E-Mail: jmodell@anest.ufl.edu.

MODZELESKI, WILLIAM, former federal agency administrator; BA in Polit. Sci., U. Bridgeport; MPA, C.W. Post Coll. Juvenile justice and corrections specialist US Dept. Justice, staff dir. coordinating coun. on juvenile justice and delinquency prevention, dir. family violence programs, fed. coord. High Impact Cities Program; exec. dir. Nat. Commn. on Drug-Free Schs. US Dept. Edn., Washington; assoc. dep. under sec. US Dept. Edn. Office of Safe and Drug-Free Schs., acting asst. dep. sec., 2011; sr. cons. SIGMA Threat Mgmt. Associates., Alexandria, Va. Contbr. articles to profl. jours. With US Army, Vietnam. Office: SIGMA Threat Mgmt Associates 1800 Diagonal Rd Alexandria VA 22314*

MOEHLMAN, MICHAEL SCOTT, lawyer; b. Columbus, Ohio, Apr. 11, 1938; s. Arthur Henry and Marguerite Caroline M.; m. Carol Jean Shafer, Sept. 28, 1963; 1 son, Matthew. BA, Harvard U., 1960; LLB, U. Tex., 1963. Bar: Tex. 1963. With Strasburger & Price, Houston. Bd. dirs. St. Martin's Episcopal Children's Ctr. Fellow Tex. Bar Found.; mem. ABA (com. bank securities), Internat. Bar Assn., Tex. Bar Assn. (com. revision corp. law), Houston Bar Assn. (judicature com.), Tex.-Mex. Bar Assn., Am. Judicature Soc., Houston Bar Found. (chmn. bd. dirs.), Phi Delta Phi. Clubs: Houston (chmn. fin. com., bd. dirs., pres.), Houston Racquet, Houston Yacht, Harvard (Boston), Harvard (NYC), St. Charles Bay Hunting, Colonneh Club. Episcopalian. Office: Strasburger & Price 909 Fannin St Ste 2300 Houston TX 77010-1036 Office Phone: 713-951-5684. Business E-Mail: michael.moehlman@strasburger.com.

MOEHRING, MARY BETH, food service executive; b. Balt., Md. m. Bill Moehring. Grad., Bryn Mawr Sch.; BS in Hotel & Restaurant Mgmt., U. Houston. Joined Sysco Corp., 1980, various positions, v.p., learning and orgnl. capability. Mem. Exec. Woman's Partnership, Woman's Foodservice Forum; mem., Conrad N. Hilton Coll. U. Houston. Avocations: travel, hiking, cooking. Office: SYSCO Corp 1390 Enclave Pky Houston TX 77077-2099 Office Phone: 281-584-1390. Office Fax: 281-584-2721. Business E-Mail: mary.moehring@corp.sysco.com.

MOELING, WALTER GOOS, IV, lawyer; b. Quantico, Va., Feb. 16, 1943; s. Walter Goos III and Dorothy M.; m. Nell Frances Askew, Aug. 27, 1965; children: Charles H., Christine E. BA, Duke U., 1965, JD, 1968. Bar: Ga. 1968. Assoc. Bryan Cave, Atlanta, 1968-75, ptnr., 1975—. Bd. dirs. So. Banking Law and Policy Conf., 1989-96, Southeastern Conf. for Bank Dirs., 1996—, Children's Rehab. Ctr., Atlanta, 1982—, Gatchell Home, Atlanta, 1983-99; bd. dirs. Frazer Ctr., 1989—, chmn. bd. dirs., 1993. Mem. ABA (mem. banking com. 1986—), Ga. C. of C. (bd. dirs. 1998-2000), Ga. Bar Assn., Ga. Bankers Assn. (assoc., chairperson bank counsel sect. 1992-95, bd. dirs. 1998-2000), Cmty. Bankers Assn. (assoc.), Capital City Club, Willow Point Country Club. Democrat. Unitarian Universalist. Avocations: golf, fly fishing. Office: Bryan Cave LLP One Atlantic Ctr 1201 W Peachtree St Atlanta GA 30309-1740 Office Phone: 404-572-6629. Business E-Mail: watt.moeling@bryancave.com.

MOELLER, DADE WILLIAM, environmental engineer, educator; b. Grant, Fla., Feb. 27, 1927; s. Robert A. and Victoria (Bolton) M.; m. Betty Jean Radford, Oct. 7, 1949 (dec. Oct. 1998); children: Garland Radford, Mark Bolton, William Kehne, Matthew Palmer, Elisabeth Anne. BSCE, Ga. Inst. Tech., 1947, MS in Environ. Engring., 1948; PhD in Nuc. Engring., N.C. State U., 1957. Commd. jr. asst. san. engr. USPHS, 1948, advanced through grades to san. engr. dir., 1961; rsch. engr. Los Alamos (N.Mex.) Sci. Lab., 1949-52; staff asst. Radiol. Health Program, Washington, 1952-54; rsch. assoc. Oak Ridge Nat. Lab., 1956-57; chief radiol. health tng. Taft San. Engring. Ctr., Cin., 1957-61; officer charge Northeastern Radiol. Health Lab., Winchester, Mass., 1961-66; assoc. dir. Kresge Ctr. Environ. Health, Harvard Sch. Pub. Health, 1966-83, prof. engring. in environ. health, head dept. environ. health scis., 1968-83, dir. Office of Continuing Edn., 1982-84, assoc. dean continuing edn., 1985-93; environ. cons., 1993—; pres. Dade Moeller & Assocs., Inc., 1993—2003, chmn. bd., 2005—; prof. emeritus Harvard Sch. Pub. Health, 2006—. Cons. radiol. health. Author: (textbook) Environmental Health, 3rd edit., 2005; contbr. articles to profl. jours. Chmn. Am. Bd. Health Physics, 1967-70; mem. com. 4 Internat. Commn. on Radiol. Protection, 1978-85; chmn. nat. air pollution manpower devel. adv. com. U.S. EPA, 1972-75; mem. adv. com. reactor safeguards U.S. NRC, 1973-88, chmn., 1976, chmn. adv. com. nuc. waste, 1988-93; chmn. sci. and tech. rev. panel Office of Civilian Radioactive Waste Mgmt., U.S. Dept. Energy, 2003-. Recipient Disting. Engring. Alumnus award, N.C. State U., 2001, Disting. Prof. Emeritus award of merit, Sch. Pub. Health, Harvard U., 2006, honored, Nat. Coun. Radiation Protection and Measurement, 2008; named to Ga. Inst. Tech. Engring. Hall of Fame, 1999. Fellow Am. Pub. Health Assn., Am. Nuc. Soc.; mem. AAAS, Am. Acad. Environ. Engrs., Nat. Coun. Radiation Protection and Measurements (hon.), NAE, Am. Acad. Health Physics Soc. (pres. 1971-72, Robley D. Evans Commemorative medal 2003, William McAdams Outstanding Svc. award 2005).

MOELLERING, JOHN HENRY, aviation maintenance company executive; b. Ft. Wayne, Ind., Feb. 4, 1938; s. Robert Charles and Irene Pauline (Nolde) M.; m. Karla Louise Fritzsche, Dec. 21, 1963; children: John Henry, Matthew C., Ann Elizabeth. BS, U.S. Mil. Acad., 1959; MS, U. Calif., Berkeley, 1962; postgrad., Army Command and Gen. Staff Coll., 1971-72, Army War Coll., 1976-77. Registered profl. engr., La. Commd. 2d lt. U.S. Army, 1959, advanced through grades to lt. gen., 1985; aide de camp Combat Devel. Command, 1961-63; command and staff 24th Inf. Div., Fed. Republic Germany, 1964-67; ops. officer Engr. Group, Vietnam, 1967-68; instr. civil engring., asst. prof. history U.S. Mil. Acad., 1968-71; with Office Army Chief of Staff, Pentagon, 1972-73; White House staff, 1973-74; bn. comdr. 101st Airborne Div., 1974-76; dist. engr. Vicksburg, Miss., 1977-79; exec. to Army Chief of Staff, Pentagon, 1979-81; asst. div. comdr. 9th Inf. Div., Ft. Lewis, Wash., 1981-82; commandant West Point, NY, 1982-84; comdg. gen. Ft. Leonard Wood, Mo., 1984-85; asst. to chmn. Joint Chiefs of Staff, Pentagon, Washington, 1985-87; corp. v.p. Automatic Data Processing, Inc., San Ramon, Calif., 1987-90; pres., chief exec. officer Lear Siegler Mgmt. Svcs. Corp., Oklahoma City, 1990-93; pres. UNC Aviation Svcs., Annapolis, Md., 1993-97; pres., CEO Lear Siegler Svcs., Inc., Annapolis, Md., 1997—2002, JM Associates, Chapel Hill, NC, 2002—. Bd. dirs. USAA, 1996—, chmn., 2007—; bd. dirs. Lear Sigeler Svcs., Inc., Indsl. Coll. of the Armed Forces; frequent lectr. Nat. Def. U.; mem. adv. bd. Sch. Bus. Adminstrn. The Citadel; adj. faculty Kenan-Flagler bus. sch. U. NC, 2006—. Editor, contbr.: Evolution of Modern Warfare, 1969, Battalion Commanders Speak Out, 1977. Mem. Sci. Def. Bd., The Pentagon; chmn. Class of '59 fund com. U.S. Mil. Acad., 1984—89. Decorated Def. DSM, Army DSM, Legion of Merit, Bronze Star; White House fellow, 1973-74. Mem.: Nat. Def. Indsl. Assn. (bd. dirs.), Phi Kappa Phi. Office: 50130 Manly Chapel Hill NC 27517-8565 Personal E-mail: johnmoellering@hotmail.com.

MOESER, JAMES CHARLES, music educator, former academic administrator; b. Colorado City, Tex., Apr. 3, 1939; s. Charles Victor and Virginia (James) M.; m. Jesse Kaye Edwards, Jan. 26, 1963 (div. July 1984); children: James Christopher, Kathryn Carter; m. Susan Kay Smith Dickerson, June 21, 1987. B.Mus., U. Tex., 1961, M.M., 1964; postgrad. (Fulbright grantee), Hochschule fur Musik, Berlin, 1961-62; D.MA (Univ. fellow), U. Mich., 1966. Chmn. dept. organ, asst. prof. organ U. Kans., 1966-69, assoc. prof., 1969-74, prof., 1974-86, dean Sch. Fine Arts, 1975-86, Carl and Ruth Althaus disting. prof. organ, 1985-86; organist, choirmaster Plymouth Congl. Ch., Lawrence, Kans., 1967-86; organist nat. conf. Music Tchrs. Nat. Assn., Portland, Oreg., 1972, LA, 1974; dean Coll. Arts and Architecture, Pa. State U., State College, 1986—91; v.p., academic affairs & provost U. SC, 1991—96; chancellor U. Nebr., Lincoln, Nebr., 1996—2000, U. NC, Chapel Hill, 2000—08; prof. music Inst. for Arts and Humanities, U. NC, 2008—. Concert organist, on tour, W. Ger., 1977, Lisbon (Portugal) Festival, 1978, 81, recitals for, Musica Festiva da Costa Verde, Portugal, 1981; organist concerts, W. Ger., 1982, 86, 87; world premier Paul Creston's 3d Symphony for Organ and Orchestra, Kennedy Ctr., Washington, 1982. Bd. govs. Josephson Inst. Ethics, 1998-2002; trustee N.C. Symphony Soc., Inc., 2001—09; mem. vis. com. Meml. Ch., Harvard U. Recipient Palmer Christian award U. Mich., 1981, Disting. Alumnus awrd Grad. Sch. U. Tex., 2001; Kent fellow Danforth Found.; Danforth Assoc. Mem. Am. Guild Organists (past dean chpt., nat. dir. student groups 1973-75, nat. chmn. com. on profl. edn. 1983—, chmn. 2d nat. conf. on organ pedagogy 1984, 3d nat. conf. 1986, v.p. 1986—); fellow Am. Acad. Arts & Scis. Episcopalian. Office: Inst Arts and Humanities Campus Box 3322 Chapel Hill NC 27599-3322 Home: 505 N Boundary St Chapel Hill NC 27514 Office Phone: 919-843-2558. E-mail: james_moeser@unc.edu.

MOFFATT, JOYCE ANNE, performing company executive; b. Grand Rapids, Mich., Jan. 3, 1936; d. John Barnard and Ruth Lillian (Pellow) M. BA in Lit., U. Mich., 1957, MA in Theatre, 1960; HHD (hon.), Profl. Sch. Psychology, San Francisco, 1991. Stage mgr., lighting designer Off-Broadway plays; costume, lighting and set designer, stage mgr. stock cos., 1954-62; nat. subscription mgr. Theatre Guild/Am. Theatre Soc., NYC, 1965-67; subscription mgr. Theatre, Inc.-Phoenix Theatre, NYC, 1963-67; cons. NYC Ballet and NYC Opera, 1967-70; asst. house mgr. NY State Theater, 1970-72; dir. ticket sales City Ctr. of Music and Drama, Inc., NYC, 1970-72; prodn. mgr. San Antonio's Symphony/Opera, 1973-75; gen. mgr. San Antonio Symphony/Opera, 1975-76, 55th St. Dance Theater Found., Inc., NYC, 1976-77, Ballet Theatre Found., Inc./Am. Ballet Theatre, NYC, 1977-81; v.p. prodn. Radio City Music Hall Prodns., Inc., NYC, 1981-83; artist-in-residence CCNY, 1981—; propr. mgmt. cons. firm for performing arts NYC, 1983—; exec. dir. San Francisco Ballet Assn., 1987-93; mng. dir. Houston Ballet Assoc., 1993-95; gen. mgr. Chgo. Music and Dance Theater, Inc., 1995—2004. Cons. Ford Found., NY State Coun. on Arts, Kennedy Ctr. Performing Arts., Lensic Performing Arts Ctr., Santa Fe, Bloomington Cultural Dist., Ill., Sheboygan Theater Found., Wis., The Arts Partnership Spartanburg, SC; mem. dance panels NY State Coun. on Arts, 1979-81; mem. panels for Support to Prominent Orgns. and Dance, Calif. Arts Coun., 1988-92. Appointee San Francisco Cultural Affairs Task Force, 1991; chmn. bd. dir. Tex. Inst. Arts in Edn., 1994—; trustee Internat. Alliance of Theatrical Stage Employees Local 16 Pension and Welfare Fund, 1991-94; bd. dir. Rudolf Nureyev Dance Found., Chgo., 1998—, Tryon Fine Arts Ctr., NC, St. Luke's Hosp. Found., COlumbus, NC. Mem. Assn. Theatrical Press Agts. and Mgrs., Actors Equity Assn., United Scenic Artists Local 829, San Francisco Visitors and Conv. Bur. (bd. dirs.). Office Phone: 864-457-4575.

MOFFETT, JAMES ROBERT, mining executive; b. Houma, La., Aug. 16, 1938; s. Robert E. and Mary G. (Pollack) M.; m. Louise C. Hohmann, June 5, 1960; children: Crystal Louise, James R. BS, U. Tex., 1961; MS, Tulane U., 1963. Cons. geologist oil and gas industry, New Orleans, 1964-69; v.p. founding ptnr. McMoRan Exploration Co., New Orleans, 1969-74; pres., chief exec. officer McMoRan Oil & Gas Co., New Orleans, 1974-81, 81-85, chmn., chief exec. officer, 1985—97, dir., from 1974; vice-chmn. Freeport McMoRan Inc., New Orleans, 1981-85, chmn., chief exec. officer, 1984—97, chmn., 1997—; co-chmn. McMoRan Exploration Co. Mem. Nat. Petroleum Council, Washington, 1979, Commn. on the Future of South, 1986; bd. dirs. La. Energy Nat. PAC, Metairie, La., 1979, World Trade Ctr., New Orleans, Am. Cancer Soc. Greater New Orleans, Bus. Task Force Edn., Inc.; chmn. bd. La. Coun. Fiscal Reform; chmn. bus. coun. New Orleans and River Region, 1985-87. 2nd lt. U.S. Army, 1961-68, capt. Res. ret. Recipient T award Ex Students Assn. U. Tex., 1960, Hornblower Yr. award Pub. Relations Soc. Am., 1986, Vol. Yr. award Urban League Greater New Orleans, 1987; Minnie Stevens Piper Found. scholar U. Tex., 1960, Jacques E. Yenni, S.J. award Loyola U. of New Orleans for Outstanding Community Svc., Jr. Achievement Bus. Hall of Fame award, 1987, Loyola U. of New Orleans' Integritas Vitae award, 1988; named One of Ten Outstanding Persons of 1985 Inst. for Human Understanding, New Orleans Mem. All Am. Wildcatters, New Orleans Geol. Soc., Petroleum Club New Orleans, Greater New Orleans Mktg. Com. (exec. com. 1987), Geology Found U. Tex. (adv. council 1972-85), Devel. bd. U. Tex., La. Ind. producers Royalty Owners Assn. South La. Mid-Continent Oil Gas Assn. (v.p.), Dinner Steering Com. (Disting. Citizen award 1983, 85 Boy Scouts Am. New Orleans div.), Green Wave Club. Republican. Mailing: Freeport-McMoRan Copper & Gold Co PO Box 61119 New Orleans LA 70161

MOFFITT, TIM D., state legislator; 3 children. Founder, CEO Moffitt Internat.; mem. Dist. 116 NC House of Representatives, 2008—. Republican. Office: 3182 Sweeten Creek Rd Asheville NC 28803 Address: North Carolina House of Representatives 16 W Jones St Room 1025 Raleigh NC 27601-1096 Office Phone: 828-651-8550, 919-715-3012. Business E-Mail: Tim.Moffitt@ncleg.net.

MOGLIA, JOSEPH H., college football coach, brokerage house executive; b. Apr. 1, 1949; m. Amy Jardine; 4 children from previous marriage. BA, Fordham U., Bronx, NY, 1971; MA, U. Del., 1974. Asst. football coach Fordham Prep. Sch., Bronx, 1968—70; economics, polit. sci. & European history tchr., head football & wresting coach and freshman baseball coach Archmere Acad., Claymont, Del., 1971—74; economics & European history tchr., head football & baseball coach Penncrest HS, Media, Pa., 1975—78; defensive secondary & spl. teams coach, recruiting coord. Lafayette Coll. Leopards, Easton, Pa., 1978—80; def. coord. Dartmouth Coll. Big Green, Hanover, NH, 1981—83; positions including bond salesman, head NY & global fixed income sales and head mcpl. divsn. Merrill Lynch & Co., Inc., 1983—97, sr. v.p., head investment performance & product group, 1997—2001; CEO TD Ameritrade Holding Corp., Omaha, 2001—08, non-exec. chmn., 2008—; exec. advisor to head football coach Bo Pellini U. Nebr. Cornhuskers, Lincoln, 2008—10; head coach, pres. Omaha Nighthawks, United Football League, Nebr., 2011; head football coach Coastal Carolina U. Chanticleers, Conway, SC, 2011—. Bd. dirs. TD Ameritrade Holding Corp., 2001—, AXA Financial, Inc., 2002—, MONY Life Ins. Co. Author: Perimeter Attack Offense, 1981. Bd. dirs. Nat. Italian American Found. Recipient Ellis Island Medal of Honor. Office: Coastal Carolina Univeristy Football Program c/o Athletics Dept 132 Chanticleer Dr W Conway SC 29528 also: TD Ameritrade Holding Corp 4211 S 102nd St Omaha NE 68127-1031

MOHAMADI, MASOUD, retired surgeon; b. Tehran, Iran, June 8, 1937; arrived in U.S., 1962; children: Hooman, Michele, Robert; m. Soheila Emami, 1990. MD, U. Tehran, 1961. Diplomate Am. Bd. Surgery. Intern Coney Island Hosp., NYC, 1962-63; resident in gen. surgery Maimonides Med. Ctr., Bklyn., 1963-67; fellow in vasc. surgery SUNY, Bklyn., 1967-68. Mem. AMA. Personal E-mail: mmohamadi@tampabay.rr.com.

MOHLER, RICHARD ALBERT, JR., academic administrator, theologian; b. Lakeland, Fla., Oct. 9, 1959; s. Richard Albert Sr. and Janet Rae (Johnson) M.; m. Mary Ann Kahler, July 16, 1983; children: Mary Katherine, Christopher Albert. BA magna cum laude, Samford U., 1980; MDiv, So. Bapt. Theol. Sem., Louisville, 1983, PhD, 1989; postgrad., St. Meinrad Sch. Theology, 1985, Oxford U., Eng., 1986. Ordained min. So. Bapt. Ch. Pastor Union Grove Bapt. Ch., Bedford, Ky., 1982-87; asst. to pres., coord. found. support, dir. capital funding So. Bapt. Theol. Sem., Louisville, 1983-89, pres., 1993—; editor The Christian Index, Atlanta, 1989-93, prof. christian theology, 1996—, Joseph Emerson Brown prof. Christian theology, 2005—. Assoc. dir. The So. Sem. Found., 1983-89; rsch. fellow Ethics and Religious Liberty Commn., 1998—; bd. dirs. Focus on the Family; lectr. in field. Assoc. editor Preaching, 1985-93, contbg. editor, 1993—; gen. editor: The Gods of the Age of the God of the Ages?, 1993; editor-in-chief The So. Bapt. Jour. Theology, 1997—; columnist Religion News Svc., 1998—; sr. corr. World Mag., 1997—; mem. editl. bd. Salem Broadcasting, 1999—; host (radio programs) Truth On the Line, 2001—10, The Albert Mohler Program; author daily Crosswalk Commentaries, Engaging Current issues with Timeless Truth, 2008, A Christian Confronts the New Atheists, 2008, Desire & Deceit: The Real Cost of New Sexual Tolerence, 2008, He is not Silent: Preaching in a Postmodern world, 2008, The Dissappearance of God: Dangerous Beliefs in the New Spiritual Openness, 2009, Words from the Fire: Hearing the Voice of God in the ID Commandants, 2009; contbr. articles to profl. jours. Pres., chmn. Coun. of Sem. Pres. of So. Bapt. Conv., 1996—, chmn., Greater Louisville Billy Graham Crusade, 2001. Named one of 40 Rising Evang. Leaders, Christianity Today, 1996, one of 96 Southerners to Watch, Atlanta Jour. and Constitution, 1996, one of 50 Young Leaders Under 40 years of age TIME Mag., one of Emerging Leaders in Edn. CHANGE Mag., 1998. Mem. Am. Acad. Religion, Soc. Biblical Lit., Evang. Theol. Soc., Evang. Philos. Soc., So. Bapt. Hist. Soc., Bapt. Pub. Rels. Assn., So. Bapt. Press Assn., Evang. Press Assn., Nat. Assn. Evangs., Ga. Bapt. Hist. Soc., Rotary Internat., Phi Kappa Phi, Omicron Delta Kappa. Achievements include being named one of 50 young leaders under 40 years of age TIME Mag. Office: So Bapt Theol Sem 2825 Lexington Rd Louisville KY 40280-0001 Home Phone: 502-897-4121; Office Phone: 502-897-4121. Personal E-mail: mail@albertmohler.com. Business E-Mail: presoffice@sbts.edu, mohler@sbts.edu.

MOHR, LAWRENCE CHARLES, physician; b. S.I., NY, July 8, 1947; s. Lawrence Charles Sr. and Mary Estelle (Dawsey) M.; m. Linda Johnson, June 14, 1970; 1 child, Andrea Marie. AB with highest honors, U. N.C., 1975, MD, 1979. Diplomate Am. Bd. Internal Medicine. Commd. 2d lt. U.S. Army, 1967, advanced through grades to col., 1989; med. intern Walter Reed Army Med. Ctr., Washington, 1979-80, resident in medicine, 1980-82, chief resident, 1982-83, attending physician, 1984-86, pulmonary fellow, 1986-87; command surgeon 9th Inf. Div., Ft. Lewis, Wash., 1983-84; med. cons. Madigan Army Med. Ctr., Tacoma, 1983-84; White House physician Washington, 1987-93; asst. prof. medicine Uniformed Svcs. U. of the Health Scis., Bethesda, Md., 1984-91; assoc. prof. medicine Uniformed Svcs. U. Health Scis., Bethesda, Md., 1991-94; assoc. clin. prof. medicine George Washington U., Washington, 1990-94; prof. medicine Med. U. S.C., Charleston, 1994—, dir. environ. bioscis. program, 1995—. Attending physician Med. U. Hosp., Charleston, 1994—, Charleston Meml. Hosp., 1994—; mem. Working Group on Disability in U.S. Presidents, 1995—. Editor: International Case Studies in Risk Assessment and Magagement, 1997, Biomarkers, Medical and Workplace Applications, 1998; contbr. articles to profl. jours. and books. Bd. dirs. Internat. Lung Found., Washington; mem. adv. bd. Nat. Mus. Health and Medicine, Washington; mem. sci. adv. bd. Consortium in Environ. Risk Evaluation; prin. investigator Consortium in Molecular Epidemiology and Biomarker Rsch. Decorated Silver Star, Bronze Star with 2 V devices and 3 oak leaf clusters, Purple Heart, Meritorious Svc. medal with oak leaf cluster, Air medal, Army Commendation medal with oak leaf cluster, D.S.M.; recipient Erskine award Walter Reed Army Med. Ctr., 1982; named Outstanding Med. Resident, 1982. Fellow ACP, Am. Coll. Chest Physicians; mem. AMA, Army and Navy Club, Order Mil. Med. Merit, Harbour Club, Phi Beta Kappa. Episcopalian. Avocations: mountain climbing, skiing. Home: 673 Lake Francis Dr Charleston SC 29412-4345 Office: Med U S C Environ Bioscis Program 171 Ashley Ave Charleston SC 29425-0001

MOJTABAI, ANN GRACE, author, educator; b. NYC, June 8, 1937; d. Robert and Naomi (Friedman) Alpher; m. Fathollah Mojtabai, Apr. 27, 1960 (div. 1966); children: Chitra, Ramin. BA in Philosophy, Antioch Coll., 1958; MA in Philosophy, Columbia U., 1968, MS in Libr. Sci., 1970. Lectr. philosophy Hunter Coll., CUNY, 1966-68; libr. CCNY, 1970-76; fellow Radcliffe Inst. Ind. Study, Cambridge, Mass., 1976-78; Briggs-Copeland lectr. on English Harvard U., 1978-83; writer-in-residence U. Tulsa, 1983—2005, Yaddo Found., Saratoga, NY, 1975, 76. Author: Mundome, 1974, The 400 Eels of Sigmund Freud, 1976, A Stopping Place, 1979, Autumn, 1982, Blessed Assurance, 1986, Ordinary Time, 1989, Called Out, 1994, Soon: Tales From Hospice, 1998, All That Road Going, 2008. Recipient Richard and Hinda Rosenthal award Am. Acad. and Inst. Arts and Letters, 1983, Lillian Smith award So. Regional Coun., 1986, Lit. Acad. award AAAL, 1993; Guggenheim fellow, 1981-82 Mem.: PEN, Mark Twain Soc., Tex. Inst. Letters, Phi Beta Kappa. Home: 2329 Woodside Drive Amarillo TX 79124-1036 Personal E-mail: agmojtabai@aol.com.

MOKRASCH, LEWIS CARL, neurochemist, educator; b. St. Paul, May 9, 1930; s. Lewis and Anna (Dvorak) M.; m. Jane Carolyn Church, Apr. 20, 1974. BS magna cum laude, Coll. St. Thomas, 1952; PhD, U. Wis., 1955. Rsch. assoc. dept. psychiatry and neurology La. State U. Med. Center, New Orleans, 1956-57, assoc. prof. dept. biochemistry, 1971-76, prof., 1976-92, prof. emeritus, 1992—, acting head dept., 1978-79. Instr. medicine U. Kans. Med. Center, Kansas City, 1957-59, assoc. in medicine, dir. neurochemistry lab., 1959-62; asst. biochemist McLean Hosp., Belmont, Mass., 1960-64, assoc. biochemist, 1964-71; assoc. dept. biol. chemistry Harvard Med. Sch., Boston, 1964-67; asst. prof., 1967-71; adj. assoc. prof. biology Hellenic Coll., Brookline, Mass., 1969-71; staff scientist Neurosciences Rsch. Programs, Brookline, 1970-71; vis. prof. neurology Duke U. Med. Ctr., 1981-82; grant reviewer neurological diseases and blindness NIMH, 1969-92; lectr. in field Co-author: Myelin, 1971; contbr. articles to profl. jours., 1952-94; reviewer: jours. Sci., FASEB, Jour. Biol. Chemistry, 1956-92. Pres. Belmont Preservation Soc., 1969; candidate Bd. Selectman, Belmont, 1969; insp. Forsyth County Adult Care Home Cmty. Adv. Com., Hospice, Sr. Fin. Care, Winston-Salem, Sr. Svcs. Program, Winston Salem, 1992-, Citizens Quality Nursing Home Care, New Orleans, 1987-92; sr. leader Duke Long Term Care Program Edn. Com., 1999; edn. com. Shepherd Ctr., 1996; Reynolda House Mus. Am. Art, 2007-, Reynolda Gardens. Grantee NIMH, 1973-74, Nat. Inst. Neurol. Disability and Blindness, 1957-90, Schlieder Found., 1971-72, 83-84, La. Bd. Regents, 1986-88. Fellow Am. Assn. Clin. Chemists; mem. Am. Soc. Neurochemistry (local chmn. 1974), Am. Soc. Biol. Chemists, Soc. Neurosci. (founder, pres. local chpt. 1974-75), Soc. Rsch. Adminstrs. (membership chmn. New Eng. sect.), Nat. Citizens Coalition Nursing Home Reform, Am. Assn. Individual Investors (founder, past pres., sec. Piedmont chpt.). Libertarian. Achievements include first demonstration of adaptive enzyme regulation in animals and allosteric control of fructose bisphosphatase, of incorporation of hydrouracil into transfer RNA, of thermogenic mechanism for arousing hibernators, of metabolic control in hibernation, of altered hydrophobic proteins in neurological disorders, of biosynthesis of hydrophobic proteins and mitochondrial proteins in brain in vitro, of altered transport processes in cells of neurological disease victims, of defective transport of acetylcholine precursors into cells of Alzheimer's victims and that such transport is modulatable; development of coestimation method for ketoses, aldoses, and pentoses; first isolation in pure form of receptor hydrophobic proteins from mammalian brain. Home: 3609 Bechler Ln Winston Salem NC 27106 Personal E-mail: drlemokrasch@bellsouth.net.

MOLAY, HILARY S., lawyer; b. 1954; BA cum laude, Brandeis U.; JD cum laude, U. Miami. Bar: 1980. Law clk. to Judge Rita C. Davidson Md. Ct. of Appeals; trial atty. civil div. US Dept. Justice, Washington; assoc. Shank, Irwin & Conant, Finley, Kumble, Wagner, Heine, Underberg, Manley, Myerson & Casey; counsel JCPenney Co., Inc.; v.p., gen. counsel, sec. Zale Corp., Irving, Tex., 2000—05, sr. v.p., gen. counsel, corp. sec., 2005—. Mem., adv. bd. corp. counsel symposium Southern Meth. U., 2004; mem., gen. counsel forum Nat. Retail Fedn. Mem.: ABA, Am. Soc. of Corp. Secretaries (mem. corp. practices comm.). Office: Zale Corp 901 W Walnut Hill Ln Irving TX 75038 Office Phone: 972-580-4000. Office Fax: 972-580-5547. Business E-Mail: hmolay@zalecorp.com.

MOLBECK, JOHN N., JR., insurance company executive; Attended Advanced Mgmt. Program, Harvard U.; grad., U. Houston; MBA, Pepperdine U. CPA. Mng. dir. Aon Natural Resources Group; pres., COO Houston Casualty Co. (subs. of HCC Insurance Holdings, Inc.), 1997—2002; CEO Jardine Lloyd Thompson LLC, 2003—05; pres., COO HCC Ins. Holdings Inc., 1997—2002, COO, 2006—09; pres. HCC Insurance Holdings, Inc., 2006—11, CEO, 2009—. Bd. dirs. HCC Ins. Holdings Inc., 2005—. Former officer, bd. dirs. Tex. Surplus Lines Assn.; former chmn. Marine Ins. Seminar. Office: HCC Insurance Holdings Inc 13403 NW Fwy Houston TX 77040 Office Phone: 713-690-7300. Office Fax: 713-462-2401. Business E-Mail: john.molbeck@hcch.com.

MOLEN, JOHN KLAUMINZER, lawyer; b. Gary, Ind., June 13, 1952; s. Franklin B. and Jane Anne (Klauminzer) M.; m. Susan Wilson Blair, Aug. 10, 1985; children: Mary Wilson, Elisabeth Blair. AB with honors, U. NC, 1974, MBA, 1978, JD with honors, 1978. Bar: Ala. 1978. Assoc. Bradley Arant Boult Cummings LLP, Birmingham, Ala., 1978—84, ptnr., 1984—. Mem. Rotary Club Birmingham-Sunrise. Presbyterian. Avocations: sailing, swimming. Office: Bradley Arant Boult Cummings LLP One Federal Pl 1819 5th Ave N Birmingham AL 35203-2104 Office Phone: 205-521-8238. Business E-Mail: jmolen@babc.com.

MOLER, EDWARD HAROLD, retired lawyer; b. Oklahoma City, May 26, 1923; s. Harold Stanley and Rosemary (Callahan) M.; m. Donna Blocksom Cram, Sept. 12, 1964; children: John Frederick, Shelley Elizabeth, Christopher Bryan. BA, U. Okla., 1947, LLB, 1948. Bar: Okla. 1948, U.S. Supreme Ct. 1951. Pvt. practice law, Oklahoma City, 1948-52, 61—; asst. mcpl. counselor, 1952-59; mcpl. counselor, 1959-61; spl. justice Okla. Supreme Ct., 1977. Trustee Oklahoma City Mcpl. Improvement Authority, 1960-61, Dolese Found, 2007-; bd. dirs. Mummers Theatre, Inc., 1969—; bd. dirs. Greater Oklahoma City YMCA, 1981-91. 2d lt. USAAF, 1943-45. Mem. ABA, Okla. Bar Assn., Oklahoma County Bar Assn. (bd. dirs. 1963-67, pres. 1968), Rotary, Phi Delta Phi, Phi Gamma Delta (pres. local chpt. 1946, pres. Nu Omega Housing Assn. 1963-65). Home: 2540 NW Grand Blvd Oklahoma City OK 73116-4110 E-mail: demoler@cox.net.

MOLER, ELIZABETH ANNE, retired utilities executive; b. Salt Lake City, Jan. 24, 1949; d. Murray McClure and Eleanor Lorraine (Barry) M.; m. Thomas Blake Williams, Oct. 19, 1979; children: Blake Martin Williams, Eleanor Bliss Williams. BA, Am. U., 1971; postgraduate student, Johns Hopkins U., Balt., 1972; JD, George Wash. U., 1977. Bar: DC 1978. Chief legis. asst. Senator Floyd Haskell, Washington DC, 1973-75; law clk. Sharon, Pierson, Semmes, Crolius & Finley, Washington DC, 1975-76; profl. staff mem. com. on energy and natural resources US Senate Com. on Energy and Natural Resources, Washington DC, 1976—77, counsel, 1977—86, sr. counsel, 1987-88; mem. FERC, Washington DC, 1988-93, chair, 1993-97; dep. sec. Dept. Energy, Washington DC, 1997-98, acting sec., 1998; ptnr. Vinson & Elkins, Washington DC, 1999; sr. v.p. govt. affairs and policy Unicom Corp. (now Exelon Corp.), 2000—02, exec. v.p., 2002; exec. v.p. govt. and environ. affairs and pub. policy, mem. exec. com.; ret. 7/2010 Exelon Corp., Washington DC. Bd. dirs. Henry M. Jackson Found. Recipient Disting. Svc. award, Nat. Energy Resources Orgn., Energy Daily Ann. Pub. Policy Leadership award, Woman of Yr. award, Women's Coun. Energy and the Environment. Mem. ABA, DC Bar Assn. Democrat. Office Phone: 202-347-7500.

MOLHOEK, KERRINGTON RAMSEY, research scientist; d. Carlton Lee and Linda Ford Ramsey; m. Charles Conrad Molhoek, June 12, 2004. PhD, U. Va., Charlottesville, 2004. Rsch. faculty U. Va. Sch. Medicine, Charlottesville, 2004—. Mem.: U. Va. Alumni Assn. (life), Colonnade Club (life), Nat. Soc. Collegiate Scholars (life), Delta Delta Delta (life). Office: U Va 409 Lane Rd MR-4 Rm 3038 Charlottesville VA 22908 Business E-Mail: klr5w@virginia.edu.

MOLHOLM, KURT NELSON, retired federal agency administrator; b. Denver, June 24, 1937; s. Ervin Maurice and Helen Pauline (Nelson) M.; m. Sonja Dell Williams, Aug. 17, 1967; children: Kevin William, Paul Nelson. BS, U. Oreg., 1959; MS, George Washington U., 1974; grad., Indsl. Coll. Armed Forces, 1974. Computer specialist D.L.A. Adminstrv. Support Ctr., Alexandria, Va., 1963-65; with Hdqrs. Def. Logistics Agy., Alexandria, 1965-85, chief planning and policy office, 1975-76, chief ADP/T tech. div., 1984-85; adminstr. Def. Tech. Info. Ctr., Alexandria, 1985—2005; ret., 2005; pvt. practice, 2007—. Pres. Nat. Fedn. Abstracting and Info. Svcs., Phila., 1993-94, treas., 1990-93; del. Va. Govs. Conf. Librs. Info. Svcs., 1990, Fed. Libr. Pre-White House Conf. On Librs. Info. Sci., 1990; vice chmn. Fed. Libr. and Info. Ctr. Com., 1992-93, 2002-03; chmn. CENDI Group, 1991-94, 99-2001; mem. NATO Agard Tech. Info. Panel, 1985-91, Internat. Coun. Sci. and Tech. Info., 1993—, treas., 1998-2001, chair editl. bd., 1999-2001, pres. 2001—04; mem. Info. Infrastructure Task Force, 1993-97; chair panel 2 U.S. Nat. Commn. on Librs. and Info. Sci. Comprehensive Assessment of Pub. Info. Dissemination, 2000; mem. Handle Sys. Adv. Com., 2001-05; NFAIS Conrad Meml. lectr., 2003; cons. in field, 2006-. 1st lt. U.S. Army, 1960-63. Recipient Meritorious award William A. Jump Meml. Found., 1973, Civilian Svc. award, Def. Logistics Agy., 1991, Exceptional Civilian Svc. award, DLA, 1985, Exceptional Civilan Svc. award, Def. Info. Systems Agy., 2005. Methodist. Personal E-mail: kmolholm@verizon.net.

MOLINAS, GALYA FRAYMAN, soft drinks manufacturing company executive; 2 children. Grad., Bosphorus U. Product mgr. Unilever, 1989—96; consumer mktg. mgr., Trademark Coca-Cola Coca-Cola Pazarlama, 1996—2000; exec. asst. to Ahmet Bozer pres., Eurasia and Middle East Divsn. Coca-Cola Co., 2000—01, mktg. mgr. Turkey, 2001—04, dep. mktg. dir., Ctrl. Europe Divsn., 2004—05, dep. mktg. dir. Russia, 2004—05, mktg. dir., Eurasia and Middle East Divsn., 2005—07, mktg. dir., Eurasia Group, 2007—08, dep. pres., bus. unit. Turkey, 2008—09, pres., bus. unit, 2009—. Founding mem. Coca-Cola Life Plus Fouund., chmn., Turkey; mem. Women's Leadership Coun. Office: The Coca-Cola Co 1 Coca-Cola Plz Atlanta GA 30313-2499 Office Phone: 404-676-2121. Office Fax: 404-676-6792. Business E-Mail: gfrayman.molinas@na.ko.com.

MOLINEAUX, CHARLES BORROMEO, lawyer, arbitrator, columnist, poet; b. NYC, Sept. 27, 1930; s. Charles Borromeo and Marion Frances (Belter) M.; m. Patricia Leo Devereux, July 2, 1960; children: Charles, Stephen, Christopher, Patricia, Peter, Elizabeth. BS cum laude, Georgetown U., 1950; JD, St. Johns U., 1959. Bar: N.Y. 1959, Mass. 1981, D.C. 1988. From assoc. to ptnr. Nevius, Jarvis & Pilz and successor firms, NYC, 1959-77; ptnr. Gadsby & Hannah, NYC, 1978-80; v.p., gen. counsel Perini Corp., Framingham, Mass., 1980-87; pvt. practice Washington, 1987—. Adj. faculty Internat. Law Inst., Washington, 1989—. Author numerous poems. Mem. adv. bd. Inst. for Transnat. Arbitration; committeeman Rep. Party, Nassau County, NY, 1965—71, mem. exec. com., committeeman Fairfax County, Va., 1989. 1st lt. US Army, 1954—56. Fellow Am. Bar Found.; mem. ASCE, Am. Arbitration Assn. (constrn. ADR task force 1994—), Chartered Inst. Arbitrators, Fedn. Internat. Engrs.-Conseils (Assoc. Gen. Contractors del. constrn. contract com., Louis Prangey award for svc. to profession cons. engring. 1996), Soc. Constrn. Arbitrators London, Del. Hist. Soc., London Ct. Internat. Arbitration, Fellowship Cath. Scholars. Roman Catholic. Home: 8321 Weller Ave Mc Lean VA 22102-1717 Office: 8201 Greensboro Dr Ste 300 Mc Lean VA 22102 Personal E-mail: cmlnx@aol.com.

MOLITERNO, DAVID J., cardiologist, educator; b. Flint, Mich., Oct. 29, 1960; m. Judith Ann Delp; children: Nathaniel, Benjamin. BS with honors, U. Mich., 1982; MD, Med. Coll. Va., 1987. Diplomate Am. Bd. Internal Medicine, Am. Bd. Cardiovascular Medicine, Am. Bd. Interventional Cardiology. Intern Vanderbilt U. Hosps., Vanderbilt U. Med. Ctr., Nashville, 1987—88; resident Vanderbilt U. Hosps. and Nashville VA Med. Ctr., 1988—90; fellow Parkland Meml. Hosp. and Dallas VA Med. Ctr., U. Tex. Southwestern Med. Ctr., 1990—93; fellow in interventional cardiology The Cleve. Clinic Found., 1993—94, staff physician sect. interventional cardiology dept. cardiovascular medicine, 1994—2003; vice chmn., internal medicine, chief, divsn. cardiology, Jefferson M. Gill prof. cardiology Univ. Ky.,

2003—. Contbr. numerous articles to profl. jours.; reviewer: jours. in field, sect. editor: Jour. Thrombosis and Thrombolysis, mem. editl. bd.: Jour. Am. Coll. Cardiology. Named one of Best Doctors in Am., 2007. Fellow: ACP, European Soc. Cardiology, Am. Coll. Cardiology; mem.: AMA, Am. Heart Assn. Office: Gill Heart Inst U Ky Health-Care 800 Rose St Lexington KY 40536 Address: U Ky Divsn Cardiovascular Medicine Wethington Bldg Rm 317 900 S Limestone St Lexington KY 40536-0200 Office Phone: 859-323-5843. Office Fax: 859-257-3537. Business E-Mail: moliterno@uky.edu.

MOLL, GEORGE WILLIAM, pediatrician, educator; b. Milw., Nov. 23, 1947; s. George William, Sr. and Laverne Delores (Klein) M.; m. Susana Valdez Ramos, June 24, 1978; children: Christina, Teresa. BA in Chemistry cum laude, Carleton Coll., 1969; PhD in Biochemistry, U. Chgo., 1975, MD, 1977. Diplomate Nat. Bd. Med. Examiners; diplomate in pediatrics and pediat. endocrinology Am. Bd. Pediatrics; cert. PALS, CPR. Pediatric resident Mott Children's Hosp., U. Mich., Ann Arbor, 1977-79; pediatric endocrinology fellowship Wyler Children's Hosp., U. Chgo., 1979-81; asst. prof. pediatrics U. Chgo., 1981-85, Emory U. Sch. Medicine, Atlanta, 1985-87; assoc. prof. pediatrics U. Miss. Med. Ctr., Jackson, 1987-93, prof. pediatrics, 1993—; assoc. staff pediatric endocrinology Little Co. of Mary Hosp., Evergreen Park, Ill., 1981-85, The Meth. Hosps., Gary and Merrillville, Ind., 1981-85; staff pediatric endocrinologist The Emory Clinic, Atlanta, 1985-87, Henrietta Egleston Hosp. for Children, Atlanta, 1985-87, Grady Meml. Hosp., Atlanta, 1985-87; staff Emory Univ. Hosp., 1987, dir. pediatric endocrinology; staff U. Miss. Med. Ctr., Jackson, 1987—. Contbr. articles to profl. jours. Active Diabetes Found. of Miss., Inc., 1998, Juv. Diabetes Found. Internat., 1998, Filipino-Am. Assn. of Miss., 1990—, Chronic Disease Coalition of Miss., 1996—. Recipient med. scientist NIH scholarship/grant U. Chgo., 1970-77, Andrew Mellon Found. fellowship, 1981-82, Med. Excellence award So. Med. Assn., 1995; grantee Am. Lung Assn., 1987-89, Eli Lilly Co., Mobil Oil Co., 1991, Diabetes Rsch. and Edn. Found., Inct., 1992, Pharmacia & Upjohn, 1998, others. Fellow Am. Acad. Pediatrics, Am. Coll. Endocrinology; mem. AAAS, Nat. Bd. Med. Examiners (comprehensive task force for reprodn./endocrinology 1989-90), Chgo. Endocrine Club (sec. 1984-85), N.Y. Acad. of Sci., Am. Fedn. for Med. Rsch., Lawson Wilkins Soc. for Pediat. Endocrinology, Midwest and So. Soc. for Pediatric Rsch., Miss. State Med. Assn., Cen. Miss. Med. and Pediatric Soc., The Endocrine Soc. (regional rep. U.S. Pharmacopeia Quinquennial), Am. Diabetes Assn., Juv. Diabetes Found., Sigma Xi, others. Achievements include isolation of a bovine brain protein kinase and establishment of a protein kinase assay employing a novel PEI-cellulose thin-layer system as part of a PhD Biochemistry; established a novel modified flow-dialysis system for steady state hormone action studies; assisted the delineation of a LH-receptor defect related to precocious puberty and a novel genetic mutation in thyroid binding globulin in males; novel genetic mutation in succinate dehydrogenase subunit B gene for malignant paraganglioma. Avocations: carpentry, general handicrafts, electronics, computer repair work. Office: Univ Miss Med Ctr 2500 N State St Jackson MS 39216-4500 Business E-Mail: gmoll@ped.umsmed.edu.

MOLLEN, EDWARD LEIGH, pediatrician, allergist, clinical immunologist; b. Richmond, Va., May 13, 1946; s. Irving Roth and Ruth (Damsky) M.; m. Mary Viola Jeffrey, Dec. 14, 1975; children: Shawn, Michael, Eric, Christopher. BS in Chemistry, Coll. William and Mary, 1968; MD, Med. Coll. Va., 1972. Diplomate Am. Bd. Pediatrics, Am. Bd. Allergy and Immunology. Resident in pediatrics Med. Coll. Va., Richmond, 1972-75, fellow in allergy and immunology, 1975-77; practice allergy and pediatric allergy and clin. immunology Allergy Assocs. of Richmond, 1977-85; pvt. practice allergy/pediatric allergy and clin. immunology Richmond, 1985—. Fellow Am. Acad. Allergy, Asthma and Immunology, Am. Acad. Pediatrics; mem. Med. Soc. Va., Richmond Acad. Medicine, Asthma and Allergy Soc. Va. Avocations: bicycling, running. Office: 5855 Bremo Rd Ste 702 Richmond VA 23226-1926 Home Phone: 804-353-8353; Office Phone: 804-288-5216. E-mail: elmollenmd@aol.com.

MONAGHAN, CRAIG THOMAS, automotive executive; b. Phila., Feb. 16, 1957; m. Mary Lou Murphy, Jul. 25, 1981; children: Shannon, Connor, Rand. BS industrial engr., Lehigh U., 1980; MBA in fin., Wharton U. Pa., 1985. Cert. mgmt. acct. Financial analyst General Motors Corp., NYC, 1985-87, mgr. overseas fin., 1987-88; dir. corp. fin. Squibb, Princeton, NJ, 1988-90; dir. internat. fin. Bristol-Myers Squibb Co., NYC, 1990-91; asst. treas. Reader's Digest, Pleasantville, NY, 1991-92, controller europe, 1992—98; CFO iVillage.com, 1998-2000; exec. v.p., CFO AutoNation, Inc., Fort Lauderdale, Fla., 2000—06; CFO Sears Holdings Corp., Hoffman Estates, Ill., 2006—07; sr. v.p., CFO Asbury Automotive Group, Inc., NYC, 2008—11, pres., CEO, 2011—. Capt. US Army, 1980—83. Mem.: Inst. Mgmt. Accts. Avocations: fishing, golf, reading. Office: Asbury Automotive Group 622 3d Ave New York NY 10017

MONAHAN, PAUL EDWARD, pediatrician; b. Winchester, Va., July 3, 1963; AB, Princeton U., 1986; MD, U. Va., 1990. Cert. in pediat. hematology, oncology. Prof. pediat. U. NC at Chapel Hill Sch. Medicine, 1998—, dir. pediat. hemostasis, 1998. Regional dir. region IV-N US Hemophilia Treatment Ctr. Network, 2005. Recipient Rsch. award, Nat. Hemophilia Found., 2013; grants, NIH, numerous grants. Office: Physicians Office Bldg CB#7326 1185 1st Fl Chapel Hill NC 27599-7236 Office Fax: 919-966-0907. Business E-Mail: paul_monahan@med.unc.edu.*

MONAHAN, THOMAS PAUL, accountant; b. Pitts., Feb. 27, 1951; s. Thomas Andrew and Patricia (Tompkins) M.; m. Ellen McKeithan Easterby, Aug. 2, 1975; children: Kelley Kathleen, Thomas Patrick, Kyle Easterby, Tessa Elizabeth. BS in Acctg., U. S.C., 1973. CPA SC. Staff acct. Rogers, Brigman, Peterson & Co., Columbia, S.C., 1972-75, ptnr., 1975-82; chmn., treas., prin. GMK Assocs., Columbia, 1982—. Chmn., bd. dirs., treas. Devel. Properties, Inc.; trustee, pres. Town Theater Trust, 2000—. Mem. bus. coun. S. Dems., 1986—; bd. dirs. Cultural Coun. of Richland and Lexington Counties; active Com. of 100. Mem. AICPA, CGMA, SC Assn. CPAs, Columbia Stage Soc. (trustee, bd. dirs.), Spring Valley Country Club, Capital City Club, Palmetto Club, Zeta Beta Tau (trustee emeritus). Office: GMK Assoc Ste 2100 1201 Main St Columbia SC 29201-3263 Home: 701 Abelia Rd Columbia SC 29205-2012 Office Phone: 803-256-0000. Business E-Mail: tmonahan@gmka.com.

MONCARZ, RAUL, economist, researcher; s. Sara Percal and Isaac Moncarz; m. Elisa Elisa Shafran, May 31, 1973; children: Felippe Henley, Roger Jonathan, Benjamin David Benjamin. PhD, Fla. State U., Tallahassee, 1969. Prof. Fla. Internat. U., Miami, 1972—, asst. v.p. academic affairs, 1986—87, vice-provost, 1999—2006; chairperson FIU-Dept. Econs., Miami, 1989—95. Adv. bd. mem. North Am. Econs. and Fin. Assn., Washington, D.C., 1979—2001; pres. Internat. Soc. for the Intercommunication of New Ideas, Mexico City, 2001—02; bd. mem. Social and Econ. Coun., Dade County, Miami, 2002—08; pres. Internat. Trade and Fin. Assn., Columbus, 2006—07; bd. mem., ednl. dir. Our Elder Bros. and Sisters Found., Miami, 2007—. Contbr. articles to profl. jours. Manuscript reviewer Jour. Devel. Entrepreneurship, Rochester, 2002—08; editl. bd. Problemas del Desarrollo, Mexico City, 2002—08; adv. coun. Indian Inst. Fin., New Delhi, 2003—06; vol. Internat. Trade and Fin. Assn., Miami, 2006—07. Recipient Editl. Bd., Global Econ. Jour., Since 2005, Frontiers in Fin. and Economics, Since 2004, Pres., Internat. Soc. for New Ideas, 2004, Vis. Prof., Fulbright Commn., 1971, Fulbrigth Commn., 1997, Outstanding Africanist award, 2007, Raul Moncarz award, 2006, Outstanding Svc. award, Service award. Mem.: Internat. Soc. New Ideas (treas. 2003—05), Internat. Trade and Fin. Assn. (dir. 2004—07), Collegium Cuban Economists (treas. 2000—08), Am. Econ. Assn., Internat. Trade and Fin. Assn. (pres. 2006—07). Achievements include editorial board, several academic journals; leadership medallion; Prominent Hispanics. Avocations: reading, swimming, walking, travel. Office Fax: 305-919-5478. Business E-Mail: moncarz@fiu.edu.

MONCRIEF, MICHAEL JOSEPH, former Mayor, Fort Worth, former state legislator; b. Houston, Sept. 5, 1943; s. Richard Barto Sr. and Mary Daisy (Wiley) M.; m. Rosemary Brewer, Dec. 31, 1980; children: Troy L., Mitchell K. BS, Tarleton State U., 1968. Ind. oil prodr., Ft. Worth, 1969—; mem. Tex. Ho. of Reps., 1971—72, mem. appropriations com., 1970-72; judge Tarrant County, Tex., 1974—86; mem. Tex. State Senate, 1991—2003; pres. pro tempore Tex. Senate, 2001; mayor City of Ft. Worth, 2003—11. Past mem. Tarrant County Drug Abuse Bd., Lone Star Transp. Authority, N. Central Tex. Council of Govts., Appropriations Com.; mem. Gov.'s Blue Ribbon Commn. on Criminal Justice, many other groups. Bd. dirs. Assn. Retarded Citizens (hon. chmn.), chmn. Neighborhood Resources Devel. Coun., Tarrant County Med., Edn. and Rsch. Found., Tarrant County Mental Health Assn., Drug Treatment Ctr., Tarrant County Juvenile Bd., Ft. Worth State Sch., Inst. Pub. Svc. Tarleton State U., Tex. Affiliate Adv. Com., AHA, Alliance for Children (hon.), Paul Quinn Coll., Tex. Preservation Bd., US Olympic Com., and several others; pres. Neighborhood Health Horizons; past bd. dirs. Gill Children Svcs., Inc., Ft. Worth Libr. Bd., Longhorn Coun. Boy Scouts Am., Tex. Soc. for Prevention of Blindness, North Tex., many others; dir. North Tex. Commn., 2003-; affiliated with Ft. Worth C. of C., Tex. Arts Alliance, Muscular Dystrophy Assn., Inc. and several others. Named Outstanding Cmty. Leader Am., 1970, Outstanding Young Man Am., 1971, Newsmaker of Yr., 1974, 78, Freshman Legislator of Yr., Tex. Legislature, 1971, AARP award, 1997, Common Cause Star of Tex. Pub. Svc. award, 2000, Kiwanis Club ' Community Builder" award, 2002, many other honors. Mem. Tarleton Alumni Assn. (Disting. Alumni 1977), Ind. Petroleum Assn. Am., Am. Judicature Soc., Nat. Coll. Probate Judges, Ft. Worth Res. Police Officers, other profl. orgns. Avocations: skiing, tennis, golf, hunting rattlesnakes and alligators. Business E-Mail: Mayor@fortworthgov.org.

MONCRIEF, WILLIAM ALVIN, JR., oil and gas producer; b. Little Rock, Mar. 27, 1920; d. William Alvin and Elizabeth (Bright) Moncrief; m. Deborah Beggs, Jan. 30, 1947; children: William A. III, R.W., C.B., T.O. BS in Petroleum Engring., U. Tex., Austin, 1942. Registered profl. engr., Tex. Ptnr. Moncrief Oil, Ft. Worth, 1945—; dir. First Republic Bank, Dallas. Regent, U. Tex. sys. Served to ensign USNR, 1944-45, PTO. Named Disting. Engring. Grad. U. Tex.-Austin, 1983; named one of Forbes 400: Richest Americans, 2006-. Mem.: Shady Oaks of Ft. Worth (pres.); Eldorado (Indian Wells, Calif.); Brookhollow (Dallas). Republican. Episcopalian. Office: Moncrief Oil Moncrief Bldg 950 Commerce St at 9th Fort Worth TX 76102

MONCURE, JOHN LEWIS, lawyer; b. Houston, Nov. 4, 1930; s. Walter Raleigh Daniel and Margaret (Atkins) M.; m. Norma Steed, Dec. 29, 1954 (dec. June 1982); children: John Carter, Michael Lewis, Douglas Lee, Stuart Richard, Mary Margaret; m. Margaret Edmonston, Nov. 12, 1983. BBA, U. Houston, 1953; JD, U. Tex., 1956. Bar: Tex. 1956. Assoc. Butler, Binion, Rice, Cook & Knapp, Houston, 1956-68; ptnr. Prappas, Moncure & Eidman, Houston, 1969-86, John L. Moncure and Assocs., Houston, 1987—. Lectr. bus. law U. Houston, 1958-59, 68-69 Mem. sch. bd. St. Thomas Episcopal Sch., Houston, 1965-78; mem. vestry St. Thomas Episc. Ch., 1975-78. Named Distinguished Alumni Coll. Bus., U. Houston, 1968 Fellow Am. Coll. Probate Counsel; mem. Am., Tex., Houston bar assns., Assn. Christian Schs. (trustee), Coll. Bus. Alumni Assn. U. Houston (pres., dir.), U. Houston Alumni Fedn. (treas., dir.), Sigma Alpha Epsilon. Republican. Home: 1220 W Clay Houston TX 77019 Office: 1656 Townhurst Dr Ste D Houston TX 77043 Home Phone: 713-528-9870; Office Phone: 713-880-8285. Personal E-mail: johnlmoncure@yahoo.com.

MONDELLO, MARK T., electronics executive; BSME, U. South Fla. Former project mgr. on comml. and def.-related aerospace programs Moog, Inc.; prodn. line supr. Jabil Circuit, Inc., St. Petersburg, Fla., 1992—93, project mgr., 1993—97, v.p. bus. devel., 1997—99, sr. v.p. bus. devel., 1999—2002, COO, 2002—. Bd. dirs. All Children's Hosp. Office: Jabil Cir 10560 9th St N Saint Petersburg FL 33716

MONG, ROBERT WILLIAM, JR., publishing executive, newspaper editor; b. Fremont, Ohio, Jan. 22, 1949; s. Robert William and Betty (Dwyer) Mong; m. Carla Beth Sweet, July 25, 1975 (div. 1979); m. Diane Elizabeth Reischel, Jan. 23, 1988; children: Eric Robert, Elizabeth Diana. BA, Haverford Coll., Pa., 1971; graduate exec. bus. program, Stanford U., 1997. Reporter Cin. Post, 1973-75, Capital Times, Madison, Wis., 1975-77; city editor Madison Press Connection, 1977-79; asst. city editor Dallas Morning News, 1979-80, bus. editor, 1980-81, projects editor, 1981-83, asst. mng. editor, 1983-88, dep. mng. editor, 1988-90, mng. editor, 1990-96, gen. mgr., 1998-2001, pres., 1998—, editor, 2001—; pub., CEO Owensboro Messenger-Inquirer, Ky., 1996-97; exec. v.p. pub. divsn. A.H. Belo Corp., Dallas, 1997-98. Mem. exec. com. American Press Inst., 2001—. Chair Dallas Morning News Charities campaign, 1998—; pres. bd. visitors Manship Sch. Mass Comm., La. State U., 1999—. Recipient Empathy award, Volunteers America, 2004, J.B. Buck Marryat award for meritorious svc., Dallas Press Club, 2005. Mem.: Religion Newswriters Assn. (bd. dirs.), Southern Newspaper Publishers Assn., Newspaper Assn. America, American Soc. Newspaper Editors. Office: The Dallas Morning News PO Box 655237 508 Young St Dallas TX 75202-4828 Home Phone: 214-521-1952; Office Phone: 214-977-8222. Business E-Mail: bmong@dallasnews.com.

MONGEAU, LUC, consumer products company executive; Grad. in Bus., Universite de Sherbrooke; MBA, U. Western Ontario, 1997. Asst. brand mgr. Procter & Gamble Co., 1997—98; brand mgr. Mars Can. Inc., 1998—2000, mktg. dir., 2000—04, sales dir., 2004—05, v.p., supply chain, 2005—06, pres., 2006—08, Mars Petcare North America, 2008—. Office: Mars, Inc 6885 Elm St Mc Lean VA 22101 Office Phone: 703-821-4900. Office Fax: 703-448-9678.

MONK, SUZANNE RENEE, academic administrator; d. Samuel William and Evelyn Sue Monk. M, Ohio U., Athens, 1986. Mng. editor Meridian Star, Miss., 1998—2007; dir. pub. info. East Miss. CC, Scooba, 2007—. Pvt. practise, Miss., 2007—. Recipient numerous awards, Miss. Press Assn., 1994—2008. Office: East MS CC 1512 Kemper St Scooba MS 39358 Business E-Mail: smonk@eastms.edu.

MONNET, BEVERLY C., corporate financial executive; b. Tulsa, Okla. 2 children. B in Acctg., U. Okla., Norman, 1980. CPA. With Southport Exploration Co., Tulsa; revenue acct. ONEOK, Inc., 1987, mgr., revenue acctg., 1988—95; mgr., gas acctg. ONEOK, Inc. (Okla. Natural Gas Co.), 1995—97; mgr., acctg. ONEOK, Inc. (ONEOK Resources Co.), 1997—2001; chief acctg. officer ONEOK, Inc., 2001—04, v.p., contr., Okla. natural gas, kans. gas svc. & Tex. gas svc., 2001—. Bd. dirs. Tulsa Chpt. of the Petroleum Accountants Soc., Okla., 1992-96, chmn., Okla., 1994; mem. AICPA, Okla. Soc. Cert. Pub. Accountants, Okla. Ind. Petroleum Assn., Kans. Ind. Oil and Gas Assn. Office: ONEOK Inc 100 W 5th St Tulsa OK 74103 Office Phone: 918-588-7000. Office Fax: 918-588-7960. Business E-Mail: beverly.monnet@oneok.com.

MONROE, FREDERICK LEROY, chemist; b. Redmond, Oreg., Oct. 13, 1942; s. Herman Sylvan Monroe and Mary Roberta (Grant) Emery. BS in Chemistry, Oreg. State U., Corvallis, 1964; MS in Environ. Engring., Wash. State U., Pullman, 1974. Control specialist Air Pollution Control Authority, Centralia, Wash., 1969-70; asst. chemist Wash. State U., 1970-74; environ. engr. Ore-Ida Foods, Inc., Idaho, 1974-77; cons. Idaho, 1977-78; applications engr. AFL Industries, Riviera Beach, Fla., 1979-80; mgr. chem. control PCA Internat., Matthews, NC, 1980—85; quality assurance mgr. Stork Screens Am., Charlotte, NC, 1985—99; grade IV NC wastewater treatment operator. Pres. Unity Ch., 1982-84. Served with USAF, 1964-68, maj. Res. ret.; served with N.G., 1973-78. Decorated Air Force Commendation medal, Vietnam Era Svc. Commemorative medal; recipient Blue Thumb award Charlotte-Mecklenburg Utility Dist., 1993. Fellow AIChE. Republican. Home and Office: 207 Summermore Dr Charlotte NC 28270 Home: 1661 Vista De Montana Cottonwood AZ 86326 Personal E-mail: fredmonroe@aol.com.

MONROE, HASKELL MOORMAN, JR., chancellor emeritus, retired history professor, dean; b. Dallas, Mar. 18, 1931; s. Haskell M. and Myrtle Marie (Jackson) Monroe; m. Margaret Joan Phillips, June 15, 1957; children: Stephen, Melanie, Mark, John. BA, Austin Coll., Tex., 1952, MA, 1954; PhD, Rice U., Houston, 1961; D (hon.), Austin Coll., 1984. From instr. to prof. Tex. A&M U., 1959-80, asst. dean Grad. Sch., 1965-68, asst. v.p. acad. affairs, 1972-74, dean faculties, 1974-80, assoc. v.p. acad. affairs, 1977-80, dean faculties emeritus College Station, 1997—; pres. U. Tex., El Paso, 1980-87; chancellor U. Mo., Columbia, 1987-91, prof. history, 1987-97, chancellor emeritus, prof. history, 1997—. Instr. Schreiner Inst., Kerrville, Tex., 1959; vis. lectr. Emory U., 1967, 1972; faculty lectr. Tex. A&M U., 1972; alumni lectr. Austin Coll., 1980; bd. dirs. City Nat. Bank, Southwestern Bell Corp., Boone County Nat. Bank, SBC Comms., Inc.; history adv. com. Sec. Air Force, 1987; orientation com. Dept. Def.-Joint Chiefs, 1986. Contbr. articles, revs. to profl. jours.; editor: Papers of Jefferson Davis, 1964—69; adv. editor: Texana, 1964—71; mem. bd. editl. advisers Booker T. Washington Washington Papers, 1965—85. Bd. dirs. Brazos Valley Rehab. Ctr., 1975-77, Salvation Army, El Paso, 1984-87, Columbia, Mo., 1988-97, Crime Stoppers of El Paso, United Way Columbia, 1988-94, Keep Brazos Beautiful, 1999-2003, Washington-on-the-Brazos State Park Assn., 2002-; trustee Bryan Hosp., 1976-79, chmn., 1979; bd. ch. visitors Austin Coll., 1977-78; deacon First Presbyn. Ch., Bryan, 1961-63, elder, 1965-67, 69-71, 73-74, clk. of session, 1973-74, chmn. pulpit nominating com., 1971-72; mem. presbytery's coun. Presbytery of Brazos, 1969-71, mem. resources for the 80s steering com., 1978-80; elder 1st Presbyn. Ch., El Paso, 1984-87, 1st Presbyn. Ch., Columbia, 1994-96; mem. exec. bd. Great Rivers coun. Boy Scouts Am., 1990-97; mem. Pres. Coun. NCAA, 1986-87; chmn. Jefferson Davis award com. Confederate Mus., 1996-97; bd. dirs. Salvation Army, 1989-97, Schreiner U., 1998-2007 Recipient Citation of Appreciation, LULAC, 1982, Honor award Salvation Army, 1997, Faculty Disting. Achievement award Tex. A&M U., 1964, U. Mo. Alumni award for tchg., 1995, also numerous achievement awards; grantee Social Sci. Rsch. Coun., Tex. A&M U., Huntington Libr., Intrafraternity and Sorority Outstanding Tchr. award, U. Mo., 1997; named Ky. Col., 1967; named to Legends of Aggieland, 1998. Mem. Am. Hist. Assn., Orgn. Am. Historians, So. Hist. Assn. Hist. Found. Presbyn. and Reformed Chs. (pres. 1970-72), Coll. Football Assn. (chmn. bd. 1989-90, bd. dirs.), Truman Scholarship Panel, Soc. Conf. Deans Faculties and Acad. V.P.s (pres. 1978), Rotary (El Paso, hon. Columbia, Mo., Bryan, Tex., Paul Harris fellow 1986, 2000). Home: 1005 Sonoma Cir College Station TX 77845-7907 Office: Tex A&M U 6B15 Evans Libr College Station TX 77843 Office Phone: 979-324-4546. Personal E-mail: mjomonroe@aol.com.

MONROE, JOSEPH M., oil industry executive; B in Chem. Engring., NC State U.; M in Chem. Engring., U. Calif., Berkeley; MBA, U. So. Calif. V.p. pipelines and terminals, pres. Unocal Pipeline Co. Unocal Corp., 1999—2002; sr. v.p. supply and distbn. Tesoro Refining and Mktg. Co. Tesoro Corp., San Antonio, 2002—04, sr. v.p. strategic planning and bus. devel., sr. v.p. orgnl. effectiveness, sr. v.p. bus. intergration & analysis, sr. v.p. bus. devel. & logistics, sr. v.p. corp. devel., sr. v.p. logistics and marine. Office: Tesoro Corp 19100 Ridgewood Pkwy San Antonio TX 78259-1828 Office Phone: 210-283-2464.

MONROE, JUDITH ANN, public health service officer; b. Dayton, Ohio, Apr. 4, 1953; m. Robert Lubitz; 3 children. BS, Eastern Ky. Univ., 1975; MD, U. Md., 1983. Residency U. Cin., 1983—86; physician Nat. Health Svc. Corps, Morgan County, Tenn., 1986—90; dir. clinics Ind. U. Dept. Family Med., Indpls., 1990—92; dir. primary care ctr. & family med. residency prog. St. Vincent Hosp. & Health Svc., Indpls., 1992—2005; commr. Ind. Dept. Health, Indpls., 2005—10; dep. dir. Centers for Disease Control & Prevention (CDC), Atlanta, 2010—, dir. state, tribal, local & territorial support, 2010—. Chairwoman Tobacco Prevention and Cessation Exec. Bd.; mem. Ind. Health Info. Exch. Bd.; pres. Assn. State and Territorial Health Officials. Recipient Merit Award, Ind. Hosp. Assn., 2009, McGovern award, 2010, MVP Award, Peyton Manning Children's Hosp., 2011, Governor's Disting. Svc. Medal, State of Ind., 2011; named a Woman of Influence, Indpls. Bus. Journal, 2009; fellow, Eastern Tenn. State U., 1990, U. Wis., 1993. Office: Centers for Disease Control (CDC) 1600 Clifton Rd Atlanta GA 30333

MONROE, ROBERT RAWSON, national security consultant; b. Oakland, Calif., Sept. 25, 1927; s. Robert Ansley and Muriel Estelle (Burnham) M.; m. Charlotte Boies Anderson, Oct. 16, 1951; children: Robert Anderson, Nancy Lynn Monroe Sims, Susan Leslie Monroe Gordon. BS in Naval Sci., U.S. Naval Acad., 1950; MA in Internat. Rels., Stanford U., Calif., 1962. Commd. ensign USN, 1950, advanced through grades to vice-admiral, 1977; dir. Navy Systems Analysis, 1972-73; comdr. South Atlantic Force, 1973-74; comdr. Operational Test and Evaluation Force USN, 1974-77; dir. Def. Nuclear Agy., 1977-80; dir. Navy Rsch., Devel., Test and Evaluation, 1980-83; ret., 1983; joined Bechtel Nat., Inc., San Francisco, 1984, mgr. def. and space, 1984-89, v.p., 1985, sr. v.p., ptnr., 1987, mgr. mktg. and govt. ops., 1989-91, mgr. spl. projects, 1992-93, mgr. govt. ops. Washington, 1993—2002, sr. counselor, 2002—05; ret., 2005; nat. security cons., 2006—. Mem. nat. security adv. bd. Los Alamos (N.Mex.) Nat. Lab., 1983—88; mem. tech. evaluation panel U.S. Dept. Energy, 1983—88; mem. engring. adv. com. Oak Ridge Nat. Lab., 1986—89, Rensselaer Poly. Inst., 1990—91; mem. bd. advisors Office Tech. Assessment, Washington, 1987—89, Nat. Contract

Mgmt. Assn., 1986—91; mem. task forces Def. Sci. Bd., Washington, 1983—89; corp. mem. Charles Stark Draper Lab., Cambridge, Mass., 1983—99, mem. emeritus, 1999—; affiliate mem. Ctr. for Internat. Security and Cooperation, Stanford U., 1989—93; chmn. space transp. subcom. NASA's Adv. Coun., 1995—2001; mem. strategic adv. bd. Nev. Test Site, 1995—99; mem. Nat. Security adv. panel Sandia Nat. Labs., 1996—2011; mem. threat reduction adv. com. (nuc. panel) Dept. Def., 1998—2010; mem. Enhanced Test Readiness External Rev. Group, 2002—03; mem. threat reduction adv. com. (sys. & tech. panel) Dept. Def., 2004—10, mem. U.S. Nuc. Strategy Forum, 2004—; mem. mil. com. Ctr. for Security Policy, 2004—; mem. adv. bd. arms control and nonproliferation State Dept., Washington, 2005—06, chmn. task force on nat. strategy to combat weapons of mass destruction, 2006—07, mem. internat. security adv. bd., 2006—09; pres. US Naval Acad. Class 1950, 2009—; mem. Coalition Common Def., 2011—; mem., bd. advisors Task Force on Nat. Homeland Security, 2013—; mem. Workshop on Nuclear Multipolarity & Stability, 2013—. Decorated Def. DSM, Navy DSM, Legion of Merit, Bronze Star medal with combat device, Joint Svcs. Commendation medal, USN Commendation medal with combat device; Legion of Honor (France). Avocations: golf, hiking, reading. Home: 2313 Sawdust Rd Vienna VA 22181-3044 Personal E-mail: rrmonroe@cox.net.

MONROE, WILLIAM LEWIS, human resources executive; b. Detroit, May 11, 1941; s. Lewis Stewart and Ada Jeanette (Williams) Monroe; m. Sharon Lynne Kahal, June 30, 1967; children: Andrea M. Dunk, William J. BA, Western Mich. U., 1963, MA, 1964. Rsch. analyst Chrysler Corp., Detroit, 1965-72, labor economist, 1972-77, mgr. retirement, savs. and unemployment benefit plans, 1977-81; dir. employee benefits W. R. Grace & Co., NYC, 1981-87, v.p. human resources, 1987-2001, bd. trustee, v.p. coun. on employee benefits, 1989-2001, pres. coun. on employee benefits, 1995-96; cons. AON, Boca Raton, 2001—02. Adj. prof. mgmt. FAU Univ., Boca Raton, 2001; corp. bd. dirs. Internat. Found. Employee Benefits, 1986—88; mem. bus. rsch. adv. coun. U.S. Dept. Labor/Bur. Labor Stats., 1987—96; mem. Human Resources Policy Inst. Boston U., 1993—96. Co-chmn. closing com. PTSA Sch., Birmingham, Mich., 1977; chmn. pers. com. Wilton Presbyn. ch., Wilton, Conn., 1982—86; officer, bd. dirs. Forest Hills Property Owners Assn., Birmingham, 1974—80; mem. exec. bd. Gulf Stream coun. Boy Scouts Am., 1993—99. Served USAR, 1965—71. Mem.: Soc. for Human Resources & Mgmt., Boca Raton Resort and Club, Royal Palm Yacht & Country Club. Independent. Presbyterian. Avocations: tennis, golf. Personal E-mail: billmonroe03@yahoo.com.

MONSKY, JOHN BERTRAND, investment company executive; b. Montgomery, Ala., May 17, 1930; s. Harry and Belle (Golding) M.; m. Joan Gilbert, June 8, 1952; children: Leslie Joy, John Richard, Harry Robert. BA, Yale, 1952; MBA, Harvard, 1954. Sec. Devoe & Raynolds Co., Inc., Louisville, 1956-65; v.p., dir. Universal Marion Corp., Jacksonville, Fla., 1965-69, pres., chmn. bd., chief exec. officer, 1969-71, cons., 1971—; vice chmn. ServAmerica, Inc., Jacksonville, 1972-74, co-chmn. bd. dirs., 1974-80, chmn. bd. dirs., 1980—; pres., chmn. bd. dirs. First Fla. Capital Corp., 1985—; affilate ptnr. Lindsay Goldberg, NYC, 2009—. Dir. Fla. Wire & Cable Co., Jacksonville, 1975-82 Past pres. bd. trustees Jacksonville Country Day Sch. Prior Affiliations Include; bd. dirs. Jacksonville Art Mus.; trustee Bolles Sch., Jacksonville, Jacksonville Symphony Assn. Served with USAF, 1954-56. Mem. Jacksonville Area C. of C. (com. of 100), Harvard Bus. Sch. Club of Ky. (exec. com. 1964-65), Phillips Acad. Andover Alumni Club of Ky. (pres. 1963-64), Epping Forest Cmty. Master Assn. (bd. dirs. 1994—), Yale Club N.E. Fla. (bd. dirs. 1987—), Yale Club of NYC, Harvard Club (Jacksonville), Assn. Yale Alumni (del. 1996—, schs. com.), AYA (sch. com.), Ponte Vedra Club, Epping Forest Yacht Club, Harvard Bus. Sch. Alumni Club (Jacksonville) Home: Epping Forest 7015 Gaines Ct Jacksonville FL 32217-2672 Office: 132 Harbourmaster Ct Ponte Vedra Beach FL 32082 Office Phone: 904-396-0348. Personal E-mail: jbmonsky@aol.com. Business E-Mail: jbmonsky@firstfloridacapital.com.

MONSOUR, ALEX, state legislator; b. Lake Charles, La., May 5, 1962; m. Amanda McCool Monsour. Attended La. State U. Bus. owner; realtor; mem. Dist. 54 Miss. House of Reps., 2008—. Republican. Catholic. Office: PO Box 1018 Jackson MS 39215 Home: 112 Villanova Dr Vicksburg MS 39183-9551 Office Phone: 601-415-7274. E-mail: amonsour@house.ms.gov.

MONTAG, TOM (THOMAS KELL MONTAG), bank executive; b. 1957; m. Janet Montag. BA, Stanford U., 1979; MBA, Northwestern U., 1982. Mgmt. positions First National Bank of Chicago; pres., dir. Goldman Sachs Mitsui Marine Derivative Products, 1993, ptnr., exec. v.p., 1996; gen. ptnr., v.p. Goldman Sachs & Co., mng. dir., co-pres. Japanese Ops., 2002—07, co-head global securities bus., 2006—08; exec. v.p., head global sales & trading Merrill Lynch & Co., Inc., NYC, 2008; pres., global markets Bank of America Corp., Charlotte, NC, 2009, pres., global banking & markets, 2009—11, co-COO, 2011—. Bd. dirs. BlackRock, Inc., 2011—. Bd. trustees Riverdale Country Sch. Office: Bank of America Corp 100 N Tryon St Charlotte NC 28202 Office Phone: 704-386-5681. Office Fax: 704-386-6699. Business E-Mail: tom.montag@bankofamerica.com.

MONTALVO, FRANK, judge; 4 children. BS with honors, U. PR, 1976; MS in Bioengring., U. Mich., 1978; JD, Wayne State U., 1985. Engr. Chrysler Corp., Mich., 1978, Gen. Motors, Mich., 1978—88; assoc. atty. Groce, Locke & Heboon, P.C., San Antonio, 1988—91, Ball & Weed, P.C., San Antonio, 1991—94; judge 288th Jud. Dist. Ct. Bexar County, San Antonio, 1995—2003, US Dist. Ct. (we. dist.) Tex., 2003—, US dist. judge, El Paso Divsn., 2003. Office: 525 Magoffin Ave Ste 461 El Paso TX 79901 Office Phone: 915-534-6600.

MONTANARO, DONATO A., JR., brokerage house executive; BA in Govt. & Internat. Rels., U. Notre Dame, Ind., 1988; JD, Cath. U. America, 1991. V.p. electronic trading Quick & Reilly, 1991—97; founder, pres. SureTrade Inc. (subs. Quick & Reilly), 1997—2000; spl. cons. Am. Stock Exch., 2002—05; chmn., CEO TradeKing, Charlotte, NC, 2005—. Office: TradeKing PO Box 49050 Charlotte NC 28277-3432 E-mail: donato@tradeking.com.

MONTEITH, LARRY KING, chancellor emeritus; b. Bryson City, NC, Aug. 17, 1933; s. Earl and Essie (King) M.; m. Nancy Alexander, Apr. 19, 1952; children: Larry, Carol, Steve. BSEE, N.C. State U., 1960; MSEE, Duke U., 1962, PhD in Elec. Engring., 1965. Registered profl. engr., N.C. Mem. tech. staff Bell Tel. Labs., Burlington, NC, 1960-62, Rsch. Triangle Inst., Raleigh, NC, 1962-66, group leader rsch. sect., 1966-68; adj. asst. prof. elec. engring. N.C. State U., Raleigh, 1965-68, assoc. prof., 1968-72, prof., 1972—, head dept. elec. engring., 1974-78, dean of engring., 1978-89, interim chancellor, 1989-90, chancellor, 1990-98, chancellor emeritus, 1998—. Contbr. articles to profl. jours. With USN, 1952-56. Recipient Disting. Engring. Alumnus award Duke U., 1984, Outstanding Engring. Achievement award N.C. Soc. Engrs., 1990, Disting. Engring. Alumnus award N.C. State U., 1999. Fellow IEEE, Am. Soc. for Engring. Edn.; mem. NSPE (edn. adv. group), Raleigh C. of C. (bd. dirs.), Rotary Internat. (Paul Harris fellow Rotary Found. 1991), Phi Beta Kappa, Sigma Xi, Sigma Iota Rho, Phi Kappa Phi, Eta Kappa Nu, Tau Beta Pi, Sigma Beta Delta. E-mail: lmonteith@nc.rr.com.

MONTELL, BRAD, state legislator; BA, MA, Western Ky. U. Fin. adv., broker W. Brad Montell Investments; mem. Dist. 58 Ky. House of Reps., 2003—. Mem.: Shelby County C. of C. (pres. 1993), County Econ. Devel. (pres. 1994—95), Nat. Fedn. Internat. Bus. Chmn. Republican. Mailing: 543 Main St Shelbyville KY 40065-1119 Office: Capitol Annex Rm 432C Frankfort KY 40601 Office Phone: 502-564-8100 ext. 609. Fax: 502-633-6812.

MONTFORD, WILLIAM J., III, state legislator; b. Marianna, Fla., Aug. 22, 1947; m. Jane Gard Montford; children: Katherine Montford Peters, William IV. AA, Chipola Jr. Coll., 1967; BS in Math. Edn., Fla. State U., 1969, MS in Adminstrn. & Supervision, 1971; LLD (hon.), Flagler Coll., St. Augustine, Fla. Math tchr. Belle Vue Mid. Sch., Tallahassee; supt. Leon County Schools, Fla.; CEO Fla. Assn. Dist. Sch. Superintendents; mem. Dist. 6 Fla. State Senate, 2011—. Democrat. Baptist. Avocations: reading, sports, Family activities. Office: 56 Market St Apalachicola FL 32320 also: Florida State Senate 208 Senate Office Bldg 404 S Monroe St Tallahassee FL 32399-1100 Office Phone: 850-653-2656, 850-487-5004. Business E-Mail: montford.bill.web@flsenate.gov.

MONTGOMERIE, COLIN STUART, professional golfer; b. Glasgow, Troon, Ayrshire, Scotland, June 23, 1963; children: Olivia Rose, Venetia, Cameron. Profl. golfer, 1987—; mem. Team Great Britain & Ireland Walker Cup, 1985, 87; mem. Team Europe Ryder Cup, 1991, 93, 95, 97, 99, 2002, 2004, 2006, capt. Team Europe, 2010; mem. Team Scotland Alfred Dunhill Cup, 1988, 91-2000, World Cup, 1988, 91-93, 97-99, 2007; playing capt. Team Great Britain & Ireland Seve Trophy, 2000, 2002, 2003, 2005, mem. Team Great Britain & Ireland, 2007; mem. World Team UBS Cup, 2003, 2004; playing capt. Team Europe Royal Trophy, 2010. Decorated European Order of Merit; winner Scottish Stroke Play, 1985, Scottish Amateur Championship, 1987, European Tour Rookie of Yr., 1988, Portuguese Open, 1989, Scandinavian Masters, 1991, 99, 2001, Heineken Dutch Open, 1993, Volvo Masters, 1993, 2002, Spanish Open, 1994, English Open, 1994, Volvo German Open, 1994-95, Alfred Dunhill Cup, 1995, Trophee Lancome, 1995, Dubai Desert Classic, 1996, Murphy's Irish Open, 1996-97, 2001, Canon European Masters, 1996, Million Dollar Challenge, 1996, Compaq European Grand Prix, 1997, World Cup Individual, 1997, Andersen Cons. World Champion, 1997, King Hassan II Trophy, 1997, Brit. Masters, 1998, German Masters, 1998, Benson & Hedges Internat. Open, 1999, BMW Internat. Open, 1999, Std. Life Loch Lomond, 1999, Volvo PGA Championship, 1998-2000, Cisco World Matchplay Championship, 1999, The Skins Game (USA), 2000, Novotel Perrier Open de France, 2000, Ericsson Australian Masters, 2001, European Open, 2007; 2d pl. US Open, 1994, 97, TCL Classic 2002, Macau Open, 2003, Caltex Singapore Masters, 2004, Hong Kong Open, 2005, Smurfit Kappa European Open, 2007; leader European Tour Merit, 1993-99, 2005. Achievements include member of Ryder Cup winning Team Europe, 1995, 1997, 2002, 2004, 2006, 2010; member of Alfred Dunhill Cup winning Team Scotland, 1995; member of World Cup winning Team Scotland, 2007; member of Seve Trophy winning Team Great Britain & Ireland, 2002, 2003, 2005, 2007; member of Royal Trophy winning Team Europe, 2010. Avocations: music, cars, films. Mailing: PGA Tour 112 PGA Tour Blvd Ponte Vedra Beach FL 32082

MONTGOMERY, CHARLES HARVEY, lawyer; b. Spartanburg, SC, Jan. 28, 1949; s. Dan Hugh and Ann Louise (Gasque) M.; m. Renée Jean Gubernot, Mar. 27, 1971; children: Charles Scott, Marie Renée. BA, Duke U., 1971; JD, Vanderbilt U., 1974. Bar: NC 1974, US Dist. Ct. (ea. dist.) NC 1974, US Supreme Ct. 1979, US Dist. Ct. (mid. dist.) NC 1991; cert. family law specialist, NC, 1995. Assoc. Jordan Morris & Hoke, Raleigh, NC, 1974-75; atty. Wake County Legal Svcs., Raleigh, 1975-76; pvt. practice, Raleigh, 1977; ptnr. Montgomery & Montgomery, Cary, NC, 1978-79, Sanford Adams McCullough & Beard, Raleigh, 1979-86, Adams McCullough & Beard, Raleigh, 1986-88, Toms Reagan & Montgomery, Cary, 1989-92, Toms & Montgomery, Cary, 1992-93; pvt. practice, Cary, 1993—. NC super lawers 2009, bd. dirs. Br. Bank and Trust, Cary, 1980-Councilman Town of Cary, 1977-81, 83-87; vice-chmn. Wake County Dem. party, Raleigh, 1991-92; commr. Wake County, Raleigh, 1992; bd. dirs. East Cen. Cmty. Legal Svcs., Inc., 1997-2003, State Capitol Found., 1994—; past-chair, family law sect. NC Advs. Justice, 1996-98. Mem.: ABA, Cary Bar Assn. (organizer 1993—), Wake County Bar Assn. (bd. dirs. 1999—2001), NC Bar Assn. (chmn. pub. info. com. 1994—96, dir. family law coun. 1994—97, 2006—09, vice chair family law sect. 2011—12, chair family law sect. 2012—13). Methodist. Avocation: sailing. Office: PO Box 1325 Cary NC 27512-1325 also: 590 New Waverly Pl Ste 110 Cary NC 27512-1325 Office Phone: 919-816-9002. Personal E-mail: charles@montlylaw.com. Business E-Mail: charles@montgomeryfamilylaw.com.*

MONTGOMERY, DENISE KAREN, nurse; b. NYC, Dec. 23, 1951; d. Thomas Cornell and Dorothy Marie (Castine) Simons; m. Timothy Bruce Montgomery, July 19, 1974 (div. Feb. 1981); m. Joseph Samuel Montgomery, Aug. 20, 1983. A in Nursing, San Jacinto Coll., 1971. RN, Tex. Charge nurse Aarons Womens Clinic, Houston, 1977; rsch. asst. dept. ob-gyn. Baylor Coll. Medicine, Houston, 1977-81, nursing supr., 1979-81, program coord. population control program, 1979-81; nurse Dr. Eric J. Haufrect, Houston, 1982-83; office mgr., supr. Dr. Samuel Law, Houston, 1983-84, Dr. J.S. Montgomery III, 1987—. Contbr. articles to profl. jours. Recipient Disting. Pub. Svc. award Am. Heart Assn., 1976; numerous rsch. grants. Mem. Nat. Assn. Coll. Ob-Gyn. Republican. Mem. Christian Ch. Home: 8202 N Tahoe Dr Houston TX 77040-1256 Office Phone: 281-955-5300. E-mail: denmnt@hotmail.com.

MONTGOMERY, DIRK A., corporate financial executive; Undergraduate degree in Acctg., Miami U., Ohio; MBA, U. Chgo. CPA, Ohio. CFO, Retail Group ConAgra Foods Inc.; fin. auditor, corp. fin. specialist Ernst & Young LLP; with Limited Brands, Sara Lee Corp.; CFO, sr. v.p. OSI Restaurant Partners, LLC, 2005—. Office: OSI Restaurant Partners LLC 2202 N West Shore Blvd Ste 500 Tampa FL 33607 Office Phone: 813-282-1225. Office Fax: 813-282-1209. Business E-Mail: dmontgomery@osirestaurantpartners.com.

MONTGOMERY, HASKINS, state legislator; b. Bay Springs, Miss., Feb. 12, 1952; m. Diana McDonald; children: Heather Hunt, Salli Hobson; 1 child, Anna Haskin Patton. Attended, Jones County Jr. coll., Miss. State U. Econ. developer; businessman; farmer; alderman Bay Springs, Miss.; mayor; mem. Dist. 34 Miss. State Senate, 2008—. Democrat. Methodist. Home: PO Box 611 Bay Springs MS 39422 Office: PO Box 1018 Jackson MS 39215 Home Phone: 601-764-3068; Office Phone: 601-764-2700, 601-359-3244. E-mail: hmontgomery@senate.ms.gov.

MONTGOMERY, JIM, lawyer; BS, Bowling Green State U., OH, 1974; JD, Case Western Res. U., Cleveland, 1980. Bar: Tex. 1980. Founder, mgr. SafeTScribe LLC, 2006; mng. ptnr. DLA Piper. Bd. dirs. SigmaTel Inc., 1997—2003, Sapling Systems, 2007, Austin C. of C., 2007—09, Austin Exec. Com., 2007—09, CallSpace Inc., 2009. Bd. of advisors Ronal McDonald House; bd. dirs. Breakthrough, 2001—09, Found. for the Homeless. Named one of America's Leading Lawyers for Bus., Chambers USA. Office: DLA Piper 401 Congress Ave Ste 2500 Austin TX 78701-3799 Office Phone: 512-457-7100. E-mail: jim.montgomery@dlapiper.com.

MONTGOMERY, JOHN RICHARD, pediatrician, educator; b. Burnsville, Miss., Oct. 24, 1934; s. Guy Austin and Harriet Pauline (Owens) M.; m. Dottye Ann Newell, June 26, 1965; children: John Newell, Michelle Elizabeth. BS, U. Ala., 1955, MD, 1958. Cert. Am. Bd. Pediat. Intern U. Miss., Jackson, 1958-59, resident in pediat., 1959-60, Baylor Coll. Medicine, Houston, 1960-61, fellow in pediat. infectious diseases and immunology, 1964-66, asst. prof. pediat., 1966-70, assoc. prof., 1970-75; chief pediat. programs U. Ala. Sch. Medicine, Huntsville, 1975-95, prof., 1975-97, prof. emeritus, 1997—. Bd. dirs. State Bd. Health, Ala. Bd. Med. Examiners; adv. com. Ala. EMS for Children. Contbr. articles to books and profl. jours. With AUS, 1961—62, Korea, ret. col. USAR, 1999. Mem. Soc. Pediat. Rsch., Am. Assn. Immunologists, Infectious Diseases Soc., N.Y. Acad. Scis., Am. Acad. Pediats. (pres. Ala. chpt. 1991-93), Sigma Xi, Phi Beta Kappa. Achievements include assisting in inplementing germ-free environmental bubble to protect patient with no natural immunity (patient later subject of movie The Boy in the Plastic Bubble, 1976 and PBS documentary on American Experience, 2006). Home Phone: 256-883-9029; Office Phone: 256-551-4600. Personal E-mail: dnjrmont@bellsouth.net.

MONTGOMERY, JOSEPH WILLIAM, financial consultant; m. Linda Montgomery; children: Joseph, Madeline. BBA, Coll. William and Mary, Williamsburg, Va., 1974. CFP; cert. portfolio mgr. Account exec. Wheat, First Securities, Inc., Lynchburg, Va., 1975-79, Williamsburg, Va., 1979-81, v.p., investment officer, 1981-82, sr. v.p., investment officer, 1982-90; mng. dir. investments Wells Fargo Advisors (formerly Wachovia Securities), Williamsburg, Va., 1990—, head Optimal Svc. Group. Mem. nat. nominating com. Outstanding Young Am. Program, 1998; bd. dirs. Future Hampton Roads, Inc., 1995—; mem. nat. campaign steering com. Campaign of 4th Century, William & Mary, 1992, United Way Williamsburg, 1993-95; bd. vis., 1995-99; mem. commn. tercentenary observanced Coll. William & Mary, 1992; sec. William & Mary Endowment Assn., 2000-05; mem. nat. campaign steering com. William & Mary, 2001; mem. adv. coun. Peninsula White Sox, 1986; bd. dirs. Nat. Conf. Christians & Jews, peninsula chpt., 1986-91; mem. Williamsburg Cmty. Health Found., 1998; dir., treas. Franklin & Gladys Clark Found.; mem. Greater Williamsburg Cmty. Trust, 1999-2008; mem. Jamestown Yorktown Found., 1999-2009, v.p., 2000, sr. v.p., 2001; bd. trustees Hamptons Rds. Acad., 2003-09; mem. nat. adv. coun. Colonial Williamsburg, 2006-; mem. adv. com. Va. Retirement System, 2001-05, bd. trustees, 2014. Named one of Top 300 Fin. Advisors in Country, Worth Mag., 1998, Top 100 Fin. Advisors, Worth Mag., 1999-, Top 10 Ace Advisers, Ticker Mag., 2000, Nation's 100 Most Exclusive Wealth Advisors, 2004, Worth Mag., Top Ranked Teams in Am. Rsch. Mag., 2004, 05, 06, 07, 08, Top 100 Fin. Advisors Barron's Mag., 2004-, Top 100 Wealth Advisors Worth Mag., 2005, 06, 08; named to Broker Hall of Fame, Rsch. mag., 1996, The Chancellor's Cir., Coll. William and Mary, 1998; recipient Best Brokers in Am. award Reg. Rep. Mag., 2002, Am. Top 50 Brokers award Reg. Rep. Mag., 2003, 05, Top Wirehouse Rep. Am., 2007, 08, 11; named State of Va. Top Fin. Advisor Va. Bus. Mag., 2005-08, 09; featured advisor The Winner's Cir. Book, 2002, Winner's Cir. IV Book, 2005. Mem. Internat. Assn. Fin. Planning, Inst. Cert. Fin. Planners, Investment Mgmt. Cons. Found., 1998, Soc. of Alumni William & Mary (pres. 1992, treas. 1991, sec. 1990, bd. dirs. 1989, Alumni Medallion 1996, Wachovia Way award, 2004). Office: Wells Fargo Advisors 428 McLaws Cir Williamsburg VA 23185 Office Phone: 757-220-1782.

MONTGOMERY, RICHARD (JOHNNY), state legislator; b. Sevierville, Tenn., Oct. 24, 1946; m. Anna Montgomery; 1 child. Mem. Sevier County Sch. Bd., 1982—98; state rep. Dist. 12 Tenn., 1999—; mgr. Lockheed Martin Energy Resource. Mem.: Nat. Assn. Sportsmen Legislators, Tenn. Walking Horse Assn., Nat. Rifle Assn., Tenn. Farm Bur., Tenn. Sch. Bd. Assn., Tenn. Vocat. Assn. Republican. Baptist. Office: 1582 Broad River Ln Sevierville TN 37876 also: 201 War Memorial Bldg Nashville TN 37243-0112 Office Phone: 865-453-1218, 615-741-5981. Office Fax: 615-253-0303. Business E-Mail: rep.richard.montgomery@capitol.tn.gov.

MONTGOMERY RICE, VALERIE, dean, reproductive endocrinologist, infertility specialist, medical educator; BS in Chemistry, Ga. Inst. Tech., 1983; MD, Harvard U., 1987. Intern Dept. Gynecology and Obstetrics Emory U. Sch. Medicine and Affiliated Hospitals, Atlanta, 1987—88, resident, 1988—91; fellowship reproductive endocrinology and infertility Hutzel Hosp., Detroit, 1991—93; clin. instr. Wayne State U., 1991—93; asst. prof. U. Kans. Sch. Medicine, Kansas City, 1993—97, vice chmn. Dept. Obstetrics and Gynecology, 1996—97, med. dir. Clin. Trials Divsn., Clin. Rsch. Inst., 1996—97, divsn. head reproductive endocrinology and infertility, 1998—2003; sr. staff physician Divsn. Reproductive Endocrinology Henry Ford Med. Ctr., Troy, Mich., 1997—98; assoc. prof., dir. Divsn. Reproductive Endocrinology and Infertility U. Kans. Med. Ctr., 1998—2003; prof., chair Dept. Obstetrics and Gynecology Meharry Med. Coll., Nashville, 2003—06, program dir. OB-GYN Residency Training Program, 2004—06, Joy McCann prof., 2004—06, exec. dir. Ctr. for Women's Health Rsch., 2005—, prof., 2006—, sr. v.p. health affairs, dean Sch. Medicine, 2006—09; prof. radiology, clin. prof. obstetrics and gynecology Vanderbilt U. Med. Ctr., Nashville, 2006—11; dean, exec. v.p. Morehouse Sch. Medicine, Atlanta, 2011—. Chair Wal-Mart Healthcare Insights Panel, 2007—; mem. Nat. Aids Fund Bd. Trustees, 2007—, chair Every Life Matters, Every Dollar Counts Campaign, 2009—; mem. FDA Panel for Reproductive and Urological Drugs; spkr. in field. Contbr. articles to med. jours. Recipient John D. Thompson Resident Rsch. Day First Place Award, Emory U., 1989, 1991, Michelle Marrs Vision Award, Matthew Walker Comprehensive Health, 2005, Bridge of Honor Award, Women in NAACP, 2006, YM Acad. for Women of Achievement Award, 2007, Disting. Svc. Award, NAACP, 2007, Tenn. Ladies of Distinction Svc. Award, 2007, Dr. Dorothy Brown Humanitarian Award, Minerva Found., Delta Sigma Theta Sorority, 2008, Freedom's Sister Awardee, Ford Found., 2010, Nat. Nefertiti Award, Nat. Societas Docta, Inc., 2010, Multicultural Women's Legacy award, Working Mother Media, 2011; Commonwealth Fund Med. Fellowship, 1986—87, Nat. Med. Fellowship, 1986—87. Fellow: American Coll. of Obstetrics and Gynecology; mem.: AMA, Internat. Women's Forum, Ctrl. Assn. Obstetricians and Gynecologists, North American Menopause Soc., Nat. Med. Assn., Clay-Platte County Med. Soc., Kansas City Med. Soc., Kansas City Gynecological Soc., American Med. Women's Assn. (Elizabeth Blackwell Award 2011), Soc. Reproductive Endocrinology and Infertility, Soc. Gynecological Investigation, American Soc. Reproductive Medicine, Aesculapian Club of Harvard Med. Sch., Omicron Delta Kappa. Office: Morehouse School of Medicine 720 Westview Dr SW Atlanta GA 30310 Office Phone: 404-752-1720. Office Fax: 404-752-1594.

MONTONEY, MARK R., medical officer; BA in Psychology magna cum laude, Case Western Res. U., Cleve.; MBA, Regent U., Virginia Beach, VA; MD, U. Cin. Cert. in internal medicine and geriatric medicine. Practiced, internal medicine & geriatric medicine, 1986—98; med. dir., primary care Riverside Meth. Hosp., chief resident, internal medicine, v.p., quality & clin. support, 2000—05; v.p., physician consulting OhioHealth Corp., system v.p. & chief med. officer, 2005—08; exec. v.p., chief med. officer Vanguard Health Sys., Inc., 2008—. Past chmn. Ohio Partnership for Excellence; examiner Malcolm Baldrige Nat. Quality award; bd. mem. Tenn. Ctr. for Performance Excellence Recipient Malcolm Baldrige Quality award. Mem.: Am. Coll. Physician Execs., Phi Beta Kappa Honor Soc. (elected mem. 1978). Office: Vanguard Health System Inc Ste 100 20 Burton Hills Blvd Nashville TN 37215 Office Phone: 615-665-6000. Office Fax: 615-665-6099. Business E-Mail: mmontoney@vanguardhealth.com.

MONTONI, RICHARD A., management consultant; BS, Boston U.; MS, Northeastern U., MA in Acctg. Audit ptnr. KPMG LLP; CFO, exec. v.p. & bd. dirs. CIBER, Inc., Englewood, Colo., 1996—2000; CFO, exec. v.p. Managed Storage Internat., Inc., Broomfield, Colo., 2000—01; CFO, treas. MAXIMUS, Inc., Reston, Va., 2002—06, pres., CEO & bd. dirs., 2006—. Bd. dirs. CIBER, Inc. Office: MAXIMUS Inc 11419 Sunset Hills Rd Reston VA 20190-5207 Office Phone: 703-251-8500. Office Fax: 703-251-8240. Business E-Mail: richardmontoni@maximus.com.

MONTOUCET, JACK, state legislator; Alligator farmer; owner Jacques' Croc's & Farm Pride Processors; ret. chief Lafayette Fire Dept.; mem. Dist. 42 La. House of Reps., 2008—, mem. natural resources and environment com., retirement com., transp., hwys. and pub. works com. Democrat. Office: State Capitol Po Box 44486 Baton Rouge LA 70804 also: 112 E Hutchinson Ave Crowley LA 70526-4449 Office Phone: 225-342-6945, 337-783-2999. Office Fax: 337-788-4957. Business E-Mail: montoucj@legis.state.la.us.

MONTOYA, JUAN PABLO, professional race car driver; b. Bogota, Colombia, Sept. 20, 1975; m. Connie Freydell; children: Sebastian, Paulina. Race car driver Formula One Williams, 2001—04, McLaren, 2005—06; race car driver NASCAR Chip Ganassi Racing, 2007—. 2nd pl. Spanish Grand Prix, 2001, 2002, European Grand Prix, 2001, 2003; 1st pl. Italian Grand Prix, 2001, 2005, 2nd pl., 2003, Japanese Grand Prix, 2001, Australian Grand Prix, 2002, 2003, Malaysian Grand Prix, 2002, 2004; 3rd pl. Austrian Grand Prix, 2002, Brit. Grand Prix, 2002, 2nd pl., 2003, 1st pl., 2005; 2nd pl. German Grand Prix, 2002, 2005, 1st pl., 2003; 3rd pl. Belgian Grand Prix, 2002; 1st pl. Monaco Grand Prix, 2003, 2nd pl., 2006; 3rd pl. Can. Grand Prix, 2003; 2nd pl. French Grand Prix, 2003; 3rd pl. Hungarian Grand Prix, 2003, San Marino Grand Prix, 2004, 2006; 1st pl. Brazilian Grand Prix, 2004, 2005; 3rd pl. Turkish Grand Prix, 2005; 1st pl. Toyota/Save Mart 350 Infineon Raceway, 2007; 1st pl. Heluva Good! Sour Cream Dips at the Glen Watkins Glen Internat., 2010. Founder Formula Smiles Found.; goodwill amb. UN. Recipient Lorenzo Bandini trophy, 2002; named Newcomer of Yr., Laureus World Sports Awards, 2002, NASCAR Nextel Cup Rookie of Yr., 2007. Avocations: video games, snowboarding, golf. Mailing: Ganassi Racing 8500 Westmoreland Dr Concord NC 28027

MONTROSE-GRAEM, DOUGLASS, museum director, poet painter, music maker; b. Budapest, Hungary, July 6, 1924; came to U.S., 1954, naturalized, 1965; s. Col. Hugh Merton and Ellen Charlotte (Baroness Podmaniczky) G.; children: Robert, Christopher, Anabel, Ian, Isis Marina. BA, Piarist Fathers Coll., 1942; MBA, NY Inst. Fin. (now NYU), 1958. Lic. real estate broker Acad. Real Estate Denver, 1975. Sr. officer INTEL, 1942—60; various position through ptnr. R.W. Pressprich; ptnr. Mitchell, Hutchins & Co., NYC; co-founder William D. Witter Inc., NYC; founder, dir. Turner Mus., Denver, 1973—; endownment fund organisor. Bank owner, Lafayette, Colo.; organizer, govt. securities com. Investment Assn. NY, 1955; non-exec. dir. Midwestern Fin., Denver, exec. bd. chmn.; organizer Internat. Bank Colo.; bd. dirs. Turner Soc. London; patron H.R.H. The Prince of Wales, 1978—2002; treas. Sarasota County Veterans Commn., 2011—13. Author: Durer and Domjan, 1972, Turner's Cosmic Optimism, 1990, Turner's Angels, 1991, Turner's Rainbows, 1992, Turner's Children--So Much Love, 1993, Turner's Powerful Allegories, 1994, Ascendent Turner, 2002, Triple Turner Treat, 2003, Turner in Italy, 2009, Moran & Turner A New Appraisal in the 21st Century, 2010, Collector with a Vision, Busness Plan of J.M. Turner, 2012. Cited as founder of one of Am.'s 99 Finest Museums, 1973, founder of first virtual art mus. in the world, 2001; recipient Papal Blessing, Pope John 23, One Thousand Great Americans, 2005. Mem.: DAV (life nominated Disabled Am. Vet. of Yr. 2004), St. Andrew's Soc. Colo. (life). Business E-Mail: turnermuseum@gmail.com.

MONTROSS, ERIC SCOTT, sportscaster, retired professional basketball player; b. Sept. 23, 1971; s. Scott and Janice M.; m. Laura, Aug. 27, 1994. Student in Speech Comm., U. N.C. Ctr. Boston Celtics, 1994-96, NJ Nets, 1996-97, Phila. 76ers, 1997-98, Detroit Pistons, 1998—2001, Toronto Raptors, 2001—03; ret. NBA, 2002; color analyst, U. NC basketball games Tar Heel Sports Network, 2005—. Named All-Am. Second team AP, All-ACC First team, All-Tournament teams ACC, NCAA East Region, NCAA Final Four, All-Rookie Second team, Schick, 1994-95. Achievements include member of NCAA national championship winning University of North Carolina Tar Heels, 1993. Avocations: reading, fishing, skeet shooting, travel, music. Office: Tar Heel Sports Network c/o Univ NC Athletic Dept PO Box 2126 Chapel Hill NC 27515

MONTUPET, JEAN-PAUL LEON, printing company executive; b. Paris, Dec. 24, 1947; s. Jean Pierre and Janine Paule (Poggi) Montupet; m. Isabelle Yvonne Heidt, June 19, 1973; 1 child, Pauline James. MBA, Hautes Etudes Commerciales, France, 1970. Cert. ITP Harvard Bus. Sch., 1971. Assoc. prof. Hautes Etudes Commerciales, Jouy en Josas, France, 1970—73; comptroller Fonderies Montupet, Nanterre, France, 1973—96, chmn., CEO, 1976—81; chmn., dir., N.Am. Ops. Moteurs Leroy Somer, Canada, 1990; exec. v.p., Indsl. Automation Bus. Emerson Electric Co., 2000—, pres., Europe, 2002, exec. v.p., Indsl. Motors & Drives Business, 1990. Bd. dirs. PartnerRe Ltd., King Bearing, Inc., Costa Mesa, Lexmark Internat. Inc., 2006—. Roman Catholic. Home: 24 Brentmoor Park Saint Louis MO 63105-3070 Office: Lexmark International Inc Bd Directors 740 W New Cir Rd Lexington KY 40550 Office Phone: 859-232-2000. E-mail: jlmontupet@lexmark.com.

MOOD, FRANCIS P., JR., lawyer, utilities executive; BA, The Citadel, 1960, LLD (hon.), 1985; LLB, U. Va., 1963; LLD (hon.), U. SC, 2004. Bar: SC 1963. Ptnr. Haynsworth Sinkler Boyd, Columbia, SC, 1967—2004, pres., 1984—92; sr. v.p., gen. counsel, asst. sec. SCANA Corp., Columbia, SC, 2005—. Permanent mem. Judicial Conf., US Ct. Appeals (4th cir.); interim dean Univ. SC Sch. Law, 2003; chmn. SC Bd. Law Examiners, 1973—82. Mem. bd. vis. The Citadel, 1973—79, 1994—2000, chmn., 1997—2000; bd. dir. The Citadel Develop. Found., 1980—88, 1990—94, 2001—, pres., 1982—86; mem. Univ. SC Sch. Law Partnership Bd., 1991—94, pres., 1991—93; mem. Ctrl. Carolina Cmty. Found., 1992—98, pres., 1995—97; bd. dir. Liberty Fellowship, 2004—, Columbia Urban League. Served US Army, 1964—66. Mem.: ABA, State Bar SC, Richland County Bar Assn. Office: SCANA Corp 1426 Main St Columbia SC 29218

MOODY, DIXON MCGUIRE, radiologist; b. Tyler, Tex., Jan. 12, 1937; s. Dwight Lyman Moody and Helen Blaine McGuire; m. Lucinda L. Blitz, Aug. 15, 1964; children: Abigail Ann (Moody) Sinwell, Susan Eloise (Moody) Prieto, Sarah Katherine (Moody) Bialas. MD, U. of Tex. Southwestern, Dallas, 1963. Diplomate Diagnostic Radiology Am. Bd. of Radiology, 1971, Neuroradiology Am. Bd. of Radiology, 1995. Resident physician Stanford U. Sch of Medicine, Palo Alto, Calif., 1963—70; asst. physician Cornell U. Sch of Medicine, NYC, 1970—71; asst. prof. U. of N.Mex Sch Medicine, Albuquerque, 1971—73; prof. and chief of neuroradiology Wake Forest U. Sch. Medicine, Winston-Salem, NC. Mem. Nat. Adv. Coun. NINDS, NIH, Bethesda, Md., 1994—97, Ctr. for Sci. Rev., NIH, Bethesda, Md., 1998—2004; mem., sci. program com. Radiol. Soc. of N.Am., Oak Brook, Ill. Capt. US Army, 1966—67. Decorated Bronze Star Medal US Army; recipient Established Investigator, Clin. Sci. Award, Wake Forest U. Sch. of Medicine, 2002; grantee Jacob K Javits Neurosci. Investigator, NIH, 1984—2008, Clin. Hypotheses in Neuroscience Imaging Rsch., Charles A Dana Found., 1996-1999. Fellow: Am. Coll. of Radiology; mem.: Am. Soc. of Neuroradiology (Outstanding Contributions in Rsch. award 2005), Soc. for Neurosci., Radiol. Soc. of N.Am. (Outstanding Rschr. award 2005), Forsyth Country Club, Cornell Club NY, Hillsboro Club, Alpha Omega Alpha. Achievements include research in Brain injury during heart surgery due to fat emboli; brain hemorrhage in neonates due to rupture of veins; dementia due to obstruction of veins and loss of capillaries; significant vascular disease in Alzheimer's brains; cause and prevention of brain injury during cardiopulmonary bypass. Avocation: tennis. Office Phone: 336-716-2463. Business E-Mail: dmmoody@wfubmc.edu.

MOODY, FRANK G., surgeon; b. Franklin, NH, May 3, 1928; BA, Dartmouth Coll., 1953; attended, Dartmouth Med. Sch., 1952—54; MD, Cornell Univ., 1956. Cert. FACS, 1967, Am. Bd. Surgery, 1980. Asst. prof. Univ. Calif. Med Sch., San Francisco, 1965—66; assoc. prof. through prof. Univ. Ala. Med. Sch., 1966—71; prof., chmn. dept. surgery Univ. Utah Sch. Med., 1971—82; staff surgeon Vet. Adminstrn. Hosp., Salt Lake City, 1971—82; chmn. dept. surgery Univ. Tex. Med. Sch., Houston, 1982—94, Denton A. Cooley prof. surgery, 1982—. Recipient Sci. Achievement award AMA, 1995. Mem.: Soc. U. Surgeons (Lifetime Achievement award), Soc. Surgery of the Alimentary Tract (pres. 1981), AMA, Am. Gastroenterological Assn., Am. Pancreatic Assn. (pres. 1979), Am. Physiological Soc., Am. Surgical Assn., Phi Beta Kappa, Alpha Omega Alpha. Office: U Tex Med Sch Dept Surgery 6431 Fannin St Houston TX 77030-1501 Home Phone: 713-664-3047; Office Phone: 713-500-7241. Business E-Mail: frank.g.moody@uth.tmc.edu.

MOODY, JAMES MAXWELL, JR., (JAY MOODY), federal judge; b. El Dorado, Ark., 1964; BBA, U. Ark., 1986; JD, U. Ark. Bowen Sch. Law, 1989. Assoc. Wright, Lindsey & Jennings LLP, 1989—94, ptnr., 1994—2003; cir. judge Sixth Judicial Dist. Ark. (3rd Divsn.), 2003—14; judge US Dist. Ct. (eastern dist.) Ark, 2014—. Office: US District Court 500 West Capitol Ave Little Rock AR 72201 Office Phone: 501-604-5351.*

MOODY, JAMES SHELTON, JR., federal judge; b. Tampa, Fla., Mar. 31, 1947; s. James Shelton and Irma (Cone) Moody; m. Carol Still, June 19, 1971; children: Ashley Brooke, James Shelton III, Patricia Noel; m. Kelli Ossi, Nov. 1993. BS, U. Fla., Gainesville, 1969; JD, U. Fla. Coll. Law, 1972. Bar: Fla. 1972, US Dist. Ct. (mid. dist.) Fla. 1972. Ptnr., officer Trinkle, Redman, Moody & Swanson PA, Plant City, Fla., 1972-94; cir. judge Thirteenth Jud. Cir. Ct. Hillsborough County, Fla., 1995—2000; judge US Dist. Ct. (mid. dist.) Fla., Tampa, 2000—. Mem. Hillsborough County Law Libr. Com., 1978—85, chair, 1983—85; mem. cmty. adv. bd. United Way Tampa; bd. trustees U. Fla. Law Ctr.; bd. dirs. Hillsborough County Bar Found., 2000—08, Hillsborough County United Way. Named to U. Fla. Hall of Fame. Mem.: ABA, American Law Inst., Fla. Trial Lawyers Assn., Assn. Trial Lawyers America, Hillsborough County Bar Assn. (v.p. 1986—87, pres. 1987—88, Robert Patton Outstanding Jurist award 2003), Fla. Bar Assn. (Outstanding Jurist award, Young Lawyer's divsn. 2007), Lions (past pres., Golden Chain award 1980—82), Fla. Blue Key, Omicron Delta Kappa, Beta Gamma Sigma, Phi Kappa Phi, Order of the Coif. Democrat. Presbyterian. Office: Sam M Gibbons US Courthouse 801 N Florida Ave Tampa FL 33602 Office Phone: 813-301-5680.

MOODY, LIZABETH ANN, lawyer, educator; b. Johnson City, Tenn., July 11, 1934; d. Robert Alexander and Clara Pauline (Fine) M.; m. Alan Paul Buchmann, Sept. 5, 1959. AB, Columbia U., 1956; LLB, Yale U., 1959. Bar: Conn. 1959, Ohio 1960, U.S. Dist. Ct. Conn. 1960, U.S. Supreme Ct. 1977, U.S. Dist. Ct. (no. dist.) Ohio 1961. Assoc. Goldstein & Peck, Bridgeport, Conn., 1959-60, Slough & Slough, Cleve., 1960-61, 63-66, Ginsberg, Guren & Meritt, Cleve., 1962; ptnr. Metzenbaum, Gaines, Finley & Stern, Cleve., 1967-71; assoc. prof. Cleve. State U., 1970-73, prof., 1973-94, interim dean and prof., 1987-88; vis. prof. U. Toledo, 1976-77; v.p., dean Coll. Law, prof. Stetson U., 1994-99, Disting. univ. prof., 1998—. Rev. authority on civil rights HEW, Washington, 1973—79; vis. prof. Nat. Law Ctr. George Washington U., 1981—82, U. Hawaii, Honolulu, 1988, So. Meth. U., 2004, Bklyn. Law Sch., 2007; Wallace S. Fugiama Disting. prof. U. Hawaii, Honolulu, 2002; CEO Law Sch. Admission Svcs., Newtown, Pa., 1991—93; v.p. Stetson U., 1994—99; dir., sec., mem. exec. com. Fla. Health Scis. Ctr., Tampa Gen. Hosp., Fla., 1998—2002; chair drafting com. to revise MoDel Non-Profit Corp. Act, 2009. Author: Smith's Review of Corps, 1987, Smith's Review of Estates, 1987; contbr. articles to profl. jours. Pres. Cuyahoga County Econ. and Cmty. Devel., Cleve., 1984-88, Task Force on Violent Crime, Cleve., 1987-88; chmn. audit com. Law Sch. Admission Coun., New Town, Pa., 1988-89, bd. trustees Law Sch. Admission Coun., 1989-94, exec. dir., 1991-93, pres., CEO, dir. Law Sch. Admission Svc., 1991-93; commr. Ohio Ethics Commn., Columbus, Ohio, 1988-91, Ohio Pub. Defender Commn.; v.p., trustee Gt. Lakes Theatre Festival, Cleve., 1972-90; dir., sec. exec. com. Fla. Health Scis. Ctr., 1997—; dir. Cleve. Growth Assn., 1987-88; trustee Acad. Prep., St. Petersburg, Fla., 1999—; lay reader Cathedral Ch. of St. Peter's, St. Petersburg, Fla., 2000— Recipient New Frontier award Ams. for Dem. Action, 1977, YWCA Women of Distinction award, 1988, Josephine Irwin award, 1990, award for Excellence in Governance Fl. Health Sci. Ctr., 2002; Day named in her honor, May 8, 1990, Cleve. Mem.: AAUP, ABA (chair bus. law sect., non-profit corp. com. 1987—91, bus. law sect. coun. mem. 1993—94, house of dels. 1994—99, mem. accreditation com. 1994—2000, chair internat. programs com. 1995—99, sr. lawyers divsn. coun. 1997—2001, chair accreditation com. 1999—2000, sect. legal edn. coun. 2000—, specialization standing com. 2001—04, chair sr. lawyers divsn. coun. 2003—04, chair 2003—04, standing com. libr. mem., Congress Law Libr., Glass Cutter award 1997, Bus. Law Sect. Authors award 2009), English Speaking Union (trustee 1986—89), Cleve. Bar Assn. (pres. 1987—88, meritorious svc. award 1987), Ohio State Bar Assn. (coun. of dels. 1981—91, Ohio Bar medal 1992), Am. Law Inst. (ALI-ABA com. 1998—2001, adv. com. 2001—, elected mem.), Assn. Am. Law Schs. (exec. com. 1977—81), St. Petersburg Yacht Club (Stetson U. Hall of Fame). Office: 1401 61st St S Saint Petersburg FL 33707-3246 Office Phone: 727-562-7848. Business E-Mail: moody@law.stetson.edu.

MOODY, ROBERT LEE, insurance company executive; b. 1936; Chmn. Am. Nat. Ins. Co., Galveston, Tex., 1982—91; chmn., CEO American National Insurance Co., Galveston, Tex., 1991—, Nat. Western Life Ins. Co., Austin, Tex., Moody Nat. Bank of Galveston; pres. Moody Bancshares, Inc. Bd. dirs. Am. Nat. Ins. Co., 1960—, Nat. Western Life Ins. Co.; trustee Moody Found. Office: Am Nat Ins Co 1 Moody Plz Galveston TX 77550

MOON, JOHN HENRY, SR., banker; b. Van Buren, Ark., Aug. 19, 1937; s. B.R. and Alma (Witte) M.; m. Agnes Rose Dickens, Aug. 16, 1958; children: John Henry, Randall Allen. AA, Delmar Coll., Corpus Christi, Tex., 1956; BBA cum laude, Tex. A&M U., Kingsville, 1958. Sr. acct. Tex. Eastern Transp. Co. and subs., 1958-63; exec. v.p., dir. Houston Rsch. Inst., 1963-68; sr. v.p., asst. to chmn. bd., dir. Main Bank, 1968—69; vice chmn. bd., dir. N.E. Bank, 1969; CEO, chmn. bd., dir. Pasadena Nat. Bank, Tex., 1970-81; gen. ptnr. Moon and Assocs., Ltd., 1977—. Chmn. bd., pres. Interservice Life Ins. Corp., Phoenix, Cmty. Bank, Houston, 1975-81, Interstate Bank, Houston, 1977-81, Moon Credit Corp., Pasadena, 1975—, pres., Moon Rentals, LLC, 2007-, Peoples Bank, Houston, 1983-93; chmn. bd. Cmty. Nat. Bank, Friendswood, Tex., 1981-93, Peoples Nat. Bank, Pasadena, Tex., 1984-93; chmn., pres. Sam Houston Pky. Transp. Corp., 1991-93; bd. dirs. Quality Wire Rope Corp., chmn., 1999-2005; bd. dirs., Abilene Oil Gas Inc., 2011-; pres. Sure Found. Inc., 1987—. Past bd. dirs. Pasadena Heart Assn., Salvation Army, Tex. Assn. Prevention of Blindness; past chmn. City of Pasadena Bd. Devel.; past chmn. adv. bd. Pasadena Civic Ctr.; past dir. S.E. Econ. Devel., Inc.; bd. dirs., Tex. Rangers Law Enforcement Assn., San Jacinto Coll. Found., 2000-03, chmn., 2002-03. Named Outstanding Young Man of Yr., Pasadena Jr. C. of C., 1973; named to Pasadena Hall of Fame, 1988. Mem. AICPA, Pasadena C. of C. (bd. dirs. S.E. Econ. Devel., CCC Club, Citizen of Yr. 1994), Tex. Soc. CPAs, Tex. Bankers Assn., Rotary (pres. Pasadena Rotary found. 2001-07). Home: 310 Del Monte Dr Friendswood TX 77546 Office: PO Box 3487 Pasadena TX 77501 Office Phone: 713-943-7777. Business E-Mail: jhmoon@mooncapitalcorp.com.

MOON, NORMAN K., federal judge; BA, U. Va., 1959, JD, 1962, LLM, 1988. Bar: (Va.) 1962. With firm Edmunds & Williams (formerly Williams, Robertson & Sackett), Lynchburg, Va., 1962—74; judge 24th Jud. Cir., 1974—84, chief judge, 1982—85; judge Ct. of Appeals of Va., 1985—93, chief judge, 1993—97; judge US Dist. Ct. (western dist.) Va., 1997—2010, sr. judge, 2010—. Vis. lectr. U. Va. Law Sch., Charlottesville, 1975—88. Office: PO Box 657 Lynchburg VA 24505-0657

MOONEY, DIANNE, food products executive; Various positions through v.p., Bus. Devel., v.p., Custom Pub. Southern Progress Corp.; founder Southern Living at Home, 1999, sr. v.p., 1999—2007. Bd. dirs. Sanderson Farms, Inc., 2007—. Bd. dirs. United Way of Ctrl. Ala. Office: Sanderson Farms Inc 127 Flynt Rd Laurel MS 39440 Office Phone: 601-649-4030. Office Fax: 601-426-1461. Business E-Mail: dmooney@sandersonfarms.com.

MOONEY, JOHN BRADFORD, JR., oceanographer, engineer, consultant; b. Portsmouth, NH, Mar. 26, 1931; s. John Bradford and Margaret Theodora (Akers) M.; m. Martha Ann Huntley, Dec. 25, 1953 (dec. May 1990); children: Melinda Jean, Pamela Ann, Jennifer Joan; m. Jennie Marie Duca, Nov. 24, 1990. BS, U.S. Naval Acad., 1953; postgrad., George Washington U., 1970, 71, 76; grad. sr. execs. nat./internat. security, Harvard U., 1980. Commd. ens. USN, 1953, advanced through grades to rear adm., 1979; chief staff officer Submarine Devel. Group 1, 1971-73; commdr. Bathyscaphe Trieste II, 1964-66, Submarine Menhaden, 1966-68; comdg. officer Naval Sta., Charleston, SC, 1973-75; dep. dir. Deep Submergence Systems Div., Office Chief Naval Ops., Washington, 1975-77; comdr. Naval Tng. Ctr., Orlando, Fla., 1977-78; dir. Total Force Planning Div., Office Chief Naval Ops., Washington, 1978-81; oceanographer USN, 1981-83, chief naval rsch., 1983-87, ret., 1987; pres. Harbor Br. Oceanographic Instn., Inc., Ft. Pierce, Fla., 1989-92, marine bd., 1991-94. Mem. marine programs adv. coun. Grad. Sch. Oceanography, U. R.I., Narragansett, 1989—; chmn. study panel on undersea vehicles and nat. needs NRC, 1993—96, mem. adv. com. for postdoctoral and sr. rsch. associateship programs, 1995—2001; mem. panel to visit the former Soviet Union to evaluate undersea tech. for U.S. govt., 1993; chair, 1995. At controls of Trieste II when hull of Thresher was found on floor of Atlantic, 1964; coordinated deep search and recovery of hydrogen bomb lost off coast of Spain, 1966; condr. recovery operation from depth of 16,400 feet in Mid-Pacific, 1972. Decorated Legion of Merit with 1 gold star; recipient spl. citation Armed Forces Recreation Assn., 1975, Dist. Eagle Scout award, 1986. Fellow Marine Tech. Soc. (pres. 1991-93), Explorers Club; mem. NAE, Am. Soc. Naval Engrs., Soc. Naval Architects and Marine Engrs., U.S. Naval Inst., Nat. Geog. Soc., Smithsonian Assocs., Masons, Shriners, Order of DeMolay (Legion of Honor), Tau Beta Pi. Avocations: swimming, grandchildren. Home: 2500 Barton Creek Blvd Apt 2508 Austin TX 78735-1629 Office Phone: 512-263-2799. Personal E-mail: jbradmooney@austin.rr.com.

MOONEY, ROBBI GAIL, consumer products company executive; b. Hobbs, N.Mex., Dec. 11, 1955; d. Wilson Henry and Geneva Ann (Ober) Teague; divorced; children: Daymond, Ginger; m. Timothy G. Mooney, Oct. 18, 1991. Student, Ark. Valley Vocat.-Tech. Sch., 1977. Exec. sec. Jacuzzi, Inc., Little Rock, 1977-80; chief ops. officer Mid South Roller Co., Clarksville, Ark., 1981—, Sun Roller Corp., Arlington, Tex., 2002—. Mem. adv. coun. Ark. Valley Vocat. Sch., Ozark, 1990—. Mem. Am. Bus. Women (pres. 1986-89, Woman of Yr. award 1987), Rubber Roller Group (v.p. 1998-2000, pres. 2000-02, chmn. bd. 2002-04), Clarksville C. of C. (bd. dirs. 2002-05), Rotary, Beta Sigma Phi. Home: PO Box 1072 Clarksville AR 72830-1072 Office: Mid South Roller Co PO Box 130 Clarksville AR 72830-0130 Business E-Mail: msrc@cswnet.com.

MOONEYHAM, BOBBY R., educational association administrator; D, U. Okla., 1975. Tchr., Yukon, Okla.; dir. Beaver County Cooperative Guidance Prog., Okla.; supt. Corn Pub. Schs., Okla., Okemah Pub. Schs., Okla.; exec. dir. Okla. State Sch. Bds. Assn., 1975—2000, Nat. Rural Edn. Assn., 2002—; adj. instr. dept. ednl. leadership and policy studies U. Okla., Norman. Creator Okla. Edn. Coalition, 1998. Named a Friend of Edn., Okla. Edn. Assn., 2004; named to Okla. Educators Hall of Fame, 2000. Office: U Okla 112 Fourth St Box 2 Norman OK 73019 E-mail: bmooneyham@ou.edu.

MOORADIAN, ARSHAG DERTAD, internist, educator; b. Aleppo, Syria, Aug. 20, 1953; arrived in U.S., 1981; s. Dertad and Araxi (Halajian) Mooradian; m. Deborah Lynn Miles, June 25, 1985; children: Arshag Dertad, Jr., Ariana Araxie. BS, Am. U., Beirut, 1976, MD, 1980. Diplomate Am. Bd. Internal Medicine. Asst. prof. medicine UCLA, 1985-88; assoc. prof. U. Ariz., Tucson, 1988-91; prof. St. Louis U., 1991—2006; prof. medicine, chmn. dept. medicine U. Fla.,

2006—. Contbr. articles to profl. jours. Grantee VA, 1985—97. Mem.: Am. Diabetes Assn. (chmn. task force micronutrients 1990—91, chmn. coun. nutrition and metabolism 2000—02), Endocrine Soc., Gerontol. Soc. Am., Am. Fedn. Clin. Rsch., Phi Kappa Phi, Alpha Omega Alpha. Mem. Armenian Orthodox Ch. Achievements include identification of a potential biomarker of aging; research in on age-related changes in the blood-brain barrier; on age-related changes in thyroid hormone action; on diabetes related changes in the central nervous system; regulation of the apoA-I gene expression. Office: U Fla Coll Medicine Dept Medicine 653-1 West Eighth St Jacksonville FL 32209 Business E-Mail: arshag.mooradian@jax.ufl.edu.

MOORE, ALECIA BETH See PINK

MOORE, ALISOUN, information technology executive; BA in Polit. Sci. and Biology, U. Albany, 1978—82; MPA in Info. Tech., U. Balt., 1988—91; MBA in Healthcare Mgmt. and Bus., Johns Hopkins U. With State of Maryland, 1999—2001, Montgomery County, 2001—06; dir. health and human svcs. state and local Northrop Grumman, 2007—09; dir. healthcare sys. mgmt. Northrop Grumman Info. Sys., 2007—11; v.p. health svcs. divsn. Computer Sciences Corp., 2011—, gen. mgr. health svcs. divsn., 2011—. Office: Computer Sciences Corporation 3170 Fairview Park Drive Falls Church VA 22042 Office Phone: 703-876-1000.

MOORE, BARRY, state legislator; b. Enterprise; m. Heather Moore; children: Jeremy, Kathleen, Claudia, Jeb. AS, Enterprise State Jr. Coll., Ala.; BS, Auburn U., Ala., 1992. Owner Barry Moore Industries, Enterprise; mem. Dist. 91 Ala. House of Representatives, 2011—. Mem., tchr., deacon Hillcrest Bapt. Ch., Enterprise. Served with US Army Nat. Guard. Republican. Office: 561 County Rd 623 Enterprise AL 36330 also: Ala House of Reps Rm 630-B 11 S Union St Montgomery AL 36130 Office Phone: 334-393-4264, 334-242-7773. Business E-Mail: barry@barrymooreindustries.com.

MOORE, CHARLES A., lawyer; b. Houston, Nov. 17, 1950; BA, U. Houston, 1972, JD magna cum laude, 1975. Bar: Tex. 1975, U.S. Dist. Ct. (no., so. and we. dists.) Tex., U.S. Ct. Appeals (5th, 10th and D.C. cirs.), U.S. Supreme Ct. Gen. counsel Fed. Energy Regulatory Commn., 1981-83.; ptnr., chmn. Energy & Converging Industries Group Akin, Gump, Strauss, Hauer & Feld, L.L.P., Houston; co-mng. ptnr. Houston office Dewey & LeBoeuf (formerly LeBoeuf, Lamb, Greene & MacRae LLP), ptnr. Houston. Energy advisor to Gov. of Tex., 1983-86; Tex. ofcl. rep. Interstate Oil Compact Commn., 1983-86. Mem. ABA, Fed. Energy Bar Assn., Houston Bar Assn, Maritime Law Assn. of US. Office: Dewey & LeBoeuf 1000 Main St Ste 2550 Houston TX 77002-5009 Office Phone: 713-287-2086. Office Fax: 718-287-2100. Business E-Mail: cmoore@dl.com.

MOORE, DANIEL J., health products executive; Grad., Harvard U.; MBA, Boston U. With Procter and Gamble; pres., internat. distbr. mgmt. Boston Scientific Corp., pres., inter-continental, various sales, mktg. and sr. mgmt. positions, US and Europe, 1989; pres., CEO Cyberonics, Inc., 2007—. Bd. dirs. Cyberonics Inc., 2007—. Office: Cyberonics Inc 100 Cyberonics Blvd Houston TX 77058 Office Phone: 281-228-7200. Office Fax: 281-218-9332. Business E-Mail: daniel.moore@cyberonics.com.

MOORE, DARLA DEE, investment company executive; b. Lake City, SC, Aug. 1, 1954; d. Eugene and Lorraine Moore; m. Richard Edward Rainwater, Dec. 13, 1991; stepchildren: Courtney, Todd, Matthew. BA in Polit. Sci., U. SC, 1975; MBA, George Washington U., 1981. Summer intern to Senator Strom Thurmond US Senate; rschr. Republican Nat. Com., 1976; mng. dir. Chase Manhattan Bank, N.A., NYC, 1982—94; ptnr. Rainwater, Inc., 1993—95, pres., ptnr., 1995—. Bd. dirs. The South Financial Group, Inc., 2005—09, Martha Stewart Living Omnimedia, Inc., Magellan Health Services, Inc. Bd. trustees NY U. Sch. of Medicine Found.; chmn., founder Palmetto Inst.; bd. trustees U. SC. Named one of The Top 50 Women in Business, Fortune mag., 1998, 1999. Mem.: Augusta National Golf Club (One of Two First Female Members Admitted 2012). Office: Rainwater Inc 777 Main St Fort Worth TX 76102 Office Phone: 817-878-0401.

MOORE, EDDIE N., JR., college president; BS, Pa. State U., 1968; MBA, U. Pitts., 1975; HDL (hon.), Va. State U. Cert. acct., Tex., Va. Various acctg. positions, 1971-85; asst. comptroller Commonwealth of Va./Dept. of Accounts, Richmond, 1985-88; asst. treas., registered agt. Endowment Assn./Coll. of William and Mary, Inc., 1988-90; comptroller Coll. of William and Mary, Williamsburg, Va., 1988-90; state treas. Commonwealth of Va./Dept. of Treasury, Richmond, 1990-93; pres. Virginia State University, Petersburg, Va., 1993—. Bd. dirs. Universal Corp., Richmond, Va., 2000—, Owens & Minor, Mechanicsville, Va. 1st lt. U.S. Army. Recipient Key to the City of Phila., Mayor W. Wilson Goode, others; decorated Bronze Star, Meritorious Achievement award, Army Commendation medal. Mem. Fiscal Officers of Colls. and Univs. (former v.p.). Office: Va State Univ PO Box 9085 Petersburg VA 23806-0001

MOORE, EDWARD WARREN, lawyer; b. Odessa, Tex., July 21, 1959; s. Edward Warren and Gloria (Schroeter) M.; m. JoAnne Bisso; children: Peggy, Barbara. BA in Econs., Princeton U., 1981; JD, So. Meth. U., 1984. Bar: Tex. 1984, US Dist. Ct. (no. dist.) Tex. 1984, US Dist. Ct. (we. dist.) Tex. 2003, US Ct. Appeals (5th cir.) 1984, US Ct. Appeals (10th cir.) 1985, US Dist. Ct. (eastern dist.) 2009. Dir. Tissue Gen, Inc.; sec., dir. E.N. Bisso & Son, Inc.; ptnr. Bell Nunnally & Martin LLP. Chmn. U. Park Comty. League; chmn. bd. adjustment park City of U. Park; v.p. Princeton Alumni Assn. Ft. Worth. Auction host, annual convention Safari Club Internat.; chmn. exhibitor registration com. Dallas Safari Club. Fellow Am. Bar Found.; mem. ABA (mem. bus. law, environment energy and resources, real property, trust and estate law, taxation), State Bar Tex., Dallas Bar Assn., Dallas Country Club, Safari Club Internat. (life), Dallas Safari Club (life), DSC 100 (vol.), Order of Flags, Salesmanship Club (Dallas) Roman Catholic. Office: Bell Nunnally & Martin LLP 3232 McKinney Ave Ste 1400 Dallas TX 75204-2429 Office Phone: 214-740-1478, 214-740-1400. Business E-Mail: eddym@bellnunnally.com.

MOORE, FAY LINDA, systems engineer; b. Houston, Apr. 7, 1942; d. Charlie Louis and Esther Mable (Banks) Moore; m. Noel Patrick Walker, Jan. 5, 1963 (div. 1967); 1 child, Trina Nicole Moore. Student, Prairie View Agrl. and Mech. Coll., 1960-61, Tex. So. U., 1961, Our Lady Lake U., 1993, U. Phoenix, 2003. Cert. ISO 9001 Internal Auditor, 1994-97. Instr. Internat. Bus. Coll., Houston, 1965; keypunch operator IBM Corp., Houston, 1965-67, sr. keypunch operator, 1967-70, programmer technician, 1970-72, asst. programmer, 1972-73, assoc. programmer, 1973-74, sr. assoc. programmer, 1984-87, staff programmer, 1987-92, staff sys. analyst, 1992-96; sr. software quality engr. Loral Space Info. Sys., Houston, 1994—96; owner, pres. AFT Co., Houston, 1993—2000; sr. software quality engr. Lockheed Martin Corp., Houston, 1996-97; software quality engr. Motorola, Inc., Austin, 1998-2001, cert. quality sys. rev. assessor, 1998—2001, info. tech. quality engr., 2000-2001; prin. sys. engr., L-3 Comm. Titan Corp., Houston, 2001—12, ISO 9001 lead internal auditor, 2005—09. Space shuttle flight support team IBM, 1985—92, mem. space sta. team, 1992—93. Recipient Apollo Achievement award, NASA, 1969, Quality and Productivity award, 1986, 1992, Cert. of Recognition, NASA Office of Space Flight, 2004, L-3 Comm. Team Excellence award, 2011, Program Mgrs. Commendation, Space Shuttle, 2011, Shuttle IV & V Project Completion award, 2012, Gravity Recovery and Interior Lab. (GRAIL) IV & V Project Completion award, 2012, Group Achievement award, Space Shuttle IV&V Team, 2012, NASA Group Achievement award, 2012. Democrat. Avocation: personal computing.

MOORE, GARY W., state legislator; b. 1948; married; 2 children. State rep. Dist. 50, Tenn., 2005—. Former mem. Dist. 1 Davidson County Dem. Exec. Com. Mem.: Muscular Dystrophy Assn. (former mem. exec.com.), RURAL (former sec.), Bellevue Exch. Club, Goodlettsville, Madison and Bellevue C. of C., Nashville & Mid. Tenn. Ctrl. Labor Coun., Southern Fedn. of Profl. Fire Fighters (pres.), Nashville Firefighters Union IAFF Local 140 (v. p., pres.), Tenn. Profl. Fire Fighters Assn. (pres.), Tenn. AFL-CIO, Tenn. State Employees Assn., Whites Creek Cmty. Club, Joelton Civitan Club. Democrat. Baptist. Office: 2946 Morgan Rd Joelton TN 37080 also: 35 Legislative Plz Nashville TN 37243-0150 Office Phone: 615-741-4317. Office Fax: 615-253-0360. Business E-Mail: rep.gary.moore@capitol.tn.gov.

MOORE, GEORGE CRAWFORD JACKSON, lawyer; b. Tenn. BA, U. Fla., 1963; PhB in Soviet Law, U. St. Andrews, Scotland, 1966; MA in English Law with honors, Cambridge U., Eng., 1968, LLM in Internat. Law, 1969. Bar: Eng. (Barrister, Inner Temple) 1970, Jamaica 1971, Fla. 1973, Turks & Caicos Islands 1974, U.S. Supreme Ct. 1976, Antigua and Barbuda, Brit. V.I., Grenada, Montserrat, St. Lucia 1977, Anguilla 1999. Legis. asst. to U.S. sen., Washington, 1970-72; asst. pub. defender Palm Beach County, Fla., 1973; pvt. practice West Palm Beach, Fla., 1973—. Founding pres. World Trade Coun. of Palm Beach County, 1981—; chmn. Fla. Coun. Internat. Devel., 1983—84, 2000—03, Fla. Gov.'s Conf. on World Trade and Investment, 1989, Fla. Export Coun. of U.S. Dept. Commerce, 1991—92, Free Trade Agreement of Americas. Editor spl. issues Fla. Bar Jour., 1982, 87, chmn. editorial bd., 1988-89; mem. editorial bd. The Internat. Lawyer jour. of ABA, 1979-84; contbr. articles to profl. jours. Chmn. Fla. Econ. Growth and Internat. Devel. Commn., 1989-90. Fellow: Ctr. Internat. Legal Studies, Soc. Internat. Bus. Fellows (v.p.); mem.: ABA, Fla. Bar (chmn. internat. law sect. 1994—95, bd. cert. specialist in internat. law 1999—, chmn. internat. law cert. bd. 2004—). Office: 105 S Narcissus Ave Ste 812 West Palm Beach FL 33401-5530 also: 11 King's Bench Walk, Temple London EC4Y 7EQ England Office Phone: 561-833-9000, 44-20-7632-8500. Business E-Mail: barrister@barrister.law.com.

MOORE, HUGH LESLIE, retired pediatrician; b. Dallas, Jan. 6, 1939; s. Robert Leslie and Maybeth (Thompson) Moore; m. LeAnn Kridelbaugh, May 25, 1996; children: Gwen Moore Holliday, Carolyn Moore Becker, Hugh Samuel. BA, U. Colo., 1960; MD, U. Tex.Southwestern Med. Sch., 1964. Diplomate Am. Bd. Pediat., Am. Bd. Pediat. Nephrology. Resident in pediat. Cin. Children's Hosp., Cin., 1964—67; fellow in pediat. nephrology U. Minn. Hosp., Mpls., 1969—71; pediatrician Clin. Pediat. Assoc., Dallas, 1971—; clin. prof. pediat. U. Tex. Southwestern Med. Sch., Dallas, 1982—2005; ret. Pediat. tchr. Childrens Med. Ctr., Dallas, 1971—, bd. trustees, 1984—. Lt. comdr. USN, 1967—69. Recipient Outstanding Tchr. award, Children's Med. Ctr., Mead Johnson Pediat. Lifetime Achievement award, 2006; named one of Top Doctors, D Mag., 1992, 1996, 1999, 2002, Best Doctor's in Am., 2000—01, 2001—02, 2003—04, 2004—05. Mem.: Tex. Pediat. Soc., Dallas County Med. Soc., Tex. Med. Assn. Avocations: travel, photography, birdwatching, motorcycling. Office: 7547 Greenbrier Dr Dallas TX 75225 Business E-Mail: hlalk@aol.com.

MOORE, J. STROTHER, computer scientist, educator; b. Seminole, Okla., Sept. 11, 1947; s. J. Strother and Jessie Louise Moore; m. Jo Anne O'Neil; children: Lisa, Jonathan, Chris. BS in Math., MIT, 1970; PhD in Computational Logic, U. Edinburgh, Scotland, 1973. Programmer dept. computational logic U. Edinburgh, 1971—72, rsch. fellow, 1973; rsch. mathematician Xerox Palo Alto Rsch. Ctr., Calif., 1973—76, SRI Internat., Menlo Park, Calif., 1976—78, sr. rsch. mathematician, 1979—81, staff scientist, 1981; assoc. prof. dept. computer scis. U. Tex., Austin, 1981—84, Gottesman Family Centennial prof., 1985—88, Adm. B.R. Inman prof. computing theory, 1997—, chair dept. computer scis., 2001—09. Founder, chief scientist Computational Logic, Inc., Austin, 1987—96, bd. dirs., 1987—. Co-author: (software) Boyer-Moore Theorem Prover, 1971, A Computational Logic, 1979, A Computational Logic Handbook, 1988, Computer-Aided Reasoning: An Approach, 2000; co-editor: The Correctness Problem in Computer Science, 1981; mem. editl. bd.: Jour. Automated Reasoning, Formal Methods in Sys. Design; contbr. articles to profl. jours. Co-recipient John McCarthy prize for program verification, 1983, Current prize in automatic theorem proving, Am. Math. Soc., 1991, Herbrand award, Conf. on Automated Deduction, 1999. Fellow: Assn. Computing Machinery (Software Sys. award 2005), Am. Assn. Artificial Intelligence; mem.: NAE. Avocations: rock climbing, backpacking. Office: U Tex Dept Computer Sci 1616 Guadalupe Ste 2 408 Austin TX 78701-1188 also: Computational Logic Inc 1717 W Sixth St Ste 290 Austin TX 78712 Office Phone: 512-471-9590. Office Fax: 512-471-8885. Business E-Mail: moore@cs.utexas.edu.

MOORE, JACK B., oil industry executive; b. 1953; BBA in Fin. and Mktg., U. Houston, 1977; grad. Advanced Mgmt. Program, Harvard Bus. Sch. Dir. materials Baker Hughes, Inc., dir. market rsch., dir. HR, v.p. Latin Am. Ops., v.p. Eastern Hemisphere, v.p. Western Hemisphere; v.p., gen. mgr. western hemisphere Cameron International Corp., 1999—2002, pres., Drilling and Prodn. Sys. Group Houston, 2002—06, pres., COO, 2007—08, pres., CEO, 2008—11, chmn., pres., CEO, 2011—. Exec. adv. bd. CT Bauer Coll. Bus.; dir., mem. audit com. Maverick Tube Corp., 2005—; bd. dirs. Cameron Internat. Corp. (formerly Cooper Cameron Corp.), 2007—. Office: Cameron Internat Corp 1333 W Loop S Ste 1700 Houston TX 77027-9109 Office Phone: 713-513-3300. Office Fax: 713-513-3355.

MOORE, JACKSON WATTS, retired bank executive; b. Birmingham, Ala., Nov. 2, 1948; s. Joseph Watts and Shellye Louise (Jackson) M.; m. Elizabeth Wilson, June 12, 1971; children: Jackson Jr., Wilson, Shellye. BS, U. Ala., 1970; JD, Vanderbilt U., 1973. Bar: Supreme Ct. Tenn. 1973, Supreme Ct. US 2000. Assoc. Martin, Tate, Morrow and Marston, Memphis, 1973-77; mng. ptnr. Wildman, Harrold, Allen, Dixon and McDonnell, Memphis, 1977-89; pres., COO Union Planters Corp., Memphis, 1989, also bd. dirs., chmn., CEO, 2000—04; pres. Regions Financial Corp., 2004—, CEO, 2005—06, exec. chmn., 2006—07. Bd. dirs. Union Planters Nat. Bank, Mid-South Pub. Comms. Network, Memphis Devel. Found., PSB Bancshares, Clanton, Ala. Bd. dirs. Boy Scouts Am., Memphis Emmaus Comty.; trustee Vanderbilt Univ.; chmn. bd. Vanderbilt Law Sch.; bd. trustees pres.'s cabinet U. Ala. Capt. U.S. Army, 1973. Mem. Memphis Country Club, Memphis Hunt and Polo Club. Republican. Methodist. Avocations: golf, tennis, reading. Personal E-mail: jackmoore0@gmail.com.

MOORE, JAMES E., former state supreme court justice; b. Laurens, SC, Mar. 13, 1936; s. Roy Ernest and Marie (Hill) M.; m. Mary Alicia Deadwyler, Jan. 27, 1963; children: Erin Alicia, Travis Warren. BA, Duke U., 1958, JD, 1961; D of Humanities (hon.), Lander Univ., 1997. Bar: S.C. 1961, U.S. Dist. Ct. S.C. 1961. Pvt. practice, Greenwood, S.C., 1961-76; mem. SC Ho. of Reps., Columbia, SC, 1968—76; cir. judge 8th Jud. Cir. SC, Greenwood, 1976-91; assoc. justice SC Supreme Ct., 1992—2008. Supreme ct. liaison S.C. Bd. of Law Examiners, Bd. of Commn. on Jud. Conduct, Bd. of Commn. on Atty. Conduct; chmn. Chief Justice's Commn. on Profession. Recipient Outstanding Contribution to Justice award, S.C. Trial Lawyers Assn., 1996. Mem. S.C. Bar Assn., ABA, Am. Judicature Soc.; First Baptist Church of Greenwood. Baptist. Home: 148 Amherst Dr Greenwood SC 29649-8901 Office Phone: 864-942-8559.

MOORE, JANET L.S., music educator, dean; d. Wallace Milton and Roberta Lee Schulze; m. Marvin Lynn Moore; children: Gregory Scott, Kellia Lynne. MusB, Ea. Ky. U., 1974; MusM, U. N.C., Greensboro, 1977, EdD, 1984. Choral and keyboard instr. Rockingham County Sr. H.S., Wentworth, NC, 1977—80; fine arts supr., cultural arts coord. Rockingham County Schs., Wentworth, 1978—80; elem. music specialist Price Traditional Sch., Greensboro, 1984; asst. prof. music edn. Rutgers U., New Brunswick, NJ, 1985—88, Northwestern U., Evanston, Ill., 1988—89; asst. prof. music Sch. Music U. South Fla., Tampa, 1989—95, coord. music edn., 1995—98, assoc. prof. music, 1995—, assoc. dean Coll. Visual and Performing Arts, 1998—2003, assoc. dean undergrad. studies, 2003—. Pres. faculty senate U. South Fla., Tampa, 1997—99; external evaluator Hillsborough County Sch. Sys., Tampa, 2002—07. Author: (music textbook) Understanding Music Through Sound Exploration and Experiments; contbr. music textbook On the Nature of Musical Experience; editor: (state curriculum guide) Introduction to Music Performance. Recipient Tchg. Incentive Program award, Fla. State Legislature and State U. Sys., 1994; grantee, U. South Fla. Rsch. Coun., 1990—97, U. South Fla. Ctr. Tchg. Enhancement, 1998; internat. travel grantee, Inst. on Black Life, U. South Fla., 1993, 1997, summer fellow, Rutgers U. Rsch. Coun., 1987. Mem.: Coun. Colls. Arts and Scis., Fla. Music Educators Assn. (Leadership award 1998), Am. Orff Schulwerk Assn., Internat. Soc. Music Edn. (nat. adv. bd. 1991—94, world conf. adv. bd. 1991—94), Soc. Gen. Music, Soc. Rsch. in Music Edn., Music Educators Nat. Conf. (nat. mem.-at-large Soc. Gen. Music 1997—99, editor Gen. Music Today jour. 2000—03, editl. bd. Soc. Gen. Music), Phi Kappa Phi (life), Pi Kappa Lambda (life; founding pres., Eta Lambda chpt. 1992—94). Office: U South Fla 4202 E Fowler Ave UGS SVC 2002 Tampa FL 33620-6920 Office Phone: 813-974-4051.*

MOORE, JOHN L., state legislator; b. Aug. 19, 1954; m. Elizabeth Kim Prince Moore; children: Kimberly, Melanie, Joni. Mem. Dist. 60 Miss. House of Reps., 1996—, mem. agr. com., corrections com., judiciary B com., judiciary en banc com., pub. property com., rules com., ways and means com. Mem.: Assn. Life Underwriters. Republican. Baptist. Mailing: PO Box 20 Brandon MS 39043 Office Phone: 601-591-4100, 601-359-2432. Business E-Mail: jmoore@house.ms.gov.

MOORE, JOHN NORTON, lawyer, educator, diplomat; b. NYC, June 12, 1937; s. William Thomas and Lorena (Norton) M.; m. Barbara Schneider, Dec. 12, 1981; children: Victoria Norton, Elizabeth Norton. AB in Economics, Drew U., 1959; LLB with honors, Duke U., 1962; LLM, U. Ill., 1965; postgrad., Yale U., 1965-66. Bar: Fla. 1962, Ill. 1963, Va. 1969, D.C. 1972, U.S. Supreme Ct. 1972. Tchg. fellow U. Ill., 1962—63; asst. prof. U. Fla., 1963—65, assoc. prof., 1965—66, asst. dean, 1964—66; assoc. prof. U. Va. Sch. Law, Charlottesville, 1966—69, prof., 1969—76, Walter L. Brown prof. law, 1976—, dir. grad. program, 1968—93, dir. Ctr. Oceans Law and Policy, 1976—, dir. Ctr. Nat. Security Law, 1984—. Counselor on internat. law Dept. State, Washington, 1972-73; chmn. Nat. Security Coun. Task Force on Law of Sea and dep. spl. rep. of Pres. and amb. Law of Sea Conf., 1973-76; fellow Woodrow Wilson Internat. Ctr. for Scholars, Washington, 1976; adj. prof. Georgetown Law Ctr., 1978—; mem. Nat. Adv. Com. on Oceans and Atmosphere, 1984-85; mem. U.S. del. Conf. Security and Coop. in Europe, 1984; spl. counsel, dep. agt. for U.S. to World Ct.; former cons. to the Pres.'s Intelligence Oversight Bd., Arms Control and Disarmament Agy., U.S. Info. Agy.; chmn. bd. dirs. U.S. Inst. Peace, 1985-91; co-chmn. with the U.S. dep. atty. gen. Moscow Seminar on the Rule of Law, 1990; legal advisor during Gulf crisis Kuwait's Amb. to U.S., Kuwait Rep. to UN Boundary Commn., 1991-94. Author: Law and the Indo-China War, 1972 (Phi Beta Kappa award); editor: Law and Civil War in the Modern World, 1976, Readings in International Law, 1979, The Arab-Israeli Conflict, 3 vols., 1976, 4th vol., 1991, Nat. Security Law, 1990, 2d edit., 2005, Crisis in the Gulf, 1992, Nat. Security Law Documents, 1995, Treaty Interpretation, The Constitution and the Rule of Law, 2001, The National Law of Treaty Implementation, 2001, Solving the War Puzzle, 2003; editor: The Real Lessons of the Vietnam War, 2002, Civil Litigation Against Terrorism, 2003; mem. editl. bd. Am. Jour. Internat. Law; contbr. articles to profl. jours. Sesquicentennial assoc. Ctr. Advanced Studies, U. Va., 1971-72; adv. bd. law of sea State Dept., 1977-80, adv. bd. internat. law, 1982; chmn. bd. dirs. U.S. Inst. Peace, 1986-89, 89-91; chmn. oceans policy com. Rep. Nat. Com.; com. on exploration of the seas Nat. Acad. Nat. Rsch. Coun., 2002; active Consortium on Intelligence. Recipient Alumni award in arts Drew U., 1976, award, Marine Tech. Soc., 1982; Compass Disting. Achievement award for significant contbns. to art and sci. of oceanography and marine tech., 1994; NIH fellow Yale U., 1965-66. Mem. ABA (past vice-chmn. sect. internat. law, past 4-term chmn. com. on law and nat. security, Leibman award for Nat. Security Law, 2013), Am. Law Inst., Am. Oceanic Orgn. (past exec. coun.), Marine Tech. Soc. (past exec. coun.), Rhodes Acad. Oceans Law and Policy (founding dir.), Coun. Fgn. Rels., Order of Coif, Cosmos Club, N.Y. Yacht Club, DiaFtel, Cmty. Democracies, Freedom House (bd. dirs., chmn., governance and ethics com. mem., exec. com. mem. 2008-14), US Masters Powerlifting Team for World Bench Press Championships, 2012, 2013, Phi Beta Kappa. Republican. Episcopalian. Office: U Va Sch Law 580 Massie Rd Charlottesville VA 22903-1789 Office Phone: 434-924-7441. Business E-Mail: jnm9s@virginia.edu.

MOORE, JUNE B., gas industry executive; BA in Edn., U. NC, Chapel Hill. Tchr. Charlotte-Mecklenburg Sch. Sys.; IT mgmt. positions Photo Corp. America Internat.; various mgmt. positions through v.p. info. services Piedmont Natural Gas Co., Inc., 1986—2004, v.p., customer svc., 2004—09, v.p., enterprise quality mgmt., 2009—. Past chmn., info. tech. com. Southern Gas Assn. Bd. mem. Summit House Charlotte. Recipient Women in Bus. Achievement award, Charlotte Bus. Jour., 2004. Office: Piedmont Natural Gas 4720 Piedmont Row Dr Charlotte NC 28210 Mailing: Piedmont Natural Gas PO Box 33068 Charlotte NC 28233 Office Phone: 704-364-3120.

MOORE, JUSTIN COLE, musician; b. Poyen, Ark., Mar. 30, 1984; m. Kate Moore, 2007; children: Ella Kole, Kennedy Faye. Musician: (albums) Justin Moore, 2009, Outlaws Like Me, 2011, Off the Beaten Path, 2013. Named New Artist of Yr., Acad. Country Music Awards, 2014. Office: Big Machine Records 1219 16th Ave South Nashville TN 37212-2901*

MOORE, KEVIN MICHAEL, federal judge; b. Coral Gables, Fla., 1951; BA, Fla. State U., 1972; JD, Fordham U., 1976. Bar: Fla. 1976. Asst. US atty. US Atty.'s Office (so. dist.) Fla., 1976—81; supervisory asst. US atty. US Atty.'s Office (no. dist.) Fla., 1981—82, chief asst. US atty., 1983—87, US atty. Tallahassee, 1987—89; dir. US Marshals Svc., Arlington, Va., 1989—92; judge US Dist. Ct.(so. dist.) Fla., Miami, 1992—. Office: US Dist Ct Ferguson US Courthouse 400 N Miami Ave Rm 13-1 Miami FL 33128-1812

MOORE, LAURENCE JOHN, business educator; b. Greeley, Colo., May 7, 1938; s. John Harold and Ruth Anderson M.; m. Nancy Kay Hibbert, Aug. 31, 1963 (div. Apr. 1996), m. Ivy Carol Hoy Dec. 23, 2006; children: Rebecca Ann, John Andrew, Stefani Ruth. BA in Econs., Monmouth Coll., Ill., 1962; MS in Econs., Ariz. State U., 1965, PhD in Mgmt. Sci., 1970. Dist. mktg. rep. Standard Oil Co. (Ind.), Chgo., 1962-63; sr. analyst long range and capital planning, 1964-66; head quantitative studies Continental Ill. Bank, Chgo., 1966-67; mem. faculty dept. mgmt. sci. Coll. Bus. Va. Poly. Inst. and State U., Blacksburg, 1970—2007, prof. Coll. Bus., 1977-85, C&P Disting. prof. bus., 1985-96, head dept. Coll. Bus., 1976-83, dir. univ. fin. planning and analysis, 1983-84, dir. univ. planning, 1988-89, Bell Atlantic-Va. prof. of bus., 1996—2002, Verizon prof. bus., 2002—07, emeritus, 2007. Cons. in field. Author: (with S.M. Lee, B.W. Taylor) Management Science, 1981, 4th edit., 1993, (with S.M. Lee) Introduction to Decision Sciences, 1975, (with E.R. Clayton) GERT Modeling and Simulation: Fundamentals and Applications, 1976. Served with U.S. Army, 1957-59. Recipient Disting. Service award SE region Am. Inst. Decision Scis., 1977 Fellow Am. Inst. Decision Scis. (pres. 1983-84, Disting. Svc. award 1986); mem. Inst. Mgmt. Sci. (Disting. Svc. award SE region), Inst. for Ops. Rsch. and Mgmt. Sci., Alpha Iota Delta, Beta Gamma Sigma, Omicron Delta Epsilon, Sigma Phi Epsilon. Presbyterian. Home: 1013 Chateau Ct Blacksburg VA 24060-3676 Business E-Mail: ljmoore@vt.edu.

MOORE, LEWIS H., state legislator; b. Carbondale, Ill., Dec. 22, 1958; m. Patti Moore; children: Hansen, Micah, Nathan, Jackson. AS, N. Mex. Mil. Inst.; BA, U. Ark. Rep. Federated Ins., 1997—2004; consultant CFR Ins. & Risk Mgmt., 2004—07, Guardian Life Ins., 2007—; dist. mgr. Colonial Life & Accident Ins., 2007—; mem. Dist. 96 Okla. House of Representatives, 2008—. Republican. Christian. Office: Oklahoma House of Representatives 2300 N Lincoln Blvd Rm 329-A Oklahoma City OK 73105 also: 10100 Sunday Dr Arcadia OK 73007 Office Phone: 405-557-7400. Business E-Mail: lewis.moore@okhouse.gov.

MOORE, LOIS JEAN, health science facility administrator; married; 1 child. Grad., Prairie View Sch. Nursing, Tex., 1957; BS in Nursing, Tex. Woman's U., 1970; MS in Edn., Tex. So. U., 1974. Nurse Harris County (Tex.) Hosp. Dist., 1957—; pres., chief exec. officer Harris County Hosp.; adminstr. Jefferson Davis Hosp., Houston, 1977-88, exec. v.p., chief ops. officer, 1988—2001; chief adminstr. U. Tex. Harris County Psychiat. Hosp., Houston, 2001—. Mem. adv. bd. Tex. Pub. Hosp. Assn. Contbr. articles to profl. jours. Mem. Mental Health Needs Council Houston and Harris County, Congressman Mickey Leland's Infant Mortality Task Force, Houston Crackdown Com., Gov.'s task force on health care policy, 1991; chairperson Tex. Assn. Pub. and Nonprofit Hosps., 1991, subcom. of Gov.'s task force to identify essential health care svc., 1992; bd. dirs. ARC, 1991—, Greater Houston Hosp. Coun., March of Dimes, United Way. Recipient Pacesetter award North-East C. of C., 1991; named Nurse of Yr. Houston Area League Nursing, 1976-77, Outstanding Black Achiever YMCA Century Club, 1974, Outstanding Women in Medicine YWCA, 1989. Mem. Am. Coll. Hosp. Adminstrs., Tex. Hosp. Assn. (chmn. pub. hosp. com.), Young Hosp. Adminstrs., Nat. Assn. Pub. Hosps. (bd. dirs., mem. exec. com. Tex. assn.), License Vocat. Nurses Assn., sigma Theta Tau. Home: 3730 S Macgregor Way Houston TX 77021-1506 Office: Univ Texas Harris County Psychiatric Ctr 2800 S Macbryor Way Houston TX 77021 Office Phone: 713-741-7803.

MOORE, MARY A., state legislator; b. Birmingham, Ala., July 23, 1948; 1 child, Michael. BS, Tuskegee U., Ala., 1970; MBA in Human Resource Devel., Ala. A&M U., Normal, 1983. Cert. med. tech. U. Ala., 1971. Ret. med. technologist VA Hosp., Birmingham; mem. Dist. 59 Ala. House of Reps., Montgomery, 2002—. Mem. Evergreen Missionary Bapt. Ch.; chmn. ACIPCO Finley Adv. Com., 1989—90; pres. ACIPCO Finley Neighborhood, 1991—94. Democrat. Baptist. Office: 1622 36th Ave N Birmingham AL 35207 also: Ala House of Reps Ala State House 11 S Union St Rm 539-D Montgomery AL 36130 Office Phone: 334-242-7608. Business E-Mail: mamoor48@bellsouth.net.

MOORE, MATT, political organization administrator; m. Meg Moore. BS in Indsl. Engring., Ga. Inst. Tech., Atlanta. State dir. for Senator Tim Scott US Senate, SC; exec. dir. SC Rep. Party, Columbia, 2011—12, chmn., 2013—. Mem. Nat. Youth Adv. Bd. Rep. Nat. Com. Mem. Shandon Bapt. Ch., Columbia; bd. mem. Palmetto Family Coun. Republican. Office: SC Republican Party PO Box 12373 Columbia SC 29211 Office Phone: 803-988-8440. E-mail: chairman@scgop.com.

MOORE, MICHAEL JONATHAN, federal prosecutor; b. Atlanta, 1968; BA, Mercer U., Atlanta, 1989, JD, 1993. Bar: Ga. 1993, Ga. Ct. Appeals 1993, Supreme Ct. Ga. 1993, US Dist. Ct. (mid. dist.) Ga. 1997, US Ct. Appeals (11ht cir.) 1997. Ins. fraud/claims investigator Equifax Services, Inc., Atlanta, 1989—90; law clk. US Dist. Ct. (middle dist.) Ga., Macon, 1991—92, Dist. Atty's Office, Houston Jud. Cir., Perry, Ga., 1992—93, chief/asst. dist. atty., 1993—97; ptnr. Clarke, Moore & Hall, P.C., Warner Robins, Ga., 1997—2005; pvt. law practice Warner Robins, Ga., 2005—10; mem. Dist. 18 Ga. State Senate, 2002—03; US atty. (middle dist.) Ga. US Dept. Justice, Macon, 2010—. Adminstrv. law judge City of Warner Robins, 2004—. Contbr. articles to profl. jours. Sec., CFO Kids Need Moore, Inc., Perry, 2000—10; candidate Houston County Dist. Atty., 2004. Mem.: ABA, Ga. Trial Lawyers Assn., Houston County Bar Assn., State Bar Ga., William Augustus Bootle Am. Inn of Ct., Phi Alpha Delta. Office: US Attorneys Office Gateway Plz PO Box 1702 Macon GA 31202-1702 Office Phone: 478-752-3511. Office Fax: 478-621-2604.*

MOORE, MICHAEL S., retail executive; BS, Mo. So. State Coll. Asst. mgr. Wal-Mart Stores, Inc., Carthage, Mo., 1988, co-mgr., store mgr. and dist. mgr. Okla., Nebr., regional v.p. Tex., Fla., sr. v.p. of ops. for west divsn., 2004, sr. v.p. of merchandising, 2010, pres. ctrl. USA, 2011—. Recipient Sam M. Walton Entrepreneur of the Year award, 2005. Office: Wal-Mart Stores, Incorporated 702 SW 8th St Bentonville AR 72716 Office Phone: 479-273-4000. Office Fax: 473-273-4053.

MOORE, OSCAR KENNEY, small business owner, state representative; b. Marion County, Miss., Apr. 5, 1933; m. Helen Duncan. Grad. h.s., Marion County, Miss. With U.S. Army; owner, mgr. Moore's Auto Svc. Ctr., Columbia, Miss.; rep., mem., Agrl., Juvenile Justice, Penitentiary, Pub. Utilities and Transp. coms. Ho. Reps. State of Miss., 2000—. With US Army, with USAR. Democrat. Bapt. Home: 79 Jackson Dr Columbia MS 39429 Office: Mississippi House of Representatives 400 High St Jackson MS 39215 Office Phone: 601-359-3360. Office Fax: 601-359-3728. E-mail: kmoore@mail.house.state.ms.us.

MOORE, PRESTON, bank executive; m. Cheryl Moore; children: Preston, Kathryn, Kristen. BA, Wash. and Lee U.; MBA in Fin., U. Tex., Austin. Exec. v.p., mgr., Investment Investment divsn. Amegy Bank, Tex.; pres., CEO Encore Bank, 2009—. Mem. Meml. Dr Presbyn. Ch.; vol. Neighborhood Centers, Inc.; bd. mem. Kinkaid Sch.; bd. dirs. Houston Country Club. Office: Encore Bank Ste 1000 9 Greenway Plz Houston TX 77046-0900 Office Phone: 713-787-3100. Business E-Mail: pmoore@encorebank.com.

MOORE, RENEE ALMA, English educator; b. Highland Park, Mich., June 29, 1955; d. Fred L. and Pualine A. (Robbins) W.; m. Clernest G. Moore; children: Shasaebra, Doris, Tyrone, Vietta. BS in Edn., Delta State U., Cleveland, Miss., 1991; MA, Middlebury (Vt.) Coll. Tchr. East Side H.S., Cleveland, Miss., 1991—, Broad St. H.S., Shelby, Miss.; instr. Miss. Delta Cmty. Coll., Moorhead, Miss. Edn. dir. Nu Delta Ministries, Inc., Cleveland, 1984—. Contbr. articles to profl. jours. Named Milken Family Found. Educator of Yr., 2001, Miss. Tchr. of Yr., 2002; fellow Carnegie Acad. for the Scholarship of Teaching and Learning Program for K-12 Teachers. Fellow Delta Area Writing Project; mem. NEA, Nat. Coun. Tchrs. English, Phi Delta Kappa. Avocation: freelance writing. Office: Broad St High Sch PO Box 149 Shelby MS 38774

MOORE, ROBERT, JR., state legislator, lawyer; b. Jan. 1, 1945; BA, Ouachita Baptist Univ., 1966; JD, Univ. Ark., 1973. Owner Moore Farms, 1974—; asst. atty. gen. Office of Ark. Atty. Gen., 1973—75; criminal law instr. Hartford Coll., 1975—76; workers comp. law judge, 1976—77; atty. in private practice, 1981—85; spl. asst. to Gov. Bill Clinton, 1986—87; dir. Ark. Alcoholic Beverage Control, 1987—; mem. Dist. 12 Ark. House of Reps., 2007—. Served as pilot, airborne co. comdr. & ROTC instr. US Army, 1966—71, Vietnam. Democrat. Baptist. Address: PO Box 446 Arkansas City AR 71630 Office Phone: 870-877-1210. Business E-Mail: moorer@arkleg.state.ar.us.

MOORE, ROBERT HENRY, writer, editor, communications consultant; b. Madisonville, Ky., Sept. 16, 1940; s. William Lee Moore and Robbie (Pritchett) Ruby; m. Diana Churchill, Aug. 17, 1963 (div. 1978); children: Randall Lee, Robin Churchill; m. Patricia Mary George, Oct. 4, 1981; 1 child, Christopher Robert. BA, Davidson Coll., NC, 1962; MA, U. N.C., 1964; PhD, U. Wis., 1972. Asst. dir. admissions Davidson Coll., 1963-64; teaching asst. U. Wis., Madison, 1965-68; staff and faculty U.S. Mil. Acad., West Point, NY, 1968-70; lectr., asst. prof. U. Md., College Park, 1970-76, assoc. prof., 1976; cons. U.S. Congress, Washington, 1976-77; emerging issues coordinator The Conf. Bd., NYC, 1977-79; dir. govt. relations Benefacts, Inc., Washington, 1977-78; v.p. Alexander & Alexander, Inc., Washington, 1978-81, Alexander & Alexander Svcs. Inc., NYC, Washington, 1981-85, sr. v.p. corp. rels., 1985-95, sr. v.p. (inactive), 1995-97; chmn., pres. A & A Govt. and Industry Affairs Inc., Washington, 1990-94, Aon Corp., Vienna, Va., 1997—2005; pres. PMR Comm. Group, Vienna, Va., 2005—, sr. editor; with US Army Res., West Point, 1971—72; exec. sec. Faulkner Concordance West Point, 1971—75. Del. Nat. Security Affairs Conf., Washington, 1978-82; mem. adv. bd. Career Opportunities Inst., U. Va., Charlottesville, 1982-86, Ctr. for New Am. Work Force, 1992-96; mem. corp. adv. bd. Queens Coll., CUNY, 1985-96; mem. V.P.'s Forum, 1989-94; mem. coun. Conf. Bd. Corp. Comm. Execs., 1990-94; mem. Pub. Rels. Sem., 1993-97; editl. advisor Ctr. for Mind-Body Medicine, Washington, 1998-2000; adv. coun. Mindfulness Practice Ctr. of Fairfax, 1998—; bd. visitors Dictionary of Am. Regional English, 1999—; adv. to chmn. NEH, 1999-2001; Mayo Legacy, 2004-. Co-author: (with others) School for Soldiers: West Point and the Profession of Arms, 1974 (NYT award 1974), Spreading the Risks: Insuring the American Experience, 2003 (Washington Book Pubs. award 2003), Risk Management, 2004 (Book of the Year), Revised Edit., 2005; columinist Raleigh Telegram, 2008-, Beaufort Nat., 2009-; contbr. articles to profl. jours.; contbr. interviews to nat. mags., newspapers, radio and TV. Mem. kitchen cabinet Points of Light Found., 1991-95. With U.S. Army, 1968-70, capt. USAR, 1970-72. Ops. Crossroads Africa fellow, 1960; U. Md. rsch. grantee, 1972, 76. Mem. Nat. Assn. Ins. Brokers (exec. com., bd. dirs., pres. 1985-86, chmn. past presidents adv. coun. 1989-93). E-mail: rhmcrm9@aol.com.

MOORE, RODNEY GREGORY, lawyer; b. Birmingham, Ala., Sept. 1, 1960; s. Jethroe and Tommie (Feagin) M.; m. Yalsyn Moore; children: Nyosha, Rodney II, Imari. BA, U. Wash., 1982; JD, Santa Clara U., Calif., 1985. Bar: Calif. 1987, Ga. 2000, US Ct. Appeals (9th, 11th cir.), US Supreme Ct. Concert promoter Clanagan & Moore/Class "A", Seattle and San Jose, Calif., 1984-87; ptnr. Williams, Robinson & Moore, San Jose, 1987-89; prin. Moore Law Firm, San Jose, 1989-97; gen. counsel East Side Union HS Dist., San Jose, 1997-2000; gen. counsel, chief legal officer Atlanta Pub. Schs., 2000—05; of counsel Greenberg Traurig LLP, Atlanta, 2005—08; ptnr. Adorno & Yoss, Atlanta, 2008—10, Baker Donelson Bearman Caldwell & Berkowitz, PC, Atlanta, 2010—. Disc jockey Sta. KCMU, Seattle, 1980-82; assoc. prof. contract law Lincoln Law Sch., 1992-94. Assoc. editor: Santa Clara U. Computer Law Jour., 1984—85, chmn. editl. bd.: Nat. Bar Assn. Jour., 1997—99. Mem. sch. bd. East Side Union HS Dist. Named one of Best Lawyers in America, 2007—, 50 Most Influential Minority Lawyers in America, Nat. Law Jour., 2008; scholar, Santa Clara U., 1982—85. Mem. Nat. Bar Assn. (chpt. pres. 1989, gen. counsel 1997-99, v.p. 2002-04, pres. 2008-09), Santa Clara County Bar Assn. (trustee 1990), Assn. Trial Lawyers Am., NY Sports and Entertainment Soc., Santa Clara County Black Lawyers Assn. (pres. San Jose chpt. 1989-90), Calif. Assn. Black Lawyers (pres. 1993-94, Loren Miller Atty. of Yr., 1997), Calif. Sch. Lawyers Assn., Ga. Sch. Lawyers Assn., Nat. Alliance Black Sch. Educators, Nat. Coun. Sch. Attys. Office: Baker Donelson Bearman Caldwell & Berkowitz PC Monarch Plz Ste 1600 3414 Peachtree Rd NE Atlanta GA 30326 Office Phone: 404-223-2209. Office Fax: 404-238-9649. Business E-Mail: rgmoore@bakerdonelson.com.

MOORE, RODNEY W., state legislator; b. Wilmington, NC, July 12, 1963; A, Cape Fear Tech. Inst. Prin. RM Investments, LLC, 1998—; loan officer Fairway Mortgage Corp., 2001—03; prencinct chmn. 126 Mecklenburg Dem. Party, 2003—05; life mem. NAACP-Charlotte Mecklenburg, 2004—; br. mgr. Citizens Home Loans, 2005—06; fellow NC Inst. of Polit. Leadership, 2005—06; state delegate, Mecklenburg County State Exec. Com. NCDP, 2005—10; ptnr. Aski Svcs. Co., 2005—; vice chmn. Charlotte Housing Authority, 2006—09, commr., 2006—; bd. dirs. Charlotte Mecklenburg Sr. Centers, 2006—; prencinct chmn. 146 Mecklenburg Dem. Party, 2008—09; alumni FBI Citizens Acad., 2008—09; pres., CEO Connections Unlimited, Inc., 2008—; bd. dirs. Urban League of Ctrl. Carolinas, 2010; mem. Dist. 99 NC House of Representatives, 2011—. Democrat. Baptist. Home: PO Box 44107 Charlotte NC 28215-0036 Office: North Carolina House of Representatives 16 W Jones St Room 1211 Raleigh NC 27601-1096 Office Phone: 704-597-2419, 919-733-5606, 704-449-6201. Business E-Mail: Rodney.Moore@ncleg.net.

MOORE, ROY DEAN, retired judge; b. Chickasha, Okla., Jan. 15, 1940; s. Frank B. and Delia Pauline (Morgan) M.; m. Carolyn Kaye Wood, Aug. 10, 1962; children— Darla Kaye, Jared Dean, Amy Darise. BA, Central State U., 1962, M. Teaching, 1966; JD, Oklahoma City U., 1970; grad., Nat. Coll. State Trial Judges, 1972. Bar: Okla. 1970. Coach debate, instr. dramatics Kingfisher (Okla.) High Sch., 1962-67; instr. English and journalism, head dept. lang. arts. Jarman Jr. High Sch., Midwest City, Okla., 1967-70; pros. atty. City of Lawton, Okla., 1970; spl. dist. judge 5th Jud. Dist. Okla., 1971-72; pvt. practice law Lawton, 1973-90; dist. judge 5th Jud. Dist. Okla., 1990—2002. Pres. Swinney PTA, 1975-76; Editor: Problems in Teaching in the Secondary School, 1966. Pres. Comanche County Mental Health Assn., 1973-74, bd. dirs., 1972-76; co-chmn. Kingfisher County Reps. for Congressman James V. Smith, 1966; mem. state exec. com. Okla. Republican Com., 1973-74, chmn. auditing com., 1977-78; del. Rep. Nat. Conv., 1976; chmn. cts. com. Assn. South Central Okla. Govts. Crime Commn.; chmn. Comanche County Reps. for Reagan for Pres., 1973-83; mem. adv. bd. Jim Taliferro Mental Health Center, 1977-78; del. Nat. Mental Health Assn. Conv., 1975; bd. dirs. Lawton Campfire Girls; elder N.W. Ch. of Christ, 1977-2004; dir. Back to Bible Campaigns, 1976-2002. Named Outstanding Dist. Judge in State of Okla., Okla. Trial Lawyers Assn., 1999. Mem. Am., Okla., Comanche County bar assns., Okla. Trial Lawyers Assn., Lawton Antique Auto Club, Ford Retractible Club Am., Alpha Psi Omega, Delta Theta Phi. Republican. Mem. Ch. of Christ (elder). Clubs: Fraternal Order of Police, Lion. Home: 2114 NW Atlanta Ave Lawton OK 73505-3923

MOORE, ROY S., state supreme court chief justice; m. Kayla Moore; children: Heather, Roy, Caleb, Micah. BS, U.S. Mil. Acad., 1969; JD, U. Ala., 1977. Dep. dist. atty. Etowah County, Ala., 1977—82; pvt. practice Gadsden, Ala., 1982—92; cir. judge 16th Judicial Cir., Gadsden, 1992—2001; chief justice Ala. Supreme Ct., 2001—03, 2013—; pres. Found. for Moral Law, Montgomery, Ala., 2003—12. Captain Military Police Corps US Army. Recipient George Washington Honor medal, Nat. Freedom Found., 1995, Bill of Rights award, 1997, God and Country award, Am. Family Assn., 1997, Spirit of Am. Founders award, 1997, Liberty & Union award, N.H. Ctr. for Constitutional Studies, 1998, Nat. Spirit of Life award, African Am. Family Assn., 1999, Nat. Hero of Faith award, Vision Am. Houston, 2002, Stonewall Jackson award, Vision Forum, 2003, Warriors Medal of Valor, Native Am. Nations of the U.S., 2004. Republican. Baptist. Office: Ala Supreme Ct 300 Dexter Ave Montgomery AL 36104-3741*

MOORE, RYAN, professional golfer; b. Tacoma, Dec. 5, 1982; Grad., U. Nev. Las Vegas. Mem. PGA Tour, 2006—. Recipient Haskins Award, Haskins Commn., 2005. Achievements include PGA Tour wins: Wyndham Championship, 2009. Mailing: 100 PGA TOUR Blvd Ponte Vedra Beach FL 32082

MOORE, SAM, singer; b. Winchester, Ga., Oct. 12, 1935; Formerly with The Majestics, The Gales, The Mellonaires, 1954—62; co-founder & singer Sam & Dave, 1962—82. Singer: (albums) (with Sam & Dave) Hold On, I'm Comin, 1966, Double Dynamite, 1967, Soul Men, 1967, I Thank You, 1968, Back At'cha! the United Artists Album, 1976, (solo) Plenty Good Lovin: The Lost Solo Album, 2002, Overnight Sensational, 2006, (songs) Soul Man, 1966 (Best R&B Group, Vocal or Instrumental, Grammy Awards, 1967); performer: (films) Tapeheads, 1988, Blues Brothers 2000, 1998. Recipient Pioneer award, Rhythm & Blues Found., 1991, Lifetime Achievement Living Legend award, MOBO Awards, 2006; named to Rock and Roll Hall of Fame (with Sam & Dave), 1992. Office: c/o Buddy Lee Attractions 38 Music Square E #300 Nashville TN 37203

MOORE, STANLEY RAY, lawyer; b. Dallas, July 20, 1946; s. Elzey and Heloise M.; m. Sherri Boren; children: Natalie, William, Julie, Colin, Brendan. BSME, So. Meth. U., 1969, JD, 1973. Bar: Tex. 1973, U.S. Dist. Ct. (no. dist.) Tex. 1974, U.S. Ct. Appeals (fed. cir.). Assoc. Clegg, Cantrell, Crisman, Dallas, 1973-75; ptnr. Crisman & Moore, Dallas, 1975-80, Schley Cantrell & Moore, Dallas, 1980-83, Schley, Cantrell, Kice & Moore, Dallas, 1983-87, Johnson & Wortley, P.C., Dallas, 1987-94, Jenkens & Gilchrist, Dallas, 1995—, head IP dept., 2005. Patentee in field. Foster parent Hope Cottage, Dallas, 1982-90; fund raiser Am. Heart Assn., YMCA, rep. Orgn. Recipient Outstanding Leadership commendation ASME, 1969. Mem. ABA, IAPLA, INTA, Dallas Bar Assn. (chair IP sect. 2004) Home: 1 Victoria Cir Rowlett TX 75088-6059 Office: Jenkens & Gilchrist 1445 Ross Ave Ste 3200 Dallas TX 75202-2785 Home Phone: 972-475-3945. E-mail: smoore@jenkens.com.

MOORE, THOMAS J., lawyer; b. Montclair, NJ, 1947; AB, U. Calif., Berkeley, 1971; JD magna cum laude, U. Minn., 1974. Bar: Minn. 1974, Colo. 1982, Tex. 2004. Ptnr. Faegre & Benson, Denver; co-mng. ptnr. Houston office Dewey & LeBoeuf (formerly LeBoeuf, Lamb, Greene & MacRae LLP), Tex., 2004, ptnr. Houston. Assoc. prof. law U. Minn., 1977—79. Note & article editor Minn. Law Rev., 1973—74. Mem.: Order of Coif. Office: Dewey & LeBoeuf 1000 Main St Ste 2550 Houston TX 77002-5009 Office Phone: 713-287-2066. Office Fax: 713-287-2100. Business E-Mail: tmoore@dl.com.

MOORE, THURSTON ROACH, lawyer; b. Memphis, Dec. 10, 1946; s. Richard Charlton Moore and Halcyon Hall (Roach) Lynn; m. Corell Luckhardt Halsey, Sept. 26, 1998. BA with distinction, U. Va., 1968, JD, 1974. Bar: Va. 1974. Rsch. analyst Scudder, Stevens & Clark, NYC, 1968—71; ptnr. Hunton & Williams LLP, Richmond, Va., 1974—91, mng. partner, 1991—2006, chmn., 2006—12, chmn. emeritus, 2012—. Mem.: ABA (chmn. com. on partnerships & unincorporated bus. organizations 1992—96, bus. law coun. 1999—2003, bus. law sect., fed. regulation securities com. mem.), St. Christopher's Sch. (chmn. bd. govs.), Colonial Williamsburg Found. (trustee, bd. dirs. 1992—), Richmond Bar Assn., Va. State Bar, Va. Bar Assn., Va. Commwealth U. Sch. Bus. Found. (trustee, bd. dirs.), Nature Conservancy Va. (trustee 1992—2009, chmn. 2003—09), Mary Morton Parsons Found. (pres., bd. dir., trustee), Va. Found. Ind. Coll. (trustee, bd. dirs.), Met. Bus. Found. (pres. 1995—2001, dir.), Va. Mus. Fine Arts (pres., trustee), Omricron Delta Kappa, Phi Beta Kappa. Office: Hunton & Williams Riverfront Plz E Tower 951 E Byrd St Richmond VA 23219-4074 Office Fax: 804-788-8218. Business E-Mail: tmoore@hunton.com.

MOORE, TIM, lawyer; b. Lafayette, La., Sept. 4, 1957; BS in geology, Stephen F. Austin State U., 1979; JD summa cum laude, U. Houston, 1990. Bar: Tex. 1990. Geologist Placid Oil Co., New Orleans, 1980—84, Jackson, Miss., 1980—84; regional geologist Gulf Coast Kaiser Energy Inc., New Orleans, 1984—87; assoc. Weil, Gotshal & Manges, Houston, 1990—94; gen. counsel - corp. TransTex. Gas Corp., 1994—2000; v.p., gen. counsel, sec. Plains Resources, 2000—01, Plains All American Pipeline, LP, Houston, 2000—. Mem.: Am. Corp. Counsel Assn., State Bar Tex., Order of the Barons, Order of the Coif, Omicron Delta Kappa. Office: Plains All Am Pipeline 333 Clay St Ste 1600 PO Box 4648 Houston TX 77210-4648

MOORE, TIM, state legislator; b. Kings Mountain, NC, Oct. 2, 1970; m. Juli Moore; children: McRae, Wilson. State rep. Dist. 111, NC, 2002—; atty. Flowers, Martin & Moore, Pa., 1995—. Mem.: Rotary Club. Republican. Baptist. Office: North Carolina House of Representatives 16 W Jones St Rm 1326 Raleigh NC 27601-1096 Office Phone: 919-733-4838, 704-739-1221. E-mail: Tim.Moore@ncleg.net.

MOORE, TIM, state legislator; b. July 25, 1966; BS, US Air Force Acad.; MS, U. Ark. Pilot, instr. pilot UPS; mem. Dist. 26 Ky. House of Reps., 2007—. Served with USAF, 1984—98, pilot Ky. Air Nat. Guard USAFR, 1998—. Named US Air Force Acad. Admissions Liaison Officer of Nation, 2003. Mem.: NRA, Vine Grove C. of C., Radcliff C. of C. Republican. Office: Ky Legislature Annex Rm 413H 702 Capitol Ave Frankfort KY 40601 Mailing: 417 Bates Rd Elizabethtown KY 42701 Office Phone: 502-564-8100 ext. 702. Business E-Mail: tim.moore@lrc.ky.gov.

MOORE, WILLARD S., oceanographer, educator; s. Ross H. and Alice Sutton Moore; m. Virginia Saunders, June 13, 1980. BS, Millsaps Coll., Jackson, 1962; MA, Columbia U., NYC, 1965; PhD, SUNY Stony Brook, 1969. Oceanographer US Naval Oceanog. Office, Chesapeake Beach, Md., 1969—76; post-doc. fellow Tata Inst. Fundamental Rsch., Bombay, 1970—71; prof. U. SC, Columbia, SC, 1976—2000, rsch. prof., 2000—, disting. prof. emeritus, 2000—; adj. scientist Woods Hole Oceanog. Instn., Mass., 2001—04; faculty mem. Semester Sea, Pitts., 2004. Dept. chair U. SC, 1980—84; sci. steering com. NSF Future Ocean Chemistry in US, Arlington, Va., Coastal Ocean Processes, Washington; advisor IAEA, Vienna; com. reference materials ocean sci. Nat. Acad. Sci., Washington. Contbr. articles to profl. jours. Recipient B.H. Ketchum award, Woods Hole Oceanog. Instn., 1999, Disting. Alumni, SUNY, Stony Brook, 2007, Edn. Found. award, U. SC, 1993; vis. scholar, Xiamen China & East China Normal U. Shanglia, China, 2009—; Fellow, Am. Geophys. Union, 2006, Hanse-Wissenschaftskolleg, 2008—10, Rsch. Grants, NSF, 1975—2012. Fellow: Am. Geophys. Union, Explorers Club (chair, greater piedmont chpt. 1995—96); mem.: AAAS, Geol. Soc. Am., Oceanog. Soc. (life), Geochem. Soc. Achievements include patents for fibrous filtering material and preparation thereof. Home: 1300 Louis LeConte Rd Hopkins SC 29061 Business E-Mail: moore@geol.sc.edu.

MOORE, WILLIAM THEODORE, JR., federal judge; b. Bainbridge, Ga., May 7, 1940; s. William T. and Mary (Talbert) M.; m. Jane Hodges, July 18, 1964; children: Sarah S., Mary T. William T III. AA, Ga. Mil. Coll., 1960, Law (hon.), 1978; LLB, U. Ga., Athens, 1964; LLM, U. Va., Charlottesville, 2001. Bar: Ga. 1964, US Dist. Ct. (so. dist.) Ga. 1964, US Ct. Appeals (5th and 11th cirs.) 1979, US Supreme Ct. 1980. US atty. US Dist. Ct. (So. Dist.) Ga., Savannah, 1977-81; ptnr. Corish, Smith, Remler & Moore, Savannah, 1967-77, Sparkman, Harris & Moore, Savannah, 1981-87, Oliver Maner & Gray, Savannah, 1988-94; judge US Dist. Ct. (so. dist.) Ga., Savannah, 1994—2004, 2010—, chief judge, 2004—10. Atty. Savannah-Chatham County Bd. Pub. Edn., 1975-77, mem. U.S. Atty. Gen's. Adv. com. D.C. 1978-81. Recipient Spl. Appreciation award Ga. Bur. of Investigation, 1980, US Dept. Treasury Bur. of Alcohol, Tobacco & Firearms, D.C., 1980; Extraordinary Svc. award Savannah Chapt. Fed. Bar Assn., 1980. Fellow Am. Bd. Criminal Lawyers (pres. 1993); mem. NACDL, Nat. Assn. Former US Attys. (bd. dirs. 1984—), Jud. Conf. US (com. on criminal law, sentencing subcomittee, 11th cir. jud. coun.), Ga. Assn. Criminal Def. Lawyers (v.p. 1986—), Ga. Bar Assn. Democrat. Epsicopalian. Avocations: jogging, weight training, golf, reading. Office: US Dist Ct PO Box 8286 Savannah GA 31412 Office Phone: 912-650-4173.

MOORE, WISTAR, cardiovascular surgeon; b. Feb. 16, 1959; BA, U. N.C., 1981, MD, 1985. Bd. cert. gen. surgery, thoracic surgery. Gen. surgery resident Mass. Gen. Hosp., 1985-90; cardiothoracic resident The Emory Clinic, 1990-93; cardiovasc. surgeon Watson Clinic, Lakeland, Fla., 1993-2000; chief divsn. cardiovasc. thoracic surgery Lakeland Regional Med. Ctr., 1996-2000; cardiovasc. surgeon Cardiovasc. Surgeons, Orlando, Fla., 2000—04, Leesburg-Ocala Heart Inst., 2004—. Fellow ACS, Am. Coll. Chest Physicians; mem. Fla. Soc. Thoracic and Cardiovasc. Surgeons, So. Thoracic Surg. Assn., Soc. Thoracic Surgeons. Office: 700 Doctors Ct Leesburg FL 34748

MOOREFIELD, JOHN A., insurance company executive; B, M, NC State U. Prin. ApproxiCom, LLC; mng. dir. BearingPoint; various leadership positions Cap Gemini Ernst & Young LLP, Fidelity Investments, NationsBank; joined AFLAC, Inc., 2005, chief info. officer Japan, sr. v.p., strategic mgmt., Japan, 2008—, sr. v.p., strategic mgmt., 2008—. Office: Aflac Inc 1932 Wynnton Rd Columbus GA 31999 Office Phone: 706-323-3431. Office Fax: 706-324-6330. Business E-Mail: JMoorefield@aflac.com.

MOORMAN, CHARLES W., transportation executive; b. Hattiesburg, Miss. Grad., Ga. Tech. Univ., Harvard Bus. Sch. Joined Norfolk Southern Corp., 1970, v.p. employee rels., 1992—93, v.p. info. tech., 1993—99; pres. Thoroughbred Tech. & Telecommunications, 1999—2003; sr. v.p. corp. planning & svc. Norfolk Southern Corp., 2003—04, pres., 2005—, CEO, 2005—, chmn., 2006—. Office: Norfolk Southern Corp 3 Commercial Pl Norfolk VA 23510-2191

MOORMAN, JOHN A., library administrator; m. Ileen Mary Geiger, Dec. 20, 1968; children: Johanna, Jessica Trinoskey, John A. Moorman Jr. AB, Guilford Coll., Greensboro, NC, 1969; MSLS, U. N.C., 1972; postgrad., U. N.C., Greensboro, 1974-75; PhD, U. Ill., 2002. Pub. svcs. and circulation libr. Guilford Coll., 1972-75; dir. Elbert Ivey Meml. Libr., Hickory, NC, 1975-80, Brazoria County Libr. System, Angleton, Tex., 1980-86, Oak Lawn (Ill.) Pub. Libr., 1986-88; exec. dir. Cumberland Trail Libr. System, Flora, Ill., 1989-92; city libr. Decatur (Ill.) Pub. Libr., 1992-2000; dir. Williamsburg (Va.) Regional Libr., 2000—. Adj. faculty Cath. U., 2003—. Author: Managing Small Library Collections in Businesses and Community Organizations: Advice for Non-Librarians, 1989, Running a Small Library: A How-To-Do-It Manual, 2006. Grad. Decatur Leadership Inst., 1993, Leadership Hist. Triangle, 2003; treas. Rotary Club James City County, 2009—; mem. Exec. Com. Greater Williamsburg Chamber & Tourism Alliance, 2010—; mem. bd. dirs. Literacy for Life, 2000—. Mem.: ALA (intellectual freedom roundable rep. coun. 2009—), Va. Libr. Assn. (pres. 2009—10). Mem. Soc. Of Friends. Avocations: travel, reading, woodworking, sports. Home: 8216 Old Mill Ln Williamsburg VA 23188-1135 Office: Williamsburg Regional Libr 7770 Croaker RD Williamsburg VA 23188 Office Phone: 757-259-7777. Business E-Mail: jmoorman@wrl.org.

MOORMAN, RICHARD HAL, IV, lawyer; b. Waco, Tex., Mar. 2, 1950; s. George R. and Billie (Scoggin) M.; m. Lucy Baker, May 24, 1974; children: Theodore Clark, Lydia Anne, Peter Baker. BCE, MIT, 1971; JD, So. Meth. U., 1976. Bar: Tex. 1976, U.S. Dist. Ct. (so. dist., we. dist., ea. dist.) Tex. 1976, U.S. Ct. Appeals (5th cir.) 1976; Bd. Cert. Civil Trial Law and Estate Planning and Probate Law, Tex. Bd. of Legal Specialization. Engr. Turner Collie & Braden, Houston, 1971-72, P.G. Bell Co., Houston, 1972-73; ptnr. Moorman Tate Haley Upchurch & Yates, LLP (formerly Moorman Tate Urquhart Haley, LLP), Brenham, Tex., 1976—; bd. mem. Tex. Bd. Legal Specialization, 2010—. Bd. dirs. Washington County Abstract Co., Brenham; bd. mem. Scott & White Brenham; past examiner (2002) Tex. Bd. of Legal Specialization; course dir. State Bar of Tex. Advanced Estate Planning and Probate Seminar; former editor Real Property Probate and Trust Law Jour. Mem. Tex. Air Control Bd., Austin, 1980-86; past pres. Washington on Brazos State Pk. Assn., Brenham, Brenham Downtown Assn. Named one of Tex. Superlawyers. Fellow Am. Coll. Trust and Estate Counsel, State Chair Regent Tex. Bar Found.; mem. ABA (estate gift tax com.), State Bar of Tex. (coun. mem. real estate probate and trust sect.), Washington County C. of C. (pres.); Main St. Bd. Avocations: antiques, hunting, fishing, theology, bicycling. Office: Moorman Tate Haley Upchurch & Yates LLP 207 E Main St Brenham TX 77833-3754 Office Phone: 979-836-5664. Business E-Mail: hmoorman@moormantate.com.

MORA, ALBERTO J., food products executive, lawyer; b. Boston, 1952; BA with honors, Swarthmore Coll., 1974; JD, U. Miami, 1981. Bar: Fla., D.C. Fgn. svc. officer US Dept. State, 1975—78; gen. counsel US Info. Agy., 1989—93, mem. broadcasting bd. governors, 1995—2001; counsel internat. law Greenberg Traurig LLP, Washington; gen. counsel Dept. Navy US Dept. Def., Washington, 2001—05; v.p., gen. counsel Internat. Divsn. Wal-Mart Stores, Inc., 2006—09; v.p., sec., gen. counsel Mars, Inc., 2009—. Bd. dirs. Nat. Coun. for Internat. Visitors, Radio Free Asia, Radio Free Europe/Radio Liberty. Editor-in-chief: Law of the Ams.: U. Miami Jour. of Internat. Law; appeared in (documentaries) Taxi to the Dark Side, 2008. Recipient John F. Kennedy Profile in Courage award, John F. Kennedy Library Found., 2006; named one of The Most Influential Lawyers, The Nat. Law Jour., 2011; fellow, Orgn. of Am. States. Mem.: Coun. Fgn. Rels. Office: Mars, Inc 6885 Elm St Mc Lean VA 22101 Office Phone: 703-821-4900.

MORAITIS, GEORGE R., JR., state legislator; b. Fort Lauderdale, Fla., Oct. 29, 1970; m. Heather Thompson; children: Alexis, Catherine. BS in Polit. Sci., US Naval Acad., Annapolis, Md., 1992; JD, U. Fla., Gainesville, 2002. Ptnr. Moraitis Cofar Karney & Moraitis; mem. Dist. 91 Fla. House of Representatives, 2011—. Submarine officer USN, 1992—2000, active USNR, 2000—. Republican. Office: 2132 E Oakland Park Blvd Fort Lauderdale FL 33306-1109 also: Fla House of Reps 1101 The Capitol 402 S Monroe St Tallahassee FL 32399-1300 Office Phone: 954-762-3757, 850-488-0635.

MORAITIS, KAREN KARL, real estate broker; b. Orange, Tex., Sept. 28, 1943; d. Richard Louis and Betty (Crandall) Karl; m. George Reynold Moraitis, Aug. 14, 1965; children: George Reynold Jr., Alexandra. BS in Advt., U. Fla., 1965; MEd, Fla. Atlantic U., 1968, EdS, 1974. Cert. real estate broker. Welfare worker State of Fla., Ft. Lauderdale, 1967; guidance counselor Broward County Pub. Schs., Ft. Lauderdale, 1968-70; adj. faculty Fla. Atlantic U., Boca Raton, 1971-74; real estate assoc. Blackwell Realty, Ft. Lauderdale, 1976-77; real estate broker Karen Moraitis Realty, Inc., Ft. Lauderdale, 1978—. Editor: Official Florida Publications, 1966. Mem. Pres.'s Council U. Fla., 1980—, scholarship ptnr. Gator Boosters, 1983—; pres. Harborside at Hillsboro Beach (Fla.) Condominium Assn., 1982, Parent Tchr. Student Orgn. Ft. Lauderdale High Sch., 1985-91. pres., 1986-88, Parent Tchr. Student Assn. Sunrise Middle Sch., Ft. Lauderdale, 1981-87. pres., 1982-84; v.p. PTA Bayview Elem. Sch., Ft. Lauderdale, 1980; chmn. Winter Cotillion, Ft. Lauderdale, 1986-88; bd. dirs. Sunrise Intracoastal Homeowners Assn., 1977, 96—, Broward County Zoning Bd., 1980-81, Imperial Village Condominium Assn., Ft. Lauderdale, 1983; ambassador edn. City of Ft. Lauderdale, 1986-88. Served with USN, 1965. Mem. Nat. Assn. Realtors, Fla. Assn. Realtors, Ft. Lauderdale Bd. Realtors, Humane Soc. Broward County (life), Navy League (life), Ft. Lauderdale H.S. Boosters (pres. 1984-85, 87-88), Broward County Athletic Assn. (waiver rev. com. 1992-96), Nat. Football Found. and Coll. Hall of Fame (bd. dirs. Brian Piccolo chpt. 1992-96). Republican. Avocation: travel. Office: Karen Moraitis Realty Inc 631 Middle River Dr Fort Lauderdale FL 33304-3509

MORAN, BARBARA BURNS, librarian, educator; b. Columbus, Miss., July 8, 1944; d. Robert Theron and Joan (Brown) Burns; m. Joseph J. Moran, Sept. 4, 1965; children: Joseph Michael, Brian Matthew. AB, Mount Holyoke Coll., S. Hadley, Mass., 1966; MLS, Emory U., Atlanta, 1973; PhD, SUNY, Buffalo, 1982. Head libr. The Park Sch. of Buffalo, Snyder, NY, 1974-78; prof. Sch. Info. and Libr. Sci. U. N.C., Chapel Hill, 1981—, asst. dean, 1987-90, dean, 1990-98, prof. and dir. internat. programs, 1999—, Louis Round Wilson disting. prof., 2010—. Bd. govs. U. N.C. Press, 1998—; Fulbright sr. specialist Charles U., Prague, 2006; participant various seminars; evaluator various edn. progs.; cons. in field. Author: (book) Academic Libraries, 1984; author: (with Robert D. Stueart and Claudia Morner) Library Information Center Management, 2013; author: Continuity and Change: The Integration of Oxford University's Libraries, 2005; editor (with Gary Marchionini): Information Professionals 2050: Educational Possibilities and Pathways, 2012; contbr. articles to profl. jours., chapters to books; mem. editl. bd.: Jour. Acad. Librarianship, 1992—94, Coll. and Rsch. Librs., 1996—2002, Jour. Edn. Info. and Libr. Sci., 2001—06. Mem. Chapel Hill Public Libr. Bd., 2004—13. Recipient Mount Holyoke Coll., Elizabeth Topham Kennan award, 2011; grantee Univ. Rsch. Coun., 1983, 1989, Coun. Libr. Resources, 1985, ALISE/H.W. Wilson Scholar, State Acad. Culture, St. Petersburg, Russia, 1996, IMLS, 2004, 2010; others, Fulbright sr. specialist, Charles U., Prague, 2006. Mem.: ALA, N.C. Libr. Assn., Assn. Libr. And Info. Sci. Edn., Soc. for History of Authorship, Reading, and Publishing, Popular Culture Assn., Beta Phi Mu. Home: 1307 Leclair St Chapel Hill NC 27517-3034 Office: University North Carolina School Information & Libr Sci Chapel Hill NC 27599-0001 Office Phone: 919-962-8067. Business E-Mail: moran@ils.unc.edu.

MORAN, BRIAN J., state official, former state legislator; b. Natick, Mass., Sept. 9, 1959; m. Karyn Kranz Moran; 2 children. BA, Framingham State Coll.; JD, Cath. U. of America, 1988. Sr. asst. atty. Commonwealth of Va., sec. pub. safety, 2014—; mem. Dist. 46 Va. House of Delegates, 1996—2008, mem. Courts of Justice Com., Transp. Com. and Health, Welfare and Institutions Com.; chair Dem. Party of Va., 2011—12. Mem. Secure Va. Panel, Health Care Reform Task Force, 2007. Chmn. Budget & Fiscal Affairs Adv. Coun. City of Alexandria; bd. mem. Stop Child Abuse Now. Recipient Tech. 10 award, 1998. Mem.: Alexandria C. of C., Alexandria Jaycees, Alexandria United Way (vice chmn.). Democrat. Roman Catholic. Office: Secretary of Public Safety 1111 E Broad St Richmond VA 23219 Office Phone: 804-644-1966. Office Fax: 804-343-3642.*

MORAN, DONALD WILL, consulting company executive; b. Chgo., Nov. 27, 1951; s. William Frederick and Violette Mae (Tillman) M.; m. Catherine Anne Court, Nov. 26, 1977(div. 1988); 1 child, John Savage, m. Gymhia Calcott Root, Jan 29, 1989, children: Jeanne Tillman BS, U. Ill., 1973; postgrad., Southwest Mich. Coll., 1973-74, U. Mich., 1976-77. Adminstrv. asst. Cass County Bd. of Commns., Cassopolis, Mich., 1974-75; planning cons. Mich. Employment Sector Commn., Dowagiac, 1975-76; exec. dir. Barry-Branch St. Joseph Employment & Tng. Consortium, Coldwater, Mich., 1976-77; legis. asst. U.S. Congressman David A. Stockman, Washington, 1977-81; assoc. dir. Exec. Office of Pres. Office of Mgmt. and Budget, Washington, 1981-82, exec. assoc. dir., 1982-85; v.p. ICF, Inc., Washington, 1985—98; founder & pres. The Moran Com. LLC, 1998—. Contbr. articles to profl. jours. Vice chmn. Republican Campaign Commn., Cassopolis, 1976 Mem. Am. Contract Bridge League Republican. Avocations: golf, bridge, woodworking. Home: 502 Canterbury Ln Alexandria VA 22314-4704 Office: The Moran Companies LLC 1655 North Fort Myer Dr Ste 1250 Arlington VA 22209 Business E-Mail: dwmoran@themorancompany.com.

MORAN, JIM (JAMES PATRICK MORAN JR.), United States Representative from Virginia; b. Buffalo, May 16, 1945; s. James Patrick and Dorothy (Dwyer) Moran; m. Mary Craig, Dec. 27, 1967 (div. 1974); children: Jimmy, Mary; m. Mary Howard, 1988 (div. 2003); children: Patrick, Dorothy; m. LuAnn L. Bennett, 2004. BA in Economics, Coll. Holy Cross, Worcester, Mass., 1967; MPA, U. Pitts., 1970. Comptr., budget analyst US Dept. Health, Edn. and Workforce (HEW), Washington, 1968—74; budget and fiscal policy specialist, Congl. Rsch. Svc., Libr. Congress, Washington, 1974-76; sr. staff mem. US Senate Com. Appropriations, Washington, 1976-79; investment broker A.G. Edwards & Sons, Alexandria, Va., 1979; councilman Alexandria City Coun., 1979—82, vice mayor, 1982-84, mayor City of Alexandria, 1985—90; mem. US Congress from 8th Va. dist., 1991—. Recipient Outstanding Citizenship award, YMCA, 1983. Democrat. Roman Catholic. Office: US House of Representatives 2252 Rayburn House Office Bldg Washington DC 20515 also: 333 N Fairfax St Ste 201 Alexandria VA 22314 Office Phone: 202-225-4376.*

MORAN, JOHN ARTHUR, hotel executive; b. LA, Mar. 22, 1932; s. Benjamin Edward and Louise (Chisholm) M.; m. Mary Darlene Whittaker, Aug. 14, 1954 (div. Oct. 1984); children— Kelli, Marisa, Elizabeth BS in Banking & Fin., U. Utah, 1954; postgrad., NYU, 1959, U. Southern Calif., 1960. Assoc. Blyth & Co., Inc, 1958-64, Los Angeles, 1958—64, v.p., 1964-67, The Dyson-Kissner-Moran Corp., NYC, 1967-74, exec. v.p., 1974-75, pres., 1975-84, chmn., 1984—94. Bd. dirs. Bessemer Securities, Rutherford Moran Oil Corp., The Coleman Co. Chmn. Rep. Nat. Fin. Com., 1993-95; mem. nat. adv. bd. U. Utah. Lt. USNR, 1955-58. Mem. Chief Execs. Orgn. Clubs: Metropolitan, Racquet and Tennis (N.Y.C.); Larchmont Yacht (N.Y.); Winged Foot Golf, (Mamaroneck, N.Y.), Vintage Club, Indian Wells Club (Calif.). Republican. Roman Catholic. Office: Wynn Resorts Ltd 3131 Las Vegas Blvd S Las Vegas NV 89109 Office Phone: 702-770-7555. Business E-Mail: john.moran@wynnresorts.com.

MORAN, PHILIP, state legislator; b. Bay St. Louis, Miss., Mar. 6, 1961; m. Sheila Morris; children: Loni, Alan. Attended, Pearl River CC, Poplarville, Miss., Miss. State U. Owner Philips Pest Control, LLC; mem. Dist. 46 Miss. State Senate, Jackson, 2012—. Mem.: KC, Hancock C. of C., Miss. State U. Alumni Assn., Hancock Rotary Club. Republican. Roman Catholic. Office: Miss State Senate PO Box 1018 Jackson MS 39215 Business E-Mail: pmoran@senate.ms.gov.

MORAN, WILLIAM A., real estate company executive; b. US, 1947; BBA, Cleve. State U. Founder Craftmark Group; pntr. Legend Mgmt.; prin. Elm Street Development, Inc., chmn., 1996—. Former bd. dirs. Craftmark, Inc., Craftstar Inc.; bd. dirs. ESD Inc.; founder NVR Inc., bd. dirs., 1993—. Bd. dirs. Northern Va. Bldg. Industry Assn.; pres. Fairfax County Chapter. Office: Elm Street Development Inc 1355 Beverly Rd Ste 240 Mc Lean VA 22101 also: NVR Inc Bd Directors 11700 Plz America Dr Ste 500 Reston VA 20190 Office Phone: 703-956-4000, 703-734-9730. Office Fax: 703-956-4750, 703-734-0322. Business E-Mail: wmoran@elmstreetdev.com.

MORANO, MARC PETER, editor, former legislative staff member; b. Washington, Oct. 11, 1968; s. Carl J. and Leonore (Leone) M. BA in Govt. and Polit. Sci., George Mason U., 1991. Campaign mgr. Ted Dykes for Va. Senate, Great Falls, 1991, Taxpayers for Howard Phillips, Vienna, Va., 1992; correspondent, prodr., reporter Rush Limbaugh TV Show, Washington, 1992-96; freelance journalist Mid-Atlantic Media's Washington Newsline, Vienna, 1992; investigative reporter, documentary prodr., nationally syndicated, 1997—2001; investigative reporter Cybercast News Svc., 2001—06; comm. dir. to Senator James Inhofe US Senate, Washington, 2006—09; exec. editor, chief correspondent Climate Depot.com, Washington, 2009—. Mem. bd. dirs. Citizens for Sensible Taxation, Great Falls, 1989—; commr. Cmty. Action Adv. Bd., Fairfax, Va., 1994-96. Recipient Reed Irvine Accuracy in Media award, Conservative Polit. Action Conf., 2010. Mem. White House Press Corps, Capitol Hill Press Corps, Pi Sigma Alpha. Republican. Roman Catholic. Avocations: skiing, hiking, four wheeling. Office: Climate Depot 1875 Eye St NW 5th Fl Washington DC 20006 Office Phone: 202-536-5052. E-mail: morano@climatedepot.com.

MORANT, BLAKE, dean, law educator; b. Hampton, Va. m. Paulette Morant. BA, U. Va., Charlottesville, 1975, JD, 1978; LLD, Pepperdine U., 2010. Legal intern Office the Gen. Counsel NASA, Hampton, Va., 1976, Washington, 1977; atty. 18th Airborne Corps US Army Judge Advocate Gen., Ft. Bragg, NC, 1979—82, atty. Corps Profl. Recruiting Office Ft. Belvoir, Va., 1982—84, adminstrv. law atty. Washington, 1984—85; instr. bus. law Campbell U., Buies Creek, NC, 1980—82; sr. assoc. Marguiles & Rephan, Washington, 1985—87; asst. gen. counsel Washington Met. Transit Authority, 1987—92; adj. faculty mem., instr. legal methods Am. U. Washington Coll. Law, 1988—92; assoc. prof. law U. Toledo Coll. Law, Ohio, 1992—94, Ohio, 1995—96, Ohio, 1997; vis. assoc. prof. law U. Mich. Law Sch., Ann Arbor, 1994; Roy L. Steinheimer prof. law, dir. Frances Lewis Law Ctr. Washington and Lee U. Sch. Law, 1997—2007, assoc. dean academic affairs; John S. Stone vis. prof. law U. Ala. Sch. Law, Tuscaloosa, 2002; dean, prof. law Wake Forest U. Sch. Law, Winston-Salem, NC, 2007—. Vis. fellow Oxford U., England, 2001; mem. task force to study gender bias in Va. courts Va. Supreme Ct. Mem. editl. bd.: Jour. Legal Edn.; contbr. articles to profl. jours. 2d. lt. US Army, capt. US Army Judge Advocate Gen. Corps. Decorated Meritorious Svc. medal 1st Oak Leaf Cluster US Army; vis. fellow, Univ. Coll., U. Oxford, 2001. Mem.: ABA, Assn. American Law Schools (mem. profl. devel. com. 2005—07, mem. nominating com. 2009, mem. com. on libraries & tech., mem. adv. com. 2011, mem. exec. com. 2012—). Office: Wake Forest School Law 1834 Wake Forest Rd Winston Salem NC 27109 Office Phone: 336-758-5435. Business E-Mail: morantbd@wfu.edu.*

MORD, IRVING CONRAD, II, lawyer; b. Mar. 22, 1950; s. Irving Conrad and Lillie Viva (Chapman) M.; m. Julia Ann Russell, Aug. 22, 1970 (div. Apr. 1980); children: Russell Conrad, Emily Ann; m. Kay E. McDaniel, Aug. 31, 1985 (div. Aug. 6, 2010); children: Kurt August, Clayton Troy; m. Cindy King Smith, Dec. 31, 2010. BS, Miss. State U., 1972; JD, U. Miss., 1974. Bar: Miss. 1974, U.S. Dist. Ct. (no. dist.) Miss. 1974, U.S. Dist. Ct. (so. dist.) Miss. 1984. Counsel to bd. suprs. Noxubee County, Miss., 1976-80, Walthall County, Miss., 1980—, Bd. Edn., Walthall County, 1982—. County pros. atty. Noxubee County, Macon, Miss., 1974—80, Walthall County, Tylertown, Miss., 1982—88, Tylertown, 1991—96. Bd. dirs. East Miss. Coun., Meridian, 1978-80, Trustmark Nat. Bank, Tylertown, 1986—, chmn., 2002-; v.p. Macon coun. Boy Scouts Am., 1978, mem. coun., 1979; county crusade chmn. Am. Cancer Soc., Macon, 1976-78, county pres., 1979; chmn. fund dr. fine arts complex Miss. State U.,

Macon, 1979; Walthall County family master, 1996—, Walthall County Youth referee, 1996—; mem. Local Workforce Investment Bd., 2000—. Recipient Youth Leadership award Miss. Econ. Coun., 1976. Mem. Miss. Assn. Bd. Attys. (v.p. 1985, pres. 1986), Miss. Assn. Sch. Bd. Attys., Miss. State Bar, Am. Judicature Soc. (Torts award 1972), Nat. Fed. Ind. Bus., Miss. State U. Alumni Assn., Walthall County C. of C., Phi Kappa Tau (bd. govs. 1976-80, grad. coun. 1972—, pres. grad. coun. 1977-80, pres. house corp. 1977-80, Alumnus of Yr. Alpha Chi chpt. 1979), Rotary (sec.-treas. 1977, v.p. 1978, pres. Macon 1979, pres. Tylertown club 1986-87), Phi Delta Phi. Office: 729 Beulah Ave Tylertown MS 39667-2709 E-mail: icmord@bellsouth.net.

MOREAN, WILLIAM D., manufacturing executive; s. William E. Morean and Audrey Peterson; m. Kelly Morean; 4 children. Student in Aviation, Western Mich. U. Joined Jabil Circuit, Inc., St. Petersburg, Fla., 1977, various mgmt. and operating positions, v.p. and pres., 1978—88, dir., 1978—, chmn., 1988—, CEO, 1988—2000. Bd. dirs. Eagle's Wing Found., St. Petersburg. Named one of 400 Richest Ams., Forbes mag., 2006. Office: Jabil Circuit 10560 Dr Martin Luther King Jr St N Saint Petersburg FL 33716 Office Phone: 727-577-9749. Office Fax: 727-579-8529. Business E-Mail: william.morean@jabil.com.

MOREAU, CLAUDE P., oil industry executive; Degree in fin., Laval U., Quebec, Can. Mktg. and bus. devel. positions Texaco Can., Inc., Texaco Internat. Ltd., Alimentation Couche Tard Inc.; v.p. mfg. & mktg. Chevron Texaco Latin America Products Co., 2001—03; chief comml. officer, the Americas Trafigura AG, 2003—07; v.p. mktg. Tesoro Corp., San Antonio, 2007—. Office: Tesoro Corp 19100 Ridgewood Pkwy San Antonio TX 78259-1828 Office Phone: 210-828-8484.

MOREAU, JAY MICHAEL, manufacturing executive; b. Indiana, Pa., Oct. 31, 1965; s. William Edward and Mary Katherine (Farrell) M. BS in Mktg., Juniata Coll., 1988. Divsn. pres. Martin Marietta Materials, Inc., mktg. analyst Raleigh, 1988-89, sales rep. Atlanta, 1989—. Mem. Ga. Crushed Stone Assn. (com. mem. 1989—). Republican. Roman Catholic. Avocations: weightlifting, golf, tennis. Home: 425 Stonebridge Dr Roswell GA 30075-4512 Office Phone: 919-781-4550. Office Fax: 919-783-4695. E-mail: jay.moreau@martinmarietta.com.

MORECROFT, MICHAEL JOHN, housewares company executive; b. Gloucester, UK, Mar. 4, 1942; came to U.S., 1988; s. Donald William and Miriam (Smith) M.; m. Joan Morgan, Aug. 13, 1966; children: Guy Morgan, Emma Louise. BS, U. Wales, 1963, PhD, 1966. Metal finishing mgr., quality mgr. Parkinson Cowan Ltd., Eng., 1967-70; Q&R dir., engring. dir. Hotpoint Ltd., Eng., 1970-77; engring. dir. Russell Hobbs Ltd., Eng., 1977-88; v.p. engring. Hamilton Beach, Washington, N.C., 1988-90; v.p. engring. & new product design Hamilton Beach & Proctor Silex, Richmond, Va., 1990—98, sr. v.p. engring. and product develop., 1998—2001; pres., CEO Hamilton Beach Brands, Inc. (subs. of NACCO Industries, Inc., formerly Hamilton Beach & Proctor Silex Inc.), 2001—10; vice-chmn. Hamilton Beach Brands, Inc., 2010—, Kitchen Collection, Inc. (subs. of NACCO Industries, Inc.), 2010—. Patentee in field. Avocations: sailing, skiing, golf. Office: Hamilton Beach Brands Inc 4421 Waterfront Dr Glen Allen VA 23060 Office Phone: 804-273-9777. Office Fax: 804-527-7142. Business E-Mail: mmorecroft@nacco.com.

MOREE, F. SCOTT, apparel executive; Attended, U. Miami. Mgr. Arthur Andersen & Co.; v.p., internal audit VF Corp. Office: VF Corp 05 Corporate Ctr Blvd Greensboro NC 27408 Office Phone: 336-424-6000. Office Fax: 336-424-7631. Business E-Mail: scott.moree@vfc.com.

MOREFIELD, JAMES W., JR., (WILL MOREFIELD), state legislator; b. Bluefield, W.Va., Jan. 10, 1984; s. Rebekah Peery. Attended, King Coll., Bristol, Tenn., 2002—03; BA, Midwestern State U., Wichita Falls, Tex., 2007. Small bus. owner; mem. Dist. 3 Va. House of Dels., Richmond, 2010—. Mem. Fincastle Bapt. Ch. Mem.: United Mine Workers America (assoc.), Tazewell Area C. of C. (Mem. of Yr. 2008—09). Republican. Office: Va House of Dels Gen Assembly Bldg Rm 714 PO Box 406 Richmond VA 23218 also: PO Box 828 North Tazewell VA 24630 Office Phone: 804-698-1003, 276-345-4300. Office Fax: 804-698-6703. Business E-Mail: deljmorefield@house.virginia.gov.

MORELAN, PAULA KAY, choreographer; b. Lafayette, Ind., Nov. 24, 1949; d. Dickie Booth and Marian Maxine (Fetterhoff) M.; m. Kerim Sayan, Aug. 10, 1974. Student, U. Utah, 1968-69; BFA, Tex. Christian U., 1972; postgrad., El Centro Coll., 1969-70. Tchr. Rosello Sch. Ballet, Dallas, 1972-74; mgr., tchr. Ballet Arts Ctr., Dallas, 1974-76; owner, tchr. Ballet Classique, Garland, Tex., 1976-87, Garland Ballet Acad., 1977-87; resident choreographer Garland Civic Theatre, 1988—, lifetime mem., 1998. Asst. to Mythra Rosello Tex. Civic Ballet, Dallas, 1972—74; assoc. artistic dir. Dance Repertory Theatre Dallas, 1974—75, artistic dir., 1975—76, Garland (Tex.) Ballet Assn., 1977—90, Classical Ballet Acad., Performing Arts Sch., 1987—90, Aerial Work, 1988—2004, Metropex Gynyuatium, 2005—07, Elite Champion Gymnatics, 2009; artistic dir. musical theatre dept. KD Actors Conservatory, 2005—; founder, chairperson Act IV Guild, 2002—05. Bd. dirs. Garland Civic Theatre, 2000—05. Recipient Leon Rabin award Best Choreography, Dallas Theatre League, 1996, 1998, 2000—01, 2004, Choreographer of Yr. award, 2001—04, Best Choreographer award, 2003, Column award, 2004; nominee Best Choreography award, 2006, Best Choreographer award, 2006. Office Phone: 972-240-2536. Personal E-mail: pkm@att.net.

MORELAND, ELLEN D., mathematics professor; m. Patrick; 1 child. BS in Math., MS in Math., Clarkson Coll. Tech., Potsdam, NY. Tchr. in overseas divsn. Boston U., U. Md.; faculty mem. Angelo State U., San Angelo, Tex., 1988—, sr. instr. math. Faculty mem. West Tex. Mid. Sch. Math Partnership. Recipient Chancellor's Coun. Disting. Tchg. award, Tex. Tech U. Sys., 2009; named Tex. Prof. of Yr., Carnegie Found. for Advancement of Tchg. and Coun. for Advancement and Support of Edn., 2009. Office: Angelo State University MCS 220C 2601 W Avenue N San Angelo TX 76909 Office Phone: 325-942-2317 ext. 233. Business E-Mail: ellen.moreland@angelo.edu.

MORELAND, W. BENJAMIN, telecommunications industry executive; b. 1962; BBA, U. Tex., Austin, 1984; MBA, U. Houston, 1988. Corp. fin. and real estate investment banking positions Chase Manhattan Bank, 1984—99; sr. v.p. Crown Castle International Corp., 1999—2004, treas., 1999—2004, exec. v.p., 2004—08, CFO, 2008, bd. dirs., 2006—, pres., CEO, 2008—. Former bd. dirs. FiberTower Corp.; bd. dirs. PCIA, Calpine Corp., 2008—. Office: Crown Castle International Corp 1220 Augusta Ste 500 Houston TX 77057 Office Phone: 713-570-3147. Office Fax: 713-570-3100. Business E-Mail: benjamin.moreland@crowncastle.com.*

MORENO, KAREN R., publishing executive; Joined USA TODAY (Owned by Gannett Co., Inc.), 1981, purchasing mgr.; mgr., dir. Gannett Supply Corp. (subs. of Gannett Co., Inc.), v.p., pres., 1997—. Office: Gannett Co Inc 7950 Jones Branch Dr Mc Lean VA 22107-0150 Office Phone: 703-854-6000. Office Fax: 703-854-2053. Business E-Mail: kmoreno@gannett.com.

MORENO, NIBERTO L., cardiologist; MD, Am. U., Plymouth, Monserratt, 1979. Fellowship Loyola U. Med. Ctr., Maywood, Ill., The Children's Meml. Hosp.; residency tng. Met. Group Hosps., U. Ill.; med. staff Baptist and South Miami Hosps., 1987; chief, cardio-thoracic surgery, Cardiac & Thoracic Chirurg. Group Baptist Health, 2009—. Named A Physician Who Cares award, Fla. Med. Assn., 2007. Office: Baptist Health 9601 Interstate 630 Exit 7 Little Rock AR 72205-7299 Office Phone: 501-202-2000. Office Fax: 501-202-1115. Business E-Mail: niberto.moreno@baptisthospital.com.

MORENO BLANCO, JUAN S., bank executive; Degree in Bus. Adminstrn., U. Houston. With Bankinter, 1987—94, Booz, Allen & Hamilton, 1994—97; dir., bus. devel., America's Divsn. Santander BanCorp; various positions including gen. dir., Wholesale and Instl. Banking Banco Santander México, 1997—2005; vice chmn., pres., CEO Banco Santander Puerto Rico, 2008—09, pres., CEO, bd. dirs.; vice chmn., pres., CEO Santander BanCorp, 2008—09, pres., CEO, bd. dirs., 2009—. Bd. dirs. Santander Asset Mgmt., Santander Securities Corp., Island Ins. Corp., Santander Ins. Agy., Inc., Crefisa, Inc., Santander Overseas Bank, Inc., Santander Internat. Bank, Santander Fin. Svcs., Inc. Office: Santander BanCorp 207 Ponce de Leon Ave Hato Rey PR 00917 Office Phone: 787-777-4100. Office Fax: 787-766-1437.

MORÉTEAU, OLIVIER, law educator; DEA in Comparative Law, Université Jean Moulin, 1978, DEA in French Pvt. Law, 1981, PhD summa cum laude, 1990. Tchg. and rsch. asst. Université Jean Moulin, Lyon, France, 1980—90, dir. internat. rels., 1993—95, v.p. internat. rels., 1997—99, assoc. dir. Edouard Lambert Institute of Comparative Law, 1985—2000, dir., 2000—05, assoc. prof., 1990—98, prof. comparative law, 2000—05; prof. pvt. law Université Pierre Mendes, Grenoble, France, 1998—2000; prof. law, Russell B. Long Eminent Scholars Academic Chair, dir. Ctr. of Civil Law Studies La. State U., Baton Rouge, 2005—. Vis. prof. U. Minn., 1992, Boston U., 1993—2000, 2002—04, U. Melbourne, 2002, 2004; editor-in-chief Jour. Civil Law Studies, 2008—. Contbr. articles to profl. jours. Mem.: Am. Law Inst., Société de Législation comparée, European Centre of Tort and Insurance Law, European Group on Tort Law, Internat. Acad. Comparative Law. Office: La State U Paul M Herbert Law Ctr W326C Law Ctr Baton Rouge LA 70803-1000 Office Phone: 225-578-0067. Office Fax: 225-578-3677. Business E-Mail: moreteau@lsu.edu.

MOREY, DARYL R., professional sports team executive; b. Sept. 14, 1972; m. Ellen Morey; children: Karen, Scott. BS in Computer Sci., Northwestern U., 1996; MBA, MIT, 2000. Statis. cons. STATS, Inc.; prin. cons., dir. knowledge mgmt. Parthenon Grp.; tech. lead MITRE Corp.; sr. v.p. ops. & info. Boston Celtics, 2003—06; asst. gen. mgr. Houston Rockets, 2006—07, gen. mgr., 2007—. Tchr. MIT Sloan Sch. Mgmt. Contbr. articles to profl. publs. Office: Houston Rockets 1510 Polk St Houston TX 77002

MORGAN, ALISHA THOMAS, state representative; b. Miami, Fla., Sept. 5, 1978; m. David Morgan; 1 child, Lailah. BA in Sociology, Theatre, Spelman Coll., Atlanta, 2000. Mem. children and youth, edn., health and human svcs., and govtl. affairs coms. Ga. House of Reps., state legislator, 2002; membership mgr. Young Elected Officials Network; mem. Harvard U. Black Policy Conf., Yale U. Women's Campaign Sch. Author: (book) No Apologies: Powerful Lessons in Life and Politics, 2010. Recipient People's Champion award, Cobb County Dem. Party, Champion for Choice award, All Children Matter, Legis. Leadership award, Nat. Bd. Profl. Tchg. Stads.; named Excellence in Svc., Brightest 40 under 40, Georgia Trend Mag., Nation's 30 Leaders who are under 30, Ebony Mag., Legis. of Yr., GLBC, 2008, America's Young Civil Rights Heoreos; named one of New Power Generation, Essence Mag. Mem.: NAACP (life), Family Life Restoration Ctr. (resouce bd. mem.), Austell Cmty. Taskforce, Ga. Coalition for Peoples' Agenda (mem. steering com.), Joseph E. Lowery Inst. (bd. mem.), Spl. Advs. (CASA) (adv. bd. mem.), Cobb County Ct. (apptd. mem.), Rho Zeta Omega Chpt., Alpha Kappa Alpha. Democrat. Achievements include launched the Closing the Achievement Gap Campaign. Mailing: Legis Office Bldg # 404 Atlanta GA 30334 Office: 1967 Abbey Province Austell GA 30168 Office Phone: 404-656-0109. Business E-Mail: alisha@AlishaMorgan.com.

MORGAN, CATHERINE MARIE, psychologist, writer; b. Duluth, Minn., Mar. 27, 1947; m. Ralph Morgan, 1967; 1 child, Andrew. BS, U. Nebr., 1968; MEd, U. Okla., 1973; PhD, Okla. State U., 1987; postgrad. Menninger Found., Psychotherapy Tng. Program, 1987-89. Child devel. specialist Southwest Guidance Ctr., Wheatland, Okla., 1973-74; pvt. practice Family Counseling Assocs., San Antonio, 1974-75; psychol. asst. Edmond Guidance Ctr., Okla., 1975-82; psychol. asst. supr. Southeast Guidance Ctr., Del City, Okla., 1982-86; psychol. intern Cleve. County Health Dept., Moore, Okla., 1986-87; psychologist Cen. State Hosp., Norman, Okla., 1987-89; pvt. practice assocs. in psychology Edmond, Okla.; vice chair bd. mgrs. Integris Mental Health; pres. Assocs. in Psychology, 1988—. Mem. AAUW, APA, Okla. Psychol. Assn., Am. Bus. Women's Assn., P.E.O., Kappa Delta Pi. Avocations: writing, reading, knitting, racquetball. Office: 11212 N May Ste 302 Oklahoma City OK 73120

MORGAN, DANNY, state legislator; b. Prague, Okla., Feb. 24, 1959; s. Charlie O. and Mattie Burnett Morgan; m. Debbie Hicks Morgan; children: Zachary, Danielle. BBA, Ctrl. State Univ., 1981. Former mayor, Prague, Okla.; pres. Morgan Well Svc. Inc.; mem. Dist. 32 Okla. House of Representatives, 2003—. Mem.: Last Frontier Coun. Boy Scouts America, Stroud C. of C., Davenport C. of C., Chandler C. of C., Prague C. of C., Lincoln County Dem. Party, Marginal Well Commn. Advisor Com., Okla Ind. Petroleum Assn., Assn. Energy Svc. County (state pres., nat. bd. mem., nat. polit. affairs chmn.), Prague Munic Hosp., Prague Lions Club. Democrat. Office: 2300 N Lincoln Blvd Rm 501 Oklahoma City OK 73105 Mailing: 4706 NBU Prague OK 74864 Office Phone: 405-567-4786. Business E-Mail: dannymorgan@okhouse.gov.

MORGAN, EDWARD A., oil industry executive; BS in acctg., Miss. State Univ.; M in acctg., Univ. Tenn. CPA. Acctg. positions Deloitte & Touche, 1993—97; dir. treas. ops. Am. Homepatient Inc., 1997—2002; fin. mgmt. positions Delek US Holdings, Brentwood, Tenn., 2002—03, treas., 2003—05, v.p., treas., 2005—06, v.p., CFO, 2006—09; CFO, treas. CVR Energy Inc., CVR Partners LP, Sugar Land, Tex., 2009—12; exec. v.p. investor relations Gary-Williams Energy Corp., CVR Energy, Inc., 2012—. Mem.: Am. Inst. CPAs, Assn. Fin. Professionals, Tenn. Soc. CPAs. Office: CVR Energy Inc Ste 500 2277 Plaza Dr Sugar Land TX 77479

MORGAN, ELIZABETH ANN, lawyer; d. Cyril Charles and Ann Howard Morgan; m. Matthew J. Bokor, May 1984 (div. Feb. 1999). BA, U. Fla., 1979; JD, Emory U., 1990. Bd. cert. bus. litigation: Fla. 1997. Ptnr. Powell Goldstein Frazer & Murphy LLP, Atlanta, 2000—03, Hunton & Williams LLP, Atlanta, 2003—06, Epstein Becker and Green PC, Atlanta, 2006—. Vice chair litigation com. U.S. Intellectual Property Owners Assn., Washington, 2006—08; vice chair bus. litig. certification com. Fla. Bar, Tallahassee, 1998—2005; mem. Fla. Bar Standing Com. on Professionalism, 1993—2002. Mem. Leadership Atlanta, 2002; dir. ACLU of Ga., Atlanta, 2003—05. Recipient Ga.'s Legal Elite, Ga. Trend Mag., 2006; named one of Top 50 Women Attys. in Atlanta, Atlanta Mag. and Ga. Super Lawyers Mag., 2005, Ga.'s Legal Elite, Ga. Trend Mag., 2003, 2004, 2005, Top 5% Ga. Intellectual Property Litig. Attys., Atlanta Mag. and Ga. Super Lawyers Mag., 2004, 2005, 2006, 2007. Master: Bleckley Inn of Ct.; mem.: FBA, ATLA (chair bus. torts 2005—06), ABA, Fla. Assn. for Women Lawyers (pres. Miami chpt. 1995), Internat. Trademark Assn. (chair U.S. legis.subcom. 2002—03, chair polit. action com. 2003—07, mem. Preliminery Relief Comn. 2008—), Licensing Execs. Soc., Nat. Assn. for Women Lawyers, Ga. Assn. for Women Lawyers, Atlanta Bar Assn., Copyright Soc. of U.S., Am. Intellectual Property Law Assn. (chair trademark legis. com. 2007, women in intellectual property law com.), Acad. of Fla. Trial Lawyers, Atlanta Lawyer's Club. Office: Epstein Becker and Green PC Resurgens Plaza 945 E Paces Ferry Rd Ste 2700 Atlanta GA 30326-1380 Office Fax: 404-869-5415, 404-923-9099. Business E-Mail: eamorgan@ebglaw.com.

MORGAN, G. KENNETH, association executive; b. Farmville, Va., Dec. 2, 1947; s. Raymond Henry and Evelyn (Healy) M.; m. Winnie Williams, Mar. 17, 1989; 1 child, Rebecca. BA, U. Richmond, 1974; MEd, Va. Commonwealth U., 1978. Cert. fundraising exec.; cert. assn. exec., CAE, CFRE. Program dir. Va. affiliate Am. Heart Assn., Richmond, 1970-79, mgmt. cons. nat. office Dallas, 1979-82, exec. v.p. N.C. Chapel Hill, 1982-93; nonprofit cons. Morgan & Assocs., Chapel Hill, 1993—98, NAIFA NC, 1995—. Mem. bd. advisors U. N.C. Sch. Pub. Health, Chapel Hill, 1984-93. Vol. Orange County chpt. ARC; bd. dirs. Orange County United Way, Triangle United Way. Mem. Nat. Health Agy. (pres. 1989-90), Am. Soc. Assn. Execs., Va. Assn. Rescue Squads (life, past pres.), N.C. Assn. Life Underwriters (exec. dir. 1995—), Rotary (bd. dirs. 2004-2006, Service Above Self award, Disting. Svc. award). Presbyterian. Home: PO Box 16067 Chapel Hill NC 27516-6067

MORGAN, HENRY COKE, JR., judge; b. Norfolk, Va., Feb. 8, 1935; s. Henry Coke and Dorothy Lea (Pebworth) M.; m. Margaret John McGrail, Aug. 18, 1965; children: A. Robertson Hanckel Jr., Catherine Morgan Stockwell, Coke Morgan Stewart. BS, Washington and Lee U., 1957, JD, 1960; LLM in Jud. Process, U. Va., 1998. Bar: Va. 1960, US Dist. Ct. (ea. dist.) Va. 1961, US Ct. Appeals (4th cir.) 1964. Asst. city atty. City of Norfolk, 1960-63; ptnr. Pender & Coward, Virginia Beach, Va., 1963-92; vice chmn., gen. counsel Princess Anne Bank, 1986-92; judge U.S. Dist. Ct. (ea. dist.) Va., 1992—2004, sr. judge, 2004—. Served with US Army, 1958-59. Episcopalian. Office: US Dist Ct Eastern Dist Va Walter E Hoffman US Courthouse 600 Granby St Ste 307 Norfolk VA 23510-1915 E-mail: henry_morgan@vaed.uscourts.gov.

MORGAN, JAMES H., food services company executive, former investment company executive; m. Peggy Morgan. Grad., Vanderbilt U., 1969. With Hornblower & Weeks, Bach Halsey Stuart Shields, Interstate/Johnson Lane, Charlotte, NC, 1986-89; pres. Morgan Investments, Inc., 1989—90; pres., COO Interstate/Johnson Lane, Charlotte, NC, 1990-94, pres., CEO, 1994-99, Wachovia Securities, Inc., 1999, cons. Winston-Salem, NC, 2000—01; chmn., chief investment officer Covenant Capital, LLC (formerly Morgan Semones Associates, LLC), 2001—08; vice chmn. Krispy Kreme Doughnuts, Inc., Winston-Salem, 2004—05, chmn., 2005—, pres., CEO, 2008—. Bd. dirs. Krispy Kreme Doughnuts, Inc., Winston Salem, NC, 2000—. Lt. USN. Recipient One-Yr. Investing Derby, Smart Money mag. Office: US Morgan Semones Assocs 4201 Congress St #155 Charlotte NC 28209 Mailing: Chairman of the Bd Kripsy Kreme Doughnuts Inc 370 Knollwood St Ste 500 Winston Salem NC 27103

MORGAN, JEAN ELIZABETH, plastic surgeon; b. Washington, July 9, 1947; d. William James and Antonia (Bell) Morgan; 1 child, Elena. BA magna cum laude, Harvard U., 1967; postgrad. (fellow), Oxford U., 1967, postgrad. (fellow), 1970; MD, Yale U., 1971; PhD in Psychology, U. Canterbury, Christchurch, New Zealand, 1995; MPH in Health Scis., UCLA, 2009. Cert. Am. Bd. Plastic Surgery, Am. Bd. Surgery, 1988. Intern Yale-New Haven Hosp., 1971-72, resident, 1972-73, 76-77, Tufts-New Eng. Med. Center, Boston, 1973-76, Harvard-Cambridge Hosp., Mass., 1977-78; columnist Cosmopolitan mag., 1973-80; pvt. practice specializing in cosmetic plastic surgery Washington, 1978-87, McLean, Va., 1998—2006, Chevy Chase, Md., 1998—2006; chief plastic surgery Beverly Hills Physicians, Calif., 2006—07; asst. clin. prof. dept. plastic surgery UCLA, 2006—09; clin. chief surgery U. Medicine & Health Scis., 2010. Faculty dept. psychology U. Md., 1995; assoc. faculty dept. law, justice and soc. Am. U., 1998. Author: The Making of A Woman Surgeon, 1980, Solo Practice, 1982, Custody, A True Story, 1986, The Complete Book of Cosmetic Surgery for Men, Women and Teens, 1988. Fellow: ACS, Am. Soc. Plastic Surgeons; mem.: APA, APA, Am. Pub. Health Soc., Am. Soc. Aesthetic Plastic Surgery. Avocations: ballet, opera, exercise, writing, travel. Home: 2210 Fairhaven Cir NE Atlanta GA 30305 Office: 2045 Peachtree St #412 Atlanta GA 30305 Business E-Mail: drmorgan@drelizabethmorgan.com.

MORGAN, JOHN K., chemicals executive; BS in Engring. Tech., Purdue U.; MBA, Ind. U. Various sr. mgmt. positions Lithonia Lighting, 1977—99, exec. v.p. sales & mktg., 1999—2001; exec. v.p. Acuity Brands, Inc., 2001—02, sr. exec. v.p., COO, 2002—04, pres., chief devel. officer, 2004—05, pres., CEO Acuity Brands Lighting (subs.), 2005—07, pres., CEO Acuity Splty. Products, 2007; chmn., pres., CEO Zep, Inc., 2007—. Bd. dirs. Zep, Inc., 2007—, WESCO Internat., Inc., 2008—. Office: Zep Inc 1310 Seaboard Industrial Blvd Atlanta GA 30318 Office Phone: 404-352-1680. Personal E-mail: john.morgan@zepinc.com.

MORGAN, KEN, state legislator; b. Columbia, Miss., Sept. 10, 1951; m. Wanda G. Stringer. Mem. Dist. 100 Miss. House of Reps., 2007—, mem. agr. com., conservation and water resources com., forestry com., juvenile justice com., transp. com. Republican. Baptist. Home: 1650 Hwy 587 Morgantown MS 39483 Home Phone: 601-736-9688; Office Phone: 601-736-4136. E-mail: kmorgan@house.ms.gov.

MORGAN, LARRY RONALD, minister; b. Springhill, La., Mar. 12, 1936; s. Woodrow Wilson Morgan and Alma Elizabeth (Dunn) Burch; m. Elizabeth Dianne Baker, May 24, 1958; children: Elizabeth Denise Morgan Davis, Dennis Kevin. ADiv, Bapt. Missionary Assn. Theol. Sem., Jacksonville, Tex., 1990. Ordained to ministry Bapt. Ch., 1971. Clk., carrier U.S. P.O., Springhill, La., 1956-71; assoc. pastor Webb Chapel Bapt. Ch., Dallas, 1971-72, pastor, 1972-99, First Bapt. Ch., Springhill, La., 1999—. Clk., trustee Bapt. Missionary Assn. Sem., Jacksonville, 1983-86; chmn. bd. trustees Bapt. Progress, Dallas, 1984-87. Pres. PTA Browning Elem. Sch., Springhill, 1969-70. With USAR, 1959-66. Mem. Bapt. Missionary Assn. Am. (v.p. hdqrs. Little Rock 1985-86, pres. 1986-88, v.p. Am. 1996-98, pres. 1998-2000), Dallas County Bapt. Assn. (moderator 1982-84), Bapt. Missionary

Assn. of La. (moderator 2000—)., Springhill Baptist Assn. (moderator 2001-). Baptist. Home: 611 Butler St Springhill LA 71075-2519 Office Phone: 318-539-2610. Personal E-mail: ronaldmorgan1@cmaaccess.com.

MORGAN, LUCY WARE, senior correspondent, journalist; b. Memphis, Oct. 11, 1940; d. Thomas Allin and Lucile (Sanders) Keen; m. Alton F. Ware, June 26, 1958 (div. Sept. 1967); children: Mary Kathleen, Andrew Allin; m. Richard Alan Morgan, Aug. 9, 1968; children: Lynn Elwell, Kent Morgan AA, Pasco Hernando C.C., New Port Richey, Fla., 1975; student, U. South Fla., 1976-80. Reporter Ocala Star Banner, Fla., 1965-68, St. Petersburg Times, Fla., 1967-86, capitol bur. chief, 1986—2006, sr. corr., 2006—. Assoc. editor and bd. dirs. Times Pub. Co., 1991—2006. Recipient Paul Hansel award Fla. Soc. Newspaper Editors, 1981, First in Pub. Service award Fla. Soc. Newspaper Editors, 1982, First Place award in pub. service Fla. Press Club, 1982, Pulitzer award for investigative reporting Columbia U., 1985, First Place award in investigative reporting Sigma Delta Chi, 1985; named to Kappa Tau Alpha Hall of Fame, 1992, Fla. Women's Hall of Fame, 2006; named Fla. Senate Press Gallery in Morgan's honor, 2005, 1st Pl. Non deadline Reporting, Sigma Delta Chi, 2009., 1st Pl. Fla. SOc. Newspaper Editors, 2011. Home: 7030 Spencer Dr Tallahassee FL 32312-3548 Home Phone: 850-668-8817. Personal E-mail: lucytimes@gmail.com.

MORGAN, RAYMOND VICTOR, JR., mathematics professor; b. Brownwood, Tex., May 10, 1942; s. Raymond Victor and Lovey Lucile (Tate) M.; m. Mary Jane Folks, Aug. 13, 1967; children: Jason Wesley (dec.), Jeremy Victor. BA, Howard Payne U., 1965; MA, Vanderbilt U., 1966; PhD, U. Mo., 1969. Asst. prof. So. Meth. U., Dallas, 1969-75; assoc. prof. Sul Ross State U., Alpine, Tex., 1975-82, math. dept. chmn., 1976-85, prof., 1982—, dean of scis., 1979-86, exec. asst. pres., 1985-90, pres., 1990—2009. Author textbook: Agricultural Mathematics, 1978; author articles. Bd. dirs. Texas Rural Cmtys., 1998-2006, chair, 2003—04, Marfa Pub. Radio, 2005-, Tex. Internat. Edn. Consortium; founder regional commr. Alpine Soccer League, 1984; v.p. coach Alpine Baseball League, 1983; pres. Alpine PTA, 1982-83; founder, pres. So. Meth. U. Faculty Club, 1973-75; mem. exec. com. Tex. Assn. Coll. and Univ. Student Pers. Adminstrs., 1990-92; commr. So. Assn. Colls. and Schs., 1999-2003, mem. commn. on colls. class of 2003, 2003. NSF grantee, 1979. Mem. Am. Assn. Higher Edn., Tex. Assn. Coll. Tchrs. (chpt. v.p. 1978-79), Math. Assn. Am. (chmn. Tex. sect. 1985-86), Chihuahuan Desert Rsch. Inst. (bd. dirs.), Lions Club (pres. 1979-80, 2010-, Lion of Yr. 1980, 83), Alpine Country Club. Republican. Mem. Ch. Of Christ. Avocations: motorcycling, golf, hunting, sports. Home: PO Box 1341 Alpine TX 79831-1341 Office: Sul Ross State U E Highway 90 PO Box C114 Alpine TX 79831-0114 Office Phone: 432-837-5739. Business E-Mail: rvmorgan@sulross.edu.

MORGAN, RUTH PROUSE, academic administrator, educator; b. Berkeley, Calif., Mar. 30, 1934; d. Ervin Joseph and Thelma Ruth (Pccesang) Prouse; m. Vernon Edward Morgan, June 3, 1956; children: Glenn Edward, Renée Ruth. BA summa cum laude, U. Tex., 1956; MA, La. State U., 1961, PhD, 1966. Asst. prof. Am. govt., politics and theory So. Meth. U., Dallas, 1966-70, assoc. prof., 1970-74, prof., 1974-95; prof. emeritus, 1995—; asst. provost So. Meth. U., Dallas, 1978-82, assoc. provost, 1982—86, provost ad interim, 1986-87, provost, 1987-93, provost emerita, 1993—; v.p. Chem. Abatement Tech., Inc., 1995—. Tex. state polit. analyst ABC, N.Y.C., 1972-84. Author: The President and Civil Rights, 1970, Governance By Decree: The Impact of the Voting Rights Act in Dallas, 2004; mem. editl. bd. Jour. of Politics, 1975-82, Presdl. Studies Quar., 1980-2006; contbr. articles to profl. jours. Active Internat. Women's Forum, 1987—, City of Dallas Redistricting Commn., 2001, Greater Dallas Planning Coun, 1997—; trustee Hockaday Sch., 1988-94, Kilby Awards Found., 1993-95; bd. dirs. United Way, Met. Dallas, 1993-99; adv. com. US Army Command and Gen. Staff. Coll., 1994-97; founder Archives of Women of the Southwest, 1992, chmn. adv. com. 1995-99; mem. Dallas Women's Found.; adv. bd. Cary M. Maguire Ctr. for Ethics and Pub. Responsibilty, 1998—; mem., Photographic Soc. America. Named to Austin HS Hall of Honor. Mem. Am. Polit. Sci. Assn., So. Polit. Sci. Assn. (exec. coun. 1979-84), Southwestern Polit. Sci. Assn. (pres. 1982-83, exec. coun. 1981-84), The Dallas Assembly, The Dallas Forum of Internat. Women's Forum (pres. 1996-97), Charter 100 Club (pres. 1991-92), Ctr. for the Study of the Presidency, The Women's Mus (charter), Dallas Summit Club (pres. 1992-93), Phi Beta Kappa, Pi Sigma Alpha, Phi Kappa Phi, Theta Sigma Phi. Avocations: photography, travel. Personal E-mail: morgan_ruth@yahoo.com.

MORGAN, SUSIE (DONNA SUE MORGAN), federal judge; b. Winnsboro, La., Apr. 22, 1953; BA, Northeast La. U., Monroe, La., 1974, MA, 1976; JD, La. State U. Paul M. Hebert Law Ctr., 1980. Law clk. to Hon. Henry Anthony Politz US Ct. Appeals (5th Cir.), 1980—81; assoc. Wiener, Weiss & Madison, Shreveport, 1981—85, ptnr., 1985—2005, Phelps Dunbar LLP, New Orleans, 2005—12; judge US Dist. Ct. (eastern dist.) La., 2012—. Office: US District Court 500 Poydras St Rm C-151 New Orleans LA 70130 Office Phone: 504-589-7600. Office Fax: 504-589-7697.

MORGAN, WILLIAM NEWTON, architect, educator; b. Jacksonville, Fla., Dec. 14, 1930; s. Thomas and Kathleen (Fiske) M.; m. Bernice E. Leimback, July 31, 1954; children: William Newton, Dylan Thomas. AB magna cum laude, Harvard Coll., 1952, MArch Grad. Sch. of Design, 1958. Pres. William Morgan Architects, P.A., Jacksonville, Fla., 1961—. Critic various archtl. schs.; lectr. in field; adj. prof. of art history, Jacksonville U., 1995-96, U. North Fla., 1997; Beinecke-Reeves Disting. Prof. Architecture, U. Fla., 1998-99. Prin. works include Fla. State Mus., Jacksonville Police Meml. Bldg., Pyramid Condominium, Ocean City, Md., Fed. Cts. and Offices, Ft. Lauderdale, Fla., Westinghouse World Hdqs., Orlando, Fla., Neiman-Marcus store, Ft. Lauderdale, 1st Dist. Ct. Appeal, Tallahassee, Fla., Conf. Ctr., Tallahassee, U.S. Embassy, Khartoum, Sudan, U.S. Courthouse, Tallahassee; author: Prehistoric Architecture in the Eastern United States, 1980, Prehistoric Architecture in Micronesia, 1988, Ancient Architecture of the Southwest, 1994, Precolumbian Architecture in Eastern North America, 1999, Earth Architecture, 2008. Subject of The Architecture of William Morgan (Paul Spreiregen) 1987, Images Master Architect Series: William Morgan (Robert McCarter), 2002; Fulbright grantee to Italy, 1958-59; grantee Graham Found. Advanced Studies in the Fine Arts, 1973; Lehman fellow Harvard U., 1957, Wheelwright fellow 1964-65, fellow NEA, 1991; Sam Gibbons Eminent scholar Fla. A&M U. and U. South Fla.; recipient numerous nat. and regional awards for excellence in design, Disting. Svc. award U. Fla. Sch. Architecture, 2010. Fellow AIA (past chmn. com. design) AIA Inst. honor for rsch. into the beginnings of archtl. creativity 1998, Fla. 2000 Millenium award honor for design 2000). Office: William Morgan Architects 1945 Beach Ave Atlantic Beach FL 32233-5936 Personal E-mail: wnmorgan@aol.com.

MORGANTHALL, FREDERICK S., II, retail executive; Worked Proctor & Gamble; held mgmt. positions Spartan Stores Inc., 1978—86; exec. positions, Harris Teeter Ruddick Corp., sr. mgmt. positions, Harris Teeter, pres., Harris Teeter Charlotte, NC, 1997—. Bd. dirs. Spartan Stores Inc., 2006—. Office: Ruddick Corp Ste 1800 301 S Tryon St Charlotte NC 28202 Office Phone: 704-372-5404. Office Fax: 704-372-6409. Business E-Mail: fmorganthall@ruddickcorp.com.

MORIN, ROGER PAUL, bishop; b. Lowell, Mass., Mar. 7, 1941; BA, St. John's Sem. Coll., 1966; MDiv, Notre Dame Sem., 1970; MS, Tulane U., 1974. Ordained priest Archdiocese of New Orleans, La., 1971; ordained bishop, 2003; aux. bishop Archdiocese of New Orleans, La., 2003—09; bishop Diocese of Biloxi, Miss., 2009—. Roman Catholic. Office: Diocese of Biloxi PO Box 1189 1790 Popps Ferry Rd Biloxi MS 39532-2118 Office Phone: 228-702-2112. Office Fax: 228-702-2125.

MORLEY, LLOYD ALBERT, electrical engineering educator; b. Provo, Utah, Oct. 28, 1940; s. John Jr. and Dorothea (Nielsen) M.; m. Jo Ann Bryant, Feb. 22, 1975; 1 child, Paul Loring. BS in Mining Engring., U. Utah, 1968, PhD in Mining Engring., 1972. Tchg. asst., rsch. assoc. U. Utah, Salt Lake City, 1968-71; asst. prof. mining engring. Pa. State U., University Park, 1971-75, assoc. prof., 1975-80, prof., 1980-85; prof., head dept. mineral engring. U. Ala., Tuscaloosa, 1985-93, endowed chair mining engring., 1993-99, prof. elec. engring., 1996—2006, assoc. dept. head elec. and computer engring., 1997-99, interim head, 1999-2000, head, 2000—04, prof. emeritus, 2007—. Cons. Jim Walter Resources, Inc., Brookwood, Ala., 1987-98, Pitts. and Midway Coal Mining Co., Englewood, Colo., 1990-98, Drummond Co., Inc., Birmingham, Ala., 1991-98. Author: Mine Power Systems, 1990; contbr. articles to profl. jours. Staff sgt. USNG, 1958-66. Recipient Wilson Outstanding Tchg. award Pa. State U., 1980; Outstanding Rsch. Report awards U.S. Bur. Mines, 1983-84, Hackney Faculty Leadership award, U. Ala., 2000, HKN Outstanding Tchg. award, U. Ala., 2004. Fellow IEEE (life) (bd. dirs. 1991-92, 94, 97-99, v.p. publs. 1994, 99, v.p. tech. activities 1997, 98, corp. integrity officer 2006—11, Richard M. Emberson award 2005); mem. Industry Applications Soc. IEEE (Mining Best Paper awards 1984, 88, 90, pres. 1988, Disting. lectr. 1991, Disting. Svc. award 1995), Power Engr. Soc., Computer Soc., Phi Kappa Phi, Eta Kappa Nu. Avocations: high-fidelity systems, classic sports cars, rose growing, music. Home Phone: 205-758-8551.

MOROMIZATO, SHINOBU, professional golfer; b. Okinawa, Japan, July 16, 1986; Profl. golfer LPGA Japan Tour, 2005—, LPGA Tour, 2006—. Achievements include winning LPGA of Japan Tour event: AXA Ladies Golf Tournament, 2008; Golf5 Ladies, CAT Ladies, Promise Ladies Cup, Suntory Ladies Open, Salonpas Cup, 2009; winning LPGA of Japan Tour major Championship: Japan LPGA championship Konica Minolta Cup, 2009. Office: LPGA 100 International Golf Dr Daytona Beach FL 32124-1092

MORONEY, JAMES MCQUEEN, III, publishing executive; b. 1957; s. James McQueen Jr. and Helen Claire (Wilhoit) Moroney; m. Barbara Moroney; 5 children. BA in American Studies, Stanford U., 1978; MBA, U. Tex., Austin, 1983. With Belo Corp. (formerly A.H. Belo Corp.), Dallas, 1978—, acct. exec. WFAA-TV, KFDM-TV Beaumont, Tex., 1978—84, local sales mgr. WFAA-TV Dallas-Ft. Worth, 1985, gen. sales mgr. KOTV Tulsa, Okla., 1985—89, contr. Belo Corp., 1989—92, v.p., gen. mgr. KOTV, 1992—93, pres., gen. mgr., 1993, v.p. broadcast divsn. Belo Corp., 1993—95, v.p. TV group, 1995—97, pres. TV group, 1997—98, exec. v.p. Belo Corp., 1998—99, 2007—, founding pres. Belo Interactive, Inc., 1999—2001, pub., CEO Dallas Morning News, 2001—. Bd. dirs. Belo Corp., 2008—, TV Bur. Advt. Mem. Dallas Citizens Coun.; bd. dirs. Goodwill Industries, Dallas, Tulsa, United Way Tulsa, Cath. Charities Tulsa, Jr. Achievement Tulsa, Cistercian Prep. Sch. Dallas, Dallas C. of C., State Fair Tex., The Dallas Found. Named Pub. of Yr., Editor & Pub. mag., 2004. Mem.: Newspaper Assn. America (bd. dirs., chmn. 2012—), Southern Newspaper Publishers Assn. (bd. dirs.). Office: Dallas Morning News 508 Young St Dallas TX 75202 also: Belo Corp PO Box 655237 Dallas TX 75265-7526 Business E-Mail: jmoroney@dallasnews.com.

MORONEY, JOHN RODGERS, economist, educator; b. Dallas, Jan. 29, 1939; s. John Rodgers and Irene (Lewis) M.; m. Margaret Cecil Kearny, May 30, 1959; children: John Rodgers, Stephen Kearny, Helen, Michael Edward; m. Carmen Lambert, May 22, 1993 BA, So. Meth. U., Dallas, 1960; PhD, Duke U., Durham, NC, 1964. Asst. prof. econs. Fla. State U., 1964—66; assoc. prof. econs. Mich. State U., 1966—69; mem. exec. com. Inst. Pub. Utilities, 1968—69; prof. econs., chmn. dept. Tulane U., New Orleans, 1969—81; prof., head dept. econs. Tex. A&M U., College Station, 1981—. Vis. prof. econs. MIT, 1975-76; Schmidt internat. prof. A.B. Freeman Sch. Bus., Tulane U., New Orleans, 1998—; pres. Moroney Econ. Rsch. Assocs., 1992— Author: The Structure of Production in American Manufacturing, 1972, Exploration, Development, and Production: Texas Oil and Gas, 1997, Energy and Sustainable Development in Mexico, 2005, Power Struggle: World Energy in the 21st Century, 2008; editor, contbr.: Income Inequality: Trends and Internat. Comparisons, 1979, Economic Aspects of New Technology, 1980, Formal Energy and Resource Models, 1982; editor: Econometric Models of the Demand for Energy, 1984; editor, contbr.: Energy, Capital, and Technological Change, 1987, Energy, Growth, and the Environment, 1992, Energy Prices and Production, 1994, Sustainable Economic Growth, 1995, Energy Supply and Demand, 1997, Fuels for the Future, 1999; mem. editl. bd. Bus. Topics, 1968-69, So. Econ. Jour, 1975— Social Sci. Rsch. Coun. faculty rsch. fellow, 1969; NSF rsch. fellow, 1975-76, 77-79 Mem. Am. Econ. Assn., So. Econ. Assn. (exec. com. 1975—, v.p. 1980), Royal Econ. Assn., Econometric Soc., Phi Beta Kappa Home: 210 Fireside Cir College Station TX 77840-1877 Office: Dept Econs Tex A&M U College Station TX 77843-4228 Office Phone: 979-845-1363. Business E-Mail: jmoroney@econmail.tamu.edu.

MOROWITZ, HAROLD JOSEPH, biophysicist, educator; b. Poughkeepsie, NY, Dec. 4, 1927; s. Philip Frank and Anna (Levine) M.; m. Lucille Rita Stein, Jan. 30, 1949; children: Joanna Lynn, Eli David, Joshua Alan, Zachary Adam, Noah Daniel. BS, Yale U., 1947, MS, 1950, PhD, 1951. Physicist Nat. Bur. Stds., 1951-53, Nat. Heart Inst., Bethesda, Md., 1953-55; mem. faculty Yale U., 1955-88, assoc. prof. biophysics, 1960-68, prof. molecular biophysics and biochemistry, 1968-88, master Pierson Coll., 1981-86; mem. faculty George Mason U., Fairfax, Va., 1988—, Robinson prof. biology and natural philosophy, 1988—; dir. Krasnow Inst. for Advanced Study, 1993-98. Chmn. com. on models for biomed. rsch. NRC, 1983-85, mem. bd. on basic biology, 1986-92. Author: Life and the Physical Sciences, 1964, (with Waterman) Theoretical and Mathematical Biology, 1965, Energy Flow in Biology, 1968, Entropy for Biologists, 1970, (with Lucille Morowitz) Life On The Planet Earth, 1974, Ego Niches, 1977, Foundations of Bioenergetics, 1978, The Wine of Life, 1979, Mayonnaise and the Origin of Life, 1985, Cosmic Joy and Local Pain, 1987, The Thermodynamics of Pizza, 1991, Beginnings of Cellular Life, 1992, (with James Trefil) The Facts of Life, 1992, Entropy and the Magic Flute, 1993, The Kindly Dr. Guillotin, 1997, The Emergence of Everything, 2002; editor Complexity, 1994-2002; contbr. articles to profl. jours. Mem. sci. adv. bd. Santa Fe Inst., 1991-97, co-chmn. sci. adv. bd., 2000-06, chmn. emeritus, sci. adv. bd., 2007-. Recipient Biol. Scis. award, Washington Acad. Scis., 2004. Mem. Biophys. Soc. (exec. com. 1965), Nat. Ctr. for Rsch. Resources (coun. 1987-92). Office: George Mason U Mail Stop 2A1 Krasnow Inst Advanced Study Fairfax VA 22030 Office Phone: 703-993-4334.

MORREIM, E. HAAVI, medical ethics educator; b. 1950; d. Paul and Florence Morreim. BA in Philosophy, St. Olaf Coll., 1972; PhD, U. Va., 1980; JD, U. Memphis, 2009. Med. philosopher program in human biology and soc. U. Va. Sch. Medicine, Charlottesville, 1980-82, asst. prof. philosophy in medicine, 1982-84; from asst. to assoc. prof. dept. human values and ethics U. Tenn. Coll. Medicine, Memphis, 1988—93, prof. dept. human values and ethics, 1993—2009, prof. dept. internal medicine, Health Sci. Ctr., 2009—. Adj. prof. philosophy Va. Commonwealth U., Richmond, 1980; vis. prof. philosophy St. Olaf Coll., Northfield, Minn., 1982; Andrew Mellon vis. asst. prof. humanities and medicine Georgetown U. Sch. Medicine, Washington, 1983; sr. vis. rsch. scholar Kennedy Inst. Ethics, Georgetown U., 1983; manuscript reviewer; presenter and lectr. in field. Author: Balancing Act: The New Medical Ethics of Medicine's New Economics, 1991, Holding Health Care Accountable: Law and the New Medical Marketplace, 2001; bd. editors: Jour. Law, Medicine and Ethics, IRB: Ethics and Human Research, Accountability in Research; contbr. articles to profl. jours. Active Hastings Ctr. Mem. Am. Health Lawyers Assn., Am. Soc. Law, Medicine, and Ethics, Am. Soc. for Bioethics and Humanities, Phi Beta Kappa. Avocations: running, high-performance automobile driving, photography, skiing. Office: University Tenn Coll Medicine 956 Ct G 212 Memphis TN 38163-2814 Office Phone: 901-448-5725. Business E-Mail: hmorreim@uthsc.edu.

MORRELL, DEAN SCOTT, pediatric dermatologist; b. Norwich, NY, May 11, 1965; s. Edward Arthur and Clarissa (Hyuck) M.; m. Karen Anne Hendrix, Sept. 12, 1989. BS magna cum laude, Wake Forest U., Winston-Salem, NC, 1987; M Phys. Therapy, Hahnemann U., Phila., 1989; MD, U. NC Sch. Medicine, Chapel Hill, 1997. Lic. phys. therapist Md., cert. in dermatology 2001, in pediatric dermatology 2006. Staff phys. therapist Burch, Rhoads, Loomis, P.A., Balt.; internship in pediat. U. NC Hosps., Chapel Hill, 1997—98, residency in dermatology, 1998—2000; fellow in pediatric dermatology Children's Hosp. Wis., Med. Coll. Wis., Milw., 2000—01; asst. prof. dermatology U. NC Sch. Medicine, 2001—06, assoc. prof., program dir., dir. pediatric and adolescent dermatology, dept. dermatology, 2006—. Contbr. articles to profl. jours., chapters to books. Coach YMCA Ladies Baseball Team, Towson, Md., 1990. Mem. Am. Phys. Therapy Assn. Democrat. Methodist. Avocations: running, basketball, volleyball. Office: U NC Sch Medicine Dept Dermatology 3100 Thurston-Bowles Bldg CB 7287 Chapel Hill NC 27599-7287 Office Phone: 919-966-0785. Office Fax: 919-966-3898.

MORRELL, JEAN-PAUL J., state legislator; Mem. Dist. 97 La. House of Reps., 2006—08; mem. Dist. 3 La. State Senate, 2009—, chair local and mcpl. affairs com., mem. environ. quality com., ins. com., revenue and fiscal affairs com. Democrat. Office: 6305 Elysian Fields Ave Ste 405 New Orleans LA 70122 also: Capitol Office PO Box 94183 Baton Rouge LA 70804 Office Phone: 504-942-5996, 504-284-4794. Fax: 504-942-5998. E-mail: larep097@legis.state.la.us, morrelljp@legis.state.la.us.

MORRILL, RICHARD LESLIE, academic administrator, former foundation administrator; b. Weymouth, Mass., June 4, 1939; s. Duncan Russel and Violet Erma (Gibson) M.; m. Martha Leahy, June 24, 1964; children: Katie, Amy. AB in History magna cum laude, Brown U., 1961; B.D. in Religious Thought, Yale U., 1964; PhD in Religion, Duke U., 1968. Instr. Wells Coll., Aurora, N.Y., 1967-68; asst. prof. Chatham Coll., Pitts., 1968-74, assoc. provost and asst. to pres., 1973-77, assoc. prof., 1974-77; assoc. provost Pa. State U., University Park, 1977-79; pres. Salem Coll. and Acad., Winston-Salem, N.C., 1979-82, Centre Coll., Danville, Ky., 1982-88, U. Richmond, Va., 1988-98, chancellor, Disting. Univ. prof. ethics & Democratic values, 1998—; pres. The Teagle Foundation, 2010—13. Bd. dirs. Ctrl. Fidelity Banks, Inc.; v.p. Southern Univ. Conf., 1993—; chmn. Assoc. Colleges of the South, 1993-94; v.p. Southern Univ. Conf., 1993—; mem. governing coun. Wye Faculty Seminar, 1994—; mem. presdl. adv. com. KPMG Peat Marwick, 1989—; cons. edn. divsn. Lilly Endowment, 1990—.bd. dirs., Albemarle Corp., 2002-. Author: Teaching Values in College, 1980; contbr. articles to profl. jours. Bd. dirs., mem. program com. Teagle Found., 1989—; mem. nat. bd. visitors Ind. U. Ctr. on Philanthropy, 1991—; mem. commn. on leadership devel. American Coun. on Edn., 1992-94; trustee Williamsburg Investment Trust, 1993—; mem. Richmond Symphony Coun., 1995—; mem. Va. Coun. for Internat. Edn., 1995-96; bd. dirs. Assn. American Colleges & Universities, 1996—. Woodrow Wilson fellow, 1961-62; James B. Duke fellow Duke U., 1964-67 Mem. Soc. for Values in Higher Edn. (dir. 1981-84), American Acad. Religion, American Soc. for Christian Ethics, American Assn. Higher Edn., Southern Assn. Colleges & Schools (commr. 1985—), Coll. Athletic Conf. (chmn. 1985-87), Council Ind. Ky. Colls. & Universities (sec. 1984-86, v.p. 1986-88, exec. com. 1984-86), Assn. Presbyn. Colls. & Universities (exec. com. 1984-86), Phi Beta Kappa. Clubs: University. Lodges: Rotary. Office: University of Richmond 28 Westhampton Way Richmond VA 23173 Office Phone: 804-289-8100.*

MORRIS, CLIFTON H., JR., finance company executive; b. Ft. Worth, Tex., 1936; Grad., U. Tex., 1958. CPA. Various fin. positions including v.p. & treas. Svc. Corp. Internat., Inc., 1966—71; CFO Cash America Internat. Inc.; pres. AmeriCredit Corp., 1988—96, CEO, 1988—2000, 2003—05, chmn. bd. dirs., 1988—. Bd. dirs. Svc. Corp. Internat., Inc., 1990—. Vol. Cmty. Found. North Tex. Named Bus. Exec. of Yr., Ft. Worth Bus. Hall of Fame, 2001. Mem.: AICPA (hon.), Tex. Soc. CPA's (life). Office: AmeriCredit Corp 801 Cherry St Ste 3500 Fort Worth TX 76102 Office Phone: 817-302-7000. Office Fax: 817-336-9519.

MORRIS, DOUGLAS CLAUDE, cardiologist, educator; b. Marietta, Ga., Apr. 18, 1942; BA in Chemistry, Duke U.; MD, Baylor Coll. Medicine, Houston, 1968. Cert. Internal Medicine, Cardiovascular Disease, Interventional Cardiology. Intern, internal medicine Vanderbilt U. Hosp., Nashville, 1968—69, resident, cardiology, 1969—70, 1972—73; fellow Emory U. Hosp., 1973—75; faculty staff mem., dept. medicine, divsn. cardiology Emory U. Sch. Medicine, 1973—, J. Willis Hurst prof. medicine, 1996—; dir., Carlyle Fraser Heart Ctr. Crawford Long Hosp., 1986; dir. Emory Heart Ctr., 1993; vice-chair, dept. medicine Emory U., 1999. Named one of Ten Best Doctors in Cardiovascular Disease, Atlanta Mag., 1999—. Mem.: Soc. Cardiac Angiography, Am. Coll. Cardiology (co-chair scientific sessions 1996—2000), ACP. Avocation: running. Office: Emory U Rm A2205 Emory Clinic 1365A Clifton Rd NE Atlanta GA 30322 Office Phone: 404-778-5310. Office Fax: 404-778-5320. Business E-Mail: douglas.morris@emoryhealthcare.org.

MORRIS, G. RONALD, automotive executive; b. East St. Louis, Ill., Aug. 30, 1936; s. George H. and Mildred C. M.; m. Margaret Heino, June 20, 1959; children: David, Michele, James. BS in Metall. Engring, U. Ill., 1959. Metall. engr. Delco-Remy divsn. Gen. Motors Corp., 1959-60; factory metallurgist Dubuque Tractor Works, John Deere Co., Iowa, 1960-66; with Fed.-Mogul Corp., 1966-79, v.p., group mgr. ball and roller bearing group, 1979; pres. Tenneco

Automotive divsn. Tenneco, Inc., Deerfield, Ill., 1979-82; pres., CEO PT Components, Inc., Indpls., 1982-88; vice-chmn. Rexnord Corp., Indpls., 1988-89; chmn., pres., CEO CTP Holdings Inc., 1986-88; chmn. Integrated Technologies, Inc., Indpls., 1990-92, also bd. dirs.; pres., CEO Western Industries, Inc., Milw., 1991-99. Bd. dirs. NN, Inc., Erwin, Tenn., 1994—, non-exec. chmn., 2013—; bd. dirs. Prism Capital Inc., Savannah Philharmonic, Salvation Army & Veritas Acad. Mem. Pres.'s Coun., U. Ill., mem. and chmn. sr. adv. bd. Dept. Materials Sci. and Engring, U. Ill.; mem. U. Ill. Found. Mem. ASM, SAE, The Landings Club (Savannah, Ga.), Masons, Scottish Rite, Kiwanis Internat. Republican. Presbyterian. E-mail: savannahronm@yahoo.com.

MORRIS, GERALD MICHAEL, lawyer, educator; b. Endicott, NY, July 17, 1951; s. John Philip and Rita Cathrine Morris; m. Lynn Carol (Baker), Apr. 12, 1980; children: David, Kathrine, Mary. BA in History, LeMoyne Coll., 1973; JD with honors, Nova So. Ea. U. Law Ctr., 1977; LLM, U. Houston Law Ctr., 2002. Cert.: Fla. Bar (health law) 1995, bar: Fla. 1977, US Dist. Ct. (so. dist.) Fla. 1977, US Dist. Ct. (mid. dist.) Fla. 1983, US Ct. Appeals (5th cir.) Fla. 1981, US Ct. Appeals (11th cir.) Fla. 1981, US Supreme Ct. 1981. Law clk. Saunders, Curtis, Ginestra & Gore, Ft. Lauderdale, Fla., 1975—77, assoc., 1977—82, ptnr., 1982—86; sr. assoc. Finley, Kumble, Wagner, Heine, Underberg, Manley, Myerson & Casey and successor firm Tew, Jordon & Schulte, 1986—88, Heinrich, Gordon, Batchelder, Hargrove, Weihe & James, 1989, ptnr., 1990—92; gen. coun. Holy Cross Hosp., Inc., 1992—. Mem. Fla. Bar Young Lawyers, 1977—88, bd. governors rep., 1984—87; mem. Fla. Bar Health Law Com., 1983—87, Fla. Bar Health Law Sect., 1989—; grievance com. mem. Fla. Bar 17th cir., 1987—90, grievance chmn., 1990; mem., bd. govs. Shepard Broad Law Ctr. Nova South Eastern U., 1990—2013; adj. prof. Nova So. Ea. U., 1992—; spkr. various seminars, 1989—. Bd. dirs. Boys and Girls Club Broward County, 1987—2001; mem. FDA Instl. Review Bd., Holy Cross Hosp., Fla., 1986—92; profit magazine editl. bd. mem. Greater Ft. Lauderdale C. of C., Fla., 1987—88, selection com. mem. Youth Leadership Broward, 1988—90, mem., 1988—92, chmn. legis. action sub-com., 1989—91, co-chmn. A1A Beach Redevel. Task Force, 1990, chmn., 1991, vice-chair com. affairs, 1992, exec. com. mem., 1992—93, chmn. Health Care Com., 1992—94, bd. govs., 1992—94; past mem. Am. Health Lawyer Assn., Am. Soc. for Law, Medicine and Ethics; lector, extraordinary min. St. David Catholic Ch., Davie, Fla., 1974—2001. Recipient Vision Broward award, Greater Ft. Lauderdale C. of C., 1990; nominee Alumus of Yr., NSU, 2006. Mem.: Broward County Bar Assn. (Young Lawyers Sect.) (exec. com. 1983—88, sec., treas. 1985—86, pres.-elect 1986—87, pres. 1987—88), Broward County Bar Assn. (law day com. 1985—88, chmn. 1986—87, exec. com. 1986—88, legal/medical com. 1997—99, President's award 1987), Phi Alpha Delta (legal frat.) (chpt. vice justice 1976—77). Office: Holy Cross Hosp Inc Legal Affairs Dept 4725 N Fed Hwy Fort Lauderdale FL 33308 Office Phone: 954-229-8500. Business E-Mail: gerald.morris@holy-cross.com.*

MORRIS, GREG, state legislator; House rep., Ga.; state rep. Dist. 155 Ga., 1999—2002; mem. Game Com., Fish Com., Pks. Com., Natural Resources Com., Environ. Com., Transp. Com., 1999—; state rep. Dist. 120 Ga., 2003—04; state rep. Dist. 155 Ga., 2004—. Democrat. Mailing: 601 Legis Office Bldg Atlanta GA 30334 Office: PO Box 1749 Vidalia GA 30475 Office Phone: 404-656-0254, 912-538-1062.

MORRIS, HERMAN, JR., pharmaceutical executive, lawyer; b. Memphis, Jan. 16, 1951; s. Herman and Reba (Garrett) M.; m. Brenda Partee; children: Amanda, Patrick, Geoffrey. BA in Economics, Rhodes Coll.; JD, Vanderbilt U. Bar: Tenn. 1977, U.S. Dist. Ct. Tenn. 1980, U.S. Ct. Appeals (6th cir.) 1980, U.S. Supreme Ct. 1980. Law clk. Tenn. Commn. on Human Devel., Nashville, 1976, Ratner, Sugarmon & Lucas, Memphis, 1976; assoc. Ratner & Sugarmon, Memphis, 1977-82, ptnr., 1982; mng. ptnr. Sugarmon, Salky & Morris, 1982-86; pvt. practice Herman Morris & Assocs., Memphis, 1986-88; prin. Morris & Noel, Attys. at Law, Memphis, 1988; gen. counsel Memphis Light, Gas and Water Divsn., 1989, pres., CEO, 1997—2004; ptnr. Baker, Donaldson, Bearman, Caldwell and Berkowitz, Memphis, 2004—06; city atty. City of Memphis, 2006—09; v.p., gen. counsel Pinnacle Airlines, 2006. Jud. referee Shelby County Juvenile Ct., Memphis, 1987-89; divorce referee Shelby County, 1984-87; vice chmn. bd. profl. responsibility Tenn. Supreme Ct., 1995, mem. disciplinary bd. of heargin officers, mem. state disciplinary bd.; mem. adv. com. Jud. Criminal Justice Ctr.; mem. Tenn. Jud. Selection Commn.; presenter workers' compensation law Am. Pub. Power Assn., 1993; presenter ethics in profession of law Rhodes Coll., 1994; presenter deposition strategies and tactics Profl. Edn. Sys., Inc., 1994; bd. dirs. Memphis Riverfront Devel. Corp., Perrigo Co., 1999-. Pres., mem. exec. bd. Memphis br. NAACP, 1992-96; Shelby County Homerule Commn., 1982; mem. bd. govs. Jobs Conf. Memphis; mem. bd. commrs. bd. edn. Memphis City Schs., mem. strategic planning steering com.; pres., chmn. bd. dirs. Dixie Homes Boys Club; bd. dirs. NCCJ, Memphis Landmark Commn., Goals for Memphis, Ch. and Cmty. Investment Fund, Associated Cath. Charities, Bd. of Theater, Memphis, Blues City Cultural Ctr., Memphis Pub. Edn. Fund.; mem. Primary Health Care Adv. Bd. Tenn., Cmty. Found. Greater Memphis. Recipient Appreciation award Memphis Health Ctr., 1980, Dixie Homes Boys Club, 1988, Clues City Cultural Ctr., 1988, LeMoyne Owen Coll. chpt. NAACP, 1993, Silver Sch. Bell award Memphis City Schs., 1984. Mem. ABA, ATLA (bd. dirs.), Tenn. Bar Assn. (presenter on ethics 1993), Tenn. Trial Lawyers Assn. (bd. dirs.), Memphis Bar Assn. (bd. dirs., chmn. com. on opportunities for minorities in legal profession), Nat. Bar Assn. (pres. Ben F. Jones chpt.), Temm. Black Caucus of State Legislators, Inc. (mem. com.), Rhodes Coll. Alumni Assn. (mem. exec. bd.), Southwestern at Memphis Alumni Assn. (mem. exec. bd.), Omicron Delta Kappa (bd. dirs. Southwestern at Memphis chpt.). Office: Memphis Light Gas Water Div 220 S Main St Memphis TN 38103-3917 also: Perrigo Co 515 Eastern Ave Allegan MI 49010 Office Phone: 269-673-8451. Office Fax: 269-673-9128. Business E-Mail: hmorris@perrigo.com.

MORRIS, JAMES BRUCE, internist; b. Rochester, NY, May 13, 1943; s. Max G. and Beatrice Ruth (Becker) M.; m. Susan Carol Shencup, July 31, 1966; children: Carrie, Douglas, Deborah, Rebecca. BA, U. Rochester, 1964; MD, Yale U., 1968. Diplomate Am. Bd. Internal Medicine, Am. Bd. Infectious Diseases. Intern SUNY, Buffalo, 1968-69, resident, 1969-70, 72-73, chief resident, 1973; pvt. practice medicine & infectious diseases Plantation, Fla., 1974—. Chmn. infection control com. Lauderdale Lakes Gen. Hosp., 1974-76; chmn. infection control com. Plantation Gen. Hosp., 1976-80, 83-85, chmn. pharmacy com., 1980-81, chmn. tissue com., 1982; sec., program chmn. dept. medicine Bennett Community Hosp., 1978-80, chmn. dept. medicine, 1980-81, vice chief staff, 1981-83; chmn. infection control com. Fla. Med. Center, 1980-82; chief staff Humana Hosp. Bennett, 1983-85, trustee, 1983-88, chmn. infection control com., 1985-87; bd. trustees Westside Regional Med. Ctr., 2008-. With USAR, 1970-72. Recipient Recognition, Town & Country Guide to Primary Care Physicians; named one of Top Docs in South Fla., Miami Metro; fellow, U. Miami, 1974. Fellow ACP; mem. AMA, Am. Soc. Microbiology, Infectious Diseases Soc. Am., Am. Soc. Internal Medicine, Fla. Med. Assn., Broward County Med. Assn. Office: Morris Sklaver Mestre & Perez MD PA 7353 NW 4th St Plantation FL 33317-2202 Office Phone: 954-584-9111.

MORRIS, JAMES H., state legislator; BSE, Henderson State U., 1976. Mem. Dist. 1 La. House of Reps., 2007—, mem. appropriations com., labor and indsl. rels. com., natural resources and environment com., house exec. com., joint legis. com. on the budget, mem. house com. on homeland security. Republican. Office: State Capitol PO Box 44486 Baton Rouge LA 70804 Mailing: PO Box 217 Oil City LA 71061 Office Phone: 318-995-6852, 225-342-6945. Office Fax: 318-995-6890. Business E-Mail: larep001@legis.state.la.us.

MORRIS, JAMES MALACHY, lawyer; b. Champaign, Ill., June 5, 1952; s. Walter Michael and Ellen Frances (Solon) M.; m. Mary Delilah Baker, Oct. 17, 1987; children: James Malachy Jr., Elliot Rice Baker, Walter Michael, Nicholas Aidan. Student, Oxford U., Eng., 1972; BA, Brown U., 1974; JD, U. Pa., 1977. Bar: NY 1978, US Dist. Ct. (so. and ea. dists.) NY 1978, Ill. 1980, US Tax Ct. 1982, US Supreme Ct. 1983; admitted to Barristers Chambers, Manchester, Eng., 1987. Assoc. Reid & Priest, NYC, 1977-80; sr. law clk. Supreme Ct. Ill., Springfield, 1980-81; assoc. Carter, Ledyard & Milburn, NYC, 1981-83; sole practice NYC, 1983-87; counsel FCA, Washington, 1987—2006; acting sec., gen. counsel FCS Ins. Corp., McLean, Va., 1990-98, exec. asst., bd. chmn., 2005—06, gen counsel, 2006—13, sole practice, 2013—. Cons. Internat. Awards Found., Zurich, 1981—2002, Pritzker Architecture Prize Found., NYC, 1981—2002, Herbert Oppenheimer, Nathan & VanDyck, London, 1985—2004. Contbr. articles to profl. jours. Recipient FCA Trust award, 2001, FCS Ins. Corp. Funding award, 2012. Mem. ABA, Ill. Bar Assn., NY State Bar Assn., NY County Lawyers Assn., Assn. Bar City NY, Brit. Inst. Internat. and Comparative Law, Am. Inst. Parliamentarians, Brown U. 1764 Soc., Brown U. Assn. Class Leaders, Emory U. Parent Leadership Bd., Lansdowne Club (London), Penn Club (NYC), Brown Club Wash. Office: PO Box 1407 Mc Lean VA 22101-1407

MORRIS, JOHN C., III, state legislator; BA, La. State U., 1980, JD, 1983. Atty., La.; mem. Dist. 14 La. House of Reps., Baton Rouge, 2012—. Republican. Office: 2309 Oliver Rd Rm 1&2 Monroe LA 71201 also: La House of Reps 900 N 3rd St Baton Rouge LA 70804 Office Phone: 318-362-4270. Business E-Mail: morrisjc@legis.la.gov.

MORRIS, JOHN HARVEY, retired investment company executive, board member; b. Daytona Beach, Fla., Jan. 25, 1944; s. Claude and Lorena Mary (Bracey) Morris; m. Sharon Irene Lewis Morris, Apr. 5, 1969; 1 child, Jennifer Lynn. BS in Indsl. Engring., Ga. Inst. Tech., 1966; MBA in Fin., Ga. State U., 1970. CPA Ga.; cert. mgmt. cons. Officer First Nat. Bank Atlanta, 1967—70; cons. Booz Allen Hamilton, Atlanta, 1970—71; mgr. Touche Ross & Co., Atlanta, 1971—80; CFO Peterson Group, Atlanta, 1980—81; pres., CEO LBO Capital Corp., Atlanta, 1984; v.p. Kelso & Co. Inc., Atlanta, 1985—87, gen. ptnr., 1987—89, mng. dir., 1989—92; with StoneCreek Capital, 1992—2008, ret. as co-chair, 2003. Bd. dirs. Ark. Best Corp., 1988—, Treadco, Inc., 1991—99. Mem.: AICPA, Inst. Mgmt. Cons., Planning Execs. Inst., Ga. Soc. CPA's. Office: Arkansas Best Corp Bd Directors 3801 Old Greenwood Rd Fort Smith AR 72903 Office Phone: 479-785-6000. Office Fax: 479-785-6004. Business E-Mail: jmorris@arkbest.com.

MORRIS, MALCOLM STEWART, title company executive, lawyer; b. Houston, May 8, 1946; s. Carloss M.; m. Rebecca Ann Simmons, June 14, 1969; children: Matthew William, Andrew James. BBA, So. Meth. U., 1968; JD, U. Tex., 1970, MBA, 1972. Bar: Tex. 1970. Legis. aide to Charles Wilson Tex. State Senate, Austin, 1969-70; examiner Stewart Title Austin Inc., 1970-71; analyst Bank of the S.W., Houston, 1973-74; bus. mgr. Richard Hogue Evangelism, Inc., Houston, 1974-75; cons. Morris, Lendais, Hollrah & Snowden, Houston; v.p. ops. Stewart Title Guaranty Co., Houston, 1975-87, sr. exec. v.p., asst. chmn., 1987-91, pres., CEO, 1991—2004, chmn., CEO, 2004—11; chmn., co-CEO Stewart Info. Services Corp., Houston, 2000—11, vice chmn., 2011—. Mem. bd. Stewart Title Ins. Co., N.Y.C., Stewart Title Ins. Co. U.K.; past pres. Tex. Land Title Assn., Am. Land Title Assn. Past chmn. Deacons, 1st Bapt. Ch., Houston; past chmn. Living Water Internat.; chmn. Millennium Water Alliance. Fellow Am. Bar Found., Houston Bar Assn.; mem. ABA, State Bar Tex., Houston Bar Assn., Phi Delta Phi. Baptist. Office: Stewart Info Services Corp 1980 Post Oak Blvd Houston TX 77056

MORRIS, MATTHEW W., insurance company executive; BBA in Orgnl. Behavior & Bus. Policy, So. Meth. U., Dallas; MBA in Fin., U. Tex. Former dir. for a strategic litig. consulting firm; sr. v.p. planning and devel. Stewart Info. Svcs. Corp., Houston, 2004—07, pres. profl. solutions, sr. exec. v.p., 2007—11, CEO, 2011—. Office: Stewart Title Guaranty Co Fl 8 1980 Post Oak Blvd Houston TX 77056-3899 Office Phone: 713-625-8100. Business E-Mail: matthew.morris@stewart.com.*

MORRIS, OWEN GLENN, engineering corporation executive; b. Shawnee, Okla., Feb. 3, 1927; s. Vestus and Myrtle (Lindsey) M.; m. Joyce Gast; children: Deborah Moree, Janine Inez. BS in Mech. Engring, U. Okla., 1947, M.Aero. Engring., 1948; postgrad., U. Va., 1952-53, Va. Poly. Inst., 1955-56, Coll. William and Mary, 1957-58. Aero., research scientist NASA, Langley Field, Va., 1948-61, mgr. lunar module, 1968—71, mgr. sys. integration space shuttle, 1974—80, mgr. Apollo spacecraft program, 1971—72; pres. Eagle Engring., 1980-86; pres., chief exec. officer Eagle Aerospace, Houston, 1987-90, chmn., chief exec. officer, 1990-93, chmn. bd., 1992—. Served with USNR, 1944-46. Recipient Presdl. Medal of Freedom, 1972, NASA Disting. Svc. medal, 1973, NASA Exceptional Svc. medal, 1969, Outstanding Leadership medal, NASA, 1979. Asso. fellow Am. Inst. Aeros. and Astronautics; mem. Am. Astronautical Soc., Acad. Model Aeros., Tau Beta Pi, Tau Omega. Presbyterian (elder 1964—). Club: Rotary. Home: 14914 Timberland Ct Houston TX 77062-2922

MORRIS, RAHEEM, professional football coach; b. Irvington, NJ, Sept. 3, 1976; BS in Phys. Edn., Hofstra U., Hempstead, NY, 1998. Grad. asst. Hofstra U. Pride, 1998, defensive backs coach, 2000—01; defensive backs coach, spl. teams asst. Cornell U. Big Red, Ithaca, NY, 1999; defensive internship NY Jets, 2001; defensive quality control coach Tampa Bay Buccaneers, 2002, defensive asst., 2003, asst. defensive backs coach, 2004—05, defensive backs coach, 2007—08, head football coach, 2009—11; defensive coord. Kansas State U. Wildcats, 2006; defensive backs coach Washington Redskins, 2012—. Achievements include member of Super Bowl XXXVII Championship winning Tampa Bay Buccaneers, 2003. Office: Washington Redskins 21300 Redskin Park Dr Ashburn VA 20147

MORRIS, RANDY G., small business owner; b. Waynesboro, Tenn., Sept. 7, 1953; m. Katherine Morris; children: Julianne, Sarah. AS in Pre- Bus., Columbia State CC, 1977; BS in Accounting, Tenn. Technol. U., Cookeville, 1979. Accountant Tenn. Dept. Corrections, 1983—85; controller Wayne County Gen. Hosp., 1985—96; owner Shake Raq, Inc. (64-Mart), 1996—. Aircraft repairman USAF, 1971—75. Democrat. Mem. Christian Ch. (Disciples Of Christ). Office: Shake Raq Inc 64-Mart 1023 Savannah Hwy Waynesboro TN 38485 Office Phone: 931-722-6464.

MORRIS, RICHARD L., state legislator; b. Fort Polk, La., Nov. 6, 1968; m. Cristina E. Morris; children: Courtney, Truman, Trenton, Ryan. BA in Sociology, Saint Leo U., 1998; JD, Regents Univ. Sch. Law, 2002. Mem. Dist. 64 Va. House of Delegates, 2012—, mem. Courts of Justice Com., Counties Cities and Towns Com. & Militia Policy and Pub. Safety Com. Officer USN, 1988—2010. Republican. Office: General Assembly Building PO Box 406 Richmond VA 23218 also: PO Box 128 Carrollton VA 23314 Office Phone: 804-698-1064. Office Fax: 804-698-6764. E-mail: DelRMorris@house.virginia.gov.

MORRIS, STEVEN, gastroenterologist, educator; b. Atlanta, Ga. MD, SUNY, Buffalo, 1973; JD, Georgia State U. Coll. Law. Cert. Internal Medicine, Gastroenterology. Intern, gastroenterology Emory U. Affiliated Hosps., Atlanta, 1973—74, resident, 1974—76; fellow, digestive diseases U. Miami, 1976—78; clin. assoc. prof. Emory U. Sch. Med., Atlanta; former chief of staff Emory Crawford Long Hosp.; CEO Atlanta Gastroenterology Assocs., Ga. Fellow: Am. Coll. Gastroenterology, ACP; mem.: Ga. Gastrointestinal Soc. (past pres.), Med. Assn. Ga., Med. Assn. Atlanta, Am. Gastroenterology Assn., AMA, Phi Beta Kappa. Office: Atlanta Gastroenterology Assocs Emory Crawford Long Med Office Tower 550 Peachtree St NE Ste 1600 Atlanta GA 30308 Office Phone: 404-881-1094. Office Fax: 404-874-1249.

MORRIS, STEWART, JR., title insurance company executive; b. Houston, Oct. 14, 1948; s. Stewart Sr. and Joella (Mitchel) M. BA, Rice U., 1971; MBA, U. Tex., 1973. Joined Stewart Title Co. (subs. Stewart Information Services Corp.), 1973, v.p. Houston, 1975-87, sr. exec. v.p., asst. to pres., 1987-91, chmn., pres., 1991—; adv. dir. Stewart Information Services Corp., 1997—2000, pres., co-CEO, 2000—11, vice chmn., 2011—. Bd. dirs. Southern Nat. Bank, Houston. Bd. dirs. Houston chpt. Cystic Fibrosis Found., 1985—. Mem. Am. Land Title Assn., Am. Driving Soc. (bd. dirs. 1984—), Houston Area Carriage Assn. (pres. 1995—), Carriage Assn. Am. (pres. 1995—). Office: Stewart 1980 Post Oak Blvd Ste 800 Houston TX 77056-3826

MORRIS, STUART R., lawyer; b. Bklyn. married; 3 children. BA with honors, U. Fla., Gainesville, 1986, MA with honors in Acctg., JD with honors, 1989. CPA Fla., 1989; bar: Fla. 1989, cert.: Fla. Bar Bd. Legal Specialization and Edn. (wills, trusts and estates and elder law). Founding ptnr. Morris Law Grp., Boca Raton, Fla., 1991—. Mem. adv. bd. First United Bank. Mem. profl. adv. com. Am. Friends of Hebrew U.; bd. dirs. SOS Children's Village Fla., Inc., Coconut Creek; v.p. Finance, bd. dir. Temple Beth Am, Margate, Fla. Recipient Top 100 Attys., Worth mag., 2007; named Fla. Super Lawyer, Law & Politics, 2007; named one of Top 100 Attys., Worth mag., 2006. Mem.: ABA, Fla. Inst. CPA, Alzheimer's Assn. (S.E. Fla. chpt.). Office: Morris Law Group 7000 W Palmetto Park Rd Ste 205 Boca Raton FL 33433 Office Phone: 561-750-3850. Office Fax: 561-750-4069.

MORRIS, TRACY L., corporate financial executive; BSBA, Millersville U. Pa. CPA. With Spector, Way & Co.; contr. Best Mcht. Ptnrs., LP, Silverleaf Resorts, Inc.; joined Capital SW Corp., 2007, contr., 2007—08, CFO, treas., chief compliance officer, corp. sec., 2008—. Office: Capital Southwest Corp Ste 700 12900 Preston Rd Dallas TX 75230 Office Phone: 972-233-8242. Office Fax: 972-233-7362. Personal E-mail: tmorris@capitalsouthwest.com.

MORRIS, VALERIE BONITA, dean; b. Beverly, Mass., May 22, 1947; d. Glen Franklin and Helen (Benjamin) M.; m. Boris Bohun-Chudyniv, Jan. 7, 1975; children: Alexander, Anya. BA, Am. U., 1968; MA, U. Mich., 1972. Promotions dir. McCarter Theatre, Princeton, N.J., 1972-73; assoc. mgr. Jorgensen Auditorium, Storrs, Conn., 1973-74; dir. art mgmt., chair performing arts Am. U., Washington, 1974-98, chair faculty senate, 1989-91; dean Sch. Arts Coll. of Charleston, S.C., 1998—. Exec. editor Jour. Arts Mgmt., Law and Soc., 1982-88, 90—2009; co-editor: Future of the Arts, 1990, The Arts in an New Millennium, 2003. Bd. dirs. Everyday Theatre, Washington, 1990—93, The Support Ctr., 1980—98, The Theatre Lab, 1994—2004, Charleston Symphony, 1998—, Charleston Stage Co., ABC Project, 1999—, ICFAD, 2003—05, Charleston Ballet Theatre, Charleston Concert Assn., Rotary Club Charleston; chair SC Alliance for Arts Edn. Recipient TWIN award, YWCA, 2006; named Women of Distinction, Girl Scouts Eastern SC; named one of Outstanding Women of Am., 1983; finalist Influential Women in Bus., 2013. Mem. Assn. Arts Adminstrv. Edn. (sec. treas. 1989-91, pres. 1997-98), Am. Coun. for Arts (rsch. adv. coun.), Assn. Performing Arts Presenters, Internat. Coun. Fine Arts Deans, Omicron Delta Kappa, Phi Kappa Phi. Home: 710 Willow Lake Rd Charleston SC 29412-9164 Office: Coll of Charleston 66 George St Charleston SC 29424-1407 Home Phone: 843-762-9116; Office Phone: 843-953-8222. Business E-Mail: morrisv@cofc.edu.

MORRISEY, MARENA GRANT, museum director; b. Newport News, Va., May 28, 1945; BFA in Interior Design, Va. Commonwealth U., 1967, MA in Art History, 1970, MA. With Orlando (Fla.) Mus. Art, 1970—, exec. dir., 1976—. Former v.p., chmn. mus. svcs. com., mem. ad hoc com. on collections sharing and long range planning com., past chmn. exhbns. and edn. com. Am. Fedn. Arts; former mem. nat. adv. coun. George Washington U. Clearinghouse on Mus. Edn.; former mem. accreditation com. Nat. Found. for Interior Design Edn. Rsch.; bd. dirs. Winter Pk. Art Festival, City Orlando Historic Bldg. Commn.; sec. Carroll McKenney Steck Found. Pub. Media; mem. non-profit mgmt. adv. bd. UCF Med. Sch. Fire Program Mentor. Former mem. strategic planning adv. coun. Orange County Sch. Dist.; former mem. advt. rev. bd. BBB; former mem. Orlando Pub. Art Adv. Bd., Orlando Leadership Coun., Orlando Hist. Bldg. Commn.; former chmn. art selection com. Orlando Internat. Airport, former mem. bd. dirs. WMFE-TV; bd. dirs. New World Sch. of Arts; mem. internat. arts and culture com. Metro Orlando Internat. Affairs Commn.; pub. art review com. Orange County; exec. com. Uptown Dist. Named Orlando's Outstanding Woman of Yr. in Field of Art; recipient Fla. State of Arts award, Excellence award Orlando Peabody Alliance Arts and Culture, 2004, Women's Achievement award Women's Exec. Coun., 2009. Mem. Am. Assn. Mus. (former mem. governing bd., accreditation commn., profl. stds. and practices com., internat. coun. of mus.), Assn. Art Mus. Dirs. (mem. profl. issues com., future directions com., membership com., edn. com.), Southeastern Mus. Conf. (past pres.), Fla. Art Mus. Dirs. Assn. (past pres.), Fla. Assn. Mus. (former bd. dirs.), Greater Orlando C. of C. (past mem. steering com. Leadership Orlando), Jr. League Orlando-Winter Park, Rotary Club Orlando (bd. mem., Paul Harris fellow). Office: Orlando Museum of Art 2416 N Mills Ave Orlando FL 32803-1483 Office Phone: 407-896-4231. Business E-Mail: mgmorrisey@omart.org.

MORRISEY, PATRICK, state attorney general; b. Brooklyn, NY, Dec. 21, 1967; married; 1 stepchild. BA in History and Political Sci. with honors, Rutgers Coll., 1989; JD, Rutgers Law Sch., Newark, NJ, 1992. Lic.: W.Va., Pa., NJ, DC. Ptnr. King & Spalding LLP, 1992—99; private law practice; deputy staff dir., chief health care counsel US House Energy & Commerce Com., 1999—2004, principal liaison on health care issues to the White House, US Senate, House of Representatives, HHS & Centers for Medicare & Medicaid Services; ptnr., health care atty. Sidley Austin LLP, 2004—12; atty. gen. State of W.Va., Charleston, 2013—. Served on Jefferson County Republican Executive Com. Mem.: Eastern Panhandle Business Assn. Republican. Roman Catholic. Office: Office of the Attorney General State Capitol Complex 1900 Kanawha Blvd E Building 1 Room E-26 Charleston WV 25305 Office Phone: 304-558-2021. Office Fax: 304-558-0140.*

MORRISH, DAN, state legislator; b. Oct. 20, 1950; m. Kathy Morrish. Pilots Vessel Traffic, Lake Charles; info. svc. coord.; mem. Dist. 37 La. House of Reps., 1983—2007; mem. Dist. 25 La. State Senate, 2008—, vice chair natural resources com., mem. ins. com., environ. quality com., revenue and fiscal affairs com., select com. on coastal restoration and flood control. Republican. Roman Catholic. Address: Dist Off 119 W Nezpique St Jennings LA 70546 Fax: 337-824-5898. E-mail: morrishd@legis.state.la.us.

MORRISON, GEANIE W., state legislator; b. 1950; Mem. Dist. 30 Tex. House of Representatives, 1999—. Recipient of several awards and honors. Republican. Address: Room CAP GS.06 Capitol PO Box 2910 Austin TX 78768 Mailing: 1908 N Laurent Ste 500 Victoria TX 77901 Office Phone: 361-572-0196, 512-463-0456.

MORRISON, GREGORY BERNARD, information scientist; b. Washington, Dec. 19, 1959; s. Carl Edward and Evelyn Patricia (Goodwin) M.; m. Patrice Hinton, May 20, 1981 (div. June 1989); children: Krystina, Michael, Matthew; m. Debra Dobson, 1993. BS in Math. and Physics magna cum laude, SC State U., 1982; MS in Indsl. Engring., Northwestern U., 1987. Mgr. info. svcs. Prudential Ins. Co. Am., Newark, 1989-90, v.p., info. sys. Roseland, NJ, 1989—2000, dir., group sys. exec. Newark, 1990-93, dir. info. svcs. Roseland, NJ, 1993—2000; COO, chief info. officer RealEstate.com, 2000; v.p. Cox Enterprises, Inc., Atlanta, 2002, sr. v.p., chief info. officer, 2002—. Bd. dirs. Met. YMCA, West Orange, N.J., 1990—, Minority Interchange, Inc., Newark, 1989-93. Capt. U.S. Army, 1982-89. Fellow U.S. Army, 1986. Mem. Ops. Rsch. Soc. Am., 100 Black Men N.J., Masons, Phi Beta Sigma. Avocations: golf, gardening. Office: Cox Enterprises Inc 6205 Peachtree Dunwoody Rd Atlanta GA 30328 Office Phone: 678-645-0000. Office Fax: 678-645-1079. Business E-Mail: gregory.morrison@cox.com.

MORRISON, HEATH E., school system administrator; b. Andrews AFB, Md. m. Jennifer Morrison; 2 children. B in Govt., Coll. William and Mary, Williamsburg, Va.; MEd in Ednl. Adminstrn., U. Md., College Park, PhD in Ednl. Policy & Planning; completed, Broad Supt. Acad., 2009. Prin. John Hanson Mid. Sch., Charles County, Md., Thomas Stone HS, Charles County; cmty. supt., Down County Consortium Montgomery County Pub. Sch. Sys., Md., 2007—09; supt. Washoe County Sch. Dist., Reno, 2009—12, Charlotte-Mecklenburg Schools, NC, 2012—. Adjunct instr. McDaniel Coll. Recipient Outstanding New Profl. award, U. Md., Disting. Ednl. Leader award, Wash. Post; named Md. Prin. of Yr., 2004, Supt. of Yr., Nev. Assn. Sch. Superintendents and Nev. Assn. Sch. Boards, 2011. Mem.: Nat. Assn. Secondary Sch. Principals (former co-chmn. task force on prin. preparation), American Assn. Sch. Administrators (Nat. Supt. of Yr. 2012). Office: Charlotte-Mecklenburg Schools 600 E Fourth St Charlotte NC 28202 Office Phone: 980-343-6270. Office Fax: 980-343-7135.*

MORRISON, JAMES IAN, management consultant; b. Irvine, Scotland, Dec. 22, 1952; came to U.S., 1985; s. James Morrison and Janet Miller (McCondach) Munro; m. Nora Cadham, Dec. 6, 1980; children: David, Caitlin. PhB, U. Newcastle-upon-Tyne, Eng., 1976; MA, U. Edinburgh, Scotland, 1974; PhD, U. BC, Can., 1985. Chmn. Health Futures Forum Andersen Consulting; isntr. BC Inst. Tech., Vancouver, 1980—85; rsch. assoc. U. BC, Vancouver, 1980—85; rsch. fellow Inst. for the Future, Menlo Park, Calif., 1985—86, dir. health care rsch. program, 1986—91, pres., 1990—96, cons. & pres. emeritus, 1996, sr. fellow Menlo Park, Calif., 1996. Bd. dirs. Interim Svcs., Ft. Lauderdale, Fla., Oceania, Palo Alto, Calif., HRET, Chgo.; mem. corp. adv. bd. Bristol-Myers Squibb, Princeton, N.J., 1992—; mem. UNIS Press Adv. Bd., 1990—. Co-author: Looking Ahead at American Health Care, 1988, Directing the Clinical Laboratory, 1990, System in Crisis: The Case for Health Care Reform, 1991, Reforming the System: Containing Health Care Costs in an Era of Universal Coverage, 1992, Future Tense: The Business Realities of the Next Ten Years, 1994, The Second Curve: Managing the Velocity of Change, 1996; contbr. articles to profl. jours. Mem. environ. scanning com. United Way of Am., 1990-92. Social Sci. Rsch. Coun. scholar U. Newcatle-upon-Tyne, 1974-76. Avocation: golf. Office: SFN Group Inc Bd Directors 2050 Spectrum Blvd Fort Lauderdale FL 33309 Office Phone: 954-308-7600. Office Fax: 954-308-7666. Business E-Mail: jamesmorrison@sfngroup.com.

MORRISON, JOHN M., bank executive; Owner, CEO, chmn. Ctrl. Bank Group, Golden Valley, Minn.; CEO, sole shareholder Central Bancshares Inc., Stillwater, 1988; interim chmn., CEO Allina Health Sys., 2001—02, vice chmn., 2003, chmn., 2004—. Mem. Fairview U. Med. Ctr. Bd., Fairview Health Sys. Corp. Bd.; chmn., exec. com. bd. trustees U. St. Thomas; former mem. bd. govs., chmn. bd.'s fin. com. U. Minn. Acad. Health Ctr.; former mem. Johns Hopkins Medicine bd. visitors Johns Hopkins U.; bd. dirs. Fingerhut Companies Inc., 1996; bd. dirs Heritage Bank (subs. United Fin. Corp.), 1994. Mem.: U. St. Thomas Sch. Law (mem. bd. govs., founder John. M. Morrison Ctr. Entrepreneurship). Mailing: Central Bancshares Inc PO Box 1360 Lexington KY 40588-1360 Office Phone: 859-253-6222. Office Fax: 859-253-6003.

MORRISON, ROBERT J., critical care specialist; MD, U. Tex. Southwestern Med. Ctr., Dallas, 1988. Cert. internal medicine 2001, pulmonary disease 2004, critical care medicine 2005, sleep medicine 2007. Resident in internal medicine Duke Univ. Med. Ctr., Durham, NC, 1988—91; fellow in pulmonary critical care medicine Baylor Univ. Med. Ctr., Houston, 1992—95; hosp. affiliation includes Univ. Med. Ctr. Brackenridge. Office: University Medical Center Brackenridge 601 E 15th St Ste 400 Austin TX 78705 Office Phone: 512-324-7000.

MORRISON, SCOTT DAVID, management consultant, small business owner; b. Duluth, Minn., May 8, 1952; s. Robert Henry and Shirley Elaine (Tester) M. (dec. 1990); m. Jana Louise Bergeron, May 29, 1976; children: Robert Scott (dec. 1999), Matthew John. Cert. in welding, Duluth Area Inst. Tech., 1971; student, U. Wis.-Superior, 1976-77; A in Mfg. Mgmt., N. Hennepin C.C., 1985; BA, Concordia Coll., St. Paul, 1988; MBA, St. Thomas U., St. Paul, 1991. Cert. in quality tech., Am. Soc. Quality, 1985, Dell Computer, Inc. instr. Six Sigma; lic. vocat. instr., Minn. Cert. welder Litton Ship Systems, Pascagoula, Miss., 1971-72, Barko Hydraulics, Superior, Wis., 1972-76, Am. Hoist and Derrick Co., Mpls., 1977-79, cert. level II non-destructive exam. insp., 1979-80; quality supr. Colight Inc., Mpls., 1980, Tol-O-Matic, Inc., Mpls., 1980-82; quality assurance engr. ADC Telecomm., Mpls., 1982-84, design assurance engr., 1985-86, product assurance engr., 1986-87, sr. product assurance engr., quality improvement facilitator, 1987-88, product engr. supr., 1988-90, mgr. design assurance, quality assurance, component engring., 1990-92; dir. quality and reg. affairs Waters Instruments, Inc., 1992-96, sr. quality engr., 1996, corp. quality sys. mgr., 1996-98; corp. mfg. and quality Compaq Computer Corp., Houston, 1996-98; sys. engr., sr. cons. Dimension Product Group, 1998—2001, Dell Computer Corp., Round Rock, Tex., 1998—, quality engr., sr. cons. Transactional Line of Bus., 1999—2000, mgr. quality sys. application team project, 2000, supplier quality engr., sr. cons., 2000—01; sr. cons. ABS Cons. Mgmt. Sys. divsns., Houston, 2001—03; rschr. Urban Edn. Bd. Found., LA, 2000, 2002—04; mgr. Mgmt. Sys. Cons., 2002—03; owner Dimensions in Quality, LLC, 2003—; contract mgmt. sys. auditor cons. Intertek Moody, 2004—, auditor quality, environ. and health and safety mgmt. sys., 2006—, Platinum Registration, 2010—; environ. and quality auditor DQS-UL, 2010—; sr. cons. Sirius Solutions LLC, 2009—, Whittincton & Assocs., 2012—, Frontline Resources, 2007—. Judge U.S. Amateur Boxing Fedn., Mpls., 1978-87, 95-97; examiner Minn. Quality Award Minn. Coun. for Quality, 1993, 95, Tex. Quality Award, 1997; mem. quality coun. Am. Electronics Assn., 1994-95; mem. bd. dirs. Rochester Quality Coun., 1994-95; examiner Malcolm Baldridge Nat. Quality award Nat. Inst. Standards and Technology, 1994-95, sr. examiner, 1996-97, alumni examiner, 1999-2000; reviewer fellowship grant applications ASQ, 1996; adj. instr. Riverland Tech. Coll., Rochester, Minn., 1995; lic. profl. boxing judge Tex. Dept. Licensing and Regulation, 1996—2008; cert. lead quality auditor Brit. Standards Internat., 1996, cert. lead environ. sys. auditor, 2001; facilitator Malcolm Bridge Nat. Quality Award Regional Conf., 1997; cons. in field. Recipient Tech. Excellence award ADC Telecoms., 1987, 88. Mem. ASTM, Am. Soc. Quality (cert. quality engr. cert. quality auditor, cert. quality mgr., cert. six sigma black belt, chmn. host and attendance subcom. 1986-87, RABQSA cert. prin. auditor 2010-), Am. Welding Soc., Soc. Mfg. Engrs., Internat. Platform Assn. Roman Catholic. Home and Office: 18 Seneca Pl The Woodlands TX 77382-5353 Office Phone: 713-201-3725. Personal E-mail: diminq@att.net.

MORRISSETTE, RICHARD DANIEL, state legislator, lawyer; b. Rochester, NH, Apr. 28, 1956; s. Joseph Robert and Teresa Nadeau Morrissette; 1 child. BA, Univ. NH, 1979; JD, Univ. Tulsa, 1984. Bar: Okla. 1985. Staff mem. Okla. State Senate, 1985—86; atty. Western Okla. Legal Aid Pub. Defender Office, 1986—92; of counsel Haupt Brooks Vandruff & Cloar, Okla. City.; mem. Dist 92 Okla. House of Representatives, 2005—. Democrat. Catholic. Address: 1316 S Melinda Edmond OK 73034 Mailing: 6609 S Harvey Ave Oklahoma City OK 73139 Office: 2300 N Lincoln Blvd Rm 543 Oklahoma City OK 73105 Office Phone: 405-634-7166, 405-557-7404. E-mail: richardmorrissette@okhouse.gov.

MORRISSEY, CHARLES THOMAS, historian, educator; b. Newton, Mass., Nov. 11, 1933; s. Leonard Eugene and Margaret (McCarthy) M. AB, Dartmouth Coll., 1956; MA, U. Calif., Berkeley, 1957. Instr. Dartmouth Coll., Hanover, N.H., 1961-62; oral historian Harry S. Truman Library, Independence, Mo., 1962-64; chief oral history project John F. Kennedy Libr., Washington, 1965-66; dir. Vt. Hist. Soc., Montpelier, 1966-71, 73-75; dir. oral history project Ford Found., 1971-73; adj. prof. history U. Vt., Burlington, 1969-73, 75-85; dir. Oral History and Archives Office Baylor Coll. Medicine, Houston, 1985—97, cons., 1997—. Vis. instr. oral and pub. history Portland State U., 1979—82, 1984—2001, 2003—05, Vt. Coll., Montpelier, 1985—2000, 2002—06; lectr. in field. Author: Vermont: A Bicentennial History, 1981, (with others) Vermont, 1985; editor: Oral History Assn. Newsletter, 1968-71, Vermont History, 1967-71, 73-76, Internat. Jour. Oral History, 1985-89; contbg. editor: Vermont Life mag., 1969-81, editor, 1982-83; contbr. chpts. to books; contbr. articles to profl. jours.; radio commentator Sta. WDEV, Waterbury, Vt., 1982—; columnist Hardwick (Vt.) Gazette, 1997—. Recipient Harvey Kantor award New England Assn. Oral History, 1980. Mem. Ctr. for Rsch. on Vt., Oral History Assn. (pres. 1971-72), Nat. Coun. on Pub. History (coun. 1980-82), Assn. Oral History Educators, Cosmos Club (Washington). Office Phone: 713-798-5130.

MORRISSEY, JOSEPH DEE, state legislator; b. Washington, Sept. 23, 1957; s. William Fitzgerald and Jean Noel (Manning) M. BA in Econs., U. Va., 1979; JD, Georgetown U., 1982. Bar: Va. Asst. atty. Richmond (Va.) Commonwealth's Atty.'s Office, 1984-87; ptnr. Morrissey & Hershner, Richmond, Va., 1987; commonwealth's atty. City of Richmond, 1990—93; pvt. law practice, 1993—2000; tchr. law sch., Ireland, 2001—06, 2001—06; mem. Dist. 74 Va. House of Delegates, 2008—. Co-chmn. Supt.'s Com. on Drug Awareness, Richmond, 1987—. Mem. Assn. Trial Lawyers Am., Va. Trial Lawyers Assn. Republican. Office: Dist 74 605 East Nine Mile Rd Highland Springs VA 23075 Office Phone: 804-238-1466.

MORROW, BRUCE WILLIAM, retired military officer academic administrator, management consultant; b. Rochester, Minn., May 20, 1946; s. J. Robert and Frances P. Morrow; m. Jenny Lea Morrow. BA, U. Notre Dame, 1968, MBA in Mgmt. with honors, 1974, MA in Comparative Lit., 1975; grad., U.S. Army Command and Gen. Staff Coll., 1978. Cert. project mgmt. profl. Project Mgmt. Inst., 2003. Chmn. elem. German U. Notre Dame, 1973—75; co-mgr. Wendy's Old Fashioned Hamburgers, South Bend, Ind., 1976—77; adminstrn. mgr. Ea. States Devel. Corp., Richmond, Va., 1977; v.p. JDB Assocs., Inc., Alexandria, Va., 1976—78; sr. cons. Data Base Mgmt., Inc., Springfield, Va., 1979—80; owner Aardvark Prodns., Alexandria, Va., 1980—82; sys. analyst, staff officer Hdqrs., Dept. Army, Washington, 1980—84; chmn. bd. Commonwealth Dominion Corp., Sierra Vista, Ariz., 1982—2010. Strategic planner, dep. comdr. Fort Pickett, Blackstone, Va., 1986—89; dir. continuing edn. Southside Va. C.C., Alberta, 1989—91; co-founder S.W. Bus. Group, Tucson, 1995—99; pres. Sierra Vista Golf, Inc., Ariz., 1994—95; Cochise County team leader Ariz. Coun. Econ. Conversion, 1994—95; mem. com. Ariz. Small Bus. Initiative, 1994—99; internet webmaster, 1996—; exec. dir. Southea. Ariz. Contrs. Assn., 1997—98; corp. adminstr. Garcia Cos., Sierra Vista, Tucson, Phoenix, 1997—99; property adminstr. Brown & Root Svcs., Ft. Huachuca, Ariz., Land Between the Lakes, Ky., 1999—2000, logistics coord., 2000—02; dir. assessment ctr. Transport. Security Agy. NCS Pearson, Nashville and Fresno, 2002; project advisor Dyncorp Internat., Irving, Tex., 2004. Author: (radio series) Survival in the Computer Jungle, 1986, (classroom text) Introduction to Computers, 1988, 2d edit., 1993, Defense Conversion Handbook, 1995, Business Assessment Manual, 1996, Employee Manual Guide, 1996, Business Plan Guide, 1996, Marketing Plan Guide, 1996, (screenplay) Gray Rock, 2000; contbg. columnist Notre Dame mag., 1974—86; exec. prodr.: (motion picture) Beneath the Law, 1995—96; composer songs. Active Boy Scouts Am., 1960—69; firefighter Roanoke Wildwood Vol. Fire Dept., 1991—93. Lt. col. USAR, ret. Decorated Bronze Stars, Army commendation medals, Army Achievement medal, Meritorious Svc. medals, Parachutist's badge, Army Gen. Staff badge. Mem. VFW (life), Nat. Eagle Scout Assn., Lake Gaston C. of C. (bd. dirs.), Am. Legion, Sierra Vista Area C. of C., Lions (v.p. local club), Friends Internat. (Am. v.p. 1969-71, Boeblingen, Germany), Order of DeMolay, Beta Gamma Sigma, Delta Phi Alpha. E-mail: cdc@theriver.com.

MORROW, JOHNNY M., state legislator; b. Vina, Ala., Nov. 25, 1942; m. Connie Morrow. BS in Agrl. Econs., Miss. State U.; MBA, Samford U., Birmingham, Ala. Bus. and econs. instr. Northwest Jr. Coll.; mem. Dist. 18 Ala. House of Reps., Montgomery, 1990—. Mem. First Bapt. Ch., Red Bay. Mem.: Ala. Edn. Assn., Franklin County Cattlemen's Assn. (pres.), Russellville Civitan Club, Cahaba Shrine Temple. Democrat. Baptist. Office: 1895 Highway 28 Red Bay AL 35582 also: Ala House of Reps Ala State House 11 S Union St Rm 628-B Montgomery AL 36130 Office Phone: 334-242-7698.

MORROW, JOSEPH J., metal products executive; With KPMG Peat Marwick; founder, pres Morrow & Co., Inc; CEO Morrow & Co., LLC, 1972—, Proxy Services Corp., 1972—92, chmn., 1992—, North American Galvanizing & Coatings, Inc., 1999—. Bd. dirs. Warwick Valley Tel. Co., 2004—07. Trustee Golfer's in Support of the Troops. Office: North American Galvanizing & Coatings Inc 3100 W 7th St Ste 500 Fort Worth TX 76107-8701 Office Phone: 918-488-9420. Office Fax: 918-488-8172. Business E-Mail: jj@morrowco.com.

MORSE, JOHN B., JR., retired publishing executive; b. 1946; BA in History, U. Va.; MBA, Wharton Sch., U. Pa. Ptnr. Pricewaterhouse-Coopers, LLP; v.p., contr. Washington Post Co., 1989, sr. v.p. fin., CFO, 1989—2008, ret., 2008. Bd. dirs. Barcelo Crestline Corp., 1998—, Host Hotels & Resorts LP, 2003—, HSN, Inc., 2008—, AES Corp., 2008—, Northern Va. Tech. Coun. Trustee U. Va. Coll. Found. Mem.: AICPA, Inst. Newspaper Fin. Execs. Office: AES Corp Bd Directors 4300 Wilson Blvd 11th Fl Arlington VA 22203 Office Phone: 703-522-1315. Office Fax: 703-528-4510. Business E-Mail: jmorse@aicpa.org.

MORSE, MARVIN HENRY, retired judge; b. Mt. Vernon, NY, July 19, 1929; s. Frank Irving and Lillian (Seeger) M.; m. Betty Anne Hess, Dec. 27, 1953; children: Martin Albert, Michael Howard, Lee Anne. AB, Colgate U., 1949; LLB, Yale U., 1952. Bar: N.Y. 1952, Ky. 1956, Md. 1964, U.S. Supreme Ct. 1960, U.S. Ct. Appeals (6th cir.), U.S. Dist. Ct. (we. dist.) Ky., U.S. Ct. Mil. Appeals, U.S. Ct. Claims, U.S. Ct. Appeals (D.C. cir.), U.S. Ct. Appeals (fed. cir.), U.S. Dist. Ct. (no. dist.) Tex., U.S. Dist. Ct. Hawaii. Pvt. practice, Louisville, 1956-62; asst. counsel Office of Gen. Counsel Dept. Navy, Washington, 1962-65, Office of Gen. Counsel Office Sec. Def., Washington, 1965-68; asst. gen. counsel GSA, Washington, 1968-70, U.S. Postal Svc., Washington, 1970-73; adminstrv. law judge Fed. Energy Regulatory Commn., Washington, 1973-75, Postal Rate Commn., Washington, 1975-77, CAB, Washington, 1977-80; dir. adminstrv. law judges Office Pers. Mgmt., Washington, 1980-82; chief adminstrv. law judge SBA, Washington, 1982-87, asst. adminstr. hearings and appeals, 1985-87; adminstrv. law judge Exec. Office of Immigration Rev. Dept. Justice, Washington, 1987—2002; temp. mem. Bd. of Immigration Appeals, 1998—2002; ret., 2002. Mem. Adminstrv. Conf. of U.S., 1980-84, govt. mem., 1985-86, 87-95, liaison mem.; faculty and faculty coord. The Nat. Jud. Coll., 1977, 79-80. Author: (with S. Groner) ABA Handbook chpt. on adminstrv. law, 1981, (with Lucy Moran) Troubling the Waters: Human Cargos, 2002. Trustee Washington area chpt. Am. Digestive Disease Soc., 1976-87. With JAGC, USAF, 1952-56, to col. USAFR, ret. 1979. Decorated USAF Legion of Merit; recipient Disting. Svc. award Am. Digestive Disease Soc., 1980. Mem. ABA (exec. com. 1977-82, 84-87, chmn. 1980-81, conf. adminstrv. law judges, del. ho. of dels. 1984-87, lawyers in govt. com. 1985-86, jud. selection, tenure and compensation com. 1987-93, govt. pub. sect. lawyers divsn., coun. 1996-02), Fed. Bar Assn. (nat. coun. 1976—, chmn. career svc. sect. 1983-86, chmn. judiciary sect. 1986-88, sect. coord. 1988-90, sec. 1991-92, del. to ABA ho. of dels. 1992-93, 97-99, v.p. 1993-94, pres.-elect 1994-95, pres. 1995-96), Am. Law Inst., Fed. Adminstrv. Law Judges Conf. (exec. com. 1975-77, 82-96, 2000-01), Nat. Assn. Adminstrv. Law Judges (hon.), Fed. Am. Inn of Ct. (coun. 1990-92, pres. 1992-94), Longboat Key Democratic Club, Fla. (pres. 2006-08). Home: 1241 Gulf Of Mexico Dr Unit 303 Longboat Key FL 34228-4619 Home Phone: 941-383-4707. Personal E-mail: bhmmhm@comcast.net.

MORTENSEN, ROBERT HENRY, landscape and golf course architect; b. Jackson, Mich., June 9, 1939; s. Henry and Charlotte Marie (Brown) Mortensen; m. Linda McGinnis, 2005; children: Phillip(dec.), Paul, Susan, Julia, Lee McGinnis, Charles McGinnis, Laurel Corridon. B in Landscape Architecture, Ohio State U., 1961; M in Landscape Architecture, U. Mich., 1965. Registered landscape arch., Va., Md. Landscape arch. various firms, Louisville, 1960, 61-63; with Ohio Divsn. Pks., Columbus, 1960-61; landscape arch. various firms, Toledo, 1963, 65-67; pvt. practice Ann Arbor, Mich., 1963-65; ptnr. firms Toledo, 1967-78; pres. Harvey Jones and Assocs., Clearwater, Fla., 1979-81; owner Mortensen Assocs., Toledo and Falls Church, Va., 1979-85; prin. Mortensen, Lewis & Scully, Inc., Vienna, Va., 1985-93; owner Mortensen Assocs., McLean, Va., 1993—. Assoc. prof. U. Mich. Grad. Sch., 1973; vis. lectr. Ohio State U., 1965—, Bowling Green State U., Ohio, 1969—, U. Mich., 1971, Purdue U., 1971, Mich. State U., 1973—, U. Mass., 1986—, U. Cath., Cordoba, Argentina, 2007, U. Buenus Aires, 2007, Beijing Forestry U., 2008; archtl. environ. rev. com. Ohio Arts Coun., 1974-78; adj. prof. Dept. Landscape Architecture, U. Md., 1992-96; chmn. Merrifield Master Plan Task Force, 1998-2001. Editor: Handbook of Professional Practice, 1972, Marketing Landscape Architectural Services to the Federal Government, 1974. Mem. Ohio Bd. Unreclaimed Strip Mined Lands, 1973-76; mem. Lucas County facilities rev. com. Health Planning Assn. N.W. Ohio, 1972-76, chmn. maternal and child health subcom., 1972-74; bd. dirs. No. Va. Cmty. Appearance Alliance, 1988-, chair, 1991, pres., 1994. Recipient Disting. Svc. award Health Planning Assn. N.W. Ohio, 1973, Disting. Alumni award U. Mich. Sch. Natural Resources, 1985, Disting. Alumnus award Ohio State U. Coll. Engring., 1985. Fellow Am. Soc. Landscape Architects (trustee 1977-82, v.p. 1982-83, pres.-elect 1983-84, nat. pres. 1984-85, del. to Internat. Fedn. Landscape Architects 1987-92, del. Internat. Landscape Alliance 1994-2000); mem. Ohio Soc. Landscape Architects (pres. 1969-74), Landscape Inst. U.K. (hon. corr.), Toledo C. of C. (chmn. sts. and hwys. transit com. 1972-73), Greater Merrifield Bus. and Profl. Assn. (bd. dirs. 1993-2002, chmn. bd. dirs. 1998, pres. 1997), Nat. Bldg. Stone Inst. (mem. adv. bd.), Va. Cmty. Revitalization & Reinvestment Adv. Group (Fairfax county bd. mem. 2009-), Washington Golf and Country Club (officer, bd. dirs. 1999-2003, pres. 2002-03), Rotary Internat., Sigma Phi Epsilon, Staunton Augusta Arts Coun.(bd. mem., 2014-); Staunton Downtown Devel. Assn., (bd. mem. 2014-) Home and Office: Mortensen Assocs 107 Smithleigh Cir Staunton VA 24401 Office Phone: 571-259-1620. Office Fax: 540-885-1362. Personal E-mail: rhmort@gmail.com.

MORTON, HARVEY LEON, lawyer; b. Sweetwater, Tex., May 9, 1941; s. William Allen and Lenora Elizabeth Morton; m. Betty Catherine Morton, Jan. 30, 1965; children: Allison Pritchard, Kimberly Hendrix, Craig. BA, McMurry Coll., Abilene, Tex., 1964; JD, U. Tex., Austin, 1967. Bar: Tex. 1967. Pvt. practice, Lubbock, 1970—; ptnr. Brock, Morton & Pigg, Lubbock, Tex., 1978—88. Atty. City of Slaton, Tex., 1970—; panel trustee US Trustee Program, Dallas, 1982—; pres. West Tex. Bankruptcy Bar, Lubbock, 1999; pres., chmn. bd. dirs. Dreyer Music Co., San Angelo, Tex., 1990—95, InstaChek San Angelo, 1998—2000, Queen City Land Devel. Co. San Angelo, 1999—2000. Chmn. bd. dirs. Lubbock Regional Mental Health Bd., 1995—97; dist. dir. McMurry Coll. Alumni, 1973—74; mem. criminal justice planning coun. South Plains Assn. Govts., 1973—74; county chmn. State Dem. Party, Lubbock County, 1982—88, mem. exec. com. Tex., 1978—82; long range planning chmn. St. Luke's United Meth. Ch., 1988—95, former charge lay leader, youth sponsor, chmn. adminstrv. bd., Sunday sch. tchr.; bd. dirs. Meth. Home, Waco, Tex., 1988—92, Tex. Coun. Risk Mgmt. Fund, Lubbock, 1991—, chmn. bd. dirs., 1995—97; bd. dirs. Wesley Found., Tex. Tech U., 1974, Marion Moss Found., 1986. Recipient Scrappy award for vol. svc., Lubbock Regional Mental Health Bd., 1995; named Man of Yr., Slaton C. of C., 1991. Mem.: Lubbock County Bar Assn. (treas. 1997—98), West Tex. Bankruptcy Bar Assn. (pres.-elect 1998—99, pres. 1999—2000, 2008—), State Bar Tex., Rotary (pres. Slaton chpt. 1995—2000). Office: PO Box 10305 Lubbock TX 79408

MORTON, JAMES CARNES, JR., retired automotive executive; b. Duncan, Okla., May 8, 1945; s. James Carnes and Syble Lyda (Looney) Morton; m. Susan Phillips, May 25, 1968; children: James III, Terrissa Anne, Scott Thomas. BA, Westminster Coll., 1967; JD, U. Mo., 1972. Bar: Mo. 1972. Tax acct. Arthur Andersen Co., St. Louis, 1972—74; tax atty. Gen. Dynamics Corp., St. Louis, 1974—76; asst. gen. counsel Michelin Tire Corp., Greenville, SC, 1976—86; gen. counsel Michelin Tire Corp. and Michelin Tires (Can.) Ltd., Greenville, 1990—92; dir. pub. rels. and govt. affairs Michelin Tire Corp., Greenville, 1986—92; exec. dir. external rels. Michelin N.Am., Inc., Greenville, 1992—96, v.p. pub. rels. and govt. rels., 1996—2000; sr. v.p. fin. and adminstrn., bd. dirs., mem. mgmt. com. Nissan N.Am., Inc., LA, 2000—06, vice chmn. Nashville, 2006—07, asst. to CEO, sr. advisor govt. affairs, 2007—08; pres. Morton Consulting Inc., 2007—12. Adv. bd. Trent Lott Leadership Inst., U. Miss., 2006—, Hollings Cancer Ctr. Med. U. SC, 2005—12, vice chmn., 2008—12. Bd. dirs. Greenville Symphony Orch., 1986—89, United Way Greenville, 1987—88, Greenville YMCA, 1988—89, Greenville Tech Found., 2007—, vice chmn., 2009—10, chmn., 2010—12; mem. S.C. Reorganization Commn., 1985—98; trustee S.C. Gov.'s Sch. Sci. and Math., 1996—99; mem. sch. bd. Christ Ch. Episcopal Sch., Greenville, 1997—2000; vice chmn. S.C. Ports Authority, 1999—2000; pres. Nissan Found., 2003—07; bd. trustees Greenville Health Sys., 2008—, Westminster Coll., Fulton, Mo., 2011—, chmn., Planning Fin. Commn., 2012—; joint bd. liaison com. U. SC Sch. Medicine, Greenville, 2011—14. Lt. US Army, 1967—70, capt. Mo. Army N.G., 1970—72. Recipient Alumni Achievement award, Westminster Coll., 2003. Mem.: ABA, Mo. Bar Assn., Alliance Automobile Mfrs. (bd. dirs. 2000—03), Rubber Mfrs. Assn. (bd. dirs. 1995—2000, govt. affairs com., tire mgmt. com.), Assn. Internat. Automobile Mfrs. (exec. com. 2000—07, chmn. bd. dirs. 2005—07), Nat. Urban League (trustee 2004—07), Greater Greenville C. of C. (bd. dirs. 1990—93, chmn. legis. affairs com. 1996—98), S.C. C. of C. (exec. com. 1981—84, 1986—95, pres. 1993—94, chmn. 1994—95, bd. dirs.), Calif. C. of C. (bd. dirs. 2001—04), L.A. Urban League (bd. dirs. 2001—05), Poinsett Internat. Club, Kiawah Island Club, Greenville Country Club (bd. govs. 2008—13, v.p. 2009, pres. 2010—11). Presbyterian. Avocation: golf. Office Phone: 864-232-5841. Personal E-mail: jmorton5841@att.net.

MORTON, JOHN TEMPLETON, bank executive, former federal agency administrator; b. Inverness, Scotland, 1966; Trial atty. US Dept. Justice, 1994, spl. asst. to gen. counsel, Immigration & Naturalization Svc. (INS), then counsel to dep. atty. gen., 1996—99, asst. US atty. (eastern dist.) Va. major crimes & terrorism unit, 1999—2006, acting chief domestic security sect., sr. counsel to asst. atty. gen. criminal divsn., 2007—09, acting dep. asst. atty. gen. criminal divsn., 2009; asst. sec. for immigration & customs enforcement (ICE) US Dept. Homeland Security, 2009—13; sr. v.p., head compliance Capital One, Va., 2013—. Office: Capital One 1680 Capital One Dr Mc Lean VA 22101 Office Phone: 703-720-1000.*

MORTON, MARSHALL NAY, finance executive; b. Chgo., Oct. 3, 1945; s. Frederick Samuel and Margaret Elizabeth (Burke) Morton; m. Caroline Sanders, Sept. 13, 1969; children: Marshall Burke, Margaret Elizabeth. BA, U. Va., 1970, MBA, 1972. Fin. analyst West Point Pepperell Inc., Ga., 1972—73, budget dir., 1973—74, fin. mgr., 1974—75, asst. treas., 1975—81, treas., 1981—86, v.p., contr., 1986—89; sr. v.p., CFO Media Gen., Inc., Richmond, Va., 1989—. Pres. Valley United Fund, West Point, 1982; pres. West Point chpt. Am. Cancer Soc., 1985—87; v.p. fin. Lanier Council Boy Scouts Am., 1986—87, pres. Robert E. Lee Coun.; past pres. Metro Bus. Found.; former bd. dirs. Commonwealth Girl Scout Coun., Va.; bd. govs. St. Catherine's Sch. Served with USN, 1966—68, Vietnam. Mem.: Richmond Metro C. of C. (former bd. dirs.), Commonwealth Club, Country Club Va., Union League Club NYC. Episcopalian. Avocations: tennis, sailing. Office: Media Gen Inc 333 E Grace St Richmond VA 23293-1000

MORTON-YOUNG, TOMMIE, psychology professor, writer; b. Nashville; BA cum laude, Tenn. State U., Nashville, 1951; MA, Peabody Vanderbilt U., 1955; PhD, Duke U., Durham, NC, 1977; postgrad., U. Okla., Norman, 1967, U. Nebr., 1968. Coord. Young Adult Program Lucy Thurman br. YWCA, 1951-52; instr. edn. Tenn. State U., Nashville, 1956-59; instr. coord. media program Prairie View Coll., Tex., 1959-61; asst. prof. edn., assoc. prof. English, dir. IMC Ctr. U. Ark., Pine Bluff, 1965-69; asst. prof. English and edn., dir. learning lab NC Ctrl. U., Durham, 1969-74; prof., dir./chairperson libr. /dir. Afro-Am. Family Project, prof. philosophy sociol. found. NC Agrl. and Tech. State U., Greensboro, 1975—92; adj. prof. langs., lit. and philosophy, dir. schs. history project Tenn. State U., Nashville, 1994—. Dir. workshops, grants; pres., dir. Ednl. Cons. Svcs.; owner Historic Black Nashville Tours; with Tenn. Judicial Coun., 2008-. Author: Afro-Am. Genealogy Sourcebook, 1987, Oral Histories of Former All-Black Public Schs., 1991, After School Program for At-Risk Youth and Their Families, 1997, Sable Scenes, 1996, Genealogist's Guide to Discovering Your African Ancestors, 1997, A Sister Speaks, 1998, Nashville, Tennessee, 2000, Fabulous You: Women Celebrating the Fabulous Self, 2005, Ride a Dark Horse, 2007, 10; contbr. poem to Poetry: American Heritage; contbr. rsch. papers, articles to profl. jours., pub. ten books. Nat. chmn. Com. to Re-Elect the Pres.; past sec. Fedn. Colored Women's Clubs; bd. dirs. Southwestern div. ARC, Nashville area, 1994-, dir. Volun-Teens; chairperson schs. div. Durham County Unit Am. Cancer Soc.; past adv. bd., bd. dirs. YMCA, Atlanta; chair Guilford County Commn. on Needs of Children; bd. advisors NIH, NC Coun. of the Arts; mem. Guilford County Involvement Coun.; chmn. NC adv. com. US Civil Rights Com.; exec. planning com. Greensboro; hon. staff 54th Legis. Dist., Nashville, 1996; pres. Davidson County Dem. Women, 2003-04; rep. dist. 1 exec. com. Davidson County Dem. Party; chair resolutions com. Nat. Fedn. Dem. Women; disting. alumi Peabody Coll. Vanderbilt U., 2010; spkr. Commencement, 2010; human rights adv., U. Nebr., 2011. Recipient awards ARC, 1968, 73, NAACP, 1973, HEW, 1978, US Commn. on Civil Rights, 1982, cert. of Accomplishement Contributing to Youth Devel. Bus. and Profl. Women, 2000, Extraordinary Cmty. Svc. award Tenn. Coun. Women, 2005, Civic and Bus. Leaders Enterprising award, 2006, Civil Rights Leadership award Tenn. Dem. Party, 2006, Athena award, Governing Body Athena Internat. Powerlink, Nashville, 2006, Legacy award, Scarritt-Bennett Ctr., 2010-11, Women of Legend and Merit award, Tenn. State U., 2010-11; named Disting. Alumni Tenn. State U., 1994, Peabody Colls. Gift to the World, Peabody Coll. Alumna, 2010, Disting. Peabody Alumni award, 2010-11, Commencement Address, 2010, Disting. Human Rights Svc. award UN, 2010, US Commn. & Coun., Freedoms Sisters award, Ford Motor Co., 2010-11, Human Rights Adv. award, UN-Human Rels. Commn., 2010-11, Human Rights award, Tenn. Human Rights Commn., 2013; Tenn. Crossroads TV, 2013. Mem. AAUW (honor award 1983, pres. Greensboro br., chairperson internat. rels. com.), ALA (divsn. coll. and rsch. librs., past chair), NAACP (life, 1st v.p. Durham br., exec. bd. Greensboro br. dir. parent edn./child advocacy program, chair exec. com. Nashville, Woman of Yr. 1992, Dedicated Svc. to Civil Rights, 2005, President's award Nashville br. 2006), NEA, LWV (bd. dirs. Nashville), Assn. Childhood Ednl. Internat., Comperative and Internat. Edn. Assn., Archives Assoc., Internat. Platform Assn., Nat. Hist. Soc., Greenboro Jr. League (community adv. bd. 1991—), African Am. Gen. Soc. Tenn. (founder 1994), Zeta Phi Beta (chairperson polit. action com. eastern region, nat. grammateus, Polit. and Civic Svc. award 1974, Outstanding Social-Polit. Svc. award 1982, Woman of Yr. 1977), Comm. on Status of Women (Woman of Achievement 1991), Phi Kappa Phi (Disting. Alumni award Tenn. State U. 1994, Disting. Alumni NAFEO award, 1995, Carl Rowan-Oprah Winfrey lectr. Tenn. State U., 1995, Excellence in Journlism award SPJ, 1995, Tenn. Outstanding Achievement award, 1997), 100 Black Women, Steering Com., Tenn. Trust for Historic Preservation, 1999 (named Woman of Distinction Top Ladies, 2001, named Peabody/Vanderbilt Jnin Great, 2005, nominee Athena award 2005). Achievements include being the first African American to graduate from Peabody College (Vanderbilt University); having a community Service award named in her honor by Vanderbilt University, 2006. Home: PO Box 281613 Nashville TN 37228-8506

MORUKOV, BORIS V., cosmonaut; b. Moscow, Oct. 1, 1950; s. Vladimir D. Morukov and Lidia F. Khromova; m. Nina M. Morukova; children: Olga, Ivan. MD, Moscow Med. U., 1973; PhD in Space, Aviation and Naval Medicine, 1979; student, Gagarin Cosmonaut Tng. Ctr., 1990—92; grad. advanced course in emergency med. care, 1995, grad. tng. course in endocrinology and hematology, 1996; attended Flight-Surgeon Tng. Course, NASA, Johnson Space Ctr., Houston, 1998—99. Rschr. Inst. for Biomed. Problems, 1978—84, sr. rschr., 1984—88, chief. dept. metabolism and regulation, 1988—89, cosmonaut, rschr., chief lab. metabolism and immunology, 1989—94; cosmonaut, rschr., chief Divsn. of State Rsch. Ctr. RF Inst. for Biomed. Problems, 1995—98; cosmonaut Inst. for Biomed. Problems, 1998—; mem. crew STS-106 to Internat. Space Sta., 2000. Med. support for space sta. Salut-6, mem. staff Mission Control Ctr., 1979—80; human life-scis. expts. coord. NASA-Mir Sci. Program, 1995—98. Contbr. over 100 articles to sci. jours. Recipient Leader in Pub. Med. Svc. award, 1989, Medal for Merits to Motherland of 2d degree, 1996. Achievements include patents for 4 inventions; research in calcium metabolism correction; logging 11 days, 19 hours in space. Avocations: reading, movies, cooking. Office: NASA Johnson Space Ctr Astronaut Office/CB Houston TX 77058

MOSBY, HOWARD, state legislator; Former state rep. Dist. 59, Ga.; state rep. Dist. 90 Ga., 2004—; mem. Adminstrn. Svcs., Govt. Affairs Coms., Health & Ecology & State Planning & Cmty. Affairs Coms.; house reps. Ga.; asst. v.p. Grady Health Sys. Democrat. Address: 2101 Sugar Creek Falls Atlanta GA 30316 Mailing: Legislative Office Bldg # 608 Atlanta GA 30334 Business E-Mail: hmosby@legis.state.ga.us. E-mail: mosbyfordist59@aol.com.

MOSCHETTA, ROBERT P., safety engineering administrator; b. Pitts., Dec. 10, 1955; s. Robert C. and Frances (Katich) M.; m. Cynthia J. McGuirk, Aug. 20, 1981. BA in Environ. Studies, Calif. U., Pa., 1978; MS in Safety Studies, W. Va. U., 1980. V.p., health safety environment Oceaneering International, Inc.; underground coal miner J & L Steel Corp., Waynesburg, Pa., 1977-82; safety supr. Beaver Creek Coal Co., Price, Utah, 1982-85; safety mgr. West Elk Coal Co., Somerset, Colo., 1985. Vol. disaster action team ARC, Price chpt., 1983-85. Mem. Am. Soc. Safety Engrs., Nat. Safety Mgmt. Soc., Am. Mining Congress (ad hoc diesel com.), Nat. Fire Protection Assn., Colo. Mining Assn. (health and safety com.). Lodges: Elks, KC. Democrat. Roman Catholic. Avocations: scuba diving, swimming, running, camping, bicycling. Office: Oceaneering International Inc 11911 FM 529 Houston TX 77041 Office Phone: 713-329-4500. Office Fax: 713-329-4951. Business E-Mail: rmoschetta@oceaneering.com.

MOSELEY, JAMES FRANCIS, lawyer; b. Charleston, SC, Dec. 6, 1936; s. John Olin and Kathryn (Moran) M.; m. Anne McGehee, June 10, 1961; children: James Francis Jr., John McGehee. AB, The Citadel, 1958; JD, U. Fla., 1961. Bar: Fla. 1961, U.S. Supreme Ct. 1970. Pres. Moseley, Prichard, Parrish, Knight & Jones, Jacksonville, Fla., 1963—. Chmn. jud. nominating com. 4th Jud. Cir., 1978-80 Editor: American Maritime Cases; contbr. articles on admiralty, transp. and ins. law to legal jours. Pres. Jacksonville United Way, 1979; chmn. bd. dirs. United Way Fla., 1992-93, S.E. regional coun. United Way, 1992-96; trustee Jacksonville Cmty. Found.; chmn. bd. trustees Jacksonville Pub. Libr.; trustee Libr. Found., sec., 1987-91; trustee CMI Am. Found.; chmn. Jacksonville Human Svcs. Coun., 1989-91; chmn. bd. trustees United Way N.E. Fla., 1995-97; bd. govs. United Way Am., 1996-2002. Recipient Meritorious Pub. Svc. award/medal & Svc. award U.S. Dept. Transp./USCG, 1998. Fellow Am. Coll. Trial Lawyers, Am. Bar Found.; mem. ABA (house of del. 2002-08), Jacksonville Bar Assn. (pres. 1975), Fla. Coun. Bar Pres. (chmn. 1979), Maritime Law Assn. U.S. (exec. com. 1978-81, chmn. navigation com. 1981-88, v.p. 1992-96, pres. 1996-98), Comm. Maritime Internat. (titulary), Com. on Collision (Lisbon Rules), Fed. Ins. Corp. Counsel (chmn. maritime law sect.), Internat. Assn. Def. Counsel (chmn. maritime com. 1989-91), Am. Inns of Ct. (master of bench), Assn. of Citadel Men (bd. dir. 1989-93, exec. com. 1994, Man of Yr. award 1992, S.C. Palmetto medal and award 2001, Citadel Inn of Ct. sr. bencher), Deerwood Club, River Club, India House (NYC), Army Navy Club (Washington), St. John's Dinner Club (pres. 1988). Office: Moseley Prichard Parrish Knight & Jones 501 West Bay Bldg 1887 Jacksonville FL 32202 Office Phone: 904-356-1306. Office Fax: 904-354-0194. Business E-Mail: jfmoseley@mppks.com.

MOSELEY, KAREN FRANCES FLANIGAN, educational consultant, retired school system administrator, educator; b. Oneonta, NY, Sept. 18, 1944; d. Albert Francis and Dorothy (Brown) Flanigan; m. David Michael McLaud, Sept. 8, 1962 (div. Dec. 1966); m. Harry R. Lasalle, Dec. 24, 1970 (dec. Feb. 1990); 1 child, Christopher Michael; m. Kel Moseley, Jan. 22, 1994. BA, SUNY, Oneonta, 1969; MS, SUNY and Hockerill Coll., Eng., 1970. Cert. secondary edn. tchr., Fla., Mass., NY. Tchr. Hanover (Mass.) Pub. Schs., 1970-80; lobbyist Mass. Fed. Nursing Homes, Boston, 1980-84; tchr., dept. chair Palm Beach County Schs., Jupiter, Fla., 1985-95; ret., 1996; chair of accredidation Jupiter H.S., 1990-91. Fulbright tchr., Denmark, 1994-95. Author: How to Teach About King, 1978, 10 Year Study, 1991. Mem., spkr. PBC chpt. ARC; disaster team vol. Palm Beach County Red Cross; vol. Pace Ctr. for Girls, PACE Ctr. for Girls; del. Dem. Conv., Mass., 1976-84; campaign mgr. Kennedy for Senate, NY, 1966, Tsongas for Senate, Boston, 1978; dir. Plymouth County Dems., Marshfield, Mass., 1978-84; mem. Sch. Accountability Com., 1991-95; polit. cons. Paul Tsongas U.S. Senate, Boston, 1978-84, Michael Dukakis for Gov., Boston, 1978-84. Mem. AAUW (North Palm Beach County, officer, Ednl. Found. Honor award 2003), NEA (life), Nat. Honor Soc. Polit. Scientists, Classroom Tchrs. Assn., Palm Beach County Classroom Tchrs. Assn., Mass. Coun. Social Studies (bd. dirs. Boston chpt. 1970-80), Mass. Tchrs. Assn. (chair human rels. com. Boston chpt. 1976-80), Plymouth County Social Studies (bd. dirs. 1970-80), Mass. Hosp. Assn. (bd. dirs. Boston chpt. 1980-84), Nat. Coun. for Social Studies, Fulbright Alumni Assn., Prologue Soc., Forum Club of the Palm Beaches, Fla. History Ctr., Marine Life Ctr., Norton Mus. Art, Winslow Hist. Assn., Pilgrim Hall, Plimoth Plantation, Hispanic Human Resources Coun., Mus. Fine Arts Boston. Roman Catholic. Avocations: reading, fishing, travel, art collector, snorkeling. Home: 369 River Edge Rd Jupiter FL 33477-9350 Office Phone: 561-744-6286. Personal E-mail: moseleykaren@comcast.net.

MOSER, KENNETH ALLEN, lawyer; b. Rowan County, NC, Sept. 8, 1942; BA, Wake Forest U., 1965, JD cum laude, 1968. Bar: NC 1968. Former mng. mem. Winston-Salem office Womble Carlyle Sandridge & Rice PLLC. Former mem. faculty Grad. Sch. Banking of South, Baton Rouge, La., 1987-89; pres. Wake Forest Law Rev., 1967-68. Named one of The Best Lawyers in Am., in Banking Law and Real Estate Law, Chambers USA, Am.'s Bus. Lawyers. Mem.: ABA (chair loan practices and lender liability com. 1988—93, mem. books and media com. 1995—99, real estate, probate and trust law sect.), Wake Forest U. Sch. Law (Bd. Visitors 2008—), Wake Forest U. Law Alumni Coun. (pres. 1998), Am. Counsel Assn., Forsyth County Bar Assn., NC Bar Assn., Am. Coll. Mortgage Attorneys, Am. Coll. Real Estate Lawyers. Office: Womble Carlyle Sandridge & Rice PLLC One West Fourth St Winston Salem NC 27101 Home Phone: 336-761-0127; Office Phone: 336-721-3504. Business E-Mail: kmoser@wcsr.com.

MOSES, ALFRED HENRY, lawyer, writer, diplomat; b. Balt., July 24, 1929; s. Leslie William and Helene Amelia (Lobe) Moses; m. Carol Whitehill, Nov. 24, 1955 (dec.); children: Barbara, Jennifer, David, Amalie; m. Fern Magonet Schad, Aug. 28, 2005. BA, Dartmouth, 1951; postgrad., Woodrow Wilson Sch., Princeton U., 1951-52; JD, Georgetown U., 1956, LHD (hon.), 2013; LLD (hon.), Yeshiva U., 2010. Bar: D.C. 1956. Assoc. Covington & Burling, Washington, 1956-65, ptnr., 1965—94, 1997—99, sr. counsel, 1999—. Co-founder, sr. ptnr., chief strategy officer Promontory Fin. Group LLC and affiliates, Washington, 2001—; legal advisor minority rights Dem. Nat. Com., Washington, DC Commn. Urban Renewal; commr. Pub. Housing Fairfax County, Va., 1971—72; spl. advisor, spl. counsel Pres. Jimmy Carter, Washington, 1980—81; amb. U.S. Dept. State, Romania, 1994—97; spl. Presdl. emissary Cyprus conflict Pres. William J. Clinton, 1999—2001; chmn. UN Watch, Geneva, 2001—; chmn. nat. bd. Hebrew Coll., Newton Ctr., Mass., 2002—09; bd. chair Project on Ethnic Rels., Inc., Princeton, NJ, 2006—12; chair Internat. Coun.; co-chair, bd. govs. Beit Hatfutsot; mem. Diplomatic Coun. Energy Security; bd. trustees Romanian Am. Found., Harry S Truman Rsch. Inst. Advancement of Peace Hebrew U. Jerusalem; bd. advisors Am. Friends of Mid. East Media Rsch. Inst., Internat. Bd. Atidim; chair, internat. bd. trustees Inst. Nat. Security Studies, Tel Aviv; lectr. in field. Contbr. articles to profl. jours. Pres. Am. Jewish Com., 1991—94, chmn. centennial com., 2005—07, chmn. adv. coun., 1997—; bd. dirs. Paralysis Cure Rsch. Found., 1978—81; trustee Phelps Stokes Fund, NYC, 1978—84, Jewish Publ. Soc., 1989—94, Haifa U., 1988—90; co-chmn. legal divsn. United Givers Fund, Washington, 1975—76; active Coun. Fgn. Rels., NYC, 1977—; pres. Nat. Children's Island, Washington, 1975—76, Golda Meir Assn., 1986—88, nat. chmn., 1988—93; bd. regents Georgetown U., 1986—92. Recipient Frizis award, Nat. Coordinated Effort of Helenes, 1999, Pentru Merit award, Govt. of Romania, 2002, Yakir award, Beit Hatfutsot, 2012. Mem.: ABA, D.C. Bar Assn., Econ. Club Washington, Met. Club. Democrat. Jewish. Home: 7710 Georgetown Pike Mc Lean VA 22102-1431

MOSES, DANIEL, writer, singer; b. Hartsville, SC, Dec. 4, 1954; s. Paul Henry and Maggie (James) M.; m. Burlean Smith, May 10, 1980; 1 child, Brian Ashley. BS in Bus. Mgmt., Coker Coll., 1978; M in Human Resources, Kennedy We. U., 1997; PhD, Kennedy Western U., 1999; studied with Amelia Smith, U. S.C., 1974-84, studied with Richard Conant; studied with Shirley Goins, studied with Laurence Siegel, studied with Betty Swenson; studied with William Vessels, Kennedy Western U., 1999. Mgr. Jewel Cos., Jacksonville, Fla., 1981-85, Pharmor Drug Store, Columbia, SC, 1985-88; agent Lincoln Benefit Life, Columbia and Lincoln, Nebr., 1989-97; cons. Bridge Counseling Ctr. Benedict Coll., Columbia, 1989-92; recruiter Edward Waters Coll., Jacksonville, Fla., 1995-96; co-founder Project Heritage Quest Inc.; publ., rschr., genealogist Daniel Moses Inc., Delaware, SC, 1994—, Daniel Moses & Co. Inc., 2006—; dir. Diamonds in the Rough Prodn., Daytona Beach, Fla.; founder Diamonds Rough Reductions Inc., Daytona Beach. Former prof. Jones Coll., Jacksonville; prof. Phoenix U., Jacksonville; bd. dirs. Theatre Works. Author: (poems) Poetic Living: The Mind of Young America, 1980, The James Family: A Historical Perspective 1770-1980s, 1989, A Descroptive Study of Issues Associated with Sexual Harassment in the Workplace, 2001; co-author 2 books; contbr. poems to anthologies; operatic debut Othello Opera A'La Carte, Jacksonville, Fla., 1981; appeared in Samson and Delilah, Barber of Seville, Pagliacci, Cavalleria Rusticana, Carmen, Arpad Darazs; with S.C. Philharmonic Chorus, Columbia Choral Soc., Town Theatre's Show Stoppers; performances (with Butler H.S. Chorus) Concerts Abroad, Graz, Austria, for HM Queen Elizabeth the Queen Mother, Montreal, Can., Maria Isabel Sheraton, Mexico City, Internat. Platform Assn. Conv. Capitol Hill, Washington, Jerusalem 3000, 1996, Ramses Hilton, Cairo, 2000, Dimonds In The Rough Productions, Daytona Beach, Fla., 2011. Recipient Towney award Town Theater, Columbia, S.C., 1987, Merit award Internat. Music Festival, 1993, Jr. Achievement, Carolina Music Acad., 1992-94, Ramses Hilton award. Mem. SHRM, Am. Parliamentary Assn., Internat. Platform Assn. (chmn. poetry program 1977—, Disting. Mem. 1985, mem. bd. govs.), Am. Inst. Parliamentarians, S.C. Philharmonic Orch., WWII Tank Destroyer Soc., Southside Businessmen's Club, Fort Mose Hist. Soc., African-Am. Cmty. of Freedom, Inc., Congress World Poets, World Acad. Arts and Scis., Honorable Order of Ky. Col., Columbia (S.C.) C. of C. (amb. 1992—), Jacksonville (Fla.) C. of C., Southside Bus. Mens Club. Avocations: writing, horticulture, travel, photography. Home: PO Box 2403 Jacksonville FL 32203-2403 Office Phone: 904-662-3554.

MOSJIDIS, JORGE, agricultural studies educator, researcher; b. Santiago, Chile; arrived in U.S., 1976; d. Georgios and Aliky Mosjidis; m. Cecilia O'Hara Mosjidis, Mar. 23, 1986; children: Christina Zoe Wood, Alexis Georgios. B in Agronomy, U. Chile, Santiago, 1970; PhD, U. Calif., Riverside, 1981. Asst. prof. Auburn (Ala.) U., assoc. prof., 1986—96, prof., 1996—2012, prof. emeritus, 2012—. Chair clover crop germplasm com. USDA, 2005—08, sec., 2002—05; assoc. editor Crop Sci., 1995—2000; editor Diversity, 2009—. Contbr. articles to profl. jours. Recipient Dir.'s Rsch. award, Ala. Agr. Exptl. Sta., 2005; grantee, USDA-CSREES-NRI, 2003—06, CSREES, Integrated Organic Program, 2005—08, So. Region SARE, 2005—10, 2005—10. Mem.: Nat. Acad. Inventors, Am. Forage and Grassland Coun., Am. Genetic Assn., Am. Soc. Agronomy, Crop Sci. Soc. Am. (assoc. editor 2000, chair G.O. Mott. 2008), Gamma Sigma Delta, Sigma Xi. Greek Orthodox. Achievements include patents for utilization of a plant to control gastrointestinal parasites in ruminants; obtained a certificate of plant variety protection for 18 years for a sericea lespedeza cultivar. Avocations: yoga, flower and vegetable gardening, tai chi, qi kung. Office: Auburn Univ 202 Funchess Hall Auburn University AL 36849-5412

MOSKOWITZ, JAY, health science association administrator, educator, dean; b. NYC, Jan. 9, 1943; s. Murray and Helene Moskowitz; m. Joanne Cathy Schindelheim, Dec. 27, 1970; children: Michael Bradley, Andrew Cory. BS, Queens Coll., 1964; postgrad., CUNY, 1965; PhD, Brown U., 1969. From research assoc. in pharmacology to dep. dir. NIH, Bethesda, Md., 1969—93, dep. dir. sci. policy and tech. transfer, prin. dep. dir., 1993; with Nat. Heart, Lung and Blood Inst., Bethesda, 1976—86; acting dir. Nat. Inst. Deafness and Other Comm. Disorders, Bethesda, 1988—90, dep. dir., 1993—95; sr. assoc. dean rsch. devel., prof. pub. health scis. Wake Forest U. Sch. Medicine, Winston-Salem, NC, 1995—2001, sr. assoc. dean, 1997—2001; assoc. v.p. health sci. rsch. Pa. State U., University Park, 2002—, vice dean rsch. coll. medicine, 2002—07, prof. medicine, 2002—07; chief sci. officer Milton Hershey Med. Ctr., Pa., 2004—07; pres., CEO Health Scis. SC, Columbia, 2007—; prof. medicine Med. U. SC, 2007—; prof. pub. health U. SC, 2007—; adj. prof. Clemson U. Contbr. articles to profl. jours. Served to lt. comdr. USPHS. Recipient Meritorious award William A. Jump Meml. Found., 1977, Dir.'s award NIH, 1978, Superior Svc. award USPHS, 1980, performance awards Sr. Exec. Svc., Presdl. Meritorious Exch. Rank award 1989, Disting. Svc. award HHS, 1991, Disting. Svc. award Nat. Inst. on Deafness and Other Comm. Disorders, 1994. Mem. AAAS, Soc. Exptl. Biology and Medicine, N.C. Inst. Medicine. Jewish. Office: 1320 Main St Ste 625 Columbia SC 29201 Office Phone: 803-576-5902. Business E-Mail: jmoskowitz@healthsciencesc.org, jmoskowitz@sc.edu.

MOSKOWITZ, PAUL T., human resources specialist; 4 children. BA, Princeton U., 1986; MBA, Rice U. Sr. dir., Internat. Human Resources, Caribbean and L.Am. Tricon Global Restaurants (now Yum! Brands); compensation cons. Towers Perrin, 1988—92; various Human Resources positions Brinker Internat., Inc., 1992—94, Darden Restaurants, Inc., 1994—96; dir., Global Human Resources PepsiCo Food Sys., 1996; various positions Yum! Brands, Inc., 1996—2007; v.p., Field Human Resources and Tng. Pizza Hut, Inc.(divsn. of Yum! Brands, Inc.), 2001—04, chief people officer, 2004—07; exec. v.p., Human Resources Dean Foods Co., 2007—. Avocations: travel, running, theater. Office: Dean Foods Co 2515 McKinney Ave Ste 1200 Dallas TX 75201 Office Phone: 214-303-3400. Office Fax: 214-303-3499. Business E-Mail: paul_moskowitz@deanfoods.com.

MOSS, BILL RALPH, lawyer; b. Amarillo, Tex., Sept. 27, 1950; s. Ralph Voniver and Virginia May (Atkins) M.; 1 child, Brandon Price. BS with honors, West Tex. A&M U., 1972, MA, 1974; JD, Baylor U., 1976; cert. regulatory studies program, Mich. State U., 1981. Bar: Tex. 1976, U.S. Dist. Ct. (no. dist.) Tex. 1976, U.S. Dist. Ct. (we. dist.) Tex. 2005, U.S. Tax Ct. 1979, U.S. Ct. Appeals (5th cir.) 1983. Briefing atty. Ct. Appeals 7th Supreme Jud. Dist. Tex., Amarillo, 1976-77; assoc. Culton, Morgan, Britain & White, Amarillo, 1977-80; hearings examiner Pub. Utility Commn. Tex., Austin, 1981-83; asst. gen. counsel State Bar Tex., Austin, 1983-87; founder, owner Price & Co. Publs., Austin, 1987-97; asst. gen. counsel Tex. Ethics Commn., Austin, 1997—2004; asst. atty. gen. antitrust and civil medicaid fraud div. Office Atty. Gen., Tex., 2004—11; atty. at law, 2011—. Instr., lectr. West Tex. State U., Canyon, Ea. N.Mex. U., Portales, 1977-80; spkr. in field. Election inspector State of Tex., 1998—. Mem. ABA (panel dir. & issues facing profession), Am. Assn. Individual Investors(dem. nat. com. mem.), Fed. Bar Assn., Tex. Bar Assn., Nat. Orgn. Bar Counsel, Nat. Coun. Prescription Drug Programs, Internat. Platform Assn., Capitol of Tex. Rotary Club, Am. Assn. Individual Investors, Nature Conservancy, Alpha Chi, Lambda Chi Alpha, Omicron Delta Epsilon, Phi Alpha Delta, Sigma Tau Delta, Pi Gamma Mu. Episcopalian. Address: 506 Explorer St Lakeway TX 78734-3447 Office Phone: 512-799-3520.

MOSS, DENNIS CARROLL, state legislator; b. Union, Jan. 13, 1954; s. James Edward and Mary Ivey Moss; m. Janet Ellis; 1 child, Brandon Lindsay. Attended, Spartanburg Meth. Coll. Mem. Dist. 29 SC House of Reps., 2007—, mem. Agr., Natural Resources and Environ. Affairs Com. Mem.: Hejaz Shrine Temple, Sertoma Internat., Cherokee Shrine Club, Lions Internat. Club, Gaffney #186 Masonic Lodge. Democrat. Home: 306 Silver Circle Gaffney SC 29340 Office: 418A Blatt Building Columbia SC 29201 Home Phone: 864-487-2121; Office Phone: 864-761-6353. E-mail: MossD@schouse.org.

MOSS, MADISON SCOTT, retired editor; b. Charlotte, NC, May 23, 1948; s. James Madison and Nellie Lee (Jenkins) M. BA in English, U. N.C., 1970. Editl. aide NASW, Inc., Washington, 1974, promotions specialist, 1974-79, assoc. editor, 1979-80, editor, 1980-90, mng. editor, 1990—2008. Campaign coord. Eugene McCarthy for Pres., Rutherford County, N.C., 1968. Recipient award for Pub. Excellence Comms. Concepts, 1993, 94, 95, 96, 97, 98, Bronze award newspaper gen. excellence Soc. Nat. Assn. Publs., 1996, Silver award, 1997, Bronze awards, 2005, 06. Mem. Am. Assn. Ret. Persons, U. N.C. Gen. Alumni Assn., Flight 93 Nat. Meml. (founding sponsor 2008). Democrat.

MOSS, ROBERT WILLIAMS, real estate developer; b. Balt., May 16, 1942; s. Ambler Holmes and Dorothea (Williams) M.; m. Marguerite McKee, Jan. 30, 1971; children: Dorothy Williams, Lucile Aycock. BA, MCP, Yale U., 1967. V.p. Howard R&D Corp. subs. The Rouse Co., Balt., 1967-73; dir. devel. Flower Mound New Town Raymond D. Nasher Co., Dallas, 1973-76; regional dir. Campaign for Yale U., Dallas, 1976-78; dir. devel. Tecon Realty (Murchison Interests), Dallas, 1978-85; exec. v.p. Cityplace Devel. Corp. subs. The Southland Corp., Dallas, 1985-91; prin. Moss & Assocs., Dallas, 1991-96; pres., CEO City of Dallas Bus. Devel. Corp., 1996—2006; dir. real estate adv. svcs. HDR, Inc., 2007—. Dir. Historic Landmarks, Inc. Mem. Urban Land Inst., Yale Club Dallas (pres. 1984-86). Episcopalian. Avocations: reading, tennis, skiing, jogging. Home: 4319 Allencrest Ln Dallas TX 75244-7406 Office: PO Box 570417 Dallas TX 75357 Office Phone: 214-960-4150. Personal E-mail: mossdbdc@airmail.net.

MOSS, SANTANA TERRELL, professional football player; b. Miami, Fla., June 1, 1979; s. Lloyd, Natalie; married; children: Santana Jr., Saniya. BA in Liberal Arts, U. Miami, Fla., 2000. Wide receiver NY Jets, 2000—04, Wash. Redskins, 2005—. Recipient Offensive and Special Teams Player Yr. awards, Big East Conf., 2000; named to Nat. Football Conf. Pro Bowl Team, NFL, 2005. Office: Washington Redskins 21300 Redskin Park Dr Ashburn VA 20147

MOSS, SHAD GREGORY (BOW WOW, LIL' BOW WOW), rap artist, actor; b. Columbus, Ohio, Mar. 9, 1987; s. Teresa and Alfonso Moss, Rodney Caldwell (Stepfather); 1 child, Shai. Singer: (albums) Beware of Dog, 2000, Doggy Bag, 2001, Unleashed, 2003, Wanted, 2005, Signal Fire, 2006, The Price of Fame, 2006, New Jack City II, 2009, Underrated, 2013, (with Omarion) Face Off, 2007, (songs) Bounce With Me, 2000, Let Me Hold You, 2005, Fresh Azimiz, 2005, Like You, 2006, (featured on film soundtracks) Hardball, 2001, Like Mike, 2002; actor: (TV films) Carmen: A Hip Hopera, 2001; (films) All About the Benjamins, 2002, Like Mike, 2002, Johnson Family Vacation, 2004, Roll Bounce, 2005, The Fast & the Furious: Tokyo Drift, 2006, Hurricane Season, 2009, Lottery Ticket, 2010, Madea's Big Happy Family, 2011, Allegiance, 2013, Scary Movie 5, 2013; TV appearances Entourage, 2008—09. Office: Bow Wow Foundation Ste 307 6555 Sugarloaf Pkwy PMB 223 Duluth GA 30097 also: c/o Jeff Frasco or Ken Stovitz Creative Artists Agency LCC 2000 Avenue of the Stars Los Angeles CA 90067 Office Fax: 678-376-5911.

MOSS, STEPHEN BRUCE, lawyer; b. Jacksonville, Fla., July 14, 1943; s. Rudy and Betty (Sobel) M.; m. Rhoda Goodman, Nov. 24, 1984; children: Kurt, Shannon. BA, Tulane U., 1964; JD, Cumberland Sch. Law, 1968. Bar: Fla. 1968, U.S. Dist. Ct. (So. Dist.) Fla., U.S. Tax Ct. 1971. From assoc. to ptnr. Heiman & Crary, Miami, Fla., 1971-74; pvt. practice law So. Miami, Fla., 1974-75; ptnr. Glass, Schultz, Weinstein & Moss P.A., Coral Gables, Fla., 1975-78, Ft. Lauderdale, Fla., 1978-80, Holland & Knight, LLP, Ft. Lauderdale, 1980—, mem. dir. com., 2004—06. Lectr. in the field. Mem. pro bono com. 17th Jud. Cir., 2000; co-founder, co-chair Broward County Child Welfare Initiative, 2001. Capt. U.S. Army, 1968-70, Vietnam. Named Outstanding Kiwanian, Miami, Fla., 1974, Child Advocate of the Yr., Broward County, Fla., 2003, Role Model, 2004, Legal Elite, Fla. Trend Mag., 2004; named an Olympic torchbearer, 1996; named one of Best Lawyers in Am., 2007, 2008, 2009—11. Fellow: Am. Bar Found., Fla. Bar Found.; mem.: Broward County Chpt. Fla. Resturant Lodging Assn. (bd. dir. 2007—11), Internat. Law Moot Ct., Broward County Bar Assn., Legal Aid Svc. of Broward County (bd. dirs. 2000), Fla. Bar Assn. (real property, probate and trust law sect.), Greater Ft. Lauderdale C. of C. (gen. counsel 1991—92, chmn. bd. dirs., bd. govs. 1995, past chair 1995, trustee rep. 2005—11, Ft. Lauderdale centinnial com., Chmn.'s award 1991, 2000, Sr. Exec. Alumni of Year 2003), Tower Forum (pres. 1993—94, bd. dirs. 1995—2005), Phi Alpha Delta. Democrat. Jewish. Avocations: baseball, child welfare, spinning. Office: Holland & Knight LLP 515 E Las Olas Blvd Ste 1200 Fort Lauderdale FL 33301 Office Phone: 954-468-7857. Business E-Mail: stephen.moss@hklaw.com.

MOSS, THOMAS WARREN, JR., county official; b. Norfolk, Va., Oct. 3, 1928; s. Thomas Warren Moss and Laura Burckard Moss; m. Lorna Payne; three c.: Elizabeth Ann, Susan Bruce, Thomas Warren, III BS, Va. Poly. Inst.; LLB, U. Richmond. Mem. House of Dels., Richmond, Va., 1966, majority leader, 1980, speaker of the house, 1991; atty., owner, pres. Thomas W. Moss, Jr. PC; treas. City of Norfolk, Va., 2001—. Mem. bd. dirs. Commonwealth Bankshares Inc., 1999—. Mem. lay adv. bd. DePaul Hosp.; former chmn. Am. Cancer Soc.; mem. bd. dirs. Va. chpt. Cystic Fibrosis Assn.; former mem. Tidewater Vocat. Ctr.; bd. trustees Jamestown-Yorktown Found., Va. Mus. Fine Arts; ex-officer chmn. Commn. on Militia and Police, Commn. on Gen. Laws, Commn. on Corps., Ins. and Banking; del. Dem. Nat. Conv., 1980; active Commn. on Preservation of Capitol, Jud. Coun. Va. Recipient Disting. Svc. to Humanity award Va. Assn. Optometrists, 1983, Disting. Svc. award Alumni U. Richmond, Class '56, 1984, Va. Crime Prevention Assn. award, 1986, Va. State Sheriffs' Assn. award, 1987, Svc. award Med. Coll. Hampton Roads, 1988, Disting. Svc. award Louise W. Eggleston Ctr., 1988, Spl. Legis. award Edn. Assn. Norfolk, 1989; named Legis. of Yr., Va. Assn. Locally Elected Constl. Leaders, 1989. Mem. ABA, Va. Trial Lawyers Assn., Norfolk-Portsmouth Bar Assn., Va. Bar Assn., Va. Poly. Inst. Alumni Assn. (Tidewater chpt. former pres., bd. dirs.), Sertoma Club of Norfolk, Mason (32 degree). Lutheran. Office: Commonwealth Bankshares Inc 403 Boush St Norfolk VA 23510 Office Phone: 757-446-6900. Office Fax: 757-446-6911. Business E-Mail: thomas.moss@norfolk.gov.

MOSS, V. STEPHEN (STEVE MOSS), state legislator; b. Feb. 3, 1950; m. Cheryl Moss; children: Elizabeth, Jessica, Emily. BA, Clemson U., 1972. Mem. Cherokee County Sch. Bd., 1990—94; mem. Dist. 30 SC House of Reps., 2009—, mem. Agr., Natural Resources and Environ. Affairs Com. Bd. mem. SC Banker's Assn. Office: 418D Blatt Bldg Columbia SC 29201 Mailing: 104 Rains Rd Blacksburg SC 29702 Office Phone: 803-212-6885. E-mail: StephenMoss@schouse.org.

MOSSBERGER, KAREN, political science professor, director; BA summa cum laude in honors polit. sci., Wayne State U., Detroit, 1991, MA in polit. sci., 1992, PhD in polit. sci., 1996. Academic visitor U. Strathclyde, Glasgow, Scotland, 1992—93; lectr. Eastern Mich. U., 1996—97; asst. prof. dept. polit. sci. Kent State U., 1997—2003, assoc. prof. dept. polit. sci., 2003—05; assoc. prof. pub. adminstrn. U. Ill., Chgo., 2005—09, prof. pub. adminstrn., 2009—13, assoc. dean for faculty affairs Coll. Urban Planning and Pub. Affairs, 2010—11, head dept. pub. adminstrn., 2011—13; dir. Sch. Pub. Affairs, prof. pub. affairs Ariz. State U., Phoenix, 2013—. Author: (books) The Politics of Ideas and the Spread of Enterprise Zones, 2000; co-author: Virtual Inequality: Beyond the Digital Divide, 2003, Digital Citizenship: The Internet, Society, and Participation, 2008; co-author: (with Caroline Tolbert and William Franko) Digital Cities: The Internet and the Geography of Opportunity, 2012; co-editor: Oxford Handbook of Urban Politics, 2012. Mem.: American Polit. Sci. Assn. (pres. Urban Politics Sect. 2009—10). Office: School Public Affairs University of Arizona 411 N Central Ave Ste 400 Phoenix AZ 85004-0687 E-mail: karen.mossberger@asu.edu.

MOSSINGHOFF, GERALD JOSEPH, lawyer, educator; b. St. Louis, Sept. 30, 1935; m. Jeanne Carole Jack, Dec. 29, 1958; children: Pamela Ann Jennings, Gregory Joseph, Melissa M. Ronayne. BSEE, St. Louis U., 1957; JD with honors, George Washington U., 1961. Bar: Mo. 1961, DC 1965, Va. 1981. Project engr. Sachs Electric Corp., 1954-57; dir. congl. liaison NASA, Washington, 1967-73, dep. gen. counsel, 1976-81; asst. Sec. Commerce, commr. patents and trademarks U.S. Patent Office, 1981-85; pres. Pharm. Rsch. and Mfrs. Am., Washington, 1985-96; Cifelli prof. intellectual property law George Washington U., Washington, 1996—; sr. counsel Oblon, Spivak, McClelland, Maier & Neustadt, Arlington, Va., 1997—. Amb. Paris Conv. Diplomatic Conf. Recipient Exceptional Svc. medal, NASA, 1971, DSM, 1980, Outstanding Leadership medal, 1981, Jefferson medal, 2000, Disting. Pub. Svc. award, Sec. of Commerce, 1983; named Disting. Alumnus, George Washington U., 1996, presdl. rank of meritorious exec., 1980. Fellow: Am. Acad. Pub. Adminstrn.; mem.: Reagan Alumni Assn. (bd. dirs.), Cosmos Club, Knights of Malta, Order of Coif, Pi Mu Epsilon, Eta Kappa Nu. Home: 1530 Key Blvd Penthouse 28 Arlington VA 22209-1532 Office: Oblon Spivak McClelland Maier and Neustadt 1940 Duke St Alexandria VA 22314

MOSTERT, PAUL STALLINGS, retired mathematician; b. Morrilton, Ark., Nov. 27, 1927; s. Johannes F. T. and Lucy (Stallings) Mostert; m. Kathleen Gray, 1947 (div. 1989); children: Paul Theodore, Richard Stallings, Kathleen, Kristina; m. Barbara Bond, 1990. AB in Math., Rhodes Coll., Memphis, 1950; MS in Math., U. Chgo., 1951; PhD in Math., Purdue U., Lafayette, Ind., 1953. Mem. faculty Tulane U., 1953-70, prof. math., 1962-70, chmn. dept., 1968-70; prof. U. Kans., 1970-91, prof. emeritus math., 1991—, chmn. dept., 1970-73; pres. Equix, Inc., NY, 1984—85, Pennfield Biomechanics Corp., Inc., Erwinna, Pa., 1985—89, Equix Biomechanics, Lexington, Ky., 1989—97, Equix Rsch. Corp., Lexington, 1989—2005; proprietor Mostert Group, Lexington, 1997—2003; dir. rsch. Mostert-Group LLC dba Equix Biomechanics, Lexington, 2003—06; mgr. MSRCO, LLC, Lexington, 2004—. Vis. prof. U. Tubingen, Germany, 1962—63; mem. Inst. Advanced Study, Princeton, 1967—68; vis. prof. math. U. Ky., 1984—85; chmn. Rhodes Coll. Sci. Initiaitve Task Force, 1989—90. Author: Analytic Trigonometry, Prentice Hall, 1960, Sheaf Theory, Tulane Lecture Notes, 1968; co-author (with K.H. Hofmann): Splitting in Topological Groups, 1963; co-author: 3d edit., 1993, Elements of Compact Semigroups, Charles E. Merrill, Columbus, 1966, The Cohomology Ring of Finite and Compact Abelian Groups, Deutscher Verlag der Wissenschaften, Berlin, 1973; editor: Proc. Conf. Transformation Groups at New Orleans, 1967, Springer Verlag, Berlin-Heidelberg, 1968, Clifford Wallace Commemorative Volumes of the Semigroup Forum, Springer Verlag, NY, 1974; creator 11 software programs one of which selected matings that produced Kentucky Derby winners Lil E.T. and Big Brown; contbr. articles to profl. jours. Mem. Ky. Statewide Exptl. Program Stimulate Competitive Rsch. Com., 1994—96, Rhodes Coll. Sci. Initiative Task Force, 1989—90. With USN, 1945—46. Recipient Rsch. awards, Small Bus. Innovative Rsch., Dept. Homeland Security, 2006—08; NSF Sr. Postdoc. fellowship, 1967—68, grant, PI NSF STTR, 2008—09, Nat. Sci. Found., Ford Found., Tulane U., U. Kansas. Mem.: Assn. Mems. Inst. Advanced Studies, Am. Math. Soc. (mem. at large coun. 1972—75, chmn. com. acad. freedom, tenure and employment security 1973—76), Thoroughbred Owners and Breeders Assn. Achievements include patent for methods and computer-readable medium for tracking motion; patent for navigating between a plurality of discrete images. Office: 3298 Roxburg Dr Lexington KY 40503-3432 Office Phone: 859-223-1490. Personal E-mail: mostert.paul@gmail.com, psmostert@twc.com.

MOST-LEVIN, CAROL LYNN, physician, geriatrician; b. LI, NY, Sept. 1, 1959; d. Herbert Jules and Jean (Friedman) Most; m. Ronald Mitchell Levin, June 17, 1979; children: Jay Samuel Levin, Marc Andrew Levin, Eric Brian Levin. BA magna cum laude, La Salle Coll., Phila., 1981; MD, Med. Coll. Pa., 1985. Diplomate Nat. Bd. Med. Examiners; diplomate in internal medicine and geriatric medicine Am. Bd. Internal Medicine, diplomate in geriatric medicine, 2014-. Intern and resident Abington Meml. Hosp., Pa., 1985-88, internist, 1995—2011, mem.-at-large med. exec. com., 1999—2002; pvt. practice, 1988—95, 2001—03; staff physician W.G. (Bill) Hefner VA Med. Ctr., Salisbury, NC, 2003—06, West Palm Beach Va. Med. Ctr., Fla., 2006—, clin. exec. bd. elected mem. at large, 2013—, Champion Move program WPB VAMC, 2010—; affiliate asst. prof. of medicine U. Miami Miller Sch. Medicine, 2010—; "MOVE" program champion West Palm Beach VA Med. Ctr., Fla., 2010—. Med. dir. US Homecare, Phila., 1991-94; clin. instr. Temple U., Phila., 1995-96; instr. Jefferson U., 1996-2003; med. sch. interviewer Alleghany U., 1995-97; spkr. in field. Contbr. articles to mag., jours. Recipient First prize Eleanor Dixon Writing/Rsch. Competition, 1988; named Clin. Employee of Yr., VA Med. Ctr., 2004, Appreciation award, Fla. Chpt. Am. Legion. Fellow ACP; mem. AMA (Physician's Recognition award 1991, 94, 97, 2000, 03, 06, 09, 12), Am. Geriatrics Soc. Avocations: travel, cooking. Office: West Palm Beach Va Med Ctr 7305 N Military Trail West Palm Beach FL 33410 Home: 10124 Cobblestone Creek Dr Boynton Beach FL 33472 Personal E-mail: cmlmdfacp@aol.com.

MOTES, JOSEPH MARK, retired cruise and convention promotion company executive; b. Leesburg, Fla., Oct. 12, 1948; s. Lewis Jackson and Yolanda (Fernandez) M. AA in Computer Sci., Miami-Dade Community Coll., 1976. Promoter Trekruise & Seatrek, 1975—; conv. promoter Trekon & Vulkon, Fla., 1977—; v.p. Seatrek Ent., Inc., Cooper City, Fla. Pres. Genesis Prodns., Inc., 1992—. Sgt. USMC, 1967—74, Vietnam. Named Broward County Vet. Yr. Mem.: DAV, VFW, Disabled Am. Vet., AmVets, Vet. Fgn. Wars, Sons Confederate Vets., Sons the Am. Revolution, 9th Marines Assn., 1st Bat., 3rd Marine Divsn. Assn., Am. Legion, Marine Corps League. Conservative. Roman Catholic. Avocations: water sports, travel, boating, photography. Home and Office: 2133 NW 208th Ter Pembroke Pines FL 33029-2320 Personal E-mail: joemotes@aol.com.

MOULIN, HERVÉ, economics professor; b. Paris, Aug. 1, 1950; s. Robert Moulin and Monique Huard; m. Anna Bogomolnaia, Nov. 15, 2001; children: Daniel Bogomolnyi-Moulin, Philip Moulin-Bogomolnyi; m. Renee Marie Bouquier, Oct. 15, 1980 (div. Sept. 10, 2000). PhD, U. Paris, 1975. Prof., math. U. Paris, Dauphine, 1975—84; prof., economics Va. Poly. Inst. and State U., Blacksburg, 1984—89, Duke U., Durham, NC, 1989—99, Rice U., 1999—. Author: (scholarly book) The Strategy of Social Choice, Game Theory for the Social Sciences, Axioms of Cooperative Decision Making, Cooperative Microeconomics, Fair Division and Collective Welfare. Microeconomic rsch., NSF, 1987—89, 1992—93, 1998—2001, 2001—07. Fellow: Econometric Soc.; mem.: Soc. Social Choice and Welfare (pres. 1998—99), Game Theory Soc. (coun. mem. 2000—08). Office: Rice Univ 6100 Main St Houston TX 77005 Business E-Mail: moulin@rice.edu.

MOULTON, GRACE CHARBONNET, retired physicist; b. New Orleans, Nov. 1, 1923; d. Wilfred J. and Louise A. (Hellmers) Charbonnet; m. William Gates Moulton, June 1, 1947; children: Paul Charbonnet Moulton, Nancy Gates Moulton. BA, Tulane U., 1944; MS, U. Ill., 1948; PhD, U. Ala., 1962. Asst. prof. physics U. Ala., Tuscaloosa, 1962-65, Fla. State U., Tallahassee, 1965-74, assoc. prof. physics, 1974-80, prof. physics, 1980-91, prof. emerita, 1991. Cons. State Bd. Regents, Fla., 1985-90, Fla. Univ. System, 1985, 90. Referee jour. articles Jour. Chem. Physics, Radiation Rsch.; contbr. many sci. rsch. articles to profl. jours. Scholar, U. Ill.; Four Yr. Undergrad. scholar, Tulane U., rsch. grantee, NIH. Mem. Am. Phys. Soc., (mem. coun. southeastern sect. 1988-92). Avocations: gardening, music (classical and folk), birding. Personal E-mail: gmoulton@phy.fsu.edu.

MOULTON, JAMES ROGER, small business owner; b. Washington, Dec. 9, 1950; s. Roger Daniels and Vivian (Marshall) M.; m. Lynne Fellman, Feb. 5, 1977 (div. Aug. 12, 1984); m. Diane Marthe Allard, Jan. 6, 1986; children: Melissa Jane, Justin Roger. BS in Computer Sci., N.C. State U., 1972; MS in Computer Sci, U. Md., 1981. Computer specialist U.S. Naval Acad., Annapolis, Md., 1973—75; mem. tech. staff Computer Scis. Corp., Arlington, Va., 1975—78; sys. developer Sys. Devel. Corp., McLean, Va., 1978—81; computer specialist Nat. Bur. of Stds., Gaithersburg, Md., 1981—86; dist. mgr. Bell Comm. Rsch. Inc., Red Bank, NJ, 1989—90; pres. Open Network Solutions, Inc., Sterling, Va., 1981—, ATN Software Ltd., Sterling, Va., 1998—. Cons. Protocol Stds. and Comm., Ottawa, Can., 1986-88, ORS Assocs., McLean, Va., 1989-93, Open Network Solutions, Inc., Sterling, Va. Co-author (with others) Internat. Computer Standards, 1980-88; contbr. numerous articles to profl. jours. Recipient Dept. of Commerce Bronze medal, 1981. Democrat. Avocations: flying, mountain climbing. Personal E-mail: moulton@ons.com.

MOUNTAIN, JANET M., foundation administrator, former computer company executive; b. Oct. 19, 1967; BBA, U. Tex., Austin; MBA, Harvard Bus. Sch. Former sr. consultant Andersen Consulting, Houston; v.p., gen. mgr., US consumer divsn. Dell Inc., Round Rock, Tex., 1993—2003; exec. dir. The Michael & Susan Dell Found.,

Austin, Tex., 2003—. Named a Young Global Leader, Forum of Young Global Leaders, 2006. Office: The Michael & Susan Dell Found PO Box 163867 Austin TX 78716*

MOUNTCASTLE, WILLIAM WALLACE, JR., retired philosophy and religion educator; b. Hanover, NH, July 10, 1925; s. William Wallace and Grace Elizabeth (Zottarelli) M.; m. Ila M. Warner (div.); children: Christine, Susan, Gregory, Eric; m. Barbara Kaye Teelin, Oct. 19, 1979; 1 child, Cathleena; stepdaughter, Dasha Teelin. BA, Whittier Coll., 1951; STB, Boston U., 1954, PhD, 1958. Ordained to ministry United Meth. Ch. Asst. prof. philosophy and religion High Point Coll., NC, 1958—60; mem. So. Calif. Ann. Conf. United Meth. Ch., 1954—60; assoc. prof., head dept. philosophy Nebr. Wesleyan U., Lincoln, 1960—63, prof., head dept. philosophy, 1963—67; mem. Nebr. Ann. Conf. United Meth. Ch., 1960—95; prof. philosophy Fla. So. Coll., Lakeland, 1967—68; assoc. prof. philosophy and religion U. West Fla., Pensacola, 1968—79, prof. philosophy and religion, 1979—, M.L. Tipton prof. philosophy and religion, 1980—2003, emeritus M.L. Tipton prof., 2003. Author: Religion in Planetary Perspective, 1979, Science Fantasy Voices and Visions of Cosmic Religion, 1996, The Secret Ministry of Jesus, 2007; contbr. articles to profl. jours. Fighter pilot USAAF, 1942-48, PTO. Mem. NEA/United Faculty Fla., Am. Assn. Religion, Am. Philos. Assn., Democrat. Office: U West Fla Dept Phil-Religious Studies Pensacola FL 32514 Office Phone: 850-474-2678.*

MOUNTS, L. DAVID, corporate financial executive; b. 1963; married; 3 children. BSBA in Fin. & Mgmt. Info., U. Nev.; MBA, U. Pa. Wharton Sch. Bus., 2004. Joined UPS Inc., 1983, v.p., mergers & acquisitions, 1999—2002, CFO, Supply Chain Solutions Group, 2002—04, corp. contr., US ops., 2004—05; exec. v.p., CFO Domino's Pizza, Inc., Ann Arbor, Mich., 2005—07, exec. v.p., supply chain svcs., 2007; CEO Inmar, Inc. Bd. dirs. Procuri Inc., 2006—. Bd. dirs. The Genesis Shelter. Office: Inmar Inc 2601 Pilgrim Court Winston Salem NC 27106 Office Phone: 336-631-2500.

MOUNTZ, WADE, retired healthcare executive; b. Winona, Ohio, Nov. 19, 1924; s. Lowell J. and Ethel M. (Coppock) M.; m. Betty G. Wilson, June 3, 1946; children: David John, Timothy Wilson. BA, Baldwin-Wallace Coll., Berea, Ohio, 1948; MHA, U. Minn., Mpls., 1951; LHD (hon.), Ky. Wesleyan Coll., Owensboro, 1991. With Norton Meml. Infirmary, Louisville, 1951—58, asst. adminstr., 1958—69, adminstr., 1969—81; pres. Norton-Children's Hosps., Inc., Louisville, 1981—87, NKC, Inc., Louisville, 1981-85, vice chmn., 1985-87; pres. emeritus Norton Healthcare, 1987—. Vice chmn. Comprehensive Health Planning Council Ky., 1968-73, chmn., 1973-79; bd. dirs. Louisville chpt. ARC, 1961-74; trustee Blue Cross Hosp. Plan, 1959-72; trustee Am. Hosp. Assn., 1971-76, chmn. bd., 1975. Served with A.C., USNR, 1943-45. Recipient Disting. Service award Ky. Hosp. Assn.; Disting. Layman award Ky. Med. Assn. Fellow Am. Coll. Healthcare Execs. (life, gold medal), Modern Health Hall of Fame 2008, Masons. Home and Office: Betty & Wade Mountz 8021 Christian Ct # 401 Louisville KY 40222-9023 Home Phone: 502-426-5478. Personal E-mail: wmountz@insightbb.com.

MOURNING, ALONZO, professional sports team executive, retired professional basketball player; b. Chesapeake, Va., Feb. 8, 1970; m. Tracy Mourning; children: Alonzo III, Myka. BA in Sociology, Georgetown U., Washington, DC, 1992. Ctr. Charlotte Hornets, 1992—95, Miami Heat, 1995—2003, 2005—09, v.p. player programs, 2009—; ctr. NJ Nets, 2003—04; ret. NBA, 2009. Mem. Dream Team II, 1994. Co-author (with Dan Wetzel): Resilience: Faith, Focus, Triumph, 2008. Founder Alonzo Mourning Charities; founding mem. Athletes for Hope. Recipient J. Walter Kennedy Sportsmanship award, NBA, 2002, Cmty. Assist award, 2006, Outstanding Cmty. Svc. award, Nat. Urban League, 2003, Silver Medallion Cmty. Svc. award, Nat. Conf. for Cmty. and Justice, 2003, Excellence award for pub. policy, Children's Trust, 2007; named First Team All-NBA, 1999, Defensive Player of Yr., NBA, 1999, 2000; named to All-Rookie First Team, 1993, Ea. Conf. All-Star Team, 1994—97, 2000—02, All-Defensive First Team, 1999, 2000. Achievements include leading the NBA in: blocked shots, 1999, 2000; member of the NBA Finals championship winning Miami Heat, 2006. Office: Miami Heat 601 Biscayne Blvd Miami FL 33132-1801

MOURTON, KENNETH R., lawyer; BSBA, U. Ark., 1970, JD. CPA 1975; bar: Ark. 1975, US Dist. Ct. Ea & We. Ark., US Ct. Appeals 6th, 8th & 10th Cir., US Tax Ct., US Supreme Ct. Atty., law, mng. prin. atty. Ball and Mourton, Ltd., PLLC, Fayetteville, Ark.; part owner Emerald Travel Svcs., Ltd., Fayetteville, Ark.; pres. E.J. Ball Plz., Inc., Fayetteville, Ark., Coors of Western Ark., Inc., Fayetteville, Ark. Bd. dirs. & chmn. Wholesale Beer Distbrs. of Ark.; bd. dirs. Southwestern Energy Co., 1995—, Ark. Rural Endowment Fund, Inc. Chmn., gen. counsel Fayetteville C. of C. Named one of Ark. Best Lawyers, Ark. Times, 1998. Mem.: AICPA, Ark. Soc. of CPAs, Razorback Found. Office: Ball & Mourton Ltd PLLC 2575 N Keystone Crossing PO Box 1948 Fayetteville AR 72702-1948 Office Phone: 479-442-6213. Office Fax: 479-442-6233. Business E-Mail: kmourton@ballandmourton.com.

MOUTON, CHARLES PETER, dean, physician, educator; b. New Orleans, Jan. 9, 1960; m. Yvette Mouton. BS, Howard U., 1981, MD, 1986; MS, Harvard U., 1997. Diplomate Am. Bd. Family Practice. Resident Prince George's Hosp. Ctr., Cheverly, Md., 1987-90; fellow George Washington U. Med. Ctr., D.C., 1990-92; asst. prof. Sch. Medicine U. Medicine and Dentistry N.J., Newark, 1992-97; asst. prof. Health and Sci. Ctr. U. Tex., San Antonio, 1997—2004; prof. cmty. and family medicine Howard U., Washington, 2004—10; prof. family medicine Mehary Med. Coll., 2010—, dean Sch. Medicine, 2010—, sr. v.p. health Affairs, 2010—. Adv. bd. Guardianship Svcs., San Antonio, 1997-2001. Contbr. articles to profl. jours., chpts. to books. Fellow Am. Acad. Family Physicians, Assn. Am. Med. Colls.; mem. AMA, Am. Geriatrics Soc., Nat. Med. Assn., Gerontol. Soc. Am., Soc. Tchrs. Family Medicine, Knights Peter Claver. Avocations: reading, sports, Judo, music. Office: Meharry Med Coll 1005 Dr DB Todd Jr Blvd Nashville TN 37208 Home: 1320 Beddington Park Nashville TN 37215-5811 Office Phone: 615-327-6204. Business E-Mail: cmouton@mmc.edu.

MOW, ROBERT HENRY, JR., lawyer; b. Cape Girardeau, Mo., Dec. 10, 1938; s. Robert H. Sr. and Ann Elise (Beck) M.; m. Jody K. Boggs, Aug. 29, 1987; children: Robert M., Brynn A., W. Brett, Rebecca M., W. Kirk, Allison M. Student, Westminster Coll., 1956-57; AB with distinction, U. Mo., 1960; LLB magna cum laude, So. Meth. U., 1963. Bar: Tex. 1963, US Dist. Ct. (no. dist. Tex.) 1965, US Dist. Ct. (so. dist. Tex.) 1969, US Dist. Ct. (ea. and we. dists. Tex.) 1976, US Ct. Appeals (5th cir.) 1972, US Ct. Appeals (11th cir.) 1981, US Ct. Appeals (fed. cir.) 1994, US Supreme Ct. 1978. Assoc. Carrington, Johnson & Stephens, Dallas, 1963-69; ptnr. Carrington, Coleman, Sloman & Blumenthal, Dallas, 1970-85, Hughes & Luce, LLP (merged with K&L Gates LLP), Dallas, 1985—2007, mng. ptnr., 2003—07; ptnr. K&L Gates LLP, Dallas, 2008—. Editor-in-chief Southwestern Law Jour., 1962-63. Trustee First Bapt. Acad., chair, 1999-2002. Served to 1st lt. US Army, 1963-65. Recipient Disting. Alumni award, Pvt. Practice, SMU Sch. Law, 2008; named Top 100 Atty. award, Dallas Ft. Worth Region, 2012; named one of Best Lawyers in America, Comml. Litigation Legal Malpractice, 1984—, Best Lawyers in Dallas, 2005, 2008. Fellow: Am. Coll. Trial Lawyers; mem.: Dallas Bus. Jour. Defenders, Chambers & Ptnrs. Gen. Litig., Tex., Chambers USA, Dallas Bar Assn. (Dallas Bar Trial Lawyer of Yr. 2003), ABA (first chair intellectual property com. litig. sect.), State Bar Tex., Dallas Bar Fellows (chmn. com. qualified judiciary 2003—04), Am. Bd. Trial Advs. (pres. Dallas chpt. 1983—84), Tex. Assn. Def. Counsel (v.p. and dir. 1981—82), Dallas Assn. Def. Counsel. Republican. Baptist. Office: K & L Gates 1717 Main St Ste 2800 Dallas TX 75201 Office Phone: 214-939-5448. Office Fax: 214-939-5849. Business E-Mail: bob.mow@klgates.com.

MOWERY, ANNA RENSHAW, state legislator; b. Decatur, Tex., Jan. 4, 1931; d. Lafayette William and Virginia Bobo Renshaw; m. Wesley Harold Mowery; children: Jeanette, Mark William, Timothy Dean, Marianne. Mem. Tex. House Rep.; vice chmn. Tarrant County Rep. Com., Tex., 1973—75, chmn., 1975—77; del. State Conv., 1970—2000, Rep. Nat. Conv., 1976; chmn. Permanent Orgn. Com. State Rep. Party, 1976; committeewoman Dist. 12 Rep. Com., Tex., 1980—84; chmn. Tex. State Rep. Ele Code Review Com., 1981—82; candidate co. commr., 1982; chmn. Tarrant County Reagan-Bush Campaign, 1984; state rep. Dist. 97 Tex. Named Outstanding Rep. Woman of Tex., 1975; nominee Newsmaker of Yr., 1975, 1977. Mem.: Baylor Alumni, Women's Policy Forum, Ft. Worth Rep. Women's Club. Republican. Baptist. Office: Capitol 1N 05, Box 2910 Austin TX 78768 Address: 4108 Hildrine Dr W Fort Worth TX 76109 Office: 6421 Camp Bowie Blvd Suite 310 Fort Worth TX 76116 Office Phone: 512-463-0608, 817-732-1372, 817-921-2169. Office Fax: 512-463-8342. Business E-Mail: anna.mowery@house.state.tx.us.

MOYER, R. CHARLES, finance company executive, educator, dean emeritus; b. Reading, Pa., July 11, 1945; s. Ralph Charles and Jane Anne (Huls) M.; m. Sally Louise Prizer, May 19, 1973; children: Laura Prizer, Craig Prizer. BA in Econs., Howard U., 1967; MBA, U. Pitts., 1968, PhD in Fin., 1971. Asst. prof. fin. U. Houston, 1971-76; fin. economist U.S. Maritime Adminstrn., Washington, 1973-74; assoc. prof. Lehigh U., Bethlehem, Pa., 1976-77; from assoc. prof. to prof. U. N.Mex., Albuquerque, 1977-80; prof., chmn. fin. dept. Tex. Tech U., Lubbock, 1980-87; GMAC ins. chair in fin., Babcock Grad. Sch. Wake Forest U., Winston-Salem, NC, 1988—2004, dean Babcock Grad. Sch. of Mgmt., 1996—2003, dean emeritus, 2003—; dir. King Pharm., Inc., Bristol, Tenn., 2000—11; dean Coll. Bus. U. Louisville, 2005—13, dean emeritus, 2013—; dir. Summit Bioscis., 2011—, Direct Kypha Pharmaceuticals, 2011—12; bd. mem. Louisville & Southern Indiana Bridges Authority, 2010—; dir. Capitala Investment Group, 2013—. Pres., founder R.O.E. Cons. Group, Lubbock, 1978; cons. Pub. Svc. Co. N.Mex., 1978—, KN Energy, Denver, 1979—, Gas Co. N.Mex., 1985—, San Diego Gas Electric Co., 1986—, Source Gas LLC, 2007-; mem. adv. bd. Amarr Garage Door Co., Winston-Salem, 2001-05; bd. dirs. Kty. Seed Capital Fund, Capital South Ptnrs., LLC, Louisville & Southern Ind. Bridges Authority, 2010-. Author: Financial Management with Lotus 1-2-3, 1986, Contemporary Financial Management, 13th edit., 2014, Contemporary Financial Management Fundamentals, 2d edit., 2007, Managerial Economics, 13th edit., 2014; contbr. numerous articles to profl. jours. Vice-chmn. Lubbock Gen. Hosp. Found., 1985-88; bd. mem. Enterprise Corp., GLI, Louisville; Capt. US Army, 1972-74. Fed. Res. Bank Cleve. fellow, 1970-71. Mem.: Enterprise Angel Group (bd. mem.), Ea. Fin. Assn., So. Fin. Assn. (v.p. 1990—93, pres. 1993), Am. Fin. Assn., Fin. Mgmt. Assn. (bd. dir. ombudsman 1985—87, v.p. 1988—, sec.-treas. 1994—2002), Louisville Country Club, Beta Gamma Sigma, Phi Beta Kappa. Avocations: tennis, golf, bicycling. Office Phone: 502-852-5007. Business E-Mail: charlie.moyer@louisville.edu.

MOYERS, SYLVIA DEAN, retired medical librarian; b. Independence, W.Va., Oct. 22, 1936; d. Wilkie Russell and Ina Laura (Watkins) Collins; m. Paul Franklin Moyers, June 29, 1957; children: Tammy Jeanne, Thomas Paul, Tara Sue. Student, Am. Med. Record Assn., 1977—79. Sec. Teets Lumber Co., Terra Alta, W.Va., 1954-58, Preston County News, 1958-60; med. record clk. med. record dept. Hopemont (W.Va.) Hosp., W.Va., 1960-75, dir., 1975-88; sec. The Terra Alta Bank, 1990-95; ret., 1995. Charter mem., past mother advisor Order of Rainbow Girls (Terra Alta Assembly No. 26), past grand editor Mountain Echoes; vol. Preston Meml. Hosp., ARC, Salvation Army, Am. Cancer Soc., Boy Scouts Am.; active Kingwood Fire Dept. Aux. Named Kingwood Citizen of Yr., 2005; named one of 100 Most Influential Persons, 2004. Mem.: Preston County Hist. Soc., Kingwood Red Hat Mamas (charter), Preston Meml. Hosp. Aux., Kingwood Women's Civic Club. Republican. Methodist. Home: 260 Windy Ln Bruceton Mills WV 26525-6270

MOYLAN, JAMES E., JR., communications executive; b. Savannah, Ga., Feb. 3, 1951; s. James Emmett and Annette (Durrence) M.; m. Joanne Connie Shuman, Aug. 24, 1974; children: Lindsay Marie, Michelle Kathleen, Laura Elizabeth. BS in Indsl. Engring., Ga. Tech Inst. Tech., 1972; MBA, Harvard U., 1976. CPA, Tex. Indsl. engr. Westinghouse Electric Corp., Tampa, Fla., 1972-74; planning analyst Sonat Offshore Drilling, 1976-77, mgr. planning, 1977-79, contracts & sales rep., 1979-82; asst. v.p. Sonat Inc., Birmingham, Ala., 1982-84; v.p., comptroller Sonat, Inc., Birmingham, Ala., 1984; sr. v.p., CFO SCI Sys., Inc. (merged Sanmina), 1999—2002; exec. v.p. composite panels distbn. & adminstrn. Georgia-Pacific Corp., 2002—03; exec. v.p., CFO PRG-Schultz Internat., 2004—06, Swett & Crawford, 2006—07; sr. v.p., CFO Ciena Corp., 2007—. Mem. acctg. adv. coun. U. Ala., Birmingham, 1987—; bd. dirs. Jr. Achievement Brimingham, 1986—; bd. dirs. Birmingham Children's Theater, 1989—. Mem. AICPA, Fin. Execs. Inst. (bd. dirs. Birmingham chpt. 1985-90, v.p. 1987-88, pres. 1988-89). Clubs: Mountain Brook Swim & Tennis, Downtown (Birmingham). Roman Catholic. Avocations: tennis, jogging, golf, reading. Office: Ciena Corporation 7035 Ridge Rd Hanover MD 21076-1426 Office Phone: 410-694-5700. Office Fax: 410-694-5750. Business E-Mail: jmoylan@ciena.com.

MOYNIHAN, BRIAN THOMAS, bank executive; b. Marietta, Ga., Oct. 9, 1959; m. Susan Berry; 3 children. BA, Brown U., 1981; JD, U. Notre Dame Law Sch., 1984. Assoc. Edwards & Angell LLP, 1984—91, ptnr., 1991—93; dep. gen. coun. FleetBoston Financial Corp., 1993—94, mng. dir. corp. strategy & devel., 1994—2000, sr. v.p., 1998—99, exec. v.p., 1999—2000, exec. v.p. brokerage & wealth mgmt., 2000—04; pres. global wealth & investment mgmt. Bank of America Corp., Charlotte, NC, 2004—07, exec. v.p., gen. counsel, 2008—09, pres. global corp. & investment banking, 2007—09, pres. global banking, global wealth & investment mgmt., 2009, head consumer banking, 2009—, pres., CEO, 2010—; CEO Merrill Lynch Bank of America, 2009. Bd. dirs. Bank of America Corp., 2010—. Bd. dirs. YouthBuild Boston, Boys & Girls Clubs of Boston; past chmn. Travelers Aid Soc., Rhode Island, Providence Haitian Project, Inc. Office: Bank of America Corp 100 N Tryon St Charlotte NC 28255 Office Phone: 704-386-5681. Office Fax: 704-386-6699. Business E-Mail: brian.t.moynihan@bankofamerica.com.*

MOYNIHAN, GARY PETER, industrial engineering educator; b. Little Falls, NY; s. Peter H. and Frances S. (Ferjanec) M.; m. Eleanor T. McCusker, Mar. 10, 1984; children: Andrew Ross, Keith Patrick. BS in Chemistry, Rensselaer Polytech. Inst., 1978, MBA in Opsl. Mgmt., 1980; PhD in Indsl. Engring., U. Ctrl. Fla., 1990. Cert. project mgmt. profl. 2013. Prodn. supr. Am. Cyanamid, Bound Brook, N.J., 1978-79, Nat. Micronetics, Kingston, N.Y., 1980-81; assoc. mfg. engr. Martin Marietta Aerospace, Orlando, Fla., 1981-82, indsl. engr., 1982-85, sr. indsl. engr., 1985-87, group indsl. engr., 1987-90; asst. prof. indsl. engring. U. Ala., Tuscaloosa, 1990-96, assoc. prof., 1996—2001, prof., 2001—; asst. dir. Ala. Indsl. Assessment Ctr., 2006—. Cons. in field. Contbr. articles to profl. jours. Regents scholar N.Y. State Bd. Regents, 1974-78; rsch. fellow NASA, 1992-93, 98-99; rsch. grant BellSouth Telecomm., 1994-96; recipient Outstanding Tchg. award AMOCO Found., 1993-94, Ralph R. Teetor Nat. Engring. Educator award Soc. Automotive Engrs, 2000, Cert. of Recognition, NASA Inventions and Contbns. Bd., 2008, US Dept. Energy Ctr. Excellence award, 2011. Mem.: IEEE (sr.), Aerospace and Def. Soc. (v.p. fin. and adminstrn. 1994—97), Inst. Indsl. Engrs. (sr.; chpt. dir. 1991—95, chpt. pres. 1996—97, regional v.p. 2004—06, Outstanding Faculty Adv. SE Region award 2004, 2006, Nat. Outstanding Faculty Adv. award 2007). Achievements include design and development of information systems applications for the aerospace and foundry industries; 5 software copyrights. Office: University Ala Dept Civil Construction Environ Engring Tuscaloosa AL 35487-0205

MOYNIHAN, WILLIAM J., retired museum executive; b. Little Falls, NY, Apr. 8, 1942; s. Bernard J. and Mary A. (Flynn) M.; m. Irene A. Sheilds, July 2, 1966; children: Patricia, Erin, Sean. BA, SUNY, Binghamton, 1964; MA, Colgate U., 1966; PhD, Syracuse U., 1973. From asst. to assoc. prof. Colgate U., Hamilton, NY, 1973—77, from asst. to assoc. dean faculty, 1977—80, dean students, 1980—83, dean coll., 1983—88; v.p.m. dir. Am. Mus. Natural History, NYC, 1988—95; pres., CEO Milw. Pub. Mus., 1995—2002; ret., 2002. Bd. dirs. N.Y. State Mus.; adv. com. arts and culture Congressman J. Nadler, N.Y.C., 1993-95. Adv. editor Curator jour., 1991-95. Mem. Am. Mus. Assn., Am. Assn. Museums (mem. ethics com., bd. dirs.), Wis. Acad. of Scis., Arts and Letters (councillor-at-large 1995-02), Univ. Club. Home: 4685 Kirkpatrick Ln Alexandria VA 22311-4915

MOYSE, HERMANN, III, banker; b. Baton Rouge, Dec. 28, 1948; s. Hermann Jr. and Marie Louise (Levy) M.; m. Janet Lee Doise; children: Allison Leze, David Hermann, Aaron Lewis. BA, Coll. of Emporia, 1970; MSW, La. State U., 1973. Asst. dir. Capital Area Health Planning Agy., 1973-74; research assoc. La. State U., Baton Rouge, 1974-78; trainee to v.p. City Nat. Bank, Baton Rouge, 1978—, sr. v.p., 1985-94, also bd. dirs., chmn., 1994-98; owner, pres. HM3 Corp., 1999—. Sec.-treas. Melrose Devel. Corp., Baton Rouge, 1986-87; bd. dirs. La. Cos., Charter Chambers, LLC, First NBC Bank, New Orleans, Bizzuka, Inc.; CEO Health Net One, 1999; adv. bd. Iberia Bank, 2004-05; pres. WRKF Radio, 2003-04. Active Capital Area United Way Agy. Svcs. Div., Baton Rouge, 1979-86, 88-91, vice chmn. 1981, bd. dirs., 1987—, chmn., 1989-90; v.p. Arts Coun. Greater Baton Rouge, 1990—; 1st v.p. La. Arts & Sci. Ctr., Baton Rouge, 1985—, pres., 1988; mem. Community Funds for Arts, 1989-90; mem. Arts & Humanities Coun., 1990—, v.p., 1991—, treas., 1992; mem. Cmty. Funds for the Arts, 1989—, vice-chmn., 1992; pres. Cath. Cmty. Life Office, Baton Rouge, 1981, Baton Rouge Speech and Hearing Found., 1986, pres. 1983, treas., 1981; v.p. St. Joseph's Acad. Adv. Bd., 1986-88, pres., 1987-88; bd. dirs. St. James Place; treas. Baton Rouge Crisis Intervention Ctr., 1984-85, v.p., 1987, pres., 1987; sec. St. Joseph's Children's Home, 1980; bd. dirs. Crime Stoppers, Inc., 1986—, v.p., 1989, pres. 1991—; pres. Mid City Devel. Alliance, 1991-93, 97—; adv. bd. Tau Ctr., 1990-93; trustee Episc. HS, 1990-92; treas. La. Delta Svc. Corps. Inc., 1995—; bd. trustees Gen. Health Sys., Inc, 1994-98, La. Nature Conservancy, 2001—, Our Lady of Lake Coll., 2001—09, sec., 2003-05; chmn. fin. com. Baton Rouge Crimestoppers, 1997—; chmn. First Commerce Cmty. Devel. Corp., 1993-99, La. State U. Health Care Svcs. Found., 2002—. Mem. La. Bankers Assn. (fed. affairs com. 1990—), La. Coun. Econ. Edn. (trustee 1987, regional v.p. 1990—, Community Vol. Activist award 1988), NCCJ (chpt. bd. dirs. 1988, treas. 1995), City Club, Baton Rouge Country Club. Democrat. Jewish. Office Phone: 225-926-1600. Personal E-mail: hmoyse3@yahoo.com.

MOZLEY, PAUL DAVID, retired obstetrics and gynecology educator; b. Decatur, Ala., Oct. 27, 1928; s. James Howard and Ruth Dianne (Brindley) Mozley; m. Mary Dale Goss, Aug. 30, 1983; children from previous marriage: Susan Ruth, Paul David Jr., Sally Robin. BA, U. Ala., 1950; MD, Med. Coll. Ala., 1955. Diplomate Am. Bd. Ob-Gyn, Am. Bd. Psychiatry and Neurology. Commd. lt. USN, 1955, advanced through grades to capt., 1970; resident ob-gyn Corona (Calif.) and San Diego Naval Hosp., 1956-59; resident in psychiatry Bethesda, Md., 1964-66, Phila. Naval Hosp., 1969-70; staff gynecologist U.S. Naval Hosp., Yokosuku, Japan, 1959-62, chief gynecologist Memphis, 1962-64, dir. med. services Naples, Italy, 1966-68, comdg. officer, 1969; chmn. neuropsychiatry Naval Regional Med. Ctr., Portsmouth, Va., 1970-75; ret., 1975; assoc. prof. psychiatry Eastern Va. Med. Sch., Norfolk, 1975-77, prof., interim chmn. dept., 1977-78, vice chmn. psychiatry, 1978-79; prof., dir. undergrad. edn. Dept. Ob-Gyn Sch. Medicine, East Carolina U., Greenville, 1979-84; prof. ob-gyn, chmn. dept., Coll. Community Health Scis. U. Ala., Tuscaloosa, 1984-99, prof. ob-gyn, assoc. chmn. dept. Sch. Medicine, 1984-99, prof., chmn. emeritus Sch. Medicine, prof. emeritus obstetrics, 1999—; ret., 2002. Dir. psychiat. svcs. Norfolk Gen. Hosp., 1975—79; chmn. dept. ob-gyn DCH Regional Med. Ctr., Tuscaloosa, 1986—; obstetrician Baldwin Clinic; cons. med. liability law legal firms, Ala., Tenn., 1980—. Contbr. articles to profl. jours. Mem. Regional Parental Adv. Coun., Montgomery, Ala., 1986—87; sponsor Tuscaloosa Symphony Assn. Recipient Meritorious Svc. medal, US Pres., 1975, Surgeon Gen.'s Merit award, 1975, Attending of the Yr. award, Resident's in Psychiatry, 1979, Clin. Sci. Course award, Dept. Ob-Gyn grad. class 1982, Eastern Va. Sch. Medicine; named one of Outstanding Young Men in Am., Jaycees, 1964. Fellow: ACS, ACOG (life; chmn. various programs 1974, 1976, 1977, Chmn.'s award clin. rsch. 1969), Am. Psychiat. Assn. (life Continuing Med. Edn. Stds. award 1977); mem.: LWV, AMA (Physician's Recognition award 1986), Am. Bd. Physician Specialist (bd. mem. 2007—), Ala. Psychiat. Assn., Med. Assn. Ala., Pitt County Med. Soc., NC Neuropsychiatric Assn., Va. Med. Soc., Assn. Acad. Psychiatry, Va. Ob-Gyn. Soc., Am. Soc. Psychosomatic Ob-Gyn (founding mem., pres. 1979—80, chmn. nominating com. 1981, mem. permanent steering com. 1982), United Meth. Ch., Torch Club (Portsmouth), Alpha Epsilon Delta. Methodist. Avocations: cabinetry, goldsmithing. Home: 563 N Mobile St Fairhope AL 36532-2609 Personal E-mail: pmoz@bellsouth.net.

MRACHEK, LORIN LOUIS, lawyer; b. Fairmont, Minn., Jan. 5, 1946; s. Louis L. and Kathleen (Loring) M.; m. Elizabeth Moss, Aug. 31, 1968; children: Kathleen Elizabeth, Louis Moss. BA with honors, Fla. State U., 1968; MBA, JD, Columbia U., 1974. Bar: Fla. 1974, Va. 1977, U.S. Ct. Mil. Appeals 1977, U.S. Dist. Ct., U.S. Ct. Appeals (5th cir.), U.S. Ct. Appeals (7th cir.), U.S. Ct. (11th cir.), U.S. Supreme Ct. 1978, U.S. Bankruptcy Ct. (so. dist.) Fla., U.S. Bankruptcy Ct. (mid. dist.) Fla., U.S. Bankruptcy Ct. (no. dist.) Fla.; cert. in civil trial law, 1985, bus. litigation, 1997, Fla. Bar Bd. Certification; cert. in bus. bankruptcy law Am. Bd. Bankruptcy Certification, 1992; cert. in civil trial advocacy Nat. Bd. Trial Advocacy, 1995. Commd. 2d lt. USMC, 1969, advanced through grades to capt., 1974, chief def. counsel Marine Corps. Recruit Depoit, Paris Island, 1975-77, resigned, 1977;

spl. asst. to gen. counsel U.S. Ry. Assn., Washington, 1977-78; shareholder Gunster, Yoakley, Valdes-Fauli & Stewart, P.A., West Palm Beach, Fla., 1978-2000; founding shareholder Page, Mrachek, Fitzgerald & Rose, West Palm Beach, Fla., 2000—. Editor-in-chief Columbia Jour. Law and Social Problems, 1973-74; contbr. articles to profl. jours. Named one of Best Lawyers in Am.; Harlan Fiske Stone scholar. Fellow Am. Coll. Trial Attys.; mem. ABA, Am. Bankruptcy Inst., So. Fla. Bankruptcy Bar Assn. Avocations: travel, golf. Office: 505 S Flagler Dr Ste 600 West Palm Beach FL 33401-5941 Office Phone: 561-655-2250. Business E-Mail: lmrachek@pm-law.com.

MRKONIC, GEORGE RALPH, JR., hotel executive; b. Lawrence, Kans., July 13, 1952; s. George Ralph and Ruth (Clayton) M.; m. Barbara Machmer, June 22, 1974; children: Matthew George, John William, Kelsey Margaret. BA and MA in Econs., Stanford U., 1975; MBA, Harvard U., 1978. Fin. analyst WR Grace/Retail Group, NYC, 1978-79, group mgr., 1979-80, dir. fin. planning, 1980-81, v.p., chief fin. officer, 1981, Herman's Sporting Goods Inc., Carteret, N.J., 1981-85, sr. v.p., chief fin. officer, 1985-87, exec. v.p., dep. chief exec. officer, 1986-87, pres., chief exec. officer, 1987; pres. Eyelab, Inc, River Edge, N.J., 1987-90; exec. v.p. splty. retailing K Mart Corp., Troy, Mich., 1990-94; pres. Borders Group, Inc., Ann Arbor, Mich., 1994—97, vice chmn., 1994—2002. Bd. dirs. Borders Group, Inc., 1994-2004, Champion Enterprises, Syntel, Inc., Paperchase, 2004-, Pacific SunWear of Calif., Inc., Autozone, Inc., Brinker Internat. Office: Brinker International Inc Bd Directors 6820 LBJ Freeway Dallas TX 75240 Office Phone: 972-980-9917. E-mail: george.mrkonic@brinker.com.

MUCHMORE, ROBERT CHARLES, JR., oil industry executive; BBA with honors, So. Meth. U., 1975. CPA Tex., 1977. Teller, mail rm. clk. Preston State Bank (not Bank One), 1971—75; staff auditor Arthur Andersen LLP, Dallas, 1975—78; internal auditor Otis Engring Corp. (not Halliburton Energy Svcs.), 1978—79, fin. reporting supr., 1979—80, internat. acctg. coord., 1980—82, internat. controller, 1982—83, internat. tax mgr., 1983—84, mgr., L.Am. fin. & adminstrn., 1984—85; mgr. internat. fin. systems Halliburton Energy Svcs., Houston, 1985—87, mgr. internat. fin. svcs., 1987—89, mgr. Europe/Africa regional fin. and adminstrn., 1989—96; v.p., controller Halliburton Co., 1996—2003, v.p. fin. controls, 2003—. Mem.: AICPA, Fin. Exec. Inst., Tex. Soc. CPA's. Office: Halliburton Co 10200 Bellaire Blvd Houston TX 77020-5299 Office Phone: 281-575-3000. Business E-Mail: charles.muchmore@halliburton.com.

MUCKLEY, RONALD, aerospace and defense manufacturing company executive; B in Elec. Engring., Purdue U.; MBA, U. Detroit. Various product and mfg. positions Chrysler Corp., 1976, engring. supr., 1986—89, engring. mgr., 1989; dir., engring. TRW Automotive Holdings Corp., 1992, v.p., gen. mgr., safety/security electronics bus., v.p., gen. mgr., North American braking and suspension bus.; v.p., engring. and materiel Vought Aircraft Industries, Inc., 2008—. Office: Vought Aircraft Industries Inc 9314 W Jefferson Blvd Dallas TX 75211 Office Phone: 972-946-2011. Business E-Mail: Ronald_Muckley@voughtaircraft.com.

MUELLER, BERNDT, physics professor; b. Markneukirchen, Germany, Feb. 8, 1950; came to US, 1990; Dr.Phil.Nat., U. Frankfurt, Fed. Republic Germany, 1973. Prof., physics U. Frankfurt, 1976-89, Duke U., Durham, NC, 1990—; assoc. lab. dir. Brookhaven Nat. Lab., 2013—. Author: Structured Vacuum, 1985, Quark-Gluon Plasma, 1985, Neural Networks, 1990; contbr. articles to profl. jours. Recipient Roentgen prize U. Giessen, 1975, Sr. Scientist award Humboldt Found., 1998, Jesse Beams award SESAPS, 2007. Fellow AAAS, Am. Phys. Soc. (chair divsn. nucl. physics, 2013, ORAU bd. dirs., 2012). Office Phone: 919-660-2570.*

MUELLER, EDWARD ALBERT, retired transportation engineer; b. Madison, Wis., May 12, 1923; s. Edward F. and Lulu (Wittl) M.; m. Margaret Wetzel, Sept. 12, 1953; children: Lynn, Karen. Student, U. Wis., 1941-43; BCE, Notre Dame U., 1947; cert. in traffic, Yale U., 1953, postgrad., 1952—53, Fla. State U., 1955-62; MCE, Catholic U. Am., 1967. Registered profl. engr., Fla. Project engr. Carl C. Crane, Inc., 1947-50; engr. Ammann & Whitney, Inc., Milw., 1950-52; rsch. asst. Yale U., 1953-55; asst. dir., dir. traffic and planning div. Fla. State Rd. Dept., Tallahassee, 1955-63; engr. traffic and ops. Transp. Rsch. Bd., Washington, 1963-70; sec. Fla. Dept. Transp., Tallahassee, 1970-72; exec. dir. Jacksonville (Fla.) Transp. Authority, 1972-80; mgr. transp. div. Reynolds, Smith & Hills, 1980-83; v.p. Morales and Shumer Engrs., Inc., 1983-95. Occasional lectr. U. Fla., 1971-76, U. N.Fla., 1974-76 Author: Steamboating on the St. Johns, 1979, Ocklawaha River Steamboats, 1983, St. Johns River Steamboats, 1986, Perilous Journeys, 1990, Upper Mississippi River Rafting Steamboats, 1995, Steamships of the Two Henrys, 1996, Images of St. Johns and Ocklawaha River Steamboats, 1999, Queen of Sea Routes, 2000, The Savannah Line, 2001, First Coast Steamboat Days, 2005, St. Johns Steamboat Days, 2006, (DVD) Suwannee River Steamboats, 2007, (DVD) Ocklawaha River Steamboats, 2008, (DVD) The Suwannee River in Song, (DVD) Henry Bradley Plant's Transportation Empire, Fla., (DVD) The Sunshine State in Song, (DVD) Maritime Music, (DVD) The Spanish American War in Song, 2010, (DVD) The Lusitania & the U-20, (DVD) Brunel's Great Ships, Railroad Music DVD, Sounds of the East Coast, Amazing Grace, Jacob Brook and the St. Johns Block; contbr. engring. articles to profl. jours. Mem. Fla. Com. of 100, 1970-72; bd. dirs. Luth. Social Svcs., Jacksonville, 1982-94, v.p., 1981-91; regional v.p. Fla.-Ga. dist. Luth. Laymen's League, 1982-92; curator Jacksonville Maritime Mus., 1990-99, mem. exec. com., 1989-95, 2008-10, pres., 1993-95, exec. dir., 1995-99. Recipient Disting. Svc. award Coll. Engring., U. Fla., 1975, Samuel Ward Stanton award for life achievement Steamship Hist. Soc. Am., 2001; named one of top 10 pub. works ofcls. in U.S., 1978. Mem. Southeastern Assn. State Hwy. Ofcls. (pres., v.p. 1971-72), Engrs. in Govt. (chmn., vice-chmn. sec.), Fla. Engring. Soc. (pres. Northeast chpt. 1982-83, Engr. of Yr. Tallahassee chpt. 1972, Jacksonville chpt. 1974, award for outstanding tech. achievement 1976, outstanding svc. to engring. profession 1989, James Shivler award 1993), Inst. Transp. Engrs. (pres. 1977, disting. svc. award Fla. sect. 1976), Fla. Transit Assn. (pres. 1974-75), Fla. Engring. Found. (sec. 1986-95). Lutheran. Home: 4734 Empire Ave Jacksonville FL 32207-2136 Home Phone: 904-398-9687.

MUELLER, NANCY SCHNEIDER, retired biology professor; b. Wooster, Ohio, Mar. 8, 1933; d. Gilbert Daniel and Winifred (Porter) Schneider; m. Helmut Charles Mueller, Jan. 27, 1959; 1 child, Karl Gilbert. AB in Biology, Coll. of Wooster, Ohio, 1955; MS in Zoology, U. Wis., Madison, 1957, PhD in Zoology, 1962. Instr. zoology U. Wis., Madison, 1966; asst. prof. poultry sci. and zoology N.C. State U., Raleigh, 1968-71; vis. prof. biology N.C. Ctrl. U., Durham, 1971-73, assoc. prof., 1973-79, prof., 1979-93; ret., 1993. Vis. scientist U. Vienna, Austria, 1975. Contbr. articles, abstracts to profl. publs. Mem. Soc. for Integrative and Comparative Biology, Wis. Acad. Sci., Arts and Letters, N.C. Acad. Sci., Sigma Xi. Home: 409 Moonridge Rd Chapel Hill NC 27516-5576 Business E-Mail: hmueller@email.unc.edu.

MUELLER, STEVEN L., energy executive; BS in Geol. Engring., Colo. Sch. Mines, 1975. Sr. v.p., exploration and prodn. Belco Oil & Gas Corp., joined, 1996; worked in geol. and engring. positions Tenneco Oil Co., 1975—88; exploration mgr., South La. Fina Oil & Chem. Co., 1988—92; v.p., exploitation American Exploration Co., 1992—96; sr. v.p., gen. mgr., Onshore The Houston Exploration Co., 2001—04; exec. v.p., COO Houston Exploration Co., 2004—; exec. v.p. CDX Gas LLC, 2007—08; COO Southwestern Energy Co., 2008, pres., 2009—, CEO, 2009—. Bd. dirs. Southwestern Energy Co., 2009—. Office: Southwestern Energy Co Ste 125 2350 N Sam Houston Pky E Houston TX 77032 Office Phone: 281-618-4700. Office Fax: 281-618-4820. Business E-Mail: steven_mueller@swn.com.

MUELLER, TRISH, marketing professional; AS, Adirondack Cmty. Coll., Queensbury, NY, 1982; BA, SUNY Plattsburgh, 1984. Dir. mktg. Montgomery Ward, 1995—97, dir. mktg. planning & advt. ops., 1997—99; sr. v.p. broadcast sales ShopNBC, ValueVision Media, 1999—2004; v.p. advt. American Signature Inc., 2004—06; sr. v.p. mktg. & advt. Sports Authority Inc., 2006—09; v.p. advt. The Home Depot, Inc., 2009—11, chief mktg. officer, 2011—. Named a Woman to Watch, Advertising Age, 2011. Office: The Home Depot Corp Hdqs 2455 Paces Ferry Rd Atlanta GA 30339

MUELLER-HEUBACH, EBERHARD, medical educator; b. Berlin, Feb. 24, 1942; came to U.S., 1968; s. Heinrich Gustav and Elisabeth (Heubach) M.; m. Cornelia Rosemarie Uffmann, Sept. 6, 1941; 1 child, Oliver Maximilian. MD, U. Koeln, 1966. Intern U. Koeln (Germany) Women's Hosp., 1967-68, Middlesex Gen. Hosp., New Brunswick, NJ, 1968-69; rsch. fellow Columbia U., 1969-71; resident Columbia-Presbyn. Med. Ctr., NYC, 1971-74, chief resident, 1974-75; asst. prof. Magee-Women's Hosp. U. Pitts., 1975-81, assoc. prof. Magee-Women's Hosp., 1981-89; prof., chmn. ob-gyn. Sch. Medicine Wake Forest U., Winston-Salem, 1989—2002, prof. ob-gyn., 2002—07, prof. emeritus, 2007—. Mem. editl. bd.: Ob-Gyn, 1999—2002. Mem. Am. Gyn.-Ob. Soc. (asst. sec. 1999-2001, sec. 2002-04, pres.-elect 2004-05, pres. 2005-06), Soc. Gynecol. Investigation, The Perinatal Rsch. Soc., Coun. Univ. Chairs Ob-Gyn. (pres. 1998-2000). Avocations: travel, art. E-mail: emueller@wfubmc.edu.

MUENCH, KARL HUGO, clinical geneticist; b. St. Louis, May 3, 1934; MD, Washington U., St. Louis, 1960. Diplomate Am. Bd. Med. Genetics. Intern Barnes Hosp., St. Louis, 1960-61; fellow in biological chemistry Stanford U. Sch. Medicine, 1961-65; staff mem. Jackson Meml. Hosp., Miami, Fla.; prof. medicine U. Miami Sch. Medicine. Mem. AMA, ACP, Am. Coll. Med. Genetics. Office: U Miami Sch Med Divsn Endocrinology Diabetes and Metabol PO Box 16960 Miami FL 33101-6960 Office Phone: 305-243-5950. Business E-Mail: kmuench@med.miami.edu.

MUENCH, ROBERT WILLIAM, bishop; b. Louisville, Dec. 28, 1942; s. William Anthony Muench and Mary Kathryn Allgeier. BA in Philosophy, Notre Dame Sem., New Orleans; MA in Edn., Cath. U. Am., Washington, 1968, grad. in Theol. Sem. Studies, 1968. Ordained priest Archdiocese of New Orleans, 1968, vicar, christian formation, 1977—81, archdiocesan vocations dir., 1981—83, dir., Pope John XXIII House for Vocation Discernment, 1983—90; various positions through rector St. John Vianney Prep Sch., 1969—76; assoc. pastor to co-pastor St. Matthias Parish, New Orleans, 1976—82; ordained bishop, 1990; aux. bishop Archdiocese of New Orleans, 1990—96; bishop Diocese of Covington, Ky., 1996—2001, Diocese of Baton Rouge, 2001—. Faculty mem. St. John Vianney Prep Sch., 1969—77. Named a Prelate of Honor, 1985. Roman Catholic. Office: Diocese of Baton Rouge PO Box 2028 1800 S Acadian Thruway Baton Rouge LA 70821 Office Phone: 225-387-0561. Office Fax: 225-336-8789.

MUFSON, MAURICE ALBERT, infectious diseases physician, educator; b. NYC, July 7, 1932; s. Max and Faye M.; m. Diane Cecile Weiss, Apr. 1, 1962; children: Michael Jeffrey, Karen Andrea, Pamela Beth. AB, Bucknell U., 1953; MD, NYU, 1957. Intern Bellevue Hosp., NYC, 1957-58, resident, 1958-59; chief resident Cook County Hosp., Chgo., 1965-66; sr. surgeon USPHS Lab. Infectious Diseases, NIH, 1961-65; from asst. prof. medicine to prof. U. Ill., 1965-76; prof. Marshall U., 1976—2002, prof. emeritus, 2002—, chmn. dept. medicine, 1976—2000, chmn. emeritus, 2000—. Vis. scientist Karolinska Inst., 1984-85. Contbr. articles to profl. jours. Served with U.S. Navy, 1959-61. WHO grantee, 1967; recipient Meet-the-Scholar award Marshall U., 1986, Rschr. of Yr. award Sigma Xi, Marshall U., 1989, Solomon A. Berson Alumni Achievement award in health sci. NYU Sch Medicine, 1997; co-recipient Louis Weinstein award Jour. Clin. Infectious Diseases, 1994; named to Greater Huntington Wall of Fame, 2002. Master ACP (traveling scholar 1987, Laureate award W.Va. chpt.), Infectious Diseases Soc. Am.; mem. AMA, Soc. Exptl. Biology and Medicine, Ctrl. Soc. Clin. Rsch., So. Soc. Clin. Investigation, W.Va. State Med. Assn., Assn. Profs. Medicine (counselor 1992-95, pres.-elect 1995-96, pres. 1996-97, past pres. 1997-98), Marshall U. Joan C. Edwards Sch. Medicine Alumni Assn. (hon.), Alpha Omega Alpha. Office: Marshall U Sch Medicine 1249 15th St 2nd Fl Huntington WV 25701 Home Phone: 304-522-9357; Office Phone: 304-691-1050. Personal E-mail: maurymufson@comcast.net. Business E-Mail: mufson@marshall.edu.

MUGAVERO, THOMAS COLLIER, lawyer; b. Greenwich, Conn., Nov. 1, 1962; s. Thomas Franklin and Ann Collier Mugavero; m. Patricia Lynn Scott, May 6, 1995. BA, Yale U., New Haven, Conn., 1985; M, JD, Georgetown U., Washington, 1989. Bar: Va. 1989, US Ct. Appeals (4th cir.) 1989, US Ct. Appeals (DC cir.) 1992, US Dist. Ct. (ea. dist.) Va. 1992, US Dist. Ct. DC 1993, US Dist. Ct. (we. dist.) Va. 1993, US Ct. Appeals (DC cir.) 1993, Md. 1995, US Dist. Ct. Md. 1997. Assoc. Tanaka Ritger Middleton, Washington, 1989—92; assoc., then ptnr. Montedonico, Hamilton & Altman, 1992—2002; staff counsel Hartford Ins. Co., Alexandria, Va., 2002—05; of counsel Whiteford, Taylor & Preston, LLP, Washington, 2005—. Mem.: ACLU, ABA, Fairfax Bar Assn., Fairfax C. of C., Fed. Bar Assn., Italian-Am. Bar Assn., Fairfax Bar Assn., Amnesty Internat. Liberal. Lutheran. Avocations: music, cooking. Office: Whiteford Taylor & Preston LLP 3190 Fairview Park Dr Ste 200 Falls Church VA 22042 Home: 4511 Brookside Dr Alexandria VA 22312 Office Fax: 202-327-6171. Business E-Mail: tmugavero@wtplaw.com.

MUHAMMAD, MUHSIN, II, investment company executive, retired professional football player; b. Lansing, Mich., May 5, 1973; s. Muhsin & Marian Muhammad; Christa Muhammad; children: Jordan Taylor, Chase Soen, Muhsin III, Kennedy Rain; 2 adopted children Grad, Mich. State U., 1996. Wide receiver Carolina Panthers, 1996—2004, 2008—10, Chgo. Bears, 2005—08; ret. NFL, 2010; mng. ptnr. Axum Capital Partners, Charlotte, 2008—. Color analyst, NFL Europe Fox Sports, 2002, 2003; post-season corr. NFL Network, 2004; team rep. NFL Players Assn., 2006—10. Founder, pres., The M2 Found. for Kids, 1999-, Ruckus House Learning Ctr., 2005-; bd. dirs. Big Brothers Big Sisters Charlotte, NC; spokesperson Men For Change, Ronald McDonald House Found. Recipient Chgo. Emmy award, Outstanding Achievement for Sports Programs, 2005; named Man of Yr., Carolina Panthers, 1999, First Team All-Pro, NFL, 2004; named to Nat. Football Conf. Pro Bowl Team, 1999, 2004. Christian. Achievements include leading the NFL in: receptions, 2000, receiving yards, 2004, receiving yards per game, 2004, receiving touchdowns, 2004. Office: Axum Capital Partners 6100 Fairview Rd Ste 1156 Charlotte NC 28210-4260 Office Phone: 704-334-3334.

MUHL, SHAUNA SULLIVAN, lawyer; BA magna cum laude, Cornell Univ.; M, Univ. Calif.; JD, Univ. Pa. Assoc. Willkie, Farr & Gallagher, NYC, Bond, Schoeneck & King, Syracuse, NY; counsel Cox Enterprises, Inc., Atlanta, 1994—2007, asst. v.p. governance, 2007—10, v.p. legal, corp. sec., 2010—. Editor: Univ Pa. Law Rev. Trustee The Atlanta Acad., Spruill Ctr. for the Arts. Mailing: Cox Enterprises Inc PO Box 105357 Atlanta GA 30348 Office Phone: 678-645-0000.

MUIR, DOUGLAS R., food service executive; BS in Bus. Adminstrn. & Acctg., Washington & Lee U., 1976. CPA. Various positions to audit ptnr. Price Waterhouse, Charlotte, NC, 1976—93; various sr. mgmt. roles to exec. v.p. and CFO Oakwood Homes, 1993—2004; cons. Krispy Kreme Doughnut Corp., 2004—05, chief acctg. officer, 2005—07; CFO Krispy Kreme Doughnuts, Inc., 2007—. Office: Krispy Kreme Doughnut Corp PO Box 83 Winston Salem NC 27102 Office Phone: 336-725-2981. Office Fax: 336-733-3794. Business E-Mail: DMuir@krispykreme.com.

MUIR, WARREN ROGER, chemist, educator; b. NY, 1945; s. Ernest Roger and Phyllis (Stirn) M.; children: Amy, Douglas, Michael, Gregory, Daniel. AB in Chemistry cum laude, Amherst Coll., 1967; MS in Chemistry, Northwestern U., Evanston, Ill., 1968, PhD in Chemistry, 1971; postgrad. in epidemiology, Johns Hopkins U., 1975-77. Sr. staff mem. environ. health Council on Environ. Quality, EPA, Washington, 1971-78; dir. Office of Toxic Substances, EPA, 1978-81; pres. Hampshire Rsch. Assocs., Inc., 1981-99, Hampshire Rsch. Inst., 1987-99; exec. dir. divsn. earth and life studies NRC/Nat. Acad. Scis., 1999—2013. Assoc. environ. health scis. Johns Hopkins U., 1981-99; rsch. prof. biology Am. U., 1985; sr. fellow INFORM, 1982-95; mem. Nat. Conf. Lawyers and Scientists, 1987-89; bd. environ. scis. and toxicology NRC, 1997-99. Contbr. articles on environ. quality to profl. jours. Mem., chair several Nat. Rsch. Coun. coms.; pres. Children's Friendship Project for No. Ireland, 1997-99, bd. dirs. 1995-2007, chair 1997-2002, bd. dirs. HasNa, Inc., 2003—, chair, 2009-, exec. dir., 2010-, Cyprus Friendship Program. Recipient NSF Acad. award, 1966, Howard Waters Doughty prize Amherst Coll., 1967, Forris Jewett Moore fellow, 1967; comdr., 1996, officer brother Most Venerable Order of St. John, 1992; co-recipient Adminstrs. award U.S. EPA, 1992, Cmty. Svc. award Nat. Acads., 2003. Mem.: AAAS, Am. Chem. Soc. Home: PO Box 981 Wolfeboro NH 03894-0981

MUKHERJEE, ANN (ANINDITA MUKHERJEE), marketing executive; b. Kolkata, India, Oct. 26, 1965; m. Dipu Mukherjee; 2 children. BA in Economics, U. Chgo., 1987, MBA in Fin., 1994. Product devel. Citibank Diners Club; joined mktg. team Kraft Foods Inc.; group v.p. mktg. Frito-Lay North America, Inc., 2006—09, sr. v.p., chief mktg. officer, 2009—. Named Marketer of the Yr., Brandweek, 2007; named a Woman to Watch, Advt. Age, 2007. Office: Frito-Lay PO Box 660634 Dallas TX 75266-0634 Office Phone: 972-334-7000.

MUKHTAR, SAQIB, agricultural engineer, educator; BS in Agrl. Engring., U. Agriculture, Faisalabad, Pakistan, 1981; MS in Agrl. Engring., Iowa State U., 1984, PhD in Agrl. Engring., 1989. Lic. Engr., Tex. Rsch. officer On Farm Water Mgmt. Rsch. Project, U. Agriculture, Faisalabad, Pakistan, 1981; civil engr. Fort Dodge Area Office USDA Natural Resources Conservation Svc., 1990—91, civil engr. Engring. Project Office Centerville, Iowa, 1991—93; rsch. asst., dept. agrl. & biosystems engring. Iowa State U., Ames, 1982—89, postdoctoral rsch. assoc., dept. agrl. & biosystems engring., 1989—90, agrl. engring. field specialist, 1993—98; extension agrl. engr. Texas A&M U., College Station, 1998—, asst. prof., 1999—2004, assoc. prof., 2004—. Faculty, Ctr. for Agrl. Air Quality Engring. and Sci. Texas A&M U., College Station, 2002—, faculty water mgmt. and hydrologic sci. interdisciplinary grad. degree program, 2008—; several committee memberships at Tex. A&M U. and Iowa State U. Contbr. several articles to profl. jours. Coord. Tex. Animal Manure Mgmt. Issues, 1998—; chair Tex. Animal Manure Mgmt. Conf., 1999, 2009. Recipient USDA Cert. of Merit, 1992, Governor's Citation-State of Iowa, 1995—96. Mem.: Am. Soc. Agrl. and Biol. Engineers (awards com., Iowa sect. 1994—95, Educational Aids Blue Ribbon Award in the Comprehensive Publication Category for Publication-Managing Contaminated Animal and Plant Materials-Field Gu 2009), Gamma Sigma Delta. Office: Dept Biological & Agricultural Engring Texas A&M U 207A Scoates Hall College Station TX 77843-2117 Office Phone: 979-458-1019. Office Fax: 979-847-8828. Business E-Mail: mukhtar@tamu.edu.

MULFORD, CLAY (ROSS CLAYTON MULFORD), think-tank executive, lawyer; b. Bethesda, Md., Mar. 13, 1956; s. Ross Leonard and Diane (Clayton) M.; m. Nancy Elizabeth Perot, June 6, 1987; children: Ross Clayton, Price Perot, Benjamin Fell. BA cum laude, Amherst Coll., 1978; MBA, JD, U. Va., 1982. Bar: Tex. 1982. From assoc. to ptnr. Hughes and Luce, LLP, Dallas, 1982—2004; ptnr. Jones Day, Dallas, 2004—07; COO Nat. Math & Sci. Initiative (NMSI), Dallas, 2007. Fellow Inst. Politics, vis. lectr. John F. Kennedy Sch. Govt., Harvard U., 1995; trustee Citizens Rsch. Found., 1994—; gen. counsel, sr. advisor Perot '92 Presdl. Campaign, Dallas, 1992; mem. nat. adv. com. Money, Politics and the Pub. Voice project LWV, 1995—; fellow Brit.-Am. Project Johns Hopkins Sch. Advanced Internat. Studies and the Royal Inst. Internat. Affairs, 1995. Contbr. articles to profl. jours. Dir. Dallas Zoo, 1990—, Episcopal Sch., Dallas, 1991—, Ctr. for Human Nutrition S.W. Med. Sch., U. Tex., 1993—, Baylor Hosp. Found., 1997—; gen. counsel Perot 96, 1996. Mem. ABA (spl. select com. Coalition for Justice 1993-94, adv. commn. on election law 1994-95, 99-2001, standing com. on election law 1995-99), State Bar Tex. Episcopalian. Office: National Math & Science Initiative (NMSI) 325 N St Paul St Ste 2900 Dallas TX 75201 Office Phone: 214-665-2548.

MULHERN, MARK F., electric power company executive; b. 1960; Grad., St. Bonaventure U., 1982; grad. nuclear exec. program, MIT. CPA, cert. Mgmt. Acct., Internal Auditor. Acctg. positions Price Waterhouse, Syracuse, NY; CFO Hydra Co. Enterprises (subs. Niagara Mohawk); v.p., contr. Progress Energy, Inc., 1996—97, v.p., treas., 1997—2000, v.p., strategic planning, 2000—03; sr. v.p., competitive comml. ops. Progress Ventures (subs. Progress Energy), 2003—05, pres., 2005—08; sr. v.p., fin. Progress Energy, Inc., 2007—08, sr. v.p., CFO, 2008—11; exec. v.p. & chief adminstrv. officer Duke Energy Corp., Charlotte, NC, 2011—. Bd. dir. Microcell Corp.; mem. fin. adv. com. Edison Elec. Inst. Served in a number of vol. and leadership roles St. Michaels Elementary Sch., Leadership NC, Planning Inst. Ctrl. NY. Office: Duke Energy Corp 550 S Tryon St Charlotte NC 28202

MULKEY, JACK CLARENDON, retired library director; b. Shreveport, La., Oct. 31, 1939; s. Jack Youmans and Hilda Lillian (Beatty) Mulkey; m. Mary Lynn Shepherd, Jan. 30, 1971; 1 child, Mary Clarendon. BA, Centenary Coll., 1961; postgrad. (Rotary scholar), U. Dijon, France, 1961-62, Duke U. Law Sch., 1962-63; MS,

La. State U., 1969. Jr. exec. Lykes Bros. S.S. Co., 1964-66; asst. dir. admissions Centenary Coll. of La., 1966-67; head reference services and acquisitions Shreveport Pub. Library, 1968-71; dir. Green Gold Library System of N.W. La., 1971-73; mgmt. cons. Miss. Library Commn., 1973-74, asst. dir., 1974-76, dir., 1976-78, Jackson Met. Library System, 1978-85; assoc. dir. Ark. State Library, 1986-2000; State Librarian of Ark., 2000—05; ret., 2005. Adj. prof. U. So. Miss. Grad. Sch. Libr. Sci., 1979—; treas., bd. dirs. Southeastern Library Network (SOLINET), 1985-86; cons. in field; mem. White House Conf. Taskforce on Libraries and Info. Services, 1980—. Chmn. Miss. Govs. Conf. on Libraries, 1979; chmn. Miss. delegation White House Conf. on Libraries, 1979; hon. del. White House Conf. on Librs., 1991. Served with USAF, 1963-64. Mem. ALA (chmn. state libr. agy. sect. 1995-97), Southeastern Libr. Assn. (bd. dirs. 1994—), Miss. Libr. Assn. (pres. 1981-82), Ark. Libr. Assn. (exec. bd. dirs. 1994—), Chief Officers of State Libr. Agys., Phi Alpha Delta, Beta Phi Mu, Omicron Delta Kappa, Phi Kappa Phi. Episcopalian. Home: 1805 Martha Dr Little Rock AR 72212-3840 Office: 1 Capitol Mall Little Rock AR 72201-1049 Personal E-mail: jmulkey@webtv.net.

MULKEY, KIM, women's college basketball coach; b. Santa Ana, Calif., May 17, 1962; children: Makenzie, Kramer. B, La. Tech U., 1984. Asst. coach La. Tech U. Lady Techsters, 1985—96, assoc. head coach, 1996—2000; head coach Baylor U. Lady Bears, 2000—. Mem. women's nat. team USA Basketball, 1982—84. Co-author (with P. May): (autobiography) Won't Back Down, 2007. Recipient Gold medal, Pan Am. Games, 1983, Summer Olympic Games, 1984, James Corbett award, La., 1984; named Naismith Small Player of Yr., 1984, Nat. Coach of Yr., Real Sport Mag., 2000, Big 12 Coach of Yr., Dallas Morning News, 2001, Waco Tribune-Herald, 2001, Sr. Coll. Coach of Yr., Tex. Assn. Basketball Coaches, 2002, Big 12 Conf. Coach of Yr., 2005, 2012, 2013, Nat. Coach of Yr., AP, 2012; named to Nat. HS Hall of Fame, 1985, La. HS Hall of Fame, 1986, La. Sports Writers Hall of Fame, 1990, La. Tech Athletics Hall of Fame, 1992, Women's Basketball Hall of Fame, 2000, Academic Hall of Fame, Coll. Sports Info. Directors America, 2003, Baylor Athletic Hall of Fame, 2007. Achievements include head coach of the NCAA Women's Final Four Division I National Championship winning Baylor University Lady Bears, 2005, 2012. Office: Baylor Univ Athletics 1500 S University Parks Dr Waco TX 76706 Office Phone: 254-710-3947. Business E-Mail: kim_mulkey@baylor.edu.

MULLANE, JOHN FRANCIS, pharmaceutical executive; b. NYC, Mar. 10, 1937; s. John Gerard and Rita Ann (Hoben) Mullane; m. Ruth Ann Cecka, Nov. 17, 1962; children: Rosemarie, Michael, Kathleen, Therese, Thomas. MD, SUNY Med. Ctr., 1963; PhD, SUNY, 1968; JD, Fordham U., 1977. Bar: NY 1978, DC 1979. Assoc. med. dir. Ayerst Labs. div. Am. Home Products Corp., NYC, 1973-75, dir. clin. research, 1975-76, v.p. clin., 1977, v.p. sci., 1978-82, sr. v.p., 1982, exec. v.p., 1983-88; pres. Mullane Health Care Cons., NYC and Sarasota, Fla., 1989—; dir. drug devel. DuPont Med. Products, Wilmington, Del., 1990; sr. v.p. DuPont-Merck, Wilmington, 1991-94; exec. v.p. Amylin Pharms., 1994-96. Contbr. articles to profl. jours. Served to lt. col. US Army, 1970-73 Recipient Upjohn Achievement award, 1970; NY Heart Assn. Crawford-Maynard fellow, 1966-68 Fellow Am. Coll. Clin. Pharmacology; mem. ABA, Am. Soc. Clin. Pharmacology and Therapeutics, Am. Assn. Study of Liver Diseases, Misty Creek Country Club (pres. 2004-2005). Roman Catholic. Achievements include development of major drugs including Inderal, Premarin, Lodine, Coumadin, Cozaar. Avocation: golf. Home and Office: 9047 Misty Creek Dr Sarasota FL 34241-9542 E-mail: johnmullane9047@comcast.net.

MULLANY, HANK, retail executive; m. Jane Mullany; children: Mark Mullany, John Mullany. BBA in Acctg. & Mgmt., Temple U., MBA in Fin.; Exec. Devel. Program, Harvard U. With Fleming Companies, Inc. (Phila. Divs.), Oklahoma City, 1981—87, Coopers & Lybrand LLP, Phila.; pres., family markets, former bd. dirs. Genuardi's; exec. v.p, COO Kimmel Ctr., 2003—06; sr. v.p., pres., Northeast Divsn. Wal-Mart Stores, Inc., exec. v.p., pres., Walmart North, 2010; CEO ServiceMaster Co., 2011—. Bd. dirs. ServiceMaster Global Holdings, Inc. Bd. trustees Temple U.; vol. Woodlynde Sch., Strafford; bd. mem. Memphis Tomorrow, Memphis Shelby Growth Alliance; co-chair Saint Joseph's U. Loyola Soc. Exec. Coun; bd. visitor Saint Joseph's U. Erivan K. Haub Bus. Sch.; mem. adv. bd. Archbishop Carroll HS Recipient Seashore House Vol. of the Yr. award, The Children's Hosp. Office: ServiceMaster Co 1929 Allen Pkwy Houston TX 77019 Office Phone: 713-522-5141.

MULLEN, DAN, college football coach; b. Manchester, NH, Apr. 27, 1972; m. Megan West; 1 child, Canon. BS in Exercise and Sport Sci., Ursinus Coll., Collegeville, Pa., 1994; MEd, Wagner Coll., Staten Island, NY, 1996. Wide receivers coach Wagner Coll. Seahawks, 1994—95, Columbia U. Lions, 1996—97; grad. asst., offensive Syracuse U. Orange, 1998, U. Notre Dame Fighting Irish, 1999—2000; quarterbacks coach Bowling Green State U. Falcons, 2001—02, U. Utah Utes, 2003—04; offensive coord., quarterbacks coach U. Fla. Gators, 2005—08; head football coach Miss. State U. Bulldogs, 2008—. Office: Miss State Univ Football PO Box 5327 Mississippi State MS 39762 Office Phone: 662-325-2539.

MULLEN, GRAHAM CALDER, federal judge; b. Charlotte, NC, 1940; BA, Duke U., 1962, JD, 1969. Bar: NC 1969. Ptnr. Mullen, Holland, Cooper, Morrow, Wilder & Sumner, 1969-90; judge US Dist. Ct. (we. dist.) NC, Charlotte, 1990—98, chief judge, 1998—2005, sr. judge, 2005—. Lt. USN, 1962—66. Mem.: Mecklenburg County Bar Assn., NC Bar Assn. (bd. gov. 1983—88). Office: US Courthouse 401 W Trade St Rm 230 Charlotte NC 28202-1619 Office Phone: 704-350-7450. Business E-Mail: graham_mullen@ncwd.uscourts.gov.

MULLEN, RON, insurance company executive, wealth manager; b. Tex., Aug. 8, 1939; s. Durward Lacy and Blanche V. (Coulson) M.; m. Carole King, Dec. 29, 1959; children: Lacy Lynne Holcomb, Misty Kay. Student, Abilene Christian Coll., 1957-58, San Antonio Coll., 1958-59; BBA, S.W. Tex. State U., 1965. C.L.U., Chartered Fin. Cons. City council mem. City of Austin, 1977-83, mayor, 1983-85; mgr. Prin. Fin. Group, Austin, 1965-98, Ron Mullen & Assocs. Inc., Austin, 1966—, InNet Fin. Group; prin. Small Employer Benefits L.P. Chmn. TML Ins. Trust Fund Com., 1983—; mem. Gov.'s Task Force on State Employees Health Ins. Benefits, Austin, 1984 Chmn. Austin Transp. Study Com., Austin, 1983—, Greater Austin-San Antonio Corridor Coun., 1984—, Social Policy Adv. Com., Austin, 1979-80, March of Dimes campaign, Austin, 1974-75; co-chmn. Consumers United for Rail Equity, Austin, 1983—; v.p. Austin Symphony Orch., 1974-75; mem. exec. com. Capital Area Planning Coun., Austin, 1976—, exec. bd. Tex. Mcpl. League, Austin, 1983—, Gov.'s Task Force on Indigent Health Care, Austin, 1984, Tex. Adv. Commn. on Intergovtl. Rels., Austin, 1981—; chmn. Infant Parent Tng. Ctr., 1985-98; bd. dirs., chmn. South MoPac Transp. Com., 1986-87; life mem. Austin Jaycees, bd. dirs., 1974-75; vice-chmn. Mental Health Mental Retardation Bd.; vice chmn. South Tex. Audio Reader Svc.; bd. dirs. BBB, Inc., Hyde Park Bapt. Sch., 1999—.deacon, Austin Baptist Ch. Recipient Road Hand award Tex. Dept. Hwys. and Transp., 1985, award for regional statesmanship Greater Austin-San Antonio Corridor Commn.; named Boss of Yr., Treaty Oaks chpt. Am. Bus. Women's Assn., 1978, Nat. Mgr. of Yr., Bankers Life Ins. Co., 1977, 82, 84-85, Alumnus of Yr. Austin Jaycees, 1988-90. Mem. Am. Coll. Life Underwriters (pres.), Tex. Assn. Life Underwriters (pres. 1997-98), Austin Assn. Life Underwriters (pres. 1974-75), Austin Gen. Agts. and Mgrs. Assn. (pres. 1978-80), Sales and Mktg. Execs. of Austin (pres. 1972-73), Downtown Rotary (pres. 1996-97), Tex. Assn. Ins. and fin. Advisors (nat. committeeman). Baptist. Home: 6902 Mesa Dr Austin TX 78731-2822 Personal E-mail: ron9991@msn.com.

MULLEN, TIMOTHY W., food service executive; V.p. info. svcs. Cracker Barrel Old Country Store, Inc. Office: Cracker Barrel Old Country Store Inc 305 Hartmann Dr Lebanon TN 37088-0787 Office Phone: 615-444-5533. Office Fax: 615-443-9818.

MULLENDORE, WALTER EDWARD, retired economist; b. Harrah, Okla., Apr. 22, 1940; s. Newton and Ida Minnie (Lohmann) M.; m. Edra Janell Havenstrite, July 4, 1963; children: Matthew Edward, Karen Kay, Mark Andrew. BS, Okla. State U., 1961, MS, 1963; PhD in Econs., Iowa State U., 1968. Grad. asst. Okla. State U., 1961-63; instr. Iowa State U., 1965-67; mem. faculty dept. econs. U. Tex., Arlington, 1968—2002, prof., 1975—2002, dean Coll. of Bus., 1980—93; ret., 2002. Contbr. articles to profl. jours. Served with U.S. Army, 1963-65. Mem. Mo. Valley Econ. Assn. (v.p. 1980-81, pres. 1982-83), Gt. S.W. Rotary (pres. 1989-90), Omicron Delta Epsilon. Methodist. Home: 8003 John T White Rd Fort Worth TX 76120-3611

MULLENIX, LINDA SUSAN, law educator; b. NYC, Oct. 16, 1950; d. Andrew Michael and Roslyn Marasco; children: Robert Bartholomew, John Theodore, William Joseph. BA, CCNY, 1971; M Philosophy, Columbia U., 1974; PhD Pres.'s fellow, 1977; JD, Georgetown U., 1980. Bar: DC 1981, US Dist. Ct. DC 1981, US Ct. Appeals (DC cir.) 1981, US Supreme Ct. 1986, Tex. 1991, US Ct. Appeals (5th cir.) 1995. U. Md. European divsn., Ramstein, Germany, 1974; adj. instr. Fordham U., NYC, 1975—76, adj. asst. prof., 1977; instr. NY Inst. Tech., NYC, 1976; assoc. prof., lectr. George Washington U., Washington, 1977-80; asst. prof. Am. U., Washington, 1979; assoc. Pierson, Ball & Dowd, Washington, 1980-81; clin. prof. Loyola U. Law Sch., LA, 1981-82; asst. prof. Cath. U. Law Sch., Washington, 1983—86; assoc. prof., 1986-90; prof., 1990; Reuschlein disting. vis. chair Villanova Law Sch., 2000. Vis. asst. prof. CCNY, 1977, Cooper Union Advancement Sci., Art, NYC, 1977, Loyola U. Law Sch., LA, 1982-83; jud. fellow U.S. Supreme ct. and fed. Jud. Ctr., 1989-90; Bernard J. Ward Centennial prof. U. Tex., 1991-2001, Morris and Rita Atlas chair in advocacy, 2001—; vis. prof. Harvard Law Sch., 1994-95, Mich. Law Sch., 1996; resident scholar Rockefeller Found. Bellagio (Italy) Study Ctr., 2002; Fulbright scholar Disting. Chair in Law, Trento, Italy, 2007. Author: Mass Tort Litigation: Cases and Materials, 1996, 2d cd 2008, Civil Procedure Roadmap, 1997, 2d cd 2006, Casenotes: Federal Courts, 1997, ExamPro: Civil Procedure, 1998, 2d cd 2007, State Class Actions: Practice and Procedure, 2000, Civil Procedure, 2004, Leading Cases in Civil Procedure, 2010; co-author: Understanding Federal Courts, 1998, Federal Courts in the Twenty-First Century, 1996, 3d edit., 2007; Moore's Federal Practice and Procedure, 1991, 97, and annual updates; editor bibliographies Polit. Theory, A. Jour. Polit. Philosophy, 1972-74, The Tax Lawyer Jour., 1978-80; columnist The National Law Jour., 1998—; contbr. editor preview of U.S. Supreme Ct. Cases; co-reporter Report and Plan of Civil Justice Reform Act Adv. Group, S.d., Tex., 1991; assoc. reporter ALI, Restatement of the Law Governing Lawyers; contbr. articles to profl. jours. Alt. del. Dem. State Conv., 1980. Fellow NDEA, 1971-74; NY State Regents Scholar, 1967-71. Fellow Tex. Bar Found.; mem. ABA (reporter task force on class actions 1995-97), Internat. Assn. Procedural Law, Am. Law Inst., DC Bar Assn. (com. on ethics, CLE and the Model Rules 1987), Am. Assn. Law Schs. (exec. com. sect. on civil proc. 1987-88, exec. com. sec. on conflicts of law 1991-92, chair prof. devel. com. 1991-93), Jour. Legal Edn. (editl. bd. 1997-1999), Revista Processo-(editl. bd. mem.), Phi Beta Kappa. Home: 722 Crystal Creek Dr Austin TX 78746-4730 Office: U Tex Sch Law 727 E Dean Keeton St Austin TX 78705-3224 Office Phone: 512-232-1375. Business E-Mail: lmullenix@law.utexas.edu.

MULLER, EDWARD ROBERT, energy executive, lawyer; b. Phila., Mar. 26, 1952; s. Rudolph E. and Elizabeth (Steiner) M.; m. Patricia Eileen Bauer, Sept. 27, 1980; children: Margaret Anne, John Frederick. AB summa cum laude, Dartmouth Coll., 1973; JD, Yale U., 1976. Assoc. Leva, Hawes, Symington, Martin & Oppenheimer, Washington, 1977-83; dir. legal affairs Life Scis. group Whittaker Corp., Arlington, Va., 1983-84; v.p. Whittaker Health Svcs., Arlington, Va., 1984-85; v.p., gen. counsel, sec. Whittaker Corp., LA, 1985-93, chief adminstrv. officer, 1988-92, CFO, 1992-93, bd. dirs., 1993-99; v.p., gen. counsel, sec. BioWhittaker, Inc., Walkersville, Md., 1991-93; pres., CEO, bd. dirs. Edison Mission Energy, Irvine, Calif., 1993-2000; chmn., pres., CEO Mirant Corp., Atlanta, 2005—10; chmn., CEO GenOn Energy (merger of Mirant & RRI Energy), Houston, 2010—. Bd. dirs. Oasis Residential, Inc., Las Vegas, 1995—98, Global Marine, Inc., Houston, 1997—2001, GlobalSantaFe Corp., Houston, 2001—07, Interval, Inc., Marina del Rey, Calif., 2000—05, Strategic Data Corp., Santa Monica, Calif., 2001—05, The Keith Cos., Inc., Irvine, Calif., 2001—05, RigNet, Inc., Houston, 2002—05, RealEnergy, Inc., Woodland Hills, Calif., 2003—05, Ormat Tech., Inc., Sparks, Nev., 2004—05, Transocean Ltd., Zug, 2007—; mem. Brookings Task Force on Civil Justice Reform, 1988—89; chmn. U.S.-Philippines Bus. Com., 1998—2000; adv. bd. Tennenbaum Capital Ptnrs., LLC, LA, 1997—2003; mem. Coun. on Fgn. Rels., 1998—, Pacific Coun. on Internat. Policy, 1998—; dep. chmn. Contact Energy Ltd., Wellington, New Zealand, 1999—2000. Trustee Exceptional Children's Found., L.A., 1988-94, treas., 1988-93; co-chair Internat. Energy Devel. Coun., Washington, 1993-00; bd. govs. Jr. Achievement of Orange County and the Inland Empire, 1995-96; mem. Pres. Leadership Coun., Dartmouth Coll., 2003—; trustee Riverview Sch., East Sandwich, Mass, 2004—, chmn., 2008-; bd. advisors The Pathway Program UCLA Ext., LA, 2004—; bd. councilors Carter Ctr., Atlanta, 2008-. Office: GenOn Energy 1000 Main St Houston TX 77002 Office Phone: 832-357-3000.

MULLER, KIRK, professional hockey coach, former professional hockey player; b. Kingston, Ont., Canada, Feb. 8, 1966; m. Stacey Muller; children: Brittney, Kourtney, Bryelle, Kira. Left wing NJ Devils, 1984—91, Montreal Canadiens, 1991—95, capt., 1994—95; left wing NY Islanders, 1995, Toronto Maple Leafs, 1995—97, Fla. Panthers, 1997—99, Dallas Stars, 1999—2003; head coach Queen's U. Golden Gaels, Kingston, Ont., Canada, 2005—06; asst. coach Montreal Canadiens, 2006—11; head coach Milwaukee Admirals, 2011, Carolina Hurricanes, 2011—. Mem. Team Canada, Olympic Games, Sarajevo, 1984. Achievements include being a member of Stanley Cup Champion Montreal Canadiens, 1993. Office: Carolina Hurricanes Hockey Club RBC Center 1400 Edwards Mill Rd Raleigh NC 27607

MULLER, PATRICIA ANN, nursing administrator, educator; b. NYC, July 22, 1943; d. Joseph H. and Rosanne (Bautz) Felter; m. David G. Smith, Mar. 19, 1988; children: Frank M. Muller III, Kimberly M. Muller. BSN, Georgetown U., 1965; MA, U. Tulsa, 1978, EdD, 1983. RN. Coord. staff devel. St. Francis Hosp., Tulsa, 1978—79, asst. dir. for nursing svc., nursing edn., 1979—82, dir. dept. edn., 1982—98, St. Francis Health Sys., 1998—2002, cons., 2002—; CEO Smith Assocs. LLC, 2002—. Mem. faculty Okla. U., Northeastern U., Tulsa U.; presenter at confs. and convs. Contbg. editor JOPAN, 1992-2001; contbr. articles to profl. jours. Mem. Leadership Tulsa, 1991; bd. dirs. Am. Heart Assn., Ronald McDonald House. Mem. ANA, Nat. League for Nursing, Am. Soc. for Nursing Svc. Adminstrs., Am. Soc. for Health Manpower Edn. and Tng., Okla. Nurses Assn., Okla. Orgn. of Nurse Execs. (pres. 1992-93), Sigma Theta Tau. Home and Office: 6203 W Utica Ct Broken Arrow OK 74011 Office Phone: 918-671-7767. E-mail: mullsmi@aol.com.

MULLIGAN, JOHN J., tobacco company executive; Student, Holy Cross Coll.; BA in Liberal Arts, St. John's U., NYC, 1976; M in Bus. and Acctg., Fordham U., NYC, 1981. With Mfrs. Hanover Leasing Corp., 1979—86; mgr. lease financing Philip Morris Capital Corp., 1986—87, dir. structured fin., 1987—94, v.p. lease/structured fin., 1994—2001, pres., CEO, 2001—. Office: Altria Corperate Services 615 Maury St Richmond VA 23224-4121

MULLIKIN, THOMAS WILSON, mathematics professor; b. Flintville, Tenn., Jan. 9, 1928; s. Houston Yost and Daisy (Copeland) M.; m. Mildred Virginia Sugg, June 14, 1952; children: Sarah Virginia, Thomas Wilson, James Copeland. Student, U. South, 1946-47; AB, U. Tenn., 1950; postgrad., Iowa State U., 1952-53; A.M., Harvard, 1954, PhD, 1958. Mathematician Rand Corp., Santa Monica, Calif., 1957-64; prof. math. Purdue U., 1964-93, interim v.p., dean grad. sch., 1991-93, dean grad. sch., prof. math emeritus, 1993—. Served with USNR, 1950-52. Mem.: AAAS, Am. Math. Soc. Home: 104 Club Ct Cape Carteret NC 28584-9736 Personal E-mail: tmullikin@ec.rr.com.

MULLIN, BERNARD JAMES, sport management and marketing consultant; b. Liverpool, Eng., May 3, 1949; came to US, 1973; s. Bernard F. and Mary A. Mullin; m. Valerie Mullin; children: Julie, Lara, Steven 1 stepchild, Chad. BA in Bus. Studies, Coventry U., Eng., 1972; MS in Mktg., U. Kans., 1974, MBA, 1976, PhD in Bus., 1978. Mgr. mktg. rsch. Brit. Leyland Motor Corp., Oxford, England, 1970—73; mktg. devel. mgr. Serck Tubes Ltd., Birmingham, England, 1973; instr. U. Kans., Lawrence, 1974-77; prof. sport mgmt. U. Mass., Amherst, 1977-86; pres. NSM Mgmt. Cons., Amherst, 1979-86; sr. v.p. bus. Maj. League Baseball Pitts. Pirates, 1986—91; sr. v.p. bus. ops. Maj. League Baseball Colo. Rockies, 1991—93; pres., gen. mgr. Internat. Hockey League Denver Grizzlies, 1993; vice chancellor athletics U. Denver; sr. v.p. mktg. and team bus. ops. NBA, 2000—04; pres., CEO Atlanta Spirit, LLC (parent co. of NBA Atlanta Hawks, NHL Atlanta Thrashers and Philips Arena), 2004—08; founder, prin. The Aspire Group, Inc., Atlanta, 2008—. Author: Sport Marketing. Chmn. bd. mgmt. YMCA Pitts., 1988; bd. mem. Ctrl. Atlanta Progress, Atlanta Sports Coun., Metro Atlanta C. of C. Mem. Rotary Internat., Beta Gamma Sigma. Roman Catholic. Avocations: golf, tennis, soccer, reading. Office: The Aspire Group Inc 3340 Peachtree Rd NE Ste 1800 Atlanta GA 30326 Office Phone: 404-814-5250. Business E-Mail: bernie.mullin@theaspiregroupinc.com.

MULLIN, JOHN HATCHMAN, III, board member; b. Atlanta, June 15, 1941; s. John Hatchman and Dorothy (Ewing) M.; m. Susan Spaulding, July 8, 1967; children: John Hatchman, Harrison Spaulding. BA, Washington & Lee U., 1963; MBA, U. Pa., 1969. Assoc. Dillon, Read & Co., Inc., 1969-73, v.p., 1973-76, sr. v.p., 1976-78, mng. dir., 1978—89; chmn. Ridgeway Farm LLC, Brookneal, Va., 1989—. Bd. dir. Ryland Group, Columbia, Md., 1982-83, Crystal Brands, Inc., Southport, Conn., Sonoco Products Co., 2002-. Served to lt. (j.g.) USNR, 1963-67. Mem. Beta Gamma Sigma Clubs: Piedmont Driving (Atlanta); Blooming Grove Hunting and Fishing (Hawley, Pa.); Hights Casino (Bklyn.) (gov.). Office: Sonoco Products Co Bd Directors 1 N 2nd St Hartsville SC 29550-3305 Office Phone: 843-383-7000. Office Fax: 843-383-7008. Business E-Mail: john.mullin@sonoco.com.

MULLIN, MARKWAYNE, United States Representative from Oklahoma, plumber, rancher; b. Tulsa, July 26, 1977; m. Christie Mullin, 1998; children: Jim, Andrew, Larra. Attended, Mo. Valley Coll., 1996; AAS in Construction Technology, Okla. State U. Inst. Technology, 2010. Owner Mullin Plumbing, Mullin Farms, Mullin Properties, Mullin Services, 1997—; radio host "House Talk"; mem. US Congress from 2nd Okla. Dist., 2013—, US House Transp. & Infrastructure Com., 2013—, US House Natural Resources Com., 2013—. Mem.: Cherokee Natoin. Republican. Pentecostal. Office: US House of Representatives 1113 Longworth House Office Bldg Washington DC 20515 also: 104 S Muskogee Ave Claremore OK 74017 Office Phone: 202-225-2701, 918-341-9336. Office Fax: 202-225-3038, 918-342-4806.*

MULLINAX, A. R., energy executive; b. Cameron, Tex., 1954; BBA in Acctg., Tex. A&M; grad. Exec. Program, Stanford U. CPA Tex. Internal audit staff, sr. analyst corp. planning. Tex. Eastern Corp., Tex., 1977—80, supr., mgr. natural gas acctg. area, v.p. info. svcs. and controls Tex., 1985—96; sr. v.p., shared svcs. Duke Power Co., 1997—99; pres., CEO DukeNet Comm., 2002; exec. v.p., bus. svcs. Duke Energy Corp., Charlotte, NC, 2003, sr. v.p., chief info. officer. Mem.: AICPA, Tex. Soc. CPAs. Office: Duke Energy Corp 526 S Church St Charlotte NC 28202-1803 Office Phone: 704-594-6200. Office Fax: 704-382-4964. Business E-Mail: amullinax@duke-energy.com.

MULLINS, KEM M., healthcare company executive; B in Health Care Mgmt., Marshall U., Huntington, W.Va.; M in Fin., Morehead State U., Ky. COO Atlanta Med. Ctr., Atlanta, Ga., Regional Med. Ctr. of NE Ark., Jonesboro, Ark; assoc. adminstr. U. Med. Ctr., Lebanon, Tenn., Williamson Memorial Hosp., Williamson, W.Va.; CEO St. Francis Hospital, Bartlett, Tenn., 2006—. Chmn., Economic Devel. Plan Bartlett Area C. of C. Recipient Cir. of Excellence award, Tenet Healthcare Corp., 2005. Office: Tenet Healthcare Corp 1445 Ross Ave Ste 1400 Dallas TX 75202 Office Phone: 469-893-2200. Office Fax: 469-893-8600.

MULLINS, PAT, political organization administrator, insurance company executive; m. Jackie Mullins; children: Cathy, Steve, Mike, Debbie. BA, Columbia U.; JD, George Washington U. Dir. assn. devel. Markel Insurance, Glen Allen, Va. Chmn. Fairfax County Rep. Com., 1990—96, Louisa County Rep. Com., Rep. Party of Va., 2009—; pres. Fairfax County Coun. of PTA, Turnpike Basketball League. Mem.: Certified Horsemanship Assn., Annandale C. of C. (pres.), Annandale Rotary Club (pres.), Nat. Therapeutic Riding Assn. (pres.). Republican. Office: Republican Party of Virginia Richard D Obenshain Ctr 115 E Grace St Richmond VA 23219 Office Phone: 804-780-0111. Office Fax: 804-343-1060.*

MULLIS, JEFF E., state legislator; m. Teresa Mullis; 3 children. Exec. dir. NW Ga. Joint Develop. Agy.; chief Walker County Fire & Rescue; mem. Dist. 53 Ga. State Senate, 2001—. Republican. Office: 212 English Rd Chickamauga GA 30707 Office Phone: 706-375-1776. Business E-Mail: jeff.mullis@senate.ga.gov.

MULVA, JAMES JOSEPH (JIM MULVA), corporate board member, retired oil industry executive; b. Oshkosh, Wis., June 19, 1946; m. Miriam Mulva; 2 children. BBA in Finance, U. Tex., 1968, MBA in Finance, 1969; DEng (hon.), Colo. Sch. Mines, 2010. Mgmt. trainee, treas. Phillips Petroleum Co., Bartlesville, Okla., 1973, asst. treas. London, 1974—76, mgr. fgn. exchange & investment Bartlesville, Okla., 1976—80, v.p., treas. Europe/Africa divsn. London, 1980—84, mgr. corporate planning Bartlesville, Okla., 1984—85, asst. treas., 1985—86, treas., 1986—88, v.p., treas., 1988—90, CFO, 1990—99, pres., COO, 1994—99, vice-chmn., pres., CEO, 1999, chmn., CEO, 1999—2002; pres., CEO ConocoPhillips, Houston, 2002—04, chmn., CEO, 2004—12. Bd. dirs. ConocoPhillips, 2002—12, General Electric Co., 2008—, Gen. Motors Co., 2012—, Statoil ASA, 2013—. Served in Navy USN, 1969—73. Roman Catholic.*

MULVA, PATRICK T., oil industry executive; b. Green Bay; BBA, Notre Dame U.; MBA, U. Tex. Fin. analyst ExxonMobil Corp., Baton Rouge, 1976, exec. asst. to pres. U.S. affiliate, 1987, asst. contr. internat. affiliate, fin. dir. Malaysia, 1991, upstream to asst. contr., 1993, v.p. investor rels. and sec., 2002—04, v.p., contr., 2004—; contr. Imperial Oil Ltd., 1996, sr. v.p. fin. and adminstrn., 1998—2002, contr., 2000—02. With USAF, 1972—75. Office: Exxon Mobil Corp Hdqs 5959 Las Colinas Blvd Irving TX 75039-2298

MULVANEY, MICK (JOHN MICHAEL MULVANEY), United States Representative from South Carolina, former state legislator; b. Alexandria, Va., July 21, 1967; s. Michael and Kathleen Mulvaney; m. Pamela West, 1998; children: Caroline, James, Finnegan. BS with honors, Georgetown U. Sch. Fgn. Svc., 1989; JD, U. NC, Chapel Hill, 1992; grad. owner's and presidents mgmt. program, Harvard Bus. Sch., 2006. Atty. James, McElroy & Diehl, Charlotte, NC, 1992—97, Mulvaney & Fisher PA, Charlotte, NC, 1997—2000; mem. Dist. 45 SC House of Reps., Columbia, 2007—09; mem. Dist. 16 SC State Senate, Columbia, 2009—11; mem. US Congress from 5th SC Dist., Washington, 2011—, US House Budget Com., Washington, 2011—, US House Small Bus. Com., Washington, 2011—. Franchise owner-operator Salsarita's Fresh Cantina, 2009—. Youth baseball coach Lancaster County Parks & Recreation; bd. visitors U. SC, Lancaster. Mem.: Indian Land Rotary (founding mem.). Republican. Roman Catholic. Office: US House of Representatives 1207 Longworth House Office Bldg Washington DC 20515 Office Phone: 202-225-5501. Office Fax: 202-225-0464.

MULVEY, W(ILLIAM) MICHAEL, bishop; b. Houston, Tex., Aug. 23, 1949; BA, St. Edward's Univ., Austin, Tex.; STB, Angelicum Univ., Rome; STL, Pontifical Gregorian Univ., Rome. Ordained priest Diocese of Austin, Tex., 1975; assoc. pastor St. Mary's parish, Taylor, Tex., St. Louis parish, Austin; chaplain Reicher Catholic High. Sch., Waco, Tex.; spiritual dir., vice rector St. Mary's Seminary, Austin; pastor St. Thomas Aquinas parish, College Station, Tex.; staff mem. Focolari Movement, NYC; pastor St. Helen's parish, Georgetown, Tex.; chancellor, vicar gen. & moderator of the Curia Diocese of Austin, adminstr., 2009—10; ordained bishop, 2010; bishop Diocese of Corpus Christi, Tex., 2010—. Roman Catholic. Office: Diocese of Corpus Christi 620 Lipan St Corpus Christi TX 78401 Mailing: Diocese of Corpus Christi PO Box 2620 Corpus Christi TX 78403-2620 Office Phone: 361-882-6191. Office Fax: 361-882-1018.

MUMMA, ALBERT GIRARD, JR., architect; b. Long Beach, Calif., July 2, 1928; s. Albert Girard and Carmen (Braley) M.; m. Janeal Thomas Woolf, Dec. 24, 1973; children: Eugenia M. Villagra, Albert Girard III, Peter Brenaman. B.Arch., U. Va., 1951. Designer McLeod & Ferrara, Architects, Washington, 1951-56; assoc. Deigert & Yerkes, Architects, 1956-62; prin. Mumma & Assocs., Washington, 1962—. Archtl. designer hotel div. Marriott Corp., 1980-82 Prin. archtl. works include Nat. Arboretum Hdqrs. Bldg, 1961, Finnmark Sq., Silver Spring, Md., 1964, Inverness townhouses, Potomac, Md., 1971, Post Office and Fed. Bldg., Elkins, W.Va., 1971, U.S. Trade Fairs in Spain, Finland, Japan, El Salvador, Poland 1963-72, Fallswood housing project, Falls Church, Va., 1972, Bristow Village townhouses, Annandale, Va., 1972-73, Marriott Hotel, Dayton, Ohio, 1982, Plaza Venetia, Biscayne Bay, Miami, Fla., 1983, Houston Med. Ctr. Hotel, Newark Airport Hotel, 1984, pvt. residences, No. Neck, Rappahanock River, Lancaster County, Va., 1993-2004, subdivision and townhouse projects, Washington, Md., Va., Pa., 1962—. Served with USMC, 1945-47. Recipient Design award Washington Bd. Trade, 1964; winner Newark Airport Hotel Competition, 1981. Mem. AIA (medal 1951), Rappahannock River Yacht Club, Indian Creek Yacht and Country Club, Moran Creek Yacht Club.

MUMPOWER, CARL, III, councilman; b. London, Dec. 4, 1952; m. Lisa Mumpower; children: Kristen, Matthew. AA in Gen. Studies, Okaloosa-Walton Jr. Coll., Fla., 1973; BA in Psychology, St. Leo Coll., Fla., 1974; MA in Counseling, Western Carolina U., Cullowhee, NC, 1975; MSW in Clin. Social Work, U. Ga., Athens, 1976; PhD in Clin. Psychology, Union Inst. & Univ., Cin., 1985. Lic. practicing psychologist NC, health care provider in psychology NC, practicing psychologist NC; LCSW NC. Chmn. United Services Credit Union; vice mayor City of Ashville, NC, councilman. Mem. NC Marriage and Family Therapy Lic. Bd.; chmn. NC Social Work Lic. Bd. Founder Top-A-Stop Bus Shelter Program; chair For Our Kids... Pub. Housing Initiative; chmn. Meml. Stadium Restoration Comm., Asheville-Buncombe Drug Commn., Asheville Civic Ctr. Commn.; mem. First Bapt. Ch.; bd. dirs. John Locke Found. Served with USAF, 1970—73, Vietnam. Republican. Office: c/o Asheville City Coun 70 Court Plz PO Box 7148 Asheville NC 28802 Office Phone: 828-251-1122.

MUNAVALLI, GIRISH S. (GILLY MUNAVALLI), dermatologist; BS in Biology minor in Chemistry, 1987—92; M in Health and Sciences, Immunology and Infectious Disease, Johns Hopkins U., Balt., 1993—94; MD, Morehouse Coll., Atlanta, 1994—98. Diplomate Am. Bd. Dermatology, 2002, lic. Ga., cert. Calif., Md., NC. Transitional year internship Mayo Clinic Mayo Grad. Sch. of Medicine, Scottsdale, Ariz., 1998—99; dermatology residency tng. Emory Univ. Sch. of Medicince, Atlanta, 1999—2002; fellowship mohs micrographic surgery and cosmetic dermatologic surgery San Francisco Sch. of Medicine Univ. of Calif., San Francisco, 2002—03; fellowship advanced lasers and vein surgery Maryland Laser, Skin and Vein Inst. LLC, Hunt Valley, Md., 2003—04; clin. faculty dermatology dept. Johns Hopkins Sch. of Medicine, Balt., 2004—; clin. faculty dermatology dept. Balt. Sch. of Medicince Univ. of Md., 2004—06; part-time faculty Veterans Adminstrn. Md. Health Care System, Balt., 2004—06; med. dir. The Goslen Aesthetic and Skin Ctr.; assoc. Md. Laser, Skin, and Vein Inst. Co-author: (textbooks chpts.) Presentations of Venous Disease, 2005, Sclerotherapy and Lasers for the Treatment of Leg Veins, 2004, Intense Pulsed Light, 2004, Computers in Mohs Surgery, 2004, Laser Treatment of Leg Veins, Ambulatory Phlebectomy, (sci. jours.) Advances in Techniques for Endovenous Ablation of Truncal Veins, Our Approach to Non-ablative Treatment of Photoaging, Photoaging and Nonablative Photorejuvenation in Ethnic Skin, and numerous others. Fellow: Am. Acad. of Dermatology (bd. dirs. 2003—); mem.: Md. Dermatology Soc., Johns Hopkins Univ. Sch. of Hygiene and Pub. Health Alumni Assn., Mayo Alumni Assn., Am. Pathology Imaging, Informatics, and the Internet, Internat. Soc. of Dermatologic Surgery, Internat. Transplant Skin Cancer Collaborative, Am. Coll. of Mohs Micrographic Surgery and Cutaneous Oncology (website and CME com. 2005—), Am. Soc. for Dermatologic Surgery (online CME com. 2003—, website com. mem. 2003—), Am. Soc. for Lasers and Surgery in Medicine (website com. 2005—, CME com. 2005—), Alpha Omega Alpha Nat. Med. Honor Society (Gamma chpt.). Office: Midtown Medical Plaza Ste 550 1918 Randolph Rd Charlotte NC 28207 Office Phone: 704-375-6766. Office Fax: 704-332-6552.

MUNCEY, JAMES ARTHUR, JR., architect; b. Dallas, July 9, 1933; s. James Arthur and Thelma (Bush) M.; m. Virginia Diers, Aug. 12, 1955; children: James G., Leah V., Laura E. BArch, Tex. A & M U., 1956. Registered arch., Tex. Design assoc. Wright Rich Assoc. Architects, Dallas, 1958—70; ptnr. Manos & Muncey Architects, Dallas, 1970—80. 1st lt. US Army, 1956—58. Mem.: AIA, Tex. Soc. Architects. Republican. Episcopalian. Avocation: investments. E-mail: jm@beecreek.net.

MUNDT, BARRY MAYNARD, management consultant; s. Kenneth Francis and Janet (Doughty) M.; m. Sally Hanscom, June 13, 1960; children: Kevin Warren, Trevor Stevens, Stacey Corbin BS in Indsl. Engring., Stanford U., 1959; MBA, Santa Clara U., 1964. Registered indsl. engr., Calif. Statistician Aerojet-Gen., Sacramento, 1957-58; reliability engr. Lockheed Missiles, Sunnyvale, Calif., 1959-61; mgmt. engr. C-E-I-R, Inc., Los Altos, Calif., 1961-65; sr. cons. Peat, Marwick, Livingston & Co., Los Angeles, 1965-68; mgr., prin. Peat, Marwick, Mitchell & Co., Atlanta, 1968-84; ptnr.-in-charge, ops. mgmt. cons. KPMG Peat Marwick Main & Co., NYC, 1984-88; internat. mgmt. cons. ptnr. KPMG Internat., NYC and Amsterdam, The Netherlands, 1988-92; mgmt. cons., ptnr. KPMG Peat Marwick U.S., Montvale, NJ, 1992-95; prin. The Strategy Facilitation Group, Asheville, NC, 1995—. Bd. dirs. Adjusters Internat., Inc., 2005—, Mosaic Acctg., Inc., 2005—. Author-editor: Managing Public Resources, 1982; co-author Il Manager Pubblico (Italy), 1986; mem. editl. bd., contbg. author Handbook of Industrial Engineering, 3rd edit., 2001; contbr. articles to profl. jours. Mem. ann. campaign Atlanta Symphony Orch., 1974-82, Atlanta Arts Alliance, 1976-81; del. to assembly United Way of Met. Atlanta, 1974-84; bd. chmn., mem. Brandon Hall Sch., Atlanta, 1980—2002; chmn., mem. steering coun., NC Ctr. Creative Retirement, 2007-. Fellow Inst. Indsl. Engrs. (treas. 1976-81, pres. 1982-83, asst. treas. 1985-92); mem. Asheville Country Club. Independent. Home and Office: 175 Windsor Rd Asheville NC 28804 Office Phone: 828-254-2769. Personal E-mail: bmundt@charter.net.

MUNISTERI, JOSEPH GEORGE, construction executive; b. Rome, Sept. 24, 1930; arrived in USA, 1934; s. Peter P. and Inez Gertrude (Ziniti) Munisteri; m. Theresa Grasso, June 7, 1952 (div. Dec. 2000); children: Joanne, Robert, Laura, Stephen, James, Richard; m. Barbra Coffman, Nov. 30, 2001. BE, Yale U., 1952. With Bechtel Corp., San Francisco, 1952-59; with The Lummus Co., NYC, London and Houston, 1959-67, gen. mgr., 1967—70; sr. v.p. sales Brown & Root, Inc., Houston, 1970—75, group v.p. power div., 1975-80, group v.p. corp. devel., 1980-81, also bd. dirs.; pres. Enserch Engrs. & Constructors, Inc., Houston, 1981-85; exec. v.p. Ford, Bacon & Davis, Inc., Dallas, 1985-87; chmn., pres., CEO Comstock Group, Inc., Danbury, Conn., 1987-88; pres. Joseph G. Munisteri Co., Houston, 1989—, MBJ Water Corp., Houston, 2012. Former chmn. bd. Pine-O-Pine. Former mem. Bd. dirs. Atomic Indsl. Forum; Bd. dirs. Am. Nuclear Energy Council. Mem. Atomic Indsl. Forum, Am. Inst. Chem. Engrs., Am. Nuclear Soc., Atomic Indsl. Forum, ASTM, Council Engring. Law, ASCE, Assn. Iron and Steel Engring., Assoc. Builders and Contractors (dir.), Yale Club of Houston, Yale Club of N.Y. Office: 4265 San Felipe St Ste 1100 Houston TX 77027-2998 Home Phone: 713-877-0240; Office Phone: 713-960-1272, 713-557-5084. Business E-Mail: jmunisteri@comcast.net.

MUNISTERI, STEPHEN P., political organization administrator, lawyer; BBA, JD, Univ. Tex., Austin. Bar: Tex. 1982. Atty. private practice; founder Munisteri Sports & Entertainment Inc.; vice chmn. Tex. Young Americans for Freedom, 1976, state chmn., 1977—80; founder Young Conservatives of Tex., 1980; mem. Tex. State Rep. Com.; chmn. Tex. Rep. Party, 2010—. Republican. Presbyterian. Office: Texas Rep Party Ste 500 1108 Lavaca Austin TX 78701 Office Phone: 512-477-9821. Office Fax: 512-480-0709.*

MUNK, ZEV MOSHE, physician, researcher; b. Stockholm, July 14, 1950; m. Susan Deitcher; 4 children. BS, McGill U., 1972; MD, C.M., 1974. Licentiate Med. Coun. Can.; diplomate Am. Bd. Internal Medicine, Am. Bd. Allergy and Clin. Immunology. Intern Royal Victoria Hosp., Montreal, 1974-75, resident, 1975-76; resident in clin. immunology and allergy Montreal Gen. Hosp., 1976-78; practice medicine specializing in allergy/clin. immunology Houston, 1978—; founder, CEO Pharm-Olam Internat. Contbr. articles to med. jours. Pres. Young Israel Synagogue of Houston, 1994-96; founder Allergy Ctr., P.A., Houston, Breco Rsch., Houston; founder, past pres. Torah and Outreach Resource Ctr. of Houston. McGill U. scholar, 1968-74. Fellow ACP, Am. Acad. Allergy Asthma and Immunology, Am. Coll. Allergy and Immunogy, Royal Coll. Physicians (Can.); mem. Tex. Med. Assn., Que. Med. Assn., Tex. Allergy Soc., Harris County Med. Soc., Houston Allergy Soc. Office: 450 N Sam Houston Pwky Ste 250 Houston TX 77060

MUNN, CECIL EDWIN, lawyer; b. Enid, Okla., Aug. 8, 1923; s. Cecil Edwin and Margaret (Kittrell) M.; m. Carolyn Taylor Culver, May 8, 1948; children: Franklin Culver, Charlotte Munn Forswall. BA, U. Okla., 1945; JD cum laude, Harvard U., 1947. Bar: Okla. 1948, Tex. 1956. Practice in, Enid, 1947-54, Ft. Worth, 1954—; partner firm Cantey & Hanger, Ft. Worth, 1960-91, of counsel, 1992—. With Champlin Petroleum Co., 1954-60, v.p., atty., 1958-60, dir., 1962-75. Fellow Am. Coll. Trial Lawyers, Am. Bar Found.; mem. ABA (chmn. natural resources law sect. 1970-71), Southwestern Legal Found. (past dir.), Tex. Bar Found., Phi Delta Theta, Phi Delta Phi. Presbyterian. Office: Cantey Hanger LLP 600 W 6th St Ste 300 Fort Worth TX 76102-6899

MUNNERLYN, ELIZABETH ROGERS, state legislator; b. Bennettsville, SC, June 20, 1969; d. John Irby and Carolyn (Budd) Rogers; m. Jerry Ronald Munnerlyn, Jr., Dec. 29, 1990.; Mary Catherine, William Ford. BA in fin. Magna Cum Laude, Converse Coll., 1990; JD, U. S.C., 1993. Bar: S.C., 1993. Law clk. to Cir. Judge James Lockeny, Dillon, SC, 1993-94; asst. solicitor 4th Cir. Solicitor's Office, Darlington, SC, 1994-96; atty. Rogers & Munnerlyn, P.A., Bennettsville, 1996—; mem. Dist. 54 SC House of Representatives, 2010—. Mem.: ABA. Democrat. Home: 611 E Main St Bennettsville SC 29512-3217 Office: Rogers & Munnerlyn PA P O Box 1175 207 W Main St Bennettsville SC 29512-1175 Address: 333A Blatt Bldg Columbia SC 29201 Office Phone: 843-479-9577, 803-212-6896, 843-479-9577. Office Fax: 843-479-0685.

MUÑOZ, CALISE ILEEN, healthcare company executive, lawyer; b. 1970; BA, U. So. Calif.; JD, Georgetown U. Law Ctr., 1995. Bar: Calif. Law clk. Office Wash. State Atty. Gen.; legal clk., legis. asst. fed. affairs health team American Assn. Ret. Persons; dep. dir. policy, Office Intergovernmental Affairs US Dept. Health and Human Svcs., 2001—04, regional rep. San Francisco, 2004—06; v.p. govt. rels. Amerigroup Corp., 2006—. Office: Amerigroup Corp 4425 Corporation Ln Virginia Beach VA 23462 Office Phone: 757-490-6900. Office Fax: 757-222-2330.

MUNOZ, HENRY R., III, architectural firm executive; Positions up to pres., CEO Munoz & Company, San Antonio, 1983—. Chmn. Futuro Fund; founding chmn. Alameda Nat. Ctr. for Latino Arts and Culture; chmn. VIA Transp. Bd., San Antonio; trustee Cooper Hewitt Nat. Design Mus., San Antonio Mus. Art; commr. Tex. Dept. Transp., 1991—94; nat. fin. com. chair Dem. Nat. Com., 2013—; mem. nat. bd. Smithsonian Instn., 1999; mem. nat. com. Latino Mus. of Nat. Mall; mem. nat. com. for performing arts John F. Kennedy Ctr. Recipient Philanthropist of the Yr. Award, 2000, Cmty. Svc. Award, San Antonio Hispanic C. of C., 2007, Diversity FIRST Award, Tex. Diversity Coun., 2007; named one of Entrepreneurs of the Yr., Hispanic Bus. Mag., 2002. Democrat. Office: Munoz & Company 1017 N Main Ste 300 San Antonio TX 78212 Office Phone: 210-349-1163. Office Fax: 210-525-1038.

MUNOZ, OSCAR, corporate financial executive; BS, U. So. Calif., 1982; MBA, Pepperdine U., 1986. Fin. analyst, acctg. mgr., mgr. fin. control Pepsico Inc., L.A. and Purchase, NY, 1983—86; divsn. contr., dir. fin. ops., asst. corp. contr. Coca-Cola Enterprises, Inc., L.A. and Atlanta, 1986—91, CFO, region v.p. Hollywood, Calif., 1991—96; exec. dir. Coca-Cola Co., Atlanta, 1996—97; v.p. fin., contr. USWEST Comms. Inc., Denver, 1997—99; CFO, v.p. U.S. West Retail Markets, Denver, 1999—2000; sr. v.p. fin. and adminstrn. Qwest Comms. Internat. Inc., Denver, 2000; CFO, v.p. AT&T Consumer Svcs. AT&T Corp., Basking Ridge, NJ, 2001—03; exec. v.p., CFO CSX Corp., Jacksonville, Fla., 2003—. Mem.: Fin. Execs. Inst. Office: CSX Corp 500 Water St 15th Floor Jacksonville FL 32202

MUÑOZ-SOLÁ, HAYDEÉ SOCORRO, retired library administrator; b. Caguas, PR, Dec. 27, 1943; d. Gilberto Muñoz and Carmen Haydeé (Solá) de Muñoz; m. Juan M. Masini-Soler, Jan. 8, 1966 (div. 1979); children: Juan Martín Masini-Muñoz, Haydeé Milagros Masini-Muñoz. BA in Psychology, U. P.R., Río Piedras, 1965, MLS, 1970; D in Libr. Sci., Columbia U., 1985. Asst. libr. U. P.R., Río Piedras, 1964-67; dir. libr. Interam. U., Aguadilla, PR, 1974-75; head svcs. to pub. U. P.R., Aguadilla, 1975-76; cataloguer Cath. U., Ponce, PR, 1976-79, U. P.R., Río Piedras, 1983—84, 1987, head libr. and info. sci. libr. Río Piedras, 1984-85, prof. grad. libr. sch., 1986, 99, dir. libr. sys., 1986—99, coord. external resources libr. sys., 1994-97, dir. of libr. Ponce, PR, 1997, collection devel. officer Río Piedras, 1998, sabbatical leave, 2000-01; compiler, editor Puerto Rican Bibliography, 2001—07. Dir. P.R. Newspaper Project, Río Piedras, 1986-90; mem. Adv. Com. on Pub. Librs., San Juan, 1987-93; proposal reviewer NEH, 1990-2007; chmn. Puerto Rican Del. to Nat. White House Conf. on Libr. and Info. Svcs., 1991. Author: La Información y la Documentación Educativa/Informe Sobre la Situación Actual en Puerto Rico, 1991, Memorias: Sequnda Pre-Conferencia de Casa Blanca Sobre Bibliotecas y Servicios de Información en Puerto Rico, 1991, Lineamientos para Colecciones Bibliograficas Nacionales, 1997, Premio por Excelencia en Investigación Aplicada y Publicación, 1997; contbr. articles to profl. jours. Mem. Ponce Sport Club, 1976—83, ARC, Ponce, 1978. Recipient plaque White House Pre-Conf. on Libr. and Info. Sci., 1990, others, Leccion Magistral Josefina del Toro Fulladosa, 2002; French Alps Study Tour scholar Assn. Caribbean Univ. Rsch. and Instl. Libr., 1989, Germany Study Tour scholar Fgn. Rels. Office, Germany, 1991, coord. So. area 1974, Lauro award 1989, Leccion Magistral Josefina del Toro Fulladosa award, 2002. Mem. ALA, Am. Mgmt. Assn., Grad. Sch. Libr. and Info. Sci. Alumni Assn. (pres. 1988-90), Seminar for Acquisitions L.Am. Libr. Materials, Iberoamerican Nat. Libr. Assn. (pres. 1992-93), Puerto Rican Libr. Soc., Assn. Caribbean U. Rsch. and Instnl. Libr. (Parchment award 1988), Asoc. para las Comunicaciones y Tecnología Educativa, Mid. States Assn. Coll. and Sch. (collaborator), Am. Women Assn., Nat. Commn. P.R. Women, PR Libr. Assn., Phi Delta Kappa (chair P.R. com. 1988-90, Kappan of Yr. 1990), Eta Gamma Delta. Roman Catholic. Avocations: reading, crewel work, embroidery, knitting, movies. Personal E-mail: hms@onelinkpr.net.

MUNRO, DONALD WILLIAM, JR., non-profit organization executive; b. Phila., Dec. 27, 1937; s. Donald William and Emily McCoy (Graham) M.; m. Joyce Eleanor Thomas, Sept. 9, 1961; children: Deborah Joy, Mark William. BS, Wheaton Coll., 1959; MS, Pa. State U., 1963, PhD, 1966. Prof. biology Houghton (N.Y.) Coll., 1966-94; exec. dir. Am. Sci. Affiliation, Ipswich, Mass., 1994—2005. Adj. prof. biology Gordon Coll., Wenham, Mass., 1995-2004; chmn. biology dept. Houghton Coll., 1972-94. Capt. U.S. Army, 1960-69. Predoctoral fellow NIH, 1964-66. Mem. Am. Philatelic Soc., Houghton Stamp Club (pres. 1988-90). Republican. Baptist. Avocations: piano, hiking, stamp collecting/philately.

MUNSEY, VIRDELL EVERARD, JR., retired utilities executive; b. Washington, Sept. 25, 1933; s. Virdell Everard and Mildred Lovenia (Wood) M.; m. Bernice Ann Wilson, Sept. 20, 1956; children: Wanda Louise, Allan Coll, Andrew Everard, Carolyn Jane. BA magna cum laude, Yale U., 1955; M.P.A., Harvard U., 1967. Reporter Washington Post, 1957-63; legis. asst. Rep. Henry S. Reuss, Washington, 1963-68; info. dir. United Democrats for Humphrey, Washington, 1968; asst. dir. public affairs Dem. Nat. Com., 1968; with Nat. Planning Assn., Washington, 1969-77, exec. v.p., 1974-76; dep. asst. sec. for public affairs Dept. Treasury, Washington, 1977-81; cons. World Bank, 1981; with Va. Electric and Power Co., 1981-86, mgr. corp. communications, 1982-83, exec. dir. pub. policy, 1983-86, v.p. pub. policy, 1986, Dominion Resources Inc., 1986-96; cons., 1996—2002. Mem. Va. Coal and Energy Commn., 1983-95. Chmn. Arlington County Dem. Party, 1967-69; mem. Arlington County Bd., 1972-75, chmn., 1973; vice chmn. No. Va. Transp. Commn., 1973, chmn., 1974; bd. dirs. Washington Met. Area Transit Authority, 1975; mem. transp. planning bd. Met. Washington Coun. Govts., 1973-75; treas. Competitive Power Policy Forum, 1990-96. Served with U.S. Army, 1955-57, treas Pilgrim Henry Samson Kindred, 2005-11, asst. Pilgrim Hopkins Heritage Soc., 2005-11. Recipient Am. Political Sci. Assn. award Disting. Reporting of Public Affairs, 1962; Am. Polit. Sci Assn. Fellow, 1966—67. Mem. United Ch. Christ. Personal E-mail: everard1933@yahoo.com.

MUNTZ, DAVID S., healthcare company executive; AB in Premedicine, Columbia U., NYC, 1971; attended, Southern Methodist U., 1988. Data sys. dir., info. svc. Presbyterian Healthcare System, Dallas, v.p., info. svcs. & telecom., 1996, v.p., chief info. officer, 1996—97; sr. v.p., chief info. officer Texas Health Resources (formed in merger with Presbyn. Healthcare Sys., others), 1990—2006; sr. v.p., Info. Sys., chief info. officer Baylor Health Care System, 2006—. Office: Baylor Health Care System 3500 Gaston Ave Dallas TX 75246-1901 Office Phone: 214-820-0111. Office Fax: 214-820-7499. Business E-Mail: david_muntz@baylorhealth.edu.

MURAI, NORIMOTO, plant molecular biologist, educator; b. Sapporo, Japan, Mar. 4, 1944; came to U.S., 1968; s. Nobuo and Hideko (Odagiri) M.; m. Andreana Lisca, Nov. 14, 1977; 1 child, Naoki. BS, Hokkaido U., 1966, MS, 1968; PhD, U. Wis., 1973. Rsch. assoc. dept. botany U. Wis., Madison, 1974-78, project assoc. dept. bacteriology,

1979, postdoctoral fellow dept. plant pathology, 1980-82; lab. head dept. molecular biology Nat. Inst. Agrobiol. Resources, Tsukuba, Japan, 1983-84; assoc. prof. plant pathology and crop physiology La. State U., Baton Rouge, 1985-92, prof., 1992—. Adj. prof. biochemistry, full mem. grad. faculty and interdept. studies in plant physiology and genetics La. State U.; mem. study sect. on minority biomed. rsch. support program NIH, 1993; grant reviewer USDA, NSF, NIH. Reviewer manuscripts Genome, Protein Engring., Plant Cell, Plant Physiol., Planta, Plant Molecular Biology, Plant Cell Report, Australia Jour. Plant Physiol. Named Honors Rschr., Phi Delta Kappa, 1989; grantee Fulbright Found., 1968, Sci. and Tech. Agy., Tokyo, 1984, La. Edn. Quality Support Fund, 1988, 89, 91, 94, 95, 97, 98, Monsanto Co. Fund, 1992, 93, US Dept. Agr., 1995, 2008, Rockefeller Found., 1995-96; Fulbright scholar. Mem. AAAS, Am. Soc. Plant Biologists, Internat. Soc. Plant Molecular Biology, Japan Molecular Biology Assn., Crop Sci. Soc. Am., Fulbright Assn., Sigma Xi, Gamma Sigma Delta, Phi Delta Kappa. Avocations: running, skiing, gardening, golf, tennis. Office: La State Univ Dept Plant Pathology & Crop Physiology Baton Rouge LA 70803-1720 Office Phone: 225-578-1380. Business E-Mail: nmurai@lsu.edu.

MURANO, ELSA A., agricultural studies educator, former academic administrator; b. Havana, Cuba, Aug. 14, 1959; m. Peter S. Murano. BS in Biol. Sci., Fla. Internat. U., 1981; MS in Anaerobic Microbiology, Va. Polytechnic Inst., 1987, PhD in Food Sci. & Tech., 1990. Rsch. lab technician Florida International U., 1981—83; researcher, teaching asst. Va. Tech. U., Blacksburg, Va., 1984—90; asst. prof. dept. microbiology, immunology & preventive medicine Iowa State U., Ames, 1990—92, prof. in charge rsch. programs linear accelertor facility, 1992—95; various positions including dir. food safety Texas A&M University, College Station, Tex., 1995—2001, assoc. prof. animal sci., 1995—2000, prof. dept. animal sci., 2000—01; under sec. for food safety USDA, Washington, 2001—04; dir. Tex. Agrl. Experiment Station, 2005; vice chancellor, dean agrl. & life scis. Texas A&M University, 2005—08, pres., 2008—09, pres. emerita, 2009—, prof. animal sci., 2009—. Chair food safety state initiative com. Tex. Agr. Ext. Sta., 1999—2001; nat. adv. com. meat and poultry inspection USDA, 2001; mem. Nat. Alliance for Food Safety Ops. Com., 1998—2001, chair, 2000—01; bd. dirs. Hormel Foods Corp., 2006—. Named one of The 100 Most Influential Hispanics, Hispanic Bus. mag., 2002; named to The Alumni Hall of Fame, Hispanic Scholarship Fund, 2005. Mem.: Intenat. Assn. Food Protection, Poultry Sci. Assn., Inst. Food Technologists, Assn. Meat Sci., Am. Soc. Microbiology. Avocations: astronomy, drums. Office: Tex A&M U Mailstop 2471 College Station TX 77843 Office Phone: 979-845-2217. Office Fax: 979-845-5027. E-mail: president@tamu.edu, emurano@tamu.edu.

MURCHISON, DAVID RODERICK, lawyer; b. Washington, May 28, 1948; s. David Claudius and June Margaret (Guilfoyle) M.; m. Kathy Ann Kohn, Mar. 15, 1981; children: David Christopher, Benjamin Michael. BA cum laude, Princeton U., 1970; JD, Georgetown U., 1975. Bar: D.C. 1975, Fla. 1993. Legal asst. to vice chmn. CAB, Washington, 1975-76, enforcement atty., 1976-77; sr. atty. Air Transport Assn., Washington, 1977-80, asst. v.p., sec., 1981-85; sr. assoc. Zuckert, Scoutt and Rasenberger, Washington, 1980-81; v.p., asst. gen. counsel Piedmont Aviation, Inc., Winston-Salem, NC, 1985-88; v.p., gen. counsel, sec. Braniff, Inc., Dallas, 1988-89, chief exec. officer Orlando, 1990-94; fed. adminstrv. law judge Office of Hearings and Appeals, Charleston, W.Va., 1994-96, chief adminstrv. law judge Mobile, Ala., 1996-99, adminstrv. law judge, 1999—. Lectr. continuing legal edn. program Wake Forest U., Winston-Salem, 1988. Contbr. articles to legal jours. Lt. USNR, 1970-72. Mem. ABA, Met. Club Washington. Republican. Roman Catholic. Office: Hearings & Appeals Office 550 Government St #200 Mobile AL 36602 Office Phone: 866-593-1648.

MURCKO, MARY, publishing executive; b. 1964; Grad., Purdue U., Ind., 1986. Advt. sales rep. New York mag., 1987—91; beauty market mgr. Self mag., 1991—95; gen. mgr., group pub. Hachette Filipacchi Post Co., Bangkok, 1995—2001; assoc. pub. W mag. Fairchild Publications Inc., 2001—03, pub. Elegant Bride, 2003—04, pub. W Jewelry, 2004; founding pub. Best Life mag. Rodale Inc., 2004—06, exec. v.p., group pub., 2010—11; v.p., pub. Women's Health Rodale Magazines Inc., 2006—09, sr. v.p., pub. Prevention, 2009—10; pres. sales Gannett Co., Inc., McLean, Va., 2012—. Bd. mem. Cosmetic Exec. Women. Named Sales Team Leader of Yr., MinOnline mag., 2008; named a Woman to Watch, Advt. Age, 2009. Mem.: Advt. Women of NY. Office: Gannett Co Inc 7950 Jones Branch Dr Mc Lean VA 22107

MURDOCK, GLENN, state supreme court justice; b. Enterprise, Ala., June 25, 1956; s. Billy A. and Marita H. Murdock; m. Margaret Gilchrist; children: Emily, Bailey, John Taylor. BA summa cum laude, U. Ala., 1978; JD, U. Va. Law Sch., 1981. Law clk. United Dist. Judge (No. Ala. dist.) Clarence W. Allgood; atty. Wallace, Jordan, Ratliff & Brandt, Birmingham/Montgomery, Ala., 1992—; judge Ala. Ct. Civil Appeals, 2001—07; assoc. justice Ala. Supreme Ct., 2007—. Mem.: Ala. Bar Assn., Birmingham Bar. Assn., Birmingham Rotary Club, Phi Beta Kappa. Office: Ala Supreme Ct 300 Dexter Ave Montgomery AL 36104*

MURDOCK, JOHN CAREY, economics professor, investor; b. Blackwell, Okla., Dec. 10, 1922; s. Frank Elbert and Nannine (Watt) M.; m. Jean Boardman, Oct. 15, 1949 (dec.); children: John B., Robert C.; m. Betty Lassiter, Nov. 14, 2000. BS, U. Okla., 1947; MS, U. Wis., 1951, PhD, 1955. Faculty U. Mo., Columbia, 1951—, prof. econs., 1958—, chmn. dept., 1962-64; dean U. Mo. (Grad. Sch.), dir. research adminstrn., 1967-71. Project dir. NASA study location of research, 1964-67; cons. to industry, 1962—; vis. prof. Massey U., New Zealand, 1972-73. Author: (with J. Graves) Regions and Research, 1966; contbr. articles to profl. jours. Chmn. Mid-Am. State Univs. Assn. Grad. Schs., 1970-71; active Wyo. Coun. for the Humanities, 1981-84, vice chmn., 1984; bd. dirs. Wyo. Centennial Cmty. Found., 1990—. Gulf Refining Co. fellow, 1957; U. Mo. fellow, 1958; Community Studies fellow, 1960-61 Mem. Am. Econs. Assn., Econ. History Assn., Royal Econs. Soc. Home: 360A Nc Highway 902 Pittsboro NC 27312-8063 Office Phone: 919-542-3680. Business E-Mail: jmurdock@nc.rr.com.

MURDOCK, REGINALD, state legislator; m. Willie Murdock; 1 child. Degree in indsl. engring., U. Ark., Fayetteville. Engr., contractor; mem. Dist. 52 Ark. House of Representatives, 2011—. Democrat. Office: PO Box 1071 Marianna AR 72360 Office Phone: 870-295-3208. Office Fax: 870-295-3162. Personal E-mail: rkm_72360@yahoo.com.

MURKISON, EUGENE COX, finance educator; b. Donalsonville, Ga., July 2, 1936; s. Jeff and Ollie Mae (Shores) Murkison; m. Marilyn Louise Adams, July 3, 1965; children: James, David, Jennifer. Grad., US Army JFK Spl. Warfare Sch., 1967, US Naval War Coll., 1972, US Army Command/Staff Coll., 1974; BS, U. Ga., Athens, 1959; MBA, U. Rochester, NY, 1970; PhD, U. Mo., 1986. Surveyor USDA, Donalsonville, 1956—59; commd. 2d lt. US Army, 1959, advanced through grades to lt. col., 1974, inf. bn. leader Vietnam, 1967—68; mechanized comdr. (G-3), ops. officer Brigade Exec. Officer, Korea, Europe and US, 1968—70; prof. leadership & psychology West Point, NY, 1970—73; ops. officer (J-3) Office of Chmn. Joint Chiefs of Staff, Washington, 1974—77; prof. mil. sci. and leadership Kemper Mil. Coll., 1977—81; ret. US Army, 1981; instr. U. Mo., Columbia, 1981—84; asst. prof. Ga. So. U., Stateboro, 1984—89, assoc. prof., 1989—94, prof., 1995—, chair grad. curriculum & programs task force, 1996—99. Vis. prof. mgmt. and bus. U. Tirgoviste, Romania, 1994—96, 1998—2000; vis. prof. human resource mgmt. Tech. U. Romania, Cluj-Napoca, 1998—2000; chmn. grad. programs curriculum com. GSU, 1998—2002. Author (with Gheroghe Ionescu): Human Behavior in Organizations, 2000; contbr. articles to profl. jours., chapters to books. Rep. Bulloch county FT Stewant/ HUnter AAF Joint land Use Com., 2009—11; adminstrv. bd. Pittman Pk. Meth. Ch., Statesboro, 1986—, trustee, 1992—99, chmn., trustee, 1995—96, mem. staff parish com., 2000—04, chair memls. com., 2005—, adminstrv. bd., 2006—; chair, safe sancturies com. Pittman Pk. UMC, 2009—11; vice chair Kiwanis Ogeachae Regional Fair, 2008—. Decorated Bronze Star with oak leaf cluster; recipient Tchg. award, U. Mo., 1983, Devel. award, Ga. So. U., 1990, Albert Burke Rsch. award, 1992, Internat. Educator of the Yr. award, Rutherford award for Excellence in Grad. Rsch. and Edn., 2006, Grad. Instrn. and Svc. award, McIntosh, 2006, others; grantee, IREX, 1994, SOROS, 1995, 1996. Mem.: VFW, Acad. Bus. Disciplines, Ga. Hist. Soc., Bus. History Conf., Acad. Mgmt., Internat. Acad. Bus. (program chair 1994, 1995, Best Paper award 10th Ann. Conv., McGregor Grad. Tchg. award 2006), Inst. Info. and Mgmt. Sci., So. Mgmt. Assn., Inst. Mgmt. Sci., Mil. Order World Wars (Statesboro VFW Chapt.), Newcomen Soc., Kiwanis Club Statesboro, Scabbard & Blade, Blue Key, Alpha Zeta, Beta Gamma Sigma. Republican. Avocations: history, hiking, boating, farming. Office: Ga So U Coll Bus Adminstrn Statesboro GA 30460-8154

MUROFF, LAWRENCE ROSS, nuclear medicine physician, educator; b. Phila., Dec. 26, 1942; s. John M. and Carolyn (Kramer) M.; m. Carol R. Savoy, July 12, 1969; children: Michael Bruce, Julie Anne. AB cum laude, Dartmouth Coll., Hanover, NH, 1964, B of Med. Sci., 1965; MD cum laude, Harvard U., Cambridge, Mass., 1967. Diplomate Am. Bd. Radiology, Am. Bd. Nuclear Medicine. Intern Boston City Hosp., Harvard, 1968; resident in radiology Columbia-Presbyn. Med. Ctr., NYC, 1970-73, chief resident, 1973; instr. dept. radiology, asst. radiologist Columbia U. Med. Ctr., NYC, 1973-74; dir. dept. nuc. medicine, computed tomography and MRI Univ. Cmty. Hosp., Tampa, Fla., 1974-94, H. Lee Moffitt Cancer Hosp., Tampa, 1994—; pres. Edn. Symposia Inc., Tampa, 1975-2001; pres., CEO Imaging Cons. Inc., Tampa, 1994—, chmn. bd. Am. Phys. Ptnrs. Inc. (Radiologix), Dallas, 1996—98. Clin. asst. prof. radiology U. South Fla., 1974-78, clin. assoc. prof., 1978-82, clin. prof., 1982—; clin. prof. U. Fla., 1988—, bd. dirs., Radiology Leadership Inst., 2011-. Contbr. articles to profl. jours. Lt. comdr. USPHS, 1968-70. Fellow Am. Coll. Nuclear Medicine (disting. fellow., Fla. del.), Am. Coll. Nuclear Physicians (regents 1976-78, pres.-elect 1978, pres. 1979), Am. Coll. Radiology (councilor 1979-80, 91-96, 2001-06, 08-, chancellor 1981-87, chmn. commn. on nuclear medicine 1981-87, bd. dirs., Gold medal, 2013); mem. Am. Assn. Acad. Chief Residents Radiology (chmn. 1973), AMA, Boylston Soc., Fla. Assn. Nuclear Physician (pres. 1976), Fla. Med. Assn., Hillsborough County Med. Assn., Radiol. Soc. N.Am., Soc. Nuclear Medicine (coun. 1975-90, trustee 1980-84, 86-89, pres. Southeastern chpt. 1983, vice chmn. correlative imaging coun. 1983), Fla. Radiol. Soc. (exec. com. 1976-91, treas. 1984, sec. 1985, v.p. 1986, pres. elect 1987, pres. 1988, gold medal 1995), West Coast Radiol. Soc., Soc. Magnetic Resonance Imaging (bd. dirs. 1988-91, chmn. ednl. program 1989, chmn. membership com. 1989-93), Clin. Magnetic Resonance Soc. (pres.-elect 1995-98, pres. 1998-2000, bd. dirs. 1995—2011), Am. Coll. Radiology Leadership Inst.(bd. dirs. 2011-), ACR Health Policy Inst. (bd. dirs. 2012-). Office: 16804 Avila Blvd Tampa FL 33613-5220 Personal E-mail: lrmuroff@hotmail.com.

MURPHEY, ARTHUR GAGE, JR., law educator; b. Macon, Miss., June 16, 1927; s. Arthur Gage and Elizabeth (Crutcher) Murphey; m. Linda Chaney, May 17, 1975 (dec. June 2007); children: Mason Alexander, Arthur Nesbit 1 stepchild, Leslie Jo Pafford. Student, Vanderbilt U., 1947—48; AB, U. N.C., 1951; JD, U. Miss., 1953; postgrad., London Sch. Econs., U. London, 1953—54; LLM, Yale U., 1962. Assoc. Satterfield, Ewing, Williams and Shell, Jackson, Miss., 1953; asst. prof. U. Ga., Athens, 1956-58, Emory U., Atlanta, 1958-61, U. Akron, 1962—63, assoc. prof., 1963—67; prof. U. Ark., Little Rock, 1967—75, 1975—97, asst. dean Sch. Law, 1970—73, Ark. Bar Found. prof., 1996—97, Ark. Bar Found. prof. emeritus, 1997—. Vis. lectr. Case Western Res. U., Cleve., 1966; vis. prof. U. Miss., 1977. Faculty editor: Jour. Pub. Law, 1958—61; faculty advisor Ga. Bar Jour., 1958—61; contbr. articles to profl. jours. With Air Corps US Army, 1945—47. Fulbright scholar, 1953—54. Mem.: ABA, Anglican Mission in America, Phi Beta Kappa, Beta Theta Pi, Phi Delta Phi. Anglican. Home: 1918 Old Forge Dr Little Rock AR 72227-5515 Office: U Ark Sch Law 1201 McMath Ave Little Rock AR 72202-5142

MURPHEY, JASON, state legislator; m. Raleah Murphey, 1996; children: Jarod, Jarel. BA, Charter Oak State Coll., 2006. Business owner; city councilman Guthrie, Okla.; mem. Dist. 31 Okla. House of Representatives, 2007—. Mem.: NRA. Republican. Office: Okla House of Reprs 2300 N Lincoln Blvd Rm 437 Oklahoma City OK 73105 Home: 1521 Olison Turn Trl Guthrie OK 73044-7406 Office Phone: 405-557-7350. E-mail: jason.murphey@okhouse.gov.

MURPHREY, ELIZABETH HOBGOOD, retired history professor, librarian; b. Rocky Mount, NC, Mar. 22, 1947; d. Isaac Green and Ernestine Ragsdale (Hobgood) Murphrey. BA, U. N.C., Greensboro, 1969; MA, Duke U., 1971, PhD, 1976; postgrad., U. Fla., 1984; MLS, U. N.C., Chapel Hill, 1993. Vis. instr. history Wake Forest U., Winston-Salem, NC, 1976; asst. prof. history N.C. A&T State U., Greensboro, 1977—81; intelligence rsch. specialist U.S. Army, Fayetteville, NC, 1982—89; adj. prof. history Fayetteville State U., 1989—90; adj. instr. history Everest U. South Campus, Orlando, 2000—03, adj. history, instr. Columbia Coll. Orlando divsn., 2005; libr. Everest U., South Orlando, 1998—2011, co-dir., 2004—11; adv. bd. mem. Seminole County Libr., 2012—13. Vis. asst. prof. of history Elizabeth City State U., NC, 1993—96. Editor (guidebook): Socialist Party of America Papers, microfilm edit., 2 vols., 1973—77. Apptd. Seminole County Disiability Adv. Coun., 2005, vice chair, 2008. Recipient award, NEH, 1994, 1996, 2000. Mem.: LWV (bd. dirs. Guilford County chpt. 1978—82, bd. dirs. Seminole County chpt. 2001—08), Seminole County League Women Voters (bd. dir. 2012—, sec. 2012—). Home: 424 Windmeadows St Altamonte Springs FL 32701 Personal E-mail: ehmurphrey@hotmail.com.

MURPHY, BEN CARROLL, retired engineering company executive; b. Aug. 21, 1931; s. Benjamin Franklin and Effie (Lett) M.; m. Vivian Inez Hancock, March 3, 1950; children: Lanny Carroll, Debra Kay Murphy Soffitri, Kathy M. Murphy David, Gregory Lynn, Jon Patrick. BS, Delta State U., 1969, MBA, 1974; grad., United Electronic Inst., 1962. CCL-PHD candidate. With US Gypsum Co., Greenville, Miss., 1951-54, 55-56, Atlantic & Pacific Tea Co., Greenville, Miss., 1954-55; cost acct. Baxter Labs., Cleveland, Miss., 1966-69; project engr. mfg. US Gypsum Co., Danville, Va., 1969-72; plant personnel and safety mgr. Cook Industries, Inc., Memphis, 1972-73, divsn. safety dir., plant personnel mgr., 1973-75, corp. compensation sr. analyst, 1976, div. indsl. rels. and personnel mgr., 1975-76, corp. compensation mgr., 1976-79; divsn. asst. personnel mgr. Robertson CECO Corp., Columbus, Miss., 1979-80, structural supt., 1980-82, mgr. prodn. control sys., 1982-92, divsn. prodn. control, schedule mgr., 1992-97; with doctoral program Miss. State U., 2009—, 2009—. Ret. night instr. bus. and econs. NW Jr. Coll., Southaven, Miss., 1975-79, East Miss. CC, 1980—; cons. in compensation SE Memphis Mental Health Center, 1978-82. Bd. dirs. Cmty. Water Assn. Mem. Mid-South Compensation and Benefits Assn. (dir. 1977-80, mem. organizing team 1976), Univ. for Women (adv. com. for extended studies of Miss. U.), Am. Compensation Soc., Soc. Mfg. Engrs. (sr., 3d v.p. chpt.), Miss. Mfg. Assn., Am. Mgmt. Compensation Soc., Carmack Cmty. Club (pres.). Baptist. Home: 2066 Attala Rd 3989 Vaiden MS 39176-9606 Home Phone: 662-289-3415; Office Phone: 662-243-1900. Personal E-mail: bencm@bellsouth.net.

MURPHY, CHRIS J., state legislator; s. Patrick J. Murphy and Barbara A. Murphy; m. Maite Murphy. BA, Citadel Grad. Coll., 1990; PhD in Jurisprudence, Miss. Coll. Sch. Law, 1995. BAR, Summerville. Atty. Murphy Law Firm LLC; sr. asst. solicitor to solicitor Walter M. Bailey, Jr.; spl. asst. US Atty. Multi-County Violent Crime and Drug Task Force; with Charleston Area Transp. Com.; founding mem. Summerville Miracle League; pres. Summerville Rotary Club, Summerville Citadel Club; chmn. Dorchester County Coun., 2003; mem. Dist. 98 SC House of Representatives, 2010—. With USN; with SC Army Nat. Guard, US Army. Republican. Office: 136 W Richardson Ave Summerville SC 29483 Address: 310A Blatt Bldg Columbia SC 29201 Office Phone: 843-563-0196. Business E-Mail: cmurphy@dorchestercounty.net.

MURPHY, DANIEL KENNEDY, corporate financial executive; m. Cathleen Murphy; children: Tom, Catie. BBA, Univ. Notre Dame, 1988; MBA, Northwestern Univ., 1995. CPA; cert. CFA. Acct. Coopers & Lybrand; fin. mgmt. positions through dir. investor rels., internat. treas. & v.p. corp. fin. Heller Fin. Inc.; sr. v.p., fin. and investor rels. Fidelity National Financial, Inc., 2000—08, sr. v.p., treas., 2008—. Chmn. Gator Bowl Assn.; bd. dir. Sulzbacher Ctr. Office: Fidelity National Financial Inc 601 Riverside Ave Jacksonville FL 32204 Office Phone: 904-854-8100. Office Fax: 904-357-1007. Business E-Mail: dkmurphy@fnf.com.

MURPHY, DOUGLAS A., cardiothoracic surgeon; b. Mpls., Minn., Oct. 14, 1949; BS, Middlebury Coll., Middlebury. Vt., 1971; MD, U. Pa., 1975. Cert. Am. Bd. Thoracic Surgeons, Am. Bd. Surgery. Intern, internal medicine Mass. Gen. Hosp., Boston, 1975—76, resident, internal medicine, 1976—77, intern, gen. surgery, 1977—78, resident, gen. surgery, 1978—81; resident, cardiothoracic surgery Emory U. Affiliated Hosps., Atlanta, 1981—83; with Peachtree Cardiothoracic and Thoracic Surgeons, PA, Atlanta, 1983—; chief, cardiothoracic surgery St. Joseph's Hosp., Atlanta; chair St. Joseph's Heart and Vascular Inst., Ga., 2007—. Hosp. appointment St. Joseph's Hosp., Atlanta, 1987—, Piedmont Hosp., Atlanta. Address: Peachtree Cardiovascular and Thoracic Surgeons PA 5665 Peachtree Dunwoody Rd Ste 150 Atlanta GA 30342 Office Phone: 404-847-9683, 404-252-6104. Office Fax: 404-257-1808. E-mail: dmurphy407@aol.com.

MURPHY, EWELL EDWARD, JR., lawyer; b. Washington, Feb. 21, 1928; s. Ewell Edward and Lou (Phillips) M.; m. Patricia Bredell Purnell, June 26, 1954 (dec. 1964); children: Michaela, Megan Patricia, Harlan Ewell. BA, U. Tex., 1946, LLB, 1948; DPhil, Oxford U., Eng., 1951. Bar: Tex. 1948. Assoc. Baker & Botts, Houston, 1954-63, ptnr., 1964-93, head internat. dept., 1972-89. Pres. Houston World Trade Assn., 1972-74; trustee Southwestern Legal Found., 1978—2003; chmn. Houston Com. on Fgn. Rels., 1984-85, Inst. Transnat. Arbitration, 1985-89, Internat. and Comparative Law Ctr., 1986-87; mem. J. William Fulbright Fgn. Scholarship Bd., 1991-96, vice chmn., 1992-93, chmn., 1993-95; vis. prof. U. Tex. Law Sch., 1993-97; disting. lectr., U. Houston Law Ctr., 1996-2006, adj. prof., 2007-. Contbr. articles to profl. jours. Served to lt. USAF, 1952—54. Recipient Carl H. Fulda award U. Tex. Internat. Law Jour., 1980; Rhodes scholar, 1948-51. Mem.: ABA (chmn. sect. internat. law 1970—71), Internat. Law Inst. (bd. dirs. 1994—2008), Houston Bar Assn. (chmn. internat. law com. 1963—64, 1970—71), Coun. on Fgn. Rels., Philos. Soc. Tex., Houston C. of C. (chmn. internat. bus. com. 1964—65), Fulbright Assn. (bd. dirs. 1999—2004, v.p. 2002—04). Home and Office: 17 W Oak Dr Houston TX 77056-2117 Home Phone: 713-622-3840; Office Phone: 713-622-3840.

MURPHY, HAROLD LLOYD, federal judge; b. Haralson County, Ga., Mar. 31, 1927; s. James Loyd and Georgia Gladys (McBrayer) M.; m. Jacqueline Marie Ferri, Dec. 20, 1958; children: Mark Harold, Paul Bailey. Student, West Ga. Coll., 1944-45, U. Miss., 1945-46; LLB, U. Ga., 1949. Bar: Ga. 1949. Pvt. practice, Buchanan, Ga., from 1949; ptnr. Howe & Murphy, Buchanan and Tallapoosa, Ga., 1958-71; judge Superior Cts., Tallapoosa Circuit, 1971-77, US Dist. Ct. (no. dist.) Ga., Rome, 1977—. Rep. Gen. Assembly of Ga., 1951-61; asst. solicitor gen. Tallapoosa Jud. Circuit, 1956; mem. Jud. Qualifications Commn., State of Ga., 1977 With USNR, 1945-46. Fellow Am. Bar Found.; mem. ABA, Ga. Bar Assn., Dist. Judges Assn. for 11th Cir. Bar Assn., Am. Judicature Soc., Tallapoosa Cir. Bar Assn., Old War Horse Lawyers Club, Am. Inns Ct. (past pres. Joseph Henry Lumpkin sect.), Fed. Judges Assn. Methodist. Home: 3 Haley Dr SE Rome GA 30161 Office: 600 E 1st St Rm 311 Rome GA 30161-3187

MURPHY, JACK, state legislator; b. June 9, 1941; m. Wendy Murphy (dec.); 6 children. Attended, Univ. Del. V.p. Orkin Inc.; founder, pres., CEO Radar Exterminating Co.; pres., CEO private real estate investment co.; mem. Ga. House Reps., 2003—06; mem. Dist. 27 Ga. State Senate, 2007—. Served USAF. Republican. Episcopal. Mailing: 3830 Adams Rd Cumming GA 30041 Office Fax: 770-205-0602. Business E-Mail: jack.murphy@senate.ga.gov.

MURPHY, JIM, state legislator; m. Kathleen Murphy; children: Robert, Pace. Exec. dir., pres. Dist. Mgmt. Svcs., 1986—; mem. Dist. 133 Tex. House of Representatives, 2007—08, 2011—. Former mem. bd. West Houston Med. Ctr., Houston West C. of C.; mem. adv. coun. John Ben Shepperd Pub. Leadership Inst. Active Greater Houston Partnership; mem. bd. trustees Houston Realty Breakfast Club, Houston CC, 1997—2006. Named one of Outstanding Young Texans, 1995. Mem.: Assn. Comml. Real Estate Profls. (former chmn.), Urban Land Inst., Houston Assn. Realtors, Alief Edn. Found. (founder, former vice chmn.), Jaycees (former pres., former state pres.). Republican. Roman Catholic. Office: 1 E Greenway Plz Ste 225 Houston TX 77046 also: Room E2.606 Capitol Extension PO Box 2910 Austin TX 78768 Office Phone: 713-526-3399, 512-463-0514, 855-597-0662. Office Fax: 512-463-8715.

MURPHY, JOHN JOSEPH, manufacturing executive; b. Olean, NY, Nov. 24, 1931; s. John Joseph and Mary M.; m. Louise John; children: Kathleen A. Murphy Bell, Karen L. Murphy Rochelli, Patricia L. Murphy Smith, Michael J. AAS in Mech. Engring., Rochester Inst. Tech., 1952; MBA, So. Meth. U., 1981. Engr. Clark div. Dresser Industries, Olean, 1952-67, gen. mgr. roots blower div. Connersville, Ind., 1967-69, pres. crane, hoist and tower div. Muskegon, Mich., 1969-70, pres. machinery group Houston, 1970-75, sr. v.p. ops. Dallas, 1980, exec. v.p., 1982, pres., 1982-92, CEO, 1983—95, chmn. bd., 1983-96; mng. dir. SMG Mgmt. L.L.C., Dallas, 1997-2000. Bd. dirs. W.R. Grace & Co.,emeritus mem. Bus. Coun. With US Army, 1954—56. Office: 3838 Oak Lawn Ave Ste 777 Dallas TX 75219

MURPHY, MARK R., plastic surgeon; BA in English Lit., Tulane U., 1989—93, MD, 1994—98. With gen. surgery Columbia Univ., 1998—99; fellow in facial plastic surgery Tulane Univ., New Orleans, 2003—04; with med. missions for children Antigua, Guatemala, 2002; with NY Presbyn. Hosp., The Univ. Hosps. of Columbia & Cornell, Meml. Sloan Kettering Cancer Ctr. Contbr. (book) Masters of Facial Rejuvenation, 2006, (publs.) "Balanced" orbital decompression for severe Graves orbitopathy: Technique with treatment algorithm, Cost Effective Diagnosis of Acoustic Neuromas: A Philosophical, Macroeconomic, and Technological Decision, The Extended Columellar Strut-Tip Graft, Hypopharyngeal perforation "near misses" during traditional (blind) transesophageal echocardiography superior safety of optically-guided transesophageal echocardiography, Laparoscopic incisional hernia repair after transverse rectus abdominis myocutaneous flap reconstruction, Breast cancer in reduction mammoplasty: case reports and a survey of plastic surgeons. Mem.: AMA, Am. Acad. of Otolaryngology, Am. Acad. of Facial Plastic & Reconstructive Surgery. Office: Palm Beach Facial Plastic Surgery Suite 310 4280 Professional Center Dr Palm Beach Gardens FL 33410 Office Phone: 561-659-9766. Office Fax: 561-799-4090.

MURPHY, PATRICK ERIN, United States Representative from Florida, accountant; b. Miami, Mar. 30, 1983; BS in Acctg. & Finance, U. Miami, 2006. CPA. Accountant Deloitte & Touche; v.p. Coastal Construction Group (CCG); mem. US Congress from 18th Fla. Dist., Washington, 2013—, US House Financial Services Com., 2013—, US House Small Bus. Com., 2013—. Democrat. Roman Catholic. Office: US House of Representatives 1517 Longworth House Office Bldg Washington DC 20515 also: 2000 PGA Blvd Suite A3220 North Palm Beach FL 33408 Office Phone: 202-225-3026, 561-253-8433. Office Fax: 202-225-8398, 561-253-8436.*

MURPHY, QUINCY, state legislator; State rep. Dist. 97, Ga., 2003—04; state rep. Dist. 120 Ga., 2004—; sec. Intragovt. Coordination Com.; mem. Higher Edn., Ins., & Transportation Coms., Ins. Fin. Svcs. Democrat. Office: 1510 Avalon Ave Augusta GA 30909 also: 512 Legislative Office Bldg Atlanta GA 30334 Mailing: 3238 Peach Orchard Rd Augusta GA 30909 Office Phone: 706-790-4600, 404-656-7859. Business E-Mail: qmurphy@legis.state.ga.us.

MURPHY, RANDALL KENT, writer, educator, consultant; b. Laramie, Wyo., Nov. 8, 1943; s. Robert Joseph and Sally (McConnell) M.; m. Cynthia Laura Hillhouse, Dec. 29, 1978; children: Caroline, Scott, Emily. Student, U. Wyo., 1961—65; MBA, So. Meth. U., 1983. Dir. mktg. Wycoa, Inc., Denver, 1967—70; dir. Comm. Resource Inst., Dallas, 1971—72; account exec. Xerox Learning Sys., Dallas, 1973—74; regional mgr. Systema Corp., Dallas, 1975; pres. Performance Assocs.; pres., dir. Acclivus Corp., Dallas, 1976—; founder, chmn. Acclivus Inst., 1982—. Author: Performance Management, Coaching and Counseling and Performance, 1980, Managing Development and Performance, 1982, Acclivus Performance Planning System, 1983, (with others) BASE For Performance, 1983, Acclivus Coaching, 1984, Acclivus Negotiation, 1985, R3 Service, 1997, BASE for Effective Presentations, 1987, BASE for Strategic Presentations, 1988, The New BASE for Excellence, 1988, Major Account Planning and Strategy, 1989, Strategic Management, 1989, Building on the BASE, 1992, Negotiation Mastery, 1995, R3 Service, 1997, Co-creating R3 Value, 2002, Getting the Meeting, 2004, R3 Interaction, 2005, R3 Negotiation, 2009, R3 Transaction Online, 2010; co-inventor The Randy-Band multi-purpose apparel accessory, 1968. Vice chmn. bd. trustees The Winston Sch., 1994-96, chmn. bd. trustees, 1997-2000; mem. adv. bd. The Women's Ctr. of Dallas, 1995-98. With AUS, 1966. Mem. ASTD, Inst. Mgmt. Scis., Soc. Applied Learning Tech., Assn. Mgmt. Cons., Am. Assn. Higher Edn., World Future Soc., Soc. for Intercultural Edn., Tng. and Rsch., Internat. Fedn. Tng. and Devel. Orgns., Inst. Noetic Scis., Nat. Peace Inst., Amnesty Internat., Acad. Polit. Sci., The Nature Conservancy, Theosophical Soc. Am., So. Meth. U. Alumni Assn., U. Wyo. Alumni Assn, Assn. Humanistic Psychology, Assn. Conflict Resolution. CG Jung Found., NY Hist. Soc., Southern Poverty Law Ctr., Internat. Soc. Performance Improvement, United Nations Assn., Soc. Human Resource Mgmt., Am. Mus. Natural History, Jane Goodall Inst., Human Soc. US, Norman Rockwell Mus., US Holocaust Meml. Mus., Neuroleadership Inst. Office Phone: 972-385-1277. Business E-Mail: randall.murphy@acclivus.com.

MURPHY, ROBIN ROBERSON, computer scientist, robotics engineer; b. Mobile, Ala., Aug. 25, 1957; d. Fred Blakely and Ada Lee (Wills) Roberson; m. Kevin Eddy Murphy, Aug. 27, 1982; children: Kathleen Freebern(dec.), Allan Roberson. BME, Ga. Inst. Tech., 1980, MS in Computer Sci., 1989, PhD in Computer Sci., 1992. CIMS rsch. asst. Sch. Info. and Computer Sci., Ga. Inst. Tech., Atlanta, 1987—88, grad. tchg. asst., 1989; project engr. Dow Chem. USA, Plaquemine, La., 1980-84; software project engr. Turbitrol Co., Atlanta, 1984-86; asst. prof. dept. math. and comp. sci. Colo. Sch. Mines, Golden, 1992—98, assoc. dir. Ctr. Robotics and Intelligent Systems, 1994—98; assoc. prof. Dept. Computer Sci. and Engring. and Dept. Psychology U. South Fla., Tampa, 1998—2003, dir. Inst. Safety Security Rescue Tech. (formerly Ctr. Robot-Assisted Search and Rescue), 2002—, prof., 2003—, founder, site dir. Inst. Safety, Security, Rescue Tech. Ctr., 2002—; founder NSF Industry Univ. Cooperative Rsch. Ctr. on Safety, Security and Rescue Tech., 2003; with Tex. A&M Univ., Dept. Computer Sci. and Engring. Cons. Defense Sci. Study Group Inst. for Defense Analyses, 1998—99, cons., 2000—; ad hoc mem. USAF Sci. Adv. Bd., 2001, mem., 2001—05; mem. study on unmanned ground vehicles Nat. Rsch. Coun., 2001—02; mem. tech. adv. panel USMC Chem. Biological Incident Response Force, 2002—; mem. DARPA Info. Sci. and Tech. Study Group, 2004—07, Nat. Rsch. Coun. Study on Using Info. Tech. to Enhance Disaster Mgmt., 2005—; bd. dirs. Space Fla., 2006—; adv. bd. mem. NSF, Computer & Info. Sci. & Engring., 2006—; spkr. in field. Author: (with others) The Handbook of Brain Theory and Neural Networks, 1995, Artificial Intelligence for Mobile Robots, 1997, AI for Mobile Robots, 1997, (textbook) Introduction to AI Robotics, 2000; spl. column editor Robotics and Autonomous Systems, 1997-; contbr. articles to profl. jours. Rsch. grantee NSF, 1993—, Advanced Rsch. Projects Agy., 1994—, NASA, 1994—, Northrop Grumman, 1997—; Rockwell Internat. Doctoral fellow; recipient Colo. Inst. Equity Excellence award, Colo. Inst. for Gender Equity, 1997, Nils Nilsson Technical Achievement award, Am. Assn. for Artificial Intelligence, 2000, Eagle award, Nat. Inst. for Urban Search and Rescue, 2001, Phi Kappa Phi, Univ. South Fla. Chpt. Artist and Scholar of the Yr. award, 2004, US Air Force Exemplary Civilian Svc. award for Distinguished Svc. on the Air Force Scientific Adv. Bd., 2005; named one of TIME Mag. Innovators, 2004. Mem.: IEEE, Am. Assn. for Artificial Ingelligence, Soc. Women Engrs., Soc. Photo-Optical Instrumentation Engrs., Fla. Fire Chiefs' Assn., Assn. for Unmanned Vehicle Sys. Internat., Assn. Computing Machinery. Achievements include being the founder of rescue robotics; participated in the following disasters: World Trade Center, 2001, Hurricanes Charley, 2004, Dennis, 2005, Katrina, 2005, and Wilma, 2005, La Conchita California Mudslides, 2005 and others. Office: Computer Sci and Engring U S Fla 4202 E Fowler Ave ENB342 Tampa FL 33620-5399 also: Texas A&M Univ Dept Computer Sci and Engring 333 Harvey R Bright Building College Station TX 77843-3112 Business E-Mail: murphy@cs.tamu.edu. E-mail: murphy@cse.usf.edu.

MURPHY, SUSAN (JANE MURPHY), small business owner, real estate broker; b. Williamsport, Pa., Dec. 26, 1950; d. Jack W. and Edythe J. (Grier) M.; m. Michael J. Sanchez, Dec. 30, 1979. BBA, Pa. State U., 1978. Gen. mgr. Murphy Swift Homes, Hummelstown, Pa., 1970-75; owner, operator Murphy's Home Ctr., Hummelstown, 1975-79, 85-91; mgr. Builder's Emporium, San Diego, 1979-80; entrepreneur Castle in the Sand, San Diego, 1980-83; adminstr. Sohio Constrn., Prudhoe Bay, Alaska, 1983-85; fin. systems analyst Blue Shield, San Francisco, 1991-93; pres. San Francisco Mgmt. Svcs., Inc., San Francisco, 1993-99; entrepreneur Blue Skies Inn and Island Place of Olde Key West, Key West, Fla., 1999—, An Island Oasis, Key West, 2005; broker, owner An Island Oasis Realty Svcs., LLC; owner Murphy's Home Ctr., Hummelstown, Pa., 2007—. Cons. in field; owner Murphy's True Value Home Ctr. Photographs displayed at San Diego Art Inst. Vol. Hershey (Pa.) Free Ch. Donald MacIntyre scholar, 1979, Class of 1920 scholar, 1979, Congressman Kunkel scholar, 1979. Mem.: Mem. Pa. Hardware Assn., Hummelstown C. of C., Better Bus. Bur. Evangelical Christian. Avocations: sailing, scuba diving, photography. Home: 2120 58th Ave 114 Vero Beach FL 32966

MURPHY, THOMAS MILES, pediatrician, educator; m. Priscilla Rollin Coit. AB in Math., Harvard Coll., 1969; MD, U. Rochester, 1973. Diplomate Am. Bd. Med. Examiners, Am. Bd. Internal Medicine, Am. Bd. Pediatrics, subbd. pulmonology; lic. physician, N.C. Intern Georgetown U. Med. Divsn., D.C. Gen. Hosp., Washington, 1973-74; resident in internal medicine Georgetown U. Med. Ctr., Washington, 1974-76, fellow pediat. pulmonary medicine, 1976-78; asst. prof. pediat. Georgetown U. Sch. Medicine, Washington, 1979-80, asst. prof. clin. pediat., 1980-85, U. Chgo., 1985-87, asst. prof. pediat. and medicine, 1990-93; asst. prof. pediat. U. Chgo. Pritzker Sch. Medicine, 1987-90, chief sect. pulmonary medicine dept. pediat., 1992-93; assoc. prof., chief divsn. pediat. pulmonary diseases Duke U., Durham, NC, 1993—. Assoc. dir. Pediatric Pulmonary and Cystic Fibrosis Ctr., Georgetown U., 1978-80; asst. prof. child health and devel. George Washington U. Sch. Medicine and Health Scis., Washington, 1980-85; assoc. chmn. dept. pulmonary medicine, co-dir. Cystic Fibrosis Ctr. for Care, Teaching and Rsch., Children's Hosp. Nat. Med. Ctr., Washington, 1980-85; dir. pediatric pulmonary fellowship tng. program U. Chgo., 1990-93, dir. Cystic Fibrosis Ctr., 1991-93, assoc. chief sect. allergy, immunology and pulmonology, dept. pediatrics, 1991-92; editor ATS Pediat. Assembly Website, 2000—; ad hoc mem. lung biology and pathology study sect. NIH, 2002. Contbr. articles to profl. jours., chpts. to books; cons. referee editor New Eng. Jour. Medicine, 1989, Am. Rev. Respiratory Disease, 1989—, Am. Jour. Physiology: Lung Cellular and Molecular Physiology, 1990—, Pediatric Rsch., 1991—, Jour. Applied Physiology, 1991—, Pediat. Pulmonology, 1993—, mem. editl. bd., 1996—; contbg. editor The Hudson Monitor. Mem. ctr. com. Cystic Fibrosis Found., 1992-97, 2000-2002; chmn. childhood lung disease com. D.C. Lung Assn., 1980-83, lung disease com., 1984; mem. adv. coun. D.C. Sudden Infant Death Syndrome, 1981-83, chmn. med. adv. com., 1982-83. Recipient Cmty. Svc. award So. Md. Lung Assn., 1980, Media award Am. Acad. Pediatrics, 1980, Svc. award homicide br. Met. Police Dept. D.C., 1983, Svc. award Met. D.C. chpt. Cystic Fibrosis Foun., Washington, 1985, Nat. Cystic Fibrosis Found., 1997; Rsch. grantee Am. Lung Assn., N.Y.C., 1992, NIH, Bethesda, Md., 1993, 98. Mem.: AAAS, European Respiratory Soc., Am. Thoracic Soc. (program com. assembly on respiratory structure and function 1993—96, chair long range planning com. 2000—02, chair subcom. on physician scientists, pediat. assembly 1997—, liaison officer pediat. assembly 2000—), N.Y. Acad. Scis., Am. Physiol. Soc., Soc. Pediatric Rsch. Avocations: refereeing soccer, jazz. Office: Duke U Med Ctr PO Box 2994 Durham NC 27710-2994

MURPHY, THOMAS PATRICK, lawyer; b. Syracuse, NY, Feb. 12, 1952; s. George Edward and Sara Eileen (Murphy) M.; m. Susan Hollis Francher, Oct. 19, 1976 (div. Oct. 1992); m. Lise M. Adkins, Aug. 6, 1994; children: Casey Marie, Matthew Thomas. BS, Clarkson U., 1974; JD, Vt. Law Sch., 1978. Bar: N.Y. 1978, D.C. 1981, Md. 1988, Va. 1989. Asst. U.S. atty. U.S. Atty.'s Office, Washington, 1982—85; assoc. Highsaw & Mahoney, Washington, 1985—87, McGuire, Woods, Battle & Boothe, Washington, 1987—90; ptnr. Reed Smith Shaw & McClay, McLean, Va., 1990—99, Hunton & Williams, McLean, 1999—. Contbr. articles to profl. jours. Chmn. bd. profl. responsibility DC Ct. Appeals; mem. planning com. Va. CLE Found. With USN, 1978—82, lt. USN, 1978—81, with USNR, 1978—90. Recipient Spl. Achievement award US Dept. Justice, 1984; named one of Best Lawyers in Am. for employment law; Legal Elite Va. Bus. Mag. 2004, 05, 06, America's Leading Lawyers for Bus. Chamber's USA, Va. Super Lawyers. Mem. ABA, Fed. Bar Assn., NY State Bar Assn., DC Bar Assn. (chmn. pro se litigants com.), Md. Bar Assn., Va. Bar Assn., Fairfax County Bar Assn., Asst. US Attys., Bd. Profl. Responsibility DC Ct. Appeals (hearing com.). Office: Hunton & Williams 1751 Pinnacle Dr Ste 1700 Mc Lean VA 22102-3836 Home Phone: 202-333-9745; Office Phone: 703-714-7533. Business E-Mail: tpmurphy@hunton.com.

MURPHY, TIMOTHY JAMES, lawyer; b. Topeka, Sept. 30, 1946; s. Miles J. and Norine D. Murphy; m. Patricia MacKinnon, Apr. 7, 1990. BA, U. Ga., 1968; JD with honors, Washington & Lee U., 1970; LLM, Harvard U., 1976. Bar: Va. 1970, Fla. 1972. Atty. Anderson, Mori & Rabinowitz, Tokyo, 1970—71, Shutts & Bowen, Miami, Fla., 1976—. Contbr. articles to profl. jours. Mem. Fla. Ho. of Reps., 1982-84; bd. dirs. Cath. Charities, Inc., 1982-97, pres., 1994-97, Cath. Charities Legal Svcs., Inc., Miami, 2000—; pres., 2008-11, The Barnacle soc., 1991-2002, pres. 2000-02; mem. adv. bd. Miami-Dade County Pub. Libr., 1988-2002. Col. JAG Corps USAFR, 1971-95. Mem.: Biscayne Bay Yacht Club, Army and Navy Club (Washington). Democrat. Roman Catholic. Office: Shutts & Bowen 201 S Biscayne Blvd Ste 1500 Miami FL 33131-4308 Office Phone: 305-379-9137. Business E-Mail: tmurphy@shutts.com.

MURPHY, WILLIAM ALEXANDER, JR., diagnostic radiologist, educator; b. Pitts., Apr. 26, 1945; s. William Alexander and LaRue (Eshbaugh); m. Judy Marie Lang, June 18, 1977; children: Abigail Norris, William Lawrence, Joseph Ryan. BS, U. Pitts., 1967; MD, Pa. State U., 1971. Diplomate Am. Bd. Radiology. Intern Barnes Hosp., St. Louis, 1971-72, staff radiologist, 1975-93; radiology resident Washington U., St. Louis, 1972-75, prof. radiology, 1983-93; sec. chief Mallinckrodt Inst. Radiology, St. Louis, 1975-93; cons. Office Med. Examiner City and County St. Louis, 1993—. Radiologist, prof. radiology, John S. Dunn Sr. prof., disting. chair MD Anderson Cancer Ctr. U. Tex., 1993—, v.p. hosp. and clinics, 1996-97, COO, 1997; chmn. bd. dirs. MD Anderson Physicians Network Corp., 2001—. Fellow Am. Acad. Forensic Scis., Am. Coll. Radiology; mem. Radiol. Soc. N.Am. (1st. v.p. 1997-98), Am. Roentgen Ray Soc., Am. Soc. Bone and Mineral Rsch., Internat. Skeletal Soc., Assn. Univ. Radiologists. Methodist. Home: 4808 Bellview St Bellaire TX 77401-5306 Office: University Tex Anderson Cancer Ctr Divsn Dx Imaging 1475 1515 Holcombe Blvd Houston TX 77030-4009 Office Phone: 713-792-4916. Business E-Mail: wmurphy@mdanderson.org.

MURPHY, WILLIAM PARRY, JR., mechanical engineer; b. Boston, Nov. 11, 1923; s. William Parry and Harriet Adams Murphy. BS, Harvard Coll., 1946; MD, U. Ill., 1947. Intern St. Francis Hosp., Honolulu; rsch. fellow in medicine Peter Bent Brigham Hosp., Boston; physiologic instrumentation rschr. MIT; founder, pres., CEO, chmn. Cordis Corp. (formerly Med. Devel. Corp.), Miami, Fla., 1957—85; founder, chmn. Small Parts Inc., 1964—2005. Bd. dirs. Hyperion, Inc., 1986—2003, chmn., CEO, 1999—2003; bd. dirs. Bioheart, Inc., 2003—. Contbr. articles to profl. jours. Co-founder, mem. exec. adv. bd. Found. Inspiration & Recognition of Sci. & Tech. (FIRST), 1989—. Recipient FIRST Founder's award, 2000, Lemelson-MIT Lifetime Achievement award, 2003, Disting. Svc. award, N.Am. Soc. Pacing & Electrophysiology, Jay Malina award, Beacon Coun. Miami; named to Nat. Inventors Hall of Fame, 2008. Fellow: Am. Inst. Med. & Biol. Engring. (founding fellow 1993). Achievements include development of a flexible sealed blood bag for the transfusion of whole blood first used during the Korean War; design of a series of inexpensive medical trays equipped with drugs and sterilized tools that can be discarded after use, reducing cross-contamination of patients; patents in field. Mailing: c/o FIRST 200 Bedford St Manchester NH 03101 also: Bioheart Inc 13794 NW 4th St Ste 212 Fort Lauderdale FL 33325

MURRAH, CHARLIE, manufacturing executive; B in Indsl. Engirng., Ga. Inst. Tech., 1984. Registered profl. engr., Ga.; CERT. prodn. & inventory mgr. Various engring. & mgmt. positions, energy cable & copper ops. Southwire Co., v.p., supply chain, exec. v.p., pres., Energy Divsn., indsl. engr., carrollton utility products plant, 1984. Recipient Coun. of Outstanding Young Engring. Alumni award, Ga. Tech, 1996. Office: Southwire Co 1 Southwire Dr Carrollton GA 30119 Office Phone: 770-832-4242. Business E-Mail: charlie_murrah@southwire.com.

MURRAY, CYNTHIA, retail executive; Retail mgmt. positions Charming Shoppes, Saks Fifth Ave.; retail mgmt. positions through sr. v.p., Merchandising Stores and Catalog Talbot's, 1989—2004; exec. v.p., gen. mdse. mgr. Stage Stores Inc., 2004—06, exec. v.p., chief merchandising officer, Stage Divsn., 2006—09; brand pres. Chico's FAS, Inc., 2009—. Office: Chico's FAS Inc 11215 Metro Pky Fort Myers FL 33966 Office Phone: 239-277-6200. Office Fax: 239-277-5237. Business E-Mail: cynthia.murray@chicos.com.

MURRAY, DAVID GEORGE, retired architect; b. Tulsa, Nov. 9, 1919; s. Lee Cloyd and Marion (Bennett) M.; m. Margaret Elizabeth Oldham, Sept. 23, 1944 (dec. Mar. 08, 2010); children: Michael Allen, Lucy Margaret (Mrs. Norman Scheer), Patrick David. BArch, Okla. State U., Stillwater, 1942. Registered architect, Okla. Ptnr. Atkinson & Murray, Tulsa, 1949-52; prin. David G. Murray & Assocs., Tulsa, 1952-56; pres. Murray, Jones, Murray, Inc., Tulsa, 1957-85, chmn., 1986-89. Chmn., bd. govs. Licensed Architects, Oklahoma City, 1964-74. Prin. works include Cities Service Technology Ctr., Broken Arrow, Okla., Terminal Bldg. Tulsa Internat. Airport, St. Patrick's Ch., Oklahoma City, Coll. of Osteopathic Medicine and Surgery, Tulsa, First Nat. Tower, Tulsa, Hillcrest Med. Ctr., Tulsa, Thomas Gilcrease Mus., Tulsa, Tulsa Civic Ctr. Bldgs. Chmn., dir. Goodwill Industries of Tulsa, 1966-87; chmn., exec. com. Downtown Tulsa Unltd., 1975-87; v.p., exec. com., dir. Met. Tulsa C. of C., 1979-85. Served to 1st lt. USAF, 1942-45. Named to Hall of Fame Coll. Engring. Okla. State U., 1969. Fellow AIA (pres. Tulsa chpt. 1964, mem. com. office practice 1983-87). Republican. Methodist. Avocations: travel, golf. E-mail: davidmurray1@cox.net.

MURRAY, EDWIN RENE, state legislator; b. Aug. 6, 1960; Atty.; coord. Summer Youth Employment Program, 1982—85; mem. State Democratic Ctrl. Com., 1984—88; mem. Dist. 96 La. House of Reps., 1992—2004; mem. Dist. 4 La. State Senate, 2004—, vice chair labor and indsl. rels. com., interim mem. ins. com., local and mcpl. affairs com., mem. fin. com., judiciary A com., senate and govtl. affairs com. Mem.: Coun. State Govts. (chmn. bus. & fin. com.), Nat. Conf. Black State Legislators, Nat. Coun. Ins. Legislators, Faubourg/St. John Neighborhood Assn., La. Bar Assn., Treme Improvement Polit. Soc., New Orleans Com. Judicial Reform, Cmty. Access Corp. Democrat. Baptist. Address: 1200 Park Island Dr New Orleans LA 70122 Mailing: 1540 N Broad New Orleans LA 70119 Home Phone: 504-288-3015; Office Phone: 504-945-0042. Office Fax: 504-902-5968.

MURRAY, JAMES E., managed health care company executive; Ptnr. Coopers & Lybrand, Louisville; joined Humana, Inc., Louisville, 1989, interim CFO, until 1997, CFO, 1997-2000, COO Health Plan Div., 2000—01, COO svc. ops., 2001—02, COO Market and Bus. Segments Ops., 2002—06, COO, 2006—. Office: Humana Inc 500 West Main St Louisville KY 40202

MURRAY, JAMES J., textiles executive; b. 1961; CPA. Tax acct. pvt. industry; mng. dir. KPMG Corp. Trans. Svc. Practice; exec. v.p., CFO, sec. Johnston Industries, Inc., 1997—. Office: Johnston Textiles Inc 300 General Colin Powell Pkwy Phenix City AL 36869-6953 Fax: 706-641-3159.

MURRAY, PAMELA J., pediatrician, educator; Spl. tng. in Biophysics, Pa. State U., 1972; spl. tng. in Nutrition, Columbia Univ., NYC, 1974; spl. tng. in Health Planning, U. NSW, Australia, 1986; MD, Drexel U., Phila., 1978. Diplomate Am. Bd. Pediatrics, 1983, Am. Bd. Pediatrics-adolescent medicine, 2009. Resident pediat. Children's Hosp., Phila., 1979—81; fellow pub. health Univ. NSW, Sydney, 1986—87; chief adolescent medicine W.Va Univ., co-chief divsn. of gen. pediat. and adolescent medicine, vice chmn. dept. of pediat., prof. pediat. Office: West Virginia University Department Pediatrics PO Box 9214 Morgantown WV 26506-9214 Office Phone: 304-293-1225. Office Fax: 412-692-6677.

MURRAY, PATRICK BRIAN, lawyer; b. Chgo., Jan. 16, 1964; s. Robert Joseph and Sharon Ann (Edmunds) Murray; m. Michelle Terese Rust, Aug. 5, 1989; 4 children. BA in Hist., Creighton U., Omaha, 1986; JD, DePaul U. Coll. Law, Chgo., 1989. Bar: Ill. 1989, US Dist. Ct. (no. dist.) Ill. 1989. Assoc. Clausen Miller Gorman Caffrey & Witous P.C., Chgo., 1989-90; asst. US atty. criminal divsn. US Atty.'s Office (no. dist.) Ill., 1990—95; counsel US House Com. on Judiciary, Washington, 1995—96; dep. chief counsel US House Com. Internat. Rels., Washington, 1996—97; chief counsel US House Permanent Select Com. Intelligence, Washington, 1997—2001, chief counsel, staff dir., 2003—04; assoc. dep. atty. gen. US Dept. Justice, Washington, 2001—03; chief of staff to dir. CIA, 2004—06; sr. counsel Verizon Wireless, Verizon Comm. Inc., 2007—. Mem.: Federalist Soc. Law & Pub. Policy, Chgo. Bar Assn. Roman Catholic. Office: Verizon Wireless Hdqs PO Box 105378 Atlanta GA 30348

MURRAY, ROBERT CHARLES, retired electric power industry executive; b. Washington, Nov. 10, 1945; s. Thomas F. and Margaret (Regan) M.; m. Ellen Meehan, June 22, 1969; children: Erin E., Griffin R. BA, Holy Cross Coll., Worcester, Mass., 1968; MBA,

Dartmouth Coll., 1970. Hmn., interim CEO Pantellos Corp.; analyst Conn. Gen. Life, Bloomfield, 1972-75; assoc., analyst Morgan Stanley & Co., NYC, 1976-79, v.p., 1980-81, prin., 1982-86, mng. dir., 1987-91; sr. v.p., CFO Pub. Svc. Enterprise Group, Newark, 1991. Bd. dirs. Riverside Health Care System, Inc., Mirant Corp., 2006, GenOn Energy, Inc., 2010—. Bd. trustees St. John's Riverside Hosp. Lt. USAF, 1970—72. Home: Riverview Rd Irvington NY 10533-1307 Office: GenOn Energy Inc Bd Directors 1000 Main St Houston TX 77002 Office Phone: 832-357-3000. Office Fax: 832-357-0140. Business E-Mail: rob.murray@genon.com.

MURRAY, ROBERT J., retired board member; b. Aug. 2, 1941; s. Andrew M.; m. Judith; children: Maura Murray Locke, Judith, Robert Jr., Jennifer, Caitlyn, Karyn. BA, Boston Coll., BS, 1962; MBA, Northeastern U., Boston, 1966; Advanced Mgmt. Program, Harvard U., 1990. Chmn. New England Bus. Svc., Inc.; product mgr., mktg. The Gillette Co.-Safety Razor Div., Boston, 1967-69; exec. asst. to pres. Gillette N.Am. Hdqrs., Boston, 1969-73; sales assignments Paper Mate Div., Boston, 1974-78; group gen. mgr. Braun U.K., London, 1978-80; group gen. mgr., Anglo Am. Braun AG, Germany, 1980-82; pres. Paper Mate Div., Boston, 1982-85; chmn. Braun AG, Germany, 1985-90; exec. v.p. Gillette North Atlantic, Boston, 1990. Bd. dirs. Delhaize Group, IDEXX Labs., Inc., LoJack Corp., The Hanover Ins. Group, Inc., Tupperware Brands Corp.; bd. trustees Boston Coll., Mass., 1990—. Bd. of overseers Boston (Mass.) Symphony Orch., 1991. Mem. Scituate Yacht Club, Hatherly Country Club. Office: Tupperware Brands Corp Bd Directors 14901 S Orange Blossom Trail Orlando FL 32837 Office Phone: 407-826-5050. Office Fax: 407-826-8268. Business E-Mail: robertmurray@tupperware.com.

MURRAY, SUSAN LYONS, library director; b. Barksdale Air Force Base, La., Feb. 23, 1948; BA, Trinity Coll., Washington, 1971; MSLS, Fla. State U., 1976; MBA, Rosary Coll., 1989. Pub. svcs. libr. St. Mary's Coll., Moraga, Calif., 1976-79; head pub. svcs. Hood Coll., Frederick, Md., 1979-85, Dominican U. (formerly Rosary Coll.), River Forest, Ill., 1985-87; dir. libr. Aurora (Ill.) U., 1987-97; dir. libr. and acad. info. svcs. Trinity Coll. Libr. (now Trinity U.), Washington, 1997—2005; dir. libr. Valencia Cmty. Coll., Winter Park, Fla., 2005—. Adj. assoc. prof Rosary Coll. Grad. Sch. Libr. and Info. Sci., 1990-97. Mem. ALA, Assn. Coll. and Rsch. Librs. (nat. adv. com., rep. Ill. chpt. 1991-95), Pvt. Acad. Librs. of Ill. (pres. 1994-96), Ill. Libr. Assn. (del. pre-White House Conf., Chgo., 1989-90), Beta Phi Mu, Phi Eta Sigma (hon.). Office: Winter Park Campus Valencia Cmty Coll 850 W Morse Blvd Winter Park FL 32789 Office Phone: 407-582-6815. Personal E-mail: susanmurray238@yahoo.com. Business E-Mail: smurray27@valenciacc.edu.

MURRAY-RUST, CATHERINE, library director; B in Polit. Sci. and History, Mt. Holyoke Coll.; studies in African politics and internat. rels., U. Dar es Salaam, Tanzania, 1971—72; grad. diploma in libr. and info. studies, U. London, 1974; completed grad. studies in internat. nutrition, Cornell U., Ithaca, NY, 1976. Chartered in librarianship Libr. Assn. Great Britain, 1976. Intern UN Econ. Commn. for Africa, Addis Ababa, Ethiopia, 1969; news libr. Reuters News Agency, London, 1973—77; reference bibliographer SUNY, Cortland, 1977; various positions including reference libr., tng. & implementation libr. and coord. reference and instrn. Cornell U., 1978—87, asst. univ. libr., 1987—93, assoc. univ. libr., 1993—97, dir. campus delivery, 1998; assoc. univ. libr. pub. services and innovative tech. Oreg. State U., 1999—2003; dean libraries Colo. State U., Fort Collins, 2003—05, Ga. Inst. Tech., Atlanta, 2008—, vice provost learning excellence, 2012—. Mem.: ALA, Libr. Adminstrn. and Mgmt. Assn., Libr. Assn. Great Britain and No. Ireland. Office: Georgia Institute of Technology Library 704 Cherry St Atlanta GA 30332-0900 Office Phone: 404-894-8914.

MURRELL, JERRY (VICTOR JEROME MURRELL), restaurant chain executive; b. 1944; m. Janie Murrell; children: Ben, Tyler;children from previous marriage: Matt, Jim, Chad. BA in Economics, U. Mich. Insurance salesman AXA Equitable; co-founder, CEO Five Guys Enterprises, LLC, Lorton, Va., 1986—. Office: Five Guys Enterprises, LLC 10440 Furnace Rd Lorton VA 22079

MURRIAN, ROBERT PHILLIP, retired federal judge, educator; b. Knoxville, Tenn., Apr. 1, 1945; s. Albert Kinzel and Mary Gilbert (Eppes) M.; m. Jerrilyn Sue Boone, Oct. 29, 1983; children: Kimberley Ann, Jennifer Rebecca, Albert Boone, Samuel Robert. BS, U.S. Naval Acad., 1967; JD, U. Tenn., 1974. Bar: Tenn. 1974, U.S. Dist. Ct. (ea. dist.) Tenn. 1975, U.S. Dist. Ct. (mid. dist.) Tenn. 2005, U.S. Ct. Appeals (6th cir.) 1982. Law clk. to judge US Dist. Ct. (ea. dist.) Tenn., Knoxville, 1974-76, magistrate judge, 1978—2002; assoc. Butler, Vines, Babb & Threadgill, Knoxville, 1976-78; ptnr. Kramer Rayson LLP, Knoxville, 2002—08, Reeves, Herbert & Murrian, P. A., Tenn., 2008—. Adj. prof. U. Tenn. Coll. Law, 1990-93, 95-96, 2002; trial lawyer, arbitrator, mediator, spl. master litigation. Lt. USN, 1967-71. Green scholar, 1973-74, Nat. Moot Ct. scholar, 1974; named one of Best Lawyers in America ADR, 2005-10. Fellow Tenn. Bar Found.; mem. ABA, Tenn. Bar Assn., Knoxville Bar Assn. (bd. govs. 1994, 2002—), Sixth Cir. Jud. Conf. (life), Order of Coif, Am. Inn of Ct. (master of the bench, pres. 1997-98), Phi Kappa Phi. Presbyterian (Elder). Office: Reeves Herbert & Murrian PA Tyson Pl 2607 Kingston Pike Ste 130 Knoxville TN 37919 Office Phone: 865-540-1977. Business E-Mail: rmurrian@arclaw.net.

MURRISH, CHARLES HOWARD, oil and gas exploration company executive; b. Rochester, Mich., Dec. 27, 1940; s. Richard John and Emily Louise (Marsh) M.; m. Brigitte Marie Furlotte, Oct. 23, 1965; children: Stephanie, Stephen, Brian. Student, Mexico City Coll., 1962; BS, Mich. State U., 1963, MS, 1966. Exploration geologist and geophysicist Chevron, New Orleans, 1966-71; mgr. exploration Odeco, New Orleans, 1971-77; v.p. McMoRan Offshore Exploration Co., Metairie, La., 1977-79, sr. v.p., 1979-81; pres. McMoRan-Freeport Oil Co., Metairie, 1981-83, McMoRan Exploration Co., Metairie, 1983-86; exec. v.p. McMoRan Oil & Gas Co., 1986, sr. exec. v.p., 1986-90, Freeport-McMoRan Oil & Gas Co., 1990-92; ptnr. CLK Co., 1992-94; pres., COO McMoRan Oil & Gas Co., New Orleans, 1994—2001, McMoRan Oil & Gas LLC, New Orleans, 1998-2001; exec. v.p. McMoRan Exploration Co., New Orleans, 1998—, vice-chmn., 2001—. Chmn. bd. Hysell Ballet Arts, Inc., New Orleans, 1982-83; chmn. petroleum majors campaign United Way, 1996, 98; bd. dirs. Lenpac, Metairie, 1983; chmn. citizenship com. McMoRan Exploration Co., 2000—. Mem. New Orleans Geol. Soc., Geol. Soc. Am., Am. Assn. Petroleum Geologists, Petroleum Club of New Orleans (bd. dirs. 1988, 89, 90), Houston Geol. Soc., La. Assn. Ind. Producers, Mid-Continent Oil and Gas Assn. also: PO Box 60004 New Orleans LA 70160-0004 Office: McMoran Exploration Co 1615 Poydras St New Orleans LA 70112-1254

MURROW, WAYNE LEE, retired minister, communications educator, dean; b. Alva, Okla., Jan. 23, 1935; s. Everett Emmet Murrow and Stella Jean McGlothlin; m. Marti L. Rogers, Aug. 19, 1956 (dec. Sept. 1966); children: Sherri, Randal, Cynthia, Jeffrey; m. Nila Arlene West, Jan. 19, 1968. BA, Bethany Nazarene Coll., 1956; M of Tchg., Ctrl. State U., 1968; PhD, U. Okla., 1972. Min. Ch. of the Nazarene, Tex., Okla.; prof. So. Nazarene U., Bethany, Okla., 1968-80, dean, prof., 1980—2002; ret. emeritus prof., 2002—. Evaluation team mem. Okla. State Dept. Edn., Oklahoma City, 1980-94. Mem. Nat. Comm. Assn, Ctrl. States Comm. Assn. (adv. coun. 1977-90), Okla. Theatre Speech Comm. Assn. (pres. 1976-77, Outstanding Tchr. award 1980), Christian Adult Higher Edn. Assn. (coun. mem. 1994-2000, pres. 1997-98), North Ctrl. Assn. (evaluation team mem. 1968-80, cons.-evaluator for colls. and univs. 1994—2002). Independent. Avocation: family history. Home: 8105 Bridgeport Ln Bethany OK 73008 Personal E-mail: murrow@cox.net.

MURRY, J. WARREN, surgeon, educator; b. Kansas City, Mo., Mar. 28, 1925; BS in Medicine, U. Ark., 1946; MD, U. Ark., Little Rock, 1947. Diplomate Am. Bd. Surgery. Intern Charity Hosp., New Orleans, 1947-48; resident in surgery Univ. Hosp., Little Rock, 1948-53; instr. family medicine dept. U. Ark. for Med. Sci., Little Rock, 1993—2002, instr. N.W. Ark. A.H.E.C. Family Med. Ctr. Fayetteville; pvt. practice Fayetteville, Ark., 1957—89, Heber Springs, Ark., 1989—92; ret., 2002. Fellow ACS; mem. AMA, So. Med. Assn.

MURRY, THOMAS O., state legislator; m. Tamara Murry; children: Ella Murry, Gretchen Murry. Lic. pharmacist. Mem. Triangle Coun. of Govts., Morrisville, Cmty. Emergency Response Team, Morrisville; exec. dir. Pharmacy Compounding Accreditation Bd.; mem. Dist. 41 NC House of Representatives, 2011—. Republican. Mailing: PO Box 1054 Morrisville NC 27560 Address: North Carolina House of Representatives 16 W Jones St Rm 2121 Raleigh NC 27601-1096 Office Phone: 919-824-5753, 919-733-5602, 919-865-9993. Business E-Mail: murry4house@live.com, Tom.Murry@ncleg.net.

MURTAGH, GREG, marketing executive, entrepreneur; BS in Mktg. Mgmt., U. Conn., Storrs, 1984; MBA, So. Meth. U., Dallas, 1991. Sales mgr. Proctor & Gamble / Richardson-Vicks, 1984—86; regional sales mgr. American Cyanamid / Shulton Group, 1986—91; brand mgr. Dial Corp., 1991—94; mktg. cons. Reach Mktg., 1994—97; founder, ptnr. eMarketing, Inc., 1997—2003; founder, CEO Triad Retail Media, Tampa, Fla., 2004—. Bd. dirs. Dunedin Fine Arts Ctr., Fla. Named a Media Maven, Advt. Age, 2011. Office: Triad Retail Media 100 Carillon Pkwy Ste 100 Saint Petersburg FL 33716-1208 Office Phone: 813-286-6586.

MUSA, SAMUEL ALBERT, university executive; m. Judith Friedman; children: Gregory, Jeffrey. BA, BSEE, Rutgers U., 1961; MS in Applied Physics, Harvard U., 1962, PhD in Applied Physics, 1965. Rsch. scientist Gen. Precision Inc., Little Falls, NJ, 1965-66; asst. prof. elec. engring. U. Pa., Phila., 1966-71; project leader Inst. for Def. Analyses, Arlington, Va., 1971-78; dep. dir. Office of Under Sec. Def., Washington, 1978-83; dir. rsch. and advanced tech. E-Systems, Inc., Dallas, 1983-86, v.p. rsch. and advanced tech., 1986-95; exec. dir. Ctr. Display Tech. and Mfg. U. Mich., 1995-99; assoc. v.p. for strategic initiative, prof. elec. and computer engring. Northwestern U., Evanston, Ill., 1999—2007; sr. rsch. fellow ctr. tech. and nat. security Nat. Def. U., chmn., Homeland Security Sci. Tech., 2005—12. Mem. sci. adv. bd. USAF; mem. sci. bd. Def. Intelligence Agy., Army Sci. Bd. Contbr. articles to profl. jours. Recipient Exceptional Civilian Svc. award, Sec. of Air Force, cert. of appreciation, Sec. Def. Fellow IEEE; mem. AIA (tech. and ops. coun. 1986-95, vice chmn. 1993, chmn. 1994), Sigma Xi, Tau Beta Pi, Pi Mu Epsilon.

MUSACCHIA, X(AVIER) J(OSEPH), physiology and biophysics educator; b. Bklyn., Feb. 11, 1923; s. Castrense and Orsolina (Mazzola) M.; m. Betty Cook, Nov. 23, 1950; children: Joseph, Mary, Thomas, Laura Ann. BS, St. Francis Coll., Bklyn., 1944; MS, Fordham U., 1947, PhD, 1949. Instr. biology Marymount (N.Y.) Coll., 1948-49; from instr. to prof. biology St. Louis U., 1949-65; prof. physiology U. Mo., Columbia, 1965-78; prof. physiology and biophysics U. Louisville, 1978-91, prof. emeritus, 1991—, dean Grad. Sch., 1978-89, assoc. provost for rsch., 1985-89. Bd. dirs. Coun. Grad. Schs., 1986-89. Author: Depressed Metabolism, 1969, Regulation of Depressed Metabolism and Thermogenesis, 1976, Survival in Cold, 1981; also articles. Bd. govs. J. Graham Brown Cancer Ctr., Louisville, 1978-83; bd. dirs. Oak Ridge Associated Univs. Served with AUS, 1943-45. Research grantee NIH; Research grantee NASA. Fellow AAAS; mem. Am. Physiol. Soc., Am. Soc. Zoologists, Am. Soc. for Space and Gravitational Biology (v.p. 1988-89, pres. 1989-90), Soc. Exptl. Biology and Medicine, Corp. Marine Biol. Lab., Sigma Xi. (past chpt. pres.) Home: 1770 East Overland Loop Fayetteville AR 72703-5202

MUSACCHIO, MARILYN JEAN, nurse midwife, administrator, educator; b. Louisville, Dec. 7, 1938; d. Robert William and Loretta C. (Liebert) Poulter; m. David Edward Musacchio, May 13, 1961; children: Richard Peter, Michelle Marie. BSN cum laude, Spalding Coll., 1968; MSN, U. Ky., 1972, cert. in nurse-midwifery, 1976; PhD, Case Western Res U., 1993; diploma, St Joseph Infirmary Sch, 1959. RN; cert. nurse-midwife; advanced registered nurse practitioner. Staff nurse gynecol. unit St. Joseph Infirmary, Louisville, 1959-60, staff nurse male gen. surgery unit, 1960; instr. St. Joseph Infirmary Sch. Nursing, Louisville, 1960-71; from asst. prof. to assoc. prof., dir. dept. nursing edn. Ky. State U., Frankfort, 1972-75; asst. prof. U. Ky. Coll. Nursing, Lexington, 1976-79, assoc. prof., coord., 1979-92, acting coordinator nurse-midwifery, 1982-84, coordinator for nurse-midwifery, 1987-92; assoc. prof., dir. nurse-midwifery U. Ala., Birmingham, 1992-96, assoc. prof., 1997-98; dean, prof. Tenn. Technol. U., Cookeville, 1998—2005; prof. Spalding U., Louisville, 2005—09, chmn.; dir. RN to BSN Program Aquinas Coll., Nashville, 2008—09; dean & prof. nursing edn. Sullivan U. Spencerian Coll., Louisville, 2009—. Cons. in field, dean nursing edn. Sullvian U. Mem. editorial bd. Jour. Obstet., Gynecol. and Neonatal Nursing, 1976-82; author pamphlet; contbr. articles to profl. jours. Mem.Louisville Safety Coun., 1973-80. Brig. Gen. Army Nurse Corps, USAR, 1992-95. Recipient Disting. Citizen award City of Louisville, 1977, Jefferson Cup award Jefferson County, Ky., 1991; named Outstanding Alumna, Mercy Acad., 1993; named to Hall of Disting. Alumni, U. Ky., 1995; recipient scholarships and fellowships, other awards. Fellow Am. Acad. Nursing; mem. AWHONN, ANA, Nurse Assn. Am. Coll. Ob-Gyn. (charter; nat. sec. 1970-72, chmn. dist. V 1969), Am. Coll. Nurse-Midwives, Res. Officers Assn., Assn. Mil. Surgeons U.S., Sr. Army Res. Comdr. Assn., Assn. U.S. Army, Army Nurse Corps. Assn., Army War Coll. Alumni Assn. (life). Roman Catholic. Avocations: reading, candy making, cake decorating, cooking, sewing. Home: PO Box 4907 Louisville KY 40204-4907 Office Phone: 502-413-8853. Personal E-mail: mjmusacchio@gmail.com.

MUSCHAMP, WILL, college football coach; b. Rome, Ga., Aug. 3, 1971; m. Carol Muschamp; children: Jackson, Whit. B, U. Ga., Athens, 1994; M, Auburn U., Ala., 1996. Grad. asst. Auburn U. Tigers, 1995—96, defensive coord., secondary coach, 2006—07; secondary coach U. West Ga. Wolves, 1998, Eastern Ky. U. Colonels, 1999; defensive coord. Valdosta State U. Blazers, 2000; linebackers coach La. State U. Fighting Tigers, 2001, defensive coord., linebackers coach, 2002—04; asst. head coach def. Miami Dolphins, 2005; defensive coord., linebackers coach U. Tex. Longhorns, 2008—10; head football coach U. Fla. Gators, 2010—. Finalist Frank Broyles award, Rotary Club Little Rock, 2007. Achievements include defensive coordinator of NCAA football BCS National Championship winning Louisiana State University Fighting Tigers, 2003. Office: University Fla Football Ben Hill Griffin Stadium Univ Ave & North South Dr Gainesville FL 32611

MUSCI, MICHAEL N., JR., pediatrician, healthcare company executive; DO, Mich. State U., 1975; MBA, St. Joseph U., 1994. Cert. neonatal/perinatal medicine, pediatrics. Med. dir. Virtua Health, 1993—96; chief med. officer Paradigm Health, 1998—2002; nat. med. dir. Amerigroup Corp., 2002—05; chief med. officer CarePlus Health Plan, 2005—06, UnitedHealth Group, Inc., 2006—07; CEO, Amerigroup Cmty. Care SC Amerigroup Corp., 2007—09, CEO, SC, 2009—. Office: Amerigroup Corp Ste 100 4425 Corporation Ln Virginia Beach VA 23462 Office Phone: 757-490-6900. Office Fax: 757-518-3600. Business E-Mail: mmusci@amerigroupcorp.com.

MUSE, JOHN R., investment company executive; b. Ft. Worth, Feb. 24, 1951; s. Arthur C. and Betty L. (Smith) M.; m. Lyn A. Reynolds, Aug. 10, 1975; children: Michael J., J. Tyler, Whitney J. BS, USAF Acad., 1973; MBA, UCLA, 1974. Commd. 2d lt. USAF, 1973, advanced through grades to capt., resigned, 1978; sr. v.p., corp. fin. dir. Schneider, Bernet & Hickman, Dallas, 1980-84; mng. dir. Prudential Bache Capital Funding, Dallas, 1984—89; co-founder, ptnr., mem. mgmt. com. HM Capital Partners (formerly Hicks, Muse, Tate & Furst Inc.), Dallas, 1989—, chmn., 2005—. Bd. dirs. Dean Foods Co., 1997—, Swift & Co., 2002—. Bd. visitors UCLA Anderson Sch. Mgmt. Presbyterian. Office: HM Captial Ste 1600 200 Crescent Ct Dallas TX 75201 Office Phone: 214-740-7300. Office Fax: 214-720-7888. E-mail: jmuse@hmcapital.com.

MUSGRAVES, KACEY LEE, musician; b. Mineola, Tex., Aug. 21, 1988; Musician: (albums) Movin' On, 2002, Wanted: One Good Cowboy, 2003, Kacey Musgraves, 2007, Same Trailer Different Park, 2013 (Grammy award for Best Country Album, 2014, Acad. Country Music award for Album of Yr., 2014), (songs) Merry Go Round (Grammy award for Best Country Song, 2014). Named New Artist of Yr., Country Music Assn. Awards, 2013. Office: Sandbox Entertainment 54 Music Square East Suite 200 Nashville TN 37203*

MUSHER, DANIEL MICHAEL, medical educator, researcher, epidemiologist, director; b. NYC, Feb. 27, 1938; s. Sidney and Hadassah Musher; m. Karol Sue Katz; children: Rebecca Gross, Benjamin, Deborah. AB magna cum laude, Harvard Coll., 1959; MD, Columbia U. Coll. Physicians and Surgeons, 1963; postgrad., MIT, 1969-70. Cert. Am. Bd. Internal Medicine, 1970, diplomate infectious diseases specialist Am. Bd. Internal Medicine, 1974. Intern, jr. med. resident first med. divsn. Bellevue Hosp., NYC, 1963—65; chief internal medicine 3640 USAF Hosp., Laredo AFB, Tex., 1965—67; instr. medicine Tufts U., Boston, 1970—71; chief infectious diseases Michael E. DeBakey Veterans Hosp., Houston, 1971—; asst. to assoc. prof. mmicrobiology and immunology Baylor Coll. Medicine, 1972—78, prof. medicine, 1979—, prof. microbiology and immunology, 1979—, prof. microbiology and molecular virology, 2000—. Chief infectious diseases Michael E. DeBakey Veterans Hosp., Houston, 1971—; mem. editl. bd. Sexually Trasmitted Diseases, 1979—83, Infection and Immunity, 1996—2000, Clin. Infect OIS, 2010; assoc. editor Jour. Infectious Diseases, 1983—88; head infectious diseases Baylor Coll. Medicine, 1992—99, mem. curriculum com., 1999—2004; mem. adv. bd. treatment of STD's Centers for Disease Control, 1995—2001, mem. working group on drug resistant pneumococci, 1996—. Contbr. more than 490 chpts. to books, articles to profl. jours. Bd. mem., v.p. and pres. Houston Friends of Music, 1975—2012; mem. Tex. State Commn. on Judicious Use of Antibiotics; bd. mem. Congregation Beth Yshurun; mem. Hillel, Jewish Fedn. Gtr. Houston; chmn. edn. William Malev Schs. of Congregation Beth Yeshurun, 1993—95; bd. mem. and past pres. I. Weiner Jewish Secondary Sch., 1979—89; bd. mem., consert master Tex. Med. Ctr. Orch., 2000—. With USAF, 1965—67. Recipient Outstanding Faculty Member award, Baylor Coll. Medicine Grad. Class, 1988, 2003, Dir.'s Profl. Leadership award, Michael E. DeBaket Veterans Hosp., 1991, Physician's Recognition award, AMA, 1991—, Nakano citation Outstanding Paper Epidemiology, Ctrs. Disease Control, 1993, Excellence in Tchg. award, Baylor Coll. Medicine, 1997—2002, Outstanding Tchr. award, Baylor Dept. Medicine, 1999, DeBakey medal excellence in Rsch., Baylor Coll. Medicine, 1990—99, Outstanding Tchr. Basic Scis., Baylor Coll. Medicine 2d Yr. Students, 1995, 1999, 2001—07, Outstanding Faculty Member award, Baylor Coll. Medicine Grad. Class, 1994, 2000, 2002, 2004—06, Most Outstanding Tchr., VA Med. Ctr. Med. Residents, 1992, 1998, 1999, 2002—11, Barbara and Corbin J. Robertson Pres. award, Baylor Coll. Medicine, 2003, John P. McGovern Outstanding Tchg. award, 2003; named to Baylor Hall of Fame Excellence in Tchg., 2003, Baylor Tchg. Hall of Fame, 2006; nominee Outstanding Contbn. Pub. Health, Centers for Disease Control, 2001. Fellow: ACP; mem.: AAAS, Am. Fedn. Clin. Rsch., Infectious Diseases Soc. Am. (Louis Weinstein prize Best Clin. article 1994, Clin. Tchr. award 2007, De Bakey medal 1999), Am. Soc. Microbiology, Am. Soc. Clin. Investigation, Am. Assn. Immunologists. Avocations: string quartet player, reading, music. Office: Michael E DeBakey VA Hosp 2002 Holcombe Blvd Houston TX 77030-4211 Office Fax: 713-794-7045. E-mail: Daniel.Musher@med.va.gov.

MUSICK, GERALD JOE, retired entomology educator; b. Ponca City, Okla., May 24, 1940; s. Arlie A. and Leona (Beier) M.; m. Florene Ione Thompson, May 11, 1962; children: Linda Kaye, Mary Louise. BS, Okla. State U., 1962; MS, Iowa State U., 1964; PhD, U. Mo., 1969. Grad. asst. Iowa State U., 1962-64; instr. U. Mo., 1964-69; asst. prof. Ohio State U., Wooster, 1969—76, assoc. prof., 1971-76; dept. head U. Ga., Tifton, 1976-79; prof., dept. head U. Ark., Fayetteville, 1979-86, interium dir. agrl. exptl. sta., 1986-87, dean, assoc. v.p. agrl. rsch., 1987-93, univ. prof. entomology, 1993—2002, chmn.-elect faculty coun. Dale Bumpers Coll. Agrl., Food and Life Scis., 1997, chmn., 1998, prof. emeritus, 2002—, ret., 2002—; chmn. faculty coun. Dale Bumpers Coll. of Agrl. Food and Life Scis., 1998; gen. mgr. Razerback Pk. Golf Course, Fayetteville, Ark., 2003—. Author and co-author numerous publs. Vice-chairperson com. Coop. States Rsch. Svc., 1993, So. Expt. Sta.; chairperson steering com. Midwest Food Safety Consortium, 1991-93; mem. U. Ark. Faculty Senate, 1994-2002, chair campus faculty, 1998-99, chair faculty sentate 1999-2000, faculty exec. com., 1999-2001; coord. Pest Mgmt. Programs, 1998—. Mem. Entomol. Soc. Am. (pres. S.E. br. 1983-84), Ark. Acad. Sci., Ctrl. States Entomol. Soc. (v.p. 1995-96, pres. 1996-97), Sigma Xi, Gamma Sigma Delta. Lutheran. Avocation: golf. Office: Razorback Park Golf Course Fayetteville AR 72704 Personal E-mail: gjmfim@cox.net.

MUSLIH, KHALID A., oil industry executive; Various positions Coastal States Mgmt. Corp., 1993—94, Coastal States Refining and Mktg., Inc., 1994—98; dir., legis. and regulatory affairs The Coastal Corp., 1999—2000; dir., mcht. and internat. regulatory affairs El Paso Corp., 2001—02; comml. officer, mergers and acquisitions NuCoastal Corp., 2002—05; v.p., corp. devel. Pacific Energy Mgmt. LLC, 2005; pres., devel. and logistics segment Buckeye Partners, LP, 2009—, v.p., corp. devel., 2010—. Office: Buckeye GP Holdings LP One Greenway Plz Ste 600 Houston TX 77046 Office Phone: 832-615-8600. Business E-Mail: Kmuslih@buckeye.com.

MUSS, HYMAN BERNARD, oncologist, educator; b. Bklyn., Apr. 18, 1943; m. Loretta Anne Lassam; children: Sarah, Jonathan, Daniel. BA in Chemistry cum laude, Lafayette Coll., 1964; MD summa cum laude, SUNY, 1968. Diplomate Am. Bd. Internal Medicine, sub-splty. med. oncology, Am. Bd. Hematology, Am. Bd. Oncology. Intern Peter Bent Brigham Hosp., Boston, 1969-69, jr. asst. resident, 1969-70, rsch. fellow in medicine, 1972-73, rsch. fellow in hematology, 1973-74, Children's Hosp. Med. Ctr., Boston, 1972-73; fellow in oncology Dana Farber Cancer Inst., Boston, 1973-74; asst. prof. medicine, hematology/oncology Wake Forest U., Winston-Salem, N.C., 1974-78, assoc. prof., 1978-85, assoc. dir. clin. rsch. Comprehensive Cancer Ctr., 1979-96, prof. medicine, 1985-96, U. Vt., 1996—2009; assoc. dir. U. Vt. Cancer Ctr., 1996—2009; prof. medicine, breast cancer & geriatric oncology Lineberger Comprehensive Cancer Ctr., U. NC. Sch. Medicine, Chapel Hill, 2009—. Peer review com. Health Scis. Consortium, Inc., 1978-80; sci. adv. com. black/white survival study, 1985-96; com.consulting staff Forsyth Meml. Hosp., Winston-Salem, N.C., N.C. Bapt. Hosp., Winston Salem. Mem. editl. bd. Am. Jour. Med. Sci., 1986—, Jour. Clin. Oncology, 1994, Nat. Cancer Insts. Computerized, 1986-91, Contemporary Oncology, 1990—; reviewer New Eng. Jour. Medicine, Jour. Clin. Oncology, Archives of Internal Medicine, Breast Cancer Rsch. & Treatment, Cancer, Gynecologic Oncology, Surg. Neurology, Jour. Nat. Cancer Inst., Jour. Immunotherapy, Clin. Chemistry; contbr. articles, abstracts to profl. jours., chpts. to books. Active Am. Cancer Soc., 1978—, bd. dirs., 1985-87; trustee Blumenthal Jewish Home, 1992-93, chair med. ethics com., chair HIV/infectious disease com. Maj. U.S. Army, 1970-72, Vietnam. Decorated Bronze Star U.S. Army; recipient Cooper Meml. award Wake County, 1979; Jr. Faculty fellow Am. Cancer Soc., 1975-79. Fellow ACP; mem. AMA, Am. Coll. Obstetricians and Gynecologists (com. human rsch.), Internal Soc. Geriatric Oncology, Vt. State Med. Soc., New England Cancer Soc., Am. Bd. Internal Medicine, Internat. Soc. Breast Disease, Am. Soc. Hematology, Am. Fedn. Clin. Rsch., Am. Soc. Clin. Oncology, Am. Assn. Cancer Rsch., Internat. Gynecologic Cancer Soc., Internat. Assn. Breast Cancer Rsch., So. Assn. Oncology (edn. com. 1988—), So. Med. Assn., So. Soc. Clin. Rsch., N.C. Med. Soc. (cancer com.), Forsyth County Med. Soc. (chmn. cancer com. 1977-80, med. adv. com. 1977-79), Cancer and Acute Leukemia Group B, Gynecologic Oncology Group (sarcoma com. 1977-79, endometrial com. 1978-90, quality control com. 1978-90, chemotherapy com. 1977—, chmn., 1980—, protocol com. 1980-90, new drug liaison com. 1980—, exec. comb. 1991—, quality of life com. 1993—, cervix com. 1993—), Piedmont Oncology Assn. (chmn. 1991—), Phi Beta Kappa, Alpha Omega Alpha. Office: University of North Carolina Chapel Hill 170 Manning Dr CB #7305 Chapel Hill NC 27599 Office Phone: 919-966-3856. E-mail: muss@email.unc.edu.

MUSSER, CHERRI M., information technology executive; m. Jack Musser. BA in Math., Miss. State Univ., 1973; MBA, Southern Methodist Univ. Various positions from programmer to dir. bus. sys. Texas Instruments, 1973—94, v.p. R&D, TI software, 1994—96; process information officer, supply chain GM, 1996; group v.p., CIO GMAC, Detroit, 2003—08; v.p., CIO Electronic Data Systems, Plano, Tex., 2008—. Recipient Coll. of Arts & Scis. Alumnus of Yr., Miss. State Univ., 1999. Mem.: Mich. Coun. Women in Tech. (pres. 2005—08). Office: EDS 5400 Legacy Dr Plano TX 75024 Office Phone: 313-665-5906, 972-605-1959. Business E-Mail: cherri.musser@gm.com, cherri.musser@eds.com.

MUSSETT, RICHARD EARL, city official; b. Erie, Pa., June 24, 1948; s. Clarence Harold and Elva (Brueckner) M.; m. Alaine Kathleen Rau, Aug. 14, 1971; children: Matthew, Mark. BPA, U. N.D., 1974; M of Urban Planning, U. Mich., 1975. Chief planner City of Largo, Fla., 1976-77; chief long-range planning Pinellas County Planning Dept., Clearwater, Fla., 1977-80; planning dir. City of St. Petersburg, Fla., 1980-85, dep. city mgr., adminstr. Fla., 1987—2014; adminstr. cmty. devel. City of Bloomington, Minn., 1985-87. Chmn. Pinellas County Planners Adv. Com., 1982. Alternate del. N.D. Dem. Conv., 1972; mem. Tampa Bay Study Commn., 1984-85; mem. environ. quality com. Fla. League of Cities, 1984-85, devel. strategies legis. policy com., 1986; bd. dirs. Mahaffey Theater, 1994-2007, Tampa Bay Partnership, 1997-2007. Rackham grantee, 1975. Mem. Am. Inst. Cert. Planners (charter), Am. Planning Assn. (chmn. Suncoast sect. 1984, mem. legis. policy com. Fla. chpt. 1984-85, editor Suncoast sect. newsletter 1985). Lutheran. Avocations: reading, sports, politics. Office: City of St Petersburg 175 5th St N Saint Petersburg FL 33701-3708

MUSTARD, LEWIS WILLIAMS, management consultant, educator; b. Durham, NC, Sept. 4, 1942; s. Harry S. and Elizabeth (Williams) M.; m. Athena Frangoulis; children: Juliana Janice, Lewis Williams Jr.; step children: Christina Frangoulis, Victoria Frangoulis AB in English, U. NC, Chapel Hill, 1966; cert. in hosp. adminstrn., Duke U., 1970; LLB, La Salle U., Chgo., 1974; D Bus. Adminstrn., Western Coll. U., 1976; PhD in Health Adminstrn., Union Grad. Sch., Cin., 1992; MA in Humanities, Calif. State U., Dominguez Hills, 1995. Hosp. adminstr. Woodruff (S.C.) Hosp., 1968-70; exec. dir. AID, Inc., Bryn Mawr, Pa., 1970-73; sr. hosp. cons. Summerour & Assocs., Atlanta, 1975-76; regional v.p. Qualicare, Inc., New Orleans, 1976-78; regional adminstr., v.p. Triage Corp., Clearwater, Fla., 1978-80; CEO Healthcare Negligence Control, Inc., Chapel Hill, NC, 1998—; faculty UCLA, 2012—. Legal cons., solo practitioner, 1992-; adj. prof. Ctrl. Mich. U., Mt. Pleasant, 1993-99, Webster U., St. Louis, 1994-99, MBA program, NY Inst. Tech., 2004-05, Bellevue U., Nebr., 2005-, Strayer U., 2005-09, MPH program, A.T. Still U., 2002-04; adj. charter New Britain, Conn., 2003-12; faculty mem., UCLA, 2012-, Park U., Kansas City, 2012-, Excesior Coll. Served with USNR Res., 1959-68. Vis. scholar, U. Cin. Sch. Med. Sch., 2011—. Mem.: American Coll. Healthcare Execs. Episcopalian. Personal E-mail: executivehealthcare@yahoo.com.

MUTH, RICHARD FERRIS, economics professor; b. Chgo., May 14, 1927; s. Merlin Arthur and Margaret Ferris Muth; m. Helene Louise Martin, Dec. 23, 1955; children: Lisa Helene, Laurianne Love. Student, USCG Acad., 1945-47; AB, Washington U., St. Louis, 1949, MA, 1950; PhD, U. Chgo., 1958; M of Theol. Studies, Emory U., 1995. Lectr. polit. economy Johns Hopkins U., Balt., 1955-56; economist Resources for Future, Washington, 1956-58; assoc. prof. urban econs. U. Chgo., 1959-64; economist Inst. Def. Analyses, Arlington, Va., 1964-66, cons., 1966-69; prof. econs. Washington U., St. Louis, 1966-70, Stanford U., Calif., 1970-83; Callaway prof. econs. Emory U., Atlanta, 1983—2001, chmn. dept., 1983-90, prof. emeritus, 2001—. Vis. assoc. prof. econs. Vanderbilt U., 1958—59; vis. sr. fellow Urban Inst., Washington, 1976—77; vis. prof. Sch. Bus. U. Calif., Berkeley, 1991. Author (with others): Regions, Resources and Economic Growth, 1960, Cities and Housing, 1969, Public Housing, 1974, Urban Economic Problems, 1975; co-author (with Allen C. Goodman): The Economics of Housing Markets, 1989. Mem. Presdl. Task Force on Urban Renewal, 1969, Presdl. Task Forces on Urban Affairs and Housing, 1980—81, Presdl. Commn. on Housing, 1981—82. With USCG, 1951—52. Libertarian. Methodist. Business E-Mail: rmuth@emory.edu.

MUTOMBO, DIKEMBE (DIKEMBE MUTOMBO MPOLONDO MUKAMBA JEAN JACQUE WAMUTOMBO), retired professional basketball player; b. Kinshasa, Zaire, June 25, 1966; m. Rose Mutombo; children: Carrie Biamba Wamutumbo, Jean Jacques Dikembe Mutombo Mplombo Jr.; 4 adopted children. BA in Linguistics and Diplomacy, Georgetown U., 1991; LHD, SUNY, Cortland, 2004. Ctr. Denver Nuggets, 1991—96, Atlanta Hawks, 1996—2001, Phila. 76ers, 2001—02, NJ Nets, 2002—03, NY Knicks, 2003—04, Chgo. Bulls, 2004, Houston Rockets, 2004—09; ret., 2009. Founder Dikembe Mutombo Found., Inc., 1997—; youth emissary UN Devel. Program, 1999; founder Biamba Marie Mutombo Hosp. and Rsch. Ctr., Kinshasa, Democratic Republic of Congo, 2001; adv. bd. mem. NIH Fogarty Internat. Ctr., 2003. Recipient Most Caring Athlete award, USA Weekend, 1999, President's Svc. award, Points of Light Found., 1999, Henry P. Iba Citizen Athlete award, 1999, J. Walter Kennedy Citizenship award, NBA, 2001, Trailblazer award, Constituency for Africa, 2001, Internat. Health Sect. award, Am. Pub. Health Assn., 2002, Samuel J. Halsey award, Georgetown U., 2002, Coach John Thompson Jr. Legacy of a Dream award, 2010, European Hero award, TIME mag., 2003, Helen Hayes MacArthur award, Helen Hayes Hosp. Found., NY, 2003, African-Am. Legacy Coun. Creed medal, Cmty. Found. Greater New Haven, 2005, Jackie Robinson Humanitarian award, US Sports Acad., 2007, Order of the Eagle Exemplar, 2007; named NBA Defensive Player of Yr., 1995, 1997, 1998, 2001; named to We. Conf. All-Star Team, NBA, 1992, 1995, 1996, Ea. Conf. All-Star Team, 1997, 1998, 2000—02, All-Rookie Team, 1992. Achievements include leading the NBA in: total rebounds, 1995, 1997, 1999, 2000; defensive rebounds, 1999, 2000; offensive rebounds, 2001; blocked shots, 1994-1998; ranking second all-time in blocked shots (3,289); fluent in English, French, Spanish, Portuguese and five African dialects. Office: Dikembe Mutombo Found Inc PO Box 250225 Atlanta GA 30325-1225 Office Phone: 404-262-2109. Office Fax: 404-262-2168.

MUTRYN, THOMAS A., information technology executive; b. Schenectady, NY; BArch, Cornell U., MS in Structural Engring., MBA. Various sr. fin. positions American Airlines, 1983—89; dir. fin. analysis, v.p. revenue mgmt. United Airlines, 1989—95, v.p., treas., 1995—98; sr. v.p. fin., CFO US Airways, 1998—2002; sr. v.p., CFO GTSI Corp., 2003—06; exec. v.p. corp. devel. CACI International, Inc, 2006—07, exec. v.p., CFO, treas., 2007—. Named Corp. Exec. Dealmaker of Yr., Assn. Corp. Growth, 2008; named one of Ten CFO's to Watch in 2010, ExecutiveBiz.com. Office: CACI International Inc 1100 N Glebe Rd Arlington VA 22201 Office Phone: 703-841-7800. Office Fax: 703-841-7882. E-mail: tmutryn@caci.com.

MUTZ, OSCAR ULYSSES, manufacturing and distribution executive; b. Edinburg, Ind., Feb. 12, 1928; s. Harold Winterberg and Laura Belle (Sawin) M.; m. Jean Greiling, Aug. 22, 1948; children: Marcia, H. William. BS, Ind. U., 1949. Vice pres. Peerless Corp., Indpls., 1954-63; v.p., gen. mgr. Space Conditioning, Inc., Harrisonburg, Va., 1964-66; v.p., treas. Cosco, Inc., Columbus, Ind., 1966-67; exec. v.p., 1967-69; pres., 1969-71; chmn. bd. Court Manor Corp., Columbus, 1971-73; pres. Jenn Air Corp., Indpls., 1973-75; pres., CEO Mutz Corp., 1975-81; pres., dir. Haag Drug Co., 1977-78; pres. Forum Group, Inc. (merger Mutz Corp. and Excepticon, Inc.), Indpls., 1981-91; chmn., CEO, bd. dirs. Capital Industries, Inc., Indpls., 1991-96; chmn. Lakeland Auto Mall, 1996—2011. Pres. Ct. Manor Corp., co-chmn. bd. dirs. Sargent & Greenleaf, Safemasters; pres. Security Group, Inc., 1991-2004, also bd. dirs. Nat. trustee Fellowship Christian Athletes, 1985-91, chmn. nat. conf. ctr., 1994-96; mem. pres. coun. and dean's adv. coun. Ind. U., elder Presbyn. Ch. Mem. Ind. Mfrs. Assn. (chmn. 1980), Acad. Alumnae Fellows Ind. U. Sch. Bus., Lakeland Yacht Club, Grasslands Country Club, Lone Palm Country Club. Republican. Presbyterian. Office: Mutz Corporation 5119 Lake in the Woods Blvd Lakeland FL 33813-2942

MYERS, DAVID W., state legislator; b. McComb, Miss., Dec. 30, 1961; m. Brenda K. Sibley; children: Lakisha, Micheal. Former self-employed contractor, fireman & policeman; mem. Dist. 98 Miss. House of Reps., 1996—; bd. dir. Boys & Girls Club, Project Forward; mem., bd. selectman City of McComb. Mem.: NAACP (bd. dir.), Parent Tchr. Assn., Masons Lodge. Democrat. Baptist. Address: 808 N Cherry St McComb MS 39648 Mailing: State Capitol Rm 201M PO Box 1018 Jackson MS 39212-1018 Office Phone: 601-684-4000, 601-359-3371. Business E-Mail: dmyers@house.ms.gov.

MYERS, ELISSA MATULIS, publishing executive, professional society administrator; b. Munich, Aug. 4, 1950; (parents Am. citizens); d. Raymond George and Anne Constance (Moley) Matulis; m. John Wake Myers, Sept. 13, 1967 (div. 1972); 1 child, Jennifer Anne Myers Bick. BA in English Lit., George Mason U., 1972, MA in English Lit., 1982. Dir. rsch. and info. Am. Soc. Assn. Execs., Washington, 1972-80, dir. mem. svcs., 1980-88, v.p., pub. Assn. Mgmt. mag., 1988-97; pres., CEO Nat. Infomercial Mktg. Assn., Washington, 1997—98, Electronic Retailing Assn., Washington, 1998—2003; chmn. Assn. Internet Radio Network; CEO ERA, 1998—2003. Chmn. Assn. Internet Radio Network, 2004; pres. Advice & Consensus, 2007—; host weekly radio show Assn. Nation, Assn. Power and Politics; advisor Mcpl. Fin. Officers Assn., Republic of Georgia. Pub. Principles of Association Management, 1976, 3d edit., 1996; columnist Footnotes, 1988-97. Bd. dirs. Ethics Resource Ctr., Washington, 1982-86; mem. Universal Postal Union Adv. Group 2000-; mem. Fed. Adv. Commn. on e-commerce; appointee DofC 1fac-4 Ecommerce, 2001-. Mem. Am. Soc. Assn. Execs. (cert.), Assn. Conv. Mktg. Execs., Greater Washington Soc. Assn. Execs. (bd. dirs. 2000—), Nat. Assn. Hispanic Mktg. Profls. (adv. bd.), Soc. Nat. Assn. Publs., Com. of 100 U.S. C. of C., Soc. Scholarly Pubs. Roman Catholic. Avocations: running, scuba diving. Home: 5315 Moultrie Rd Springfield VA 22151-1915 Office: AIR 5673 Ravnel Ln Springfield VA 22151 Office Phone: 703-626-9087. E-mail: elissa@elissamyers.com.

MYERS, ELLEN HOWELL, historian, educator; b. Bryan, Tex., Feb. 16, 1941; d. Douglas Wister and Ann Olive (Emory) Howell; m. William Allen Myers, Dec. 23, 1967; 1 child, William Webb. Student, Mt. Vernon Jr. Coll., 1959—61, U. Madrid, 1961—62; BA, Sophie Newcomb Coll. of Tulane U., 1963; MA, U. Va., 1965, PhD, 1970. Lectr. U. Houston, 1966—67; instr. Okla. State U., Stillwater, 1967—70; asst. prof. San Antonio Coll., 1970—73, assoc. prof., 1973—77, prof. history, 1977—. Author: (student's rev. manuals, instrs. manuals) The American Nation, 1975, 1977, 1979, 1983, 1987, Test Bank for the West Transformed, 2000; contbr. articles to profl. jours. Mem. S.W. Conf. Commn. on Higher Edn. and Campus Ministry Meth. Ch., 1978—81; bd. dirs. Family Svc. Assn., 1978—85, pres., 1983—84; bd. dirs. San Antonio Area Red Cross, 1979—85, Laurel Heights Weekday Sch., 1980—83, chmn., 1982—83. Mem.: AAUP (exec. com. San Antonio Coll. 1973—74), Conf. on L.Am. History, S.W. Conf. on L.Am. Studies (exec. com. 1974—75), Tex. C.C. Tchrs. Assn., Tues. Musical Club, Jr. League of San Antonio (bd. dirs. 1977—79), Kappa Alpha Theta, Phi Alpha Theta. Democrat. Methodist. Home: 307 Arcadia Pl San Antonio TX 78209-5950 Office: 1300 San Pedro Ave San Antonio TX 78212-4201

MYERS, FRANKLIN, oil industry executive; b. Pensacola, Fla., Nov. 2, 1952; m. Elizabeth A. Berner; children: Amanda C., Adam F., Anne Marie M., Mary Lauren Miller, Zachary J., Thomas J. BS, Miss. State U., 1974; JD, U. Miss., 1977. Bar: Miss. 1977, Tex. 1978. Ptnr. Fulbright and Jaworski, Houston, 1978-88; sr. v.p., gen. counsel Baker Hughes Inc., Houston, 1988-95; sr. v.p. Cooper Cameron Corp., Houston, 1995—2008, CFO, 2002—08. Adj. prof. U. Tex. Sch. Law, 1990—2003; bd. dirs. InPut Output Inc., Comfort Sys., Inc., Frontier Oil Corp.; operating advisor Paine Ptnrs. Fellow: Houston Bar Assn., Miss. Bar Assn., Tex. Bar Assn., Houston Bar Found.; mem.: Tex. Bar Found.

MYERS, HANCE, energy executive; B, La. State U., 1982; JD, South Tex. Coll. Law, 1992. Equity rsch. analyst, v.p., mem. instl. sales team Howard Weil Inc., 1997—2005; mng. dir. Tudor Pickering Holt & Co., 2005—08; v.p. investor rels. Plains Exploration and Production Co., 2008—. Office: Plains Exploration & Production Co Ste 3100 700 Milam Houston TX 77002 Office Phone: 713-579-6291. Office Fax: 713-579-6611. Business E-Mail: hmyers@pxp.com.

MYERS, PHILLIP FENTON, corporate financial and technology executive; m. Hope Gail Strum, Aug. 13, 1961 B in Indsl. Engring., Ohio State U., 1958, MBA, 1960; D in Bus. Adminstrn., Harvard U., 1966. Staff indsl. engr. Procter & Gamble Co., Cin., 1958; sr. cons. Cresap, McCormack & Paget, NYC, 1960—61; staff assoc. Mitre Corp., Bedford, Mass., 1961; cons. Sys. Devel. Corp., Santa Monica, Calif., 1963—64; dir. long range planning Electronic Splty. Co., LA, 1966—68; chmn. Atek Industries, 1968—72; pres. Myers Fin. Corp., 1973—82; chmn. Amvid Comm. Svcs., Inc., 1975—79, Omni Resources Devel. Corp., 1979—83; chmn., pres. Am. Internat. Mining Co., Inc., 1979—83; pres. Advent Internat. Mgmt. Co., Inc., 1982—; chmn. Global Bond Mktg. Svcs., Inc., 1987—90; pres., CEO Whitehall Container Mfg. Corp., 1988—91; pres. Whitehall Motors Co., 1989—97, Allied Metamatter Tech. Corp., 1994—96; chmn. U.S. Water Resources, Inc., 1994—96. Pres. Turbogen, Inc., 1995-98, Blue Star Material Techs. Inc., 1997-2000, Advent Power Systems, 2006-12; founding dir. Warner Ctr. Bank, 1980-83; bd. dirs., pres. Cyber Security Systems, Inc., 2000—03; lectr. bus. adminstrn. U. So. Calif., L.A., 1967-74; prof. Grad. Sch. Bus. Adminstrn. Pepperdine U., 1974-81. Trustee, treas. Chamber Symphony Soc. Calif., 1971-78; mem. campaign issues com. Reagan for Pres., 1976, 80; pub. safety commr. City of Hidden Hills, Calif., 1976-83, chmn., 1982-83; co-chmn. budget adv. com. Las Virgenes Sch. Dist., 1983-86; mem. Mayor's Blue Ribbon Fin. Com., 1981-82; mem. dean's select adv. com. Coll. Engring., Ohio State U., 1984-94; mem. state exec. com. Calif. Libertarian Party, chmn. region 61, 1989-90, chmn. strategic planning com.; dep. chmn. Los Angeles County Libertarian Party, 1991-92; chairperson campaign issues com. Marrou for Pres., 1991-92; chmn. bd. trustees WWII Hist. Soc., 1992—; first v.p. Armed Forces Cmty. Rels. Coun. Ctrl. Ohio, 2001-04. Capt. USAF, 1958-60. Ford Found. fellow, 1961-64 Mem. Soc. Automotive Engrs., Harvard Bus. Sch. Assn., Ohio State Alumni Assn., Harvard Bus. Club Columbus (bd. dirs. 1998-2005, pres. 1996-98), Ohio State Alumni Club (pres. 1998-99), Harvard Club Ctrl. Ohio (bd. dirs.), Harvard Club of Broward County (bd. dirs.), Wynmoor Republican Club (dir. 2008-), Broward County Republican Club (mem. exec. com. 2010-).

MYERS, ROBERT JAY, retired aerospace executive; b. Bklyn., Oct. 15, 1934; s. John J. and Clara S. (Martinsen) M.; m. Carolyn Erland, Aug. 10, 1963; children: Susan, Kenneth. BCE, NYU, 1955, post-grad., 1957-65; P.MD, Harvard U., 1972. With Grumman Corp., Bethpage, NY, 1964-94, v.p. resources, 1980-83, sr. v.p. bus. and resource mgmt., 1983-85, sr. v.p. corp. svcs., 1985-86; pres. Grumman Data Systems Corp., Bethpage, 1986-90; pres., chief operating officer, bd. dirs. Grumman Corp., 1991-94, ret., 1994. Sci. adv. coun. Ala. Space and Rocket Ctr., 1986-91. Adv. panel on econ. devel. N.Y. State Project 2000, 1985-86; mem. L.I. Project 2000; adv. bd. L.I. Youth Guidance, 1986-91; bd. dirs. Poly. U., 1991-98, North Shore Health System, 1994—, L.I. Mus. of Sci. and Tech., 1994-96; chmn. Huntington Hosp., 1996—2000. 1st lt. U.S. Army, 1955-57. Fellow Poly. U., 1987, Disting. Alumni award, 1989. Mem. Am. Def. Preparedness Assn. (dir. 1992-94), Navy League, Industry Exec. Bd., Nat. Space Club (bd. govs. 1986-89), Huntington Country Club (N.Y.), Audubon Country Club (Naples, Fla.). Presbyterian. Home: 200 Cheshire Way Naples FL 34110 Personal E-mail: rjm34@aol.com.

MYERS, ROBERT MANSON, language educator, writer; b. Charlottesville, Va., May 29, 1921; s. Horwood Prettyman and Matilda Manson (Wynn) M. BA summa cum laude, Vanderbilt U., 1941; MA, Columbia, 1942, Harvard, 1943; PhD, Columbia, 1948. Instr. English Yale, 1945-47; asst. prof. Coll. William and Mary, 1947-48, Tulane U., 1948-54; tchr. English Brearley Sch., NYC, 1954-56; chmn. dept. English Osbourn High Sch., Manassas, Va., 1956-59; mem. faculty U. Md., College Park, 1959—, prof. English, 1968-86, prof. emeritus, 1986—. Author: Handel's Messiah, 1948, From Beowulf to Virginia Woolf, 1952, rev., 1984, Handel, Dryden, and Milton, 1956, Restoration Comedy, 1961, The Children of Pride, 1972, abridged edit., 1984 (Carey-Thomas award 1972, Nat. Book award 1973), A Georgian at Princeton, 1976, Quintet: Five Plays, 1991, Sixes and Sevens: Three Plays, 2004, The Bostonians: A Play, 2005, Poynton Park: A Play, 2005, Ars Amatoria: An Anthology, 2009. Mem. bd. visitors Winthrop U. Fulbright Postdoctoral Research fellow U. London, 1953-54; Fulbright lectr. Rotterdam, Netherlands, 1958-59; recipient Medal of Honor in Arts Winthrop U., 2003. Mem. Modern Lang. Assn. Am., Am. Soc. 18th Century Studies, Jane Austen Soc. N.Am., Phi Beta Kappa. Home: 3804 Deckford Pl Charlotte NC 28211-3408

MYRICK, BISMARCK, diplomat, history professor; b. Portsmouth, Va., Dec. 23, 1940; m. Marie Pierre Mbaye; children: Bismarck Jr., Wesley Todd, Allison Elizabeth. BA, U. Tampa, 1972; MA, Syracuse U., 1973, postgrad., 1979-80; LHD (hon.), Spelman Coll., 2002. Enlisted U.S. Army, 1959; desk officer for Somalia, U.S. Dept. State, Washington, 1980-82; advanced through grades to maj., 1975; ret., 1979; polit. officer Am. Embassy, Monrovia, Liberia, 1982-84; action officer office strategic nuclear policy bur. politico-milit. affairs U.S. Dept. State, 1985-87, dep. dir. policy plans and coordination bur. inter-Am. affairs, 1987-89, Una Chapman Cox fellow US-African Policy, 1988-90; consul gen. Am. Consulate Gen., Durban, South Africa, 1990-93, Capetown, South Africa, 1993-95; amb. to Lesotho, Am. Embassy, Maseru, 1995-98; diplomat-in-residence Atlanta U. Ctr. at Spelman Coll., 1998-99; U.S. amb. to Liberia Dept. of State, Monrovia, Liberia, 1999—2002; univ. lectr. internat. affairs Old Dominion U., 2002—; sr. fellow Joint Forces Staff Coll., Norfolk, Va., 2002—. Adj. prof. history and polit. sci. Old Dominion U., 2002—03, amb.-in-residence. Author: Three Aspects of Crisis in Colonial Kenya, 1975; contbr. chpt. to book. Goodwill amb. for West Africa, Graceland, Senegal, 2008. Decorated Silver Star, Purple Heart, 4 Bronze Stars; named to U.S. Army Hall of Fame, 1996; named Ambassador Bismarck Myrick Days, City of Portsmouth, Va., 2000; named one of Portsmouth Notable, 2006; Bismarck Myrick St. and Bismarck Myrick Crescent St. named in his honor, 2002. Mem.: World Affairs Coun. Hampton Rds. (bd. dirs. 2004—). Address: 1200 Mill Run Chesapeake VA 23322 Personal E-mail: myrickbx@hotmail.com.

MYRICK, SUE WILKINS, former United States Representative from North Carolina, former mayor; b. Tiffin, Ohio, Aug. 1, 1941; d. William Henry and Margaret Ellen (Roby) Wilkins; m. Jim Forest (div.); children: Greg, Dan; m. Wilbur Edward Myrick Jr., Sept. 11, 1977. Student, Heidelberg Coll., 1959-60, LLD (hon.), 1995. Exec. sec. to mayor and city mgr. City of Alliance, Ohio, 1962-63; dir. branch office Stark County Ct. Juvenile & Domestic Rels., Alliance, Ohio, 1963-65; pres. Myrick Advt. & Public Relations, Charlotte, NC, 1971-95; at-large councilman City of Charlotte, Charlotte, NC, 1983—85, mayor, 1987-91; pres. Myrick Enterprises, 1992—94; mem. US Congress from 9th NC Dist., 1995—2013. Chmn. Republican Study Com., 2003—05. Active Heart Fund, Multiple Sclerosis, March of Dimes, Arts & Sciences Fund Dr.; bd. dirs. NC Inst. Politics; v.p. Sister Cities Internat.; mem. Pres. Bush's Affordable Housing Commn.; founder, coord. Charlotte vol. tornado relief effort; lay leader, Sunday sch. tchr. 1st United Meth. Ch.; treas. Mecklenburg Ministries. Recipient Woman of Yr. award Harrisonburg, Va., 1968; named one of The Outstanding Young Women of America, 1968, Public Svc. Leadership award, 2002, Small Bus. Survival Com. award, 2004, Oncology Medal of Honor award, 2005. Mem. Women's Polit. Caucus, Beta Sigma Phi. Republican. Methodist.

MYUNG, GIGI L., retail executive; B in Petroleum Engring., U. Tulsa; M in Internat. Mgmt., Am. Grad. Sch. Internat. Mgmt., Glendale, Ariz., MBA. Regional v.p. W.W. Grainger, Inc.; various positions Toyota Motor Sales & Nissan Motor Co., 1987—94; v.p., purchasing Group 1 Automotive, Inc., 2007—. Office: Group 1 Automotive Inc 800 Gessner Rd Ste 600 Houston TX 77024-4538 Office Phone: 713-647-5700. Office Fax: 713-647-5858. Business E-Mail: gmyung@group1auto.com.

NABERS, DRAYTON, JR., retired state supreme court chief justice, insurance company executive; b. Birmingham, Ala., Dec. 2, 1940; s. Drayton Sr. and Jane (Porter) N.; m. Fairfax Smathers, Dec. 31, 1965; children: Drayton III, Mary James, Fairfax Virginia. BA, Princeton U., 1962; LLB, Yale U., 1965. Law clk. to justice Hugo Black U.S. Supreme Ct., Washington, 1965-66; assoc. Cabaniss, Johnston, Gardner, Dumas & O'Neal, 1967-71, ptnr., 1971-79; sr. v.p. ops., gen. counsel Protective Life Ins. Co., 1979; pres. Empire Gen. Life Ins. Co., 1980-82; pres., COO Protective Life Corp./Protective Life Ins. Co., 1982-92; pres., CEO Protective Life Ins. Co, Birmingham, Ala., 1992-94, chmn., pres., CEO, 1994—2002; fin. dir. State of Alabama, 2002—04; chief justice Alabama Supreme Ct., 2004—06; chmn., CEO ProAssurance Corp.; atty. Maynard, Cooper and Gale, P.C., Birmingham. Bd. dirs. Protective Life Corp., Protective Life Ins. Co., Am. Found. Life Ins. Co., Energen, Inc., Nat. Bank of Commerce. bd. dirs. Infinity Property & Casualty Corp., bd. dirs. ProAssurance Corp., 2007- Chmn. Leadership Birmingham, United Way Ctrl. Ala., Am. Council Life Insurers, Cornerstone Schools of Ala. Mem. Ala. Acad. Honor, Birmingham Bar Assn., Ala. Bar Assn. Office: ProAssurance Corp 2400 Regions Harbert Plz 1901 Sixth Ave N Birmingham AL 35203 Office Phone: 205-254-1000. Office Fax: 205-254-1999. Business E-Mail: dnabers@proassurance.com.

NACCARATO, BEN, corporate financial executive; B in Commerce & Fin., U. Toronto, 1985. Cert. mgmt. acct. Various corp. and operational positions, including dir., fin. planning and analysis USPCI Inc., Laidlaw Environ. Svcs. Inc., Safety-Kleen Corp., 1998—2002; v.p., CFO Culp Petroleum Co., Inc., 2002—04; v.p., fin., indsl. segment Perma-Fix Environ. Svcs., Inc., 2004—06, treas., 2006—08, v.p., corp. contr., 2006—09, interim CFO, 2008—09; sec. Perma-Fix Environmental Services, Inc., 2008—, v.p., CFO, 2009—. Office: Perma-Fix Environmental Services Inc 8302 Dunwoody Pl Ste 250 Atlanta GA 30350 Office Phone: 770-587-9898. Office Fax: 770-587-9937. Personal E-mail: bnaccarato@perma-fix.com.

NACHMAN, RONALD JAMES, chemist, researcher; b. Takoma Park, Md., Feb. 1, 1954; s. Joseph Frank and Rosemary (Anderson) N.; m. Lita Rose Wilson, Dec. 18, 1976 (div. 1987); m. Isidora Austria Panis, May 6, 1989. BS in Chemistry, U. Calif., San Diego, 1976; PhD in Organic Chemistry, Stanford U., 1981. Rsch. asst. Scripps Inst. Oceanography, La Jolla, Calif., 1974-76; chemist Western Regional Rsch. Ctr., USDA, Berkeley, Calif., 1981-89, Vet. Toxicology and Entomology Rsch. Lab., College Station, Tex., 1989—. Vis. scientist dept. molecular biology Salk Inst., La Jolla, 1985, Scripps Rsch. Inst., La Jolla, 1988-89. Mem. editl. adv. bd. Pesticides, The Jour. Peptides, guest editor, 2001-07; mem. organizing com. Ann. Invertebrate Neuropeptide Conf.; contbr. sci. articles to profl. jours. Recipient USDA Cert. of Merit, 1988, 1991, 1994—2007, Arthur S. Flemming award for sci. achievement, 1994. Fellow Internat. Neoropeptide Soc. (bd. dirs. 2000—), Am. Assoc. Advancement Sci.; mem. AAAS, Internat. Neuropeptide Soc., Am. Chem. Soc., N.Y. Acad. Scis., Sigma Xi. Avocations: travel, photography, jogging, racquetball. Home: 14891 Pollux Dr Willis TX 77318-5079 Office: USDA Southern Plains Agrl Rsch Ctr 2881 F And B Rd College Station TX 77845-4988

NADEAU, ROBERT BERTRAND, JR., lawyer; b. Miami Beach, Fla., July 15, 1950; s. Robert B. and Ernestine Inez (Nicholson) N. BBA magna cum laude, U. Notre Dame, 1972; JD with honors, U. Fla., 1975. Bar: Fla. 1975, U.S. Dist. Ct. (mid. dist.) Fla. 1976, U.S. Dist. Ct. (so. dist.) Fla. 1982, U.S. Ct. Appeals (11th cir.) 1982. Asst. to pres. The Fla. Bar, Tampa, 1975-76; ptnr. Akerman, Senterfitt & Eidson, P.A., Orlando, Fla., 1976—. Arbitrator Am. Arbitration Assn., Orlando, 1987—. Mem. ABA, The Fla. Bar (chmn. student edn. and admission to bar com., vice chmn. 9th cir. grievance com.), Notre Dame Club Greater Orlando (pres. 1979-80). Avocations: golf, running. Office: Akerman Senterfitt 420 S Orange Ave 1200 Orlando FL 32801 Home Phone: 407-834-5059; Office Phone: 407-423-4000. Business E-Mail: robert.nadeau@akerman.com.

NADERI, SHERVIN, plastic surgeon; B in Psychology, minor in Chemistry, Boston U., M in Med. Sciences; MD, Drexel U.(formerly Med. Coll. Pa - Hahneman U. Sch. of Medicine). Diplomate Am. Bd. Facial Plastic and Reconstructive Surgery (ABFPRS), Am. Bd. Otolaryngology, Am. Bd. Medical Specialties. Intern gen. surgery Ind. Univ. Sch. of Medicine, resident otolaryngology - head and neck surgery, clin. assoc. prof. facial plastic surgery; fellow facial plastics and reconstructive surgery under Dr. Stephen Perkins Meridian Plastic Surgery Ctr.; pvt. practice The Naderi Ctr. For Cosmetic Surgery and Skin Care. Med. bd. examiner ABFPRS; guest lectr. dept. of surgery Sch. of Medicine George Washington Univ. Author multiple chpts. in major facial plastic surgery and head and neck surgery textbooks on nose surgery and facelift surgery techniques, multiple med. papers. Fellow: ACS; mem.: Am. Acad. of Facial and Reconstructive Surgery (past pres., officer). Office: The Naderi Center Rhinoplasty and Cosmetic Surgery 297 Herndon Pky Ste 101 Herndon VA 20170 also: 5454 Wisconsin Ave Ste 1655 Chevy Chase MD 20815 Office Phone: 703-481-0002, 301-222-2020.

NAESER, NANCY DEARIEN, geologist, researcher; b. Morgantown, W.Va., Apr. 15, 1944; d. William Harold and Katherine Elizabeth (Dearien) Cozad; m. Charles Wilbur Naeser, Feb. 6, 1982. BS, U. Ariz., 1966; PhD, Victoria U., Wellington, New Zealand, 1973. Geol. field asst. U.S. Geol. Survey, Flagstaff, Ariz., 1966; sci. editor New Zealand Jour. Geology and Geophysics, New Zealand Dept. Sci. and Indsl. Rsch., Wellington, 1974-76; postdoctoral rsch. assoc. U. Toronto, 1976-79, U.S. Geol. Survey, Denver, 1979-81, geologist, 1981—2006, scientist emeritus, 2006—. Adj. prof. Dartmouth Coll., Hanover, NH, 1985—97, U. Wyo., Laramie, 1984—91. Editor: Thermal History of Sedimentary Basins--Methods and Case Histories, 1989, Debris-Flow Hazards - Mechanics, Prediction and Assessment, 2000; contbr. articles on fission-track analysis to profl. jours. Docent, Denver Zoo, 1991-99. Fulbright fellow, New Zealand, 1967-68. Fellow Geol. Soc. Am.; mem. Geol. Soc. New Zealand, Mortar Board, Phi Kappa Phi. Methodist. Office: US Geol Survey Mail Stop 926A 12201 Sunrise Valley Dr Reston VA 20192-0002 Office Phone: 703-648-5328. Business E-Mail: nnaeser@usgs.gov.

NAGEL, VERNON J., chemicals and electronics executive; BBA, U. Mich. CPA. V.p. fin., CFO, treas., sec. Stericycle Inc.; exec. v.p., CFO, treas. Kuhlman Corp., 1993—99; prin. Jepson Assocs., Inc., 1999—2001; CFO Acuity Brands, Inc., Atlanta, 2001—04, vice chmn., 2004, chmn., pres., CEO, 2004—. Office: Acuity Brands Inc 1170 Peachtree St NE Atlanta GA 30309

NAGERA, HUMBERTO, psychiatrist, psychoanalyst, educator, writer; b. Havana, Cuba, May 23, 1927; m. Gloria Maria Hernandez, Sept. 8, 1952; children: Lisette Maria, Humberto Felipe, Daniel. B.Sc., U. Havana, 1945; MD, Havana Med. Sch., 1952. Intern, resident in psychiatry Havana U. Hosp., 1950-55; sr. staff, chmn. research Anna Freud's Clinic, London, 1958-68; prof. psychiatry U. Mich., Ann Arbor, 1968-87, chief youth services, 1973-79, prof. emeritus, 1987; prof. psychiatry U. South Fla., 1987—2010, prof. emeritus, 2010, dir. adolescent inpatient unit and children's inpatient unit, 1987-97, dir. Carter Jenkin Ctr., 2002—. Lectr. in field. Author: Early Childhood Disturbances, Problems of Developmental Psychoanalytic Psychology, 1966, Vincent Van Gogh, 1966, Basic Psychoanalytic Concepts on the Libido Theory, 1969, Basic Psychoanalytic Concepts on the Theory of Instincts, 1970, Basic Psychoanalytic Concepts of Metapsychology Conflicts, Anxiety, and Other Subjects, 1970, Female Sexuality and the Oedipus Complex, 1975, Obsessional Neurosis: Developmental Psychopathology, 1977, 2nd edit., 1993, The Developmental Approach in Child Psychopathology, 1981; Contbr. articles to profl. jours. Mem. Am. Psychiat. Assn., Internat. Psychoanalytic Assn., Mich. Psychoanalytic Inst. (pres. 1975-77), Am. Assn. Child Psychoanalysis, Cuba Med. Assn. in Exile, South Fla. Tampa Bay Psychoanalytic Soc. (pres. 1992-93). Home: 5202 Dwire Ct Tampa FL 33647-1016 Office: 1325 W Fletcher Ave Tampa FL 33612 Office Phone: 813-908-8686.

NAGUEH, SHERIF F., cardiologist, educator; BA in Chemistry, Cairo U., Egypt, MD, 1986. Diplomate Am. Bd. Internal Medicine, 2003, Am. Bd. Internal Medicine-cardiovasc. disease, 2007. Resident pediat. Cairo Univ. Hosps., Cairo; resident internal medicine Baylor Coll. of Medicine, Houston, 1991—93, fellow cardiovasc. disease, 1993—96, asst. prof. medicine dept., 1996, assoc. prof. medicine dept., 2001, chair clin. cardiology T.L.L. Temple/William H. Spencer, MD, 2004—05; sr. mem. The Meth. Hosp. Rsch. Inst.; assoc. dir. echocardiography lab. The Meth. Hosp.; prof. medicine Weill Cornell Med. Coll./Cornell Univ. Co-author: (publs.) Cardiac resynchronization therapy in heart failure with narrow QRS complexes, 2007, Left ventricular untwisting rate by speckle tracking echocardiography, 2007, Hemodynamically tailored therapy in congestive heart failure: alive and well, 2007, American Society of Echocardiography. American Society of Echocardiography recommendations for performance, interpretation, and application of stress echocardiography, 2007, Outcome of surgical myectomy after unsuccessful alcohol septal ablation for the reatment of patients with hypertrophic obstructive cardiomyopathy, 2007. Office: The Methodist Hospital 6565 Fannin St Houston TX 77030 Office Phone: 713-441-2850. Office Fax: 713-793-7034. Business E-Mail: snagueh@tmhs.org.

NAHAI, FOAD, plastic surgeon, educator; b. Teheran, Iran, Sept. 23, 1943; came to U.S., 1970; m. Shahnaz Mossanen, Aug. 4, 1969; children: Farzad, Fariba BSc with honors, U. Bristol, Eng., 1966, MB ChB, 1969. Diplomate Am. Bd. Surgery, Am. Bd. Plastic Surgery (dir. 2001-2007); lic. Eng., Ga. Med. and surg. intern United Bristol Hosps., Bristol, England, 1969-70; intern in surgery Balt. City Hosps., 1970-71; resident in surgery Johns Hopkins Hosp., Balt., 1971-72; resident in gen. surgery Emory U. Affiliated Hosps., Atlanta, 1972-74, chief resident, gen. surgery, 1974-75, fellow in hand surgery and microsurgery, 1975-76, resident in plastic surgery, 1976-77; instr. in surgery Emory U., Atlanta, 1975—76, 1978, asst. prof. surgery (plastic surgery), 1978—83, assoc. prof. surgery (plastic surgery), 1983—91, prof. plastic surgery, 1991—97; pvt. practice Paces Plastic Surgery, Atlanta, 1998—. Invited spkr. in field; vis. prof. at various universities, colleges and institutions, domestically and internationally. Co-author (with S.J. Mathes) Clinical Atlas of Muscle and Musculocutaneous Flaps, 1979, Clinical Applications for Muscle and Musculocutaneous Flaps, 1982, Reconstructive Surgery: Principles Anatomy and Technique, 1996, (with others) Microvascular Surgery in Reconstruction of the Head and Neck, 1989, Plastic and Reconstructive Breast Surgery, 1990, Grabb's Encyclopedia of Flaps, 1990, Chirurgie Due Cancer Due Sein Diagnostique, 1997, (with Bostwick and Eaves) Endoscopic Plastic Surgery, 1995; mem. editl. bd. Annals Plastic Surgery, 1984-88, Outlook Plastic Surgery, 1988-97, Perspectives in Plastic Surgery 1994-97, Plastic and Reconstructive Surgery 1998, Aesthetic Plastic Surgery, 1999, Aesthetic Surgery Jour., 2000, Roundtables in Plastic Surgery, 2003; author Art of Aesthetic Surgery Principles and Techniques, 2005; co-editor Vertical Scar Mammoplasty, 2005; contbr. articles to profl. jours.; co-prodr. (movies) Breast Reconstruction After a Radical Mastectomy with Latissimus Dorsi Musculocutaneous Flap, 1978, The Tensor Fascia Lata Free Flap, 1979; prodr. (videotapes) TFL Neurosensory Flap for Coverage of Greater Trochanteric and Ischium, Rectus Abdominis Flap for Sternal Coverage, Gastrocnemius Muscle Flap for Coverage of Tibia, others; contbr. chpts. to books. Recipient Russell Cooper prize, U. Bristol, Eng., 1968, Gold Medal Paper Presentation Southeastern Surg. Conf., 1976, Best Paper award Atlanta Clin. Soc., 1980, award Am. Med. Writers Assn., 1983; named one of Best Doctors in Am., Best Doctors in the US, Top Plastic Surgeon Good Housekeeping, More Mag., Atlanta Mag., Top Plastic Surgeon in the World, W Mag. Fellow ACS (3d Ann. Residents Competition award Ga. chpt. 1977); mem. Am. Soc. Plastic Surgeons (President's award, 2005), Am. Assn. Plastic Surgeons (James Barrett Brown award 1982), Am. Soc. for Aesthetic Plastic Surgery (jud. coun. 1997, bd. dirs. 1999-, tchg. course subcommittee chmn., 1999-2002, sec. 2002-04, edn. commn. co-chair, 2002-05 chair 2005, v.p. 2005, pres.elect 2006, pres. 2007-2008), Am. Soc. Plastic and Reconstructive Surgeons (rsch. grantee ednl. found.), Ga. Soc. Plastic Surgeons, Med. Assn. Ga., Ga. Surg. Soc., Med. Assn. Atlanta, Southeastern Soc. Plastic and Reconstructive Surgeons (Outstanding Resident award 1977), Internat. Assn. Univ. Plastic Surgeons, Plastic Surgery Rsch. Coun. (program chmn. 1988, chmn. 1989), Soc. Residents and Ex Residents of Inst. Reconstructive Surgery (hon.), Sociedad Jaime Planas de Cirurgia Plastica (hon.), Internat. Soc. Aesthetic Plastic Surgery (1st term course dir. 1999, sec. gen. 2000-2004, 2d v.p. 2004-06, 1st v.p. 2006-07, pres.-elect 2007, pres. 2008), Am. Soc. for Laser Medicine and Surgery, Plastic Surgery Ednl. Found. (bd. dirs. 2003-05), Internat. Plastic & Reconstructive Surgery Found. (v.p. 1999), Am. Soc. for Reconstructive Microsurgery (sec. 1986-89); corr. mem. Brazilian Coll. Surgeons, Brazilian Soc. Plastic Surgeons, Italian Soc. Plastic, Reconstructive and Aesthetic Surgery, Fla. Soc. Plastic and Reconstructive Surgeons, Israeli Assn. Plastic and Cosmetic Surgeons, Japanese Soc. Plastic and Reconstructive Surgery, Assn. Plastic and Reconstructive Surgeons So. Africa (also hon.), Lebanese Soc. Plastic, Reconstructive, and Aesthetic Surgery (hon.), New Eng. Soc. Plastic Surgeons (hon.). Office: Paces Plastic Surgery 1411 Grayson Pt Buckhead GA 30625-2237 Office Phone: 404-351-0051. Office Fax: 404-351-0632. Business E-Mail: nahaimd@aol.com. E-mail: pacesplasticsurgery@aol.com.

NAHATA, BABU L., economics professor, researcher; b. Sardarshahr, Rajasthan, India, June 2, 1944; s. Bhikam Chand and Manohari Nahata; m. Kusum Lodha, Aug. 8, 1949; children: Ritu Nahata Rowland, Rohit. BS, Birla Inst. Tech., Ranchi, India, 1967; MS, Ill. Inst. Tech., Chgo., 1970, Poly. U., Bklyn., 1974; PHD, No. Ill. U., Dekalb, 1977. Prof., co-dir., ctr. emerging market economies U. Louisville, 1978—. Vis. exch. prof. Hiroshima Shudo U., Japan, 1986—87. Fellow, Fukuoka U., Japan, 1992, Japan Soc. Promotion Sci., Tokyo, 1996—97; scholar, Indian Inst. Mgmt., Calcutta, 1989, Fukuoka U., 2000. Mem.: Am. Econ. Assn., Sigma Xi. Office: U Louisville Dept Econs COB Louisville KY 40292 Office Fax: 502-852-7672. Business E-Mail: nahata@louisville.edu.

NAHMAD, ALBERT H., manufacturing executive; b. Oct. 15, 1940; m. Jane Davis; 2 children. BS in Mech. Engring., U. N. Mex., 1962; MS in Indsl. Adminstrn., Purdue U., 1963. Mgmt. cons. Arthur Young, NYC; group v.p. W.R. Grace & Co.; chmn. pres., CEO Watsco, Inc., Coconut Grove, Fla., 1973—. Bd. dirs. Am. Bankers Ins. Group, Mayor's Jewelers. Mem. Fla. Coun. 100; chmn. bd. of trustees Miami Children's Hosp.; past chmn. Fla. chpt Young Presidents' Org.; bd. dir. Cmty. Partnership for the Homeless Inc. Mem. Chief Executives Org., World Presidents' Org. Office: Watsco Inc 2665 S Bayshore Dr Ste 901 Miami FL 33133

NAHMAD, MICHEL HENRY, thoracic surgeon; b. Nov. 7, 1938; married; 4 children. BSc in Biology, U. NM, Albuquerque, 1960; MD, Tulane U. Med. Sch., New Orleans, 1964. Diplomate Am. Bd. Surgery, 1971, Am. Bd. Thoracic and Cardiac Surgery, 1971, cert. spl. competence pediatric surgery 2005. Internship in mixed medicine Charity Hosp. La., Tulane Svc., New Orleans, 1964—65, residency in gen. surgery, 1965—66; residency in gen. surgery, assoc. resident in surgery Bronx Mcpl. Hosp., the Albert Einstein Coll. Medicine, NY, 1966—67, clin. instr., surgery, 1966—70, surg. rsch. fellow, 1967—68, residency in surgery, 1968—69, chief resident in surgery, 1969—70; clin. instr., surgery Ohio State U. Coll. Medicine, Columbus, 1967—70, thoracic surgery specialist, U. Hosp., 1970—71, instr. surgery, 1970—72, pediatric surgery specialist, gen., thoracic and urologic surg. tng., Children's Hosp., 1971—72; attending pediatric surgeon, chief thoracic surgery Miami Children's Hosp. Pediatric and Thoracic Surgery, Fla., 1972—; pvt. practice in pediatric and thoracic surgery Dade and Broward Counties, Fla. Active Bapt. Hosp., Miami, 1972—; cons. Mt. Sinai Hosp., Miami, 1972—. Contbr. articles to profl. jours. Former med. bd. mem., treas. Miami Children's Hosp., vice chmn. bd. trustees; mem. Soc. Hosp. Founders. Grantee Gen. Rsch. Support, CHRF NIH, 1972. Fellow: ACS, Am. Acad. Pediat.; mem.: AMA, Greater Miami Pediatric Soc., Fla. Assn. Pediatric Surgeons, Dade County Med. Assn., Fla. Med. Assn. Office: Miami Children's Hosp 3200 SW 60th Ct Ste 201 Miami FL 33155 Office Phone: 305-662-8320. Office Fax: 305-665-2467.

NAHMIAS, DAVID ERICH, state supreme court justice, former prosecutor; b. Atlanta, Sept. 11, 1964; s. Andre and Brigitte Nahmias; m. Catherine M. O'Neil; 2 children. BA summa cum laude, Duke U., 1986; JD magna cum laude, Harvard U., 1991. Bar: Ga. 1991. Law clerk to Hon. Laurence H. Silberman US Ct. Appeals (DC cir.), 1991—92; law clerk to Justice Antonin Scalia US Supreme Ct., 1992—93; assoc. Hogan & Hartson LLP, Washington, 1993—95; asst. US atty. (no. dist.) Ga. US Dept. Justice, Atlanta, 1995—2001, counsel for the asst. atty. gen. criminal divsn. Washington, 2001—03, dep. asst. atty. gen. criminal divsn., 2003—04, US atty. (no. dist.) Ga. Atlanta, 2004—09; justice Ga. Supreme Ct., Atlanta, 2009—. Editor: Harvard Law Review. Recipient Nat. Award for Superior Performance by a Asst. US Atty., US Dept. Justice, 2002, Common Cause of Ga. Democracy award, 2007; named an "On the Rise" Ga. Atty., Fulton County Daily Report, 2004; named one of The 100 Most Influential Atlantans, Atlanta Bus. Chronicle, 2005, 2006, 2007, 2008. Office: Georgia Supreme Court 244 Washington St SW Atlanta GA 30334 Office Phone: 404-656-3474. Office Fax: 404-656-2253.*

NAIFEH, JAMES (JIMMY) O., state legislator; b. Covington, Tenn., June 16, 1939; m. Betty Taylor, 1962; children: Jim, Beth, Sameera. Past chmn. Rural West Tenn. Dem. Caucus; bd. dir. St. Jude Children Rsch. Hosp., FSB, Inc.; state rep. Dist. 81 Tenn., 1974—; spkr., 1992—2008; spkr. emeritus, 2009—. Mem.: Am. Legion, Tipton County U. Tenn. Alumni Assn. (founding mem., former pres.), South Tipton C. of C., Covington Rotary (former pres.), Covington-Tipton County C. of C. (former pres.), Tenn. Wholesale Grocers Assn. (founding mem.). Democrat. Episcopal. Mailing: PO Box 97 Covington TN 38019 Office: G19A War Memorial Bldg Nashville TN 37243-0181 Office Phone: 901-476-9593, 615-741-3774. Office Fax: 615-741-0944. Business E-Mail: spk.eme.jimmy.naifeh@capitol.tn.gov.

NAIMOLI, VINCENT JOSEPH, diversified financial services company executive; b. Paterson, NJ, Sept. 16, 1937; s. Ralph A. and Margaret R. (Calabrese) N.; children— Christine, Tory Ann, Alyson, Lindsey. BSM.E., U. Notre Dame, 1959; MSM.E., N.J. Inst. Tech., 1962; MBA, Fairleigh Dickinson U., 1964; grad. Advanced Mgmt. Program, Harvard Bus. Sch., 1974. With Continental Group, 1965-77, v.p., gen. mgr. ops., 1975-77; pres., chief oper. officer Allegheny Beverage Corp., Balt., 1977-78; sr. v.p., group exec. Jim Walter Corp., Tampa, Fla., 1978-81; group v.p. packaging Anchor Hocking Corp., Lancaster, Ohio, 1981-83; chmn. bd., pres., chief exec. officer Anchor Glass Container Corp., Lancaster, 1983-89; chmn., pres., CEO Anchor Industries Internat., Tampa, Fla., 1990—; chmn., chief exec. officer Electrolux Corp., Atlanta, 1990-91; chmn., CEO Doehler Jarvis Corp., Toledo, 1991-95; CEO Ladish, Inc., Milw., 1992-95; chmn., pres., CEO Harvard Industries, 1993-97; mng. gen. ptnr., CEO Tampa Bay Devil Rays, 1992—2005, chmn., 2006—. Bd. dirs. Strategic Materials, Inc. Roman Catholic. Office: Anchor Industries Internat 1 Tropicana Dr Saint Petersburg FL 33705-1703

NAIR, GANESH KUMAR VENUGOPALAN, endocrinologist, internist; arrived in U.S., 1995; s. Venugopalan and Sreekumari Nair; m. Usha Kartha, Jan. 21, 1996; 1 child, Nikhil. Student, U. Kerala, 1981—83, MBBS, 1989. Diplomate in endocrinology, diabetes and metabolism Am. Bd. Internal Medicine, 2008, cert. in thyroid ultrasound and guided biopsy, clin. densitometrist, lic. Jamaican Med. Coun. Intern Kerala U., Trivandrum, Kerala State, India, 1990—91; sr. ho. surgeon Gastroenterology Med. Coll. Trivandrum, 1991, rsch. asst. Gastroenterology, 1991—92; intern Ministry Health, Kingston, Jamaica, 1992; jr. resident Kingston Pub. Hosp., 1993—95; resident internal medicine Conemaugh Valley Meml. Hosp. Program Temple U., Johnstown, Pa., 1995—98, chief resident, internal medicine Conemaugh Valley Meml. Hosp. Program, 1998—99; fellow endocrinology, diabetes and metabolism U. Ark., 1999—2001, asst. prof. medicine, 2002—05; staff physician Ctrl. Ark. Vets. Healthcare Sys., Little Rock, 2002—05; attending endocrinologist Little Rock Diagnostic Clinic, 2005—. Assoc. program dir. endocrinology, diabetes and metabolism fellowship program U. Ark., Little Rock, 2003—05. Contbr. articles to profl. jours. Recipient Cert. of Merit, Sahodara Samajam Nair Sanodara Samajam. Karayogam, 1981, 1983, Clin. award, Internal Medicine Residency, Temple U., 1998, Chief Resident Award, 1999, Excellence award, U. Ark. Med. Sci., 1999—2001, Outstanding Svc. award, Appreciation Cert., Dept. Vets. Affairs, Ctrl. Ark. Vets. Healthcare System, Little Rock, 2005; named one of Best Drs. in America, 2011—13. Fellow: ACP, Am. Coll. Physicians, Am. Coll. Endocrinology; mem.: Am. Diabetes Assn., Internat. Soc. Clin. Densitometry, The Endocrine Soc., Am. Assn. Clin. Endocrinologists (Best Drs. in America 2011—14). Office: 10001 Lile Dr Little Rock AR 72205 Office Phone: 501-227-8000.*

NAISHTAT, ELLIOTT, state legislator; b. NYC, Feb. 15, 1945; s. Sidney and Doris Naishtat. MSW, JD, U. Tex. Staff counsel to Senator Gonzalo Barrientos Tex. State Senate; pvt. practice atty.; chmn. Austin Cmty. Development Commission; dir. U. Tex. Sch. of Social Work Legislative Training Program; mem. Dist 49 Tex. House of Representatives, 1990—. Adj. prof. St. Edwards U. Author: (book) The 74th Legislature, The Austin Lawyer. VISTA vol. Lyndon B. Johnson's War on Poverty Campaign. Recipient Blind Access award, America Found., Tex. Outstanding Pub. Servant, People First award; named Legislator of Yr., Tex. Apt. Assn., Tex. Coun. Family Violence. Mem.: Nat. Assn. Jewish Legislators, Travis County Bar Assn., Nat. Assn. Social Workers (nat. pub. elected official 1999), Environ. Def. Fund, Common Cause (award), Sierra Club (award). Democrat. Jewish. Office: Room GW.16 Capitol Bldg PO Box 2910 Austin TX 78768 Office Phone: 512-463-0668. Office Fax: 512-463-8022.

NAKAHARA, MORIHIKO, conductor; Grad., Andrews U., Berrien Springs, U. Cin. Conducted symphonies including Toledo, Lansing, Peoria, Lubbock, SW Mich., Billings, and Missoula; guest condr. Lexington Philharm., Chgo. Pro Musica, Chattanooga Symphony Orch., Green Bay Symphony Orch.; assoc. condr. Jacksonville Symphony Orch., 2007—08, Spokane Symphony Orch., resident condr., 2010—11; music dir. Holland Symphony Orch., SC Philharm., 2008—. Tchr. Eastern Washington Univ., Andrews Univ. Named a Brilliant Young Condr., Free Times. Office: South Carolina Ste B 721 Lady St Columbia SC 29201 Office Phone: 803-771-7937. Office Fax: 803-254-0268.

NALBANDIAN, DAVID, professional tennis player; b. Cordoba, Argentina, Jan. 1, 1982; s. Norbeto and Alda. Jr. champion Jrs.-US Open, 1998; finalist Wimbledon, 2002; semi-finalist US Open, 2003, French Open, 2004; mem. Argentina Davis Cup team, 2002—04; winner Estoril Open, 2006, Mutua Madrilena Masters Madrid, 2007, BNP Paribas Masters, Paris, 2007, Copa Telmex, Buenos Aires, 2008, If Stockholm Open, 2008, Medibank Internat., 2009. Named World Newcomer Yr.; nominee, Laureus World Sports Awards, 2003. Achievements include highest world ranking #4, 2004. Avocations: fishing, soccer. Office: c/o Assn Tennis Profl 201 ATP Blvd Ponte Vedra Beach FL 32082

NALLEY, ELIZABETH ANN, chemistry professor; b. Catron, Mo., July 8, 1942; d. Arthur E. and Thelma L. (King) Frazier; m. Robert L. Mullican, Jan. 2, 1986; 1 child, George L. BS, Northeastern Okla. State U., 1965; MS, Okla. State U., 1969; PhD, Tex. Woman's U., 1975. High sch. tchr. Muskogee (Okla.) Ctrl. High Sch., 1964-65; instr. Cameron U., Lawton, Okla., 1969-72, asst. prof., 1972-75, assoc. prof., 1975-78, prof., 1978—2012, Clarence Page endowed chair of sci. and math. edn. Contbr. articles to profl. jours. Recipient Disting. Svc. award Cameron U., 1995, Alumni Hall of Fame award, 1996; named Okla. Sci. Tchr. of Yr., Okla. Sci. Tchrs. Assn., 1999, named to Okla. Higher Edn. Hall of Fame, 2010, Named one of top ten Female University Faculty- 2013, S.W. Tech. Disting. Rsch. award, 2001, Disting. Alumnus Tex. Woman's U., 2001, Profl. Excellence award, Iota Sigma Phi, 2005, Disting. Rsch. award, U. Oklahoma Sigma Xi, 2005, Fellow ACS, 2009, AAAS, 2013, DaVinci, 2013. Mem. AAAS, Assn. for Advancement of Computers in Edn., Am. Chem. Soc. (councilor 1980-97, sec. div. profl. rels. 1987-, sec. divsn. profl. rel. 1987-96, chair-elect divsn. profl. rels. 1996, chair divsn. profl. rels. 1997, nat. bd. dirs. 1997-2003, Okla. Chemist award 1992, divsn. profl. rels. Henry Hill award, 1996), Am. Inst. Chemists (nat. bd. dirs.), Phi Kappa Phi (regent 1981-89, nat. v.p. 1989-92, nat. pres.-elect 1992-95, nat. pres. 1995-98, Disting. Faculty award 1978), Sigma Xi, Sigma Pi Sigma, Iota Sigma Pi. Home: 2718 County St 2864 Chickasha OK 73018-9544 Office: Cameron U Dept of Chemistry 2800 W Gore Blvd Lawton OK 73505-6320 E-mail: annn@cameron.edu.*

NAM, CHARLES BENJAMIN, demographer, sociologist, genealogist, writer; b. Lynbrook, NY, Mar. 25, 1926; s. Samuel and Yetta (Huff) N.; m. Marjorie Lee Tallant, Jan. 1, 1956; children: David Wallace, Rebecca Jane. BA, NYU, 1950; MA, U. N.C., 1957, PhD, 1959. Statistician U.S. Bur. Census, Washington, 1950-53, chief edn. and social stratification br., 1957-64; statistician USAF, Montgomery, Ala., 1953-54; rsch. asst. U. N.C., Chapel Hill, 1954-57; prof. sociology Fla. State U., Tallahassee, 1964—96, chmn. dept. sociology, 1968—71, disting. rsch. prof., 1994—96, disting. rsch. prof. emeritus, 1996—; founder & rsch. assoc. Ctr. for Demography and Population Health, 1967—, dir., 1967—82; mem. population adv. com. U.S. Bur. Census, 1978-81. Cons. population divsn. Orgn. for Econ. Coop. and Devel., 1968-70, UNESCO, 1978-83, Indonesian Ministry of Population and Environment, Jakarta, 1988-90; Social Sci. Rsch. Coun., 1981-88. Author: (with John K. Folger) Education of the American Population, 1967, Population and Society, 1968, (with Susan Gustavus) Population: The Dynamics of Demographic Change, 1976, Nationality Groups and Social Stratification, 1981; (with Susan Philliber) Population: A Basic Orientation, 1983; (with Mary Powers) The Socioeconomic Approach to Status Measurement, 1983, Our Population: The Face of America, 1988, Understanding Population Change, 1994; (with Richard Rogers and Robert Hummer) Living and Dying in the USA, 2000; (with Janusz Balicki and Ewa Fratczak) Mechanisms of Population Changes and Population Policy (in Polish), 2003, The Golden Door, 2006; editor: Demography, 1972-75; co-editor: (with David Sly, William Serow) International Handbook of Internal Migration, 1990, Handbook of International Migration, 1990; mem. editl. bd. Population Research and Policy Review, 1993-94. Fellow AAAS (rep. sect. K 1999-2004); mem. Am. Sociol. Assn. (chmn. sect. on population 1976-78), Population Assn. Am. (pres. 1979), Internat. Union for Sci. Study Population, Am. Statis. Assn. (chmn. social statistics sect. 1974, fellow 1980), So. Sociol. Soc. (pres. 1981-82), So. Demographic Assn. (vice chmn. 1974-75; fellow 2001; hon. pres. 2007), Soc. Study Social Biology (bd. dirs. 1996-2006, exec. com. 1998-99). Home: 4147 Diplomacy Cir Tallahassee FL 32308 Personal E-mail: charlesbnam@gmail.com.

NAMATH, JOE (JOSEPH WILLIAM NAMATH), retired professional football player; b. Beaver Falls, Pa., May 31, 1943; s. John Andrew and Rose (Juhasz) N.; m. Deborah Lynn Mays, Nov. 7, 1984 (div. June 28, 1999); children: Jessica Grace, Olivia Rose BA in Interdisciplinary Studies, U. Ala., 2007. Quarterback NY Jets, 1965-77, LA Rams, 1977; co-owner Joe Namath Instructional Football Camp, Dudley, Mass. Actor: (films) C.C. and Company, 1970, Avalanche Express, 1978, Chattanooga Choo Choo, 1984, Going Under, 1990, Green Visionary, 1993; (TV films) Marriage is Alive Well, 1980, Our Voices Ourselves, 1982; (TV series) The Waverly Wonders, 1978; (TV appearances) The Merv Griffin Show, 1967, Toast of the Town, 1969, Rowan & Martin's Laugh-In, 1971,'72, The Flip Wilson Show, 1971, '72, '73, Dinah's Place, 1972, Here's Lucy, 1972, The Sonny & Cher Comedy Hour, 1973, The Brady Bunch, 1973, The Dean Martin Show, 1974, The Captain and Tennille, 1976, Disneyland, 1978, The Love Boat, 1980, 1981, The Big Show, 1980, Fantasy Island, 1981, The A-Team, 1986, ALF, 1986, Kate and Allie, 1988, Married...With Children, 1993, The John Laroquette Show, 1993, The Simpsons (voice), 1997, 2002; (stage appearances) Picnic, 1979, Li'l Abner, 1980, Damn Yankees, 1981, The Caine Mutiny Court-Martial, 1983, Sugar, 1984; host: The Joe Namath Show, 1969; announcer: ABC Monday Night Football, 1985-86; co-author: (with Dick Schapp) I Can't Wait Until Tomorrow... 'Cause I Get Better-Looking Every Day, 1969, (with Bob Oates Jr.) Namath: A Matter of Style, 1973; author: (autobiography): Namath, 2006 Past chmn. Leukemia Soc. Coin Campaign; hon. chmn. Am. Hungarian Soc.; established scholarship for women athletes U. Ala. Named Am. Football League Rookie of Yr., Sporting News, 1965, Am. Football League MVP, 1968-69, Super Bowl III MVP, 1969, Am. Football League All-Pro, 1966-68, NFL All-Pro, 1969, 1972; recipient Hickock Belt for Profl. Athlete of Yr., 1969, George Halas Most Courageous Athlete award, 1972, NFL Comeback Player of Yr. award, 1974; named one of the 100 Greatest Football Players, The Sporting News, 1999; named to Am. Football League Pro Bowl Team, 1965, 1967-68, Am. Football Conf. Pro Bowl Team, 1969, 1972, Ala. Sports Hall of Fame, 1981, Pro Football Hall of Fame, 1985. Achievements include being a member of Super Bowl III Champion New York Jets, 1969.

NAMNOUM, ANNE BRAWNER, obstetrician, gynecologist; b. Balt., Apr. 26, 1960; m. James Daniel Namnoum; children: Timothy Spencer, Anne Addison, Reed Daniel, Hannah Paine, Eliza Stewart, Isabelle Austin. MD, Johns Hopkins U., Balt., 1987. Diplomate Am. Bd. Ob-Gyn., cert. in Reproductive Endocrinology/Infertility. Ob-gyn. intern Johns Hopkins U., 1987-88, residnet in ob-gyn., 1988-91, fellow in reproductive endocrinology, 1991-93, asst. prof., 1993-95, Emory U. Sch. Medicine, Atlanta, 1995—. Contbr. articles to profl. jours. Mem.: Am. Coll. Ob-Gyn. Office: 2001 Peachtree Rd NE Ste 545 Savannah GA 30309

NAMNOUM, JAMES DANIEL, plastic surgeon; b. Hartford, Conn. m. Anne Brawner Namnoum; 6 children. MD, John Hopkins Sch. Medicine, 1987. Cert. Am. Bd. Plastic Surgery. Resident, surgery John Hopkins Hosp., Baltimore, Md., 1987—93, resident, plastic surgery, 1993—95; fellow, plastic surgery Reconstructive Surgery Found., Atlanta, 1996; co-dir. Atlanta Breast Symposium; chief, plastic surgery St. Joseph's Hosp.; med. dir. AYA Med. Spa; private practice Atlanta Plastic Surgery. Lectr. in field; cons. to companies specializing in products for cosmetic surgery. Mem.: Med. Assn. Ga., Med. Assn. Atlanta, Ga. Soc. Plastic Surgery, Southeastern Soc. Plastic Surgery, Am. Soc. Aesthetic Plastic Surgery, Am. Soc. Plastic Surgeons. Avocations: cooking, reading, fitness tng., wine enthusiast. Office: Atlanta Plastyic Surgery PC STE 100 975 Johnson Ferry RD NE Atlanta GA 30342-1618 Office Phone: 404-256-1311. Office Fax: 404-256-5487. Business E-Mail: aps@atlplastic.com.

NANCE, CYNTHIA ELEANOR (CYNDI NANCE), law educator, former dean; b. Chgo., Sept. 3, 1958; d. Eual Dean and Fern Elizabeth Nance. BS in Econs., Chgo. State U., 1986; JD with distinction, U. Iowa, 1990, MA in Fin., 1991, ABD in Indsl. Rels., 1993. Lic.: Iowa Supreme Ct. 1990. Law clk. Glasson, Grove, Sole & McMannus, Cedar Rapids, Iowa, 1989; program coord. U. Iowa Labor Ctr., 1989—91; tchg. asst. U. Iowa Coll. Bus., 1991—93; faculty fellow U. Iowa Coll. Law, 1993—94; asst. prof. to prof. law U. Ark. Sch. Law, Fayetteville, 1994—, dean, 2006—11, Nathan G. Gordon prof. law, 2011—. Mem. audit com. Law Sch. Admissions Coun., Newtown, Pa., 1994—98, fin. and legal affairs com., 1998—, chair fin. and legal affairs com., 2003—, CEO search com.; mem. sect. on minorities in the law Am. Assn. Law Schools, Washington, 1994—, chair labor and employment law sect., 2000—01, chair employment discrimination sect., 2001—02. Co-chair Greensboro Massacre Truth and Reconciliation Commn. Adv. Com., NC, 2001—; pres. Ozark Mountain Masters Swim Team, Springdale, Ark., 1999—2001; women of the ELCA anti-racism trainer Evang. Luth. Ch. America, Chgo., 1996—2002, mem. adv. com. on corp. social responsibility, 1999—; mem. ch. coun. Good Shepherd Luth. Ch., Fayetteville, 2002—03; bd. dirs. Sources for Ind. Living, Ark., 1994—99, ACLU, Little Rock, 1998—99, Nat. Interfaith Com. Worker Justice, Chgo., 1999. Recipient Martin Luther King Jr. Individual Achievement award, 2004, Woman of Distinction award, Girl Scouts N.W. Ark., Heritage award for profl. achievement, NIA, 2006; fellow Grad. Opportunities for Advanced Level Studies Found., U. of Iowa Coll. of Bus., 1990—92; Tchg. Fellow, U. of Iowa, Coll. of Law, 1993—94. Mem.: ABA (co-chair labor and employmentlaw sect. ethics and professionalism com. 2001—, mem. pro bono com. labor and employment law sect. 2003—, Outstanding Lawyer), Indsl. Rels. Rsch. Assn., Ark. Bar Assn. (jurisprudence and law reform com. 1995—, lawyer assistance program com. 1999—, com. on diversity 2000—, labor law sect.), W. B. Putman Am. Inn of Ct., Nat. Bar Assn., Alpha Kappa Alpha (chpt. pres. 1999—2002, faculty advisor 2001—, Outstanding Svc. award 2000), Beta Gamma Sigma, Phi Delta Phi. Liberal. Evangelical Lutheran. Avocations: swimming, travel, cooking. Office: University of Arkansas School Law 128 Waterman Hall Fayetteville AR 72701 Office Phone: 479-575-2403. E-mail: cnance@uark.edu.

NANDA, NAVIN CHANDAR, cardiologist, educator; came to U.S., 1971; s. Balwantrai and Maya (Vati) N.; m. Kanta Kumari Markan, Sept. 13, 1967; children: Nitin, Anil, Anita. Inter Sci. cert., Bombay U., 1956, MD, 1962. Resident house officer King George IV Hosp., Nairobi, Kenya, 1962; med. registrar King Edward Meml. Hosp., Bombay, 1963-64, sr. med. registrar, 1964-67; fellow Inst. Cardiology and Nat. Heart Hosp., London, 1967-68; sr. house physician, registrar Rotherham (Eng.) Hosp., 1968-71; instr., trainee in cardiology U. Rochester (N.Y.) Sch. Medicine, 1971-73; asst. prof. medicine and radiology, assoc. physician U. Rochester Sch. Medicine and Strong Meml. Hosp., Rochester, 1971-73, assoc. prof. medicine, dir. noninvasive cardiology labs.; cons. cardiology Genesee Hosp., Rochester Gen. Hosp., 1979—84; prof. of medicine div. cardiovascular disease U. Ala., Birmingham, 1984—2011, disting. prof. medicine and cardiovascular disease, 2011—. Dir. heart sta. and echocardiography labs. U. Ala.-Birmingham Hosp., 1984—, past pres. soc. geriat. cardiology, 2008-09; hon. vis. dean Dr. Navin C. Nanda Nat. Inst. Echocardiography and Cardiac Rsch., Mool Chand K.R. Hosp., New Delhi, 1988—; hon. vis. cons. dept. cardiology Bombay Hosp. Inst. of Med. Scis., 1988—; overseas vis. cons. P.D. Hinduja Hosp. and Med. Rsch. Ctr., Bombay, 1989—. Author: (with R. Gramiak) Clinical Echocardiography, 1978; editor: Doppler Echocardiography, 1985, 2d edit., 1993; author: Atlas of Color Doppler Echocardiography, 1989 and Textbook of Color Doppler Echocardiography, 1989; co-editor: Advances in Echo Imaging Using Contract Enhancement, 1993, Atlas of Transesophageal Echocardiography, 1998, Atlas of Three-Dimensional Echocardiography, 2002; co-author: Live/Real Time 3D Echocardiography, 2010; editor: Comprehensive Textbook of Echocardiography, 2014; (videotapes) Videotextbook of Two-Dimensional and Doppler Echocardiography, 1982-88; Case Studies in Doppler Echocardiography, 1985, Case Studies in Color Doppler Echocardiography; mem. editorial bd. numerous jours.; contbr. numerous articles, abstracts, revs. to profl. publs. Recipient Ellis Island medal of honor, Nat. Ethnic Coalition of Orgns., 2006; named Father of Echocardiography, Russian Soc. Cardiology, Chinese Med. Assn., Mexican Soc. Echocardiography, Emirates Cardiology Soc., Indian Coll. Cardiology, Indian Soc. Cardiology, Cardiol. Soc. India, Indian Acad. Echocardiography, Indian Assn. Cardiovasc. and Thoracic Anesthesiologists, World Congress Clin., Preventive and Geriatric Cardiology, Punjab Med. Coun. Fellow Am. Coll. Angiology, Am. Coll. Cardiology (mem. com., Internat. Svc. award 2010), Am. Heart Assn. (coun. on clin. cardiology), Internat. Coll. Angiology, Soc. Geriatric Cardiology, Rochester Acad. Medicine, N.Y. Cardiol. Soc., Soc. Geriat. Cardiology (past pres.); mem. AAAS, AMA, Am. Inst. Ultrasound Medicine, Am. Soc. Echocardiography (bd. dirs. 1978-80), Assn. Acad. Minority Physicians, Inc., Ala. Acad. Sci., Internat. Soc. Cardiovasc. Ultrasound (pres.), Am. Assn. Cardiologists Indian Origin (founding pres.), Am. Assn. Physicians Indian Origin (past pres.), numerous others. Hindu. Achievements include pioneering use of new innovative technique of color Doppler flow mapping. Office: U Ala Birmingham Heart Sta Swb S 102 Birmingham AL 35249 Office Phone: 205-934-8256. Business E-Mail: nanda@uab.edu.

NANNEY, WENDY K., state legislator; b. Greenville, SC, Apr. 16, 1965; d. Bob and Barb Taylor; m. Timothy Lee Nanney, Dec. 12, 1986; children: Meredith, Taylor, Kacey, Travis, Maggie. BS, Bob Jones U., 1987. Upstate rep. Women's Club, 2003—06; chmn. Greenville Co. Rep. Party, Greenville, SC, 2006—07; former staff asst. Chief Legal Counsel for Senator Jesse Helms; credit mgr. Interfilm Holdings; mem. Dist. 22 SC House of Reps., SC, 2008—. Republican. Office: Capitol Office 312D Blatt Bldg Columbia SC 29201 Home: 124 Birnam Ct Greenville SC 29615-3612 Office Phone: 864-569-4690, 864-292-1523, 803-212-6877. E-mail: wendynanney@schouse.org.

NAOR, DANIEL, food products executive; b. Paris, July 1, 1960; s. Shlomo and Sarah (Puderbeutel) N.; 1 child, Nathalie. BS in Elec. Engring., MIT, 1981, MS in Elec. Engring. and Computer Sci., 1981; MBA, INSEAD, 1990. Cert. engr. Project mgr. ELOP, Rehovot, Israel, 1985-87, mktg. mgr., 1988—89; assoc. McKinsey & Co., Paris, 1990—95, prin., 1995—98, Dallas, 1998—2002; group v.p. strategy, planning and bus. devel. Frito Lay N.Am., Plano, 2002—05, sr. v.p. bus. innovation, chief strategist, 2005—09; sr. v.p. bus. innovation PepsiCo Americas Foods, 2009—10, sr. v.p. & gen. mgr. growth ventures, 2011—. Contbr. articles to profl. jours. Mem. bd. dirs. Dallas Theater Ctr. Bd., 1999-2002, Variety, 1997—. Capt. Israeli Air Force, 1981-85. Mem. IEEE, Tau Beta Pi, Sigma Xi (assoc.). Jewish. Avocations: films, theater, ballroom and Latin dancing. Office: Frito Lay N Am 7701 Legacy Dr 2B-265 Plano TX 75024 Business E-Mail: Daniel.Naor@FritoLay.com.

NAPIER, CAMERON MAYSON FREEMAN, historic preservationist; b. Shanghai, Dec. 5, 1931; d. Hamner Garland and Cameron Middleton (Brame) Freeman; m. John Hawkins Napier III, Sept. 11, 1964. Student, L'Ecole des Artes Municipale, Paris, 1950-51, Westhampton Coll./U. Richmond, 1951—53; BA, U. Ala., 1955. Photographer's asst. Scott, Demott & Perry, Montgomery, Ala., 1951; art dir. WCOV-TV, Montgomery, 1955; self-employed graphic designer Dallas, 1956-64; self-employed designer Alexandria, Va., 1965-71; restoration chmn. White House Assn. Ala., Montgomery, 1973-76, 1st vice regent, 1976-80, regent, 1980—2009, hon. regent, 2009—. Co-founder Friends of Stratford Hall for No. Va., Alexandria, late 1960s; docent chmn. Lee's Boyhood Home, late 1960s; bd. dirs. Landmarks Found., Montgomery, 1971-75; advisor Conde Charlotte House, Mobile, Ala., 1994-95. Author, designer booklet: The First White House of the Confederacy, 1978 (nat. printers award 1979), The Struggle to Preserve the First White House of the Confederacy, 1982; contbr. to Ency. of So. Culture, 1989, Ency. of Ala.-online, 2006. Bd. dirs. English Speaking Union, Montgomery, 1980—83. Recipient Award of Excellence, Advt. Artists Assn., Dallas, 1960—62, disting. svc. award, Ala. Hist. Commn., Montgomery, 1977, Cert. of Commendation, Gov. Ala., 1986, Gov. Bob Riley, 2009, So. Patriot award, 1997, Lifetime Achievement award, Ala. Preservation Alliance, 2001, Jefferson Davis award, 1984, Winnie Davis award, United Daus. of Confederacy, 1985; named Hon. First Lady, by the Gov.'s wife, Montgomery, Ala., 1985. Mem.: Antiquarian Soc. (pres. 1981—82), Sojourners Lit. Club (pres.), Order of Merovingian Dynasty, Militi Templi Scotia, Daus. of Barons Runnymede, Nat. Soc. Colonial Dames in Am. (hist. properties com. 1994—95, state bd. mgrs. 1998—2000, ctr. vice chmn. 1998—2000), Am. Soc. Most Venerable Order of the Hosp. St. John of Jerusalem (assoc. officer sister 1995, named Comdr. Sister 2002), Soc. Descs. of Colonial Clergy, Order of the Crown in Am., Kappa Delta. Episcopalian. Avocation: crossword puzzles.

NAPIER, JOHN HAWKINS, III, historian; b. Berkeley, Calif., Feb. 6, 1925; s. John Hawkins and Lena Mae (Tate) Napier; m. Harriet Elizabeth McGehee, Aug. 30, 1950 (dec.); m. Cameron Mayson Freeman, Sept. 11, 1964. BA, U. Miss., 1949; MA, Auburn U., 1967; postgrad., Georgetown U., 1971; D (hon.), Napier U., Edinburgh, 2000. Journalist, tchr. Picayune (Miss.) H.S., 1946; commd. 2d lt. U.S. Air Force, 1949, advanced through grades to lt. col., 1966; ret., 1977. Staff dir. Congressional Com. on S.E. Asia, 1970; faculty Air War Coll., 1971-74; Air U. Command historian, 1974-77; asst. to exec. dir. Ala. Commn. on Higher Edn., Montgomery, 1977-78; adj. history faculty Auburn U., Montgomery, 1980-85; columnist Montgomery Advertiser, 1980-87; lectr. in field. Author: Lower Pearl River's Piney Woods: Its Land and People, 1985; The Air Force Officers Guide, 30th edit., 1995, Dr. Patrick Napier: His Ancestors and Some Descendants, 1991; contbr. articles to profl. jours. Sgt. USMC, 1943-46, col. Ala. State Defense Force, 1991-97, brig. gen., dep. comdr., 1997-99. Decorated Legion of Merit; Comdr. Order of St. John of Jerusalem, Comdr. Milit. and Hospitaller Order of St. Lazarus of Jerusalem Grand Cross, Grand Cross Sovereign Mil. Order of Temple of Jerusalem; recipient award of merit Ala. Hist. Commn., 1976, Ala. Disting. Svc. medal, 1999, merit award English-Speaking Union U.S., 1983, Hon. Alumnus, Oxford U., 2010; Taylor medal and grad. fellow U. Miss., 1949; Storrs scholar Pomona Coll., 1942-43. Fellow: Soc. Antiquaries Scotland; mem.: S.R. SAR (pres. 1974—75), SCV (vice comdr. Ala. 1979—80), Krewe of Phantom Host, Ala. Hist. Assn. (pres. 1979—80), Royal Order Scotland, English-Speaking Union (pres. 1978—87, nat. dir. 1980—86, 1987—90, 1991—94), Scabbard and Blade, Mil. Order Carabao, Soc. Colonial Wars, Soc. War of 1812 (pres. Ala. 1980—82), St. Andrews Soc., Clan Napier in N.Am. (lt. to chief 1985—), Order 1st Families Va., Jamestowne Soc., Soc. Cincinnati, Ala. Assn. (pres. 1998—2001), Aztec 1847, Soc. Pioneers Montgomery (pres. 1979—80), Montgomery Country Club, Masons (32d degree), Pi Sigma Alpha, Phi Alpha Theta, Omicron Delta Kappa, Phi Kappa Phi, Sigma Chi. Democrat. Episcopalian. Home: Kilmahew 158 Mt Zion Rd Ramer AL 36069-6505

NAPIER, LANHAM (A. LANHAM NAPIER), web services company executive; b. 1970; s. Albert Napier. BA in Economics, Rice U., 1993; MBA, Harvard U., 1997. With Dobson; analyst Merrill Lynch and Co., 1993—95; CFO Rackspace Hosting, Inc. (formerly Rackspace Managed Hosting Corp.), 2000—03, pres., 2001—06, pres., CEO, 2006—. Bd. dirs. Silver Brands Partners, 1997—2000, Rackspace Hosting, Inc., 2001—. Named one of America's 15 Most Powerful CEO's 40 and Under, Forbes mag., 2010. Office: Rackspace Hosting Inc 5000 Walzem Rd San Antonio TX 78218 Office Phone: 210-312-4000. Office Fax: 210-447-4300. Business E-Mail: Lanham.Napier@rackspace.com.

NAPIER, LONNIE, state legislator; b. May 24, 1940; Realtor; farmer; auctioneer; newspaper editor; mem. Dist. 36 Ky. House of Reps., 1985—. Former mem. Garrard County Fiscal Ct. Named Ky. Res. Champion Auctioneer, 1982—83, Garrard County Businessman of Yr., 1983. Mem.: Garrard County Beef Cattle Fair Bd., Nat. Rifle Assn., Dix River Bd. Realtors, Ky. Assn. Realtors, Nat. Auctioneers Assn., Ky. Auctioneers Assn., Garrard County C. of C. (former pres.). Republican. Baptist. Mailing: 302 Danville St Lancaster KY 40444 Office: Capitol Annex Rm 405E Frankfort KY 40601 Home Phone: 859-792-4860; Office Phone: 859-792-2535, 502-564-8100 649. E-mail: lonnie.napier@lrc.ky.gov.

NARDELLI, ROBERT LOUIS, firearms and ammunition manufacturing company executive; b. Old Forge, Pa., May 17, 1948; m. Sue Nardelli, 1971; 4 children. BS in Bus., Western Ill. U., 1971; MBA, U. Louisville, 1975; D in Bus. Adminstrn. (hon.), U. Louisville, 2001; LLD (hon.), Siena Coll., 2001; LHD (hon.), Western Ill. U., 2002. With General Electric Co., 1971-88; exec. v.p., gen. mgr. worldwide parts & components Case Corp., Racine, Wis., 1988-91; pres., CEO Can. Appliance Mfg. Co. subs. GE, Toronto, Ont., Canada, 1991-92, GE Transp. Sys., Erie, Pa., 1992-95, GE Power Sys., 1995-2000, Home Depot, Inc., Atlanta, 2000—07, chmn., 2002—07; CEO, Cerberus Ops. and Adv. Co. LLC Cerberus Capital Management, LP, 2007—12, advisor, Cerberus Ops. and Adv. Co. LLC, 2012; chmn., CEO Chrysler LLC, Auburn Hills, Mich., 2007—09; CEO Remington Arms Co. and Freedom Group, Inc. (parent co.), 2012—. Bd. dirs. The Home Depot, 2000—07, The Coca-Cola Co, 2002—05, Chrysler LLC, 2007—09; bd. dirs., non-exec. chmn. NewPage Corp., 2010—. Pres. Bush's Coun. Savannah Coll., Art and Design, chmn., atlanta bd. visitors; mem. The Bus. Coun.; bd. advisors. U. Louisville Grad. Sch. Bus.; mem. advisory bd. We. Ill. U. Coll. Bus. & Tech. Recipient Disting. Pennsylvanian Award, Gannon U., 1995, Disting. Alumni Award, Western Ill. U. Coll. Bus. & Tech., 1998; named Exec. of Yr., Schenectady County C of C, 2000, Alumnus of Yr., U. Louisville, 2001. Mem.: The Bus. Coun., President's Coun. on Service and Civic Participation, 2003. Office: Remington Arms Co LLC 870 Remington Dr PO Box 700 Madison NC 27025-0700 Office Phone: 212-891-2100. Office Fax: 212-891-1540. Business E-Mail: rnardelli@cerberuscapital.com.

NARSAVAGE, GEORGIA ROBERTS, nursing educator, researcher; b. Pittston, Pa., Jan. 1, 1948; d. George H. Roberts and Betty (Smith) Brown; m. Peter P. Narsavage, Oct. 26, 1968; children: Peter A., Paul J., Marea L. BSN, U. Md., Washington DC, 1969; MSN, Misericordia U., 1984; PhD in Nursing, U. Pa., Phila., 1990. RN, W.Va.; cert. adult nurse practitioner, Ohio, Ga., W.Va., cert. adult nurse practitioner Case Western Res. U. Sch. Nursing, Cleve., 2002, clin. nurse specialist, Comm. Pub. Health. Staff nurse Mercy Hosp., Scranton, Pa., 1970-72; pvt. duty nursing Pa., 1972-79; clinical instr. Lackawanna County Vo-Tech Practical Nursing Program, Dunmore, Pa., 1979-82; clinical and theoretical instr. Mercy Hosp. Sch. of Nursing, Scranton, Pa., 1982-84; asst. prof. nursing dept. U. Scranton, Pa., 1984-93, assoc. prof., 1993—99, chmn. dept., 1991-94, dir. RN program dept. nursing, 1990-92, assoc. dean Panuska Coll. Profl. Studies, 1998—99; assoc. prof. Case Western Res. U., Cleve., 1999—2005, dir. MSN program Sch. Nursing, 1999—2004, assoc. dean Academic Programs, 2003—05; prof. and assoc. dean academic affairs Med. Coll. Ga., 2005—07; dean, prof. W.Va. U., Sch. Nursing, Morgantown, 2007—12; prof., dir. W.Va. U., Inter-Profl. Edn. Health Sci. Ctr., 2013—. Postdoctoral fellow U. Pa., Phila., 1995-97, mem. bd. dirs., W.Va. U Hosp., mem. W.Va. Rural Health Adv. Bd.; cons. in field. Contbr. articles to profl. jours. Gifted program mentor Scranton Sch. Dist.; active in ch. and civic choirs; bd. mem. Pitts. Symphony Orchestry, Morgantown. Grantee U. Scranton, 1989, 91, 94-98, NIH NRSA, 1995-97, Health Resources and Svcs. Adminstrn. Divsn. Nursing, 2004-, NIH NCI, 2010-13, Claude Worthington Benedum Found., Josiah Macy Jr. Found.; recipient Rsch. award European Respiratory Soc., 2002, Ednl. Rsch. award Midwest Nursing Rsch. Soc., 2004, Alumni award Nursing Edn. Coll. Misericordia, 2005, award WVU Acad. Excellence in Tchg. and Learning, 2013. Fellow Am. Acad. Nursing(expert panel global health mem.), Nat. Acad. Practice, Nursing (disting. fellow 2000); mem. ANA, APHA, AAUW (W. Va. chair coll. u. commn., 09-, Morgantown br. pres., 2010-)Am. Thoracic Soc./Am. Lung Assn. (chmn. nursing assembly 2004—06, edn. commn., 08-10, bd. dirs., Abstract award 2002), Pa. Nurses Assn. (bd. dirs., chmn. com., conv. del., Excellence award 1996), Lackawanna Nurses Assn. (bd. dirs., com. chmn., dist. pres.), Nat. League for Nursing, Coun. Nursing Informatics (chair nominating com. 1993-95), Pa. League for Nursing (chair nominating com.), Ohio Nurses Assn. (chmn. practice com.), Midwest Nursing Rsch. Soc. (chmn. membership com., vice chmn. conf. com.), U. Md. Nurses Alumnae Assn., Ea. Nursing Rsch. Soc. (mem.-at-large bd. dirs., interim treas., rsch. grantee 1994), Southern Nursing Rsch. Soc. (co-chair rsch. com., mem. legis. Com.), Am. Assn. Colls. Nursing (elect Nominating com. mem. 2011-), Respiratory Nursing Soc. (bd. mem., Rsch. award, 2011), Theta Phi, Sigma Theta Tau (Rsch. award 1994), Iota Omega (Mentor award 2002). Office: W Va University Health Sciences Ctr 3602 PO Box 9600 Morgantown WV 26506-9600 Office Phone: 304-293-6729. Personal E-mail: narsavageg1@hotmail.com. Business E-Mail: gnarsavage@hsc.wvu.edu.

NASH, DAVID J., engineering and construction company executive, retired military officer; Student in Exec. Prog., Carnegie Mellon U., Pitts.; BSEE, Ind. Inst. Tech., Ft. Wayne, 1965; PhD (hon.), Ind. Inst. Tech.; MS in Fin. Mgmt., Naval Postgraduate Sch., Monterey, Calif., 1977. Advanced through ranks to rear adm. USN, comdr., Naval Constrn. Bn. Ctr. Port Hueneme, Calif., comdr., Pacific Divsn., Naval Facilities Command, comdr., naval facilities engring., chief civil engrs.; with Parsons Brinkerhoff Constrn. Svcs., dir., automotive & indsl. divsn.; prog. dir., tech. ctr. campus GM, Warren, Mich.; project cons. Dave Nash & Assocs., LLC; pres. PB Bldgs., 2002; dir. Iraq Prog. Mgmt. Office, 2003—04, Iraq Reconstruction Mgmt. Office, 2004, Project and Contracting Office, 2004; chmn. BE&K Fed. Group, LLC; v.p., govt. ops. BE&K, 2003—04, pres., govt. group Birmingham, Ala., 2004—. Recipient Henry L. Michel award for Industry Advancement of Rsch., 2001, John I. Parcel-Leif J. Sverdrup award for Civil Engring. Mgmt., ASCE, 2004, Golden Eagle award, Soc. Am. Mil. Engrs., 2005, Golden Beaver award, 2005; named one of Top 25 Newsmakers, Engring. News-Record, 2004. Mem.: Nat. Acad. Constrn., NAE. Office: BE&K Govt Grp 2000 International Park Dr Birmingham AL 35243

NASH, ELISABETH G., funeral services company executive; BBA in Acctg., Tex. A&M U. Various acctg. and fin. positions Pennzoil Corp.; mng. dir., strategic planning and process improvement Svc. Corp. Internat., 2002—04, v.p., process and tech., 2004—10; sr. v.p. ops. services Service Corp. International, 2010—. Office: Service Corporation International 1929 Allen Pkwy Houston TX 77019 Office Phone: 713-522-5141. Office Fax: 713-525-5586.

NASH, HENRY WARREN, marketing educator; b. Tampa, Fla., Sept. 19, 1927; s. Leslie Dikeman and Mildred (Johnson) N.; m. Frances Lora Venters, Aug. 20, 1950; children: Warren Leslie, Richard Dale. BS in Bus. Adminstrn, U. Fla., 1950, MBA, 1951; postgrad., Ind. U., 1951-53; PhD, U. Ala., 1965. Student asst. U. Fla., 1948-50, grad. asst., 1950-51, Ind. U., 1951-53; salesman Field Enterprises, Inc., Chgo., 1953; assoc. prof. bus. and econs. Miss. Coll., 1953-57; assoc. prof. marketing Miss. State U., 1957-66, prof., head dept., 1966-96; emeritus prof. mktg.; emeritus head dept. mktg., quantitative analysis, bus. law; dir. Coll. Bus. and Industry Acad. Advising Ctr., 1995-2000; ptnr. Southland Cons. Assos., 1968-84; bd. dirs. Govt. Employees Credit Union, 1969-92, v.p., 1969-73, pres., 1973-78; ret., 2000. Author: (with others) Principles of Marketing, 1961 Served with USNR, 1945-46, USNR, 1953-63. Loveman's Merchandising fellow U. Ala., 1961-62 Mem. Am. Mktg. Assn., Am. Acad. Advt., Acad. Internat. Bus., So. Econ. Assn., Am. Legion, So. Mktg. Assn. (sec. 1974-75, pres. 1976-77), Sales and Mktg. Execs. (internat. chmn. educators com. 1967-70), Miss. Retail Mchts. Assn. (bd. dirs.), Pi Sigma Epsilon (nat. educator, v.p. 1967-69, nat. pres. 1969-71), Kiwanis (treas. Starkville club 1969-70, v.p. 1973-74, pres. 1974-75, lt. gov. 1977-78, gov. 1982-83), Blue Key, Beta Gamma Sigma, Omicron Delta Kappa, Mu Kappa Tau (nat. v.p. 1977-79, 86-88, pres. 1979-81, 88-90), Alpha Kappa Psi, Phi Kappa Phi (v.p. Miss. State U. 1990-91, pres. 1991-92), Shepherd's Ctr. (Tupelo) (v.p. 2009-10, pres. 2011), Am. Legion. Baptist (tchr., deacon). Home: 2800 W Main St Cottage 302B Tupelo MS 38801-3027

NASH, JAMES E., JR., bank executive; m. Linda Nash. B in Bus, U. Va. Credit analyst NC Nat. Bank; mng. dir. & group head, sports fin. & advisory Banc of America Securities LLC. Chmn. Charlotte Regional Visitors Authority, NC. Named one of Most Influential People in the World of Sports, Bus. Week, 2008. Office: Banc of America Securities LLC Sports Fin & Advisory 101 S Tryon St Charlotte NC 28280

NASH, MELVIN SAMUEL, lawyer; b. Atlanta, Aug. 26, 1949; s. Ralph Samuel and Mary Pauline (Quarles) Nash; m. Cynthia Joanna Hamrick, Aug. 21, 1980 (dec.); m. Kristine Marie Clark, Nov. 22, 1997. AB, Ga. State U., 1974; JD, U. Fla., 1976. Bar: Ga. 1977, US Ct. Claims 1983, US Ct. Internat. Trade 1983, US Tax Ct. 1982, US Ct. Appeals (5th cir.) 1978, US Ct. Appeals (11th cir.) 1981, US Supreme Ct. 1985. Asst. solicitor State Ct., Cobb County, Marietta, Ga., 1977—78; assoc. Milam & Smith, Austell, 1978; ptnr. Milam, Smith & Nash, Austell, 1978—79; sole practice Marietta, 1979—; spl. master Cobb Superior Ct., 1982—; dir. Nash Trucking Co., Inc., Marietta, Security Fidelity Mortgage, Nash Properties. Magistrate Prohac Vice State Ct. Cobb County, Marietta, 1980—82; candidate state rep. Dist. 21, Ga., 1982. With USAF, 1967—71. Mem.: ABA, Atlanta Track (Marathon finisher), State Bar Ga. (fee arbitrator 1982—), Cobb Criminal Def. Bar Assn. (sec., Seminar award 1984), Cobb County Bar Assn. (com. 1983—84), Ga. Assn. Criminal Def. Lawyers, Nat. Assn. Criminal Def. Lawyers, Assn. Trial Lawyers Am., Acad. Fla. Trial Lawyers, Atlanta Lawyers Club, Atlanta Ski Club. Democrat. Presbyn. Office Phone: 770-422-0878. E-mail: melvinsnash@msn.com.

NASH, ROSS W., dentist, educator; Attended, NC State U.; DDS, U. NC, 1978. Faculty mem. sch. dentistry The Med. Coll. Ga.; dir. contemporary dentistry The Inst. for Advanced Studies, Charlotte, NC. Named one of World's Finest Cosmetic Dentists. Fellow: Am. Acad. of Cosmetic Dentistry; mem.: Am. Acad. of Cosmetic Dentistry, The Charlotte Dental Soc., Acad. of Gen. Dentistry, NC Dental Soc., ADA. Office: The Nash Institute for Dental Learning 403 Gilead Rd Ste E Huntersville NC 28078-6814 Office Phone: 888-442-0242.

NASHMAN, ALVIN ELI, computer company executive; b. NYC, Dec. 16, 1926; s. Joseph and Fay (Portnoy) N.; m. Honey Weinstein, May 29, 1960; children: Jessica Rachel, Pamela Wynne, Stephanie Paige. BEE, CUNY, 1948; MEE, NYU, 1951; ScD (hon.), Pacific U., 1968, George Washington U., 1986. With Ketay Mfg. Corp., NYC, 1951-52; dir. missile systems lab, dir. rsch. and devel. programs ITT Fed. Labs., Nutley, N.J., 1952-62; dir. ops., systems engring. and tech. advisor Defense Comms. Agency ITT Intelcom, Inc., Falls Church, Va., 1962-65; pres. Computer Scis. Corp., Falls Church, 1965-67, bd. dir., 1968-95, v.p., 1969-92. Patentee in field; contbr. articles to profl. jours. Trustee Inova Hosp. System Found. With USN, 1944-46. Fellow IEEE; mem. Armed Forces Communications and Electronics Assn. (dir., internat. v.p. 1976-79, chpt. pres. 1979-80, exec. com. 1980-84, chmn. bd. 1984-86), AIAA, Nat. Space Club, Nat. Security Indsl. Assn., Tau Beta Pi, Eta Kappa Nu. Republican. Jewish. Home: 3609 Ridgeway Ter Falls Church VA 22044-1308

NASSETTA, CHRISTOPHER J., hotel executive; b. 1962; m. Paige Nassetta; 6 children. BS in Fin., U. Va., 1984. Various positions, including chief devel. officer Oliver Carr Co., 1984-91; co-founder, pres. Bailey Realty Corp., 1991-95; exec. v.p. Host Hotels & Resorts Inc., 1995—97, COO, 1997—2000, pres., CEO Bethesda, Md., 2000—07, Hilton Worldwide Inc. (formerly Hilton Hotels), Beverly Hills, Calif., 2007—. Bd. dirs. CoStar Group Inc.; trustee Prime Group Realty Trust. Bd. adv., McIntire Sch. Commerce U. Va.; bd. dirs. Wolf Trap Found. for the Performing Arts, The Real Estate Roundtable (RER); mem. Fed. City Coun.; various positions Arlington Free Clinic; vice chmn., corp. fund John F. Kennedy Ctr. for the Performing Arts. Office: Hilton Worldwide Inc 7930 Jones Branch Dr Ste 1100 Mc Lean VA 22102 Office Phone: 703-883-1000. Business E-Mail: christopher.nassetta@hilton.com.

NATALE, PATRICK J., professional society administrator; m. Sheila Natale; 2 children. BS in Civil Engring., Newark Coll.of Engring.; MS in Engring. Mgmt., NJ Inst. of Tech.; grad., exec. mgmt. program, Yale U. Lic. profl. engr., NJ; cert. Assn. Exec. (CAE). Gen. mgr. PSE&G, NJ; v.p., northeast region Nat. Soc. Profl. Engr., exec. dir., 1999—2002; exec. dir., chief staff officer, sec. American Society Civil Engineers, Reston, Va., 2002—. Pres. Am. Soc. Civil Engr. Found., 2003—. Chmn. Goodwill Ind. of NJ; bd. dir. C. of C., Am. Red Cross; asst. dist. commr. Boy Scouts of Am. Office: American Society of Civil Engineers 1801 Alexander Bell Dr Reston VA 20191-4400

NATALICIO, DIANA SIEDHOFF, academic administrator; b. St. Louis, Aug. 25, 1939; d. William and Eleanor J. (Biermann) Siedhoff. BS in Spanish summa cum laude, St. Louis U., 1961; MA in Portuguese lang., U. Tex., 1964, PhD in Linguistics, 1969; PhD (hon.), Smith Coll., Universidad Autonoma de Nuevo Leon. Chmn. dept. modern langs. University of Texas, El Paso, 1973-77, assoc. dean liberal arts, 1977-79, acting dean liberal arts, 1979-80, dean Coll. Liberal Arts, 1980-84, v.p. acad. affairs, 1984-88, pres., 1988—. Bd. dirs. El Paso br. Fed. Res. Bd. Dallas, chmn., 1989; mem. Presdl. Adv. Commn. on Ednl. Excellence for Hispanic Ams., 1991; bd. dirs. Sandia Corp., Trinity Industries; bd. dirs. Nat. Action Coun. for Minorities in Engring., 1993—; mem. Nat. Sci. Bd. 1994-2006; mem. NASA Adv. Coun., 1994-96; bd. mem. Fund for Improvement of Post-Secondary Edn., 1993-97; bd. dirs. Fogarty Internat. Ctr. of NIH, 1993-96; bd. chair Am. Assn. Higher Edn., 1995-96; bd. dirs. U.S.-Mexico Commn. for Ednl. and Cultural Exch., 1994—. Co-author: Sounds of Children, 1977; contbr. articles to profl. jours. Bd. dirs. United Way El Paso, 1990-93, chmn. needs survey com., 1990-91, chmn. edn. divsn., 1989; chmn. Quality Edn. for Minorities Network in Math. Sci. and Engring., 1991-92; chairperson Leadership El Paso, Class 12, 1989-90, mem. adv. coun., 1987-90, participant, 1980-81; mem. Historically Black Colls. and Univs./Minority Instns. Consortium on Environ. Tech. chairperson, 1991-93; trustee Rockefeller Found. Recipient Harold W. McGraw. Jr. prize in edn., 1997, Torch of Liberty award Anti-Defamation League B'nai B'rith, 1991, Conquistador award City of El Paso, 1990, Humanitarian award El Paso chpt. NCCJ, 1990, Disting. Alumnus Award, U. Tex. Austin, 2006; named to El Paso Women's Hall of Fame, 1990, Tex. Women's Hall of Fame, 1998. Mem. Philos. Soc. Tex. Avocations: hiking, bicycling, skiing, skating. Office: U Tex at El Paso Office of the Pres 500 W University Ave El Paso TX 79968-0001

NATHAN, JOE (JOSEPH MICHAEL NATHAN), professional baseball player; b. Houston, Nov. 22, 1974; m. Lisa Lemoncelli; 1 child, Cole. Grad. in bus. mgmt., SUNY, Stony Brook, 1997. Pitcher San Francisco Giants, 1999—2003, Minn. Twins, 2003—11, Tex. Rangers, 2011—. Mem. US nat. team World Baseball Classic, 2006. Recipient Univ. medal, SUNY Stony Brook, American League Rolaids Relief Man award, 2009; named to American League All-Star Team, Maj. League Baseball, 2004, 2005, 2008, 2009, 2012, 2013. Mem.: Golden Key Internat. Honor Soc. Office: Tex Rangers 1000 Ballpark Way Arlington TX 76011*

NATHANSON, IAN THOMAS, pediatric pulmonologist; b. NYC, Nov. 22, 1948; BA, SUNY Buffalo, MD, 1974. Cert. Am. Bd. Pediat., 1979, in pediatric pulmonology Am. Bd. Pediat., 2003, in sleep medicine Am. Bd. Pediat., 2007. Internship in pediat. Buffalo Gen. Hosp., 1974; residency in pediatric pulmonology Children's Hosp., Buffalo, 1976—77, fellowship in pediatric pulmonology, 1977—79; rsch. fellowship U. Calif. Med. Sch., San Farancisco; pediat. staff Arnold Palmer Hosp. Women & Children, Jacksonville, Fla.; assoc. prof. Mayo Med. Sch., Fla.; med. dir. Nemours Children's Clinic, Orlando, Fla. Contbr. articles to profl. jours. Office: Nemours Childrens Clinic 496 Delaney Ave Ste 408 Orlando FL 32801-3851 Office Phone: 407-650-7000. Office Fax: 407-650-7124.

NATIONS, HOWARD LYNN, lawyer; b. Dalton, Ga., Jan. 9, 1938; s. Howard Lynn and Eva Earline (Armstrong) Lamb; m. Ella Lois Johnson, June 4, 1960 (div. Nov. 1976); children: Cynthia Lynn Nations Garcia, Angela Jean Gordon Hernandez. BA, Fla. State U., 1963, JD, 1966. Bar: Tex. 1966; cert. trial atty. Tex. Bd. Legal Specialization. Assoc. Butler, Rice Cook & Knapp, Houston, 1966-71; pres. Nations & Cross, Houston, 1971—; v.p., dir., co-founder Ins. Corp. Am., Houston, 1972—; pres. Caplinger & Nations Galleries, Houston, 1973—, Nations Investment Corp., Houston, 1975—, NCM Trade Corp., Houston, 1975; v.p. Delher Am. Inc., Houston, 1975—; pres. Howard L. Nations, PC, Houston, 1971—, Trial Focus, Inc., 1995—. Founder Nations Found.; adj. prof. So. Tex. Coll. Law, Houston, 1967—; speaker in field. Author: Structuring Settlements, 1987; co-author: Texas Workers' Compensation, 1988, (with others) The Anatomy of a Personal Injury Lawsuit, 3rd rev. edit. 1991; editor: Maximizing Damages in Wrongful Death and Personal Injury Litigation, 1985; contbr. articles to profl. jours. Chmn., trustee Nat. Coll. Advocacy, Washington, 1985-92. With M.I. Corps, U.S. Army, 1957-60. Recipient Gene Cavin Excellence award State Bar Tex., 2000, STLA War House award, 2009, Clarence Darrow award, 2010; named to Trial Lawyer Hall of Fame, 2012, fellow, Litig. Counsel America, 2012. Fellow Tex. Bar Found., Houston Bar Found. (life); mem. AAJ (exec. com. mem. 1991-95, 2010), Nat. Bd. Trial Advocacy (diplomate civil trial advocacy), Southern Trial Lawyers Assn. (pres. 1994-95, Warhorse award 2009), Tex. Trial Lawyers Assn. (pres. 1992-93), Melven Belli Soc. (pres. 2007-08, The Mel award 2010), Alethia Inst.(pres. 2010), Nat. Trial Lawyers Assn. (pres. 2011). Office: The Nations Law Firm 3131 Briarpark Dr # 208 Houston TX 77042-3793 Office Phone: 713-807-8400, 800-269-3050. Office Fax: 713-807-8423. Business E-Mail: andrea@howardnations.com.

NAUGLE, JAMES (JIM) THOMAS, former mayor, Ft. Lauderdale, Florida; b. Fort Lauderdale, Fla., Feb. 24, 1954; m. Carol-Lisa Phillips; 1 child, Rachel Elizabeth. BA in Bus. Adminstrn., Fla. Atlantic U., 1975. Realtor Jim Naugle & Co., Fort Lauderdale, 1974—; commr. City of Ft. Lauderdale, 1985-91, mayor, 1991—2008. Bd. dirs. Nat. League Cities, Washington, chair environ. energy and nat. resources, 1998—99, mem. nominating com.; former pres. Fla. League of Cities, Tallahassee. Avocations: sailing, yard work, restoring antique cars, restoring old homes. Office Phone: 954-761-5003.

NAVAR, LUIS GABRIEL, physiology educator, director, researcher; b. El Paso, Tex., Mar. 24, 1941; s. Luis and Concepcion (Najera) N.; m. Randa Ann Bumgarner, Oct. 15, 1965; children: Tonia, Tess, Gabriel, Daniel. BS, Tex. A&M U., 1962; PhD, U. Miss., 1966, postdoctoral study, 1966-69. Instr. dept. physiology/biophysics U. Miss., Jackson, 1966-67, asst. prof., 1967-71, assoc. prof., 1971-74, U. Ala., Birmingham, 1974-76, prof., 1976-88, assoc. prof. Nephrology Rsch. and Tng. Ctr., 1979-83, prof., 1983-88; prof., chmn. dept. physiology Tulane U. Med. Sch., New Orleans, 1988—, co-dir. Hypertension and Renal Ctr. of Excellence, 2001—. Vis. scientist Duke U. Med. Ctr., Durham, N.C., 1972-73; adv. bd. NIH Ctr. Sci. Rev., 1998-99; bd. dirs. Fedn. Am. Socs. Exptl. Biology, 1997-01. Assoc. editor News in Physiol. Scis., 1994-2000, Am. Jour. Physiology, 1983-89, mem. editl. bd., 1982-83, 97—; mem. editl. bd. Kidney Internat., 1976-87, Kidney, 1992—, Clin. Sci., 1994-99, Jour. Am. Soc. Nephrology, 1996-2001, Jour. Am. Soc. Nephrology, 1996-2001, Am. Jour. Kidney Disease, 1997-2001, Am. Jour. Hypertension, 1999—, Hypertension, 1980-83, 2002-04, assoc. editor, 1993-2000, cons. editor, 2006—; contbr. chpts. to books, articles to profl. jours. Cardiovascular and renal study sects. NIH, 1998—2000, chmn., 2000—02; bd. dirs. Consortium for Southeastern Hypertension Control, 1998—2000. Recipient Rsch. Career Devel. award, Nat. Heart, Lung and Blood Inst., 1974—79, Merit award, 1988—97, Bodil M. Schmidt Nielson Disting. Mentor and Scientist award, 2006, Lifetime Achievement award, COSEHC, 2006, Robert W. Berliner award for excellence in renal physiology, 2007, Daggs award, 2008, Disting. award, 2009, Michael A. Kirschenbaum Meml. Lectr. award, 2009, 6th Ann. Sourirajan Lectr., U. Ottawa, Kidney Rsch. Ctr., 2009, 15th Ann. Carl W. Gottschalk Lectr., U. NC, 2011, Walter B. Cannon award, Am. Physiol. Soc., 2012, Excellence award Hypertension Rsch., CHBPR, 2012, Thomas E. Andreoli Lectr., U. Ala. Birmingham, 2012, Inaugural Oliver Fund award, Tulane U., 2013; named First Urlich Hopfer Lectr., Case Western Res. U., 2013; vis. scholar Pfizer/ACF, 2002. Fellow: AAAS; mem.: Nat. Kidney Found., Microcirculation Soc., Internat. Soc. Pathophysiol. (internat. adv. bd. 2001—02), Internat. Soc. Hypertension (prog. adv. com. 2001—02, internat. adv. bd. 2012), Coun. High Blood Pressure Rsch. Am. Heart Assn., Assn. of Am. Med. Coll. (administrv. bd. of coun. of academic soc. 2004—), Assn. Chmn. Depts. Physiology (councillor 1993—95, pres.-elect 1995—96, pres. 1996—97, Disting. Svc. award 2003), Inter Am. Soc. Hypertension (chair pub. com. 1998, chair awards com. 2003—, organizing com. 2004—05, pres. exec. com. 2010—11), Am. Soc. Hypertension (coun. 1992—94, exec. coun. 1992—95, chmn. basic. sci. com. 1997, treas. 1997—2001, prog. com. 1994—96, 2004—05, chair pub. com. 2003—12, Richard Bright award 2001), Internat. Soc. Nephrology, Am. Soc. Nephrology, Am. Heart Assn. (chmn. cardiorenal rsch. study com. 1994—95, nat. rsch. com. 1994—99, Lewis K. Dahl Lectr. 1997, profl. and pub. edn. com. 1999—, chmn. coun. high blood pressure rsch. 2006—, kidney, high blood pressure couns., vice chmn. leadership com. coun. high blood pressure rsch., Sci. Coun. Disting. Achievement award 1999, Corcoran Lectr. award 2001), Am. Physiol. Soc. (coun. 1991—94, Gottschalk Disting. Lectr. Renal Physiology 1997, pres.-elect 1997—98, pres. 1998—99, Bodil M. Schmidt-Nielson Disting. Mentor and Sci. award 2006, Robert W. Berliner award 2007, Ray G. Daggs award 2008, Walter B. Cannon award 2012), Sigma Xi. Democrat. Roman Catholic. Home: 10020 Hyde Pl New Orleans LA 70123-1522 Office: Tulane U Med Sch Dept Physiology 1430 Tulane Ave New Orleans LA 70112-2699 Home Phone: 504-738-5547; Office Phone: 504-988-5251. Business E-Mail: navar@tulane.edu.

NAVIAUX, LAREE DEVEE, retired psychologist, academic, director; b. Lewellen, Nebr., Aug. 18, 1937; d. Prosper Leo and Dorothy DeVee (Walters) Naviaux; m. Frank Anthony D'Abreo, June 16, 1973. BS, U. Nebr., 1959; MS, Iowa State U., 1963; PhD, Duquesne U., 1973. Instr. Iowa State U., Ames, 1963—65; asst. prof. Kans. State U., Manhattan, 1965—66; grad. faculty part-time assoc. Margaret Morrison Coll. Carnegie-Mellon U., Pitts., 1966—69; asst. prof. West Ga. Coll., Carrollton, 1969—72; regional dir. Children's Mental Health, Charleston, W.Va., 1973—80; asst. clin. prof. W.Va. U., 1977—87; therapist, educator Cmty. Mental Health Ctr., Charleston, 1980—82; pvt. practice, 1982—2004; ret., 2004; assoc. spiritual dir. W.Va. Inst. Spirituality, pres., 2001—04, supr. final projects, 2004—. Creator (CD) In This Moment Meditation, 2008, Tribute to World YWCA, 2011; contbr. articles to profl. jours. and books. Bd. dirs. Parents Anonymous W.Va., 1979—82, Creative Arts Clinic, 1981—83, Charleston Chamber Music, 2004—12, W.Va. Pub. Broadcasting Friends, 2004—, Collectors Club Clay Ct., 2009—, YWCA, 1991—97, v.p., 1995—97. Recipient Outstanding Vol. Leadership award, 1994; grantee, Humanities Found. W.Va., 1978—79, 1981—82, 1982, 2005. Mem.: W.Va. Free, Friends Libr. Found. Ka C., Friends W.Va. Culture and History, W.Va. Humanities Coun., Collectors Club Clay Ctr., Mental Health Assn. (life), Am. Psychol. Assn. (life), Iowa State U. Alumni (life), U. Nebr. Alumni (life), Indian Assn., Gourmet Club. Democrat.

NAYFEH, ALI HASAN, engineering educator; arrived in U.S., 1958; s. Hasan Ahmad and Khadrah (Said) N.; m. Inam A. Zibdeh, Aug. 4, 1965; children: Mahir, Tariq, Samir, Nader. BS in Engring. Sci. with Great Distinction, Stanford U., Palo Alto, Calif., 1962, MS in Aeronautics and Astronautics, 1963, PhD in Aeronautics and Astronautics, 1964; Doctorate (hon.), Marine Tech. U., St. Petersburg, Russia, 1996, Tech. U. Munich, Germany, 1999, Poly. Szczecinska, Poland, 2004. Prin. research scientist KMS Industries, Van Nuys, Calif., 1964-68, Accurex, Mountain View, Calif., 1968-71; prof. Va. Poly. Inst. and State U., Blacksburg, 1971-76, disting. prof., 1976—2012, U. Jordan, 2012—. Dean Sch. Engring.; Disting. prof., v.p. Yarmouk U., Irbid, Jordan, 1980-84. Author: Perturbation Methods, 1973, Russian edit., 1976, (with others) Nonlinear Oscillations, 1979, Introduction to Perturbation Techniques, 1981, Russian edit., 1984, Problems in Perturbation, 1984, Method of Normal Forms, 1993, Applied Nonlinear Dynamics, 1995, Perturbation Methods with Mathematica, 1999, Pertubation Methods with Maple, 1999, Nonlinear Interactions, 2000, Linear and Nonlinear Structural Mechanics, 2004; also more than 485 archival articles. Editor-in-chief Nonlinear Dynamics, Jour. Vibration and Control. Recipient The Kuwait Science prize, 1981, Pendray Aerospace Literature award Am. Inst. of Aeronautics and Astronautics, 1995, ASME J.P. Den Hartog award, 1997, Va. Life Achievment Sci. award, 2005, ASME Lyaponuv award, 2005, Gold medal Honor Acad. Trans-Disciplinary Learning & Advanced Studies, 2007, ASME Thomas Caughey award, 2008, Benjamin Franklin medal, 2014. Fellow Soc. Design and Process Sci., Am. Phys. Soc., Am. Acad. Mechanics, AIAA. Muslim. Home: 13591 Bathgate Dr Herndon VA 20171 Office: University Jordan Al Jamia Al Urduniyya Amman 24061 Jordan Office Phone: 540-231-5453. Personal E-mail: anayfeh@yahoo.com.

NAZAREWICZ, WITOLD, nuclear scientist, educator; b. Warsaw, Dec. 26, 1954; s. Ryszard and Hanna Nazarewicz; m. Krystyna Kustosik, Apr. 11, 1977; children: Pawel, Natalia. MS in Engring., Warsaw U. Tech., 1977, PhD, 1981. Cert. habilitation Warsaw U., 1986, tchr. Poland, 1994. Prof. Warsaw U. Tech., 1977—90, assoc. dean faculty tech. physics & applied math., 1987—90, prof. physics, 1991—, U. Tenn., Knoxville, 1995—; Holifield radioactive ion beam facility sci. dir. Oak Ridge Nat. Lab., Tenn., 1995—. Mem. program adv. com. EUROGAM, Strasbourg, France, 1990—94; mem. nuc. physics bd. European Phys. Soc., 1992—95; mem. spl. emphasis panel on evaluation of sflow-energy nuc. physics accelerator labs. NSF, 1993; mem. hribf program adv. com. physics divsn., ORNL, Oak Ridge, Tenn., 1994—96; mem. vivitron pac CNRS, Strasbourg, 1994—96; mem. nat. adv. com. Inst. Nuc. Theory, Seattle, 1995—98; mem. nscl pac Nscl, Msu, E.Lansing, Mich., 1995—98; mem. com. nuc. physics Bd. Physics and Astronomy, US NRC, DC, 1996—99; mem. atlas pac Argonne Nat. Lab., Ill., 1996—99; mem. 1988 cyclotron pac Lawrence Berkeley Nat. Lab., Calif., 1996—2000; mem. rev. com. for physics divsn. of anl U. Chgo., 1996—2004; mem. steering com. for nat. nuc. physics summer sch. divsn. nuc. physics, APS, 1998, aps divsn. of nuc. physics nominating com., 1999—2000, vice-chair, 2000, mem. dissertation award com., 2000—01, mem. dnp program com., 2007—, mem. dnp fellowship com., 2008—; mem. jihir directorate Joint Inst. Heavy Ion Rsch., Oak Ridge, Tenn., 1999—; mem. nuc. sci. adv. com. DOE/NSF, DC, 2000—03; chair RIA Working Grp. Steering Com., 2000—04; mem. program adv. com. NSCL, Mich. State U., E.Lansing, 2001—02; mem. acot com. NRC, Canada, 2001—05; dir., co-dir. RIA Summer Sch., 2002—05; chmn. Warsaw U., 2002—; chair, mem. exec. com. RIA Users Orgn., 2004—; mem. rare isotope sci. assessment com. US NRC, DC, 2005—07; mem. internat. adv. panel EURISOL Design Study Grp., France, 2005—; mem. of the steering com. of justipen Japan U.S. Theory Inst. for Physics with Exotic Nuclei, Tokyo, 2006—; mem. program adv. com. Jefferson Lab., Newport News, Va., 2006—; sci. expert, sci. adv. bd. for Finnish Ctr. Excellence in Nuc. and Accelerator Based Physics Acad. Finland, Jyvaskyla, Finland, 2006—. Co-editor, editl. bd. mem. European Phys. Jour., 2006—; contbr. articles to profl. jours. Recipient Individual Sci. award, Polish Phys. Soc., 1986, Rsch. and Creative achievement award, U. Tenn., 2004; named one of Most Highly-cited Physicists, ISI; grantee Rsch. and travel grants, NSF, 1992—, Rsch. grants, Dept. Energy, 1993—; fellowship, Inst. Physics, 2004. Fellow: Inst. Physics (mem. editl. bd. 2001—06), Am. Phys. Soc. (mem. editl. bd. 1994—96, nuc. physics assoc. editor 2006—); mem.: European Phys. Soc., Wash. Map Soc., Internat. Map Collector's Soc. Achievements include research in nuclear structure. Avocations: collecting ancient maps, history. Office: Univ Ten 401 Nielsen Physics Bldg Knoxville TN 37996 Business E-Mail: witek@utk.edu.

NEAL, GERALD A., state legislator; b. Sept. 22, 1945; State senatoe Dist. 33, Ky., 1989—; mem. Appropriations & Revenue Com.; mem. edn. com.; mem. judiciary com.; mem. seniors; mem. Mil. Affairs & Pub. Safety Com.; state senator Ky.; atty. Ky. Recipient Crime Prevention award, West Louisville, Sterling award, Minority Bus., Region VI award, Nat. Bar Assn., Disting. Svc. award, City Louisville & Jefferson County. Mem.: Urban League, Ky. & Nat. Bar Asns. Democrat. Catholic. Office: Capitol Annex Rm 251 Frankfort KY 40601 Home: 462 S 4th St Ste 1270 Louisville KY 40202-3500 Home Phone: 502-778-1178; Office Phone: 502-584-8500, 502-564-8100 ext. 718. Fax: 502-584-1119.

NEAL, JAMES M., state legislator, retired principal; b. Kershaw, SC, Apr. 30, 1943; s. James N. Neal and Annie Neal Smith; m. Harriett Hawkins Neal, July 17, 1966; children: Bryant, Scott. BS, Clemson U., 1965; MEd, Winthrop U., 1978. Ret. principal; mem. Dist. 44 SC House of Reps, 1999—, mem. Edn. and Pub. Works Com. Mem. Lancaster County Lit. Coun., Lancaster County Election Commn., 1990—98. Democrat. Baptist. Office: State Capitol 422C Blatt Bldg Columbia SC 29211 Home: 5148 Sandy Ln Kershaw SC 29067 E-mail: jmn@scstatehouse.net.

NEAL, JAY, state legislator; b. July 02; married; 2 children. Pastor Gordon Lake Wesleyan Ch., LaFayette, Ga., 1989—2009; mem. Dist. 1 Ga. House of Reps., 2005—. Republican. Office: District Office PO Box 645 La Fayette GA 30728 also: Ga House of Reps 401 Coverdell Legis Office Bldg Atlanta GA 30334 Office Phone: 706-375-9200, 404-656-0152. Business E-Mail: jay.neal@house.ga.gov.

NEAL, JOSEPH H., state legislator, minister, computer company executive; b. Aug. 31, 1950; s. Choatte R. Neal Sr. and LaVerne K. Neal; m. Beverly Johnson; children: Edward, Noelle. BA, Benedict Coll., 1972; postgrad., Colgate Divinity, Pittsburg Theol. Sem.; DD (hon.), Benedict Coll. Minister; v.p. New Horizons Sys., Inc.; mem. Dist. 70 SC House of Reps., 1993—, mem. Edn. and Pub. Works Com., mem. Rules Com. Chmn. Citizens for Hopkins Commn. Orgn.; bd. dirs. S.C. Fair Share, Citizens Local Environ. Action Network; mem. S.C. Environ. Watch; bd. dirs. Area Communities Econ. Develop.; mem. Sumter Area Econ. Develop.; bd. dirs. Funds So. Coms.; chmn. S.C. Legis. Black Caucus, 2000—02; dep. Dem. Leader. Mem.: NAACP, Am. Soc. Software Engrs., Moving Forward Commn. Assn., Kappa Alpha Psi. Democrat. Baptist. Office: State Capitol 309B Blatt Bldg Columbia SC 29211 Home: PO Box 5 Hopkins SC 29061 Address: 1326 Clarkson Rd Hopkins SC 29061 Office Phone: 803-734-2804. E-mail: JN@schouse.org.

NEAL, YASMIN, state legislator; b. Jonesboro, Ga. Attended, Valdosta State U., Clayton Coll. and State U. Writer Clayton Daily News, Henry Daily Herald Newspaper; hiring investigator, fugitive unit investigator Clayton County Sheriff's Dept.; detective major felony unit Clayton County Police Dept.; mem. Dist. 75 Ga. House of Representatives, 2008—. Office: Georgia House of Reps 604 Coverdell Legis Office Bldg Atlanta GA 30334 Home: 6033 Morrow Cv Morrow GA 30260-1015 Office Phone: 678-656-6589, 404-656-0265. Business E-Mail: yasmin.neal@house.ga.gov.

NEAL BLIXT, DIANNE M., former tobacco company executive; b. Dec. 3, 1959; BS in Acctg., U. NC, Greensboro, 1981, MBA, 1988. CPA NC. Acctg. positions Forsyth Mem. Hosp., Winston Salem, NC; fin. mgmt. positions R.J. Reynolds Tobacco, Winston Salem, NC, 1988—94, dir. fin. planning & acctg., 1994—97, v.p., contr., 1997—99, v.p. investor rels., 1999—2003; exec. v.p., CFO R.J. Reynolds Tobacco Holdings & R.J. Reynolds Tobacco, Winston Salem, NC, 2003—04, Reynolds American Inc., Winston Salem, NC, 2004—08. Bd. dirs. LandAmerica Fin. Group, Inc., 2006—09, Metaventa Holding Co., 2007—09, Lorillard, Inc., 2011—. Bd. dirs. Reynolda House Mus. American Art.

NEAVEL, CELIA BETH, medical association administrator; b. Blommington, Ind., Aug. 30, 1959; d. Richard Charles and Nancy Trager Neavel; m. Jose Carlos Cortez; children: Elizabeth, Elena, Geordi. BA with honors in liberal arts, U. Tex., 1981; MD, Baylor Coll. of Medicine, 1985. Diplomate Am. Bd. of Family Medicine, cert. Added Qualification, Adolescent Medicine. Asst. prof. Dept. of Family Medicine, Cin., 1989—91; contract physician Austin Regional Clin., Austin, Tex., 1991—92; clin. asst., prof. of Pediat. Scott and White, Temple, Tex., 1991—95; physician adv. Easter Seals Ctrl. Tex., Austin, Tex., 1995—; faculty Austin Med. Edn. Program, Austin, Tex., 1995—2006; dir., adolescent medicine Ctr. for Adolescent Health at People's Cmty Clin., Austin, Tex., 1994—. Med. dir. Lifeworks St. Outreach Clin., Austin, Tex., 1996—, RGK Downtown Ctr. for Health Clin., Austin, Tex., 1996—, Phoenix Acad. Off-Site Clin., Austin, Tex., 2003—; dir. Devel. Behavioral Primary Care Program, People's Cmty. Clin., Austin, Tex., 2004—; clin. asst. prof. pediat. UTMB, Austin, 2006—. Co-author: (monograph) Integrating Child and Adolescent Mental Health Into Primary Care, 2002. Vol. lectr. Camp Disabled Children, Center Point, Tex., 1990—2005, physician, 1990—2005. Recipient Amb. award, St. Lukes Episcopal Health Charities, 2007; named Tex. Super Doctor, Tex. Monthly Mag., 2004; fellow, Soc. Adolescent Medicine, 2007; grant, Healthy Tomorrows from HRSA, 2005. Mem.: AMA, Physicians for Social Responsibility, Soc. of Adolescent Medicine, Tex. Med. Assn., Travis County Managed Care Regional Adv. Com. Office: Ctr for Adolescent Health Peoples Cmty Clin 2909 NIH 35 Austin TX 78722 Office Phone: 512-478-4939. Office Fax: 512-320-0702. E-mail: ibappmd@aol.com.

NEDOM, H. ARTHUR, petroleum consultant; b. Lincoln, Nebr., Aug. 19, 1925; s. Henry Arthur and Pearle Bertrick (Swan) N.; m. Patricia Margaret Rankin, July 4, 1974; children: Richard A., Robert L., Nicole C. BS, U. Tulsa, 1949, MS, 1950; postgrad. in bus. adminstrn., Northwestern U., Evanston, Ill., 1968. Chief engr. Amerada Petroleum Corp., Tulsa, 1961-65, v.p., 1965—, Natomas Co., San Francisco, 1971-74; v.p, dir. pres. Norwegian Oil Co., Houston, 1974-75; pres., mng. dir. Weeks Petroleum Ltd., Westport, Conn., 1975-82; chmn. bd. arbitration Prudhoe Bay Unit. Chmn. Offshore Tech. Conf., 1971; bd. dirs. Engrs. Joint Council, 1978 Served with inf. U.S. Army, 1943-45, ETO. Decorated Bronze Star; named Disting. Alumnus U. Tulsa, 1972 Mem. Soc. Petroleum Engrs. (dir. 1965-68, pres. 1967, Disting. Lectr. 1973, Disting Svc. award 1978, DeGolyer Disting. Svc. medal 1981, Disting. mem. 1983, Disting. lectr. emeritus 1989, Legion of Honor 1998, v.p. SPE Found. 1988-89), AIME (dir. 1966-69, 76-79, pres. 1977, hon. mem. 1982, Disting. Svc. award 1993), Am. Assn. Engring. Soc. (dir. 1980-82, chmn. 1981, Spl. award 1979, Engring. Svc. award 1980). Home: 9924 S Sandusky Ave Tulsa OK 74137-5311 Personal E-mail: artnedom@aol.com.

NEDZBALA, MICHAEL, lawyer; b. Washington, Feb. 2, 1962; BA in Econs. and Govt., U. Va., 1984; JD, U. NC, 1987. Mng. ptnr. Charlotte office Hunton & Williams LLP, Charlotte, NC, 1995—, co-head asset securitization group, mem. global capital mkts. team. Mem.: Va. State Bar Assn., NC State Bar Assn., Mecklenburg Co. Bar Assn., UNC Banking Inst. (bd. adv.). Office: Hunton & Williams LLP Bank of America Plz Ste 3500 101 S Tryon St Charlotte NC 28280 Office Phone: 704-378-4703. Office Fax: 704-378-4890. Business E-Mail: mnedzbala@hunton.com.

NEDZBALA, PAUL, health products executive; COO, health sciences Constella Group Inc. (acquired SRA Internat. Inc.); v.p., health programs SRA International, Inc., 1993—. Office: SRA International Inc 4300 Fair Lakes Ct Fairfax VA 22033 Office Phone: 703-803-1500. Office Fax: 703-803-1509. Business E-Mail: paul_nedzbala@sra.com.

NEEDHAM, WENDY BEALE, retired investment company executive, board member; b. 1953; married. BS in Journalism, Temple U.; MBA in Fin., Columbia U. Rsch. analyst Smith Barney, 1981—94, mng. dir. automotive rsch., 1989—94; prin. automotive rsch. Donaldson, Lufkin and Jenrette, 1994—2000; mng. dir. global automotive rsch. Credit Suisse First Boston, 2000—03; ret., 2003. Former bd. dirs. Asahi Tec; bd. dirs. Genuine Parts Co., 2003—, Metaldyne Corp., 2004—. Office: Genuine Parts Co c/o Bd Directors 2999 Cir 75 Pky Atlanta GA 30339 Office Phone: 770-953-1700. Office Fax: 770-956-2211.

NEEDLEMAN, ALAN, mechanical engineering educator; b. Phila., Sept. 2, 1944; s. Herman and Hannah (Goodman) N.; m. Wanda Sapolsky, Apr. 12, 1970; children: Deborah, Daniel BS, U. Pa., 1966; MS, Harvard U., 1967, PhD, 1970; PhD (hon.), Ecole Normal Superoir de Cachan, 2006; PhD Honoris Causa (hon.), Tech. U. Denmark, 2006. Instr. applied math. MIT, Cambridge, 1970-72, asst. prof., 1972-75; asst. prof. engring. Brown U., Providence, 1975-78, assoc. prof., 1978-81, prof., 1981—2009, dean engring., 1988-91, Florence Pirce Grant Univ. prof., 1996—2009, Florence Pirce Grant Univ. prof. emeritus, 2009—; prof. U. North Tex., 2009—. Vis. asst. prof. Tech. U. Denmark, Lyngby, 1973; vis. fellow Clare Hall, U. Cambridge, Eng., 1978; vis. prof. MIT, Cambridge, 1991. Contbr. articles to profl. jours. Guggenheim fellow, 1977; recipient award Nat. Acad. Engring., 2000, Am. Acad. Arts & Scis., 2007, Prager medal Soc. Engring. Scis., 2006. Fellow: ASME (Timoshenko medal, 2011), Am. Acad. Mechanics, Danish Ctr. for Applied Math. and Mechanics (fgn.), Groupe Francais de Macanique des Matériaux (hon.), Am. Acad. Arts & Scis.; mem.: NAE. Office: Univ North Tex 1155 Union Circle # 305310 Denton TX 76203-5017 Business E-Mail: needle@unt.edu.

NEEL, RICHARD EUGENE, economist, educator; b. Bluefield, Va., Jan. 7, 1932; s. Charles Richard and Zell LaVerne (Bowling) Neel; m. Binnie Jo LeFever, June 10, 1961; children: Jeffrey Richard, Cynthia Jo. BS, U. Tenn., 1954, MS, 1955; PhD, Ohio State U., 1960. Instr. econs. Ohio State U., 1958-60; asst. prof. econs. Coll. William and Mary, 1960-61; asst. prof. U. South Fla., 1961-63, assoc. prof., 1963-66, chmn. econs. and fin. programs, 1964-66, acting chmn. grad. program Coll. Bus Adminstrn., 1965-66; dir. instl. planning Fla. Tech. U., 1966-68, chmn. dept. econs., prof. econs., 1968-69; assoc. dean Sch. Bus. Adminstrn. Ga. State U., 1969-77, dean grad. studies Sch. Bus. Adminstrn., 1973-77, prof. econs. Sch. Bus. Adminstrn., 1969-78; dean Coll. Bus. Adminstrn. U. NC, Charlotte, 1978-93, prof. econs., 1978-97, dean emeritus Belk Coll. Bus., 1997—, prof. econs. emeritus, 1997—. Editor: (book) Readings in Price Theory, 1973; contbr. chapters to books, articles and monographs to profl. publs. Mem.: Beta Gamma Sigma, Phi Kappa Phi. Presbyterian. Office: U NC at Charlotte Dept Economics Charlotte NC 28223 Business E-Mail: reneel@uncc.edu.

NEELEY, DELMAR GEORGE, mediator, pastoral counselor; b. Charleston, Ill., June 4, 1937; s. Glenn Truman and Gladys Bernice (Dittman) N.; m. Terry Anne Barbour, Aug. 28, 1971; children: Robert James, Stephen Edward. BA in Philosophy, Olivet Nazarene U., 1965, MA in Bibl. Lit., 1969; EdD, U. Sarasota, 1996. Cert.: Fla. Bar Assn. (mediator); cert. clin. pastor, counselor corp. chaplain. Mgr. mgmt. devel. Rauland Divsn. Zenith Corp., Chgo., 1967-70; sr. personnel cons. Mid. West Svc. Co., Chgo., 1971-73; dir. human resources Nichols-Homeshield Inc., West Chicago, Ill., 1974-76, Gould Inc./Ind. Battery Divsn., Langhorne, Pa., 1976-81; pres., owner Barbour-Neeley Inc., Sarasota, Fla., 1982-91. Stephen Ministries leader. Min. of visitation, United Ch. of Christ. Recipient Meritorious Svc. award Chgo. Boys Club, 1970, Svc. award Chgo. Jaycees, 1967-71. Mem.: Fla. Assn. Christian Counselors (cert.), Fla. Acad. Profl. Mediators, Fla. Assn. Profl. Chaplains (cert. corp. chaplain). Congregationalist. Home: 4213 Copenhagen St Sarasota FL 34234 Personal E-mail: dgn2040@aol.com.

NEELY, EDDIE W., mining executive; CPA. Various acctg. and fin. positions Pittston Coal Co. (subs. of The Brink's Co.); dir. acctg. The Brink's Co., 1996—97; contr. Hunt Assisted Living LLC., 1997—99; CFO White's Fresh Foods Inc., 1999—2002; asst. sec. Alpha Natural Resources Inc., sec., 2002, v.p., contr., 2004—09, CFO, 2009; exec. v.p., chief risk officer Alpha Natural Resources, Inc., 2009—. Office: Alpha Natural Resources Inc One Alpha Place Abingdon VA 24212 Office Phone: 276-619-4410. Office Fax: 276-628-9025.

NEELY, GINA, chef, restaurant manager; m. Patrick Neely, 1994; children: Spenser, Shelbi. Events coord. Carter Malone Group; branch mgr. Nat. Bank of Commerce, Memphis; co-owner, co-mgr. Neely's Bar-B-Que, Memphis; mgr. Neely's Bar-B-Que catering bus.; co-host, chef At Home With the Neelys, 2008—; co-host Road Tasted with the Neelys, 2008; co-owner Neely's Barbecue Parlor, NYC, 2011—. Co-author (with Pat Neely & Paula Disbrowe): Down Home with the Neelys: A Southern Family Cookbook, 2009; co-author: (with Pat Neely) The Neelys Celebration Cookbook: Down Home Meals for Every Occasion, 2011, Back Home with the Neelys: Comfort Food from Our Southern Kitchen to Yours, 2014; guest appearances Paula's Home Cooking, Paula's Party, Road Tasted, BBQ with Bobby Flay and several other Food Network Specials. Mem. Cummings St. Missionary Bapt. Ch., mem. Hospitality and Greeters ministries; mem. steering com. Women's Empowerment Summit, Memphis Housing Authority; mem. Parent Tchr. Student Assn. Cordova High Sch.; mem. Dreamers Club Nat. Civil Rights Mus. Recipient 2007 Bus. of Yr. (Neely's Bar-B-Que), Memphis MED-Week, Blue Ribbon Small Bus. (Neely's Bar-B-Que), US C. of C. Mem.: Memphis Restaurant Assn. Office: Neelys Bar B Que 585 S Cooper St Memphis TN 38104-5358*

NEELY, PATRICK, chef, restaurant manager; m. Gina Neely, 1994; children: Spenser, Shelbi. Co-owner, co-mgr. (with brothers) Neely's Bar-B-Que, Memphis, 1988—, East Memphis, 1992—, 2001—; co-host, chef Down Home With the Neelys, 2008—; co-host Road Tasted with the Neelys, 2008; co-owner Neely's Barbecue Parlor, NYC, 2011—. Co-author (with Gina Neely & Paula Disbrowe): Down Home with the Neelys: A Southern Family Cookbook, 2009; co-author: (with Gina Neely) The Neelys Celebration Cookbook: Down Home Meals for Every Occasion, 2011, Back Home with the Neelys: Comfort Food for Our Southern Kitchen to Yours, 2014; guest appearances with Gina Neely Paula's Home Cooking, Paula's Party, Road Tasted, BBQ with Bobby Flay and several other Food Network Specials. Bd. mem. Memphis Regional C. of C., Shelby Farms

Conservancy; bd. chmn. Memphis Conv. and Visitors Bur. Recipient 2007 Bus. of Yr. (Neely's Bar-B-Que), Memphis MED-Week, Blue Ribbon Small Bus. (Neely's Bar-B-Que), US C. of C.; named Restaurateur of Yr., Memphis Restaurant Assn., 2007. Office: Neelys Bar B Que 585 S Cooper St Memphis TN 38104-5358 Office Phone: 901-521-9798. Office Fax: 901-521-7252.*

NEELY, RICHARD, lawyer; b. Aug. 2, 1941; s. John Champ and Elinore (Forlani) N.; m. Carolyn Elaine Elmore, 1979; children: John Champ, Charles Whittaker. AB, Dartmouth Coll., 1964; LLB, Yale U., 1967. Bar: W.Va. 1967. Practiced in, Fairmont, W.Va., 1969-73; chmn. Marion County Bd. Pub. Health, 1971-72; mem. W.Va. Ho. of Dels., 1971-73; justice, chief justice W.Va. Supreme Ct. of Appeals, Charleston, 1973-95; ptnr. Neely & Hunter, Charleston, 1995—2007, Neely & Callaghan, Charleston, 2007—. Chmn. bd. Kane & Keyser Co., Belington, W.Va., 1970-88. Author: How Courts Govern America, 1980, Why Courts Don't Work, 1983, The Divorce Decision, 1984, Judicial Jeopardy: When Business Collides with the Courts, 1986, The Product Liability Mess: How Business Can Be Rescued from State Court Politics, 1988, Take Back Your Neighborhood: A Case for Modern-Day Vigilantism, 1990, Tragedies of our Own Making: How Private Choices have Created Public Bankruptcy, 1994; contbr. articles to nat. mags. Mem. bd. advisors BNA Class Action Litigation Report. Capt. US Army, 1967-69. Decorated Bronze Star, Vietnam Honor medal 1st Class. Mem.: Am. Legion, VFW, Internat. Brotherhood Elec. Workers, W.Va. Bar Assn., Fourth Cir. Jud. Conf. (life), Moose, Phi Sigma Kappa, Phi Delta Phi. Episcopalian. Office: Neely & Callaghan 159 Summers St Charleston WV 25301-2134 Office Phone: 304-343-6500. Business E-Mail: rneely@neelycallaghan.com.

NEFF, CAROLE CUKELL, lawyer; b. Geneva, NY, Aug. 3, 1951; d. Samuel and Hannah (Schoenfeld) C.; m. Richard Theodore Neff, Dec. 28, 1976; children: Alex Ryan, Hilary Shayna. BS magna cum laude, SUNY, Buffalo, 1973; JD, Tulane U., 1977. Bar: La. 1977. Law clk. La. State Supreme Ct., New Orleans, 1977—78; assoc. Session & Fishman, New Orleans, 1978—83; ptnr. Session, Fishman, Nathan & Israel, LLC, New Orleans, 1983—. Co-author: (with Max Nathan, Jr.) Louisiana Estate Planning, Will Drafting and Estate Administration 2nd ed., 2000; mem. bd. editors Tulane U. Law Rev. Bd. dir., pres. Jewish Endowment Found., New Orleans, 2006—. Named Achiever, Am. Coun. Career Women, 1990, Woman of Yr., New Orleans Bus. and Profl. Women, 1991, YWCA Role Model, 1992; named one of Top 25 Women Lawyers, Top 50 Lawyers, La. Super Lawyers, 2007; recipient Young Family Profl. Excellence award Jewish Endowment Found., 1989. Fellow Am. Coll. Trust and Estate Counsel; mem. NCJW, La. Bar Assn., New Orleans Bar Assn. (CLE chair 1987-89, 3d v.p. 1989-90, probate chair 1991-2000), Women's Profl. Coun. (bd. dirs., 1st v.p. 1989-90, pres. 1990-91), Profl. Fin. Planners of Greater New Orleans (sec. 1982-83, pres. 1983-84), New Orleans Estate Planning Coun. (pres. 2002-03), Jewish Endowment Found. (pres. 2007-09), Order of Coif, Rotary Internat. (bd. dirs. 1994-96), New Orleans Project (successions chair 2007-, AUODAH adv. com. chair 2009-), Hadassah, Sisterhood Shir Chadash (v.p. 2006—). Democrat. Jewish. Avocations: cooking, piano playing, travel. Office: Session Fishman & Nathan LLP 201 Saint Charles Ave Ste 3500 New Orleans LA 70170-3500 Office Phone: 504-582-1500. Business E-Mail: cneff@sessions-law.com.

NEFF, SEVERINE, music educator; b. Waterbury, Conn., Dec. 17, 1949; d. Victor and Evangeline Josephine Neff; m. Joel Stanley Feigin, June 7, 1986. AB, Barnard Coll., 1971; MA, Yale U., 1972; MFA, Princeton U., NJ, PhD, 1979. Asst. prof. Bates Coll., Lewiston, Maine, 1979—80, U. Hawaii, Honolulu, 1980—81, Barnard Coll., NYC, 1983—91; fellow Cornell U., Ithaca, NY, 1981—83; assoc. prof. Cin. Coll.-Conservatory, 1991—92, prof., 1993—95; prof. music U. NC, Chapel Hill, 1995—2003, Eugene Falk disting. prof., 2004—. Mem. adv. bd. Ind. Theory Rev. Music Contemporary Culture U. Haifa, 2009—, Musicologica Austriaca, Vienna; vis. endowed chair U. Ala., 2013. Author: Coherence, Counterpoint, Instrumentation, Instruction in Form, 1994, The Musical Idea, 1995, 2nd edit., 2006, Chinese edit., 2011, Norton Critical Score, Second String Quartet, Op. 10 by Arnold Schoenberg, 2006; editor: Theory and Practice, 1991—93, Music Theory Spectrum rev. edit., 1999—2001; editor chief: Music Theory Spectrum, 2009—13; editor chief Schoenberg Words, Oxford U. Press, 2009—. Grantee, NEH, 1993, Arnold Schoenberg Ctr., 2004, 2009—14, Korea Found., 2005; scholar, Fulbright Found., 1998—99; fellowship, Mellon Found., 1981, 2011—13, Tchg. fellowship, Mannes Inst., 2005—07, 2011, Acad. Arnold Schoenberg Ctr., 2009—12, 2012—14, grant, Ctrl. Conservatory Beijing, 2010, Mellon Found. Conf., 2011, Sichuan Conservatory, 2012, Moscow State Conservatory, 2013. Mem.: Soc. Music Theory (sec. 1991—94, bd. dirs.), Coll. Music Soc. (theory rep. 2001—04, bd. dirs.). Achievements include discovery of two unknown works of Arnold Schoenberg. Avocation: antiques. Office: U NC CB 3320 Chapel Hill NC 27599 Business E-Mail: sneff@email.unc.edu.

NEGRON, JOSEPH, JR., state legislator; b. West Palm Beach, Fla., Oct. 9, 1961; m. Rebecca Horton Negron; children: David, Jonathan, Becca. BA, Stetson U., 1983; JD, Emory U., Atlanta, 1986; MPA, Harvard U., 2009. Bar: Fla. 1986. Mem. Fla. House of Reps., 2000—06, co-chair Fla. house taxpayer protection caucus, 2003—06, chair appropriations com., 2005—06; mem. Dist. 28 Fla. State Senate, 2009—; of counsel Akerman Senterfitt; ptnr. Gunster, Yoakley & Stewart P.A., West Palm Beach, Fla., 2010—. Chmn. Safe Fla. Found. Recipient Freshman Legislator of Yr. award, Fla. Med. Assn., 2001, Legis. Leadership Award, Trust for Pub. Lands, 2001, Faith and Family Award, Christian Coalition of Fla., 2003, Fla. Bar Pres.'s Legis. Award, 2003, 2004, Legis. Voice for Children award, 2005. Republican. Avocations: basketball, softball, golf, architecture. Office: 3500 SW Corporate Pky Ste 204 Palm City FL 34990 also: 10795 Civic Ln Port Saint Lucie FL 34986 also: 306 Senate Office Bldg 404 S Monroe St Tallahassee FL 32399-1100 also: Gunster Yoakley & Stewart PA 777 S Flagler Dr Ste 500 E West Palm Beach FL 33401 Office Phone: 772-219-1665, 772-345-3951, 850-487-5088, 561-650-0768. Office Fax: 561-671-2469. E-mail: negron.joe.web@flsenate.gov, jnegron@gunster.com.

NEHR, PETER, state legislator; b. Kapfenburg, Austria, June 29, 1952; m. Anita Nehr; children: Christopher, Brian, Clifford. BA in Polit. Sci. summa cum laude, U. South Fla., Tampa, 2000. Owner Am. Spirit Flag Shop; mem. Dist. 48 Fla. House of Reps., Tallahassee, 2006—, dep. whip, 2008—09, mem. gen. govt. policy coun., health care appropriations com., health care regulation policy com., ins., bus. and fin. affairs policy com. Commr. City of Tarpon Springs, 2002—06. Recipient Champion for Bus. award, Associated Industries Fla., 2008; named Legislator of Yr., Fla. Assisted Living Affiliation, 2007, Friend of Free Enterprise, Associated Builders and Contractors, 2008. Mem.: Tarpon Springs Hist. Soc., Republican Club North Pinellas County, Rotary, Tarpon Springs, Kiwanis Club, Pinellas County (Kiwanian of Yr. 1981). Republican. Roman Catholic. Office: Tarpon Tower 905 E Martin Luther King Jr Dr Ste 430 Tarpon Springs FL 34689-4829 also: 400 House Office Bldg 402 S Monroe St Tallahassee FL 32399-1300 Office Phone: 727-943-4880, 850-488-5580.

NEHRBASS, SETH MARTIN, lawyer; b. Lafayette, La., Nov. 10, 1960; s. Neil Martin Nehrbass and Janet (Himbert) Nehrbass; m. Mary Elizabeth Dennis, Aug. 12, 2000; children: Gabriel, Fabian. Student in French Lang., U. Catholique de l'Ouest, Angers, France, 1980, U. Paul Valéry, Montpellier, France, 1981; BS in Physics summa cum laude, U. La., Lafayette, 1982; JD cum laude, Loyola U., Coll. Law, New Orleans, 1990. Bar: Supreme Ct. US, 1999, US Patent & Trademark Office, 1984, Supreme Ct. La., 1990, US Dist. Cts. (ea, middle, and we. dists.) La., 1990, US Ct. Appeals (fed. cir.), 1990, US Ct. Appeals (5th cir.), 1990, Notary Pub., State La., 1991. Patent examiner U.S. Patent & Trademark Office, 1982-84; patent agt. with law firm New Orleans, 1986-87; patent agent with pravel Gambrell, Hewitt, Kimball & Krieger, New Orleans, 1987—90, Hewitt & Kimball, New Orleans, 1990—98; patent atty. Garvey, Smith, Nehrbass & North, L.L.C., New Orleans, 1998—. Adj. law faculty Tulane Law Sch., 1997—; judge practice round moot ct. teams Loyola Law Sch., 1992—; preparer questions patent bar exam PTO Q & A Bd., 1992-93; presenter in field. Contbr. articles to profl. jours. Den leader 2d grade Cub Scouts, Boy Scouts Am., Lusher Sch., Audubon Dist., 1991-92, 3d grade, 1994-95, asst. den leader 3d grade, 1992-93, 4th grade, 1993-94; soccer coach Carrollton Booster Club, New Orleans, 1993-95, Lakeview Soccer Club, New Orleans, 1995-96; adv. mem. La. Ctr. for Law and Civic Edn., 1996-98; mem. New Orleans Citizen Diplomacy Coun., 2000—. Recipient Hornbook award West Pub. Co., 1986-87, 87-88, Corpus Juris Secundum award, 1986-87, Am. Jurisprudence awards (2), 1986; scholar La. State U. Alumni Fedn., 1978, Coun. Devel. French La./French Govt., 1980-81, Loyola Law Sch., 1986. Mem. ABA (sect. law, sci., tech. 1988-91, law student divsn. liaison patent trademark and copyright law 1988-90, intellectual property law sect. 1988—, chmn. law student com. 1996-98, chmn. spl. com. drug crisis 1990-93, co-chmn. ann. meeting arrangements com. 1993-94, internat. treaties and laws com. 1994—, co-chmn. young lawyers com. 1998-99), Am. Intellectual Property Law Assn. (ADR com., internat. and fgn. law com., patent law com. 1994-2000), La. Bar Assn. (internat. law sect. 1992—, intellectual property law sect. 1996—, vice chmn. 1997-98, chair-elect 1998-99, chair 1999-2000), New Orleans Bar Assn. (interim chmn. ad hoc com. drug crisis 1991-92, chmn. intellectual property law com. 1991-95, chmn. law related edn. com. 1995-97), Round Table Club, Plimsoll Club, Rotary Club New Orleans (newsletter editor, 2009-2010); East Jefferson Bus. Assn. (bd. mem. 2009-), Loyola Law Sch. Moot Ct. Alumni Assn., Sigma Pi Sigma, Pi Delta Phi, Alpha Sigma Nu. Democrat. Roman Catholic. Avocations: gardening, photography, travel, hunting, fishing. Home: 453 Audubon Blvd New Orleans LA 70125-3503 Office: 3838 N Causeway Blvd Ste 3290 Metairie LA 70002 Office Phone: 504-835-2000. Business E-Mail: nehrbass@gsnn.us. E-mail: SNehrbass@gmail.com.

NEIDICH, GEORGE, lawyer; b. NYC, Feb. 22, 1950; s. Hyman and Rosalyn N.; m. Alene Wendrow, Jan. 10, 1982; 1 child, Hannah Lauren. BA, SUNY, Binghamton, 1971; JD magna cum laude, SUNY, Buffalo, 1974; MLT, Georgetown U., 1981. Bar: N.Y. 1975, D.C. 1979, Va. 1996, Conn. 1990. Assoc. Runfola & Birzon, Buffalo, 1973-75, Duke, Holzman, Yaeger & Radlin, Buffalo, 1975-77; gen. counsel subcom. on capital, investments and bus. opportunity, com. on small bus. US House of Representatives, Washington, 1977-79, subcom. on gen. oversight, 1979-80; sr. legal advisor Task Force Product Liability and Accident Compensation Office of Gen. Counsel, Dept. Commerce, Washington, 1980-81; assoc. Steptoe & Johnson, Washington, 1981-86, of counsel, 1986-89; gen. counsel, sr. v.p. Preferred Health Care, Ltd., Wilton, Conn., 1989-93; COO Value Behavioral Health, Inc., Falls Church, Va., 1993-95; counsellor at law, 1995—. Adj. prof. Georgetown U. Law Ctr., 1985—87. Office: 1600 Tysons Blvd 8th Fl Mc Lean VA 22102 Office Phone: 703-757-2820. Personal E-mail: gneidich@aol.com.

NEIKIRK, WILLIAM ROBERT, retired journalist; b. Irvine, Ky., Jan. 6, 1938; s. Lewis Byron and Nancy Elizabeth (Green) N.; m. Ruth Ann Clary, Sept. 10, 1960; children: Paul Gregory, John Stuart, Christa Lynn. BA in Journalism, U. Ky., 1960. Reporter Lexington (Ky.) Herald, 1959-60; state capital corr. AP, Frankfort, Ky., 1961-66, Baton Rouge, 1966-69; econ. corr. AP (Washington Bur.), 1970-74; nat. econ. writer Chgo. Tribune, Washington, 1974-83, White House corr., 1977, 94-98—, econ. columnist, 1980—94, news editor Washington bur., 1983, fin. editor, 1988-91, sr. writer, 1991—2008, chief Washington corr., 1998—2008. Author: The Work Revolution, 1983, Volcker: The Money Man, 1987. Recipient Beck award Chgo. Tribune, 1975, Bus. Writing award U. Mo., 1978, 80, Bus. Writing award Amos Tuck Grad. Sch. Bus., Dartmouth Coll., 1980, John Hancock Bus. Writing award Wharton Sch. Fin., U. Pa., 1979, finalist, 1990, 91, John Hancock Bus. Writing award U. Houston, 1980, Loeb Bus. Writing award UCLA Grad. Sch. Mgmt., 1979, Chgo. Headliner Club award, 1979, 84, Raymond Clapper Meml. award, 1981, Barnet Nover award, 1994, Merriman Smith award, 1995, White House Correspondents Assn.; named to Ky. Journalism Hall of Fame, 1998, One of Top 100 Bus. News Luminaries of the Century, TJFR mag., 2000; co-recipient Pulitzer Prize, 2001. Mem.: Gridiron Club (pres. 2007). Mem. Christian Ch. (Disciples Of Christ). Home: 5121 38th St N Arlington VA 22207-1827

NEILSON, DENNY WOODALL, state legislator; d. d Lawrence W Woodall Woodall and Lula Denny W., Lawrence W. Woodall and Lula Denny W.; m. David Neilson Neilson; 1 child, David Neilson; m. David Neilson Neilson. BS, Coker Coll., 1973; MS, Winthrop U., 1975. Mem. Darlington City Coun., 1975—83; mem. Dist. 56 SC House of Reps., 1984—, mem. Rules Com. & Ways and Means Com. Recipient Human Relations award, SC. Edn. Assn., 1978, SC. Disting. Tchr.-Citizen award, 1979, Goodfellow award, Darlington Lions Club, 1985, Woman of Year, Darlington Bus. & Prof. Women Assn., 1985, Svc. award, SC. Ret. Educators, 1988, Wilson Group Healthcare, 1989. Mem.: Nat. Assn. Accredited Talent and Beauty Judges (pres. 1970—71), Darlington County Edn. Assn. (tres. 1976—77), Area Classroom Tchr. Assn. (pres. 1978—79), charter mem. Darlington Bus. & Prof. Women, Darlington C. of C. (bd.dir. 1980, bd. dir. 1980—), Darlington Pilot Club (former. pres.). Democrat. Baptist. Address: 109 Carol Dr Darlington SC 29532 Mailing: 530B Blatt Bldg Columbia SC 29201 Office Phone: 803-734-3097. E-mail: dwn@legis.lpitr.state.sc.us.

NEILSON, WILLIAM S., economics professor; s. John and Mary Jane Neilson; m. Elizabeth Neilson; 1 child, Henry. BA, Rice U., Houston, 1983; PhD, U. Calif. San Diego, La Jolla, 1988. Prof. Tex. A&M U., College Station, 1988—2006; J. Fred Holly chair of excellence U. Tenn., Knoxville, 2006—. Editor: (acad. jour.) Economic Inquiry, 1997—2001; author: (textbook) Personnel Economics, 2007. Achievements include research in the economics of risk and uncertainty, behavioral economics and game theory.

NEIMAN, JOHN, JR., lawyer; B in Economics, with highest honors, U. NC, Chapel Hill; JS magna cum laude, Harvard U., Mass. Law clk. to Hon. Paul Niemeyer US Ct. Appeals (4th Cir.); law clk. to Hon. Anthony Kennedy US Supreme Ct., Washington; ptnr. Bradley Arant Boult Cummings LLP, Birmingham; solicitor gen. Office of Atty. Gen., Ala., 2011—. Law sch. instr. U. Ga., Cumberland U., Tenn., U. Ala. Office: Ala Atty General's Office 501 Washington Ave Montgomery AL 36130 Office Phone: 334-242-7300. Business E-Mail: jneiman@ago.state.al.us.

NEIMS, ALLEN HOWARD, pediatrician, educator, dean, researcher; b. Chgo., Oct. 24, 1938; s. Irving Morris and Ruth (Geller) N.; m. Myrna Gay Robins, June 18, 1961; children: Daniel Mark, Susan Roberta, Nancy Elizabeth. BA, BS, U. Chgo., 1957; MD, Johns Hopkins U., 1961, PhD, 1966. Intern, resident in pediatrics Johns Hopkins Hosp., 1961-62, 66-68; research asso. Lab. Neurochemistry, NIH, 1968-70; asst. prof. physiol. chemistry and pediatrics Johns Hopkins Med. Sch., 70-72; assoc. prof. McGill U., 1972-77, prof. pharmacology and pediatrics, 1977-78; dir. Roche developmental pharmacology unit, 1972-78; prof., chmn. dept. pharmacology and therapeutics, prof. pediatrics U. Fla., Gainesville, 1978-89, dean Coll. Medicine, 1989-96, prof. pharmcology, pediat., 1996—2007; dir. Ctr. for Spirituality and Health, 2002—07, prof. emeritus, 2007—. Dir. Ctr. Spirituality and Health; Fulton Bequest prof. U. Melbourne, Australia, 1974; mem. human embryology and devel. study sect. NIH, 1979-83; sci. cons. Can. Found. for Study of Sudden Infant Death, 1974-77, Nat. Soft Drink Assn., 1976-78, Internat. Life Scis. Inst., 1978-89; bd. sci. counsellors Nat. Inst. Child Health and Human Devel., 1984-89. Contbr. chpts. to books, articles to med. jours. Served to comdr. USPHS, 1968-70. NIH, Can. Med. Research Council grantee. Mem. Can. Assn. Research in Toxicology (pres. 1976-78), Am. Soc. Pharmacology and Exptl. Therapeutics (past mem. exec. coms. clin. pharmacology and drug metabolism), Am. Pediatric Soc., Am. Acad. Pediatrs. Democrat. Jewish. Office: U Fla Coll Medicine PO Box 100267 Gainesville FL 32610-0267 Office Phone: 352-392-0687. Personal E-mail: ahneims@aol.com. Business E-Mail: ahneims@ufl.edu.

NEITZKE, ERIC KARL, lawyer; b. Mobile, Ala., Dec. 10, 1955; s. Howard and Otti S. Neitzke; m. Kathryn Sloan; children: Kyle, Blake, Blaire. BA, U. Fla., 1979, JD, 1982. Bar: Fla. 1982, U.S. Dist. Ct. (mid. dist.) Fla. 1987. Asst. state atty. 7th Jud. Cir., State Atty., Daytona Beach, Fla., 1982; assoc. Dunn, Smith & Withers, Daytona Beach, 1982—88, Monaco, Smith, Hood and Perkins, Daytona Beach, 1988—2003; sole practice Daytona Beach, 2003—. Adj. faculty family law and criminal law Daytona C.C.; chmn. adv. com. Juvenile Detention Ctr. Contbr. articles to profl. jours. Mem. ATLA, Fla. Acad. Trial Lawyers, Volusia Bar Assn., Fla. Assn. Criminal Def. Lawyers, Phi Beta Kappa. Avocations: water sports, shooting, travel. Home: 19 Lost Creek Ln Ormond Beach FL 32174-4840 Office: Eric K Neitzke PA 412 N Wild Olive Ave Daytona Beach FL 32118 Office Phone: 386-323-1900. Personal E-mail: knightmas@aol.com.

NELON, ROBERT DALE, lawyer; b. Shawnee, Okla., Aug. 8, 1946; s. Cecil Eugene and Neata Madelyn (Fox) N.; m. Freddie Anne Tipton, Aug. 2, 1975; children: Lindsay Anne, Gregory Tipton. BA, Northwestern U., 1968; JD, U. Okla., 1971. Bar: Okla. 1971, U.S. Dist. Ct. (we., no. and ea. dists) Okla. 1971, U.S. Ct. Appeals (10th cir.) 1971, (8th cir.) 1992, (2d cir.) 1993, U.S. Ct. Appeals for the Armed Forces 1972, U.S. Supreme Ct. 1989. Law clk. Okla. Atty. Gen., Oklahoma City, 1966-70; mem. Andrews, Davis, Legg, Bixler, Milsten & Price, Oklahoma City, 1971-95, Hall Estill Hardwick Gable Golden & Nelson, Oklahoma City, 1995—. Served to capt. USMCR, 1972-74. Mem. ABA, Okla. Bar Assn., Am. Judicature Soc. Democrat. Methodist. Office: Hall Estill Hardwick Gable Golden & Nelson Chase Tower Suite 2900 100 N Broadway Ave Oklahoma City OK 73102-8865 Home Phone: 405-721-8501; Office Phone: 405-553-2828. Business E-Mail: bnelon@hallestill.com.

NELSEN, HART MICHAEL, sociologist, educator; b. Pipestone, Minn., 1938; s. Noah I. and Nova Nelsen; m. Anne Kusener, June 13, 1964; 1 dau., Jennifer. BA, U. No. Iowa, 1959, MA, 1963; M.Div., Princeton Theol. Sem., 1963; PhD (NSF faculty fellow), Vanderbilt U., 1972. Asst. prof. sociology Western Ky. U., Bowling Green, 1965-70, assoc. prof., 1970-73, Catholic U. Am., 1973-74, prof., 1974-81, chmn. dept. sociology, 1974-77, mem. Boys Town Ctr. for Study Youth Devel., 1974-81; prof. sociology La. State U., Baton Rouge, 1981-84, chmn. dept. sociology, head dept. rural sociology, 1981-84, coordinator rural sociology research, 1981-84; dean Coll. Liberal Arts Pa. State U., 1984-90, prof. sociology, 1984—2004, prof. emeritus, 2004—. Author: (with Anne K. Nelsen) Black Church in the Sixties, 1975; co-author: The Religion of Children, 1977, Religion and American Youth, 1976; editor: (with others) The Black Church in America, 1971; adv. editor: Sociol. Quar, 1976-82; assoc. editor: Sociol. Analysis, 1977-80, Rev. Religious Research, 1977-80, 84—, editor, 1980-84; mem. editorial bd.: Social Forces, 1983-86. Co-rec. sec. Capitol Hill Restoration Soc., 1979-80, v.p., 1980-81; mem. exec. bd. Lafitte Hills Assn., 1983-84; pres. Midtown Sq. Condo. Assn., 1996-99, treas., 1999-2001; v.p. Market Sq. West Condominium Assn., 2006-. Presbyterian Chs. grantee, 1966-69; NIMH co-grantee, 1969-72; Russell Sage Found. co-grantee, 1972-73; La. Gov.'s Commn. on Alcoholism and Drug Abuse grantee, 1982 Mem. Assn. Sociology Religion (exec. coun. 1974-76, 78-82, v.p. 1978-79, pres. 1980-81), Religious Rsch. Assn. (dir. 1977-80, pres.-elect 1985-86, pres. 1987-88), Soc. Sci. Study Religion (coun. 1981-83, exec. sec. 1984-87), Am. Sociol. Assn., So. Sociol. Soc. (chmn. membership com. 1983-85), AAAS (rep. 1984-2000). Mem. United Ch. Of Christ. Home: 909 5th Ave 603 Seattle WA 98164 Personal E-mail: hmnelsen@mindspring.com.

NELSEN, ROBERT STEVEN, academic administrator, literature and language professor; b. Brigham City, Utah, Jan. 21, 1952; s. Robert Secrist and Geraldine (Jensen) N.; m. Joellyn Hawkins, Feb. 14, 1975; 1 child, Robert Seth. BA, Brigham Young U., 1978, MA in Polit. Sci., 1979; PhD, U. Chgo., 1989. Adminstrv. asst. U. Chgo., 1989-90; instr. U. Ill., Chgo., 1989-90; assoc. prof., dir. creative writing program U. Tex. at Dallas, 1990—2008, assoc. provost than vice provost, 2005—08; assoc. v.p. academic affairs, pres. English Texas A&M U.-Corpus Christi, 2008—09; pres. U. Tex.-Pan Am., 2010—. Guest rsch. assoc. U. Frankfurt, Fed. Republic Germany, 1987-88. Author short stories; exec. editor Common Knowledge, 1991—. Mem. AWP. Office: U Tex Pan-Am Office of Pres 1201 W University Dr Edinburg TX 78539 Home: 9808 Las Palmas McAllen TX 78504-6035 Office Phone: 956-381-2100. E-mail: president@utpa.edu.

NELSON, ALLEN W., lawyer; b. 1964; m. Amy Nelson; children: Katie, Teddy. BA with honors, Duke U., Durham, NC, 1986, JD, 1989. Assoc. Troutman, Sanders, Lockerman & Ashmore, Atlanta, 1989—91; atty. Hawkins & Parnell, Atlanta, 1991—97; chief compliance counsel BellSouth Corp., 1997—2005; sr. v.p. Crawford & Co., chief adminstrv. officer, exec. v.p., gen. counsel & corp. sec., 2005—. Bd. mem. Ga. Trust for Hist. Preservation, Atlanta Ballet. Office: Crawford & Co 1001 Summit Blvd Atlanta GA 30319 Office Phone: 404-256-0830. Office Fax: 404-300-1905. Business E-Mail: allen_nelson@us.crawco.com.

NELSON, BILL (CLARENCE WILLIAM NELSON), United States Senator from Florida; b. Miami, Fla., Sept. 29, 1942; s. C.W. and Nannie (Merle) N.; m. Grace H. Cavert, Feb. 19, 1972; children: C. William, Nan Ellen. BA, Yale U., 1965; JD, U. Va., 1968. Bar: Fla.

1968. Atty. Nelson, Normile & Dettmer, Melbourne, Fla., 1970-79, Maguire, Vorrhis & Wells, Pa., 1991—94; mem. Fla. House of Reps., Tallahassee, 1972-78, US Congress from 9th Dist. Fla., Washington, 1979—83, US Congress from 11th Dist. Fla., Washington, 1983—91; payload specialist 1 Space Shuttle Columbia seventh orbital mission, 1986; treas., ins. commr. State of Fla., Tallahassee, 1995—2000; US Senator from Fla., 2001—; chmn. US Senate Space, Aeronautics & Related Sciences Subcommittee, 2007—, US Senate Spl. Com. on Aging, 2013—. Author: Mission: An American Congressman's Voyage to Space, 1988. Bd. dirs. American Astronautical Soc.; mem. Fla. Space Bus. Roundtable. Served to capt. USAR, 1965—75, served with US Army, 1968—70. Recipient Public Svc. award, Nat. Crystallography Assn., 1988, Debus award, Nat. Space Club, Fla. Com., 1993, President's award, Fla. State Conf. NAACP, 2001. Mem.: Fla. Bar Assn., Brevard County Bar Assn., Assn. Space Explorers. Democrat. Episcopalian. Office: US Senate 716 Hart Senate Office Bldg Rm 716 Washington DC 20510 Address: Landmark Ctr Two Ste 410 225 E Robinson St Orlando FL 32801 Office Phone: 202-224-5274, 407-872-7161. Office Fax: 202-228-2183, 407-872-7165.*

NELSON, BRYAN, state legislator; b. Orlando, Fla., Sept. 14, 1958; m. Debbie Nelson; children: Reed, Linda. BS in Ornamental Horticulture, U. Fla., 1979. Ins. agent; mem. Dist. 38 Fla. House of Reps., 2006—, vice chair gen. govt. policy coun., mem. econ. devel. policy com., govt. ops. appropriations com., ins., bus. and fin. affairs policy com. Mem. Orange County Citizens Rev. Bd., 1998—2002, Orange County Zoning Bd., 2002—, chmn., 2006; mem. Cmty. Action Bd., 2007—. Mem. Habitat for Humanity, 2007—. Mem.: Apopka Area C. of C. (pres. 2003), Florida Foliage Assn. (pres. 1992), Apopka Rotary Club (Rotarian of Yr. 1998). Republican. Methodist. Office: 409 S Park Ave Apopka FL 32703-5261 also: 214 House Office Bldg 402 S Monroe St Tallahassee FL 32399-1300 Office Phone: 407-880-4414, 850-488-2023.

NELSON, CALEB EDWARD, law educator; b. Cleve., Sept. 20, 1966; s. David Aldrich and Mary Dickson Nelson; m. Elizabeth Kristol, Aug. 11, 1991; children: Maxwell David, Katherine Ellen. AB, Harvard U., 1988; JD, Yale U., 1993. Bar: Ohio 1993. Mng. editor and other editl. positions The Pub. Interest, Washington, 1988—90; law clk. to judge Stephen F. Williams U.S. Ct. of Appeals for the D.C. Circuit, Washington, 1993—94; law clk. to justice Clarence Thomas U.S. Supreme Ct., Washington, 1994—95; assoc. litig. dept. Taft, Stettinius & Hollister, Cin., 1995—98; prof. U. Va. Sch. Law, Charlottesville, 1998—. Vis. prof. Harvard Law Sch., 2006. Author: Statutory Interpretation, 2011; contbr. articles to profl. jours. Recipient Paul M. Bator award, Federalist Soc., 2006, All-U. Tchg. award, 2008; named Winner Scholarly Papers Competition, Assn. Am. Law Schs., 2000. Mem.: Phi Beta Kappa. Republican. Office: Univ Virginia School Law 580 Massie Rd Charlottesville VA 22903-1789

NELSON, DAVID DANIEL, lobbyist, former ambassador; b. Minn., 1956; m. Gloria Nelson; 1 child, Alex. BA in Economics & Internat. Rels., U. Wis., 1978; MA in Economics, U. Md., 1987. Economics officer US Embassy, Quito, Ecuador, 1987—89, Bonn, Germany, 1990—93, Madrid, 1993—97; dir. Office of Monetary Affairs, Bur. Economics, Energy & Bus. Affairs US Dept. State, Washington, 1997—2000; min. counselor for economics US Embassy, Berlin, 2001—03; sr. coord. for the G-8 NSC, Washington, 2003—04; dir. Office Terrorism Finance & Econ. Sanctions US Dept. State, Washington, 2004—07, exec. asst. to under sec. for econ., energy & agrl. affairs, 2007—08, prin. dep. asst. sec. for economics, energy & bus. affairs, 2008—09, acting asst. sec. for economics, energy & bus. affairs, 2009, US amb. to Republic of Uruguay Montevideo, 2009—11; sr. mgr. global govt. affairs & policy-Americas Gen. Electric Co., Washington, 2011—.

NELSON, DAVID LEONARD, business executive; b. Omaha, May 8, 1930; s. Leonard A. and Cecelia (Steinert) N.; m. Jacqueline J. Zerbe, Dec. 26, 1952; 1 child, Nancy Jo. BS, Iowa State U., 1952. Mktg. adminstr. Ingersoll Rand, Chgo., 1954-56; with Accuray Corp., Columbus, Ohio, 1956-87, exec. v.p., gen. mgr., 1967, pres., 1967-87, chief exec. officer, 1970-87; pres. process automation bus. unit Combustion Engring., Inc., Columbus, 1987-90; pres. bus. area process automation Asea Brown Boveri, Stamford, Conn., 1990-91, v.p. customer satisfaction Ams. region, 1991-93, v.p. customer support Ams. region, 1994-95; chmn. bd. dirs. Herman Miller Inc., Zeeland, Mich., 1995-2000, counsel, 2000—04. Served to capt. USMCR, 1952-54. Mem. IEEE, Instrument Soc. Am., Newcomen Soc. N.Am., Tau Beta Pi, Phi Kappa Phi, Phi Eta Sigma, Delta Upsilon. Achievements include patents in field. Home: 1113 Roundhouse Ln Alexandria VA 22314-5935 Office Phone: 703-299-4588. Business E-Mail: david-nelson@hermanmiller.com.

NELSON, DAVID LOREN, geneticist, educator; b. Washington, June 25, 1956; s. Erling Walter and Marlys Joan (Jorgenson) N.; m. Claudia Jane Hackbarth, July 31, 1982; children: Jorgen William, Erik Alexander. BA, U. Va., 1978; PhD, MIT, 1984. Staff fellow NIH, Bethesda, Md., 1985-86; sr. assoc. Baylor Coll. Medicine, Houston, 1986-89, instr., 1989-90, asst. prof., 1990-94, assoc. prof., 1994-99, prof., 1999—. Dir. Human Genome Ctr., 1995-96. Editor: Genome Data Base, 1992-2000; assoc. editor Genomics, 1994-2002. Mem.: Am. Soc. Human Genetics (sec. 2002—10). Achievements include development of Alu PCR; discovery of fragile X syndrome gene (FMR-1), new form of genetic mutation (simple repeat expansion); identification of gene defects in Lowe Syndrome and Incontinentia Pigmenti. Office: Baylor Coll Dept Medicine Molecular & Human Genetics 1 Baylor Plz MSBCM0225 Houston TX 77030-3411 Personal E-mail: nelson@bcm.edu.

NELSON, DEAN B., wholesale distribution executive; Process control engr. Shell Oil Co., 1981—83; with Boston Consulting Group, Inc., 1985—98, sr. v.p., 1998—2000; founder, CEO Capstone Consulting LLC, 2000—; chmn. PRIMEDIA Inc., 2003—, pres., CEO, 2005—. Bd. dirs. PRIMEDIA Inc., 2003—. Office: PRIMEDIA Inc 3585 Engineering Dr Ste 100 Norcross GA 30092 Office Phone: 678-421-3000. Business E-Mail: dean@primedia.com.

NELSON, DONNIE, professional sports team executive; b. Sept. 10, 1962; s. Don Nelson; m. Lotta Nelson; children: Christie, D.J. Grad., Wheaton Coll., Ill., 1986. Regional scout Milw. Bucks, 1984—86; asst. coach Golden State Warriors, 1986—94, Phoenix Suns, 1994—97; asst. coach, dir. player pers. Dallas Mavericks, 1998—2002, acting head coach, 2001, 2002, pres. basketball ops., 2002—, gen. mgr., 2005—. Asst. coach Lithuanian Nat. Team, 1990—; scout at World Championships USA Basketball, Toronto, Canada, 1994; founder Global Games, Dallas; hon. amb. League of Industries; chief advisor Chinese Nat. Basketball Team. Founder Assist Youth Found. (now combined with Heroes), 2002. Recipient Grand Cross of the Comdr., Pres. of Lithuania, 2004; named to Wheaton Coll. Hall of Honor, 1997. Office: Dallas Mavericks The Pavilion 2909 Taylor St Dallas TX 75226 E-mail: dcn@dallasmavs.com.

NELSON, EDWARD GAGE, brokerage house and bank executive, consultant; b. Nashville, May 17, 1931; s. Charles and Polly (Prentiss) N.; m. Carole Olivia Frances Minton, Sept. 17, 1960; children: Carole Gervais, Emily Minton, Ellen Prentiss BA in Polit. Sci., U. of South, Sewanee, Tenn., 1952. Exec. v.p. Clark, Landstreet & Kirkpatrick, Inc., Nashville, 1955-64, Commerce Union Bank, Nashville, 1968-72, pres., 1972-82, cons., 1985—, chmn., CEO, 1982-84; chmn., pres. Nelson Capital Corp., Nashville, 1985—. Hon. consul gen. Japan; bd. dirs. Werthan Packaging, Consumers Ins., Franklin Industries, Trans Arabian Investment Bank, Ctrl. Parking Sys., Ohio Star Forge, Bucyrus Internat., Inc.; mem. 1st adv. coun. Japan/Tenn. Soc. Trustee Vanderbilt U., Nashville, 1979—, chmn. med. ctr. bd., 1984-2003. Spl. agt. U.S. Army, 1955, Japan. Mem. Belle Meade Country Club, River Club (N.Y.C.). Republican. Episcopalian. Home: 103 Westhampton Pl Nashville TN 37205-3438

NELSON, EDWARD SHEFFIELD, retired utilities executive, lawyer; b. Keevil, Ark., Feb. 23, 1941; s. Robert Ford and Thelma Jo (Mayberry) N.; m. Mary Lynn McCastlain, Oct. 12, 1962; children: Cynthia, Lynn (dec.), Laura. BS, U. Cen. Ark., 1963; LLB, Ark. Law Sch., 1968; JD, U. Ark., 1969. Mgmt. trainee Ark. La. Gas Co., Little Rock, 1963-64, sales engr., 1964-67, sales coordinator, 1967-69, gen. sales mgr., 1969-71, v.p., gen. sales mgr., 1971-73, pres., dir., 1973-79, pres., chmn., chief exec. officer, 1979-85; ptnr., chmn. bd., chief exec. officer House, Wallace, Nelson & Jewel, Little Rock, 1985-86; pvt. practice law Little Rock, 1986—; of counsel Jack, Lyon & Jones, P.A., 1991—; ptnr. Jack, Nelson & Jones, Pa., 2008—, Jack, Nelson, Jones, & Bryant, Pa., 2011. Bd. dirs. Fed. Res. Mem. N.G., 1957-63, Fellowship Bible Ch.; bd. dirs. U. Ark., Little Rock, vice chmn. bd. visitors, 1981; bd. dirs. Philander Smith Coll., 1981; chmn. Ark. Indsl. Devel. Commn., 1987, 88; past chmn. Little Rock br. Fed. Res. Bd. St. Louis; chmn. Econ. Expansion Study Commn., 1987—; bd. dirs. Ark. Ednl. TV Found., Ark. Game and Fish Commn. Found.; founder, 1st pres. Jr. Achievement Ark., 1987-88; Rep. nominee for Gov. of Ark., 1990, 94; co-state chmn. Ark. Reps., 1991-92, nat. committeeman Ark. GOP, 1993-2000; mem. Ark. Higher Edn. Coord. Bd., 1997-99; apptd. commr. Ark. Game and Fish Commn., 2000-07, chmn., 2007-. Named Ark.'s Outstanding Young Man Ark. J. C. of C., 1973; One of Am.'s Ten Outstanding Young Men U.S. Jr. C. of C., 1974; Citizen of Yr. Ark. chpt. March of Dimes, 1983; Humanitarian of Yr. NCCJ, 1983; Best Chief Exec. Officer in Natural Gas Industry Wall Street Transcript, 1983; recipient 1st Disting. Alumnus award U. Cen. Ark., 1987, Outstanding Svcs. award, Ducks Unlimited, 2007, First Legacy award Jr. Achievement, Ark., 2008, Best Citizen award Ark. Times Readers, 2009, Living Legend award Arks. Bus., 2009. Mem. Am., Ark., Pulaski County Bar Assns., Ark. C. of C. (dir.), Little Rock C. of C. (dir., pres. 1981), Sales and Mktg. Execs. Assn. (pres. 1975, Top Mgmt. award 1977), U. Ark. Law Sch. Alumni Assn. (pres. 1980), Sigma Tau Gamma (Ben T. Laney Leadership award for leadership and achievement 2000), Ark. Wildlife Fedn. (Conservationist of Yr. 2002), Am. Lung Assn. (chmn., Philanthropist of Yr. 2003, Jerry Jones Sportman's award 2007, Ducks Unlimited, Arks. Mpcl. League(Mpcl. Law award, 2008), Easter Seals (Arkansan of Yr. award, 2010). Fellowship Bible Ch. Office: 2800 Ctrl Rd Ste 500 Little Rock AR 72202 Home Phone: 501-372-4900; Office Phone: 501-375-1122.

NELSON, ERIN MULLIGAN, social commerce industry executive, marketing professional; BBA in Internat. Bus. and Mktg., U. Tex., Austin. Asst, brand mgr. Procter & Gamble Co., 1991—93; mgmt. cons. A.T. Kearney, 1994—98; mem. corp. strategy team Frito-Lay N.Am., Inc. (now PepsiCo, Inc.), 1998—99; sr. mktg. mgr. Dell Inc. (formerly Dell Computer Corp.), 1999—2001, dir. mktg., 2001—03, dir. sales, 2003—05, dir. eBusiness, EMEA (Europe, Middle East, Africa) home/small bus., 2006—07, dir. mktg., EMEA small/medium bus., 2007, v.p. mktg. EMEA, 2008—09, v.p. mktg., chief mktg. officer, 2009—10; chief mktg. officer Bazaarvoice, Inc., 2010—. Office: Bazaarvoice Inc 3900 N Capital of TX Hwy Ste 300 Austin TX 78746 Office Phone: 512-338-4400. Office Fax: 512-728-3653.

NELSON, GORDON LEIGH, chemist, educator; b. Palo Alto, Calif., May 27, 1943; s. Nels Folke and Alice Virginia (Fredrickson) N. BS in Chemistry, U. Nev., 1965; MS, Yale U., 1967, PhD, 1970; DSc (hon.), William Carey Coll., 1988. Staff research chemist corp. research and devel. Gen. Electric Co., Schenectady, NY, 1970-74, mgr. combustibility tech. plastics div. Pittsfield, Mass., 1974-79, mgr. environ. protection plastics div., 1979-82; v.p. materials sci. and tech. Springborn Labs. Inc., Enfield, Conn., 1982-83; prof., chmn. dept. polymer sci. U. So. Miss., Hattiesburg, 1983-89; dean Coll. Sci. and Liberal Arts, prof. chemistry Fla. Inst. Tech., Melbourne, 1989—, v.p. academic affairs, 2011—, mem. coun. sci., soc. pres., sec. Melbourne, 1989-90, chair-elect, 1991, chair, 1992. Cons. in field. Author: Carbon-13 Nuclear Magnetic Resonance for Organic Chemists, 1972, Carbon-13 Nuclear Magnetic Resonance for Organic Chemists, 2d edit., 1980; co-author: Polymeric Materials-Chemistry for the Future, 1989, Carbon Monoxide and Human Lethality, 1993; editor: Fire and Polymers-Materials and Tests for Hazard Prevention, 1990, 1995; co-editor: Fire and Polymers-Materials and Solutions for Hazard Prevention, 2001, Fire and Polymer IVs-Materials and Solutions for Hazard Prevention, 2005, editor books on coating sci. tech.; contbr. articles to profl. jours. Mem.: ASTM (E5 cert. of appreciation 1985, D1 1997), Soc. Advancement of Scandinavian Study, Coun. Colls Arts and Scis., Soc. Plastics Industry (structural plastics divsn., Man of Yr. 1979), Internat. Electrotech. Commn. (U.S. tech. adv. group on info. processing equipment), Ctr. Sci. Tech. and the Media (bd. dir. 1991—94), Info. Tech. Industry Coun. (chmn. plastics task group), Am. Chem. Soc. (bd. dirs. 1977—85, 1987—89, pres. 1988, bd. dirs. 1992—94, 1st Nelson award Orlando sect. 1996, Charles Holmes Herty medal Ga. sect. 1998), Am. Inst. Chemists, Nev. Hist. Soc., Yale Chemists Assn. (pres. 1981—), Sigma Xi. Republican. Presbyterian. Avocations: travel, western U.S. history. Office: Fla Inst Tech Academic Affairs 150 W University Blvd Melbourne FL 32901-6975 Office Phone: 321-674-8480.

NELSON, JAMEER, professional basketball player; b. Chester, Pa., Feb. 9, 1982; s. Pete Nelson and Linda Billings; 1 child, Jameer Jr. B in Sociology, St. Joseph's U., Phila., 2004. Point guard Orlando Magic, 2004—. Recipient Adolph Rupp award, 2004, Oscar Robertson award, 2004, Francis Pomeroy Naismith award, 2004, Naismith Men's College Player of Yr. award, 2004, John R. Wooden award, 2004; co-recipient Player of Yr. award, Nat. Assn. Basketball Coaches, 2004; named Player of Yr., Atlantic 10 Conf., 2004, AP, 2004, 1st Team All-Am., 2004, Coll. Basketball Player of Yr., The Sporting News, 2004; named to Ea. Conf. All-Star Team, NBA, 2009. Office: Orlando Magic 8701 Maitland Summit Blvd Orlando FL 32810

NELSON, JANE GRAY, state legislator; b. Oct. 5, 1951; m. J. Michael Nelson; children: Brian, Elizabeth, Christina, Michelle, Jennifer. BS, U. North Tex., Denton. Former pub. sch. tchr.; businesswoman; mem. Tex. State Bd. Edn., 1989—92; mem. Dist. 22 Tex. State Senate, 1995—2002, mem. Dist. 12, 2003—. Mem. health com. Nat. Conf. State Legislatures. Bd. dirs. Tex. Women's Alliance, Tex. Conservative Coalition; mem. bd. advisors Free Enterprise PAC, Texans for Safe Roads; mem. Tex. Tech U. Edn. Adv. Coun., Baylor U. Med. Ctr. Grapevine Women's Adv. Coun. Recipient Jane Nelson Friend Cmty. Edn. award, Nat. Cmty. Edn. Citizen Leadership award, Outstanding Alumni award, U. North Tex., 1993, Nat. Disting. Advocacy award, Am. Cancer Soc., 2008; named Legislator of Yr., Tex. Coun. Child Welfare Boards, 2009; named one of Tex. Top Ten Legislators, Free Market Found., 1993, 1995; named to Tex. Women's Hall of Fame. Mem.: Inst. Rep. Women, Caring Children Found. Tex. Inc. (co-chair), Am. Enterprise Forum (bd. trustees), C. of C., Texas Art Coun., Texas Cancer Coun., Cmty. Action League Lewisville. Republican. Methodist. Office: 1235 S Main St Ste 280 Grapevine TX 76051 also: PO Box 12068 Capitol Station Austin TX 78711 Office Phone: 512-463-0112, 817-424-3446.

NELSON, JANIE RISH, health facility administrator; b. Mar. 1, 1941; d. William Hubert and Essie Dell (Davis) Rish; m. John Preston Nelson, Aug. 19, 1984. Student, S.W. Miss. Jr. Coll., 1959—61, Stephens Coll., 1981—. Accredited record tech. Admissions clk. Field Hosp., Centreville, Miss., 1963—68, asst. dir. med. records, 1968—73; dir. med. records West Feliciana Parish Hosp., St. Francisville, La., 1976—2000; ret., 2000. Med. records cons. Beverly Enterprises & Centreville Health Care, 1983—84. Mem. U.S. Congl. Adv. Bd. for La., 1985; fund raiser Rep. Com., 1984; mem. nat. adv. bd. Am. Security Coun., 1984—85. Mem.: NAFE, Tumor Registration Assn. La., La. Med. Records Assn., Am. Med. Records Assn., Miss. Sheriffs Assn. (hon.), Civic Club. Republican. Presbyterian. Avocations: reading, public speaking, gardening. Home: PO Box 374 Centreville MS 39631-0374

NELSON, JASON, state legislator; m. Lori Nelson; children: Benjamin, Grace. Owner Pub. Rels. Firm, Wood Furniture Building, Repair, Restoration; legis. liaison to Gov. Frank Keating; mem. Dist. 87 Okla. House of Reps., 2008—. Republican. Baptist. Office: 2300 N Lincoln Blvd Rm 301 Oklahoma City OK 73105 also: PO Box 22371 Oklahoma City OK 73123 Office Phone: 405-557-7335. Business E-Mail: jason.nelson@okhouse.gov.

NELSON, LARRY A., statistics educator, consultant; b. Omaha, Oct. 28, 1932; s. Rudolph Lawrence and Elizabeth Coleman (Lewis) N. BS in Agronomy, Iowa State U., 1954; MS in Soil Sci., Tex. A&M U., 1958; PhD in Soil Sci.-Stats., N.C. State U., 1961. Soil scientist Iowa Agrl. Exptl. Sta., Ames, 1954-55; soils instr. Tex. A&I Coll., Kingsville, 1955; rsch. soil scientist Tex. A&M Rsch. Found., College Station, 1956; soils lab. instr. Tex. A&M U., College Station, 1956-58; rsch. asst. N.C. State U., Raleigh, 1959-61; asst. specialist in land classification Land Study Bur., U. Hawaii, Honolulu, 1961-64; asst. prof. exptl. stats. N.C. State U., Raleigh, 1964-66, assoc. prof. exptl. stats., 1966-71, prof. stats., 1971-89, prof. emeritus stats., 1989—, coord. Concade Project (Bolivia), 1999—2003, interim coord. internat. programs Coll. Agr. and Life Scis., 2002—03, asst. dean for internat. programs Coll. Agr. and Life Scis., 2003—07. Spl. advisor head dep. stats. Kasetsart U., Bangkok, Thailand, 1973; evaluator quantitative skills IADS, Bangladesh, 1984; mem. rev. team Ctr. for Agrl. Econs. and Ctr. for Data Processing, Winrock Internat., Indonesia, 1985; statis. cons. PROCAFE, El Salvador, 1993-96, ICRAF, Nairobi, Kenya, 1991-95; cons. Potash and Phosphate Inst. Can., China and India, 1990, 94, 96; ptnr. Statis. Rsch. Assocs., Honolulu, 1962-63; bd. dirs. Meadowlands Environ. Rsch. Inst., NJ, 2005-; lectr., tchr., cons. in field. Assoc. editor Geoderma, 1976-84, Agronomy Jour., 1981-87; contbr. numerous articles to profl. publs. Mem. bd. NC-Bolivia Ptnrs. of Ams., 2007—12, GDC Corp., 2007—12. NATO fellow Data Analysis Lab., Lyngby, Denmark, 1978. Fellow AAAS, Am. Statis. Assn. (mem. biometrics sect. com. 1989-90, mem. com. on internat. rels. in stats. 1996-98), Am. Soc. Agronomy, Soil Sci. Soc. Am.; mem. Statis. Assn. Thailand (life), Internat. Biometric Soc. (bus. mgr. and treas. 1969-79, awards com. 1987-94, chmn. 1990-93, com. on edn. 1997-99, Rob Kempton award 2008), Internat. Statis. Inst., Sigma Xi, Gamma Sigma Delta (internat. pres. 1984-86, award of merit 1973-74, rep. to AAAS 1978-86), Phi Kappa Phi, Sigma Iota Rho. Baptist. Avocations: music, genealogy, diving, bicycling, travel. Home: 2816 Wycliff Rd Raleigh NC 27607-3035 Office: NC State University Dept Statistics SAS Hall Raleigh NC 27695 Personal E-mail: lnelson44@nc.rr.com. Business E-Mail: larry_nelson@ncsu.edu.

NELSON, MARILYN CARLSON, energy executive; b. Mpls. m. Glen Nelson; children: Diana, Curtis C., Wendy. Student, U. Sorbonne, Paris, Inst. Hautes Etudes Econ., Geneva; BA in Internat. Econs. with honors, Smith Coll., 1961; D in Bus. Adminstrn., Johnson & Wales U.; DHL (hon.), Coll. St. Catherine, Gustavus Adolphus Coll. Securities analyst Paine Webber, Mpls.; pres., COO, vice chmn. & sr. v.p. Carlson Companies, Inc., Minnetonka, 1998—2003, CEO, 1998—2008, chmn., 2008—. Co-chair Carlson Holdings, Inc., 2000—; co-chair Carlson Wagonlit Travel, 1994-2003; disting. vis. prof. Johnson & Wales U.; bd. dirs. Exxon Mobil Corp., 1991-; Mayo Clinic Found., Com. to Encourage Corp. Philanthropy, Rezidor Hotel Group; chmn. Nat. Women's Bus. Coun., 2002-05; vice chair U.S. Travel and Tourism Adv. Bd.; bd. mem. Singapore Tourism Bur. Author: How We Lead Matters Reflections on A Life of Leadership, 2008. Pres. United Way Mpls., campaign chair, 1984; bd. dirs. United Way Am., 1984-90, U.S. Nat. Tourism Orgn., 1996-98, Ctr. for Internat. Leadership, 1989-2003; mem. disting. adv. coun. Coll. of St. Catherine, 1991-94; hon. bd. dirs. Svenska Inst., Stockholm, 1993—; mem. adv. bd. Hubert H. Humphrey Inst. Pub. Affairs, 1992-96; co-founder Minn. Women's Econ. Roundtable, 1974—; chair Minn. Super Bowl Task Force, 1984-92; chair, founder Midsummer Internat. Festival of Music, 1992; co-chair New Sweden '88; past bd. dirs. Guthrie Theatre, Greater Mpls. Girl Scout Coun., Jr. Achievement, Jr. League Mpls., KTCA Pub. TV, Minn. Econ. Assn., Minn. Congl. Award, Minn. Opera Co., Women's' Assn. Minn. Symphony Orch.; trustee Smith Coll., Northampton, Mass., 1980-85, Macalester Coll., St. Paul, 1974-80; mem. adv. bd. Minn. Women's Yearbook; trustee Curtis L. Carlson Family Found. Recipient Minn. Congl. award for initiative and svc. to cmty., Commendation cert., State of Minn., Cmty. Svc. award, YWCA, Independence award, Vinland Nat. Ctr., Cmty. Svc. award, Park-Nicollet Med. Ctr., Outstanding Mktg. Exec. of Yr. award, Minn. Distributive Edn. Club Am., Career Achievement award, Sales and Mktg. Execs. Mpls., Outstanding Achievement award, United Way Mpls., Extraordinary Leadership award, Greater Mpls. C. of C., Disting. Svc. award, United Way of Am., 1984—90, Nat. Caring award, Caring Inst., 1995, Outstanding Bus. Leader award, Northwood U., 1995, Disting. Svc. award (highest vol. honor), United Way Minn., 1998, Good Neighbor award, WCCO Radio, 1999, Caring Heart award, Larry King Cardiac Found., 1999, Svc. Above Self award, Rotary Club Downtown, Minn., 1999, Northwest Airlines Disting. World Traveler award, Hospitality Sales and Mktg. Assn. Internat., 2000, Responsible Capitalism award, FIRST mag., 2001, Glass Ceiling award, Minn. Women's Consortium, 2001, Great Swedish Heritage award, Swedish Coun. Am., 2002, Lifetime Achievement award, Internat. Investment Forum, 2002, Athena award, Athena Found., 2004, Lifetime Achievement award, Hospitality Sales and Mktg. Assn. Internat., 2004, 18th Ann. Lucia Travel award, 2005, Chevalier knight, French Legion Honor, 2006, Icon award, Nat. Bus. Travel Assn., 2006, Leadership award, Multicultural Devel. Ctr., 2006, Lifetime Achievement award, 2007; named Sales Exec. of Yr., Sales and Mktg. Exec. Mpls., Woman of Yr., Minn. Exec. Women in Tourism, 1991—92, Outstanding Individual in Tourism, Minn. Office Tourism, 1992, Woman of Yr., Roundtable Women in Food Svc., 1995, #1 Most Powerful Women in Travel, Travel Agent Mag., 1997—2003, Businesswoman of World, Bus. Women's Network, 2001, Swedish Am. of Yr., King and Queen of Sweden, 2003,

Minnesotan of Yr., Minn. Monthly mag., 2003, Businesswoman of Yr., US Commerce Dept. Small Bus. Adminstrn., 2005, Life Dir., Minn. Orchestra, 2006, Hall of Fame, Am. Soc. Travel Agents, 2007, Entrepreneur of Decade, Women Pres. Orgn., 2007, 100 Most Influential People in Bus. Ethics, Ethisphere Mag., 2007, Bus. Hall of Fame Layreate, 2008; named one of Exec. Yr. Corp. Report Minn., 1999, Forbes 400: Richest Americans, 2006—, Am.'s Best Leaders, US News and World Report, 2006, 100 Most Powerful Women, Forbes mag., 2007; named to Hall of Fame, Sales and Mktg. Execs. Mpls., 2003. Mem. World Econ. Forum, World Travel and Tourism Coun., Travel Industry Assn. Am. (bd. dirs.), Hennepin County Med. Soc. Aux., Bus. Roundtable, Smith Coll. Alumni Assn., Smith Club Mpls., Woodhill Country Club, Mpls. Club, N.W. Tennis Club, Nat. Ctr. Social Entrepreneurs, Com. of 200, Hospitality Sales and Mktg. Assn. Internat. (Lifetime Achievement award 2004), Minn. Orchestral Assn., Orphei Dranger, Alpha Kappa Psi. Office: Exxon Mobil Corp Bd Directors 5959 Las Colinas Blvd Irving TX 75039-2298 Office Fax: 972-444-1350. Business E-Mail: marilyn.c.nelson@exxonmobil.com.

NELSON, PAT, state legislator; Attended, Copiah-Lincoln CC, Wesson, Miss., Miss. State U., Tulane U., New Orleans. Ret. regional customer svc. mgr. Entergy Corp.; mem. Dist. 40 Miss. House of Reps., Jackson, 2012—. Republican. Office: Miss House of Reps PO Box 1018 Jackson MS 39215 Business E-Mail: pnelson@house.ms.gov.

NELSON, RALPH ERWIN, investment company executive; b. Chgo., July 30, 1946; s. Vernon Leslie and Astrid Lorene (Seagren) Nelson; m. Elarie Marie Fletcher, Oct. 14, 1967; 1 child, Anne Marie. BS, McPherson Coll., 1971; MBA, U. Sarasota, 1980, MFM, 1981, MHS, 1983; PhD, Columbia Pacific U., 1984. Chief planning dept. Roberts & Zoller Inc., Bradenton, Fla., 1971—76; v.p., supr. planning divsn. Dan Zoller Engring. Inc., Bradenton, 1976—78; pres. Ralph Nelson & Assocs., Inc.; pvt. practice Bradenton, 1978—88; with Nelson Investments, Inc., 1981—. Baptist. Address: PO Box 14777 Bradenton FL 34280-4777

NELSON, RALPH STANLEY, lawyer; b. Mpls., Mar. 15, 1943; s. Stanley L. and Louise M. Nelson; m. Judy E. Nelson, July 8, 1867; children: Sara C., Amy E., David A. BS in Bus. Adminstrn., U. Minn., 1966; JD with honors, Drake U., 1972. Bar: Minn. 1973, Wash. 1982, Tex. 1985, Ga. 2003. Assoc. Wiese and Cox, Ltd., Mpls., 1973-76; atty. Burlington No. R.R., St. Paul, 1976-81; sr. corp. counsel Burlington No. Inc., Seattle, 1981-85; v.p. law and adminstrn. Burlington Motor Carriers Inc., Ft. Worth, 1985-88, exec. v.p. and gen. counsel, 1988-93, sr. v.p., gen. counsel Daleville (Indpls.), Ind., 1993-96, Trism Inc., Kennesaw, Ga., 1996-2001, exec. v.p., gen. counsel, 2001—03; sr. v.p., gen. counsel Tango Transport Inc., Shreveport, La., 2003—. Mem. law rev. Drake U. Mem. Order of the Coif. Office: 6009 Financial Plz Shreveport LA 71129-2615 Office Phone: 318-683-6605. Personal E-mail: ralphnelso@yahoo.com.

NELSON, RICK, state legislator; b. June 11, 1954; Tchr. Bell County Sch. Sys.; mem. Dist. 87 Ky. House of Reps., 2001—. Mem.: Gideons Ky. Edn. Assn. Democrat. Baptist. Mailing: Rt 3 Box 686 Middlesboro KY 40965 Office: Capitol Annex Rm 358 702 Capitol Ave Frankfort KY 40601 Office Phone: 502-564-8100 ext. 612. Business E-Mail: rick.nelson@lrc.state.ky.us.

NELSON, S. JAMES, JR., oil industry executive; b. Minneapolis, Minn., Apr. 11, 1942; s. Stanley J. Nelson; children: Christian, Erik, Gretchen, Scott. BS in Acctg., Coll. Holy Cross, 1964; MBA, Harvard U., 1966. CPA. Former bd. dirs., v.p., CFO & vice chmn. Cal Dive International (now Helix Energy Solutions Group); mem. staff Arthur Andersen & Co., 1966-70, mgr., 1970-76, ptnr., 1976-80; v.p., CFO Apache Corp., 1980-85; sr. v.p., CFO Diversified Energies, Inc., 1985. Bd. dirs. ION Geophysical Corp. (formerly Input/Output, Inc.), W&T Offshore, Inc., Oil States Internat., Inc., 2004—. Trustee Ucross (Wyo.) Found., 1981—. Mem. Am. Inst. CPA's, Harvard Bus. Sch. Alumni Club (bd. dirs. Minn. chpt. 1980—). Home: 3016 Amherst St Houston TX 77005-3008 Office: Oil States International Inc Bd Directors 3 Allen Ctr 333 Clay St Ste 4620 Houston TX 77002 Office Phone: 713-652-0582. Office Fax: 713-652-0499. Business E-Mail: s.nelson@oilstatesintl.com.

NELSON, SCOTT REYNOLDS, historian, educator; b. Nyack, NY, Mar. 28, 1964; s. John Reynolds and Carole Brown Nelson; m. Cindy Hahamovitch, Dec. 28, 1985; children: Annie Nelson Hahamovitch children: Reynolds Nelson Hahamovitch. BA in History (highest honors and Magna Cum Laude), U. NC, Chapel Hill, 1987, MA & PhD in US History, 1995. Asst. prof. history Coll. of William and Mary, Williamsburg, Va., 1994—2001, assoc. prof. history, 2001—07, Leslie and Naomi Legum Prof. History, 2007—. Sr. network arch. Dylex Ltd, Toronto, Ont., Canada, 1993—94; vis. rsch. fellow agrarian studies Yale U., 1999—2000; mem. Mellon Advisory Bd. Project TORCH: The Online Resource Center in the Humanities, 2003—04; invited spkr. in field. Author: Iron Confederacies: Southern Railways, Klan Violence, and Reconstruction, 1999, Steel Drivin' Man: John Henry, the Untold Story of American Legend, 2006 (Merle Curti award: Best Book in US Social and Cultural History, Organization of American Historians, 2007, Anisfield-Wolf Literary Prize for Nonfiction, 2007, Nat. award for Arts Writing, 2007, Virginia Literary award for Nonfiction, 2007), A Nation of Deadbeats: An Uncommon History of America's Financial Disasters, 2012; co-author (with Carol Sheriff): A People at War: Civilians and Soldiers in America's Civil War, 2007; co-author: (with Marc Aronson) Ain't Nothing But A Man: My Quest to Find the Real John Henry, 2008 (Best of 2008 from Booklist, Publishers Weekly, Chicago Public Library, Aesop prize: Best Book in Folklore, American Folklore Soc., 2008, NCSS-NCB Notable Social Studies Trade Book for Young People, 2009, Notable Book & Best Book for Young Adults, American Library Assn., 2009, Children's Book in the Language Arts, Nat. Ctr. for Teachers of English, 2009, James Addams Prize, Women's Internat. League for Peace & Freedom, 2009); contbr. of several articles to profl. publications; assoc. editor Journal of the Gilded Age and Progressive Era, 2003—11, mem. editl. bd. Virginia Magazine of History & Biography, 2007—11, Labor: Studies of Working Class History of the Americans, 2007—. Named Disting. Lecturer, Organization of American Historians, 2008—11; George E. Mowry Dissertation Fellow, U. NC, 1994, Alternate American Coun. of Learned Societies Fellow, 2003, C. Ballard Breaux Vis. Fellow, Filson Historical Soc., Louisville, Kentucky, 2003, Commonwealth of Virginia Disting. Scholar, 2007—, Lloyd Lewis Fellow in American History, Newberry Library, 2009—10, Charles Warren Fellow, Harvard U., 2010—11. Mem.: Soc. for the History of the Gilded Age and Progressive Era (editl. bd. mem. 1998—2001), Labor and Working Class History Assn. (electronics communications chair 1998—2001), Phi Beta Kappa. Office: Department of History Blair 340 College of William & Mary Williamsburg VA 23187-8795 Home: 110 Hermitage Rd Williamsburg VA 23188-2530 Office Phone: 757-221-3720. Office Fax: 757-221-2111.

NELSON, STEVE, dean, pulmonologist, educator; b. NYC, Nov. 26, 1952; s. Ivar Stanley and Maggie Louise Nelson; m. Julie Anne Noone, July 14, 1984; children: David, Karen, Kevin. BS in Biology, SUNY at Stony Brook, 1974; MD, McGill U., 1978. Diplomate Nat. Bd. Med. Examiners, in internal medicine, pulmonary diseases and critical care medicine Am. Bd. Internal Medicine. Attending physician, med. intensive care unit Johns Hopkins Hosp., Balt., 1983—84; staff physician, div. pulmonary/critical care Univ. Hosp., New Orleans, 1984—, Charity Hosp. of New Orleans, 1984—; asst. prof., medicine La. State U. Med. Ctr., New Orleans, 1984—89; assoc. med. staff Tulane Med. Ctr., New Orleans, 1985—; asst. prof., physiology La. State U. Med. Ctr., New Orleans, 1988—89, dir., rsch. labs., div. pulmonary/critical care, 1988—, assoc. prof. physiology, 1989—94, assoc. prof., medicine, 1989—94, assoc. prof., sch. grad. studies, 1989—94, prof., sch. grad. studies, 1994—, prof., physiology, 1994—, prof. medicine, 1994—, John H. Seabury prof. of medicine, 1995—; clin. asst. prof., medicine and pediat. Sch. Medicine, Tulane U., New Orleans, 1985—89, clin. assoc. prof., medicine and pediat., 1989—94; dir., critical care units Univ. Hosp., New Orleans, 1990—96; staff physician, section of pulmonary/critical care medicine Ochsner Clinic and Hosp., New Orleans, 1994—; clin. prof., pediat. Sch. Medicine, Tulane U., New Orleans, 1994—; dir. Alcohol Rsch. Ctr. La. State U. Health Scis. Ctr., New Orleans, 2000—, sect. chief pulmonary/critical care medicine, 2005—, vice chair rsch. dept. medicine, 2005—, dean, 2007—. Author: Cytokines in Pulmonary Disease. Infection and Inflammation., 2000; contbr. articles to profl. jours. Scholar Univ., 1976-1978. Fellow: Am. Coll. Chest Physicians; mem.: AMA (Physician's Recognition award 1984), Am. Thoracic Soc. (program com. chmn. 1994—96), Phi Beta Kappa, Alpha Omega Alpha. Office: La State University Health Sciences Ctr School of Medicine 2020 Gravier St 5th Fl New Orleans LA 70112 Office Phone: 504-568-4007. Office Fax: 504-568-2189. Business E-Mail: snelso1@lsuhsc.edu.

NELSON, STUART OWEN, agricultural engineer, researcher, educator; b. Pilger, Nebr., Jan. 23, 1927; s. Irvin Andrew and Agnes Emilie (Nissen) N.; m. Carolyn Joye Fricke, Dec. 27, 1953 (dec. Nov. 1975); children: Richard Lynn, Jana Sue; m. Martha Ellen White Fuller, Apr. 8, 1979. BS in Agrl. Engring., U. Nebr., 1950, MS in Agrl. Engring., 1952, MA in Physics, 1954; PhD in Engring., Iowa State U., 1972; DSc (hon.), U. Nebr., 1989. Grad. asst. U. Nebr., Lincoln, 1952-54, rsch. assoc., 1954-60, assoc. prof., 1960-72, prof., 1972-76. Project leader Farm Electrification Rsch., Agrl. Rsch. Svc., USDA, Lincoln, 1954-59, rsch. investigations leader, 1959-72, rsch. leader 1972-76, rsch. agrl. engr. Russell Rsch. Ctr., Athens, Ga., 1976—2007, collaborator 2007-, adj. prof., U. Ga., 1976-; sci. adv. coun. Am. Seed Rsch. Found.; mem. CAST Task Force on Irradiation for Food Preservation and Pest Control; adv. com. grain moisture measurement Nat. Coun. Weights and Measures; mem. sci. bd. 4th Internat. Conf. on Phys. Properties Agrl. Materials, Prague, 1985. Assoc. editor Jour. Microwave Power 1975-76, 95-2000; contbr. more than 700 articles to sci. and tech. jours. Optimist internat. pres. lt. gov. Waste Water Treatment Adv. Com., Athens-Clarke County, Georgia. With USN, 1946—48. Recipient HM Crops and Soils award Am. Soc. Agronomy, 1966, Founders Gold medal Fed. Engr. of Yr. NSPE, 1985, Superior Svc. award USDA, 1986, Profl. Achievement Citation Engring. award Iowa State U., 1987, Ga. Engring. Found. medal of honor, 1999; named to U. Nebr. Biol. Systems Engring. Hall of Fame, 1999, USDA-ARS Sci. Hall of Fame, 2002. Fellow IEEE, Am. Soc. Agrl. Engrs. (Tech. Paper award 1965, 94, 2005, 06, 07, 12 Engr. of Yr. award Ga. sect. 1988, chmn. Ga. sect. 1988-89, Cyrus Hall McCormick-Jerome Increase Case Gold Medal award 2000), Internat. Microwave Power Inst. (Decade award 1981), AAAS; mem. The Electromagnetics Acad., Internat. Soc. Agromaterials Sci. and Engring., Internat. Dielectric Soc., Ga. Soc. Profl. Engrs. (Engr. of Yr. in Govt. award 1991, Engr. of Yr. 1998), Nat. Acad. Engring., Nat. Soc. Profl. Engrs., Orgn. Profl. Employees of Dept. of Agrl. (pres. Athens area chpt. 1984-86, nat. coun. rep. 1988-95, Profl. of Yr. award 1987), Athens Optimist (pres. 1980-81, 2000-2001, lt. gov. Ga. dist. 1983-84, Optimist of Yr. award 1982, disting. and outstanding lt. gov. Ga. dist. 1985), Assn. for Microwave Power in Europe for Rsch. and Edn., Sigma Xi, Sigma Tau, Gamma Sigma Delta, Tau Beta Pi. Methodist. Avocations: music, photography. Home: 270 Idylwood Dr Athens GA 30605-4635 Office: USDA Agrl Rsch Svc Russell Rsch Ctr 950 College Station Rd Athens GA 30604-5677

NELSON, THOMAS C., manufacturing executive; BS in Indsl. Engring., Stanford U., Calif., 1984; MBA, Harvard U., 1988. Formerly with Morgan Stanley & Co., NYC, San Francisco; spl. asst. to sec. of def. US Dept. Defense, 1992—93; exec. v.p., CFO National Gypsum Co., Charlotte, NC, 1995—99, vice chmn., 1996—99, pres., CEO, 1999—, chmn., 2005—; co-founder, gen. ptnr. Wakefield Group, Charlotte, 1998—2009. Bd. dirs. Belk, Inc., 2003—, Yum Brands, Inc., 2006—, A4 Health Systems, Inc. Bd. dirs. Found. Carolinas, United Way Ctrl. Carolinas, Bus. Roundtable, Blumenthal Performing Arts Ctr., Mecklenburg County Coun. Boy Scouts America. Office: Nat Gypsum Co 2001 Rexford Rd Charlotte NC 28211 Business E-Mail: tnelson@nationalgypsum.com.

NEMEC, MICHAEL LEE, lawyer; b. Tulsa, Aug. 1, 1949; s. Milton L. and Betty D. (Lawrence) N.; m. Vivian Strobel, Dec. 26, 1970; children: Adam, Jennifer, David. BA in Polit. Sci., U. Tulsa, 1971, JD, 1976. Bar: Okla. 1976. Pvt. practice law, Tulsa, 1976-78; dir. deferred giving Okla. State U. Found., Stillwater, 1978-80; asst. v.p., trust officer Bank Okla. N.A., Tulsa, 1980; v.p., trust officer Bank Commerce & Trust Co., Tulsa, 1980-85; pvt. practice law Tulsa, 1985-89; assoc. Hall, Estill, Hardwick, Gable, Golden & Nelson P.C., Tulsa, 1989-93, shareholder, 1993—. Fin. com. Monte Cassino Sch., Inc., Tulsa, 1987; vol. Boy Scouts Am., Tulsa, 1984—86, 1997—2001; mem. long-range planning com. U. Tulsa Coll. Law, 2005—08; mem. major gifts com. Am. Heart Assn., 1998—99; participant U.S. Naval Acad. Fgn. Affairs Conf., 1971. Recipient Outstanding Senior Alumnus, U. Tulsa Coll. Law, 2013; named Family of Yr., LDS Ch., Tulsa, 1985. Mem.: ABA, Tulsa Tax Forum (pres. 1994, 1995), Tulsa Estate Planning Forum (bd. dirs. 2000—03), Tulsa Title and Probate Lawyers (bd. dirs. 2001—, sec. 2003, v.p. 2004, pres. 2005), Tulsa County Bar Assn. (sec. tax sect. 1988, Golden Rule award 2006), Okla. Bar Assn., U. Tulsa Coll. Law Dean's Cir., U. Tulsa Coll. Law Alumni Assn. (bd. dirs. 2002—, sec. 2007, treasurer 2008, v.p. 2009, pres. elect. 2010, pres. 2011). Roman Catholic. Office: Hall Estill Hardwick Gable Golden & Nelson PC 320 S Boston Ave Ste 200 Tulsa OK 74103-3706

NEMEROFF, CHARLES BARNET, neurobiology and psychiatry educator; b. Bronx, NY, Sept. 7, 1949; s. Philip Peace and Sarah (Greenberg) N.; m. Melissa Ann Pilkington, May 24, 1980 (div.); children: Matthew P. (dec. 1997), Amanda P., Sarah-Frances P.; m. Gayle Applegate, June 11, 2001. BS, CCNY, 1970; MS, Northeastern U., 1973; PhD, U. N.C., 1976, MD, 1981. Diplomate Am. Bd. Psychiatry and Neurology; lic. physician, N.C., Ga. Rsch. asst. ichthyology Am. Mus. Natural History, NYC, 1968-71; neurochemistry lab. McLean Hosp., Belmont, Mass., 1971-72; rsch. assoc. surgery Beth Israel Hosp., Boston, 1972-73; tchg. asst. biology Northeastern U., 1972-73; postdoctoral fellow Biol. Scis. Rsch. Ctr., U. N.C., Chapell Hill, 1976-77, rsch. fellow, 1977-83, clin. instr. psychiatry, 1983; resident psychiatry N.C. Meml. Hosp., Chapel Hill, 1981-83; asst. prof. dept. psychiatry and pharmacology Duke U., Durham, NC, 1983-85, assoc. prof. psychiatry, 1985-89, assoc. prof. pharmacology, 1986-89, prof. depts. psychiatry and pharmacology, 1989-91, chief divsn. biol. psychiatry, 1988-91; prof., chmn. dept. psychiatry and behavioral scis. Emory U. Sch. Medicine, Atlanta, 1991—2008, Reunette W. Harris prof. psychiatry and behavioral scis., 1994—2009; leonard M. Miller prof. chmn. dept. psychiatry & behavioral scis. U. Miami, Fla., 2009—; dir. Ctr, Aging U. Miami, 2011—. Vis. prof. physiology Cath. U., Santiago, Chile, 1978; sci. coun. Nat. Alliance for Rsch. Schizophrenia and Depression, 1997—; mem. coun. NIMH, 1999-2002; mem. biomed. rsch. coun. NASA, 2000-03; bd. dirs. George West Mental Health Found., 1999—2009, Cypress Bioscis. Inc., 2001—05, NovaDel Pharma, 2005—. Editor: (with A.J. Prange Jr.) Neurotensin, a Brain and Gastrointestinal Peptide, 1982, (with A.J. Dunn) Peptides, Hormones and Behavior, 1984, (with P.T. Loosen) Handbook of Clinical Psychoneuroendocrinology, Neuropeptides in Psychiatric and Neurological Disorders, 1987, Neuropeptides in Psychiatric Disorders, 1991, Neuroendocrinology, 1992, (with P. Kitabgi) The Neurobiology of Neurotensin, 1992, (with A.F. Schatzberg) Textbook of Psychopharmacology, 1995, 4th edit., 2009, (with A. F. Schatzberg) Recognition and Treatment of Psychiatric Disorders, 1999, The Corsini Encyclopedia of Psychology and Behavioral Science, 3d edit., vols. 1-4, 2001, (with W.E. Craighead) concise edit. 2004, (with Dennis S. Charney) The Peace of Mind Prescription, 2004 (Ken award Nat. Alliance of The Mentally Ill), (with David Purselle and Arthur Jongsmia) The Psychopharmacology Treatment Planner, 2003, (with Jeffrey Kelsey and D. Jeffrey Newport) Principles of Psychopharmacology for Mental Health Professionals 2006; editor-in-chief: Depression, 1993-00, Psychopharmacology Bull., 2001-02, Neuropsychopharmacology, 2001-06; co-editor-in-chief: Critical Revs. in Neurobiology, 1992-01; contbr. chpts. to books and articles and abstracts to profl. jours. Recipient Michiko Kuno award U. N.C., 1978, 79, Merck award for acad. excellence, 1981, Merck award for young investigators Am. Geriatrics Soc., 1985, 2nd prize Anna Monica Found. for Rsch. in Endogenous Depression, 1987, Merit award NIMH, 1987, rsch. prize World Fedn. Socs. Biol. Psychiatry, 1991, Edward J. Sachar award Columbia U., 1993, Edward A. Strecker prize Instnl. Pa. Hosp., 1993, Outstanding Alumni award in health scis. Northeastern U., 1995, Disting. Alumni award U. NC Sch. Medicine, 1999, George Ham Alumni award dept. psychiatry U. NC, 2000, Charles Burlingame prize Inst. Living, 2002, Alumni award U. NC, 2006; grantee Nat. Inst. Aging, 1982-83, NIMH, 1983—, NIDA, 1996-98; predoctoral fellow Schizophrenia Rsch. Found., Soc. Scottish Rite, Lexington, Mass., 1975-76, postdoctoral fellow Nat. Inst. Neurol., Communicative Disorders and Stroke, 1977, Nanaline Duke fellow Duke U. Med. Ctr., 1985-87. Fellow Am. Coll. Neuropsychopharmacology (Mead Johnson Travel award 1982, Efron award 1987, coun. 1993—99, pres. 1997), Am. Coll. Psychiatrists (chmn. contbns. com. 1991-93, 95—, edn. com. 1993-96, 96—, bd. regents 1994-97, 1st v.p. 1999, pres.-elect 2000, pres. 2001, chair sci. program com. 2005-07, 2009, Mood Disorders Rsch. award 1998, Bowis award 1999, Dean award 2004); mem. AAAS, AMA, Soc. Neurosci. (program com. 1993-95), Internat. Soc. Psychoneuroendocrinology (pres. 1993-96, Curt P. Richter award 1985), Internat. Soc. Neuroendocrinology, Internat. Soc. Neurochemistry, Am. Soc. Neurochemistry (Jordi-Folch-Pi award 1987), Endocrine Soc., Soc. Neuroendocrinology, Soc. Biol. Psychiatry (A.E. Bennett award 1979, Gold medal award 1996), Am. Fedn. Clin. Rsch., Am. Pain Soc., Am. Psychiat. Assn. (coun. rsch. 1993-98, 02-04, chmn. 1994-95, bd. dirs. rsch. inst. 1999—2007, chair coun. rsch. subcom. on psychiat. treatments 1999-2003, chair, subcom. rsch. tng. 2006-, Kempf award 1989, Samuel Hibbs award 1991, Rsch. prize 1996, Judson Marmor award, 2008, Vestermark award 2006, Disting. Psychiatrist lectr. Ann. Meeting 1999, 2003, Rsch. Mentoring award 2008), Am. Coll. Physicians (William C. Menninger award 2000), Argentine Assn. Psychoneuroendocrinology (sci. coun.), Nat. Depressive and Manic Depressive Disorders Assn. (vice chair 1996-98, bd. dirs. 1999—2002, chair 1999-2000, Gerald L. Klerman Lifetime Achievement award 1997), Anxiety Disorder Assn. Am. (chmn. sci. adv. bd. 2001-2003), NY Acad. Scis., Am. Found. for Suicide Prevention (sci. adv. bd. 1997—, bd. dirs. 1998—, v.p. 2006, pres. Sci. Coun. 2007—, pres. 2008-,Rsch. prize 2001), Inst. Medicine, Sigma Xi, Alpha Omega Alpha. Democrat. Jewish. Office: University Miami Sch Medicine Dept Psychaitry & Behavioral Scis 1120 NW 14th St Miami FL 33136 Office Phone: 305-243-6400. Business E-Mail: cnemero@emory.edu, cnemero@med.miami.edu.

NEMES, MICHAEL J., state legislator; 4 children. Mem. Dist. 38 Ky. House of Reps., Frankfort, 2011—. Republican. Roman Catholic. Office: Kentucky House of Reps Annex Rm 413C 702 Capitol Ave Frankfort KY 40601 Office Phone: 502-564-8100 ext. 670. Business E-Mail: mike.nemes@lrc.ky.gov.

NEMHAUSER, GEORGE L., industrial engineer, systems engineer, educator, operations research specialist; b. NYC, July 27, 1937; s. Martin and Rose (Schwartz) N.; m. Ellen Krupsaw, Sept. 14, 1959; children: Wendy, Dennis. B.Chem.Engring., CCNY, 1958; MS, Northwestern U., 1959, PhD, 1961. Asst. prof. ops. rsch. and indsl. engring. Johns Hopkins U., Balt., 1961—69; prof. ops. rsch. and indsl. engring. Cornell U., Ithaca, NY, 1970—84, Leon C. Welch prof. engring., 1984-85, dir. Sch. Ops. Research and Indsl. Engring., 1977-83; A. Russell Chandler III chaired prof. indsl. and systems engring. Ga. Inst. Tech., 1985—, inst. prof., 1991—, co-dir. Logistics Engring. Ctr. Vis. prof. U. Leeds, U.K., 1963-64; vis. prof., dir. research Center for Ops. Research and Econometrics, U. Louvain, Belgium, 1975-77; cons. NSF, Nat. Inst. Standards and Tech., Nat. Rsch. Coun.; ptnr. Sports Scheduling Group 2000-; tech. adv. bd. CombineNet 2004-2012. Author: Introduction to Dynamic Programming, 1966, Integer Programming, 1972, Integer and Combinatorial Optimization, 1988; editor-in-chief: Ops. Research, 1975-78, Ops. Research Letters, 1981-2002; founding editor Operations Research Letters; editor of Handbooks of Operations Research and Management Science; contbr. articles to profl. jours. NSF sr. faculty fellow, 1969-70; recipient Engr. Alumnus of 1999, Northwestern U., Disting. Alumni award, Dept. Indsl. Engring., Northwestern U., 2007. Fellow INFORMS (pres. 1981-82, Lanchester prize 1977, 90, George E. Kimball medal 1988, von Neumann prize 2012), Soc. Indsl. and Applied Math.; mem. NAE (com. mem. 2013-), Math. Programming Soc. (chmn. 1989-1992), Ops. Rsch. Soc. of America (coun. mem., pres., editor Operations Research), Sports Scheduling Group. Home: 195 14th St NE Ste 7 Atlanta GA 30309-2682 Office: H Milton School of Industrial and Systems Engineering Georgia Inst Technology 765 Ferst Dr Atlanta GA 30332-0205 Office Phone: 404-894-2306. Office Fax: 404-894-2301. Business E-Mail: george.nemhauser@isye.gatech.edu.

NEMIROVSKI, ARKADI, mathematics professor; b. Moscow, Mar. 14, 1947; emigrated to Israel in 1993. married; 1 child. MSc in Math., Moscow State U., 1970, PhD in Math., 1974, soviet degrees in Physical & Math. Sci., 1990. Cert. Supreme Attestation Bd. Soviet Coun. Ministers. Faculty, indsl. engring. and mgmt. Technion Israel Inst. Tech., 1993—2005, chaired full professor, 1999—2005; John Hunter chair and prof., sch. indsl. and sys. engring. Ga. Inst. Tech., 2005—. Vis. prof., faculty of technical math. Technical U. of Delft, 1998; Stieltjes vis. professorship Stieltjes Inst., Netherlands, 2001; adj. professorship, dept. discrete and combinatorial optimization, faculty of math. U. Waterloo, 2000—04; vis. prof., sch. indsl. and sys. engring. Ga. Inst. Tech., 2003—05; presenter in field. 5 monographs, 94 papers in referred journals, several papers and book chapters in proceedings and collections; associated editor Mathematics of Operations Research. Co-recipient Fulkerson prize, Math. Programming Soc. and Am. Math. Soc., 1982, Dantzig prize, Math. Programming Soc. and Soc. for Indsl. and Applied Math., 1991, John von Neumann Theory prize, Inst. for Ops. Rsch. and the Mgmt. Sciences (INFORMS), 2003; Einstein Vis. Fellowship, Israel Acad. Sciences, 1992. Office: Ga Inst Tech Sch of Indsl and Sys Engring Groseclose 0205 Rm 446 765 Ferst Dr NW Atlanta GA 30332-0205 Office Phone: 404-385-0769. Office Fax: 404-894-2301.

NEREM, ROBERT MICHAEL, engineering educator, consultant; b. Chgo., July 20, 1937; s. Robert and Borghild Guneva (Bakken) Nerem; m. Jill Ann Thomson, Dec. 21, 1958 (div. 1977); children: Robert Steven, Nancy Ann; m. Marilyn Reed, Oct. 7, 1978; stepchildren: Christina Lynn Maser, Carol Marie Maser. BS, U. Okla., 1959; MS, Ohio State U., 1961, PhD in Aero. and Astronautical Engring., 1964; D (hon.), U. Paris, 1990, Imperial Coll. London, 2010, Ill. Inst. Tech., 2010. Asst. prof. Ohio State U., Columbus, 1964-68, assoc. prof., 1968-72, prof., 1972-79, assoc. dean Grad. Sch., 1975-79; prof. mech. engring., chmn. dept. U. Houston, 1979-86; Parker H. Petit prof. Ga. Inst. Tech., Atlanta, 1987—2010, Inst. prof., 1991—, dir. Parker H. Petit Inst. for Bioengring. and Biosci., 1995—2009; dir. Ga. Tech/Emory Ctr. pregenetive medicine NSF Engring. Rsch. Ctr., Atlanta, 1998—, inst. prof. emeritus, 2010—. Mem. Ga. Gov.'s Adv. Coun. on Sci. and Tech. Devel., Atlanta, 1992—95; Alza disting. lectr. Biomed. Engring. Soc., 1991; ASME Thurston lectr., 1994; mem. sci. bd. FDA, 2000—03; sr. adv. for bioengring. Nat. Inst. Biomed. Imaging and Bioengring., 2003—06. Contbr. articles to profl. jours. Fellow: AAAS, ASME, Instn. Mech. Engrs. UK (hon.), Am. Inst. Med. and Biol. Engring. (founding pres. 1992—94); mem.: NAE (Founders award 2008), Royal Swedish Acad. Engring. Scis., Polish Acad. Scis., US Nat. Com. on Biomechanics (chmn. 1988—91), Japanese Soc. for Med. & Biol. Engring. (hon.), Internat. Fedn. for Med. and Biol. Engring. (pres. 1988—91), Internat. Union for Phys. and Engring. Scis. in Medicine (pres. 1991—94), Inst. Medicine, Biomed. Engring. Soc., Am. Acad. Arts and Scis. Home: Park Springs 9435 Creekside Trail Stone Mountain GA 30087 Office Phone: 404-894-2768. Business E-Mail: robert.nerem@ibb.gatech.edu.

NERHOOD, ROBERT CLARKE, obstetrician, gynecologist; b. Altoona, Pa., Aug. 27, 1944; s. Albert and Jeanne (VanOrmer) N.; m. Carolyn Haught, Aug. 27, 1965; children: Robert, Timothy; m. Deborah Brooks, Nov. 30, 1984. Student, W.Va. U., 1962-65, MD, 1969. Diplomate Am. Bd. Ob-Gyn. Intern Polyclinic Hosp., Harrisburg, Pa., 1969-70; resident in ob-gyn. W.Va. Hosp., Morgantown, 1970-73, Kessler Air Force Med. Ctr., 1973-75; clin. assoc. prof. Sch. Medicine Marshall U., Huntington, 1977-87; dir. resident edn. Allegheny Gen. Hosp./Med. Coll. Pa.; assoc. prof. ob-gyn. Med. Coll. Pa., 1989-92; chief ob-gyn. Berkshire Health Sys.; assoc. prof. Med. Sch. U. Mass.; with Mass. Bd. Perinatal Medicine; chmn. bd. Cabell Huntington Hosp., 2002—; prof. chmn. ob-gyn. divsn. Sch. Medicine Marshall U., Huntington, W.Va., 1992—2010, emeritus faculty mem., 2010—, interim dean Joan C. Edwards Sch. Medicine, 2011—12. Mem. W.Va. Bd. Perinatal Medicine, 1977-87. Ob-gyn. editor Postgraduate Medicine, 1997—. Maj. USAF, 1973-75. Mem. Am. Coll. Ob-Gyn. (vice chair W.Va. sect. 1992-95, chair W.Va. sect. 1995-98, 2001-, mem. adv. coun. dist. IV 1992-98, 2001-). Office: Marshall University Joan C Edwards Sch Medicine 1600 Medical Center Dr Huntington WV 25701-3655 Office Phone: 304-691-1400. Office Fax: 304-691-1453.*

NESBIT, KELLY MCDADE, US marshal; b. 1961; BS in Polit. Sci., cum laude, U. NC, 1982. Dep. US marshal US Dept. Justice, 1983, various positions on increasing responsibility, then chief dep. US marshal (we. dist.) NC, 2006—10, US marshal (we. dist.) NC, 2010—. Office: US Marshal 401 W Trade St 401 W Trade St Ste 210 Charlotte NC 28202-1619 Office Phone: 704-344-6234.

NESBIT, ROBERT RAYMOND, JR., surgeon; b. New Haven, Apr. 1, 1939; BA, Harvard U., 1961; MD, U. Rochester, 1965. Diplomate Am. Bd. Surgery. Intern Strong Meml. Hosp., Rochester, 1965-66, resident in surgery, 1966-67, 69-74; chief vascular surgery Med. Coll. Ga. Hosps., Augusta, 1994-2000; prof. surgery Med. Coll. Ga., 1994-2000, prof. surgery emeritus, 2000—, dir. med. student edn. dept. surgery, 2002—. Fellow ACS; mem. Am. Assn. for Vascular Surgery, So. Surg. Assn., Assn. VA Surgeons, So. Assn. Vascular Surgery, Augusta-Richmond County Hist. Soc. (pres. 2003-05), Am. Osler Soc., Atlanta Vascular Soc., (pres. 2004-06), So. Assn. History Medicine and Sci. (pres. 2006-08, sec. treas., 2009-), Assn. Surg. Edn. (chair surgery clerkship dirs. com. 2006-08), Phi Beta Kappa, Alpha Omega Alpha. Office: Med Coll Ga Dept Surgery Augusta GA 30912 Home Phone: 706-733-8861; Office Phone: 706-721-1967. Business E-Mail: rnesbit@georgiahealth.edu.

NESBITT, DEETTE DUPREE, small business owner, investor; b. Houston, May 5, 1941; d. Raymond Benjamin DuPree and Alice Lula (Cade) Foster; children: Alice L., Charles S. Massey Nesbitt; m. Ernest V. Nesbitt, Aug. 20, 1971 (dec.). Student, Sam Houston State U., 1960-61, U. Houston, 1961-62, 81-83. Contbr. articles to various publs. Former trustee Pace Soc. Am., Inc., 1992-95, Inc.; bd. dirs. Evergreen Friends, Inc., 1991-92; dir., sec. competitive swim team Dad's Club YMCA, Houston, 1981-83; vol. adminstrv. asst. numerous orgns., Houston; patron Houston Jr. League, River Oaks Chamber Orchestra, Daus. of Republic Tex., San Jacinto Chpt., Life Mem., Daus. of Cin., NY, Life Mem. Recipient Varina Howell Davis medal Mil. Order Stars and Bars, 1992, Silver Good Citizenship medal SAR, 1992, Honor award Tex. SCV, 1992; featured on Eyes of Texas, NBC, 1992, Nat. Honor award Hereditary Soc. Cmty., 2003; Ky. Col., The Soc. First Families of SC 1670-1700 Mem.: Order of Crown Charlemagne USA (hon.), 100 Living Descs. Blood Royal (hon.), Pilgrims United States (NYC) (life), HSC Adv. Coun. (life; cons. 2007—09), Hereditary Soc. (cmty. cons. 2006—), Harris County Hist. Commn., Freedoms Found. Valley Forge (George Washington Honor medal 1994), United Daus. Confederacy (Confederate Ball com. 1985—95, co-chmn. ball 1988, adv. to chmn. 1989, 1990, hon. chmn. Houston's confederate ball 1995, So. Heritage Ball com. 2005—, Charleston chpt. #4, Jefferson Davis Hist. award, Winnie Davis medal, Spl. Recognition award), Daus. Rep. Tex. (Appreciation award 1996), Huguenot Soc. Am., S.C. Soc. Descs. of Colonial Clergy, Nat. Soc. Magna Charta Dames (Houston colony historian 1992—95), Plantagenet Soc., Am. Royal Descent, Nat. Jamestown Soc. (mem. coun. 1993—95, auditor gen. 1995—97, lt. gov. gen. 1997—98, gov. gen. 1998—2000, Resolution of Appreciation, Outstanding Leadership 2000), First Tex. Co. Jamestowne Soc. (lt. gov., gov. 1985—93, hon. gov. emerita), Nat. Gavel Soc., Dames of Colonial Cavaliers 1640-1660 (organizing dep. gov. gen. 2001—03, gov. gen. 2003—05, life hon. gov. gen. emerita), Soc. First Families of S.C. 1670-1700 (life; sec. 2003—05, 3rd v.p. 2005—07, pres. gen. 2007—09), Order of First Families of Va. 1607-1624 (life; mem. coun. 2001—, rec. sec. 2005—), Order of First Families of Miss. 1699-1817 (life), Nat. Soc. DAR, Colonial Dames Am. (pres. chpt. VIII 1995—97), Sons and Daus. of Pilgrims (nat. com. 1993—97), Nat. Soc. Sons and Daus. Antebellum Planters 1607-1861, Nat. Soc. Colonial Dames Am. in Commonwealth of Va., Galveston Yacht Club, Petroleum Club Houston, Order Descendants Colonial Cavaliers (life; organizing gov. gen. and hon. gov. gen. 2007). Republican. Episcopalian. Home: 15411 Old Stone Trail Houston TX 77079-4206

NESLER, FRED, state legislator; b. Aug. 2, 1944; Realtor Chapman-Nesler Real Estate; state rep. Dist. 2 Ky., 1993—; mem. Agr. & Natural Resources & Appropriations & Revenue Com. Named Realtor of Yr., 1978. Mem.: Mayfield-Graves County C. of C. & Bd. Realtors, Mayfield Rotary Club. Democrat. Baptist. Office: Capitol Annex Rm 316D Frankfort KY 40601 Address: PO Box 308 Mayfield KY 42066-0029 Home Phone: 270-247-8557; Office Phone: 270-623-6184, 502-564-8100 ext. 638. E-mail: fred.nesler@lrc.ky.gov.

NESNOW, STEPHEN C., research scientist; BS in Chemistry, Bucknell U., Lewisburg, Pa., 1963; MS in Chemistry, NYU, 1968, PhD in Organic Chemistry, 1968. Postdoc. fellow Sloan Kettering Inst. Cancer Rsch., NYC, 1968—70, McArdle Inst. Cancer Rsch., Madison, Wis., 1970—74; asst. scientist U. Wis., Dept. Human Oncology, Madison, 1974—77; chief, Biochemistry and Pathobiology Br. US EPA, Rsch. Triangle Park, NC, 1977—99, sr. rsch. scientist, 1999—; asst. prof. U. NC, Dept. Pathology, Chapel Hill, 1977, adj. prof., 1999—. Author sci. papers to profl. jours. Recipient Bronze medal, US EPA, 1980, 2007. Office: US Environmental Agency 109 TW Alexander Dr Durham NC 27711 Personal E-mail: snesnow@pobox.com. Business E-Mail: nesnow.stephen@epa.gov.

NESPOLI, PAOLO ANGELO, astronaut; b. Milan, Apr. 6, 1957; s. Luigi and Maria Nespoli. BS in Aerospace Engring., Poly. U. N.Y., 1988, MS in Aeronautics and Astronautics, 1989; laurea in ingegneria meccanica, U. degli Studi di Firenze, Italy, 1990. Registered profl. engr.; lic. pvt. pilot, advanced scuba diver, NitrOx diver, master parachutist, cert. parachutist instr., jump master, demolition expert. Non-commd. officer, parachute instr. Scuola Militare de Paracudutismo, Pisa, Italy, 1977—80; spl. forces operator 9° Btg d'Assalto "Col Moschin", Livorno, Italy; mem. multinat. peacekeeping force Italian Army, Beirut, 1982—84, ret., 1987; design engr. Proel Tecnologie, Florence, Italy, 1989—91; mem. astronaut tng. divsn., European Astronaut Ctr. European Space Agy., Cologne, Germany, 1991—98; mem. EUROMIR project European Space Tech. Ctr., Noordwijk, Netherlands, 1995—96; mem. spaceflight tng. divsn. NASA, Johnson Space Ctr., Houston, 1996—98; astronaut Italian Space Agy., 1998; joined European Space Agy. European astronaut corps European Astronaut Ctr., Colonge, Germany, 1998; astronaut, mission specialist candidate NASA, Johnson Space Ctr., Houston, 1998—. Temporary assignment Gagarin Cosmonaut Tng. Ctr., Star City, Russia, 2004; mission specialist STS-120 to Internat. Space Station, 2006; mission specialist, European Space Agy. astronaut STS-120 Discovery Mission to Internat. Space Station, 2007; flight engr. Expedition 26-Soyuz TMA-20, 2010. Avocations: scuba diving, aircraft piloting, assembling computer hardware and electronic equipment, computer software. Office: Astronaut Office NASA Johnson Space Ctr Houston TX 77058

NESS, NORMAN FREDERICK, retired astrophysicist, educator, administrator; b. Springfield, Mass., Apr. 15, 1933; s. Herman and Eva N.; children: Elizabeth Ann, Stephen Andrew. BS, Mass. Inst. Tech., 1955, PhD, 1959. Space physicist, asst. prof. geophysics UCLA, 1959-61; NAS-NRC postdoctoral rsch. assoc. NASA, 1960-61; rsch. physicist in space scis. Goddard Space Flight Center, Greenbelt, Md., 1961-86, head extraterrestrial physics br., 1968-69, chief Lab. for Extraterrestrial Physics, 1969-86; pres. Bartol Rsch. Inst. U. Del., Newark, 1987—2000, prof. Bartol Rsch. Inst., 1987—2005, prof. emeritus, 2005—; dir. NASA Space Grant Coll. Consortium, Del., 1991—2005. Lectr. math. U. Md., 1962-64, assoc. rsch. prof., 1965-67; vis. prof. U. Rome, 1968-69; liasion scientist US Office Naval Rsch., London, 1984-85. Contbr. articles profl. jours. Recipient Exceptional Sci. Achievement award NASA, 1966, 81, 86, Arthur S. Flemming award, 1968, Space Sci. award AIAA, 1971, Disting. Svc. medal NASA, 1986, Nat. Space Club Sci. award, 1993, Emil Wiechert medal German Geophys. Soc., 1993, Space Sci. award COSPAR, 1996. Fellow Am. Geophys. Union (John Adam Fleming award 1965); mem. US-NAS, Acad. Nat. dei Lincei. Achievements include research in publications reporting on experimental studies of interplanetary and planetary magnetic fields by satellites and space probes. Personal E-mail: nfnudel@yahoo.com. Business E-Mail: nfness@udel.edu.

NESTLER, JOHN EDWIN, endocrinology educator; b. Passaic, NJ, Sept. 24, 1952; m. Michelle Dumont, Dec. 29, 1990. BA in Chemistry (with honors) and German, Haverford Coll., Pa., 1975; MD, U. Pa., Phila., 1979. Diplomate Am. Bd. Internal Medicine, Am. Bd. Endocrinology and Metabolism; cert. Nat. Bd. Med. Examiners. Intern Med. Coll. Va., Richmond, 1979-80, resident, 1980-82, chief med. resident, instr. in medicine, 1982-83, fellow in endocrinology, 1985-86, asst. prof. medicine, 1986-91, assoc. prof. medicine, 1991—, dir. med. affairs, BioClin, 1991-95, prof. medicine, 1995—, chmn. divsn. endocrinology and metabolism, 1997—, vice chmn. dept. internal medicine, 2003—; fellow in endocrinology U. Pa., Phila., 1983-85. Reviewer various profl. jours.; vis. prof. Dalhousie U., Halifax, N.S., 1991; invited speaker several major confs. including NIH/NICHD Conf. on Polycystic Ovary Syndrome, Bethesda, Md., 1990. Author numerous original publs., book chpts., abstracts. Recipient Sandra Tate Russell Meml. Rsch. award Am. Diabetes Assn. Va. affiliate, 1986, Clin. Assoc. Physician award NIH, 1985-87, rsch. trainee awards Phila. Endocrine Soc., 1984, 85. Fellow Am. Coll. Physicians; mem. AAAS, Internat. Diabetes Found., European Assn. for Study of Diabetes, Cen Va. Assn. Diabetes Educators, Am. Assn. Diabetes Educators, Am. Diabetes Assn. (pres. 1990—), Am. Fedn. Clin. Rsch., Internat. Soc. for Androgenic Disorders, The Endocrine Soc., So. Soc. for Clin. Investigation. Achievements include research on diabetes, polycystic ovary syndrome, steroids, and insulin. Home: 5800 Three Chopt Rd Richmond VA 23226-2337 Office: Med Coll Va Div Endocrinology PO Box 980111 Richmond VA 23298-0111 Office Phone: 804-828-9696. Business E-Mail: jnestler@mcvh-vcu.edu.

NESTOR, DANIEL MARK, professional tennis player; b. Belgrade, Yugoslavia, Sept. 4, 1972; m. Natasha Nestor, July 24, 2005. Profl. tennis player ATP, 1991—. Mem. Canadian nat. tennis team Summer Olympic Games, Sydney, 2000. Founder Daniel Nestor Celebrtiy Charity event. Recipient Gold medal, men's doubles, Summer Olympic Games, 2000; named ATP Doubles Team of Yr. (w/Knowles), 2002, 2004. Achievements include winning 80 career doubles titles, ATP; winner Grand Slam doubles championships: Australian Open, 2002; US Open, 2004; French Open, 2007, 2010-12; Wimbledon, 2008, 2009; winner Grand Slam mixed doubles championships: Australian Open, 2007, 2011; Wimbledon, 2013. Avocations: football, hockey. Office: ATP Americas 201 ATP Tour Blvd Ponte Vedra Beach FL 32082*

NETHERLAND, JOSEPH H., energy executive; BS in Indsl. Engring., Ga. Inst. Tech.; MBA, U. Pa. Bus. planner, machinery group FMC Technologies, Inc., 1973—78, ops. mgr., ordnance divsn., 1978—83, mgr., fluid control divsn., 1983—84, mgr., wellhead divsn., 1984—85, gen mgr., wellhead divsn., 1985—89, gen. mgr., specialized machinery group, 1989—99, pres., CEO, 2001—06, chmn., 2001—08. Bd. dirs. Am. Petroleum Inst. Mem. adv. bd. Dept. Engring. Tex. A&M Univ.; mem. Pres. Council Ga. Inst. Tech. Recipient Don E. Waggener Butch Griffin award, Spindletop Internat., 2002. Office: Newfield Exploration Co 363 N Sam Houston Pky E Ste 2020 Houston TX 77060 Office Phone: 281-847-6000. Office Fax: 281-405-4242. Business E-Mail: jnetherland@newfield.com.

NETTELS, ELSA, English language educator; b. Madison, Wis., May 25, 1931; d. Curtis Putnam and Elsie (Patterson) Nettels. BA, Cornell U., 1953; MA, U. Wis., 1955, PhD, 1960. From instr. to asst. prof. English Mt. Holyoke Coll., South Hadley, Mass., 1959—67; from asst. prof. to prof. English Coll. William and Mary, Williamsburg, Va., 1967—97, prof. emeritus, 1997—. Author: James and Conrad, 1977 (South Atlantic MLA award, 1975), Language, Race and Social Class in Howells' America, 1988, Language and Gender in American Fiction: Howells, James, Wharton, and Cather, 1997; contbr. articles to profl. jours. Fellow, NEH, 1984—85. Mem.: MLA, South Atlantic MLA (mem. editl. bdl. 1977—83), Henry James Soc. (mem. editl. bd. 1983—2013). Home: 3002 Tanglewood Cove Williamsburg VA 23185

NETTLES, WILLIAM N. (BILL NETTLES), federal prosecutor; b. Sumter, SC, 1961; BA, The Citadel Mil. Coll., Charleston, SC, 1992; JD, Widener U. Sch. Law, Harrisburg, Pa., 1995. With sales dept. AC Elfman Constrn., Doylestown, Pa., 1983—84; owner RGH-Group Mfg. Co., Forest Grove, Pa., 1984—90; sales positions Napco Pipe, Worcester, Mass., 1989—90; law clk. Chesapeake Bay Found., Harrisburg, 1990—91, Mellon, Webster & Shelley, Doylestown, 1991—92; atty. Richland County Pub. Defender Office, Columbia, SC, 1992—95; ptnr. Banks & Nettles, LLC, Camden, SC, 1995—97; pvt. practice atty. Columbia, 1997—2005; ptnr. Sanders & Nettles, LLC, Columbia, 2005—10; US atty. Dist. SC US Dept. Justice, 2010—. Head sailing instr. Corinthian Yacht Club, Cape May, NJ, 1990. Democrat. Office: US Courthouse 1441 Main St Ste 500 Columbia SC 29201 also: US Courthouse 151 Meeting St Ste 200 Charleston SC 29401*

NEU, CHARLES ERIC, historian, educator; b. Carroll, Iowa, Apr. 10, 1936; s. Arthur Nicholas and Martha Margaret (Frandsen) N.; m. Deborah Dunning, Sept. 2, 1961 (div. 1978); children: Hilary Adams, Douglas Bancroft.; m. Sabina deWerth Tuck, Mar. 27, 1999. BA, Northwestern U., 1958; PhD, Harvard U., 1964. Instr. history Rice U., 1963-64, asst. prof., 1964-67, asso. prof., 1968-70; asso. prof. history Brown U., Providence, 1970-76, prof., 1976—2003, prof. emeritus, 2003—, chmn. dept. history, 1995—98, 1999—2002. Dir. summer seminar NEH, 1979, 1986—87, 1989, 1992, 2005; adj. prof. history U. Miami, 2004—. Author: An Uncertain Friendship: Theodore Roosevelt and Japan, 1906-1909, 1967, The Troubled Encounter: The United States and Japan, 1975, America's Lost War: Vietnam, 1945-1975, 2005; co-editor: The Wilson Era: Essays in Honor of Arthur S. Link, 1991, Artists of Power: Theodore Roosevelt, Woodrow Wilson, and Their Enduring Impact on U.S. Foreign Policy, 2006; editor: After Vietnam: Legacies of a Lost War, 2000. Adv. coun. Vietnam Ctr. Tex. Tech. U.; adv. bd. mem. Theodore Roosevelt Assn., 2008—. Recipient, Woodrow Wilson Found. fellowship, 1958—59, Am. Coun. Learned Socs. fellowship, 1975—76, Charles Warren Ctr. fellowship, 1971—72, Howard Found. fellowship, 1976—77, Guggenheim fellowship, 1981—82, Barrett Hazeltine citation for disting. undergrad. tchg., 1998; fellow, NEH, 1968—69; guest scholar, Woodrow Wilson Ctr., 1988, Pub. Policy scholar, 2007. Mem. Am. Hist. Assn., Orgn. Am. Historians, Soc. Historians of Am. Fgn. Policy, Phi Beta Kappa. Democrat. Home: 4929 SW 71st Place Miami FL 33155 Home Phone: 305-668-7978. Personal E-mail: cneu@bellsouth.net.

NEUGEBAUER, RANDY (ROBERT RANDOLPH NEUGEBAUER), United States Representative from Texas; b. St. Louis, Dec. 24, 1949; m. Dana Collins; 2 children. BBA in Acctg., Tex. Tech U., Lubbock, 1972. Mgr. Sentry Property Mgmt., Lubbock, 1972—75; v.p. First Nat. Bank, Lubbock, 1975—82; pres. Prestige Homes, Lubbock, 1983—87; pres., CEO Lubbock Land Co., 1987—2003; mem. US Congress from 19th Tex. dist., 2003—. Instr. South Plains Coll., Lubbock, 1975—78; councilman Lubbock City Coun., 1992—98, mayor pro tempore, 1994—96; chair Ports-to-Plains Trade Coalition, 1996—2003. Mem.: West Tex. Home Builders Assn. (pres. 1990). Republican. Baptist. Office: US House of Representatives 1424 Longworth House Office Bldg Washington DC 20515 also: 611 University Ave Ste 220 Lubbock TX 79401 Office Phone: 202-225-4005.*

NEUMAN, SUSAN CATHERINE, public relations and marketing consultant; b. Detroit, Jan. 29, 1942; d. Paul Edmund and Elsie (Goetz) N. AB, U. Miami, Fla., 1964; MBA, Barry U., Miami Shores, Fla., 1985. Journalist, writer The Miami Herald, 1962-65; editor Miamian Mag., 1965-69; pres. Susan Neuman Inc., Miami, 1969—; ptnr. Neuman Enterprises Unltd., 1994—. Mem. Fla. Gov.'s Pub. Rels. Adv. Coun., 1978-86. Mem. Pub. Rels. Soc. Am. (accredited, past officer, bd. dirs.), Miami C. of C., Counselors Acad., Miami City Club (founder, bd. govs.), Miami Internat. Press Club (charter, founder, pres. 1985-86), Com. of One Hundred (bd. dirs., sec.). Democrat. Roman Catholic. Home: 13540 NE Miami Ct Miami FL 33161-2739 Office: Susan Neuman Inc Venetia 25th Fl 555 NE 15th St Ste 25K Miami FL 33132-1404 Office Phone: 305-372-9966. E-mail: susan@miamipr.net.

NEUMANN, DAVID A., investment company executive, former councilman; m. Frances Neumann; children: Ivy, Corbin. BS in Bus., Ind. U., Bloomington, 1982. Co-founder, pres., CEO Ivy Jane, Dallas, 1989—; banking officer InterFirst Bank Dallas, 1982—84; v.p., gen. mgr. Fidelity Investments, 1984—89; pres., CEO F.L. Malik, Inc., 1989—2011; pres. gen. partnership IJN CJN Investments, Ltd., 1998—; councilman Dist. 3 Dallas City Coun., 2007—11, chmn. fin., audit & accountability com., legis. com., pub. safety com., quality of life & govt. svcs. com. Chmn. Dallas Zoning Ordinance Adv. Com., Stemmons Corridor Bus. Assn., Dallas, North Oak Cliff Weed & Seed Initiative; v.p. bd. gov.'s Dallas Apparel Mart; trustee Dallas Police and Fire Pension Sys., 2008—11. Treas. Kessler Neighbors United; active Kessler Park United Meth. Ch.; bd. dirs. Trinity Commons Found., Dallas, Greater Dallas Planning Coun., Dallas Friday Group. Mem.: Dallas Apparel Mfr.'s Assn. (past treas.), Oak Cliff C. of C. (bd. dirs.), Oak Cliff Lions Club. Office: PO Box 1139 Mont Belvieu TX 77580 Office Phone: 214-670-0776. Office Fax: 214-670-5115.

NEUMANN, HENRY W., JR., energy executive; B in Acctg. and Bus. Adminstrn., Ill. State U., Normal. Joined Kinder Morgan, Inc., Houston, 1976; various positions in acctg. and info. tech. Kinder Morgan, v.p. sys. devel., v.p., chief info. officer. Office: Kinder Morgan 500 Dallas St Ste 1000 Houston TX 77002 Office Phone: 713-369-9000.

NEVAREZ, MIGUEL A., academic administrator; Pres. U. Tex.-Pan Am., Edinburg, 1981—. Office: U Tex-Pan Am 1201 W University Dr Edinburg TX 78539-2909 E-mail: info@panam.edu.

NEVERS, BEN W., state legislator; Former mem. Wash. Parish Sch. Bd.; mem. Dist. 75 La. House of Reps., 1999—2003; mem. Dist. 12 La. State Sente, 2003—, chair edn. com., mem. agr., forestry, aquaculture and rural devel. com., health and welfare com., retirement com.; marine store operator. Democrat. Mailing: 61596 Little Southern Village Rd Bogalusa LA 70427 Address: 724 Avenue F Bogalusa LA 70427 Home Phone: 504-732-4062. E-mail: neversb@legis.state.la.us.

NEVILL, WILLIAM ALBERT, retired chemistry professor; b. Indpls., Jan. 1, 1929; s. Irwin Lowell and Mary Marie (Barker) N.; m. Nancy Neiman (Roll), May 19, 1979; children: Paul David, John Michael, Steven Joseph, Anne Marie, Deborah Ruth. BS, Butler U., 1951; PhD, Calif. Inst. of Tech., 1954. Rsch. chemist Procter and Gamble, Cin., 1954; chemistry prof., chmn. dept. Grinnell Coll., 1956-67; prof. chemistry Ind. U., Purdue, Indpls., 1967-83, chmn. dept., 1967-72, dean sch. sci., 1972-79, dir. grad. studies, 1979-83; pres. B and N Cons. Co., 1972-93; vice chancellor acad. affairs La. State U., Shreveport, La., 1983-85, prof., 1983-94; pres. Catoctin Assoc., 1993—. Arbitrator, mediator, Ind. Employment Rels. Bd., 1975-83. Author: Gen. Chemistry, 1967, Expt. in Gen. Chemistry, 1968. Bd. dir. Indpls. Sci. and Engring. Found., 1972-75, 79-82, Westminster Found., Lafayette, Ind., 1972-74, Am. Chem. Soc., 1986-92. With U.S. Army, 1954-56; col., USAR, 1956-84. Grantee NSF, 1959-74; Grantee NIH, 1963-70; Grantee Office Naval Rsch., 1953 Mem. Ind. Acad. Sci., Am. Chem. Soc., chmn. sect. 1972, counselor 1973-92. Presbyterian.

NEVIN, HUGH WILLIAMSON, JR., lawyer; b. Sewickley, Pa., Dec. 9, 1946; s. Hugh Williamson and Eleanore (George) N.; m. Eliza Scott Nevin, June 16, 1972; 1 child, John Irwin. BA, Harvard U., 1968, JD, 1974. Bar: Pa. 1975, U.S. Dist. Ct. (We. Dist.) Pa. 1975. Pres., CEO, chmn. internat. bus. group Cohen & Grigsby, Pitts., 1986—2001, Bonita Springs, Fla., 2001—, Naples, Fla., 2004—. With U.S. Army, 1968-70. Mem. Phi Beta Kappa. Presbyterian. Office: Cohen & Grigsby 27200 Riverview Center Blvd Bonita Springs FL 34134 Office Phone: 239-390-1900. Business E-Mail: hnevin@cohenlaw.com.

NEVINS, JOHN JOSEPH, bishop emeritus; b. New Rochelle, NY, Jan. 19, 1932; Student, Iona Coll., NYC, Cath. U. Washington; MA, Tulane U., 1969. Ordained priest Archdiocese of Miami, Fla., 1959; ordained bishop, 1979; aux. bishop Archdiocese of Miami, 1979—84; first bishop Diocese of Venice, 1984—2007, bishop emeritus, 2007—. Roman Catholic. Office: 1000 Pinebrook Rd PO Box 2006 Venice FL 34292 Office Phone: 941-484-9543. Office Fax: 941-486-4761. E-mail: mcgrath@dioceseofvenice.org.

NEVOLA, ROGER, lawyer; b. NYC, Apr. 30, 1947; m. Molly Cagle; children: Adrienne L., Jake F. Student, U. Notre Dame, 1964-66; BSME, Stanford U., 1968; JD, U. Tex., 1974. Bar: Tex. 1974. Assoc. Vinson & Elkins, Houston, 1974-79, Austin, 1979-81, ptnr., 1981-95; pvt. practice Austin, 1995—. Fellow Tex. Bar Found. (life). Home: 4304 Bennedict Ln Austin TX 78746-1940 Office: 1723 Palma Plz PO Box 2103 Austin TX 78768-2103 Office Phone: 512-499-0500. E-mail: roger@nevola.com.

NEW, WILLIAM, JR., engineer, physician, investor; BS, Stanfor U., MS in Elec. Engring., 1966; PhD in Physiology, UCLA, 1971; MD, Duke U., 1972; MS in Mgmt., Stanford U., 1981. Clin. assoc. prof. Dept. Anesthesia Stanford U. Sch. Medicine, 1975—2000; co-founder, chmn. Nellcor Corp., Hayward, Calif., 1981—88; pres., CEO, chmn. The Novent Group, Palo Alto, Calif., 1988—; pres., chmn., chief tech. officer Natus Med., Inc., San Carolos, Calif., 1989—2004; co-founder, chmn., chief mktg. officer Adigy Corp., Durham, NC, 2005—. Venture ptnr. Aurora Funds, Inc.; assoc. dean bioengineering Oreg. Grad. Inst., Oreg. Health & Scis. U. Chmn. bd. visitors Duke U. Med. Ctr., 1994—98. Kaiser Found. Fellow, 1980—81. Mem.: Nat. Acad. Engring. Office: Adigy Corporation 3412 Olney Dr Durham NC 27705 Office Phone: 650-328-4000.

NEWBERN, WILLIAM DAVID, retired state supreme court justice; b. Oklahoma City, May 28, 1937; s. Charles Banks and Mary Frances (Harding) N.; m. Barbara Lee Rigsby, Aug. 19, 1961 (div. 1968); 1 child, Laura Harding; m. Carolyn Lewis, July 30, 1970; 1 child, Alistair Elizabeth. BA, U. Ark., 1959, JD, 1961; LL.M., George Washington U., 1963; MA, Tufts U., 1967; degree, Fletcher Sch. Law & Diplomacy. Bar: Ark. 1961, U.S. Dist. Ct. (we. dist.) Ark. 1961, U.S. Supreme Ct. 1968, U.S. Ct. Appeals (8th cir.) 1983. Commd. 1st lt. advanced to maj. U.S. Army JAGC, 1961-70; Prof. law U. Ark., Fayetteville, 1970-84; adminstr. Ozark Folk Ctr., Mountain View, Ark., 1973; judge Ark. Ct. Appeals, Little Rock, 1979-80; assoc. justice Ark. Supreme Ct., Little Rock, 1985-99; commr. Ark. Pub. Svc. Commn., 2008. Mem. faculty sr. appellate judges seminar NYU, 1987-91; panel chmn. com. on profl. conduct Ark. Supreme Ct., 2001—05. Editor Ark. Law Rev., 1961; author: Arkansas Civil Practice and Procedure, 1985, (with John J. Watkins) 4th edit., 2006, (with John J. Watkins and Denzil Price, Marshar II)5th edit., 2010. Mem. Fayetteville Bd. Adjustment, 1972-79; bd. dirs. Decision Point, Inc., Springdale, Ark., 1980-85, Hot Springs Music Festival, 2000—03, Little Rock Wind Symphony, 1993-2001, pres. 1993-95. Named a Disting. Alumnus, Fulbright Coll. Arts and Scis., U. Ark., 2004. Fellow Ark. Bar Found.; mem. Ark. Bar Assn., Am. Judicature Soc. (bd. dirs. 1985-89), Inst. Jud. Adminstrn., Ark. IOLTA Found. (bd. dirs. 1985-87). Democrat. Avocations: string band-guitar, mandolin, banjo and brass band quintet-tuba. Personal E-mail: wdnewben@sbcglobal.net.

NEWBERRY, DAN, state legislator; b. Nov. 22, 1975; m. Laura Newberry; children: Claire, Paige, Eva. Pres.,CEO mortgage bus.; mem. Dist. 37 Okla. State Senate, 2008—. Youth pastor Victory Christian Ctr. Republican. Christian. Office: 2300 N Lincoln Blvd Rm 414 Oklahoma City OK 73105 Office Phone: 405-521-5600. Business E-Mail: newberry@oksenate.gov.

NEWBERRY, JIM, former mayor; m. Cheryl Ann Newberry, 1979; children: Drew, Will. Co-founder, atty. Newberry, Hargrove and Rambicure, 1990; former ptnr. Wyatt, Tarrant and Combs; former v.p., gen. mgr. Airdrie Stud, Ky.; former exec. officer agr., econ. develop., health care Office Lt. Gov., Ky.; acting sec. Natural Resources and Environ. Protection Cabinet, Ky.; mayor City of Lexington, Ky., 2007—11. Exec.-in-residence U. Ky. Coll. Agr., 2011—. Former v.p. Health Ky., Bluegrass Cmty. Found.; former chmn. Bus. Com. for Character Coun. of Ctrl. Ky. Named Lexington's Outstanding Young Leader, 1992. Democrat. Baptist. Office: University of Kentucky College of Agriculture Ag Science North Lexington KY 40546 Office Phone: 859-258-3100. Fax: 859-258-3194. E-mail: mayor@lfucg.com.

NEWBY, PAUL MARTIN, state supreme court justice; b. Asheboro, NC, May 5, 1955; s. Samuel O. and Ruth (Parks) Newby; m. Macon Tucker, Apr. 16, 1983. BA in Pub. Policy studies, magna cum laude, Duke U., Durham, NC, 1977; JD, U. NC, Chapel Hill, 1980. Bar: NC 1980, US Dist. Ct. (we. dist.) NC 1981, US Dist. Ct. (mid. dist.) NC 1983, US Dist. Ct. (ea. dist.) NC 1985, US Ct. Appeals (4th cir.) 1986. Rsch. & tchr. asst. U. NC Sch. Law, 1979—80; assoc. Van Winkle, Buck, Wall, Starnes & Davis, Asheville, NC, 1980-84; v.p., gen. counsel Cannon Mills Realty & Devel. Corp., Kannapolis, NC, 1984-85; asst. atty. (ea. dist.) N.C. US Dept. Justice, Raleigh, 1985—2004, chief fin. litigation (ea. dist.) N.C., 1994—99; assoc. justice Supreme Ct. NC, Raleigh, 2004—. Chmn. bd. dirs. Pregnancy Life Care Ctr., Raleigh, 1986. Mem.: NC Bar Assn., Christian Legal Soc. Avocation: tennis. Office: NC Supreme Ct PO Box 2170 Raleigh NC 27602*

NEWELL, CHARLDEAN, public administration educator; b. Ft. Worth, Oct. 14, 1939; d. Charles Thurlow and Mildred Dean (Looney) Newell. BA, U. North Tex., Denton, 1960, MA, 1962; PhD, U. Tex., 1968; cert., Harvard U., Cambridge, Mass., 1988. Instr. U. North Tex., Denton, 1965-68, asst. prof., 1968-72; assoc. prof., dir. Fedn. North Tex. Area Univs., Denton, Dallas, 1972-74; assoc. prof., assoc. v.p. acad. affairs U. North Tex., Denton, 1974-76, assoc. prof., chair dept. polit. sci., 1976-80, prof. polit. sci., 1980-92, assoc. v.p., spl. asst. to chancellor, 1982-92, regents prof. pub. adminstrn., 1992—2002, prof. emerita, 2002—. Cons. Miss. Bd. Trustees State Instns. Higher Learning, Jackson, 1983—84, Ednl. Testing Svc., Princeton, NJ, 1980, Princeton, 1982, Princeton, 1985, Spear Down & Judin, Dallas, 1994—95, North Tex. Inst. Edn. Visual Arts, Denton, 1993—94; bd. regents Internat. City/County Mgmt. Assn., Washington, 1994—98, vol. credentialing adv. bd., 2002—; trainer Emerging Leaders Program, 2005—, Mid Career Mgmt. Program, 2012—. Author (with others): City Executives: Leadership Roles, Work Characteristics and Time Management, 1989, The Effective Local Government Manager, 2004; author: Essentials of Texas Politics, 2007; co-author: Texas Politics, 2013; editor: Effective Local Government Management: Cases in Decision Making, 2008; contbr. articles to profl. jours. Chmn. Denton Charter Rev. Com., 1978—79; mem. Denton CSC, 1989—97, chmn., 1992—97; active Denton Blue Ribbon Capital Improvements Com., 1995—96; mem. Denton Devel. Plan Com., 1996—97, Denton Pub. Utilities Bd., 1997—2009, chmn., 2002—09; v.p. Denton Christian Pre-Sch. Bd., 2001—02, pres., 2002—05, mem., 2005—07, City Coun. Ethics Com., 2004; bd. mem. Our Daily Bread, 2005—08, vice-chair, 2005—06; mem. exec. coun. Episcopal Diocese Dallas, 1985—88. Recipient Elmer Staats Career Pub. Svc. award, Nat. Assn. Sch. Pub. Affairs Adminstrn., 1993. Fellow: Nat. Acad. Pub. Adminstrn.; mem.: Am. Soc. for Pub. Adminstrn. (sect. chmn. 1982—83, mem. editl. bd. 1985—88, Donald C. Stone award 2004), Internat. City/County Mgmt. Assn. (hon.), Pi Alpha Alpha (exec. coun. 1995—99), Pi Sigma Alpha (exec. bd. 1988—92). Democrat. Episcopalian. Avocations: spectator sports, reading. Home: 2008 Tremont Cir Denton TX 76205-7408 Business E-Mail: newellc@verizon.net.

NEWELL, PAUL HAYNES, JR., engineering educator; b. Nashville, July 1, 1933; s. Paul Haynes Newell; m. Martha A. Newell; children: Paul Haynes III, Mike, Nan. B.M.E., U. Tenn., 1958, M.M.E., 1961; Mech.E., Mass. Inst. Tech., 1964, PhD, 1966. Registered profl. engr., Ala., Tenn., Tex., N.J. Student asst. mech. engring. U. Tenn., 1957, instr. mech. engring., 1958-62; NSF sci. faculty fellow MIT, 1962-65; asso. prof. U. Ala. Coll. Engring., 1966-69; prof. mech. Tex. A&M U., 1969-72, asso. dean engring., 1972, prof., head indsl. engring. dept., 1972-74, prof., head combined programs of behavioral engring., bioengring., cybernetic engring., hygiene and safety engring., indsl. engring., 1972-74; prof. biomed. engring., dept. phys. medicine Baylor Coll. Medicine, 1969-74, prof. biomed. engring., dept. physiology, 1970-74, prof. biomed. engring., dept. community medicine, 1972-74, prof. biomed. engring., dept. rehab., 1972—, mem. grad. faculty, 1970-74, prof. Houston, from 1971; pres., prof. Newark Coll. Engring., NJ Inst. Tech., 1974-78; prof. Adminstrn. Prosthetics Ctr., NY, 1973-75, VA Hosp., Houston, 1972-75; pres. Newell Engring., Greenbrier, Tenn., 1979—. Bd. dirs. NJ Bell Tel. Co., Mid Atlantic Nat. Bank, Thomas-Betts Corp. Contbr. articles to profl. jours., chapters to books. Mem. liaison com. NSF, Newark Transp. Coun., N.J. Safety Coun.; sec. exec. com. coun. Boy Scouts Am., Birmingham, Ala., 1966—68; bd. dirs. N.J. State Opera, United Hosps. Newark. With USMCR, Korea. NSF Sci. Faculty fellow. Mem.: NSPE, ASME, AAAS, N.J. Soc. Engrs., Am. Fluid Power Soc., Pres.'s Assn., Soc. Engring. Sci., Soc. Advanced Med. Sys., Internat. Soc. Prosthetics and Orthotics, Inst. Engring. Deans, Biomedical Engring. Soc., Am. Soc. Engring. Edn., Am. Soc. Artificial Internal Organs, Am. Inst. Indsl. Engrs., Am. Heart Assn., Am. Congress Rehab. Medicine, Ala. Acad. Scis., N.Y. Acad. Scis., Am. Soc. Tool and Mfg. Engrs., Rotary, Sigma Xi, Pi Tau Sigma, Phi Kappa Phi, Tau Beta Pi. Home and Office: Newell Engring 1855 Lake Rd Greenbrier TN 37073-4619

NEWELL, RICHARD G., economics professor, educator, former federal agency administrator; b. 1965; BA in Philosophy, Rutgers U., NJ, 1988, BS in Materials Engring., 1988; MPA, Princeton U., NJ, 1990; PhD in Environ. and Resource Econs., Harvard U., Mass., 1997. Sr. assoc. ICF Inc., Fairfax, Va., 1990—93; tchg. fellow Harvard U., Cambridge, Mass., 1993—97; fellow Resources for the Future, Washington, 1997—2005, sr. fellow, 2005—06, univ. fellow, 2007—; Ian Axford fellow New Zealand Fulbright Program, Wellington, 2004; sr. economist for energy and environment Pres.'s Coun. Econ. Advisors, 2005—06; Gendell assoc. prof. energy & environ. economics Duke U. Nicholas Sch. Environment, Durham, NC, 2007—; rsch. assoc. Nat. Bur. Econ. Rsch., 2008—; affiliated prof. bus. adminstrn. and corp. sustainability Duke U. Fuqua Sch. Bus., 2009—; adminstr. Energy Info. Adminstrn. US Dept. Energy, Washington, 2009—11; assoc. prof. economics Duke U., 2011—, dir. Duke U. Energy Initiative, 2011—. Affiliate Motu Econ. and Pub. Policy Rsch., Wellington, 2003—09; mem. com. on benefits of energy R & D NAS, 2005—07, mem. com. on NSF innovation inducement prizes, 2006—07, mem. com. on energy efficiency stds., 2007—09, mem. com. on energy externalities, 2008—09, chair workshop on econs. of climate change, 2008; mem. com. on geopolitics and policy Nat. Petroleum Coun. Global Oil and Gas Study, 2006—07; mem. adv. bd. Progressive Automotive X-Prize, 2006—09, Princeton Carbon Mitigation Initiative, 2007—, Study on the Energy Efficiency Potential of the Appalachian Region, 2007—09; bd. mem. Assn. Environ. and Resource Economists, 2008—; bd. dirs. Resources for Future, 2011—. Mem. editl. bd.: profl. jours. Energy Econs., 2003—09, mem. editl. coun.: profl. jours. J. Environ. Econs. and Mgmt., 2007—09. Office: Duke U Nicholas Sch Environment 106 Old Chemistry Bldg Box 90227 Durham NC 27708 Office Phone: 919-681-8663. Office Fax: 919-684-5833. Business E-Mail: richard.newell@duke.edu.

NEWGARD, CHRISTOPHER B., medical educator; B in Botany and Zoology, Duke U.; PhD, U. Tex., 1984. Prof. dept. biochemistry, dept. internal medicine U. Tex. Southwestern Med. Ctr., Dallas, Gifford O. Touchstone and Randolph G. Touchstone Disting. chair, prof., 1994—2002, co-dir., Touchstone Ctr. for Diabetes Rsch.; dir., Sarah W. Stedman Nutrition and Metabolism Ctr. Duke U. Sch. Medicine, 2002—, W. David and Sarah W. Stedman Disting. Prof., 2002—, prof. pharmacology and cancer biology, 2002—, prof. medicine, 2002—. Contbr. several articles to profl. jours. Trustee Insulin-Free World Found. Mem.: NIH (mem. metabolism study sect.), Am. Diabetes Assn. (mem. grant rev. bd., Outstanding Sci. Achievement award 2001). Office: Duke U Med Ctr Duke Independence Park Facility 4321 Medical Park Dr Durham NC 27704 Office Phone: 919-668-6059. Business E-Mail: christopher.newgard@utsouthwestern.edu, newga002@mc.duke.edu.

NEWHALL, DAVID, III, retired federal official; b. Phila., Dec. 6, 1937; s. David, Jr. and Jane Martyn (Dunn) Newhall. AB in Politics, Princeton U., 1961. Mgr. Bell Tel. Co. of Pa., Norristown, 1961-63; adminstrv. asst. U.S. Rep. R.S. Schweiker, Washington, 1963-69; chief of staff U.S. Senator R.S. Schweiker, Washington, 1969-81, HHS, Washington, 1981-83; pres. Marmion Plantation Co., King George, Va., 1983—85; prin. dep. asst. sec. def.(health affairs) U.S. Dept. Def., Washington, 1985-90, acting asst. sec. def. (health affairs), 1989-90; gen. ptnr. Marmion Partnership Restorations, 1990—. Bd. dirs. Western Healthcare Alliance, Phoenix, 1995—97; chmn. compliance com., lead dir. TrailBlazer Health Enterprises, LLC, Dallas, 1997—2007; outside dir. 1st Coast Svc. Options, Inc., Jacksonville, 2007—10, C2C Solutions Inc., Jacksonville, 2010—11. Mem.: Princeton Tower Club. Republican. Episcopalian. Home and Office: 7382M Marmion Ln King George VA 22485-7300

NEWKIRK, INGRID, animal rights organization administrator; b. Surrey, Eng., June 11, 1949; m. Steve Newkirk, 1967 (div. 1980). Former animal protection officer, dep. sheriff State of Md.; poundmaster Washington, 1978; chief animal disease control Commn. Public Health, Washington; dir. cruelty investigations Washington Humane Soc., 1978-80; pres., co-founder (with Alex Pacheco) People for the Ethical Treatment of Animals (PETA), Washington, 1980—. Author: Kids Can Save the Animals! 101 Easy Things You Can Do, 1991, The Compassionate Cook: Please Don't Eat the Animals, 1993, 250 Things You Can Do To Make Your Cat Adore You, 1998, You Can Save the Animals: 251 Simple Ways to Stop Thoughtless Cruelty, 1999, Free the Animals: The Amazing True Story of the Animal Liberation Front, 2000, Making Kind Choices: Everyday Ways to Enhance Your Life Through Earth and Animal-Friendly Living, 2005, Let's Have a Dog Party!: 20 Tail-Wagging Celebrations to Share With Your Best Friend, 2007, One Can Make a Difference: How Simple Actions Can Change the World, 2008, The PETA Practical Guide to Animal Rights - Simple Acts of Kindness to Help Animals in Trouble, 2009; appearance in documentary I Am an Animal: The Story of Ingrid Newkirk and PETA, 2007. Recipient Courage of Conscience award, The Peace Abbey, Sherborn, Mass., 1995; named Washingtonian of Yr., 1980. Office: People for the Ethical Treatment of Animals (PETA) 501 Front St Norfolk VA 23510 E-mail: ingridn@peta.org.*

NEWLIN, KIMREY DAYTON, SR., retired international trade and political consultant, personal computer analyst; b. Greensboro, NC, Jan. 27, 1944; s. Dayton Gilbert and Pearl (Kimrey) N.; m. Beverly Jane Agnew, Mar. 9, 1968; children: Kim, Jr., Stephanie, Laurie. BS in Physics, Guilford Coll., 1966; MS in Agrl. Econs., Clemson U., 1969; ME in Engring., Texas A&M U., Coll. Sta., 1970. Cert. profl. logistician, cost analyst, cert. profl. estimator. Gen. engr., lifetime staff and faculty mem. Army Logistics Mgmt. Coll./Darcom/Dept. of Def., Ft. Lee, Va., 1968-71; chief economist Army Procurement Rsch. Office/Army Logistics Mgmt. Coll./Darcom/Dept. of Def., Ft. Lee, Va., 1971-75, ops. rsch. analyst, 1975-78; statistician fisheries mgmt. S.E. Fisheries Ctr./Nat. Marines Fisheries Svc./Nat. Oceanographic Atmospheric Adminstrn./Dept. Commerce, Miami, 1978—2005, environ. compliance officer fisheries mgmt., 1992—98; ret., 2005. Keeper The LOG, Crew of the S.S. Fellowship, Crew Roster US Jr. C. of C., 2008—. Author: Treatment of Textile Waste, 1971, How to Run Successful Projects, 1976—90, Handbook for Chapter Plan Guide, 1976—90, DT LCC, Logistics Spectrum, 1978, 64 seafood dealer directories, 1987—2003; contbr. more than 200 articles to profl. jours. Ctr. rep. S.E. Fisheries Sci. Ctr. So. Fla. Fed. Exec. Bd., 1986—2005, chair steering com., 1999—2000, mem. policy bd., 2001—05; life mem., col. Fla. Gator Corps, 1993—; set up charitable remainder trust for the Lord homeless hosps./med. rsch. and scholarships, 25 yr. charities, 1997; cmty. bd. trustee Miami-Dade Am. Heart Assn., 2003—08. Recipient Miami Fed. Volunteerism Cert. Exec. Bd., 1993—97, Pullen Soc.(The R Stanhope Pullen Soc.) (Lifetime Giving Soc.), NC State U. Found., 1997, Heritage League Am. Cancer Soc., 1997, Heritage Soc., Diabetes Rsch. Inst. Found., 1997, Heritage Soc., Guilford Coll., 1997, Amb. of Mercy Hosp., Mercy Found., 1997, Champions of the Heart Legacy award Paul Dudley White Legacy, Am. Heart Assn., 1998, Heritage Members of A&M Legacy Soc.(Forsyth Soc.), Texas A & M U., 2001, award, Founders Gp., Bapt. Health Found., 1997, Founders Soc., Alzheimers Found., 2003, Clemson Legacy Soc., Clemson Univ. Found., 2010, Legacy Learning Soc., FL Intl. Univ. Found., 2009, Chairman's Circ., Greenville Hosp. Sys Univ. Found., 2010, JCI Found., Henry Giessenbier fellowship Jaycees Intl. Found., 1997, Diamond JCI Senators Found. (FL JCI Sen. Found.), 1997, No One Left Homeless Legacy Soc., Miami Rescue Mission Found., 2011, Nat. Parkinson Found. Legacy Soc. Nat. Parkinsons Found., 2009. Fellow Soc. Logistics Engrs. (life, corp.); mem. AARP, NARFE (life), FL JCI Senate (life), US JCI Senate (life), Coconut Grove Jaycees (life), The CREW of SS Fellowship (life). Libertarian. Presbyterian. Avocations: woodworking, flea markets, personal computers, travel, yard sales. Home: 12455 SW 97th Ct Miami FL 33176-4909 Office Phone: 305-361-9362. Personal E-mail: jcisenator@msn.com.

NEWMAN, ANDREA FISCHER, air transportation executive; AB, U. Mich., Ann Arbor, 1979; JD, George Washington U., 1983. With Patton, Boggs, Washington; dept. asst. to V.P. George Bush The White House; spl. counsel to asst. sec. def. for acquisitions and logistics Dept. Def.; sr. ptnr Miller, Canfield, Paddock and Stone, Detroit; v.p. state and local affairs NW Airlines Corp., sr. v.p. govt. affairs Detroit, 2001—08, Delta Air Lines, Inc., Atlanta, 2008—. Bd. regents U. Mich., Ann Arbor, 1994—; vice chmn. George W. Bush for Pres. Campaign, co-chmn. fin. com. Mich., 2000; bd. dirs. Mich. Econ. Devel. Corp. Found., Mich. Thanksgiving Day Parade Found., Isiah Thomas Found. Mem.: Detroit Econ. Club (v.p.). Mailing: Delta Air Lines 1030 Delta Blvd Atlanta GA 30320-6001 Office Phone: 404-715-2600.

NEWMAN, BOBBI, library and information scientist; BA in History, Spanish, Anthropology, U. No. Iowa, Cedar Falls, 1998; MA in Info. Resources & Libr. Sci., U. Ariz., Tucson, 2002; grad. student in pub. policy and adminstrn., Iowa State U., Ames, 2011—. Libr. II Raytheon, 2002—05; digital services libr. Mo. River Regional Libr., 2005—09; self -employed cons., spkr., trainer, author Librarian by Day, 2008—; digital br. mgr. Chattahoochee Valley Libr., Columbus, Ga., 2009—11; staff learning engagement mgr. Richland County Pub. Libr., Columbia, SC, 2011—. Adj. instr. U. Mo., 2009. Founder, coord. Libr. Day in the Life Project; co-founder, writer Libraries and Transliteracy Project. Named to Movers & Shakers, Libr. Jour., 2011. Mem.: ALA (councilor-at-large 2011—). Office: Richland County Pub Library 1431 Assembly St Columbia SC 29201 Office Phone: 803-799-9084.

NEWMAN, BRUCE MURRAY, retired antiques gallery owner, designer author; b. NYC, Jan. 27, 1930; s. Meyer and Evelyn (Kantor) Newman; m. Judith S Brandus, June 26, 1965; 1 child, Emily Rachel. BA, Pratt Inst., 1953, D (hon.), BFA (hon.), 1998, degree (hon.) in fine arts, 1997. Pres. Newel Art Galleries Inc., NYC, 1975—2001. Lectr mus and univs; mem regional adv bd Chase Manhattan Bank; mem regional adv bd J P Morgan Chase Bank. Author: Fantasy Furniture, 1989, Don't Come Back Until You Find It, 2006; featured numerous TV & radio programs, mags, and other publs, guest CBS Morning Show, 1988; guest: Lifestyles of the Rich and Famous. Assoc mem Mt Sinia Med Ctr, 1988—; founder Kravis Ctr.; bd dirs New York City Ctr, 1988—90; lifetime trustee Pratt Inst., Bklyn., 1983—. Recipient Designer Award, Art Dirs. Club, 1984; named Man of the Yr., Pratt Inst., 1993. Mem.: Victorian Soc Am, Am Soc Interior Designers (bd dirs 1989—). Avocations: golf, reading, travel.

NEWMAN, CHARLES FORREST, lawyer; b. Grenada, Miss., Jan. 15, 1937; s. Wiley Clifford and Lurene (Westbrook) Newman; m. Jeannette Kay Bailey, May 26, 1973. BA magna cum laude, Yale Coll., 1959; JD, Yale Law Sch., 1963; Postgrad., U. Bonn, Fed. Republic Germany, 1959—60. Bar: Tenn. 1964, US Supreme Ct. 1981. Law clk. US Dist. Judge Bailey Brown, Western Dist, Tenn., 1963—64; mem. firm Burch Porter & Johnson; attys. Memphis, 1965—; ptnr., 1966—; mem. exec. com. Yale U. Law Sch. Assn., 1984—88; chair Pres.'s Coun. Rhodes Coll., 1994—95; commr. Memphis Landmarks Commn., 1983—87; mem. class coun. Class of '59, Yale Coll., 1980—90, Memphis Bar Assn.; former bd. dirs./trustees Lemoyne-Owen Coll., Memphis Coll. Art, Tenn. Nature Conservancy, Nat. Civil Rights Mus., Memphis Met. Interfaith Assn., Memphis Pub. Lib. Found. Recipient Disting. Svc. medal, Rhodes Coll., Best Lawyers in Am.; Adenauer fellowship, U. Bonn, 1959—60, Paul Harris fellow, Rotary Internat. Fellow: Tenn. Bar Found.; mem.: ABA, Am. Inns Ct. (master bench), Memphis Bar Assn. (bd. dirs. 1990—96, pres. 1996), Tenn. Bar Assn., Yale Club NY, Yale Club Memphis (past pres.), Phi Beta Kappa. Home: 3880 Poplar Ave Memphis TN 38111-7614 Office: Burch Porter & Johnson 130 N Court Ave Memphis TN 38103-2288 Office Phone: 901-524-5103.

NEWMAN, JOEL S., law educator; b. Valley Stream, NY, Oct. 21, 1946; AB, Brown U., 1968; JD, U. Chgo., 1971. Assoc. Shearman & Sterling, NY, 1971—73, Fredrikson Law Firm, Mpls., 1973—76; prof. Wake Forest U. Sch. Law, 1976—. Author: Federal Income Taxation, 2008. Fellow, Am. Bar Found., Fulbright Tchg. fellowship, 1995. Mem.: Am. Law Inst. Office: 3307 Worrell Professional Bldg 1834 Winston Salem NC 27109 Business E-Mail: newmanjs@wfu.edu.

NEWMAN, LAWRENCE GRAHAM, lawyer; b. Dallas, July 7, 1947; s. Frank Gene and Frances Helen (Graham) Newman; m. Nancy Lynn Vanderkolk, June 14, 1969; children: Courtney Kolk, Torrey Peyton. BA cum laude, Colo. Coll., 1969; JD, U. Chgo. Law Sch., 1972. Bar: Colo. 1973, Tex. 1973, US Dist. Ct. (no. dist.) Tex. 1973, US Supreme Ct. 1979, US Ct. Appeals (5th cir.) 1982, cert. mediator: 1989. Law clk. to Judge Alfred A. Arraj US Dist. Ct., Denver, 1972—73; ptnr. Newman, Shook & Newman, Dallas, 1973-79; founder, pres. Law Firm of Lawrence G. Newman, PC, Dallas, 1980—. Past chmn. bd. dirs. Legal Services North Tex. Author: Texas Corporation Law (updated annually), 1986, The Complete Guide to Nonprofit Corporations, 2009. Mem.: ABA, American Law Inst., Dallas Bar Assn., Tex. Bar Assn., Colo. Bar Assn. Avocations: musician, skiing, athletics, artist. Office: Law Firm of Lawrence G Newman PC 3402 Mcfarlin Blvd Ste 200 Dallas TX 75205-5700 Office Phone: 214-522-7444. Office Fax: 214-522-7715. E-mail: lgn@newman-law.com.

NEWMAN, RYAN JOSEPH, race car driver; b. South Bend, Ind., Dec. 8, 1977; m. Krissie Boyle. BS in Vehicle Structure Engring., Purdue U., 2001. Race car driver NASCAR Penske Racing South, 2001—08, Stewart-Haas Racing, 2009—. 1st pl. NH 300 NH Motor Speedway, 2002, 1st pl. Sylvania 300, 2005, 1st pl. Lenox Indsl. Tools 301, 2011; 1st pl. Samsung/Radio Shack 500 Tex. Motor Speedway, 2003; 1st pl. MBNA Armed Forces Family 400 Dover Internat. Speedway, 2003, 1st pl. Dover 400, 2003, 1st pl. MBNA Am. 400, 2004; 1st pl. Tropicana 400 Chicagoland Speedway, 2003; 1st pl. Pa. 500 Pocono Raceway, 2003; 1st pl. GFS Marketplace 400 Mich. Internat. Speedway, 2003, 1st pl. DHL 400, 2004; 1st pl. Chevy Rock and Roll 400 Richmond Internat. Raceway, 2003; 1st pl. Banquet 400 Kans. Speedway, 2003; 1st pl. Daytona 500 Daytona Internat. Speedway, 2008; 1st pl. Goody's Fast Relief 500 Martinsville Speedway, 2012. Co-founder Ryan Newman Found. Named NASCAR Rookie of Yr., 2002, NASCAR Driver of Yr., 2003, Am. Driver of Yr., SPEED Channel, 2003. Office: Stewart-Haas Racing 6001 Haas Way Kannapolis NC 28081 Office Phone: 704-652-4227.

NEWMAN, SLATER EDMUND, psychologist, educator; b. Boston, Sept. 8, 1924; s. Max and Gertrude (Raphael) N.; m. Corrine Lois Siften, June 18, 1950 (div. 1968); children: Kurt Douglas, Jonathan Mark, Eric Bruce; m. Patricia Ellen Christopher Thomas, July 2, 1969; 1 stepchild, Arthur C. Thomas III. BS, U. Pa., 1947; MA, Boston U., 1948; PhD, Northwestern U., 1951. Research psychologist U.S. Air Force, 1951-57; mem. faculty N.C. State U., Raleigh, 1957—2003, prof. emeritus psychology, 2003—. Vis. fgn. mem. Exptl. Psychology Soc. U.K., 1973-74, 82-83, 90. Contbr. chpts. to books, articles to profl. publs. Bd. dirs. ACLU, 1992—97, mem. biennial conf. com., 1994—97, mem. task force internat. human rights, 1994—2005, mem. spl. nominating com., 1996, mem. constn. com., 1996—97, mem. youth affairs com., 1997, mem. nat. adv. coun., 1998—; organizing com. NC Civil Liberties Union, 1965, pres., 1980—82, exec. com., 1986—87, bd. dirs., 1969—73, 1976—82, 1984—90, 1992—97; chair Com. on Internat. Human Rights, 1988—; chair founding com. Wake County chpt. ACLU, 1969, pres., 1969—72, 1984—86, bd. dirs., 1969—73, 1976—82, 1984—90, life mem., 2002—; founding mem. North Carolinians Against the Death Penalty, 1967, bd. govs., 1967—73; mem. Mayor's Com. UN Week, Raleigh, 1986—95; active Amnesty Internat., 1984—; co-founder, mem. steering com. North Carolinians Against Apartheid, 1985—87; mem. Wake County Com. Bicentennial US Constn., 1987—89; co-founder, co-chair NC Com. for Celebration of Human Rights, 1989—97; mem. Human Rights Week Com., NC State U., 1993—99, founder, 1993, chair, 1993—96; co-founder Human Rights Coalition NC, 1997—, co-chair, 1997—; co-founder North Carolinians for Ratification, Convention on Elimination of All Forms of Discrimination Against Women, 1997, chair, 1998—2009; mem. civil rights adv. bd. NC Mus. History, 2001—05, adv. bd. mem., Women NC, 2009—; co-founder To Release the Arms Race. Served with USAAC, 1943—46, 2d lt. USAF, 1952—53. USPHS spl. rsch. fellow U. Calif.-Berkeley, 1965-66; U. London hon. rsch. fellow, 1973-74, 82-83, 90; recipient W.W. Finlator award ACLU of Wake County, 1997, Norman Smith award ACLU of NC, 1998; recipient Frank Porter Graham Award, ACLU of NC, 2004, Human Rights award, Wake County and West Triangle Chpts., UN Assn., 2007, Slater E. Newman Scholarship Endowment, NC State U., Dept. Psychology, 1997; Slater Newman annual debate established by Wake County ACLU, 2006, Peacemaker award NC Peace Action, 2010, Carolyn and Cy King Peace and Justice award Cmty. United Ch. Christ, Raleigh, 2014. Fellow: APA, AAAS, Psychonomic Soc., Assn. for Psychol. Sci.; mem.: AAUP (pres. N.C. State U. chpt. 1968—69), Vets. Peace, Carolinas Conf. for Undergrad. Rsch. in Psychology (co-founder 1976), N.C. Cognition Group (founder 1972), S.E. Psychol. Assn. (exec. com. 2001—07, sec.-treas. 2004—07), S.E. Workers in Memory (founder 1969), NC Peace Action, UN Assn. (bd. dirs. Wake County chpt. 1991—95), Psi Chi (v.p. southea. region 1990—94, nat. coun. 1990—94, nat. pres.-elect 1996—97, nat. coun. 1996—99, nat. pres. 1997—98, nat. past pres. 1998—99), Sigma Xi. Home: 315 Shepherd St Raleigh NC 27607-4031

NEWMAN, STEPHEN D. (STEVE NEWMAN), state legislator; b. Stuart, Va., Oct. 15, 1964; m. Kimberly Newman. Fin. counselor; owner SDN Co.; state del. Dist. 23 Va., 1992—96; state senator Dist. 23 Va., 1996—; mem. Edn. & Health Com., Local Govt. Com., Transp. & Rehabilitation & Soc. Svcs. Com., Va. State Senate. Mem.: America Cancer Soc. Republican. Baptist. Address: Lynchburg VA Mailing: PO Box 2209 Lynchburg VA 24501-0209 Office: Dist Off PO Box 480 Forest VA 24551 Office Phone: 804-385-1065. E-mail: snewman@inmind.com, district23@sov.state.va.us.

NEWMAN, STEPHEN MICHAEL, lawyer; b. Buffalo, Jan. 12, 1945; s. Howard A. and Mildred (Ballow) N.; m. Gayle Mallon, May 24, 1969; children: Holly, Deborah. AB, Princeton U., 1966; JD, U. Mich., 1969. Bar: N.Y. 1969, Fla. 1976. Assoc. Hodgson, Russ, Andrews, Woods & Goodyear, Buffalo, 1969-73; ptnr. Hodgson Russ, LLP (formerly Hodgson, Russ, Andrews, Woods & Goodyear), Buffalo, 1973—2004, Nixon Peabody, LLP, Buffalo, 2005—. Lectr. in field. Bd. dirs. Leukemia Soc., United Jewish Fedn. Buffalo Inc., Jewish Ctr. Greater Buffalo Inc., Temple Beth Zion; bd. dirs., chpt. chmn., exec. com. Am. Jewish Com., Buffalo chpt.; bd. advisors Am. Lung Assn., Southeast Fla. chpt. Fellow Am. Coll. Trusts and Estates Coun.; mem. ABA (personal svc. corps. com. tax sect.), N.Y. State Bar Assn. (chair trusts and estates law sect. 2001), Princeton Club of Fla. Home Phone: 561-626-4621; Office Phone: 561-691-5424. Business E-Mail: snewman@nixonpeabody.com.

NEWMAN, STEVEN L., healthcare executive; BA, Rutgers U., NJ; MBA, Tulane U., New Orleans; MD, U. Tenn. Intern to resident to fellow Emory U. Sch. Medicine, Atlanta; assoc. prof. pediat. and medicine Wright State U. Sch. Medicine, Dayton, Ohio, 1979—90; dir. gastroenterology and nutrition support Children's Med. Ctr., Dayton, Ohio, 1979—90; sr. v.p., chief med. officer Touro Infirmary, New Orleans, 1990—97; pres., CEO Louisville Healthcare Network Columbia/HCA, 1997—98, pres. Omega Divsn., 1998—99; CEO Audubon Hosp., 1997; v.p. ops. Gulf States Region in Ala., La. and Miss. Tenet Healthcare Corp., 1999—2000, sr. v.p. ops., 2000—03, sr. v.p. Calif. ops., 2003—07, COO, 2007—. Mem. exec. com. of bd. dirs. Calif. Hosp. Assn. Office: Tenet Healthcare Corp 1445 Ross Ave Ste 1400 Dallas TX 75202-2703 Office Phone: 469-893-2200. Office Fax: 469-893-8600.

NEWMAN, TERRIE LYNNE, advertising and marketing executive; b. Boston; d. Joseph and Clara (Bistry) N.; m. Fredric Aron Kerstein, June 18, 1978. BA in English, U. Mass., Boston, 1973. Copywriter Vanda Beauty Counselor, Inc., NYC, 1973-75, creative dir., 1975-76; sr. writer Avon Products, Inc., NYC, 1976-79; copywriter Hume, Smith, Mickelberry Advt., Inc., Miami, Fla., 1979-80, Beber, Silverstein & Ptnrs., Advt., Miami, 1980-81; pres., creative dir. Terrie Lynne Newman, Inc., Miami, 1981-92, Terrie Newman Communs., Miami, 1992—. Recipient Internat. Gold Echo award Direct Mktg. Assn., 1987, 88, Internat. Bronze Echo award, 1987, Gold Award for Excellence in Mktg., Gold Coast chpt. Am. Mktg. Assn., 1987, First Place Gold medallion Broadcast Promotion & Mktg. Execs., 1986, Clio award, 1981, Emmy award, 1981, others. Home: 6970 SW 125th St Miami FL 33156-6240

NEWMARK, EMANUEL, ophthalmologist; b. Newark, May 25, 1936; s. Charles Meyer and Bella (Yoskowitz) Newmark; m. Tina Steinberg, Aug. 25, 1957; children: Karen Beth, Heidi Ellen, Stuart Jeffrey. BS in Pharmacy, Rutgers U., Newark, 1959; postgrad., U. Amsterdam, The Netherlands, 1960-63, Armed Forces Inst. Pathology, Washington, 1971; MD, Duke U., Durham, NC, 1966; postgrad., Harvard U., Cambridge, Mass., 1967. Diplomate Am. Bd. Ophthalmology. Intern George Washington U. Hosp., Washington, 1966; trainee NIH rsch. U. Fla., Gainesville, 1967—70; resident ophthalmology U. Fla. Hosp., 1967—70; instr. dept. ophthalmology U. Fla., 1970; cons. ophthalmology Gainesville VA Hosp., 1970; clin. instr. ophthalmology U. Tex. Med. Sch., San Antonio, 1971—72; cons. ophthalmology Kerrville VA Hosp., Tex., 1971—72; asst. chief ophthalmology svc. Brooke Army Gen. Hosp., Fort Sam, Tex., 1971—72. Clin. asst. prof. ophthalmology Bexar County Hosp. and Clinics, San Antonio, 1971—72; tchg. faculty Joint Commn. Allied Health Pers. in Ophthalmology, commr., 2004—09; sec., treas. Palm Beach Eye Assocs., Atlantis, Fla., 1973—98; pharm. adv. com. Agy. Health Care Adminstrn. Bd. Optometry, 1991—2013; chief ophthalmology JFK Med. Ctr., 1984, chmn. CME and edn. com., 2004—07; staff ophthalmologist West Palm Beach VA Hosp., 2005—, Regional Eye Inst., 1998—2006. Exec. editor Ophthalmic Medical Assisting: An Independent Study Course, 2006, Cert. Ophthalmic Asst. Exam Study Guide, 2010; contbr. chapters to books, articles to profl. jours. & publs.; co-editor: Ophthalmic Medical Assisting An Independent Study Course 5th Edit., 2012. Alumni assoc. Rutgers Coll. Pharmacy, 1990—, chmn. reunion, 1986, 2001, Duke U. Med. Alumni Assn., NC, 1967—; centurian Davison Club-Duke U. Med. Sch., NC, 1982—; campaign chmn., nat. vice chmn. Israel Bonds, Palm Beach County, Fla., 1988—90; participant charitable orgns.; v.p. Palm Beach Liturgical Culture Found., 1994—2000, pres., 2000—01, Jt. Commn. Allied Health Personal Opthal. Statesmanship Award, 2010. Decorated Lion of Judea State of Israel; recipient Gates of Jerusalem medal, 1991, Jerusalem medal, 1996, Recognition award, Joint Commn. Allied Health Personnel in Ophthalmology, 2001, 2006, US Army Commendation medal, Joint Commn. Fellow: ACS, Am. Acad. Ophthalmology (del. to coun. 1996—2001, allied health edn. com. 1997—2002, editor Refinements 1998—2000, rep. to joint com. allied health pers. in ophthalmology 2004—09, Fla. state chmn. ednl. trust, Achievement award 2001, Councillors award 2001, Secretariat award 2005, 2010); mem.: AMA, Fla. Soc. Ophthalmology (ethics chmn. 1985—90, pres. 1990—91, James W. Clower Jr. Cmty. Svc. award 1995, Shalar Richardson, MD Svc. to Medicine award 2007, John R. Brayton Leadership award 2012), Palm Beach County Ophthal. Soc. (pres. 1984—85, Ophthalmologist of Yr. 2004), Palm Beach County Med. Soc. (chair ethics com. 1997—2000, vice chair ethics com. 2002, bd. dirs. 2003, bd. dirs. mem.-at-large 2003—06, svcs. bd. mem. 2004—10, coun. on ethical and jud. affairs 2004—, trustee 2005, v.p. svcs. bd. 2008—09, Heroes in Medicine award 2009, Svc. award 2011), Fla. Med. Assn. (ho. dels. 1993—95, 2001—06, 2008—), Am. Orgn. for Rehab. Through Tng. Fedn. (nat. exec. com.-campaign cabinet 1987, pres. 1987—90, hon. del. 1993—95, 2001—03, Palm Beach Men's Achievement award 1988, Pres. award 1989), Founder's Soc. Duke U. Jewish. Avocation: travel. Home: 180 Palm Cir Atlantis FL 33462-6627 Office: West Palm Beach Vets Med Ctr 7305 Military Trail West Palm Beach FL 33410 Personal E-mail: mannynewmark@msn.com.

NEWSOME, GARY D., hospital operations company executive; BS, Bluefield State Coll., W.Va.; MBA, Butler U., Indpls.; advanced studies, U. Mich. Sch. Bus. Hosp. ops. Humana, Inc.; divisional v.p. group ops., asst. v.p. group ops., hosp. CEO Health Mgmt. Associates, Inc., 1993—98; v.p. group ops. Cmty. Health Systems, Inc., divsn. pres. hosp. ops.; pres., CEO Health Management Associates, Inc., 2008—. Bd. dirs. Health Mgmt. Associates, Inc., 2008—. Office: Health Mgmt Associates Inc 5811 Pelican Bay Blvd Ste 500 Naples FL 34108 Office Phone: 239-598-3131.

NEWSOME, KENNETH R., manufacturing executive, venture capitalist; BS in Fin., U. Va., MBA. COO MedSurg Industries (acquired by Microtek Med. Inc.); pres., CEO AMF Automation Technologies Inc., 1996—. Bd. dirs. Med. Action Industries Inc., 2006—. Office: AMF Automation Technologies Inc 2115 W Laburnum Ave Richmond VA 23227-4315 Office Phone: 804-355-7961. Office Fax: 248-737-9110. Business E-Mail: knewsome@amfautomation.com.

NEWTON, ALEXANDER WORTHY, lawyer; b. Birmingham, Ala., June 19, 1930; s. Jeff H. and Annis Lillian (Kelly) N.; m. Sue Aldridge, Dec. 22, 1952; children: Lamar Aldridge Newton, Kelly McClure Newton Hammond, Jane Worthy Newton, Robins Jeffry Newton. BS, U. Ala., 1952, JD, 1957. Bar: Ala. 1957. Pvt. practice law, Birmingham; assoc. Hare, Wynn & Newell, Birmingham, 1957; ptnr. Hare, Wynn, Newell & Newton, Birmingham, 1961—. Del. U.S. Ct. Appeals (11th cir.) Jud. Conf., 1988, 89, 90, 91; mem. Jefferson County Jud. Nominating Com., 1983-89; mem. Birmingham Airport Authority, 1991-2006; founding dir. First Comm. Bank. Co-author: (with others) Federal Appellate Procedure, 11th Circuit, 1996. Vice chmn. Birmingham Racing Commn., 1984-87; v.p. U. Ala. Law Sch. Found., 1978-79, pres., 1980-82, exec. com., 1987—; mem. Leadership Ala. Class IV; trustee Ala. Trust Fund, 2002; bd. dirs. St. Vincent Hosp. Found.; mem. Jefferson Met. Healthcare Authority, 2005-06. Capt. inf. U.S. Army, 1952-54. Recipient Disting. Alumnus award Farrah Law Soc. U. Ala., 1984, Sam W. Pipes Disting. Alumnus award 1982 Fellow Am. Coll. Trial Lawyers (state chmn. 1983-84, regents' nominatin com. 1984-85), Internat. Soc. Barristers (bd. dirs. 1974-75, sec.-treas. 1976-77, v.p. 1977-78, pres. 1979-80), Internat. Acad. Trial Lawyers (bd. dirs. 1998—); mem. ABA, ATLA, Am. Bar Found., Ala. State Bar (chmn. practices and procedures subsect. 1965, governance com. and pres.'s task force 1984-86, pres.'s com. 1987-88), Birmingham Bar Assn. (exec. com. 1967), Ala. Trial Lawyers Assn. (sec.-treas. 1958-65), Am. Judicature Soc., 11th Cir. Hist. Soc. (trustee 1988-2007), Birmingham Bar Assn. (Lawyer of Yr.), Shoal Creek Club, Birmingham Country Club, Capital City Club (Atlanta), Garden of the Gods Club (Colorado Springs, Colo.), Univ. Club (N.Y.C.), Sigma Chi. Democrat. Presbyterian. Home: 2837 Canoe Brook Ln Birmingham AL 35243-5908 Office: Hare Wynn Newell & Newton 800 Massey Bldg 2025 3d Ave N Ste 800 Birmingham AL 35203-3330 Office Phone: 205-328-5330.

NEWTON, CAM (CAMERON JERRELL NEWTON), professional football player; b. College Park, Ga., May 11, 1989; s. Cecil and Jackie Newton. Attended, U. Fla., Gainesville, 2007—08, Blinn Coll., Brenham, Tex., 2009, Auburn U., Ala., 2010—11. Quarterback U. Fla. Gators, 2007—08, Blinn Coll. Buccaneers, 2009, Auburn U. Tigers, 2010—11, Carolina Panthers, 2011—. Recipient Davey O'Brien Nat. Quarterback award, Davey O'Brien Found., 2010, Maxwell award, Maxwell Football Club, 2010, Walter Camp Player of Yr. award, Walter Camp Football Found., 2010, Heisman Meml. Trophy, Heisman Trophy Trust, 2010, Manning award, Sugar Bowl Com., 2010; named Offensive Player of Yr., Southeastern Conf., 2010, 1st Team All-American, SI.com, 2010, AP, 2010, Coll. Football Player of Yr., 2010, NFL Offensive Rookie of Yr., 2011; named to Nat. Football Conf. Pro Bowl Team, NFL, 2011. Achievements include member of National Junior College Athletic Association national championship winning Blinn College Buccaneers, 2009; one of only three players in NCAA Football Bowl Subdivision history with at least 20 touchdowns both rushing and passing in a season, 2010; member of the BCS National Championship winning Auburn University Tigers, 2010; being the first overall pick in the NFL Draft, 2011; setting the NFL record for: passing yards by a rookie in his regular season opener (422 yards), 2011; rushing touchdowns by a quarterback in a single-season, 2011; first player in NFL history to pass for more than 4,000 yards and rush for more than 500 yards, 2011. Office: Carolina Panthers 800 S Mint St Charlotte NC 28202

NEWTON, CHARLES OLIVER, state legislator; b. Greenville, Ala., July 11, 1947; s. James and Arthurine Newton; m. Jan Newton; children: Ollie, Seth, Lila. BA, U. Ala., 1968, MA, 1970. Pres. Newton Oil Co., 1975—; councilman City of Greenville, Ala., 1984—89; mem. Dist. 90 Ala. House of Reps., Montgomery, 1989—. Bd. dirs. Greenville Bank. Mem. Greenville C. of C., First Bapt. Ch., Greenville. Mem.: Ala. Cattlemen's Assn., Ala. Hist. Assn., Rotary, Phi Eta Sigma, Beta Theta Pi. Democrat. Baptist. Office: 1216 S Conecuh St Greenville AL 36037 also: PO Box 246 Greenville AL 36037 also: Alabama House of Reps Alabama State House 11 S Union St Rm 541-E Montgomery AL 36130 Office Phone: 334-382-8700, 334-242-4460.

NEWTON, DEMETRIUS C., state legislator; b. Fairfield, Ala., Mar. 15, 1928; m. Beatryce; children: Deirdre & Demetrius, Jr. BA, Wilberforce U., Ohio; JD, Boston U. Pvt. practice atty., Birmingham; former pres., CEO Birmingham Urban League, Inc.; mem. Dist. 53 Ala. House of Reps., Montgomery, 1986—, spkr. pro tempore. Recipient Outstanding Lawyer award Ala. Lawyer Assn., Outstanding Legislature award Ala. Poultry & Egg Assn. Mem.: ABA, Ala. Bar Assn., NAACP, Am. Judicature Soc., Nat. Bar Assn., 101 Black Men, Wilberforce U. Alumni Assn., Vulcan Gold Club, Phi Beta Sigma. Democrat. Baptist. Office: PO Box 2525 Birmingham AL 35203 also: 1820 7th Ave N Ste 10 Birmingham AL 35202 also: Ala House of Reps Ala State House 11 S Union St Rm 516-B Montgomery AL 36130 Office Phone: 205-252-9203, 334-242-7663.

NEWTON, DON ALLEN, economic development consultant; b. Laurel, Miss., Oct. 19, 1934; s. Wilfred L. and Mary (McMullan) N.; m. Coleta Farrell, Oct. 11, 1958; children: Don Jr., Coleta Midge Rast. AA, Meridian CC, Miss., 1954; BA, U. Ala., 1956; postgrad. in Assn. Mgmt., U. NC; postgrad. in Econ. Devel., U. Okla. Asst. mgr. Meridian C. of C., 1956; mgr. Winston County C. of C., Louisville, Miss., 1960—61; asst. dir. Delta Coun. Indsl. and Cmty. Devel. Bd., Stoneville, Miss., 1961—62, dir., 1963—70; exec. v.p. Met. Devel. Bd., Birmingham, Ala., 1970—74; pres. Birmingham Regional C. of C., 1974—99; pub. Birmingham Mag., Birmingham Bus. Mag., 1974—99; pres. Birmingham Area C. of C. Found., Inc., 1988-99, Devel. Assocs. Econ. Devel., 1999. Contbr. articles to profl. jours., newspapers. Former appointee Ala. Export Coun.; bd. dirs. Birmingham Met. Devel. Bd., Ala. Sports Found. Lt. USNR, 1957-60. Named Ala. Mktg. Man of Yr., 1972. Mem.: Sigma Chi. Home: 4156 Glenbrook Dr Birmingham AL 35213 Office: Development Assocs PO Box 530093 Birmingham AL 35253-0093 Home Phone: 205-879-9088.

NEWTON, ELDON SHARPE, III, (E.S. NEWTON, BUCK NEWTON), state legislator, lawyer; b. Wilson, NC, July 5, 1968; s. Eldon Sharpe Newton Jr. and Beatrice Lee Newton; m. Hope Taylor Edmondson, June 25, 1994; children: Eldon Sharpe IV, Thomas Winfield, Virginia Grey. JD, Campbell U., Buies Creek, NC, 1999. Bar: NC 1999, US Dist. Ct. (ea. dist.) NC 1999. Staff asst. US Senate Com. Fgn. Rels., Washington, 1990—91; mng. ptnr. Newton, Lee & Boyd, Wilson, 1999—; mem. Dist. 11 NC State Senate, 2011—. Treas. Arts Coun. Wilson, 2002—04; past pres. Wilson Downtown Devel. Corp.; county chmn. Elizabeth Dole For Senate, Wilson, 2002; county co-chair Richard Burr For Senate, Wilson, 2004. Mem.: ABA, NC Acad. Trial Lawyers, Rotary Club. Methodist. Avocations: hunting, sailing, travel, reading, skiing. Office: Newton Lee & Boyd Attorneys At Law PO Box 2047 Wilson NC 27894-2047 Mailing: NC Senate 300 N Salisbury St Rm 410 Raleigh NC 27603 Office Phone: 252-291-3443, 919-715-3030. Office Fax: 252-291-3491. E-mail: leelaw1@earthlink.net, Buck.Newton@ncleg.net.

NEWTON, FLOYD CHILDS, III, lawyer; b. Griffin, Ga., Feb. 4, 1955; s. Floyd Childs Jr. and Jean (Hunt) N.; m. Katrina Dalton, Aug. 30, 1986; children: Stephanie, Amanda, Natalie. BA, Princeton U.,

NJ, 1977; JD, U. Ga., 1980. Bar: Ga. 1980, U.S. Dist. Ct. (no. dist.) Ga. 1980, U.S. Ct. Appeals (11th cir.) 1980. Ptnr. King & Spalding, Atlanta, 1980—. Mem. Nat. Assn. Bond Lawyers (pres. 1998-99). Office: King & Spalding 1180 Peachtree St Atlanta GA 30309 Office Phone: 404-572-4600. Business E-Mail: fnewton@kslaw.com.

NEWTON, LLOYD WARREN, board member; b. Ridgeland, SC; BS in Aviation Edn., Tenn. State U., 1966; postgrad., Armed Forces Staff Coll., Norfolk, Va., 1978, Indsl. Coll. Armed Forces, Washington, 1985; MPA, George Wash. U., 1985; postgrad., Harvard U., 1987. Congl. liaison officer House of Representatives, Washington, 1978—82; comdr., 883rd Air Division Holloman AFB, N.Mex., 1991, comdr., 49th Fighter Wing N.Mex., 1991—93; comdr. Air Edn. Tng. Command, Randolph AFB, Tex., 1997—2000; commd. 2d lt. USAF, 1966, advanced in grades to gen., 1997, F-4D pilot and sys. operator Da Nang Air Base, Vietnam, 1968—69, F-4D pilot 523rd Tactical Fighter Squadron Clark Air Base, Philippines, 1969—73, F-4D flight instr. pilot Luke AFB, Ariz., 1973—74, narrator, slot pilot Thunderbirds Nellis AFB, Nev., 1974—78, right wingman, narrator Thunderbirds, 1978, asst. dep. comdr. for ops., 8th Tactical Fighter Wing, 1982—83, asst. dep. comdr. for ops., 388th Tactical Fighter Wing Hill AFB, Utah, 1983—84, asst. dep. dir. for ops. and tng. Hdqrs. Washington, 1985—86, asst. dir. spl. projects, directorate of plans Hdqrs., 1986—88, comdr., 71st Air Base Group Vance AFB, Okla., 1988—89, comdr., 71st Flying Tng. Wing, 1989—90, comdr., 12th Flying Tng. Wing Randolph AFB, Tex., 1990—91; dir. ops, J-3, U.S. Special Ops Command MacDill, AFB, Fla., 1993-95; asst. vice chief staff USAF, Washington, 1995—97, ret., 2000; exec. v.p., Mil. Engines Pratt & Whitney, 2000—06. Bd. dirs. Goodrich Corp., Sonocco Products Co., Torchmark Corp., 2006—. Decorated D.S.M. with oak leaf cluster, Legion of Merit with oak leaf cluster, DFC with oak leaf cluster, Air medal with 16 oak leaf clusters. Office: Torchmark Corp Bd Directors 3700 S Stonebridge Dr Mc Kinney TX 75070-8080 Office Phone: 808-569-4000. Business E-Mail: lnewton@torchmarkcorp.com.

NEWTON, VIRGINIA, archivist, historian, librarian; d. John Walter and Reba Newton; m. Alvin Ellis Schmid, 2003. Student, Inst. Tecnológico y de Estudios Superiores de Monterrey, Nuevo Leon, Mex., 1957; AA in Bus. Adminstrn., Stephens Coll., 1958; BA in History, Okla. State U., 1960; M of Librarianship, U. Wash., 1963; cert. in libr. sci., U. Tex., 1968, MA in Latin Am. Studies, History, Archives and Libr. Sci., 1975, PhD in Latin Am. Studies, History, Archives and Libr. Sci., 1983. Libr. Inst. Pub. Affairs U. Tex., Austin, 1963-65, libr. Art Libr., 1965-67; coord. Sr. Cmty. Svcs. Program Econ. Opportunities Devel. Corp., San Antonio, 1968-69; archivist, spl. collections libr. Trinity U., San Antonio, 1969-73; spl. collections and reference libr. Pan Am. U., Edinburg, Tex., 1974-77; archivist, records analyst Alaska State Archives and Records Svc., 1983-84, dep. state archivist, 1984-87; state archivist Alaska State Archives & Records Mgmt. Svcs., 1988-93; dir. Columbus Meml. Libr. OAS, Washington, 1993—2001. Archives cons. Ford Found. for Brazilian Archivists Assn., 1976, Soc. for Ibero-Latin Thought, 1980, Project for a Notarial Archives Computerized Guide, 1980; chair Alaska State Hist. Records Adv. Bd., 1988-93, coords. steering com., 1991-93; cons. Puerto Rican Hist. Records Adv. Bd., 1997-99. Author: An Archivists' Guide to the Catholic Church in Mexico, 1979. Founder jail libr. Bexar County Jail, San Antonio; hon. dep. sheriff Bexar County, 1972-75; mem. Dem. party; chair Dems. Abroad in Mex., 1979-81; mem. Dems. Abroad Del. The Dem. Nat. Conv., N.Y., 1980; vice- chair Bill Egan Forum Greater Juneau Dem. Precinct, 1986-88 Recipient Commendation award Gov. of Alaska William Sheffield, 1985, Disting. Alumnae award U. Tex. Sch. Libr. and Info. Sci., 1998; Masonic Scholarship for internat. rels. George Washington U., 1960-61; univ. fellow U. Tex.-Austin, 1982-83, post masters fellow U.S. Dept. Edn.-U. Tex., Austin, 1967-68; scholar Orgn. Am. States, 1980, 81, Fulbright-Hays scholar, 1979, 80, scholar Nat. Def. Fgn. Lang.-U. Tex., Austin, 1978-79, scholar Calif. State Libr., 1962-63. Mem. AAUW (bd. dirs. 1983-86, scholar 1983), Nat. Assn. Govt. Archives and Records Adminstrs. (bd. dirs. 1989-93, chair membership com. 1989-93), Alaska Hist. Soc. (bd. treas. 1988-94), Alaska Libr. Assn., Acad. Cert. Archivists (cert. 1989), Rotary, Phi Kappa Phi. Democrat. Avocations: skiing, dance, researching, reading, hiking. Office: 206 Laurel Heights Place San Antonio TX 78212

NEWTON, WAYNE (CARSON WAYNE NEWTON), entertainer, actor, recording industry executive; b. Norfolk, Va., Apr. 3, 1942; s. Patrick and Evelyn (Smith) N.; m. Elaine Okamura, June 1, 1968 (div. 1985); 1 child, Erin; m. Kathleen McCrone, April 9, 1994; 1 child, Lauren Ashley. L.H.D. (hon.), U. Nev.-Las Vegas, 1981; Doctorate (hon.), William Woods U. Owner Tamiment Internat. Resort. Appearances include Sands, Caesar's Palace, Desert Inn, Flamingo and Frontier hotels, Las Vegas, Harrah's Club, Reno and Lake Tahoe, I Love N.Y. Concert, Americana Hotel, N.Y.C., Talk of the Town, London, London Paladium, Grand Ole Oprey House, Nashville, 4th of July, Washington, Astrodome, Houston, Hollywood (Calif.) Bowl, Melodyland, Anaheim, Calif., Circle Star, San Francisco, Sea World, Orlando, Fla., Sherman House, Chgo., Wis. State, Iowa State fairs, Valley Forge Music, Westbury Music fairs, Deauville and Eden Roc hotels, Miami Beach, Carlton Club, Bloomington, Minn., hotels Atlantic City, N.J., before U.S. troops, Vietnam, Beirut, & Persian Gulf; TV appearances include Red, White & Wow, A Christmas Card, (TV miniseries) North and South: Book II, 1986, TV spls. Opryland, 1973, Joys, 1976, Happy Birthday, Las Vegas, 1977, The Wayne Newton Special, 1982, The Real Las Vegas (TV series), 1996, Las Vegas on Ice, 1997, Feed the Children, 1997, Elvis Meets Nixon, 1997, VH1 Divas Las Vegas, 2002; film appearances in 80 Steps to Jonah, 1969 (also composer), Licence to Kill, 1989, The Adventures of Ford Fairlane, 1990, The Dark Backward, 1991, Best of the Best II, 1993, Night of the Running Man, 1994, Vegas Vacation, 1997, Ocean's Eleven, 2003, Smokin' Aces, 2006, (voice) Hoodwinked Too! Hood VS. Evil, 2010; video appearances in Who's Your Daddy?, 2003; host, prodr. The Entertainer, 2005; guest appearances include Jackie Gleason and His American Scene Magazine, 1962. 1964, The Mike Douglas Show, 1964, The Lucy Show, 1965, Bonanza, 1966, Here's Lucy, 1968, 1970, The Tonight Show Starring Johnny Carson, 1971, 1972, The Dean Martin Show, 1971, 1974, Switch, 1976, Vega$, 1979, 1981, The Highwayman, 1988, Full House, 1990, L.A. Law, 1991, Roseanne, 1991, Perfect Strangers, 1992, Renegade, 1994, 1995, Tales from the Crypt, 1994, The Fresh Prince of Bel-Air, 1995, Ellen, 1997, Ally McBeal, 1998, The Pretender, 2000, Las Vegas, 2003, 7th Heaven, 2004, The Tonight Show with Jay Leno, 2004, Larry King Live, CBS This Morning, E! Entertainment Television, Entertainment Tonight and others; albums include Danke Schoen, 1963, In Person!, 1964, Wayne Newton in Person!, 1964, Summer Wind, 1965, Red Roses for a Blue Lady, 1965, Now!, 1966, It's Only the Good Times, 1967, Old Rugged Cross, 1966, One More Time, 1968, Walking on New Grass, 1968, Can't You Hear the Song?, 1972, Change of Heart, 1978, Daddy Don't You Walk So Fast, 1972, Coming Home, 1989, God Is Alive, 1991, Showstoppers, 1992, Rock of Ages, 1992, A Merry Little Christmas, 1992, Moods & Moments, 1992, Christmas Song, 1995, Branson City Limits, 1998, Real Thing, 2004, Song of the Year: Wayne Newton Style, Tomorrow; author (with Dick Maurice): Once Before I Go, 1989; performer Dancing With the Stars, 2007. A supporter St. John's Indian Mission, Levene, Ariz.; chmn. USO Celebrity Cir.; mem. Patawomeck Indian Tribe, Va. Recipient citation as distinguished recording artist and humanitarian, 1971; Freedom Lantern award Commonwealth of Mass., 1979, Entertainer of Yr. award Variety Clubs So. Nev., 1973, Gov.'s award Commonwealth of Mass., 1976, cert. of appreciation Gov. of Nev., 1978, Founders award St. Judes Childrens Hosp., Humanitarian award Am. Cancer Soc. Cancer Research Ctr., Lifetime Achievement award, First Am. in the Arts, 2000, Congl. medal, Honor Soc. Citizenship award, medal of honor, Dept. Def., US Legion of Valor's Citizen award, Jimmie E. Howard Meml. award, Medal of Honor, City Las Vegas, Ellis Island Medal of Honor, 1999, American Legend award, Washington, D.C., 1999, VFW Hall of Fame award, Am. Legion Exceptional Citizen award, star on the Hollywood Walk of Fame, award for Daddy Don't Walk So Fast ASCAP, platinum record for Danke Schoen, also gold album and gold records; named one of 10 Outstanding Young Men of Am. Nat. Jaycees, 1976; named Most Disting. Citizen of Yr. NCCJ, Outstanding Indian Entertainer of Yr. Navajo Nation, 1980, Entertainer of Yr., Nev. Mag., Casino Player Mag., 1999, Top Three Entertainers of the Century in Nev. and Around the World, Reno Gazett Jour., Amb. Goodwill, State of Nev, Veteran Fgn. Wars of US, Hon. Vietnam Veteran, Hon. Green Beret, 1999; knighted, 1998; renamed in his honor Las Vegas' McCarran Internat. Airport main thouroghfare Wayne Newton Blvd.; inducted Gaming Hall of Fame, Am. Gaming Assn.

NEXSEN, JULIAN JACOBS, lawyer; b. Kingstree, SC, Apr. 14, 1924; s. William Ivey and Barbara (Jacobs) N.; m. Mary Elizabeth McIntosh, Jan. 28, 1948; children: Julian Jacobs Jr. At, The Citadel, Charleston, SC, 1941—43; BS magna cum laude, U. SC, Columbia, 1948, JD magna cum laude, 1950. Bar: S.C. 1950, U.S. Supreme Ct. 1960. Ptnr. firm Nexsen Pruet, LLC, Columbia, SC. Trustee Richland County Pub. Libr., chmn., 1976-77; trustee Providence Hosp., chmn., 1984-86; trustee Providence Found., Providence Ministries, Sisters of Charity of St. Augustine Health Sys.; past bd. dirs. Columbia Music Festival Assn., ARC Richland-Lexington Counties, Ctrl. Carolina Cmty. Found.; mem. U.S.C. Law Sch. partnership bd.; elder Eastminster Presbyn. Ch., trustee Congaree Presbytery, 1967-87, Synod, S.C., 1969-74, mem. Trinity Presbytery Coun. Lt. inf. AUS, 1943-46, ETO, capt., 1950-51, Korea. Decorated Bronze Star with oak leaf cluster; recipient Compleat Lawyer award U. SC Sch. Law, Disting. Pub. Svc. award Order of Coif, 2007. Mem. ABA, SC Bar (treas., bd. govs. 1974-79, House of Dels. 1980-92), Richland County Bar Assn. (pres. 1974-75, Disting. Svc. award 1987), Am. Bar Found., SC Bar Found. (pres. 1971-72), SC Law Inst. (coun., exec. com. 1986—), Am. Law Inst., Am. Coll. Trust and Estate Counsel (regent 1973-82), Am. Judicature Soc., Forest Lake Country Club, Palmetto Club, Kiwanis (bd. dirs. 1972-74, 77-79), Phi Beta Kappa. Home: 2840 Sheffield Rd Columbia SC 29204-2332 Office Phone: 803-771-8900. Business E-Mail: jnexsen@nexsenpruet.com.

NGUYEN, CHARLES CUONG, engineering educator, researcher, dean; b. Danang, Vietnam, Jan. 1, 1956; arrived in U.S., 1978, naturalized, 1978; s. Buoi and Tinh Thi Nguyen; m. Kim-Bang Pham, Aug. 5, 1989 (div.); children: Carissa Kim Thuy Duong, Olivia Quynh Duong, Dylan Nhat Khang, Parker Duy Khang. Diploma, Konstanz U., Fed. Rep. Germany, 1978; MS with distinction, George Washington U., 1980, DSc with superiour performance, 1982. Engr. Siemens Corp., Erlangen, Germany, 1977-78; lectr. George Washington U., Washington, 1978-82; asst. prof. engring. Cath. U. Am., Washington, 1982-85, assoc. prof. elec. engring., 1985-92, prof., 1992—, chmn. dept. elec. engring. and computer sci., 1997-2001, dean Sch. Engring., 2001—; mem. Inst. de La Providence Hue Vietnam, 1971, Fgn. Svc. Selection Bd. US Nepetusenr State, 2010, 2013. Cons. Mitre Corp., Meridian Corp., Jet Propulsion Lab., others; dir. Ctr. Artificial Intelligence and Robotics, 1985—; mem. organizing coms. various robotics confs.; sr. rsch. assoc. NAS, 1990—; program vice chair IEE-Internat. Conf. Robotics 2d Automation, 1997, Internat. Symposium and Robotic Automation, 1997; chmn. organizing com. Robotics Internat., Internat. Symposium Robotics and Mfg.; elected bd. mem. Fgn. Svc. Selection Bd., US Dept. State, 2010. Founding editor, editor-in-chief: Jour. Intelligent Automation and Soft Computing (10th Anniversary award, 2006); editor: (book) Robotics and Manufacturing, Vol. 5, 1994, Intelligent Automation and Soft Computing, Vol. 1, 1994, Intelligent Automation and Soft Computing, Vol. 2, 1994; mem. editl. bd.: Jour. Intelligent and Fuzzy Sys., Engring. Design and Automation, assoc. editor: Computers and Elec. Engring.: An Internat. Jour., 1992—, guest editor: Jour. Robotic Sys., —; contbr. scientific papers to profl. jours. Apptd. by Pres. Bus to bd. dirs. Vietnam Edn. Found., 2004—07. Recipient Leadership award, Internat. Network Engring. Rsch., Excellence in Cmty. Svc. award, Vietnamese Med. Rsch. Found., 2007, Rsch. Initiation award, Engring. Found., 1985, Disting. Alumni Scholar award, George Wash. U., 2002, Lifetime Achievement award, World Automation Congress, 2004, Cmty. Svc. award in Edn., Asia Entertainment Inc., 2004, Lifetime Achievement award, Dist. Columbia Coun. Engring. and Archtl. Socs., 2009; fellow, NASA-Am. Soc. Elec. Engring., 1985, 1986, Goddard Space Flight Ctr., 1994. Fellow: AAAS; mem.: IEEE (sr.; program v.p. Washington chpt.), IEEE Sys. Jour. (mem. editl. adv. bd. 2009—), Soc. Mfg. Engrs. (sr. Robotics Internat.), Internat. Soc. Mini-and Microcomputers, Tau Beta Pi (faculty advisor), Sigma Xi. Roman Catholic. Avocations: guitar, singing, tennis, skiing, ping pong/table tennis. Business E-Mail: nguyen@cua.edu.

NIBLOCK, ROBERT A., consumer home products company executive; b. Fla., 1962; m. Melanie Niblock; 2 children. BA in Acctg., U. NC. Acct. Ernst & Young LLP, 1986—93; dir. tax Lowe's Companies, Inc., Mooresville, NC, sr. dir. tax Mooreville, NC, v.p., treas., 1997—99, sr. v.p. fin. Mooresville, NC, 1999—2000, sr. v.p., CFO, 2000—01, exec. v.p., CFO, 2001—03, pres., 2003—06, chmn., CEO, 2005—11, chmn., pres., CEO, 2011—. Bd. dirs. Lowe's Companies Inc., 2004—, ConocoPhillips, 2010—, Retail Industry Leaders Assn., vice chmn., 2006—07, chmn., 2008—09. Office: Lowe's Companies Inc 1000 Lowe's Blvd Mooresville NC 28117*

NICELEY, FRANK S., state legislator; b. Knoxville, Tenn., Mar. 3, 1947; m. Cyndie Niceley; 3 children. Former vice chmn. Jefferson County Planning Coun.; state rep. Dist. 17 Tenn., 2005—; supr. Jefferson County Soil Conservation Dist.; farmer. Mem.: Jefferson County Farm Bur. Republican. Methodist. Office: 1023 Creek Rd Strawberry Plains TN 37871 also: 113 War Memorial Bldg Nashville TN 37243-0117 Office Phone: 615-741-4419. Office Fax: 615-253-0347. Business E-Mail: rep.frank.niceley@capitol.tn.gov.

NICHOL, GENE RAY, JR., law educator, former academic administrator; b. Dallas, May 11, 1951; s. Gene R. and Dolores (Dumas) N.; m. Janet Castle, Aug. 20, 1973 (div. 1978); m. Glenn George, Nov. 25, 1984. BA in Philosophy, Okla. State U., 1973; JD, U. Texas, 1976. Bar: Alaska 1978. Assoc. Ely, Guess and Rudd, Anchorage, 1976-78; asst. prof. W.Va. U., Morgantown, 1978-80, assoc. prof., 1980-82; prof. law U. Fla., Gainesville, 1983-84; Cutler prof. law, dir. Inst. of Bill of Rights Law Coll. William & Mary, Williamsburg, Va., 1984-88, pres., 2005—07; dean U. Colo. Law Sch., 1988-95; dean, Burton Craige prof. law U. NC Sch. of Law, Chapel Hill, 1999—2005, prof. law, 2008—. Host Culture Wars, KBDI T.V., Denver, 1995-96. Author: (with M. Redish) Federal Courts; columnist: Rocky Mt. News, 1999-2000, Raleigh News and Observer, 2000-04; contbr. articles to profl. jours. Posten research grantee U. W.Va., 1980, 81, 82. Mem. Nat. Lawyers Guild (coms. 1978, vice chair Colo. reapportionment commn.), Am. Law Inst., ACLU (coms. 1978—), Am. Bar Found. Fellows, Order of Coif. Roman Catholic. Avocation: back packing. Office: U NC Sch of Law 5106 Van Hecke-Wettach Hall 100 Ridge Rd Chapel Hill NC 27599 E-mail: gnichol@email.unc.edu.

NICHOLAS, NICKIE LEE, retired industrial hygienist; b. Lake Charles, La., Jan. 19, 1938; d. Clyde Lee and Jessie Mae Nicholas. BS, U. Houston, 1960, MS, 1966. Tchr. sci. Pasadena (Tex.) Ind. Sch. Dist., 1960-61; chemist FDA, Dallas, 1961-62, VA Hosp., Houston, 1962-66, NASA Johnson Spacecraft Ctr., 1968-73; chief biochemist Baylor U. Coll. Medicine, 1966-68; analytical chemist TVA, Muscle Shoals, Ala., 1973-75; indsl. hygienist, compliance officer OSHA, Dept. Labor, Houston, 1975-79, area dir. Tulsa, 1979-82, mgr. Austin, Tex., 1982-96, ret. Faculty VA Sch. Med. Tech., Houston, 1963—66. Recipient award for Outstanding Achievement, German Embassy, 1958, Suggestion award, VA, 1968, Group Achievement award, Skylab Med. Team NASA, 1974, Personal Achievement award, Dept. Labor Fed. Women's Program, 1984, Career Achievement award, Federally Employed Women Inc., 1988, Meritorious Performance award, DOL-OSHA, 1990, Asst. Sec.'s Leadership award, 1992, 1996, Disting. Career Svc. award, Dept. Labor, 1991, Sec.'s Exceptional Achievement award, 1991, cert. of Appreciation, OSHA, 1991. Mem.: Fed. Exec. Assn. (pres. 1984—85), Am. Harp Soc., Am. Soc. Safety Engrs., Am. Indsl. Hygiene Assn., Am. Conf. Govtl. Indsl. Hygienists, Am. Assn. Clin. Chemists, Am. Chem. Soc. (dir. analytical group Southeastern Tex. and Brazosport sects. 1971, chmn. elect 1973), Order Eastern Star, Kappa Epsilon. Home: 1603 LCR 706 Kosse TX 76653

NICHOLL, JEFFREY SCOTT, neurologist, educator; b. Stamford, Conn., Aug. 13, 1949; s. Robert George and Helen Holmes (Wilson) N.; m. Katherine Maris Mattes, Mar. 2, 1996; 1 child, Colleen Marie. BA, U. Pa., 1970; MD, Georgetown U., 1974. Diplomate in psychiatry, neurology, and clin. neurophysiology Am. Bd. Psychiatry and Neurology, Am. Bd. Emergency Medicine, Am. Bd. Clin. Neurophysiology. Intern Hosp. of the Good Samaritan, LA, 1974—75; resident in psychiatry UCLA, 1975—77, 1978—79, fellow in epilepsy, 1998—2000; fellow in consultation-liaison psychiatry U. Calif., Irvine, 1979—80; emergency physician various instns, Calif., 1979—87, Kaiser-Permanente, San Diego, 1987—95; resident in neurology Tulane U., New Orleans, 1995—98, assoc. prof. clin. neurology and psychiatry, 2000—; clin. instr. neurology UCLA, 1998—2000; dir. Residency Program and Med. Student Edn., 2008—11; fellow forensic psychiatry Tulane U., New Orleans, 2011—12. Avocations: sailing, swimming. Office: Tulane U Sch Medicine 1430 Tulane Ave #8065 New Orleans LA 70112 Office Phone: 504-988-6669. Personal E-mail: jsnichollmd@yahoo.com.

NICHOLLS, TIM S., paper company executive; BBA, Univ. SC, Spartansburg; MBA, Univ. Ga. Fin. mgmt. positions Union Camp Co., 1991—99; various mgmt. positions International Paper Co., Memphis, 1999—2007, gen. mgr. emerging markets, dir. fin. indsl. packaging, v.p., CFO IP Europe Brussels, pres. Weldwood Canadian pulp & wood bus. Vancouver, v.p. spl. assignment Memphis, sr. v.p., CFO, 2007—, sr. v.p. printing & comm. papers, the Americas, 2011—. Office: Internat Paper 6400 Poplar Ave Memphis TN 38197

NICHOLS, BUFORD LEE, JR., pediatrician, nutritionist; b. Ft. Worth, Dec. 12, 1931; married; 3 children. BA, Baylor U., 1954, MS, 1958; MD, Yale U., 1960. Diplomate Am. Bd. Pediatrics, Am. Bd. Nutrition. Instr. pediatrics Baylor U. Coll. Medicine, Houston, 1956-57, instr. physiology and pediatrics, 1964-66, from asst. prof. to assoc. prof. pediatrics, 1966-67, instr. physiology, 1967-74, chief sect. nutrition and gastroenterology, dept. Pediatrics, 1970-78, assoc. prof. community medicine, 1975—, prof. physiology and pediatrics, 1977—, head sect. nutrition and physiology, 1979-92; intern in pediatrics Yale-New Haven Med. Ctr., 1960-61, chief resident in pediatrics, 1963-64; resident in pediatrics Johns Hopkins Hosp., 1961-63; instr. pediatrics Yale U. Sch. Medicine, 1963-64; dir. USDA Children's Nutritional Rsch. Ctr., Houston, 1979-92, emeritus dir., 1992—2010, emeritus prof., 2010. Recipient award Bristol-Myers, 1984, Nutrition award, Am. Acad. Pediats., 1998, Shwachman award, N.Am. Soc. for Pediat. Gastroenterology, Hepatology and Nutrition, 2002. Mem. Am. Acad. Pediatrics, Am. Soc. Clin. Nutrition, Am. Coll. Nutrition (v.p. 1975-76, pres. 1977-79). Baptist. Achievements include research in environmental effects upon growth and development in the infant especially alterations in body composition and muscle physiology in malnutrition, chronic diarrhea and malnutrition; cloned, sequenced and expressed recombinant intestinal maltase-glucoamylase gene, knocked out the maltase-glucoamylase gene in mice to determine its role in digestion and glucose homeostasis. Office: Baylor Coll Medicine Childrens Nutrition Rsch Ctr 1100 Bates Ave Houston TX 77030-2600 Office Phone: 713-798-7018. Personal E-mail: blnjr@sbcglobal.net. Business E-Mail: bnichols@bcm.tmc.edu.

NICHOLS, EUGENE DOUGLAS, mathematics professor; b. Rovno, Poland, Feb. 6, 1923; came to U.S., 1946, naturalized, 1951; s. Alex and Anna (Radchuk) Nichiporuk; m. Alice Bissell, Mar. 31, 1951. BS, U. Chgo., 1949, postgrad., 1949-51; MEd, U. Ill., 1953, MA, 1954, PhD, 1956. Instr. math. Roberts Wesleyan Coll., North Chili, N.Y., 1950-51, U. Ill., 1951-56; assoc. prof. math. edn. Fla. State U., 1956-61, prof., head dept., 1961-73; dir. Project for Mathematical Devel. of Children, 1973-77; dir. math program NSF, 1958-61; dir. Math. Inst. Elem. Tchrs., 1961-70; pres. Nichols Schwartz Pub., 1992—; prof. math. edn. Fla. State U., 1974-90. Chmn. U. Ill. Com. on Sch. Math., 1954-55; cons. editor math McGraw-Hill Book Co., 1956 Co-author: Modern Elementary Algebra, 1961, Introduction to Sets, 1962, Arithmetic of Directed Numbers, 1962, Introduction to Equations and Inequalities, 1963, Introduction to Coordinate Geometry, 1963, Introduction to Exponents, 1964, Understanding Arithmetic, 1965, Elementary Mathematics Patterns and Structure, 1966, Algebra, 1966, Modern Geometry, 1968, Modern Trigonometry, 1968, Modern Intermediate Algebra, 1969, Analytic Geometry, 1973, Holt Algebra 1, 1974, 78, 82, 86, 92, Holt Algebra 2, 1974, 78, 82, 86, 92, Holt Geometry, 1974, 78, 82, 86, Holt School Mathematics, 1974, 78, 81, Holt Pre-Algebra Mathematics, 1980, 86, Holt Mathematics, 1981, 85, Elementary School Mathematics and How to Teach It, 1982, Geometry, 1991, Holt Pre-Algebra, 1992, Mathematics Dictionary and Handbook, 1993, 95, 98, 99; author: Pre-Algebra Mathematics, 1970, Introductory Algebra for College Students, 1971, Mathematics for the Elementary School Teacher, 1971, College Mathematics, 1975, College Mathematics for General Education, rev. edit., 1975. Named Fla. State U. Disting. Prof., 1968-69; recipient Disting. Alumni award U. Ill. Coll. Edn., 1970. Mem. Am. Math. Soc., Math. Assn. Am., Sch. Sci. and Math. Assn., Nat. Coun. Tchrs. Math., Coun. Basic Edn., Text and Acad. Authors Assn., Pi Mu Epsilon, Phi Delta Kappa. Home: 3386 Lakeshore Dr Tallahassee FL 32312-1305 Home Phone: 850-385-9218; Office Phone: 570-253-9362. Personal E-mail: eunichols@aol.com.

NICHOLS, JAMES RICHARD, civil engineer, consultant; b. Amarillo, Tex., June 29, 1923; s. Marvin Curtis and Ethel (Nichols) N.; m. Billie Louise Smith, Dec. 24, 1944; children: Judith Ann, James Richard Jr., John M. BS in Civil Engring., Tex. A&M U., 1949, MS in Civil Engring., 1950; DHum (hon.), Tex. Wesleyan U., 1990. Registered profl. engr., Tex., Okla., N.Mex. Ptnr. Freese & Nichols, Inc., Cons. Engrs., Fort Worth, 1950-76, pres., 1977-88, chmn., 1988—. Former chmn., dir. emeritus Tex. Bd. Profl. Engrs. Former chmn. Ft. Worth Conv. and Visitors Bur., Baylor All Saints Hosp.; bd. dirs. Pub. Comm. Found. North Tex., Tex. A&M Rsch. Found., Tex. Wesleyan U.; co-chmn. Metroplex Mission with Billy Graham. With US Army, 1943—46. Fellow: Am. Cons. Engrs. Coun.; mem.: NSPE, ASCE (hon.), Tex. Water Conservation Assn., Ft. Worth C. of C. (bd. dirs., adv. coun., former chmn.), Rotary, Ft. Worth Club, Exch. Club. Methodist. Office: Freese & Nichols Inc 4055 Internat Plz Ste 200 Fort Worth TX 76109-4895 Home: 1600 Texas St Apt 21602 Fort Worth TX 76102-7512 Office Phone: 817-735-7300. Personal E-mail: jm@freese.com.

NICHOLS, JONATHAN, state legislator; b. Nov. 14, 1965; m. Talitha Nichols; 1 child, Jessica. BA, Northeastern State Univ.; JD, Univ. Okla. Asst. atty.; project dir. Multi-Jurisdictional Drug Task Force Dist. 21; mem. Dist. 15 Okla. State Senate, 2001—. Mem.: Purcell C. of C., Norman C. of C. Republican. Episcopalian. Address: 2300 N Lincoln Blvd Rm 428 Oklahoma City OK 73105 Mailing: 3901 Annalane Dr Norman OK 73072 Office Phone: 405-521-5535. Business E-Mail: nichols@oksenate.gov.

NICHOLS, MICHAEL COOPER, food products executive, lawyer; b. Birmingham, Ala., Feb. 4, 1952; s. F.W. and Jeanette (Cooper) N.; m. Marcia Couch, Sept. 23, 1976; children: Joshua, Jessica, Zachary, Anna. BA with honors, Brown U., 1974; JD, Emory U., 1977. Bar: Ga. 1977, Tex. 1981. Mem. Georgia House of Reps., Atlanta, 1977-81; chief adminstrv. officer Appletree Mktg., Houston, 1988-91; gen. counsel Sysco Corp., Houston, 1981-88, v.p., 1991—98, v.p., sec., gen. counsel, 1998—, sr. v.p., gen. counsel, corp. sec., 2006—09, sr. v.p. adminstrn., gen. counsel, 2009—. Pres. Houston Food Bank, Houston, 1990—92; trustee Houston Police Officer Pension Fund; chmn. Houston Civil Svc. Commn.; bd. dirs. Congregation Beth Israel, 1986. Office: Sysco Corp Office Gen Counsel 1390 Enclave Pkwy Houston TX 77077-2099 Office Phone: 281-584-1471. E-mail: nichols.mike@corp.sysco.com.

NICHOLS, ROBERT, state legislator; m. Donna Nichols; children: Brittney, Joshua, Collynn'rae. BS in Indsl. Engring., Lamar U., 1968. Former mem. Jacksonville City Coun.; former mayor City of Jacksonville, Tex.; mem. Dist. 3 Tex. State Senate, 2007—. Bd. dirs. Nan Travis Hosp. Found., East Tex. Med. Ctr., Lon Morris Coll. Republican. Methodist. Office: 2040 N Loop 336 W Ste 107 Box 7 Conroe TX 77304 also: PO Box 12068 Capitol Station Austin TX 78711 also: 329 Neches St Jacksonville TX 75766 also: 2915 Atkinson Dr Lufkin TX 75901 Office Phone: 512-463-0103. Office Fax: 936-756-5168, 936-756-5170.

NICHOLS, RONALD LEE, surgeon, educator; b. Chgo., June 25, 1941; s. Peter Raymond and Jane Eleanor (Johnson) N.; m. Elsa Elaine Johnson, Dec. 4, 1964; children: Kimberly Jane, Matthew Bennett. MD, U. Ill., 1966, MS, 1970. Diplomate Am. Bd. Surgery (assoc. cert. examiner, New Orleans, 1991), Nat. Bd. Med. Examiners. Intern U. Ill. Hosp., Chgo., 1966-67, resident in surgery, 1967-72, instr. surgery, 1970-72, asst. prof. surgery, 1972-74; assoc. prof. surgery U. Health Scis. Chgo. Med. Sch., 1975-77, dir. surg. edn., 1975-77; William Henderson prof. surgery Tulane U. Sch. Medicine, New Orleans, 1977—2002, vice chmn. dept. surgery, 1982-91, staff surgeon, 1977—2002, prof. microbiology, immunology, 1979—, William Henderson prof. surgery emeritus, 2003—; sr. vis. surgeon Med. Ctr. La., New Orleans, 1988—2009, hon med. staff, 2009—. Cons. surgeon VA Hosp., Alexandria, La., 1978-93, Huey P. Long Hosp., Pineville, La., 1978-2002, Lallie Kemp Charity Hosp., Independence, La., 1977-85, Touro Infirmary, New Orleans, Monmouth Med. Ctr., Long Branch, NJ, 1979-88; sr. vis. surgeon Med. Ctr. La., New Orleans, 1988—2009; mem. VA Coop. Study Rev. Bd., 1978-81, VA Merit Rev. Bd. in Surgery, 1979-82; sci. program com. 3d Internat. Conf. Nosocomial Infections, Ctr. Disease Control, sci. program and fundraising com. 4th Internat. Conf.; bd. dirs. Nat. Found. Infectious Diseases, 1988-2003, v.p., 1994-97, pres.-elect., 1997-99, pres., 1999-2001, trustee, 2003-2008, bd. dirs., 2008-; hon. fellow faculty Kasr El Aini Cairo U. Sch. Medicine, 1989; adv. com. on infection control Ctrs. for Disease Control, 1991-97; disting. guest, vis. prof. Royal Coll. Surgeons Thailand, 1989, 1992; infectious diseases adv. bd. Roche Labs., 1988-95, Abbott Labs., 1990-92, Kimberly Clark Corp., 1990-99, SmithKline Beecham Labs., 1990-95, Fujisawa Pharm., chmn., 1990-99, Bayer Pharm., 1994-2001, Merck Sharpe Dohme, 1996, Depotech, 1996, Zeneca Pharm., 1997-2000, Rhone-Poulenc Rorer, 1997-99, Wyeth-Ayrest Labs., 1998-2003, Pfizer Pharm., 1999, Searle Pharm., 1999-2001, GlaxoWellcome, 1999, Aventis, 1999-2000, Cubist Pharm., 2000—05, Regent Med., 2003—06, others; study group Prophylaxis Antibiotic Project La. Health Care Rev., Inc., 1995-2000, Nat. Com. Study Blood Borne Disease Transmission make Nat. Policy, Rockefeller Brothers Fund, 2001-03; apptd. by gov. La. commn. HIV and AIDS, 1999-2007; lectr. Royal Coll. Physicians and Surgeons, Can., 1998, Internat. Infectious Disease Soc. Ob-gyn., 1998, 20th NY State Surg. Symposium, 1998, Dept. Surgery, U. Ark., 1998; nat. policy com. study innovative surgery reg. Greenwall Found., 2003—06; lectr. in field. Author: (with Gorbach, Bartlett and Nichols) Manual of Surgical Infection, 1984; author, guest editor: (with Nichols, Hyslop Jr. and Bartlett) Decision Mking in Surgical Sepsis, 1991; guest editor, author: Surgical Sepsis and Beyond, 1993; mem. editl. bd. Current Surgery, 1977-2006, Hosp. Physician, 1980—2006, Infection Control, 1980-86, Guidelines to Antibiotic Therapy, 1976-81, Am. Jour. Infection Control, 1981-99, Internat. Medicine, 1983—, Confronting Infection, 1983-86, Current Concepts in Clin. Surgery, 1984—, Fact Line, 1984-91, Host/Pathogen News, 1984—, Infectious Diseases in Clin. Practice, 1991—2005, surg. sect. editor, 1992-2005, Surg. Infections: Index and Revs., 1991—, So. Med. Jour., 1992-97, ANAEROBE, 1994—2010, Surg. Infections, 1998—, Clin. Infectious Diseases, 1999-2010; editl. adv. bd. MD Consult Infectious Diseases, 2002-04; mem. adv. bd. Physician News Network, 1991-95; patentee (with S.G. schoenberger and W.R. Rank) Helical-Tipped Lesion Localization Needle Device; patentee in field. Elected faculty sponsor graduating class Tulane Med. Sch., 1979-80, 83, 85, 87, 88, 91-92; apptd. La. Commn. HIV and AIDS, 1999-2007. Maj. USAR, 1972-75. Recipient House Staff tchg. award U. Ill. Coll. Medicine, 1973, rsch. award bd. trustees U. Health Scis., Chgo. Med. Ctr., 1977, Clin. Prof. of Year U. Health Sci., 1977, Tchg. award Owl Club, 1980-86, 90, Douglas Stubbs Lectr. award Nat. Med. Assn. Surg. Sect., 1987, Prix d'Elegance award Men of Fashion, New Orleans, 1993; named Prof. of Yr. U. Health Sci., Chgo. Med. Sch., 1977, Clin. Prof. of Yr. Tulane U. Sch. Medicine, 1979, Brit. Jour. Surgery Lectr., 1997, 1st Ann. Warren Cole Lectr., 2001; elected to Wall of Fame, Lakeview HS, Chgo., 2006. Fellow Infectious Disease Soc. Am. (mem. FDA subcom. to develop guidelines in surg. prophylaxis 1989-93, co-recipient Joseph Susman Meml. award 1990), Am. Acad. Microbiology, Internat. Soc. Univ. Colon and Rectal Surgeons, ACS (mem. oper. rm. environ. com. 1978-80, vice chair oper. rm. environ. com. 1980-81, chmn. oper. rm. environ. com. 1981-83, sr. mem. oper. rm. environ. com. 1983-87, mem. internat. rels. com. 1987-93, sr. mem. internat. rels. com. 1993-97); mem. Joint Commn. on Accreditation of Health Care Orgn. (Infection Control adv. group, 1988-98, sci. program com. 3d internat. conf. nosocomial infections CDC/Nat. Found. Infectious Diseases 1990, FDA Subcom. to Develop Guidelines in Surg. Prophylaxis, 1989-93; prophylactic antibiotic study group La. Health Care Rev. Inc. 1996-2000, clin. advisor, mem., 2001-08, AIDS commr. State of La. 1992-94, mem. 1999-2007), 5th Nat. Forum on AIDS (sci. program com.), US Pharmacopeial Convention Inc. (adv. panel surg. drugs and devices 1995-2000, nominating com. The Heinz Awards 1995-96), Assn. Practitioners in Infection Control (physician adv. coun. 1991-98), Internat. Soc. Anaerobic Bacteria, So. Med. Assn. (vice chmn. sect. surgery 1980-81, chmn. 1982-83), Assn. Acad. Surgery, NY Acad. Sci., Warren H. Cole Soc. (pres.-elect 1988, pres. 1989-90), Assn. VA Surgeons, Soc. Surgery Alimentary Tract, Inst. Medicine Chgo., Midwest Surg. Assn., Ctrl. Surg. Assn., Ill. Surg. Soc., European Soc. Surg. Rsch., Collegium Internationale Chirugiae Digestivae, Chgo. Surg. Soc. (hon.), New Orleans Surg. Soc. (bd. dirs. 1983-87), Soc. Univ. Surgeons, Surg. Soc. La., Southeastern Surg. Soc., Phoenix Surg. Soc. (hon.), Hellenic Surg. Soc. (hon.), Ctrl. NY Surg. Soc. (hon.), Tulane Surg. Soc., Alton Ochsner Surg. Soc., Am. Soc. Microbiology, Soc. Internat. de Chirugie, Surg. Infection Soc. (sci. study com. 1982-83, fellowship com. 1985-87, ad hoc sci. liaison com. 1986-89, program com. 1986-87, chmn. ad hoc com. rels. with industry 1990-93, mem. sci. liaison com. 1995-96), Soc. for Intestinal Microbial Ecology and Disease, Soc. Critical Care Medicine, Am. Surg. Assn., Kansas City Surg. Soc., Bay Surg. Soc. (hon.), Cuban Surg. Soc. (hon.), Panhellenic Surg. Soc. (hon.), Tacoma Surg. Club (hon.), Sigma Xi, Alpha Omega Alpha. Episcopalian. Home: 1521 7th St New Orleans LA 70115-3322 Office: 1430 Tulane Ave New Orleans LA 70112-2699 Office Phone: 504-988-5168. Personal E-mail: rlnmd@yahoo.com. Business E-Mail: ronald.nichols@tulane.edu.

NICHOLS, STEVEN PARKS, mechanical engineer, educator, academic administrator, lawyer; b. Cody, Wyo., July 1, 1950; s. Rufus Parks Nichols and Gwen Sena (Frank) Keyes; m. Mary Ruth Barrow, Aug. 5, 1990; 1 child, Nicholas Barrow Nichols. PhD, U. Tex., Austin, 1975, JD, 1983. Assoc. dir. Tex. Space Grant Consortium, Austin, 1989-91, dir. Design Projects Program, 1989—2002; dep. dir. Ctr. for Energy Studies, U. Tex., Austin, 1988-91, dir. of Ctr., 1991-99, acting dir. Ctr. for Electromechanics, 1994-99, assoc. prof. mech. engring., 1996—2000, prof. mech. engring., 2004—, assoc. chair dept. mech. engring., 1999—2002, dir. Ctr. for Energy and Environ. Resources, 1998—, fellow Ctr. for Nano and Molecular Scis., 1998—, dir. Chair of Free Enterprise, 2001—, fellow, 2001—, assoc. v.p. rsch., 2002—06, ASME Internat. vision and strategy task force, 2006—, prof. IC2, 2006—, fellows dir. Advanced Mfg. Ctr. Bd. dirs. Assn. Mfg. Excellence; chmn. Nat. Coun. Space Grant Dirs., NASA, 1989-92; bd. dirs. So. Coalition for Advanced Transp., 1994-99, chair elect 1998-99, chair 1998-00; bd. dirs. Nat. Inst. for Engring. Ethics, 1996-; chmn. mgmt. divsn. ASME Internat., 1999-01, exec. com. engring. and tech. mgmt., 1999-; rsch. integrity officer, 2004-2006. Patentee (with others) pulsed welding techniques, railgun igniter, inert burner, rail thruster, other patents pending. Recipient Olympus Innovation award, 2005. Fellow ASME (Disting. Lectr. award 2004-06, strategic vision com, 2007-), IC2 Inst. (sr.), Ctr. Nano and Biotech.; mem. NSPE, ABA, ASCE (anti-corruption task force 2006-), Am. Soc. Engring. Edn. (Fred Merryfield Design award 2001, Kauffman Outstanding Entrepreneurship award 2007), Nat. Inst. Engring. Ethics (bd. govs. 1987-93, 96-01), NY Acad. Scis. (Tex. gov.'s task force on technology communicalization, 2006—, dir. global idea product program, 2003—). Home: 1400 Lorrain St Austin TX 78703-4023 Office: U Tex Dept Mech Engring Austin TX 78712

NICHOLS, WILLIAM CURTIS, clinical psychologist, educator, marriage and family therapist, consultant; b. Fayette, Ala., Apr. 16, 1929; s. William Curtis and Eva (Hargett) N.; m. Alice Louise Mancill, May 29, 1954 (dec. 1990); children: Alice Camille, William Mancill, David Paul; m. Mary Anne Pace, Feb. 29, 1992. AB, U. Ala., 1953; EdD, Columbia U., 1960. Diplomate Am. Bd. Profl. Psychology. Asst. prof. sociology U. Ala., Birmingham, 1960-63; postdoctoral fellow Merrill-Palmer Inst., 1963-64, mem. psychotherapy faculty, 1965-69; prof. sociology Samford U., Birmingham, Ala., 1963-65; pvt. practice clin. psychology and marital and family therapy Grosse Pointe, Mich., 1969-73, 76-87; pvt. practice psychology, marital and family therapy Birmingham, Mich., 1976-87; prof. home and family life, dir. marriage and family counseling Fla. State U., 1973-76; exec. dir. Gov.'s Constituency Children, Fla., 1987-89; pvt. practice marital and family therapy S.E. Family Inst., 1989-90; pres. William Nichols Assocs., Organizational Cons., 1990-91; cons., marital and family therapist Atlanta, 1992—97; cons. in field, 1997-98; with The Nichols Group, Inc., 1998. Adj. prof. clin. psychology U. Detroit, 1976-83; adj. prof. family therapy Fla. State U., 1990-91; adj. prof., grad. faculty child and family devel. dept. U. Ga., 1992-05, founder, chair adv. com. Family Therapy Archives, 1993—, The Nichols Group, Inc., 1998-99. Author: Treating People in Families: An Integrative Framework, 1996, Marital Therapy: An Integrative Approach, 1988, Treating Adult Survivors of Childhood Sexual Abuse, 1992, The AAMFT: Fifty Years of Marital and Family Therapy, 1992, Family Therapy Around the World: A Festschrif to Florence Kaslow, 2004; co-author: Systematic Family Therapy, 1986; editor: (with others) Handbook of Family Development and Intervention, 2000; editor The Family Coord., 1970-75, Jour. Marriage and Family Counseling, 1974-76, Contemporary Family Therapy: An Internat. Jour., 1986-2006, Family Therapy News, 1986-91, The Internat. Connection, 1996-99; mem. editl. bd. Internat. Jour. Family Therapy, 1977-85, Jour. Divorce and Remarriage, 1976-83, 85—, Sage Family Studies Abstracts, 1977-99, Family Systems Medicine, 1982-96, Jour. Marital and Family Therapy, 1984—, Jour. Family Psychotherapy, 1990—, Jour. Family Psychology, 1986-90. Mem. mental health and health coms. Detroit Mayor's Commn. on Children and Youth, 1966-69; bd. dir. Family and Children's Svc., Oakland, Mich., 1977-87, chmn., 1984-86, dir. emeritus, 1987—. With C.E., U.S. Army, 1948-49. Recipient Svc. award Ala. Assn. for Mental Health, 1962, Spl. award for Outstanding Contbns. Fla. Assn. Marriage and Family Therapy, 1977, 82, 90; NSF fellow U. Colo., 1963, Disting. Svc. Families award Southeastern Coun. on Family Rels., 1996. Fellow: Am. Assn. Marriage and Family Therapy (dir. 1969—72, founding editor Jour. Marital and Family Therapy 1974—76, chmn. accreditation com. 1976—77, pres.-elect 1979—80, dir. 1979—83, pres. 1981—82, Spl. awards 1976, 1978, Disting. Leadership awards 1982, 1983, Disting. Leadership award 1991, Orgnl. Contbns. award 1992), Am. Psychol. Soc.; mem.: APA, Soc. for Family Psychology (Disting. Contbn. award 2010), Am. Family Therapy Acad., Internat. Family Therapy Assn. (bd. dirs. 1996—98, editor Internat. Connections 1996—99, pres. 1999—2001, 2009—11), Ga. Assn. for Marriage and Family Therapy (pres.-elect 1994—95, pres. 1996), Mich. Bd. Marriage Counselors (chmn. 1980—87), Nat. Coun. on Family Rels. (bd. dir., exec. com. 1969—78, pres. 1976—77), Mich. Assn. Marriage Counselors (pres. 1969—71, chmn. profl. liaison com. 1972—73), Mich. Inter-Profl. Assn. on Marriage, Divorce and Family (com. chmn. 1968—71, 1976—86, trustee 1977—80, Orgnl. Contbn. award 1992), Assn. Marital and Family therapy Regulation Bds. (MFT examination adv. bd. 1989—92), Am. Assn. Marriage and Family Therapy Edn. and Rsch. Found. (trustee 1992—94). Home: 755 W Lake Dr Athens GA 30606 Personal E-mail: nicholsw@aol.com.

NICHOLSON, FLOYD, state legislator; b. Greenwood, SC, July 26, 1949; s. Marion N. and Nona Nicholson; m. Mamie W. Nicholson, 1977; children: Douglas Anthony, Cedric Antonio, Floyd Michael. BS, SC State U., 1972. Chmn. Upper Savannah Coun. of Govts., 1990—92; mem. Greenwood City Coun., 1982—93; hon. dr. of humanities Lander U., 1997; pres. SC Mcpl. Assn., 2001; transition team mem. Jim Rex Supt. of Edn., 2006; mayor City of Greenwood, 1994—2008; mem. Dist. 10 SC State Senate, 2008—. Democrat. Address: PO Box 1777 Greenwood SC 29646 Office: Capitol Office 610 Gressette Bldg Columbia SC 29201 Mailing: 527 Bryte St Greenwood SC 29649 Home Phone: 864-223-9460; Office Phone: 864-223-0400, 803-212-6040. E-mail: floydnicholson@scsenate.org.

NICHOLSON, HENRY HALE, JR., retired surgeon; b. Statesville, NC, June 22, 1922; s. Henry Hale and Martha Haseltine (Miller) N.; m. Freda Hyams, Sept. 24, 1956; children: Henry Hale III, Thomas Dalton Miller, John Christie, Michael Witherspoon, Freda Amanda, W. Stuart Cooper. BA in Chemistry, Duke U., 1944, MD, 1947; grad., USAF Sch. Aviation Medicine, 1952. Diplomate Am. Bd. Gen. Surgery, Am. Bd. Colon and Rectal Surgery. Rotating intern U. Wis. Gen. Hosp., Madison, 1947-48; resident in gen. surgery Med. Coll. Va., Richmond, 1948-49, Alton Ochsner Hosp. and Clinic, New Orleans, 1949-51, 53-55, inaugeral resident in colon and rectal surgery, 1955-56; pvt. practice gen., colon and rectal surgery, aerospace medicine Charlotte, NC, 1956—2002; sr. surg. staff mem. Carolinas Med. Ctr. and Mercy Hosp., Charlotte; ret., 2002. Sr. surg. staff Presbyn. Hosp., Charlotte, 1956-2002; sr. active teaching staff Carolinas Med. Ctr., 1956-85, cons. staff, 1985—; surg. cons. Surgeon Gen. USAF, 1971-82. Mem. Airport Authority Charlotte/Douglas Internat. Airport, 1992-2009, chmn., 2008-09; mem. Mayor's Com. of 100 to study regional transp. and make appropriate recommendations, 1993-94; sr. examiner FAA, 1952-2007, active pilot; mem. athletic-med. bd. N.C. Shrine Bowl, 1980-2003. With U.S. Army, 1943-46. Maj. flight surgeon USAF, 1951-53, Korea; col. USAFR, 1961-82, NCANG, command air surgeon 1961-1982. Decorated Legion of Merit, Disting. Svc. medal USAF NC; named Flight Surgeon of Yr., USA N.G., 1981, 1st Alternate Flight Surgeon of Yr. award USAF, 1982. Fellow ACS, Am. Soc. Colon and Rectal Surgeons; mem. Mecklenberg County Med. Soc. (pres. 1972), Charlotte Surg. Soc. (pres. 1987), Shriners, Masons (32 degree), Jesters, Alton Ochsner Surg. Soc., Hazel Creek Trout Club, Rotary Internat., Robert Burns Soc. (pres. 1963-64), St. Andrews Soc. of Carolina, Air Force Assn., Hound Ears Club (Blowing Rock, N.C.), Charlotte Country Club, Alpha Tau Omega, Phi Chi, Omicron Delta Kappa. Methodist. Avocations: golf, skiing, fly fishing, travel, painting.

NICHOLSON, LELAND ROSS, retired utilities executive, energy consultant; b. Carrington, ND, Feb. 21, 1924; s. Malcom and Lena May (Kerlin) N.; m. Virginia E. Blair, Mar. 16, 1946, (dec. Oct 10, 2002); children: Heather Le Nicholson Studebaker, Leland B., Holly Kay, Nicholson Sites. Student, Northwestern U., 1940-41; BSEE, U. N.D., 1949; postgrad. in utility mgmt., U. Minn., 1952. Planning and mktg. engr. Minkota Power Coop., Grand Forks, ND, 1949-54; dir. new bus. Kans. Power & Light Co., Topeka, 1954-64, v.p. mktg., 1964-76, sr. v.p., 1976-80, exec. v.p., 1980-83, also bd. dirs.; pres. Kans. Power & Light Gas Service, Topeka, 1985-88, ret., 1988; pres., chief operating officer The Gas Service Co., Kansas City, Mo., 1983-85. Pres. Indsl. Devel. Corp., Topeka; chmn. Kans. Coun. on Electricity and Environment; exec. com. Kansas City Labor Mgmt. Coun., 1986-89; mem. Mktg. Execs. Conf.; bd. dirs. Gas Service Energy Corp., Kansas City, Merchants Nat. Bank, Topeka, bd. dir. CM Hosp. Southitill, 2010- Idea innovator heat pump water heater, photo cell controlled yard light, hydrogen fuel cell, electric grill. Bd. dirs., area relations com. Kansas City Area Econ. Devel. Coun., Mo., 1983-89; bd. dirs. Kansas City Pvt. Industry Coun., 1986-89, Kansas City Downtown Coun.; trustee U. Mo., Kansas City, 1984-91; mktg. chmn. Kansas City Full Employment Council; past chmn., mem. Topeka-Shawnee County Planning Commn.; adult adv. com. Sea Scouts. Master sgt. USMC, 1942-46. Mem. Am. Gas Assn., Midwest Gas Assn. (bd. dirs. 1985-89), Mo. Valley Electric Assn. (chmn. 1979-81), Edison Electric Inst. (mktg. chmn. 1978-80), Assoc. Industries of Mo., Kans. Assn. Commerce and Industry, Greater Kansas City (Mo.) C. of C. (bd. dirs. 1979-82), US Marine Corps League (life), Shawnee Yacht Club (Topeka) (commodore 1972-74), Lake Gaston Assn. (pres. 1993-97), Kansas City Club, Rotary. Republican. Methodist. Avocations: sailing, canoeing, fishing, reading.

NICHOLSON, MYREEN MOORE, artist, researcher; d. William Chester and Illeen (Fox) Moore; m. Roland Quarles Nicholson Jr., Jan. 9, 1965 (dec. 1986); children: Andrea Joy, Ross (dec. 1965); m. Harold Wellington McKinney II, 1981; 1 child, Cara Isadora. AA, William and Mary Coll., 1960; BA, Old Dominion U., 1962, MA, 1997; PhD, 1988; MLS, U. N.C., Chapel Hill, 1971; grad., The Citadel, 1968—69, Hastie Sch. Art, 1968, Chrysler Mus. Art Sch., 1964, Contemporary Art Ctr., Va., 1964, Old Dominion U., 2000. LSW Va., 1965, SC, 1967; cert. tchr. English, art and media Va. English tchr., Chesapeake, Va., 1962-63; dept. head Portsmouth Bus. Coll., Va., 1963-64; tech. writer City Planning/Art Commn., Norfolk, 1964-65; art tchr. Norfolk pub. schs., 1965-67; prof. lit. art Palmer Jr. Coll., Charleston, S.C., 1968; tchr. John's Island, SC, 1968; libr. Charleston Schs., 1968-69; asst. to asst. dir. City Libr. Norfolk, 1970-72; head model city program, 1970—71; art and audio-visual libr., 1972-75; rsch. libr., 1975-83; libr. dept. fiction, 1983-90; asst. Pulitzer poet WD Snodgrass, 1978—80; prof. Ctrl. Tex. Coll., 1998—; dir. W. Ghent Arts Alliance, Norfolk, 1978—, Grader SAT's, 2006—. Poet-in-schs., Virginia Beach, Va., 1987. Book reviewer Art Book Revs., Libr. Jour., 1973-76; editor, illustrator Acquisitions Bibliographies, 1970—, (play) Eldorado: The Poes in Norfolk, 1996; editor West Ghent newsletter, 1995-96; juried exhibits various cities including Grand Hyatt, Mayflower, Washington, by Joan Mondale, Nohra Haime, curator of Freer Gallery, by sr. curator Nat. Mus. Am. Art, curator Phillips Collection, asst. curator, White House and by dir. of Nat. Portrait Gallery; group shows include Contemporary Art Ctr., Va., Va. Beach, 1993, 98, Yorktown Small Works Show, 1996, Tidewater Artists Assn. Portfolio Show, 1996, Portfolio Show, D'Art Ctr., 2011, Portfolio Show Suffolk Art Mus., 2012, Andy Warhol Exhibit Mus. Contemporary Art, 2012, Theme Show Suffolk Art Mus., 2012, Suffolk Artists and Writers Invitational Exhibit, 1996, What in the Word Art, Suffolk Art Gallery, 2011, Artists in Virginia, 1996, Peninsula Ann., Juried Art Exhibit, 1996, Hampton Bay Day Juried Art Exhibit, 1996, Trinity Ch. Stations of the Cross, Portsmouth Mus., 1996-97, Hermitage Mus., 1996, 2010-11, Yorktown, Va. On-The-Hill, 1997, 98 (First Place, IPA Printmaking, Washington), Wakefield Art Ctr., 1998, Portlock So No, 2009, 2010, Hampton Art League, 2009-10, 2013, The Warehouse, 2009, Spirits, 2009, Miniature Show One Eleven Gallery, 2013, Renewal, Metamorphosis, 2010-11, Tiny Treasures, Ill. Gallery, 2009-10, Miniature Show, One-Eleven Gallery, 2013; one-man show: Norfolk Internat. Airport, 2002-04, Poet's Domain: Halley's Comet, 2008, Norfolk Drawing Group, 2009-, Riverview Gallery, 2010, Va. Mus. Contemporary Art, 2013; contbr. art and poetry to various publs. and anthologies. Mem. Charleston Artists Guild, 1968-70, Virginia Beach Arts Ctr., 1978-98,

Suffolk Art League, 1990-2003; dir. W. Ghent Art/Lit. Festival, 1979, Better Block Art Statue City Norfolk, 2013; poetry reader Poetry Soc. Va., Va. Ctr. for Creative Arts, Sweetbriar, 1989, Walden Books, 1991, Christopher Newport U., 1994-95, J.M. Prince Books and Coffeehouse, 1995—, Statues St. Mark's Cath. Ch., 1991-92, Statue City of Hampton Va. Devel., 2004-05, Statue of St. Bridget, Oreg., 2005; coral Andy Warhol Show, Va. Mus. Contemporary Arts, 2013; graphics of hundreds of celebrities from life; curator Va. Winter Show Life Saving Mus., 1991-92; judge Bornstein art scholarship Chrysler Mus., 1992, Drawtoberfest Com., 2013-, Va. Mus. Contemporary Art, 2013; mem. staff Mid-Atlantic Antiques Mag., 1993-2008; Nat. Endowment Arts grantwriter, 1975; bd. dirs. Tidewater Literacy Coun., 1971-72, Maine Antiques Digest, 2007, co-organizer World Peace Day; poetry reader GaiaFest, 2006-09, 11-. Recipient awards various art and poetry contests; Coll. William and Mary art scholarship, 1958, William & Mary Tricentenial award for Contbns. to the Arts in Va., 1993; recipient Cert. for Vol. Contbns. to Va. by Gov., 1984; named Precinct Capt.-at-Large, 2002-03. Mem. ALA (poster sessions rev. com. 1985-96, pub. relations judge, subcom. com. 1988-90), Pub. Libr. Assn. (com. bylaws and orgns. 1988-90), Va. Libr. Assn. (pub. rels. com. 1984-86, grievance and pay equity com. 1986-88, co-winner Paraprofl. Logo award 1985, chair Pub. Documen ts Forum 1992-93), Southeastern Libr. Assn. (Rothrock award com. 1986-88, com. on coms. 1991-92), Poetry Soc. Va. (v.p. 1986-89, nominating com. 1989-90, editor newsletter 1990-93, dir. publicity 1993-95, 70th Anniversary poster for Wren Bldg., commn. 75th anniversary poster, Poetry, Prose and Pints-Officer The Paid Poet, 2010-), Art Librs. Soc. N.Am., Tidewater Artists Alliance (bd. dirs. 1989—, chair grantwriting com. 1990—, pres. 1991-92, Historian, 2009-), Norfolk Hist. Soc., Old Dominion U. Alumni Assn. (artistic dir. Silver Reunion), Ikara (pres. 1989—), D'Art Ctr. (bd. dirs. 1991-92), Va. Writers Club. Home and Office: Dir Moore Nicholson Arts West Ghent Arts Office 1404 Gates Ave Norfolk VA 23507-1131 Office Phone: 757-282-6982. E-mail: Myreen7@gmail.com.

NICKEL, RICHARD, finance company executive; BA in Telecom., U. Ky. With Education One Group Bank One; v.p., pres. Southwest Student Svcs. Corp. (subs. SLM Corp.); sr. v.p., pres., U.S.A. Funds Svcs. Sallie Mae - SLM Corp., 2008—. Office: SLM Corp 12061 Bluemont Way Reston VA 20190 Office Phone: 703-810-3000. Office Fax: 703-810-5074.

NICKELS, JIM, state legislator; b. Hot Springs, Ark., Sept. 10, 1947; m. Kathy Nickels; children: Kris, Justin. BA in Sociology, Henderson State U., 1970, MS in Sociology, 1976; JD, U. Ark., 1981. Bar: Ark. Vocat. evaluator Hot Springs Rehab. Ctr., 1972—77; adj. prof. Henderson State U., 1977; prof. U. Ark., Little Rock, 1977—; atty. Nickels Law Firm, 1981—; mem. Dist. 43 Ark. House of Reps., 2008—. Sec. U. Ark. Fed. Credit Union, 1998—2001, chmn., 2002; exec. bd. Little Rock Workforce Investment Bd., 2005—. With US Army, 1970—72. Mem.: ABA, Am. Assn. U. Professors, Am. Assn. for Justice, Labor & Employment Rels. Assn., Ark. Bar Assn., Nat. Employment Lawyers Assn., Ark. Trial Lawyers Assn., Am. Fedn. Labor-Congress Indsl. Orgs. (mem. Lawyers Coord. Com. 1998—). Democrat. Methodist. Office: State Capitol Rm 350 Little Rock AR 72201 also: PO Box 6564 Sherwood AR 72124 Office Phone: 501-682-6211, 501-682-7771, 501-833-2424. Business E-Mail: nickelsj@arkleg.state.ar.us.

NICKENS, HARRY CARL, medical association administrator; b. Monterey, Tenn., June 25, 1944; s. Van B. and Martha (Winningham) N.; m. Alicia Beck, Aug. 26, 1967; children: Kimberly, Cassidee, Brad. BS, Tenn. Tech. U., 1966, MS, 1968; EdD, U. Tenn., 1972. Counselor Va. Western C.C., Roanoke, 1972-76, dir. student devel., 1977-78, dean students, 1979-84, exec. dir. community devel. and tng., 1985-89; pres. Coll. Health Scis., Roanoke, 1989—2001; v.p. cmty. rels. and devel. Ephraim McDowell Health, Danville, Ky., 2002—07. Chair Roanoke Valley Chamber's Sch., originator Grad, Ctr.; pres. Ephraim McDowell Health Care Found., 2003-06. Pres. Roanoke Valley Career Edn.; bd. dirs. Va. Cares, Adult Care Ctr., Am. Heart Assn., Va. Amateur Sports, Salvation Army; bd. suprs. Roanoke County; trustee St. Catherine Coll. Mem. Kiwanis (pres. Roanoke chpt. 1990, pres. Danville chpt. 2006). Baptist. Avocation: gardening. Home: 107 Patrick Henry Ct Danville KY 40422 Office: Ephraim McDowell Health 217 South 3rd St Danville KY 40422 Office Phone: 859-239-2632. Business E-Mail: hnickens@emhealth.org.

NICKENS, TIM, editor; m. Bridget Nickens; 2 children. BA in Journalism, Indiana University, 1982. With Journal-Gazette, Fort Wayne, Ind., 1982—83; editorial writer, political editor and asst. managing editor/metro Miami Herald, 1990—95; asst. managing editor/Metro Saint Petersburg Times, 2001—04, deputy editor of editorials, 2004—08; reporter Tampa Bay Times, 1983—90, editor of editorials, 2008—. Co-recipient Pulitzer Prize for Editorial Writing, 2013. Office: Tampa Bay Times 490 First Ave South Saint Petersburg FL 33701*

NICKERSON, GARY W., lawyer; BA in Psychology, U. Va., 1979; JD, Coll. William & Mary, 1984. Bar: W.Va. Mem. Steptoe & Johnson PLLC, Bridgeport, W.Va., 1984—. Fellow: W.Va. Bar Found.; mem.: W.Va. State Bar (bd. govs. 2001—03, 2006—09, mem. Workers' Compensation Com., pres. 2010—11), W.Va. Bar Assn., Harrison County Bar Assn. Office: Steptoe & Johnson PLLC 400 White Oaks Blvd Bridgeport WV 26330 Office Phone: 304-933-8163. E-mail: gary.nickerson@steptoe-johnson.com.

NICKLAUS, JACK WILLIAM, sports apparel executive, retired professional golfer; b. Columbus, Ohio, Jan. 21, 1940; s. Louis Charles, Jr. and Helen (Schoener) N.; m. Barbara Bash, July 23, 1960; children: Jack William II, Steven Charles, Nancy Jean, Gary Thomas, Michael Scott. Student, Ohio State U., 1957-62, D (hon.) of Athletic Arts, 1972; LLD (hon.), U. St. Andrews, 1984. Chmn., CEO Golden Bear Internat., Inc.; ptnr. Nicklaus Design; owner Nicklaus Golf Equipment Co. Player U.S. Ryder Cup Team, 1969, 1971, 1973, 1975, 1977, 1981, 1983, 1987. Author: My 55 Ways to Lower Your Golf Score, 1964, Take a Tip From Me, 1968, The Greatest Game of All, 1969, Jack Nicklaus' Lesson Tee, 1972, Golf My Way, 1974, Jack Nicklaus' Playing Lessons, 1976, On and Off the Fairway, 1978, Play Better Golf, Vols. 1-3, 1980, 81, 83, The Full Swing, 1982, My Most Memorable Shots in the Majors, 1988. Chmn. Ohio divsn. Am. Cancer Soc., 1967; chmn. sports divsn. Nat. Easter Seal Soc., 1967. Recipient Byron Nelson award, 1964, 65, 72, 73, Bob Jones award, 1975, Presdl. Medal of Freedom, The White House, 2005, Congressional Gold Medal, 2012; named PGA Player of Yr., 1967, 72, 73, 75, 76, Dunlop Profl. Athlete of Yr., 1972, Golfer of Yr. Profl. Golfers Assn., 1973, Sportsman of Yr., Sports Illus. mag., 1978, Athlete of the Decade for 1970-79, 1979, Golfer of the '70s, 1979, Golfer of the Century, 1988; named to World Golf Hall of Fame, 1974; named one of Most Influential People in the World of Sports, 2008. Mem. President's Club Ohio State U., Phi Gamma Delta. Achievements include playing on over 105 golf courses on 5 continents, 12 ranked in US Top 100; hosted 185 profl. tournaments 1973—; won 73 ofcl. tournaments; maj. tournaments won include Tournament of Champions, 1963, 64, 71, 73, 77, US Amateur, 1959, 61, US Open, 1962, 67, 72, 80, US Masters, 1963, 65, 66, 72, 75, 86, Brit. Open, 1966, 70, 78, PGA Championship, 1963, 71, 73, 75, 80, Internat. Pro-Amateur, 1973, Tournament Players Championship, 1974, 76, 78, Australian Open, 1964, 68, 71, 75, 76, 78, World Series of Golf, 1962, 63, 67, 70, 76, PGA Seniors Championship, 1991, US Sr. Open, 1991, 93. Office: Golden Bear Golf Inc 11780 US Hwy #1 North Palm Beach FL 33408

NICKLE, DENNIS EDWIN, electronics engineer, consultant, deacon; b. Sioux City, Iowa, Jan. 30, 1936; s. Harold Bateman and Helen Cecilia (Killackey) H. BS in Math., Fla. State U., 1961. Cert. software configuration mgmt. specialist, software configuration mgmt. mgr.; ordained deacon Roman Cath. Ch., 1979. Reliability mathematician Pratt & Whitney Aircraft Co., West Palm Beach, Fla., 1961-63; br. supr. Melpar Inc., Falls Church, Va., 1963-66; prin. mem. tech. staff Xerox Data Sys., Rockville, Md., 1966-70; sr. tech. officer WHO, Washington, 1970-76; software tech. mgr. Melpar divsn. E-Sys., Inc., Falls Church, 1976-95; software process improvement mgr. Bell Atlantic, Arlington, Va., 1996-97; sr. software mgr. Litton Denro, Gaithersburg, Md., 1997—2001; cons., 2001—; bd. dirs., treas. BARK Enterprises LLC, 2006—14. Lectr. in field; coord. D.C. Software Process Improvement Network, 1995—2001, chair, 1997—2002. Author: Stress in Adolescents, 1986; co-author: Handbook for Handling Non-Productive Stress in Adolescence, Standard for Software Life Cycle Processes, IMPEESA Junior Leader Training Guide, Standard for Software Quality Assurance, 1984-91, Standard for Developing Software Life Cycle Processes, Configuration Management Procedures, Software Quality Assurance Procedures, Software Development Procedures; editor: Mama's Good Italian Cookbook, 2004; contbr. to profl. jours. Chief judge for computers Fairfax County Regional Sci. Fair, 1964-88; scoutmaster, commr. Boy Scouts Am., 1957-92; youth custodian Fairfax County Juvenile Ct., 1973-87; chaplain No. Va. Regional Juvenile Detention Home, 1978-88; moderator Nocturnal Adoration Soc.; parochial St. Michael's Ch., Annandale, Va., 1979-89, Christ the Redeemer, Sterling, Va., 1990-93; mem. Vol. Income Tax Assistance Program, 2004—08; counselor Va. Ins. Councellry and Assistance Program, 2004—08. With U.S. Army, 1958-60. Recipient Eagle award, Silver award, Silver Beaver award, other awards Boy Scouts Am.; Ad Altare Dei, St. George Emblem, Diocese of Richmond. Mem. Assn. Computing Machinery, Computer Soc., Am. Soc. for Quality Control, CODSIA (chmn. working groups), ORLANDO II (Govt./industry working group), Old Crows Assn., Rolm Mil-Spec Computer Users Group (internat. pres.), San Antonio I (select industry coord. group), Nat. Security Indsl. Assn. (conv. com. 1985-96, software quality assurance subcom., regional membership chmn. 1981-89, nat. exec. vice-chmn. 1989-94, chmn. 1994-96), Am. Security Coun., IEEE (sr., stds. working group in computers 1983—, Outstanding Vol. award 1993, Golden Core 1996), Def. Software Devel. Stds. Adv. Bd. (chmn. 1991-96), Soc. Software Quality, Hewlett-Packard Users Group, Smithsonian Assn., Internat. Platform Assn., NRA (endowment), Nat. Eagle Scout Assn. (life), KC (4 deg.), Alpha Phi Omega (life), Sigma Phi Epsilon. Home: 43245 Preston Ct Ashburn VA 20147-5307 Office Phone: 703-729-2653.

NICKON, ALEX, chemist, educator; b. Poland, Oct. 6, 1927; came to Can., 1929, US, 1955, naturalized, 1961; s. Steve and Maria (Nickon); m. Beulah Monica Godby, Aug. 22, 1950; children— Dale Beverly, Linda Cheryl, Leanne Marie. B.Sc., U. Alta., 1949; MA, Harvard U., 1951, PhD, 1953. Vis. lectr. Bryn Mawr Coll., 1953; postdoctoral fellow Birkbeck Coll., U. London, England, 1953-54, NRC, Ottawa, Canada, 1954-55; NSF sr. fellow; Imperial Coll., London, 1963-64; U. Munich, Germany, 1971-72; mem. faculty Johns Hopkins, 1955—, prof. chemistry, 1964-94, Vernon K. Krieble prof. chemistry, 1975-94, prof. emeritus, 1994—. Vis. assoc. Am. Chem. Soc. on Profl. Tng., 1975-95; mem. medicinal chem. panel NIH, 1966-70; postdoctoral panel NRC, 1968-69. Sr. editor Jour. Organic Chemistry, 1965-71; Am. exec. editor: Tetrahedron Reports, 1978-96. Recipient Md. Chemist award, 1990; Sloan Found. fellow, 1957-61 Fellow N.Y. Acad. Scis.; mem. Am. Chem. Soc. (nat. awards com. 1974-76), Brit. Chem. Soc. Home: 770 Knoll Rd Copper Canyon TX 75077-4802 Personal E-mail: nickontx@yahoo.com.

NICOLADIS, MICHAEL F., engineering company executive; b. New Orleans, Aug. 15, 1960; s. Frank and Peggy (Yemelos) N. B in Engring. magna cum laude, Vanderbilt U., 1982; MBA, Duke U., 1984. Assoc. N-Y Assocs., Inc., Metairie, La., 1984-85, v.p., 1985-97, COO, prin., 1997—. Mem. Holy Trinity Greek Orthodox Cathedral, New Orleans. Fuqua Scholar, Conoco Scholar Duke U. Mem.: ASCE, St. Martin's Episcopal Sch. (chair, bd. trustees), Am. Pub. Works Assn., Am. Coun. Engring. Cos., Soc. Am. Mil. Engrs., Chi Epsilon, Tau Beta Pi. Avocations: tennis, reading, travel. Office: N-Y Assocs Inc 2750 Lake Villa Dr Metairie LA 70002-6786 Office Phone: 504-885-0500. Business E-Mail: mnicoladis@n-yassociates.com.

NICOLETTI, PAUL LEE, retired veterinarian, educator; b. Goodman, Mo., Oct. 26, 1932; s. Felix and Clarice N.; m. Earlene Blackburn, June 6, 1954(dec.); children: Diana (dec.), Julie, Nancy. BS in Agr., U. Mo., 1956, DVM, 1956; MS, U. Wis., 1962. Diplomate Am. Coll. Vet. Preventive Medicine. Veterinarian USDA, Mo., Wis., NY, 1956-68, UN FAO, Tehran, Iran, 1968-72, USDA, Jackson, Miss., 1972-75, Gainesville, Fla., 1973-78; prof. vet. medicine U. Fla., Gainesville, 1978—2003, prof. emeritus, 2003—. Recipient awards from Fla. Cattleman's Assn., 1978, Dairy Farmers, Inc., 1978, Borden award, 1979, Gold Star award Fla. Veterinary Medicine Assoc., 1981, 86, U. Austral, Chile, 1981, P.R. Dairy Assn., 1978, faculty alumni award U. Mo., 1987; named Basic Scis. Tchr. of Yr. Nat. Student Am. Vet. Med. Assn., 1994, Alumnus of Yr. award, U. Mo., 2000, U. Fla. Disting. Svc. award, 2008, Karl Meyer-James Steele Gold Headed Cane award, Am. Vet. Epidemiology Soc., 2010; inductee Fla. Agrl. Hall of Fame, 2013. Mem. AVMA (12th Internat. prize 1991), Fla. Vet. Medicine Assn. (pres. 1995-96, veterinarian of yr. 1994, Disting. Svc. award 1999, Lifetime Achievement award 2004), Am. Coll. Vet. Preventive Medicine (pres. 1997-98), Phi Zeta (nat. pres. 1997-99). Home: 2552 SW 14th Dr Gainesville FL 32608-2042 Office: Univ of Fla Coll Vet Medicine PO Box 110880 Gainesville FL 32611-0880 Office Phone: 352-294-4289. Business E-Mail: nicolettip@ufl.edu.

NICOLIN, MAGNUS R., consumer products company executive; BA, Stockholm Sch. of Economics; MBA, U. Pa. Various leadership positions McKinsey & Co., Bayer Diagnostics, Pitney Bowes; worked J. W. Childs; pres., CEO Esselte; cons., fine writing, pres., Europe Sanford Brands, 2006; pres. Sanford Brands Europe, 2006; joined Newell Rubbermaid Inc., 2006, pres., Europe, Middle East & Africa, 2007—, pres., Asia Pacific, 2009—. Office: Newell Rubbermaid Inc 3 Glenlake Pky Atlanta GA 30328 Office Phone: 770-418-7000. Business E-Mail: mnicolin@newellrubbermaid.com.

NIE, ZENON STANLEY, manufacturing executive; b. Chgo., Nov. 19, 1950; m. Carol Ann Klockowski, Mar. 27, 1970; 1 child, Andrea Nicole. BS, U Ill., Chgo., 1971; MBA, Loyola U., Chgo., 1974. Mgr. sales stats. Zenith Electronics, Chgo., 1971-74; mktg. mgr. Hollister, Inc., Chgo., 1974-79; dir. market devel. Sealy, Inc., Chgo., 1979-81; sr. v.p. Serta, Inc., Chgo., 1981-89, exec. v.p., 1988-89, pres., 1989-91, The Bibb Co., Macon, Ga., 1991-93; chmn., pres., CEO, COO Simmons Co., 1993—2000; founded CEO Adv. Bd. LLC, 2000, chmn., pres., CEO, 2000—; oper. ptnr. Tri-Artisan Partners, 2001—. Instr. Coll. of Lake County, Ill., 1978-81; bd. dirs. Ladd Furniture Co. bd. dirs. Crown Crafts Inc., 2001- Bd. dirs. Cottage Sch. Mem. Internat. Sleep Products Assn. (chmn. stats. com. 1985—), Young Presidents Orgn., Bus. Execs. for Nat. Security. Avocations: scuba diving, fishing, skiing, jogging. Office: Tri-Artisan Partners LLC 37th Fl 110 E 59th St New York NY 10022 Office Phone: 212-610-1500. Office Fax: 212-610-1501.

NIEDERHUBER, JOHN EDWARD, medical researcher, surgeon, former federal agency administrator; b. Steubenville, Ohio, June 21, 1938; s. William Henry and Helen (Smittle) Niederhuber; m. Tracey J. Williamson (dec. Dec. 2001); children: Elizabeth Ann, Matthew John. BS, Bethany Coll., W.Va., 1960; MD, Ohio State U. Coll. Medicine, 1964. Diplomate Am. Bd. Surgery. Intern surgery Ohio State U. Hosp., Columbus, 1964-65; vis. fellow divsn. immunology Karolinska Inst., Stockholm, 1970—71; resident surgery U. Mich. Med. Ctr., Ann Arbor, 1971—73, faculty, 1973—87, prof. surgery, prof. microbiolog/immunology, 1980-87, assoc. dean rsch., 1982—85, sr. assoc. dean med. sch., 1983—85, chief divsn. surg. oncology, 1983—86; vis. prof. molecular biology & genetics Johns Hopkins U. Sch. Med., Balt., 1986—87, prof. surgery, oncology, molecular biology & genetics, 1987-91; chief surgery Stanford U. Hosp., Calif., 1991-95; Emile Holman prof. surgery, chair dept. surgery, head sect. surg. scis. Stanford U. Sch. Medicine., 1991-95, prof. microbiology/immunology, 1991-97; asst. dean oncology, dir. Comprehensive Cancer Ctr. U. Wis. Sch. Medicine, Madison, 1997—2002, prof. surgery/oncology, 1997—2005; dep. dir. translational & clin. scis., COO Nat. Cancer. Inst. (NCI), NIH, Bethesda, Md., 2005—06; acting dir. Nat. Cancer Inst., NIH, 2006, dir., 2006—10; exec. v.p., CEO Inova Inst. Translational Rsch. and Personalized Medicine Inova Health Sys., Falls Church, Va., 2010—. Cons. Wayne County Gen. Hosp., Mich., 1973—84, Ann Arbor VA Hosp., 1973—87; vis. prof. Howard Hughes Med. Inst., Chevy Chase, Md.; bd. dirs. Emergent BioSolutions Inc., 2010—. Mem. editl. bd. Jour. Immunology, 1981—85, Current Opinion in Oncology, 1989—95, Annals of Surgery, 1991—97, Surg. Oncology, 1991—, Jour. Clin. Oncology, 1993—95, Annals of Surg. Oncology, 1993—, The Oncologist, 1995—, Surgery, 1999—2004; contbr. articles to profl. jours., chapters to books. Mem. awards assembly GM Cancer Rsch. Found., 1988—92, 1998—2003; mem. rsch. adv. com. Burroughs-Wellcome Found., 1999—2006. Capt. US Army, 1965—67. Recipient Disting. Faculty Svc. award, U. Mich., 1978, Alumni Achievement award, Ohio State U. Coll. Medicine, 1989, Disting. Alumni award in medicine, Bethany Coll., 1989, Career Devel. award, USPHS. Fellow: ACS; mem.: Soc. Clin. Surgery, Am. Soc. Clin. Oncology, Am. Assn. Cancer Rsch., Soc. Surg. Oncology (v.p. 1999—2001, pres. 2001—02, 2001—03), Assn. Acad. Surgeons, Soc. Univ. Surgeons, Coller Surg. Soc., Am. Assn. Cancer Insts. (v.p. 1999—2001), Am. Soc. Transplant Surgeons, Am. Assn. Immunologists, Am. Surg. Assn., Transplantation Soc., Inst. Medicine. Avocations: golf, gardening. Office: Inova Health System 8110 Gatehouse Rd Falls Church VA 22042

NIEHOFF, KARL RICHARD BESUDEN, financial industry executive; b. Cin., May 11, 1943; s. Karl George and Jean (Besuden) N.; children: K. Richard B. Jr., Kelly B. BA, U. Cin., 1967. Corp. trust ops. officer 5th-3d Union Trust, Cin., 1968-74; v.p., gen. mgr. Sabina Water Co., Ohio, 1974-76; v.p., sec. Weil, Roth and Irving, Inc., 1974-76; co-mgr., mcpl. fin. dept. Thomson McKinnon Securities, Cin. and NYC, 1976—78; chmn. Cin. Stock Exch., Inc., Cin., 1975, pres., trustee, seat owner, mem., 1976—89; exch. rep., founding mem. Consol. Quote, Consol. Tape Oper. Coms., 1979-90, alt., 1991-92; pres. Fin. Instruments Svcs. Corp., Cin., Chgo., London, 1985-90; sr. v.p. Trading, Trans. and Market Svcs. NASDAQ, Inc., 1990—92; v.p. D.E. Shaw & Co., NYC, 1992-94; pres. D.E. Shaw Securities, LLC, NYC, 1992—94; pres., mng. ptnr. Niehoff and Assocs., NYC, 1994-99; mng. dir., chief of party, developer MDTS OTC Capital Mkt. Devel. Project, CeTO (Subs. Warsaw Stock Exch., Warsaw, 1994—96; advisor Ministry Mass Privatization, Republic of Poland, Warsaw, 1994—96; v.p., dir. Third Market Trading Corp., Chicago, 1994-98; pres., dir. SBX Inc., Cin., Princeton, NJ, 1997-2000; mng. dir. trading and tech. Unified Mgmt. Corp., Indpls., 1999—2000; pres. VSX Techs. Inc., NYC, Indpls., 1999—2000, Mark Securities, Inc., Pelham Manor, NY, 2002—05; pres., CEO Webix, Inc., NYC, 2000—02; chmn. The X-Change Corp., NYC, 2002, pres., 2002; founder, chmn. US OTC Markets, Inc., NYC, 2005—; dir., pres., sec., treas. Schuyler Pk. Manor Inc., Pelham Manor, NY, 2000—12; dir. Entrex, Inc., Chgo., 2006—09; mem. Internat. Stock Exchange Exec. Emerite, 2010—; CEO Nat. Bd. Trade Inc., NYC, 2008—; mem. small bus. fin. crisis Task Force ISEEE, 2010—; pres. Mark Securities Inc., 2002—05; mem. ISEEE, 2010—; curator History Cin. Stock Exch. Inc. In Conjunction with U. Cin. Coll. Jours., 2010—; pres. Municipal Bond Club, Queen City, 1974, mem., 1972—78; pres. Cin. Stock & Bond Club, 1975, mem., 1972—85, Cleve. Ohio Securities Tragedy Assn., 1975—85; dir. Fin. Com. Dayton Nat. History Soc. & Boonshoft Mus. Dayton, Ohio, 2013—, Atlas Holdings, LLC, 2013—, Global Bull. Bd. Inc., 2013—. Witness US House Reps. Consumers Protection and Fin. Com., 1977, other gen. oversight, GAO com. panels and inquiries, 1987—94; panelist to numerous sec. & excellence commn. divsn. conf., 1987—2009; developer DMX-Direct Market Axcess Sys., DMX ON-Line Order Routing Sys., 1987—88; v.p. Wit Capital Corp., NYC, 1998—99; pres., COO Digital Stock Market, 1998—99; seat owner, mem. Phila. Stock Exch., 1974—76; mem. Cin. Stock Exch., 1974—89, trustee, 1974—90, chmn. bd. trustees, 1975; developer Nat. Securities Trading Sys., 1976—89; founding mem. dir. Composite Quote Sys., 1977—91, Consolidated Tape Operating Com., 1977—91; mem. oper. com. Inter-Market Trading Sys., 1980—90; mem. chief execs. com. Stock Exch., 1988—90; mem. task force com. GLOBEX, 1988—89; founding charter mem. Easdaq, Brussels, 1994—96; vis. lectr. U. Cin. Coll. Bus. Adminstrn., U. Cin. Coll. Journalism, Xavier U. Bus. Adminstrn. Coll., Cin.; long-term planning com. rep. Chgo. Bd. Options Exch., 1987—88; allied mem. NY Stock Exch., 1996—98; pres. Digital Stock Market, NYC, 1998—99; vis. com. US Info. Agy., NYC, 1992—95; mng. dir. trading and tech. Unified Mgmt. Corp., Inc., Indpls., 1999—2000, NYC, 1999—2000; pres. WEBIX, Inc., 1999—2002; bd. dirs., audit com. Equity Analysts Mutual Funds, LLC, Cin., 2002—05; instl. trading com. Boston Stock Exch., instl. adv. com., 2004, mem., 2005—09, Securities Traders Assn. Chgo., 1984—94; pres. Mark Securities Inc., 2002—05; disting. alumni U. Cin., 2011. Trustee, sec. Contemporary Arts Ctr., Cin., 1975-83; bd. mem. Fin. Com., Boonshoft Mus., D.S.N.H., 2013-, Young Mens Mercantile Libr. Assn., 1974-90, adv. com., 1974-77; devel. com. Tangeman Gallery of Art, 1981-82; pres., dir. Bermuda High Condominium Assn., Delray Beach, Fla., 1999-06; mem. NY Stock Exch. Luncheon Club, 1979-2008, Boston Securities Traders Assn., 2000-05; granter, donor Niehoff Collection, Boonshoft Mus., Dayton, Ohio, Pre-Historic Native Am. Indian Ceramic Pottery, mem. UNESCO, World Heritage Com., Hopewell Ceremonial Earthwork, 2013-; commissioned a Ky. col. Gov. Edward T. Breathitt, 1996. Nominee, Great Living Cincinnatian, 2008. Mem.: Dayton Soc. Natural History, Archeol. Soc. Ohio, Securities Traders Assn. NY (chmn. listed trading com. 1993—95, OTC Bull. Bd. 2002—04, com. chmn. STA trading subcom. 2002—04), India House, Keeneland Assn., Stone House Club, Cin. Stock and Bond Club (trustee and 1st v.p. 1974—90), NY Athletic Club, NYAC Yacht Club (Pelham Manor), Nat. Arts Club, Queen City Mcpl. Bond Club (trustee 1974—80), Phi Alpha Theta. Achievements include development of DMX Direct Market Axcess System and DMX online Trading System 1987-88; CeTo OTC Real

Time Trading System, the Warsaw Stock Exchange Poland 1997; National Securities Trading System, the First Securities and Exchange Commision approved Regulation NMS System. Home: 2324 Madison Rd Cincinnati OH 45208

NIELSEN, KENNETH ANDREW, chemical engineer; b. Berwyn, Ill., Oct. 10, 1949; s. Howard Andrew and La Verne Alma (Wentzer) N.; m. Linda Kay Miller, Aug. 22, 1970; children: Annette Marie, Kirsten Viola. BS in Chem. Engring., Iowa State U., 1971, MS in Chem. Engring., 1974, PhD in Chem. Engring., 1977. Sr. engr. Union Carbide Corp., Charleston, W.Va., 1976-80, project scientist, 1980-87, rsch. scientist, 1987-94, sr. rsch. scientist, 1994—. Contbr. articles to profl. jours. Co-founder Forest Hills Asns., Charleston, 1981; advisor Boy Scout Explorer Post, Charleston, 1992. Recipient Fellowships NDEA Title IV, Procter and Gamble Co., Am. Oil Co., Elias Singer award Troy Chem. Co., 1990, Kirkpatrick Chem. Engring. Achievement award Chem. Engring. mag., 1991, Profl. Progress in Engring. award Coll. Engring. Iowa State U., 1992. Mem. AIChE, Soc. Rheology, Inst. Liquid Atomization and Spraying Sys. Achievements include discovery of a fundamentally new type of spray atomization known as a decompressive spray; invention of UNICARB system for spray coating which is a recognized major new pollution-prevention technology; SERT process for applying mold release agents in polyurethane foam manufacture; patents in field. Home: 108 Stratford Pl South Charleston WV 25303-2819 Office: Union Carbide Corp PO Box 8361 South Charleston WV 25303

NIELSEN, NIELS CHRISTIAN, JR., retired religious studies educator; b. Long Beach, Calif., June 2, 1921; s. Niels Hansen and Frances (Nofziger) N.; m. Erika Kreuth, May 10, 1958; children: Camilla Regina, Niels Albrecht. BA, George Pepperdine Coll., LA, 1942; BD, Yale U., 1946, PhD, 1951. Ordained to ministry Meth. Ch., 1946. Pastor Woodbury (Conn.) Meth. Ch., 1944-46; instr. religion Yale U., New Haven, 1948-51; faculty Rice U., Houston, 1951—, J. Newton Rayzor prof. religious studies., prof. emeritus, 1991—; Amax presdl. prof. humanities Colo. Sch. Mines, Golden, 1982-83. Author: Philosophy and Religion in Contemporary Japan, 1957, Geistige Landerkunde USA, 1960, A Layman Looks at World Religions, 1962, God in Education, 1966, Solzhenitsyn's Religion, 1975, The Religion of Jimmy Carter, 1977, The Crisis of Human Rights, 1978, Religions of the World, 1982, Revolutions in Eastern Europe: The Religious Roots, 1991, Fundamentalism, Mythos and World Religions, 1993; editor: Religion After Communism in Russia, 1994, God in the Obama Era, president's religion & ethics from George Washington to Barack Obama 2009; contbr. articles to profl. jours. Mem. Am. Acad. Religion, Am. Philos. Soc., Am. Soc. Study Religion (sec. 1977-89), Soc. European Culture, Soc. for Values in Higher Edn. Democrat. Home and Office: 2424 Swift Blvd Houston TX 77030-1806 Business E-Mail: niels@rice.edu.

NIEMAN, VALERIE GAIL, writer, language educator, journalist; b. Jamestown, NY, July 6, 1955; d. Warner Ernest and Eleanor A. (Aiken) Student, Jamestown CC, NY, 1975—76; BS in Journalism, W.Va. U., Morgantown, 1978; MFA in Creative Writing, Queens U., Charlotte, NC. Staff writer W.Va. U News Svc., Morgantown, W.Va., 1978; reporter Dominion Post, Morgantown, 1978, Times West Virginian, Fairmont, W.Va., 1979-92, city editor, 1992-95, exec. editor, 1995-97; asst. city/state editor News & Record, Greensboro, NC, 1997—2004; instr. dept. journalism and mass comm. NC A&T State U., Greensboro, 2000—04, asst. prof. English, journalism, 2004—09, assoc. prof., 2009—. Tchr. basic newswriting W.Va. U., Morgantown, 1990, tchr. sci. fiction writing, 1995; lectr., vis. writer Appalachia & SE, 1998; co-founder, co-dir. Kestrel Writers Conf., Fairmont, 1993-97; dir. HBCU Nat. Newspaper conf., 2006; instr. John C. Campbell Folk Sch., Brasstown, NC, 2008-. Author: (novel) Neena Gathering, 1988, Survivors, 2000, Blood Clay, 2011, (short story collection) Fidelities, 2004, (poetry chpts.) How We Live, 1996, Slipping Out of Old Eve, 1988, (poetry collection) Wake Wake Wake, 2006, e-book and Audiobook, 2013; founding co-editor: Kestrel lit. jour., Fairmont, 1992-1997, poetry editor, Prime Number, 2010-, poet facilitator Life Verse, 2009. W.Va. cir. writer W.Va. Humanities Commn., 1994; mem. Leadership Marion, Fairmont, 1995-96; judge United Arts Coun., NC, 2009, 11; presenter Poetry GSO, 2005-. Recipient award in letters Fairmont Arts and Humanities, 1988, 94, Elizabeth Simpson Smith prize, 1998, 2002, Greg Grummer award in poetry George Mason U., 1999, Eric Hoffer Book award, 2012, named NC Touring Artists Directory, 2012, others; fellow in poetry NEA, 1991, fellow in fiction Ky. Found. for Women, 1991, fellow in fiction W.Va. Commn. on Arts, 1992. Mem.: Authors Guild, NC Poetry Soc., NC Writers Conf., NC Writers Network (instr. 2007—), Am. Sailing Assn., Lake Townsend Yacht Club (chmn Mayor's Cup Regatta 2006, 2009). Democrat. United Ch. Of Christ. Avocations: gardening, hiking, travel, sailing. Office: NC AT&T State U 1601 E Market St Greensboro NC 27411 Business E-Mail: vgnieman@ncat.edu.*

NIEMI, ALBERT WILLIAM, JR., economics professor; b. Worcester, Mass., Aug. 30, 1942; s. Albert William and Helen Josephine (Powers) N.; m. Maria de Sano, Feb. 4, 1967; children: Albert III, Edward. AB, Stonehill Coll., 1964; MA, U. Conn., 1965, PhD, 1969. Asst. prof. Terry College of Bus., U. Ga., Athens, 1968-71, assoc. prof., 1971-75, prof., 1975—96, dir. rsch., 1975-96, assoc. dean, 1976-78, chmn. dept. econs., 1981-82, acting dean, 1982-83, dean, 1983—96; dean Coll. Bus. Adminstrn. U. Ala., Birmingham, 1996—97; dean, Tolleson Chair in bus. leadership Edwin L. Cox Sch. Bus., So. Meth. U., 1997—. Author: State and Regional Patterns in American Manufacturing, 1974, Gross State Product and Productivity in the Southeast, 1975, U.S. Economic History, 1975, 80. Mem. exec. com., bd. dirs. World Affairs Coun. of Dallas; mem. internat. adv. coun. Greater Dallas C. of C.; bd. mem. Children's Med. Ctr.; adv. coun. Cath. Found.; pres. coun. Dallas Ctr. for Performing Arts; bd. trustees Stonehill Coll. Mem. Assn. for Univ. Bus. and Econ. Rsch. (sec. 1982-84, pres. 1986), Am. Econ. Assn., Econ. History Assn., So. Econ. Assn., Athens Area C. of C., Beta Gamma Sigma, Phi Kappa Phi, Delta Epsilon Sigma. Office: So Meth U Cox Sch Bus Fincher Bldg, Rm 200 PO Box 750333 Dallas TX 75275 Office Phone: 214-768-3012.

NIETO, JUAN MANUEL, emergency medicine physician; b. Alpine, Tex., Sept. 24, 1949; s. Edmundo Miguel and Socorro; children: Ana Raquel, Cristina Marie. BS, U. Notre Dame, 1970; MD, U. Colo., 1974. Intern LA County, U. So. Calif. Med. Ctr., 1974-75; physician Cmty. Health Found., LA, 1975-77; physician emergency dept. Physicians Med. Group, Marina Del Ray, Calif., 1977-78; resident in emergency medicine Denver Gen.-St. Anthony Hosp. Sys., 1978-80; mem. staff North Colo. Med. Ctr., Greeley, 1980-83; emergency physician, med. dir. emergency dept. Brackenridge Hosp., Austin, Tex., 1984-85; practice medicine Austin, 1983—. Emergency physician Emergency Physicians Affiliates, 1986-89; assoc. prof. U. Tex. Health Sci. Ctr., San Antonio, 1994—; mem. planning com. Starflight Helicopter Air Transport, 1985; instr. advanced cardiac life support, 1977; bd. dirs. Nat. Chicano Health Orgn., 1971-74; advisor East Los Angeles Hypertension Screening Program, 1978; med. advisor Weld County Ambulance Service, 1980-83; med. dir. Air Life, 1980-83; med. dir. Alamo Heights Emergency Med. Svc., 1988-90, med. dir. AMR Ambulance, 1991-98; amb. Nat. Health Svc. Corps, 2003—. Del. Colo. Med. Soc., 1983. Fellow: Nat. Hispanic Med. Assn., Am. Acad. Emergency Medicine, Am. Coll. Emergency Physicians, NYU Wagner Sch. (leadership fellow 2001); mem.: APHA, Nat. Hispanic Medicine Assn., Soc. Academic Emergency Medicine, Physicians for a Nat. Healthcare Program, Nat. Hispanic Med. Assn., Travis County Med. Soc., Tex. Med. Assn., Nat. Hispanic Med. Assn. (leadership fellow, advisor, board mem. 2001—, mem. adv. bd. 2003—, Leadership award 2006), Amnesty Internat. Personal E-mail: jnietomd@sbcglobal.net, juan-nieto@msn.com.

NIETSCH, ELISABETH, information technology executive; CIO, v.p., constrn. SRA Internat., Inc. Office: SRA International Inc 4300 Fair Lakes Ct Fairfax VA 22033 Office Phone: 703-803-1500. Office Fax: 703-803-1509. Business E-Mail: elisabeth_nietsch@sra.com.

NIGBOR, DONALD E., electronics executive; BS in Engring., MS in Engring., Rensselaer Poly. Inst.; MBA, Dartmouth Coll. Analyst Digital Equipment Corp.; mfg. analyst Intermedics, 1980—84; gen. mgr. Benchmark Electronics Inc., 1984—90, pres., 1986—2001, CEO, 2001—05; chmn. Benchmark Electronics, Inc., 2001—. Office: Benchmark Electronics 3000 Technology Dr Angleton TX 77515 Office Phone: 979-849-6550. Office Fax: 979-848-5270. Business E-Mail: don.nigbor@bench.com.

NIHILL, JULIAN DUMONTIEL, lawyer; b. Nairobi, Kenya, Apr. 17, 1950; Student, Ampleforth Coll., Eng., 1967; LLB with honors, Exeter U., Eng., 1972; barrister at law, Inner Temple, Eng., 1973; JD, Boston U., 1977. Bar Tex. 1984. Assoc. McDermott, Will & Emory, Chgo., 1977-79, Baker & McKenzie, Chgo., 1979-83; ptnr. Gardere & Wynne, Dallas, 1984—; pvt. practise Dallas. Home: 901 Main St Ste 4400 Dallas TX 75202-3729 Office Phone: 214-522-2167.

NIIMI, ATSUSHI, automotive executive; b. Aichi, Japan, July 30, 1947; m. Michiko Niimi; 2 children. Degree in Aero. Engring., Nagoya U., 1971. Joined Toyota Motor Corp., 1971, gen. mgr. various divsns., 1995—99, dir., 2000, mng. officer, plant gen. mgr., 2003, sr. mng. dir., 2004, exec. vice pres., rep. dir., 2009; pres. Toyota Motor Mfg. North America, Inc., 2002—05. Avocations: golf, swimming, driving. Office: Toyota Motor Mfg NAm Inc 25 Atlantic Ave Erlanger KY 41018 also: 1 Toyota-Cho 471-8571 Toyota Japan

NILL, JAMES, professional sports team executive, former professional hockey player; b. Hanna, Alberta, Can., Apr. 11, 1958; m. Bekki Nill. Attended, U. Calgary. Right wing St. Louis Blues, 1982, Vancouver Canucks, 1982—84, Boston Bruins, 1984—85, Winnipeg Jets, 1985—88, Detroit Red Wings, 1988—91; ret., 1991; amateur to profl. scout Ottawa Senators, 1991—94; scout, v.p., asst. gen. mgr. Detroit Red Wings, 1994—2013; gen. mgr. Dallas Stars, 2013—. Achievements include being on the management team for the Stanley Cup Champion Detroit Red Wings, 1997, 1998, 2002, 2008. Office: Dallas Stars American Airlines Ctr 2500 Victory Ave Dallas TX 75201*

NIMER, STEPHEN DAVID, physician, leukemia researcher; b. Chgo., May 20, 1954; m. Georgia Takigawa, Oct. 18, 1987. BS, MIT, 1975; MD, U. Chgo. Sch. Medicine, 1979. Diplomate Am. Bd. Internal Medicine, Am. Bd. Hematology, Am. Bd. Med. Oncology. Intern, internal medicine UCLA Sch. Medicine, 1979—80, resident, hematologic oncology, 1980—82, fellow, 1983—86, asst. prof. medicine, 1987-92; dir. transplantation biology Jonsson Compr. Cancer Ctr., LA, 1991-92; assoc. mem. Sloan-Kettering Inst., NYC, 1993-99, mem., 1999—; chief hematology svc. Meml. Hosp., NYC, 1993—2010; head, divsn. hematologic oncology Meml. Sloan-Kettering Cancer Ctr., NYC, 1996—2008, vice chair faculty devel., 2008—12; prof. medicine Weill Medical Coll., 2000—; chair Alfred P. Sloan, 2008—12; dir. Syhester Comprehensive Cancer Ctr., 2012—; prof. medicine, biochemistry and molecular biology U. Miami, Miller Sch. Medicine, 2012—. Funded investigator NIH, 1990—. Mem. editl. bd.: Blood, 1997—2002; co-editor: Hematologic Complications of Cancer, 1996; contbr. over 200 sci. articles to profl. jours. Chmn. med. adv. bd. Gabrielle's Angel Found. for Cancer Rsch., 1998-; bd. dirs. Bone Marrow Found., Aplastic Anemia, Myelodysplastic Syndrome Internat. Found., Inc.; chmn. Myelodysplastic Syndrome (MDS) Found., 2010-. Recipient Irma T. Hirschl Career Scientist award Cornell U. Med. Sch., 1995. Fellow ACP; mem. Am. Soc. for Clin. Investigation, Am. Soc. for Hematology, Am. Soc. Clin. Oncology, Am. Assn. for Cancer Rsch., Leukemia Soc. Am. (bd. trustees NY chpt. 1998-2004), Alpha Omega Alpha. Office: Sylvester Comprehensive Cancer Ctr Clinical Research Bldg 660A 1120 NW 14th St Miami FL 33136 Office Phone: 305-243-1775. Business E-Mail: snimer@med.miami.edu.*

NIMMER, CHAD, state legislator; b. Blackshear, Ga., July 16; m. Amy Rigdon; children: Gracie, JC. Timber broker, mgr. Pierce Timber Co.; co-owner Suwannee Forest Products; mem. Dist. 178 Ga. House of Reps., Atlanta, 2011—. Mem., former Sunday sch. tchr. Emmanuel Bapt. Ch., Ga. Republican. Office: 3401 Twin Lake Rd PO Box 312 Blackshear GA 31516 also: Ga House of Reps 607-C Coverdell Legis Office Bldg Atlanta GA 30334 Office Phone: 912-449-6190, 404-656-0287. Business E-Mail: chad.nimmer@house.ga.gov.

NIMMER, RAYMOND T., law educator, former dean; b. Chgo., May 2, 1944; s. Raymond O. and Helen (Barscz) Nimmer. BA in Math., Valparaiso U., 1966, JD with distinction, 1968. Bar: Ill 1968, Tex. 1984, US Ct. Appeals (5th Cir.) 1984, US Supreme Ct. 1985, US Ct. Appeals (11th Cir.), US Ct. Appeals (Fed. Cir.). Rsch. atty. Am. Bar Found., 1968—75; assoc. dean U. Houston Law Ctr., 1975—85, Leonard H. Childs prof. law, 1979—, acting dean, 1993—95, co-dir. Intellectual Property and Info. Law Program, 1997—, Leonard Childs prof. law, 1998—, interim dean, 2006—08, dean, 2008—13; counsel Sheinfeld, Maley & Kay, Houston, 1985—91, Weil, Gotshal & Manges, Houston, 1992—99. Cons. Law Social Scis. Program NSF, 1979—92; vis. prof. law U. Tex., Austin, 1985, U. Mich. Law Sch., Ann Arbor, 1987, U. Maine Sch. Law, 2001—; cons. US State Dept. Legal Advisors Office, 1990—2001; vis. prof. law Sydney U., Australia, 2003, 2008; cons. US Office Tech. Assessment, Washington, 1991—95; chmn. Twenty-Second Century Found., 2004—; chair Annual Computer and Info. Law Inst., 2001—; Fulbright-Fladd disting. chair internat. Commercial law Universidad Catholica Sch. Law, Lisbon, Portugal, 2007—08, disting. chair in residence, 2008—; spkr. in field. Author: Commercial Asset-Based Financing, 1989, The Law of Computer Technology, 2d edit., 1993; co-author: Secured Financing in Personal Property, 1992, Bankruptcy and Creditors Rights, 1992, Modern Licensing Law, 2005-08; bd. editors The Cyberspace Lawyer, 1995-, Computer and Recht Internat., 1999-, Contracts Law Jour., 2008-; mem. bd. advisors Internat Law and Regulation Jour., 1998-; contbr. articles to prof. jours. Recipient 5th Nat. Prize Nathan Burkan Copyright Competition, ASCAP, 1970; Best New Book in Law, Assn. Am. Publishers, 1985; Faculty Svc. Award, U. Houston, 2004 Fellow: Tex. Bar Found., Am. Coll. Comml. Fin. Lawyers; mem.: Computer Law Assn. (bd. dirs. 1994—99), Law and Soc. Assn., Licensing Law Execs. Soc., Am. Law Inst., Am. Intellectual Property Law Assn. Office: University of Houston Law Center 201 TUII 100 Law Ctr Houston TX 77204 Office Phone: 713-743-2100. Office Fax: 713-743-2122. E-mail: lawdean@uh.edu.*

NIRSCHL, ROBERT PHILLIP, orthopedic surgeon; b. South Milwaukee, Wis., Aug. 28, 1933; s. Boyd A. and Helen (Wozny) N.; m. Mary Ann Oleniczak, June 21, 1958; children: Suzanne, Robert C., Julie. Student, Coll. Holy Cross, 1951-53, Marquette U., 1953-54; MD, Med. Coll. Wis./Marquette U., 1958; MS, U. Minn., 1965. Diplomate Am. Bd. Orthop. Surgery. Intern St. Mary's Hosp., Duluth, Minn., 1958-59; resident in orthop. Mayo Clinic, Rochester, Minn., 1959-63; lt. comdr. USN, Washington, 1963-65; pvt. practice Arlington, Va., 1965—. Attending orthop. surgeon Va. Hosp. Ctr., Arlington, dir. Hand Surgery Svc., 1975—85, v.p. med. staff, 1980—83, mem. hosp. med. exec. com., 2006—12; chief orthop. surgery No. Va. Cmty. Hosp., 1971—82; founding dir. Nirschl Orthop. Ctr. for Sports Medicine and Joint Reconstrn., 1974—, Nirschl Orthop. Sport Med. Ctr. Orthop. Sports Medicine Fellowship Program Va. Hosp. Ctr., Arlington, 1987—2013; mem. clin. faculty Georgetown U. Med. Ctr., 1965—2013; orthop. cons. Pres.'s Coun. Phys. Fitness, Washington, 1981—87; mem. sports sci. com. USTA, NYC, 1987—94; founding chmn. Nirschl Orthp. Sports Medicine Rsch. Found., 2005—; chief orthopedic sports med. cons. Athletic Dept. Marymount U., 2006—; course dir. numerous symposia in field. Author: Arm Care, 1981, rev. edit., 1996, Isoflex Exercise System, 1983; chief med. editor Orthop. Today, 1983-93; mem. editl. bd. The Physician and Sportsmedicine, 1992-2005, The Med. Sentinel, 1996-02, Orthopedics Today, 2003-13; creator 10 video programs; contbr. 48 chpts. to books and over 125 articles to profl. publs.; patentee in field. Chmn. Jeffersonian Health Policy Found., Williamsburg, Va., 1994—97; mem. Va. Bd. Medicine, 2000—04; trustee Marymount U., Arlington, 2005—. Grantee Pfizer Inc., 1992-93, Sano Corp, 1993-94, Iomed Corp., 1999-2000, Travanti Pharma Inc, 2008-09. Mem.: AMA, Am. Orthop. Assn., VA Orthop. Soc. (Lifetime Career award 2005), Arlington County Med. Soc. (pres. 1977, chmn. legis. com. 1987—2004, Welburn award 1995), Med. Soc. Va. (chmn. sports medicine com. 1973—84, trustee polit. action com. 1990—2002, legis. com. 1995, liability com. 2005—06, trustee polit. action com. 2006—11), Va. Orthop. Soc. (pres. 1998—99, career award 2005), Washington Orthop. Soc., Ea. Orthop. Assn., Soc. Tennis Medicine and Sci. (exec. com.), Am. Orthop. Soc. Sports Medicine (ethics com. 1992—97, bd. dels. 2002—08), Am. Acad. Orthop. Surgery (health fin. com. 1994—2000, comm. and state soc. coms. bd. of counselors 2000—03, bd. counselors 2000—06), Washington Golf and Country Club. Republican. Roman Catholic. Avocation: fitness activities. Office: Nirschl Orthop Ctr Sports Medicine & Joint Reconstrn 1715 N George Mason Dr Ste 504 Arlington VA 22205-3670 Home Phone: 703-237-8706; Office Phone: 703-525-2200. Personal E-mail: nirschlorthopaedics@comcast.net.

NISENBAUM, LAYNE D., dermatologist, educator; Attended, U. Fla., 1976—80; DO, Southeastern U. of Health Sciences. Diplomate Nat. Bd. of Examiners for Osteo. Physician and Suregeons of the USA, 1986, Am. Osteopathic Bd. of Dermatology, 1992. Intern Doctors Green Hosp., 1985; resident dermatology Dr. Edwin H. Cohen (preceptor/dir.), 1987—90; dir. and dermatologist Cocoanut Creek Dermatology Ctr., 1990—98; with Good Samaritan Hosp.; med. dir. of dermatology Island Dermatology and Laser Inst., 1998—. Clin. assoc. prof. dermatology Southeastern Univ. of Health Sciences. Fellow: Am. Soc. of Laser Medicine and Surgery; mem.: Am. Soc. of Anti-Aging Medicine, North Am. Soc. of Phlebology, Fla. Osteo. Medicine Assn., Am. Osteo. Assn., Am. Osteo. Coll. of Dermatology, Fla. Soc. of Dermatology, Am. Acad. of Dermatology. Office: Island Dermatology and Laser Institute 50 Cocoanut Row 120 Palm Beach FL 33480 Office Phone: 561-832-1950.

NISHI, MASAO, supply chain executive; m. Wendy Nishi; 2 children. BS in Engring., Washington U., St. Louis, 1969, MBA, 1974. Pres., Logistics Resource Leaseway Transp. Corp., Cleve.; v.p., transp. products Manugistics, Phila.; v.p. Sabre Group, Dallas; ptnr. KPMG Consulting, Dallas; v.p., supply chain mgmt. Sysco Corp., Houston, 2003—. Office: Sysco Corp 1390 Enclave Pky Houston TX 77077-2099 Business E-Mail: nishi.masao@corp.sysco.com.

NISHIYAMA, ASAHIKO, tire manufacturing company executive; Degree in Comml. Sci., Keio U. Chmn., CEO and pres. BATO, 2009; joined Bridgestone Tire Co. Ltd., 1977; pres., human resources dept. Bridgestone Americas, Inc., mgr.; gen. mgr., human resources Bridgestone Corp., Japan; dir., bus. planning Bridgestone Firestone Inc., 1997; dir., Americas and Europe Ops. Divsn. Bridgestone Corp., 2004; vice chmn., pres. Bridgestone Americas Holding, Inc., 2005; CEO, pres., Bridgestone Americas Tire Ops. Bridgestone Americas Inc., 2009—10; chmn. Bridgestone Americas, Inc., 2010—. Bd. dirs. Bridgestone Americas Tire Ops., LLC, Bridgestone Retail Ops., LLC, BFS Brands, LLC, Firestone Polymers, LLC, Firestone Diversified Products, LLC, Morgan Tire & Auto, LLC. Mem. Japanese Supplementary Sch. of Mid. Tenn., Mid. Tenn. Japan Soc., Habitat for Humanity; exec. com. mem. Bridgestone Workers Union, 1991. Office: Bridgestone Americas Inc 535 Marriott Dr Nashville TN 37214 Office Phone: 615-937-1000. Office Fax: 615-937-3621. Business E-Mail: nishiyamaasahiko@bfor.com.

NISSENBAUM, ROBERT JAY, law librarian, educator; b. NYC, July 31, 1952; s. I. Joseph and Lillian E. (Spingeld) N. BA in internat. affairs, George Washington U., 1973; MLS, Pratt Inst., 1976; JD, Western New Eng. Coll., 1980. Bar: Mass. 1980, Tex. 1982, NY, 2007, U.S. Dist. Ct. (fed. dist.) Mass. 1981, U.S. Dist. Ct. (fed. dist.) Conn. 1981, U.S. Ct. Appeals (1st cir.) 1981, U.S. Ct. Appeals (5th cir.) 1984. Law/legis. ref. libr. Conn. State Libr., Hartford, 1980-81; law libr. ref. dept. U. Tex., Austin, 1981-82, libr. collection mgmt./reference, lectr. law, 1982-83, head reference svc., lectr. law, 1983-84; dir. law libr., assoc. prof. law Cleve. State U., 1984-88; dir. law libr., prof. law Loyola Law Sch., LA, 1988—2004; prof. law, dir. Leo T. Kissam Meml. Libr. Fordham U. Sch. Law, NYC, 2004—. Vis. prof. law U. Tex., Austin, summer 1992, U. Internat. Bus. and Econs., Beijing, 1995; chmn. govt. documents spl. interst sect. Ad Hoc Com. on Citation Reform, 1983-94. Author: (with Saltalamachia) Fundamentals of Legal Research Assignments and Instructor's Manual, 3d edit., 1985; book rev. editor Criminal Law Bull., 1995%; contbr. articles to profl. jours., chpts. to books. Matthew Bender scholar, 1984. Mem. Assn. Am. Law Schs. (law libr. jour. com. 1983-84, chmn. com. on stds. 1985-87, rep. to Am. Nat. Stds. Inst. 1986-87, mem. nat. com. law libr. resources 1985-87, chmn. spl. com. citation form 1986-87), Assn. Jesuit Colls. and Univs. (treas. conf. law librs. 1993-94, chmn.-elect conf. 1994-95), Order of Coif, Beta Phi Mu. Jewish. Avocations: theater, classical music, rare books. Office: Fordham University School Law 140 W 62nd St New York NY 10023 Office Phone: 212-636-7609. Office Fax: 212-930-8818. E-mail: rnissenbaum@law.fordham.edu.

NIVICA, GJON NELSON, JR., lawyer; b. Boston, June 21, 1964; s. Gjon Nelson Sr. and Lynne Rose Nivica; m. Erica Kristin Schlegel. BS, Fla. State U., 1986; JD magna cum laude, Boston U., 1989; TGMP, Harvard Bus. Sch., 2000. Bar: Calif. 1989. Assoc. Gibson Dunn & Crutcher, LA, 1989-94; sr. counsel AlliedSignal Aerospace, Torrance, Calif., 1994-96; v.p., gen. cousnel AlliedSignal Engines, Phoenix, 1996-99; v.p., gen. counsel Honeywell Engines & Sys., Phoenix, 1999—2002, Honeywell Aerospace Electronic Systems, 2002—05, Honeywell Transp. Systems, 2005—09; dep. gen. counsel, asst. sec. Honeywell Internat., Inc., 2005—09; sr. v.p., corp. sec., gen. counsel Celanese Corp., Dallas, 2009—. Mem. Defenders of Wildlife,

Ctr. for Marine Conservation, Greater Phoenix C. of C. (bd. dirs. 1998). Christian. Office: Celanese Corp 1601 W LBJ Freeway Dallas TX 75234-6034 Office Phone: 972-443-4435.

NIX, JERRY W., automotive executive; Sr. v.p. fin., CFO Genuine Parts Co., Atlanta, 1979—2000, exec. v.p. fin., CFO, 2000—05, vice-chmn., exec. v.p. fin., CFO, 2005—. Office: Genuine Parts Co 2999 Circle 75 Pkwy SE Atlanta GA 30339-3050

NIX, KEMIE RICHARDS, educational association administrator, editor; b. Atlanta, Dec. 10, 1938; d. James McDowell and Evelyn Knight Richards; m. John Arthur Nix, July 22, 1961; children: Mary Evelyn Nix Hollowell, John Arthur Jr. EdB, Emory U., 1960, EdM, 1970. Tchr. Westminster Schs., Atlanta, 1961—87; founder, dir. Children's Lit. for Children, Atlanta, 1986—2002, Reader-to-Reader, Atlanta, 1986—2002; co-founder, co-dir. Reader-to-Patient, Atlanta, 1990—2000; co-founder Biblioteca Juvenil de Mayaguez, PR, 1991—2001; dir. Reader-to-Reader: Africa, 1990—; co-dir. Adamsville Elem. Sch., Atlanta, 2008—. Children's book editor Atlanta Jour./Constn., 1976—91, Parents' Choice, 1978—, corr. editor Jour. African Youth and Children's Lit., 1995—. Bd. dirs. US Bd. Books Young People, Wilmington, Del., 1996—98, Children's Lit. Children, Atlanta, 1996—, Mt. Kenya Acad., Nyeri, Kenya, 2002—. Named to Coca-Cola Centennial Olympic Wall, Atlanta, 1996, Kemie Nix Libr. named in her honor, Primary Sch., Nyeri, 1992, Mt. Kenya Acad., Nyeri, 2001. Mem.: ALA (Newbery com. 1994, Notable Books com. 1998—99, Newbery com. 2002, Caldecott com. 2006), Internat. Reading Assn. Democrat. Presbyterian. Avocations: birdwatching, reading. Home and Office: Reader-to-Reader: Africa 104 Madison Ave Peachtree City GA 30269 Personal E-mail: kemienix@aol.com.

NIX, RANDY, state legislator; b. June 19; m. Debra Nix; children: Jess, Julie. State rep. Dist. 69, Ga., 2007—; mem. Banks and Banking Com., 2007—, Econ. Devel. and Tourism and Natural Resources and Environ. Com., 2007—; sec. Info. and Audits Com., 2007—. Republican. Methodist. Home: 371 S Grayson Trl Hogansville GA 30230-2460 Home Phone: 706-845-9853. E-mail: ronix@charter.net.

NIXON, JOHN TRICE, federal judge; b. New Orleans, Jan. 9, 1933; s. H. C. and Anne (Trice) N.; children: Mignon Elizabeth, Anne Trice. AB cum laude, Harvard Coll., 1955; LL.B., Vanderbilt U., 1960. Bar: Ala. bar 1960, Tenn. bar 1972. Individual practice law, Anniston, Ala., 1960-62; city atty., 1962-64; trial atty. Civil Rights Div., Dept. Justice, Washington, 1964-69; staff atty., comptroller of Treasury State of Tenn., 1971-76; pvt. practice law Nashville, 1976-77; cir. judge, 1977-78; gen. sessions judge, 1978-80; judge US Dist. Ct. (mid. dist.) Tenn., Nashville, 1980—91, 1991—98, sr. judge, 1998—. Served with U.S. Army, 1958. Mem. Fly Club (Cambridge), Harvard-Radcliffe Club (Nashville). Democrat. Methodist. Office: US Dist Ct 770 US Courthouse 801 Broadway Nashville TN 37203

NIXON, SAMUEL ANTHONY, JR., state agency administrator, former state legislator; b. Martinsville, Va., Nov. 9, 1958; m. Carol Gibbs Nixon; 1 child, Jonathan. BBA in Mktg., James Madison U., Harrisonburg, Va. Dir. bus. devel. TLSC, Va.; mem. Dist. 27 Va. House of Delegates, 1994—2010, chmn. Republican caucus, 2008—10; sr. cons. CapTech Ventures, Richmond, Va.; CIO Commonwealth of Va., 2010—, Va. Info. and Technologies Agency, 2010—. Mem. Chesterfield Local Emergency Planning Com.; mem. adv. bd. St. Francis Hosp. Recipient Tech-Ten Legislator award. Mem.: Data Processing Mgmt. Assn., Chesterfield Bus. Coun., Chesterfield Jaycees (life; pres., former treas.). Republican. Church Of Nazarene. Office: Va Info Technologies Agency 11751 Meadowville Ln Chester VA 23836

NOBER, ROGER PAUL, rail transportation executive, lawyer; b. 1964; married; 3 children. BA, Haverford Coll., Pa., 1986; JD, Harvard Law Sch., 1989. Assoc. Skadden, Arps, Slate, Meagher & Flom, LLP, NYC, 1991—93; various positions US House Transp. & Infrastructure Com., 1993—97, chief counsel, 1997—2001; counselor to dep. sec. Michael Jackson US Dept. Transp.; chmn. US Surface Transp. Bd. (STB), Washington, 2002—06; ptnr. Steptoe & Johnson, LLP, Washington, 2006; exec. v.p. law, sec. Burlington Northern Santa Fe Corp., Fort Worth, Tex., 2007—10; exec. v.p. law, govt. affairs & corporate rels. Burlington Northern Santa Fe LLC (subs. Berkshire Hathaway), Fort Worth, Tex., 2010—. Republican. Office: Burlington No Santa Fe Corp PO Box 961056 Fort Worth TX 76161-0056 Office Phone: 817-352-1460.*

NOBLE, MARY C., state supreme court justice; b. Jackson, Ky., 1949; m. Larry Noble. B., Austin Peay State U., Clarksville, Tenn., 1971, M., 1975; JD, U. Ky. Coll. Law, 1981. Pvt. practice, 1981—91; domestic rels. commr., 1989—91; cir. judge for Fayette County Fayette Cir. Ct., 1991—2006, chief regional cir. judge, 1998—2002; co-founder, judge Ky. Drug Courts, 1996—2006; justice Supreme Ct. Ky., 2007—, dep. chief justice, 2010—. Mem.: Nat. Assn. Drug Ct. Professionals (mem. & former pres. congress state drug cts., bd. dirs.). Office: Supreme Court Of Kentucky 300 W Vine St Ste 2201 Lexington KY 40507-1810 Office Phone: 859-246-2220.*

NOCERO, MICHAEL A., cardiologist; MD, NYU, 1966. Diplomate Am. Bd. Internal Medicine, 1972, Am. Bd. Internal Medicine-cardiovasc. disease, 1976. Resident internal medicine Bellevue Hosp. Ctr., NYC, 1968—71, fellow cardiovasc. disease, 1971—73; hosp. affiliation includes Fla. Hosp., Orlando. Office: Florida Hospital Ste 100 1745 N Mills Ave Orlando FL 32803 Office Phone: 407-841-7151.

NOEL, RANDALL DEANE, lawyer; b. Memphis, Oct. 19, 1953; s. D.A. and Patricia G. Noel; m. Lissa Johns, May 28, 1977; children: Lauren Elizabeth, Randall Walker. BBA with honors, U. Miss., 1975, JD, 1978. Bar: Miss. 1978, U.S. Dist. Ct. (no. and so. dists.) Miss. 1978, Tenn. 1979, U.S. Dist. Ct. (we., mid. and ea. dists.) Tenn. 1979, U.S. Ct. Appeals (5th and 6th cirs.) 1984, U.S. Supreme Ct. 1986. Assoc. Armstrong/Allen, PLLC, Memphis, 1978-85, ptnr., 1985—, mgr. litig. practice group, 1990-94; mgmt. com. Armstrong, Allen, Prewitt, Gentry, Johnston & Holmes, Memphis, 1994—97; chief mem. Armstrong/Allen, PLLC, Memphis, 2002—04; ptnr. Butler, Snow, O'Mara, Stevens & Cannada, 2004—, litig. dept. chair, 2007—. Fin. com. Memphis in May Internat. Festival, 1980-81; pres. Carnival Memphis, 1996; bd. dirs. Christ United Meth. Ch., Memphis, 1984-87, 89-91, chmn. bd. trustees, 1995; mem. Leadership Memphis, 1994-95. Fellow Am. Bar Found., Tenn. Bar Found., Memphis Bar Found.; mem. ABA (young lawyers divsn., fellow dir. 1988-90, editor The Affiliate newsletter 1987-88, dir. Affiliate Outreach project 1988—, vice-chmn. Award of Achievement com. 1986, ALI-ABA bd. 1992-97, div. dir. litig. sect., 2002, coun. litig. sect., mem. House of Dels., standing com. fed. judiciary), Am. Counsel Assn. (pres. 1997), Tenn. Bar Assn. (pres. young lawyers divsn. 1990, pres. litig. sect. 1988, bd. govs. 1989—, pres. 1999, Pres.'s Disting. Svc. award 1988-89), So. Conf. Bar Pres. (pres. 2000), Memphis and Shelby Bar Assn. (mem. jud. recommendations, law week nominations and membership coms.), Miss. Bar Assn., Def. Rsch. Inst., Tenn. Def. Lawyers Assn., Am. Judicature Soc. (bd. dirs. 1992-96), Tenn. Legal Cmty. Found. (pres. 1999-2001), Tenn. Supreme Ct. Hist. Soc. (bd. dirs. 2005). Home: 2938 Tishomingo Ln Memphis TN 38111-2627 Office: Butler Snow O'Mara Stevens & Cannada PLLC Ste 500 Crescent Ctr 6075 Poplar Ave Memphis TN 38119 Business E-Mail: randy.noel@butlersnow.com.

NOGUCHI, SOICHI, astronaut; b. Yokohama, Japan, Apr. 15, 1965; married; 3 children. Bachelor in Aero. Engring., U. Tokyo, 1989, M in Aero. Engring., 1991. Flight instructor cert. as CFII and MEI. Mem. mfg. dept. Ishikawajima-Harima Heavy Industries Co., Ltd., Japan, 1991—96; astronaut Nat. Space Devel. Agy. Japan (merged with Inst. of Space & Astronautic Sci. and Nat. Aerospace Lab. of Japan and renamed Japan Aerospace Exploration Agy. in 2003), 1996—; tech. specialist Astronaut Office Space Sta. Br. Johnson Space Ctr., Houston, 1996, qualified mission specialist, 1998—, assigned tech. duties to support Japanese Experiment Module (Kibo) develop. tests, mission specialist, STS-114/ULF-1(Utilization and Logistics Flight), 2001; participated in the basic tng. course for Russian manned space systems Gagarin Cosmonaut Tng. Ctr., 1998; flight engr., Expedition 20 Internat. Space Station mission on Soyuz spacecraft Baikonur Cosmodrome, Kazakhstan, 2009. Mem.: Japan Soc. Aero. and Space Scis. Will serve as MS-1 (mission specialist) and EV-1 on the Return To Flight Mission of STS-114 (Discovery), during which the crew will test and evaluate new procedures for flight safety and shuttle inspection and repair techniques in July, 2005; second Japanese astronaut ever to walk the void of three spacewalks. Office: NASA Johnson Space Ctr Astronaut Office/CB Houston TX 77058

NOHRNBERG, JAMES CARSON, language educator; b. Berkeley, Calif., Mar. 19, 1941; s. Carson and Geneva Gertrude (Gibbs) N.; m. Stephanie Payson Lamport, June 14, 1964; children: Gabrielle L., Peter Carson L. Student, Kenyon Coll., 1958-60; BA, Harvard Coll., 1962, postgrad., 1965-68; PhD, U. Toronto, 1970. Tchg. fellow dept. English U. Coll., U. Toronto, 1963-64; jr. fellow Soc. of Fellows Harvard U., 1965-68; acting instr. dept. English Yale U., New Haven, 1968-69, lectr., 1969-70, asst. prof., 1970-75, assoc. prof., 1975; prof. English U. Va., Charlottesville, 1975—2011; emeritus prof. U. Va, Charlottesville, 2011—. Adj. instr. English Harvard U., Cambridge, 1967; Gauss Seminars in Criticism lectr. Princeton U., 1987; lectr. various univs., 1974—; Kathleen Williams lectr. Kalamazoo Medieval Conf., 2012; mem. Northeast Milton Seminar, 2012. Author: The Analogy of The Faerie Queene, 1976, 80, Like Unto Moses: The Constituting of an Interruption, 1995; mem. editl. bd. Spenser Ency., 1977-90, Spenser Studies, 1977—, Manchester Spenser, 2007—; contbr. articles to profl. jours. and poems to mags.; editor vols. on myth, exegesis, allegory, Bible, Homer, Dante, Boiardo, Spenser, Raleigh, Shakespeare, Milton, Tennyson, Thomas Pynchon, Northrop Frye, among others. Recipient Robert Frost poetry prize, Kenyon Coll., 1960, Am. Acad. Poets prize Harvard U., 1962; Woodrow Wilson fellow, 1962, jr. fellow Harvard U., 1965-68, Morse fellow Yale U., 1974-75, U. Va. Ctr. for Advanced Studies fellow, 1975-78, Guggenheim fellow, 1981-82, Ind. U. Inst. for Advanced Studies fellow, 1991, U. Va. Sesquicentennial fellow, 2003-2004, Hon. award Renaissance Prose Conf., Purdue U., 2009, Internat. Spenser Soc. Colin Clout Lifetime Achievement award, 2011; Hon. membership, Harvard Coll. Chpt. Phi Beta Kappa, 2012. Mem.: MLA, Northeast Milton Seminar, Am. Comparative Lit. Assn., Milton Soc., Spenser Soc., Phi Beta Kappa. Presbyterian. Avocations: poetry, collecting books and records. Home: 1874 Wayside Pl Charlottesville VA 22903-1631 Office: U Va Dept English Bryan Hall Charlottesville VA 22903 Business E-Mail: jcn@virginia.edu.

NOKES, JIM W., retired oil industry executive; b. McCook, Nebr., 1946; BA, Fort Hayes State Univ., Kans.; MBA, Univ. Ark. With ConocoPhillips Co., Houston, 1970—2006, v.p. North American refining and mktg. ops., 1994—99, pres. North American refining and mktg. ops., 1998—99, exec. v.p. worldwide refining and mktg. ops., 1999—2002, exec. v.p. refining, mktg., supply and transp., 2002—06, ret., 2006. Bd. dirs. Chevron Phillips Chem. Co. LLC, 2002—06, Tesoro Corp., 2007—, Albemarle Corp., 2009—. Mem. adv. bd. Yellowstone Pk. Found., Jr. Achievement Southeast Tex. Office: Albemarle Corp Bd Directors 451 Florida St Baton Rouge LA 70801 Office Phone: 225-388-8011. Office Fax: 225-388-7686. Business E-Mail: james.nokes@albemarle.com.

NOLAN, CHRISTOPHER P., beverage company executive; b. 1964; BA, Emory U. Goizueta Bus. Sch., 1986. Auditor Cooper & Lybrand; various positions in corp. auditing & corp. treasury, mgr. financial risk mgmt. & corp. finance The Coca-Cola Co., Atlanta, 1992—2004, dir. insurance risk mgmt. & investments, 2008—09, v.p., treas., 2009—; treas. Coca-Cola Hellenic Bottling Co., Athens, Greece, 2004—08. Office: The Coca-Cola Co 1 Coca-Cola Plz Atlanta GA 30313

NOLAN, JOHN MICHAEL, lawyer; b. Conway, Ark., June 21, 1948; s. Paul Thomas and Peggy (Hime) N. BA, U. Tex., 1970, JD, 1973; LLM in Taxation, George Washington U., Washington, DC, 1976. Bar: Tex. 1973, DC 1975, US Ct. Mil. Appeals 1973, US Ct. Appeals (DC cir.) 1975, US Tax Ct. 1975, US Supreme Ct. 1975. Chief counsel to chief judge US Ct. Mil. Appeals, Washington, 1976-77; assoc. Winstead, McGuire, Sechrest & Minick PC, Dallas, 1977-81; shareholder Winstead Sechrest & Minick PC, Dallas, 1981—2006, Winstead, Dallas, 2007—. Editor in chief The Advocate, 1973-76. Capt. JAGC, US Army, 1973-76. Named one of Outstanding Young Men in Am. US Jaycees, 1976; Keeton fellow Chancellor Coun.; named among Best Lawyers in Am. Tex. Super Lawyer. Fellow Dallas Bar Found. (life), Tex. Bar Found. (life); mem. ABA (real property, probate and trust sect., real property com., partnerships, joint ventures, and other investment vehicles), Tex. Bar Assn. (real property, probate and trust sect.), DC Bar Assn., Dallas Bar Assn. (real estate group), Tex. Coll. Real Estate Lawyers, Am. Coll. Real Estate Lawyers, Coll. State Bar Tex., Real Estate Coun. (bd. dirs.), Salesmanship Club Dallas, Royal Oaks Country Club. Presbyterian. Home: 35 Downshale Cir Dallas TX 75230 Office: Winstead 5400 Renaissance Tower 2728 N Harwood St Ste 500 Dallas TX 75201-1743 Office Phone: 214-745-5251. Business E-Mail: jnolan@winstead.com.

NOLAN, KEVIN F., consumer products company executive; B in Mech. Engring., U. Conn., 1989. Held various leadership positions, GE Consumer & Indsl. GE Co., gen. mgr., sourcing, GE Consumer & Indsl., gen. mgr., new product intro., 2002—06; v.p., tech., GE consumer & industrial General Electric Co., 2007—. Office: GE Consumer & Industrial Appliance Pk AP3-232 Louisville KY 40225 Office Phone: 502-452-4311. Office Fax: 502-452-0352. Business E-Mail: kevin.nolan@ge.com.

NOLAN, MIKE, professional football coach; b. Balt., Mar. 7, 1959; s. Dick Nolan; m. Kathy Nolan; children: Michael, Christopher, Laura, Jennifer. Attended, U. Oreg. Asst. coach U. Oreg. Ducks, 1981—82, Stanford U. Cardinal, 1982—83, Rice U. Owls, 1984—85; head coach La. State U. Fighting Tigers, 1986; linebackers coach, spl. teams asst. Denver Broncos, 1987—92; defensive coord. NY Giants, 1993—96, Wash. Redskins, 1997—99, NY Jets, 2000; wide receivers coach Balt. Ravens, 2001, defensive coord., 2002—04; head football coach San Francisco 49ers, 2005—08; defensive coord. Denver Broncos, 2009—10, Miami Dolphins, 2010—11, Atlanta Falcons, 2012—. Office: Atlanta Falcons 4400 Falcon Pky Flowery Branch GA 30542

NOLAN, RICHARD THOMAS, clergyman, educator, writer; b. Waltham, Mass., May 30, 1937; arrived in Ireland, 2014; s. Thomas Michael and Elizabeth Louise (Leishman) N.; life partner, Robert C. Pingpank, 1955-2009, m. June 4, 2009 BA, Trinity Coll., 1960; Diploma in Theol. Studies, Berkeley Div. Sch., 1960; MDiv. in Theol. Studies, Hartford Sem. Found., 1963; postgrad. in Religious Edn., Union Theol. Sem., 1963; MA in Religion, Yale U., 1967; PhD in Religion, NYU, 1973; rsch. fellow in Biomed. Ethics, Harvard U., 1991. cert. in Classical Piano; ordained deacon Episcopal Ch., 1963, priest, 1965; cert. in clinical pastoral edn. Conn. Valley Hosp., 1962, cert. in death, dying and bereavement Waterbury Hosp. Health Ctr., Conn., 1977, cert. in career assessment, Ctr. Career Devel. and Ministry, Mass., 1987. Instr. Latin and English Watkinson Sch., Conn., 1961-62; instr. math. Choir Sch. of Cathedral of St. John the Divine, NYC, 1962-64; instr. math. and religion, assoc. chaplain Cheshire Acad., Conn., 1965-67; instr. philosophy & edn. Hartford Sem. Found., Conn., 1967-68, asst. acad. dean, lectr. philosophy and edn., 1968-70; instr. Mattatuck C.C., Waterbury, Conn., 1969-70, asst. prof. philosophy and history, 1970-74, assoc. prof., 1974-78, prof. philosophy and social sci., 1978-92, prof. emeritus, 1992—; part-time vicar St. Paul's Parish, Bantam, Conn., 1974-88, pastor emeritus, 1988—; pres. Litchfield Inst., Conn. and Fla., 1984-96; adj. lectr. in philosophy Palm Beach C. C., Fla., 2000—02. Ethics com. Waterbury Hosp. Health Ctr., 1984—88; vis. and adj. prof. philosophy, theology and religious studies Trinity Coll., Conn., L.I. U., U. Miami, St. Joseph Coll., Conn., Pace U., Teikyo Post U., U. Conn., Hartford Grad. Ctr., Ctrl. Conn. State U., 1964—95, Broward C.C., Fla.; lectr. philosophy and theology Barry U., Fla., 1973, 1989—92, 1997—98; adj. assoc. in continuing edn. Berkeley Div. Sch. Yale U., 1987—89; Rabbi Harry Halpern Meml. lectr., Southbury, Conn., 1987; adj. prof. philosophy Fla. Atlantic U., 1998—99; adj. prof. The Union Inst., Fla., 1999; faculty of cons. examiners Charter Oak State Coll., Conn., 1990—93; assoc. for edn. Christ Ch. Cathedral, Hartford, Conn., 1988—94, hon. canon, 1991—; cons. Dept. Def. Activity Non-Traditional Ednl. Support, Ednl. Testing Svc., Princeton, NJ, 1990; vis. scholar Coll. Preachers, Washington Nat. Cathedral, 1994; supply priest Episcopal Diocese of S.E. Fla., 1994—2002; ret. priest-in-residence St. Andrew's Ch., Lake Worth, Fla., 2002—; soc. regents Cathedral Ch. St. John the Divine, 2002—; rsch. fellow med. ethics Yale U., 1978; guest spkr. Trinity Coll. Chapel, 2012; lectr. philosophy and religious studies John Knox Village Fla., 2012—. Author (with H. Titus and M. Smith): Living Issues in Philosophy, 7th edit., 1979, Indonesian edit., 1984, 8th edit., 1986, 9th edit., 1995; author: (with F. Kirkpatrick) Living Issues in Ethics, 1982, 2d edit., 2000, Chinese edit., 1988 (Honored Author for Books Exceeding 100,000 Copies award Wadsworth Pub. Co., 1986); author: (with Robert C. Pingpank) Soul Mates: More Than Partners (online), 2004; author: Commentary on the Catechism Episcopal Book Common Prayer Polish Translation Online, 2012, Chinese edit., 2014; editor, contbr. Diaconate Now, 1968, online; TV host Conversations With..., 1987—89. Notary pub., Fla. Recipient Founder's Day award, NYU, 1973; co-recipient Marital award with Robert C. Pingpank, Cathedral St. John Divine, 2005, award Exceptional Leadership and Cmty. Svc., ACLU Palm Beach Chpt., 2008. Mem. Am. Acad. Religion, Am. Philos. Assn., Authors Guild, Hemlock Soc. Fla. (adv. bd. 1998-), Interfaith Alliance, Integrity, 1635 Soc. Boston Latin Sch. Alumni Assn., Elizabeth S. Taber Soc. Tabor Acad. Alumni Assn., ELMS Soc. Trinity Coll., Yale Legacy Partners, Harwood Soc. Cheshire Acad., Society of The Torch of NYU, Founders Soc. of the Wash. Nat. Cathedral, Planned Parenthood, Lambda Legal, Compassion & Choices, Conn. Episcopal Clergy Assn., SAGE(NYC & South Fla.), PFLAG, People Am. Way, ACLU, GLAAD, Pride Ctr, Ft. Lauderdale, Equality Fla., Human Rights Campaign, Flagler Mus., Norton Mus. Art, Friends of St. Patrick's Cathedral (Dublin), Phi Delta Kappa. Independent. Episcopalian. Avocation: piano. Home: John Knox Village 451 Heritage Dr Apt 1014 Pompano Beach FL 33060-7777 Personal E-mail: canon@rtnolan.com.

NOLAN, STANTON PEELLE, surgeon, educator; b. Washington, May 29, 1933; s. James Parker and Ellen Dubose (Peelle) N.; m. Marion Faro, June 16, 1955; children: Stanton Peelle Jr., Tiphanie Ravenel Clarke. BA, Princeton U., NJ, 1955; MD, U. Va., Charlottesville, 1959, MS, 1962. Diplomate Am. Bd. Surgery, Am. Bd. Thoracic Surgery. Intern U. Va. Med. Ctr., Charlottesville, 1959-60, asst. resident gen. surgery, 1960-61, research fellow surgery, 1961-62, sr. asst. resident gen. surgery, 1962-64, chief resident gen surgery, 1964-65, chief resident thoracic cardiovascular surgery, 1965-66; sr. rsch. assoc. Clinic of Surgery Nat. Heart Inst., NIH, Bethesda, Md., 1966-68; asst. prof. surgery U. Va. Med. Ctr., Charlottesville, 1968-70, assoc. prof. surgery, 1970-74, surgeon in charge div. thoracic cardiovascular surgery, 1970-93, prof. surgery, 1974-81, Claude A. Jessup prof. surgery, 1981-98, clin. prof. surgery, 1998—2004, prof. surgery, 2004—06, med. dir. Thoracic Cardiovascular post-operative unit, 1989-93, prof. emeritus of surgery, 2006—, vis. prof. surgery, 2011—. Established Investigator Am. Heart Assn., 1969-74; mem. surgery A study sect. NIH, Washington, 1972-76, surgery and bioengring. study sect. 1984-87, chmn. 1985-87; cons. thoracic cardiovascular surgery VA Hosp., Salem, Va., 1968-98, Am. Bd. Surgery cons. to qualifying examination com., 1988-91; surg. cons. Bur. Crippled Children, Charlottesville, 1968-93; vis. cons. cardiothoracic surgery Aga Khan U., Karachi, Pakistan, 1995, vis cons. Vol. Health Svcs., Madras, India, 1997, cons. So. Petrochem. Industries Corp. SPIC, Chennai, India 2000; vis. prof. U. Hanover, Germany, 1990; vis. prof. Cardiac Surgerey, U. Wis. 1992; keynote spkr., assoc. surg. physician asst., 2000. Mem. editl. bd. Jour. Surg. Rsch., 1973-79, Annals of Thoracic Surgery, 1979-88; mem. sci. adv. bd. Jour. for Heart Valve Disease, 1993—2006; mem. editl. adv. bd. ECRI Operating Rm. Risk Mgmt., 1992-2006; co-editor: Comprehensive Thoracic Surgery Curriculum, TSDA, 1995; contbr. 171 articles to profl. jours., 21 chpts. to books. Bd. mgrs. Ctrl. Va. Health Network, 2000—05, Westminster Canterbury Blue Ridge, chmn. Residents' Assn., 2004—06, Westminster Canterbury Found. bd., 2007—, chmn. found. bd., 2010—12; bd. dirs. Piedmont Liability Trust, 1989—2005, emeritus mem., 2006—, chmn. claims com., 1989—2006, chmn. bd., 1991—2004, emeritus mem., 2007—. Recipient John Horsley Meml. prize U. Va. Med. Sch., 1962, Merit award Rsch. Forum of Am. Coll. Chest Physicians, 1968, Clyde Watson Disting. Svc. award Pastoral Care and Edn., 2006, Stanton P. Nolan Professorship Thoracic and Cardiovascular Surgery, U. Va. Bd. Visitors, 2006; Rsch. fellow Va. Heart Assn., 1961-62, Am. Cancer Soc., 1963-64; grantee NIH, 1968-84, Am. Heart Assn., 1970-73, Medtronic Corp., 1975-81. Fellow ACS (com. allied health pers. 1996—2004, exec. com. 1997-2000, vice chair), Am. Coll. Cardiology, Am. Surg. Assn., Am. Assn. Thoracic Surgery; mem. Am. Heart Assn. (coun. on cardiovasc. surgery 1969-99, anesthesiology, radiology and surgery study com. 1991-94), Andrew G. Morrow Soc., Assn. Acad. Surgery, Assn. Advancement of Med. Instrumentation (chair 1998-2000, co-chmn. cardiac valve prostheses stds. com. 1974-2005, internat. stds. strategy com. 1989—2005, bd. dirs. 1990-2000, stds. bd. 1991—2005, edn. com. 1992-93, nominating com. 1996-2000, chair 1998-2000, exec. com. 1996-2000, govt. rels. com. 1996-2000), Internat. Stds. Orgn. (chmn. subcom. on cardiovascular surg. implants 1982-2004), Assn. Clin. Cardiac Surgeons, Halsted Soc. (exec. com. 1985-89), Coord. Com. on Perfusion Affairs (chmn. 1990-2000), Internat. Assn. Cardiac Biol. Implants (sci. com. 1994), Am. Assn. for Vascular Surgery, Muller-Jones Surg. Soc. (pres. 1979), Soc. Internat. de Cirurgie, Soc. Vascular Surgery, Soc. Thoracic Surgeons (ad hoc com. on industry rels. 1992-97, stds. and ethics com. 1993-95, 98-2001, edn. and resources com. 1996-97), Soc. Univ. Surgeons, Southeastern Surg. Congress, So. Surg. Assn. (2d v.p. 1982), Thoracic Surgery Found. Rsch. and Edn. (chair New Century Soc. com. 1997-2000), Va. Surg. Soc. (v.p. 1980-83, pres. 1984), Va. Vascular Soc. (exec. coun. 1985-86), Soc. Critical Care Medicine, Raven Soc., Assn. Am. Med. Colls. (rep. coun. acad. socs. 1992-01), Chevy Chase Club, Alpha Omega Alpha, Omicron Delta Kappa, Commn. on Accreditation Allied Health Education Programs (Award for Exceptional Svc. 2007). Home: #5204 250 Pantops Mountain Rd Charlottesville VA 22911-8702 Office: U Va TCV Surgery PO Box 800679 Charlottesville VA 22908-0679 Business E-Mail: snolan@virginia.edu.

NOLEN, ROY LEMUEL, retired lawyer; b. Montgomery, Ala., Nov. 29, 1937; s. Roy Lemuel Jr. and Elizabeth (Larkin) N.; m. Evelyn McNeill Thomas, Aug. 28, 1965; 1 child, Rives Rutledge. BArch, Rice U., 1961; LLB, Harvard U., 1967. Bar: Tex. 1968, U.S. Ct. Appeals (5th cir.) 1969. Law clk. to sr. judge U.S. Ct. Appeals (5th cir.), 1967-68; assoc. Baker Botts LLP, Houston, 1968-75, ptnr., 1976-2000; co-head Corp. Dept., 1985-90; mem. exec. com., 1988-91; adminstrv. ptnr., 1997-2000; ret., 2001. Cmty. rep. instnl. animal care and use com. M.D. Anderson Cancer Ctr., 2001—06. Bd. dirs. Houston Ballet Found., 1980-92, Rice Design Alliance, 1995-96; exec. com. Contemporary Arts Mus., 1990-96, 97-2002; exec. com. Houston Symphony Soc., 1994-99, gen. counsel, 1994-98; trustee Menil Found. (Menil Collection), 1999—, sr. warden Christ Ch. Cathedral, 1991-92, chancellor, 2003-08; chmn. Houston area devel. initiative Episcopal Diocese of Tex., 1997. 1st lt. USMC, 1961-64. Mem.: State Bar Tex., Briar Club, Paul Jones Dancing Club, Allegro, Coronado Club. Episcopalian. Office: Baker Botts LLP One Shell Plz 910 Louisiana St Houston TX 77002-4995 Office Phone: 713-229-1216. Personal E-mail: roynolen@aol.com.

NOLEN, WILLIAM GILES, lawyer, accountant; b. Fayetteville, Ark., Aug. 4, 1931; s. William Jefferson and Marie (Giles) N.; m. Carole Turner, Aug. 25, 1957; children: Kathy, Thomas (dec.). BSBA, U. Ark., Fayetteville, 1960; JD, U. Houston, 1980. Bar: Tex. 1980; CPA, Tex. Auditor Arthur Anderson & Co., Houston, 1960-66; sec., treas. Brown & Root (U.K.) Ltd., London, 1966-69; v.p. Highlands Ins. Co., Houston, 1969-73, sr. v.p., 1973-80, dir., 1973-88; v.p. Halliburton Co., Dallas, 1980-82; sr. v.p. Brown & Root, Inc., Houston, 1982-86; exec. v.p. Highlands Ins. Co., Houston, 1986-88; of counsel Whitmore, Sheppard & Pollicoff, Houston, 1988-92, Policoff, Smith & Myres LLP, Houston, 1992-95, Policoff, Smith, Myres & Remels LLP, Houston, 1995-2000, Pollicoff, Smith & Remels, Houston, 2000—02. Maj. USAF, 1951-56. Mem. Am. Assn. Atty. CPAs (past pres., bd. dirs.), Tex. Soc. CPAs (Tex. CPA of Yr. 1961), Mensa. Presbyterian.

NOLL, RICHARD A., apparel executive; BBA, Pa. State Univ.; MBA with distinction, Carnegie Mellon Univ. CEO U.S. sock bus. Sara Lee Corp., Chgo., 1992—2002, COO bakery group, 2002—03, CEO bakery group, 2003—05, sr. v.p., pres. & COO branded apparel, 2005—06, CEO branded apparel, 2006; CEO Hanesbrands, Inc., Winston Salem, NC, 2006—09, chmn., CEO, 2009—. Bd. dirs. Office: Hanesbrands Inc 1000 E Hanes Mill Rd Winston Salem NC 27105

NOLLY, ROBERT J., pharmacist, educator, health facility administrator; married; 3 children. BS in Pharmacy, Albany Coll. Pharmacy, NY, 1970; MS in Hosp. Pharmacy, Ohio State U., Columbus, 1979. Pharmacist Park Row Drugs, Canajoharie, NY, 1970—71, asst. mgr., 1971—72; staff pharmacist Mary Imogene Bassett Hosp., Cooperstown, NY, 1972—74, 1975—77; med. svc. rep. Dista Products Co., Eli Lilly and Co., Indpls., 1974-75; resident hosp. pharmacy Grant Hosp., Columbus, Ohio, 1977-79; asst. dir. pharmacy svcs. City of Memphis Hosp., 1979-81, U. Tenn. Bowld Hosp., Memphis, 1982, dir. pharmacy svcs. and materials mgmt., 1982-85, asst. adminstr. pharmacy svcs. and materials mgmt., 1985—90, adminstr., 1991—92, adminstr. ops., 1992—98, exec. dir., 1999—2002. Asst. prof. Coll. Pharmacy U. Tenn., Memphis, 1979-92, assoc. prof. 1992-2005; prof. 2005; bd. dir. Tenn. Hosp. Assn. Solution Group, 1997-2000; trustee, Diversified Svcs., Inc., Tenn. Hosp. Assn., 1990-94, mem. pharmacy adv. com., 1990; bd. dirs. Ava Marie Nursing Home, chmn. nom. com., 1988, 89, mem. long-range planning com., 1989, 90, mem. constn. and by-laws com., 1990, mem. govtl. rels. com., 1991-93; presenter in field. Editor U. Tenn. Bowld Hosp. Pharmacy Newsletter, 1987-91; mem. editl. bd. Drug and Therapeutics Newsletter, U. Tenn. Coll. Pharmacy, 1989, 90. Mem. adv. bd. Trinity Home Care and Hospice, Memphis Managed Care Formulary, Memphis and Shelby County Pub. Libr.; mem. cmty. adv. bd. Hope Health Care. Recipient Med. Staff Disting. Svc. award, U. Tenn. Bolwd Hosp. Mem. Parenteral Drug Assn., Am. Assn. Pharmaceutical Scientists, Tenn. Soc. Health Sys. Pharmacists (mem. com. 1980, constn. and by-laws com. 1985, 88, 89, 90, chmn. nominating com. 1989, orgn. and goals com. 1991, strategic planning com. 1992, 98, 2005, pharmacy tech. task force 1988, 89, 90, chmn. tech. curriculum com. 1991, tech. edn. accreditation com. 1994, 95, Technician Edn. Com. 1991, 92, 93), Memphis Area Soc. Hosp. Pharmacists (pres.-elect 1984, pres. 1985, past pres. 1986, chmn. nominating com. 1991), Memphis Area Pharmacists Society, Tenn. Hosp. Assn. (liaison Tenn. Med. Assn. com. 1993), Kappa Psi, Rho Chi. Office Phone: 901-448-1144. Business E-Mail: rnolly@utmem.edu.

NOONAN, JACQUELINE ANNE, pediatrician, educator; b. Burlington, Vt., Oct. 28, 1928; BA (hon.), Albertus Magnus Coll., New Haven, Conn., 1950, degree (hon.), 2010; MD, U. Vt., Burlington, 1954, DSc (hon.), 1980. Diplomate Am. Bd. Pediatrics, Am. Bd. Pediatric Cardiology. Intern N.C. Meml. Hosp., Chapel Hill, 1954-55; resident in pediatrics Children's Hosp., Cin., 1955-57; rsch. fellow Children's Med. Ctr., Boston, 1957-59; asst. prof. pediatrics State U. Iowa Sch. Medicine, 1959-61; asst. prof. pediatrics cardiology U. Ky. Coll. Medicine, Lexington, 1961-64, assoc. prof., 1964-69, prof., 1969-99, chmn. dept. pediatrics, 1974-92, emeritus prof., 1999—. Mem. embryology and human devel. study sect. NIH, 1973-78; mem. US-USSR Symposium on Congenital Heart Disease, 1975; mem. sub. bd. pediatric cardiology Am. Bd. Pediatrics, 1977-82; examiner, mem. test. com. Nat. Bd. Med. Examiners, 1984-90, exec. com., 1991-95; participant various confs. in field; vis. prof. Vanderbilt U., Nashville, 1987-; spkr. in field. Contbr. articles, revs. to med. publs.; mem. editl. bd. Am. Jour. Diseases Children, 1970-80, Am. Jour. Med. Edn., 1975-78, Pediatric Cardiology, 1978-90, Am. Heart Jour., 1994-96, Clin. Pediatrics, 1990-99. Recipient Lifetime Achievement award, Castle Connolly, 2008, Bradley Soule award, 2009. Fellow: Royal Coll. Irish Physicians (hon.); mem.: AMA, So. Soc. Pediat. Rsch. (pres. 1972), Soc. Pediat. Rsch., NIH Alumni Assn., Ky. State Med. Assn., Irish-Am. Pediat. Soc. (pres. 1999—2001), Fayette County Pediat. Soc., Am. Pediat. Soc., Assn. Med. Sch. Pediatrics (dept. chmn. exec. com. 1978—81), Am. Coll. Cardiology (gov. Ky. chpt. 1989—92, Gifted Tchr. award 2014), Am. Acad. Pediatrics (chmn. cardiol. sect. 1972—74). Business E-Mail: jnoonan@uky.edu.

NOONAN, JOHN GERARD, bishop; b. Limerick, Ireland, Feb. 26, 1951; s. John and Margaret Purcell Noonan. BA, St. John Vianney Coll. Sem., Miami, 1977—79; MDiv, St. Vincent de Paul Regional Sem., Boynton Beach, 1979—83; MEd, Boston Coll., 1993—96. Ordained priest Archdiocese of Miami, 1983; parochial vicar St. Elizabeth of Hungry, Pompano Beach, 1983—89; chaplain Youth Ministry, Broward County, 1985—87; dean of men St. John Vianney Coll. Sem., 1989—93; supervising prin. Msgr. Edward Pace High Sch., 1993—94, St. Brendan High Sch., Miami, 1994—96; pres., rector St. John Vianney Coll. Sem., 1996—2010; dir. Priestly Life and Ministry, 2001—10; ordained bishop, 2005; aux. bishop Archdiocese of Miami, 2005—10, vicar for religious, 2008—10, vicar gen., 2010; bishop Diocese of Orlando, Fla., 2010—. Bd. dir. Nat. Assn. Coll. Rectors, 1998—99. Roman Catholic. Mailing: Diocese of Orlando PO Box 1800 Orlando FL 32802-1800 Office: Diocese of Orlando 50 E Robinson St Orlando FL 32801 Office Phone: 407-246-4800. Office Fax: 407-246-4817.

NOONAN, PATRICK FRANCIS, conservation executive; b. St. Petersburg, Fla., Dec. 2, 1942; s. Francis Patrick and Henrietta (Donovan) Noonan; m. Nancy Elizabeth Peck, Aug. 15, 1964; children: Karen Elizabeth(dec.), Dawn Wiley. BA, Gettysburg Coll., 1965; M in City and Regional Planning, Catholic U. Am., 1967; MBA, Am. U., 1971. V.p., pres. The Nature Conservancy, 1968—80; founder, dir., chmn. Am. Farmland Trust, 1980—97; founder, chmn., pres. The Conservation Fund, 1985—2003, chmn. emeritus, 2003—; founder, vice chmn. Chesepk Conservancy, 2007—. Trustee Nat. Geog. Soc., 1990—; vice chmn. Nat. Geog. Edn. Found., 1995—; trustee Gettysburg Coll., 1978—91, Duke U. Sch. Environment, 1979—, Ind. Sector, 1984—91, Am. Conservation Assn., 1986—, Natural Resources Coun. Am., 1996—2002; dir. Ashland, 1991—2006, Internat. Paper, 1993—2004, Saul Ctrs., 1993—; mem. Pres.' Commn. on Am. Outdoors, 1985—87, Pres.' Commn. on Environ. Quality, 1991—93, Pres.' Commn. on White House Fellows, 2001—08. MacArthur Found. fellow, 1985—90. Office: The Conservation Fund 1655 Fort Myer Dr Ste 1300 Arlington VA 22209-3199 Office Phone: 703-908-5812.

NOONAN, PATRICK SUTTON, author management educator; b. Springfield, Ill., July 11, 1955; s. Patrick Arthur and Julia Ann (Sutton) N.; m. M. Jo Howarth, Apr. 27, 1985; children: Paul Howarth, William Prindiville. BS in Engring. Sci., Yale U., 1977, MBA, 1984; MS in Engring. Sci., Harvard U., 1989, PhD in Decision Scis., 1992. Dir. and gen. mgr. East River Consort, Boston, 1977—80; pres. Greenpeace New Eng., Boston, 1980-82; assoc. McKinsey & Co., Inc., NYC, 1984-88; prin. Planning Techs. Group, Inc., Lexington, Mass., 1990—98; prof. and assoc. dean Emory U., 1993—. Author, Decision and Info. Analysis, 2009; Prodr. record albums, including Laurasia, 1978, Undiscovered Country, 1988, Beat Noir, 1996, Scott's Red Star, 2000; prodr. film Journey to Georges Bank, 1982. Office Phone: 404-727-0549. Business E-Mail: pnoonan@emory.edu.

NOOR, AHMED KHAIRY, engineering educator, researcher; b. Cairo, Aug. 11, 1938; s. Mohamed Sayed and Fatma Mohamed (El-Zeini) Noor; m. Zakia Mahmoud Taha Noor, Aug. 18, 1966; 1 child, Mohamed. BS with honors, Cairo U., Egypt, 1958; MS, U. Ill., Urbana, 1961; PhD, U. Ill., 1963. Asst. prof. aero. and astronautics Stanford U., 1963—64; sr. lectr. structural mechanics Cairo U., 1964—67; vis. sr. lectr. structural mechanics U. Baghdad, Iraq, 1967—68; sr. lectr. structural mechanics U. NSW, Australia, 1968—71; NRC sen. resident postdoct. res. assoc. NASA Langley Rsch. Ctr., Hampton, Va., 1971—72; prof. engring. and applied sci. George Washington U., Hampton, 1972—90; Ferman W. Perry prof. aerospace structures and applied mechanics U. Va., dir. advanced computational tech. ctr.; eminent scholar, William E. Lobeck prof. engring. & dir. Ctr. Advanced Engring. Environments, Old Dominion U., Norflok, Va., 1991—; mem. coms. computational mechanics and large space sys. Nat. Acad. Engring. Editor-in-chief Jour. Advances in Engineering Software, Ctrl. European Jour. Engring.; mem. editorial bd. numerous tech. jours. Contbr. articles to profl. jours.:, editor books on structures and solids and computational mechanics. Fellow: ASME, ASCE (Aerospace Structures and Materials award 1989), AIAA, Nat. Inst. Aerospace, US Assn. Computational Mechanics, Internat. Assn. for Computational Mechanics (founder mem.), Am. Acad. Mechanics; mem.: Sigma Xi. Avocation: reading. Home: 31 Towler Dr Hampton VA 23666-2659 Office: 600 Butler Farm Rd Hampton VA 23666

NORBY, RICHARD JAMES, plant physiologist; b. Chgo., Oct. 6, 1950; s. William C. and Camilla (Edbrooke) N.; m. Ellen D. Smith, Apr. 25, 1977; 1 child: Karl. BA in Chemistry, Carleton Coll., Northfield, Minn., 1972; PhD in Forestry and Botany, U. Wis., Madison, 1981. Rsch. asst. dept. botany U. Wis., Madison, 1977—78, rsch. asst. dept. forestry, 1978—81; US Dept. Energy postdoctoral rsch. tng. program Environmental Sciences Divsn., Oak Ridge Nat. Lab., 1981—83, U. Tenn. Rsch. Assoc., 1983—85, rsch. assoc., 1985—87, rsch. staff mem., 1987—96, sr. rsch. staff mem., 1996—2001, disting. R&D staff mem., 2001—07, U. Tenn.-Battelle Corp. Fellow, 2007—. Adj. prof. Dept. Ecology & Evolutionary Biology U. Tenn., Knoxville, 1988-; task leader, Global Change and Terrestrial Ecosytems, Focus 1, 1997-2003; sci. steering group for the N.Am. Carbon Program, 2005-; scientific steering com., Terrestrial Ecosystem Responses to Atmospheric and Climate Change, 2001-. Reviewer for several publications, environment sect. editor and mgr. of US office The New Phytologist, 1997—, mem. editl. bd. Ecological Applications, 1998—2002, Journal of Plant Ecology, 2007—, editl. review bd. Tree Physiology, 1986—; contbr. of several articles to profl. jours. Recipient Soc. of Technical Communications, Award of Merit for Technical Publication, 1989, 1998, U. Tenn. Battelle award for Outstanding Accomplishment in Sci. and Technology, 2004; E.B. Fred Fellow, U. Wis.-Madison, 1977. Fellow AAAS; mem. Ecol. Soc. Am., Sigma Xi, Xi Sigma Pi Office: Environmental Sciences Divsn Oak Ridge National Lab One Bethel Valley Rd Bldg 1062 MS 6422 Oak Ridge TN 37831-6422 also: Oak Ridge National Lab Bldg 1062 MS 6422 PO Box 2008 Oak Ridge TN 37831-6422 Office Phone: 865-576-5261. Office Fax: 865-576-9939. Business E-Mail: norbyrj@ornl.gov, rjn@ornl.gov.

NORCROSS, GARY A., diversified financial services company executive; Mgmt. positions Systematics, Inc. (acquired by ALLTEL Info. Svcs.), 1988—91; tech. mgmt. positions ALLTEL Info. Svcs. (acquired by Fidelity Nat. Info. Svcs.), 1991—96, pres., Integrated Fin. Solutions divsn., sr. v.p., gen. mgr. cmty. bank segment, 1996—2003; pres., integrated fin. solutions Fidelity National Information Services, Inc., 2003—06, exec. v.p., integrated fin. solutions, 2006—07, pres., COO, transaction processing svcs., 2007, corp. exec. v.p., COO, 2007—. Office: Fidelity National Information Services Inc 601 Riverside Ave Jacksonville FL 32204 Office Phone: 904-854-5000. Office Fax: 904-357-1105. Business E-Mail: gary.norcross@fnf.com.

NORD, WALTER ROBERT, business administration educator, researcher, consultant; b. Mt. Kisco, NY, July 2, 1939; s. Arthur William and Elizabeth (Reimstedt) N.; m. Ann Feagan, June 10, 1967. BA in Econs., Williams Coll., 1961; MS in Organizational Behavior, Cornell U., 1963; PhD in Social Psychology, Washington U., St. Louis, 1967. Asst. prof. organizational psychology Washington U., 1967-70, assoc. prof., 1970-73, prof., 1973-89; prof. mgmt. U. South Fla., 1989—, Disting. Univ. prof., 2001; vis. prof. faculty commerce Northwestern U., 1981, U. B.C. (Can.), Vancouver, 1975-76. Author: (with S. Tucker) Implementing Routine and Radical Innovations, 1987; editor: Concepts and Controversy in Organizational Behavior, 1972, rev. edit, 1976; (with P. Frost and V. Mitchell) Organizational Reality, 1978, rev. edit., 1982, 86, 92; (with H. Meltzer) Making Organizations Humane and Productive, 1982; (with P. Frost and V. Mitchell) Managerial Reality, 1989, HRM Reality, 1992; (with A. Brief) Meanings of Occupational Work, 1990, (with S. Clegg and C. Hardy) Handbook of Organization Studies, 1996 (George Terry Book award 1997), 2d edit., 2006, (with P. Frost and L. Krefting) Managerial and Organization Reality, Stories of Life and Work, 2004, (with S. Clegg, C. Hardy and T. Lawrence) Sage Handbook of Organization Studies, 2006. Fellow APA; mem. Acad. Mgmt. (named Disting. Educator 2002). Home: 6004 Pratt St Tampa FL 33647-1043 Office: U South Fla Sch Bus Tampa FL 33620-5500 Office Phone: 813-974-1787. Business E-Mail: wnord@coba.usf.edu.

NORDEN, ERNEST ELWOOD, retired foreign language educator; b. Chgo., July 11, 1938; s. Ernest and Jeleste Katherine (Diggle) N.; m. Janet Louise Burke, June 22, 1963; children: Brent C., Keith R. BS, Purdue U., 1961; MA, U. Oreg., 1963; PhD, U. Calif., Berkeley, 1974. Asst. prof. U. Colo., Boulder, 1969-71, Northeast La. U., Monroe, 1971-72, 73-75; assoc. prof. Baylor U., Waco, Tex., 1975-85, prof., 1985—2006; prof. emeritus, 2006—. Contbr. articles to profl. jours. Vol. Dept. Pub. Health, Waco, 1993-96. Lectr. Fulbright Commn., 1972-73; fellow NEH, 1975, 87, Woodrow Wilson fellowship, 1961. Mem. Am. Assn. Tchrs. Spanish and Portuguese (v.p. Lone Star chpt. 1978-79, pres. 1979-80), Modern Lang. Assn. Am. (bibliographer Spanish sect. 1981-2007, mem. advisory com., 2004-07), AARP Tax Aide. Home Phone: 469-467-6938. Personal E-mail: ernest_norden@baylor.edu.

NORDEN, JED L., human resources specialist; BSBA, Ctrl. Mich. U. Various positions, human resources Ingersoll-Rand PLC, May Department Stores, Payless Shoesource, Inc., Ultimate Electronics, Inc.; exec. v.p., human resources, chief adminstrv. officer Retail Ventures, Inc., 2004—08; sr. v.p., human resources Servicemaster Co., Servicemaster Global Holdings, 2008—. Bd. dirs. Boston U. Human Resources Policy Inst., Brigham Young U., U. Kans., Washburn U.; founding bd. mem. Corp. Leadership Bd., Washington. Office: The ServiceMaster Co 860 Ridge Lake Blvd Memphis TN 38120 Office Phone: 901-597-1400. Office Fax: 630-663-2001. Business E-Mail: jed.norden@servicemaster.com.

NORDEN, MARK, mining executive; V.p., gen. mgr. Mideast divsn., Va. dist. Martin Marietta Materials, Inc., Richmond, Va. Mem.: Va. Transp. Constrn. Alliance (bd. dirs., aggregate producers rep.), Md. Transp. Builders and Materials Assn. (bd. dirs.), Nat. Stone, Sand & Gravel Assn. (chmn. mining, reclamation and dredging com.). Office: Martin Marietta Materials Inc Mideast Divsn Va Dist 9513 Hull Street Rd Ste A Richmond VA 23236 Office Phone: 804-674-9517. Office Fax: 804-675-9261.

NORDGREN, BECKY, state legislator, marketing professional; b. Gadsden, Ala., May 25, 1961; m. Eric Nordgren; children: Eric, Miles, Millicent. Attended, Snead State Jr. Coll., 1980, Auburn U., 1982, U. Ala., 1985. Sales rep. Cable Advantage, 1987—93, WQEN FM Radio, 1993—94; agent Attaway Advt., 1994—99; co-owner Clear Images-Advt.; mktg. rep. Lincare Respiratory Services; mem. Dist. 29 Ala. House of Representatives, 2002—. Bd. dirs. Southern Little League, 1999-, Rams Pee-Wee Football, 1999-; mem. Etowah-Gadsden C. of C., 2000-02. Republican. Office: 930 Keith Ave Anniston AL 36207 also: Ala House of Reps Rm 522-E 11 S Union St Montgomery AL 36130 Office Phone: 334-353-9032. Business E-Mail: clearimages4@earthlink.net.

NORELID, JAN A., construction materials company executive; b. Sweden, 1953; naturalized; married; 2 children. Grad., Stockholm Sch. Econs. Various fin. and mgmt. positions various multinat. corps.; CFO U.S. oper. subs. of Swedish med. equipment mfr.; owner printing co.; v.p., CFO Devcon International Corp., Deerfield Beach, Fla., 1997—. Office: Ste 201 1350 E Newport Center Dr Deerfield Beach FL 33442

NORIEGA, MELISSA, councilwoman, educator; b. Phila., 1954; d. Charles and Connie Meisgeier; m. Richard J. Noriega, Feb. 14, 1991; 1 child, Richard J. Jr. 1 stepchild, Alex. BS in Psychology, U. Houston, 1977; MEd, U. Houston Coll. Edn., 1983. Adminstr. Houston Ind. Sch. Dist., 1981—2005, 2007—, various positions including data analyst Title I rsch., mgr. Spl. Projects and Dist. Initiatives, mgr. Profl. Devel. Svcs.; mem., Dist. 145 Tex. House of Reps., 2005—06; councilwoman-at-large, Position 3 Houston City Coun., 2007—. Mem. exec. com. Parents for Pub. Sch.'s. Active Christ Ch. Cathedral. Recipient Joe E. Moreno Svc. award, Tex. House Reps., 2005, Recognition award, Greater Houston Partnership, 2005, Cmty. Svc. award, Am. Jewish Com., 2006; named Freshman of Yr., Dem. Caucus, 2005. Mem.: East End C. of C. (Svc. award 2005), Eastwood Civic Assn. (past pres.), U. Houston Alumni Assn. (life). Office: City Hall Annex 900 Bagby 1st Fl Houston TX 77002 Office Phone: 832-393-3005. Office Fax: 832-393-3251. Business E-Mail: atlarge3@cityofhouston.net.

NORIEGA, RICK (RICHARD JOEL NORIEGA), state legislator; b. Jan. 8, 1958; m to Melissa Meisgeier; children: Alexander & Rick Jr. Grad., U. Houston, 1984; MPA, Harvard U. John F. Kennedy Sch. Govt., 1999. Texas State Representative, District 145, 1999-, member, Human Serv & Transportation Committees, 1999-, Corrections, Def Affairs & State-Fed Relations Committees, currently, Texas House Representative.Sr state relations specialist, currently; project manager, Communities in Schools Inc, formerly; teacher, Houston Independent Sch District & Houston Community Col Syst, formerly; joined Houston Industries Inc (now CenterPoint Energy), 1993-, manager economic development, 1998-; director, Catholic Charities, currently. Mem. human svc. & transportation, corrections, def. affairs and state-fed. rels. coms. Tex. House Representatives. Mem. Christ Ch. Cathedral, Houston; Laredo border sector comdr. Operation Jump Start, 2006; incident comdr., Houston's Hurricane Katrina relief efforts George R. Brown Convention Ctr. Named Legislator of Year, Hispanic Journal, 2001; Awards from: Texas Association of Bilingual Educators (TABE), Texas League of United Latin America Citizens (LULAC); selected by the Texas Association of Chicanos in Higher Education (TACHE) and the Hispanic Journal as "2001 Legislator of the Year"; Nat awards included the Legislature Leaders in Education Award from the Nat Col Bd, 2002 and Hispanic Caucus of the America Association for Higher Education (AAHE) for Outstanding Support of Hispanic Issues In Higher Education, 2003; Govt of

Mexico, honored with OHTLI Award. Democrat. Mailing: PO Box 230324 Houston TX 77023 Address: 2900 Woodridge Ste 305 Houston TX 77087 Office: Capitol Ext E2 718 Austin TX 78701 Fax: 512-463-5896, 713-649-6454.

NORMAN, ALBERT GEORGE, JR., lawyer; b. Birmingham, Ala., May 29, 1929; s. Albert G. and Ila Mae (Carroll) N.; m. Catherine Marshall DeShazo, Sept. 3, 1955; children: Catherine Marshall, Albert George III. BA, Auburn U., 1953; LLB, Emory U., 1958; MA, U. NC, 1960. Bar: Ga. 1957. Assoc. Moise, Post & Gardner, Atlanta, 1958-60, ptnr., 1960-62, Hansell & Post, Atlanta, 1962-86, Long, Aldridge & Norman, Atlanta, 1986-2000. Dir. Atlanta Gas Light Co., 1976-2000. Served with USAF, 1946-49. Mem. ABA, Ga. Bar Assn., Atlanta Bar Assn., Lawyers Club Atlanta (pres. 1973-74), Am. Law Inst., Am. Judicature Soc. (dir. 1975-78), Old War Horse Lawyers Club, (pres. 1991-92), Cherokee Town and Country Club. Episcopalian. Office: 134 Peachtree St NW Atlanta GA 30303-1802 Personal E-mail: almarnorman@att.net.

NORMAN, JIM, state legislator; b. Jacksonville, Fla., Sept. 3, 1953; m. Mearline Norman. Attended, U. North Fla., Jacksonville. Legis. analyst Salvation Army, Tampa, Fla.; commr. Hillsborough County Bd. County Commissioners, 1992—2010; mem. Dist. 12 Fla. State Senate, 2011—. Republican. Office: 14031 N Dale Mabry Blvd Tampa FL 33618 also: Florida State Senate 214 Senate Office Bldg 404 S Monroe St Tallahassee FL 32399-1100 Office Phone: 813-265-6260, 850-487-5068. Business E-Mail: norman.jim.web@flsenate.gov.

NORMAN, RALPH W., state legislator; b. Rock Hill, SC, June 20, 1953; m. Elaine Norman; children: Warren III, Caroline, Anne, Mary Catherine. BS, Presbyterian Coll., 1973. Mem. SC House of Reps., 2004—06, mem. Dist. 48, 2009—. Bd. visitors Med. Univ. of SC. Mem.: Young Men's Christian Assn. (bd. dirs.). Office: 404A Blatt Bldg Columbia SC 29211 Home: 907 Maple Hill Lane Rock Hill SC 29732 Office Phone: 803-212-6888.

NORMAN, THENA MONTS DURHAM, microbiologist, researcher, health facility administrator; b. Bradenton, Fla., July 10, 1945; d. Turner and Silverrene (Taylor) M.; m. Millard Durham, Aug. 30, 1969 (div. 2001); children: Bryce Vincent-Barnard, Brittanie Yvonne; m. Herman H. Norman, August 6, 2005. BS, Fisk U., 1966; MS, Purdue U., 1968. Rsch. microbiologist Ctrs. for Disease Control, Atlanta, 1968-86, assoc. dir. for programs Nat. Ctr. for Prevention Svcs., 1988-95; program analyst Office Dir. Ctr. for Health Promotion and Edn., 1986-88; dir. exec. secretariat Ctrs. for Dis. Control and Prevention, Atlanta, 1995—2001; dep. dir. for policy Nat. Ctr. for HIV, STD, and TB Prevention for CDC, Atlanta, 2001—05; ret., 2005. Cons. FDA; mem. alumnae adv. com., pres. coun. dept. biol. scis. Purdue U.; bd. dirs. Balm in Gilead, Inc. Contbr. articles to profl. jours. Mem. NAACP, Neighborhood Planning Unit, SCLC/Women Adv. Coun., So. Christian Leadership Council/Women, Atlanta, 2005; bd. dirs. Cmty. Advanced Practices Nurses, Atlanta, 2004, Three Star Fitness Inc. Recipient Sec.'s award for Disting. Svc. Dept. HHS, 2001. Mem. AAAS, Sci. Rsch. Soc., Am. Soc. Microbiologists, CDC Assn. Exec. Women (founder, co-chmn.), Women in Sci. and Engring., Alumni Adv. Com., Nat. Assn. Broaden and Enchance Images (bd. dirs.), Three-Star Youth Fitness, Inc. (bd. dirs.). Democrat. Office Phone: 404-753-1322, 678-613-6265. Personal E-mail: thena1@bellsouth.net.

NORMENT, THOMAS K., state legislator; b. Richmond, Va., Apr. 12, 1946; m. Mary Carlisle Humelsine. Atty.; mem. Dist. 3 Va. State Senate, 1992—, minority leader, 2008—; mem. Agr. Com., Conservation & Natural Resources Com., Commerce & Labor Com., Courts of Justice & Privileges & Elections Com., 1992—. Mem.: James City County Rotary, Williamsburg & Peninsula C. of C., Williamsburg & Newport News Bar Asns., Va. State Bar. Republican. Episcopal. Office: Po Box 6205 Williamsburg VA 23188 also: Capitol Office Senate of Virginia Rm 427 PO Box 396 Richmond VA 23218 Office Phone: 804-698-7503, 757-259-7810. Office Fax: 757-259-7812, 804-698-7651. E-mail: district03@senate.virginia.gov.

NORONA, MIKE, automotive parts company executive; married; 2 children. B in Commerce, U. BC. Head fin. Future Shop, Canada; v.p. fin. svcs. Best Buy Co., Inc., pres. fin. svcs., 2007—08; exec. v.p., CFO Advance Auto Parts, Inc., Roanoke, Va., 2008—. Adv. com. mem. MasterCard, First Data; former bd. mem. World Wide Retail Exchange. Mem.: Certified Gen. Accountants of Can. Office: Advance Auto Parts Inc 5008 Airport Rd Roanoke VA 24012

NORQUIST, DAVID LUTZ, financial services company executive, former federal agency administrator; b. Concord, Mass., Nov. 24, 1966; s. Warren Elliott and Carol (Lutz) Norquist; m. Stephanie Rae Kristich; children: Warren, Elise, Vivian. BA in Polit. Sci., U. Mich., 1989, MA in Pub. Policy, 1989; MA in Nat. Security Studies, Georgetown U., 1995. Program/budget analyst Dept. Army, US Dept. Def., 1989—93, CCP program/budget analyst, 1993—95; dir. resource mgmt. US Army Intelligence & Security Command, 1995—97; staff mem. US House Appropriations Com., 1997—2002; dep. under sec. for fin. mgmt., comptr. US Dept. Def., 2002—04, acting prin. under sec., comptr., 2004—05, dep. under sec. for budget & appropriations affairs, comptr., 2004—06; CFO US Dept. Homeland Security, 2006—08; prin. Kearney & Co. Recipient Army Commander's award for Civilian Svc. medal, 1996, Joint Meritorious Unit award, US Dept. Def., 2003, Superior Honor award, US Dept. State, 2003, 2004, Secretary of Defense medal for Exceptional Pub. Svc., US Dept. Def., 2004. Office: Kearney & Co 1701 Duke St Alexandria VA 22314-3415 Office Phone: 703-391-5600. Office Fax: 703-391-3655.

NORRIS, CHARLES HEAD, lawyer, manufacturing executive; b. Boston, Sept. 14, 1940; s. Charles Head and Martha Marie N.; m. Diana D. Strawbridge, July 27, 1974 (div. 1994); children: Margaret Dorrance, Cecilia Walker; m. Ceil T. Walker, Oct. 13, 2001 (div. Feb. 2011). BA, U. Pa., 1963; JD, 1968; MA, U. Wash., 1965. Mem. Morgan, Lewis & Bockius, Phila., 1968-77; pres., chief exec. Artemis Corp., 1978-79; chmn. bd., chief exec., 1979-91; chmn. exec. com., vice-chmn. bd. Remington Rand Corp., 1979-81; ptnr. Artemis Energy Co., 1980-92; chmn., CEO Norris Investment Co., 1992—. Chmn. Norris Mfg. Co., 1994—, Garret Precision Products, 1996-11; chmn., CEO AmTech Engring. Co., 1996—2012, CEO Cactus Productions LLC, 2013-, Cactus Entertainment LLC; trustee maj. stockholders' voting trust Campbell Soup Co., 1987-90; bd. dirs. SBSF Funds, Inc., 1988-91, Del. Trust, 1987-91. Mem. Harvard U. Overseas Com. to Visit Libr., 1989—; mem. Pa. Commn. to Crime and Delinquency, 1980-84; mem. Thouron Award Selection Com., 1985-90; mem. Pa. Electoral Coll., 1980; mem. West Pikeland Twp. Suprs., 1969-72; mem. bd. visitors Carnegie Mellon U. Sch. Urban and Pub. Affairs, 1988-90; corp. mem. Belmont Hill Sch., 1990—. Served officer USAF, 1960. Mem. ABA, Pa. Bar Assn., Am. Econ. Assn., Phila., Knickerbocker, Vicmead Hunt, Everglades (bd. dirs. 1986-91), Bath and Tennis Club (treas., bd. dirs. 1985-91), Sunningdale Golf Club, The Brookline (Mass.) Country Club, Coral Beach and Tennis Club, Mid Ocean Club, Rolling Rock Club. Avocations: golf, reading, fishing. Office: Norris Family Office PO Box 772719 Memphis TN 38177-2719 Address: PO Box No 772719 Memphis TN 38177 Office Phone: 901-322-6049. Business E-Mail: bfoust@norrisinvestmentco.com.*

NORRIS, CHUCK (CARLOS RAY NORRIS), actor; b. Ryan, Okla., Mar. 10, 1940; s. Ray and Wilma Norris; m. Dianne Holochek, Dec. 29, 1958 (div. 1988), children: Mike, Dina, Eric; m. Gena O. Kelly, Nov. 28, 1998; children: Dakota Alan, Danilee; stepchildren: Kelley, Tim. Weekly syndicated columnist World Net Daily, Townhall Human Events. Actor: (films) The Wrecking Crew, 1969, Return of the Dragon, 1972, The Student Teachers, 1973, Slaughter in San Francisco, 1974, Breaker!, Breaker!, 1977, Good Guys Wear Black, 1978, Force of One, 1979, The Octagon, 1980, An Eye for an Eye, 1981, Silent Rage, 1982, Forced Vengeance, 1982, Lone Wolf McQuade, 1983, Missing in Action, 1984, Missing in Action II: The Beginning, 1985, Code of Silence, 1985, Delta Force, 1986, Firewalker, 1986, Hero and the Terror, 1988, Delta Force 2: Operation Stranglehold, 1990, The Hitman, 1991, Hellbound, 1994, Top Dog, 1995, Forrest Warrior, 1996, Bells of Innocence, 2003, Dodgeball: A True Underdog Story, 2004The Expendables 2, 2012; actor, co-screenwriter: (films) Invasion, U.S.A., 1985, Braddock: Missing in Action III, 1987; actor, co-exec. prodr. (films) Sidekicks, 1993; actor, exec. prodr.: (TV films) Logan's War: Bound by Honor, 1998, The President's Man, 2000, The President's Man: A Line in the Sand, 2001, Walker, Texas Ranger: Trial By Fire, 2005; actor: (TV series) Walker, Texas Ranger, 1993-2001; actor, exec. prodr.: (films) The Cutter, 2005, (TV series) Walker, Texas Ranger, 1993-2001, Sons of Thunder, 1999; exec. prodr. (films) Birdie and Bogey, 2004; author: The Secret Power Within: Zen Solutions to Real Problems, 1996, Black Belt Patriotism: How to Reawaken America, 2008; co-author: (with Joe Hyams) The Secret of Inner Strength: My Story, 1988, (with Ken Abraham) Against All Odds: My Story, 2004; (novels) (with Ken Abraham & Aaron Norris) The Justice Riders, 2006, Threat to Justice, 2007; host: The Ultimate Stuntman: A Tribute to Dar Robinson. Founder, chmn. United Fighting Arts Fedn.; founder, chmn. Kick Start Found., Houston, 1992; founder, World Combat League, 2005. Profl. world middleweight karate champion, 1968-74; Named Fighter of the Yr., Black Belt mag., 1969, Veteran of the Yr., American Veteran awards, 2000; recipient Golden Lifetime Achievement award World Karate Union Hall of Fame, 2000; named to Martial Arts History Mus. Hall of Fame, 1999; named an Honorary Tex. Ranger, State of Tex., 2010. Republican. Address: Kick Start Foundation Ste 203 427 W 20th St Houston TX 77008

NORRIS, JOHN DAVID, lawyer; b. El Dorado, Ark., Aug. 26, 1947; s. Jerome Clark and Mildred Rose (Leroux) N.; m. Sandra Kay Watts, Jan. 11, 1986; children: Millicent Mae, Clark Edward. BSChemE with high honors, U. Ark., 1969; JD with honors, George Washington U., 1977. Bar: Va. 1977, Tex. 1979, D.C. 1980, U.S. Dist. Ct. (so. dist.) Tex. 1980, U.S. Ct. Appeals (Fed. cir.) 1983, U.S. Supreme Ct. 1990. Law clerk to chief judge U.S. Ct. Appeals (Fed. cir.), Washington, 1977-79; chem. engr. Exxon Rsch. Laboratories; assoc. Arnold, White & Durkee, Houston, 1979-84, ptnr., 1984—2000, chmn. bd., 1990-93; ptnr., mem. exec. com. Howrey Simon Arnold & White LLP (formerly Arnold, White & Durkee), Houston, 2000—07. Adj. prof. U. Houston Law Ctr., 2007—08. Editor: Intellectual Property Law Review, 1988-91. Fellow (life) Houston Bar Found.; mem. ABA (patent, trademark and copyright sect.), State Bar Tex. (treas. intellectual property law sect. 1986-87) Houston Intellectual Property Law Assn. (pres. 1996-97), Am. Intellectual Property Law Assn., A.A. White Dispute Resolution Inst., U. Houston (bd. advisors 1996-1999). Presbyterian. Office: Howrey LLP 1111 Louisiana Fl 25 Houston TX 77002 Office Phone: 713-787-1505. Business E-Mail: NorrisJ@howrey.com.

NORRIS, JOHN W., manufacturing executive; Founding chmn. Environmental Funders Network; co-founder Maine Network Ptnrs.; co-founder, pres. Borealis, Inc., 1988—2000; joined Lennox International, Inc., 1960; pres. Lennox Internat. Inc. (Lennox Industries (Can.) Ltd.); v.p., Mktg. Lennox International, Inc., corp. sr. v.p., pres., 1977, pres., CEO, 1980, chmn., 1991. Bd. dirs. Air Conditioning and Refrigeration Inst., chmn., 1986; bd. dirs. AmerUs Life Holdings, Inc., Metroplex Regional Adv. Bd., Chase Bank Tex., NA. Assoc. dir., Philanthropy The Nature Conservancy, 2000—05; vol. Peace Corps, Jamaica, 1985—87. Mem. Gas Appliance Mfrs. Assn. (bd. mem., chmn. 1980-81). Office: Lennox International Inc 2140 Lake Park Blvd Richardson TX 75080 Office Fax: 972-497-5292. E-mail: john.norris@lennoxintl.com.

NORRIS, PAUL J., retired manufacturing executive; Grad., Mt. St. Mary's Coll.; MBA, U. Md. Various exec. positions, including pres., catalysts & chemicals Engelhard Corp., 1981—89, sr. v.p., gen. mgr., catalysts, v.p. & bus. dir., petroleum catalysts, 1981—89; pres. fluorine products Allied Signal Inc. (now Honeywell), 1989—94, pres., Chemicals & Catalysts, 1989—94, pres., Polymers Divsn., 1994—97, sr. v.p., pres., splty. chems. unit & chmn. UOP, 1997-98; with, Mktg. & Bus. Devel. Divsns. W. R. Grace & Co., 1971—81, pres. Columbia, Md., 1998—2003, CEO, 1998—2005, chmn., 1999—2005, Sealy Corp., 2008—. Former bd. dirs. Borden Chemicals, Inc.; bd. dirs. Nalco Holding Co. Office: Sealy Corp 1 Office Pky at Sealy Dr Trinity NC 27370 Office Phone: 336-861-3500. Office Fax: 336-861-3501. Business E-Mail: pnorris@sealy.com.

NORTH, JULIA B., manufacturing executive; V.p., customer svcs. Bellsouth Telecom., Atlanta; pres., consumer svcs. BellSouth Corp.; pres., CEO VSI Enterprises, Inc. Bd. dirs. Acuity Brands, Inc. Office: Acuity Brands Inc Bd Directors 1170 Peachtree St NE Ste 2300 Atlanta GA 30309-7676 Office Phone: 404-853-1400. E-mail: julia.north@acuitybrands.com.

NORTH, MARJORIE MARY, writer; b. Mt. Clemens, Mich., Oct. 21, 1945; d. Robert Haller and Hilla Beryl (Willard) Wright; m. William B. Hirons; children: Laura, Christina, Angela. Features editor Elizabeth City (N.C.) Daily Advance, 1966-69; news/mng. editor Brandon (Fla.) News, 1977-78; city editor Leesburg (Fla.) Comml., 1978-79; metro editor Sarasota (Fla.) Herald Tribune, 1979-80, Fla. West editor, 1980-85, daily columnist, 1985—2009. Host Weekly Interview Show, SNN-TV, 1997—2005. Author: Sarasota: A City For All Seasons, 1994, (plays) With the Best Intentions, 1994, Back in the Game, 1998. Recipient Layout, Creativity and Overall Publ. awards Fla. Press Assn., numerous comty. awards and citations; winner Fla. shorts competition Fla. Studio Theater New Play Festival, 1994, 98; Paul Harris fellow. Avocations: tennis, theater. E-mail: mnorth456@gmail.com.

NORTH, OLIVER LAURENCE (OLLIE NORTH), syndicated columnist, retired military officer; b. San Antonio, Oct. 7, 1943; m. Betsy Stuart, Nov. 13, 1968; children: Tait, Dornin, Sarah, Stuart. Student, SUNY, Brockport; BA, US Naval Acad., Annapolis, 1968. Commd. lt. USMC, 1966, advanced through ranks to lt. col., 1983, ret., 1990; dep. dir. polit.-mil. affairs NSC, Washington, 1981—83, counter-terrorism coord., 1983—86; host nat.-syndicated radio program Oliver North Radio Show/Common Sense Radio, 1995—2003; host War Stories with Oliver North, Fox News Channel, 2001—. Founder, hon. chmn. Freedom Alliance, Dulles, Va., 1990—; former co-host Equal Time, MSNBC; regular commentator Hannity & Colmes. Author: Under Fire: An American Story, 1991, War Stories: Operation Iraqi Freedom, 2003, American Heroes: In the Fight Against Radical Islam, 2008, Heroes Proved, 2012; co-author: (with David Roth) One More Mission: Oliver North Returns to Vietnam, 1993, (with Brian Smith) True Freedom: The Liberating Power of Prayer, 2004, (with Sara Horn) A Greater Freedom: Stories of Faith from Operation Iraqi Freedom, 2004, (with Joe Musser) War Stories II: Heroism in the Pacific, 2004, War Stories III: The Heroes Who Defeated Hitler, 2005, Mission Compromised: A Novel, 2002, Jericho Sanction, 2003, The Assassins, 2005. Decorated Silver Star, Bronze Star, Purple Hearts (2). Mem.: NRA (mem. bd. dirs. 1998—). Republican. Office: Freedom Alliance 22570 Markey Ct Ste 240 Dulles VA 20166 Office Phone: 703-444-7940. Office Fax: 703-444-9893.

NORTHAM, RALPH SHEARER, Lieutenant Governor of Virginia, former state legislator; b. Nassawadox, Va., Sept. 13, 1959; s. Wescott B. and Nancy B. (Shearer) Northam; m. Pam Northam; children: Wes, Aubrey. BS, Va. Mil. Inst., 1981; MD, Eastern Va. Med. Sch., 1984. Maj. US Army; asst. prof. neurology Eastern Va. Med. Sch.; resident Brooke Army Med. Ctr.; pediatric neurologist Children's Hosp. of the King's Daughters, 1992—; mem. Dist. 6 Va. State Senate, 2008—14; lt. gov. Commonwealth of Va., Richmond, 2014—. Democrat. Office: Lieutenant Governor 102 Governor St Richmond VA 23219 Office Phone: 804-786-2078. Office Fax: 804-786-7514.*

NORTHCUTT, CLARENCE DEWEY, lawyer; b. Guin, Ala., July 7, 1916; s. Walter G. and Nancy E. (Homer) Northcutt; m. Gwen Barton, Feb. 2, 2009. AB, U. Okla., 1939, LL.B., 1938. Bar: Okla. 1938. Pvt. practice, Ponca City, 1938—. Mem. bd. visitors U. Okla. Served with AUS, 1941-46. Decorated Bronze Star, Air medal with oak leaf cluster, Order St. John of Jerusalem; named Outstanding Citizen of Ponca City, 1982; inducted to Okla. Hall of Fame, 2001. Fellow Am. Coll. Trial Lawyers, Am. Coll. Trust and Estate Attys., Am. Bar Found.; mem. Acad. Univ. Fellows, Internat. Soc. Barristers, Am. Bd. Advocacy, Internat. Acad. Trial Lawyers, Okla. Bar Assn. (pres. 1975, bd. govs.), Ponca City C. of C. (past pres.). Clubs: Mason (32 Degree), Kiwanian. Democrat. Baptist. Office: PO Box 1669 Ponca City OK 74602-1669 Office Phone: 580-762-1655. Business E-Mail: cdnorth@northcuttlawfirm.com.

NORTHEN, CHARLES SWIFT, III, retired bank executive; b. Birmingham, Ala., Jan. 25, 1937; s. Charles Swift and Jennie Hood (Hunt) S.; m. Margaret Carson Robinson, Dec. 27, 1959 (div. 1972); children: Margaret Allen, Charles Swift IV, Bryce Robinson; m. Betty Jean Taylor, Oct. 3, 1981. BA cum laude, Vanderbilt U., 1959, MA, 1961. Chartered fin. analyst. Mem. staff trust dept. Birmingham Trust Nat. Bank, 1960-64; with First Ala. Bank Birmingham, 1964-80, sr. v.p., trust officer, 1975-80, Central Bank of South, Birmingham, 1981-85; exec. v.p. Regions Fin. Corp., 1985—95, corp. investment officer, 1993-95; mng. dir. Sterne, Agee & Leach, Inc., Birmingham, 1995-98, investment cons., 1998—2001; ret. Lectr. So. Trust Sch., Birmingham So. Coll.; pres. First Ala. Investments Inc.; dir. Hubbard Press, Findlay, Ohio. Bd. dirs. United Presbyn. Found., N.Y.C., 1977-86; mem. Birmingham Com. Fgn. Rels., 1970—. Mem. Ala. Security Dealers Assn. (pres.), Ala. Soc. Fin. Analysts (pres.), Inst. Chartered Fin. Analysts, Newcomen Soc., SAR, Kiwanis, Mountain Brook Club, The Club, Soc. Colonial Wars (Ala. gov. 2005-06). Presbyterian. Home: 3024 N Woodridge Rd Birmingham AL 35223-2748

NORTHERN, RICHARD, lawyer; b. Louisville, Dec. 17, 1948; s. James William and Mary Helen (Barry) Northern; m. Mary Lou Grundy, Aug. 28, 1971; children: James Barry, Nancy Hope, Mary Grace. BA in English, U. Louisville, 1970, JD, 1976; MPA, Harvard U., 1977; LHD (hon.), Spalding U., 2006. Bar: Ky. 1976, U.S. Dist. Ct. (we. and ea. dists.) Ky. 1977. Staff writer Courier-Jour., Louisville, 1970-72; dir. planning devel. Jefferson County Govt., Louisville, 1972-76; legis. dir. Office of U.S. Rep. Romano Mazzoli, Washington, 1977-78; spl. asst. U.S. Sec. of Interior, Washington, 1979-80; ptnr. Wyatt, Tarrant & Combs, Louisville, 1980—. Bd. dirs. Nugent Sand Co. Chmn. Louisville Devel. Authority, 2005—; dir. Jewish Hosp. Found., 2006—, Stock Yards Bank & Trust Co., 2011—. White House fellow, 1979, U.S.-Japan Leadership fellow, Japan Soc., Inc., 1988. Democrat. Roman Catholic. Office: Wyatt Tarrant & Combs 2800 Citizens Plz Louisville KY 40202-2898 Office Phone: 502-562-7234. Business E-Mail: rnorthern@wyattfirm.com.

NORTHRUP, HOPE A., clinical geneticist, pediatrician; MD, Med. U. SC, 1983. Lic. Tex., 1988, cert. Am. Bd. Clin. Genetics-Med. Genetics, Am. Bd. Clin. Biochemical/Molecular Genetics-Med. Genetics, diplomate Am. Bd. Pediatrics. Resident Children's Med. Ctr., 1984, Dallas, 1986; fellow Inst. Molecgene, Baylor, 1989; hosp. affiliation includes Shriners Hosp., Lyndon B. Johnson Gen. Hosp., Meml. Hermann Hosp. System. Office: Memorial Hermann Hospital 6410 Fannin St Ste 500 Houston TX 77030 Office Phone: 713-500-5760. Office Fax: 713-500-5760.

NORTON, BARBARA M., state legislator; Legal course, La. State U. Ret. AT&T; mem. Dist. 3 La. House of Reps., 2008—, mem. adminstrn. of criminal justice com., mcpl., parochial and cultural affairs com., transp., hwys. and pub. works com. Democrat. Office: State Capitol PO Box 44486 Baton Rouge LA 70804 Mailing: 3245 Hollywood Ave Shreveport LA 71108 Office Phone: 225-342-6945, 318-632-5887. Office Fax: 318-632-5889. Business E-Mail: nortonb@legis.state.la.us.

NORTON, DAVID C., federal judge; b. Washington, July 25, 1946; s. Charles Edward and Louise Helen (Le Feber) N.; children: Phoebe Elizabeth, Christine Baron. BA in History, U. of the South, 1968; JD, U. S.C., 1975. Assoc. Holmes & Thomson, Charleston, S.C., 1975-77, 80-82, ptnr., 1982-90; dep. solicitor 9th Jud. Ct., Charleston, 1977-80; judge US Dist. Ct. SC, Charleston, 1990—2007, chief judge, 2007—. Fourth cir. dist. ct. rep. U.S. Jud. Conf., 2003—; mem. adv. com. Halls of Evidence, 1996—2002. With USN, 1969—72. Mem. Fed. Judges Assn., Charleston County Bar Assn. (sec.-treas. 1983-90), S.C. Def. Trial Attys. Assn. (exec. com. 1988-90), S.C. Bar Assn. (Ho. Dels. 1986-90). Episcopalian. Avocations: boating, racquet ball. Office: Hollings Judicial Ctr PO Box 835 Broad & Meeting Sts 3rd Fl Charleston SC 29402-0835

NORTON, PIERCE H., gas industry executive; With Delhi Gas Pipeline, 1982, Am. Oil and Gas Co.; v.p. KN Energy; gen. mgr. Heartland Region; v.p. bus. devel. Bear Paw Energy, pres., 2002; exec. v.p. natural gas ONEOK Inc., pres. distbn. companies, 2009—, COO, 2011—. Bd. mem. Tulsa Cmty. Coll. Found. Mem.: Ind. Petroleum Assn. of Mountain States (past bd. mem.), ND Petroleum Coun. (past bd. mem.), Tex. Pipeline Assn. (past bd. mem.), Interstate Natural Gas Assn. of America (past bd. mem.), Am. Gas Assn. (leadership coun. mem.). Office: ONEOK Incorporated ONEOK Plz 100 W 5th St Tulsa OK 74103 Office Phone: 918-588-7000.

NORTON, ROBERT HOWARD, entertainer, writer, music arranger; b. NYC, July 19, 1946; s. Howard R. and Lena (Triano) N.; m. Eileen Williams, Sept. 29, 1966 (div. 1976); children: Brian, Lelania.

Student, Broward C.C., Ft. Lauderdale, Fla., 1970-75; community antenna TV engr. cert., Nat. Cable TV Inst., 1976. Rec. session artist Motown and various other recording labels, 1964—; entertainer various concerts, 1964—; systems technician Selkirk Communications, Ft. Lauderdale, Fla., 1979-81; cable TV engr. Gen. Instrument Corp., Hatboro, Pa., 1985—; entertainer (with Leilani Chandler) The Sophisticats, Ft. Pierce, Fla., 1984—; owner, author, software writer Norton Music, Ft. Pierce, Fla., 1990—. Author: The Artist's and Entertainer's Tax Bible, 1990, Entertainer's Guide to Cruising, 1991—; writer mus. software: 900 User Styles, 1991—, Band-in-a-Box Supercharger, 1993—, 32 Band-in-a-Box Fake Disks, 1994—, 28 Band-in-a-Box User Style Disks, 1993—, 900 After Market Styles for Microsoft Songsmith, software 475+: Gen. MIDI Sequences, 1993—; composer: numerous songs, —, arranger of more then 500 songs, —. Mem. Internat. Wind Synthesis Assn. Home and Office: Norton Music PO Box 13149 Fort Pierce FL 34979-3149 E-mail: norton@nortonmusic.com.

NORWOOD, BERNARD, economist; s. Hyman and Rose (Fink) N.; m. Janet Lippe, June 25, 1943; children: Stephen Harlan, Peter Carlton. BA, Boston U., 1947; MA, Fletcher Sch. Law and Diplomacy, 1948, PhD, 1957; degree in Nat. Security, Nat. War Coll., Washington, 1968. Internat. economist State Dept., 1949-58; joined U.S. Fgn. Svc., 1955; 1st. sec. U.S. mission to European Communities, Brussels, Belgium, 1958-62; asst. chief comml. policy and treaties divsn. Dept. State, 1962; chmn. trade staff com. Office Spl. Rep. for Trade Negotiations, Exec. Office Pres., 1963-67; assigned The Nat. War Coll., 1967-68; advisor divsn. internat. fin. bd. govs. Fed. Res. Sys., 1968-75; prin. assoc., sr. cons. Nathan Assocs., Inc., 1975-94. Mem. U.S. del. to negotiations and confs. GATT, Geneva, 1953-67. Served with AUS, 1943-46. Home: 2500 Barton Creek Blvd Apt 2315 Austin TX 78735-1627

NORWOOD, DEBORAH ANNE, law librarian; b. Honolulu, Nov. 12, 1950; BA, U. Wash., 1972, M in Law Librarianship, 1979; JD, Willamette U., 1974. Bar: Wash., U.S. Dist. Ct. (we. dist.) 1975, U.S. Ct. Appeals (9th cir.) 1980. Ptnr. Evans and Norwood, Seattle, 1975-79; law libr. U.S. Courts Libr., Seattle, 1980-89; state law libr. Wash. State Law Libr., Olympia, 1989—2002, reporter of decisions, 1994-2001; asst. dir. pub. svcs. Jacob Burns Law Libr. George Washington U., Washington, 2002—. Mem. Freedom to Read Found. Mem. Am. Assn. Law Librs. (chmn. state, ct. and county spl. interest sect. 1995-96, chair legal info. svcs. to pub. spl. interest sect. 2001-02). Office: Jacob Burns Law Libr George Washington U 716-20th St NW Washington DC 20052 Office Phone: 202-994-7338. Business E-Mail: dnorwood@law.gwu.edu.

NORWOOD, JANET LIPPE, economist; b. Newark, Dec. 11, 1923; d. M. Turner and Thelma (Levinson) Lippe; m. Bernard Norwood, June 25, 1943; children: Stephen Harlan, Peter Carlton. BA, Douglass Coll., 1945; MA, 1946; PhD, Fletcher Sch. Law and Diplomacy, 1949; LLD (hon.), Fla. Internat. U., 1979, Carnegie Mellon U., Pitts., 1984, Harvard U., Cambridge, Mass., 1997, Rutgers U., 2003; D, State US. Instr. Wellesley Coll., 1948-49; economist William L. Clayton Ctr., Tufts U., 1953-58; with Bur. Labor Stats., U.S. Dept. Labor, Washington, 1963-91; dep. commr., then acting commr. Bur. Labor Stats. Dept. Labor, Washington, 1975-79, commr. labor stats., 1979-92; sr. fellow The Urban Inst., Washington, 1992-99; counselor, sr. fellow N.Y. Conf. Bd., 2001—09. Dir. Nat. Opinion Rsch. Ctr., chair adv. coun. unemployment compensation, 1993—96; pres. COSSA, 2001—02; mem. bd. sci. counselors Nat. Ctr. Health Stats., 1975—77; chair panel on offshoring Nat. Acad. Pub. Adminstrn., 2005—07. Author: Organizing to Count: Change in the Federal Statistical System, 1995; contbr. scientific papers in field. Recipient Disting. Achievement award, Dept. Labor, 1972, Spl. Commendation award, 1977, Philip Arnow award, 1979, Elmer Staats award, 1982, Pub. Svc. award, 1984, Presdl. Disting. Exec. Rank, 1988, Elizabeth Scott award, Com. Pres.'s Statis. Assns., 2002; named Hall Disting. Alumni, Rutgers U., 1987. Fellow: AAAS, Nat. Assn. Bus. Economists, Royal Statis. Soc., Am. Statis. Assn. (pres. 1989, Founder's award 1997); mem.: Nat. Inst. Statis. Sci. (bd. trustees 1991—2000), Nat. Acad. Sci. (assoc.), Nat. Acad. Pub. Adminstrn., Internat. Assn. Ofcls. Stats., Internat. Statis. Inst., Douglass Coll. Soc. Disting. Achievement, Cosmos Club (pres. 1995—96). Home: 2500 Barton Creek Blvd Apt 2315 Austin TX 78735-1627 Home Phone: 301-951-8581. Personal E-mail: janetnor@aol.com.

NOSANOW, BARBARA SHISSLER, museum director, curator; b. Roanoke, Va. d. Willis Morton and Kathryn Sabin (Bradford) Johnson; m. John Lewis Shissler Jr., July 28, 1957 (dec. May 1972); children: John Lewis Shissler III, Ada Holland Shissler; m. Lewis Harold Nosanow, Oct. 15, 1973. AB, Smith Coll., 1957; MA, Case Western Res. U., 1958; ABD, U. Minn., 1972. Asst. mng. editor Jour. Aesthetics and Art Criticism, Cleve. Mus. Art, 1958-63; dir. publs. and rsch. Mpls. Inst. Arts, 1963-72; dir. U. Minn. Art Mus., Mpls., 1972-76; dir. exhbns. and edn. Nat. Archives, Washington, 1976-79; curator Smithsonian Instn., Washington, 1979-82; asst. dir. Nat. Mus. Am. Art, Smithsonian Instn., 1982-88; dir. Portland (Maine) Mus. Art, 1988-93, Art Spaces, 1993—; study leader, lecturer Smithsonian Study Tours of France and Russia, 1997—. Lectr. in field. Past mem. various rev. panels NEH, Washington. Bd. dirs. Md. Com. for Humanities, Balt., 1980-83. Mem. Internat. Women's Forum. Avocation: travel. Home: 100 Ansonborough Ln Ste 402 Athens GA 30605-6815 Office Phone: 760-559-4465. Personal E-mail: bsnosanow14530@yahoo.com.

NOSEF, JOSEPH D., III, political organization administrator, lawyer; B in Acctg., U. Miss., 1991, M in Acctg., 1994, JD, 1995; LLM, U. Fla., Gainesville, 1996. Chief counsel to Haley Barbour Office of Gov., Miss., 2004—06; campaign mgr. Haley Barbour's Gubernatorial Re-Election Campaign, 2007; chief of staff to Phil Bryant Office of Lt. Gov., Miss., 2007—08; counsel Watkins & Eager PLLC; chmn. Miss. Rep. Party, 2012—. Mem. Lt. Gov. Commn. on Effectiveness and Efficiency in Govt.; officer, outside counsel Miss. Disaster Recovery Fund. Mem. exec. com. Hinds County Rep. Party; mem. St. Richard Cath. Ch.; bd. mem. Marsha Barbour Cmty. Ctr., Metro YMCA; bd. trustees Hinds County Econ. Devel. Dist., 2001—03; mem. adv. bd. Metro Salvation Army; bd. dirs. Ballet Miss., SafeCity. Mem.: Jackson Young Lawyers Assn., Capital Area Bar Assn., Miss. Bar Assn., Phi Kappa Phi. Republican. Office: Watkins & Eager PLLC The Emporium Bldg 400 E Capitol St Jackson MS 39201 also: Miss Republican Party PO Box 60 Jackson MS 39205 Office Phone: 601-965-1884. Office Fax: 601-965-1901. Business E-Mail: jnosef@watkinseager.com.*

NOTHAFT, FRANK EMILE, economist; b. Jersey City, Apr. 10, 1956; s. Frank Emil and Rita Johanna (Laer) N.; m. Lisa Beth Greenfield, June 13, 1981; children: Frank Austin, Daniel Blake, John Paul. BA, N.Y.U., 1976; MA, Columbia U., 1977, MPhil, 1979, PhD, 1986. Economist Bd. Govs. Fed. Reserve System, Washington, 1983-86; sr. economist Freddie Mac, McLean, Va., 1986-88, dep. chief economist, 1988-90, dir., office of chief economist, 1990—2001, chief economist, 2001—, v.p., 2004—. Contbr. articles to profl. jours. Sec., bd. dirs. Falls Church Housing Corp., Va., 1988-91. Sloan Found. grantee, 1982; Columbia U. fellow, 1976-79; recipient Founders' Day award, N.Y.U., 1976. Mem. Am. Real Estate Urban Econs. Assn. (bd. dirs. 1990-92, 2002-04, v.p. 2006-08, pres. 2008—09, 06-11), Real Estate Rsch. Inst. (adv. bd. mem., 2009-), Fin. Mgmt. Assn. (bd. dirs. 2006-08), Am. Real Estate Soc., Nat. Assn. Bus. Economists (chair real estate com.). Office: Freddie Mac 8200 Jones Branch Dr Mail Stop 484 Mc Lean VA 22102-3110

NOUJAIM, FARES DOURID, investment company executive; b. Kuwait, 1964; arrived in US, 1972; married; 3 children. BS in Quantitative Economics, Pace U., NYC. Analyst Goldman Sachs & Co., 1985—87; fin. mgmt. positions through vice chmn. & global head of capital markets group The Bear Stearns Companies Inc., 1987—2008; pres. Middle East & No. Africa Merrill Lynch & Co. Inc., NYC, 2008—09; vice chmn. corp. & investment banking Bank of America Corp., 2009—. Office: Bank of America Corp 100 N Tryon St Charlotte NC 28255

NOVA, CRAIG, writer; b. LA, July 5, 1945; s. Karl and Elizabeth (Sinclair) N.; m. Christina Barnes, July 2, 1977; children: Abigail, Tate. BA, U. Calif.-Berkeley, 1967; M.F.A., Columbia U., 1969. Disting. prof. humanities U. N.C., Greensboro, 2005—. Author: Turkey Hash, 1972, The Geek, 1975, Incandescence, 1978, The Good Son, 1982, The Congressman's Daughter, 1986, Tornado Alley, 1989, Trombone, 1992, The Book of Dreams, 1994, The Universal Door, 1997, Brook Trout and the Writing life, 1999, Wetware, 2001, Cruisers, 2004. Recipient Harper-Saxton prize Harper and Row, Pubs., 1972; recipient award in lit. Am. Acad. and Inst. Arts and Letters; Guggenheim Found. fellow, 1977; fellow Nat. Endowment for Arts, 1973, Nat. Endowment for Arts, 1975, Creative Artists Pub. Service, 1976; NEA fellow, 1985; story included in Best Am. Short Stories, 1987. Office Phone: 919-732-1857. E-mail: nova@sover.net.

NOVAK, DAVID C., restaurant company executive; b. 1952; m. Wendy Novak. BA, U. Mo., 1974. Sr. v.p., mktg. Pizza Hut, 1986—90; exec. v.p., mktg. and nat. sales Pepsi-Cola Co., 1990—92, COO, N. Am., 1992—94; pres., CEO N. Am. Kentucky Fried Chicken, 1994—97; group pres., CEO, Pizza Hut, KFC Tricon Global Restaurants, Inc. (now Yum! Brands Inc.), Louisville, 1996—97; vice-chmn. Yum! Brands, Inc. (formerly TRICON Global Restaurants, Inc.), Louisville, 1996—97, pres., 1997—2000, pres., CEO, 2000—01, chmn., pres., CEO, 2001—12, chmn., CEO, 2012—. Bd. dirs. Yum Brands, Inc., 1997—, J.P. Morgan Chase & Co., 2001—12. Co-author (with John Boswell): The Education of an Accidental CEO: Lessons Learned from the Trailer Park to the Corner Office, 2007. Named one of The Bus. People of Yr., Fortune mag., 2010. Office: Yum Brands Inc 1441 Gardiner Ln Louisville KY 40213-1914*

NOVAK, GORDON S., JR., computer scientist, educator; b. Colo., 1947; m. Susan Raye Strawn, May 7, 1977; children: Genevieve, Courtney. BSEE, U. Tex., 1969, MA in Computer Sci., 1971, PhD in Computer Sci., 1976. Mgr. sys. programming Tracor Inc., Austin, Tex., 1966-76; instr. U. Tex., Austin, 1976-77, asst. prof., 1978-81, 83-84, assoc. prof., 1984-98; prof., 1998—; dir. Artificial Intelligence Lab. U. Tex., Austin, 1984-99; computer sci. SRI Internat., Menlo Park, Calif., 1977-78. Vis. asst. prof. Stanford (Calif.) U., 1981-83. Contbr. articles to profl. jours. Office: U Tex Dept Computer Sci Austin TX 78712

NOVAK, JOSEPH DONALD, science educator; b. Mpls., Dec. 2, 1930; s. Joseph Daniel and Anna (Podany) N.; m. Joan Owen, July 18, 1953; children: Joseph Mark, Barbara Joan, William John BS, U. Minn., 1952, MA, 1954, PhD, 1958; D (hon.), U. Comanhue, Neuquen, Argentina, 1998, Pub. U. Navarra, 2002, U. Urbino, 2006. Teaching asst. U. Minn., Mpls., 1952-56, instr., 1956-57; asst. prof. Kans. State Tchrs. Coll., 1957-59, Purdue U., West Lafayette, Ind., 1959-62, assoc. prof., 1962-67; prof. Cornell U., Ithaca, NY, 1967-95, prof. emeritus, 1995—; pres. Joseph D. Novak Knowledge Consultants, Inc.; sr. rsch. scientist Inst. for Human and Machine Cogniion, Pensacola, Fla. Knowledge constrn. and orgn. cons. to Procter & Gamble and other cos.; cons. to over 400 schs. and colls., 1975—; vis. fellow Harvard U., 1965-66; disting. vis. prof. U. N.C., Wilmington, 1980, U. West Fla., 1987-88; vis. prof. U. South Fla., 1995; sr. rsch. scientist Fla. Inst. Human and Machine Congition, 1996—. Author: Learning How to Learn, 1984, in 10 langs., 1984—96, Educational Psychology: A Cognitive View, 1978, A Theory of Education, 1977, Aprendizaje Significativo: Techieas y Aplicaciones, 1997, Learning, Creating and Using Knowledge: Concept Maps as Facilitative Tools for Schools and Corporations, 1998, Teaching Science for Understanding, 1998, Assessing Science Understanding, 2000, Una aportacion a la mejora de la calidad de la docentia universitaria: Los mapas Conceptuales, 2000, Errores Conceptuales: Diagnosis, Tratamientoy Reflexiones, 2001, Learning, Creating and Using Knowledge, Routledge, 2010, 22 others; contbr. over 40 chpts. to books, over 130 articles to profl. jours. Recipient Charles E. Bessey award Bot. Soc. America, 2003; fellow Tozer Found., Lydia Anderson, 1955-56; research assoc. Harvard U., 1965-66; Fulbright-Hayes Sr. Scholar, Australia, 1980 Fellow: AAAS (sec. sect. Q); mem.: NSTA, Coun. Sci. Soc. Presidents (1st hon. award for rsch. in sci. edn. 1998), Nat. Assn. Biology Tchrs. (Hon. Mem. award), Nat. Assn. Rsch. in Sci. Tchr. (pres. 1968, Outstanding Contbns. Sci. Tchg. Through Rsch. award 1990), Sigma Xi. Avocations: hiking, swimming, dance, music. Office: Cornell University 40 S Alcaniz St Pensacola FL 32502 Personal E-mail: jnovak@ihmc.us. Business E-Mail: jdn2@cornell.edu.*

NOVAK, KENT, computer company executive; BS in Indsl. Engring., MS in Indsl. Engring., Purdue U. Digital switching sys. engr. AT&T Bell Labs., 1988; joined Texas Instruments, Inc., 2003, v.p., gen. mgr., med. and High Reliability, various positions, Wireless Infrastructure Bus. Unit & High Speed Comm. Group, sr. v.p., gen. mgr., DLP products, 2008—. Bd. mem. Metroplex Tech. Bus. Coun. Office: Texas Instruments Inc 12500 TI Blvd Dallas TX 75266 Office Phone: 972-995-2011. Office Fax: 972-927-6377. Business E-Mail: kent.novak@ti.com.

NOVAK, MICHAEL (JOHN), religion educator, author, editor; b. Johnstown, Pa., Sept. 9, 1933; s. Michael John and Irene (Sakmar) N.; m. Karen Ruth Laub-Novak, June 29, 1963; children: Richard, Tanya, Jana. AB summa cum laude, Stonehill Coll., North Easton, Mass., 1956; BT cum laude, Gregorian U., Rome, 1958; MA, Harvard U., 1966; LLD, Keuka Coll., NY, 1970, Stonehill Coll., Mass., 1977, Thomas More Coll., 1992; LHD, Davis and Elkins Coll., W.Va., 1971, LeMoyne Coll., NY, 1976, Sacred Heart U., 1977, Muhlenberg Coll., 1979, D'Youville Coll., 1981, Boston U., 1981, New Eng. Coll., 1983, Rivier Coll., 1984, Marquette U., 1987; D en Ciencias Sociales, U. Francisco Marroquin, Guatemala, 1993, Jacksonville U., 1994; HHD, Saint Xavier U., 1995. Tchg. fellow Harvard U., 1961-63; asst. prof. Stanford U., 1965-68; assoc. prof. philosophy and religious studies SUNY, Old Westbury, 1968-71; assoc. dir. humanities Rockefeller Found., NYC, 1973-75; provost Disciplines Coll., SUNY, Old Westbury, 1969-71; vis. prof. Jan. session Carleton Coll., Northfield, Minn., 1970, Immaculate Heart Coll., Hollywood, Calif., 1971, U. Calif., Santa Barbara, 1972, Riverside, 1975; Ledden-Watson disting. prof. religion Syracuse U., 1977-79; journalist nat. elections Newsday, 1972; writer in residence The Washington Star, 1976, syndicated columnist, 1976-80, 84-89; columnist Forbes Mag., 1989—94; resident scholar Am. Enterprise Int., Washington, 1978—83; George Frederick Jewett chair pub. policy and religion Am. Enterprise Inst., Washington, 1983—, dir. social and polit. studies, 1987—; chmn. working seminar on family and Am. welfare policy Ind., 1986; faculty U. Notre Dame, Ind., 1986-87, vis. W. Harold and Martha Welch Prof. Am. Studies Ind., 1987, 88. Judge Nat. Book awards, 1971, DuPont Broadcast Journalism awards, 1971-80; speechwriter nat. polit. campaigns, 1970, 72; mem. Bd. Internat. Broadcasting, 1983—; mem. Presdl. Task Force Project Econ. Justice, 1985-87, Council Scholars Library of Congress, 1986—; mem. monitoring panel UNESCO, 1984; vice chmn. Lay Commn. Cath. Social Teaching and U.S. Economy, 1984-86; U.S. Ambassador to Experts Meeting on Human Contacts of the Conf. On Security and Cooperation in Europe, Bern, Switzerland, 1986; U.S. rep. to human rights commn. UN, 1981-83; hon. prof. U. Cuyo, Argentina, 1992. Author: (novel) The Tiber was Silver, 1961, A New Generation, 1964, The Experience of Marriage, 1964, The Open Church, 1964, Belief and Unbelief, 1965, 3d edit., 1994, A Time to Build, 1967, A Theology for Radical Politics, 1969, American Philosophy and the Future, 1968, Story in Politics, 1970, (with Brown and Herschel) Vietnam: Crisis of Conscience, 1967, Naked I Leave, 1970; Politics: Realism & Imagination, 1971, Ascent of the Mountain, Flight of the Dove, 1971, A Book of Elements, 1972, All the Catholic People, 1971, The Experience of Nothingness, 1970, The Rise of the Unmeltable Ethnics, 1972, Choosing Our King, 1974, The Joy of Sports, 1976, The Guns of Lattimer, 1978, The American Vision, 1978, Rethinking Human Rights I and II, 1981, 82, The Spirit of Democratic Capitalism, 1982, Confession of a Catholic, 1983, Moral Clarity in the Nuclear Age, 1983, Freedom with Justice, 1984, Human Rights and the New Realism, 1986, Will It Liberate? Questions About Liberation Theology, 1986, Character and Crime, 1986, The New Consensus on Family and Welfare, 1987, Taking Glasnost Seriously: Toward an Open Soviet Union, 1988, Free Persons and the Common Good, 1989, This Hemisphere of Liberty, 1990, The Spirit of Democratic Capitalism, 1991 (Anthony Fisher award 1992), Choosing Presidents, 1992, The Catholic Ethic and the Spirit of Capitalism, 1993, Awakening from Nihilism, 1995, Joy of Sports, rev. 1995; Belief and Unbelief, rev., 1995; Business as a Calling, 1996, The Fire of Invention, 1997, with daughter Jana Novak, Tell Me Why: A Father Answers His Daughter's Questions About God, 1998, On Cultivating Liberty, 1999, To Empower People, anniv. ed, 1995, A Free Society Reader, 2000, Three in One, 2001 (essays on Dem. Capitalism 1976-2000), On Two Wings, 2002; numerous other articles and books transl. into all maj. langs.; assoc. editor Commonweal mag., 1966-69; contbg. editor Christian Century, 1967-80, Christianity and Crisis, 1968-76, Jour. Ecumenical Studies, 1966-77, This World, 1982-89, First Things, 1990; religion editor Nat. Rev., 1979-86; founder, pub. Crisis, 1982-1996, editor-in-chief, 1993-95. Decorated K.M.G., Soverign Mil. Order of Malta, 1987, Order of the Byzantine Cross Republic of Slovakia, 1996; Kent fellow, 1961-65; fellow Hastings Inst., 1970-76; named Most Influential Prof. Sr. Class Stanford U., 1967, 68; Man of Yr. Johnstown, Pa., 1978; recipient Faith and Freedom award Religious Heritage Am., 1978, HIAS Liberty award, 1981, Friend of Freedom award, 1981; Newman Alumni award CCNY, 1984; George Washington Honor medal, 1984; award of Excellence, Religion in Media, 8th annual Angel Awards, 1985, Ellis Island Honor medal, 1986, Anthony Fisher award, 1992, Wilhelm Weber Prize, 1993, Templeton prize for progress in religion, 1994, Internat. prize Inst. World Capitalism, 1994, Award for the Arts City of Bratislava, 1998, Gold Medal Slovak Acad. Scis., 2000, Masaryk award Czech Republic, 2000, IDI Award for Econs., Fondazione Istituto Dirigenti, Rome, 2000, Cezanne medal City of Aix-en-Provence, 1998, Boyer award Am. Enterprise Inst., 1999, Internat. Prize for Cath. Culture, Italy, 1999, Gold medal Pa. Soc., 2001, Milan R. Stefanik award Slovak-Am. Cultural Ctr., 2002, Maritain medal for Scholarly Excellence, Am. Maritain Assn., 2002; diploma as vis. prof. U. Francisco Marroquin, 1985; named acad. corr. mem. from U.S., Argentina Nat. Acad. Scis., Morals & Politics, 1985, others. Mem. Soc. Religion in Higher Edn. (ctrl. com. 1970-73), Am. Acad. Religion (prog. dir. 1968-72), Coun. Fgn. Rels., Cath. Theol. Soc., Soc. Christian Ethics, Inst. Religion and Democracy (dir. 1981—), Nat. Ctr. Urban and Ethnic Affairs (dir. 1982-86). Office: Am Enterprise Inst 5050 Ave Maria Blvd Ave Maria FL 34142-9505 E-mail: mnovak@aei.org.

NOVAK, RAYMOND FRANCIS, research director, pharmacology educator; s. Joseph Raymond and Margaret A. (Cerutti) N.; m. Frances C. Holy, Apr. 12, 1969; children: Jennifer, Jessica, Janelle, Joanna. BS in Chemistry, U. Mo., St. Louis, 1968; PhD in Phys. Chemistry, Case Western Res. U., 1973. Assoc. in pharmacology Northwestern U. Med. Sch., Chgo., 1976-77, asst. prof. pharmacology, 1977-81, assoc. prof., 1981-86, prof., 1986-88; prof. pediat., divsn. clin. pharmacology Wayne State U. Sch. Medicine, Children's Hosp. Mich., Detroit, 1988—; dir. Inst. Environ. Health Scis. Wayne State U., Detroit, 1988—2008, dir. EHS Ctr. in Molecular and Cellular Toxicology with Human Application, 1994—2009, dir. interdisciplinary grad. program in Molecular and Cellular Toxicology, 1994—2008; bd. sci. counselors Nat. Toxicology Program, NIH Nat. Inst. Environ. Sci., 2008—11; chair Bd. Sci. Counselors NTP NIEHS, 2010; corp. dir. rsch. programs Shriners Hosps. Children Internat., 2010—. Mem. toxicology study sect. NIH, Bethesda, Md., 1984-88, mem. and chair numerous grant review com.; adj. sci. Inhalation Toxicology Rsch. Inst., Lovelace Biomed. and Environ. Rsch. Inst., 1991-98; program leader Epidemiology and Environ. Carcinogenesis, Karmanos Cancer Inst. and Comprehensive Cancer Ctr., 1996-98. Assoc. editor Toxicol. Applied Pharmacology, 1992-96, Toxicol. Scis., 2004—09; editor Drug Metabolism and Disposition, 1994-2000; mem. editorial bd. Jour. Toxicology and Environ. Health, 19 87-92, In Vivo, 1986—, Toxic Substances Jour., 1993-98; mem. bd. pub. trustees Am. Soc. Pharmacology and Experimental Therapeutics, 1994-2000; publr. over 140 sci. manuscripts, review articles and book chpt. in profl. jour. and books. Co. comdr., field grade officer (Major) USAR, 1968—99. Recipient Disting. Alumni award U. Mo., St. Louis, 1988; grantee Nat. Inst. Environ. Health Sci., 1979—2010, Gen. Medicine sect. NIH, 1979-82, 89-94. Mem. Am. Soc. for Biochem. and Molecular Biology, Soc. Toxicology (councilor 1996-98, chmn. cont. edn. com. 1995-96), Am. Assn. for Cancer Rsch., Am. Soc. for Pharmacology and Exptl. Therapeutics (bd. publ. trustees 1994-99), Am. Soc. Hematology, Internat. Soc. for Study Xenobiotics. Achievements include patents in field. Office: Shriners Hosps Children Internat 2900 Rocky Point Dr Tampa FL 33607 Office Phone: 813-281-8157. Business E-Mail: rnovak@shrinenet.org.

NOVAKOVIC, PHEBE N., defense industry manufacturing executive; b. 1957; Grad., Smith Coll., Northampton, Mass., 1979; MBA in Strategic Planning & Finance, Wharton Sch., U. Pa., 1988. Dep. assoc. dir. Office Mgmt. & Budget, Exec. Office of the Pres., Washington, 1992—97; spl. asst. to sec. & dep. sec. US Dept. Def., Washington, 1997—2001; dir. strategic planning & devel. General Dynamics Corp., Falls Church, Va., 2001—02, v.p. strategic planning, 2002—05, sr. v.p., planning & devel., 2005—10, exec. v.p. marine systems, 2010—12, pres., COO, 2012, chmn., CEO, 2013—. Bd. dirs. Abbott Labs., 2010—, General Dynamics Corp., 2013—. Named one of The 50 Most Powerful Women in Bus., Fortune mag., 2010—13, The 100 Most Powerful Women, Forbes mag., 2013. Office: General Dynamics Corp 2941 Fairview Park Dr Ste 100 Falls Church VA 22042-4513 Office Phone: 703-876-3000. Office Fax: 703-876-3125. Business E-Mail: phebe.novakovic@generaldynamics.com.*

NOVELLO, ANTONIA COELLO, pediatric nephrologist, former state health commissioner, former United States Surgeon General; b. Fajardo, PR, Aug. 23, 1944; d. Antonio and Ana D. (Flores) Coello; m. Joseph R. Novello, May 30, 1970. BS, U. P.R., Rio Piedras, 1965; MD, U. P.R., San Juan, 1970; MPH, Johns Hopkins Sch. Hygiene, 1982; DrPh, Johns Hopkins U., 2000; DSc (hon.), Med. Coll. Ohio, 1990, U. Ctrl. Caribe, Cayey, PR, 1990, Lehigh U., 1992, Hood Coll., 1992, U. Notre Dame, Ind., 1991, N.Y. Med. Coll., 1992, U. Mass., 1992, Fla. Internat. U., 1992, Cath. U., 1993, Washington Coll., 1993, St. Mary's Coll., 1993, Ea. Va. Med. Sch., 1993, Ctrl. Conn. State U., 1993, Georgetown U., 1993, U. Mich., 1994, Mt. Sinai Sch. Medicine, 1995; LHD (hon.), Alvernia Coll., 1996; HHD (hon.), Kings Coll., 1996; D in Health Sci. (hon.), Ponce Sch. of Medicine, 1996; D in Law (hon.), Gannon U., 1997; LHD (hon.), Loyola U., 1997; DSc (hon.), U. North Tex., Ft. Worth, 2002, Howard U., 2003, NYU, 2003, Pace U., 2003, Coll. New Rochelle, NY, 2003, Chatham Coll., Pitts., 2005; LHD (hon.), Coll. St. Rose, NY, 2004, Setton Hall U., 2006, Nova Southeastern U., 2007. Diplomate Am. Bd. Pediatrics. Intern in pediatrics U. Mich. Med. Ctr., Ann Arbor, 1970-71, resident in pediatrics, 1971-73, pediatric nephrology fellow, 1973-74, Georgetown U. Hosp., Washington, 1974-75; project officer Nat. Inst. Arthritis, Metabolism and Digestive Diseases NIH, Bethesda, Md., 1978-79, staff physician, 1979-80; exec. sec. gen. medicine B study sect., div. of rsch. grants NIH, Bethesda, 1981-86; dep. dir. Nat. Inst. Child Health & Human Devel., NIH, Bethesda, 1986-90; surgeon gen. US Dept. Health & Human Services, Washington, 1990-93; spl. rep. for health and nutrition UNICEF, NYC, 1993—96; vis. prof. health policy and mgmt. Johns Hopkins U. Sch. of Hygiene and Pub. Health, 1996—99; commr. of health State of NY, 1999—2007; v.p. Women and Children's Health and Policy Affairs, Fla. Children's Hosp., 2008—; exec. Disney Children's Hosp., Orlando, Fla., 2009—; exec. dir. Pub. Health Policy Fla. Hosp., 2010. Clin. prof. pediatrics Georgetown U. Hosp., Washington, 1986, 89, Uniformed Svcs. U. of Health Scis., 1989; adj. prof. pediatrics and communicable diseases U. Mich. Med. Sch., 1993; adj. prof. internat. health Sch. Hygiene and Pub. Health, Johns Hopkins U., Balt.; prof. dept. health policy mgmt. and behavior SUNY, 1999—; clin. prof. pediats. U. Rochester, N.Y., 1999—; mem. Georgetown Med. Ctr. Interdepartmental Rsch. Group; legis. fellow U.S. Senate Com. on Labor and Human Resources, Washington, 1982-83; mem. Com. on Rsch. in Pediatric Nephrology, Washington; participant grants assoc. program seminars Nat. Inst. Arthritis, Diabetes and Digestive and Kidney Diseases, NIH, Bethesda, 1980-81; pediatric cons. Adolescent Medicine Svc., Psychiat. Inst., Washington, 1979-83; nephrology cons. Met. Washington Renal Dialysis Ctr. affiliate Georgetown U. Hosp., Washington, 1975-78; phys. diagnosis class instr. U. Mich. Med. Ctr., Ann Arbor, 1973-74; chair Sec.'s Work Group on Pediatric HIV Infection and Diseases, DHHS, 1988; cons. WHO, Geneva, 1989; mem. Johns Hopkins Soc. Scholars, 1991. Contbr. numerous articles to profl. jours. and chpts. to books in field; mem. editorial bd. Internat. Jour Artificial Organs, Jour. Mexican Nephrology. Served in USPHS, 1978-99. Recipient Intern of Yr. award U. Mich. Dept. Pediatrics, 1971, Woman of Yr. award Disting. Grads. Pub. Sch. Systems, San Juan, 1980, PHS Commendation medal HHS, 1983, PHS Citation award HHS, 1984, Cert. of Recognition, Divsn. Rsch. Grants, NIH, 1985, PHS Outstanding medal HHS, 1988, PHS Unit Commendation, 1988, PHS Surgeon Gen.'s Exemplary Svc. medal, 1989, PHS Outstanding Unit citation, 1989, DHHS Asst. Sec. for Health Cert. of Commendation, 1989, Surgeon Gen. Medallion award, 1990, Alumni award U. Mich. Med. Ctr., 1991, Elizabeth Blackwell award, 1991, Woodrow Wilson award for disting. govt. svc., 1991, Congl. Hispanic Caucus medal, 1991, Order of Mil. Med. Merit, 1992, Washington Times Freedom award, 1992, Charles C. Shepard Sci. award, 1992, Golden Plate award, 1992, Elizabeth Ann Seton award, 1992, Ellis Island Congl. Medal of Honor, 1993, Legion of Merit medal, 1993, Athena award Alumnae Coun., 1993, Nat. Citation award Mortar Bd., 1993, Disting. Pub. Svc. award, 1993, Healthy Am. Fitness Leaders award, 1994, Pub. Leadership Edn. Network Mentor award, 1994, Disting. Svc. award Nat. Coun. Cath. Women, 1995, James E. Van Zandt Citizenship award, 1995, Ronald McDonald Children's Charities Excellence award, 1995, Hispanic Heritage Leadership award, 1998, Disting. Alumnus award Am. Assn. of State Colls. and Univs., 1997, Humanitarian award Am. Cancer Soc., 2001, James Smithson Bicentenial medal Smithsonian Inst., 2002; named Health Leader of Yr., COA, 1992; inductee Nat. Women's Hall of Fame, 1994, Internat. Pediatric Hall of Fame Miami Children's Hosp., 1996, Am. Med. Women Assn. Hall of Fame, 2002, Don Quijote Life Achievement award, 2011, Women Bus. award, 2013, 50 Women Am. Health award, 2013. Fellow Am. Acad. Pediatrics (Excellence Pub. Svc. award 1993); mem. AMA (Nathan Davis award 1993, Meritorious Svc. award 1993, Luther L. Terry award, 2000), Inst. Medicine Nat. Acad. Scis., Internat. Soc. Nephrology, Am. Soc. Nephrology, Latin Am. Soc. Nephrology, Soc. for Pediatric Rsch., Am. Pediatric Soc., Assn. Mil. Surgeons U.S., Am. Soc. Pediatric Nephrology, Pan Am. Med. and Dental Soc. (pres.-elect, sec. 1984), D.C. Med. Soc. (assoc.), Johns Hopkins U. Soc. Scholars, Nat. Govs. Assn. (Disting. Svc. to State Govt. award 2005), Scis. Smithsonian Latino Ctr. (Legacy award, 2008), Alpha Omega Alpha. Achievements include being the first woman and first Hispanic to serve as surgeon general. Avocation: collecting antique furniture. Office Phone: 407-303-1760. Business E-Mail: antonia.novello.md@flhosp.org.

NOWAK, JERZY, educational association administrator, horticulture professor, director; m. Jocelyne Couture-Nowak (dec.); children: Francine Dulong, Sylvie Couture-Nowak. MSc in Plant Biochemistry, Agrl.-Tech. U., Olsztyn, Poland, 1968, PhD in Plant Physiology & Biochemistry, 1973, Dr. Habil in Biochemistry, 1980. Jr. rsch. asst. Inst. Potato Rsch., Gdansk, Poland, 1968—69, rsch. asst., 1971—73; postdoctoral fellow molecular biology Max-Planck Soc., Goettingen, Germany, 1974—75; postdoctoral fellow enzyme tech. Alex v. Humboldt Found., Braunschweig, Germany, 1977—78; adj. prof. Agrl.-Tech. U., Olsztyn, Poland, 1980; Alex v. Humboldt rsch. fellow GBF, Braunschweig, Germany, 1980—83; vis. sr. lectr. U. Lagos, Nigeria, 1980—82; vis. rsch. sci. U. Alberta, Edmonton, Alta., Canada, 1983—84; assoc. prof. Nova Scotia Agrl. Coll., Truro, NS, Canada, 1984—88, prof. plant sci., 1988—2000, dept. head plant sci., 1997—2000; hon. rsch. fellow Biology Dept. Dalhousie U., Halifax, NS, Canada, 1985—91, adj. prof., 1991—2001; prof. horticulture Va. Tech. U., Blacksburg, 2000—, dept. head horticulture, Coll. Agrl. and Life Scis., 2000—08, founding dir. Ctr. for Peace Studies and Violence Prevention, 2008—; founder Inst. Sustainable and Renewable Resources, Danville, Va., 2001—05, co-dir., 2003—05; interim dir. rsch., tech. devel. and transfer Inst. Advanced Learning and Rsch., Danville, Va., 2005. Contbr. articles to profl. jours. Office: Va Tech U 301 Saunders Hall Blacksburg VA 24061 Office Phone: 540-231-9836. E-mail: jenowak@vt.edu.

NOWITZKI, DIRK WERNER, professional basketball player; b. Würzburg, West Germany, June 19, 1978; s. Joerg and Helen Nowitzki. Forward Dallas Mavericks, 1998—. Served in German Army, 1997—98. Named NBA MVP, 2007, NBA Player of Yr., The Sporting News, 2007, NBA Finals MVP, 2011; named to All-NBA Second Team, 2002, 2003, 2008, All-NBA First Team, 2005—07, 2009, Western Conf. All-Star Team, NBA, 2002—12. Achievements include winner of the NBA All-Star Weekend Three-Point Shootout, 2006; member of the NBA Finals Championship winning Dallas Mavericks, 2011. Avocations: reading, saxophone. Mailing: Dallas Mavericks 2500 Victory Ave Dallas TX 75219

NOWLIN, JAMES ROBERTSON, federal judge; b. San Antonio, Nov. 21, 1937; s. William Forney and Jeannette (Robertson) N. BA, Trinity U., 1959, MA, 1962; JD, U. Tex., Austin, 1963. Bar: Tex. 1963, Colo. 1993, U.S. Dist. Ct. D.C. 1966, U.S. Ct. Claims 1969, U.S. Supreme Ct. 1969, U.S. Dist. Ct. (we. dist.) Tex. 1971. Assoc. Kelso, Locke, & King, San Antonio, 1963-65; assoc. Kelso, Locke & Lepick, San Antonio, 1966-69; legal counsel U.S. Senate, Washington, 1965-66; propr. Law Offices James R. Nowlin, San Antonio, 1969-81; mem. Tex. Ho. of Reps., Austin, 1967-71, 73-81; judge US Dist. Ct. (we. dist.) Tex., Austin, 1981-99, chief judge, 2000—03, sr. judge, 2003—. Instr. Am. govt. and history San Antonio Coll., 1964-65, 71-73. Capt. U.S. Army, 1959-60, USAR, 1960-68. Fellow State Bar Found (life); mem. San Antonio Bar Assn., Colo. Bar Assn. Republican. Presbyterian. Avocations: pilot, skiing, hiking, jogging. Office: US Courthouse 200 W 8th St Austin TX 78701-2325 Office Phone: 512-916-5675. Business E-Mail: james_r_nowlin@trwd.uscourts.gov.

NTAIMO, LEWIS, engineering educator, researcher; b. Kitwe, Zambia, May 21, 1973; s. Laso and Alice Bwalya Ntaimo; m. Chloe Agnes Balfour; children: Joseph Mulenga, Claire Mumba, Ceanah Bwalya. PhD in Systems and Indsl. Engring., U. Ariz., Tucson, 2004. Rsch. asst. dept. mining and geol. engring. U. Ariz., Tucson, 1999—2000, rsch. asst. dept. sys. and indsl. engring., 2001—04; asst. prof. dept. indsl. and sys. engring. Tex. A&M U., College Station, 2004—. Grantee, NSF, 2005—. Mem.: Inst. Indsl. Engrs. (assoc.; faculty advisor student chpt. 2005—06). Office: Tex A&M U 3131 Tamu College Station TX 77843 Office Fax: 979-847-9005. Business E-Mail: ntaimo@tamu.edu.

NUERNBERG, WILLIAM RICHARD, lawyer; b. Pitts., July 7, 1946; s. William W. and Frances (Hubler) N. BA cum laude, Denison U., 1968; JD cum laude, U. Mich., 1971. Bar: Pa. 1971, U.S. Dist.Ct. (we. dist.) Pa. 1971, Fla. 1995. Mem. Eckert Seamans Cherin & Mellott LLC, 1981-98; ptnr. Duane Morris LLP, Miami, 1999—. Bd. govs. Big Bros. Big Sisters Greater Miami. Pitt fellow U. Pitts. Sch. Bus., 1987-88. Mem. ABA, Pa. Bar Assn., Fla. Bar Assn., Miami City Club. Office: Duane Morris LLP 200 S Biscayne Blvd Ste 3400 Miami FL 33131-2318

NUGENT, GEORGE ROBERT, neurosurgeon; b. Yonkers, NY, Feb. 6, 1921; s. George Fitzsimmons and Alberta Belle (Wolven) N.; m. Virginia Ellen Hayes, July 3, 1947; children: Dana A., Robert W., Leslie Ellen, Barnes L., Courtney A. BA, Kenyon Coll., 1950; MD, U. Cinn., 1953. Diplomate Am. Bd. Neurol. Surgery. Resident Duke U. Med. Ctr., Durham, 1958, instr. of neurosurgery, 1957-58; asst. dir. Divsn. Neurosurgery U. Cinn. Coll. Medicine, 1958-61; asst. prof. neurosurgery to prof. neurosurgery W. Va. U. Med. Ctr., Morgantown, 1961—, chmn. dept. neurosurgery, 1970-85, prof. neurosurgery, 1985—, adj. prof. neurosurgery. Cons. VA Hosp., Clarksburg, W.Va., 1961-93, Pa. Trauma Found., Pittsburgh, 1991-92; participant seminars in field; guest prof. various univs. Exhibitor various sci. exhibits, 1973-79; contbr. articles to profl. jours. and publs. Team physician W. Va. U. Mountaineers, Morgantown, 1966—. Lt. (j.g.) U.S. Maritime Svc., 1943-45. Fellow Am. Bd. Neurol. Surgery; mem. Am. Assn. Neurol. Surgeons, Congress Neurol. Surgeons, So. Neurosurg. Soc. (v.p. 1970-96), Soc. Neurol. Surgeons. Democrat. Avocations: tennis, woodworking, travel, cooking, reading. Office: Robert Byrd Health Scis Ctr Morgantown WV 26506 Fax: 304-292-4944.

NUGENT, RICHARD BYRON, United States Representative from Florida, former sheriff; b. Evergreen Park, Ill., May 26, 1951; m. Wendy Nugent, 1975; children: Ryan, Kyle, Casey. BA in Criminology, St. Leo U., 1991; MPA, Troy State U., Ala., 1995; grad., FBI Nat. Acad., Quantico, Va. Police officer, Ill., 1972—84; police officer, ops. bur. comdr. Hernando County Sheriff's Office, Fla., 1984—2000, sheriff, 2000—10; mem. US Congress from 5th Fla. Dist., Washington, 2011—13, US Congress from 11th Fla. Dist., 2013—, US House Adminstrn. Com., 2011—, US House Rules Com., 2011—, US House Armed Services Com., 2013—. Youth soccer coach Spring Hill Soccer Club, Fla.; coach, dir. Spring Hill Dixie Baseball League; mem. First United Meth. Ch., Spring Hill, 1985—; chmn. YMCA Capital Campaign; bd. dirs. Hernando County Fair, 2003—09; v.p. bd. dirs. Dawn Center Domestic Violence Shelter. Served with Ill. Air Nat. Guard, 1969—75. Mem.: Spring Hill Rotary Club. Republican. Methodist. Office: US House of Representatives 1727 Longworth House Office Bldg Washington DC 20515 also: 115 Southeast 25th Ave Ocala FL 34471 Office Phone: 202-225-1002, 352-351-1670. Office Fax: 202-225-6559, 352-351-1674.*

NUGTEREN, CORNELIUS, air force officer; b. Colton, SD, Feb. 7, 1928; s. Adrian Joe and Marie Johanna N.; m. Liane Albrecht, Sept. 22, 1956; children: Cecile, Aneli. BA, Central Coll., Pella, Iowa, 1951. Commd. 2d lt. USAF, 1953, advanced through grades to maj. gen., 1980; advisor Vietnam Air Force, 1970-71; served in Germany, 1971-77; vice comdr. (Air Logistics Center), Utah, 1977-79; comdr. (Aerospace Rescue and Recovery Service), Scott AFB, Ill., 1979-81; chief (Joint U.S. Mil. Aid Group), Greece, 1981-82; comdr. Air Logistics Ctr., Robins AFB, Ga, 1983-88; ret.; cons. for def. industries Warner Robins, Ga., 1988-94; v.p. Chem. Tech. Internat., Warner Robins, Mercer U. Engring. Rsch. Ctr., Warner Robins, 1996—. Decorated D.S.M., Legion of Merit, Bronze Star, Superior Service medal; recipient USAF EEO award, 1979; named to Ga. Aviation Hall of Fame, 2004. Mem. Air Force Assn., Order Daedalians, Internat. Order Hansen, Order of the Sword. Office: 114 Holly Dr Warner Robins GA 31088-6615 Office Phone: 478-953-6810. Personal E-mail: gennewt@aol.com.

NULL, GARY G., lawyer; b. Lakehurst, NJ, June 25, 1950; AB summa cum laude, Dartmouth Coll., 1972; JD cum laude, Harvard U., 1975. Bar: Tex. 1975. Ptnr. Hughes & Luce LLP (merged with K&L Gates LLP), Dallas; ptnr., corp. fin. practice K&L Gates LLP, Dallas, 2008—. Recipient Best Lawyers in Am., 1995, Tex. Super Lawyer, 2003—06. Mem. ABA, State Bar Tex., Tex. Bar Found., Dallas Bar Assn., Phi Beta Kappa. Office: K&L Gates LLP Ste 2800 1717 Main St Dallas TX 75201 Office Phone: 214-939-5508. Office Fax: 214-939-5849. Business E-Mail: gary.null@klgates.com.

NUNEZ, JEANETTE M., state legislator; b. Miami, Fla., June 6, 1972; m. Adrian Nunez; children: Jason, Justin, Megan. BA in Internat. Rels. & Polit. Sci., Fla. Internat. U., Miami, 1994, MPA, 1998. Legis. aide to Alex Diaz de la Portilla Fla. State Senate, 1995—2004; v.p. external affairs Aventura Med. Ctr.; v.p. govt. affairs Jackson Health System; v.p. external affairs Kendall Regional Med. Ctr.; mem. Dist. 112 Fla. State House of Representatives, 2011—. Adj. prof. grad. program Fla. Internat. U. Coll. Pub. Health; advisor healthcare MBA program Fla. Internat. U. Coll. Bus. Republican. Roman Catholic. Office: 2450 SW 137th St Miami FL 33175-6312 also: Fla Haouse of Reps 1003 The Capitol 402 S Monroe St Tallahassee FL 32399-1300 Office Phone: 305-227-7630, 850-488-7897.

NUNN, CHARLES BURGESS, retired religious organization administrator; b. Richmond, Va., May 1, 1931; s. Charles Burgess Sr. and Virginia Atkinson (Goode) N.; m. Helen Agnes Parker, Sept. 1, 1957; children: Patsy Virginia, Catherine Louise, Stephen Charles, Stewart Gavin. BA in Econs., Randolph Macon Coll., 1953; BD, Southwestern Bapt. Theol. Sem., 1959, MDiv, 1969; DMin, Pitts. Theol. Sem., 1979. Ordained to Gospel ministry, 1954. Pastor Warwick Rd. Bapt. Chapel, Richmond, Va., 1952-53, Garrett's Bluff Bapt. Ch., Arthur City, Tex., 1954-56, Plymouth Haven Bapt. Ch., Alexandria, Va., 1959-68, First Bapt. Ch., Bluefield, W.Va., 1968-77; exec. dir. missions Richmond (Va.) Bapt. Assn., 1977-97; adminstr., treas. So. Bapt. Conf./Assoc. Dirs. Missions, 1997—2003, ret., 2003. Trustee Bluefield (Va.) Coll., 1972-82, U. Richmond, Va., 1989-93; first v.p. Va. Bapt. Gen. Bd., Richmond, 1974-75; dir. Home Mission Bd., So. Bapt. Conv., Atlanta, 1976-84. Author: (children's book) Following Jesus, 1968; (autobiography) The Life and Times of a Baptist Nunn, 2010. Commr. Bluefield (W.Va.) Urban Renewal Authority, 1971-74; chmn. Bluefield (W.Va.) Beautification Commn., 1972-73; pres. North Chamberlayne Civic Assn., Richmond, 1989-91. Recipient Disting. Svc. award City of Bluefield, 1970, Disting. Alumnus award Alumni Soc. Randolph Macon, Ashland, Va., 1992, Vol. Missions award Richmond Regional Devel. Coun. of the Fgn. Mission Bd., So. Bapt. Conv., 1995. Mem. Richmond Rotary Club, Omicron Delta Kappa. Avocations: travel, fishing, photography, baseball. Personal E-mail: cbnunnjr@aol.com.

NUNN, GRADY HARRISON, retired political science professor; b. Arlington, Tex., Apr. 12, 1918; s. William Roy and Floy Brooke (Dugan) N.; m. Ann Torrey Welsh, June 15, 1951 (dec. 1980); 1 child, Therese von Hohoff.; m. Virginia Cotton Chivington, Dec. 18, 1982 (dec. 2009). BA, U. Okla., 1939, MA, 1941; PhD (Penfield fellow), N.Y.U., 1961. Instr. N.Y.U., 1946-49; from instr. to asso. prof. U. Ala., Tuscaloosa, 1949-65, prof., chmn. dept. polit. sci. Birmingham, 1969-83, prof. emeritus, 1983—; vis. asst. prof. Ind. U., 1960-61; asst. prof., asso. prof. U. Pitts. at Ahmadu Bello U., Nigeria, 1964-68; assoc. prof. U. Pitts., 1968, Auburn U., 1968-69. Bd. dirs. Unitarian Universalist Service Com., 1978-84, v.p., 1981-82 Assoc. editor: Background on World Politics, 1957-62; Contbr. to: Readings in Government in American Society, 1949, Federalism in the Commonwealth, 1963, The Politics and Administration of Nigerian Government, 1965; editorial bd.: Jour. of Politics, 1971-74. Mem. Birmingham Regional Planning Commn., 1995-2000. pvt to Capt. F.A., AUS, 1942-46. Ford Found. Fgn. Area fellow, 1956-57 Mem. Am. Polit. Sci. Assn., So. Polit. Sci. Assn. (exec. council 1974-77), Royal African Soc., AAUP (pres. Ala. conf.), Phi Beta Kappa, Pi Sigma Alpha, Phi Eta Sigma, Alpha Tau Omega, Omicron Delta Kappa. Unitarian Universalist. Home: 5723 Belmont Place Birmingham AL 35210 Personal E-mail: ghnunn@aol.com.

NUNNELEE, ALAN (PATRICK ALAN NUNNELEE), United States Representative from Mississippi, former state legislator; b. Tupelo, Miss., Oct. 9, 1958; m. Tori Bedells Nunnelee; children: Reed, Emily, Nathan. BS, Miss. State U., 1980. Mem. Dist. 6 Miss. State Senate, 1995—2011; mem. US Congress from 1st Miss. Dist., Washington, 2011—, US House Appropriations Com., Washington, 2011—. Founder, pres. Allied Funeral Assocs. Mem.: Nat. Assn. Ins. and Fin. Advisors (mem. NE Chap.), Chesterville Baseball Assn., Nebr. Miss. Assn. Life Underwriters. Republican. Baptist. Office: US House of Representatives 1427 Longworth House Office Bldg Washington DC 20515 Office Phone: 202-225-4306.*

NUSSBAUM, BENNETT L., food products executive; BS in Econs., U. Pa. Wharton Sch. Bus., Phila., 1969; MBA, Columbia U., 1971. Exec. PepsiCola Internat.; sr. v.p., CFO Kinko's Inc., Ventura, Calif.; exec. v.p., CFO Burger King Corp., 2001—03; sr. v.p., CFO Winn-Dixie Stores, Inc., 2003—. Office: Winn Dixie Stores Inc 5050 Edgewood Ct Jacksonville FL 32254 Office Phone: 904-370-6655. Business E-Mail: bennettnussbaum@winn-dixie.com.

NUSSBAUM, MICHAEL SCOT, physician, medical educator; b. Cleve., Nov. 4, 1956; s. Fritz S. and Elaine (Sukenik) N.; m. Sue Ellen Weinstein, Aug. 6, 1983; children: Jaclyn, Rachel. BA, Northwestern U., 1977; MD, U. Pa., 1981. Intern dept. surgery U. Cin., 1981-82, resident dept. surgery, 1982-86, chief resident dept. surgery, 1985-86; dir. surg. edn. Jewish Hosp., Cin., 1986-90; asst. prof. surgery U. Cin., 1986-96, asst. prof. molecular and cellular physiology, 1991—96, assoc. prof. surgery, 1996—2006, prof. surgery, 2006—08; attending physician dept. parenteral and enteral nutrition U. Cin. Hosp., 1989—2008, dir. surg. endoscopy and laparoscopy, 1993—2000, chief sect. gen. surgery, 1999—2003, chief of staff, 2000—08, vice chmn. clin. affairs, 2003—08, asst. dean for hosp. affairs, 2003—06, interm chair dept. surgery, 2006—07; prof. U. Fla. Coll. Med. Jacksonville Dept. Surgery, 2008—, chair, 2008—. Med. records com. Jewish Hosp. Cin., 1986-88, med. incident rev. com., 1986-92, intensive care com., 1986-2000, CPR com., 1986-92, course dir. ACLS, 1987-92, chmn. nutrition support com., 1988-2000; chmn. adverse drug reaction com. U. Cin. Hosp., 1988-92, edn. coordinating com., 1990-93, oper. rm. adv. com. 1992-2000, patient care rev. com., 1992-2000, chmn. pharmacy and therapeutics com., 1992-2000, med. co-dir. collaborative care unit, 1993—, clin., tech. and support design team, 1994—, others; ACLS subcom. Am. Heart Assn.-Southwestern Ohio Chpt., 1988-95, affiliate faculty ACLS, 1988-95; assoc. examiner The Am. Bd. Surgery, 1990, 94, 96; trauma adv. com. Ohio Emergency Med. Svcs. Bd., 1993-2000. Editor-in-chief: The Mont Reid Handbook, The University of Cincinnati Surgical Manual, 1987; editl. bd. mem. Current Summaries in the Jour. Parenteral and Enteral Nutrition, 1991-97; contbr. chpts. to books and articles to profl. jours. Bd. mem. Yavneh Day Sch., Cin., 1992-95. Fellow ACS (com. on trauma, instr. advanced trauma life support 1987—, Ohio chpt. chmn. resident essay contest 1994—, sec. Ohio chpt. 1997-2000, chair local arrangements 1996 annual meeting); mem. Am. Soc. for Parenteral and Enteral Nutrition (liaison com. 1993-95), Am. Trauma Soc., Assn. for Acad. Surgery (com. on edn. 1989-91, nominating com. 1992, com. on issues 1992-94, councilor 1994-96), Assn. for Surg. Edn., Ctrl. Surg. Assn. (sec. 2006-2009, pres. elec. 2009-10, pres. 2010-11), Cin. Acad. Medicine, Cin. Surg. Soc. (treas. 1990-92), Mont Reid Surg. Soc. U. Cin., Ohio Soc. for Parenteral and Enteral Nutrition (dir.-at-large 1990, pres.-elect 1991, pres. 1991-92), Ohio State Med. Assn., Pancreas Club, Inc., Soc. Am. Gastrointestinal Endoscopic Surgeons (resident edn. com. 1998-2006, rsch. com. 1998-2005, 2001-2006, membership com. 2001-), Am. Bd. Surgery, 2000-2006, Soc. Critical Care Medicine, Soc. for Parenteral Alimentation, Soc. for Surgery of the Alimentary Tract, Surg. Infection Soc., Soc. Univ. Surgeons (com. on surg. edn. 1998-2002, chair 1999-2002), Am. Surg. Assn., Halsted Soc., Alpha Omega Alpha, Southern Surg. Assn. Office: University Fla Coll Medicine Jacksonville Dept Surgery 653 W 8th St 3rd Fl Faculty Clinic Jacksonville FL 32209 Home: 1401 Riverplace Blvd Apt 713 Jacksonville FL 32207 Office Phone: 904-244-5502. Business E-Mail: michael.nussbaun@jax.ufl.edu.

NUTI, WILLIAM R., computer services company executive; married; 1 child. BS in Fin. & Economics, Long Island U., 1986. Various sales positions to sr. sales staff mem. IBM Corp., 1982—88; sales mgr. Network Equipment Technologies, 1988—90, Netrix Corp., 1990—92; v.p. then pres. Greater Asia Pacific region Cisco Sys., Inc., with, 1992—2002, sr. v.p., pres., Europe, Middle East & Africa Ops.

London, 1999—2001, sr. v.p., worldwide svc. provider bus. & US theatre ops., 2001—02; pres., COO Symbol Technologies, Holtsville, NY, 2002—03, pres., CEO, 2003—05, NCR Corp., 2005—, chmn., 2007—. Bd. dirs. Opus 360, 1999—, Sprint Nextel Corp., 2008—. Bd. dir. Fair Media Council; trustee Long Island U. Office: NCR Corp 3097 Satellite Blvd Duluth GA 30096-5810 Office Phone: 937-445-1936. Office Fax: 937-445-5541. Business E-Mail: william.nuti@ncr.com.

NUTT, RONALD, electrical engineer; b. Apr. 24, 1938; BSEE, U. Tenn., Knoxville, 1961, MSEE, 1962, PhD in Elec. Engring., 1969; MD (hon.), U. Essen, Germany, 2008. Rschr. Oak Ridge Nat. Lab., Tenn.; elec. engring. instr. U. Tenn.; v.p. EG&G Ortec, 1969—79; co-founder Tech. for Energy Corp., Radio Systems Corp., Delta M Corp.; co-founder, v.p. R&D, tech. dir. CTI Molecular Imaging Inc., Knoxville, 1983—98, pres., CEO, 2002—05, CTI PET Systems, Inc. (joint venture between CTI, Inc. & Siemens Med. Systems), Knoxville, 1998—2003; founder, chmn., CEO ABT Molecular Imaging, Inc., Louisville, Tenn., 2006—09, chmn., 2009—. Recipient Nathan Dougherty award, U. Tenn. Coll. Engring., 1997; named Disting. Scientist of Yr., Inst. Clin. PET, 1999. Fellow: IEEE (Outstanding Engr. award 1999, Medal for Innovations in Healthcare Tech. 2010); mem.: Acad. Molecular Imaging (Disting. Scientist of Yr. 1999). Achievements include with physicist David Townsend, implementing design, commercial development and clinical implementation of hybrid PET/CT scanners, named TIME Magazine's Invention of the Year in 2000; patents in field. Mailing: ABT Molecular Imaging Inc 3024 Topside Business Pk Louisville TN 37777

NUTTER, SUSAN K., librarian, academic administrator; b. Boston, Aug. 9, 1944; m. Joe Hewitt, 1982; stepchildren: Kirsten Elizabeth Hewitt(dec.), Stephen A. Hewitt. BS, Colby Coll., Waterville, Maine, 1966; MLIS, Simmons Coll., Boston, 1968. Libr. intern to libr. Project INTREX MIT, 1966—73, assoc. head engring. libraries, assoc. dir. libraries collection mgmt. and technol. services, 1980—87; Coun. on Libr. Resources Academic Libr. Mgmt. Intern U. NC, Chapel Hill, 1979—80; dir. libraries NC State U., Raleigh, 1987—, vice provost, 1995—. Mem. steering com. NC Libraries for Virtual Edn. (NC LIVE); mem. exec. com., governing bd. Triangle Rsch. Libraries Network. Recipient Alumni Achievement Award, Simmons Coll., 1995, Hugh C. Atkinson Meml. Medal, Assn. College & Rsch. Libraries, 1999; named Libr. of Yr., Libr. Jour., 2005. Mem.: Assn. Rsch. Libraries (pres. 1993). Office: DH Hill Libr NC State U Campus Box 7111 Raleigh NC 27695-7111 Office Phone: 919-515-7188. Office Fax: 919-515-3628. Business E-Mail: susan_nutter@ncsu.edu.

NWOKE, BEN U., engineering educator, consultant; s. Uduma Nwoke and Susannah Ogbeyalu Amogu; children: Steven B., Joane B., Susan N. BS, 1966; MS, Iowa State U., Ames, 1972, PhD, 1984. Cert. Soc. Mfg. Engrs., 1987, mech. insp., Am. Soc. Quality Passing Prescribed Exam. Assoc. prof. U. ND, Grand Forks, 1992—97; full prof. Engring. & Tech., Va. State U., Petersburg, 1997—. Cons. Dumak Engring. Co., Ohafia, Abia State, 2003—. Contbr. articles to profl. jours. including indsl. engring. Mem.: Richmond Joint Engrs. Coun., Am. Soc. Quality, Soc. Mfg. Engrs. (vice chair 2008, Pres.'s Cir. 1998). Conservative. Presbyterian. Achievements include development of graduate programs at UND and VSU. Avocations: travel, tennis, ballroom dancing, soccer. Office: Virginia State Univ Engineering & Technology Dept Petersburg VA 23806 Office Fax: 804-524-6372. Business E-Mail: bnwoke@vsu.edu.

NYBERG, DONALD ARVID, oil industry executive, educator; b. Ridgewood, NJ, Aug. 23, 1951; s. Arvid H. and Rita T. (Tenwick) N.; m. Susan Radis, Feb. 16, 1985; children: Matthew D., Ryan T. BA, St. Lawrence U., 1973; MBA, Harvard U., 1975. Mgr. marine ops. Standard Oil, LA, 1982-83, mgr. ops. planning Cleve., 1984-85, dir. strategic studies, 1986; divsn. mgr. Brit. Petroleum, Ltd., London, 1987-88; v.p., gen. mgr. U.S. gas bus. BP Exploration, Houston, 1989, v.p., gen. mgr. tech., 1990, v.p. comml., 1991-94; pres., CEO BP Pipelines, Anchorage, 1991-94; pres. Marya Resources, Houston, 1994—; v.p. MAPCO, Tulsa, 1996; pres. Tesoro Marine Svcs., Houston, 1996—2003; CEO, bd. dirs. McDonough Marine, 2004—07; CEO Champion Elevators, 2005—07, bd. dirs., 2004—07; prof. mgmt., program dir. bus. mgmt., maritime, long-term care San Jacinto Coll., 2008—. Bd. dirs., Boys and Girls Country Houston, Boys and Girls Harbor Houston, Asst. League Houston. Mem. Forest Club, Bentwater Country Club. Avocations: running, weightlifting, reading. Office Phone: 713-553-1880. Personal E-mail: don.nyberg@yahoo.com.

NYBERG, KAREN L., astronaut; b. Parkers Prairie, Minn., Oct. 7, 1969; d. Kenneth and Phyllis Nyberg. BS in Mech. Engring. (summa cum laude), U. ND, 1994; MS in Mech. Engring., U. Tex., Austin, 1996, PhD in Mech. Engring., 1998. Co-op working in a variety of areas Johnson Space Ctr., 1991—95; environ. control sys. engr. Crew and Thermal Sys. Divsn., 1998—2000; mission specialist NASA, 2000—. Technical duties, crew support astronaut (Expedition 6 crew), astronaut office station ops. br. NASA, 2002, duties with space shuttle and exploration branches; mission specialist STS-124 Mission (Discovery), mission to Internat. Space Station to launch components to complete Japanese Kibo Lab., 2008. Recipient U. ND Sch. Engring. & Mines Meritorious Svc. award, 1991—92, D.J. Robinson award for Academic Achievement, 1992, Space Act award, 1993, NASA Tech Briefs award, 1993, NASA Johnson Space Ctr. Patent Application award, 1993, Joyce Medalen Soc. Women Engrs. award, 1993—94, NASA Johnson Space Ctr. Cooperative Edn. Spl. Achievement award, 1994, U. ND Young Alumni Achievement award, 2004. Achievements include patents for Robot Friendly Probe and Socket Assembly, 1991; being the 50th woman to fly in space (STS-124 Mission aboard the Discovery, 2008). Avocations: art, running, volleyball, sewing, backpacking, piano. Office: Astronauts Office/CB NASA Lyndon B Johnson Space Ctr 2101 NASA Pkwy Houston TX 77058

NYCE, JOHN DANIEL, lawyer; b. York, Pa., Sept. 7, 1947; s. Harry Lincoln and Dorothy (Wagner) Nyce; m. Deborah Dvorak; children: Joshua David, Laura Kimberly. BA, SUNY, Buffalo, 1970; JD, U. Miami, 1973. Bar: Fla. 1973, U.S. District Ct. (so. dist.) Fla. 1973, U.S. Dist. Ct. (middle dist.), Fla. 1973, U.S. Ct. Appeals (5th and 11th cirs.) 1986, U.S. Supreme Ct. 1984. Assoc. Ralph P. Douglas, Pompano Beach, Fla., 1974, Coleman, Leonard & Morrison, Ft. Lauderdale, Fla., 1975-78; sole practice Ft. Lauderdale, 1979—. Adj. prof. bus. law, inernat. bus. law Lynn U., Boca Raton, Fla., 2001—. Author: Proof of God's Existence in the Seven C's and Christian Handbook of Lists, 2003, ApoloVangelism, 2006. Mem. Social Register Ft. Lauderdale; mem. Broward County Right to Life, Operation Rescue, South Fla., Beach Street Aid to the Homeless of Ft. Lauderdale, Legis. Adv. Coun. on Adoptions, Am. Assn. Adoption Attys., Nat. Right to Life Com., Inc.; founder Broward County Christian Lawyers Assn., past pres., bd. dirs.; mem. Christian Legal Soc.; mem. exec. com. Broward County Rep. Party; Broward Citizens bd. U. Miami; mem. The Right God Soc.; bd. dirs. Shepherd Care Ministries, Inc.; co-founder Christian Adoption Svcs. of Shepherd Care Ministries, Inc.; cert. trainer Evangelism Explosion III Internat., Inc.; legal counsel and evangelism trainer Coral Ridge Presbybn. Ch., Christ the Rock Cmty. Ch., First Bapt. Ch., West Hollywood, Fla., Calvary Chapel of Ft. Lauderdale Ch., New Covenant Presbyn. Ch., Good News Ch.; bd. dirs. Alliance for Responsible Growth, Inc. Mem.: Nat. Rifle Assn., Am. Assn. Adoption Attys., Nat. Acad. Elder Law Attys., Attys. Title Ins. Fund, NRA, S.D. Rifle and Hunting Assn., SUNY Buffalo Alumni Assn., U. Miami Alumni Assn., Am. Numismatic Assn., Holiday Park Tennis Ctr., U.S. Tennis Assn., Crystal Lake Golf & Country Club, U. Miami Hurricane Club, Sports Fitness Clin. Republican. Presbyterian. Home: 3051 NE 48th St Apt 102 Fort Lauderdale FL 33308 Mailing: PO Box 11022 Fort Lauderdale FL 33339-1022 Office Phone: 954-801-0073, 954-567-3305. Personal E-mail: miamijd73@gmail.com.

NYE, C. HOWARD (WARD), construction executive, lawyer; B, Duke U., 1984; JD, Wake Forest U., 1987. V.p., bus. devel. Hanson Bldg. Materials America, 1997—2000; gen. counsel Hanson Aggregates East, pres., 2000—03; exec. v.p. Hanson Aggregates N.Am., 2003—06; pres., COO Martin Marietta Materials, Inc., 2006—10, pres., CEO, 2010—. Bd. dirs. Romeo Guest Assocs., Inc., Martin Marietta Materials, Inc., 2010—. Mem., gubernatorial NC Mining Commn.; mem., alumni bd. Duke U.; bd. dirs. Am. Road & Transp. Builders Assn., Nat. Stone, Sand & Gravel Assn. Office: Martin Marietta Materials Inc 2710 Wycliff Rd Raleigh NC 27607-3033 Office Phone: 919-781-4550. Office Fax: 919-783-4695.

NYE, ERLE ALLEN, hotel executive, lawyer; b. Ft. Worth, June 23, 1937; s. Ira Benjamen N.; m. Alice Ann Grove, June 5, 1959; children: Elizabeth Nye Janzen, Pamela Nye Schneider, Erle Allen Jr., Edward Kyle, Johnson Scott. BEE, Tex. A&M U., 1959; JD, Southern Meth. U., 1965. With Dallas Power & Light Co., 1960—75, v.p., 1975—80, Tex. Utilities Co. (dba TXU Corp.), Dallas, 1980, exec. v.p., 1980—87, pres., 1987—95, pres., CEO, 1995—97, chmn., CEO, 1997—2004, chmn., 2004—05; chmn. emeritus TXU Corp., 2005—. TU Svcs., 1982-97, chmn., CEO, 1997—, Tex. Utilities Properties Inc., 1994, Tex. Utilities Commn., Dallas, 1995-97, chmn., CEO, 1997—, pres. Tex. Utilities Fuel Co., 1982-97, chmn., CEO, 1997—, chmn. Tex. Utilities Australia Pty., Ltd., 1996—, chmn. and CEO ENSERCH Corp., Enserch Devel. Corp., Dallas, 1997—, chmn. Enserch Energy Svcs. Inc., 1997—, bd. dirs. The Energy Group PLC, London, 1998—, chmn. and CEO Tex. Energy Industries Inc., Dallas, 1997—, Southwestern Electric Svc. Co., 1997—, chmn. Lufkin-Conroe Comm. Co., 1997—, chmn. bd., CEO Tex. Utilities Integrated Solutions Inc., 1997—, bd. dirs. TXU Corp., 1987-95, S&C Electric Co., U. Tex. Investment Mgmt. Co., Brinker Internat. Inc. Bd. dirs. Dallas Bar Found., 1980-83, Dallas Cen. Bus. Plan Com., 1980-83, Inroads/Dallas-Ft. Worth Inc., 1984-88, trustee Baylor Dental Coll., Dallas, 1985-94; mem. Dallas Together Forum, 1989—, Dallas Com. Fgn. Rels., 1991—, Bd. of Boys & Girls Clubs of Am., 1991—; The Dallas Found., 1994—; The Science Pl., Dallas, 1995-99; The Salvation Army's Dallas County Adv. Bd., 1995-99. Mem. ABA, Dallas Bar Assn., Tex. State Bar Assn., Dallas C. of C. (bd. dirs. 1991-95, vice chmn. 1992-95). Clubs: Engineers (pres. 1982-83), Northwood (Dallas). Methodist. Office: Brinker International Inc 6820 LBJ Freeway Dallas TX 75240 Home: 6924 Desco Dallas TX 75225 Office: TXU Corp 1601 Bryan St Fl 41 Dallas TX 75201-3411 Office Phone: 972-980-9917. E-mail: erle.nye@brinker.com.

NYERGES, ALEXANDER LEE, museum director; b. Rochester, NY, Feb. 27, 1957; s. Sandor Elek and Lena (Angeline) N.; m. Kathryn Gray; 1 child, Robert Angeline. BA, George Washington U., 1979, MA, 1982. Intern The Octagon, Washington, 1976-79; archeol. asst. Smithsonian Instn., Washington, 1977; curatorial intern Nat. Mus. Am. History, 1978-79; adminstrv. asst. George Washington U., Washington, 1979-81; exec. dir. DeLand Mus. Art, Fla., 1981-85, Miss. Mus. Art, Jackson, 1985-92; dir. Dayton Art Inst., 1992—2006, Va. Mus. Fine Arts, Richmond, 2006—. Mem. grants panel Nat. Endowment for the Arts, 1988—; field surveyor Inst. Mus. Svcs., Washington, 1985-88, nat. review panel, 1990-92; treas., bd. dirs. Volusia County Arts Coun., Daytona Beach, Fla., 1983-85. Author: Selections from the Permanent Collection, 1999, In Praise of Nature: Ansel Adams and Photographers of the American West, The Harold W Shaw Collection: Pre Columbian Treasures, 2003, Edward Weston: A Photographer's Love of Life, 2004; contbr. articles to profl. jours. Bd. dirs. West Volusia Hist. Soc., 1984-85; pres. Miss. Inst. Arts and Letters, 1987-88; trustee Cultural Arts Ctr., DeLand, 1984-85, Miami Valley Cultural Alliance, 1993-95, Intermus. Conservation Lab., 1993-99, Montgomery County Arts and Culture Dist., 1994-2001; trustee, chmn. Dayton-Montgomery County Conv. and Visitors Bur.; bd. trustees Assn. Art Mus. Dirs., 2007—. U.S. Dept. Edn. scholar, 1973. Mem. DeLand Area C. of C. (bd. dirs., tourist adv. com. 1984-85), Assn. Art Mus. Dirs. (bd. trustees 2008-, program chair 2008-), Am. Assn. Mus. (S.E. regional rep. to non-print media com. 1983-85, nat. legis. com. 1986-93), Miss. Mus. Assn., Southeastern Mus. Conf. (bd. dirs. 1991-92), Fla. Mus. Assn., Fla. Art Mus. Dirs. Assn., Cultural Roundtable (pres. 1993-95), Va. Ctr. for Creative Arts (bd. trustees), Ohio Mus. Assn. (trustee 1993-98), Phi Beta Kappa. Avocations: photography, music, writing, sports, scuba diving. Office: Virginia Mus Fine Arts 200 N Blvd Richmond VA 23220 Office Phone: 804-340-1504. E-mail: anyerges@aol.com.

NYIKOS, STACY ANN, publishing executive; d. Michael J. and Martha Nyikos; m. Rainer Kohrs, Dec. 1, 1994; children: Alysia Bella Kohrs, Sophia Johanna Kohrs. BA, U. Notre Dame, 1990; MA, Christian Albrecht U., Germany, 1994; PhD, U. Va., 2000; MFA, Vt. Coll. Fine Arts, 2011. Gen. mgr. Stonehorse Pub., Tulsa, Okla., 2004—07; stats. lab coord. U. Okla., Tulsa, 2004—06. Author: (children's lit.) Squirt, 2005, Shelby, 2006, Dizzy, 2007, Dragon Wishes, 2008; co-author (with Kane Milter): Rope Em, 2011 (Read Across Okla. Book award, 2011). Organizer Okla. involvement Screentime Awareness, Internat. TV Turnoff Week. Recipient Moms Choice award, 2007, Nautilus award, San Francisco Book Festival, 2009; named winner, Ariz. Author's Literacy Contest, 2006; finalist Foreword Bk. of Yr. award, 2006; grantee, Fulbright Com., 1998—99; Dissertation Improvement grantee, NSF, 1999—2001, President's fellow, U. Va., 1995—98, Dumas Malone Traveling fellow, 1998—99. Liberal. Roman Catholic. Avocations: running, travel. Office: Stonehorse Pub LLC Ste D1 Rm 296 6528 E 101st St Tulsa OK 74133 Office Fax: 888-867-1927. Business E-Mail: snyikos@stonehorsepublishing.com.

OAAS, ERIC, insurance company executive; Ptnr. Stewart Info. Svcs. Corp. Office: Stewart Information Services Corp 1980 Post Oak Blvd Ste 800 Houston TX 77056 Office Phone: 713-627-1310. Office Fax: 713-629-2244. Business E-Mail: eoaas@stewart.com.

OATES, JAMES CALDWELL, rheumatologist, physician, research scientist; b. Nashville, Jan. 5, 1964; s. John Alexander III and Meredith (Stringfield) O; m. Jennifer Goodwin; children: Evan Edward, Aubrey Elizabeth. BS in Chemistry, Bates Coll., 1986; MD, Johns Hopkins U., 1991. Intern Duke U. Med. Ctr., Durham, N.C., 1991-92, resident, 1992-94, fellow in rheumatology, 1994-96, Med. U. S.C., Charleston, 1996-97, asst. prof. medicine, 1997—2000, assoc. prof. medicine, 2000—, assoc. dir., Clin. Translational Rsch. Ctr., 2007—; chief rheumatology Ralph H. Johnson VA Med. Ctr., 2007—. Mem. Am. Coll. Rheumatology, Am. Fedn. Med. Rsch., Southern Soc. Clin. Rsch., Nitric Oxide Soc., Soc. Free Radical Biology and Medicine. Office: Med U SC MSC 637 Charleston SC 29425-6370

OATES, JOHN ALEXANDER, III, medical educator and biomedical scientist; b. Fayetteville, NC, Apr. 23, 1932; s. John Alexander and Isabelle (Crowder) O.; m. Meredith Stringfield, June 12, 1956; children: David Alexander, Christine Larkin, James Caldwell. BS magna cum laude, Wake Forest Coll., 1953; MD, Bowman Gray Sch. Medicine, 1956. Intern, asst. resident medicine N.Y. Hosp.-Cornell U. Med. Center, NYC, 1956-58, 61-62; from clin. assoc. to sr. investigator Nat. Heart Inst., 1958-63; faculty Vanderbilt U. Sch. Medicine, Nashville, 1963—, prof. medicine and pharmacology, 1969—, Werthan prof. investigative medicine, 1974-84, chmn. dept. medicine, 1983-97, Thomas F. Frist Sr. prof. medicine, 1984—. Drug rsch. bd. Nat. Acad. Scis.-NRC, 1967-71; chmn. pharmacology and toxicology tng. com. Nat. Inst. Gen. Med. Scis., 1969-70; adv. coun. Nat. Heart, Lung and Blood Inst., 1985-89. Master ACP; fellow Am. Acad. Arts and Scis., Am. Assn. Advancement Sci.; mem. Am. Fedn. Clin. Rsch. (pres. 1970-71), Am. Soc. Clin. Investigation (v.p. 1976-77), Assn. Am. Physicians (pres. 1981-82), Am. Soc. Pharmacology and Exptl. Therapeutics (chmn. exec. com. divsn. clin. pharmacology 1967-69), Inst. of Medicine, Am. Clin. & Climatological Assn. (pres. 2010-11). Achievements include co-discovery of antihypertensive effect of methyldopa, elucidation of a number of interactions between drugs in humans; research in biochemistry, pharmacology and pathophysiology of eicosanoids. Home: 2032 Sunset Hills Terr Nashville TN 37215 Office: Vanderbilt Med Ctr 536 RRB Nashville TN 37232-6602 Home Phone: 615-665-1976; Office Phone: 615-343-4845. Business E-Mail: john.oates@vanderbilt.edu.

O'BANNON, JOHN M., III, state legislator; b. Richmond, Va., Feb. 14, 1948; m. Patricia Anne Steinmetz O'Bannon; children: John Harding, Virginia Louise Deasy, Andrew Hill. Former chief staff Richmond Metro Hosp., Henrico Drs Hosp.; mem. Gov. Warner's Secure Va. Panel; bd. trustees, vice chmn. Hargrave Mil. Acad.; state del. Dist. 73 Va., 2001—; bd. trustee Henrico Drs. Hosp. Recipient Caravati Svc. award, MCV Alumni Assn. Mem.: AMA, Va. Tobacco Settlement Found., Rotary West Richmond, Med. Soc. Va., Richmond Acad. Medicine, River Rd. Bapt. Ch. Republican. Baptist. Mailing: Dist Off PO Box 70365 Richmond VA 23255 Office: Gen Assembly Bldg Rm 518, PO Box 406 Richmond VA 23218 Office Phone: 804-282-8640, 804-698-1073. Fax: 804-786-6310. E-mail: Del_Obannon@house.state.va.us.

OBENSHAIN, MARK DUDLEY, state legislator; b. Richmond, Va., June 11, 1962; s. Richard Dudley and Helen Wilkins Obenshain; m. Suzanne Obenshain. Former lt. gov. 4th Jud. Cir.; co-chmn. Young Virginians for Warner, 1978, 1984; del. Rep. Nat. Conv., 1980; vice chmn. Coll. Rep. Va. Tech., 1981—82, Va. State Coll. Rep. Fed., 1982—83, chmn., 1983—; youth coord. Paul Trible US Senate Campaign, 1982; mem. Va. State Rep. Exec. Com., 1982—; state senator Dist. 26 Va., 2004—; atty. Walton, Alhizer & Weaver. Mem.: Am. Bar Assn. Republican. Presbyterian. Mailing: 1062 Wyndham Dr Harrisonburg VA 22801 Office: Dist Off PO Box 555 Harrisonburg VA 22801 Office Phone: 540-437-3126. E-mail: district26@sov.state.va.us, mobenshain@ntelos.net.

OBERHOUSEN, BRAD A., state legislator; m. Anna Ward. B, Miss. State U.; JD, Miss. Coll., Clinton. Owner, atty. Oberhousen Law Firm, PLLC; mem. Dist. 73 Miss. House of Reps., Jackson, 2012—. Mem. Lakeshore Congl. Meth. Ch. Democrat. Office: Miss House fo Reps PO Box 1018 Jackson MS 39215 Business E-Mail: boberhousen@house.ms.gov.

OBERMAYER, HERMAN JOSEPH, newspaper publisher; b. Phila., Sept. 19, 1924; s. Leon J. and Julia (Sinsheimer) O.; m. Betty Nan Levy, June 28, 1955 (dec. Jan. 26, 2013); children: Helen O. Levy-Myers, Veronica O. Atnipp, Adele O. Malpass, Elizabeth O. Weintraub. Student, U. Geneva, Switzerland, 1946; AB cum laude, Dartmouth Coll., Hanover, NH, 1948. Reporter L.I. Daily Press, Jamaica, NY, 1950-53; classified advt. mgr. New Orleans Item, 1953-55; asst. to pub. Standard-Times, New Bedford, Mass., 1955-57; editor, pub. Long Branch Daily Record, NJ, 1957-71, Northern Va. Sun, Arlington, 1963-89; adj. prof. journalism U. Md., 1989-93; vis. lectr. U. West Indies, Jamaica, 1994-95; publ. com. Commentary Mag., 1989—2006. Pulitizer Prize juror, 1983, 84; lectr. publs. mgmt. Hungary, Poland, Lithuania, Latvia, Estonia, Ukraine, Moldova, Slovenia, Macedonia, Russia, Croatia, Serbia, 1990-2002, Internat. Ctr. Journalists, 1992-2002. Author: Jews in the News: British and American Newspaper Articles About Jews 1665-1800, 2002, Soldiering for Freedom: A GI's Account of World War II, 2005, REHNQUIST: A Personal Portrait of the Distinguished Chief Justice of the US, 2009, America Navy Party in Arlington 1958-1984, 2012, in Chinese, 2012; contbr. articles to popular mags., newspapers. Bd. dirs. Monmouth Med. Ctr., 1958-71; exec. coun. Monmouth Boy Scouts America, 1958-71, exec. com. Nat. Capital coun., Boy Scouts America, 1971-79, v.p., 1974-77; mem. Va. Legis. Alcohol Beverage Control Study Commn., 1972-74, Arlington Arts Ctr., 2008-10; trustee Arlington (Va.) Bicentennial Commn., Am. Jewish Com. Cmty. Svc. award, 1986, nat. bd. govs., 1989-96, nat. coun., 1996—2008; trustee Jewish Inst. for Nat. Security Affairs, 1996-2011. Staff sgt. US Army, 1943-46, ETO. Rhineland Campaign Star; Recipient Silver Beaver award Boy Scouts Am., 1977, Knight Internat. Press fellow, 1994-95. Mem. American Soc. Newspaper Editors, So. Newspaper Pubs. Assn. (dir. 1981-84), Mont Pelerin Soc., Nat. Press Club (Washington), Cosmos Club (Washington), Washington Golf and Country Club (Arlington, Va.), Dartmouth Club (NYC), Sigma Chi. Jewish. Rotarian.

OBERNDORF, MEYERA E., former mayor, Virginia Beach, Virginia; m. Roger L. Oberndorf; children: Marcie, Heide. BS in Elem. Edn., Old Dominion U., 1964, LLD (hon.), 1999. Broadcaster Sta. WNIS, Norfolk, Va.; chair Pub. Libr. bd., Va.; mem. city coun. City of Virginia Beach, Va., 1976—88, vice-mayor Va., 1986—88, mayor Va., 1988—2008. Mem. exec. bd. Tidewater coun. Boys Scouts Am.; bd. dirs. Va.Beach Pub. Libr., 1966-76, chmn. bd., 1967-76; past pres. Va. Muncipal League; bd. dir. Hampton Roads Partnership; Econ. Develop. Alliance; adv. com. Va. Inst. of Gov. Recipient Women's Achievement award, Zonta Club of Hampton Roads, 2002; named Outstanding Woman of Va., Am. Legion Aux., Newsmaker of the Yr., Va. Press Women, 1997; named one of 25 Most Dynamic Mayors in the US, Newsweek. Mem. AAUW, U.S. Conf. Mayors (trustee), Va. Mcpl. League (exec. bd.), Nat. League Cities (vice-chmn., mem. adv. bd., past chair Energy, Environ., and Natural Resources Steering Com.), Princess Anne Women's Club; chair Standing Com. on Internat. Affairs. Jewish.

O'BRIEN, BILL, professional football coach, former college football coach; b. Dorchester, Mass., Oct. 23, 1969; m. Colleen O'Brien; children: Jack, Michael. BA, Brown U., Providence, 1993. Tight ends coach Brown U. Bears, 1993, inside linebackers coach, 1994; offensive graduate asst. Ga. Inst. Tech. Yellow Jackets, 1995—97, running backs coach, 1998—2000, recruiting coord., 1999—2000, offensive coord., quarterbacks coach, 2001—02, asst. head coach, 2002; running backs coach U. Md. Terrapins, 2003—04; offensive coord., quarterbacks coach Duke U. Blue Devils, 2005—06; coaching asst. New Eng. Patriots, 2007, wide receivers coach, 2008, quarterbacks coach, 2009—10, offensive coord., quarterbacks coach, 2011—12; head coach Pa. State U. Nittany Lions, University Park, 2012—13,

Houston Texans, 2014—. Recipient Paul "Bear" Bryant Coll. Coach of Yr. award, Nat. Sportscasters & Sportswriters Assn., 2012; named Maxwell Coach of Yr., Maxwell Football Club, 2012, Big Ten Conf. Coach of Yr., 2012. Office: Houston Texans 2 Reliant Park Houston TX 77054*

O'BRIEN, CONAN, talk show host, writer; b. Brookline, Mass., Apr. 18, 1963; s. Thomas and Ruth (Reardon) O'Brien; m. Liza Powel, Jan. 12, 2002; children: Neve, Beckett. BA in American Hist. & Lit., Harvard U., 1985. Staff mem. The Harvard Lampoon, 1981-85 (pres. 1983, 84) Stage appearances with: The Groundlings (L.A.) 1985-87; writer, performer The Happy Happy Good Show (LA, Chgo.) 1988; writer (TV series) Not Necessarily the News (HBO) 1985-87, Saturday Night Live, 1988-91 (NBC, Emmy Outstanding Writing in Comedy series 1989), Lookwell (NBC) 1991; writer, prodr. The Simpsons (Fox) 1991-93, The Wilton North Report (syndicated) 1987; writer, prodr., host Late Night with Conan O'Brien (NBC) 1993-2009 (Best Writing in Comedy/Variety Show Writer's Guild award 1997, TV award Writers Guild America 2000, 2002, 2003, 2005, 2006, Primetime Emmy for Outstanding Writing for a Variety, Music or Comedy Prog., Acad. TV Arts & Sciences, 2007); host Tonight Show with Conan O'Brien (NBC), 2009-10, Conan (TBS), 2010-; film appearances include Tomorrow Night, 1998, Barenaked in America, 1999, Vanilla Sky, 2001, Bewitched, 2005, The Great Buck Howard, 2008; TV appearances include (voice only) The Simpsons, 1994, The Single Guy, 1996, Arli$$, 1996, (voice only) Dr. Katz, Professional Therapist, 1997, Veronica's Closet, 1998, Spin City, 1998, LateLine, 1999, Space Ghost Coast to Coast, 1999, (voice) Futurama, 1999, Tomorrow Night, 1998, (voice) Robot Chicken, 2005. Named Favorite Talk Show Host, People's Choice Awards, 2011; named one of The 100 Most Influential People in the World, TIME mag., 2010. Democrat. Irish Catholic. Office: TBS 1 CNN Ctr 100 International Blvd Atlanta GA 30303

O'BRIEN, DAVID MICHAEL, law educator; b. Rock Springs, Wyo., Aug. 30, 1951; s. Ralph Rockwell and Lucile O'Brien; m. Claudine M. Mendelovitz, Dec. 17, 1982; children: Benjamin, Sara, Talia. BA, U. Calif., Santa Barbara, 1973, MA, 1974, PhD, 1977. Fulbright lectr. Oxford (Eng.) U., 1987-88; lectr. U. Calif., Santa Barbara, 1976-77; asst. prof. U. Puget Sound, Tacoma, Wash., 1977-79; Spicer prof. U. Va., Charlottesville, 1979—. Fulbright rschr., Tokyo, Kyoto, Japan, 1993-94, Fulbright chair, Bologna, Italy, 1999; jud. fellow U.S. Supreme Ct., Washington, 1982-83; Fulbriht lectr., Oxford U., England, 1987-1988; vis. postdoctoral fellow Russell Sage Found., NYC, 1981-82; lectr. USIA, Burma, Japan, France, 1994-95. Author: Supreme Court Watch, 1991—, Constitutional Law and Politics, 2 vols., 6th edit., 2005, Storm Center: The Supreme Court in American Politics, 7th edit., 2005, To Dream of Dreams: Constitutional Politics in Postwar Japan, 1996, To Dream of Dreams: Religious Freedom in Postwar Japan, 1996, Animal Sacrifice & Religious Freedom, 2004; editor: Views from the Bench, 1985, Judges on Judging, 1997, Government by the People, 22nd edit., 2005. Rappatour, jud. selection 20th Century Fund Task Force, N.Y., 1986-87. Tom C. Clark Jud. Fellow, Jud. Fellows Commn., Washington, 1983. Mem. ABA (Silver Gavel award 1987), Am. Judicature Soc., Am. Polit. Sci. Assn., Supreme Ct. Hist. Soc. (editl. bd. 1982—), Internat. Polit. Sci. Assn. Democrat. Avocations: painting, travel. Home: 916 Tilman Rd Charlottesville VA 22901-6338 Office: U Va 232 Cabell Hall Charlottesville VA 22901 Office Phone: 434-994-3358.

O'BRIEN, GREGORY MICHAEL ST. LAWRENCE, academic administrator; b. NYC, Oct. 7, 1944; s. Henry Joseph and Mary Agnes (McGoldrick) O'B.; m. Mary K. McLaughlin, Dec. 28, 1968; children: Jennifer Jane, Meredith Kathleen. BA with honors, Lehigh U., 1966; MA, Boston U., 1968, PhD, 1969. Assoc. in psychology Lab. Community Psychology, Harvard Med. Sch., Boston; dir. Human Svcs. Design Lab., Sch. Applied Social Scis., Case Western Res. U., Cleve., 1970-74; dean, prof. Sch. Social Welfare, U. Wis., Milw., 1974-78; provost, prof. psychology U. Mich.-Flint, 1978-80; prof. social work and psychology, v.p. acad. affairs U. South Fla., Tampa, 1980-83, provost, 1983-87, prof. mgmt., 1986-87; chancellor U. New Orleans, 1987—2003; interim supr. New Orleans Paris Schs., 1999; pres. Argosy U. Sys., 2004—07, pres. emeritus, 2008—. Bd. dirs. WLAE-TV (PBS), Bank One New Orleans Region, Entergy New Orleans, Nat. Coalition for Advanced Mfg., Nat. Assn. State Univs. and Land-Grant Colls. Contbr. chpts. to books, articles to profl. jours. State of La. Econ. Devel. Coun., 1997—; vice chmn. State of La. Film and Video Commn., 1993-94, mem., 1993-2003; chmn. Metro. Coun. Govts. MetroVision, 1992-1994; adv. mem. Bus. Coun. New Orleans and the River Region; bd. dirs. The Chamber/New Orleans and the River Region, 1988-2003; mem. Kellogg Commn. on Future of Land Grant Colls. and State Univs., 1996-1998. NIMH fellow, 1968-69 Fellow Am. Coll. Mental Health Adminstrs. (founding fellow, pres. 1984-86); mem. NCAA (chair pres. commn. 1992-93), Nat. Assn. Social Workers, Nat. Conf. Social Welfare, Soc. Gen. Systems Research, Am. Psychol. Assn., Am. Public Health Assn., Metrovision Partnership Found. (1992-93), Council Social Work Edn. (presdl. task force on structure of assn.), Indsl. Relations Research Assn. Roman Catholic. Office: 900 Gulf Shore Dr # 1022 Destin FL 32541 Home: 900 Gulf Shore Dr Unit 1022 Destin FL 32541-3208

O'BRIEN, JAMES J., manufacturing executive; b. Circleville, Ohio; Degree in Acctg., Fin., Ohio State U., MBA. Exec. asst. to chmn. Ashland, Inc., 1992—94; v.p., gen. mgr. branded mktg. Ashland Petroleum Co., 1994; v.p. Ashland, Inc.; pres. Valvoline, 1995—2001; joined Ashland, Inc., 1976, sr. v.p., 1997, group oper. officer, pres., COO, 2002, chmn., CEO, 2002—. Bd. dir. Humana Inc., 2006—. Nat. bd. dirs. Big Bros. Big Sisters Am.; adv. bd. sch. bus. Ohio State U.; chmn. bd. trustees Midway Coll. Ky. Mem.: Am. Chemistry Coun., Assn. Governing Bds. Univ. Colls. Office: 50 E River Ctr Blvd Covington KY 41012-0391

O'BRIEN, JAMES K. (JAY O'BRIEN), state legislator; b. Nuremberg, Germany, Dec. 10, 1951; m. Sevea Grace Staves; children: Kerry Maureen, James Kenneth III, Benen Patrick, Sean Patrick, Kiernan Kevin. State del. Dist. 40, Va., 1992—2002; state senator Dist. 39, 2003—; co-chmn. Mining & Mineral Resources Com.; mem. Fairfax County Rep. Com., Edn. Com., Gen. Laws Com., Counties Cities & Towns Com., Labor Com., Commerce Com. Recipient Sec. award, Dept. Health & Human Svcs. Mem.: West Point Assn., Occoquan Watershed Coalition, KofC, Res. Officers Assn., Fairfax County C. of C., Rotary Club, Jaycees. Republican. Catholic. Mailing: 7903 Clifton Hunt Ct Clifton VA 20124 also: Senate of Va PO Box 396 Richmond VA 23218 Office: Dist Off PO Box 5 Clifton VA 20124 E-mail: district39@sov.state.va.us.

O'BRIEN, JIM, professional basketball coach; b. Phila., Feb. 11, 1952; m. Sharon Ramsay; children: Jack, Shannon, Caitlyn. B in Mgmt. & Mktg., St. Joseph's U., 1974; MBA, U. Md., 1981. Asst. coach Wheeling Jesuit Coll. Cardinals, 1974—75, head coach, 1982—87; asst. coach Pembroke State Coll. Braves, 1975—76, U. Md. Terrapins, 1976—77, St. Joseph's U. Hawks, 1977—78, U. Oreg. Ducks, 1978—82, NY Knicks, 1987—88, U. Ky. Wildcats, 1994—97; head coach U. Dayton Flyers, 1989—94; interim head coach Boston Celtics, 2001, head coach, 2001—04, Phila. 76ers, 2004—05, Ind. Pacers, 2007—11; asst. coach Dallas Mavericks, 2012—. Recipient Markward award, 1970; named to St. Joseph's U. Hall of Fame, 1988, Big Five Hall of Fame, 1989. Office: Dallas Mavericks 2909 Taylor St Dallas TX 75226*

O'BRIEN, KEVIN JAMES, museum director; b. St. Cloud, Minn., 1954; m. Grace Benedict. BFA, U. Notre Dame, 1977; MFA, Tulane U., 1979. Dir. Community Ctr. for Arts, Michigan City, Ind., 1981-85, So. Ohio Mus. and Cultural Ctr., Ohio Arts Coun., 1985-88, Pensacola (Fla.) Mus. Art/Fla. Arts Coun., 1988-91, Everhart Mus., Scranton, Pa., 1991, Pa. Coun. Arts, 1994; exec. dir. Key West Art & Hist. Soc., 1995—2000, Tippecanoe County Hist. Assn., Lafayette, Ky. Mus. Art and Craft, Louisville, 2006—. Office: Ky Mus Art and Craft 715 W Main St Louisville KY 40202 Office Phone: 502-589-0155 ext. 201. Business E-Mail: kevinobrien@kentuckyarts.org.

O'BRIEN, MARK STEPHEN, pediatric neurosurgeon; b. West New York, NJ, Jan. 2, 1933; s. Mark Peter and Hannah (Dempsey) O'B.; m. Mary Morris Johnson, June 3, 1961 (div.); children: David, Derek, Marcia; m. Karen-Marie Sampson, June 1, 1984; children: Blythe, Blake, Lauren-Blair, Connor. AB cum laude, Seton Hall U., 1955; MD, St. Louis U., 1959. Diplomate Am. Bd. Neurol. Surgery, Am. Bd. Pediat. Neurol. Surgery. Intern St. John's Hosp., St. Louis, 1959-60, resident in surgery, 1960; resident in neurology Charity Hosp., New Orleans, 1962-63; resident in neurosurgery St. Vincent's Hosp., NYC, 1963-64, resident in surgery, 1965; sr. resident, chief resident Cin. Children's Hosp., U. Cin., 1965-68, research fellow in neurosurgery, 1966-67, 67-68; NIH spl. fellow in neuroradiology Albert Einstein Coll. Medicine, NYC, 1968-69; mem. faculty dept. surgery Emory U. Sch. Medicine, Atlanta, 1969—2003, prof. surgery, assoc. prof. pediatrics, 1979—2003; chief neurosurgery Henrietta Egleston Hosp. for Children, Atlanta, 1971—2003; prof. neurosurgery U. Ark. for Med. Scis., Little Rock, 2005—. Trustee Elaine Clark Center for Exceptional Children; mem. med. adv. bd. Nat. Found., March of Dimes; trustee Henrietta Egleston Hosp. for Children; mem. profl. adv. panel Spina Bifida Assn. Am. Editorial bd. Pediatric Neurosurgery; contbr. chpts. to books, articles to med. jours. Served with USNR, 1960-62. Mem. Am. Assn. Neurol. Surgeons, Soc. Neurol. Surgeons, Congress Neurol. Surgeons, Internat. Soc. Pediatric Neurosurgery, Greater Atlanta Pediatric Soc., Med. Soc. Atlanta, AMA, ACS, Ga. Neurosurg. Soc., Am. Acad. Pediatrics, Am. Soc. Pediatric Neurosurgery, Pediatric Oncology Group, Am. Bd. Pediatric Neurol. Surgery (sec.), Acad. Pediatric Neurosurgeons. Home: 5720 Hawthorne Rd Little Rock AR 72207 Office: Ark Childrens Hosp 1 Children's Way 800 Marshall St Slot 838 Little Rock AR 72202 Office Phone: 501-364-1448. Personal E-mail: mobrien33@mac.com. Business E-Mail: obrienmark@uams.edu.

O'BRIEN, ROBERT JAMES, financial consultant, small business owner; b. Waterbury, Conn., Nov. 22, 1940; s. Stephen Joseph and Ada Florence (Schiaroli) O'B.; m. Janyce Leah Bruni, Sept. 24, 1966; children: Gayle Elizabeth O'Brien Blachura, Julie Maureen O'Brien Orlando. BA, U. Conn., 1964. Registered investment advisor SEC; CFP; CLU; CFC; cert. chartered advisor for sr. living. Commd. ensign USN, 1964, advanced through grades to comdr., ret., 1984; fin. cons. Davenport-Dukes Assocs., Virginia Beach, Va., 1984—97, prin., ptnr., 1992—97, 2011; prin., mng. ptnr. Fin. Security Group, Inc., 1997—; pres. Fin. Security Adv., Inc., chmn. bd., 2011—. Elder Kempsville Presbyn. Ch., Virginia Beach, 1987—; bd. dirs. Edmarc Children's Hospice, Portsmouth, Va., 1988-92, pres. bd. dirs., 1992; bd. dirs. Bethany Christian Svcs., Virginia Beach, 1995-96. Mem. Nat. Assn. Life Underwriters (Million Dollar Round Table 1994-2007). Republican. Avocations: golf, reading, chess. Home: 4841 Kempsville Greens Pkwy Virginia Beach VA 23462-6438 Office: Fin Security Group Inc 575 Lynnhaven Pky Ste 310 Virginia Beach VA 23452-7331 Office Phone: 757-431-1414. Business E-Mail: bob@gofsg.com.

O'BRIEN, SOLEDAD, broadcast executive, journalist; b. St. James, NY, Sept. 19, 1966; m. Brad Raymond; children: Sofia, Cecilia, Charlie, Jackson. Degree in English and Am. Lit., Harvard U.; hon. degree, Siena Coll., Mercy Coll.; LHD (hon.), Cornell U., 2007. Prodr. Second Opinion, reporter Health Week in Review Sta. KISS-FM, Boston; assoc. prodr., newswriter Sta. WBZ-TV, Boston; field prodr., Nightly News and Today NBC News, 1991—93; co-host The Know Zone Discovery Channel; local reporter, bur. chief Sta. KRON-TV, San Francisco, reporter, The Know Zone, 1993—96; anchor, The Site MSNBC, 1996—97; contributed reports for Today Show and weekend editions of NBC Nightly News NBC, 1999, anchor, Weekend Today, 1999—2003; co-anchor, American Morning CNN, 2003—07; anchor, spl. corr. CNN: Spl. Investigations Unit; anchor, Early Start CNN (Cable News Network), 2011—12, anchor, Starting Point, 2012—13; founder, chmn. Starfish Media Group, 2013—; spl. correspondent, America Tonight Al-Jazeera America, 2013—; co-anchor Real Sports with Bryant Gumbel, 2013—. Exec. prodr., moderator National Geography Bee; vis. disting. fellow Harvard Grad. Sch. of Education, 2013—14; bd. dirs. Foundation for The National Archives, Washington, 2013—; bd. chair The After School Corp. Co-author: Latinos in America, 2009; author: (memoir) The Next Big Story: My Journey Through the Land of Possibilities, 2010; host (documentaries) Black in America, 2007—, Latinos in America (RTDNA/UNITY award, Edward R. Murrow awards, 2010). Bd. dirs. Harlem Sch. the Arts. Recipient Emmy award as a co-host on Discovery Channel's The Know Zone, Women of Power award, Nat. Urban League, 2006, Mickey Leland Humanitarian award, Nat. Assn. Minorities in Cable, 2006, President's award, NAACP Image Awards, 2007, Clara Barton Humanitarian award, Am. Red Cross, Mass. Bay, 2007, Gracie Allen award, Found. Am. Women in Radio and TV, 2007, Soledad O'Brien Freedom's Voice award, Cmty. Voices at the Morehouse Sch. Medicine, 2007, John Hopkins Bloomberg Sch. of Public Health Goodermote Humanitarian award, 2008, Emmy award for Crisis in Haiti (Anderson Cooper 360) in the category of Outstanding Live Coverage of a Current News Story-Long Form, 2011; named Groundbreaking Latina of the Year, Catalina Mag., 2005; named one of 50 Most Beautiful People, People Mag., 2001, People en Español, 2004, 15 People Who Make America Great, Newsweek, 2006, Crain's Bus. Reports', Essence Mag. & Black Enterprise, "40 under 40", Top 100 Irish Americans (several times), Irish American Mag.; named to Black Enterprise Hot List, 2005. Mem.: Nat. Assn. Hispanic Journalists, Nat. Assn. Black Journalists (Journalist of the Yr. 2010), Delta Sigma Theta (hon.).*

O'CALLAGHAN, WILLIAM LAWRENCE, JR., lawyer; s. William Lawrence and Martha Kathryn (Fitzpatrick) O'Callaghan; m. Bonnie Faye Whitmire, Dec. 18, 1964; children: Diana Lee, John Patrick, Michael Lawrence. BBA, U. Ga., 1963, JD cum laude, 1965; LLM in Taxation, Georgetown U., 1968. Bar: Ga. 1965, U.S. Supreme Ct. 1971. Assoc. Sutherland, Asbill & Brennan, Atlanta, 1965; ptnr. Gambrell, Russell et al, Atlanta, 1968-74; chmn. O'Callaghan, Saunders & Stumm, Atlanta, 1974-90; ptnr. Branch, Pike, Ganz & O'Callaghan, Atlanta, 1990—93, O'Callaghan & Stumm LLP, 1993—2002, Alston & Bird, LLP, Atlanta, 2002—09; pvt. practice Atlanta, 2010—. Cons. bd. dirs. Atlanta Jr. Golf Assn., 2009—, pres., 1987—88; bd. dirs. Phoenix Soc. Atlanta, 1985—87. Served to capt. US Army, 1965—68. Mem.: AAC Jones Rm. Found. (chair 1995—), ABA (chmn. 1985—89, mem. com. fed. tax real property sect., mem. real property sect., mem. tax sect.), State Bar Ga., Atlanta Bar Assn., Atlanta Estate Planning Coun., Sandy Springs (Ga.) C. of C. (bd. dirs. 1982—83), Atlanta Athletic Club (bd. dirs. 1987—96, pres. 1992—94), Optimists (pres. Sandy Springs chpt. 1978), Rotary (v.p. Sandy Springs chpt. 1986, mem. Robert T. Jones, Jr. scholarship com. 1992—). Conservative. Presbyterian. Avocations: golf, travel, railroading, genealogy. Office: PO Box 921995 Norcross GA 30010-1995 Home Phone: 770-448-8485; Office Phone: 678-480-1900. Business E-Mail: wloclaw@comcast.net.

OCHOA, ARMANDO XAVIER, bishop; b. Oxnard, Calif., Apr. 9, 1943; Attended, Ventura Coll., Calif., St. John's Coll., Camarillo, Calif. Ordained priest Archdiocese of LA, 1970; ordained bishop, 1986; aux. bishop, vicar gen. Archdiocese of LA, 1986—96; bishop Diocese of El Paso, Tex., 1996—. Roman Catholic.

OCHOA, ELLEN, astronaut; b. L.A., May 10, 1958; d. Roseanne Ochoa; m. Coe Fulmer Miles; 1 child BS in Physics, San Diego State U., 1980; MSEE, Stanford U., 1981, PhD in EE, 1985. Rsch. engr. Sandia Nat. Labs., Livermore, Calif., 1985—88; chief intelligent systems tech. br. NASA/Ames Rsch. Ctr./Moffet Field Naval Air Sta., Mountain View, Calif.; astronaut NASA, Houston, 1991—, dep. dir., flight crew ops., 2002—06, dir. flight crew ops., 2006—12, dir., Lyndon B. Johnson Space Ctr., 2012—. Flew in shuttle missions STS-56, 1993, STS-66, 1994, STS-96, 1999, STS-110, 2002. Recipient two Space Act Tech Brief Awards, 1992, Space Flight Medals 1993, 1994, 1999, 2002; Outstanding Leadership Medal, 1995, Exceptional Svc. Medal, 1997, Women in Aerospace Outstanding Achievement Award, the Hispanic Engr. Albert Baez Award for Outstanding Tech. Contribution to Humanity, the Hispanic Heritage Leadership Award, San Diego State U. Alumna of the Year. Mem. Optical Soc. America, American Inst. Aeronautics & Astronautics, Phi Beta Kappa, Sigma Xi, Pres. Commn. on the Celebration of Women in American History. Achievements include being the first Hispanic director and second female director for Space Shuttle program. Office: NASA Johnson Space Ctr 2101 NASA Parkway Houston TX 77058

OCHOA, LORENA, retired professional golfer; b. Guadalajara, Mex., Nov. 15, 1981; d. Javier and Marcela Ochoa; m. Andres Conesa Labastida, 2009. Student, U. Ariz. Profl. golfer LPGA Tour, 2003—10. Five-time U.S. 8-12 Jr. World Championship winner; NCAA Player of Yr., 2001; NCAA Freshman of Yr., 2001; finished second NCAA Championships, 2001; finished first place Futures Tour money list, 2002. Founder The Lorena Ochoa Found., Mexico, 2004—. Recipient Nat. Sports award, Mex., 2001, Nancy Lopez award for Outstanding Amateur Accomplishments, 2002, Louise Suggs Rolex Rookie of Yr. award, LPGA, 2003, Rolex Player of Yr. award, 2006, 2007, 2008, 2009, ESPY award, Best Female Internat. Athlete, ESPN, 2008, Mickey Wright award, Golf Digest, 2008; named Female Player of Yr., Golf Writers Assn. of America, 2006, Female Athlete of Yr., AP, 2006, 2007; named one of 100 Most Influential People in the World, TIME mag., 2008, 100 Most Powerful Celebrities, Forbes.com, 2008. Achievements include winner LPGA Tour events including Franklin Am. Mortgage Championship, 2004, Wachovia LPGA Classic, 2004, Wegmans LPGA, 2005, 07; LPGA Takefuji Classic, 2006, Sybase Classic, 2006, 07, Wendy's Championship for Children, 2006, Corona Morelia Championship, 2006, Samsung World Championship, 2006, 07, Tournament of Champions, 2006; Safeway Internat., 2007, Women's British Open, 2007, Can. Women's Open, 2007, Safeway Classic, 2007, ADT Championship, 2007, Kraft Nabisco Championship, 2008. Avocations: triathalons, marathons, mountain climbing, tennis, basketball, accordion.

OCHOA-BRILLEMBOURG, HILDA MARGARITA, investment banker; b. July 8, 1944; BS in Econs., U. Catolica Andres Bello, Caracas, Venezuela; MPA, Harvard U.; postgrad. in fin., Harvard Bus. Sch. Chief investment officer, pension investment div. World Bank, 1976—87; mng. dir. Emerging Markets Investment Corp.; founder, pres., CEO Strategic Investment Group, 1987—. Bd. dirs. Harvard Mgmt. Co., Gen. Mills, Inc., McGraw-Hill Inc.; treas. C.A. Luz Electrica de Venezuela, Caracas, 1967—71; lectr. U. Catolica Andres Bello, 1970; ind. cons. in econs. and fin. Published articles in Fin. Analyst Jour. and Pensions & Investments. Bd. dirs. Washington Nat. Opera; chmn. bd. dirs. Youth Orch. of the Americas; vice chair, Group of 50 Carnegie Endowment for Internat. Peace; mem. adv. com. Rockefeller Ctr. for Latin Am. Studies; bd. dirs. Fulbright Found., Atlantic Coun. US. Fulbright-Hays fellow. Office: 1001 19th St N 16th Fl Arlington VA 22209-1722 Office Phone: 703-243-4433.

OCHS, WALTER J., civil engineer, consultant; b. Springfield, Minn., May 20, 1934; s. Walter Minrod and Cleo (Schultz) O.; m. Connie Mae Strate, Sept. 15, 1956; children: Julie, Brian. BS in Agrl. Engring., South Dakota State U., 1957. Registered profl. civil engr., Mich. Engr. in training USDA, Soil Conservation Svc., Watertown, S.D., 1957-58, project engr. Britton, S.D., 1958-61, area engr. Sioux Falls, S.D., 1961-63, asst. state conservation engr. East Lansing, Mich., 1963-66, state conservation engr., 1966-69, asst. state conservationist Saint Paul, Minn., 1969-71, nat. drainage engr. Washington, 1971-86; drainage adviser World Bank, Washington, 1986-96; internat. ind. water mgmt. cons., 1996—98; co-owner Water Mgmt. Engrs., LLC, 1998—2012. Bd. dirs. Internat. Inst. for Land Reclamation and Improvement Postgrad Land Drainage Course, The Netherlands, 1990-98; particpated in project work over 30 countries; mem. Internat. Commn. Irrigation and Drainage. Contbr. to profl. jours. Named Fed. Engr. of Yr., NSPE, 1982; recipient Outstanding Alumnus award S.D. State U., 1977, Outstanding Contbn. award Corrugated Plastic Tubing Assn., 1981, Svc. to the Profession award U.S. Com. on Irrigation and Drainage, 2004; named to Internat. Drainage Hall of Fame, 1996. Fellow: Am. Soc. Agrl. Engrs.; mem.: ASCE (chmn. drainage com. 1975—76, Royce J. Tipton award 2001). Home: 7418 Spring Village Dr Apt 206 Springfield VA 22150-4933 E-mail: wochs@hotmail.com.

OCHSNER, JOHN LOCKWOOD, thoracic-cardiovascular surgeon; b. Madison, Wis., Feb. 10, 1927; s. Edward William Alton and Isabel (Lockwood) O.; m. Mary Lou Hannon, Mar. 20, 1954; children: John L., Joby Hannon, Katherine Lockwood, Frank Hannon. MD, Tulane U., 1952; hon. diploma (hon.), U. Delgado, San Salvador, El Salvador, 1999. Diplomate Am. Bd. Thoracic Surgery (chmn. 1993-95), Am. Bd. Surgery, Am. Bd. Vascular Surgery. Intern Univ. Mich. Hosp., Ann Arbor, 1952-53, resident, 1953-54, Baylor U. Affiliated Hosp., Houston, 1956-58, 1958-59; chief surg. resident Tex. Children's Hosp., 1959-60; instr. Baylor U., Houston, 1960-61; mem. staff Ochsner Clinic, New Orleans, 1961—, chmn. dept. surgery, 1966-87, chmn. emeritus dept surgery, 1987—; clin. asst. prof. Tulane U., New Orleans, 1961-65, clin. assoc. prof., 1965-70, clin. prof. surgery, 1970—. Vis. prof. to more then 40 univs. and colls. Author: (with others) Coronary Artery Surgery, 1978. Pres. Tennis Patrons Assn. New Orleans, 1972; image amb. City of New Orleans, 1982; bd. dirs. Internat. Trade Mart, New Orleans, 1983. Capt. USAF, 1954-56. Recipient award, Life Mag., 1961, Golden Plate Acad. Achievement award, 1962, award of distinction, Am. Heart Assn. La., 1976, Svc. award, Cystic Fibrosis Rsch. Found., 1977—78, medal of honor, Ecuador, 1981, Crystal Achievement award, Child's Wish of Greater New Orleans, 1987, Young Leadership Coun. award, 1987, medal of honor, Czechoslovakian Surg. Soc., 1996, Honor of Achievement, Am. Heart Assn., 1997, Internat. Recognition award, Denton A.

Cooley Cardiovasc. Surg. Soc., 1998, Outstanding Alumnus award, Tulane Sch. Medicine, 1998, Spirit of Love award, Ronald McDonald House Charities, 1999, DeBakey award, DeBakey Internat. Surg. Soc., 2000, Outstanding Physician award, Orleans Parish Med. Soc., 2002, Weiss Brotherhood award, New Orleans chpt. Nat. Conf. for Cmty. and Justice, 2002, Outstanding Person award, Family Svc. Greater New Orleans, 2004, DeBakey medal, Covenant Heart Inst., 2007, Order of the Plimsoll Mark, World Trade Ctr.; named Rex, King of Carnival, Mardi Gras, New Orleans, 1990, Grand Marshall, Oktoberfest, 1990, 1992. Mem. Am. Assn. Thoracic Surgery (sec. 1979-83, pres. 1992-93), New Orleans Surg. Soc. (pres. 1977-78), So. Surg. Assn. (pres. 1991), So. Assn. for Vascular Surgery (pres. 1983), Boston Club, La. Club, New Orleans Country Club, City Club, Alpha Omega Alpha. Republican. Office: Ochsner Clinic Found 1514 Jefferson Hwy BH 231 New Orleans LA 70121-2483 Home: 170 Walnut St 9-H New Orleans LA 70118

O'CONNELL, EDWARD JAMES, JR., psychologist, educator, systems administrator, consultant; b. Sterling, Ill., Aug. 15, 1932; s. Edward James and Elizabeth E. (Clapham) O.; m. Pamelia Canon Floyd, Aug. 21, 1959; children— Edward James III, John Matthew BS in Psychology, Ill. Inst. Tech., 1958; MA in Psychology, Northwestern U., 1961, PhD in Psychology, 1962. Carnegie Inst. Tech. NSF predoctoral fellow, Pitts., 1959—62; NSF postdoctoral fellow Carnegie Inst. Tech., 1962—63, asst. prof. psychology, 1963-65; psychology faculty Syracuse (N.Y.) U., NY, 1965-93, prof., 1975-93, prof. emeritus, 1993—. Cons. Rand Corp., Santa Monica, Calif., 1962-64, Abt Assocs., Boston, 1970-73, Marcy Psychiat. Hosp., N.Y., 1979-82 Served to cpl. U.S. Army. Mem. Sigma Xi. Democrat. Avocations: billiards, computer programming. Address: PO Box 570 Cashiers NC 28717-0570 Office Phone: 828-743-3257. Personal E-mail: ejoconn@dnet.net.

O'CONNELL, MATTHEW MCGOWAN, telecommunications industry executive, lawyer; b. NYC, Sept. 12, 1952; s. John Joseph and Patricia (Smith) O'C.; m. Elizabeth Stanton Haight, June 10, 1978; children: Charles, Lucy. BA, Trinity Coll., Hartford, Conn., 1974; JD, U. Va., 1978. Bar: N.Y. 1980. Sr. v.p., legal and bus. affairs, Sony Worldwide Networks, Divsn. Sony Corp.; mng. dir. Crest Advisors; assoc. Winthrop, Stimson, Putnam & Roberts, NYC, 1979-84; asst. gen. counsel Cablevision Systems Corp., Woodbury, 1984-88, assoc. gen. counsel, 1988-90; sr. v.p.,gen. counsel Osborn Comm. Corp., NYC, 1990-94; sr. v.p., gen. counsel Sony Worldwide Networks, 1994-97; gen. counsel Crest Comms. Holdings, 1997; CEO ORBIMAGE, 2001—06; pres., CEO and dir. GeoEye Corp., 2006—. Mem.: University (N.Y.C.). Democrat. Avocations: violin, piano, guitar. Office: GeoEye Corp 2325 Dulles Corner Blvd Ste 1000 Herndon VA 20171-6123 Office Phone: 703-480-7500. Office Fax: 703-450-9570. Business E-Mail: matthew.oconnell@geoeye.com.

O'CONNELL, ROBERT FRANCIS, physics professor; b. Athlone, Ireland, Apr. 22, 1933; came to U.S., 1958; s. William and Catherine (O'Reilly) O'C.; m. Josephine Molly Buckley, Aug. 3, 1963; children: Adrienne Molly, Fiona Catherine, Eimear Kathleen. BSc, Nat. U. Ireland, Galway, 1953, DSc, 1975; PhD, U. Notre Dame, 1962. Telecommunications engr. Dept. Posts and Telegraphs, Dublin, Ireland, 1954-58; scholar Inst. Advanced Studies, Dublin, 1962-63; systems analyst IBM, Dublin, 1963-64; sr. rsch. assoc. Inst. Space Studies, NYC, 1966-68; asst. prof. physics La. State U., Baton Rouge, 1964-66, assoc. prof., 1966-69, prof., 1969-86, Boyd prof., 1986—. Editor for theoretical physics Hadronic Jour.; former bd. mem. Phys. Rev. A; contbr. articles to profl. jours. Named Disting. Rsch. Master, La. State U., 1975; NAS-NRC fellow, 1966-68, Sci. Rsch. Coun. (Eng.) sr. vis. fellow, 1976. Fellow Am. Phys. Soc.; mem. Am. Astron. Soc., Internat. Astronomy Union, Internat. Soc. Gen. Relativity and Gravitation. Republican. Roman Catholic. Avocation: tennis. Home: 522 Bancroft Way Baton Rouge LA 70808-4807 Office: La State Univ Dept Physics And Astronomy Baton Rouge LA 70803-0001 Business E-Mail: oconnell@phys.lsu.edu.

O'CONNELL, WILLIAM EDWARD, JR., retired finance educator; b. NYC, Sept. 16, 1937; s. William Edward and Helen Margaret (Brazel) O'Connell; m. Janet Elinor Shields, Aug. 15, 1965; children: William Edward III, Cathleen Anne. AB, Manhattan Coll., Riverdale, NY, 1959; MBA, Columbia U., NYC, 1961; DBA with honors, Ind. U., Bloomington, 1967; JD, Coll. William and Mary, Williamsburg, Va., 1974. Fin. analyst Pfizer, Inc., NYC, 1962-64; asst. prof. U. Conn., Storrs, 1967-69; Morris prof. banking U. Va., Charlottesville, 1988; Chessie prof. bus. Coll. William and Mary, Williamsburg, Va., 1969—2005. Mem. faculty Va. Bankers Sch., Charlottesville, 1975—99, Stonier Grad Sch. Banking, Newark, 1977—91, Bank Adminstrn. Inst., Madison, Wis., 1978—97; bd. dirs. C. & F Fin. Corp., 1994—2010, Citizens & Farmers Bank, 1994—2010. Author: Asset & Liability Management, 1979, Advanced Financial Planning, 1984, Financial Planning for Credit Unions, 1989, Strategic Financial Managment for Commercial Banks, 1993. Mem.: Fin. Mgmt. Assn., Am. Fin. Assn., Omicron Delta Epsilon, Beta Gamma Sigma. Roman Catholic. Home: 112 Meadowbrook Williamsburg VA 23188-9211

O'CONNOR, BRIAN, college baseball coach; b. Council Bluffs, Iowa, Apr. 21, 1971; m. Cindy Petratis; children: Ellie, Maggie, Dillon. B in Mktg., Creighton U., Omaha, Nebr., 1993. Minor league pitcher Martinsville Phillies, Appalachian League, Va., 1993; pitching coach Creighton U. Bluejays, 1993—95; asst. coach U. Notre Dame Fighting Irish, 1995—2001, assoc. head baseball coach, 2001—03; head baseball coach U. Va. Cavaliers, 2003—. Named Nat. Asst. Coach of Yr., Am. Baseball Coaches Assn., Baseball America, 2001, AFLAC Nat. Asst. Coach of Yr., 2003, Atlantic Region Coach of Yr., Am. Baseball Coaches Assn., 2004, 2009, Coach of Yr., Atlantic Coast Conf., 2004, Coll. Baseball Found., 2006, Nat. Coach of Yr., Nat. Collegiate Baseball Writers Assn., 2009. Office: Univ Va Baseball University Hall PO Box 400839 Charlottesville VA 22904-4839 Office Phone: 434-982-5092. Business E-Mail: uvabaseball@virginia.edu.

O'CONNOR, BRIDGET, bank executive; b. 1964; A, Middlesex County Coll., NJ. With AT&T Bell Labs, 1985—91; joined Lehman Brothers, 1991, chief info. officer, head global bus., 2002—09; mng. dir., chief tech. officer Depository Trust & Clearing Corp. (DTCC), 2009—10; chief tech. officer Consumer & Small Bus. Banking (CSBB) Bank of America Corp., Charlotte, NC, 2010—. Contbr. articles to profl. jours. Named one of The 100 Most Influential Women in NYC Bus., Crain's NY Bus., 2007. Mem.: YWCA NYC Acad. Women Leaders. Office: Bank of America Corp 100 N Tryon St Charlotte NC 28255

O'CONNOR, CHRISTOPHER M., cardiologist; b. Dec. 8, 1957; MD, U. Md., 1983. Cert. Internal Medicine, 1988, Cardiovasc. Disease, 1989. Resident in internal medicine/cardiology Duke U. Med. Ctr., Durham, NC, 1983—86, 1986—87, 1988—89, exec. dir. cardiology, dir. Heart Ctr. Office: Duke Sch Medicine 129 Davison Bldg DUMC 3356 Durham NC 27710 Office Phone: 919-681-5816, 919-681-3447. Office Fax: 919-681-7755.

O'CONNOR, DORIS JULIA, not-for-profit fundraiser, consultant; b. Apr. 30, 1930; 1 child: Kim C. BA cum laude in Econs., U. Houston, 1975. Adminstrv. asst. Shell Cos. Found. Inc., NYC, 1966-71, asst. sec. Houston, 1971-73, sec., 1973-76, sr. v.p., dir., mem. exec. com., 1976-93; prin. Doris O'Connor & Co., 1993—. Corp. assoc. United Way of Am., Washington, 1976-93; corp. advisor Bus. Com. of Arts, N.Y.C., 1976-91, del., 1982-87; dir. Ind. Sector, Washington, 1981-89, vice chmn., 1983-87; mem. contbns. coun. Conf. Bd., N.Y.C., 1976-93; advisor Coun. of Better Bus. Burs., Washington, 1975-94, vice chmn., 1983-87; commr. adv. commn. on work-based learning, Dept. Labor, 1991-93; mem. Houston/Harris County Arts Task Force, 1991-93, Houston Ind. Sch. Dist. Task Force, 1991-93; trustee Houston Grand Opera, 1993-99, Houston Symphony Soc., 1993-99, Soc. Performing Arts, 1993-99, Cultural Arts Coun., 1993-96, Greater Houston Coalition Edn. Excellence, 1993-96; mem. adv. bd. Houston Zool. Soc., 1993-99; mem. Mus. Fine Arts, Houston, Houston Mus. Natural Sci. Mem. Houston Com. Fgn. Rels., Houston World Affairs Coun., Houston Philos. Soc., Plaza Club (bd. givs. 1987-89), Omicron Delta Epsilon. Office Phone: 713-522-3278.

O'CONNOR, KAREN LENDE, Olympic athlete, sports association administrator; b. Feb. 17, 1958; m. David O'Connor, 1993. Mem. US Equestrian Olympic Team, Seoul, Korea, 1988, Atlanta, 1996, Sydney, 2000, US Equestrian Team, Pan Am. Games, 2003; with Olympic Team, 2008. Co-chmn. instr. cert. prog. US Eventing Assn.; bd. dir. US Equestrian Fedn.; mem. athlete adv. bd. US Olympic Comm. Winner CCI, Boekelo (Holland), 1984, CCI, Chesterland (Pa.), 1985, placed 1st Role/Kentucky Internat. CCI Three Day Event, 1991, 1st Tetbury (Eng.) Horse Trials, 1991, 1st Fair Hill (Md.) Horse Trials, 1991, 3rd Burghley Three Day Event CCI (Eng.), 1991, 6th World Three Day Event Rider Rankings L'Annee Hippique, 1991, 3rd CCI, Loughanmore (Ireland), 1992, 6th Blenheim Audi Internat. Horse Trials (Eng.), 1993, 1st CCI, Punchestown (Ireland), 1993, 10th CCI Internat. de Saumur, 1994; recipient Silver medal, Olympic Games, Atlanta, 1996, Team Bronze medal, Olympic Games, 2000, Silver medal, Pan Am. Games, 2003, Gold medal, 2007; winner Foxhall Cup, 2001; named U.S. Combined Tng. Assn. Lady Rider of the Year, 1989, 90, 91, 95, 96, 97, 98, Female Equestrian Athlete of the Year Olympic Com., 1993, USET spring champion, winning Kentucky CCI, USET FAll Reserve champion, 2nd Fair Hill, 1999, World Equestrian Games Bronze Medal Team, 1998, USET spring champion, winner Kentucky CCI, 1997, Equestrian of Yr. UEST, 2007, US Fall Champion, 2009; grantee USET, 1991. Office: OCET PO Box D The Plains VA 20198

O'CONNOR, MARY, marketing executive; BA, U. Notre Dame, Ind., 1996; MBA, Ind. U. Kelley Sch. Bus., 1999. Mktg. analyst Gen. Motors Pontiac Brand Team, 1999—2001; Olympic comm. dir. Gen. Motors Chevrolet Advt. & Sales Promotion, 2001—02, customer relationship mktg. mgr., 2002, sales promotion mgr., 2003—04; dir. Carat Sponsorship Solutions, 2004—05; dir. Olympic mktg. The Mktg. Arm, 2005—. Named one of Forty Under 40, Street & Smith's SportsBus. Jour., 2009. Office: The Mktg Arm 1999 Bryant St Ste 1800 Dallas TX 75201 Office Phone: 214-259-3200. Office Fax: 214-259-3201.

O'CONNOR, RALPH STURGES, investment company executive; b. Pasadena, Calif., Aug. 27, 1926; s. Thomas Ireland and Edith Masury (Sturges) O'Connor; m. Alice Maconda Brown, Apr. 28, 1950 (div. 1993); children: George Rufus, Thomas Ireland III, Nancy Isabel, John Herman; m. Becky Miller Gorham, Mar. 22, 2008. BA, Johns Hopkins U., Balt., 1951; postgrad., Harvard U., Cambridge, Mass., 1967. With Highland Resources, Inc., Houston, 1951-87, exec. v.p., 1961-64, pres., 1964-87; pres., CEO Ralph S. O'Connor and Assocs., Houston, 1987—. Trustee Salk Inst.; chmn. bd. dirs. Arnaud's Restaurant, New Orleans. Trustee emeritus Rice U., Johns Hopkins U., Oldfields Sch., Glencoe, Md. With USAAF, 1943—46. Mem.: NAS, Presdl. Counselors, Houston Landmen's Assn. (past pres.), All Am. Wildcatters, Am. Assn. Petroleum Landmen, Johns Hopkins Instns., River Oaks Country Club, Bayou Club. Office: Ralph S O'Connor & Assocs 10000 Memorial Dr Ste 510 Houston TX 77024-3422 Office Phone: 713-682-3441.

O'CONNOR, REED CHARLES, federal judge; b. Houston, 1965; BS, U. Houston, 1986; JD, South Tex. Coll. Law, 1989. Bar: Tex. 1990. Assoc. Vinson & Elkins, LLP, 1989—94; asst. dist. atty. Tarrant County Dist. Atty.'s Office, 1994—98; asst. US atty. (no. dist.) Tex. US Dept. Justice, 1998—2007; mem. US Senate Com. on Judiciary, 2003—07; judge US Dist. Ct. (no dist.) Tex., 2007—. Mem.: South Tex. Law Review. Office: US Dist Ct 1100 Commerce St Rm 1520 Dallas TX 75242

O'CONNOR, ROD, chemist, consultant, inventor; b. Cape Girardeau, Mo., July 4, 1934; s. Jay H. and Flora (Winters) O'C.; m. Shirley Ann Sander, Aug. 7, 1955; children: Mark Alan (dec.), Kara Ann, Shanna Suzanne, Timothy Patrick. BS, S.E. Mo. State Coll., 1955; PhD, U. Calif., Berkeley, 1958. Asst. prof. chemistry U. Omaha, 1958-60, Mont. State Coll., 1960-63; assoc. prof. chemistry Mont. State U., Bozeman, 1963-66; assoc. prof., coordinator gen. chemistry Kent (Ohio) State U., 1966-67; prof., dir. 1st year chemistry U. Ariz., Tucson, 1968-72; staff assoc. Adv. Council on Coll. Chemistry Stanford (Calif.) U., 1967-68; vis. prof. Wash. State U., Pullman, 1972-73; prof. chemistry Tex. A&M, College Station, 1973-86; pres. Texas ROMEC Inc., College Station, 1983-98; prof. environ. studies Baylor U., Waco, Tex., 1996-99. Cons. insect venoms Hollister-Stier Labs., Spokane, Wash., 1963-67; lab. separates editor W.H. Freeman Co., 1968-78; ednl. cons. TUCARA-4 Media Resources, Inc., 1971-74; mem. Coll. Chemistry Cons. Service; vis. scientist, tour lectr. Am. Chem. Soc., 1970-86. Author: (with T. Moeller) Ions in Aqueous Systems, 1972, Fundamentals of Chemistry, 1981, (with C. Mickey and A. Hassell) Solving Problems in Chemistry, 1981, (with L. Peck and K. Irgolic) Fundamentals of Chemistry in The Laboratory, 1981, (with T.E. Taylor and P. Glenn) Toward Success in College, 1981, (with A. Hassell and C. Mickey) Advanced Problems in Applied Chemistry, 2000; films Laboratory Safety, 1971; Contbr. articles to profl. jours.; patentee in field Recipient nat. teaching award Mfg. Chemists Assn., 1978; 4 regional teaching awards. Fellow AAAS, Am. Inst. Chemists, Sigma Xi; mem. Internat. Soc. Toxinology, Am. Chem. Soc. Office: Chem Consulting Svcs 1300 Angelina Cir College Station TX 77840-4855 Office Phone: 979-693-5804. E-mail: docroc34@hotmail.com.

O'DAY, DENIS MICHAEL, ophthalmologist, educator; b. Melbourne, Victoria, Australia, Dec. 10, 1935; came to U.S., 1967; s. Kevin John and Bernadette John (Hay) O'D.; m. Ann Georgina Despard, May 28, 1966; children: Luke Gerard, Simon Patrick, Edward Daniel. Diploma, Xavier Coll., 1953; MBBS, Melbourne U., 1960. Diplomate Am. Bd. Ophthalmology. Intern St. Vincent's Hosp./U. Melbourne, 1961; resident in internal medicine St. Vincent's Hosp., 1962-64, chief resident dept. medicine, 1964, clin. asst. medicine, 1965-66; 3d asst., mem. asst. Royal Victoria Eye & Ear Hosp., Melbourne, 1967-70; resident in ophthalmology U. Calif., San Francisco, 1970; Wellcome rsch. fellow in corneal disease Inst. Opthalmology, London, 1970-72; asst. prof. ophthalmology Vanderbilt U. Sch. Medicine, Nashville, 1972-74, assoc. prof. ophthalmology, 1974-77, prof. ophthalmology, now chmn., 1977-92, chmn. ophthalmology dept., 1992—; exec. dir. Am. Bd. Ophthalmology, Bala Cynwyd. Cons. ophthalmologist Royal Commonwealth Soc. of Blind, Nigeria, 1972; cons. VA Hosp., 1973-74, active staff, 74; mem. active staff Nashville Gen. Hosp., 1974, Park View Hosp., 1980, Vanderbilt Hosp., 1972; mem. cons. staff St. Thomas Hosp.; bd. dirs. Am. Bd. Ophthalmology, Phila., 1988-, current exec. dir.; proctor lectr. U. Calif., San Francisco, 1993; co-med. dir. Lions Eye Bank and Sight Svc., 1973-86, med. dir. 1986—; bd. dirs. Lions Eye Bank Mid. Tenn., 1987—; ad-hoc mem. NIH Visual Sci. Study Sect., 1977. Author: Management of Functional Impairment due to Cataract, 1993; contbr. numerous articles, abstracts to profl. publs., chpts. to books. Chair ethics com. Cath. Pub. Policy Commn., Nashville, 1991—. Joyn Hayden rsch. fellow, 1965; recipient Felton Bequest and Potter Found. awards, 1967, recognition award Alcon Rsch. Inst., 1983, Sr. Sci. Investigator award Rsch. to Prevent Blindness, 1987, Health Profl. of Yr. award Tenn. chpt. Assn. for Edn. and Rehab. of Blind and Visually Impaired, 1990. Fellow ACS, Royal Australia Coll. Physicians, Royal Soc. Medicine, Am. Acad. Ophthalmology (sec. quality of care com. 1993—, Honor award for Ednl. Contbns. 1981-85, dir. clin. alert program, pub. health com. 1985-88); mem. AMA, AAUP, Am. Ophthalmol. Soc., Assn. for Rsch. in Vision and Ophthalmology, Nashville Acad. Medicine, Nashville Acad. Ophthalmology (v.p. 1980-81), Oxford Ophthalmol. Soc., Royal Australasian Coll. Physicians, Tenn. Acad. Medicine, Tenn. Acad. Ophthalmology. Roman Catholic. Avocation: sailing. Office: Vanderbilt U Med Ctr East Dept Ophthalmology Med Ctr Fl 8 Nashville TN 37232-0001

O'DAY, PAUL THOMAS, trade association executive; b. May 2, 1935; s. James Thomas and Jeannette Irene (Deschenes) O'D.; m. Nancy Frances Eitler, June 16, 1962; children: Kathleen, Maureen, Michael, Ellen. BA, Am. Internat. Coll., Springfield, Mass., 1958; JD, Georgetown U., 1963; MPA, Am. U., 1967; D of Pub. Adminstrn. honoris causa, Am. Internat. Coll., 1997. Bar: D.C. 1964, Va. 2005, U.S. Supreme Ct. 1974. Patent examiner US Patent Office, Washington, 1959-62; exec. sec. panel high-speed ground transp., auto. air poll. Dept. Commerce, Washington, 1965-66, staff asst. to sec., 1967-69, exec. asst. to sec., 1969-71, dep. dir. bur. domestic commerce, 1972-74; dep. dir. Nat. Bus. Coun. for Consumer Affairs, Washington, 1971-72; cons. to Gen. Counsel GE, Fairfield, Conn., 1974-75; asst. trade rep. Exec. Office of the Pres., Washington, 1975-77; dep. asst. sec. US Dept. Commerce, Washington, 1978-84; pres. Am. Fiber Mfrs. Assn., Washington, 1984—. Chmn. Fiber Econs. Bur., 1984—; pres. Eisenhower World Affairs Inst., 1993-99, exec. com., 2000-06. Corporator Am. Internat. Coll., 1974—; mem. governing coun. Shakespeare Theater Guild, 1989-2001; exec. planning team Am. Writers Mus., 2013-. Recipient Constl. Law award Georgetown U. Law Ctr., 1962; Alumni award Am. Internat. Coll., 1970; Pres.'s Meritorious Exec. award., 1984; Nat. Inst. Pub. Affairs fellow Princeton U., 1964 Mem.: AAAS, Robert Benchley Soc., Am. Constitution Soc., Nat. Assn. Mfrs. Coun. (bd. dirs. 2006—10, Leadership award 2009), Am. Chem. Soc., Jussi Bjorling Soc. USA (charter), O'Dea Clan Assn. (Corofin, Ireland), Cosmos Club. Home: 8261 Private Ln Annandale VA 22003-4471 Office: Am Fiber Mfrs Assn 1530 Wilson Blvd Ste 690 Arlington VA 22209 Home Phone: 703-425-7727.

O'DAY, STEPHEN EDMUND, lawyer; b. Indpls., Nov. 8, 1953; s. George R. and M. Kate (Harrington) O'D.; m. Fran Bold, Dec. 16, 1973; children: Jeremy, Kelly, Rory, Curry. Student, Ga. Inst. Tech., 1971-72; BA summa cum laude, Furman U., 1976; JD cum laude, Harvard U., 1979. Bar: Ga. 1979, US Dist. Ct. (no. dist.) Ga. 1979, US. Ct. Appeals (5th cir.) 1979, US Ct. Appeals (11th cir.) 1981, US Claims Ct. 1981, US Supreme Ct. 1986. Assoc. Hurt, Richardson, Garner, Todd & Cadenhead, Atlanta, 1979-85, former ptnr.; now mem. Smith, Gambrell & Russell, Atlanta, ptnr. Trustee Ga. Conservancy, Atlanta, 1981-91, sec. 1984-85, vice chmn. 1986; bd. dirs. Southern Environ. Law Ctr., Charlottesville, Va., 1985—, sr. litig. counsel., chmn. Environ. Adv. Coun. for Ga. Lt. Gov., Solid Waste Task Force, Ga., part-time instr. Ga. Tech. Youth dir. Episcopal Ch. of St. Peter and St. Paul, Marietta, Ga., 1982-84, vestry, 1984-85; bd. trustees Upper Chattahoochee River Keeper, 1996-, mem. Met. Atlanta C. of C. (water quality task froce), Leadership Atlanta. Recipient River Guardian award; named Ga. Super Lawyer, Atlanta Mag. and Law & Politics Media, Inc, Am. Leading Lawyers for Bus., Chambers USA, Best Environ. Lawyer, Corp. Counsel. Mem. ABA (natural resources, energy and environ. sect., litigation, tort trial & ins. practice sects.), Ga. Bar Assn. (chmn. com. on the handicapped, 1980-81, mem. young lawyers sect., vice chmn. environ. sect. 1995), Phi Beta Kappa, Phi Eta Sigma, Pi Gamma Mu. Democrat. Chmn. Harvard Environ. Law Soc. Office: Smith Gambrell & Russell LLP Ste 3100 1230 Peachtree St NE Promenade II Atlanta GA 30309 Office Phone: 404-815-3527. Office Fax: 404-815-6827. Business E-Mail: soday@sgrlaw.com.

O'DEA, MARITA, human resources specialist; Grad., U. Portland, Oreg. Various positions, human resource divsn. Gimbels, Inc.; v.p., human resources Bergdorf Goodman, 1984—95, sr. v.p., human resources, 1995—2001; v.p., human resources The Neiman Marcus Group, Inc., 2001—02, sr. v.p., chief human resource officer, 2002—, Neiman Marcus, Inc., 2005—. Office: Neiman Marcus Inc 1618 Main St Dallas TX 75201 Office Phone: 214-743-7600. Business E-Mail: marita_odea@neimanmarcus.com.

ODEEN, PHILIP A., energy company executive; b. SD, 1935; BA in Govt., U. SD, 1957; MA in Polit. Sci., U. Wis., 1959. V.p. Wilson Sporting Goods Co., 1973—78; mng. ptnr. Coopers & Lybrand, 1978—92; pres., CEO BDM Internat., Inc., 1992—97; exec. v.p., gen. mgr. TRW Systems & Info. Tech., 1997—99; exec. v.p. Wash. ops. TRW, Inc., 1998—2000, interim CEO, 2001—02, chmn., 2002; acting CEO, chmn. Reynolds & Reynolds Co., 2004—05, acting CEO, 2004—05, non-exec. chmn., 2004—06; CEO QinetiQ North America, 2005—06; chmn. Avaya, Inc., 2006—07, The AES Corp., 2009—. Bd. dirs. Convergys Corp., 2000—, Avaya, Inc., 2002—07, Northrop Grumman Corp., 2003—08, The AES Corp., 2003—, Booz Allen Hamilton Holding Corp., 2008—, XStream Systems, Inc., 2008—. Office: The AES Corp 4300 Wilson Blvd Arlington VA 22203 Office Phone: 703-522-1315.

ODELL, PATRICK LOWRY, retired mathematics professor; b. Watonga, Okla., Nov. 29, 1930; s. Max Vernon and Pamela (Massey) Odell; m. Norma Lou Maddox, Aug. 16, 1958 (dec. May 1980); children: James M., David L., Michael R.L., Julie K., Patricia L., Deborah L.; m. Dovalee Dorsett, Aug. 3, 1985. BS, U. Tex., 1952; postgrad., UCLA, 1953-54; MS, Okla. State U., 1958, PhD, 1962. Mathematician White Sands (N.Mex.) Proving Grounds, 1952-53, Kaman Nuclear, Albuquerque, 1958-59, U.S. Naval Nuclear Ordnance Evaluation Unit, 1959-62, Ling-Temco Vought Aeros., 1962; asst. prof. math. U. Tex., Austin, 1962-66; prof., chmn. dept. math. Tex. Technol. U., Lubbock, 1966-71, coordinator insts., dir. rsch., Coll. Arts and Sci., 1971-72; prof math. scis. and environ. scis. U. Tex., Dallas, 1972-88, prof. emeritus, 1988—; prof. emeritus math. sci. Baylor U., Waco, Tex., 1988—2001; exec. dean grad. studies and rsch. U. Tex., Dallas, 1972-75. Assoc. dir. Tex. Ctr. for Rsch., Austin, 1964—66; rsch. scientist Def. Rsch. Lab., 1963—65; cons. math.

statistician, 1962—. Capt. USAF, 1953—57. Fellow: Am. Statis. Assn., Tex. Acad. Sci. (Disting. Tex. Scientist award 1994). Home: 1117 Deer Run Rd Valley Mills TX 76689 Personal E-mail: pat_odell@baylor.edu.

O'DELL, RICHARD, trucking executive, board member; With Yellow Corp., 1987—95, v.p., fin. and adminstrn., WestEx subs., 1995—97; CFO Saia Motor Freight Line, Inc., v.p., fin. & adminstrn. Duluth, Ga., 1997—99, pres., CEO, 1999—; CEO Saia, Inc., 2007—, pres., bd. dirs., 2006—. Office: Saia Inc 11465 Johns Creek Pky Ste 400 Duluth GA 30097 Office Phone: 770-232-5067. Office Fax: 770-232-4066. Business E-Mail: ro'dell@saia.com.

O'DELL, WILLIAM H., state legislator; b. Ware Shoals, SC, Oct. 11, 1938; s. William B. and Sara Francis William O'Dell; m. Aedra Gayle Tisdale, 1965; children: William B., Patricia Michelle. BA, The Citadel, 1960. Pres. O'Dell Mop Co., Inc.; vice chmn. Greenwood Sch. Dist. 51, SC, 1974—81; mem. Dist. 4 SC State Senate, 1989—, mem. Banking and Ins. Com., Fin. Com., Gen. Com., Invitations Com. & Labor, Commerce and Industry Com. Mem.: SC C. of C. (dir. 1985—88), United Fund (chmn. 1986), Ware Shoals C. of C. (pres. 1985). Democrat. Baptist. Mailing: PO Box 540 Ware Shoals SC 29692 Office: 610 Gressette Bldg PO Box 142 Columbia SC 29201 Home Phone: 803-252-0845, 864-943-0905; Office Phone: 803-212-6040, 864-861-2222. E-mail: WHO@scsenate.org.

ODEN, GREG, professional basketball player; b. Buffalo, Jan. 22, 1988; s. Greg Oden, Sr. and Zoe Oden. Student in Bus. Adminstrn., Ohio State U., Columbus, 2006—07. Center Portland Trail Blazers, Oreg., 2007—12, Miami Heat, Fla., 2013—. Mem. USA Basketball Men's Sr. Nat. Team, 2007. Recipient Arthur L. Trester Mental Attitude award, Ind. Boy's Basketball Class 4A, 2005—06, Morgan Wootten award (McDonald's All-Am. Player of Yr.), 2006; named USA Today Player of Yr., 2005, 2006, Parade Mag. Player of Yr., 2005, 2006, Gatorade Ind. and Nat. Player of Yr., 2005, 2006, Gatorade Nat. HS Male Athlete of Yr., 2006, Player of Yr., Nat. HS Coaches Assn., 2006, Ind. Mr. Basketball, Indpls. Star, 2006, Atlanta Tipoff Club 2006 Naismith Prep Player of Yr.; named a McDonald's All-Am., 2006. Achievements include being the first overall pick in the NBA Draft, 2007. Office: Miami Heat 601 Biscayne Blvd Miami FL 33132

ODEN, JEREMY H., state legislator; b. Oct. 7, 1968; BA, Ashbury Coll.; post grad., Ashbury Theol. Sem. CFO Delta Discount Corp.; mem. Dist. 11 Ala. House of Reps., Montgomery, 1998—. Mem. Eva United Meth. Ch. Mem. Eva Lion's Club, Arrites Oden Masonic Lodge, Huntsville Scottish Rite, Decatur York Rite, Huntsville Shrine Assn., Ashbury Alumni Assn. (bd. mem.). Republican. Methodist. Office: PO Box 9 Eva AL 35621 also: Ala House of Reps Ala State House 11 S Union St Rm 527-D Montgomery AL 36130 Office Phone: 256-734-4236, 334-242-7722. Office Fax: 256-739-9119.

ODEN, JOHN TINSLEY, engineering educator, mathematician, consultant; b. Alexandria, La., Dec. 25, 1936; s. John James and Sara Elizabeth (Lyles) O.; m. Barbara Clare Smith, Mar. 19, 1965; children: John Walker, Elizabeth Lee. BS, La. State U., 1959; MS, Okla. State U., 1960, PhD, 1962; DSc (hon.), Tech. U. Lisbon, Portugal, 1986; Doctorate (hon.), Polytechnique de Mons, Belgium, 2000, Tech. U. Krakow, Poland, 2001, Ecole Normale Superior Cachan, 2006. Registered profl. engr., Tex., La. Teaching asst. La. State U., Baton Rouge, 1959; asst. prof. Okla. State U., Stillwater, 1961-63; sr. structures engr. Gen. Dynamics, Fort Worth, 1963-64; prof., head dept. engring. mechanics U. Ala., Huntsville, 1964-73; prof. U. Tex., Austin, 1973—, Carol and Henry Groppe prof. engring., Ernest and Virginia Cockrell chair in engring. Austin, 1987-93, Cockrell Family Regents chair engring., 1993—. Prof. Coope U. Fed., Brazil, 1974; dir. Inst. Computational Engring and Sci., 2003, assoc. v.p. for rsch., 2003—; mem. Sci. Rsch. Coun. vis. scholar Brunel U., Eng., 1981; com. on computational mechanics NRC; chmn. U.S. Nat. Com. on Theoretical and Applied Mechanics, 1992-94; founder, CEO computational Mechanics Co., Inc., 1982-96; Peter O'Donnell Jr. chair in computer sys., 2003. Author, editor 45 books; editor Jour. Computer Methods in Applied Mechanics and Engring., 1980—; contbr. over 500 articles to profl. jours. Decorated Chevalier Ordre des Palms Academique (France); recipient rsch. award Southeastern Conf. on Theoretical and Applied Mechanics, 1978, Lohmann medal Okla. State U., 1991, Hocott Rsch. award, 1992, Computational Mechanics Medal Japan Soc. Mech. Engrs., 1993, Presdl. Citation, U. Tex. Austin, 2004 Fellow ASCE (life; Outstanding Svc. award 1968, Walter Huber rsch. award 1973, Theodore von Karman medal 1992, Joe J. King Prof. Engring. award 1994), ASME (hon. mem., Worcester Reed Warner medal 1990, Timoshenko medal 1996), NAE, Soc. Engring. Sci. (pres. 1978, Eringen medal 1991), Am. Acad. Mechanics (pres. 1990-94, Disting. Svc. medal 1995), Internat. Assn. Computational Mechanics (pres. 1990-94, Congress-Gauss-Newton medal 1994), Am. Acad. Arts and Sciences; mem. Soc. Indsl. and Applied Math., U.S. Assn. Computational Mechanics (pres. 1990-92, John Von Neumann medal 1993), Soc. Natural Philosophy, Nat. Acad. Engring. Mex., Nat. Acad. Engring. Brazil, World Innovation Found. (hon. 2004), Polish Assn. Computational Mechanics (Zienkiewicz medal, 2007). Office: Univ Tex Austin ICES Campus Code CO200 Austin TX 78712 Home: 7403 W Rim Dr Austin TX 78731-2044

ODEN, WILLIAM BRYANT, bishop, educator; b. McAllen, Tex., Aug. 3, 1935; s. Charles Alva and Evea (Bryant) O.; m. Marilyn Brown, July 12, 1957; children: Dena Lee Oden Bowen, William Dirk, Valerie Lyn, Charles Bryant. BA, Okla. State U., 1958; MDiv, Harvard U., 1961, postgrad., 1964; ThD, Boston U., 1968; DD (hon.), Oklahoma City U., 1980; LHD (hon.), Centenary Coll., 1990. Ordained to ministry Meth. Ch., 1961. Pastor Aldersgate United Meth. Ch., Oklahoma City, 1963-69, St. Stephen's United Meth. Ch., Norman, Okla., 1969-76, Crown Heights United Meth. Ch., Oklahoma City, 1976-83; prof. Phillips Grad. Sem., Enid, 1976-88; pastor 1st United Meth. Ch., Enid, 1983-88; bishop United Meth. Ch., La., 1988-96, Dallas area, 1996—2004, Ecumenical del. to Lambeth Conf., 1998. Pres., United Meth. Coun. Bishops, 2000-01; pres. SCJ Coll. of Bishops, 1989-90; del. Gen. Conf., 1976, 80, 84, 88; chmn. Okla. Del. to Gen. and Jurisdictional Confs., 1984, 88; Jackson lectr. Perkins Sch. Theology, So. Meth. U., 1975, Wilson lectr. SCJ Bishop's Week, 1989; co-chair World Meth.-Anglican Dialogue, 1991-95; bd. dirs. Wesley Works Project; pres. Gen. Bd. Higher Edn. & Ministry, 1996-01; pres. comm., United Meth. Comm., 2000-04; Ecumenical officer, head communion, 2004-. Author: Oklahoma Methodism in the Twentieth Century, 1968, Liturgy as Life Journey, 1976, Wordeed: Evangelism in Biblical and Wesleyan Perspective, 1978; contbr.: Send Me: The Iteneracy in Crisis, 1991, Vision and Supervision, 2003. Trustee Oklahoma City U., 1980-88, Southwestern U., Winfield, Kans., 1983-88, Centenary Coll., 1988-96, Dillard U., 1988-96, So. Meth. U., 1996—2004. Recipient Outstanding Alumni award, Harvard Divinity Sch., 2005; named to U. Hall of Fame, Okla. State, 2003; Charles E. Merrill fellow, Harvard U., 2003. Mem. Am. Acad. Homiletics. Methodist. Avocations: writing, reading biographies, mountain climbing, backpacking. Home: PO BOX 866188 Plano TX 75086-6188 Personal E-mail: wbo8@earthlink.net.

ODOM, FLOYD CLARK, surgeon; b. Cisco, Tex., 1946; MD, U. Tex., San Antonio, 1972. Diplomate Am. Bd. Colon & Rectal Surgery, Am. Bd. Surgery. Intern Bexar County Hosp., San Antonio, 1972-73, resident in gen. surgery, 1973-77; fellow in colon & rectal surgery Baylor Med. Ctr., Dallas, 1977-78; colorectal surgeon Presbyn. Hosp., Dallas, 1997—. Fellow ACS, Am. Soc. Colon and Rectal Surgeons. Office: 8220 Walnut Hill Ln Dallas TX 75231-4406 Home Phone: 214-360-0364; Office Phone: 214-739-5758.

ODOM, GARY, state legislator; b. Elizabethton, Tenn., Nov. 1, 1951; m. Sue Odom; 2 children. BS in Law Enforcement Svcs., East Tenn. State U., 1973; MS in Criminal Justice, Eastern Ky. U., 1975. Former spl. investigator, state atty. gens. office, Tenn.; vice chmn., conservation & environment com.; mem. Fiscal Rev., Health & Human Resources Com., Metro Nashville Coun. Dist. 23; dem. leader; faculty mem. Aquinas Jr. Coll.; exec. dir. Tenn. Optometric Assn.; house rep. mem. Dist. 55 Tenn., 1987—. Recipient Outstanding Conservation Advisor award, Tenn. Environment Coun., 1998; named Legislator of Yr., Nat. Rural Health Assn., Tenn. Recreation & Pks. Assn., Tenn. Environment Coun. & Nat. Wildlife Fedn. Mem.: Metro Coun. Sch. Com. (chmn. 1986—87), Tenn. Soc. Assn. Exec. (pres. 1987), Bellevue C. of C., Kiwanis, Bellevue Exch. Club. Democrat. Baptist. Office: 18A Legislative Plz Nashville TN 37243-0155 also: 119 Dunham Springs Ln Nashville TN 37205 Office Phone: 615-741-4410, 615-356-5096. Office Fax: 615-741-7528. Business E-Mail: rep.gary.odom@capitol.tn.gov.

ODOM, ROD D., JR., telecommunications industry executive; b. Miami; Grad., U. Fla. Comm. cons. So. Bell, West Palm Beach, Fla., 1972—83; dir., new venture planning Bellsouth Corp., 1983—2000, exec. v.p., network ops., 2000—02; pres., network svcs. Bellsouth Corp, 2002; pres. BellSouth Telecom., Inc. Bd. dirs. Oglethorpe U., Sheltering Arms, Piedmont Hosp., Fla. Found.; mem. engring. adv. bd. U. Fla. Methodist. Office: BellSouth Telecommunications Inc 357 Nw Broad St Lyons GA 30436-1105 Office Phone: 912-526-3440.

O'DONNELL, MICHAEL PAUL, restaurant executive; b. Phila., Mar. 17, 1956; s. John Gerald and Marjorie Ann (Wheeler) O'D; m. Deane Jonas, Oct. 25, 1978. BA in English, Rollins Coll., 1978. Chmn., pres. & CEO Ground Round Restaurants, Inc.; CEO Sbarro, Inc.; pres., CEO, New Bus. & pres., Roy's Outback Steakhouse, Inc.; pres., COO Miller's Ale House; mgr. Saga Food Svc., Winter Park, Fla., 1975-78; banker Kidder Peabody & Co., 1978-79; area supr. Pizza Hut Inc., 1979-81, franchise operator, Mid-Atlantic region, 1981-82, dir., major franchise projects, 1982-84; pres. Pollo Food Svc., Jacksonville, Fla., 1984-86; v.p. T.G.I. Fridays, Inc., 1986; chmn., pres. & CEO Champps Entertainment, Inc., 2005—07; pres., CEO & bd. dirs. Ruths Hospitality Group Inc., 2008—. Republican. Roman Catholic. Avocations: golf, running. Home: 288 Deer Run Dr S Ponte Vedra Beach FL 32082-3507 Office: Ruths Hospitality Group Inc 1030 W Canton Ave Ste 100 Winter Park FL 32789-3050 Office Phone: 407-333-7440. Office Fax: 407-833-9625. Business E-Mail: mo'donnell@rhgi.com.

O'DONNELL, PETER, JR., foundation administrator; m. Edith O'Donnell. LHD (hon.), So. Meth. U., 2008. Co-founder, pres. O'Donnell Found., Dallas, 1956—; former dir. Dallas Biomedical Corp., Interfirst Bank, Stadium Associates; dir., exec. com. Univ. Med. Ctr., Inc. Recipient Disting. Svc. award, U. Tex. Austin Alumni Assn., 2003. Fellow: Am. Acad. Arts and Sciences; mem.: Acad. Medicine, Sci. and Engring. of Tex. (founding mem.), Nat. Acad. Medicine (Pres.'s cir.). Office: O'Donnell Found Ste 1660 100 Crescent Ct Dallas TX 75201

O'DONOVAN, CORMAC A., neurologist, educator; 2 children. BS, U. Coll. Galway, Ireland, 1982, MD, 1985. Assoc. prof. neurology Wake Forest U. Sch. Medicine, Winston-Salem, NC, 1995—. Med. dir., dir. eeg and evoked potential labs., assoc. prof. internal medicine-cardiology Wake Forest U. Sch. Medicine. Fellow: Am. Clin. Neurophysiology; mem.: AMA, Am. Acad. Sleep Medicine, Irish Neurol. Assn., So. Epilepsy and Ctrl. EEG Soc., Am. EEG Soc., Am. Epilepsy Soc., Am. Acad. Neurology. Office: Wake Forest Univ Sch of Medicine Medical Center Blvd Winston Salem NC 27157 Business E-Mail: odonovan@wfubmc.edu.

ODUM, MARVIN E., oil industry executive; b. 1958; married; 3 children. BS in Mech. Engring., U. Tex., 1982; MBA, U. Houston. Engr. Shell Oil Co., 1982, gas and power dir. for Americas London, 2001; v.p. bus. devel. & tech. Shell Exploration & Prodn., Houston, exec. v.p. Americas, 2005—; pres. Shell Oil Co., 2008—; CEO InterGen, 2003—05; bd. dirs. upstream Americas unit Royal Dutch Shell, 2009—. Adv. bd. mem. U. Tex. Coll. Engring.; bd. dirs. Am. Petroleum Inst., chmn. upstream com.; mem. deans coun. Harvard U. JFK Sch. Govt. Bd. dirs. Palmer Drug Abuse Prog.; bd. visitors Univ. Cancer Foundation, M.D. Anderson Cancer Center. Office: Shell Oil Co 910 Louisiana St Houston TX 77210 Office Phone: 713-241-6161. Office Fax: 713-241-4044.

OEHLERT, WILLIAM HERBERT, JR., cardiologist, administrator, educator; b. Murphysboro, Ill., Sept. 11, 1942; s. William Herbert Sr. and Geneva Mae (Roberts) O.; m. L. Keith Brown, Mar. 14, 1976; children: Emily Jane, Amanda Elizabeth. BA, So. Ill. U., 1967; MD, Washington U., St. Louis, 1967; M in Med. Mgmt., Tulane U., 1998. Diplomate Nat. Bd. Med. Examiners, Am. Bd. Internal Medicine, Am. Bd. Cardiovascular Disease, North Am. Soc. Pacing and Electrophysiology, Am. Coll. Physician Execs. Med. intern Union Meml. Hosp., Balt., 1967-68, resident, 1968-69, U. Iowa, Iowa City, 1969-70, cardiology fellow, 1970-72; asst. prof. medicine, dir. coronary care units U. Okla. Health Sci. Ctr., Oklahoma City, 1972-74, asst. clin. prof. medicine, 1974-82, assoc. clin. prof. medicine, 1982-88, clin. prof. medicine, 1988—2010; chmn. dept. cardiology Bapt. Med. Ctr., 1992-95; pvt. practice Oklahoma City, 1974—. Med. dir. cardiovasc. svcs. Integris Bapt. Med. Ctr., 1993-98; pres. Cardiovasc. Clinic, Oklahoma City, 1987-91, chmn. exec. com., 1987-91; med. dir. Cardiovasc. Imaging Svcs. Corp., Oklahoma City, 1987-92; v.p. Plaza Med. Group, 1992-93; CEO W.H. Oehlert, MD, P.C., 1993—; prin. clin. coord Okla. Found. Med. Quality, 1998-2002, med. clin. coord., 2002-06. Author: Arrhythmias, 1973, Cardiovascular Drugs, 1976; contbr. articles to profl. jours. Fellow ACP, Am. Heart Assn. (nat. program com. 1979-82, pres. Okla. affiliate 1985-86, bd. dirs. 1974-88, ACLS nat. affiliate faculty 1987-90, bd. dirs. Oklahoma City 1999-2005), Am. Coll. Cardiology; mem. AMA (del. 2007—), ACP-Am. Soc. Internal Medicine, Nat. Assn. Residents and Interns, Am. Coll. Physician Execs. (cert.), Am. Diabetes Assn. (western coun. 2000-03, ea. coun. 2000-01), Okla. State Med. Assn. (pres., 2007—08, trustee 2001—, chmn. Physicians Campaign for Healthier Okla., 2003-04, chmn. CME accreditation rev. com. 2003—04, chmn. CME planning com. 2004-07), Okla. City Clin. Soc., Okla. Cardiac Soc. (pres. 1978-79), Osler Soc., Soc. Nuc. Medicine, Okla. Found. for Med. Quality (bd. dirs. 1995-98), Okla. County Med. Soc. (chmn. quality of care com. 1990-91, pres. 2006), Wilderness Med. Soc., Stewart Wolf Soc., Sportman's Club (bd. dirs. 2003-09), Okla. Blood Inst. (bd. dirs. 2006-, exec. com. mem. 2010-), Phi Eta Sigma, Phi Kappa Phi. Home: 3017 Rock Ridge Pl Oklahoma City OK 73120-5713 Personal E-mail: woehlert@cox.net.

OELBERG, DAVID GEORGE, neonatologist educator, researcher; b. Waukon, Iowa, May 26, 1952; s. George Robert and Elizabeth Abigail (Kepler) O.; m. Debra Penuel, Aug. 4, 1979; children: Anna Elizabeth, Benjamin George. BS with highest honors, Coll. William and Mary, 1974; MD, U. Md., 1978. Diplomate in pediat. and in neonatal-perinatal medicine Am. Bd. Pediat. Intern U. Tex. Med. Br., Galveston, 1978-79, resident, 1979-81, house pediat. staff, 1978-81; postdoctoral fellow in neonatal medicine U. Tex. Med. Sch., Houston, 1981-84, asst. prof. dept. pediat., 1984-90, assoc. prof., 1990-93; assoc. prof. pediat., head perinatal rsch. Ctr. Pediat. Rsch. Ea. Va. Med. Sch., 1993-2001, prof., interim chmn. dept. pediat. Ctr. Pediat. Rsch., 2001—, dir. divsn. neonatal-perinatal medicine. Mem. hosp. staff Hermann Hosp., Houston, 1983-93; physician Crippled Children's Svcs. Program, Houston, 1985-93; mem. hosp. staff Lyndon B. Johnson County Hosp., 1990-93; vis. prof. Wyeth-Ayerst Labs., 1992; med. dir. Office Rsch., Children's Hosp. of King's Daus., 1993—, v.p. for acad. devel., 2001—; med. dirs. Office of Rsch., Sentara-Norfolk Gen. Hosp., 1993—, pres. med. staff. Mem. editl. adv. bd. jour. Neonatal Intensive Care; contbr. articles to profl. jours.; ad hoc reviewer profl. jours.; patentee in field. Physician cons. Parents of Victims of Sudden Infant Death Syndrome, Houston, 1984; chmn. Instl. Animal Care and Use Com., bd. mem. Fund for William Mary Recipient award in analytical chemistry Am. Chem. Soc., 1974, NIH Clin. Investigator award NHLBI, 1989-94, Founders award SSPR, 2012; rsch. grantee Am. Lung Assn., 1989-90, NIH, 1989-94. Fellow Am. Acad. Pediat. NY Acad. Scis.; mem. AMA, NAS, Soc. Exptl. Biology and Medicine, So. Soc. Pediatric Rsch. (councilor, pres., sec.-treas.), Soc. Pediatric Rsch. Achievements include development of a method for optical measurement of bilirubin in tissue and ion channel proteins in pulmonary surfactant. Home: 1624 W Little Neck Rd Virginia Beach VA 23452-4720 Office: Ea Va Med Sch Ctr Pediatric Rsch 855 W Brambleton Ave Norfolk VA 23510-1005 also: Neonatal Medicines CHKD 601 Childrens Lane Norfolk VA 23507 Office Phone: 757-668-7456. Business E-Mail: doelberg@chkd.org.

OELRICH, STEVE, state legislator; b. Pensacola, Fla., Sept. 29, 1945; m. Rose Mary Treadway; children: Ivan, Kenneth, Nick(dec.). AA, St. Petersburg Jr. Coll., 1968; BS, Fla. State U., 1970. Spl. agent Fla. Dept. Law Enforcement; sheriff Alachua County, Fla., 1992—2006; mem. Dist. 14 Fla. State Senate, Tallahassee, 2006—, chair higher edn. com., vice chair mil. affairs and domestic security com., mem. commerce com., comm., energy and pub. utilities com., gen. govt. appropriations com., select com. on Fla.'s inland waters. Mem. adv. bd. U. Fla. Procurement Orgn., Juvenile Assessment Ctr.; chmn. NSA Gift of Life Found.; bd. dirs. United Network Organ Sharing. Mem. Nat. Sheriffs' Assn., Fla. Sheriffs' Assn., Big Brothers Big Sisters, Alzheimer's Assn., Gainesville Rotary Club. Republican. Office: 314 Senate Office Bldg 404 S Monroe St Tallahassee FL 32399-1100 also: 19372 S County Road 325 Hawthorne FL 32640-8408 Office Phone: 352-375-3555, 850-487-5020. Business E-Mail: oelrich.steve.web@flsenate.gov.

OESTERREICHER, JAMES E., insurance company executive; b. 1941; m. Patricia Ann Oesterreicher; children: Scott, Tom, David. BS in Mktg., Mich. State U., 1964. Joined J. C. Penney Co. Inc., 1964, pres., Western Region, 1987-88, exec. v.p., 1988-94, dir., stores, 1988—92, pres., stores and catalog, 1992—95, vice-chmn., 1995—97, CEO, 1995—2000, chmn., 1997—2000. Bd. dirs. The Dial Corp., TXU, Brinker Internat., Inc., 1994—, HCC Ins. Holdings Inc., 2007—. Bd. dirs. Tex. Health Resources, Circle Ten Coun., Boy Scouts Am., March Dimes, Spina Bifida Birth Defects Found. Office: HCC Insurance Holdings Inc 13403 NW Fwy Houston TX 77040-6094 Office Phone: 713-690-7300. Office Fax: 713-462-2401. Business E-Mail: joesterreicher@hcc.com.

OESTREICH, CHARLES HENRY, retired university president; b. Columbus, Ohio, June 8, 1932; s. Henry F. and Martha (Schwartz) O.; m. Rhoda J. Haseley, Aug. 26, 1957; children: Martha, Mary, David. BS, Capital U., 1954; MS, Ohio U., 1956, PhD, 1961; LLD, Capital U., 1986. Instr. chemistry Va. Mil. Inst., 1956-57, Capital U., Columbus, 1960-62, asst. prof., 1962-64, assoc. prof., 1965-69; acad. dean Tex. Luth. U., Seguin, 1969-76, interim pres., 1976-77, pres., 1977-94, pres. emeritus Seguin, 1995—. Postdoctoral rsch. fellow Vanderbilt U., 1965-66 Bd. dirs., past pres. Mid-Tex. Symphony; past bd. dirs. Eden Home, Inc. Mem. Rotary (past pres. Seguin). Home and Office: 2269 S Abbey Loop New Braunfels TX 78130-8965 E-mail: charleso@satx.rr.com.

OETTINGER, MARION, JR., museum director, anthropologist; m. Jill Oettinger; children: Julia, Helen. BA in Anthropology, U. Americas, Mex., 1967; PhD in Anthropology, U. NC, Chapel Hill, 1974. Vis. asst. prof. anthropology Cornell U., 1974—76, U. NC, Chapel Hill, 1977—78, 1979—81; vis. asst. prof. anthropology, sociology Occidental Coll., 1976—77; rsch. affiliate Nat. Autonomous U. Mex., 1978—79, rsch. assoc. ethnology, 1981—83; project dir. Mexican folk art exhbn. and symposium Meridian House Internat., Washington, 1983—85; curator folk art and Latin Am. art San Antonio Mus. Assn., 1985—93; guest curator, project dir. Visiones del Pueblo: The Folk Art of Latin America, Mus. Am. Folk Art, NY, 1988—92; sr. curator, curator Latin Am. art San Antonio Mus. Art, 1994—2005, interim dir., 2004, Betty and Bob Kelso dir., 2005—; installation project dir. Nelson A. Rockefeller Ctr. for Latin Am. Art, 1996—98. Rsch. in field; lectr. in field; chmn. colloquium com. Cornell U., 1974—76, U. NC, 1982; co-founder Friends of Latin Am. Art, 1985; mem. Steering Com., Tex. Folklife Festival, Inst. Texan Cultures, 1986—90, Visual Arts Panel, Tex. Com. for Arts, 1988—90; founder lectr. series on Latin Am. art, 1987; mem. bd. dirs. Partnership for Hope, 1988—91; mem. editl. adv. bd. Latin Am. Art, 1990—95; mem. adv. bd. Instituto Cultural Mexicano, 1990—95; sec. Antiquities Com., State of Tex., 1991—96; cons. Nat. Geographic Soc., 1994; mem. review panel Nat. Endowment for Humanities, 2000; spl. lectr. Speakers Bur., Tex. Coun. for Humanities, Austin, 2000—05; arts advisor San Fernando Cathedral Restoration, 2002—03. Author: Folk Treasures of Mexico: The Nelson A. Rockefeller Collection, 1990, The Folk Art of Latin America: Visiones del Pueblo, 1992, Rostros de Mexico: Celebrating 50 Years of UNAM in San Antonio, 1994, The Folk Art of Spain and the Americas: El Alma del Pueblo, 1997, Retratos: 2000 Years of Latin American Portraits, 2004. Mem. Cultural Arts of San Antonio, 2007; vestry St. Marks Episcopal Ch., San Antonio, 2006; bd. mem. San Antonio River Oversight Commn., 2007, San Antonio Area Tourism Coun., 2007. Recipient Gold Medallion award for Contributions toward Better Understanding of Puerto Rican Culture, 1993, San Antonio Pub. Libr. Arts and Letters award, 1993, Best and Brightest award, U. Roundtable, 2005, Imagineering award, Mind Sci. Found., 1992. Mem.: Tex. Assn. Mus., Coll. Arts Assn., Am. Art Museum Dirs., AAM. Office: San Antonio Mus Art 200 W Jones Ave San Antonio TX 78215 Office Phone: 210-978-8111. Business E-Mail: Marion.Oettinger@samuseum.org.

OGBUANU, IKECHUKWU UDO, physician; b. Arochukwu, Abia, Nigeria, Feb. 28, 1974; s. Sebastian Njoku and Veronica Chinyere Ogbuanu; m. Chinelo Amarachukwu Ezeh; children: Joseph Chiedozie, Hannah Chinyere, Olivia Chiamaka. MD, U. Nigeria, Nsukka, 1998; MPH, U. SC., Columbia, 2006, PhD, 2009. House officer, intern Nigerian Army Reference Hosp., Kaduna, Nigeria, 1999—2000; med. officer, corp. physician Imaobong Missionary Outreach Med. Ctr.,

Uyo, Akwa-Ibom, Nigeria, 2000—02; med. officer St. Luke's Hosp. Dept. Surgery, Anua, Akwa-Ibom, 2002—03; med. dir. Faith Med. Ctr., Uyo, 2003—04; grad. rsch. asst. Arnold Sch. Pub. Health, Columbia, SC, 2006—09; rsch.-grad. asst. Dept. Internal Medicine, U. SC., Sch. Medicine, Columbia, 2006—09; epidemic intelligence svc. officer Ctrs. Disease Control & Prevention, Atlanta, 2009—11, med. epidemiologist, 2011—. Contbr. chapters to books, articles to profl. jours. Deacon Winners Chapel Internat., Atlanta, 2004—. Program Excellence Sci. fellow, Am. Assn. Advancement Sci., 2010. Mem.: SAS Users Group, Nigerian Med. Assn., APHA, Delta Omega Honors Soc., Nat. Scholars Honor Soc., Golden Key Internat. Honor Soc. Office: Ctrs Disease Control & Prevention 1600 Clifton Rd MS A-04 Atlanta GA 30333 Personal E-mail: dr_iyke@yahoo.com. Business E-Mail: ige2@cdc.gov.*

OGDEN, STEVE, state legislator; b. Sept. 21, 1950; m. Beverly Ogden, 1973; children: Michael, Stephanie, Kristen, Charles. BS, US Naval Acad., Annapolis, Md., 1973; grad., Naval Nuc. Power Sch., 1974; MBA, Tex. A&M U., 1987. Oil and gas exploration businessman; pres. Ogden Resource Corp., Bryan, Tex.; mem. Dist. 14 Tex. House of Representatives, 1990—97; mem. Dist. 5 Tex. State Senate, 1997—. Officer submarine fleet USN. Republican. Office: 3740 Copperfield Dr Ste 103 Bryan TX 77802 also: PO Box 12068 Capitol Station Austin TX 78711 Office Phone: 979-776-0521, 512-463-0105. Office Fax: 979-776-8951, 512-463-5713.

OGDEN, THOMAS D., finance company executive; B, MBA, Mich. State U. Exec. v.p. Comerica Bank, 2001—07, dir., Global Corp. Banking; exec. v.p. Comerica, Inc., 2007—; pres., Michigan Market Comerica Bank, 2008—. Office: Comerica Inc Comerica Bank Tower 1717 Main St Dallas TX 75201 Office Phone: 214-462-4831. Business E-Mail: thomas_d_ogden@comerica.com.

O'GEARY, DENNIS TRAYLOR, retired engineering company executive; b. Waverly, Va., Feb. 20, 1925; s. King William and Mary Virginia (Traylor) O'G.; m. Alice Stuart Baum, Aug. 3, 1947; children: Dennis Patrick, Mary Alice O'Geary Eisenbarth, Elizabeth Christina O'Geary Bernstorf. Surveying degree, Tri-State U., 1943; BS in Civil Engring., Ill. Inst. Tech., 1947. Resident engring trainee Va. Hwy. Dept., Richmond, 1947-50; civil engring. supt. Wiley Jackson Co., Roanoke, Va., 1950-57; engr., asst. estimator, project mgr., v.p. and asst. to area mgr. S.J. Groves & Sons Co., Mpls. and Springfield, Ill., 1957-77, v.p., area mgr., 1978-82, v.p., asst. divsn. mgr., divsn. estimator Atlanta, 1982-84; pres. Peabody S.W., Inc., Houston, 1984-85; v.p. Houston ops. J.D. Abrams, Inc., Austin, Tex., 1985-99; ret., 1999. Cons. J.D. Abrams, Inc. With USNR, 1943—46, with USNR, 1958. Mem. ASCE (life), Am. Concrete Inst. (50 yr. mem.), Soc. Am. Mil. Engrs. (50 yr. mem.), Nat. Maritime Hist. Soc. Christian (Disciples Of Christ). Home: 15402 Cresent Oaks Ct Houston TX 77068-2079 Personal E-mail: dennisalice@gmail.com.

OGIE, ELIZABETH C., investor; BA, Columbus Coll., Ga., Ga. State U. Bd. dirs. Synovus Fin. Corp., 1993—. Mem. nominating com. Med. Coll. Ga. Found., 2008—; former chair bd. trustees Andrew Coll., Cuthbert, Ga., Muscogee County Libr. Found.; mem. St. Luke United Meth. Ch.; bd. dirs. Girls Inc., Columbus; trustee/bd. dirs. Bradley-Turner Found., Ga. Health Scis. Found., 2008—, Pitts Found., Wesleyan Coll., Hist. Columbus Found. Recipient Woman of Achievement award, Columbus Girl Scouts, 1993, Guardian Angel award, Girls, Inc., 2001. Mailing: c/o Synovus Financial Corp Ste 500 1111 Bay Ave Columbus GA 31901 Office Phone: 706-649-2311. Office Fax: 706-641-6555.

OGLE, ROY CLINTON, cell biologist, educator; s. Roy Ray and Helen Ruth Ogle, Virgil Atwell Motely (Stepfather); m. Rebecca Elizabeth Adams, Apr. 1977; children: Molly Elizabeth, Katharine Adams. PhD, U. Va., Charlottesville, 1985. Prof. Med. U. SC, Charleston, 1987—90, U. Va., Charlottesville, 1990—. Sci. advisor Stemgent, Charlottesville, 2007—. Author: (book) Crainiofacial Surgery. Mem.: Am. Soc. Cell Biology. Achievements include patents for menningeal stem cells; the production of osteoclasts from adipose tissues; fabrication of laminin nanofiber meshes; research in pathoetiology of craniosynostosis; discovery of dura mater stem cells. Avocations: fly fishing, gardening, bird watching. Office: Univ Va Box 800568 HSC Charlottesville VA 22908 Business E-Mail: royogle@virginia.edu, rco2j@virginia.edu.

OGLESBY, HAROLD MICHAEL, federal marshal; b. 1950; Patrolman Mena Police Dept., Ark., 1976; dep. sheriff Polk County, Ark., 1976—80, sheriff, collector, 1989—2010; justice of the peace Polk County Quorum Ct., 1982—89; US marshal (we. dist.) Ark. US Mashals Svc., US Dept. Justice, 2010—. Served in Ark. Army NG, 1969—76. Office: Judge Isaac C Parker Fed Bldg 30 S 6th St Rm 243 Fort Smith AR 72901 Office Phone: 479-424-5000.

OGLETREE, POWELL G., JR., lawyer; m. Holly Ogletree; 2 children. BS, U. So. Miss., Hattiesburg, 1977; JD, U. Miss. Sch. Law, 1980. Bar: Miss., Ala. Ptnr. Adams and Reese LLP, Jackson, Miss., 1997—, founding ptnr. & co-leader forestry team, chmn. exec. com. Adj. prof. real estate fin. and devel. Miss. Coll. Sch. Law. Recipient Disting. Svc. award, Miss. State Bar Assn.; named one of The Best Lawyers in America, Natural Resources, Real Estate and Timber Law. Mem.: ABA (mem. bd. dirs. environment, energy and resources sect., mem., former chmn. timber resources com.), Miss. Forestry Assn., Miss. Manufactured Housing Assn., Rankin County C. of C. Office: Adams and Reese LLP 300 Renaissance 1018 Highland Colony Pky Ste 800 Ridgeland MS 39157 Office Phone: 601-292-0740. Office Fax: 601-355-9708. Business E-Mail: gee.ogletree@arlaw.com.

OGLIARUSO, MICHAEL ANTHONY, retired chemist, educator, actor; b. Bklyn., Aug. 10, 1938; s. Andrea and Anna (Bianco) O.; m. Basila Gallo, Apr. 2, 1961; 1 child, Michael Dana. BS, Poly. Inst. Bklyn., 1960, PhD, 1965. Postdoctoral rsch. assoc. UCLA, 1965-67; asst. prof. chemistry Va. Poly. Inst. and State U., Blacksburg, 1967-72, assoc. prof., 1972-78, prof., 1978-95, assoc. dean Coll. Arts and Scis., 1984-95; ret. Coll. Arts and Scis.; profl. actor. Contbr. articles to profl. jours. Served with C.E. U.S. Army, 1960-61. Mem. Am. Chem. Soc., Va. Acad. Sci., Sigma Xi, Phi Lambda Upsilon.

OGNIBENE, ANDRE JOHN, retired military officer, internist, educator; b. NYC, Nov. 18, 1931; s. Morris S. and Josephine C. (Macaluso) O.; m. Margaret A. Haug, Apr. 21, 1957; children: Judy, Andrea, Adrienne, Marc, Eric. BA cum laude, Columbia U., 1952; MD, NYU, 1956. Diplomate Am. Bd. Internal Medicine, Am. Bd. Geriatrics, Am. Bd. Med. Mgmt. Intern in medicine Bellevue Hosp., NYC, 1956-57, resident in medicine, 1957-59; commd. capt. US Army M.C., 1957, advanced through grades to brig. gen., 1978; resident in medicine Manhattan VA Hosp., NYC and chief resident in medicine, 1959-60; chief med. service US Army Hosp., Nurnburg, Germany, 1961-62, chief dept. medicine, 1962-64; fellow in cardiology Walter Reed Gen. Hosp., Washington, 1964-65, asst. in cardiology, 1965-66, asst. chief dept. medicine, 1969-72; chief dept. medicine, chief profl. services US Army Hosp., Ft. Meade, Md., 1966-68; cons. in medicine Hdqrs. US Army, Vietnam, 1969; asst. chief dept. medicine Walter Reed Army Med. Ctr., 1970-72; from chief dept. medicine to dir. med. edn. Brooke Army Med. Ctr., Ft. Sam Houston, Tex., 1972-78, dir. med. edn., 1976-78, dep. comdr. and chief profl. services, 1976-78, comdr., commanding gen., 1978-81; hosp. dir. San Antonio State Chest Hosp., 1981-85; program dir. internal medicine Canton, Ohio, 1985-95; prof. medicine NE Ohio U., Rootstown, 1985-98, prof. emeritus, 1998—, chmn. dept. medicine, 1989-98, assoc. dean for med. edn., 1989—98; med. dir. Mercy Med. Ctr., 1995—98; v.p., treas. Majomed Corp., San Antonio, 1999—2008. Instr. medicine NYU, 1960; assoc. clin. prof. Georgetown U., 1970-72; clin. prof. U. Tex. Health Sci. Ctr., San Antonio, 1973-85, mem. postgrad. adv. com., 1977-78; mem. Instl. Rev. Bd., 1981-85; pres. Bexar Met. unit Am. Cancer Soc., 1984; dir. Eisenhower Nat. Bank; bd. dirs. Cancer Therapy and Rsch. Ctr.; chmn. South Tex. Epilepsy Found., 1985. Contbr. articles to med. publs. and chpts. to books; editor, prin. author Internal Medicine in Vietnam, Vol. II, 1982; editor-in-chief: Internal Medicine in Vietnam, vol. I, 1977. Trustee Regina Health Ctr., 1992-97; mem. med. adv. bd. Access Health Inc., 1998-2000. Decorated DSM, Legion of Merit; named among Am. Top Physicians, Consumer Rsch. Coun., 2003-05. Master ACP (laureate, master tchr.); fellow Am. Coll. Physician Execs. (cert.), Am. Coll. Angiology; mem. NY Acad. Scis., Am. Fedn. Clin. Rsch., Bexar County Med. Soc., Stark County Med. Soc., Assn. Profs. Medicine, Tex. Med. Found., Alpha Omega Alpha. Home and Office: 193 Shores Point Canyon Lake TX 78133 Business E-Mail: aognibene@clear.net.

O'GRADY, LIAM, federal judge; b. Newark, 1950; BA, Franklin & Marshall Coll., 1973; JD, George Mason U., 1977. Pvt. practice, Va., 1979—82; asst. commonwealth's atty. Commonwealth of Va., 1982—86; asst. US atty. (ea. dist.) Va. US Dept. Justice, 1986—92; ptnr. Finnegan, Henderson, Farabow, Garrett, & Dunner, LLP, 1992—2003; magistrate judge US Dist. Ct. (ea. dist.) Va., Alexandria, 2003—07, judge, 2007—. Office: Albert V Bryan US Courthouse 401 Courthouse Sq Alexandria VA 22314 Office Phone: 703-299-2121.

O'GRADY, RICHARD T., science administrator; Grad. in Zoology, McGill U., Montreal; PhD, U. BC, Vancouver, 1987. Postdoctoral fellow Smithsonian Instn. Nat. Mus. Natural History; pub. Bio-Science; exec. dir. Am. Inst. Biol. Scis., Washington, 1997—. Office: 1900 Campus Commons Dr Ste 200 Reston VA 20191 also: Am Inst Biol Scis 1444 I St NW Ste 200 Washington DC 20005 Office Phone: 202-628-1500 ext. 258. Office Fax: 202-628-1509. E-mail: rogrady@aibs.org.

OGUN, TOYIN, retail executive; Dir. human resources Pepsi Co., Borden; sr. v.p. human resources Limited Brands, Sears, Leon Leonwood Bean, Zale Corp., 2011—, sr. v.p. customer svcs., 2011—. Office: Zale Corporation 901 W Walnut Hill Lane Irving TX 75038-1003 Office Phone: 972-580-4000.

O'HAIR, SEAN, professional golfer; b. Lubbock, Tex., July 11, 1982; s. Marc and Brenda O'Hair; m. Jackie Lucas, 2002; children: Molly, Luke. Profl. golfer, 1999—. Mem. US team Presidents Cup, 2009. Writer (blog) pgatour.com, 2008. Achievements include winning PGA Tour events: John Deere Classic, 2005; PODS Championship, 2008; Quail Hollow Championship, 2009; RBC Canadian Open, 2011. Office: PGA Tour 100 PGA Tour Blvd Ponte Vedra FL 32082

O'HARA, KEVIN M., gas industry executive; b. Ft. Wayne, Ind. BA in Economics, U. Notre Dame; MBA, DePaul U. With Andersen Consulting (now Accenture), Chgo.; joined Piedmont Natural Gas Co., Inc., Charlotte, NC, 1987, v.p., corp. planning, 1993—2003, v.p., bus. devel. & ventures, 2003—06, sr. v.p., corp., & cmty. affairs, 2006—. Bd. dirs. Energy Transfer Ptnrs., L.P. Bd. dirs. Charlotte C. of C., Charlotte Regional Partnership. Mem.: Am. Gas Assn., So. Gas Assn. Office: Piedmont Natural Gas 4720 Piedmont Row Dr Charlotte NC 28210 Mailing: Piedmont Natural Gas PO Box 33068 Charlotte NC 28233 Office Phone: 704-364-3120. Office Fax: 704-365-8515.

O'HARE, JAMES RAYMOND, energy executive; b. Evergreen Park, Ill., July 20, 1938; s. Raymond Clarence and Helen (Nickel) O'H.; m. Nan Jane Raleigh, Sept. 18, 1965; children: Joan, Daniel, Colleen, Patrick. BS, Marquette U., 1960; MBA, U. Calif. at Los Angeles, 1961. C.P.A., Ind., Ill., Ky., Calif., Tex. Mgr. Peat, Marwick, Mitchell & Co., Chgo., 1961-68, South Bend, Ind., 1968-69; controller Essex Internat., Inc., Fort Wayne, Ind., 1969-76, Am. Air Filter Co., Inc., Louisville, 1976-80; fin. v.p. and treas. Petrolane Inc., Long Beach, Calif., 1980-85; treas. Tex. Eastern Corp., Houston, 1985-87, v.p., treas., 1987-88; sr. v.p. fin. and adminstrn. Tex. Ea. Gas Transmission Co., Houston, 1988—89; v.p., CFO Enclean Inc., Houston, 1991—93; fin. cons., 1993—97; v.p., CFO Ascendant Healthcare Group, Inc., Houston, 1997, John March Ptnrs., Inc., Houston, 1998—2004, Sensor Microsystems, Inc., San Antonio, 2004; gen. ptnr. Connemara Ventures, LLC, The Woodlands, 2004. Controller Afras USA, Inc., 2005. Served with USNR, 1962-68. Mem. Evans Scholars, Fin. Execs. Inst., The Woodlands Country Club, Beta Gamma Sigma. Personal E-mail: jamesohare40@yahoo.com.

OHM, SEONG K., consumer products company executive; b. South Korea; m. Michael Ohm; children: Jessica, Nicholas. BS in Neurosci., U. Rochester, NY, MBA in Fin. and Mktg. Mktg. consumer divsn General Electric Co.; dir. product mgmt. and sales ops. AT&T Inc.; dir. sales ops. Agere Systems; v.p., divisional mdse. mgr. electronics and tech. products Sam's Club/Wal-Mart Stores, Inc., 2003—05, sr. v.p., gen. mdse. mgr., 2005—. Office: Wal Mart Stores Inc Hdqs 702 SW 8th St Bentonville AR 72716 Office Phone: 479-273-4000. Office Fax: 479-277-1830.

OHMAN, E. MAGNUS, cardiologist, educator; s. Karl-Erik Ohman and Maj-Britt Borjeson; m. Elspeth O'Reilly-Hyland, June 12, 1987; children: Edward, Elsa-Maria, Henry. MB, BCh, MD, Royal Coll. of Surgeons in Ireland, Dublin, 1981. Resident gen. internal med. St. Laurence's Hosp., St. Vincent's Hosp., Dublin, 1981—84; rsch. fellow in cardiology St. Laurence's Hosp., Dublin, 1984—87; fellow in cardiology Duke U. Med. Ctr., Durham, NC, 1987—91, asst. prof. medicine, 1991—96, assoc. prof. medicine, 1996—2001; prof. medicine U. NC, Chapel Hill, NC, 2001—05, Duke U. Med. Ctr., Durham, NC, 2005—. Dir. Heart Ctr. U. of N.C., Chapel Hill, 2001—05. Contbr. articles to profl. jours.; editor (assoc.): Am. Heart Jour. Recipient Edith Walsh award, Brit. Med. Assn., 1985. Fellow: Am. Coll. Cardiology, European Soc. Cardiology, Royal Coll. Physicians of Ireland, Soc. of Cardiac Angiography and Intervention; mem.: Am. Coll. Chest Physicians (chmn. Peer Rev. Com.), AMA (chmn. Acute Cardiac Care Com.). Achievements include patents for Methods patent for assessing reperfusion in heart attacks. Office: Duke Univ Med Ctr DUMC 3126 Erwin Rd Durham NC 27710 Office Phone: 919-681-2069. Office Fax: 919-681-0811.

OHRN, NILS YNGVE, chemistry and physics educator; b. Avesta, Sweden, June 11, 1934; came to U.S., 1966; s. Nils E. and Gerda M. (Akerlund) O.; m. Ann M.M. Thorsell, Aug. 24, 1957; children: Elisabeth, Maria. MS, Uppsala U., 1958, PhD, 1963, FD., 1966. Research assoc. Uppsala (Sweden) U., 1963-66; assoc. prof. U. Fla., Gainesville, 1966-70, prof. chemistry and physics, 1971—, assoc. dir. Quantum Theory Project, 1976-77, dir. Quantum Theory Project, 1983-98, chmn. dept. chemistry, 1977-83. Editor: Internat. Jour. Quantum Chemistry, 1970—. Fulbright grantee Com. for Internat. Exchange of Scholars, Washington, 1961-63; recipient Bicentennial Gold medal King of Sweden, 1980; Fla. Acad. Scis. medal, 1984; named Tchr./Scholar of Yr., U. Fla., 2003-04. Fellow Am. Phys. Soc., Chaire Francqui Interuniversitaires Belgium; mem. Am. Chem. Soc. (Fla. award 1997), Royal Acad. Scis. Uppsala Sweden (fgn.), Finnish Acad. Scis. (fgn.), Royal Danish Acad. Scis. (fgn.), Sigma Xi, Phi Beta Kappa. Home: 1823 NW 11th Rd Gainesville FL 32605-5323 Office: U Fla Quantum Theory Project 2301 NPB Bldg # 92 Gainesville FL 32611-8435 Business E-Mail: ohrn@qtp.ufl.edu.

OJAKLI, ZIAD S., lobbyist, automotive executive; b. Brooklyn, NY, June 28, 1967; BA in American Govt., Georgetown U., 1989; MA in American Govt., Johns Hopkins U. Legis. asst. to Senator Dan Coats US Senate, Washington, 1988—94, policy dir. & chief of staff to Senator Paul Coverdell, 1998—2000; chief of staff to Rep. Mark Souder US Congress, Washington, 1995—98; Senate liason Bush-Cheney Transition Team, Washington, 2000; dep. asst. to the Pres. for legis. affairs The White House, Washington, 2001—02, prin. dep. asst. to Pres. for legis. affairs, 2002—03; group v.p. govt. & cmty. rels. Ford Motor Co., Dearborn, Mich., 2004—. Bd. mem. Alliance of Automobile Manufacturers, Arab-Am. Mus. Adv. Bd., Arab-Am. Ctr. for Econ. & Social Services, Fabretto Children's Found., Henry Ford Learning Inst., NAM; del. World Econ. Forum's Young Global Leaders; bd. mem. Mich. Manufacturers Assn., Washington Ctr. for Internships. Republican. Office: Ford Motor Co 1 American Rd Dearborn MI 48126

OJEDA EISELEY, JAIME DE, former Spanish ambassador, educator; b. Aug. 5, 1933; BL maxima cum laude in Law, U. Madrid, Spain, 1957; grad., Internat. Acad. of The Hague, The Netherlands; student, Naval War Coll. and Sr. Ctr. for Nat. Def. Studies, Madrid, Spain. Prof. polit. law Complutense U. Madrid, Spain, 1958; joined diplomatic svcs., 1958; served Embassy of Spain, Washington, 1962—69; min. counselor Peking, China, 1973—76; consul-gen. of Spain Hong Kong and Macao, 1976-79; fellow Ctr. Internat. Rels., Harvard U., Cambridge, Mass., 1979-80; dep. permanent rep. NATO, 1982-83, permanent rep., 1983-90; amb. to U.S.A., Spanish Embassy, Washington, 1990-97; pres. high level coun. fgn. affairs Min. F.A. Madrid, 1997. Vis. scholar Johns Hopkins U., Washington, 1997; amb.-in-residence Shenandoah U., Winchester, Va., 1997—; disting. adj. fellow CSIS, Washington, 1997. Translator: Alice in Wonderland and Through the Looking Glass, by Lewis Carroll, 1971—74, Spain and America: The Past and Future, 1994, El 98 en el Congreso y en la Prensa de los Estados Unidos, 1999. Lt. Reserve Marine Corps. Spanish Navy, 1957. Decorated Great Cross Mil. Merit, Great Cross of Civil Merit, Order of Charles III. Home: PO Box 57 3770 Leeds Manor Rd Markham VA 22643-1817

O'KEEFE, EDWARD FRANKLIN, lawyer; b. SI, NY, June 9, 1937; s. Francis Franklin and Bertha (Hall) O'K.; m. Toni Lynne McGohan; children: Kira Kathleen, Douglas Franklin, Andrew Franklin, Alison Elizabeth, Theadore William, Nigel Francis. AB, U. N.C., 1959; JD, U. Denver, 1961. Bar: Colo. 1962, N.C. 2000. Law clk. Colo. Supreme Ct., Denver, 1962-63; assoc. gen. counsel Hamilton Mgmt. Corp., Denver, 1966-69, sec., 1968-76, v.p. legal, gen. counsel, 1969-76; ptnr. Moye White, Denver, 1976—2006; pvt. practice Southport, NC, 2006—12. Assoc. gen. counsel, sec. ITT Variable Annuity Ins. Co., Denver, 1969, v.p. legal, gen. counsel, 1969-70; sec. Hamilton Funds Inc., Denver, 1968-76 With USNR, 1963—66. Mem. Nat. Assn. Security Dealers (dist. conduct com., chmn. 1976), Colo. Assn. Corporate Counsel (pres. 1974-75) Office Phone: 757-962-4800.

O'KEEFE, EDWARD PETER, bank executive, lawyer; b. 1955; BS in Bus. Adminstrn., U. RI; JD, Fordham U., 1981. Bar: NC, NY, NJ. Pvt. practice, 1981—87; joined Chemical Bank, 1987; atty. real estate, employment and tech. Chase Manhattan Corp.; head global staff support legal functions outside of Germany Deutsche Bank AG; joined Bank of America Corp., Charlotte, NC, 2004, dep. gen. counsel for staff support, sr. privacy exec., global compliance & operational risk exec., dep. gen. counsel, head litig., interim gen. counsel, 2009, gen. counsel, mem. exec. mgmt. team, 2009—. Bd. mem. Mental Health Assn. of Ctrl. Carolinas; mem. Tocqueville Com. United Way of the Carolinas. Mem.: NJ Bar Assn., NY Bar Assn., NC Bar Assn., South Charlotte Soccer Assn. (mem. Oversight Bd.). Office: Bank of America Corp 100 N Tryon St Charlotte NC 28255*

O'KEEFE, PATRICK SHAW, retired manufacturing executive; b. Troy, NY, Dec. 25, 1952; s. John J. and Jennie (Shaw) O'K.; m. Edwina Zylka, June 2, 1979; children: Megan, Caitlin, Patrick Shaw Jr. BS, Canisius Coll., 1975; MBA, Northwestern U., 1981. CPA, N.Y., Ill.; cert. managerial acct. Sr. cons. Price Waterhouse & Co., Buffalo, 1975-79; asst. to pres. Mark Controls Corp., Skokie, Ill., 1981-82, mgr. ops., 1982-83, v.p. sales and mktg., 1983-84, v.p. ops., 1984-85, sr. v.p., 1985-86; chief oper. officer Clayton Mark Inc., Rogers, Ark., 1986-88; gen. mgr., pump accessory group Amtrol, Inc., West Warwick, 1989; pres., CEO Crane Can. (subs. Crane Co.), 1994—96, Huttig Building Products, 1996—97; CEO Zep Mfg., 1997—99; pres., CEO & bd. dirs. Indsl. Distbn. Group, 1999—2001, Watts Water Technologies Inc. (formerly Watts Industries Inc.), 2002—11. Office: Industrial Distribution Group 1575 1 Atlanta Plaza PO Box 1127 Belmont NC 28012-1127

O'KEEFE, SEAN CHARLES, aerospace transportation executive, former academic administrator; b. Monterey, Calif., Jan. 27, 1956; s. Patrick Gordon and Patricia Carlin O'Keefe; m. Laura Jean McCarthy, Oct. 7, 1978; children: Lindsey, Jonathan, Kevin. BA, Loyola U., New Orleans, 1977; MPA, Syracuse U., 1978. Budget analyst US Dept. Def., Washington; profl. staff mem. US Senate Appropriations Com., Washington, 1981—89; staff dir. US Def. Appropriations Subcommittee, Washington; comptr., CFO US Dept. Def., Washington, 1989—92, acting sec. Dept. Navy, 1992—93; asst. to sr. v.p. for rsch., dean grad. sch. Pa. State U., 1993—96, prof. bus. adminstrn. University Park, 1993—96; Louis A. Bantle Prof., business and govt. policy Maxwell Sch. Citizenship and Pub. Affairs, Syracuse U., 1996—2001, endowed chair, 1996—2001; dir., Nat. Security Studies Partnership, Syracuse U. and John Hopkins U., 1996; dep. dir. Office of Mgmt. & Budget, Exec. Office of the Pres., Washington, 2000—01; adminstr. NASA, Washington, 2001—05; chancellor La. State U. and A&M Coll., Baton Rouge, 2005—08; v.p. Washington ops. GE Aviation, Washington, 2008—09; CEO EADS North America, 2009—. Bd. dirs. E. I. du Pont de Nemours & Co., 2005-08, Sensis Corp., 2005-, EADS North America, 2009-; vis. scholar Wolfson Coll. U. Cambridge. Co-author: The Defense Industry in Post Cold War Era: Corporate Strategies and Public Policy Perspectives, 1998, Keeping the Edge: Managing Defense for the Future, 2000; contbr. articles to profl. jours.; chpts. to books. Staff rep. platform com. Rep. Nat. Com., New Orleans, 1988, advisor, Washington, 1994-97, mem. bd. adv. Naval Postgraduate Sch. Recipient Disting. Pub. Svc. award, US Dept. Def., 1993, Chancellor's award for Pub. Svc., Syracuse U., 1999, Pub. Svc. award, Dept. Navy, 2000, Navigator award, Potomac Inst. for Policy Studies, 2005, Honorary Engr. of the Yr. award, Engrs. Coun., 2005; named one of The Top 100 Irish Americans, Irish American Mag., 2003—04, The Stars of the South, 2006; named to, The La. Polit. Hall of Fame, 2007. Fellow Nat. Acad. Pub. Adminstrn., Internat. Acad. Astronautics; mem. Ft. Ticonderoga Assn., Cavalry

Club. Republican. Roman Catholic. Avocations: golf, fishing. Office: EADS North America 1616 N Ft Meyer Dr Ste 1600 Arlington VA 22209 Office Phone: 703-236-3300.

O'KELLEY, WILLIAM CLARK, federal judge; b. Atlanta, Jan. 2, 1930; s. Ezra Clark and Theo (Johnson) O'K.; m. Ernestine Allen, Mar. 28, 1953; children: Virginia Leigh O'Kelley Wood, William Clark Jr. AB, Emory U., 1951, LLB, 1953. Bar: Ga. 1952. Pvt. practice atty., Atlanta, 1957—59; asst. US atty. US Atty.'s Office (no. dist.) Ga., 1959-61; ptnr. O'Kelley, Hopkins & Van Gerpen, Atlanta, 1961-70; judge US Dist. Ct. (no. dist.) Ga., Atlanta, 1970—88, 1994—96, chief judge, 1988—94, sr. judge, 1996—. Mem. com. on adminstrn. of criminal law Jud. Conf. U.S., 1979-82, exec. com., 1983-84, subcom. on jury trials in complex criminal cases, 1981-82, dist. judge rep. 11th cir., 1981-84, mem. adv. com. of fed. rules of criminal procedure, 1984-87; bd. dirs. Fed. Jud. Ctr., 1987-91, adv. com. history program, 1989-91, com. on orientation of newly appointed dist. judges, 1985-88; mem. Com. Jud. Resources, 1989-94; mem. Jud. Coun. 11th Cir., 1990-96, exec. com., 1990-96; mem. Fgn. Intelligence Surveillance Ct., 1980-87; mem. Alien Terrorist Removal Ct., 1996—; corp. sec., dir. Gwinnett Bank & Trust Co., Norcross, Ga., 1967-70. Mem. exec. com., gen. counsel Ga. Republican Com., 1968-70; mem. fin. com. Northwest Ga. Girl Scout Coun., 1958-70; trustee Emory U., 1991-97, mem. fin. com., 1994-2007; mem. Emeritus Adv. Com. to pres. and chmn. bd., 2008-. Served as 1st lt. USAF, 1953-57; capt. USAFR. Mem. Fed. Bar Assn., Ga. State Bar, Atlanta Bar Assn., Dist. Judges Assn. 5th Cir. (sec.-treas. 1976-77, v.p. 1977-78, pres. 1978-80), Lawyers Club Atlanta, Kiwanis (past pres.), Atlanta Athletic Club, Sigma Chi (named Significant Sig 1983), Phi Delta Phi, Omicron Delta Kappa. Baptist. Home: 550 Ridgecrest Dr Norcross GA 30071-2158 Office: US Dist Ct 1942 US Courthouse 75 Spring St SW Atlanta GA 30303-3309 Office Phone: 404-215-1530.

OKUN, NEIL JEFFREY, vitreoretinal surgeon; b. St. Louis, Nov. 21, 1957; s. Edward and Barbara J. (Braham) O.; m. Joan A. Sosnoff, May 19, 1984; children: David E., Sarah E. AB, Dartmouth Coll., 1980; MD, Washington U., 1984. Diplomate Am. Bd. Ophthalmology. Intern internal medicine Jewish Hosp. at Washington U., St. Louis, 1984-85; resident ophthalmology Washington U. Med. Ctr., St. Louis, 1985-88; fellow vitreoretinal Retina Cons., Ltd., Washington U., St. Louis, 1988-89; vitreoretinal surgeon Fla. Retina Inst., Jacksonville, Fla., 1990-91, Retina Assocs. Ctrl. Fla., Orlando, 1991—2004, Ctrl. Fla. Retina, Orlando, 2004—08, Eye Specialists Mid-Fla., Winter Haven, Fla., 2008—. Instr. dept. ophthalmology Washington U. Sch. Medicine, St. Louis, 1988-89; clin. asst. prof. dept. ophthalmology U. South Fla., Tampa, 1992—; chmn. dept. ophthalmology Fla. Hosp. Orlando, 1996-97 Recipient Upjohn Achievement award for endocrinology and metabolism Washington U. Sch. Medicine, St. Louis, 1984. Fellow ACS, Am. Acad. Ophthalmology; mem. AMA (Physicians's Recognition award for continuing med. edn. 1992—), Am. Soc. Retina Specialists, Assn. for Rsch. in Vision and Ophthalmology, Fla. Med. Assn., Fla. Soc. Ophthalmology, Ctrl. Fla. Soc. Ophthalmology, Polk County Med. Soc., Vitreous Soc., Paul Cibis Club. Avocations: music, art. Office: Eye Specialists Mid-Fla 407 Ave K SE Winter Haven FL 33880 Office Phone: 863-294-3504.

OLAJUWON, HAKEEM ABDUL, retired professional basketball player; b. Lagos, Nigeria, Jan. 21, 1963; s. Salaam and Abike Olajuwon. Student, U. Houston, 1980—84. Ctr. Houston Rockets, 1984—2001, Toronto Raptors, 2001—02; ret. NBA, 2002; co-founder Islamic Da'wah Ctr., Houston, 2002—. Named 1st Team All-NBA, 1987—89, 1993—94, 1st Team All-Def., NBA, 1987—88, 1990, 1993—94, NBA MVP, 1994, NBA Defensive Player of Yr., 1993, 1994, NBA Finals MVP, 1994, 1995; named to 1st Team All-American, Sporting News, 1984, NBA All-Rookie Team, 1985, We. Conf. All-Star Team, NBA, 1985—90, 1992—97, Naismith Meml. Basketball Hall of Fame, 2008. Achievements include member of NBA Finals championship winning Houston Rockets, 1994, 1995. Office: Islamic Da'wah Ctr 201 Travis at Franklin Houston TX 77002

OLDER, JAY JUSTIN, ophthalmic plastic surgeon; b. Jersey City, Feb. 7, 1940; m. Lois Rosner; children: Benjamin, Jessica. AB, Rutgers U., 1961; MD, Stanford U., 1966. Diplomate Am. Bd. Ophthalmology. Intern, resident in internal medicine Cornell U./Bellevue Hosp. Ctr., NYC, 1968; resident in ophthalmology Stanford (Calif.) U., 1973; fellow in ophthalmic plastic and reconstructive surgery Stanford U., San Francisco, 1974; pvt. practice Tampa, Fla., 1974—. Clin. prof. ophthalmology U. South Fla. Coll. Medicine, Tampa, 1975—, dir. oculoplastic svc., 1974—99. Author: Eyelid Tumors: Clinical Diagnosis and Surgical Treatment, 1987, 2d edit., 2003. Fellow Am. Acad. Ophthalmology (Sr. Honor award 1995), Am. Soc. Ophthalmic Plastic and Reconstructive Surgery (pres. 1987, sec. 1983-84), ACS; mem. Phi Beta Kappa (v.p. Greater Tampa Bay Assn. 1995-96). Office: Older & Slonim Eyelid Inst 4444 E Fletcher Ave Ste D Tampa FL 33613-4937 Home: 16631 Sedona De Avil Tampa FL 33613

OLDHAM, DARIUS DUDLEY, lawyer; b. Beaumont, Tex., July 6, 1941; s. Darius Saran and Mary Francis (Carraway) O.; m. Judy J. White, Jan. 23, 1965; children: Steven, Michael BA, U. Tex., Austin, 1964; JD, U. Tex., 1966. Bar: Tex. 1966, U.S. Dist. Ct. (so., no., ea. and we. dists.) Tex. 1966, U.S. Supreme Ct. 1974, U.S. Ct. Appeals (3rd, 5th and 11th cirs.) 1968; cert. arbitrator and mediator. Assoc. Fulbright & Jaworski, Houston, 1966—74, ptnr., 1974—2006, of counsel/ret. ptnr., 2007—, mem. exec. and policy com., 1980—2004, mem. former chair litigation mgmt. com., 1998—2004; mem. adv. coun. UT Med. Sch. Mem. faculty grad. litigation program U. Houston; former mem. adv. com. Nat. Ctr. State Cts.; mem. chancellors coun. exec. com. U. Tex.; lectr. in field. Former mem. bd. editors Aviation Litigation Reporter, Personal Injury Def. Reporter, Internat. Ins. Law Rev.; contbr. articles to profl. jours. Former mem. adv. coun. Nat. Jud. Coll., 2009—; chair adv. coun. Inst. Molecular Medicine, U. Tex. Health Sci. Ctr.; life mem. Liberal Arts Adv. Coun., U. Tex.; past bd. dirs. FDCC Found., Houston Pops Orch. Fellow Am. Coll. Trial Lawyers (chair complex litigation and judiciary com.), Tex. Bar Found. (life), Am. Bar Found. (life), Houston Bar Found. (life), Am. Bd. Trial Advs. (pres. Houston chpt. 1999); mem. ABA (mem. ho. of dels. 1996-98, chair tort and ins. practice sect. 1994-95, mem. coun. tort and ins. practice sect. 1988-98, presdl. emissary 1993-95, chmn. Standing Com. on Independence of the Judiciary 2001-04, chmn. Select Commn. on Jud. Campaign Fin. 2000-01, standing com. fed. jud. improvements, chmn. John Marshall award selection com. 2004-05), U. Tex. Law Sch. Alumni Assn. Exec. Com., 2003—09, Tex. Bar Assn. (chmn. liaison fed. jud. com. 1989-90, pattern jury charges Vol. IV com. 1988-92), Tex. Young Lawyers Assn. (bd. dirs., chmn.), Fed. Def. and Corp. Counsel (pres. 1989-90, chmn. bd. 1990-91, exec. com. 1988-91), Tex. Assn. Def. Counsel, Maritime Law Assn. U.S., Am. Counsel Assn. (bd. dirs. 1982-83, 89-94), Def. Rsch. Inst. (chmn. aerospace com. 1984-87, Presdl. Achievement award 1987, bd. dirs. 1989-92, exec. com. 1991-92), Lawyers for Civil Justice (bd. dirs. 1988-98, chmn. 1998, exec. com. 1990-98, pres. 1997), Nat. Ctr. for State Cts. Lawyers Commn., U. Tex. Health Sci. Ctr. (chair adv. coun., Inst. Molecular Medicine), River Oaks Country Club, Sigma Chi (Significant Sig), Phi Delta Phi., Warren Burger Soc. Office: Norton Rose Fulbright 1301 Mckinney St 51st Fl Houston TX 77010-3031 Home Phone: 713-465-5804; Office Phone: 713-651-5397. Personal E-mail: dudley.oldham@nortonrosefulbright.com.

OLDHAM, JOHN MICHAEL, physician, psychiatrist, educator; b. Muskogee, Okla., Sept. 6, 1940; s. Henry Newland and Alice Gray (Ewton) O.; m. Karen Joan Pacella, Apr. 24, 1971; children: Madeleine Marie, Michael Clark. BS in Engring., Duke U., 1962; MS in Neuroendocrinology, Baylor U., 1966, MD, 1967. Licensed physician NY, SC, Tex.; diplomate in psychiat. and forensic psychiatry Am. Bd. Psychiatry and Neurology; cert. Am. Psychoanalytic Assn. Intern pediatrics St. Luke's Hosp., NYC, 1967-68; resident psychiat. Columbia U. Dept. Psychiat., N.Y.S. Psychiatric Inst., NYC, 1968-70; chief resident in psychiatry Columbia U., NY State Psychiat. Inst., 1970-71; grad. Columbia Psychoanalytic Ctr., NYC, 1977; dir. psychiatric emergency svcs. Roosevelt Hosp., NYC, 1973-74, dir. residency tng. dept. psychiat., 1974-77; dir. short term diagnostic and treatment unit NY Hosp. Westchester Divsn., White Plains, NY, 1977-80, dir. divsn. acute treatment svcs., 1980-84; deputy dir. NY State Psychiatric Inst., NYC, 1984-89, acting dir., 1989-90, dir., 1990—2002; assoc. chmn. dept. psychiatry Columbia U. Coll. Physicians & Surgeons, NYC, 1986-96, vice chmn., 1996-2000, acting chmn., 2000—02; chief med. officer NY State Office Mental Health, Albany, 1989—2002; prof. psychiatry Med. U. SC, 2002—07, chmn. dept. psychiatry and behavioral sci., 2002—07, exec. dir. Inst. Psychiatry, 2002—07; sr. v.p., chief of staff The Menninger Clinic, 2007—; prof., exec. vice chmn. Menninger dept. psychiatry & behavioral scis. Baylor Coll., 2007; pres. Am. Coll. Psychiatrists, 2009—10, 2011—12, Am. Psychiat. Assn., 2010—12. From instr. clin. psychiatry to prof. clin. psychiatry Columbia U. Coll. P&S, 1974-96, 1988-96, Elizabeth K. Dollard profl clin. psychiatry medicine and law, 1996-2002; asst. prof. psychiatry Cornell U. Med. Coll., NYC, 1977-83, assoc. prof. clin. psychiatry, 1983-84; attending staff dept. psychiatry Roosevelt Hosp., NYC, 1973-77; assoc. attending in psychiatry, NY Hosp., 1977-84, Presbyn Hosp., NYC, 1984-88, attending in psychiatry, 1988-2002; tng. and supervising psychoanalyst Columbia Psychoanalytic Ctr., NYC, 1983-2002; coord. med. student edn., dept. psychiatry Cornell U. Med. Coll., Westchester Divsn., White Plains, NY, 1977-84; coord. clin. clerkships in psychiatry Roosevelt Hosp., Columbia U. Coll. P&S, NYC, 1974-77; spl. adv. bd. Freedom From Fear, Inc.; examiner Am. Bd. Psychiatry and Neurology; chmn. acute divsn. rsch. group, Westchester Divsn., NY Hosp., 1981-84, co-project dir. borderline rsch. group, 1982-84, co-prin. investigator familial transmission DSM III personality disorders, 1982-84; prin. investigator personality disorders in bulimia, NYS. Psychiat. Inst., 1985-90, structured DSM III assessment psychoanalytic patients, Columbia Psychoanalytic Ctr., 1986-91; co-prin. investigator validity DSM III R personality disorders, NY State Psychiat. Inst., 1987-94; co-investigator NIMH, 1996-2002; Hall-Mercer vis. scholar, dept. psychiatry, U. Pa., 2004; Judge Bernard Thompson Meml. Lectr., dept. psychiatry, North Shore U. Hosp., 2004; Albert M. Biele MD vis. prof. in psychiatry, Jefferson Med. Coll., 2005; Wolfe-Adler Lectr., SHeppard Pratt Health Sys., 2006; Ferald R. Klerman MD Meml. Lectr., Payne Whitney Clinic, NYC, 2007; Stanton lectr., McLean Hosp., Harvard Med. Sch., 2008; Frederick Weniger MD lectr., Western Psychiat. Inst. & Clinic, U. Pittsburgh Med. Ctr., 2011; vis. prof. Pub. Psychiatry, Dept. Psychiatry, U. SC, 2011. Author: (with L.B. Morris) The Personality Self-Portrait, 1990; editor Jour. Psychia. Practice; editor bd. Jour. Personality Disorders; dep. editor Am. Psychiat. Pub., Inc.; reviewer Arch Gen. Psychiatry, Am. Jour. Psychiatry, Psychiat. Svcs.; contbr. numerous articles to profl. jours.; presentations in field. Major USAF, 1971—73. Recipient John J. Weber prize Excellence in Psychoanalytic Rsch. Columbia Psychoanalytic Ctr., 1990, Dorothea Dix Award Mental Illness Found., 1996, Spl. Comm.'s award NY State Office Mental Health, 1997, Spl. Presdl. commendation Am. Psychiat. Assn., 1999, 2005, Payne Whitney Clin. award for Extraordinary Pub. Svc., 2002; Spl. Citation conferred by Governor George E. Pataki, State of NY, 2002; Paul Hoch award for Disting. Leadership, NY State Office Mental Health, 2002, Annual award The Borderline Personality Disorder Resource Ctr., NY Presbyn. Hosp., 2007; Ed Hornick Meml. Lectr. award, NY Acad. Medicine, 2010; Exemplary Psychiatrist award, Nat. Alliance on Mental Illness, 2010; Assembly Spkrs. award, Am. Psychiat. Assn., 2012; Psychiat. Excellence award, Tex. Soc. Psychiat. Physicians, 2012. Fellow Am. Coll. Psychiatrists (pres. 2010-, Bowis award 2007), Am. Psychiat. Assn. (pres. NY County dist. br., 1989-90, com. rsch. psychiat. treatment 1987-93, coun. rsch., steering com. practice guidelines, chmn. sci. program com. 1992-95, chmn. com. quality indicators 1999-2003, chmn. coun. quality care 2003—06, pres. elect 2010-2011, pres. 2011-2012.), Am. Psychopath. Assn., NY Acad. Medicine; mem. AMA, Am. Psychoanalytic Assn. (cert.), Assn. Psychoanalytic Medicine (pres. 1989-91), Internat. Psychoanalytical Assn., NY Acad. Sci., Assn. Rsch. Personality Disorders (bd. dirs.), Internat. Soc. for Study of Personality Disorders (pres. 2000—03), SC Psychiat. Assn. (pres. 2006-07), Houston Psychiatric Soc. Office: Menninger Clinic 12301 Main St Houston TX 77035 Office Phone: 713-275-5016. Office Fax: 713-275-5117. Business E-Mail: joldham@menninger.edu.

O'LEARY, GEORGE JOSEPH, college football coach; b. Ctrl. Islip, NY, Aug. 17, 1946; m. Sharon Littlefield; children: Chris, Tim, Trish, Marty. BS in Phys. Edn., U. NH, Durham, 1968. Asst. coach Ctrl. Islip HS, 1968-76; head coach Liverpool HS, NY, 1977-79; asst. head coach, defensive line coach Syracuse U. Orange, 1980-86; defensive coord. Ga. Inst. Tech. Yellow Jackets, 1987-91, head football coach, 1994—2001; defensive line coach San Diego Chargers, 1992-93; defensive coord. Minn. Vikings, 2002—04; head football coach U. Ctrl. Fla. Knights, 2004—. Recipient Bobby Dodd Coach of Yr. award, Bobby Dodd Found., 2000; named Atlantic Coast Conf. Coach of Yr., 1998, 2000, Conf. USA Coach of Yr., 2005, 2007, 2010, American Athletic Conf. Coach of Yr., 2013. Office: University Ctrl Fla Football c/o UCF Athletics Assn Inc 4000 Central Florida Blvd Orlando FL 32816-3555 Office Phone: 407-823-5397.*

O'LEARY, HAZEL ROLLINS, academic administrator, former United States Secretary of Energy, lawyer; b. Newport News, Va., May 17, 1937; d. Russell E. and Hazel (Palleman) Reid; m. John F. O'Leary, Apr. 23, 1980 (dec. Dec. 19, 1987); 1 child, Carl G. Rollins. BA, Fisk U., Nashville, 1959; JD, Rutgers U., Newark, 1966. Bar: NJ 1967, DC 1985; cert. fin. planner. V.p., gen. counsel O'Leary & Associates, Inc., Washington, 1981-89, pres. Chevy Chase, Md., 1997—; exec. v.p. corp. affairs No. States Power Co., Mpls., 1989-93; adminstr., dep. adminstr. econ. regulatory commn. US Dept. Energy, Washington, 1977—81, sec., 1993-97; COO Blaylock & Partners LLP, NYC, 1997—2002; pres. Fisk U., 2004—. Trustee AES Copr., ICF Kaiser, Inc. Trustee Morehouse Coll., Africare, Ctr. Democracy, Keystone Ctr. Mem. Phi Beta Kappa. Office: Fisk U 1000 17th Ave N Nashville TN 37208-3051 Office Phone: 615-329-8555.

O'LEARY, PATRICK J., manufacturing executive; BS in Acctg. and Law, U. Southampton, England. From acct. to ptnr. Boston (Mass.) Office Deloitte & Touche, 1978—88, ptnr. Boston (Mass.) Office, 1988—94; CFO, dir. Carlisle Plastics, Inc., 1994—96; v.p. fin., treasurer, CFO SPX Corp., Charlotte, NC, 1996—2004, exec. v.p., CFO, 2004—. Bd. dir. Pulte Homes Inc. Office: SPX 13320 Ballantyne Corporate Pl Charlotte NC 28277-3607

O'LEARY, ROBERT C., publishing and media executive; BA magna cum laude, Boston Coll., MBA. Fin. & mgmt. positions GE; v.p. fin. Cox Cable Comm., 1982, sr. v.p. fin., 1982—86, sr. v.p. fin. & adminstrn., 1986—89, sr. v.p. ops., 1989—96; sr. v.p., CFO Cox Enterprises Inc., Atlanta, 1996—99, exec. v.p., CFO, 1999—. Vice-chmn. Ga. Chpt. Nat. Multiple Sclerosis Soc.; trustee Woodruff Arts Ctr., Atlanta. Named to Boston Coll. Athletic Hall of Fame. Office: Cox Enterprises Inc PO Box 105357 Atlanta GA 30348-5357

OLENCHAK, FRANK RICHARD, retired music educator, musician; b. Scranton, Pa., Aug. 5, 1928; s. Francis Richard and Helen Anita Olenchak; m. Patricia Maye Ingram, June 15, 1949; children: Francis Richard III, Rebecca Lynn, Jeffrey Stuart. MusB, James Madison U., 1950; MEd, Pa. State U., 1957; CASE, PhD candidate, Johns Hopkins U., 1965; PhD in Music: Music Edn., U. Mich., 1977. Cert. music tchr. Md., Va. Supr. of music, band dir. Galax Pub. Schs., Va., 1950—54; dir. h.s. band Harford County Schs., Bel Air, Md., 1954—58, Balt. City Schs., 1958—61; tchr. elem. instrumental music Balt. County Schs., Towson, Md., 1961—66; emeritus prof. edn. and profl. devel. We. Mich. U., Kalamazoo, 1966—84; adj. coord. student tchg. Ea. Mich. U., Ypsilanti, 1984—85; dir., CEO Music on the Move of Mich., Ann Arbor, 1985—87; chair dept. of music Allen U., Columbia, SC, 1989—2005, ret., 2005; CEO, record prodr. Myrtle Records, Columbia, 1997—. Postdoctoral rschr. Columbia U., 1981; vis. scholar U. Mich., Ann Arbor, 1981—82. Editor: (newsletter) Michigan Association of Teacher Educators; author: (exploratory music) The Instructor, 1968; editor: (books) SchoolMATES, 3 vols., 1981, 1982. Choir dir. Trinity Luth. Ch., Columbia, 1999—2002; dir. of music 3d Luth. Ch., Balt., 1960—62. Recipient doctoral tchg. fellowship, U. of Mich., 1969—70, acad. scholarship, Shenandoah Conservatory of Music, 1947. Mem.: Am. Fedn. Musicians (life), Assn. Tchr. Educators (life; pres., comms. chair 1978—83, Meritorious Svc. award 1980), Phi Delta Kappa (life; pres. 1978—87, 1991—94, Disting. Svc. Key 1985). Achievements include creating NUMCOMPO, a system for teaching musical notation to children with no prior knowledge of music. Avocations: sports, bridge, checkers, record collecting, travel. Personal E-mail: myrtrec@hotmail.com.

OLENS, SAMUEL SCOTT, state attorney general; b. Miami, Fla., July 8, 1957; s. Louis and Gertrude (Kramer) O.; m. Lisa Zellinger; children: Lauren Tracy, Jonathan William. BA, Am. U., 1978, MA, 1980; JD, Emory U., 1983. Bar: Ga. 1983, DC 1986, US Supreme Ct. 1987, US Ct. Appeals (11th cir.) 1983, US Dist. Ct. (no. dist.) Ga. 1983. Ptnr. Olens & Ezor (formerly Rand, Ezor & Olens), Atlanta, 1983—2010; atty. gen. State of Ga., 2011—. Treas. East Cobb Civic Assn., 1991-93, past pres.; mem. Leadership Cobb, 1995-96; mem. bd. Cobb County PAL; mem. Cobb County Housing Authority; mem. Dist. 3 Cobb County Bd. Commissioners., 1999-2002, chmn. 2002-10, Atlanta Regional Commn., 2004-09; rep. 6th Congl. dist. Ga. Dept. Cmty. Affairs Bd., 2003-10; vice chmn. Met. North Ga. Water Planning Dist., 2005-10. Mem. ABA, ATLA, Ga. Trial Lawyers Assn., Atlanta Bar Assn., Cobb County Bar Assn., Cobb County C. of C. Republican. Office: Office of the Attorney General 40 Capitol Square SW Atlanta GA 30334-1300 Office Phone: 404-656-3300. Office Fax: 404-657-8733.*

OLIKER, VLADIMIR, mathematician, educator; b. Ulianovsk, Russia, Oct. 7, 1945; came to U.S. 1975, naturalized 1980; s. Yosef and Sonia (Bakelman) Oliker; m. Elena Matis, Mar. 20, 1969; children: Olga, Aviva, Yosef Matis. MS, Leningrad U., Russia, 1967; PhD, Leningrad U., 1971. Sr. researcher Hydrometeorological Inst., Leningrad, Russia, 1970-72; group leader Dept. Transportation, 1972-74; vis. prof. Temple U., Phila., 1975-77; assoc. prof. to prof. U. Iowa, Iowa City, 1977-80, 80-84; prof. math. Emory U., Atlanta, 1984—. Vis. mem. Math Scis. Research Inst., Berkeley, Calif., 1983; vis. prof. U. Florence, Italy, 1983, Technische U., Berlin, 1982, U. Heidelberg, Fed. Republic Germany, 1981 Contbr. articles to profl. jours. Jewish. Home: 1565 Adelia Pl NE Atlanta GA 30329-3805 Office: Emory U Dept Math And Computer Sci Atlanta GA 30322-0001 Business E-Mail: oliker@mathcs.emory.edu.

OLIN, MARILYN, secondary school educator; b. Rochester, NY; BA in English, Nazareth Coll. Rochester, 1965; MS in English Edn., SUNY, Brockport, 1971. Nat. bd. cert. tchr. 1999. Tchr. Rochester Diocese Cath. Schs., 1965—68, Rochester Pub. Schs., 1968—71, Duval County (Fla.) Pub. Schs., 1972—, Paxon Sch. for Advanced Studies, Jacksonville, Fla., 1996—. Mem.: Nat. Forensic League, Nat. Bd. for Profl. Tchg. Stds. Office: Paxon Sch for Advanced Studies 3239 Norman E Thagard Blvd Jacksonville FL 32254 Office Phone: 904-693-7583 ext 161.

OLIN, ROBERT FLOYD, mathematician educator, administrator, researcher; b. Evanston, Ill., Oct. 8, 1948; s. Floyd Thomas and Anne Elanor (Knutson) O.; children: Kristopher Robert, Susan Michelle. BSc, Ottawa U., 1970; PhD, Ind. U., 1975. Asst. prof. math. Va. Poly. Inst. and State U., Blacksburg, 1975-80, assoc. prof., 1980-87, prof., 1987-2000, dept. head, 1994-2000; prof. math., dean arts and scis. U. Ala., Tuscaloosa, 2000—. Vis. assoc. prof. Ind. U., Bloomington, 1985; Virginia B. Smith Innovation Leadership Award, 2002; rschr. NSF, 1975-94, grad. chmn., 1993-94, Dept. of Energy, 1997-2001, Eisenhower, 1997-2001; chmn. rsch. commn., 1993-94. Co-author: A Functional Calculus for Subnormal Operators II, 1977, Subnormal Operators, and Representations of Bounded Analytic Functions and Other Uniform Algebras, 1985. Pres. Southwestern Va. Soccer Assn., Blacksburg, 1989-90; tchr. Sunday Sch. Blacksburg Bapt. Ch., 1983-99; treas. Margaret Beeks PTA, 1993-95; chmn. steering com. Southeastern Analysis Meeting, 1984-89. Named Hon. Faculty Mem., Sichuan U., Chengdu, China, 1988; recipient cert. Math. Edn. Devel. Ctr., Ind. U., Bloomington, 1976. Mem. Coun. Coll. of Arts and Scis., Am. Coun. Edn., N.Y. Acad. Scis., Va. Acad. Scis., Am. Math. Soc. (chmn. com. on sci. 2005—, mem. edn. com. 2005—), Math. Assn. Am., Nat. Coun. Tchrs. Math., Coun. Undergrad Rsch., Am. Assn. Higher Edn., Tuscaloosa (Ala.) C. of C., Rotary, Sigma Xi, Pi Mu Epsilon. Avocations: racquetball, cooking, computers, soccer. Office: U Ala Coll Arts & Scis Box 870268 Tuscaloosa AL 35487-0268 Home: 1337 Greystone Dr Tuscaloosa AL 35406-2697 Home Phone: 205-247-7799; Office Phone: 205-348-5972. Business E-Mail: olin@as.ua.edu.

OLIVA, JOSE, state legislator; b. Elizabeth, NJ, Jan. 6, 1973; m. Jeanne Oliva; children: Benjamin, Sabrina, Celeste. Attended, St. Thomas U., Miami, Fla., 1993—94. CEO Oliva Cigar Co.; mem. Dist. 110 Fla. House of Reps., Tallahassee, 2011—. Mem. Census Bd. Hialeah, 0199; commr. Hialeah Housing Commn., 2001—05; dir. Cuban Liberty Coun. Mem.: Kiwanis Club. Republican. Roman Catholic. Office: 3798 W 12th Ave Ste A Hialeah FL 33012-4126 also: Fla House of Reps 1301 The Capitol 402 S Monroe St Tallahassee FL 32399-1300 Office Phone: 305-364-3114, 850-487-2197.

OLIVEIRA, RENE ORLANDO, state legislator; b. Brownsville, Tex., Mar. 14, 1955; s. Antonio and Gloria Gonzalez Oliveira; m. Katherine Sunde, 1982; 1 child, Rene Orlando Jr. Ptnr. Wiech, Black, Fleming, Hamilton, Roerig, Oliveira & Fisher, 1979—; chmn. Cameron County Dem. Com., Tex., 1980—81; mem. Dist. 39 Tex. House of Representatives, 1989—90, mem. Dist. 37, 1981—85, 1991—.

Recipient Russell Long award, Disting. Svc. award, Tex. Southmost Coll., 1982, Rex Braun award, 1983; named Citizen of Week, KGBT-TV, 1981, KELT Radio, 1981. Mem.: Tex. County Chmn. Assn., Assn. Immigration & Nationality Lawyers, Tex. Criminal Def. Lawyers Assn., Cameron County Bar Assn., Am. Bar Assn., Sierra Club Internat. Democrat. Roman Catholic. Office: 855 W Price Rd Ste 22 Brownsville TX 78520 also: Room CAP 3N.06 Capitol PO Box 2910 Austin TX 78768 Office Phone: 956-542-1828, 512-463-0640.

OLIVER, GARY J., psychologist, educator; b. Great Falls, Mont., Sept. 20, 1947; m.Linda Ellen Motz, April 3, 2010; children: Nathan, Matthew, Andrew. MDiv, Talbot Sem, 1974; ThM, Fuller Sem., 1977; MA, U. Nebr., 1980, PhD, 1984. Cert. clin. psychology, Nebr., Colo., Ark. Sr. staff psychologist Lincoln Family Med. Group, Nebr., 1984—86; clin. dir. SW Counseling Assocs., Littleton, Colo., 1986—98; exec. dir., prof. psychology and practical theology The Ctr. for Relationship Enrichment, John Brown U., Siloam Springs, Ark., 1998—. Acad. dir., prof. Denver Sem., 1998-2010; sr. fellow Coun. Christian Colls. and Univs., 1999-2007. Co-author: (with Carrie Oliver) Raising Sons...And Loving It!, 2000, Mad About Us, 2007, A Woman's Forbidden Emotion, 2005; author: Fears, Doubts, Blues & Pouts, 1999, Real Men Have Feelings Too, 1993; editor Marriage and Family Christian Jour.; contbr. over 300 articles to profl. jours. and popular mags. Mem. APA, ACA, Am. Assn. Christian Counselors (bd. mem.), Am. Assn. for Marriage and Family Therapy, Assn. for Psychol. Type, Nat. Coun. on Family Rels., Christian Assn. for Psychol. Studies, Ctr. Relationship Enrichment. Achievements include Dr. Gary J. Oliver endowed chair for marriage family & relationship studies. Office: Ctr for Relationship Enrichment John Brown Univ 2000 W University St Siloam Springs AR 72761-2112 Office Phone: 479-524-7105. Business E-Mail: cre@jbu.edu, goliver@jbu.edu.*

OLIVER, GEORGIANNA WHITE, technology consulting company executive; b. Tulsa, Okla., Sept. 14, 1966; m. Jack Oliver; 1 adopted child, Teddy. BS in Polit. Sci., Okla. State U. Legis. asst. US House Ways and Means Com., 1991; with The Nat. Affordable Housing Mgmt. Assn.; v.p. for real estate mgmt. firm; founder, CEO Evergreen Solutions, Washington, DC, 2000—. Gov. Okla. Intercollegiate Legislature; congl. aide Congressman Bill K. Brewster. Mem.: Vistage. Democrat. Methodist. Office: 1325 E 15th St Ste 205 Tulsa OK 74120 Office Phone: 918-585-8886. Office Fax: 918-585-8889. Personal E-mail: gwoliver2008@gmail.com. Business E-Mail: info@oliverforuscongress.com.

OLIVER, HARRY MAYNARD, JR., retired brokerage house executive; b. Kansas City, Mo., Jan. 21, 1921; s. Harry Maynard and Marie (Curtin) O. BA, Williams Coll., 1943. Pres. M.A. Gesner & Co., Marsh & McLennan Co., Chgo., 1947-88. Chmn. Chgo. Commn. for Sr. Citizens, 1960-69; mem. Chgo. Bd. Edn., 1966-69; pres. Vol. Agys. Chgo., 1956-86; mem. vis. com. Sch. Edn. and div. of social scis., U. Chgo.; pres., bd. dirs. Benton House Settlement, 1953-58; bd. dirs. Adult Edn. Council Greater Chgo., Nat. Fedn. Settlements and Community Centers, 1961-67; trustee Old Peoples Home Chgo., Pub. Sch. Tchrs. Pension and Retirement Fund Chgo., 1966-69, George M. Pullman Ednl. Found., Field Mus. Natural History, 1971-75. Served to lt. (j.g.) USNR, World War II. Mem. Chgo. Club, Racquet Club, Onwentsia Club (Lake Forest, Ill.), Chi Psi. Home: 1948 N Lincoln Ave Chicago IL 60614-5476 also: PO Box 1319 Big Pine Key FL 33043 also: New Richmond PO Box 100 Fennville MI 49408-0100

OLIVER, MARY, poet; b. Maple Heights, Ohio, Sept. 10, 1935; d. Edward William and Helen Mary (Vlasak) O. Student, Ohio State U., 1955—56, Vassar Coll., 1956—57. Chmn. writing dept. Fine Arts Work Ctr., Provincetown, Mass., 1972-73, mem. writing com., 1984; Banister poet-in-residence Sweet Briar Coll., 1991-95. William Blackburn vis. prof. creative writing Duke U., 1995; Catharine Osgood Foster prof. Bennington Coll., 1996-2001. Author: No Voyage and Other Poems, 1963, enlarged edit., 1965, The River Styx, Ohio, 1972, The Night Traveler, 1978, Twelve Moons, 1979, American Primitive, 1983, Dream Work, 1986, House of Light, 1990, New and Selected Poems, 1992, Vol. 2, 2005, A Poetry Handbook, 1994, White Pine, 1994, Blue Pastures, 1995, West Wind, 1997, Rules for the Dance, 1998, Winter Hours, 1999, The Leaf and the Cloud, 2000, What Do We Know, 2002, Owls and Other Fantasies, 2003, Why I Wake Early, 2004, Long Life, 2004, Blue Iris, 2004, New and Selected Poems, Vol. 2, 2005, Thirst, 2006, Our World, 2007, Red Bird, 2008, the Truro Bear and Other Adventures, 2008, Evidence, 2009, Swan, 2010, A Thousand Mornings, 2012, Dog Songs, 2013; contbr. to Yale U. Rev., Kenyon Rev., Poetry, Atlantic, Harvard mag., others. Recipient Shelley Meml. award, 1970, Alice Fay di Castagnola award, 1973, Cleve. Arts prize for lits., 1979, Achievement award Am. Acad. and Inst. Arts and Letters, 1983, Pulitzer prize for poetry, 1984, Christopher award, 1991, L.L. Winship award, 1991, Nat. Book award, 1992, Lannan award, 1998; Nat. Endowment fellow, 1972-73; Guggenheim fellow, 1980-81. Mem. PEN.

OLIVER, MARY MARGARET, state legislator, lawyer; b. Mar. 7, 1948; Atty., Decatur, Ga.; adminstrn. law judge; assoc. magistrate judge DeKalb County, Ga.; state rep. Dist. 53 Ga., 1987—92; state rep. Dist. 56, 2002—04; state rep. Dist. 83, 2004—; state senator Dist. 42 Ga., 1993—98. Vis. prof., Barton child law and policy clinic Emory U. Sch. Law. Vol. Druid Hills Civic Assn.; Sunday sch. tchr. All Saints Episc. Ch.; bd. mem. Jr. League. Recipient Woman of Achievement award, YWCA; named Legis. of Yr., Garden Club. Mem.: Decatur Rotary. Democrat. Episcopal. Mailing: 150 E Ponce de Leon Ave Suite 350 Decatur GA 30030 Office: Ga Gen Assembly Legis Office Bldg 18 Capitol Sq Ste 604 Atlanta GA 30334 Office Phone: 404-656-0265. Office Fax: 404-656-2634. Business E-Mail: marymargaret.oliver@house.ga.gov.

OLIVER, PATRICIA, lawyer, executive secretary; b. Erie, Pa. m. Jim Oliver; 3 children. BA in Polit. Sci. magna cum laude, Allegheny Coll.; JD, Case Western Res. U., Cleve. Atty., ptnr. Squire, Sanders & Dempsey, Cleve.; corp. sec. BB&T Corp. (Branch Banking and Trust Co.), gen. counsel Winston Salem, NC, 2004—. Founder Women in Family Bus. Seminar Series, Cleve. Pres. Children's Aid Soc. Recipient Rainmaker (community svc.), No. Ohio Live Magazine, 2003, Profl. Woman of Excellence, Cleve. YMCA. Office: BB&T Corp 200 W 2nd St Winston Salem NC 27101 Office Phone: 336-733-2000. Office Fax: 336-721-3499.

OLIVER, ROBERT BRUCE, retired investment company executive; b. Brockton, Mass., Aug. 1, 1931; s. Stanley Thomas and Helen (Sabine) O.; m. Sylvia E. Bell, Feb. 17, 1954; children: Susan Pamela, Robert Bruce. AB, Harvard U., 1953; postgrad., Bus. Sch., 1971, Boston U. Law Sch., 1955-57; MA, Mich. State U., 1958. Ret. chmn., pres., chief exec. officer John Hancock Income Securities Trust, Boston, 1989. Ret. chmn., pres. chief exec. officer John Hancock Investors Trust, John Hancock Bond Trust, John Hancock Growth Trust, John Hancock Tax Exempt Cash Mgmt. Trust, John Hancock Govt. Securities Trust, John Hancock Tax Exempt Income Trust, John Hancock Cash Mgmt. Trust, John Hancock Spl. Equities Trust, John Hancock Global Trust, John Hancock World Trust, John Hancock High Income Trust, John Hancock Tax Exempt Series Trust; chmn., dir. John Hancock Distbrs.; vice chmn., chief exec. officer John Hancock Advisers, Inc.; chmn., mng. dir. John Hancock Advisers Internat. Ltd. 1st lt. USMCR, 1953-55. Home: 9271 SW 29th Ave Gainesville FL 32608 Personal E-mail: gandg811@gmail.com.

OLIVER, SUSAN M., human resources specialist; b. Des Moines, Iowa, July 6, 1947; married; 3 children. BS, George Washington U., 1970; JD, U. Denver, 1980. Atty. Kempell, Huffman and Ginder, 1983—84; asst. counsel Wein Airlines, 1984—85; labor rels. cons. City of Reno, 1985—86; counsel, employee rels. American Airlines, Inc., 1986—90, mng. dir., flight svcs., 1990—96, mng. dir., strategic planning, 1996—97, v.p., employee rels., 1997—2000, sr. v.p., human resources, 2000—04; sr. v.p., human resources & labor Walmart Stores, 2004—08; founder, pres. Katana Ptnrs., 2009—. Office: Katana Partners 17304 Preston Rd Ste 800 Dallas TX 75252 Office Phone: 682-325-4161. Business E-Mail: sue.oliver@katanapartners.com.

OLIVERA, ARMANDO J., electric power industry executive; BS in Electrical Engring., Cornell U.; MBA, U. Miami. Sr. v.p., power sys. FPL Group, Inc., 1999—2003; pres. Florida Power & Light Co., 2003—, CEO, 2008—. Bd. dirs. Nicor Inc. Office: Florida Power & Light Co 700 Universe Blvd Juno Beach FL 33408 Office Phone: 561-694-4000. Business E-Mail: armando_olivera@fpl.com.

OLIVERA, CHRIS, retail executive; Attended, The Coll. William & Mary; BA in English & Comm., The Coll. Santa Fe, 1989. Pub. affairs mgr. & found. dir. Regents of Univ. Calif., 1990—2001; dir., corp. affairs RadioShack Corp., 2001—03; asst. v.p., mng. dir. MWW Group, 2003—05; v.p., corp. comm. and pub. affairs GameStop Corp., 2005—. Office: GameStop Corp 625 Westport Pky Grapevine TX 76051 Office Phone: 817-424-2000. Office Fax: 817-424-2002. Business E-Mail: ChrisOlivera@gamestop.com.

OLIVERI, EUGENE ALFRED, gastroenterologist; b. NYC, Apr. 30, 1937; children: Gregory, Lisa, Michelle. Student, Bklyn. Coll., 1954-56, 58-60; DO summa cum laude, Kansas City Coll., 1964; LHD, U. Health Scis., 2000; MSc, Trinity So. U., 2003; D of Osteopathic Edn., U. New Eng., Biddeford, Maine, 2007. Diplomate Am. Bd. Internal Medicine, Am. Bd. Gastroenterology. Intern Detroit Osteo. Hosp., 1964-65; resident in internal medicine Botsford/Ziegler Hosps., 1965-67; fellowship in gastroenterology VA Hosp., East Orange, NJ, 1967-68; asst. dean Coll. Osteo. Medicine Mich. State U. Prof. dept. internal medicine sect. of gastroenterology Botsford Gen. Hosp., assoc. program dir. gastroenterology residency emeritus; mem., courtesy staff emeritus dept. of internal medicine Huron Valley Hosp. Trustee Pikeville (Ky.) Coll., 1998—2004, U. New Eng., Biddeford, Maine, 2001—. With US Army, 1956—58. Recipient Highest Acad. Achievement award K.C.U. U. Medicine, 1964, Mead-Johnson, 1964, Outstanding Alumni Achievement award U. for Health Scis., Coll. Osteo. Medicine, 1991, Dr. J.O. Watson Disting. Lecr. Ohio Osteo. Assn., 1991, Walter Patenge medal for humanitarian svc. MSU, 1999, Galusha Meml. lectr., 1999, FSMB A.T. Still Meml. Lecture award, AOA, 2009, Phillips medal Pub Svc., Ohio U., 2002; named Physician of Yr. Mich. chpt. Ileitis and Colitis Found., 1985, Botsford Profl. Staff, 1994, Riland medal, Pub. Svc. NYIT, 2011. Fellow Am. Coll. Osteo. Internists (pres. 1982-83, Disting. Svc. award 1982, Disting. Lectr. award 1983, Presdl. Leadership award 2010); fellow Am. Coll. Internists (master); mem. Am. Osteo. Assn. (pres. 1999-2000, trustee mem. bd., Disting. Svc. certificat 2005, pioneer medicine 2008), Mich. Assn. Osteo. Physician and Surgeons (pres. 1991-92), Oakland County Osteo. Assn., Am. Coll. Gastroenterology, Am. Soc. Gastrointestinal Endoscopy, Am. Soc. Addiction Medicine, Am. Osteo. Found. (bd. dirs., past pres. bd. dirs., com. on awards), Mich. Osteo. Coll. Found. (chair, trustee, bd. dirs.), Crohn's and Colitis Found. Am. (Physician of Yr. 1991), Psi Sigma Alpha, Sigma Sigma Phi Med. Honor Fraternities. Avocations: cooking, health policy. Home: 7653 Lexington Club Blvd Apt A Delray Beach FL 33446-3442 Personal E-mail: picooliveri@aol.com.

OLSEN, EDGAR OLIVER, economics professor; b. New Orleans, La., Mar. 13, 1942; s. Edgar Oliver and Georgie Walker (Thompson) Olsen; children: Robert Buckner, Melanie Guerry. BA, Tulane U., 1963; PhD, Rice U., 1968. Postdoctoral fellow Ind. U.-Bloomington, 1967—68; from asst. prof. to assoc. prof. U. Va., Charlottesville, 1970—83, prof., 1983—, chmn. dept. econs., 1993—96. Vis. assoc. prof. econs. U. Wis., Madison, 1975—76, vis. prof., 1982—84; economist Rand Corp., Santa Monica, Calif., 1968—70; vis. scholar HUD, Washington, 1978—79, cons., 1973—2003; bd. editors Am. Econ. Rev., Princeton, NJ, 1985—91; cons. GAO, Washington, 1999—2001; v.p. So. Econ. Assn., 2003—05; bd. dirs. Am. Real Estate and Urban Economics Assn., 1998—2000, 2005—07. Contbr. articles to profl. publs. Congl. Testimony, 2001, 2003, 2006, 2008. Recipient Cert. Spl. Achievement, HUD, 1979; NIH fellow, 1983. Mem.: Am. Real Estate and Urban Econ. Assn., Am. Econ. Assn., Assn. Pub. Policy Analysis and Mgmt., So. Econ. Assn. Home: 1606 Jamestown Dr Charlottesville VA 22901 Office: Univ Va Dept Economics PO Box 400182 Charlottesville VA 22904-4182 Office Phone: 434-924-3443. Business E-Mail: eoo@virginia.edu.

OLSEN, KATHIE LYNN, neuroscientist; b. Portland, Oreg., Aug. 3, 1952; d. Roland Berg and Gladys Elizabeth (Eldreth) O. BS, Chatham Coll., 1974; PhD, U. Calif., Irvine, 1979. Postdoct. fellow Harvard Med. Sch., Boston, 1979-80; rsch. scientist Long Island Rsch. Inst., Stony Brook, N.Y., 1980-83; rsch. asst. prof. SUNY, Stony Brook, 1982-85, asst. prof., 1985-89; assoc. program dir. NSF, Washington, 1984-86, program dir., 1988, leader neurosci., 1991; legis. fellow Brookings Instn., Washington, 1996—97; chief scientist NASA, 1999—2002; acting assoc. adminstr. Enterprise in Biological and Physical Research, 2000—02; assoc. dir. for tech. Office Science & Tech. Policy, Exec. Office of the Pres., Washington, 2002—05; dep. dir. NSF, Arlington, 2005—09, sr. adv., Office Info. & Resource Mgmt., 2009—. Adj. assoc. prof. George Washington U., Washington, 1989—; cons. editor Hormones and Behavior, 1988—. Contbr. articles to profl. jours, chapters to books. Recipient Dir. Superior Accomplishmentaward, NSF, Barry M. Goldwater Educator award, Am. Inst. of Aeronautics & Astronautics -Nat. Capital Section, Outstanding Leadership medal, NASA, Internat. Behavioral Neuroscience Soc. award, Soc. for Behavioral Endocrinology award, Barnard medal of Distinction. Mem. Soc. Neurosci., Endocrine Soc., Women in Neurosci., Sod. Study of Reproduction, Internat. Acad. Sex Rsch. Office: National Science Foundation 4201 Wilson Blvd Arlington VA 22230

OLSEN, KIRK (GEORGE KIRK OLSEN), healthcare company executive; BA in Comm., Brigham Young U.; MS in Orgn. Behavior, U. Utah, 1976. V.p. Salt Lake Regional Med. Ctr., 1986—90; pres. through CEO Molina Healthcare Utah, 1998—2007; corp. v.p. Molina Healthcare Inc., 1999—2007; pres. Utah market IASIS Healthcare, LLC, 2007—, exec. v.p. Mountain region, 2008—. Office: Iasis Healthcare LLC Bldg E 117 Seaboard Ln Franklin TN 37067 Office Phone: 615-844-2747. Office Fax: 615-846-3006.

OLSEN, MARTIN E., gynecologist, educator, inventor; b. Morgantown, W.Va., 1959; m. Natalie Ann Maschmann, June 25, 1985; 1 child, Karen Rebeca. BS, Muskingum Coll., New Concord, 1981; MD, Med. Coll. Ohio, Toledo, 1981. Diplomate Am. Bd. Ob-Gyn. Resident in family practice Akron (Ohio) Gen. Med. Ctr., 1985-88; resident in ob-gyn. U. Tenn., Chattanooga, 1989-91; mem. faculty E. Tenn. State U., Johnson City, 1992—, chmn. dept. ob-byn., 1999—2009; dir. residency program Johnson City Med. Ctr., 1994—. Textbook editor; contbr. articles to profl. jours. Office: PO Box 70569 Johnson City TN 37614-1707 Office Phone: 423-439-8755. Business E-Mail: olsen@etsu.edu.

OLSEN, RICHARD JAMES, artist, educator; b. Milw., Nov. 15, 1935; s. Edward Marinus and Ann Frances (Keymar) Olsen; m. Nina Marsh Civilette-Olsen, July 25, 1969; children: Dayna Kim, Dawn Beth(dec.), Josh Keymar. BS, U. Wis., 1958, MFA in Painting and Printmaking, 1966. Tchg. asst. U. Wis., 1965-66; art tchr. grade 8 Winnequah Grade Sch., Monona, Wis., 1966-67; instr. printmaking Oper. Area Arts, Green Bay, Wis., 1967-69; from instr. painting and drawing to prof. emeritus U. Ga., Athens, 1969—2000, Gen. Sandy Beaver tchg. prof., 1998—2000, emeritus prof., 2001—; represented by Berman Gallery, Atlanta, 1986-97, Novus Inc., Atlanta, 1990—, Maurine Littleton Gallery, Washington, 1990, Miriam Perlman Gallery, Chgo., 1991, EDL & Assocs., Atlanta, 1994, Elements of Art, Columbus, Ohio, 1995, Ellen Wallace-Paushter, Art Cons., Chgo., 1999, Mercury Art Works, Athens, Ga., 2001—, Tew Galleries Atlanta, 2012. Wrestling coach Monona Grove (Wis.) H.S., 1966-67; panelist Steinham Arts Festival St. Lawrence U., N.Y., 1987, Crossroads in Cultural Studies, Tampere, Finland, 1996; head praparator Reflexes and Reflections Russell Rotunda Capitol Hill, Washington, 1983, Lincoln Ctr., N.Y.C., 1984. One-man shows include Claywork Gallery, Atlanta, 1986, H. Smith Gallery U. SC, Spartanburg, 1991, Nat. Vietnam Vets. Art Mus., Chgo., 1999, Mercury Art Works, Athens, Ga., 2003, 2008, Floataway Complex, Atlanta, 2005, Augusta State U., Ga., 2007, Monroe Art Guild, 2010, Large Format Wall Painting The Gallery, Madison Ga., 2011, Vietnam Revisited III: Another Focus, Steffen Thomas Mus. Art, Buckhead, Ga., 2012, numerous group shows including most recently, exhibited in group shows at Peace Mus., Chgo., 2002, Aurora (Ill.) Pub. Art Ctr., 2003, U. N.Mex., 2004, Children of War, Nat. Vietnam Vets. Art Mus., 2005, Wis. Vets. Mus., Madison, 2006—10, Athens Acad., Ga., 2007, War and the Veteran, Milk. Art Mus., 2009, Terraverte, Hotel Indigo, Athens, Ga., 2009, Operation Area Arts, Neville Pub. Mus., Green Bay, Wis., 2010, 35th Juried Exhbn., Lyndon House Art Ctr., Athens, 2010, 37th Juried Exhibition Lyndon House Art Center Athens Ga., 2012, 38th Juried Exhib, Lydon House Art Ctr., Athens, Ga., 2013, LZ Lambeau Heritage Hill State Pk., Green Bay, Wis., 2010, Represented in permanent collections Nat. Vietnam Vets. Art Mus., Chgo., Nat. Mus. Fine Art, Hanoi, Vietnam., Ga. World Congress Ctr., Atlanta, U. Ga. Complex Carbohydrate Rsch. Ctr., Bank South Ga., Tifton, Ga., Western Carolina U., Cullowhee, NC, Chastain Bldg., Athens, Ga, Chastain Ins. Agy. Collection, Keller, Crymes, Demarco Optical, Athens, Athens Eye Doctors, Doctors & Surgeons, Balentine, Fin. Investment Firm, Sovereign Bldg. Atlanta, Jamestown Properties L.F., Manhattan, NY; featured (in over 150 mags.); Exhibited in group shows at LZ Lambeau Heritage Hill State Park, Green Bay, Wis., 2010, Here and Now and than, 5 Decade UW Alum Show, Art Lofts Gallery, Madison, Wis., 2010, Defrance of Tradition Nat. Vietnam Vets Mus., 2006, exhibited in group shows at Seige of Khe Sahn Neville Pub. Mus. Green Bay, 2010, Timothy Tews Top 25 TEW Galleries Atlanta, 2012, exhibitions include Lyndon House Art Ctr. Athens, Ga., 2011—13, 'Woman' Madison Art Group, Town 220 Gallery, Madison, 2013, "Tenacity and Truth: People, Places and Memories", Nat. Vets. Art Mus., Chgo., 2013, Above and Beyond: War through the Eyes of American Veterans (War Point), Mus. Polit. History, St. Petersburg, 2013, Defiance of Tradition Nat.Vets. Art Mus. Chgo., 2006, Siege of Khe Sahn Neville Pub. Mus. Green Bay, Wis., 2010, Timothy Tews Top 25 TEW Galleries Atlanta, 2012, Above and Beyond: War through the Eyes of American Veterans, Mus. Polit. History in St. Petersburg, Russia, 2013, Tenacity and Truth: People, Places, and Memories, Nat. Vets. Art Mus., 2013. With U.S. Army, 1959-63, Vietnam. Decorated Purple heart, 1963; Visual Arts fellow So. Arts Fdn./NEA, 1988; Sr. Faculty grantee U. Ga. Rsch. Found., Inc., 1991-93, 96-98, Individual Artist grantee Ga. Coun. Arts, 1993-94; recipient Purchase award 8th Annual Maine/Maritime Internat. Flatworks Exhibn., 1990, Merit award Three Works 29th Juried Exbhn., Lyndon House Arts Center, Athens, Ga., 2004. Mem. VFW, Mil. Order of the Purple Heart (comdr. 1999-2000), Vietnam Helicopter Pilots Assn. Home: 165 Springdale St Athens GA 30605-1237

OLSON, CHERYL KAY, public health consultant, educator; b. Mpls., Jan. 29, 1960; d. Harley and Renae Olson; m. Lawrence Alan Kutner, Oct. 30, 1988; 1 child, Michael S. Kutner. BA, U. Minn., Mpls., 1981, MPH, 1986; ScD, Harvard Sch. of Pub. Health, Boston, 1995. Cert. in pharmaceutical medicine European Ctr. of Pharm. Medicine, 2001. Co-founder Health Comm. Consultants, Inc., Belmont, Mass., 1985—; co-dir. Harvard Med. Sch. Ctr. Mental Health and Media, Waltham, 2001—; instr. pub. health dept. of psychiatry Mass. Gen. Hosp. Harvard Med. Sch., Boston, 2000—; strategic comm. cons. F. Hoffmann-La Roche Ltd., Basel, Switzerland; prof. Harvard Med. Sch.; co-dir Harvard Med. Sch. Ctr. for Mental Health and Media. Young scholar Johann Jacobs Found., Zurich, Switzerland, 1992, liaison young scholar program, 1993; columnist Parents Mag., NYC, 1993—98; evaluation cons. Calif. Dept. Health, Berkeley, 1996—99; vis. prof. pediatric neuropsychiatry U. Medicine and Pharmacy, Timisoara, Romania, 1997—97; vis. scholar Elliot-Pearson Dept. Child Devel. Tufts U., Medford, Mass., 2004—; cons. in field. Co-author: Real-World Fitness, 1999; co-author: (with Lawrence Kutner) Grand Theft Childhood: The Surprising Truth About Violent Video Games and What Parents Can Do, 2008; editor: Proactive Parenting: Guiding Your Child from Two to Six, 2003, If You Decide to Quit Smoking., 2004; contbr. articles to profl. jours. Recipient 2 CINE Golden Eagle awards; grantee prin. investigator, Office of Justice Programs U.S. Dept. of Justice, 2003—. Office Phone: 781-392-2201. E-mail: colson@ckolson.com.

OLSON, DENNIS OLIVER, lawyer; b. Seminole, Tex., Oct. 19, 1947; s. Edwin and Beulah Matilda (Strang) O.; m. Leonee Lynn Claud, Jan. 30, 1971; children: James Edwin, Stacy Rae. BA in English, U. Tex., 1969; JD, Tex. Tech U., 1974. Bar: Tex. 1974, U.S. Ct. Mil. Appeals 1974, U.S. Dist. Ct. (no. dist.) Tex. 1978, U.S. Dist. Ct. (we. dist.) Tex. 1978, U.S. Ct. Appeals (5th cir.) 1984, U.S. Supreme Ct. 1985, U.S. Dist. Ct. (ea. dist.) Tex. 2002. Commd. USMC, 1969, advanced through grades to capt., 1973, infantry officer various locations including Vietnam, 1969—74, judge advocate various locations, 1974—78, resigned, 1978; assoc. Carr, Evans, Fouts & Hunt, and predecessor, Lubbock, Tex., 1978—81, ptnr., 1981—85; pvt. practice Dallas, 1985—88; shareholder, co-chmn. bankruptcy sect. Godwin & Carlton, P.C., Dallas, 1989—94; ptnr. Olson Nicoud & Gueck, LLP and predecessor, Dallas, 1994—. Bd. dirs. Presbyn. Ctr. Doctors Clinic, Lubbock, 1983-85, United Campus Ministry, Tex. Tech U., Lubbock, 1984-85, Discovery Sch.of Canyon Creek, Richardson, 1999-2002; elder Preston Hollow Presbyn. Ch., Dallas; treas., bd. dirs. Lubbock chpt. ARC, 1981-83; vol. Lubbock United Way, 1978-80. Decorated Bronze Star Combat V; named Outstanding Young Man of Am., 1983. Fellow: Tex. Bar Found. (sustaining life), Dallas Bar Assn., Dallas Bar Found., Lubbock County Bar Assn. (bd. dirs. 1983-85), Tex. Young Lawyers Assn. (bd. dirs. 1981-83), Judge Advocates Assn. (bd. dirs. 1976-78), Lubbock C. of C. (grad.

Leadership Lubbock program 1981), U. Tex. NROTC Alumni Found., (bd. dirs. 2001-09), Phi Delta Phi. Home: 313 Forest Grove Dr Richardson TX 75080-1937 Office Phone: 214-979-7302. Business E-Mail: dennisо@dallas-law.com.

OLSON, MARK A., corporate financial executive; BA in Acctg. & Spanish, Lewis U.; MBA, DePaul U. CPA. With Nortel, Johnson & Johnson; group contr. Andrew Corp., 1993—98, corp. contr., 1998—2000, v.p., corp. contr., 2000—03, v.p., corp. contr., chief acctg. officer, 2003—07; v.p., contr. Andrew, LLC, 2007—09; sr. v.p., contr. CommScope, Inc., 2009—12, exec. v.p., CFO, 2012—. Mem.: AICPA, Ill. CPA Soc. Office: CommScope Inc 1100 CommScope Pl SE Hickory NC 28603 Office Phone: 828-324-2200. Office Fax: 828-328-3400.

OLSON, PETER GRAHAM (PETE OLSON), United States Representative from Texas; b. Ft. Lewis, Wash., Dec. 9, 1962; m. Nancy Olson; children: Kate, Grant. BA in Computer Sci., Rice U., Houston, 1985; JD, U. Tex. Sch. Law, Austin, 1988. Naval liason officer US Senate, 1995—98, legis. aide to Senator Phil Gramm Washington, 1998—2002, chief of staff to Senator John Cornyn, 2002—07; mem. US Congress from 22nd Tex. Dist., Washington, 2009—, US House Homeland Security Com., Washington, 2009—, US House Science & Tech. Com., Washington, 2009—, US House Transp. & Infrastructure Com., Washington, 2009—, US House Energy & Commerce Com., Washington, 2011—. Naval aviator USN, 1988—97. Decorated Joint Chiefs of Staff Badge, Southwest Asia Svc. medal, Armed Forces Expeditionary medal, Navy & Marine Corps Achievement medal, Joint Svc. Achievement medal, Joint Svc. Commendation medal. Mem.: NRA, Tex. State Soc., Rice U. R Assn., Tex. Lyceum (dir.), Littlefield Soc. Republican. Methodist. Office: US House of Representatives 312 Cannon House Office Bldg Washington DC 20515 also: 1650 Hwy 6 Ste 150 Sugar Land TX 77477 Office Phone: 202-225-5951, 281-240-3700. Office Fax: 202-225-5241, 281-240-2959.*

OLSON, RICHARD DAVID, psychology professor; b. Reading, Pa., Oct. 10, 1944; s. Milton Stuart and Sarah Ellen (Moyer) O.; m. M. Gayle Augustine, Aug. 26, 1967. BA, U. Redlands, 1966; MS, St. Louis U., 1968, PhD, 1970. Lic. psychologist, La. Asst. prof. psychology U. New Orleans, 1970-74, assoc. prof., chmn. dept. psychology, 1974-79, prof., chmn. dept., 1979-81, assoc. dean Grad. Sch., 1981-82, dean, 1982-88, vice chancellor, 1984-88, rsch. prof., 1988—2000, prof. emeritus, 2000—; chmn. dept. psychology, 1995—2000. Cons. psychologist, New Orleans, 1973—2002; pres. Statis. Cons. of New Orleans, 1977-82 Editor: Learning in the Classroom, 1971, The Comma After Love, The Selected Poems of Raeburn Miller, 1994, The Collected Poems of Raeburn Miller, 1997; contbr. articles to profl. jours. Grantee HEW, 1976-81 Fellow APA, Am. Psychol. Soc.; mem. Soc. for Neuroscis., Am. Statis. Assn. Home: 40 Infinity Dr Poplarville MS 39470 Office: U New Orleans Dept Psychology Lake Front New Orleans LA 70148 Office Phone: 601-795-4838. Business E-Mail: richardolson@hughes.net.

OLSON, ROBERT EUGENE, physician, biochemist, educator; b. Minn., Jan. 23, 1919; s. Ralph William and Minnie (Holtin) O.; m. Catherine Silvoso, Oct. 21, 1944; children: Barbara Lynn, Robert E., Mark Alan, Mary Ellen, Carol Louise. AB, Gustavus Adolphus Coll., 1938; PhD, St. Louis U., 1944; MD, Harvard, 1951; MD (hon.), Chiang Mai U., Thailand, 1983. Diplomate: Nat. Bd. Med. Examiners, Am. Bd. Nutrition (pres. 1962-63). Postgrad. research asst. biochemistry St. Louis U. Sch. Medicine, 1938-43, asst. biochemistry, 1943-44, Alice A. Doisy prof. biochemistry, chmn. dept. biochemistry, 1965-82, asso. prof. medicine, 1966-72, prof. medicine, 1972-82; vis. prof. (sabbatical) dept. biochemistry U. Freiburg, Breisgau, West Germany, 1970-71; also Hoffman-La Roche Co., Basel, Switzerland, 1970-71; instr. biochemistry and nutrition Harvard Sch. Pub. Health, 1946-47; research fellow Nutrition Found., 1947-49, Am. Heart Assn., 1949-51, established investigator, 1951-52; house officer Peter Bent Brigham Hosp., Boston, 1951-52; prof., head dept. biochemistry and nutrition Grad. Sch. Pub. Health U. Pitts.; lectr. medicine Sch. Medicine, 1952-65; mem. panel malnutrition Japan-U.S. Med. Scis. Program, 1965-69; dir. Nutrition Clinic, Falk Clinic, 1953-65; mem. sr. staff Presbyn. Hosp., dir. metabolic unit, 1960-65; mem. staff St. Louis U. Hosp., 1965-81; prof. biochemistry, prof. medicine, assoc. dean acad. affairs U. Pitts. Sch. Medicine, 1982-84; prof. medicine, prof. pharm. scis. SUNY-Stony Brook, 1984-90, prof. emeritus, 1990—; prof. pediatrics U. South Fla., Tampa, 1994—. Cons. Mercy Hosp., U. Pitts. Med. Center; assoc. in medicine St. Margaret's Meml. Hosp., Pitts., dir. metabolic unit, 1954-60; cons. divsn. rsch. grants USPHS, 1954-69, 72-76; dir. Anemia and Malnutrition Center, Chiang Mai, Thailand, 1967-77; vis. scholar dept. biochemistry Oxford (Eng.) U., 1961-62; vis. prof. dept. biochemistry U. Freiburg, West Germany, 1970-71; food and nutrition bd. NRC, 1977-83; adv. council Nat. Inst. Arthritis, Diabetes, Digestive and Kidney Diseases, 1981-85; William A. Noyes lectr. U. Ill., Urbana, 1980. Author: Perspectives in Biological Chemistry, 1970, Methods in Medical Research, 1970, Protein-Calorie Malnutrition, 1975, Balanced Nutrition, 1989; assoc. editor Nutrition Revs., 1954-56, editor, 1978-88; assoc. editor Am. Jour. Medicine, 1956-65, Circulation Rsch., 1956-76, Am. Heart Jour., 1958-65, Am. Jour. Clin. Nutrition, 1960-66, Methods in Med. Rsch., 1963-70, Biochem. Medicine, 1967-90, Molecular and Cellular Cardiology, 1967-78, Ann. Rev. Nutrition, 1979-84, editor, 1984-94; co-editor: Vitamins and Hormones, 1975-81; author 236 original sci. papers in peer-reviewed jours.; contbr. 114 chpts. in books and major reviews to profl. jours. Bd. dirs. Nat. Nutrition Consortium, 1977-81, Am. Council on Sci. and Health, 1984-91. Lt. (j.g.) USNR, 1944-46. Recipient Fulbright award, 1961-62, Guggenheim Found. award, 1961-62, 70-71, McCollum award, 1965, Joseph Goldberger award, 1974; named Atwater Meml. lectr., 1978; Geiger Meml. lectr., 1979, William A. Noyes lectr. U. Ill., 1980, H. Brooks James lectr. N.C. State U., 1981, Virginia Beal lectr. U. Mass., 1990. Fellow ACP, Internat. Acad. Cardiovasc. Scis., Am. Pub. Health Assn. (chmn. food and nutrition sect. 1960-61), Am. Inst. Nutrition (pres. 1981-82, Conrad Elvehjem award 1998), Assn. Am. Physicians; mem. AAAS (sec. med. scis. N. sect. 1965-67), Am. Assn. Cancer Research, Am. Heart Assn., AMA (mem. council food and nutrition 1959-67, vice chmn. 1962-67), Royal Soc. Health (London), N.Y. Acad. Scis., Am. Fedn. Clin. Research, Am. Soc. Clin. Investigation, Boyleston Med. Soc., Am. Chem. Soc. (pres. biochemistry group Pitts. sect. 1960-61), Am. Soc. Biol. Chemists, Soc. Exptl. Biology and Medicine, Am. Soc. Clin. Nutrition (pres. 1961-62, McCollum award 1965, Herman award 2002), Assn. Med. Sch. Depts. Biochemistry (pres. 1979-80), Pa., St. Louis, Allegheny County med. socs., Am. Soc. Study Liver Diseases, Phi Beta Kappa, Sigma Xi, Phi Lambda Upsilon, Alpha Omega Alpha, Alpha Sigma Nu. Clubs: Cosmos (Washington), Countryside Country Club (Clearwater, Fla.). Office: U South Fla Dept Pediatrics 17 Davis Blvd Ste 200 Tampa FL 33606-3438 Office Phone: 813-259-8700. Business E-Mail: rolson@hsc.usf.edu.

OLSON, WALTER JUSTUS, JR., management consultant; b. Paterson, NJ, July 27, 1941; s. Walter Justus and Viola Patricia (Trautvetter) O. BS, BA, Brown U., 1964; MBA, Columbia U., 1967. CPA Va. Design engr. Rockwell Internat., Inc., Downey, Calif., 1964-65; mgmt. officer CIA, Washington, 1969-73; sr. cons. Booz, Allen and Hamilton, Inc., Washington, 1973-78; corp. planning coordinator Washington Gas Light Co., Washington, 1978-82; prin. Walter J. Olson & Assoc., McLean, Va., 1982-83; dep. asst. sec. for export adminstrn. U.S. Dept. Commerce, Washington, 1983-86; prin. Walter J. Olson & Assoc., Washington, 1986—; sr. rsch. analyst U.S. House Select Com. Technology Transfer to PRC, Washington, 1998-99. Vice-chmn. fin. com. Fairfax County Reps., Va., 1982-83. Served to 1st lt. USAF, 1967—69. Mem. AICPA, Greater Wash. Soc. CPAs, Strategic Leadership Forum (pres. Washington chpt. 1990-91). Republican. Episcopalian. Office: 370 Maple Ave West Ste 4 Vienna VA 22180-5615 Home: 7326 Dartford Dr Mc Lean VA 22102-7326 Office Phone: 703-356-6919. Personal E-mail: walterolson@mindspring.com.

OLUM, BETSY, management consulting executive; BA in Sociology, Colgate U., 1976—80; MBA, U. Pennsylvania The Wharton Sch., 1982—84. Bd. dirs. CEW (Cosmetic Exec. Women); with Avon, Charles of the Ritz, Erno Laszlo; owner Prema Nolita Day Spa, NY; dir. Living Proof Inc.; creative dir. Escada Beaute, v.p. global mktg., gen. mgr. n. Am.; brand cons. Sephora; sr. v.p. mktg. Sephora USA Inc., 1999—2009; pres. Betsy Olum Mktg., 2009—; gen. mgr. beauty & merchandising strategy HSN Inc., 2011—. With Fragrance Found. Recipient CEW Achiever award, 2008. Office: HSN Inc 1 HSN Dr Saint Petersburg FL 33729 Office Phone: 727-872-1000.

O'MALLEY, BERT WILLIAM, cell biologist, educator, physician; b. Pitts., Dec. 19, 1936; s. Bert Alloysius O'M.; m. Sally Ann Johnson; children: Sally Ann, Bert A., Rebecca, Erin K. BS, U. Pitts., 1959, MD summa cum laude, 1963; DSc (hon.), N.Y. Med. Coll., 1979, Nat. U. Ireland, 1985; MD (hon.), Karolinska Inst., Stockholm, 1984. Intern, resident Duke U., Durham, N.C., 1963-65; clin. assoc. Nat. Cancer Inst., NIH, Bethesda, Md., 1965-67, head molecular biology sect., endocrine br., 1967-69; Lucius Birch prof., dir. Reproductive Biology Ctr. Vanderbilt U. Sch. Medicine, Nashville, 1969-73; Tom Thompson prof., chmn. dept. cell biology Baylor Coll. Medicine, Houston, 1973—. Disting. Svc. prof., 1985, dir. Baylor Ctr. for Reproductive Biology, 1973—. Mem. endocrine study sect., NIH, 1970-73, chmn., 1973-74; chmn. CETUS-UCLA Symposium on Gene Expression, 1982; con., mem. coun. rsch. and clin. investigation awards Am. Cancer Soc., 1985-87. Author: (with A.R. Means) Receptors for Reproductive Hormones, 1973, (with L. Birnbaumer) Hormone Action, vols. I and II, 1977, vol. III, 1978, (with A.M. Gotto) The Role of Receptors in Biology and Medicine, 1986; co-author: Methods in Enzymology: Hormone Action: Calmodulin and Calcium-Binding Proteins, 1983, Mechanism of Steriod Hormone Regulation of Gene Transcription, 1994; editor: Gene Regulation: UCLA Symposium on Molecular Cellular Biology, 1982; contbg. author to over 400 publs. Lt. comdr. USPHS, 1965-69. Recipient Ernst Oppenheimer award Am. Endocrine Soc., 1975, Gregory Pincus medal, 1975, Lila Gruber Cancer award, 1977, Disting. Achievement in Modern Medicine award, 1978, Borden award Assn. Am. Med. Colls., 1978, Dickson prize for Basic Med. Rsch., 1979, Philip S. Hench award U. Pitts., 1981, Axel Munthe Reproductive Biology award, Capri, Italy, 1982, Bicentennial Medallion of Distincton U. Pitts., 1987, Carl G.Hartman award, 2007, 2007 Nat. Medal Sci. Mem. AAAS, NAS, Inst. Med. NAS, Am. Soc. Biol. Chemists, Am. Acad. Arts and Scis., Endocrine Soc. (pres. 1985, Fred Conrad Koch medal 1988), Am. Soc. Clin. Investigation, Am. Inst. Chemists, Fedn. Clin. Rsch., Harvey Soc., Alpha Epsilon Delta, Phi Beta Kappa, Alpha Omega Alpha. Democrat. Roman Catholic. Office: Baylor Coll Medicine Interdepartmental Program in Cell & Molecular Biology One Baylor Pla Houston TX 77030 Office Phone: 713-798-6205. Office Fax: 713-798-5599. Business E-Mail: berto@bcm.edu.

O'MALLEY, THOMAS ANTHONY, gastroenterologist, retired internist; b. St. Helens, Lancashire, Eng., Jan. 21, 1932; s. Michael and Margaret (Melia) O'M.; m. Margaret Mary O'Kane, Apr. 7, 1958 (dec. Apr. 1985); m. Marianne Rapier, Jan. 23, 1988; children: Anne, Patricia, Katherine, Jane, Margaret. MBChB, U. Liverpool, Eng., 1956; Lic. Medicine, U. State N.Y., 1964. Diplomate Am. Bd. Internal Medicine, State Bd. Med. Examiners Fla. House physician Royal Infirmary, Liverpool, 1956-57; house surgeon Royal Liverpool Children's Hosp., 1957; resident in medicine C.S. Wilson Meml. Hosp., Johnson City, NY, 1957-58; fellow internal medicine Lahey Clinic, Boston, 1958-59; USPHS trainee in gastroenterology U. Rochester (N.Y.), Strong Meml. Hosp., 1959-60; chief resident medicine/Segal Watson fellow gastroenterology Genesee Hosp., Rochester, 1960-61; gastroenterologist Cancer Clinic, Regina, Sask., Canada, 1963; asst. dir. med. edn. Genesee Hosp., U. Rochester, 1964—66; pvt. practice Rochester, NY, 1967—72; clin. asst. prof. medicine U. Rochester, 1967—72; clin. assoc. prof. medicine U. South Fla., Tampa, 1972—2008. Chief medicine Sarasota (Fla.) Meml. Hosp., 1973, Doctors Hosp., Sarasota, 1985. With RAF, 1961-62. Recipient Physician of Yr. award Doctors Hosp. Sarasota, 1985; listed among Best Dr.'s of Am., 1998, Lifetime Achievement award, Sarasota Meml. Hosp, Fla., 2008. Fellow: ACP, Am. Coll. Gastroenterology; mem.: Cavalieri del Vini Nobili (amb. 1989—, pres. 1997—, past pres. 2009), Chevalier du Tastevin (comdr. 1985—2011, officieur comdr. 2001—11). Personal E-mail: t.omalley10@comcast.net.

O'MEILIA, DAVID E., lawyer; b. July 1951; Grad. Okla. State U.; grad. in Law, Tulsa Coll. Atty. Tulsa County Dist. Atty.'s Office, 1980—84; asst. US atty. US Atty.'s Office, Tulsa, Okla., 1986—96; atty. Nichols, Wolfe, Stamper, Nally, Fallis & Robertson, 1996—99; ptnr. Lyons, Clark, Danielson & O'Meilia, Tulsa, Okla., 1999—2001; US atty. (no. dist.) Okla. US Dept. Justice, 2001—09; ptnr. Richards & Connor PLLP, Tulsa, 2009—. Office: Richards & Connor PLLP ParkCentre Bldg 12th Fl 525 S Main St Tulsa OK 74103-4509 Office Phone: 918-585-2394. Office Fax: 918-585-1449. Business E-Mail: domeilia@richardsconnor.com.

O'NEAL, LARRY E., state legislator; b. Jacksonville, Fla., May 5, 1949; m. Kathy O'Neal; children: Megan, Lawrence Jr. Mgr. Drs. Clinic Warner Robins, 1974—75; ptnr. O'Neal, Long & Hall, 1976—; bd. dir. Cb&T Bank Mid. Ga., 1998—; mem. Banks & Banking Com., Jours. & Judiciary Com., Houston County Rep. Exec. Com., 2001—; house rep. Ga.; former state rep. Dist. 117 Ga., 2004—. Mem.: Houston County Bar Assn. (former pres.), America & Ga. Bar Assns., United Way, Salvation Army (bd. dir.), Warner Robins Rotary Club, Houston Drug Action Coun. (bd. dir.). Republican. Methodist. Office: 109 State Capitol Atlanta GA 30334 also: 200 Winllingham Dr Bonaire GA 31005 Office Phone: 478-953-4557, 404-656-0126. Office Fax: 404-463-6612. Business E-Mail: loneal@legis.state.ga.us.

O'NEAL, SHAQUILLE RASHAUN, sportscaster, retired professional basketball player; b. Newark, Mar. 6, 1972; s. Philip A. Harrison and Lucille O'Neal; m. Shaunie Nelson, Dec. 26, 2002 (separated 2007); children: Shareef Rashaun, Amira Sanaa, Shaquir Rashuan, Me'arah Sanaa. BS, La. State U., Baton Rouge, 2000; MBA, U. Phoenix, 2005; student in broadcasting, Sportscaster U. at Syracuse U. S.I. Newhouse Sch. Pub. Comm., NY, 2009; EdD, Barry U., 2012. Ctr. Orlando Magic, Fla., 1992—96, LA Lakers, 1996—2004, Miami Heat, Fla., 2004—08, Phoenix Suns, 2008—09, Cleve. Cavaliers, 2009—10, Boston Celtics, 2010—11; ret. NBA, 2011; NBA analyst Turner Sports, 2011—. Mem. US men's basketball team World Championships, Toronto, Canada, 1994, Olympic Games, Atlanta, 1996; owner, clothing line and record label TWIsM. Actor: (films) Blue Chips, 1994, Kazaam, 1996, Steel, 1997, The Wash, 2001, After the Sunset, 2004, The Year of the Yao, 2004, Scary Movie 4, 2006; performer: (albums) Shaq Diesel, 1993, Shaq Fu: Da Return, 1994, You Can't Stop the Reign, 1995, The Best of Shaquille O'Neal, 1996, Shaquille O'Neal Presents his Superfriends, Vol. 1, 2002; co-author (with Jackoe Macmullan): Shaq Uncut: My Story, 2011. Res. officer Miami Beach Police Dept., Fla.; vol. Tempe Police Dept., Ariz.; res. dep. officer Bedford County Sheriff's Dept., Va., 2004—07; spl. dep., col. Maricopa County Sheriff's Dept., Ariz., 2006—08. Recipient Gold medal, men's basketball, World Championships, 1994, Atlanta Olympic Games, 1996; named 1st Team All-Am., Sporting News, 1991, 1992, NBA Rookie of Yr., 1993, NBA All-Star Game MVP, 2000, 2004, NBA All-Star Game co-MVP, 2009, NBA MVP, 2000, NBA Player of Yr., The Sporting News, 2000, 2005, NBA Finals MVP, 2001, 2002; named one of 50 Greatest Players in NBA History, 1996, The Most Influential People in the World of Sports, Bus. Week, 2007, 100 Most Powerful Celebrities, Forbes.com, 2008; named to Eastern Conf. All-Star Team, NBA, 1993—96, 2005—07, Western Conf. All-Star Team, 1997, 1998, 2000—04, 2009, All-NBA 2nd Team, 1995, 1999, All-NBA 1st Team, 1998, 2000—06, NJ Hall of Fame, 2008. Achievements include being first overall pick in the NBA Draft, 1992; member of NBA Championship winning: Los Angeles Lakers, 2000-2002; Miami Heat, 2006; leading the NBA in: field goals, 1994, 1995, 1999-2001; field goal attempts, 1995; field goal percentage, 1994, 1998-2002, 2004-06; free throw attempts, 1995, 1999-2002, 2004; points, 1995, 1999, 2000; points per game, 1995, 2000. Office: Turner Sports 1015 Techwood Dr Atlanta GA 30303

O'NEIL, JAMES F., III, telecommunications industry executive; BCE, Tulane U., New Orleans, 1980. Worked Haliburton Co.; joined Quanta Services, Inc., 1999, v.p., Ops Integration, 1999—2002, sr. v.p., Ops. Integration and Audit, 2002—08, pres., COO, 2008—11, pres., CEO, 2011—. Office: Quanta Services Inc Ste 2100 1360 Post Oak Blvd Houston TX 77056 Office Phone: 713-629-7600. Office Fax: 713-626-7676. Business E-Mail: joneil@quantaservices.com.

O'NEILL, ALBERT CLARENCE, JR., lawyer; s. Albert Clarence and Sue Virginia O'N.; m. Vanda Marie Nigels, Apr. 26, 1969; 1 child, Heather Marie. BA with high honors, U. Fla., 1962; LL.B. magna cum laude, Harvard U., 1965. Bar: Fla. 1965. Law clk. to judge U.S. Dist. Ct. (mid. dist.) Fla., Jacksonville, 1965-66; assoc. Fowler, White, Collins, Gillen, Humkey & Trenam, Tampa, Fla., 1966-69; ptnr. Trenam, Simmons, Kemker, Scharf & Barkin, Tampa, 1970-77; mem. firm Trenam, Kemker, Scharf, Barkin, Frye, O'Neill & Mullis (P.A.), Tampa, 1977—, also bd. dirs. Vis. lectr. law Stetson Law Sch., 1970-73; mem. adv. coun. IRS, 2001-03. Exec. editor Harvard Law Rev., 1964-65; contbr. articles to profl. jours. Bd. dirs. Fla. Gulf Coast Symphony, Inc., 1975-86, U. Fla. Found., Inc., 1976-84, 97-2001, 03-11, 12-. Fla. Orch., 1988-2005, Gator Boosters, Inc., 2002—11. Mem. ABA (chmn. tax sect. 1992-93), Am. Law Inst., Am. Coll. Tax Counsel, Fla. Bar (chmn. tax sect. 1975-76), Am. Bar Retirement Assn. (pres. 2000-01, bd. dirs. 1995-04), Phi Beta Kappa. Office: Trenam Kemker Scharf Barkin Frye O'Neill & Mullis 101 E Kennedy Blvd Ste 2700 Tampa FL 33602-5150 Home: 2529 SW 50th Blvd Gainesville FL 32608-3975 Office Phone: 813-227-7437. Business E-Mail: aconeill@trenam.com.

O'NEILL, HARRIET, lawyer, retired state supreme court justice; b. Apr. 20, 1957; m. Kerry Cammack; children: Carolina, Hailey. BA, Converse Coll., 1978; studied, U. Coll., Oxford, England; JD, U. S.C., 1982; PhD (hon.), Converse Coll., 2001. Practice law, Houston; atty. Porter & Clements, Morris & Campbell; pvt. practice, 1982-92; judge 152d Dist. Ct., Houston, 1992—95; justice 14th Ct. Appeals, Houston, 1995—98, Tex. Supreme Ct., Austin, 1998—; pvt. practice Austin, Tex., 2010—. Lectr. continuing edn. courses; adv. bd. CLE Inst., 1996; panelist Tex. Ctr. Advanced Jud. Studies., Austin, 1993. Contbr. articles to profl. publs. Mem. U. S.C. academic honors soc.; founder Jud. Outreach for Literacy Training. Named Appellate Justice of Yr., Tex. Assn. of Civil Trial & Appellate Specialists, 2002, 2006. Mem.: Harris County Bar Assn., ABA. Republican. Office: 919 Congress Ave, Suite 1400 Austin TX 78701 Office Phone: 512-944-2222. Office Fax: 512-476-6441.

O'NEILL, MOLLY ANN, information technology executive, former federal agency administrator; d. Vincent and Pam O'Neill. BS in Biology, Va. Tech. U., 1988. Mgr. A.T. Kearney, 1989—97; dir. state practice TechLaw, Inc., 1997—98; prin. American Mgmt. Systems, Inc., 1998—2002; with Environ. Coun. of the States, 2002—06, state dir. Nat. Environ. Info. Exchange; chief info. officer, asst. adminstr. for environ. info. EPA, Washington, 2007—09; v.p. fed. energy & environmental industry lead CGI Federal, Inc., Fairfax, Va., 2009—. Chief info. officer CIO Council's Architecture & Infrastructure Com., 2008; assoc. prof. George Mason U., 2010—. Named Civilian IT Exec. of Yr., Govt. Computer News, 2007. Fellow: Nat. Acad. Pub. Adminstrn. (NAPA). Office: CGI Federal 12601 Fair Lakes Cir Fairfax VA 22033 Office Phone: 703-227-6000. E-mail: moneill@gmu.edu.

O'NEILL, ROBERT EDWARD (BOBBY O'NEILL), consulting firm executive, former federal prosecutor; b. Bronx, NY, 1957; BA, Fordham U., 1979; JD, NY Law Sch., 1982. Asst. dist. atty. NY County's (Manhattan) Dist. Attorney's Office, 1982—86; asst. US atty. (southern dist.) Fla. US Dept. Justice, 1986—90; trial atty. Kramer, Dillof, Tessel, Duffy & Moore, NYC, 1990—92; assoc. ind. counsel, Office Spl. Prosecutor US Dept. Justice, Washington, 1992—93, assoc. ind. counsel, Office Spl. Prosecutor, Alexandria, 1997, asst. US atty. Tampa, 1993—2010, dep. chief in charge of litigation narcotics & dangerous drugs section Washington, 1998—99, chief spl. prosecution section & pub. corruption section Tampa, 1999—2001, chief criminal divsn. (middle dist.) Fla., 2002—07, 1st asst. US atty., 2001—02, 2007, interim US atty. (middle dist.) Fla., 2007—08, US atty., 2010—13; mng. dir. Freeh Group Internat. Solutions, LLC (FGIS), Miami, 2013—. Co-owner Four Green Fields. Fellow: American Coll. Trial Lawyers; mem.: DC Bar Assn., Fla. Bar Assn. Independent. Office: Freeh Group International Solutions LLC (FGIS) 350 Fifth Ave Ste 3100 New York NY 10118 Office Phone: 646-558-3632. Office Fax: 302-824-7148.*

O'NEILL, WILLIAM WALTER, dean, cardiologist, educator; b. Nov. 24, 1951; BS, U. Mich., 1972; MD, Wayne State U., 1977. Diplomate Am. Bd. Internal Medicine, Am. Bd. Cardiology. Intern internal medicine U. Wis., Madison, 1977—78; resident internal medicine Wayne State U., Detroit, 1978—80; fellow U. Mich., Ann Arbor, 1980-82, instr. internal medicine, 1982-83, asst. prof., 1983-86, assoc. prof., 1986-87; dir. cardiac catheterization lab. U. Mich. Hosp., Ann Arbor, 1984-87; dir. divsn. cardiovascular disease William Beaumont Hosp., Royal Oak, Troy, Mich., 1987—2006, corp. chief cardiology, 2002—06, vice chair Dept. Internal Medicine for Rsch., 2003; co-dir. Beaumont Heart Ctr., 1999—2006; prof. medicine, exec. dean clin. affairs Miller Sch. Medicine, U. Miami, 2006—. Attending cardiologist VA Hosp., Ann Arbor, 1982-90; chmn. govt. rels. subcom. Nat. Cardiovasc. Network; rsch. peer rev. com. Am. Heart Assn. Mich., 1988-89; chmn. publs. com. Mansfield Scientific Balloon Valvuloplasty Registry; bd. govs. William Beaumont Hosp. Rsch. Inst.; presenter in field. Author: Myocardial Revascularization by Coronary Angioplasty or Bypass Surgery During MI in Acute Myocardial Infarction: New Approaches to Evaluation and Therapy, 1986, (chpt.) Acute Coronary Intervention, 1987, Current Perspective in Coronary Care, 1987, Interventional Cardiovascular Medicine, 1994, Acute Coronary Care, 2d edit., 1995; co-author: (chpts.) Cardiovascular Review, 6th edit., 1985, 8th edit., 1987, Tissue Plasminogen Activator in Thrombolytic Therapy, 1987, Techniques and Applications in Interventional Cardiology, 1991, Atherectomy, 1992, Emergency Medicine: A Comprehensive Study Guide, 3d edit., 1992, Adjunctive Therapy for Acute Myocardial Infarction, 1992, Manual of Interventional CArdiology, 1992, Cura Intensiva Cardiologica, Primary Coronary Angioplasty in Acute Myocardial Infarction; author, co-author: (chpt.) Interventional Cardiovascular Medicine, 1994; editl. cons. Jour. Intervention Cardiology; mem. editl. bd. Catheterization Cardiovasc. Diagnosis; contbr. over 400 articles to profl. publs. Grantee Smith/Kline Beecham, 1989-90, 90—, Advanced Cardiovasc. Sys., Inc., 1988-90, 90—, Midwest Heart Rsch. Found., Abbott Labs., 1990—, Duke U., 1990—, William Beaumont Hosp. Rsch. Inst., 1990—. Fellow Am. Coll. Cardiology (chpt. sec.-treas. 1993-94, reimbursement com.), Am. Coll. Chest Physicians, Coun. Clin. Cardiology; mem. AMA, ACP, Internat. Andreas Gruentzig Soc. Office: U Miami Clin Affairs 1600 Nw 10TH Ave RMSB 1122A Miami FL 33136 Office Phone: 305-243-9483. E-mail: woneill@med.miami.edu.

ONG, LAUREEN E., broadcast executive; b. NYC, Sept. 24, 1952; d. Douglas and Marion (Chin) Ong; m. Richard Ong. BA in Math. & Speech Theater Arts, Montclair State Coll., NJ, 1974; MA in Comm., Columbia U., NYC, 1977. Mgr. sales MTM TV Distbn. Group; acct. exec. WPVI-TV, Phila.; sales mgr. KRON-TV, San Francisco; sr. exec. Rainbow Programming, 1994—96; v.p., gen. mgr. KSAZ-TV, Phoenix, 1997—98, WTTG-TV, Washington, 1998—2000; pres., CEO Nat. Geog. Channel, Washington, 2000—07; COO STAR GROUP Ltd., Hong Kong, 2007—10; pres. The Travel Channel LLC Scripps Networks Interactive, Knoxville, Tenn., 2010—. Mem.: Cable TV Adminstrv. and Mktg. Execs., Women in Comm., Women in Cable, Nat. Cable TV Assn. Lutheran. Office: Scripps Networks Interactive 9721 Sherrill Blvd Knoxville TN 37932 Office Phone: 865-694-2700.

ONSANIT, TAWACHAI, physician; b. Trang, Thailand, Jan. 14, 1940; arrived in U.S., 1965; s. Toon and Tanomchit (Kongsong) O.; m. Bubpha Janturagit, May 8, 1966; children: Krittika, Addie. MD, Chulalongkorn Med., Bangkok, 1964. Rotating intern Queens Gen. Hosp., NYC, 1965-66; resident in gen. surgery Med. Coll. of Ohio, Toledo, 1966-70; resident in colon and rectal surgery Allentown (Pa.) Gen. Hosp., 1970-72; mem. staff Coaldale (Pa.) Hosp., 1973-77, Sentara Hosp., Virginia Beach, Va., 1977—; pvt. practice, 1973—; asst. prof. clin. surgery Ea. Va. Med. Sch., Norfolk, Va., 1993. Fellow ACS, Am. Soc. Colon and Rectal Surgery; mem. Soc. Am. Gastrointestinal Endoscopic Surgeons. Avocations: photography, ballroom dancing, reading. Home: 1201 Witchduck Bay Ct Virginia Beach VA 23455-5620

ONSTEAD, R. RANDALL RANDALL, JR., retail executive; m. Pam Onstead; 2 children. B in Mktg., Tex. Tech U., 1978; completed program for mgmt. devel., Harvard U., Mass. Various mgmt. positions Randall's Food Markets, Inc., Houston, 1978—86, pres., COO, 1986—96, pres., CEO, 1996—98, chmn., CEO, 1998—99; mng. dir. Chapman Partners, LLC, Chgo; pres., CEO Garden Ridge Corp., Houston; pres. Dominick's Finer Foods, Oak Brook, Ill.; founding prin. Lone Star Retail Partners, LLC; pres., CEO Bi-Lo/Winn Dixie BI-LO, LLC, Jacksonville, Fla., 2012—. Bd. mem. Metro YMCA, York Christian Coll., York, Nebr., Randall's Food Markets, Topco Assoc., Inc., Mem. Care Sys. Office: Bi-Lo LLC 5050 Edgewood Ct Jacksonville FL 32254-3699

ONUFRIYENKO, YURI, cosmonaut; b. Ryasnoe, Ukraine, Feb. 6, 1961; m. Valentina Mikhailovna Ryabovol; 3 children. Pilot/engr. diploma, V.M. Komarov Eisk Higher Mil. Aviation Sch., 1982; degree in cartography, Moscow State U., 1994. Commd. Russian Air Force, 1994, advanced through grades to col.; cosmonaut candidate Y.A. Gagarin Cosmonaut Tng. Ctr., Russia, 1989—91, test cosmonaut, 1991—, comdr. MIR-21, 1996. Crew mem. STS-100 Endeavour Mission, 2001, Soyuz TMA-1 to ISS, 2002; comdr. Expedition-18 to ISS, 2008. Decorated medals (2) Russian Armed Forces; named Chevalier, French Honor Legion. Office: NASA/Johnson Space Ctr co Astronaut Office/CB Houston TX 77058

ONUNKWO, EMMANUEL NWAFOR, retired economics professor; b. Ogbunike, Anambra, Nigeria, July 21, 1933; came to U.S., 1966; s. Justin Binyelum and Susannah (Anoma) O.; m. Hazel Herbalene Johnson, June 7, 1969. BA in Econs., U. Durham, Eng., 1960; M Pub. and Internat. Affairs, U. Pitts., 1968; MA in Econs., Georgetown U., 1970, PhD in Econs., 1973. Sr. asst. sec. Ministry of Econ. Planning, Enugu, Nigeria, 1971-73, prin. asst. sec., 1973-74, chief planning officer, 1974, acting asst. contr. of planning, 1974-75; asst. prof. econ. Ft. Valley State Univ., Ga., 1975-78; asst. prof. econs. S.C. State U., Orangeburg, SC, 1978-82, assoc. prof. econs., 1982—87, prof. econs., 1987—2003, dept. chmn., 1988—92. Mem. Nigerian delegation World Bank, 1971; dir. Ctr. for Econ. Edn., 1986-88, S.C. State Coun. on Econ. Edn., DEEP adv. com., 1988-90. Mem. Nat. Econ. Assn., Nigerian Econ. Soc. Anglican/Methodist. Avocations: photography, reading, music. Personal E-mail: eno1427@aol.com.

OPPENHEIM, MARTHA KUNKEL, pianist, educator; b. Port Arthur, Tex., June 25, 1935; d. Samuel Adam and Grace (Moncure) Kunkel; m. Russell Edward Oppenheim, June 18, 1960; children: Lauren Susan, Kristin Lee Oppenheim Mortenson. MusB with honors, U. Tex., 1957, MusM, 1959; diploma in piano, Juilliard Sch. Music, 1960; student, Am. Conservatory, Fontainebleau, France, 1956, student, 1958. Soloist Amarillo (Tex.) Symphony, Austin (Tex.) Symphony, U. Tex. Orch., San Antonio Symphony, Dallas Symphony, Heilbronner Kammer Orch., Heilbron, Germany. Solo and chamber music recitals in Tex., N.Y., France; mem. Halcyon Trio, 1974—77; tchg. asst. U. Tex., 1957—59, 1968—69; pvt. piano tchr., San Antonio, 1962—; pianist in duo with cellist Dan Zollars, 1991—. Recipient 1st place award, Internat. Piano Rec. Festival, Nat. Guild Piano Tchrs., 1956, 1956, Tuesday Mus. Club Young Artist Competition, 1956, 1st place award Young Artist Competition, Amarillo Symphony, 1959, 1st place award G.B. Dealey competition, Dallas Symphony and Dallas Morning News, 1959; scholar, U. Tex., Juilliard Sch. Music. Mem.: San Antonio Music Tchrs. Assn., Tex. Music Tchrs. Assn., Music Tchrs. Nat. Assn., Tuesday Musical Club (San Antonio, bd. dirs.), Pi Kappa Lambda, Sigma Alpha Iota. Presbyterian. Home and Office: 9118 E Valley View Ln San Antonio TX 78217-5160 E-mail: moppenheim@satx.rr.com.

O'QUINN, ISRAEL D., state legislator; b. Abingdon, Va., Mar. 5, 1980; m. Emily Lauren Gentry. BA in Polit. Sci., Emory & Henry Coll., 2002. Mem. Dist. 5 Va. House of Delegates, 2012—, mem. Privileges and Elections Com., Fin. Com. & Militia Policy and Pub. Safety Com. Commr. Va. Tobacco Commn. Bd. mem. Va. Pub. Safety Found. Republican. Office: General Assembly Building PO Box 406 Richmond VA 23218 also: PO Box 16325 Bristol VA 24209 Office Phone: 804-698-1005. Office Fax: 804-698-6705. E-mail: DelIOQuinn@house.virginia.gov.

O'QUINN, WILLIAM L., JR., wholesale distribution executive, lawyer; b. 1968; AB, Duke U., Durham, NC; JD, U. NC, Chapel Hill. Bar: 1994. Asst. gen. counsel, asst. sec. Alliance One International, Inc. Mem.: ABA. Office: Alliance One International Inc 8001 Aerial Ctr Pkwy Morrisville NC 27560-2009 Office Phone: 919-379-4300. Office Fax: 919-379-4346.

ORBACH, RAYMOND LEE, physicist, researcher, former federal agency administrator; b. L.A., July 12, 1934; s. Morris Albert and Mary Ruth (Miller) O.; m. Eva Hannah Spiegler, Aug. 26, 1956; children: David Miller, Deborah Hedwig, Thomas Randolph. BS, Calif. Inst. Tech., Pasadena, 1956; PhD, U. Calif., Berkeley, 1960; PhD in Policy Analysis (hon.), The Rand Grad. Sch., Santa Monica, Calif., 2002; PhD in Engring. (hon.), Colo. Sch. Mines, Goldon, 2005. NSF postdoctoral fellow Oxford U., 1960-61; asst. prof. applied physics Harvard U., 1961-63; prof. physics UCLA, 1963-92, asst. vice chancellor acad. change and curriculum devel., 1970-72, chmn. acad. senate L.A. divsn., 1976-77, provost Coll. Letters and Sci., 1982-92; chancellor U. Calif., Riverside, 1992—2002, chancellor emeritus, Disting. prof. physics emeritus, 2002—; dir. Office Sci. US Dept. Energy, Washington, 2002—09, under sec. for sci., 2006—09; dir. Energy Inst., U. Tex., Austin, 2009—. Mem. physics adv. panel NSF, 1970-73; mem. vis. com. Brookhaven Nat. Lab., 1970-74; mem. materials rsch. lab. adv. panel NSF, 1974-77; mem. Nat. Commn. on Rsch., 1978-80; chmn. 16th Internat. Conf. on Low Temperature Physics, 1981; Joliot Curie prof. Ecole Superieure de la Physique et Chimie Industrielle de la Ville de Paris, 1982, chmn. Gordon Rsch. Conf. on Fractals, 1986; Lorentz prof. U. Leiden, Netherlands, 1987; Raymond and Beverly Sackler lectr. Tel Aviv U., 1989; faculty rsch. lectr. UCLA, 1990; Andrew Lawson lectr. U. Calif., Riverside, 1992; mem. external rev. com. Nat. High Magnetic Fields Lab., 1994-01. Author: (with A.A. Manenkov) SpinLattice Relaxation in Ionic Solids, 1966; divsn. assoc. editor Phys. Rev. Letters, 1980-83, Jour. Low Temperature Physics, 1980-90, Phys. Rev., 1983-87; contbr. articles to profl. jours. Recipient Whitney M. Young Humanitarian award Urban League of Riverside and San Bernardino, 1998, El Sol Azteca award La Prensa Hispana, 2000, Disting. Alumni award Calif. Inst. Tech., 2005; Alfred P. Sloan Found. fellow, 1963-67; NSF sr. postdoctoral fellow Imperial Coll., 1967-68; Guggenheim fellow Tel Aviv U., 1973-74. Fellow AAAS (chairperson steering group physics sect.), Am. Phys. Soc. (chmn. nominations com. 1981-82, counselor-at-large 1987-91, chmn. divsn. condensed matter 1990-91); mem. NSF (mem. rsch. adv. com. divsn. materials 1992-93), Phys. Soc. (London), Univ. Rsch. Assn. (chair coun. pres. 1993), Sigma Xi, Phi Beta Kappa, Tau Beta Pi. Office Phone: 512-471-2993. Personal E-mail: rorbach@earthlink.net.

ORBEN, ROBERT, writer; b. NYC, Mar. 4, 1927; s. Walter August and Marie O.; m. Jean Louise Connelly, July 25, 1945. Humor and speech writer for entertainment personalities, bus. execs., politicians, 1946—; writer Jack Paar Show, NYC, 1962-63, Red Skelton Hour, Hollywood, Calif., 1964-70; editor Orben's Current Comedy, Wilmington, Del., 1971-89; cons. to Vice Pres. Gerald R. Ford, Washington, 1974; speechwriter Pres. Gerald R. Ford, Washington, 1974-75; spl. asst. to pres., dir. White House speechwriting dept., Washington, 1976-77; speaker on uses of humor in communication, 1977—. Author: 2500 Jokes to Start 'Em Laughing, 1979, 2100 Laughs for All Occasions, 1983, 2400 Jokes to Brighten Your Speeches, 1984, 2000 Sure-Fire Jokes for Speakers, 1986, Speechwriter's Handbook of Humor, 2007, others. Recipient World Humor award Workshop Libr. on World Humor, 1992, Humor award Gliner Humor Ctr., U. Md., 2005; Literary fellow Acad. Magical Arts, 1996, Master of Influence award, Nat Speakers Assn., 2013 Mem. Writers Guild Am. Clubs: Nat. Press (Washington). Unitarian Universalist. Avocations: travel, theater. Home: 3709 S George Mason Dr Apt 205E Falls Church VA 22041-3700

ORDAN, MARK S., personal care industry executive; s. Harry and Doris Ordan; m. Kathryn Ann Sklar, Nov. 12, 1983. BA, Vassar Coll., 1979; MBA, Harvard Bus. Sch. Equities divsn. Goldman Sachs & Co.; co-founder, pres. then CEO Fresh Fields (sold to Whole Foods Market for $135 million in 1996), Md., 1991—96; co-founder (with Ken Brody) Chartwell Health Mgmt., Bethesda, Md., 1997; chmn. Federal Realty Investment Trust, Arlington, Va., 2003—06; CEO Sutton Place (changed name to Balducci's), Bethesda, Md., 2003—06; COO The Mills Corp., Chevy Chase, Md., 2006, CEO, pres., 2006—08; chief adminstrv., investment officer Sunrise Sr. Living, Inc., McLean, Va., 2008; CEO Sunrise Senior Living, Inc., 2008—. Bd. dirs. Fidelity & Trust Bank, Federal Realty Investment Trust, Sunrise Sr. Living. Exec. com. bd. trustees Vassar Coll.; bd. dirs. Cystic Fibrosis Found. Met., Washington. Mem.: Young President's Assn. Office: Sunrise Sr Living 7900 Westpark Dr Ste T900 Mc Lean VA 22102-4217 Office Phone: 703-273-7500. Office Fax: 703-744-1601.

ORDEMANN, WILLIAM, energy executive; BSChemE, Va. Tech. U., Blacksburg. V.p. Shell Midstream Enterprises, 1997—98, Tejas Natural Gas Liquids, LLC, 1998—99, Enterprise GP Holdings, LP, 1999—2001, sr. v.p., 2001—07, Tex. Ea. Products Pipeline Company, LLC, 2005; exec. v.p., COO Enterprise GP Holdings, LP, 2007—10; exec. v.p. Enterprise Products Holdings LLC, 2010—. Office: Enterprise Products Holdings LLC 1100 Louisiana St Houston TX 77002 Office Phone: 713-381-6500.

OREN, RAM, science educator; BS in Forest Resource Mgmt., Humboldt State U., Calif., 1978; MS in Forest Ecology, Oreg. State U., Corvallis, 1980, PhD in Physiological Ecology, 1984. Asst. forester Simpson Timber Co., Korbel, Calif., 1977; rsch. asst. Israel Nat. Park Authority, Tel-Aviv, 1978, Dept. Forest Sci., Oreg. State U., Corvallis, 1979—84; project scientist ecophysiological group, Acid Rain Project, dept. plant ecology U. Bayreuth, Germany, 1985—86, scientist, dept. plant ecology, 1986—93; scientist Jet Propulsion Lab., Calif. Inst. Tech., 1990—97; invited short term visitor Smithsonian Tropical Rsch. Inst., 1993; asst. prof. ecology/ecophysiology Duke U., 1986—92, assoc. prof. ecology/ecophysiology, 1993—2002, prof. ecology/ecophysiology, 2002—, Nicholas Prof. Earth Sys. Sci., chair environ. sci. and policy divsn., 2007—. Invited spkr. in field. Mem. editl. bd. Oecologica, Tree Physiology, reviewer for several publications. Mem.: AAAS, Union of Concerned Scientists, Ecological Soc. Am., Am. Inst. Biol. Sciences. Office: Duke U A319 LSRC Box 90328 Durham NC 27708 Office Phone: 919-613-8032. Office Fax: 919-684-8741. Business E-Mail: ramoren@duke.edu.

ORENDER, DONNA, marketing executive, former sports association executive; b. 1957; m. M.G. Orender; children: Jacob, Zachary stepchildren: Morgan, Colleen. BA, Queens Coll., NY, 1978; LLD (hon.), Adelphi U., 2007. Player (Women's Profl. Basketball League) NY Stars, 1978—79, NJ Gems, 1979—80, Chgo. Hustle, 1980—81; with ABC Sports, SportsChannel; owner Primo Donna Prodns.; with NBA Entertainment, PGA Tour, 1988—2001, sr. v.p. strategic devel., 2001—05; pres. WNBA, NYC, 2005—10; founder Orender Unlimited, 2010—; cons. PGA of America, 2011—. Prodr.: Insided the PGA Tour. Bd. mem. Beth El - The Beaches Synagogue, Monique Burr Found. for Children, Inc., Jacksonville Film & TV Adv. Coun., Maccabi USA/Sports for Israel. Named one of The Most Influential People in the World of Sports, Bus. Week, 2007, The 10 Most Popular Women in Sports, FoxSports.com, 2005; named to The Power 100, The Sporting News, 2005. Mem.: Women's Basketball Coaches Assn. (bd. dirs.). E-mail: donna@orenderunlimited.com.

ORGEBIN-CRIST, MARIE-CLAIRE, retired biology professor, department chairman; b. Vannes, France, Mar. 20, 1936; License Natural Scis., License Biology, Sorbonne, U. Paris, 1957; D. Scis., Lyons U., France, 1961. Stagiaire dept. biochemistry faculty medicine, Paris, 1957—58; stagiaire Centre Nat. de la Recherche Scientifique, Paris, 1958—60, attachee de recherche, 1960—62; research assoc. Population Council (Med. Div.), NYC, 1962—63; research assoc. dept. ob/gyn Vanderbilt Sch. Medicine, 1963—64, research instr., 1964—66, asst. prof., 1966—70, assoc. prof., 1970—73, Lucius E. Burch prof. reproductive biology, 1973—2005, prof. dept. anatomy, 1975—2005; dir. Vanderbilt Sch. Medicine (Center Reproductive Biology Research.), 1973—2005, prof. emeritus, 2005—. Editor-in-Chief Jour. Andrology, 1983-89 Recipient Career Devel. award NIH, 1968-73, NIH Merit award, 1986,; Fogarty Internat. sr. fellow, 1977; Disting. Scientist award Am. Soc. Reproductive Medicine, 1996. Mem. Am. Assn. Anatomists, Am. Soc. Cell Biology, Am. Soc. Andrology (v.p. 1994-95, pres. 1995-96, Disting. Svc. award 1997, Disting. Andrologist award 1990), Internat. Com. on Andrology, Endocrine Soc., Soc. for Study Fertility (Eng.), Soc. for Study Reprodn., N.Y. Acad. Scis. Office: Vanderbilt U Sch Med Ctr Reproductive Biology Rsch Rm R-1215 MCN Nashville TN 37232-0001 E-mail: m-c.orgebin-crist@vanderbilt.edu.

ORLIN, KAREN J., lawyer; b. Washington, Apr. 2, 1948; d. Hyman and Lenore O.; 1 child. AB Summa Cum Laude, in math., U. Pa., 1969; JD, Harvard U., 1972. Bar: NY 1973. US Dist. Ct. (so. and ea. dists.) NY 1973, US Ct. Appeals (2d cir.) 1973, Fla. 1982. Former assoc. Kronish, Lieb, Weiner & Hellman LLP, NYC, 1972-81; former sr. assoc. Valdes-Fauli, Bischoff, Kriss and Mandler, Miami, Fla., 1981-82, ptnr., 1982-83; former sr. assoc. Ruden, Barnett, McClosky, Smith, Schuster & Russell, P.A., Ft. Lauderdale, Fla., 1983-85, Shea & Gould, NYC and Miami, Fla., 1985-87; former of counsel Thomson, Muraro, Razook and Hart P.A., Miami, Fla., 1987—88; sr. v.p.-assoc. counsel, former asst. sec. Am. Savs. of Fla., F.S.B., Miami, Fla., 1988—95; former ptnr. Berman, Rennert Vogel & Mandler P.A., Miami, Fla., 1995—97; former mem. Zack Kosnitzky, Miami, Fla., 1997—99; former of counsel Akerman Senterfitt & Eidson P.A., Miami, 1999—2002; former counsel Stearns Weaver Miller Weissler Alhadeff & Sitterson P.A., Miami, 2002—03; former sr. atty. Rutherford Mulhall P.A., Boca Raton, Fla., 2004—05; former ptnr. Wasserstrom Newbreb & Wealcatch PL, Hollywood, Fla., 2005—06; pvt. practice & expert corp. gov., corp. & securities legal malpractice, fiduciary duty, legal ethics, 2006—; v.p. & gen. legal counsel Pacific Nat. Bank, Miami, Fla., 2007; former ptnr. Rothstein Rosenfeldt Adler P.A., Ft. Lauderdale, Fla., 2007—08. Instr. bus. law various inst. South Fla. and NYC; presenter in fields. Contbr. articles to profl. jours. Mem. Fla. Bar (corps., securities & fin. svcs. com. 1999—, chair 2004-06, vice chair, 2001-04), Fla. Bar Com. with CPAs & FICPA (vice chair 2007-08), Am. Mensa Ltd., Phi Beta Kappa, ABA (bus. law sect.), NY City Bar Assn., Coral Gables C. of C., U. Pa. Dade Alumni Club (sec., 1991-93, pres., 1993-95) Office: PO Box 430620 Miami FL 33243-0620 Office Phone: 305-794-6387. Office Fax: 305-668-7072. Personal E-mail: kjorlin@bellsouth.net. Business E-Mail: karen@orlinlaw.com.

ORLOWSKY, MARTIN L., tobacco company executive; b. NYC, Dec. 7, 1941; s. Solomon and Sylvia (Levine) O.; m. Carolyn Louise Brady, Mar. 25, 1973; children— Daniel, Keith, Matthew. BA, Long Island U., NYC, 1963. Media planner Compton Advertising, 1968—69, Young & Rubicam, Inc, 1969—71; v.p., media Grey Advt., 1971—76; sr. v.p., media and mktg. svcs. Needham, Harper & Steers, NYC, 1976—77; media dir. R.J. Reynolds Tobacco Co., Winston-Salem, NC, 1977—80, dir., mktg. services, 1980—82, v.p., brand mktg., 1982—84, sr. v.p., mktg., 1984—85, exec. v.p., 1986; pres. Grocery div. Nabisco Brands, U.S.A., Parsippany, NJ, 1986, DKM Holdings, 1988—90, Planters and Life Savers div. Nabisco Brands, U.S.A., Parsippany, NJ, 1997; sr. v.p. mktg. Lorillard Tobacco Co., 1990—92, exec. v.p. mktg. and sales, 1992—95, pres., 1995—2008, CEO, 1999—2008; pres., CEO Lorillard, Inc., Greensboro, NC, 1999—2010; chmn. Lorillard Tobacco Co., 2001—08, Lorillard, Inc., 2001—10. Vol., Peace Corps, Bolivia, 1963-65. Served to sgt. U.S. Army, 1966-68 Avocations: fishing, tennis. Home: 90 Beach Rd S Wilmington NC 28411-9217

O'ROURKE, BETO (ROBERT FRANCIS O'ROURKE), United States Representative from Texas, former city councilman; b. El Paso, Tex., Sept. 26, 1972; s. Pat and Melissa O'Rourke; m. Amy Hoover Sanders, Sept. 24, 2005; 3 children. BA in English Lit., Columbia U., 1995. Singer, guitarist Foss, Los Dregtones; co-founder Stanton Street Technology Group, El Paso, 1999—; city councilman Dist 8 City of El Paso, Tex., 2005—11; mem. US Congress from 16th Tex. Dist., Washington, 2013—, US House Homeland Security Com., 2013—, US House Veterans' Affairs Com., 2013—. Singer, guitarist (albums with Foss) The El Paso Pussycats, 1993, Fewel St., 1994. Democrat. Roman Catholic. Office: US House of Representatives 1721 Longworth House Office Bldg Washington DC 20515 also: 303 N Oregon St Ste 210 El Paso TX 79901 Office Phone: 202-225-4831, 915-541-1400.*

O'ROURKE, ROBERT A., cardiologist, educator; b. San Francisco, Calif., June 12, 1936; m. Suzann Reiter, June 8, 1963; children: Michael, Kevin, Sean, Kathleen, Ryan. Student, Santa Clara U., 1954-55; BS, Creighton U., 1957, MD, 1961. Diplomate Am. Bd. Internal Medicine, 1968, Am. Bd. Cardiology, 1969. Straight med. internship Georgetown U. Hosp., Washington, 1961-62, jr. asst. resident internal medicine, 1962-63, sr. asst. resident internal medicine, 1963-64, med. houseofficer internal medicine, 1961-65, fellow cardiology dept., 1964-65; fellow U. Calif Cardiovasc. Rsch. Inst., Washington, 1965-66; staff cardiologist Madagan Army Hosp., Washington, 1966-68; instr. in medicine cardiology Georgetown U. Hosp., Washington, 1968-69; asst. prof. medicine cardiology coll. medicine U. Ariz., Tucson, 1969-70; asst. prof. medicine cardiology, dir. clin. cardiology section, dir. heart station U. Calif., San Diego, 1970-73, assoc. prof. medicine cardiology, dir. clin. cardiology section, dir. coronary care unit, assoc. dir. myocardial infarction rsch. unit, 1973-76; acting chief medicine Audie L. Murphy Vets. Adminstrn. Hosp., 1977-78; Charles Conrad Brown disting. prof. cardiovasc. disease, dir. cardiovasc. divsn. U. Tex. Health Sci. Ctr., San Antonio, 1976—. Cons. in field for various hosps.; vis. professorships to various med. ctrs./univs. Mem. editl. bd.: Jour. Am. Coll. Cardiology, 1983-87, Am. Jour. Cardiology, 1976-81, 83—, Am. Heart Jour., 1980—, Clin. Cardiology, 1985—, Jour. Intensive Care Medicine, 1985—, Internat. Jour. Cardiology, 1981—, Annals of Internal Medicine, 1979-82, Med. Month, 1983—, Weekly Update: Cardiology, 1978-80, Cardiovasc. Medicine, 1976-80, Cardiologic Consultation, 1980—, Cardiovasc. Drugs and Therapy, 1989-90, Coronary Artery Disease, 1990—, Cardiology, 1990—, Jour. Heart Valve Disease, 1992, Current Problems in Cardiology, 1975—, assoc. editor, 1980-83, editor-in-chief, 1984—, Circulation, 1977-80, 81-83, 83-86, 86—, consulting editor, 1993, Yr. Book Cardiology, 1986-92, assoc. editor, 1986-92; assoc. editor: Jour. Applied Cardiology, 1985-90, Am. Jour. Cardiovasc. Pathology, 1985—. Recipient Sinsheimer award for

Cardiovasc. Rsch., 1969-70; grantee from various sponsors. Fellow Am. Coll. Physicians, Am. Coll. Cardiology; mem. Am. Soc. Clin. Investigation, Am. Fedn. Clin. Rsch., Am. Heart Assn., Am. Physiological Soc., Assn. Army Cardiologists, Southern Soc. Clin. Rsch., Am. Soc. Echocardiography, Assn. U. Cardiologists, Alpha Omega Alpha, others. Office: The Univ Tex Health Sci Ctr VAH Rm C644 7703 Floyd Curl Drive San Antonio TX 78229-3900 Office Phone: 210-617-5100. Office Fax: 210-567-4687.

ORR, ARTHUR WOOTEN, state legislator, lawyer; b. Decatur, Ala., May 25, 1964; s. Rufus Wilson and Florence Blythe (Patton) Orr; m. Amy Wallace Bethshares; 1 child, Jack. BA in English, Wake Forest U., 1986; JD, U. Ala., Tuscaloosa, 1989. Bar: Ala. 1989, D.C. 1991, U.S. Dist. Ct. (no. dist.) Ala. 1992, U.S. Ct. Appeals (11th cir.) 1993. Instr. English U. Ala., Tuscaloosa, 1988-89; ednl. cons. US Peace Corps, Katmandu, Nepal, 1989-91; ptnr. Harris Caddell & Shanks, Decatur, 1992—; gen. counsel Cook's Pest Control; mem. Dist. 3 Ala. State Senate, Montgomery, 2006—. Contbr. articles to profl. jours. Pres. Vol. Ctr. of Morgan County, Decatur, 1997; chmn. bd. Decatur Heritage Christian Acad., Decatur, 1996-97. Recipient Heritage award Decatur Heritage Christian Acad., 1997, Comms. award Points of Light Found., 1996. Mem. Morgan County Bar Assn. (pres. young lawyers divsn. 1995-96), Rotary Club of Decatur, Jaycees (pres. 1993-94), Decatur C. of C. (bd. dirs. 1993-94). Republican. Presbyterian. Avocations: reading, writing, jogging. Office: Harris Caddell & Shanks 214 Johnston St SE Decatur AL 35601-2516 also: Ala State Senate Ala State House 11 S Union St Montgomery AL 36130 Office Phone: 256-345-3861, 334-242-7800.

ORR, EMMA JANE, pharmacist, educator; b. Pennington Gap, Va., Sept. 30, 1956; d. Clyde Wilson and Monnie Lee (Daugherty) O.; m. Allen Emerson Clark, Oct. 24, 1981; 1 child, Katherine Wilson. BS in Pharmacy, Med. Coll. Va., 1979; D of Pharmacy with highest hons., U. Ky., 1981. Registered pharmacist, Va., Ky., Tenn. Asst. dir. pharmacy St. Mary's Hosp., Norton, Va., 1980-84, Norton Community Hosp., 1984-90; clin. coord. Hoston Valley Hosp., Kingsport, Tenn., 1990—; asst. clin. preceptor Sch. Pharmacy, East Tenn. State U., Johnson City; ch. choir dir. 3 bells Units Methodist Ch. Adj. faculty Mountain Empire C.C., Big Stone Gap, Va., 1981—; asst. clin. prof. dept. pharmacy and pharmaceutics Med. Coll. Va., Richmond, 1982—; clin. prof. So. Sch. Pharmacy Mercer U.; mem. pharmacy coll. admission and curriculum coms. East Tenn. State U., 2005—. Tchr., children's spkr. Ch. United Meth. Ch., Duffield, Va., Mountain Empire Older Citizens, Wise, Va., 1983-85; leader Girl Scouts, Duffield, Va. Named Young Career Woman of Yr. Bus. and Profl. Women's Club, 1983. Mem.: Va. Soc. Hosp. Pharmacists, Am. Soc. Hosp. Pharmacists. Methodist. Avocations: reading, needlecrafts, skiing, swimming. Home: 192 Cecil D Quillen Dr Duffield VA 24244 Office Phone: 423-224-5601. Personal E-mail: ejo@adelphia.net. Business E-Mail: ejane.orr@wellmont.org.

ORR, KENNETH BRADLEY, academic administrator; b. Charlotte, NC, Mar. 15, 1933; s. Frank Wylie and Kate Harriett O.; m. Ruth Douglas Currie; children: Kevin, Jeffrey, Jonathan. BA, Duke U., 1954; MDiv, Union Theol. Sem., 1960, ThM, 1961; PhD, U. Mich., 1978; LittD, Carroll Coll., 1990; DD, Presbyn. Coll., 1997. Ordained to ministry, Presbyn. Ch., 1961. Minister West End Presbyn. Ch., Roanoke, Va., 1961-64; asst. to pres. Union Theol. Sem., Richmond, Va., 1964-68, v.p., 1968-74; pres. Presbyn. Sch. Christian Edn., Richmond, 1974-79, Presbyn. Coll., Clinton, S.C., 1979-97, pres. emeritus, 1997—; sr. v.p. John McRae & Assocs., Atlanta, 1997—. Past mem. coun. presidents Nat. Assn. Intercollegiate Athletics, Kansas City, Mo., chmn. S. Atlantic Conf., 1989—91; mem. nat. adv. com. on instnl. quality and integrity U.S. Dept. Edn., 1995—2001. Contbr. to religious and ednl. publs. With USAF, 1955—57. Mem. Assn. Presbyn. Colls. and Univs. (pres. 1994, exec. com.), Coun. Ind. Colls. (bd. dirs. 1993-96), Laurens County C. of C. (past pres.), Kiwanis. Democrat. Avocations: reading, travel, classical music. Personal E-mail: kb003@bellsouth.net.

ORR, M. ALAN, oil industry executive; BS in Engring., US Mil. Acad., West Point, 1973. Roughneck Helmerich & Payne, Inc., 1975, v.p., chief engr. Helmerich & Payne Internat. Drilling Co., 1991—2005, exec. v.p. engring. & devel., 2006—. Named Contractor of Yr., Internat. Assn. Drilling Contractors, 2005. Office: Helmerich & Payne Inc 1437 S Boulder Ave Tulsa OK 74119 Office Phone: 918-742-5531. Office Fax: 918-742-0237.

ORR, ROB, state legislator; b. Dec. 20, 1955; m. Pam Orr; children: Chelsea, Randi, Michael, Taylor, James. Owner, broker Orr & Associates Real Estate, Burleson; mem. Dist. 58 Tex. House of Representatives, 2004—. Mem.: Nat. Assn. of Realtors (bd. dirs.), Tex. Assn. of Realtors (bd. dirs.), Greater Fort Worth Assn. of Realtors (pres.). Republican. Presbyterian. Office: 201 W Ellison Ste 201 Burleson TX 76028 also: Room EXT E1.414 PO Box 2910 Austin TX 78768 Office Phone: 817-295-5158, 512-463-0538. Office Fax: 817-295-5319.

ORR-CAHALL, ANONA CHRISTINA, museum director, art historian; b. Wilkes-Barre, Pa., June 12, 1947; d. William R.A. and Anona (Snyder) Boben; m. Richard Cahall. BA magna cum laude, Mt. Holyoke Coll., 1969; MA, Yale U., 1974, MPhil, 1975, PhD, 1979. Curator of collections Norton Gallery Art, West Palm Beach, Fla., 1975-77; asst. prof. Calif. Poly. State U., San Luis Obispo, 1978-81, Disting. prof., 1981; dir. art div., chief curator Oakland (Calif.) Mus., 1981-88; chief exec. officer Corcoran Gallery Art, Washington, 1988-90; dir. Norton Mus. Art, West Palm Beach, 1990—. Author: Addison Mizner: Architect of Dreams and Realities, 1974, 2d printing, 1993, Gordon Cook, 1987, Claude Monet: Am Impression, 1993; editor: The Art of California, 1984, The American Collection at the Norton Museum of Art, 1995. Office: Norton Museum of Art 1451 S Olive Ave West Palm Beach FL 33401-7162 Fax: 561-832-6529.

ORROCK, NANCY (NAN) GROGAN, state legislator; b. Abingdon, Va., Nov. 8, 1943; c Jesse & Daniel. BA, Mary Washington Coll., Univ. Va., 1965. Legal sec. Emory Legal Aid Soc., 1969—71; mgmt. positions Nabisco Inc., 1971—87; exec. dir. Fund for So. Communities Found., 1987—93; program dir. Women's Action for New Directions, 1997—; mem. Dist. 30 Ga. House Reps., 1987—92, mem. Dist. 56, 1993—2002, mem. Dist. 51, 2003—04, mem. Dist. 56, 2005—06; mem. Dist. 36 Ga. State Senate, 2007—. Republican. Unitarian-Universalist. Mailing: 1070 Delaware Ave SE Atlanta GA 30316-2470 Office Phone: 404-524-5999. Office Fax: 404-622-0486. Business E-Mail: nan.orrock@senate.ga.gov.

ORROCK, ROBERT DICKSON (BOBBY ORROCK), state legislator; b. Fredericksburg, Va., Nov. 13, 1955; s. Welford Orrock and Cornelia Houck; m. Betsy Malinda Massey Orrock, 1978 (dec.); children: Robert D. Jr., Lila Joanna, Welford Thomas. Attended, Germanna CC, Locust Grove, Va., 1975—76; BS in Agr. Edn., Va. Polytechnic Inst. and State U., Blacksburg, 1978; MEd in Agr. Edn., Va. State U., Petersburg, 1988. Sales rep., New Holland, Va., 1985—86; vocat. agr. instr. Hanover County, Va., 1986—91; broadcaster Sta. WFLS Radio, Fredericksburg, 1988—; mem. Dist. 54 Va. House of Delegates, 1990—; agr. edn. instr. Spotsylvania HS, Va., 1991—. Hunter safety instr. Va. Game Commn., 1980—; deacon, trustee Bethany Bapt. Ch.; bd. dirs. Rappahannock Area Emergency Med. Svc., 1984—96; trustee Ladysmith Vol. Rescue Squad, Va. Recipient Outstanding Vocat. Agr. Instr. award, Va. State Dairyman's Assn., 1983, Va. Farm & Home Electrification Coun., 1987, Outstanding Young Virginian award, Va. Jaycees, 1994, Disting. Svc. award, Fredericksburg Jaycees, 1994, Pub. Svc. award, Fredericksburg Area Bldg. Assn., 1994, Friend Extension award, 1996, Outstanding Svc. award, Nat. Agrl. Educators & Assn., 1998; named Dist. Tchr. of Yr., Tri-County Soil & Water Conservation, 1980—83, Legis. of Yr., Va. Vocat. Assn., 1993. Mem.: Fredericksburg Area C. of C., Va. Vocat. Agr. Tchrs. Assn. (former pres.), Rappahannock Area Assn. Retarded Citizens (bd. mem. 1990—96), Spotsylvania Lions, Phi Delta Kappa, Rappahannock Chpt. Republican. Baptist. Office: PO Box 458 Thornburg VA 22565 Office Phone: 540-891-1322. Business E-Mail: DelBOrrock@house.virginia.gov.

ORTEGA, CHARLES L., state legislator; m. Margaret Ortega; 2 children. Mem. Dist. 52 Okla. House of Representatives, 2008—. Republican. Office: 2300 N Lincoln Blvd Rm 537 Oklahoma City OK 73105 Mailing: 1509 N Main PMB 292 Altus OK 73521 Office Phone: 405-557-7369, 580-482-0259. Business E-Mail: charles.ortega@okhouse.gov.

ORTEGO, STEPHEN J., state legislator; BArch, MArch, Tulane U., New Orleans. Co-founder, home builder and contractor Ecolafayette, La.; mem. Dist. 39 La. House of Reps., Baton Rogue, 2012—. Active Make It Right Found.; bd. dirs. World Studies Inst. La. Democrat. Office: La House of Reps 900 N 3rd St PO Box 94062 Baton Rouge LA 70804 Business E-Mail: ortegos@legis.la.gov.

ORTH, DAVID NELSON, endocrinologist, educator, sculptor, potter; b. East Orange, NJ, Mar. 5, 1933; s. John Joseph and Marjorie Adelaide (Wauters) O.; m. Linda Diana D'Errico, June 9, 1979; children by previous marriage: John Randall (dec.), Jennifer Stewart, Julie Thomas. ScB in Chemistry, Brown U., 1954; MD, Vanderbilt U., 1962. Intern, Osler med. service Johns Hopkins Hosp., Balt., 1962-63, fellow in medicine, 1962-65; asst. resident John Hopkins Hosp., Balt., 1963-65; mem. faculty dept. medicine Vanderbilt U. Sch. Medicine, Nashville, 1965—, prof., 1975-98, prof. emeritus, 1998—, joint dir. endocrinology div. dept. medicine, 1968-81, dir. cancer research and treatment ctr., 1972-77, dir. div. endocrinology, 1984-96; sculptor and potter, 1998—. Scholar-in-residence Rockefeller Found. Bellagio Study and Conf. Ctr., Italy, 1989; vis. scientist Vollum Inst. for Advanced Biomed. Rsch., Oreg. Health Scis. U., Portland, 1993-94. Contbr. numerous articles in field of endocrinology to med. jours. Served with U.S. Navy, 1954-57. John and Mary R. Markle scholar, 1968-73; Howard Hughes Med. Inst. investigator, 1969-75 Mem. AAUP, AAAS, ACP, Assn. Am. Physicians, Am. Soc. Clin. Investigation, Endocrine Soc. (sec.-treas. 1989-94, pres. 1997-98), N.Y. Acad. Scis., Am. Fedn. Clin. Rsch., So. Soc. Clin. Investigation. Personal E-mail: orth@comcast.net.

ORTIZ, ALVARO, legislative staff member; b. Madrid; Degree in Journalism, Complutense U., Madrid, 1996; MA in Journalism, U. Mo., 2003. Asst. chief editor on-line newspaper Estrella Digital, Madrid, 1997—2000; reporter EFE Spanish News Agy., Madrid, 2000—01; reporter, anchor sta. KOMU Channel 8, Columbia, Mo., 2002—03; reporter, prodr. news divsn. Azteca America, Washington, 2003—04, Tex. News Bur. chief Houston, 2004—09; press sec. Office US Rep. Al Green, Houston, 2010—. Democrat. Office: Dist Office US Rep Al Green 3003 S Loop W Ste 460 Houston TX 77054 Office Phone: 713-383-9234. Office Fax: 713-383-9202.

ORTIZ, JUAN CARLOS, marketing executive; b. 1968; Asst. copywriter Leo Burnett Worldwide, Inc., Colombia, creative dir., 1996—99, gen. mgr., 1999—2002, worldwide creative dir. Chgo., 2002—05, pres. Latin American region, 2005—07; co-pres. Leo Burnett North Am., 2007; pres. Latin ops. DDB Worldwide Comm. Grp., Inc., Miami, Fla., 2007—. Pres. of jury FIAP awards show, 2008. Recipient Cannes Gold Lion, 2000; named to AAF's Advt. Hall of Achievement. Office: DDB Worldwide Comm Grp Inc 806 Douglas Rd 11th Fl Miami FL 33134

ORTIZ-TAYLOR, SHEILA, retired English language educator; b. LA, Sept. 25, 1939; d. John Santray and Juanita Loretta (Shrode) T.; m. John Leonard Clendenning, Aug. 27, 1958 (div. 1971); m. Joy Lynn Lewis, Mar. 16, 1991; children: Andrea, Laura, Jessica, Will, Lynn. BA, Calif. State U., Northridge, 1963; MA, UCLA, 1964, PhD, 1973. Lectr. Calif. State U., Northridge, 1964-70; prof. emerita English Fla. State U., Tallahassee, 2006—. Author: (novels) Faultline, 1982, Spring Forward/Fall Back, 1985, Southbound, 1990, Coachella, 1998, Outrageous, 2006, Assisted living, 2007, Homestead, 2011, (book of poetry) Slow Dancing at Miss Polly's, 1989 (memoir) Imaginary Parents, 1996. Recipient Fulbright fellowship Fulbright Assn., 1991; fellowship Nat. Endowment for the Arts, 2008. Democrat. Home: 4146 Diplomacy Cir Tallahassee FL 32308 Business E-Mail: sortiztaylor@fsu.edu.

ORTON, JEFF, retail executive; BA in English, Allegheny Coll., 1978; MA in English Lit., Penn State U., 1981. Chief info. officer, chief logistics officer Wilsons Leather, 1993—2007; chief info. & logistics officer Genesco, Inc., 2010—. Office: Genesco Inc Genesco Park 1415 Murfreesboro Rd Nashville TN 37217-2895 Office Phone: 615-367-7000. Office Fax: 615-367-8278. Business E-Mail: jorton@genesco.com.

ORTON, KYLE, professional football player; b. Altoona, Iowa, Nov. 14, 1982; s. Byron. BA in History, Purdue U., 2005. Quarterback Chgo. Bears, 2005—09, Denver Broncos, 2009—11, Dallas Cowboys, 2012—. Named Big Ten Offensive Player Yr., Sporting News, 2004. Office: Dallas Cowboys One Cowboys Pky Irving TX 75063

ORWIG, MATTHEW DANE, lawyer, former prosecutor; b. Ardmore, Okla., Jan. 2, 1959; s. Richard R. and Mary E. (Pyle) O.; m. Melissa L. Vaughan, July 11, 1981; children: Joshua Matthew, Rachel Elizabeth, Jacob Andrew. BS, Tex. Tech. U., 1981, JD, 1984. Bar: Tex. 1985, US Dist. Ct. (no. dist.) Tex. 1985, US Ct. Appeals (5th cir.) 1985. Legal intern for no. dist. Tex. US Dept. Justice, Dallas, 1983; briefing atty. for judge US Dist. Ct., Lubbock, Tex., 1984-86; ptnr. Jones, Flygare, Galey, Moody and Brown, Lubbock, Tex., 1986-89; asst. US atty. (ea. dist.) Tex. US Dept. Justice, Dallas, 1989—2001, US atty., 2001—07; mng. ptnr., nat. chair govt. litig. & investigations group Sonnenschein Nath & Rosenthal LLP, Dallas, 2007—. Adj. prof. So. Meth. U. Law Sch, 1990—, Tex. Wesleyan U. Sch. Law, 1990—; legal advisor Exec. Office of U.S. Attys., Office of Legal Counsel, 1997—. Mem. ABA, State Bar Tex., Lubbock County Bar Assn., Lubbock County Young Lawyers Assn. (bd. dirs. 1987-89), Tex. Trial Lawyers Assn. Methodist. Office: Sonnenschein Nath & Rosenthal LLP 2000 McKinney Ave Ste 1900 Dallas TX 75201-1957 Office Phone: 214-259-0990. Business E-Mail: morwig@sonnenschein.com.

ORY, MARCIA GAIL, public health researcher; b. Dallas, Feb. 8, 1950; d. Marvin Gilbert and Esther (Levine) O.; m. Raymond James Carroll, Aug. 13, 1972. BA magna cum laude, U. Tex., 1971; MA, Ind. U., 1972; PhD, Purdue U., 1976; MPH, Johns Hopkins U., 1981. Rsch. asst. prof. U. N.C., Chapel Hill, 1976-77, from adj. asst. prof. to assoc. prof. sch. pub. health, 1978-88; rsch. fellow U. Minn., Mpls., 1977-78; asst. prof. Sch. Pub. Health U. Ala., Birmingham, 1978-80; program dir. biosocial aging and health Nat. Inst. on Aging, Bethesda, Md., 1981-86, chief social sci. rsch. on aging, 1987—2001; prof. Sch. Rural Pub. Health Tex A&M U. Sys., College Station, 2001—, regent prof., 2007—. Dir. RWJF Nat. Program Office on Increasing Phys. Activity in the 50 Plus, 2001—09. Contbr. more than 250 articles to profl. jours. Mem. several nat. task forces on aging and health issues; leadership coun., Healthy Aging Rsch. Collaborative, Health Found. South Fla.; bd. dirs. Ctr. for Health Improvement; local bd. mem. Am. Cancer Soc. Recipient Dept. HHS award, 1984, 1985, 1988, Dir.'s award, NIH, 1995, Merit award, 1999, 2001, Dir's Lifetime Achievement award, 2000, Polisher award, Gerontol. Soc. Am., 2001, Excellence in Program Innovation award, Archstone Found., 2005, Excellence in Rsch. award, Sch. Rural Pub. Health, 2005—06, Disting. Mentor award, Gerontological Soc. Am., 2007, Betty J. Cleckley Excellence in Minority Health and Ageing Hon. Mention award, 2007, Erickson Found. Excellence Rsch. award, 2009, Philip G. Weiler Leadership in Aging award, 2010, Tex. A&M Health Sci. Ctr. Presdl. Rsch. award, 2012; named Disting. Alumna, Purdue U.; named one of 5 Industry Innovators in Active Aging, Internat. Coun. on Active Aging, 2003; named to McKnights Long Term Care News 100, 1997; fellow, Inst. Advanced Study Latrobe U., Melbourne, Australia, 2004. Fellow: Am. Acad. Health Behavior, Soc. Behavioral Medicine (program chmn. pub. health track 1988—89, program com. 1991—92, program chair lifespan/devel. track 2001—02), Acad. for Behavioral Medicine Rsch., Gerontol. Soc. Am.; mem.: APHA (program chmn. 1986, gov. coun. 1986—88, chmn.-elect 1989—91, chmn. 1992—93, leadership group 1996—, chair, Polisher Award Com. 2009—, chair, Womens Group 2009—, chair older women's interest group 2000—10, chair rural and environ. health group 2010—, Philip G. Weiler Leadership award 2010), Am. Sociol. Assn. (regional reporter 1984—94, program com. 1986, nominations com. 1987, councilor-at-large 1992—93), Delta Omega, Omicron Nu, Phi Kappa Phi. Avocations: walking, birding, travel. Office: Sch Rural Pub Health 1266 TAMU College Station TX 77843-1266

ORY, STEVEN JAY, physician, educator; b. Houston, Aug. 4, 1950; s. Edwin Marvin and Norma Gertrude O.; m. Kathleen Higgins, Jan. 10, 1981; children: Eleanor Claire, Edward Michael. BA, Washington and Lee U., 1972; MD, Baylor Coll., 1976. Diplomate Am. Bd. Obstetrics and Gynecology, subsplty. cert. in Reproductive Endocrinolgy and Infertility. Asst. prof. Duke U., Durham, NC, 1981-82, Northwestern U., Chgo., 1982-85; assoc. prof., cons. Mayo Clinic, Rochester, Minn., 1985-95, chmn. sect. reproductive endocrinology and infertility, 1985-95; pvt. practice reproductive endocrinology and infertility; mem. ob-gyn. staff Internat. U., Margate, Fla., 1995—; prof. ob-gyn. Fla. Internat. U., Miami, 2008—; vol. assoc. prof. obstets. and gyn. U. Miami, Fla., 1999—. Assoc. dir. Am. Soc. Reproductive Medicine, Birmingham, Ala., 1986-87; bd. trustees Northwest Med. Ctr., Margate, Fla., 2003—09. Asst. editor: Fertility and Sterility, 1988-96, assoc. editor, 2009-11, editor in chief, surveillance editor, 2011-; contbr. articles to profl. jours. Mem.: Ft. Lauderdale Ob-Gyn. Soc. (pres. 1998—2000), Soc. Reproductive Endocrinologists (sec.-treas., pres. 2001—02), Am. Soc. Reproductive Medicine (chmn. practice com. 1998—2000, bd. dirs. 1999—2002, v.p. 2004—05, pres.-elect 2005—06, pres. 2006—07, past pres. 2008—09, bd. dirs. 2010—), Soc. for Humanism in Medicine (bd. dirs. 1999—2002, v.p. 2004—05, pres.-elect 2005—06, pres. 2006—07). Office Phone: 954-247-6200.

ORZEL, DENNIS J., aerospace and defense parts manufacturing company executive; B in Biology & Chemistry, Ctrl. Conn. State U.; Exec. Edn. Program, Darden Sch. Mgmt. Various positions, including gen. mgr., turbine module ctr., plant mgr., north haven facility Pratt & Whitney; v.p., ops., distbn., Transp. Divsn. Exide Technologies Corp., 2003; v.p., mfg. ops. Vought Aircraft Industries, Inc., 2006, v.p., Integrated Aerosystems Divsn., 2008—. Office: Vought Aircraft Industries Inc Tower 1 Ste 900 201 E John Carpenter Freeway Irving TX 75062 Office Phone: 972-946-2011. Business E-Mail: dennis_orzel@voughtaircraft.com.

OSAKWE, CHRISTOPHER, lawyer, educator; b. Lagos, Nigeria, May 8, 1942; arrived in U.S., 1970, naturalized, 1979; s. Simon and Hannah (Morgan) Osakwe; m. Maria Elena Amador, Aug. 19, 1982; 1 child, Rebecca E. LLB, Moscow State U., Lomonosov, 1967; PhD, Moscow State U., 1970; JSD, U. Ill., 1974. Bar: Moscow 1967, Kazakhstan 1997. Prof. sch. law Tulane U., New Orleans, 1972-81, 86-88; Eason-Weinmann prof. comparative law, dir. Tulane U., Eason-Weinmann Ctr. Comparative Law, New Orleans, 1981-86; ptnr. Riddle and Brown, New Orleans, 1989—. Vis. prof. U. Pa., 1978, U. Mich., 1981, Washington and Lee U., 1986, Lomonosov Moscow State U., 1999—; vis. fellow St. Anthony's Coll. Oxford (Eng.) U., 1980, vis. fellow Christ Ch. Coll., 1988—89; cons. U.S. Dept. Commerce, 1980—85. Author: The Participation of the Soviet Union in Universal International Organizations, 1972, The Foundations of Soviet Law, 1981, Joint Ventures with the Soviet Union: Law and Practice, 1990, Soviet Business Law, 2 vols., 1991, The Russian Civil Code Annotated: Translation and Commentary, 2000, Comparative Law in Diagrams: General and Special Parts, 2000, 2d edit., 2002, Comparative Law: Diagrammatic Commentary, 2008, Russian Civil Code: Text and Analysis, 2008; author: (with others) Comparative Legal Traditions in a Nutshell, 1982, Comparative Legal Traditions - Text, Materials and Cases, 1985, 2d edit., 1994; editor: Am. Jour. Comparative Law, 1978—86, Jour. Fgn. Legis. and Comparative Law, 2006—; mem. editl. bd.: Am. Jour. Legal Edn., 1983—85. Carnegie fellow, Hague Acad. Internat. Law, 1969, Russian Rsch. fellow, Harvard U., 1972, USSR Sr. Rsch. Exch. fellow, 1982, Rsch. fellow, Kennan Inst. Advanced Russian Studies, 1988. Mem.: ABA, Soc. de Legis. Comparée, Supreme Ct. Hist. Soc., Am. Soc. Internat. Law, Am. Law Inst., Order of Coif. Republican. Roman Catholic. Home: 339 Audubon Blvd New Orleans LA 70125-4124 Office: 201 S Charles Ave Ste 3100 New Orleans LA 70170 Office Phone: 504-861-1272. Personal E-mail: osakwec@aol.com.

OSBAHR, ALBERT J., hospital administrator; s. Albert J. and Jeanne Osbahr. BA, MD, U. NC; MS in Cmty. Medicine, Marshall U., W.Va. Cert. American Bd. Family Medicine, in occpl. medicine and preventive medicine/pub. health American Bd. Preventive Medicine, American Bd. Ind. Med. Examiners, med. rev. officer American Assn. Med. Rev. Officers. Resident in family medicine Marshall U. Joan C. Edwards Sch. Medicine; resident in occupl./preventive medicine U. Ky.; pvt. practice family health practitioner in preventive medicine; occupl. health dir. Haywood Regional Med. Ctr., Clyde, NC; med. dir. occupl. health services Catawba Valley Med. Ctr., Hickory, NC. Lab dir., med. cons. Haywood County Health Dept.; med. reviewer Carolinas Ctr. Med. Excellence, ExamWorks, Inc., NC Dept. Disability Services. Mem. fed. motor carriers safety adminstrn. med. rev. bd. US Dept. Transp.; mem. rev. panel NC Med. Bd.; mem. NC Gov. Task Force on Pub. Health; bd. dirs. One Health Commn. Mem.: AMA (NC del. 1988—, mem. coun. sci. and health 2004, 2008, chmn. coun. sci. and health 2010—11, bd. trustees 2011—, mem. coun. on med. svc.), NC Med. Soc. (pres. 2008—09, mem. indsl. commn. liaison com., mem. hosp. med. staff com.). Office: Catawba Valley Med Ctr 810 Fairgrove Ch Rd SE Hickory NC 28602 Office Phone: 828-326-3800.

OSBORN, JOHN SIMCOE, JR., lawyer; b. Louisville, Jan. 14, 1926; s. John S. and Ruby (Pinnell) O.; m. Mary Jo Fishback, Sept. 6, 1947; children— Robert, John, Donna LLB, U. Louisville, 1949. Bar: Ky. 1949, U.S. Dist. Ut. (ea. and we. dists.) Ky. 1952. Exec. v.p., gen. counsel Louisville Title Ins. Co., 1954-72; ptnr. Tarrant Combs & Bullitt (name changed to Wyatt Tarrant & Combs 1980), Louisville, 1972—. Chmn. bd. Beargrass Corp. Capt. JAGC, U.S. Army, 1952-54. Fellow Am. Bar Found.; mem. Ky. Bar Assn., Louisville Bar Assn., ABA, Am. Land Title Assn., Am. Coll. Real Estate Lawyers, Rotary. Democrat. Lutheran. Office: Wyatt Tarrant & Combs 2800 Citizens Plz Louisville KY 40202 Office Phone: 502-562-7584, 502-589-5235. Business E-Mail: josborn@wyattfirm.com.

OSBORN, JUNE ELAINE, pediatrician, microbiologist, educator, foundation administrator; b. Endicott, NY, May 28, 1937; d. Leslie A. and Dora W. (Wright) Osborn; children: Philip I. Levy, Ellen D. Levy, Laura A. Jana. BA, Oberlin Coll., Ohio, 1957; MD, Western Res. U., 1961; DSc (hon.), U. Med. Dental Sch. N.J., 1990, Emory U., 1993, Oberlin Coll., 1993, Rutgers U., 1994, Case Western Res. U., 1997, SUNY, Stony Brook, 1999, U. Wis., 2004; DMS (hon.), Yale U., 1992; LHD (hon.), Med. Coll. Pa., 1994. Intern, resident in pediatrics Harvard U. Hosp., 1961—64; fellow Johns Hopkins, 1964—65, U. Pitts., 1965—66; prof. med. microbiology and pediat. U. Wis. Med. Sch., Madison, Wis., 1966—84, prof. pediat. and microbiology, 1974—84, assoc. dean Grad. Sch., 1975—84; dean Sch. Pub. Health U. Mich. Sch. Pub. Health, 1984—93; prof. epidemiology, pediat. and communicable diseases U. Mich. Sch. Pub. Health and Med. Sch., 1984—96, prof. emeritus, 2008—. Pres. Josiah Macy, Jr. Found., 1997—2007; pres. emeritus, 2008—; mem. rev. panel viral vaccine efficacy FDA, 1973—79, mem. vaccines and related biol. products adv. com., 1981—85; mem. exptl. virology study sect. Divsn. Rsch. Grants, NIH, 1975—79; mem. med. affairs com. Yale U. Coun., 1981—86; mem. life scis. associateships rev. panel NRC, 1981—84; mem. U.S. Army Med. R&D Adv. Com., 1983—85; chmn. working group on AIDS and the Nation's Blood Supply NHLBI, 1984—89; chmn. WHO Planning Group on AIDS and the Internat. Blood Supply, 1985—86. Contbr. articles to profl. jours.; mem. editl. bd.: Jour. AMA, 2002—11. Active task force in AIDS, Inst. of Medicine, 1986; adv. com. Robert Wood Johnson Found. AIDS Health Svcs. Program, 1986—91; nat. adv. com. on health of pub. program Pew and Rockefeller Founds.; active Global Commn. on AIDS, WHO, 1988—92; chmn. Nat. Commn. on AIDS, 1989—93; trustee Kaiser Found., 1990—98, Case Western Reserve U., Cleve., 1993—97; nat. vaccine adv. com. HHS, 1995—98; adv. coun. Nat. Inst. on Drug Abuse, 1995—98; internat adv. bd. Nat. Acads., 2002—05; bd. dirs. Legal Action Ctr., 1994—2001, Ctr. for Health Care Strategies, 1998—2003, The Mind Inst., 2003—05, US Pharmacopeia Bd., 2005—10. Recipient NIH Pub. Svc. award, 2000, Scientific Freedom and Responsibility award, AAAS, 1994, Lifetime Achievement award, Nat. Med. Fellowships, 2008; grantee NIH, 1969, 1972, 1974—75, Nat. Multiple Sclerosis Soc., 1971. Fellow: Infectious Diseases Soc. Am., Am. Acad. Microbiology, Am. Acad. Arts and Scis., Am. Acad. Pediat.; mem.: Inst. Medicine (health promotion and disease prevention bd. 1987—90, coun. mem. 1995—2000), Soc. Pediat. Rsch., Am. Assn. Immunologists. Personal E-mail: june.e.osborn@gmail.com.

OSBORN, LESLIE, state legislator; Mem. Dist. 47 Okla. House of Representatives, 2008—. Republican. Office: 2300 N Lincoln Blvd Rm 303-B Oklahoma City OK 73105 Mailing: PO Box 1200 Mustang OK 73064 Office Phone: 405-557-7333. Business E-Mail: leslie.osborn@okhouse.gov.

OSBORN, MARVIN GRIFFING, JR., educational consultant; b. Baton Rouge, Sept. 7, 1922; s. Marvin Griffing and Mamie (Hester) Osborn; m. Sarah Fleming Osborn, Aug. 3, 1945; children: Jane Fleming, Charles Porter. BA, La. State U., 1942, MA, 1946; LLD, St. Xavier U., 1971; DHum, Phillips U., 1977. Pub. relations counsel La. State U., 1945-47, acting dir. bur. pub. service, 1947; assoc. prof., chmn. dept. journalism and dir. pub. relations Howard Coll. (now Frank Samford U.), 1947-49; dir. pub. relations, lectr. journalism Miss. State Coll. (now Miss. State U.), 1949-53; dir. information Washington U., 1953-58, pub. relations adviser, 1955-58, dir. Devel. Funds, 1958-61; cons. coll. and univ. adminstrn., 1961—, Drake U., Phillips U., Duke U., Tex. Christian U., Hendrix Coll., Bethany Coll., others, Christian Ch. Found., Nat. Meth. Found. Christian Higher Edn., Lexington Theol. Sem., Memphis Theol. Sem., Nat. Benevolent Assn. Christian Ch., Sisters of Loretto; interim pres. St. Xavier Coll. (now St. Xavier U.), 1968—69; pres. Marvin Osborn, Inc., 1979—94. Mem. planning com. Conf. Advancement Understanding and Support Higher Edn., White Sulphur Springs, W.Va., 1958. Mem., co-chair Cypress Village Devel. Coun., Jacksonville, 1992—98; chair first trustee ballot com. Cypress Village Residents Coun., 2005; mem. Fiers-Brown Soc. Christian Ch. Found., 1991; mem. nat. fundraising com. Disciples World, 2002—04; treas. Cypress Village Christian Worship, 2011—; mem. exec. com. program and arrangements com. Gen. Assembly Christian Ch., 1977, 1987—89; trustee National City Christian Ch. Corp., 1981—85; bd. dirs., mem. exec. com., sec. divsn. higher edn. Christian Ch., 1973—77; mem. panel study fin. procedures Disciples of Christ, 1987—89; bd. dirs. St. Louis Heart Assn., 1969—75, Fla. Christian Ctr., 1986—88. Capt. US Army, 1942—45, ETO. Recipient Harry T. Ice Disting. Svc. award for Excellence in Philanthropy, Christian Ch. Found., 1991. Mem.: Soc. Profl. Journalists, Nat. Benevolent Assn. (amb. 1992—98), Coun. for the Advancement and Support Edn. (v.p. dists. 1951—52, v.p. membership 1952—53, sec.-treas. 1953—55, pres. 1959—60), Sigma Chi, Omicron Delta Kappa. Home: 13655 Myrica Ct Jacksonville FL 32224-6626

OSBORNE, CAROLINE L., law librarian, educator; BA in Polit. Sci. and Psychology, U. NC, Chapel Hill, 1988; JD, U. Richmond, 1991; LLM in Taxation, Emory U., 1992. Atty. Cadwalader Wickersham & Taft, Kennedy Covington Lobdell & Hickman, LLP, Hunter, Maclean, Exley & Dunn, P.C., Womble Carlyle Sandridge and Rice PLLC; reference and rsch. svcs. libr. U. Richmond Sch. Law; rsch. and instrnl. svcs. libr., lectr. law Washington and Lee Sch. Law, 2007—09, dir. Burks Scholars legal rsch. program, interim dir. Law Libr., 2009—10, dir. Law Libr., 2010—. Office: Washington and Lee University School Law 326 Sydney Lewis Hall 1 Denny Circle Lexington VA 24450 Office Phone: 540-458-8545. Office Fax: 540-458-8488. E-mail: osbornecl@wlu.edu.

OSBORNE, DAVID, state legislator; b. Mar. 27, 1964; BS, U. Ky. Farmer; real estate profl.; mem. Dist 59 Ky. House of Reps., 2005—. Mem.: Ky. Assoc. of Realtors, Prospect Christian Ch., Thoroughbred Club America, Oldham Co. C. of C. Republican. Christian. Mailing: PO Box 8 Prospect KY 40059 Office: Ky Legislature Rm 405B 702 Capitol St Frankfort KY 40601 Office Phone: 502-564-8100 ext. 679. Business E-Mail: david.osborne@lrc.ky.gov.

OSBORNE, ROBERT STEPHEN, lawyer; b. Montreal, Que., Can., Oct. 21, 1954; m. Martha Osborne; children: Tom, Sarah. AB magna cum laude, Harvard U., 1976, JD magna cum laude, 1979. Bar: Ill., 1979. Assoc. Kirkland & Ellis LLP, Chgo., 1979-85, ptnr., 1985—2002, Jenner & Block LLP, Chgo., 2002—06, 2009—10; group v.p., gen. counsel Gen. Motors Corp., Detroit, 2006—09; exec. v.p., exec. gen. counsel Booz Allen Hamilton, 2010—. Gen. counsel, Lands' End, Inc., Dodgeville, Wis., 1986-95, corp. sec., spl. asst. to bd. dirs., 1995-2002; adj. prof., U. Chgo. Law Sch., 2002-. Bd. dirs. Chgo. Shakespeare Theater, The Nature Conservancy of Alaska. Mem. ABA, Am. Soc. Corp. Secs., Internat. Bar Assn. Avocations: fly fishing, hiking. Office: Booz Allen Hamilton 8283 Grrensboro Dr Mc Lean VA 22101

OSBURN, CHARLES BENJAMIN, retired librarian, dean; b. Pitts., May 25, 1939; s. C. Benjamin and Lydia (Harmon) O.; divorced; 1 child, Christopher Bart; m. Sharon Tuffendsam, June 12, 1987; 1 stepchild, Bradley Alan Tuffendsam. BA, Grove City Coll., 1961; MA, Pa. State U., 1963; MS, U. N.C., 1971; PhD, U. Mich., 1978. Instr. French Pa. State U., University Park, 1963-66; asst. prof. U. Wis.-Whitewater, 1966-69; humanities bibliographer U. N.C., Chapel Hill, 1969-74; asst. dir. libraries SUNY-Buffalo, 1974-76; asst. univ. librarian Northwestern U., Evanston, 1976-80; dean, univ. librarian U. Cin., 1980-86; dean libraries U. Ala., Tuscaloosa, 1986—2001, prof. library sci., 1986—2001, dean, prof. emeritus univ. libraries, 2001—. Bd. dirs. Ctr. for Research Libraries, Chgo., SOLINET, Atlanta, Assn. Rsch. Librs., 1987-93; mem. rsch. libr. adv. counc. to Online Computer Library Ctr., Dublin, Ohio; adj. prof. Sch. Libr. and Info. Studies, U. Ala., Tuscaloosa, 2001-. Author: The Social Transcript: Uncovering Library Philosophy, 2009, Academic Research and Library Resources: Changing Patterns in America, 1979 (award ALA 1980), The Western Devaluation of Knowledge, 2014; compiler: Research and Reference Guide to French Studies, 2d edit., 1981; mem. editorial bd. Literary Research: A Journal of Scholarly Method and Technique, 1986—; co-editor: (with R. W. Atkinson) Collection Management: A New Treatise, 2 vols., 1991. Mem. ALA, MLA, Assn. Rsch. Librs., Phi Sigma Iota, Beta Phi Mu. Office: Univ Ala Sch Library and Info Studies Tuscaloosa AL 35487-0252 Business E-Mail: cosburn@bama.ua.edu.

OSGOOD, NANCY JEAN, medical educator, writer; b. July 6, 1951; d. Jack Kent and Lois Emma (Stober) Luttrell; m. Raymond Clifford Jordan, Jr., Oct. 13, 1984. BA in Sociology and Spanish, Yankton Coll., 1972; MA in Sociology, Drake U., 1974; cert. in gerontology, Syracuse U., 1979; PhD in Sociology, 1979. Rsch. assoc. Syracuse Rsch. Corp., NY, 1975—78; asst. prof. SUNY, Cortland, 1979—80, Med. Coll. Va., Richmond, 1980—92, prof., 1992—. Mem. Nat. Com. on Vital and Health Stats., Washington, 1982—84. Author: Senior Settlers: Social Integration in Retirement Communities, 1982, Suicide in the Elderly: A Practitioner's Guide to Diagnosis and Mental Health Intervention, 1985, Suicide Among the Elderly in Long-Term Care Facilities, 1991; editor: Life after Work: Retirement, Leisure, Recreation and the Elderly, 1982; co-author: Seniors on Stage: The Impact of Applied Theatre on the Elderly, 1985, Suicide and the Elderly: An Annotated Bibliography and Review, 1986; co-editor: Dynamic Leisure Programming with Older Adults, 1987, The Science and Practice of Gerontology: A Multi-disciplinary Guide, 1989, Alcoholism and Aging: An Annotated Bibliography and Review, 1995, Treating Alcohol and Drug Abuse in the Elderly, 2002. Selection com. King William HS, Va., 1985; active Va. State Rehab. Bd., Am. Cancer Soc. Recipient acad. scholarship, Yankton Coll., 1969—72, N.Y. State Dept. Mental Hygiene Rsch. fellowship, 1974—75, Nat. Inst. Edn. award, 1975—78, NIMH award, 1977—79, Presdl. Invitation to White House, 1984, 1991; grantee Va. Commonwealth U., 1981—82. Fellow: Gerontol. Soc. Am.; mem.: Internat. Platform Assn., So. Gerontol. Soc., Am. Sociol. Assn., Am. Assn. Suicidology. Avocations: playing piano and clarinet, gourmet cooking, parrots. Home: PO Box 245 Manquin VA 23106-0245

OSGUTHORPE, JOHN DAVID, medical educator; b. Fairbanks, Alaska, June 15, 1948; MD, U. Utah, 1973. Cert. Am. Bd. Otolaryngology, 1978. Prof. Med. U. SC, 1979—. Accreditation coun. Skull Base fellowship U. Zurich. Fellow: Am. Rhinologic Soc. (residence rev. comm. 1998—2004, chair, residence rev. comm. 2002—04, bd. mem. 2004—06), Am. Laryngol. Assn. (bd. dir. 1998—, pres. 2004), ACS, Am. Acad. Otolaryngic Allergy (bd. dirs. 1997—, coord. continuing edn. 2000—08, Pres.'s award 1999, 2003, Golden Apple award 2006, Pres.'s award 2008, pres.'s award 2011), Am. Acad. Otolaryngology-Head and Neck Surgery (rep. speciality soc. adv. com., Disting. Svc. award 1994, Bd. Govs. award 1999, 2001, Disting. Svc. award 2004, Pres.'s award 2004, Bd. Govs. award 2007). Avocations: scuba diving, fishing, hunting, gardening. Office: Dept Surgery Veteran's Administration Hosp 1109 Bee St Charleston SC 29401 Office Fax: 843-937-6110. Business E-Mail: osguthjd@musc.edu.

O'SHEA, DONALD C., physicist, educator, optical engineer; b. Akron, Ohio, Nov. 14, 1938; s. Donald Joseph and Sarah O'S.; m. Helen Rose Spustek, Oct. 20, 1962; children: Kathleen Susan, Sean Stanley, Sheila Sarah, Patrick Donald. BS, U. Akron, 1960; MS, Ohio State U., 1963; PhD in Physics, Johns Hopkins U., 1968. Rsch. fellow McKay Lab., Harvard U., Cambridge, Mass., 1968-70; asst. prof. Ga. Inst. Tech., Atlanta, 1970-75, assoc. prof., 1975-87, prof. physics, 1987—2004, prof. emeritus, 2004—. Author: Elements of Modern Optical Design, 1985; co-author: Introduction to Lasers and Their Applications, 1978; editor Optical Engring., 1998-99, 2001-09; co-author Diffractive Optics, 2004; contbr. some 40 articles to profl. jours. Fellow Internat. Soc. Optical Engring. (sec. 1997, v.p. 1999, pres. 2000), Optical Soc. Am. (Esther Hoffman Beller award 1996). Democrat. Roman Catholic. Achievements include creation of the optics discovery kit for children; 3 patents in optical design. Business E-Mail: doshea@prism.gatech.edu.

OSHMAN, GENE JAY, lawyer; b. Wharton, Tex., Jan. 21, 1958; s. Ben J. and Esther B. O.; m. Karen Eve Appel, May 30, 1982; children: Stephen, Katherine. BA summa cum laude, hist., Yale U., 1980, JD, 1983. Bar: Tex. 1984. Law clk. to Hon. M. Joseph Blumenfield US Dist. Ct. Conn., Hartford, 1983-84; assoc. Baker Botts LLP, Houston, 1984-90, ptnr., 1990—. Sr. editor: Yale Law Jour., 1982—83. Recipient Best Lawyers in America, Woodward White, Inc., 2001—, Tex. Super Lawyer, Tex. Monthly and Law & Politics, 2003—; named Guide to World's Leading Mergers and Acquisitions Lawyers, Experts Guides, 2004—06, Chambers USA, 2009—, Tex. Lawyer Dealmaker of Week, 2011, Lawyer of Yr., Houston Securities, Capital Markets Law, 2012; named one of Best Lawyers; named to BTI Client Svcs. All-Star Team for law firms. Mem. Coronado Club, Phi Beta Kappa, Houston Bar Assn., Houston Ballet (mem., bd. trustees, 2007-) Office: Baker Botts LLP 910 Louisiana St 1 Shell Plaza Houston TX 77002 Office Fax: 713-229-7778. Business E-Mail: gene.oshman@bakerbotts.com.

OSIAS, RICHARD ALLEN, corporate financial executive; b. NYC, Nov. 13, 1941; s. Harry L. and Leah (Schank) O.; children: A. Kimberly, Alexandra Elizabeth. Student, Columbia U., 1963; PhD, David Lipscomb U., 1988. Owner Osias Enterprises, Inc., numerous locations, 1953—98. Mem. bus. cabinet David Lipscomb U.; bd. dirs. Am. 21. Prin. works include city devel., residential and apt. units, developer City of Deer Park, LI, NY, founder, developer City North Lauderdale, Fla., founder, developer City of Lauderhill, Fla., complete residential housing communities, shopping centers, country clubs, golf courses, hotel chains, comprehensive housing communities; contributed Greystone Raquet and Tennis Club to Nolensville, Tenn.; owner, operator Coolsprings Exec. Plz., landmark office bldg., Internat. Common Market Shopping Complex and other office bldgs., shopping ctrs. in mid-southern region; co-author: South Florida Uniform Building Code; author: Prenuptial Bliss, 2003; columist: New York Daily Mirror, 1960s, 74-83, New York Herald Tribune, 1974-84. Mem. North Lauderdale City Coun., 1967—, mayor, 1968, police and fire commr., 1967—; hon. police chief NYC, Ft. Lauderdale, and Nashville Met. Police, 1994—; mem. Gold Cir., Atlanta Ballet; benefactor Atlanta Symphony Soc.; founder Boys Clubs Broward County, Tower coun. Pine Crest Prep. Sch.; v.p., bd. dirs. LaCiel Park Tower Condominium Assn.; bd. dirs. Tenn. Children's Home, MADD, Tenn. chpt., Tenn. Children's Home, Agape Children's Care Ctr., Nashville, 1993—; founding bd. dirs. AGAPE, Broward County chpt. Boys Club Am.; advisor to bd. dirs. Aviculture Microbiology Found., Inc. Recipient Best Am. House award Am. Home mag., 1962, Westinghouse award, 1968, Cert. of Merit for outstanding achievement and contbn. to City of Atlanta by Mayor Andrew Young, 1982; named Builder of Yr., Sunshine State Info. Bur., Fla. and Sunshine State Sr. Citizen, Fla., 1967-73, Builder of Month, Builder/Arch. Mag., 1992, Hon. Police Chief, Nashville, Tenn., 1995, N.Y.C., 1980; profiles on nat. and internat. media, including Dateline/CBS TV, NBC TV, CBS TV and Fuji Network (Japan). Mem. Fla. Sheriff's Assn., Ft. Lauderdale BBB, N.Y. BBB, Nashville BBB, Offshore Power Boat Racing Assn., Fraternal Order Police Assn. (pres.), U.S. C. of C., Fla. C. of C., Margate C. of C., Ft. Lauderdale C. of C., Smithsonian Instn., Soc. Founders U. Miami, Tower Coun., Columns Soc., Pinecrest Prep. Sch. (founder), Nat. Assn. Home Builders, Bankers Club (Miami, Fla.), Bankers Top of First Club, Quarter Deck Club (Galveston, Tex.), Boca Raton (Fla.) Yacht and Country Club, Maunalua Bay Club (Honolulu), Tryall Golf and Country Club (Jamaica), Top of the Home Club, Svc. Plus Club (France), Ensworth Red Gables Soc., Hawaii Loa Ridge Assn., Cannes Island Yacht Club, Canary Islands Yacht Club, Collier's Reserve Country Club (Naples, Fla.), Grey Oaks Country Club (Naples), Le Ciel Club (Naples; v.p. bd. dirs.), Hawaii Loa Ridge Assn. Personal E-mail: osias1@aol.com.

OSMAN, EDITH GABRIELLA, lawyer; b. NYC, Mar. 18, 1949; d. Arthur Abraham and Judith (Goldman) Udem; children: Jacqueline, Daniel. BA in Spanish, SUNY, Stony Brook, 1970; JD cum laude, U. Miami, 1983. Bar: Fla. 1983, U.S. Dist. Ct. (so. dist.) Fla. 1984, US Dist. Ct. (mid. dist.) Fla. 1988, US Ct. Appeals (11th cir.) 1985, Fla. Supreme Ct. 1987, US Ct. Mil. Appeals 1990; cert. family law mediator Fla. Supreme Ct., civil mediator, Fla. Assoc. Kimbrell & Hamann, PA, Miami, 1984-90, Dunn & Lodish, PA, Miami, 1990-93; pvt. practice Miami, 1993-98; shareholder Carlton Fields, Miami, 1998—, practice group leader, family law divsn. Bd. dirs. Miami City Club, Supreme Ct. Historic Soc., So. Legal Coun., Fla. Women of Achievement (bd. dirs. leading atty). Mem. adv. com. for Implementation of the Victor Posner Judgement to Aid the Homeless, 1986-89. Recipient Breaking the Glass Ceiling award Ziff Mus., 2000, In the Company of Women award Dade County, 2000, Judge Mattie Belle Davis award, 2000, FAWL's Rosemary Barkett Achievement award, 1997, Outstanding Past Vol. Bar Pres.'s award, 1996, Women's Park Founders and Wall of Honor award, 2001; selected for photographic exhibit Florida Women of Achievement, 2000, South Fla.'s Top 250 Lawyers South Fla. Legal Guide, 2001, 02, 03, 04, 05, 06, 07; Women of Impact award Women's History Coalition Miami-Dade County, 2007, named 100 Women to Watch MIA Metro Mag., Fla. Trend, 2000, Women's Park Hall of Fame, 2001, Super Lawyers 2006, 07. Fellow Am. Bar Found., Fla. Bar Found.; mem. ABA (family law, alternate dispute resolution, Ho. of Dels. 1998—, standing com. on independence of judiciary 2000-03, standing com. bar svs. 2003-, house select com., 2004-, bd. govs., 2010-), The Fla. Bar (budget com. 1989-92, 97-98, voluntary bar liaison com. 1989-90, spl. com. on formation of All-Bar Conf. 1988-89, chair mid-yr. conv. 1989, long range planning com. 1988-90, bd. govs. 1991-98, spl. commn. on delivery of legal svcs. to the indigent 1990-92, bus. law cert. com. 1995-96, practice law mgmt. com. 1995-96, chair program evaluation com., 1993-94, exec. com. 1992-93, 96-2000, rules and bylaws com., 1993-94, vice-chair disciplinary rev. com. 1994-95, investment com. 1994-95, vice-chair rules com. 1994-95, All-Bar Conf. chair 1997, chair grievance mediation com. 1997-99, pres.-elect 1998-99, pres. 1999-2000, exec. coun. family law sect. 2001—, vice-chair legis. 2001-2002, co-chair alternative dispute resolution com. 2003—, chair commn. legal needs of children, 2003-04, spl. commn. on disciplinary rev., 2003—, family law rules procedure com. 2003—,spl. com. succession planning), Dade County Bar Assn. (fed. ct. rules com. 1985-86, chmn. program com. 1988-91, bd. dirs., 1988—, 96-97, exec. com. 1987-88), Fla. Assn. Women's Lawyers Assn. (Dade County chpt. bd. dirs. 1984-85, treas. 1985-86, v.p. 1986-87, pres. 1987-88), Fla. Assn. Women Lawyers (v.p. 1988-89, pres. 1989-90), Fla. Bar Found. (dir. 1998-2001), Nat. Conf. Women's Bar Assn. (dir. nat. conf. 1990-91), Cuban Am. Bar Assn., Fla. Acad. Trial Lawyers, Dade County Trial Lawyers Assn., Nat. Conf. Bar Pres., So. Conf. Bar Pres., Leading Attys. (bd. dirs. 2000—), Iron Arrow Honor Soc., First Family Inns of Ct. Office: Carlton Fields PA 100 SE 2nd St Ste 4000 Miami FL 33131-2148 Office Phone: 305-530-0050. E-mail: eosman@carltonfields.com.

OSSOFF, ROBERT HENRY, otolaryngologist, surgeon; b. Beverly, Mass., Mar. 25, 1947; s. Michael Max and Eve Joan (Kladky) G.; m. Lynn Spilman, 1984; 2 children: Leslin, Jacob. BA, Bowdoin Coll., Brunswick, Maine, 1969; DMD, Tufts U., Medford, Mass., 1973, MD, 1975; MS in Otolaryngology, Northwestern U., Evanston, Ill., 1981. Diplomate Am. Bd. Otolaryngology. Intern Northwestern Meml. Hosp., Chgo., 1975-76; resident in otolaryngology and maxillofacial surgery Northwestern U. Med. Sch., Chgo., 1976—80, NIH rsch. fellow dept. otolaryngology and maxillofacial surgery, 1977-78, clin. fellow in head and neck surgery, 1980-81; jr. faculty clin. fellow Am. Cancer Soc. Northwestern Med. Sch., Chgo., 1981-84; faculty practice, otolaryngology, head and neck surgery, laryngology and care of profl. voice Northwestern Med. Sch., Chgo., 1981—86, Vanderbilt U. Med. Ctr., Nashville, 1986—, prof., otolaryngology, 2008—; exec. med. dir. Vanderbilt Voice Ctr., 1991—. Attending physician Cook County Hosp., Chgo., 1981—83, cons. physician, 1983—86; attending physician Northwestern Meml. Hosp, Chgo., 1981—86, Children's Meml. Hosp., Chgo., 1981—86; attending physician, chief otolaryngology svc. VA Lakeside Hosp., Chgo., 1982—85; attending physician, head divsn. otolaryngology head and neck surgery Evanston Hosp., 1983—86, chief divsn. otolaryngology, 1983—86; asst. prof. Northwestern U. Dental Sch., Chgo., 1980—86, Northwestern U. Med. Sch., Chgo., 1981—85, assoc. prof., 1985—86; attending surgeon, otolaryngologist-in-chief Vanderbilt U. Hosp., Nashville, 1986—, chief staff, 1995—97; attending surgeon VA Hosp., Nashville, 1986—; Guy M. Maness prof., chmn. dept. otolaryngology Vanderbilt U. Med. Ctr., Nashville, 1986—2008, assoc. vice chancellor health affairs, 1995—2005; assoc. dir. Vanderbilt Free-Electron Laser Ctr. Med. and Materials Rsch., Nashville, 1992—95; dir. Vanderbilt Bill Wilkerson Ctr. Otolaryngology Communication Scis., Nashville, 1997—2008; asst. vice chancellor, compliance and corp. integrity Vanderbilt Med. Ctr., 2008—; asst. vice chancellor, 2008—13; spl. asst. to vice-chacellor for health affairs, 2013—14. Sr. editor Lasers in Surgery and Medicine, 1987—94, editor-in-chief, 1995—2005, laryngology sect. editor Otolaryngology-Head and Neck Surgery, 2005—, mem. editl. bd. Clin. Laser Monthly, 1984—, Jour.

Voice, 1987—, The Laryngoscope, 1988—2003, Jour. of Laser Applications, 1988—2004, Otolaryngology-Head and Neck Surgery, 1988—, mem. editl. adv. bd. Gen. Surgery News, 1990—97, mem. editl. bd. Archives of Otolaryngology, 2006—, assoc. editor Diagnostic and Therapeutic Endoscopy, 1992—2000; co-editor: Complications in Head and Neck Surgery, W.B. Saunders Co., 1993, The Larynx, Lippincott Williams and Wilkins, 2002; contbr. over 160 articles to profl. jours., 60 chpts. in books; editor, co-editor (8 books in field). Bd. dirs. Laser Inst. Am., 1984—90; trustee Midwest Biolaser Inst., Chgo., 1981—86, Leadership Nashville, 1988—89, Nashville Leadership Music, 2008—09; bd. dirs. MDR, Performing Arts Ctr., 2010—, MDR, HCCA, 2011—. Recipient Nat. Rsch. Svc. award, NIH, 1977-78; Francis L. Lederer-Norval H. Pierce award, Chgo. Laryngol. and Otol. Soc., 1978, Hon. mem., 1986; Guest of Honor, First European Carbon Dioxide Laser Surgery Course and Workshop in Otolaryngology Head and Neck Surgery, Roskilde, Denmark, 1984; named a Prin. Investigator, NIH, 1977-78; Am. Cancer Soc., Ill. Divsn., 1981-82; VA Merit Rev., 1884-85; Nat. Cancer Inst., 1985-88; Office Naval Rsch., 1987-90, 91-94; A. Ward Ford Found., 1989-90. Fellow: ACS (bd. govs. 1996—2002, adv. coun. Otorhinolarygology 1996—2003), Am. Laryngol. Assn. (chmn. rsch. support task force 1994—96, coun. mem. 1996—2008, sec. 1998—2003, Daniel C. Baker Jr. lectr. 2001, v.p., pres. elect 2003—04, pres. 2004—05, presdl. citation 2008, historian 2010—, coun. mem. 2010—, Guest of Honor 2002, Presdl. citation 2003, DeRoaldes medal 2004, James Newcomb award 2007), The Triological Soc. (nat. nominating com. 1993, coun. mem. 1996—99, thesis adv. com. 1998—99, v.p. so. sect. 2002—03, coun. mem. 2002—03, 2005—, dir., CME 2005—11, Presdl. Citation 2008, pres. elect 2010, pres. 2011, Presdl. Citation 2006), Am. Soc. Head and Neck Surgery (coun. mem. 1991—94); mem.: AMA, Soc. Univ. Otolaryngologists Head and Neck Surgeons (coun. mem. 2002—05, pres.-elect 2004—05, pres. 2005—06), Assn. Academic Depts. Otolaryngology Head Neck Surgery (sec.-treas. 1996—98, pres. elect 1998—2000, pres. 2000—02, coun. mem. 2002—04), Am. Laryngol. Voice Rsch. Edn. Found. (bd. dirs. 1996—2007, sec. 1998—2003), Am. Bd. Otolaryngology (task force for new materials mem. 1985—89, assoc. examiner 1994—97, dir. 1995—2007), Cartesian Soc., Am. Broncho-Esophagological Assn. (coun. mem. 1987—90, treas. 1990—94, pres.-elect 1994—95, pres. 1995—96, Chevalier Jackson award 1997, Guest of Honor 2000, Presdl. Citation 2012), Soc. Head and Neck Surgeons, Am. Soc. Laser Medicine and Surgery (bd. dirs. 1985—88, chmn. program com. 1986—87, pres.-elect 1988—89, pres. 1989—90, nominating com. 1990—91, William B. Mark award 1992, Presdl. citation 2003), Am. Acad. Otolaryngology-Head and Neck Surgery (chmn. laser surgery com. 1983—89, chmn. self instl. package com. 1990—96, bd. dirs. 1992—95, coord. for devel. 2001—06, Cert. of Honor 1984, Disting. Svc. award 1995, Presdl. citation 1999, Disting. Svc. award 2004, Presdl. citation 2005), Am. Acad. Oral Pathology, Am. Acad. Oral Medicine, Sigma Xi, Omicron Kappa Upsilon. Achievements include reestablishment of department of otolaryngology at Vanderbilt University Medical Center in 1986; establishment of the Vanderbilt Voice Center in 1991; establishment of an advanced training laryngology fellowship program at Vanderbilt University Medical Center in 1992. Avocations: boating, skiing, fly fishing, golf, photography. Office Phone: 615-343-0429. Business E-Mail: robert.ossoff@vanderbilt.edu.

OSTBYE, TRULS, medical and public health researcher, epidemiologist; b. Norway, Dec. 15, 1954; arrived in U.S., 1999; m. Hemali Kulatilaka, 1984; children: Trevor, Adrian. MD, U. Bergen, 1979; MPH, Harvard U., 1983; PhD, U. Bergen, 2000; MBA, Edinburgh Bus. Sch., 2000. Exec. officer Directorate of Orgn. and Mgmt., Norway, 1981—84; spl. med. officer Nat. Inst. Pub. Health, Norway, 1984—85; lectr. U. Otago, New Zealand, 1985—86; Lalia B. Chase rsch. fellow Dalhousie U., Halifax, N.S., Canada, 1986—88; asst. prof. to prof. U. We. Ont., London, Canada, 1988—99; prof., dir. global health Dept. Cmty. and Family Medicine Duke U., Global Health Inst., Durham, NC, 2000—; prof. Duke-NUS Grad. Med. Sch., Singapore, 2008—; prof., dept. global pub. health and primary care U. Bergen, Norway. Contbr. more than 310 articles to profl. jours. Achievements include research in the epidemiology of aging and obesity. Office: Duke U Dept Cmty and Family Medicine DUMC 104006 Durham NC 27710 E-mail: truls.ostbye@duke.edu.

OSTEEN, JOEL, minister; b. Houston, Mar. 5, 1963; s. John and Dodie Osteen; m. Victoria Iloff, 1987; children: Jonathan, Alexandria. Student, Oral Roberts U., 1981—82. Ordained 1992. Prodr., creator John Osteen TV Program, 1982—99; pres., co-owner Sta. KTBU Channel 55, Houston, 1998—; sr. pastor Lakewood Ch., Houston, 1999—. Author: Your Best Life Now: 7 Steps to Living at Your Full Potential, 2004, Living the Joy Filled Life (Six Easy Steps to Living a Life of Victory Abundance and Blessing, 2005, Scriptures and Meditations for Your Best Life Now, 2006, Become a Better You: 7 Keys to Improving Your Life Every Day, 2007 (Publishers Weekly bestseller), Your Best Life Begins Each Morning: Devotions to Start Every New Day of the Year, 2008, It's Your Time: Activate Your Faith, Achieve Your Dreams and Increase in God's Favor, 2009 (Publishers Weekly bestseller), Every Day a Friday: How to Be Happier 7 Days a Week, 2011, I Declare: 31 Promises to Speak Over Your Life, 2012, Break Out!: 5 Keys to Go Beyond Your Barriers and Live an Extraordinary Life, 2013; co-author (with Dodie Osteen): Choosing Life: One Day at a Time, 2006; several compact discs titles and journals/devotional books. Named Most Influential Christian, Ch. Report Mag., 2006; named one of Barbara Walters 10 Most Fascinating People, 2006. Achievements include minister to the one of the largest and most diverse congregations in America; weekly television program appears on six cable networks and internationally in over 100 nations. Office: Lakewood Church PO Box 4600 Houston TX 77210*

O'STEEN, WENDALL KEITH, anatomist, neurologist, educator; b. Meigs, Ga., July 3, 1928; s. Wellna Hubert and Lillian (Powell) O'S.; m. Sandra Lynn Kraeer, July 30, 1983; children: Lisa Diane, Kerry Keith, Buckley Powell. BA, Emory U., 1948, MS, 1950; PhD, Duke U., 1958. Asst. prof. Emory U. Jr. Coll., Valdosta, Ga., 1948-49; instr. Emory U., Atlanta, 1950-51; prof. Emory U. Sch. Medicine, Atlanta, 1968-77; from asst. prof. to prof. med. br. U. Tex., 1958-67; asst. prof. Wofford Coll., Spartanburg, SC, 1951-53; prof., chmn. dept. neurobiology and anatomy, Bowman Gray Sch. Med. Wake Forest U., Winston-Salem, NC, 1977-93, prof. emeritus, 1993—. Mem. anatomy com. Nat. Bd. Med. Examiners, Phila., 1982-87. Contbr. over 150 articles to books, nat. and internat. jours. Lt. col. USAR. Recipient Golden Apple teaching award Med. Br. U. Tex., Galveston, 1967, Outstanding Tchr. award Emory U., 1973, Williams Disting. Teaching award Emory U., 1974, award for teaching excellence Bowman Gray Sch. Medicine, Wake Forest U. Mem. Am. Assn. Anatomists (exec. com. 1980-84, v.p. 1990-92), Assn. Anatomy Chairmen (exec. com. 1982-84, pres. 1990-91), So. Soc. Anatomists (pres. 1975-76), Soc. for Neurosci., N.C. Soc. Neurosci. (pres. 1980-81), Western N.C. Soc. Neurosci. (pres. 1987-88), Assn. Rsch. in Vision and Ophthalmology, Alpha Omega Alpha. Republican. Methodist. Avocations: gardening, music. Office: Wake Forest U Bowman Gray Sch Medicine Dept Neurobiology and Anatomy Winston Salem NC 27157-0001 Office Phone: 336-716-4368.

OSTEEN, WILLIAM LINDSAY, JR., federal judge; b. Greensboro, NC, Aug. 8, 1960; BS, U. NC, 1983, JD, 1987. Bar: NC 1987. Assoc. Osteen, Adams, Tilley & Walker, Greensboro, NC, 1987—91; ptnr. Adams & Osteen, Greensboro, NC, 1991—2007; judge US Dist. Ct. (mid. dist.) NC, Greensboro, NC, 2007—. Office: US Dist Ct Mid Dist of NC 324 W Market St Greensboro NC 27401 Office Phone: 336-332-6090.

OSTERBERG, EDWARD CHARLES, JR., lawyer; b. Honolulu, Jan. 1, 1942; s. Edward Charles and Emily Julia (Preston) O.; m. Susan Rhea Snider, Aug. 26, 1967; 1 child, Edward Charles III. BA, Northwestern U., Evanston, Ill., 1963, JD cum laude, 1966; LLM in Taxation, So. Meth. U., Dallas, 1972. Bar: Tex. 1966, Ill. 1966. Assoc. Vinson & Elkins, Houston, 1967-73, ptnr., 1974—. Reporter Internat. Fiscal Assn., Sydney, Australia, 1978, Barcelona, Spain, 1991. Contbr. articles to profl. publs. Mem. ABA (chmn. taxation com.), Houston Bar Assn. (chmn. taxation sect. 1987), Petroleum Club, Houston Racquet Club. Methodist. Home: 11222 Wilding Ln Houston TX 77024-5308 Office: Vinson & Elkins LLP 1001 Fannin St Ste 3300 Houston TX 77002-6760 Office Phone: 713-758-2192. Business E-Mail: eosterberg@velaw.com.

OSTERBERG, MARK WILLIAM, air transportation executive; b. Lincoln, Nebr., Aug. 11, 1950; s. William Harry and Lorraine (Schmalz) Osterberg; m. Nancy Stribling, Mar. 7, 1981; children: Kristin Michelle, Kimberly Ann. BBA, So. Meth. U., 1972; MA in Econs., Rice U., 1973; MBA in Acctg., U. Fla., 1974. CPA Tex. Chief acctg. officer Quinta Corp., Northwest Airlines; CFO Sun Country Airlines; with Deloitte Haskins & Sells (known as Deloitte & Touche USA LLP), audit mgr., airline specialist Dallas, 1974-84; v.p. fin., controller Braniff, Inc., Dallas, 1984—; v.p., chief acctg. officer AirTran Airways, Inc., 2006—. Fin. acctg. stds. adv. coun.,Sr. Adv. Group Fin. Acctg. Stds. Bd. Mem.: Air Transport Assn. America (fin. coun. 1986—87), Tex. Soc. CPA's. Avocations: golf, photography, sports. Office: AirTran Airways 2702 Love Field Dr Dallas TX 75235-1908 Office Phone: 407-318-5600. Office Fax: 407-318-5900. Business E-Mail: mark.osterberg@airtran.com.

OSTERGARD, PAUL MICHAEL, retired foundation executive; b. Akron, Ohio, Apr. 1, 1939; s. Paul and Janette Beryl O. AB magna cum laude, Case-Western Res. U., 1961; JD, U. Mich., 1964; MPA, Harvard U., 1969; diploma in hispanic studies, U. Madrid, Spain, 1960. Bar: Ohio 1964. Atty. US Steel Corp., Pitts., 1967—69; gen. atty. TWA Inc., NYC, 1969—71; v.p. adminstrn., sec., counsel Pa. Co. (now Penn Ctrl. Corp.), 1971—74, and subs. Buckeye Pipe Line Co., NYC, 1972—74; pub. affairs exec. GE, Fairfield, Conn., 1974—84; pres. GE Found., Fairfield, 1984—90; chmn., CEO, bd. dirs. Citigroup Found., NYC, 1990—99; pres. Com. to Encourage Corp. Philanthropy, NYC, 1999—2001; pres., CEO Jr. Achievement Internat., 2001—04; pres. Hispanic Scholarship Fund, San Francisco, 2006—07. Bd. mem. Red Cross Greater NY, Operation Smile, Jr. Achievement Internat., Am.s for Arts; bd. dirs. Master Card Found., Securities Industry Fin. Markets Found., Hispanic Scholarship Fund; trustee emeritus Case Western Res. U. Decorated Bronze Star medal, Littauer fellow, 1968-69. Mem. Harvard Club NYC, Wexford Plantation Club, Phi Beta Kappa, Omicron Delta Kappa. Episcopalian. Home: 29 Oxford Dr Hilton Head Island SC 29928

OSTROW, STUART, theatrical producer, educator, author; b. NYC; m. Ann Elizabeth Gilbert; children: Julie Elizabeth, Katherine Ann, John Stuart. Disting. univ. prof. theater U. Houston. Pres. Stuart Ostrow Found., Inc., Mus. Theater Lab.; founding mem. opera-mus. theatre panel NEA; mem. bd. overseers com. to visit Loeb Drama Ctr. Harvard U. Prodr.: We Take the Town, 1961, The Apple Tree, 1966, 1776, 1969, Scratch, 1971, Pippin, 1972, The Moony Shapiro Songbook, 1981, American Passion, 1983, M. Butterfly, 1988, La Bête, 1991, Face Value, 1993; prodr., dir.: Here's Love, 1963, Swing, 1980; author, producer: Stages, 1978; assoc. dir.; Chicago, 1975; author: A Producer's Broadway Journey, 1999, Thank You Very Much, 2002, Present At the Creation, Leaping in the Dark and Going Against the Grain, 2005, Booklist Top Ten Arts Books, 2006. Mem. Pulitzer Prize Drama Jury; chmn. bd. trustees Inst. for Advanced Study in Musical Theatre. With USAF, 1952—55.

O'SULLIVAN, FRANCES K., computer company executive; BS, U. Va., 1980. Gen. mgr., PC Divsn. IBM Corp., 1981—2005; sr. v.p., COO, Product Group Lenovo Corp., Purchase, NY, 2005—. Mem. engring. industry adv. bd. Univ. Va. Office: Lenovo 1009 Think Pl Morrisville NC 27560-9002 Business E-Mail: fosullivan@lenovo.com.

OTHERSEN, HENRY BIEMANN, JR., surgeon, physician, educator; b. Charleston, SC, Aug. 26, 1930; s. Henry and Lydia Albertine (Smith) Othersen; m. Janelle Lester, Apr. 4, 1959; children: Megan, Mandy, Margaret, Henry Biemann III. BS, Coll. Charleston, 1950; MD, Med. Coll. S.C., 1953. Diplomate Am. Bd. Surgery, Am. Bd. Thoracic Surgery, Am. Bd. Pediatric Surgery. Intern Phila. Gen. Hosp., 1953-54; postgrad. U. Pa., 1956-57; resident in gen. surgery Med. Coll. S.C., Charleston, 1957-62; resident in pediatric surgery Ohio State U. and Columbus Children's Hosp., 1962-64; research fellow Harvard U., Mass. Gen. Hosp., Boston, 1964-65; from asst. prof. to assoc. prof. pediat. surgery Med. U. SC, Charleston, 1965—72, prof., 1972—, chief pediat. surgery, 1972-98; med. dir. Med. U. S.C. Hosp., 1981-85, Children's Hosp., 1985—2001, med. dir. profl. staff, 1996—2001, physician liaison documentation, 2002—03; acting chief surgery VA Hosp., 2002—04. Editor: The Pediatric Airway; mem. editl. bd. Jour. Pediatric Surgery, Jour. Parenteral and Enteral Nutrition; contbr. articles to profl. jours. Bd. Children's Hosp. Fund; bd. dirs., pres. S.C. divsn. Am. Cancer Soc., 1977—79; bd. dir. SC Safe Kids. With USN, 1954—56, Korea. Fellow: ACS, Am. Acad. Pediat.; mem.: Charleston County Med. Soc. (pres. 1981—83), Am. Trauma Soc., SC Surg. Assn. (pres. 1991—92), Am. Surg. Assn., Brit. Assn. Pediatric Surgeons (overseas coun. 1995—99), Am. Pediatric Surg. Assn. (pres. 1998—99), Alpha Omega Alpha (councilor 1978—93). Republican. Lutheran. Achievements include first academic pediat. surgeon in SC; first to establish divsn. pediat. surgery and children's hosp., H. Biemann Othersen, Jr. chair, pediat. surgery, Med. U. SC. Avocation: water sports. Home: 3 West St Charleston SC 29401-1929 Home Phone: 843-722-5939. Personal E-mail: jnbothersen@bellsouth.net.

OTIS, CLARENCE, JR., restaurant chain company executive; b. Vicksburg, Miss., Apr. 11, 1956; s. Clarence Otis; m. Jacqueline Bradley, 1983; children: Calvin, Allison, Randall. BA magna cum laude, Williams Coll., 1977; JD, Stanford Univ., 1980. Atty., NY; v.p. First Boston, 1987—90; investment banker Kidder Peabody; mng. dir., co-head Mcpl. Securities group Chem. Securities, 1992—95; v.p., treas. Darden Restaurants Inc., Orlando, Fla., 1995-97, sr. v.p. investor rels., treas., 1997-98, sr. v.p. fin., 1998-99, sr. v.p., CFO, 1999—2002, exec. v.p., CFO, 2002, exec. v.p., pres. Smokey Bones div., 2002—04, CEO, 2004—05; chmn., CEO Darden Restaurants, Inc., Orlando, Fla., 2005—. Bd. dirs. VF Corp., 2004—, Darden Restaurants Inc., 2004—, Verizon Communications Inc., 2006—; mem. Exec. Leadership Council. Trustee Williams Coll.; bd. mem. Enterprise Fla. Inc., Preserve Eatonville Inc. Named to Power 150, Ebony mag., 2008. Mem.: Phi Beta Kappa. Avocation: Art Collecting. Office: Darden Restaurants Inc 1000 Darden Center Dr Orlando FL 32837-4032

OTIS, LEE (SARAH) LIBERMAN, lawyer, educator; b. NYC, Aug. 19, 1956; d. James Benjamin and Deen (Freed) L.; m. William Graham Otis, Oct. 24, 1993. BA, Yale U., 1979; JD, U. Chgo., 1983. Bar: N.Y. 1985, D.C. 1994. Law clk. US Ct. Appeals (DC cir.), Washington, 1983-84; spl. asst. to asst. atty. gen., civil div. US Dept. Justice, Washington, 1984-86, dep. assoc. atty. gen., 1986, assoc. dep. atty. gen., 1986; law clk. to Justice Antonin Scalia US Supreme Ct., Washington, 1986-87; asst. prof. law George Mason U., Arlington, Va., 1987-89; assoc. counsel to the Pres. Exec. Office of the Pres., Washington, 1989-92; assoc. Jones, Day, Reavis & Pogue, Washington, 1993-94; chief judiciary coun. US Sen. Spence Abraham, 1995-96; chief counsel subcom. on immigration Com. on the Judiciary, US Senate, 1997-2000; gen. counsel US Dept. Energy, 2001—05; assoc. dep. atty. gen., 2005—07; sr. v.p., dir. faculty div. Federalist Soc. Law and Pub. Policy, 2007—. Adj. prof. law Georgetown Law Sch., 1995, 96, 2008-10 Mem. Federalist Soc. for Law and Pub. Policy (founder). Republican. Jewish. Avocations: sailing, computers. Office Phone: 202-822-8138.

O'TOOLE, AUSTIN MARTIN, lawyer, mediator, arbitrator; b. New Bedford, Mass., Oct. 5, 1935; s. John Brian, Jr. and Helen Veronica O'T.; m. Valerie Sherlock O'Toole; children: Erin Ann, Austin Martin Jr. BBA, Coll. Holy Cross, 1957; JD, Georgetown U., 1963. Bar: NY 1965, DC 1963, Tex. 1975; cert. disting. mediator, Tex. Mediator Credentialing Assn. Law clk. to judge U.S. Ct. Appeals, Washington, 1962-63; assoc. White & Case, NYC, 1963-74; sr. v.p., sr. counsel, sec. Coastal Corp., Houston, 1974—2001. Bd. editors Georgetown Law Jour., 1962-63. Bd. dirs. Nat. Coun. on Alcoholism and Drug Dependency, Inc., 2001—; charter mem., certificated mediator Inst. for Responsible Dispute Resolution, Houston, 2000—; bd. dirs. Houston Marathon Com., 1973—2002, Houston Dispute Resolution Ctr., 2007—. Officer USMC, 1957—60. Mem. ABA, Am. Soc. Corp. Secs. (bd. dirs. 1982-85), State Bar of Tex., Houston Bar Assn. (past chmn. corp. counsel sect. 1979-80, chair ADR sect. 2007-08), Assn. Atty.-Mediators, Tex. Assn. Mediators (bd. dirs. 2007-). Home: 3711 San Felipe 8H Houston TX 77027 Office Phone: 713-628-3079. Personal E-mail: austinotoole@msn.com.

O'TOOLE, H. MARLENE, state legislator; b. Somerville, Mass., Feb. 18, 1945; m. Ed O'Toole; 5 children. Ret. regional mgr. IBM; mem. Dist. 42 Fla. House of Reps., 2008—, vice chair state univs. and pvt. colls. policy com., mem. civil justice and courts policy com., edn. policy coun., fin. and tax council, state univs. and pvt. colls. appropriations com. Dir. Take Stock in Children, 1999, mentor; mem. Lake County Rep. Exec. Com., 2007; bd. mem. Cornerstone Hospice, 2008; vol. Beverly Shores Sch. & Rimes Elem. Student Reading Programs. Mem.: United Way Lake & Sumter Counties. Republican. Catholic. Office: House Office Bldg 402 S Monroe St Rm 210 Tallahassee FL 32399-1300 also: 916 Avenida Central The Villages FL 32159-5704 Office Phone: 850-488-5991, 352-315-4445. Business E-Mail: marlene.otoole@myfloridahouse.gov.

O'TOOLE, LAURENCE JOSEPH, public administration and policy educator, researcher; b. Syracuse, NY, Dec. 7, 1948; s. Laurence Joseph and Marjorie Rose (Weinheimer) O.; m. Mary Irene Gilroy, June 26, 1971; children: Conor Gilroy O'Toole, Kathleen Easton O'Toole. BS with high honors, Clarkson U., 1970; MPA, Syracuse U., 1972, PhD, 1975. Asst. prof. polit. sci. U. Va., Charlottesville, 1975-79; assoc. prof. polit. sci. Auburn U., Ala., 1979-85, prof. polit. sci., 1985-92, U. Ga., Athens, 1992—, M. Hughes and Robert T. Golembiewski prof. pub. adminstrn., 2000—, head dept. pub. adminstrn. and policy, 2002—08. Vis. rschr. Internat. Inst. Mgmt. Sci. Ctr., Berlin, 1978; prof. comparative sustainability policy studies Ctr. for Clean Tech. and Environ. Policy, Twente U., The Netherlands, 1994—; sr. rsch. assoc. Carl Vinson Inst. of Govt., U. Ga., Athens, 1994-2002; mem., bd. editors Administrn. and Society, Blacksburg, Va., 1995—, Administrv. Theory and Praxis, San Francisco, 1995-2002, Beleidswetenschap Groningen, The Netherlands, 1997—, Evaluation and Program Planning, 2000—, Jour. Pub. Affairs Edn., 2001—, Jour. Pub. Admin. Rsch. Theory, 2005-, Chinese Pub. Admin. Review, 2006-. Author: Institutions, Processes and Outputs for Acidification, 1998; co-author: American Government: Origins, Institutions and Public Policy, 1984, Regulatory Decision Making: The Virginia State Corporation Commission, 1984, Implementation Theory and Practice, 1990, Bureaucracy in a Democratic State, 2006; editor: American Intergovernmental Relations, 1985, 2d rev. edit., 1993, 3d edit., 2000, 4th edit., 2006; co-editor: International Comparative Policy Research, 1992, Networks for Water Policy, 1995, Participation and the Quality of Environmental Decision Making, 1998, Advancing Public Management, 2000, Johns Hopkins Studies in Governance and Public Management, 2001—, Jour. Policy and Mgmt., 2004—, Public Services Performance, 2006; contbr. articles to profl. jours. Recipient outstanding prof. award Ga. Students for Pub. Adminstrn., Athens, 1994, 95; vis. scholar Erasmus U., Rotterdam, The Netherlands, 1989, 94, Calif. U. Wales, 2003. Fellow: Nat. Acad. Pub. Adminstrn.; mem.: ASPA (Burchfield award 1979, Mosher award 1987, Stone award 1999, Levine award 2002, Wholey award 2004, Waldo award 2005), Pub. Mgmt. Rsch. Assn. (bd. dirs. 2001—, pres. 2005—), So. Polit. Sci. Assn., Am. Polit. Sci. Assn. (chair pub. adminstrn. sect. 1985, Gaus award 2009). Home: 190 Avalon Dr Athens GA 30606-3235 Office: Univ Ga Sch Pub and Internat Affairs Dept Pub/Adminstrn Policy/Baldwin Hall Athens GA 30602 E-mail: cmsotool@uga.edu.

OTT, HARRY L., state legislator; b. Orangeburg, SC, Oct. 2, 1952; m. Linda Ott; 2 children. BS, Clemson U., SC, 1974. Former pres., state dir. Calhoun County Farm Bur.; mem. Calhoun County Sch. Bd., 1980—88, chmn., 1992—96; mem. Dist. 93 SC House of Reps., 1998—. Democrat. Methodist. Office: 335B Blatt Bldg Columbia SC 29201 also: 461 Bull Swamp Rd Saint Matthews SC 29135 Home Phone: 803-874-1042; Office Phone: 803-734-2998. Business E-Mail: HLO@schouse.org.

OTT, WALTER RICHARD, information technology executive, writer; b. Bklyn., Jan. 20, 1943; s. Harold Vincent and Mary Elizabeth (Butler) Ott; m. Carla M. Narrett, May 27, 2000; children: Regina Winter Burrell, Christina W. Chiappetta, Walter R. Jr. BS in Ceramic Engring., Va. Poly. Inst. and State U., 1965; MS in Ceramic Engring., U. Ill., 1967; PhD in Ceramic Engring., Rutgers U., 1969; DSc (hon.), Alfred U., 2001. Registered profl. engr., Pa. Process engr. Corning Inc., Buckhannon, W.Va., 1965-66; staff rsch. engr. Champion Spark Plug Co., Detroit, 1969-70; prof. engring. Rutgers U., New Brunswick, NJ, 1970-80; dean, assoc. provost N.Y. State Coll. Ceramics, Alfred, 1980-88; provost, chief acad. officer Alfred U., Alfred, 1988-2000; pres. Predictive Edge, Inc., Punta Gorda, Fla., 1999—; v.p. enrollment mgmt. Caldwell (N.J.) Coll., 2002—04. Rsch. assoc. Atomic Energy Commn.-E.I. duPont de Nemours, Aiken, SC, 1971; cons. Haight & Hofeldt Inc., Chgo., 1984-88, Pillsbury, Mpls., 1977-79, Ctr. for Profl. Advancement, New Brunswick, 1971-79, Hammond Lead Products, Ind., 1970-80; bd. dirs. Victor Insulator Inc., NY, UNIPEG, 1987-88; treas. Alfred Tech. Resources NY; bd. dirs. Grads Found., NYC, 1988-2002. Contbr. articles to profl. jours.; patentee in field. Recipient Ralph Teetor award Soc. Automotive

Engrs., 1973, PACE award Nat. Inst. Ceramic Engrs., 1975, Ann. award Ceramic Assn. N.J., 1980; named to Greaves Walker Roll, Keramos, 1991. Fellow Am. Ceramic Soc. (trustee 1980-83, v.p. 1988-89); mem. Ceramic Ednl. Coun. (pres. 1976-77), Ceramic Assn. N.Y. (treas. 1980-88, bd. dirs.), Ceramic Assn. N.J. (bd. dirs. 1974-80), Keramos (pres. 1982-84, Greaves-Walker Roll of Honor 1991), Tau Beta Pi. Avocations: reading, golf. Home: 2156 Charlotte Amalie Ct Punta Gorda FL 33950 Personal E-mail: wrottsr@comcast.net.

OTTERBOURG, ROBERT KENNETH, public relations consultant, writer; b. NYC, Jan. 26, 1930; s. Albert Marcus and Frances (Roset) O.; m. Susan Delman, Apr. 14, 1957; children— Laura Ann, Kenneth Douglas. BA, Colgate U., 1951; MS, Columbia U., 1954. Reporter, editor Fairchild Publs., NYC, 1953-57; editor McGraw-Hill Pub. Co., 1957-59; v.p. pub. rels. Charles Mathieu & Co., 1959-61; pres. pub. rels. Otterbourg & Co., NYC, 1962-69, 71—. Sr. v.p. Daniel J. Edelman, 1970. Author: It's Never Too Late, 1993, Retire and Thrive, 1995, 4th edit., 2006, Switching Careers, 2001; contbr. articles to profl. and consumer jours. Legis. asst. N.Y. State Senate, 1962-64; mem. exec. com. Columbia U. Sch. Journalism, N.Y.C., 1980-93, pres. exec. com., 1985-87; trustee Flat Rock Nature Ctr., pres., 1991-92; trustee Planned Parenthood Bergen County, 1985-88, v.p., 1986-88; trustee Urban League for Bergen County, 1988-93; chmn. Durham County Libr., 1997-99, Exec. Svc. Corps of the Greater Triangle; bd. dirs. Colgate U. Alumni Corp., 1969-73; bd. dirs., pres. Threshold, 2003; pres. Triangle Radio Reading Svc., 2004, trustee, Reth Conf. Libr. Found., 2010, Rurman County Libr. Found., 2010. 1st lt. USAF, 1951-53. Mem. Columbia U. Grad. Sch. Journalism Alumni Assn. (pres. 1985-87, bd. mem., sr. pharmassist 2008). Democrat. Jewish. Home: 1201 Clover St Winston Salem NC 27101-2416 Office Phone: 919-489-9591. Personal E-mail: rkotter@aol.com.

OTTMAN, BOB, insurance company executive; B, Ea. Conn. State U., Willimantic. Cert. flexible compensation instrn. Employers Coun. Flexible Compensation. V.p. Frank Gates USA (formerly Acordia of Dallas); mgmt. position AFLAC, Inc., Columbus, Ga., 1999, various leadership positions including v.p. adminstrv. svcs., new bus. & underwriting and new account set-up, sr. v.p. account implementation and mgmt., sr. v.p. claims, AFLAC benefit services & NY adminstrn., sr. v.p. sales ops. mgmt., sr. v.p. strategic transformation, 2010—. Office: AFLAC Inc 1932 Wynnton Rd Columbus GA 31999 Office Phone: 706-323-3431.

OTTO, JOHN C., state legislator; b. Oct. 14, 1948; m. Nancy Otto, Dec. 1969; children: Bryan, Jason. BBA in Acctg., Texas A&M U., 1970. CPA. Mem. audit staff KPMG, Houston; dir. for bus. development Ryan & Co., Dallas, 2006—; former city councilman Dayton; mem. Dist. 18 Tex. House of Representatives, 2004—. Recipient of several awards and honors. Republican. Office: PO Box 965 Dayton TX 77535 also: Room E2.706 Capitol Extension Austin TX 78768 Office Phone: 936-258-8135, 512-463-0570.

OTTO, PAMELA, diagnostic radiologist, educator; MD, U. Mo., 1988. Diplomate Am. Bd. Radiology-diagnostic radiology, 1993. Resident diagnostic radiology Univ. Tex. Health Sci. Ctr., 1990—93, fellow breast imaging, 1993; assoc. prof. radiology Univ. Tex.; hosp. affiliations include Univ. Hosp., South Tex. Veterans Health Care Sys. Office: South Texas Veterans Health Care System Mail Code 7800 7703 Floyd Curl Dr San Antonio TX 78229 Office Phone: 210-567-3448.

OVECHKIN, ALEXANDER, professional hockey player; b. Moscow, Sept. 17, 1985; s. Mikhail and Tatiana Ovechkin. Left wing Dynamo Moscow (Russian Super League), 2001—05, Washington Capitals, 2005—, capt., 2010—. Mem. Team Russia, World Junior Championships, 2003—05, Team Russia, World Championships, 2004, 2005, Team Russia, World Cup of Hockey, 2004, Team Russia, Olympic Games, Torino, Italy, 2006, Vancouver, 2010. Recipient Calder Meml. Trophy, 2006, Art Ross Trophy, 2008, Maurice Richard Trophy, 2008, 2009, 2013, Lester B. Pearson Award, 2008, 2009, Ted Lindsay Award (formerly Lester B. Pearson Award), 2010, Hart Meml. Trophy, 2008, 2009, 2013, Wayne Gretzky award, The Hockey News, 2013; named NHL Rookie of Yr., Sporting News, 2006, NHL Player of Yr., 2008, 2009; named one of 50 Most Powerful People in DC, GQ mag., 2009; named to First All-Star Team, NHL, 2006—10, NHL All-Star Game, 2007, 2008, 2009, 2011, All-NHL Team, Sporting News, 2009, 2010, Second All-Star Team, NHL, 2011. Achievements include being a member of gold medal Team Russia, World Junior Championships, 2003; being the first overall draft pick in NHL entry draft, 2004. Office: c/o Washington Capitals Verizon Center 601 F St NW Washington DC 20004 also: 627 N Glebe Rd Ste 850 Arlington VA 22203*

OVELMEN, RICHARD J., lawyer; b. LaPorte, Ind., July 26, 1952; BA cum laude, Butler U., 1974; JD, Yale U., 1979. Bar: Fla., US Ct. of Appeals (11th Cir.), US Dist. Ct. (so. and mid. Dists.) Fla., US Supreme Ct. Adj. prof. law U. Miami, 1986-87; lectr. U of Miami Coll. of Liberal Arts; mem. Baker & McKenzie, Miami; ptnr. Jorden Burt LPP, Miami, Fla. Judge moot court finals; spkr. in field. Contbr. articles to profl. jour. Named Fla. Legal Elite, Fla. Trend Mag., Fla. Super Lawyer, Super Lawyer, Best Lawyer in America; named one of South Fla.'s Top Lawyers and Law Firms, South Fla. Legal Guide. Mem. ABA (chmn. media law and defamation com., sect. tort and ins. practice 1989-90), Fla. Bar Assn. Office: Jorden Burt LPP 100 SE 2nd St Ste 4200 Miami FL 33131-2113 Office Phone: 305-347-6805. Office Fax: 305-372-9928. Business E-Mail: rjo@jordenusa.com.

OVERBEY, BETTY, state legislator; m. George Overbey; 3 children. Ret. state revenue agt.; mem. Dist. 69 Ark. House of Representatives, 2011—. Democrat. Office: PO Box 177 Lamar AR 72846 Office Phone: 479-885-6479. Business E-Mail: betty.overbey@arkansashouse.org.

OVERBEY, DOUG, state legislator; b. Kingsport, Tenn., Dec. 11, 1954; m. Kay S. Overbey; children: Elizabeth, Hannah, Kathleen. Assoc. ptnr. Fowler & Robertson, 1979—82; ptnr. Robertson, Ingram & Overbey, 1982—; commr. Blount County Planning Commn., 1982—89, Blount County Bd. Commrs., 1982—90; mem. Dist. 20 Tenn. House of Reps., 2001—08; mem. Dist. 8 Tenn. State Senate, 2009—; Dist. bd. dir. Blount County Children's Advocacy Coun.; exec com. mem. Success by Six of Blount County; Chancellor Diocese of East Tenn. Mem.: Blount County United Way, Blount County C Of C, Blount County Bar Assn., Knoxville Bar Assn., Tenn. Bar Assn., America Bar Assn., Kiwanis Club Maryville. Republican. Episcopalian. Office: 1105 North Heritage Dr Maryville TN 37803 also: 4 Legislative Plz Nashville TN 37243 Office Phone: 615-741-0981, 865-681-8236. Business E-Mail: sen.doug.overbey@capitol.tn.gov.

OVERHOLT, HUGH ROBERT, lawyer, retired military officer; b. Beebe, Ark., Oct. 29, 1933; s. Harold R. and Cuma E. (Hall) O.; m. Laura Annell Arnold, May 5, 1961; children: Sharon, Scott. Student, Coll. of Ozarks, 1951-53; BA, U. Ark., 1955, LL.B., 1957. Bar: Ark. 1957. Commd. 1st lt. U.S. Army, 1957, advanced through grades to maj. gen., 1981; chief Criminal Law Div., JAG Sch., Charlottesville, Va., 1971-73; chief personnel, plans and tng. Office of JAG, U.S. Army, Washington, 1973-75; staff judge adv. XVIII Airborne Corps, Ft. Bragg, NC, 1976-78; spl. asst. for legal and selected policy matters Office of Dep. Asst., 1978-79; asst. judge adv. gen. for mil. law Office of JAG, Washington, 1979-81, asst. judge adv. gen., 1981-85, judge adv. gen, 1985-89; atty. Ward & Smith, New Bern, NC, 1989—. Notes and comment editor Ark. Law Rev, 1956-57. Decorated Army Meritorious Service medal with oak leaf cluster, Army Commendation medal with 2 oak leaf clusters., Legion of Merit, Def. Meritorious Service medal, D.S.M. Mem. ABA, N.C. Bar Assn., Ark. Bar Assn., Assn. U.S. Army, Delta Theta Phi, Omicron Delta Kappa, Sigma Pi. Presbyterian. Office: Ward and Smith 1001 College Ct New Bern NC 28562-4972 Office Phone: 252-672-5462. Business E-Mail: hro@wardandsmith.com.

OVERINGTON, JOHN, state legislator; b. Laurel, Md., June 5, 1946; s. Robert Bruce and Helen (Besley) O.; m. JoAnn Elizabeth Bertaux, Nov. 29, 1975. BS in Chemistry, Washington Coll., 1969. Tchr. Oxon Hill Sr. HS, Md., 1969-72; editor, pub. Cmty. Sentinel, Hagerstown, Md., 1976-78; prodn. supr. Harry Kahn Assocs., Hagerstown, 1978-81; comm. asst. Grove Mfg. Co., Shady Grove, Pa., 1981-82; mem. Dist. 55 W.Va. House of Delegates, Charleston, 1984—, ranking minority mem. Constl. Revision Com. Mem. judiciary com., agr. and natural resources, industry and labor, enrolled bills com., minority chmn. constl. revision com., chmn. Rep. caucus, 1994. Bd. dirs. Ea. Panhandle Mental Health, Martinsburg, W.VA., 1985, So. Regional Edn. Bd., 1988-91; newsletter chmn. W.Va. Rep. Exec. Com., Charleston, 1992; mem. Berkeley County Rep. Exec. Com. Recipient Vol. Svc. award W.Va. Rep. Party, 1992, Pub. Svc. award Marsh Inst., 2006, Humane State Legis. award HSUS, 2007. Mem. NRA, Jefferson County C. of C., Berkeley County C. of C. (Outstanding Chmn. award 1988), W.Va. Rifle and Pistol Assn., Jefferson County Hist. Soc., Berkeley County Hist. Soc., SAR (sec. treas. 1973, Good Citizenship award 1984), Berkeley County Farm Bur., Soc. War of 1812, Mensa, Berkeley County Humane Soc., Izaak Walton League, Nat. Rep. Legislators Assn., Nat. Taxpayers Union, Am. Legis. Exch. Coun., Bedington Ruritan (bd. dirs.), Rotary, James Ramsey Torch Club. Republican. Episcopalian. Mailing: 491 Hoffman Rd Martinsburg WV 25404-7208 Office: WV House of Dels 1900 Kanawha Blvd E State Capitol Complex Rm 258M Bldg 1 Charleston WV 25305 Home Phone: 304-274-1791; Office Phone: 304-274-1791, 304-340-3148. Business E-Mail: john@overington.com.

OVERLY, SANNIE, state legislator; b. Millersburg, Ky., July 2, 1966; BS in Civil Engring., U. Ky., 1989; JD, U. Louisville Coll. Law, 1993. Civil engr. Ky. Trans. Cabinet, 1989—93; asst. Ky. Transp. Sec. Don Kelly, 1993; atty. Jackson & Kelly, 1993—99, pvt. practice, 1999—2001; ptnr. Overly & Johnson, 2001—; mem. Dist. 72 Ky. House of Reps., 2008—. Democrat. Office: 702 Capitol Ave Rm 332A Frankfort KY 40601 also: 340 Main St Paris KY 40361 Office Phone: 502-564-8100 Ext.752, 859-987-9879. Business E-Mail: sannie.overly@lrc.ky.gov.

OVERTON, JEFFREY LAURENCE, professional golfer; b. Evansville, IN, May 28, 1983; BA in Sports Mgmt., Ind. U., 2005. Profl. golfer PGA Tour, 2006—. Mem. US team Walker Cup, 2005, Palmer Cup, 2005, Ryder Cup, 2010. Mailing: 100 PGA TOUR Blvd Ponte Vedra Beach FL 32082

OVITT, KIMBERLY, medical researcher; AA in Communication, Ctrl. Ariz. Coll.; BA in Communicatio, Ariz. State U. Accredited in Pub. Rels. (APR) Pub. Rels. Soc.of Am. (PRSA). Mktg./pub. rels. mgr. Baptist Hosps. and Health Sys., 1983—86; mktg./pub. rels. coord. City of Mesa, Ariz., 1986—95; communication dir. Phoenix Children's Hosp., 1995—2004; communication dir., the Biodesign inst. Ariz. State Univ., 2004—10, dir. strategic affairs, the Biodesign inst., 2004—10, communication dir., complex adaptive sys. initiative, 2010—11; sr. v.p. pub. rels. St. Jude Children's Rsch. Hosp., 2011—. Mem. Green Collar Ariz. Recipient four nat. collegiate speaking awards, 1978—79. Mem.: Ariz. Tech. Coun., Ariz. BioIndustry Assn. (AZBio), Publ. Rels. Soc. of Am. (PRSA Nat.) (PERCY award 1993), Econ. Club of Phoenix. Office: St Jude Children's Research Hospital 262 Danny Thomas Pl Memphis TN 38105 Office Phone: 901-595-3300.

OWEN, CYNTHIA CAROL, retired sales executive; b. Ft. Worth, Oct. 16, 1943; d. Charlie Bounds and Bernice Vera (Nunley) Rhoads; m. Franklin Earl Owen, Oct. 20, 1961 (div. Jan. 1987); children: Jeffrey Wayne, Valeria Ann, Carol Darlena, Pamela Kay; m. John Edward White, Jan. 1, 1988 (div. Sept. 1991), m. John Wayne Napier, Nov. 26, 2002. Cert. Keypuncher, Comml. Coll., 1963; student, Tarrant County Jr. Coll., 1974-77; BBA in Mgmt., U. Tex., Arlington, 1981; diploma, Stratford Career Inst., 2011. Keypunch operator Can-Tex. Industries, Mineral-Wells, 1966-67; sec. Electro-Midland Corp., Mineral-Wells, 1967-68; exec. sec. to v.p. sales Pangburn Co., Inc., Ft. Worth, 1972-78; bookkeeper, sec. CB Svc., Ft. Worth, 1978-82; project mgr. Square D Co., Carrollton, Tex., 1982—2009; cons. Natural Health Cons. Mem.: NAFE, NOW, AAUW. Baptist. Home: 1221 Pine Ridge Rd Roanoke TX 76262

OWEN, DUNCAN SHAW, JR., internist, retired educator; b. Fayetteville, NC, Oct. 24, 1935; s. Duncan S. and Mary Gwyn (Hickerson) O.; m. Irene Lacy Rose, Oct. 22, 1966; children: Duncan Shaw III, Robert Burwell, Frances Gwyn. BS in Medicine, U. N.C., 1957, MD, 1960. Diplomate Am. Bd. Internal Medicine (proctor 1977-97). Intern Med. Coll. Va., Richmond, 1960-61; jr. asst. resident in medicine N.C. Meml. Hosp., Chapel Hill, 1961-62; asst. resident in medicine Med. Coll. Va., Richmond, 1964-65, fellow in rheumatic diseases, 1965-66; internal medicine and rheumatology physician Richmond, Va., 1966—; from instr. in medicine to assoc. prof. Med. Coll. Va., Richmond, 1966-78, prof. dept. internal medicine, 1978—; Taliaferro/Scott Disting. prof. internal medicine Med. Coll. Va., Va. Commonwealth U., 1989-2000, emeritus prof., 2000—; dir. residency tng. Med. Coll. Va. Hosp.; dir. rheumatology clinics. Dir. clin. tng. divsn. rheumatology, allergy, immunology, 1975-98, chmn. clin. activities comm., dept. internal medicine, 1970-90; chmn. med. adv. com. Richmond br. Arthritis Found., 1966-75, nat. patient edn. com., 1979-80; med. advisor Social Security Adminstrn., HHS, 1967-2004; co-chmn. arthritis project Va. Regional Med. Program, 1975-76; prodr. Your Health TV series Va. Ednl. TV, 1978-79; prodr. Update in Medicine, Good Morning Virginia TV show, 1980; cons. McGuire VA. Contbr. articles to profl. jours.; assoc. editor: Va. Med., 1978-98; edtl. reviewer Jour. AMA, 1979—, Arthritis Rheumatism, 1981-2004, Jour. Rheumatology, 1984—. Mem. usher's guild First Presbyn. Ch., Richmond, Va., 1966-70, deacon, 1974-77, chmn. of diaconate, 1976-77, elder, 1978—, chmn. witness com., 1978-80; co-chmn. physicians statewide capital funds campaign Va. Commn. U., 1986-87; bd. dirs. Mooreland Farms Assn., 1971-73, 77-81, Va. chpt. Arthitis Found., 1970-85; mem. Va. Mus., Richmond Symphony; bd. dirs. Richmond Area Health Care Coalition, 1980-84. Med. officer US Army, 1962—63, Womack Army Hosp., Fort Bragg, NC, post surgeon, asst. divsn. surgeon US Army, 1963—64, Camp Kaiser, Korea. Decorated Army Commendation medal; recipient Gerard B. Lambert award, 1974-75, Disting. Svc. award Arthritis Found., 1971, U. N.C., Chapel Hill, 1999; Nat. Inst. Arthritis and Metabolic Diseases fellow, 1965-66 Fellow ACP (Laureate award 1997), Am. Coll. Rheumatology; mem. AMA (expert on diagnostic and therapeutic tech. assessment program 1990-99), Am. Rheumatism Assn. (exec. com. 1979-80), Richmond Acad. Medicine (pres. 1982, chmn. bd. 1983, parliamentarian 1988-99), Med. Soc. Va. (com. on aging 1980-89, v.p. 1973, 75, del. 1972-99, scholarship com. 1980-89), Richmond Soc. Internal Medicine (bd. dirs. 1971-73), Met. Richmond C. of C. (bd. dirs. 1981-84), Jr. Clin. Club (emeritus), Custis Hunting and Fishing Club, Alpha Omega Alpha Honor Med. Soc. Presbyn. Achievements include development of techniques for arthrocenteses; cellophane tape polarizing microscopic compensator for identifying crystals in joint fluid. Avocations: hunting, fishing, photography, amateur radio. Home: 8910 Brieryle Rd Richmond VA 23229-7704 Personal E-mail: dowen75089@aol.com.

OWEN, JOHN ATKINSON, JR., internist, educator; b. South Boston, Va., Sept. 24, 1924; s. John Atkinson and Mary Helen (Carrington) O.; m. Wanda Earle Reamy, Nov. 29, 1952; children: John Atkinson III, Ryland R. BS, Hampden-Sydney Coll., 1944; MD, U. Va., 1948. Intern Cin. Gen. Hosp., 1948-49; resident, fellow U. Va. Hosp., 1950-52; rsch. fellow Duke Med. Center, 1954-56; asst. prof. medicine Med. Coll. Ga., 1956-58, George Washington U. Med. Sch., 1958-60; mem. faculty U. Va. Sch. Medicine, 1960-96, prof., 1970-96, vice chmn. dept. internal medicine, 1972-74, James M. Moss prof. diabetes, sr. assoc. dean, 1995-96, prof. emeritus, 1997—. Mem. Va. Vol. Formulary Bd.; mem. exec. com. U.S. Pharmacopeia, 1970-75, pres., 1975-80, trustee, 1975-85. Mem. editorial bd.: Jour. Clin. Pharmacology, 1971-84; editor-in-chief: Hosp. Formulary, 1974-83. Capt. MC, USNR, 1942-45, 48-50, 52-53, ret. Recipient Raven award U. Va., 1948; co-recipient Horsley Research prize, 1962, Walter Reed Disting. Achievement award, 1998; laureate ACP, 1998. Mem. AMA, ACP, Am. Fedn. Clin. Rsch., So. Soc. Clin. Investigation, Med. Soc. Va. (pres. 1990-91), Am. Diabetes Assn., Endocrine Soc. Presbyterian. (elder 1965—). Home: 106 Tally Ho Dr Charlottesville VA 22901-2034

OWEN, JOHN B., bank executive; b. 1960; BS in Aerospace Mgmt. and Engring., Auburn U., 1982. Worked in info. sys. American Airlines, Inc., 1983, McDonnell-Douglas; chief info. officer, North Am. ops. Arrow Electronics; sr. v.p., global sys. devel. Citicorp Credit Svcs.; sr. v.p., info. tech. Assurant Splty. Property, 1998, CIO, 2000, exec. v.p. consumer mktg. services, 2001, COO, Property and Solutions Group, 2003—05, pres., CEO, 2005—07; sr. exec. v.p., ops. and tech. Regions Financial Corp., Birmingham, Ala., 2007—, mem. exec. coun., 2009—. Office: Regions Financial Corp 1900 Fifth Ave N Birmingham AL 35203 Office Phone: 205-944-1300. Office Fax: 334-832-8419.

OWEN, PRISCILLA RICHMAN, federal judge, former state supreme court justice; b. Palacios, Tex., Oct. 4, 1954; BA, Baylor U., 1975; JD, Baylor U. Sch. of Law, 1977. Bar: Tex. 1978, US Ct. Appeals (4th, 5th, 8th and 11th cirs.). Law clerk Sheehy, Lovelace & Mayfield, 1976—77; assoc. Andrews, Kurth, Campbell & Jones, 1978—85, ptnr., 1985—94; justice Supreme Ct. Tex., Austin, 1995—2005; judge US Ct. Appeals (5th cir.), New Orleans, 2005—. Liaison to Tex. Legal Svcs. for Poor Spl. Supreme Ct. Tex., Supreme Ct. Adv. Com. on Ct.-Annexed Mediations. Bd. mem. Tex. Hearing & Service Dogs, A.A. White Dispute Resolution Inst.; advisory bd. mem. Federalist Soc. (Houston & Austin Chapter). Named Young Lawyer of Yr., Baylor U., Outstanding Young Alumna. Mem.: ABA, Am. Judicature Soc., Am. Law Inst. Office: US Courthouse 903 San Jacinto Blvd Rm 434 Austin TX 78701-2450

OWEN, RANDY YEUELL, country musician, cattle rancher; b. Ala., Dec. 13, 1949; married; 3 children. Vocalist, guitarist with group Alabama, 1973—, also songwriter; albums include My Home's in Alabama, 1980, Feels So Right, 1981, Mountain Music, 1982 (Grammy award), The Closer You Get, 1983 (Grammy award), Roll On, 1984, Forty Hour Week, 1985, The Touch, 1986, Just Us, 1987, Alabama "Live", 1988, American Pride, 1992, Cheap Seats, 1993, Country Side of Life, 1993, Gonna Have A Party...Live, 1993, Greatest Hits, Vol. II, 1994, In Pictures, 1995, Super Hits, 1996, Dancin' on the Boulevard, 1997, 20th Century, 1999, Alabama for the Record, 2000, When It All Goes South, 2001, The Farewell Tour (live), 2003, Lady Down on Love, 2005, One One One, 2008. Group awards include: Country Music Assn. Instrumental Group Yr., 1981, 1982, Vocal Group Yr., 1981-83, Entertainer Yr., 1982-84 Acad. Country Music Vocal Group Yr., 1981-86, Entertainer Yr., 1982-86, Artist of Decade, 1989, Pioneer Award 2003, Am. Music Awards for Country Group Yr. & Favorite Country Group 1983, 1985, 1986, 1988-99, 2003, Recording Industry Assn. Am. Country Group of the Century, 1999, Am. Music Merit award, Spirit of Alabama medal, Pentagon 9/11 Medallion, 2003, named to Country Music Assn. Hall of Fame, 2005. Office: care Morris and Assocs 818 19th Ave S Nashville TN 37203-3202

OWEN, ROBERT HUBERT, lawyer, real estate broker; b. Birmingham, Ala., Aug. 3, 1928; s. Robert Clay and Mattie Lou (Hubert) O.; m. Mary Dane Hicks, Mar. 14, 1954; children: Mary Kathryn, Robert Hubert. BS, U. Ala., 1950; JD, Birmingham Sch. Law, 1956. Bar: Ala. 1957, Ga. 1965. Methods and procedures analyst, supr. Ala. Power Co., Birmingham, 1952-58; assoc. Martin, Vogtle, Balch & Bingham, Birmingham, 1958-63; asst. sec. So. Services, Atlanta, 1963-69; sec. Southern Co. Svcs. Inc., 1969—77, Southern Co., Atlanta, 1969-71, sec., asst. treas., house counsel, 1971—77; exec. v.p., sec., gen. counsel, dir. Proverbs 31 Corp., Atlanta, 1978-81, 90-97; broker Bob Owen Realty, Atlanta, 1990-97; pvt. practice law Marietta, 1978-85; v.p., gen. counsel Hubert Properties, 1985-86. Atlanta area rep. Inst. Basic Life Principles, 1970-80; elder Calvary Bapt. Ch., 1997—. Served to maj. USAF, 1951-52, 61-62. Mem.: Jasons, Phi Eta Sigma, Beta Gamma Sigma, Omicron Delta Kappa, Delta Chi, Delta Sigma Pi. Home and Office: 6590 Bridgewood Valley Rd NW Sandy Springs GA 30328-2906 Personal E-mail: roberthowen@bellsouth.net.

OWEN, SUE ANN, retired poet; b. Clarinda, Iowa, Sept. 5, 1942; d. Theodore Reynold and Elizabeth (Roderick) Matthews; m. Thomas Charles Owen, Aug. 29, 1964. BA in English, U. Wis., 1964; MFA in Writing, Goddard Coll., 1978. Poet in schs. Arts and Humanities Coun., Baton Rouge, 1980—92; artist fellowship La. Divsn. of Arts, 1993, 2001; instr. La. State U., 1992—98, poet-in-residence, 1998—2005. Author: Nursery Rhymes for the Dead, 1980, The Book of Winter, 1988 (Ohio State Univ. Press/The Jour. award, 1988), My Doomsday Sampler, 1999; contbr.: poems to mags., anthologies, including Harvard Mag., Iowa Rev., The Nation, Poetry, Ploughshares, So. Rev., The Best of Intro, The Poetry Anthology: 1912-2002, USA Poetry (Sweden), readings in: Boston, N.Y.C., Washington, San Francisco, New Orleans, Moscow, London; author: The Devils Cookbook, 2007. Named Profl. Artist of Yr., La. State Arts Coun., 1998. Mem.: Poets and Writers, Arts and Humanities Coun., Associated Writing Programs, Poetry Soc. Am. Home: 7825 Rue Cache CT Baton Rouge LA 70808

OWENS, CHRISTINE M., delivery service executive; b. Phila. BS, Shippensburg U., Pa. Part-time temp. helper United Parcel Service of America, Inc. (UPS), Phila., 1979—80, driver, 1980—81, numerous ops. mgmt. positions Metro Phila. dist., 1981—89, dist. mgr. NE Tex., 1989, mgr. Metro Chgo. dist., then West region mgr., 1997—2000, SE region mgr., 2000—04, v.p. transp., 2004—05, sr. v.p. comm. & brand mgmt. Atlanta, 2005—. Trustee UPS Found. Bd. dirs. Nat. Coun. La Raza, Women Presidents' Orgn.; former mem. Ill. Gov.'s Commn. Status of Women. Named one of Who's Who in B2B Advt., BtoB Mag., 2008, 2009, The 25 Best Marketers, 2009. Office: UPS Corp 55 Glendale Pky NE Atlanta GA 30328 Business E-Mail: COwens@ups.com.

OWENS, DARRYL T., state legislator; b. Nov. 10, 1937; BA, JD, Howard U. Pvt. practice atty.; mem. Dist. 43 Ky. House of Reps., 2005—. Served with US Army. Mem.: NAACP, Nat Bar Assn., Ky. Bar Assn., Urban League. Democrat. Baptist. Office: 332A Capitol Annex Frankfort KY 40601 Home: 1018 S 4th St Louisville KY 40203-4224 Office Phone: 502-584-6341, 502-564-8100 ext. 685. Fax: 502-584-6342.

OWENS, GEORGE J., marketing professional; BA in Polit. Sci., Calif. State U., Northridge, 1993; MBA, Pepperdine U., Malibu, Calif., 2004. Various positions including dir. retail, office sys. & tech. practice, product rsch. mgr. and sr. analyst JD Power & Associates, 1995—2007; mng. dir. mktg. Service Corp. International, 2007—. Adj. prof. mktg. rsch. Pepperdine U. Mem.: Mktg. Rsch. Assn., Am. Mktg. Assn. Office: Service Corp International 1929 Allen Pky Houston TX 77019 Office Phone: 713-522-5141. Office Fax: 713-525-5586.

OWENS, LAURA LEWIS, lawyer; b. Atlanta, Sept. 27, 1960; BA cum laude, Furman U., 1982; JD cum laude, U. Ga., 1985. Bar: Ga. 1985. Ptnr. Alston & Bird L.L.P., Atlanta. Mem. editl. bd. Ga. Jour. Internat. and Comparative Law, 1983-85, editor-in-chief, 1984-85; author: Annual Survey of Developments in International Trade Law, 1983. Mem. Atlanta Bar Assn., State Bar of Ga. Office: Alston & Bird 1 Atlantic Ctr 1201 W Peachtree St NW Atlanta GA 30309-3424 Office Phone: 404-881-7363. Office Fax: 404-881-7777. Business E-Mail: lowens@alston.com.

OWENS, MICHAEL HOWARD, otolaryngologist; b. Evanston, Ill., Jan. 15, 1958; MD, U. South Fla., Tampa, 1984. Diplomate Am. Bd. Otolaryngology, 1990. Intern in otolaryngology U. South Fla., 1984—86, resident in gen. surgery and otolaryngology, 1986—90; otolaryngologist Miami Children's Hosp., Bapt. Health South Fla.; clinical asst. prof. U. Miami. Office: Miami Childrens Hosp #204 6705 SW 57th Ave Ste 704 South Miami FL 33143-3652 Office Phone: 305-666-0203. Office Fax: 305-666-0535.

OWENS, PHILLIP DRAYTON, state legislator; b. Pickens, SC, Mar. 20, 1951; s. Fred William and Lillian Parsons Owens; m. Lynn Catherine Southerland; children: Lori Jill, Kathryn Diana. Mem. Dist. 5 SC House of Reps., 2003—; mem. Agr. Com., Natural Res. & Environ. Affairs Com.; bd. dir. Pickens County Salvation Army, 1995—98, Pickens County YMCA, 1995—, Pickens County Mfrs.1 Assn., 1996—97; pres. Pickens County YMCA, 1997—98; bd. dir. Easley Econ. Devel. Corp., 1997—2000; advisor bd. First Union-Wachovia Bank Upstate, 1998—; bd. dir. YMCA Blue Ridge Assembly, 2000—. Mem.: St. Andrew United Meth. Ch. (chmn. vision com., past chmn. adminstrn. bd., lay mem. to ann. conf.), Palmetto Bapt. Med. Ctr. Found. (bd. dir. 1999—, treas., fin. com. chmn. 2001—), Greater Easley C. of C. (bd. dir. 1993—98, chmn. 1994, 2001—). Republican. Office: 429 Blatt Bldg Columbia SC 29201 Office Phone: 803-734-3053. E-mail: owensp@scstatehouse.net.

OWENS, ROBERT HUNTER, mathematics professor; b. Phila., Apr. 9, 1921; (married); 4 children. BS, Webb Inst., 1944; MA, Columbia, 1948; PhD in Math, Cal. Inst. Tech., 1952. Instr. math. Stevens Inst. Tech., 1946-48; asst. Cal. Inst. Tech., 1949-52; research asso. in applied math. Brown U., Providence, 1952-53; phys. sci. coordinator Office of Naval Research, Pasadena, Cal., 1953-54, mathematician Washington, 1954-56; asst. prof. math. U. N.H., 1956-59, asso. prof., 1959-62; acting head math. sci. sect. NSF, 1963-64; prof., chmn. dept. applied math. and computer sci. U. Va., Charlottesville, 1964-74, prof., 1974—, acting chmn. dept. applied math. and computer sci., 1978-79. Liaison scientist Office Naval Research, London, 1970-71 Served with USNR, 1943-46. Mem. Am. Math. Assn., Am. Soc. Indsl. and Applied Math. Office: U Va Sch Engring and Applied Sci Charlottesville VA 22901

OWENS, TYLER BENJAMIN, chemist; b. Norfolk, Va., Aug. 28, 1944; s. Arthur Samuel and Julia Tyler (Downs) O.; m. Brenda Anne Coates, Sept. 5, 1980; children: Brooks Downs, Elizabeth Tyler. BA in Chemistry, Campbell U., Buies Creek, NC, 1967; postgrad., N.C. State U., 1967-69. Sanitarian State of Va. Health Dept., Manassas, Va., 1971-72; chief chemist Goodmark Foods, Raleigh, N.C., 1972-75; real estate broker Nadine Hodge Realty, Raleigh, 1976-77; sales engr. Hewlett Packard Co., Palo Alto, Calif., 1977-80; sales rep. Sperry Univac Corp., Blue Bell, Pa., 1980-81; sales engr. Spectra Physics Corp., San Jose, 1981-83; pres. Batchelor & Owens, Inc., Raleigh, 1983-88; territory mgr. Extrel Corp., Pitts., 1988-90; sales mgr. Delsi Nermag Instruments, Paris, 1990-91, Viking Instruments Corp., Reston, Va., 1989-93; account exec. Dean Witter, Raleigh, 1993-95, Bodman Industries, Raleigh, 1995—; organic sales engr. Leco Corp., 1998—, Bruker Daltonics, 2004—. Active YMCA, Raleigh, 1989—; bd. dirs. Stonebridge Homeowners Assn., Raleigh, 1990-93, pres., 1993; bd. govs. Friends of the Children, Wake Meml. Hosp., Raleigh, 1990-93; precinct del. Wake County Rep. Party, Raleigh, 1985; vestry Episcopal Ch. of the Nativity, Raleigh, 1988-90, sr. warden, 1988-89. Mem. Am. Soc. Mass Spectrometry, N.C. Real Esate Commn., Triangle Mass Spectrometer Discussion Group, Wake County Rep. Men's Club. Mem. Anglican Ch. Avocations: running, flying, amateur radio, bridge. Home and Office: 1009 Carrington Dr Raleigh NC 27615-1212

OWENS, WILLIAM ARTHUR (BILL OWENS), telecommunications industry executive, retired military officer; b. Bismarck, ND, May 8, 1940; s. Earl and Ruth (Arthur) O.; m. Monika Bastian, Sept. 30, 1967; 1 child, Todd. BA in Math., US Naval Acad., 1962; MA in Politics, Philosophy & Economics, U. Oxford, Eng., 1974; M in Mgmt., George Washington U., 1976. Registered profl. engr. Founder Extend America; commd. ensign USN, 1962, multiple assignments in nuclear submarines, 1962-77, adm., 1996; comdg. officer USS Sam Houston (SSBN609), Honolulu, 1977-80, USS Corpus Christi (SSN705), New London, Conn., 1980-81, Submarine Squadron 4, Charleston, SC, 1984-85, Submarine Group 6, Charleston, SC, 1987-88; dir. office of program appraisal, Dept. of Navy US Dept. Def., Washington, 1988, sr. mil. asst. to sec., 1988—91; comdr. US 6th Fleet, Gaeta, Italy, 1990—91; dep. chief naval ops. for resources, warfare requirements and assessments USN, Washington, 1991—93; vice-chmn. Joint Chiefs of Staff US Dept. Def., Washington, 1993—96; vice chmn., pres., COO Sci. Applications International Corp., 1996-98; chmn., CEO Teledesic LLC, 1998—2003; vice chmn., pres., & CEO Nortel Networks Corp., Brampton, Ont., Canada, 2004—05; chmn., CEO & mng. dir. AEA Holdings Asia, 2006—; mng. dir., chmn. & CEO AEA Investors Asia, 2006; chmn. Intelius, Inc., 2006—; former bd. dirs. EMBARQ (now part of CenturyLink); chmn. CenturyLink, Inc. (formerly CenturyTel, Inc.), 2009—. Bd. dirs. Daimler Chrysler AG, Nortel Networks Corp., 2002—05, Polycom, Inc., 2005—, Wipro Ltd., 2006—. Author: Future of the Maritime Strategy, 1988, High Seas, 1994, Lifting the Fog of War, 2000; contr. articles on national security. Bd. dirs. Carnegie Corp., Carnegie Found.; mem. Brookings Instn., Fred Hutchinson Cancer Rsch. Ctr., Can. Coun. Chief Execs. Decorated 4 Stars; recipient Intrepid Salute award, Intrepid Foundation, 2004; named 50 Most Powerful People in Networking, Network World, 2004. Mem. Oxford Soc., Coun. Fgn. Rels. Episcopalian. Avocations: golf, skiing. Office: CenturyLink Inc 100 CenturyTel Dr Monroe LA 07120 Office Phone: 318-388-9000. E-mail: william.owens@centurylink.com.

OWENS, WILLIAM CLARENCE, state legislator; b. Elizabeth City, NC, Apr. 2, 1947; s. William Clarence and Hazel Markham C. Owens; m. Cynthia Owens. Mgr. W. W. Owens & Sons Moving & Storage, 1967—; 3rd vice chmn. Pasquotank Dem. Party, NC, 1974—76, chmn., 1976—78; ptnr. Linda's Hairstyling, 1977—; chmn. Pasquotank Dem. Party, 1981—84; sec. Albemarle Mini-Warehouses Inc., 1982—; state rep. Dist. 1 NC, 1995—; chmn., local bd. mem. People's Bank & Trust Co., 1979—. Served with NC Army Nat. Guard, 1967—96. Recipient Disting. Svc. award, Elizabeth City Jaycees, 1975, Appreciation award, Elizabeth City Coun., 1977, Red Cross Blood Program, 1979; named Man of Yr., VFW, 1975. Mem.: Jaycees, Elks, Moose, Redmen, Rotary Club. Democrat. Baptist. Address: PO Box 537 Elizabeth City NC 27909 Office: North Carolina House of Representatives 300 N Salisbury St Rm 611 Raleigh NC 27603-5925 Office Phone: 919-733-0010. Fax: 919-338-1648. Business E-Mail: Bill.Owens@ncleg.net.

OWINGS, MALCOLM WILLIAM, retired management consultant; b. Cin., Feb. 5, 1925; s. William Malcolm and Margaret (Benvie) O.; m. Margie M. Gehiker, Sept. 4, 1948 (dec. June 2000); children: Lynn A., Sandra S., Wendy K., Cheryl M; m. Doris Marie Gorman, Aug. 23, 2002, (dec. Dec, 2008) BS in Bus. Adminstrn., Miami U., Oxford, Ohio, 1950, LL.D., 1976; A.M.P., Harvard U., 1975. With Continental Can Co., 1950-83, corp. v.p., from 1971; v.p., gen. mgr. pub. affairs Continental Packaging Co (Continental Group, Inc.), 1982-83; owner, pres. Owings Assocs., Inc., Pinehurst, NC, 1983-92; ret., 1992. Dir. First Bank, Pinehurst, N.C.; adviser to Am. del. Internat. Tin Coun., 1978-82; bd dir RockPamley Lecture Series 2010-. Columnist The Pilot, Southern Pines, N.C., 1997-2004. Dean's assoc. exec. in residence Sch. Bus., Miami U., 1973, mem. alumni coun., 1958-65, mem. pres.'s devel. coun., 1965-69, meem. resource devel. bd., 1982; trustee Village of Thiensville, Wis., 1956-59; mem. N.C. Clean, 1985-94, chmn., 1986-93; bd. dirs. Barrington Area Devel. Coun., 1974-79, Sales Mgmt. Execs. Grad. Sch., Am. Soc. Environment, 1976, Keep Am. Beautiful, 1980-81, also chmn., 1990; chmn. Keep N.C. Beautiful Coun., Raleigh, 1988-92, Moore Meml. Hosp. Found., Pinehurst, N.C., 1986-89; mem. Moore Regional Hosp. Scroll Soc., 1991-94, chmn., 1992-93; chmn. Moore County (N.C.) Rep. Party, 1986-88; co-founder Rep. Presdl. Task Force; mem. U.S. Senate Bus. Adv. Bd., 1981-91; commr. Moore County, 1988-96, Youth Svcs., 1993-95; apptd. to N.C. Watershed Protection Adv. Com. by N.C. Environ. Mgmt. Commn., 1990-92; bd. dirs. Pub. Edn. Found., 1994-99, Ptnrs. for Children and Family, 1994-97, Drug-Free Moore County Inc., 1995-98, Dispute Settlement Ctr. of Moore County, 1995-97, Keep Moore County Beautiful, 1997—; mem. Moore County Bd. of Health, 1994-97; pres. Belle Meade Residents Assn., 2000, rep. precinct chairs East Knollwood Precinct, 2009, chmn. Recipient Cert. of Meritorious Svc. Miami U., 1967, Meritorious Svc. award Keep Moore County Beautiful, Inc., 1993-94; named Alumnus of Yr. Miami U., 1970; 1st Am. recipient Order of Apteryx Earth Awareness Found., 1971, Order of Long Leaf Pine. Mem. Ill. C. of C. (bd. dirs. 1976-78), Miami U. Alumni Assn. (nat. pres. 1964-65), Omicron Delta Kappa, Sigma Chi, Delta Sigma Pi Clubs: Pinehurst Country, Country of N.C. (Pinehurst). Home: 105 Gossman Rd Ste 119 Southern Pines NC 28387-2275 E-mail: mowings1@nc.rr.com.

OWNBEY, PAT, state legislator; m. Kathy Ownbey, June 12, 1976; children: Scott, Susan Perkins. BS, Univ. Okla. Former vice pres. & gen. mgr. KKAJ-KVSO Radio; former owner & gen. mgr. KICM Radio; pres. & gen. mgr. On the Air Property Mgmt.; mem. Dist. 48 Okla. House of Representatives, 2008—. Former chmn. deacons First Bapt. Ch., Ardmore. Mem.: Okla. Cattleman's Assn., Ardmore Kiwanis Club. Republican. Baptist. Office: 2300 N Lincoln Blvd Rm 301 Oklahoma City OK 73105 also: 2303 Cloverleaf Pl Ardmore OK 73401 Office Phone: 405-557-7326. Business E-Mail: pat.ownbey@okhouse.gov.

OWNBY, DENNIS RANDALL, pediatrician, allergist, educator, researcher; b. Athens, Ohio, July 14, 1948; s. Dillard Ralph and Miriam (Lee) Ownby; m. Helen Louise Engelbrecht, May 24, 1970; children: David Randall, Kathryn Louise. BS, Ohio U., 1969; MD, Med. Coll. Ohio, 1972. Diplomate Am. Bd. Allergy and Immunology (bd. dirs. 1993-98, chair 1998, residency rev. com. 1995-2000), Am. Bd. Pediat., Nat. Bd. Med. Examiners. Intern and resident Duke U. Sch. Medicine, Durham, NC, 1972—74, asst. prof., 1977—80; staff physician Henry Ford Hosp., Detroit, 1980—97, dir. Allergy Rsch. Lab., 1986—97; prof. pediat. Case Western Res. U., Cleve., 1997; prof. pediat. and medicine Med. Coll. Ga., Augusta, 1998—. Clin. asst. prof. pediat. U. Mich., Ann Arbor, 1980—86, clin. assoc. prof. pediat., 1986—95. Contbr. articles to med. jours., chpts. to books. Fellow: Am. Acad. Allergy, Am. Acad. Pediat. Office: Med Coll of Georgia Sect Allergy & Immunology BG-1019 Augusta GA 30912-3790 Home Phone: 706-651-9229; Office Phone: 706-721-3531. Business E-Mail: downby@mcg.edu.

OXFORD, HUBERT, III, lawyer; b. Beaumont, Tex., Sept. 25, 1938; s. Hubert Burton and Virginia Mary (Cunningham) O.; m. Cynthia Lynn Culp, Apr. 25, 1987; children: Mary Francelia, Hubert IV, Mary Cunningham, Virginia Barrett, Alaina Danielle, Adriana Victoria, Gabriella Elizabeth. BSME, Tex. A&M U., 1960; LLB, U. Tex., 1963. Bar: Tex., 1963, Mont. 1996, Wyo. 1996, Okla. 1996, DC 1998, Colo. 1998, U.S. Ct. Appeals (5th cir.) 1967, U.S. Dist. Ct. (ea., so., no., we. dists.) Tex., U.S. Supreme Ct. 1975, U.S. Dist. Ct., Okla., Mont., 1996, Wyo., 1996, DC 1998, Colo. 1998. Briefing atty. to U.S. dist. judge Eastern Dist. Tex., Beaumont, 1966; asst. dist. atty. Jefferson County, Tex., 1967; mng. ptnr. firm Beckenstein & Oxford, L.L.P., Beaumont, 1966; gen. counsel Sabine-Neches Navigation Dist., Lower Neches Valley Authority. Mem. Gov. Reorganization Commn. Tex. 70th Legislature, 1987-88, Tex. Oil Spill Commn.; U.S. Commr. Ea. Dist. Tex., 1968-70; mem. Tex. Bd. Registration for Profl. Engrs., 1994-2000. Assoc. editor Tex. Law Rev., 1962-63. Bd. dirs. Ducks Unltd., 1978-86, Gulf Coast Conservation Assn., 1978-86; sec. bd. regents Lamar U., 1978-84, gen. counsel, 1986-92; mem. Tex. Air Control Bd., 1984-90; chmn. Tex. Clean Air Study Com., 1989. Capt. JAGC, USAF, 1963-66. Fellow ABA, Tex. Bar Assn., Internat. Soc. Barristers; mem. ATLA, Southeastern Admirality Law Inst., Internat. Assn. Def. Counsel, Tex. Assn. Def. Lawyers, Nat. Bd. Trial Advocacy, Best Lawyers in Am., State Bar Tex. (chmn. CLE com. 1979-81, course dir. admirality and maritime seminar 1991, 96, grievance com. Dist. 3A, dir. Dist. 3 1997-2000), Maritime Law Assn., Jefferson County Bar Assn. (pres. 1987-88, Outstanding Young Lawyer 1972), Def. Rsch. Inst., Beaumont C. of C. (dir. 1978-84), Phi Delta Theta, Tau Beta Pi, Phi Kappa Phi, Phi Delta Phi. Roman Catholic. Home: 4810 Calder Rd Beaumont TX 77706 Office: Benckenstein & Oxford LLP 3535 Calder Ave Ste 300 Beaumont TX 77706-5087 Office Phone: 409-833-9182. Personal E-mail: hubertoxford@benoxford.com.

OXFORD, PATRICK C., lawyer; b. Beaumont, Tex., Aug. 15, 1942; BBA, U. Tex., 1966, JD with honors, 1967. Bar: Tex. 1967. Former mng. ptnr. Bracewell & Giuliani LLP (formerly Bracewell & Patterson LLP), Houston, chmn. of firm. Mem. bd. dirs. BioHouston, Inc., M.D. Anderson Services Corp., Tex. Med. Ctr. Mng. editor Tex. Law Rev., 1966-67. Mem. Am. Coll. Mortgage Attys., State Bar Tex. Office: Bracewell & Giuliani LLP S Tower Pennzoil Pl 711 Louisiana St Ste 2300 Houston TX 77002-2781 Office Fax: 713-224-8888. Business E-Mail: pco@bgllp.com.

OXFORD, VAYL STANLEY, consulting firm executive, former federal agency administrator; b. 1952; BS in Gen. Engring., US Mil. Acad, West Point, NY, 1974; MS in Aeronautical Engring., USAF Inst. Tech., 1975. Asst. prof. aeronautics USAF Acad., 1982—86; dir. counterproliferation Def. Nuc. Agy., Def. Spl. Weapons Agy., 1993—98; dep. dir. tech. devel. Def. Threat Reduction Agy.; dir. counter proliferation NSC; dir. Office Domestic Nuc. Detection US Dept. Homeland Security, Washington, 2005—09; dir. WMD Countermeasures Northrop Grumman Corp., 2009; sr. policy adv. The Tauri Group, Alexandria, Va., 2009—. With USAF. Office: The Tauri Group 6361 Walker Ln Ste 100 Alexandria VA 22310-3280 Office Phone: 703-683-2883. Office Fax: 703-683-2866.

OXLEY, JAMES GRIEVE, mathematics professor; b. Sale, Victoria, Australia, Feb. 4, 1953; s. William A. and Dilys C. (Grieve) O.; m. Judith Danute Surkevicius; children: Margaret Catherine (dec.), David Grieve (dec.). BSc, U. Tasmania, 1974; MSc, Australian Nat. U., 1975; PhD, U. Oxford, 1978. Lectr., rsch. fellow Australian Nat. U., 1978—82; asst. prof. La. State U., Baton Rouge, 1982—85, assoc. prof., 1985—90, prof., 1990—99, alumni prof., 1999—2012, Boyd prof., 2012—. Vis. instr. U. N.C., Chapel Hill, 1978; vis. rsch. fellow Merton Coll., Oxford, England, 2005. Author: Matroid Theory, 1992, 2nd edit., 2011; mem. editl. bd. Combinatorics, Probability and Computing, Soc. Indsl. and Applied Math. Jour. on Discrete Math., Jour. Combinatorial Theory Series B; reviewer Mathematical Reviews, Zentralblatt für Mathematik; contbr. chpts. to books, articles to profl. jours. Grantee NSF, 1985-87, 89-91, La. Edn. Quality Support Fund, 1987-94, Nat. Security Agy., 1994—2013, others; Fulbright fellow U. N.C., 1980; named Disting. Rsch. Master of Engring, Sci. and Tech., La. State U., 1999. Fellow Am. Math. Soc.; mem. London Math. Soc. Office: La State U Math Dept Baton Rouge LA 70803-4918 Home Phone: 225-769-9106; Office Phone: 225-578-1577. Business E-Mail: oxley@math.lsu.edu.

OZERDEN, HALIL SULEYMAN (SUL), federal judge; b. Hattiesburg, Miss., Dec. 5, 1966; 1 child. BS in Fgn. Svc. magna cum laude, Georgetown U.Sch. Fgn. Svc., 1989; Grad., Navy Flight Sch., Pensacola, Fla., 1989—90; JD, Stanford Law Sch., 1998. Bar: Miss., Fla., La., Ala., US Ct. Appeals (5th Cir.), US Dist. Ct. (no. & so. dist.) Miss., US Dist. Ct. (ea. dist.) La., US Dist. Ct. (no. dist.) Fla. 1988. Law clk. to Hon. Eldon E. Fallon US Dist. Ct. (ea. dist.) La., 1998—99; ptnr. Dukes, Dukes, Keating & Faneca, P.A., Gulfport, Miss., 1999—2003, shareholder, 2003—07; judge US Dist. Ct. (so. dist.) Miss., Gulfport, 2007—. Mem. Rotary Club Gulfport, 1999—; mentor Gulfport Pub. Schools, 1999—2005; exec. com., v.p. pub. affairs Gulfport C. of C., 2000—03, chmn.-elect, 2005; v.p. Gulfport Bus. Club, 2004—05; vestry mem. St. Peter's By-the-Sea Episcopal Church, 2002—04. Served in USN, 1989—95. Recipient Johnson & Gibbs Law Review award, Outstandsing Contribution as an Assoc. Editor, 1998, Volunteer of Yr., Gulfport C. of C., 2003; named one of Top Ten South Miss. Bus. Leaders Under 40, 2004. Mem.: Am. Inns of Ct., Harrison County Young Lawyers Assn., Harrison County Bar Assn., Ala. Bar Assn., Fla. Bar Assn., Miss. Bar Assn. Office: US Dist Ct PO Box 23552 Jackson MS 39225

OZUNA, LETICIA, councilwoman; BA in Latin American Studies, U. Tex., Austin; MA, Tex. A&M, College Station. Councilwoman Dist. 3 San Antonio City Coun., 2012—. Bd. mem. Highland Park Neighborhood Assn.; mem. City of San Antonio Parks Bond Com. Grantee NSF. Office: City Hall PO Box 839966 San Antonio TX 78283 also: 3319 Sidney Brooks, Bldg 510 San Antonio TX 78235 Office Phone: 210-207-7064. Office Fax: 210-207-0969.

PABON CHARNECO, MILDRED G., territorial supreme court justice; b. San Juan, Nov. 27, 1957; d. Julio Pabon Maldonado and Charneca Aida Villanueva; 3 children. BS with highest honors, Univ. PR, JD, 1983. Bar: PR 1985, US Dist. Ct. PR Dist. 1987. With Bufete Troncoso Fuentes-Agostini; legal adv. Office of Legis. Services, PR Legis., 1989—92, dir. legal div., 1992; dep. dir. & asst. gov. PR Gov. Office of Legis. Affairs, 1992—95; judge PR Cir. Ct. Appeals, 1995—2009; assoc. justice PR Supreme Ct., 2009—. Mailing: Rama Judicial de Puerto Rico PO Box 9022392 San Juan PR 00902-2392 Office Phone: 787-723-6033.*

PACE, ANDREW K., information technology library director; BA in Rhetoric & Communication Studies, U. Va., 1991; MSLS, Cath. U. of Am., 1996. Libr. asst. Cath. U. of Am. Libraries, 1994—96; systems libr. Innovative Interfaces, Inc., 1996—99; sys. libr., digital projects NC State U. Libraries, 1999, asst. head, sys., 1999—2001, head, info. tech., 2001—. Named Libr. of Yr., DRA Users' Group, 2002; Frye fellowship, 2006. Mem.: Nat. Info. Standards Orgn. (co-chair metasearch initiative 2003—05), Assn. Coll. & Rsch. Libraries, Libr. and Info. Tech. Assn. (dir.-at-large 2004—07, pres.-elect 2007—). Office: NC State U DH Hill Libr Raleigh NC 27695-7111 Office Phone: 919-515-3087. Office Fax: 919-513-3330. Business E-Mail: andrew_pace@ncsu.edu.

PACE, G. MICHAEL, JR., lawyer; b. Roanoke, Va., Mar. 11, 1957; BA, Hampden-Sydney Coll., 1979; JD, Washington & Lee U., 1984. Bar: Va. 1984. Mng. ptnr. Gentry Locke Rakes & Moore LLP, Roanoke, Va. Mem. adv. bd. SunTrust, Roanoke, Va.; bd. mem., chmn. Roanoke Regional C. of C., 2002—04; pres. Roanoke Valley Econ. Devel. Partnership, 2002—04; exec. com. Roanoke Valley Bus. Coun.; chmn. Bus. Leadership Fund; bd. mem. Fifth Planning Dist. Regional Alliance, Va. Western Cmty. Coll. Found.; mem. Roanoke Regional Airport Alliance; bd. trustees Hampden-Sydney Coll.; pres. Hampden-Sydney Coll. Alumni Assn.; trustee Hampden Sydney Coll. Recipient Gold Best Local Lawyer award, The Roanoker Mag., 2004; named one of Legal Elite in field of corp. law, Va. Bus. Mag., 2000—02, Legal Elite in field of real estate/construction, 2003—04, Legal Elite in field of bus., 2005—06, Va. Super Lawyers, 2007, Best lawyers in Am. Mem.: Roanoke Valley Econ. Devl. Partnership (pres. 2002—05), Roanoke Regional C. of C., Va. We. Cmty. Coll. Found. (bd. mem.), Bus. Coun. (chair elect.), Bus. Leadership Fund (chmn.), Va. State Bar (past chmn. real property sect.), Va. Bar Assn. (pres.-elect 2006—07, pres. bd. govs. 2008, chmn. bd. gov.), Roanoke Bar Assn. (pres. 2000—01, Presidents Volunter Svc. award, Silver level 2006). Mailing: Gentry Locke Rakes & Moore PO box 40013 Roanoke VA 24022-0013 Office: Gentry Locke Rakes & Moore 10 Franklin Rd SE Roanoke VA 24011 Office Phone: 540-983-9312. Office Fax: 540-983-9400. E-mail: mike_pace@gentrylocke.com.

PACE, NICHOLAS JOSEPH, insurance company executive, lawyer; b. Cleve., Ohio, Oct. 10, 1970; BS in Acctg. and Fin., Miami U., Ohio, 1993; JD, MBA, U. Richmond, Va., 1996. Bar: Va. 1996, Calif. 2001. Cons. Ernst & Young LLP, Richmond, 1996—98; assoc. LeClair Ryan PC, Richmond, 1998—2000; sr. assoc. Morrison & Foerster LLP, Palo Alto, Calif., 2000—03; asst. gen. counsel CarMax Inc., 2003—06; sr. v.p., dep. gen. counsel, asst. sec. Amerigroup Corp., 2006—10, exec. v.p., gen. counsel, sec., 2010—. Mem.: ABA, Calif. Bar Assn., Va. Bar Assn. Office: Amerigroup Corp 4425 Corp Ln Virginia Beach VA 23462 Office Phone: 757-490-6900. Office Fax: 757-222-2330.

PACIFICO, ALBERT DOMINICK, cardiovascular surgeon; b. Bklyn., Sept. 24, 1940; s. Dominick Vincent and Amelia Catherine (Jannelli) P.; m. Vicki Lynne Overton, May 16, 1980; children: Albert D., Nicole M., Paul V. BS, St. Johns U., 1960; MD, N.J. Coll. Medicine, 1964. Diplomate Am. Bd. Surgery, Am. Bd. Thoracic Surgery. Med. intern Jersey City Med. Ctr., Seton Gall Coll. Medicine, 1964-65; asst. resident in surgery Mayo Clinic, Rochester, Minn., 1965-67; research fellow in surgery U. Ala., Birmingham, 1967-69, sr. resident, then chief resident surgery, resident in thoracic and cardiovascular surgery, 1968-72, mem. faculty dept. surgery, 1970—2006, prof. surgery, 1978-83, John W. Kirklin prof. cardiovascular surgery, 1983—2006, vice chmn. dept. surgery, 1990, dir. divsn. cardiothoracic surgery, 1984—2006, dir. Congenital Heart Disease Diagnosis and Treatment Ctr., 1985—2006; ret., 2006. Mem. staff gen., thoracic and cardiovascular surgery Univ. Hosp., Birmingham, 1972-2006, VA Hosp., Birmingham, 1972-2006; mem. staff Children's Hosp., Birmingham, 1971-2006, chief gen., thoracic and cardiovascular surgery, 1984-2006. Author: (with others) Pediatric Cardiac Surgery, 1985, Cardiology, 1985, Textbook of Surgery, 13th edit., 1986, The Treatment of Congenital Cardiac Anomalies, 1986, Perspectives in Pediatric Cardiology, 1988, Current Therapy in Cardiothoracic Surgery, 1989, Decision Making in Surgery of the Chest, 1989, Cardiac Surgery: Cyanotic Congential Heart Disease, 1989, Reoperation in Cardiac Surgery, 1989, others; mem. editorial bd. Am. Jour. Cardiology, 1983-2006, Heart and Vessel, 1985-2006, Jour. Cardiac Surgery, 1985-2006; cons. editorial referee Ala. Jour. Med. Scis., 1974-75; contbr. articles to med. jours. Fellow ACS, Am. Coll. Cardiology, Am. Surg. Assn.; mem. AMA, Ala. State Med. Soc., Jefferson County Med. Soc., Am. Heart Assn. (Paul Dudley White Internat. Svc. Citation 1977), Am. Assn. Thoracic Surgery, Soc. Thoracic Surgeons, Am. Surg. Soc., Internat. Coll. Pediatrics, John Kirklin Soc., Congentital Heart Surgeons Soc., Assn. Acad. Surgery, Ala. chpt. Mayo Clinic Alumni Assn., Panamanian Soc. Cardiology (hon.), Peruvian Soc. Thoracic and Cardiovascular Surgery (hon.), Soc. Nat. Inst. Cardiology Mex. (hon.), Cardiac Soc. Australia and New Zealand (corr.), Peruvian Soc. Cardiology (corr.), Alpha Omega Alpha. Republican. Roman Catholic.

PACKER, GARY D., gas industry executive; Grad. in Petroleum Engring. & Natural Gas Engring., Pa. State U. Worked Amerada Hess, Tenneco Oil Co.; gen. mgr., Rocky Mountains Newfield Exploration Co., mgr., acquisitions and devel., Gulf Mexico, joined, 1995, pres., v.p., Rocky Mountains, 2004, exec. v.p., COO, 2009—. Exec. dir. Ind. Petroleum Assn. Mountain States (IPAMS); mem. The Soc. Petroleum Engrs. Mem.: The Ind. Producers Assn. America. Office: Newfield Exploration Co Ste 100 363 N Sam Houston Pkwy E Houston TX 77060 Office Phone: 281-847-6000. Office Fax: 281-405-4242. Business E-Mail: gpacker@newfld.com.

PADALINO, MICHAEL L., mortgage company executive; 2 children. BS, U. Ala., Tuscaloosa, Ala.; MBA, U. Ala., Birmingham, 1982; grad., Northwestern U., Chgo. Pres., COO AmSouth Mortgage Co., Birmingham; pres. Molton, Allen & Williams Corp., Birmingham; pres., CEO Synovus Mortgage Corp., Birmingham. Named Outstanding Alumnus, U. Ala. Birmingham, 2005. Mem.: Mortgage Bankers Assn. (mem. residential bd. governors), Mortgage Bankers Assn. Ala. (pres. 1986—87). Office: Synovus Mortgage Corp Ste 350 800 Shades Creek Pky Birmingham AL 35209 Office Phone: 205-874-1459. Office Fax: 205-874-1516.

PADDACK, SUSAN, state legislator; m. Gary Paddack; children: Elizabeth, Geoffrey. BS in Edn., Univ. Colo.; ME in Secondary Edn., Ea. Ctrl. Univ. Former tchr. in middle and junior high schools in Tex., Colo. and Okla.; adj. faculty mem. East Ctrl. U.; mem. Dist. 13 Okla. State Senate, 2004—. Recipient of several awards and honors. Mem.: Okla. State Med. Assn. Alliance (pres. 1991—92), American Med. Assn. Alliance (pres. 2000—01). Democrat. Presbyterian. Mailing: 500 Southeast County Rd Ada OK 74820 Office: 2300 N Lincoln Blvd Rm 533A Oklahoma City OK 73105 Office Phone: 405-521-5541, 580-332-7607. Business E-Mail: paddack@oksenate.gov.

PADDEN, ANTHONY ALOYSIUS, JR., retired federal government official, US immigration hearings and court policy and procedures advisor; b. Kearny, NJ, Apr. 3, 1949; s. Anthony Aloysius and Harriet Margaret Padden. PBA, Fairleigh Dickinson U., 1970, MA in Pub. Adminstrn., 1980; postgrad., U. Tenn. Sch. Law, 1970. Cert. hist. preservation NOVA, 2012. Employment interviewer N.J. Dept. Labor, Trenton, 1970—76, prin. procedure analyst, 1976—79; nat. procedure coord. Interstate Compendium Employment Svc. Activities Project, Trenton, 1979—80; mgmt. analyst Dept. Justice, Washington, 1980—83; chief clk. ct. U.S. Immigration Ct., Falls Church, Va., 1983—. Adj. faculty Nat. Judicial Coll., Reno, 1998—2003; cons., Dumfries, Va., 1978—. Author: Dept. Labor tech. report, 1980; contbr. and editor: other profl. studies. Presdl. mgmt. intern, 1980, Logan Chambers grantee, Internat. Assn. Pers. in Employment Security, 1979. Mem.: Pi Alpha Alpha (Adminstr. of Yr. 1991).

PADGETT, JOHN, political organization administrator; m. Mary Padgett; 3 children. Grad., U. Ga., Athens. Chmn. Athens-Clarke County Rep. Party, 11th and 12th Congl. Dist.; owner SE Ambulance Svc., Athens; sec., mem. exec. com. Ga. Rep. Party, chmn. Atlanta, 2013—. Co-chair Athens-Clarke County Bush Campaign, 2000, 2004. Chair Athens Downtown Devel. Authority; pres. Oconee County C. of C., Athens Downtown Coun.; bd. mem. Athens Area C. of C., Athens Hist. Soc. Republican. Office: Georgia Republican Party PO Box 550008 Atlanta GA 30355

PADGETT, JOHN DAVID, lawyer; b. Norfolk, Va., July 8, 1958; s. Royal Claytor and Phyllis (Hunt) Padgett; m. Lee Ann Hagy. BA with distinction, U. Va., 1980; JD, Washington & Lee U., 1983. Bar: Va. 1983, US Bankruptcy Ct. Ea. Dist. 1983, US Dist. Ct. Ea. Dist. Va. 1983, US Ct. Appeals 4th Cir. 1983. Ptnr. Jett, Berkley, Furr & Padgett (merged with McGuireWoods LLP), Norfolk, Va., 1983—93, McGuireWoods LLP, Norfolk, Va., 1993—, mng. ptnr. Norfolk office. Escheator City of Norfolk, Va., 1994—2003; gen. counsel Rep. Party of Va. Vice chair Hampton Rd. YMCA, 2005—; chmn. State Coun. of Higher Edn., Va., 1998—2001. Mem. Maritime Law Assn., Southeastern Admiralty Law Inst., Hampton Roads C. of C.(chmn. 2003), Phi Delta Phi., Hampton Roads Fgn. Commerce Club (pres.), Norfolk Rotary Club. Presbyterian. Avocations: baseball, golf, book collecting, politics. Office: McGuireWoods LLP World Trade Ctr Ste 9000 101 W Main St Norfolk VA 23510-1655 Office Phone: 757-640-3779. Office Fax: 757-640-3968. Business E-Mail: jpadgett@mcguirewoods.com.

PADRÓN, EDUARDO JOSE, academic administrator; b. 1944; BA summa cum laude, Fla. Atlantic U., 1966; MA, U. Fla., PhD in Econs. Faculty mem. Miami Dade Coll., 1971—, asst. prof., academic dean, pres., 1995—. Chmn. Fla. CC Coun. of Pres., 1999—2000; mem. White House Commn. on Ednl. Excellence; bd. dirs. Am. Coun. on Edn., Am. Assn. Hispanics in Higher Edn., US Congl. Hispanic Caucus Inst., Bus.-Higher Edn. Forum, 2009—; bd. dirs. Miami Br. Fed. Reserve Bank of Atlanta, 2009. Editl. bd. mem. Univ. Bus., The Hispanic Outlook in Higher Edn., The Presidency; contbr. articles to profl. jours. Adv. bd. mem. Holocaust Documentation and Edn. Ctr.; bd. trustees Carnegie Found. for the Advancement of Tchg. Recipient Hispanic Achievement Award in Edn., Hispanic Mag., 2004, Paul A. Elsner Internat. Excellence in Leadership Award, 2005, Excellence in Edn. Award, Poder-Boston Consulting Group, 2008; named Nat. CEO of Yr., Assn. CC Trustees, 2002, Comdr. in Ordre des Palms Académiques, Republic of France, Order of San Martin, Republic of Argentina, Order of Queen Isabella, Spain; named one of The 10 Best Coll. Presidents, TIME mag., 2009. Mem.: Assn. Am. Colls. and Univs. (vice chair, chair-elect bd. dirs. 2008, chair 2009). Office: Miami Dade College 300 NE 2nd Ave Miami FL 33132-2204 Office Phone: 305-237-8888.

PADRON, JOSHUA BEN MICHAEL, academic administrator; BA in Religion, Palm Beach Atlantic U., Fla., 1991; MBA, U. Phoenix, 2006. Gen. mgr. Devash Judaica Internat., Inc., Ft. Lauderdale, Fla.; sr. sales mgr. CTI Bus. Mgmt. Systems, Inc., Houston; dir. admissions Internat. Acad. Design & Tech., Orlando, Fla., 2003—05; v.p. admissions & mktg. Lehigh Valley Coll., Center Valley, Pa., 2005—06; campus dir. Brooks Coll., Sunnyvale, Calif., 2006—07; pres. Collins Coll., Tempe, Ariz., 2007—09; pres. South Fla. metro campuses DeVry U., 2009—. Office: DeVry U Miramar Campus 2300 SW 145th Ave Hollywood FL 33027 Mailing: DeVry U 1 Tower Ln Ste 1000 Oakbrook Terrace IL 60181-4624 Office Phone: 630-706-3527. E-mail: jpadron@devry.com.

PAES, LEANDER, professional tennis player; b. Goa, India, June 17, 1973; s. Vence and Jennifer. Profl. tennis player WTA Tour, 1991—. Mem. Indian nat. team Davis Cup, Summer Olympic Games. Recipient Arjuna award, 1990, Bronze medal, tennis, Atlanta Olympic Games, 1996, Rijiv Gandhi Khel Ratna award, 1996—97, Padma Shri award, 2001; named Male MVP, World Team Tennis, 2009, 2011. Achievements include winning 1 career singles title, 33 career doubles titles, ATP; Grand Slam men's doubles champion: Wimbeldon, 1999, French Open, 1999, 2001, 2009, US Open, 2006, 2009, 2013, Australian Open, 2012. Office: ATP Americas 201 ATP Tour Blvd Ponte Vedra Beach FL 32082*

PAFFORD, MARK S., state legislator; b. Apr. 11, 1966; m. Tracy Pafford; children: Audrey, Brendan. BA in Pub. Adminstrn., Fla. Internat. U., 1988. Mem. Dist. 16 US House of Representatives, 1989—92; US Congl. aide Congressman Lawrence J. Smith; sr. coord. Cultural Ctr., Royal Palm Beach, 1993—96; legis. asst. Rep. Lois Frankel, 1996—97; exec. dir. & CEO Alzheimer's Assn., 1998—2007; dir. planning & policy Area Agy. on Aging, 2007—08; dir. leadership giving & resource devel. Lord's Place; mem. Dist. 88 Fla. House of Reps., 2008—, mem. elder and family svcs. policy com., mil. and local affairs policy com., natural resources appropriations com. Mem. Youth Conservation Corps, 1980; interpretive guide & naturalist Arch Creek Park Miami-Dade Parks & Recreation, 1986—89; vol. Foster Care Rev. Bd., 2001; pres. Palm Beach County Partnership For Aging, 2005—06. Mem.: Dem. Exec. Com., Democracy For Palm Beach County, Palm Beach County Young Dem., Century Village United Dem. Club, West Palm Beach Dem. Club, North County Haitian Am. Dem. Club, Mid-County Dem. Club (former v.p.), Lake Worth West Dem. Club, Golden Lakes Dem. Club, Cypress Lakes Dem. Club. Democrat. Jewish. Office: 402 S Monroe St Rm 1401 Tallahassee FL 32399-1300 also: 2240 Palm Beach Lakes Blvd Ste 102 West Palm Beach FL 33409-3403 Office Phone: 850-488-0175, 561-682-0156. Business E-Mail: mark.pafford@myfloridahouse.gov.

PAGALIA, CONSTANTINO, information technology executive; Diploma in Mgmt., Australian Inst. Mgmt., Crontonville Leadership Inst. GE; B in Computer Sci., U. Sydney. Leader, applications divsn. General Electric Capital, Western Australia, Australia, 1995—98; account exec. BHP Billiton, 1998—2003, regional mgr., global accts., 2003, delivery mgr., global enterprise applications, account Australia; joined Computer Sciences Corp., 1999, gen. mgr., mng. dir., pres., Latin America operations, 2008—; regional mgr., global accts. Newmont Mining Corp., 2003. Mng. dir., prin. cons. Infolink, Australia. Office: Computer Sciences Corp 3170 Fairview Park Dr Falls Church VA 22042 Office Phone: 703-876-1000. Business E-Mail: cpagalia@csc.com.

PAGAN, JOHN RUSTON, law educator; b. Little Rock, Aug. 4, 1951; s. John Frank and Betty (Hardin) P. BA, Coll. of William and Mary, 1973; MLitt, Oxford U., 1975; JD, Harvard U., 1978; DPhil, Oxford U., 1997. Bar: Ark. 1979, Va. 1982, D.C. 1984, N.Y. 1996. Clk. hon. Ozell M. Trask US Ct. of Appeals (9th cir.), Phoenix & San Francisco, 1978—79; from asst. to assoc. prof. Marshall-Whyte Sch. of Law Coll. of William and Mary, Williamsburg, Va., 1979-84; assoc. prof. Sch. of Law U. Ark., Little Rock, 1984-86, prof. Sch. of Law, 1986-95; global prof., dir. (global law sch. prog.) NYU, 1996—97; dean, prof. of law U. Richmond Sch Law, Richmond, Va., 1997—2003, u. prof., 2003—. Author: Anne Orthwoods Bastard: Sex and Law in Early Virginia (Prize in Atlantic History, 2003) Contbr. articles to profl. jours. Ark. state senator, Little Rock, 1991-92; legislator Pulaski County Quorum Ct., Little Rock, 1987-90. Mem. Assn. of Marshall Scholars, Phi Beta Kappa. Democrat. Avocation: historical research. Office: U Richmond Sch Law 28 Westhampton Way Rm 216 Richmond VA 23173 Office Phone: 804-289-8188. Office Fax: 804-289-8992.

PAGE, FRANK S., religious organization administrator; b. Greensboro, NC, 1952; m. Dayle Page; children: Melissa, Lauren, Allison. BS in Psychology, Gardner Webb Univ.; MDiv., PhD, Southwestern Baptist Theological Seminary. Former pastor So. Bapt. Conv. Ch. (SBC Ch.) Tex., SBC Ch. NC, Warren Baptist SBC Ch. Ga., Taylor's First SBC Ch. SC; pres. So. Bapt. Conv., 2006—08, v.p. evangelism for N.Am. mission bd., 2009—10, pres., CEO exec. com., 2010—. Office: Southern Baptist Convention 1 Lifeway Plz MSN 146 Nashville TN 37234-1001

PAGE, JOHN GARDNER, toxicologist, consultant; b. Milw., Wis., Sept. 14, 1940; s. Raymond G. and Leone B. (Churchill) P.; m. Joyce Ann Krueger, July 7, 1962; children: Teresa Ann, Kimberly Christine. BS, U. Wis.-Madison, 1963, MS, 1966, PhD, 1967. Diplomate Am. Bd. Toxicology. Sr. scientist NIH, Bethesda, Md., 1967-69, Eli Lilly Co., Indpls., 1969-77; dir. toxicology and pathology Rhone Poulenc, Inc., Ashland, Ohio, 1977-79; dir. toxicology Toxigenics, Inc., Decatur, Ill., 1979-83; sr. rsch. advisor Battelle Meml. Inst., Columbus, Ohio, 1983-87; dir. preclin. toxicology So. Rsch. Inst., Birmingham, Ala., 1987—2004; dir. NGVL-Nat. Toxicology Ctr., 2001—06; disting. scientist So. Rsch. Inst., Birmingham, Ala., 2004—06; CEO, chief scientist Rockhill Toxicology Cons. LLC, 2006—. Adj. prof. U. Ill., 1981-83, ctr. for AIDS rsch., U. Ala., Birmingham, 1987—, sch. pub. health, 1988—, sch. medicine, 1997—. Contbr. articles to profl. jours. Bd. dirs. Am. Cancer Soc., Greenfield, Ind., 1973-77. Recipient Rennebohm Outstanding Tchr.'s award U. Wis., 1964. Mem. AAAS, Fedn. Am. Socs. Exptl. Biology, Am. Soc. Pharm. Exptl. Therapeutics, Soc. Toxicology, Am. Coll. Toxicology, Internat. Soc. for Study Xenobiotics, Sigma Xi, Rho Chi. Avocations: photography, hiking, fishing. Home and Office: 3700 Rockhill Rd Birmingham AL 35223-1562 Office Phone: 205-967-2776.

PAGE, LARRY KEITH, neurosurgeon, educator; b. Rayville, La., July 7, 1933; s. Ardie Lee and Edris Estelle (Chaney) P.; m. Joan Marie Doherty, Aug. 27, 1960; children: Matthew, Elizabeth, Jennifer. BS, La. State U., 1955, MD, 1958. Diplomate: Am. Bd. Neurol. Surgery. Intern Grad. Hosp., U. Pa., Phila., 1958-59; resident Children's Hosp. and Peter Bent Brigham Hosp., Boston, 1962-66; assoc. neurosurgeon Children's Hosp., assoc. surgeon Peter Bent Brigham Hosp., 1966-71; cons. Beverly Hosp., Mass., Robert Breck Brigham Hosp., Boston, Pondville Hosp., Boston, West Roxbury VA Hosp., Boston VA Hosp.; clin. instr. neurosurgery Harvard U., Boston, 1966-71; prof., vice chmn. dept. neurosurgery U. Miami, Fla., 1971-95, prof. emeritus Fla., 1995—, chief div. pediatric neurosurgery Fla., 1971-95; neurosurgeon VA Hosp., Miami, 1971-88, Jackson Meml. Hosp., Miami, 1971-95, dir. neurosurgery, 1994-95; chief neurosurgery Mt. Sinai Hosp., Miami, 1990-94. Chmn. CSF Shunt Standard Com. for ASTM, ISO, AANS & CNS, 1974-86, cons. neurosurg. FDA, 1976-79, NASA, 1979-80 Mem. editorial bds., contbr. articles to profl. jours. Served to lt. USN, 1959-62. Mem. ACS, Am. Acad. Pediatrics, Am. Assn. Neurol. Surgeons, Internat. Soc. Pediatric Neurosurgery, Am. Soc. Pediatric Neurosurgery, Congress Neurol. Surgeons, Fellowship of Acad. Neurosurgeons, Internat. Neurosurg. Forum, Royal Soc. Medicine, Soc. for Rsch. in Hydrocephalus and Spina Bifida, New Eng. Neurosurg. Soc., Fla. Neurosurg. Soc. (pres. 1989-90), Mass. Med. Soc., Dade County Med. Assn., Internat. Palm Soc., Alpha Omega Alpha. Roman Catholic. Home and Office: 13845 SW 73rd Ct Miami FL 33158-1213

PAGE, RANDALL, state official; b. Mt. Vernon, Ohio, Feb. 18, 1967; s. James and Nancy Page; m. Melissa Rohrman, Feb. 16, 1991; children: Julie Anne, Jason Ryan. BS, Bob Jones U., Greenville, 1990. Dir. of pub. events Office of the Gov., Columbia, SC, 1995—99; exec. v.p. Jordan and McCallum Co., Greenville, SC, 1999—2001; legislative affairs dir. Office of the Lt. Gov., Columbia, SC, 2001—03, chief of staff, 2003—04; campaign mgr. Beasley for Senate, Columbia, SC, 2004; pres. South Carolinians for Responsible Govt., Columbia, 2005—13; sr. assoc. Richard Quinn & Assocs., Columbia, SC, 2004—05; second congressional dist. chmn. SC Rep. Party Columbia, 2012—13; del. Rep. Nat. Convention, 2012; dir. pub. rels. Bob Jones U., 2013—. Bd. dirs. Insights, Greenville, SC, 1994—2001; exec. bd. SC Citizens for Life, Columbia, 2001—. Cons. George W. Bush for Pres., Columbia, SC, 2000; fourth dist. chmn. SC Rep. Party, Columbia, 2001—03, co-chair, platform-resolutions com., 2013—; mem. Lexington County Rep. Exec. Com., 2007—13; dist. vice chair Lexington County Rep. Party, 2011—13; mem. platform commn. Republician Nat. Coun., 2012; mem. Electoral Coll., 2012; bd. dirs. Kennerly Rd. Bapt. Ch., Irmo, SC, 2003—06, 2008—10, chmn., 2004—06, 2008—10; mem. exec. bd. Greenville County Libr. Sys., SC, 1999—2001; bd. dirs. Palmetto Family Coun., 2006—. Recipient Order of the Palmetto, Gov. David M. Beasley, SC., 1998, Hon. Order of Ky. Colonels, Gov. Paul Patton, Ky., 2003, Disting. Svc. award, Bob Jones U. Alumni Assn., 2006. Republican. Baptist. Avocation: swimming. Personal E-mail: randypagesc@gmail.com.

PAGNANI, MICHAEL JOSEPH, orthopaedic surgeon; b. Endicott, NY, Apr. 23, 1961; s. Bruno and Patricia Ann Connors P.; m. Kelly Jackson, May 14, 1988; children: Sarah, Connor. MD, Vanderbilt U., 1987. Diplomate Am. Bd. Orthopaedic Surgery. Intern Baylor U., Dallas, 1987-88; resident in orthop. surgery The Hosp. for Spl. Surgery-Cornell U., NYC, 1988-92, fellow in sports medicine, 1992-93; pvt. practice The Lipscomb Clinic, Nashville, 1993, Nashville Knee & Shoulder, Nashville; attending orthop. surgeon Centennial Med. Ctr., Nashville, 1993—, St. Thomas Hosp., Nashville, 1993—; clin. asst. prof., orthop., rehabilitation Vanderbilt U., Nashville, 1993—2002. Bd. dir. Nashville Sports Coun., 1997-2002; asst. orthop. cons. St. John's U., 1992-93; orthop. cons. Tenn. Technological U., 1993-94, Nashville Xpress Baseball Team, 1994, Chgo. White Sox Baseball Orgn., 1995-97, Pitts. Pirates Baseball Orgn., 1998-2003, Miami Dolphins, 2001-; team physician NY Pub. Sch. Athletic League, 1988-92, numerous Nashville area high schools, 1993-, Elite Runners, Country Music Marathon, 2000-2003; orthop. team physician, Nashville Sounds Baseball team, 1994-2003; asst. team physician, NY Giants Football team, 1992-93, NY Mets, 1992-93; med. cons. Ohio Valley Conf. Basketball Tournament, 1994-2000, NCAA Sectional Basketball Tournament, 2000; med. staff mem. US Open Tennis Championships, 1989-92; US Figure Skating Championships, 1997; head team physician, Nashville Kats arena football team, 1997-2002, Tenn. State Univ., 1993-, Nashville Predators Hockey team, 1997-2007. Cons. Am. Journal of Sports Medicine, Journal of Bone and Joint Surgery. Named Tenn. Sports Medicine Person of Yr., Tenn. Athletic Trainers' Soc., 2004. Fellow, Am. Acad. Orthop. Surgeons (mem. program com.), mem. Am. Orthop. Soc. Sports Medicine (rsch. com., 1997-), Nat. Hockey League Team Physicians' Soc., Arthroscopy Assn. N. Am., Nashville Acad. Medicine, Tenn. Med. Assn., Am. Shoulder and Elbow Surgeons (mem. program com.). Office: Nashville Knee And Shoulder Center Pllc 345 23rd Ave N Ste 301 Nashville TN 37203-1513 Office Fax: 615-329-3530.

PAIGE, HILLIARD WEGNER, corporate executive, consultant; b. Hartford, Conn., Oct. 2, 1919; s. Joseph Wegner and Ruth (Hill) P.; m. Dorothea Magner, Dec. 8, 1945; children: Elizabeth, Deborah, Hilliard, Jr. BSME, Worcester Poly. Inst., 1941, D (hon.) of Engring., 1971. Sr. v.p. for aerospace and computer ops. GE, NYC, 1941—71; pres. Gen. Dynamics, St. Louis, 1971—73; CML Satellite Bus. Sys., Inc., Washington, 1973—76; vice-chmn. bd. Internat. Energy Assocs., Ltd., Washington, 1976—85; chmn. bd. H.A. Knott, Ltd., Silver Spring, Md., 1984—89. Vice-chmn. The Atlantic Coun. of U.S., 1987—, Gallager Marine Systems, Inc., 1993—. Patentee in field; contbr. articles to profl. jours. Mem. Def. Sci. Bd. U.S. Dept. Def., Washington, 1973-78; trustee Worcester Poly. Inst., Mass., 1974—. Recipient Pub. Service award NASA, 1969, Space Reconnissance Pioneer award NRO, 2008, Order of Merit Italy, 1970, Engr. of Year award Greater Phila. Engring Council, 1960, named Hall of Fame, Del. Valley Engring., 2010 Fellow AIAA (founding dir.), Explorers Club (nat.); mem. NAE. Clubs: Metropolitan, Chevy Chase (Washington); Conquistadores del Cielo. Republican. Congregationalist. Avocations: skiing, tennis, scuba diving, golf. Home and Office: 5834 Williamsburg Landing Dr Williamsburg VA 23185 Office Phone: 757-220-2797.

PAINTER, JACK TIMBERLAKE, civil engineer; b. Kincaid, W.Va., July 23, 1930; s. Troy Earl and Nannie Bell (Proffit) P. BSCE, W.Va. U., 1950, MSCE, 1955. Instr. civil engring. W.Va. U., 1950-51, 53-55; mem. faculty La. Tech U., Ruston, 1955—; prof. civil engring. La. Tech. U., 1962-92; Alumni Found. prof. La. Tech U., 1977-78; prof. emeritus La. Tech. U., 1992—. Vis. lectr. Manhattan Coll., Coll. Forestry, SUNY, Syracuse, Cornell U., U. Wis., 1954-60 Nat. pres. Circus Fans Assn. Am., 1967; lic. eucharistic min. Episcopal Ch.

active mem. USNR, 1951-52, comdr. res., 1966- Recipient Mech. Engring. program Outstanding Svc. award, 2008; named Man of Year Omicron Delta Kappa, 1972, Jack T. Painter Scholarship in his honor, 1998, The Jack T. Painter Professorship in Engring. in his honor, 2003, Super Computer Painter, 2008; Faculty fellow NSF, 1958—59. Fellow Nat. ASCE (life), La. Tech. ASCE (11 Outstanding Prof. awards 1969-90); mem. La. Engring. Soc. (Charles M. Kerr Pub. Rels. award 1990), Am. Soc. Engring. Edn., Tau Beta Pi (Outstanding Prof. awards 1963, 68, 74, 78), Chi Epsilon (Nat. Excellent Tchg. award 1985). Address: 101 Biel Lane New Bern NC 28562

PAINTER, JOHN HOYT, engineer; b. Winfield, Kans., Mar. 27, 1934; s. John Paul and Marjorie Marietta (Slack) P.; m. Joy Lou Vaughan, June 7, 1955; children: John Mark, Paul Burton, William Vaughan, Joy Lynn. BS, U. Ill., 1961, MS, 1962; postgrad., Coll. William and Mary, 1967—69; PhD, So. Meth. U., 1972. Apollo comm. engr., tchr. astronauts Manned Spacecraft Ctr. NASA, Houston, 1962—65; sr. engr. Motorola Govt. Electronics divsn., Scottsdale, Ariz., 1965—67; rsch. engr. NASA Langley Rsch. Ctr., Hampton, Va., 1967—74; assoc. prof. elec. engring. Tex. A&M U., College Station, 1974—79, prof. elec. engring., 1979—, prof. computer sci., 1989—, prof. aerospace engring., 1999—. Pres. ALTAIR Corp. cons., College Station, 1980—2010; tchr. Christian eschatology seminars; adj. instr. Nat. Emergency Response and Rescue Training Ctr., 2003-06. Author: The Church Visited, 2002; patentee digital signal processing and fuzzy logic. With USAF, 1953—58, Navigator. Recipient Recognition cert. NASA, 1975; GE Found. fellow, 1962. Mem.: IEEE (life; sr. mem.). Avocation: radio operating. Office Phone: 979-696-0429. Business E-Mail: painter@tamu.edu.

PAINTER, THEOPHILUS SHICKEL, JR., internist, allergist; b. Austin, Tex., Apr. 29, 1924; s. Theophilus Shickel and Anna Mary (Thomas) P.; m. Dorothy Bulkley, July 11, 1957; children: Dana Parkey, Amy Hur, Theophilus III. BA, U. Tex., 1944, MD, 1947. Diplomate Am. Bd. Internal Medicine, Am. Bd. Allergy and Immunology. Rotating intern Univ. Hosp., U. Mich., Ann Arbor, 1947-48, resident in internal medicine, 1948-51, fellow, jr. clin. instr., 1956-58; pvt. practice, Austin, Tex., 1958—. Capt. USAF, 1951-53. Fellow ACP, Am. Coll. Allergy and Immunology, Am. Acad. Allergy and Immunology. Avocations: fishing, carving, hunting, painting. Home: 3222 Tarryhollow Dr Austin TX 78703-1639 Office: 800 W 34th St Ste 201 Austin TX 78705-1146 Office Phone: 512-454-5821. Personal E-mail: tspainterjr@gmail.com.

PAISLEY, BRAD, musician; b. Glen Dale, W.Va., Oct. 28, 1972; m. Kimberly Williams, Mar. 15, 2003; children: William Huckleberry, Jasper Warren. Grad., Belmont U., 1995. Musician: (albums) Who Needs Pictures, 1999, Part II, 2001, Mud On The Tires, 2003, Time Well Wasted, 2005 (Album of Yr., Acad. Country Music Awards, Country Music Assn. Awards, 2006), A Brad Paisley Christmas, 2006, 5th Gear, 2007, Play, 2008, American Saturday Night, 2009, Hits Alive, 2010, This is Country Music, 2011, Wheelhouse, 2013, (songs) He Didn't Have to Be, 1999 (Song of Yr., Single of Yr. & Video of Yr., Country Music Assn., 2000), I'm Gonna Miss Her, 2001 (Song of Yr., Single of Yr. & Video of Yr., Country Music Assn., 2002, Grammy award for Best Male Country Vocal Performance, 2003), Celebrity, 2003 (Song of Yr., Single of Yr., Video of Yr., Country Music Assn., 2003), Online, 2007 (Music Video of Yr., Country Music Assn., 2007, Comedy Video of Yr., Country Music TV, 2008, Video of Yr., Acad. Country Music, 2008), Throttleneck, 2007 (Grammy award for Best Country Instrumental Performance, 2008), Letter to Me, 2007 (Grammy award for Best Male Country Vocal Performance, 2009), Cluster Pluck, 2009 (Grammy award for Best Country Instrumental Performance, 2009), (with Chely Wright) Hard to be a Husband, Hard to be a Wife, 2001 (Vocal Event of Yr., Country Music Assn., 2001), (with Alison Krauss) Whiskey Lullaby, 2003 (Video of Yr., Event of Yr., Country Music Assn., 2004, Video of Yr., Event of Yr., Acad. Country Music, 2005, Collaborative Video of Yr., Country Music TV, 2005), (with Dolly Parton) When I Get Where I'm Going, 2005 (Inspiring Video of Yr., Country Music TV, Video of Yr. & Vocal Event of Yr., Acad. Country Music, Musical Event of Yr., Country Music Assn., 2006), (with Andy Griffith) Waitin' on a Woman, 2007 (Music Video of Yr., Country Music Assn., 2008, Video of Yr., Acad. Country Music, 2009), (with Keith Urban) Start a Band, 2008 (Vocal Event of Yr., Acad. Country Music, 2009), (with Carrie Underwood) Remind Me, 2011 (Collaborative Video of Yr., CMT Music Awards, 2012); author: Diary of a Player, 2011. Founder The Brad Paisley Foundation, 2001—. Recipient Male Vocalist of Yr. award, Country Music Assn., 2000—03, 2007—09, Entertainer of Yr. award, 2010, Top Male Vocalist award, Acad. Country Music, 2007—11, Favorite Male Country Artist award, American Music Awards, 2008, 2010. Office: c/o William Morris Agency 1600 Division St Ste 300 Nashville TN 37203-2755

PAK, B.J., state legislator; b. Seoul, Republic of Korea, Oct. 24; m. Sandra Pak; 2 children. B in Acctg., Stetson U., DeLand, Fla.; JD with honors, U. Ill. CPA. Atty. Alston & Bird LLP; asst. US atty. No. Dist. Ga. Criminal Divsn.; ptnr. Schiff Hardin, LLP; mem. Dist. 102 Ga. House of Representatives, 2011—. Republican. Office: 1201 W Peachtree St NW Ste 2300 Atlanta GA 30309 also: Georgia House of Reps 301 Coverdell Legis Office Bldg Atlanta GA 30334 Office Phone: 404-656-0254. Personal E-mail: bj.pak@house.ga.gov.

PAK, SE RI, professional golfer; b. Daejeon, Korea, Sept. 28, 1977; Profl. golfer Korea LPGA Tour, 1996—98, LPGA Tour, 1998—. Recipient Tiger of Order, Korean Govt., 1998, Blue Dragon of Order of Sports Merits, 2010, Vare trophy, 2003, LPGA, 2003, Heather Farr award, 2006; named LPGA Rookie of Yr., 1998, Female Athlete of Yr., AP, 1998, Player of Yr., Golf Writers Assn. America, 1998; named to World Golf Hall of Fame, 2007. Achievements include winning Korea LPGA Tour events: Dong-Il Renown Ladies Classic, Fila Women's Open, SBS Women's Professional Golf Challenge, Seoul Women's Open, 1996, 1997, Chief Industries Rose Women's Open, 1997; winning LPGA Tour major championships: McDonald's LPGA Championship, 1998, 2002, 2006, US Women's Open, 1998, Weetabix Women's British Open, 2001; winning LPGA Tour events: Jamie Farr Kroger Classic, 1998, 1999, 2001, 2003 Giant Eagle LPGA Classic, 1998; ShopRite LPGA Classic, Samsung World Championship of Women's Golf, PageNet Championship, 1999; YourLife Vitamins LPGA Classic, AFLAC Champions, 2001; The Office Depot Championship, First Union Betsy King Classic, Mobile LPGA Tournament of Champions, Sports Today CJ Nine Bridges Classic, 2002; Safeway PING, Chick-fil-A Charity Championship, 2003; Michelob ULTRA Open at Kingsmill, 2004, Jamie Farr Owens Corning Classic, 2007; Bell Micro LPGA Classic, 2010. Avocations: video games, shopping, watching television, Tae Kwon Do. Address: LPGA 100 International Golf Dr Daytona Beach FL 32124-1082 Office Phone: 386-274-6200. Office Fax: 386-274-1099.

PALAZZO, STEVEN MCCARTY, United States Representative from Mississippi, former state legislator; b. Gulfport, Miss., Feb. 21, 1970; m. Lisa M. Belvin Palazzo; 3 children. BA in Acctg., U. Southern Miss., 1994, MPA, 1996. Mem. Dist. 116 Miss. House of Reps., 2007—11; mem. US Congress from 4th Miss. Dist., 2011—, US House Sci., Space & Tech. Com., 2011—, US House Armed Services Com., 2011—. Mem.: NRA, AICPA, Miss. Soc. CPA, Marine Corps Assn., Rotary Club. Republican. Roman Catholic. Office: US House of Representatives 331 Cannon House Office Bldg Washington DC 20515 Office Phone: 202-225-5772. Office Fax: 202-225-7074.*

PALLADINO-CRAIG, ALLYS, museum director, educator; b. Pontiac, Mich., Mar. 23, 1947; d. Stephan Vincent and Mary (Anderson) Palladino; m. Malcolm Arnold Craig, Aug. 20, 1967; children—Ansel, Reed, Nicholas. BA in English, Fla. State U., 1967; grad., U. Toronto, Ont., Can., 1969; MFA, Fla. State U., 1978, PhD in Humanities, 1996. Editorial asst. project U. Va. Press, Charlottesville, 1970-76; instr. English Inst. Franco Americain, Rennes, France, 1974; adj. instr. Fla. State U., Tallahassee, 1978-79, dir. Four Arts Ctr., 1979-82, dir. U. Mus. of Fine Arts, 1982—, prof. mus. studies. Mem. grad faculty Mus. Studies Cert. Program Fla. State U. Curator, contbg. editor: Nocturnes and Nightmares, Monochrome/Polychrome, Chroma, High Roads & Low Roads-Anthems, Dirges, Myths; contbg. editor: Body Language; guest curator, author: Mark Messersmith: New Mythologies; curator, editor Albert Paley--Sculpture, Drawings, Graphics and Decorative Arts, Trevor Bell: A British Painter in America, and Trial by Fire: Contemporary Glass; curator, author: The Abridged Walmsley--Selections from the Career of William Aubrey Walmsley, co-curator, contbg. author: Terrestrial Forces; author: Jack Nichelson: Micro-Theatres, Alexa Kleinbard: Talking Leaves, Jake Fernandez--Ethereal Journeyman, Jim Roche-Sense of Place; editor: Athanor I-XXXII, 1980—; author: Gabrielle Wu Lee. Individual artist fellow Fla. Arts Coun., 1979 Mem. Am. Assn. Mus., Fla. Art Mus. Dirs. Assn. (sec. 1989-91), Assn. Academic Museums & Galleries, Phi Beta Kappa. Democrat. Avocations: antiques, accordion. Home: 1410 Grape St Tallahassee FL 32303-5636 Office: Fla State U Mus of Fine Arts 250 Fine Arts Bldg Tallahassee FL 32306-1140 Home Phone: 850-224-4188. Business E-Mail: apalladinocraig@fsu.edu.

PALMAZ, JULIO C., cardiologist, radiologist, educator; b. Buenos Aires, Dec. 13, 1945; m. Amalia Palmaz; children: Florencia, Christian. MD, Nat. Univ. La Plata, Argentina, 1971. Vascular radiologist, chief of angiography San Martin Univ. Hosp., La Plata, Argentina, 1974—77; radiology tng. Martinez VA Med. Ctr., U. Calif., Davis, 1977—80, chief spl. procedures, 1981; chief of angiography & spl. procedures U. Tex. Health Sci. Ctr., San Antonio, 1983—99, Stewart R. Reuter disting. prof., chief cardiovasc. & interventional radiology rsch., 1999—2005, Ashbel Smith prof., 2006—. Co-owner Palmaz Vineyards, Napa, Calif., 1997—; co-founder Advanced Bio Prosthetic Surfaces Ltd, San Antonio, 1999; co-founder, chief scientist, chmn. bd. dirs. Palmaz Scientific Inc., Dallas, 2008—. Mem. editl. bd. Circulation; contbr. articles to profl. jours., chapters to books. Recipient Presdl. Disting. Scholar award, U. Tex. San Antonio, 2003; named a Disting. Scientist, Am. Heart Assn., 2005; named to Nat. Inventors Hall of Fame, 2006. Fellow: Am. Inst. Med. & Biol. Engring.; mem.: Internat. Soc. Endovascular Surgery, Soc. Interventional Radiology. Achievements include invention of a balloon-expandable stent (the Palmaz-Schatz stent), a tiny, expandable stainless steel tube which holds heart arteries open following angioplasty; patents in field. Office: U Tex Health Sci Ctr Dept Radiology 7703 Floyd Curl Dr MS 7800 San Antonio TX 78229 also: Palmaz Vineyard 4029 Hagen Rd Moraga CA 94556 Office Phone: 210-567-5544. Office Fax: 210-567-5541. E-mail: palmaz@uthscsa.edu.

PALMER, ANTHONY J., health products executive; BS in Mktg., Monash U., Melbourne, Australia, 1986; MBA, Internat. Mgmt. Inst., Geneva, 1989. Bus. devel. mgr. PA Consulting Group, 1986—91; sr. cons. LEK Partnership, 1991—92; mktg. mgr. Mars Confectionery, Australia, 1992—95, CSR Refined Sugars, Australia, 1995—96; mktg. and gen. mgmt. positions Minute Maid divsn. Coca-Cola Co., 1996—2000, region dir. Australia; pres. natural, frozen and warehouse club businesses Kellogg Co., mng. dir. UK; sr. v.p., chief mktg. officer Kimberly-Clark Corp., 2006—. Office: Kimberly-Clark Corp PO Box 619100 Dallas TX 75261-9100 Office Phone: 972-281-1200. Office Fax: 972-281-1435. Business E-Mail: tony.palmer@kcc.com.

PALMER, CHRIS, professional football coach; b. Brewster, NY, Sept. 23, 1949; m. Donna Palmer; children: Mark, Kristin. BS, MS, So. Conn. State U., New Haven. Defensive line, wide receivers coach U. Conn. Huskies, 1972—74; wide receivers coach Lehigh U. Mountain Hawks, 1975; offensive coord. Colgate U. Red Raiders, 1976-82; offensive line coach Montreal Concords, 1983-84; wide receivers coach NJ Generals, 1984, quarterbacks coach, offensive coord., 1985; head football coach U. New Haven Chargers, 1986-87, Boston U. Terriers, 1988-89; wide receivers coach Houston Oilers, 1990-92, New Eng. Patriots, 1993—95, quarterbacks coach, 1996; offensive coord. Jacksonville Jaguars, 1997—98; head coach Cleve. Browns, 1999—2000; offensive coord. Houston Texans, 2001—05; quarterbacks coach Dallas Cowboys, 2006, NY Giants, 2007—09; head coach, gen. mgr. Hartford Colonials, Conn., 2010; offensive coord. Tenn. Titans, Nashville, 2011—. Named to The Southern Conn. State Univ. Athletic Hall of Fame, The Univ. New Haven Hall of Fame, The Immaculate HS Hall of Fame. Office: Tennessee Titans One Titans Way Nashville TN 37213

PALMER, DAVE RICHARD, retired military officer, academic administrator; b. Ada, Okla., May 31, 1934; s. David Furman and Lorena Marie (Clardy) P.; m. LuDelia Clemmer, Apr. 13, 1957; children: Allison, J. Kersten. BS, U.S. Military Acad., 1956; MA in History, Duke U., 1966; postgrad., Army War Coll., 1972-73; PhD (hon.), Duke U., 1990. Commd. U.S. Army, 1956, advanced through grades to lt. gen.; mem. faculty dept. history U.S. Mil. Acad., 1966-69; mem. staff (Pentagon), 1973-76, Joint Chiefs of Staff, 1979-81; comdr. Baumholder Mil. Community, W. Ger., 1981-83; dep. comdt. Command and Gen. Staff Coll., Ft. Leavenworth, Kans., 1983-85; comdg. gen. 1st Armored Div., W.Ger., 1985-86; supt. U.S. Mil. Acad., 1986-91, ret., 1991; pres. Walden U., 1995-99; CEO Walden Corp., 1999-2000. Author: The River and the Rock, 1969, The Way of the Fox, 1975, Summons of the Trumpet, 1978, 1794-America, Its Army, and The Birth of the Nation, 1994, First in War, 2000, Provide for the Common Defense, 2001, Washington and Arnold, 2006, George Washington Military Genius, 2012. Bd. dirs. Walden U., 1992-2001. Decorated Legion of Merit (3); Bronze Star (2), D.S.M.(2); named Disting. Grad., U.S. Mil. Acad., 2005, Outstanding Alumnus Army War Coll., 2007, Named to Hall of Fame, Command and Gen. Staff Coll., 2013- Mem. Assn. U.S. Army, Armor Assn., Mil. History, Soc. Cin. Personal E-mail: dpalmer1956@yahoo.com.

PALMER, EDWARD L., psychologist, educator, writer; b. Hagerstown, Md., Aug. 11, 1938; s. Ralph Leon and Eva Irene (Brandenburg) P.; children: Edward Lee, Jennifer Lynn. BA, Gettysburg Coll., 1960; BD, Luth. Theol. Sem., Gettysburg, 1964; MS, Ohio U., 1967, PhD, 1970. Asst. prof. Western Md. Coll., Westminster, 1968-70, Davidson Coll., NC, 1970-77, assoc. prof. NC, 1977-86, chair, 1985—99, prof. NC, 1986—, Watson prof. NC, 1991—, Watson prof. chair, 2009—11, Watson prof. chair emeritus, 2011—. Guest rschr. Harvard U., Cambridge, Mass., 1977; vis. scholar UCLA, 1984, UNC Chapel Hill, 1991, U. Exeter, 2000, U. Ala., 2005; cons. Council on Children, Media, Merchandising, 1978-79, 1st Union Bank Corp., Charlotte, N.C., 1975-79; NSF proposal reviewer, 1978—. Editl. reviewer Jour. Broadcasting and Electronic Media, 1978—, editl. bd. Media Psychology; editor: Children and the Faces of TV, 1980, Faces of Televisual Media, 2003; author: Children in the Cradle of TV, 1987; contbr. to Wiley Ency. of Psychology, 1984, 2002, Lawrence Erlbaum Assocs., 1991, Sage Pub., 1993-96; author jour. articles and book chpts. Sec. Mecklenburg Child Devel. Assn., Davidson and Cornelius, N.C., 1974-78; bd. mem. pub. radio Sta. WDAV, 1970-90, Telecomms. task force Rutgers U., 1981. Recipient Thomas Jefferson Tchg. award Robert Earl McConnell Found., 1993, Deptl. Psychology in Svc. award, 2007. Mem. APA, Am. Psychol. Soc., Assn. Heads Depts. Psychology (chair 1994-96), Am. Psychol. Assn. (task force on advt. and children 2001-03), Southeastern Psychol. Assn., Southeastern Soc. Social Psychologists, Phi Beta Kappa (pres. Davidson chpt. 1985-86). Avocations: sunrise and sunset walks, poetry, hiking, birdwatching, music. Office: Davidson Coll PO Box 7007 Davidson NC 28035-7007 Office Phone: 704-408-4592. E-mail: edpalmer@davidson.edu.

PALMER, FORREST CHARLES, librarian, educator; b. Burlington, Wis., Oct. 17, 1924; s. Forrest Blaire and Marie Florence (Rubach) P.; m. Lois Mae Davis, June 12, 1946; children: Forrest Charles Jr., Beth Elaine, Janet Lorrayne. Student, U. Pitts., 1943-44; BA, Valparaiso U., 1948; BS in Libr. Sci., George Peabody Coll., 1949, MS in Libr. Sci., 1953. Head catalog dept. Janesville (Wis.) Pub. Library, 1949-50; serials cataloger N.C. State U., Raleigh, 1950-51, head serials dept., 1951-55; dir. libraries Miss. State U., State College, 1955-62; librarian, head dept. library sci. James Madison U., Harrisonburg, Va., 1962-70, head librarian, 1970-74, prof. library sci., documents librarian, 1973-89, ret., 1989, prof. emeritus, 1990—, faculty senate, 1982-86, faculty marshall, 1983-85, treas. senate, 1985-86. Mem. libr. com. Va. Higher Edn. Study Commn.; sec. joint law libr. com. Laird L. Conrad Meml. Law Libr., Harrisonburg, 1974-89; adv. com. Va. Coun. Higher Edn.; Madison Coll. rep. libr. affairs Va. U. Ctr Editor: Virginia Librarian, 1963-65. Contbr. articles to profl. publs. Mem. edn. com. Starkville (Miss.) Youth Ctr., 1956; chmn. adv. bd. YMCA, State College, Miss., 1957-59; vice-chmn. Rep. city com., Harrisonburg, 1979-81; mem. land use adv. com. Ctrl. Shenandoah Planning Dist. Commn., 1979; mem. Bd. Zoning Appeals, Harrisonburg, 1981-91, vice chmn., 1983-85, chmn., 1985-91; ruling elder Presbyn. Ch. U.S., clk. of session; mem. task force on maintenance Synod of Mid-Atlantic, Presbyn. Ch., Massanetta Springs, 1991; mem. Ft. Delaware Soc., 1992, life mem., 1995—; mem. LaPorte County Hist. Steam Soc., Inc., 1996—; mem. Massanetta Springs Heritage Soc., 1997—; mem. Peabody Pioneers, Vanderbilt U., 2003—. With Signal Corps AUS, PTO, 1943-46; vol. Keister Elem. Sch., Harrisonburg, Va., 1992—. Recipient Outstanding Libr. Sci. student award, George Peabody Coll.,1949, Golden Triangle award YMCA. Mem. ALA (liaison com. Library Instrn. Round Table 1978-80, com. on instrn. in use of libraries 1977-79, mem. Govt. Documents Round Table 1983-89), Southeastern Library Assn. (chmn. coll. sect. 1960-62, treas., mem. exec. bd. 1975-76, budget com. 1974-80, hdqrts. liason com., 1987-91), Miss. Library Assn. (chmn. standards and planning com. 1958-59, chmn. coll. sect. 1959-60), Va. Library Assn. (activities com. 1962-65, chmn. publs. com. 1963-65, 1st v.p. 1968, pres. 1969-70), WWII Meml. Soc. (charter), Pi Gamma Mu, Alpha Beta Alpha (adviser 1962-70), Beta Phi Mu. Republican. Presbyterian. Home: 60 E Weaver Ave Harrisonburg VA 22801-3041

PALMER, JAMES DANIEL, information technology educator; b. Washington, Mar. 8, 1930; s. Martin Lyle and Sarah Elizabeth (Hall) P.; m. Margret Kupka, June 21, 1952; children: Stephen Robert, Daniel Lee, John Keith. AA, Fullerton Jr. Coll., 1953; BS (Alumni scholar), U. Calif., Berkeley, 1955, MS, 1957; PhD, U. Okla., 1963; DPS (hon.), Regis Coll., Denver, 1977. Chief engr. Motor vehicle and Illumination Lab. U. Calif., Berkeley, 1955-57; assoc. prof. U. Okla., Norman, 1957-63, prof., 1963-66, asst. to dir. Rsch. Inst., 1960-63, cons. Rsch. Inst., 1966-69, dir. Sch. Elec. Engring., 1963-66, dir. Systems Rsch. Center, 1964-66; dean sci. and engring., prof. elec. engring. Union Coll., Schenectady, 1966-71; pres. Met. State Coll., Denver, 1971-78; rsch. and spl. programs adminstr. Dept. Transp., Washington, 1978-79; v.p., gen. mgr. rsch. and devel. div. Mech. Tech., Inc., Latham, NY, 1979-82; exec. v.p. J.J. Henry Co., Inc., Moorestown, NJ, 1982-85; BDM internat. prof. info. tech. George Mason U., Fairfax, Va., 1985-95, prof. emeritus, 1995—; software cons., 1995—. Bd. dirs. J.J. Henry Co., Inc.; cons. Sym Mgmt. Co., Boston, Higher Edn. Exec. Assocs., Denver, PERI, Princeton; adj. prof. U. Colo. Co-author: (with A.P. Sage) Software Systems Engineering, (with Aseltine, Beam and Sage) Introduction to Computer Systems, Analysis, Design and Application. Bd. dirs., exec. v.p. adv. com. USA Vols. Internat. Tech. Assistance, 1967-83, exec. v.p., 1970-71, chmn. exec. com.; trustee, vice chmn. Nat. Commn. on Coop. Edn.; mem. exec. policy bd. Alaska Natural Gas Pipeline, 1978-79; trustee Auraria Higher Edn. Program, Denver; mem. Fulbright fellow Selection Com., Colo.; bd. mgrs., mem. exec. com. Hudson-Mohawk Assn. Colls. and Univs., trustee, chmn. bd., 1970-71; adv. com. USCG Acad., 1972-82, chmn. adv. com., 1979-82; mem. Colo. Govs. Sci. and Tech. Adv. Coun.; pres. Denver Cath. Cmty. Svcs. Bd.; mem. Archdiocesan Cath. Charities and Cmty. Svcs.; bd. dirs. U. Okla. Rsch. Inst.; chair bd. dirs. Tri-City Vols. Inc., 2004-; mem. adv. com. Mile-Hi Red Cross; mem. Tri-City Vols., chair. With USMC, 1950—51. Recipient Outstanding Contbns. award, Inst. Elec. and Electronics Sys. Man and Cybernetics Soc., Joseph Wohl Outstanding Career award, 1983, US Coast Guard medal, 1983, St. Vincent de Paul Svc. and Spirituality Honor award, 2010; named James D. Palmer scholarship in his honor, George Mason U., 2002; Centennial scholar, Case-Western Res., 1981. Fellow IEEE (exec. and adminstrv. coms., v.p. long-range planning and finance, chmn. com. on large scale systems, Joseph E. Wahl Outstanding Career Achievement award 1993, Millennium medal 2000); mem. Systems, Man and Cybernetics Soc. (pres., Outstanding Contbns. award 1981), alumni assns. U. Calif. and U. Okla., Inst. Internat. Edn. (bd. dir. Rocky Mt. sect.), Soc. Naval Architects and Marine Engrs., Am. Soc. Engring. Edn., Am. Mil. Engrs., N.Y. Acad. Sci., Navy League, Sigma Xi, Eta Kappa Nu, Pi Mu Epsilon, Alpha Gamma Sigma. Home: 860 Cashew Way Fremont CA 94536-2646 Office: George Mason U Sch of Info Tech & Engring Fairfax VA 22030 Personal E-mail: jdpalmer@ix.netcom.com.

PALMER, JAMES F., aerospace transportation executive; BS, Southeast Mo. State, 1971. Sr. v.p., CFO McDonnell Douglas Corp., 1995—97; pres., Boeing Shared Services Group Boeing Co., 1997—2000, sr. v.p.; pres. Boeing Capital Corp., 2000—04; exec. v.p., CFO Visteon Corp., 2004—07; corp. v.p., CFO Northrop Grumman Corp., LA, 2007—. Office: Northrop Grumman Corp 2980 Fairview Park Dr Falls Church VA 22042-4511 Office Phone: 734-710-2020.

PALMER, LARRY GARLAND, music educator, writer, musician; b. Warren, Ohio, Nov. 13, 1938; s. Gerald Leroy and Esther Garland Palmer. MusB, Oberlin Coll., Ohio, 1960; MusM, Eastman Sch. Music, U. Rochester, NY, 1961, MusD, 1963. Head Dept. Fine Arts St. Paul's Coll., Lawrenceville, Va., 1963—65; prof. music Norfolk (Va.) State U., 1965—70; prof. harpsichord and organ So. Meth. U., Dallas, 1970—. Author: Hugo Distler and his Church Music, 1967, Harpsichord in America: A 20th-Century Revival, 1989, paperback 2nd edit., 1993, Letters from Salzburg: A Music Student in Europe 1958-1959, 2006; contbg. author: The New Grove Dictionary of Music, The

Grove Dictionary of Opera, Twentieth-Century Organ Music, 2012; musician: The Harpsichord Now and Then, 1975, Organ Works of Hugo Distler, 1978, Dedication Recital, Fisk Organ opus 101, 1993, Larry Palmer /Harpsichord/ Bach, 1994, Harpsichord Recital, 1997, Music of Rudy Davenport, 1999, Dos Prados: Larry Palmer Plays the 1762 Oldovini Organ in the Meadows Museum, SMU, 2001, Hommages: Music for Harpsichord, 2008; harpsichord editor: The Diapason, 1969—; author: Twentieth Century Organ Music Herbert Howells, 2012. Mem.: Hist. Keybd. Soc. N.Am., Am. Guild Organists (dean Norfolk chpt. 1968—70, dean Dallas chpt. 1977—79), Southeastern Hist. Keyboard Soc. (pres. 2004—08), Pi Kappa Lambda. Avocations: reading, cooking. Office: Southern Methodist University Meadows School of the Arts Dallas TX 75275 E-mail: lpalmer@smu.edu.

PALMER, MARILYN JOAN, English composition educator; b. Mahoning County, Ohio, Mar. 3, 1933; d. Rudolph George and Marian Eleanor Wynn; m. Richard Palmer, Nov. 10, 1956 (dec. 1987); children: Ricky, Larry, Kevin. Phys. therapy cert., UCLA, 1954, BS, 1955; MA in Philosophy, Ohio State U., 1969; PhD, U. Okla., 1996. Phys. therapist Neil Ave. Sch. for Handicapped, Columbus, Ohio, 1968-69; instr. philosophy Ohio State U., Columbus, 1969; instr. English Youngstown (Ohio) State U., 1970-71; writer, editor The Economy Co., ednl. publs., Oklahoma City, 1977-81; grad. asst. in English U. Okla., Norman, 1981-87, lectr. in English, 1988-90, tech. writing instr. ind. studies, 1988-97. Free-lance editing and cons.; cons. for on-line CD-ROM to accompany a textbook, 2002. Author: Technical Writing for Science, Business and Industry, 1988, An Enthymeme as a Platform for Understanding Audience Values, 1997; editor: Kindergarten Keys Teacher's Guidebook, 1982, author parochial supplement, 1982. Fund-raiser Easter Seal Soc., 1965-68; den mother coord. Boy Scouts Am., 1966, 67. Dept. Energy grantee, 1976. Mem. AAUP, Am. Phys. Therapy Assn., Soc. for Women in Philosophy, Alpha Xi Delta (nat. editor Quill 1984-86). Office Phone: 405-447-6495. Personal E-mail: doclynn@userenewableenergy.com.

PALMER, R.J., II, state legislator; b. Dec. 15, 1970; State rep. Dist. 73, Ky., 1999—2002; mem. Agr. Com., Natural Resources Com., Banking Com., Ins. Com., 1999—2002; house rep. Ky.; state senator Dist. 28 Ky., 2001—; mem. Conv. & Tourism Commn.; acct. rep. Ctr. Ky. Corrugated Specialists. Mem.: Leadership Winchester, Clark County C of C (dir.), Winchester-Clark County Recreation, Winchester Rotary Club. Democrat. Address: 126 Shanahan Lane Winchester KY 40391 Mailing: 1391 McLure Rd Winchester KY 40391 Office: Capitol Annex Rm 214 Frankfort KY 40601 Home Phone: 859-737-2945; Office Phone: 502-564-8100 ext 714. Business E-Mail: rj.palmer@lrc.state.ky.us.

PALMER, VICKI R., management consultant; b. Memphis; m. John E. Palmer; 1 child, Alexandria. B in Economics & Bus. Adminstrn., Rhodes Coll., 1975; MBA in Fin., U. Memphis, 1980. Pres. The Palmer Group, LLC; corp. loan officer First Tenn. Bank.; head pension investment FedEx, mgr., corp. fin.; mgr., pension investments Coca-Cola Co., 1983—86; asst. treas. Coca-Cola Enterprises, Inc., 1986—93, treas., 1993, v.p., 1993—99, sr. v.p., spl. asst. to CEO, 1999—2004, bd. dir., 2001, exec. v.p., fin. svcs. & adminstrn., 2004—09. Bd. dirs. Haverty Furniture Companies, Inc., First Horizon Nat. Corp., 1993—. Bd. dirs. Spelman Coll., Rhodes Coll., Woodward Acad., First Tenn. Nat. Corp. Recipient Disting. Alumni award, U. Memphis Alumni Assn.; named one of 20 Women of Power and Influence in Corp. Am., Black Enterprise Mag., 100 Black Women of Influence, Atlanta Bus. League, 1998. Office: The Palmer Group LLC 3600 Market St Ste 530 Philadelphia PA 19104 also: First Horizon National Corp Bd Directors 165 Madison Memphis TN 38103 Office Phone: 215-243-2590, 901-523-4444. Office Fax: 215-243-2593. Business E-Mail: vpalmer@palmer-group.com.

PALMISANO, DONALD J., general and vascular surgeon, medical educator; b. New Orleans, 1939; m. Robin Palmisano; 3 children. MD, Tulane U., 1963; JD, Loyola U., 1982. Diplomate Am. Bd. Surgery; bar: La. Intern Charity Hosp., New Orleans, 1963-64, resident in surgery, 1964-68, Lallie Kemp Charity Hosp., Independence, 1967-68; pvt. practice; clin. prof. surgery, clin. prof. med. jurisprudence Tulane U. Sch. Medicine; founder, pres. Intrepid Resources. Mem. Gov.'s Commn. on organ donations; chair La. Med. Disclosure Panel; founding mem. La. Med. Mutual Ins. Co., bd. dirs. 1982-89; commr. on the bd. Joint Com. on Accreditation of Healthcare Organizations, 1999-2003; selected as one of 60 Americans "opinion-leaders" chosen by Dept. Def. to participate in the Joint Civilian Orientation Conf. (JCOC 63), 2000; bd. dirs. Nat. Patient Safety Found., chair develop. com. responsible for fund raising; bd. govs. Tulane U. Health Svcs. Ctr., 2005-, The Doctors Company, 2004-; mem. Nat. Advisory Council, Annenberg Ctr. Health Sci.; adj. prof., dept. health sys. mgmt., Tulane Sch. Pub. Health and Tropical Medicine, 2005; lectr. in field; keynote spkr. on leadership. Author On Leadership: Essential Principals for Success, 2008; chair comm. prog., 2000; editl. bd. Journal of Patient Safety; guest appearances on Good Morning America, Today Show, debate on Nightline. World News Tonight, CNN Talk Back Live, Hardball with Chris Matthews, CNN Crossfire, John McLaughlin One on One, Fox News with Tony Snow, Aaron Brown's NewsNight; featured on CNN The Capital Gang; contbr. articles to profl. publs. With USAF. Recipient Air Force Commendation medal, award for the Advancement of Patient Safety, The Doctors Co., 2005, Dr. Edward Annis Med. Leadership award, Honolulu, 2007; named one of top doctors in New Orleans, 2001. Fellow ACS, AMSUS, SAFCS; mem. AMA (bd. trustees 1996-2005, chair devel. com., Physician Outreach awards, exec com. mem. 1999, sec-treas. 2001, pres-elect 2002, pres. 2003-04, chair La. delegation), La. State Med. Soc. (pres. 1984-85, elected to Hall of Fame 2000), Tulane Sugical Soc. (pres. 2000). Republican. Achievements include playing a key role in the passage of the landmark Louisiana Medical Malpractice Act of 1975. Avocation: photography. Office: Intrepid Resources 5000 W Esplanade Ave #432 Metairie LA 70006 Office Phone: 504-455-5895. Office Fax: 504-455-9392. Business E-Mail: djp@intrepidresources.com.

PALMORE, JOHN STANLEY, JR., retired lawyer; b. Ancon, C.Z., Aug. 6, 1917; s. John Stanley and Antoinette Louise (Gonzalez) P.; m. Eleanor Anderson, July 31, 1938 (dec. 1980); 1 child, John Worsham (dec.); m. Carol Pate, Jan. 1, 1982. Student, Western Ky. State Coll., 1934-36; LL.B. cum laude, U. Louisville, 1939. Bar: Ky. 1938. Practice law, Henderson, 1939-42, 47-59; judge Ct. Appeals Ky. (name changed to Supreme Ct. Ky. 1975), 1959-82, chief justice, 1966, 73, 77-82; practice law Frankfort, Ky., 1983-84; ptnr. Palmore & Sheffer, Henderson, 1984-86; sr. counsel Jackson & Kelly, Lexington, Ky., 1986-92; ret., 1992. City pros. atty., Henderson, 1949-53, city atty., 1953-55; commonwealth's atty. 5th Circuit Ct. Dist. Ky., 1955-59 Served to lt. USNR, 1942-46, 51-52. Mem. VFW, Ky. Bar Assn., Am. Legion, Ky. Hist. Soc., Frankfort Country Club, Lexington Club, Frankfort Rotary Club (pres. 1993-94), Masons, Shriners, Elks, Phi Alpha Delta. Episcopalian (past vestryman, sr. warden). Home: 2310 Peaks Mill Rd Frankfort KY 40601-9437

PALMS, JOHN MICHAEL, academic administrator, physicist; b. Rijswijk, The Netherlands, June 6, 1935; naturalized, 1956; s. Peter Joannes and Mimi Adele (DeYong) P.; m. Norma Lee Cannon, June 2, 1958; children: John Michael, Danielle Maria, Lee Cannon. BS in Physics, The Citadel, 1958, DSc (hon.), 1980; MS in Physics, Emory U., 1959; PhD, U. N.Mex., 1966. Commd. 2d lt. USAF, 1958, retired capt. Res., 1970; lectr. physics dept. U. N.Mex., 1959-60; instr. physics dept. USAF Acad., 1961-62; staff mem. Western Electric Sandia Lab., 1961-62, U. Calif. Los Alamos Sci. Lab., 1962-66, Oak Ridge Nat. Lab., 1966; asst. prof. Emory U., Atlanta, 1966-69, assoc. prof., 1969-73, chmn., assoc. prof. dept. physics, asso. prof. radiology dept. Med. Sch., 1973-74, prof., chmn. dept. physics, 1969-74, dean Coll. Arts. and Scis., 1974-80, acting chmn. dept. math. and computer sci., 1976-77, v.p. arts and scis., acting chmn. dept. anthropology, 1979-80, acting dean Emory Coll., 1979-80, acting dir. Emory U. Computing Ctr., 1980-82, v.p. acad. affairs, 1982-88, interim dean Grad. Sch., 1985-86, Charles Howard Candler prof. nuclear, radiation and environ. physics, 1988-90; pres., prof. physics Ga. State U., Atlanta, 1989-91, U. S.C., Columbia, 1991—92. Chmn. bd. Assurant Inc., 2003-2010, Inst. for Def. Analyses; bd. dirs. Fortis, Inc., N.Y.C., Exelon Corp., Chgo., NCAA, Simcom Internat. Holdings, Inc., Atlanta, Computer Task Group, Assurant, 1990-; adv. com. Oak Ridge Nat. Lab., 1985-89; mem. nat. nuclear accredititng bd. Inst. Nuclear Power Ops., 1985-91, mem. nat. adv. coun., 1997-2001; mem. panel for semicondr. detectors NAS/NRC, 1963-74; cons. Acad. Natural Scis., Phila., Hughes, Inc., Santa Barbara, Calif., Tennelec, Inc., Three Mile Island Environ. Study, TRW Space Sys. Divsn., L.A., Ga. Dept. Human Resources, Nat. Cancer Inst.; mem. high tech. task force Atlanta C. of C. Contbr. articles on nuclear, atomic, med. and environ. physics to profl. jours. Mem. adv. bd. The Citadel, Oak Ridge Nat. Lab.; mem. exec. bd. Atlanta Area Coun. Boy Scouts of Am., 1989-90; mem. cmty. rels. bd. U.S. Penitentiary, Atlanta; trustee, chmn. Inst. Def. Analyses, Wesleyan Coll., 1984-89, Pace Acad., 1984-89, St. Joseph's Hosp., Atlanta, 1987-89, Ga. Rsch. Alliance, 1988-89; mem. S.C. Univs. Edn. Found., Devel. Found. and Rsch. Found., S.C. Rsch. Inst. Bds.; bd. dirs. Civic-Atlanta Partnership Bus. and Edn., Inc., 1988-90, United Way; chair Rhodes scholar selection com., 1987, S.C., 1995-99; bd. dirs. Nat. Merit Scholarship Corp. Mem. AAAS, Am. Phys. Soc., Am. Assn. Physics Tchrs., IEEE (Nuclear Sci. Group), Am. Nuclear Soc., Am. Coun. Edn., Coun. Provosts and Acad. V.P.s, Am. Conf. Acad. Deans, Soc. Nuclear Medicine, Health Physics Soc., Greater Columbia C. of C. (bd. dirs.), Rotary, Columbia C. of C., Phi Beta Kappa, Sigma Xi, Phi Kappa Phi, Omicron Delta Kappa, Sigma Pi Sigma. Home and Office: Pres U SCO Osborne Bldg Columbia SC 29208-0001

PALUMBO, BENJAMIN LEWIS, public relations executive, consultant; b. Boston, Mar. 4, 1937; s. Guido Americo and Stella Marie (Lombardo) P.; m. Magdalene Julia Palinczar, Nov. 18, 1961; children: Matthew, Jason, Guy. BA, Rutgers U., 1959, MA, 1961. Adminstrv. asst. to Gov. Richard J. Hughes, NJ, 1963-65; dir. rsch. NJ Dem. Com., Trenton, 1965-66; asst. to commr. NJ Dept. Transp., Trenton, 1966-70; asst. dean Woodrow Wilson Sch., Princeton U., NJ, 1970—71; adminstrv. asst. to Senator Harrison Williams, US Senate, Washington, 1971-73, staff dir. US Ho. Dem. caucus, 1975-77, Ho. subcom. on govt. activities and transp., 1977-78; nat. campaign dir. Bentsen for Pres., Washington, 1973-75; dir. fed. govt. rels. Phillip Morris, Inc., Washington, 1978-83; chmn. The Palumbo Co. LLC; bd. dirs. Caths. Alliance for Common Goog, Cath. United. Bd. dirs., past pres. Nyumbani Child of God Hospice and Orphanage; treas., bd. dirs. John Mott Found. Mem.: NJ State Soc., Am. League Lobbyists, Nat. Dem. Club, Rutgers Club Washington, Nat. Press Club. Democrat. Roman Catholic. Business E-Mail: bpalumbo@covad.net.

PALUMBO, RUTH ANN, state legislator; b. Lexington, Ky., July 7, 1949; d. James Keith and Dorothy Calvin (Carrier) Baker; m. John Anthony Palumbo II, June 29, 1974; children: John A. III (dec.), Joseph Edward, James Thomas, Stephen Baker. BA in Secondary Edn., U. Ky., 1972. Sales Chez Lissette Boutique, Leysin, Switzerland, 1966; sales, shoes Purcell's Dept. Store, Lexington, Ky., 1966-70; organist Ctrl. Bapt. Ch., Lexington, Ky., 1968; clk. Good Samaritan Hosp., Lexington, Ky., 1968-73; sec. Dr. Joseph Keith, Lexington, Ky., 1971-73; senate clk. aide Ky. Gen. Assembly, Frankfort, Ky., 1974; pub. rels. Palumbo Properties, Lexington, 1974-92; mem. Dist. 76 Ky. House of Reps, 1990—. Mem. LWV, Lexington, 1990-92, Ky. Women's Polit. Caucus, Louisville, 1991-92, NAt. Order Women Legislators, Washington, 1992; sec. Ctrl. Ky. Caucus, Lexington, 1991-92. Mem. Greater Lexington Dem. Women, fin. v.p., 1982; mem. Nat. Order of Women Legislators, Washington, 1992; legis.liaison ACS Breast Cancer Detection Task Force, Ky., 1992; adv. coun. Bryan Sta. Youth Svcs. Ctr., Lexington, 1992; ball chmn. Lexington Philharmonic Women's Guild, 1990; govt. affairs Am. Symphony Orch. League Vol. Coun., Washington, 1992; bd. dirs. Philharmonic Women's Guild, pres., 1986-88; bd. dirs. Am. Cancer Soc., pres., 1988-89; bd. dirs. Lexington Phulharmonic Soc. Recipient Dorothy Moomaw Miles Svc. award Sayre Sch., 1986, Govs. Vol. Activist award Gov. Wallace G. Wilkinson, 1989, named Lexington's Outstanding Young Woman Bluegrass Jr. Woman's Club, 1982, Leadership Lexington, C. of C., 1988, Leadership Am. Found. for Women's Resources, Washington, 1989. Fellow U. Ky. Devel. Coun.; mem. Jr. League LExington (sec. 1989-90), Prof. Women's Forum, Gamma Phi Veta (pres. 1980-82). Democrat. Baptist. Avocations: singing, music boxes, stamp collecting/philately, piano. Home: 10 Deepwood Dr Lexington KY 40505-2106 Office: House of Reps State Capitol Annex Rm 370B Frankfort KY 40601

PAMPLIN, ROBERT BOISSEAU, JR., manufacturing company executive, minister, writer; b. Augusta, Ga., Aug. 3, 1941; s. Robert Boisseau and Mary Katherine (Reese) P.; m. Marilyn Joan Hooper; children: Amy Louise, Anne Boisseau. Student, Va. Poly. Inst., 1960-62; BS in Bus. Ad., Lewis & Clark Coll., 1964, BS in Acctg., 1965, BS in Econs., 1966; BS (hon.), Va. Tech., 1964; LHD (hon.), Va. Poly. Inst., 1995, Pacific U., 2001; DHL (hon.), Va. Poly. Inst., 1995; MBA, U. Portland, 1968, LLD (hon.), 1972, MEd, 1975; MA, Western Conservative Bapt. Sem. (name now Western Sem.), 1978, DMin, 1982, D (hon.) of Sacred Letter, 1991, MA, 2000; PhD, Calif. Coast U.; DHL (hon.), Warner Pacific Coll., 1988; LLD (hon.), Western Baptist Coll., 1989, George Fox U., 2005; cert. in wholesale mgmt., Ohio State U., 1970; cert. labor mgmt., U. Portland, 1982; cert. in advanced mgmt., U. Hawaii, 1975; DD (hon.), Judson Baptist Coll., 1984; DBA (hon.), Marquis Giuseppe Scicluna Internat. U. Found., 1986; LittD (hon.), Va. Tech. U., 1987, LHD (hon.), BS (hon.) in Bus. Adminstrn., 2001; LHD (hon.), Western Seminary, 1991; DD, Western Evang. Sem., 1994; DBA (hon.), U. S.C., 1996; D Pub. Svc., DHL (hon.), U. Puget Sound, Pacific U., 1999, 2001. Pres., CEO R.B. pamplin Corp., Portland, Oreg., 1964—. Chmn. bd., CEO Columbia Empire Farms Inc., Lake Oswego, Oreg., 1976—, Pamplin Comms.; chmn. bd., CEO Mt. Vernon Mills Inc.,; pres., CEO Ross Island Sand & Gravel; lectr. bus. adminstrn. Lewis and Clark Coll., 1968-69; adj. asst. prof. bus. adminstrn., U. Portland, 1973-76; pastor Christ Cmty. Ch., Lake Oswego; lectr. in bus. adminstrn. and econs. U. Costa Rica, 1968, Va. Tech. Found., 1986; chmn. bd. dirs. Christian Supplly Ctrs. Inc.; prof. with tenure U. Portland, 1999. Author: Everything is Just great, 1985, The Gift, 1986, Another Virginian: A Study of the Life and Beliefs of Robert Boisseau Pamplin, 1986; author: (with others) A Portrait of Colorado, 1976, Three in One, 1974, The Storybook Primer on Managing, 1974, One Who Believed, Vol. I, 1988, vol. II, 1991, Climbing the Centuries, 1993, Heritage the Making of an American Family, 1994, American Heroes, 1995, Prelude to Surrender, 1995, Alaska Gold, 1998, Robert Reese, 1998; editor: Oreg. Mus. Sci. and Industry Press, 1973; trustee Oreg. Mus. Sci. and Industry Press, 1971, 1974—; editor: Portrait of Oregon, 1973; editor: (with others) Oregon Underfoot, 1975. Trustee Lewis and Clark Coll., 1989—, chmn. bd. trustees, 1988-96, life trustee 1996-; hon. life pres. Western Conservative Bapt. Sem.; chmn. regents Western Sem., 1994; mem. nat. adv. coun. on vocat. Edn., 1975—; mem. Western Interstate Com. on Higher Edn., 1981-84; co-chmn. Va. Tech. $50 Million Campaign for Excellence, 1984-87, Va. Tech. Found., 1986—, Va.-Oreg. State Scholarship Commn., 1974—, chmn. 1976-78; mem. Portland dist. adv. coun. SBA, 1973-77; mem. rewards rev. com., City of Portland, 1973-78, chmn., 1973-78; bd. regents U. Portland, 1971-79, chmn. bd., 1975-79, regent emeritus, 1979—; trustee Oreg. Episc. Schs., 1979, Linfield Coll., U. Puget Sound, 1989—; dr. pub. svc., U. Puget Sound, 1999; chmn. bd. trustees Portland Art Mus., 2003-05. Recipient Disting. Alumnus award, Lewis and Clark Coll., 1974, ROTC Disting. Svc. award, USAF, 1974, bronze medal, Albert Einstein Acad., 1986, Disting. Leadership medal, Freedoms Found., Disting. Bus. Alumnus award, U. Portland, 1990, Nat. Caring award, Caring Inst., 1991, Pride of Portland award, Portland Lions Club, Hero Athlete award, 1994, Herman Lay Entrepreneurship award, 1995, Thomas Jefferson award, Oreg. Hist. Soc., 1998, Aubrey R. Watzek award, Lewis and Clark Coll., 1998, Leadership award, Portland Living Mag., 1998, Unique Contbns. to Comms. award, Portland Advt. Fedn., 2001, Oliver Wendell Holmes, Jr. award for Civil War Preservationalist of Yr., 2001, Govs. Arts award, 2001, Legacy award, Civil War Preservation Trust, 2003, Gov.'s Gold award as Oregonian of Achievement, 2003, Corp. Citizenship award, Woodrow Wilson Internat. Ctr. for Scholars, 2005, Nat. Vol. Outstanding Svc. award, Vol. Am., 2006, Deans Leadership award, OSU Excellence Family Bus., 2009, Excellence Leadership award, OSU, 2009, Reaching and Empowering All People award, 2013; named Outstanding Philanthropist of Yr. award, Nat. Soc. Fund Raising Execs., 1997, Western Conservative Bapt. Sem. Lay Inst. for Leadership, Edn. Devel. and Rsch. named for R.B. Pamplin Jr., 1988, Textile World's Top 10, 1999, Portland First Citizen, Portland Met. Assn. Realtors, 1999, Parents of Yr., Juvenile Diabetes Found., 2001, Entrepreneur of Yr., Oreg. Entrepreneur Forum, 2001, Va. Tech. Coll. Bus. Adminstrn. renamed R.B. Pamplin Coll. Bus. Adminstrn. in his honor, U. Portland Sch. Bus. renamed Dr. Robert B. Pamplin, Jr. in his honor, Civil War Preservationalist of Yr., Civil War Preservation Trust, 2003, Nat. Vol. of Yr., Vols. of Am., 2006; named one of 20 Most Influential Execs. Past 20 Yrs., Bus. Jour.; named to Hall of Fame, U. Portland Sch. Bus., 2009. Mem. Acad. Mgmt., Delta Epsilon Sigma, Beta Gamma Sigma (Bus. Achievement award 2012), Sigma Phi Epsilon, Waverley Country Club (pres. 2003-04), Arlington, Multnomah Athletic Clulb, Capitol Hill Club, Greenville Country Club, Poinsett Club, Eldorado Country Club, Thunderbird Country Club, Rotary. Republican. Episcopalian. Office: RB Pamplin Corp Inc Ste 2400 805 SW Broadway Portland OR 97205-3341

PAN, CHAI-FU, engineering educator; b. Loshon, Szechwan, China, Sept. 8, 1936; arrived in US, 1960; s. I-Chen Pan, Shih-Liang Shih; m. Maria Chia-Yao Shih, Aug. 18, 1962; children: Lawrence, Mariette. BS in Chem. Engring., Nat. Taiwan U., 1956; PhD in Phys. Chemistry, U. Kans., Lawrence, 1966. Assoc. prof. Ala. State U., Montgomery, 1966—71, prof., 1971—91, prof. emeritus, 1991—. Contbr. numerous articles to profl. jours. Recipient Rsch. award, Ala. State U., 1985; grantee MISIP grantee, NSF, 1985. Fellow: Am. Inst. Chemists; mem.: Am. Chem. Soc. (referee), Phi Lambda Upsilon. Achievements include development of Pan equations; research in methods to study hydrophilic and hydrophobic phenomena in electrolyte solutions. Avocations: reading, writing, gardening, photography. Home: 2420 Wentworth Dr Montgomery AL 36106 Personal E-mail: ppan@charter.net.

PAN, YI, computer science educator; b. Wujiang, Jiangsu, China, May 12, 1960; came to U.S., 1987; s. Jun and Xiuzhen (Fei) P.; m. Hong Miao, Aug. 4, 1986; children: Marissa, Anna. BEng, Tsinghua U., Beijing, 1982, MEng, 1984; MSc, U. Pitts., 1988, PhD in Computer Sci., 1991. Rsch. asst. Tsinghua U., 1982-86; tchg. asst. U. Pitts., 1987-89, tchg. fellow, 1989—91; asst. prof. computer sci. U. Dayton, Ohio, 1991-96, assoc. prof. Ohio, 1996-2000; assoc. prof. computer sci. Ga. State U., Atlanta, 2000—, now chair computer sci. Director of Graduate Studies in Computer Science University of Dayton, Dayton, 1998—2000. Contbr. articles to profl. jours. Recipient Rsch. Opportunity award NSF, 1995, Investment Competition Fund award Ohio Bd. Regents, 1996, World Acad. Scis. Achievement award, 2002; Mellon Found. fellow 1990, Summer Rsch. fellow U. Dayton Rsch. Coun., 2000, Air Force Office for Sci. Rsch., JSPS fellow, 1998. Mem.: IEEE (sr.; Secretary of the IEEE Computer Society Dayton Chapter 1996—97, BIBE Outstanding Achievement award 2007, IEEE Computer Soc. Disting. Visitor Program Spkr. 2000). Home: 615 Summer Breeze Ter Alpharetta GA 30005-6431 Office: Ga State U Computer Sci Dept 34 Peachtree St Ste 1450 Atlanta GA 30303 Office Phone: 404-413-5719. E-mail: pan@cs.gsu.edu.

PANGELINAN, JULIE ANNA, hotel company executive; b. 1964; BBA, San Francisco State U., 1987. CPA. Staff acct. Ernst & Young LLP, 1987—89; audit ptnr. BDO Seidman, LLP., 1990—2000; v.p., acctg. policy Marriott International, Inc. (formerly Marriott Corp.), 2000—06; chief acctg. officer Sunrise Sr. Living, Inc., 2006—09, acting CFO, 2007; CFO Sunrise Senior Living, Inc., 2009—11, Interstate Hotels & Resorts, Inc., Arlington, Va., 2011—. Mem.: AICPA. Office: Interstate Hotels & Resorts Inc 4501 N Fairfax Dr Arlington VA 22203 Office Phone: 703-273-7500. Office Fax: 703-744-1601. Business E-Mail: julie.pangelinan@sunrise-al.com.

PANGLE, THOMAS LEE, political scientist; b. Gouverneur, NY, Nov. 29, 1944; AB with distinction, Cornell U., Ithaca, NY, 1966; PhD in Polit. Sci., U. Chgo., 1972. Lectr., asst. to assoc. prof. Yale U., New Haven, 1971—79; fellow, Victoria Coll. U. Toronto, Canada, 1979—84, apptd. to grad. sch. with tenure, 1979, assoc. prof. polit. sci., 1979—83, prof. polit. sci., 1983—2001, fellow, St. Michael's Coll., 1985—2004, univ. prof. in polit. sci., 2001—04; Joe R. Long endowed chair in dem. studies, dept. govt. U. Tex. at Austin, 2004—. Author: Montesquieu's Philosophy of Liberalism, 1973, The Spirit of Modern Republicanism: The Moral Vision of the American Founders and the Philosophy of Locke, 1988, The Ennobling of Democracy: The Challenge of the Postmodern Age, 1992, (with Lorraine Pangle) The Learning of Liberty: The Educational Ideas of the American Founders, 1993, (with Peter Ahrensdorf) Justice Among Nations: On the Moral Basis of Power and Peace, 1999, Political Philosophy and the God of Abraham, 2003, Leo Strauss: An Introduction, 2006, The Theological Basis of Liberal Modernity in Montesquieus Spirit of the Laws, 2010; editor: The Rebirth of Classical Political Rationalism: An Introduction to the Thought of Leo Strauss, 1989, The Roots of Political Philosophy: Ten Forgotten Socratic Dialogues, 1987; polit. theory editor The Ency. of Democracy, 4 vols., 1995; gen. editor The Agora Editions; sr. adv. editor Books in Canada: The Canadian Review of Books, 1995-98; mem. editl. bd. Polit. Rsch. Quar. and Polis, Jour. the Soc. the Study of Greek Polit. Thought; contbr. numerous articles to various jours. Recipient Robert Foster Cherry award, 1992; NEH fellow, 1975-76, 1985-86, 1993, 2001-02; Guggenheim fellow, 1981-82; Connaught fellow, 1994; Siemens fellow, 1997-98; Killam fellow, 2002-04. Fellow: Royal Soc. Can.; mem.: Phi Beta Kappa. Office: Univ Tex at Austin Dept Govt 1 University Sta A1800 Austin TX 78712-0119 Office Phone: 512-232-1529. Office Fax: 512-471-1061. Business E-Mail: tpangle@austin.utexas.edu.*

PANKEY, GEORGE ATKINSON, internist, educator, researcher; b. Shreveport, La., Aug. 11, 1933; s. George Edward and Annabel (Atkinson) P.; m. Patricia Ann Carreras, Sept. 22, 1972; children: Susan Margaret, Stephen Charles, Laura Atkinson, Edward Atkinson. Student, La. Poly. Inst., 1950-51; BS, Tulane U., 1954, MD, 1957; MS, U. Minn., 1961. Diplomate Am. Bd. Internal Medicine, Am. Bd. Infectious Disease. Intern U. Minn. Hosps., 1957-58, resident in internal medicine, 1958-60, Mpls. VA Hosp., Mpls. Gen. Hosp., 1960-61; asst. vis. physician Charity Hosp. La., New Orleans, 1961-62, vis. physician, 1962-75, sr. vis. physician, 1975-95; ptnr. Ochsner Clinic, New Orleans, 1968—99; head sect. infectious diseases Ochsner Clinic Found., 1972—94, dir. infectious disease training program, 1972—94, dir. infectious disease rsch., 1999—; instr. dept. medicine, div. infectious diseases Tulane U. Sch. Medicine, New Orleans, 1961-63, clin. instr., 1963-65, clin. asst. prof. medicine, 1965-68, clin. assoc. prof., 1968-73, clin. prof., 1973—. Dir., founder Century Nat. Bank, New Orleans; medicine test com. Nat. Bd. Med. Examiners, 1979-83; infectious diseases adv. bd. Hoffman-LaRoche, 1982-92; dir. Nat. Found. Infectious Diseases, 2004—10, 2012-, trustee, 2010-12. Author: A Manual of Antimicrobial Therapy, 1969; co-author: (with Charles W. Gross and Michael G. Mendelsohn) Contemporary Diagnosis and Management of Sinusitis, 1997, 4th edit., 2004; (with Julia Garcia-Diaz and Layne O. Gentry) Contemporary Diagnosis and Management of Diabetic Foot Infections, 2006; editor: Infectious Diseases Digest, 1983-95, So. Med. Assn. Program for Infectious Diseases Dial-Access, 1983-92, Ochsner Clinic Reports on Serious Hosp. Infections, 1985-2005, Ochsner Clinic Reports on Geriatric Infectious Diseases, 1990-93, Ochsner Clinic Reports on the Mgmt. of Sepsis, 1991-93, Infectious Disease Clinics of N.Am., 1994; co-editor: (with Geoffrey A. Kalish) Outpatient Antimicrobial Therapy - Recent Advances, 1989; contbg. editor: Antimicrobial Therapy Guide, 18th edit., 2006; mem. editl. bd. Patient Care, 1969-75, Today in Medicine, 1990, Nat. Infectious Disease Info. Network, 1983, Compendium Continuing Edn. in Dentistry, 1984-2004, Quinolones Bull., 1985-93, Ochsner Jour., 1999-2003, Infectious Disease News, 2001—; contbr. articles to profl. jours. Dir. Camp Fire Inc.; Pres. New Orleans Young Republican Club, 1969-71; adv. bd. Angie Nall Sch. Hosp., Beaumont, Tex.; trustee Nall Found. for Children, Beaumont. Recipient cert. merit Am. Acad. Gen. Practice, 1969, 70, 2002. Master ACP-ASIM (laureate award La. chpt. 1997); fellow Am. Coll. Preventive Medicine, Infectious Disease Soc. Am. (Clinician award 1996), Am. Coll. Chest Physicians, Royal Soc. Medicine; mem. Am. Soc. of Transplantation, Assn. Contamination Control (chpt. pres. 1968-70), Am. Fedn. Med. Rsch., So. Med. Assn. (certificate of award 1970), Am. Soc. Internal Medicine (del. ann. meeting 1971-72), Am. Soc. Microbiology, Am. Thoracic Soc., New Orleans Acad. Internal Medicine (pres. 1977-78, 96-97), AMA, Aerospace Med. Assn., Am. Soc. Tropical Medicine and Hygiene, Am. Venereal Disease Assn., Am. Soc. Parasitologists, Internat. Travel Medicine Soc., La. Soc. Internal Medicine (pres. 1972-73), La. Med. Soc., La. Thoracic Soc. (chmn. program com. 1968, governing council 1976-80), Surg. Infection Soc., Immunocompromised Host Soc., Musser Burch Soc., Orleans Parish Med. Soc., N.Y. Acad. Scis., Pan Am. Med. Assn. (diplomate mem. sect. internal medicine 1971, sect. pres. infectious diseases and virology 1978-85), SAR, Huguenot Soc. Founders Manakin in Colony of Va., Aviation Med. Examiner, Federal Air Surgeon(inf. dis cons.), Masons (32 deg), Shriners. Home: 5910 Prytania St New Orleans LA 70115-4348 Office: Ochsner Clinic Found 1514 Jefferson Hwy New Orleans LA 70121-2483 Office Phone: 504-842-4006. Personal E-mail: gpankey@ochsner.org.

PANNELL, CHARLES A., JR., federal judge; b. DeKalb County, Ga., 1946; BA, U. Ga., Athens, 1967, JD, 1970. Asst. US atty. (northern dist.) Ga. US Dept. Justice, 1971—72; pvt. law practice Ga., 1972—76; spl. asst. atty. gen. Ga. Dept. Law, 1974—76; dist. atty. Conasauga Jud. Cir., Ga., 1977—79, superior ct. judge, 1979—99; judge US Dist. Ct. (northern dist.) Ga., Atlanta, 1999—2013, sr. judge, 2013—. Mem. JAG Corps USAR, 1970—98. Office: US Dist Ct 2367 US Courthouse 75 Spring St SW Atlanta GA 30303-3309 Office Phone: 404-215-1580.

PANOS, TAS, lawyer; b. 1955; BA, U. Nev., Las Vegas; JD, U. San Diego Sch. Law. Pvt. practice, Calif., 1985—2002; litigation, labor & employment group counsel Affiliated Computer Services, Inc. (ACS) (acquired by Xerox Corp.), sr. v.p., group counsel, 2002—08, exec. v.p., gen. counsel, 2008—10. Adj. prof. U. San Diego Sch. Law.

PAOLILLO, JOSEPH GUY PETER, management professor, researcher; b. Bklyn., Feb. 2, 1948; m. Toni Mae Peterson, Mar. 14, 1981; children: Guy Joseph, Marya Louise. PhD, U. Oreg., Eugene, 1977. Prof. mgmt. U. Miss., University, 1986—. Contbr. articles to profl. jours. With US Army, 1971—72, MDW. Mem.: Acad. of Mgmt. Business E-Mail: jpaolillo@bus.olemiss.edu.

PAPA, MARK GARY, oil and gas industry executive; b. Monroeville, Pa., Sept. 16, 1946; s. Mark W. Papa and Jean Feiler; m. Susan Berryman, Dec. 21, 1970; 1 child, Christine. BS in Petroleum Engring., U. Pitts., 1968; MBA in Econs./Fin., U. Houston, 1980. Registered profl. engr., Tex. Various petroleum engring., supervisory & engring. positions Conoco, Inc., various locations, 1968-81; divsn. prodn. coord. Belco Petroleum, Houston, 1981-82, mgr. ops., 1982-83; v.p. drilling and prodn. Belnorth, Houston, 1983-84, sr. v.p. drilling and prodn., 1984-85; sr. v.p. ops. Enron Oil & Gas, Houston, 1986—94, pres. N.Am. ops., 1994—98, pres., 1996—99, COO, 1997—98, CEO, 1998—99; chmn., CEO EOG Resources, Inc., 1999—. Bd. dir. Oil States Internat., Magellan Midstream Partners; chmn. U.S. Oil & Gas Assn. Mem. Soc. Petroleum Engrs., Am. Assn. Petroleum Geologists, Natural Gas Supply Assn., Tex. Ind. Prodrs. Royalty Orgn. Avocation: tennis. Office: EOG Resources 333 Clay St PO Box 4362 Houston TX 77002

PAPANICOLAOU, ANDREW C., neuroscientist, educator; b. Sikyon, Greece, July 8, 1950; U.S. s. Constantinos A. and Photeini C. Papanicolaou; m. Nora Kapouralis, Nov. 21, 1950; children: Constantinos, Anastasia. Student, U. Athens, 1968—70; BS, Xavier U., 1972, MA, 1974; PhD, So. Ill. U., 1978. Asst. prof. U. Tex., Galveston, 1980—86, assoc. prof., 1986—90, prof. neurosurgery, 1990—93; prof., dir. divsn. clin. neurosci. U. Tex., Houston Med. Sch., 1993—. Dir. Vivian L. Smith advanced studies Inst. Internat. Neuropsychol. Soc., Houston, Xylocastro, Greece. Author: Emotion: A Reconsideration of the Somatic Theory, 1989; editor: Bergson and Modern Thought: Towards A Unified Science, 1987; author: Fundamentals of Functional Brain Imaging, 1998, Plato: 4 Critique of Pragmatism (in Greek), 2002; co-author: The Amnesias: A Clinical Textbook of Memory Disorders, 2006. Grantee, NIH, 1999—, 2000—, NSF, 2001—. Mem.: APA, AAAS, Soc. Psychophysiological Rsch., NY Acad. Sciences, Internat. Neuropsychological Soc., Hellenic Psychological Assn., Am. Soc. Neurophysiological Monitoring. Office: Univ Tex Houston Med Sch 1333 Moursund Ste H114 Houston TX 77030

PAPANTONIO, MIKE (JAMES MICHAEL PAPANTONIO), lawyer, talk radio host; b. Oct. 24, 1953; married; 1 child. Grad., U. Fla.; JD, Samford U. Cumberland Sch. Law, Birmingham, Ala. Bar: Fla. 1982, US Dist. Ct. (mid. dist.), Fla. 1983. Sr. ptnr. Levin, Papantonio, Thomas, Mitchell, Echsner & Proctor, P.A., Pensacola, Fla., 1983—; co-host weekly radio program Ring of Fire, Air America Radio, 2004—. Founder legal edn. orgn. Mass Torts Made Perfect, Pensacola, 1983. Author: In Search of Atticus Finch, A Motivational Book for Lawyers, 1996, Clarence Darrow, the Journeyman: Lessons for the Modern Lawyer, 1997, Resurrecting Aesop: Fables Lawyers Should Remember, 2000; contbr. articles to profl jours. Co-founder Emerald Coastkeepers, Inc., 1998. Fellow: Internat. Acad. Trial Lawyers, Internat. Soc. Barristers; mem.: Acad. Fla. Trial Lawyers, Southern Trial Lawyers Assn., Am. Trial Lawyers Assn., Am. Bd. Trial Advocates. Office: Levin, Papantonio, Thomas, Mitchell, Echsner & Proctor 316 South Baylen St Ste 600 Pensacola FL 32502 Office Phone: 850-435-7001. Office Fax: 850-435-7020.

PAPITTO, RALPH RAYMOND, manufacturing executive; b. Providence, Nov. 1, 1926; s. John and Maria (David) P.; m. Norma J. Ewart, June 10, 1943 (div.); children: Andrea (Mrs. Harry Crump), Aurelia (Mrs. William Young), David John; m. Barbara Auger, Apr. 1982. BS in Finance, Bryant Coll., Providence, 1947, DSc Bus. Adminstrn. (hon.), 1987; student, Boston U. Law Sch., 1948-49; DSc Bus. Adminstrn. (hon.), Roger Williams Coll., 1985; LLD (hon.), New Eng. Inst. Tech., 1985, Suffolk U., 1986, New England Inst. Tech. With Arthur Andersen & Co. and Ernst & Ernst, Providence, 1948-51; exec. v.p. fin. Ritz Products, Inc., Providence, 1951-55; founder, pres., chmn., dir. Glass-Tite Industries, Inc., Providence, 1956-63, chmn. bd., 1963—, also bd. dirs.; founder, chief exec. officer, pres., chmn. Nortek Inc., Providence, 1967-90, bd. dirs.; Chair and CEO AFC Cable Systems, Inc., Providence, 1993—. Bd. dirs. Hi-G, Inc. Fin. dir. Town of Johnston, R.I., 1955-59; trustee Roger Williams U., Bristol, R.I., chmn. bd. trustees, 1972-2007; bd. dirs. Meeting St. Sch. Retarded; mem. Gov.'s Blue Ribbon Commn., Roger Williams Hosp.; mem. Aurora Civic Assn. Named Man Yr. in R.I., R.I. C. of C., 1961. Mem. Alpine Country Club (pres. 1966-68, 92—), Jockey Club, Surf Club, LaGorce Country Club (Fla.). Office: AFC Cable Systems Inc 1020 Park Ave Ste 108 Cranston RI 02910 Home Phone: 401-828-5751; Office Phone: 401-453-2000, 401-275-1925. Fax: 401-453-2009, 401-828-0613.

PAPPAS, ALCESTE THETIS, consulting company executive, educator; b. Dix Hills, NY, May 5, 1945; d. Costas Ernest and Thetis (Hero) P.; m. Sylvan V. Endich, Sept. 13, 1987. AB, U. Calif.-Berkeley, 1967, PhD, 1978; EdM, Harvard U., 1969. Cert. guidance counselor, Mass., secondary sch. tchr., Mass. Dir. student-young alumni affairs Calif. Alumni Assn., Berkeley, 1969-71; dir. residential programs U. Calif., Berkeley, 1971-73, dir. housing and childcare, 1973-79; sr. cons., mgr. Peat, Marwick, Mitchell & Co., NYC, 1979-80, 80-82, sr. mgr., 1982-84; ptnr. in charge edn., other instns. KPMG, NYC, 1984-93; pres., CEO Pappas Cons. Group, Inc., Palm Beach Gardens, Fla., 1992—. Spkr. in field. Author: Reengineering Your Non-Profit Organization: A Guide to Strategic Transformation, 1996; contbr. articles to profl. jours., author monographs. Mem. Merola Opera Bd., San Francisco, 1978-80, Calif. Alumni Council, 1976-79; bd. overseers Regents Coll., 1986-89; bd. dirs., mem. fin. com. Hellenic Coll. and Holy Cross Sch. Theology, Brookline, Mass., 1983-87, Seabury Western Theol. Sem., Evanston, Ill., 1983-89; bd. dirs. N.Y. Chiropractic Coll., 1986-88, Com. on Econ. Devel., 1986-88, Greek Orthodox Archdiocese Council, N.Y.C., 1985-89; bd. dirs., vice chmn. St. Basil Acad., 1983-87; bd. dirs., mem. exec. com. YWCA, N.Y.C., 1985-90, Catalyst, 1988-90; chairperson capital campaign com. U. Calif., Berkeley, exec. v.p. exec. coun. Coll. Letters and Sci.; trustee Clark U., 1993-95, U. Calif. Found., 1993-99; bd. dirs. Nat. Coun. for Rsch. on Women, 1996-98; mem. adv. bd. Grad. Sch. Edn. U. Calif., Berkeley, 2005—. Named mem. Acad. Women Achievers, YWCA, N.Y.C., 1984; recipient award Nat. Mgmt. Assn., 1997. Mem. Mid. States Assn. Schs. and Colls. (bd. dirs., fin. com. 1984-89, planning com. 1988-89), Order of the Ky. Colonels, Mortar Bd., Pi Lambda Theta, Prytanean. Avocations: travel, photography, gourmet cooking. Office: 117 Island Cove Way Palm Beach Gardens FL 33418 Office Phone: 561-624-5653. Personal E-mail: pappas01@aol.com.

PAPPAS, JAMES PETE, university administrator; b. Price, Utah, June 30, 1939; s. Pete S. and Dia P. (Metrakis) P.; m. Peggy Ann Kunz, Aug. 30, 1964; children: C. Jennifer, Peter T. AS in Psychology, Coll. Eastern Utah, 1959; BA in Psychology, U. Utah, 1961; MS in Counseling Psychology, Ohio U., 1964; PhD in Clin. Psychology, Purdue U., 1968; cert. in Mgmt., Stanford U., 1979; cert. in adminstrn., Harvard U., 1985. Asst. dir. counseling ctr. U. Utah, Salt Lake City, 1969-72, dir. ctr. for acad. advising, assoc. dean liberal edn., 1975-78, assoc. dean divsn. of continuing edn., 1978-87; prof. ednl. psychology and liberal studies U. Okla., Norman, 1987—, v.p. for univ. outreach; dean Coll. of Continuing Edn., 1994-00, Coll. of Liberal Studies, 2000—. Author: (book) Windows of Opportunity: Preparing University Based Residential Continuing Education for the Twenty-First Century, 1992, The University's Role in Economic Development: From Research to Outreach, 1997; co-author: (workbook) Promotional Techniques, 1987. Mem. Norman Econ. Devel. Coalition, 1996—; state chmn. Utah Endowment for Humanities, 1985-88; pres. Norman Arts and Humanities Coun., 1994-95. Recipient St. Paul award Greek Orthodox Ch. of N. Am., Denver, 1990, Christopher Outstanding Leadership and Bittner Svc. awards U. Continuing Edn. Assn.; inductee Internat. Adult and Continuing Edn. Hall of Fame, 1997. Fellow Assn. Grad. Liberal Studies; mem. Am. Assn. Counseling and Devel. (nat. senator 1975-77), Assn. Acad. Affairs Adminstr. (bd. dirs. 1977-78), Adult Edn. Assn. Utah (bd. dirs. 1979-82), Univ. Continuing Edn. Assn. (pres. 1996-97, Julius M. Nolte award 2006), Nat. Assn. State Univs. and Land Grant Colls. (bd. dirs. 1994-97), Assn. Grad. Liberal Studies Programs (bd. dirs. 2000—), Assn. Continuing Higher Edn. (exec. v.p. 2008-), Assn. Grad. Liberal Studies. Avocations: reading, community service, writing, sports, travel. Office: Coll Continuing Edn 1700 Asp Ave Rm 111 Norman OK 73072-6407 Office Phone: 405-325-6361. Business E-Mail: jpappae@ok.edu.

PAPPAS, PHILO T., retail executive; Sr. v.p., merchandising Staples, Inc., 1993—2003; sr. v.p., chief merchandising officer Tweeter Home Entertainment Group Inc., 2003—08; exec. v.p., category mgmt. Michaels Stores, Inc., 2009—. Office: Michaels Stores Inc 8000 Bent Branch Dr Irving TX 75063 Office Phone: 972-409-1300. Office Fax: 972-409-1556. Business E-Mail: pappasp@michaels.com.

PAQUETTE, WILLIAM ARTHUR, historian, educator; b. Lawrence, Mass., Aug. 6, 1947; s. Arthur Conrad Paquette and Dorothy Lucille Root; m. Sylvia Lois Kreps, June 14, 1969 (div. 1987). BA, Grove City Coll., Pa., 1969; MA, Duquesne U., Pitts., 1971; PhD, Emory U., Atlanta, 1994. Tchr. Acad. Holy Cross, Kensington, Md., 1972—75, chmn. dept. social sci., 1973—75; from adj. prof. to prof. history Tidewater C.C., Portsmouth, Va., 1975—94, prof., 1994—. Grad. tchg. asst. Duquesne U., Pitts., 1969—71; adj. prof. history Old Dominion U., Norfolk, Va., 1975—78, Spelman Coll., Atlanta, 1983—84, adj. prof., 1989—90; adj. prof. history Ga. Perimeter, Atlanta, 1983—84; adj. prof. edn. Emory U., Atlanta, 1989—90; project historian NEH, 1979—82, 1995—96, 2000—02, grant reviewer, 2012; reviewer ETS, 1995—2002; chmn. chancellor's prefix review com. Va. CC. Sys., Richmond, 1998—2000; nat. editor history Merlot Project, 2000—10; mem. adv. bd. history digital project Nat. Humanities Alliance, 2000—, Gale Group Pubs., 2003—, ProQuest Pubs., 2004—, Prentice-Hall, 2004—, Houghton Mifflin, 2005—; cons. in field; grants reviewer Dept. Edn., 2004—; edn. reviewer Nat. Gallery of Art, 2004—; editor, spl. issue chair Landmark Pilgrims and Wampoanoog, Plymouth, Mass.; reviewer NEH Grants, 2012—; spkr. in fields. Author: U.S. Colored Troops from Lower Tidewater in the Civil War, 1992, Encyclopedia of African-American Civil Rights, 1992, Ready Reference: Censorship, 1997, Great Events from History, North America Series, 1997, The War of 1812: An Encyclopedia, 1998, Dictionary of World Biography: 20th Century, 1999, Biographical Encyclopedia of Twentieth Century World Leaders, 1999, Encyclopedia of the U.S. Supreme Court, 2000, Encyclopedia of America's Historic Sites, 2000, Putting the World into World History textbooks, Teaching History, 2001, Great Events: 1900-2001, 2002, World Education Encyclopedia, 2002, World Press Encyclopedia, 2003, A Taste of Merlot: The Multimedia Resources for Historians and Others, Perspectives, 2003; co-author: Instructor's Guide to the Teaching of American History, 1979, Readings in Black and White, 1982, Suffolk: A Pictorial History, 1987, Dictionary of World Biography: Renaissance, 1998, Encyclopedia of North America, 1998, Teaching History, A Journal of Methods, 2001; photographer Fashion Doll Wardrobe, 2002, Suffolk: A Celebration of History, 2006, Instructor's Manual, Western Civilization, 2007; author: Great Events From History Modern Scandals, 2005, Great Events from History: Modern Scandals, 2010, City As Living Organism: The Case Study Of Bolivar NY, 2008, Teaching the Latin American Survey, 2009, Genealogy of Houses and Public Buildings, Mayflower Quarterly, 2010; co-author: Universalist Churches in Western New York State, Mayflower Quarterly, 2010, Great Lives From History: The Incredibly Healthy, 2011, The Thirties in America, 2011, The Twenties in America, 2011; contbr. ency., articles to mags., to profl. jours.; editor: Special Issue CCHR Plymouth MA Landmark Pilgrims & Wampanoag, 2011; author: BRAG Historical Society: The Curious Case of Bishop Root, Finding Penelope Root, 2014. Mem. adv. bd. US Com. World Food Day, 1999—; commr. Mus. Fine Arts, Portsmouth, Va., 1997—2002; mem. adv. bd. Ba. Fest. of the Book, 1998—2004; project dir. NEH Grant, Pilgrims and the Wampanuag Indians, 2010, NEH: Thomas Jefferson: Legacies and Landmarks, 2011; adv. bd. H-NET, 2005. Recipient Disting. Svc. award, Gen. Soc. Mayflower Descendants, 2011, Disting. Alumni award, Duquesne U., 2011; grantee Am. Cities and Pub. Spaces, NEH, 2005—09, Alamo, John Adams, 2007, Transcendentalists, 2008, Nat. Lyceum Rutherford B. Hayes, 2009; fellow, NEH, 1985; grant, 2010, Gilder-Lehrman fellow, U. Va., 2005, Landmark grants, NEH Inst., 2007—08, Grad. fellowship, Brown U., 2011, grant, NEH, 2009, 2011, Lyceum Movement, the Gilded Age, Tuning grant, AHA, 2012—. Mem.: Va. Political Scientists, History of Edn. Soc., Comparative and Internat. Edn. Soc., US Capitol Hist. Soc., Internat. Standing Conf. History Edn., Am. Ednl. Rsch. Assn., Am. Coun. Quebec Studies, Cmty. Coll. Humanities Assn. (v.p. 1991—93, bd. dirs. 1993—97, Disting. Svc. award 1997, Merlot award Tchg. Distinctive Use & Devel. of Online Materials 2008), Orgn. Am. Historians (com. cmty. coll. 2002—, chmn. 2004—05), Am. Hist. Assn. (Nancy Roelker Mentorship com. 1997—2000, chmn. 1999—2000, joint com. adj. 2000—04), Mayflower Soc. Va. (asst. historian 1992—93, historian 1993—98, dep. gov. 2004—07, gov. 2007—10, GSMD Edn. chair 2008—). Avocations: stamp collecting/philately, photography, travel, genealogy. Home: 13644 Bridlewood Dr Gainesville VA 20155 Office: Tidewater CC 120 Campus Dr Portsmouth VA 23701 Business E-Mail: wpaquette@tcc.edu.

PARADA, LUIS FERNANDO, science educator; b. Santa Fe de Bogota, Colombia, July 18, 1954; s. Alfonso and Clara Parada. BS in Molecular Biology, U. Wis., Madison, 1979; PhD in Biology, MIT, 1985. Damon Runyon postdoc. fellow Pasteur Inst., Paris, 1985—86, Helen Hay Whitney postdoc. fellow, 1986—87; head molecular embryology group Mammalian Genetics Lab., Nat. Cancer Inst., Frederick, Md., 1987—94; prof., dir. Ctr. Devel. Biology, U. Tex. Southwestern Med. Ctr., Dallas, 1994—2006, dir. Kent Waldrep Ctr. Nerve Regeneration, 1995—, Southwestern Bell disting. chair basic neurosci. rsch., 1998—, Amer. Cancer Soc. rsch. prof., 2003, Dana & Richard C. Strauss disting. chmn. devel. biology, 2006—. Mem. nat. adv. coun. Nat. Inst. Neurol. Disorders & Strokes; mem. sci. adv. bd. Rett Syndrome Rsch. Trust; sci. rev. bd. Howard Hughes Med. Inst.; adv. bd. Pews Scholars Found. Recipient Peter A. Steck Memorial ward, Soc. Neuro-Oncology, 2000, Friedrich von Recklinghausen award, Children's Tumor Found., 2009, Javits Neuroscience Investigator award, NIH. Fellow: AAAS; mem.: NAS, American Assn. Cancer Rsch., Soc. Devel. Biology, Soc. Neuroscience, Inst. Medicine, American Acad. Arts & Scis. Achievements include research in the elucidation of regulatory pathways that control the complex process of nervous system development and the consequences of inappropriate development which can include behavioral and mood disorders as well as cancer. Office: U Tex Southwestern Med Ctr 5323 Harry Hines Blvd Dallas TX 75390-9133 Office Phone: 214-648-1822. E-mail: luis.parada@utsouthwestern.edu.

PARADISE, LOUIS VINCENT, education educator, dean; b. Scranton, Pa., Apr. 19, 1946; s. Louis Benjamin and Lucille P.; children: Christopher, Gabrielle,Victoria. BS, Pa. State U., 1968; MS, Bucknell U., 1974; PhD, U. Va., 1976. Lic. psychologist, profl. counselor; cert. sch. psychologist. Assoc. prof. Cath. U. Am., Washington, 1976-83; prof. edn., chmn. edn. leadership U. New Orleans, 1983-90, dean Coll. Edn., 1990-92, univ. vice chancellor, provost, 1992-94, exec. vice chancellor, provost, 1994—2003, prof. Dept. Ednl. Leadership, Counseling, and Found., 2003—. Author: Ethics in Counseling and Psychotherapy, 1979, Questioning: Skills for the Helping Process, 1979, Counseling in Community College, 1982. 1st lt. U.S. Army, 1968-72. DuPont scholar U. Va., 1974. Mem. APA, ACA (ethics com. 1986-89), Am. Edn. Rsch. Assn., So. Assn. Counselor Edn. (chmn. ethics com. 1988-89), Acad. Counseling Psychology, Chi Sigma Iota (founding chpt. pres. 1985-87). Roman Catholic. Avocations: running, bicycling, music. Office: U New Orleans Dept Ednl Leadership Counseling & Found New Orleans LA 70148-0001 Office Phone: 504-280-6026. Business E-Mail: louis.paradise@uno.edu.

PARDUE, DWIGHT EDWARD, venture capitalist; b. North Wilkesboro, NC, Aug. 3, 1928; s. Gilbert F. and Nina (Glass) P.; m. Annie Eller, Mar. 24, 1951; children: Richard S., Dwight E. Cert., Clevenger Bus. Coll., 1956. Dir. warehousing Lowe's Co., Inc., North Wilkesboro, 1956-57, store mgr. Sparta, NC, 1957-59, Richmond, Va., 1959-70, regional v.p. North Wilkesboro, 1970-75, sr. v.p. store ops., 1975-78, exec. v.p. sales and store ops., 1978-86, sr. exec. v.p., 1986-90; pres., investor D. Pardue & Assocs., Wilkesboro, NC, 1990—. Mem. steering com. Home Ctr. Leadership Coun., Nat. Home Ctr. Home Improvement Congress and Exposition, 1983—86; bd. dirs. Northwestern Nat. Bank, Inc., Wilkesboro, NC, Integrity Fin. Corp., Hickory, NC; chmn. bd. Cmty. Bancshares, Inc., Wilkesboro, 1992—2002. Served with U.S. Army, 1950-52. Mem. Jefferson Landing Golf Club, Masons. Office Phone: 336-667-9411. Personal E-mail: dep0013@aol.com.

PAREN, DENNIS A., wholesale distribution executive; MBA in Fin., U. Toledo, 1980. V.p., internat. risk Alliance One International, Inc., 2004—. Office: Alliance One International Inc 8001 Aerial Ctr Pky Morrisville NC 27560-2009 Office Phone: 919-379-4300. Office Fax: 919-379-4346.

PARENT, DAVID HILL, investment company executive; b. Salem, Oreg., Apr. 13, 1940; s. Donald Allan and Pauline Louise (Lyons) P.; m. Christine Hedwige Marie Thérèse Wielezynski, Sept. 25, 1976; children: Marc Alexander Lair Thompson, Nathalie Jacqueline Marie Pauline. BS, U. Calif. Berkeley, 1963; MBA, Columbia U., 1965. Internat. fellow Columbia U., NYC, 1963; dir. mktg. Europe Vendo Internat., Brussels, 1965-69; exec. v.p. T.S.I., Hempstead, N.Y., 1969-70; v.p. mktg. Gateway-Globus, Forest Hills, N.Y., 1970-72; mgr. Ctrl. Africa, Leon Tempelsman & Son, NYC, 1972-79; pres. The Parent Co., Plano, Tex., 1979—. Advisor to pres. of Gabon, Libreville, 1976-79. Charter rep. troop 285 Boy Scouts Am., Plano. Mem. Rockwall Citizens's Counc. (exec. com.), Rockwall C. of C., Plano C. of C. Republican. Roman Catholic. Avocations: travel, skiing, scuba diving. Home and Office: 4948 Stony Ford Dr Dallas TX 75287-7235

PARENT, ELENA C., state legislator; b. Washington, Dec. 27, 1975; m. Briley Brisendine; 1 child, Brooks. BA in Psychology, U. Va., 1998, JD in Law, 2002. Litigator Sutherland Asbill & Brennan LP, 2002—08; chief staff to David Adelman Ga. State Senate, 2009; dir. devel. HOPE Atlanta; mem. Dist. 81 Ga. House of Reps., 2011—. Democrat. Episcopalian. Office: PO Box 81502 Atlanta GA 30366-1502 also: Georgia House of Reps 511 Coverdell Legis Office Bldg Atlanta GA 30334 Office Phone: 404-229-9596, 404-656-6372. Business E-Mail: elena@elenaparent.com, elena.parent@house.ga.gov.

PARENT, KEN, travel company executive; Various positions including exec. v.p., CFO, COO The Mills Corp.; sr. v.p. ops./mktg. and human resources Pilot Flying J (formerly Pilot Travel Centers, LLC). Office: Pilot Flying J 5508 Lonas Dr Knoxville TN 37909

PARESKY, DAVID S., travel company executive; b. Boston, Sept. 27, 1938; s. Paul and Ada (Rudnick) P.; m. Linda Kotzen, Aug. 18, 1963; children: Pamela, Laura, Mark. BA, Williams Coll., 1960; JD, Harvard U., 1963, MBA, 1965. Bar: Mass. Pres., chmn. bd. Crimson Travel Svc., Inc., Cambridge, Mass., 1965-89; pres., CEO, chmn. bd. Thomas Cook Travel, Cambridge, Mass., 1989-94. Mem. Bd. Higher Edn., Boston, 1980; trustee New Eng. Med. Ctr., 1982-83; mem. Bd. Regents of Higher Edn., Boston, 1980-86. Mem. Young Pres. Orgn. (chmn. New Eng. chpt. 1985), Chief Execs. Orgn., Phi Beta Kappa, Fisher Island Club (bd. dirs. 1998-01).

PARFITT, DIANE, state legislator; b. 1946; BS in Nursing, M in Maternal Child Nursing. Owner City Ctr. Gallery and Books, Fayetteville, NC; state rep. Dist. 44, 2010—. Mem. Appropriations com., Appropriations Subcom. on Transp., Commerce, Small Bus. and Entrepreneurship com., Edn. com., Health com.; vice chmn. Edn. Subcom. on Universities. Democrat. Office: North Carolina House of Representatives 16 W Jones St Rm 1017 Raleigh NC 27601-1096 Office Phone: 919-733-9892. E-mail: Diane.Parfitt@ncleg.net.

PARHAM, BOBBY EUGENE, state legislator; b. Nov. 6, 1941; m. Juanita Norris Parham; children: Alisa, Audra, Robbie. Pharmacist; commr. Baldwin County, 1969—75; mem. Ga. House Rep.; state rep. Dist. 105 Ga., 1975—92; state rep. Dist. 122, 1993—2002; state rep. Dist. 94, 2003—04; state rep. Dist. 141, 2004—09; chmn. motor vehicles com.; mem. health com.; mem. ecol. com.; mem. rules com.; chmn. bd. dir. First Nat. Bank, Baldwin County; mem. Dist. 12 Ga. State Transp. Bd., 2009—. Recipient Disting. Svc. award, U. Ga., Meritorius Svc. award, Ga. Pharma. Assn., Cmty. Svc. award, Merk, Sharp & Dhome; named A. H. Robbins Bowl of Hygea. Mem.: Jaycees (bd. mem., Disting. Svc. award). Democrat. Baptist. Office: Ga Dept Transp One Georgia Ctr 600 W Peachtree NW Atlanta GA 30308 Office Phone: 404-631-1990.

PARIENTE, BARBARA J., state supreme court justice; b. NYC, Dec. 24, 1948; m. Frederick A. Hazouri; children: David, Leslie, Josh. Grad. with highest honors, Boston U., 1970; JD with highest honors, George Washington U., 1973. Bar: Fla. 1973; cert. civil trial lawyer Fla. Bar; cert. Nat. Bd. Trial Advocacy. Law clk. to hon. Norman C. Roettger, Jr. US Dist. Ct. (so. dist.) Fla., 1973-75; assoc. Cone Wagner and Nugent, 1975—77, ptnr., 1977—83, Pariente & Silber, P.A., 1983; pvt. practice, 1983—2001; judge US Ct. of Appeals (4th dist.), 1993-97; justice Fla. Supreme Ct., Tallahassee, 1997—, chief justice, 2004—06, liaison, task force on treatment-based drug cts., 1999—2004, chair, steering com. families and children in cts., 2002—04, faculty mem., Justice Tchg. Inst. Participant Twenty-First Century Justice Conf.; mem. Jud. Cir. Grievance Com., 1989-92, chair, 1990-92; appointee gov.'s adv. com. character edn., 1999; second v.p. Conf. of Justices, 2005-06; mem. 15th jud. cir. nominating commn.; mem. nat. judges adv. com. balanced and restorative justice project, Dept. of Justice; bd. dirs. Fla. Bar Found., Legal Aid Soc., Palm Beach County Bar Assn.; conf. organizer in field; spkr. in field. Contbr. articles to profl. jours. in field. Mentor Take Stock in Children, 1992-2003, Communities in Schs.; mentoring program mem. Cities in Schs., 1993; mem. Palm Beach County Commn. on Status of Women; program vol. judge Palm Beach County Youth Ct. Recipient Disting. Svc. to Arts award Palm Beach County Bar Assn., 1987, Civil Litig. Pro Bono award Legal Aid Soc., 1993, Lifetime Achievement award Palm Beach County Jewish Fedn., 1998, Disting. Jud. Svc. award Fla. Coun. Crime and Delinquency, 2000, Breaking the Glass Ceiling award Jewish Mus. Fla., 2002, Good Govt. award Palm Beach County LWV, 2005, Lifetime Achievement award Fla. Assn. Sch. Social Workers, 2005, Disting. Alumni award George Washington U., 2006, Jurist of Yr. award Fla. Chpt. Am. Acad. Matrimonial Lawyers, 2006, award Fla. Assn. Women Lawyers, Palm Beach Chapter, 2007, Lifetime Achivement award Fla. Justice Assn., 2007, Fla. Women's Hall Of Fame Governor Charlie Crist, 2008. Master Am. Inns of Ct. (Palm Beach County chpt.); mem. ABA (mem. coalition for justice com. 2000-03, Law Day Speech award 1998), Nat. Assn. Women Judges, Am. Inns of Ct. (founding mem. Palm Beach County chpt.), Acad. Fla. Trial Lawyers (bd. dirs., chair spkr.'s bur. program 1984-87, outreach com. 1991-92, co-chair workhorse seminar 1991-92), Assn. Trial Lawyers Am. (vice chair profl. rsch. and devel. dept. 1980-82, chair comml. litig. sect. 1984-85, women's trial lawyer caucus 1986-87, mem. ethics com. 1989-90, conv. planning com. 1992-93), Fla. Assn. Women Lawyers (Lifelong Dedication award 2000), Fla. Bar Assn. (civil rules com. 1981-87, commn. legal needs of children 2000-02, Family Law Visionary award 2004, William M. Hoeveler Jud. Professionalism award 2004, Hugh S. Glickstein Child Adv. of Yr. award 2005), Order of Coif. Office: State Supreme Ct of Florida 500 S Duval St Tallahassee FL 32399-1925 Business E-Mail: supremecourt@flcourts.org.*

PARIS, MIRIAM, state legislator; b. June 30; Lic. realtor; mem. Ward IV Macon City Coun., Ga.; mem. Dist. 26 Ga. State Senate, Atlanta, 2011—. Bd. dirs. New Town Macon, Macon C. of C., Cmty. Partnership, Macon, Manna Ministries, Assn. Informed and Dedicated Sisters. Democrat. Office: PO Box 14056 Macon GA 31203 also: Ga State Senate 305B Coverdell Legis Office Bldg Atlanta GA 30334 Office Phone: 478-737-3036, 404-656-5035.

PARISER, DAVID MICHAEL, dermatologist, educator; b. Norfolk, Va., Sept. 8, 1946; s. Harry and Alice Pariser; m. Carol Odessky, Mar. 25, 1975; children: Michael Steven, Jana Robin. MD, Med. Coll. Va., Richmond, 1972. Cert. Am. Bd. Dermatology, 1977, Va. State Bd. Med. Examiners, Nat. Bd. Med. Examiners, Am. Bd. Pathology, spl. competence in dermatopathology. Intern Med. Coll. Va., Richmond; resident Univ. Miami Sch. Medicine/Jackson Meml. Med. Ctr., 1973—76; prof., dept. dermatology Ea. Va. Med. Sch., Norfolk, 1995—; sr. physician Pariser Dermatology Specialists, Ltd., Norfolk, Va. Spkr. in field. Contbr. articles to profl. jours.; review coms. of several peer-reviewed jours., mem. editl. bds. of several peer-reviewed jours. Pres. Ea. Va. Dermatology Found., Norfolk, 2001—07, bd. dirs., Sentara Health Mgmt., Dermatology Services, Inc., Nat. Psoriasis Found. Recipient Gold Triangle award, Am. Acad. Dermatology, 2007. Fellow: Am. Soc. for Laser Medicine and Surgery, Am. Soc. for Dermatologic Surgery, Am. Acad. Dermatology (secretary-treasurer 2003—06, pres. elect 2008—, pres. 2009—10, bd. dirs., Gold Triangle award for outstanding dedication to isotretinoin awareness initiatives 2002, (9) Continuing Med. Edn. award, (4) Presdl. Citations); mem.: Am. Dermatol. Assn. (pres. 2011—12), Med. Soc. Va., Am. Soc. for Dermatologic Surgery, AMA (Physician's Recognition award 2004), Internat. Hyperhidrosis Soc. (pres., founding mem., bd. dirs. 2003—). Office: Ea Va Med Sch Pariser Dermatology SpecialistsLtd 601 Medical Tower Norfolk VA 23507 Office Fax: 757-625-6940.

PARISH, RICHARD LEE, engineer, consultant; b. Kansas City, Mo., May 31, 1945; s. Charles Lee and Ruth (Duncan) P.; m. Patricia Ann Erickson, June 2, 1968; children: Christie Lynn White, Kerry Anne Parish-Philp. BS in Agrl. Engring., U. Mo., 1967, MS in Agrl. Engring., 1968, PhD, 1970. Registered profl. engr., Ohio. Asst., then assoc. prof. engring. Univ. Ark., Fayetteville, 1969-74; mgr. mech. research and devel. O.M. Scott & Sons Co., Marysville, Ohio, 1974-83; assoc. prof., then prof. La. State U., Baton Rouge, 1983-97; prof. Hammond Rsch. Sta., 1995—2008, resident coord. Coastal area rsch. sta., 2005—08; prof. emeritus Agrl. Engring. La. State U., 2008—. Cons. in equipment patents, equipment safety, product liability, personal injury, design and evaluation; expert witness testimony in agrl. and hort. equipment, patents, 1984—. Contbr. over 120 articles to profl. jours.; patentee in field. Bd. dirs. Agrl. Devel. Found. Recipient Quality award, ITT, 1979, Doyle Chambers award for excellence in rsch., La. State U. Agrl. Ctr., 2001; NSF fellow, 1967—69. Mem. Am. Soc. Agrl. Engrs. (chmn. agrl. chem. application com. 1982-83, chmn. power and machinery divsn. program com. 1986-87, chmn. cultural practices equipment com. 1994-95, chmn. fruit and vegetable prodn. engring. com. 1999-2001), Am. Soc. Hort. Sci. Republican. Baptist. Avocations: old tractors, gardening, woodwork, bicycling. Home: 21135 Highway 16 Amite LA 70422-4733 Office: Richard L Parish PE LLC 21135 Hwy 16 Amite LA 70422 Business E-Mail: parish@agmachineryengr.com.

PARK, ANTHONY J., corporate financial executive; m. Debbie Park; children: Justin Park, Tyler Park. BA in Bus. Economics, U. Calif., Santa Barbara; MBA, Jacksonville U. Contr., asst. contr. Fidelity National Financial, Inc., 1991—2000, chief acctg. officer, 2000—05, exec. v.p., CFO, 2005—. Office: Fidelity National Financial Inc 601 Riverside Ave Jacksonville FL 32204 Office Phone: 904-854-8100. Office Fax: 904-357-1007. Business E-Mail: Anthony.Park@fnf.com.

PARK, CHRISTOPHER S., city manager; b. Bedford, NY, Mar. 27, 1950; BA, Stetson U., 1972, MBA, 1973. With Barnett Banks of Fla., 1973-77; investment banker, 1977-82; v.p., real estate The Haskell Co., 1982—; chmn. civil svc. bd. City of Jacksonville, Fla., 1995—; exec. v.p. Haskel Enterprise Group, Jacksonville, 1999—. Mem. Jacksonville Com. of 100, Fla., 1983—. Mem. Nat. Assn. Office Indsl. Parks, Fla. Chambers. Office: The Haskell Co 111 Riverside Ave Fl 1 Jacksonville FL 32202-4950 Business E-Mail: cspark@thehaskellco.com.

PARK, HEE-JUNG (GLORIA PARK), professional golfer; b. Seoul, Republic of Korea, Feb. 27, 1980; Profl. golfer Korean LPGA, 1998—2000, LPGA Tour, 2000—. Winner Australian Jr. Championship, 1996, 1997, 1998. Achievements include winning Korea LPGA event: Sports Seoul Ladies Open, 1998; winning the Indonesian Ladies Open, 1999; winning LPGA events: Williams Championship, 2001, Sybase Big Apple Classic, 2002. Avocations: movies, music, video games. Office: LPGA 1000 International Golf Dr Daytona Beach FL 32124-1092

PARK, INBEE, professional golfer; b. Republic of Korea, July 12, 1988; d. Song Kim. Grad., KwangWoon U., Republic of Korea. Profl. golfer Futures Tour, 2006, LPGA Tour, 2007—. Recipient Vare trophy, LPGA, 2012. Achievements include winning LPGA Tour major championships: US Women's Open Championship, 2008, 2013; Kraft Nabisco Championship, 2013; LPGA Championship, 2013; winning LPGA Tour events: Evian Masters, Sime Darby LPGA Malaysia, 2012; Honda LPGA Thailand, North Texas LPGA Shootout, Walmart NW Arkansas Championship, 2013; winning LPGA of Japan Tour events: Nishijin Ladies Classic, Japan LPGA Tour Championship Ricoh Cup, 2010; Daikin Orchid Ladies, 2011; Fundokin Ladies, 2012. Office: c/o Ladies Profl Golf Assn 100 International Golf Dr Daytona Beach FL 32124-1092*

PARK, JUNG CHUL, finance educator; married. MBA, Binghamton U. SUNY, 2003; PhD, U. South Fla., Tampa, 2007. Adj. instr., grad. asst. U. South Fla., 2003—07; asst. prof., fin. and humana found., Mike McCallister endowed prof. La. Tech. U., Ruston, 2007—11; assoc. prof., fin. and McLain family prof. Auburn U., Ala., 2011—. Mem.: Korea Am. Fin. Assn., Fin. Mgmt. Assn., Am. Fin. Assn. Office: Auburn University 303 Lowder Hall Auburn AL 36849 Office Fax: 334-844-4960. Business E-Mail: jzp0023@auburn.edu.*

PARK, LELAND MADISON, retired librarian; b. Alexandria, La., Oct. 21, 1941; s. Arthur Harris and Jane Rebecca (Leland) P. Student, McCallie Sch., 1957—59; AB, Davidson Coll., 1963; MLS, Emory U., 1964; postgrad., Simmons Coll., 1968; AdvM in Libr. Sci., Fla. State U., 1973, PhD, 1974. Reference libr. Pub. Libr. of Charlotte and Mecklenburg County, NC, 1964-65; head reference and student pers. Davidson (N.C.) Coll. Libr., 1967-70, asst. dir., 1970-75, dir., 1975—2006. Cons. coll. cons. network So. Assn. Colls and Schs.; vis. lectr. Emory U., summer 1972; temporary instr. Fla. State U., 1973; libr. cons.; conf. spkr.; chmn. state adv. com. Libr. Svcs. and Constrn. Act, 1975-79; mem. N.C. State Libr. Commn., 1983-85, 87-92, chmn., 1989-92; mem. Davidson (N.C.) Town Appearance Commn., 1986-93, design rev. bd. 98-, Hist. Preservation Commn., 1994-96; mem. editl. bd. CHOICE, 2003-06. Editor Southeastern Librarian, 1976-78; acad. sect. editor N.C. Libraries, 1972-77; contbr. articles to profl. jours. Mem. Wake County Citizens for Better Librs., N.C., 1965-67; sec. com. libr. affairs Piedmont U. Ctr., 1969-70, chmn., 1970-72; mem. nat. bd. cons. NEH, 1976-2006; clk. mission com. St. Alban's Episcopal Mission, Davidson, N.C., 1969-72, layreader, 1970-75, treas., 1975-86; bd. dirs. statewide computer libr. resource network NC-LIVE, 1997—2006. Recipient H.W. Wilson Libr. periodical award, 1979, Alumni Achievement award The McCallie Sch., 1989, Order of Long Leaf Pine presented by N.C. Gov. James G. Martin, 1993, Jack Burney Pub. Svc. award Town Davidson, 2012, Alumni Svc. award Davidson Coll., 2013. Mem. ALA, Southeastern Libr. Assn. (chmn. coll. and univ. sect. 1976-78, exec. bd. 1976-78), N.C. Libr. Assn. (2d v.p. 1975-77, 1st v.p. 1981-83, pres. 1983-85), Metrolina Libr. Assn. (pres. 1969-71), Mecklenburg County Libr. Assn. (treas. 1969-70), Soc. of Cin. (2d v.p Ga. Soc. 1982-83), SAR, Mil. Order World Wars, Raleigh Jaycees (chmn. libr. com. 1965-67), Res. Officer Assn., SCV, Soc. Colonial Wars, S.C. Huguenot Soc., Rotary, Beta Phi Mu, Sigma Nu, Omicron Delta Kappa, Davidson Coll. (bd. visitors). Home: PO Box 777 235 Ney Circle Davidson NC 28036-0777 E-mail: lepark@aol.com.

PARK, YONG-MOON, preventive medicine physician, educator; b. Seoul, Republic of Korea, Mar. 1, 1969; s. Kyun-Hee Park and Young-Sun Lee; m. Janette Heejin, July 5, 2003; children: Edward Jiho, Clara Jimin, Olivia Seyoung. MD in Medicine, Cath. U. Korea, 1996, MMSc in Preventive Medicine, 1999, PhD, 2005; MS in Genetic Epidemiology, Washington U., St. Louis, 2008. Diplomate Korean Bd. Preventive Medicine. Instr. dept. preventive medicine Cath. U. Korea, 2003—05, asst. prof. dept. preventive medicine, 2005—10, assoc. prof. dept. preventive medicine, 2011—. Mem. com. on diabetes treatment Korean Diabetes Assn., 2005—07; mem. institutional review bd. Catholic Med. Ctr., 2009—; bd. dirs. Korean Soc. Epidemiology, 2009—, Korean Diabetes Assn., Korea Soc. Genomic Epidemiology, Korea Genome Orgn., Internat. Genetic Epidemiology Soc., Am. Heart Assn., Korean Soc. Preventive Medicine; bd. mem. Korean Soc. Hypertension, Korean Soc. Cardiovascular Disease Prevention, Am. Diabetes Assn.; ad-hoc reviewer Korean Jour. Occupl. Health, Korean Jour. Epidemiology, Tohoku Jour. Exptl. Medicine, Jour. Preventive Medicine and Pub. Health, Blood Pressure, Experimental and Molecular Medicine, Epidemiology & Health; statis. advisor Jour. Korean Soc. Endocrinology, Korea Ctr. Disease Control and Prevention, Diabetes and Metabolism Jour.; ad-hoc reviewer African J. Biotechnology, Jour. Korean Pub. Health Assn.; mem. Cardiovascular Diabetology, Jour. Nutrition and Metabolism, N.Am. Jour. Med. Sci., Digestive Disease and Scis., Diabetes Care. Pub. health doctor Ministry of Health and Welfare, 2000—03, Republic of Korea. Recipient award, Washington U., 2008; Alumni grant, Cath. U. Korea, 2005, grant, Korean Med. Assn., 1998, Korea Inst. Health and Social Affairs, 2005, Korea Rsch. Found., 2005. Mem.: Sanofi-aventis Korea, Cath. Med. Ctr. Rsch. Found. Achievements include research in epidemiologic characteristics of obesity hypertension, metabolic syndrome, and diabetes mellitus in Korean population; the identification of genetic epidemiologic characteristics of metabolic syndrome. Avocations: travel, golf, Go, classical music, photography. Office: University SC Dept Epidemiology and Biostat/Sch Pub He 915 Greene Columbia SC 29208 Office Phone: 803-800-4549. Office Fax: 803-777-2524. Personal E-mail: markympark@gmail.com.*

PARKE, DAVID WILKIN, II, ophthalmologist, educator, health facility administrator; b. Columbus, Ohio, May 19, 1951; s. David William Parke and Eunice Joyce Erikson; m. Julie Diane Thorne, Sept. 15, 1975; children: David W. III, Laura Thorne, Lindsey Diane. AB, Stanford U., 1973; MD, Baylor Coll. Medicine, 1977. Diplomate Am. Bd. Ophthalmology. Resident in internal medicine Baylor Coll. Medicine, Houston, 1977-78, resident in ophthalmology, 1978-81, fellow in med. retina, 1981-82, asst. prof., 1983-90, assoc. prof., 1990-92; fellow diseases and surgery of the retina and vitreous Med. Coll. of Wis., 1982-83; prof., chair dept. ophthalmology U. Okla., Oklahoma City, 1992—; pres., CEO McGee Eye Inst., Oklahoma City, 1992—. Chmn., bd. dirs. Medem, Inc., 2004—; vice chair Ophthalmic Mut. Ins. Co., 2005—. Active Okla. Econ. Devel. Found., 1992, Okla. Health Ctr. Found., 1992—; trustee Presbyn. Health Found., 1995-2006, Casady Sch., 1997-2004, vice chair, 1999-2004; mng. dir. Stephenson Laser Ctr., 1996—; bd. mgrs. Okla. Health Alliance, 1995-97; dir. Oklahoma City C. of C. Fellow: Am. Acad. Ophthalmology (assoc. sec. 1983—92, trustee 2000—, sr. sec. for ophthalmic practice 2002—, pres. 2007—08, Honor award 1980, Sr. Honor award 1998); mem.: Am. Soc. Ret. Specialists, Retina Soc., Assn. Univ. Profs. Ophthalmology (trustee 1997—2003, pres. 2001—02), Greater Oklahoma City C. of C. (bd. dirs. 1998—99, 2004—), Alpha Omega Alpha. Office: Dean A McGee Eye Institute 608 Stanton L Young Blvd Oklahoma City OK 73104-5065 E-mail: david-parke@ouhsc.edu.

PARKER, ANNISE DANETTE, mayor, Houston; b. Houston, Tex., May 17, 1956; life ptnr. Kathy Hubbard; 2 adopted children. BA in Anthropology, Psychology and Sociology, Rice U., 1978. With Mosbacher Energy, Houston; at-large mem. Houston City Coun., 1998—2004; contr. City of Houston, 2004—10, mayor, 2010—. Former co-owner Inklings Bookshop. Adv. bd. mem. Holocaust Mus. Houston; pres. Houston GLBT Polit. Caucus, 1986; bd. dirs. Houston - Galveston Area Coun. & Tex. Environ. Rsch. Consortium; adv. bd. Trees for Houston, Houston Zoo Found., Montrose Counseling Ctr., Ctr. Houston's Future. Recipient Good Brick Award, Greater Houston Preservation Alliance, Disting. Local Elected Official award, Tex. Recreation & Park Soc.; named Coun. Mem. of the Yr., Houston Police Officers Union; named one of Houston's Most Influential Women, Houston Woman mag., 2008, The 100 Most Influential People in the World, TIME mag., 2010. Mem.: Neartown Civic Assn. (pres. 1995—97). Democrat. Office: City of Houston PO Box 1562 Houston TX 77251 Business E-Mail: mayor@houstontx.gov.*

PARKER, DAVID RAYMOND, finance company executive; b. Corpus Christi, Tex., July 6, 1943; s. Jesse Raymond P. and Mary Jane (Valentine) Arrington; m. Judith Evans, Aug. 2, 1969. BS in Engring., U. Tex., 1966; MBA, Harvard U., 1972. COO The Archstone Partnerships; dist. ops. mgr. AT&T Long Lines div., Dallas, 1968-70; mgr. Boston Cons. Group, 1972-76; v.p., strategic planning Am. Can Co., Greenwich, Conn., 1976-78, sr. v.p. metal container packaging, 1978-81, sr. v.p. & sector exec. metal container packaging, 1981-83, exec. v.p., packaging, 1983-84; sr. exec. v.p., COO, Bus. Svcs. Group Ryder System, Inc., Miami, Fla., 1984-89, pres., Vehicle Leasing & Svcs. Divsn., 1989. Bd. dir. SFN Group, Inc., Tupperware Brands Corp., Am. Can of Can., Am. Can (U.K.) Ltd., Envases Venezolanos, 1983—; bd. dirs. Can. Mfrs. Inst., 1981—, Sun Bank/Miami N.A., Sun Banks, Inc. Active Nat. Planning Assn., Washington, 1982, Internat. Mgmt. and Devel., 1982, U.S. Coun. Internat. Bus., N.Y.C., 1982; bd. dirs. Exec. Coun. on Fgn. Diplomats, Armonk, N.Y., Inst. for Ednl. Leadership, Inc., Washington; bd. trustees Fla. Internat. U. With USAR, 1968-74. Harvard U. Fredrich Sheldon fellow, 1972; Baker scholar Harvard U., 1972 Mem.: Harvard Faculty, Harvard Bus. Episcopalian. Avocation: golf. Office: The Archstone Partnerships 360 Madison Ave 20th Fl New York NY 10017 Office Phone: 212-201-0500. Business E-Mail: davidparker@tupperware.com.

PARKER, ELLIS D., retired military officer; b. Adams, Tenn., Nov. 1, 1932; s. Ellis A. and Lorene P.; m. Judy C. Matthews, Dec. 24, 1952; children: Donald S., Phillip R., David B. BS in Psychology, U. Nebr., 1972; MPA, Shippensburg U., 1979; LLD (hon.), Miles U., 1989. Rated aviator FAA. Commd. 2d lt. U.S. Army, 1957, advanced through ranks to lt. gen., 1992, aviation officer, comdr. 17th aviation brigade Republic of Korea, 1978-80; dir. requirements army staff Pentagon, Washington, 1980-83; asst. divsn. comdr. 101st airborne divsn. U.S. Army, Ft. Campbell, Ky., 1983-84, commdg. gen. Army

Aviation Ctr. Sch. Ft. Rucker, Ala., 1984-89; dir. army staff Pentagon, Washington, 1989-92; bd. dirs. Can. Aviation Electronics, 1993—2008, chmn., CEO Can., 1993—2001, chmn. govt. security com., 2001—08; co-chmn., bd. dirs. Doss Aviation. Bd. dirs. Doss Aviation, Colorado Springs; chmn., bd. dirs. Hammer Constrn. Co., Samson, Ala., Aereus Internat., Enterprise, Ala. Contbr. articles to profl. jour. Chmn. Fort Rucker Mus. Found., 1995—; adv. bd. Troy U., Dotham, 1992—2002; chair retiree coun. for chief of staff U.S. Army, 1993-99; co-chair Dept. of Def. Retiree Coun., 1994-99. Decorated D.S.M. with oak leaf cluster, D.F.C., Legion of Merit, Bronze Star with two oak leaf clusters, Meritorious Svc. medals, 23 Air medals; named to Hall of Honor Bd. by Gov. Ala., 1993-; named to USAF Gathering of Eagles, Maxwell, AFB, Ala. Mem.: C. of C., Army Assn. Am., Enterprise C. of C. (chmn bd. dirs. 1993—95), Assn. U.S. Army (mem. exec. com. Ft. Rucker chpt. 1994, named to Army Aviation Hall of Fame 1994), Ret. Officers Assn. (bd. mem.), Army Aviation Assn. Am. (pres.,, Order of St. Michel, Gold 1992), Enterprise Rotary Club (Paul Harris fellow). Republican. Avocations: flying, hunting, fishing, volunteering in community. Home and Office: 128 Deer Run Strut Enterprise AL 36330-7812

PARKER, FRANK LEON, environmental engineering educator, consultant; b. Somerville, Mass., Mar. 23, 1926; s. Benjamin James and Bertha (Cohen) Parker; m. Elaine Marilyn Goldman, Aug. 22, 1954; children: Nina Madeline, Aaron Bennet, Stephan Alexander, David Seth. BS, MIT, 1948; MS, Harvard U., 1950, PhD, 1955. Registered profl. engr., N.Y. Engr. U.S. Bur. Reclamation, Riverton, Wyo., 1948; field engr. Rockland Light & Power Co., Nyack, NY, 1949—50; cons. Howard M. Turner, Boston, 1955; sect. chief IAEA, Vienna, 1960—61; chief radioactive waste disposal rsch. sect. Oak Ridge Nat. Lab., 1956—66; prof. environ. engring. Vanderbilt U., Nashville, 1967—89, disting. prof. environ. and water resources engring., 1989—, Alexander Heard Disting. prof., 1988; Westinghouse Savannah River Disting. Sci. prof. Clemson (S.C.) U., 1991—96, emminent scientist prof., 1997—. Harvie Branscomb Disting. prof., 1994—95; sr. rschr. Beijer Inst., 1983—87, Internat. Inst. Applied Sys. Analysis, 1995—; chmn. bd. radioactive waste mgmt. NAS, 1985—91; commr. Monitored Retrievable Storage Rev. Commn., 1988—89. Co-author: Physical and Engineering Aspects of Thermal Pollution, 1970, Engineering Aspects of Thermal Pollution, 1969, Biological Aspects of Thermal Pollution, 1969. Mem. Port Authority Nashville, 1979—90, Nashville Appeals Bd., 1979—88, Jewish Cmty. Rels. Coun., Nashville, 1981—87. With US Army, 1943—46. Mem.: AAAS, NAE, Soc. Risk Analysis, Nat. Coun. Radiation Protection and Measurements (consociate), Health Physics Soc., Am. Geophys. Union, Am. Nuc. Soc. Home: 4400 Iroquois Ave Nashville TN 37205-3832 Office: Vanderbilt U Station B PO Box 1596 Nashville TN 37235 Home Phone: 615-298-2578; Office Phone: 615-343-2371. Business E-Mail: parkerfl@vuse.vanderbilt.edu.

PARKER, GERALD M., osteopath, researcher; b. Olean, NY, Nov. 20, 1943; s. Richard and Kathleen (Manwaring) P.; m. Linda Kay Stuart, Dec. 28, 1968; children: Kimberly, Gerald, Cassandra, Kevin. BA, Western Wash. U., 1965; DO, Kirksville Coll. Osteopathy & Surgery, 1969. Intern Art Centre Hosp., Detroit, 1969-70; ptnr. Doctor's Clinic, Amarillo, Tex., 1970. Dir. S.W. Inst. Preventive Medicine, Amarillo, 1978—, Hyperbaric Oxygen Ctr., Amarillo, 1979—; appeared on That's Incredible TV show, 1982. Contbr. articles to profl. jours. Pres. S.W. Amarillo Little Dribblers Assn., 1979—; coach Girls Nat. Champion Basketball Teams, 1981, 83-87, 89. Named Physician of Yr., Nat. Rep. Com. Physician Adv. Bd., 2003. Fellow Am. Acad. Med. Preventics; mem. S.W. Acad. Preventive Medicine (pres. 1980—), Am. Osteo. Assn. Methodist. Avocation: athletics. Office: Doctors Clinic 4714 S Western St Amarillo TX 79109-5950 Office Phone: 806-355-8263.

PARKER, JEFFREY SCOTT, law educator; b. Alexandria, Va., Sept. 6, 1952; s. Clarence Franklin and Mary Florence (Partlow) P. B in Indsl. Engring., Ga. Inst. Tech., 1975; JD, U. Va., 1978. Bar: N.Y. 1979, U.S. Dist. Ct. (ea. and so. dists.) N.Y. 1979, U.S. Ct. Appeals (3d cir.) 1981, U.S. Ct. Appeals (2d cir.) 1984, U.S. Supreme Ct. 1984, U.S. Ct. Appeals (fed. cir.) 1985, U.S. Ct. Appeals (4th cir.) 1992, U.S. Ct. Appeals (D.C. cir.) 1997. Assoc. Sullivan & Cromwell, NYC, 1978-86, Sacks Montgomery, NYC, 1986-87; dep. chief counsel U.S. Sentencing Commn., Washington, 1987-88; of counsel Sacks Montgomery, NYC, 1988-90; assoc. prof. law George Mason U Sch. Law, Arlington, Va., 1990-94; prof. George Mason U. Sch. Law, Arlington, Va., 1994—, assoc. dean acad. affairs, 1994-96. Cons. counsel U.S. Sentencing Commn., Washington, 1988-89. Contbr. articles to law revs.; mem. editorial bd. Va. Law Rev., 1976-78. Mem. ABA, Assn. of Bar of City of N.Y., N.Y. State Bar Assn., Am. Law and Econs. Assn., Am. Econs. Assn., Am. Judicature Soc. Office: George Mason U Sch of Law 3401 Fairfax Dr Arlington VA 22201-4411 E-mail: jparke3@gmu.edu.*

PARKER, JOHN R., JR., food products executive, lawyer; b. Anderson, S.C., 1951; BA, Univ. Ga.; JD, Univ. NC, 1973. Bar: Ga., US Ct. Appeals, 11th Cir. Atty. Coca-Cola Co., 1987—92; v.p., gen. counsel The Coca-Cola Bottling Co. of N.Y., 1992—95; counsel for Nordic and No. Eurasia Divsn. Coca-Cola Co., 1995; gen. counsel. European group Coca-Cola Enterprises, Inc., 1996—99, sr. v.p., gen. counsel, 1999—2004, v.p., gen. mgr. west ctrl. region, 2004—05, sr. v.p. strategic initiatives, 2005—08, sr. v.p., gen. counsel and strategic initiatives, 2008—. Editor (articles): UNC Law Rev. Mem.: State Bar Ga., ABA, Order of the Coif. Office: Coca-Cola Enterprises 2500 Windy Ridge Pkwy Atlanta GA 30339

PARKER, JOHN VICTOR, federal judge; b. Baton Rouge, Oct. 14, 1928; m. Mary Elizabeth Fridge, Sept. 3, 1949; children: John Michael, Robert Fridge, Linda Anne. BA, La. State U., 1949, JD, 1952. Bar: La. 1952. Atty. Parker & Parker, Baton Rouge, 1954-66; asst. parish atty. City of Baton Rouge, Parish of East Baton Rouge, 1956-66; atty. Sanders, Downing, Kean & Cazedessus, Baton Rouge, 1966-79; chief judge US Dist. Ct. (mid. dist.) La., Baton Rouge, 1979—98, sr. judge, 1998—. Vis. lectr. law La. State U. Law Sch. With JAG US Army, 1952—54. Mem.: ABA, Baton Rouge Bar Assn. (past pres.), La. State Bar Assn. (past mem. bd. govs.), Am. Arbitration Assn., Am. Judicature Soc., Baton Rouge Country Club, Kiwanis (past pres.), Masons (32 degree), Order of Coif, Phi Delta Phi. Democrat. Office: Russell B Long Fed Bldg and Courthouse 777 Florida St Ste 355 Baton Rouge LA 70801-1717 Office Phone: 225-389-3568.

PARKER, KATHLEEN, syndicated columnist; b. Winter Haven, Fla., Sept. 26, 1951; d. J. Hal Jr. and Martha Ayer (Harley) Connor; m. Sherwood McKissick Cleveland, Nov. 12, 1988; 1 child, John Connor Parker stepchildren: Sherwood McKissick Jr., Samuel Henry Edmunds. Attended, Converse Coll., Spartanburg, SC; BA in Spanish Lit., Fla. State U., 1973, MA in Spanish Lit., 1976. Staff writer Charleston Evening Post, SC, 1978-80, Fla. Times-Union, Jacksonville, 1980-82, Birmingham Post-Herald, Ala., 1982-83, San Jose Mercury News, Calif., 1983-87; staff writer, columnist Orlando Sentinel, Fla., 1987-88; writer, contbr. Weekly Standard, TIME, Town & Country, Cosmopolitan, Fortune Small Bus.; nat. syndicated columnist Tribune Media Svcs., 1995—2006, Washington Post Writers Group, 2006—; co-host Parker Spitzer CNN, 2010—11. Instr. U. SC Coll. Journalism, Columbia, 1988—89; consulting faculty mem. Buckley Sch. Pub. Speaking, Camden, SC, 1991—; mem. Forum page bd. contributors USA Today, 1996—. Author: Save the Males: Why Men Matter, Why Women Should Care, 2008; regular appearances include The O'Reilly Factor, Chris Matthews Show. Recipient H.L. Mencken writing award, Balt. Sun, 1993, Pulitzer prize for Commentary, 2010. Mailing: c/o Washington Post Writers Group 1150 15th St NW Washington DC 20071

PARKER, KEVIN T., information technology executive; BS in Acctg., Clarkson U. With O'Neil Data Sys., Toshiba Am. Info. Sys., CalComp, Price Waterhouse; contr., sys. product divsn. Std. Microsystems; sr. v.p. fin. and adminstrn. Fujitsu Computer Products Am., 1996—99; sr. v.p., CFO Aspect Comm. Corp., 1999—2000, PeopleSoft, Inc., Pleasanton, Calif., 2000—02, exec. v.p. fin. & adminstrn., 2002—04, co-pres., 2004; chmn., pres. & CEO Deltek Systems, Inc., Herndon, Va., 2004—. Bd. dirs. Polycom, Inc. Fellow, Henry Crown Aspen Inst. Office: Deltek Inc 2291 Wood Oak Dr Herndon VA 20171-2823 Office Phone: 703-734-8606. Office Fax: 703-734-1146. Business E-Mail: KevinParker@deltek.com.

PARKER, LEE BRYAN, retired physician; b. Dermott, Ark., May 10, 1929; s. Lee Bryan and Viola Lee Parker; m. Beverly Edith Brosell, Dec. 23, 1951; children: Susan Leigh Brewer, Elizabeth Ann Beecher, Steven Lee, Edith Lynn Hegwood. BS, U. Ark., Fayetteville, 1950; MD, U. Ark., Little Rock, 1954. Lic. physician Ark., 1954. Intern Crawford Long Hosp., Atlanta, 1954—55; pvt. practice Dermott, 1957—59, McGehee, Ark., 1959—67; gen. practice Doctor's Bldg., Fayetteville, Ark., 1967—74; dir. U. Ark. Med. Scis., Area Health Edn. Ctr. NW, Fayetteville, 1974—96; ret., 1996. Chief med. staff S.t Mary's Hosp., Dermott, 1964—65, McGehee Desha Hosp., Ark., 1965—67, Fayetteville City Hosp., 1975—76, Wash. Regional Med. Ctr., Fayetteville, 1980—81; vis. prof. Kaohsiung Med. U., Taiwan, 1986; bd. dirs. Ark. Regional Med. Program, Little Rock, 1967—70, Butterfield Trail Village, Fayetteville, 2001—06; dir. continuing med. edn. U. Ark. Sch. Medicine, Little Rock, 1970—74, adj. prof., 1996—; adv. bd. U. Ark. Sch. Medicine, Area Health Edn. Ctr. NW, Fayetteville, 2004—. Sec. Wash. County Med. Soc., Fayetteville, 1973—74. Capt. USAF, 1955—57. Recipient Disting. Svc. award, McGehee Jaycees, 1963, Distinguised Svc. award, U. Ark. for Med. Scis. Coll. Medicine, 1992, Founders Soc. award, U. Ark. for Med. Scis., 1996, Eagle award, Wash. Regional Med. Found., 1999, Diamond Soc. award, Ark. Cmty. Found., 2004, Doyne Soc. award, U. Ctrl. Ark., 2004, Legacy Soc. award, U. Ark. for Med. Scis., 2005. Mem.: Ark. Acad. Family Physicians (life; bd. dirs. 1962—67, chmn. continuing edn. com. 1971—89, pres. 1982—83, alt. del. 1984—89, Family Dr. of Yr. 1993), Ark. Med. Soc. (life; councilor 4th dist. 1965—67, jour. editor 1993). Independent. Methodist. Avocations: hunting, fishing, golf, gardening. Office: University Ark Med Sci 1125 N Coll Fayetteville AR 72703

PARKER, MARIAN F., law librarian, educator; BA, U. NC, Greensboro; MSLS, U. NC, Chapel Hill, 1979; JD, Wake Forest U., 1978. Rsch. libr., instr,and Instructor Duke U., 1979—80; assoc. dir. pub. svcs., asst. prof. SUNY, Buffalo, 1980—83; dir. Law Libr., asst. prof. law U. Tulsa, 1983—86; mgr. legal quality, competitive analysis mgr. Mead Data Ctrl., 1986—90; assoc. law libr. rsch. svcs. Harvard U., 1990—92; dir. Law Libr., prof. law NYU, 1992—94; spl. asst. edn. tech. NC Dept. Human Resources, 1994—96; dir. profl. rels. Lexis-Nexis/Matthew Bender & Co., 1996—99; dir. Profl. Ctr. Libr., prof. law Wake Forest U. Sch. Law, Winston-Salem, NC, 1999—, assoc. dean info. svcs. Office: Wake Forest U Sch Law PO Box 7206, Reynolda Station Winston Salem NC 27109 Office Phone: 336-758-4879. Office Fax: 336-758-4301. E-mail: parkermf@law.wfu.edu.

PARKER, RICHARD WILSON, retired rail transportation executive, lawyer; b. Cleve., June 14, 1943; s. Edgar Gael and Pauline (Wilson) P.; m. Helen Margaret Shober, Jan. 3, 1998; children from previous marriage: Brian Jeffrey, Lauren Michelle, Lisa Christine. BA in Econs. cum laude, U. Redlands, 1965; JD cum laude, Northwestern U., 1968. Bar: Ohio 1968, Va. 1974. Assoc. Arter & Hadden, Cleve., 1968—71; asst. gen. atty. Norfolk & Western Ry. Co., Cleve. and Roanoke, Va., 1971-74, asst. gen. solicitor Roanoke, 1974-78, gen. atty., 1978-84, Norfolk So. Corp., 1985-88, sr. gen. atty., 1988-93, asst. v.p. real estate, 1993-99, v.p. properties, 1999-2000, v.p. real estate, 2000—03. Mem. Va. State Bar. Presbyterian. Office: 3 Commercial Pl Norfolk VA 23510-2108

PARKER, SARAH ELIZABETH, state supreme court chief justice; b. Charlotte, NC, Aug. 23, 1942; d. Augustus and Zola Elizabeth (Smith) Parker. AB, U. NC, 1964, JD, 1969; LHD (hon.), Queens Coll., 1998. Bar: NC 1969, US Dist. Ct. (mid., ea. and we. dists.) NC. Vol. US Peace Corps, Ankara, Turkey, 1964-66; pvt. practice Charlotte, 1969-84; judge NC Ct. Appeals, Raleigh, 1985—92; assoc. justice Supreme Ct. NC, Raleigh, 1993—2005, chief justice, 2006—. Bd. visitors U. NC, Chapel Hill, 1993—97; pres. Mecklenburg County Dem. Women, Charlotte, 1973; NC ct. commr., 1999—; bd. dirs. YWCA, Charlotte, 1982—85. Recipient Woman of Achievement award, Nat. Fedn. Women's Clubs, 1997, Disting. Woman of NC award, 1997, Humanitarian award, NC Assn. Black County Officials, 2003; named Judge of Yr., NC Women Attorneys Assn., 2002. Mem.: ABA, Women Attys. Assn. (Gwyneth David Pub. Svc. award 1986), NC Internat. Women's Forum, Wake County Bar Assn., NC Bar Assn. (v.p. 1987—88), Mecklenburg County Bar (sec.-treas. 1982—84), Inst. Jud. Adminstrn. Episcopalian. Office: NC Supreme Ct PO Box 2170 Raleigh NC 27602-2170*

PARKER, SCOTT JEROME, US marshal; With Nashville Police Dept., NC, 1987—89; asst. comdr. Roanoke Chowan Narcotics Task Force, Hertford County, NC, 1989—95; rose through ranks to lt., dir. narcotics divsn. Nash County Sheriff's Office, NC, 1995—2010; US marshal (ea. dist.) NC US Dept. Justice, 2010—. Office: Terry Sanford Fed Bldg & Courthouse 310 New Bern Ave Raleigh NC 27601 Office Phone: 919-856-4153.

PARKER, STEVE, state legislator; b. Miss., May 27, 1951; s. Luther and Gracie (Scrimpshire) Parker; m. Rita Kay Hammett, 1976; children: Christy, Kevin. BA, Newberry Coll., 1973; MAT, Converse Coll., 1975; grad, U. SC, 1979. Educator Aiken and Cherokee Sch. Districts Spartanburg County Schools., 1973—93; mem. Dist. 2 Spatanburg County Coun. Sch. Bd., 2002—04; owner Steve Parker Painting Inc., 1973—; mem. Dist. 37 SC House of Reps., SC, 2008—. Republican. Bapt. Office: Dist/Home Office 330 Farm Lake Rd Spartanburg SC 29316 also: Capitol Office 404C Blatt Bldg Columbia SC 29201 Home Phone: 864-578-6298; Office Phone: 864-978-0195, 803-212-6878. E-mail: steveparker@schouse.org.

PARKER, TAN, state legislator; m. Beth Parker; children: Lauren, Ashley. B, U. Dallas; M, London Sch. Economics. Former intern to Pres. George H.W. Bush The White House, Washington; former intern US Dept. Commerce, London; former fin. advisor Dean Witter Reynolds; with Computer Scis. Corp., former regional v.p.; exec. v.p. Trivac Ltd.; former chmn. Tex. Indsl. Devel. Corp.; mem. Dist. 63 Tex. House of Representatives, 2007—. Mem.: Denton County Young Reps. (co-founder). Republican. Office: 800 Parker Sq Ste 245 Flower Mound TX 75028-7434 also: Room E2.608 Capitol Extension PO Box 2910 Austin TX 78768 Office Phone: 972-724-8477, 512-463-0688.

PARKER, TOM, state supreme court justice, lawyer; b. Montgomery, Ala., Aug. 19, 1951; s. Tom Parker and Gloria Parker Pennington; m. Dottie James. BA, Dartmouth Coll., 1973; JD, Vanderbilt U., 1978; attended, U. Sao Paulo Sch. of Law, Brazil. Prtnr. Parker & Kotouc; asst. atty. gen. State of Ala.; legal adviser, to Chief Justice Ala. Supreme Ct.; dep. administrative dir., gen. counsel Ala. Ct. System, 2001—03; assoc. justice Ala. Supreme Ct., 2004—. Former special projects mgr. Found. for Moral Law. Founding exec. dir. Ala. Family Alliance (now Alabama Policy Institute), Ala. Family Advocates. Grantee Rotary Internat. Fellowship, U. São Paulo Sch of Law, Brazil. Office: Ala Supreme Ct 300 Dexter Ave Montgomery AL 36104-3741*

PARKER, TONY (WILLIAM ANTHONY PARKER II), professional basketball player; b. Bruges, Belgium, May 17, 1982; s. Tony Parker and Pamela Firestone; m. Eva Longoria, July 7, 2007 (div. 2011). Degree in Econ., Nat. Inst. Physical Edn., Paris. Guard San Antonio Spurs, 2001—. Mem. French nat. team FIBA European Championships, Turkey, 2001, Sweden, 2003, Serbia and Montenegro, 2005, Spain, 2007, Poland, 2009, Lithuania, 2011, Summer Olympic Games, London, 2012. Singer: (albums) Top of the Game, 2007. Decorated Chevalier French Legion of Honor; recipient Bronze medal, FIBA European Championships, 2005, Silver medal, 2011; named Champion of French Champions, L'Equipe, 2003, NBA Finals MVP, 2007; named to All-Rookie First Team, NBA, 2002, Western Conf. All-Star Team, 2006, 2007, 2009, 2012, 2013. Achievements include member of NBA Championship winning San Antonio Spurs, 2003, 2005, 2007; winner of the NBA All-Star Weekend Skills Challenge, 2012. Office: San Antonio Spurs 1 AT&T Center Parkway San Antonio TX 78219

PARKER, WILLIAM, education educator; b. Savannah, Ga., May 23, 1965; s. William Robert and Carolyn Parker; m. Maria Susanne Meza-Keuthen, Aug. 4, 1989. PhD, U. Nebr., 1992. Asst. prof. Duke U. Med. Ctr., Durham, NC, 1993—. Co-author: more than 90 sci. articles. Grantee, NIH. Mem.: Fedn. Am. Socs. for Exptl. Biology, Protein Soc., Sigma Xi Sci. Rsch. Soc., AAAS, Am. Soc. Transplant Surgeons, Am. Chem. Soc. Achievements include discovery of new model for host-bacterial interactions in the gut, the apparent function of the cecal appendix in humans and a variety of other mammals; new model for evaluation of the hygiene hypothesis; evidence for universal protein folding mechanism proposed by Valery Lim; new member of the family of antibodies that includes isohemagglutinins. Home: 1023 Wells St Durham NC 27707 Office: Duke Univ Med Ctr DUMC Box 2605 Durham NC 27710 Business E-Mail: bparker@duke.edu.

PARKERSON, GEORGE ROBERT, JR., medical educator; s. George Robert and Nettie Sue Parkerson; m. Mary McCowen, June 4, 1949 (dec. 2006); children: Sue, George Robert III, Ann Jones, Lyn Carpenter. MD, Duke U. Sch. Medicine, Durham, NC, 1953; MPH in Epidemiology, U. NC Sch. Pub. Health, Chapel Hill, 1977. Diplomate Am. Bd. Family Practice, 1984. Pvt. practice, Winder, Ga., 1955—73; dir. family practice residency program Med. Ctr. Ctrl. Ga., Macon, 1973—74. Asst. prof. family practice Med. Coll. Ga., Augusta, 1973—74; asst. prof. cmty. family medicine Duke U. Sch. Medicine, Durham, NC, 1974—80, assoc. prof. cmty. family medicine, 1980—88, chmn., 1985—94, prof., 1988—; adj. asst. prof. U. NC Sch. Pub. Health, 1978—83, adj. assoc. prof., 1983—89, adj. prof., 1989—; chmn. Instl. Rev. Bd. Clin. Investigations, Duke U. Health Sys., Durham, NC, 2000—. Contbr. scientific papers. Seaman first class USN, 1945—46, Bainbridge, Newport, Boston, destroyer duty on USS Robert L. Wilson. Mem.: North Am. Primary Care Rsch. Group, NC Acad. Family Physicians, Soc. Teachers Family Medicine, Am. Acad. Family Physicians (life). Office: Duke Univ Med Ctr Durham NC 27710

PARKHILL, KAREN, diversified financial services company executive; B in Bus. Adminstrn. and Math., So. Meth. U., Dallas; MBA, U. Chgo. Securities analyst Rauscher Pierce Refsnes, Inc. (now called Dain Rauscher), Dallas; from assoc. in mergers and acquisitions group to mng. dir. investment banking coverage group JP Morgan Chase & Co., 1992—2006, CFO comml. banking, 2007—11; vice chmn., mem. mgmt. policy com. Comerica, Dallas, 2011—, CFO, 2011—. Founder, chmn. Leadership Coun. for Mercy Home for Boys and Girls, Chgo. Named one of The 25 Women to Watch, American Banker, 2011. Office: Comerica Corp Hdqs Comerica Bank Tower 1717 Main St Dallas TX 75201

PARKHILL, SUSAN, finance company executive; BA in Mktg., Cameron U. Joined SLM Corp., 1990, sr. dir., call ctr. ops.; v.p., call ctr. ops. Sallie Mae - SLM Corp., 2008—. Office: SLM Corp 12061 Bluemont Way Reston VA 20190 Office Phone: 703-810-3000. Office Fax: 703-984-5042. Business E-Mail: susan.d.parkhill@salliemae.com.

PARKINS, FREDERICK MILTON, dental educator, dean; b. Princeton, NJ, Sept. 8, 1935; s. William Milton and Phyllis Virginia (Plyler) P.; m. Carolyn V. Rude; children: Bradford, Christopher, Eric. Student, Carleton Coll., 1953-56; D.D.S., U. Pa., 1960; MSD. in Pedodontics, U. N.C., Chapel Hill, 1965; PhD in Physiology, 1969. Instr. pedodontics U. N.C., 1965-67; asst. prof. pedodontics U. Pa., 1967-68, dir. Dental Aux. Utilization program, chmn. pedodontics, 1968-69; assoc. prof., head pedodontics U. Iowa, Iowa City, 1969-72, prof., head pedodontics, 1972-75; asst. dean acad. affairs U. Iowa (Coll. Dentistry), 1974-75, asso. dean acad. affairs, 1975-79, dir. continuing edn., 1975-77; prof. pedodontics, dean Sch. Dentistry, U. Louisville, 1979-85, prof. pediatric dentistry, 1985—2003, prof. pediatric dentistry emeritus, 2003—. Mem. Hillenbrand Fellowship adv. com. Am. Fund Dental Health, 1980-85; cons. Div. Dental Health USPHS, 1969-72; dental cons., med. staff Children's Hosp. Phila., 1968-71; med. staff Kosair Children's Hosp. Louisville, 1983—; cons., mem. pedodontic adv. com. Council Dental Edn., 1974-80, chmn. pedodontic adv. com., 1978-80, cons. council on legislation, 1978-79; dental cons. Aux. Utilization VA, 1968-69; cons. Bur. Health Resources Devel., 1974-76, Dept. Army, 1980-, numerous others Assoc. editor Jour. Preventive Dentistry, 1973-79, mem. editl. bd., 1980-83; editl. reviewer Jour. Pediatrics, 1969-, Jour. Dental Edn, 1978-, Jour. AMA, 1979-; assoc. editor Jour. Clin. Preventive Dentistry, 1979-84; mem. editl. bd. Jour. Clin. Laser Medicine and Surgery, 1999-; contbr. chpts. to textbooks, articles to profl. publs. Bd. govs. Youth Performing Arts Coun., Louisville-Jefferson County Sch. Dist., 1980-89, pres., 1986-88; bd. govs. Regional Cancer Ctr., U. Louisville, 1979-84, Univ. Hosp., 1979-84; mem. human studies com. U. Louisville, 1988-90. Robert Wood Johnson Congl. fellow Inst. of Medicine, 1977-78; USPHS postdoctoral fellow, 1963-67; NIH grantee, 1971-75; Recipient Earle Banks Hoyt Teaching award, 1969 Fellow AAAS, Am. Acad. Pediat. Dentistry (chmn. rsch. com. 1972-73, Ann. Rsch. award 1968, chmn. advanced edn. com. 1974-75, chmn. dental care programs com. 1978-80); mem. ADA, Am. Coll. Dentistry, Am. Soc. Dentistry for Children (exec. bd. Iowa unit 1969-75, award com. 1973-76, edn. com. 1974-77, chmn. rsch. adv.

com. 1973-76), Biophys. Soc., Internat. Assn. Dental Rsch., N.Y. Acad. Dentistry, Ky. Dental Assn. (exec. bd. 1979-84), Am. Assn. Dental Schs. (coun. deans 1979-85, chmn. pedodontics sect. 1976, chmn. continuing edn. sect. 1979, legis. com. 1978-83), Louisville Dental Alumni Assn. (bd. govs. 1979-84), Am. Assn. Dental Rsch. (nat. affairs com. 1978-85), Acad. Laser Dentistry (co-chmn. rsch. and edn. 1997, chair 1998-2003, bd. dirs. 1997-2003, cert. com., T.H. Maiman award for excellence in dental laser rsch.), U.S. Power Squadron (bd. govs. 1987-93, sec. 1989, adminstrv. officer 1990, exec. officer 1991, comdr. 1992), Aircraft Owners and Pilots Assn., Omicron Kappa Upsilon (pres. Wa. chpt. 1991-92), Rotary. Unitarian Universalist. Home: 6424 Marina Dr Prospect KY 40059-8846 Office: U Louisville Sch Dentistry Dept Orth and Pediatric Dentistry Rm 240N Louisville KY 40292 Office Phone: 502-228-3389. Business E-Mail: fmpark01@louisville.edu.

PARKS, JOHN SCOTT, pediatric endocrinologist; b. Washington, Oct. 14, 1939; s. John Louis and Mary Dean (Scott) P.; m. Georgia Bigley, May 7, 1959, (dec.) Sept 25, 2008; children: Stephanie Dean, Paige Wallace Parks Adams, John Thurston. AB in Am. Studies magna cum laude, Amherst Coll., 1961; MD, U. Pa., 1966, PhD in Biochemistry, 1971. Diplomate Nat. Bd. Med. Examiners, Am. Bd. Pediat. Intern in pediat. Children's Hosp. Phila., 1967-68, resident in pediat., 1968-69; clin. assoc. endocrinology br. Nat. Cancer Inst. NIH, Bethesda, Md., 1969-71; endocrinology fellow Children's Hosp. Phila., 1971-73; from instr. pediat. to assoc. prof. pediat. U. Pa., 1971-83; asst. physician, asst. endocrinologist Children's Hosp. Phila., 1972-74, assoc. physician, assoc. dir. endocrinology, 1974-80, assoc. endocrinologist, 1974-82, dir. hypothyroidism program, 1978-81, sr. physician, dir. adolescent medicine, 1980-82; prof. pediat. Emory U., Atlanta, 1982—, assoc. prof. biochemistry, 1983—, dir. divsn. pediat. endocrinology and diabetes, 1982—; pediat. endocrinologist Henrietta Egleston Hosp., 1982—, Grady Meml. Hosp., 1982—. Lectr. in field. Author books; contbg. author over 50 book chpts.; contbr. over 65 articles to profl. jours. Bd. dirs. Spruce Hill Cmty. Assn., 1967-69, Hill Top Prep. Sch., 1977-81. Recipient fellowship NIH, 1963-64, 66-67, 75-80, GM Nat. scholarship, 1957-61, Ford Found. fellowship, 1960-61, Am. Cancer Soc. fellow, 1962-63, Morton McCutcheon award, 1963, Merck award, 1966, numerous rsch. awards, 1964—. Mem. Am. Pediat. Soc., Endocrine Soc. (organizing com. 1990), Soc. for Pediat. Rsch., Coll. Physicians and Surgeons of Phila., Lawson Wilkins Pediat. Endocrine Soc. (program com. chair 1983-87, bd. dirs. 1990-93, pres. 1996-97), Spinx Soc., Scarab Soc., Phi Beta Kappa, Psi Upsilon. Office: Emory U Sch Medicine Dept Pediat 2015 Uppergate Dr NE Atlanta GA 30322 Office Phone: 404-778-2400. Office Fax: 404-727-9834. Business E-Mail: jparks@emory.edu.

PARKS, JULIA ANNE, state legislator; b. Greenwood, SC, Jan. 1, 1955; d. James Lloyd and Julia Arnold Parks. BS, Johnson C. Smith U., 1976. Mem. Dist. 12 SC House of Reps., 1999—; mem. Med. Com., Mil. Com., Pub. Com.; mortician & funeral dir. Parks Funeral Home; real estate agent. Mem.: Stop the Violence Commn., Greenwood City Coun. Democrat. Address: PO Box 181 Greenwood SC 29648 Mailing: 434D Blatt Bldg Columbia SC 29201 Office Phone: 803-734-3069, 864-229-3206. Business E-Mail: jap@legis.lpitr.state.sc.us.

PARKS, LLOYD LEE, oil industry executive; b. Kiefer, Okla., Dec. 9, 1929; s. Homer Harrison and Avis Pearl (Motes) P.; m. Mary Ellen Scott, Aug. 20, 1948 (dec. 2008); children: Connie Jo, Karyn Ann, Rebecca Lee; m. Dena M. Pierce, Apr. 11, 2009. Student, Okla. State U., 1948-50, Tulsa U., 1950-51, Harvard U. Bus. Sch., 1965. Acct. Deep Rock Oil Corp., 1951-54; chief acct. Blackwell Oil & Gas Co., Tulsa, 1954-60, sec. treas., 1960-62; v.p., controller Amax Oil & Gas Inc., Houston, 1962-67, pres., CEO, 1968—92; v.p. Amax, Inc., 1975-92; pvt. practice oil and gas and real estate investment Salado, Tex., 1992—. Served with AUS, 1946-48, 50-51. Mem.: Lions Club. Republican. Office: PO Box 1021 Salado TX 76571-1021 Personal E-mail: llparks9@aol.com.

PARKYN, JOHN WILLIAM, editor, writer, columnist; b. London, Dec. 7, 1931; came to U.S., 1967; citizen, 1973; s. James R. and Eva M. (Dix) P.; m. Sybil (Judy) Hetherington; 1 child, Elaine. Student, Dulwich Coll., 1943-48. Staff writer Bus. Mag., London, 1954-56; writer-editor Amalgamated Press, London, 1956-58; features editor Woman's Illustrated mag., London, 1958-60; staff writer Internat. Pub. Corp., London, 1960-61; editor Westward mag. Daily News Ltd., London, 1961-64; assoc. editor Daily Telegraph mag., London, 1964-66; features editor King mag. Europress, Ltd., London, 1966-67; assoc. editor Tropic mag. Miami Herald, 1967-69; editor Tropic mag., 1969-77; editor Calif. Today mag. San Jose Mercury News, Calif., 1977-83; editor Sunshine: The Mag. of South Fla. Sun-Sentinel Co. (subs. Tribune Co.), Ft. Lauderdale, Fla., 1983-96; columnist S. Fla. Sun-Sentinel, 1997—2005; exec. editor, sr. writer Vero Beach Mag., Fla., 1998—; columnist, feature writer City & Shore mag., 2000—05. Cons. Het Parool newspaper, Amsterdam, 1965. Contbr. numerous articles to Am. and European mags. Chmn. Sunday Mag. Editors Conf., Louisville, 1973. With RAF, 1950-52. Recipient Outstanding Use of Editl. Color award Editor & Pub. mag., 1974, 75, 77, Nat. Headliner award, 1976, 79; named Editor Best Weekly Mag. in State Fla. Press Club, 1985-93, 95. Personal E-mail: johnparkyn@aol.com.

PARMAM, LARRY VANCE, state official, lawyer; b. 1947; m. Darlene Parmam; children: Alexandra Parman Pitts, Scott Parman. BS in Bus. & Public Adminstrn., U. Mo., Columbia, 1969; JD, U. Mo. Kansas City Sch. Law, 1974. Lic.: US Supreme Ct.; accredited estate planner Nat. Assn. of Estate Planners and Councils, cert. Family Wealth Counselor. CEO Parman & Easterday LLP, Oklahoma City, 1984—; sec. of state State of Okla., Oklahoma City, 2013, sec., exec. dir. commerce, 2013—. Ptnr. Notch It Up Strategies LLC, 2008—; pres. The Hawthorn Group, Alexandria, Va., 2001—03; pres., CEO Trencor, Inc., Okla.; CEO Maestro, 2006—; bd. managers Comp-Source Oklahoma, 1999—2002, 2011—13, chmn.; bd. dirs. BancInsure; frequent guest on radio and TV talk shows; featured spkr. on educational video, Living Trusts. Author and co-author of multiple articles on estate planning, financial planning and business; co-author: Estate Planning Basics: A Crash Course in Safeguarding Your Legacy, Guiding Those Left Behind in Oklahoma: Settling Affairs of Your Loved Ones; author: Above the Fray: Leading Yourself, Your Business and Others During Turbulent Times, 2013. Bd. dirs. Oklahoma Council on Economic Development, Research Inst. for Economic Development; bd. dirs, also chmn. Junior Achievement of Oklahoma City. Capt. US Army. Mem.: American Academy of Estate Planning Attorneys, Mo. Bar Assn., Oklahoma Bar Assn. Republican. Office: Oklahoma Dept Commerce 900 N Stiles Ave Oklahoma City OK 73104 E-mail: larry_parman@okcommerce.gov.*

PARMLEY, RICHARD TURNER, pediatric hematologist, oncologist; b. Madison, Wis., Sept. 10, 1949; BA, U. Va., 1970; MD, Med. U. SC, 1973. Diplomate in pediatrics and in pediatric hematology/oncology Am. Bd. Pediatrics; diplomate in hematopathology Am. Bd. Pathology, active med. licences, Fla. Ala., SC, NC, ND. Intern Med. U. SC, Charleston, SC, 1973, resident in pediats., 1974-75; fellow in pediat. hematology-oncology St. Jude Children's Rsch. Hosp., Memphis, 1976-77, U. Ala., Birmingham, 1977; clin. fellow in med. oncology bone marrow transplant svc. Fred Hutchinson Cancer Rsch. Ctr., Seattle, 1986; dir. electron microscopy and histology unit inst. dental rsch. U. Ala., Birmingham, 1978-83, assoc. scientist Comprehensive Cancer Cancert Ctr., 1978-83, asst. prof. pediats. and pathology, 1978-82, assoc. prof. pediats., 1982-83; assoc. prof. pediats. and pathology U. Tex. Health Sci. Ctr., 1983-88, prof. pediats., 1988-94; dir. divsn. pediat. hematology/oncology Carolinas Med. Ctr., Charlotte, NC, 1994—2000; clin. prof. pediat. U. NC, Chapel Hill, 1994—2000; mem. med. staff Spartanburg Reg. Med. Ctr., SC, 2000—07; clin. prof. pediat. Med. U. SC, Charleston, 2000—07; pediat. hematologist-oncologist Nemours Children's Clinic, Pensacola, Fla., 2007—; clin. prof. Fla. State U., 2007—. Mem. Am. Soc. Pediatric Hematology/Oncology, Am. Acad. Pediat., Childrens Oncology Group, Alpha Omega Alpha. Office Phone: 850-505-4790.

PARMLEY, ROBERT JAMES, lawyer, consultant; b. Madison, Wis., Oct. 23, 1950; s. Loren Francis and Dorothy Louise (Turner) Parmley; m. Debra Paliszewski, Dec. 23, 1982; children: Michelle Hope, Matthew Turner. BA, U. Va., 1972; JD, U. SC, 1975. Bar: Tex. 1976, US Dist. Ct. (so. dist.) Tex. 1976, US Dist. Ct. (we. and no. dists.) Tex. 1980, US Ct. Appeals (5th cir.) 1978, US Tax Ct. 1976, US Supreme Ct. 1980. Staff atty., Vista vol. Tex. Rural Legal Aid, Inc., Alice, 1975-76, mng. atty. Kingsville, 1976-79, sr. staff atty. Kerrville, 1979-81; sole practice Kerrville, 1981—. Bd. dirs. Kerr County Skeet and Trap Club, 2003—12, Salvation Army, Kerrville, Tex., 1991—. Mem. State Bar Tex., Kerr County Bar Assn. Episcopalian. Office: 222 Sidney Baker St Ste 615 Kerrville TX 78028-5900 Office Phone: 830-896-4900. Business E-Mail: law@ktc.com.

PARMON, EARLINE W., state legislator; Edn. cons.; state rep. Dist 72 NC, 2003—. Mem. Appropriations com., Health com., Judiciary II com., Juvenile Justice com., Mental Health Reform com.; vice chmn. Appropriations Subcom. on Edn., Edn. com.; chmn. Edn. Subcom. on Presch., Elem. and Secondary Edn. Served with USAR. Democrat. Mailing: 3873 Barkwood Dr Winston Salem NC 27105 Office: North Carolina House of Representatives 300 N Salisbury St Rm 509 Raleigh NC 27603-5925 Office Phone: 919-733-5829. E-mail: Earline.Parmon@ncleg.net.

PARR, ROBERT GHORMLEY, chemistry professor; b. Chgo., Sept. 22, 1921; s. Leland Wilbur and Grace (Ghormley) P.; m. Jane Bolstad, May 28, 1944; children: Steven Robert, Jeanne Karen, Carol Jane. AB magna cum laude with high honors in Chemistry, Brown U., 1942; PhD in Phys. Chemistry, U. Minn., 1947; D (hon.), U. Leuven, 1986, Jagiellonian U., 1996. Asst. prof. chemistry U. Minn., 1947-48; mem. faculty Carnegie Inst. Tech., 1948-62, prof. chemistry, 1957-62, Johns Hopkins U., 1962-74, chmn. dept., 1969-72; William R. Kenan, Jr. prof. theoretical chemistry U. N.C., Chapel Hill, 1974-90, Wassily Hoeffding prof. chem. physics, 1990—. Vis. prof. chemistry, mem. Ctr. Advanced Study, U. Ill., 1962; disting. vis. prof. SUNY, Buffalo, Pa. State U., 1967; vis. prof. Japan Soc. Promotion Sci., 1968, 79, U. Haifa, 1977, Free U., Berlin, 1977, Duke U., 1996-97; Firth prof. U. Sheffield, 1976; Coochbehar prof. Indian Assn. Cultivation of Sci., 1990; Sandoval Vallarta prof. UAM-Iztapalapa, 1992; chmn. com. postdoctoral fellowships in chemistry NAS-NRC, 1961-63; chmn. panel theoretical chemistry Westheimer com. survey chemistry NAS, 1964; mem. coun. Gordon Rsch. Conf., 1974-76; mem. Commn. on Human Resources, NRC, 1979-82; mem. coun. Inst. for Molecular Sci., Okazaki, Japan, 1986-88; bd. trustees Inst. for Fundamental Chemistry, Kyoto, Japan, 1988—. Author: Quantum Theory of Molecular Electronic Structure, 1963, Density-Functional Theory of Atoms and Molecules, 1989, also numerous articles.; Assoc. editor: Jour. Chem. Physics, 1956-58, Chem. Revs, 1961-63, Jour. Phys. Chemistry, 1963-67, 77-79, Am. Chem. Soc. Monographs, 1966-71, Theoretica Chimica Acta, 1966-69, 92-96; Chinese Chem. Letters, 1998—; bd. editors: Jour. Am. Chem. Soc, 1969-77; adv. editorial bd.: Internat. Jour. Quantum Chemistry, 1967—, Chem. Physics Letters, 1967-79. Recipient Outstanding Achievement award U. Minn., 1968, N.C. Disting. Chemist award, 1982; fellow U. Chgo., 1949; research asso., 1957; Fulbright scholar U. Cambridge, Eng., 1953-54; Guggenheim fellow, 1953-54; NSF sr. postdoctoral fellow U. Oxford (Eng.) and Commonwealth Sci. and Indsl. Research Orgn., Melbourne, Australia, 1967-68; Sloan fellow, 1956-60, N.C. award in sci., 1999, North Carolina Govs. Alumni Sci. award, 1999. Fellow AAAS, Am. Phys. Soc. (chmn. divsn. chem. physics 1963-64); mem. NAS (award in chem. scis., 2004), AAUP, Am. Chem. Soc. (chmn. divsn. phys. chemistry 1978, Irving Langmuir award in chem. physics 1994, theoritical chemistry award 2009), Am. Acad. Arts and Sci., Indian Nat. Sci. Acad., Internat. Acad. Quantum Molecular Sci. (pres. 1991-97), Phi Beta Kappa, Sigma Xi, Phi Lambda Upsilon, Pi Mu Epsilon. Home: 701 Kenmore Rd Chapel Hill NC 27514-2019 Office: U NC Dept Chemistry Chapel Hill NC 27599-3290 Business E-Mail: rgparr@email.unc.edu.

PARRA, RO (ROSENDO G. PARRA), hotel executive; b. Ecuador, Nov. 12, 1959; m. Cheryl L. Parra; 4 children. BA in Mktg., U. Md., 1982. Various sales, mgmt. positions, bus. prod. divsn. Tandy Corp.; various sales, gen. mgmt. positions GRiD Sys. Corp.; v.p. Dell USA, 1993—94; group v.p. sales, mktg. & services Dell, Inc., 1994—97, v.p. pub. & Americas internat., 1997—98, sr. v.p. Americas pub. & Americas internat., 1998—2001, sr. v.p., gen. mgr. Americas, 2002—06, sr. v.p., worldwide home & small bus. group, 2006—07; ptnr., founder Daylight Partners, 2007—. Bd. dirs. NII Holdings, Inc., Pacific Gas & Electric, Dell Inc., 2004—07, Brinker Internat. Inc., 2004—. Named one of Most Important Hispanics in Tech., Bus., Hispanic Engineer and Info. Tech. mag., 2005. Office: Brinker International Inc 6820 LBJ Freeway Dallas TX 75240 Office Phone: 972-980-9917. E-mail: rosendo.parra@brinker.com.

PARRAMORE, BARBARA MITCHELL, education educator; b. Guilford County, NC, Aug. 29, 1932; d. Samuel Spencer and Nellie Gray (Glosson) Mitchell; m. Lyman Griffis Worthington, Dec. 23, 1956 (div. 1961); m. Thomas Custis Parramore, Jan. 22, 1966 (dec. Jan. 13, 2004); children: Lisa Gray, Lynn Stuart. AB, U. N.C., Greensboro, 1954; MEd, N.C. State U., 1959; EdD, Duke U., 1968. Counselor, tchr. Raleigh City Schs., 1954-59, sch. prin., 1959-65; prof. dept. of curriculum and instrn. N.C. State U., 1970-96, prof. emeritus, 1996—. Acad. specialist Office Internat. Edn., U.S. Info. Svcs., sec. sch. initative program, The Philippines, 1987. Author: The People of North Carolina, 1972, 3rd edit. 1983. Japan Inst. Social and Econ. Affairs fellow, 1980; N.C. AAUW award for juvenile lit., 1973, Holladay medal for excellence N.C. State U., 1994. Mem. ASCD, N.C. ASCD (pres. 1994-96), N.C. Coun. for Social Studies (pres. 1985-87), Assn. Tchr. Educators, Delta Kappa Gamma, Kappa Delta Pi. Home: 5012 Tanglewood Dr Raleigh NC 27612-3135

PARRETT, DENNIS L., state legislator; b. Oct. 30, 1959; s. Denver Parrett; m. Lisa Thomas Parrett; children: Devan, Dayna, Kristen. BS in Agrl. Economics, U. Ky. Co-owner Cecilia Farm Svc.; mem. Dist. 10 Ky. State Senate, Frankfort, 2011—. Democrat. Roman Catholic. Office: Kentucky State Senate Annex Rm 255 702 Capitol Ave Frankfort KY 40601 Office Phone: 502-564-8100 ext. 645. Business E-Mail: dennis.parrett@lrc.ky.gov.

PARRISH, CHARLES S., lawyer, oil industry executive; BA in History with honors, U. Va.; JD, U. Houston Law Sch. Pvt. practice, Houston and San Antonio; v.p., asst. gen. counsel, sec. Tesoro Corp., San Antonio, 1994—2005, 2005—06, sr. v.p., gen. counsel, sec., 2006—09, exec. v.p., gen. counsel & sec., 2009—. Mem.: ABA, State Bar Tex. Office: Tesoro Corp 19100 Ridgewood Pky San Antonio TX 78259 Office Phone: 210-626-6000. Office Fax: 210-745-4494. Business E-Mail: charles.s.parrish@tsocorp.com.*

PARRISH, JOHN WESLEY, JR., biology professor; b. Dennison, Ohio, Mar. 5, 1941; s. John Wesley Parrish Sr. and Dorothy Irene (Dickinson) Price; m. Paula Schmanke, July 9, 1966; children: Corinne Danelle, Wesley Allen. BS, Denison U., 1963; MA, Bowling Green State U., Ohio, 1970, PhD, 1974. Tchr. sci. Northwood Jr. HS, Norfolk, Va., spring 1967; vis. instr. dept. biology Kenyon Coll., Gambier, Ohio, 1973-74; postdoctoral fellow dept. zoology U. Tex., Austin, 1974-76; asst. prof. dept. biol. sci. Emporia State U., Kans., 1976-82, assoc. prof. Kans., 1982-88, assoc. chairperson dept. biol. sci. Kans., 1987-88; prof. Ga. So. U., Statesboro, 1988—2008, chairperson dept. biology, 1988-94; emeritus prof. biology, 2008. Vis. rsch. assoc. prof. dept. physiology Cornell U., Ithaca, NY, fall 1986. Author: (with others) Field and Laboratory Biology, 1985; editor: Activities in the Environ. and Life Sci., 1986, Annotated Checklist of Georgia Birds, 2003, Birds of Georgia, 2005; mem. editorial bd. Oriole, 1991-98, co-editor, 1999—2005; contbr. numerous articles to profl. jour. Officer USNR, 1964—67. Grantee Josselyn Van Tyne Meml. Fund, 1968, Emporia State U., 1977-85, 87-88, NSF, 1984, Kans. Fish and Game Commn., 1985, Kans. Dept. Wildlife and Pk., 1987, Quail Unltd., 1988, Arcadia Wildlife Preserve, Inc., 1994—, Ga. Dept. Nat. Resources, 1994, 95, 2004—; Outstanding Faculty award Emporia State Univ., 1985, Merit award Georgia So. Univ., 1999, 2005, Outstanding Biology Faculty award, Ga. Southern U., Disting. Alumnus award, Canton Lincoln HS, Ohio, 2008. Mem.: KOS, GOS, AOU, Sigma Xi (life). Avocations: birding, bicycling, computers, photography, tennis. Office: Ga So U Dept Biology PO Box 8042 Statesboro GA 30460-8042 Business E-Mail: jparrish@georgiasouthern.edu.

PARRISH, LARRY J. (BUTCH), state legislator; b. Nov. 14, 1941; m. Linda P. Wood; children: Lynn, Randy. Mem., city coun., Swainsboro; house rep. Ga.; ex-officio state rep. Dist. 109 Ga., 1984—92; ex-officio state rep. Dist. 144, 1993—2002; state rep. Dist. 102 Ga., 2003—04; state rep. Dist. 156, 2004—; chmn., banks & banking com.; mem., appropriations & rules com.; mem. Emanuel County Coun. Alcohol & Drug Abuse; pharmacist; pres. Shoprite Drug Inc.; v.p. Swainsboro Ford-Lincoln Inc.; mem., alumni adv. coun. Sch. Pharmacy U. Ga.; bd. mem. First Liberty Bank, Swainsboro. Recipient Outstanding Citizen award, Woodmen of World, Disting. Alumnus award, U. Ga. Coll. Pharmacy, Pres.'s Citation award, Ind. Ins. Agt. Ga.; named Pharmacist of Yr., Phi Delta Chi Pharm. Frat. Mem.: Acad. Durable Med. Equipment Suppliers, Nat. Assn. Ind. Med. Equipment Suppliers, Nat. Assn. Retail Druggists, Ga. Pharmacy Assn., Ga. Pharm. Assn. (former pres.), Swainsboro & Emanual County C. of C., Swainsboro Exch. Club (former pres.), U. Ga. Pharmacy Alumni Assn. (former pres.), Ga. Sheriff's Assn. (life). Democrat. Methodist. Mailing: 224 W Main St Swainsboro GA 30401-2352 Office: 218 State Capitol Atlanta GA 30334 Office Phone: 404-656-5096, 478-237-7032. Business E-Mail: lparrish@legis.state.ga.us.

PARRISH, LORI NANCE, property appraiser; b. Evansville, Ind., July 31, 1948; m. Geoffrey Cohen; children: Gary Brown, Brandi Schmidt. Student, Fin. Inst. Sch., 1968, Fla. Atlantic U., 1969, Clemson U., 1982, Fla. Internat. U., 1988; LHD (hon.), Keiser Coll., 1996; postgrad., U. Ctrl. Fla., 1996—98. Cert. Retail Nurseryman Nova/Davie Cmty. Sch., Fla., 1975, in Credit and Collections Broward CC, Fla., 1980, in Quality Cir. Fla. Atlantic U., 1986, in Target Mgmt. Selection Fla. Internat. U., 1988, County Commrs. Cert. in Fin. Mgmt. Fla. Counties Found., Fla. Assn. Counties, 1997, County Commrs. Cert. in County Govt. Law Fla. Counties Found., Fla. Assn. Counties, 1998, County Commrs. Cert. in Ethics Fla. Counties Found., Fla. Assn. Counties, 1998. Toll operator So. Bell Telephone Co., 1966-68; adminstrv. asst. appraisal and constrn. Loan Dept. Hollywood Fed. Savings & Loan Assn., 1968—72; acct., qualifying agt. Victor Purdo Painting Co., 1972-81; fin. mgr. CRG, Inc., 1982-83; bookkeeper I county and vocat. Sch. Bd. Broward County, South Plantation HS, 1983-84; commr. dist. 5 Broward County, Fla., 1988—2004, vice-chair, 1989—90, 1996—97, chair, 1990—91, 1997—98, 2001—02, property appraiser, 2005—. Citizen's adv. bd. City of Cooper, 1976-77, pers. rev. bd., 1976-77; mem. Property Appraisal Adjustment Bd., 1984-90, 91-94, vice chair, 1987-88, chair 1989-90, 1993-94, 95-96; mem. South Fla. Coordinating Coun., 1985-, Criminal Justice Planning Coun., 1985-90, Nat. Assn. Counties, 1988-2004, Human Svcs. Com., 1988-2004, Broward Econ. Devel. Bd., 1988-89, chair 1991-92; mem. Courthouse Security Com., 1990-93, Pub. Health Trust Com., Environment, Energy Land Use Steering Com., 1991-2004, Health Steering Com. 1989-90, 94-95, Overall Econ. Devel. Planning Com., 1988-90, Met. Planning Orgn., 1988-90, 92-2004, HIV Health Planning Coun., 1992-93, Broward Edn. Planning Initiative Com., Legal, Legis. Subcommittee, 1993, Resource Recovery Bd. 1994-95, 2002-03, vice chair, 1992, chair, 1993, Tourist Devel. Coun. 1997, 2001; mem. select com. water policy, Fla. Assn. Counties', 1995-96, elderly task force mem., 1995; bd. govs. Fort Lauderdale C. of C., 1987-88, 90-91; adv. bd. mem. Water Supply, 1988-94, chair 1991-92; Brady Brigade recruiter, Nat. Orgn. Disability, 1991-93; chair NACO's Subcommittee on Aging, 1993; chair Cooper City Election Reform Com., 1993-94; bd. dirs. Cmty. Health Purchasing Alliance, 1993-96, Fla. Assn. Counties, 1988-2001, South Fla. Regional Transp. Authority, Tri-County Commuter Rail Authority, 1988-2004, vice chair, 1996-97, chair 1997-98; vice chair Broward County Planning Coun., 1991-92, mem. 2002-; spl. projects coord. Davie/Cooper City C. of C.; adminstrv. asst. to bldg. ofcl. City of Cooper City, 1972-81; landscape contractor, owner Earthy Interiors; v.p. Lake Shore Motel and Swap Shop, Inc., 1994-2003, 3290 Sunrise Investments, Inc., 1994-2003, 3291 Sunrise Investments, Inc. (dba Swap Shop), 1994-2003, Fla. Drive-In Theater Mgmt., Inc. 1994-2001, COO Millennium Hollywood's City Pl., 1994-2003; v.p., sec., treas. Swap Shop Mgmt. LLC, 2001-; founder Broward Workshop Criminal Justice Com. Regional Transp. Orgn. Bd. 1996-2003. Adv. bd. Broward County Libr., 1979-85, Mommas and Poppas of Cooper City High, 1982-90, Broward C.C. Women's Programs Adv. Com., 1981-82; sec. Cooper City Elem. Sch. Adv. Com., 1979-80, chair 1980-82, South Ctrl. Area Adv. Com., 1982-83, sec., 1981-82; legis. chair Broward County Libr. Adv. Bd., 1982-84; active Broward County Sch. Bd., 1984-88, vice-chair, 1986-87, chair, 1987-88; bd. dirs. Pembroke Pines Human Resource Ctr. Adv. Com., 1984-88. Recipient Lifetime Membership award Broward County Phys. Edn. Tchrs., 1988, VIP Female award West Broward Dem. Club, 1988, Lifetime Membership award Young Dems., 1988, Outstanding Svc. award Lauderhill Regular Dem. Club, 1988, Disting. Svc. award Plantation Dem. Club, 1988, Disting. and Dedicated Svc. award Broward County Deputies Assn., 1989, 92, Spl. Achievement award Jefferson-Jackson, 1990, Friend of ARC award Assn. Retarded Citizens of Broward, 1990, Tribute to Success award Pembroke Pines Dem. Club, 1991, Leadership and Dedication award Children's Svcs. Bd., 1991, Desert Storm Family Support award 1991, Disting. Svc.

award Women in Distress, 1991-92, Appreciation award Mus. Archaeology, 1992, Ann. Appreciation award N.W. Federated Woman's Club, 1992, Mother's Day award Rainbow Crusaders, 1992, Environ. Appreciation award Sunshine Ranches Homeowners Assn., 1992, Woman Leadership award Assn. Retarded Citizens, 1992, Coconut Creek Disting. Svc. award, 1994, Conservation Legislator of Yr. award Broward County Airboat, Halftrack, Conservation Club, 1994, Honoree Sunrise Regular Dem. Club, 1994, Legislator of Yr. award Broward County Fire Fighters and Paramedics, 1994, Woman of Yr. award Plantation Dem. Club, 1995, Humanitarian of Yr. award Sorel Jewish Cmty. Ctr., 1995, Pres.'s award Broward County Fair, 1996, award Manatee Survival Found. 1996, Dream Maker award Jr. League Greater Fort Lauderdale, 1996, Jesse Portis Helms award Dolphin Dem. Club, 1996, Par Excellence award Miramar High Cmty. Sch., 1997, Recognition award North Dade C. of C., 1997, Par Excellence award Miramar High Cmty. Sch., 1997, Criminal Justice Image award Cmty. Reconstruction Inst., 1998, Govtl. Dream Builder award Children's Harbor, 1999, Ray Lisanti Meml. award Gays United to Attack Repression and Discrimination, 1999, Gracias award Hispanic Unity, 1999, Polit. Leader of Yr. award The Vanguard Chronicle, 1999, Environ. Merit award EPA, 2000, Third Ann. Student Life Achievement Corp. Ptnr. of Yr. award Nova Southeastern U., 2002, 2002 Arts Collaboration award 13th Ann. ArtServe Encore awards, Karl Clark Cmty. Involvement award, 2002, Commr. Leadership award Fla. Local Environ. Resource Agencies, 2002, Spirit of Excellence award South Broward Chpt. Am. Bus. Women's Assn., 2002, Edee Greene Good Egg award, 2002, Humanitarian award LWV, 2002, Medallion award Unsung Heroine People with AIDS Coalition Broward County, 2002, Dem. Elected Women Honoree N.W. Dem. Club, 2002, Contbn. to Cmty. award, Pine Island Ridge Civic Orgn. award, 2003, Outstanding Svc. award Engring. Profession Broward Chpt. Fla. Engring. Soc., 2003, Women of Valor Broward County award David Posnack Jewish Cmty. Ctr., 2003, Outstanding Svc. award Washington Pk. Neighborhood Preservation and Enhancement Dist., 2003, South Fla. Commuter Svcs. Transp. Leadership award, 2004, David Posnack Hebrew Day Sch. Lifetime Achievement award, 2004, Outstanding Pub. Ofcl. award Fla. Assn. Mus., 2004-05, Pub. Svc. award Davie Merchants and Indsl. Assn., 2005, Cert. Appreciation Coral Springs C. of C., 2005, Cert. Appreciation Poinsettia Heights Civic Assn., 2005; nominee Feminist of Yr. Fedn. Pub. Employees, 1987; finalist Woman of Yr. Govt., 1987; named Woman of Yr. Sunrise Lakes Phase III Women's Club, 1987, Woman of Yr. City of Hope, 1989, Hon. Conch and Citizen of Fabulous Fla. Keys, 1991, Woman of Yr. Metro Broward Fire Fighters, 1992, Dem. of Yr. Jefferson-Jackson, 1992, 2002, Woman of Yr. Women in Distress, 1993, Environ. Legislator of Yr. Environ. Coalition of Broward County, 1993, Polit. Alliance of Yr. Dolphin Dem. Club, 1999, Humanitarian of Yr. E.A.S.E. Found., 2001, Woman of Yr. South Fla. Mus. Natural History and Pyramid Soc., 2002; named to Broward County Women's Hall of Fame, 1997; Paul Harris fellow Rotary Found. Rotary Internat. Davie Rotary Club, 1997. Mem. ALA, Southeastern Libr. Assn., Davie/Cooper City Friends of Libr. (founder), Ft. Lauderdale Friends of Libr., Broward County Friends of Libr., Amalgamated Transit Union (hon. life, Naval Air Sta., Ft. Lauderdale Hist. Assn. (hon.), Broward County Police Benevolent Assn. (hon.). Office: Broward County Property Appraiser 115 S Andrews Ave Ste 111 Fort Lauderdale FL 33301-1801 Home Phone: 954-236-5537; Office Phone: 954-357-6904. Business E-Mail: lori@bcpa.net.

PARRY, TIMOTHY R., lawyer; b. Syracuse, NY, July 28, 1954; s. Edward Lee and Ruth (Thomas) P.; children: Ryan Edward, Ian Andrew, Erika Isabella. BS, Ariz. State U., 1976; JD, U. Cin., 1980. Bar: Ohio 1980, Fla. 1983, US Dist. Ct. (so. dist.) Ohio 1981, US Dist. Ct. (so. and mis. dists.) Fla. 1983, US Ct. Appeals (11th cir.) 1984. Law clk. to judge John D. Holschuh US Dist. Ct. (so. dist.) Ohio, Columbus, 1980-81; asst. atty. gen. Ohio Atty. Gen.'s Office, Columbus, 1981-83; assoc. Harter, Secrest & Emery, Naples, Fla., 1983-88, ptnr., 1989—96; div. v.p., asst. gen. counsel Health Mgmt. Associates, Inc., Naples, Fla., 1996—97, sr. v.p., gen. counsel, sec., 1997—. Past pres., Cath. Social Svcs. Collier County, Naples, Fla. 1988—; dir. Econ. Devel. Coun. Collier County, 2004-; mem. pres.'s adv. coun. Internat. Coll., Naples, Fla., 2005-. Mem. Fla. Bar Assn. (20th jud. cir. bar grievance com. 1989-91), Collier County Bar Assn. (bd. dirs. 1989—). Office: Health Mgmt Associates 5811 Pelican Bay Blvd Naples FL 34108-2710 Home Phone: 239-598-1717; Office Phone: 239-598-3131.

PARSHALL, GERALD, journalist; b. St. Paul, Apr. 24, 1941; s. William Elmer and Evelyn (Steckling) P.; m. Sandra Grant, Dec. 20, 1970. BA, U. Minn., 1963; MA, U. Mich., 1964; grad. fellow, U. Chgo., 1966-67. Reporter York (Pa.) Gazette and Daily, 1968, Balt. Evening Sun, 1968-71; Capitol Hill staff U.S. News & World Report, Washington, 1971-77, sr. editor, 1977-79, asst. mng. editor, 1979-90, sr. writer, 1990-99, contbg. editor, 1999—2004. Mem. Exec. Com. of Periodical Corrs., U.S. Congress, 1974-80, chmn., 1979-80 Served to 1st lt. U.S. Army, 1964-66. Recipient Front Page award Washington-Balt. Newspaper Guild, 1971, Silver Gavel award ABA, 1983 Home: 1004 Congress Ln Mc Lean VA 22101-2116 Personal E-mail: gparshall@verizon.net.

PARSHALL, KAREN VIRGINIA HUNGER, mathematician; b. Virginia Beach, Va., July 7, 1955; d. Maurice Jacques and Jean Kay (Wroton) Hunger; m. Brian J. Parshall, Aug. 6, 1978. BA, U. Va., 1977, MS, 1978; PhD, U. Chgo., 1982. Asst. prof. math. Sweet Briar (Va.) Coll., 1982-87, U. Ill., Urbana, 1987-88; asst. prof. math. and history U. Va., Charlottesville, 1988-93, assoc. prof. math. and history, 1993—99, prof. math. and history, 1999—, assoc. dean social scis., 2009—. Author: (with David Rowe) Emergence of American Mathematics Research Community, 1994; (with others) Experiencing Nature, 1997, James Joseph Sylvester: Life and Work in Letters, 1998, (with others) Mathematics Unbound: The Emergence of an International Mathematical Community, 1800-1945, 2002, James Joseph Sylvester: Jewish Mathematician in a Victorian World, 2006, Episodes in the History of Modern Algebra, 2007; Years Ago editor Mathematical Intelligencer, N.Y.C., 1990-93; book rev. editor Historia Mathematica, San Diego, 1990-93, mng. editor, 1994-95, editor, 1996-99; contbr. articles to Archive for History Exact Scis., History of Sci., Jour. of the History of Biology, Archives internationales d'histoire des sciences, Annals of Sci., Historia Mathematica, Notices of the Am. Math. Soc., Am. Math. Mo., Revue d'histoire des mathématiques. Scholars award NSF, 1986-87, 90-93, NSF VPW award, 1996-97; John Simon Guggenheim Found. fellow, 1996. Mem. Am. Math. Soc., History Sci. Soc., Académie Internationale d'histoire des sciences (corr.), Internat. Commn. for History Math. (past-chair), Phi Beta Kappa. Office: U Va Depts Math and History Dept Mathematics P O Box 400137 Charlottesville VA 22904

PARSLEY, BRANTLEY HAMILTON, librarian; b. Oct. 15, 1927; s. Clarence Elroy and Florence Sally (Barnes) P.; m. Loyce Marie Franklin, Apr. 18, 1951; children: Linda Marie, Brantley Hamilton; m. Bettye Abercrombie, 1996. AA, Balt. Jr. Coll., 1950; BA, U. Md., 1952; BD, New Orleans Bapt. Theol. Sem., 1955, MRE, 1958; M in Librarianship, Emory U., 1965. Ordained to ministry Bapt. Ch., 1956. Pastor Calvary Bapt. Ch., Albany, Oreg., 1955-57; libr. asst. New Orleans Pub. Libr., 1958-61; supt. night circulation and stacks Theology Libr., Emory U., 1961-65; dir. libr. Campbellsville (Ky.) Coll., 1965-82; dir. Genealogy Workshop, Ch. History Writing Workshop. Dir.: (radio broadcast series) Kentucky Authors, 1976, Study of Black Literature, 1978; coll. page editor Ala. Libr., 1985-87. Bd. dirs. Taylor County Cmty. Concerts, Mobile (Ala.) Coll., 1982-93; pres. Cen. Ky. Arts Series, 1975-78; dir. Sch. Merger Workshop, 1976; sec. ACTS of Mobile, bd. dirs., 1985-88; mem. Ala. Sch. Libr. Task Force, 1990-93; mem. bd. dirs. Habitat for Humanity, 1993-99, west covenant adv. coun., mem. family selection com. constrn. crew; outreach vol., team leader, workshop trainer Widowed Persons Svcs., 1993; pres. Widowed Persons Svcs. of Greater Mobile, 2007; mem. Helpline Mobile, 1994-2007; mem. adv. coun. Ret. Sr. Vol. Program; tchr. Adult Men's Sunday Sch.; hospice chaplain Mobile Infirmary, 1998—. Recipient Sch. award Am. Legion, 1947. Mem. ALA, Southeastern Libr. Assn., Ky. Libr. Assn. (chmn. coll. and rsch. sect. 1970-71, sec. treas. edn. sect. 1972-73), Ala. Libr. Assn. (chmn. project com. coll., univ. and spl. libr. divsn.), Bay Area Libr. Assn. (pres.-elect 1984), Ala. Assn. Coll. and Rsch. Librs. (chmn. 1986-87), Coun. Ind. Ky. Colls. (chmn. 1970-75), Taylor County Hist. Soc. (dir. 1970), Taylor County Bapt. Assn. (dir. tng. 1968-70), Taylor County Bapt. Sunday Sch. Assn. (supt. 1968-70). Home: 808 Montfort Rd E Mobile AL 36608-3576 Home Phone: 251-342-7530. Personal E-mail: hamilton_53@bellsouth.net.

PARSONS, DANIEL LANKESTER, pharmaceutics educator; b. Biscoe, NC, Sept. 10, 1953; s. Solomon Lankester and Doris Eva (Bost) P. BS in Pharmacy, U. Ga., Athens, 1975, PhD, 1979. Asst. prof. pharmaceutics U. Ariz., Tucson, 1979-82; asst. prof. Auburn U., Ala., 1982-86, assoc. prof. Ala., 1986-91, chmn. divsn. Ala., 1990—2008, prof. Ala., 1991—. Cons. Wyeth-Ayerst, Phila., 1989—93, Technomics, Ardsley, NY, 1990—93, Murty Pharm., Lexington, Ky., 1996—99; presenter in field. Author (with G.V. Betageri and S.A. Jenkins): Liposome Drug Delivery Systems, 1993. Named Disting. Alumni, Sandhills Coll., 1990, Tchr. of Yr., Pharmacy Student Coun., 1987, Grad. Faculty Mem. of Yr., Grad. Student Orgn., 1994, Hargreaves Faculty Mentor award, 2008, Outstanding Faculty mem. award, Harrison Sch. Pharmacy Student Govt. Assn., 2013. Mem. Am. Assn. Pharm. Scientists, Phi Kappa Phi, Kappa Psi (advisor 1990-95, nat. grad. devel. com. 1993-95, nat. scholarship com. 1995-99, nat. grand coun. dep. com. 1997-05, Svc. award 1990, 95, Advisor award 1992, Prof. of Yr., 2000, Outstanding Faculty award, 2007, Svc. award 2013, Legends award, 2014, Faculty award 2014). Achievements include research in plasma protein binding of drugs, effects of perfluorochemical blood substitutes on such binding, and development of orally disintegrating tablets. Office: Auburn U Harrison Sch Pharmacy Auburn AL 36849 Business E-Mail: parsodl@auburn.edu.

PARSONS, DON L., state legislator; m. Jo Parsons. Former state rep. Dist. 40; house rep. Ga.; state rep. Dist. 29 Ga., 2003—04; state rep. Dist. 42 Ga., 2004—; mem. Appropriations Com., Health Com., Ecol. Com., Indsl. Com.; ops. mgr. Republican. Office: 3167 Sycamore Lane Marietta GA 30066-4173 Mailing: State Capitol 611 Legis Off Bldg Atlanta GA 30334 Office Phone: 404-656-0314, 770-997-4426. Fax: 770-509-0897. Business E-Mail: don@donparsons.net.

PARSONS, LEONARD JON, marketing educator, consultant; b. Pitts., Sept. 1, 1942; s. Leonard J. and Marion Jane (Williams) P.; m. Julia Grieve, Jan. 23, 1965; children: Lorelei, Leonard Jon Jr. BSChemE, MIT, 1964; MS in Indsl. Adminstrn., Purdue U., 1965, PhD in Indsl. Adminstrn., 1968. Asst. prof. Ind. U., Bloomington, 1968-70; assoc. prof. Claremont (Calif.) Grad. Sch., 1970-77; prof. marketing Ga. Inst. Tech., 1977—. Vis. scholar MIT, Cambridge, fall 1973; Fulbright-Hays sr. scholar Cath. U. Leuven, Belgium, spring 1977; vis. prof. INSEAD, France, fall 1984, Norwegian Sch. Mktg., Oslo, fall 1989, UCLA, spring 1990, Advt. Edn. Found., Anheuser Busch, St. Louis, summer 1993, CREER/FUCAM, Belgium, Fall 1995; mem. rsch. and test devel. com. Grad. Mgmt. Admissions Coun., 1988-90. Author: Using Microcomputers in Marketing, 1986; co-author: Marketing Management, 7th edit., 2000, Market Response Models, 2d edit., 2001, others; edtl. bd. Jour. Mktg. Rsch., 1970-80, 83-85, Jour. Bus. Rsch., 1973-79, Jour. Mktg., 1978-80; assoc. editor: Decision Scis., 1976-79; mktg. dept. editor: Mgmt. Sci., 1980-82; contbr. numerous chpts. to books, articles to profl. jours. Recipient first prize rsch. design contest Am. Mktg. Assn., 1971-72. Mem. Am. Mktg. Assn. (mem. adv. bd. mktg. rsch. spl. interest group 1998), Am. Statis. Assn. (chmn. stats. in mktg. sect. 1995), European Mktg. Acad. (mem. exec. com. 1981-84), Theta Delta Chi, Beta Gamma Sigma, Phi Kappa Phi. Office: Ga Inst Tech Coll Mgmt Atlanta GA 30308-0520 Office Phone: 404-894-4381. Business E-Mail: len.parsons@mgt.gatech.edu.

PARSONS, VINSON ADAIR, retired computer company executive; b. Frankfort, Ky., Oct. 22, 1932; s. Richard Adair and Nina (Mefford) P.; m. Elizabeth Ann Peltier, June 2, 1956. AS, Mitchell Coll., 1959; BS, U. Conn., 1960; Advanced Mgmt. Program cert., Harvard U., 1985. Auditor, Price Waterhouse & Co. (C.P.A.s), Hartford, Conn., 1960-65; controller Pervel Industries Inc., Plainfield, Conn., 1965-70; v.p., controller Akzo Am. Inc., Asheville, NC, 1970-71, 73-83, v.p., chief fin. officer, 1983-86, System Software Assocs. Inc., Chgo., 1986-89, also bd. dirs.; ret., 1990. Bd. dirs. Am. Tape Co., BRIntec Co., Control Tech. Corp. Elected commr. Town of Weaverville Bd. Commrs., 1994-2000. With USN, 1953-57. Mem. Am. Mgmt. Assn., Fin. Execs. Inst., Inst. Mgmt. Accts. (pres. local chpt. 1969-70) Clubs: Asheville Country; University (NYC); Bilt. Forest CC. Personal E-mail: vinsonparsons@gmail.com.

PARSONS, WILLIAM JONATHAN, cardiologist; b. Apr. 3, 1955; married; 3 children. BA, Dartmouth Coll., 1977, MD, 1980. Diplomate Am. Bd. Internal Medicine, Am. Bd. Cardiovascular Diseases, Am. Bd. Nuclear Cardiology, Nat. Bd. Echocardiography; registered physician in vascular interpretation. Resident in internal medicine Strong Meml. Hosp. U. Rochester (N.Y.), 1983-85; cardiology fellow Duke U. Med. Ctr., Durham, 1985-88, asst. prof., 1988-91; asst. prof. medicine Southwestern Med. Ctr. U. Tex., Dallas, 1991-93; attending cardiologist Baylor U. Med. Ctr., Dallas, 1993—2001, WakeMed Health & Hosps., Raleigh, NC, 2001—. Contbr. articles to profl. jours. Gen. med. officer USPHS-IHS, 1981-83. Fellow Am. Coll. Physicians, Am. Coll. Cardiology, Am. Soc. Echocardiography, Am. Soc. Nuc. Cardiology. Office: Carolina Cardiology WakeMed 3324 Six Forks Rd Raleigh NC 27609 Home Phone: 919-845-6743; Office Phone: 919-781-7772. Personal E-mail: sereneparsons@aol.com.

PARTAIN, CLARENCE LEON, radiologist, nuclear medicine physician, educator, health facility administrator; b. Memphis, July 12, 1940; s. Archie Leon and Vergie (Young) P.; m. Judith Stafford, Jan., 1964; children: David Blane, Teri Ellyn, Amy Leigh. BSNE, U. Tenn., 1963; MSNE, Purdue U., 1965, PhD in Nuc. Engring., 1967; MD, Washington U., St. Louis, 1975. Diplomate Am. Bd. Nuc. Medicine, Am. Bd. Radiology; registered profl. engr., Mo. Asst. prof. nuc. engring. U. Mo.-Columbia, 1968-71, assoc. prof., 1971-75; resident NC Meml. Hosp., Chapel Hill, 1975-79; assoc. prof. radiology U. NC-Chapel Hill, 1978-79; assoc. prof. Vanderbilt U., Nashville, 1980-85, prof. radiology and biomed. engring., 1985—, vice chmn. radiology, 1989-92, dir. nuc. medicine, 1981-85, dir. magnetic resonance imaging, 1983-92, chmn. radiology, radiologist in chief, 1992-2000, dir. Ctr. for Imaging Rsch., 2000—; cons. NIH, Bethesda, Md., 1980—; Carol D. and Henry P. Pendegrass prof. radiology and radiol. scis. Vanderbilt U., 1997—. Pres. SE chpt., Soc. Nuc. Medicine, 1984—85; editor, jour. MRI Internat. Soc. Magnetic Resonance Imaging, 2000—; bd. dirs. Internat. Soc. MRI, 2000—, Rad Soc. N.Am., Rsch. and Edn. Found., 2003—09; pres. Radiology Rsch. Alliance, Assoc. U. Radiologists, 2004—05; Paul Ross lectr. U. Mich. Author: Nuclear Magnetic Resonance (NMR) Imaging, 1983, NMR Imaging: Clinical Utility and Correlation, 1984, Thyroid and Parathyroid Imaging, 1986, Magnetic Resonance Imaging, 2d edit., 1988, Correlative Image: Nuclear Medicine, Magnetic Resonance, Computer Tomography, Ultrasound, 1988; editl. bd. Acad. Radiology, Magnetic Resonance Imaging, Jour. Magnetic Resonance Imaging, Jour. Nuclear Medicine; editor-in-chief Jour. of Magnetic Resonance Imaging. Scientific adv. coun. Whitaker Found. AEC Spl. fellow, 1964-66; grantee Nat. Inst. Neurosci., Communicative Diseases and Stroke, 1977-78 Fellow Am. Coll. Nuc. Physicians, Am. Coll. Radiology, Soc. Magnetic Resonance Imaging (bd. dirs.), Internat. Soc. of Magnetic Resonance in Medicine, Accreditation Coun. for Grad. Med. Edn., Residency Rev. Com. Nuc. Medicine; mem. AMA, IEEE, Radiol. Soc. N.Am. (chair rsch. devel. com., trustees, R&E Found.), Assn. Univ. Radiologists (exec. com.), Radiology Rsch. Alliance (pres.), Soc. Nuc. Medicine (trustee, Benedict Casson lectr. 1981), Am. Roentgen Ray Soc. (exec. coun.), Soc. Magnetic Resonance in Medicine (trustee), Internat. Soc. Magnetic Resonance in Medicine (governance coun., bd. dirs.), Soc. Chmn. Acad. Radiology Depts. (bd. dirs.), Am. Bd. Radiology (examiner in nuc. medicine, Disting. Svc. award), Sigma Phi Epsilon. Baptist. Avocation: travel. Office: Vanderbilt U Med Ctr Dept Radiology RM RR-1223 MCN Nashville TN 37232-0001 Home: 6224 Belle Rive Dr Brentwood TN 37027

PARTLETT, DAVID FREDERICK, law educator; b. 1947; LLB, U. Sydney Sch. Law, 1970; LLM, U. Mich. Law Sch., 1972-74; JSD, U. Va. Sch. Law, 1980. Bar: New South Wales 1971. Solicitor Messrs Sly & Russell, Sydney, 1969—71; vis. asst. prof. U. Ala. Sch. Law, Tuscaloosa, 1972-73; sr. legal officer Commonwealth Atty. General's Dept., Canberra, Australia, 1974—75; prin. law reform officer Australian Law Reform Commn., 1975—77; lectr. Australian Nat. U., Canberra, 1978-80, sr. lectr., 1980-87, assoc. dean, 1982—85; vis. assoc. prof. Vanderbilt U. Sch. Law, Nashville, 1987-88, prof. law, 1988-2000, acting dean, 1996-97; prof. law, v.p., dean Washington & Lee U. Sch. Law, Lexington, Va., 2000—06; Asa Griggs Candler prof. law, dean Emory U. Sch. Law, Atlanta, 2006—11, prof. law, 2011—. Sparkman disting. vis. prof. Ala. U., 1986—87; vis. prof. U. Sydney Law Sch., 2008; mem. adv. bd. LexisNexis Law Sch., 2009—. Co-author: Professional Negligence, 1985, Suing for Medical Malpractice, 1993, Child Mental Health and the Law, 1994, Modern Remedies: Cases, Practical Problems and Exercises, 1997, Torts: Cases and Materials (11th edit.), 2005, The Right to Speak Ill: Defamation, Reputation and Free Speech, 2006; co-editor: Compensation for Personal Injuries, 1985; contbr. articles to profl. jours. Recipient Paul J. Hartman Award for excellence in tchg., Vanderbilt U., 1992—93, Disting. Svc. award, 1996, Thomas Jefferson award for disting. svc., 1997. Mem.: ABA, American Law Inst., American Soc. Law & Medicine, Southeastern Assn. American Law Schools (treas., past pres.), Selden Soc. Office: Emory Univ School Law 1301 Clifton Rd Atlanta GA 30322 Office Phone: 404-727-9569. Business E-Mail: david.partlett@emory.edu.

PARTON, DOLLY, singer, composer, actress; b. Sevier County, Tenn., Jan. 19, 1946; d. Robert Lee and Avie Lee (Owens) P.; m. Carl Dean, May 30, 1966. D in Humane & Musical Letters (hon.), U. Tenn., Knoxville, 2009. Country music singer, rec. artist, composer, actress, radio and TV personality. Entrepreneur, owner entertainment park Dollywood, established 1985; founder Dixie Stampede, 1988; built Dollywood Splash Country, Tennessee's largest water park, 2001. Established Velvet Apple Music (BMI); owner of record company Blue Eye Records; radio appearances include: Grand Ole Opry, WSM Radio, Nashville, Cass Walker program, Knoxville; TV appearances include: Porter Wagoner Show, from 1967, Cass Walker program, Bill Anderson Show, Wilburn Bros. Show, Barbara Mandrell Show; rec. artist, Mercury, Monument, RCA, CBS record cos.; (albums) Here You Come Again (Grammy award 1978), Real Love, 1985, Just the Way I Am, 1986, Portrait, 1986, Think About Love, 1986, Trio (with Emmylou Harris, Linda Ronstadt), 1987, (Grammy award 1988), Heartbreaker, Great Balls of Fire, Rainbow, 1988, White Limozeen, 1989, Home for Christmas, 1990, Eagle When She Flies, 1991, Slow Dancing with the Moon, 1993, (with Tammy Wynette and Loretta Lynn) Honky Tonk Angels, 1994, The Essential Dolly Parton, 1995, Just the Way I Am, 1996, Super Hits, 1996, (with others) I Will Always Love You & Other Greatest Hits, 1996, Hungry Again, 1998, Trio II, 1998, Grass is Blue, 1999 (Grammy award for Best Bluegrass Album), Best of the Best-Porter & Doll, 1999, Halos and Horns, 2002, For God and Country, 2003, Makin' Believe, 2003, Live and Well, 2004, Those Were the Days, 2005, Backwoods Barbie, 2008, Better Day, 2011; appears on song "Creepin' In" with Norah Jones, 2004; composer numerous songs including Nine to Five (Grammy award 1981); actress: (films) Nine to Five, 1980, The Best Little Whorehouse in Texas, 1982, Rhinestone, 1984, Steel Magnolias, 1989, Straight Talk, 1991, Frank McKlusky, C.I., 2002, (voice) Gnomeo & Juliet, 2011, Joyful Noise, 2012; (TV films) A Smoky Mountain Christmas, 1986, Wild Texas Wind, 1991, Unlikely Angel, 1996, Blue Valley Songbird, 1999; (TV series) Heavens to Betsy, 1994, Mindin My Own Business, 1996, Reba, 2005, Hannah Montana, 2006-10; author: Dolly, 1994; music and lyrics (Broadway plays) 9 to 5, 2009; (autobiography) My Life and Other Unfinished Business, 1994, Dream More: Celebrate the Dreamer in You, 2012, (cookbook) Dolly's Dixie Fixin's: Love, Laughter and Lots of Good Food, 2006. Began Dollywood Found., 1988. Recipient (with Porter Wagoner) Vocal Group of Yr. award, 1968, Vocal Duo of Yr. award All Country Music Assn., 1970, 71, Nashville Metronome award, 1979, Am. Music award for Best Duo Performance (with Kenny Rogers), 1984, Grammy awards for Best Female Country Vocalist, 1978, 81, for Best Country Song, 1981, for Best Country Vocal Performance with Group, 1987, People's Choice award, 1980, 88, Icon award, Broadcast Music, Inc., 2003, US Libr. of Congress Living Legend award, 2004, Nat. Medal of Arts Nat. Endowment for the Arts, 2005, Kennedy Ctr. Honor, John F. Kennedy Ctr. for Performing Arts, 2006, Johnny Mercer award, Songwriter's Hall of Fame, 2007, Grammy Lifetime Acheivement award, 2011; co-recipient (with Emmylou Harris and Linda Ronstadt) Acad. Country Music award for album of the yr., 1987, (with Brad Paisley) Most Inspiring Video of Yr. for When I Get Where I'm Going, CMT Awards (Country Music TV), 2006, Video of Yr. and Vocal Event of Yr., Acad. Country Music award, 2006; Cliffie Stone Pioneer award, Acad. Country Music, 2008, Jim Reeves Internat. award, 2009; named Female Vocalist of Yr., 1975, 76, Country Star of Yr., Sullivan Prodns., 1977, Entertainer of Yr., Country Music Assn., 1978, Female Vocalist of Yr., Acad. Country Music, 1980; Dolly Parton Day proclaimed, Sevier County, Tenn., designated Oct. 7, 1967, Los Angeles, Sept. 20, 1979; named to Small Town of Am. Hall of Fame, 1988, East Tenn. Hall of Fame, 1988, Country Music Hall of Fame, 1999, Nat. Acad. of Popular Music Songwriters Hall of Fame, 2001, Gospel Music Hall of Fame, 2009, Music City Walk of Fame, 2009, Country Gospel Music Hall of Fame,

2010; Star on Hollywood Walk of Fame, 1984; bronze statue, Courthouse lawn, Sevierville, Tennessee Address: RCA 6 W 57th St New York NY 10019-3901 Office: Dollywood Co 1020 Dollywood Ln Pigeon Forge TN 37863-4101

PARTOYAN, GARO ARAKEL, lawyer; b. Toledo, Dec. 6, 1936; s. Garo and Vartoohi Partoyan; m. Beverly Meadows Partoyan; 1 child, Williams; children: Garo Linck, Elizabeth Margaret 3 children. BS in Chem. Engring., Northwestern U., 1959; JD, U. Mich., 1962; LLM, NYU, 1964. Bar: N.Y. 1963, U.S. Dist. Cts. (so. dist.) N.Y. 1964, U.S. Ct. Claims 1966, U.S. Ct. Appeals (2nd cir.) 1966, U.S. Dist. Ct. (ea. dist.) N.Y. 1968. Ptnr. Curtis, Morris & Safford, NYC, 1962-76; gen. counsel mktg. and tech. Mars, Inc., McLean, Va., 1976-98; pres. Mgmt. of Intellectual Property, Inc., Sarasota, Fla., 1998—. Mem. Dobbs Ferry (N.Y.) Bd. Edn., 1972-76, pres., 1975-76; chmn. Fairfax Citizens Group, Fairfax County, Va., 1988-90. Mem. ABA, Licensing Execs. Soc., Am. Intellectual Property Law Assn., N.Y. Intellectual Property Law Assn., Internat. Trademark Assn. (pres. 1990-91, bd. dirs. 1983-2006), Intellectual Property Owners (bd. dirs. 1992-99), Armenian Bar Assn. Avocations: sailing, curling, croquet. Office: 419 MacEwen Dr Osprey FL 34229 Home Phone: 941-918-0720; Office Phone: 941-918-0595. Fax: 941-966-8020. E-mail: partoyanga@aol.com.

PARTRIDGE, WILLIAM FRANKLIN, JR., lawyer; b. Newberry, SC, July 16, 1945; s. William F. and Clara (Eskridge) P.; m. Ilene S. Stewart, Aug. 16, 1969; children: Allison, William F. BA in History, The Citadel, 1967; JD, U. S.C., 1970. Bar: S.C. 1970, U.S. Ct. Claims 1971, U.S. Ct. Mil. Appeals 1971, U.S. Tax Ct. 1971, U.S. Supreme Ct. 1973, U.S. Dist. Ct. S.C. 1980. Instr. internat. law Chapman Coll., 1973-74; pub. issue com. S.C. Bar, 1982-83. Lt. Col. USAFR. Mem. Newberry Bar Assn. (pres. 1982-83), Palmetto Club, County of Newberry Club, Cotillion Club, Assn. Citadel Men Club, Masons, Phi Delta Phi. Democrat. Methodist. Home: 2029 Harrington St Newberry SC 29108-3055 Office: 1201 Boyce St Newberry SC 29108-2705 Office Phone: 803-276-5968.

PASANO, MICHAEL S., lawyer; b. Kansas City, Mo., Mar. 10, 1951; s. Angelo S. and Rachel (Young) P. AB summa cum laude, Georgetown U., 1973; JD, Yale U., 1976. Bar: Fla., Mo., DC, US Ct. Appeals (5th, 11th & DC circuits), US Supreme Ct, US Ct. Appeals (1st, 2nd, 6th, and 8th cir.), US Dist. Ct.(middle & southern dist.) Fla., US Dist. Ct. DC. Lawy clk. US Dist. Ct. DC, Washington, 1976-77; asst. US atty. DC US Dept. Justice, Washington, 1977-81, asst. U.S. atty. (southern dist.) Fla. Miami, Fla., 1981-85, chief fraud section, 1983—85; atty. Zuckerman Spaeder LLP (formerly Zuckerman, Spaeder, Taylor & Evans), Miami, Fla., 1985—2008; shareholder Carlton Fields, Miami, Fla., 2008—. Recipient Charles R. English award, ABA Section on Criminal Justice, 2008; named one of The Nation's Top Litigators, The Nat. Law Journal, 2009, Florida's Super Lawyers, 2008, 2009, 2010. Mem. ABA, Fla. Bar Assn., Fla. Assn. Criminal Def. Lawyers, 11th Cir. Lawyer Disciplinary Com., 11th Cir. Fed. Pub. Defender Com., Southern Dist. Criminal Justice Act Panel Com. Office: Carlton Fields Miami Tower 100 SE Second St Ste 4200 Miami FL 33131 Office Phone: 305-530-4064. Office Fax: 305-530-0055. E-mail: mpasano@carltonfields.com.

PASCHE, BORIS CLAUDE ROGER, hematologist, oncologist, educator; b. Lausanne, Vaud, Switzerland, Aug. 5, 1961; arrived in US, 1989; s. Rene Charles Edouard and Marina (Guidetti) Pasche. MD, Karolinska Inst., Stockholm, 1986, PhD, 1989; MD, U. Lausanne, Switzerland, 1987. Diplomate Am. Bd. Internal Med., Am. Bd. Med. Oncology, Am. Bd. Hematology, lic. NY, Ill., Ala. Rsch. fellow cardiovasc. medicine Brigham & Women's Hosp./Harvard Med. Sch., Boston, 1989-92; intern medicine NY Hosp./Cornell Med. Ctr., NYC, 1992-93, resident medicine, 1993-94; fellow hematology/oncology Meml. Sloan-Kettering Cancer Ctr., NYC, 1994—97; rsch. fellow cell biology Howard Hughes Med. Inst., Chevy Chase, 1996—2000; asst. prof. medicine Northwestern U. Feinberg Sch. Medicine, Chgo., 2001—05, assoc. prof. medicine, 2006—08; prof. medicine, dir. divsn. hematology/oncology U. Ala., Birmington, 2008—, Martha Ann & David L. May endowed chair cancer rsch., 2008—; assoc. dir. transnational rsch. U. Ala. Comprehensive Cancer Ctr., 2008—09, dep. dir., 2009—. Asst. physician NY Hosp./Meml. Sloan-Kettering Cancer Ctr., 1993—2000; attending physician Northwestern Meml. Hosp., 2001—08; co-leader cancer genes & molecular targeting program Robert H. Lurie Comprehensive Cancer Ctr., Chgo., 2006—07. Editor: Oncology, Genetics & Molecular Medicine, 2003—, Jour. Exptl. & Clin. Cancer Rsch., 2004—; contbr. articles to profl. jours. Recipient K12 Physician Scientist award, Nat. Cancer Inst., 1995—98, Human Cancer Genetics Program Commemorative Medal, Ohio State U., 2005; grantee Swiss Academic Soc. fellowship, 1983, Rsch. fellowship, Lausanne Academic Soc., 1984—86, Clin. Oncology fellowship, Am. Cancer Soc., 1994. Fellow: ACP; mem.: AMA, AAAS, Am. Soc. Clin. Investigation, Am. Fedn. Clin. Rsch., Am. Soc. Human Genetics, Am. Assn. Cancer Rsch., Am. Soc. Clin. Oncology, Am. Soc. Hematology, Internat. Soc. Thrombosis & Haemostasis (Young Scientist Merit award 1989, Young Investigator Merit award 1991), Bioelectromagenetics Soc., Nat. Inst. Electromed. Info., European Bioelectromagnetics Soc. Achievements include invention of electronic system for influencing cellular functions. Avocations: skiing, windsurfing, classical music, fine arts. Office: U Ala Divsn Hematology Oncology 1802 6th Ave S NP 2566 Birmingham AL 35294 Office Phone: 205-934-9591. Business E-Mail: uifcftu@uab.edu.

PASCOE, B. LYNN (BURTON LYNN PASCOE), former international organization official, former ambassador; b. Mo., July 7, 1943; m. Diane Pascoe; 2 children. BA, U. Kans., 1965; MA, Columbia U., 1967. Spl. asst. to dep. sec. US Dept. State, dep. exec. sec.; dep. chief of mission US Embassy, Beijing; prin. dep. asst. sec. for East Asian & Pacific US Dept. State; dir. American Inst. Taiwan, Taipei, 1993—96; US spl. negotiator, Nagorno-Karabakh & regional conflicts, US co-chair, Orgn. Security & Cooperation in Europe's Minsk Group US Dept. State, 1997—98, US amb. to Malaysia Kuala Lampur, 1999—2001, dep. asst. sec. for European & Eurasian Affairs Washington, 2001—04, US amb. to Indonesia Jakarta, 2004—07; under-sec. gen. polit. affairs UN, NYC, 2007—12.

PASCOE, RANA S., physician, family medicine, adolescent medicine; MD, U. Southern Calif., 1987. Cert. Adolescent Medicine 2001, family medicine 2002. Resident family medicine Kaiser Found. Hosp., 1988—90; fellow adolescent medicine Children's Hosp., LA, 1990; physician Baylor Med. Ctr. at Garland. Office: Baylor Medical Center at Garland Ste 100 890 Rockwall Pkwy Rockwall TX 75032 Office Phone: 214-771-3712.

PASSARO, PAUL CHARLES, business executive, management consultant; b. Ridgewood, NJ, June 6, 1967; s. Richard Paul and Barbara (Brown) Passaro; m. Kristi-Anne Tolo, June 25, 1994; children: Peter James, Anne Marie, Charles Andrew. BA in History cum laude, Williams Coll., Williamstown, Mass., 1989; MBA, U. N.C., 1993. Mcpl. bond trader and salesman Roosevelt & Cross, Inc., NYC, 1989—91; v.p. The Fraser Co., Hilton Head, SC, 1992—94; CFO Pine Needles and Mid Pines Resorts, Southern Pines, NC, 1994—2003; COO EastWest Ptnrs. Club Mgmt., Chapel Hill, NC, 2003—06; ptnr. Brown-Locy Advisors, 1992—. Bd. dirs. small bus. adv. bd. NC Citizens for Bus. and Industry, Raleigh, 1999—2002; v.p. The Toppers, NYC, 1991; founder Habitat for Humanity Charity Golf Classic, Chapel Hill, 1992—2013; mem. fin. com. Trinity Sch., Durham, Chapel Hill, 1999—2002; bd. dirs. Leadership NC, 1999—2005; mem. audit com. NC Rep. Party, Raleigh, 1999—2003, chmn., 2001—03; alt. del. 2004 Rep. Nat. Conv.; elder Christ Cmty. Ch., Chapel Hill, 1994—2010. Mem.: Theodore Roosevelt Assn. Republican. Avocations: bible study, golf, reading history, bird hunting. Home Phone: 919-932-6404. Personal E-mail: paul@brown_locy.com.

PASSEY, GEORGE EDWARD, psychologist, educator; b. Stratford, Conn., Sept. 28, 1920; s. Henry Richard and Elizabeth (Angus) P.; m. Algie Aldridge Ashe, Nov. 18, 1950; children— Richard Ashe, Elizabeth Aldridge, Mary Louise. BS, Springfield Coll., 1942; MA, Clark U., 1947; PhD, Tulane U., 1950. Asst. prof. U. Ala., Tuscaloosa, 1952-55, assoc. prof., 1955-56, 57-59, prof., 1959-63, prof. psychology, chmn. div. social and behavioral scis. Birmingham, 1967-73, prof. engring., 1969-84, Disting. Service prof. psychology, 1984-85, Disting Service prof. emeritus, 1985—; dean U. Ala. (Sch. Social and Behavioral Scis.), Birmingham, 1973—84. Research scientist Lockheed Ga. Co., Marietta, Ga., 1956-57, 63-65, cons., 1965-67; prof. Ga. Inst. Tech., 1965-67 Served with USNR, 1942-46, PTO; with USAF, 1951-52, lt. col. USAF, 1980 Lt. col. USAR. Fellow Am. Psychol. Assn.; mem. So. Soc. for Philosophy and Psychology, Southeastern Psychol. Assn., Ala. Psychol. Assn., Sigma Xi. Home: 3746 Colchester Rd Mountain Brook AL 35223-2829 E-mail: gpassey3299@charter.net, gpassey@connectedliving.com.

PASSIDOMO, KATHLEEN C., state legislator; b. Jersey City, May 19, 1953; m. John Passidomo; children: Francesca, Gabriella, Catarina. BA, Trinity U., Washington, 1975; JD, Stetson U., Fla., 1978. Cert.: Fla. Bar Bd. (real estate lawyer). Ptnr. Kelly, Passidomo & Alba LLP; mem., Dist. 76 Fla. House of Representatives, 2011—. Republican. Avocations: hiking, trekking. Office: 3299 Tamiami Trail E Ste 304 Naples FL 34103 also: Florida House of Reps 324 The Capitol 402 S Monroe St Tallahassee FL 32399-1300 Office Phone: 239-417-6200, 850-488-4487.

PASSONNO STOTT, NICOLE MARIE, astronaut, engineer; b. Albany, NY; BS in Aeronautical Engring., Embry-Riddle Aeronautical U., 1987; MS in Engring. Mgmt., U. Ctrl. Fla., 1992. Structural design engr. Pratt and Whitney Govt. Engines, West Palm Beach, Fla., 1987; ops. engr., Orbiter Processing Facility NASA Kennedy Space Ctr., Fla., 1988, detailed to the Dir. of Shuttle Processing, 1988, lead for joint AMES/Kennedy Space Ctr. software project to develop intelligent scheduling tools, 1988, mem., Space Station Hardware Integration Office, NASA project lead for the Internat. Space Station truss elements under construction at the Boeing Space Station facility. Huntington Beach, Calif.; several positions, vehicle ops engr. NASA convoy comdr.; shuttle flow dir. for Endeavour and orbiter project engr. for Columbia. NASA Shuttle Processing; mem., NASA Aircraft Ops. Divsn., serving as a Flight Simulation Engineer (FSE) on the Shuttle Training Aircraft (STA) NASA Johnson Space Ctr., 1998; mission specialist, astronaut NASA, 2000—. Tech. duties in the Astronaut Office Station Ops. Br. NASA; support astronaut for the Expedition 10 crew and as an ISS CAPCOM; crew mem. on the NEEMO 9 mission (NASA Extreme Environment Mission Ops.), 2006; flight engr. ISS Expeditions 20 and 21; mission specialist on mission to International Space Station with the crew of STS-128 and will return with STS-129 crew, 2009; mission specialist STS-133-Final Flight of Discovery, 2011. Recipient Aircraft Ops. Divsn., Newt Myers Team Spirit award, Kennedy Space Ctr. Pub. Affairs Cert. Appreciation for Svc., NASA Exceptional Achievement medal, NASA Cert. Commendation, NASA Performance award, NASA On-the-Spot award, Lockheed Cert. Appreciation. Avocations: flying, snow skiing, scuba diving, woodworking, painting, gardening. Office: Lyndon B Johnson Space Ctr Astronaut Office 2101 NASA Pwy Houston TX 77058

PASSTY, JEANETTE NYDA MENDELSSOHN, literature and language professor, writer, editor; b. LA, Jan. 19, 1947; d. Walter Isaac and Mollie Sarah Nyda; m. Gregory Bohdan Passty, June 18, 1976; children: Benjamin and Jocelyn. AA, L.A. Valley Coll., 1966; BA, UCLA, 1968; MA, U. So. Calif., 1974, PhD, 1982. Cert. CC instr., Calif. Tchg. asst., lectr., assoc. dir. Freshman English program U. So. Calif., 1971—78; vis. scholar English dept. Tex. State U., San Marcos, 1982—83; lectr. English dept. U. Tex., Austin, 1983—85; vis. asst. prof., adj. assoc. prof. Tex. Luth. U., Seguin, 1983, 1985—87; from instr. to asst. prof. St. Philip's Coll., San Antonio, 1988—92, assoc. prof., 1992—. Lectr. UCLA, U. Tex., Austin, Western Mich. U., U. Louisville, Salisbury State U., Morehead State U., Tex. Tech. U., U. Wales, Bangor, U. London; humanities book reviewer CHOICE (ALA Jour.), 1985—86; manuscript reviewer Fairleigh Dickinson U. Press, 1991—; editl. cons. CONNECTIONS: Online Distance Learning Faculty Forum, 2002—10; coll. English cons. Scholar Strategies Korean Program, 2008—11; lectr. U. C. Berkeley, 2012. Author: Eros and Androgyny: The Legacy of Rose Macaulay, 1988, The Lion Tells Her Story: A Biography of the Honorable N.P. Brooks Hinton, 1998, Bringing Denis Home: The Hero from Hope, Kansas, 2001, Creating the Spark, 2009, Hard Times and Great Expectations, 2010, The Music of the Spheres, 2011, Conquering Diabetes, 2012; annotator: Alice Crawford's Paradise Pursued, 1995; contbr. articles to encyclopedia, profl. and lit. jours., chpts. to books; guest Sta. KSPL Radio in Touch With, 1989; appearance Sta. KENS-TV, 1992; Channel 12 Morehead, KY, 1998; CNN, 1998, Roadside (entr'acte with G.S. Bailey), 2000. Mem. Nat. Abortion Rights Action League, Audubon Soc., Environment Tex., Greenpeace, Environ. Def. Fund, The Nature Conservancy, NOW, Sierra Club, Handgun Control, Orgn. Internat. Conf. on the Holocaust, San Antonio, 2000. Recipient Elizabeth K. Pleasants Tchg. award, U. So. Calif., 1974, letters of appreciation, Lord Bonham-Carter, 1987, HRH Princess Margaret, 1989—90, Oustanding Acad. Book award, ALA, 1989, Women Honoring Women award, Am. Assn. Women in C.C.s, 1997, Katherine Anne Porter Lit. prize, 1999, NISOD Internat. Conf. on Tchg. and Leadership Excellence Award, 2003, St. Philip's Coll. Tchg. Excellence award, 2003—04; named to Alamo Colls. Women's Hall of Fame, 2009; nominee Minnie Stevens Piper Prof., 2012. Mem. AAUW, MLA, Nat. Coun. Tchrs. English, South Ctrl. Soc. 18th Century Studies, Victorian Studies Inst., Virginia Woolf Soc. Avocations: Tae Kwon Do, travel. Office: Saint Philip's Coll 1801 Martin Luther King Dr San Antonio TX 78203-2098 Office Phone: 210-486-2377. Business E-Mail: jpassty@alamo.edu.

PASSY, CHARLES, writer; b. NYC, Jan. 9, 1964; s. Victor and Beverly (Green) P.; m. Leslie M. Olsen, Dec. 15, 1989; two children: Jacob E., Emma F. BA, Columbia U., 1985. Assoc. Jay K. Hoffman and Assocs., NYC, 1983-87; sr. editor, mng. editor Ovation Mag., NYC, 1988-89; editor Classical Mag., NYC, 1989-91; editor-in-chief Musical Am. Pub., NYC, 1991-92; staff writer The Palm Beach Post, West Palm Beach, Fla., 1992—2010; writer Dow Jones, 2010—. Announcer, prodr. WNYC FM, N.Y., 1984-85; entertainment stringer N.Y. Newsday, 1987-92. Author (with others): New Voices: Selected University and College Prize Winning Poems, 1989, The New Grove Dictionary of Jazz, 1988, The New Grove Dictionary of American Music, 1986, The New Grove Dictionary of Music and Musicians, 2d edit., 2001; editor: The Letters of Virgil Thomson, 1988; contbr. numerous articles to publs. in field, columns in newspapers, articles to various newspapers and mags. Recipient Poetry award Acad. Am. Poets Columbia U., 1985, Criticism & Writing awards Soc. Profl. Journalists, 1995, 97, 99, 2001, 03, 05, Fla. Press Club, 1993, 2004, Fla. Soc. Newspaper Editors, 1993, 2001, Cox Newspapers, 2001, Am. Assn. Sunday and Feature Editors, 2002, 05, award Mo. Lifestyle Journalism, 2005, Assn. Food Journalists, 2008; fellow Knight Ctr. for Specialized Journalism, 1993. Office: Palm Beach Newspapers Inc 2751 S Dixie Hwy West Palm Beach FL 33405-1298 Home: 365 W 28 St 3B New York NY 10001 Office: 1211 Ave of Americas New York NY 10036 Office Phone: 561-820-4589. Personal E-mail: chazpbg@aol.com. Business E-Mail: charles_passy@pbpost.com.

PASTERNAC, ANDRÉ, cardiologist, educator; b. Toulouse, France, July 22, 1937; came to Can., 1971, naturalized, 1978. s. Jacques and Régine P. Adv. math., Lycée Henri IV, Paris, 1956; BA in Polit. Sci., Toulouse U., 1963, MD Med. Sch., 1968; grad. in Mgmt. Program, Columbia U., 2000. Cert. Ins. and Disability Assessment U. Montreal, 2002. Intern Toulouse Univ. Hosp., 1962-63, resident, 1963-64, Edouard-Herriot Hosp., Lyon, France, 1965-66; Fulbright scholar in cardiology Harvard U., 1968-71; research fellow Peter Bent Brigham Hosp., Boston, 1968-69; Milton fellow Children's Hosp., Boston, 1969-71; fellow in cardiology Toronto (Ont., Can.) U., 1971-72; staff cardiologist Montreal (Que., Can.) Heart Inst., 1972—2008; asst. prof. medicine U. Montreal, 1972-78, clin. assoc. prof., 1978—87, clin. prof. medicine, 1987—2008. Vis. lectr. U. Liège (Belgium), 1977, U. Madrid, 1977, U. Warsaw, 1979, 83; cons. Harley St. Clinic, Cromwell Hosp., Wellington Hosp., London; vis. assoc. prof. McGill U., Montreal, 1975-76; medico-legal and ins. expert U. Montreal, 2002. Contbr. articles to profl. jours. Bd. dirs. Heart-Brain Rsch. Found. Inc., NYC, Cardiostat Canada Inc., Montreal, Cardiostat USA Inc., West Palm Beach, Fla. Recipient Physician of Yr. award, Fla., 2004, Man of the Yr. award, Am. Biographical Inst., 2012, Am. Field Svc. grantee, Oreg., 1954-55. Mem. French Cardiac Soc., European Soc. Cardiology, Canadian Cardiovasc. Soc., Am. Coll. Cardiology, Am. Heart Assn., Internat. Soc. Heart Rsch., Am. Fedn. Clin. Rsch., NY Acad. Scis. Research in stress-related myocardial ischemia and dysfunction, mitral valve prolapse, cardiovascular drugs, cardiomyopathies, catecholamines, neuroendocrine control of the heart, stress and the heart, prevention of cardiovascular disease. Office: Ctr for Cardiovascular Disease Prevention 200 Butler St Ste 61 West Palm Beach FL 33407 also: Cardiovascular Disease Prevention Ctr 1045 95th St Ste 10 Bay Harbor Islands FL 33154 also: Westmount Square Health Group 1 Westmount Square Suite 550 Westmount PQ H3Z2PG Canada Office Phone: 561-659-6756, 561-644-3999. Personal E-mail: apartemac@gmail.com.

PASTERNACK, STEFAN ALAN, psychiatrist, psychoanalyst; b. Jersey City, Nov. 5, 1939; BA, Cornell U., 1961; MD, Georgetown U., 1965. Diplomate in psychiatry Am. Bd. Neurology and Psychiatry; lic. physician, D.C., Md. Resident in psychiatry U. Cin. Gen. Hosp., 1966-69; psychiat. cons. North Cmty. Mental Health Ctr., Washington, 1971-97; asst. prof. psychiatry Georgetown U. Sch. Medicine, Washington, 1971-79, assoc. clin. prof. psychiatry, 1979-86, clin. prof. psychiatry, 1986—, co-dir. advanced studies prog. in psychiatry/psychoanalysis, 1995—; clin. prof. biomed. sci. Fla. Atlantic U., 2007—; tchg. analyst Fla. Psychoanalytic Inst., 2008—. Pvt. practice psychiatry and psychoanalysis, Washington, 1978-2005; Fla., 2005; faculty, Fla. Psychoanalytic Inst., 2006; clin. prof. psychiatry, Fla. Atlantic U., 2007. Editor: Violence and Victims, 1975; contbr. articles to profl. jours. Bd. dirs. Nat. Capital Med. Found., Washington, 1973-76, Forum for Psychoanalytic Study of Film, Washington, 1989—, vol. clin. prof. psychiatry U. Miami Miller Sch. Medicine, 2007-. Lt. comdr. USN, 1969-71. Mem.: Fla. Psychiat. Soc., Washington Psychiat. Soc. (mem. coun. 1987—99), Am. Psychoanalytic Assn., Am. Psychiat. Assn. (disting. life fellow), Cosmos Club. Avocations: motorboating and yachting, piano, writing. Home: 6924 Balboa Island Ct Delray Beach FL 33446-5641 Office: Ste 2004 950 Pa Corp Cir Boca Raton FL 33487 Office Phone: 561-706-9584. Personal E-mail: drsp39@gmail.com.

PASTIDES, HARRIS, academic administrator; m. Patricia Moore, Aug. 27, 1980; children: Katharine, Andrew. BS in Biological Scis., U. Albany, 1975; MPH, Yale U., PhD in Epidemiology. Sr. Fulbright rsch. fellow U. Athens, Greece, 1987—88; prof. epidemiology, chmn. Dept. Biostatistics and Epidemiology U. Mass., Amherst; dean Arnold Sch. Pub. Health U. SC, Columbia, 1998—2003, v.p. rsch. and health scis., exec. dir. rsch. found., 2003—08, pres., 2008—. Cons., advisor WHO, 1994, 1995. Author: Foundations of Cancer Epidemiology; contbr. articles to profl. jours. Office: University of South Carolina Office of President Osborne Administration Building, Suite 2 Columbia SC 29208 Office Phone: 803-777-5458. Office Fax: 803-777-5457. E-mail: pastides@sc.edu, president@sc.edu.*

PASTIN, MARK JOSEPH, health science association administrator, educator; b. Ellwood City, Pa., July 6, 1949; s. Joseph and Patricia Jean (Camenite) Pastin; m. Joanne Marie Reagle, May 30, 1970 (div. Mar. 1982); m. Carrie Patricia Class, Dec. 22, 1984 (div. June 1990); m. Christina M. Brecto, June 15, 1991. BA summa cum laude, U. Pitts., 1970; MA, Harvard U., 1972, PhD, 1973. Asst. prof. Ind. U., Bloomington, 1973-78, assoc. prof., 1978-80; founder, bd. Compliance Resource Group, Inc., 1983—; chmn., CEO, pres. Coun. Ethical Orgns., Alexandria, Va., 1986—; prof. mgmt., dir. Ariz. State U., Tempe, 1988-92, prof. emeritus, 1996—; chair Health Ethics Trust, 1995—. Dir. Learned Nicholson, Ltd., 1990-91; bd. Japan Am. Soc. Phoenix, Found. for Ethical Orgns.; cons. GTE, Interim Healthcare, 1997-2000, U.S. Dept. Edn., 2002, Tex. Instruments, MicroAge Computers, Med-Tronic, Blood Sys., Inc., Opus Corp., GTE, NyNex, Am. Express Bank, Kaiko Bussan Co., Japan, Arex Co., Japan, Century Audit Co., U.S. Dept. Edn., Japan, Scottsdale Meml. Hosp., Cosanti Found., Lincoln Electric Co., Tenet Healthcare, The Williams Co.; vis. faculty Harvard U., 1980; presenter Australian Inst. Mgmt., Nippon Tel. & Tel., Hong Kong Commn. Against Corruption, 1984, Young Pres.'s Orgn. Internat. U., 1990, Nat. Assn. Indsl. & Office Parks, 1990, ABA, 1991, Govt. of Brazil, 1991; columnist Jour. Clin. Medicine. Author: Hard Problems of Management, 1986 (Book of Yr. Armed Forces Mil. Comtrs. 1986, Japanese edit. 1994), The Hotline Handbook, 1996, Planning Forum, 1992, Make An Ethical Difference, 2013, Best Practice Standards For Compliance Programs, 2013; editor: Public-Private Sector Ethics, 1979; mem. editl. bd. Report on Medicare Compliance; pub. Pastin Report on Best Compliance Practices, 1998—, Columnist jours. clin. medicine; Guerin Lect. on Philanthropy, 1996. Founding bd. mem. Tempe Leadership, 1985-89; bd. mem. Ctr. for Behavioral Health, Phoenix, 1986-89, Tempe YMCA, 1986—, Valley Leadership Alumni Assn., 1989-92; mem. Clean Air Com., Phoenix, 1987-90. Nat. Sci. Found. fellow, Cambridge, Mass., 1971-73; Nat. Endowment for the Humanities fellow, 1975; Exxon Edn. Found. grant, 1982-83. Mem.: Found. Ethical Orgns. (chmn. 1988, pres.), Am. Soc. Assn. Execs. (presenter 1987—97), Potomac Pitt Club, Chesapeake Club, Harvard Club D.C., Phi Beta Kappa, Golden Key. Avocations: golf, running. Office: 214 S Payne St Alexandria VA 22314-3530 Home: 7205 Regent Dr Alexandria VA 22307-2044 Office Phone: 703-683-7916. Personal E-mail: councile@aol.com, markpastin@gmail.com.

PASTNER, JOSH, men's college basketball coach; s. Hal Pastner; m. Kerri Pastner; 1 child, Payten Sydney. B in Family Studies, U. Ariz., Tucson, 1998, M in Tchg. and Tchg. Edn., 1999. Video & recruiting coord., adminstrv. asst. U. Ariz. Wildcats, 2001—02, asst. coach, 2002—08, U. Memphis Tigers, 2008—09, head basketball coach, 2009—. Head coach Houston Hoops, AAU, 1999—2000. Active Boys and Girls Clubs, Tucson, Boy Scouts America, Leukemia and Lymphoma Soc., Naval Spl. Warfare Found., Spl. Olympics. Named Conf. USA Coach of Yr., 2013; named to 40 Under 40, Tucson Bus. Edge, 2007. Achievements include member of the NCAA Men's Basketball National Championship winning University of Arizona Wildcats, 1997. Office: Univ Memphis Athletics Dept 570 Normal Athletic Office Bldg Rm 230 Memphis TN 38152

PASTOREK, PAUL G., aerospace company executive, lawyer; b. Anchorage, Alaska, June 27, 1954; m. Kathy Pastorek; children: Ryan, Jeffery, Kaitlin. BA, Loyola U., 1976, JD, 1979. Bar: La. 1979. Litig. atty., ptnr. Adams & Reese LLP, New Orleans, 1979—2002, ptnr. spl. bus. svcs., 2004—07; gen. counsel NASA, Washington, 2002—04; supt. edn. La. Dept. Edn., Baton Rouge, 2007—11; chief adminstrv. officer, chief counsel, corp. sec. EADS North America, Arlington, Va., 2011—. Bd. mem. La. State Bd. Elem. & Secondary Edn., 1996—2004, pres., 2000—04. Mem.: La. State Bar Assn. Office: EADS North America Suite 9000 2550 Wasser Terrace Herndon VA 20171 Office Fax: 225-342-0193. E-mail: paulpastorek@la.gov.

PASTRICK, HAROLD LEE, aeronautical engineer; b. Ambridge, Pa., June 28, 1936; s. Samuel and Mary (Makara) P.; m. Vivienne Lee Nusser Heinricher, June 3, 1961; children: Tracy Lee, Gregory Harold, Michael Joseph Samuel. BSEE, Carnegie-Mellon U., 1958; postgrad., Rutgers U., 1959-61, CCNY, 1961-63, U. Ala. Huntsville, 1964-66, 68-73; student, MIT, summers 1961-63; MS in Aeronautics & Astronautics, Stanford U., 1967, engr. in Aeronautics & Astronautics, 1972; PhD in Engring., Calif. Western U., 1977. Registered prof. engr., Ala. Metallurgical engring. aide Jones & Laughlin Steel Corp., Aliquippa, Pa., 1955-56; asst. engr., designer Am. Bridge Divsn., U.S. Steel Corp., Ambridge, 1957; electronics engr. Avionics Divsn., U.S. Army Signal R&D Labs., Ft. Monmouth, N.J., 1958-63; aerospace engr., Inertial Systems Team Missile R&D Labs., Redstone Arsenal, Ala., 1963-64; tech. dir. Army Inertial Guidance & Tech. Ctr., Redstone Arsenal, 1964-66; project engr. Inertial Guidance Br., Redstone Arsenal, 1967-71; rsch. aerospace engr. Guidance & Control Br., Redstone Arsenal, 1971-73; group leader Terminal Homing Missile Analysis, Redstone Arsenal, 1973-79; staff specialist, asst. to dir., land warfare Office of Under Sec. Def., Rsch. and Engring., Washington, 1979-80; chief, guidance and control analysis U.S. Army Missile Command, Redstone Arsenal, Ala., 1980-81; v.p. engring. Control Dynamics Co., Huntsville, 1981-83; asst. v.p., engring. analysis divsn. Sci. Applications Internat. Corp., Huntsville, 1983-86; v.p. theater missile def. and system analysis operation, 1986-91; corp. v.p., gen. mgr. SRS Technologies, Huntsville, 1991—2004. Acting pres. and COO SRS Techs., 1994, mem. corp. exec. mgmt. com., 1991-2004, mem. profit sharing and 401(k) com., 1993-2004; CEO, Pastrick Engring. and Mgmt. Cons., 2005—; lectr. Sch. of Sci. and Engring., U. Ala., Huntsville, 1967-83; lectr. dept. continuing edn. George Washington U., 1985-87; engring. seminar dir. Applied Tech. Inst., Frankfurt, Germany, 1984, Singapore, 1986; tech. tng. dir. Tech. Tng. Corp., Tel Aviv, 1988; lectr. Advanced Tech. Internat., Ltd., London, 1985; guidance and control cons. various labs Dept. of Def., Washington, 1971-2001; lectr., rsch. advisor Southeastern Inst. Tech., Huntsville, 1978-84; lectr., seminar leader Guidance and Control Technologies, U.S., Europe, Asia, Mex., 1980-94. Contbr. over 120 articles to profl. jours. Chmn. combined fed. campaign ARDEC United Way, Redstone Arsenal, 1976; mem. Huntsville Econ. Devel. Com., 1994; chmn. indsl. contbns. Armed Forces Week C. of C. Huntsville-Madison County, 1993—96, 1999, vice chmn. mil. affairs. com., 1994—95, chmn. mil. affairs com., 1996; program chmn. tech. and bus. symposium and exhbn. Huntsville, 1994—95; gen. chmn., 1995—96; chmn. adv. com., 1997—98; founding trustee Ala. Constn. Village Found., 2001—; mem. All-Peoples Meml. for All Vets., Madison County, 2001—; mem. elec. and computer engring. adv. bd. The Citadel, Charleston, SC, 2001—; pres. St. Michael's Orthodox Ch., 2002—09, 2013—; pathfinder chmn., mem. exec. cabinet Huntsville Madison County (Ala.) United Way, 2005—07; pres. Greek Orthodox Ch., 1967, 1973, chmn. planning com., 1993—2000. Capt. US Army, 1958—64. Recipient Eminent Engr. Disting. Tau Beta Pi, 1998. Fellow: AIAA (assoc.; vice-chmn. Huntsville chpt. 1979, guest editor Jour. Guidance and Control 1981, missile tech. com. 1989—91); mem.: Ala. Acad. Sci. (vice chmn. 1978—79, engring. chmn. 1979—81), Inst. Navigation, Assn. U.S. Army, IEEE (sr.; chpt. program chmn. 1972—73), Soc. Computer Simulation, Am. Def. Preparedness Assn. (vice-chmn. Huntsville chpt. 1974—75), Huntsville Assn. Tech. Socs. (adv. com. 1997—98, pres. 1998—99, chmn.), Redstone Golf Club, Greenwhyche Club (v.p. 1979), Heritage Club, Rotary (sec. 1994—95, pres.-elect. 1995—96, pres. 1996—97, asst. gov. dist. 6860 1997—2000, dist. task force dir. 2000—01), Greater Huntsville Rotary Found. (dir. internat. svc. 1992—94, CEO 1998—2000). Achievements include pioneering hardware in the loop simulations for testing laser semi-active guided missiles. Avocations: golf, weightlifting, choral music, reading, running. Office Phone: 256-509-6700. Personal E-mail: hpastrick@bellsouth.net.

PATCH, DARCY L., finance company executive; Attended, U. Calif., Irvine, 1985. V.p., Mktg., mortgage information & services. divsn. & LSI Fidelity National Financial, Inc., 2003—04, sr. v.p., mktg. & comm., enterprise office, 2004—06; sr. v.p., mktg., real estate & mortgage information services Fidelity National Information Services, Inc., 2006—08, sr. v.p., mktg., v.p., mktg. Fidelity National Information Solutions, Inc.; sr. v.p., mktg., real estate information services. Fidelity National Financial, Inc., 2000—; sr. v.p., mktg., real estate information services Fidelity National Real Estate Solutions, 2001—; sr. v.p., mktg. Lender Processing Services, Inc., 2008—. Office: Lender Processing Services Inc 601 Riverside Ave Jacksonville FL 32204 Office Phone: 904-854-5100. Office Fax: 904-854-4124. Business E-Mail: darcy.patch@fnis.com.

PATE, LOUIS MILFORD, state legislator; b. Duplin County, NC, Sept. 22, 1936; s. Louis Milford and Mary Best Pate; m. Joyce Cameron Garner, 1966; children: Louis M. III, Frances D. BS, Golden Gate U., San Francisco, 1978, MBA, 1980. Pres. Garner Bros. Inc., 1982—90; mayor Town of Mt. Olive, NC, 1991—94, 1999—2002; mem. Dist. 11 NC House of Representatives, 1995—96, 2003—08; mem. Dist. 5 NC State Senate, 2011—. Commr. Mt. Olive Bd. Commissioners, 1987—89; dir. NC Global Transpark Authority, 1997—2001. Del. Rep. Nat. Conv., 2008. Officer USAF, 1962—82. Mem.: VFW, American Legion, Mt. Olive Rotary Club (pres. 1986). Republican. Baptist. Mailing: Dist Address PO Box 945 Mount Olive NC 28365 also: Capitol Address 300 N Salisbury St Rm 406 Raleigh NC 27603 Office Phone: 919-658-3637, 919-733-5621. E-mail: Louis.Pate@ncleg.net.

PATE, ROBERT HEWITT, JR., retired counselor educator; b. Abingdon, Va., Apr. 5, 1938; s. Robert Hewitt and Esther Frances (Kirk) P.; m. Ellen O'Neal Pope, Dec. 11, 1960; children: Robert Hewitt III, Mary Ellen Pate Barton. AB, Davidson Coll., 1960; MEd, U. Va., 1965; PhD, U. N.C., 1968. Lic. prof. counselor, Va. Marketer Sinclair Refining Co., Abingdon, Va., 1960-61, 63-64; counselor St. Andrews Presbyn. Coll., Laurinburg, NC, 1965-66; counselor educator U. Va., 1968—2008, interim dean, 1994-95, assoc. dean, 1995—2007, prof. edn., emeritus, William Clay Parrish Jr. prof. edn., 2003—08. Author: Being A Counselor, 1983. Sr. warden, St. Paul's Ivy, Va., 2010. 1st lt. U.S. Army 1961-63. Mem. ACA, Va. Counselors Assn. (pres. 1983-84), Ctr. Credentialing and Edn.(dir., chair 2012-), Nat. Bd. Cert. Counselors (chair 1996-97). Avocation: reading. Home: 552 Dryden Pl Charlottesville VA 22903-4666

PATE, RUSSELL R., exercise physiologist; b. NY; BS in Physical Edn., Springfield Coll., 1968; MS, U. Oreg., 1973, PhD in Exercise Physiology, 1974. Faculty Arnold Sch. Pub. Health, U. SC, Columbia, 1974—, prof. dept. exercise sci., assoc. v.p. health scis., dir. Children's Phys. Activity Rsch. Group. Apptd. mem. SC Gov.'s Coun. Phys. Fitness, 1988—; panel mem. US Dietary Guidelines Adv. Com., NAS Inst. Medicine, 2003—04; past pres. Nat. Coalition Promoting Phys. Activity; past faculty mem. U. Va., Med. Coll. Ga. Author: Scientific Foundations of Coaching, 1984, Training for Young Distance Runners, 1996; editor: Health & Fitness through Physical Education, 1994; contbr. articles to profl. jours. Recipient Alliance Scholar award, Am. Alliance Health, Phys. Edn., Recreation & Dance, 1999, Sci. Honor award, Pres.'s Coun. Phys. Fitness & Sports, 2008. Fellow: Am. Acad. Kinesiology & Phys. Edn.; mem.: Am. Coll. Sports Medicine (pres. 1993—94, Citation award 1996), Am. Dietetic Assn. (hon.), Carolina Marathon Assn. (bd. dirs., past. pres.). Achievements include coordinating the effort leading to the development of the recommendation on physical activity and public health of the US Centers for Disease Control and Prevention and the American College of Sports Medicine; competing in three US Olympic Trials marathons and placing twice among the top ten finishers in the Boston Marathon. Office: Arnold Sch Pub Health U SC 800 Sumter St Columbia SC 29208 Office Phone: 803-777-5032. Office Fax: 803-777-4783. Business E-Mail: rpate@mailbox.sc.edu.

PATE, THOMAS R., food service executive; Attended, East Tenn. State U., Johnson City. V.p. tng. and mgmt. devel. Cracker Barrel Old Country Store, Inc. Office: Cracker Barrel Old Country Store Inc 305 Hartmann Dr Lebanon TN 37087 Office Phone: 615-444-5533. Office Fax: 615-443-9476.

PATE, WILLIAM, information technology executive; BA in Journalism, Ga. State U., 1981. Pub. rels. specialist ARC, Goodwill Industries; with Knapp Inc., Atlanta; prodr. advt. and mktg. programs S.E. Dairy Assn.; supr. domestic and internat. advt. and pub. rels. MCI, sr. dir., Mktg. & Advt., 1992—96; chief mktg. officer BellSouth Corp., Atlanta, 1996—2007, v.p. advt. & Pacific rels., 1997; pres. Career Sports & Entertainment, Inc., 2007—08, CSE; pres., CEO Atlanta Convention & Visitors Bureau, 2008—. Chmn. Atlanta Conv. and Visitors Bur., The Chick-Fil-A Peach Bowl; mem. bd. trustees Ga. State U.; bd. dirs. Alliance Theatre Co., The Ad Coun. Recipient Ad Campaign of Yr. for Gramercy Press campaign, Advt. Age mag., Campaign of Yr. award for Chatsford, Am. Mktg. Assn. Mem.: Pub. Rels. Soc. Am., Assn. Nat. Advertisers, Am. Advt. Fedn. Office: Atlanta Convention & Visitors Bureau 233 Peachtree St NE Ste 1400 Atlanta GA 30303 Office Phone: 404-521-6000. Office Fax: 404-577-3293.

PATE, WILLIAM PATRICK, city manager; b. Duplin County, NC, July 30, 1962; s. William Atlas and Bonny Lou (O'Leary) P.; m. Sandra Martin, Aug. 17, 1985; children: William Glenn, Andrew Patrick. BA in Polit. Sci. and Religion, U. N.C., 1984, MPA, 1986. Budget and evaluation analyst intern City of Winston-Salem, NC, 1985-86, budget and evaluation analyst NC, 1986-87, lead budget and evaluation analyst NC, 1987; budget and rsch. mgr. City of Greensboro, NC, 1987-90, budget and evaluation dir. NC, 1990-99; asst. city mgr. City of High Point, NC, 1999—. Inst. of Govt. intern N.C. Office Coastal Mgmt., Raleigh, N.C., 1984; rsch. asst. U. N.C., Chapel Hill, 1984-85. Mem. Chmns. Soc. United Way of High Point, 1998—; mem. Leadership Greensboro, 1993-99, Leadership High Point, 2000—; elder, clk. session Faith Presbyn. Ch., Greensboro; mem. Salem Presbyn. World Ministries Cluster, 1997-99; chair staff parish rels. team Covenant Ch., 2005-07, adminstrn. bd., 2005-07, pres. SW Guilford HS Baseball Booster Club, 2008-. Recipient Disting. Svc. award Alpha Phi Omega, 1984. Mem. Internat. City Mgrs. Assn., Am. Soc. Pub. Adminstrn. (pres. Piedmont Triad chpt. 1994), Gov. Fin. Officers Assn. U.S. and Can. (exec. bd. 1998-2004, nat. com. on govtl. budgeting and mgmt. 1993-98, nat. com. on debt and fiscal policy 1998-2001, pres. 2002-03, Disting. Budget Presentation award reviewer, Disting. Budget Presentation award 1992-98), N.C. Local Govt. Budget Assn. (bd. dirs. 1990-92, 95, 1st v.p. 1992-93, pres. 1993-94), N.C. City/County Mgrs. Assn., U. N.C. MPA Alumni Assn. (program chmn. 1992, pres-elect 1993, pres. 1994, Scholarship award 1985), U. N.C. Gen. Alumni Assn. (bd. dirs. 1994-95, v.p. 2006-07, pres. 2008-), Kiwanis Club (v.p. 2006—, pres., 2008-09, Disting.Club award, 2008-09). Methodist. Home: 4509 Calabria Ct High Point NC 27265-9595 Office: City of High Point PO Box 230 High Point NC 27261-0230 E-mail: pat.pate@highpointnc.gov.

PATEL, AJAY, finance educator; m. Aparna Patel; 2 children. BS, St. Joseph's Coll., India; MBA, U. Balt.; PhD, U. Ga. Faculty appointments U. Mo., Bentley Coll.; faculty mem. Babcock Grad. Sch. Mgmt., Wake Forest U., 1993, Babcock rsch. prof. fin., 2001—08, interim dean, 2003—04, dean, 2004—08, GMAC chair in fin., 2008—, prof., 2008—; dir. Ctr. Enterprise Rsch. and Edn., 2009—. Office: Wake Forest University School of Business Farrell Hall Winston Salem NC 27106 Home Phone: 336-815-8035; Office Phone: 336-758-5575. Business E-Mail: ajay.patel@mba.wfu.edu.

PATEL, UPTAL DINESH, nephrologist, researcher; BA, U. Calif. San Diego, 1993; MD, U. Calif. San Francisco, 1997. Diplomate Am. Bd. Internal Medicine, 2001, Diplomate, Subspecialty in Nephrology Am. Bd. Internal Medicine, 2005, Diplomate Am. Bd. Pediat., 2001, Diplomate, Subspecialty in Pediat. Nephrology Am. Bd. Pediat., 2005. Robert Wood Johnson clin. scholar U. Mich., Ann Arbor, 2003—05; asst. prof. medicine and pediat. Duke U., Sch. Medicine, Durham, NC, 2005—11, assoc. prof. medicine and pediat., 2012—. Assoc. editor Am. Heart Jour.; mem. editl. bd.: Jour. Am. Soc. Nephrology, 2007—, Clinical Medicine: Cardiology, 2007—. Rsch. Career Devel. award, NIH, 2006—11. Mem.: Nat. Kidney Disease Edn. Program NIH (chair, Health Info. Tech. Working Group), Am. Soc. Nephrology (chair chronic kidney disease working group, mem. bd. advisors 2012—, Carl W. Gottschalk Rsch. scholar 2009—12).

PATRICK, ANDREW S., state legislator; b. Warsaw, NY, Aug. 5, 1969; s. Leon and Joy Patrick; m. Amee Patrick, June 27, 1998; children: Sasha Patrick, Emma Patrick, Hannah Patrick, Vlademir Patrick, Joel Patrick. BS, SUNY, Brockport, 1995. CEO Advance Point Global; with mil. svc. US Air Force, 1987—92; sergeant US Navy, 1987—92; staff sergeant, security specialist NY Air Nat. Guard, 1992—95; trooper NY State Police, 1996—97; special agent US Secret Svc., 1997—2007; mem. Dist. 123 SC House of Representatives, 2011—. Republican. Office: South Carolina House of Representatives District 123 308A Blatt Bldg Columbia SC 29201 Address: PO Box 22676 Hilton Head Island SC 29925 Office Phone: 803-212-6928.

PATRICK, CHARLES WILLIAM, JR., lawyer; b. Monroe, NC, Oct. 9, 1954; s. Charles William and Louise (Nisbet) P.; m. Celeste Hunt, June 5, 1976; children: Laura Elizabeth, Charles William III. BA magna cum laude, Furman U., 1976; JD, U. SC, 1979. Bar: S.C. 1979, U.S. Dist. Ct. S.C. 1981, U.S. Ct. Appeals (11th cir.) 1981, U.S. Ct. Appeals (10th cir.) 1983, U.S. Ct. Appeals (4th cir.) 1986. Law clk. to presiding judge 9th Cir. Ct. State of S.C., Charleston, 1979—80; assoc. Ness, Motley, Loadholt, Richardson and Poole and predecessor firm Blatt and Fales, Charleston, 1980—2002, 1980—2002; ptnr. Ness, Motley, Loadholt, Richardson & Poole & Predecessor firm Blatt & Fales, Charleston, 1984—2009, Richardson, Patrick, Westbrook & Brickman, LLC, Charleston, 2002—. Exec. editor S.C. Law Review, 1978; contbr. articles to profl. jours. Mem. ABA, Assn. Trial Lawyers Am., S.C. Assn. Trial Lawyers, Trial Lawyers for Pub. Justice, Phi Beta Kappa. Democrat. Presbyterian. Avocations: boating, skiing, jogging. Office: Richardson Patrick Westbrook & Brickman LLC PO Box 879 174 East Bay St Charleston SC 29402-0879 Home: 12 Murray Blvd Charleston SC 29401-2742 Home Phone: 843-853-8601; Office Phone: 843-727-6500. Business E-Mail: cpatrick@rpwb.com.

PATRICK, CONNIE L., federal agency administrator; m. John Patrick; 4 children. BA in Criminal Justice, U. Ctrl. Fla.; Grad., FBI Nat. Acad., Fla. Criminal Justice Exec. Inst., Fed. Exec. Inst. Dep. Sheriff's Office Brevard County, 1976—81; various positions including spl. agent, spl. agent supr., asst. spl. agent in charge of Tampa reg. ops. bur., dir. Fla. Criminal Justice Inst. Fla. Dept. Law Enforcement, 1981—95, dir. divsn. human resources & training, 1995—96; dir. gen. training Fed. Law Enforcement Training Ctr., 1996—98, assoc. dir. planning & resources, 1998—2001, assoc. dir. planning & workforce devel., 2001—02, dir., 2002—. Recipient Presdl. Meritorious Rank award, 2001. Office: Fed Law Enforcement Training Ctr 1131 Chapel Crossing Rd Brunswick GA 31524*

PATRICK, DAN, state legislator; b. Balt. m. Janetlea Patrick; children: Ryan, Shane. BA in English, U. Md. Balt. County. Radio sta. owner, operator, talk show host, Dallas, Houston; mem. Dist. 7 Tex. State Senate, 2007—. Author: The Second Most Important Book You Will Ever Read, 2002; prodr.: (Christian film) The Heart of Texas. Mem.: Clout (founder 2003). Republican. Office: 11451 Katy Freeway Ste 209 Houston TX 77079 also: PO Box 12068 Capitol Station Austin TX 78711 Office Phone: 713-464-0282, 512-463-0107. Office Fax: 713-461-0108, 512-463-8810.

PATRICK, DIANE, state legislator; m. Ned Patrick, 1965; children: Craig, Claire. BA in Elem Edn., Baylor U., Waco, Tex.; MEd, U. North Tex., Denton, PhD in Ednl. Adminstrn., 1999. Tchr., Waco, Tex., Richardson Ind. Sch. Dist., Birdville Ind. Sch. Dist.; dir. ednl. programs to two psychiatric hospitals; mem. Tex. State Bd. Edn., 1992—96; former bd. trustees & pres. Arlington Ind. Sch. Dist., v.p. edn. found. bd.; clin. assoc. prof. U. Tex., Arlington, 1994—2007; lectr. Tex. Christian U.; mem. Dist. 94 Tex. House of Representatives, Tex., 2007—. Adv. bd. mem. Consortium State Orgns. Tex. Tchr. Educators, Tex. Ctr. Ednl. Rsch.; former bd. dir. Arlington Mus. Art, Children's Advocacy Network. Mem.: Women's Policy Forum Tarrant County, Jr. League Arlington, Am. Assn. U. Women, Assn. Tex. Profl. Educators. Republican. Office: 318 W Main St Ste 102 Arlington TX 76013 also: Room EXT E2.610 Capitol Extension PO Box 2910 Austin TX 78768 Office Phone: 817-548-9091, 512-463-0624.

PATRICK, JAMES DUVALL, JR., lawyer; b. Griffin, Ga., Dec. 28, 1947; s. James Duvall and Marion Wilson P. BS in Indsl. Mgmt., Ga. Inst. Tech., 1970; JD, U. Ga., 1973. Bar: Ga. 1973, U.S. Dist. Ct. (mid. dist.) Ga. 1973, U.S. Dist. Ct. (so. dist.) Ga. 1983, U.S. Ct. Appeals (5th cir.) 1974, U.S. Ct. Appeals (11th cir.) 1981, U.S. Tax Ct. 1985, U.S. Supreme Ct., 1977. Assoc. Cartledge, Cartledge & Posey, Columbus, Ga., 1973-74; ptnr. Falkenstrom, Hawkins & Patrick, Columbus, 1975, Falkenstrom & Patrick, Columbus, 1975-77; sole practice Columbus, 1977—. Instr. bus. law Chattahoochee Valley C.C., Phenix City, Ala., 1975-77; instr. paralegal course Columbus Coll., 1979, 84; del. U.S./China Joint Session on Trade, Investment, and Econ. Law, Beijing, 1987, Moscow Conf. on Law and Bilateral Econ. Rels., Moscow, 1990; U.S. del. U.S./Cuba Law Initiative, Havana, 2000. Mem. Hist. Columbus Found., Mayor's Comn. for the Handicapped, 1987-88; local organizer, worker Joe Frank Harris for Gov. Campaign, Columbus, 1982; bd. dirs. Columbus Symphony Orch., 1988-94. Fellow Am. Bar Found.; mem. ATLA, ABA (fellow found.), Am. Judicature Soc., State Bar Ga., Fed. Bar Assn., Ga. Trial Lawyers Assn., Columbus Lawyers Club, Columbus Kappa Alpha Alumni Assn. (sec.), Civitan (bd. dirs. 1975-77), Country Club of Columbus, Georgian Club (Atlanta), Buckhead Club, Chattahouchee River Club, Phi Delta Phi, Kappa Alpha. Methodist. Office: PO Box 2745 Columbus GA 31902-2745

PATRICK, RUSS, retail executive; Joined The Neiman Marcus Group, Inc., 1990; various mdse. positions Neiman Marcus Direct, Neiman Marcus Stores; divisional mdse. mgr., men's sportswear The Neiman Marcus Group, Inc.; v.p., gen. mdse. mgr., Neiman Marcus stores Neiman Marcus Group, Inc., 2004—. Office: The Neiman Marcus Group Inc 1618 Main St Dallas TX 75201 Office Phone: 214-743-7600. Office Fax: 214-573-5320. Business E-Mail: Russ_Patrick@neimanmarcus.com.

PATRICOT, HUBERT, beverage company executive; Mktg. dir. Coca-Cola Enterprises, Inc., France, v.p., sales and mktg.; product mgr., French arm Coca-Cola Enterprises Inc, France; sales & mktg. dir. Coca-Cola Enterprises, Inc., 1997—2002, asst. gen. mgr., 2002—03, v.p., gen. mgr. France, 2003—08, exec. v.p., pres., European Group, 2008—. Office: Coca-Cola Enterprises Inc 2500 Windy Ridge Pky Atlanta GA 30339 Office Phone: 770-989-3000. Office Fax: 770-989-3788. Business E-Mail: HPatricot@na.cokecce.com.

PATRONIS, JIMMY T., state legislator; b. Panama City, Fla., Apr. 13, 1972; m. Katie Patronis; 1 child, Jimmy Theo III. AS in Restaurant Mgmt., Gulf Coast CC, Panama City, 1994, AA in Gen. Edn., 1994; BS in Pub. Adminstrn., Comm., Polit. Sci., Fla. State U., Tallahassee, 1996. Intern Fla. State Senate, Tallahassee, 1995; rsch. asst. House of Commons, London, 1996; restaurateur Capt. Anderson's, Panama City; mem. Dist. 6 Fla. House of Reps., Tallahassee, 2006—, mem. agr. and natural resources policy com., Fla. legis. com. on intergovernmental rels., roads, bridges and ports policy com., transp. and econ. devel. appropriations com. Mem. Fla. Coun. on Vocat. Edn., 1996—97, Fla. State Elections Commn., 1998—2003, Bay County Airport Authority, 2004—06; past chmn. Bay County-Panama City Internat. Airport and Indsl. Dist. Mem. St. John's Greek Orthodox Ch. Republican. Greek Orthodox. Office: 455 Harrison Ave Ste A Panama City FL 32401-2775 also: 1102 The Capitol 402 S Monroe St Tallahassee FL 32399-1300 Office Phone: 850-914-6300, 850-488-9696.

PATTERSON, AUBREY BURNS, JR., banker; b. Grenada, Miss., Sept. 25, 1942; s. Aubrey Burns and Elizabeth (Staten) P.; m. Ruby Kathryn Clegg, Dec. 12, 1964; children: Aubrey B. III, Clayton H., Jennifer L. BBA, U. Miss., 1964; MBA, Mich. State U., 1969. Joined Bancorp South (formerly Bank of Mississippi), Tupelo, 1972, pres., 1983—90, chmn., chief exec. officer, 1990—. Chmn., CEO Bancorp-South, Inc. Former chmn. bd. dirs. Salvation Army, Tupelo; bd. dirs. Cmty. Devel. Found., chmn. bd., 1994-95; bd. dirs. Columbia Theol. Sem., Decatur, Ga., Fin. Svs. Roundtable, Presbyn. Ch. U.S.A. Found., New Covenant Trust Co.; former chmn. CREATE, Inc.; bd. dirs. Miss. Econ. Coun., Jackson, 1986—, chmn., 1994; chmn. bd. dirs. North Miss. Health Svcs. Inc., 1987—, also exec. com.; bd. dirs. Miss. Partnership Econ. Devel.; bd. dir. Furniture Brands Internat. and Miss. Instns. Higher Learning; moderator St. Andrews Presbytery Presbyn. Ch. USA; chmn., bd. dirs. U. Miss. Found.; laureate Miss. Bus. Hall of Fame; bd. dirs. Journal Pub. Co.; mem. exec. com. Miss. Pub. Edn. Forum. Capt. USAF, 1965-72. Decorated Air Force Commendation medal, Meritorious Svc. medal, Nat. Def. Svc. medal. Mem. ABA (govt. rels. coun.), Am. Bankers Assn. (chmn. 2002-2003), U. Miss. Hall of Fame, Miss. Bankers Assn. (pres. 1995—), Soc. Internat. Bus. Fellows, Conf. of State Bank Supr., Bankers Adv. Coun. (chmn.), Tupelo Country Club, Univ. Club, Kiwanis (pres. Tupelo 1987), Beta Gamma Sigma, Beta Alpha Psi, bd. dirs. Furniture Brand Internat. and Miss. Power Co., bd. trustees Miss. instns. Higher Learning. Presbyterian. Office: BancorpSouth PO Box 789 Tupelo MS 38802-0789

PATTERSON, CHRISTOPHER NIDA, circuit judge; b. Washington Courthouse, Oh., Apr. 17, 1960; s. Right Reverend Donis Dean and JoAnne (Nida) Patterson; m. Vicky Patterson; children: Travis, Kirsten. BA in psychology, Clemson U., SC, 1978—82; JD, Nova U., Ft. Lauderdale, Fla., 1982—85. Bar: Fla. 1985, U.S. Dist. Ct. (mid. dist.) Fla. 1985, U.S. Ct. Mil. Rev. 1986, U.S. Ct. Appeals Armed Forces 1987, U.S. Dist. Ct. (ea. dist.) Va. 1987, U.S. Supreme Ct. 1989, U.S. Ct. Appeals (11th cir.) 1992, U.S. Dist. Ct. (no. dist.) Fla. 1992, U.S. Dist. Ct. (so. dist.) Tex. 1995; cert. criminal trial specialist Fla. Bar., 1995-2013, cert. criminal trial advocate Nat. Bd. Trial Advocacy, 1995-2009; cert. dependency mediator, family law mediator, 1998-2010, county ct. mediator, arbitrator 1995-2010. Cert. legal intern Fla. 9th circuit State Atty. Office, Orlando, Fla., 1985; judge advocate gen. corps. U.S. Army, 1986—90; special asst. U.S. atty. US Dist. Ct. (ea. dist.) Va, 1987—90; pvt. practice, 1991—2010; asst. public defender 14th Judicial Circuit, 2010, circuit judge, 2010. Adj. prof. law Gulf Coast Coll., 1995—2009; mem. Fla. Supreme Ct. Mediators Qualifications Bd., 2000—10; on-air legal analyst Next Media Radio-WYOO-FM, 2002—09; juvenile rules com. Fla. Bar., 2005—06; cert. dependency mediator, 1999—2009; cert. family law mediator, 1998—2009; dependency mediation coord. Bay Co., 2004—06. Author: Queen's Pawn, 1996, Treasure Trove, 1997, Krysha, 2006; contbr. Nat. DAR Mag., Fla. Defender mag, The End of Privacy, 1998; contbg. editor, Fla. Assn. Criminal Defence Lawyers, Defender Mag., 2000-2003, The Army Lawyer, Commercial Activities, 1989, The Fla. Bar Jour., Bay Co. Teen Ct., 1995; Ct. TV Asst. gov. district 6940 Rotary Internat., 2008-2010; Paul Harris Fellow; Former Chancellor St. Thomas Episcopal Ch.; former bd. dirs. Bay County Teen Ct., Inc., Gulf Coast Triathalon Girls Inc. Svc. Orgn., Widowed Persons Svc., The Unlimited Path, Inc. Captain, commission U.S. Army, 1982, service dates U.S. Army, 1986—91. Recipient Clemson Disting. Military Grad., 1982, U.S. Army Chief of Staff award for legal excellence, 1989, US Army CECOM Legal Achievement award, 1989, Pro Bono Svc. award, Fla. Bar, 1995, Guardian ad litem commendation, Fla. Supreme Ct., 1999, Jefferson award finalist, 1999, Fla. Super Lawyer, 2006, 2007, 2008, 2009, 2010. First Families Gallia Co., Oh.; former mem. ABA, FBA, SAR, NACDL, Am. Coll. Barristers, Fla. Assn. Criminal Def. Lawyers, Acad. Fla. Trial Lawyers, Assn. Fed. Def. Attys., Fla. Acad. Profl. Mediators, Fla. Bar Spkrs. Bur.; Fla. Bar Pres. Pro Bono Svc. award; Nominee Jefferson award for Pub. Svc., 1999; Bay Co. Bar Assn.; former mem., The Ret. Officers' Assn., Christian Legal Soc., Am. Legion, Fellowship of Christian Athletes, Nat. Triathlon Fedn., Soc. Colonial Wars, Mil. Order Fgn. Wars. Episcopalian. Avocations: history, genealogy, athletics, travel, writing, photography, music. Office: 111 Moonlight Dr Panama City FL 32413 also: Washington County Courthouse 1293 Jackson Ave Chipley FL 32428

PATTERSON, DENNIS M., bank executive; Grad., Ga. Inst. Tech., Atlanta, 1971. Corp. exec. v.p. corp. sales adminstrn., mem. mgmt. com. SunTrust Banks, Inc. Mem. adv. bd. Ga. Inst. Tech. Coll. Mgmt. Named to Acad. Disting. Alumni, Ga. Inst. Tech. Coll. Mgmt., 2006. Office: SunTrust Banks Inc PO Box 4418 Atlanta GA 30302-4418 Office Phone: 404-588-7711. Office Fax: 404-827-6173.

PATTERSON, DONALD ROSS, lawyer, educator; b. Sept. 9, 1939; s. Sam Ashley and Marguerite (Robinson) P.; m. Peggy Ann Schulte, May 1, 1965; children: D. Ross, Jerome Ashley, Gretchen Anne. BS, Tex. Tech U., 1961; JD, U. Tex., 1964; LLM, So. Meth. U., 1972. Bar: Tex. 1964, U.S. Ct. Claims 1970, U.S. Ct. Customs and Patent Appeals 1970, U.S. Ct. Mil. Appeals 1970, U.S. Supreme Ct. 1970, U.S. Dist. Ct. (ea. dist.) Tex. 1982, U.S. Ct. Appeals (5th cir.) 1991, U.S. Ct. Appeals (D.C. cir.) 1994; bd. cert. in immigration and naturalization law, Tex. Commd. lt. (j.g.) USN, 1964, advanced through grades to lt. comdr., 1969; asst. officer in charge Naval Petroleum Res., Bakersfield, Calif., 1970-72; staff judge adv. Kenitra, Morocco, 1972-76; officer in charge Naval Legal Svcs. Office, Whidbey Island, Wash., 1976-79; head mil. Justice divsn., Subic Bay, The Philippines, 1979-81; ret. USN, 1982; pvt. practice Tyler, Tex., 1982—. Former instr. U. Md., Chapman Coll., U. LaVerne, Tyler Jr. Coll., Jarvis Christian Coll., U. Tex., Tyler. Mem. East Tex. Estate Planning Coun. Mem. Coll. of State Bar of Tex., Tex. Bar Assn., Smith County Bar Assn., Am. Immigration Lawyers Assn., Masons, Rotary (past pres.), Shriners, Toastmasters (past pres.), Phi Delta Phi. Republican. Baptist. Home: 703 Wellington St Tyler TX 75703-4666 Office: 1021 ESE Loop 323 Ste 200 Tyler TX 75701 Office Phone: 903-592-8186. Personal E-mail: oneworldtogether@sbcglobal.net.

PATTERSON, DOUGLAS MACLENNAN, finance educator; b. Jan. 16, 1945; s. Thomas and Ruth (MacLennan) P.; m. Sara Louise Lucas; children: Cara Beth, John Douglas. BSEE, U. Wis., 1968, MBA, 1972, PhD, 1978. Elec. engr. Westinghouse Electric, Balt., 1968—71; asst. prof. U. Mich., Ann Arbor, 1976—80, Va. Tech., Blacksburg, 1980—86, assoc. prof., 1986—98, prof., 1998—. Vis. prof. U. Calif., Santa Barbara, 1989; vis. scholar U. Tex., Austin, 1994; dir. PhD program fin. Va. Tech., 1991—95; invited spl. spkr. Statis. Inference and Non-Linear Dynamics in Time Series conf., Bressanone, Italy, 2005; presenter, spkr. in field; dir. program on free markets Pampin Coll. Bus., 2007—; vis. scholar U. Calif., Santa Barbara, 2008. Co-author: A Nonlinear Times Series Workshop: A Tool Kit for Detecting and Identifying Nonlinear Serial Dependence; contbr. articles to profl. jours Mem. ad hoc com. Detroit Area Hosp. Assn., 1978-79 Recipient Tchg. Excellence award Va. Tech., 1983; U. Mich. fellow, 1979; USN grantee, 1984, 85, 90 Mem. Am. Fin. Assn., Am. Econ. Assn. Methodist. Home: 702 Crestwood Dr Blacksburg VA 24060-6006 Office: Va Poly Inst Dept Finance 0221 Blacksburg VA 24061 Business E-Mail: amex@vt.edu.

PATTERSON, ELIZABETH JOHNSTON, former United States representative, South Carolina; b. Columbia, SC, Nov. 18, 1939; d. Olin DeWitt and Gladys (Atkinson) Johnston; m. Dwight Fleming Patterson, Jr., Apr. 15, 1967; children: Dwight Fleming, Olin DeWitt, Catherine Leigh. BA, Columbia Coll., 1961; postgrad. in polit. sci., U. S.C., 1961, 62, 64; LLD (hon.), Columbia Coll., 1987; D Pub. Svc. (hon.), Converse Coll., 1989, M in Liberal Arts, 1999; LLD (hon.), Wofford Coll., 1999. Pub. affairs officer Peace Corps, Washington, 1962-64, VISTA, OEO, Washington, 1965-66; D Pub. Svc. Head Start and VISTA, OEO, Columbia, 1966-67; tri-county dir. Head Start, Piedmont Community Actions, Spartanburg, SC, 1967-68; mem. Spartanburg County Coun., 1975-76, S.C. State Senate, 1979-86, 100th-102nd Congresess from 4th S.C. dist., 1987-93; dir. continuing edn., converse II program Converse Coll., 1993—2003; ret. Adj. prof. Spartanburg Meth. Coll., 1993—2001. Trustee Wofford Coll., 1978—90, Columbia Coll., 1991—2003, Spartanburg Meth. Coll., 2004—; pres. Spartanburg Dem. Women, 1968; v.p. Spartanburg County Dem. party, 1968—70, sec., 1970—75, pres., 2004—08; bd. dirs. S.C. Ind. Colls. and Univs., 1995—99, Charles Lea Ctr., 1978, Spartanburg Coun. on Aging; chmn., bd. dirs. Bethlehem Cmty. Ctr., 1998—, Gen. Conf. United Meth. Ch. and Southeastern Jurisdictional Conf., U.M.A., 2008. Mem.: Bus. and Profl. Women's Club, Alpha Kappa Gamma. Democrat. Methodist.

PATTERSON, GARY, college football coach; b. Larned, Kans., Feb. 13, 1960; m. Kelsey Patterson; children: Josh, Cade, Blake. BS in Phys. Edn., Kans. State U., Manhattan, 1983; MEd, Tenn. Technol. U., Cookeville, 1984. Grad. asst. Kans. State U. Wildcats, 1982; linebackers coach Tenn. Technol. U. Golden Eagles, 1983—84, U. Calif.-Davis Aggies, 1986, Pitts. State U. Gorillas, Kans., 1988; defensive coord. Calif. Luth. U. Kingsmen, 1987, Sonoma State U. Seawolves, Calif., 1989—91; coach Oreg. Lightning Bolts, 1992; secondary coach Utah State U. Aggies, 1992—94, US Naval Acad. Midshipmen, 1995; defensive coord., safeties coach U. N.Mex. Lobos, 1996—97, Tex. Christian U. Horned Frogs, 1998—2000, head football coach, 2000—. Recipient George Munger award, Maxwell Football Club, 2009, Woody Hayes trophy, Touchdown Club Columbus, 2009, Bobby Dodd Coach of Yr. award, Bobby Dodd Coach of Yr. Found., 2009, Eddie Robinson Coach of Yr. award, Football Writers Assn. America, 2009, Walter Camp Coach of Yr. award, Walter Camp Football Found., 2009, Coach of Yr. award, American Football Coaches Assn. (AFCA), 2009; named Coach of Yr., Mountain West Conf., 2005, Conf. USA, 2002, Mountain West Conf., 2009, Liberty Mutual, 2009, Sporting News, 2009, AP, 2009; finalist Bobby Dodd award, 2003, Eddie Robinson award, 2003. Office: TCU Athletics PO Box 297600 Fort Worth TX 76129

PATTERSON, JAMES M., JR., state legislator; b. Huntsville, Ala., Apr. 2, 1950; m. Susan Patterson; 3 children. BS in Bus., Jacksonville State U., 1972. Broker Thompson MC Kerrior, 1976—80; retired pharm. rep. Bristol Myers Squibb, 1980—2008; owner, operator Patterson Properties, 1999—; ptnr. AJ Fuel City LLC, Regional Spine & Wrist Ctr., Huntsville; mem. Dist. 21 Ala. House of Reps., 2011—. Mem., deacon Flint River Bapt. Ch., Meridianville, Ala.; bd. dirs. Madison County Sch., 1988—2000, former pres. Capt. US Army, 1972—76, comdr. D-926th engr. bn. USAR. Republican. Baptist. Office: PO Box 286 Meridianville AL 35759 also: Ala House of Reps Rm 526-B 11 S Union St Montgomery AL 36130 Office Phone: 256-828-4291, 334-242-7531. Business E-Mail: jimpattersonhd21@gmail.com.

PATTERSON, JAN POWELL, former judge; b. Austin, Tex., 1948; BA, U. Tex., Austin, 1969; JD, U. Tex. Sch. Law, 1973; MA in Jud. Process, U. Va. Law Sch., 2004. Bar: Tex. 1974. Law clk. US Dist. Ct. (so. dist.) NY, NYC, 1973-74; assoc. Sullivan & Cromwell, NYC, 1975-80; asst. US atty. US Dept. Justice, NYC, Austin, 1981-86; vis. prof. U. Tex. Sch. Law, Austin, 1987-88; staff Office Ind. Counsel, US Ct. Appeals, Washington, 1995; shareholder Johnson & Gibbs, Dallas, Sneed Vine & Perry, Austin; judge US Ct. Appeals (3d cir.), Austin, 1999—2010. Mem. Tex. State Commn. Jud. Conduct, 2007—10, vice chair, 2009—10; vis. prof. Baylor U. Sch. Law, Waco, Tex. Bd. trustees Tex. Ctr. Legal Ethics & Professionalism. Recipient Outstanding Achievement award, Travis County Women Lawyers' Assn., 2003; named Friars Outstanding Alumna, U. Tex., 2003. Fellow: Tex. Bar Found. (life); mem.: FBA (pres Austin chpt. 1988—89), American Law Inst., Austin Inns of Ct. (pres. 1995—96), Coll. State Bar Tex. Methodist. Mailing: c/o Sheila & Walter Umphrey Law Ctr Baylor U One Bear Place #97288 1114 S University Parks Dr Waco TX 76798 E-mail: jan_patterson@baylor.edu.

PATTERSON, MICHAEL A., lawyer; m. Christine Lipsey; 1 child. BA, La. State U., 1968, JD, 1971; LLM in Dispute Resolution, Pepperdine U., 2008. Bar: La. 1971, DC 1988. Ptnr. Long Law Firm, L.L.P., Baton Rouge. Judge pro tempore La Ct. Appeals (1st cir.), 2002; adj. prof. trial advocacy and evidence La. State U. Paul M. Herbert Law Ctr.; panel mem. US Dist. Ct. Middle Dist. Register of Neutrals. Contbr. articles to profl. jours. Vice chair then chair La. State U. Paul M. Herbert Law Ctr. Chancellor's Coun. Grantee Excellence in Dispute Resolution Scholarship, Calif. Dispute Resolution Coun., 2007. Fellow: Baton Rouge Bar Found. (life; chair bd. trustees 1991—92); mem.: ABA, La. Assn. Justice, American Inn of Ct., Baton Rouge Bar Assn. (pres. 1984—85), American Arbitration Assn. (mem. Construction Panel and Mediation Panel), La. State Bar Assn. (mem. House of Del. 1978—82, bd. govs. 1987—89, chair Lawyers in Transition Com. 2007—, pres.-elect 2009—10, pres. 2010—11, Pres.'s Award 1999). Office: Long Law Firm LLP One United Plaze Suite 500 4041 Essen Lane Baton Rouge LA 70809-7319 Office Phone: 225-922-5110. Office Fax: 225-922-5105. E-mail: map@longlaw.com.

PATTERSON, MIKE, state legislator; Realtor Piggott Realty County; mem. Dist. 79 Ark. House of Reps., 2007—. Democrat. Address: PO Box 283 Piggott AR 72454 Office Phone: 870-598-3142. Office Fax: 870-598-8080. Business E-Mail: pattersonm@arkleg.state.ar.us.

PATTERSON, OSCAR, III, retired academic administrator; b. July 25, 1945; s. Oscar Jr. and Frances (Killian) P.; m. Kathy E. Gibson, June 6, 1966 (div. Apr. 1979); 1 child, Elizabeth Anne Patterson Cassel; m. Julie Ann Holmes, Dec. 28, 1990. BA, Pfeiffer U., Misenheimer, NC, 1967; MFA, U. Ga., Athens, 1973; PhD, U. Tenn., 1982. Asst. prof. architecture and fine arts Auburn (Ala.) U., 1972-75; chairperson BFA in Theatre program Western Carolina U., Cullowhee, NC, 1975-79; dir. telecom. U. NC, Pembroke, NC, 1984—98; prof. and chair comm. and visual arts U. North Fla., Jacksonville, Fla., 1998—2006, prof. comm., 2006—07; ret., 2007. Juvenile probation officer Cleveland Ct. Sys., Shelby, NC, 1967-68; gen. mgr., news dir. WNCP-TV, NC, 1984-98. Contbr. articles to profl. jours.; host pub. tv program, 1989-98. Served US Army, 1968—75, Vietnam. Mem. SAR, AEJMC, Mason, 32nd Degree Mason, Soc. Profl. Journalists, Phi Kappa Phi. Independent. Avocations: research, writing. Personal E-mail: opatters@comcast.net.

PATTERSON, RANDALL H., state legislator; b. Biloxi, Miss., Feb. 4, 1948; m. Vickie Lackey Patterson; children: Grand, Randi. Mem. Dist. 115 Miss. House of Reps., 2004—, vice chair ports, harbors and airports com. Democrat. Methodist. Address: 1352 Kensington Dr Biloxi MS 39530 Home Phone: 228-348-2170; Office Phone: 228-432-8480. Business E-Mail: rhpatterson@house.ms.gov.

PATTERSON, RICKEY LEE, clergyman; b. Indpls., Sept. 24, 1952; s. William Irving and Wanda (Calbert) P.; m. Sharon Rose Leonard, May 4, 1974; children: Rachel L., Rickey L. BA, Ind. U., 1976; postgrad., U. Miami, 1976-80; ThM, Internat. Bible Inst. and Sem., 1983; ThD, Christian Leadership U., 1995; PhD, Miami Christian U., 1997. Cert. pvt. pilot FAA, realtor MEI, II, Internat. Realtor Assoc., TRC, hypnotherapist, NLP master practitioner, NAET practioner, internat. property specialist 2014. Pres. Pat-Cat Enterprises, Inc., Miami, 1977-81; pastor, 1972—; founder, pres. Jesus Students Fellowship, Inc., 1973—; pastor, 1979—; radio broadcast spkr., 1978—; dir. J.S.F. Cassette Ministries, 1978—; pres. Jesus Fellowship, Inc., 1981—, Miami Christian U., 1982—; with Metanet Mktg. Grp., Inc., 1993—; CEO, Churches Dot Network, 1995—, Christian Internet Radio Network, 1996—, Christian Internet TV Network, 1997—; CEO Patterson Aviation; travel agt. Global Travel Internat., 2002—; sr. pastor Christ Life Ctr., Miami, 2006—, pastor, 2002—; pres Patterson Investment Gr., Inc., 2006—, 2007—; real estate agent RE/MAX, 2014. Ordained to minstry Internat. Conv. Faith Chs. and Ministers, Inc., 1980; coll. unit dir., Northwestern Mutual Life Ins. Co., Milw., 1980-83; founder, supt. Jesus fellowship Christian Sch., 1983—, CEO, pres., Metanet Mktg. Grp., Inc., pres. Dade County Pvt. Sch. Sys., Inc., 1983—; instr. Bible, Ind. U., 1973-76; instr. Bible, U. Miami, 1976—, also guest lectr., dept. religion; pres. Miami Bible Inst., 1984—, pres., Christian Internet Radio; guest lectr. Miami North Community Correctional Ctr., Dade County Correctional Inst., Fed. Inst. Corrections; adv. Miami chpt. Women Aglow, 1980-82; campus minister Ind. U., Miami, Fla. internat. U., Miami-Dade C.C., U. P.R.; exec. bd. mem. Internat. Congress of Local Chs., 1988—; dir. Christian Benefactor, 1990—, charter mem. Rep. Presdl. Task Force; sustaining mem. Rep. Nat. Com.; bd. govs. Am. Coalition Traditional Values, 1984—, keynote spkr. Iceland Healing The Healers Conf. Mem. Pershing Rifles Mil. Frat., 1970—73; capt. Civil Air Patrol, 2008—; bd. dirs. San Francisco Timle, St. Louis, 2011—; keynote spkr. Icel and Healing The Healers Conf., 2011—12. Mem. Bur. Bus. Practice, Aircraft Owners and Pilots Assn., Nat. Audubon Soc., Am. Entrepreneurs Assn., Inst. Cert. Fin. Planners, Am. Security Counc., U.S. Senatorial Club, Zool. Soc. Fla., Adult Congregate Living Facility (pres. Naples chpt. 1988-90), Christian Booksellers Assn., Nat. Assn. Life Underwriters, Am. Mktg. Assn., Full Gospel Businessman's Fellowship Internat. Coalition of Local Chs. (mem. exec. bd. 1988-99), Ind. U. Alumni Assn., Sigma Pi. Republican. Avocations: dance, computers, travel, skydiving, scuba diving, sailing. Office: PO Box 565490 Miami FL 33256 Business E-Mail: rick@patterson.org.

PATTERSON, SAMUEL C., retired political science professor; b. Omaha, Nov. 29, 1931; s. Robert Foster and Garnet Marie (Jorgensen) P.; m. Suzanne Louise Dean, June 21, 1956; children— Polly Ann, Dean Foster, Grier Edmund. BA, U. S.D., 1953; MS, U. Wis., 1956, PhD, 1959. Asst. prof. polit. sci. Okla. State U., Stillwater, 1959-61; asst. prof. U. Iowa, Iowa City, 1961-64, assoc. prof., 1964-67, prof., 1967-85, Roy J. Carver prof., 1985-86; prof. Ohio State U., Columbus, 1986-98, prof. emeritus, 1998—; ret., 1998. Vis. prof. U. Wis., 1962, U. Okla., 1968-78, U. Essex, Colchester, Eng., 1969-70, U. S.D., 2001. Co-author: (with others) Representatives and Represented, 1975, A More Perfect Union, 4th edit., 1989, The Legislative Process in the United States, 4th edit., 1986, Comparing Legislatures, 1979, Great Theatre: The American Congress in the 1990s, 1998; editor: American Legislative Behavior, 1968; co-editor: Comparative Legislative Behavior: Frontiers of Research, 1972, Handbook of Legislative Research, 1985, Political Leadership in Democratic Societies, 1991, Parliaments in the Modern World, 1994, Senates: Bicameralism in the Contemporary World, 1999; editor Am. Jour. Polit. Sci., 1970-73; co-editor Legis. Studies Quar., 1981-85; mng. editor Am. Polit. Sci. Rev., 1985-91. Served with U.S. Army, 1953-55 Recipient Disting. Scholar award Ohio State U., 1990; fellow Social Sci. Rsch. Coun., 1961, 67, Guggenheim, 1984-85; vis. fellow Brookings Instn., 1984-85, Ctr. Advanced Study in Behavioral Scis., 1993-94; Fulbright Bologna chair, 1995. Mem. Am. Polit. Sci. Assn. (Frank J. Goodnow award, 2000), Midwest Polit. Sci. Assn. (pres. 1980-81), Phi Beta Kappa, Phi Kappa Phi, Pi Sigma Alpha. Home Phone: 239-395-2784. Personal E-mail: patpat851@embarqmail.com.

PATTERSON, SUZANNE D., food products executive, accountant; B, Colby Coll., Waterville, Maine; MS, MBA, Northeastern U., Boston. Various positions Deloitte & Touche, LLP; joined Sun Microsystems, Inc., 1997, v.p. internal audit, 2004—06, Coca-Cola Enterprises, Inc., 2006—09, v.p., contr., chief acctg. officer, 2009—. Office: Coca Cola Enterprises Inc 2500 Windy Ridge Pky Atlanta GA 30339 Office Phone: 770-989-3000. Office Fax: 770-989-3790. Business E-Mail: spatterson@cokecce.com.

PATTERSON, WILLIAM BROWN, retired dean, history professor; b. Charlotte, NC, Apr. 8, 1930; s. William Brown and Eleanor Selden (Miller) P.; m. Evelyn Byrd Hawkins, Nov. 27, 1959; children: William Brown Patterson, Evelyn Byrd Donatelli, Lucy Patterson Murray, Emily Patterson Higgs. BA, U. South, 1952; MA, Harvard U., 1954, PhD, 1966, cert. ednl. mgmt., 1982; BA, Oxford U., Eng., 1955, MA, 1959; MDiv, Episc. Div. Sch., Cambridge, Mass., 1958; DLitt, 2012. Ordained to ministry Episcopal Ch. as deacon, 1958, as priest, 1959. Asst. prof. history Davidson (N.C.) Coll., 1963-66, assoc. prof., 1966-76, prof. history, 1976-80, U. of South, Sewanee, Tenn., 1980—2005, dean Coll. Arts and Scis., 1980-91; Francis S. Houghteling prof. hist., 2001. Author: (with others) Discord, Dialogue, and Concord, 1977, This Sacred History: Anglican Reflections for John Booty, 1990, Richard Hooker and The Construction of Christian Community, 1997, King James VI and I and the Reunion of Christendom, 1997, A Companion to Richard Hooker, 2008, Sewanee Perspectives on the History of the University of the South, 2008, The Liberal Arts At Sewanee: A History of Teaching and Learning at the University of the South, 2009, Lutheran and Anglican: Essays in Honour of Egil Grislis, 2009; mem. bd. editors St. Luke's Jour. Theology, Sewanee, 1982-90; contbr. numerous articles to profl. jours. Trustee U. South, 1968-71; mem. internat. adv. com. U. Buckingham, Eng., 1977-93; pres. So. Coll. and Univ. Union; organizer Associated Colls. of South, 1988-89. Danforth Found. grad. fellow, 1952, Mellon Appalachian fellow U. Va., 1992-93, rsch. fellow NEH, 1967, Folger Shakespeare Libr., Washington, 1975, Inst. for Rsch. in Humanities, U. Wis., Madison, 1976, Newberry Libr., Chgo., 1979; Rhodes scholar, 1953. Mem. Am. Hist. Assn., Am. Soc. Ch. History (Albert C. Outler prize for best book in ecumenical ch. history 1999), N.Am. Conf. on Brit. Studies, Eccles. History Soc. Eng., Royal Hist. Soc. Eng., So. Hist. Assn., Soc. for Values in Higher Edn., Episcopal Div. Sch. Alumni/ae Assn. (mem. exec. com. 1984-87), Phi Beta Kappa, Beta Theta Pi. Avocations: gardening, tennis. Home: 195 N Carolina Ave Sewanee TN 37375-2040 Business E-Mail: bpatters@sewanee.edu.

PATTERSON, WILLIAM S., lawyer; b. Kings Mountain, NC, July 16, 1947; BA, Wake Forest U., 1969; JD with honors, U. NC, 1973. Bar: N.C. 1973. Staff atty. interpretive divsn. Office Chief Counsel U.S. Dept. Treasury, 1973-75, staff atty. tax ct. litigation divsn.,

1975-77; mng. ptnr. Raleigh office Hunton & Williams LLP, NC. Office: Hunton & Williams 1 Hanover Sq Ste 1400 421 Fayetteville St Raleigh NC 27601-2997 Office Phone: 919-899-3022. Office Fax: 919-833-3233. Business E-Mail: bpatterson@hunton.com.

PATTON, ALTON DEWITT, electrical engineering consultant; b. Corpus Christi, Tex., Feb. 1, 1935; s. Alton G. and Civilia Louise (Taylor) P.; m. Nancy Jo Elder, Mar. 1, 1959; children: Elizabeth, Carolyn. BEE, U. Tex., 1957; MEE, U. Pitts., 1961; PhD in Elec. Engring., Tex. A&M U., 1972. Registered profl. engr., Tex. Engr. Westinghouse Electric Corp., Pitts., 1957-65; prof. elec. engring. dept. Tex. A&M U., College Station, 1965-79, 82-2000, head elec. engring. dept., 1992-96, Brockett prof., 1986, Dresser prof., 1987, dir. Electric Power Inst., 1976-79, 85-92, prof. emeritus, 2005—; rsch. fellow Tex. Engring. Expt. Sta., College Station, 1985, dir. Ctr. for Space Power, 1987-92; pres. Associated Power Analysts Inc., College Station, 1973—. Mem. panel for assessment of NIST Elec. and Electronics Engring. Lab., 1995-2000, NRS, ind. mem., bd. dirs. Electric Reliability Coun. Tex., Inc., 2008-2011, Tex. Regional Entity, 2008-10, mem. bd. dirs. Contbr. articles to elec. engring. jours. Fellow IEEE (life, tech. com., Prize Paper award 1975, 94, Richard Harold Kaufmann award 2000); mem. NSPE. Republican. Presbyterian. Avocations: fishing, hunting, photography, stamp and coin collecting. Home: 8411 Spring Crk College Station TX 77845-4608 Office: Associated Power Analysts Inc 303 Anderson St College Station TX 77840-3114 Home Phone: 979-693-1918; Office Phone: 979-696-0010. Business E-Mail: adewittpatton@msn.com.

PATTON, CARL VERNON, retired academic administrator; b. Coral Gables, Fla., Oct. 22, 1944; s. Carl V. and Helen Eleanor (Benkert) Patton; m. Gretchen West, July 29, 1967. BS in Cmty. Planning, U. Cin., 1967; MS in Urban Planning, U. Ill.-Urbana, 1969, MS in Pub. Adminstrn., 1970; MS in Pub. Policy, U. Calif.-Berkeley, 1975, PhD in Pub. Policy, 1976. From instr. to prof. U. Ill., 1968—83, dir. Bur. of Urban and Regional Planning Rsch., 1977—79, prof., chmn. dept., 1979—83; prof., dean Sch. Architecture and Urban Planning U. Wis., Milw., 1983—89; v.p. acad. affairs, prof. polit. sci., geography and urban planning U. Toledo, 1989—92; pres. Ga. State U., Atlanta, 1992—2008. Author: Academia in Transition, 1979; co-author: The Metropolitan Midwest, 1985; co-author: (with David Sawicki) Basic Methods of Policy Analysis and Planning, 1986, rev. 2d edit., 1993 Chinese translations, 2001, 2002; co-author: (with Kathleen Reed) Guide to Graduate Education in Urban and Regional Planning, 1986, 1988; editor: Spontaneous Shelter: International Perspectives and Prospects, 1988; co-editor (with G. William Page): Quick Answers to Quantitative Problems: A Pocket Primer, 1991; assoc. editor: Jour. of Planning Edn. and Rsch., 1983—87, editl. bd.: Habitat International, 1993—99, Intertrade and Investment (formerly Atlanta Internat. Mag.), 1993—2000; contbr. articles to profl. jours. Fellow U. Ill. Ctr. Advanced Studies, 1973—74; chmn. Cmty. Devel. Commn., Urbana, 1978—82; mem. Civic Design Ctr., Milw., 1983—87, City Milw. Art Commn., 1988—89, Toledo Vision, 1989—92, City Toledo Bd. Cmty. Rels., 1990—92, Ga. Rsch. Alliance, Atlanta Convention Vis. Bur., 1995—2005, Woodruff Art Ctr., 1996—2006, Fulton-Dekalb Hosp. Authority, 2008—, DBA Grady Meml. Hosp., 2008—, Fox Theatre, Ga. Coun. Econ. Edn., Atlanta Neighborhood Devel. Partnership; chair Centennial Olympic Park Area Inc., 1998—2000, Grady (Hosp.) Healthcare, Inc., 1998—2000, Atlanta Reg. Coun., 1998—, Ctrl. Atlanta Progress, 2000—03; co-chair Atlanta Belt Line Task Force, 2004—05; bd. dirs., chair The Atlanta Downtown Partnership, 1997—2000. Fellow, NIMH, 1973—75. Fellow: Am. Inst. Cert. Planners; mem.: Met. Atlanta C. of C., Assn. Collegiate Schs. of Planning (v.p. 1985—87, pres. 1989—91), Am. Planning Assn. Avocations: racquetball, gardening, travel. Office Phone: 404-413-1300. Business E-Mail: cpatton@gsu.edu.

PATTON, JOSEPH DONALD, JR., management consultant; b. Washington, Pa., Jan. 4, 1938; s. Joseph Donald and Priscilla Ann (Johnson) P.; m. Susan Oertel, June 3, 1967; children: Jennifer Ann, Joseph Donald III (dec.). BS in Phys. Scis. and Math. Edn., Pa. State U., 1959; MBA in Mktg., U. Rochester, NY, 1974. Registered profl. quality engr., Calif.; cert. profl. logistician; cert. quality engr.; cert. reliabilty engr. Tchr. Aschaffenburg (W.Germany) Am. Sch., 1963-64; with Xerox Corp., Rochester, 1964-75, mgr. field engring., 1975—93; CEO Patton Cons., Inc., Rochester, NY, 1976—93, Hilton Head, SC, 1993—. Chmn., Mgmt. Metrics Svcs., Inc., 1996-2001; mem. adj. faculty Rochester Inst. Tech., SUNY, Geneseo. Author 8 textbooks; contbr. over 200 articles to profl. jours. Capt. U.S. Army, 1959-63. Recipient Leadership and Svc. award, Pa. State U. Coll. Edn., 1999, Lifetime Achievement award, Svc. Industry Assn., 2007, Guild of the Seven Seals award. Fellow Am. Soc. Quality (reliability and maintainablity tech. award 1982), Internat. Soc. Logistics (SOLE Armitage medal 1980, 82, 97); mem. Instrument Soc. Am. (sr.), Assn. Svcs. Internat. (AFSMI publs. award 1981, Pres.'s Club 2005), Nat. Assn. Svc. Mgrs. (life cert. svc. exec.). Republican. Presbyterian (elder). Office: Patton Consultants Inc 36 Blue Heron Pt Hilton Head Island SC 29926-1209 Personal E-mail: JoePatton@pattonconsultants.com.

PATTON, PAUL EDWARD, academic administrator, former Governor of Kentucky; b. Fallsburg, Ky., May 26, 1937; s. Ward and Irene Patton; m. Carol Cooley (div. Feb. 25, 1977); children: Nikki, Christopher; m. Judi Jane Conway, 1977. BS in Mech. Engring., U. Ky., 1959; D in Public Service, U. Louisville. Dep. sec. transp. State of Ky., 1979; judge-exec. Pike County, 1981; lt. gov. State of Ky., Frankfort, 1991-95, gov., 1995—2003; chmn. Ky. Council on Post-secondary Edn., 2009—11; pres. U. Pikeville, Ky., 2009—13, chancellor, 2013—. Bd. overseers Bellarmine Coll., bd. trustees Pikeville Coll.; chmn. Ky. Democrats, 1981-83 Democrat. Presbyterian. Office: University of Pikeville 147 Sycamore St Pikeville KY 41501 Office Phone: 606-218-5261. E-mail: pep@upike.edu.*

PATTON, ROBERT J., lawyer, electronics executive; B in Economics, Southern Conn. State U.; JD, Mich. State U. Legal positions through assoc. gen. counsel Xerox Corp.; corp. counsel Lexmark International, Inc., 2001—08, acting gen. counsel, 2008, v.p., gen. counsel, sec., 2008—. Office: Lexmark International Inc One Lexmark Ctr Dr 740 W New Cir Rd Lexington KY 40550 Office Phone: 859-232-2000. Business E-Mail: RPatton@lexmark.com.

PATTY, CLAIBOURNE WATKINS, JR., lawyer; b. Cleve., Feb. 19, 1934; s. Claibourne Watkins and Eleanor (Todd) P.; m. Barbara Benton, May 4, 1968; children— Claibourne Watkins III, William Jordan. BA, U. of South, 1955; JD, U. Ark., 1961. Bar: Ark. 1961. Law clk. U.S. dist. judge, Ft. Smith, 1961-63; pvt. practice Little Rock, 1963-68; asst. ins. commr. State of Ark., 1968-69; trust officer Union Nat. Bank of Little Rock, 1969-77; asst. dean U. Ark. Sch. Law, Little Rock; also exec. dir. Ark. Inst. for Continuing Legal Edn., 1977-86; law clk. 2d Div. Chancery Ct., Pulaski County, 1986-89; of counsel Gruber Law Firm, North Little Rock, 1989-2001; prin. Patty Law Firm, North Little Rock, 2001—. Lectr. law Ark. Sch. Law, 1965; bd. dirs., chmn. Pulaski County Legal Aid Bur., 1966—69; mem. com. on civil practice Ark. Supreme Ct., 1998—2004. Bd. dirs., pres. Family Svc. Agy. of Ctrl. Ark., 1976—81, 1986—93, 1999—2004, 2009—, Good Shepherd Ecumenical Retirement Ctr., 1975—2002; mem. Ark. adv. com. U.S. Commn. on Civil Rights, 1985—89; bd. dirs. Am. Diabetes Assn., Ark. Affil., 1996—2005, Ark. Gerontol. Soc., 1996—2010. With AUS, 1955—57. Mem.: Phi Alpha Delta, Beta Theta Pi. Office: Patty Law Firm 315 N Broadway St North Little Rock AR 72114-5379 Home Phone: 501-663-0604; Office Phone: 501-375-5061. Personal E-mail: clairgpm@swbell.net.

PATURIS, E(MMANUEL) MICHAEL, lawyer; b. Akron, Ohio; s. Michael George and Sophia (Manos) P.; m. Mary Ann Toompas, Febr. 28, 1965. BS, U. N.C., 1954, JD with honors, 1959. Bar: NC 1959, DC 1969, Va. 1973; CPA, NC. Acct., Charlotte and Wilmington, N.C., 1960-63; assoc. Poyner, Geraghty, Hartsfield & Townsend, Raleigh, N.C., 1963-64; atty. advisor Chief Counsel's Office, Washington, 1964-66, sr. trial atty. Richmond, Va., 1966-69; ptnr. Reasoner, Davis & Vinson, Washington, 1969-78; sole practitioner Alexandria, 1978—. Acctg. lectr. U. N.C., Chapel Hill, 1959-60; acctg., econs. lectr. N.C. State U., Raleigh, 1963-64; business law lectr. George Mason U., Fairfax County, Va., 1978-79. Mem. bd. editors U. N.C. Law Rev. With U.S. Army, 1954-56. Recipient U. N.C. Law Sch. Block award, 1959. Mem.: Washington Golf and Country Club, Beta Gamma Sigma, Phi Beta Kappa. Home: 6326 Stoneham Ln Mc Lean VA 22101-2345 Office: Law Offices of E Michael Paturis 431 N Lee St Alexandria VA 22314-2301 Office Phone: 703-836-2501.

PATZ, EDWARD F., diagnostic radiologist, educator; MD, U. Md., 1985. Diplomate Am. Bd. Radiology-diagnostic radiology, 1990. Resident diagnostic radiology Brigham & Women's Hosp., Boston, 1986—90, fellow thoracic radiology, 1989—90; prof. radiology Sch. of Medicine Duke Univ., prof. pathology Sch. of Medicine, prof. pharmacology and cancer biology Sch. of Medicine; hosp. affiliation includes Duke Univ. Med. Ctr. Co-author: (publs.) Estimate of lung cancer mortality from low-dose spiral computed tomography screening trials: implications for current mass screening recommendations, 2004, Guidelines for management of small pulmonary nodules detected on CT scans: a statement from the Fleischner Society, 2005, Tumor infiltrating Foxp3+ regulatory T-cells are associated with recurrence in pathologic stage I NSCLC patients, 2006, Panel of serum biomarkers for the diagnosis of lung cancer, 2007, Validation of two models to estimate the probability of malignancy in patients with solitary pulmonary nodules, 2008, Isolation of novel EGFR-specific VHH domains, 2009, and numerous others. Office: Duke University Medical Center Radiology Dapartment Box 3808 Durham NC 27710 Office Phone: 919-684-7999.

PAUKEN, THOMAS WEIR, venture capital executive, mediator; b. Victoria, Tex., Jan. 11, 1944; s. Thomas N. and Patricia (Weir) P.; m. Ida Ayala; children: Thomas II, Michelle, Angela, Elizabeth, Daniel, Victoria, Monica. AB in Polit. Sci., Georgetown U., 1965, postgrad., 1966-67; JD, So. Meth. U., 1973. Bar: Tex., 1975. White House staff asst., dep. dir. White Ho. fellows, Washington, 1970-71; pvt. practice atty. Dallas, 1974-80; dir. ACTION, Washington, 1981-85; pres. Sta. KRZI-Radio, Waco, Tex., 1985-86; v.p., corp. counsel Garvon, Inc., Dallas, 1986-91; pres. TWP, Inc., Dallas, 1991—. Bd. dirs. TOR Minerals, Inc. Author: The Thirty Years War - The Politics of the 60s Generation, 1994. Mem. Reagan transition team Counsel's Office, Washington, 1980-81; Tex. Rep. State chmn., 1994-97; chmn. Gov.'s Tex. Task Force on Appraisal Reform, 2006-07, chmn Tex. Workforce Commn., 2008-. With US Army, 1967—70. Recipient Drug Edn. Leadership award PRIDE, 1985, Dir.'s award U.S. Office of Personnel Mgmt., 1985; Weaver fellow 1965. Mem. State Bar Tex., VFW (life). Roman Catholic. Avocation: reading. Office Phone: 214-378-9340. Business E-Mail: twpauken@sbcglobal.net.

PAUL, GORDON LEE, behavioral scientist, psychologist; b. Marshalltown, Iowa, Sept. 2, 1935; s. Leon Dale and Ione Hickman (Perry) P.; m. Joan Marie Wyatt, Dec. 24, 1954; children: Dennis Leon, Dana Lee, Joni Lynn. Student, Marshalltown Community Coll., 1953-54, San Diego City Coll., 1955-57; BA, U. Iowa, 1960; MA, U. Ill., 1962, PhD, 1964. Social sci. analyst VA Hosp., Danville, Ill., 1962; counseling psychologist U. Ill., Urbana, 1963; clin. psychologist VA Hosp., Palo Alto, Calif., 1964-65; pvt. practice clin. psychology, 1964-65; asst. prof. psychology U. Ill., Champaign-Urbana, 1965-67, assoc. prof., 1967-70, prof., 1970-80; Cullen disting. prof. psychology U. Houston, 1980—2011, Cullen disting. prof. emeritus psychology, 2011—; pvt. practice psychology Champaign, 1965-80, Houston, 1980—. Psychotherapy rsch. cons., Palo Alto, 1964-65; cons. Ill. Dept. Mental Health, 1965-73, 78-82, NIMH, 1968-78; adviser Ont. (Can.) Mental Health Found., 1968-69, NSF, 1968-69, Can. Coun., 1969-75, VA, 1972, 80—, APA, 1970—, UCLA/VA Med. Ctr./Camarillo Schizophrenia Rsch. Ctr., 1978-93, Alliance for Mentally Ill, 1980—. Author: Insight vs. Desensitization in Psychotherapy, An Experiment in Anxiety Reduction, 1966, Anxiety and Clinical Problems, 1973, Psychosocial Treatment of Chronic Mental Patients, 1977, Assessment in Residential Treatment Settings, Part 1, 1986, Observational Assessment Instrumentation for Service and Research, Part 2, 1987, Part 3, 1988; mem. editl. bd. Behavior Therapy, 1969-75, Behavior Therapy and Exptl. Psychiatry, 1969—, Schizophrenia Bull., 1971-99, Jour. Abnormal Psychology, 1972-76, Jour. Behavioral Residential Treatment, 1983—96, Jour. Psychopathology and Behavioral Assessment, 1985—; cons. editor Jour. Applied Behavior Analysis, 1966-77, 81—, Psychol. Bull., 1967—, Jour. Abnormal Psychology, 1970-72, 76—, Psychosomatic Medicine, 1971-77, Psychophysiology, 1971—77, Archives Gen. Psychiatry, 1973-74, Behavior Therapy, 1976-87, Profl. Psychologist, 1977-87, Psychiat. Svcs. (formerly Hosp. Cmty. Psychiatry), 1980—, Biobehavioral Revs., 1980-84, Jour. Cmty. Psychology, 1983, Am. Psychologist, 1983—, Brit. Jour. Clin. Psychology, 1985-87, Jour. Nervous and Mental Disease, 1992, Current Directions in Psychol. Sci., 1992—, Psychology Scis., 2012-; contbr. articles to profl. jours. Served with USN, 1954-58. Recipient Creative Talent award Am. Inst. Rsch., 1964, Teaching award U. Ill., 1968, 75; rsch. award Mental Health Assn., 1985; listed one of 327 Best Mental Health Experts in Nation, Good Housekeeping, 1994; NIMH fellow, 1963-64. Fellow APA (corr. com. 1965-70, pres. sect. III div. 12 1972-73, exec. coun. div. 12 1974-77, Disting. Scientist award sect. III, div. 12 1977, Disting. Sci. Contbns. to Clin. Psychology award Soc. Clin. Psychology divsn. 12 1999), recipient Trail Blazer award for lifetime achievment in schizophrenia and serious mental illness Assoc. for Cognitive and Behavioral Therapy, 2007 Am. Psychol. Soc., Assn. Clin. Psychosocial Rsch., Am. Assn. Applied and Preventive Psychology; mem. Midwestern Psychol. Assn., Tex. Psychol. Assn. (Outstanding Sci. Contbn. award 2010), Houston Psychol. Assn., Assn. for Advancement Psychology, Phi Beta Kappa, Chi Gamma Iota. Achievements include being subject of NIMH sci. report monograph, 1981: Treating and Assessing the Chronically Mentally Ill: The Pioneering Research of Gordon L. Paul. Office: U Houston Dept Psychology 126 Heyne Bldg Houston TX 77204-5022 Home: 3402 Parkside Dr Pearland TX 77584 Home Phone: 281-692-9543; Office Phone: 713-743-8564. Business E-Mail: gpaul@uh.edu.

PAUL, MAURICE MITCHELL, federal judge; b. Jacksonville, Fla., 1932; BSBA, U. Fla., 1954, LLB, 1960. Bar: Fla. 1960. Sssoc. Sanders, McEwan, Mims & MacDonald, Orlando, Fla., 1960-64; ptnr. Akerman, Senterfitt, Eidson, Mesmer & Robinson, Orlando, 1965-66, Pitts, Eubanks, Ross & Paul, Orlando, 1968-69; judge US Cir. Ct. (9th cir.) Fla., 1973-82, US Dist. Ct. (no. dist.) Fla., Gainesville, 1982—93, chief judge, 1993—97, sr. judge, 1997—. Office: US Dist Ct 401 SE 1st Ave Gainesville FL 32601-6816

PAUL, RAND (RANDAL HOWARD PAUL), United States Senator from Kentucky, ophthalmologist; b. Pitts., Jan. 7, 1963; s. Ronald Ernest and Carol Wells Paul; m. Kelley Ashby, 1991; children: William, Duncan, Robert. BS, Baylor U.; MD, Duke U., 1988. Intern surgery Ga. Bapt. Med. Ctr., 1989; resident ophthalmology Duke U. Med. Ctr., 1990—93; staff mem. Greenview Regional Hosp., Bowling Green, Ky., Bowling Green Med. Ctr., Logan County Meml. Hosp., Russellville, TJ Sampson Hosp., Glasgow; ophthalmologist Graves-Gilbert Clinic; pvt. practice Bowling Green, 1993—; US Senator from Kentucky Washington, 2011—; mem. US Senate Energy & Natural Resources Com., Washington, 2011—, US Senate Homeland Security & Governmental Affairs, Washington, 2011—, US Senate Small Bus. & Entrepreneurship Com., Waashington, DC, 2011—, US Senate Health, Edn., Labor, & Pensions Com., Washington, 2011—. Founder, chmn. Ky. Taxpayers United (KTU), 1994—. Author: The Tea Party Goes to Washington, 2011. Founder Southern Ky. Lions Eye Clinic, 1995. Recipient Outstanding Svc. and Commitment to Seniors, Twilight Wish Found., 2002; named one of The 100 Most Influential People in the World, TIME mag., 2013, 2014. Mem.: Lions Clubs Internat. (former pres., Melvin Jones Fellow Award for Dedicated Humanitarian Svcs., Lion of Yr. Award, Bowling Green Lions, Fines E. Davis Fellow Award for Dedicated Humanitarian Svc., Govs. Appreciation Award for Sight Conservation). Republican. Presbyn. Office: US Senate 124 Russell Senate Office Bldg Washington DC 20510 also: 600 Dr Martin Luther King Pl Rm 1072B Louisville KY 40202 Office Phone: 202-224-4343, 502-582-5341. Office Fax: 202-228-1373.*

PAUL, RUSSELL KENT (RUSTY PAUL), state legislator, marketing executive; b. Greenwood, SC, June 23, 1952; m. Jan Foran; 5 children. BS in Journalism/English Lit., Samford U., 1974; postgrad., NYU, 1984, Ga. State U., 1982-89. Reporter Cullman (Ala.) Times, 1974; editor Dixie Contractor Mag., 1974-83; dir. pub. rels. Lanier Bus. Products Inc. div. Harris Corp., 1983-87; mgr. corp. communications Sci.-Atlanta, Inc., 1987-89; intergovtl. rels. officer HUD, 1989, liaison Fed. Housing Fin. Bd., 1989, dep. asst. sec. for grant programs, 1990-91, asst. sec. congl. and intergovernmental rels., 1991-98; owner iSquared Communications/PR Prose, Inc, Sandy Springs, Ga.; mem. Ga. Senate from 40th dist., Atlanta, 2001—. Cons. pub. rels. Rep. House and Senate Caucuses, Ga. Gen. Assembly, 1981. Mem. exec. com. DeKalb County Reps., 1974-86, chmn. 55th Dist. Reps., 1979-80, alt. del. Rep. Nat. Conv., 1980, press aide Ga. del. Rep. Nat. Conv., 1984; mem. Stone Mountain (Ga.) City Coun., 1977-85; mayor pro tem City of Stone Mountain, 1984-85; chmn. policy com. DeKalb Head Start, Econ. Opportunity Authority, Ga., 1979-81, bd. dirs., 1980-81; dir. communications Ga. area Reagan for Pres. of U.S. Com., 1979-80; mem. steering com. Bell for Gov. campaign, Ga., 1981-82, Mattingly for U.S. Senate re-election, Ga., 1985-86; polit. dir. Ga. area Kemp for Pres. of U.S. campaign, 1987-88; chmn. Hoffman for U.S. Congress campaign, Ga., 1988; mem. steering com. Ga. area Bush for Pres. of U.S. gen. election campaign, 1988. Mem. Cable TV Pub. Affairs Assn., Pub. Rels. Soc. Am. (pub. svc. com. Ga. chpt. 1986—, chmn. edn./mini-seminar com. 1985, Best Audio/Visual Prodn. awards Ga. chpt. 1986, Best Feature Writing award 1986), Am. Acad. Polit. Sci., Associated Constrn. Publs. (chmn. editors group 1981-82), 4th Congl. Dist. Mcpl. Assn. (2d vice chmn. 1980, 1st vice chmn. 1981, chmn. 1982), Ga. Mcpl. Assn. (transp. com. 1981, bd. dirs. 1982-83). Office: Ga Senate 303B Legislative Office Bldg Atlanta GA 30334 Home: 1005 Riverside Trce Nw Atlanta GA 30328-3642

PAUL, WILLIAM DEWITT, JR., (BILL PAUL), retired art educator, collector, artist; b. Wadley, Ga., Sept. 26, 1934; s. William Dewitt and Sonoma Elizabeth (Tinley) Paul; m. Dorothy Hefling Paul, Sept. 2, 1962; children: Sarah Elizabeth, Barbara Susan, Dorothy Ann. Student, Emory U., Atlanta, summer 1952, U. Rome, summer 1953, Ga. State Univ., Atlanta, 1953—; BFA, Atlanta Coll. Art, 1955; AB, U. Ga., Athens, 1958, MFA, 1959. Instr. art and art history Park Coll., Parkville, Mo., 1960-61; dir. exhbns., instr. art history Kansas City Art Inst., 1959-64, curator study collections, asst. prof. art, 1964-65; coordinator basic courses dept. art, asst. prof. art U. Ga., Athens, 1965-67; curator Ga. Mus. Art, assoc. prof. art, 1967-69, dir., asso. prof., 1969-80, prof., 1997—2002, gen. Sandy Beaver tchr. prof., 2000—02, prof. emeritus, 2002—. Lectr. Boston, LA, New Orleans, San Antonio, Memphis, Birmingham; chmn. visual arts rev. panel Ga. Council for Arts and Humanities, 1976-77, organizer ICO Exhbns., HCAI; v.p. Arts Festival Atlanta, 1982, 84, 85, trustee, 1982-93; guest artist Arts Festival Atlanta, 1987; mem. parents council Randolph-Macon Woman's Coll., Lynchburg, Va., 1986-87. Exhibited in one man shows at Ga. Mus. Art, 1959, Atlanta Art Assn., 1959, Unitarian Gallery, Kansas City, 1960, Palmer Gallery, Kansas City, 1965, Heath Gallery, Atlanta, 1976, Hunter Mus. Art, Chattanooga, 1976, Forum Gallery, NYC, 1977, Madison, Ga., Morgan Cultural Ctr., 1980, Columbus, Ga., Mus. Arts and Scis., 1980, Macon, Ga., Mus. Arts and Sci., 1980, Banks Haley Gallery, Albany, Ga., 1980, Augusta Richmond County, Ga., Mus., 1980, Heath Gallery 1982, Moon Gallery, Berry Coll., Rome, Ga., 1983, Bathhouse Gallery, Atlanta, 1987, MIA Gallery, Seattle, 1988, Valencia CC, Orlando, Fla., 1991, Gasperi Gallery, New Orleans, 1993, Contemporary Arts Ctr., New Orleans, 1994, Lyndon House Art Ctr., Athens, Ga., 2005, Averitt Art Ctr., Statesboro, Ga., 2006, Splitbeard Gallery, Athens, 2008-10; numerous site-specific installations, 1986-97; exhibited group shows, New Arts Gallery, Atlanta, 1961, Kansas City Art Inst., 1960-64, Park Coll., 1960, Mulvane Art Ctr., Topeka, 1965, Palazzo Venezia, Rome, 1984, Elaine Benson Gallery, Bridgehampton, LI, NY, 1986, Dulin Gallery Art, Knoxville, Tenn., 1986, 1987 Atlanta Biennale, Nexus Contemporary Art Ctr., Atlanta, Valencia CC, Orlando, 1988, Greg Kucera Gallery, Seattle, 1992, King Plow Arts Ctr., Atlanta, 1994, Leslie-Lohman Found., NYC, 1995, Mus. Fine Arts, Tallahassee, 1996, Art Ctr., Miami Beach, Fla., 1997, Lebanon Valley Coll., Annville, Pa., 1998, others; represented in permanent collections Gen. Mills, Inc., Mpls., Hallmark Cards, Kansas City, Little Rock Arts Ctr., Ga. Mus. Art, U. Ga., The Kinsey Inst., Ind. U., Calif. State U., Tom of Finland Found. Ford Found. faculty enrichment grantee, 1978; recipient numerous awards for paintings. Mem. Am. Fedn. Arts (trustee 1969-81), Coll. Art Assn., Am. Assn. Museums (coun. 1981), Lovis Corinth Meml. Found., Ga. Alliance Arts Edn. (dir. 1975-77), Phi Kappa Phi. Home: 150 Bar H Ct Athens GA 30605-4702 Office: 4900 Barnett Shoals Rd Athens GA 30605 Office Phone: 706-613-2312. Business E-Mail: bp@uga.edu.

PAUL, WILLIAM GEORGE, lawyer; b. Pauls Valley, Okla., Nov. 25, 1930; s. Homer and Helen (Lafferty) P.; m. Barbara Elaine Brite, Sept. 27, 1963; children: George Lynn, Alison Elise, Laura Elaine, William Stephen. BA, U. Okla., 1952, LL.B., 1956. Bar: Okla. bar 1956. Pvt. practice law, Norman, 1956; ptnr. Oklahoma City, 1957-84; with Crowe & Dunlevy, 1962-84, 96—; sr. v.p., gen. counsel Phillips Petroleum Co., Bartlesville, Okla., 1984-95; ptnr. Crowe & Dunlevy, Oklahoma City, 1996—. Assoc. prof. law Oklahoma City U., 1964-68; adv. bd. Martindale Hubbell, 1990—. Author: (with Earl Sneed) Vernon's Oklahoma Practice, 1965. Bd. dirs. Nat. Ctr. for State Cts., 1993-99, Am. Bar Endowment, 1986—, Bank 2, 2005-; trustee Nat.

Constitution Ctr., 2000—. 1st lt. USMCR, 1952-54. Named Outstanding Young Man Oklahoma City, 1965, Outstanding Young Oklahoman, 1966, Okla. Hall of Fame, 2003. Fellow Am. Bar Found. (chmn. 1991), Am. Coll. Trial Lawyers; mem. ABA (bd. govs. 1995—, pres. 1999), Okla. Bar Assn. (pres. 1976), Oklahoma County Bar Assn. (past pres.), Okla Lottery Commn., Nat. Conf. Bar Pres. (pres. 1986), U. Okla. Alumni Assn. (pres. 1973), Order of Coif, Phi Beta Kappa, Phi Delta Phi, Delta Sigma Rho. Democrat. Presbyterian. Home: 13017 Burnt Oak Rd Oklahoma City OK 73120-8919 Office: Crowe & Dunlevy 20 N Broadway Ave Ste 1800 Oklahoma City OK 73102-8273 Office Phone: 405-239-6676.

PAULEY, BRUCE FREDERICK, retired history professor; b. Lincoln, Nebr., Nov. 4, 1937; s. Carroll Righter and Blanche Marie (Hulsebus) P.; m. Marianne Barbara Utz, Dec. 21, 1963; children: Mark Allan, Glenn Hamilton. BA, Grinnell Coll., 1959; MA, U. Nebr., 1961; PhD, U. Rochester, 1966. Instr. history Coll. of Wooster, Ohio, 1964-65, U. Nebr., Lincoln, 1965-66; asst. prof. history U. Wyo., Laramie, 1966-71; from assoc. prof. to prof. history U. Ctrl. Fla., Orlando, 1971—2006, chmn. faculty senate, 1978-79, prof. emeritus, 2006. Vis. prof. history U. Nebr., Lincoln, 2002, 06; cons., expert witness war crimes divsn. Can. Justice Dept., 1998-99. Author: The Habsburg Legacy, 1867-1939, 1972, Hahnenschwanz und Hakenkreuz: Steirischer Heimatschutz und österreichischer Nationalsozialismus, 1918-1934, 1972, Hitler and the Forgotten Nazis: A History of Austrian National Socialism, 1981, Der Weg in den Nationalsozialismus: Ursprünge und Entwicklung in Österreich, 1988, From Prejudice to Persecution: A History of Austrian Anti-Semitism, 1992 (Charles Smith prize So. Hist. Assn. best book European history, 1992, best book Austrian studies Austrian Cultural Inst., 1993), Eine Geschichte des österreichischen Antisemitismus: Von der Ausgrenzung zur Auslöschung, 1993, Hitler, Stalin and Mussolini: Totalitarianism in the Twentieth Century, 1997, 2d edit., 2003, 3rd edit., 2009. Chmn. parents' adv. com. Oviedo (Fla.) High Sch., 1981-82; established Carroll R. Pauley Lecture Series U. Nebr., Lincoln, 1997, Pauley Family Speaker Series on Global Affairs, U. Ctrl. Fla., Orlando, 2000. Named Disting. Alumnus, U. Nebr., Lincoln, 1996; Fulbright fellow, 1963-64, rsch. fellow NEH, 1972, 87, Honor Cross scholarship, Govt. of Austria, 2010, Lifetime Achievement award, U. Nebr., Lincoln, 2005. Mem.: Soc. Austrian and Habsburg Historians, German Studies Assn. (exec. com. 1986—89). Avocations: traveling to historical sites, photography, golf. E-mail: bfpauley4@msn.com.

PAUL-NOEL, KARLS, firefighter; b. 1957; AA in Fire Sci. Tech., Miami Dade Coll., Fla.; BA in Pub. Adminstrn., Barry U., Miami; MPA, Fla. Internat. U. Cert. firefighter, paramedic, fire svc. instr., rescue scuba diver, marine firefighter. Active mem. urban search & rescue team Miami-Dade County Fire Rescue Dept., 1987—, various positions including recruit instr. & training captain, now asst. fire chief, tech. & supportive svcs. Adj. med. prof. Miami Dade Coll., Fla. Internat. U. Named one of The 100 Most Influential People in the World, TIME mag., 2010. Mem.: Haitian Am. Leadership Orgn. Achievements include recognition as the highest-ranking Haitian-American firefighter in the nation; responding to disasters worldwide, including earthquakes in Turkey and Haiti, the Mozambique Floods, and numerous hurricanes. Office: Miami Dade Fire Rescue Dept 9300 NW 41st St Miami FL 33178

PAULSEN, JAMES WALTER, law educator; b. Eau Claire, Wis., Feb. 17, 1954; s. Walter Henry and Doris Antoinette (Babington) P.; m. Robin Russell, Apr. 23, 1988 BFA, Tex. Christian U., 1976; JD, Baylor U., 1984; LLM, Harvard U., 1992. Bar: Tex. 1984, U.S. Dist. Ct. (no. dist.) Tex. 1985, U.S. Dist. Ct. (so. dist.) Tex. 1986, U.S. Ct. Appeals (5th cir.) 1985. Asst. debate coach U. Utah, Salt Lake City, 1976-78; acting debate coach Brigham Young U., Provo, Utah, 1978-79; briefing atty. Supreme Ct. Tex., Austin, 1984-85; assoc. Liddell, Sapp, Zivley, Hill & LaBoon, Houston, 1985-91; prof. law South Tex. Coll. Law, Houston, 1992—. Editor-in-chief Baylor Law Rev., 1984; contbr. articles to legal jours. Mem. ABA, State Bar Tex. (vice chmn. legal svcs. com. 1987-88, 90-91), Tex. Bar Found., Tex. Assn. Bank Counsel (bd. dirs. 1990-93), Houston Bar Assn., Houston Vol. Lawyers Assn., Tex. State Hist. Assn., Nat. Order Barristers. Lutheran. Avocations: writing, hiking. Home: 2815 Wroxton Rd Houston TX 77005-4022 Office Phone: 713-646-1894. Business E-Mail: jpaulsen@stcl.edu.

PAULSON, BERNARD ARTHUR, oil industry executive, consultant; b. Lakeview, Mich., July 12, 1928; s. Arthur Bernard and Genevieve Talbard (Bushley) P.; m. Dec. 4, 1954; children: James, Joseph (dec.), Ann, Thomas (dec.), Bernadette, Patricia, Steven. BS in Chem. Engring., Mich. State U.-East Lansing, 1949. Registered profl. engr., Tex. Process engr. Mid-West Refineries Inc., Alma, Mich., 1949-57; plant mgr. Kerr-McGee Corp., Cleve. and Wynnewood, Okla., 1957-66; v.p. Coastal States Petrochemical, Corpus Christi, Tex., 1966-71, Koch Industries Inc., St. Paul and Wichita, 1971-88, cons. Corpus Christi, Tex., 1988-94; pres. Koch Refing Co., Wichita, 1981-88; chmn. The Automation Group Inc.; chmn., CEO The Inspection Group Inc. Chmn. Tor Minerals Internat., 1997, also bd. dirs; dir. Orion Refining Corp., 1999—, chmn. bd. dir., Torminerals Internat. Inc., 1999-. Chmn., pres. Cleve. Area Hosp. Corp., 1962; bd. govs. Water Devel. Bd. Tex. Region 10 Water JCom.; pres. Corpus Christi Bd. Trade; commr. Port of Corpus Christi Authority, vice chmn., 1997; bd. dirs. Ada Wilson Hosp. Found., Driscoll Hosp. Found., Coastal Bend Cmty. Found., Del Mar Coll. Found., Tex. A&M U. Corpus Christi Found., Art Mus. South Tex. 1st lt. USAF, 1955—57. Recipient Claud R. Erickson Disting. Alumnus award Mich. State U., 1994. Mem.: AIChE (fuels and petrochem. award 1989), Yacht Club, Elks. Home: 8580 Woodway Dr Apt 1108 Houston TX 77063-2464

PAULSON, JEROME AVROM, pediatrician; b. Balt., July 31, 1949; s. Robert R. and Edna (Brenner) P.; m. Susan Miller, 1973 (div. 1986); m. Gwen Victor Gampel, July 2, 1989. BS in Biochemistry, U. Md., 1971; MD, Duke U., 1974. Diplomate Am. Bd. Pediatrics, Nat. Bd. Med. Examiners. Resident in pediatrics Johns Hopkins Hosp., Balt., 1974-76, Sinai Hosp., Balt., 1976-77, fellow in ambulatory pediatrics, 1977-78; asst. prof. pediatrics Case Western Res. U., Cleve., 1978-86; dir. sci. rsch. and pub. policy devel. Joseph P. Kennedy Jr. Found., Washington, 1986-87; dir. pediatrics Regional Inst. for Children and Adolescents, Rockville, Md., 1987-89; clin. assoc. prof. pediat. Georgetown U., Washington, 1989—2000; exec. dir. Research!America, Alexandria, Va., 1989-90; assoc. prof. medicine (formerly healthcare scis.) George Washington U., Washington, 1990—2002, assoc. prof. pediats., 1991—2000, fellow Ctr. Health Policy Rsch., 1991—98, assoc. prof. prevention and cmty. health, 1997—2012, assoc. rsch. prof. environ. health sci. & policy, 2003—12, prof. pediats., Sch. Medicine, 2012, prof. environ. & occupl. health, Sch. Pub. Health, 2012; dir. Mid-Atlantic Ctr. for Children's Health and the Environment Children's Nat. Med. Ctr., 2000—; med. dir. Nat. Global Affairs, Children's Health Adv. Inst., 2008—. Mem. conf. on methodology and std. definitions for childhood injury rsch. Nat. Inst. Children & Human Devel., 1989; health adv. com. Congressman James Moran, 8th Congl. Dist., Va., 1992—94; mem. benefits working group Nat. Drinking Water Adv. Coun. EPA, 1989—99; adv. Health Pages, 1994—97; spl. asst. to dir. Nat. Ctr. for Environ. Health, Ctrs. for Disease Control, Washington, 1999—2001; Soros advocacy fellow Children's Environ. Health Network, 2000—02; bd. dirs. Creative Glass Ctr. Am. Author: Pediatrics: Review for New National Boards, 2000; editor Pediat. Clinics N.Am., 2001, 07; contbr. articles to profl. jours., chpts. to books. Profl. adv. bd. Nat. Safety Town Ctr., Cleve., 1981-85; bd. dirs., pres. James Renwick Alliance, Washington, 1986-93, 95-98; bd. dirs. Jewish Social Svcs. Agy Greater Washington, 2002—08, chmn. No. Va. com., 2002—08, mem. Child Health Protect Adv. Com., USEPA, 2007-. Recipient Cert. for Ednl. and Pub. Policy Activity, Ohio State Senate/Ho. of Reps., 1985; Robert Wood Johnson Health Policy fellow, 1985-86, Soros Advocacy fellowship 2000-02, 4th Annual Gianides Lecturerships award, Mt. Sinal Med. Ctr., 2013. Fellow Am. Acad. Pediat. (chair exec. com., coun. on environ. health 2011-); mem. Acad. Pediatric Assn. Jewish. Office: Children's Health Adv Inst 2233 WI Ave NW Washington DC 20007 Home Phone: 703-461-7683; Office Phone: 202-471-4891. Business E-Mail: jpaulson@childrensnational.org.

PAULY, JOHN EDWARD, retired anatomist; b. Elgin, Ill., Sept. 17, 1927; s. Edward John and Gladys (Myhre) P.; m. Margaret Mary Oberle(dec.), Sept. 3, 1949; children: Stephen John (dec.), Susan Elizabeth, Kathleen Anne, Mark Edward; m. Dola S. Thompson, Jan. 7, 2006. BS, Northwestern U., 1950; MS, Loyola U., Chgo., 1952, PhD, 1955. Grad. asst. gross anatomy Stritch Sch. Medicine, Loyola U., 1953-54; rsch. asst. anatomy Chgo. Med. Sch., 1952-54, rsch. instr., 1954-55, instr. in gross anatomy, 1955-57, assoc. in gross anatomy, 1957-59, asst. prof. anatomy, 1959-63, asst. to pres., 1960-62; assoc. prof. anatomy Tulane U. Sch. Medicine, 1963-67; prof., head dept. anatomy U. Ark. for Med. Scis., Little Rock, 1967-83, prof., head dept. physiology and biophysics, 1978-80, vice chancellor for acad. affairs and sponsored rsch., 1983-92, assoc. dean Grad. Sch., 1983-92, prof. anatomy, 1967—95, prof. emeritus, 1995—. Flight instr. Ctrl. Flying Svc., Little Rock, 1997—2002; tech. adviser Ency. Brit. Films, 1956; mem. safety and occupl. health study sect. Nat. Inst. Occupl. Safety and Health, Ctr. for Disease Control, 1975—79; vis. prof. faculty medicine Kuwait U., 1993, 1994; vis. prof. anatomy U. Nev., 1996; chief of staff Ark. wing Civil Air Patrol, 2002—05. Author: (with Hans Elias) Human Microanatomy, 1960, 3d edit. 1966, (with Elias and E. Robert Burns) Histology and Human Microanatomy, 1978; editor: (with Lawrence E. Scheving and Franz Halberg) Chronobiology, 1974, (with Heinz von Mayersbach and Lawrence E. Scheving) Biological Rhythms in Structure and Function, 1981, The American Association of Anatomists, 1888-1987. Essays on the History of Anatomy in America and a Report on the Membership-Past and Present, 1987, (with Lawrence E. Scheving) Advances in Chronobiology, 1987, (with Dora K. Hayes and Russel J. Reiter) Chronobiology: Its Role in Clinical Medicine, General Biology and Agriculture, 1990; editor Am. Jour. Anatomy, 1980-92; co-mng. editor Advances in Anatomy, Embryology and Cell Biology, 1980-95; mem. adv. editl. bd. Internat. Jour. Chronobiology, 1973-83; contbr. articles to profl. jours. Chief of staff, mission pilot, instr. pilot and check pilot Ark. Wing Civil Air Patrol, 2002—05. With USNR, 1945—47. Recipient merit certificates AMA, 1953, 59; Bronze award Ill. Med. Soc., 1959; Lederle Med. Faculty award, 1966, Coll Medicine Hall of Fame, U. Ark. medical Sci., 2007. Fellow AAAS, Am. Assn. Anatomists (sec.-treas. 1972-80, pres. 1982-83, Centennial award 1987, Henry Gray award 1995); mem. So. Soc. Anatomists (pres. 1971-72), Assn. Anatomy Chmn. (sec.-treas. 1969-71), Am. Physiol. Soc., Internat. Soc. Chronobiology, Pan-Am. Assn. Anatomy, Internat. Soc. Electrophysiol. Kinesiology, Internat. Soc. Steriology, Consejo Nacional de Profesores de Ciencias Morfologicas (hon.), Quiet Birdmen, Sigma Xi, Sigma Alpha Epsilon. Roman Catholic. Personal E-mail: flydoc1@comcast.net.

PAVSEK, DANIEL ALLAN, banker, educator; b. Cleve., Jan. 18, 1945; s. Daniel L. and Helen A. (Femec) P. AB, Maryknoll Coll., Glen Ellyn, Ill., 1966; MA, Maryknoll Sch. Theology, Ossining, NY, 1971, Cleve. State U., 1972; PhD, Case Western Res. U., 1981; MS, George Washington U., 2000. Pres. Coun. Richmond Heights, Ohio, 1972-75; lectr. econs. Cleve. State U., 1972-75; asst. prof. Baldwin-Wallace Coll., Berea, Ohio, 1975-81; v.p., economist Ameritrust Co., Cleve., 1981-91; dean, prof. econs. Harry F. Byrd Jr. Sch. Bus. Shenandoah U., Winchester, Va., 1992-99, Durell prof. money and banking H.F. Byrd Jr. Sch. Bus., 1999—2007, prof. emeritus, econs., 2007—; pres. Chinese-Am. Ednl. Consultants, Ltd., 2007—. Adj. prof. bus. adminstrn. Baldwin-Wallace Coll., Berea, Ohio, 1981-91 Mem. Am. Econ. Assn., Nat. Assn. Bus. Econs. Democrat. Home: 21343 Sawyer Sq Ashburn VA 20147-4728 Personal E-mail: dpavsek@dkdp.net.

PAXTON, KEN, state legislator; b. Dec. 23, 1962; m. Angela Paxton; children: Tucker, Abby, Madison, Katie. BA in Psychology, Baylor U., 1985, MBA, 1986; JD, U. Vir., 1991. Mgmt. cons. Arthur Anderson; with Strasburger & Price LLP; in-house legal counsel JC Penny Co., Inc.; ptnr. Pittenger, Paxton, Nuspl & Crumley; owner title company McKinney; mem. Dist. 70 Tex. House of Representatives, 2004—. Republican. Office: Room GW.04 Capitol PO Box 2910 Austin TX 78768 also: 206 S Kentucky St # 200 McKinney TX 75069-5439 Office Phone: 972-562-4543, 512-463-0356.

PAYNE, ARTHUR LEE, state legislator; b. Trussville, Ala., June 5, 1946; s. Hansel Bernard and Venie (Martin) Payne; children: Mark, Marty. BS in Bus. Adminstrn., Auburn U., Ala., 1968; MBA, U. Ala. Birmingham, 1974, MA in Edn. Adminstrn., 1975. Accountant Owens-Corning Fiberglass, Anderson, SC, 1968—68; lectr. in acctg. U. Ala. Birmingham, 1971—72, asst to the dean, Sch. Nursing, 1972—77, asst. dir. planning, 1977—82; mem. Dist. 44 Ala. House of Reps., Montgomery, 1978—; former owner Arthur Payne Sporting Goods. Mem. First Bapt. Ch., Trussville, Ala. E-5 US Army, 1970, Germany. Recipient Merit award United Way America, 1972, 1976, 1977, Club Honor Key Southside Civitan Club, 1977; named Most Outstanding Grad. Student U. Ala. Birmingham, 1976. Mem.: Ctr. Point Civitan Club. Republican. Baptist. Office: 7763 Peppertree Highlands Cir Trussville AL 35173-2695 also: Ala House of Reps Ala State House 11 S Union St Rm 627-B Montgomery AL 36130 Office Phone: 334-242-7753.

PAYNE, BILLY PORTER (WILLIAM PORTER PAYNE), golf course and tournament executive; b. Athens, Ga., Oct. 13, 1947; m. Martha Payne. BA in polit. sci., U. Ga.; JD, U. Ga. Joseph Henry Lumpkin Sch. of Law; D (hon.), U. SC, Emory U., Mercer U., Oglethorpe U., Presbyn. Coll., U. Ga. Comml. real estate atty. in pvt. practice; dir. Healtheon/WebMD, Premiere Technols.; vice chmn. NationsBank, Bank of America Corp.; head Atlanta Com. for the Olympic Games 1996, 1992; ptnr. Gleacher Ptnrs.; chmn. Augusta Nat. Golf Club & The Masters, Augusta, Ga., 2006—. Founding mem. Ga. State Games; adv. bd. Nat. Distbg. Co.; chmn. Centennial Investment Properties; bd. dirs. Crown Crafts, Atlanta C. of C., Commerce Club, Convex Grp., Atlanta Falcons, ILD Telecom., Lincoln Financial Grp. (was Jefferson-Pilot Corpn.), Cousins Properties, Anheuser-Busch, 1997—; head The Masters media com., 2000—06; pres., CEO Ga. Amateur Athletic Found. Trustee U. Ga. Found.; mem. State of Ga. Internat. Edn. Task Force; bd. deacons, ruling elder St. Luke's Presbyn. Ch. Recipient Nat. Sports Marketeer of Yr., Washington, DC Touchdown Club, 1990, Presdl. citation, Morehouse Coll., 1996, Theodore Roosevelt award, NCAA, 1997, Olympic Order in Gold, Internat. Olympic Com., Disting. Svc. award, Martin Luther King, Jr. Ctr. for Non-violent Social Change, Cmty. Svc. Governor's award for Unique and Outstanding Vol. Svc. Mem.: ABA. Achievements include induction to Ga. Sports Hall of Fame, 1996. Office: Augusta National Golf Club 2604 Washington Rd Augusta GA 30904 Office Phone: 404-262-3900. Office Fax: 404-262-3912.

PAYNE, GEORGE FREDERICK, academic administrator; b. Summerville, SC, Jan. 29, 1941; s. Fred N. and Lota (Griffith) Payne; m. Kay Martin, June 23, 1963; children: John F., Mark C., Janet E. Student, Ga. Inst. Tech., 1959-60, U.S. Naval Acad., 1960-62; BS, U. S.C., 1963, MA, 1966; MRE, Luth. Theol. Sem., 1968; postgrad., U. Ga., 1969-71; LLD (hon.), Lincoln Meml. U., 1988. Cert. fund raising exec. 2000. From instr. to asst. prof. Ga. So. Coll., Statesboro, 1966-78; dir. admission Brewton-Parker Coll., Mt. Vernon, Ga., 1978-80; v.p. devel. North Greenville Coll., Tigerville, SC, 1980-86; pres. Limestone Coll., Gaffney, SC, 1986-91, dir. various grants, 1976-91; spl. agt., registered rep. Prudential Fin. Svcs., 1991-92; dir. ITT Tech. Inst., Greenville, SC, 1992-95; exec. dir. Inst. Adv. Greenville Tech. Coll., 1996—2006; cons. Greenville Tech. Found., 2007—; exec. dir. GTF McAlister LLC, 2003—, GTF Student Housing LLC, 2004—, Brashier Charter LLC, 2007—, Greenville County Coun., Dist. 28. Author: An Introduction to the Principles of Geography: Facts, Skills, Concepts, and Models, 1973; contbr. articles to profl. jours. Active Leadership Greer, SC, 1980—81, regent, 1982—84; active AACTion Consortium, 1980—82, Leadership Greenville, 1982—83; bd. dirs. Greenville County unit Am. Cancer Soc., 1985—86; advisor Cherokee County Arts Coun., 1986—91; trustee Rolling Green Village Continuing Care Ret. Cmty., 1996—2006, sec., 1998, 2003; trustee Baptist Found. S.C., 2001—05, 2007—, Oakwood Sch., Va., 2002—; bd. dirs. Greenville Redevel. Authority, 2005—06, chair adminstrn. com., 2006. With USN, 1960—62. Recipient Disting. Svc. award, Brewton-Parker Coll., 1980, North Greenville Coll., 1986. Mem.: Coun. Advancement Support Edn. (Circle of Excellence award for ednl. fund-raising 2001, 2004), Assn. Fund-Raising Profls. (cert. fund-raising exec.), Greater Greer C. of C. (bd. dirs. 1981—84), Rotary. Baptist. Avocation: reading. Office: Greenville Tech Found McAlister Ste E-11 225 S Pleasantburg Dr Greenville SC 29607 Office Phone: 864-884-8899. Business E-Mail: Fred.Payne@GvlTec.edu. E-mail: fpayne@greenvillecounty.org.

PAYNE, JAMES HARDY, federal judge; b. Lubbock, Tex., Mar. 5, 1941; BS, U. Okla., 1963, JD, 1966. Bar: Okla. Bar Assn. 1966, Am. Bar Assn. 1966, Muskogee Bar Assn. 1970. Asst. U.S. atty. for ea. dist. Okla., U.S. Dept. Justice, Muskogee, 1970-73; ptnr. Sandlin & Payne, Muskogee, 1973-80, Sandli, Payne & Grober, Muskogee, 1980-86, Sandlin & Payne, Muskogee, 1986-88; magistrate judge for ea. dist. Okla., US Magistrate Ct., Muskogee, 1988—2001; judge US Dist. Ct. (ea. dist.) Okla., 2001—. With JAGC USAF, 1966—70, with Res. USAF, 1975—92. Office: US District Courthouse PO Box 2459 Muskogee OK 74402-2459 Office Phone: 918-684-7940. Office Fax: 918-684-7941.

PAYNE, JAMES L., oil industry executive; BS in Geophysical Engring., U. Colo., 1959; MBA, Golden State U., 1974. Various positions Chevron Oil; sr. v.p., exploration and land Santa Fe Energy Co. (subs. Santa Fe Pacific Corp.), Houston, 1982—86, pres., 1986—91, chmn., CEO, 1990—99; chmn., pres., CEO Santa Fe Energy Resources, Inc., Houston, 1991; CEO, chmn. Santa Fe Snyder Corp., 1999—2000; vice chmn. Devon Energy Corp., 2000—01; chmn., pres. & CEO Nuevo Energy Co., 2001—04; chmn., CEO Shona Energy Co., 2005—. Bd. dirs. Global Industries, Ltd., Nabors Industries Ltd., BJ Svcs. Co., 1999—2010, Baker Hughes Inc., 2010—. Office: Shona Energy Co 1770 Saint James Pl Ste 360 Houston TX 77056 Office Phone: 713-622-8809. Office Fax: 713-622-8819. Business E-Mail: jarmendariz@shonaenergy.com.

PAYNE, ROGER LEE, geographer; b. Winston-Salem, NC, Oct. 26, 1946; s. Irvin Lee and Gladys Odel (Binkley) P.; m. Sara Lucinda Parker, Aug. 16, 1970 (div. Feb. 1992); 1 child, Jennifer Nicole; m. Anne F. Remen, June 11, 1995. BA, East Carolina U., 1969, MA, 1972. Geographer, chief geog. names U.S. Geol. Survey, Reston, Va., 1974—2006; instr. geography and history Pan Am. Inst./U.S. Geog. Survey, 1989—; exec. sec. U.S. Bd. Names, U.S. Geol. Survey, Washington, 1990—2006, emeritus, 2006—12. Instr. East Caroline U., Greenville, N.C., 1969-71, George Washington U., Washington, 1977-90, George Mason U., Fairfax, Va., 1979-83, 1998—2003, Benjamin Franklin U., Washington, 1985-87, Old Dominion U., 2005-08; del. UN, N.Y.C., 1987—2006, instr., 1995—; mem. scientist exch. Geol. Survey, Beijing, 1989; instr. Nat. Black Colls., Howard U., 1985; book reviewer AAAS, 1975—; mem. Antarctica Sci. Field Program, 1999-2000; cons. in field. Author: Urban Development in South Africa, 1972, Place Names of Outer Banks, 1985, Manuals on Auto Names, 1987, 89, 97; coord., editor: (book series) National Gazetter U.S., 1982—2006; contbr. articles to profl. jours. Chmn. E. Carolina Blood Dr., Greenville, 1969. Lt. USAF, 1970-72. Recipient Guy Buzzard award Gamma Theta Upsilon, 1970; Superior Svc. award Geol. Survey, 1988, Outstanding Achievement award, 1985, 86, 88, 97, 2004, Diversity Achievement award, 2010. Fellow Explorers Club; mem. Assn. Am. Geographers (various coms. 1969-95, pres. mid-Atlantic divsn. 1981-82, treas., sec.), Am. Name Soc. (pres. 1989), Am. Nat. Std. Inst. (rep. 1986-2001), Cosmos Club (cons. 1994—, manuscript reviewer 1975—). Achievements include Mount Payne, Antarctica, named in his honor. Avocation: hiking. Home: 137 Sir Thomas Lunsford Dr Williamsburg VA 23185-3394 Personal E-mail: y2dkinv@gmail.com.

PAYNE, ROY STEVEN, lawyer; b. New Orleans, Aug. 30, 1952; s. Fred J. and Dorothy Julia (Peck) P.; m. Laureen Fuller, Sept. 8, 1973; children: Julie Elizabeth, Kelly Kathryn, Alex Steven, Michael Lawrence. BA with distinction, U. Va., 1974; JD, La. State U., 1977; LLM, Harvard U., 1980. Bar: La. 1977, US Dist. Ct. (we. dist.) La. 1980, US Ct. Appeals (5th cir.) 1980, US Supreme Ct. 1983. Law clk. to judge U.S. Dist. Ct., Shreveport, La., 1977-79; assoc. Blanchard, Walker, O'Quin & Roberts, Shreveport, 1980-83, ptnr., 1984-87; U.S. Magistrate judge We. Dist. La., Shreveport, 1987—2005; pvt. practice Shreveport, 2005—. Instr. New Eng. Sch. Law, Boston, 1979-80. Contbr. articles to profl. jours. Chmn. Northwest La. Legal Svcs. Assn., Shreveport, 1984-85; pres. Shreveport Bar Found., 2003-06. Mem. 5th Cir. Bar Assn., 5th Cir. Jud. Coun. (magistrate judges com. 1992-2000), La. State Bar Assn. (editl. bd. Forum jour., 1983-87, legal aid com.), Fed. Magistrate Judges Assn. (circuit dir. 2003-05), Shreveport Bar Assn. (pres. 2010), La. Assn. Def. Counsel (bd. dirs. 1987), Harry V. Booth Am. Inn of Ct. (pres. elect 1994-95, pres. 1996-98), Order of Coif, Rotary, Phi Kappa Phi, Phi Delta Phi. Republican. Methodist. Home: 12494 Harts Island Rd Shreveport LA 71115-8505 Office: Gregorio Gregory & Payne 7600 Fern Ave Bldg 700 Shreveport LA 71105 Home Phone: 318-798-0814; Office Phone: 318-865-8680. Office Fax: 318-865-8565.

PAYNE, TIMOTHY D., information technology executive; b. Oct. 25, 1958; BS, Univ. Calif., Santa Barbara, 1981. Pres., CEO Openware Technologies Inc., 1994—97; pres., COO Modis Inc., 1997—2000; pres., CEO MPS (Modis Professional Services) Group,

Inc. (acquired by Adecco), Jacksonville, Fla., 2001—. Bd. dir. ITFlorida.com Inc. Office: MPS Group Inc 10151 Deerwood Park Blvd Ste 200 Jacksonville FL 32256-0557

PAYTON, SEAN (PATRICK SEAN PAYTON), professional football coach; b. San Mateo, Calif., Dec. 29, 1963; m. Beth Payton; children: Meghan, Connor Thomas. BS in Comm., U. Ea. Ill., 1987. Quarterback Arena Football League Chgo. Bruisers, 1987, Chgo. Bears, 1987; grad. asst. San Diego State U., 1988—89, running backs coach, 1992—93; offensive coach Ind. State U., 1990—91; quarterbacks coach, co-offensive coord. Miami U., Ohio, 1994—95; quarterbacks coach U. Ill., 1996, Phila. Eagles, 1997—98, NY Giants, 1999—2000, offensive coord., 2000—03; quarterbacks coach Dallas Cowboys, 2003, asst. head coach, offensive coord., 2004—05; head coach New Orleans Saints, 2006—. Co-author (with Ellis Henican): Home Team: Coaching the Saints and New Orleans Back to Life, 2010. Named NFL Coach of Yr., AP, 2006, The Sporting News, 2009; named to U. Ea. Ill. Hall of Fame, 2000. Achievements include head coach of Super Bowl XLIV championship winning New Orleans Saints, 2010. Office: New Orleans Saints 5800 Airline Dr Metairie LA 70003

PEACE, BERNIE KINZEL, art educator, artist; b. Williamsburg, Ky., Oct. 20, 1933; s. Edgar and Ida M. (Miller) P.; m. Sylvia A. Hitchcock, Dec. 19, 1956; children: Anthony P., Tracy A. Peace-Gantzer. AB in Art, Berea Coll., 1954; MFA in Painting, Ind. U., 1957. Prof. art West Liberty (W.Va.) State Coll., 1960-95, prof. emeritus, 1995—. Invitee arts and letters series Gov.'s Mansion, 1993. One-man shows include Oglebay Inst., Wheeling, W.Va., 1963, Washington & Jefferson Coll., Washington, Pa., 1968, Huntington (W.Va.) Galleries, 1969, W.Va. U., Morgantown, 1971, Weirton (W.Va.) Community Ctr., 1973, N.E. Mo. State U., Kirksville, 1987, Mus. Fine Arts, Oak Ridge, Tenn., 1988, The Art Store, Charleston, W.Va., 1992; group shows include Ky. State Fair, Louisville, 1960, Upper Ohio Valley Art Show, Wheeling, 1961, Grove City (Pa.) Coll. Invitational, 1962, 63, Bethany (W.Va.) Coll. Art Exhbn., 1963, 68, Steubenville (Ohio) Art Assn. Ann. Exhibit, 1964, 65, 69, 88, 91, Mint Mus. Art., Charlotte, N.C., 1967, 70, 71, Butler Inst. Am. Art, Youngstown, Ohio, 1967, Charleston (W.Va.) Art Gallery, 1970, 71, 72, 74, 77, Westmoreland County Mus. Art, Greensburg, Pa., 1970, 71, 74, Purdue U., 1972, New Orleans Mus. Art, 1973, Richard Hackett Galleries, Parkersville, W.Va., 1974, Pitts. Watercolor Soc., 1974, 75, The Country Studio, Hadley, Pa., 1976, 3-Rivers Arts Festival, Pitts., 1976, Upshur County Ctr. Creative Arts, Buckhannon, W.Va., 1976, Erie Art Ctr., 1977, Wayne County Arts Coun., Ceredo, W.Va., 1978, Delf Norona Mus., Moundsville, W.Va., 1979, Stifel Fine Arts Ctr., Wheeling, W.Va., 1979-80, 83-85, 88-89, 91-93, Gallery G, Pitts., 1979, 42d Ann. Exhbn. Contemporary Am. Paintings, Palm Beach, 1980, Nat. Competitive Exhbn. Painting and Sculpture, 1981, Owensboro (Ky.) Mus. Art, 1982, Art Store Gallery, Charleston, 1984, 90-93, Cultural Ctr., Charleston, 1985, 87, 89, 93, W.Va. State Coll., 1986, 87, Washington & Jefferson Coll., Washington, Pa., 1991, Sunrise Mus. Downtown, Charleston, 1991, USX Bldg. Lobby Tower, Pitts., 1992, 93, State Capitol Bldg., Charleston, 1993, West Liberty State Coll., 1995, 2002, 2005 (Purchase award, 2002, Cert. Excellence, 2005), Wheeling Area Photography Club, 2003, 2004, (Fine Arts award, 2003, 2004). With U.S. Army, 1957-60. Recipient numerous awards including 1st prize Steubenville Art Assn., 1965, Grumbacher Medal of Merit, 1989, 92, Albert and Jane Wilson Meml. award, 1993, Best of Show award Upper Ohio Valley Art Show, Wheeling, 1967, 82, award State W.Va. Permanent Collection, 1972, Judges' Choice award Bethany Coll. Fall Ann., 1976, Best of Show award, 1991, award of Excellence Allied Artists of W.Va., 1990. Mem. Allied Artists of W.Va., Silver Eye Ctr. Photography. Avocations: backgammon, walking. Home: 1214 Washington Farms Wheeling WV 26003

PEACE, CHRISTOPHER KILIAN, state legislator; b. Richmond, Va., Nov. 16, 1976; m. Ashley Hopkins. State del. Dist. 97, Va., 2006—; mem. Courts of Justice Com., 2006—, Health Com., 2006—, Welfare and Inst. and Sci. and Tech. Com., 2006—; atty. Multi-State Govt. Relations Cons. Recipient Leadership Metro Richmond award, 2005; named Style Weekly, Top Forty Under 40, 2005. Mem.: DC Bar Assn., Hanover Safe Place, Mechanicsville Businessmen's Assn., Caroline County ChfC, New Kent County ChfC, Coun. Human Rights, Hanover Assn. Bus & ChfC, Hanover Ruritan, Fraternal Lodge No 168. Republican. Episcopalian. Office: PO Box 819 Mechanicsville VA 23111 Home Phone: 804-559-8039; Office Phone: 804-730-3737. E-mail: DelCPeace@house.state.va.us.

PEACE, H. W., II, small business owner, retired oil industry executive; b. Clinton, Okla., May 21, 1935; s. Herman Wilbern and Bernice (Mitchell) P.; m. Norma June Williams; children: Hugh William, Susannah Lee. BS in Geology, U. Okla., 1959, MS in Geology, 1964; postgrad., U. S.W. La., 1968. Jr. geologist Union Oil Co. Calif., Houston, 1964-65, area geologist Lafayette, La., 1965-70, geologist dist. exploration Oklahoma City, 1970-77, mgr. Rocky Mountain exploration Casper, Wyo., 1977-80; mgr. divsn. exploration Cotton Petroleum Corp., Tulsa, 1980-83; v.p. exploration Hadson Petroleum Corp., Oklahoma City, 1983-85, exec. v.p., COO, 1985-88, also bd. dirs.; exec. v.p., COO Mosswood Oil and Gas Co., Oklahoma City, 1985-88, Anadarko Supply Co., Oklahoma City, 1986-88, also bd. dirs.; mng. ptnr. EXAD, Oklahoma City, 1988-91, owner, 2006—; pres., CEO, dir. Panhandle Royalty Co., Oklahoma City, 1991—2006; pres., CEO Wood Oil Co. subs. Panhandle Royalty Co., 2001—06. Mgmt. com. PLC Energy Data, LLC, 1994—2001; bd. dirs. OIL Law Recs. Corp., chmn. bd. dirs., 2006—12, Energy Lib. Online, 2008—10; bd. dir. Farmers Royalty Co., 2009—; adv. dir. Energy Lib. Online, 2010—13. Dir. sch. geology adv. com. U. Okla., Norman, 1984—, vice chmn. 1988-89, chmn. 1989-90, exec. com. 1990—. Lt. USN 1959-63, capt. USNR, 1963-82, ret. list 1995. Mem. Am. Assn. Petroleum Geology (rep. del. or alt. 1984—, mid-continent sect. bd. sec. 2011-13), Soc. Exploration Geophysicists, Soc. Econ. Paleontologists and Mineralogists, Petroleum Assn. Wyo. (v.p. 1979-80), Tulsa Geol. Soc., Oklahoma City Geol. Soc. (chmn. profl. affairs 1976-77, rep. to mid. continent sec. 2007—), Naval Res. Assn., Cherokee Hills Homeowners Assn. (pres. 1971-73), Fieldstone Homeowners Assn. (pres. 1983), Navy League, Okla. Corp. Commn. (royalty adv. com. 1998—), Okla. Nat. Royalty Owners (assoc.) (bd. dirs. 2006-12, 13-, pres, 2007—09, bd. dirs., 2013-), Am. Assn. Petroleum Geologist (sec. mid continent sect., 2011-13, v.p. 2013-), Rotary. Republican. Avocations: golf, swimming, hiking. Office: EXAD Bradley Sq Ste 22 2932 NW 122d St Oklahoma City OK 73120 Office Phone: 405-286-5538.

PEACE, KARL E., biostatistician, scientist, educator, philanthropist; BS in Chemistry, Ga. Southern U., 1963; MS in Math., Clemson U., 1964; PhD in Biostats., Med. Coll. Va. Commonwealth U., 1976. Health sci. cert. Vanderbilt U., 1974. Instr. math. Ga. Southern Coll., 1964—67, Clemson U., 1967—69; assoc. prof. math. Randolph Macon Coll., 1969—78; sr. statistician Burroughs Wellcome, 1977—80; mgr., clin. stats. A. H. Robins, 1980—82; assoc. dir., biostats. SmithKline & French Labs., 1982—83, assoc. dir., statis. svcs., 1984—85, dir., rsch. stats., 1985—86; dir., G.I. clin. studies, data mgmt. & analysis G.D. Searle & Co., 1986—87, sr. dir., G.I. clin. studies worldwide data info. mgmt., 1987—88; v.p., worldwide tech. ops. Park Davis Warner-Lambert Co., 1988—89; founder, pres. & CEO Biopharm. Rsch. Consultants Inc., 1989—96, chief security officer, CFO, 1996—2000; sr. rsch. scientist, founding dir. Ctr. Biostats. Ga. Southern U., 2000—. Adj. faculty Va. Comonwealth U., Med. Coll. Va., Univ. NC, Duke U., Temple U., Mich. U., 1970—2000; founder, chair Biopharm. Applied Stats. Symposium, 1994—2008. Author: (books) Introductory Probability Theory and Statistical Inference, 1976, Stochastic Processes and Markov Chains with Applications, 1977, Biopharmaceuticals Statistics for Drug Development, 1987, Statistical Issues in Drug Research & Development, 1989, Biopharmaceutical Sequential Statistical Applications, 1991, Clinical Trials with Time to Event Endpoints, 2008—; editor: Champan-Hall Biostats. Series, 2006—; contbr. articles to profl. jours., chapters to books. Recipient Ralph Macon - Mednick Meml. Fund award, 1974, Meritorious Svc. award, ASQC, 1983, 1985, 1988, Pres. medal, Ga. Southern U., 2005, Founders Soc. medal, Med. Coll. Va., 2005, Meritorious Svc. award, Ga. Cancer Coalition, 2005, Biopharm. Applied Stats. Symposium, 2006, Deen Day Smith Humanitarian Svc. award, 2007, Outstanding Rschr. award, Ga. Southern U., 2007, Shining Star award, 2008, Alumnus of Yr. in pvt. enterprise, 2004; named Star Alumnus, Med. Coll. Va., 1991, Featured Alumnus, 1993, Alumnus of Yr., Ga. Southern U., 1998, Greatest Living Benefactor, 2005; Shell grant, 1974—77. Fellow: Am. Statis. Assn.; mem.: SW Ga. Cancer Coalition (sr. sci. adviser 2006—, Meritorious Svc. award 2007), GA-CORE of GCC, Va. Acad. Scis., Regulatory Affairs Profl. Soc., Ga. Soc. Clin. Oncology, Drug Info. Assn. (Meritorious Svc. award 1995), Internat. Chinese Statis. Assn. (life Pres. award 2004), ASA (life), Philippine Statis. Assn. (life), Pharm. Mfrs. Assn., Biometrika, Biometric Soc., Am. Soc. Clin. Pharmacology and Therapeutics, Am. Pub. Health Assn. (Stats. Sect. award 2007), Omicron Delta, Chi Beta Phi. Office: GA Southern Univ JP Hsu Coll Pub Health PO Box 8015 Statesboro GA 30460-8015 Office Phone: 912-486-7905. Business E-Mail: kepeace@georgiasouthern.edu.

PEACOCK, BARROW, state legislator; m. Melanie Fuller; children: Russell, William, Henry. BBA, So. Meth. U., Dallas; MBA, La. State U., Baton Rogue. Lic. cert. internal auditor; in real estate La., La. notary public. Ptnr. BHP Properties, La.; mem. Dist. 37 La. State Senate, Baton Rogue, 2012—. Auxiliary dep. sheriff Caddo Parish, La.; mem. First Meth. Ch., Shreveport, La.; bd. dirs. Christus Schumpert Health Sys. Found., La. Assn. for Blind; fin. chair Biomedical Rsch. Found. NW La. Mem.: NRA, Shreveport Rotary Club. Republican. Methodist. Office: 1619 Jimmie Davis Hwy Bossier City LA 71112 also: La State Senate 900 N 3rd St Baton Rouge LA 70804 Office Phone: 318-741-7180. Business E-Mail: peacockb@legis.la.gov.

PEACOCK, ERLE EWART, JR., surgeon, lawyer, educator; b. Durham, NC, Sept. 10, 1926; s. Erle Ewart and Vera Louise (Ward) P.; m. Mary Louise Lowrey, Apr. 17, 1954; children: James Lowrey, Susan Louise, Virginia Gayle. Cert. in Medicine, U. N.C., 1947, BS, 1990, JD, 1999; MD, Harvard U., 1949. Bar: N.C. 1993. Intern, asst. resident surgery Roosevelt Hosp., NYC, 1949-51; from asst. resident gen. surgery U. N.C. Hosps., Chapel Hill, 1953-54, chief resident gen. surgery, 1954-55; resident in plastic surgery Barnes Hosp., St. Louis, 1955-56; mem. faculty dept. surgery U. N.C., Chapel Hill, 1956-69, prof. surgery, head divsn. plastic surgery, 1965-69; prof., chmn. dept. surgery U. Ariz., Tucson, 1969-77; prof. surgery Tulane U., New Orleans, 1977-82; pvt. practice surgery Chapel Hill, 1982-93; vis. prof. surgery U. Va., Charlottesville, 1988-97; clin. prof. surgery U. N.C., Chapel Hill, 1996—. Chief hand surgery Valley Forge Army Hosp., Phoenixville, Pa., 1951-53. Author: Wound Repair, 1977, 3d edit., 1982; assoc. editor: Am. Jour. Surgery, 1967—, Surgery Yearbook, 1970-89, Plastic and Reconstructive Surgery, 1972-78; asst. editor: Jour. Surg. Rsch., 1970-76. Served with U.S. Navy, 1945-46; served to capt. M.C. U.S. Army, 1951-53. Recipient Yandell medal Louisville Surg. Soc., 1972, McGraw medal Detroit Surg. Soc., 1973, Disting. Svc. award U. N.C., 1979, Jacob Markowitz award Acad. Surg. Rsch., 1993, Lifetime Achievement award Wound Healing Soc., 1994. Mem. AAAS, ACS, ABA, Womack Sur. Soc. (pres. 1979-80), Soc. U. Surgeons (treas. 1965-68), Plastic Surgery Rsch. Coun. (pres. 1966), Am. Surg. Assn., Am. Bd. Plastic Surgery (pres. 1976), Am. Bd. Gen. Surgery, Am. Assn. Plastic Surgeons (Clinician of Yr. 1985), Am. Soc. Surgery Hand, Internat. Soc. Surgeons, So. Surg. Assn., Am. Coll. Legal Medicine, Rotary, Alpha Omega Alpha. Republican. Methodist. Mailing: 425 Cedar Club Cir Chapel Hill NC 27517 Home Phone: 919-967-0347. E-mail: eepeacockmd@aol.com.

PEACOCK, PENNE KORTH, ambassador; b. Hattiesburg, Miss., Nov. 3, 1942; m. Fritz-Alan Korth, Dec. 15, 1965 (div. 1997); children: Fritz-Alan Jr., Maria Korth Chieffalo, James Frederick; m. Andrew Peacock, Sept. 21, 2002. Student, U. Tex., 1960—64. Sr. Washington assoc., client liaison and rep. trust and estate div. Sotheby's, 1986-89; amb. to Mauritius, Port Louis, 1989-92; pres. Firestone and Korth Ltd., Washington, 1993-97; commr. US Adv. Commn. Pub. Diplomacy, 1997—. Bd. dir. Chevy Chase Bank, 1993—2009; rep. Sotheby's Internat., 1997—; adv. com. Sydney Cancer Ctr., 2003—09; adv. bd. mem. Harry Ransom Ctr., U. Tex., 2008—. Sr. advisor Ptnrs. in Performance Internat., 2005—; co-chmn. Am. Bicentennial Presdl. Inauguration, Washington, 1988—99; mem. adv. bd. Washington Ballet, 2002—; bd. dirs. Hillwood Mus. and Gardens; counselor Meridian Internat. Ctr.; bd. dirs. Coun. of Am. Ambs., 1994—. Mem.: Assn. for Diplomatic Studies and Tng. (bd. dir. 1996—2002). Office: 3604 Mt Bonnell Rd Austin TX 78731

PEAK, KENNETH RAYMOND, energy executive; b. Cleve., July 17, 1945; s. Harold Raymond and Marirose (Wolf) Peak; 1 child, Mari-Clare. BS in Physics, Ohio U., 1967; MBA, Columbia U., 1972. Asst. v.p., energy industry divsn. First Nat. Bank Chgo., 1973—80; v.p., treas. Tosco Corp., 1980—82; sr. v.p., dir., CFO Tex. Internat. Co., 1982; chmn., CEO & CFO Contango Oil & Gas Co., 1999—. Bd. dirs. Patterson-UTI Energy, Inc., 2000—. With USN, 1968—71, lt. comdr. res. USN. Mem.: Am. Petroleum Inst. Office: Contango Oil & Gas Co 717 Texas St Ste 2900 Houston TX 77002-2836 Office Phone: 713-960-1901. Office Fax: 713-960-1065. Personal E-mail: kpeak@contango.com.

PEAKE, ALLEN, state legislator; b. Macon, Ga., Feb. 17; s. George and Ann Peake; m. Betsy Peake; 3 children. State rep. Dist. 137, Ga., 2007—; mem. Banks and Banking Com., 2007—, Health and Human Svc. Com., 2007—, Ways and Means Com., 2007—, Children and Youth Com., 2007—. Republican. Presbyterian. Office: 103 Colony Ct Macon GA 31210 Home Phone: 478-474-9105; Office Phone: 478-474-5633. E-mail: allen@allenpeake.com.

PEAKE, JAMES BENJAMIN, information technology executive, former United States Secretary of Veterans Affairs; b. St. Louis, June 18, 1944; m. Janice M. Peake; children: Kimberly, Thomas. BS, U.S. Mil. Acad., 1966; MD, Cornell U., 1972; grad., U.S. Army War Coll., 1988. Commd. 2nd lt. inf. US Army, 1972, advanced through grades to lt. gen., 1995, ret., 2004; gen. surgery resident Brooke Army Med. Ctr., Ft. Sam Houston, asst. chief cardiothoracic surgery; staff gen. surgeon, chief gen. surgery clinic DeWitt Army Hosp., Ft. Belvoir, Va.; dep. comdr. for clin. svcs. Tripler Army Med. Ctr., Honolulu; comdr. 18th Med. Command and 121st Evacuation Hosp. US Army, Seoul, Republic of Korea, dep. dir., profl. svcs. chief, cons. Office Surgeon Gen., commdg. gen. 44th Med. Brigade/Corps Surgeon XVIII Airborne Ft. Bragg, NC; commdg. gen. Madigan Army Med. Ctr./N.W. Health Svc. Support Activity, Tacoma; dep. comdr. US Army Med. Command, 1996-97; installation comdr. US Army, Ft. Sam Houston, 1996; comdr. US Army Med. Dept. Ctr. & Sch., 1996-2000, US Army Med. Command, Ft. Sam Houston, Tex., 2000—04; surgeon gen. US Army, 2000—04; exec. v.p., COO Project HOPE, 2004—06; chief med. officer, COO QTC Mgmt. Inc., 2006—07; sec. US Dept. Veterans Affairs, Washington, 2007—09; sr. v.p. for health industry CGI Group, Inc., Fairfax, Va., 2009—. Chmn. Med. Advisory Bd. The BrainScope Co., Inc., 2009—. Contbr. articles to profl. jours. Decorated Order of Mil. Med. Merit, Silver Star, Def. Superior Svc. medal, Legion of Merit with three oak leaf clusters, Bronze Star with V device and oak leaf cluster, Purple Heart with oak leaf cluster, Meritorious Svc. medal with two oak leaf clusters, Air medal, Joint Svc. Commendation medal, Army Commendation medal with V device and oak leaf cluster, Humanitarian Svc. medal, Armed Forces Expeditionary medal, Joint Meritorious Unit award with oak leaf cluster. Fellow ACS, Soc. Thoracic Surgeons, Am. Coll. Cardiology; mem. Korean Med. Assn. (hon.), Assn. Mil. Surgeons U.S., Soc. Med. Cons. of the Armed Forces. Republican. Office: CGI Group Inc 12601 Fair Lakes Cir Fairfax VA 22033

PEARCE, JENNIFER SUE, real estate appraiser; b. Jacksonville, Fla., Nov. 1, 1954; d. Marvin William and Betty Mae (White) Robinson; m. James Zenous Pearce Jr., Mar. 30, 1974; children: Keith Bryan, Kevin Patrick. Student, Baylor U., 1983, U. Ga., 1985; cert., Jacksonville U., 1986. Cert. residential and comml. real estate appraiser, Fla. Broker, sales Watson Realty Corp., Jacksonville, 1979-82; sr. resdl. appraiser Page Aspinwall Appraiser, Jacksonville, 1982-90; owner Jennifer Pearce Appraiser, Jacksonville, 1991—; with Pearce Appraisals Inc., 2012. Instr. real estate appraisal Fla. Community Coll., 1987; commissioned by Ednl. Testing Svc. to establish exam for certification of appraisers in state of Fla. Mem. Appraisal Inst., Nat. Assn. Realtors, Better Bus. Bur., Jax (Fla.) Home: 4807 Avon Ln Jacksonville FL 32210-7505 Office: 4556 Lexington Ave Jacksonville FL 32210-2038 Office Phone: 904-387-5550. Business E-Mail: jennifer@pearceappraisals.com.

PEARL, IRA G., gas industry executive; B in Chemical Engring., Ga. Inst. of Tech., 1985; post grad. in Nuc. Engring. Exec. positions Delta Air Lines, Inc.; joined AGL Resources, Inc., 2005, v.p., engring svcs., supply chain, 2005—08, v.p., tech. and environ. sustainability, 2009—. Bd. dirs. Atlanta Bot. Garden, Ga. Conservancy, Southface Energy Inst. Nuc. submarine officer USN. Mailing: AGL Resources Inc P O Box 4569 Atlanta GA 30302-4569 Office: AGL Resources Inc Ten Peachtree Pl NE Atlanta GA 30309 Office Phone: 404-584-4000. Office Fax: 404-584-3945. Business E-Mail: IPearl@aglresources.com.

PEARLMAN, JERRY KENT, electronics company executive; b. Des Moines, Mar. 27, 1939; s. Leo R. Pearlman; married; children: Gregory, Neal. BA cum laude, Princeton U., 1960; MBA, Harvard U., 1962. With Ford Motor Co., 1962-70; v.p. fin. dir. Behring Corp., 1970-71; from contr. to chmn. Zenith Electronics Corp., Glenview, Ill., 1971-95. Bd. dirs. Smurfit-Stone Container Corp., Nanophase Techs., Northshore U. Health Sys. Home: 202 Indian Rd Palm Beach FL 33480-3022 E-mail: jerry@pearlmanoffice.com.

PEARSALL, GEORGE WILBUR, materials scientist, mechanical engineer, consultant; b. Brentwood, NY, July 13, 1933; s. Milo Dickerson and Margaret Elizabeth (White) P.; m. Patricia Louise Stevens, Oct. 11, 1962 (dec.), Margaret Mary Feeney, Oct. 2, 2010. B. Metall. Engring., Rensselaer Poly. Inst., 1955; Sc.D. (Am. Soc. Metals fellow), MIT, 1961. Registered profl. engr., NC. Rsch. engr. Dow Chem. Co., Midland, Mich., 1955-57; rsch. fellow MIT, 1957—59, rsch. asst., 1959-60, asst. prof. metallurgy, 1960-64; assoc. prof. mech. engring. Duke U., 1964-66, prof., 1966-81, prof. mech. engring. and materials sci., 1981—2001, prof. pub. policy studies, 1982—2001, acting dean Sch. Engring., 1969-71, dean, 1971-74, 82-83, prof. emeritus, 2001—; adj. prof. materials sci. and engring. Rensselaer Poly. Inst., 2010—. Trustee Triangle Univ. Ctr. for Advanced Studies, 1976-92, chmn. exec. com., 1983-88; dir. Duke-IBM Product Safety Inst., 1979-90; rsch. fellow Hashemite Kingdom of Jordan; vis. scientist Mid-Pacific Marine Lab., Eniwetok Atol, Marshall Islands. Author: (with W.G. Moffatt and J. Wulff) The Structure and Properties of Materials, 1964; mem. editl. bd. Jour. Products Liability, 1977-92, Jour. Products and Toxics Liability, 1993-96, Proceedings of the IEEE, 1994-96; contbr. articles to profl. jour. Mem. Durham C. of C., 1970—80, Coll. CAD/CAM Consortium Nat. Steering Com., 1982—86, Nat. Steering Com. Sloan Found. and State U. NY Dept. Tech. and Soc., 1985—86. With US Army, 1956. Recipient Honoree of George W. Pearsall Disting. Lecture Series, Duke U. Mem.: ASME (life; Triodyne Safety award 2001), Am. Soc. Metals (life; Rsch. fellowship, 1957-59), Phi Lambda Upsilon, Tau Beta Pi, Pi Tau Sigma. Office: 2941 Welcome Dr Durham NC 27705-5555 Office Phone: 518-785-1240. Personal E-mail: page1212@msn.com.

PEARSALL, JOHN WESLEY, lawyer; b. Richmond, Va., Aug. 21, 1914; BS, Randolph-Macon Coll., 1935; LLB, U. Richmond, 1941. Bar: Va. 1940. Assoc. McGuire, Riely & Eggleston, Richmond, 1941-50; ptnr. McGuire, Eggleston, Bocock & Woods, Richmond, 1950-53; gen. counsel Va.-Carolina Chem. Corp., Richmond, 1953-56; pvt. practice Richmond, 1956-60; ptnr. McCaul, Grigsby & Pearsall, Richmond, 1960-86, Pearsall & Pearsall, 1986—2008; dir. Estes Express Lines, 1972—. Chpt. chmn. ARC, Chesterfield County, Va., 1944-49, campaign chmn., 1949, campaign chmn. Richmond, Henrico, and Chesterfield, Va., 1950, nat. vice chmn. fund dr., 1956, nat. gov., 1953-55; mem. budget com. Richmond Area Cmty. Chest, 1946-47, mem. exec. com., 1947-55, trustee, 1946-50, campaign chmn., 1951, pres., 1955, United Giver's Fund, 1970; v.p. Children's Aid Soc., Richmond, 1950-55, trustee, 1948-55; active Boy Scouts Am., 1953-56; mem. exec. com. Randolph-Macon Coll., 1958-76, chmn. long range plan com., 1960-76, trustee, 1955-76, mem. alumni bd., 1994-99, trustee emeritus, 2006; mem. Chesterfield County Welfare Bd., 1951-55; trustee Sheltering Arms Hosp., Richmond, 1949-80; dir. Jr. Achievement, 1975-81; vestryman St. Stephens Ch., 1967-70, ch. bearer, 1986-87; mem. exec. com. Hist. Richmond Found. (1965-70), Falls of James adv. bd., 1979-08, Chesterfield Hist. Soc., 1985-95. Served to lt. j.g. USNR, 1944-46. Mem. ABA, Va. Bar Assn., Richmond Bar Assn., Chesterfield County Bar Assn. (pres. 1963-64), Am. Judicature Soc., Va. State Bar Council (chmn. judicial ethics com. 1970-71), Am. Archaeol. Soc. (local chpt., pres. 1976), Phi Beta Kappa (pres. Richmond area chpt. 1976-77), Jr. C. of C. (Disting. Svc. award 1948, state pres. 1948-49), Omicron Delta Kappa, Lambda Chi Alpha. Office: Ellen Glasgow House 1 W Main St Richmond VA 23220-5623 Home: 1 W Main St Richmond VA 23220-5623 Home Phone: 804-200-1189; Office Phone: 804-644-5491. Personal E-mail: jwpearsall@comcast.net.

PEARSALL, SAMUEL HAFF, III, ecologist, geographer, foundation administrator; b. Nashville, Sept. 2, 1949; s. Sam H. Jr. and Margaret Isabelle (Ikard) P.; m. Patricia Davenport, July 1973 (div. 1978); 1 child, Rachel Claire; m. Linda Louise Parrish, Sept. 4, 1982; 1 child, Paul Samuel. BS, U. Tenn., 1942; M of Prof. Studies, Cornell U., 1982; PhD, U. Hawaii, 1993. Exec. dir. Coastal Resources Ctr.,

Bar Harbor, Maine, 1975-77; program dir. Natural Areas and Natural Heritage Survey Tenn. Dept. Conservation, Nashville, 1978-81, dir. Ecol. Svcs. divsn., 1982-85; dir. Pacific Sci. The Nature Conservancy, Honolulu, 1989-91, dir. sci. and stewardship Durham, NC, 1992-99, dir. sci. and Roanoke River Project, 2000—07, dir. sci. and climate change adaptation, 2007—08; southeast regional mgr. land, water and wildlife Environ. Def. Fund, Raleigh, NC. Adj. faculty U. NC, 1993—, Nicholas Sch. Environment Duke U., 1999—, founder Pacific Sci. program Nature Conservancy, 1989, founding mem. conservation com., 1994-96, Ecoregions working group, 1996-97; mem. So. Blue Ridge Ecoregional Planning Team, 1996-97; leader Mid-Atlantic Coastal Plain Ecoregional Planning Team, 1997—; founding mem. Ga.-Pacific/Nature Conservancy Roanoke Ecosys. Partnership, 1995-97; sci. and tech. adv. com. Albermarle-Pamlico Nat. Estuari Program, 2004-05; adv. com. coastal elevations and sea level rise US EPA, 2007-09; mem. Nat. Park Svc. Cape Hatteras Regulatory Negotiation Com., 2007-08, NC Marine Fisheries Commn. Habitat & Water Quality Adv. Com., 2009-. Author: Terrestrial Coastal Environments and Tourism in Western Samoa, 1993, Managing for Future Change on the Albemarle Sound, 2005, Adapting Coastal Lowlands to Rising Seas, 2005; (with others) Wildlife Conservation Evaluation Methods in U.S., 1985; contbr. articles to profl. jours. Bd. dirs. Tenn. Environ. Coun., Nashville, 1980-85, Natural Areas Assn., Rockford, Ill., 1984-87, Bend, Oreg., 97-2000, treas., 1999-2000; counselor Conservation Trust for N.C., 1993-98; founder Tenn. Protection Planning Com.; student fellow East-West Ctr., 1985-90. Recipient Hodgson award Assn. Am. Geographers, 1988, Wiens award U. Hawaii, 1993, Conservation by Design award Nature Conservancy, 2003. Achievements include research in nature conservation, adaptive ecosystem management and landscape ecology in Western Samoa and North Carolina, coastal climate change and sea level rise in North Carolina; co-author FERC Lic. Settlement among Dominion Generation, Inc. and stakeholders at Lake Gaston and Roanoke Rapids dams. Home: 1307 Chaney Rd Raleigh NC 27606-2736 Office: 4000 Westchase Blvd #510 Raleigh NC 27607 Home Phone: 919-859-6297. Business E-Mail: spearsall@edf.org.

PEARSON, CHARLES THOMAS, JR., lawyer, director; b. Fayetteville, Ark., Oct. 14, 1929; s. Charles Thomas and Doris (Pinkerton) P.; m. Wyma Lee Hampton, Sept. 9, 1988; children: Linda Sue, John Paddock. BS, U. Ark., 1953, JD, 1954; postgrad., U.S. Naval Postgrad. Sch., 1959; A.M., Boston U., 1963. Bar: Ark. bar 1954. Practice in, Fayetteville, 1963—. Dir. officer N.W. Comms., Inc., Dixieland Devel., Inc., Jonlin Investments, Inc., World Wide Travel Svc., Inc., Okliania Farms, Inc., N.W. Arl. Land & Devel., Inc., Garden Plaza Inns, Inc, Word Data, Inc., M.P.C. Farms, Inc., Fayetteville Enterprises, Inc., NWA Devel.Co., Delta Comm., Inc.; past. dir., organizer N.W. Nat. Bank. Adviser Explorer Scouts, 1968—; past pres. Washington County Draft Bd.; past pres. bd. Salvation Army. Served to comdr. Judge Adv. Gen. Corps USNR, 1955-63. Mem. ABA, Ark. Bar Assn., Washington County Bar Assn., Judge Advs. Assn., N.W. Ark. Ret. Officers Assn. (past pres.), Methodist Men (past pres), U. Ark. Alumni Assn. (past dir.), Sigma Chi (past pres. N.W. Ark. alumni, past chmn. house corp.), Alpha Kappa Psi, Phi Eta Sigma, Delta Theta Phi. Clubs: Mason (32 deg., K.T., Shriner), Moose, Elk, Lion, Metropolitan. Republican. Methodist. Office: 9 N College Ave Fayetteville AR 72701-5301 Office Phone: 479-521-4300. Personal E-mail: tpesq1101@aol.com. Business E-Mail: tpesq@cox.net.

PEARSON, DANIEL R., electronics executive; BSEE, Univ. Pitts. Joined Harris Corp., Melbourne, Fla., 1977, v.p., gen. mgr. strategic develop., pres. network support divsn., 2000—03, group pres. Dep. of Defense programs, 2003—06, group pres. defense comm., 2006—07, group pres. defense comm. & elec., 2007—08, group pres. govt. comm. systems, 2008—10, exec. v.p., COO, 2010—. Mem.: Security Affairs Support Assn., Nat. Defense Indsl. Assn., Armed Forces Comm. & Elec. Assn., Aerospace Industries Assn., Air Force Assn., Assn. US Army. Office: Harris Corp 1025 W NASA Blvd Melbourne FL 32919

PEARSON, J. KEVIN, state legislator; Attended, Devry Inst., U. New Orleans Coll. Fin. Planning. Fin. advisor; mem. Dist. 76 La. House of Reps., 2008—, mem. appropriations com., ins. com., retirement com., joint legis. com. on the budget. Republican. Office: Capitol Office PO Box 44486 Baton Rouge LA 70804 also: 1349 Corporate Square Dr Ste 6 Slidell LA 70458-3157 Office Phone: 985-646-6487, 225-342-6945. Office Fax: 985-646-6489. E-mail: pearsonk@legis.state.la.us.

PEARSON, JOHN YEARDLEY, JR., lawyer; b. Norfolk, Va., July 23, 1942; BA, Washington & Lee U., 1964; JD, U. Va., 1971. Bar: Va. 1971. Atty. Willcox & Savage P.C., Norfolk. Mem edit!. bd.: Va. Law Rev., 1969—71. Fellow Am. Coll. Trial Lawyers; mem. ABA (litig. sect.), Internat. Assn. Def. Counsel, Order of Coif. Office: Willcox & Savage PC 1800 Bank of America Ctr Norfolk VA 23510-2197 Office Phone: 757-628-5503. Business E-Mail: jpearson@wilsav.com.

PEARSON, PAUL HOLDING, insurance company executive; b. Worcester, Mass., Feb. 14, 1940; s. Malcolm D. and Myra L. (Holding) P.; m. Judith N. Howe, July 13, 1958 (div. June 1974); children: Scott D., Todd E.; m. Anne Beck, July 26, 1974. BA in Bus. and Econs., U. Maine, 1961. C.L.U., 1971. Jr. life underwriter State Mut. Am., Worcester, 1961-63, life underwriter, 1963-67, sr. life underwriter, 1967-69; dir. life underwriting Security Mut. Life Ins. Co., Binghamton, NY, 1969, 2d v.p. underwriting, 1970, v.p., 1971-75, sr. v.p. ins. services div., 1975-79, exec. v.p., 1979-81, pres., 1981-96, chief exec. officer, 1987-97; chmn. Security Mutual Life Ins. Co. of N.Y., Binghamton, 1996-97. Chmn., CEO, bd. dirs. SML Properties corp., Binghamton, Security Equity Life Ins. Co., Binghamton, 1987-93; vice chmn. Generalife, 1997-99. Trustee, treas. Lourdes Meml. Hosp., Binghamton, 1978-92; mem. SUNY Found., Binghamton, 1982-89; trustee, chmn. fin. com. Elmira Coll., 1983-87; bd. dirs. Broome C.C. Found., 1982-91, pres. 1985-86; pres. New Industries for Broome, Binghamton, 1985-95, N.Y. State Bus. Devel. Coun., 1987-96; bd. dirs. Valley Devel. Found., 1987-91, Bus. Coun. N.Y., 1988-97, Am. Coun. Life Ins., 1990-96; bd. dirs., treas. Fiddlesticks C.C., 2002-05. Mem. Assn. for Advanced Life Underwriting, Nat. Assn. Life Underwriters, Broome County C. of C. (bd. dirs. 1980-88, chmn. 1986), Binghamton C/C Live Wire Club, Fiddlesticks Country Club (bd. dirs., treas. 2002-05). Office Phone: 239-768-0162. Personal E-mail: phapearson@aol.com.

PEARSON, RICHARD DALE, internist, infectious disease specialist, educator; MD, U. Mich., Ann Arbor, 1973. Diplomate Am. Bd. Internal Medicine, 1976, Am. Bd. Internal Medicine-infectious disease, 1980. Intern Strong Memorial Hosp., Rochester, Minn., 1974, resident internal medicine, 1974—76, fellow infectious disease, 1978—79; assoc. dean student affairs sch. of medicine Univ. Va. Health System, prof. medicine and pathology dept. of medicine divsn. of infectious diseases and internat. health and pathology, physician. Office: University of Virginia Health System School of Medicine PO Box 800466 Charlottesville VA 22908-0466 Office Phone: 434-924-5579. Office Fax: 434-982-4073. E-mail: rdp9g@virginia.edu.*

PEARSON, ROBERT LAWRENCE, executive recruiter; b. Chgo., Apr. 19, 1939; s. Jonas Peter and Caroline Margaret (Reilly) P.; m. Norma Eloise Dale, April 27, 1963; children: Jill C., Keith D. BSEE, Mich. State U., 1961; MS magna cum laude, MIT, 1963. Cons. McKinsey and Co., Inc., Chgo., 1964-68; v.p. Raymond James and Assoc., St. Petersburg, Fla., 1968-70; pres. Pearson Wade and Co., Inc., Ft. Lauderdale, Fla., 1970-71, Pearson, Inc., Racine, Wis., 1971-81; exec. dir. Russell Reynolds Assoc., Inc., Dallas, 1981-83; mng. dir. Lamalie Assoc., Inc., Dallas, 1984-89, chmn., 1989-94; pres. Lamalie Amrop Internat., Dallas, 1994-98, chmn., CEO, 1994—99; CEO Pearson Ptnrs. Internat., Inc., 1999—; mem., bd. dirs. Tatum CFO Inc., 1999—2003; mem. bd. dirs. Pentagon Techs. Inc., 2000—, Baird Capital Ptnrs. Inc., 2000—. Mem. fund raising com. Dallas Mus. of Art, 1983-85; mem. Dallas Mus. Natural History, 1985—, bd. dirs., 1988-90; mem. YMCA, Dallas; patron Ronald McDonald House of Dallas; speech writer Gov.'s Campaign, Chgo., 1968. Contbr. articles to profl. jours. Mem. MIT Enterprise Forum, Dallas C. of C., Phi Delta Theta (pres. 1959-61), Tower Club (Dallas), MIT (Dallas, pres. 1993-96), Gilda's Club North Tex. (founding sponsor), Dallas Nat. Golf Club, Broadmoor Golf Club. Episcopalian. Avocations: squash, jogging, deep sea fishing, hunting, marathon running. Office: Pearson Ptnrs Internat Inc Ste 1200 8080 N Central Expy Dallas TX 75206 Home: Apt 9D 3510 Turtle Creek Blvd Dallas TX 75219 Office Phone: 214-292-4130. Business E-Mail: rpear@pearsonpartners.intl.com.

PEARSON, ROY LAING, business administration educator; b. Victoria, Hong Kong, Oct. 18, 1939; s. Roy Ross and Martha Ann L.; m. Louise Elliott Johns, June 11, 1960; 1 child, Cynthia Laing. BS in Commerce, U. Va., 1961, PhD in Econs., 1968. Asst. prof. U. Ark. Sch. Bus. Adminstrn., Fayetteville, 1964-68; assoc. prof. Centenary Coll. La., Shreveport, 1968-71; assoc. prof. bus. adminstrn. Coll. William and Mary, Williamsburg, Va., 1971-76, prof. bus. adminstrn., 1976-87, dir. Bur. Bus. Rsch., 1985-98, Chancellor prof. bus. adminstrn., 1987—2005, prof. emeritus, 2005. V.p. Wessex Group, Inc., Williamsburg, Va., 1979—; sec.-treas. McKinley Land Co., Inc., Williamsburg, 1969-2001. Editor, author: (newsletter) Virginia Business Report, Virginia Outlook, 1984-99, Foresight: The Internat. Jour. Applied Forecasting, editl. bd. mem., 2005-, forecasting intelligence editor., 2007-, assoc. editor, 2012-. Bd. dirs. Williamsburg Community Hosp., 1985-90; gov.'s adv. bd. economists Commonwealth of Va., Richmond, 1984-98, 2002-10; mem. trust fund adv. com. Va. Employment Comm., 1984—2011. NSF fellow, 1963. Mem. Va. Assn. Economists (pres. 1990-91, bd. dirs. 1985-91, disting. fellow 1998), Assn. for Univ. Bus. and Econ. Rsch. (bd. dirs. 1991-92, v.p. 1992-94, pres. 1994-95, hon. mem. 1999—), Nat. Assn. Bus. Economists, Internat. Inst. Forecasters (bd. dirs. 2001-2004), Nat. Bus. and Economics Soc. (v.p. 2004-13), World Future Soc., Techcast (expert panel mem. 2008-). Avocations: scuba diving, underwater photography, science fiction. Home and Office: 4400 Chickasaw Ct Williamsburg VA 23188-8020 Business E-Mail: roy.pearson@mason.wm.edu.

PEARSON, WALTER DONALD, editor, columnist; b. Pittsfield, Mass., Feb. 5, 1916; s. Edgar C. and Edna (Scott) P.; divorced; children: Florence, Donald, Sharon; m. Elsa Swanson (dec.); 1 child, Richard Scott. Student, Dartmouth Coll., 1941-43. Advt. salesman, 1935-41; securities broker Charles A. Day Co., Boston, 1947-55; founder, owner, mgr. First New Eng. Securities Co., Inc., Southbridge, Mass., 1955-71; now owner, editor Pearson Investment Letter, Dover, Fla.; ptnr. Pearson Capital Inc.; fin. columnist World Intelligence Rev., CDL Report, Nationalist Times; free-lance columnist various publications; fin. advisor, investment mgr. Author: Investing for the Millions, 1990, Bridge Made Easy, 1995 With inf. U.S. Army, 1943-45, ETO. Decorated Bronze star, Croix de Guerre (France), Combat Infantry badge. Home: 3608 Casey Jones Dr Valrico FL 33594 Office Phone: 813-662-4114. Personal E-mail: PearsonCap@aol.com.

PEART, SANDRA JOAN, dean; b. Stratford, Canada, Apr. 4, 1959; d. Donald MacLean and Beverley Joan Peart; m. Craig Warren Heinicke, June 4, 1988; children: Nathan Casey Heinicke-Peart, Matthew Warren Heinicke-Peart. BA, U. Toronto, Ont., Can., 1982, PhD, 1989. Asst. prof. Coll. William and Mary, Williamsburg, Va., 1989—91; prof. econs. Baldwin-Wallace Coll., Berea, Ohio, 1991—2007; dean Jepson sch. leadership studies U. Richmond, Va., 2007—. Vis. scholar Ctr. Study of Pub. Choice George Mason U., Fairfax, Va., 2004—05, dir. Summer Inst. Ctr. Study of Pub. Choice, 2004—. Co-author (with David Levy): The Vanity of the Philosopher: From Equality to Hierarchy in Post-Classical Economics, 2005, The Street Porter and the Philosopher Conversations on Analytical Egalitarianism, 2008; contbr. articles to profl. jours. Fellow, Am. Coun. Edn., 2005—06. Mem.: History Econs. Soc. (exec. com. 2000—05, pres. 2007—, Best Dissertation award 1990). Achievements include research in the transition from egalitarian thinking to notions of race and hierarchy in economics; the role of sympathy in economics and social science; the role of the expert in social science. Office: Jepson Sch Leadership Studies Univ Richmond Richmond VA 23173 Personal E-mail: sandrajpeart@gmail.com. Business E-Mail: speart@richmond.edu.

PEAY, J.H. BINFORD, III, academic administrator, retired career military officer; b. Richmond, Va., May 10, 1940; m. Pamela Jane Pritchett; children: James, Ryan. BS, Va. Mil. Inst., 1962; MA, George Washington U., 1975; grad., U.S. Army Command and Gen. Staff Coll., U.S. Army War Coll. Commd. 2d lt. US Army, 1962, advanced through grades to gen., 1993, commd. gen., 101st Airborne Divsn., 1989—91, vice chief staff Washington, 1993; comdr. in chief US Ctrl. Command, MacDill AFB, Fla., 1994-97; ret., 1997; chmn. bd. Allied Def. Group, 2001—; supt. Va. Mil. Inst., 2003—. Served in Viet Nam, 1967-68, 71-72, Desert Storm, 1991. Decorated Def. D.S.M., Silver Star, Legion of Merit with oak leaf cluster, Army D.S.M. with three oak leaf clusters, Def. D.S.S.M., Purple Heart, Bronze Star medal with three oak leaf clusters. Office: Virginia Military Institute Office of Superintendent 201 Smith Hall Lexington VA 24450 Home: 412 VMI Parade Lexington VA 24450-2115*

PECK, ABRAHAM JOSEPH, historian; b. Landsberg, Fed. Republic of Germany, May 4, 1946; came to U.S., 1949. s. Shalom W. and Anna (Koltun) P.; m. Jean Marcus, June 21, 1969; children: Abby, Joel. BA, Am. U., 1968, MA, 1970; PhD, U. East Anglia, Eng., 1977; postgrad., U. Hamburg, Fed. Republic Germany, 1973-74. Adminstrv. dir. Am. Jewish Archives, Cin., 1976—; exec. dir. Holocaust Mus., Houston, 1997—; dir. academic coun. U. South Marrl, 2001—; prof. Holocaust Gen. Human Rights Studies, 2009—, 2009—; exec. dir. adj. prof. Ctr. Cath. Jewish Studies Saint Leo U. Lectr. in Judaic studies U. Cin., 1980—; mem. internat. adv. bd. Internat. Ctr. for Holocaust Studies, 1986—; mem. adv. bd. Nat. Cath. Inst. for Holocaust Studies, 1988—; founding mem. Greater Cin. Interfaith Holocaust Found., 1986—. Author: Radicals and Reactionaries, 1978; editor Jews and Christians After the Holocaust, 1982, The Holocaust and History, 1998; co-editor Am. Rabbinate: A Century of Continuity and Change 1883-1983, 1985, Studies in the American Jewish Experience II, 1984, Queen City Refuge: An Oral History of Cincinnati's Jewish Refugees from Nazism, 1989, Sephardim in the Americas: Studies in Culture and History, 1993; editor: The German-Jewish Legacy in America: From Bildung to the Bill of Rights, 1989, Selected Documents of World Jewish Congress, 1936-50, 2 vols., 1991, Holocaust and History, 1998, Maine's Jewish Heritage, 2007; coauthor: Our Zero Hours Germans & Jews After 1945, Family History, Holocaust & New Beginnings German, 2006, Unwanted Legacies: Shaging the Burden of Post Genocide Generations, 2013; contbr. articles to profl. jours. Spl. advisor U.S. Holocaust Meml. Coun., Washington, 1982-86; bd. dirs. Am. Jewish Com., Cin., 1978-84, Anti-Defamation League of Ohio, Ind. and Ken., Columbus, 1982-86, Jewish Community Rels. Coun., Cin., 1980-86; mem. Am. Hist. Found., Orgn. Am. Historians. Fullbright Found. fellow, 1973-74; Ohio Program in the Humanities grantee, 1980, 83, 85. Mem. Assn. Jewish Studies, Soc. Scholarly Pub., Soc. Am. Archivists, Internat. P.E.N. Centre of German-Speaking Writers Abroad. Avocations: travel, raising dogs. Home: 27443 Mistflower Dr Wesley Chapel FL 33544 Office Phone: 352-588-7298. Business E-Mail: apeck@maine.edu.

PECK, CHRISTOPHER, newspaper editor; b. Wyo., Aug. 2, 1950; m. Kate Duignan Peck; children: Sarah, Cody. Degree in comms., Standord U., 1972. Editor The Wood River Jour., Sun Valley, Idaho; city editor, edtl. oage editor, mng. editor Times-News, Twin Falls, Idaho, 1975-79; columnist, 1979; editor The Spokesman Rev., Spokane, Wash., 1982—2001, Memphis (Tenn.) Comml. Appeal, 2002—. Chmn. journalism So. Meth. U., Dallas, 2001—02. Mem.: Soc. Am. Soc. Newspaper Editor (Pulitzer prize nominating judge), Nat. AP Mng. Editors Assn. (dir.). Office: The Commercial Appeal PO Box 364 Memphis TN 38101-0364

PECK, DIANNE KAWECKI, architect; b. Jersey City, June 13, 1945; d. Thaddeus Walter and Harriet Ann (Zlotkowski) Kawecki; m. Gerald Paul Peck, Sept. 1, 1968; children: Samantha Gillian Gildersleeve, Alexis Hilary Cognazzo. BArch, Carnegie-Mellon U., 1968. Architect P.O.D. R&D, 1968, Kohler-Daniels & Assocs., Vienna, Va., 1969-71, Beery-Rio & Assocs., Annandale, Va., 1971-73; ptnr. Peck & Peck Architects, Occoquan, Va., 1973-74, Peck Peck & Williams, Occoquan, Va., 1974-81; corp. officer Peck Peck & Assocs., Inc., Woodbridge, Va., 1981—. CEO interior design group Peck Peck & Assocs., 1988—; mem. archtl. rev. bd. Prince William County, 1998—, chair 2000-2005, mem., 1998—2009. Work pub. in Am. Architecture, 1985. V.p. Vocat. Edn. Found., 1976; chmn. architects and engrs. United Way, Indsl. Devel. Authority of Prince William, 1976, vice chair, 1977, mem. 1975-79, chmn. Prince William County Arch-Rev. Bd., 2001-04, mem., 2004—; mem. Health Sys. Agy. of No. Va., commendations 1977, Washington Profl. Women's Coop.; developed rsch. project Architecture for Adolescents, 1987-88; mem. inaugural class Leadership Am., 1988, Leadership Greater Washington, D.C. Coun. Metrication, 1992—, D.C. Hist. Preservation League, Rep. Nat. Com. Recipient commendation Prince William Bd. Suprs., 1976, State of Art award for Contel Hdqrs. design, 1985, Best Middle Sch. award Coun. of Ednl. Facilities Planners Internat., 1989, Creativity award Masonry Inst. Md., 1990, First award, 1990, Detailing award, 1990, Govt. Workplace award for renovations of Dept. of Labor Bldg., 1990, Creative Use of Materials award Inst. of Bus. Designers, 1991, Proclamation award DC Mayor, 1st award Brick Inst. Md., 1993, award Brick Inst. Va., 1994, Bull Elephant award Prince William County Young Reps., 1995, Detailing & Craftsmanship award Washington Builder's Congress, 1998, Pres.'s citation AIA, Atlanta, 2005, Excellence in Design award, Environ. Design and Constrn. Mag., 2006, Presdl. award AIA; Archtl. Design Competition winner Vis. Pavillion Bur. Engraving and Printing, 2002; named Best Instl. Project Nat. Comml. Builders Coun.; subject of PBS spl.: A Success in Howard Co., Shaping the Skyline award, DC Mayor Fenty. Mem. Soc. Am. Mil. Engrs., Prince William C. of C. (bd. dirs.), Soroptimist Club. Roman Catholic. Research on inner-city rehab., adolescents and the ednl. environ. Office: 2050 Old Bridge Rd Woodbridge VA 22192-2447 Office Phone: 703-690-3121 ext. 142. Personal E-mail: dpeck@peckpeck.com.

PECK, MARYLY VANLEER, retired academic administrator, chemical engineer; b. Washington, June 29, 1930; d. Blake Ragsdale and Ella Lillian (Wall) VanLeer; m. Jordan B. Peck, Jr., June 15, 1951; children: Jordan B. III, Blake VanLeer, James Tarleton VanLeer, Virginia Ellaine.; m. 2d, Walter G. Ebert, Sept. 3, 1983 (dec. June 1990); m. 3d Edwin L. Carey, Apr. 13, 1991. Student, Ga. Inst. Tech., 1948, 55-58, Duke U., 1947-48; B.Ch.E., Vanderbilt U., 1951; MSE., U. Fla., 1955, PhD, 1963. Chem. engr. Naval Research Lab., Washington, 1951-52; chem. engr. Med. Field Research Lab., Camp LeJeune, NC, 1952; asso. research and instr. U. Fla., Gainesville, 1953-55; chem. engr., research asso. Ga. Tech. Expt. Sta., Atlanta, 1956-58; lectr. Ga. State Coll., Atlanta, 1957-58; lectr. math. East Carolina Extension, Camp Lejeune, 1959; sr. research engr. Rocketdyne div. N.Am. Aviation Co., 1961-63; self-employed as lectr., 1963; assoc. prof. Campbell Coll., Buie's Creek, NC, 1963-66, prof., 1966; acad. dir. St. John's Episcopal Sch., Upper Tumon, Guam, 1966-68; chmn., prof. phys. scis. U. Guam, Agana, 1968-73, dean Coll. Bus. and Applied Tech., 1973-74, dean Community Career Coll., 1974-77; pres. Cochise Coll., Douglas, Ariz., 1977-78; systems planning analyst Urban Pathfinders, Inc., Balt., 1978-79; dean undergrad. studies U. Md. Univ. Coll., College Park, 1979-82; pres. Polk Community Coll., Winter Haven, Fla., 1982-97, pres. emeritus, 1997—; headmaster All Saints' Acad., 1997-99. Cons. in field. Founder, pres. Guam Acad. Found., 1972-77; bd. dirs. Cochise Coll. Found., 1977-78; charter bd. dirs. Turnaround Inc., 1987-91, chmn. 1990-93; bd. dirs. United Way Ctrl. Fla., 1986-95, vice-chmn., 1992, chair elect, 1993, chmn. 1994; founding mem. Prince George's Ednl. TV Cable Coalition; mem. Prince George's Cable TV Ednl. Adv. Group, 1980-82, Polk County Coun. Econ. Edn., 1982; sec. Polk C.C. Found., 1982-97; mem. Polk County Coord. Coun. Vocat. Edn., 1982-91, PRIDE Adv. Coun.; vice-chmn. Fla. Job Tng. Coord. Coun., 1983-87, Fla. Edn. Fund Bd., 1988-93; active Girls Inc. Bd., 1992—, pres., 2000-2001, hon. mem., 2005; trustee All Sts.'s Acad. 1994-2002; trustee Vanguard Sch., 2001—06, mem. Fdn. Bd., 2001—06; bd. dirs. Theater Winter Haven, 2000—, chair, 2002-03. Recipient She Knows Where She's Going award Girls Inc. of Winter Haven, 1995, Cmty. Svc. award Jr. League Winter Haven, 2002, Disting. Citizen award Lake Region dist. Gulf Ridge coun. Boy Scouts Am., 2005, NDAR Cmty. Svc. award, 2005, Vanderbilt Disting. Alumna award, 2008; named Disting. Alumnus U. Fla., 1992, Woman of Distinction Girls Scouts, 1994, Woman of Distinction, 1997; fellow NSF, 1961-63; named to Fla. Women Hall of Fame, 2007, PCC Sports Hall of Fame, 2008. Fellow Soc. Women Engrs. (nat. v.p. 1962-63); mem. AAUW, AIChE, DAR (Cmty. Svc. award 2005), Am. Chem. Soc., NSPE, Am. Assn. for Higher Edn., Am. Assn. Cmty. and Jr. Colls., Am. Assn. Univ. Adminstrs., Rotary of Winter Haven (hon., sec. 1999-2000, pres.-elect 2003-04, centennial pres. 2004-05, hon. mem 2005), Rotary of Palm Beach Gardens, Sigma Xi, Tau Beta Pi, Chi Omicron Gamma, Phi Kappa Phi, Delta Kappa Gamma. Episcopalian. Home: 5390 Woodland Lakes Dr 206 Palm Beach Gardens FL 33418-3959 E-mail: marylypeck@bellsouth.net.

PECK, PATRICK F., management consultant; BS in Info. Sys. Mgmt., U. Md., 1980; MS in Tech. & Mgmt., American U., 1984. Joined Booz Allen Hamilton Holding Corp., 1984, co-chmn., CIO Leadership Coun., exec. v.p, 2008—. Active, Nat. Capital Area Jr. Achievement. Recipient Performance Excellence award, Booz Allen

Hamilton Holding Corp., IRS Commr. award. Office: Booz Allen Hamilton Holding Corp 8283 Greensboro Dr Mc Lean VA 22102 Office Phone: 703-902-5000. Office Fax: 703-902-3333. Business E-Mail: peck_patrick@bah.com.

PECORA, DAVID VICTOR, retired surgeon; b. Yonkers, NY, Oct. 2, 1916; s. Cavaliere Michele and Tulia (Muzi) Pecora; m. Dorothy Edith Beavers, July 22, 1944; children: Ann Charlene Diamond, Michele. BA, Columbia U., 1937; MD, Yale U., 1941. Diplomate Am. Bd. Gen. Surgery, Am. Bd. Thoracic Surgery. Intern Lakeside Hosp., Western Res. U., Cleve., 1941-42; grad. fellow in surgery NY Med. Coll., NYC, 1946-47; asst. resident in surgery Sch. Medicine, Yale U., New Haven, 1947-49, resident surgeon in thoracic surgery Uncas-on-Thames, Conn., 1949-51; chief thoracic surgery, sect. chief second surg. svc. VA Hosp., Providence, 1951-54, McGuire VA Hosp., Richmond, Va., 1967-72; prin. thoracic surgeon Ray Brook State Tb Hosp., NY, 1954-65; chief surgery Sunmount VA Hosp., Tupper Lake, NY, 1964-65, VA Hosp., Altoona, Pa., 1965—67; chief surg. svc. VA Ctr., Wilmington, Del., 1972-82; pvt. practice in thoracic, vascular and gen. surgery Newark, Del.; mem. staff Med. Ctr., Wilmington, Del., Cmty. Hosp., Chester, Pa., Crozer-Chester Hosp., Pa., Union Hosp., Elkton, Md., Riverside Hosp., Wilmington; ret., 1995. Instr. in surgery Boston U., 1953-54; clin. assoc. prof. in surgery SUNY, Syracuse, NY, 1961-70; asst. prof. surgery Med. Coll. Va., Richmond, 1967-70, assoc. prof. surgery, 1970-72; prof. surgery Thomas Jefferson U., Phila., 1972—; adj. prof. surgery Hahnemann U., Phila., 1988—; supv. tng. surg. residents numerous hosps. Mem. editl. bd. Del. Med. Jour.; author: Memoir: Between the Raindrops, 1998; contbr. over 130 articles to sci. jours. Capt. med. corps U.S. Army, 1942-46. Fellow ACS (instr. advanved trauma life support); mem. AMA, IEEE, Am. Assn. for Thoracic Surgery, Am. Coll. Chest Physicians, Am. Thoracic Soc., Am. Soc. Microbiology, Am. Med. Writers Assn., Am. Lung Assn. (eastern sect.), Royal Soc. Medicine, Pa. Assn. Thoracic Surgery, Del. Valley Vascular Soc., Md. State Med. Assn., Del. State Med. Assn., Del. Acad. Medicine, Va. Thoracic Soc., New Castle County Med. Assn., Phila. Acad. Surgery, Phila. Coll. Physicians, So. Thoracic Surg. Assn., Soc. Thoracic Surgeons (founder), Soc. Laparoendoscopic Surgeons, Soc. Neurovascular Surgery, Upstate NY Soc. Thoracic Surgery (past pres.), Saranac Lake Med. Soc. (past pres.).

PEDERSEN, GEORGE J., information technology executive; b. 1935; Attended, Rutgers U., 1953. Contracts mgr. VitroLabs, West Orange, NJ, 1953—68; co-founder ManTech International Corp., Fairfax, Va., 1968—, chmn., 1979—, pres., 1995—2004, CEO, 1995—, interim pres., 2010—. Bd. dirs. GSE Sys. Inc. Bd. dirs. Nat. Defense Indsl. Assn., Assn. For Enterprise Integration. Recipient James Forrestal Industry Leadership award, Nat. Defense Indsl. Assn., 2005. Office: ManTech Internat Corp 12015 Lee Jackson Hwy Ste 300 Fairfax VA 22033 Office Phone: 703-218-6000. Office Fax: 703-218-8296. Business E-Mail: george.pedersen@mantech.com.

PEDERSON, WILLIAM CHRISTOPHER, plastic surgeon; b. Texas City, Tex., July 15, 1952; s. Alton Curtis and Lucy Vernor (Windham) P.; m. Cynthia Lea Anderson, June 17, 1978; children: Liv, Anton, Candice. BA, U. Tex., 1974, MD, 1978. Hand fellow U. Louisville, 1984; rsch. fellow Duke U. Med. Ctr., Durham, N.C., 1985; microsurgery rsch. fellow St. Vincent's Hosp., Melbourne, 1986; asst. prof. plastic surgery Duke U. Med. Ctr., Durham, 1087-89; chief of plastic surgery U. Tex. Health Sci. Ctr., San Antonio, 1989—; intern, resident surgery U. Tex., San Antonio, 1978—83, resident plastic surgery, 1983—85; pres. Am. Soc. Reconstructive Microsurgery, 2005—06. Contbr. articles to profl. jours. Fellow ACS (assoc.); mem. Am. Soc. Plastic and Reconstructive Surgery, Am. Assn. Hand Surgery, Am. Soc. Reconstructive Microsurgery.

PEDRAZAS, XIMO, hotel executive; Team leader, maintenance IBM Global Services, 1988—95; chief engr. Hosteleria Cremades, 1995—97, HUSA, 1997—99, InterContinental Hotels Group, 1999—2007, Marriott Hotels, 2007—09, Hilton Worldwide, Inc., 2009—. Office: Hilton Worldwide 7930 Jones Branch Dr Ste 1100 Mc Lean VA 22102 Office Phone: 703-883-1000. Business E-Mail: ximo.pedrazas@hilton.com.

PEEBLER, ROBERT PAUL, energy executive; b. Great Bend, Kans., June 22, 1947; s. John Warren and Eleanor (Marion) P.; m. Patricia Marie Malone, June 8; children: Bryan Robert, Michael John. BSEE, U. Kans., 1970. Field engr. Schlumberger Ltd., Woodward, Okla., 1970-73, tech. staff engr., 1973-75, dist. mgr. New Iberia, La., 1975-76, div. mgr. Corpus Christi, 1976-78, wireline coord., 1978-79, mktg. mgr., N.Am., 1979-81, v.p. ops., N.Am., 1981-86; pres. Peebler & Assocs., Inc., 1987-89; founder, pres. & CEO Energy Virtual Ptnrs.; v.p., mktg. Landmark Graphics Corp. (acquired by Halliburton Co.), 1989—92, CEO, 1992; v.p., e-Bus. Strategy & Ventures Halliburton Co., joined, 1996; bd. dirs. ION Geophysical Corp., 1999—, pres., 2003—08, CEO, 2003—, pres., 2010—. Mem. com. Mus. Natural History, Houston, 1989-90. Mem. Soc. Prof. Well Analysts, Soc. Petroleum Engrs., Am. Mktg. Assn. Republican. Avocations: reading, golf, jogging, music, aquarium. Home: 5607 Court Of Lions St Houston TX 77069-2744 Office: ION Geophysical Corp 2105 City-West Blvd Houston TX 77042-2839 Office Phone: 281-933-3339. Office Fax: 281-879-3626. Business E-Mail: robert.peebler@iongeo.com.

PEEBLES, PEYTON ZIMMERMANN, JR., retired electrical engineer, educator; b. Columbus, Ga., Sept. 10, 1934; s. Peyton Zimmermann Peebles Sr. and Maida Erlene Dials; m. Barbara Ann Suydam, Sept. 6, 1969; children: Peyton Zimmermann III, Edward Arlen. BSEE, Evansville Coll., 1957; MSEE, Drexel Inst., 1963; PhD, U. Pa., 1967. Design engr. RCA, Moorestown, NJ, 1958-64, systems engr., 1966-69; prof. U. Tenn., Knoxville, 1969-75, 76-81; vis. prof. U. Hawaii, Honolulu, 1975-76; prof. U. Fla., Gainesville, 1981-84, 90-96, assoc. chmn., 1984-90, prof. emeritus, 1996—. Cons. in field. Author: Communication System Principles, 1976, Probability, Random Variables and Random Signal Principles, 1980, 4th edit., 2001, Digital Communication Systems, 1987; prin. author: Principles of Electrical Engineering, 1991, Radar Principles, 1998; contbr. articles to profl. jours.; patentee in field, artist:(painting)(oil portrate)for numerous commns. Capt. USAFR, 1957-61. David Sarnoff fellow, 1964-66. Fellow IEEE (life); mem. Sigma Xi, Eta Kappa Nu, Tau Beta Pi, Sigma Pi Sigma, Phi Beta Chi. Methodist. Avocations: fishing, painting, woodworking. Home Phone: 352-375-3764. Personal E-mail: peytonpeebles@cox.net.

PEEBLES, R. DONAHUE, real estate company executive; b. Washington, Mar. 2, 1960; m. Katrina Peebles; children: Donahue III, Choe. Attended, Rutgers U.; D in Hospitality Mgmt. (hon.), Johnson & Wales U. Real estate agent/appraiser, Washington, 1979—83; appt. mem. DC Bd. Equalization and Rev., 1983, chmn., 1984—88; founder RDP Corp., 1983, RDP Assessment Appeals Svcs., Inc., Washington, 1988; founder, chmn., CEO Peebles Corp. (formerly Peebles Atlantic Devel. Corp.), 1997—. Spkr. in field. Author: The Peebles Principles, Tales and Tactics from an Entrepreneur's Life of Winning Deals, Succeeding in Business and Creating a Fortune from Scratch, 2007, The Peebles Path to Real Estate Wealth, 2008; featured in NY Times, Washington Post, Forbes, Wall St. Jour., Black Enterprise, Ebony and others; appeared on: CNBC, CNN, ABC, Fin. Network and others. Named Black Enterprise Co. of Yr., 2004; named to Power 150, Ebony mag., 2008. Achievements include development of the first 5-star Black-owned convention hotel (Royal Palm Crowne Plaza Hotel) in American history, 2002. Office: Peebles Corp 1 Alhambra Plz Ste 1400 Coral Gables FL 33134-5247 Office Phone: 305-442-4342. Office Fax: 305-442-4345.

PEEK, MICHAEL S., lawyer; b. Paducah, Ky., May 12, 1948; AB summa cum laude, Murray State U., 1970; JD, Vanderbilt U., 1974. Bar: Tenn. 1974. Mem. Bass, Berry & Sims, Nashville. Assoc. editor: Vanderbilt Law Rev., 1973-74. Former mem., Alumni Bd. Vanderbilt Law Sch.; former chmn. Murray State U. Found.; former pres. Murray State U. Alumni Assn. Mem. ABA (mem. corp., banking and bus. law sect.), Tenn. Bar Assn. (mem. real estate sect.), Nashville Bar Assn., Alpha Chi. Office: Bass Berry & Sims PLC 150 3rd Ave S Ste 2800 Nashville TN 37201 Business E-Mail: mpeek@bassberry.com.

PEELER, HARVEY SMITH, JR., state legislator; b. Gaffney, SC, Sept. 8, 1948; s. H. Smith Peeler and Sally Bratton P.; m. Ila LaDonna Caudill, 1969; 3 children. V. p. Peeler Jersey Farms, Inc., Gaffney; councilman Cherokee County, SC, 1977—80; mem. Dist. 14 SC State Senate, 1981—, chair Fin. Com., 1977—80. Mem.: Woodmen of World, SC Dairy Assn., America Legion, Kiwanis, Mason, Shriner, Rotary Club. Republican. Baptist. Mailing: PO Box 742 Gaffney SC 29342 Office: 213 Gressette Bldg Columbia SC 29201 Home Phone: 864-489-3766; Office Phone: 864-489-9994, 803-212-6430. Office Fax: 803-212-6434. Business E-Mail: sfg@legis.lpitr.state.sc.us.

PEEPLES, DONNA N., gas industry executive; m. William Peeples; children: Darla Peeples, Dawn Peeples. Degree in Mgmt., Troy U. With Optimum Energy Sources; v.p., sales and mktg. Peachtree Natural Gas; cons. Shell Energy LLC, Shell Oil Co.; ter. mgr. Lennox Industries, Inc.; mgr., NGV sales Atlanta Gas Light (subs. of AGL Resources Inc.); owner Motivated, Inc., founder, 1996; v.p., sales and mktg. comm. AGL Resources, Inc., mng. dir., sales and mktg., dir., bus. devel., v.p., corp. comm., chief mktg. officer, 2008—. Chmn. Coun. for Responsible Energy, Am. Gas Assn., Ga. C. of C.; active mem. Southern Gas Assn., CMO Coun., Habitat for Humanity, Advt. and Mktg. Com., Am. Pub. Gas Assn., Tenn. Gas Assn., Fla. Natural Gas Assn., Atlanta Press Club, Susan B. Komen Breast Cancer Found., Project Open Hand, Tocqueville soc. United Way Met. Atlanta; bd. dirs. Southeastern Energy Efficiency Alliance, NGV America, Energy Solutions Ctr., Clean Air Campaign. Recipient Mktg. Best Practices awards, Southern Gas Assn., 2004, 2005, 2006, 2007, 2008, Show South Addy award, 2006, MarCom Gold award, 2007, Telly awards, 2007, Southern Gas Assn, 2008. Office: AGL Resources Inc 10 Peachtree Place NE Atlanta GA 30309 Office Phone: 404-584-4000. Office Fax: 404-584-3714. Business E-Mail: DPeeples@aglresources.com.

PEEPLES, WILLIAM DEWEY, JR., mathematics professor; b. Bessemer, Ala., Apr. 19, 1928; s. William Dewey and Thelma Jeannette (Chastain) P.; m. Katie Ray Blackerby, Aug. 30, 1956; children: Mary Jeannette, William Dewey III, Gerald Lewis, Stephen Ray. BS, Samford U., 1947; MS, U. Wis., 1949; PhD in Math., U. Ga., 1951. Rsch. mathematician Ballistics Rsch. Lab., Aberdeen, Md., summer 1951; mem. faculty Samford U., Birmingham, Ala., 1951-56, prof. math., 1959-95, head dept., 1967-95; prof. emeritus, 1995; mem. faculty Auburn U., 1956-59. Cons. Hayes Internat. Corp. Co-author: Modern Mathematics for Business Students, 1969, Finite Mathematics, 1974, Modern Mathematics with Applications to Business and the Social Sciences, 4th edit, 1986, Finite Mathematics with Applications to Business and the Social Sciences, 1981, 2d edit., 1987; Contbr. articles to profl. publs. Served to 1st lt. AUS, 1954-56. Mem. Am. Math. Soc., Math. Assn. Am., Nat. Council Tchrs. Math., Ala. Coll. Tchrs. Math. (pres. 1969), Sigma Xi, Pi Mu Epsilon, Phi Kappa Phi (pres. 1977), Lambda Chi Alpha. Baptist (deacon, chmn. 1986). Club: Mason (Shriner). Home: 419 Poinciana Dr Birmingham AL 35209-4129 E-mail: wdpeeples@peoplepc.com.

PEETS, TERRY R., retail executive; MBA with honors, Pepperdine U. Exec. v.p. Vons Grocery Co.; group v.p., store ops. Ralphs Grocery Co., 1987—88, group v.p., merchandising, 1988—90, sr. v.p., merchandising, 1990—91, sr. v.p., mktg., 1991—94, exec. v.p., 1994—95, Vons Companies, Inc., 1995—97; pres., CEO, bd. dirs. PIA Merchandising Svcs., Inc., 1997—99; chmn. Bruno's Supermarkets, Inc., Birmingham, Ala., 2000—03; sr. advisor J.P. Morgan Ptnrs., 2000—07; chmn. WKI Holding Co. Inc., 2003, World Kitchens, LLC. Former bd. dirs. QRS Corp., Diamond Brands Oper. Corp.; bd. dirs. Diamond Brands Inc., Andronico, Inmar, Inc.; vice chmn. City of Hope, Ruiz Foods, Inc.; bd. dirs., SuperMarkets Online divsn. Catalina Mktg. Corp.; bd. dirs. Park City Group, Hostess Brands, Inc. (formerly Interstate Bakeries Corp.), Datalogic Scanning, Inc., 2000—, Doane Pet Care Co. (subs. Doane Pet Care Enterprises Inc.), 2001—, Doane Pet Care Enterprises Inc., 2001—, WKI Holding Co. Inc., 2003; former bd. dirs. Pinnacle Foods Fin. LLC, 2004, Berry Plastics Corp., 2004, BPC Holding Corp., 2004; bd. dirs. Pinnacle Foods Group Inc., 2004—; former bd. dirs. Aurora Foods, Inc., 2004; bd. dirs. Winn-Dixie Stores Inc., 2006—. Vice chmn. Children's Mus. of Orange County; chmn. City of Hope Nat. Cancer Ctr., Arnold Beckman Rsch. Inst. Office: Winn-Dixie Stores Inc 5050 Edgewood Ct Jacksonville FL 32254-3699 Office Phone: 904-783-5000. Office Fax: 904-370-7224. Business E-Mail: tpeets@winn-dixie.com.

PEFANIS, HARRY N., oil industry executive; b. Buffalo, 1957; Grad., U. Okla., 1979. Spl. asst. corp. planning Plains Resources, 1983—87, mgr. product mktg., 1987—88, v.p. product mktg., 1988—96, sr. v.p., 1996—98, exec. v.p. midstream, 1998—2001; pres., COO Plains All American Pipeline, LP, Houston, 1998—; vice chmn. PAA Natural Gas Storage LP, 2010—. Office: Plains All American Pipline LP 333 Clay St Ste 1600 Houston TX 77002

PEFLEY, CHARLES SAUNDERS, real estate broker; b. Portsmouth, Va., Sept. 4, 1943; s. William R. and Dorothy (Everett) P.; m. Audrey Diane Bennett, Aug. 15, 1977 (div. Sept. 1983); m. Marie Frances Servonsky, Mar. 3, 2003. BA in Polit. Sci., Old Dominion U., 1967; JD, U. Balt., 1971; postgrad., Johns Hopkins U., 1972. Lic. real estate broker. V.p. Saxis Island Devel. Corp., Virginia Beach, Va., 1965-72, Pefley, Inc., Virginia Beach, Va., 1972-77; ptnr. Pefley Realty Co., Virginia Beach, 1977—95, Pefley Realty Corp., Camden, 1983—2008, Mickey Properties, Virginia Beach, 1983-87, C.J.S. Enterprises, Virginia Beach, 1986—, Pefzar Realty, Rockville, Md., 1986—, Kelben Properties, Rockville, Md., 1983—; owner Charles S. Pefley and Assocs., Realtors, 2006—. Pres. Pefley Realty Corp., Camden, N.C., Bold Realty and Realty Co., Inc., Fair Rental Group, Inc., Centurian Residential Realty Corp., a Va. Corp., Budget Realty Devel. Corp. Served with U.S. Army, 1968-69. Mem. Tidewater Bd. Realtors, Albermarle Area Assn. Realtors, Rein Network Democrat. Roman Catholic. Avocations: boating, camping. Home: 2021 Pefley Ln Virginia Beach VA 23457-1223 Office: Charlie S Pefley and Assocs Realtors 1808 Arctic Ave Virginia Beach VA 23451-3306 Office Phone: 757-425-6916. Personal E-mail: charliepefley@yahoo.com.

PEIRCE, MARY MCCABE, publishing executive; d. Margaret Scripps Buzzelli. Bd. dirs. Scripps Networks Interactive, Inc., 2008—, The E. W. Scripps Co., 2008—. Former bd. dirs. Visiting Nurse Svcs., Long Island, NY; trustee The Edward W. Scripps Trust. Office: The E W Scripps Co Bd Directors 312 Walnut St Cincinnati OH 45202 also: Scripps Networks Interactive 9721 Sherrill Blvd Knoxville TN 37932 Office Phone: 865-694-2700, 513-977-3000. Office Fax: 865-985-7778, 513-977-3024.

PEISER, ROBERT ALAN, board member; b. NYC, Apr. 17, 1948; s. Donald Edward and Natalie (Phillips) Peiser; m. Nancy McCormick; children: Karyn, Brian, Craig, Scott. BA, U. Pa., 1969; MBA, Harvard U., 1972. Dir. corp. fin. TWA, NYC, 1972-77, sr. v.p. fin., CFO, 1983-86, exec. v.p. fin., CFO, 1994-96; treas. Hertz Corp., NYC, 1977-80; staff v.p., treas. ops. RCA Corp., NYC, 1980-81; v.p., treas. Trans World Corp., NYC, 1981-83; sr. v.p., CFO ALC Comm. Corp., Birmingham, Mich., 1986-88; sr. v.p. fin., CFO Borman's Inc., Detroit, 1988-89; pres., CEO Orange-Co. Ic., Bartow, Fla., 1989-92; with BBK, Ltd., Southfield, Mich., 1992-94; vice chmn., CEO FoxMeyer Drug Co., Carrollton, Tex., 1996; pres., CEO Western Pacific Airlines, Colorado Springs, Colo., 1996-98; chmn. CVSI, Inc., Bedford, Mass., 1998-99; chmn., CEO Vitality Beverages, Tampa, Fla., 1999—2002; pres., CEO Imperial Sugar Co., Sugar Land, Tex., 2002—08; CEO Omniflight Helicopters, Inc., Addison, Tex., 2008—10. Bd. dirs. Kitty Hawk, Inc., 2002—05, Pinnacle Airlines Corp., 2003—05, Team, Inc., 2006—12, Solutia, Inc., 2008—12, Signature Group Holdings, 2010—11, USA Truck, Inc., 2012—. Bd. pres. Houston Symphony. Mem.: League of Am. Orchs., Houston Area Women's Ctr., Nat. Assn. Corp. Dirs. (mem. Tex. Tricities chpt.), Lakeside Country Club (Houston).

PELFREY, D. PATTON, lawyer; b. Ky., 1941; BA, Calif. State U., LA, 1963; JD, U. Louisville, 1968. Bar: Ky. 1968. Trial atty. region 9 NLRB, Cin., 1968-72; mem. Frost Brown Todd LLC, Louisville, 1972—. Prof. labor law sch. law U. Louisville. Fellow Coll. Labor and Emloyment Lawyers; mem. ABA (sect. labor and employment law), Ky. Bar Assn. (labor sect.), Louisville Bar Assn. (mem. labor com. 1983—), Delta Theta Phi. Office: Frost Brown Todd LLC 400 W Market St Ste 3200 Louisville KY 40202-3363 Office Phone: 502-589-5400. E-mail: ppelfrey@fbtlaw.com.

PELHAM, ANN, publishing executive, department chairman; BA in history, Duke U., 1974. Reporter The News & Observer, Raleigh, NC, Congl. Quarterly, Washington, Governing Mag.; reporter through exec. editor Legal Times, Washington, 1988—96, assoc. pub., 1996—98, publisher, 1998—; v.p. Duke U. Alumni Assn., 2004—; chmn. Duke Student Pub. Co., 2003—. Editor: The Chronicle (Duke Univ. newspaper). Office: Duke Student Publishing Co Inc 101 W Union Bldg Durham NC 27708-0001 Office Phone: 919-684-3811. Office Fax: 919-684-8295.

PELL, JONATHAN LAURENCE, performing company executive; b. Memphis, Oct. 20, 1949; s. Burton Marshall and Eleanor (Leopold) P. BA, U. So. Calif., 1971. Interior designer Gene Morse Assocs., Wichita, Kans., 1971-77; mgr. Internat. Artists Mgmt., NYC, 1977-79, Robert Lombardo Assocs., NYC, 1979-80; TV producer Sta. WNET, NYC, 1980-83; dir. publicity John Curry Skating Co., NYC, 1983; prodr. Jerome Kern Centennary Gala Town Hall, NYC, 1984; dir. artistic adminstrn. Dallas Opera, 1984—2009, dir. artistic, 2009—. Vocal competition judge Met. Opera Nat. Coun. Auditions, Pavarotti Competition, Bidu Sayao Internat. Competition, Brazil, Ottavio Ziino Internat. Competition, Rome, Patronesses of the Opera Competition, Miami, Fla., George London Awards, Ctr. for Contemporary Opera, Jensen Found. Competition, Dallas Opera Guild, Denver Lyric Opera Guild, Ft. Worth Opera, Marguerite McCammon Competition, San Antonio Opera Guild, Shreveport Opera, Richard Tucker Award, others; tchr. master classes for young singers Opera Am., Nat. Opera Assn., Can. Opera Co., S.W. Chpt. NATS, Performing Arts Assistance Corp., U. North Tex., Internat. Sch. Performing Arts, Amarillo Opera, So. Meth. U.; host Dallas Opera Radio Hour, WRR, 1994—97; guest Inside the Dallas Opera, WRR, 2004—; lectr. on opera Crystal Cruises. Bd. dirs., chmn. nat. auditions com., mem. award selection com. Richard Tucker Music Found., 1996-2009; former mem. adv. bd. Awards Recognizing Individual Artistry; former advisor to singer svcs. com. Opera Am. Named Singer of Yr. Office: Dallas Opera Campbell Ctr I LBI-11 2403 Flora St # 500 Dallas TX 75201-2415 Office Phone: 214-443-1086. Business E-Mail: jonathan@dallasopera.org.

PELLOCK, JOHN MICHAEL, child neurologist; b. Passaic, NJ, Dec. 25, 1943; s. John and Laura (Holubko) P.; m. Mary Lee Miller, June 27, 1970; children: Mary Kathryn, John Michael. BA, Johns Hopkins U., 1965; MS, Fairleigh Dickinson U., 1967; MD, St. Louis U., 1971. Diplomate Nat. Bd. Med. Examiners, Am. Bd. Psychiatry and Neurology, Am. Bd. Pediatrics; lic. physician, Mo., N.J., N.Y., Md., Va. Intern, resident in pediatrics Med. Coll. Va., Richmond, 1971-73, asst. prof. neurology, 1978, asst. prof. pediatrics, 1979; fellow Columbia Presbyn. Med. Ctr., NYC, 1973-76; instr. neurology and pediatrics U. Health Scis., Bethesda, Md., 1976-78; assoc. prof. neurology and pediatrics Va. Commonwealth U., Richmond, 1984-88, prof. neurology and pediatrics, 1988—, chmn. epilepsy divsn., 1993—; prof. pharmacy and pharms. Med. Coll. Va./Va. Commonwealth U., Richmond, 1994, chmn. child neurology divsn., 1995. Mem. academic staff D.C. Children's Hosp., Nat. Med. Ctr., Washington, 1976-78; mem. staff Med. Coll. Va. Hosp., 1978—, Children's Hosp., Richmond, 1986-2007, St. Mary's Hosp., Richmond, 1988-2006, Nat. Naval Med. Ctr., Bethesda, 1976-78; cons., lectr. and presenter in field. Editor: Neurologic Emergencies in Infancy and Chlidhood, 1984, Pediatric Epilepsy, Diagnosis and Therapy, 1993, Neurologic Emergencies in Infancy and Childhood, 2d edit., 1993, A Textbook of Epilepsy, 5th edit., 1997, Pediatric Epilepsy, 3d edit., 2008; guest editor Seizure Disorders, Pediatric Clinics North America, 1989, Promise and Progress in the Treatment of Epilepsy, Neurology, 34, 1993, Seminars in Child Neurology; editor jours. Practice of Pediatrics, 1980-88, Drug Evaluations, 1991-96; (newsletter) Child Neurology Soc., 1986-88; mem. editl. bd. Jour. Child Neurology, 1997—; contbr. numerous articles and abstracts to profl. jours. Eucharistic minister St. Edward's Cath. Ch., Bon Air, Va., 1980—; profl. advisor Va. Capital of March of Dimes, 1980-86; bd. dirs. Cath. Charities of Richmond, 1981-93 (Cert. of Appreciation 1993). Lt. comdr. USNR, 1968-78, hon. discharge. Recipient Cert. of Appreciation, S.C. Epilepsy Assn., 1985; named Best Drs. in Am., Woodward/White Inc., 1993-, Am. Men and Women of Sci., 1994-; Am. Acad. Pediatrics fellow, 1972; grantee NIH, 1972-74, 78, 84, 87—, Burroughs Wellcome Co., 1980-82, 84-86, 91—, Boots Pharms., Inc., 1984-85, Ciba-Geigy, 1988, 92-93, A.H. Robins, 1984-85, GD Searle Co., 1986, Abbott Labs., 1986-88, 90—, Parke Davis/Warner Lambert/Pfizer, 1988—, Carter-Wallace, 1991-95, multiple others DHHS, 1986—, Med. Coll. Va., 1989-93, Janssen Rsch. Found., 1989-97, others. Fellow Am. Acad. Neurology, Am. Acad. Pediatrics, Am. Neurol. Assn.; mem. AMA, Am. Epilepsy Soc. (J. Kiffin Perry award Excellence Epilepsy Care 2004, treas. 2005-08, v.p. 2009-10, pres. 2010-), Epilepsy Found. Am., Epilepsy Assn. Va. (bd. dirs. 1979—, profl. adv. bd. 1983—, chmn. 1983-88), Va. Neurol. Soc., Med. Soc. Va., Va. Pediat. Soc., Child Neurology Soc. (exec. com. 1988-90, editor newsletter 1986-88, membership com. 1982-86,

88-90), Itnernat. Child Neurology Assn., Itnernat. League Against Epilepsy (commn. 1994-), Richmond Pediatric Soc., Richmond Acad. Medicine, USN Neurol. Soc. Office: Med Coll Va/Va Commonwealth PO Box 980211 MCV Station Richmond VA 23298 Office Phone: 804-828-0442. Business E-Mail: jpellock@mcvh-vcu.edu.

PELTON, ELOIS BLEIDT, retired physical education educator; b. Corpus Christi, Tex., Apr. 3, 1939; d. Hodge Lester and Valena (Lee) Bleidt; m. Scott Horton Pelton, July 23, 1961 (div. June 1967); 1 child, Shawn Scott. BS in Edn., U. Ark., 1961; MS in Edn., U. Central Ark., 1967; EdD, Northwestern State U. La., 1972. Phys. edn. tchr. East Side Jr. HS, Little Rock, 1963-65, Searcy Jr. HS, Ark., 1965-68; prof. phys. edn. Ctrl. Mo. State U., Warrensburg, 1968—2000, prof. emeritus, 2000—; lay spkr. Christ United Methodist Ch. Hot Spring Village, Springs Village, 2013—. Phys. edn. curriculum cons. Ctrl. Mo. State U., Warrensburg, 1965—2000. Mem. Park Bd., City of Warrensburg. Mem. AAHPER and Dance (nat. del. 1988—), Mo. Asns. Health, Phys. Edn., Recreation and Dance (pres. 1989, presidential award 1987). Avocations: exercise, golf, tennis, reading. Home: 39 Letrista Dr Hot Springs AR 71909-6603 Personal E-mail: ebpelton@sbcglobal.net.

PELTON, JAMES RODGER, retired library director; b. St. Louis, Mar. 21, 1945; s. Norman C. and Leona V. (Schulte) Pelton; m. Sandra Lee Birdsell, Mar. 29, 1969; children: Joni Lee, Vicki Sue. BA, U. Mo., 1967, MLS, 1969. Br. libr. Scenic Regional Libr., Union, Mo., 1968—71; adminstr. Daniel Boone Regional Libr. - Columbia Ctr., Mo., 1971—78; cons. La. State Libr., Baton Rouge, 1978—80; dir. Shreve Meml. Libr., Shreveport, La., 1980—2009, ret., 2009. Mem.: ALA, La. Libr. Assn. Office Phone: 318-226-5897. Office Fax: 318-226-4780. E-mail: jpelton@shreve-lib.org.

PEÑA, AARON, JR., state legislator; b. Austin, Tex., June 8, 1959; s. Lionel Aron and Sylvia (Alamia) P.; m. Monica Solis, Mar. 29, 1991; children: Adrienne, Aaron, John, Alyssa, Anthony. BA in Liberal Arts, U. Tex., 1984; JD, Tex. So. U., 1987. Bar: Tex. 1988. Legis. asst. Tex. Legislature, Austin; mem. staff Tex. Dem. Party, Austin; mem. staff to Senator Bob Krueger US Senate, Austin; tchr. Austin Ind. Sch. Dist.; ptnr. Peñna, McDonald, Prestia & Ornelas, Edinburg, Tex., 1988-90, Aaron Peña & Associates, Edinburg, 1990—; mem. Dist. 40 Tex. House Representatives, 2002—. Author, spkr. published rec.: Million Dollar Arguments, 1997. Mem. ABA, ATLA, State Bar Tex., Nat. Employment Lawyers Assn. Democrat. Roman Catholic. Avocations: travel, golf. Office: Aaron Peña & Associates 1110 S Closner Blvd Edinburg TX 78539-5662 also: PO Box 1637 Edinburg TX 78540 also: Room E1.304 Capitol Extension PO Box 2910 Austin TX 78768 Office Phone: 956-383-7444, 512-463-0426.

PENA, RAYMUNDO JOSEPH, bishop; b. Corpus Christi, Tex., Feb. 19, 1934; s. Cosme A. and Elisa (Ramon) P. DD, Assumption Sem., San Antonio, 1957. Ordained priest Roman Cath. Ch., 1957. Ordained priest Diocese of Corpus Christi, Tex., 1957; asst. pastor St. Peter's Ch., Laredo, Tex., 1957—60, St. Joseph's-Our Lady of Fatima, Alamo, Tex., 1960—63, Sacred Heart, Mathis, Tex., 1963—67, Christ the King and Our Lady of Pillar Parishes, Corpus Christi, 1967—69; pastor Our Lady of Guadalupe Parish, Corpus Christi, 1969—76; v.p. Corpus Christi Diocesan Senate of Priests, 1970—76; ordained bishop, 1976; aux. bishop Archdiocese of San Antonio, 1976—80; bishop Diocese of El Paso, 1980—95, Diocese of Brownsville, Tex., 1995—2009, bishop emeritus, 2009—. Mem. secretariat Prep. Synod of Bishops for Am., 1996—97; Synodal Father Synod of Bishops for Am., 1995. Mem.: US Conf. Cath. Bishops (chmn. bishops' com. for Hispanic affairs 1987—90, bishops' com. for ch. in L.Am. 1994—97, 2000). Roman Catholic. Home: 741 Bowie Alamo TX 78516 Office: PO Box 2279 Brownsville TX 78522-2279 Office Phone: 956-542-2501. Business E-Mail: rjpena@cdob.org.

PENA, RICHARD, lawyer; b. San Antonio, Feb. 13, 1948; s. Merced and Rebecca (Trejo) P.; m. Carolyn Sarah Malley, May 25, 1979; 1 stepchild, Jason Charles Schubert. BA, U. Tex., 1970, JD, 1976. Bar: Tex. 1976, Colo. 1986. Atty. Law Offices of Richard Pena, Austin, Tex., 1976—. Instr. bus. law St. Edwards U., Austin, 1983, Austin CC, 1981-82; broker Tex. Real Estate Commn., 1980—; sports editor Austin Light, 1982. Bd. dirs. Ctr. for Battered Women, Austin, 1979-82, Austin Assn. Retarded Citizens, 1980-82; chmn. Austin Travis County Mental Health/Mental Retardation Pub. Responsibility Com., 1979-84; chmn. pvt. facilities monitoring com. Austin Assn. Retarded Citizens, 1981; bd. dirs. Boys Club of Austin, 1987-88; chair Homeless Task Force Austin, 1999—. Named one of Outstanding Young Men of Am., 1982. Fellow Tex. Bar Found. (sustaining life; trustee 1994, sec., treas. 1994, vice-chmn. 1995, chmn. 1996); mem. ABA (house dels., nominating com. 1998—, immigration bono com. 2000—, chair 2004-07, vice chair credentials com. 2001, state del. 2002-07, bd. govs. 2007—10), Am. Bar Found. (bd. dirs. 2000, fellows officer 2003-04, chair 2004-05, vice pres. 2006), Nat. Conf. Bar Pres. (exec. com. 2001-03), State Bar Tex. (bd. dirs. Dist. 9 1991-94, exec. com. 1992—, chmn. minority representation com. 1991-92, chair James Watson Inn 1997-98, pres. 1998-99, chmn. profl. devel. com. 1991-92, policy manual com. 1993, fed. jud. appts. com. 1984-86, opportunities for minorities in the profession com. 1990-91, mem. advt. rev. com., pres.-elect 1997, pres. 1998-99), Travis County Bar Assn. (trustee lawyer referral svc. 1984-85, bd. dirs. 1986-88, sec. 1988, pres. 1990-91, chmn. jud. screening com. 1987, chmn. 1988-89, ins. com. 1988, 89, chmn. law day banquet com. 1988-89, lawyer referrel svc. com. 1983-84, trustee 1984-86, membership com. 1989), Capitol Area Mex. Am. Lawyers (pres. 1985, Outstanding Hispanic Lawyer Austin 1989), Legal Aid Soc. Ctrl. Tex. (bd. dirs. 1984), Austin Young Lawyers Assn., Tex. Trial Lawyers Assn., Austin C. of C. (Leadership Austin 1985-86). Democrat. Office: Law Offices of Richard Pena 1701 Directors Blvd Ste 110 Austin TX 78744-1096 Office Phone: 512-327-6884. Business E-Mail: richard@rpenalaw.com.

PENALVER, MANUEL A., gynecologic oncologist; MD, U. Miami, 1977. Diplomate Am. Bd. Ob-Gyn, Am. Bd. Ob-Gyn-gynecologic oncology, lic. Fla., 1978. Intern pathology Sch. of Medicine Univ. Miami/Jackson Meml. Med. Ctr., 1978, resident ob-gyn. dept., 1982, fellow gynecologic oncology, 1984; joined faculty dept. ob-gyn. Univ. Miami, 1984, prof. dept. ob-gyn., 1999—2004, chmn. dept. ob-gyn., 1999—2004; co-ptnr. South Fla. Gynecologic Oncology Group; hosp. affiliations include Baptist Health South Fla. Hosp., Aventura Hosp. and Med. Ctr., Broward Gen. Med. Ctr., Cleveland Clinic Hosp., Healthsouth Doctors Hosp., Hialeah Hosp., Mercy Hosp. Inc., Mt. Sinai Med. Ctr., Palmetto Gen. Hosp., South Miami Hosp., Univ. Miami Hosp. and Clinic, Baptist Hosp. of Miami, Doctors Hosp. Author: various publs. Mem.: Soc. of Gynecologic Surgeons, Soc. of Gynecologic Oncologists, Soc. of Pelvic Surgeons, ACOG. Office: Doctors Hospital 5000 University Dr Coral Gables FL 33146 Office Phone: 786-308-3000.

PENCE, IRA WILSON, JR., engineering executive, researcher; b. Pontiac, Mich., June 18, 1939; s. Ira Wilson and Fern Elizabeth (Fraser) P.; m. JoAnna Springer, Sept. 5, 1959; children: Ira W. III, Teresa Ann, Deidre Lynn. BS, U. Mich., 1962, MSEE, 1964, PhD, 1970. Rsch. engr. Willow Run Labs., Ypsilanti, Mich., 1960-67, Dow Lab., Ann Arbor, Mich., 1967-70, GE, Schenectady, NY, 1970-80, engring. mgr. Charlottesville, Va., 1980-83; v.p. engring. Unimation, Inc., Danbury, Conn., 1983-87; dir. MHRC Ga. Inst. Tech., Atlanta, 1987-97, dir., pres. Intelligent Integrated Info. Sys., 1999—2009; chair Camp Wesley Bldg. Com., 2010, 2008—. Cons. Superior Motor, Hartford, 1987—89; bd. dirs. Wesley Found.; mem. adv. coun. Westinghouse, Pitts., 1983—87; treas. Wesley Comm. Ctrs., Inc., 1999—2007; exec. pres. Intelligent Integrated Info. Sys., 1999—2008; dir. 21iii.com, 2000—. Editor: Progress in Material Handling and Logistics, 1988; Material Handling for 90's, 1990. Trustee United Meth. Ch., 1988—, Camp Wesley, Inc. 1998— (treas. 2003-); cons. West Africa Theol. Sem., 2008-. Recipient New Product of Yr. award Innovation Today, 1985. Mem. IEEE (sr., sect. chmn. 1978), ASME (Materials Handling Engring. divsn. chair 1994). Republican. Methodist. Avocations: cabinet making, golf. Office Phone: 770-435-3183. Business E-Mail: ipence@isye.gatech.edu.

PENCE, LORENZO L., dean, osteopath, educator; BS, Bluefield State Coll., W.Va.; MD, W.Va. Sch. Osteo. Medicine, Lewisburg, 1985. Resident in family medicine Parkview Hosp., Toledo; dir. med. edn. The Toledo Hosp., St. Vincent Mercy Med. Ctr., Toledo, Greenbrier Valley Med. Ctr., Ronceverte, W.Va.; prof. family medicine W.Va. Sch. Osteo. Medicine, assoc. dean grad. med. edn., 2003—, v.p. academic affairs, dean, 2011—, chief academic officer Mountain State Osteo. Postdoctoral Tng. Institutes; chmn. bd. dirs. Southeastern Area Health Edn. Ctr. Office: WVa Sch Osteo Medicine C203 C Bldg 400 N Lee St Lewisburg WV 24901 Office Phone: 304-647-6237. Office Fax: 304-793-6810. Business E-Mail: lpence@osteo.wvsom.edu.*

PENDERGRAFT, PHILIP A., diversified financial services company executive; BA in Economics, Trinity U., San Antonio, Tex. Securities industry profl.; co-founder, various exec. officer and dir. positions with certain affiliated entities Penson Financial Services, Inc., 1995—; exec. v.p., COO Penson Worldwide, Inc., 2000—05, CEO, 2005—. Bd. dirs. Penson Worldwide, Inc., 2000—, The Options Clearing Corp., 2009—. Office: Penson Worldwide Inc 1700 Pacific Ave Ste 1400 Dallas TX 75201 Office Phone: 214-765-1100. Office Fax: 214-217-4978. Business E-Mail: PPendergraft@penson.com.

PENDERGRASS, EWELL DEAN, retired communications executive; b. Houston, Dec. 24, 1945; s. Ewell Burl and Mary LaVerne (Sharp) P.; m. Linda Jo Williams, 1973; children: William Dean, Douglas Aaron, Nagaya Jo. AAS, Westark C.C., 1979. Comm. technician Murdock Comm., Ft. Smith, Ark., 1966-73; electronics technician City of Ft. Smith, Ft. Smith, 1973—2010, now electronics supr.; co-owner LED Comms., 1975—. Broadcast engr. Sta. KWHN, 1972-73, Sta. KFSA, 1975-76; mem. Ark. Dept. Pollution and Ecology Wastewater Licensing Bd.; mem. Ark. Licensing Commn. Mem. Am. Water Works Assn., Ark. Water Works and Pollution Control Assn. (chmn., Western dist. dir.), Border Amateur Radio Club (prs. 1974-75). Democrat. Methodist. Avocation: amateur radio. Home: 1106 Country Meadow Ln Cedarville AR 72932-9524 Personal E-mail: ledcomm.mail@gmail.com, edpbub@gmail.com.

PENDLETON, JOEY, state legislator; b. Hopkinsville, Ky., May 3, 1946; s. Allen Pendleton and Josephine; m. Diane Wood. State senator Dist. 3, Ky., 1993—; Minority Whip, 2005—; Farmer, farm op. mgr. Murray State U.; bd. mem. Pennyrile Area Devel. Dist. Recipient Outstanding Young Dairy Farmer, SE, 1977, Conrad Feltner 4-H Alumni award, Distinguished Svc. award, Ky. Mental Health Coalition award, Ky. Assn. Conserv Dist., STAR award, Ky. Brain Injury Assn., Better Life award, Ky. Assn. Health Care Facil, Agr. Support award, Murray State U.; named Outstanding Layperson of Yr., Ky. Optometrist Assn. Mem.: Christian County Democratic Assn., Am. Jersey Cattle Assn. (nat. bd. mem.), Fraternal Order Eagles, Christian County Ext. Coun., North Am. Internat. Livestock Expn. (exec. com. mem.), Kiwanis, Friends of 4-H. Democrat. Baptist. Mailing: 905 Hurst Dr Hopkinsville KY 42240 Office: Capitol Annex Rm 257 Frankfort KY 40601 Home Phone: 270-885-1639; Office Phone: 502-564-2470. Fax: 270-885-0640. E-mail: jpendleton@mail.lrc.state.ky.us.

PENDLETON, MARY CATHERINE, retired foreign service officer; b. Louisville, June 15, 1940; d. Joseph S. and Katherine R. (Toebbe) Pendleton. BA, Spalding Coll., 1962; MA, Ind. U., 1969; cert., Nat. Def. U., 1990; D (hon.), U. N. Testemitanu, Moldova, 1994. Cert. secondary tchr. Ky. Tchr. Presentation Acad., Louisville, 1962-66; vol. Peace Corps, Tunis, Tunisia, 1966-68; employment counselor Ky. Dept. for Human Resources, Louisville, 1969-75; gen. svcs. Am. Embassy, Khartoum, Sudan, 1975-77, counsular officer Manila, 1978-79, adminstrv. officer Bangui, Central African Republic, 1979-82, Lusaka, Zambia, 1982-84; post mgmt. officer Dept. of State Bur. European and Can. Affairs, Washington, 1984-87; adminstrv. counselor Am. Embassy, Bucharest, Romania, 1987-89; dir. adminstrv. tng. divsn. Fgn. Svc. Inst., Arlington, Va., 1990-92; ambassador Am. Embassy, Chisinau, Moldova, 1992-95, adminstrv. counselor Brussels, 1995-98; consul gen. U.S. Consulate Gen., Montreal, 1998-2001; mgmt. counselor Am. Embassy, Cairo, 2001—04; diplomat in residence U. Memphis, 2004—05; ret., 2005. Bd. dirs. Cairo Am. Coll., 2001—04; vol. instr. Presdl. Classroom, 2006—09; bd. dirs. Am. Sch. Bucharest, 1987—89; vol. evaluator Am. Couns. Internat. Edn., 2009—; vol. fin. asst. Encore Svc. Corps., 2009—; election official Arlington County Va., 2008—; sec. treas. Condominium Owners Assn., 2006—. Named to, Hon. Order Ky. Cols., 1988. Democrat. Roman Catholic. Avocation: outdoor activities. Home: 1946 N Cleveland St Arlington VA 22201 Personal E-mail: pendletonmc@gmail.com.

PENDLETON, TERRY LEE, professional baseball coach, retired professional baseball player; b. LA, July 16, 1960; m. Catherine Grindulo Marquey, Oct. 27, 1984; children: Stephanie, Terry, Trinity. Student, Oxnard Coll., Calif., Fresno State U. Infielder St. Louis Cardinals, 1982-90, Atlanta Braves, 1991-94, 1996, batting coach, 2001—10, first base coach, 2011—; infielder Fla. Marlins, 1995-96, Cin. Reds, 1997, Kansas City Royals, 1998. Recipient Gold Glove award, 1987, 89, 92; named Nat. League Comeback Player of Yr. The Sporting News, 1991, Nat. League MVP Baseball Writers' Assn. Am., 1991; named to Nat. League All-Star Team Maj. League Baseball, 1992. Achievements include leading the National League in: batting average (.319), 1991. Office: Atlanta Braves Turner Field 755 Hank Aaron Dr Atlanta GA 30315

PENDLETON, TODD, telecommunications industry executive; Grad., Northeastern U., Boston, 1994. Account exec. Saatchi & Saatchi, 1994—96; advt. mgr. Nike, Inc., 1996—2001, brand mgr., 2001—04, mktg. dir. Germany, Austria, Switzerland, Slovenia, 2004—05, brand comm. dir. Asia Pacific, 2007—08, brand comm. dir. US, 2008—09, global brand comm. dir., 2009—11; chief mktg. officer Samsung Telecommunications America, LLC, 2011—. Office: Samsung Telecommunications America 1301 E Lookout Dr Richardson TX 75082

PENDLEY, WILLIAM TYLER, military officer, educator; b. Paris, Ky., June 21, 1936; s. Louis Tyler and Virginia Lorene (Poplin) P.; m. Anne Carroll Cooke, Dec. 13, 1958; children: Stephen Tyler, Robert Randolph, Lisa Carroll, Leslie Brooks. BS in Engring., U.S. Naval Acad., 1958; MA, Am. U., Washington, 1965. Commd. ensign USN, 1958, advanced through grades to rear adm., 1983; comdg. officer Patrol Squadron 45, Jacksonville, Fla., 1975-76; ops. officer Patrol Wing 11, U.S. Atlantic Fleet, Jacksonville, 1976-78, comdr., 1979-81; exec. sec. for joint chief of staff matters Chief Naval Ops., Washington, 1978-79, planner for joint chief of staff matters, 1981-82, dir. plans policy and strategy divsn., 1985-86; exec. asst. to comdr. in chief U.S. Pacific Fleet, Pearl Harbor, Hawaii, 1982-83; comdr. patrol wings U.S. Atlantic Fleet, Brunswick, Maine, 1983-85; commdr. Naval Forces Korea, Seoul, 1986-89; sr. mem. UN Mil. Armistice Commn., 1986-89; dir. strategic plans and policy USCINCPAC, Camp H. M. Smith, Hawaii, 1989-91; dep. asst. sec. def. for East Asia and Pacific affairs Dept. Def., Washington, 1992-93; prof. internat. rels. Air War Coll., Maxwell AFB, Ala., 1993-98. Lectr. and cons., 1998—; fellow Georgetown U. Leadership Seminar, Washington, 1985. Co-author: Nuclear Coexistence, 1987; contbr. articles to profl. jours. Decorated Def. D.S.M. with oak leaf cluster, Legion of Merit with 4 gold stars; named hon. Ky. Col., 1975; recipient Def. medal for disting. pub. svc., 1993. Mem. Phi Kappa Phi, Pi Gamma Mu. Methodist. Avocations: golf, travel. Home: 10 Walden Ln Bluffton SC 29909 Office Phone: 843-705-2334. E-mail: pendleyw@yahoo.com.

PENG, SYD S., mining engineer, educator; arrived in US, 1965; Diploma in Mining Engring., Taiwan; M, SD Sch. Mines; PhD in Mining Engring., Stanford U., Calif., 1970. Mining engr. Twin Cities Rsch. Ctr. US Bur. Mines, 1970—74; asst. prof. mining engring. W.Va. U., Morgantown, 1974—78, chmn. dept. mining engring., 1978—2006, dir. Longwall Mining and Ground Control Rsch. Ctr., 1985—, Charles T. Holland disting. prof., 1987—, Charles E. Lawall chair mining engring. Morgantown, 2006—. Contbr. articles to sci. jours.; author: Coal Mine Ground Control, 1978, Longwall Mining, 1984, Surface Subsidence Engring., 1992. Recipient Instn. Overseas Medal award, Instn. Mining Engrs., UK, 1992, Howard N. Eavenson award, Soc. Mining, Metallurgy and Exploration, 1999, Donald S. Kingery Meml. award, Pitts. Coal Mining Inst. Am., 2001, Erskine Ramsey Medal award, AIME, 2002, Medal for Excellence, Inst. Materials, Minerals and Mining, UK, 2004, R & D 100 award, R & D Mag., 2004, 2005, 2006. Mem.: NAE. Achievements include patents in field. Office: Dept Mining Engring PO Box 6070 365 Mineral Resources Bldg Morgantown WV 26506-6070 Office Phone: 304-293-7680 ext. 3301. E-mail: sspeng@mail.wvu.edu.

PENN, LORETTA A., human resources specialist; BS, U. North Tex. Regional exec. (sales & mktg.) IBM Corp.; recruiting & staffing positions Olsten Svcs.; v.p., east coast ops. Temporaries Inc.; mgmt. positions comml. staffing bus. group Spherion Corp., exec., legal staffing divsn., v.p., nat. accounts, 2000—06, v.p., chief svc. excellence advocate, 2006—07, pres. staffing svcs., 2008—, sr. v.p., chief svc. excellence officer, 2007—. Bd. dirs. TECO Energy, 2005—. Office: Spherion Corp 2050 Spectrum Boulevard Fort Lauderdale FL 33309 Office Phone: 954-308-7600. Office Fax: 954-351-8117. Business E-Mail: lorettapenn@spherion.com.

PENNARTZ, TRACY, state legislator; BA, Univ. Ark., 1973, MA, 1974. Assoc. dir. We. Ark. Counseling & Guidance Ctr., 1975—2006; pres. Pennartz & Associates; adj. prof. Webster Univ.; mem. Dist. 65 Ark. House of Reps., 2007—. Mem. Fort Smith Art Ctr., Ark. Mental Health Planning Adv. Coun., Fort Smith League of Women Voters. Democrat. Roman Catholic. Mailing: PO Box 10441 Fort Smith AR 72917 Office Phone: 479-285-4800. Business E-Mail: pennartzt@arkleg.state.ar.us.

PENNETTA, FLAVIA, professional tennis player; b. Brindisi, Italy, Feb. 25, 1982; Profl. tennis player WTA, 2000—. Named Knight of Order of Merit of the Republic, Italy, 2007. Achievements include patents in field of winner 9 career singles titles, 11 career doubles titles, WTA; winner 7 career singles titles, 9 career doubles titles, ITF. Office: c/o WTA Tour Ste 1500 One Progress Plaza Saint Petersburg FL 33701

PENNIMAN, NICHOLAS GRIFFITH, IV, retired newspaper publisher; b. Balt., Mar. 7, 1938; s. Nicholas Griffith Penniman III and Esther Cox Lony (Wight) Keeney; m. Linda Jane Simmons, Feb. 4, 1967; children: Rebecca Helmle, Nicholas G. V. AB, Princeton U., 1960; MA, Washington U., 1999. Asst. bus. mgr. Ill. State Jour. Register, Springfield, 1964-69, bus. mgr., 1969-75; asst. gen. mgr. St. Louis Post-Dispatch, 1975-84, gen. mgr., 1984-86, pub., 1986-99; sr. v.p. newspapers ops. Pulitzer Pub. Co., 1986-99; pres., CEO Pulitzer Comm. Newspapers Inc., 1997-99; chmn. bd. Penniman & Browne, Inc., Balt., 2001—08. Chmn. Downtown St. Louis, Inc., 1988-90, Mo. Health and Ednl. Facilities Adminstrn., 1982-85, Ill. State Fair Bd., Springfield, 1973-75, Forest Pk. Forever, 1991-93, Pks. and Open Space Task Force St. Louis 2004, 1996-00, St. Louis Sports Com., 1992-93, Gateway Pks. and Trls. 2004, 1999-04; pres. Caring Found. Children, 1988-91; trustee St. Louis Country Day Sch., 1983-86, Nat. Recreation Found., 2003—, Merc. Libr. St. Louis, 1997-00; bd. dirs. Mo. Coalition for Environment, 1997-2000, Randall Rsch. Ctr., Pineland, Fla., 2001—, Friends of Rookery Bay, 2004—09; bd. mem. Everglades Found., 2009-, chmn. bd. Am. Rivers, 2004-06, Conservancy of SW Fla., 2007—13; mem. Sons of Am. Revolution, 1982-, Collier County Environ. Adv. Coun., Fla., 2005-09, adv. commn. Collier County Coastal, 2014-, bd. mem. Valleys Planning Coun. Md., 2010-, Preservation Md., 2010-, treas., 2013- With US Army, 1962—67. Mem.: Moorings Country Club, Elkridge Club, Grey Oaks Country Club. Home: 611 Portside Dr Naples FL 34103-4118 E-mail: ngpiv@aol.com.

PENNINGER, FRIEDA ELAINE, retired literature educator; b. Marion, NC, Apr. 11, 1927; d. Fred Hoyle and Lena Frances (Young) Penninger. AB, U. N.C., Greensboro, 1948; MA, Duke U., 1950, PhD, 1961. Copywriter Sta. WSJS, Winston-Salem, NC, 1948-49; asst. prof. English Flora Macdonald Coll., Red Springs, NC, 1950-51; tchr. English Barnwell, SC, 1951-52, Brunswick, Ga., 1952-53; instr. English U. Tenn., Knoxville, 1953-56; instr., asst. prof. Woman's Coll., U. N.C., Greensboro, 1956-58, 60-63; asst. prof., assoc. prof. U. Richmond (Va.), 1963-71; chair. dept. English Westhampton Coll., Richmond, 1971-78; prof. English U. Richmond, 1971-91, Bostwick prof. English, 1987-91, ret., 1991. Author: William Caxton, 1979, Chaucer's "Troilus and Criseyde" and "The Knight's Tale": Fictions Used, 1993, (novel) Look at Them, 1990; compiler, editor: English Drama to 1660, 1976; editor: Festschrift for Prof. Marguerite Roberts, 1976. Fellow Southeastern Inst. of Mediaeval and Renaissance Studies, 1965, 67, 69. Mem.: Friends of The Libr. U. NC Greensboro. Democrat. Presbyterian. Home: 2701 Camden Rd Greensboro NC 27403-1438

PENNINGTON, JODIE A., education outreach educator; b. Danville, Ky., Oct. 27, 1949; s. Emmett Clair and Edna Davis Pennington; m. Melinda Snider Pennington, June 10, 1972; children: Sara E., Ellen M. Pennington Steinmiller. BS, Western Ky. U., Bowling Green, 1971; MS, U. Ill., Urbana-Champaign, 1974, PhD, 1976. Asst. prof. animal sci. U. Wisconsin-River Falls, 1976—81, Purdue U., West

Lafayette, Ind., 1981—85; asst. to assoc. prof. agr. Western Ky. U., Bowling Green, 1986—92; prof./dairy specialist Univ Ark. Coop Ext. Svc., Little Rock, 1993—. Contbr. more than 400 articles to profl. jours. Active United Meth. Ch., Conway, Ark., 1993—. Capt. USAR, 1971—83. Rsch. grantee, 1976—92, various grants, 1993—. Mem.: Nat. Mastitis Coun., Dairy Shrine (state coord. 2000—), Am. Dairy Sci. Assn. (3 com. chairmanships, bd. dirs. So. region), Am. Dairy Sci. Assn. Found. (charter mem.), Holstein Assn. Am., Ark. Assn. Registered Profl. Animal Scientists (pres. 1998—99), Ark. Assn. Coop. Ext. Specialists (pres., bd. mem. 1998—2002), Omicron Delta Kappa (life), Epsilon Sigma Phi (life), Gamma Sigma Delta (life), Sigma Xi (life), Phi Eta Sigma (life; advisor 1981—86), Alpha Gamma Rho (life; chpt. advisor 1976—81, Cert. of Merit 1981). Methodist. Avocations: gardening, landscaping, cattle and goat shows. Home Phone: 501-336-8986; Office Phone: 501-671-2190. Office Fax: 501-671-2185. Business E-Mail: jpennington@uaex.edu.

PENNINGTON, OLIVER, councilman, lawyer; b. Houston; m. Beverly Buzzini, 1968; children: Oliver, Sarah. Grad., Rice U., 1960; JD, U. Tex., 1963. Ptnr. Fulbright & Jaworski, LLP, Houston, 1973—2002; councilman, Dist. G Houston City Coun., 2010—. Former chmn. Houston Civil Svc. Commn. Mem.: North Houston Assn. (bd. dirs.), Greater Houston Partnership, Houston Bar Assn. Office: City Hall Annex 900 Bagby, 1st Fl Houston TX 77002 Office Phone: 832-393-3007. Office Fax: 832-395-9571. Business E-Mail: distinctg@houstontx.gov. E-mail: districtg@cityofhouston.net.

PENSEC, JOHN, manufacturing executive; BA in Journalism, Wash. and Lee U., 1983. Account supr. Hill and Knowlton, 1989—93; mgr. mktg. comm. TW Design, 1993—94; v.p. corp. comm. and cmty. rels. John H. Harland Co., 1994—2007; corp. affairs cons., 2007—08; dir. corp. comm. & pub. affairs Mueller Water Products, Inc., 2008—. Mem.: Internat. Assn. Bus. Communicators. Office: Mueller Water Products Inc Ste 1200 1200 Abernathy Rd NE Atlanta GA 30328 Office Phone: 770-206-4200. Office Fax: 770-206-4235. Business E-Mail: jpensec@muellerwp.com.

PEPE, GERALD J., physiologist, educator; b. RI; m. Catherine Pepe; 2 children. BA, Providence Coll., 1965; MS, Northeastern U., 1967; PhD, U. Kans., 1970. Sr. staff fellow Divsn. Child Health NIH, Bethesda, Md., 1972—78; assoc. prof. physiology Eastern Va. Med. Sch., Norfolk, Va., 1978—84, interim chmn. dept. physiology, 1982—84, prof. and chmn. dept. physiology, 1985—2004, assoc. dean rsch., 1995—97, prof., chmn. physiol. sciences, 1997—2005, 2011—, interim dean and provost, 2004—05, dean and provost, 2005—12. Office: East Virginia Medical School Physiological Sciences Dept PO Box 2020 Norfolk VA 23501-1980 Office Phone: 757-446-5616. E-mail: pepegj@evms.edu.*

PEPPAS, NICHOLAS ATHANASSIOU, chemical and biomedical engineering educator, consultant; b. Athens, Greece, Aug. 25, 1948; s. Athanassios Nikolaou Peppas and Alice Petrou Rousopoulou; m. Lisa Brannon, Aug. 10, 1988; children: Katherine, Alexander. Diploma in Engring., Nat. Tech. U., Athens, 1971; ScD, MIT, 1973; PhD honoris causa, U. Parma, Italy, 1999, U. Ghent, Belgium, 1999, Nat. and Capodistrian U. of Athens, 2000, U. Ljubljana, Slovenia. Asst. prof. chem. engring. Purdue U., West Lafayette, Ind., 1976-78, assoc. prof., 1978-81, prof., 1981—2002, Showalter Disting. prof. of chem. and biomed. engring., 1993—2002; prof. chem. engring. U. Tex., Austin, 2003—, prof. biomed. engring., 2003, prof. pharmaceutics, 2003—, Fletcher S. Pratt Chair in Engring., Prof. chemical and biomedical engineering and pharmacy, 2003—, chair biomed. engring., 2009—. Vis. prof. U. Geneva, 1982—83, Calif. Inst. Tech., Pasadena, 1983, U. Paris, 1986, Hoshi U., Tokyo, 1994, Hebrew U., Jerusalem, 1994, U. Naples, 1995, Free U., Berlin, 2001, Couplentense U. Madrid, 2001, Santiago de Compostela, U. Hacettepe, Ankara, Nanyang U., Singapore, 2007; adj. prof. U. Parma, Italy, 1987; cons. in field; mem. adv. bd. several cos. Author: Biomaterials, 1982, Hydrogels in Medicine and Pharmacy, 1987, One Hundred Years of Chemical Engineering, 1989, Pulsatile Drug Delivery, 1993, Biopolymers, 1993, Superabsorbent Polymers, 1994, Biomaterials for Drug and Cell Delivery, 1994, Polymer/Inorganic Interfaces, 1995, Physicochemical and Cellular Foundations of Biomaterials, 2004, Nanotechnology in Therapeutics, 2007; contbr. over 1100 articles and over 450 abstracts to jours.; editor: Biomaterials, 1982-2002; assoc. editor: AIChE Jour., 2008-, Biomedical Microdevices, 2007-, Pharmaceutical research, 2004-, and Biomedical Engring. Series of Books of Cambridge U. Press Active Austin Symphony Orch., Transfiguration Orthodox Ch. Austin. Recipient APV medal, Herbert McCoy award Purdue U., 2000, Hamilton Book award, 2004; Career Rsch. Excellence award U. Tex., 2007, Maurice Marie Janot award, Pharmaceutical Sciences, 2009, 2010, Southeastern Universities Rsch. Assn. Disting. Scientist award, 2010, William Hall award, SFB, 2010 Fellow: ASEE, AIChE (chmn. materials divsn. 1988—90, dir. bioengring. divsn. 1994—97, bd. dirs. 1999—2002, Inst. lectr. 2007, elected engr. modern era 2008, Materials Engring. Sci. award 1984, Bioengring. award 1994, Best Paper award 1994, William Walker award 2006, Jay Bailey award 2006, Founders award 2008, Top 100 Engrs. Modern Era 2008, Founders award 2008), Biomed. Engring. Soc. (Best Rsch. award 2002, Disting. Rsch. award 2010), American Soc. Engring. Edn. (AT&T award 1982, Curtis McGraw award 1988, G. Westinghouse award 1992, GE Sr. Rsch. award 2002, Dow Chem. Engring. award 2006, Benjamin Garver Lamme award for Teaching 2013), American Phys. Soc., Italian Soc. Medicine and Scis., Controlled Release Soc. (pres. 1987—88, Founders award 1991, Eurand award 2002), Soc. Biomaterials (pres. 2002—03, 2003—04, Clemson award 1992, Founders award 2005, W. Hall award 2010), American Inst. Med. Biol. Engineers (chair of College of Fellows, Pierre Galletti award 2008), American Assn. Pharm. Scientists (Rsch. Achievements Pharm. Tech. award 1999, Dale Wurster award 2002); mem.: Internat. Union of Societies of Biomaterial Science and Engring. (pres. 2008), Acad. of Medicine, Engring. and Sciences of Texas, Acad. of Medicine, Royal Nat. Acad. of Pharmacy of Spain, Acad. Biomaterial (Gold medal 2010), Nat. Acad. Engring. (Simon Ramo Founders award 2012), Inst. Medicine, Tex. Acad. Scis., French Acad. Pharmacy, Polymer Pioneer, Soc. Biomaterials, American Chemical Soc. (Newsmaker of Yr. award 2002), Sigma Xi (South U. Rsch. award 2010, Maurice Janot award 2010). Achievements include patents in field. Avocations: linguistics, opera, rare maps, classical record collecting. Office: U Texas at Austin Department Chemical Engineering CPE 3.46 200 E Dean Keeton St Stop C0400 Austin TX 78712-1589 Office Phone: 512-471-6644. Business E-Mail: peppas@che.utexas.edu.*

PERDIKIS, GALEN, plastic surgeon; MB BCh, U. Witwatersrand, South Africa, 1988. Assoc. prof. dept. plastic surgery Mayo Clinic, Jacksonville, Fla., 2001—. Contbr. articles to profl. jours. Recipient Trubshaw prize, Coll. of Medicine, South Africa, 1993, Golden Apple, Student Body, Creighton U., 1999; Herbert Davis scholarship, Creighton U., 1999. Fellow: ACS; mem.: Southeastern Soc. of Plastic and Reconstructive Surgeons, Greater Jacksonville Soc. of Plastic Surgeons, Am. Soc. of Plastic Surgery, Alpha Omega Alpha. Office: Mayo Clinic 4500 San Pablo Rd Jacksonville FL 32224

PERDUE, DAVID A., JR., retail executive; b. Macon, Ga., Dec. 10, 1949; s. David A. Sr. and Gervaise (Wynn) P.; m. Bonnie Dunn Perdue, Aug. 26, 1972; children: David A. III, Blake R. BS, Ga. Inst. Tech., 1972, M in Ops. Rsch., 1975. Registered securities principal; cert. fin. planner; cert. mgmt. cons. Staff cons. Kurt Salmon Associates, 1972-75, ptnr., 1976—83; v.p. Profl. Planning Assocs., 1983-86, Paul R. Ray and Co., 1986-87; pres. Westar Holding Co., 1987—92; sr. v.p., ops. Sara Lee Corp., Hong Kong, China, 1992—94; sr. v.p. Haggar Inc., 1994—98; sr. v.p., Global Supply Chain Reebok Intern. Ltd., 1998—99, exec. v.p., Global Oper. Units, Reebok Brand, 1999—2001, exec. v.p., Global Supply Chain, 2001—02, pres., CEO, Reebok Brand, 2001—02; chmn., CEO Pillowtex Corp., 2002—03, Dollar General Corp., 2003—07; CEO Aquila Group, LLC, Sea Island, Fla., 2007—. Mem. investor liaison com. Mortgage Banking Assn., Atlanta, 1989—; bd. dirs. Carl R. Young Sr. Trust, Johnson City, Tenn., Alliant Energy Corp., 2001-, Ga. Tech. Adv. Bd., Jo-Ann Stores, Inc., 2008-, Liquidity Services, Inc., 2009-. Mem. Ga. Coun. on Youth, Atlanta, 1972, Atlanta Care Adv. Bd., 1983-85, Atlanta Athletic Club House Com., 1988—. Mem. Mortgage Banking Assn., Inst. Cert. Fin. Planners, Inst. Mgmt. Cons., Atlanta Athletic Club. Republican. Baptist. Avocations: tennis, golf, sailing, reading. Office: Jo-Ann Stores Inc Bd Directors 5555 Darrow Rd Hudson OH 44236 Office Phone: 330-656-2600. Office Fax: 330-463-6675. Business E-Mail: david.perdue@joann.com.

PERDUE, WENDY COLLINS, dean, law educator; BA, Wellesley Coll., Mass., 1975; JD, Duke Law Sch., NC, 1978. Law clk. to the Hon. Anthony M. Kennedy US Ct. Appeals Ninth Cir., 1978—79; assoc. Hogan & Hartson, Washington, 1979—82; faculty mem., prof. law Georgetown U. Law Ctr., Washington, 1982—2011, assoc. dean rsch., 1998—99, assoc. dean for JD program, 1999—2004, 2010—11, assoc. dean grad. programs, 2005—10; dean, prof. law U. Richmond Sch. Law, Va., 2011—. Vice chair Montgomery County Planning Bd.; commr. Md. Nat. Capitol Planning Commn. Co-author (with R. Freer): Civil Procedure: Cases, Materials, and Questions, 1996; co-author: (with S. Symeonides & A. von Mehren) Conflicts of Law: American, Comparative, International, 1998; mem. editl. bd.: Jour. on Legal Edn., 2001—04; contbr., articles to profl. jours. Mem. bd. visitors Duke Law Sch.; mem. law sch. publications adv. bd. Lexis/Nexis, 2005—07. Mem.: ABA (mem. com. on law sch. adminstrn. 2002—04), Assn. American Law Schools (mem. exec. com., sect. on civil prcedure 1999—2001, chmn. sect. on civil prcedure 2000, chmn. membership rev. com. 2002—04, mem. nominations com. 2005, chmn. sect. on conflict of laws 2008), Order of Coif (mem. exec. com. 2006—11, v.p. 2009—11). Office: University of Richmond 202-B School of Law 28 Westhampton Way Richmond VA 23173 Office Phone: 804-289-8740. Office Fax: 804-289-8992. Business E-Mail: wperdue@richmond.edu.*

PEREZ, BEATRIZ R., marketing executive; b. 1969; BS in Mktg., U. Md., 1991. Event svc. coord. US Hispanic Chamber of Commerce, Washington, 1991—94; account exec. DMB&B/Sosa, Bromley, Aguilar, Noble & Associates, San Antonio, 1994—96; various positions including assoc. brand mgr. Coca-Cola Co., Atlanta, 1996—99, dir. motor sports mktg. & NASCAR, 1999—2002, v.p. sports & entertainment mktg., 2005—06, chief mktg. officer, 2010—11, chief sustainability officer, 2011, v.p., chief sustainability officer, 2011—; sr. v.p. integrated mktg. Coca-Cola North America, 2007—10, v.p. sports & entertainment, 2006—07. Bd. dirs. HSBC North America Holdings Inc., 2007—. Bd. dirs. Grammy Found., Children's Healthcare Atlanta Found., Victory Junction Gang Camps, Abu Dhabi Investment House. Named Most Promising Mgr. of Yr., Nat. Hispanic Employees Assn., 1997; named one of The Top 25 Women in Bus., Sports Bus. Jour., 2000, 2005, The 40 Under 40, 2001—03; named to The Sports Bus. Jour. Hall of Fame, 2003, The Advt. Hall of Fame, American Advt. Fedn., 2009. Office: The Coca Cola Co PO Box 1734 Atlanta GA 30301 Business E-Mail: bperez@na.ko.com.

PEREZ, CARMEN M., telecommunications industry executive; BBA, Fla. Internat. U. CPA. Acct. Deloitte & Touche LLP, 1982—89; dir., corp. acctg., asst. contr. FPL Group, Inc.; dir., revenue recovery Fla. Power & Light Co. (subs. FPL Group, Inc.); joined FPL FiberNet, LLC (subs. of FPL Group, Inc.), 2004, v.p., sales, contr. and dir., acctg., pres., 2007—. Office: FPL FiberNet LLC 9250 W Flagler St Miami FL 33174 Office Phone: 305-552-3539. Office Fax: 305-229-5959.

PEREZ, DENNISE, legislative staff member; Press sec. Pedro Pierluisi for Congress, 2008; press sec. to Rep. Pedro Pierluisi US House of Representatives, Washington, 2009—. Office: Office of RC Pedro Pierlusi 1213 Longworth House Office Bldg Washington DC 20515-5401 also: 250 Calle Fortaleza San Juan PR 00901 Office Phone: 202-225-2615, 787-723-6333. Office Fax: 202-225-2154, 787-729-7738. E-mail: dennise.perez@mail.house.gov.

PEREZ, JORGE M., real estate developer; b. Argentina; arrived in U.S., 1968; BS in Economics summa cum laude, Long Island U.; MS in Urban Planning, with highest honors, U. Mich. Mng. gen. ptnr. Related Group of Fla., Miami, 1979, chmn., CEO & founder. Bd. dirs. Regions Fin. Corp. Author: Powerhouse Principles: The Billionaire Blueprint for Real Estate Success, 2008. Past. mem. Dem. Nat. Com.; trustee Univ. Miami; vice chmn. Miami Dade Cultural Affairs Council; dir. Miami Film Festival, Miami Downtown Develop. Authority. Recipient Miami Bus. Leader of Yr. award, 2000, Ernst & Young Entrepreneur of Yr. award, 2002, Multifamily Exec. Builder of the Yr., 2003, Citizen of Yr. award, Miami C. Of C., 2004; named one of The 25 Most Influential Hispanics, TIME mag., 2005, Forbes' Richest Americans, 2006. Democrat. Avocations: art collecting, especially Latin Am. contemporary art, tennis. Office: Related Group of Florida 315 S Biscayne Blvd Ste 300 Miami FL 33131-2380 Office Phone: 305-460-9900. Office Fax: 305-460-9911.

PEREZ, JOSEPHINE, psychiatrist, educator; b. Tijuana, Mex., Feb. 10, 1941; came to the U.S., 1960, U.S. citizenship, 1968. BS in Biology, U. Santiago de Compostela, Spain, 1971, MD, 1975. Nuc. medicine technician, EEG technician, supr. Electrographic Labs., Encino, Calif., 1963—69; clerkships in internal medicine, gen. surgery, otorhinolaryngology, dermatology and venereology Gen. Hosp. of Galicia, Spain, 1972-75; resident in gen. psychiatry U. Miami, Jackson Meml. Hosp. and VA Hosp., Miami, Fla., 1976-78; practice medicine specializing in psychiatry, marital and family therapy, individual psychotherapy Miami, 1979—. Emergency room physician Miami Dade Hosp., 1975; attending psychiatrist Jackson Meml. Hosp., 1979—, asst. dir. adolescent psychiat. unit, 1979-83; mem. clin. faculty U. Miami Sch. Medicine, 1979—, clin. instr. psychiatry, 1979—. Mem. AMA (Physicians' Recognition award 1980, 83, 86, 89, 98, 2000, 01, 05), Am. Assn. for Marital and Family Therapy (cert. clin. mem., treas. 1982-84, pres.-elect 1985-87, pres. 1987-89), Am. Psychiat. Assn., Am. Med. Women's Assn., Assn. Women Psychiatrists, Fla. Psychiat. Soc., South Dade Women Physicians Assn. Office: 420 S Dixie Hwy Ste 4A Coral Gables FL 33146-2228 Office Phone: 305-666-7766, 305-857-9250.

PÉREZ, LOUIS A., JR., history professor; MA, U. Ariz., 1966; PhD, U. N.Mex., 1970. J. Carlyle Sitterson prof. history U. NC at Chapel Hill, dir. Inst. for the Study of the Americas. Author: Cuba: Between Reform and Revolution, 1995, The War of 1989: The United States and Cuba in History and Historiography, 1998, On Becoming Cuban: Identity, Nationality and Culture, 2000 (Bolton-Johnson prize, Conf. Latin Am. History, 2000), Winds of Change: Hurricanes and the Transformation of 19th-Century Cuba, 2001 (George Perkins Marsh prize, Am. Soc. Environ. History, 2001), Cuba and the United States: Ties of Singular Intimacy, 2003, To Die in Cuba: Suicide and Society, 2005 (Elsa Goveia prize, 2007), Cuba in the American Imagination, 2008. Fellow John Simon Guggenheim Meml. Found., 2000. Fellow: Am. Acad. Arts and Sciences. Office: U NC Chapel Hill Dept History CB 3195 Hamilton Hall Chapel Hill NC 27599-3195 Office Phone: 919-962-6880. E-mail: perez@email.unc.edu.

PEREZ, TONY (ATANASIO PEREZ), professional sports team executive, retired professional baseball player; b. Ciego De Avila, Cuba, May 14, 1942; arrived in U.S., 1960; m. Pituke Perez; children: Orlando, Eduardo. Third baseman, first baseman Cin. Reds, 1964—76, first baseman, 1984—86, Montreal Expos, Canada, 1977—79, Boston Red Sox, 1980—82, Phila. Phillies, 1983; batting coach Cin. Reds, first base coach, mgr., 1993; spl. asst. Miami Marlins (formerly Fla. Marlins), Miami, 1993—, mgr., 2001. Recipient Lou Gehrig Meml. award, 1980, Sports award, Hispanic Heritage Found., 2007; named All-Star MVP, 1967; named to Nat. League All-Star Team, 1967—70, 1974—76, Baseball Hall of Fame, 2000. Office: Miami Marlins 501 Marlins Way Miami FL 33125

PÉREZ DAMERA, MYRA M., lawyer; b. Havana, Cuba, Sept. 15, 1952; arrived in US, 1959; d. Genovevo Pérez and Mirtha Acosta; AA, Miami Dade Jr. Coll., Fla., 1973; BS, Fla. Internat. U., Miami, 1987; JD, Cath. U. PR, Ponce, 1993. Legal asst. Lehman Brothers Inc., 1993—96; ptnr. Damera & Dreize, PA, Miami, 1996—. Spkr. Dade County Bar Assn., 2004; pres., CEO, founder Fla. Traffic Atty. Com., Miami, 2004—06; trainer, guest spkr. Traffic Magistrate Orientation, Miami, 2005—06. Mem.: Fla. Bar Assn. Avocations: tennis, boating, skiing. Office: Damera & Dreize PA 901 Ponce de Leon Blvd #506 Coral Gables FL 33134 Office Phone: 305-446-6760. Business E-Mail: briefdc@aol.com.

PEREZ-GIMENEZ, JUAN MANUEL, federal judge; b. San Juan, Mar. 28, 1941; s. Francisco and Elisa (Gimenez) P.; m. Carmen R. Ramirez, July 16, 1964; children: Carmen E., Juan C., Jorge E., Jose A., Magdalena. BBA, U. P.R., 1963, JD, 1968; MBA, George Washington U., 1965. Bar: P.R. 1968. Ptnr. Goldman, Antonetti & Davila, San Juan, 1968-71; asst. U.S. atty. San Juan, 1971-75; magistrate US Dist. Ct. PR, San Juan, 1975-79, judge, 1979—84, 1991—2006, chief judge, 1984—91, sr. judge, 2006—. Mem. ABA, Fed. Bar Assn., Colegio de Abogados. Roman Catholic. Office: US Dist Ct Toledo US Courthouse Rm 129 300 Recinto Sur St San Juan PR 00901

PEREZ-POLO, JOSE REGINO, editor-in-chief, educator; s. Jose Regino Perez-Menedez and Fabiola Lopez-Calderon; m. Karin Werrbach, June 25, 1976; children: Gabriela Cristina Foster-Brown, Adriana Regina Perez. BS, Cornell, NYC, 1965, MS, 1966; PhD, Stanford, Calif., 1970. Asst. prof. Univ. Tex., Austin, 1973—77; prof. Univ. Tex. Med. Br., Galveston, 1977—, chair, 1977—. Editor chief Int. J. Dev. Neurosci., Oxford, 1981—. Office: UTMB 301 Univ Blvd Galveston TX 77555 Business E-Mail: regino.perez-polo@utmb.edu.

PERICH, THOMAS J., lawyer; b. Galveston, Tex., 1945; BS, Georgetown U., 1967; MA with honors, in Economics, U. Tex., 1971, JD with honors, 1975. Bar: Tex. 1976, admitted to practice: US Ct. Appeals (5th Cir.), bar: US Ct. Appeals (11th Cir.). Ptnr. Dept. Bus. Transactions Andrews & Kurth LLP, Houston, mem. policy com. Mem. Tex. Law Rev., 1974—75. Mem.: Tex. Assn. Bank Counsel (dep. mng. ptnr. houston office), Houston Comml. Lawyer Forum, Houston Bar Assn., State Bar Tex., ABA, Order of Coif. Office: Andrews & Kurth LLP 600 Travis St Ste 4200 Houston TX 77002-3090 Home Phone: 713-818-3650; Office Phone: 713-220-4268. Office Fax: 713-238-7175. Personal E-mail: tperich@akllp.com. Business E-Mail: tperich@andrewskurth.com.

PERKIN, RONALD MURRAY, pediatrician, educator; b. Denver, July 31, 1948; s. Robert Murray and Marion Kathryn (Thompson) P.; m. Susan Renee Sheer; children: Matthew Murray, Jeffrey Jay, Nickolas James, Thomas Mitchell, Benjamin Sheer, Savannah Paige. BS in Engring., U. Colo., 1970; postgrad., Johns Hopkins U., 1970-71; MD, U. South Fla., 1976; MA, Loma Linda Univ., 1997. Diplomate Am. Bd. Pediatrics. Resident in pediatrics Children's Med. Ctr., Dallas, 1976-79, fellow in pediatric intensive care, 1979-81, asst. dir. pediatric intensive care, 1981; clins. asst. prof. pediatrics U. Tex. Health Sci. Ctr. Southwestern Med. Sch., Dallas, 1981; asst. adj. prof. pediatrics U. Calif. Sch. Medicine, San Diego, 1982-84, co-dir. pediatric intensive care, 1982-84; dir. pediatric ICU attending physician Childrens Hosp. Orange (Calif.) County Hosp., 1984-88; attending physician newborn ICU St. Joseph's Hosp., Orange, 1984-88; assoc. prof. pediatrics Loma Linda Univ., 1988-90, prof. pediatrics, 1990-2000; prof., chmn. dept. pediats. Brody Sch. Medicine, East Carolina U., Greenville, NC, 2000—. Cons. Naval Hosp., San Diego, 1983-84; asst. adj. prof. pediatrics U. Calif., Irvine, 1984-88; dir. pediat. intensive care fellowship program U. Calif. Irvine and Children's Hosp. Orange County, 1984-88; critical care adv. com., critical care coun., Extra Corporeal Membrane Oxygenation found. So. Calif., emergency dept. com., ethics com., ethics cons. svc. critical care com., resident evaluation sub-com., respiratory care com.; dir. pediat. critical care Loma Linda U. Children's Hosp., 1988-2000, assoc. chair pediat. Sch. Medicine, 1993-2000; lectr. in field. Editor: (with others) Brain Insults in Infants and Children: Pathophysiology and Management; Emergency Management of the Critically Ill Child; Pediatric Hosp. Medicine: A Textbook of Inpatient Care, 2003, 2d edit., 2008, Primer on Pediatric Palliative Care, 2005, Pediatric Emergency Medicine Manual, 2007, The PICU Book, 2012; reviewer Capistrano Press, Ltd., 1982-84, Jour. Pediatrics, 1982—; contbr. articles to profl. jours. With USN, 1971—73. Recipient student awards U. South Fla. Coll. Medicine, faculty awards U. Calif., Irvine, Lange Ann. award Lange Book Co., 1974; Mosby scholar Mosby Book Co., 1975-76. Fellow Am. Acad. Pediatrics, Am. Coll. Critical Care Medicine, Am. Acad. Sleep Medicine; mem. Soc. Critical Care Medicine, Calif. Children Svcs. (adv. com. rev. pediatric ICU's 1986-2000). Office: 3E-142 Brody Med Scis Bldg Greenville NC 27858-4354 Office Phone: 252-744-2540. Office Fax: 252-744-1376. Business E-Mail: perkinr@ecu.edu.

PERKINS, BRADLEY A., surgical hospital company executive; BA in Microbiology, U. Mo., Columbia, MD; MBA, Emory U. Chief med. resident Houston Vet. Adminstrn. Med. Ctr.; internal medicine residency Baylor Coll. of Medicine; capt. US Pub. Health Svc., 1997; prin., chief, meningitis, spl. pathogens br. & assoc. dir., bioterrorism Centers for Disease Control and Prevention, chief, office, strategy & innovation, epidemic intelligence svc. officer, 1989, worked, rsch. officer group, 2003, dep. dir., office, strategy & innovation, 2004—05, chief strategy officer & chief innovation officer, 2005—09; exec. v.p., strategy, innovation & chief transformation officer Vanguard Health Sys., Inc., 2009—. Office: Vanguard Health Systems Inc Ste 100 20 Burton Hills Blvd Nashville TN 37215 Office Phone: 615-665-6000. Office Fax: 615-665-6099. Business E-Mail: bperkins@vanguardhealth.com.

PERKINS, CHRIS (CARL CHRISTOPHER PERKINS), pastor, former United States Representative from Kentucky; b. Washington, Aug. 6, 1954; s. Carl Dewey and Verna (Johnson) P.; m. Janet Neville, Apr. 1987 (div.); children: Carl Andrew, Megan; m. Bunny Perkins, 2001 AB in Economics, Davidson Coll., 1976; JD, U. Louisville Louis D. Brandeis Sch. Law, 1978; MDiv, Louisville Presbyterian Theological Seminary, 2003, ThM, 2008. Asst. commonwealth atty. 30th Jud. Dist., Frankfort, Ky., 1979; ptnr. Weinberg, Perkins & Campbell, Hindman, Ky., 1979-84; mem. Ky. House of Reps., Frankfort, 1981—84, US Congress from 7th Ky. Dist., Washington, 1984—93; supply pastor Ezel United Presbyterian Church, Ky., 2002—05; pastor 1st Presbyterian of Carmi, Ill., 2005—09, Enslow Park Presbyterian Church, Huntington, W.Va., 2009—. Democrat. Presbyterian. Office: Enslow Park Presbyterian Church 1338 Enslow Blvd Huntington WV 25701 Office Phone: 304-523-9920.*

PERKINS, EDWARD JOSEPH, political science professor, retired ambassador; b. Sterlington, La., June 8, 1928; m. Lucy Liu; children: Katherine, Sarah. Student, U. Calif., Lewis and Clark Coll.; BA, U. Md., 1967; MPA, U. So. Calif., 1972, DPA, 1978; studied French, Fgn. Service Inst., 1983; LLD (hon.), U. Md., 1990, St. John's U., 1990, Lewis and Clark Coll., 1988; LHD (hon.), Winston-Salem State U., 1990, Bowie State Coll., 1993; HHD (hon.), St. Augustine Coll., 1991, Beloit Coll., 1990, U. So. Calif., 1995. Chief pers. Army and Air Force Exch. Svc., Taipei, Taiwan, 1958-62, dep. chief Okinawa, Japan, 1962-64; chief pers. & adminstrn. Army and Air Force Exchange Service, Okinawa, Japan, 1964-66; asst. gen. services officer Far East bur. US Agy. Internat. Devel. (USAID), 1967-69, mgmt. analyst, 1969-70; asst. dir. for mgmt. US Ops. Mission to Thailand, 1970-72; staff asst. Office of Dir. Gen. Fgn. Svc., 1972, personnel officer, 1972-74; adminstrv. officer Bur. Near Eastern & South Asian Affairs US Dept. State, 1974-75, mgmt. analysis officer Office Mgmt. Ops., 1975-78, counselor for polit. affairs Accra, Ghana, 1978-81, dep. chief of mission Monrovia, Liberia, 1981-83, dir. Office of West African Affairs, Bur. African Affair, 1983-85, US amb. to Liberia, 1985-86, US amb. to South Africa, 1986-89, dir. gen., dir. pers. Fgn. Svc. Washington, 1989-92, US amb. to UN NYC, 1992-93, US amb. to Australia Canberra, 1993-96. William J. Crowe prof. and exec. dir. Internat. Programs Ctr., U. Okla., Norman 1996-; mem. adv. bd. Inst. Internat. Pub. Policy, 1997-; mem. adv. coun. Univ. Office of Internat. Programs, Pa. State U., 1997; mem. White House Adv. Com. on Trade Policy and Negotiations, 2003-. Contbr. articles to profl. publs.; editor (with David Boren) Preparing American's Foreign Policy for the 21st Century, 1999, with (Joseph Ginat) Palestinian Refugees: Traditional Positions and New Solutions, 2001, (with David Boren) Democracy, Morality, and the Search for Peace in America's Foreign Policy, 2002, (with Joseph Ginat and Edwin G. Corr) Middle East Peace Process: Vision Versus Reality, 2002, (with Connie Cronley) Mr. Ambassador: Warrior For Peace, 2008 Trustee Lewis and Clark Coll., 1994—, Woodrow Wilson Nat. Fellowship Found., 1999—; bd. govs. Joint Ctr. for Polit. and Econ. Studies, 1996-2003; mem. steering com. Ctr. for Australian and New Zealand Studies, Georgetown U., 1996—; bd. Cranlana Programme; bd. visitors Nat. Def. U., 2002-. Recipient Superior Honor award US Dept State, 1983, Presdl. Meritorious Svc. award, 1987, Presdl. Disting. Svc. award, 1989, Meritorious Honor award US Agy. for Iinternat. Devel. (USAID), 1967, Award for Outstanding Svc. as Fgn. Svc. Officer Una Chapman Cox Found., 1989, Living Legend award The Links, Inc., 1989, Disting. Alumni award U. So. Calif., 1991, Achievement award So. U., 1991, Statesman of Yr. award George Washington U., 1992, Dir. General's Cup, US Dept. State, 2001; honoree U. Okla. chpt. Beta Gamma Sigma, 1998. Fellow Nat. Acad. Pub. Adminstrn.; mem. VFW, ASPA, Navy League, Am. Polit. Sci. Assn., Fgn. Policy Assn. (ambassadorial fellow), Internat. Studies Assn., Coun. on Fgn. Rels., Am. Acad. Diplomacy, Am. Consortium Internat. Pub. Adminstrn., Am. Fgn. Svc. Assn., Am. Legion, Ctr. Study of Presidency, Chester A. Arthur Soc., Pub. Svc. Comm., World Affairs Couns. Okla. and Washington, Am. Acad. Diplomacy, Pacific Coun. on Internat. Policy, Assn. for Diplomatic Studies and Tng. (bd. dirs. 1998—), Kappa Alpha Psi (Laurel Wreath award,1993, C. Rodger Wilson Leadership Conf. award, 1990, Disting. Svc. award 1989, Outstanding Achievement award for Fgn. Svc. 1986), Phi Kappa Phi. Office: U Okla Internat Programs Ctr 339 W Boyd St Rm 400 Norman OK 73019-5144 E-mail: eperkins@ou.edu.

PERKINS, JOE BOB, energy executive; Cons. McKinsey & Co.; dir. bus. develop. Tejas Gas, 1994—95; v.p. bus. develop. Coral Energy LLC, 1995—96; v.p. corp. planning Houston Industries, 1996—98; pres. & COO wholesale & power generation Reliant Resources, 1998—2002; ptnr. RTM Media, 2002—03; pres. Targa Resources Corp., Houston, 2004—11, dir., CEO, 2012—. Office: Targa Resources Inc Ste 4300 1000 Louisiana Houston TX 77002

PERKINS, RAY, college football coach, former professional football coach; b. Mt. Olive, Miss., Nov. 6, 1941; m. Carolyn Martin; children: Tony, Mike. BS, U. Ala., 1967. Wide receiver Balt. Colts, 1967-71; asst. coach Miss. State U. Bulldogs, Starkville, 1973, New Eng. Patriots, 1974-77, San Diego Chargers, 1978; head coach N.Y. Giants, 1979-82; head football coach U. Ala. Crimson Tide, Tuscaloosa, 1983-86; head coach, v.p. football ops. Tampa Bay Buccaneers, 1987-90; head coach Ark. State U. Red Wolves, Jonesboro, 1992; offensive coord. New Eng. Patriots, 1993—96, Oakland Raiders, 1996; tight ends coach Cleve. Browns, 1999, running backs coach, 2000; head coach Jones County Jr. Coll. Bobcats, Ellisville, Miss., 2011—. Named First Team All-American, AP, 1966, Southeastern Conf. (SEC) Player of Yr., 1966; named to The Ala. Sports Hall of Fame, 1990, The Miss. Sports Hall of Fame, 1998, The Sr. Bowl Hall of Fame, 2005. Achievements include being a member of the Super Bowl Winning Baltimore Colts, 1970. Office: Jones County Junior College 900 South Court St Ellisville MS 39437 Office Phone: 601-477-4000.

PERKINS, ROBBIE, real estate company executive, former mayor, Greensboro, North Carolina; AB, Duke U., Durham, NC, 1977, MBA, 1979. CCIM designation Nat. Assn. Realtors, 1986. Comml. real estate broker; dir., pres., ptnr. NAI Piedmont Triad, Greensboro, NC; councilman Greensboro City Coun., NC, 1993—2005, 2007—; mayor City of Greensboro, 2011—13. Mem. Greensboro Bd. Realtors, 1979—; bd. dirs. NC League Municipalities, 1999—2001, FNB Southeast, 2005—07, New Bridge Bank, 2007—. Mem. Crescent Rotary Club, 1985—2007; moderator Triad CCIM/NAIOP Market Forecasts, 2002, 2004—06; mem. alumni admissions adv. com. Duke U., 1979—; pres. NC CCIM Chpt., 1994; chmn. bd. dirs. One Step Further, 1999—; co-chmn. steering com. Heart of Triad, 2005—07; mem. regionalism com. Greensboro C. of C., 2006—08; bd. trustees Bennett Coll., 2006—, Piedmont Area Regional Transp., 2007—; chmn. Greensboro Met. Planning Orgn. Transp., 2007—. Office: NAI Piedmont Triad 500D State St Greensboro NC 27405-5659*

PERKINS, THOMAS P., JR., lawyer; b. 1953; BA, Harvard U.; JD, Loyola Univ., New Orleans. Bar: La., Tex. 1979. Former staff atty. Dallas regional office FTC; former spl. asst. atty. gen., chief of antitrust and consumer protection divisions Tex. Atty. Gen.'s Office; pvt. practice atty.; atty. Dallas City Atty. Office, 1999—, former 1st asst. city atty., litig. divsn., city atty., 2005—. Adj. professor law So. Methodist Univ. Dedman Sch. Law, LSU Law Sch. Bd. mem. Tex. Appleseed. Mem.: Tex. State Bar Assn. (dir. Antitrust & Bus. Litig. Sect., formerly). Office: Dallas City Atty Office 1500 Marilla St Suite 7-BN Dallas TX 75201-6622

PERKINS, WILLIE J., state legislator; b. Oct. 21, 1952; m. Sheriel Faye Walker; children: Ashaki Niambi Osborne, Willie James, Takiyah Herminone, Jamilah Akilah, Jamal Walker. Former city judge, city prosecuting atty. & city pub. defender; bd. atty. Leflore County Bd. Supr.; mem. Dist. 32 Miss. House of Reps., 1993—. Mem.: NAACP, Magnolia & Leflore County Bar Assn. Democrat. Baptist. Address: 806 South Blvd Greenwood MS 38930 Mailing: PO Box 8404 Greenwood MS 38935-8404 Office Phone: 662-455-1211, 601-359-3014. Fax: 662-453-9159. Business E-Mail: wperkins@house.ms.gov.

PERKOWSKI, JAN LOUIS, language, literature and folklore educator; b. Perth Amboy, NJ, Dec. 29, 1936; m. Liliana Asenova Daskalova, May 24, 1989. AB magna cum laude, Harvard U., 1959, AM, 1960, PhD, 1965. Asst. prof. U. Calif., Santa Barbara, 1964-65; assoc. prof. U. Tex., Austin, 1965-74; prof. U. Va., Charlottesville, 1974—2009, prof. emeritus, 2009—. Author: A Kashubian Idiolect in U.S., 1969, Vampires, Dwarves & Witches Among the Ontario Kashubs, 1972, Vampires of the Slavs, 1976, Gusle & Ganga Among the Hercegovinians of Toronto, 1978, The Darkling-A Treatise on Slavic Vampirism, 1989, Vampire Lore, 2006; contbr. over 65 articles to profl. jours. Grantee, fellow Ford Found., Harvard U., Kościuszko Found., U. Tex., Am. Philos. Soc., Nat. Mus. Man, U. Va., NEH, Kennan Inst., I.R.E.X., Fulbright, others. Mem. The South East European Studies Assn., Am. Assn. S.E. European Studies, Bulgarian Studies Assn.

PERLIN, GARY LAURENCE, diversified financial services company executive; b. Chgo., May 8, 1951; s. Maurice and Berna (Bardige) P.; m. Amy R., July 4, 1976; children: Jonah, Jacob. BS in Fgn. Svc., Georgetown U., 1972; MS, London Sch. Econs., 1974; MPA, Princeton U., NJ, 1975. Staff aide to US Senator Adlai Stevenson III, Washington, 1972-73; economist The World Bank, Washington, 1975-78, dir. fin. sector devel. dept., 1993—96, v.p., treas., 1996—99, sr. v.p., CFO, 1999—2003; trader J. Aron & Co., NYC, 1978-80; cons., v.p. Hadley Lockwood, NYC, 1980-82; v.p. risk mgmt. Fed. Nat. Mortgage Assn. (Fannie Mae), Washington, 1982-85, sr. v.p. fin., treas., 1985—93; exec. v.p., CFO, prin. acctg. officer Capital One Financial Corp., McLean, Va., 2003—. Mem. Commodity Futures Trading Commn., Fin. Products Adv. Com., Washington, 1986-91; dir. Future Industry Assn., 1991—; treas. The European Inst., 1991—. Office: Capital One Fin Corp 1680 Capital One Dr Mc Lean VA 22102

PERLIN, JONATHAN BRIAN, hospital administrator; b. 1961; s. Seymour Perlin; m. Donna Perlin; 2 children. MS in Health Adminstrn., Va. Commonwealth U., Ph.D in Pharmacology & Toxicology, MD. Med. dir., quality improvement, Med. Coll. Va. Hosps. Va. Commonwealth U., assoc. dir., internal medicine residency tng. prog., adj. prof., health adminstrn.; CEO Veterans Health Adminstrn. (VHA); chief quality officer & chief performance officer US Dept. Veterans Affairs, Washington, 1999—2002, dep. under sec. health, 2002—04, acting chief rsch. officer & chief devel. officer, 2003—04, acting under sec. for health, Veterans Health Adminstrn., 2004—05, under sec., health, 2005—06; sr. v.p. quality HCA Inc., 2006, pres., clin. svcs., chief med. officer, 2006—. Adj. prof., medicine & biomedical informatics Vanderbilt U. Contbr. articles to profl. jours. Bd. dirs. Nat. Quality Forum, Joint Commn., Meharry Med. Coll., Am. Health Info. Cmty.; fellow Am. Coll. of Physicians, Am. Coll. of Med. Informatics. Recipient Disting. Alumnus, Founders Medal, Assn. of Mil. Surgeons of the US; named one of 15 Most Influential Physician Execs. in US, Modern Healthcare, nine hon. mems., Spl. Forces Assn. & Green Berets. Fellow: ACP. Office: HCA Inc One Park Plz Nashville TN 37203 Office Phone: 615-344-9551. Business E-Mail: jonathan.perlin@hcahealthcare.com.

PERLMAN, MIKE, mortgage company executive; b. Haifa, Israel, Apr. 2, 1951; BEME, CCNY, 1973; MBA, NYU, 1976. Cert. mgmt. cons., cert. systems profl. Mech., nuc. engr. Ebasco Svcs., NYC, 1973-76; treasury analyst Consol. Edison, NYC, 1976-78; cons., ptnr. Deloitte & Touche, NYC, Washington; founding ptnr. fin. services group AT&T Solutions; mng. dir. Morgan Stanley, 1997—2007; exec. v.p. ops., and tech. Freddie Mac - Federal Home Loan Mortgage Corp., 2007—. Office: Freddie Mac 8200 Jones Br Dr Mc Lean VA 22102-3110 Office Phone: 703-903-2000.

PERLMUTTER, DAVID, neurologist, writer; b. Coral Gables, Fla., Dec. 31, 1954; married; 2 children. Attended, Fla. State U., 1972—73; AB in Biology, Lafayette Coll., 1976; MD, U. Miami Sch. of Medicine, 1981. Diplomate Nat. Bd. of Med. Examiners, 1982, lic. Fla., 1982, cert. American Bd. of Psychiatry and Neurology, founding diplomat American Bd. of Holistic Medicine. Instr. microneurosurgery, dept. neurosurgery U. Fla., 1976—77; researcher, microvascular reconstruction Centro Ramon Y Cajal, Madrid, 1978; resident, gen. surgery Mt. Sinai Hosp., Miami Beach, Fla., 1981—82; resident, neurosurgery U. Miami Sch. of Medicine, 1982—83, resident, neurology, 1983—86, assoc. prof.; private practice Naples, Fla.; pres., dir. Perlmutter Health Ctr., Naples, Fla.; med. dir. Perlmutter Hyperbaric Ctr., Naples, Fla.; founder Perlmutter Brain Found., Naples, Fla., 2006—, bd. dirs. Presenter in field at institutions such as Harvard U., U. Ariz., Scripps Inst., NYU, and Columbia U.; adj. faculty The Inst. for Functional Medicine; chief neuroscience officer XYMOGEN, Inc; pres. iNutritionals, Inc.; co-founder, pres. The Better Brain Found.; co-founder, pres., CEO National Living Will Registry. Frequent contributor to Huffington Post, The Daily Beast and Mind Body Green, guest appearances 20/20, Larry King Live, CNN, Fox News, Fox and Friends, The Today Show, Oprah, Dr. Oz, Montel Across America, and the CBS Early Show, medical advisor (TV series) Dr. Oz; contbr. articles to many peer-reviewed publications; author: LifeGuide, Volume I-Your Guide to a Longer and Healthier Life, 1993, BrainRecovery.com-Powerful Therapy for Challenging Brain Disorders, 2000, Grain Brain: The Suprising Truth About Wheat, Carbs, & Sugar-Your Brain's Silent Killers, 2013; co-author (with Carol Coleman): The Better Brain Book: The Best Tool for Improving Memory and Sharpness and Preventing Aging of the Brain, 2004, Raise a Smarter Child by Kindergarten: Raise IQ by up to 30 Points and Turn On Your Child's Smart Genes, 2006; co-author: (with Alberto Villoldo) Power Up Your Brain-The Neuroscience of Enlightenment, 2011; chief cons. Food Cures-Breakthrough Nutritional Prescriptions, Reader's Digest, 2007; editor: Food and Nutrients in Disease Management, Chapter 28-Parkinson's Disease, 2009; host (blog-www.DrPerlmutter.com), mem. editl. bd. Integrative Medicine-A Clinician's Journal, mem. editl. adv. bd. Healthy Aging Magazine, mem. editl. review panel The Journal of the American Nutraceutical Assn., bd. mem. IntegrativePractitioner.com, creator, host (TV series) LifeGuide. Recipient Physician's Recognition award with Commendation for Self-Directed Learning, 1999, Denham Harmon award, American Coll. for Advancement in Medicine, 2002, Linus Pauling Functional Medicine award, 2002, Clinician of the Yr. award, Nat. Nutritional Foods Assn., 2006; McKelvy Scholar. Fellow: American Coll. of Nutrition (Humanitarian of the Yr. award 2010); mem.: AAAS, AMA, The Oxygen Soc., Undersea and Hyperbaric Medicine Soc., American Acad. of Neurology (sr.), American Holistic Med. Assn., Physician's Com. for Responsible Medicine. Avocations: flying, running, scuba diving, fishing, guitar. Office: Commons Medical and Surgical Centre 800 Goodlette Rd N Suite 270 Naples FL 34102 Office Phone: 239-649-7400.*

PERMAN, STEVEN M., state legislator; b. Queens, NY, Mar. 26, 1957; s. William and Eileen Perman; m. Irene Budd; children: Benjamin, Arielle. Attended, Emory U., Atlanta; grad., NY Chiropractic Coll., 1979. Cert. chiropractic sports physician, clin. nutritionist, registered dietician/nutritionist NY. Chiropractic physician, Fla.; mem. Dist. 78 Fla. House of Representatives, 2011—. Democrat. Jewish. Office: The Shoppes at Boca Greens 19365 S State Rd 7 Ste Unit 43 Boca Raton FL 33498-4771 also: Fla House of Reps 1401 The Capitol 402 S Monroe St Tallahassee FL 32399-1300 Office Phone: 561-470-6596, 850-488-5588.

PEROT, ROSS (H. ROSS PEROT, HENRY ROSS PEROT), real estate company, investment company, data processing executive; b. Texarkana, Tex., June 27, 1930; s. Gabriel Ross and Lulu May Perot; m. Margot Birmingham, 1956; children: Ross Jr., Nancy, Suzanne, Carolyn, Katherine. Ed., US Naval Acad., 1949—53. Data processing salesman IBM Corp., 1957-62; founder Electronic Data Systems Corp., Dallas, 1962-84, sold to GM, 1984, chmn., CEO, also dir., to 1986; founder The Perot Group, Dallas, 1986—, Perot Systems Corp., Washington, 1988—, bd. mem. Dallas, 1988—94, Plano, 1997—, chmn. Dallas, 1988—92, Plano, 2000—04, chmn. emeritus, 2004—. Ind. candidate US Presdl. Election, 1992, Reform Party candidate, 1996. Author (books) United We Stand: How We Can Take Back Our Country, 1992, Not for Sale at Any Price: How We Can Save America for Our Children, 1993, Intensive Care: We Must Save Medicare and Medicaid Now, 1995, Preparing Our Country for the 21st Century, 1995, Ross Perot: My Life & the Principles for Success, 1996; co-author (with Pat Choate) Save Your Job, Save Our Country: Why NAFTA Must Be Stopped-Now!, 1993, (with Senator Paul Simon) The Dollar Crisis: A Blueprint to Help Rebuild the American Dream, 1996. Served with USN, 1953-57. Recipient Winston Churchill Award, 1986, Internat. Disting. Entrepreneur Award, U. Man., 1988, Raoul Wallenberg Award, Jefferson Award, Patrick Henry Award, Nat. Bus. Hall of Fame Award, Sarnoff Award, Eisenhower Award, Smithsonian Computerworld Award, Horatio Alger Award.; named one of Forbes 400: Richest Americans, 1999-, World's Richest People, Forbes mag., 1999—. Office: Perot Systems Corp 2300 W Plano Pkwy Plano TX 75075 also: Perot Family Trust PO Box 269014 Plano TX 75026-9014*

PEROT, ROSS, JR., (HENRY ROSS PEROT JR.), real estate developer, professional sports team executive; b. Arlington, Tex. m. Sarah Fullinwider, 1984. BBA, Vanderbilt U., 1981. With Petrus Oil Co., Okla., 1981-83; mng. ptnr. The Perot Group, 1983—; owner Hillwood Devel., Dallas, 1988—; majority owner Dallas Mavericks basketball, 1996—2000; pres., CEO Perot Systems, Dallas, 2000—04, chmn., 2004—. Exec. com. Prince of Wales Bus. Leaders' Forum, Winston Churchill Found. Pilot, USAFR, 1983-1991. Achievements include completing first flight around the world in a helicopter. Office: Perot Systems 2300 W Plano Pkwy Plano TX 75075

PERREAULT, WILLIAM DANIEL, JR., business administration educator; b. NYC, Apr. 7, 1948; s. William Daniel Sr. and Barbara Louise (Peckham) P.; m. Pamela Pittard, May 27, 1972; children: Suzanne Elizabeth, William Daniel III. BS, U. N.C., 1970, PhD, 1973. Asst. prof. U. Ga., Athens, 1973-76, U. N.C., Chapel Hill, 1976-79, assoc. prof., 1979-81, prof., 1981-83, Hanes prof., 1983-88. Vis. prof. Stanford (Calif.) U., 1986-87, assoc. dean, 1988-92. Kenan prof., 1988—; vis. prof. Cambridge (Eng.) U., 1997. Co-author: Essentials Marketing, 2013, The Marketing Game, 2001; editor: Jour. Mktg. Rsch., 1982-85; contbr. articles to profl. jours. Chmn. adv. com. Bur. Census, Washington, 1982—86. Mem. Am. Mktg. Assn. (v.p. 1986, 95, bd. dirs. 1986-89, 94-95, Odell award 1985, Disting. Educator award 1997, Churchill award 1997, Stern award, 2007, Lifetime Achievement award, Sales Rsch., 2008, 13), Acad. Mktg. Sci. (Outstanding Edn. award 1995), Decision Scis. Inst. (coun. 1977), Assn. Dir. Consumer Rsch. Conf. (chmn. 1976—), Mktg. Sci. Inst. (trustee 1989-94), Phi Beta Kappa. Republican. Presbyterian. Office: U NC CB 3490 Mccoll Bldg Chapel Hill NC 27599-3490 Office Phone: 919-619-2436. Business E-Mail: bill_perreault@unc.edu.

PERRIN, ROBERT, writer, consultant; b. Ann Arbor, Mich., Aug. 21, 1925; m. Barbara J. Groom, June 25, 1949; children: Stephen, Jennifer Perrin Hummel. BS, U. Minn., 1945. Reporter United Press Assn., Detroit, 1948-49, Detroit Free Press, 1949-55; adminstrv. asst. U.S. Senate, Washington, 1955-66; asst. dir. U.S. Office Econ. Opportunity, Washington, 1966-68, dep. dir., 1968-70; v.p. Mich. State U., East Lansing, 1970-79; vice-chancellor SUNY System, Albany, 1979-85; exec. v.p. Tchrs. Ins. and Annuity Assn.-Coll. Retirement Equities Fund, NYC, 1987-92; cons. Dept. State, 1993-94. Author: Piggy's Luck and More Tales of Evildoing, 1998, Keeping in Practice, 2001, To Talk of Many Things, 2008; contbr. articles to mags., newspapers. Mem. U.S.-Mex. Commn. on Border Devel., Washington, 1967-68. Lt. USNR, 1943-46, PTO. Fellow Reid Found., 1954; Pulitzer prize nominee Detroit Free Press, 1956.

PERROT, PAUL NORMAN, museum director; b. Paris, July 28, 1926; came to US, 1946, naturalized, 1954; s. Paul and K. Norman (Derr) P.; m. Joanne Stovall, Oct. 23, 1954; children— Paul Latham, Chantal Marie Claire, Jeannine, Robert. Student, Ecole du Louvre, 1945-46, N.Y. U. Inst. Fine Arts, 1946-52. Asst. The Cloisters, Met. Mus. Art, 1948-52; asst. to dir. Corning (NY) Mus. Glass, 1952-54, asst. dir. mus., 1954-60, dir., 1960-72; editor Jour. Glass Studies, 1959-72; asst. sec. for mus. programs Smithsonian Instn., Washington, 1972-84; dir. Va. Mus. Fine Arts, 1984-91, Santa Barbara Mus. Art, 1991-94, mus. cons., 1995—. Lectr. glass history, aesthetics, museology; past pres., NY State Assn. Mus.; past v.p. Internat. Coun. Mus. Found.; past pres. N.E. Conf. Mus.; past pres. Internat. Centre for Study of Preservation and Restoration of Cultural Property, Rome, mem. coun., 1974-88. Author: Three Great Centuries of Venetian Glass, 1958, also numerous articles on various hist. and archael. subjects. Former trustee Winterthur Mus.; former trustee, treas. Mus. Computer Network; former mem. Internat. Cons. Com. for the Preservation of Moenjodaro; former chmn. adv. com. World Monuments Fund; former chmn. vis. com. Getty Conservation Inst. Mem. Am. Assn. Mus. (past v.p., coun. 1967-78, named to Centennial Honor Roll, 2006), NY State Assn. Mus. (past pres.), Internat. Assn. History Glass (past v.p.) Corning Friends of Library (past pres.), So. Tier Library System (past pres.), Glass Cir. (hon. v.p.). E-mail: paulnperrot@comcast.net.

PERRY, A. MICHAEL, banker; b. Huntington, W.Va., May 31, 1936; s. Austin Lee and Virginia (Cole) P.; m. Henriella Mylar, 1958; children— Michele, Melanie, Audy BA, Marshall U., 1958; LL.B., W.Va. U., 1961. Ptnr. Huddleston, Bolen, Beatty, Porter, Copen, Huntington, 1961-81; chmn. bd., CEO 1st Huntington National Bank, 1981-88, chmn. bd., 1981—; pres., CEO Key Bancshares W.Va., Inc., Huntington, 1983-85, Key Centurion Bancshares, Inc., 1985—; CEO

Bank One, W. Va., 1983—2001, chmn., 1993. Bd. dirs. Champion Industries, Inc., Portec Rail Products, Inc., Arch Coal, Inc., 1998—. Trustee Alderson Broaddus Coll., 1984-89, Greater Ashland Found. Inc.; bd. dirs. Tri-State Cultural Devel. Plan; mem. adv. bd. Marshall Artists Series, Huntington, 1987-89; mem. bd. trustees U. W.Va. system, vice chairperson. Recipient Advocate of Yr. award SBA, 1985, Citizen of Yr. award Huntington newspaper, 1987. Mem. W.Va. Research League (bd. dirs., v.p.), W.Va. Bankers Assn. (bd. dirs., chmn. govt. and legis. com., chmn. interstate banking task force), W.Va. C. of C. (mem. exec. com., chmn.-elect 1989), Order of Coif, Omicron Delta Kappa Clubs: Rotary (past pres.). Baptist. Avocations: farming, collecting farm and kitchen implements. Home: 3350 Harvey Rd Huntington WV 25704-9112 Office: Arch Coal Inc Bd Directors 1 City Pl Dr Ste 300 Saint Louis MO 63141 Office Phone: 314-994-2700. Office Fax: 314-994-2878. Business E-Mail: aperry@archcoal.com.

PERRY, CYNTHIA NORTON SHEPARD, retired ambassador; b. Terre Haute, Ind., Nov. 11, 1928; d. George William and Flossie (Phillips) N.; m. James O. Shepard, Nov. 2, 1946 (div. June 1970); children: Donna Ross, James O. Jr., Milo Kent, Mark; m. James O. Perry, Mar. 20, 1971; children: Paula Lucille, James O. Jr. BS in Polit. Sci., Ind. State U., 1967, DCL (hon.), 1987; EdD, U. Mass., 1972; LLD (hon.), U. Md., 1984, Coppin State Coll., 1991; LHD (hon.), Chatham Coll., 1988; D of Pub. Svc., U. Mass., 1989. Sec. Nichols Investment Corp., Terre Haute, 1956-61; ednl. rep. Ohio region IBM Corp., Terre Haute, 1962-68; dir. nat. tchrs. corps U. Mass. Sch. Edn., Amherst, 1968-71; assoc. prof. edn. Tex. So. U., Houston, 1971-74; cons., lectr., U. Nairobi U.S. Peace Corps, Kenya, 1974-76; staff devel. officer UN Econ. Com. for Africa, Addis Ababa, Ethiopia, 1976-78; dean internat. student affairs Tex. So. U., Houston, 1978-82; chief edn. and human resources div. USAID, Washington, 1982-86; amb. to Sierra Leone Am. Embassy, Freetown, 1986-89, amb. to Burundi Bujumbura, 1989-93; dir. internat. investment adv. svcs. FCA Corp., Houston, 1996—2001; US dir. African Develop. Bank, Abidjan, Côte d'Ivoire, 2001—08; ret., 2008. Author (memoir) All Things Being Equal: One Women's Journey, 2000; contbr. articles to profl. jours. Bd. dirs. Inst. for Internat. Edn. Bd. Bols., 1984, World Affairs Coun., 1984, Houston Internat. Festival, 1994, Houston Model UN, 1994, Nat. Coun. for Internat. Vis., 1994; mem. Houston Commn. on Fgn. Rels., 1984, Houston Consular Corps, 1984, Greater Houston Partnership, 1993-96; diplomat in residence Furr H.S., 1993-96. Recipient Disting. Alumni award U. Mass., 1981, Ind. State U., 1987, Exceptional Diplomacy award U. Burundi, Ctrl. Africa, 1993, Superior Honor award U.S. Dept. State, 1993, Hon. Consul Republic of Senegal, 1994—. Mem. Praeclarus, Nat. Bus. and Profl. Women, Internat. Coun. for Edn l. Devel. (bd. dirs. 1984-86), Altrusan Soc. (bd. dirs. 1981-82), Delta Sigma Theta (pres. Houston chpt. 1982-83). Republican. Avocations: painting, creative writing, landscaping, gardening. Home and Office: 1601 Blodgett St Houston TX 77004-5016

PERRY, GEORGE, dean, neuroscientist, educator; s. George Richard and Mary Arlene (George) P.; m. Paloma Aguilar, May 21, 1983; children: Anne, Elizabeth. AA in Liberal Arts, Allan Hancock Coll., Santa Maria, Calif., 1973; BA in Zoology with high honors, U. Calif., Santa Barbara, 1974; PhD in Marine Biology, U. Calif., San Diego, 1979; PhD (hon.), Arturo Prat, Iquique, Chile, 2007. Postdoctoral fellow Baylor Coll. Medicine, Houston, 1979-82; from asst. prof. to prof. pathology Case Western Res. U., Cleve., 1982-94, prof., 1994—2005, interim chair dept., 2001—05; affiliated prof. chemistry and biochemistry U. Alaska, Fairbanks, 2001—; dean Coll. of Sciences U. Tex., San Antonio, 2006—. Tchg. asst. U. Calif., San Diego, 1977, Stanford U., 1978—79; memory task force on Alzheimer's disease Ohio Gov., 1987, 1990; mem. sci. adv. bd. Familial Alzheimer's Disease Rsch. Found., 1988—; mem., chair neurology scis. study sect. NIH, Bethesda, Md., 1989—95; cons. Nymox, Inc., Panacea Pharms., Inc., Prion Devel. Labs., Voyager, Takeda Pharms., Neurotez Labs., Avia Neuroscis., IOS Press, Alzheimer Rsch. Disease and Regeneration Forum, Alzheimer Found. America; mem. Faculty of 1000 Biology, Neurobiology Sect., 2004—; spkr. in field; mem. numerous rev. bds. nationally/internationally. Author: The Neuronal Cytoskeleton, 1992, numerous publs. in field; co-author: Frontiers in Biosciences, 2002, Neurosignals, 2002, Brain Pathology, 2004, Microscopy Rsch. and Technique, 2005, Internat. Jour. Exptl. Pathology, 2005; assoc. editor: Am. Jour. Pathology, 1994-2000, Jour. Biomedicine and Biotechnology, 2004—; sr. assoc. editor: Microscopy Rsch. and Technique, 2002—; mem. editl. bd. Am. Jour. Pathology, 1992—, Alzheimer Disease and Associated Disorders, 1994—, Alzheimer's Disease Rev., 1995-98, Jour. Alzheimer's Disease, 1997—, Jour. Exptl. Neurol., 1997-99, Molecular Chem. Neuropathology, 1997-99, Jour. Neural Transmission, 1998-2003, Investigational Drugs Jour., 1998—, Brain Pathology, 1999—, Jour. Molecular Neurosci., 1999-2001, Antioxidant and Redox Signaling, 2000—, Research Signpost, 2000, Lab. Investigation, 2000—06, Brain Rsch., 2002—, Current Medicinal Chemistry, 2002—, Neurobiology of Lipids, 2003—, Jour. Biomed. Biotech., 2002—, Pathology, 2003—, Pharm. Devel. Regime, 2003—, Med. Chemistry Rev.-Online, 2003-05, Current Alzheimer Rsch., 2003—, NeuroSignals, 2003—, Disease Markers, 2003—, Neurobiology Disease, 2004—, Lett Drug Design Discovery, 2004—; reviewer: Expert Review of Neurotherapeutics, 2004—, Mini-Reviews in Medicinal Chemistry, 2005—, Future Neurology, 2005—, Jour. Biological Chemistry, 2006—, Developmental Microbiology and Molecular Biology, 2006—, CNS Agents in Medicinal Chemistry, 2006—, Jour. Clin. Pathology, 2007—, Molecular Neurodegeneration, 2007—, Open Medicinal Chemistry Jour., 2007—, Acta Neuropathol., Alan Liss Publ. Co., Am. Jour. Pathol., Ann Neurol, others; contbr. articles to Exptl. Cell Rsch., Jour Cell Biology, Devel. Biology, Brain Rsch., Am. Jour. Pathology, Jour. Neurosci., European Jour. Cell Biology, Nature, Annals Neurology, Lancet, Acta Neuropathology, Jour. Neurochemistry, Neurosci. Letters, Neuroreport, Med. Hypotheses, Nature Medicine, Neurodegeneration, Sci., others. Pres. Serra Club, 1995-97; sr. investigator Internat. Coll. Geriat. Psychoneuropharmacology. Tng. corps. USAR, 1972—74, U. Calif. Santa Barbara. Recipient Bausch and Lomb medal, 1971, Rsch. Career Devel. award, NIH, 1988—93, Temple award, Alzheimer's Assn., 1999, Disting. Am. Portuguese Ancestry award, Portuguese-Am. Hist. Found., Inc., 2001, Mensch award, Alzheimer Rsch. Forum, 2003, Cmty. Svc. award, Cleve. Area Chpt. Alzheimer's Assn., 2004, Zenith award, Alzheimer Assn., 2007, Nat. Honor Plaque Panama, 2011, Sr. Investigator award, Internat. Coll. Geriatric Psychoneuropharmacology, 2011; grantee, NIH, 1985—, Am. Health Assistance Found., 1988—90, 1997—99, Alzheimer's Assn., 1989—90, 1998—2002, 2004—09, 2010—13, United Mitochondrial Disease Fund, 2000—02; fellow, Kennecott Copper, 1974—75, Muscular Dystrophy Assn., 1980—82, Philip Morris, USA, 2003—06. Fellow AAAS, Microscopy Soc. America, Acad. Scis. Lisbon (corr.), Portuguese Tribune (Semmes found. endowed chair 2013; named Scientist of Yr., 2012), Linnean Soc., Royal Soc. Medicine, Biology Soc. (fellow, CBiol, CSci), Iberoam. Molecular Biology Orgn., ISI Highly Cited Com. Neurosci.; mem. AAUP (case chapter exec. com. 1996—2006, membership chair 1996-98, v.p. 1998-99, pres. 1999—2006), Am. Soc. Cell Biology, Royal Acad. Spain (corr.; fgn. corr. mem. 2009), Electron Microscopy Soc. N.E. Ohio (treas. 1986-88, trustee 1988-90, pres. 1990-91), Soc. Neurosci., Am. Assn. Neuropathologists (awards com. 1992-93, 95-2002, chmn. 2001-02, internat. congress neuropathology concilator 1995-2000, 2013-, sec.-treas. 2003-08, pres. elect. 2007-08, pres. 2008-, past pres. 2009-10, mem. non com. 2010-13, chair 2010), Am. Soc. Investigative Pathology (program com. 1998-2001, 12-), Am. Soc. Neurochemistry, U.S. and Can. Acad. of Pathology, Hispanic Med. Assn. (com. on status of Portuguese in medicine and sci.), Soc. for Neurosci., Sigma Xi (pres. chpt. 2004-06; Martin Golland award 2013), Iberoamerican Molecular Biology Orgn., Am. Aging Assn.(Harman Research award, 2008), Soc. Advancements Chicanos and Native Ams. in Scis. (Disting. Profl. Mentor award 2010, Alzheimer award 2010, Fulbright Sr. scholar 2012), Dana Alliance Brain Initiatives., Mex. Acad. Scis. (Corr.), Royal Soc. Chemists (fellow CChemt), Nat. Orgn. Portuguese Am. (bd. mem. 2009-, chair 2013-), Royal Coll. Pathologists (fellow), Phi Kappa Phi. Democrat. Roman Catholic. Avocation: genealogy. Office: U Tex San Antonio Coll Scis One UTSA Circle San Antonio TX 78249-0661 Office Phone: 210-458-4450. Business E-Mail: george.perry@utsa.edu.

PERRY, JAMES E.C., state supreme court justice; b. New Bern, NC; m. Adrienne M. Perry, 1971; children: Willis, Jaimon, Kamilah. BA, St. Augustine's Coll., 1966; JD, Columbia Univ., 1972. Sr. ptnr. Perry & Hicks PA; judge Fla. 18th Jud. Cir., 2000—09, chief judge, 2003—05; assoc. justice Fla. Supreme Ct., 2009—. Founder, pres. Jackie Robinson Sports Assn.; trustee Carter CME Tabernacle Church; treas. bd. trustees St. Augustine's Coll. Recipient Humanitarian award, Seminole County NAACP, Paul C. Perkins award, Orange County NAACP, Key to the City, New Bern, NC, 2004, Martin Luther King Drum Major award for social just., 2005, Williams-Johnson Outstanding Jurist award, Brevard & Seminole County Bar Associations, 2006. Office: Fla Supreme Ct 500 S Duval St Tallahassee FL 32399-1925 Office Phone: 850-921-1096.*

PERRY, JAMES FREDERIC, philosophy educator, writer; b. Washington, Jan. 21, 1936; s. Albert Walter and Helene Anna Maria (Neumeyer) P.; m. Sandra Jean Huizing, Feb. 18, 1957 (div. May 1972); children: Sandra Elaine, James Frederic Jr., Bartholomew; m. Roberta Schofield, June 6, 1984. Student, Princeton U., 1953-56, Marietta Coll., Ohio, 1958-60; BA with honors in Philosophy, Ind. U., 1962, PhD in Philosophy of Edn., 1972. NDEA fellow in philosophy U. N.C., 1962—65; instr. N.C. State U., Raleigh, 1965-66; Univ. fellow Ind. U., 1971, adj. lectr. Bloomington, 1972-75; prof. philosophy Hillsborough C.C., Tampa, Fla., 1975-97, 2005—11, honors prof. philosophy, 1997—2005. Adj. prof. U. South Fla., 2000—, adj. honors prof., 2006—. Author: Random, Routine, Reflective, 1989; contbr. articles to profl. jours. Precinct committeeman Dem. Party, Tampa, Fla., 1988—2004. Mem. AAUP (pres. Fla. conf. 1986-89, chair com. "A" on acad. freedom 1989-2002), C.C. Humanities Assn. (so. divsn. exec. bd. 1981-89), Am. Philos. Assn., Fla. Philos. Assn. (pres. 2004-05), Internat. Soc. Philos. Enquiry, Internat. Congress for Critical Thinking and Moral Critiques (founding mem. S.E. coun. 1991), World Congress Philosophy (Boston 1998, Istanbul 2003, Seoul 2008, Athens 2013), Princeton Alumni Assn. of Fla. Suncoast (sec. 1983-86, pres. 1986-95), Mensa, Authors Guild, Textbook and Acad. Authors Assn. Avocations: travel, genealogy. Office: PO Box 10561 Tampa FL 33679-0561 Business E-Mail: philart@gte.net.*

PERRY, JONATHAN W., state legislator; m. Christine LeBeouf; children: Molli, Meredith, Major, Marlee Perry. BA Criminal Justice & Sociology, Northeast La. U., 1995; JD, Southern Law Ctr. Atty.; mem. Dist. 47 La. House of Reps., 2008—11, mem. adminstrn. of criminal justice com., agr., forestry, aquaculture and rural devel. com., ways and means com., joint legis. com. on capital outlay; mem. Dist. 26 La. State Senate, 2011—. Republican. Office: State Capitol PO Box 94183 Baton Rouge LA 70804 Office Phone: 225-342-2040. E-mail: perryj@legis.state.la.us.

PERRY, KENNY (JAMES KENNETH PERRY), professional golfer; b. Elizabethtown, KY, Aug. 10, 1960; s. Ken Perry; m. Sandy Perry; children: Lesslye, Justin, Lindsey. Grad., Western Ky. U., Bowling Green, 1982. Profl. golfer, 1982—; mem. US Team Presidents Cup, 1996, 2003, 2005, 2009, Ryder Cup, 2004, 2008. Deacon Ch. of Christ, Franklin, Ky. Achievements include winning PGA Tour events: New England Classic, 1994, Bob Hope Chrysler Classic, 1995, Buick Open, 2001, 2008, Bank of America Colonial, 2003, 2005, Meml. Tournament, 2003, 2008; Greater Milw. Open, 2003, Pres. Cup, 2003, Bay Hill Invitational, 2005, Ryder Cup, 2008, John Deere Classic, 2008, FBR Open, 2009, Travelers Championship, 2009. Avocation: auto racing. Office: PGA Tour 100 PGA Tour Blvd Ponte Vedra FL 32082

PERRY, KIMBERLY, musician; b. Miss., July 12, 1983; Lead singer The Band Perry, 2005—. Musician: (albums) The Band Perry, 2010, Pioneer, 2013, (songs) If I Die Young, 2010 (USA Weekend Breakthrough Video of Yr., CMT Music Awards, 2011, Single of Yr., Song of Yr., New Artist of Yr., Country Music Assn. Awards, 2011). Named New Vocal Duo/Group, Acad. Country Music Awards, 2011, Top New Artist, 2011, Vocal Group of Yr., 2014. Office: Major Bob Music Inc 1111 17th Avenue S Nashville TN 37212*

PERRY, MARK, state legislator; Mem. Dist. 44 Ark. House of Reps., 2009—. Democrat. Office: State Capitol Rm 350 Little Rock AR 72201 also: PO Box 97 Jacksonville AR 72078 Office Phone: 501-682-6211, 501-682-7771, 501-982-4561. Business E-Mail: mperry@windstream.net.

PERRY, MURVIN HENRY, communications educator; b. Bruce, SD, Apr. 28, 1922; s. Earl Henry and Lorraine (Eichel) P.; m. Rita Clare Kaefring, Aug. 23, 1952; children— Gail, Mark, Scott, Todd, Chris. BS, S.D. State Coll., 1950; MA, U. Iowa, 1954, PhD in Mass Communications, 1959. High sch. tchr., Gregory, S.D., 1947-48; publicist, tchr. S.D. State Coll., 1949-51; with VA, 1952-56; asst. to dir. Sch. Journalism, State U. Iowa, 1956-59; asst. prof. journalism Kans. State U., 1959-63; prof., dir. journalism Kent State U., 1963-79; chmn. dept. communication E. Tenn. State U., Johnson City, 1979-88, ret., 1988. Mem. Early Ford V8 Club. Author: (short stories) Murv's Motoring Memories, 1993; editor: 1935 Ford convertible, 1965 Ford Mustang convertible, Disciple, Monthly parish Newsletter, St. Marys Cath. Ch., Johnson City. Served with USNR, 1943-46, South Pacific Theater. Recipient Lifetime Adv. award, Tenn. Right to Life, 2004, Lifetime Achievement award, East Tenn. State U., 2008. Mem. Soc. Profl. Journalists. Home: 307 Oak Ln Johnson City TN 37604-3109 Business E-Mail: mhpjctn@embarqmail.com.

PERRY, NEIL, musician; b. Miss., July 23, 1990; Drummer The Band Perry, 2005—. Musician: (albums) The Band Perry, 2010, Pioneer, 2013, (songs) Hip to My Heart, 2009, If I Die Young, 2010 (USA Weekend Breakthrough Video of Yr., CMT Music Awards, 2011, Single of Yr., Song of Yr., New Artist of Yr., Country Music Assn. Awards, 2011), You Lie, 2011. Named Top New Vocal Duo/Group, Acad. Country Music Awards, 2011, Top New Artist, 2011, Vocal Group of Yr., 2014. Office: Major Bob Music Inc 1111 17th Avenue S Nashville TN 37212 Office Phone: 615-329-4150.*

PERRY, REID, musician; b. Miss., Nov. 17, 1988; Bassist, background vocals The Band Perry, 2005—. Musician: (albums) The Band Perry, 2010, Pioneer, 2013, (songs) If I Die Young, 2010 (USA Weekend Breakthrough Video of Yr., CMT Music Awards, 2011, Single of Yr., Song of Yr., New Artist of Yr., Country Music Assn. Awards, 2011). Named Top New Vocal Duo/Group, Acad. Country Music Awards, 2011, Top New Artist, 2011, Vocal Group of Yr., 2014. Office: Major Bob Music Inc 1111 17th Avenue S Nashville TN 37212 Office Phone: 615-329-4150.*

PERRY, RICK (JAMES RICHARD PERRY), Governor of Texas; b. Paint Creek, Tex., Mar. 4, 1950; s. Joseph Ray and Amelia June (Holt) Perry; m. Anita Thigpen, Nov. 6, 1982; children: Griffin, Sydney. BS in Animal Sci., Tex. A&M U., 1972. Farmer/rancher; mem. Dist. 64 Tex. House of Reps., Austin, 1985—91; commr. agrl. State of Tex., Austin, 1991—99, lt. gov., 1999-2000, gov., 2000—. Chmn. Republican Governors Assn., 2007—08, 2010—11, finance chmn., 2008—09; candidate for Republican nomination 2012 US Presdl. Election. Author: On My Honor: Why the American Values of the Boy Scouts Are Worth Fighting For, 2008, Fed Up!: Our Fight to Save America from Washington, 2010. Capt. USAF, 1972—77. Recipient Disting. Eagle Scout award, Boy Scouts America, 1992, Gerald W Thomas Agriculturist award; named Man of Yr. in Tex. Agrl., Tex. County Agrl. Agents Assn., 1990; named an Outstanding Tex Leader, John Ben Shepperd Pub. Leadership Inst., 1996; named one of The Most Effective Legislators, Dallas Morning News, 1989. Mem.: Tex. & Southwestern Cattle Raisers Assn., Tex. Firemen & Fire Marshals Assn. (life), Nat. Future Farmers of America Alumni Assn., American Legion Post #75 (life), Eagle Scouts. Republican. Methodist. Office: Office of the Governor PO Box 12428 Austin TX 78711 Office Phone: 512-463-2000. Office Fax: 512-463-1849.*

PERRY, STEVEN L., lawyer; b. Okla. City, June 24, 1952; s. Ed and Marilyn Vick Perry; divorced; 1 child, Kyle Kubecka. BA in Polit. Sci., U. Okla., 1974; JD, Okla. City U., 1977. Claims, collection Trans-South, 2001—02; govt. claims CMR, 2003—05; atty. Wheat and Assocs., 2005—06; landman, atty. Triad Energy Inc., 2006—. Mem.: Okla. Bar Assn. Democrat. Methodist. Office: PO Box 18721 Oklahoma City OK 73154-8721 Office Phone: 405-605-0590. Business E-Mail: steveperry@steveperry08.com.

PERRY, W. KEITH, state legislator; b. Tallahassee, Fla., Dec. 3, 1958; m. Amy S. Cekander; children: Alexis, Amanda. Owner, contractor Perry Roofing Contractors; mem. Dist. 22 Fla. House of Representatives, 2011—. Pres. House of Hope. Republican. Avocations: hiking, boating, fishing. Office: 2440 SW 76th St Ste 120 Gainesville FL 32608-6544 also: Florida House of Reps 1301 The Capitol 402 S Monroe St Tallahassee FL 32399-1300 Office Phone: 352-313-6544, 850-488-0887.

PERRY, WILLIAM BRIAN, colorectal surgeon; b. Natchitoches, La., Dec. 18, 1963; s. William Nathaniel and Joyce Hargis Perry; m. Holly Christine Hundemer, June 27, 1987; children: Katherine Mitchell, Patrick William, Austin Joseph. BS, La. State U., 1986; MD, Duke U., 1990. Lic. colon and rectal surgery Am. Bd. of Colon and Rectal Surgery, gen. surgery Am Bd. of Surgery, Tex. State Bd. of Med. Examiners. Chief of colorectal surgery Wilford Hall Med. Ctr., Lackland AFB, Tex., 1997—2006, gen. surgery residency program dir., 2002—06. Cons. to USAF surgeon gen. for colorectal surgery USAF Med. Corps, Bolling AFB, DC, 1997—2004; chief med. ops., chief of staff 4407th Med. Group, Prince Sultan Air Base, Saudi Arabia, 1998; chief trauma surgeon 332d Expeditionary Med. Group, Balad Air Base/LSA Anaconda, Iraq, 2005, 2007. Contbr. articles to med. jours. and texts. Lt. col. USAF, 1990—2008. Decorated Commendation Medal USAF Bronze Star. Fellow: ACS, Am. Soc. of Colon and Rectal Surgeons; mem.: VFW, Soc. of Air Force Clin. Surgeons (pres. 2004—06), Delta Tau Delta (treas. 1983—84). E-mail: william.perry.1@us.af.mil.

PERRYMAN, MARLIN RAY, economist, educator; b. Tyler, Tex., Dec. 25, 1952; s. Merrill A. and Oneta (Davis) Perryman; m. Nancy Beth Satterwhite, July 14, 1973. BS In Math, Baylor U., 1974; PhD in Econs., Rice U., 1978. Founder dir., Ctr. for the Advancement of Econ. Analysis Baylor U., Waco, Tex., 1979—, dir. honors program, 1980—, mem. grad. faculty, 1978—, Herman Brown prof. econs., 1980—, mem. publ. com. Baylor Bus. Studies, 1977—, dir. econs. div. Inter-U. Consortium for Polit. and Social rsch., 1978—, sr. asso. ctr. for comm. rsch., 1981—, Resource Econs. and Mgmt. Assos. Dir. State of Tex. Econometric Model Project, 1979—; founder, dir. Baylor U. Forecasting Svc.; econ. cons. to Comptr. Pub. Accts. State Tex., 1979—; reviewer numerous acad. jours. and rsch. grant orgns., 1978—; guest lectr. econs. various radio and TV programs, 1977. Author: Trends in the Texas Economy, 1982—, Fluctuations in Economic Activity: Analysis and Forecasting, 1983; author: (with Nancy B. Perryman) Problems in Economic Forecasting, 1983; editor: Time Series Analysis, 1981, Applied Time Series Analysis, 1981, Econometric Modelling, 1981; contbr. numerous articles on economics analysis and theory to scholarly jours. Mem. urban and regional policy planning bd. Heart of Tex. Coun. of Govts., 1978, 1979, 1980. Recipient Outstanding Young Economist and Social Scientist in U.S., NSF, 1979, 1980, Disting. Prof. award, Hankamer Sch. Bus., 1979, Tchg. Excellence citation, Baylor U., 1978—81; named Outstanding Alumni in Econs. Rsch., Rice U., 1979, Most Popular Prof., Hankamer Sch. of Bus., 1979; Nat. Merit scholar, 1971—74. Mem.: AAAS, Sherlock Holmes Soc. London, Southwestern Social Sci. Assn., Southwestern Econ. Assn., Assn. Evolutionary Econs., History of Econs. Soc., La. Acad. Scis., Royal Econ. Soc. of Eng., Am. Acad. Arts and Scis., Beta Gamma Sigma, Phi Eta Sigma, Omicron Delta Kappa, Omicron Delta Epsilon, Alpha Chi. Baptist. Home: 309 Brookwood Dr Waco TX 76712-3208 Office: Baylor U Dept of Econs Waco TX 76798

PERSELLIN, ROBERT HAROLD, physician; b. Fargo, ND, July 3, 1930; s. James Harry and Bessie (Hoffman) P.; m. Bonnie Feibleman, June 27, 1957 (dec. 1983); children: Kathleen, Jamie; m. Diane Cummings, June 14, 1986 BS, Northwestern U., 1952, MD, 1956, MS, 1959. Diplomate: Am. Bd. Internal Medicine, Am. Bd. Rheumatology. Intern Charity Hosp., New Orleans, 1956-57; resident in internal medicine Northwestern U. Med. Center, 1957-60; fellow in rheumatology Southwestern Med. Sch., 1962-64; asst. prof. medicine U. Oreg. Med. Sch., 1964-68; prof. medicine, head div. rheumatology U. Tex. Health Sci. Ctr., San Antonio, 1968—81, prof. family practice, 1993—2003. Cons. rheumatology VA Hosps., U.S. Army, Internat. Med. Corps, Kosovo and Republic of Moldova; vis. prof. rheumatology Kingstown Med. Coll.; vis. scholar Corpus Christi Coll., Cambridge U., 1979-80; vis. scientist Strangeways Rsch. Lab., Cambridge. Contbr chpts. to books, articles to profl. jours. Bd. dirs. San Antonio Chamber Music Soc., 1970-75, 80-96, pres., 1983-85; bd. dirs. Friends of Strings, 1972-75, San Antonio Bot. Soc., 1985-87; Dem. precinct committeeman Washington County, Oreg., 1966-68. Served to capt. M.C. U.S. Army, 1960-62. Fellow ACP, Am. Coll. Rheumatology (exec. com. mem.); mem. Arthritis Found. (chmn. med. and sci. com. South Ctrl. Tex. chpt.), Heberden Soc., Am. Fedn. Clin. Rsch., So. Soc. Clin. Investigation, Tex. Rheumatism Assn. (pres.), Nat. Soc. Clin. Rheumatology, Mex. Rheumatology Soc. (hon.). Office: 635 E Olmos Dr San Antonio TX 78212-2504

PERSOFF, MYRON MAYER, plastic surgeon; b. West Palm Beach, Fla., Apr. 26, 1941; BS, U. Fla., Gainesville, 1963; MD, U. Miami, Fla., 1967. Cert. Am. Bd. Plastic Surgery, 1977. Rotating-2 intern

Phila. Naval Hosp., 1967—68; resident gen. surgery U. South Fla. Sch. Medicine, Tampa, 1971—73, St. Joseph Hosp., Houston, 1973—74, resident plastic surgery, 1974—76; fellow Cronin-Brauer Clin. Assn., Houston, 1974—76; staff mem. North Broward Hosp., 1976—90, West Boca Med. Ctr., 1985—94, Northridge Med. Ctr., Ft. Lauderdale, Fla., 1993—95, Mercy Hosp., Coconut Grove, Fla., 1994—, Coral Gables Hosp., Fla., 1998—2001; active staff mem. Boca Raton Cmty. Hosp., Fla., 1976—93; clin. asst. U. Miami Sch. Medicine, 1977—2001. Contbr. articles to med. jours.; featured: magazines Plastic Surgery Products. Orthopedic surgeon USN, 1968—69, Navy Hosp., Pensacola, Fla., sea duty USN, 1968, USS Speigel Grove, attended Flight Surgeons Sch. USN, 1969, Pensacola, Fla., served in USN, 1969—71, US Naval Air Sta., Cubi Point, Philippines. Fellow: Am. Coll. Surgeons; mem.: AMA, Broward County Soc. Plastic Surgeons, Lipolysis Soc. N.Am., Miami Soc. Plastic Surgeons, Dade County Med. Assn., Palm Beach County Med. Soc., Fla. Med. Assn., Palm Beach County Soc. Plastic and Reconstructive Surgeons, Fla. Soc. Plastic and Reconsructive Surgeons, Southeastern Soc. Plastic and Reconstructive Surgeons, Am. Soc. Plastic and Reconstructive Surgeons, Am. Soc. Aesthetic Plastic Surgery. Office: Coconut Grove Plastic Surgery Mercy Output Ctr 4011 Hardie Ave Miami FL 33133-6344 Office Phone: 305-858-5255. Office Fax: 305-858-5235. Business E-Mail: info@drpersoff.com.

PERSON, CURTIS S., JR., judge, former state legislator, lawyer; b. Nov. 27, 1934; married; 6 children. BS, Memphis State U., 1956; LLB, U. Miss., 1959. Chief legal officer Juvenile Ct. Memphis and Shelby County; former mem. Tenn. Ho. Reps.; mem. Tenn. Senate, 1969—2007, Senate Rep. whip, 1973-76, minority caucus chmn., 1976-82; judge Juvenile Ct. Memphis and Shelby County, Tenn., 2006—. Chmn. Senate Judiciary com. 95th-104th Gen. Assemblies. Pres. Memphis-Shelby County Mental Health Assn., 1969-73, Handicapped Inc., 1972-74; chmn. Memphis Commn. Drug Abuse, 1970-71; charter pres. Memphis State Tiger Rebounders; past trustee Memphis State U.; exec. committeeman St. Jude's Memphis Open Golf Classic; co-chmn. Shelby County Legis. Del., 1973-74, vice chmn., 1970, 75, 76, 85-88; chmn. Shelby Rep. Del., 1977, 83-84; mem. adv. bd. Jr. League Memphis, 1995-98; vice chmn. Select Com. Children and Youth, 1997-2002, ex officio Senate Mem., Juvenile Justice Reform Commn., 1998. Named Memphis and Tenn. Outstanding Young Man of Yr., Jaycees, 1969, Outstanding Legis. of Yr., Govt. Leader Against Drunk Driving, Tenn. MADD, 1988, Legis. of Yr., Tenn. Alcohol and Drug Assn., 1988, Legislator of Yr. Tenn. Juvenile Svcs. Yr., 2001; recipient Liberty Bell Freedom award Memphis/Shelby County Bar Assn., 1969, Tenn. Adv. of Yr. Handicapped Children, 1978, Outstanding Svc. Children award Tenn Coun. Juvenile Ct. Judges, 1981, Pres.' Svc. award Tenn. Juvenile Ct. Svcs. Assn., 1981, Americanism award Memphis Civitan Club, 1986, Disting. Svc. award County Ofcls. Assn. Tenn., 1989, Cmty. Svc. award Tenn. Med. Assn., 1989, Eagle award Eagle Forum, 1994, Bill Bates Legis. award United Tenn. League, 1994, Champion for Children award Tenn. Assn. Child Care, 1995, Outstanding Legis. award County Ofcls. Assn. Tenn., 1996, Tenn. Juvenile Svcs. Assn. Pres. Svc. award, 1997, Tenn. Trial Lawyers Assn. Legis. of Yr. award, 1997, Shelby County Rep. Party Chmn. of Yr. award, 1999, Am. Lung Assn. Tenn. Legis. of Yr. award, 1999, Tenn. Task Force Against Domestic Violence Outstanding Legis. of Yr. award, 1999, Tenn. Dispensing Opticians Assn. Legis. of Yr. award, 2000, award Tenn. Juvenile Ct. Svcs. Assn., 2001, Spl. Honor Elvis Presley Meml. Martial Arts Hall of Fame, 2002, Lifetime Achievement award Defenders of Freedom, 2002, Animal Advocacy award Metro Animal Svcs., 2002, Legislator of Yr. award Tenn. Trial Lawyers Assn., 2003; named Legislator of Yr. Tenn. Devel. Dists., 2003, Hon. Fellow and Legislator of Yr., Opticians Assn. Am., 2003, Legislative Leadership award, Tenn. Cable Telecommunications Assn., 2003-2004, Friend of the Family award Tenn. Home Edn. Assn., 2004, Humane Legislator award Humane Soc. U.S., 2004, Thomas B. Murphy Longevity of Svc. award Southern Legislative Conf., 2004, Legislator of Yr., Animal Control Assn. of Tenn., 2004, award of appreciation Tenn. Silica Justice Coalition, 2006; named Champion Tenn. Disability Coalition, 2003-04, Outstanding Legislator, Co. Ofcls. Assn. Tenn., 2004. Office: 616 Adams Ave Memphis TN 38105 Home Phone: 901-767-8659; Office Phone: 901-405-8574.

PERSONS, (W.) RAY (W. RAY PERSONS), lawyer, legal association administrator; b. Talbottan, Ga., July 22, 1953; s. William and Frances (Crowell) P.; m. Wendy-Joy Mottley, Sept. 24, 1977; children: Conrad Ashley, April Maureen. BS cum laude, Armstrong State Coll., 1975; JD, Ohio State U., 1978. Bar: Ga. 1979, US Dist. Ct. (so. dist.) Ga. 1980, US Dist. Ct. (no. dist.) Ga. 1986, US Ct. Appeals (11th cir.) 1986. Assoc. Troutman, Sanders, Lockerman & Ashmore, Atlanta, 1978-79; atty. NLRB, Atlanta, 1980-82; legis. counsel U.S Ho. Reps., Washington, 1983-86; atty. Mack & Bernstein, Atlanta, 1986-87; ptnr. Arrington & Hollowell LLP, Atlanta, 1987-95, Swift, Currie, McGhee & Hiers LLP, Atlanta, 1995-99, Hunton & Williams LLP, Atlanta, 1999—2001, King & Spalding LLP, Atlanta, 2001—. Adj. prof. litigation Ga. State U., Atlanta, 1989—; spl. asst. atty. gen. State of Ga., Atlanta, 1988—. Master Am. Inns of Ct. (Lamar chpt.); fellow Am. Coll. Trial Lawyers; mem. ABA, Internat. Soc. Barristers, Am. Bd. Trial Advocates, State Bar Ga., Atlanta Bar Assn. (bd. dirs., 1996-97, 2000-, sec., 2003-04, treas., 2004-05, 2nd v.p., 2005-06, pres.-elect, 2006-07, pres., 2007-) Lawyers Club of Atlanta. Roman Catholic. Office: King & Spalding 1180 Peachtree St NE Atlanta GA 30309 Business E-Mail: rpersons@kslaw.com.

PERSZYK, ANTHONY ANDREW, clinical geneticist; MD, U. Wis., 1985. Lic. Fla., 1993, diplomate Am. Bd. Pediatrics, 2004, cert. Am. Bd. Med. Genetics-clin. genetics, 2004. Intern pediat. Med. Coll. of Wis., 1986, resident pediat., 1986—88; fellow clin. genetics Univ. Wash. Hosp., 1988—90; hosp. affiliation includes Methodist Hosp., Memphis, Univ. Fla., Baptist Med. Ctr., Meml. Hosp., jacksonville, St. Vincent's Med. Ctr., Univ. med. Ctr., Wolfson Children's Hosp. Office: Baptist Medical Center 820 Prudential Dr Ste 405 Jacksonville FL 32207 Office Phone: 904-633-0920.

PESKA, DON N., dean, surgeon, educator; b. NY; m. Judith Peska; 3 children. BS in Biology, Bklyn. Coll.; DO, Des Moines Osteo. Coll. Rotating internship and gen. residency Oakland Gen. Hosp; residency in cardiovascular and thoracic surgery Detroit Osteo. and Bi-County Hospitals; clin. practice in thoracic and vascular surgery Ft. Worth, 1982—; assoc. prof. surgery U. North Tex. Health Sci. Ctr. Tex. Coll. Osteo. Medicine, Ft. Worth, 1995—2008, asst. dean clin. edn., 2003, assoc. dean academic affairs, 2003—04, assoc. dean ednl. programs, 2004—, prof. surgery, 2008—, dean, 2009—; dir. osteo. med. edn. John Peter Smith Hosp.; adminstrv. dir. med. edn. Plz. Med. Ctr. Contbr. articles to profl. jours. Mem.: American Coll. Osteo. Surgeons (President's Svc. award 2003, Disting. Osteo. Surgeon award 2007), American Osteo. Assn., Tex. Osteo. Med. Assn., Tarrant County Med. Soc., Tex. Med. Assn., Tex. Med. Found. Studio: University North Tex Health Sci Ctr Tex Coll Osteo Medicine Med Edn Tng Bldg 3500 Camp Bowie Blvd PCC4 Fort Worth TX 76107 Office Phone: 817-735-2244. Office Fax: 817-735-0623. Business E-Mail: don.peska@unthsc.edu.

PESTANA, CARLOS, surgeon, retired dean, educator; b. Tacoronte, Tenerife, Canary Islands, Spain, June 10, 1936; came to U.S., 1968, naturalized, 1973; s. Francisco and and Blanca (Suarez) P.; m. Myrna Lorena Serrato, Aug. 25, 1966; children— Becky Elizabeth, George Byron. BS, Nat. U. Mex., 1952, MD, 1959; PhD in Surgery, U. Minn., 1965. Intern St. Mary of Nazareth Hosp., Chgo., 1959-60; resident Mayo Clinic, Rochester, Minn., 1961-65; surgeon Hosp. 20 de Noviembre Mexico City; asst. prof. surgery Nat. U. Mex., 1966-67, U. Tex. Med. Sch. at San Antonio, 1968-70, asso. prof., 1970-74, prof., 1974—, asso. dean for acad. devel., 1971-73, asso. dean for student affairs, 1973-86, assoc. dean acad. affairs, 1986-97, clin. prof. surgery, 1998-2000, prof. emeritus, 2000—. Recipient Edward John Noble Found. award, 1965, Piper Prof. award Minnie Stevens Piper Founds., 1972, Nat. Golden Apple award Am. Med. Student Assn., 1999. Mem. Alpha Omega Alpha (Robert J. Glaser Disting. Tchr. award 1997). Home: 10123 N Manton Ln San Antonio TX 78213-1932 Office: 7703 Floyd Curl Dr San Antonio TX 78284-6200 Office Phone: 210-567-5700.

PETER, JACK E., museum administrator; married; 1 child. Grad., Loyola U. With Airfax Productions, Optimus, Inc.; gen. mgr. & v.p. Post Group, Disney-MGM Studios; dir. prodn. PGA TOUR Productions, Ponte Vedra Beach, Fla., 1994—95, v.p., 1995—2000; gen. mgr. World Golf Hall of Fame, St. Augustine, Fla., 2000—01, v.p., 2000—04, COO, 2001—, sr. v.p., 2004—. Office: World Golf Hall Of Fame 12173 Ripken Cir N Jacksonville FL 32224-4638 Office Phone: 904-940-4000.

PETERS, CALVIN RONALD, plastic and reconstructive surgeon; b. New Orleans, Jan. 27, 1940; s. Arthur Henry and Christine Cecile (Moldaner) P.; m. Pamela Alice Orth, Sept. 4, 1965; children: Brandon Scott, Kendall Kyle. BS, La. State U., 1961, MD, 1964. Diplomate Am. Bd. Surgery, Am. Bd. Plastic Surgery. Intern USN Hosp., Portsmouth, Va., 1964-65; gen. surg. resident Ochsner Clinic, 1968-72; plastic surgery resident Duke U. Med. Ctr., Durham, 1972-75, asst. prof. plastic surgery, 1975-78; program dir., plastic surgery Cleve. Clinic, 1978-79; pres., founder Ctr. for Plastic and Reconstructive Surgery, Orlando, Fla., 1979—. Chmn. dept. plastic surgery, Orlando Regional Med. Ctr., Orlando, 1981-86, Fla. Hosp. Med. Ctr., Orlando, 1981-86. Contbr. numerous articles, chpts. to profl. jours. and textbooks. With USN, 1965-68. Recipient Sr. Resident award Plastic Surgery Ednl. Found., Chgo., 1975. Fellow Am. Coll. Surgeons (bd. govs. 1980-86); mem. Am. Soc. Plastic and Reconstructive Surgeons, Am. Assn. Plastic Surgeons, Am. Soc. Maxillofacial Surgeons, Am. Soc. Aesthetic Plastic Surgeons, Orange County Med. Soc. (pres. 1989—), Fla. Soc. Plastic and Reconstructive Surgeons (pres. 1989—), Fla. Cleft Palate Soc. (pres. 1987-88), Interlachen Country Club, Winter Park Racquet Club. Republican. Episcopalian. Avocations: running, skiing, swimming, boating, golf. Home: 467 Lakewood Dr Winter Park FL 32789-3939 Office: Ctr Plastic/Recon Surgery 2501 N Orange Ave Ste 442 Orlando FL 32804-4642

PETERS, DOUGLAS ALAN, appeals nurse manager; b. Portsmouth, Va., Oct. 4, 1968; s. Terrance Gene and Pamela P. BA in Philosophy, Va. Poly. Inst. and State U., 1992; BSN summa cum laude, James Madison U., 1995; JD, U. Md., Balt., 2003. RN Tenn.; cert. case mgr., legal nurse cons. Photojournalist CVNI/The Greene County Record, Stanardsville, Va., 1992; nursing asst. Rockingham Meml. Hosp., Harrisonburg, Va., 1993-95; clin. nurse Bapt. Hosp., Pensacola, Fla., 1995-96; nurse mgr. quality assurance Escambia County Jail Infirmary, Pensacola, 1996-97; case mgr./U.R. Total Health Care, Balt., 1997-98; case mgr. Blue Cross/Blue Shield of Md., Balt., 1998-2000, appeals analyst, 2000—01, sr. appeals analyst, 2001—04; jud. law clk. 23d Jud. Cir., W.Va., 2004—05; legal cons. CareFirst Blue Cross Blue Shield, 2005; nurse, case mgr. George Washington U. Hosp., 2006—07, Medicare Part D Appeals Grievances Healthspring Inc., Nashville, 2007—09, appeals nurse supervisor, 2009—10, appeals nurse manager, 2011—. Mem.: Greater Nashville Darts Assn., Am. Assn. Legal Nurse Cons., Phi Alpha Delta, Sigma Theta Tau, Alpha Chi Sigma. Avocation: darts. Personal E-mail: dapeters2006@yahoo.com.

PETERS, JEAN S., diversified financial services company executive; BS in Journalism, Northwestern U., Evanston, Ill. Bus. writer Louisville Courier-Jour., 1982—84; bus. editor Dayton Daily News/Jour. Herald, Ohio, 1984—86; asst. v.p. corp. comm. Capital Holding Corp., 1986—89, second v.p. investor rels., 1989—94; v.p. investor rels. Allmerica Fin. Corp., 1994—99; sr. v.p. investor rels. John Hancock Financial Services, Inc., 1999—2004; sr. v.p. investor rels. & corp. comm. Genworth Financial, Inc., 2004—07, sr. v.p. corp. comm. & external rels., 2007—. Bd. dirs. Nat. Investor Rels. Inst., Boston Chapter. Office: Genworth Financial Inc 6620 W Broad St Richmond VA 23230 Office Phone: 804-281-6000. Office Fax: 804-662-2414. Business E-Mail: jean.peters@genworth.com.

PETERS, KEVIN, consumer products company executive; BSBA, U. LaVerne; MBA, Northwestern U. Held positions (phys. distbn. ops., purchasing, inventory mgmt.) McMaster-Carr Supply Co.; v.p., supply chain and merchandising. Home Depot Inc., Toronto, v.p., gen. mgr., home depot comml. direct San Diego; v.p. inventory mgmt. W.W. Grainger Inc., sr. v.p. supply chain and merchandising, 2004—07; exec. v.p., supply chain & info. tech. Office Depot, Inc., 2007—10, pres., N.Am. retail, 2010—11, pres. No. America, 2011—. Office: Office Depot Inc 6600 N Military Trail Boca Raton FL 33496 Office Phone: 561-438-4800. Office Fax: 561-438-4001. Business E-Mail: Kevin.Peters@officedepot.com.

PETERS, RONALD GREGORY, state legislator; b. Tulsa, Sept. 28, 1944; s. Stanley Ray and Margie (Smith) Peters; m. Bonnie LaVerne Swenke, June 12, 1965; children: Gregory James, Ronda JoAnn. BBA, Tulsa U., 1966. Cert. in mgmt. Tulsa U., 1974. Market analyst Sunray DX Oil Co., Terre Haute, Ind., 1966; mgr. planning and analysis LP Gas Divsn., Tulsa, 1967, mktg. rsch. and economics analyst, 1968, mgr. sales promotion, 1969; sr. staff assoc. Sun Oil Co., Phila., 1970; mktg. rsch. coord. Cities Svc. Co., Tulsa, 1971—74, mgr. internal comm., 1974—81, mgr. policy devel., 1981—83, dir. govt. & industry affairs, 1983—86, dir. state rels., 1986, dir. govt. & pub. affairs, 1987—2005; pres. Relations, Inc.; mem. Dist. 70 Okla. House of Representatives, 2005—. Bd. dirs. Hospice Green Country; dr. coord. Tulsa Area United Way, 1977. Recipient Jefferson Fellow award, Rogers State U., Everyday Hero award, ARC (Tulsa chpt.), Dream Catcher award, Tulsa Cmty. Svc. Coun., Great Spirit award, March of Dimes, Guardian Angel award, Parent Child Ctr Tulsa, Marion Jacewitz award, State Interagency Child Abuse Prevention Task Force, 2003; named Editor of Yr. award, Am. Petroleum Inst., 1979. Mem.: Tinker Soc. Profl. Engrs. and Scientists (Cert. of Appreciation), Am. Mktg. Assn. (past pres. Tulsa chpt., Outstanding Svc. citation). Republican. Office: 2300 N Lincoln Blvd Rm 328 Oklahoma City OK 73105 also: 4432 S Atlanta Pl Tulsa OK 74105 Office Phone: 405-557-7359, 918-749-2658. E-mail: ronpeters@okhouse.gov.

PETERSEN, CATHERINE HOLLAND, lawyer; b. Norman, Okla., Apr. 24, 1951; d. John Hays and Helen Ann (Turner) Holland; m. James Frederick Petersen, June 26, 1973 (div.); children: T. Kyle, Lindsay Diane; m. Lester E.R. Doty, Apr. 17, 2004. BA, Hastings Coll., 1973; JD, Okla. U., 1976. Bar: Okla. 1976, U.S. Dist. Ct. (we. dist.) Okla. 1978. Legal intern, police legal advisor City of Norman, 1974-76; sole practice Norman, 1976-81; ptnr. Williams Petersen & Denny, Norman, 1981-82; pres. Petersen Assocs., Inc., Norman, 1982—2004; ptnr. Petersen, Henson & Meadows, PC, Norman, 2004—08, Petersen, Henson & Meadows, Pecore & Poet, PC Norman, 2008—. Adj. prof. Oklahoma City U. Coll. Law, 1982, U. Okla. Law Ctr., 1987; instr. continuing legal edn. U. Okla. Law Ctr., Norman, 1977, 79, 81, 83, 84, 86, 89-95; instr. Okla. Bar Assn., ABA, Am. Acad. Matrimonial Lawyers. Bd. dirs. United Way, Norman, 1978-84, pres., 1981; bd. dirs. Women's Resource Ctr., Norman, 1975-77, 82-84; mem. Jr. League, Norman, 1980-83, Norman Hosp. Aux., 1982-84; trustee 1st Presbyn. Ch., 1986-87. Named among Outstanding Okla. Women of 1980s, Women's Polit. Caucus, 1980, Outstanding Young Women of Am., 1981, 1983, named Best Lawyers in America, 1997-. Fellow Am. Acad. Matrimonial Lawyers (pres. Okla. chpt. 1990-91, bd. govs. 1991-95, 2010-2012, parliamentarian, 2011); mem. ABA (family law sect., faculty Family Law Inst. 1993-2007, 2009-), Cleveland County Bar Assn., Okla. Bar Assn. (chmn. family law sect. 1987-88), Phi Delta Phi. Republican. Office: PO Box 1243 314 E Comanche St Norman OK 73069-6009 Home: 5300 180 Noble OK 73068 Office Phone: 405-329-3307.

PETERSEN, CHAP, state legislator; b. Washington, Mar. 27, 1968; m. Sharon Petersen; children: Eva, Mary, Thomas. BA, Williams Coll.; JD, U. Va. Ptnr. Surovell, Markle, Issacs, & Levy PLC; mem. Fairfax City Coun., 1998—2001, Va. House of Delegates, 2002—05; mem. Dist. 34 Va. State Senate, 2008—. Democrat. Office: PO Box 1066 Fairfax VA 22038 also: Senate of Virginia PO Box 396 Richmond VA 23218 Office Phone: 703-349-3361, 804-698-7534. Office Fax: 800-635-9417, 804-698-7651. E-mail: district34@senate.virginia.gov.

PETERSON, BUZZ (ROBERT BOWER PETERSON), men's college basketball coach; b. Asheville, NC, May 17, 1963; m. Jan Peterson; children: Nicole, Olivia, Rob. BA in Geography, U. NC, Chapel Hill, 1985. Asst. coach Appalachian State U. Mountaineers, 1987—89, head basketball coach, 1996—2000, 2009—10; asst. coach East Tenn. State U. Buccaneers, 1989—90, NC State U. Wolfpack, 1990—93, Vanderbilt U. Commodores, 1993—96; head basketball coach U. Tulsa Golden Hurricane, U. Tenn. Volunteers, 2001—05, Coastal Carolina U. Chanticleers, 2005—07; dir. player pers. Charlotte Bobcats, 2007—09; head basketball coach U. NC Wilmington Seahawks, 2010—. Named So. Conf. Coach of Yr., 1998, 2000. Achievements include member of NCAA Final Four national championship winning University of North Carolina Tar Heels, 1982; head coach of National Invitational Tournament championship winning Tulsa University Golden Hurricane, 2001. Office: University NC Wilmington Basketball Program 601 S College Rd Wilmington NC 28403-3297 Office Phone: 910-962-3045. Business E-Mail: buzz@uncw.edu.

PETERSON, COLEMAN HOLLIS, consulting firm executive, retired retail executive; b. Birmingham, Ala., Apr. 6, 1948; s. George Bell and Doris Mae (Wilson) P.; m. Shirley Ann Hardy, May 31, 1975; children: Rana, Collin. BA in English Lit., Loyola U., Chgo., 1972, MS in Indsl. Rels., 1977. Mgmt. trainee Osco Drug, Inc., Oakbrook, Ill., 1972-74, coll. recruiter, 1974-75, dir. coll. recruiting, 1975-77, mgr. recruit and devel., 1977-78, dist. personnel officer, 1978-79; regional personnel mgr. Venture Stores, Inc., Chgo., 1979-82, v.p. orgn. devel. O'Fallon, Mo., 1982-84, sr. v.p. human resources, 1984—94; exec. v.p., human div. Wal-Mart Stores, Inc., Bentonville, Ark., 1994—2004; founder, pres., CEO Hollis Enterprises, LLC, 2004—. Bd. dirs. J.B. Hunt Transport Services, Inc., 2004—, The ServiceMaster Co., 2004—07, Build-A-Bear Workshop, Inc., 2005—, Cracker Barrel Old Country Store, Inc., 2011—. Bd. mem. Urban League Met. St. Louis, United Way Greater St. Louis; bd trustees Northwest Ark. Cmty. Coll. Recipient Meritorious Svc. award United Negro Coll. Fund, St. Louis, 1986, Award for Profl. Excellence Soc. for Human Resources Mgmt., Martin Luther King Lifetime Achievement award Northwest Ark. MLK Planning Com., 2007, Volunteer of the Yr. award U. Ark., 2007, Nat. Assn. African Americans in Human Resources Professionals Trail Blazer award, 2008, Lifetime Achievement award Ark. Soc. for Human Resources Mgmt. State Coun., 2008 Mem. Kappa Alpha Psi (life), Nat. Coun. La Raza; fellow Nat Acad. Human Resources Avocations: jogging, creative writing, music. Office: Hollis Enterprises LLC 44 Gull Point Hilton Head Island SC 29928 Office Phone: 843-671-7442. Office Fax: 843-671-7444. E-mail: chp@hollisent.com.

PETERSON, DAVID FREDERICK, retired government agency administrator; b. Washington, Apr. 4, 1937; s. Victor Henry and Alice Augusta (Vogle) P.; m. Laurie A. Cadigan, June 11, 1988. AB, Harvard U., 1959; LL.B., Cornell U., 1962. Bar: D.C. 1963. With Metromedia Inc., NYC and Los Angeles, 1963—70; exec. dir. consumer info. ctr. GSA, Washington, 1970—76, dir. consumer affairs, 1976—82, assoc. archivist for mgmt. Nat. Archives and Records Service, 1982—83; asst. archivist for Fed. Records Ctrs. Nat. Archives and Records Adminstrn., Washington, 1983—96; asst. archivist Presdl. Librs., 1996—2001; ret., 2001. Served with U.S. Army, 1963 Home: 2730 NE Sewalls Landing Way Jensen Beach FL 34957 Personal E-mail: lcdfpeterson@aol.com.

PETERSON, EDWARD ADRIAN, lawyer; b. St. Louis, May 19, 1941; s. Adrian J. and Virginia (Hamlin) P.; m. Catherine Frances Younghouse, Dec. 17, 1960; children: Kristin, Kendra. BSBA, Washington U., St. Louis, 1963; LLB, So. Methodist U., 1966. Bar: Tex. 1966, U.S. Dist. Ct. (no. and so. dists.) Tex. Instr. bus. law and acctg. Midwestern U., Wichita Falls, Tex., 1966-67; assoc. Schenk & Wesbrooks, Wichita Falls, 1966-67, Newman & Pickering, Dallas, 1967-72; ptnr. Moore & Peterson, Dallas, 1972-89, Winstead PC, Dallas, 1989—. Spkr. in field. Contbr. articles to legal jours. Bd. dirs. Leukemia Soc., 1970-71, North Tex. Commn., 1992-96, South Dallas/Fair Park Trust Fund, 1992, Tex. Ch. Extension Fund, Tex. Dist., Tex. Dist. Luth. Ch. Mo. Synod., 2002-07, Dallas Luth. Sch., 2007—10. Fellow Am. Coll. Real Estate Lawyers (title ins. com., common interest com.), Am. Coll. Mortgage Attys., Tex. Bar Found. (life), Dallas Bar Found., Coll. State Bar Tex.; mem. ABA, State Bar Tex., Dallas Bar Assn., Phi Alpha Delta, Sigma Alpha Epsilon. Lutheran. Home: 131 Hilton Head Island Dr Mabank TX 75156 also: 3701 Turtle Creek Blvd Dallas TX 75219 Office: Winstead PC 500 Winstead Bldg 2728 N Harwood Dallas TX 75201 Office Phone: 214-745-5642. Business E-Mail: epeterson@winstead.com.

PETERSON, ERIC V., retail executive; BA in Bus., Calif. State U., Sacramento, 1971; degree in Bus. Adminstrn., Sacramento State Coll. Sr. v.p. Diamond Internat.; joined Home Depot, Inc., 1993, various positions, regional mdse. mgr., dist. mgr., mcht., divisional merchandising mgr., v.p., merchandising Canada, regional v.p., ops., South Atlantic Region, sr. v.p., merchandising svcs., pres., NW divsn., 2003, pres., strategic market stores, 2003—06, sr. v.p., lumber and bldg. materials, 2006—07, sr. v.p., merchandising bldg. materials, 2007—11. Office: The Home Depot Inc 2455 Paces Ferry Rd NW Atlanta GA 30339 Office Phone: 770-433-8211. Office Fax: 770-384-2356. Business E-Mail: Eric_Peterson@homedepot.com.

PETERSON, GEORGE P. (BUD PETERSON), academic administrator; b. Prairie Village, Kans. BS in Mech. Engring. and Math., Kans. State U., 1975, MS in Engring., 1980; PhD, Tex. A&M U., 1985. Engring. prof. Tex. A&M U., College Station, 1981—2000; provost Rensselaer Poly. Inst., Troy, NY, 2000—06; chancellor U. Colo., Boulder, 2006—09; pres. Ga. Inst. Tech., 2009—. Mem. Nat. Sci. Bd., NSF, 2008—. Editor: Jour. Exptl. Thermal and Fluid Scis.; assoc. editor: ASME Jour. Heat Transfer, AIAA Jour. Thermophysics and Heat Transfer, Internat. Jour. Heat and Fluid Flow, Microscale Thermophysical Engring.; contbr. articles to profl. jours. Recipient Best Paper award, AIAA, 1990, award for outstanding mgmt., NSF, 1994, Ralph James and the O. L. (Andy) Lewis awards, ASME, Dow Outstanding Young Faculty award, ASEE, Pi Tau Sigma Gustus L. Larson Meml. award, ASME, Thermophysics award, AIAA, Meml. award, ASME, Sustained Svc. award, AIAA; fellow, Tex. Engring. Expt. Sta., 1986, 1988; sr. fellow, 1989. Fellow: Am. Inst. of Aeronautics and Astronautics, Am. Soc. of Mech. Engrs.; mem.: Phi Kappa Phi, Sigma Xi, Tau Beta Pi, Pi Tau Sigma. Office: Georgia Institute of Technology Office of President 225 N Ave NW Carnegie Bldg Atlanta GA 30332 E-mail: bud.peterson@gatech.edu.*

PETERSON, KAREN CARTER, state legislator, political organization administrator; b. New Orleans, Nov. 1, 1969; BBA, Howard U.; attended, U. Va. Law, Boston Coll. Law Sch.; JD, Tulane Law Sch. Atty.; mem. Dist. 93 La. House of Reps., 1999—2010, spkr. pro tempore, 2008—10; mem. Dist. 5 La. State Senate, 2010—; chair La. Dem. Party, 2012—. Democrat. Office: Capitol Office PO Box 94183 Baton Rouge LA 70804 also: 1010 Common St Ste 2510 New Orleans LA 70112 Office Phone: 504-568-8346, 225-342-6945. Office Fax: 504-568-8405. E-mail: lare093@legis.state.la.us.*

PETERSON, MARK F., business educator; b. Phila., May 23, 1953; s. Eugene F. Jr. Peterson, June R. Peterson; m. Susan M. Mende; children: Janice M., Daniel F. BA, Duke U., 1975; PhD, U. Mich., 1979. Prof. mgmt. U. Miami, 1980—85, Tex. Tech. U., Lubbock, 1985—96, Fla. Atlantic U., Boca Raton, 1996—, Internet Coast Adams prof. mgmt., 2000—06. John R. Galvin vis. prof. Fletcher Sch. Law and Diplomacy, Tufts U., 2002—03; Hofstede chair cultural diversity U. Maastricht, Netherlands, 2006—; vis. rsch. prof. Aarhus U., 2010; vis. prof. Peking U., 2011. Author: Cross Cultural Management: Essential Concepts, 2nd edit., 2014; editor: Handbook of Organizational Culture and Climate, 2001 (Outstanding Academic Title, ALA, 2001), 2nd edit., 2011, Handbook of Cross Cultural Management Research, 2008, Foundations of Cross Cultural Management Research, 2008; assoc. editor Jour. Orgnl. Behavior, 2001—, Jour. Internat. Bus. Studies, 2004—. Fulbright fellowship, Osaka U., Japan, 1996, McMaster U., Can., 2008. Mem.: Internat. Assn. Cross Cultural Psychology, Acad. Internat. Bus., Acad. Mgmt. Presbyterian. Office: Fla Atlantic U Coll Bus Dept Mgmt Boca Raton FL 33431 Office Phone: 561-297-3669. Business E-Mail: mpeterso@fau.edu.*

PETERSON, MARK W., janitorial service company executive; BS in Econ., Augustana Coll., Rock Island, Ill., 1972. Various positions, including investment banking, risk mgmt., treasury KPMG Peat Marwick, Enron Corp., First City Nat. Bank Houston, Continental Bank; v.p., asst. treas. Sprint; v.p. Cin. Bell, Inc., treas., 1999—2007; sr. v.p., treas. The ServiceMaster Co. Mem.: Nat. Assn. Corp Treasurers (bd. dirs. 2004—05). Office: The ServiceMaster Co 860 Ridge Lake Blvd Memphis TN 38120 Office Phone: 901-597-1400. Office Fax: 630-663-2001. Business E-Mail: Mark.Peterson@servicemaster.com.

PETERSON, PAM, state legislator; b. NYC, June 28, 1955; m. Paul Peterson; children: Matthew, Audra. BA in Communications, Oral Roberts Univ., 1977. TV spokesperson, assoc. TV producer; former Tulsa County Republican Chmn.; former 1st Congressional Dist. vice-chmn. for Republican Party; mem. Dist. 67 Okla. House of Representatives, 2005—, majority whip, 2005—06. Republican. Mailing: 6528 E 101st PMB 422 Tulsa OK 74133 Office: 2300 N Lincoln Blvd Rm 303 Oklahoma City OK 73105 Office Phone: 405-557-7341. E-mail: pampeterson@okhouse.gov.

PETERSON, ROGER, community bank executive, retired international investment banker, manufacturing executive, air force general; b. Chgo., June 7, 1929; s. Milton Albert and LaVergne P.; m. Sally Ann Alder, Apr. 25, 1952; children: Bruce Roger, Dale Alder, Drew Alan. BS in Acctg., UCLA, 1955; MS in Mgmt., U. Colo., 1964; grad., Air Command and Staff Coll. Air U., Ala., 1965; grad. Exec. Program for Internat. and Nat. Security, J.F. Kennedy Sch. Govt., Harvard U., Cambridge, Mass., 1983. Cert. in indsl. engring. Exec. Program, Calif. Inst. Tech., 1984. Joined USAF, 1950, advanced through grades to maj. gen., 1981, pilot, 1956-61, mgr. tactical missile site constrn., 1961; air officer comdg. 11th Cadet Squadron, Air Force Cadet Wing USAF Acad., 1961-64; asst. sec. Joint Chiefs of Staff and NSC matters for Hdqrs. Pentagon, 1965-68; transport pilot USAF, Vietnam, 1968, asst. chmn. US-Japan Joint Com., Adminstrn. of US Japan Status of Forces Agreement, 1968-73, chief program cost, dir. budget, 1973-76, chief plans, comptroller of Air Force, 1976-78, dir. mgmt. analysis, 1978-79, dir. programs, asst. chief of staff for research and devel., 1979-81; asst. dir. plans, policies and programs Def. Logistics Agy., Alexandria, Va., 1981-82, dep. dir., 1982-83; asst. dep. chief staff for logistics and engring. Hdqrs. USAF, Washington, 1983-84; pres., chief exec. officer advanced tech. rsch. & devel. firm, 1984—85; strategic planner United Techs. Corp., 1985-88; v.p., chief oper. officer Sikorsky Support Svcs. Inc., 1988-90; exec. asst. to mng. ptnr. O'Connor & Assocs., 1990-92; mng. dir. global ops. and svcs. Swiss Bank Corp., Zurich, 1992-96, chief of staff Chgo., 1996-99, br. mgr. Chgo. N.Am. and S.Am., 1996-99; mng. dir. UBS A.G. (formerly Swiss Bank Corp.), NY, 1996-99, UBS AG, NYC, 1999—2001, br. mgr., Resolved Holocaust Issue Between Swiss Banks NY State Banking Commn.; mng. dir. mktg. and strategic planning SunSouth Bank, Dothan, Ala., 2002—. Decorated D.S.M., Legion of Merit, Air medal with oak leaf cluster, Joint Service Commendation medal, Air Force Commendation medal with two oak leaf clusters. Mem. Air Force Assn., Beta Gamma Sigma, Sigma Iota Epsilon. Presbyterian. Achievements include designing and negotiating consolidation of US Air Force bases in Tokyo, 1970-73; negotiating mil. and civil aviation agreement for return of Okinawa to Japan; created global bus. mgmt. system for Swiss Bank Corp. resolved Holocaust Issues with Swiss Banks And NY State Banking Commission. Home: 1602 Deerpath Rd Dothan AL 36303-2173 Office: SunSouth Bank 108 Jamestown Blvd Dothan AL 36302 Business E-Mail: rpeterson@sunsouthbank.com.

PETERSON, SUSAN, political science professor, dean; d. Phillip (Stepfather) and Janet Chalke, Jack Peterson; life ptnr. Heather Scully; 1 child, Norah. BA, St. Lawrence U., Canton, NY, 1983; PhD, Columbia U., NYC, 1992. Vis. asst. prof. govt. Smith Coll., Northampton, Mass., 1991—93; vis. asst. prof. Sch. Internat. Rels. U. So. Calif., LA, 1993—94; asst. prof. govt. Coll. William and Mary, Williamsburg, Va., 1994—98, assoc. prof. govt., 1998—2004, prof. govt., 2004—, dean ednl. policy arts and scis., 2005—07, dean under grad. studies, 2007—; prof. govt. Wendy Emery Reves Internat. Relations. Exec. editor Security Studies, 2003—05, editor-in-chief, 2005—06. Author: Crisis Bargaining and the State: The Domestic Politics of International Conflict; co-editor: Altered States: International Relations, Domestic Politics, and Institutional Change; contbr. articles to profl. jours. Mem. Peninsula AIDS Found., Newport News, Va., 1997—2000, Our Own Cmty. News, Norfolk, Va., 1997—98; chair Williamsburg AIDS Network, 1998—2000. Recipient Outstanding Internat. Studies Faculty award, Coll. of William and Mary, 2002, 2003; Nat. Security fellow, John M. Olin Inst. Strategic Studies Harvard U., 1989—91, Dwight Eisenhower/ Clifford Roberts fellow, World Affairs Inst., 1990—91. Mem.: Women in Internat. Security, Am. Polit. Sci. Assn., Internat. Studies Assn. Unitarian Universalism. Home: 112 Barrows Mount Williamsburg VA 23185 Office: Coll William and Mary 127 Ewell Hall Williamsburg VA 23187-8795 Office Fax: 757-221-2464. Business E-Mail: smpete@wm.edu.

PETES, THOMAS DOUGLAS, geneticist, educator; b. Washington, Mar. 27, 1947; s. Joseph and Helen Barbera Petes; m. Rosann Farber, July 20, 1974; children: Laura Christine, Diana Elizabeth. BS in Biology, Brown U., Providence, RI, 1969; Phd in Genetics, U. Washington, 1973. Postdoc rsch. assoc. Nat. Inst. Med. Rsch., London, 1973—75, MIT, Cambridge, 1975—77; prof. U. Chgo., 1977—88, U. NC, Chapel Hill, 1988—2004, Duke U. Sch. Medicine, Durham, NC, 2004—, chair, 2004—. V.p. to pres. Genetics Soc. of Am., Rockville, Md., 2001—02. Named Minnie Geller Prof. Rsch. in Genetics, Duke U. Sch. Medicine, 2006—; named one of Kenan Disting. Prof., U. NC, 2002—05. Mem.: AAAS, Genetics Soc. of Am. (v.p. to pres. 2001—02). Democrat. Achievements include research in the mechanisms of recombination and DNA repair. Avocations: running, travel. Office: Duke Univ Sch Medicine Box 3054 Durham NC 27710

PETIT, PARKER HOLMES, investment company executive; b. Decatur, Ga., Aug. 4, 1939; s. James Percival and Ethel (Holmes) P.; m. Janet Lewis; children: William Wright, Patricia Monique, Meredith Katherine. BS in Mech. Engring., Ga. Inst. Tech., 1962, MS in Engring. Mechanics, 1964; MBA, Ga. State U., 1973. Engr. Gen. Dynamics Corp., Fort Worth, Tex., 1966-67; engring. project mgr. Lockheed-Ga. Co., Marietta, 1967-71; pres., founder, CEO Healthdyne, Inc., Marietta, 1971—2008; founder, pres. The Petit Group, Roswell, Ga., 2008—. Bd. dirs. Atlantic S.E. Airlines, Atlanta, Healthdyne Technologies, Inc., Atlanta, Healthdyne Info. Enterprises, Inc., Marietta, Ga., Matria Healthcare, Inc., Marietta, Logility Corp., Atlanta, Intelligent Sys., Norcross, Ga. Author: Primer on Composite Materials, 1968; patentee in field Chmn. bd. dirs. Sudden Infant Death Syndrome Alliance, Washington, 1986; active nat. adv. coun. Emory U. Med. Sch., Coun. fellows for the Emory, Ga. Tech. Biomed. Tech. Rsch. Ctr.; bd. dirs. Ga. Rsch. Alliance, 1995. 1st lt. U.S. Army, 1964-67. Recipient Humanitarian award La Societe Francaise de Bienfaisance, 1981; named Ga. Tech. Acad. Disting. Alumni, 1994; named to Tech. Hall of Fame Ga., 1994, Ga. State Bus. Sch. Hall of Fame, 2007; Internat. Bus. fellow, 1986. Mem. NAE, Health Industry Mfrs. Assn., Cobb County C. of C. (bd. dirs. 1980-82), Atlanta C. of C. (bd. dirs. 1997—), Pi Kappa Phi. Republican. Methodist. Avocations: flying, painting, golf, tennis. Office: The Petit Group 3550 George Busbee Pkwy NW Ste 175 Kennesaw GA 30144-5428 Office Phone: 770-650-7570. Office Fax: 770-650-7569. Business E-Mail: pete.petit@thepetitgroup.com.

PETITT, ANTHONY B., corporate financial executive; BS in Accountancy cum laude, Wake Forest U., 1993. CPA. Mgr. Arthur Andersen LLP., 1993—2002; dir., acctg. ops. Watkins Motor Lines, Inc., 2002—05; v.p., chief acctg. officer Kforce Inc., 2005—07; asst. corp. contr. Whirlpool Corp., 2007—08, v.p., contr., chief acctg. officer, 2008—10, Lorillard, Inc., 2010—. Office: Lorillard Inc 714 Green Valley Rd Greensboro NC 27408-7018 Office Phone: 336-335-7000. Office Fax: 336-335-7550. Business E-Mail: apetitt@lorillard.com.

PETRANEK, STEPHEN LYNN, editor; b. Wash., Aug. 19, 1944; s. Chester J. and Mabel Oleta (Mercer) P. Student, U. Okla., Norman, 1962-63; BS, U. Md., 1970; postgrad., U. Mo., Columbia, 1971. Editor-in-chief The Diamondback, U. Md., 1969-70; reporter Democrat and Chronicle, Rochester, NY, 1972, financial writer, 1972-73, asst. Sunday editor, 1973; editor Upstate mag., 1974—77; editor-in-chief Tropic Mag. The Miami Herald, 1977-78; dep. editor The Washington Post Mag., 1978-81, mng. editor, 1982-90; sr. editor LIFE mag., 1990-96; editor-in-chief This Old House mag., 1996—99, Discover mag., 1999—2006, editor-at-large, 2006—07; group editor-in-chief Weider History Mags., 2006—. Author: newspaper series Decline and Fall of Stirling Homex, 1972. Recipient John Hancock award for fin. writing, 1972, Bus. Journalism award U. Mo., 1973, Frank Tripp Newswriting award, 1973; finalist Nat. Mag. award, 1997, 2000, 03. Mem. Sigma Delta Chi, Kappa Tau Alpha, Omicron Delta Kappa, Pi Delta Epsilon. Mem. United Ch. of Christ. Office: 741 Miller Dr SE Ste D-2 Leesburg VA 20175 Home: 4110 Ruckle St Indianapolis IN 46205-2721 Office Phone: 703-779-8389. Business E-Mail: steve@weiderhistorygroup.com.

PETRANOVA, LUDMILA, electric power industry executive; Undergraduate in Nuclear & Phys. Engring., Czech Tech. U. Dir., econ. fin., sec. & gen. mgr. CEPS, Czech Republic, CEO, mem. exec. bd., 2002—09; dir. gen. Lumen Energy Corp.; chmn. Lumen Energy A.S., 2009—. Mem.: Internat. Assn. Energy Econ. Office: Lumen Energy Corp 20 E 5th S Tulsa OK 74103 Office Phone: 918-764-0204.

PETRICK, MICHAEL JOSEPH, journalism educator; b. Antigo, Wis., Sept. 6, 1942; BS, U. Wis., Milw., 1965, MS, 1967; PhD, U. Wis., Madison, 1970. News editor Milw. South Times Star, 1966-67; disting. teaching fellow U. Wis., Madison, 1969-70; from asst. to assoc. prof. U. Md., College Park, 1970-78; copy editor Evening Star, Washington, 1974-75; chairperson dept. journalism Ctrl. Mich. U., Mt. Pleasant, 1978-84, prof., 1984-2000, prof. emeritus, 2000—. Writing and editing coach Ctrl. Mich. Newspapers, 1984-85; writing and reporting coach Greenville (Mich.) Daily News, 1997-99; chair bd. in control of student media Ctrl. Mich. U., 1997-99 Co-author: Using the Mass Media, 1975; contbr. articles to profl. jours Named to Ctrl. Mich. Jour. Hall of Fame, 2006. Mem. Md.-Del.-D.C. Press Assn. (chmn. freedom of info. com. 1972-73), Soc. Profl. Journalists (campus chpt. adviser 1970-99), Nat. Coun. Editl. Writers, Assn. for Edn. in Journalism and Mass Communication Home: 4930 Swiss Ave Dallas TX 75214-5234 Business E-Mail: michael.petrick@cmich.edu.

PETRIE, WILLIAM MARSHALL, psychiatrist; b. Louisville, Oct. 19, 1946; s. Garner McReynolds and Claire (Samuels) P.; children: Christopher W., Ellen P. Edwards, Shelley P. Serafin; m. Lori L. Molchin, Oct. 1, 1994; 1 child, Halle C. BA, Vanderbilt U., 1968, MD, 1972. Research psychiatrist NIMH, Rockville, Md., 1975-77; asst. prof. dept. psychiatry Vanderbilt Med. Ctr., Nashville, 1977-81, assoc. prof., 1981-82, assoc. clin. prof., 1982-87, clin. prof., 1992—, prof. clin. psychiatry, dir. geriat. psychiatry, 2011; pvt. practice psychiatry Psychiat. Cons., P.C., Nashville, 1982—, pres., 1996—; med. dir. Pavtham Pavilian, 2007—08, Rolling Hills Hosp., 2009—11; prof. clin. psychiatry Vanderbilt Med. Ctr., 2011—. Bd. dirs Psychiat. Solutions, Inc.; clin. instr. Georgetown U. Med. Ctr., 1975—77; cons. psychopharmacology rsch. br. NIMH, 1977—80; rschr. in geriatric psychopharmacology; med. dir. memory Study Ctr., 1987—; chmn. of psychiatry Parthenon Pavilion, 1994—96; bd. trustees Centennial Mutual Ctr., 1994—2000, vice-chmn. bd. trustees, 1998—2000; pres. Columbia Psychiat. Care Network, 1997—98, Psychiat. Cons., PC, 1999—2005; med. dir. Parthenon Pavilion, 2007—, Rolling Hills Hosp., 2009—11; bd. dirs. Acadia Health Care, 2012—. Mem. editl. bd. Audio Digest Psychiatry, 1996-99, editl. bd. mem.; contbr. articles to profl. jours.; chpts. to books. Named US News Top Doctors, 2012—13. Fellow Am. Psychiat. Assn. (disting. fellow, pres. mid. Tenn. dist. br. 1986-87); mem. AMA, Tenn. Med. Assn., Am. Assn. Geriatric Psychiatrists, Am. Coll. Psychiatrists, Tenn. Psychiat. Assn. (pres. 1999-2000). Democrat. Methodist. Office Phone: 615-936-3555. Business E-Mail: william.petrie@vanderbitt.edu.

PETRIK, MICHAEL THOMAS, lawyer; b. Chgo., Jan. 13, 1957; s. Thomas J. and Bette J. (Sarich) P.; m. Susan Renée Prince, June 2, 1979; children: Michael Ray, Stephanie Renée. BS in Bus. Mgmt., Ea. Ill. U., 1979, BA in Econs., 1979; JD, Duke U., 1983. Bar: Ga. 1983, US Tax Ct. 1985. Assoc. Alston & Bird LLP, Atlanta, 1983—90, ptnr., 1991—, leader state and local tax group. Instr. constnl. law and tax, Atlanta Law Sch., 1984-92, state and local tax law, Ga. State U., 1992-98; tech. cons. Sales and Use Tax Alert, 1991-92. Edit. adv. bd.: State Income Tax Alert, 1991—, Ga. corr. State Tax Notes, Arlington, Va., 1990-97, Interstate Tax Rep., 1996—, Corp. Bus. Taxation Monthly, 1999-; contbr. articles to profl. jours. Mem. United Way, Atlanta, 1984-90, bd. dirs. 1995-04; mem. Met. Atlanta Mentoring Coun., 1992-95, One-to-one Atlanta Leadership Coun., 1993-96; St. Joseph's Mercy Found. Leadership Coun., 2005-; bd. adv. United Way 211, 1992-03, chair; bd. advisors St. Pius Catholic HS, 2004-; Big Bros./Big Sisters, Atlanta, 2004-; United Way Pub. Policy Com.,2006-; United Way Cmty. Impact Coun., Atlanta, 2006-; active Vol. DeKalb, Atlanta, 1984-86; bd. dirs. Arrive Alive, Inc., Atlanta, 1987-91; bd. dirs. Duke Law Alumni Assn., 2005-; Delta Sigma Phi Found., 2006-; bd. trustees Brother Rice HS, Chgo., 2006-; trustee Lawyers Comm. Civil Rights, 2001-, United Way Pub. Policy Com., 2007-; bd. of trustees Vasser Woolley Found., 2002-, Leadership Atlanta, 2001-, chair, 2004-05; adv. bd. The Salvation Army of Metro Atlanta, 2007-, Ga. C. of C. Tax Com., 2008-. Mem. KC, Ga. Bar Assn. (state coun. 1983—), Atlanta Bar Assn., Federalist Soc., St. Thomas More Soc., Serra Internat., Commerce Club, Delta Mu Delta, Omicron Delta Epsilon, Ga. C. of C. Tax Cmty. Roman Catholic. Avocations: religion, literature, music. Office: Alston & Bird LLP 1201 W Peachtree St One Atlantic Ctr Atlanta GA 30309-3424 Office Phone: 404-881-7479. Office Fax: 404-253-8784. Business E-Mail: mike.petrik@alston.com.

PETRINO, BOBBY (ROBERT PATRICK PETRINO), college football coach; b. Lewistown, Mont., Mar. 10, 1961; m. Becky Schaff; children: Kelsey, Nick, Bobby, Katie. BS in Math & Phys. Edn., Carroll Coll., Helena, Mont., 1983. Grad. asst. Carroll Coll. Fighting Saints, 1983, offensive coord., 1985—86; grad. asst. Weber State U. Wildcats, Utah, 1984, wide receiver, tight ends coach, 1987—88; quarterbacks coach U. Idaho Vandals, 1989, offensive coord., 1990—91; quarterbacks coach Ariz. State U. Sun Devils, 1992—93; offensive coord. U. Nev. Wolf Pack, 1994, Utah State U. Aggies, 1995—97, U. Louisville Cardinals, 1998; quarterbacks coach Jacksonville Jaguars, 1999—2000, offensive coord., 2001, Auburn U. Tigers, 2002; head coach U. Louisville Cardinals, 2003—06, 2014—, Atlanta Falcons, Flowery Branch, Ga., 2007, U. Ark. Razorbacks, Fayetteville, 2008—12, Western Ky. U. Hilltoppers, Bowling Green, 2013. Office: Louisville Cardinals c/o Athletics Dept SAC Bldg 2100 S Floyd St Louisville KY 40292 Office Phone: 270-745-0111.*

PETROSKI, HENRY, engineering educator, writer; b. NYC, Feb. 6, 1942; s. Henry and Victoria Petroski; m. Catherine, July 15, 1966; children: Karen, Stephen. B Mech. Engring., Manhattan Coll., Riverdale, NY, 1963, DP (hon.), 2003; MS, U. Ill., 1964, PhD, 1968; DSc (hon.), Clarkson U., Potsdam, NY, 1990; DHL (hon.), Trinity Coll., Hartford, Conn., 1997; DSc (hon.), Valparaiso U., Ind., 1999. Registered profl. engr., Tex.; chartered engr., Inst. of Engrs. of Ireland. Instr. U. Ill., Urbana, 1965-68; asst. prof. U. Tex., Austin, 1968-74; engr. Argonne Nat. Lab., Ill., 1975-80; assoc. prof. civil engring. Duke U., Durham, NC, 1980-87, prof., 1987-93, Aleksandar S. Vesic prof., 1993—, prof. history, 1995—, chmn. dept. civil and environ. engring., 1991-2000, dir. grad. studies, 1981-86. Author: To Engineer is Human, 1985, Beyond Engineering, 1986, The Pencil, 1990, The Evolution of Useful Things, 1992, Design Paradigms, 1994 (Best Book award in engring., Am. Assn. U. Presses, 1994), Engineers of Dreams, 1995, Invention by Design, 1996, Remaking the World, 1997, The Book on the Bookshelf, 1999, Paperboy, 2002, Small Things Considered, 2003, Pushing the Limits, 2004, Success Through Failure, 2006, The Toothpick, 2007, The Essential Engineer, 2010, (documentary) To Engineer is Human, 1987; columnist: Am. Scientist, 1991—, ASEE Prism, 2000—. Fellow NEH, 1987-88, Nat. Humanities Ctr., 1987-88, Guggenheim fellow, 1990-91; recipient Outstanding Engring. Grad. award Manhattan Coll., 1992, Alumni award for disting. svc. Coll. Engring. U. Ill. at Urbana-Champaign, 1994, Washington award Western Soc. Engrs., 2006, Disting. Svc. award Engring. Alumni Assn. Duke U., 2007. Fellow ASME (Ralph Coats Roe medal 1991), Am. Acad. Arts and Sci., Am. Philos. Soc., Inst. Engrs. Ireland, NAE, Soc. History Tech., The Moles (hon.), Sigma Xi, Tau Beta Pi; mem. ASCE (disting. mem., Civil Engring. History and Heritage award 1993). Office: Duke U Sch Engring PO Box 90287 Durham NC 27708-0287 Office Phone: 919-660-5203. Business E-Mail: petroski@duke.edu.

PETROVICH, DUSHAN, food products executive; b. Chgo. BA in Economics, Knox Coll.; M in Acctg. Sci., Roosevelt U.; grad. Exec. Program, U. Mich. CPA. Adj. prof., MBA Program Dominican U.; pres. Wrigley Found.; first officer, leader, orgnl. devel. Wm. Wrigley Jr. Co. (subs. of Mars, Inc.), various positions, fin. dept., 1975, treas., 1992—93, v.p., 1993—99, contr., 1996—99, v.p., orgnl. devel., 1999—2000, sr. v.p., people, learning & devel., 2001—04, sr. v.p., chief adminstrv. officer, 2004—08, pres., 2008—; pres., Wrigley Gum & Confections Mars, Inc., 2008—. Mem., Belgrade Com. Chicago's Sister Cities; bd. dirs. Chicago Shakespeare Theater, Nat. Found. For The Improvement of Edn.; bd. trustee Adler Planetarium, Knox Coll., Galesburg, Ill., 2005-. Office: Mars Inc 6885 Elm St Mc Lean VA 22101 Office Phone: 703-821-4900. Office Fax: 703-448-9678. Business E-Mail: dushan.petrovich@mars.com.

PETROVICH, NEAL A., corporate financial executive; Grad., U. Va., ABA Grad. Sch. Bank Investments & Fin. Mgmt.; BBA with honors, James Madison U. CPA. Exec. v.p., CFO Bank of Tidewater, 1995—2002; fin. officer Southtrust Bank, Va., sr. v.p., 2002—04; various positions, including sr. v.p., CFO, treas., prin. acctg. officer and sec. Am. Nat. Bankshares, Inc.; cashier Am. Nat. Bank and Trust Co. (subs. Am. Nat. Bankshares, Inc.), 2004—05, sr. v.p., CFO through prin. acctg. officer, treas. and sec., 2004—09, exec. v.p., 2005—09; exec. v.p., CFO Hampton Roads Bankshares, Inc., 2009—10. Office: Hampton Roads Bankshares Inc 999 Waterside Dr Ste 200 Norfolk VA 23510 Office Phone: 757-217-1000. Office Fax: 757-217-3656.

PETROVICH, STEPHEN CHRISTOPHER, lawyer; b. Kirkwood, Mo., Apr. 25, 1966; s. John Paul and Mardo Catherine (Wonder) P.; m. Emilie Melissa Koers, May 16, 1992; 3 children BA, DePauw U., 1988; JD, U. Ga. Sch. Law, 1991. Bar: Ga. 1991. Summer assoc. Morris, Manning & Martin LLP, 1990; law clk. to Hon. Harold L. Murphy US Dist. Ct. (northern dist.) Ga., 1991-93; assoc. Nelson,

Mullins, Riley & Scarborough, Atlanta, 1993-95, Kelly Law Firm, PLLC, Atlanta, 1995—97; litigation counsel Charter Behavioral Health Systems, 1997—2000; sr. v.p., gen. counsel, sec. AHS Medical Holdings LLC, Nashville, 2000. Author: DNA Fingerprinting: A Rush to Judgement, 1990; exec. notes editor Ga. Law Rev., 1991. Office: AHS Medical Holdings LLC 1 Burton Hills Blvd Nashville TN 37215 Office Phone: 615-296-3000.

PETTERSSON, CARL, professional golfer; b. Gothenburg, Sweden, Aug. 29, 1977; s. Lars Pettersson; m. DeAnna Pettersson, 2003; children: Carlie, Chase. Grad., NC State U., Raleigh. Profl. golfer, 2000—; mem. World Cup team, 2002, 2006. Mem. bd. dirs. Wyndham Championship, 2008. Achievements include winning European Tour events: Algarve Open Portugal, 2002; winning PGA Tour events: Chrysler Championship, 2005, Memorial Tournament, 2006, Wyndham Championship, 2008, RBC Canadian Open, 2010, RBC Heritage, 2012. Office: PGA Tour 100 PGA Tour Blvd Ponte Vedra FL 32082

PETTEWAY, SAMUEL BRUCE, college president; b. Fayetteville, NC, July 18, 1924; s. Walter Bernard and Margaret Maysie (Cole) P.; m. Eleanor Glenn Sugg, Nov. 27, 1948; children— Margaret Petteway Small, Samuel Bruce. BS, N.C. State U., 1949, MEd, 1966, EdD, 1968. Gen. mgr. Homeowners Ins. and Realty Co., 1960-63; engring. tech. dept. chmn., dean occupational and transfer programs, dir. evening programs Lenoir County Community Coll., 1963-68; pres. Coll. of the Albemarie, Elizabeth City, NC, 1968-75, N.C. Wesleyan Coll., Rocky Mount, 1975-86; br. mgr. Sherwin Williams, 1953—60; first class radio engr. Radio WFTC-AM, 1949—53. Prof. Va. Poly. Inst. and State U., 1973-75, East Carolina U., 1994-99; pres. Philanthropic Cons., Inc., Kinston, N.C., 1986-96; sec. Coll. Mgmt. Svcs., Inc., Raleigh, N.C., 1989; lic. amateur radio operator, 1992—. Pres. chpt. Am. Cancer Soc., 1960-61, Boys' Club Lenoir County, 1987-91, Westminster Homeowners Assn., 1997; bd. dirs. Rocky Mount Acad., 1979-80, Triangle East, Inc., 1985-86, Cypress Glen Retirement Home, chmn. 1996; chmn. deferred giving com. N.C. Meth. Found., 1979-86; chmn. coun. on ministries 1st United Meth. Ch., Rocky Mount, 1980-81, Westminster United Meth. Ch., 1989-90, chmn. bd. trustees, 1994-99, chmn. adminstrv. bd., 2001-03; chmn. bd. trustees Art Edn. Found., 1980; mem. Nash County Bd. Health, 1985-86; bd. trustees United Meth. Retirement Homes, Inc., 1996-99; treas. Meth. Home for Children, 1997-2002. With USN, 1943—46, with USNR, 1946—51. Named Tar Heel of Week News and Observer, 1975, Today's Outstanding N.C. Citizen WNCT-TV, 1975; NSF fellow U. Ill., 1963 Mem. Nat. Assn. for Hosp. Devel., N.C. Assn. Colls. and Univs., N.C. Conf. United Meth. Ch. (chmn. bd. trustees 1973-79), Nat. Soc. Fund Raising Execs. (cert.), Rocky Mount C. of C. (bd. dirs. 1980-84), Rotary (scholarship com. dist. 7730 1995-2004), Phi Kappa Phi, Theta Alpha Phi. Clubs: Benvenue Country, Galaxy Social; Kinston Country. Lodges: Rotary (pres. 1980-81, bd. dirs. Kinston chpt. 1988-92). Republican. Office: 708 Westminster Ln Kinston NC 28501-2770 Home Phone: 252-527-7982. Personal E-mail: bpetteway@suddenlink.net.

PETTIT, DONALD R., astronaut, flight engineer, researcher; b. Silverton, Oreg., Apr. 20, 1955; m. Micki Pettit; 2 children. BSChemE, Oreg. State U., 1978; PhD in Chemical Engring., U. Ariz., 1983. Staff scientist Los Alamos Nat. Lab., Los Alamos, N.Mex., 1984—96, mem. synthesis group, slated with assembling the technology to return to the moon and explore Mars, 1990, mem. Space Station Freedom Redesign Team, 1993; mission specialist, Lyndon B. Johnson Space Ctr. with technical duties in the Astronaut Office Computer Support Branch NASA, Houston, 1996—. Projects included: Reduced gravity fluid flow and materials processing experiments aboard the NASA KC-135 airplane, atmospheric spectroscopy measurements on noctolucent clouds seeded from sounding rocket payloads, volcano fumarole gas sampling on active volcanos, investigated problems in the detonation physics applied to weapons systems; completed first space flight as NASA ISS science officer and flight engineer aboard the International Space Station, Expedition-6 (launched in the STS-113 Space Shuttle Endeavour and returned to Earth on Soyuz TMA-1), Nov. 23, 2002 to May 3, 2003, logged over 161 days in space and 2 EVAs (spacewalks) totalling 13 hours and 17 minutes. During the 5 1/2 months aboard the ISS, the crew worked with numerous US and Russian science experiments; crew mem. for STS-126 Endeavour Mission, 2008. Avocations: photography, swimming. Office: NASA Johnson Space Center 2101 NASA Pwky Houston TX 77058

PETTY, JAMES C., retail executive; With Gap, Inc.; pres., gen. mgr., Ltd. Too Divsn., exec. v.p., Stores and Real Estate, sr. v.p., Stores, v.p., Stores, Ltd. Too Divsn. Tween Brands, Inc. (formerly Too, Inc.), 1997—2004; pres., CEO PureBeauty, Inc., 2005—06; pres., Retail Stores Carter's, Inc., 2007—. Office: Carter's Inc 1170 Peachtree St NE Ste 900 Atlanta GA 30309 Office Phone: 404-745-2700. Office Fax: 404-892-0968. Business E-Mail: james.petty@carters.com.

PETTY, MARTY, publishing executive; b. 1953; m. Mark Petty; children: Lindsay, Skip. BJ, U. Mo., 1975; MS in Mgmt., Harvard Grad. Ctr., 1989. Asst. mng. editor Kansas City Star and Times; mng. editor The Hartford Courant, 1983-86, v.p., dep. exec. editor, 1986-89, assoc. pub. for projects and planning, 1989, sr. v.p., gen. mgr., pub., CEO, 1997—2000; exec. v.p. St. Petersburg Times, Fla., 2000—09, pub., 2004—09; CEO Creative Loafing, Tampa, 2009—. Bd. dirs. St. Petersburg Times, Tampa, Fla.; chmn. Barnes Scholarship com. St. Petersburg Times Fund; trustee Poynter Inst. Media Studies, Congl. Quarterly, Governing mag., Fla. Trend mag., Tampa Bay Newspapers, Inc. Editor The Electronic Times, 1991-92. Mem. journalism bd. Wm. Randolph Hearst Found., 1987-89; mem. CEO adv. bd. Greater Hartford Arts Coun.; pres. bd. Camp Courant; bd. dirs. Hartford Courant Found., Hartford Hosp. Holding Co.; mem. The MetroHartford Growth Couns. millennium mgmt. com.; bd. dirs. Tampa Bay Partnership, Leadership Fla.; trustee Jr. Achievement, Acad. Prep, Kids Voting USA; mem. pres.'s coun. Eckerd Coll. Named Disting. Bus. Woman of Yr., St. Petersburg Area C. of C., 2005, Bus. Woman of Yr., Tampa Bay Bus. Jour., 2005; named a Woman of Distinction, Girl Scouts of Suncoast Coun., 2004. Mem. Newspaper Assn. of Am. (Ptnrs. 2000 com., Copyright Clearance Ctr. adv. bd.), Soc. Newspaper Design (pres. 1985, active cons.), Am. Soc. Newspaper Editors, Am. Press Inst. (adv. bd.), AP Mng. Editors, Poynter Inst., Fla. Press Assn. (bd. dirs.), Nat. Assn. Minority Media Execs. Office: Creative Loafing 1911 N 13th St Ste W200 Tampa FL 33605 Office Fax: 813-739-4800, 813-739-4801. Business E-Mail: marty.petty@creativeloafing.com.

PETTY, ROY WILLIAM, orthopedist; b. Little Rock, Oct. 18, 1942; s. Roy H. and Mary Lee (Harrell) Petty; m. Betty Petty; 1 child, David M.; m. Betty Blackmon, Dec. 27, 1963; children: David William, Mark Aaron, Julie Allison. BS, U. Ark., 1962, MD, 1966, MS, 1968. Diplomate Am. Bd. Orthopaedic Surgery. Intern Tampa Gen. Hosp., Fla., 1966—67; fellow in orthopedics Mayo Clinic, Rochester, Minn., 1970—74; orthopedic surgeon Naples, Fla., 1974—75; asst. prof. U. Fla., Gainesville, 1975—79, assoc. prof., 1979—84, prof. & chmn. dept. orthopedics, 1981—; chief orthopaedic surgeon VA Hosp., Gainesville, 1979—84, pres., 2002—07; founder, chmn. & CEO Exactech Inc. Author: Total Joint Replacement; contbr. articles to profl. jours. Mem., hosp. bd. Shands Hosp., Gainesville, Fla.; examiner Am. Bd. of Orthopaedic Surgery; mem., orthopaedic residency review com. Am. Med. Assn.; editl. bd. Jour. of Bone & Joint Surgery; exec. bd. Am. Acad. of Orthopaedic Surgeons. Capt. USAF, 1967—69. Recipient Kappa Delta award, Am. Acad. of Orthopaedic Surgeons. Mem.: AMA, NY Acad. Sci., Cmty. Med. Svcs. Assn. Inc., Alachua County Med. Soc., Fla. Med. Assn., Fla. Orthopedic Soc., Orthopedic Rsch. Soc., Am. Acad. Orthopedic Surgeons, Alpha Omega Alpha, Sigma Xi. Methodist.

PETZEL, FLORENCE ELOISE, textiles educator; b. Crosbyton, Tex., Apr. 1, 1911; d. William D. and Eloise Petzel. PhB, U. Chgo., 1931, AM, 1934; PhD, U. Minn., 1954. Instr. Judson Coll., 1936—38; asst. prof. textiles Ohio State U., 1938—48; assoc. prof. U. Ala., 1950—54; prof. Oreg. State U., Corvallis, 1954—61, 1967—75, prof. emeritus, 1975—, dept. head, 1954—61, 1967—75; prof., divsn. head U. Tex., 1961—63; prof. Tex. Tech. U., 1963—67. Vis. instr. Tex. State Coll. for Women, 1937; vis. prof. Wash. State U., 1967 Author: Textiles of Ancient Mesopotamia, Persia and Egypt, 1987; contbr. articles to profl. jours. Effie I. Raitt fellow, 1949—50. Mem. Met. Opera Guild, Sigma Xi, Phi Kappa Phi, Omicron Nu, Iota Sigma Pi, Sigma Delta Epsilon, New Eng. Hist. & Geneal. Soc. Home: 26B Health Ctr 500 Downs Loop Clemson SC 29631

PEVERLEY, RICH, professional hockey player; b. Kingston, Ont., Canada, July 8, 1982; m. Nathalie Peverley; 1 child, Bella. Grad., St. Lawrence U., 2004. Center Nashville Predators, 2007—09, Atlanta Thrashers, 2009—11, Boston Bruins, 2011—13, Dallas Stars, 2013—. Achievements include being a member of Stanley Cup Champion Boston Bruins, 2011. Office: Dallas Stars American Airlines Ctr 2500 Victory Ave Dallas TX 75201*

PEW, JOHN GLENN, JR., lawyer; b. Dallas, Apr. 18, 1932; s. John Glenn Sr. and Roberta (Haughton) P. BA, U. Tex., 1954, LLB, 1955. Bar: Tex. 1955, U.S. Dist. Ct. (no. dist.) Tex. 1959, U.S. Supreme Ct. 1959, U.S. Ct. Appeals (5th cir.) 1961, U.S. Ct. Appeals (10th cir.) 1982. Ptnr. Jackson Walker LLP, Dallas, 1964—. With USNR, 1955-58. Mem.: Order of Coif, Phi Beta Kappa. Republican. Presbyterian. Office: Jackson Walker LLP 901 Main St Ste 6000 Dallas TX 75202-3797 Office Phone: 214-953-6000. E-mail: jpew@jw.com.

PEWITT, JAMES DUDLEY, retired academic administrator; b. Franklin, Tenn., July 28, 1930; s. James Isaac and Eleanor (Dudley) P.; m. Betty Louise Hightower, Oct. 31, 1952; children: Ransom D., James P., Thomas E. Attended, Battle Ground Acad., 1948; student, Vanderbilt U., 1948-51; MBA, MS, U.S.C., 1964, D in Bus. Adminstrn., 1967. Commd. lt. USAF, 1952, advanced through grades to col., 1969; AMC test pilot, 1958—62; spl. asst. for econ. analysis Office of Sec. of Air Force, 1967; exec. to asst. sec. Air Force for Fin. Mgmt. Nat. War Coll., 1971; asst. Da Nang Air Base, Vietnam, 1972; dep. comdr. for ops. Vietnam, 1972; vice comdr. Gunfighters, 1972; chief linebacker ops. Staff of Dir. of Ops., Vietnam, 1972; dir. mgmt. analysis USAF, 1973, ret., 1973; dir. grad. sch. bus. U. Ala., Birmingham, 1973-74, asst. v.p. ops. and planning, 1974-77, v.p. adminstrn., 1977-84, sr. v.p. adminstrn., 1984-90, Disting. prof., 1990—94, emeritus, 1994—. Bd. dir. Birmingham Cable Communications, Allied Products Co. Mem. Birmingham Airport Authority, 1986-93; chmn. bd. So. Mus. of Flight, 1993-2005; faculty rep. Sun Belt Conf., 1983-90, pres., 1989-90; mem. NCAA Coun., 1990-94. Decorated D.F.C. with 3 oak leaf clusters, Bronze Star, Legion of Merit with 2 oak leaf clusters, Air medal with 11 oak leaf clusters, 10 other awards and fgn. decorations; named to Ala, Aviation Hall of Fame, 2003, Battle Ground Acad. Hall of Fame, 2011. Mem.: Birmingham C. of C. (bd. dirs. 1977-84, pres. 1983, chmn. 1984), Birmingham Country Club, Skull & Dagger, Phi Kappa Phi, Beta Gamma Sigma, Sigma Xi, Omicron Delta Kappa, Kappa Alpha, Order of Daedalians, QB's Order of Quiet Birdmen. Avocations: flying, golf. Home Phone: 205-870-5470.

PEYTON, JOHN, former mayor, Jacksonville, Florida; b. July 28, 1964; m. Kathryn Pearson; children: John Conner, Kent Thomas. Grad. Exec. Edn. Program, Harvard Bus. Sch.; BA, Mercer U., 1986. V.p. Gate Petroleum Co., Fla.; mayor City of Jacksonville, Fla., 2003. Mem. Harry S. Truman Scholarship Found., 2007—. Past pres. Greenscape of Jacksonville, 1998—99; chmn. Jacksonville Symphony Assn.; mem. St. John's Episcopal Ch.; bd. mem. Jacksonville Transp. Authority, 1996—99, chmn., 1999—2003. Recipient James Patterson Pageturner award, 2005, Children's Champion award, Episcopal Children's Services, 2005. Republican. Office: Gate Petroleum Co 9540 San Jose Blvd Jacksonville FL 32241

PEZZELLA, JERRY JAMES, JR., investment and real estate company executive; b. Chesapeake, Va., Sept. 30, 1937; s. Jerry James, Sr. and Mabel (Aydlett) Pezzella; m. Carolyn Blades; children: James M., Stanley J., Julie Pezzella Scanlon. BS, U. Richmond, 1963; MBA, U. Pa., 1964; grad., ABA Sch. Bank, Norfolk, VA, 1965, Ohio State U., 1965—66. Asst. v.p. Va. Nat. Bank (now Bank of Am.), Norfolk, 1964-68; chmn. bd., pres. First Am. Investment Corp., First Ga. Investment Corp., Atlanta, 1968-74; v.p. Great Am. Investment Corp., Atlanta, 1974-78, dir., 1983—85, sr. exec. v.p., 1983—85; dir. Firstate Savings Bank, Orlando, Fla., 1983—85; v.p. SFC Virginia Army Nat. Guard, Chesapeake, Va., 1955—61; exec. v.p. Equity Fin. & Mgmt. Co., Chgo., 1978-99; pres., chmn. bd. First Capital Fin. Corp., Chgo., 1983-85; pres. GAFGI Holdings Inc., Chgo., 1983-98; chmn. bd. 1st Property Mgmt. Corp., 1990-92; dir., fin. officer, treas., vice chairman Bear Paw Svc. Dist., 2002—08. Instr. fin. Old Dominion U., 1965—67, Ga. State U., 1970—73; adj. prof. U. Richmond, 1975—77; real estate cons., 1997—2001; bd. dirs. Great Am. Mgmt. and Investment, Inc.; pres. Southeast Small Bus. Investment Co. Assn., 1972—73; dir. Nat. Assn. Small Bus. Investment Co., 1971—73. Mem. exec. com. Nat. Multi Housing Coun., 1991—93, bd. dirs., 1992—94. Mem.: Met. Club (Chgo.). Home: 1240 Village Rd Murphy NC 28906-1763

PFAFF, WILLIAM WALLACE, medical educator; b. Rochester, NY, Aug. 14, 1930; s. Norman Joseph and Eleanor Blakesley (Wells) P.; m. Patricia Ann Clark; children: Nancy, Karen, Margaret, Mary Catherine. AB, Harvard U., 1952; MD, SUNY, 1956. Intern U. Chgo., 1956-58; sr. asst. surgeon NIH, Bethesda, Md., 1958-60; resident Stanford U. Med. Ctr., Palo Alto, Calif., 1960-65; asst. prof. U. Fla., Gainesville, 1965-68, assoc. prof., 1968-71, prof. surgery, 1971-95, prof. emeritus, adj. prof., 1995—, dir. organ transplant programs, 1971-95. Bd. dirs. United Network for Organ Sharing, Richmond, Va., pres. elect, 1997-98, pres., 1998-99; pres., com. chmn. Southeastern Organ Procurement Found., Richmond, 1973-95. Fellow Am. Coll. Surgeons; mem. Am. Surg. Assn., Am. Soc. Transplant Surgeons, So. Surg. Assn., Transplantation Soc., Alachua County Med. Soc. (pres. 1977-78). Home: 2445 NW 15th Pl Gainesville FL 32605-5148 Office: U Fla Dept Surgery PO Box 100286 Gainesville FL 32610-0286 Personal E-mail: puffer12@aol.com.

PFEIFER, MICHAEL DAVID, bishop; b. Alamo, Tex., May 18, 1937; s. Frank and Alice (Savage) P. Student, Oblate Sch. Theology. Ordained priest Missionary Oblates of Mary Immaculate, 1964; priest Roman Cath. Ch., Mexico City, 1964-1981, provincial-superior of Oblate Southern US Province San Antonio, 1981-85; ordained bishop, 1985; bishop Diocese of San Angelo, Tex., 1985—. Roman Catholic. Address: PO Box 1829 804 Ford St San Angelo TX 76902 Office Phone: 325-651-7500. Office Fax: 325-651-6688. Business E-Mail: mdpomi@aol.com.

PFEIFER, THOMAS J., legislative staff member; b. Copaigue, NY, Apr. 5, 1954; married; twin daughters. AS in Journalism, Moorpark Coll., 1983. Reporter, editor-in-chief Simi Valley (Calif.) Mirror, 1983; reporter, news editor, mng. editor Simi Valley Enterprise, 1984-92; city editor, team leader, bur. chief Ventura County (Calif.) Star, 1992-98; press sec., dir. comm. US Rep. Elton Gallegly, Washington, 1998—. Office: Office of Rep Elton Gallegly 2309 Rayburn House Office Bldg Washington DC 20515-0524 Office Phone: 202-225-5811. Business E-Mail: thomas.pfeifer@mail.house.gov.

PFEIFFER, ERIC ARMIN, psychiatrist, gerentologist, author; b. Rauental, Germany, Sept. 15, 1935; came to U.S., 1952; naturalized, 1957; s. Fritz and Emma (Saborowski) P.; m. Natasha Maria Emerson, Mar. 21, 1964; children: Eric Alexander, Michael David, Mark Armin. AB, Washington U., 1956, MD, 1960. Intern Albert Einstein Coll. Medicine, Bronx, NY, 1960-61; resident in psychiatry U. Rochester, NY, 1961-64; practice medicine specializing in psychiatry Durham, NC, 1966-76, Denver, 1976-78; asst. prof. Duke U., Durham, 1966-69, assoc. prof., 1969-72, prof., 1973-76, project dir., 1971-76, assoc. dir., 1974-76; dir. Davis Inst. Care and Study Aging, Denver, 1976-77; prof. psychiatry U. Colo., Denver, 1976-78; prof. psychiatry, chief div. geriatric psychiatry U. South Fla. Coll. Medicine, Tampa, 1978—2008, dir. Suncoast Gerontology Ctr., 1980—2008. Chief psychiatry svc. Tampa VA Med. Ctr., 1979-80; cons. in field; chmn. bd. Social Systems, Inc., 1975-76; chmn. com. on mental health and mental illness of elderly HEW, 1976-77. Author: Disordered Behavior, 1968, (with E.W. Busse) Behavior and Adaptation in Late Life, 1970, 3d edit., 1977, Successful Aging, 1974, Multidimensional Functional Assessment, 1977, Alzheimer's Disease, 1989, Winning Strategies for Successful Aging, 2012, Under One Roof: Poems, 2010, The Art of Caregiving in Alzheimer Disease, 2011. With USPHS, 1964-66. Markle Found. scholar acad. medicine, 1968-73; Eric Pfeiffer Chair in Alzheimer's Disease Rsch. named in his honor, U. S. Fla., 1985. Fellow Gerontol. Soc. (chmn. clin. medicine sect. 1975-76), Am. Psychiat. Assn.; mem. Am. Geriatrics Soc. (Allen Gold medal 1977), So. Psychiat. Soc., Phi Beta Kappa. Office Phone: 813-839-5769.

PFEIFFER, PHILIP JOHN, of counsel, retired lawyer; b. Houston, Aug. 16, 1947; BS, Sam Houston State U., 1969; JD, So. Meth. U., 1972. Bar: Tex. 1972. Ptnr. Fulbright & Jaworski LLP, San Antonio, 1979—2011, former ptnr.-in-charge, of counsel; ret. Editor-in-chief Employment Discrimination Law (Second Supplement to Lindemann and Grossman). Named a Super Lawyer, Tex. Monthly Mag., 2003—13. Fellow Am. Coll. Labor and Employment Lawyers; mem. ABA, State Bar Tex., San Antonio Bar Assn., San Antonio Bar Found., Tex. Bar Found., Order of Coif, Phi Alpha Delta.

PFENNIGER, RICHARD CHARLES, JR., lawyer, healthcare company executive; b. Akron, Ohio, July 26, 1955; s. Richard Charles Pfenniger and Phyllis Irene (Rutan) Gatto. BBA, Fla. Atlantic U., 1977; JD, U. Fla., 1982. Bar: Fla. 1982; CPA, Fla. Acct. Price Waterhouse & Co., Ft. Lauderdale, Fla., 1977-79; assoc. Stearns, Weaver, Miller, Weisller, Alhadeff & Sitterson, P.A., Miami, Fla., 1982-86; mem. Greer, Homer, Cope & Bonner P.A., Miami, 1986-89; sr. v.p., legal affairs, gen. counsel IVAX Corp., Miami, 1989—94, COO, 1994—97; CEO, vice chmn. Whitman Edn. Group, Inc., Miami, Fla., 1987—2002; chmn. Continucare Corp., 2002—, pres., CEO, 2003—. Bd. dirs. N.Am. Vaccine, Inc. Mem. ABA, AICPA. Office: Continucare Corp 7200 Corporate Center Dr Ste 600 Miami FL 33126 Office Phone: 305-500-2000. Office Fax: 305-500-2080.

PFIFFNER, JAMES PRICE, university professor; b. Stevens Point, Wis., June 24, 1946; s. James Sturtevant and Alice Price Pfiffner; m. Debra Ann Jones, Aug. 11, 1979; children: Megan Cyr, Katherine Courtney, Morgan Meehan. BA in Polit. Sci., U. Wis., 1968, MA in Polit. Sci., 1972, PhD in Polit. Sci., 1975. Tchg. asst. U. Wis., Madison, 1971-74; rsch. fellow Brookings Inst., Washington, 1974-75; asst. prof. U. Calif., Riverside, 1975-78, Calif. State U., Fullerton, 1978-80, assoc. prof. polit. sci., 1980-84, John Brown Mason prof., 1983-84; spl. asst. to dir. Office Pers. Mgmt., Washington, 1980-81; assoc. prof. govt. and pub. policy George Mason U., Fairfax, Va., 1984-87, prof., 1987—, univ. prof., 2003—; S.T. Lee Profl. fellow Sch. Advanced Study, U. London, 2007. Author: The President, the Budget, and Congress: Impoundment and the 1974 Budget Act, 1979, The Strategic Presidency: Hitting the Ground Running, 1988, 2d edit., 1996, The Modern Presidency, 1998, 5th edit., 2007, The Character Factor: How We Judge America's Presidents, 2004, (book) Power Play: The Bush Presidency Constitution, 2008, Torture as Public Policy, 2010; editor: The President and Economic Policy, 1986, The Managerial Presidency, 1991, 2d edit., 1999, Governance and American Politics: Classic and Current Perspectives, 1995; co-editor: The Presidency in Transition, 1989, The Presidency and the Gulf War, 1993, Understanding the Presidency, 1997, 5th edit., 2008, The Future of Merit, 2000, Intelligence Nat. Security Policy Making on Iraq, British Am. Perspectives, 2008. With U.S. Army, 1969-70, Vietnam. Decorated Army Commendation medal for Valor, Vietnam/Cambodia, 1970; Brookings Instn. fellow, 1974-75, vis. scholar, 1983, 97; Nat. Assn. Sch. Pub. Affairs and Adminstrn. faculty fellow, 1980-81; S. T. Lee Professorial fellow Sch. for Advanced Study, U. London, 2007. Mem. Nat. Acad. Pub. Adminstrn., Cosmos Club. Office: George Mason University Sch Pub Policy 3351 Fairfax Dr Arlington VA 22201

PHAM, SI MAI, cardiothoracic surgeon; b. Ninh Hoa, Khanh Hoa, Vietnam, Oct. 6, 1955; arrived in US, 1975; s. Tro Pham and Nhung Thi Mai; m. Marie Christine Pham, Sept. 9, 1987; children: Benjamin Bartley, Anthony Ninh, Vivienne Elisabeth, Victoria B.H. Student, U. Saigon Sch. Pharmacy, Vietnam, 1973-75; BS in Chem. magna cum laude, Lebanon Valley Coll., Annville, Pa., 1979; MD, U. Pitts., 1983; D (hon.), U. Morón, 2002. Diplomate, surg. critical care Am. Bd. Surgery, Am. Bd. Thoracic Surgery. Intern, resident gen. surgery U. Pitts., 1983-86, rsch. fellow, cardiothoracic surgery, 1986-87, sr. and chief resident gen. surgery, 1987-89, resident cardiothoracic surgery, 1989-92, asst. prof. surgery, Sch. Medicine, 1992—98, dir. adult cardiac transplant program, Sch. Medicine, 1993-97, assoc. dir. heart transplant and artificial heart program, 1997-98, dir. cardiothoracic transplant rsch., 1997-98; dir. extracorporeal membrane oxygenation svc. Presbyn. U. Hosp., Pitts., 1993-98; dir. cardiopulmonary transplantation and artificial heart program, divsn. cardiothoracic surgery U. Miami Sch. Medicine, 1998—; assoc. prof. surgery U. Miami Sch. Medicine, 1998—2002, prof. surgery, 2002, prof. surgery & biomed. engring., 2010. Reviewer various med. jours. Contbr. articles to profl. jours., chapters to books, scientific papers. Recipient Am. Chem. award, 1979, Radiology award U. Pitts., 1983, Dalsemer rsch. scholar award Am. Lung Assn., 1997-99; ACS Faculty fellowship award, 1994-96, Health Care Heroes award Greater Miami C. of C., 2007; grantee Children's Hosp. Pitts., 1987, Am. Heart Assn., 1987-89, 94-96, 96-99, Thoracic Surgery Found., 1996-97, 97-98, Am. Lung

Assn., 1997—, Presbyn. U. Hosp., 1987-89, NIH, 1999—, Vietnamese Am. Med. Rsch. Found. sci. award, 2005. Fellow Am. Coll. Surgeons, Am. Heart Assoc. (cmty. bd. mem.); mem. Am. Soc. Artificial Internal Organs, Internat. Soc. Heart and Lung Transplantation, Soc. Critical Care Medicine, Am. Assn. Advancement of Sci., Am. Soc. Transplant Surgeons, Soc. Thoracic Surgeons, Am. Assn. Thoracic Surgery, Extracorporeal Life Support Organization, Assn. for Acad. Surgery, Phi Alpha Epsilon, Transplant Found. South Fla. (adv. bd. mem.). Avocations: reading, gardening. Office: U Miami Sch Medicine Highland Profl Bldg 1801 NW 9th Ave Ste 5th Fl Miami FL 33136 Office Phone: 305-355-5070. Personal E-mail: simaipham@gmail.com. Business E-Mail: spham@med.miami.edu.

PHARIS, RUTH MCCALISTER, retired bank executive; b. San Diego, Feb. 13, 1934; d. William L. and Mary E. (Beuk) McC.; m. E. Edwin Pharis, Mar. 14, 1953; children: Beth, Tracey, Todd. Banking course Del Mar Coll., Corpus Christi, Tex., 1979, Sr. Human Resources Profl. Asst. cashier Parkdale State Bank, Corpus Christi, 1970-72, asst. v.p., 1972-76, v.p., 1976-79, Cullen Center Bank & Trust, Houston, 1979-81, sr. v.p., 1982-93; dir. human resources Scooter Store, Inc., New Braunfels, Tex., 2001—03. Instr. Am. Inst. Banking, 1977—79. Mem. adv. coun. Houston CC; vice chmn. Comal County Rep. Party; organizer and pres. Hill Country Tea Party Patriots; past pres. New Braunfels Rep. Women; choir Puppet Ministry. Mem. Human Resource Mgmt. Assn., Bank Adminstrn. Inst. (v.p. Coastal Bend chpt. 1979), Nat. Assn. Bank Women (ednl. chmn. Coastal Bend group), Am. Inst. Banking (rep.), Tex. Bankers Assn. (coun. 1983-84, instr.), Coastal Bend Personnel Soc. (v.p.), Houston Personnel Assn., New Braunfels (Tex.) Rep. Women (pres. 1999-2002), Corpus Christi C. of C. (mem. women's com. 1976-79), Order Eastern Star. Republican. Baptist. Avocation: oil painting. Home: 2779 Morning Star New Braunfels TX 78132-4722

PHELAN, ANDY, legislative staff member; Grad., Coll. Charleston, SC. Web prodr. The State, Columbia, SC; weekend editor The Sumter Item; web designer Atlanta Jour.-Constitution; reporter The Champion, Decatur, Ga.; comm. dir. to Rep. Hank Johnson US House of Representatives, Washington, 2009—. Office: Office of Rep Hank Johnson 1133 Longworth House Office Bldg Washington DC 20515-1004 also: Office of Rep Hank Johnson Ste 205 3469 Lawrenceville Hwy Tucker GA 30084-5866 Office Phone: 770-939-2016. Office Fax: 770-939-3753. E-mail: andy.phelan@mail.house.gov.

PHELAN, EDWARD, defense and space services executive; BS in Biol. Sciences & Chemistry, North Dakota State U.; MS in Logistics Mgmt. Sci., Fla. Inst. Tech.; MBA Exec. Seminars Program, Pepperdine U., Los Angeles. Various positions, adminstrv., logistics, comm., and info. tech. svcs. United Nations; joined DynCorp Internat. LLC., 2001, sr. v.p., strategic bus. devel. Col. US Army. Office: DynCorp International LLC 3190 Fairview Park Dr Ste 700 Falls Church VA 22042 Office Phone: 571-722-0210. Office Fax: 571-722-0252.

PHELAN, MARILYN ELIZABETH, law educator; b. Tex., July 12, 1938; m. Harold L. Phelan, Sept. 1, 1960; children: Pat, Scott, Kimberly. BA, Tex. Tech U., 1959, MBA, 1967, PhD, 1971; JD, U. Tex., 1972. Bar: Tex. 1961. Assoc. prof. Tex. Tech U., Lubbock, 1971-77, prof. law, 1977—2011, Paul Whitfield Horn prof. law, 1993—2011, emeritus prof., 2011—. Author: Law of Cultural Property, 1998, Nonprofit Enterprises--Corporations, Trusts, and Associations, 2008, Nonprofit Organizations: Law and Taxation, 2010, Representing Tax Exempt Organizations, 2010, Museum Law., 2007, 4th edit., 2014, Nonprofit Organizations, 2003, 3rd edit, 2010. Mem. ABA (Academic award, 2011), AICPA, Nat. Conf. Commrs. Uniform State Laws, Am. Law Inst., State Bar Tex., Internat. Coun. Mus. (legal affairs com. mem. 2005-11). Home Phone: 817-579-5179. E-mail: marilyn.phelan@ttu.edu.

PHELAN, ROBIN ERIC, lawyer; b. Steubenville, Ohio, Dec. 28, 1945; s. Edward John and Dorothy (Borkowski) P.; m. JoAnn Keach, June 27, 1970 (dec. May 18, 1994); children: Travis McCoy, Tiffany Marie, Trevor Monroe; m. Melinda Jo Ricketts, May 27, 1995; 1 child, Taezja Monet. BSBA, Ohio State U., 1967, JD, 1970. Bar: Tex. 1971, U.S. Ct. Appeals (5th cir.) 1981, U.S. Ct. Appeals (11th cir.) 1981, U.S. Ct. Appeals (6th cir.) 1986, U.S. Ct. Appeals (10th cir.) 1988, U.S. Supreme Ct. Ptnr. Haynes and Boone, Dallas, 1970—. Co-author: Bankruptcy Practice and Strategy, 1987, Cowans Bankruptcy Law and Practice, 1987, Annual Survey of Bankruptcy Law, 1988, Bankruptcy Litigation Manual; contbr. articles to profl. jours. Mem. ABA (chmn. insolvency and secured transactions com. internat. law sect.), Internat. Bar Assn., Internat. Insolvency Inst. (bd. dirs.), Am. Bankruptcy Inst. (dir., past pres.), Am. Coll. Bankruptcy, State Bar Tex. (chmn. bankruptcy law com. sect. bus. law 1989-91), Dallas Bar Assn. Roman Catholic. Avocation: athletics. Home: 4214 Woodfin Dr Dallas TX 75220-6416 Office Phone: 214-651-5612. Business E-Mail: robin.phelan@haynesboone.com.

PHELPS, JOHN BRIDGES, legislative official; With Fla. Ho. of Reps., Tallahassee, 1974—, exec. asst. to spkr., 1978-80, staff dir. com. on rules and calendar, 1980-82, dep. clk., 1982-86, clk., 1986—. Cons. Assocs. in Rural Devel., Inc., Burlington, Vt., Am.-Mideast Ednl. and Tng. Svcs., Inc., USIA/Nat. Conf. State Legislatures, others; spkr. in field. Contbr. articles to profl. jours. Recipient Davis Productivity award Fla. TaxWatch, Inc., 1989, numerous certs. of appreciation. Mem. Nat. Conf. State Legislatures (staff vice chair 1998-99, chair, 1999-2000), Am. Soc. Legis. Clks. and Secs. (exec. com. 1989-95, pres. 1992-93, award 1997), Assn. Ctrl. Am. Legis. Technicians. Office: 327 The Capitol Tallahassee FL 32399-1300

PHILBECK, JOHN HEYDT, lawyer; BA, Elon U., 1989; JD, Valparaiso U. Sch. Law, 1992. Bar: NC 1992, US Dist. Ct., NC 1993, US Dist. Court (ea. and mid. dist.) NC 2000, US Dist. Ct. (we. dist.) NC 2000, US Ct. Appeals (4th cir.) 2000, US Tax Ct. 2000, US Ct. Internat. Trade 2000, US Supreme Ct. 2000, All NC State Trial and Appellate Cts. Atty. J. Heydt Philbeck, Atty. at Law, Raleigh, NC, 1992—96, Murphy & Philbeck, PLLC, Raleigh, 1996—2000, Allen & Pinnix, P.A., Raleigh, 2000—06, Bailey & Dixon LLP, Raleigh, 2006. Pres. Craven Everett Am. Inn Ct., Duke Law Sch., 2009—10. Recipient 40 Under 40 Leadership award, Triangle Bus. Jour., 2005, Best Lawyers in America, 2010—; named NC Super Lawyers, Law and Politics Mag., 2006—, Top 100 Lawyers, NC Super Lawyers, 2009, 2014, Leaders in Law, NC Lawyers Weekly, 2014; named one of Legal Elite, Bus. NC, 2007—. Fellow: Litig. Counsel America (charter mem., hon. trial lawyer), NC Inst. Polit. Leadership; mem.: Nat. Employment Lawyers Assn., Am. Inn Law, Southern Trial Lawyers Assn., Am. Advs. Justice, Leadership NC, Nat. Employment Lawyer's Assn., NC Assn. Justice, Wake County Bar Assn. (bd. dirs.), NC Bar Assn. Office: Bailey & Dixon LLP 434 Fayetteville St Ste 2500 Raleigh NC 27601 Office Fax: 919-828-6592.

PHILBIN, GARY M., retail executive; Various positions, store ops. and merchandising Kroger Co., 1973; sr. v.p., merchandising, Walbaum A&P, 1993—96; exec. v.p., ops. and merchandising, Cub Foods SuperValu, 1996—97; various positions, including pres., CEO, chief merchandising officer, bd. dirs. Grand Union (sale to C&S Wholesale Grocers), NJ, 1997; sr. v.p., stores Dollar Tree Stores, Inc., 2001—07, COO, 2007—. Office: Dollar Tree Inc 500 Volvo Pky Chesapeake VA 23320 Office Phone: 757-321-5000. Office Fax: 757-855-5555. Business E-Mail: gphilbin@dollartree.com.

PHILBIN, JOE (JOSEPH A. PHILBIN), professional football coach; b. Springfield, Mass., July 2, 1961; m. Diane Philbin; children: Matthew, Michael(dec.), John, Kevin, Timothy, Colleen. B, Wash. and Jefferson Coll., Washington, Pa., 1984; MEd, Tulane U., New Orleans, 1986. Grad asst. Tulane U. Green Wave, 1984—85; offensive line coach Worcester Poly. Inst. Engineers, Mass., 1986—87, US Merchant Marine Acad. Mariners, Kings Point, NY, 1988—89; asst. coach Allegheny Coll. Gators, Meadville, Pa., 1990—93; offensive line coach Ohio U. Bobcats, Athens, 1994; offensive coord., offensive line coach Northeastern U. Huskies, Boston, 1995—96, Harvard U. Crimson, Cambridge, Mass., 1997—98; offensive line coach U. Iowa Hawkeyes, Iowa City, 1999—2002; asst. offensive line coach Green Bay Packers, Wis., 2003, tight ends, asst. offensive line coach, 2004—05, offensive line coach, 2006, offensive coord., 2007—11; head coach Miami Dolphins, Fla., 2012—. Achievements include member of Super Bowl XLV championship winning Green Bay Packers, 2011. Office: Miami Dolphins 7500 SW 30th St Davie FL 33314

PHILBIN, PEGGY (MARGARET M. PHILBIN), federal agency administrator; b. 1950; Grad., Coll. Mt. St. Vincent, 1972, St. John's U., 1976. Bar: N.Y., Fla. Trial atty. Immigration & Naturalization Svc. US Dept. Justice, Miami, Fla., 1988-90; assoc. gen. counsel Exec Office for Immigration Rev. (EOIR), Falls Church, Va., 1990-95, gen. counsel, dep. dir.; exec. dir. Bur. Adminstrn. & Info. Resources Mgmt. US Dept. State, Washington; dep. dir. US Trade & Devel. Agy., Arlington, 2010—. Adj. prof. law criminal justice dept. L.I. U. Office: US Trade & Development Agency 1000 Wilson Blvd Ste 1600 Arlington VA 22209 Office Phone: 703-875-4357. Office Fax: 703-875-4009.*

PHILIPS, BRIAN D., delivery service executive; b. Toledo, 1967; Grad., Miami U., Oxford, Ohio, 1988; MBA, Ind. U., 1992. With mktg. dept. Kimberly Clark Corp.; with svc. devel. mktg. dept. FedEx Express, mng. dir. mktg. Latin Am. and Caribbean divsn., mng. dir. segment and sponsorship mktg.; v.p. US mktg. FedEx Services; exec. v.p., COO FedEx Office, pres., CEO, 2008—. Mem. exec. com. The United Way Met. Dallas. Office: FedEx Office 13155 Noel Rd Ste 1600 Dallas TX 75240

PHILLIPS, ANITA, food service executive; m. Jim Phillips; children: Marie, Nicole. BS in Acctg., St. Cloud State U. CPA. Asst. corp. controller Carlson Restaurants, Mpls., 1989—91, v.p. Travel Group, group fin. dir. Carlson Leisure Group England, v.p. corp. fin. svcs. and bus. risk mgmt. Mpls., 1999, CFO mktg., v.p. fin. and strategic sourcing, sr. v.p., CFO, 2005; interim pres., COO T.G.I. Friday's USA, Carrollton, Tex., 2010—11, pres., COO, mem. exec. com., 2011—. Office: TGI Friday's Restaurants 4201 Marsh Lane Carrollton TX 75007

PHILLIPS, BARRY, lawyer; b. Valdosta, Ga., Feb. 16, 1929; s. W. Otis and Gypsy (Mercer) P.; m. Grace Greer, Aug. 3, 1957; children: Mary Grace, Barry Jr., Greer, Quinton. AB, U. Ga., 1949, LLB, 1954. Bar: Ga. 1951, D.C. 1977. Assoc. Kilpatrick Stockton, Atlanta, 1954-60, ptnr., 1960-97, of counsel, 1997—. Bd. dirs., mem. exec. com., credit com. Bank South Corp., 1978-96. Mem. bd. regents Univ. Sys. Ga., 1988-94, vice chmn., 1991-93, chmn., 1993-94; trustee U. Ga. Found., Atlanta, 1983-87, treas., 1985-87; mem. bd. visitors U. Ga. Law Sch., 1983-87, chmn., 1985; dir. Ctrl. Atlanta Progress, 1985-86; dir. USA-ROC Econ. Coun., 1985-91; bd. dirs. Ga. Coun. Internat. Visitors, Atlanta, 1986-93, sec., 1986-87, pres., 1987-88; bd. dirs. Atlanta Conv. and Visitors Bur., 1986-91, sec., 1986-87, v.p., 1987-88; bd. dirs. Ga. Region NCCJ, 1980-98, co-chair, 1982-83; chmn. Met. Atlanta Olympic Games Authority, 1990-91; bd. dirs. Ga. Sports Hall of Fame, 1990—, vice chmn., 1993-95, chmn., 1995-96; attache Can. Olympic Team for 1996 Olympics, 1995-96. 1st lt. U.S. Army, 1951-53, Korea. Decorated Air medal; recipient Brotherhood-Sisterhood award Ga. Regional NCCJ, 1993. Fellow Am. Coll. Investment Counsel (bd. dirs. 1986-88), Ga. Bar Found., Soc. Internat. Bus. Fellows; mem. Ga. Bar Assn. (chmn. corp. and banking law sect. 1977-78), Atlanta Bar Assn., D.C. Bar Assn., Lawyers Club Atlanta, U. Ga. Law Sch. Alumni Assn. (trustee 1979-84, pres. 1982-83), Can. Am. Soc. (bd. dirs. 1981-90, pres. 1981-83), Brit. Am. Bus. Group (bd. dirs. 1985-95), Sphinx, Gridiron, Phi Beta Kappa, Phi Kappa Phi, Omicron Delta Kappa. Democrat. Methodist. Avocations: reading, travel. Home: 4850 Tanglewood Ct NW Atlanta GA 30327-4558 Office: Kilpatrick Stockton 1100 Peachtree St NE Ste 2800 Atlanta GA 30309-4530 Home Phone: 404-255-6521; Office Phone: 404-815-6380. Business E-Mail: bphillips@kilstock.com. E-mail: bphilatl@aol.com.

PHILLIPS, BAXTER FRANCIS, JR., energy executive; b. 1946; s. Baxter Francis and Frances (Walker) Phillips; m. Sharon Lee; 1 child, Baxter Francis III. BS in Bus. & Mgmt., Va. Commonwealth U., 1975, MBA, 1976. Group head, corp. banking divsn. American Security Bank, Wash., DC; cash mgmt. officer United Va. Bankshares, Inc., Richmond, Va.; with A.T. Massey Coal (now Massey Energy), 1981—92, v.p. purchasing & risk mgmt., 1992—2000; v.p., treas. Massey Energy Co., 2000—03, sr. v.p., CFO, 2003—04, exec. v.p., chief adminstrv. officer, 2004—08, pres., 2008—10, pres., CEO, 2010—. Bd. dirs. Massey Energy Corp., 2007—. Office: Massey Energy Corp PO Box 16429 Bristol VA 24209-6429 Office Phone: 804-788-1800. Office Fax: 804-788-1870. Business E-Mail: baxter.phillips@masseyenergyco.com.

PHILLIPS, BETTY LOU (ELIZABETH LOUISE PHILLIPS), writer, interior designer; b. Cleve. d. Michael N. and Elizabeth D. (Materna) Suvak; m. John S. Phillips, Jan. 27, 1963 (div. Jan. 1981); children: Bruce, Bryce, Brian; m. John D.C. Roach, Aug. 28, 1982. BS, Syracuse U., 1960; postgrad. in English, Case We. Res. U., 1963—64. Cert. elem. and spl. edn. tchr., NY; cert. interior designer, Calif. Tchr. pub. schs., Shaker Heights, Ohio, 1960—66. Sportswriter Cleve. Press, 1976-77; spl. features editor Pro Quarterback Mag., NYC, 1976-79; bd. dirs. Cast Specialties Inc., Cleve., 1960-2007. Author: Chris Evert: First Lady of Tennis, 1977, Picture Story of Dorothy Hamill, 1978 (ALA Booklist selection), American Quarter Horse, 1979, Earl Campbell: Houston Oiler Superstar, 1979, Picture Story of Nancy Lopez, 1980 (ALA Notable book), Go! Fight! Win! The NCA Guide for Cheerleaders, 1981 (ALA Booklist), Something for Nothing, 1981, Brush Up on Your Hair, 1981 (ALA Booklist), Texas.The Lone Star State, 1989, Provençal Interiors-French Country Style in America, 1998, French by Design, 2000, French Influences, 2001, Villa Décor: Decidedly French and Italian Style, 2002 (Foreword Mag. Best Non-Fiction Book, 2003), Unmistakably French, 2003, Emily Goes Wild, 2003 (Tex. Inst. Letters Best Children's Book, 2004), Secrets of French Design, 2004, The French Connection, 2005, Emily Works Out, 2005, Emily's Manners, 2005, Inspirations From France & Italy, 2007 (Forward Mag. Silver medal), The French Room, 2008, French Impressions, 2010, The Allure of French & Italian Decor, 2012, The Night Before Christmas in Paris, 2012, Interiors by Design, 2013, The Night Before Christmas in NY, 2013, Night Before Christmas in Texas, 2013, The French Way with Design, 2014; contbr. articles popular mags. Mem.: American Soc. Interior Designers (profl. mem., cert.), Soc. Children's Book Writers, Delta Delta Delta. Republican. Roman Cath. Home: 4200 Saint Johns Dr Dallas TX 75205

PHILLIPS, CHARLES DAVID, gerontologist, health services researcher, public health professional; b. Abilene, Tex., Nov. 3, 1948; s. Willie Everette and Mary Charlene Phillips; m. Catherine Hawes, June 2, 1978; 1 child, Anna Michelle Tankersley. BA, Tarleton State U., Stephenville, Tex., 1971; MPH, U. NC, Chapel Hill, 1987; PhD, U. Tex., Austin, Tex., 1979. Asst. prof., dept. polit. sci. U. N.C., Chapel Hill, 1980—87; rsch. scientist RTI Internat., Rsch. Triangle Park, NC, 1988—96; dir. Myers Rsch. Inst., Beachwood, Ohio, 1996—2000; regents prof. dept. health policy and mgmt. Sch. Rural Pub. Health, Coll. Sta., Tex., dir. health svcs. rsch. program, 2000—, head doctoral studies, 2001—07. Mem. grad. faculty Tex. A&M U., 2000—. Mem. editl. bd.: The Gerontologist, 2000—09. Recipient Pub. Svc. award, Nat. Citizens Coalition Nursing Home Reform, 2005, Alumni Academic Forum honoree, Tarleton State U., 2006, Regents Prof. award, TAMU Sys, Bd. Regents, 2008; named Gerontologist of Yr., U. Tex., Houston Ctr. Aging, 2001; named to Rschr. Honor Roll, Nat. Citizens Coalition Nursing Home Reform, 2000, ISI Highly Cited Authors Social Scis. Fellow: Gerontol. Soc. Am., interRAI; mem.: APHA, Nat. Pub. Health Honor Soc., Academy-Health, Delta Omega. Democrat. Office: Sch Rural Pub Health TAMUSHSC 1266 Tamu College Station TX 77843 Business E-Mail: phillipscd@srph.tamhsc.edu.

PHILLIPS, CHARLES E., JR., computer software company executive; b. Little Rock, Ark., 1959; m. Karen Phillips; 1 child, Chas. BS in Computer Sci., USAF Acad., 1981; MBA in Fin., Hampton U., Va., 1986; JD, NYU Law Sch., 1993. CFA; bar: Ga., DC. Prin. Morgan Stanley & Co., Inc., 1994—95, mng. dir., 1995—2003; exec. v.p. strategy, partnerships & bus. devel. Oracle Corp., Redwood City, Calif., 2003—04, co-pres., 2004—10, PeopleSoft, Inc., 2004; CEO Infor Global Solutions, Alpharetta, Ga., 2010—. Bd. dirs. Oracle Corp., 2004—10, Viacom Corp., 2004—, Morgan Stanley, 2006—10, Infor, 2010—; mem. President's Econ. Recovery Advisory Bd., 2009—. Trustee Joint Ctr. Polit. & Econ. Studies, Washington, NY Law Sch.; bd. dirs. Jazz at Lincoln Ctr., NYC. Capt. USMC. Named one of The 50 Who Matter Now, Business 2.0, 2007, The 50 Black Professionals on Wall Street, Black Enterprise Mag. Office: Infor 13560 Morris Rd Ste 4100 Alpharetta GA 30004 Office Phone: 678-319-8000. Office Fax: 678-319-8682.

PHILLIPS, CLIFFORD DOUGLAS, radiologist, educator; b. Elkins, W.Va., Oct. 3, 1959; s. Clifford R. and Angelia E. Phillips. MD, Marshall U., Huntington, W.Va., 1984. Lic. in diagnostic radiology Am. Bd. Radiology, 1988, cert. in neuroradiology added qualifications Am. Bd. Radiology, 2005. Prof., dept. radiology, neurosurgery and otolaryngology-head and neck surgery U. Va. Health Sys., Charlottesville, 1998—, dir. divsn. neuroradiology, 2000—. Fellow: Am. Coll. Radiology. Office: Univ Va Health Sys Dept Radiology 1215 Lee St Charlottesville VA 22908

PHILLIPS, DAVID P., grocery company executive; CFO Publix Super Markets, Inc., Lakeland, Fla., 1999—, treas. Office: Publix Super Markets PO Box 407 Lakeland FL 33802-0407 Office Phone: 863-688-1188.

PHILLIPS, HARRY R., III, cardiologist; MD, Duke U., 1975. Diplomate Am. Bd. Internal Medicine, 1978, Am. Bd. Internal Medicine-cardiovasc. disease, 1979, Am. Bd. Internal Medicine-interventional cardiology, 2001. Resident internal medicine Mass. Gen. Hosp., Boston, 1976—77, fellow cardiovasc. disease, 1977—79; assoc. dir. Duke Heart Ctr., Durham, NC, chief med. officer. Office: Duke University Medical Center PO Box 3126 Durham NC 27710 Office Phone: 919-681-4804. Office Fax: 919-681-2990.

PHILLIPS, JOHN, communications executive; Pres., COO Advanced Telecoms. Corp., 1985-88; CEO Resurgens Comms. Group, Inc., 1989-93; pres., CEO Actava, 1994-95; pres., CEO, dir. Metromedia Internat. Group Inc. (formerly Actava), 1995-96; chmn., CEO Resurgens Comms., 1997-99; pres., CEO World Access, Atlanta, 1999—. Office: World Access Inc 945 E Paces Ferry Rd NE Atlanta GA 30326-1376

PHILLIPS, JOHN L., astronaut; b. Fort Belvoir, Va., Apr. 15, 1951; m. Laura Jean Doell; 2 children. BS in Math. and Russian, U.S. Naval Acad., Annapolis, Md., 1972; MS in Aero. Systems, U. W. Fla., 1974; MS in Geophysics and Space Physics, UCLA, 1984, PhD in Geophysics and Space Physics, 1987. Commd. ensign USN, Annapolis, 1972; advanced through grades to Capt. USNR; Navy Corsair pilot USN, Lemoor, Calif., 1975—76, resigned, 1982; postgrad studies UCLA, 1982—89; Oppenheimer fellow Los Alamos Nat. Lab., N.Mex., 1987—89, rschr., 1989—93; prin. investigator Solar Wind Plasma Experiment aboard Ulysses Spacecraft, 1993—96; navy reservist, as A-7 pilot, 1982—2002; ret. as Capt. USNR, 2002; astronaut NASA, Houston, 1996—; ascent/entry flight engr. STS-100 Endeavour, 2001; flight engr., NASA sci. officer Expedition 11, 2005; mission specialist STS-119 Discovery Mission, 2009. Contbr. scientific papers on plasma environs. of sun, earth, other planets, comets etc, 1992. Recipient NASA Space medal, 2000, Disting. Performance award, Los Alamos Nat. Lab., 1996. Avocations: exercise, hiking, kayaking, skiing. Office: Astronauts Office NASA Johnson Space Ctr 2102 NASA Parkway Houston TX 77058

PHILLIPS, LARRY, state legislator; b. Apr. 5, 1966; m. Robin Phillips. Mem. Dist. 62 Tex. House of Representatives, 2004—. Republican. Office: 421 N Crockett Sherman TX 75090 also: Room E2.602 Capitol Extension PO Box 2910 Austin TX 78768 Office Phone: 512-463-0297, 903-891-7297.

PHILLIPS, LARRY EDWARD, lawyer; b. Pitts., July 5, 1942; s. Jack F. and Jean H. (Houghtelin) P.; m. Karla Ann Hennings, June 5, 1976; 1 child, Andrew H.; 1 stepchild, John W. Dean IV. BA, Hamilton Coll., Clinton, NY, 1964; JD, U. Mich., 1967. Bar: Pa. 1967, Fla. 2004, US Dist. Ct. (we. dist.) Pa. 1967, US Tax Ct. 1969. Assoc. Buchanan Ingersoll & Rooney PC, Pitts., 1967—73, shareholder, 1973—2010. Mem. Am. Coll. Tax Counsel, Fla. Bar, Tax Mgmt. Inc. (adv. bd.). Republican. Presbyterian. Business E-Mail: larryephillipsh2@gmail.com.

PHILLIPS, LINDA GOODE, state legislator; b. Mullen, W.Va., Oct. 21, 1952; d. Jack, Mary Lee; m. Ron Phillips; children: Kate Phillips-Black, John Paul, Justin. BA, MA, Marshall U. Mem. Dist. 22 W.Va. House of Delegates, 2008—, mem. Fin. Com., Health and Human Resources Com., Natural Resources Com. Mem.: NRA, Nat. Edn. Assn. Democrat. Methodist. Office: State Capitol Complex Rm 230E, Bldg 1 Charleston WV 25305 Mailing: PO Box 505 Pineville WV 24874 Office Phone: 304-340-3163, 304-732-6298. E-mail: lgphill@mail.wvnet.edu.

PHILLIPS, OWEN P., clinical geneticist, educator; MD, U. Miss., Jackson, 1980. Cert. Am. Bd. Clin. Genetics-Med. Genetics, 2006, diplomate Am. Bd. Ob-Gyn., 2006. Resident ob-gyn. Univ. Miss.,

Jackson, 1981—84; fellow reproductive genetics Univ. Tenn. Health Sci. Ctr., 1989—90, prof. ob-gyn. dept., dir. pathology lab. maternal serum screening program; hosp. affiliation includes Univ. Tenn. Med. Group, Regional Med. Ctr., Memphis, Baptist Meml. Hosp. Recipient Huffman-Capraro award, Charles Hunter award; named one of the Best Doctors in America. Fellow: ACOG; mem.: Soc. Gynecol. Investigation, Memphis and Shelby County Med. Obstet., Ctrl. Assn. Ob-Gyn., Profs. Ob-Gyn. Assn., Am. Soc. Human Genetics, AMA, Am. Coll. Med. Genetics. Office: University Tennessee Medical Group Center for High Risk Pregnancies 6215 Humphreys Blvd Ste 201 Memphis TN 38120-2382 Office Phone: 901-866-8085. Office Fax: 901-302-2085.

PHILLIPS, RANDY E., corporate financial executive; Grad. Tuck Exec. Program, Dartmouth Coll., 1997; BS in Computer Sci. & Sys., Wright State U., Ohio; completed, Harvard U. Program for Sr Exec. in Nat. and Internat. Security. Dir., corp. devel. Alcoa, Inc., NY, pres., China corp. devel; v.p., corp. devel. TRW Inc., 1996—2003; joined Computer Sciences Corp., 2007, v.p., corp. devel., 2008—. Trustee Wright State U. Found.; trustee, external adv. bd. Coll. Engring. and Computer Sci. Office: Computer Sciences Corp 3170 Fairview Pk Dr Falls Church VA 22042 Office Phone: 703-876-1000. Business E-Mail: randy.phillips@csc.com.

PHILLIPS, RICHARD B., education educator; b. Raleigh, 1942; BS in Sci., NC State U., 1964, M in Sci., 1970, PhD in Chem. Engring., 1970. Joined International Paper Co., Stamford, Conn., 1971, v.p., tech., sr. v.p., tech., 1996—2005; adj. prof., exec. in residence, wood and paper sci. dept. NC State U., 2005—. Bd. dirs. Gruppa Ilim OAO, 2007—. Office: NC State University Campus Box 8005 Raleigh NC 27695 Office Phone: 919-515-5807. Business E-Mail: Richard_Phillips@ncsu.edu.

PHILLIPS, ROBERT GLENN, gas industry executive, lawyer; b. Midland, Tex., Oct. 9, 1954; s. Glenn Sterling and Mary Ruth (McGee) P.; m. Shirley Jean Davanay, July 14, 1979; children: Brittany Kyle, Cameron Sterling, Christian Victoria, Courtland Price, Mallory Blair. AB, Tyler Jr. Coll., 1974; BBA, U. Tex., 1977; JD, South Tex. Coll., 1981. Contract adminstr. Gulf Oil Co., 1977-78; with, hydrocarbon sales Anadarko Prodn. Co., 1978-79; gas purchase rep. Tenn. Gas Transmission Co., 1979-80; gas supply mgr. Tex. Gas Corp., 1980-81; v.p., gen. mgr. Eastex Gas Transmission Co., 1981-83; pres., chmn. & CEO Eastex Energy Inc., 1983—95; various sr. mgmt. positions El Paso Corp.; pres. El Paso Field Svc. Co. (subs. El Paso Corp.), 1996—2004; chmn., pres. & CEO GulfTerra Energy Ptnr. LP (acquired by Enterprise Products Ptnr. LP), 1999—2004; COO Enterprise Products Ptnr. LP, 2004—05, bd. dirs., 2004—07, pres., CEO, 2005—07; founder Crestwood Midstream Partners LP (formerly Quicksilver Gas Services LP), 2007, chmn., pres. & CEO, 2010—. Bd. dirs. Triten Corp., Pride Internat., Inc., 2007—. Mem. Nat. Gas Assn. Houston, Tex. Lyceum Assn., United Shareholder Assn. (chmn. Houston chpt. 1988—). Avocations: golf, hunting. Office: Crestwood Midstream Partners LP 700 Louisiana St Ste 2060 Houston TX 77002-2830 Office Phone: 832-519-2200. Office Fax: 832-519-2250. Business E-Mail: rphillips@prde.com.

PHILLIPS, ROBERT JAMES, JR., lawyer, corporate financial executive; b. Houston, 1955; s. Robert James. BBA, So. Meth. U., 1976, JD, 1980. Bar: Tex. 1980. Vp., gen. counsel Aegis Shipping Ltd., London, 1980-81; assoc. Bishop, Larrimore, Lamsens & Brown, 1981-82; pres. Phillips Devel. Corp., Ft. Worth, 1982—; pvt. practice Ft. Worth, 1982—87; assoc. Haynes and Boone, Ft. Worth, 1988-89; sr. v.p. Am. Real Estate Group, 1989-93, Am. Savs. Bank, N.A., New West Fed. Savs. and Loan Assn., 1989-93, Am. Savs. Bank, Ft. Worth, 1991-92; chmn., CEO creative risk control Environ. Risk Mgmt. Inc., Ft. Worth, 1992-94; chmn., CEO Pangburn Candy Co., 1996-99; exec. v.p. Ancor Holdings, 1999—2002; chmn., CEO Am. Staff Resources Corp., 1999—2004; pres. InterProm Capital L.L.C., 2003—04, Fund Corp., Inc., 2004—. Bd. dirs. Tex. Heritage, Inc. Bd. dirs., exec. com. Ft. Worth Ballet Assn., 1984-85, Van Cliburn Found.; v.p. planning, bd. dirs., exec. com. Ft. Worth Symphony Orch., 1984-85; bd. dirs. Mus. Modern Art, 1986; bd. dirs., exec. com., chmn. investment com. Tex. Boys Choir, 1983-85. Mem. ABA, Tex. Bar Assn., Ft. Worth Bd. Realtors, Phi Delta Phi, Kappa Sigma, Beta Gamma Sigma.

PHILLIPS, T. DANNY, insurance company executive; Acct. Condley and Co.; various fin. mgmt. positions Harken Energy Corp.; CFO Aloha Petroleum, Ltd., AdvancePCS, Irving, Tex., 1992—2002, sr. exec. v.p., 2003—, bd. dirs. Office: AdvancePCS Inc 750 W John Carpenter Freeway Ste 1200 Irving TX 75039

PHILLIPS, THOMAS WADE, federal judge; b. Oneida, Tenn., July 6, 1943; s. W.T. and Lucille (Lewallen) P.; m. Dorothy Mills, Jan. 2, 1971; children: Lori Ann, Wade Thomas. BA, Berea Coll., Ky., 1965; JD, Vanderbilt U. Law Sch., 1969; LLM in Labor Law, George Washington U., 1973. Bar: Tenn. 1969, U.S. Supreme Ct. 1972, U.S. Ct. Appeals (6th cir.) 1980. Assoc., ptnr. Baker, Worthington, Crosley, Stansberry & Wolfe, Huntsville, Tenn., 1973—77; ptnr. Phillips & Williams, P.C., Oneida, Tenn., 1977—91; magistrate judge US Dist. Ct. (eastern dist.) Tenn., Knoxville, Tenn., 1991—2002, judge, 2002—13, sr. judge, 2013—. County atty. Scott County, Huntsville, 1976-91; city atty. Town of Oneida, 1978-91. Capt. JAGC, U.S. Army, 1969-73. Mem. ABA, Tenn. Bar Assn. (house of dels. 1989-91), Scott County Bar Assn. Office: US District Court Howard H Baker Jr Courtho 800 Market St Knoxville TN 37902-2327*

PHILLIPS, WADE, professional football coach; b. Orange, Tex., June 21, 1947; s. Oail Andrew (Bum) and Helen Phillips; m. Laurie Phillips; children: Tracey, Wesley. Student, U. Houston, 1965—68. Grad. asst. U. Houston Cougars, 1969; defensive coord. West Orange-Stark HS Mustangs, Orange, Tex., 1970-72; linebackers coach Okla. State U. Cowboys, 1973-74; defensive line coach U. Kans. Jayhawks, 1975; linebackers coach Houston Oilers, 1976, defensive line coach, 1977-80; defensive coord. New Orleans Saints, 1981-85, interim head coach, 1985; defensive coord. Phila. Eagles, 1986-88, Denver Broncos, 1989-93, head coach, 1993-94; defensive coord. Buffalo Bills, 1995—97, head coach, 1998—2000; defensive coord. Atlanta Falcons, 2001—04, interim head coach, 2003; defensive coord. San Diego Chargers, 2004—07; head coach Dallas Cowboys, 2007—10, defensive coord., 2009—10, Houston Texans, 2011—, interim head coach, 2013—. Office: The Houston Texans Two Reliant Pk Houston TX 77054*

PHILLIPS, WINFRED MARSHALL, academic administrator, professor, mechanical engineer; b. Richmond, Va., Oct. 7, 1940; s. Claude Marshall and Gladys Marian (Barden) P.; children: Stephen, Sean. BSME, Va. Poly. Inst., 1963; MA in Engring., U. Va., 1966, DSc, 1968. Mech. engr. U.S. Naval Weapons Lab., Dahlgren, Va., 1963; NSF trainee, tchg. and rsch. asst. dept. aerospace engring. U. Va., Charlottesville, 1963—67, rsch. scientist, 1966—67; asst. prof. dept. aerospace engring. Pa. State U., University Park, 1968-74, from assoc. prof. to prof., 1974—80, assoc. dean rsch. Coll. Engring., 1979—80; head Sch. Mech. Engring. Purdue U., West Lafayette, Ind., 1980-88; dean Coll. Engring. U. Fla., Gainesville, 1988-99, assoc. v.p. engring., 1989—99, v.p. rsch. and Don and Ruth Eckis prof. biomed. engring., 1999—2011, sr. v.p., COO, 2011—. Bd. dir. Wells Fargo Bank, Gainesville; vis. prof. U. Paris, 1976—77; adv. com. Nimbus Corp., 1985—90, Hong Kong U. Sci. and Tech., 1990—93, AvMed Inc.; co-founder, v.p. CEO Inc., 1990—; acad. adv. coun. Indsl. Rsch. Inst., 1990—93; exec. com. Accreditation Bd. on Engring. and Tech., 1991—96; sci. adv. com. Electric Power Rsch. Inst., 1994—99; vice-chmn. Southeastern Coalition Minorities Engring., 1995—2011; chmn. Southeastern Coalition for Minorities in Engring., 2001—04; internat. revs. for univs. in Saudi Arabia, Russia, Netherlands, Kuwait, Mexico, China, France Accreditation Bd. on Engring. and Tech., 1995—; bd. dirs Oak Ridge Associated Univs., 2002—12, chair coun., mem. exec. com., 2002—12, chmn. bd., 2009—12; mem. US Pres.'s Commn. on Nat. Medal of Sci., 2003—08. Sect. editor Am. Soc. Artificial Internal Organs Jour., 1985-99; contbr. over 175 articles to profl. jours., chpts. to books. Mem. Ind. Boiler and Pressure Vessel Code Bd., 1981—88; bd. dirs. Ctrl. Pa. Heart Assn., 1974—80, U. Fla. Found., 1989—91, 1995—2001. Recipient Career Rsch. award, NIH, 1974—78, NIH Surgery and Bioengring. Study sect., 1988—91, Fla. High Tech. and Industry Coun., 1990—94, Nat. Engring. award, Am. Assn. Engr. Socs., 2000, Linton Grinter award, 2000, Global Messenger award, Southeastern Consortium for Minorities in Engring., 2003; named Disting. Hoosier Ind., 1987, Sagamore of the Wabash, 1988. Fellow AAAS, AIAA, ASEE (vice chair 2001-02, chmn. bd. 2002-03, Lamme award 2003), ASME (hon. sr. v.p. edn. 1986-88, bd. dirs. 1995-2000, pres. 1998-99, Dedicated Svc. award 2001, Ralph Coates Roe medal 2005), Biomed. Engring. Soc.(fellow, 2005), NY Acad. Scis., Am. Astron. Soc., Am. Inst. Med. and Biol. Engring. (founding fellow, chair coll. fellows 1994-95, pres. 1996-97), Am. Soc. Engring. Edn. (past chmn. long range planning soc. awards 1990-92, vice chmn. engring. deans coun. 1991-93, chair 1993-95, bd. dirs. 1994-98, 1st v.p. 1994-95, pres. 1996-97), Royal Soc. Arts, Am. Soc. Artificial Internal Organs (trustee 1982-90, sec.-treas. 1986-87, pres. 1988-89, adv. bd. 1998—), ABET (pres. 1996-97); mem. Nat. Assn. State Univs. and Land-Grant Colls. (com. quality of engring. edn.), Univ. Programs in Computer-Aided Engring., Design and Mfg. (bd. dirs. 1985-91), Wash. Accord (chair 2007-11), IEA (chair 2010-11), Am. Phys. Soc., Internat. Soc. Biotheology, Fla. Engring. Soc., Cosmos Club, Fla. Blue Key, Rotary (pres. Lafayette 1987-88), Sigma Xi, Phi Kappa Phi, Phi Tau Sigma, Sigma Gamma Tau, Tau Beta Pi (eminent engr.). Achievements include research in artificial heart pumps; reentry aerodynamics; blood rheology; modeling blood flow; fluid dynamics of artificial hearts; use of smooth blood contacting surface; prosthetic valve fluid dynamics; laser Doppler studies of unsteady biofluid dynamics. Home: 4140 NW 44th Ave Gainesville FL 32606-4518 Office: University Fla SVP Coo 204 Tigert Hall Gainesville FL 32611 Office Phone: 352-392-9122.

PHILP, RICHARD NILSON, writer, editor, journalist, historian; b. Plainfield, NJ, July 7, 1943; s. Lester Perry and Gladys Emma Linea (Nilson) P. BA in English and Theater cum laude, U. N.C., 1965; MFA in Theater Lit. and Playwriting, Yale U., 1968. Lectr. Yale U., Princeton U., Fordham U., Juilliard, U. Utah, U. Wyo., others; faculty Summer Dance Festival U. Wyo., 1995-97. Author 8 plays, produced 1963-72; author: To Move, To Learn, 1973, Danseur: The Male in Ballet, 1977, Romeo and Juliet, Romeos Dancing, Shakespeare Without Words, 2003, Vladimir Malakov, 2003, Dracula the Ballet, 2004, Peter Pan: A Ballet Scenario, 2005, Alice in Wonderland: A Ballet Scenario, 2005, Village, A Biocentennial Celebration of the Village of Catskill, 2006, Catskill Village, 2009; editor and contbg. author: Memoirs of a Dancer: Shadows, Dreams, Memories, 1979, The Gospel According to Dance, 1980, Alvin Ailey American Dance Theater, 1993, Passion & Line, 1997; exec. editor: Dance Books, 1981-86; founding bd. dirs. World Dance Alliance, 1993; chmn. Dance Mag. Prize for Reportage, Video Danse, 1992, 93, 96, 99; mng. editor Dance Mag., 1970-88, editor-in-chief, 1989—99, exec. editor, 2000-02, editor-in-chief emeritus, 2002-; assoc. editor Critics Choice, 1969-70, assoc. editor After Dark, Magazine of Entertainment, 1970-75; contbr. monthly column Kickoff, 1989—2002; contbr. articles to profl. jours. Treas. Dance Mag. Found., 1984-93; co-chmn. internat. adv. bd. Jackson Ballet Competition, Miss., 1989-2004; selection com. ann. Broadway Astaire awards, 1989-2005; bd. dirs. Israel Dance Collection Libr., 1989—95, Joffrey Ballet Sch., 1994—, Video Danse, Paris, Lively Art Christ Ch. Episcopal, Hudson, NY; treas., bd. dirs. Beattie-Powers Pl., 2006-, Beattie-Powers Pl. historian, 2006-; adv. bd. Juilliard Sch., 1994-2002; bd. advisors Thomas Cole's Cedar Grove, 1999-2008; docent Thomas Cole's Cedar Grove, 2001—; active Catskill Bicentennial Com., 2006; historian Catskill Village, 2006—, Town of Catskill Historian, 2008-, curator Catskill River Views, 2009, Pleshakov Piano Found., 1995-, bd. chmn., 2008-. Recipient Spl. citation Soc. Illustrators, Bronze medal 28th Internat. Film and TV Fest, NYC, 1985, Silver medal Chgo. Internat. Film Festival, 1985, TV Documentary Writing award Am. Film Festival, 1986, Nijinsky award, 1994, Ellen Rettus Planning Achievement award for cmty. svc., 2006. Mem. Catskill Writers Group (founder 1978), Devon Beekeepers Assn. (Eng.), Mountain Beekeepers Assn., 2006-. Home and Office: 166 Bridge St Catskill NY 12414-1404 Home: The Towers Apt 22 33-15 80th St Jackson Heights NY 11372 also: Vista Harbor Apt 10C 2800 Indian River Blvd Vero Beach FL 32960 Office Phone: 518-943-5308. Personal E-mail: richardphilp@mhcable.com.

PHIPPS, BENJAMIN KIMBALL, II, lawyer; b. Boston, Jan. 16, 1933; s. Benjamin Kimball and Bertha Elizabeth (Forsyth) P.; m. Phyllis Jarrett Anderson, Jan. 10, 1962; children: Lisa Jarrett, Christina Caroline. BS in Commerce, U. Va., 1955, LLB, 1958. Bar: Fla. 1964, U.S. Dist. Ct. (no. dist.) Fla., U.S. Claims Ct., U.S. Ct. Appeals (5th and 11th cirs.), U.S. Tax Ct.; cert. Inst. Profls. in Taxation, 2004. Pvt. practice, Tallahassee, 1965—; chmn. & sr. ptnrs. Phipps & Howell. Counsel tax com. Fla. Ho. of Reps., 1966-72, counsel to spkr., 1973-74, mem. adv. com. fin. & tax com., 1983-84; mem. Legis. Task Force Taxpayers' Bill Rights, 1989-91; elected dir. Fla. Coun. Property Tax Lawyers, 2003 Contbr. articles to profl. jours.; columnist Tallahassee Democrat. Chmn. Hist. Tallahassee Preservation Bd., 1970-91; mem. Tallahassee Trust for Hist. Preservation, 1997—, treas., 1998—. Served to capt., U.S. Army, 1958-64. Mem. ABA (tax sect. state and local tax com.), Tallahassee Bar Assn., Fla. Bar Assn. (treas., vice chmn., chmn. tax sect. 1985-86, editl. bd. Fla. Bar Jour. News, chmn. 1975-76), Inst. Profls. Taxation, CMI, Gov.'s Club, Univ. Ctr. Club, Cosmos Club, Exch. Club, Tiger Bay Club (dir.), Fla. Econ. Club, St. Andrews Soc. (pres. 1978-79), Sigma Alpha Epsilon, Phi Alpha Delta, Pi Delta Epsilon. Republican. Episcopalian. Office: PO Box 1351 Tallahassee FL 32302-1351 Office Phone: 850-222-7000. Business E-Mail: bkp@thephippsfirm.com.

PHUNG, NGUYEN DINH, medical educator; b. Ninh Binh, Vietnam, Sept. 25, 1950; came to U.S., 1975; s. Thu Dinh Nguyen and Minh Tuyet Le; m. Thuy Thanh Tran, Sept. 25, 1974; children: The-Ngoc, Khoi-Nguyen, Thien Huong. MD, Saigon Med. Sch., 1973. Diplomate Am. Bd. Internal Medicine, Am. Bd. Allergy and Immunology. Clin. instr. medicine, staff physician U. Okla. Health Scis. Ctr. & Vets. Hosp., Oklahoma City, 1982-84; clin. asst. prof. medicine U. Tex. Med. Sch., Houston, 1989—. Co-author: Practical Allergy & Immunology, 1983; contbr. articles to profl. jours. Mem. ACP, Am. Acad. Allergy and Immunology. Avocations: writing, music. Office: Allergy and Asthma Clinic 2905 Milam St Houston TX 77006-3609

PIANKA, ERIC RODGER, population biologist, educator; b. Hilt, Calif., Jan. 1939; s. Walter and Virginia P.; m. Helen Dunlap, Dec. 20, 1965 (div. Dec. 1980); children: Karen, Gretchen. BA, Carleton Coll., 1960; PhD (NIH fellow), U. Wash., 1965; DSc, U. We. Australia, 1990. NIH postdoctoral fellow Princeton U., 1965-68, U. Western Australia, Nedlands, 1966-67; asst. prof. zoology U. Tex., Austin, 1968-72, assoc. prof., 1972-77, prof., 1977—, Denton A. Cooley Centennial prof. zoology, 1986—. Vis. prof. U. Kans., 1978, U. P.R., 1981 Author: Evolutionary Ecology, 6th edit., 2000, also Greek, Japanese, Spanish, Polish and Russian transl., Ecology and Natural History of Desert Lizards, 1986, The Lizard Man Speaks, 1994; co-editor: Lizard Ecology: Studies of a Model Organism, 1983, Lizard Ecology: Historical and Experimental Perspectives, 1994, Lizards: Windows to the Evolution of Diversity, 2003, Varanoid Lizards of the world, 2004; mng. editor The Am. Naturalist, 1971-74; mem. edit. bd. BioSci, 1975-80; bd. editors Nat. Geog. Rsch., 1985—; contbr. articles to profl. publs. Named Disting. Herpetologist, 2004, Disting. Tex. Scientist, 2006; Fulbright Sr. Rsch. scholar, 1990-91; Guggenheim fellow, 1978-79; NSF grantee, 1966-94; Nat. Geog. Soc. grantee, 1975-79, 89-90, 95-96; Fellow, Ecol. Soc. America, 2013. Fellow AAAS; mem. Am. Soc. Naturalists, Ecol. Soc. Am., Am. Soc. Ichthyologists and Herpetologists, Soc. for Study Evolution, Herpetologists League, Western Australian Naturalists Club, French Varanid Assn. (hon.). Research on ecology and diversity of desert lizards.

PIASSICK, JOEL BERNARD, lawyer; b. Atlanta, June 2, 1940; s. Louis S. and Sarah (Freeman) P.; m. Karen Pevow, Aug. 11, 1963; children: Joan, Louis. BA in Polit. Sci., Tulane U., 1962; LLB, U. Va., 1965. Bar: Va. 1965, Ga. 1966, Colo. 1999. Ptnr. Smith, Gambrell & Russell, Atlanta, 1967-90; ptnr., of counsel Kilpatrick Stockton LLP, Atlanta, 1990—; exec. v.p. Harbert Mgmt. Corp, Birmingham, Ala., 1998—. Fellow Am. Coll. Bankruptcy. Office: Harbert 2100 3rd Ave N Ste 600 Birmingham AL 35203-3416

PICARD, DENNIS J., retired electronics company executive; b. Providence, Aug. 25, 1932; m. Dolores Picard; 5 children. BBA, Northeastern U., 1962; doctorate (hon.), Merrimack Coll., Bentley Coll. With RCA, 1954—55; from elec. engr. to pres. Raytheon Co., 1955—91, corp. v.p., 1976, CEO, 1989—99, Rayth of dirs., 1989—2001, chmn. emeritus, 1989—. Dir. State St. Boston Corp.; trustee Northeastern U.; trustee emeritus Bentley Coll.; dir., mem. bus. coun. Discovery Mus., Acton, Mass. Active Def. Policy Adv. Com. on Trade, Pres.'s Export Coun., Pres.'s Nat. Security Telecomms. Adv. Coun. With USAF, 1951—53. Decorated Environ. Achievement award Nat. Security Indsl. Assn., Fleet Admiral Cheser W. Nimitz award Navy League of U.S., Intrepid Salute award Intrepid Mus. Found., John R. Allison award USAF Assn., John W. Dixon medal Assn. U.S. Army; recipient New Englander of Yr., New England Coun., 1997, Indsl. Leadership award, Nat. Def. Indsl. Assn., 1998, Rear Admiral John J. Bergen Leadership medal, Navy League, 1998. Fellow: AIAA (hon.; pres., adv. bd.); mem.: IEEE, NAE, Armed Forces Commns. and Electronics Assn., Bus. Coun., Mass. Bus. Roundtables, Algonquin Club of Boston. Office: AIAA Ste 500 1801 Alexander Bell Dr Reston VA 20191-4344

PICAZIO, KIM LOWRY, lawyer; b. Greenville, NC, Jan. 8, 1969; d. Harry Etheridge and Marion Thomas Lowry; m. Michael James Picazio, Mar. 25, 1995. BS, U. Miami, 1991; JD, Fla. State U., 1995. Bar: Fla. 1995. Lawyer Heinrich, Gordon, Hargrove, Weihe & James, P.A., Ft. Lauderdale, Fla., 1995-96; atty. Law Offices of Robert D. Hertzberg, P.A., Miami, Fla., 1996—2007, pvt. practice, 2007—. Recipient: Corpus Juris Secundum award (Contract Law), Am. Jurisprudence award (Contract Law); named on of Top Lawyers, South Fla. Legal Guide., 2005-07. Mem. ATLA, Am. Acad. Matrimonial Lawyer, Dade County Bar Assn., First Family Law Inns Ct., Fla. Bar (Family Law Sect.), Fla. Acad. Matrimonial Lawyers. Office: Law Office Kim L Picazio PA One Fin Plaza 1 Financial Plz Ste 2024 Fort Lauderdale FL 33394-0013 Office Phone: 954-467-5558. Office Fax: 954-462-1335. Personal E-mail: picazio@bellsouth.net. Business E-Mail: kim@picaziolaw.com.

PICI, FRANK A., corporate financial executive; Bachelor's Degree, Clarion U. of Pa.; MBA, U. Pitts. CPA. Sr. financial mgmt. positions Cabot Oil & Gas Corp.; v.p, CFO Mariner Energy, Inc.; exec. v.p., CFO Penn Va. Corp.; CFO Penn Va. GP Holdings, LP, Penn Va. Resources Partners, LP; CFO, treas. CVR Energy, Inc., 2012—; mng. gen. ptnr. CVR Partners, LP. Office: CVR Energy Inc Ste 500 2277 Plaza Dr Sugar Land TX 77479*

PICKARD, FRANK CLEMENCE, III, corporate financial executive; b. Albuquerque, Dec. 30, 1944; s. Frank Clemence and Manson (Meriweather) P.; m. Nancy Dewitt Thompson, June 28, 1991; 1 child, Frank C. IV. BA, Northwestern U., 1967; M in Internat. Bus., Am. Grad. Sch. Internat. Mgmt., 1969; MBA, Dartmouth Coll., 1971. Officer comml. banking The Northern Trust Co., 1971-75; joined VF Corp., 1976, various fin. positions, including mergers & acquisitions, employee benefits & taxes, asst. treas., 1985-87, asst. sec., treas., 1987—, v.p., 1999—. Episcopalian. Office: VF Corp 105 Corporate Ctr Blvd Greensboro NC 27408 Office Phone: 336-424-6000. Business E-Mail: frank_pickard@vfc.com.

PICKENS, RUPERT TARPLEY, III, French language educator; b. High Point, NC, Feb. 20, 1940; s. Rupert T. Jr. and Ida (Munyan) P.; m. Nancy Shore Clinard, May 13, 1942; children: John Armfield, Edward Munyan. AB, U. N.C., 1961; postgrad., U. de Rennes (France), 1961-62; MA, U. N.C., 1964, PhD, 1966. Asst. prof. French U. N.C., Chapel Hill, 1966-69, U. Ky., Lexington, 1969-70, assoc. prof. French, 1970-78, prof. French, 1978—, chair dept. French, 1984-92, 1998—2001. Author: The Welsh Knight, 1977; editor: The Sower and His Seed, 1983, In Honor of Hans-Erich Keller, 1993, The French Canon, 1994; editor, co-author: The Songs for Jaufre Rudel, 1978, Perceval by Chrétien de Troyes, 1990; translator: The Story of Merlin, 1993. Vestry mem. Ch. of St. Michael the Archangel, Lexington, 1978-82, 87-90, 2005, 08, sr. warden, 1980-82, 88-90, 2008-. Fulbright fellow U.S. Govt., 1961-62; rsch. grantee Nat. Endowment for the Humanities, 1989-90. Mem. Soc. Guillaume IX (pres. 1992-94), Internat. Marie de Franco Soc. (pres. 2007-09), Fulbright Assn., Internat. Arthurian Soc., Internat. Country Literature Soc., Soc. Rencesvals. Episcopalian. Office: U Ky 1021 Patterson Towers Lexington KY 40506-0006 Home: 968 Hammock Oak Ln Lexington KY 40515-6455 Office Phone: 859-257-3133. E-mail: rtpickens@insightbb.com.

PICKENS, T. BOONE (THOMAS BOONE PICKENS JR.), hedge fund manager, former oil industry executive; b. Holdenville, Okla., May 22, 1928; s. Thomas Boone Pickens and Grace Molonson; m. Lynn O'Brien, 1949 (div. 1971); 4 children; m. Beatrice Louise Carr, Apr. 21, 1972 (div.); 1 adopted child; m. Nelda Cain, 2000 (div. 2004); m. Madeleine Paulson, July 16, 2005. Student, Tex. A&M U.; BS in Geology, Okla. State U., Stillwater, 1951. Geologist Phillips Petroleum Co., 1951-54; co-founder Mesa Petroleum Co. (formerly Petroleum Exploration, Inc.), 1956, chmn. bd. dirs., pres., 1964—96; gen. ptnr., CEO Mesa Ltd. Partnership, 1985—96; founder, chmn. BP Capital Mgmt., 1996—. Mem. Nat. Petroleum Coun.; founder, chmn. United Shareholders Assn.; bd. dirs. Clean Energy Fuels Corp., 2001—, Exco Resources Inc., 2005—. Author: Boone, 1987, The

Luckiest Guy in the World, 2001, The First Billion is the Hardest: Reflections on a Life of Comebacks and America's Energy Future, 2008. Adv. Nat Campaign for Drug Free America; founder, chmn. T. Boone Pickens Found. Recipient Disting. Am. award, Nat. Football Found., 2008, Bower award for bus. leadership, Franklin Inst., Phila., 2009, Horatio Alger award, US Dept. Energy Clean Cities Nat. Partner award, INFORM's Corp. Environmental Leadership award, Honda Environmental Citizen award; named Texan of Yr., Tex. Legis. Conf., 2008; named one of Forbes 400: Richest Americans, 2006—, 25 Most Influential Republicans, Newsmax Mag., 2008, The World's Most Influential People, TIME mag., 2009. Republican. Office: BP Capital 8117 Preston Rd Ste 260 Dallas TX 75225

PICKERING, JAMES HENRY, III, academic administrator, educator; b. NYC, July 11, 1937; s. James H. and Anita (Felber) P.; m. Patricia Paterson, Aug. 18, 1962; children: David Scott, Susan Elizabeth. BA, Williams Coll., 1959; MA, Northwestern U., 1960, PhD, 1964. Instr. English Northwestern U., 1963-65; mem. faculty Mich. State U., East Lansing, 1965-81, prof. English, 1972-81, grad. and assoc. chmn. dept., 1968-75, dir. Honors Coll., 1975-81; dean Coll. Humanities and Fine Arts U. Houston, 1981-90, sr. v.p., provost, 1990-92, pres., 1992-95, Martha Gano Houstoun prof. lit. criticism, 2008—10; historian laureate Estes Park, Colo., 2006. Author: The Spy, 1971, The Harper Reader, 1971, Fiction 100, 1974, 1978, 1982, 1985, 1988, 1992, 1995, 1998, 2001, 2004, 2007, 2010, 2012, The World Turned Upside Down: Prose and Poetry of the American Revolution, 1975, The Spy Unmasked, 1975, The City in American Literature, 1977, Concise Companion to Literature, 1981, Literature, 1982, 86, 90, 94, 97, Mountaineering in Colorado, 1987, Wild Life on the Rockies, 1988, A Mountain Boyhood, 1988, The Spell of the Rockies, 1989, Purpose and Process, 1989, Poetry, 1990, In Beaver World, 1990, Rocky Mountain Wonderland, 1991, A Summer Vacation in the Parks and Mountains of Colorado, 1992, Fiction 50, 1993, Knocking Round the Rockies, 1994, Drama, 1994, Frederick Chapin's Colorado, 1995; This Blue Hollow: Estes Park, The Early Years, 1859-1915, 1999, Mr. Stanley of Estes Park, 2000, In the Vale of Elkanah, 2003, 07, The Ways of the Mountains, 2003, Early Estes Park Historical Narratives, 4 vols., 2004, America's Switzerland: Estes Park and Rocky Mountain National Park, The Growth Years, 2005, Enos Mill's Colorado, 2005, Estes Park and Rocky Mountain National Park, Then and Now, 2006, Rocky Mountain Celts, 2006, The MacGregors of Black Canyon: An American Story, 2008, Bob Flame, Rocky Mountain Ranger, 2009, William Allan White: The Moraine Park Years, 2010, Lost Links: The Search for Estes Park 's Oldest Golf Course, 2010, Shared Moments: Rocky Mountain National Park and Estes Park Remembered in Postcards, 2011. Historian laureate Town of Estes Park. Mem. Coll. English Assn. (pres. 1980-81), Phi Beta Kappa, Phi Kappa Phi, Omicron Delta Kappa. Office: U Houston Dept English Houston TX 77204-0001 Personal E-mail: jhpick@earthlink.net.

PICKERING, LARRY KENNETH, pediatrician, researcher; m. Margaret Jane Thompson, July 8, 1967; children: Margaret Anne, Andrew Michael. MD, W.Va. U. Sch. Medicine, 1970. Diplomate Am. Bd. Pediat. in Pediats., Nat. Bd. Med. Examiners. Intern pediat. svc. St. Louis Children's Hosp., 1970-71, resident pediat. svc., 1971-72; fellow pediat. infectious diseases St. Louis Children's Hosp. and Washington U. Sch. Medicine, 1972-74; asst. prof. pediat. U. Tex. Med. Sch., Houston, 1974-77, assoc. prof. pediat., 1977-82, prof. pediat. dept. pediat. divsn. infectious diseases, 1982-92, prof. program in immunology, 1982-92. Cons. M.D. Anderson Hosp. and Tumor Inst., Houston, 1974-78, St. Joseph Hosp., Houston, 1975-89, Meml. Hosp. Sys., Houston, 1977-92, AMA; assoc. prof. pediat. M.D. Anderson Hosp. and Tumor Inst., U. Tex. Cancer Ctr., 1978-83, prof. pediat., 1983-92; infection control med. advisor Speech and Hearing Inst., U. Tex. Health Sci. Ctr., Houston, 1978-87, prof. Grad. Sch. Biomed. Scis., 1982-89; adj. prof. pharmaceutics dept. pharmaceutics Coll. Pharmacy, U. Houston, 1983-92; dir. Ctr. for Pediat. Rsch., Ea. Va. Med. Sch., Children's Hosp. of The King's Daus., Norfolk, 1992-2001; David R. Park prof. pediat., 1989-92, dir. divsn. infectious diseases dept. pediat., 1975-1992; prof., CHKD chair in pediatric rsch. Ea. Va. Med. Sch., Norfolk, 1992-2001; prof. pediats. dept. pediats. Emory U. Sch. Medicine, Atlanta, 2001-; external examiner and reviewer dept. pediat. U. Jordan, Amman, 1984; mem. subboard pediat. infectious diseases Am. Bd. Pediat., 1991-96; mem. planning com. First Internat. Pediat. Infectious Diseases Conf., Monterey, Calif., 1995; mem. sci. com. First World Congress of Pediat. Infectious Diseases, 1995; mem. steering com. E. Mead Johnson Award for Rsch. in Pediat., 1996-99; presenter in field; assoc. dir. spl. projects, Nat. Immunization Program, Ctrs. Disease Control & Prevention, Atlanta, 2000-01, sr. advisor to dir. Nat. Ctr. for Immunization and Respiratory Diseases, 2001-, exec. sec. Adv. Comm. Immmir Practices Ctr. Disease Ctrl. & Prevention, Atlanta, 2005-. Author: (with H.L. DuPont) Infections of the Gastrointestinal Tract, 1980, Infectious Diseases of Children and Adults; editor: (with R.R. Howell and F.H. Morriss) Human Milk in Infant Nutrition and Health, 1986, (with M.T. Osterholm, J.O. Klein and S.S. Aronson) Infectious Diseases in Child Day Care: Management and Prevention, 1987, Infections in Day Care Centers Seminars in Pediatric Infectious Diseases, 1990, Diarrheal Disease, 1994, (with S. Long and C. Prober) Principles and Practice of Pediatric Infectious Diseases, 1997, 3rd edit., 2008; contbg. editor: Infectious Disease Clinics in North America, 1992; editor-in-chief Pediat. Infectious Diseases: Clin. Updates, Nat. Found. for Infectious Diseases, 1994-2000; mem. editl. bd. Infectious Diseases Newsletter, 1985-89, Infection, 1988, Pediat., 1990-93, Report on Pediat. Infectious Diseases, 1990-95, co-editor, 1993-95, Pediatric Infectious Disease Jour., 1987-96, 2001--, Seminars in Pediat. Infectious Diseases, 1997—2001, Vaccine Bull., 1997-2001, Infectious Diseases in Children, 1997-09; editor; contbr. articles to profl. jours. Med. adv. com. Met. Houston chpt. March of Dimes, 1974-76, bd. dirs., 1975-80, chmn. profl. adv. com., 1977-79; mem. rsch. com. Nat. March of Dimes, 1999-2004. Named Disting. Alumnus, W.Va. U. Sch. Medicine, Morgantown, 1995, Edward J. van Liere Rsch. award. Fellow Infectious Diseases Soc. Am. (exec. com. Emerging Infections Network 1997-2000, mem. coun. 2003--06); mem. AAAS, Am. Acad. Pediats., Intersci. Conf. on Antimicrobiol Agts. and Chemotherapy, Internat. Soc. for Rsch. in Human Milk and Lactation, Am. Soc. for Clin. Pharmacology and Therapeutics, Am. Soc. for Tropical Medicine and Hygiene, Am. Pediat. Soc., Am. Soc. Microbiology, Am. Acad. Pediat. (com. on infectious diseases 1990-96, assoc. editor RedBook 1990-97, editor 1997-, exec. com. sect. breastfeeding 2001—03), Am. Fedn. for Clin. Rsch., Nat. Found. of Infectious Diseases (bd. dirs. and treas. 1997—, chair continuing med. edn. com. 1999—2003), Va. Pediat. Soc., Tex. Pediat. Soc., Tex. Med. Assn., Tex. Infectious Diseases Soc. (coun. mem. 1982-84), Harris County Pediat. Soc. (edn. com. 1975-79), Harris County Med. Soc., Houston Acad. Medicine, Houston Pediat. Soc. (constn. and by-laws com. 1978-82), So. Soc. for Pediat. Rsch. (coun. mem. 1981-83, Founder's award 1994), Soc. for Pediat. Rsch. (chair infectious diseases subspecialty sect. 1995, co-chair seminar Epidemiology 1995), Pediat. Infectious Diseases Soc. (pres.-elect 1993-95, pres. 1995-97, Disting. Physician award, 2007), The Milk Club (exec. com. 1995-99), ICAAC (program com. 1997-2002), AAP (chair rsch. com. and exec. com. sect. on breastfeeding), Infectious Diseases Soc. Am. (coun. mem. 2003-06, sci. program com., 2007-10, chair panel on immunization guideline devel., 2008-12, IDSA awards com. mem., 2012-, co-chair Infectious Diversity Guidelines Level, 2011, 21st Edward H Kans lectr., 2010), AAP (Lifetime Contbr. Infectious Disease Edn. award) Avocations: tennis, biking, reading, travel. Office: CDC and Prevention Nat Ctr Immunization Respiratory Disease 1600 Clifton Rd NE # MsA 27 Atlanta GA 30333 Office Phone: 404-639-8562. Business E-Mail: LPickering@cdc.gov.

PICKETT, JOE C., state legislator; b. Dec. 6, 1956; m. Denise Pickett; 4 children. Lic. real estate broker Tex. Real estate instructor; tchr. ethics and law in continuing edn. programs; mem. El Paso City Coun., Tex.; mem. Dist. 79 Tex. House of Representatives, 1995—. Recipient of several awards and honors. Democrat. Office: 1790 Lee Trevino Ste 307 El Paso TX 79936 also: Room 1W.05 Capitol PO Box 2910 Austin TX 78768 Office Phone: 915-590-4349, 512-463-0596.

PICKHOLTZ, RAYMOND LEE, electrical engineering educator, consultant; b. NYC, Apr. 12, 1932; s. Isidore and Rose (Turkish) P.; m. Eda Rebecca Mittler, June 30, 1957; children: Robin, Andrew, Julie. BEE, CUNY, 1954, MEE, 1958; PhD, Poly. U. N.Y., 1966. Research engr. RCA Labs., Princeton, NJ, 1954-57, ITT Labs., Nutley, NJ, 1957-61; assoc. prof. Poly. Inst. Bklyn., 1962-71; prof. elec. engring., chmn. dept. George Washington U., Washington, 1977-80, prof., 1971—2004, prof. emeritus, 2004—; pres. Telecommunication Assocs., Fairfax, Va., 1963—; cons. Inst. Def. Analyses, 1971-90, IBM Research, Yorktown Heights, NY, 1968-72; del. Union Radio Scientifique, Geneva, 1979—, vice chmn., 1987; del. NRC, Washington, 1980-83; cons. Motorola, CBC, NAB, USADR, Lucent, Verizon, 1996—. Vis. prof. U. Que., 1977; vis. scholar U. Calif., 1983; chmn. U.S. Nat. Commn. C, Union Radio Sci. Internat., 1990-92; mem. sci. and indsl. adv. bd. Telecom. Inst. Ont., Can. and Inst. Nacionale de la Recherches Scientique; vice chair, wireless panel World Tech. Evaluation Ctr. Editor: book series Computer Science Press, 1979—; IEEE Trans., 1975-80; editor-in-chief Jour. of Comms. and Networks, 2005—; author: Local Area and Multiple Access Networks, 1986; contbr. articles to profl. jours.; patentee in field. Recipient rsch. award RCA Labs., 1955; rsch. grantee Office of Naval Research, Washington, 1982, E-Systems, Falls Church, Va., 1983-96, MCI, Falls Church, Va., Instelsat, Washington, Nortel Networks, 1996—, DARPA, NSF, 1999—, IEEE Com. Thy. Svc. award, 2010. Fellow IEEE (bd. govs. 1979-82, digital comm. com., Centennial medal 1984, Cmty. Phys. Svc. award 2010), AAAS, Washington Acad. Scis.; mem. IEEE Comm. Soc. (v.p. 1986-88, pres. 1990-92, Donald W. McLellan award, 1994, Erskine fellow New Zealand 1997, Third Millennium medal 2000, ACM MSWIN prize paper award, 1999, Best paper of 1999 in Jour. of Comms. and Networks, 2000, gen. chair, Infocom, Kobe, Japan 1997, gen. chair, ACM Mobicom Y2K, Boston, 2000, named to GW Engring. Hall of Fame 2010), Math. Assn. Am., Cosmos Club, Sigma Xi, Eta Kappa Nu. Home: 3613 Glenbrook Rd Fairfax VA 22031-3210 Office: George Washington U Dept Elec Computer Engring Washington DC 20052-0001

PICKLER, KELLIE DAWN, singer; b. Albemarle, NC, June 28, 1986; d. Cynthia Morton and Clyde Pickler; m. Kyle Jacobs, Jan. 1, 2011. Singer: (albums) Small Town Girl, 2006, Kellie Pickler, 2008, 100 Proof, 2012, The Woman I Am, 2013, (songs) I Wonder, 2006 (Breakthrough Video of Yr., Tearjerker Video of Yr., Performance of Yr., CMT Music Awards, 2008); TV appearances Extreme Makeover: Home Edition, 2009, performer, contestant Dancing With the Stars, 2013 (winner, Mirror Ball Trophy, 2013). Supporter St. Jude Children's Rsch. Hosp. Office: c/o Fitzgerald Hartley Co 1908 Wedgewood Ave Nashville TN 37212*

PIDOT, WHITNEY DEAN, retired lawyer; b. NYC, Mar. 2, 1944; s. George B. and Virginia (Ulrich) P.; m. Jeanne Stoddard, April 23, 1973; children: Whitney Dean Jr., Philip Martin, Seth Thayer. AB magna cum laude, Harvard U., 1966; JD, MBA, Columbia U., 1970. Bar: N.Y. 1971. Ptnr. Shearman & Sterling, NYC, 1970, global mng. ptnr., 1998—2002, mem. exec. goup, 1998—2003, Asia mng. ptnr., 2001—03, of counsel, 2004—05; chair, CEO Goelet Co. LLC, 2004—11. Mem. adv. bd. Barclays Bank N.Y., 1989-92, Molecular Tool, Inc. (biotech.) Balt., 1991-96, Equine Genetic Rsch. Ptnrs., Balt., 1991-95; trustee, vice chair Winthrop Univ. Hosp., Mineola, NY. Mayor, Village of Matinecock, Locust Valley, N.Y., 1977-92; vice chmn. North Shore Mayors Com., Long Island, N.Y., 1980-92; bd. dirs. Nassau County (N.Y.) Village Officials Assn., 1978-80; commr. Locust Valley Fire Dist., 1979-93. Mem. N.Y. Bar Assn., Piping Rock Club (pres. 1988-94), Jupiter Island Club (pres. 2006-), Union Club N.Y.C., Phi Delta Phi. Republican. Home: 370 S Beach Rd Hobe Sound FL 33455-2608 Business E-Mail: wpidot@goeletcorp.com.

PIEPHO, LEE (EDWARD LEE PIEPHO), humanities educator; b. Detroit, Jan. 10, 1942; s. Edward Ernest and Dolores Faye (Dowis) P.; m. Susan Brand, June 13, 1964. AB, Kenyon Coll., 1964; MA, Columbia U., 1966; PhD, U. Va., 1972. Instr. Sweet Briar Coll., Va., 1969—72, asst. prof., 1972—78, assoc. prof., 1978—83, prof., 1983—94, Shallenberger Brown prof., 1994—2006, rsch. prof., 2006—, dept. chmn., 2000—01, coord. European civilization program, 1986—89. Author: Holofernes' Mantuan, 2001; translator, editor: Adulescentia: The Eclogues of Mantuan, 1989; contbr. articles to profl. jours. Grantee, NEH, 2007; fellow, SIMRS, 1979, NEH, 1985, 1997; Dulin fellow, Folger Shakespeare Libr., 1989—90, Mednick fellow, 1996. Mem. Internat. Assn. for Neo-Latin Studies, Modern Lang. Assn. Am., Renaissance Soc. Am. Avocations: golf, scuba diving. Home: 137 Woodland Rd Sweet Briar VA 24595 Office: Sweet Briar Coll Dept English Sweet Briar VA 24595 Business E-Mail: lpiepho@sbc.edu.

PIERCE, ANGELA, information technology executive; BBA, MBA, The U. of Texas, Austin. Sr. credit analyst fin. svcs. Deutsche Bank; assoc. corp. banking The Bank of Tokyo Mitsubishi Ltd.; contr. Web America Networks Inc.; v.p. fin. Level 3; v.p. fin. planning and treasury Convio Inc.; CFO Trillion Ptnrs. Inc., AirStrip Technologies. Office: AirStrip Technologies 335 E Sonterra Blvd Ste 200 San Antonio TX 78258-4385 Office Phone: 210-805-0444. Office Fax: 210-805-0446.

PIERCE, BOBBY, state legislator; Owner Telebooth Inc., Sheridan True Value; mem. Dist. 19 Ark. House of Reps., 2007—. Served Ark. Nat. Guard. Democrat. Methodist. Address: 587 Grant 758 Sheridan AR 72150 Office Phone: 501-888-4390.

PIERCE, DONALD FAY, lawyer; b. Bexley, Miss., Aug. 28, 1930; s. Percy O. and Lavada S. (Stringfellow) Pierce; m. Norma Faye Scribner, June 5, 1954; children: Kathryn Pierce Tuttle, D. F. Jr., John S., Jeff G. BS, U. Ala., 1956, JD, 1958. Bar: Ala. 1958, U.S. Ct. Appeals (5th cir.) 1958, U.S. Dist. Ct. (no., mid. and so. dists.) Ala. 1958, U.S. Ct. Appeals (11th cir.) 1982. Law clk. to presiding judge U.S. Dist. Ct. (so. dist.) Ala., 1958—59; ptnr. Hand, Arendall, Bedsole, Greaves & Johnston, Mobile, Ala., 1964—91, Pierce, Carr, Alford, Ledyard & Latta, P.C., 1991—; pvt. practice; of counsel Butler Pappas LLP. Mem. Products Liability Adv. Coun., 1990—; bd. overseers Vanderbilt Cancer Ctr., 1994—. Contbr. articles to profl. jours. Trustee UMS Prep Sch., 1980—87. 1st lt. US Army, 1951—53. Mem.: Def. Research Inst. (pres. 1987, chmn. 1988), Def. Counsel Trial Acad. (bd. dir. 1983—84), Internat. Assn. Def. Counsel, Am. Acad. Hosp. Attys., Fedn. Ins. and Corp. Counsel, Ala. Def. Lawyers Assn. (past pres.). Baptist. Home: 4452 Winnie Way Mobile AL 36608-2221 Office: Butler Pappas LLP 1110 Montlimar Dr Ste 1050 Mobile AL 36608 Home Phone: 251-344-0170; Office Phone: 251-338-1313. Business E-Mail: d.pierce@butlerpappas.com.

PIERCE, GARLAND E., state legislator; Minister; state rep. Dist. 48 NC, 2005—. Mem. Commerce, Small Bus. and Entrepreneurship com., Ins. com.; vice chmn. Aging com., Appropriations com., Fed. Rels. and Indian Affairs com.; chmn. Appropriations Subcom. on Natural and Econ. Resources. With US Army, 1971—74. Democrat. Baptist. Mailing: 21981 Buie St Wagram NC 28396 Office: North Carolina House of Representatives 16 W Jones St Room 1204 Raleigh NC 27601-1096 Office Phone: 919-733-5803, 910-369-2844. E-mail: Garland.Pierce@ncleg.net.

PIERCE, JERRY EARL, publishing executive; b. Hindsdale, Ill., Aug. 3, 1941; s. Earl and Adeline A. (Zaranski) P.; m. Carol Louise Martin, Aug. 15, 1964; children: Patricia, Barbara, Linda. Bradley. BS, U. Ill., 1964. With R.R. Donnelley & Sons, Chgo., 1964-70, Western Pub. Co., Racine, Wis., 1970—, nat. pubs. acct. exec., 1975—. Chair bd. Pierce Sale Co., Inc., Restaurant Equipment World, Inc., Heat Transfer Engring. Inc.; chmn. bd. Tech Industries & Millwork, Inc., 1989-93; pres. B.J. Installation Co., Inc., 1989-91, ROI World Equipment, 1993—; v.p., sec. Savers Clubs Am., Inc.; v.p. Pierce Aviation, 2000—; chmn. adv. bd. Greater Winter Park, Bankfirst Bank, Winter Park, Fla. Chmn. Leadership Trust of Nat. Fedn. Ind. Bus. 1st lt. US Army, 1968—70. Recipient Gov.'s Bus. Amb. award, Fla., 2013; named Small Bus. Humanitarian of Yr., Small Bus. Coun. America, 2011. Mem.: Stetson U. Family Enterprise Ctr. (chmn. adv. bd. 2010), Nat. Fed. Ind. Bus. Fla. (chmn. safe trust, chmn. leadership coun. Fla. 2012—, Small Bus. Person of Year 2006), Goldenrod C. of C. (bd. dirs. 2007—08), Nat. Bus. Aviation Assn., Food Equipment Distbrs. Assn. (bd. dirs. 1997—98), Food Svc. Cons. Soc., Cleve. Advt. Club, Interlachen Country Club (treas. Winter Pk., Fla. 2009—10), Ctrl. Fla. Veterans Mem. Found. (chmn. 2008—), Ctrl. Fla. Vets. Inc. (past pres.). Republican. Episcopalian. Achievements include patents for refrigeration-to-water utility cost control system; invention of E-Commerce business model. Office: 2413 N Forsyth Rd Orlando FL 32807-6455 Home: 566 Genius Dr Winter Park FL 32789-5135 Office Phone: 407-679-9004.

PIERCE, RANDY G., state supreme court justice; 3 children. BS in acctg., Univ. So. Miss., 1987, MBA; JD, Univ. Miss. CPA; bar: Miss. 1997. Atty. private practice, 1997—2005; mem., Dist. 105 Miss. House Reps., 2000—05; chancery ct. judge Miss. 16th Dist.; assoc. justice Miss. Supreme Ct., 2009—. Bd. mem. Jones County Jr. Coll. Found. Mem.: Am. Inst. CPAs, Miss. Soc. CPAs, Miss. Bar Assn. Baptist. Office: Miss Supreme Ct 450 High St Jackson MS 39201 Office Phone: 601-359-2093.*

PIERCE, SUSAN RESNECK, author, consultant, retired academic administrator; d. Elliott Jack and Dory (Block) Resneck; 1 child, Alexandra Siegel. BA, Wellesley Coll., 1965; MA, U. Chgo., 1966; PhD, U. Wis., 1972. Lectr. U. Wis., Rock County, 1970-71; from asst. prof. to prof. English Ithaca (N.Y.) Coll., 1973-82, chair dept., 1976—79; vis. assoc. prof. Princeton (N.J.) U., 1979; program officer Nat. Endowment for Humanities, 1982-83, asst. dir., 1983-84; dean Henry Kendall Coll. Arts and Scis. U. Tulsa, 1984-90; v.p. acad. affairs, prof. English Lewis and Clark Coll., Portland, Oreg., 1990-92; pres. U. Puget Sound, Tacoma, 1992—2003, Boca Raton Comty. Hosp. Found., 2004—05, SRP CONSULTING, LLC, 2005—. Author: The Moral of the Story: Literature, Values and American Higher Education, On Being Presidential, 2011, Governance Reconsidered, 2014; co-editor: Approaches to Teaching Ellison's invisible Man. Bd. dirs. Arts and Humanities Coun., Tulsa, 1984-90, Mizener Pk., 2004-; trustee Hillcrest Hosp., Tulsa, 1986-90; mem. cultural series com., community rels. com. Jewish Fedn., Tulsa, 1986-90; bd. dirs. Tulsa chpt. NCCJ, 1986-90, Kemper Mus. 1996—, Seattle Symphony, 1993-96, St. Joseph Hosp., 1992-93, Portland Opera, 1990-92, Ctr. for Arts, Boca Raton, 2004—. Recipient Best Essay award Arix. Quar., 1979, Excellence in Teaching award N.Y. State Edn. Council, 1982, Superior Group Service award NEH, 1984, other teaching awards; Dana scholar, Ithaca Coll., 1980-81; Dana Research fellow, Ithaca Coll., 82-83; grantee Inst. for Ednl. Affairs, 1980, Ford Found., 1987, NEH, 1989. Mem. MLA (adv. com. on job market 1973-74), South Ctrl. MLA, NIH (subcom. on college drinking), Assn. Governing Bds. (coun. of pres.), Nat. Inst. on Alcohol Abuse (presl. advisory group), Soc. Values in Higher Edn., Assn. Am. Colls. (bd. dirs.), Am. Conf. Acad. Deans (bd. dirs. 1988-91, presenter), The Annapolis Group (mem. exec. com.), NAICU (presenter), CIC, ACE, Phi Beta Kappa, Phi Kappa Phi, Phi Gamma Kappa. Jewish. Office Phone: 561-212-5103. Business E-Mail: srpconsulting@comcast.net.*

PIERGALLINI, ALFRED A., board member; b. Easton, Pa., Aug. 1, 1946; BA in Economics cum laude, Lafayette Coll., 1968; MBA in Mktg. & Fin., U. Chgo., 1970. Regional dir. Beverage Mgmt. Inc.; sales and brand mgr. Procter & Gamble Co.; pres., CEO Shasta Beverages Inc., Hayward, Calif., 1985-90; chmn., pres., CEO, COO Gerber Products Co., Fremont, Mich., 1989—99; cons. Desert Trail Consulting. Bd. dirs. Comerica Inc., 1991—. Office: Comerica Inc Bd Directors 1717 Main St Dallas TX 75201 Office Phone: 214-969-6476. Business E-Mail: apiergallini@comerica.com.

PIERLUISI, PEDRO R., Resident Commissioner from Puerto Rico, United States House of Representatives; b. San Juan, PR, Apr. 26, 1959; s. Jorge A. and Doris (Urrutia) Pierluisi; m. María Elena Carrión; children: Anthony, Michael, Jacqueline, Rafael. BA, Tulane U., New Orleans, 1981; JD, George Washington U., 1984. Bar: DC 1984, U.S. Dist. Ct. (dist. DC) 1985, US Ct. Appeals (DC cir.) 1985, PR 1990, US Dist. Ct. (dist. PR) 1990, US Supreme Ct. 1990, US Ct. Appeals (1st cir.) 1993. Assoc. Verner, Liipfert, Bernhard, McPherson & Hand, Washington, 1984—85, Cole, Corette & Abrutyn, Washington, 1985—90; ptnr. Pierluisi Pierluisi & Mayol-Bianchi, San Juan, 1990—93; atty. gen. Govt. of PR, 1993—96; ptnr. O'Neill & Borges, San Juan, 1997—2007; resident commr. US Congress from Puerto Rico, 2009—; mem. US House Ethics Com., 2011—, US House Judiciary Com., 2011—, US House Natural Resources Com., 2011—. Mem.: ABA (mem. house of delegates 1995—96, state membership chmn. 2000—03), Am. Arbitration Assn., Internat. Ctr. Dispute Resolution, George Washington U. Internat. Law Soc. (pres. 1982—83), Nat. Assn. Attys. Gen. (chair ea. region 1996), Jose Jaime Pierluisi Found. (pres. 2003—06), Puerto Rico Homebuilders Assn. (bd. dirs. 1999—2003), Phi Alpha Delta (hon.). Democrat. Avocation: jogging. Office: US House of Representatives 1213 Longworth House Office Building Washington DC 20515 also: 250 Calle Fortaleza Viejo San Juan PR 00901 Office Phone: 202-225-2615, 787-723-6333. Office Fax: 202-225-2154.*

PIERONI, ROBERT EDWARD, internist, educator, military officer; b. Portland, Maine, June 20, 1937; s. Ansel Kirby and Agnes Mary (Dumais) P.; m. Dorothy Louise McDonnell, Oct. 3, 1970; children: Michelle Kirby, Robert Francis. BS, Boston Coll., 1959; MD, Pa. State U., 1971. Diplomate Am. Bd. Internal Medicine, Am. Bd. Family Practice, Am. Bd. Allergy and Immunology, Am. Bd. Quality Assurance, Am. Bd. Geriatric Medicine. Chemist Mass. Dept. Pub. Health, Boston, 1962-71, sr. bacteriologist, 1971-74; asst. prof.

internal medicine U. Ala., Tuscaloosa, 1974-76, assoc. prof. dept. internal medicine and family practice, 1976-81, prof. internal medicine and family practice, 1981—; enlisted U.S. Army, 1961, advanced through grades to col., 1981. Prior cons. VA Hosp., Tuscaloosa, T. Hardin Med. Facility and Partlow State Hosp., Tuscaloosa, 1974—; cons. FDA, Dept. Def. Contbr. articles to profl. jours., chapters to books. Decorated Bronze Star, 1991, Commendation for Valor; recipient Golden Stethoscope award, 1982, Faculty Recognition award, 1986, Ala. Golden Eagle Humanitarian award Ala. Sr. Citizens Hall of Fame, 1988 and Physicians award, 1998, Wright A. Garner scientist award Ala. Acad. Sci., 1997, Designator A Proficiency award Army Surgeon Gen., 2001. Mem. AMA, ACP, Am. Coll. Allergy, Asthma and Immunology, Am. Geriatric Soc., Gerontol. Soc. Am., Am. Acad. Family Physicians, Physicians for Human Rights, VFW, Am. Legion. Democrat. Roman Catholic. Avocations: mountain trekking, scuba diving, studying medical and military history, reading. Home: 398 Riverdale Dr Tuscaloosa AL 35406-1814 Office: U Ala Dept Internal Medicine PO Box 870326 Tuscaloosa AL 35487-0001 Office Phone: 205-348-1287. Personal E-mail: dp398@comcast.net.

PIERRE, JUAN, professional baseball player; b. Mobile, Ala., Aug. 14, 1977; Attended, Galveston Coll., Tex., U. South Ala., Mobile. Outfielder Colo. Rockies, 2000—02, Fla. Marlins, 2003—05, Chgo. Cubs, 2006, LA Dodgers, 2007—09, Chgo. White Sox, 2009—11, Phila. Phillies, 2012, Miami Marlins, 2013—. Recipient Cool Papa Bell award, Negro Leagues Baseball Mus., 2003; named Player of Yr., Sun Belt Conf., 1998. Achievements include leading the National League in: stolen bases, 2001, 03; singles, 2001, 03, 04, 06, 07; games played, 2003-07; at-bats, 2003, 04, 06; hits, 2004, 06; triples, 2004; member of the World Series championship winning Florida Marlins, 2003; leading the American League in: stolen bases, 2010; singles, sacrifice hits, 2011. Office: Miami Marlins 501 Marlins Way Miami FL 33125*

PIERRE, VINCENT J., state legislator; Attended, So. U., Baton Rogue. Small bus. co-owner; mem. Dist. 44 La. House of Reps., Baton Rogue, 2012—. Democrat. Office: La House of Reps 900 N 3rd St PO Box 94062 Baton Rouge LA 70804 Business E-Mail: pierrev@legis.la.gov.

PIERSON, AL See PIZZAMIGLIO, ALBERT

PIETSCH, VONNIE, state legislator; m. Bill Pietsch (dec.). State rep. Dist. 22, ND, 2005—; mem. Human Svc. Com., Polit. Subdivision. Republican. Lutheran. Home: 8501 Lullwater Dr Apt 1402 Dallas TX 75238-4704 Office Phone: 888-635-3447, 701-347-4958. Business E-Mail: vpietsch@nd.gov.

PIGOTT, BILL, state legislator; b. Tylertown, Miss., Oct. 13, 1946; m. Doris Revette. BS, Miss. State U.; attended, Pearl River CC. Farmer; mem. Dist. 99 Miss. House of Reps., 2008—, vice chair forestry com., mem. agr. com., conservation and water resources com., juvenile justice com. Republican. Baptist. Home: 92 Pigott Easterling Rd Tylertown MS 39667 Office: PO Box 1018 Jackson MS 39215 E-mail: bpigott@house.ms.gov.

PIGOTT, MELISSA ANN, social psychologist; b. Ft. Myers, Fla., Jan. 28, 1958; d. Park Trammell and Leola Ann (Wright) P.; m. David H. Fauss, Jan. 1, 1988. BA in Psychology, Fla. Internat. U., Miami, 1979; MS in Social Psychology, Fla. State U., 1982, PhD in Social Psychology, 1984. Rsch. asst. Fla. Internat. U., 1978-79, Fla. State U., Tallahassee, 1980-84; dir. mktg. rsch. Bapt. Med. Ctr., Jacksonville, Fla., 1984-89; rsch. assoc. Litigation Scis., Inc., Atlanta, 1989-91; sr. litigation psychologist Trial Cons., Inc., Miami, 1991-93; dir. rsch. Magnus Rsch. Cons. Inc., Ft. Lauderdale, 1993—. Adj. prof. psychology U. North Fla., Jacksonville, 1985-89, Nova Southeastern U., Ft. Lauderdale, 1995—. Author: Social Psychology: Study Guide, 1990, Social Psychology: Instructors Manual, 1990; contbr. articles to profl. jours. Mem. ACLU, Am. Psychol. Assn., Am. Psychol. Law Soc., Amnesty Internat., Civitan Internat., Southeastern Psychol. Assn., Soc. for Psychol. Study of Social Issues, Soc. Personality and Social Psychology, Greenpeace, Psi Chi. Democrat. Avocations: concerts, playing piano, going to the beach, bass guitar. Office: Magnus Rsch Cons Inc 1305 NE 23rd Ave Ste 1 Pompano Beach FL 33062-3748

PIJEAUX, LAWRENCE J., JR., museum director; b. New Orleans, 1944; m. Maxine J. Pijeaux; 5 children. BS, Southern U., Baton Rouge; MA in Tchg., Tulane U., New Orleans; EdD, U. Southern Miss., Hattiesburg. Mgr., Lila Wallace Grant Indpls. Mus. Art; pres., CEO Birmingham Civil Rights Inst., Ala., 1995—. Mem. Nat. Museum & Library Services Bd., 2010—. Mem. adv. bd. Ala. Bur. Tourism and Travel; bd. dirs. United Way of Ctrl. Ala., Inc., Ala. Symphony Orchestra, Birmingham Internat. Festival, Ala. Sch. Math. and Sci., 2007—. Recipient Mus. Leadership award, Smithsonian Inst., Am. Hero in Edn. award, Reader's Digest; named Ala. Tourism Exec. of Yr., 2006. Mem.: Ala. Mus. Assn., Am. Assn. Mus., Am. Assn. for State and Local History, Assn. African-Am. Mus. (pres., Svc. and Achievement award), 100 Black Men of Birmingham, Rotary Internat., Omega Psi Phi (Edn. Leader of Yr. award). Office: Birmingham Civil Rights Inst 520 Sixteenth St N Birmingham AL 35203 Office Phone: 205-328-9696. Office Fax: 205-251-6104. Business E-Mail: lpijeaux@bcri.org.

PIKE, LARRY SAMUEL, lawyer; b. Savannah, Ga., Feb. 23, 1939; s. Abram and Ida (Feinberg) P.; m. Bonnie Jo Haykin, June 21, 1959; children: Douglas, Stacey, Scott. BA, Emory U., 1960, LLB, 1963; postgrad., Leeds U., Eng., 1960-61. Assoc. L. Jack Swertfeger Jr. Atty., Decatur, Ga., 1963-65; ptnr. Swertfeger, Scott, Pike & Simmons, Decatur, 1966-75, Simmons, Pike & Warren, Decatur, 1975-76, Lefkoff, Pike & Sims, Atlanta, 1976-85, Branch, Pike & Ganz, Atlanta, 1985-95, Holland & Knight LLP, Atlanta, 1995—. Pres. Ansley Park Civic Assn., Atlanta, 1977-79, Northshore Homeowners Assn., Tybee Island, Ga., 1992-95, The Temple, Atlanta, 1979-81, trustee, 1977—, Am. Cancer Soc., DeKalb County, Ga. unit, 1970-71, crusade chmn., 1969-70; trustee Ansley Park Beautification Found., Inc., Atlanta, 1984—, treas., 2000-06, v.p. 2006—; trustee The Temple Endowment Fund, Atlanta, 1979-87, Atlanta Jewish Cmty. Ctr., 1973-76; bd. dirs., Soc. Classical Reform Judaism, 2010-; bd. overseers Hebrew Union Coll., Cin., 1987-93; alumni coun. Emory U., Atlanta, 1966-72; bd. trustees Union of Am. Hebrew Congregations, 1991-99; mem. Rabbinical Placement Commn., 1994-2000; mem. St. Joseph's Hosp. Leadership Coun., 2003—; mem. planned giving adv. bd. Cmty. Found. Greater Atlanta, 2005-08; mem. gift planning adv. coun. Emory U., 2006—. Editor-in-chief law jour. and newspaper; contbr. articles to profl. jours. Named Outstanding Young Man of Yr., North DeKalb Jaycees, 1968, Super Lawyer, Atlanta Mag.; named one of Legal Elite, Ga. Trend mag.; Fulbright fellow, 1960—61. Mem. ABA, State Bar Ga. (exec. coun. Young Lawyers sect. 1968-72), Atlanta Bar Assn., Decatur-DeKalb Bar Assn. (sec. 1965-66), Atlanta Legal Aid Soc. (pres. 1974-75, past bd. dirs.), Atlanta Tax Forum, Lawyers Club Atlanta, B'nai B'rith (pres. Atlanta lodge 1970-71, Ga. pres. 1974-75, dist. 5 bd. govs. 1973-76, chair Youth Orgn. Bd. 1971-73), Bryan Soc., Phi Beta Kappa, Omicron Delta Kappa. Office: Holland & Knight LLP 2000 One Atlantic Ctr Atlanta GA 30309 Business E-Mail: larry.pike@hklaw.com.*

PIKE, LYNN A., bank executive; Grad., Duke U. Fuqua Sch. Bus. Exec. Sch. Mktg., Durham, NC. With Bank of Boston; mgr., Fla., NY and NJ cmty. banking units First Nationwide Bank; dir. nat. sales GMAC Mortgage Corp.; exec. v.p., regional pres. LA met. divsn. Wells Fargo Bank; mng. dir. consumer banking & distbn. FleetBoston, 2002—04; pres. banking bus. Bank of America Corp., 2004—07; pres. Bank of America Calif., 2004—07; COO banking bus. Capital One Financial Corp., McLean, Va., 2007, pres. banking, 2007—. Mgmt. operating com. Bank of America; dir. Capital One Nat. Assn.; mem. br. bd. Fed. Res. Bank San Francisco. Mem. Calif. Businesses Edn. Excellence, Calif. Bus. Roundtable; bd. trustees Bank of America Found.; mem. exec. com. Operation HOPE, mem. nat. bd. dirs., 2001, northeastern bd. mem., 2007—, vice chair, 2010—; bd. dirs. Phoenix Houses Calif.; bd. trustees Autry Mus. Named one of 25 Women to Watch, US Banker, 2007, 2008, 25 Most Powerful Women in Banking, 2009, 2010. Office: Capital One Financial Corp 1680 Capital One Dr Mc Lean VA 22102 Office Phone: 703-720-1000.

PIKE, RALPH WEBSTER, chemical engineer, educator, academic administrator; b. Tampa, Fla., Nov. 10, 1935; s. Ralph Webster and Macey (Adams) P.; m. Patricia Jennings, Aug. 23, 1958. B in Chem. Engring., Ga. Inst. Tech., 1957, PhD, 1962. Rsch. chem. engr. Exxon R & D Co., Baytown, Tex., 1962—64; Paul M. Horton prof. chem. engring. and sys. sci. La. State U., Baton Rouge, 1964—, assoc. vice chancellor rsch., 1967—96, dir. La. Mineral Inst., 1979—, dean engring., 1999—2001. Cons. to chem. and petroleum refining industry, fed. govt. and State of La., 1964—. Author: Formulation and Optimization of Mathematical Models, 1970, Optimization for Engineering Systems, 1986, Optimizacion en Ingenieria, 1989, Computational Transport Phenomena for Engineering Analyses, 2009, Chemicals from Biomass: Integrating Bioprocesses into Chemical Production Complexes, 2011. Active various civic, ch. and cmty. orgns., Baton Rouge, 1964—. 2d lt. U.S. Army, 1958-60. Recipient more than 100 rsch. grants, including NASA, NSF, Dept. Energy, Dept. Interior, Dept. Def., EPA, NOAA, state agys. and pvt. industry, 1964—. Fellow AIChE (chmn. nat. program com. 1984, local sect. 1985); mem. Am. Chem. Soc. (Charles E. Coates Mem. Award, 1994), Sigma Xi. Democrat. Methodist. Avocation: skiing. Home: 6053 Hibiscus Dr Baton Rouge LA 70808-8844 Office: La State U 1139 Energy Coast and Environment Bldg Baton Rouge LA 70803-0001 Office Phone: 225-578-3428. Business E-Mail: pike@lsu.edu.

PILEGGI, DOMINIC J., electronics executive; BA, Rutgers U. Sales & mgmt. positions Thomas & Betts Corp., Memphis, 1979—88, pres. electronics, 1988—94, pres. elec. products group, 1994—95; sr. exec. positions with Casco Plastic, Inc., Jordan Telecommunications, 1995—98; pres. EMS div. Viasystems Inc., 1998—2000; sr. v.p. Thomas & Betts Corp., Memphis, 2000—02, group pres. electrical, 2000—03, pres., COO, 2003—04, pres., CEO, 2004—05, chmn., CEO, 2006—12, chmn., 2012—. Office: Thomas & Betts 8155 T&B Blvd Memphis TN 38125 Office Phone: 901-252-8000.

PILGRIM, LONNIE (BO PILGRIM), food products executive; b. May 8, 1928; married. Ptnr. Pilgrim's Pride Corp., Pittsburg, Tex., 1953-68, CEO, 1968—98, chmn., CEO, 1998—2004, chmn., 2004—10. Chmn. First State Bank Pitts. Served with U.S. Armed Forces, 1951-53. Office: Pilgrim's Pride Corp 4845 US Hwy 271 N Pittsburg TX 75686 Mailing: Pilgrim's Pride Corp PO Box 93 Pittsburg TX 75686-0093

PILLSBURY, HAROLD CROCKETT, III, otolaryngologist; b. Balt., Dec. 5, 1947; m. Carol Higgins Pillsbury; children: Matthew, Benjamin, Thomas. BA, George Washington U., Washington, 1970, MD, 1972. Diplomate Nat. Bd. Med. Examiners, Am. Bd. Otolaryngology; lic. Conn., N.C. Resident gen. surgery U. N.C., Chapel Hill, 1972-73, resident otolaryngology, 1973-76; fellow Kantonsspital, Zurich, Switzerland, 1977; asst. prof. otolaryngology Yale U., New Haven, Conn., 1977-81, assoc. prof. otolaryngology, 1981-82; assoc. prof. surgery, otolayngology, head and neck surgery U. N.C. Sch. Medicine, Chapel Hill, 1982-86, prof. surgery, otolaryngology, head and neck surgery, 1986—, Thomas J. Dark Disting. Prof., 1991—. Civilian cons. USAF Surgeon Gen. for Otolaryngology-Head and Neck Surgery, 1993; hon. guest lectr. Alpha Omega Alpha Induction Ceremonies, U. N.C., Chapel Hill, 1990, 91, Sch. of Medicine Commencement Ceremony, U. N.C., 1990., Whitehead lectr. Whitehead Med. Soc., U. N.C., 1994. Countbr. numerous articles to profl. jours. Recipient John A Kirchner Tchg. award, 1980, Disting. Alumni Achievement award George Washington U., 2006. Mem. Am. Acad. Otolaryngology-Head and Neck Surgery (past pres. 1998-99, Honor award 1985, Disting. Svc. award 1994, Harris Mosher award 1986), Am. Bd. Otolaryngology (pres. 2004-06), Am. Laryngol., Rhinol. and Otol. Soc. (pres. 2007), Am. Laryngol. Assn. (past pres. 2000-01), Soc. Univ. Otolaryngologists (past pres. 1997-98), Alpha Omega Alpha, Triological Soc. (pres. 2008). Office: Univ NC Dept Otolaryngology Head & Neck Surgery G125 Physicians Office Bldg 170 Manning Dr Chapel Hill NC 27599-7070 Office Phone: 919-966-3342.

PILON, NATHALIE, corporate financial executive; BBA, U. Montreal. Chartered Accountant. Sr. mgr., profl. practice KPMG LLP, 1999; mem., Can. exec. com. Thomas & Betts Corp., v.p., fin. & info. tech. Canada, 1996—2008, pres., Can., 2008—. Recipient Young Achievers Award U. Montreal Haute Etudes Commerciales Network, 1999. Mem.: Can. Inst. Chartered Accountants. Office: Thomas & Betts Corp 8155 T&B Blvd Memphis TN 38125 Office Phone: 901-252-8000. Office Fax: 901-680-5112.

PILON, RAY, state legislator; b. Pontiac, Mich., Jan. 11, 1945; m. Kathleen Pilon; 2 children. BS, No. Mich. U., Marquette, 1968. Commr. Sarasota County, 1996—2000; dir. cmty. and govt. affairs Peace River Manasota Regional Water Supply Authority; mem. Dist. 69 Fla. House of Representatives, 2011—. Mem. Sarasota County Rep. Exec. Com., 1996—2000. Republican. Presbyterian. Avocations: golf, hunting, music, travel, fishing. Office: 1660 Ringling Blvd Ste 310-311 Sarasota FL 34236-6808 also: Fla House of Reps 1101 The Capitol 402 S Monroe St Tallahassee FL 32399-1300 Office Phone: 941-955-8077, 850-488-7754.

PIMENTEL, ARMANDO, energy executive; BS in Acctg., Fla. State U., Tallahassee. Profl. acctg. fellow Office the Chief Accountant, US Securities and Exch. Commn., 1996—98; ptnr. acctg. rsch. dept. Deloitte & Touche LLP, audit ptnr., head power & utilities segment, sr. ptnr., regulatory and pub. policy group; sr. engagement ptnr. FLP Group, Inc., Miami, Fla., exec. v.p. fin., CFO, 2008—. Spkr. in field. Office: FPL Group Inc PO Box 025576 Miami FL 33102

PIMM, STUART L., conservationist biologist, educator; b. Derbyshire, Eng., Feb. 27, 1949; naturalized, U.S. m. Julia Killeffer, June 2, 1990; children: Stephanie, Shana. BA second class honors, Oxford, United Kingdom, 1971; PhD, New Mex. State Univ., 1974. Asst. prof. Clemson Univ., SC, 1974—75, Tex. Tech Univ., Lubbock, 1975—79, assoc. prof., 1979—82; assoc. prof. ecology and evolutionary biology Univ. Tenn., Knoxville, 1982—86, prof., 1986—99; prof., Ctr. for Environmental Rsch. and Conservation Columbia Univ., NYC, 1999—2002; Doris Duke chair of conservation ecology Duke Univ., NC, 2002—. Vis. prof. Griffith Univ., Queensland, Australia, 1983—84, Inst. for Nonlinear Sci., Univ. Calif., San Diego, 1987, Sch. of Ecosystem Mgmt., Univ. New Eng., Australia, 1987, Ctr. for Population Biology, Imperial Coll., Silwood Park, England, 1990, Mammal Rsch. Inst., Pretoria, South Africa, 1996, Pretoria, 2000; and several others; sr. vis. scholar Nat. Rsch. Coun., 1995; disting. assoc. in rsch. Bernice P. Bishop Mus., Honolulu, 1997—; extraordinary prof. U. Pretoria, South Africa, 2001—. Contbr. articles several articles to profl. journals, chapters to books; mem. of several editl. boards. Recipient Pew Fellowship, 1993—96, Kempe prize for Disting. Ecologists, 1994, Aldo Leopold Leadership Fellow, 1999, Marsh prize, Zoological Soc. London, 2004, Edward T. LaRoe III Meml. award, 2006, Dr. A.H. Heineken prize for Environmental Sciences, Royal Netherlands Acad. Arts & Sciences, 2006, William Proctor prize for Scientific Achievement, Sigma Xi, 2007; named Highly Cited Researcher, Inst. Scientific Info., 2002, Alumnus of Yr., New Mexico State U., Coll. Arts & Sciences, 2005. Fellow: Am. Acad. Arts & Sci. Office: Nicholas Sch Environ and Earth Sci Duke Univ Box 90328 A301 LSRC Durham NC 27708 Office Phone: 919-613-8141. Office Fax: 919-684-8741. E-mail: stuartpimm@aol.com.

PINCKNEY, CHARLES COTESWORTH, lawyer; b. Richmond, Va., Oct. 23, 1939; s. Thomas and Charlotte (Kent) P.; m. Helen Raney, Aug. 13, 1966; children: Sarah Whitley, Thomas. BA, Yale U., 1961; LLB, U. Va., 1967. Bar: Va. 1967. Assoc. Mays, Valentine, Davenport & Moore, Richmond, 1967-72; ptnr. Mays & Valentine, LLP, Richmond, 1972-2000, Troutman Sanders LLP, Richmond, 2001—07, counsel, 2008—10. Bd. dirs. Sweet Briar Coll., 1996-2000; pres. Sheltering Arms Hosp., Richmond, 1986-87, bd. dirs., 1970-99, 2004-09; trustee William H.-John G.-Emma Scott Found., 1974-, sec., 1994-99, 2008-, v.p., 1999-2004, pres. 2005-08; campaign chmn. United Way Svcs., 1998, bd. dirs., 1997-2009; vestry St. Stephen's Episcopal Ch., Richmond, Va., 1970-72, 1975-77, 1984-86, 2010-12. Lt. (j.g.) USNR, 1961—64. Mem. Country Club of Va., Commonwealth Club (bd. govs. 1986-92, pres. 1991-92), Richmond German (pres. 1996-98, sec.-treas. 2006-11), Soc. of Cin., fellow Va. Law Found. Republican. Episcopalian. Home: 2 Roslyn Rd Richmond VA 23226-1610 Office: Troutman Sanders LLP 1001 Haxall Pt PO Box 1122 Richmond VA 23218-1122 Home Phone: 804-288-3367; Office Phone: 804-697-1383. Business E-Mail: cotes.pinckney@troutmansanders.com.

PINCKNEY, CLEMENTA CARLOS, state legislator; b. Beaufort, SC, Oct. 30; s. John and Theopia Aiken Pinckney. BA, Allen U., 1995; MPA, U. SC, 1999. Pastor Mt. Horry AME Ch., Younges Island, SC; mem. Dist. 112 SC House of Reps., 1977—2000; mem. Dist. 45 SC State Senate, 2001—, mem. Banking and Ins. Com., Corrections and Penology Com., Fin. Com. and Med. Affairs Com. Democrat. Office: 512 Gressette Bldg Columbia SC 29201 Mailing: PO Box 507 Ridgeland SC 29936 Home Phone: 843-726-3849; Office Phone: 843-726-6019, 803-212-6148. E-mail: CCP@scsenate.org.

PINELLI, DONNA M., gynecologic oncologist, director, gynecologist; married; 3 children. Undergrad., U. Va.; MD, Va. Commonwealth U. Diplomate Am. Bd. Ob-Gyn, 1997, Am. Bd. Ob-Gyn-gynecologic oncology. Resident ob-gyn. dept. Univ. South Fla., fellow gynecologic oncology, Tampa Gen. Hosp., Moffitt Cancer Ctr.; pvt. practice Palm Beach County, Fla.; pvt. practice Palm Beach, Pa., Jupiter and Wellington offices Ob-Gyn. Specialists; on staff several area hosps.; on staff Jupiter Med. Ctr., 1996—, med. dir. Robotic Surgery Program. Active Gynecologic Cancer Found., Jupiter Med. Ctr. Found. Fellow: ACOG; mem.: AMA, Palm Beach County Med. Soc., Fla. Med. Assn., Fla. Obstet. and Gynecologic Soc., Fla. Soc. of Gynecologic Oncologists, Soc. of Gynecologic Oncologists, Am. Cancer Soc. (bd. mem. Jupiter Br.). Avocations: boating, swimming. Office: Jupiter Medical Center 1210 S Old Dixie Hwy Jupiter FL 33458 Office Phone: 561-263-2234.

PINGREE, BRUCE DOUGLAS, lawyer; b. Salt Lake City, June 6, 1947; s. Howard W. and Lois (Ivie) P.; m. Lorraine Bertelli, Oct. 11, 1981; children: Christian James, Matthew David, Alexandra Elizabeth, Meredith Gillian, Lauren Ashley, Geoffrey Nicholas. BA in Philosophy, U. Utah, 1970, JD, 1973. Bar: Ariz. 1973, Tex. 1990. Ptnr. Snell & Wilmer, Phoenix, 1973—89; shareholder Johnson & Gibbs, Dallas, 1989—93; ptnr. Gardere & Wynne, Dallas, 1993—95, Baker Botts, LLP, Dallas, 1995—2012. Lectr. in field. Contbr. articles to profl. jours. Served to capt. USAR Fellow Am. Coll. Employee Benefit Counsel, Inc. (charter); mem. ABA (tax sect., past chair employee benefits com., past vice chair, past chmn. various subcoms., 1993-94, chair joint com. on employee benefits 1994-95), Tex. State Bar Assn. (chair, tax sect. benefits and compensation com. 2000), Dallas Bar Assn. (chair employee benefits sect. 2001-2002), S.W. Benefits Conf., Nat. Assn. Stock Plan Profls., Order of Coif. Episcopalian. Office: Baker Botts LLP 2001 Ross Ave Ste 600 Dallas TX 75201-2900 Home: 4218 Rosa Ct Dallas TX 75220 Office Phone: 214-953-6878. Business E-Mail: bruce.pingree@bakerbotts.com.

PINION, PHILLIP E., state legislator; b. Martin, Tenn., May 19, 1952; m. Linda Pinion; children: Chip, Chad. Former Tenn. state rep. Dist. 17; former asst. majority whip; former majority whip; wholesale food distbr.; house rep. Tenn.; tchg. elder Cumberland Presbyn. Ch.; del. Gen. Assembly; Tenn. state rep. Dist. 77, 1989—. Named Legislator of Yr., Nat. Assn. Self-employed, 1992, Tenn. Devel. Dist. Assn., 1996. Mem.: Masons, Obion County C. of C., Rotary. Democrat. Presbyterian. Office: 2103 Stonewall Union City TN 38261 Mailing: Capitol Off 24 Legislative Plaza Rm D77 Nashville TN 37243-0177 also: PO Box 87 Union City TN 38281 Office Phone: 901-885-9175. E-Mail: rep.phillip.pinion@legislature.state.tn.us.

PINK, (ALECIA BETH MOORE), singer; b. Doylestown, Pa., Sept. 8, 1979; d. James and Judy (Kugel) Moore; m. Carey Hart, Jan. 7, 2006; 1 child, Willow Sage Hart. Model, spokesperson CoverGirl, 2012—. Singer: (albums) Can't Take Me Home, 2000, M!ssundaztood, 2001, Try This, 2003, I'm Not Dead, 2006, Funhouse, 2008, Greatest Hits...So Far!!!, 2010, The Truth About Love, 2012, (songs) There U Go, 2000, Most Girls, 2000, You Make Me Sick, 2001, Get the Party Started, 2001 (Best Female Video, Best Dance Video, MTV Video Music Awards, 2002, Favorite Song, Nickelodeon Kids' Choice Awards, 2002), (with Mya, Lil' Kim, & Christina Aguilera) Lady Marmalade, 2001 (Video of Yr., Best Video from a Film, MTV Video Music Awards, 2001, Best Pop Collaboration with Vocals, Grammy Awards, 2002), Don't Let Me Get Me, 2002, Just Like a Pill, 2002, Family Portrait, 2002, Trouble, 2003 (Best Female Rock Vocal Performance, Grammy Awards, 2004), God is a DJ, 2003, Stupid Girls, 2006 (Best Pop Video, MTV Video Music Awards, 2006), Who Knew, 2006 (BMI Pop award, Broadcast Music, Inc., 2008), Ur + Ur Hand, 2006 (BMI Pop award, Broadcast Music, Inc., 2008), Sober, 2008, So What, 2008, Please Don't Leave Me, 2009, Raise Your Glass, 2010, F**kin' Perfect, 2010; film appearances Ski to the Max, 2000, Rollerball, 2002, Charlie's Angels: Full Throttle, 2003, Catacombs, 2007, Get Him to the Greek, 2010; actress: (films) Happy Feet II (voice), 2011, Thanks for Sharing, 2012. Co-recipient Best Collaboration with Nate Ruess for the song Just Give Me a Reason, MTV Video Music awards, 2013; named Best Pop New Artist, Billboard Music Awards, 2000, Favorite Female - New Artist, Blockbuster

Entertainment Awards, 2001, Favorite Female Artist, Nickelodeon Kids' Choice Awards, 2002, Best Internat. Female Solo Artist, Brit Awards, 2003, Best Selling American Pop Female Artist, World Music Awards, 2003; named one of The 100 Sexiest Artists, VH1, 2002, The World's Most Powerful Celebrities, Forbes Mag., 2010, Top Accomplished Women Entertainers, CEOWORLD Mag. Office: La Face Records 1 Capital City Plz 3350 Peachtree Rd Ste 1500 Atlanta GA 30326

PINKERTON, ROBERT BRUCE, mechanical engineer; b. Detroit, Feb. 10, 1941; s. George Fulwell and Janet Lois (Hedke) P.; m. Barbara Ann Bandfield, Aug. 13, 1966; 1 child, Robert Brent. BSME, Detroit Inst. Tech., 1965; MA in Engring., Chrysler Inst. Engring., 1967; JD, Wayne State U., 1976. From mech. engr. to emissions and fuel economy planning specialist Chrysler Engring. Office Chrysler Corp., Highland Park, Mich., 1967-80; dir. engring. Replacement div. TRW, Inc., Cleve., 1980-83; v.p. engring. TRW Automotive Aftermarket Group, 1983-86; v.p. engring. and rsch. Blackstone Corp., Jamestown, NY, 1986-89, pres., CEO, 1989-90, Athena Corp., Beaufort, SC, 1990—, Cedar Crest Corp., Beaufort, SC, 1990—; chmn., CEO Beaufort Land Co., 1998—. Bd. dirs. VRI, LLC, Coastal Banking Co., Inc., Low Country Nat. Bank, Village Renaissance, Inc., Carpenters Hall, Coastal Banking Co., Inc.; chmn. redevelopment commn. City Beaufort, 2004—. Mem. exec. com. Beaufort Schs. Oversight Com., 1995-99, Pvt. Industry Coun., 1996-99. Mem.: Greater Beaufort C. of C. (bd. dirs. 1997—98), Beaufort Roundtable (pres. 2000—02), Rotary (asst. dist. gov. 1997—98). Episcopalian. Home: 5-D Rising Tide Dr Beaufort SC 29902 Office: PO Box 2115 1203 Boundary St Beaufort SC 29902 Business E-Mail: rbp@athenacorp.com.

PINNELL, MATT, political organization worker; BS, Oral Roberts Univ., 2002. Mgr. legis. affairs AIADA, 2003—04; PAC mgr. Am. Assn. Orthopedic Surgeons, 2004—05; campaign mgr. Scott Pruitt for Lt. Gov., 2005—06; Okla. exec. dir. Am. Majority, 2009; dir. ops. Okla. Rep. Party, 2006—08, chmn., 2010—13; state party dir. Rep. Nat. Com., Ohio, 2013—. Republican. Office: Okla Republican Party 4031 N Lincoln Blvd Oklahoma City OK 73105 Office Phone: 405-528-3501. Office Fax: 405-521-9531.*

PINNIX-RAGLAND, HILDA, electric power industry executive; m. Al; children: Katherine. B in Acctg. magna cum laude, A&T State U., NC, 1977; MBA, Duke U., 1986. Acct. Colgate-Palmolive, New York; auditor Arthur Anderson & Co., New York; joined Progress Energy, Inc., 1980, various positions, v.p., northern region, v.p., corp. pub. affairs. Chair NC State Bd. Cmty. Colls., NC Inst. Medicine; past nat. chair Am. Assn. Blacks Energy; bd. dirs. RTI Internat. Recipient Distinguished Alumni award, A&T State U., 2003, Disting. Alumni Citation of the Yr. award, Nat. Assn. for Equal Opportunity in Higher Edn., 2004, Kappa Psi Phi, Distinguished Citizen award, 2005, NC Women of Distinction, 2005, Sisters Delany Honor Soc. Achievement award, 2005, Women of Achievement award, Gen. Fedn. Women of NC, 2006, L.Richardson Preyer Alumni award, Leadership NC, 2006, James E. Stewart award, Am. Assn. of Blacks, 2007, NC 4-H Lifetime Achievement award, 2008. Office: Progress Energy Inc 410 S Wilmington St Raleigh NC 27601 Office Phone: 919-546-6789. Office Fax: 919-546-2920. Business E-Mail: Hilda.Pinnix-Ragland@pgnmail.com.

PINSON, CHARLES WRIGHT, surgeon, educator, academic administrator; b. Albuquerque, May 29, 1952; s. Ernest Alexander and Jean Elizabeth Pinson. Student, Miami U., Oxford, Ohio, 1970-72; BA, U. Colo., Boulder, 1974, MBA, 1976; MD, Vanderbilt U., 1980. Diplomate Am. Bd. Surgery, Am. Bd. Surg. Critical Care, Nat. Bd. Med. Examiners. Resident in gen. surgery Oreg. Health Sci. U., Portland, 1980-86; fellow gastrointestinal surgery Lahey Clinic, Burlington, Mass., 1986-87; fellow transplant surgery Harvard U., Boston, 1987-88; dir. liver transplant program VA Western region, Portland, 1989-90, Oreg. Health Sci. U., Portland, 1988-90; interim chmn. dept. surgery Vanderbilt U., Nashville, 1993-95, chief divsn. hepatobiliary surgery and liver transplantation, 1990—2004, vice-chmn. dept. surgery, 1995-2001; dir. Vanderbilt Transplant Ctr., Nashville, 1993—; chmn. med. bd. Vanderbilt U. Med. Ctr., Nashville, 1997-99; chief of staff Vanderbilt U. Hosp., Nashville, 1997—2004; H. William Scott prof., chmn. dept. surgery Vanderbilt U., Nashville, 2001—04; chief med. officer, assoc. vice chancellor for clin. affairs Vanderbilt U. Med. Ctr., Nashville, 2004—09; dep. vice chancellor health affairs CEO Vanderbilt Hosp. & Clinics; pres. Vanderbilt Health Svc.; sr. assoc., dean Vanderbilt Med. Ctr. Adv. bd. Pacific N.W. Transplant Bank, Portland, 1989—90, Tenn. Donor Svcs., Nashville, 1991—, sec., 2003—05. Mem. editl. bd. Annals Surgery, Jour. Gastronintestinal Surgery, Liver Transplantation, HPB; contbr. articles to profl. jours., chapters to books. Chair liver and intestine allocation com. United Network Organ Sharing, 2003—05; bd. dirs. ARC, Nashville, 1992—94, Am. Liver Found., 1992—96, Ronald McDonald House, 2002—, United Network Organ Sharing, 2000—02, Hosp. Hospitality House, Nashville, 2005—. Fellow, Am. Heart Assn., 1983—84. Mem.: Internat. Hepatopancreatobiliary Assn. (mem. sci. com. 2000—03, mem. exec. com. 2003—, treas. 2004—08, pres. elect. 2008—), Internat. Liver Transplantation Soc., Soc. Surgery Alimentary Tract, Assn. Acad. Surgery, N. Pacific Surg. Assn. (mem. sci. program 1990—92), Western Surg. Assn., So. Surg. Assn., Am. Surg. Assn., So. Med. Assn. (chmn. sect. surgery 1997—2001), Am. Physiologic Soc., Am. Hepatopancreatobiliary Assn. (mem. exec. com. 1997—, treas. 1999—2003, pres. elect 2001—03, pres. 2003—05), Am. Gastroent. Assn., Am. Soc. Study Liver Diseases, Am. Soc. Transplant Surgeons, Soc. Surg. Oncology, Halsted Soc., Soc. Univ. Surgeons, Phi Beta Kappa, Sigma Xi, Alpha Omega Alpha. Office: Vanderbilt U Med Ctr D3300 MCN Nashville TN 37232-5545

PINSON, LEWIS EUGENE, state legislator; b. Greenwood, SC, Nov. 2, 1949; s. Thomas R. and Ruth P. Pinson; m. Carol V. Metger Pinson, Aug. 3, 1974; children: Brian, Emliy, Neal. BS, The Citadel, 1972. Mem. Dist. 13 SC House of Reps., 2003—, mem. Labor, Commerce and Industry Com. & Rules Com. Master: Masonic Lodge; mem.: Greenwood Ret. Guardsman, America Legion Post (comdr.), Citadel Alumni Assn. (past leader), Scout Main St. Bapt. Ch. (deacon), Cub Scout Leader, Greater Greenwood Citadel Club, Ret. Officers Club Assn. Republican. Office: 522A Blatt Bldg Columbia SC 29201 Office Phone: 864-388-9433. E-mail: pinsong@scstatehouse.net.

PINSON, WILLIAM MEREDITH, JR., pastor, writer, administrator, professor; b. Ft. Worth, Aug. 3, 1934; s. William Meredith and Ila Lee (Jones) P.; m. Bobbie Ruth Judd, June 4, 1955; children: Meredith Pinson Creasey, Allison Pinson Hopgood. BA, U. N. Tex., 1955; BD, Southwestern Bapt. Theol. Sem., Ft. Worth, 1959, ThD, 1963, MDiv, 1973; LittD (hon.), Calif. Bapt. Coll., Riverside, 1978; DD (hon.), U. Mary Hardin-Baylor, Belton, Tex., 1984; LHD (hon.), Howard Payne U., Brownwood, Tex., 1986; LittD (hon.), Dallas Bapt. U., 1990; LLD (hon.), Hardin Simmons U., 1999. Ordained to ministry Bapt. Ch., 1955. Assoc. sec. Christian Life Commn., Dallas, 1957-63; prof. Christian ethics Southwestern Bapt. Theol. Sem., Ft. Worth, 1963-75; pastor First Bapt. Ch., Wichita Falls, Tex., 1975-77; pres. Golden Gate Bapt. Theol. Sem., Mill Valley, Calif., 1977-82, pres. emeritus, 2000—; vol. dir. Tex. Bapt. Heritage Ctr., 2000—; disting. prof. Dallas Bapt. U., 2001—; disting. vis. prof. Baylor U., 2001—. Exec. dir. Bapt. Gen. Conv. Tex., 1982—2000, exec. dir. emeritus, 2000—; chmn. program com. Christian Life Commn. So. Bapt. Conv., spl. rschr. for home mission bd., nat. task force planned growth in giving, 1984—94, stewardship commn., 1986—96; bd. dirs. T.B. Maston Found.; adj. prof. Southwestern Bapt. Theol. Sem., 1976—77; chmn. study commn. freedom, justice and peace Bapt. World Alliance, 1975—80, study commn. on ethics, 1990—95, commn. on racism, 1992—, com. polity and heritage, 2000—10, com. Baptist heritage & identity, 2010—; v.p. Bapt. Gen. Conv. Tex., 1972—73, state missions commn., 1976—77, vice chmn. urban strategy com., chmn. order of bus. com., 1976, chmn. steering com. Good News Tex., 1976—77, chmn. resolutions com.; spkr. in field; bd. dirs., chair centennial com. Baylor U. Health Care Sys., 2002—03, trustee, 2010—. Contbr. articles to profl. jours., chapters to books;, author numerous books on ethics, history. Adv. bd. Bapt. History and Heritage Soc., 2002—; mem. adv. com. Sch. Leadership Dallas Bapt. U., 2003—. Named Lilly Found. scholar Southwestern Bapt. Theol. Sem., 1960-62; recipient Disting. Alumni award Southwestern Bapt. Theol. Sem., 1979, U. North Tex., 1980, Mosaic Missions award Home Mission Bd., 1984, Parabolani award Tex. Bapt. Men, 1999, Spirit of Excellence award Houston Bapt. U., 2000, Tex. Bapt. Missions award State Missions Commn., 2000, Pinson Endowed Lectrs. award, 2000-, Pioneer award Tex. Bapt. Missions Found., 2001, W. Winfred Moore award for lifetime achievement in ministry Baylor U., 2001, Pro Ecclesia award, 2010, Officers' award Bapt. History and Heritage Soc., 2003, Elder Statesman award Independence. Assn., 2005, George W. Truett award, Baylor U., 2008. Mem. So. Bapt. Assn. Colls. and Schs., So. Bapt. Assn. of State Exec. Dirs. (pres. 1996-97). Baptist. Avocations: travel, reading. Office: Bapt Gen Conv Tex 333 N Washington Ave Dallas TX 75246-1782 Home Phone: 972-298-7371; Office Phone: 214-370-9471. Office Fax: 214-370-0228. Business E-Mail: william.pinson@texasbaptists.org.

PINTO, NICHOLAS JOAQUIM, physics professor; s. Thomas Celstino Pinto and Agatha Louie Fernandes; m. Carmen Ines Sanchez, Aug. 30, 1997; 1 child, Victoria Ines. BSc in Physics, Bombay U., 1985; MS in Physics, Bowling Green State U., Ohio, 1987; PhD in Physics, Mont. State U., Bozeman, 1992. Postdoctoral rschr. Wichita State U., Kans., 1992—94; prof. U. PR, Humacao, 1995—; vis. scientist U. Pa., 2001—02. Mem.: AAAS, Am. Chem. Soc., Am. Phys. Soc. Achievements include patents for conducting polymers. Home: Urb Santa Cecilia # 55 C/Stma Trinidad Caguas PR 00725 Office: PR 100 Rd # 908 Humacao PR 00791 Business E-Mail: nicholas.pinto@upr.edu.

PIOLI, SCOTT, professional sports team executive; b. Washingtonville, NY, Mar. 31, 1965; m. Dallas Pioli; 1 child, Mia Costa Pioli. BA in Comm., Ctrl. Conn. State U., New Britain, 1988; MA, Syracuse U. S.I. Newhouse Sch. Pub. Comm., NY. Grad. asst. Syracuse U. Orange, 1988—90; offensive line coach Murray State U. Racers, 1990, defensive line coach, 1991; pro pers. asst. Cleve. Browns, 1992—95; dir. pro pers. Balt. Ravens, 1996, NY Jets, 1997—99; pers. dir. New Eng. Patriots, 2000—01, v.p. player pers., 2002—08; gen. mgr. Kansas City Chiefs, 2009—12; host Sirius XM NFL Radio, 2013—14; asst. gen. mgr. Atlanta Falcons, 2014—. Founder Rose Pioli Scholarship; bd. dirs. Coll. for Every Student Found. Recipient George Young NFL Exec. of Yr. award, The Sporting News, 2003, 2004, Award for Exec. Achievement, NFL Players Assn., 2004; named NFL Exec. of Yr., Dallas Morning News, 2001, 2007, Pro Football Weekly, 2003, 2007, Sports Illus., 2003, USA Today, 2004, San Francisco Chronicle, 2004, 2007, SI.com, 2004; named to The Ctrl. Conn. State U. Hall of Fame, 2005. Achievements include member of Super Bowl XXXVI, XXXVIII, XXXIX Championship winning New England Patriots. Office: Atlanta Falcons One Georgia Dome Dr NW Atlanta GA 30313*

PIPER, DON COURTNEY, political scientist, educator; b. Washington, July 29, 1932; s. Don Carlos and Alice (Courtney) Piper; m. Rowena Inez Wise, July 6, 1956; children: Sharon, Valarie. BA, U. Md., 1954, MA, 1958; PhD (James B. Duke fellow), Duke U., 1961. Research assoc. Duke U., 1961-62; exec. sec. Commonwealth-Studies Center, 1962-64; asst. prof. dept. govt. and politics U. Md., College Park, 1964-67, assoc. prof., 1967-69, prof., 1969-97, prof. emeritus, 1997—, head dept. govt. and politics, 1968-74, dir. grad. studies dept., 1982-95, mem. coun. of system faculty, 1989-90; chmn. faculty council College Park Faculty Assembly, 1974-75, chmn. campus senate, 1975-77, 89-90, univ. marshal, 1981-97, mem. Athletic Council, 1986-93, mem. senate ad hoc com. on undergrad. edn., 1986-88, chmn. chancellor's ad hoc com. on campus ceremonies, 1986-87, chmn. acad. com. of Athletic Council, 1986-89; chmn. campaign for College Park, 1988-89; chmn. retention review com. U. Md., 1990-91, chmn. budget and facilities com. athletic coun., 1991-93, chmn. senate com. on programs courses and curriculi, 1991-93, co-chair Mid. States self-study exec. com., 1995-97; tchg. fellow Lilly Ctr. for Tchg. Excellence, 1994—95. Rsch. asst. Am. Coun. Edn., 1966—68; mem. faculty adv. com., mem. adv. com. Md. State Bd. Higher Edn., 1977—82. Author: International Law of Great Lakes, 1967; co-author: International Law Standard and Commonwealth Developments, 1966, De Lege Pactorum, 1970, Foreign Policy Analysis, 1975; editor (with R. Taylor Cole): Post-Primary Education and Political and Economic Development, 1964; editor, author (with Ronald Terchek): Interaction: Foreign Policy and Public Policy, 1983; bd. editors World Affairs, 1971—94, mem. editl. adv. com. Internat. Legal Materials, 1977—78. Served to 1st lt. USAF, 1955—58. Mem.: Phi Beta Kappa (pres. Gamma chpt. 1978—79), Pi Sigma Alpha, Omicron Delta Kappa (faculty advisor 1990—97), Phi Kappa Phi (chpt. pres. 1982—83). Methodist. Home: 6312 Oakview Ct Hillsborough NC 27278

PIPER, LLOYD LLEWELLYN, II, engineer, government and service industry executive; b. Wareham, Mass., Apr. 28, 1944; s. Lloyd Llewellyn and Mary Elizabeth (Brown) P.; m. Jane Melonie Scruggs, Apr. 30, 1965; 1 child, Michael Wayne. BSEE, Tex. A&M U., 1966; MS in Indsl. Engring, U. Houston, 1973. Registered profl. engr., Tex.; bd. cert. hazardous waste mgmt. Am. Acad. Environ. Engrs. With Houston Lighting & Power Co., 1965—74; project mgr. Dow Chem. Engring. & Constrn Svcs., Houston, 1974—78, Ortloff Corp., Houston, 1978, mgr. engring., 1979—80, v.p., 1980—83; pres., CEO Plantech Engrs. & Constructors, Inc. subs. Dillingham Constrn. Corp., Houston, 1983—86; pres. Delta Plantech Co., Houston, 1985—86; dir. on-site tech. devel. Chem. Waste Mgmt., Inc., Oak Brook, Ill., 1986—88, mgr. projects Houston, 1988—94, dir. facility devel., 1994—95; asst. mgr. Richland Ops. U.S. Dept. Energy, Wash., 1995—96, dep. mgr., 1996—99, adminstr., 1999—2002, asst. mgr., 2002—03; dep. mgr. Carlsbad Field Office US Dept. Energy, 2003—07; mgr. Piper & Associates, LLC, 2007—. Bd. dirs., pres. Harris County Water Control and Improvement Dist., 1973—83; bd. dirs. Environ. Sci. and Tech. Found., 1997—99, United Way, 1998—2003, exec. com., 1998—2001, treas., 2000—01, bd. dirs., 2004—07, Ponderosa Joint Powers Agy. Harris County, 1977—83, pres., 1977—83; pres. bus. and industry adv. coun. North Harris Montgomery C. C. Dist., 1991—92. Contbr. articles to profl. jours. Recipient Disting. Svc. award Engrs. Coun. Houston, 1970; named Tex. Young Engr. of Yr., 1976, Nat. Young Engr. of Yr., 1976. Mem. IEEE (Outstanding Svc. award Houston sect. 1974), NSPE (chpt. pres. 1978, nat. chmn. engrs. in industry divsn. 1977, nat. v.p. 1977, chmn. nat. polit. action com. 1979-82, vice chmn. nat. engrs. week 1988-92, nat. trustee edn. found. 1988-90), Phi Kappa Phi, Tau Beta Pi. Office: Piper & Assoc LLC PO Box 6353 Bryan TX 77805

PIPES, PAUL RAY, county commissioner; b. Truscott, Tex., Oct. 1, 1928; s. David and Maggie (Brown) Pipes; m. Linda Mullins, Dec. 17, 1961; children: Dana, Tricia. BBA, Sam Houston U., Huntsville, Tex., 1956, MEd, 1971. Acct. Pan Am. Petroleum Corp., Thibodaux, La., 1956-61; bus. tchr. Brenham H.S., Tex., 1962-90; county commr. Washington County, Brenham, 1991-98. With US Army, 1951-53, Korea. Decorated Def. Disting. Svc. medal. Republican. Methodist. Avocations: gardening, nature study. Home: 2106 Jane Ln Brenham TX 77833-5331 Personal E-mail: plpipes@academicplanet.com, plpipes@yahoo.com. Business E-Mail: plpipes@att.net.

PIPKIN, GREGORY W., corporate financial executive; BBA, Tex. Tech. U. CPA. Contr., v.p., acctg. & reporting Alamosa Holdings, Inc., 2001—06; dir., fin. reporting Patterson-UTI Energy, Inc., 2006—07, chief acctg. officer, asst. sec., 2007—. Office: Patterson-UTI Energy Inc 450 Gears Rd Ste 500 Houston TX 77067 Office Phone: 281-765-7100. Office Fax: 281-765-7175.

PIRKEY, LOUIS THOMAS, lawyer; b. Ft. Worth, Dec. 6, 1937; s. Louis F. and Juanita (Copeland) Pirkey; m. Jewell Katherine Buchanan, Oct. 19, 1940; children: Julia Hope, Jeffry Thomas. BSChE, U. Tex., 1960; JD with honors, George Washington U., 1964. Bar: Tex. 1964, US Supreme Ct. 1981, US Ct. Appeals (5th and 11th cirs.), US Dist. Ct. (we., so. and ea. dists.) Tex. Mem. Arnold, White & Durkee, Houston, 1964—, 1969—; chmn. intellectual property law sect. State Bar Tex., 1982—83; mem. US delegation Diplomatic Conf. Rev. Paris Conv., 1982. Fellow: Tex. Bar Found.; mem.: Order Coif, Internat. Assn. Protection Intellectual Property, Travis County Bar Assn., Houston Patent Law Assn., Houston Bar Assn., Am. Patent Law Assn., ABA, US Trademark Assn., U. Club, Capital, Headliners, Westwood Country (Austin), Phi Alpha Delta. Office: 600 Congress Ave Ste 2300 Austin TX 78701-2977

PIRKLE, GEORGE EMORY, photographer, instructional media producer; b. Sept. 3, 1947; s. George Washington and Glanna Adeline (Palmer) P.; m. Karen Leigh Horn, Oct. 20, 1973; 1 child, Charity Caroline. Student, North Ga. Coll., 1965-66; BA in Journalism, U. Ga., 1969, MA, 1971. Photography cert. U. North Ga., 2013. Radio announcer, sportscaster various radio stations, North Ga. area, 1968-70; TV prodr., dir. Instructional Resources Ctr., Athens, Ga., 1969-70; Vietnam era vet. US Army, U.S. Army, 1971—73; pub. info. officer Ga. Dept. Revenue, Atlanta, 1973-78; coord. TV prodn. svcs. So. Co. Svcs., Inc., Birmingham, Ala., 1978-88; exec. v.p. Mgmt. and Human Devel. Assocs., Inc., Birmingham, Ala., 1984-86; prodr. Prodn. Works, Birmingham, Ala., 1984-88; owner Talking Rock Prodns., Cumming, Ga., 1989—. Actor for various radio and TV commercials, corp. TV programs, radio dramas, stage plays, 1968—; comml. acting instr. elan Casablancas Modeling Career Ctr., 1988—1992; instr., Cliff Osmond Acting Program, 1989-92; anchor This Week Banking Bankers TV Network, 1990-92; adj. instr., computer sci., Lanier Tech. Coll., 2001. Editor monthly newsletter Ga. Revenews, 1973-78; editor, dir. Bankers TV Network, 1990-92; writer, prodr., dir., exec. prodr. more than 500 corp. and pub. svc. TV and film programs; exec. prodr. videotape for Birmingham Film Coun., 1985; prodr., dir. Highway in Crisis, 1986; writer, prodr., dir. campaign film Birmingham Area United Way, 1981, 86, 87; writer, prodr., narrator, 1987 campaign film; anchor This Week in Banking, 1990-92, Before They Fall, Sunrise, Sunset, We Must Remember. Master of ceremonies, gov.'s vet. awards presentation World Peace Luncheon, 1981, 82, 84, Birmingham; bd. directors Birmingham Internat. Ednl. Film Festival, 1987—91; dir., campaign film United Way, Pensacola, 1989; chmn. Sadie award com.; dir. student video competition; comml. acting instr. elan/Casablancas Modeling/Career Ctr., 1988—92; mem. tech. steering com. Forsyth Bd. Edn., 1995; bd. dirs. United Way of Forsyth County, 1995—2004; vol. Am. Cancer Soc. Relay for Life, 1996—2002; permanent mem. allocations com. United Way Forsyth County, 2000—04, v.p. allocations, 2003; chair Forsyth County Bd. Ethics, 2002—12; mem. Comms. com. Birmingham Area Couns. Boy Scouts Am., 1983—85, City Parks Recreation Bd., 1996—; mem. adv. bd. Sawnee Mtn. Preserve; bd. dirs. Leadership Forsyth, 2005—08; comm. bd. dirs. Bald Ridge Lodge, 2005—10; historian, archivist Hist. Soc. Forsyth County, 2011—. 1st lt. US Army, 1971—73, 2nd. lt. US Army, 1969, with US Army, 1972, with US Army, 1973. Recipient So. Superlative Outstanding employee award, So. Co. Svcs., 1986, Battles award 1988, various others, Internat. Television Assn. Paddlewheel award, 1986, Birmingham Internat. Ednl. Film Festival Battles award, 1988, Small Bus. Mem. of Yr., Cumming Forsyth County, 2002, Captained winner, 2004. Mem.: So. Electric Sys. Visual Comms. Subcom. (founding), Internat. TV Assn. (pres. pro tem 1984, charter pres. Birmingham chapter 1984—85, editor newsletter Freeze Frame), Hist. Soc. Forsyth County (pres. 1996), Ga. Hist. Soc., Rotary Club Forsyth County (pres. 2012—, Dist. 6910 Literacy chair 2013—, Paul Harris fellow 2001, 2013), Cumming/Forsyth C. of C. (Bus. Mem. of the Yr. 2002). Achievements include introduced first series of performances "The Reach of Song" at Cumming Playhouse newly rescued and restored school building. Avocations: photography, astronomy, genealogy, history, archaeology, model railroading. Home and Office: Talking Rock Productions PO Box 2218 Cumming GA 30028 Home Phone: 770-841-4396. Business E-Mail: trvideo@bellsouth.net.

PIRODSKY, DONALD MAX, psychiatrist, educator; b. Freeport, NY, Feb. 2, 1945; s. Max and Doris Geilhard (Biedermann) P.; m. Gail Giufre Pallotta, Jan. 4, 1997(div.); children: Laura Anne, Jason Donald. BA, Hofstra U., Hempstead, NY, 1966; MD, SUNY, Syracuse, 1970. Diplomate Am. Bd. Psychiatry and Neurology, Nat. Bd. Med. Examiners. Intern Northwestern U. Med. Ctr., Chgo., 1970-71; resident in psychiatry Strong Meml. Hosp., Rochester, NY, 1973-74, U. Ariz. Med. Ctr., Tucson, 1974-76; instr. psychiatry SUNY Health Sci. Ctr., Syracuse, 1976-78, attending psychiatrist, 1976-91, asst. prof. psychiatry, 1978-85, mem. exec. com. of med. coll. assembly, 1979-82, clin. assoc. prof., 1985—2006, adj. attending psychiatrist, 1991—2006; pvt. practice psychiatrist Syracuse and Fayetteville, NY, 1976—2006; staff psychiatrist, dir. consultation/liaison svc. Syracuse VA Med. Ctr., 1976-87, chmn. pharmacy rev. and therapeutic agts. com., 1980-86. Psychiat. cons. Ariz. Sch. Deaf and Blind, Tucson, 1975-76, Syracuse Devel. Ctr., 1977-2006, Rochester Sch. Deaf, 1978-81; ex-officio mem. Family Counseling Agy., Tucson, 1975-76; adj. attending psychiatrist SUNY Health Sci. Ctr., Syracuse, 1991-2006. Author: Primer of Clinical Psychopharmacology: A Practical Guide, 1981, (with Jerry S. Cohn) Clinical Primer of Psychopharmacology: A Practical Guide, 2d edit., 1992; contbr. articles to profl. jours., chpts. to med. books. Lt. comdr. USPHS, 1971-73. Fellow Am. Psychiat. Assn. (Disting., mem. cen. NY dist. br.); mem. Am. Psychosomatic Soc., Am. Assn. Mental Retardation, Med. Soc. State of NY, NY State Psychiat. Assn., Onondaga County Med. Soc., Assn. Am. Physicians & Surgeons. Episcopalian. Avocations: sports, collecting baseball cards and other sports memorabilia. Home and Office: 5393 Cambiago St Sarasota FL 34238-4771 Office Phone: 315-247-9681.

PISANO, ETTA D., radiologist, educator; AB cum laude, Dartmouth Coll., 1979; MD, Duke U. Cert. Diagnostic Radiology Am. Bd. Radiology, 1988. Radiology resident Beth Israel Hosp., Boston, 1984—88, chief resident, 1986—87, dir. mammography, 1988—89; med. dir. Carolina Screening Mammography, 1989—93; residency program dir. Dept. Radiology U. NC Sch. Medicine, 1992—96, section chief Breast Imaging Sect., 1989—2005, program dir. Post-grad. Continuing Med. Edn. Course in Breast Imaging, 1989—2005, Kenan prof. radiology and biomedical engring., dir. Biomed. Rsch. Imaging Ctr., 2003—, vice dean academic affairs, 2006—. Contbr. articles to profl. jours. Recipient Francis W. Gramlich Philosophy Prize, 1979, Health Breakthrough award, Ladies' Home Jour., 2006; named one of 20 Most Influential People in Radiology, Diagnostic Imaging, 2002, America's Best Breast Cancer Doctors, Redbook, 2001. Fellow: Soc. Breast Imaging; mem.: Inst. Medicine, Assn. Profl. Women in Medicine and Sci. (mem. Nominating and Salary Equity Com. 1994—), Assn. Univ. Radiologists, Am. Coll. Radiology, Am. Assn. Women's Radiologists, Am. Med. Women's Assn. (Women in Sci. Award 2005), Radiological Soc. North Am., Internat. Digital Mammography Devel. Group (chair 1996—, pres. pro tem 2001—), Am. Roentgen Ray Soc. Office: U NC Chapel Hill Sch Medicine 503 Old Infimary Chapel Hill NC 27599-7510 Home: 1319 Cove Ave Sullivans Island SC 29482-9769 Home Phone: 919-942-1166; Office Phone: 919-966-4397. E-mail: etpisano@med.unc.edu.

PISARCZYK, RICHARD V., oil industry executive; m. Mary Pisarczyk; 1 child, Michael. B in Chem. Engring., Mich. State U., 1968. Engr. Mobil Oil Corp., 1968, mgr. Ferndale Refinery Wash., 1984—86, v.p., gen. mgr. olefins and aromatics, petrochemicals divsn., Mobil Chem. Co., 1986—88, mgr. planning and fin. analysis, mfg. Fairfax, Va., 1988, mgr. Chalmette Refinery La., 1989, mgr. planning coordination, corp. planning and economics Fairfax, 1992, mng. dir. Mobil Oil Australia Pty Ltd., 1994—97, v.p. East/Gulf Coast bus., North America mktg. & refining, 1997—99; regional dir. Americas, ExxonMobil Chem. ExxonMobil Corp., 1999—2001, sr. v.p. basic chemicals, 2001—03, sr. v.p. basic chemicals and intermediates, 2003—05, pres. ExxonMobil Rsch. & Engring. Co., 2005—. Rep. Indsl. Rsch. Inst.; mem. Rsch., Innovation and Enterprise Coun. Recipient Red Cedar Cir. award in Chem. Engring. and Materials Sci., Mich. State U., 2007. Avocations: golf, woodworking. Office: Exxon Mobil Corp Hdqs 5959 Las Colinas Blvd Irving TX 75039-2298

PISCITELLI, FELICIA ANN, librarian, musician, musicologist; b. Tinker Air Force Base, Oklahoma City, Okla., Sept. 21, 1956; d. Domenic Ralph and Frankie Lee Piscitelli. BA in Fine Arts, U. N.Mex, 1979, MusM, 1983; MLS, U. Ariz., 1990. Piano tchr., Albuquerque, 1982—84; libr. tech. asst. U. N.Mex, Albuquerque, 1984—89; original cataloger, assoc. prof. Tex. A&M U., College Station, 1991—, asst. dir. cataloging, 2004—. Contbr. articles to profl. jours., chapters to books (Walter Gerboth award music bibliography, 1994);, author program notes musical concerts. Part-time organist St. Thomas Aquinas Cath. Ch., College Station, 1993—2005. Grantee Hymnody Am. Protestantism Project, Inst. Study Am. Evangelicalism, 1998. Mem.: Am. Guild Organists, Music Libr. Assn., Brazos Valley Chorale, Sigma Alpha Iota (life). Roman Catholic. Avocations: music, travel, languages. Office: Tex A&M U Sterling C Evans Libr Cataloging College Station TX 77843-5000 Office Fax: 979-862-1166. Business E-Mail: f-piscitelli@tamu.edu.

PISTOLE, JOHN S., federal agency administrator; b. 1956; married; 2 children. BA, Anderson U., 1978; JD, Ind. U. Law Sch., 1981. Pvt. practice, Anderson, Ind., 1981—83; spl. agent Mpls. divsn. FBI, 1983—85, spl. agent NY divsn., 1985—90, supr. organized crime sect. Washington, 1990—94, field supr. white collar crime and civil rights squad, undercover coord. Indpls., 1994—99, asst. spl. agent in charge Boston, 1999—2001, inspector Washington, 2001—02, dep. asst. dir. counterterrorism divsn., 2002—03, asst. dir. counterterrorism divsn., 2003, exec. asst. dir., counterterrorism and counterintelligence, 2003—04, dep. dir., 2004—10; asst. sec., adminstr. Transp. Security Adminstrn. (TSA) US Dept. Homeland Security, Washington, 2010—. Instr. Internat. Law Enforcement Acad., Budapest, Hungary, 1995—96; FBI rep. state dept. delegation, Sofia, Bulgaria; dir. Blue Team info. soc. working group, 2001. Recipient Presdl. Rank award for Disting. Exec., 2005, Edward H. Levy award for Outstanding Professionalism & Exemplary Integrity, 2007. Office: Transportation Security Administration (TSA) 601 S 12th St Arlington VA 22202*

PITCOCK, JAMES KENT, otolaryngologist; b. Tachikawa AFB, Japan, Nov. 18, 1951; s. James Kenneth and Helen (Robertson) P.; m. Cynthia H. Zipperly. Student, U. Houston, 1974; MD, Baylor U., 1979. Diplomate Am. Bd. Otolaryngology. Resident in gen. surgery Baylor Coll. Medicine, Houston, 1979-81, resident in otolaryngology, head and neck surgery, 1981-84; clinician Kelsey-Seybold Clinic, P.A., Houston, 1984-85; lectr. head and neck surgery Inst. Laryngology and Otology, U. London, 1985-86; instr., fellow head and neck surgery U. Chgo., 1986-88; asst. prof. dept. otolaryngology, head and neck surgery, chief div. head and neck surgical oncology U. Calif.-Irvine Med. Ctr., Orange, 1988-92. Dir. head and neck oncology clin. and rsch. program Clin. Cancer Ctr. U. Calif., Irvine. Author: Oral and Maxillofacial Trauma, 1989, Musculocutaneous Flap Reconstruction of the Head and Neck, 1989, Surgery of the Skull Base, 1989. Fellow Am. Acad. Otolaryngology, Head and Neck Surgery; mem. Am. Rhinologic Soc. Office: Premier Med Grp 3701 Dauphin St Mobile AL 36608-1756 Home Phone: 251-343-9445; Office Phone: 251-341-3368.

PITINO, RICK, men's college basketball coach; b. NYC, Sept. 18, 1952; m. Joanne Pitino; children: Michael, Christopher, Richard, Ryan, Jacqueline. Grad., U. Mass., 1974. Grad. asst. U. Hawaii, 1974, asst. coach, 1975-76, Syracuse U., 1976-78; head coach Boston U., 1978-83; asst. coach NY Knicks, 1983-85, head coach, 1987-89, Providence U., 1985—87, U. Ky., Lexington, 1989-97; head coach, pres. Boston Celtics, 1997—2001; head coach U. Louisville, 2001—. Author: (with Bill Reynolds) Born to Coach: A Season with the New York Knicks, 1988, (with Dick Weiss) Full Court Pressure: A Year in Kentucky Basketball, 1992; Success Is a Choice: Ten Steps to Overachieving in Business and Life, 1997, Lead to Succeed, 2000, (with Pat Forde) Rebound Rules: The Art of Success 2.0, 2008, (with Eric Crawford) The One-Day Contract: How to Add Value to Every Minute of Your Life, 2013 Named New Eng. Coach of Yr., 1979, 1983, Nat. Assn. Basketball Coaches Nat. Coach of Yr., 1987, John Wooden Nat. Coach of Yr., 1987, Southeastern Conf. Coach of Yr., 1990, 1991, 1997, Conf. USA Coach of Yr., 2005; named to NYC Hall of Fame, 2006, Naismith Meml. Basketball Hall of Fame, 2013. Achievements include head coach of the NCAA Final Four National Championship winning University of Kentucky Wildcats, 1996; University of Louisville Cardinals, 2013. Office: Mens Basketball Program Athletics Dept University of Louisville Louisville KY 40292 Office Phone: 502-852-6651. E-mail: rick.pitino@louisville.edu.*

PITMAN, ROBERT LEE, federal prosecutor, former federal judge; b. Ft. Worth, Tex., 1962; BS, Abilene Christian U., 1984; JD, U. Tex., 1988. Legis. aide to Rep. Bob Hunter Tex. House of Reps., Austin, 1985—87; law clk. to Hon. David Belew Jr. US Dist. Ct. (northern dist.) Tex., 1988—89; assoc. Fulbright & Jaworski LLP, Austin, 1989—90; atty. advisor Executive Office for US Attorneys US Dept. Justice, Washington, DC, 1997—98; cheif Austin Div., Western Dist., Tex.; asst US atty. (western dist.) Tex. US Dept. Justice, Tex., 1991—2001, US atty. San Antonio, 2001, 2011—, dep. US atty., 2001—03; magistrate judge US Dist. Ct. (western dist.) Tex., Tex., 2003—11. Adj. prof. U. Tex., Austin, 2002—; mem. Supreme Ct. Tex. Task Force on Disciplinary Rules, 2004—05. Bd. dirs. United Cerebral Palsy, 1993—95; mem. Hill County Ride for AIDS Production Team, 2001—05. Recipient commendations from Exec. Office for US Atty, Fed. Bureau of Investigation, US Dept. of State, US Drug Enforcement Adminstrn., US Secret Service. Fellow: Tex. Bar Found.; mem.: Lloyd Lochridge American Inn of Ct. (pres. 2009—10). Office: US Attorney's Office 601 NW Loop 410 Ste 600 San Antonio TX 78216-5597 Office Phone: 210-384-7100. Fax: 210-384-7105.*

PITMAN, SHARON GAIL, retired middle school counselor; b. Dayton, Ohio, June 13, 1946; d. Finley Andrew and Lena Kay (Wells) Jennings; m. Benjamin Pitman III, Jan. 19, 1980; children: Elizabeth Ann (dec.), Emily; stepchildren: Scott, Todd. BS in Edn., Miami U., Oxford, Ohio, 1968, MEd in Edn., 1970; cert. sch. counseling, Ga. State U., 1979, MEd in Counseling, 1981, EdS in Guidance and Counseling, 1989. Tchr. pub. schs., Hamilton, Ohio, 1968—73, Gwinnett County, Ga., 1973—80; sch. counselor Buford Mid. Sch., Ga., 1981—89, Duluth Mid. Sch., Ga., 1989—96, Lanier Mid. Sch., Ga., 1998—2004. Condr. workshops in field. Mem. Am. Sch. Counseling Assn. (Nat. Mid. Sch. Counselor of Yr. 1989), Ga. Sch. Counselors Assn. (Mid. Sch. Counselor of Yr. 1988). Personal E-mail: s-pitman@charter.net.

PITMAN-GELLES, BONNIE LOUISE, former museum director; b. Stamford, Conn., Apr. 24, 1946; d. Benjamin Pitman and Margaret (Hackett) Perry; m. George Gelles, Jan. 1, 1976 (div. 1985); 1 child, David Alexander. AB, Pine Manor Coll., 1966; BA cum laude, Sweet Briar Coll., 1968; MA, Tulane U., 1971. Curator of edn. Winnipeg Art Gallery, Canada, 1968-71, New Orleans Mus. Art, 1971-75; faculty New Orleans Ctr. for Creative Arts, 1975-76; cons. Nat. Endowment for Arts, Washington, 1976-80, panelist Arts in Edn., 1978-84; cons. NEH, Washington, 1977-79, panelist, 1978-79; market rep. Parker Bros., Inc., Salem, N.Y., 1980; cons. Bklyn Ednl. Cultural Alliance, 1980-81, Lincoln Ctr., NYC, 1980-81; assoc. dir. Seattle Art Mus., 1981—, acting dir., 1986-87; mem. faculty mus. mgmt. program U. Colo., Boulder, 1986; dep. dir. U. Art Mus. U. Calif., Berkeley, 1990—95; exec. dir. Bay Area Discovery Mus., Sausalito, Calif., 1995—2000; dep. dir. Dallas Mus. of Art, 2000—08, Eugene McDermott dir., 2008—11, cons., 2011—. Mem. nat. adv. com. Getty Ctr. for Edn. in the Arts, 1988—; cons. numerous mus. Author: Watermelon, 1973, Pumpkins into Coaches: Handbook on Youth Education in Museums, 1977, Museums as Educational Instruments, 1980, Museums, Magic and Children, 1981, Taking a Closer Look: Evaluation in Art Museums, 1992. Excellence and Equity: Education & The Public Dimension of Museums, Presence of Mind: Museums and the Spirit of Learning, 1999; editor: Southeast Regional Resource Book for Museums, 1973; numerous articles in field. Panelist Office of Edn., Washington, 1976-77, Nat. Mus. Act, Washington, 1975-7; assoc. mem. bd. dirs. Children's Hosp., Seattle; Sausalito C. of C. Recipient Leadership Tomorrow award United Way, C. of C., 1985, Disting. Svc. award Music & Art Found., Seattle, 1988; named to Centennial Honor Roll, Am. Assn. Museums, 2006. Am. Assn. Mus. (councilor at large 1976-79, 85-88, chmn. edn. com. 1976-80, v.p. 1979-80, 88-92), Internat. Com. Mus. (accreditation commr. 1985—, exec. com. 1977-83), Nat. Hist. Trust, Western Mus. Assn. (Director's Chair award 1992), Phi Beta Kappa, Delta Kappa Phi. Democrat. Avocation: sailing. Office: Dallas Mus of Art 1717 N Harwood Dallas TX 75201 E-mail: bpitman@DallasMuseumofArt.org.

PITTARD, PATRICK S., investment company executive; m. Dana Pittard; 3 children. Grad., U. Ga. With Citizens and Southern Bank; chmn. Greensboro Baseball LLC; prin. Kurt Salmon Associates, PatrickPittard Advisors; with Texas Commerce Bank; oper. ptnr. Tri-Artisan Capital Ptnrs. LLC; joined Heidrick and Struggles, Inc., 1983, ptnr., mng. dir., mng. dir., N.Am., pres., CEO; chmn. Heidrick & Struggles International, Inc., 1983—2002; pres., CEO Heidrick & Struggles Internat. Inc, 1997—2001; faculty Terry School Business University Georgia, 2002—. Bd. dirs. Cbeyond, Inc., Greensboro Baseball LLC, Lincoln Fin. Advisors Corp., MCG Health System, Jefferson-Pilot Corp., 1998—, Artisan Internat. Fund, 2001—, Artisan Internat. Small Cap Fund, 2001—, Artisan International Value Fund, 2001—, Artisan Mid Cap Fund, 2001—, Artisan Mid Cap Value Fund, 2001—, Artisan Small Cap Fund, 2001—, Artisan Small Cap Value Fund, 2001—; vice chmn. Revenue Analytics Inc, 2005—; bd. dirs. Lincoln Nat. Corp., 2006—. Author: Bearfoot, A Northbounder. Former chmn. HSII, LeadersOnline, U. Ga. Found.; co-owner Minor League Baseball Team. Named Exec. Recruiter, Appalachian Trail thru-hiker, 2002; recipient Distinguished Alumnus, U. Ga. Office: Terry Collee of Business University of Georgia 335 Brooks Hall Athens GA 30602 Office Phone: 706-542-8100. Office Fax: 706-542-3835.

PITTENGER, ROBERT, United States Representative from North Carolina, former state legislator; b. Dallas, Aug. 15, 1948; m. Suzanne Pittenger; children: Robert Jr., Natalie, Amy, Grace. BA, U. Tex., 1970. Asst. to pres. Campus Crusade for Christ, 1970—85; owner Robert Pittenger Co., 1989; mem. Dist. 40 NC State Senate, 2003—04, mem. Dist 39, 2004—08; mem. US Congress from 9th NC Dist., Washington, 2013—, US House Financial Services Com., 2013—. Republican. Evangelical Christian. Office: US House of Representatives 224 Cannon House Office Bldg Washington DC 20515 also: 2701 Coltsgate Rd Ste 105 Charlotte NC 28211 Office Phone: 202-225-1976, 704-365-6234, 202-225-3389. Office Fax: 704-365-6384.*

PITTMAN, ANASTASIA, state legislator; b. Miami, Fla. d. C. Anthony and Maye B. Pittman. BA in Journalism/Public Relations, Univ. Okla.; MEd in Urban Edn. & Behavioral Sci., Langston Univ. Founder Magic Star Found, Inc.; former tutor Nat. Weed And Seed Program, US Dept. Justice; bd. dirs. YWCA, Metropolitan Better Living Ctr., Aids Walk Okla.; mem. Dist. 99 Okla. House of Representatives, 2007—. Mem.: NAACP (life). Democrat. Address: PO Box 17479 Oklahoma City OK 73136 Office: 2300 N Lincoln Blvd Rm 505 Oklahoma City OK 73105 Home Phone: 405-606-8756; Office Phone: 405-557-7393. E-mail: anastasia.pittman@okhouse.gov.

PITTMAN, CONSTANCE SHEN, endocrinologist, educator; b. Nanking, China, Jan. 2, 1929; arrived in US, 1946; d. Leo F.-Z. and Pao Kong (Yang) Shen; m. James Allen Pittman, Jr., Feb. 19, 1955; children: James Clinton, John Merrill. AB in Chemistry, Wellesley Coll., 1951; MD, Harvard U., 1955. Diplomate Am. Bd. Internal Medicine, sub-bd. Endocrinology. Intern Baltimore City Hosp., 1955-56; resident U. Ala., Birmingham, 1956-57; instr. in medicine U. Ala. Med. Ctr., Birmingham, 1957—59, fellow dept. pharmacology, 1957-59, from asst. prof. to assoc. prof., 1959-70, prof., 1970—. Prof. medicine Georgetown U., Washington, 1972—73; mem. diabetes and metabolism tng. com. NIH, Bethesda, Md., 1972—76, mem. nat. arthritis, metabolism and digestive disease coun., 1975—78, mem. gen. clin. rsch. ctrs. com., 1979—83, 1987—90; bd. dirs., mem., exec. dir. Internat. Coun. for Control of Iodine Deficiency Diseases, 1994—; mem. Iodine Deficiency Disorders Elimination Steering Com. Kiwanis Internat., 2002—. Interim editor: ICCIDD Newsletter, 2004—06. Master ACP; mem. Assn. Am. Physicians, Am. Soc. for Clin. Investigation, Endocrine Soc. (coun., 1978-79, pres. women's caucus 1978-79), Am. Thyroid Assn. (pres. 1990-91), Kiwanis (mem. iodine deficiency disorders steering com.). Achievements include research in activation and metabolism of thyroid hormone; kinetics of thyroxine conversion to triiodothyrine in health and disease states; control of iodine deficiency disorders. Emails. Office: UAB Div Endocrinology/Metab Lab Med Ctr Birmingham AL 35294-0001 Office Phone: 205-934-0800. Business E-Mail: cpittman@uab.edu.

PITTMAN, JACQUELYN, retired mental health nurse, nursing educator; b. Pensacola, Fla., Dec. 22, 1932; d. Edward Corry Sr. and Hettie Oean (Wilson) P. BS in Nursing Edn., Fla. State U., 1958; MA, Columbia U., 1959, EdD, 1974. Physician asst. Med. Ctr. Clinic, Pensacola, 1953-55; clin. instr., asst. dir. nursing svc. Sacred Heart Hosp., Pensacola, 1955-56; instr. psychiat. nurse Fla. State Hosp., Chattahoochee, 1958; instr. psychiat. nursing Pensacola Jr. Coll., 1959-60, 62-63; chmn. div. nursing Gulf Coast C.C., Panama City, Fla., 1963-66; asst. prof. U. Tex., Austin, 1970-72, assoc. prof., 1972-80; prof. nursing, coord. curriculum and tchg. grad. program La. State U. Med. Ctr., New Orleans, 1980-99, rep. faculty senate, 1997-99; pres.-elect faculty assembly Sch. Nursing La. State U. Med. Ctr. Sch. Nursing, New Orleans, 1997-98, pres., 1998-99; ret., 1999. Curriculum cons. Nicholls State U., Thibodaux, La., 1982, Our Lady of Lake Sch. Nursing, Baton Rouge, 1983; rsch. liaison So. Bapt. Hosp., New Orleans, 1987-89, Med. Ctr. La., 1992-99; mem. adv. bd. Sister Henrietta Guyot Professorship; mem. planning com. Nichols State U./La. State U. Ctr. Partnership, 1996-99. Mem. ethics com., trustee Hotel Dieu Hosp., New Orleans, 1987—91; judge Internat. Sci. and Engring. Fair Assn., 1990, 1992; del. La. State Nurses' Assn. State Conv., 1992, 1994; assoc. Libr. of Congress, Smithonian Instn.; mem. Dem. Nat. Comm., Presdl. Task Force, 1992, Ctr. for Study of Presidency; tchr. Christian edn. program for mentally retarded St. Ignatius Martyr Ch., 1979—80; tchr. initiation team Rite of Christian Initiation of Adults, Our Lady of the Lake Cath. Ch., Mandeville, La., 1983—86; v.p., bd. dirs. St. Tammany Guidance Ctr., Inc., Mandeville, 1987—91; mem. parish outreach meals-on-wheels program St. Tammany, Covington, La., 2001—02. Mem. ANA, LWV, Am. Assn. Adv. Sci. Directory, N.Y. Acad. Scis., Acad. Polit. Sci., Libr. of Congress Assocs., Nat. Trust for Hist. Preservation, La. Endowment for Humanities, La. Nurses Assn. (archivist 1987-99, state task force com. to preserve hist. documents 1987-99), So. Nursing Rsch. Soc., Nat. League Nursing, Boston U. Nursing Archives, Women's Inner Cir. Achievement N.Am. Cmtys., Internat. Order of Merit, World Found. Successful Women, Wilson Ctr. Assocs., Kappa Delta Pi, Sigma Theta Tau. Democrat. Roman Catholic. Avocations: swimming, golf, travel, reading, louisiana history. Address: 204 Woodridge Blvd Mandeville LA 70471-2604 Personal E-mail: jpit204@att.net.

PITTMAN, JAMES ALLEN, JR., endocrinologist, educator; b. Orlando, Fla., Apr. 12, 1927; s. James Allen and Jean C. (Garretson) Pittman; m. Constance Ming-Chung Shen, Feb. 19, 1955; children: James Clinton, John Merrill. BS, Davidson Coll., 1948, DSc (hon.), 1981; MD, Harvard, 1952; DSc (hon.), U. Ala., Birmingham, 1984, Chung Shan Med U., Taichung, Taiwan, 2005. Intern, asst. resident medicine Mass. Gen. Hosp., Boston, 1952—54; tchg. fellow medicine Harvard U., 1953—54; clin. assoc. NIH, Bethesda, Md., 1954—56; instr. medicine George Washington U., 1955—56; chief resident U. Ala. Med. Ctr., Birmingham, 1956—58, instr. medicine, 1956—59, asst. prof., 1959—62, assoc. prof., 1962—64, prof. medicine, 1964—92, dir. endocrinology and metabolism divsn., 1962—71, co-chmn. dept. medicine, 1969—71, also prof., physiology and biophysics, 1967—92, dean, 1973—92, Disting. prof., 1992—. Mem. endocrinology study sect. NIH, 1963—67; mem. nat. adv. rsch. resources coun. NIH, 1991—95; asst. chief med. dir. rsch. and edn. in medicine U.S. VA, 1971—73; prof. medicine Georgetown U. Med. Sch., Washington, 1971—73; mem. grad. med. edn. nat. adv. com. HEW, 1976—78; mem. HHS Coun. on Grad. Med. Edn., 1986—90; hon. prof. Chung Shan Med. and Dental Coll., Taiwan, 1994; sr. advisor Internat. Coun. on Ctrl. of Iodine Deficiency Diseases, 1994—96. Author: Diagnosis and Treatment of Thyroid Diseases, 1963; contbr. articles in field to profl. jours. Master: Am. Coll. Endocrinology; fellow: AAAS; mem.: ACP, Stearman Restorers Assn., Hist. Sci. Soc., Am. Soc. for the History of Medicine, So. Soc. Clin. Investigation (Founder's medal 1993), Am. Fedn. Clin. Rsch. (pres. So. sect., nat. coun. 1962—66), Am. Chem. Soc., Am. Diabetes Assn., Am. Ornithologists Union (life), NY Acad. Scis. (life), Endocrine Soc. Ecuador (hon.), Soc. Nuc. Medicine, Am. Thyroid Assn., Am. Assn. Clin. Endocrinologists, Endocrine Soc., Assn. Am. Physicians, Inst. Medicine of NAS, Harvard U. Med. Alumni Assn. (pres. 1986—88), Wilson Ornithol. Club (life), Alpha Omega Alpha, Phi Beta Kappa, Omicron Delta Kappa. Office: U Ala Sch Med Pittman CAMS 1924 7th Ave S Birmingham AL 35294-0007 Personal E-mail: japdoc@msn.com. Business E-Mail: japdoc@uab.edu.

PITTMAN, JAMES MORRIS (JACK PITTMAN), cartoonist, illustrator, character designer, consultant; b. Sanford, NC, Oct. 22, 1952; s. James Berdine and Merry Louise (Thomas) P.; m. Patricia Lynne Smith, Nov. 27, 1977; children: Jay Scott, Jonathan Patrick, Joy Elizabeth. B of Environ. Design in Arch. with honors, N.C. State U., 1974. Sports and editl. cartoonist, illustrator, courtroom artist The News and Observer, Raleigh, NC, 1974-83; freelance cartoonist, illustrator Raleigh, 1983—. Adj. prof. Meredith Coll., Raleigh, 1993-94; advtsg. illustrator for Am. Express, Coca-Cola, Procter & Gamble, GMC, Palace Entertainment, Kellogg's, Wendy's, Carolina Hurricanes, NHL, Ericsson, Inc., Gatorade, GlaxoSmithKline, Nortel Networks, Touchstone Energy coops. Illustrator: (book) A Dust of Snow, 1980, Are You Smart, Or What?, 2001, If You're So Smart, Prove It!, 2007, Discover Your Inner Sloth, Darren Dwayne DeBakey and His Amazing Inventions, Smart Is As Smart Does, 2010, mags. include Nat. Geographic World, Wildlife in NC, Carolina Country, Focus on the Family Publication, Reader's Digest, (CD-ROM) Heavenword Children's Bible, 1997, The Birth of Kidd Millennium, 2001, (comic strip) Kidd Millennium, 2001-05; permanent collections include The Internat. Mus. of Cartoon Art, N.C. Mus. History, 2002-03, NC Wildlife Resources Commn. Offices, NC State U. Centennial Campus, 2006—, Animation Exhibit, John E. Pechmann Fishing Edn. Ctr., 2008—, drummer, Adjustyd Bluz Band, 2006—Deacon So. Bapt. Ch. Recipient various ADDY awards Triangle Advtsg. Fedn., 1983-97, 69th Exhbn. Merit; Best in Mag. Illustration award. Mem. Nat. Cartoonists Soc. (chmn. SE chpt. 2009-13, Best in Advt. and Illustration award Reuben divsn. 1995, 98, 2004), Soc. Illustrators, Raleigh Civitan Club. Republican. Baptist. Avocations: percussion, computers. Home: PO Box 10711 Raleigh NC 27605-0711 Office: J Pittman Illustrator 1740 Brooks Ave Raleigh NC 27607-6618 Office Phone: 919-785-1966. Personal E-mail: jptoonist@aol.com. Business E-Mail: jack@jackpittman.net.

PITTMAN, LARRY G., state legislator; b. Kinston, NC, Sept. 30, 1954; AS in Religion, Mt. Olive Junior Coll., 1974; BA in English, Atlantic Christian Coll., 1976; MDiv in Pastoral Ministry/Religion, Southeastern Baptist Theological Seminary, 1981. Laborer Carolina-Dixie Grain Co., 1981; student pastor Boyd Meml. Presbyterian

Church, 1980—81, Camden/Moven Presbyterian Churches, 1981—83, pastor, 1983—86, Turner Presbyterian Church, 1986—90, McKinnon Presbyterian Church, 1990—99; shipping working, company chaplain Snyder Packaging, 1998—; stated supply pastor Royal Oaks Prebyterian Church, 2000—04; state Rep. Dist. 82 NC, 2011—. Republican. Presbyterian. Office: North Carolina House of Representatives 16 W Jones St Room 1321 Raleigh NC 27601-1096 Home: 250 Roberta Rd SW Concord NC 28027-7037 Office Phone: 704-782-3528, 919-715-2009. Business E-Mail: Larry.Pittman@ncleg.net.

PITTMAN, LISA ETTA, legislative staff member, lawyer; b. Limestone, Maine, Jan. 4, 1959; d. William Franklin and Rowena Paradis (Umphrey) Pittman. BA in English, with highest honors, U. Fla., Gainesville, 1980, MA in English, 1981, JD, 1984; LLM in Environ. Law, with highest honors, George Washington U., 1988. Bar: Fla. 1984, DC 1993, US Supreme Ct. 1993. Spl. asst. Office Gen. Counsel, Nat. Oceanic & Atmospheric Adminstrn., US Dept. Commerce, Washington, 1984-85, atty.-advisor, Office Gen. Counsel, 1985-87; Rep. counsel US House Mcht. Marine & Fisheries Com., Washington, 1987—95; dep. chief counsel US House Natural Resources Com., 1995—2001, chief counsel, 2001—, dep. chief of staff, 2002—04. Contbr. articles to profl. jour. Avocations: reading, needlepoint, filmmaking. Office: House Natural Resources Com 1324 Longworth House Office Bldg Washington DC 20515-6201 Office Phone: 202-225-2761. Office Fax: 202-225-5929. Business E-Mail: lisa.pittman@mail.house.gov.

PITTMAN, TRIP, state legislator; b. Birmingham, Ala., 1960; m. Lynn Pittman. BS in Commerce, U. Ala., BBA. Owner Pittman Tractor Company, Inc., Ala.; mem. Dist. 32 Ala. State Senate, Montgomery, 2007—. Mem. Fairhope United Meth. Ch. Republican. Avocations: fishing, hunting, golf. Office: Pittman Tractor Co Inc PO Box 1812 Daphne AL 36526 also: Ala State Senate Ala State House 11 S Union St Rm 738-B Montgomery AL 36130 Office Phone: 251-621-3555, 334-242-7897. Business E-Mail: trip.pittman@alsenate.gov.

PITTMAN, WILLIAM CLAUDE, JR., retired electrical engineer; b. Pontotoc, Miss., Apr. 22, 1921; s. William Claude and Maude Ella (Bennett) P.; m. Eloise Savage, Apr. 20, 1952 (dec. Oct 13, 2008); children: Patricia A. Pittman Ready, William Claude III, Thomas Allen. BSEE, Miss. State Coll., 1951, MSEE, 1957. Cert. svc. holder US Govt. From electronic engr. to supr. elec. engring. dept. U.S. Army Labs., Redstone Arsenal, Ala., 1951-59; supr. electronic engr. to aero. engring. supr. NASA/Marshall Space Flight Ctr., 1960; electronic engr. Army Missile Labs., 1962-82; program mgr. Army Labs. and R&D Ctr., Redstone Arsenal, 1982-99; vol. cons. Army Aviation and Missile Rsch., Devel. and Engring. Ctr., 1999—. Organizer numerous sci. and tech. confs.; mem. Launch Team First Redstone Missile Cape Canaveral, 1953. Author patents, reports, papers, Flag of United States Flown Over Capitol, 1997. Vol. emeritus US Army, 1999-2012, sgt. USMC, 1940-46, PTO. Recipient Medal of Honor, DAR, Meritorious Civilian Svc. award Dept. Army, 1993, Numerous award & Commendation Letters, award, AMRDEC Medallion, Outreach Program. Fellow AIAA (assoc.; chmn. Miss.-Ala. chpt. 1981-82, Martin Schilling award 1980); mem. IEEE (sr. life; Cert. Svc. Holder), First Marine Div. Assn., DAV, IRE (chmn. Huntsville sect. 1957-58), Madison Hist. Soc., Servic PIN SAR (pres. Tenn. Valley chpt. 1984-85, Ala. Soc. 1990-91, Cert. 1991, Patriot medal), Tau Beta Pi, Phi Kappa Phi, Kappa Mu Epsilon. Avocations: history, genealogy. Home: 704 Desoto Rd SE Huntsville AL 35801-2032 Office: US Army Aviation Missile Command Huntsville AL 35898-5000 Office Phone: 256-876-1778. Personal E-mail: bill.pittman@amrdec.army.mi, wcpittman@comcast.net.

PITTS, JAMES, gas industry executive; BSEE, Tex. Tech U. Registered profl. engr., Ill. Various ops. and engring. positions, v.p., engring. Kinder Morgan; cons. AGL Resources, 2005—07; v.p., midstream svcs. Pivotal Energy Development (divsn. of AGL Resources), 2007—. Office: Pivotal Energy Development Two Allen Ctr 1200 Smith St Houston TX 77002 Office Phone: 832-397-1700. Office Fax: 832-397-3713.

PITTS, JIM, state legislator; b. Jan. 1, 1947; m. Evelyn Pitts (dec. 2004). Atty.; mem. Dist. 10 Tex. House of Representatives, 1993—. Republican. Office: 310 W Jefferson Ste 1 Waxahachie TX 75165 also: Room CAP 1W.02 Capital PO Box 2910 Austin TX 78768 Office Phone: 972-938-9392, 512-463-0516. Business E-Mail: jim.pitts@house.state.tx.us.

PITTS, JOE, state legislator; b. Clarksville, Tenn., Aug. 15, 1958; Mem. Commerce Com., State & Local Govt. Com.; state rep. Dist. 67 Tenn., 2007—. Democrat. Baptist. Office: 544 Hay Market Rd Clarksville TN 37043 also: 109 War Memorial Bldg Nashville TN 37243-0167 Office Phone: 615-741-2043. Office Fax: 615-741-7531, 615-253-0200. Business E-Mail: rep.joe.pitts@capitol.tn.gov.

PITTS, KEITH B., surgical hospital company executive; BS, U. Fla. Ptnr., healthcare consulting practice Ernst & Young LLP; exec. v.p., CFO OrNda HealthCorp, 1992—97; chmn., CEO Paragon Health Network, Inc., 1997—99, Mariner Post-Acute Network, Inc., 1997—99; exec. v.p. Vanguard Health Sys., Inc., 1999—2001, bd dirs., 1999—2004, vice chmn., 2001—. Office: Vanguard Health Systems Inc Ste 100 20 Burton Hills Blvd Nashville TN 37215 Office Phone: 615-665-6000. Office Fax: 615-665-6099. Business E-Mail: kpitts@vanguardhealth.com.

PITTS, MICHAEL A., state legislator; b. Greenwood, SC, Dec. 31, 1955; s. Jr. Joseph C. and Lois Lollis Pitts; m. Susan W. Slay Pitts, June 28, 1974; children: Nolan, Clifton, Della. AS, Greenville Tech. Coll., 1978; BS, Lander U., 1985. Mem. Dist. 14 SC House of Reps., 2003—, sec. Ethics Com., mem. Resources Com. & Ways and Means Com. Mem.: Rocky Mountain Elk Found. Republican. Office: 327C Blatt Bldg Columbia SC 29201 Office Phone: 803-734-2830. E-mail: pittsm@scstatehouse.net.

PIZER, DONALD, author, educator; b. NYC, Apr. 5, 1929; s. Morris and Helen (Rosenfeld) P.; m. Carol Hart, Apr. 7, 1966; children—Karin, Ann, Margaret. BA, UCLA, 1951, MA, 1952, PhD, 1955. Mem. faculty Tulane U., 1957—2001, prof. English, 1964-72, Pierce Butler prof. English, 1972—2001, Mellon prof. humanities, 1978-79. Author: Hamlin Garland's Early Work and Career, 1960, Realism and Naturalism in Nineteenth-Century American Literature, 1966, The Novels of Frank Norris, 1966, The Novels of Theodore Dreiser, 1976, Twentieth-Century American Literary Naturalism: An Interpretation, 1982, Dos Passos "USA": A Critical Study, 1988, The Theory and Practice of American Literary Naturalism, 1993, American Expatriate Writing and the Paris Moment, 1996, Am. Naturalism and the Jews, 2008,; Toward a Modernist Style: John Dos Passos, 2013 Served with AUS, 1955-57. Guggenheim fellow, 1962; Am. Council Learned Socs. fellow, 1971-72; Nat. Endowment Humanities fellow, 1978-79 Mem. MLA., Am. Lit. Soc. Home: 6320 Story St New Orleans LA 70118-6340

PIZZAGALLI, JAMES, construction and real estate company executive; b. Burlington, Vt., Nov. 23, 1944; s. Angelo and Theresa (Moalli) P.; m. Judy Rock, June 21, 1969; 1 child, Michael. BS, U. Vt., 1966; JD, Boston U., 1969. Treas. PC Constrn. Co., Burlington, Vt., 1969—76, v.p., 1976—91, chmn., CEO, 1991—98, co-chmn., 1998—2013; pres. Pizzagalli Properties, LLC, 1971—. Dir. Chittenden Corp., Burlington, 1982-2007, AGC Edn. Found., Washington, 1992-2004, Shelburne (Vt.) Mus., 1983-92, 2000—; life dir. Assn. Gen. Contractors, Washington, 1976—2013, atty.-at law. Trustee U. Vt., 2000—05. Mem.: The Moles. Republican. Roman Catholic. Office: Pizzagalli Properties LLC 346 Shelburne Rd Burlington VT 05401-4935 Home: 3393 Harbor Rd Shelburne VT 05482 E-mail: jpizzagalli@pizzagalliproperties.com.

PIZZAMIGLIO, ALBERT THEODORE (AL PIERSON), conductor; b. Ill. m. Nancy Alice Gilman, Mar. 27, 1978; five children. Studied music theory and composition; BA, MA, Ill. State U.; advanced music studies, U. Ill. Condr. Al Pierson Big Band U.S.A., 1975-89, Guy Lombardo's Royal Canadians, Aubrey, Tex., 1989—. Nat. youth music dir. Am. Inst. of Cooperation; co-host, owner TV show, Bloomington, Ill.; tchr. high sch. and coll., amb. music Ill. State U. Musician, composer, arranger, vocalist, band leader; founder Al Pierson & Big Band U.S.A. (Best New Dance Band in the Country 1975, America's Number One Dance Band 1977), performed for fourteen yrs. at numerous famous ballrooms in the midwest and many prestigious pvt. parties, on twenty internat. dance tours including Europe, the Orient, the Middle East, the Caribbean, Mexico, Hawaii, Alaska and Tahiti; released 15 albums; recorded Guy Lombardo music album, 2000, now with Guy Lombardo's Royal Canadians performing throughout the continental U.S. and Can. and 44 other fgn. countries; condr. PBS TV series (past three yrs. and continuing), 1977, PBS TV spls., 1994, 95, 96, 97, 2000, Presdl. Inauguration Festivities, 1994. Mem. Pres. George Bush Inauguration, 2004, Pres. Bill Clinton's Inauguration, 1992. Recipient Superman award for helping save 32 lives in snowstorm, 1997, 98, 99, Ill. State U. Disting. Alumni award, 2004; inducted into Ballroom Dancers' Hall of Fame, 1976; named amb. Music for World pres. Ill. State U., 1998, Alumnus of Yr. Ill. State U., 2004-, Mens Club award, Ill. Club Office: Gilman Inc Artists Mgmt RR 1 Aubrey TX 76227-9801 Personal E-mail: apglo@aol.com.

PIZZO, SALVATORE VINCENT, pathologist; b. Phila., June 22, 1944; s. George J. Pizzo and Aida (Alcaro) Lepore; m. Carol Ann Kurkowski, Dec. 28, 1968 (dec. 2009); children: Steven, David, Susan. PhD, Duke U., 1972; BS, St. Joseph's Coll., 1966; MD, Duke U., 1973. Asst. prof. Duke U. Med. Ctr., Durham, NC, 1976-80, assoc. prof., 1980-85, prof., 1985—, disting. prof. pathology, 2006—, dir. med. scientist tng. program, 1987—2007, chmn., 1991—. Mem., chmn. program rev. com. NIH, Bethesda, Md., 1986-90; vice chmn. Gordon Conf. Proteases, Holderness, N.H., 1990, chmn., 1992-96; cons. in field, 1980—; mem. Cellular and Molecular Basis of Disease Rev. Com., 1990-96. Contbr. articles to profl. jours. Grantee NIH, 1976—, Am. Cancer Soc., 1976—; Disting. Faculty award, Duke U., 2004, Dean's award for excellence in mentoring, 2004; named one of the top 150 cited authors for jours. in the life sciences. Fellow AAAS; mem. Am. Heart Assn. (exec. com. Thrombosis coun. 1990, 92), Am. Chem. Soc., Am. Assn. Pathologists (program com. 1985-88, long range planning com. 1990-92), Am. Soc. Biological Chemists, Alpha Sigma Nu, Phi Beta Kappa, Alpha Omega Alpha, Sigma Xi. Achievements include patents in field; research in lipoproteins in coagulation and fibronolysis, a link to atherosclerosis, anticoagulation drug development; identification of ATP synthase as the target for Angiostatin action; research in GRP 78 in cancer progression. Office: Duke U Med Ctr PO Box 3712 Durham NC 27710-0001 Office Phone: 919-684-3528, 919-421-3058. Business E-Mail: pizzo001@mc.duke.edu.

PLAEGER, FREDERICK JOSEPH, II, lawyer; b. New Orleans, Sept. 10, 1953; s. Edgar Leonard and Bernice Virginia (Schiwetz) P.; m. Kathleen Helen Dickson, Nov. 19, 1977; children: Douglas A., Catherine E. BS, La. State U., 1976, JD, 1977. Bar: La. 1978, Tex. 1999, U.S. Dist. Ct. (ea. dist.) La. 1978, U.S. Ct. Appeals (5th cir.) 1981, U.S. Supreme Ct. 1989. Law clk. U.S. Dist. Ct. (ea. dist.) La., New Orleans, 1977-79; assoc. Milling, Benson, Woodward, Hillyer, Pierson & Miller, New Orleans, 1979-85, ptnr., 1985-89; v.p., gen. counsel, corp. sec. La. Land and Exploration Co., New Orleans, 1989-97; v.p., gen. counsel Burlington Resources Inc., Houston, 1997—2006; sr. v.p., gen. counsel EOG Resources, Inc., 2007—. Selected mem. Met. Area Com. Leadership Forum, 1986; bd. dirs. Soc. Environ. Edn., La. Nature and Sci. Ctr., 1992—94; trustee Houston Ballet, 2001—; bd. dirs. New Orleans Speech and Hearing Ctr., 1985—91, pres., 1988—90; bd. dirs. Children's Oncology Svcs. La. (Ronald McDonald Ho. of New Orleans), 1987—90. Recipient Service to Mankind award Sertoma, 1989; named Tex. Super Lawyer, Tex. Monthly Mag., 2004, 05, 06, 07, Magna Stella Lifetime Achievement award, 2007. Mem.: ABA, Am. Exploration & Production Coun. (bd. dirs. 2007—), Ctr. Am. and Internat. Law (truatee 2010—), Am. Natural Gas Alliance (mem. exec. com. 2009—10), Tex. Gen. Counsel Forum (pres. Houston chpt. 2005—06, statewide chmn. 2006—07), Am. Corp. Counsel Assn. (bd. dir. New Orleans chpt. 1995—98), La. Bar Assn., Inst. Energy Law (adv. bd. 2001—, exec. com. 2002—, chmn. 2005—08), Houston City Club. Republican. Roman Catholic. Avocations: fishing, computers. Home: 5105 Longmont Dr Houston TX 77056-2417

PLAKON, SCOTT, state legislator; b. Rochester, NY, Mar. 13, 1959; m. Susie Plakon; 6 children. BS in Psychol., Stetson U., 1981. Mem. Dist. 37 Fla. House of Reps., 2008—. Bd. mem. A Safe Harbor Pregnancy Resource Ctr., Christian Life Missions; trustee Media Rsch. Ctr.; adv. bd. mem. Pinnacle Bank; vice chmn. bd. dirs. Sanford Rescue Outreach Mission & Open Door Shelter for Women & Children; mem. Seminole County Youth Commn.; mktg. chmn. Servants of the People Com. Mem.: NRA (life), Nat. Fedn. Ind. Businesses, Markham Place Homeowners Assn. (former pres.). Republican. Office: House Office Bldg 402 S Monroe St Rm 308 Tallahassee FL 32399-1300 Home: 1855 W State Road 434 Ste 242 Longwood FL 32750-5071 Office Phone: 850-488-2231, 407-262-7520. Business E-Mail: scott.plakon@myfloridahouse.gov.

PLANCK, ROBERT DEMPSEY, food company executive; b. Texas City, July 1, 1948; s. Henry Ver and Elizabeth (Dempsey) Planck; m. Sharon Brieger, Dec. 27, 1969; 1 child, Jeffrey. BS in Hotel and Restaurant Mgmt., U. Houston, 1971. Dir. corp. food svc. Humana Hosp. Corp., Louisville, 1975—77; dir. edn. and quality assurance SYSCO Corp., Houston, 1977—81, v.p. sales and mktg. Compton Foods disvn., 1981—84, v.p. mktg., 1986—, Sysco Food Svcs., 1984—86. Chmn. bd. trustees Tau Kappa Epsilon U Houston, 1980—83, pres. Houston Area Alumni, 1980—81; v.p. Hilton Coll. Alumni Assn., 1986—; mem. dean search com. Hilton Coll., U. Houston, 1986—87; mem. Galveston Hist. Found. Served to capt. US Army, 1971—75. Recipient Outstanding Alumni award, Tau Kappa Epsilon, 1981, 1985, Pres. Emeritus award, 1986, 1st Pl. Nat. Seafood Svc. award, 1978; named one of Outstanding Young Men in Am., Hon. Alumni of Yr., Hilton Coll., U. Houston, 1982. Mem.: U. Houston Alunmi Assn., Ky. Cols., Am. Mktg. Assn., Dietitians in Bus. and Industry, Am. Soc. Food Technologists, Am. Dietetic Assn., Soc. Advancement of Foodsvc. Rsch., Coun. on Hotel Restaurant and Inst. Edn., U. Houston Taxi Squad, U. Houston Century Club, U. Houston Cougar Cagers. Republican. Home: 11406 Hambleton Way Houston TX 77065-4144

PLANK, ROGER B., energy executive; BA, Colgate Univ.; MBA, Univ. St. Thomas. Joined Apache Corp., Houston, 1981, v.p., CFO, 1997-2000, exec. v.p., CFO, 2000—09, pres., 2009—11, pres., chief corp. officer, 2011—. Bd. dir. Parker Drilling Co.; past pres. Tex. Independent Producers & Royalty Owners Assn.; dir. Okla. Independent Petroleum Assn., Domestic Petroleum Council. Bd. mem. Alley Theatre, Houston, Ucross Found. Office: Apache Corp 2000 Post Oak Blvd Ste 100 Houston TX 77056-4400

PLASIL, FRANZ, physicist; b. Prague, Czechoslovakia, May 17, 1939; came to U.S., 1960; s. Frank and Eva (Wenger) P.; m. Catherine Logan, Feb. 15, 1964 (div. Sept. 1979); two children: Maia (dec. Feb. 26, 2008), David; m. Carol Baratz, Apr. 12, 1980. BS, Queen Mary Coll., U. London, 1960; PhD, U. Calif., Berkeley, 1964. Chemist Lawrence Berkeley (Calif.) Lab., 1964-65; rsch. assoc. Brookhaven Nat. Lab., Upton, NY, 1965-67; rsch. staff physics div. Oak Ridge (Tenn.) Nat. Lab., 1967-78, group leader physics div., 1978-86, sect. head physics div., 1986-99; fellow U. Tenn.-Battelle, 1999—2002; hon. rsch. prof. dept. physics and astronomy U. Tenn., Knoxville, 2002—. Contbr. articles to Annals of Physics, Phys. Rev., Phys. Rev. Letters, Nuc. Phys., Phys. Letters. Ct. appointed spl. advocate for abused and neglected children. Recipient Alexander von Humboldt award 1985, E. Mach medal of honor Acad. of Sci. of the Czech Republic, 1998. Fellow Am. Phys. Soc. Achievements include rsch. in fission-imposed limits on the stability of rotating nuclei and rsch. in nucleus-nucleus collisions at ultrarelativistic energies. Home: 964 W Outer Dr Oak Ridge TN 37830-8607 Personal E-mail: plasil@comcast.net.

PLASKETT, THOMAS GEORGE, transportation executive, director; b. Raytown, Mo., Dec. 24, 1943; s. Warren E. and Frances S. P.; m. Linda Lee Maxey, June 8, 1968; children: Kimberly, Keith. B in Indsl. Engring., Kettering U.; MBA, Harvard U. Supr. indsl. engring. GM, Flint, Mich., 1968, supt. indsl. engring., 1969-73, sr. staff asst., treas. NYC, 1973; asst. contr. American Airlines, Inc., NYC, 1974, v.p. mktg. adminstrn., 1975-76, sr. v.p. fin., 1976-80, sr. v.p. mktg. Dallas, 1980—86; pres., CEO Continental Airlines Inc., Houston, until 1988; chmn., CEO, pres. Pan Am Corp., NYC, 1988—91; chmn. Fox Run Capital Associates, 1991—; dir., interim pres., CEO, acting CFO Greyhound Lines, Inc., Dallas, 1994-95, chmn., 1995—99; vice-chmn. Legend Airlines, Dallas, 1997—2001, exec. v.p., 1999—2001; pres., CEO Probex Corp., Dallas, 1999—2000, chmn., 1999—2000. Bd. dirs. Radioshack Corp., Ft. Worth, Novell, Inc. 2002-; Waltham, Mass., Provo, Utah, Alcon Inc., Ft. Worth, Platinum Rsch. Orgn., Dallas, non-exec. chair, 2002-08. Avocations: golf, skiing, squash. Office: PO Box 141111 Irving TX 75014-1111 Office Phone: 972-333-4751. Business E-Mail: tom@foxruncapital.com.

PLATSOUCAS, CHRIS DIMITRIOS, immunologist; b. Athens, Greece, Apr. 17, 1951; came to U.S., 1973; s. Dimitrios Evagelos and Maria (Tsonidis) P.; m. Emilia L. Oleszak, Oct. 18, 1985. BS, Patras U., Greece, 1973; postgrad., Purdue U., 1974; PhD, MIT, 1978; PhD (hon.), U. Thrace Sch. Medicine, Greece, 2009, U. Patras Sch. Scis. Greece, 2011. Rsch. fellow/assoc. Meml. Sloan-Kettering Cancer Ctr., NYC, 1978—81, asst. mem., 1982—85, asst. prof., 1981-85, head lab. biol. response modifiers, 1981-85; assoc. prof. dept. immunology M.D. Anderson Cancer Ctr., Houston, 1985-89, prof., dep. chmn., 1989-93, Ashbel Smith professorship, 1991-92, H.L. and O. Stringer professorship in cancer rsch., 1992-93; L.H. Carnell prof. dept. microbiology, immunology Temple U. Sch. Medicine, Phila., 1993—2007, chmn. dept. microbiology and immunology, 1993—2006; acting dean Coll. Sci. and Tech. Temple U., Phila., 1998-2000, dean Coll. Sci. and Tech., 2000—04, Old Dominion U., Norfolk, Va., 2007—; dean Coll. Sci.; dir. Ctr. Mol. Medicine; prof. Biol Sci. Biotech. cons., sci. reviewer study sects. NIH, Bethesda, Md., 1982—. Contbr. numerous articles to profl. jours. Nat. Rsch. Svc. award NIH, 1978-79; grantee NIH, Am. Cancer Soc., State of Tex., many others. Mem. Am. Assn. Immunologists, Am. Soc. Hematology, Am. Assn. Biochem & Molecular Biology, Soc. Investigative Pathology, Am. Assn. Cancer Rsch. Greek Orthodox. Achievements include patents in field; research on human T cell immunology, on T-cell antigen receptors, on tumor-infiltrating lymphocytes in malignant melanoma and ovarian carcinoma, on organ transplantation, on chronic rejection, on AIDS, on multiple sclerosis, schlerodema, osteoarthritis, and other autoimmune diseases. Office: Old Dominion Univ Office of Dean, Coll Sci 4600 Elkhorn Ave OCNPS Rm 143 Norfolk VA 23529 Office Phone: 757-683-3274. Business E-Mail: cplatsoucas@odu.edu.

PLATT, JAN KAMINIS, former county official; b. St. Petersburg, Fla., Sept. 27, 1936; d. Peter Clifton and Adele (Diamond) Kaminis; m. William R. Platt, Feb. 8, 1963; 1 child, Kevin Peter. BA, Fla. State U., 1958; postgrad., U. Fla. Law Sch., 1958-59, U. Va., 1962, Vanderbilt U., 1964. Pub. sch. tchr. Hillsborough County, Tampa, Fla., 1959-60; field dir. Girl Scouts Suncoast Coun., Tampa, 1960-62; city councilman Tampa City Coun., 1974-78, Fla. Constl. Revision Commn., 1976; county commr. Hillsborough County, 1978—94, country commr., 1996—2004; chmn. Hillsborough County Bd. County Commrs., 1980-81, 83-84, 98-99, ret., 1994, re-elected, 1996, chmn., 1998-99, County Charter Rev. Bd., 2005—06; cp-chair Countrywide Cultural Plan, 2006—. Chmn. Tampa Bay Regional Planning Coun., 1982, West Coast Regional Water Supply Authority, Tampa, 1985, Hillsborough County Coun. Govts., 1976, 79, Agy. Bay Mgmt., Hills Environ. Protection Commn., Sunshine Amendment Drive 7th Congrl. Dist., Tampa, 1976, Cmty. Action Agy., Tampa, 1981, 83-84,chmn. pro tem Tampa Charter Revision Commn., 1975, chmn. Prison Sitting Task Force, Tampa, 1983, Tampa Housing Study Com., 1983, Met. Planning Orgn., Tampa, 1984, Bd. Tax Adjustment, Tampa, 1984, chmn. Hartline, 2002-03, Friendship Trailbridge Oversight Com., 2002-03, Tampa Bay Water, 2003-04; appointee Constn. Revision Commn., Fla., 1977, HRS Dist. IV Adv. Coun., Fla.; mem. Hillsborough County Expy. Authority, Taxicab Commn., Ch. Hills Cmty. Youth Coun.; vice chmn. steering com. Nat. Counties Environ. Task Force; pres. Suncoast Girl Scout Coun., 1973-74, Ch. Head Start Cmty. Found., 2005-12; chmn. County Charter Rev. Bd., 2005. Bd. dirs. March of Dimes, Tampa, The Fla. Orch., Tampa, Tampa Bay Sierra, Tampa Audubon; trustee Hillsborough County Hosp. Authority, Tampa, 1984-94; pres. Citizens Alert, Tampa, Bay View Garden Club, Rose Garden Cir., 2007-13; v.p. Hillsborough County Bar Aux.; adv. bd. Northside Cmty. Mental Health Ctr.: Access House, Tampa, 2007-; active Arts Coun. Tampa-Hillsborough County, 1983-85, 96-2001, Drug Abuse Coordinating Coun. Orgn., Tampa, Bd. Criminal Justice, Tampa, Fla. Coun. on Aging, Inebriate Task Force, Tampa, Tampa Downtown Devel. Authority Task Force, Tampa Sports Authority, Tampa Area Mental Health Bd., Children's Study Commn., Manahill Area Agy. on Aging, Tampa, Athena Soc., Tampa Area Com. Fgn. Affairs, LWV; v.p. Life Enrichment Ctr.; bd. dirs. Arts Coun.; exec. com. Tampa Performing Arts Ctr., chmn. charter rev. bd.; co-founder, pres. Ybor Fresh Market; pres. Keep Hillsborough Beautiful, 2007-09, Waverly Home-owners Assn., 2007-09; mem. Com. of 100, pres. Friends of Libr. Coun., 2009-12; hon. chair Girl Scout

Coun. West Ctrl., WOD Luncheon. Recipient Athena award, Women in Comm., 1976, Spessard Holland Meml. award, Tampa Bay Com. for Good Govt., 1979, First Lady of Yr. award, Beta Sigma Phi, 1980, First Ann. Humanitarian award, Nat. Orgn. of Prevention of Animal Suffering, 1981, Women Helping Women award, Soroptimist Internat. Tampa, 1983, Good Govt. award, Tampa Jaycees, 1983, LWV, 1983, John Brooks Meml. award, Fla. Audubon Soc., 1989, Girl Scout Woman of Distinction award, 1996, Girl Scout Thanks award, 1996, Liberty Bell award, Hillsborough County Bar Assn., 2000, Black Bear award, Suncoast and Tampa Bay Groups of the Sierra Club, 2001, Eliza Wolff award, Tampa United Meth. Ctrs., Outstanding Leadership in Local Environ. Protection, Fla. Local Environ. Resource Agys., 2002, Lifetime Achievement award for outstanding leadership in local environ. protection, 2004, Communicator of Yr., Tampa Ednl. Cable Consortium, 2005, Disting. Alumna award, Fla. State U., 2005, Tampa Bay Ethics award, Tampa U. Ctr. Ethics, 2005, Dan Hanson Conservationist Yr., Frank Sergeant Fishing Expo, 2006, Zonta Status of Women award, 2006, Lifetime Time Achievement award, League of Women Voters, 2010, Herman Goldner award, Tampa Bay Regional Planning Coun., 2010; named Humanitarian of Yr., Dist IV Head Start, 2010, Fla. Head Start, 2010, Woman of Distinction, Sun City Ctr., AAUW, 2012; named to Tampa-Hillsborough Hall of Fame, Hillsborough County Human Rights Coun., 2012. Mem. Am. Judicature Soc., State Assn. County Commrs. Fla. (at-large dir.), AAUW (Women of Distinction, 2012), Mortar Bd. (Disting. Lifetime Mem. award 2006), Garnet Key, Phi Beta Kappa (past pres. local alumni), Phi Kappa Phi. Democrat. Episcopalian. Home: 3531 Village Way Tampa FL 33629-8914

PLATTS-MILLS, THOMAS ALEXANDER EVELYN, immunologist, educator, researcher; b. Colchester, Essex, Eng., Nov. 22, 1941; arrived in US, 1982; s. John Faithful and Janet Katherine (Cree) Platts-Mills; m. Roberta Rosenstock, Apr. 9, 1970; children: Eliza, Timothy, James, Oliver. BA in Animal Physiology, Balliol Coll., Eng., 1963; PhD, London U., 1982. Fellow in medicine Johns Hopkins U., Balt., 1971-74; staff mem. Med. Rsch. Coun., England, 1975—79; hon. cons. physician Northwick Park Hosp., London, 1978-82; Oscar Swineford, Jr. prof. medicine & microbiology, head divsn. allergy & immunology U. Va., Charlottesville, 1982—, dir. Asthma & Allergic Diseases Ctr., 1993—. Mem. immunological scis. study sect. NIH, 1988—92. Mem. editl. bd. Am. Jour. Respiratory Critical Care Medicine, Clin. & Exptl. Immunology, Clin. Allergy, Jour. Immunological Methods; contbr. articles to profl. jours. Fellow: Royal Soc. London, Royal Coll. Physicians; mem.: Southeastern Allergy Assn. (pres. 1987—88, Hal Davidson award 1986), Brit. Soc. Allergy & Clin. Immunology, Am. Acad. Allergy, Asthma & Immunology (v.p. 2004—05, pres.-elect 2005—06, pres. 2006—07), Assn. Am. Physicians. Office: U Va Med Sch PO Box 801335 Charlottesville VA 22908-0225 Office Phone: 434-924-2209. Office Fax: 434-924-5779. E-mail: tap2z@virginia.edu.

PLAVE, LEE JONATHAN, lawyer; BA, Clark U., 1980; JD cum laude, NY Law Sch., 1983. Bar: NY 1983, DC 1987, Va. 2004. Atty., Used Car Rule program coord. FTC, Washington, 1983—87; assoc. to ptnr. Brownstein & Zeidman, P.C., Washington, 1987—96; ptnr. DLA Piper (formerly Piper Rudnick), Washington, 1996—2007; ptnr., chmn. Domain Name practice group DLA Piper, Washington, 2005—07; co-founding ptnr. Plave Koch PLC, Va., 2007—. Assoc. editor NY Law Sch. Jour. Internat. and Comparative Law, 1982-83; contbr. articles to profl. jours. Mem. ABA, Internat. Bar Assn., Va State Bar Assn., DC Bar Assn., NY State Bar Assn., Internat. Franchise Assn. Jewish. Avocations: ice hockey, stamp collecting/philately, politics. Office: Plave Koch PLC 12005 Sunrise Valley Dr # 200 Reston VA 20191-3404 Office Phone: 703-774-1203. Office Fax: 703-774-1201. Business E-Mail: lplave@plavekoch.com.

PLAVSIC, BRANKO MILENKO, radiologist, educator; b. Zagreb, Yugoslavia, Croatia, Feb. 14, 1947; came to U.S., 1989; s. Milenko and Nevenka P. MD, U. Zagreb, 1972, MS, 1974, PhD, 1975. Asst. prof. U. Zagreb, 1986, prof. radiology, chief abdominal radiology, 1988; prof. radiology, vice-chmn., dir. abdominal radiol./rsch. Tulane U., New Orleans, 1991—2006; dir. abdominal radiology and rsch. dept. radiology Health Scis. Ctr. Tex. Tech U., El Paso, 2006—. Co-author: (with A.E. Robinson, R.B. Jeffrey) Gastrointestinal Radiology: A Concise Text, 1992; contbr. articles to profl. jours. Avocations: poetry, music. Office: Tex Tech U Health Scis Ctr Dept Radiology El Paso TX 79905

PLEACHER, DAVID HENRY, secondary school educator; b. Reading, Pa., Dec. 29, 1946; s. John K. and Isabel Kathleen (Moyer) P.; m. Carol Elizabeth Jackson, June 8, 1968; children: Amy Elizabeth, Michael David, Sarah Catherine. BA in Math., Hartwick Coll., 1968; MS in Edn., James Madison U., 1971. Cert. tchr., Va. Tchr. Arlington (Va.) County Pub. Schs., 1968, Fairfax County Pub. Schs., Herndon, Va., 1968-73; tchr., dept. chair Winchester (Va.) City Schs., 1973—. Instr. James Madison U., Harrisonburg, Va., 1982-87; lectr., instr. Lord Fairfax C.C., Middletown, Va., 1986-89; project mem. Computer Software Devel. Project, 1985-90; participant Math. Inst. Woodrow Wilson Found., Princeton, 1986. Co-editor: (computer column) Va. Math. Tchr., 1982-84; author computer programs; contbr. articles to profl. jours. Recipient Presdl. Excellence award NSF, Washington, 1985, Homer "Pete" Ice Svc. award Handley High Athletic Dept., 1991, Tandy Tech. Scholars award Tandy Corp./T.C.U., Washington, 1992, Tchr. of Influence award Rotary, 2005. Mem. NEA (life), Va. Edn. Assn., Winchester Edn. Assn., Nat. Coun. Tchrs. Math. (presenter at confs.), Va. Coun. Tchrs. Math. (presenter at confs., William Lowry Outstanding Math Tchr. 1987), Valley Va. Coun. Tchrs. Math., Coun. Presdl. Awardees in Math. Presbyterian. Avocations: model railroading, sports, games, computer programming. Office: John Handley High Sch PO Box 910 Winchester VA 22604-0910

PLEASANT, JAMES CARROLL, mathematician, computer sciences educator; b. Greenville, NC, Jan. 9, 1936; s. George Lemuel and Elizabeth Pleasant; m. Louise D. Pleasant, Feb. 22, 1957; children: Carroll, Gary, Scott. BS, East Carolina U., Greenville, NC, 1958, MA, 1960; PhD, U. S.C., 1965. Prof. math. East Carolina U., Greenville, 1960-61, 63-65, East Tenn. State U., Johnson City, 1966-85, prof. computer scis., 1985—2003; prof. math. Milligan Coll., 2003—04; tchg. prof. East Carolina U., 2004—11. Rsch. assoc. Oak Ridge (Tenn.) Nat. Lab., 1975-80. Orch. player Johnson City Symphony, 1970-85. Mem. Assn. Computing Machinery. Avocations: fishing, rv-ing, horseback riding. Home: 6 Brooklawn Ct Johnson City TN 37604-7181 Home Phone: 423-928-3594. Personal E-mail: ljplez@usit.net.

PLEASANT, JAMES SCOTT, lawyer; b. Anniston, Ala., July 14, 1943; s. James C. and Barbara (Scott) P.; m. Susan M. Pleasant, May 17, 1966; children: Deborah Kaye, Carol Ann, Julie Ruth. BS, Oreg. State U., 1965; JD summa cum laude, Williamette U., 1972. Bar: Tex. 1972, U.S. Dist. Ct. (no. dist.) Tex. 1973, U.S. Ct. Appeals (5th cir.) 1975, U.S. Supreme Ct. 1977. Ptnr. Gardere Wynne Sewell, LLP, Dallas, 1972—. Mem. Smithsonian Assn., Washington, 1985—, Dallas Mus. of Art, 1987—. Capt. U.S. Army, 1966-69, Vietnam. Mem. ABA (partnership law sect. 1969—), Tex. Bar Assn. (partnership law sect. 1989—), Vietnam Pilots Assn., Dustoff Assn. Office: Gardere Wynne Sewell LLP 1601 Elm St Ste 3000 Dallas TX 75201-4761 Office Phone: 214-999-4690. Business E-Mail: pleasant@gardere.com.

PLEICONES, COSTA M., state supreme court justice; b. Greenville, SC, Feb. 29, 1944; s. Mike and Lecha Pleicones; m. Donna Singletary; 2 children. BA in English, Wofford Coll., Spartanburg, SC, 1965; JD, U. SC, 1968. Bar: SC 1968. Pub. defender Richland County, SC; atty. Lewis, Babcock, Pleicones and Hawkins; municipal judge City of Columbia, SC; county atty. Richland County, SC; resident cir. ct. judge 5th Judicial Cir., 1991—2000; assoc. justice SC Supreme Ct., 2000—. With JAG US Army, 1968—73, with USAR, 1973—99. Office: 1231 Gervais St Columbia SC 29201-3206 also: SC Supreme Ct PO Box 11330 Columbia SC 29211*

PLENDL, HANS S., retired physicist, editor; arrived in U.S., 1948; s. Hans N. and Anna Katherina Plendl; m. Marion Setsuko Ito, Aug. 3, 1957 (div. Dec. 8, 1990); children: Konrad Alexander, David Christopher, Kathrin Francesca, Leilani Ann. BA, Harvard U., 1952; PhD, Yale U., 1958. Tchg. asst. physics dept. Yale U., New Haven, 1952—53, rsch. asst. Cyclotron Lab., 1954—56; from asst. to assoc. to prof. physics dept. Fla. State U., Tallahassee, 1956—95, prof. emeritus physics dept., 1995—. Vis. staff mem. Nuc. Rsch. Ctr. Karlsruhe and Max Planck Inst. for Nuc. Physics, Heidelberg, Germany, 1960—62; vis. prof. physics dept. Tech. U., Munich, 1985—86; guest scientist Rsch. Ctr., Juelich, Germany, 1989—98; sr. rsch. fellow, project dir. nuc. waste mgmt. & disposition Inst. Internat. Coop. Environ. Rsch., Tallahassee, 1995—; vis. scientist Oak Ridge Nat. Lab., 1957—87, Brookhaven Nat. Lab., 1985—87, Los Alamos Nat. Lab., 1985—87; program adv. com. NASA Space Radiation Effects Lab., Newport News, Va., 1969—78; edn. adv. com. US Senate, Washington, 1983—85; bd. trustees Nautilus Found., Tallahassee, 1991—99; adv. com. Internat. Conf. on Mesons and Nuclei, Dubna, Russia, 1994; co-chair Internat. Workshop on Nuc. Methods for Transmutation of Nuc. Waste, Dubna, 1996; adv. com. Internat. Symposia on Environ. Contamination in Ea. and Ctrl. Europe, Warsaw and Prague, 1998, 2000, 2003; co-chair Internat. Workshop on Techs. in Nuc. Separations, Prague, 2000; mem. Recon Inc., Tallahassee, 1965—69; writer, editor Ricordiarte and LEM Art Pubs., Milan, 2000—06; dir. German Sch. Tallahassee, 2004—; bd. dirs. U. Enterprises Internat. Inc., 1994—; chief scientist Poly Terra Innovation GmbH, Berlin, 2011—; presenter, cons. in field. Co-author: (textbook) Hands-on Astronomy; editor: Nuclear Transmutation Methods for Disposition of Long-Lived Radioactive Materials, Accelerator Driven Systems, Science and Technology without Borders, Philosophical Problems of Modern Physics; contbr. 120 articles to sci. jours. Recipient Travel award, Fulbright Found., 1963, Award for Excellence in Tchg., Amoco Found., 1975, Rsch. stipend, Deutsche Forschungsgemeinschaft, 1985. Achievements include discovery of several isomeric states in scandium and titanium isotopes and elucidation of pion-nucleus interactions. Avocations: languages, international education. Office: Fla State U Physics Dept Tallahassee FL 32306 Business E-Mail: plendl@phy.fsu.edu.

PLESS, RODNEY S., corporate financial executive; V.p., contr. & chief acctg. officer TransMontaigne; v.p. Tyson Foods, Inc., Springdale, Ark., 2000—01, contr., chief acctg. officer, 2000—, sr. v.p., 2001—. Office: Tyson Foods Inc 2200 Don Tyson Pky Springdale AR 72762-6999 Office Phone: 479-290-4000. Office Fax: 479-290-4061. Business E-Mail: rodney.pless@tyson.com.

PLON, SHARON E., clinical geneticist, educator; BS, MIT, 1980; MD, Harvard Med. Sch., 1987; PhD, Harvard U., 1987. Cert. Am. Bd. Med. Genetics, 2006. Resident internal medicine Univ. Wash., 1987—88; fellow molecular genetics Nat. Cancer Inst., 1988—90; fellow med. genetics Fred Hutchinson Cancer Rsch. Ctr., 1990—93; assoc. prof. pediat. and molecular and human genetics Baylor Coll.; chief cancer genetics clinic Tex. Children's Hospital. Mem.: Am. Coll. Med. Genetics, Am. Soc. Human Genetics. Office: Texas Children's Hospital Clinical Care Center 6701 Fannin St 14th Fl Houston TX 77030 Office Phone: 832-822-3334. Office Fax: 832-825-4276.

PLONSEY, ROBERT, electrical and biomedical engineer; b. NYC, July 17, 1924; s. Louis B. and Betty (Vinograd) P.; m. Vivian V. Vucker, Oct. 1, 1948; 1 child, Daniel. BEE, Cooper Union, 1943; MSEE, NYU, 1948; PhD, U. Calif., Berkeley, 1955; postgrad. med. sch., Case Western Res. U., 1969-71; D of Technol. Scis., Slovak Acad. Scis., 1995. Registered profl. engr., Ohio. Asst. prof. elec. engring. U. Calif., Berkeley, 1955-57, Case Inst. Tech., Cleve., 1957-60, assoc. prof., 1960-66, prof., 1966-68, dir. bioengring. group, 1962-68; prof. biomed. engring. Sch. Engring. and Sch. Medicine Case Western Res. U., 1968-83, chmn. dept., 1976-80; vis. prof. biomed. engring. Duke U., Durham, NC, 1980-81, prof., 1983-96, prof. biomed. engring., Hudson prof. engring., 1990-93, Pfizer-Inc.-Edmond T. Pratt Jr. Univ. prof. biomed. engring., 1993-96, Pfizer-Inc.-Edmond T. Pratt Jr. Univ. prof. emeritus, 1996—. Mem. biomed. fellowships rev. com. NIH, 1966-70; mem. tng. com. Engrs. in Medicine and Biology, 1972-73, cons., 1974-96; cons. NSF, 1973-93; mem. internat. sci. adv. com. Ragnar Granit Inst., Tampere (Finland) U. Tech., 1992—; ad hoc mem. sci. adv. com. Whitaker Found., 1989-91. Author: (with R. Collin) Principles and Applications of Electromagnetic Fields, 1961, Bioelectric Phenomena, 1969, (with J. Liebman and P. Gillette) Pediatric Electrocardiography, 1982, (with T. Pilkington) Engineering Contributions to Biophysical Electrocardiography, 1982, (with J. Liebman and Y. Rudy) Pediatric and Fundamental Electrocardiography, (with R.C. Barr) Bioelectricity: A Quantitative Approach, 1988, 3d edit., 2007, (with J. Malmivuo) Bioelectromagnetism, 1995; mem. editl. bd. Trans. IEEE, Biomed. Engring, 1965-70; assoc. editor, 1977-79; mem. editl. bd. TIT Jour. 1971-81, Electrocardiology Jour., 1974—, Med. and Biol. Engring. and Computing, 1987— Critical Revs. in Biomed. Engring., 1994— procs. editor Engring. in Medicine and Biology, 17th Ann., Conf., 1965. Mem. com. on electrocardiography Am. Heart Assn., 1976-82; v.p. Your Schs., Cleveland Heights, Ohio, 1968-69, 73-75; provisional trustee Am. Bd. Clin. Engrs., 1973-74, pres. 1975, trustee, 1976-85. With AUS, 1944-46. Recipient sr. postdoctoral award NIH, 1980-81, Merit award Internat. Union Phys. and Engring. Scis. in Medicine, 1997, Ragnan Granit prize, 2003. Fellow AAAS, IEEE (chmn. Cleve. chpt. group on biomed. electronics 1962-63, chmn. publs. com. group on engring. in medicine and biology 1968-70, v.p. adminstrv. com. 1970-72, pres. 1973-74, chmn. fellows com. Engring. in Medicine and Biology Soc. 1986-88, 2000, v.p. tech. and conf. activities 1991, William S. Morlock award 1979, Centennial medal 1984, co-program chair ann. conf., Paris 1992, chmn. awards com. 1996, Millennium medal 2000, Ragnar Granit prize 2004); mem. AAUP, NAE (bioengring. peer com. 1988-91, 2001-04, chair 1990-91, 2003-04, nominating com. 1991-92, mem. com. 1992-94, program adv. com. 1996-98, NRC postdoctoral rsch. associateships evaluation panel 1987-90, Russ prize com. 2000-03), Internat. Acad. Med. and Biol. Engring. (founding mem. 1997), Am. Inst. Med. and Biol. Engring. (founding fellow 1992—), Alliance for Engring. in Medicine and Biology (treas. 1976-78), Biomed. Engring. Soc. (bd. dirs. 1975-78, 79-83, pres. 1981-82, chmn. affiliations com. 1987-89, ALZA Disting. lectr. 1988, Disting. Svc. award, 2004), Am. Physiol. Soc., Am. Soc. Engring. Edn. (bd. dirs. biomed. engring. divsn. 1978-83, chmn. 1982-83, Pilkington Outstanding Educator award, 2002). Office: Duke U Box 90281 Dept Biomed Engring Durham NC 27708-0281 Office Phone: 919-660-3131. Business E-Mail: robert.plonsey@duke.edu.

PLUM, KENNETH RAY, state legislator; b. Shenandoah, Va., Nov. 3, 1941; s. John D. and Gladys May P. Plum; m. Jane Durham Meacham; children: Timothy W., David R., Helen Meacham, Augusta Meacham. BA, Old Dominion U., Norfolk, Va.; MEd, U. Va. Ret. educator Fairfax County Pub. Schools, Va.; mem. Dist. 36 Va. House of Delegates, 1978—80, 1982—; mem. commerce com.; mem. labor com.; mem. sci. & tech. com.; mem. agr. com.; mem. Chesapeake & natural resources com. Named Adult Educator of Yr., Adult Edn. Assn., Va., 1974. Mem.: Dulles Corridor Rail Assn. (chmn.), Ret. Tchrs. Assn., Reston Environ. Found., Cmty. Edn. Assn. Va., Fairfax County Edn. Assn., Nat. Va. County Edn. Assn. Democrat. United Christian. Office: 2073 Cobblestone Ln Reston VA 20191 Office Phone: 703-758-9733. Office Fax: 703-391-0865. Business E-Mail: DelKPlum@house.state.va.us.

PLUMMER, LEONARD NIEL, retired geochemist; b. Lexington, Ky., Aug. 13, 1945; s. Leonard Niel and Marjorie Sidney Wiest Plummer; m. Phyllis C. Mohney, Aug. 21, 1945; children: Philip Niel, Michael Ross, Rebecca Wiest Weaver, Kathryn Elizabeth Cartwright. BA, U. Ky., Lexington, 1967, MS, 1969; PhD, Northwestern U., Evanston, Ill., 1972. Asst. prof. SUNY, Buffalo, 1972—74; hydrologist U.S. Geol. Survey, Reston, Va., 1974—92, sr. rsch. scientist, 1992—2012, scientist emeritus, 2012—. Contbr. articles to sci. publs. Recipient Meritorious Svc. award, U.S. Dept. Interior, 1987, Disting. Svc. award, 1996, Spl. Recognition award, Assn. Ground Water Scientists and Engineers, Nat. Water Well Assn., 1990. Fellow: Geol. Soc. Am. (O.E. Meinzer award 1993); mem.: Geochemical Soc., Am. Chem. Soc., Am. Geophys. Union, Sigma Xi. Achievements include development of geochemical models for simulation of water-rock reactions; ground-water dating with chlorofluorocarbons; research in hydrochemistry of major US aquifers; contaminants in ground water such as arsenic, perchlorate, volatile organic carbon compounds; co-development of concept of stoichiometric saturation in solid-solution - aqueous solution reactions; solubility of calcium carbonate in water; application of environmental tracers to interpretation of ground-water age studies with sulfur hexafluoride, tritium/helium-3, and others. Avocation: violin.

PLUMMER, MICHAEL DAVID, mathematics professor; b. Akron, Ohio, Aug. 31, 1937; s. Lewis Benjamin and Marguerite Lizabeth Plummer; m. Sara Fletcher Lee, Aug. 17, 1968; children: Carrie Elizabeth, Ian Benjamin. BA, Wabash Coll., Crawfordsville, Ind., 1959; MS, U. Mich., Ann Arbor, 1961, PhD, 1966. Instr. math. Yale U., New Haven; asst. prof. computer sci. CUNY, 1968—70; prof. math. Vanderbilt U., Nashville, 1970—2008. Editl. bd. Utilitas Math., Thai Jour. Math. Co-author: (math. book) Matching Theory; contbr. over 100 rsch. articles pub. Recipient Niveau prize, Hungarian Acad. Scis., 1991; grantee, NSF, NAS, Internat. Rsch. Exch. Fellow: Inst. for Combinatorial Analysis (mem. coun. 2002—07); mem.: Am. Math. Soc., Pi Delta Epsilon, Tau Kappa Alpha, Sigma Xi, Sigma Pi Sigma, Phi Beta Kappa. Home: 4612 Villa Green Dr Nashville TN 37215 Office: Dept Math Vanderbilt Univ Nashville TN 37240

PLUMMER, WILLIAM HAMILTON, III, museum director, editor; b. Syracuse, NY, Sept. 3, 1944; s. William Hamilton and Anne Dorothy (Stolar) Plummer; Student, U. Maine, 1964-65; BS, Ind. U., 1973; postgrad., U. Okla., 1983-84. Scholastic sports writer Syracuse Herald-Jour., 1968-69, sports writer, summers 1968-73, Riverside (Calif.) Press-Enterprise, 1973-74, Syracuse Herald-Jour., 1975-79; dir. pub. rels., media Amateur Softball Assn., Oklahoma City, 1979—96, mgr. Nat. Softball Hall of Fame, 1996—, historian, trade show mgr. Press officer US Olympic Com., Colorado Springs, Colo. and Houston, 1979-86, Syracuse and Chapel Hill, NC, 1981-87, Baton Rouge, 1985-91, Colorado Springs, 1983-90, Mpls./St. Paul, 1990 and La., 1991, San Antonio, Tex., 1993, St. Louis, 1994, Denver, 1995, (Pan Am Games) Indpls., 1982, 87, Parana, Argentina, 1995; softball info. mgr. for 1996 Olympic Games; press officer for 1987 and 1995 Pam Am. Games, and for US Olympic Festivals 1979, 81, 82, 83, 85, 86, 87, 89, 90, 91, 93, 94, and 95; press officer for Tex. State U. Games, 1989; stringer for AP, NCAA Coll. World Series, 1991-96, 97-98, 2000-07; umpire 2 Am. Softball Assn. Regionals, selected for 1995 Am. Softball Assn. 16-under Girls' Slow Pitch Nat. Championship; voting mem. James E. Sullivan award, Dial award; sec. ISF Press Commn., 1987; mem. Olympic Results Info. Svcs. Working Grp. for softball, 2000 Olympic Games. Contbr.: The Worth Book of Softball, 1994, Encyclopedia of World Sport, 1996, The Irresistible American Softball Book, 1978, Greatest Athletes of the 20th Century, 1991, The Complete Book of Softball, The Loonies Guide to Playing and Enjoying the Game, 1984,J our. of West, 1991, The Volvo Halls of Fame Guide, 1995, The Zollner Piston Story, 1995, Inside CNY Softball, 1995-97, The Joy of Keeping Score, 1996, The Masterful Art of Fast Pitch Pitching, 1996, 2000 Sydney Olympic Games official prog.; editor, The Inside Pitch, Okla. City; scriptwriter, voiceovers, rschr. (TV series) Softball 360, Fox, 2004, scriptwriter Greatest Softball Moments, 2005; preteens and tenns book cons., 2006, author: The Game America Plays, 2008. Mem. Steering com. Sooner State Games, Oklahoma City, 1984. Sgt. USAF, 1964-68. Recipient Cert. of Merit Civil Air Patrol, 1966, Outstanding Softball Coverage, Softball Writers and Broadcasters Assn., 1970, 71, 75, So. Calif. Wrestling Assn., 1974, Cert. Appreciation, Pan Am. Games, 1987, 95, NCAA Women's Coll. Softball World Series, 1988, 89, 90, Atlanta Organizing Com., 1996, SODA President's award, 1995, Outstanding Publ. award Okla. Mus. Assn., 2006; named Outstanding Sports Reporter, USAF, 1968, Softball Writer for Atlantic Coast, Amateur Softball Assn., 1971, Softball Writer of Yr., Softball Insight Mag., 1983, Outstanding Umpire, Oklahoma City Metro Amateur Softball Assn., 1996; Ernie Pyle scholar Ind. U., 1971; named to Ind. Amateur Softball Assn. Hall of Fame (hon.), 1998, Nat. Softball Hall of Fame, 1999, NY State Amateur Softball Assn. Hall of Fame, 2003. Mem. Ind. U. Alumni Assn., Cosida, Olympic Pub. Rels. Assn., Okla. City Softball Assn. (sec., 1998), Sigma Delta Chi. Avocations: photography, jogging, umpiring, reading, freelance writing. Office: Amateur Softball Assn 2801 NE 50th St Oklahoma City OK 73111-7203 Office Phone: 405-425-3433. E-mail: dplummer@softball.org.

PLUMSTEAD, WILLIAM CHARLES, SR., quality engineer, consultant; b. Two Rivers, Wis., Nov. 2, 1938; m. Peggy Bass, July 19, 1959 (dec.); children: William Jr., Jennifer, Kevin A. (dec.), Keith M.; m. Vicki Newton, June 27, 1981. Student, U. Fla., 1956-58, Temple U., 1966-72, Albright Coll., 1973-75; BSBA, Calif. Coast U., 1985, MBA, 1989. Lic. profl. engr., Calif. V.p. U.S. Testing Co., Inc., Hoboken, N.J., 1963-76; div. mgr. Daniel Internat., Inc., Greenville, S.C., 1976-83; group mgr. Bechtel Group, Inc., San Francisco, 1983-89; prin. engr. Fluor Daniel, Inc., Greenville, 1989-94; pres. PQT Svcs., Inc., Greenville, S.C., 1994—. Author: (with others) Code/Specification Syndrome, 1976, NDT Laboratories Update, 1991, NDT in Construction, 1991, NDT-A Partner in Excellence, 1994, Maximizing NDT Training Effectiveness, Materials Evaluation (jour), 2010; contbr. articles to profl. jours. Bd. dirs. Piedmont Food Bank, 1994-97. Recipient Lifetime Achievement award, ASTM Com. E9, 2013. Fellow: Am. Soc. Nondestructive Testing (coun. chmn. 1985-88, nat. sec., treas. 1992-93, nat. v.p. 1993-94, pres. 1994-95, chmn. bd. dirs. 1995-96), ASTM (sec. 1989-93, vice chmn. 1994-96, chmn. 1996-98, Charles Briggs award 1993, award of Merit 2000); mem.: Toastmasters Internat. (pres. local chpt. 1990-91, Competent Toastmaster award 1986, Able Toastmaster award 1993, Lifetime Achievement award, 2013). Avocations: sports, wine tasting. Home and Office: Plumstead Quality and Tng Svcs 806 Botany Rd Greenville SC 29615-1608 Office Phone: 864-292-1115. Personal E-mail: wplumstead@hotmail.com. Business E-Mail: bill.sr@pqt.net.

PLUNKETT, JACK WILLIAM, writer, publisher; b. Dallas, May 17, 1950; s. Ivan Wayne and Waltina Lee (Roark) P.; m. Lynn Ann Richards (div.); 1 child, Jack W. Plunkett Jr.; m. Mary Lee Hartfelder, Dec. 8, 1972 (div.); children: Altus W., Robert L.; m. Martha Menefee Burgher, Oct. 7, 2000. Pres. Plunkett Properties Corp., Dallas, 1968-74; ind. mktg. cons. Dallas, 1974-83; mgr. ptnr. Brown-Plunkett, Waxahachie, Tex., 1983—; CEO, pub. Plunkett Rsch. Ltd., Houston, Tex., 1986—. Cons. Houston Symphony, 1996-97, The Odyssey House, Houston, 1997—. Author: The Almanac of American Employers, 1985, 8th edit., 2004, Plunkett's Health Care Industry Almanac, 1995, 7th edit., 2004, Plunkett's InfoTech Industry Almanac, 1995, 5th edit., 2004, Plunkett's Financial Services Industry Almanac, 1996, 4th edit., 2004, Plunkett's Retail Industry Almanac, 1996, 5th edit., 2004, Plunkett's Entertainment and Media Industry Almanac, 1998, 3d edit., 2002, Plunkett's Energy Industry Almanac, 1999, 3d edit., 2003, Plunkett's Telecommunications Industry Almanac, 2000, 3d edit., 2003, Plunkett's E-Commerce and Internet Business Almanac, 2000, 3d edit., 2003, Plunkett's Engineering and Research Industry Almanac, 2000, 2d edit., 2003, Plunkett's Biotech and Genetics Industry Almanac, 2001, 3d edit., 2003, Plunckett's Consulting Industry Almanac, 2003, Plunckett's Real Estate & Construction Industry Alamanac, 2003. Chmn. Mayor's Libr. Fundraising Com., Boerne, Tex., 1988-89; founding pres. Greater Boerne Area Econ. Devel. Corp., 1986-87; dir. Boerne Area Cmty. Ctr., 1983-86; area chmn. Lamar Smith for Congress, Boerne, 1986; bd. dirs. Boerne Econ. Devel. Coun., 1992-94, Galveston Hist. Found., 1996--, Sch. of Nursing, U. Tex. Med. Br., 1996—, Sch. of Bus., U. of Houston Downtown Campus, 2001—, Strand Theater, 1996—; trustee Galveston County United Way, 1996-97; bd. dirs. Houston Symphony Orch., 1999-2000; mem. Dickens on the Strand 25th Ann. Com., 1997-98; v.p. Houston Symphony Ptnrs., 1997-98, pres.-elect, 1998-99, pres., 1999-2000; founding pres. Tex. Entrepreneurs Exch., 2000—. Recipient Houston's Singular Best award Cystic Fibrosis Found., 1997, Outstanding Acad. Book of the Yr. award Choice Mag. Editors, 1996; named outstanding chmn. Boy Scouts Am., 1983, Cmty. Vol. of Yr., Boerne Area C. of C., 1989; elected to Knights of Momus, 1998. Mem. Rotary (pres. Boerne chpt. 1988-89), The Centurions, Knights of Maximillian. Republican. Office: Plunkett Rsch Ltd PO Box 541737 Houston TX 77254-1737

PLYMALE, ROBERT H., state legislator; b. Huntington, W.Va., Feb. 21, 1955; BA, Marshall U., 1978. Mem. Dist. 5 W.Va. State Senate, 1993—, chair Edn. Com., mem. Confirmations Com., Fin. Com., Pensions Com., Rules Com. & Transp. and Infrastructure Com. Mem.: Byrd. Mfg. Ctr. (bd. dir.), Huntington Regional C. of C. Democrat. Protestant. Mailing: 206 Cliffview Dr Huntington WV 25704-8810 Office: State Capitol Rm 417M, Bldg 1 1900 Kanawha Blvd E Charleston WV 25305 Home Phone: 304-453-6321. Fax: 304-595-2992. E-mail: robert.plymale@wvsenate.gov.

POCALYKO, MICHAEL NICHOLAS, investment banker, corporate director, novelist; b. Fountain Hill, Pa., Dec. 24, 1954; s. Walter and Anna Margaret (Pagats) P.; m. Barbara Wilson Snelbaker, Dec. 26, 1976; children: James Kenneth, Kathryn Laura. AB, Muhlenberg Coll., 1976; MPA, Harvard U., 1985; MBA, U. Pa., 1995. Cert. fraud examiner 2010. Commd. ensign USN, 1976, advanced through grades to comdr., 1992; aviation detachment officer in charge USS Pharris, 1983-84; mem. strategic concepts group Office of Chief of Naval Ops., Washington, 1985-86, spl. asst. to Dep. Chief of Naval Ops., 1986-87; aviation detachment officer in charge USS Boone, 1988-90; with Office of Sec. of Navy, Washington, 1990-92; sr. fellow Atlantic Coun. U.S., Washington, 1992-93; with Office of Sec. Def., Washington, 1993—95; founder, prin. M.N. Pocalyko Investment Bankers, 1995—97; mng. dir., CEO Monticello Capital, 1997—, corp. dir., chmn., 1997—. Corp. dir., audit com. chmn. Challenger Corp., 2002—08, Herley Industries, 2010—11; chmn. Advanced Environ. Resources Inc., 2003—08, Erdevel Europa S.à r.l., 2003—08, Erdevel Europa in the Kingdom of Saudi Arabia, 2004—08, Erdevel Water Sys. S.r.l. (later International Sys. S.r.l.), 2004—08, TherimuneX Pharms., Inc., 2008—; trustee Fairleigh Dickinson U., 2000—06; founder, corp. dir. Envambien, S.A., 2007—08; bd. adv. Financial Investments Inc., 2009—; bd. leadership fellow Nat. Assn. Corp. Dirs., 2011—, adv. coun., 2011—, From Battlefield to Boardroom corp. dir. develop. program, 2011—; mem. Assn. Cert. Fraud Examiners, 2012—. Co-editor, contbr.: A John Hawkes Symposium: Design and Debris, 1977; contbr.: Reconstituting America's Defense, 1992, In Support of Arab Democracy, 2005; rapporteur: The Future of Russian-American Relations in a Pluralistic World, 1992, The Future of Ukrainian-American Relations in a Pluralistic World, 1992; co-author: The NATO Infrastructure Program, 1993; author: The New Trade Order, 1994, The Navigator-a novel, 2013; contbr. articles to profl. publs., books, newspapers, on-line publs. Apptd. Fairfax County Industrial Devel. Authority, 1999—2000; apptd. mem. exec. coun. Boy Scouts Am. Nat. Capital Area Coun., 2002—; apptd. mem. Va. Commonwealth Competition Coun., 2000—03, Internat. Assn. U. Pres. UN Commn. on Disarmament Edn., Conflict Resolution and Peace, 2010—; mem. Fairfax County Rep. Com., 1996—2004, Va. Ho. Delegates 36th dist. Rep. Com., 1996—2001, chmn., 2001—06. Recipient Eagle Scout award, 1968, Vincent Astor Found. award U.S. Naval Inst., 1983, Lamb award, Evangelical Lutheran Ch. Am., 1998, Silver Beaver award, Boy Scouts Am., 2002, Fairfax County Good Scout award, 2011, Muhlenberg Coll. Alumni Lifetime Achievement award, 2011, Disting. Eagle Scout award, Boy Scouts Am., 2011; decorated Navy Commendation Medal, Navy Achievement Medal, Meritorious Svc. Medal (3 awards), 16 other decorations. Assn. Cert. Fraud Examiners, Nat. Assn. Corp. Dirs., U.S. Naval Inst., Internat. Inst. Strategic Studies, Coun. on Fgn. Rels., Assn. Naval Aviation, Muhlenberg Coll. Alumni Assn. (exec. coun. 1986-90, chmn. com. 1986-90), Metropolitan Club (New York), Cosmos Club (Wash.), Am. Legion, V.F.W., Beirut Veterans of Am., Masons, Sovereign Military Order Temple Jerusalem (gran officier), Military Order Foreign Wars, Military Order Carabao, Sigma Phi Epsilon, Sigma Tau Delta. Republican. Lutheran. Avocation: horseback riding. Office: Monticello Capital Lindbergh Ctr - Dulles Business Park 3901 Centerview Dr Ste R Chantilly VA 20151-3299 Office Phone: 703-674-0500. Business E-Mail: pocalyko@monticellocapital.com.

POCCIA, CLAUDIA, cosmetics company executive; b. 1959; Account exec. Designer Fragrance Divsn. L'Oreal, 1984; regional sales mgr., v.p. field sales Giorgio Beverly Hills; dir. spl. events, regional mktg. dir., v.p. bus. devel. The Estee Lauder Companies Inc., 1994; v.p. sales & edn. The Estee Lauder Companies Inc, 2000—03, sr. v.p., gen. mgr. Stila Cosmetics, 2003—05; global pres. mark. Avon Products, Inc., 2005—11; pres., CEO Gurwitch Products, 2011—. Recipient Achiever award, Cosmetic Exec. Women, 2010, Innovation Marketer Beauty Biz award, Women's Wear Daily, 2010. Office: Gurwitch Products, LLC 8 Greenway Plz Fl 7 Houston TX 77046-0826 Office Phone: 888-637-2437.

POCHICK, FRANCIS EDWARD, financial consultant; b. Metuchen, NJ, May 28, 1931; s. Frank Stephen and Bertha Barbara Pochick; m. Shirley Ann Elliott, Feb. 16, 1957; children: Bonnie Lynn, Keith Francis. Student, Rutgers U., 1949-50, 54-55. Agt. New Eng. Mut. Life. Ins. Co., Newark and New Brunswick, NJ, 1958-61, Lambert M. Huppeler Co., Inc., NYC, 1962-64, cons., 1964, sr. cons. employee benefits, 1967-87; fin. cons. Francis E. Pochick Assocs., NYC, 1987—. Mem. adv. bd. Mercer Fund, Cmty. Found. N.J., 1986—, Rec. for the Blind, Princeton, 1989, charitable devel. officer Nat. Found., Inc., 1992, Nat. Coun. on The Aging, Planned Giving Coun. 1994; mem. com. bd. dirs. health Princeton Coun. Planned Giving, 1993; v.p. The Benefits Planning Co., Ltd., Charlottesville, Va., 1995. With USMC, 1951-54. Mem. Am. Soc. Pension Actuaries, Nat. Assn. Life Underwriters, Fin. Planning Assn., Estate Planning Coun., Nat. Assn. Philanthropic Planners, Lions, Glenmore Country Club. Office: PO Box 518 Keswick VA 22947-0518 also: No Jersey Br 30 Two Bridges Rd Fairfield NJ 07004-1550 Home: 308 Sussex Dr Staunton VA 24401-2626 Office Phone: 434-295-7173. Personal E-mail: fepassoc@embarqmail.com.

PODGORNY, GEORGE, emergency physician; b. Tehran, Iran, Mar. 17, 1934; arrived in US, 1954, naturalized, 1973; s. Emanuel and Helen (Parsian) Podgorny; m. Ernestine Koury, Oct. 20, 1962; children: Adele, Emanuel II, George, Gregory. BS, Maryville Coll., 1958; postgrad., Bowman Gray Sch. Medicine, 1958; MD, Wake Forest U., 1962. Intern surgery NC Bapt. Hosp., Winston-Salem, 1962—63, chief resident gen. surgery, 1966—67, with, cardiothoracic surgery, 1967—69; sec.-treas. Forsyth Emergency Svcs., Winston-Salem, 1970—80; sr. med. examiner Forsyth County, NC, 1972—; dir. dept. emergency medicine Forsyth Meml. Hosp., Winston-Salem, 1974—80; chmn. residency rev. com. emergency medicine East Carolina U. Sch. Medicine, Greenville, 1980—88, clin. prof. emergency medicine, 1984—; mem. Accreditation Coun. Grad. Med. Edn. Contbr. articles to profl. publs.; editl. bd. mem. Anns. Emergency Medicine, Med. Meetings. Chmn. bd. trustees Emergency Medicine Found.; chmn. residency rev. com. emergency medicine Accreditation Coun. Grad. Med. Edn.; founder Western Piedmont Emergency Med. Svcs. Coun., 1973; trustee Forsyth County Hosp., Authority, 1974—75; bd. dirs. Medic Alert Found. Internat., NC Health Coordinating Coun., 1975—82, Piedmont Health Systems Agy., 1975—84; dir. Emergency Med. Svcs. Project Region II NC, 1975—; mem. NC Emergency Med. Svcs. Adv. Coun., 1976—81; assoc. prof. clin. surgery Bowman Gray Sch. Medicine, Wake Forest U., Winston-Salem, 1979—. Fellow: Southeastern Surg. Congress, Royal Soc. Medicine, Royal Soc. Health (Great Britain), Internat. Coll. Angiology, Internat. Coll. Surgeons; mem.: AMA (chmn. coun. sect. emergency medicine 1978—90), Am. Bd. Emergency Medicine (pres. 1976—81), Am. Coll. Emergency Physicians (charter, pres. 1978—79, alt. del. 1990—). Home: 6 Bluebird Ct Durham NC 27713-8139 Office Phone: 336-727-1161.

PODOLSKI, JOSEPH S., pharmaceutical executive; BS in Chemistry, Ill. Inst. of Tech., MSChemE. Various positions in mfg., engring., quality contr. and devel. of fine chemicals, antibiotics, pharmaceuticals and hosp. products Baxter Pharmaceuticals, Dearborn Chem. Co., Abbott Laboratory, Inc.; various positions in engring., product devel., mfg. G.D. Searle (subs. of Monsanto Co.), 1977—89; v.p. ops. Repros Therapeutics, Inc., 1989—92, pres., CEO, bd. dirs., 1992—. Office: Repros Therapeutics Inc 2408 Timberloch Pl B 7 The Woodlands TX 77380 Office Phone: 281-719-3400. Office Fax: 281-719-3446. Business E-Mail: podolski@reprosrx.com.

PODOLSKY, DANIEL K., university administrator, physician; AB, Harvard Coll., Cambridge, Mass., 1974; MD, Harvard Med. Sch., 1978. Cert. Am. Bd. Internal Medicine, subsplty. cert. in gastroenterology Am. Bd. Internal Medicine. Residency in internal medicine Mass. Gen. Hosp., 1978—80, clin. and rsch. fellow in medicine, 1980—82, joined med. staff, 1981, chief gastroenterology, 1989—2008; joined faculty Harvard Med. Sch., 1981, Mallinckrodt prof. medicine, 1998—2008; chief academic officer Partners Health-care Sys.; pres. U. Tex. Southwestern Med. Ctr., 2008—, clin. practice in digestive and liver diseases, prof., Doris and Bryan Wildenthal disting chair in med. sci., Philip O'Bryan Montgomery, Jr., MD disting. presdl. chmn. in academic adminstrn. Contbr. articles to profl. jours. Recipient MERIT award, NIH, 1998; Clin. fellow in Medicine, Harvard Med. Sch., 1978—80, Rsch. fellow in Medicine, 1980—82. Mem.: NAS Inst. Medicine, Am. Gastroenterological Assn. (pres. 2003, Disting. Achievement award 2007, Julius Friedenwald medal 2009), Am Assn. Physicians, Am. Soc. Clin. Investigation, Am. Fed. Clin. Rsch. Office: University Tex Southwestern Med Ctr Outpatient Bldg 6th Fl Ste 102 1801 Inwood Rd Dallas TX 75390-9083 Business E-Mail: daniel.podolsky@utsouthwestern.edu.

POE, GEORGE WILKINSON, literature, culture and language professor; b. Greenville, SC, Mar. 28, 1952; s. Frank Swift and Rosalie (Haynes) P.; m. Sylviane Rosello, Jan. 8, 1977. AB with high honors in French, Davidson Coll., NC, 1974; postgrad., U. Paris IV, Inst. d'études politiques de Paris, 1974—75; MA, Middlebury Coll., Vt., 1975; PhD, Duke U., 1981. Part-time instr. French Duke U., Durham, NC, 1976—78; instr. to asst. prof. Davidson Coll., 1978—82; asst. prof. Hanover Coll., 1982—87, Sewanee: The U. of the South, Tenn., 1987—, assoc. prof., 1990—97, dept. chair, 1994—2000, prof. French and French Studies, 1997—; resident fellow. Faculty dir. Jr. Yr. in France Davidson Coll., 1979-81; study abroad dir. Dept. French Hanover Coll., 1982-87; founder Sewanee in France summer prog., 1988, dir., 1989-96; elected del. Assembly of Modern Lang. Assn., 1988-1991; elected to Conseil d'Adminstrn. Soc. Marivaux, 1989-1995; Camargo Found. scholar-in-residence, vis. prog. dir., 1995., resident fellow, 1992. Author: The Rococo & 18th Century French Literature, 1987; co-editor: The French Novel, 1995; editl. bd. Synthesis: An Interdisciplinarhy Jour. and the Synthesis Book Series, 1994-2006; contbr. articles and revs. to profl. jours. Alumni coord. meml. fund Ghigo-Embry-Meeks Fund Davidson Coll., 1987-. Recipient Tchr. of Yr. award, Sewanee: The U. of the South, 2004, US Prof. of Yr. award for Tenn., Carnegie Found. for Advancement of Tchg., Coun. for Advancement and Support of Edn., 2006; named Class of 1961 Hon. Chair of Coll., Sewanee, 2010. Mem. MLA, Am. Assn. Tchrs. French, Am. Soc. 18th Century Studies, Tenn. Fgn. Lang. Tchg. Assn., South Atlantic MLA. Avocations: theater, cinema, travel, golf. Office: Dept French and French Studies Sewanee The U of the South 735 University Ave Sewanee TN 37383 Office Phone: 931-598-1522. Business E-Mail: gpoe@sewanee.edu.

POE, TED, United States Representative from Texas, former judge; b. Temple, Tex., Oct. 13, 1948; m. Carol Poe. BA in Polit. Sci., Abilene Christian U., 1970; JD, U. Houston Law Ctr., 1973. Asst. dist. atty. Harris County, Tex., 1973—81, criminal ct. judge Tex., 1981—2003; mem. US Congress from 2nd Tex. dist., 2005—. Instr. FBI Nat. Acad., Quantico, Va., US Mil. Acad., West Point, U. Houston. Bd. dirs. Nat. Children's Alliance; past bd. dirs. Children's Assessment Ctr. Houston, CASA Child Advocates, Child Abuse Prevention Coun., Parents of Murdered Children, MADD, DARE, Roseate Women's Ctr. Abused Women, Abilene Christian U. Svc. with USAFR, 1970—76. Recipient Congl. Partnership award, Southeast Tex. Regional Planning Commn., 2006, Spirit of Enterprise award, US C. of C., Social Change award, Tex. Assn. Against Sexual Assault, Morton Bard award, Nat. Orgn. Victims Assistance; named Outstanding Judge, Found. Improvement of Justice, Outstanding Instr., Tex. Dist. Atty. Assn., Best Judge, Kans. Peace Officers Assn., Outstanding Dist. Judge, Houston Police Officers Assn./Harris County Dep. Sheriffs Assn., Outstanding Young Lawyer, Houston Bar Assn. Republican. Christian. Office: US House of Represntatives 2412 Rayburn House Office Bldg Washington DC 20515 also: 1801 Kingwood Dr Ste 240 Humble TX 77339 Office Phone: 202-225-6565.*

POEHLEIN, GARY WAYNE, retired chemical engineering professor; b. Tell City, Ind., Oct. 17, 1936; s. Oscar Raymond and Eva Lee (Dickman) P.; m. Sharon Eileen Wood., Jan. 1, 1958; children: Steven Ray, Timothy Wayne, Valorie Ann, Sandra Lee. BSChemE, Purdue U., 1958, MSChemE, 1961, PhD, 1966. Design engr. Proctor & Gamble, Cin., 1958-61; from asst. prof. to assoc. prof. Lehigh U., Bethlehem, Pa., 1965-75, prof. chem. engring., 1975-78, co-dir. emulsion polymers inst., 1973-78; dir. sch. chem. engring. Ga. Inst. Tech., Atlanta, 1978-86, assoc. v.p. rsch., dean grad, studies, 1986-91, v.p. interdisciplinary programs, prof. chem. engring., 1991-95; prof. chem. engring., 1978-96; dir. Chem. and Transport Systems Divsn. NSF, 1996-2000; ret., 2000. Bd. dirs. Flexible Products Co., Marietta, Ga.; interim chair chem. engring. dept., vis. prof. Lehigh U., 2001—02. Contbr. over 100 articles to tech. publs. Mem. sch. bd. Bethlehem Area Sch. Dist., 1969-75. Recipient Honor Scroll award Phila. br. Am. Inst. Chemists, 1977, Mac Pruitt award Coun. for Chem. Rsch., 1989, Outstanding ChE Alumni award Pudue U., 2008. Fellow AIChE. Avocations: woodworking, sailing. Home: 407 S Henry St Alexandria VA 22314-5901

POEHLING, KATHERINE, pediatrician; d. Gary Poehling; m. Timothy Peters, May 4, 1996; children: Jennifer Peters children: Robert Peters. MD, Wake Forest Sch. of Medicine, Winston-Salem, NC, 1995; MPH, Vanderbilt U. Sch. of Medicine, Nashville, Tenn., 2001. Lic. NC Med. Bd., 2007, cert. Bd. Am. Acad. Pediat., 1998. Fellow Vanderbilt U., Nashville, 1999—2002, asst. prof. of pediat., 2002—07; assoc. prof. pediats. Wake Forest Sch. Medicine, Winston-Salem, NC, 2007—. Mem. NC Med. Bd., 2007. Fellow: Am. Acad. Pediat.; mem.: Soc. Pediatric Rsch., Acad. Pediat. Assn., Infectious Disease Soc. Am., Alpha Omega Alpha. Achievements include research in Clin. rsch. on pediat. respiratory infections.

POGGE, BRENDA L., state legislator; b. Norfolk, Va., Mar. 18, 1957; m. Roger Franklin; children: Sarah Pogge Duncan, David, Joshua, Timothy, Jonathan. Attended, Alpha Coll. Real Estate, 1995. Realtor; mem. Dist. 96 Va. House of Delegates, 2008—. Named Citizen of the Year, Family Found., 2000. Republican. Office: General Assembly Bldg PO Box 406 Richmond VA 23218 also: PO Box 196 Norge VA 23127-0196 Office Phone: 757-223-9690, 804-698-1096. Fax: 804-698-6796. E-mail: DelBPogge@house.virginia.gov.

POHL, MICHAEL A., lawyer; b. Cleve., Oct. 25, 1942; s. Irwin P. and Ruth B. (Bishko) P.; m. Ellen Durchslag, Dec. 12, 1970 (div. 1982); children: Matthew E., Andrew F. BA, Amherst Coll., 1965; JD, Case Western Res. U., 1968. Bar: Ohio 1968, Fla. 1972, U.S. Supreme Ct. 1974. Mem.: The Fla. Bar, Ohio State Bar Assn. Avocations: opera, golf. Home: Gulf Harbour 14971 Rivers Edge Ct #204 Fort Myers FL 33908 Office: Patterson Eskin & Ball 1420 SE 47th St Cape Coral FL 33904 Office Phone: 239-549-5551. Office Fax: 239-549-4834. Personal E-mail: michaelapohl@comcast.net.

POHLMANN, MARCUS D., political science professor; b. Davenport, Iowa, Sept. 18, 1950; s. Clement A. and Lois L. (Smith) P.; m. Barbara A. Heimann, May 27, 1972; 1 child, Justin. BA in Polit. Sci., Cornell Coll., Mt. Vernon, Iowa, 1972; MA in Polit. Sci., Columbia U., NYC, 1974, MPhil in Polit. Sci., 1975, PhD in Polit. Sci., 1976. Rsch. assoc. Met. Applied Rsch. Ctr., NYC, 1975-76; instr. The Spence Sch., NYC, 1975-76; cons. Media and Soc., NYC, 1982; Fulbright sr. lectr. Yerevan St. U., Armenia, USSR, 1982; asst. prof. Coll. of Wooster, Ohio, 1977-83; assoc. prof. Ark. State U., Jonesboro, 1983-86; prof. Rhodes Coll., Memphis, 1986—. Vis. asst. prof. Bates Coll., Lewiston, Maine, 1976-77. Author: Political Power in the Postindustrial City, 1986, Black Politics in Conservative America, 1990, 3d edit., 2007, Governing the Postindustrial City, 1993, Racial Politics at the Crossroads, 1996, Landmark Congressional Laws on Civil Rights, 2002, African American Political Thought, 2003, Opportunity Lost, 2009. Recipient Lydia C. Roberts fellowship Columbia U., NYC, 1972-76. Mem. Am. Polit. Sci. Assn., Acad. Polit. Sci., Am. Mock Trial Assn. (pres., bd. dirs.), Authors Guild. Democrat. Avocations: basketball, bridge, golf, hiking, canoeing. Home: 367 Forest Hill Irene Cordova TN 38018-4628 Office: Rhodes Coll 2000 North Pky Memphis TN 38112-1624 Office Phone: 901-843-3843. Business E-Mail: pohlmann@rhodes.edu.

POILE, DAVID ROBERT, professional sports team executive; b. Toronto, Ont., Canada, Feb. 14, 1949; s. Norman Robert and Margaret Poile; m. Elizabeth Ramey, July 4, 1971; children: Brian Robert, Lauren Elizabeth. BS, Northeastern U., 1971. Asst. mgr. Atlanta Flames, 1971-80, Calgary Flames, Alta., Can., 1980-82; gen. mgr., v.p. Washington Capitals, Landover, Md., 1982-95; exec. v.p., gen. mgr., pres. hockey ops. Nashville Predators, Nashville, 1997—. Gen. mgr. Team USA, Olympic Games, Sochi, Russia, 2014. Recipient NHL Exec. of Yr., Sporting News, 1983, 1984, Lester Patrick Trophy, 2001; named NHL Exec. of Yr., Sporting News, 2007. Office: Nashville Predators Bridgestone Arena 501 Broadway Nashville TN 37203-3932*

POINDEXTER, BYRON D., plastic surgeon; b. Beech Grove, Ind., Apr. 2, 1966; married. BA in Chemistry, Psychology summa cum laude, phi beta kappa hon. soc., Ind. U., 1984—88, MD summa cum laude, alpha omega alpha hon. soc., 1988—92. Diplomate Am. Bd. Plastic Surgery. Resident gen. surgery Univ. of Fla., 1992—96; fellow plastic surgery Univ. of Ala., 1996—98; staff surgeon Austin-Weston Ctr. for Cosmetic Surgery. Co-author: (publs.) Selection of Patients for Renal Artery Repair Using Captopril Testing, 1995, A Simple Method of Lower Extremity Arteriography in the Laboratory Rat, 1998, Microvascular Surgery Utilizing the Endoscope as the Sole Source of Visual Assistance, 1998, The Present Status of Endoscopy, 1998, Rejuvenation of the Aged Face, 2000, Surgical Treatment of the Aged Mouth, 2003, Lip Recontouring, 2005. Recipient Ray Bierstedt Memorial award, Univ. of Ala., Distinguished Alumni Svc. award, Ind. Univ. Mem.: Va. Soc. of Plastic Surgeons, Nat. Capital Soc. of Plastic Surgeons (pres.), Am. Bd. of Plastic Surgery. Achievements include research in Histopathyology of Specimens from Elective Breast Reductions; Anatomy of the Malar Fat Pads and Central Third of the Face; General and Local Anesthesia in Strabismus Surgery; C14 Labeled Leucine Uptake in the Ovine Fetus: Fed and Fasting Models of Neonatal Nutrition. Office: Austin-Weston Center for Cosmetic Surgery 1825 Samuel Morse Dr Reston VA 20190 Office Phone: 703-893-6168.

POINDEXTER, CHARLES D., state legislator; b. Roanoke, Va., Feb. 27, 1942; m. Janet Poindexter; 6 children. BS in Math., Lynchburg Coll., 1964; MSA in Mgmt., George Washington U., 1973. Software devel. various companies; farmer; mem. Dist. 9 Va. House of Delegates, 2009—. Mem. Franklin County Bd. of Suprs. Dir. Franklin County Hist. Soc.; chmn. bd. of trustees Crafts United Methodist Church; mem. Air Force Assn., Farm Bur. Republican. Methodist. Office: PO Box 117 Glade Hill VA 24092 also: Capitol Office Gen Assembly Bldg PO Box 406 Richmond VA 23218 Office Phone: 540-576-2600, 804-698-1009. Business E-Mail: DelCPoindexter@house.virginia.gov.

POITEVINT, ALEC LOYD, II, mineral company executive, political organization administrator; b. Bainbridge, Ga., Aug. 28, 1947; s. Alec Loyd and Joyce Lynn Poitevint; m. Doreen Styles, 1971. Attended, U. Ga., 1965—70. V.p. Southeastern Minerals, Inc., Bainbridge, Ga., 1973—74, exec. v.p., 1974—75, pres., 1975—; exec. v.p. Marshall Minerals, 1973—75, pres., 1975—; chmn. Decatur County Republican Com., Ga., 1975—77; vice chmn. Ga. Republican Party, 1977—79, chmn., 1989—93, 2003—07, Second Dist. Republican Com., 1981—83; chmn. com. on arrangements Republican Nat. Convention, Atlanta, 2011—. Treas. Republican Nat. Com., 1997—2001; chmn. Perdue for Gov., 2002; co-chmn. Perdue Inaugural Com., 2003; bd. dirs. United Ins. Holding Corp., 2001—09; bd. mem. Ga. Ports Authority, 2007—, chmn., 2010—. Mem.: American Fed. Mfrs. Assn. (bd. dirs. 1982—86), Nat. Feed Ingredients Assn. (bd. dirs. 1980—90), Rotary. Republican. Presbyn. Office: Southeastern Minerals Inc PO Box 1650 Bainbridge GA 31718 Home: PO Box 506 Bainbridge GA 31717*

POLAND, RICHARD CLAYTON, law educator; b. Hartland, Maine, June 23, 1947; s. Richard and Viola (Gardiner) P.; m. Judy Raithel, Feb. 2, 1978; 1 child, Brooke. BA, Taylor U., Upland, Ind., 1969; MS in Bus., Thomas Coll., 1993; JD, Northeastern U. Sch. Law, 1974. Bar: Maine, US Dist. Ct. Maine, US Supreme Ct. Sole practice law, Skowhegan, Maine, 1974-94; prof. law, dir. pre-law program Flagler Coll, St. Augustine, Fla., 1994—. Probate judge Somerset County, Skowhegan, 1977-94, Maine Family Ct. Commn., Augusta, 1981; mem. Maine Jud. Coun., Portland, 1989-93. Author: Pre-Law Handbook for Undergrads., 2000, 6th edit., 2010. Chmn. faculty welfare com. Flagler Coll. Cpl. Maine Nat. Guard, 1970-76. Mem. So. Assn. Pre-Law Advisors (pres. 2000-02, bd. dirs. 2002-06), Pre-Law Adv. Nat. Conf. (exec. bd. 2000-02). Avocations: travel, reading. Office: Flagler Coll 74 King St Saint Augustine FL 32084-4342 Office Phone: 904-819-6338. Business E-Mail: polandrc@flagler.edu.

POLEMITOU, OLGA ANDREA, accountant; b. Nicosia, Cyprus, June 28, 1950; d. Takis and Georgia (Nicolaou) Chrysanthou. BA with honors, U. London, 1971; PhD, Ind. U., Bloomington, 1981. CPA Ind. Asst. productivity officer Internat. Labor Office/Cyprus Productivity Ctr., Nicosia, 1971-74; cons. Arthur Young & Co., NYC, 1981; mgr. Coopers & Lybrand, Newark, 1981-83; dir. Bell Atlantic, Reston, Va., 1983-97; v.p. corp. auditing Columbia Energy Group, Herndon, 1997—2000; pres., CEO Aristion, Inc., Reston, Va., 2000—; CFO Leader Capital LLC, NY, 2006—. Chairperson adv. coun. Extended Day Care Cmty. Edn., West Windsor Plainsboro, NJ, 1987—88. Contbr. articles to profl. jours. Bus. cons. project bus. Jr. Achievement, Indpls., 1984—85. Mem.: AICPAs, NAFE, Princeton Network Profl. Women, Va. Soc. CPAs, N.J. Soc. CPAs (sec. mem. in industry com.), Ind. CPA Soc., Nat. Trust Hist. Preservation. Avocations: water-skiing, tennis. Home: PO Box 2744 Reston VA 20195-0744 Office: 11921 Freedom Dr Ste 550 Reston VA 20190 Business E-Mail: opolemitou@aristion.com.

POLEN-DORN, LINDA FRANCES, communications executive; b. Cleve., Mar. 23, 1945; d. Stanley and Mildred (Kain) Neuger; m. Samuel O. Dorn; children: Lanelle, Brian, Adam, Dawn. BA cum laude, U. Miami, 1967; MBA, Nova Southeastern U., 1993. Reporter Miami News, Del., 1966-67, Miamian Mag., 1967—68; dir. pub. rels. Muscular Dystrophy Assn., Miami, 1968—72; cons., adv. and pub. rels. Ft. Lauderdale, 1974—77; pub. rels. writer J. Cory and Assocs., Ft. Lauderdale, 1978—79; account supr. Maizner & Franklin, Ft. Lauderdale, 1979—86; v.p. mktg., comm. Glendale Fed. Bank, 1986—95; prod. mktg. mgr. Ryder Sys., Inc., Miami, 1995—2003; cons. Southeastern Consulting Group, LLC, Ft. Lauderdale, 2004—. Active Symphony of Ams. Soc., Ft. Lauderdale, 2004—, Symphony Soc. Ft. Lauderdale, 1987-2003—. Mem. Internat. Assn. Bus. Communicators, Am. Mktg. Assn., Broward C. of C. (vice chmn. govt. affairs 1984-85). Avocation: travel.

POLHAMUS, BARBARA, behavioral scientist; d. Helen and Leslie Polhamus. PhD, MPH, U. N.C., Chapel Hill, 1991—97. Registered dietitian Am. Dietetic Assn., 1982. Nutrition dir. Dorchester Ho. Multi-Svc. Ctr., Mass., 1982—84; nutrition dir., maternal and child health Mass. Dept. Pub. Health, Boston, 1984—91; rsch. assoc. U. N.C., Chapel Hill, 1998—2000; behavioral scientist CDC, Nat. Ctr. for Chronic Disease Prevention and Health Promotion, Divsn. Nutrition Phys. Activity & Obesity, Atlanta, 2000—. Tech. cons., Ukraine micronutrient survey CDC, Kiev, 2002. Contbr. chapters to books, articles to profl. jours., sci. material for web sites. Recipient award of Excellence Pub. Health Tng. and Nutrition Team award, 2005, Delta Omega Alumni award, U. NC, Gillings Sch. Global Pub. Health, Dept. Nutrition, 2011; grantee, Inst. Nutrition, 1994; fellow, Dannon Inst., 1998. Mem.: APHA (elected sect. mem. 2002—04). Liberal. Avocations: yoga, hiking, travel. Office: CDC 4770 Buford Hwy NE MS K-03 Atlanta GA 30341 Personal E-mail: palhamus1@earthlink.net.*

POLIAKOFF, GARY A., lawyer, educator; b. Greenville, SC, Nov. 25, 1944; s. Herman and Dorothy (Ravitz) P.; m. Sherri D. Dublin, June 24, 1967; children: Ryan, Keith. BS, U. S.C., 1966; JD, U. Miami, 1969. Bar: Fla. 1969, DC 1971, Colo. 1999. Founding prin. Becker & Poliakoff, P.A., Hollywood, Coral Gables, Naples, Sarasota, West Palm Beach, Orlando, Ft. Walton Beach, Fla., Prague and NY, 1973—, Washington, Morristown, Red Bank, NJ, Ft. Myers, Melbourne, Port St. Lucie, Tallahasse, Tampa Bay, NYC, mng. shareholder, 1973—2008. Adj. prof. condominium law and practice Nova Southeastern U.; panelist Nat. Confs. Cmty. Assn.; testified before coms. of the US Senate on Condominiums; lectr. condominium seminars Fla. Bar; participant Fla. Law Revision Council; cons. to State Legis. and the White House in drafting Condominium and Coop. Abuse Relief Act, 1980; mem. condominium study commn. State of Fla., 1990; chmn. State of Fla. Advisory Coun. on Condominiums, 1992, 93.; Atty. Emeritus Town of Southwest Ranches. Author: The Law of Condominium Operations, 1988; co-author: Florida Condominium Law and Practice, 1982, The Florida Bar Continuing Legal Education, 1982, 2007; co-author: New Neighborhoods: The Consumer's Guide to Condominium, Co-op and HOA Living, 2009, Fl Civil Circuit Mediator, 2010; contbr. articles to legal jour. Mem. pres. adv. group U. SC, U.S.C. Ednl. Found., 1999-2001. Recipient Judge Learned Hand award Am. Jewish Com. for devel. of co-ownership housing law, 1999; Legal Elite award Fla. Trend Mag., 2004, 05, 06, 08, Diamond award Honoree for Excellence in Bus. Leadership So. Fla. Bus. Jour., 2002, 04-06, 08, Gurdon Buck award, Cmty. Assn. Law, Pioneer award, Broward County Commrs., Broward County Hist. Commn.; named Outstanding Adj. Prof. of Yr., Best Lawyers of America, Best Mcpl. Law Practitioners in America; named one of Top Fla. Lawyers. Mem. ABA (adv. nat. conf., nat. conf. commr., Uniform State Laws), Fla. Bar, Coll. Cmty. Assn. Lawyers (bd. gov., Highest Achievement award, 2011), Scribes. Home Phone: 954-434-7375; Office Phone: 954-985-4150. Personal E-mail: gpoliakoff@becker-poliakoff.com.

POLIAKOFF, STEVEN R., human services administrator, gynecologic oncologist, director; BS, Cornell U., NY, 1971; MD, U. NC, Chapel Hill, 1975; MBA, U. Miami, Fla., 1994. Diplomate Am. Bd. Ob-Gyn, lic. Fla., 1979. Extern Queen Charlotte's Maternity Hosp., London, 1971, Karolinska Inst., Stockholm, 1972, Oxford Univ., England, 1973; intern Johns Hopkins Hosp., Baltimore, 1975—76, resident, 1976—79, fellow Sch. of Medicine, 1975—79; fellow Univ. Miami/Jackson Meml. Hosp., Fla., 1979—80; asst. prof. ob-gyn. dept. Univ. Miami, Fla., 1980—81; hosp. affiliations include Naples Cmty. Hosp., South Miami Hosp., Mt. Sinai Med. Ctr., Cleveland, chief women's and children's svcs. divsn. Miami Beach, 2001—. Contbr. various articles. Exec. med. dir. Women's Cancer Rsch. Found., 2000—. Recipient Guilden award Journalism, Cornell Univ., 1970, First Pl. award Eastman Rice Univ. Debates, 1971, Fgn. Fellowship award for Rsch., Univ. NC, 1972, Clin. Honors. award, 1975; named one of rhe Twelve Good Men, Ronald McDonald House, 1994, the Who's Who in Medicine, Weill Cornell Physicians, 1995, the Best Doctors in America, 1997, the Best Doctors in Miami, 2000, the Top Doctors, South Fla., 2001, the Best Doctors in South Florida, 2002, the America's Top Doctors for Cancer, Castle Connolly, 2006—11. Fellow: ACOG; mem.: ARC (bd. mem. 1995—), William A. Little Ob-Gyn. Soc., Howard A. Kelly Soc., Southern Med. Assn., Soc. of Laparoendoscopic Surgeons, North Caroline Med. Soc., Nat. Vulvodynia Assn., Nat. Assn. of Residents and Interns, Internat. Society for the Study of Vulvar Disease, Internat. Society of Gynecologic Oncologists, Internat. Soc. of Gynecologic Endoscopy, Internat. Soc. for the Advancement of Humanistic Studies in Medicines, Internat. Urogynecological Cancer Soc., Internat. Gynecologic Cancer Soc., Internat. Corr. Soc. of Ob-Gyn., Fla. Physicians Assn., Fla. Med. Assn., Fla. Obstetric and Gynecologic Soc., Fla. Soc. of Gynecologic Oncologists, Fla. Birth-Related Neurol. Injury Compensation Assn., Endometriosis Assn., Durham-Orange County Med. Assn., Dade County Med. Assn. (state delegate 1995—), Collier County Med. Assn., Am. Soc. of Clin. Oncology, Am. Med. Soc., ACP Execs. (pres.), Am. Cancer Soc. (pres., Golden award for Svc. 1974), Am. Assn. of Gynecologic Laparoscopists (state delegate), Coelio-Schauta Club. Office: Mount Sinai Medical Ctr Ste 760 4308 Alton Rd Miami Beach FL 33140 Office Phone: 305-532-1826. Office Fax: 305-661-9635.

POLICINSKI, EUGENE FRANCIS, non-profit organization executive, syndicated columnist, editor, radio and television personality, producer; b. South Bend, Ind., Aug. 31, 1950; s. E.T. and Margaret C. (O'Neill) P.; m. Kathleen Beta O'Donnell Powell, Aug. 19, 1972; children: Ryan, David. Degree in Journalism and Polit. Sci., Ball State U., 1972; student, Nashville Sch. Law, 2005—07. Reporter, Greenfield, Marion, Ind., 1969—76; corr. Gannett News Svcs., Indpls., 1976—79, Gannett News Svc., Washington, 1979-82; Wash. editor USA Today, Arlington, Va., 1982-83, page one editor, 1983-85, mng. editor sports, 1989—96; spl. asst. to chmn./CEO Freedom Forum, Arlington, Va., 1996-98; Wash. editor Freedom Forum website, 1998-99; dep. dir. First Amendment Ctr., Nashville, 1999—2004, exec. dir., 2004—, v.p., 2006—10, sr. v.p., 2010—; pres., COO Diversity Inst., 2013—. Host, commentator USA Today Sky Radio, Arlington, 1992—95; host Newseum Radio, 1998—2001; adj. faculty Winthrop U., 1999—; exec. prodr. Speaking Freely (PBS), 2001—05; host Freedom SIngs, 2003—. Founding editor USA Today Baseball Weekly, 1991. Bd. advisors Ctr. Study Sport in Soc., 1995—2007; trustee US Sports Acad., 1997—2006, Watkins Coll. Art and Design, 2001—04; dir. J-IDEAS program Ball State U., 2003—04; bd. advisor Balt. U., Ky., 2007—. Named one of 100 Most Important People in Sports Sporting News, 1992-93, 95, Sports Person of Yr., U.S. Sports Acad., 1996; named to Journalism Hall of Fame, Ball State U., 1989, Alumni of Yr., 1996. Mem. NATAI (nat. treas. 2004), Am. Soc. Newspaper Editors, Soc. Profl. Journalists, Assn. Educators in Journalism and Mass Comms, Internat. Press Inst., Newspaper Assn. Am. Found. Avocations: sailing, bicycling, golf. Office: First Amendment Ctr Newseum 555 Pennsylvania Ave NW Washington DC 20001 Home Phone: 615-460-9314; Office Phone: 202-292-6290. Business E-Mail: gpolicinski@freedomforum.org.

POLING, DANIEL, state legislator; b. Parkersburg, W.Va., Oct. 3, 1954; m. Cynthia Miller; children: Michelle, Danielle, Brian. Mem. Dist. 10 W.Va. House of Delegates, 2007—, mem. Govt. Orgn. Com., Health and Human Resources Com., Polit. Subdivisions Com. & Sr. Citizen Issues Com. Democrat. Office: State Capitol Complex Rm 223E, Bldg 1 1900 Kanawha Blvd E Charleston WV 25305 Mailing: 1007 Star Ave Parkersburg WV 26101 E-mail: dpoling@mail.wvnet.edu.

POLING, MARY MARTHA, state legislator, secondary school educator; b. Philippi, W.Va., Nov. 23, 1946; d. Boyce L. and Phyllis L. (Channel) Daugherty; m. William F. Poling, Mar. 15, 1969; children: William F. Jr., Edward Len. BS, W.Va. U., 1967, MS, 1975. Cert. math. and English tchr., W.Va. Math. tchr. Barbour County Bd. Edn., Philippi, 1968—2002, chair math. dept., 1975—2002; mem. Dist. 40 W.Va. House of Delegates, 2000—, chair Edn. Com. Vol. leader Barbour County 4-H Equestrian Team, 1980-94; sec. Barbour County Concerned Citizens (WV4-H All Stars), 1985—, life mem.; mem. Barbour County Develop. Authority, W.Va. House of Delegates, 2001-08.; chmn. House Edn. Com., 2007-08. Mem. NEA, Barbour County Edn. Assn., Lions (mem. jr. club). Democrat. Methodist. Avocation: horsemanship. Mailing: RR 1 Box 331 Moatsville WV 26405-9760 Office: Philip Barbour High School RR 2 Philippi WV 26416-9802 also: State Capitol Complex Rm 434M Bldg 1 Charleston WV 25305 Home Phone: 304-457-2206; Office Phone: 304-340-3265. Business E-Mail: marypoli@mail.wvnet.edu.

POLISH, SHELDON S., lawyer; b. Cleve., Feb. 14, 1943; BS in Acctg., Ohio State U., 1965; JD, Cleve. State U., 1969. CPA Fla., 1974; bar: Ohio 1969, Fla. 1974. Dir. tax., office mng. ptnr. Ernst & Young, Ft. Lauderdale, Fla.; shareholder, chmn. Ft. Lauderdale tax dept. Greenberg Traurig, P.A.; shareholder Berger Singerman, Ft. Lauderdale, Fla., 2003—. Grievance com. Fla. Bar, 2008—. Recipient Pres.'s award for Outstanding Svc. to the Jewish Fedn., Cmty. Svc. award, Jewish Cmty. Ctr., Esther Lowenthal Cmty. Svc. award, Jewish Fedn. Young Leadership award; named one of Top 100 Attys., Worth mag., 2005, Top Lawyers in Tax, Estates and Trusts, South Fla. Legal Guide, 2005—07. Mem.: Fla. Inst. CPA, AICPA, Fla. Bar Assn., ABA, Greater Ft. Lauderdale Tax Coun. Office: Berger Singerman 350 E Las Olas Blvd Ste 1000 Fort Lauderdale FL 33301 Office Phone: 954-712-5132. Business E-Mail: spolish@bergersingerman.com.

POLITE, KENNETH ALLEN, JR., federal prosecutor; b. New Orleans, La., 1979; BA in Gov., Harvard Coll., 1997; JD, Georgetown U. Law Ctr., 2000. Law clk. to Hon. Thomas L. Ambro US Ct. Appeals (3rd Cir.), Phila, Pa., 2001—02; assoc. Skadden, Arps, Slate, Meagher, & Flom LLP, NYC, 2002—06; asst. US atty. (southern dist.) NY US Dept. Justice, 2007—10, US atty. (eastern dist.) La., 2013—; shareholder, head white collar crime defense group Liskow & Lewis, New Orleans, 2010—13. Mem.: Nat. Assn. Criminal Defense Lawyers, New Orleans Bar Assn., La. State Bar Assn., NY State Bar Assn., Del. Bar Assn., Nat. Bar Assn., Am. Bar Assn. Office: US Attorney's Office 650 Poydras St Ste 1600 New Orleans LA 70130*

POLK, HIRAM CAREY, JR., surgeon, educator; b. Jackson, Miss., Mar. 23, 1936; s. Hiram Carey and Dorris (Hemby) P.; m. Susan Galandiuk; children: Susan Elizabeth, Hiram Cary. BS, Millsaps Coll., 1956; MD, Harvard U., 1960. Intern Barnes Hosp., St. Louis, 1960-61, resident, 1961-65; instr. in surgery Washington U., St. Louis, 1964-65; asst. prof. surgery U. Miami, Fla., 1965-69, assoc. prof., 1969-71; prof. chmn. dept. surgery U. Louisville, 1971—; pres., chmn. bd. U. Surg. Assocs., PSC, 1971—2005; chmn. bd. Clin. Services Assn., Inc. Mem. merit rev. bd. for surgery VA, 1983—85. Author: (with H.H. Stone) Contemporary Burn Management, 1971, Hospital-Acquired Infections in Surgery, 1977; (with B. Gardner, H.H. Stone and W.L. Sugg) Basic Surgery, 1978; (with H.H. Stone and B. Gardner) 2d edit., 1983, 3d edit., 1987, 4th edit., 1992, 5th edit., 1995; (with D.C. Carter) Trauma, 1982; (with J.E. Conte Jr. and L.S. Jacob) Antibiotic Prophylaxis in Surgery: A Comprehensive Review, 1984; (with J.D. Richardson and L.M. Flint Jr.) Trauma: Clinical Care and Pathophysiology, 1987; contbr. articles to profl. jours.; mem. editl. bd. So. Med. Jour., 1970-72, Jour. Surg. Rsch., 1970-72, 75-77, 78-80, Current Problems in Surgery, 1973—, Surgery, 1975-85, Current Surgery, 1977—, Current Surg. Techniques, 1977—, Emergency Surgery: A Weekly Update, 1977—, Collected Letters in Surgery, 1978—, Brit. Jour. Surgery, 1981-94; chief editor Am. Jour. Surgery, 1986-2004. Fellow Royal Coll. Surgeons Edinburgh (hon.); mem. ACS (gov. 1972-80), AMA, Allen O. Whipple Soc. (exec. coun. 1977-80), Am. Assn. Cancer Edn. (exec. coun. 1968-72), Am. Assn. Surgery of Trauma, Am. Burn Assn., Am. Cancer Soc. (pres. Ky. div. 1989-90, nat. del. dir. 1989-92, 93-95), Am. Surg. Assn. (sec. 1984-89, pres. 2005), Acad. Surgery (pres. 1975-76), Cen. Surg. Assn., Assn. Am. Med. Colls. (chmn. ad hoc com. on Medicare and Medicaid 1978-79), Collegium Internat. Chirurgiae Digestivae (sec.-treas. 1981-86, pres. 1986-87), Coun. on Public Higher Edn. (task group on health scis.), Halsted Soc., Jefferson County Med. Soc., Ky. Med. Assn., Ky. Surg. Soc. (pres. 1982-83), Louisville Surg. Soc. (pres. 1989-90), Residency Rev. Com. for Surgery (vice chmn. 1981-83, chmn. 1983-85), Soc. Internat. de Chirurgie, Soc. Surgery Alimentary Tract (treas. 1975-78, pres. 1985-86), Soc. Clin. Surgery, Soc. Surg. Chairmen, Soc. Surg. Oncology (pres. 1984-85), Soc. Univ. Surgeons (treas. 1971-74, pres. 1979-80), James IV Assn. Surgeons (v.p. 2002—), Southeastern Surg. Congress (exec. coun. for Ky. 1985-86, pres. 1994-95), So. Med. Assn. (vice chmn. sect. on surgery 1969-70, chmn. sect. 1972-73, sec. 1970-72, exec. coun. for Ky. 1971-77, 89-90), So. Surg. Assn. (pres. 1988-89), Alpha Omega Alpha. Home: 5609 River Knoll Dr Louisville KY 40222-5846 Office: U Louisville Dept Surgery Louisville KY 40292-0001 Office Phone: 502-852-1897. Business E-Mail: hcpolk01@gwise.louisville.edu.

POLK, JAMES RAY, journalist; b. Oaktown, Ind., Sept. 12, 1937; s. Raymond S. and Oeta (Fleener) P.; m. Bonnie Becker, Nov. 4, 1962; children: Geoffrey, Amy; m. Cara Bryn Saylor, June 21, 1980; 1 child, Abigail. BA, Ind. U., 1962. With A.P., Indpls., 1962-65, Milw., 1965, Madison, Wis., 1966-67, Washington, 1967-71; investigative reporter Washington Star, 1971-75; correspondent NBC News, Washington, 1975-92; sr. producer CNN Spl. Assignment, 1992—. Pres. Investigative Reporters and Editors, Inc., 1978-80, chmn. bd., 1980-82, nat. coll. chmn., 1983-90. With U.S. Navy, 1955-58. Recipient Pub. Affairs Reporting award, Am. Polit. Sci. Assn., 1961, Raymond Clapper Meml. award, 1972, 1974, Pulitzer prize for nat. reporting on Watergate, 1974, Sigma Delta Chi award, 1974, Nat. Headliner awards, 2d pl. award TV documentary, 1996, 2003, investigative reporting, 1993, Emmy award for coverage of Oklahoma City bombing, 1996, Ind. U. Disting. Alumni award, Journalism award, Nat. Air Disaster Found., 2007, Peabody award, 2007, Dupont-Columbia award, 2008; named to Ind. Journalism Hall of Fame, 1994. Mem. Phi Kappa Psi. Office: CNN Center Atlanta GA 30303

POLK, JOHN A., state legislator; b. Columbia, Miss., Mar. 18, 1949; m. Jan Barnett; children: Brian, Julie Breazeale. B, U. So. Miss., Hattiesburg, 1971. Owner, CEO Polk's Meat Products, 1974—2012; mem. Dist. 44 Miss. State Senate, Jackson, 2012—. Mem. Temple Bapt. Ch., Oak Grove, Miss. Republican. Baptist. Office: Miss State Senate PO Box 1018 Jackson MS 39215 Business E-Mail: jpolk@senate.ms.gov.

POLK, MICHAEL B., consumer products company executive; b. 1960; married. BS in Ops. Rsch. & Indsl. Engring., Cornell U., 1982; MBA in Mktg. & Gen. Mgmt., Harvard Bus. Sch., 1987. Mfg., rsch. & devel. The Procter & Gamble Co., 1982—85; joined Kraft Foods, Inc., 1987, various position brand mgmt. & sakles, 1987—97, v.p. category sales mgmt. & strategy, 1997—98, pres. Asia Pacific Region, 1999—2001, pres. biscuits, snacks, & confections segment, 2001—03; exec. v.p., gen. mgr. Post cereal divsn. Kraft Foods N.Am., 1998—99, group v.p., 2001—03, Kraft Foods Internat., 2000—01; sr. v.p. mktg., pres. Unilever Best Foods N.Am. Unilever, 2003—05; pres. Unilever USA, 2005—07, Unilever Americas, 2007—11; pres., CEO Newell Rubbermaid, 2011—. Bd. dirs. The Yankee Candle Co., Inc., 2003—, Retail Industry Leadership Assn., Grocery Mfrs. America & Food Products Assn., GS1, Yellowstone Nat. Park. Office: Newell Rubbermaid 3 Glenlake Pky Atlanta GA 30328 Office Phone: 770-418-7000.

POLLACK, LYNDA C., clinical geneticist; MD, NYU, 1970. Diplomate Am. Bd. Pediatrics, 1975, lic. Calif., 1976, Fla., 1980, cert. Am. Bd. Clin. Genetics-Med. Genetics, 1982. Intern pediat. Albert Einstein Coll., 1971; resident pediat. Montefiore Med. Ctr., 1971—73; fellow med. genetics Baylor Coll. Medicine, 1977—78; hosp. affiliation includes Orlando Regional Med. Ctr., Fla. Hosp. Office: Florida Hospital Ste D 1814 Lucerne Terrace Orlando FL 32806 Office Phone: 407-648-7802.

POLLARD, C. WILLIAM, former outsourcing company executive; b. Chgo., Ill., June 8, 1938; m. Judy Pollard; 4 children. Grad., Wheaton Coll.; JD, Northwestern U. of Law. Pvt. practice, 1963—72; v.p., faculty mem. Wheaton Coll., Ill., 1972-77; chmn. UnumProvident Corp., 2003—06; chmn., CEO SM Clean LLC, ServiceMaster Clean L; pres. The ServiceMaster Co., Downers Grove, Ill., 1983—90, chmn., CEO, 1999—2002; chmn. emeritus Servicemaster Co., Downers Grove, Ill., 2002—. Bd. dirs. Coro, Inc.; lead dir. Herman Miller, Inc., 1985—2010. Author: The Soul of the Firm, 1996. Bd. adv. Drucker Found. for Nonprofit Mgmt.; chmn. Hosp. Rsch. and Ednl. Trust. Office: The ServiceMaster Co 860 Ridge Lake Blvd Memphis TN 38120 Office Phone: 901-597-1400. Office Fax: 630-663-2001.

POLLARD, OVERTON PRICE, retired lawyer; b. Ashland, Va., Mar. 26, 1933; s. James Madison and Annie Elizabeth (Hutchinson) Pollard; m. Anne Aloysia Meyer, Oct. 1, 1960; children: Mary O., Price, John, Anne, Charles, Andrew, David. AB in Econs., Washington and Lee U., 1954, JD, 1957. Bar: Va. Claims supr. Travelers Ins. Co., Richmond, Va., 1964-67; asst. atty. gen. State of Va., Richmond, 1967, 70-72; spl. asst. Va. Supreme Ct., Richmond, 1968-70; exec. dir. Pub. Defender Commn., Richmond, 1972—2003; ptnr. Pollard & Boice and predecessor firms, Richmond, 1972-87. Bd. govs. Va. Criminal Law Sect., Richmond, 1970—72; pres. Met. Legal Aid, Richmond, 1978; chair sr. lawyers sect. Va. State Bar, 1999—2000. Del. State Dem. Conv., Richmond, 1985; mem. Va. Commn. Family Violence Prevention, 1995; bd. dirs. Henrico County Housing Corp., 1999. With USN, 1957—59. Recipient Svc. award, Criminal Law Bd. of Govs. Pub. Defender Study, 1971, Outstanding Svc. award, Pub. Defender Commn., 1998, Carrico Professionalism award, Va. State Bar Criminal Law Sect., 2005. Fellow: ABA Found., Va. Law Found.; mem.: ABA, Va. Bar Assn. (Pro Bono Publico award 1995, Walker award 2005), Nat. Legal Aid and Defender Assn. (Reginald Heber Smith award 1991), Richmond Bar Assn., Va. Bar Assn. (chmn. criminal law sect. 1991—93). Democrat. Baptist. Avocations: fishing, gardening. Home: 7726 Sweetbriar Rd Richmond VA 23229-6622

POLLEI, DANE F., museum director; b. Fond du Lac, Wis., Oct. 28, 1964; s. Gerald E. and Barbara May (Bassett) P.; m. Lynn Pollei; children: Marley, Chase, Odie BA in Anthrop., Mus. Studies, Beloit Coll., Wis., 1986; cert. in Non-Profit Mgmt., U. Wis., Parkside, 1990; cert. in Archival Adminstr., U. Wis., 1995. Mus. asst. Logan Mus. of Anthrop., Beloit, Wis., 1983-85; asst. to dir. Beloit Coll. Mus., 1985-86; dir., curator Freeport Art Mus., Ill., 1987-89; exec. dir. Kenosha County Hist. Soc., Wis., 1989-97; dir. adminstrn. John Michael Kohler Arts Ctr., Sheboygan, Wis., 1997—2004; dir. Brevard Mus. Art and Sci., Melbourne, Fla., 2004—06; dir., chief curator Mabee-Gerrer Mus. Art, Shawnee, Okla., 2006—. Instr. Highland C.C., Freeport, IL, 1988-89; adv. com. Wis. Fedn. Museums, 1990-92; cons. Font Bank On-Line, Evanston, IL, 1994. Author, editor: W.E.S.T. Word Traveller, 1992-96, co-author: Focus on Louis Thiers: A Photographers View of Kenosha, 1998 Pres. bd. dirs. Kenosha (Wis.) Unified Sch. Dist., 1993-96; mem. Hist. Preservation Commn., Kenosha; founder, pres. H.M.G.G. Festival of Arts and Culture, 1986—. Mem. Am. Assn. Museums. Populist Progressive. Office: Mabee-Gerrer Mus Art 1900 W MacArthur Dr Shawnee OK 74804 Personal E-mail: danepollei@yahoo.com.

POLSBY, DANIEL D., dean, law educator; b. Norwich, Conn., Mar. 14, 1945; BA, Oakland U., 1964; JD magna cum laude, U. Minn., 1971. Bar: Minn. 1971, DC 1972, Ill. 1977, NY 1982. Law clk. to Judge Harold Leventhal U.S. Ct. Appeals (D.C. cir.), 1971-72; assoc. Wilmer, Cutler & Pickering, Washington, 1972-74; legal adviser to commr. FCC, Washington, 1974-76; asst. prof. law Northwestern U., Chgo., 1976-78, assoc. prof., 1978-79, prof., 1979—99, Kirkland & Ellis prof., 1990—99; prof. law George Mason U. Sch. Law, 1999—, assoc. dean, 1999—2004, acting dean, 2004—05, dean, 2005—. Vis. prof. Cornell U., 1981—82, U. Mich., 1982, U. So. Calif., 1990; Chgo. corr. The Economist, 1990—94; legal counsel Beyond the Beltway with Bruce Dumont, 1995—99. Author: The False Promise of Gun Control, 1994. Mem.: ALI, ABA, Order of Coif. Office: George Mason University-Arlington Campus School of Law 3301 Fairfax Dr Room 209 Hazel Hall Arlington VA 22201-4426 Office Phone: 703-993-8087. E-mail: polsby@gmu.edu.*

POLSGROVE, CAROL CLAXON, writer, retired communications educator; b. Louisville, Feb. 19, 1945; d. William Neville and Emma Osborne Claxon; 1 child, Cora. BA, Wake Forest U., Winston-Salem, NC, 1966; MA, U. Louisville, 1969, PhD, 1973. Instr. Maysville CC, Maysville, Ky., 1973—74; asst. prof. Eastern Ky. U., Ky., 1974—77; lectr. San Jose State U., Calif., 1978—80, 1982—83, Calif. State U., Hayward, 1987—89; prof. Ind. U., Bloomington, 1989—2008; ret., 2008. Author: It Wasn't Pretty Folks, But Didn't We Have Fun? Esquire in the Sixties, 1995, Divided Minds: Intellectuals and the Civil Rights Movement, 2001, Ending British Rule in Africa: Writers in a Common Cause, 2009; editor: Mother Jones, 1983—85; assoc. editor: The Progressive, 1980—81, mem. adv. bd.: Reporting Civil Rights, 2003; contbr. articles to Sierra, The Atlantic, The Progressive, Oceans, The American Prospect, The Nation.

POLSTON, RICKY L., state supreme court chief justice; m. Deborah Ehler Polston; four children, six adopted children. BS summa cum laude, Fla. State Univ., 1977, JD with high honors, 1986. CPA 1978; bar: Fla. 1987, US Dist. Ct., No., Middle & So. Fla. Districts, US Tax Ct., US Ct. Appeals 11th Cir., US Ct. Appeals Fed. Cir., US Ct. Fed. Claims, US Supreme Ct. Pub. acctg. practice, 1977—84; private law practice, 1987—2000; judge Fla. Ct. Appeal, 1st Dist., 2001—08; assoc. justice Fla. Supreme Ct., 2008—, chief justice, 2012—. Mem.: Tallahassee Bar Assn., Tallahassee Inn of Ct., Am. Inst. CPAs, Fla. Inst. CPAs, Beta Alpha Psi, Order of the Coif. Office: Fla Supreme Ct 500 S Duval St Tallahassee FL 32399-1925 Office Phone: 850-488-2361.*

POMA, JOHN M., mining company executive, lawyer; BA, MBA, Coll. William and Mary; JD, Emory U. Atty. Jenkins Fenstermaker Krieger Kayes & Farrell, Huntington, W.Va., Midkiff & Hiner, Richmond, Va.; corp. counsel Massey Energy Co., 1996—2000, sr. corp. counsel, 2000—03, v.p., human resources, 2003—09, v.p., chief adminstrv. officer, 2009—. Office: Massey Energy Co 4 N 4th St Richmond VA 23219 Office Phone: 804-788-1800. Office Fax: 804-788-1801. Personal E-mail: john.poma@masseyenergyco.com.

POMERANTZ, MARTIN, chemistry educator, researcher; b. NYC, May 3, 1939; s. Harry and Pauline (Sietz) P.; m. Maxine Miller, June 4, 1961; children: Lee Allan, Wendy Jane, Heidi Lauren. BS, CCNY, 1959; MS, Yale U., 1961, PhD, 1964. NSF postdoctoral fellow U. Wis.-Madison, 1963-64; asst. prof. Case Western Res. U., Cleve., 1964-69; assoc. prof. chemistry Yeshiva U., NYC, 1969-74, prof., 1974-76, chmn. dept., 1971-72, 73-76; prof. chemistry U. Tex.-Arlington, 1976—2011, prof. emeritus, 2011—; co-dir. Ctr. for Advanced Polymer Rsch., 1988-91; dir. Ctr. for Advanced Polymer Rsch., 1991—2011; vis. assoc. prof. U. Wis.-Madison, 1972; vis. prof. Columbia U., NYC, 1970-75, Ben Gurion U. of the Negev, Beer Sheva, Israel, summers 1981, 85; program officer NSF, 2005—07. Expert part time program officer NSF, 2014—. Contbr. articles to sci. jours. Fellow Alfred P. Sloan Found., 1971-76, NSF and Sterling, 1962-63, Leeds and Northrup Found., 1960-62, Woodrow Wilson fellow, 1959-60; grantee NSF, Robert A. Welch Found., Def. Adv. Rsch. Projects Agy., Air Force Office Sci. Rsch., Dept. Energy, Petroleum Rsch. Fund, Tex. Advanced Tech. program, Tex. Advanced Rsch. program, Disting. Record of Rsch. award U. Tex., Arlington, 1997, also others. Mem. Am. Chem. Soc. (Wilfred T. Doherty award Dallas-Fort Worth sect. 1997), Phi Beta Kappa, Sigma Xi. Achievements include research in synthesis, reactions and properties of organo lambda-5-phosphazenes, reactions of carbenes with other molecules, with themselves and with diazo precursors; design, synthesis and study of electronically conducting polymers with enhanced properties, synthesis and study of electroluminescent (light emitting) polymers, synthesis and study of potentially planar bithiophenes and trithiophenes, preparation and study of polymeric ionic self-assembled monolayers (ISAMs), non-linear optical materials. Home: 5521 Williamstown Rd Dallas TX 75230-2127 Office: U Tex Dept Chemistry-Biochemistry PO Box 19065 Arlington TX 76019-0065 Office Phone: 817-272-3811. Business E-Mail: pomerantz@uta.edu.

PONDER, ANNE, academic administrator; b. Asheville, NC, Apr. 26, 1950; d. Herschel Doyle and Mary Eleanor (Israel) Ponder; m. John Christopher Brookhouse, Mar. 3, 1973; children: Stephen Christopher, Nathaniel. AB, U. NC, 1971, MA, 1973, PhD, 1979. Dir. honors Elon Coll., NC, 1977-85; assoc. acad. dean Guilford Coll., Greensboro, NC, 1985-89; acad. dean, prof. Kenyon Coll., Gambier, Ohio, 1989—96, v.p. info. tech.; pres. Colby-Sawyer Coll., New London, NH, 1996—2005; chancellor U. NC, Asheville, 2005—. Mem.: NC Honors Assn. (pres. 1983), Nat. Collegiate Honors Coun. (pres. 1988—89), Order of Valkyries. Episcopalian. Office: U NC - Chancellor's Office Phillips Hall, CPO # 1400 One University Heights Asheville NC 28804-8503 Office Phone: 828-251-6500. Office Fax: 828-251-6495.

PONTI, ERICH E., state legislator; BS in Constrn. Mgmt., U. La., at Monroe. Gen. contractor; mem. Dist. 69 La. House of Reps., 2008—, vice chair labor and indsl. rels. com., mem. commerce com., house and govtl. affairs com. Republican. Office: 7341 Jefferson Hwy Ste J Baton Rouge LA 70806 also: Capitol Office PO Box 44486 Baton Rouge LA 70804 Office Phone: 225-362-5301, 225-342-6945. Office Fax: 225-362-5303. E-mail: pontie@legis.state.la.us.

PONTIUS, DUANE H., JR., physics professor; BS magna cum laude, Birmingham-So. Coll., 1981; PhD in Space Physics and Astronomy, Rice U., 1988. Postdoctoral rsch. assoc. Rice U., 1987—91; rsch. scientist Bartol Rsch. Inst., 1991—99; asst. prof. Birmingham-So. Coll., Ala., 1999—2005, assoc. prof., 2005, now T. Morris Hackney prof. physics. Recipient Richebourg Gaillard McWilliams Faculty Scholarship Award, 2008; named Ala. Prof. of Yr., Carnegie Found. for Advancement of Tchg. and Coun. for Advancement and Support of Edn., 2009. Mem.: Ala. Acad. Sci., Am. Geophysical Union, Am. Astronomical Soc. Divsn. Planetary Scis., Am. Assn. Physics Tchrs., Phi Beta Kappa. Office: Birmingham-Southern College 900 Arkadelphia Rd Birmingham AL 35254 Office Phone: 205-226-4765. Office Fax: 205-226-3078. E-mail: dpontius@bsc.edu.

POOLE, DAVID P., lawyer, oil and gas executives; b. Houston, Mar. 13, 1962; s. Preston L. and Shari J. Poole; children: Aubrey, Reese. BSc in Petroleum Engring., Tex. Tech. U., Lubbock, 1984, JD, 1988. Bar: Tex. 1988, DC 1989, US Dist. Ct. (ND Tex.) 1988. Assoc. Worsham, Forsythe Woodridge, Dallas, 1988—97, ptnr., 1997—2002, mng. ptnr., 2001—02; ptnr., mng. ptnr. Hunton & Williams LLP, Dallas, 2002—04; assoc. gen. counsel, sr. v.p. TXU Corp., Dallas, 2004—06; gen. counsel, exec. v.p. Energy Future Holdings, Dallas, 2006—08; sr. v.p., gen. counsel, sec. Range Resources Corp., Fort Worth, 2008—. Mem. exec. bd. Cir. 10 Coun. Boy Scouts of Am., Dallas, 2003—. Mem.: Dallas Bar Assn. (co- chair CLE Com. 2003—04). Office: Range Resources Corporation Ste 1200 100 Throckmorton St Fort Worth TX 76102

POOLE, EVA DURAINE, librarian; d. Leonard Milton and Polly Mae (Flint) Harris; 1 child, Tommy Lynn Cole, Jr.; m. Earnest Theodore Poole; 1 child, Aleece Remelle Poole. BA in LS, Tex. Woman's U., Denton, MLS; postgrad., U. Houston, 1989. Children's libr. Houston Pub. Libr., 1974-75, 1st asst. libr., 1976-77; children's libr. Ector County Libr., Odessa, Tex., 1977-80; head pub. svcs. Lee Davis Libr. San Jacinto Coll., Pasadena, Tex., 1980-84; libr. dir. San Jacinto Coll. South, Houston, 1984-90; libr. svcs. mgr. Emily Fowler Pub. Libr., Denton, 1990-93, interim dir., 1993; dir. librs. Denton Pub. Librs., 1993—2012. Mem. Libr. Svcs. Constrn. Act Adv. Coun., 1994-97, Libr. Svcs. Tech. Act Adv. Coun., 1997-2000; mem. TEX-SHARE adv. bd. Tex. State Libr. and Archives Commn., 1999-2005, chmn., 2003-2004; bd. dirs. Denton Area Tchrs. Credit Union, 2003-06, Denton Area Tchrs. Credit Union, 2007—12; treas., 2008-, v.p., 2009-, pres. 2010-; mem. adv. bd. U. North Tex. Sch. Libr. and Info. Sci., 2000—12, chair, 2006-07; mem. members coun. Online Computer Libr. Ctr., 2004-07; mem. presdl. search adv. com. U. North Tex., 2005-06; mem. external constituent bd. Tex. Woman's U. Sch. Libr. and Info. Studies, 2005—06. Bd. dirs. Amigos Libr. Svcs., 2000-03, Girl Scouts Cross Timbers Coun., 2002-04, United Way of Denton County, 2002—12, exec. com., bd. pres., 2006-07, life mem. 2010-12, chair Strategic Planning Com., 2010; bd. dirs. Friends of Librs. U.S.A., 2003-2007. Named to Outstanding Young Women of Am., 1991. Mem. ALA (chair Loleta Fyan jury com. 1999-2000, coun.-at-large 2009-) Allied Profl. Assn.(chmn. cert. pub. libr. adminstr. program 2005-06, mem. com. orgn., 2005-06), Pub. Libr. Assn. (mem. budget and fin. com. 1999-2002, chair budget and fin. com. 2001-2002, 2004-05, nat. conf. com. 2002-04, chair bylaws and orgn. 2002-03, mem. instnl. scholarships task force 2006-2007, bd. dirs. 2006-09, bd. dir. 2011-, pres. elect. 2011-2012, pres. 2012-), mem. Instl. Scholarship Award Jury (chair 2008) Libr. Adminstrn. and Mgmt. Assn. (program com. 1994-97, mem.-at-large bd. dirs. 2000-02, chair cultural diversity com. 2000-01, com. on orgn. 2002-05, rep. to Freedom to Read Found. 2002-03, strategic planning com. 2005-06), Tex. Libr. Assn. (pub. libr. divsn. sec. 1995-96, chair 1997-98, leadership devel. com. 1995-97, leadership devel. com. chair 1996-97, alumnae 1st class Tex. Accelerated Libr. Leaders 1994, legis. com. 1997-99, Dist. 7 coun. 1996-99, exec. bd. 1998-2000, 2002-05, ad hoc comn. on pub. lib. stds. com. chair 1998-2000, 2002 conf. local arrangements com. 2001-02, chair 2000 conf. program com. 1998-2000, chair awards com. 2001-02, pres.-elect 2002-03, pres. 2003-04, chair Tocker Found. com. 2006-08, chair nominating com. 2009-10, mem. highsmith com. 2009-), Pub. Libr. Adminstrs. North Tex. (vice chair 1994-95, chair 1995-96), Tex. Mcpl. Libr. Dirs. Assn. (pres. 1995-96, grantee 1993, Libr. of Yr. 1998), Denton Rotary Club (mem. bd. dirs., 2006—10, pres.-elect, 2007-08, pres., 2008-09), Tex. Mcpl. League (bd. dirs. 1997-2000), Greater Denton Arts Coun. (bd. dir., 2008-10), Denton Regional Med. Ctr. (bd. dirs. 2009-, v.p., 2011-12), Denton Friends of Family (bd. dirs. 2009-10), Denton Pub. Sch. Found. Office: Denton Pub Libr 502 Oakland St Denton TX 76201 Office Phone: 940-349-8750. Business E-Mail: eva.poole@cityofdenton.com.

POOLE, RICHARD WILLIAM, economist; b. Oklahoma City, Dec. 4, 1927; s. William Robert and Lois (Spicer) Poole; m. Bertha Lynn Mehr, July 28, 1950; children: Richard William, Laura Lynne, Mark Stephen. BS, U. Okla., 1951, MBA, 1952; postgrad., George Washington U., 1957—58; PhD, Okla. State U., 1960. Rsch. analyst Okla. Gas & Electric Co., Oklahoma City, 1952- 54; mgr. sci. and mfg. devel. dept. Oklahoma City C. of C., 1954—57; mgr. Office of J.E. Webb, Washington, 1957-58; from instr. to prof. econs. Okla. State U., Stillwater, 1960-65, prof. econs., dean Coll. Bus. Adminstrn., 1965-72, v.p., prof. econs., 1972-88, Regents Disting. Svc. prof., prof. econs., 1988-93, emeritus v.p., dean, Regents Disting. Svc. prof./prof. econ., 1993—. Cons. to adminstr. NASA, Washington, 1961—69; adviser subcom. govt. rsch. U.S. Senate, 1966—69; lectr. Intermediate Sch. Banking, Ops. Mgmt. Sch., Okla. Bankers Assn., 1969—88; lectr. internat. off-campus programs Oklahoma City U., 1994—96. Author (with others): The Oklahoma Economy, 1963, County Building Block Data for Regional Analysis, 1965. Mem. Gov.'s Com. Devel. Ark.-Verdigris Waterway, 1970—71, Gov.'s Five-Yr. Econ. Devel. Plan, 1993; past v.p., bd. dirs., past chmn. Mid-Continent R & D Coun., 1966—78. 2d lt. arty. US Army, 1946—48. Recipient Delta Sigma Pi Gold Key award, Coll. Bus. Adminstrn. U. Okla., 1951, Tchg. award on Am. free enterprise sys., Merrick Found., 1992, Disting. Alumni award, Okla. State U., 1995, Henry G. Bennett Disting. Svc. award, 1999; named to Coll. Bus. Adminstrn. Hall of Fame, Okla. State U., 1993, Stillwater Hall of Fame, Payne county Hist. Soc. and Stillwater C. of C., 1996, Okla. Higher Edn. Hall of Fame, 1998; Henry G. Bennett fellow, Sch. Internat. Studies, Okla., 2010. Mem.: Southwestern Bus. Adminstrn. Assn. (past pres.), Nat. Assn. State Univs. and Land Grant Colls. (past chmn. commn. edn. for bus. professions), Am. Assembly Collegiate Schs. Bus. (past bd. dirs.), Southwestern Econ. Assn. (past pres.), Stillwater C. of C. (past bd. dirs., pres.), Santa Fe Trail Assn. (bd. dirs. 2001—02), Okla. C. of C. (past bd. dirs.), Okla. Heritage Assn. (bd. dirs. 2000—05), Omicron Delta Kappa, Phi Eta Sigma, Phi Kappa Phi, Beta Gamma Sigma (past bd. dirs.). Home: 14901 N Pennsylvania Apt 336 Oklahoma City OK 73134

POOLE, SCOTT, architect, educator; b. Jan. 1, 1951; MArch, U. Tex., 1983. Registered arch., Va. Faculty Va. Tech., Blacksburg, 1986—2011; prof. and dir. Sch. Arch. & Design, 2004—11; prof., dean Coll. Architecture and Design U. Tenn., 2011—. Lectr. Yale U., U. Va., Sch. arch., Aarhus, Denmark; Gilmore vis. lectr. U. Calgary, 2000; vis. prof. Royal Danish Acad. Art, Copenhagen, Royal Inst. Tech., Stockholm; bd. dirs. Va. Soc. American Inst. Archs., 2007—10. Recipient Tchg. Excellence award, Va. Tech. Coll. Arch. a, 2002; named one of America's Top 25 Architectural Educators and Administrs., DesignIntelligence, 2012; Fulbright scholar, Finland. Mem.: AIA (Disting. Achievement award 2010). Office: Sch Architecture 1715 Volunteer Blvd Knoxville TN 37996-2400 Business E-Mail: scott.poole@utk.edu.

POOLE, WILLIAM STITT, III, state legislator, lawyer; m. Niccole Poole; children: Sally, Bill. BS in Bus. Mgmt. & English, U. Ala., JD, 2004. Atty., prosecutor, Brookwood, Ala.; mgr. fed. affairs divsn. Pharm. Mfrs. of America; internat. trade analyst Sandler, Travis & Rosenberg, P.A., Washington; staff asst. US House of Ways & Means Com.; pvt. practice atty. Tuscaloosa, 2004—; mem. Dist. 63 Ala. House of Reps., 2011—. Mem. First United Meth. Ch., Tuscaloosa. Republican. Office: 1927 7th St Tuscaloosa AL 35401 also: Ala House of Reps Rm 537-D 11 S Union St Montgomery AL 36130 Office Phone: 205-752-8338, 334-242-7691. Business E-Mail: poole@g-plaw.com.

POPE, ANDREW JACKSON, JR., (JACK POPE), retired judge; b. Abilene, Tex., Apr. 18, 1913; s. Andrew Jackson and Ruth Adella (Taylor) Pope; m. Allene Esther Nichols, June 11, 1938; children: Andrew Jackson III, Walter Allen. BA, Abilene Christian U., Tex., 1934, LLD (hon.), 1980; LLB, U. Tex., 1937; LLD (hon.), Pepperdine U., Malibu, Calif., 1981, St. Mary's U., San Antonio, 1982, Okla. Christian U., Oklahoma City, 1983. Bar: Tex. 1937. Practice law, Corpus Christi, 1937-46; judge 94th Dist. Ct., Corpus Christi, 1946-50; justice Ct. Civil Appeals, San Antonio, 1950-65, Supreme Ct. Tex., Austin, 1965-82, chief justice, 1982-85; ret., 1985. Author: John Berry & His Children, 1988; chmn. bd. editors Appellate Procedures in Texas, 1974; contbr. articles to profl. jours. Pres. Met. YMCA, San Antonio, 1956—57; chmn. Tex. State Law Libr. Bd., 1973—80; trustee Abilene Christian U., 1954—2007. With USNR, 1944—46. Recipient Silver Beaver award, Alamo Coun. Boy Scouts Am., 1961, Disting. Eagle award, 1983, Rosewood Gavel award, 1962, Outstanding Alumnus award, Abilene Christian U., 1965, St. Thomas More award, St. Mary's U., San Antonio, 1982, Greenhill Jud. award, Mcpl. Judges Assn., 1980, citation, Houston Bar Found., 1985, award, San Antonio Bar Found., 1985, Disting. Jurist award, Jefferson County Bar, 1985, Oustanding Alumnus award, U. Tex. Law Alumni Assn., 1988, George Washington Honor medal, Freedom Found., 1988, Disting. Lawyer award, Travis County, 1992, Austin Groups Elderly Vital Aging award, 2007. Fellow: Tex. Bar Found. (Law Rev. award 1979—81); mem.: ABA, Tex. Ctr. for Legal Ethics and Professionalism (Outstanding Svc. award 2007, Jack Pope Professionalism award 2009), State Bar Tex., Tex. Supreme Ct. Hist. Soc. (v.p.), Tex. State Hist. Assn., Am. Judicature Soc., Tex. Philos. Soc., Bexar County Bar Assn., Travis County Bar Assn., Nueces County Bar Assn. (pres. 1946), State Bar Tex. (pres. jud. sect. 1962, Oustanding Fifty Yrs. Lawyer award 1994, Jud. Sect. Lifetime Achievement award 2010), Christian Chronicle Coun. (chmn.), KP (grand chancellor 1946), Masons, Sons Rep. of Tex., Austin Knife and Fork (pres. 1980), Order of Coif, Pi Sigma Alpha, Phi Delta Phi, Alpha Chi. Mem. Ch. Of Christ. Home: 2803 Stratford Dr Austin TX 78746-4626

POPE, C. LARRY, food products executive; BBA, Coll. William & Mary, 1975, EMBA, 1994. Controller Smithfield Foods, Inc., Smithfield, Va., 1980—99, v.p. fin., 1999—2000, CFO, 2000—01, pres., COO, 2001—06, pres., CEO, 2006—. Bd. dirs. Smithfield Foods Inc., 2006—. Bd. mem. Coll. William & Mary Bus. Sch. Found. Office: Smithfield Foods Inc 200 Commerce St Smithfield VA 23430-1204

POPE, CLAUDE E., JR., political organization administrator; m. Melissa Pope. Co-owner Getitquick.com; chmn. Wake County GOP, 2009—10; pres., CEO Maritime Market Ventures LLC, Bald Head Island, NC, 2011—; chmn. NC Rep. Party, Raleigh, 2013—. Republican. Office: North Carolina Republican Party 1506 Hillsborough St Raleigh NC 27605 also: Maritime Market Ventures PO Box 3256 Southport NC 28461 Office Phone: 910-457-7450. E-mail: claude.pope@ncgop.org.

POPE, J. ROGERS, state legislator; MEd, U. Southeastern La. Former supt. Livingston Parish; mem. Dist. 71 La. House of Reps., 2008—, mem. health and welfare com., retirement com., transp., hwys. and pub. works com. Republican. Office: PO Box 555 Denham Springs LA 70727 also: Capitol Office PO Box 44486 Baton Rouge LA 70804 Office Phone: 225-667-3588, 225-342-6945. Office Fax: 225-667-3590. E-mail: poper@legis.state.la.us.

POPE, JOHN EDWIN, editor, columnist; b. Athens, Ga., Apr. 11, 1928; s. Henry Louis and Rose (McAfee) P.; m. Eileen Pope; children: Shirley, Susan, Eddie, David. BA in Journalism, U. Ga., 1948. Sports editor Banner-Herald, Athens, Ga., 1943-48; So. sports editor UPI, Atlanta, 1948-50; sports writer Atlanta Constn., 1950-54; exec. sports editor Atlanta Jour., 1954-56; asst. sports editor Miami (Fla.) Herald, 1956-67, sports editor, 1967—2001, sports columnist, 2001—. Author: Football's Greatest Coaches, 1956, Baseball's Greatest Managers, 1960, Encyclopedia of American Greyhound Racing, 1963, Ted Williams: The Golden Year, 1970, (with Norm Evans) On the Line, 1976, The Edwin Pope Collection, 1988; contbr. articles to popular mags. and Ency. Brittanica, World Book. Recipient Bill Corum Meml. award Thoroughbred Racing Assn., 1962, top sports column award Nat. Headliners Club, 1962, 79, 82, 86, Eclipse award Thoroughbred Racing Assn., 1976, 82, 86, Red Smith award AP Sports Editors, 1989; named to Internat. Churchmen's Sports Hall of Fame, 1976; recipient Knight-Ridder editl. excellence award, 1996, Nat. Sportswriters and Sportscasters Assn. Hall of Fame, 1995, Fla. Sports Hall of Fame, 1996, Bert McGrane award Coll. Football Hall of Fame, 2000, Dick McCann award NFL Pro Football Hall of Fame, 2002, A.J. Liebling award Boxing Writers Assn. Am., 2005; named Orange Bowl Hall of Hon., 2003. Mem. Profl. Football Writers Am. (pres. 1968-69), Football Writers Assn. Am., Golf Writers Am., Nat. Turf Writers, U.S. Tennis Writers. Presbyterian. Office: Miami Herald 235 Harbor Dr Key Biscayne FL 33149 Home Phone: 305-361-9786. Personal E-mail: edwinpope@aol.com. E-mail: epope@herald.com.

POPE, JOHN MARVIN, journalist; b. Hattiesburg, Miss., Nov. 5, 1948; s. Paul M. Jr. and Mary Lee (Scott) P.; m. Diana Pinckley, May 19, 1984. BA cum laude, U. Tex., 1970, MA, 1972. Copy editor The States-Item, New Orleans, 1972-73, reporter, 1973-80, The Times-Picayune, New Orleans, 1980-86, med.-health reporter, 1986—2005, higher edn. reporter, 2005—. Hearst Found. vis. fellow U. Tex., 2005. Co-author: American First Ladies: Their Lives and Their Legacy, 1996. Recipient Med. Writing award, La. State Med. Soc., 1990, 1998, 2005, Frank Allen award, La.-Miss. AP, 1989, Louise McFarland award for excellence in pub. health comm., La. Pub. Health Assn., 2003, Pulitzer prize, Pub. Svc. Breaking News, 2006, George Polk Award, 2006, Nat. Headliner award, 2006; fellow Knight Found., Ctrs. for Disease Control and Prevention, 2001; Knight Ctr. for Specialized Journalism fellow, 1999. Fellow Phi Beta Kappa (senator 2012-); mem. Soc. Profl. Journalists, Investigative Reporters and Editors, Press Club New Orleans (4 1st pl. awards 1978-87, Alex Waller award 1987). Avocations: running, travel, aerobics. Office: NOLA Media Group 365 Canal St Ste 3100 New Orleans LA 70130 Business E-Mail: jpope@timespicayune.com.

POPE, LAWRENCE J., human resources specialist; BA in Economics, U. Tex., Austin, 1990; MBA, Rice U., 2004. Divsn. v.p., human resources, energy svcs. group Halliburton Co., 2001—03, dir., fin. & adminstrn., drilling and formation evaluation divsn., energy svcs. group, 2003—04; sr. v.p., adminstrn. Kellogg Brown & Root, Inc. (former subs. of Halliburton Co.), 2004—06; v.p., human resources & adminstrn. Halliburton Co., 2006—07, exec. v.p., adminstrn., chief human resources officer, 2008—. Office: Halliburton Co 3000 N Sam Houston Pky E Houston TX 77032 Office Phone: 281-871-2699. Business E-Mail: lawrence.pope@halliburton.com.

POPE, ROBERT DEAN, lawyer; b. Memphis, Mar. 10, 1945; s. Ben Duncan and Phyllis (Drenner) P.; m. Elizabeth Dante Cohen, June 26, 1971; 1 child, Justin Nicholas Nathanson. AB, Princeton U., 1967; Diploma in Hist. Studies, Cambridge U., 1971; JD, Yale U., 1972, PhD, 1976. Bar: Va. 1974, D.C. 1980. Assoc. Hunton & Williams, Richmond, Va., 1974-80, ptnr., 1980—. Mem. steering com. Bond Attys. Workshop, 1994—98; lectr. in law U. Va. Law Sch., 2000—02; advisor, com. on govtl. debt and fiscal policy Govt. Fin. Officers Assn., 1993—99; adj. prof. law William & Mary Law Sch., 2004—. Author: Making Good Disclosure: The Role and Responsibilities of State and Local Officials Under the Federal Securities Laws, 2001; co-author (contbg. editor): Disclosure Rules of Counsel in State and Local Government Securities Offerings, 3rd edit., 2009. Mem. adv. com. Va. Sec. of Health and Human Svcs. on Continuing Care Legislation, 1992-94; mem. Anthony Commn. on Pub. Fin.; adv. coun. dept. history Princeton U., 1987-91; mem. Mcpl. Securities Rulemaking Bd., 1996-99, vice chmn. 1998-99. Mem.: Nat. Council Cmty. Justice, Nat. Conf. Cmty. Justice (bd. dirs. Richmond), Yale Law Sch. Assn. (exec. com. 1985—88), Va. Bar Assn. (chmn. legal problems of elderly 1982—88), Am. Coll. Bond Counsel (bd. dir. 2003—, sec. 2004—06, treas. 2006—08, v.p. 2008—10, pres. 2010—), Am. Acad. Hosp. Attys., Nat. Assn. Bond Lawyers (bd. dirs. 1982—89, treas. 1984—85, sec. 1985—86, pres. 1987—88, coordinating coun. 2005—08, Bernard P. Friel medal for contbns. to pub.fin. 1994), Bond Club Va. (bd. dirs. 1990—98, v.p. 1993—94, pres. 1994—95), Phi Beta Kappa. Republican. Episcopalian. Avocations: history, golf, music, book reviews. Office: Hunton & Williams 951 E Byrd Richmond VA 23219-4074 Home: 9704 Old Country Trace Richmond VA 23238 Office Phone: 804-788-8438. Business E-Mail: dpope@hunton.com.

POPE, THOMAS E., state legislator; b. Rock Hill, July 24, 1962; s. James E. and Elizabeth Thomas Pope; m. Kimberly Greenwood, July 22, 1994; children: Kaylen Pope, Preston Pope, Jacob Pope, Logan Pope. BS, U. SC, 1984, JD, 1987. Solicitor 16th Circuit, 1993—2006; atty. Elrod Pope Law Firm; mem. Dist. 47 SC House of Representatives, 2010—. Chmn. SC Common Prosecution Coordination, 2006; bd. governors House of Delegates; chmn. Judicial Qualification Commission; chief vol. officer Boys and Girls Club of York County, 2009; bd. trustee Winthrop U., 2009—10. Recipient Silver Compleat Lawyer award, 1999. Mem.: SC Bar, SC Solicitors Assn. (pres. 2001—03), Order of Palmetto. Republican. Address: PO Box 471 York SC 29745 Office: 420A Blatt Bldg Columbia SC 29201 Home: 1322 Pampas Cir Rock Hill SC 29732-3853 Home Phone: 803-628-1611; Office Phone: 803-324-7574, 803-212-6895.

POPE, WILLIAM L., lawyer, judge; s. William E. and Maria Antonieta P.; m. Sandra Solis, May 16, 1992; children: Ana Lauren, William E.H. AA, Tex. Southmost Coll., 1980; postgrad., U. Tex., 1980-81, Tex. Christian U., 1982, U. North Tex. Health Sci. Ctr., Fort Worth, Tex., 1982; JD, Baylor U., 1986; MD (hon.), Cosmopolitan U. & Rsch. Inst., Vina del Mar, Chile, 1998. Bar: Tex. 1986, US Dist. Ct. (so. dist.) Tex. 1988, US Supreme Ct. 1990, US Tax Ct. 2007. Assoc. Adams & Graham, Harlingen, Tex., 1986-91, ptnr., 1991—; mcpl. ct. judge & state magistrate City of La Feria, Tex., 1987—; presiding judge Mcpl. Ct., Town of Laguna Vista, Tex., 2013—. Bd. trustees Episcopal Day Sch., Brownsville, Tex., 1999—2000. Mem.: Tex. Bar Jour. (bd. editors 2009—), Cameron County Bar Assn., Am. Coll. Legal Medicine, Tex. State Bar Assn. (mem. judiciary rels. com. 1999—2005). Republican. Mem. Ch. Of Christ. Office: Adams & Graham LLP 134 E Van Buren Ave Ste 301 Harlingen TX 78550 Office Phone: 956-428-7495. Business E-Mail: pope@adamsgraham.com.

POPOVIC, TANJA, physician, research scientist; b. Zagreb, Croatia, June 2, 1956; came to U.S., 1989; d. Bosko and Ivana (Poljanac) P.; m. Boris Uroic, Aug. 11, 1979; children: Igor, Iva. MD, U. Zagreb Sch. Medicine, 1979, MS, 1983, PhD, 1986. Resident in clin. microbiology U. Zagreb Hosp. Infectious Disease, 1980-83, clin. microbiologist, 1983-89; asst./assoc. prof. microbiology U. Zagreb Sch. Medicine, 1985-89; Fulbright postdoctoral fellow Ctr. Disease Control and Prevention, Atlanta, 1989-90, mem. Cholera Task Force, 1991-94, chief Diphtheria Lab., prin. investigator Diphtheria rsch., 1995-97, chief Epidemiol. Investigation Lab., 1997, assoc. dir. science, 2004—06, chief sci. officer, 2006—10, dep. assoc. dir. sci., 2010—. Prin. investigator various internat. projects; cons. WHO, 1997, Russian State Com. Sanitary and Epidemiol. Surveillance, 1994, Inst. de Salud Carlos III, Madrid, 1994; organizer and chair 8 nat. and internat. meetings, confs. and workshops; invited lectr. over 20 internat. meetings and confs.; reviewer internat. scientific projects, including Third World Acad. Scis., Trieste, Italy, Wellcome Trust, London; cons. Nat. Immunization Program in diphtheria surveillance studies in U.S.; WHO cons. meningitis in Africa. Contbr. chpts. to books, articles to numerous profl. jours. and conf. procs., including Jour. Infectious Diseases, Jour. Food Microbiology, Jour. Clin. Microbiology, European Jour. Infectious Disease and Clin. Microbiology, others; reviewer Jour. Tropical Medicine and Hygiene, Jour. Clin. Microbiology, Jour. Pediat., Jour. Infectious Diseases. Brit. Coun. scholar, Worcester (Eng.) Royal Infirmary, 1987, 88. Mem. Am. Soc. Microbiology, WHO Diphtheria Working Group, Pasteur Inst. Molecular Subtyping Database Group (Paris). Office: Ctrs Disease Control Prevention 1600 Clifton Rd Atlanta GA 30333

POPOVICH, GREGG, professional basketball coach; b. Chgo., Jan. 28, 1949; m. Erin Popovich; children: Micky, Jill. BA in Soviet Studies, USAF Acad., 1970; MA in Phys. Edn. & Sports Scis., U. Denver. Asst. coach USAF Acad., 1973—79; head coach Pomona-Pitzer Coll., Claremont, Calif., 1979—87; asst. coach San Antonio Spurs, 1988-92, gen. mgr., 1994—2002, exec. v.p. basketball ops., 1994—2008, head coach, 1996—, pres. Spurs basketball, 2008—; asst. coach Golden State Warriors, 1992—94. Asst. USA Men's Sr. Nat. Team, 2002—04. 2nd lt. USAF, 1970—75. Recipient Daily Point of Light award, Pres. George H.W. Bush, 1992, Disting. Grad. award, Air Force Acad., 2008; named NBA Coach of Yr., 2003, 2012, 2014. Achievements include winning NBA Championships as head coach of the San Antonio Spurs, 1999, 2003, 2005, 2007; one of five NBA coaches with four or more championship titles. Office: San Antonio Spurs One AT&T Ctr San Antonio TX 78219*

POPP, BERNARD FERDINAND, bishop emeritus; b. Nada, Tex., Dec. 6, 1917; s. Ferdinand and Anna Staff Popp. Attended, St. John's Sem., San Antonio. Ordained priest Archdiocese of San Antonio, 1943, sec. to archbishop Robert E. Lucey, 1945—68; rector San Fernando Cathedral; ordained bishop, 1983; aux. bishop Archdiocese of San Antonio, 1983—93, aux. bishop emeritus, 1993—. Roman Catholic.

POPPEL, HARVEY LEE, management consultant, investment banker; b. Bklyn., Dec. 18, 1937; s. Frank M. and Fannie (Axenzow) P.; m. Emily A. Daigneault, Jan. 2, 1959; children: Marc F., Clinton S. BS, Rensselaer Poly. Inst., 1958, MS, 1959. Sr. info. systems analyst Westinghouse Electric Corp., Pitts., 1959-65; mgr. industry systems Western Union, Paramus, NJ, 1965-67; from assoc. to mem. operating coun. Booz, Allen & Hamilton, NYC, 1967-84; gen. ptnr. Poptech, LLC, Palm Beach, Fla., 2003—. Bd. dirs. Larscom, Santa Clara, Calif., 1996-02; mng. dir. Broadview Assocs., Ft. Lee, 1984-96; mem. panel, lectr. on computers, comms. and info. industry; judge Entrepreneur of Yr., 1991, 93, 94, 95, 96; investor in start-ups. Co-author: Information Technology: The Trillion-Dollar Opportunity, 1987. Mem. Aspen Inst. Fellows, Inst. Mgmt. Cons., Israel Cancer Assn. (exec. com.), Rep. Jewish Coalition, Palm Beach Civic Assn. (exec. com. 2010-, bd. dirs. 2006—,), Soc. Four Arts, Banyan Golf Club, Marin Country Club, Breakers Ocean Club, Zeta Psi Personal E-mail: hpoppel@msn.com.

POPPELL, JAMES W., SR., human relations executive; JD, U. Mo. Sr. atty. Florida Power & Light Co., 2003—05, dir., employee rels., 2005—06, v.p., human resources, 2006—08, exec. v.p., human resources, 2008—; asst. sec. FPL Group, Inc., 2005, exec. v.p., human resources, 2008—. Office: FPL Group Inc 700 Universe Boulevard North Palm Beach FL 33408 Office Phone: 561-694-4000, 561-694-4999. Personal E-mail: James.Poppell@fpl.com.

PORAYKO, MICHAEL K., internist, educator; s. Peter Porayko and Anne Haley; m. Karen Manoukian, June 13, 1987; children: Chris, Caitlyn. MD, U. Ill., Rockford, 1981. Diplomate Am. Bd. Internal Medicine, cert. Am. Bd. Internal Medicine-Transplant Hepatology, Am. Bd. Internal Medicine-Gastroenterology. Intern Mich. State Univ. Associated Hospitals, 1982, resident, 1984; fellow, hepatobilary medicine Lahey Clinic Med. Ctr. and New England Deaconess Hosp., 1987; fellow Mayo Clinic, Rochester, Minn., 1988; assoc. prof. medicine, med. dir. liver transplantation Vanderbilt U., Nashville, 2002—. Designer exam. for hepatologists Am. Bd. Internal Medicine, Phila., 2004—06. Mem.: ACP (bd. dirs. 2004—06, Rsch.award 1985). Achievements include research in nutrition in Cirrhotic patients. Office Phone: 615-322-0128.

PORIES, WALTER JULIUS, surgeon, educator; b. Munich, Jan. 18, 1930; s. Theodore Francis and Frances (Lowin) P.; m. Muriel Helen Aronson, Aug. 18, 1951; children: Susan E., Mary Jane, Carolyn A., Kathy G.; m. Mary Ann Rose McCarthy, June 4, 1977; children: Mary Lisa, Michael McCarthy. BA, Wesleyan U., Middletown, Conn., 1952; MD with honors, U. Rochester, 1955. Diplomate Am. Bd. Surgery, Am. Bd. Thoracic Surgery. Intern Strong Meml. Hosp., Rochester, NY, 1955—56, resident, 1958—62; chmn. dept. surgery Wright-Patterson AFB, Ohio, 1952—67; asst. prof. surgery and oncology U. Rochester, 1967—69; prof. surgery and assoc. chmn. dept. surgery Case Western Res. U., 1969—77; prof. surgery, biochemistry, exercise and sport medicine East Carolina U., Greenville, NC, 1977—, chmn. dept. surgery, 1977—96, dir. Metabolic Inst., 2005—08; chief surgery Pitt County Meml. Hosp., 1977—96, prof. surgery U. Health Scis. of Uniformed Svcs., 1982—; founder, assoc. dir. Rochester Cancer Ctr., 1967—69; founder, dir. Cleve. Cancer Ctr., 1972—77, Hospice of Cleve., 1975; founder, chmn. bd. Hospice of Greenville, 1981; med. dir. Home Health Care of Greenville, 1978—83; pres. Surg. Rev. Corp., Raleigh, 2003—. Founder, chmn. bd. Ctr. for Creative Living, 1985-91; pres., chmn. Echo Mgmt. Orgn., 1994—; vis. scholar NIH, 1996; sec. treas., pres. N.C. Med. Bd., 1997-2003. Author: Clinical Applications of Zinc Metabolism, 1974; editor: Operative Surgery series, vols. 1-4, 1979-83, Office Surgery for Family Physicians, 1985; editor in chief Current Surgery, 1990-2005; editor Nat. Curriculum for Residency in Surgery, 4th edit., 1988—. Bd. dirs. Boy Scouts Am., Cleve., 1974-77, Greenville Arts Mus., 1980-82; pres. Sequoiah, Inc., 1999—; bd. dirs. East Carolina U. Found., United Meth. Homes, 2003-. Maj. USAF, 1955-67; col. USAR, 1979-91, comdr. USAF Hosp., Durham, N.C.; activated Desert Shield, 1990. Decorated Legion of Merit; Thorndyke scholar, 1948-51; recipient McLester award USAF, 1966, Miss. Magnolia Cross, 1989, Presdl. citation for Desert Shield, 1994; named to Hon. Order of Ky. Cols., 1965. Fellow ACS, Am. Coll. Cardiology, Am. Coll. Chest Physicians; mem. Soc. for Vascular Surgery, Soc. Surg. Oncology, Soc. Univ. Surgeons, Am. Surg. Assn., Soc. Environ. Geochemistry (past pres.), Residency Rev. Com. for Surgery (vice-chair 1992-98), So. Surg. Assn., Soc. for Thoracic Surgery, Ea. Carolina Health Orgn. (pres., chmn. bd. 1994-99), Assn. Programs Dirs. in Surgery (pres. 1995-96), N.C. Surg. Assn. (pres. 1995-96), Am. Soc. Bariatic Surgery (pres. 2002), Sigma Xi (O. Max Gardner prize), Phi Kappa Phi. Home: Deep Sun Farm 7464 NC 43 N Macclesfield NC 27852 Office: East Carolina U Dept Surgery Greenville NC 27858 Office Phone: 252-744-3290. Business E-Mail: pories@ecu.edu.

PORT, P. ALLAN, lawyer; s. Paul Port; m. Peggy Port; children: Paul Hunter, Maggie. Grad., Yale U., 1964; JD, U. Tex., 1967. Law clk. to Judge J.C. Hutcheson Jr. U.S. Circuit Ct. of Appeals; assoc. Baker Botts; ptnr. Childress, Port & Crady; mng. ptnr. Seawell & Riggs (now Gardere Wynne Seawell); exec. v.p. Orillion USA, 2000—02; exec. v.p., gen. counsel Amegy Corp., 2002—. Office: Amegy Corp 4400 Post Oak Pkwy Houston TX 77027-7459 Office Phone: 713-235-8800. Office Fax: 713-439-5949. Business E-Mail: pallan.port@amegybank.com.

PORTACCI, MICHAEL T., healthcare services company executive; CEO Cmty. Health Sys. Inc., 1988—91, group dir., 1991—94, group v.p., 1994—2001, sr. v.p., group ops., 2001—07; pres., divsn. II ops. Community Health Systems, Inc., 2007—. Office: Community Health Systems Inc 4000 Meridian Blvd Franklin TN 37067 Office Phone: 615-465-7000. Office Fax: 615-371-1068. Business E-Mail: michae_.portacci@chs.net.

PORTER, BIGGS C., corporate financial executive; B in Acctg., Duke U.; M in Profl. Acctg., U. Tex., Austin. CPA. Audit prin. Arthur Young & Co.; corp. contr., asst. treas. Vought Aircraft; CFO, integrated sys. sector Northrop Grumman, CFO, comml. aircraft divsn.; sr. v.p., corp. controller TXU Corp.; v.p., corp. controller Raytheon Co., Waltham, Mass., 2003—05, acting CFO, 2005—06; CFO Tenet Healthcare Corp., 2006—. Mem.: AICPA. Office: Tenet Healthcare Corp 13737 Noel Rd Dallas TX 75240 Office Phone: 469-893-2200. Office Fax: 469-893-8600. Business E-Mail: biggs.porter@tenethealth.com.

PORTER, BO (MARQUIS DONNELL PORTER), professional baseball coach; b. Newark, July 5, 1972; Attended, U. Iowa, Iowa City. Outfielder Chgo. Cubs, 1999, Oakland Athletics, Calif., 2000, Tex. Rangers, 2001; hitting coach Class A Greensboro Grasshoppers, South Atlantic League, NC, 2005; mgr. Class A-Advanced Jamestown Jammers, NY-Penn League, NY, 2006; third base coach Fla. Marlins, 2007—09; third base coach, bench coach Ariz. Diamondbacks, 2010; third base coach Washington Nationals, 2011—12; mgr. Houston Astros, 2013—. Office: Houston Astros 501 Crawford St Houston TX 77002*

PORTER, DANIEL J., oil industry executive; B in Chem. Engring., U. Akron, Ohio. Mgmt. positions Std. Oil Ohio, BP/Amoco; regional pres. No. Gt. Plains Region, mgr. Mandan, ND refinery Tesoro Corp., 2001—02, pres. NW region Tesoro Refining and Mktg. Co., 2002—05, mgr. Anacortes refinery, 2002—05, sr. v.p. mktg., 2005—07, sr. v.p. supply & optimization, 2007—08, sr. v.p. refining, 2008—. Office: Tesoro Corp 19100 Ridgewood Pkwy San Antonio TX 78259-1828 Office Phone: 210-283-2000.

PORTER, DUBOSE, political organization administrator, former state legislator; b. Dublin, Ga., Oct. 2, 1953; s. Lester and Katherine D. Porter; m. Carol Dodd, 1983; 4 children. BA in English, Davidson Coll., NC; JD, Samford U. Cumberland Law Sch., Calif., 1979. Former atty., Dublin; co-owner, editor Dublin Courier Herald; mem. Dist. 119 Ga. House of Reps., 1982—92, mem. Dist. 143, 1993—2011, spkr. pro tempore, 1998—2004, minority leader, 2005—11; chmn. Dem. Party of Ga., 2013—. Bd. dirs. Jekyll Island Found. Mem.: Liberty Trustees Assn., Ga. Press Assn. Democrat. Methodist. Office: Democratic Party of Georgia PO Box 20442 Atlanta GA 30325*

PORTER, ELIZABETH, state legislator; b. Lake City, Fla., Nov. 18, 1964; m. Andrew; children: Erin, Drew. AA, Lake City CC, Fla.; BA in Comm., Fla. State U., Tallahassee. Med. billing profl.; cons.; mem. Dist. 11 Fla. House of Representatives, 2008—. Republican. Office: 678 SE Baya Dr Lake City FL 32025-6038 also: Fla House of Reps 1301 The Capitol 402 S Monroe St Tallahassee FL 32399-1300 Office Phone: 386-719-4600, 850-488-9835.

PORTER, GEORGE HOMER, III, physician, medical foundation executive; b. Charlotte, NC, Sept. 7, 1933; s. George Homer Jr. and Sallie Mapp (Jacob) P.; m. Virginia Pillow, Apr. 5, 1958; 1 child, Virginia Mapp (dec.). AB magna cum laude, Duke U., 1954, MD with honors, 1958. Diplomate Am. Bd. Internal Medicine, Am. Bd. Hematology, Am. Bd. Med. Oncology. Intern internal medicine Duke U. Med. Ctr., Durham, NC, 1958-59; asst. resident medicine, instr. medicine Barnes Hosp., Washington U. Sch. Medicine, St. Louis, 1959-60; sr. resident physician The Peter Bent Brigham Hosp., Boston, 1960-61; clin. assoc. medicine, fellow hematology NIH, Bethesda, Md., 1961-64; staff hematologist-oncologist Ochsner Clinic, New Orleans, 1964—; chmn. emeritus, dept. hematology/oncology Ochsner Health Sys., New Orleans; trustee, mem. exec. com. Alton Ochsner Med. Found., New Orleans, 1973—, pres., chief exec. officer, 1980—2001; pres. Ochsner Clinic Found., New Orleans, 2001—. Prin. investigator Southeastern Cancer Study Group, 1973-78; bd. dirs. Eye, Ear, Nose and Throat Hosp., New Orleans, 1986—, Hibernia Corp., Hiberna Nat. Bank, New Orleans, 1980-92. Bd. dirs. Am. Cancer Soc., New Orleans, 1978-89, La. Cancer and Lung Trust Fund, 1980—, Leukemia Soc. Am., 1968-72, The Chamber, New Orleans, 1984-88, Bus. Task Force on Edn., New Orleans, 1985—, Bur. Govtl. Rsch., New Orleans, 1988—, Metrovision Partnership, New Orleans, 1990—. Named Tchr. of Yr., Alton Ochsner Med. Found., 1967. Fellow ACP (life), Internat. Soc. Hematology; mem. AMA, ABA (mem. sect. on med. schs.), AAAS, Internat. Assn. for Study Lung Cancer (founding), Am. Fedn. Clin. Rsch., Am. Hosp. Assn., Am. Assn. Clin. Oncology, Am. Assn. Hematology, Am. Soc. Internal Medicine, Internat. AIDS Soc., La. Med. Soc., Am. Cancer Soc., Orleans Med. Soc. Soc. Surg. Oncology, Am. Coll. Legal Medicine (assoc.-in-medicine, bd. trustees NO/AIDS Task Force, bd. dirs. Acad. Med. Ctr. Consortium), Internat. Soc. for AIDS Edn., Assn. for Health Care Rsch., Mensa, SAR, Royal Soc. St. George, Milton Soc., Confrerie chevaliers du Tastevin, New Orleans Country Club, Boston Club, Century Assn. (N.Y.C.), Pickwick Club, Phi Beta Kappa. Office: Ochsner Clinic Found 1516 Jefferson Hwy New Orleans LA 70121-2429

PORTER, JIM (JAMES W. PORTER II), advocacy group executive, lawyer; b. Birmigham, Ala., Feb. 7, 1949; s. Irvine Craig and Sarah (Sterett) Porter; m. Kathryn Porter. BA, U. Ala., 1971; JD, Samford U. Cumberland Sch. Law, 1974. Law clk. to Chief Judge Virgil Pittman US Dist. Ct. (southern dist.) Ala., 1975—77; spl. asst. atty. gen. State of Ala.; mem. Porter, Porter & Hassinger P.C., Birmingham, Ala. Trustee Ala. Trust Fund, 1998—99. Mem.: ABA, NRA (v.p. 2009—13, pres. 2013—, bd. dirs. 1998—), Internat. Mcpl. Lawyers Assn., Assn. Transp. Practicioners, Birmingham Bar Assn., Ala. Bar Assn., Ala. Mcpl. Lawyers Assn., Phi Delta Phi. Office: NRA 11250 Waples Mill Rd Fairfax VA 22030 also: Porter Porter & Hassinger PC PO Box 128 Birmingham AL 35201 Office Phone: 205-322-1744. E-mail: jwporterii@pphlaw.net.*

PORTER, PHILIP DREW, lawyer; b. Buffalo, Jan. 31, 1947; s. Verne William and Eleanor Marie Porter. BA, Canisius Coll., Buffalo, 1969; MEd, U. SC, 1974, JD, 1982. Bar: DC 1982, Va. 1996. Tchr., guidance counselor, curriculum coord. Barnwell County Schools, SC, 1969-76; coord. sec. curriculum Horry County Schools, Conway, SC, 1976-79; assoc. Shaw Pittman, Washington, 1982-86, Fenwick & West, LLP, Washington, 1986-96; ptnr. Hogan Lovells US LLP (formerly Hogan & Hartson LLP), McLean, Va., 1996—, dir. intellectual property practice group. Faculty Advanced Computer Law Inst., Georgetown U. Law Ctr., Washington, 1990—99; adj. prof. Johns Hopkins U., Balt., 2002—03. Contbr. articles to profl. jours. Mem. DC Computer Law Forum, 1992—96; bd. advisors Internet Multimedia Ctr., George Mason U., Fairfax, Va., 1998—2000. Named one of Legal Elite for Intellectual Property Law, Va. Bus. Mag., 2006, America's Leading Lawyers for Bus., Chambers USA. Mem.: Nat. Assn. Coll. & Univ. Attorneys, Computer Law Assn., DC Bar (chair steering com. 1994—97, Golden Achievement award 1995, 1992). Office: Hogan Lovells US LLP Park Place II Ninth Fl 7930 Jones Branch Dr Mc Lean VA 22102 Office Phone: 703-610-6108. Office Fax: 703-610-6200. Business E-Mail: philip.porter@hoganlovells.com.

PORTER, THOMAS WILLIAM, III, lawyer; b. Dallas, Aug. 23, 1941; s. Thomas William and Ruth Mae (Campbell) P.; m. Sally Ann Shell, May 10, 1963 (div. July 1983); children: Elizabeth Elisse, Laura Christina; m. Patty Ann Sanders, Nov. 2, 1985. BA in Fin., So. Meth. U., Dallas, 1963; LLB, Duke U., Durham, NC, 1966. Bar: Tex. 1966, U.S. Dist. Ct. (no. dist.) Tex. 1967, U.S. Dist. Ct. (so. dist.) Tex. 1975, U.S. Dist. Ct. (we. dist.) Tex. 1977, U.S. Ct. Appeals (5th cir.) 1977. Assoc. Jackson & Walker, Dallas, 1966-72; ptnr. Bracewell & Giuliani, Houston, 1972-74, Foreman & Dyess, Houston, 1974-81; sr. ptnr. Porter Hedges, LLP, Houston, 1981—2009, chmn., 2000—09, chmn. emeritus, 2010—. Bd. dirs. Helix Energy Solutions. Life mem. bd. visitors Duke U. Law Sch.; dir. Hobby Ctr. Performing Arts. Fellow: Tex. Bar Found.; mem.: ABA (fed. regulation of securities com. 1979—2011, com. on law firms 1981—2011), State Bar Tex. (securities and investment banking com. 1976—2005, coun. mem. sect. bus. law 1984—86), Coronado Club, River Oaks Country Club. Republican. Methodist. Office: Porter Hedges LLP 36th Fl 1000 Main St Houston TX 77002-6336 Business E-Mail: bporter@porterhedges.com.

PORTER, WAYNE RANDOLPH, dermatologist; b. Washington, Jan. 10, 1948; s. James Randolph and Betty Rose (Burgess) P. BS, MIT, 1970; MD, Duke U., 1973. Diplomate Am. Bd. Internal Medicine, Am. Bd. Dermatology. Intern U. Miami (Fla.) Affiliated Hosps., 1973-74; resident in internal medicine U. Miami Sch. Medicine, 1973-76, resident in dermatology, 1976-78, clin. instr., then asst. prof. dermatology (vol.), 1978-85, assoc. prof. (vol.), 1985—2005, prof., 2005—. Adj. prof. Barry U. Sch. Grad. Medicine, 2000—; practice medicine specializing in dermatology, North Miami Beach, 1978—; mem. staff U. Miami-Jackson Meml. Hosp. Mem. med. adv. bd. Dade-Broward chpt. Lupus Found. Am. Fellow Internat. Soc. for Dermatologic Surgery, Am. Acad. Dermatology, Am. Assn. Dermatologic Surgeons; mem. AMA, ACP, Internat. Soc. Pediat. Dermatology, Fla. Med. Assn., Fla. Dermatology Soc., Miami Dermatol. Soc. (pres.), Dade County Med. Assn., So. Med. Assn., Bath Club (Miami Beach), Coral Reef Yacht Club. Office: 909 N Miami Beach Blvd Miami FL 33162-3712 Home Phone: 305-285-8983; Office Phone: 305-949-4223. E-mail: wrpmd@bellsouth.net.

PORTERA, MALCOLM, academic administrator; b. Miss. m. Olivia Portera; children: John Paul Portera, Andy Portera. BA, MA, Miss. State U.; PhD in Polit. Sci., U. Ala. V.p. academic affairs and rsch., exec. asst. U. Ala.; pres. Miss. State U., 1998—2001; vice chancellor external affairs U. Ala. Sys., chancellor, CEO, 2002—; interim pres. U. Ala. Birmingham, 2002, U. Ala. Huntsville, 2011. Bd. dirs. Regions Fin. Corp., Furniture Brands Internat., Inc., Ala. Power Co., Protective Life Corp., 2003—. Co-founder Internat. Bus. Adv. Bd.; vice chmn. Ala. Rsch. Alliance; bd. dirs. The Bryant-Jordan Scholar Athlete Found., Operation New Birmingham, The Birmingham Bus. Alliance, PARCA, Ala. Tech. Network, Southern Rsch. Inst.; mem. Found. for Advanced Info. & Rsch., Japan; former chmn. Southeastern Universities Rsch. Assn. Recipient Alabama's Samuel Ullman award, Japan America Soc., Governor's award, Governor, 2003. Mem.: Internat. Bus. Adv. Bd., Japan's Found. for Advanced Info. and Rsch. Office: The University of Alabama System 401 Queen City Ave Tuscaloosa AL 35401-1551 Office Phone: 205-348-5861. Office Fax: 205-348-9788. Business E-Mail: mportera@uasystem.ua.edu.

PORTEUS, MATTHEW H., pediatric hematologist, oncologist; b. Pomona, Calif., Aug. 15, 1964; AB magna cum laude, Harvard U., 1986; MD, PhD, Stanford U. Sch. Medicine, 1994. Diplomate Am. Bd. Pediat., cert. in pediatric hematology-oncology. Pediatric internship Children's Hosp., Boston, 1994—95, pediatric residency, sr. asst. resident, 1995—96; pediatric hematology/oncology fellow Dana Farber Cancer Inst., Boston, 1996—99; postdoc. scholar Calif. Inst. Tech., 1999—2003; asst. prof. pediat. and biochemistry U. Tex. Southwestern Med. Ctr. Contbr. articles to profl. jours. Recipient Burroughs Wellcome Fund Career Devel. award, 2003; grantee Howard Hughes Med. Inst. Postdoc. Rsch. Fellowship for Physicians, 2002. Office: Childrens Med Ctr 1935 Medical District Dr Dallas TX 75235 Office Fax: 214-648-3896, 214-648-3122. E-mail: matthew.porteus@utsouthwestern.edu.

PORTH, ARI ABRAHAM, state legislator; b. Washington, Sept. 25, 1970; m. Tatyana Porth. BS, Northeastern U., Boston, 1991; JD, Nova Southeastern U., Ft. Lauderdale, Fla., 1995. Legis. aide, Senator Bob Graham US Senate, Washington; asst. state atty. Broward County, Fla.; mem. Dist. 96 Fla. House of Reps., Tallahassee, 2004—, Dem. whip, 2004—06, ranking mem. health care regulation policy com., mem. criminal and civil justice appropriations com., health and family svcs. policy coun., policy coun., select com. on stds. of ofcl. conduct. Bd. dirs. Alzheimer's Family Ctr., Nat. Safety Coun., South Fla. Chpt.; bd. mem. Hatikvah House, Nova Southeastern U. Sch. Law Alumni Assn. Mem.: Broward County Bar Assn. Democrat. Jewish. Office: 1300 Coral Springs Dr Coral Springs FL 33071 also: 405 House Office Bldg 402 S Monroe St Tallahassee FL 32399 Office Phone: 954-346-2810, 850-488-2124.

PORTIER, CHRISTOPHER JUDE, public health service officer, research scientist; b. Houma, La., Apr. 3, 1956; life ptnr. Meike Mevissen; children: Katherine Mary, Margaret Claire. BS, Nicholls State U., Thibodaux, LA, 1977; MS, U. NC, Chapel Hill, 1979; PhD, U. NC, 1981. Math. statistician NIEHS, Research Triangle Park, NC, 1978—90, head risk methodology sect., 1990—93, chief lab. computational biology and risk analysis, 1993—2005, prin. investigator, environ. sys. biology, 1993—2010, assoc. dir. risk assessment, 1996—2000, dir. environ. toxicology program, 2000—06, assoc. dir. nat. toxicology program, 2000—06, dir. office risk assessment rsch., 2006—09, assoc. dir., 2006—09, sr. advisor to the dir., 2009—10; dir. Agency Toxic Substances and Disease Registry Dept. Health and Human Services, 2010—; dir. Nat. Ctr. Environ. Health Centers for Disease Control and Prevention, Atlanta, 2010—. Com. chmn. Internat. Agy. for Rsch. Cancer, Lyon, France, 1995—2008, WHO, Geneva, 1995—2008, sci. advisor, 2006—08; mem. EPA FIFRA Sci. Adv. Panel, Washington, 1998—2004; co-chmn. health and environ. sub com. President's Nat. Com. Sci. and Tech., Washington, 2003—05, chmn. toxics and risk sub com., 2005—. Recipient James E. Grizzle Disting. Alumnus award, Dept. BioStatistics, U. NC, 1991, Spiegelman award, Am. Pub. Health Assn., 1995, Disting. Achievement award, Am. Statis. Assn., 1995, Outstanding Risk Practitioner award, Internat. Soc. Risk Analysis, 2000, Best Paper award, Soc. Toxicology, 1995, Risk Assessment Splty. Sect. Paper of Yr., 2005, 2006. Fellow: Internat. Statis. Inst., Am. Statis. Assn., World Innovation Found.; mem.: Russian Nat. Academy Natural Sci. (Foreign Corr. 1992). Office: Centers Disease Control and Prevention 1600 Clifton Rd Atlanta GA 30333

PORTIS, CHARLES MCCOLL, writer; b. El Dorado, Ark., Dec. 28, 1933; s. Samuel Palmer and Alice (Waddell) Portis. BA in Journalism, U. Ark., Fayetteville, 1958. Reporter The Comml. Appeal, Memphis, 1958, Ark. Gazette, Little Rock, 1959-60, NY Herald Tribune, NYC, 1960-64. Author: (novels) Norwood, 1966, True Grit, 1968, The Dog of the South, 1979, Masters of Atlantis, 1985, Gringos, 1991; contbr. numerous works of short fiction to profl. publs. Sgt. USMC, 1952—55, Korea. Presbyterian.

PORTMAN, GLENN ARTHUR, lawyer; b. Cleve., Dec. 26, 1949; s. Alvin B. and Lenore (Marsh) P.; m. Katherine Seaborn, Aug. 3, 1974 (div. 1984); m. Susan Newell, Jan. 3, 1987. BA in History, Case Western Res. U., 1968; JD, So. Meth. U., 1975. Bar: Tex. 1975, U.S. Dist. Ct. (no. dist.) Tex. 1975, U.S. Dist. Ct. (so. dist.) Tex. 1983, U.S. Dist. Ct. (we. and ea. dists.) Tex. 1988, Ct. of Appeals, Fifth Cir., 1998. Assoc. Johnson, Bromberg & Leeds, Dallas, 1975-80, ptnr., 1980-92, Arter, Hadden, Johnson & Bromberg, Dallas, 1992-95, Arter & Hadden LLP, Dallas, 1996—2003, Bennett, Weston, LaJone & Turner, PC, Dallas, 2003—. Chmn. bd. dirs. Physicians Regional Hosp., 1994-96; mem. exec. bd. So. Meth. U. Sch. Law, 1994—; lectr. bankruptcy topics South Tex. Coll. Law, State Bar Tex.; mem. vis. com. Coll. Arts and Scis., Case Western Res. U., 1999-2004, commr., Planning & Zoning City Coppels Tex. Asst. editor-in-chief Southwestern Law Jour., 1974-75; contbr. articles to profl. jours. Firm rep. United Way Met. Dallas, 1982-92; treas. Lake Highlands Square Homeowners Assn., 1990-93. Mem. ABA, Am. Bankruptcy Inst., State Bar Tex., Dallas Bar Assn., Turnaround Mgmt. Assn., So. Meth. U. Law Alumni Assn. (coun. bd. dirs., v.p. 1980-86, chmn. admissions com., chmn. class agt. program 1986-89, chmn. fund raising 1989-91), 500 Club Inc., Assemblage Club. Republican. Methodist. Home: 1306 Bradford Dr Coppell TX 75019 Office: 1603 LBJ Freeway Ste 280 Dallas TX 75234 Office Phone: 214-691-1776 ext. 207. Office Fax: 214-393-4007. Personal E-mail: glennportman@tx.rr.com. Business E-Mail: gportman@bennettweston.com.

POSEY, BILL (WILLIAM JOSEPH POSEY), United States Representative from Florida; b. Washington, Dec. 18, 1947; s. Walter J. and Beatrice (Tohl) P.; m. Mary Ingram, Nov. 23, 1987; children: Pamela J., Catherine L. AA, Brevard Community Coll., 1969; student, Stetson U., 1978. Quality assurance rep. McDonnell-Douglas, Cape Kennedy, Fla., 1966-69; pres., CEO Mid Fla. Racing Inc., Melbourne, 1969-71; mgr. Gay & Taylor Inc., St. Petersburg, Fla., 1971-74; broker Sherwood Realty Inc., Cocoa, Fla., 1974-78; pres., CEO Posey & Co., Rockledge, Fla., 1978—; mem. Dist. 32 Fla. House of Reps., Tallahassee, 1992-2000; mem. Dist. 15 Fla. State Senate, Tallahassee, 2001—03, mem. Dist. 24, 2003—09; mem. US Congress from 15th Fla. Dist., Washington, 2009—13, US Congress from 8th Fla. Dist., 2013—. Bd. dirs. Rockledge Land Co., Indian Oaks Corp., Rockledge, Rockledge Realty Corp., Nat. Racetrack Clearing House, Rockledge; founder Fla. Motorsports Hall Fame, 1986. Author: Race Track Promotters Handbook, 1971. Mem. Rockledge Planning Commn., 1974-76, Rockledge City Coun., 1976-86, Rockledge Econ. Devel. Commn., 1985—, Bus. and Indsl. Task Force, 1985—. Mem. Fla. Assn. Realtors (bd. dirs. 1986—), Cape Kennedy Area Bd. Realtors (pres. 1987—), Cocoa Beach C. of C. (com. 100 1974—). Clubs: Country Brevard. Lodges: Kiwanis, Masons. Republican. Methodist. Office: US House of Representatives 120 Cannon House Office Bldg Washington DC 20515 also: 2725 Judge Fran Jamieson Way Bldg C Melbourne FL 32940 Office Phone: 202-225-3671, 321-632-1776. Office Fax: 202-225-3516, 321-639-8595.*

POSEY, CLYDE LEE, business administration and accounting educator; b. Tucumcari, N.Mex., Dec. 27, 1940; s. Rollah P. and Opal (Patterson) P.; m. Dora Diane Vassar; children: Amanda Bennett, Julia Forsyth, Rebecca Posey; m. Judith James Jerry, July 31, 1991; stepchildren: David Jerry, Georgia Kenyan. BBA, U. Tex., El Paso, 1963; MBA, U. Tex., 1965; postgrad., U. So. Calif., 1968; PhD, Okla. State U., 1978. Registered investment advisor. Ret. lab. aide FBI, Washington, 1959-60; acct. Lipson, Cox & Colton (now Deloitte & Touche), El Paso, Tex., 1962; auditor Main & Co. (now KPMG), El Paso, 1963; tchg. asst. U. Tex., Austin, 1963-65; tax cons. Peat, Marwick, Mitchell & Co. (now KPMG), Dallas, 1965-66; cons. Roberson, Martin, Horg and Ryckman, Fresno, Calif., 1967; pvt. practice acctg. Fresno, 1966—78, Ruston, La., 1978—2012; asst. prof. Calif. State U., Fresno, Ruston, La., 1966—78; assoc. prof. La. Tech. U., Ruston, 1978-84, prof., 1984—2005; prof. MBA program Alcorn State U., Natchez, 2005—. Vis. asst. prof. U. Ctrl. Okla., Edmond, Okla., 1971-72, U. Okla., Norman, 1976-78; cons. J. David Spence Accountancy Corp., Fresno, 1974-76; many coms. at La. Tech. U. including acad. senator, new faculty welcoming com., acctg. scholarship chmn.; faculty senate rep.; Faculty Consortium, St. Charles, Ill., 1993; expert witness Superior Ct. Calif. and Dist. Ct., La. Author: Biblical Principles of Finance: The Cure for Financial Depression, Now That You Are Christian: What's Next? Practical Follow-Up For the New Christian; contbr. numerous articles to profl. jours., bus. mags., newspapers, also book reviews; presentations to profl. meetings. Past bd. dirs. Goodwill, Inc., Ctrl. Calif.; ch. deacon and mem. many coms.; pres., treas., state scripture coord. Gideons Internat. Ruston Camp; rep. United Way La. Tech. U., Ruston; deacon 1st Bapt. Ch., Ruston. Hon. discharge res. USCG, 1965. Recipient El Paso CPA's Outstanding Jr. scholarship, Standard Oil scholarship, Price Waterhouse scholarship, Outstanding Educator award Gamma Beta Phi, 1986. Mem. AICPA (life), Am. Acctg. Assn. (La. membership com. chmn.), Am. Inst. for Decision Scis. (program com. chmn. acctg. track), La. Soc. CPAs, Am. Tax Assn. (internat. tax policy subcom.), Beta Gamma Sigma (pres.), Beta Alpha Psi, Delta Sigma Pi. Baptist. Avocations: golf, tennis, gardening, bicycling. Home: 2700 Foxxwood Dr Ruston LA 71270-2509 Office: 9 Campus Dr Natchez MS 39120 Office Phone: 601-304-4367.

POST, GLEN FLEMING, III, telecommunications industry executive; b. El Dorado, Ark., Oct. 4, 1952; s. Glen F. Jr. and Mary L. (Tubberville) P.; children: Brad, Luke, Matt. BS in Acctg., La. Tech. U., 1974, MBA, 1976. Pvt. practice tax acctg., 1974-76; Joined CenturyTel, Inc., Monroe, La., 1976; v.p. CenturyTel Inc., Monroe, La., 1982—84, sr. v.p., treas., 1984-86, sr. v.p., CFO, 1986—88, exec. v.p. & COO, 1988—90, pres. & COO, 1990—92, vice chmn., pres., CEO, 1992—2003, chmn., CEO, 2003—09; pres., CEO CenturyLink, Inc. (formerly CenturyTel, Inc.), 2009—. Bd. dir. Yelcot Telephone Co., No. La. Regions Bank. Mem. exec. cabinet Coll. Adminstrn. & Bus., La. Tech. Univ.; bd. dir. La. Tech. Univ. Found., La. Tech. Univ. Rsch. Found. Recipient Tower Medallion award, La. Tech. Univ., 1997, Lifetime Achievement award in bus., DeGree Enterprises, 2003. Mem. Am. Mgmt. Assn., STICC (subcom. acctg.), Beta Alpha Psi. Office: CenturyLink Inc 100 CenturyLink Dr Monroe LA 71203

POST, LESLEE MILAM, state legislator; m. Andrew Post; 4 children. Grad., U. of Ozarks, Clarksville, Ark. Mem. Dist. 83 Ark. House of Representatives, 2011—. Democrat. Roman Catholic. Office: PO Box 1212 Ozark AR 72949 Office Phone: 479-518-0331. Business E-Mail: leslee.post@arkansashouse.org.

POSTOLOS, GEORGE, professional sports team executive; m. Nicole Postolos; 2 children. Clk. Tex. Supreme Ct., 1990—91; atty. Watchtell, Lipton, Rosen & Katz, NYC, 1991—96; spl. asst. to the commr. NBA, 1997—98; COO Houston Rockets, Houston, 1998—2002, pres., CEO, 2002—06; owner, pres., CEO The Postolos Group LP, Houston, 2006—; pres., CEO Houston Astros, 2011—. Office: The Postolos Group LP 4409 Montross Ste 200 Houston TX 77006 also: Houston Astros 501 Crawford St Houston TX 77002

POSTON, ANITA OWINGS, lawyer; b. Sylacauga, Ala., Sept. 24, 1949; d. John T. and Margaret Owings; m. Charles E. Poston, June 9, 1973; children: Charles Evans Jr., John W., Margaret Elizabeth. BA, U. Md., 1971; JD, Coll. William & Mary, 1974. Bar: Va. 1974. Atty. Vandeventer Black LLP, Norfolk, Va., 1974—. Substitute judge Norfolk (Va.) Gen. Dist. Cts., 1982-90; mem. Bar Examiners Bd.; mem. bd. visitors Coll. William and Mary. Mem. State Bd. C.C.s, Richmond, 1985-90, chmn. 1988-89; mem. Norfolk Sch. Bd., 1990-2002, chmn. 1998-2002; bd. dirs. WHRO Pub. Broadcasting, chair, 2002-04; bd. dirs. Access Coll. Found., Va. Symphony Orch., Towne Bank, Norfolk. Mem. ABA (law fellows), Va. Bar Assn. (pres. 2000), Norfolk-Portsmouth Bar Assn. (pres. 1998-99), Va. Law Fellows, Am. Inn of Ct. Office: Vandeventer Black LLP 500 World Trade Ctr Norfolk VA 23510-1679 Office Phone: 757-446-8600. Office Fax: 757-446-8670. Business E-Mail: aposton@vanblk.com.

POSTON, REBEKAH JANE, lawyer; b. Wabash, Ind., Apr. 20, 1948; d. Bob and April (Ogle) Poston. BS magna cum laude, U. Miami, Fla., 1970; JD, U. Miami Sch. Law, 1974. Bar: Fla. 1974, US Dist. Ct. (so. and mid. dists.) Fla., US Ct. Appeals (11th cir.). Asst. US atty. (so. dist.) Fla. US Dept. Justice, Miami, 1974—76, spl. atty. organized crime and racketeering sect. Cleve., 1976—78; ptnr. Fine, Jacobson, Schwartz, Nash & Block, Miami, 1978—94, Steel Hector & Davis, Miami, 1994—2006, Squire, Sanders & Dempsey LLP, Miami, 2006—. Adj. prof. U. Miami Law Sch. Contbr. articles to profl. jours. Named one of Florida's Legal Elite, Fla. Trend mag., 2004—11, Leading Lawyers in Field, South Fla. Legal Guide, 2007—08, Eight Women Lawyers Who've Excelled in their Legal Careers, 2008. Fellow: American Bar Found.; mem.: Dade County Bar Assn., American Immigration Lawyers Assn., Nat. Assn. Criminal Def. Attorneys, Fla. Bar Assn. Democrat. Lutheran. Avocations: power boat racing, swimming. Office: Squire Sanders & Dempsey LLP 200 S Biscayne Blvd Miami FL 33131 Office Phone: 305-577-7022. Business E-Mail: rebekah.poston@ssd.com.

POTAMKIN, ALAN, automotive company executive; CEO, chmn. Potamkin Devel. Co. LLC, NYC; co-chmn. Planet Auto Group, Inc. (formerly Potamkin Auto Group), Coral Gables, Fla. Office: Potamkin Devel Co LLC 798 Eleventh Ave New York NY 10019

POTESHMAN, MICHAEL S., consumer products company executive; b. Ill. married; 2 children. B in Acctg., U. Ill., Urbana, 1985; MBA in Fin. and Bus. Economics, U. Chgo., 1997. CPA 1985. Audit mgr. PricewaterhouseCoopers, 1985—93; various positions including asst. contr., v.p. & contr. and treas. Tupperware Brands Corp. (formerly Premark Internat., Inc.), 1993—2000; v.p. fin. and investor rels Tupperware Brands Corp., 2001—02, v.p., CFO Europe, Africa and Mid. East Nyon, Switzerland, 2002—03, sr. v.p., CFO, 2003—04, exec. v.p., CFO, 2004—. Former bd. mem. Jewish Cmty. Ctr. Greater Orlando; bd. dirs. Metro Orlando Econ. Devel. Commn. Office: Tupperware Brands Corp 14901 S Orange Blossom Trail Orlando FL 32837 Office Phone: 407-826-5050.

POTLURI, VENKATESWARA RAO, medical facility administrator; b. Krishna Dist., India, Jan. 1, 1955; came to U.S., 1983; s. Venkata Krishnaiah and Bulli Ademma (Koduru) P.; m. Padma Sree Peddu, Dec. 4, 1986; children: Vani, Vamsee Krishna, Varun. BSc, ANR Coll., Gudivada, India, 1975; MSc, AU Coll. Sci. and Tech., Waltair, India, 1977; MPhil, Delhi U., India, 1979, PhD, 1982. Diplomate Am. Bd. Med. Genetics, 1984. Postdoctoral fellow Mt. Sinai Med. Ctr., NYC, 1983-85, vis. asst. prof., 1985-87; lab. dir., adj. mem. med. staff Norwalk (Conn.) Hosp., 1987-98; lab. dir. Lab. Diagnostics (divsn. Cytogenetics), Norwalk, 1998—2001; lab dir. Ctr. for Genetic Svcs. Inc. (divsn. Lab. Corp. of Am.), Corpus Christi, Tex., 2001—03, Dynagene divsn. Lab. Corp. Am., Houston, 2003—. Fellow: Am. Coll. Med. Genetics (founding); mem.: Am. Soc. Human Genetics. Avocations: classical music, Telugu literature, home improvement. Home: 4018 Blue Bonnet Blvd Apt D Houston TX 77025 Office: Dynagene 3701 Kirby Dr Ste 528 Houston TX 77098-3942

POTTASH, A. CARTER, psychiatrist, hospital executive; b. Phila., Nov. 30, 1948; s. R. Robert and Elizabeth (Braunschweig) P. BS with high honors, Trinity Coll., Hartford, Conn., 1970; MD, Yale U., 1974. Intern Tufts U. Sch. Medicine, Springfield, Mass., 1974-75; clin. fellow Yale-New Haven Hosp., 1977-78; fellow Yale U., New Haven, 1975-78; med. dir. Psychiatric Diagnostic Labs. Am., Summit, NJ, 1979-83. Lectr., cons. in field; vis. prof. St. Elizabeth Med. Ctr., Northeastern Ohio U. Coll Medicine, 1979; clin. prof. NYU, 1989—; pres. Fla. Consultation Svcs., P.A., West Palm Beach, 1992—, Psychiatric Assocs. N.J., P.A., Summit, N.J., 1978-93, Met. Med. Group P.C., N.Y.C., 1981-92, So. Fla. Med. Group P.A., Delray Beach, 1984-93, Stony Lodge Hosp., Inc. and Stony Lodge Med. Group P.C., Briarcliff Manor, N.Y., 1985—, Hampton Med. Group, P.A., Rancocas and Summit, N.J., 1986-95; exec. med. dir. Fair Oaks Hosp., Summit, 1978-92, The Regent Hosp., N.Y.C., 1981-92, Lake Hosp of the Palm Beaches, Lake Worth, Fla., 1984-92, Fair Oaks Hosp. at Boca/Delray, Fla., 1984-92, Hampton Hosp., Rancocas, N.J., 1986-95—; chmn. Stony Lodge Hosp., Briarcliff Manor, N.Y., 1985—. Editor Psychiatry Letter, 1980-91; mem. editl. bd. Internat. Jour. Psychiatry in Medicine, 1978-87, The Psychiatric Hosp., 1982—, Jour. Nat. Assn. Pvt. Psychiatric Hosps., 1980-81, Fla. Psychiatry Newsletter, 1992—; reviewer Jour. Nervous and Mental Disorders, Alcoholism, Clin. and Exptl. Rsch., JAMA, Hosp. and Cmty. Psychiatry; contbr. articles to profl. jours. Mem. adv. bd. Mothers for More Halfway Houses, N.Y.C., 1986—; cons. com. on women and alcoholism Jr. League of N.Y.C., 1987; bd. dirs. Met. Soc. Arts, N.Y.C., 1984-87, South Fla. Sci. Mus. Fellow Am. Coll. Clin. Pharmacology, Assn. Clin. Scientists, Nat. Acad. Clin. Biochemistry, Am. Psychiat. Assn. (disting. life fellow), The Acad. Medicine N.J.; mem. AMA, Soc. Neurosci., Nat. Acad. Clin. Biochemistry, Palm Beach County Med. Soc., Am. Acad. Clin. Psychiatrists, Brit. Brain Rsch. Assn. (hon.), European Brain and Behavioral Soc. (hon.), Am. Soc. Addiction Medicine, Am. Academy of Addiction Psychiatry (founding mem. 1987), Fla. Med. Soc., Palm Beach County Psychiat. Soc., Med. Soc. State N.Y., Med. Soc. N.J., Union County Med. Soc., N.Y. Athletic Club, Canoe Brook Country Club, Beacon Hill Club, Phi Beta Kappa, Delta Phi Alpha. Office: PO Box 381 Palm Beach FL 33480-0381 Office Phone: 561-837-2215.

POTTER, PAUL EUGENE, communications educator, consultant; b. Long Beach, Calif., May 14, 1938; s. Paul and Mae Eugenia Potter; m. Tanya Gregory, Dec. 21, 1974; children: Anthony Eugene, Mark Andrew, Jonathan Criswell. AA, El Centro Coll., Dallas County CC Dist., 1968; BFA in Broadcasting and Film with honors, Southern Meth. U., Dallas, 1969, MFA in Broadcasting and Film, 1970, postgrad., 1971, Dallas Bapt. U., 1972—73; PhD in Edn. and Speech-Drama, U. North Tex., Denton, 1978. Cert. in drama & voice tng. 20th Century Fox Studios, New Talent Dept., Beverly Hills, Calif., in electronics & broadcast fundamentals Elkins Inst. Radio, Dallas, honor guard, officer records specialist US Air Force, Pers. Specialist Sch., Scott AFB, Ill., 12th Air Force Hdqs., Waco, Tex. News reporter, announcer KBOX-AM and FM, Dallas, 1966—69; postdoc. fellow U. North Tex., Coll. Edn., Denton, 1992—93; assoc. prof., TV dir. Xavier U., Cin., 1980—82; assoc. prof., asst. dir., exec. prodr. OU TV news U. Okla., Norman, 1982—85; v.p. 1st Am. Nat. Securities & Mass. Indemnity & Life Ins. Co., 1984—90; prof., journalism & mass communication dept. head Angelo State U., San Angelo, Tex., 1990—92; dir., adminstrn. & ops. Bingle Camp Ministries, Inc., Harding Lake, Alaska, 1994—95; adminstr. Door of Hope Ch., Fairbanks, Alaska, 1995—97; exec. dir. Joseph Inst.,

Maryville, Tenn., 1997—98; James Pedas prof. comm. endowed chair Thiel Coll., Greenville, Pa., 1998—2000; head, dept. comm. Hardin-Simmons U., Abilene, Tex., 2000—02, prof., dept. communication, 2000—. Exec. prodr. QUBE programming Warner Amex Cable TV, Cin., 1980; exec. dir. Joseph Inst., Maryville, Tenn., 1997—98; cons. Pub. Speaking Made Easy, Abilene, Tex., 2004—; guest spkr. Tex. Assn. Conv. and Visitors Bur., Abilene, 2006; mem. edtl. adv. bd. Pearson Allyn & Bacon; mem. bd. dirs. S.S. Golf Group, Inc. Prodr., interviewer (radio program) Top of the Mountain, WMEN Radio, prodr., editor, interviewer (syndicated radio program) Faith in Action, NBC, actor, on-screen narrator (TV Christmas spl.) The Messiah, ABC; exec. prodr.: (films) Step Back in Time, Those Who Serve; prodr.: (films) Vanishing Breed; prodr.: (dir.) Dream of The Rode. Ministry team mem., united christian fellowship Phila. Freedom, Philadelphia, Pa., 1996; adminstr. Door of Hope Ch., Fairbanks, Alaska; dir. adminstrn. and ops. Bingle Camp Ministries, Inc. Yukon Presbytery, Harding Lake, Alaska. A2c USAF, 1956—60, Waco, Tex. Tchg. fellow, U. N.Tex., 1970—71. Mem.: Tex. Blackboard Users Group, Univ. Film and Video Assn., Broadcast Edn. Assn., Nat. Press Photographers Assn., SW Edn. Coun. Journalism and Mass Comm., Speech Communication Assn., World Affairs Coun. (Dallas, Ft. Worth) (ednl. mem.), Sigma Delta Chi, Phi Delta Kappa. Avocations: reading, travel, art, coin collecting/numismatics. Office: Hardin-Simmons Univ HSU Box 16146 Abilene TX 79698 Business E-Mail: ppotter@hsutx.edu.

POTTER, ROBERT JOSEPH, technical and business executive; b. NYC, Oct. 29, 1932; s Mack and Ida (Bernstein) P.; married; children: Diane Gail, Suzanne Lee, David Craig. BS cum laude, Lafayette Coll., 1954; MA in Physics, U. Rochester, 1957, PhD in Optics, 1960. Cons. ANPA Rsch. Inst., AEC Brookhaven Nat. Lab., RCA Labs., US Naval Rsch. Labs., 1952-60; mgr. optical physics and optical pattern recognition IBM Thomas J. Watson Research Center, Yorktown Heights, NY, 1960-65; assoc. dir. Applied Rsch. Lab., Xerox Corp., Rochester, NY, 1965-67; v.p. advanced engring. Xerox Corp., 1967-68, v.p. devel. and engring., 1968-69, v.p., gen. mgr. Spl. Products and Systems divsn. Stamford, Conn., Pasadena, Calif., 1969-71, v.p. info. tech. group Rochester, 1971-73, Dallas, 1973-75, pres. Office Sys. divsn., 1975-78; sr. v.p., chief tech. officer Internat. Harvester Co., Chgo., 1978-82; group v.p. integrated office sys. Nortel Networks, Richardson, Tex., 1984—87; pres., CEO Datapoint Corp., San Antonio, 1987—90, R.J. Potter Co., Dallas, 1990—. Bd. govs., vice chmn. IIT Rsch. Inst., 1999—2002; chmn. Tatum CIO Ptnrs., LLP, 2000—02; adv. dir. Am. Nat. Bank, 2002—05; mem. rsch. adv. bd. U. Tex., Dallas, 2003—07; bd. dirs. Zebra Techs., Cree, Inc., Molex Inc., 1981—, Bradshaw Group, Speed FC. Contbr. articles to profl. jours. Life trustee Ill. Inst. Tech. Recipient IBM Outstanding Tech. Contbn. award, 1964, Disting. Achievement award Soc. Mfg. Engrs., 1981; Kroner scholar Lafayette Coll., 1954; Disting. Rochester scholar U. Rochester, 1995. Fellow Optical Soc. Am., Am. Phys. Soc.; mem. Phi Beta Kappa, Sigma Xi. Office: R J Potter Co 5215 N O Connor Blvd Ste 360 Irving TX 75039-3739 Office Phone: 972-869-8270. Office Fax: 972-869-6593. Business E-Mail: RJPotter@RJPotter.com.

POTTER, WILLIAM GRAY, JR., university librarian; b. Duluth, Minn., Feb. 18, 1950; s. William Gray and Kathryn Martha (Scheuer) P.; m. Marsha Ann Munie, Sept. 23, 1982. BA in English, So. Ill. U., Edwardsville, 1973; MLS, U. Ill., Urbana-Champaign, 1975; MA in English, U. Ill., 1976, PhD in Libr. and Info. Sci., 1984. Libr. U. Wis.-Whitewater, 1975-78; asst. dir. gen. svcs. U. Ill.-Urbana, 1978-85; assoc. dean librs. Ariz. State U., Tempe, 1985-89; univ. libr., assoc. provost U. Ga., Athens, 1989—. Editor: Serials Automation, 1980, Libr. Trends, 1981, Info. Tech. and Librs., 1984-89; Coll. and Rsch. Libr., 2002-08. Contbr. articles to profl. jours. Bd. dirs. Richard B. Russell Found., 1989— (sec., 1990—), ARL, 1996-99, SOLINET, 2001-03; trustee OCLC, 1994-2000. Recipient Hugh Atkinson Meml. award, 1997; Nix-Jones Outstanding Libr. Ga., 1998; LITA/Gaylord Award 2000; named Disting. Alumnus of Yr. So. Ill. U., Edwardsville, 2001. Office: U Ga Librs U Ga Athens GA 30602-1641 Office Phone: 706-542-0621. Office Fax: 706-542-4144. Business E-Mail: wpotter@uga.edu.

POTTLE, STEVEN L., lawyer; b. Anchorage, Nov. 3, 1960; Student, Univ. of London, Japanese Bus. and Soc. Program, Tokyo; BBA, Univ. Wash., 1983; JD, Vanderbilt Univ., 1987. CPA; bar: Ga. 1987. Acct. Ernst & Whinney; ptnr., chmn., corp. health care group Alston & Bird LLP, Atlanta. Office: Alston & Bird LLP One Atlantic Ctr 1201 W Peachtree St NW Atlanta GA 30309-3424 Office Phone: 404-881-7554. Office Fax: 404-881-7777. Business E-Mail: spottle@alston.com.

POTTS, KEVIN T., retired chemistry professor; b. Sydney, Oct. 26, 1928; married; children: Mary Ellen, Jeannette, Karen, Susan. BSc, U. Sydney, 1950, MSc, 1951; PhD in Organic Chemistry, Oxford U., Eng., 1954, DSc, 1973. Demonstrator chemistry U. Sydney, 1950, tchg. fellow, 1951; rsch. asst. organic chemistry Oxford U., 1951-54; scientist Med. Rsch. Coun. of Eng., 1954-56; rsch. asst. organic chemistry Harvard U., 1956-58; lectr. Adelaide, 1958-61; asso. prof. chemistry U. Louisville, 1961-65; assoc. prof. Rensselaer Poly. Inst., 1965-66, prof. chemistry, 1966-94; prof. emeritus Rensselaer Poly Inst., 1994—; chmn. dept. Rensselaer Poly. Inst., 1973-80. Contbr. articles in field organic chemistry to sci. jours. Grantee Nat. Cancer Inst., Nat. Heart Inst., Dept. Energy, NSF, Am. Chem. Soc.-Petroleum Rsch. Fund. Mem. AAAS, Am. Chem. Soc., Brit. Chem. Soc., Royal Soc. Chemistry. Home: 102 Pelican Cv Sneads Ferry NC 28460-9520 Office: Rennselaer Poly Inst Dept Chemistry 110 Eighth Troy NY 12180 E-mail: pottskt@charter.net.

POTTS PARKS, RITA, state legislator; b. Corinth, Miss., Dec. 18, 1962; m. Mike Parks; 1 child, Hannah. Attended, U. Miss. Quality and regulatory mgr., Miss.; mem. Dist. 4 Miss. State Senate, Jackson, 2012—. Mem.: NRA, American Soc. Quality, Kiwanis. Republican. Office: Miss State Senate PO Box 1018 Jackson MS 39215 Business E-Mail: rparks@senate.ms.gov.

POTVIN, ALFRED RAOUL, retired engineering executive; m. Janet Holm, Mar. 20, 1965 BEE, Worcester Poly. Inst., 1964; MSEE, Stanford U., 1965, Engr. in EE, 1967; MS in Bioengring., U. Mich., 1970, MS in Psychology, 1970, PhD in Bioengring., 1971. Registered profl. engr., Tex. Asst. prof. elec. engring. U. Tex., Arlington, 1966—68, assoc. prof. biomed. engring. and elec. engring., 1971—76, prof., 1976—84, chmn. biomed. engring., 1972—84; dir. med. instrumentation sys. rsch. divsn. Eli Lilly & Co., Indpls., 1984—90, dir. tech. assessment and project mgmt., 1990—92, dir. engring., med. devices and diagnostics divsn., 1992—93; prof. elec. engring. Purdue Sch. Engring. and Tech., Ind. U.-Purdue U., Indpls., 1993—96; dean engring. and tech. Ind. U.-Purdue U., Indpls., 1993—95; pres. MEECO, Melbourne, Fla., 1996—99; ret., 1999; emeritus prof. U. Tex. Arlington, 2011. Clin. prof. biophysics U. Tex. Health Sci. Ctr., Dallas, 1967-84; faculty fellow NASA, Houston, 1972-73; life scientist NASA and Moffett Field, 1974-75; founder grad. level biomed. engring. program with U. Tex., Arlington and U. Tex. Health Sci. Ctr., Dallas, 1974, med. devices rsch. divsn. Eli Lilly, Indpls., 1984; mem. phys. med. device panel FDA, Washington, 1978-84; developer NIH Rehab. Engring. Rsch. Ctr., Arlington, 1982; mem. adv. bd., reviewer Biomed. Engring. NSF, Washington, 1984-90, 93-97; founding dir. Ctr. Advanced Rehab. Engring., 1983-84, mem. adv. bd., 1984-88; mem. adv. bd. Engring. Rsch. Ctrs. NSF, Washington, 1988-92, Biomed. Engr. Worcester Polytech. Inst., Mass., 1987—2001, Coll. Engrs. Duke U., Durham, N.C., 1987-94, U. Calif., Berkeley, 1989-92, Coll. Engrs. U. Denver, 1990-93, Sch. Engr. and Tech. Ind. U.-Purdue U., Indpls, 1992-93, med. engring. Jet Propulsion Lab., Pasadena, Calif., 1989; chmn. adv. bd. NIH Resource Ctr. Case Western Res. U., Cleve., 1988-96; bd. advisors Sch. of Health and Rehab. Sci., U. Pitts., 1993-97; mem. adv. com. NIH, 1987-92, 93-95; bd. dirs. Biomed. Engring. Alliance for Engring. in Medicine and Biology; initiator biomed. engring. dept. Ind. U. and Purdue U., Indpls., 1995. Author two vol. book: (with W.W. Tourtellotte) Quantitative Examination of Neurologic Functions, 1985; co-editor: spl. issue on biosensors IEEE Trans. on Biomed. Engring., 1986, spl. issue on status and future directions in biomed. engring. Medicine and Biol. Mag., 1989; mem. editl. bd IEEE Spectrum, 1987-90, 92-95, Biomed. Sci. and Tech., 1990-93, mem. adv. bd. Biomed. Engring. Handbook, 1995, 2000; contbr. over 250 papers to profl. jours. Mem., fin. donor Worcester Poly. Inst. Founders Club, 1997—, WPI Alden Soc., 1997, Ind. U. Found., U. Tex. Arlington 1895 Soc., 2006—; charter mem. U. Tex. Arlington Edward E. Rankin Legacy Soc., 2010—; mem., fin. donor Dana Farber Cancer Inst., Chancellors Coun., U. Tex. Sys., 2009—, Tau Beta Pi 125th Club, 2010—. Recipient Life Scientist award NASA, 1974, Hall of Achievement award U. Tex. at Arlington, 2006, Svc. Industry award, Indians Electronics Mfg. Assn., 1996, Centennial Medal award, IEEE, 1984; Career Achievement award, Houston Soc. Engring. Medicine & Biology, 1993, Life Scientist award, NASA Ames Rsch. Ctr., 1974; spl. fellow NIH, 1968, fellow, Biomed. Engring. Soc., 2005, Founding fellow, Am. Inst. Med. & Biol. Engring., 1992; fellow, IEEE, 1986, Special fellow, Nat. Insts. Health, 1968; Hon. Socs. Sigma Xi, Eta Kappa Nu, Tau Beta Pi. Fellow: IEEE (life; gen. chmn. annual conf. 1982, pres. Engring. in Medicine and Biology Soc. 1983, re-elected 1984, chmn. health care engring. policy com. 1986, editl. bd. spectrum 1987—89, founding mem. steering com. symposium on computer based med. systems 1988—94, co-editor spl. issue Medicine and Biology 1989, editl. bd. Spectrum 1992—94, internat. conf. com. 1993—95, Centennial medal 1984, Life Fellow award 2008), Biomed. Engring. Soc. (chmn. edn. and pub. affairs com. 1979—83), Assn. Advancement Med. Instrumentation, Am. Inst. Med. and Biol. Engring. (bd. dirs. 1991—94, founding fellow 1992, v.p. pub. awareness 1993—94, co-pres. world congress on med. biol. engring. in Chgo. 1993—99, devel. com. 1996—99), Houston Soc. Engrs. in Medicine and Biology (Career Achievement award 1993); mem.: Ind. Elec. Mfg. Assn. (bd. dirs. 1993—96, Svc. to Industry award 1996), Assn. Advancement of Med. Instrumentation, Alliance Engrs. in Medicine and Biology (v.p. nat. affairs 1987—89, pres. 1989—92), Am. Soc. Engring. Edn. (chmn. biomed. engring. divsn. 1979—80). Avocations: boating, hiking, travel, gourmet dining, skiing. Home: 726 Palos Verde Dr Satellite Beach FL 32937 Personal E-mail: arpotvin@gmail.com.

POTVIN, WILLIAM TRACEY, management consultant; b. Milw., June 20, 1951; s. William John and Joan (Wach) P.; m. Louisa I. Vorosmarty, July 23, 1983. BS in Internat. Econs., Georgetown U., 1973; MBA, Am. U., 1975. Investment mgr. GEICO, Washington, 1973-78; mgmt. cons. Touche Ross & Co. (now Deloitte & Touch LLP), NYC, 1978-85, ptnr., 1985-2000; nat. dir. Fin. Inst. Cons., NYC, 1987-90; mng. ptnr., CEO Deloitte & Touche CIS, Moscow, 1990-96; nat. dir. Deloitte & Touche Actuarial and Ins. Cons. Group, NYC, 1996-99; ret. ptnr. Deloitte & Touche, 2000—; pres., CEO The ESP Group LLC, Arlington, Va., 1999—2007; pres. Tracy Assocs. Inc., 2007—; chmn. Budget Fin. Task Force, North Castle, NY, 2010—. Chmn. adv. group to Russian govt. on mass privatization World Bank, 1992-94, acting CFO Russian Privitization Ctr., 1996; speaker to ins. groups, N.Y.C., 1985—. Contbr. articles to profl. jours. Bd. dirs. Am. Russian Youth Orch., 1996—. Mem. Coll. of Ins. (mem. fin. industries task force 1985-90, lectr. 1985-90). Roman Catholic. also: The ESP Group LLC 76 Chestnut Ridge Rd Armonk NY 10504-3001 E-mail: william@potvin.net, potvin@msn.com.

POULOS, MICHAEL JAMES, insurance company executive; b. Glens Falls, NY, Feb. 13, 1931; s. James A. and Mary Poulos; m. Mary Kay Leslie; children: Denise, Peter. BA, Colgate U., 1953; MBA, NYU, 1963. CLU, 1970. With sales and mgmt. U.S. Life Ins. Co., NYC, 1958-70, dir., 1968, mem. exec. com., 1970; with Calif.-Western States Life Ins. Co., Sacramento, 1970-79, pres., chief exec. officer, 1975-79, dir., 1975; with Am. Gen. Corp., Houston, 1979-93, pres., 1981-91, mem. exec. com., dir., 1981-93, vice chmn., 1991-93; chmn., CEO, pres. Western Nat. Corp., Houston, 1993-98, now bd. dirs., 1998; ret., 1998. Mem. Sam Houston Area coun. Boy Scouts Am. Mem. River Oaks Country Club, Univ. Club of N.Y.C., Caston Woods County Club, Houston, Balboa Bay Club, Newport Beach Club Greek Orthodox. Home: 2121 Kirby Dr Unit 73 Houston TX 77019-6066 Office: 2727 Allen Pky Ste 450 Houston TX 77019

POUTSMA, MARVIN L., retired chemical research administrator; b. Grand Rapids, Mich., Aug. 7, 1937; m. Yolanda Arco, July 20, 1968; children: John C., Julie A. BS, Calvin Coll., 1958; PhD, U. Ill., 1962. Staff scientist corp. rsch. Union Carbide, Tarrytown, N.Y., 1961-65, group leader corp. rsch., 1965-68, sr. scientist corp. rsch., 1968-73, sr. group leader corp. rsch., 1972-78; group leader chemistry divsn. Oak Ridge (Tenn.) Nat. Lab., 1978-80, sect. head chemistry divsn., 1980-83, dir. chemistry divsn., 1984-93, dir. chem. & analytical scis. divsn., 1994-2000, ret., 2000. Contbr. chpts. to books and articles to profl. jours. Fellow AAAS; mem. Am. Chem. Soc. Office: Oak Ridge Nat Lab PO Box 2008 Oak Ridge TN 37831-6197 Office Phone: 865-576-8339. Business E-Mail: poutsmaml@ornl.gov.

POWELL, ALAN, engineering educator, research scientist; b. Buxton, Derbyshire, Eng., Feb. 17, 1928; arrived in U.S., 1956; s. Frank and Gwendolen Marie P.; m. June Sinclair, Mar. 28, 1956. Student, Buxton Coll., 1939-45; diploma in aeros., Loughborough Coll., 1948; BSc in Engring. (hon.), London U., 1949; honours diploma 1st class, Loughborough Coll., 1949; DTech (hon.), Loughborough U. Tech., 1980; PhD, U. Southampton, 1953. Chartered engr. Engr. Percival Aircraft Co., Luton, Eng., 1949-51; from rsch. asst. to lectr. U. Southampton, Eng., 1951-56; rsch. fellow Calif. Inst. Tech., Pasadena, 1956-57; engr. Douglas Aircraft Co., 1956; assoc. prof. UCLA, 1957-62, prof. engring., 1962-65, head Aerosonics lab., 1957-65; assoc. tech. dir., head acoustics and vibration lab. David Taylor Model Basin, Dept. Navy, Washington, 1965-66, tech. dir., 1966-67, David Taylor Naval Ship Research & Devel. Center, Bethesda, Md., 1967-85; mem. Undersea Warfare Research & Devel. Council, 1966-76, chmn., 1971-72; mem. council on Fed. Labs., 1972-85; prof. mech. engring. U. Houston, 1985-2000, chmn., 1985-87, prof. emeritus, 2000—. Com. on hearing bioacoustics and biomechs. NAS-NRC, 1961-85, exec. coun., 1963-65, chmn., 1965-66, advisor, 1985-95, mem. naval studies bd. 1990-95; mem. various coms. Naval Studies Bd. and Marine Bd., 1990-96; advisor Chinese U. Devel. Project, 1989-91; cons. Douglas Aircraft Co., 1956-65, others; adv. coun. Internat. Towing Tank Conf., 1981-85; mem. advisor U.S.-Japan Program Natural Resources, 1987-90, mem. Marine Facilities Panel; gen. chmn. 3d advanced vehicles conf. AIAA and Soc. Naval Archs. and Marine Engrs., 1976; chmn. internat. conf. Computer Aided Design, Manufacture and Ops. in Marine and Offshore Industries, 1987-88; cons. Sci. Applications Internat., Inc., 1987-90; governing bd. Am. Inst. Physics, 1995-97; mem. editl. bd. Internat. Jour. Aeroacoustics, 2007-. Contbr. articles to profl. jours. Recipient Navy Meritorious Civilian Service award, 1970; Brit. Empire scholar, 1945; named Meritorious Exec. Pres. of U.S., 1982; Capt. Robert Dexter Conrad gold medal for sci. achievement Sec. Navy, 1984; dedication spl. issue Internat. Jour. Aeroacoustics vol. 2 nos. 3/4, 2003. Fellow Royal Aero. Soc. London (Baden-Powell prize 1948, Wilbur Wright prize 1953), Acoustical Soc. Am. (biennial award 1962, assoc. editor Jour. 1962-67, chmn. edn. com. 1964-66, exec. coun. 1966-69, chmn. medals and awards com. 1978-81, v.p. elect 1981-82, v.p. 1982-83, pres. elect 1989-90, pres. 1990-91, past pres. 1991-92, Silver medal in engring. acoustics 1992, designated Nat. Spkr. in Engring. Acoustics 1994-98), Inst. Mech. Engrs., Inst. Acoustics (U.K.); mem. AIAA (assoc. fellow, Aeroacoustics award 1980), ASME (Rayleigh lectr. 1988, Per Brüel Gold medal 1991), Inst. Noise Control Engrs. (initial mem., dir. 1974-77, Disting. lectr. 1975, 83, v.p. 1981-84, bd. cert. 1993), Acoustics, Speech and Signal Processing Soc. (exec. com. 1969-72, awards com. 1971-73, bylaws com. chmn. 1973-75), Am. Soc. Naval Engrs. (life), Tau Beta Pi (hon. life). Office: Dept Mech Energy University Houston Houston TX 77204

POWELL, ALAN T., state legislator; b. Nov. 10, 1951; m. Bonnie Powell; children: Beau, Gabriel. Former chmn. Hart County Commn.; former state rep. Dist.23 Ga.; former vice chmn. Motor Vehicles Com.; state rep. Dist.13, 1991—92; state rep. Dist. 29 Ga., 2004—; businessman & cons. Democrat. Baptist. Mailing: PO Box 248 Hartwell GA 30643 Office: 401 State Capitol Atlanta GA 30334 Office Phone: 404-656-7856, 706-376-4422. E-mail: alanpowell23@hotmail.com.

POWELL, ALMA JOHNSON, writer, advocate, foundation administrator; b. Birmingham, Al., Oct. 27, 1937; d. Robert and Mildred Johnson; m. Colin L. Powell, Aug. 1962; children: Michael, Linda, Annemarie. BA, Fisk U., 1957; LHD (hon.), Emerson Coll., 1996. Audiologist Boston Guild Hard of Hearing, 1959—62. Author: (children's books) America's Promise, 2003, My Little Wagon, 2003. Chair nat. coun. Best Friends Found., 1989—2001; chair Alliance for Youth, 2004—. Named one of 100 Most Powerful Women in Wash., Washingtonian mag., 2001. Office Phone: 703-224-5012.

POWELL, ANNE ELIZABETH, editor-in-chief; b. Cheverly, Md., Nov. 11, 1951; d. Arthur Gorman and Barbara Anne (MacAran) P.; m. John Alan Ebeling Jr., 1972 (div. 1983). BS, U. Md., 1972; M in Profl. Studies, George Washington U., 2010. Reporter Fayetteville (N.C.) Times, 1973-75; home editor Columbus (Ga.) Ledger-Enquirer, 1976; assoc. editor Builder mag., Washington, 1977-78; architecture editor House Beautiful's Spl. Publs., NYC, 1979-81; editor Traditional Home mag., Des Moines, 1982-87, Mid-Atlantic Country mag., Alexandria, Va., 1987-89; editor in chief publs. Nat. Trust for Hist. Preservation, Washington, 1989-95; editor-in-chief Landscape Architecture Mag., Washington, 1995-98, Civil Engring. Mag., Washington, 1998—. Author: The New England Colonial, 1988. Mem. Nat. Press Club, Am. Soc. Mag. Editors. Office: American Society of Civil Engrs Civil Engring Mag 1801 Alexander Bell Dr Reston VA 20191-4344 Home: 4500 S Four Mile Run Dr Apt 803 Arlington VA 22204 Office Phone: 703-295-6213.

POWELL, BAYARD LOWERY, oncologist, educator; b. Raleigh, NC, June 22, 1954; MD, U. N.C., 1980. Diplomate Am. Bd. Internal Medicine, Am. Bd. Med. Oncology. Intern, then resident in internal medicine N.C. Bapt. Hosp., Winston-Salem, 1980-83, mem. staff; fellow hematologic oncology Bowman Gray Sch. Medicine, Winston-Salem, 1983-86, prof. hematologic oncology, sect. chief hematologic oncology, dir. leukemia svc. Named one of NC's Best Doctors, Bus. NC mag., 2002. Mem. ACP, Am. Assn. for Cancer Rsch., Am. Soc. Hematology, Am. Soc. Clin. Oncology. Office: Cancer Ctr Wake Forest Univ Sch Med Med Ctr Blvd Winston Salem NC 27157-0001 also: 2707 Buena Vista RD Winston Salem NC 27106 Office Phone: 336-713-5440, 336-716-4354. Business E-Mail: bpowell@wfubmc.edu.

POWELL, CLEO E., state supreme court justice; BA in American Govt., U. Va., Charlottesville, 1979, JD, 1982. Atty. Hunton & Williams, Richmond, Va., 1982—86; sr. asst. atty. gen. Office of Atty. Gen., Va., 1986—89; corp. counsel, dir. employee services Dominion (formerly Va. Power), 1989—93; judge Gen. Dist. Ct. Chesterfield County, Va., 1993—2000, Chesterfield County Cir. Ct., 2000—08, Ct. Appeals of Va., 2008—11; assoc. justice Supreme Ct. of Va., 2011—. Mem. Jud. Inquiry and Rev. Commn., 2008; mem. exec. com. Jud. Conf. Va., 2009—. Sheepfold leader, children's ch. instr., vol. corp instr. First Bapt. Ch., South Richmond, Va.; bd. dirs. Ctrl. Va. Foodbank, 1986—88, St. Mary's Hosp. Found., 1992—93; coord. Caritas, 1988—93; bd. dirs., v.p. Young Women's Christian Assn., 1989—93. Mem.: ABA, Va. Bar Assn., Old Dominion Bar Assn., Va. Assn. Women Judges, Nat. Bar Assn., American Judges Assn., Chesterfield/Colonial Heights Bar Assn., Met. Richmond Women's Bar Assn., Va. Assn. Black Women Attorneys, Bar Assn. of City of Richmond, John Marshall Inn of Ct., Delta Sigma Theta. Office: Supreme Court of Virginia 100 N Ninth St Richmond VA 23219*

POWELL, DON WATSON, gastroenterologist, educator; b. Gadsden, Ala., Aug. 29, 1938; s. Gordon C. and Ruth (Bennett) P.; m. Frances N. Rourke; children: Mary Paige, Drew Watson, Shawnne Margaret. BS with honors, Auburn U., 1960; MD with highest honors, Med. Coll. Ala., Birmingham, 1963. Diplomate Am. Bd. Internal Medicine, Am. Bd. Gastroenterology. Intern, resident P.B. Brigham Hosp., Boston, 1963-65; resident Yale U. Sch. Med., New Haven, 1968-69, spl. NIH fellow in physiology, 1969-71; asst. prof. medicine U. N.C., Chapel Hill, 1971-74, assoc. prof., 1974-78, prof., 1978-91; mem. external adv. bd., v.p. for rsch. U. Tex. Health Sci. Ctr., San Antonio, 2005—07; external advisor Hispanic Health Disparities Ctr., U. Tex., El Paso, 2005—07, Rehab. Rsch. Career Devel. Ctr., U. Tex. Med. Br., 2008—, Tex. Med. Ctr. Digestive Diseases Ctr., 2009—. Chief divsn. digestive diseases U. NC, 1977-91, dir. Ctr. Gastrointestinal Biol. Diseases, 1985-91, assoc. chmn. clin. affairs dept. medicine, 1989-91; mem. merit rev. bd. VA, 1977-80; cons. WHO, Geneva, 1980-82, Burroughs-Wellcome, Inc., Research Triangle Pk., N.C., 1981-82, Hoffman-LaRoche, Inc., Nutley, NJ, 1982-93, Glaxo Smith Kline, Harlow, Eng., 2004-05, Lexicon Genetics, The Woodlands, Tex., 2005-06; mem. gen. medicine A-2 study sect. NIH, 1985-89; Edward Randall and Edward Randall, Jr. Disting. chmn. U. Tex. Med. Br., Galveston, 1991-02, prof. internal medicine, neurosci. and cell biology, 1991—, assoc. dean rsch., Sch. Medicine, 2002-06, Bassel and Frances Blanton disting. prof. in internal medicine, 2008-11; mem. Nat. Inst. Diabetes Digestive and Kidney Diseases Adv. Coun., 1994-97; coun., bd. rep. adv. com. to dir. NIH, 1996-97; program dir. Gen. Clin. Rsch. Ctr., 2003-09, interim dir. gastroenterology, 2006-; dir. Inst. for Translational Scis. Clin. Rsch. Ctr., 2009-; assoc. editor Prin. Clin. Gastroenterology, 2005. Assoc. editor: Principles of Clinical Gastroenterology 1st edit., 2008, Textbook of Gastroenterology, 5th edit., 2009, Atlas of Gastroenterology, 4th edit. 2009, Cecil Textbook of Medicine, 21st-23rd edit., 2001, 2004, 2007; mem. editl. bd. Am. Jour. Physiology, Gastrointestinal and Liver Physiology, 1979-97, Am. Jour. Med. Sci., 1984-92, Regulatory Peptide Letter, 1990-2008, Annals of Internal Medicine, 1993-96, Current Treatment Options in Gastro, 1998-2005; contbr. over 85 review articles chapters to books, over 200 articles to profl. jours. Bd. dirs. Artillery Club of Galveston, 1997—2003. Capt. US Army, 1965—68. Recipient Disting. Alumnus award U. Ala. Med. Alumni Assn. 2012, Rsch. Career Devel. award NIH, 1973-78, Merit award, 1987, Outstanding Physician of Yr. award Gulf Coast chpt. Crohn's Colitis Found. Am., 1994, John P. McGovern MD award in Oslerian Medicine, 2002, Don W Powell Resident award, UTMB, 2002, Don W Powell Lectr. award, 2008, award Internal Medicine Residents, others. Master ACP (mem. med. knowledge self-assessment program VII gastroenterology com. 1983-85), ACS (Tex. chpt.) (Best Drs. in America, 1996-2012), Am. Gastroentrol. Assn. Inst. (Don W. Powell lectr., UTMB 2007, 12), UAL Med. Alumni Assoc.(Disting. Alumnus award); fellow AAAS, mem. Am. Physiol. Soc., Am. Gastroenterol. Assn. (v.p. 1991-92, pres. 1993-94, coun. acad. rep. 1999—, Julius Friedenwald medal 2001, Mentored Rsch. award 2005, fellow 2006), Gastroenterology Rsch. Group (chmn. 1988-89), So. Soc. Clin. Investigation, Federated Socs. Gastroenterology and Hepatology (chmn. 1996-98, Assn. Am. Physicians, Am. Clin. and Climatol. Assn., Alpha Omega Alpha (bd. dirs. 2000-2012). Avocations: music, literature, sports. Office: U Tex Med Br 4 106 McCullough 301 Univ Blvd Galveston TX 77555-0764 Office Phone: 409-772-1950. Business E-Mail: dpowell@utmb.edu.

POWELL, JAMES BOBBITT, health facility administrator, pathologist; b. Burlington, NC, Aug. 28, 1938; s. Thomas Edward and Sophia (Sharpe) P.; m. Pamela Oughton, Sept. 12, 1969 (div. Sept. 1979); 1 child, Daphne P. Markcrow; m. Anne Ellington, Oct. 20, 1984; children: James Bobbitt (dec.), John Banks, James Rosser, Helen Bobbitt. BA, Va. Mil. Inst., 1960; MD, Duke U., 1964. Diplomate Am. Bd. Pathology. Intern Duke U. Med. Ctr., Durham, NC, 1964-65; resident Cornell Med. Ctr., NYC, 1965-67, Englewood (N.J.) Hosp., 1967-69; founder Biomed Labs, Burlington, NC, 1969—; pres. Roche Biomed. Labs., 1982-95; pres., CEO Lab. Corp. Am. Holdings, 1995-97; CEO Tripath Imaging, Burlington, NC, 1997—2000. Bd. dirs. Vis. Internat. Faculty. Contbr. articles to sci. publs. Trustee Elon U., NC, 1979—; bd. dirs. NC Rail Rd., 2011—14, Alamance Found. Maj. M.C. US Army, 1969—72. Mem. Alamance Country Club. Republican. Methodist. Avocations: tennis, US military history. Office: 1573 York Pl Burlington NC 27215-3355

POWELL, JAY, state legislator; b. Nov. 18; m. Carole B. Powell. Atty.; mem. Dist. 171 Ga. House of Reps., 2009—. Republican. Office: 501 Coverdell Legislative Office Bldg Atlanta GA 30334 also: PO Box 188 Camilla GA 31730 Office Phone: 404-656-0177, 229-336-3962. E-mail: jay.powell@house.ga.gov.

POWELL, JERRY W., lawyer; b. Montgomery, Ala., Jan. 6, 1950; m. Carolyn Powell; children: Jennifer, Jeffrey. BA cum laude, Birmingham-So. Coll., 1972; JD, U. Ala., 1975. Bar: Ala. 1975, U.S. Dist. Ct. Ala. (No. and Mid. dist), U.S. Ct. Appeals (11th cir.). Law clk. No. Dist. Ala., 1975—76; gen. counsel, sec. Compass Bancshares, Inc., Birmingham, Ala. Mem. editl. bd.: Alabama Law Review, 1973—75. Mem.: ABA, Am. Soc. Corp. Secretaries, Am. Corp. Counsel Assn. (pres. Ala. chpt. 1984—85), Ala. State Bar Assn., Birmingham Bar Assn., Order of Coif (bench and bar). Office: Compass Bancshares Inc 15 S 20th St Birmingham AL 35233 Office Phone: 205-297-3960. Office Fax: 205-297-3043. Business E-Mail: jerry.powell@compassbank.com.

POWELL, LEWIS FRANKLIN, III, lawyer; b. Richmond, Va., Sept. 14, 1952; s. Lewis F. Jr. and Josephine (Rucker) P.; m. Lisa T. LaFata; children: Emily, Hannah, Luke. BA, Washington & Lee U., 1974; JD, U. Va., 1978. Bar: Va. 1978, U.S. Dist. Ct. (ea. and we. dists.) Va. 1979, U.S. Ct. Appeals (4th cir.) 1979, U.S. Ct. Appeals (2d cir.) 1983, U.S. Ct. Appeals (11th cir.) 1992, U.S. Supreme Ct. 1985. Law clk. to judge U.S. Dist. Ct. (ea. dist.), Richmond, 1978-79; assoc. Hunton & Williams, Richmond, 1979—86, ptnr., 1986—. Pres. young lawyers conf. Va. State Bar, 1986-87. Bd. dirs. William Byrd Cmty. Ho., Richmond, 1982-87, Boys Club of Richmond, 1984-90, Maymont Found., Richmond, 1987-92, St. Christopher's Sch., Richmond, 1989-96. Mem. Richmond Bar Assn. (chmn. improvement justice com. 1982-83), 4th Cir. Jud. Conf., Am. Law Inst. Avocations: fly fishing, mountaineering, hiking. Office: Hunton & Williams Riverfront Plz East Tower 951 E Bird St Richmond VA 23219

POWELL, MICHAEL VANCE, lawyer; b. San Diego, Sept. 30, 1946; s. Jesse Vance and Mable Louise (Cagle) P.; m. Sarada Marie Hughes, Dec. 23, 1967; children: Marilyn Jean, Michael Benjamin. AB, Davidson Coll., NC, 1968; MA, U. Tex., 1972, JD with honors, 1974. Bd. cert. civil appellate law Tex. Bd. Legal Specialization. Law clk. to judge US Ct. Appeals (9th cir.), 1974—75; assoc. Rain Harrell Emery Young & Doke, Dallas, 1975-80, ptnr., 1980-87; mem. Locke Purnell Rain Harrell, Dallas, 1987-98; ptnr. Locke Liddell & Sapp, Dallas, 1999—2007, Locke Lord, Dallas, 2007—. Elder St. Barnabas Presbyn. Ch., Richardson, Tex. Fellow: Am. Bar Found.; mem.: AAJ, Am. Coll. Trial Lawyers, Dallas Bar Found., Tex. Bar Found. Avocations: music, travel. Home: 7312 Tophill Ln Dallas TX 75248-5642 Office: Locke Lord LLP 2200 Ross Ave Ste 2200 Dallas TX 75201-6776 Office Phone: 214-740-8520. Business E-Mail: mpowell@lockelord.com.

POWELL, SARAH E., lawyer, automotive executive; b. Rocky Mount, Va., Apr. 2, 1966; BA magna cum laude, Univ. Va., 1988; JD cum laude, Washington & Lee Univ., 1993. Bar: Va. 1993, NC 2000. Asst. gen. counsel Food Lion LLC, Salisbury, NC; sr. atty. to v.p. & real estate counsel Advance Auto Parts, Inc., Roanoke, Va., 2002—07, acting gen. counsel, 2007—09, sr. v.p., corp. sec., gen. counsel, 2009—. Mem.: ABA, State Bar NC, State Bar Va., Va. Bar Assn., Roanoke Bar Assn., Phi Beta Kappa, Phi Alpha Delta, Sigma Tau Delta. Office: Advance Auto Parts 5008 Airport Rd Roanoke VA 24012 Office Phone: 540-561-1186. Office Fax: 540-561-1145.

POWELL, THOMAS EDWARD, III, biological supply company executive, physician; b. Elon College, NC, Aug. 1, 1936; s. Thomas Edward and Sophia Maude (Sharpe) Powell; m. Betty Durham Yeager, June 19, 1965; children: Frances Powell Barnes, Thomas Edward IV, Caroline Powell Rogers. AB in Biology, Va. Mil. Inst., 1957; MD, Duke U., 1961; MA, Harvard U., 1966. Surgeon USPHS, 1966—68; co-founder Biomed. Reference Labs., Inc., Burlington, NC, 1969, exec. v.p., 1969—75, chmn. exec. com., 1979—82, dir.; exec. v.p. Carolina Biol. Supply Co., Burlington, 1968—80, chmn., 1977—80, 1994—, pres., 1980—94, Wolfe Sales Corp., Burlington, 1980—84, Waubun Labs. Inc., Schriever, La., 1980—, Bobbitt Labs., Inc., Burlington, 1983—94; bd. mgrs. Wachovia Bank and Trust Co. N.A., Burlington. Contbr. articles to profl. jours. Bd. dirs. United Way Alamance County, Burlington, 1968—, Elon Coll., NC, 1968—, sec., 1975—; bd. dirs. Am. Cancer Soc., Burlington, 1971—81, Burlington Day Sch., 1973—, pres., 1974—78, 1980—84; bd. dirs. NC Citizens for Bus. and Industry, Raleigh, 1983—87, Nat. Found. for Study of Religion and Econs., Greensboro, 1984—88, Blue Ridge Sch., Dyke, Va., 1985—90. Served to capt. USAR, 1957—66. Recipient Citizens Svc. award, Elon Coll. Alumni Assn., 1980. Mem.: Am. Med. Assn., Newcomen Soc., Assn. Venture Founders, NC Med. Soc., Alamance-Caswell Med. Soc., NC Acad. Sci., Assn. Biology Lab. Edn., Greensboro City Club, Hope Valley Country Club (Durham, NC), NC Country Club (Pinehurst), Congl. Country Club (Washington), Capital City Club (Raleigh), Alamance Country Club (Burlington). Democrat. Mem. Christian Ch.

POWELL, WILLIAM COUNCIL, SR., service company executive; b. Burlington, NC, Nov. 5, 1948; s. Thomas Edward Jr. and Annabelle (Council) P.; m. Jacqueline Garrison, July 3, 1976; children: William C. Jr., Ashley C. Student, U. S.C., 1968-69; BS, Va. Mil. Inst., 1971; MBA, Wake Forest U., 1974; postgrad., Elon Coll., 1972. Lic. pilot, real estate broker. NC adminstrv. assoc. Carolina Biol. Supply Co., Inc., Burlington, 1971—91; v.p. Bobbitt Labs., Burlington, 1974-77, pres., 1977—82; owner HEADS, Inc., Elon, NC, 1978—, pres., 1984—; owner Ashwil Acres Farm, Mebane, NC, 1981—2005. Pres. Granite Diagnostics, Inc., Burlington, 1981-84, UST Specialists Inc., 1991-2000, Burlington, Warren Land Co., 1994-2005, Merrymount Property Owners Assn., Inc., 1996-2000, Merrymount Boat Slip Assn., Inc., 1996-2005, Stratonet Inc., 1996-2001, Forest Realm, Inc., 2001—, Powell Realm Inc., 2001—, Poignard Compact Inc., 2001-, Goat Island Maritime Inc., 2001—2011, chmn., 2011-; owner Powell Real Estate, Burlington, 1979-2001; bd. dirs. Excalibur Lock Co., Inc., Waubun Labs, Inc., Schriever, La.; v.p. fin. Environ. Responsible Bus. Inc., 1992-97; mem. Babcock Sch. Alumni Coun. Wake Forest U., 1981-85; mgr. Macon Farm, 1992-95; chmn. bd. Ensci Corp., Inc., 1991-95, ptnr. Port Assocs., 1987-2002, Port Assocs. II, 1992-2002; chmn. bd. Netpath Inc., 1995-96, bd. dirs.; filed for election N.C. Senate, 2000, 02. Bd. advisors Elon Coll., NC, 1984-86, bd. visitors, 1987-92; bd. advisors Duke U. Marine Lab., Beaufort, NC, 1985-92; nat. adv. coun. Baruch Marine Inst., 1998-2006; adv. panel Air Quality Compliance Panel State of NC Dept. Environ. Health and Natural Resources, 1994-2006; guardian Boy Scouts Am., Burlington, 1985; trustee Dr. T.E. Powell Jr. Trust, 1989-95; v.p. fin. Cherokee coun. Boy Scouts of Am., 1990-92, exec. bd., 1990-94, exec. bd. Old N. State coun., 1994-95; active Front St. United Meth. Ch., Burlington, NC. Capt. USAR, 1971-79. Recipient Bill Fish Cert. State of S.C., 1983, 2 Bill Fish Certs. State of N.C., 1990, Sower's award Duke U., 1985, N.C. Gov.'s Cup for Billfishing, 1991, 3rd Pl., Big Rock Blue Marlin Tourn, 1998. Mem. NRA (life), Newcomen Soc. N.Am. (life), Billiard Congress Am., Am. Angus Assn., Billiard and Bowling Inst. Assn., NC Forestry Assn. (legis. affairs com. 1994-2007), N.C. Wildlife Habitat Found. (life), Ducks Unltd. (life sponsor, area chmn. 1985-87, 1997-2005), Safari Club Internat. (state pres. 1985-88, life), Aircraft Owners and Pilots Assn., Cessna Pilots Orgn., Atlantic Coast Conservation Assn. (life), Alamance Wildlife Club (bd. dirs. 1992-95, 2000-03, pres. 1999-2000), Rolls Royce Owners Club (life), N.Am. Hunting Club (life), Found. N.Am. Wild Sheep (life), Chaine des Rotisseurs (chevalier 1991), Brotherhood of the Knights of the Vine (master knight 1991-2011), Am. Angus Assn., Nat. Wild Turkey Fedn., Quail Unltd. (life), NC Cattlemans Assn. (life), Nat. Cattlemans Assn., Inc., Ocean Green Assn., Debordieu Club, Nat. Soc. SAR, Sons Confederate Vets., Alamance County Cattleman's Assn., Citation Fishing Team (capt. 1979—2009), Alamance Country Club, Debordieu Beach Club. Home: 1109 W Front St Burlington NC 27215-3610 Office: Home Entertainment and Decor Sys Inc 945 E Haggard Ave Elon NC 27244 Office Phone: 336-584-0835, 800-275-4520. Personal E-mail: williamcpowell@bellsouth.net.

POWERS, MARC D., retail executive; BA in Comm., Auburn U., Ala. Joined Home Depot, Inc., 1986, various positions including sales assoc. and store mgr. Northern divsn., then regional v.p. Northern divsn., Jacksonville, Fla. to dist. mgr. Southern divsn., Miami, 1997—2000, regional v.p. ops., Southeast region, regional v.p., Northern divsn., dist. mgr., Southern divsn. Miami, Fla., 1997—2000, now sr. v.p. ops. nationwide. Office: The Home Depot Inc 2455 Paces Ferry Rd NW Atlanta GA 30339-4024 Office Phone: 770-433-8211. Office Fax: 770-384-2356. E-mail: Marc_Powers@homedepot.com.

POWERS, PAULINE SMITH, psychiatrist, educator, researcher; b. Sept. 23, 1941; m. Henry P. Powers; children: Jessica, Samantha. AB in Math., Washington U., 1963; MD, U. Iowa, Iowa City, 1971. Med. intern Emanuel Hosp., Portland, Oreg., 1971-72; psychiatry resident U. Iowa, Iowa City, 1972-74, U. Calif., Santa Barbara, 1974-75; from asst. prof. to assoc. prof. psychiatry Coll. Medicine U. So. Fla., Tampa, 1975-85, prof., 1985—, dir. eating disorder program, 1979—, dir. psychosomatic medicine divsn., 1979—. Author: Obesity: The Regulation of Weight, 1980; editor: The Current Treatment of Anorexia Nervosa and Bulimia, 1984; co-editor: (with J. Yager and P. Powers) Clinical Manual of Eating Disorders, 2007. Fellow: Am. Psychiat. Assn. (Rush Gold Outstanding Exhibit medal 1976, Dorfman Jour. Paper award 1987); mem.: Nat. Eating Disorders Assn. (pres.-elect 2003—05, pres. 2005—06, Lifetime Achievement award 2006), Acad. Eating Disorders (founding pres., Women Helping Women award 1995, Profl. Excellence award 1997, Outstanding Clinician award 2000). Office: U So Fla Coll Medicine Dept Psychiatry 3515 E Fletcher Ave Tampa FL 33613-4706 Home Phone: 813-971-5804; Office Phone: 813-974-2926. Business E-Mail: ppowers@health.usf.edu.

POWERS, WILLIAM CHARLES, JR., academic administrator, law educator; b. May 30, 1946; BA in Chemistry, U. Calif., Berkeley, 1967; JD, Harvard U., 1973. Bar: Wash. 1974, Tex. 1980. Law clk. to Hon. E. A. Wright U.S. Ct. Appeals (9th cir.), Seattle, 1973-74; asst. prof. Wash. U., Seattle, 1974-77, assoc. prof., 1977-78; prof. law U. Tex., Austin, 1978—, assoc. dean acad. affairs, 1984—87, 1994—95, univ. disting. prof. and Hines H. Baker and Thelma Kelly Baker chair in law, 1997—, John Jeffers Rsch. Chair in law, 2000—, dean Sch. Law, 2000—06, pres., 2006—. Chair Spl. Investigation Com. Enron Corp. Author: Texas Products Liability Law, 1992; co-author: Cases and Materials in Torts, 1998, Cases and Materials in Products Liability, 2002. Mem.: Am. Law Inst. Office: University of Texas at Austin Office of President PO Box T Austin TX 78713-8920 Home: 3600 Murillo Cir Austin TX 78703 Home Phone: 512-472-7831; Office Phone: 512-232-1120. Office Fax: 512-471-6987. E-mail: wpowers@law.utexas.edu.*

POZNER, JASON N., plastic surgeon; Grad. with distinction in rsch., Mt. Sinai Med. Sch. Diplomate Am. Bd. of Plastic Surgery, lic. Fla., NY. Resident gen. surgery Mt. Sinai Med. Ctr., NY; resident plastic surgery NY Downstate Med. Ctr.; fellow in microsurgery Montefiore Med. Ctr.; fellow in aesthetic and endoscopic plastic surgery Md.; fellow Am. Coll. of Surgeons; asst. prof. plastic surgery John's Hopkins Med. Ctr.; founder Sanctuary Plastic Surgery; co-owner Sanctuary Med. Aesthetic Ctr., Boca Raton, Fla. Adjunct clin. faculty dept. of plastic surgery Cleve. Clinic, Fla. Mem.: Am. Soc. for Lasers in Medicine and Surgery, Am. Soc. of Aesthetic Plastic Surgery, Am. Soc. of plastic Surgeons. Office: Sanctuary Medical Aesthetic Center Suite C101 4800 North Federal Highway Boca Raton FL 33431 Office Phone: 800-407-4319. Office Fax: 561-886-0981.

PRABHAKAR, ARATI, federal agency administrator; b. New Delhi, Feb. 2, 1959; came to U.S., 1962; d. Jagdish Chandra and Raj (Madan) P. BSEE, Tex. Tech U., 1979; MSEE, Calif. Inst. Tech., 1980, PhD in Applied Physics, 1984; DEng (hon.), Rensselaer Poly. Inst., 1995. Congressional fellow Office Tech. Assessment US House of Representatives, Washington, 1984-86; program mgr. electronic sci. divsn. Def. Advanced Rsch. Projects Agy. (DARPA), Arlington, Va., 1986-90, dep. dir. defense sci. office, 1990-91, dir. microelectroncs tech. office, 1991-93, dir., 2012—, Nat. Inst. Standards & Tech., US Dept. Commerce, Gaithersburg, Md., 1993-97; sr. v.p., chief technology officer Raychen, 1997—98; v.p. Interval Rsch., 1998—2000; ptnr. US Venture Partners, 2001—11. Bd. dirs. Leadis Technology, Inc., 2002—06, SRIA Internat., Inc., 2012—. Contbr. articles to profl. jours. Rsch. fellow Calif. Inst. Tech., 1979-84, grad. rsch. program for women Bell Labs., 1979, 80; named Disting. Engr. of 1994, Tex. Tech. U.; elected to Tex. Tech. Elec. Engring. Acad., 1994; recipient Disting. Alumni award Calif. Inst. Tech., 1995. Fellow IEEE; mem. Eta Kappa Nu, Tau Beta Pi. Office: Defense Advanced Research Projects Agency (DARPA) 675 N Randolph St Arlington VA 22203 Office Phone: 703-526-6630.*

PRABHUDESAI, MUKUND M., physician, educator, health facility and academic administrator, researcher; b. Lolyem, Goa, India, Mar. 17, 1942; came to U.S., 1967; s. Madhav R. and Kusum M. Prabhudesai; m. Sarita Mukund Usha, Feb. 1, 1972; 1 child, Nitin M. MB, BS (MD), G.S. Med., Bombay, 1967, postgrad., 1973-75. Diplomate Am. Bd. Pathology. Asst. pathologist Fordham Hosp., Bronx, NY, 1973-74, assoc. pathologist, 1974-76; assoc. dir. clin. pathology Lincoln Med., Bronx, 1976, dep. dir. pathology, 1977-79; chief pathology and lab. medicine svc., coord. R&D Illiana Med. Ctr., Danville, Ill., 1979—, dir. electron microscopy lab., 1987—. Senator U. Ill. Chgo.; co-investigator U. Ill. Coll. Medicine, Urbana-Champaign, clin. prof. pathology and internal medicine, 1982—. Contbr. articles to Am. Jour. Clin. Nutrition, Jour. AMA, Am. Jour. Clin. Pathology. Member Gifted Student Adv. Bd., Danville, 1984-86; v.p. Am. Cancer Soc. Vermilion County chpt., 1982, pres., 1986-88. VA rsch. grantee, 1980-82, 82-85, 83. Fellow Coll. Am. Pathology (inspector 1981-, Ill. state del. to C.A.P. Ho. Dels. 1992-, mem. reference com. 1993, chair, standard and integration com., 2000-); mem. AAAS, Am. Coll. Physician Execs., Ill. State Soc. Pathologists (bd. dirs. 1990-2011, health and wealth cons., chmn. membership com. 1990-). Achievements include development of cancer of bladder following portocarval shunting; research in adverse effects of alcohol on lung structure and metabolism; on effects of soy and bran on cholesterol, fish and coronary artery disease, endocrine response to soy protein, in induction and reversibility of atherosclerosis in trout, effects of ethanol on Vitamin A, lymphatics in atherosclerosis, iron in atherosclerosis, development of dermofluorometer for detection of P.V.D. Office: PO Box 3583 Placida FL 33946 Personal E-mail: mdesaih@aol.com. E-mail: sarita@soltec.net.

PRADHAN, NITIN VIJAY, information scientist, former federal agency administrator; b. Pune, India, 1960; married; 2 children. BS in Engring., U. Baroda, India, 1983; MBA in Mktg., U. Pune, India, 1985; MS in Accounting, Auditing & Costing, American U., 1992. Area mgr. Internat. Data Mgmt. Ltd., India, 1985—90; mng. dir. Ctr. for Innovative Tech., Va., 1995—2000; co-founder, interim CEO TechContinuum, Inc., Fairfax, Va., 2000—02; chief IT architect, dir. Office Tech. Planning & Assessment, IT exec. Fairfax County Public Schools, Fairfax, Va., 2002—09; chief info. officer, chief info. tech. adviser to sec. US Dept. Transp., Washington, 2009—12; founder public private innovations CEO-Launch Dream LLC, Reston, Va., 2012—; founder, mng. ptnr. GOVonomy, 2013—. Recipient Premier 100 Lifetime Achievement award, Computerworld.*

PRADO, EDWARD CHARLES, federal judge; b. San Antonio, June 7, 1947; s. Edward L. and Bertha (Cadena) P.; m. Maria Anita Jung, Nov. 10, 1973; 1 child, Edward C. AA, San Antonio Coll., 1967; BA, U. Tex., 1969, JD, 1972. Bar: Tex. 1972. Asst. dist. atty. Bexar County Dist. Atty.'s Office, San Antonio, 1972-76; asst. pub. defender US Pub. Defender's Office, San Antonio, 1976-80; judge US Dist. Ct. Tex., San Antonio, 1980; U.S. atty. US Dept. Justice, San Antonio, 1981—84; judge US Dist. Ct. (we. dist.) Tex., San Antonio, 1984—2003, US Ct. Appeals (5th cir.), San Antonio, 2003—. Served to capt. U.S. Army. Named Outstanding Young Lawyer of Bexar County, 1980. Mem. ABA, Tex. Bar Assn., San Antonio Bar Assn., San Antonio Young Lawyers Assn., Fed. Bar Assn. Republican. Roman Catholic.

PRADOS, JOHN WILLIAM, retired engineering educator; b. Spring Hill, Tenn., Oct. 12, 1929; s. Gustave Olivier and Elizabeth Branham Prados; m. Ruth Lynn Baird, Sept. 2, 1951; children: Elizabeth Pauline Bowman, Laura Lynn, Anne Caroline Lynch. BS in Chem. engring., U. Miss., Oxford, Miss., 1947—51; PhD, U. Tenn., Knoxville, 1954—57, MS, 1953—54. Registered ret. Profl. Engr., State Bd. of Archtl. and Engring. Examiners/Tenn., 1964. Asst. prof. chem. engring. U. Tenn., Knoxville, 1956—59, assoc. prof. chem. engring., 1959—64, prof. chem. engring., 1964—2001, assoc. dean engring., 1969—71, dean of admissions and records, 1971—73, acting chancellor, 1973—73, v.p. academic affairs, statewide sys., 1973—81, acting chancellor, martin campus Martin, 1979, v.p. academic affairs and rsch., statewide sys., 1981—88, v.p. emeritus, 1989—, univ. prof., 1989—2001, head, chem. engring. dept., 1990—93, univ. prof. emeritus, 2001—. Cons. Nuc. Divsn., Union Carbide Corp., Oak Ridge, 1957—84, Martin Marietta Energy Sys., 1984—86; vice chmn. Engring. Accreditation Commn., Accreditation Bd. for Engring. and Tech., Inc., Baltimore, Md., 1981—84, chmn., 1984—85; commr. Commn. on Colleges, So. Assn. of Colleges and Schools, Decatur, Ga., 1986—92, exec. councillor, 1986—89; dir. Accrediation Bd. for Engring. and Tech., Inc., Baltimore, Md., 1988—93; sec. Accreditation Bd. for Engring. and Tech., Inc., Baltimore, Md., 1989—90, pres., 1991—92; trustee So. Assn. of Colleges and Schools, Decatur, Ga., 1995—98; editor, jour. of engring. edn. Am. Soc. for Engring. Edn., Washington, 1996—2001; trustee F. W. Olin Coll. of Engring., Needham, Mass., 2002—09; sr. edn. assoc. NSF, Arlington, Va., 1994—97. First lt. USAF, 1951—53, Biloxi, Miss.; Albuquerque, N.Mex.; Limestone, Maine. Recipient L. E. Grinter Award for Contributions to Engring. Edn., Accreditation Bd. for Engring. and Tech., Inc., 1993, Alumni Outstanding Tchr., U. Tenn., 1967, Outstanding Engring. Alumnus, 1975, Faculty Macebearer, 1997—98, Nathan W. Dougherty award, 2010, James T. Rogers Disting. Leadership award, So. Assn. Colls. and Schs., 2004. Fellow: Am. Inst. Chem. Engrs. (dir. 1975—77, treas. 1996—2001, Knoxville-Oak Ridge Chem. Engr. of Yr. 1977, 1999), Am. Inst. of Chemists (life), Am. Soc. for Engring. Edn. (life Chem. Engring. Lifetime Achievement award 2007, Benjamin Garver Lamme award 2009); mem.: Am. Chem. Soc., Tech. Soc. of Knoxville, Torch Club, Phi Kappa Phi (Disting. Mem. 1974), Tau Beta Pi (exec. coun. 1986—90), Sigma Xi, Sci. Rsch. Soc. (pres. 1983—84, treas. 1990—2002), Alpha Tau Omega. Roman Catholic. Home: 7021 Stagecoach Trail Knoxville TN 37909-1112 Business E-Mail: jprados@utk.edu.

PRANGE, ARTHUR JERGEN, JR., psychology and psychiatry professor, neuroscientist; b. Grand Rapids, Mich., Sept. 19, 1926; s. Arthur Jergen and Martha Frances (Elliott) P.; m. Sarah Elizabeth Bowen, Feb. 4, 1950; children— Christine Anne, Martha Louise, Laura Beth, David Elliott. BS, U. Mich., 1947, MD, 1950. Intern Wayne County Gen. Hosp., Eloise, Mich., 1950-51; resident in psychiatry U. NC, Chapel Hill, 1954-57, instr., 1957-60, asst. prof., 1960-64, asso. prof., 1964-68, prof. psychiatry, 1968-83, Boshamer prof. psychiatry, 1983—, acting chmn. dept. psychiatry, 1983-85, dir. NIMH Clin. Rsch. Ctr., 1979—. Vis. scientist Med. Rsch. Coun. Unit, Epson, Surrey, Eng., 1968-69; chmn. clin. projects rsch. rev. com. HEW, NIMH, 1975-76, chmn. bd. sci. counselors, 1986-87; mem. psychopharmacologic drugs adv. com. HEW, FDA, 1979-82. Editor: The Thyroid Axis, Drugs and Behavior, 74; Contbr. articles to med. jours. Recipient NIMH Career Devel. award 1961-69, Career Scientist award, 1969-95, Gold Medal award Soc. of Biol. Psychiatry, 1992, Exemplary Psychiatrist award Nat. Alliance for the Mentally Ill, 1997, Selo prize Nat. Alliance for Rsch. in Schizophrenia and Affective Disorders, 1997. Fellow Am. Psychiat. Assn. (life, Rsch. in Psychiatry award 1996), Am. Coll. Neuropsychopharmacology (life, pres. 1987, Hoch award 1995); mem. Internat. Soc. Psychoneuroendocrinology (founding mem.), NC Neuropsychiat. Assn., Collegium Internationale Neuropsychopharmacologicum, Royal Coll. Psychiatrists (London). Home: 6503 Meadowview Rd Hillsborough NC 27278-8314 Office: Univ NC Sch Medicine Dept Psychiatry Chapel Hill NC 27599-0001

PRATHER, DONNA LYNN, psychiatrist; b. Charlotte, NC, Nov. 4, 1946; d. James Boyd and Ann (Joyner) P. BA, Queens Coll., Charlotte, 1968; MD, U. N.C., 1978. Supr. Meckenburg County Dept. Social Svcs., Charlotte, 1971-74; family practice intern Charlotte Meml. Hosp., 1978-79, resident in family practice, 1979-81; fellow in family medicine U. N.C., Chapel Hill, 1981-82; resident in psychiatry N.C. Meml. Hosp., Chapel Hill, 1982-85; pvt. practice psychiatry Chapel Hill, NC, 1985—. Psychiatrist Person Counceling Ctr., Roxboro, N.C., 1983-92; med. dir. Orange-person-Chatam Mental Health Ctr., Chapel Hill, 1992—; clin. assoc. prof. U. N.C., Chapel Hill, 1985—. Mem. N.C. Psychiat. Assn., N.C. Med. Soc., Am. Psychiat. Assn., N.C. Psychiat. Assn. (chmn., com. for women 1990-91, ethics com. 1997-99). Avocation: music. Office: 200 N Greensboro St Ste D-7 Carrboro NC 27510 Office Phone: 919-929-6519.

PRATHER, GERALD LUTHER, management consultant, retired judge, military officer; b. LaGrange, Ga., Apr. 7, 1935; s. Luther Pate and Hazel Belle (McCullough) P.; m. Carolyn Pearson, Nov. 22, 1956; children: Dean Allen, Bryan Pate, Jeri Lynn, Angela BSE.E., Auburn U., 1966; MS in Mgmt., Air Force Inst. Tech., 1972; postgrad. advanced mgmt., U. Houston, 1978; grad., SQ Officer Sch., Maxwell AFB, 1963, ICAF, Washington, 1974, Ecumenical Ctr. Religion and Health, San Antonio, Tex., 2000. Enlisted USAF, 1954-56, commd. 2d lt., 1956, advanced through grades to maj. gen., 1981, various assignments as pilot, 1956-68, served in Vietnam, 1967-68, commdr. 1963d Comm. Squadron Chanute AFB, Ill., 1968-69, comdr. 1918th Comm. Squadron Scott AFB, Ill., 1969-70, dep. dir. comm.-electronics for 15th Air Force March AFB, Calif., 1970-72, chief comm. ops. div. hdqrs. Washington, 1972-75, comdr. strategic comm. div. Offutt AFB, Nebr., 1975-77, comdr. European Comm. Div. Ramstein AFB, W. Ger., 1977-80; dir. Command Control, Comm. & Computer Systems, Hdqrs. U.S. Readiness Command MacDill AFB, Fla., 1980-81; asst. chief of staff of Info. Systems Hdqrs. USAF, Washington, 1981-84, comdr. Air Force Comm. Command Scott AFB, Ill., 1984-86, ret., 1986; pvt. practice mgmt. cons. Del Rio, Tex., 1986-1997; Justice of the Peace Val Verde County, Tex., 1987-97. Lectr. in field; also air traffic controller, parachutist; bd. dir. Del Rio Internat. Airport. Speech writer: Team America, 1983 (Freedom Found. nat. award, 1984). Scoutmaster Eagle Scout America, 1949, 2008—, Boy Scouts Am., Sacramento, 1963, chmn. com., 1964, cub master Auburn, Ala.; sponsor Explorer Troop, Boy Scouts Am., Scott AFB, Ill., 1969; chmn. Amistad Dist. Boy Scouts Am., 1988, BSA Coun. Exec. Com., 2005—08, v.p., program, 2005—07; chmn. Eagle Scout advancement, 1994—2010, Val Verde County United Way campaign, 1989, pres., bd. dirs., 1990; life mem. Nat. Eagle Scout Assn.; eucharistic min. St. James Ch., 2000—, pastoral counselor, 2002, pastoral care specialist, 2002—; chaplain Val Verde Regional Hosp., 2002—, Juvenile Detention Ctr., 1998—2006, Val Verde Vol. Firemen, 2012—; asst. pastor 1st Presbyn. Ch., 2006—09, 2011—; pastor Full Gospel Ch., 2008—10. Decorated DSM with oak leaf cluster, Legion of Merit with one oak leaf cluster, DFC, Bronze Star with V device, Air medal with two oak leaf clusters, Republic of Vietnam Gallantry Cross with Palm; recipient Gen. Edwin W. Rawlings award Air Force Inst. Tech., 1972, Comdt.'s award, 1972, Order of the Sword, 1986, Silver Beaver award Boy Scouts Am., 2003, Eagle Scout award, 2006, Nat. Distinguished Eagle Scout award, 2013; Wilma E. West fellow Boy Scouts Am., 2005, Named to Hall of Fame, Com. Info, 2008. Mem.: VFW (life), Laughlin AFB Heritage Fedn. (bd. dir. 2007—, pres. 2009—), Mil. Affairs Assn. (bd. dir. 1990—2006, v.p., life dir. 2006—, masonic citizen of yr.), Del Rio C. of C. (v.p. 1989—90, bd. dir. 1990—99, v.p. 1991—92, pres. 1995—96, bd. dir. 1999—, life dir. 2005—, Chamber Mem. of Yr. award 2005), Air Force Assn. (Jimmy Doolittle award 1984, Ira Eaker award), Telephone Pioneers of Am., Soc. Logistics Engrs., Justice of the Peace and Constables Assn., Soc. Am. Mil. Engrs., Air Traffic Control Assn., Armed Forces Comm.-Electronics Assn. (mem. com. 1981—82, chmn. ethics com. 1982—83, internat. v.p. 1982—84, assoc. dir. 1984—96, bd. dirs. 1999, Meritorious Gold medal 1976, 1983), Non-Commd. Officers Assn. (hon.), Air Force Sgts. Assn. (hon.), Army Airways Comm. Svc. Alumni Assn. (life; dir. 2000—, Hall of Honor 2002, Life Achievement award 2003, 2007), Disabled Am. Vets. (life), Ret. Officers Assn. (life), Vietnam Vets. Am. (life), Del Rio Club, Lions (dir. 1989—94, v.p. 1994, Svc. award 1992—93, 2002—03, Helen Keller fellow 2004, Dist. Chaplain 2008—09), Civitan, Am. Legion, Order of Daedalians (life). Avocations: singing, gardening, sketching, automotive mechanics, private pilot. Home: 585 Palomino Rd Del Rio TX 78840-6086 Office Phone: 830-774-4483.

PRATHER, JOHN GIDEON, JR., lawyer; b. Lexington, Ky., Sept. 10, 1946; s. John Gideon Sr. and Marie Jeanette (Moore) P.; m. Hilma Elizabeth Skonberg, Aug. 4, 1973; children: John Hunt, Anna Russell. BS in Acctg., U. Ky., 1968, JD, 1970. Bar: Ky. 1971, U.S. Dist. Ct. (ea. dist.) Ky. 1978, U.S. Dist. Ct. (we. dist.) Ky. 1984, U.S. Ct. Appeals (6th cir.) 1988, U.S. Supreme Ct. 1988. Atty., pvt. practice, Somerset, Ky., 1971—; ptnr., prin. Law Offices John G. Prather, Somerset, 1972—; dir. Ky. Higher Edn. Assistance Authority, Somerset, 2002—05. Bd. dirs. Lawyers Mutual Ins. Co. Ky., 1989—, treas., 1995—2002, chmn. bd., 2002—; chmn. Ky. Higher Edn. Assistance Authority, 2004—05, Ky. Higher Edn. Student Loan Corp., 2004—05; dir. First and Farmers Bank, 2004—, chmn. bd., 2005—. Bd. dir. United Way, 1978—; mem. state cen. com. Ky. Young. Dems., Frankfort, 1972. Served to 1st lt. USAF, 1971-72, JAG, 1972. Fellow, U. Ky., 1998—. Mem. ABA (ho. dels. 1994-2004), ATLA, Am. Bd. Trial Advs., Am. Coll. Trial Lawyers, Am. Bd. Trial Attys., Ky. Bar Assn. (ho. dels. 1984-85, bd. govs. 1985-91, v.p. 1991-92, pres.-elect 1992-93, pres. 1993-94, lectr.), Coun. Sch. Bd. Attys. (state pres., bd. dir. 1986—, lectr.), Ky. Def. Coun. (bd. dir. 1987-91), Pulaski County Indsl. Found. (bd. dir. 1982-95), Phi Delta Phi. Mem. Christian Ch. Avocations: boating, flying, developing real estate. Home: 510 N Main St Somerset KY 42501-1434 Office: PO Box 616 Somerset KY 42502-0616 Office Phone: 606-679-1626. E-mail: pratherlaw@msn.com.

PRATHER, LAURA LEE, lawyer, educator; BBA, U. Tex., 1988, JD, 1991. Jud. clk. to U.S. Dist. Judge Hayden Head Jr., Corpus Christi, Tex., 1991—92; assoc. O'Melveny & Myers, LA, 1992—93; from assoc. to ptnr. George, Donaldson & Ford, Austin, Tex., 1993—98; ptnr. Jackson Walker, Austin, 1998, Sedgwick, Detert, Moran & Arnold. Bd. dirs. KLRN, Austin; adj. prof. media and entertainment U. Tex., 2005, 2006. Editor: (e-copyright law handbook) Aspen Law and Business; contbr. articles to law jours. Mem. adv. bd. Lifeworks, Austin, Ctr. for Child Protection, Austin. Recipient Pres.'s award, Tex. Assn. Broadcasters, 2005; named Best Lawyer under 40, Austin Young Men's and Women's Alliance, 2000, Tex. Rising Star, Tex. Lawyer, 1999; named to The 45 Under 45, The American Lawyer, 2011. Mem.: ABA (mem. governing bd. forumon comms. law 2000—, mem. editl. bd. Litigation mag. 2004—), Tex. Bar Assn., Calif. Bar Assn., N.Y. Bar Assn. Office: Sedgwick Detert Moran & Arnold 919 Congress Ave Ste 1250 Austin TX 78701

PRATHER, LENORE LOVING, former state supreme court chief justice; b. West Point, Miss., Sept. 17, 1931; d. Byron Herald and Hattie Hearn (Morris) Loving; m. Robert Brooks Prather, May 30, 1957; children: Pamela, Valerie Jo, Malinda Wayne. BS, Miss. Univ. Women, 1953; JD, U. Miss., 1955; D (hon.), Miss. Univ. Women, 2003. Bar: Miss. 1955. Practice with B. H. Loving, West Point, 1955-60; sole practice, 1960-62, 65-71; assoc. practice, 1962-65; mcpl. judge City of West Point, 1965-71; chancery ct. judge 14th dist. State of Miss., Columbus, 1971-82, supreme ct. justice Jackson, 1982-92, presiding justice, 1993-97, chief justice, 1998-2001; interim pres. Miss. U. for Women, Columbus, Miss., 2001—02. V.p. Conf. Local Bar Assn., 1956-58; sec. Clay County Bar Assn., 1956-71 1st woman in Miss. to become chancery judge, 1971, and supreme ct. justice, 1982, and chief justice, 1998-2000; recipient Miss. Bar Found. Professionalism award, 2005; named Outstanding Miss. Woman, Pres.'s Commn. on Status of Women, 1986-87. Mem. Miss. State Bar Assn. (Jud. Excellence award 2000-01), DAR, Rotary, Pilot Club, Jr. Aux. Columbus Club. Episcopalian. Achievements include becoming the first female chancellor in Mississippi; the first female supreme court justice; the first female chief justice in Mississippi.

PRATS, MICHAEL, petroleum engineer, educator; b. Tampa, Fla., Dec. 18, 1925; s. Miguel and Maria (Carbó) P.; m. Mary Blanche Flaherty, Apr. 7, 1951; children: Delicia Anne, Barbara Eileen, Teresa Kaye, Steven Michael. BS in Physics, U. Tex., 1949, MA in Physics, 1951. With Shell Devel. Co., Houston, 1950—, cons. rsch. engr., then sr. rsch. assoc., 1972-89; pres. Michael Prats & Assocs., Houston, 1989—. Cons. prof. petroleum engring. dept. Stanford U., 1997—99; adj. prof. dept. geosystems petroleum engring. U. Tex., Austin, 1991—2001; participant scientist exch. Royal/Dutch Shell Lab., Amsterdam, Netherlands, 1954, 55, Shell Internat. Petroleum, The Hague, Netherlands, 1981, Maraven, S.A., Caracas, Venezuela, 1981-83. Author: Thermal Recovery, 1982, Spanish transl., 1987; contbr. articles to profl. jours.; 23 patents in field. Served to staff sgt. USAAF, 1944-46, PTO. Recipient Disting. Svc. award Rep. Honduras, 1989, KAPITSA medal Acad. Natural Scis. (Moscow), 1995; named to Internat. Hall of Fame, 1989. Mem.: NAE, AIME (hon.), Russian Acad. Nat. Scis. (fgn.), Acad. Engring. Armenia (fgn.), Assn. Petroleum Engrs. Mex., Can. Inst. Mining, Acad. Medicine, Engring. and Sci. of Tex., Mex. Nat. Acad. Engring. (corr.), Soc. Petroleum Engrs. (hon.; bd. dirs. 1976—79, sr. tech. editor 1987—90, Uren award 1974, Disting. Mem. award 1983, Enhanced Oil Recovery Pioneer 1986, Thermal Recovery Disting. Achievement award Thermal Ops. Symposium 1991, Anthony F. Lucas Gold medal 1993, Legend of Hydraulic Fracturing 2006), Pi Epsilon Tau (hon. diploma of honor 1986). Avocation: travel. Mailing: 4141 S Braeswood Blvd Ste 205 Houston TX 77025 Personal E-mail: mikep@mprats.com.

PRATS PALERM, ROBERTO L., political organization administrator; b. San Juan, 1966; m. Heddle Fernandez; 2 children. BA in Policy Analysis and Mgmt., Cornell U., Ithaca, NY, 1990; attended, Georgetown U., Washington; JD, Inter-Am. U. Sch. Law, PR, 1994. Notary pub. Aux. advisor to gov. Rafael Hernandez Colón, PR, 1990—91; staff mem. US Congress, Washington, 1991—92; econ. advisor, minority spokesman PR Senate, 1993—94, at-large senator, 2000—04; atty. Goldman, Antonetti & Córdova, 1995—97; pub. affairs & fed. rels advisor City of San Juan, 1997—99; pvt. practice atty., 2000—; chmn. PR Dem. Party, 2003—. Host Speakout, WOSO Radio. Fundraising participant Alzheimer's Assn., PR, 2002; mem. adv. bd. Cornell U., Ithaca, NY. Democrat. Office: PR Dem Party PO Box 19328 San Juan PR 00910-3939 Office Phone: 787-274-2921. Office Fax: 787-759-9075.*

PRATT, DAVID, lawyer; b. NYC, Mar. 25, 1964; BS magna cum laude in Acctg., SUNY, Albany, 1986; JD cum laude, Bklyn. Law Sch., 1991; LLM in Taxation, NYU, 1993. Bar: NY 1992, Fla. 1993, cert.: Fla. Bar Bd. Legal Specialization and Edn. (tax and wills and trusts and estates). Ptnr. Proskauer Rose, LLP, Boca Raton, Fla., 2005—. Adj. prof. U. Fla. Levin Coll. Law; faculty mem. Am. Law Inst.-ABA. Contbr. articles to profl. jours. Chair bd. trustees Jewish Cmty. Found. of Jewish Fedn. of South Palm Beach County; mem. legal com. Jewish Nat. Fund; mem. exec. com. of profl. advs. Cmty. Found. Palm Beach and Martin Counties. Named one of Top 100 Attys., Worth mag., 2006. Fellow: Am. Coll. Tax Counsel, Am. Coll. Trust and Estate Counsel; mem.: Boca Raton Estate Planning Coun., AICPA, NY State Bar Assn., Fla. Bar Assn. Office: Proskauer Rose LLP 1 Boca Pl 2255 Glades Rd Ste 340 W Boca Raton FL 33431-7360 Office Phone: 561-995-4777. Office Fax: 561-241-7145. E-mail: dpratt@proskauer.com.

PRATT, DONALD GEORGE, physician; b. Higgins, Tex., Oct. 19, 1946; s. George Horace and Esta Vici (Barker) P. BS in Biomed. Sci., West Tex. State U., 1970; MD, U. Tex., Galveston, 1974. Diplomate Am. Bd. Family Practice, Am. Bd. Radiology (Radiation Oncology). Intern Scott & White Meml. Hosp., Temple, Tex., 1974-75, resident in gen. surgery and pathology, 1975-77, physician, 1979—83; resident in family practice McLennan County Med. Edn. and Rsch. Found., Waco, Tex., 1977-79; physician Family Practice Assocs., El Paso, Tex., 1983; owner, pvt. contractor Minor Emergency Ctrs., Amarillo, Tex., 1983-85; resident in radiation therapy U. Tex., Galveston, 1985-88; ptnr. Cons. in Radiation Oncology, P.A., Amarillo, 1988—2003, pres., 1994—2003, Cons. in Radiation Oncology, 1994—2003; dir. dept. radiation oncology Harrington Cancer Ctr., Amarillo, 1994—2003, pres. staff, bd. dirs., 1995-99; prin. investigator Radiation Oncology Group, 1988-95; pres. of staff Harrington Cancer Ctr., 1995—99; ptnr. Cons. in Radiation Oncology, P.A., Amarillo, 1988—2003, pres., 1994—2003; cons. in radiation oncology, 1994—2003. Dir. Dept. Radiation Oncology Harrington Cancer Ctr., Amarillo, Tex., 1994—2003. Mem. AMA, Am. Soc. Therapeutic Radiology and Oncology, Tex. Med. Assn., Potter/Randall County Med. Soc., Tex. Radiol. Soc. Home: 261 S Timbercreek Dr Amarillo TX 79118-3751 Office Phone: 806-359-4673. Business E-Mail: dpratt@harringtonca.org.

PRATT, WALTER F., JR., law educator; BA in History magna cum laude, Vanderbilt U., 1968; D.Phil in Politics, Oxford U., 1974; JD, Yale U., 1977. Law clk. to Judge Charles Clark US Ct. Appeals (5th cir.), 1977—78; law clk. to Chief Justice Warren E. Burger US Supreme Ct., 1978—79; asst. prof. law Duke U., 1979—82, assoc. prof., 1982—86; assoc. prof. law The Law Sch., U. Notre Dame, 1986—98, co-dir. Notre Dame London Law Ctr., 1988—89, assoc. dean academic affairs, 1991—98, exec. assoc. dean, 1999—2006; dean, Ednl. Found. disting. prof. law U. SC Sch. Law, 2006—11, prof. law, 2011—. Vis. assoc. prof. law J. Reuben Clark Law Sch., Brigham Young U., 1984—85; vis. scholar law dept. Nat. U. Ireland, Galway, 1998—99. Author: Privacy in Britain, 1979, The Supreme Court Under Edward Douglass White, 1910-1921, 1999; contbr. articles to law jours. First lt. US Army, 1968—71. Recipient Spl. Presdl. Award, U. Notre Dame; grantee Rhodes Scholarship. Mem.: ABA, Am. Soc. Legal History, Assn. Am. Law Schs. Office: University South Carolina School Law Law Center 202 701 S Main St Columbia SC 29208 Office Phone: 803-777-6857. E-mail: wpratt@law.sc.edu.

PRAYSON, ALEX STEPHEN, design engineering educator; b. Tulsa, June 24, 1939; s. Stephen Alexander and Frances Prayson; m. Jacqueline Ann Prayson; children: Stephen, David, Timothy, Anthony. AS, Edison Tech., 1967; DC, Cleveland Coll., 1972; AA, Summit U., 1996, Tulsa C.C., 2002; BS, Excelsior Coll., 2003; MEd, We. Govs. U., 2004; PhD in Edn., N. Ctrl. U., 2006. Diplomate Am. Bd. Chiropractic Examiners. Owner Prayson Candies Co., Tulsa, 1963—68; cartographer Howard Needles Tammen and Bergendoff, Kansas City, Mo., 1968—71; supr. M. J. Harden Assocs., Kansas City, 1971—81; asst. prof. Tulsa C.C., 1981—2003; ret., 2003; founder, 2010—, Just Desserts Tulsa, 2009—10. Advisor Phi Theta Kappa, Tulsa, 1991-2001. Author: A Love-Hate Anthology, 1993, Cad Systems Operation, 1996; inventor Taffy-Pull. Mem. selection com. Ahepa Civic Youth Svc. Award, Tulsa, 1992—; vol. Cmty. Action Project, 2004; founder Tulsa Online Acad., 2011-. Named Most Disting. Chpt. Advisor, Phi Theta Kappa, Tulsa, 1994-95; recipient Robert Giles Disting. Advisor Internat. award, 1995-96, Continued Excellence award for advisors, 1996-97, 99-2000, Tchr. of Yr. award Tulsa C.C., 1997, Mosal Leader award Phi Theta Kappa, 2000. Mem. Nat. Assn. Realtors, Greater Tulsa Assn. Realtors, Jaquar Club of Tulsa, Kappa Delta Pi, Alpha Delta Epsilon. Avocations: bridge, travel, Scrabble. Home: 204 E 27th St Tulsa OK 74114-3912 Personal E-mail: aprayson@ymail.com.

PRECOURT, STEPHEN L., state legislator; b. Orlando, Fla., Oct. 20, 1960; m. Lisa Precourt; children: Stephanie, Michael, Heather, Samuel, Jacob. BSCE, U. Fla., 1983. Transp. engr.; small bus. owner; mem. Dist. 41 Fla. House of Reps., Tallahassee, 2006—, chair energy and utilities policy com., mem. gen. govt. policy coun., joint com. on pub. counsel oversight, natural resources appropriations com., roads, bridges and ports policy com. Past chmn. Orange County Devel. Adv. Bd.; mem. Orange County Bldg. Codes Bd. Adjustment & Appeals, West Orange-South Lake Transp. Task Force, chmn., 2004—05. Mem. ASCE (Engr. of Yr. 2004, 2006), West Orange Polit. Alliance (chmn. 2004-05), West Orange C. of C. (bd. dirs.). Republican. Roman Catholic. Office: 303 House Office Bldg 402 S Monroe St Tallahassee FL 32399-1300 also: 7009 Dr Phillips Blvd Ste 270 Orlando FL 32819-5124 Office Phone: 850-488-0256, 407-355-5784.

PREECE, BETTY P., electrical engineer, educator; b. Decatur, Ill. d. George A. and Margaret (Stock) Peters; m. Raymond G. Preece; children: Eric, George. BSEE, U. Ky., 1947; MS in Sci. Edn., Fla. Inst. Tech. Cert. Master Gardener, U. Fla. Engr. GE, various cities, 1947-50; project engr. Air Force Missle Test Ctr., Patrick AFB, Fla., 1951-54; tchr., faculty physics, math., phys. sci. Melbourne HS, Fla., 1972-90; exec. sec. Fla. Acad. Sci., Indialantic, 1991-96; accessibility coord. 45th Civil Engring. Sqd., Patrick AFB, Fla., 1990—; dir., engring. edn. cons. Jr. Engring. Tech. Soc., 2002—; dir., sec. Space Coast Ctr. for Ind. Living. Joined adj. faculty Fla. Inst. Tech., 1964; ret.; US del. Interam. Conf. on Physics Edn., 1987, 1989, 1991, 1993; presenter Internat. Conf. Women Engrs. and Scientists. Contbr. articles over 100 pub. to profl. jour. Mem. Indialantic Code Enforcement Bd., 1987—; Chair bd. and local history editor So. Brevard Hist. Soc., 1975—. Recipient Fla. Found. for Future Scientists award, 1994; named Outstanding Sci. Tchr., Sigma Xi; named to Alumni Hall of Distinction, Coll. Engring. U. Ky., 2002 Fellow Soc. Women Engrs. (sr. life mem., chartered 1st sect. at Fla. Inst. Tech., counselor, chartered U. Ctrl. Fla. Collegiate sect., past counselor U. Ctrl. Fla., Miami U., chartered Space Coast Sect., past. pres., sect. rep., career guidance com. chair., nat. conv. program chair 1992, career guidance com. chair, region D dir. 1992-94, mem. leadership coach, local past pres., liaison coord. for NSTA 1994-, editl. bd. SWE Mag. 1998-, Disting. Svc. award 2007); mem. AIAA, NSTA, IEEE (life), Sci. Ed. for Students with Disabilities, Third World Orgn. for Women in Sci., Women in Engring. Programs and Advocates Network Comm. Chairs, Assn. for Women in Sci., Am. Assn. Physics Tchr. (women in physics com. 1993—, chair 2002-04, Disting. Svc. award 1997), Fla. Hist. Soc., Missile Space and Range Pioneers, Women's Engring. Soc. UK, DAR, Daus. Am. Colonists, Daus. of War of 1812, Delta Kappa Gamma, Phi Delta Kappa, Etta Kappa Nu. Achievements include being the first female electrical engineering graduate at the University of Kentucky. Office: 615 N Riverside Dr Indialantic FL 32903-4254

PREEDOM, BARRY MASON, physicist, researcher; b. Stamford, Conn., Dec. 31, 1940; children: Bonnie Marie, Richard Lawrence. BS, Spring Hill Coll., 1962; MS, U. Tenn., 1964, PhD, 1967. Grad. fellow Oak Ridge (Tenn.) Nat. Lab., 1964-67; rsch. assoc. Mich. State U., East Lansing, 1967-70; asst. prof., then assoc. prof. U. S.C., Columbia, 1970-76, prof. physics, 1976—2006, Carolina rsch. prof., 1986-95, Carolina Disting. prof., 1995—2006, Carolina Disting. prof. emeritus, 2006—, assoc. dean for rsch., 2002—06. Vis. prof. Swiss Inst. Nuclear Rsch., Villigen, 1976; vis. staff Los Alamos (N.Mex.) Nat. Lab., 1972-91, tech. adv. panel, 1982-85; guest scientist Brookhaven Nat. Lab., Upton, N.Y., 1987—. Contbr. rsch. articles to sci. publs. Sr. teaching fellow Lilly Found., 1994-95; grantee Rsch. Corp., 1971, Office Naval Rsch., 1972-75, NSF, 1975—; recipient Mortar Bd. award for Excellence in Teaching, 1993. Mem. Am. Phys. Soc., Sigma Xi, Alpha Sigma Nu. Achievements include research and study of nuclear reaction mechanisms and nuclear structure, reaction probes including gamma rays, mesons, protons, deuterons and light ions. Office: Univ SC Dept Physics Columbia SC 29208-0001 Home Phone: 803-732-9228; Office Phone: 803-777-4121. E-mail: preedom@sc.edu.

PRENTICE, HOWARD MALCOLM, research scientist, educator; s. Roy and Doris Harvey Prentice; m. Linda Elizabeth McGrath, Mar. 31, 1978; children: Sarah Elizabeth, Christopher Andrew. MA, U. Aberdeen, Scotland, 1980; DEA, L'INSERM, Paris, 1981; MS, U. London, 1984, PhD, 1987. Fellow Stanford U. Sch. Medicine, Palo Alto, Calif., 1987—89, U. So. Calif., LA, 1989—93; lectr. U. Glasgow, Scotland, 1993—98, sr. lectr., 1998—2000; assoc. prof. biomedical sci. Fla. Atlantic U., Boca Raton, 2000—. Grant rev. com. Am. Heart Assn., Dallas, 2006—, Tampa, Fla., 2006—. Co-author (Lutz, P.L., Nilsson, G.E., Prentice H.M.): (book) The Brain Without Oxygen.; contbr. to numerous profl. jours. Team leader Am. Heart Assn. Ann. Sponsored Walk, Boca Raton, Fla., 2006—07. Grant Aid, Am. Heart Assn., 2005—08, Large Equipment grant, Fla. Dept. Health, Bankhead Coley., 2007—08, Project grant, Brit. Heart Found., 1993—95, Med. Rsch. Coun., UK., 1994—97, Brit. Heart Found., UK., 1995—99, Nat. Heart Rsch. Fund, UK., 1998—2000, Wellcome Trust, UK., 1998—99, Internat. Travel grant, 1995—99. Achievements include research in determination of regulatory characteristics of specific gene/promoter elements in normal and disease-stressed myocardial tissue, examination of the effects on altered cardiac contractility in cardiac muscle cells; investigation of mitochondria function and oxidative stress in age related disorders and in analysis of mechanisms of hypoxia and anoxia tolerance in brain. Business E-Mail: hprentic@fau.edu.

PRESBY, J. THOMAS, financial advisor, director; b. Newark, Feb. 15, 1940; s. George and Shirley (Kandel) P.; m. Elaine Merle Smith, Aug. 19, 1961; children: Philip, Terry, Mona. BSEE, Rutgers U., 1961; MBA in Indsl. Adminstrn., Carnegie-Mellon U., 1963. CPA, Ohio, N.Y. Ptnr. Touche Ross, NYC, 1972-76; regional ptnr. Touche Ross Internat., Paris, 1976-79, nat. dir. client svcs., 1979-81, exec. dir. internat., 1981-82, ptnr.-in-charge fin. svcs. ctr., 1982-90, mng. ptnr. Ea. Europe, Brussels, 1990-94, chief exec. officer Europe, Paris, 1991-95; COO Deloitte Touche Tohmatsu International, NYC, 1995—2002, dep. chmn., 1997, chief staff, mem. exec. group, 1999—2002. Bd. dirs. Am. Eagle Outfitters, Inc., Tiffany & Co., TurboChef Technologies, Inc., 2003—09, World Fuel Svcs. Corp., 2003—, Invesco Ltd., 2005, First Solar, Inc., 2006—, ExamWorks Group Inc., 2009—. Mem. bus. adv. coun. Grad. Sch. Indsl. Adminstrn., Carnegie-Mellon U., Pitts., 1984-2001; trustee Rutgers U., New Brunswick, NJ, 1985-90; bd. dirs. Tiffany & Co., Amvescap PLC, Am. Eagle Outfitters, World Fuel Services, Turbochef Technologies, German Marshall Fund., First Solar Inc. Mem. AICPA, Ohio Soc. CPAs, N.Y. Soc. CPAs, Harmonie Club. Avocations: antique autos, racquetball, squash, motorcycling, fly fishing. Office: ExamWorks Group Inc Bd Directors 3280 Peachtree Rd NE Ste 2625 Atlanta GA 30305 Office Phone: 404-952-2400. Office Fax: 404-846-1554. Personal E-mail: j.presby@examworks.com.

PRESCOTT, THOMAS J., finance company executive; BBA in Acctg., Columbus Coll., 1976. V.p. fin. Synovus Fin. Corp., 1987—91, sr. v.p. fin. and acctg., 1991—93, sr. v.p., chief acctg. officer, 1993—94, exec. v.p., treas., 1994—96; exec. v.p., CFO Synovus Financial Corp., 1996—. Bd. dirs. Columbus Country Club, Ga. Coun. on Econ. Edn.; bd. trustees Huntingdon Coll. Mem.: Ga. Soc. CPA's, Leadership Columbus, Kiwanis Club North Columbus. Office: Synovus Financial Corp Ste 500 1111 Bay Ave Columbus GA 31902 Office Phone: 706-649-2311. Office Fax: 706-641-6555.

PRESLAR, B. CLYDE, corporate financial executive; Undergraduate, Elon Coll.; MBA, Wake Forest U. CPA; cert. mgmt. acct. Dir., investor rels. RJR Nabisco, 1978—89; dir., fin. svcs., dir., investor rels. Black & Decker Corp. (merged with The Stanley Works), 1989—96; sec. Lance Inc., 1996—2005, v.p., CFO, 2002—05; exec. v.p., CFO Cott Corp., 2005—06; pvt. cons., 2006—08; CFO RailAmerica, Inc., 2008—. Former bd. dirs. Standard Comml. Corp., 1999; bd. dirs. Forward Air Corp., 2004—08, Alliance One Internat. Inc. (formerly DIMON Inc.), 2005—. Office: RailAmerica Inc 13901 Sutton Park Dr S Ste 160 Jacksonville FL 32224-0230 Office Phone: 904-538-6100. Business E-Mail: bpreslar@aointl.com.

PRESLEY, BRIAN, investment company executive; b. Evansville, Ind., Dec. 28, 1941; s. Harry and Ruth P.; m. Mary Nell Minyard, Aug. 17, 1972; children: Debra, Cynthia, David, Jeffrey, Clark, Gregory, Steven. BSBA, U. Evansville, 1963; MBA, Mich. State U., 1964; diploma, Wharton Sch., U. Pa., 1995. Market rsch. analyst Stanley Works, New Britain, Conn., 1964-68; tax shelter coord. F.I. Dupont, Memphis, 1968-73; v.p. Bullington Schas, Memphis, 1973-75; pres., mng. ptnr. Presley Assocs., Memphis, 1965-93; pres., CFO CSG, Inc., Memphis, 1975—. Gen. ptnr. various real estate and oil and gas partnerships, 1974-1986; pres. Cooper St. Group Securities, Inc., 1983-86; divsn. mgr. Advantage Capital Corp. (divsn. AIG Advisors, Inc.), 1986-89, reg. v.p., 1989, CEO 1990-94, mng. dir., mktg. strategist, 1995; pres. Presley Adv. Inc., 1995—, pub. Presley Adv. Letter; instr. fin. divsn. continuing edn. Memphis U. Bd. dirs. Apt. Coun. Tenn., 1980-86, sec.-treas., 1982-83; pres. Memphis Apt. Coun., 1983; mem., U. Evansville Nat. Alumni Bd., 1988-91; prodr. 2 daily radio stock market commentary shows, 1988; fin. commentator Sta. WEVU-TV (ABC), Ft. Myers/Naples, 1988-89; host syndicated radio show for sr. citizens, 1979-81; mem. found. bd. and fin. com. Fla. Gulf Coast U., 2001-09. Mem. Leadership Charlotte; chmn. Charlotte County Econ. Devel. Coun., 1999-2002; pres. Enterprise Charlotte Found., 2002-06; chmn. Angels Found. Charlotte County, 2002-05; fin. advisor Charlotte Symphony Orch., 2002-; bd. dirs. Charlotte County Cmty. Found., 2005—; vice chmn. Charlotte Cmty. Found., 2007—; advisor Visual Arts Ctr. Endowment Fund, 2007-, chmn., 2010-. Recipient Richard L. McLaughlin award, Econ. Devel. Coun., Fla., 2002. Mem. Internat. Assn. Fin. Planners (broker dealer adv. coun. 1993-97), Admirals Club (life, bd. dirs.), Naples Jazz Soc. (chmn. bd. dirs. 1993-96), Naples Sailing and Yacht Club (bd. dirs.1991-96), Pi Sigma Epsilon, Beta Gamma Sigma, Tau Kappa Epsilon Alumni Assn. (pres. Memphis area 1979-80), Isles Yacht Club (bd. dirs. 2001-04). Presbyterian. Home and Office: Acorn Ranch 5161 Acorn Ranch Rd Punta Gorda FL 33982-9511 Office Phone: 941-505-9017. Business E-Mail: brian@presleyadvisoryinc.com.

PRESLEY, LISA MARIE, singer; b. Memphis, Feb. 1, 1968; d. Elvis and Priscilla Beaulieu Presley; m. Danny Keough, Oct. 3, 1988 (div. 1994); children: Danielle Riley Keough, Benjamin Storm Keough; m. Michael Jackson, May 18, 1994 (div. Jan. 18, 1996); m. Nicholas Cage, Aug. 10, 2002 (div. May 16, 2004); m. Michael Lockwood, Jan. 22, 2006; children: Finley Michaela Lockwood, Harper Lisette Lockwood. Mgmt. Elvis Presley Trust; owner, chmn. bd. Elvis Presley Enterprises, Inc.; co-owner (with mother Priscilla) Elvis Presley's Memphis nightclub, operated by Presley Estate, 1997—2003. Singer: (albums) To Whom It May Concern, 2003 (cert. Gold), Lights Out, 2003, Now What, 2005, Storm & Grace, 2012; actress: (music video) You Are Not Alone, Michael Jackson, (car commercial), 1989; appeared on (cover of Vogue mag.), 1996, (cover of Vogue mag. with mother and daughter), 2004, featured in (TV) Elvis by the Presleys, 2005. Internat. spokesperson Citizens Commn. on Human Rights; co-founder (with Isaac Hayes) LEAP (Literacy, Edn., and Ability Program); involved with Fight for Kids. Recipient Humanitarian award, World Literacy Crusade, 2002. Office: Elvis Presley Enterprises Inc PO Box 16508 3734 Elvis Presley Blvd Memphis TN 38186-0508

PRESNELL, GREGORY A., federal judge; b. Tampa, Fla., Nov. 20, 1942; BA, Coll. William and Mary, 1964; JD with high honors, U. Fla., 1966. Bar: Fla. 1967. Mem. Akerman, Senterfitt & Edison, Orlando, Fla., 1966—2000; pres. Fla. Legal Services, Inc., 1977-79; judge US Dist. Ct. (middle dist.) Fla., Orlando, Fla., 2000—12, sr. judge, 2012—. Chmn. 9th Cir. Jud. Nominating Commn., 1982-83. Exec. editor U. Fla. Law Rev., 1966. Served in USAR, 1967—73. Mem. Orange County Bar Assn. (pres. 1975), Orange County Legal Aid Soc. (pres. 1974), Order of Coif. Office: US Dist Ct US Courthouse 401 W Central Blvd Rm 5750 Orlando FL 32801 Office Phone: 407-835-4301.*

PRESS, WILLIAM HENRY, physicist, computer scientist, educator; b. NYC, May 23, 1948; s. Frank and Billie (Kallick) Press; m. Margaret Ann Lauritsen, 1969 (div. 1982); 1 child, Sara Linda; m. Jeffrey Foden Howell, Apr. 19, 1991; 1 child, James Howell. AB, Harvard Coll., 1969; MS, Calif. Inst. Tech., 1971, PhD, 1972. Asst. prof. theoretical physics Calif. Inst. Tech., 1973-74; asst. prof. physics Princeton U., NJ, 1974—76; prof. astronomy and physics Harvard U., Cambridge, Mass., 1976-98, chmn. Dept. Astronomy, 1982-85; dep. lab. dir. Los Alamos Nat. Lab., N.Mex., 1998—2004, lab. sr. fellow, 2004—08, lab sr. fellow emeritus, 2008—; Warren J. and Viola M. Raymer chair computer scis. and integrative biology U. Tex. at Austin, 2007—. Mem. numerous adv. com. and panels NSF, NASA, NRC; vis. mem. Inst. Advanced Study, 1983—94; mem. Def. Sci. Bd., 1985—89; mem. sci. adv. com. Packard Found., 1988—; program com. Sloan Found., 1985—91; chmn. adv. bd. NSF Inst. Theoretical Physics, 1986—87, mem. Computer Sci. and Telecomm. Bd., 1991—96; US del. IUPAP Gen. Assembly, 1996; cons. MITRE Corp., 1977—; trustee Inst. Def. Analysis, 1988—, exec. com., 1990—; chief navel ops. Exec. Panel, 1994—2000; mem. Pres.'s Coun. of Advisors on Sci. and Tech. (PCAST), 2009—. Author: Numerical Recipes, 1986; contbr. articles to profl. jours. Sloan Found. rsch. fellow, 1974—78. Fellow: Am. Phys. Soc., Am. Acad. Arts and Scis.; mem.: NAS, Coun. on Fgn. Rels., Assn. for Computing Machinery, Internat. Soc. Relativity and Gravitation, Internat. Astron. Union, Am. Astron. Soc. (Helen B. Warner prize 1981). Office: University of Texas at Austin Department of Computer Science 1616 Guadalupe, Ste 2 408 Austin TX 78701 Office Phone: 512-232-4022. Office Fax: 512-471-8694. E-mail: wpress@cs.utexas.edu.

PRESSEL, MORGAN, professional golfer; b. Tampa, Fla., May 23, 1988; d. Kathy (Krickstein) and Mike Pressel. Profl. golfer LPGA, 2006—. Mem. US Team PING Jr. Solheim Cup, 2002, 2003, 2005; mem. East Team Cannon Cup, 2002—04. Recipient Nancy Lopez award, 2006, CoURagE award, Birdies for Breast Cancer, 2006; named Player of Yr., Am. Jr. Golf Assn., 2005. Achievements include winning the North and South Women's Amateur, 2004, US Women's Amateur, 2005; became youngest (18 years, 10 months, 9 days) major champion in LPGA history on April 1, 2007 at the Kraft Nabisco Championship; youngest (12) to qualify for the US Women's Open, 2001; won 11 events on the American Junior Golf Association circuit. Avocations: photography, computers. Mailing: LPGA 100 International Golf Dr Daytona Beach FL 32124-1092

PRESTAGE, JAMES JORDAN, consultant; b. Deweyville, Tex., Apr. 29, 1926; s. James J. and Mona (Wilkins) P.; m. Jewel Limar, Aug. 12, 1953; children— Terri, James Grady, Eric, Karen, Jay BS cum laude, So. U., Baton Rouge, 1950; MS, U. Iowa, 1955, PhD, 1959. Instr. biology Prairie View Coll., Tex., 1955-56; asst. prof. So. U., Baton Rouge, 1959, assoc. prof. biology, 1959-61, prof. biology, 1961—, dir. computer sci. ctr., 1968-71, 72-73, dean acad. affairs, v.p. acad. affairs, 1973-81, exec. v.p., 1981-82, chancellor, 1982-85, univ. disting. prof. emeritus, 1985—; univ. disting. prof. biology Dillard U., New Orleans, 1987—. Chair divsn. natural scis. Dillard U., 1990—97; asst. dir. La. Coordinating Council for Higher Edn., Baton Rouge, 1971—72; mem. commn. on scholars Ill. Bd. Higher Edn., 1975—82; mem. com. on off-campus instrn. La. Bd. Regents, 1975—; mem. La. Data Processing Coun., Baton Rouge, 1979—82; vis. prof. biology Dillard U., New Orleans; trustee Am. Coll. Testing Program, 1983—86; faculty assoc. Danforth Found., 1966—70; cons. in field. Mem. exec. bd. Istrouma council Boy Scouts Am.; vice chmn. bd. trustees Greater Mt. Carmel Baptist Ch., Baton Rouge; bd. dirs. Capital Area United Way, Baton Rouge. Served with USN, 1944-46, 50-52; ETO, Korea Named Most Outstanding Faculty Mem., So. U., 1966-67; Nat. Med. Fellowships fellow U. Iowa, Iowa City, 1956-59; NIH grantee, 1960-65 Mem. Conf. Acad. Deans So. States. NAACP, Sigma Xi, Alpha Chi, Alpha Phi Alpha (chpt. pres.), Sigma Pi Phi Democrat. Avocations: fishing, reading, gardening. Office: 11114 Wortham Blvd Houston TX 77065

PRESTAGE, JEWEL LIMAR, political scientist, educational consultant; b. Hutton, La., Aug. 12, 1931; d. Brudis L. and Sallie Bell (Johnson) Limar; m. James J. Prestage, Aug. 12, 1953; children— Terri, James, Eric, Karen, Jay. BA, So. U., Baton Rouge, 1951; MA, U. Iowa, 1952, PhD, 1954; LHD (hon.), U. D.C., 1994, Loyola U., Chgo., 1999; LLD (hon.), Spelman Coll., 1999. Assoc. prof. polit. sci. Prairie View (Tex.) Coll., 1954-55, 56; assoc. prof. polit. sci. So. U., 1956-57, 58-62, prof., 1962—, chairperson dept., 1965-83, dean pub. policy and urban affairs, 1983-89, dist. prof. emeritus, dean emeritus pub. policy, 1989—; prof. polit. sci. Prairie View U., 1989-90; dean Benjamin Banneker Honors Coll., Prairie View (Tex.) Coll., 1990-98, prof. political sci., 1998—, disting. prof. Prairie View, 2000—02. Chmn. La. adv. com. to U.S. Commn. on Civil Rights, 1975-85; mem., chmn. nat. adv. coun. on women's ednl. programs U.S. Dept. Edn., 1980-82; dist. vis. prof. U. Iowa, 1987-88. Author: (with M. Githens) A Portrait of Marginality: Political Behavior of the American Woman, 1976; contbr. articles to profl. jours. Rockefeller fellow, 1951-52; NSF fellow, 1964; Ford Found. postdoctoral fellow, 1969-70; Hon. Thurgood Marshal Scholarship Fund, 2005. Mem. NAACP, Am. Polit. Sci. Assn. (v.p. 1974-75, Frank Goodnow award 1998), So. Polit. Sci. Assn. (pres. 1975-76, Manning Dauer award 1998), Nat. Conf. Black Polit. Scientists (pres. 1976-77), Nat. Assn. African Am. Honors Programs (pres. 1993-94), Am. Soc. for Pub. Adminstrn. (pres. La. chpt. 1988-89, nat. exec. coun. 1989-90), Policy Studies Orgn. (exec. coun. 2000), Links Inc., Alpha Kappa Alpha, Congl. Black Caucus Found. (chair faculty adv. coun., 2003-04) Home: 11114 Wortham Blvd Houston TX 77065 Office: PO Box 125 Prairie View TX 77446-0125 Office Phone: 281-807-3994.

PRESTI, SAM, professional sports team executive; b. Concord, Mass. Student, Va. Wesleyan Coll., Norfolk; BA in Comm., Politics and Law, Emerson Coll., Boston, 2000. Intern San Antonio Spurs, 2000—01, basketball spl. asst., 2001—02, asst. dir. scouting, 2002—03, dir. player pers., 2003—05, asst. gen. mgr., 2005—07, v.p., 2006—07; gen. mgr. Seattle SuperSonics, 2007—08; exec. v.p., gen. mgr. Oklahoma City Thunder, 2008—. Recipient Young Alumnus award, Emerson Coll., 2005. Office: Oklahoma City Thunder Two Leadership Sq 211 N Robinson Ave Ste 300 Oklahoma City OK 73102

PRESTON, FORREST L., healthcare executive; Founder Life Care Centers of America, Cleveland, Tenn., 1970—, chmn., 2008—. Office: Life Care Centers of America 3570 Keith St NW Cleveland TN 37312 Office Phone: 423-472-9585. Office Fax: 423-476-5974. Business E-Mail: forrest_preston@lcca.com.

PRESTON, JOHN R., beverage products executive; BA in History, U. Mich., Ann Arbor, 1973; MBA, Harvard U. Bus. Sch., Mass., 1975. Exec. v.p., CFO Ripplewood Holdings, LLC; sr. v.p. Vivendi Universal; sr. v.p. treasury and strategic planning The Seagram Co. Ltd.; v.p. fin. and adminstrn. Southern Wine and Spirits America, Inc., 2004—. Office: So Wine and Spirits America 1600 NW 163d St Miami FL 33169 Office Phone: 305-625-4171.

PREWITT, LENA VONCILLE BURRELL, management educator; b. Feb. 17, 1932; BS, Stillman Coll., Tuscaloosa, Ala., 1954; MEd, Ind. U., Bloomington, 1955, EdD, 1961. Asst. prof., dept. chair Stillman Coll., 1960—66; assoc. prof., dept. chair Tex. So. U., 1967—69; assoc. prof. Florence State U., Ala., 1969—70; prof. Coll. of Commerce and Bus., U. Ala., 1970—94; core prof. Union Inst. and Univ., 1974—; interim v.p. for fiscal affairs Stillman Coll., Tuscaloosa, Ala., 1998—99, Disting. prof. mgmt., 1999—2000. Spl. rsch. cons. Tex. So. U., 1967—68; chair human resource mgmt. dept. U. Ala., 1977—83; faculty, advisor Antioch Coll., 1980—86; panel of scholars adv. com. to bd. dirs. Ind. U., 2005—; mem./chair U.S. Selective Svc. Appeals Bd., 1980—2000; presenter in field. Contbr. articles to profl. jours. Auditor Brown Meml. Presbyn. Ch., 1998; chair permanent jud. commn. Presbytery of Sheppards and Lapsley, Presbyn. Ch., 1997—, self devel. of people, 1990—; bd. dirs. Columbia Theol. Sem., Decatur, Ga., 1997—. With USAF, 1985. Recipient Outstanding Educator of Yr. award, Lucy Sheppard Art Federated Club, 1976, High Profile Prof. of Yr. award, U. Ala. Crimson White, 1991, numerous scholarships; named one of Top 5 Faculty Women, U. Ala., 1978. Mem.: Pub. Personnel Mgmt. Assn. (dissertation rsch. awards com. 1991—94), Internat. Personnel Mgmt. Assn. (publ. review bd. 1989—91), So. Mgmt. Assn., Acad. Mgmt., Omicron Delta Kappa, Phi Beta Delta. Personal E-mail: ltrewitt@netzero.net.

PREZIOSO, ROMAN W., JR., state legislator; b. June 29, 1949; s. Roman W. and Amelia A. Prezioso; m. Deborah Marie Haught; 1 child, Christopher James. Mem. Dist. 31 W.Va. House of Delegates, 1988—92, mem. Dist. 43, 1993—96; mem. Dist. 13 W.Va. State Senate, 1997—, chair Health and Human Resources Com., mem. Banking and Insurance Com., Confirmations Com., Fin. Com., Natural Resources Com. & Rules Com. Recipient W.Va. Troopers Assn. award, 1993; named Legislator of Yr., Region 1 Vocat. Assn., 1992. Mem.: C. of C. (bd. mem.), W.Va. Sch. Adminstrs. Assn., Am. Cancer Soc., Nat. W.Va. & Marion County Edn. Assns., Boy Scouts America (former pres. & bd. dir.), Elks, Moose, KofC, Kiwanis (former pres.), Toastmasters, Fairmont State Coll. Alumni Assn., W.Va. Alumni Assn. Democrat. Catholic. Mailing: 1806 Dogwood Dr Fairmont WV 26554 Home Phone: 304-366-5308; Office Phone: 304-363-7323. E-mail: roman.prezioso@wvsenate.gov.

PREZZANO, WILBUR JOHN, board member; b. Chappaqua, NY, Dec. 18, 1940; s. Wilbur J. and Adelaide J. Prezzano; m. Sheila Neary, Aug. 29, 1964; children: Timothy J., David N., E. Peter. BS in Economics, U. Pa., 1962, MBA in Indsl. Mgmt., 1964. Statistician Eastman Kodak Co., Rochester, NY, 1965-66, mem., treas.'s staff, 1966-67, fin. analyst, 1967-68, fin. analyst, bus. sys. markets div., 1968-69, coord., sales analysis and fin. info. sys., 1969-71, supr., fin. planning analysis, 1971-73, supt. acctg. analysis, 1973, staff asst. to gen. mgr., Customer Equipment Svcs. Divsn., 1973-76, mgr., field ops., 1976-78, dir., copy products, mgr., field ops., 1978-79, dir., bus. mktg. planning mktg. div., 1979-80, asst. gen. mgr., 1980, v.p., 1980-82, gen. mgr., US mktg. div., 1982-83, group v.p., gen. mgr., mktg., mgr., internat. photog. ops., 1983-84, gen. mgr., photog. products, 1985-90, gen. mgr., internat., 1990-91, pres., health, 1991-94, exec. v.p., vice chmn., chmn. and pres., greater China region, 1994-96. Bd. dirs. Can. Trust, Toronto, Can., First Fed. Savs. & Loan Assn., Rochester. Mem. Genesee Valley Club (Rochester). Office: Roper Industries Inc 6901 Professional Pky E Ste 200 Sarasota FL 34240 Office Phone: 941-556-2601. Office Fax: 941-556-2670. Business E-Mail: wprezzano@roperind.com.

PRIBRAM, KARL HARRY, neuroscience and psychology educator, brain researcher; b. Feb. 25, 1919; BS, U. Chgo., 1938, MD, 1941; PhD in Psychology (hon.), U. Montreal, Can., 1992; PhD in Philosophy (hon.), U. Bremen, 1996. Diplomate Am. Bd. Neurol. Surgery, Am. Bd. Med. Psychotherapists. Lectr. Yale U., New Haven, 1951-58; dir. rschr. Inst. Living, Hartford, Conn.; fellow Ctr. Advanced Studies Behavioral Sci., Stanford U., Calif., 1958—59, prof. Dept. Psychology and Psychiatry, 1959—89, NIH lifetime rsch. career prof., 1962—89, prof. emeritus, 1989—; eminent scholar Radford U., Va., 1989—2002, prof. emeritus, 2002—; disting. rsch. prof. dept. psychology George Mason U., 2002—07, Georgetown U., 2002—. Vis. scholar, hon. lectr. MIT, 1954, Clark U., 1956, Harvard, 1956, Haverford Coll., 1961, U. So. Calif., 1961, U. Leningrad, 1962, U. Moscow, 1962, U. Alta., Can., 1968, Ctr. for Study Dem. Insts., 1967-75, U. Coll., London, 1972, U. Chgo., 1973, Menninger Sch. Psychiatry, 1973-76, Ohio State U., 1975; vis. lectr. Grass Found., 1977; Phillips lectr., Haverford Coll., 1979; Lashley lectr., Queens Coll., 1979; Hubert Humphrey lectr. Macalester Coll., 1981; lectr. Internat. Mgmt. Inst., Geneva, Switzerland, 1987, Inst. Med. Psychology, Naples, 1988; disting. lectr. Second Annual Symposium of the Mind, Arlington, Tex., 1988; hon. lectr. Sirius Seminaries, Paris, 1988, Bielfeld, Germany, 1990-1991, numerous others. Author: Plans and the Structure of Behavior, 1960, Brain and Behavior, vol. 1-4, 1969, What Makes Man Humane, 1971, What Makes Humans Human, 2008, Languages of the Brain: Experimental Paradoxes and Principles in Neuropsychology, 1971; The Neurosciences: Third Study Program, 1971, Freuds Project Reassessed, 1976, Brain and Perception: Holonomy and Structure in Figural Processing, 1991, Rethinking Neural Networks: Quantum Fields and Biological Data, 1993, Origins: Brain and Self Organization, 1994, Scale in Conscious Experience: 1995, Learning as Self Organization, 1996, Brain and Values, 1998, The Form Within, my Point of View, 2013; editor, mem. consulting bd. Neuropsychologia, Jour. Math. Biology, Internat. Jour. Neurosci., Behavioral and Brain Scis., Jour. Mental Imagery, Jour. Human Movement Studies, Jour. Social and Biol. Structures, ReVision, STSM Quar., Indian Jour. Psychophysiology, Internat. Jour. Psychophysiology, Cognition and Brain Theory; contbr. over 600 articles to profl. jours. Recipient Lifetime Rsch. Career award in neurosci. NIH, 1962-89, Humanitarian award INTA, 1980, Realia honor Inst. Advanced Philosophic Rsch., 1986, 93, Outstanding Contbns. award Am. Bd. Med. Psychotherapists, Neural Network Leadership award Internat. Neural Network Soc., 1996, Dagmar and Vaclev Havel prize, 1989, Lifetime Achievement award Wash. Acad. Scis., 2010, Disting. Contbn. award Soc. Theoretical and Philosophical Psychology, 2012. Fellow Am. Acad. Arts and Scis., NY Acad. Scis. (hon. life); mem. AAUP, APS, AAAS, APA (pres. div. physiol. and comparative psychology 1967-68, pres. div. theoretical and philos. psychology 1979-80), Internat. Neuropsychol. Soc. (founding pres. 1967-69), Soc. Exptl. Psychologists (Anderson Lifetime Achievement award 2005), Am. Psychol. Soc., Am. Psychopathological Assn. (Paul Hoch award 1975), Am. Acad. Psychoanalysis, Soc. Biol. psychiatry (Manfred Sakel award 1976), Soc. Clin. and Exptl. Hypnosis (Henry Guze award 1991), Soc. Neurosci., Sigma Xi, Assn. Psychol. Scis. Home: PO Box 679 Warrenton VA 20188-0679 Office Phone: 202-333-6310. Business E-Mail: pribramk@georgetown.edu.

PRICE, ALAN THOMAS, business and estate planner; b. Balt., Nov. 11, 1949; s. Alvah Thompson and Doris Elaine (Cole) P.; m. Page Angela Jennings, Sept. 1978 (div. 1980); m. Lauren Ann St. Clare, Aug. 12, 1983 (div. 1992); m. Melissa Renee Ballistreri, Nov. 1997. BS, U. N.C., 1972. CLU; chartered fin. cons.; cert. estate and bus. analyst, fin. planner; registered fin. planner. Mgmt. trainee Sears, Atlanta, 1972-73; ins. agt. Aetna Life & Casualty, Atlanta, 1973-76, Pilot Life/New Eng. Life, Virginia Beach, Va., 1976-81; owner, pres. Page II Prodns., Inc., Norfolk, Va., 1981—. Founding prin. 1s Fin. Resources, 1989; veteran judge Miss U.S.A. Pageant System. Fin. columnist News-Herald, 1985-86. Active Mus. Marine Scis., Virginia Beach, 1986—, Hope Found., Windsor, N.C., 1987—, Va. Stage Co., Va. Pops Orch. Named Man of Yr., Pilot Life, Tidewater, Va., 1978, 79, 80. Fellow Life Underwriter Tng. Coun.; mem. Million Dollar Roundtable (life and qualifying), Internat. Assn. Registered Fin. Planners, Am. Coun. Ind. Life Underwriters, Am. Soc. CLU's, Internat. Assn. Fin. Planning (dir. 1987-88), Inst. Cert. Fin. Planners, Nat. Assn. Life Underwriters, Sales and Mktg. Execs., Ct. of the

Table, Tidewater Estate Planning Coun., Tidewater Builders Assn., Cen. Bus. Dist. Assn., Hampton Roads C. of C. Methodist. Avocations: painting, fishing, reading, interior decorating, sports. Home: 2645 River Rd Virginia Beach VA 23454-1224 Office: First Fin Resources Page II Prodns 2645 River Rd Virginia Beach VA 23454-1224 Office Phone: 757-481-3443. E-mail: first.financial.reserves@verizon.net.

PRICE, ALFRED LEE, lawyer, mining executive; b. Little Rock, May 19, 1935; s. Dewey Ernest and Dorothy Ava (Cooper) P.; m. Magdalena Torres, June 20, 1958; children: Gregory L., Ana Maria. BA, Hendrix Coll., 1956; JD, Tulane U., 1967. Bar: La. 1967, Miss. 1974, D.C., U.S. Supreme Ct., 1980, U.S. Tax Ct., 1977, cert. arbitrator, mediator, Am. Arbitration Assn. and Better Bus. Bur., Nat. Arbitration Forum. Office mgr., dir. personnel Petroleum Helicopters Co., Lafayette, La. and New Orleans, 1956-67; atty. Offshore Navigation and Petroleum Helicopters Co., New Orleans, 1967-74; gen. counsel First Miss. Corp., Jackson, 1974-93, corp. sec., 1988-93; commr. Miss. Employment Commn., Jackson, 1994—2002. Arbitrator Am. Arbitration Assn., 1998—. Mem. Jackson C.of C., chmn. legislative com., 1991-94. Recipient Arbitrator of Yr., Better Bus. Bureau, 1998. Mem. ABA, La. Bar Assn., Miss. Bar Assn., Hinds County Bar Assn., Miss. Mfrs. Assn. (bd. dirs.), Miss. Econ. Coun. (chmn. tort reform com.), River Hills Club. Methodist.

PRICE, ANDY, health facility company executive, accountant; B in Acctg., Fla. State U., 1984. CPA. Sr. audit mgr. BDO Seidman, Atlanta, 1989—96; sr. v.p., corp. contr. Centennial HealthCare Corp., 1996—2004; v.p. ops. acctg. HealthSouth Corp., 2004—09, chief acctg. officer, 2009—. Office: HealthSouth Corp 3660 Grandview Pky Ste 200 Birmingham AL 35243 Office Phone: 205-967-7116. Office Fax: 205-969-3543. Business E-Mail: andy.price@healthsouth.com.

PRICE, BETSY, mayor, Fort Worth, Texas; b. Fort Worth; m. Tom Price; 3 children. BS in Biology, U. Tex. Owner Price Cornelius Title Svc.; tax assessor Tarrant County, Tex., 2000—11; mayor City of Fort Worth, 2011—. Active Cowtown PTA, Tex., Camp Fire Girls, Cowtown; v.p. Red Cross, Cowtown; bd. mem. Bike Officers Citizen Support Club, Cowtown. Office: Office of the Mayor 1000 Throckmorton St Fort Worth TX 76102 Office Phone: 817-392-6118. Office Fax: 897-392-6187. Business E-Mail: betsy.price@fortworthtexas.gov.*

PRICE, DAVID EUGENE, United States Representative from North Carolina, education educator; b. Johnson City, Tenn., Aug. 17, 1940; s. Albert Lee and Elna (Harrell) Price; m. Lisa Beth Kanwit, July 27, 1968; children: Karen Elizabeth, Michael Edmond. Student, Mars Hill Coll., NC, 1957—59; BA in Am. Hist. and Math., U. NC, 1961; BD in Theology, Yale U., 1964, PhD in Polit. Sci., 1969. Legis. aide Staff of US Senator Edward Lewis Bartlett of Alaska, 1963-67; prof. polit. sci. and pub. policy Duke U., Durham, NC, 1973-86; mem. US Congress from 4th NC dist., 1987—95, 1997—, mem. appropriations com., chmn. homeland security subcommittee, mem. democracy assistance commn., co-chair Dem. budget grp. Exec. dir. NC Dem. Party, Raleigh, 1979-80, chmn., 1983-84, mem. 1983—; staff dir. nat. com. on presdl. nomination Dem. Party, 1981-82 Author: Who Makes the Laws, 1972, Bringing Back the Parties, 1984, Policymaking in Congl. Coms., 1979, The Congressional Experience: A View From the Hill, 2000. Recipient Engring. Deans Coun. award, Am. Soc. Engring. Edn., 2003, Charles Dick Medal of Merit, NC Nat Guard, Hubert H. Humphrey Pub. Svc. award, Am. Polit. Sci. Assn.; named a Champion of Sci., Sci. Coalition, 2002, 2004. Mem. Am. Polit. Sci. Assn., Soc. Values in Higher Edn., Phi Beta Kappa, Kiwanis. Democrat. Baptist. Avocations: jogging, music. Office: US House of Representatives 2162 Rayburn House Office Bldg Washington DC 20515-3304 Office Phone: 202-225-1784. Office Fax: 202-225-2014.*

PRICE, DAVID TAYLOR, professional baseball player; b. Murfreesboro, Tenn., Aug. 26, 1985; Student in sociology, Vanderbilt U., Nashville, 2005—07. Pitcher Tampa Bay Rays, 2008—. Pitcher USA Baseball Nat. Team, 2005—06. Recipient Golden Spikes award, USA Baseball, 2007, Dick Howser Trophy (Player of Yr. award), Nat. Collegiate Baseball Writer's Assn., 2007, Warren Spahn award, Okla. Sports Mus., 2010, American League Cy Young award, Baseball Writers Assn. America, 2012; named Pitcher of Yr., Southeastern Conf., 2007, Roy F. Kramer Male Athlete of Yr., 2007, Nat. Co-Player of Yr., Collegiate Baseball, 2007, Coll. Player of Yr., Baseball America, 2007, Player of Yr., American Baseball Coaches Assn., 2007, 1st Team All-American, 2007, American League Outstanding Pitcher, Maj. League Baseball Players Assn., 2010, 2012; named to American League All-Star Team, Maj. League Baseball, 2010—12. Achievements include being the first overall pick in Major League Baseball's Amateur Draft, 2007; leading the American League in: starts, 2011. Office: Tampa Bay Rays One Tropicana Dr Saint Petersburg FL 33705

PRICE, DENNIS LEE, industrial engineer, educator; b. Taber, Alberta, Can., Oct. 24, 1930; s. Walter and Wilma Harlan (Nance) P.; m. Barbara Ann Shelton; children: Denice Lynn Price Tsugawa, Philip Walter. BA, Bob Jones U., 1952; BD, MA, Am. Bapt. Sem. of the West, Berkeley, Calif., 1955; MA, Calif. State U., Long Beach, 1967; PhD in Indsl. Engring., Tex. A&M U., 1974. Cert. product safety mgr., hazard control mgr., human factors profl. Clergyman Am. Bapt. Conv., Calif., 1953-66; tech. staff autonetics divsn. Rockwell Internat., Anaheim, Calif., 1966-69; sr. engr. Martin Marietta Aerospace, Orlando, Fla., 1969-72; rsch. assoc. Tex. A&M U., College Station, 1972-74; tchg. asst. Calif. State U., Long Beach, 1963-66; asst. prof. dept. indsl. engring. and ops. rsch. Va. Poly. Inst. and State U., Blacksburg, 1974-78, assoc. prof. dept. indsl. and systems engring., 1979—83, prof., 1984-95, prof. emeritus, 1996—, dir. safety projects office, 1975-95, coord. Human Factors Engring. Ctr., 1986-95. Expert witness in safety engring. and human factors, 1978—; mem. U.S. Nuclear Waste Tech. Rev. Bd., 1989-95; U.S. tech. adv. group Internat. Stds. Tech. Com. 159 Ergonomics, 1987-94; chmn. com. on transp. of hazardous materials NRC, 1981-87; chmn. group 3 coun. emerging issues subcom. Transp. Rsch. Bd., 1987-89; chmn. task force on pipeline safety NAS, 1986 Mem. editorial bd. Human Factors, Santa Monica, Calif., 1989-95; author: (with K.B. Johns, J.W. Bain) Transportation of Hazardous Materials, 1983, (with W. Hammer) Occupational Safety Management and Engineering, 2000; author: Why Christ is the Only Way, 2003, Death, That's Life, 2005,(novel) Chasing the Fourth House, 2009 (awarded San Diego Christian Writers Guild Cert. Merit, 2010); contbr. chpts. to books, articles to profl. jours.; reviewer in field. Recipient Disting. Svc. award Nat. Rsch. Coun. NAS, 1987, 89, Outstanding Svc. commendation Transp. Rsch. Bd. NAS, 1981, Jack A. Kraft Innovator award Human Factors and Ergonomics Soc., 1996, Best Book award San Diego Christian Writers Guild, 2004; grantee NIOSH, Va. Dept. Transp. and Safety, 1977-82, 86-87, IBM, 1981-84, USN Office of Naval Rsch., 1978-80, USN Naval Systems Weapons Command, 1978-79. Mem. Inst. Indsl. Engrs. (sr.), Am. Soc. Safety Engrs. (profl.), Human Factors Soc. (rep. to rev. panel Guideline for the Preparation of Material Safety Data Sheets), System Safety Soc. (Educator of Yr. 1993), Alpha Pi Mu. Avocation: flying. Home: 15204 Moonglow Dr Ramona CA 92065-4529 Office: Va Poly Inst and State Univ Dept Indsl and Sys Engring Blacksburg VA 24061

PRICE, EDWARD J., state legislator; BA, Grambling State U., La., 1975. Supr. Diols Mfg. BASF Corp.; mem. Dist. 58 La. House of Reps., Baton Rogue, 2012—. Democrat. Office: La House of Reps 900 N 3rd St PO Box 94062 Baton Rouge LA 70804 Business E-Mail: pricee@legis.la.gov.

PRICE, HENRY ESCOE, broadcast executive; b. Jackson, Miss., Oct. 13, 1947; s. Henry E. Price Sr. and Alma Kate (Merrill) Noto; m. Maria Diane Harper, Apr. 8, 1972; children: Henry E. III, Norman Harper. BS in Radio, TV, Film, Journalism, U. So. Miss., 1972. Announcer, news dir. Sta. WROA Radio, Gulfport, Miss., 1967-69; comml. producer Sta. WJTV-TV, Jackson, Miss., 1969-73; prodn. mgr. Sta. WAAY-TV, Huntsville, Ala., 1973-77, Sta. WPEC-TV, West Palm Beach, Fla., 1977-79; dir. promotion Sta. WPTV-TV, Palm Beach, Fla., 1979-81; TV cons. Frank Magid Assoc., Marion, Iowa, 1981-83; dir. advt. and promotion Sta. WJLA-TV, Washington, 1983-84; v.p., dir. programming Sta. WUSA-TV, Gannett TV, Washington, 1984-88; pres., gen. mgr. Sta. WFMY-TV, Gannett TV, Greensboro, N.C., 1988-91, Sta. KARE-TV, Mpls., 1991-96; v.p., gen. mgr. Sta. WBBM-TV, CBS TV Stas., Chgo., 1996—2000; pres., gen. mgr. Sta. WXII-TV, Winston-Salem, NC, 2000—; sr. dir. in TV, Northwestern U. Media Mgmt. Ctr. Pres. Carolina News Network, 1988-91; sr. dir. media mgmt. Ctr. Northwestern U., 2000—. Avocations: furniture design and construction, reading, walking, bicycling. Address: 700 Coliseum Dr Winston Salem NC 27106

PRICE, ILENE ROSENBERG, lawyer; b. Jersey City, July 2, 1951; d. Irwin Daniel and Mildred (Riesberg) Rosenberg; m. Jeffrey Paul Price, Feb. 18, 1973. AB, U. Mich., 1972; JD, U. Pa., 1977. Bar: Pa. 1977, DC 1978, U.S. Dist. Ct. DC 1979, U.S. Ct. Appeals (D.C. cir.) 1979. Assoc. Haley, Bader & Potts, Washington, 1977-80; staff atty. Mut. Broadcasting System Inc., Arlington, Va., 1980-82, asst. gen. counsel, 1982-85; gen. counsel MultiComm Telecommunications Corp., Arlington, 1985-88; east coast counsel Westwood One, Inc., Arlington, 1988-91; gen. counsel Resource Dynamics Corp., Vienna, Va., 1991—2001; legal search cons. The McCormick Group, Arlington, 2001—03; gen. counsel Bluewave Resources, LLC, McLean, Va., 2003—. Mem. Fed. Communications Bar Assn., Wash. Met. Area Corp. Counsel Assn., Women's Bar Assn. D.C. (bd. dirs. 1984-87). Office: Bluewave Resources LLC Ste 310 6830 Elm St Mc Lean VA 22101 Home Phone: 703-893-6079; Office Phone: 703-448-3400. Business E-Mail: ileneprice@bwres.com.

PRICE, JOHN RANDOLPH, writer; b. Alice, Tex., Feb. 12, 1932; s. John Randolph and Eva Mae (Boney) P.; m. Janis Bryant Price, June 20, 1953; children: Susan Lynn, Leslie Anne. BS, U. Houston, 1957; PhD (hon.), Emerson Inst., 2001; DHL (hon.), Holmes Inst., 2003. Dir. advt. Gates Radio Corp., Quincy, Ill., 1957-62; v.p. Sander Rodkin, Ltd., Chgo., 1962-64; exec. v.p. Stewart, Price, Tomlin, Inc., Chgo., 1964-67; v.p. Goodwin, Dannenbaum, Littman & Wingfield, Inc., Houston, 1967-70; pres. O'Neill, Price, Anderson, Fouchard, Inc., Houston, 1970-74, John Price & Co., Houston, 1974-79, Arnan, Inc., Austin, 1979-81; chmn. bd. The Quartus Found. Inc., Boerne, Tex., 1981—. Author: The Superbeings, 1981, The Manifestation Process, 1983, The Planetary Commission, 1984, Practical Spirituality, 1985, With Wings as Eagles, 1987, The Abundance Book, 1987, Prayer, Principles & Power, 1987, A Spiritual Philosophy for the New World, 1990, Empowerment, 1992, The Angels Within Us, 1993, Angel Energy, 1995, Living a Life of Joy, 1997, The Success Book, 1998, The Wellness Book, 1998, The Meditation Book, 1998, The Love Book, 1998, The Jesus Code, 2000, The Alchemist's Handbook, 2000, Removing the Masks That Bind Us, 2001, Nothing Is Too Good to Be True, 2003. Staff sgt. USAF, 1952-56. Recipient Joseph S. Cullinan award U. Houston, 1956, Grand Prix Best Consumer Mag. Advt. award, 1970. Mem. Internat. New Thought Alliance (Humanitarian award 1992, Joseph Murphy award 1994). Achievements include organizer of first annual World Peace day on December 31, 1986. Office: The Quartus Found Inc PO Box 1768 Boerne TX 78006-6768 Office Phone: 830-249-3985. Business E-Mail: quartus@quartus.org.

PRICE, JOSEPH LEE, II, (JOE PRICE), former bank executive; b. 1961; BS in Acctg., U. NC, Charlotte, 1983. With PriceWaterhouse; mgmt. positions Bank of America Corp., Charlotte, NC, 1992—95, contr., 1995—97, gen. auditor, 1997—99, pres. consumer finance group, 1999—2002, corp. strategy & consumer spl. assets exec., 2002—03, risk mgmt. exec. global corp. & investment banking, 2003—06, CFO, 2006—10, pres. consumer, small bus. & card banking, 2010—11. Bd. dirs. Habitat for Humanity; mem. adv. bd. Belk Sch. Bus. U. NC.

PRICE, MARY KATHLEEN, law librarian, educator; b. Buffalo, Feb. 28, 1942; d. Donn Dale and Mary Elizabeth (Domedion) Price. BA with honors, U. Fla., 1963; MS, Fla. State U., 1967; postgrad., Ala. Law Sch., Tuscaloosa, 1967-70; JD with honors, U. Ill., Champaign, 1973. Bar: Ill. 1973, US Dist. Ct. (northern dist.) Ill. 1973. Tchr. Duval and Brevard County Schs., Jacksonville and Titusville, Fla., 1960-63; asst. law libr. U. Ala. Law Sch., Tuscaloosa, 1967-70, U. Ill., Champaign, 1970-73; assoc. Ross, Hardies & O'Keefe, Chgo., 1973-75; law libr., prof. law Duke U. Law Sch., Durham, NC, 1975-80; dir. law libr., prof. law U. Minn., Mpls., 1980-90, acting asst. v.p. acad. affairs, 1985-86; law libr. Libr. of Congress, 1988—94; dir. law libr., prof. law NYU Sch. Law, 1994—2003; assoc. dean libr. & tech., Clarence J. TeSelle prof. law Levin Coll. Law, U. Fla., Gainesville, 2003—. Mem. acad. adv. bd. Westlaw, St. Paul, 1984—87; vis. prof. law Uppsala U., 1987—89. Recipient Law Librarianship award, Minn. Assn. Law Libraries, 1984, Disting. Alumni award, Fla. State U., 1987. Mem.: Assn. American Law Schs. (mem. accreditation com. 1983—87, exec. bd. 1988—90), Commn. Legal Edn. Exchange with PRC (chmn. libr. subcommittee 1984—), American Assn. Law Librs. (pres. 1983—84), Order of Coif. Democrat. Roman Catholic. Office: Levin College Law University of Florida Box 117628 Gainesville FL 32611 Home: 415 NW 32nd St Gainesville FL 32607 Office Phone: 352-273-0706. Office Fax: 352-392-5093. Business E-Mail: pricek@law.ufl.edu.

PRICE, MCKINLEY, mayor, Newport News, Virginia, dentist; b. Newport News, Va. m. Valerie Scott; children: McKinley II, Marcia. BA in Biology, Hampton U., Va., 1971; DDS, Howard U., Washington, 1976. Resident in gen. anesthesia Provident Hosp., Balt.; pvt. practice dentist Va.; councilman City of Newport News, 2004, mayor, 2010—. Mem. Newport News Sch. Bd., 1984—92; apptd. mem. Va. Econ. Devel. Partnership Bd.; mem. First Ch. Newport News; former chmn. Thomas Nelson Cmty. Coll. Bd.; chmn. Riverside Health Sys. Found.; vice chmn. Riverside Health Sys. Bd. 1st lt. US Army. Recipient Presdl. Citizenship award, Hampton Univ., 1996, Humanitarian award, Nat. Conf. Cmty. and Justice, Peninsula Chpt., 1996; named Dentist of Yr., Old Dominion Dental Soc., Citizen of Yr., Alpha Kappa Alpha Sorority, 1998, Daily Press Newspaper, 2005. Fellow: Internat. Coll. Dentists, Am. Coll. Dentists, Va. Dental Assn.; mem.: Peninsula Dental Soc. (pres.), 100 Black Men, Va. Peninsula Chpt. (founding mem., President's Humanitarian award 1994). Office: Office of Mayor 2400 Washington Ave Newport News VA 23607 Office Phone: 757-926-8634.*

PRICE, RICHARD H., physics professor; b. NYC, Mar. 1, 1943; m. Betsy Mitchell, Sept. 13, 1993; 1 child, Gavrielle M. MS in Engring., Cornell U., Ithaca, NY, 1965; PhD, Caltech, Pasadena, Calif., 1971. Prof. Dept Physics, U. Utah, Salt Lake City, 1971—2004, Physics & Astronomy, U.Tex., Brownsville, 2004—. Contbr. articles to profl. jours., chapters to books. Grant, NSF, 1971—2013, NASA, 2003—08, DoD, 2011—. Fellow: AAAS, APS. Home: 13 Creekbend Dr Brownsville TX 78521 Office: Ctr Gravitational Wave Astronomy UT Brownsville 80 Fort Brown Brownsville TX 78520*

PRICE, ROBERT EBEN, judge; b. Waco, Tex., Jan. 13, 1931; s. Robert Eben and Mary Hamilton (Barnett) P.; m. Ann Hodges, June 4, 1954; children— Eben, Mary, Ann, Emily. BA, So. Methodist U., 1952, JD, 1954, LL.M., 1972; postgrad., Air War Coll., 1976. Bar: Tex. 1954, U.S. Supreme Ct., U.S. Ct. Mil. Appeals, U.S. Ct. Claims, U.S. Dist. Ct. (no. dist.) Tex. 1954. Mem. firm Taylor, Mizell, Price, Corrigan & Smith, Dallas, 1956-86; judge Dallas County Probate Ct. No. 2, 1986—2010, sr. statutory probate judge, 2011—. Lectr. continuing legal edn. program U. Houston Law Found., 1993—; lectr. law So. Meth. U. Law Sch., 1973-74, faculty paralegal cert. program Sch. Continuing Edn., 1987-89; lectr. practice skills program State Bar Tex., 1974-78. Editor-in-chief: Southwestern Law Jour., 1953-54. Trustee and sec. St. Michael and All Angels Found., 1984-88; bd. dirs. Downtown Ministry, Diocese of Dallas Episcopal, 1986-88; chmn. legis. and legal awareness subcom., vice chmn. Tex. Gov.'s Com. on Employment of Handicapped, 1978-82. Served as legal officer USAF, 1954-56; col. JAGC Res. ret. Fellow: Tex. Bar Found., Am. Coll. Trust and Estate Counsel; mem.: ABA (nat. conf. spl. ct. judges com. on probate and surrogates cts. 1992—), Tex. Coll. Probate Judges (mem. faculty), State Bar Tex. (lectr. profl. devel. program 1988—), Dallas Bar Assn., Coll. State Bar Tex., Nat. Coll. Probate Judges, Phi Delta Theta, Phi Eta Sigma, Phi Alpha Delta. Episcopalian. Home Phone: 214-528-9518.

PRICE, RONALD C., insurance company executive; b. Mar. 15, 1952; s. Floyd and Kathleen Price; m. Jean Price; children: Kristan, Scott, Jenna. BS, U. Wis. CLU, LUTCF, LLIF. V.p., agy. Farm Bur. Fin. Svcs., Des Moines; exec. v.p. Berthel Fisher & Co., Cedar Rapids, Iowa; sr. v.p., chief mktg. officer, Career Life Agencies American National Insurance Co., 2004—. Bd. dirs. Iowa Spl. Olympics, Des Moines. Office: American National Insurance Co 1 Moody Plz Galveston TX 77550-7999 Office Phone: 409-763-4661. Office Fax: 409-766-2912. Personal E-mail: ronald.price@anico.com.

PRICE, SCOTT, retail executive; BA in Bus. Adminstrn., U. NC; MA in Asian Studies, U. Va., MBA. Country mgr. Coca-Cola Co., China, country leader Japan; pres. DHL Express, Japan, CEO, Asia Pacific, CEO, Europe; pres., CEO Wal-Mart Asia, Hong Kong, 2009—14; pres. Wal-Mart China, Shenzhen, 2011—14; exec. v.p. internat. strategy Wal-Mart Stores, Inc., Bentonville, Ark., 2014—. Office: Wal Mart Stores Inc 702 SW 8th St Bentonville AR 72716 Business E-Mail: scott.price@wal-mart.com.*

PRICE, THOMAS EDMUNDS (TOM PRICE), United States Representative from Georgia; b. Lansing, Mich., Oct. 8, 1954; m. Elizabeth Clark; 1 child, Robert. BA, U. Mich., 1976, MD, 1979. Intern in surgery Emory U. Affiliated Hospitals, resident in orthop. surgery; founder Compass Orthop. (formerly North Fulton Orthop. Clinic); mem. Ga. State Senate, Atlanta, 1997—2004, majority leader, 2002—03; mem. US Congress from 6th Ga. Dist., Washington, 2005—; chmn. Republican Study Com., Washington, 2009—11, US House Republican Policy Com., Washington, 2011—13. Mem. bd. dirs. North Metro YMCA; active Roswell Presbyn. Ch., Ga. Ensemble Theatre, Chattahoochee Nature Ctr. Recipient Award for Manufacturing Legislative Excellence, Nat. Assn. Manufacturers (NAM), 2011. Mem. Rotary (bd. dirs.). Republican. Presbyterian. Office: US House of Representatives 100 Cannon House Office Bldg Washington DC 20515 also: Ste 50 3750 Roswell Rd Marietta GA 30062 Office Phone: 202-225-4501. Office Fax: 202-225-4656.*

PRICE, WILLIAM JAMES, IV, investment banker; b. Balt., Oct. 6, 1924; s. William James 3d and Frances (Robbins) P.; m. Marjorie Beard, Dec. 6, 1952; children: Marjorie, Jonathan Robbins, William James V, Juliet Robbins. BS, Yale U., 1949. Propr. Price & Co., 1949-52; with Alex. Brown & Sons, Balt., 1952-98, gen. partner, 1959-84, mng. dir., 1984-89; chmn. Vanns Spices, Ltd. Chmn. Sonitrol Security Svcs., Inc., NC. Trustee Washington Coll., St. Paul's Sch. and St. Paul's Sch. for Girls. With inf. AUS, 1943—46, ETO. Decorated Bronze Star, Purple Heart with oak leaf cluster, Combat Infantry badge. Mem.: Nat. Assn. Securities Dealers (bd. govs. 1964—66, vice chmn. 1966).

PRIDGEN, EUGENE C., lawyer; b. Asheboro, NC, Jan. 13, 1946; BS, NC State U., 1969; MBA with distinction, Wake Forest U., 1975, JD magna cum laude, 1978. Bar: NC. Atty. K&L Gates (formerly Kennedy Covington Lobdell & Hickman), Charlotte, NC, 1978—, adminstrv. ptnr.; gen. counsel Glenayre Technologies, 1979—99. Editor-in-chief Wake Forest Law Review, 1977—78. Capt. US Army, 1969—73. Fellow: American Bar Found.; mem.: ABA, NC Bar Assn. (bd. govs. 2003—06, pres-elect 2009—10, pres. 2010—11). Office: K&L Gates Hearst Tower 214 N Tryon St, 47th Floor Charlotte NC 28202-2367 Office Phone: 704-331-7476. Office Fax: 704-353-3176. E-mail: gene.pridgen@klgates.com.

PRIDGEN, GASTON L., state legislator; m. Wendy Pridgen; 4 children. Attended, Robeson Cmty. Coll. With Southern Bell Tel. Co., BellSouth Telecom. (now AT&T), CommCo., Inc., 1994; with, IS Dept. Southeastern Regional Med. Ctr., 2009; mem. Dist. 46 NC House of Representatives, 2011—. With US Army. Named Bronze Star. Republican. Address: PO Box 1924 Lumberton NC 28359 Mailing: 1044 Mercer Mill Rd Lumberton NC 28358 Office: North Carolina House of Representatives 16 W Jones St Rm 2223 Raleigh NC 27601-1096 Office Phone: 910-740-9855, 919-733-5821, 910-608-3277. Business E-Mail: Gaston.Pridgen@ncleg.net.

PRINCE, ANNA LOU, composer, music publisher, construction executive; b. Isabella, Tenn., May 28, 1935; d. Ulysses Gordon and Della Carrie (Hawkins) Prince; m. Eddie Joe McCurry; children: Sandra, Teresa, Vandi. Diploma, Carolina Sch. Broadcasting, 1966; Zion diploma, Israel Bible Sch., Jerusalem, 1970; diploma, S.W. Tech. Coll., 1970; student, United Christian Assn., 1976; MusD, London Inst. Applied Rsch., 1991; diplomatic diploma, Acad. Argentina de Diplomacia, 1993; PhD (hon.), Australian Inst. Coord. Rsch., Victoria, 1993; diploma of honors on internat. affairs, Inst. Des Affaires Internat., Paris, 1994. Lic. Bible tchr. United Christian Acad. Songwriter Hank Locklin Music Co., Nashville, 1963-70; entertainer 1982 World's Fair, Knoxville, Tenn., 1982; ptnr., owner Prince Wholesale Bait Co., Canton, NC, 1976-82, Grad Builders, Canton, 1982-86, Prince TV Co., Nashville, 1986—, Dr. Rev. Eddie Joe McCurry. Music pub. Broadcast Music, Inc., Nashville, 1982—; mem. prodn. staff, talent coord. (TV series) Down Home, Down Under, 1989-90; host TV show Real Heroes of Country Music in Nashville, 1997-2003. Songs recorded on RCA: I Feel a Cry Coming On, 1965 (#1 in Eng.), Best Part of Loving You, (#1 in Eng.), Anna, 1969 (Billboard 1970, recorded in Ireland 1974, hit in Europe and New Zealand); singer, composer I'm In Love With You, 1995; over 40 songs recorded to date; appeared Grand Ole Opry, 1970, Prince Writes Hit Songs; exec. prodr., host TV talk show, Real Hereos of Country Music, 1997—2003 (Emmy nomination 1997); author: The Strange Life of Anna Prince, 2006, Anna from Prince Mountain, 2011, Love Doctor at Nashville, 2014, 2013; singer, composer, writer numerous songs; creator host, Nash. Tenn. Candidate for county commr. Dem. Party Macon County, NC, 1984; bd. dirs. Macon County Taxpayers Assn., Inc., 1984, v.p., 1984-86; bd. dirs. Head Start, Topton, NC, 1969-73; judge Emmy Awards, Am. Registrar Ohio Valley, 2002— Nominated Disting. Women NC, NC Coun. Coun. on Status of Women, 1984, Jefferson award WYFF TV and Am. Inst. for Pub. Svc., Outstanding Bus. Woman Small Bus. Adminstrn., 1984. Mem. BMI, Internat. Parliament Safety and Peace (life, dept. fgn. affairs, dep. mem. assembly), Nashville Songwriters Assn. Internat. (moderator, tchr. 1984-86), Country Music Assn., Reunion Profl. Entertainers, Fraternal Order Police, C. of C., Order of Knight of Templars (dame) Lofsensic Order (dame), Maison Internat. des Intellectuals (Outstanding Intellectual). Independent. Personal E-mail: docaprince@gmail.com.

PRINCE, DAVID CANNON, lawyer; b. Hawkinsville, Ga., July 4, 1950; s. Carl Willis and Carobel (Cannon) Prince; m. Mary MacIntyre, June 30, 1973. BA in Econs., Clemson U., 1972; JD, St. John's U., Jamaica, NY, 1980. Bar: NY 1981, Ga. 1982, US Dist. Ct. (no. dist.) Ga. 1982. Atty. enforcement SEC, Atlanta, 1981-86; regional counsel Shearson Lehman Bros. Inc., Atlanta, 1986-92; gen. counsel Robinson-Humphrey Co., Inc., Atlanta, 1992—2001; chief legal officer SunTrust Capital Markets, Inc., 2001—06; gen. counsel Stephans Investment Mgmt. Group, LLC, Little Rock, 2006—. Capt. USAF, 1972—78. Mem.: ABA (co-chairperson young lawyers divsn. 1986—88). Democrat. Avocations: sailing, running. Office: Stephens Inc 111 Ctr St 23rd Fl Little Rock AR 72201

PRINCE, ERIK D., protective services company executive; b. Holland, Mich., June 6, 1969; s. Edgar D. and Elsa Prince; m. Joan Nicole Prince (dec. 2003); 4 children; m. Joanna Ruth Prince; 2 children. Attended, US Naval Acad.; grad., Hillsdale Coll. Intern under George H. W. Bush The White House; intern to Dana Rohrabacher Calif. Republican Rep.; co-founder Blackwater USA, 1997, chmn., CEO, 1997—2007, Blackwater Worldwide (formerly Blackwater USA), 2007—09; chmn. Xe Services LLC (formerly Blackwater USA), 2009—; chmn., CEO Prince Group. V.p. Edgar and Elsa Prince Found.; contbr. Rep. Campaign; bd. mem. Christian Freedom Internat. SEAL officer USN, 1993—96. Republican. Office: Xe Services LLC PO Box 1029 Moyock NC 27958 Office Phone: 252-435-2488. Office Fax: 252-435-6388.

PRINCE, TAYSHAUN DURELL, professional basketball player; b. Compton, Calif., Feb. 28, 1980; s. Thomas and Diane Prince; m. Farrah Brown, Apr. 11, 2005; 1 child. BA in Sociology, U. Ky., Lexington, 2002. Forward Detroit Pistons, 2002—13, Memphis Grizzlies, 2013—. Mem. US Men's Sr. Nat. Basketball Team, 2007, Beijing, 2008. Actor: Hood of Horror, 2006. Recipient Gold medal, men's basketball, Beijing Olympic Games, 2008; named to NBA All-Defensive Second Team, 2005, 2006, 2007, 2008. Achievements include being a member of the NBA Championship winning Detroit Pistons, 2004. Avocations: reading, theater. Office: Memphis Grizzlies 191 Beale St Memphis TN 38103

PRINCE, WILLIAM TALIAFERRO, retired federal judge; b. Norfolk, Va., Oct. 3, 1929; s. James Edward and Helen Marie (Taliaferro) P.; m. Anne Carroll Hannegan, Apr. 12, 1958; children: Sarah Carroll Prince Pishko, Emily Taliaferro, William Taliaferro, John Hannegan, Anne Martineau Thompson, Robert Harrison. Student, Coll. William and Mary, Norfolk, 1947-48, 49-50; AB, Williamsburg, 1955, BCL, 1957, MLT, 1959. Bar: Va. 1957. Lectr. acctg. Coll. William & Mary, 1955-57; lectr. law Marshall-Wythe Sch. Law, 1957-59; assoc. Williams, Kelly & Greer, Norfolk, 1959-63, ptnr., 1963-90; US magistrate judge US Dist. Ct. (ea. dist.) Va., Norfolk, 1990-2000; ret., 2000; recalled Ct. Appeals 4th Cir., 2000—, Ct. Appeals 10th Cir., 2002, Ct. Appeals 3d Cir., 2002, 2010—11, Ct. Appeals 6th Cir., 2003, Ct. Appeals 5th Cir., 2003, 2009; spl. assignment mem. Southern Dist. NYS, 2006, Eastern Dist. Calif., 2009. Pres. Am. Inn of Ct. XXVII, 1987-89. Bd. editors: The Virginia Lawyer, A Basic Practice Handbook, 1966. Bd. dirs. Madonna Home, Inc., 1978-93, Soc. Alumni of Coll. William and Mary, 1985-88. Fellow Am. Coll. Trial Lawyers, Am. Bar Found., Va. Law found. (bd. dirs. 1976-90); mem. ABA (ho. of dels. 1984-90), Am. Judicature Soc. (bd. dirs. 1984-88), Va. State Bar (coun. 1973-77, exec. com. 1975-80, pres. 1978-79). Roman Catholic. Personal E-mail: wtprince1@aol.com.

PRINGLE, DAVID L., insurance company executive; BA in Ins. and Risk Mgmt., Miss. State U. Sales assoc. to state sales coord. AFLAC, Inc., asst. agy. dir. West territory, dir. tng., sr. v.p. fed. rels. Sec., prin. fundraiser Aflac's Polit. Action Com. (Aflac PAC). Office: AFLAC Inc 1932 Wynnton Rd Columbus GA 31999 Office Phone: 706-323-3431. Office Fax: 706-324-6330.

PRINS, JAN F., computer science and engineering educator; BS in Math., with honors, Syracuse U., NY, 1978; MS in Computer Sci., Cornell U., Ithaca, NY, 1983, PhD in Computer Sci., 1987. Tchg. fellow Cornell U., 1980—81; instr. Johns Hopkins Ctr. Academically Talented Youth, Balt., 1984; rsch. assoc. dept. computer sci. U. Wis., Madison, 1986—87; asst. prof. dept computer sci. U. NC, Chapel Hill, 1987—93, assoc. prof., 1994—2001, prof., 2002—, chmn. dept. computer sci., 2004—09. Co-founder, computer animator Digital Effects, Inc., NYC, 1975—81; sys. programmer STSC, Inc., Rockville, Md., 1978—81; vis. prof. Inst. Theoretical Computer Sci., Swiss Fed. Inst. Tech., Zurich, 1996—97; cons., software developer 3rd Tech, Inc., Durham, NC, 2000; rsch. fellow Renaissance Computing Inst., Chapel Hill, 2010. Mem. editl. bd. Internat. Jour. High Performance Computer Graphics, Multimedia & Visualization, 2000—, Jour. Sci. Programming, 2004—; contbr. articles to numerous profl. jours. Recipient Jr. Faculty Devel. award, U. NC, 1989, Rsch. Devel. award, 1995, IBM Faculty award, 2006, 2009. Office: UNC Dept Computer Sci CB 3175 FP Brooks Bldg Chapel Hill NC 27599-3175

PRIOR, CORNELIUS BERNARD, JR., utilities executive, financial consultant; b. Hartford, Conn., Feb. 26, 1934; s. Cornelius B. Sr. and Katherine (Daly) P.; m. Trudie Yolleck, 1993; children: Elizabeth, Michael, Sarah. AB, Holy Cross Coll., Worcester, Mass., 1956; LLB, Harvard U., Cambridge, Mass., 1962. Bar: NY 1963. Assoc. atty. Sullivan and Cromwell, NYC, 1963-68; gen. counsel Private Investment Co. for Asia, Tokyo, 1969-71; v.p. Drexel Firestone, NYC, 1971-75; sr. v.p. Blythe Eastman Dillon, NYC, 1975—78; mng. dir. Paine Webber, NYC, 1978—80, Kidder, Peabody and Co., NYC, 1980-87; chmn. Atlantic Tele-Network, Inc., St. Thomas; officer US Navy, 1956—59. Bd. dirs. Atlantic Telenetwork Co., St. Thomas. Bd. dirs., mem., pres. adv. coun. and dir. Holy Cross Coll.; former mem. Harvard Law Sch., dean's adv. coun.; bd. chmn. Tropical Telecom; chmn. Tropical Aircraft; trustee, dir. emeritus Antilles Sch.; former chmn. Caribbean Assn. Nat. Telephone Orgns., former mem. adv. bd. Peter & Patricia Gruber Found.; chmn. Caribbean and C.Am. Action; dir. Kneisel Hall Music Sch. Served to lt (j.g.) USN, 1956-59. Fulbright scholar, 1962—63. Mem.: Univ. Club (NYC). Roman Catholic. Office: Atlantic TeleNetwork Inc PO Box 12030 St Thomas VI 00801 Business E-Mail: cbpriorjr@atni.com.

PRITCHARD, BILL, state legislator; m. Karen Pritchard. Owner Razorback Rentals; mem. Dist. 8 Ark. House of Reps., 2001—06; mem. Dist. 35 Ark. State Senate, 2007—, minority whip. Served USN, Vietnam. Republican. Address: 19998 Mohawk Rd Elkins AR 72727 Office Phone: 479-442-8611. Business E-Mail: pritchardb@arkleg.state.ar.us.

PRITCHARD, ROBERT O., gas industry executive; Grad. cum laude, Mars Hill Coll.; MBA, Wake Forest U. Various fin., corp. planning and regulatory affairs positions Piedmont Natural Gas Co., Inc., dir. corp. planning, 1995—2003, treas., 2003—, v.p., chief risk officer, 2006—. Chmn. Boys & Girls Clubs of Greater Charlotte. Office: Piedmont Natural Gas 4720 Piedmont Row Dr Charlotte NC 28210 Mailing: Piedmont Natural Gas PO Box 33068 Charlotte NC 28233 Office Phone: 704-364-3120. Office Fax: 704-365-3849.

PRITCHARD, RUIE JANE, English educator, director; d. Lawrence Keith and Arthelia Lutitia Pritchard. PhD in English Edn., U. Mo., Columbia, 1980. Lic. in English tchg. Mo. and NC. Supr. right to read Mo. Dept. Elem. and Secondary Edn., Jefferson City, 1978—80; prof. edn., emphasis English NC State U., Raleigh, 1981—; interim assoc. dean acad. affairs NC State Coll. Edn., Raleigh, 2003—05. Dir., capital area writing project Nat. Writing Project NC State, Raleigh, 1983—; fulbright sr. rschr. Coun. Internat. Exch. Scholars Ministry Edn., Wellington, New Zealand, 1988; dir. grad. studies NC State U. C & I Dept., 2005—. Contbr. chapters to books, articles to numerous profl. jours. Recipient NC State Alumni award; named Acad. Outstanding Faculty, NC State U., 2000; Capital Area Writing Project grant, Nat. Writing Project, 1983—. Mem.: NC Fulbright Assn. (sec. 2002—08), Nat. Coun. Tchrs. English (internat. concerns standing com. 2002—, adv. bd. English Jour. & English Edn. 1986—98), Sigma Iota Rho, Pi Lambda Theta, Phi Sigma Iota, Kappa Delta Pi (counselor), Phi Delta Kappa. Avocations: travel, writing, films. Home: 6940 Middleboro Dr Raleigh NC 27612 Office: North Carolina State Univ 402 C Poe Hall Box 7801 Raleigh NC 27695-7801 Office Fax: 919-515-6978. Business E-Mail: ruie_pritchard@ncsu.edu.

PRITCHETT, SAMUEL TRAVIS, finance and insurance educator, researcher, consultant; s. Harvey Eugene and Mary (Brown) P.; m. Bertha Yates, Feb. 20, 1960; children: John Travis, Meri Katherine. BSBA, Va. Poly. Inst. and State U., 1960, MSBA, 1967; DBA, Ind. U., 1969. CLU, ChFC, CPCU. Claim rep. Equitable Life Assurance Soc., Richmond, Va., 1960-64, asst. div. claim mgr., 1964-65; asst. prof. bus. adminstrn. U. Richmond, 1969-70; asst. prof. ins. Va. Commonwealth U., Richmond, 1970-72, assoc. prof. ins., 1972-73; assoc. prof. fin. and ins. U. S.C., Columbia, 1973-76, prof. fin. and ins., 1976-99, J.H. Fellers prof., 1981-83, W.F. Hipp prof. ins., 1983-2000, program dir., chair banking, fin., ins. and real estate, 1977-83, 99-00, acad. dir. MBA program, 1993-95, disting. prof. finance and ins., 1999-2000, disting. prof. emeritus, 2000—. Vis. prof. ins. Ind. U., Bloomington, 1995-96; chmn. Risk Theory Soc., Columbus, Ohio, 1987-88; acad. dir. internat. exec. devel. program Bamerindus Seguros, Curtiba, Brazil, 1995; mem., investment commr. S.C. Retirement Sys., 2005—. Author: Risk Management and Insurance, 7th edit., 1996, Stock Life Insurance Company Profitability, 1986, Individual Annuities as a Source of Retirement Income, 2d edit., 1982, An Economic Analysis of Workers' Compensation in South Carolina, 1994; assoc. editor Jour. Risk and Ins., 1982-86, editor, 1987-91; assoc. editor Fin. Svcs. Rev., 1989-95, 97-99; asst. editor Jour. Am. Soc. CLU and ChFC, 1993-98; mem. acad. rev. bd. Jour. Fin. Planning, 1990-91; mem. editl. bd. Jour. Bus. Rsch., 1976-83, Am. Jour. Small Bus., 1975-79; contbr. articles to profl. jours. Active S.C. Joint Ins. Study Com., 1981-86, 89-95; commr. S.C. Retirement Systems Investment Commn., 2005—, SC Treas.'s Task Force COLAs, 2007-08. Recipient Disting. Svc. award, Moore Sch. Bus. USC, 2009. Mem. Am. Risk and Ins. Assn. (pres. 1980-81), Acad. Fin. Svcs. (pres. 1987-88), So. Risk and Ins. Assn. (pres. 1977-78), Profl. Ins. Agts. Found. (named Ins. Educator of Yr. 1989), Beta Gamma Sigma (pres. chpt. 1980-81), Gamma Iota Sigma (nat. trustee 1976-92), State Retirees Assn. (bd. mem., 2004-11). Independent. Mem. Christian Ch. (Disciples Of Christ). Home: 709 Marlin Ln Charleston SC 29412-5039 Home Phone: 843-762-2645; Office Phone: 843-762-2645. Personal E-mail: tpritch@att.net.

PRITZ, MICHAEL BURTON, neurological surgeon; b. New Brunswick, NJ, Oct. 8, 1947; s. John Ernest and Helen Violet (Rockoff) P.; m. Edmay Marie Gregorcy, Feb. 18, 1973; children: Edmond Louis, Benjamin David. BS, U. Ill., 1969; PhD, Case Western Res. U., 1973, MD, 1975. Diplomate Am. Bd. Neurol. Surgery. Asst. prof. neurol. surgery U. Calif. Irvine Med. Ctr., Orange, 1981-85, assoc. prof., 1985-93; prof., 1993, U. Calif. Irvine Med. Ctr., Orange, 1993—; prof. sect. neurol. surgery Ind. U. Sch. Medicine, Indpls., 1993—, prof. neurol. surgery, 1993—. Contbr. articles to profl. jours. Recipient Herbert S. Steuer award Case Western Res. U., Cleve., 1975; NSF fellow, 1968; Edmund J. James scholar U. Ill., Champaign, 1968-69. Mem. Soc. Neurosci., Am. Assn. Anatomists, Am. Assn. Neurol. Surgeons, Congress Neurol. Surgeons, Soc. Neurol. Surgeons of Orange County (pres. 1985-86, sec.-treas. 1984-85), Ind. State Neurosurg. Soc. (pres. 1996-98). Office Phone: 317-274-5728. Business E-Mail: mpritz@iupui.edu.

PROBERT, TIMOTHY J., oil industry executive; BS in Geology & Geography, U. London, 1972. Field geologist Exploration Logging Inc.; pres., CEO Input/Output Inc.; v.p., mktg. Baker Sand Control; pres. Milpark Drilling Fluids, Eastman Teleco, Baker Hughes INTEQ, 2000—03; sr. v.p., drilling and evaluation divsn. Halliburton Co., Houston, 2003—08, exec. v.p., strategy, corp. devel., 2008—09, pres., drilling & evaluation divsn. & corp. develop., acting v.p.tech., 2009, pres. global bus. lines, chief health, safety and environment officer, 2010—11, pres. strategy & corp. develop., 2011—. Office: Halliburton 5 Houston Ctr PO Box 42807 Houston TX 77242-2807 Office Phone: 713-759-2600. Business E-Mail: tim.probert@halliburton.com.

PROCKOP, DARWIN JOHNSON, biochemist, medical educator; b. Palmerton, Pa., Aug. 31, 1929; s. John and Sophie (Gurski) Prockop; m. Elinor Sacks, Apr. 15, 1961; children: Susan Elizabeth, David John. AB, Haverford Coll., 1951; MA, Oxford U., 1953; MD, U. Pa., 1956; PhD, George Washington U., 1962; DSc (hon.) (hon.), U. Oulu, Finland, 1983, U. So. Fla., 1993. Investigator NIH, 1957—61; assoc., asst. prof., asso. prof., prof. medicine and biochemistry U. Pa., Phila., 1961—72; prof., chmn. dept. biochemistry U. Medicine and Dentistry of N.J. (Rutgers Med. Sch.), Piscataway, NJ, 1972—86; prof., chmn. dept. biochemistry and molecular biology Jefferson Med. Coll., Phila., 1986—96, dir. Jefferson Inst. Molecular Medicine, 1986—96; prof., dir. Ctr. for Gene Therapy, MCP/Hahnemann Med. Coll., Phila., 1996—2000; prof., dir. Ctr. Gene Therapy Tulane U. Med. Ctr., New Orleans, 2000—08; dir. Tex. A & M Health Sci. Ctr. Inst. Regenerative Med., Scott & White Temple, 2008—. Contbr. Served with USPHS, 1958—61. Recipient Disting. Alumnus award, George Washington U., 1991, U. Pa., 1994, Hopkins Meml. medal Brit. Biochem. Soc, 1998; named hon. companion, U. Manchester, 1999; grantee, NIH, 1961—; fellow Fulbright Found., 1951—53. Mem.: NAS, Am. Assn. Physicians, Am. Soc. Clin. Investigation, Am. Soc. Biol. Chemists, Acad. Finland, Inst. Medicine, Alpha Omega Alpha, Phi Beta Kappa. Achievements include research in on collagen and gene therapy. Home: 291 Locust St Philadelphia PA 19106-3913 Office: Ctr Gene Therapy Tulane U Med Ctr 1430 Tulane Ave New Orleans LA 70112-2699 E-mail: dprocko@tulane.edu.

PROCTOR, CLAUDE OLIVER, Russian language educator; b. Ahoskie, NC, June 9, 1938; s. Claude Oliver and Helen Louise (Lassiter) P.; m. Doris Merle Stricker, July 7, 1962; children: Christopher Michael, Gabriel Marcus. Student, Davidson Coll., 1956-58, Syracuse U., 1962-63; BGE, U. Nebr., Omaha, 1966; MA, U. Notre Dame, 1974; Tchr.'s cert. with distinction, Southwestern U., 1981; PhD, U. Tex., 1990. Commd. 2d lt. USAF, 1966, advanced through grades to maj., 1977, Russian linguist Tex., Alaska and Turkey, 1958-67, intelligence officer West Germany, 1968-70, chief fgn. lang. dept. Air Force Sch. Applied Cryptol. Scis. Tex., 1971-72, Soviet area specialist Def. Lang. Inst. Calif., 1974-77, asst. prof. Russian, chmn. strategic langs. USAF Acad. Colo., 1977-80, ret., 1980; legal edn. officer Prosecutor Coun., Austin, Tex., 1980-83; dir. S.W. Lang. Svc., Georgetown, Tex., 1983-86; asst. instr. U. Tex., Austin, 1986-88; prof. Russian Ctrl. Tex. Coll., Killeen, 1989—; faculty of sr. U. of Greater Georgetown, 1998—. Comml. Russian translator; lang. cons. Internat. Space Sta., 1998-2004. Author: Soviet Press Translation, 1980, The Analysis of Soviet Press Propaganda: A Case Study of Soviet Polemics in the Sino-Soviet Conflict, 1960-69, 73, Illustrated International Dictionary, 1990, Evaluation of Quality in a Russian-English Machine Translation System, 1990, Multilingual Dictionary of American Sign Language, 1994, Signing in Fourteen Languages, 2000. Merit badge counselor Lone Star coun. Boy Scouts Am., 1980—; booth chmn. Colorado Springs Intercultural Festival, 1979; mem. Interagy. Task Force for Indochina Refugees, 1975-76; mem. Georgetown City Charter com., 1995; commr. planning and zoning, 1996—; mem. bd. dirs. Sr. Univ. Greater Georgetown, 1997—, Georgetown Area Cmty. Found., 1996—; mem. Hist. Preservation Commn., 1998—. Mem. Am. Coun. for Tchrs. Russian, Tex. Fgn. Lang. Assn., Air Force Assn., Assn. Former Intelligence Officers, Lions, Sertoma, Rotary Internat. (dir. internat. svc. com. 1987-89, mem. world community svc. com. 1988, Paul Harris fellow 1993), Gamma Theta Upsilon, Sigma Phi Epsilon, Literacy Coun. Williamson County (instr. ESL 2007-) Lutheran. Avocations: translating, travel, relocating russian emigrees. Office: SW Lang Svcs PO Box 1131 Georgetown TX 78627-1131 Home: 106 Brazos Dr Georgetown TX 78628-2655 Personal E-mail: ProctorC@att.net, c-dproctor@suddenlink.net.

PROCTOR, ERIC, state legislator; m. Tara Proctor. AA, Tulsa Cmty. Coll.; BA, Northeastern State U. Youth minister; high school economics, history, and government tchr.; mem. Dist. 77 Okla. House of Representatives, 2007—. Mem.: NRA, Sons of American Legion. Democrat. Address: PO Box 581242 Tulsa OK 74158 Office: 2300 N Lincoln Blvd Rm 540-A Oklahoma City OK 73105 Office Phone: 405-557-7410. E-mail: eric.proctor@okhouse.gov.

PROCTOR, R. DAVID, federal judge; b. Atlanta, 1960; BA, Carson-Newman Coll., 1983; JD, U. Tenn., 1986. Law clk. to Hon. H. Emory Widener Jr. US Ct. Appeals 4th Cir., 1986—87; assoc. Sirote & Permutt PC, Birmingham, 1987—93; founding mem. Lehr, Middlebrooks & Proctor PC, 1993—2003; judge US Dist. Ct. (no. dist. Ala.), 2003—. Chmn. sch. bd. Briarwood Christian Sch. Office: US Dist Ct No Dist Ala Hugo Black Courthouse 1729 5th Ave N Birmingham AL 35203

PROCTOR, WILLIAM LEE, state legislator, academic administrator; b. Atlanta, Jan. 27, 1933; s. Samuel Cook and Rose Elizabeth (Nottingham) P.; m. Pamela Evans Duke; children: Samuel Matthews (dec.), Priscilla Nottingham. BS, Fla. State U., 1956, MS, 1964, PhD, 1968; DHL (hon.), Nova Southeastern U., 2003; LLD (hon.), Flagler Coll., 2004. Tchr. Seminole County Pub. Schs., Longwood, Fla., 1956-57, 58-62, Orange County Fla. Pub. Schs., Orlando, 1957-58; athletic coach Fla. State U., Tallahassee, 1962-65, asst. dean men, 1965-67, grad. fellow, 1967-68; supt. of schs. Rock Hill (S.C.) Sch. Dist. #3, 1968-69; dean of men U. Ctrl. Fla., Orlando, 1969-71; pres. Flagler Coll., St. Augustine, Fla., 1971-2001, chancellor, 2001—; mem. Dist. 20 Fla. House of Reps., Tallahassee, 2004—; chair House Edn. Com.; mem. House Appropriations Com. Cons. on higher edn. policy Heritage Found., Washington, 1983—, Fla. Bd. Edn., 2001-03, State Bd. Edn., 2003-2004; mem. Commn. on Colls., So. Assn. Colls. and Schs., 1995-2000; dir. Tchr. Edn. Accreditation Coun. Vice-chmn. Fla. Edn. Stds. Commn., 1995-2001; bd. dirs. Penney Retirement Cmty., chmn., 1991-2004; bd. dirs. Vicar's Landing Retirement Cmty., chmn., 1992-95, bd., 1990-96; trustee, chmn. Fla. Sch. for Deaf and Blind, St. Augustine, 1984-2001; adv. coun. Salvation Army, St. Johns County; devel. coun. First Coast Work Force, 1998-2001; mem. Bus./Higher Edn. Partnership, 2000-01; chmn. Cmtys. in Schs., St. Johns County, Fla., 2002-04. Recipient Disting. Educator award Fla. State U. Coll. Edn., 1989, Phil Carrol award Soc. for Advancement Mgmt., 1990, Disting. Svc. award Fla. Sch. for Deaf and Blind, 1990, Patrick Henry Medallion patriotic achievement Mil. Order of World Wars, 1991, Stetson S Club Achievement award, 1993, Order of the South So. Acad. Letters, Arts, and Scis., Excellence in Mgmt. award Soc. for Advancement of Mgmt., 2000, Lifetime Edn. Achievement award, 2001, Disting. Svc. award Fla. Assn. Colls. and Univs., 2002, Sec. Jim Horne's Life Edn. Leadership award; named to Fla. State U. Athletic Hall of Fame, 1988, Order of La Florida, 2001. Mem. Am. Assn. Pres. of Ind. Colls., State Hist. Assn., Ind. Colls. and Univs. of Fla. (legis. chmn. 1974-77, vice chmn. 1976-77, chmn. 1978-79, Liberty Bell award 2003), Rotary (pres. 1978-79, bd. govs. dist. 697 1988-89). Republican. Presbyterian. Avocations: history, jogging, Karate. Office: Flagler Coll Office of the Chancellor PO Box 1027 Saint Augustine FL 32085-1027 Office Phone: 904-819-6210 ext. 210. Business E-Mail: proctorw@flagler.edu.

PROEFROCK, C. KENNETH, academic medical administrator; b. Curtis, Ill., Mar. 30, 1928; s. Carl Robert and Anna Lorraine (Hagel) Proefrock; m. Margaret Muntz (dec. Apr. 1984); 3 children; m. Janelle Dillon, Sept. 8, 1988 (dec. Sept. 2001). BA, Carthage Coll., Kenosha, Wis., 1949; MDiv, Chgo. Luth. Theol. Sem., 1953. Pastor Evang. Luth. Ch. Am., 1953—66; sr. com. orgn. specialist N.Y.C. Housing and Devel. Adminstrn., 1966-68; exec. dir. Model Cities Program, Manchester, NH, 1968-70, Health Assn. Rochester and Monroe, NY, 1970-73, Mahoning Shenango Area Health Edn. Network, Youngstown, Ohio, 1973-78; spl. asst. to dean Northeastern Ohio Univs. Coll. Medicine, Rootstown, 1978-79; v.p. Med. Coll. Ohio, Toledo, 1979-88, sr. v.p. govtl. affairs, 1988-93; pres. KPA Assocs., Inc., 1993—. V.p. Found. for Applied Rsch., Washington, 1976; chmn. adv. bd. Ohio AHEC, Columbus, 1976; program adminstr. Ohio Statewide Area Health Edn. Ctr., Toledo, 1988-93. Chmn. Toledo Area Coun. Tech., 1986; spl. asst. to clergy All Saints Parish, Pawleys Island, S.C., 1998-2000. Mem. Nat. Area Health Edn. Ctrs. Assn. (bd. dir. 1988-95), Nat. Assn. Univ. Rsch. Adminstrs., Soc. Rsch. Adminstrs., Internat. Assn. Univ. Rsch. Parks, Soc. Univ. Patent Adminstrs., Nat. Assn. Health Manpower Edn. Systems, Northeastern Ohio Med.

Educators Assn. (bd. dir.), Rotary. Anglican. Home: 46 Pawleys Pl Dr Pawleys Island SC 29585-7254 Office: KPA Assocs PO Box 194 Pawleys Island SC 29585-0194 E-mail: kenkpa@cornellbox.com.

PROEHL, RICKY, professional football coach, sports complex owner, retired professional football player; b. Hillsborough, NJ, Mar. 7, 1968; m. Kelly Proehl; children: Alex, Austin, Blake. BA in Speech Comm., Wake Forest Univ., 1989. Wide receiver Phoenix Cardinals, 1990—93, Ariz. Cardinals, 1994, Seattle Seahawks, 1995—96, Chgo. Bears, 1997, St. Louis Rams, 1998—2002, Carolina Panthers, 2003—05, offensive cons., 2011—; wide receiver Indpls. Colts, 2006; ret. NFL, 2006; owner, operator Proehlific Pk. Summer Camp, Greensboro, NC. Founder Ricky Proehl Found., Greensboro, 1999—. Achievements include being a member of Super Bowl Championship winning: St. Louis Rams, 2000, Indianapolis Colts, 2007. Address: Proehlific Pk Youth Sports Complex 4517 Jessup Grove Rd Greensboro NC 27410 Office: Carolina Panthers 800 So Mint St Charlotte NC 28202 Office Phone: 336-665-5233.

PROFFIT, WILLIAM ROBERT, orthodontics educator; b. Harnett County, NC, Apr. 19, 1936; s. Glenn Theodore and Edna Marie (Queener) P.; m. Sara Thomas, Sept. 20, 1953; children: Lola Ann, Edward Thomas, Glenn Theodore. BS, U. N.C., 1956, DDS, 1959; student, Campbell Coll., Buies Creek, NC, 1952-53; PhD, Med. Coll. Va., 1962; MS, U. Wash., 1963; FDS, Royal Coll. Surgeons, 1990. Cert. Am. Bd. Orthodontics. Investigator Nat. Inst. Dental Research, Bethesda, Md., 1963-65; asst. prof. orthodontics U. Ky., Lexington, 1965-68, assoc. prof., 1968-71; prof. U.Ky., Lexington, 1971-73; prof. orthodontics U. Fla., Gainesville, 1973-75; prof., chmn. dept. orthodontics U. NC, Chapel Hill, 1975—2003, Kenan prof., 1992. Cons. NIH, Bethesda, 1974, 76— Author: Contemporary Orthodontics, 1986, 5th edit., 2012; co-author: Surgical Correction of Dentofacial Deformity, 1980, Surgical-Orthodontic Treatment, 1990, Contemporary Treatment of Dentofacial Deformity, 2003; contbr. articles to sci. jours. Served to lt. comdr. USPHS, 1963-65. Fulbright research scholar U. Adelaide, Australia, 1972 Mem. ADA, Am. Assn. Orthodontists, Internat. Assn. Dental Rsch., Phi Beta Kappa. Democrat. Presbyterian. Office: UNC Sch Dentistry Dept Orthodontics Chapel Hill NC 27599-7450 Home: 750 Weaver Dairy Rd # 229 Chapel Hill NC 27514-1468 E-mail: william_proffit@dentistry.unc.edu.

PROFFITT, WALDO, JR., newspaper editor; b. Plainview, Tex., Oct. 8, 1924; s. Waldo and Susan Ann (Smith) P.; m. Marjorie Baltzegar, Sept. 14, 1946 (div. 1963); children: Ann Herbert, Deborah, Geoffrey Harrison, Laurence Scott; m. Anne Collier Greene, Feb. 6, 1966; 1 child, Robert Waldo. BA cum laude, Harvard U., 1948. Reporter Bangor (Maine) Cochran Commercial, 1948—50; assoc. dir. Harvard News Office, Cambridge, Mass., 1952-54; city editor Charlotte (N.C.) News, 1954-58; mng. editor Journal, Lorain, Ohio, 1958-61; editorial dir. Sarasota (Fla.) Herald-Tribune, 1961-84; editor, 1984-98; columnist Sarasota-Herald Tribune, 1998—. Author: A View From Sarasota Published, 2007. Lt. U.S. Army, 1943-46, ETO, lt. USAF, 1950-52. Recipient Global Media Lifetime Achievement award, Population Inst., 2003. Mem. Am. Soc. Newspaper Editors, Fla. Soc. Newspaper Editors (pres. 1978). Democrat. Unitarian Universalist. Home: 1581 Hillview Dr Sarasota FL 34239-2047 Office: Sarasota Herald-Tribune PO Box 1719 Sarasota FL 34230-1719 Personal E-mail: wproffitt@comcast.net.

PROHM, STEVE, men's college basketball coach; b. Vienna, Va. BEd, U. Ala., Tuscaloosa, 1997. Asst. coach Centenary Coll. Gentlemen, Shreveport, La., 1998—99, SE La. State U. Lions, Hammond, 1999—2005, Tulane U. Green Wave, New Orleans, 2005—06, Murray State U. Racers, Ky., 2006—11, head basketball coach, 2011—. Named Ohio Valley Conf. Coach of Yr., 2012, Dist. IV Coach of Yr., US Basketball Writers Assn., 2012. Office: Murray State University Mens Basketball c/o Racer Athletics 217 Stewart Stadium Murray KY 42071 Office Phone: 270-809-3428. Business E-Mail: steve.prohm@murraystate.edu.

PROKASY, WILLIAM FREDERICK, academic administrator; b. Cleve., Nov. 27, 1930; s. William Frederick and Margaret Lovinia (Chapman) P.; m. Pamela Pearson; children: Kathi Lynn, Cheryl Anne; stepchildren: Lisa Wier Cauthen, Kevin Wier. BA, Baldwin-Wallace Coll., 1952; MA, Kent State U., 1954; PhD, U. Wis., 1957. Grad. asst. Kent State U., 1953-54; W.A.R.F. fellow U. Wis., 1954-55, teaching asst., 1955-57; asst. prof., then asso. prof. Pa. State U., 1957-66; prof. psychology, chmn. dept. U. Utah, 1966-69, Disting. rsch. prof., 1971-72, dean social and behavioral sci., 1968-70; dean U. Utah (Coll. Social and Behavioral Sci.), 1970-79; acting dean U. Utah (Grad. Sch. Social Work), 1979-80; prof. psychology dean Coll. Liberal Arts and Scis., U. Ill., Champaign-Urbana, 1980-88; prof., v.p. for acad. affairs U. Ga., 1988-98. Cons. in field. Editor: Classical Conditioning, 1965, (with A.H. Black) Classical Conditioning II, 1971, (with D. Raskin) Electrodermal Responding in Psychological Research, 1973, Psychophysiology, 1974-77; editor (with I. Gormezano and R. Thompson) Classical Conditioning III, 1986; assoc. editor Learning and Motivation, 1969-76; cons. editor Jour. Exptl. Psychology, 1968-80. Trustee Utah Planned Parenthood Assn., 1977—80; Utah bd. dirs. ACLU, 1978—80; v.p., bd. dirs. Champaign-Urbana Symphony, 1986—88; mem. bd. advisors Ga. Mus. Art, 1989—, U. Ga. Performing Arts Ctr., 1998—2003; mem. bd. visitors U. Ga. Librs., 1998—2007; mem. Athens-Clarke County Libr. Bd., 1999—2009; treas. Athens Opera Co. Guild, 2001—06; pres. Friends Ga. Mus. Art, 2002—03, Athens-Clarke County Libr. Bd., 2003—04, Friends of Dance, 2003—04; v.p. Athens-Clarke County Libr. Endowment Bd., 2003—07; mem. Classic Ctr. Cultural Found., 2003—, treas., 2006—07; mem. adv. bd. Franklin Coll. Arts and Scis., 2003—06; chmn. Athens chapt., Am. Wine Soc., 2007—10; del. Utah Dem. Conv., 1968—70, 1972—74; mem. Athens Regional Libr., 2002—, chmn., 2006—. Recipient Alumni Merit award Baldwin Wallace Coll., 1992, Disting. Alumni award Piedmont Coll., 1998, U. Ga. Alumni award of excellence, 1998; NSF sr. postdoctoral fellow, 1963-64. Fellow AAAS, Am. Psychol. Assn. (chmn. bd. sci. affairs 1977-78, coun. of reps. 1980-86, bd. dirs. 1983-86, bd. ednl. affairs 1993-96); mem. Fedn. Behavioral, Pyschol. and Cognitive Scis. (v.p. 1984-85, pres. 1985-87), coun. of Sci. Soc. Pres.'s (exec. bd. 1987-91, chmn. 1990), Psychonomic Soc., Coun. Rsch. Librs. (bd. dirs. 1990-96), NASULGC (exec. com. coun. on acad. affairs 1995-96), Am. Assn. Higher Edn., Soc. Psychophysiol. Rsch. (bd. dirs. 1978-84, pres. 1982-83), Utah Psychol. Assn. (exec. bd. 1968-70, pres. 1971-72), Assn. Advancement Psychology (bd. dirs. 1982-83), Sigma Xi (pres. U. Utah chpt. 1972-73), Phi Kappa Phi. Avocations: genealogy, wine tasting, reading, photography. Personal E-mail: wfp@charter.net.

PROPST, CATHERINE LAMB, biotechnology and pharmaceutical company executive; b. Charlotte, NC, Mar. 10, 1946; d. James Pinckney and Eliza M. Propst. BA magna cum laude, Vanderbilt U., 1967; M of Philosophy, Yale U., 1970, PhD, 1973. Head microbiology div. GTE Labs., Waltham, Mass., 1974-77; various sr. mgmt. positions Abbott Labs., North Chicago, Ill., 1977-80; v.p. rsch. and devel. Ayerst (Wyeth) Labs., Plainview, NY, 1980-83; v.p. rsch. and devel. worldwide Flow Gen. Inc., McLean, Va., 1983-85; pres., CEO Affiliated Sci. Inc., Ingleside, Ill., 1985-97; pres., chmn., CEO Tex. Biotech. Found., Hempstead, Tex., 1997—. Vis. prof. genetics U. Ill., Chgo., 1989—90; founder, exec. dir. Ctr. for Biotech., Northwestern U., 1990—95; pres. Ill. Biotech. Ctr., 1995—97; bd. dirs. several cos.; bd. dirs., mem. sci. adv. bd. Keystone Symposia on Molecular and Cellular Biology, 1997—2002. Author, editor Computer-Aided Drug Design, 1989, Nucleic Acid Targeted Drug Design, 1992; contbr. articles to profl. jours. Recipient many sci. and bus. awards; named to Outstanding Working Women in the U.S., 1982. Fellow: Soc. Indsl. Microbiology (bd. dirs. 1990—93), Nat. Coun. Biotech Ctrs. (bd. dirs. 1995—97); mem.: AAAS, Nat. Wildlife Fedn., Consortium for Plant Biotech. Rsch. (bd. dirs. 1994—99), Phi Beta Kappa, Sigma Xi. Episcopalian. Avocations: horseback riding, skiing, raising Black Angus and Black Brangus cattle. Office: Texas Biotech Found PO Box 17 Hempstead TX 77445-0017 Office Phone: 979-826-3075. Office Fax: 979-826-9710.

PROPST, ROBERT BRUCE, federal judge; b. Onatchee, Ala., July 13, 1931; s. Franklin Glenn and Mildred (Moore) P.; m. Elma Jo Griffin, Dec. 29, 1962; children: Stephen, David, Joanne BS, U. Ala., 1953, JD, 1957. Pvt. practice law Wilson, Propst, Isom, Jackson, Bailey & Bott, 1957-80; judge US Dist Ct. (no. dist. Ala.), Birmingham, 1980-96, sr. judge Anniston, 1996—. Served to 1st lt. U.S. Army, 1953-55 Mem. ABA, Ala. Bar Assn., Birmingham Bar Assn., Calhoun County Bar Assn., Jaycees (pres. 1954-60) Clubs: Exchange (Anniston, Ala.). Methodist. Avocation: golf. Home: 500 Webster Rd Lot 102 Auburn AL 36832-4214 Office: US Dist Ct No Dist Ala Rm 900 Hugo Black US Courthousse 1729 5th Ave N Birmingham AL 35203-2000

PROSE, NEIL STUART, pediatric dermatologist; b. NYC, 1949; MD, NYU, 1975. Cert. Am. Bd. Dermatology, 1983. Intern in pediat. San Francisco Gen. Hosp., 1975—76; resident in dermatology SUNY, 1980—83, asst. prof. pediat., 1983—84; dermatologist Duke U. Med. Ctr., Durham, NC, assoc. prof. medicine. Office: Duke U Med Ctr PO Box 3252 Durham NC 27710 Office Phone: 919-684-5146. Office Fax: 919-681-8073. Business E-Mail: prose001@mc.duke.edu.

PROSSER, MICHAEL HUBERT, communications educator; b. Indpls., Mar. 29, 1936; arrived in China, 2001; s. Marshall Herbert and Clydia Catharine (O'Dea) P.; m. Carol Mary Hogle, Nov. 27, 1958 (div. 1983); children: Michelle Ann, Leo Michael, Louis Mark; m. Joan Ann Kirkeby, Dec. 6, 1986 (div. 2001). BA, Ball State U., 1958, MA, 1959; PhD, U. Ill., 1964. Tchr. Latin Urbana Jr. HS, Ill., 1960-63; asst. prof. speech SUNY, Buffalo, 1963-69; assoc. prof. speech Ind. U., Bloomington, 1969-72; prof. rhetoric and comm. U. Va., Charlottesville, 1972-2001, chair, 1972-77, prof. emeritus, 2001—; William A. Kern prof. in comm. Rochester Inst. Tech., 1994—98; chair internat. adv. bd. Coll. English Shanghai Internat. Studies U. Intercultural Inst., 2006—, disting. prof., 2005—09; chair, internat. adv. bd. and sr. co-editor inter cultural rsch. Shanghai Internat. Studies U., 2007—. Vis. lectr. comm. CUNY Queens Coll., 1966—67; vis. assoc. prof. speech Calif. State U., Hayward, 1971; vis. prof. curriculum Meml. U., Newfoundland, St. John's U., 1972, St. Paul U., 1975, U. Ottawa, Canada, 1975; cons. U.S. Info. Agy., Washington, 1977; disting. vis. prof. speech Kent State U., Ohio, 1978; Fullbright prof. English U. Swaziland, Kwalusene, 1990—91; disting. vis. prof. comm. Rochester Inst. Tech., 1998—2001; adj prof. SUNY, Brockport, 1998—99; prof. English Yangzhou U., 2001—02, disting. prof., 2013; disting. prof. English Beijing Lang. and Culture U., China, 2002—05, Shanghai Internat. Studies U., China, 2005—09; disting. prof. com. Ocean U. China, 2011; acad. coord., lifelong learners U. Va., Semester at Sea, 2011; keynote spkr. various Chinese comm. confs. in India, Japan, Russia; editor mem. bd. Jour. Mid. Eastern & Islamic Studies, 2007—. Author: The Cultural Dialogue, 1978 (translated into Japanese 1982), translator into Chinese, 2013; co-author: Diplomatic Discourse: International Conflict at the United Nations: Addresses and Analysis, 1997; editor: An Ethic for Survival: Adlai Stevenson Speaks on International Affairs, 1936-65, 1969, Sow the Wind, Reap the Whirlwind: Heads of State Address the United Nations (2 vols.), 1970, Intercommunication Among Nations and Peoples, 1973, co-editor: Readings in Classical Rhetoric, 1969, Readings in Medieval Rhetoric, 1973, Civic Discourse: Multiculturalism, Cultural Diversity, and Global Communication, 1998, Civic Discourse: Intercultural, International and Global Media, 1999, Sino-American Compositions of Shared Topics, 2003, Intercultural Perspectives on Chinese Communication, 2007, Values at the Theoretical Crossroads of Cultures, 2012, Finding Cross Cultural Common Ground, 2013, Values Dimensions and their Conceptual Dynamics Across Cultures, 2013, CCTV Dialogue Shanghai Internat. Channel, Am. Early Pioneers of Intercultural Communication Internat. Jour. Intercultural Rels., 2012, Social Media in Asia, 2013; series editor Civic Discourse for the Third Millennium, 1998-2004, Ablex Pub. Co., Praeger, Greenwood Pub. Co., 2005, Finding Cross-Cultural Common Ground, 2013, Social Medicine in Asia, 2013; featured in China Talent Semimonthly, Chinese edit.; numerous interviews on China Radio Internat., 2007-09. Chair AFS Global Awareness Day, U. Va., 1983-90, RIT Global Awareness Day, 1995-98; bd. dirs., v.p. Assn. Rochester UN, 1996-97, pres., 1997-98; pres. Rochester Area Fulbright chpt., 1995-97; mem. Nat. Comm. Assn., Internat. Comm. Assn. Recipient Disting. Alumnus award Ball State U., 1978, Citizen of World award, SIETAR Internat., 1986, Prosser-Sitaram award, Ann. Global Fusion Conf., 2000, Spl. Recognition award, China Assn. for Intercultural Communication, 2009, 11. Mem. Internat. Soc. for Intercultural Edn., Tng. and Rsch. (pres. 1984-86, Outstanding Sr. Interculturalist 1990), Internat. Comm. Assn. (v.p., Disting. Svc. award 1978), UN Assn. U.S.A., Fulbright Assn., Nat. Comm. Assn., UN Assn. of Rochester (bd. dirs., v.p., pres.), Am. Field Svc. (pres. intercultural programs 1982-86, Charlottesville). Democrat. Roman Catholic. Avocation: travel. Office: 977 Grayson Ln Charlottesville VA 22903

PROUGH, DONALD SANDERSON, anesthesiologist; b. Huntingdon, Pa., Mar. 21, 1947; s. Donald Charles and Ruth (Sanderson) P.; m. Betty, Dec. 24, 1966; children: Stephen, Emily. BA in English, Lafayette Coll., 1969; MD, Milton S. Hershey Med. Ctr., 1973. Diplomate Am. Bd. Anesthesiology; cert. critical care. Intern in critical care medicine Nat. Naval Med. Ctr., Bethesda, Md., 1973—74, resident in critical care medicine, 1975—76, fellow in critical care medicine, 1976—77; prof. anesthesiology Wake Forest U., Winston-Salem, NC, 1980-92, critical care section head, 1982-92; Rebecca Terry White disting. prof. & chmn. in anesthesiology U. Tex. Med. Branch, Galveston, 1992—, sr. assoc. dean faculty practice, 1999—2002, interim v.p. & dean, 2011—. Adv. com. emergency med. svc. Houston Cmty. Coll., 1999. Co-editor: Critical Care Medicine: Perioperative Management, 1997, 2d edit., 2002; editl. bd. Critical Care Medicine. Pres. Forsyth County Med. Bus. coalition, Winston-Salem, 1987-90, chair, bd. mem., 1990-91; mem. Piedmont Med. Found., Winston-Salem, 1999. Capt. USNR, 1992. Recipient Distinguished Investigator award Am. Coll. Critical Care Medicine, 1999. Fellow Am. Coll. Chest Physicians; mem. Internat. Anesthesia Rsch. Soc. (bd. trustees 1996-08, B.B. Sankey award 1984, Lifetime Achievement award), Am. Soc. Critical Care Anesthesiologists (pres. 1987-88), Assn. Univ. Anesthesiologists (pres. 2002—), Soc. Critical Care Medicine, Phi Beta Kappa. Avocations: golf, jogging. Office: The Univ Texas Med Branch 301 University Blvd Ste 2A Galveston TX 77555-5302 E-mail: dsprough@utmb.edu.

PROUGH, RUSSELL ALLEN, biochemistry professor, academic administrator; b. Twin Falls, Idaho, Nov. 5, 1943; s. Elza Leroy and Beulah Elsie (Huddleston) P.; M. Betty Marie Ehlers, Dec. 26, 1965; children: Jennifer Sally, Kimberly Marie. BS in Chemistry, Coll. of Idaho, 1965; PhD in Biochemistry and Biophysics, Oreg. State U., 1969. Postdoctoral fellow VA Hosp., Kansas City, Mo., 1969-72; instr. biochemistry U. Tex. Southwestern Med. Sch., Dallas, 1972-73, asst. prof. biochemistry, 1973-77, assoc. prof. biochemistry, 1977-82, prof. biochemistry, 1982-86, U. Louisville Sch. Med., 1986—, chmn. dept., 1986—99, 2007—08, vice dean rsch., assoc. v.p. rsch., 1998—2003, 2008—, Preston Pope Joyes endowed chair biochemical rsch., 2003. Mem. NIH Toxicology Study Sect., 1984-88, State of Nebr. Smoking Disease and Cancer Rsch. Program, 1984-91, Nat. Insts. Environ. Health Scis. rsch. com., 1999-2003. Assoc. editor Drug Metabolism and Disposition, 1994—, Drug Metabolism Rev., 2002—, Pharmacology and Therapeutics, 2005—. Recipient Rsch. Career Devel. award USPHS. Mem. Am. Soc. Biochemistry and Molecular Biology, Am. Soc. Pharmacology and Exptl. Therapeutics, Internat. Soc. for Study of Xenobiotics, Sigma Xi. Lutheran. Office: U Louisville Dept Biochemistry and Molecular Biology Louisville KY 40292-0001 Office Phone: 502-852-7249. Business E-Mail: russ.prough@louisville.edu.

PROVOST, GLEN JOHN, bishop; b. Lafayette, La., Aug. 9, 1949; s. Cyrus and Sadie Marie (Blanchet) Provost. BA in English Lit., St. Joseph Sem. Coll., St. Benedict, La., 1971; BST, St. Thomas U., Rome, 1974, STL, 1975; MA in English Lit., U. La., Lafayette, 1981. Ordained priest Diocese of Lafayette, La., 1975; assoc. pastor St. Mary Magdalene, Abbeville, La., 1975—83; pastor St. Leo, Roberts Cove, La., 1983—85, St. John Cathedral, 1985—98, Our Lady of Fatima, 1998—2007; ordained bishop, 2007; bishop Diocese of Lake Charles, La., 2007—. Mem.: KC, SAR (mem. nat. chaplains com.), Equestrian Order of Knights of and Ladies of Holy Sepulchre Jerusalem (knight), Phi Eta Sigma. Roman Catholic. Office: Diocese of Lake Charles PO Box 3223 414 Iris St Lake Charles LA 70602 Office Phone: 337-439-7400. Office Fax: 337-439-7413.

PRUCINO, DIANE L., lawyer; b. Wilmington, Del., July 15, 1957; d. Lawrence Joseph and Marjorie (Lowe) P. AB summa cum laude, Duke U., 1978; JD, U. Va., 1982. Bar: Ga. 1982, US Dist. Ct. (no. dist.) Ga. 1982, US Ct. Appeals (9th cir.) 1984, US Ct. Appeals (6th cir.) 1985, US Ct. Appeals (DC cir.). Assoc. Kilpatrick & Cody, Atlanta, 1982—97; ptnr., dept. head Labor and Employment and Employee Benefits Practice Grp. Kilpatrick Stockton LLP, Atlanta, 1997—2006, mem. exec. com., co-mng. ptnr., 2007—11, Kilpatrick Townsend & Stockton LLP, 2011—. Contbr. articles to profl. jours.; mem. editl. bd. Va. Law Rev., 1980-82. Bd. dirs. Homes for Children Internat., Inc., Atlanta, 1986—; vol. atty. Atlanta Legal Aid, 1983-84. Mem. ABA, Atlanta Bar Assn. Democrat. Presbyterian. Avocation: travel. Office: Kilpatrick Townsend & Stockton LLP Ste 2800 1100 Peachtree St NE Atlanta GA 30309-4530 Office Fax: 404-541-3350. E-mail: DPrucino@KilpatrickStockton.com.

PRUDHOMME, PAUL, chef, restaurant owner; Exec. chef Commander's Palace, New Orleans, 1975; owner, chef K-Paul's Louisiana Kitchen, New Orleans, 1979—. Creator Chef Paul Prudhomme's Magic Seasoning Blends. Author: (cookbooks) Fork in the Road, Fiery Foods That I Love, Kitchen Expedition, Louisiana Kitchen, Louisiana Tastes, Pure Magic, Still Cooking!, 2007. Vol. Meals on Wheels, Easter Seals, March of Dimes, Big Brothers/Big Sisters, Chef and the Child. Recipient Restaurateur of Yr., La. State Restaurant Assn., 1983, Lifetime Achievement award, Internat. Assn. Culinary Professionals, 2008; named Culinarian of Yr., Culinary Diplomat, Am. Culinary Fedn., 1994. Office: K-Paul's Louisiana Kitchen 416 Chartres New Orleans LA 70130

PRUETT, JAMES WORRELL, librarian, educator, musicologist; b. Mt. Airy, NC, Dec. 23, 1932; s. Samuel Richard and Gladys Dorne (Worrell) P.; m. Lilian Maria-Irene Pibernik, July 20, 1957; children—Mark, Ellen. BA, U. N.C., Chapel Hill, 1955, MA, 1957, PhD, 1962. Mem. faculty U. N.C., Chapel Hill., 1961-87, prof. music, 1974-87, music librarian, 1961-76, chmn. dept. music, 1976-86; chief music div. Library of Congress, Washington, 1987-95. Vis. prof. U. Toronto, 1976; cons. in music, 1995—. Editor: Studies in the History, Style and Bibliography of Music in Memory of Glen Haydon, 1969; author: Research Guide to Musicology, 1985. Contbr. profl. jours., encys. Newberry Libr. fellow, 1966. Mem. Internat. Musicol. Soc., Am. Musicol. Soc. (chpt. chmn. 1964-66, mem. coun. 1974-77), Music Libr. Assn. (pres. 1973-75, editor jour. 1974-77), Cosmos Club (Washington). Home: 395 Carolina Meadows Villa Chapel Hill NC 27517-7522 Home Phone: 919-942-4322.

PRUETT, JIMMY, state legislator; b. Mar. 24; m. Casey Pruett. Businessman, 1974—; state rep. Dist. 144 Ga., 2007—. Mem.: Eastman Dodge Hist. Soc., Conditioned Air Assn. of Ga., Eastman-Dodge County C. of C., Citizens Bank and Trust Co. (bd. dir.), the Hosp. Authority, Heart of Ga. Airport Authority, Heart of Ga. Tech. Sch. (advisory bd.). Republican. Office: PO Box 459 Eastman GA 31023 Office Phone: 478-374-4316. Fax: 478-374-5114.

PRUETT, R.C., state legislator; b. Houston, Tex., Sept. 19, 1944; m. Barbara Pruett; 3 children. Attended, Tex. A&M Univ. Owner & operator of supermarkets in Antlers and Broken Bow; mem. Dist. 19 Okla. House of Representatives, 2005—. Mem.: Okla. Grocery Assn., Antlers Lions Club. Democrat. Mailing: PO Box 969 Antlers OK 74523 Office: Oklahoma House of Representatives 2300 N Lincoln Blvd Rm 542 Oklahoma City OK 73105 Office Phone: 405-557-7382. E-mail: rcpruett@okhouse.gov.

PRUETT, WILLIAM A., finance company executive; Various positions Columbus Bank & Trust Co.; sr. v.p., v.p. & asst. v.p. Total System Services, Inc., exec. v.p., 1993, sr. exec. v.p., pres., N.Am. Svcs. Home: PO Box 120 Columbus GA 31902-0120 Office: Total System Services Inc 1 TSYS Way Columbus GA 31902-2567 Office Phone: 706-649-2310. Office Fax: 706-649-4266. Business E-Mail: wpruett@tss.com.

PRUITT, BASIL ARTHUR, JR., surgeon, retired military officer; b. Nyack, NY, Aug. 21, 1930; s. Basil Arthur and Myrtle Flo (Knowles) P.; m. Mary Sessions Gibson, Sept. 4, 1954; children: Scott Knowles, Laura Sessions, Jeffrey Hamilton. AB, Harvard U., 1952, postgrad., 1952—53; MD, Tufts U., 1957. Diplomate Am. Bd. Surgery. Intern Boston City Hosp., 1957—58, resident surgery, 1958—59, 1961—62; commd. capt., M.C. U.S. Army, 1959, advanced through grades to col., 1972; resident Brooke Gen. Hosp., Ft. Sam Houston, Tex., 1962—64; chief clin. divsn. Inst. Surg. Rsch., Ft. Sam Houston, 1965—67; chief profl. svcs. 12th Evacuation Hosp., Vietnam, 1967—68; comdr., dir. U.S. Army Inst. Surg. Rsch., Brooke Army Med. Ctr., Ft. Sam Houston, 1968—95, ret., 1995; clin. prof. gen. surgery U. Tex. Health Sci. Ctr., San Antonio, 1975—, Dr. Ferdinand P. Herff chair surgery, 2009—; prof. surgery Uniformed Svcs. U. Health Scis., Bethesda, Md., 1978—. Mem. surgery, anaesthesiology and trauma study sect. NIH, 1978—82; mem. Shriners Burns Adv. Bd., 1985—92, Shriners Med. Adv. Bd., 1992—95, Shriners Rsch. Adv. Bd., 1996—2006, Shriners Clin. Outcomes Studies Adv. Bd., 1999—2007; merit rev. bd. for surgery VA, 1990—93; bd. dirs. Am.

Bd. Surgery, 1982—88, sr. mem., 1989—. Author med. books; contbr. chpts. to textbooks, articles to profl. jours.; mem. editl. bd. Jour. Trauma, 1975-94, editor, 1995—2011; mem. edit. bd.: Archives Surgery, 1981-93, Consultations in Surgery, Correspondence Society of Surgeons, Collected Letters, 1978-2000, Circulatory Shock, 1985-93, Jour. Burn Care and Rehab., 1984-87, Jour. Investigative Surgery, 1987-97, Shock, 1993—, Current Opinion in Surg. Infections, 1993-2001, Sepsis, 1996-2002, Injury, 1998-2003, Turkish Jour. Trauma, 2002—, English edit. Chinese Jour. Traumatology, 1998—, Med. Jour. Chinese People's Liberation Army, 2005—. Decorated Bronze Star, Legion of Merit, DSM; recipient ISS/SIC Danis prize, 1995, G. Whitaker Internat. Burns prize, 2000, US Army Med. Rsch. and Materiel Command Lifetime Achievement award, 2002, Tanner-Vandeput-Boswick Burn prize, 2006, Roswell Park medal, 2007, Disting. Alumni award, 2007, King Faisal Internat. prize, 2008. Fellow: ACS (pre and postoperative care com. 1969—79, vice chmn. 1973—75, gov. 1973—79, com. on trauma 1974—84, internat. rels. com. 1983—93, chmn. 1987—89), Am. Coll. Critical Care Medicine (Disting. Investigator award 2000); mem.: First Bolivian Burn Congress (hon. pres. 2011), Soc. Critical Care Medicine (Master Critical Care Med. award), We. Trauma Assn. (hon. life mem. 2011), Ea. Assn. Surgery Trauma, N.Am. Burn Soc. (pres. 1993—94), Shock Soc. (clin. counselor 1995—98, pres. 2007—08, chmn. 2005 program com.), Internat. Surg. Group, Surg. Infection Soc. (recorder 1980—84, pres. 1985—86), Assn. Acad. Surgery, Internat. Soc. Surgery, Surg. Biol. Club III, Am. Assn. Surgery Trauma (recorder 1976—80, bd. mgr. 1976—80, pres. 1982—83, bd. mgr. 1982—86, 1995—), Halsted Soc. (pres. 1985—86), So. Surg. Assn. (pres. 2004—05), We. Surg. Assn. (dist. rep. 1984—88, pres. 1993—94), Tex. Surg. Assn., Am. Surg. Assn. (2d v.p. 1980—81, pres. 1999—2000, Medallion 1998), Am. Burn Assn. (life; program com. chmn. 1971—73, bd. trustees 1974—79, pres. 1975—76, chmn. archives com. 1991—, hon. mem. 2002, Lifetime Achievement award 2010), Internat. Soc. Burn Injuries (hon.; nat. rep. 1974—82, co-chmn. disaster planning com. 1982—86, pres.-elect 1990—94, pres. 1994—98, life mem. 2002), Japanese Assn. Acute Medicine (hon.), Soc. Univ. Surgeons (Lifetime Achievement award 2007), Am. Trauma Soc. (pres. Tex. divsn. 1974—75, dir. 1974—, sec. 1986—88, v.p. 1988—90, pres.-elect 1990—92, pres. 1992—94), Smoke Burn and Fire Assn. (adv. coun. 1976—2008), Mediterranean Club Burns and Fire Disasters (regional rep. Ams. 1999—), Surgeons' Travel Club (pres. 2002—03). Home: 402 Tidecrest Dr San Antonio TX 78239-2517 Office: U Tex Health Sci Ctr Dept Surgery 7703 Floyd Curl Dr San Antonio TX 78229-3900 Home Phone: 210-655-4769; Office Phone: 210-567-3623. Business E-Mail: pruitt@uthscsa.edu.

PRUITT, DEAN GARNER, psychologist, educator; b. Phila., Dec. 26, 1930; s. Dudley McConnell and Grace (Garner) P.; m. France Juliard, Dec. 27, 1959; children: Andre Juliard, Paul Dudley, Charles Alexandre. AB, Oberlin Coll., 1952; MS, Yale U., 1954, PhD, 1957. Postdoctoral fellow U. Mich., 1957-59; rsch. assoc. Northwestern U., 1959-61; asst. prof., then assoc. prof. U. Del., 1961-66; assoc. prof. to prof. SUNY, Buffalo, 1966—96, disting. prof., 1996—2001, disting. prof. emeritus, 2001—, dir. grad. program in social psychology, 1969—73, 1976—77, 1985—88, 1998—2001; disting. scholar in residence George Mason U., 2001—. Author: Negotiation Behavior, 1981, (with J. Z. Rubin and S.H. Kim) Social Conflict, 1986, 94, 2004, (with P.J. Carnevale) Negotiation in Social Conflict, 1993; editor: (with R.C. Snyder) Theory and Research on the Causes of War, 1969, (with K. Kressel) Mediation Research, 1989. Grantee Office Naval Rsch., 1965, NIMH, 1969, NSF, 1969, 74, 76, 80, 83, 86, 88, 93, Guggenheim Found., 1978-79. Fellow APA, Am. Psychol. Soc., Soc. for Psychol. Study Social Issues; mem. Internat. Assn. for Conflict Mgmt. (pres. 1990-92, Lifetime Achievement award 1997), Internat. Soc. Polit. Psychology (v.p. 1984-85, Harold D. Lasswell award 1992), Soc. Study Peace, Conflict, and Violence (Lifetime Achievement award 2012), Phi Beta Kappa, Sigma Xi. Home: 9006 Friars Rd Bethesda MD 20817-3320 Office: George Mason U Sch Conflict Analysis and Resolution Fairfax VA 22030-4444 E-mail: deangpruitt@gmail.com.

PRUITT, MARY, state legislator; b. Brentwood, Tenn., Feb. 3, 1934; children: Renaldo, Marilyn. Former educator; state rep. Dist. 58 Tenn., 1985—. Mem.: Nat. Politics Congl. Black Women, Tenn. Mid. Dist. Civil Liberties League (former pres.), Nashville Urban League, Eastern Star, Rebecca Carney Temple, Nashville Club Negro Bus. & Profl. Women (former pres.). Democrat. United Methodist. Office: 25 Legislative Plz Nashville TN 37243-0158 also: 1813 Hillside Ave Nashville TN 37203 Office Phone: 615-741-3853, 615-385-0590. Office Fax: 615-741-1041. Business E-Mail: rep.mary.pruitt@capitol.tn.gov.

PRUITT, SCOTT (EDWARD SCOTT PRUITT), state attorney general, former state legislator; b. Danville, Ky., May 9, 1968; m. Marlyn Loyd; children: McKenna, Cade. BA, Georgetown Coll., 1990; JD, U. Tulsa, 1993. Bar: Okla. 1993. Atty.; mem. Dist 54, Dist. 36 Okla. State Senate, Oklahoma City, 1998—2006, republican whip, 2000—02, asst. republican floor leader, 2002—06; co-owner, mng. gen. ptnr. Triple A Okla. City Redhawks, 2002—10; atty. Latham Stall Wagner Steele & Lehman PC, Tulsa, Okla.; atty. gen. State of Okla., 2011—. Vice chmn. common ground com. Broken Arrow Public Schools, Okla.; deacon First Baptist. Ch., Broken Arrow; cons. North American Mission Bd. of Southern Bapt. Conv. Mem.: Oklahoma Bar Assn., Tulsa County Bar Assn. Republican. Avocations: baseball, tennis, collector of historical documents, family activities. Office: Office of the Attorney General 313 NE 21st St Oklahoma City OK 73105 Office Phone: 405-521-3921.*

PRYGELSKI, PETER J., III, corporate financial executive; b. Brooklyn; BBA in Fin., Stetson U., 1991. Cert. internal auditor. Former bd. dirs., asst. gen. auditor Am. Express Centurion Bank (subs. Am. Express Co.), corp fin. positions, mem., enterprise risk and assurance function through dir., audit, 1991—2003; sr. mgr., enterprise risk svcs. practice Ernst & Young LLP, 2004—06, Deloitte & Touche LLP, 2006—07; treas., prin. acctg. officer 21st Century Holding Co., bd. dirs., 2004—07, CFO, 2007—, bd. dirs., 2008—. Office: 21st Century Holding Co 14050 NW 14th St Ste 180 Sunrise FL 33323-2851 Office Phone: 954-581-9993. Office Fax: 954-316-9201. Personal E-mail: pprygelski@tchcusa.com.

PRYOR, CAROL GRAHAM, retired obstetrician, gynecologist; b. Savannah, Ga., Dec. 11, 1918; m. Louis O.J. Manganiello, June 11, 1950; children: Carol Helen, Victoria Manganiello Mudano. AB, Ga. Coll., 1939; MD, Med. Coll. Ga., 1947. Rotating intern City Hosps., Balt., 1947-48; asst. resident pathology Baroness Erlanger Hosp., Chattanooga, 1948; intern. obstetrics City Colls., Balt., 1949; coll. physician Ga. State Coll. for Women, Milledgeville, Ga., 1949-50; resident obstetrics City Hosps., Balt., 1950-51; asst. resident gynecology Univ. Hosp., Balt., 1951-52, sr. resident ob-gyn. Augusta, Ga., 1952; pvt. practice ob-gyn. Augusta, 1952—2008; chmn. ob-gyn. St. Joseph Hosp., Augusta, 1998; ret., 2008. Chair ob-gyn. dept. St. Joseph Hosp., Augusta. Mem., former pres. Iris Garden Club, Augusta; mem. coun. on maternal and infant health State of Ga., Atlanta, 1981-90; mem. edn. found. AAUW, 1961-63, state v.p., state pres., 1963-65. Recipient Cert. of Achievement-Community Leadersip, Ga. div. AAUW, 1982; named Med. Woman of Yr., Ga. br. 51 Am. Med. Women's Assn., 1961; Heritage award Ga. Coll. and State U., 2001, Achievement award, Ga. Coll. U., 1982. Fellow ACS (1st woman mem. Ga. chpt.); mem. ACOG, AMA, Richmond County Med. Soc., So. Med. Assn., So. Surg. Congress, Delta Kappa Gamma. Democrat. Methodist.

PRYOR, MARK LUNSFORD, United States Senator from Arkansas; b. Fayetteville, Ark., Jan. 10, 1963; s. David H. Pryor; m. Jill Pryor; children: Adams, Porter. BA in History, U. Ark., 1985, JD, 1988. Pvt. practice Wright, Lindsey & Jennings, Little Rock, 1988—97; mem. Dist. 57 Ark. House of Reps., Little Rock, 1991—94; atty. gen. State of Ark., Little Rock, 1999—2002; US Senator from Ark. Washington, 2003—. Contbr. articles to profl. jours. Chmn. Alliance to Save Energy; mem. cardiovascular cabinet Ark. Heart Assn.; mem. Friends of Carousel. Recipient Spirit of Enterprise award, US C. of C., 2005; named Big Brother of Yr., 1992. Democrat. Presbyterian. Office: US Senate 255 Dirksen Senate Office Bldg Washington DC 20510 also: The River Market Ste 401 500 President Clinton Ave Little Rock AR 72201-1745 Office Phone: 202-224-2353, 501-324-6336. Office Fax: 202-228-0908, 501-324-5320.*

PRYOR, STEPHEN D., oil industry executive; b. NYC; B in Biology, Lafayette Coll., Easton, Pa., 1971; MBA, Harvard U. Mktg. rep. Mobil Oil Corp., NYC, 1971, gen. mgr. Cyprus, New Zealand, v.p. Mobil Chem. Co., gen. mgr. plastics divsn., 1993, pres. Mobil Asia Pacific, 1996—98, exec. v.p. internat. downstream bus., 1998; pres. Lubricants & Specialties Co. ExxonMobil Corp., 1999—2002, exec. v.p. ExxonMobil Chem. Co., 2002—04, pres., 2004—, pres. ExxonMobil Refining & Supply Co., 2004—. Chmn. downstream com. Am. Petroleum Inst. Trustee Lafayette Coll. Mem.: NAM (mem. bd. dirs., chmn. energy/environ. policy group). Office: Exxon Mobil Corp Hdqs 5959 Las Colinas Blvd Irving TX 75039-2298

PRYOR, WILLIAM DANIEL LEE, humanities educator; b. Lakeland, Fla., Oct. 29, 1926; s. Dahl and Lottie Mae (Merchant) P. AB, Fla. So. Coll., 1949; MA, Fla. State U., Tallahassee, 1950, PhD, 1959; postgrad., U. NC, Chapel Hill, 1952—53; pvt. art studies with Florence Wilde; pvt. voice studies with Colin O'More, Anna Kaskas; pvt. piano studies with Waldemar Hille and audited piano master classes of Ernst von Dohnányi. Asst. prof. English, dir. drama Bridgewater Coll., Va., 1950-52; grad. tchg. fellow humanities Fla. State U., Tallahassee, 1953-55, 57-58; instr. English U. Houston, University Park, Houston, 1955-59, asst. prof., 1959-62, assoc. prof., 1962-71, prof., 1971-97, prof. emeritus, 1997. Vis. instr. English, Fla. So. Coll., Lakeland, MacDill Army Air Base, Tampa, Fla., summer 1951, Tex. So. U., 1961-63, humanities, govt. U. Tex. Dental Br., Houston, 1962-63; lectr. The Women's Inst., Houston, 1967-72, humanities series Jewish Cmty. Ctr., Houston, 1972-73; originator, moderator TV and radio program The Arts in Houston Stas. KUHT-TV and KUHF-FM, 1956-57, 58-63. Author: An Examination of the Southern Milieu in Representative Plays by Southern Dramatists, 1963; contbg. author: National Poetry Anthology, 1952, Panorama das Literaturas das Americas, vol. 2, 1958-60, Perspectives on Ernst von Dohnányi, 2005, Dohnányi Evkönyu 2005, 2006; assoc. editor Forum, 1967, editor, 1967-82; contbr. articles to profl. jours.; dir. Murder in the Cathedral (T.S. Elliot), U. Houston, 1965; performed in opera as Sir Edgar in Der Junge Lord (Henze), Houston Grand Opera Assn., 1967; played the title role in Aella (Chatterton), Am. premiere, U. Houston, 1970. Bd. dir., founding mem. Contemporary Music Soc., Houston, 1958-63, Houston Shakespeare Soc., 1964-67; bd. dirs., founding mem., program annotator Houston Chamber Orch. Soc., 1964-76; narrator Houston Symphony Orch., Houston Summer Symphony Orch., Houston Chamber Orch. (with Charles Rosekrans), U. Houston Symphony Orch., St. Stephen's Music Festival Symphony Orch., New Harmony, Ind.; narrator world premier of The Bells (Jerry McCathern), 1969, U. Houston Symphony Orch., 1969, Am. premier Symphony No. Seven, Antartica (Vaughn-Williams), Houston Symphony Orch. (with Andre Previn), 1967, L'Histoire du Soldat (Stravinski), U. Houston Symphony Orch., 1957, Am. premier Babar the Elephant (Poulenc-Francais), Houston Chamber Orch. (with Charles Rosekrans), 1967, Le Roi David (Honegger), 1979, Voice of God in opera Noye's Fludde (Britten), St. Stephen's Music Festival, New Harmony, Ind. 1981; bd. dir., program annotator Music Guild, Houston, 1960-67, v.p., 1963-67, adv. bd., 1967-70; mem.-at-large, bd. dir. Houston Grand Opera Guild, 1966-67; repertory com. Houston Grand Opera Assn., 1967-70; bd. dir. Houston Grand Opera, 1970-75, adv. bd. 1978-79; cultural adv. com. Jewish Cmty. Ctr., 1960-66; bd. dir. Houston Friends Pub. Libr., 1962-67, 73-75, 1st v.p., 1963-67; adv. mem. cultural affairs com. Houston C. of C., 1972-75; adv. bd. dir. The Wilhelm Schole, 1980-98, Buffalo Bayou Support Com., 1985-87, bd. dir. Moores Sch. Music Soc., 1998—, trustee, 2002-04, advisory bd. dir., 2004—; bd. dir. U. Houston Retiree Assn., 1999-2001, 2011-, v.p., 2000-2001; founding bd. dir. Internat. Dohnányi Rsch. Ctr., Inc., 2002-. Recipient Master Tchg. award Coll. Humanities and Fine Arts U., Houston, 1980, Favorite Prof. award Bapt. Student Union, U. Houston, 1991. Mem. MLA, AAUP, Coll. English Assn., L'Alliance Francaise, English-Speaking Union, Alumni Assn. Fla. So. Coll., Fla. State U., South Ctrl. MLA, Conf. Editors Learned Jours., Coll. Conf. Tchrs. English, Nat. Coun. Tchrs. English, Am. Studies Assn., Shepard Soc. Rice U., Nature Conservancy, Nat. Trust for Hist. Preservation, Inst. Internat. Edn., Century Club, Fla. So. Coll., President's Club, James D. Westcott Legacy Soc., Fla. State U., Tex. Ret. Tchrs. Assn., Phi Beta (patron), Phi Mu Alpha Sinfonia, Alpha Psi Omega, Pi Kappa Alpha, Sigma Tau Delta (Outstanding Prof. English U. Houston chpt. 1990), 1927 Soc. U. Houston, Houston Philos. Soc., Caledonian Club (London), Tau Kappa Alpha, Phi Kappa Phi. Episcopalian. Avocations: tennis, racquetball, swimming, travel. Home: 2625 Arbuckle St West University Place TX 77005-3929 Office: U Houston Dept English Univ Park 3801 Cullen Blvd Houston TX 77004-2602

PRYOR, WILLIAM HOLCOMBE, JR., (BILL PRYOR), federal judge, former state attorney general, educator; b. Mobile, Ala., Apr. 26, 1962; s. William Holcombe Sr. and Laura Louise (Bowles) Pryor; m. Kristan Camille Wilson, Aug. 15, 1987; children: Caroline Elizabeth, Victoria Camille. BA in Legal Studies with honors, N.E. La. U., 1984; JD with honors, Tulane U., 1987. Law clk. to Hon. John Minor Wisdom US Ct. Appeals (5th Cir.), New Orleans, 1987—88; assoc. Cabaniss, Johnston, Gardner, Dumas & O'Neil, Birmingham, Ala., 1988—91, Walston, Stabler, Wells, Anderson & Bains, Birmingham, 1991—95; dep. atty. gen. State of Ala., Montgomery, 1995—97, atty. gen., 1997—2004; judge US Ct. Appeals (11th Cir.), Birmingham, 2004—; commr. US Sentencing Commn., Washington, 2013—. Adj. prof. Samford U. Cumberland Sch. Law, Birmingham, 1989—94, U. Ala. Sch. Law, 2006—. Bd. student editors: Tulane Law Rev., 1985—86, editor-in-chief:, 1986—87, bd. adv. editors:, 1995—. Mem. nat. com. Young Republican Nat. Fedn., 1984—86; mem. Ala. Republican Exec. Com., 1994—95. Mem.: Federalist Soc. (assoc.), American Law Inst. (assoc.), Order of Coif, Omicron Delta Kappa, Phi Kappa Phi. Republican. Roman Catholic. Office: US Court of Appeals 900 Federal Courthouse 1729 5th Ave N Birmingham AL 35203 Business E-Mail: william_h_pryor_jr@calluscourts.gov.*

PUCCIO, LARRY, political organization administrator; Prin. Puccio & York Realty, Fairmont, W.Va.; chief of staff W.Va. Sec. of State & Gov. Joe Manchin, 2000—09; chmn. W.Va. Dem. Party, 2010—. Democrat. Mailing: WV Democratic Party Ste 214 717 Lee St Charleston WV 25301*

PUCHKOVSKY, VLADIMIR, painter; b. Margilan, Uzbekistan, 1952; m. Svetlana Shihova. Grad., Ferghana State U., 1973. With Found. of Fine and Applied Arts. Exhbns. in local and internat. venues. Mem.: Painters Assn. of Uzbekistan (Ferghana chpt.). Mailing: c/o Fine Arts of Fergana Valley Silka Gallery 7117 Enterprise Ave Mclean VA 22101

PUCKETT, ELIZABETH ANN, former law librarian; b. Evansville, Ind., Nov. 10, 1943; d. Buell Charles and Lula Ruth (Gray) P.; m. Joel E. Hendricks, June 1, 1964 (div. June 1973); 1 child, Andrew Charles; m. Thomas A. Wilson, July 19, 1985. BS in Edn., Eastern Ill. U., 1964; JD, U. Ill., 1977, MS in L.S., 1977. Bar: Kans. 1978, Ill. 1979. Acquisitions/reader services librarian U. Kans. Law Library, Lawrence, 1978-79; asst. reader services librarian So. Ill. U. Law Library, Carbondale, 1979-81, reader services librarian, 1981-83; assoc. dir. Northwestern U. Law Library, Chgo., 1983-86, co-acting dir., 1986-87; dir./assoc. prof. South Tex. Coll. Law Library, Houston, 1987-89; dir./prof. South Tex. Coll. Law Libr., Houston, 1990-94, U. Ga. Law Libr., Athens, 1994—2010, prof. emerita, 2010—. Co-author: Evaluation of System-Provided Library Services to State Correctional Centers in Illinois, 1983; co-editor Uniform Commercial Code: Confidential Drafts, 1993. Mem. ABA, Am. Assn. Law Librs. (mem. exec. bd. 1993-96). Avocations: reading, antiques. E-mail: apuckett@uga.edu.

PUCKETT, KAREN ANNE, telecommunications industry executive; b. 1960; BA, Ind. State Univ., Terre Haute, Ind.; MBA, Bellarmine Coll., Louisville, Ky. Pres. Tex. region GTE Wireless, 1996—99; sales & mktg. officer BroadStream Communications, 1999—2000; exec. v.p., COO CenturyTel, Inc., 2000—02, pres., COO, 2002—09; exec. v.p., COO CenturyLink, Inc. (formerly CenturyTel, Inc.), 2009—. Bd. dirs. US Telecom. Assn. (USTA), Harte-Hanks, Inc., 2009—. Mem. bd. dir. St. Francis Med. Ctr.; exec. bd. mem. La. Purchase Coun., Boy Scouts Am. Recipient Lewis & Clark Pioneer in Industry awards, U. Mont. Sch. Bus. Adminstrn., 2008. Office: CenturyTel Inc 100 Centurytel Dr Monroe LA 71203

PUCKETT, RUBY PARKER, food service executive, consultant, writer, dietician; b. Dora, Ala., Nov. 26, 1932; d. John Franklin Parker and Ethel V. (Short) Tuggle; m. Larry Willard Puckett, July 2, 1955; children: Laurel Lynn Puckett Brown, Hollie Kristina Puckett Walker. BS in Food and Nutrition, Auburn U., Ala., 1954; postgrad. in vocat. edn., U. Fla., 1970-80; MA in Health Sci. Edn., Cen. Mich. U., 1976. Dietitian, foodservice adminstr., food svc. exec., military traveller, evaluation of AF, Navy Marine FS. Dietetic intern Henry Ford Hosp., Detroit, 1955; staff dietitian VA Hosp., Houston, 1955-56; dietitian Matty Hersee Hosp., Meridian, Miss., 1957-58; asst. dir. U. Miss. Med. Ctr., Jackson, 1960-61; dir. dietetics Ft. Sanders Presbyn. Hosp., Knoxville, Tenn., 1961-63, Waterman Meml. Hosp., Eustis, Fla., 1963-68; dir. food and nutrition U. Fla. Shands Hosp., Gainesville, 1968-95; pres. Square One Cons. Service, Gainesville, 1979-85; pres., owner Food Svc. Mgmt. Cons., 1995—. Adv. com. on jr. coll. dietetic programs Fla. Dept. Edn., 1967-69; nominating com. Southeastern Hosp. Conf. for Dietitians, 1969, sec., 1974-75; pres. Field Agy. Nutrition, 1970; instr. U. Fla., 1972-73, 82-85, clin. and cmty. coordinated undergrad. dietetic program adv. bd., 1974-89; instr. Santa Fe Jr. Coll., Gainesville, 1977-81; adv. com. Marquis Libr. Soc., Inc., 1974; health project rev. com. North Ctrl. Fla. Planning Coun., 1974-76; named to White House Conf. on Food and Nutrition, 1976, Senate Select Com. on Food and Nutrition, 1976; com. on animal products NRC Adv. Bd. on Mil. Pers. Supplies, 1978-81; site evaluator dietetic programs in colls and univs., 1998-2008; mem. Commn. on Accrediation Dietetic Edn., 1997-2008, program reviewer for dietary mgr. tng., 2003-06; reviewer abstracts, articles Jour. Am. Dietetic Assn.; spkr. in field.; content advisor position papers ADA, editl. bd. AHF SO Connected; coun. fellows FFCSI, 2012. Author: Food Service Manual for Health Care Institutions, 1988 (Jim Rose Pub.award, 2005, 2009), 3d edit., 2004, 4th edit., 2013, Basic Nutrition and Diet Modification Shands Hospital, 1992, revised edit., 2002, Managing Foodservice Operations, 1992, HACCP The Future Challenge, Basic Food, Nutrition & Medical Nutrition Therapy Through the Life Cycle, 4th edit., 2009, Disaster and Emergency Preparedness for Food Service Operations, 2004, Dietary Managers Course by Correspondence, 14th edit., 2013—14 (Nat. U. Corr. Edn., Disting. Ind. Soc. Commn. award, 1986, 1988), Nutrition for the Elderly, Safety, Sanitation and Security for Food Services Operation, Topics in Practice: Productivity Measures for Food Service Operations, 2005, Standards of Professional Performance, 2008; mem. editl. adv. com.: Stokes Report, 1980—84, editl. advisor: Food Management, 1986—2010, Topics in Clinical Nutrition, 1988—, Aspen's Focus, 1984—91, Aspen's Hosp. Nutrition and Foodservice Forms; editl. advisor Marketlink, 2006, editl. adv. bd. FCSI-The American Quarterly Editorial ANFP, 2009—11; contbr. articles to profl. jours.; developer nutrition and older adult distance edn. course, 2013, chair, com. mem., 2013. V.p. Campus USA Credit Union, 1980—81, pres.-elect, 1981—82, chmn. elect. bd., 2013—; chmn. Shands Hosp. chpt. United Way, 1978, chmn. sellect com. for CEO, mem. speakers bur., 1985—86, chmn. bd. dirs., 2013; profl. adv. bd. Shands Home Care; vol. Mothers Supporting Daus. with Breast Cancer, 2000—; mem. Sexual Phys. Abuse Bd.; courtesy faculty appt. Divsn Youth, Family and Ext.; election clk., inspector Alachua County (Fla.) Elections, 2000—06; bd. dir. Campus USA Credit Union, 1978—, mem. budget and allocations com.; mem. adv. bd. United Way, 1983—2005, Harvest Gainesville, 1991—93, Children's Miracle Telethon, 1992—95; adv. bd. Sta. WRUF Pub. Radio, 1992; bd. dir. Fla. 4-H Found., 2000—04, North Fla. Regional Vocat. Sch.; mem. Asset-Liability Mgmt. CU Com., 2009. Recipient Community Leader award, Sta. WRUF-FM, 1972, Ivy award, Restauranteurs of Distinction, 1980, Disting. Pace Setter award, Roundtable for Women in Foodservice, 1984, Award of Distinction, Sch. Human Svc., Auburn U., 1981, Outstanding Dietitian, Fla., 1967, Robert Pacifco award, FCSI-TA, 2010; named Alumni of Yr., Auburn U. Sch. Home Econs., 1985, Disting. Woman, Alachua County, Fla., 1992; named to Woodlawn H.S. Hall of Fame, 1982, Fla. Women's Hall of Fame, 1986. Mem.: IFMA (Silver Plate award 1978), Food Svc. Consultants Internat. Soc. (N.Am. divsn. bd. trustees 2006—09, program planning com. 2007, code of ethics chair task force 2007, governance task force, other task force & cmty. appts. 2007—09, chair publ. com. 2009, mem. worldwide edn. found. 2010—, pres., worldwide editl. found. bd. 2012, Svc. award 2010, Ednl. Found. award 2010—), Fla. Coun. on Aging (sec. nutrition sect. 1974—76, adv. bd. 1974—76, chmn. 1974—76), Nat. U. Continuing Edn. Assn. (disting. ind. study course 1986, 1989), Nutrition Edn. Soc. (liaison with industry com. 1974, legis. com. 1974, charter), Dietary Mgr. Assn. Found. Fla. (steering com., Disting. Svc. award 2006), Am. Soc. Hosp. Food Service Adminstrs. (edn. com. 1968—71, nomination com. 1978, chmn. publ. com. 1981—82, chmn. legis. com. 1984, mem., Jim Rose Pub. 2005, adv. bd. Trends 2006—09, task force HACCP cert., Editl. Excellence award 2007, Jim Rose Pub. award 2009), Gainesville Dietetic Assn. (v.p. 1969, pres. 1973), Fla. Dietetic Assn. (sec.

1968—70, pres. 1973—74, del. 1980—87, chmn. by-laws com. 1985, numerous other offices, pres.), Am. Dietetic Assn. (house of delegates 1981—85, pres. practice group 41 1982—84, area III coord. 1985—88, chair DPG41 1988—91, chair practice group mgmt. in food and nutrition svc. 2001, hons. award com. 2005, emergency task force 2006—07, profl. performer 2007—09, ctrl. advisor 2009—13, developer course material execution mgmt. program 2012, mem., info. task forse 2012, chmn. stds. of profl. performance, Excellence in Mgmt. Practice award 1994, Medallion for Profl. Cmty. and Career Achievement 1996, Marjorie Hulsizer Copher award 2003, DMA Ruby P. Puckett Leadership award 2011), The Athenaeum Soc. (v.p. 2013), Internat. Gold and Silver Plate Soc. (sec. bd. trustees 1983—85), Ivy Soc., Pi Lambda Beta, Kappa Sigma Phi. Republican. Mem. Lds Ch. Achievements include Ruby P. Puckett Leadership award was named in her honor by Management Practice Group ADA. Avocations: hiking, gardening, reading, writing. Personal E-mail: rubypuckett97@gmail.com.

PUENTE, ANTONIO E., psychologist, educator, scientist; b. Habana, Cuba, Feb. 14, 1952; s. Antonio A. and Sylvia (Llanso) P.; m. Linda Newman, June 11, 1977; children: Kirsta, Antonio, Lucas. AA, Fla. Jr. Coll., Jacksonville, 1971; BA, U. Fla., 1973; PhD, U. Ga., 1978. Diplomate Am. Bd. Profl. Neuropsychology. Asst. prof. neuroanatomy St. George's U. Sch. Medicine, Grenada, W.I., 1978-79; clin. psychologist N.E. Fla. State Hosp., Macclenny, Fla., 1979-81; clin. neuropsychologist Wilmington, NC, 1982—; prof. psychology U. N.C., Wilmington, 1981—. Author: Neuropsychological Assessment of the Spanish Speaker, Handbook of Neuropsychological Assessment, others; founding editor: Neuropsychology Review. Mem. AMA (current procedural terminology panel 1994—, Ctr. Medicare and Medicade Svcs. medicare coverage adv. com. 1999-2003), APA (coun. of reps. 1994-2000, pres. divsn. neuropsychology 2002, Karl Heiser award 1995, Disting. Profl. Practice award 2011), Nat. Acad. Neuropsychology (pres. 1991, disting. svc. award 2000), N.C. Psychol. Assn. (pres. 1990), N.C. Psychol. Found. (founding pres. 1991), Hispanic Neuropsychological Soc. Republican. Roman Catholic. Avocations: surfing, tennis. Home: 1916 Lunar Ln Wilmington NC 28405-4211 Office: U NC Wilmington Dept Psychology Wilmington NC 28403 Office Phone: 910-962-3812. Business E-Mail: puente@uncw.edu.

PUFFER, JAMES C., sports medicine physician, educator, medical association administrator; married. BS, UCLA, MD, 1976. Prof., chief, divsn. family medicine UCLA; prof., family medicine Univ. Ky., Lexington; exec. dir., sec. Am. Bd. Family Medicine, Lexington, Ky., 2003—05, pres., CEO, 2005—. Physician US Winter Olympic Team, Sarajevo, 1984; head team physician US Summer Olympic Team, Seoul, 1988; mem., sports medicine, sports sci. coun. US Olympic Com., 1985—92; com. mem. NCAA Com. on Competitive Safeguards and Med. Aspects of Sports, 1983—90; cons. Pres. Coun. on Physical Fitness and Sports, 1988—90. Assoc. editor Medicine and Science in Sports and Exercise, 1989—98, editor-in-chief Sports Medicine Digest, 1992—, editl. bd. mem., peer reviewer numerous profl. jours. Recipient Duke Paoa Kahanamoku award, USA Water Polo, 2004. Fellow: Am. Coll. Sports Medicine; mem.: US Olympic Sports Medicine Soc. (bd. dir. 1993—96), Am. Med. Soc. for Sports Medicine (pres. 1996—97, founding mem.), Am. Bd. Family Medicine (bd. dir. 1989—94, exec. com. mem.-at-large 1993—94, v.p. bd. dir. 1993—94). Avocation: water polo. Office: American Board of Family Med Ste 550 1648 Mcgrathiana PKWY Lexington KY 40511-1342 Office Phone: 859-269-5626. Business E-Mail: jpuffer@theabfm.org.

PUGH, ARTHUR JAMES (JAY PUGH), retired retail executive; b. Glen Morrison, W.Va., Sept. 24, 1937; s. Arthur James and Mary Pugh; m. Sharon Hubacher, Sept. 26, 1961; children: James Gregory, Mary Elizabeth. BSBA, W.Va. U., 1959; Master of Retailing, U. Pitts., 1960. Mgmt. trainee, buyer Woodward & Lothrop, Washington, 1960-71, v.p., 1971-77, sr. v.p., 1977-80, exec. v.p., 1980-87, Coun. of Better Bus. Bur., Arlington, Va., 1987-90, bd. dir.; cons., bd. dir. Fairfax, Va., 1990—. Trustee, chmn. audit com. Calvert Mut. Funds, Washington, 1983—; bd. dirs. Acacia Capital Corp., Washington; bd. dirs., exec. com. compensation com., chmn. investment com. Acacia Fed. Savs. Bank, Falls Church, Va., 1985-2010. Chmn. bd. dirs. Better Bus. Bur. Met. Washington, 1987. Mem. Rotary Found. of Washington (pres. 1990-91), Nat. Retail Mchts. Assn. (bd. dirs. 1986), W.Va. U. Alumni Assn. (bd. dirs. 1993-98), Fairfax Country Club (bd. dirs. 1990-92), Rotary Club of Washington (Rotarian of Yr. 1982, pres. 1984). Republican. Presbyterian. Avocations: golf, skiing, swimming. Home and Office: 4823 Prestwick Dr Fairfax VA 22030-4533 Personal E-mail: jaypugh@prodigy.net.

PUGH, DOROTHY GUNTHER, performing company executive; b. Memphis, May 8, 1951; Grad. magna cum laude, Vanderbilt U., 1973; studied with Raymond Clay, studied with Donna Carver, studied with David Howard; student, Royal Acad. Dancing, London. Founder and artistic dir. Ballet Memphis, 1985—. Panelist Nat. Endowment for the Arts. Recipient Woman of Achievement award for Initiative, 1987, Gordon Holl Artistic Adminstr. of Yr. award, State of Tenn., 1999, Womens' Found. for Greater Memphis Legends award, 2012; named one of City's Influential Citizens, Memphis Mag.; grantee, National Dance Project; fellow Ctr. Social Innovation, Stanford U. Fellow: Royal Society for the Encouragement of Arts, Manufactures and Commerce. Office: Ballet Memphis 7950 Trinity Cordova TN 38018 Office Phone: 901-737-7322. E-mail: info@balletmemphis.com.

PUGH, GEORGE WILLARD, law educator; b. Napoleonville, La., Aug. 17, 1925; s. William Whitmell and Evelyn (Foley) P.; m. Jean Earle Hemphill, Sept. 6, 1952; children: William Whitmell III, George Willard Jr., David Nicholls, James Hemphill. BA, La. State U., Baton Rouge, 1947, JD, 1950; J.S.D., Yale U., New Haven, Conn., 1952; Dr. h.c., U. Aix-Marseille III, France, 1984. Bar: La. 1950. Instr. La. State U. Law Sch., 1950, mem. faculty, 1952-94, prof. law, 1959-94, Julius B. Nachman prof. law, 1984-94; prof. law emeritus, 1994—. Faculty U. Thessaloniki Greece 1974, Aix-en-Provence, France, 1985, 91; faculty U. San Diego, Paris, 1977; rsch. cons. La. State Law Inst., 1953-54; 1st jud. adminstr. Jud. Coun. Supreme Ct. La., 1954-56; vis. prof. U. Tex., 1961; vis. Doherty prof. law U. Va., 1966-67; faculty orientation program in Am. law Assn. Am. Law Schs., 1968, law teaching clinic, 1969; vis. prof. U. Aix-Marseille III, France, 1983, 1987, U. Catholique de Louvain, Belgium, 1987; cons. La. State U.S. Vietnam Legal Adminstrn. Project, 1969; coord., reporter Code of Evidence for La., 1981-95. Author: Louisiana Evidence Law, 1974, supplement, 1978; co-author: Cases and Materials on the Adminstration of Criminal Justice, 2d edit., 1969, Handbook on Louisiana Evidence Law, 1989, 22nd edit., 2010, 23rd edit., 2011. Bd. dirs. Legal Aid Soc. Baton Rouge, 1965-89, chmn., 1963-64; adv. bd. St. Alban's Episcopal Student Ctr., La. State U., 1965-68, 70-72. Served with AUS, World War II. Named George W. and Jean H. Pugh Inst. for Justice in his honor, La. State U. Law Ctr., 1997; fellow, Comparative Study Adminstrn. Justice, 1962—65. Mem. Am., La., Baton Rouge bar assns., Order of Coif, Omicron Delta Kappa, Lambda Chi Alpha. Democrat. Episcopalian. Home: 167 Sunset Blvd Baton Rouge LA 70808-5073

PUGH, STEPHEN EDMUND, SR., state legislator; b. Hammond, La., Apr. 1, 1961; s. Charles Patrick Sr. and Marion Agnes (Wadsworth) P.; m. Elizabeth Ann Dottolo, Oct. 12, 1985; children: Stephen Edmund II, Christopher Jacob. Attended, Southeastern La. U., 1979; AAMS, Coll. Fin. Planning, 2000. Accredited asset mgmt. specialist, cert. fin. cons. Owner Pugh's Florist, Ponchatoula, 1978—99, AG Edwards and Sons Inc., Hammond, 2000—05, Saint Patrick APS, 1991—; fin. advisor Your Bank, 2005—; mem. Dist. 73 La. House of Reps., 2007—, mem. commerce com., house and govtl. affairs com., mcpl., parochial and cultural affairs com. Pres. Teleflora, Inc., L.A., 1986-95. Chair, Ponchatoula Strawberry Festival, 1981-1984; pres. Tangipahoa Parish Coun. on Age, Ponchatoula, 1980-86; pres., treas. Capitol Area Agy. on Aging, 1986-90. Mem. La. State Florist Assn. (bd. dirs. Baton Rouge chpt. 1983-86). Lodges: Kiwanis (pres. elect 1986-87). Republican. Roman Catholic. Avocations: boating, water sports. Mailing: 114 Northeast Railroad Ave Ponchatoula LA 70454 Office Phone: 985-386-7844. Office Fax: 985-386-5669. E-mail: pughs@legis.state.la.us.

PUGLIESE, LUIGI, management consultant; Degree in Electronic Engring. with honors, Rome U.; MBA, Bocconi U., Milan. Ptnr., v.p. Booz Allen Hamilton Holding Corp. Office: Booz Allen Hamilton Holding Corp 8283 Greensboro Dr Mc Lean VA 22102 Office Phone: 703-902-5000. Office Fax: 703-902-3333. Business E-Mail: pugliese_luigi@bah.com.

PULGRAM, WILLIAM LEOPOLD, architect, space designer; b. Vienna, Jan. 1, 1921; came to U.S., 1940; s. Sigmund and Gisela (Bauer) P.; married, Jan. 12, 1952; children: Deirdre, Laurence, Anthony, Christopher. BS, Ga. Inst. Tech., 1949, BArch, 1950; postgrad., Ecole des Beaux Arts, Fontainebleau, France, 1951. Archtl. designer various firms, Atlanta, 1951-58; assoc., chief interior design FABR&P, Atlanta, 1958-63; exec. v.p., gen. mgr. Associated Space Design Inc., Atlanta, 1963-70, pres., CEO, 1971-85, chmn., CEO, 1985-86, chmn. emeritus, 1986-88; arch., cons. Atlanta, 1988—. Cons. UN, 1986; com. mem. NAS, 1980-84; lectr. at colls., univs., U.S. and abroad. Author: Designing the Automated Office, 1984, Japanese transl., 1985; contbr. articles to jours. in field. Mem., lectr. High Mus. Art, Atlanta, 1970—. With U.S. Army, 1943-46. With US Army, 1943—46. Named to Hall of Fame Interior Design mag., 1986. Fellow AIA (chmn. interiors 1978-84, archtl. res. coun. AIA Found. 1983-85); mem. Archs., Designers and Planners for Social Responsibility (nat. bd. dirs. 1989-93), Am. Soc. Interior Designers, Atlanta C. of C., Atlanta City Club, Lake Lanier Sailing Club. Mem. Unitarian Universalist Ch. Home: 3747 Peachtree Rd NE Apt 1425 Atlanta GA 30319-1332 Office Phone: 404-504-2345. Personal E-mail: pulgramga@comcast.net.

PULLEN, TIMOTHY L., corporate financial executive; BS, Rochester Inst. Tech.; MBA, Seattle U. Positions through v.p., fin. Hillhaven Corp., 1983—95; v.p. Tenet Healthcare Corp., Dallas, 1995—99, controller, 1995—2003, sr. v.p., 1999—2003, exec. v.p., chief acctg. officer, 2003—, interim CFO, 2005. Office: Tenet Healthcare Corp Ste 100 13737 Noel Rd Dallas TX 75240

PULLER, LINDA T., state legislator; b. Cedar Rapids, Iowa, Jan. 19, 1945; m. Lewis Burwell Puller; children: Lewis B. III, Margaret Todd. State del. Dist 44, Va., 1992—99; state senator Dist 36 Va., 1999—; mem. Edn., Transp., Fin., Privileges & Elections Com.; co-chairwoman Interstate Coop. Com.; mem. Dem. State Ctr. Com., Va. Mem.: Mt. Vernon-Lee C. of C. Democrat. Episcopal. Mailing: Dist Off Box 73 Mount Vernon VA 22121-0073 Office Phone: 804-698-7536. E-mail: district36@sov.state.va.us.

PULLIAM, LARRY G., food products executive; b. Grapevine, Tex. m. Cynthia Pulliam; 2 children. With a regional food svc. co., Ft. Worth, 1974—87, Sysco Corp., LA, 1987—91, v.p. ops., 1991—95, exec. v.p., CEO Balt., 1995—97, v.p., chief info. officer Houston, 1997—2000; pres., CEO Sysco Food Services Houston, 2000—02; sr. v.p. mdse. services Sysco Corp., 2002—05, exec. v.p. mdse. services, 2005—07, exec. v.p. sales & global supply chain, 2007—09, exec. v.p. foodservice ops., 2009—. Mem. dirs. coun. Sysco Corp.; bd. dirs. Capital Bank. Bd. dirs. End Hunger Network. Office: Sysco Corp 1390 Enclave Pky Houston TX 77077-2099

PULLIN, SUSAN, information technology executive; BBA magna cum laude, Averett Coll., Va. Cert. industry analyst rels. profl. Liaison, sci. & tech. dept., personal asst. to labor counselor British Embassy, Washington; joined Computer Sciences Corp. (sys. internat. divisn.), 1987; with Computer Sciences Corp. (Consulting Group, Southeast region); various mktg. & comm. positions, fed. & comml. bus. Computer Sciences Corp., dir., corp. comm. & mktg., Tech. Mgmt. Group Account Comm., 2000, v.p., corp. responsibility & industry analyst rels., 2008—. Mem., Bus. & Tech. Adv. Group, Sch. Continuing & Profl. Studies U. Va., Washington; mem., various svc. com. Global Internet Summit, Washington, Greater Wash. Bd. of Trade, Washington; former bd. dirs. Fairfax County C. of C. Office: CSC 3170 Fairview Pk Dr Falls Church VA 22042 Office Phone: 703-876-1000. Business E-Mail: spullin@csc.com.

PULLIN, TANYA, state legislator; b. Sept. 15, 1957; BS, JD, U. Ky.; MA, Duke U. Atty.; mem. Dist. 98 Ky. House of Reps., 2001—; bd. dir. Red Cross, Greenup County, Lewis Counties; found. dir. Our Lady Bellefonte Hosp.; bd. mem. State YMCA Ky. Mem.: Ky. Bar Assn., U. Ky. Law Sch. Alumni, Kiwanis, Boyd County C. of C., Greenup County Dem. Women's Club. Democrat. Office: Capitol Annex Rm 332C 702 Capitol Ave Frankfort KY 40601 Office Phone: 606-932-2505, 502-564-8100 ext. 678. E-mail: tanya.pullin@lrc.state.ky.us.

PURCELL, ANN RUSHING, state legislator, human services manager; b. Reidsville, Ga., May 12, 1945; d. William Robert and Katie (Dasher) Rushing; m. Dent Wiley Purcell, May 26, 1966; children: Edwin Wiley, Mieke Ann, Mikki Marie. BS in Edn., Ga. So. Coll., 1966; degree (hon.), Ga. Future Farmers Am., 1999. Cert. secondary tchr. Tchr. math. Evans H.S., Ga., 1966-68; tchr. math., earth and sci. Beaumont Jr. H.S., Lexington, Ky., 1969-70; substitute tchr. Tallahassee, 1970's; agt. Noblin Realty, Tallahassee, 1970's; office mgr. Radiation Therapy Assocs., PC, Savannah, Ga., 1979—2008, Chatham Radiation Oncology, PC, 2008—; state rep. Ga. House of Reps., Atlanta, 1991—2005, state rep. Dist. 159, 2009—. Author: Purcells of South Georgia and Other Related Families, 1976, Purcell Family History 1777-2006. Bd. dirs. Med. Assn. Ga. Polit. Action Com., Atlanta, 1988-89, Girl Scout Coun. Savannah, 1991-93, Effingham YMCA, 1999-; Effingham County fin. chmn. State YMCA, 1991-05, vice chmn. steering com., 1999, bd. dirs., 1999; trustee Ga. So. U. Found., 1992-2009, Armstrong Atlantic U. Found., 2004-05, 06, 07, 08, sec., 2005, 06, 07, Vice Chmn. Bd., 2007, 08, chmn. bd. 2008-09; mem. adv. com. Effingham County Extension Svc., 1992-2006; chmn. steering com. Effingham YMCA Bd., 2004, 05, 06, 07, chmn. fin. devel., 2005-07; mem. adv. com. Treutlin Home, 1999-04; bd. adv. Claxton Youth Detention Ctr. Hon. comdr. 165th Ga. Air Guard Airlift, 1997-04; hon. mem. Civil Air Patrol, 2001-05, Ga. State Patrol, 2001; hon. mem. Civil Air Patrol, 2010-; state bd. mem. Ga. Dept. Tech. and Adult Edn., Tech. Coll. Sys. Ga., 2005-09; co-chmn. Ga. Edn. Joint Edn. Com., 2006, 07, 08, 09; Effingham Campus of Savannah Tech. Coll., 2007, 2008, 09; mem. adv. bd. Ga. Pacific, 2006-09; bd. dirs. New Ebenezer Retreat Ctr., 2006-09, chmn. bd. trustees Armstrono Atlantic, 2008-09. Decorated WA-PO-HE award Ga. Nat. Air Guard, Minuteman award, Dept. Def. Commendation medal, Charles Dick award Nat. Guard Assn. US; recipient Friend of Medicine award, Med. Assn. Ga., 1991, 1993, 1994, 1996, Ga. Vet. award, 2003, Guardian of Small Bus. award, Nat. Fedn. Ind. Bus., 1992, 1994, 1996, Commendation cert., Ga. Emergency Mgmt. Agy., 1995, Vol. of Yr. award, Effingham 4-H, 1998, Nat. Am. hon. degree, Future Farmers Am., 1999, Friend of State 4-H award, 1999, Svc. award, Effingham Recreation Dept., 2000, Cmty. Svc. award, Guyton Masonic Lodge, 2000, Hon. Family Consumer Cmty. Leaders of Ga. award, 2001, Ga. Pub. Health award, 2003, Effingham Jr. Adv. Family Connection award, 2003, 2004, Environ. Leadership award, Ga. Conservation Voters, 2003, 2004, Pub. Rels. award, Ga. Ext. Assn. of Family and Consumer Scis., 2003, Leadership award, Ga. Water Coalition, 2003, 2004, City of Pembroke award, 2004, Bryan County Svc. award, 2004, Friend of Effingham 4-H award, 2005, Friends award, Ga. Med. Soc., 2005, Vol. Yr., Coastal Ga. YMCA, 2007, Med. Ctr. award, Meml. Health U., 2010, Ga. Nat. Guard award, 2010, award, City Rincon, 2010; named Ga.'s Legislator of Yr., Ga. Sch. Counselors Assn., 1996, Ga. Legislator of Yr., Coastal Conservation Assn. Ga., 1998, Vol. of Yr., Effingham YMCA, 2006; named to Hon. Ga. State Patrol, 2001. Mem. Aux. to the Med. Assn. Ga. (pres. 1985), Aux. to the Ga. Med. Soc. (pres. 1981-82), Ga. Salzburger Soc. (bd. dirs. 2005, 10, v.p. 2005, 06, 07, pres., 2007—09), Effingham County Pub. Ofcls. Assn., Rotary Internat. (Effingham bd. dirs., 2007-08, 2008-09, Paul Harris fellow 2003), Ga. Peace Officers Assn. (hon.), Am. Legion, (Post 322, Ga.), Rincon Noon Lions Club, Exch. Club, Salzburger Vereine V. (Berlin) (hon.). Republican. Methodist. Avocations: painting, genealogy, fishing. Office: Ga Gen Assembly 504 Coverdell Legis Office Bldg Atlanta GA 30334 Office Phone: 404-656-0188.

PURCELL, BILL, academic administrator, former mayor; b. Phila., Oct. 25, 1953; s. William Paxson, Jr. and Mary (Hamilton) Purcell; m. Deborah Lee Miller, Aug. 9, 1986; 1 child, Jesse Miller. AB, Hamilton Coll., 1976; JD, Vanderbilt U., 1979. Bar: Tenn. 1979, U.S. Ct. Appeals (6th cir.) 1985, U.S. Supreme Ct. 1988. Staff atty. W. Tenn. Legal Svcs., Jackson, 1979—81; asst. pub. defender Metro Pub. Defender, Nashville, 1981—84, sr. asst. pub. defender, 1984—85; assoc. Lionel R. Barrett, P.C., Nashville, 1985—86; ptnr. Farmer, Berry & Purcell, Nashville, 1986—90; mem. Tenn. Ho. of Reps., Nashville, 1986—96, majority leader, 1990—96; dir. child and family policy ctr. Inst. Pub. Policy Studies, Vanderbilt U., Nashville, 1996—99; mayor Met. Govt. of Nashville and Davidson County, 1999—2007; dean Coll. Pub. Svc. and Urban Affairs, Tenn. State U., 2008; dir. Harvard Inst. Politics, John F. Kennedy Sch. Govt., Cambridge, 2008—10; spl. advisor Harvard U., Holyoke Ctr., Allston, 2010—. Chmn. select com. on children and youth Tenn. Gen. Assembly, 1989—96; exec. dir. Vanderbilt Legal Aid Soc., 1978—79; chmn. NCSL Assembly State Issues, 1995; chmn. policy makers' program adv. bd. Danforth Found., 1993—2002; mem. adv. bd. U.S. Conf. Mayors, 2001—02, trustee, 2002—07, chmn. task force hunger and homelessness, 2001—05; fellow Inst. Politics Kennedy Sch. Govt., Harvard U., 2007. With Nat. League Cities, 2000—02, chmn. coun. youth, edn. and families, 2003; chmn. human svcs. com. Nat. Conf. State Legislatures, Washington, 1993; mem. exec. com. Dem. Nat. Com., 1994—97; exec. com. 6th Dist. Dems., Nashville, 1986—88; mem. Tenn. State Gen. Assembly, Nashville, 1986—96, majority leader, 1990—96; chmn. Dem. Legis. Campaign Com., 1994—96. Recipient Disting. Alumnus award, Vanderbilt Law Sch., 2004, Pub. Ofcl. of Yr., Governing mag., 2006; named Legislator of Yr., Dist. Atty.'s Gen. Conf., 1989, Tenn. Conservation League, 1991; Toll fellow, Coun. State Govts., 1988. Mem.: ABA, Nashville Bar Assn., Tenn. Bar Assn. Methodist. Office: Harvard University Holyoke Ctr Cambridge MA 02138 Office Fax: 617-495-0463. Business E-Mail: bill_purcell@harvard.edu.

PURCELL, J. NEAL, retired diversified financial services company executive; b. Ball Ground, Ga., 1942; BA in Acctg., Emory U., Atlanta, 1963. CPA. Acct. KPMG, LLP, Atlanta, 1963—72, ptnr., 1972—2002, mng. ptnr. NW and SE regions, 1993—98, vice chmn. audit ops., 1998—2002, ret., 2002. Bd. dirs. Southern Co., Atlanta, 2003—, Synovus Fin. Corp., Columbus, Ga., 2003—, Dollar Gen. Corp., 2004—07, Kaiser Found Health Plan Ga., Inc., Kaiser Found. Health Plan & Hospitals. Past chmn. Ga. C. of C., United Way Campaign Met. Atlanta, Atlanta Assoc. Developmentally Disabled, Atlanta Athletic Club, Ga.Heart Fund Campaign; charter mem. Ga. Gov. Sonny Perdue's Commn.; past chmn. bd. advisors Met. Atlanta Salvation Army; charter mem. Commn. for a New Ga.; mem. Dunwoody United Met. Ch.; trustee Emory U., 1997—. Mem.: AICPA, Ga. Soc. of CPA's, Atlanta Rotary Club (past. pres., bd. dirs.). Mailing: Southern Co 30 Ivan Allen Jr Blvd NW Atlanta GA 30308 also: Kaiser Permanente 1 Kaiser Plz Oakland CA 94612

PURCELL, MARY HAMILTON, speech educator; b. Ft. Worth; d. Joseph Hants and Letha (Gibson) Hamilton; m. William Paxson Purcell, Jr., Dec. 28, 1950; children: William Paxson III, David Hamilton. BA, Mary Hardin-Baylor Coll., 1947, HHD (hon.), 1986; MA, La. State U., 1948; HHD (hon.), U. New Eng., 2000. Instr. dept speech and dramatic arts Temple U., Phila., 1948-53, 60-61; part-time instr. speech Cushing Jr. Coll., Bryn Mawr, Pa., 1966-78. Pres. Pa. Program for Women and Girl Offend, 1968—73, Nether Providence Parent Tchr. Orgn., 1975—76; treas. Virginia Gildersleeve Internat. Fund U. Women, 1975—81, bd. dirs., 1987—93; US del. UN Commn. on Status of Women, 1996; co-chmn. NGO Com. for UNICEF, 1994—2000, mem. global forum, 2001—; bd. dirs. Wallingford-Swarthmore Sch. Dist., 1977—83, Ministers and Missionaries Fund Am. Bapt. Conv., 1985—94, pres., 1995—2003, Internat. Devel. Conf., 1986—; bd. dirs. Nat. Peace Inst. Found., 1983—86; active Big Bros./Big Sisters of Am., 1985—90; bd. dirs. Citizens Crime Commn. of Phila., 1976—, Pa. Women's Campaign Fund, 1985—88, 1993—. Recipient Eleanor Schnurr award, UNA/USA, 2000; named Outstanding Alumna, Mary Hardin-Baylor Coll., 1972, Disting. Dau. Pa., 1982, v.p., 1994—95, pres., 1995—97, Woman of Yr., DECO Women's Conf., 1998. Mem. AAUW (Pa. state pres. 1968-70, v.p. mid. Atlantic region, 1973-77, program v.p. 1979-81, pres. 1981-85, rep. to UN 1985-89), Internat. Fedn. Univ. Women (1st v.p. 1986-89, pres. 1989-92, rep. to UN 1992-2005; pres. UN Dept. Pub. Info. Non Govt. Orgn. ann. conf. 1993), Speech Assn. Am. (Zeta Phi Eta award for excellence in comm. 1983), Pi Kappa Delta, Pi Gamma Mu, Delta Sigma Rho, Alpha Psi Omega, Alpha Chi. Democrat. Baptist. Home: PO Box 60331 Nashville TN 37206-0331 Personal E-mail: mjd1926@aol.com.

PURCELL, SUSAN KAUFMAN, director; b. New York, NY, June 26, 1942; divorced; 1 child, Johanna Marguerite. BA in Spanish with honors, Barnard Coll., 1963; MA in Polit. Sci., Columbia U., 1965, PhD in Polit. Sci., 1970. Dir., Ctr., Hemispheric Policy U. of Miami; prof., polit. sci. UCLA, 1969—81; policy planning staff U.S. Dept. State, Washington, 1980-81; sr. fellow & dir., L. Am. project Coun. on Fgn. Rels., 1981-88; v.p. Americas Soc., 1989—94, Coun. of the Americas, 1994. Bd. dirs. Valero Energy Corp., 1994—. Author: Latin America: U.S. Policy After the Cold War, 1991, Europe and Latin America in the World Economy, 1995, Japan and Latin America in the new Global Order, 1992, Brazil under Cardoso, 1997, Mexico under

Zedillo, 1998, Cuba: The Contours of Change, 2000. Dir. Nat. Endowment for Democracy, Washington, Freedom House, NYC. Fullbright-Hays fellow, 1967-68, Woodrow Wilson Internat. Ctr. for Scholars fellow, 1976-77, Overseas Devel. Coun. visiting fellow, Coun. on Fgn. Rels. fellow, 1979. Mem. Coun. on Fgn. Rels. (Internat. Affairs Fellow, 1980-81, NYC), Fin. Women's Assn., the Economic Club of NY. Office: Valero Energy Corp Bd Directors 1 Valero Way San Antonio TX 78249-1112 Office Phone: 210-345-2000. Office Fax: 210-345-2646. Business E-Mail: susan.purcell@valero.com.

PURCELL, WILLIAM R., state legislator; b. Laurinburg, NC, Feb. 12, 1931; Former state rep. Dist. 17, NC; former pediatrician; state senator, Dist. 17 NC, 1999—2002; state senator, Dist. 25 NC, 2003—. Democrat. Presbyterian. Office: NC Senate 300 N Salisbury St Rm 517 Raleigh NC 27603-5925 Office Phone: 919-733-5953. E-mail: William.Purcell@ncleg.net.

PURCIFULL, DAN ELWOOD, retired plant virologist, educator; b. Woodland, Calif., July 1, 1935; s. Ernest Lee and Virginia (Margaroli) P.; m. Marcia Ann Weatherby, Sept. 7, 1966; children: Scott, Douglas. BS, U. Calif., Davis, 1957, MS, 1959, PhD, 1964. Asst. prof. plant pathology U. Fla., Gainesville, 1964-69, assoc. prof., 1969-75, prof., 1975-99, prof. emeritus, 2000—; ret., 2000. Plant virus subcom. Internat. Com. for Taxonomy of Viruses, 1973-75, mem. potyvirus study group, 1987-93; mem. plant virology adv. com. Am. Type Culture Collection, 1993-99; mem. Internat. Legume Virus Working Group, 1999. Assoc. editor Phytopathology, 1971-73, Plant Disease, 1987-89; contbr. articles to profl. jours. Mem. Morningside Nature Center Commn., City of Gainesville, 1978-81, treas., 1981. With US Army, 1957. Fellow AAAS, Am. Phytopathol Soc. (Lee Hutchins award 1981, Ruth Allen award 1992); mem. Fla. State Hort. Soc., N.Y. Acad. Sci., Am. Soc. Virology, Phytopathol. Soc. Japan, Australasian Plant Pathology Soc., U.S. Golf Assn., Block Calif. Soc. UC Davis, Nat. Wildlife Fedn. (assoc.), Nature Conservancy, Nat. Geographic Soc., Internat. Soc. Plant Pathology, Smithsonian Instn. (assoc.), Nat. Pks. Conservation Assn., Nat. Audubon Soc., Sigma Xi, Gamma Sigma Delta. Avocations: golf, birdwatching. Home: 3106 NW 1st Ave Gainesville FL 32607-2504 Home Phone: 352-376-9926. Personal E-mail: depurc@aol.com.

PURDOM, THOMAS JAMES, lawyer; b. Seymour, Tex., Apr. 7, 1937; s. Thomas Exer and Juanita Florida (Kuykendall) P.; m. Betty Marie Shoemaker, May 31, 1969; 1 son, James Robert. Student, U. Syracuse, 1956—57, U. Md., 1958—59; BA, Tex. Tech. Coll., 1962; JD, Georgetown U., 1966. Bar: Tex. 1966, U.S. Supreme Ct. 1978, U.S. Ct. Appeals (5th cir.) 1983. Ptnr. Griffith & Purdom, Lubbock, Tex., 1966-67; asst. dist. atty. 72d Jud. Dist., Lubbock, 1967-68; county atty. Lubbock County, Tex., 1968-72; pres. Purdom Law Offices, P.C., Lubbock, 1972—2010. Mem. com. for Vol. 5 pattern jury charges, 1988-97. Author: West's Texas Forms Vols. 16, 17, 18, 1984-96, Family Law, Texas Practice and Procedure, 1981. Served with USAF, 1956-60. Recipient Sam Emison award Tex. Acad. Family Law Specialists, 2000. Fellow Tex. Bar Found.; mem Lubbock County Bar Assn. (bd. dirs. 1970, Disting. Sr. Lawyer award 2000, Justice James G. Denton Disting. Lawyer award 2008), State Bar Assn. Tex. (sec. family law sect. 1974-75, chmn. family law sect. 1975-76, mem. examining commn. for family law specialization), Delta Theta Phi. Democrat. Baptist. Home: 3619 55th St Lubbock TX 79413-4713 Business E-Mail: purdom6@aol.com.

PURDY, JESSE E., psychology professor; b. Denver, Colo., Sept. 7, 1952; s. Howard E. and Mary F. Purdy; m. Karen L. Culp, June 10, 1972; children: Kristopher L., Matthew A. BS, Colo. State U., Ft. Collins, 1974, MS, 1976, PhD, 1978. Prof. psychology Southwestern U., Georgetown, Tex., 1978—; Brown disting. rsch. prof., 2000—04; vis. scientist Nat. Marine Sci. Ctr. and Southern Cross U., Coff Harbour, NSW, Australia, 2008. Assoc. nat. resource coun. Nat. Marine Fisheries Svc., Seattle, 1984—85; John H. Duncan chair, 2004—09. Author: (book) Learning and Memory, 2001; contbr. chapters to books, articles to profl. jours.; contr. to documentaries World of Wonder Discovery Channel, 1996, Kings of Camouflage Kaufmann Prodn. Inc., 2006; co-prodr.(with Randall Davis): (documentary) The World of Weddell Seals (1st Pl, 2008). Grantee, NSF, 1981, 2002; fellow, Nat. Resource Coun., 1984. Mem.: Southwestern Psychol. Assn. (pres. 1998—99), Internat. Soc. Behavioral Ecology, Animal Behavior Soc., Psi Chi (pres. 2000—01). Democrat. Office: Southwestern Univ 1001 E Univ and Maple Sts Georgetown TX 78626 Office Fax: 512-863-1846. Business E-Mail: purdy@southwestern.edu.

PURI, RAJENDRA KUMAR, business and tax specialist, consultant; b. Hoshiarpur, Punjab, India, Dec. 22, 1932; came to the U.S., 1965, naturalized, 1969; s. Harbans Lal and Satya Vati (Jerath) P.; children: Neena, Veena, Ram. BS, Agra U., 1952; diploma in Russian lang. and lit., U. Dehli, 1958; BA, U. Wash., 1968, MBA, 1969; MS in Taxation, Golden Gate U., 1982. CPA Tex. Customs officer Govt. of India, New Delhi, 1955-60; asst. treas. Merc. Bank Ltd., New Delhi, 1960-65; mem. staff Peat, Marwick, Mitchell & Co., CPAs, Seattle, 1969-70; state examiner State of Wash., Seattle, 1970-72, asst. supervising state examiner, 1972-74, supervising state examiner, 1974-77; sr. internal auditor Lockheed Corp., Sunnyvale, Calif., 1977-79; sci. programming analyst Lockheed Missile and Space Co., Sunnyvale, 1979-80, data processing specialist, 1980-84, sci. programming specialist, 1984-88; chief acct. Tex. Dept. Health, Austin, 1989-90; dir. internal audit, internal auditor Tex. Workers' Compensation Commn., Austin, 1990-95; bus. and tax cons., 1996—2003. Del. Wash. State Rep. Conv., 1976, Snohomish County Rep. Conv., 1976; Rep. nominee for state auditor, Wash., 1976; spl. advisor U.S. Congl. Adv. Bd., 1982-83. Home: 2608 Hunlac Cove Round Rock TX 78681-7107 E-mail: rkpi_2000@yahoo.com.

PURKEY, HARRY ROBERT, state legislator; b. Parsons, W.Va., June 13, 1934; m. Sonja Helene Firing; children: Harry R. Jr., Charlotte H., Gregory. Former commr. Va. Beach Rep. Com.; former dir. Indsl. Devel. Authority; house del. Va.; state del. Dist. 82 Va., 1986—; mem. Fin., Health & Welfare Insts., Corp. Ins. & Banking Com., Sci. & Tech. Com., Va. Beach Rep. Com.; v.p. & resident mgr. Merrill Lynch, Pierce, Fenner & Smith Inc.; dir. Old Dominion U. Edn. Found., Old Dominion U. Intercollegiate Found., Sanctuary Of Tidewater. Mem.: Tidewater Automobile Assn. (dir.), C. of C., Va. Pub. Beach Commn., Va. Beach & Norfolk Sports Club. Republican. Methodist. Mailing: 2352 Leeward Shore Dr Virginia Beach VA 23451 Office Phone: 757-481-1493. Business E-Mail: Del_Purkey@house.state.va.us.

PURNELL, MAURICE EUGENE, JR., lawyer; b. Dallas, Feb. 17, 1940; s. Maurice Eugene Sr. and Marjorie (Maillot) P.; m. Diane Blake, Aug. 19, 1966; children: Maurice Eugene III, Blake Maillot. BA, Washington and Lee U., 1961; MBA, U. Pa., 1963; LLB, So. Meth. U., 1966. Bar: Tex. 1966. Ptnr. Locke, Purnell, Boren, Laney & Neely, Dallas, 1966-87; shareholder Locke Purnell Rain Harrell PC, Dallas, 1987-99; ptnr. Locke Lord Bissell & Liddell LLP, Dallas, 1999—2002, of counsel, 2002—. Bd. dirs. Leggett & Platt, Inc. Bd. dirs. Dallas Summer Musicals. Mem. ABA, Tex. Bar Assn., Tex. Bar Found., Dallas Bar Assn. Am. Judicature Soc., Dallas C. of C, Brook Hollow Golf Club. Home: 4409 S Versailles Ave Dallas TX 75205-3044 Office: Locke Lord Bissell & Liddell LLP 2200 Ross Ave Ste 2200 Dallas TX 75201-6776 Office Phone: 214-740-8444.

PURRINGTON, ROBERT DANIEL, physics educator; b. Alamosa, Colo., Apr. 11, 1936; s. Robert George and Edith Brooke (Meanley) P.; m. Ethel Loraine Smith, Sept. 12, 1959; children: Jaqueline Brooke, Stpehen Daniel, Jennifer Ann, Christopher Wilson. BS in Physics, Tex. A&M U., 1958, MS, 1963, PhD, 1966. Asst. Tex. A&M Research Found., College Station, 1964-66; asst. prof. Tulane U., New Orleans, 1966-70, assoc. prof., 1970-75, prof. physics, 1975—2011, emeritus prof., 2011, chmn. dept. physics, 1979-85; dir. Tulane U. (Cunningham Obs.), 1972—2011. Editor Jour. of La. Ornithology, 1988—; author (books): (with F.E. Durham) Frame of the Universe, 1983, La Trama del Universo, 1989, (with F.E. Durham) Some Truer Method, 1990, Physics in the Nineteenth Century, 1997, The First Professional Scientist: Robert Hooke and the Royal Society of London, 2009; contbr. articles on quantum physics, ocean acoustics, history of physics, and archaeoastronomy to profl. jours. Served to 2d lt. U.S. Army, 1958-59. Woodrow Wilson fellow, 1958; NSF summer fellow, 1961; NASA, NSF, NRL, NAVO Mem. Am. Phys. Soc., Soc. History Physics, AAAS, Am. Astron. Soc., Nat. Audubon Soc., Sierra Club, Nature Conservancy, Sigma Xi, Phi Eta Sigma, Phi Kappa Phi. Democrat. Episcopalian. Home: 4700 Bissonet Dr Metairie LA 70003-1242 Business E-Mail: danny@tulane.edu.

PURSLEY, MICHAEL BADER, engineering educator, communications systems researcher, consultant; b. Winchester, Ind., Aug. 10, 1945; s. Bader E. and Evelyn L. (Bennett) P.; m. Lou Ann Hinchman, July 6, 1968; 1 child, Jessica Ann. BS, Purdue U., 1967, MS, 1968; PhD, U. So. Calif., 1974. Mem. tech. staff Hughes Aircraft Co., Los Angeles, 1967; engr. Northrop Co., Hawthorne, Calif., 1968; staff engr. Hughes Aircraft Co., Los Angeles, 1968-74; acting asst. prof. UCLA, 1974; asst. prof., then assoc. prof. elec. engring. U. Ill., Urbana, 1974-80, prof., 1980-93; Holcombe prof. elec. and computer engring. Clemson (S.C.) U., 1992—; assoc. Ctr. Advanced Study, 1980-81; vis. prof. UCLA, 1985; cons. U.S. Army, Huntsville, Ala., 1977, Ft. Monmouth, NJ, 1983-86, 91, ITT, Ft. Wayne, Ind., 1979—; pres. SIGCOM, Inc., 1986-90; prin. scientist Techno-Scis. Inc., 1990—96. Author: Random Processes in Linear Systems, 2002, Introduction to Digital Communications, 2005; contbr. chapters to books. Recipient Fred W. Ellersick award Comms. Soc., 1996, Tech. Achievement award Mil. Comm. Conf., 1999, Edwin Howard Armstrong Achievement award, 2002, Alumni award, U. So. Calif. Sch. Engrs., 2005, Purdue U. Outstanding Electrical Engr., 2008. Fellow IEEE (pres. info. theory group 1983, Centennial medal 1984, Millennium medal 2000); mem. Inst. Math. Stats. Office: Clemson U 303 Fluor Daniel Bldg Dept ECE Clemson SC 29634

PURYEAR, W.(ILLIAM) BRADFORD, lawyer; BA, Marshall Univ., 1985; JD, Univ. Ga., 1989. Bar: Ga. 1989, US Dist. Ct. No. Dist. Ga. 1989. Gen. counsel Mansfield Oil Co., Gainesville, Ga., 2006—. Pres. Gainesville Jaycees, 1998—99. Named to Marshall Univ. Athletic Hall of Fame, 2010. Avocation: soccer. Office: Mansfield Oil Co 1025 Airport Pkwy Gainesville GA 30501

PUTNAM, JOSHUA A., state legislator; b. Nov. 10, 1988; s. William and Laura. BS, North Greenville U., 2011. Landscape supervisor Printer's Touch; mem. Dist. 10 SC House of Representatives, 2011—. Mem.: North Greenville U. Student Alumni Assn. (past pres.). Republican. Address: PO Box 51542 Piedmont SC 29673 Office: 532D Blatt Office Bldg Columbia SC 29201 Home: 114 Hapsewee Dr Piedmont SC 29673 Home Phone: 864-238-9431; Office Phone: 803-212-6931, 864-238-9431.

PUTNEY, LACEY EDWARD, state legislator; b. Big Island, Va., June 27, 1928; m. Elizabeth Harlow; children: Susan K., L. Edward Jr. Atty. Putney & Putney, Bedford, Va., 1959; mem. Dist 19 Va. House of Delegates, 1962. Bd. dirs. Co. Mutual Fire Ins. Co., First Nat. Exch. Bank. Former dist. dir. Boy Scouts America. Mem.: Va. & American Trial Lawyers Assn., Bedford Co. Farm Bur., Bedford Area C. of C. (former dir.), Jaycees, Moose, Scottish Rite. Independent. Baptist. Office: PO Box 127 Bedford VA 24523 Office Phone: 540-586-0080. Office Fax: 540-586-1784. E-mail: DelLPutney@house.virginia.gov.

PYATT, EVERETT ARNO, federal official; b. Kansas City, Mo., July 22, 1939; s. Arno Doyne and Myrl Elizabeth (Osborn) P.; m. Susan Evelyn Kristal, Sept. 28, 1968; children: Jennifer, Laura, Jeffrey. B.E., BS, Yale U., 1962; MBA, U. Pa., 1977. Staff engr. office dir. def. research and devel. Office Sec. Def., Dept. Def., Washington, 1962-72; dir. acquisition planning Office Asst. Sec. Def. for Program Analysis and Evaluation, 1972-75; dir. logistics resources Office Asst. Sec. Def. for Installations and Logistics, 1975-77; prin. dep. asst. sec. for logistics Dept. Navy, Washington, 1977-79, prin. dep. asst. sec. for shipbldg. and logistics, 1981-84, asst. sec. for shipbldg. and logistics, 1984-89; exec. advisor Coopers & Lybrand, 1989—; pres. EV Ventures; dep. chief fin. officer Dept. Energy, 1979-81; dir. Dept. Energy (Office of Alcohol Fuels), 1980. Recipient Disting. Civilian Svc. medal USN, 1980-81, 87, Superior Civilian Svc. medal, 1981, Outstanding Svc. medal Dept. Energy, 1981, Pres.'s award of meritorious excellence, 1983, Disting. Civilian Pub. Svc. award Dept. Def., 1989; Office of Sec. Def. fellow, 1975-77. Mem.: IEEE, Yale Club. Home: 4560 25th Rd N Arlington VA 22207-4147 Home Phone: 703-528-5828; Office Phone: 703-841-8318. Personal E-mail: epyatt1@comcast.net.

PYCH, RICK, professional sports team executive; b. Hartford, Conn. m. Marilou Pych; 1 child, Zach. Grad. in Acctg., Fairfield U. CPA. CFO Spurs Sports & Entertainment (parent co. of NBA Spurs, Am. Hockey League Rampage and WNBA Silver Stars), San Antonio, 1993—2000, chief devel. officer AT&T Ctr., 1999—, exec. v.p. fin. and corp. devel., 2000—08, pres. bus. ops., 2008—. San Antonio Rampage repr. Am. Hockey League Bd. Govs. Bd. trustees Via Met. Transit; bd. dirs. San Antonio Sports Found., 1989—, Boys and Girls Clubs San Antonio; bd. mem. San Antonio Tax Increment Reinvestment Zone. Office: Spurs Sports and Entertainment One AT&T Ctr San Antonio TX 78219

PYKE, THOMAS NICHOLAS, JR., science administrator; b. Washington, July 16, 1942; s. Thomas Nicholas and Pauline Marie (Pingitore) Pyke; m. Carol June Renville, June 22, 1968 (dec. Oct. 2002); children: Christopher Renville, Alexander Nicholas. BS, Carnegie Inst. Tech., 1964; MS in Engring., U. Pa., 1965. Electronic engr. Nat. Bur. Standards, Gaithersburg, Md., 1964-69, chief computer networking sect., 1969-75, chief computer systems engring. div., 1975-79, dir. ctr. for computer systems engring., 1979-81, dir. ctr. programming sci. and tech., 1981-86; asst. adminstr. for satellite and info. services NOAA, Washington, 1986-92, dir. high performance computing and com., 1992-00, dir. The Globe Program, 1994—2002, chief info. officer, dir. high performance computing and comm., 2000—01; chief info. officer US Dept. Commerce, 2001—05, US Dept. Energy, 2005—10; exec. adv. Booz Allen Hamilton Inc., 2010—12, cons., 2012—14; pres. The Pyke Group, 2014—. Organizer profl. computer confs., 1970-86; mem. Presdl. Adv. Com. on Networking Structure and Function, 1980, Interagy. com. on Info. Resources Mgmt., 1983-84, bd. dirs., 1984-87, vice chmn. 1986-87 (Exec. Excellence award 1991), chmn. Interagy. Working Group on Data Mgmt. for Global Change, 1987-93; speaker in field. Mem. editl. bd. Computer Networks Jour., 1976-86; contbr. articles to profl. jours. Mem. Task Force on Computers in Schs., Arlington, 1982—85; co-pres. Jamestown Elem. Sch. PTA, Arlington, 1984—85; bd. dirs. Glebe Commons Assn., Arlington, Va., 1976—79, v.p., 1977—79. Recipient silver medal Dept. Commerce, 1973, gold medal, 1995; award for exemplary achievement in pub. adminstrn. William A. Jump Found., 1975, 76, Presdl. Rank award of Meritorious Exec., 1988, 99, Dept. Energy Exceptional Svc. award, 2010; Westinghouse scholar Carnegie Inst. Tech., 1960-64; Ford Found. fellow U. Pa., 1964-66. Fellow Washington Acad. Scis. (Engring. Sci. award 1974); mem. IEEE (sr. mem.), Computer Soc. of IEEE (Golden Core mem., bd. govs. 1971-73, 75-77, vice chmn. tech. com. on personal computing 1982-86, chmn. 1986-87), AAAS, Assn. Computing Machinery, Sigma Xi, Eta Kappa Nu, Omicron Delta Kappa, Pi Kappa Alpha (chpt. v.p. 1963-64) Episcopalian. Office: 8283 Greensboro Dr Mc Lean VA 22102 Personal E-mail: tnpyke@gmail.com.

PYLANT, STEVEN E., state legislator; b. Nov. 25, 1954; m. Rhonda Nelson. Attended, NE La. U. Sheriff Franklin Parish, La.; mem. Dist. 20 La. House of Reps., Baton Rogue, 2012—. Republican. Office: 805 Jackson St Ste A Winnsboro LA 71295 also: La House of Reps 900 N 3rd St Baton Rouge LA 70804 Office Phone: 318-435-7313. Business E-Mail: pylants@legis.la.gov.

PYLE, GERALD FREDRIC, geographer, educator; b. Akron, Ohio, Dec. 22, 1937; s. Russell Roy and Ruth (Martin) P.; m. Carole Wood, Aug. 29, 1959; children: Eric, Frances. BA, Kent State U., 1963; MA, U. Chgo., 1968, PhD, 1970. Cartographer Rand McNally, Chgo., 1962-64; rsch. geographer Ency. Brit., Chgo., 1964-65; cartographer U. Chgo., 1965-70; from asst. prof. to prof. U. Akron, 1970-80; prof. geography and earth sci. U. N.C., Charlotte, 1980-98, prof. health promotion, 1995—2002, prof. health behavior and adminstrn., 2002—04, emeritus prof. pub. health scis., 2004—. Vis. fellow Macquarie U., Sydney, 1988; rsch. dir. Ctr. for Urban Studies, Akron, Ohio, 1973—80; tech. dir. Akron Area Census File, 1974—80; vis. scholar U. SC, 1977; interim dir. health adminstrn. program U. NC, Charlotte, 2001—02; interim dir. Health Adminstrn. Program, 2008, Undergrad. Programs, 2009. Author: Heart Disease, Cancer and Stroke in Chicago, 1971, Spatial Dynamics of Crime, 1974, Applied Medical Geography, 1979, Diffusion of Influenza: Patterns and Paradigms, 1986, (with Shannon and Bashshur) The Geography of AIDS, 1990, (with shannon) Medical Atlas of the Twentieth Century, 1993; sr. editor Med. Geography, Social Sci. and Medicine, 1977-84; book rev. editor Social Sci. and Medicine, 1990-2005. Recipient Scholars medal First Citizens Bank, 1992; grantee Ill. Regional Med., 1969, Law Enforcement Adminstrn. Agy., 1972, 74, NSF, 1979, 82, Nat. Geog. Soc., 1988, NRC, 1995, Smart Start 1999-2001. Fellow Ohio Acad. Sci.; mem. APHA, Am. Coll. Epidemiology, Assn. Am. Geographers (Rsch. Honors S.E. divsn. 1994), Phi Kappa Phi, Delta Omega. Democrat. Anglican. Achievements include research in spatial diffusion of infectious diseases and health services research. Office: U NC Dept Pub Health Scis 9201 University City Blvd Charlotte NC 28223-0002 Home: 2604 Polo Club Blvd Matthews NC 28105 Home Phone: 704-846-3227; Office Phone: 704-578-7458. Personal E-mail: gfpyle@msn.com.

PYLE, GREGORY E., Chief of the Choctaw Nation of Oklahoma; b. Ft. Bragg, Calif., Apr. 25, 1949; s. Alvin Pyle and Juanita Wilmouth; m. Pat Baker, Sept. 1971; children: Andrea, Eric. Student, Murray State Coll.; BS in bus., Southeastern Okla. State U., 1972. Pers. dir. Choctaw Nation of Okla., 1982—83, asst. chief., 1983—97, chief, 1997—. Bd. mem. Nat. Indian Health Bd., Okla. Area Indian Health Bd. Named Region VI Minority Small Bus. Advocate of Yr., Small Bus. Adminstrn.; named to Okla. Hall of Fame, 2007. Mem.: Okla. State Troopers Assn. (hon.). Office: Choctaw Nation of Okla PO Drawer 1210 Durant OK 74701-1210 Office Phone: 580-924-8280.

PYLE, HOWARD, lawyer, consultant; b. Richmond, Va., Feb. 1, 1940; s. Wilfrid and Anne Woolston (Roller) P.; m. Victoria M. Sheffield; children: Elizabeth Roller Ross, Howard. AB, Princeton U., 1962; JD, U. Va., 1967. Bar: Va. 1967, D.C. 1969. Career trainee CIA, Washington, 1967-69; adminstrv. asst. to Congressman Odin Langen, US House of Representatives, Washington, 1969-70, to Congressman Hastings Keith, 1971; asst. to sec. Dept. Interior, Washington, 1971-73; Washington rep. Std. Oil Co. Ind., 1973-77; mgr. fed. pub. affairs R.J. Reynolds Industries, Inc., Winston-Salem, NC, 1977-80; dir. fed. rels. Houston Industries, Washington, 1980-99; pres. HPYLE Cons., Alexandria, Va., 1999—. Bd. mem. Torpedo Factory Condo Assn. Mem.: SAR, NRA, Torpedo Factory Condo Assn. Bd., ARRL, Assn. US Navy, Gadsbys Tavern Mus. Soc., Va. Bar, DC Bar, Order of St. John, Alexandria Assn., Res. Officers Assn., Washington Assembly, Delta Theta Phi. Republican. Episcopalian. Home: 125 N Lee St Alexandria VA 22314-3260 Office: HPYLE Cons PO Box 320817 Alexandria VA 22320-4817 Personal E-mail: hp4gk@hpyle.net.

PYLES, RODNEY ALLEN, archivist, retired county official; b. Morgantown, W.Va., June 21, 1945; s. Melford John and Luci L. (Scarcella) P.; m. Carol Louise Wrobleski, May 20, 1972; 1 child, Janessa Louise. BA, MA (Benedum scholar 1966-67, grad. research asst. 1967-68, grad. teaching fellow 1968-69), W.Va. U., 1967-69. Instr. polit. sci. Alderson-Broaddus Coll., Philippi, W.Va., 1969-71; asst. curator W.Va. U. Library, 1971-77; dir. archives and history div. W.Va. Dept. Culture and History, 1977-85; dep. chief Assessor's Office Monongalia County, 1985-88; assessor Monongalia County, 1989—2012. Mng. editor: W.Va. History quar, 1977-85 Mem. Morgantown (W.Va.) Dem. exec. com., 1966-69, Monongalia County (W.Va.) Dem. exec. com., 1972-76, state dem. exec. com., 2010-; mem. Morgantown Libr. Bd., 1988-91, Morgantown Hist. Landmarks Commn., 1986—; trustee W.Va. Pub. Theatre, 1999—, treas., 2004. Mem. Soc. Am. Archivists, W.Va. Hist. Soc. (exec. sec. 1977-90, bd. dirs. 1990—), Am. Assn. State and Local History (state awards chmn. 1980-85, state membership com. 1981-87), Monongalia Hist. Soc. (pres. 1986-88, bd. dirs. 1988—), W.Va. Polit. Sci. Assn. (treas. 1991—), W.Va. Assessors' Assn. (pres. 1992-93, bd. dirs. 2005—12), KC (pres. bowling league 1995-96, 4th deg., faithful capt. 1996—2007, faithful navigator, 2007-11, chancellor 1998-2000, dep. Grand Knight 2000-02, Grand Knight, 2002-2007), Sons of Italy (treas. 1995—2014, grand Lodge trustee 2009-13), Grand Lodge (v.p., 2013-). Roman Catholic. Home: 536 Harvard Ave Morgantown WV 26505-2157 Office: County Court House Rm 215 Morgantown WV 26505 Business E-Mail: rod.pylz@gmail.com.

QUADAGNO, JILL, sociology professor; BA, Pa. State U., 1964; MA in Sociology, U. Calif., Berkeley, 1966; PhD in Sociology, U. Kans., 1976. Fellow Nat. Insti. Mental Health, 1965—66; asst. prof. dept. sociology U. Kans., 1977—81, assoc. prof., 1981—85, prof., 1985—87; Mildred & Claude Pepper Eminent scholar in social serontology, prof. sociology Fla. State U., 1987—. NSF vis. prof. Harvard U., 1988; sr. policy advisor President's Bi-Partisan Commn. Entitlement & Tax Reform, 1994. Author: Color of Welfare: How Raism Undermined the War on Poverty, 1994, One Nation, Uninsured: Why the US Has No National Health Insurance, 2005; assoc. editor Jour. Health &Social Behavior, 2007—, mem. editl. bd. American

Sociol. Rev., 2005—07, consulting editor Jour. Gerontology, 2005—; contbr. articles to profl. jours. Named to Kans. Women's Hall of Fame, 1984; fellow, John Simon Guggenheim Meml. Found., 1994—95. Fellow: Gerontological Soc. America (pres. 1997—98); mem.: Inst. Medicine, Nat. Acad. Social Ins. (bd. dirs. 2007—), Sociol. Rsch. Assn., American Sociol. Assn. (Disting. Scholar award 1994). Office: Pepper Institute on Aging and Public Policy Florida State univ Tallahassee FL 32306 Office Phone: 850-644-8827. Office Fax: 850-644-2304. E-mail: jquadagno@fsu.edu.

QUALLS, ROBERT L., electric power industry executive; b. Burnsville, Miss., Nov. 6, 1933; s. Wes E. and Letha (Parker) Q.; m. Carolyn Morgan, Feb. 10, 1979 (dec. July 1996); 1 child, Stephanie Elizabeth; m. Nancy Martin, Sept. 11, 1999. BS in Economics, Miss. State U., 1954, MS in Economics, 1958; PhD, La. State U., 1962; LLD, Whitworth Coll., 1974; DBA with honors, U. of the Ozarks, 1984. Prof., chmn., divsn. econs. and bus. Belhaven Coll., Jackson, Miss., 1962—66, asst. to pres., 1965—66; asst. prof., fin. Miss. State U., 1967—69, adj. prof., 1969—73; sr. v.p., chmn., venture com. Bancorp South, Tupelo, Miss., 1969—73; v.p. Wesleyan Coll., Macon, Ga., 1974; pres. U. of the Ozarks, Clarksville, Ark., 1974—79; mem., cabinet Bill Clinton Gov. of Ark., 1979—80; pres., bd. dirs. First Bank Fin. Services, Inc., 1980—85, Advt. Assocs., Inc., 1980—85; exec. v.p. Bank of America Corp., Little Rock, 1980—85, chmn., CEO Harrison, Ark., 1985—86; pres., chief oper. officer Baldor Electric Co., Fort Smith, Ark., 1986—91, CEO, 1992—98, pres., 1993—98, vice chmn., 1998—2000. Bd. dirs. Baldor Electric Co., 1987—, Bank of the Ozarks, Inc., Little Rock, 1997—. Author: Entrepreneurial Wit and Wisdom, 1986; co-author: Strategic Planning for Colleges and Universities: A Systems Approach to Planning and Resource Allocation, 1979; mem. editorial adv. bd.: Bank Mktg. Mag., 1984-86. Chmn. cmty. svc. and continuing edn. com. Tupelo Cmty. Devel. Found., 1972-73; mem. Miss. 4-H adv. coun., 1969; active Boys Scouts Am.; mem. Lee County Dem. Exec. Com., 1973-74; trustee Walton Family Found., 1975-79, Oklahoma City U., 1990-95; trustee, mem. exec. com. U. Ozarks, 1982-88, chmn. bd., 2000-03; mem. Pres.'s Roundtable U. Ctrl. Ark., 1982-87; mem. exec. com. Coll. Bus. Adv. Bd., U. Ark., Little Rock, 1980-85; bd. dirs. U. Ark. Med. Sch. Found., 1991-97, Ark. Inst., 1991-94; chmn. bd. Petit Jean Youth Found., 2001-03; mem. Clarksville Light and Water Commn., 2000-01; elder Clarksville Presbyn. Ch., 1997-2000; bd. dirs. Vera Lloyd Presbyn. Home and Family Svcs., 2004-05, Thea Found., 2008-, Ark. Coun. Internat. Visitors, 2010, Lt. AUS, 1954-56. Found. for Econ. Edn. fellow, 1964; Ford Found. faculty research fellow Vanderbilt U., 1963-64; recipient Pillar of Progress award Johnson County, 1977 Mem. Am. Bankers Assn. (mktg. planning and rsch. com. 1972-73), Ark. Coun. Ind. Colls. and Univs. (chmn. 1978-79), Johnson County C. of C. (pres. 1977), Fort Smith C. of C. (dir. 1995-98), Blue Key, Omicron Delta Kappa, Delta Sigma Pi, Sigma Phi Epsilon (citation 1977), Beta Gamma Sigma, Masons (32 deg.), Clarksville Rotary (pres. 1979). Presbyterian. Office: Baldor Electric Co 5711 R S Boreham Jr St Fort Smith AR 72901 Office Phone: 479-646-4711. Office Fax: 479-648-5792. Business E-Mail: qualls@baldor.com.

QUARLES, BRANDON, law librarian; m. Debbie Quarles; children: Ashtyn, Corban. BA, Southwestern U., 1990; JD, U. Miss., 1993; MLS, U. North Tex., 1995. Atty. Passman & Jones, Dallas, 1993—94; reference/rsch. svc. libr. U. Richmond Sch. Law, Va., 1996—98; reference libr. Baylor U. Law Sch., Waco, Tex., 1998—2000, dir. Law Libr., 2000—. Contbr. articles to profl. jours. Avocations: running, skiing, bicycling. Office: Baylor Law Library 1114 S University Parks Dr One Bear Place, Box 97128 Waco TX 76798-7128 Office Phone: 254-710-4916. Office Fax: 254-710-2294. E-mail: brandon_quarles@baylor.edu.

QUARLES, CARROLL ADAIR, JR., physicist, researcher; b. Abilene, Tex., Nov. 24, 1938; s. Carroll Adair and Marguerite Marie (Vollmers) Q.; m. Sonja Gale Bandy, May 14, 1971; children: Jennifer Anne, John Patrick. BA, Tex. Christian U., 1960; PhD, Princeton U., 1964. Rsch. physicist Brookhaven Nat. Lab., Upton, NY, 1964-67; mem. faculty Tex. Christian U., Ft.Worth, 1967—, assoc. prof. physics, 1970-76, prof., 1976—2010, emeritus prof., 2010—, W.A. Moncrief Jr. prof. physics, 1986—2010, chmn. dept. physics, 1978-84, 96-99, assoc. dean Coll. Arts and Scis., 1974-78, Cecil & Ida Green Disting. emeritus tutor, 2010—. Contbr. articles to profl. jours. Mem. Am. Phys. Soc. (sec.-treas. Tex. sect. 1993-99, chair Tex. sect. 2003, mem. exec. com. Forum on Physics and Soc., 1999-2002), Am. Assn. Physics Tchrs. (pres. Tex. sect. 1984), Sigma Xi, Phi Beta Kappa (pres. Delta of Tex. chpt. 1982-84). Office: Tex Christian U Dept Physics Fort Worth TX 76129-0001 Office Phone: 817-257-7375. Business E-Mail: c.quarles@tcu.edu.

QUARLES, RYAN, state legislator; b. Oct. 20, 1983; s. Roger and Bonnie Quarles. BS in Agrl. Economics, U. Ky., BS in Pub. Svc. & Leadership, MA in Diplomacy & Internat. Commerce, MS in Agrl. Economics, JD; EdM in Higher Edn., Harvard U. Farmer; atty.; mem. Dist. 62 Ky. House of Reps., 2011—. Republican. Avocations: fishing, travel. Office: Ky House of Reps Annex Rm 424C 702 Capitol Ave Frankfort KY 40601 Office Phone: 502-564-8100 ext. 671. Business E-Mail: ryan.quarles@lrc.ky.gov.

QUARTIN, ANDREW A., critical care specialist, educator; MD, Miami U., 1991. Cert. internal medicine 1989, critical care medicine 2001. Resident in internal medicine Univ. Miami- Jackson Meml. Med. Ctr., Miami, 1986—89, fellow in critical care medicine, 1989—91; assoc. prof. Univ. Miami; assoc. chief of critical care medicine Veterans Affairs Med. Ctr.; hosp. affiliation include Univ. Miami Jackson Meml. Hosp. Office: University of Miami Jackson Memorial Hospital 1611 NW 12th Ave Miami FL 33136-1094 Office Phone: 305-585-1111.

QUBEIN, NIDO R., management consultant; MS in Bus. Edn., UNC, Greensboro, 1973; LLD (hon.). Founder Am. Bank and Trust; chmn. Great Harvest Bread Co., 2001—; pres. High Point University, High Point, NC, 2005—. Bd. dirs. BB&T Corp., 1990—, La-Z-Boy Inc., 2006—. Founder Nat. Spkrs. Found. Named Golden Gavel Medal, Toastmasters Internat., Horatio Alger Award for Disting. Americans, Ellis Island Medal of Honor, Order of the Long Leaf Pine, Amb. of Free Enterprise, Citizen of the Yr., Philanthropist of the Yr., NC Power Player, Bus. Leader Mag., 2009. Mem.: Internat. Hall of Fame. Office: High Point U 833 Montlieu Ave High Point NC 27262-3598 Personal E-mail: nqubein@highpoint.edu.

QUELLER, DAVID C., ecology and biology professor; BA in history and philosophy of sci., U. Ill., 1976; MS and PhD in biol. sciences, U. Mich., 1976—79; studied tropical ecology, U. Costa Rica, 1979. NATO postdoctoral fellow U. Sussex, 1983—84; Huxley rsch. instr. Rice U., 1984—87, rsch. assoc., 1987—88, sr. rsch. assoc., 1988—89, asst. prof., 1989—94, assoc. prof., 1994—96, prof., 1996—2005, Harry Carothers and Olga Keith Wiess prof. natural sciences, 2005—. John Simon Guggenheim fellow, 1988—89. Fellow: Am. Acad. Arts and Sciences; mem.: AAAS, Scientia, Am. Soc. Naturalists (Young Investigator award 1985), Behavioral Ecology Soc., Internat. Union Study of Social Insects, Soc. Study of Evolution (Councilor 2003—05), Sigma Xi, Phi Beta Kappa. Office: Rice U Dept Ecology & Evolutionary Biology PO Box 1892 Houston TX 77251-1892 Office Phone: 713-285-5220. Office Fax: 713-285-5232. E-mail: queller@rice.edu.

QUENCER, ROBERT M., neuroradiologist, researcher; b. Jersey City, Nov. 14, 1937; s. Arthur Bauer and Isabell (Moore) Quencer; m. Christine F. Thomas, Sept. 16, 1972; children: Kevin, Keith. BS, Cornell U., 1959, MS, 1963; MD, SUNY, Syracuse, 1967. Diplomate Am. Bd. Radiology, Nat. Bd. Med. Examiners; cert. of added qualifications in neuroradiology. Intern Jackson Meml. Hosp., Miami, Fla., 1967-68; resident in radiology Columbia U., NYC, 1968-71, fellow in neuroradiology, 1971-72; asst. prof. Downstate Med. Ctr., Bklyn., 1972-76; assoc. prof. U. Miami, 1976-79, prof., 1979-92, chmn., prof., 1992—, chief sect. neuroradiology, 1976-86, dir. divsn. magnetic resonance imaging, 1986-92, Robert Shapiro MD prof. radiology, chmn. dept. radiology. Vis. prof. U. Tenn. Coll. Medicine, Memphis, 1982, Downstate Med. Ctr. Coll. Medicine, Bklyn., 1992, U. Vt. Coll. Medicine, Burlington, 1983, NY Med. Coll., Valhalla, 1984, U. Va. Sch. Medicine, Charlottesville, 1984, U. Ky. Sch. Medicine, Lexington, 1985, Yale U. Sch. Medicine, New Haven, 1986, 2000, Columbia U. Sch. Medicine, NYC, 1986, The Mayo Clinic & Found., Rochester, Minn., 1987, Med. Coll. Va., Richmond, 1988, U. Pa. Sch. Medicine, Phila., 1988, Harvard U. Sch. Medicine/Mass. Gen. Hosp., Boston, 1989, U. Conn., Farmington, 1990, Kumamoto, Japan, 1993, U. Man., Can., 1992, Mich. State U., 1996, Mt. Sinai Med. Ctr., 1997, Cornell U. Sch. Medicine, 1998, U. Minn., 2001, U. Ky., 2002; UTMB Galveston, 2003; Dartmouth Hitchcock Med. Sch., 2003, Duke Univ. Sch. of Med., 2003, U. Calif., San Francisco, 2005, U. Mass., 2006; guest lectr. Asian Oceanic Soc. Neuroradiology, 2001, Internat. Med. Soc. Paraplegic, Lucerne, Switzerland, 2001; Phaler lectr. Phila. Roentgen Soc., 1995; dir. programs in dept. radiology U. Miami Sch. Medicine, 1984, 86, Med. Coll. Wis., 1990, 92, Kauai, Hawaii, 1991, Whistler, B.C., 1990; guest lectr. at ASEAN Congress of Radiology, Malaysia, 1992, Royal Australia Radiology Soc., Brisbane, 1993, Brazilian Congress Neurology, 1996, NY Roentgen Soc., 1997, Somerset MR course, Torquay, UK, 1998, Republic of China, 1999, Yale U., 2000, U. Minn., 2001, U. Tex., 2003, Duke U., 2003, U. Calif., San Francisco, 2005, Downstate Med. Ctr., 2007; adv. cons. NIH, 1987, 90; sci. merit reviewer V.A., 1987; presenter, lectr. in field. Author: Neurosonography, 1988; dep. editor Am. Jour. Neuroradiology, 1984-96, editor-in-chief, 1998—; assoc. editor for neuroimaging Yearbook of Neurology and Neurosurgery, 1991—; manuscript reviewer Am. Jour. Neuroradiology, 1984—, Paraplegia, 1989—, Radiographics, 1991—, Pediatrics, 1993—, Radiology, 1994—; mem. editl. bd. Jour. Clin. Neuro-Ophthalmology, 1980-90; contbr. articles to profl. jours. Pres. Am. Soc. Neuroradiology, 1994-95; prin. investigator NIH Grant on imaging/pathology of spinal cord injury; chmn. Commn. Neuroradiological Socs. World Fedn. Neuroradiology Soc., 2003-, Neuroradiology Sci. Program Com. Radiological Soc. North Am., Scientific RSNA Program, 2008-, dir. for neuroradiology, 2004-; Lt. (j.g.) USN, 1959-61. Fellow Am. Coll. Radiology, Am. Soc. Neuroradiology (pres. 1994-95, program com. 1985-89, 92, editl. com. 1984—, publs. com. 1984—, Gold medal 2007); mem. AMA, Fla. Radiology Soc. (Gold medal 2008-), Radiol. Soc. N.Am. (program subcom. on neuroradiology 1990-94, chmn. neuroradiology program 2004—, sci. program dir. 2008—), Southeastern Neuroradiol. Soc. (founder, pres. 1980-81, examiner for bd. certification in radiology and neuroradiology), Fla. Radiol. Soc. (magnetic resonance com. 1991-92, gold medal award, 2008), Alpha Omega Alpha. Avocations: golf, travel. Business E-Mail: rquencer@med.miami.edu.

QUENTEL, ALBERT DREW, lawyer; b. Miami, Fla., Nov. 27, 1934; s. Charles Edward Jr. and Alberta Amelia (Drew) Q.; m. Paula Staelin Hagar, Feb. 9, 1957 (dec. Mar. 1998); children: Albert D. Jr., Stephen C., Marshall Lee, Paul G., Peter E., Michael J. BA, U. Fla., 1956, LLB with honors, 1959, JD with honors, 1967. Bar: Fla. 1959. Assoc. Mershon, Sawyer, Johnston, Dunwody & Cole, Miami, 1959-64, ptnr., 1965-71; prin., shareholder Greenberg Traurig P.A., Miami, 1971—. Editor-in-chief U. Fla. Law Rev., 1959; contbg. author: Florida Real Property Practice, 1965, Real Estate Partnerships Selected Problems and Solutions, 1991, Commercial Real Estate Finance, 1993. Mem. Gov.'s Growth Mgmt. Adv. Com., Tallahassee, 1985-87; bd. dirs. Nat. Parkinson Found., Miami, 1980-98, v.p., 1985-97. Mem. NRA (life 1989—), Am. Coll. Real Estate Lawyers, Fla. Bar Assn. (chmn. pub. rels. com. 1970-72, chmn. editorial com. jour. 1972-73), Lions (pres. Key Biscayne, Fla. club 1973), Miami Club (pres. 1991-92), Bath Club (Fla.), Fla. Blue Key, Beta Theta Pi (pres. local chpt. 1954-55), Phi Eta Sigma, Phi Kappa Phi. Republican. Congregationalist. Avocations: reading, shooting, photography. Home: 825 Algeria Ave Coral Gables FL 33134-2401 Office: Greenberg Traurig 333 SE 2nd Ave Miami FL 33131-2207 Home Phone: 305-442-8788; Office Phone: 305-579-0505. Business E-Mail: QuentelA@gtlaw.com.

QUERREY, SAM, professional tennis player; b. San Francsisco, Oct. 7, 1987; s. Mike and Chris Querrey. Profl. tennis player ATP, 2006—. Achievements include winning jr. titles US Tennis Assn. Spring Championships, 2005, Easter Bowl, 2005; winning Tennis Channel Open Las Vegas, 2008, ATP; mem. US Men's Olympic Team, Beijing, 2008. Avocations: basketball, ping pong/table tennis, golf. Office: ATP Americas 201 ATP Tour Blvd Ponte Vedra Beach FL 32082

QUERY, LANCE D., dean, library and information scientist; BS in Edn., U. Mo., 1969; MA in Latin American History, PhD in Latin American History, Ind. U.; MLS, U. Chgo. Acting univ. libr. Northwestern U., Chgo.; asst. univ. libr., planning and adminstrn. Western Mich. U., faculty mem., dean Univ. Libraries; dean libraries and academic info. resources Tulane U., New Orleans, 2000—; interim dir. Law Libr. Tulane U. Law Sch., 2005. Mem. La. Academic Libr. Info. Network Consortium, 2000—, mem. exec. com., 2003—; bd. dirs. Amistad Rsch. Ctr., 2001—, mem. exec. com., 2002—, chmn. rsch. and edn. com., 2005—. Mem. editl. bd.: Research Strategies, Elsevier, 1999—2004; contbr. articles to profl. jours. Mem.: Assn. SE Rsch. Libraries (mem. edn. com. 2001—, pres. exec. com. 2006—). Office: Dean Libr Academic Info Resources Tulane University 6823 St Charles Ave New Orleans LA 70118-5698 Office Phone: 504-865-5131. Office Fax: 504-865-6773. Business E-Mail: lquery@tulane.edu.

QUESENBERRY, KENNETH HAYS, agronomy educator; b. Springfield, Tenn., Feb. 28, 1947; s. James William and Cora Geneva (Moore) Quesenberry; m. Joyce Ann Kaze; children: James Kenneth, Kendra Joyce. BS, Western Ky. U., 1969; PhD, U. Ky., 1975. D.F. Jones predoctoral fellow U. Ky., Lexington, 1972—75; asst. prof. U. Fla., Gainesville, 1975—80, assoc. prof. agronomy, 1980—86, prof. agronomy, 1986—2010, emeritus prof. agronomy, 2010—, interim chair agronomy dept., 2012—13. Contbr. articles to profl. jours. With US Army, 1969—71, Vietnam. Fellow: Crop Sci. Soc. Am. (chair divsn. C-8 1993—94, bd. reps. 2005—07, pres. 2009), Am. Soc. Agronomy. Achievements include research in germplasm enhancement of forages with release of four cultivars of tropical grasses and three clovers and genetic transformation of clovers; specialist Trifolium species germplasm and forage and turfgrass breeding and genetics; development of 16 forage cultivars and germplasms. Avocations: sports, antique furniture refinishing. Office: U Fla PO Box 110500 Gainesville FL 32611-0500 Office Phone: 351-392-1811. Business E-Mail: clover@ufl.edu.

QUICK, ELIZABETH L., lawyer; b. Izmir, Turkey, May 22, 1948; BA, Duke U., 1970; JD with honors, U. NC, 1974. Bar: NC 1974. Mem., trusts & estates Womble Carlyle Sandridge & Rice, Winston-Salem, NC, mem. mgmt. com. Vis. lectr. U. NC Sch. Law, 1977. Mem. U. NC Law Review, 1973—74, co-author, editor NC Estate Adminstrn. Manual, 1984; contbr. articles to profl. jours. Bd. dir. Cannon Found., Concord, NC, Reynolda House, inc., Winston-Salem, NC, Wake Forest U. Health Scis., Winston-Salem, NC. Fellow Am. Coll. Trust and Estate Counsel (past chmn.); mem. ABA, NC Bar Assn. (pres. 1997-98), Forsyth County Bar Assn. (treas.), Order of Coif. Mailing: Womble Carlyle Sandridge & Rice PLLC 1 W 4th St Winston Salem NC 27101 Office: Womble Carlyle Sandridge & Rice PLLC One West 4th St Winston Salem NC 27101 Office Phone: 336-721-3638. Office Fax: 336-733-8359. Business E-Mail: equick@wcsr.com.

QUICK, JEREMY M., corporate financial executive; Chartered acct., UK. V.p., fin. Optic Electronic, 1986—90; v.p., fin., Oldcastle Glass divsn. CRH PLC, 1995—98; CFO Invensys Bldg. Sys., Inc., 1998—2001; v.p., fin., Energy Svcs. divsn. Invensys PLC, 1998—2002, exec. v.p., ops., Climate Controls divsn., 2002—04; exec. v.p., CFO Acuity Brands Lighting, Inc., 2004—. Office: Acuity Brands Lighting Inc 1170 Peachtree St NE Atlanta GA 30309-7649 Office Phone: 770-922-9000.

QUICK, THOMAS CLARKSON, brokerage house executive; b. Westbury, NY, Feb. 26, 1955; s. Leslie Charles and Regina (Clarkson) Q. BS in Bus., Fairfield U., 1977. Br. mgr. Quick & Reilly Inc., Palm Beach, Fla., 1977-81; dir. The Quick & Reilly Group, NYC, 1981-85; v.p. Quick & Reilly Inc., Palm Beach, 1981-86, pres., dir. NYC, 1985-96, also bd. dirs.; pres., COO Quick & Reilly/Fleet Securities, Inc., 1996-98; also bd. dirs.; pres., COO Quick & Reilly Group Inc., 1998-2001. Trustee Security Industry Found. for Econ. Edn., Securities Industry Inst.; bd. dirs. Senesco Techs., corcoran.com., MindArrow Systems.com. Treas. Nat. Corp. Theater Fund, Alcoholism Coun. of N.Y.C; trustee U.S. Com.; bd. trustees Fairfield U.; mem. investment adv. bd. and endowment com. St. Jude Children's Rsch. Hosp., Memphis, 1986—; chmn. com. Wall Street Friends of St. Jude Children's Rsch. Hosp., 1979—, mem. endowment com.; bd. dirs. Best Buddies, Am. Ireland Fund. Mem. The Investment Assn. N.Y., N.Y. Stock Exch., Securities and Industry Assn. (econ. edn. com.), Am. Assn. of Sovereign Mil., Order of Malta, Young Pres.'s Orgn., Univ. Club, Friendly Sons of St. Patrick, Apawamis Country Club (Rye, N.Y.), The Beach Club (Palm Beach, Fla.), Chgo. Athletic Club., New York Yacht Club, Lotus Club, Lost Tree Club. Home: 291 El Vedado Way Palm Beach FL 33480 Office: 230 S County Rd Ste C Palm Beach FL 33480 E-mail: tquick@quick-reilly.com.

QUIJAS, LOUIS F., security firm executive, former federal agency administrator; BS in Criminal Justice Adminstrn.; MPA, Park U., Parkville, Mo., 1996; grad., FBI Nat. Acad., Sr. Mgmt. Inst. for Police; grad. sr. leadership program, Northwestern U. Kellogg Sch. Mgmt., Ill.; grad., FBI Nat. Exec. Inst.; grad. sr. exec. in state and local govt. program, Harvard U. JFK Sch. Govt., Mass. Ret. maj. Kansas City Police Dept., Mo., 1972—97; chief of police City of High Point, NC, 1997—2002; asst. dir. office law enforcement coordination FBI, 2002—08; pres. N.Am. ops. Datong Electronics, Chantilly, Va., 2008—11; asst. sec. office state and local law enforcement US Dept. Homeland Security, Washington, 2011—13; sr. v.p. strategic ventures Security Tech. Alliance, 2013—. Recipient President's award, Nat. Sheriffs' Assn., 2004, FBI Nat. Acad., 2005, Director's award, US Secret Svc., 2008; named one of Top 100 Influential Hispanics in the US, Hispanic Bus. Mag., 2002. Mem.: National Latino Peace Officers Assn. (former nat. pres.), Hispanic American Police Command Officers Assn. (former nat. bd. mem., Gil Pompa Spl. Recognition award 2003), Internat. Assn. Chiefs of Police (former mem. exec. com., former mem. civil rights and terrorism committees). Office: Security Technology Alliance 1530 Wilson Blvd Ste 670 Arlington VA 22209-240*

QUILLEN, CAROL E., academic administrator, history professor; b. St. Albans, NY, Jan. 9, 1961; d. William Tatem and Marcia Everhart (Stirling) Quillen; m. Ken Kennedy (dec. 2007); 1 child, Caitlin Lohrenz. BA in American History, U. Chgo., 1983; PhD in European History, Princeton U., 1991. Rschr. Princeton U.; asst. prof. history Rice U., Houston, 1989—96, dir. Boniuk Ctr. for Study and Advancement of Religious Tolerance, 2004—08, assoc. prof. history, 1996—2011, vice provost academic affairs, 2006—10, v.p. internat. and interdisciplinary initiatives, 2010—11; pres. Davidson Coll., 2011—. Author: Rereading the Renaissance, 1998, Petrach's Secret, 2003. Recipient Brown Tchg. Award, Brown Found., 1993; fellow Mellon Found., 1983; Whiting Fellow, MB Gilles Whiting Found., 1987. Mem.: Renaissance Soc. America, American Hist. Assn. Office: Davidson College Office of President Box 7145 Davidson NC 28035-7145 Office Phone: 704-894-2201.*

QUILLEN, MICHAEL J., state commissioner, former energy executive; Grad., Va. Tech. U. Chmn., CEO Addington Inc.; v.p. ops. NERCO Coal Corp.; v.p. AMVEST Corp.; pres. Pittston Coal Sales Corp.; v.p. ops. Pittston Coal Co.; exec. v.p. ops. Am. Metals & Coal Internat., 1998—2002; pres., CEO Alpha Natural Resources Inc., Abingdon, Va., 2004—06, chmn., CEO, 2006—09, exec. chmn., 2009—12. Commr. Va. Port Authority, 2003—, chmn., 2011—. Office: Virginia Port Authority 600 World Trade Center Norfolk VA 23510

QUILLEN, ROGER K., lawyer; BA, BS cum laude, Ohio State U., Columbus, 1975, JD with honors, 1980; MS with honors, Purdue U., Lafayette, Ind., 1977. Bar: Ga. Ptnr. Fisher & Phillips, LLP, Atlanta, mng. ptnr. and chmn. mgmt. com. Co-author: Labor and Employment Law in Georgia, 1990—2001. Named one of The Best Lawyers in America, 2006—, The Nation's 100 Most Powerful Employment Attorneys, Human Resources Exec. Mag., 2009, 2010; named to Ga. Super Lawyers, Georgia's Legal Elite. Office: Fisher & Phillips LLP 1075 Peachtree St NE Ste 3500 Atlanta GA 30309 Office Phone: 404-240-4241. Office Fax: 404-240-4249. Business E-Mail: rquillen@laborlawyers.com.

QUILLIAN, WARREN WILSON, II, pediatrician, educator; b. Miami, Fla., Jan. 21, 1936; s. Warren Wilson and Rosabel (Brown) Q.; m. Sallie Ruth Creel, July 26, 1958; children: Rutledge, Ruth, Warren C., Frances. MD, Emory U., 1961. Diplomate Am. Bd. Pediat. (examiner 1966—, bd. dirs. 1974-80, 1992-98, treas. 1978, v.p. 1979, pres. 1980). Intern in pediat. Vandertilt U., Nashville, 1961-62; resident Children's Hosp. Med. Ctr., Harvard U., Boston, 1962-63; chief resident Grady Meml. Hosp., Emory U., Atlanta, 1963-64; pvt. practice Coral Gables, Fla., 1966. Instr., asst. clin. prof., assoc. clin. prof., now clin. prof. pediat. Miller Sch. Medicine, U. Miami, 1966—; emeritus staff, bd. dirs. Miami Children's Hosp.; emeritus staff Jackson Meml. Hosp.; past chief pediat. Doctors' Hosp.; mem. hon. staff Mercy Hosp., Bapt. Hosp., South Miami Hosp.; chmn. health adv. com. Dade County Schs.; bd. dirs., v.p. Am. Bd. Pediat. Found., 1991-98; mem. adv. bd. McGlannon Sch.; cons. Fla. Divsn. Med. Svcs.; bd. dirs. Bank Coral Gables. Contbr. articles to med. jours. Hon. bd. dirs. Soc. Abused Children of Children's Home Soc., Miami, 1980-84; mem. Coral Gables Code Enforcement Bd., 1986-88; team-sch. physician Coral Gables Sr. H.G., 1980-88; bd. dirs. Dade County March of Dimes, Miami, 1968-72; bd. advisors Dade County Assn. Retarded Children, 1968-76; trustee Emory U., 1991-97; mem. coun. ministries, youth coord., mem. fin. com., Sunday Sch. tchr. United Meth. Ch. Coral Gables, 1966—; chair staff parish rels. com.; mem. bd. advisors The Growing Place; mem. Citizens Bd. U. Miami, 1997—; v.p. bd. Good Hope Equestrian Tng. Ctr. for the Handicapped, 1999-. Capt. M.C., U.S. Army, 1964-66. Recipient citation of merit Emory U., 1980, Alumni Commendation, Miami Children's Hosp., 1983, Tchg. award U. Miami Sch. Medicine, 1995, 2002, 06, Winston Churchhill medal, 1999, Commendation Key to City, City of Coral Gables, 2007, Lifetime Achievement award Miami Children's Hosp., 2007; named to CGHS Athletic Hall of Fame, 1996, Wisdom Hall of Fame, 1998; finalist Citizen of Yr., 2005. Fellow Am. Acad. Pediat.; mem. AMA, Fla. Med. Assn. (sch. health com.), Fla. Pediat. Soc. (past chmn. sch. health com.), So. Med. Assn., Dade County Med. Assn. (sch. health com., continuing edn. com.), Empirical Soc. (past pres.), Soc. for Pediat. Rsch., So. Perinatal Soc., Greater Miami Pediat. Soc. (past pres., chmn. legis. and sch. health com., Hall of Fame), Miami Med. Forum (past pres., Haverfield Cup 1985, Mansfield Trophy 1983, 88, 98), Sr. Soc. Emory U., Biscayne Bay Yacht Club (commodore, bd. govs.), DVS Sr. Honor Soc., Alpha Omega Alpha, Omicron Delta Kappa, Alpha Epsilon Upsilon, Phi Delta Theta. Democrat. Avocations: fishing, golf, boating.

QUILLIN, SUE, food products executive; b. LaCrosse, Wis. Mktg. positions Borden, Inc.; dir., mktg. Tyson Foods, Inc., various mktg. positions, 1994, v.p., mktg. svcs., 2006, chief mktg. officer, 2006—; dir., mktg. Tyson Fresh Meats, Inc. Chmn. NCC Promotions Subcommittee. Office: Tyson Foods Inc 2200 Don Tyson Pkwy Springdale AR 72762-6999 Office Phone: 479-290-4000. Office Fax: 479-290-4061. Business E-Mail: sue.quillin@tyson.com.

QUIN, LOUIS DUBOSE, chemist, educator; b. Charleston, SC, Mar. 5, 1928; s. Louis DuBose and Olga vonOven (Jatho) Q.; children: Gordon, Howard, Carol. BS, The Citadel, 1947; MA, U. N.C., 1949, PhD, 1952. Research chemist Am. Cyanamid Co., Stamford, Conn., 1949-50; research project leader FMC Corp., South Charleston, W.Va., 1952-54, 56; mem. faculty dept. chemistry Duke U., Durham, NC, 1956-86, prof., 1967-81, James B. Duke prof. chemistry, 1981-86, prof. emeritus, 1986, chmn. dept., 1970-76; prof. chemistry U. Mass., Amherst, 1986-96, prof. emeritus, 1996—, head dept., 1986-94; adj. prof., disting. vis. prof. chemistry U. N.C., Wilmington, 1996—. Mem. Durham Human Relations Commn., 1978-81 Author: Heterocyclic Chemistry of Phosphorus, 1981, (with J.G. Verkade) Phosphorus-31 NMR Spectroscopy in Stereochemical Analysis, 1987, Phosphorus-31 NMR Spectral Properties in Compound Characterization and Structural Analysis, 1994, (with A. Williams) Practical Interpretation of P-31 NMR Spectra and Computer Assisted Structure Verification, 2004; co-author: A Guide to Organophosphorus Chemistry, 2000, (with J. A. Tyrell) Fundamentals of Heterocyclic Chemistry, 2010. Served to 1st lt. U.S. Army, 1954-56. Recipient Arbusovs award in phosphorus chemistry, 1997. Fellow AAAS; mem. Am. Chem. Soc. Office: 15 Aldersgate Ct Durham NC 27705 Office Phone: 919-384-2412.

QUINCE, PEGGY A., state supreme court justice; b. Norfolk, Va., Jan. 3, 1948; m. Fred L. Buckine; children: Peggy LaVerne, Laura LaVerne. BS in Zoology, Howard U., 1970; JD, Cath. U. of Am., 1975; LLD (hon.), Stetson U., 1999, St. Thomas U., 2004. Hearing officer Rental Accomodations Office, Washington; pvt. practice Norfolk, 1977-78, Bradenton, Fla., 1978-80; asst. atty. gen. criminal divsn. Atty. Gen.'s Office, 1980; apptd. 2d Dist. Ct. of Appeals, 1994-98; justice Fla. Supreme Ct., 1998—, chief justice, 2008—10. Lectr. in field. Former asst. Sunday sch. tchr., former mem. #3 usher bd. New Hope Missionary Bapt. Ch.; active Jack and Jill of Am., Inc., Urban League, NAACP, Tampa Orgn. for Black Affairs. Recipient award Cath.'s Neighborhood Legal Svcs. Clinic, Margaret Brent Women Lawyers Achievement award, 2007, Fla. Women's Hall Of Fame. Mem. Nat. Bar Assn., Fla. Bar, Va. State Bar, George Edgecomb Bar Assn., Fla. Assn. Women Lawyers, Tallahassee Women Lawyers, William H. Stafford Inn. Ct., Alpha Kappa Alpha. Office: Fla Supreme Ct 500 S Duval St Tallahassee FL 32399-1925 Office Phone: 850-922-5624. Business E-Mail: Larryg@flcourts.org.*

QUINN, BETH J., food service executive; Attended, Western Mich. U., Kalamazoo, 1982—86. Regional v.p. retail ops. Cracker Barrel Old Country Store, Inc., 1991—. Named Regional V.P. of Yr., 2003. Office: Cracker Barrel Old Country Store Inc 305 Hartmann Dr Lebanon TN 37088-0787 Office Phone: 615-444-5533. Office Fax: 615-443-9476.

QUINN, DAVID W., building company executive; b. 1942; BA, Midwestern U. Ptnr. Arthur Andersen, Dallas, 1967-84; COO Alpert Cos., 1984-87; exec. v.p. Centex Corp., Dallas, 1987—96, CFO, 1987—97, 1997—2000. Bd. dirs. Centex Corp., 1989—, vice chmn., 1996—2002; bd. dirs. Eagle Materials Inc. Office: Centex Corp 2728 N Harwood St Ste 200 Dallas TX 75201-1591 Office Fax: 214-981-6859. Business E-Mail: dquinn@centexhomes.com.

QUINN, JOHN COLLINS, publishing executive, editor; b. Providence, Oct. 24, 1925; s. John A. and Kathryn H. (Collins) Q.; m. Lois R. Richardson, June 20, 1953; children: John Collins, Lo-anne, Richard B., Christopher A. AB, Providence Coll., 1945; MS, Columbia U. Sch. Journalism, 1946. Successively copy boy, reporter, asst. city editor, Washington corr., asst. mng. editor, day mng. editor Providence Jour.-Bull., 1943-66; with Gannett Co. Inc., Rochester, NY, 1966-90; exec. editor Rochester Democrat & Chronicle, Times-Union, 1966-71; gen. mgr. Gannett News Service, 1967-80, pres., 1980-88, v.p. parent co., 1971-75, sr. v.p. news and info., 1975-80, sr. v.p., chief news exec. parent co., editor USA TODAY, 1983-89; exec. v.p. Gannett Co., Arlington, Va., 1983-90; trustee Gannett Found., Arlington, 1988-91; dep. chmn. Freedom Forum, Arlington, 1991-97, trustee, 1991—. Named to R.I. Hall of Fame, 1975, Editor of Yr. Nat. Press Found., 1986; recipient William Allen White citation, 1987, Women in Communications Headliner award, 1986, Paul Miller/Okla. State U. medallion, 1988 Al Neuharth award for Excellence in the Media, 2007. Mem. AP Mng. Editors (past dir., nat. pres. 1973-74), Am. Soc. Newspaper Editors (dir., chmn. editorial bd., chmn. conv. program, nat. pres. 1982-83) Roman Catholic. Home: 365 S Atlantic Ave Cocoa Beach FL 32931-2719 Home Phone: 321-784-6165, 401-364-7726; Office Phone: 401-364-9282.

QUINN, NANCY K., finance company executive; b. 1953; BFA, La. State U.; MBA in Fin., U. Ark. Ltd. ptnr. Beacon Group; with S.W. Regional Banking Kidder, Peabody & Co., mng. dir., co-head natural resources, energy investment banking sect., 1982—92, mng. dir., co-head Natural Resources Group, 1990—94; exec. dir., prin. The Beacon Group, LP, 1996—2000; mng. dir., co-head Energy, Natural Resources Group PaineWebber Inc., 1994—95; co-founder, prin. Hanover Capital, LLC, 1996—; prin. Endeavor International Corp., 1996—, bd. dirs., 2004—. Bd. dirs. DeepTech Internat., 1995—98, Louis Dreyfus Natural Gas Corp. (acquired by Dominion Resources), 1999—2001, Atmos Energy Corp., 2004—, Helix Energy Solutions Group, Inc., 2009—. Mem.: YWCA Acad. of Women Achievers, Am. Gas Assn. (mem. Bankers Adv. Coun.). Office: Helix Energy Solutions Group Inc 400 N Sam Houston Pky E Houston TX 77060-3500 Office Phone: 281-618-0400. Office Fax: 281-618-0501.

QUINN, PATRICK, transportation executive; BA, U. Nebr., 1968, JD, 1971. From assoc. to ptnr. Nelson & Harding, Lincoln, Nebr., 1971-77; gen. counsel S.W. Motor Freight, Chattanooga, 1977-85; pres., co-chmn. U.S Xpress Enterprises, Inc., Chattanooga, Tenn., 1985—. Office: US Xpress Enterprises Inc 4080 Jenkins Rd Chattanooga TN 37421-1174 Office Phone: 423-510-3000.

QUINN, RICHARD M., JR., state legislator, marketing professional; b. Columbia, SC, June 22, 1965; s. Richard M. and Ruth LeJeune Quinn; m. Amy McRae Benck, July 13, 2002; children: Caroline, Trace. Student, U. SC, 1994. Owner, pres. Mail Market Strategies; campaign cons.; state rep. Dist. 71 SC House of Representatives, 1989—2004, house majority leader, 1999—2004, state rep. Dist. 69, 2010—. Chpt. chmn. SC Fed. of County Reps., state chmn. Mem.: Greater Columbia C. of C., Chapin Sertoma Club, lake Murray/Irmo Rotary Club. Republican. Office: 323A Blatt Bldg Columbia SC 29201 Home: 115 John Preston Dr Lexington SC 29072-7715 Home Phone: 803-808-3964; Office Phone: 803-799-8638, 803-212-6897. E-mail: RMQ@scstatehouse.net.

QUINN, STEPHEN F., marketing executive; m. Linda Quinn; 3 children. BA in Economics, Queens U., Can.; MBA, U. Western Ont., Can. Various mktg., sales and fin. positions The Quaker Oats Co., Johnson & Johnson, Procter & Gamble Co., Nortel Networks Corp.; various mktg. positions, including gen. mgr., convenience foods PepsiCo, Inc., 1992—2005, chief mktg. officer, Frito-Lay N.Am. divsn., head, mktg., Frito-Lay Can.; sr. v.p., mktg. Wal-Mart Stores, Inc., Bentonville, Ark., 2005—07, exec. v.p., chief mktg. officer, 2007—. Bd. dirs. Ad Coun., Assn. Nat. Advertisers, Give Kids the World. Named a Power Player, Advt. Age, 2008, 2009. Office: Wal-Mart Stores Inc 702 SW 8th St Bentonville AR 72716-8611 Office Phone: 479-273-4000. Office Fax: 479-277-1830.

QUINONES, MIGUEL A., cardiologist, educator; MD, U. Puerto Rico, San Juan, 1968. Diplomate Am. Bd. Internal Medicine, 1972, Am. Bd. Internal Medicine-cardiovasc. disease, 1974. Resident internal medicine Harlem Hosp., NYC, 1969—71; fellow cardiovasc. disease Baylor Coll. Medicine, Houston, 1971—74; chmn. cardiology dept. The Meth. Hosp., Houston; prof. medicine Weill Cornell Med. Coll. Editl. bd. several sci. jours. Co-author over 185 manuscripts in peer review jours., over 12 book chpts., and 225 pub. abstracts. Named one of The Best Doctors in America, Ctrl. Region, Woodward and White, Inc., Best of the Best, Med. Jour.-Houston, 2008. Mem.: Am. Heart Assn., Interamerican Soc. of Cardiology (exec. bd.), Soc. Pediatric Echocardiography, Soc. of Cardiovasc. Anesthesiologist, Am. Soc. of Echocardiography, Am. Heart Assn. (bd. dirs. Houston chpt., v.p. representation), Am. Coll. Cardiology (bd. trustees, v.p. representation). Office: Methodist DeBakey Cardiology Associates Smith Tower 6550 Fannin Ste 1901 Houston TX 77017 Office Phone: 713-441-1100.

QUINOY, MELISA, marketing and advertising executive; b. Puerto Rico, 1963; Grad., Cornell U., NYC, 1984. With EURO RSCG Worldwide, Australia, FCB Worldwide, Lowe & Ptnrs. Worldwide, NY; regional dir. client svcs. Ammirati Puris Lintas; sr. v.p. internat. mktg. partnerships MTV Networks Latin America, Miami, Fla., 1999—2006; exec. v.p. Viacom Brand Solutions MTV Networks Internat., London, 2006—08; CEO Dieste Harmel & Ptnrs., Dallas, 2008—. Named a Woman to Watch, Advt. Age, 2008. Office: 1999 Bryan St Ste 2700 Dallas TX 75201 Office Phone: 214-259-8000. Office Fax: 214-259-8040. Business E-Mail: CEO@dieste.com.

QUINTANILLA, CHENTE, state legislator; b. 1943; m. Gracie Quintanilla. Mem. Dist. 75 Tex. House of Representatives, 2002—. Democrat. Office: 120 N Horizon Ste A-112 El Paso TX 79927 also: Room E1.218 Capitol Extension PO Box 2910 Austin TX 78768 Office Phone: 512-463-0613, 915-859-3111.

QUINTOS, KAREN, computer company executive, marketing professional; b. 1963; BS in Supply Chain Mgmt., Pa. State U., 1985; MS in Mktg. and Internat. Bus., NYU. Various positions including dir. global supply chain mgmt. and dir. packaging Merck & Co., Inc. (formerly Schering-Plough Corp.); v.p. global ops. and tech. Citigroup, Inc.; Joined Dell, Inc., 2000, various positions including gen. mgr. small & medium bus. svcs. sales and customer care, v.p., gen. mgr. customer contact centers Americas, v.p. global pub. bus., sr. v.p., chief mktg. officer, 2010—. Bd. visitors Pa. State U. Smeal Sch. Bus.; bd. dirs. Susan G. Komen for the Cure. Office: Dell Corp Hdqs One Dell Way Round Rock TX 78682

QUIRK, RAYMOND R. (RANDY QUIRK), insurance company executive; b. 1946; m. Linda J. Quirk; 3 children. Pres. Fidelity National Financial, Inc., Jacksonville, Fla., 2002—05, CEO Fidelity Nat. Title Group, Inc., 2005—, co-pres., 2007—. Mem. bd. dirs. Fidelity Nat. Title, Alamo Title, Chgo. Title, Home Warranty subsidiaries of Fidelity Nat. Fin. Avocation: golf. Office: Fidelity Nat Fin Inc 601 Riverside Ave Jacksonville FL 32204 Office Phone: 888-934-3354.

QUITTMEYER, PETER CHARLES, lawyer; b. Charlottesville, Va., Oct. 9, 1957; s. Charles L. and Maureen (Rankin) Q.; children: Charles Lake, Laura Slater. BA with high distinction, U. Va., Charlottesville, 1979, JD, 1982. Bar: Ga. 1985. Assoc. King & Spalding, Atlanta, 1982-87; shareholder Trotter, Smith & Jacobs, Atlanta, 1987-91; ptnr. Nelson Mullins Riley & Scarborough, Atlanta, 1991—2001, Sutherland Asbill & Brennan, Atlanta, 2001—. Adj. prof. computer law Emory U. Sch. Law, Atlanta, 1996, 98, 2000; spl. asst. atty. gen. State Ga., 2002, 09-13; vice chmn. Ga. chpt. Arthritis Found., 2007-09 Author: Computer Software Agreements, 1985—; mem. editl. bd. Va. Law Rev., 1981-82; contbr. articles to profl. jours. Recipient Vol. award, Ga. chpt. Arthritis Found., 2005. Mem. ABA, Ga. Bar Assn., Raven Soc., Order of Coif, Phi Beta Kappa. Office: Sutherland Asbill & Brennan 999 Peachtree St NE Ste 2300 Atlanta GA 30309 Office Phone: 404-853-8186. Business E-Mail: peter.quittmeyer@sutherland.com.

QUNELL, KERRI WYNN, educational association administrator; b. Bastrop, Tex., Mar. 16, 1971; d. James Richard Wynn and Lu Ella Johnson; m. Jason Christopher Qunell, Sept. 25, 1999. BA, Tex. State U., San Marcos, 1993. Econ. devel. asst. Greater Austin (Tex.) C. of C., 1994—97; asst. account mgr., traffic mgr. Sicola Martin Advt., account exec. Austin, 1997—98; mktg. comm. mgr. Dell Computer Corp., Round Rock, Tex., 1998—2001; corp. devel. dir. Sta. KEYE-TV, Austin, 2001—02, cmty. rels. dir., 2002—05; v.p., comm. Capital Area Food Bank of Tex., dir., comm. Austin, 2005; dir., Mktg. Svcs. St. Edward's U., 2010—. Mktg. task force ARC Ctrl. Tex., Austin, 2002—. Bd. mem. Greater Austin Hispanic C. of C., 2002—05. Recipient Vol. of Distinction award, The Dell Found., 2001, Profiles in Power finalist, Austin Bus. Jour. & FOX TV, 2002, Austin Under 40 award, Greater Austin Hispanic C. of C., 2006. Mem.: Women in Comm. Inc., Am. Women in Radio and TV, Am. Mktg. Assn. (bd. mem. 2001—03), Young Women's Alliance Austin (life; pres. 2001—01). Methodist. Avocations: photography, camping, travel, music, interior decorating. Office: St Edward's University 3001 S Congress Ave Austin TX 78704-6425 Office Phone: 512-448-8400. Office Fax: 512-464-8851.

RAAD, VIRGINIA, pianist, educator; b. Salem, W.Va., Aug. 13, 1925; d. Joseph M. and Martha (Joseph) R. BA in Art History, Wellesley Coll., 1947; spl. student, New Eng. Conservatory Music, 1947-48; student, Berthe Bert, 1949—55, Jeanne Blancard, 1949—55, student, 1968—70, Alfred Cortot, 1950—51, Jacques Chailley, 1953—55; PhD with honors, U. Paris, 1955; diplôme, École Normale de Musique, Paris, 1950. Artist in residence Salem Coll., W.Va., 1957-70; ind. concert pianist, 1960—; musician in residence at cmty. colls. NC Arts Coun., 1971—. Adjudicator Nat. Guild Piano Tchrs., Nat. Fedn. Music Clubs; panelist, grant reviewer NEH, 1978-84, 92—; mem. com. Nat. Endowment Arts, 1978; Am. rep. Debussy Centennial Colloque, Paris, 1962. Perfomances, concerts, lectrs. master classes at West Ga. Coll., Carrollton, La Grange Coll., Ga., Columbus Coll., Ga., Young Harris Coll., Ga., U. Fla., Gainesville, Norton Gallery, Palm Beach, Fla., Alliance Française de Rollins Coll., Winter Park, Fla., Dixon Gallery and Gardens, Memphis, St. Jude Children's Rsch. Hosp., Memphis, Cleveland State CC, Tenn., Sampson Tech. Inst., Clinton, NC, Wayne CC, Goldsboro, NC, Brevard Coll., NC, Ctrl. Wesleyan Coll., SC, Ky. Wesleyan Coll., Owensboro, Coll., Alice Lloyd Coll., Pippa Passes, Ky., Coll. of William and Mary, Williamsburg, Va., Eastern Mennonite Coll., Harrisonburg, Va., The Phillips Gallery, Washington, Trinity Coll., Washington, Manhattanville Coll., Purchase, NY, Elmira Coll., NY, Fordham U., NYC, The Piano Tchrs. Congress of NY, Middlebury Coll., Vt., St. Anselm's Coll., Manchester, N.H., Mount St. Mary's Coll., Hooksett, NH, Wellesley Coll., Mass., Curry Coll., Milton, Mass., So. Conn. State U., New Haven, Slippery Rock U., Pa., Seton Hill Coll., Greensboro, Pa., Alliance Française de Pitts. and U. Pitts., Channel 13 WQED (PBS) Pitts., Lincoln U., Oxford, Pa., The Grier Sch., Tyrone, Pa., Mount de Chantal Acad., Wheeling W.Va., Wheeling Jesuit U., among other colls. and univs.; contbg. author: Debussy et l'Evolution de la Musique au XX Siècle, 1965, l'Influence: Amerique; author: The Piano Sonority of Claude Debussy, 1994; recording artist: EDUCO, 1995—, Folklore & Reminiscence in Claude Debussy in Liber amicorum Isabelle Cazeaux, NY, 2005; contbr. articles to profl. jours. Active Amnesty Internat. Urgent Action Network; alumna regional rep. Wellesley Coll.; mem bd. visitors New Eng. Conservatory of Music, 2004—. Named Outstanding W.Va. Woman Educator Delta Kappa Gamma, 1965; presented biography to Schlesinger Library on History of Women in Am. Radcliffe Coll., 1967; grantee Govt. France, Am. Coun. Learned Socs. Mem. Soc. Française de Musicologie, Am. Musicol. Soc. (regional officer 1960-65), Internat. Musicol. Soc., Music Tchrs. Nat. Assn. (adjudicator, musicology program chair 1983-87), W.Va. Music Tchrs. Assn., Audubon Activist, Alpha Delta Kappa (hon.). Roman Catholic. Avocations: hiking, gardening, birding. Home and Office: 60 Terrace Ave Salem WV 26426-1116 Personal E-mail: virginia-raad@aol.com.

RABALAIS, NANCY, marine ecologist; BS in Biology, Texas A&I U., Kingsville, 1972, MS in Biology, 1975; PhD in Zoology, U. Texas, Austin, 1983. With Louisiana Universities Marine Consortium, 1983—, exec. dir., prof. Adj. prof. Sch. of the Coast & Environment Louisiana State U.; chair Nat. Rsch. Coun. Ocean Studies Bd., 2000—05; mem. adv. bd. Nat. Sea Grant Coll. Nat. Sea Grant; past pres. Estuarine Rsch. Federation; co-chair Scientific Steering Com., Land-Ocean Interactions in the Coastal Zone, IGBP; science advisor Bjorn Carlson Found. for the Baltic Sea 2020; chair exec. bd. NOAA Coastal Restoration and Enhancement through Science and Technology; mem. Coun. for University-Naval Oceangraphic Lab. System, SCOR Working Group on Natural and Human Induced Hypoxia and Consequences for Coastal Areas, Trustees of the Consortium for Ocean Leadership, Nat. Sea Grant Program Nat. Review Panel, NSF Adv. Com. to the Environmental Rsch. and Edn. Directorate; bd. dirs. GCOOS, Gulf of Mexico Regional Assn. for IOOS. Contbr. of several articles to profl. publications; author of 3 books:; contbr. chapters to books. Recipient NOAA Environmental Hero award, 1999, 12th Bostwick H. Ketchum award for coastal rsch., Woods Hole Oceanographic Institution, 2002, Ruth Patrick award, American Soc. of Limnology and Oceanography, 2008, 17th Heinz Family Found. award, 2011, Peter Benchley Ocean award for Excellence in Science, 2012, Nat. Water Resources Inst. Clarke prize; co-recipient Blasker award for Science and Engineering, 1999; Aldo Leopold Leadership Fellow, MacArthur Fellow, John D. and Catherine T. MacArthur Found., 2012. Fellow: AAAS; mem.: NAS (nat. assoc.). Office: Louisiana Universities Marine Consortium Defelice Marine Center 8124 Highway 56 Chauvin LA 70344 Office Phone: 985-851-2801. Office Fax: 985-851-2874. Business E-Mail: nrabalais@lumcon.edu.

RABAUT, THOMAS W., private equity firm executive; b. Detroit, 1948; m. Sheila Rabaut; 3 children. BS, US Mil. Acad., West Point, NY, 1970; MBA, Harvard U., 1977. Trainee mfg. dept., drive divsn., various mfg./mgmt. positions FMC Corp., 1977-81, planning mgr., then mfg. and ops. mgr. fluid control divsn., 1982—86, mgr. steel products divsn., 1986-88, dir. ops. ground sys. divsn., 1989—93, gen. mgr. def. sys. group, 1993—94, v.p., 1994; pres., CEO United Defense Industries, Inc., Arlington, Va., 1994—2005; pres. land and armaments oper. group BAE Sys., 2005—07; sr. advisor aerospace, def. and bus./govt. svcs. group Carlyle Group, LP, Washington, 2007—. Bd. dirs. Cytec Industries Inc., 2007—, Kaman Corp., 2008—. Served with US Army, 1970—75. Mem.: Naval Surface Warfare Assn., Nat. Infantryman's Assn., US Army Ordnance Corps Assn., Assn. Indsl. Coll. Armed Forces, Aerospace Industries Assn., Navy League US, Assn. US Army, Nat. Guard Assn. US. Office: The Carlyle Group 1001 Pennsylvania Ave NW Washington DC 20004 Mailing: Cytec Industries Inc Bd Directors 5 Garret Mountain Plz Little Falls NJ 07424 Office Phone: 973-357-3100. Office Fax: 973-357-3061. Business E-Mail: thomas.rabaut@cytec.com.

RABIDEAU, PETER WAYNE, chemistry professor; b. Johnstown, Pa., Mar. 4, 1940; s. Peter Nelson and Monica (Smalley) R.; m. Therese Charlene Newquist, Sept. 1, 1962 (div.); children: Steven, Michael, Christine, Susan; m. Jennifer Lee Mooney, Nov. 15, 1986; children: Mark, Leah. BS, Loyola U., Chgo., 1964; MS, Case Inst. Tech., Cleve., 1967; PhD, Case Western Res. U., Cleve., 1968. Postdoctoral asst. U. Chgo., 1968-69, instr., 1969-70; asst. prof. Ind. U.-Purdue U., Indpls., 1970-73, assoc. prof., 1973-76, prof., 1976-90, chmn. dept. chemistry, 1985-90; dean Coll. Basic Scis. La. State U., Baton Rouge, 1990-99; dean Coll. Liberal Arts and Scis. Iowa State U., Ames, 1999—2003; provost, v.p. acad. affairs Miss. State U., 2003—09, prof. chemistry, 2010—. Program officer NSF, 1988-89. Contbr. numerous articles to profl. jours. Recipient Rsch. award Purdue Sch. Sci. at Indpls., 1982, Outstanding Alumnus award chemistry dept. Case Western U., 2001, Sch. Sci. medal, Distinction award, Ind. U.-Purdue U., Indpls., 2010, Iupui Sch. Sci. Fellow AAAS, Am. Chem. Soc. (chmn. Ind. sect. 1974, councilor 1981-90, Chemist of Yr. Miss. sect., 2011, Outstanding Alumnus award

Chemistry dept. Loyola U. Chgo. 2013). Home: 105 Derbyshire Rd Starkville MS 39759 Office: Miss State University PO Box 9573 Mississippi State MS 39762 Home Phone: 662-324-7778. E-mail: prabideau@chemistry.msstate.edu.

RABIL, ALBERT, JR., humanities educator; b. Rocky Mt., NC, May 8, 1934; s. Albert and Sophie Mae (Safy) R.; m. Janet Spain, Aug. 29, 1956; children: Albert III, J. Alison. BA, Duke U., 1957; MDiv, Union Theol. Sem., 1960; PhD, Columbia U., 1964. Instr. religion Trinity Coll., Hartford, Conn., 1964-65, asst. prof., 1965-68; asst. prof. hist. theology Chgo. Theol. Sem., 1969-71; assoc. prof. SUNY-Old Westbury, 1971-74, prof., 1974-77, disting. tchg. prof. humanities, 1977-98, emeritus prof., 1998. Program dir. NEH Summer Inst., 1992, 94, 95, 96, 98, 2000, 01, 03, 04, 05. Author: Merleau-Ponty, 1967 (Ansley award 1964), Erasmus and the New Testament, 1972, Laura Cereta, 1981, (with others) Her Immaculate Hand, 1983, Erasmus' Paraphrases of Romans and Galatians, 1983, Erasmus' Annotations on Romans, 1994, Teaching Other Voices: Women and Religion in Early Modern Europe, 2006; editor: Renaissance Humanism (3 vols.), 1988; editor, translator: Knowledge, Goodness, and Power, 1991, Henricus Cornelius Agrippa Declamation on the Nobility and Preeminence of the Female Sex, 1996; co-editor Renaissance Quarterly, 1992-97; series founding co-editor The Other Voice in Early Modern Europe, 1992—2006; mem. editl. bd. Soundings: An Interdisciplinary Jour., 1992-94. Travelling fellow Union Theol. Sem., 1960, Soc. for Values in Higher Edn., 1961; grantee Fulbright Found., 1961, NEH, 1974, 81, 92-95, 2001-05, 13. Mem. Erasmus Rotterdam Soc. (mem. editl. bd. 1980—2007), Soc. for Values in Higher Edn. (bd. dirs. 1981-90), Renaissance Soc. Am. (bd. dirs. 1991-97). Democrat. Home and Office: 2305 Honeysuckle Rd Chapel Hill NC 27514-1716 Office Phone: 919-967-0231. Personal E-mail: arabil@nc.rr.com.

RABIN, ALAN A., economics professor; b. NYC, June 16, 1947; s. Sidney and Claire Rabin. BA, Hamilton Coll., 1969; PhD, U. Va., 1977. NSF trainee U. Va., 1970—71, 1971—72; intern Coun. Econ. Advisors, 1971; instr. Calif. State U., Northridge, 1973-74, Georgetown U., Washington, 1975; asst. prof. econs. U. Tenn., Chattanooga, 1977-81, assoc. prof., 1981-86, prof., 1986—. Author: Monetary Theory, 2004; contbr. articles to profl. jours. NDEA fellow, 1969-70; U. Tenn.-Chattanooga faculty rsch. grantee, 1982. Mem. Am. Econs. Assn., So. Econs. Assn., Atlantic Econs. Soc., We. Econs. Assn., U. Tenn. Chattanooga Coun. Scholars, Omicron Delta Epsilon. Avocations: sports, stamp collecting/philately, theater. Home: 1175 Pineville Rd Apt 161 Chattanooga TN 37405-2653 Office: U Tenn-Chattanooga Dept Economics Chattanooga TN 37403 Business E-Mail: alan-rabin@utc.edu.

RABON, JEFF WARREN, state legislator; b. Durant, Okla., May 18, 1962; s. Bob and Linda Roan Rabon; m. Dana Bates; children: Jeff II, Berrie Shannon, Jackson Thomas. Former chmn. Joint Coms. Accountability Govt. & State-Tribal Rels.; state senator Dist. 5 Okla., 1997—; asst. majority fl. leader, 2004—; mem. Agr. & Rural Devel. Com., Rule Com., Fin. Com., Edn. Com.; chmn. Appropriations Subcom., Natural Resources and Regulatory Svc.; vice chmn. Tourism & Wildlife Com.; real estate agt.; appraiser; cattleman. Democrat. Episcopal. Mailing: PO Box 416 Hugo OK 74743 Home: 2727 E 2086 Rd Hugo OK 74743-4540 Office Phone: 580-326-0348. E-mail: rabon@lsb.state.ok.us.

RABON, WILLIAM PETER, state legislator; Attended, NC State U.; DVM in Vet. Medicine, U. Ga., 1976. Mem. Cape Fear Coun. BSA, Boy Scouts of America; life mem. NRA; charter mem. Southport Rotary Club; vice chmn. Brunswick Cmty. Coll.; former chmn. Brunswick County Bd. of Health, NC Nav. Commn.; ptnr. Brunswick Animal Hosp., 1976—, Southport Animal Hosp., 1984—, Oak Island Animal Hosp., 1996—; mem. Dist. 8 NC State Senate, 2011—. Republican. Office: 404 W Brunswick St Southport NC 28461 Address: NC Senate 16 W Jones St Room 2108 Raleigh NC 27601-2808 Office Phone: 910-457-5110, 919-733-5963. Business E-Mail: bill@billrabon.com, Bill.Rabon@ncleg.net.

RABUN, DANIEL W., oil and gas industry executive; BBA in Acctg., U. Houston; JD, So. Meth. U., Dallas. CPA 1976. Atty. Baker & McKenzie, 1986—2001, ptnr., 2001—06; v.p., gen. counsel, sec. Chorum Techs. Inc., 2000—01; pres. ENSCO Internat., Inc., 2006—07, pres., CEO, 2007, chmn., pres., CEO, 2007—. Chmn. Internat. Assn. Drilling Contractors. Office: ENSCO Internat Inc 500 N Akard St Ste 4300 Dallas TX 75201-3331 Office Phone: 214-397-3000.

RABUN, JOHN BREWTON, JR., criminal justice agency administrator; b. Augusta, Ga., Nov. 16, 1946; s. John Brewton and Alsie Imor (Bateman) R.; m. Anna Betsy Park, Dec. 27, 1967; children: Kerry Kristin, John Candler. BA, Mercer U., 1967; postgrad., So. Bapt. Theol. Sem., 1967—70; MSW, U. Louisville, 1971. Cert. social worker Ky., DC. Exec. dir. Ky. Civil Liberties Union, Louisville, 1971—72; dir. Cmty. Residential Treatment Svcs., Louisville, 1973—78; program mgr. Field Svcs., Louisville, 1978—80, Exploited and Missing Child Unit, Louisville, 1980—84; exec. v.p., COO Nat. Ctr. Missing and Exploited Children, Washington, 1984—2012; COO Nat. Ctr. for Missing and Exploited Children, 1984—, exec. v.p., 2006—. Mem. Alderman's Task Force on Social Svcs., Louisville, 1982, Mayor's City Youth Commn., Louisville, 1983-84; trainer and/or cons. to numerous agys. in U.S., U.K., Can., Mex., Belgium, Germany, Austria, Netherlands. Author: (book) Healthcare Guideslines Infant Abduction, 2009; contbr. articles to profl. jours., chapters to books. Recipient Key to City of Louisville, 1983, Disting. Alumnus award U. Louisville, 1985, 2003, Russell L. Colling Lit. award Internat. Assn. for Healthcare Security and Safety, 1991; named hon. chief of police City of Louisville, 1982; Alumni fellow U. Louisville, 1999. Mem. ACLU, NASW, Nat. Sheriff's Assn., Internat. Juvenile Officers Assn., Acad. Cert. Social Workers, Internat. Assn. Healthcare Safety and Security, Am. Soc. Indsl. Security, Internat. Assn. Chiefs of Police. Baptist (deacon). Avocations: photography, hunting, fishing, internet. Office: Nat Ctr for Missing and Exploited Children 699 Prince St Alexandria VA 22314-3117 Home Phone: 571-259-2112; Office Phone: 571-259-2112. Business E-Mail: jrabun@ncmec.org.

RABY, KENNETH ALAN, lawyer, retired military officer; b. Dec. 29, 1935; s. Carl George and Helen Josette (Milne) R.; m. Shirley Rae Nelson, June 2, 1957; children: Randolph Carlton, Shelly Ann. BA, U. S.D., 1957, JD, 1960; grad. with honors, Command and Gen. Staff Coll., 1975, U.S. Army War Coll., 1981. Bar: Ga., US Ct. Mil. Appeals 1961, Supreme Ct. SD 1960, US Supreme Ct. 1968, US Ct. Mil. Review 1983, DC Ct. Appeals 1983, Ga. Ct. Appeals 1988, Supreme Ct. Ga. 1988. Commd. 2d lt. US Army, 1957, chief mil. def. counsel US vs. Calley (My Lai Massacre), 1969—71, chief legal team Inf. Sch. Ft. Benning, Ga., 1969-71, advanced through grades to col. 0-6 JAGC, ret., 1987, staff judge adv. Armor Ctr. Ft. Knox, Ky., 1979—80; dep. staff judge adv. Am. Divsn., Chu Lai, Vietnam, 1968-69; team chief, acting divsn. chief adminstrv. law divsn. Dept. Army, TJAGC, 1971—74, chief criminal law divsn., 1981—84; staff judge adv. Hdqs. 24th Inf. Divsn., Ft. Stewart, Ga., 1974-79; sr. judge Army Ct. Mil. Rev., Falls Church, Va., 1984-87; staff atty. Ga. Ct. Appeals, 1987—2005; ret., 2006. Former chmn., mem. Joint Svc. Com. on Mil. Justice, 1981-84; mem. Mil. Justice Act of 1983 Adv. Commn., 1984-87; army liaison to criminal law sect. ABA, 1981-84. Eagle Scout Boy Scouts Am., 1951. Decorated Legion of Merit, Bronze Star with oak leaf cluster, Meritorious Svc. medal with 2 oak leaf clusters, Joint Svc. Commendation medal, Air medal, Army Commendation medal with oak leaf cluster, Army Achievement medal. Mem.: FBA (chmn. law enforcement liaison com. 1986—87), Ga. Bar Assn. (emeritus mem.), Masons (Scottish Rite 33 degree), Order Ea. Star (worthy grand patron 1999—2000, gen. grand chpt. Order Eastern Star parliamentarian 2003—09, 2012—), Scottish Rite, Royal Order Scotland (hon.), Arturo Reghine Lodge (Italy) (hon.), Theta Xi, Delta Theta Phi. Home: 575 Spender Trace Atlanta GA 30350-5017 Personal E-mail: kalanraby@gmail.com.

RACHOFSKY, HOWARD, retired investor, art collector, patron; m. Cindy Rachofsky, 2000; children: Meghan, Matthew. Former bd. chmn. Regal Securities Investment, L.P. Bd. dirs. Dallas Symphony Assn., Dallas Mus. Art, NYC Dia Ctr. for the Arts, East Dallas Cmty. Sch., Tate Lecture Series, So. Methodist U.; adv. dir. Booker T. Washington Magnet HS for the Performing and Visual Arts, Dallas Theater Ctr., Dallas Archtl. Found., U. Tex. Sch. Architecture; founder, bd. dirs. Dallas Ctr. for the Performing Arts Found., chair, site design com.; mem. adv. bd. Wharton Club, Dallas/Ft. Worth, Dallas Bus. Com. for the Arts; founder Howard Earl Rachofsky Found.; mem. investment com. St. Phillips Acad. Named one of Top 200 Collectors, ARTnews mag., 2003—12. Avocation: Collector of Contemporary Art. Mailing: The Rachofsky House 8605 Preston Rd Dallas TX 75225

RADA, RUTH BYERS, retired dean; b. LA, Oct. 3, 1923; d. George and Gerda Marie (Lihm) Byers; children: Kaaren Ruth, Georgene Melanie. BA, U. Southern Calif., 1944, MA, 1945; EdD, Nova South Eastern U., Davie, Fla., 1976. Asst. dean instrn. and evening East L.A. Coll., 1964-69, dean instrn., 1969-70; dean student personnel L.A. Harbor Coll., 1970-73, East L.A. Coll., 1973-77, L.A. Mission Coll., 1977-83; prof. biol. sci. East L.A. C.C., 1945-69, ret., 1983. Author: Water Biology, 1950, (with others) Human Body in Health and Disease, 1969, Structure and Function of Human Body, 1970, Laboratory Manual for Introductory Microbiology, 1963. Mem. Calif. Cmty. and Jr. Coll. Assn. (area pres. 1973-74), Calif. Woman Adminstrs. Assn., Los Angeles Coll. Adminstrs. Assn. (sec. 1973-74), Phi Beta Kappa, Phi Kappa Phi, Pi Lambda Theta, Phi Sigma. Republican. Mem. Ch. of Religious Sci.

RADEL, TREY (HENRY JUNE RADEL III), former United States Representative from Florida; b. Cin., Apr. 20, 1976; m. Amy Wegmann; 1 child, Henry June IV. BA in Comm. & Italian, Loyola U. Chgo., 1999. Comedian Second City, Chgo.; journalist CBS affiliates, Houston & Chgo.; intern CNN, Atlanta; radio talk show host 92.5 Fox News Radio; anchor WINK-TV, 2007—10, talk show host Daybreak; owner Naples Journal, Fla.; founder Trey Communications LLC; mem. US Congress from 19th Fla. Dist., Washington, 2013—14, US House Fgn. Affairs Com., 2013—14, US House Transp. & Infrastructure Com., 2013—14. Co-founder US Forces Fund. Republican. Roman Catholic. Office Phone: 202-225-2536, 239-252-6225.*

RADEMAKER, STEPHEN GEOFFREY, lobbyist, former federal agency administrator; b. Balt., July 18, 1959; s. Thomas Joseph and Ruth Virginia (Wentz) R.; m. Danielle Pletka; children: Andrew, Olivia, Sophia, Nicola. BA with highest distinction, U. Va., 1981, JD, 1984, MA in Fgn. Affairs, 1985. Bar: Va. 1984, D.C. 1985. Assoc. Covington & Burling LLP, Washington, 1984-86; law clk. to Hon. James L. Buckley US Ct. Appeals (DC Cir.), Washington, 1986; counsel to vice chmn. US Internat. Trade Commn., Washington, 1986-87; spl. asst. to asst. sec. for Inter-American affairs US Dept. State, Washington, 1987-89; dep. legal adv., assoc. counsel to Pres. NSC, Washington, 1989-92; gen. counsel Peace Corps, Washington, 1992-93; minority chief counsel US House Fgn. Affairs Com., Washington, 1993-95; chief counsel US House Internat. Rels. Com., Washington, 1995—2001, dep. staff dir., chief counsel, 2001—02; chief counsel US House Select Com. on Homeland Security, Washington, 2002; asst. sec. for arms control US Dept. State, Washington, 2002—05, acting asst. sec. for internat. security & nonproliferation, 2005—06; dir. nat. security & sr. counsel to Senator Bill Frist US Senate, Washington, 2006—07; sr. counsel BGR Govt. Affairs, Washington, 2007—11; prin. The Podesta Group, Washington, 2011—. Mem. US Commn. on the Prevention of Proliferation of Weapons of Mass Destruction & Terrorism, 2008. Recipient Raven award U. Va., 1984; S. Philip Heiner scholar U. Va., 1983. Mem. Va. Bar Assn., D.C. Bar Assn., Phi Beta Kappa, Omicron Delta Kappa. Republican. Lutheran. Avocations: skiing, bicycling, scuba diving. Office: The Podesta Group 1001 G St NW Ste 900 E Washington DC 20001 Office Phone: 202-448-5238. E-mail: srademaker@podestagroup.com.

RADER, ANGELA NICHOLE, music educator; b. Buckhannon, W.Va., Dec. 28, 1974; d. Paul Douglass and Leda Linette Koon; m. Brent David Rader, July 5, 1997; children: Jordan McKenzie, Landon Matthew. B in Music Edn., W.Va. Wesleyan Coll., 1997. Tchr. Waynesboro City Schs., Va., 1997—98; tchr., band dir. Lexington City Schs., Va., 1998—; music tchr. Fine Arts Rockbridge, 2006—09; dir. handbell choir Trinity Methodist Ch., 2006—. Advisor Waddell Svc. Club, 2004—10; music dir. Trinity United Methodist Ch., 2011—. Mem. Trinity United Meth. Handbell Choir, 2000—. Mem.: Nat. Assn. Music Edn., Va. Music Edn. Choristers Guild Assn. Republican. Methodist. Avocation: flute. Office: Waddell Elem Sch 100 Pendleton Pl Lexington VA 24450 Business E-Mail: arader@lexedu.org.*

RADER, MARIE L., state legislator; b. June 10, 1941; children: Jennifer D. Wilson, Angela D. Ernst. Former mem. McKee City Coun., Jackson County Devel. Assn. & Jackson County Indsl. Authority; former exec. dir. McKee Pub. Housing; self-employed businesswoman; mem. Dist. 89 Ky. House of Reps., 1997—. Republican. Baptist. Mailing: PO Box 323 Mc Kee KY 40447 Office: Ky State Legislature Annex Rm 413C 702 Capitol Ave Frankfort KY 40601 Office Phone: 606-287-3300, 502-564-8100 ext. 720. E-mail: marie.rader@lrc.ky.gov.

RADOVIC, MILADIN, engineering educator, researcher; s. Nedeljko and Milica Radovic. BSME, U. Belgrade, Serbia, 1992, MSME, 1997; PhD in Materials Engring., Drexel U., Phila., 2001. Tchg. asst., rsch. assoc. U. Belgrade, 1992—98; rsch. asst., assoc. dept. materials engring. Drexel U., Phila., 1998—2001; postdoctoral fellow Oak Ridge Nat. Lab., Tenn., 2001—06; asst. prof. dept. mech. engring. Tex. A&M U., College Station, 2006—. Guest scientist Nat. Inst. Stds. and Tech., Gaithersburg, Md., 1991—2001. Recipient A.W. Grosvenor award Acad. Performance, Drexel U., 2001; scholar, Ministry Sci. and Tech. Republic of Serbia, 1993, Gordon Rsch. Conf., Solid State Studies Ceramics, 2001. Mem.: ASM, European Structural Integrity Soc., Am. Ceramic Soc. Achievements include research in processing and characterization of nano-laminated MAX phases; reliability and durability of materials and components for solid oxide fuel cells; processing and characterization of the high-tempera. Office: Texas A&M Univ 3123 Tamu College Station TX 77843-3123 Home: 425 Chimney Hill Dr College Station TX 77840-1833 Office Fax: 979-845-3081. Business E-Mail: mradovic@tamu.edu.

RADVAN, MARTIN, food products executive; V.p., info. tech., Europe Info. Svcs. Internat.; pres., Mars Drinks and Developing Petcare Mars, Inc. Office: Mars Inc 6885 Elm St Mc Lean VA 22101 Office Phone: 703-821-4900. Office Fax: 703-448-9678.

RAFAJKO, ROBERT RICHARD, science administrator; b. Chgo., Sept. 3, 1931; s. Edward Michael and Mildred Eleanor (Simo) R.; m. Mary Ann Filipi, June 24, 1954 (div. 1979); children: Rorie Rae, Ronald Raymond, Robin Rene, Rod Richard, Rebecca Rae.; m. Anne Thorne Sloan, Jan. 26, 1982 (dec. May 13, 2012); 1 son, Andrew Sloan. BA, Coe Coll., Cedar Rapids, Iowa, 1953; MS, U. Iowa, Iowa City, 1958, PhD, 1960. Rsch. assoc. Merck Sharp and Dohme, West Point, Pa., 1960-61; rsch. scientist Microbiol. Assos., Bethesda, Md., 1961-66; v.p., gen. mgr. Med. Rsch. Cons., Rockville, Md., 1966-69; v.p. R & D, N.Am. Biols., Rockville, 1969-74; pres. Biofluids, Inc., Rockville, 1974-99, Bonheur Inc., Keswick, Va., 1999—. Pres. Tysan Serum, Inc., Rockville, 1974-2000, Kytaron Inc, Rockville, 1987-99; breeder thoroughbred horses, 1980—. Contbr. 23 articles to profl. jours. Chmn. PVAAU Swimming Program, Washington, Md. and Va., 1973-76; bd. dirs. Montgomery County Swim League, Montgomery County, Md., 1968-76. Served with USAF, 1954-55. Mem. AAAS, NY Acad. Scis., Am. Soc. Microbiology, Tissue Culture Assn., Am. Horse Council, Horsemans Benevolent and Protective Assn. Republican. Presbyterian. Avocations: scuba diving, photography, travel, stamp collecting/philately. Home and Office: 1349 Queenscroft Keswick VA 22947-2731 Personal E-mail: rafajko421@gmail.com.

RAFFEL, BURTON NATHAN, novelist, poet, translator; b. NYC, 1928; married, six children. BA cum laude, Bklyn. Coll., 1948; MA, Ohio State U., 1949; JD, Yale U., 1958. Lawyer Milbank, Tweed, Hadley & McCloy, NYC, 1958-60; editor Foundation News, 1960-63; instr. English SUNY, Stony Brook, 1964-65, asst. prof. of English, 1965-66, assoc. prof. English Buffalo, 1966-68; prof. English and Classics U. Tex., Austin, 1969-71; sr. tutor, dean Ont. Coll. Art, Toronto, Can., 1971-72; prof. English U. Denver, 1975-87; dir. Adirondack Mountain Found., 1987-89; Disting. prof. arts and humanities, prof. English U. La., Lafayette, 1989—2003; assoc. prof. English U. Haifa, 1968—69. Lectr. English dept. Bklyn. Coll., 1950-51; instr. Ford Found. English Lang. Tchr. Tng. program in Indonesia, resident in Makassar, 1953-55; vis. prof. Humanities York U., Toronto, 1972-75, vis. prof., prof. U. Denver, U. La., Lafayette, 2003, English Emory U., 1974; sr. editor, cons. McDonnell Douglas Computer-Based Systems Tng. Group, Denver, 1985-87; lectr. in law U. Denver, 1986-87. Author: The Development of Modern Indonesian Poetry, 1967, Mia Poems, 1968, The Forked Tongue: A Study of the Translation Process, 1971, Why Re-Create?, 1973, Four Humours, 1979, (film) The Legend of Alfred Packer, 1979, Robert Lowell, 1981, T.S. Eliot, 1982, Changing the Angle of the Sun-Dial, 1984, Grice, 1985, Evenly Distributed Rubble, 1985, Ezra Pound: The Prime Minister of Poetry, 1985, The Art of Translating Poetry, 1988, American Victorians: Exploration in Emotional History, 1984, Possum and Ole Ez in the Public Eye, 1985, After Such Ignorance, 1986, Man as a Social Animal, 1986, Artists All, 1986, Politicians, Poets, and Con Men, 1986, Founder's Fury, 1988, The Art of Translating Poetry, 1988, Founder's Fortune, 1989, From Stress to Stress: An Autobiography of English Prosody, 1992, The Art of Translating Prose, 1994, The Annotated Milton, 1999, Beethoven in Denver and Other Poems, 1999, The Annotated Hamlet, 2003, The Annotated Romeo and Juliet, 2004, Macbeth, 2005, Midsummer Night's Dream, 2005, Othello, 2005, Taming of the Shrew, 2005, The Tempest, 2006, Henry IV, Part One, 2006, The Merchant of Venice, 2006, Julius Ceasar, 2006, Twelfth Night, 2007, King Lear, 2007, Richard III, 2007, Antony and Cleopatra, 2007, Yankee Doric: America Before the Civil War, 2009, Danielle Deronde, 2012; mem. editl. bd. Oral Tradition, 1983—, Literature East and West, 1967-70, (novels) Swan Song, The Bridge Builder, Simps, The Madness of Music; adv. editor The Lit. Rev., 1987-03; reviewer/writer Asian Wall St. Jour., 1978-85; contbr. articles to profl. jours. Mem. Bar of the State of N.Y., The Nat. Faculty. Home: 203 S Mannering Ave Lafayette LA 70508-4829 Business E-Mail: bnraffel@cox.net.

RAFFEL, LEROY B., real estate developer; b. Zanesville, Ohio, Mar. 13, 1927; s. Jacob E. and Anne M. (Oliker) R.; m. Shirley Balbot, Sept. 11, 1949; children: Kenneth, Janet, James, Nancy. BS, U. Pa., 1949. Pres. Raffel Bros., Inc., Youngstown, Ohio, 1949-78, York Mahoning Co., Youngstown, 1950-64, Arby's, Inc., Youngstown, 1964-70, chmn. bd., 1971-79; pres. Brom Equity Devel., Inc., Miami, Fla., 1979—. Served with USNR, 1945-46. Home: 2141 NE 190th Ter North Miami Beach FL 33179-4352 Office: Brom Equity Devel Inc 16375 NE 18 Ave Ste 206 Miami FL 33162 Home Phone: 305-935-2187; Office Phone: 305-949-6445.

RAFUSE, NANCY E., lawyer, shareholder; b. Columbia, SC, Dec. 14, 1966; m. Mark Rafuse; 2 children. BBA cum laude, U. Ga., 1988, JD magna cum laude, 1991. Shareholder, mng. ptnr. Polsinell, Atlanta. Spkr. in field; mem. bar coun. and disciplinary com. No. Dist. Ga., 2002—05. Contbr. articles to profl. jours. Vice chair Atlanta Urban League, 2005—08, mem. bd. dirs., 2001—08, Children's Healthcare Atlanta, 2012—; mem. bd. dirs. audit com. Zoo Atlanta, 2005—12, mem. exec. com., 2010; mem. Atlanta United Way Women's Leadership Coun.; assoc. Employment Law Dept., Atlanta Office, 1991—99, ptnr., 2000—03, Paul, Hastings, Janofsky & Walker chair, 2001—03; mem. Ga. Bar Formal Adv. Opinion Bd., 2008—10. Named one of Georgia's Legal Elite, Georgia Trend mag., 2003—04, Top 40 Lawyers Under 40, Nat. Law Jour., 2005. Mem.: ABA (mem. labor and employment law sect.), Atlanta Bar Assn. (mem. labor and employment law sect.), State Bar Ga. (mem. labor and employment law sect.). Office: Polsinell 1355 Peachtree St Ste 500 Atlanta GA 30309 Office Phone: 404-253-6002. Office Fax: 404-253-6060. E-mail: nancyrafuse@polsinell.com.

RAGADA, REY HOLTBY, hotel executive; b. Amersfoort, Utrecht, Netherlands; 1 child, Jillian. BA in Hotel Mgmt. with honors, Hoge Hotelschool Maastricht, Netherlands, 1996; MA in Business, U. Ky., 2000. CPA. Beverage mgr. The Waldorf-Astoria, NYC, 2001—03; food and beverage mgr. Hilton Antwerp, 2003—09; owner, general mgr. Meriks Hotel & Spa, Paducah, Ky., 2009—; owner Meriks Inn & Suites, Fairfield, NJ. Lectr. various hotel mgmt. courses, 2007—10; cons. in field. Author: (book) Working the Hotel Industry, 2002. Vol. Time Out for Kids, Lexington, Ky., 2004—09, Habitat for Humanity, Pikeville, Ky., 2012—13. Mem.: Coq au Vin (life). Jewish. Avocations: rollerblading, writing, antique weapons. Office: Meriks Hotel & Spa 3240 Lone Oak Rd #131 Paducah KY 42003-0370

RAGAN, ROBERT ALLISON, private investment executive, financial consultant; b. Gastonia, NC, Aug. 21, 1938; s. Caldwell and Jocelyn (Sikes) R. BS in Bus. Adminstrn., U. NC, 1961; postgrad., Stonier Grad. Sch. Banking, 1968. V.p. N.C. Nat. Bank (now Bank of Am.), Charlotte, 1961-81; pres., treas. R.A. Ragan & Co., Inc., Charlotte, 1981—. Dir. Carolina Mills, Inc., Maiden, N.C., 1977—. Author, pub.: The Ragans of Gastonia (1790-1995), 1995, The Textile Heritage of Gaston County, N.C. (1848-2000), 2000, The History of Gastonia and Gaston County, NC, 2010 Founder, pres. bd. govs. The Gaston Soc. of Mecklenburg County, Charlotte, NC, 1999—; mem. North Caroliniana Soc., Chapel Hill; trustee, bd. visitors Darlington Sch., Rome, Ga., 1981—; mem. bd. visitors Daniel Stowe Bot.

Gardens, Belmont, NC, 2001—; pres. bd. trustees Gaston County Mus. Art and History, Dallas, NC, 1978—81, 1997—99. Mem. Charlotte City Club, DeBordieu Colony Country Club (Georgetown, S.C.). Republican. Presbyn. Avocations: preservation and recording of local and North Carolina history, world travel. Home: 227 Fenton Pl Charlotte NC 28207-1913 also: 407 DeBordieu Blvd Georgetown SC 29440 Home: R A Ragan & Co 227 Fenton Pl Charlotte NC 28207-1913

RAGAUSS, PETER A., oil industry executive; B. in mech. engring., Mich. State U., 1980; MBA, Harvard U., 1987. V.p. corp. devel. Tenneco Energy Inc.; v.p. fin. El Paso Energy Internat. Corp.; v.p. fin. & portfolio mgmt. Amoco Energy Internat.; asst to grp. chief exec. BP plc, 1998; CEO Air BP; segment contr. refining & mktg. BP plc, London, 2003—06; sr. v.p. & CFO Baker Hughes, Inc., Houston, 2006—. Office: Baker Hughes Inc PO Box 4740 Houston TX 77210-4740 also: Baker Hughes Inc Ste 2100 2929 Allen Pky Houston TX 77019 Office Phone: 713-439-8600. Office Fax: 713-439-8699.

RAGGIO, THOMAS LOUIS, lawyer; b. Dallas, Sept. 11, 1946; s. Grier H. and Louise (Ballerstadt) R.; m. Janice B. Savage, May 23, 1970; children: Stephen, Kristen. BA, U. Tex., 1968; JD, So. Meth. U., 1971. Bar: US Dist. Ct. (no. dist. Tex.) 1971; cert. family law specialist. Atty. Raggio & Raggio, PLLC, Dallas, 1971—, mng. ptnr., 1985—. Author, spkr. in field of family law. Named one of Best Lawyers in Dallas, D Mag., 2001—09, Best Lawyers in America, 2002—13, Tex. Super Lawyers, Tex. Top 100 Super Lawyers, 2005. Mem. Am. Acad. Matrimonial Lawyers, Tex. Bar Found. Office: Raggio and Raggio PLLC 3316 Oak Grove Ave Ste 100 Dallas TX 75204-2338 Office Phone: 214-880-7500. E-mail: tom@raggiolaw.com.

RAGON, ROBERT RONALD, clergyman; b. Flintstone, Ga., Sept. 10, 1939; s. Robert Emmett and Frances Cora (Stoner) R.; m. Judith Ann Ward, Apr. 27, 1962; children: Ronald Russell, Regina Renee. BS, U. Chattanooga, 1962; BDiv, MDiv, Columbia Theol. Sem., Decatur, Ga., 1967. Ordained to ministry Presbyn. Ch., 1967. Pastor Trion (Ga.) Presbyn. Ch., 1967-72; dir., pastor Chattooga County Presbyn. Ministries, Trion, 1971-72; pastor Brainerd Presbyn. Ch., Chattanooga, 1972—2007. Moderator Knoxville Presbytery, 1979-80; founder An Order of Slaves of Christ, Chattanooga, 1970; stated clk. Presbytery of S.E., 1990-93, moderator, 1995-96, founding bishop Christian Family Ch., 2009. Author: Covenant Agreement: O.S.C., 1970, The Journey, 1990. Trustee King Coll., Bristol, Tenn., 1983-86. Mem. Masons (Ga. chaplain 1980), KT (sec. 1991), Shriners. Republican. Presbyterian. Avocation: investments. Home: 4229 Happy Valley Rd Flintstone GA 30725-2222 Personal E-mail: ragonr@bellsouth.net.

RAHALL, NICK JOE, II, (NICK RAHALL), United States Representative from West Virginia; b. Beckley, W.Va., May 20, 1949; s. Joe and Alice Rahall; m. Melinda Ross; children: Rebecca Ashley, Nick Joe III, Suzanne Nicole. BA, Duke U., Durham, NC, 1971. Asst. to Senator Robert C. Byrd US Senate, 1971-74; sales rep. Sta. WWNR, Beckley, 1974; pres. Mountaineer Travel Co., Beckley, 1975-77; mem. US Congress from 4th W.Va. Dist., Washington, 1977—93, US Congress from 3rd W.Va. Dist., Washington, 1993—; chmn. US House Nat. Resources Com., Washington, 2007—11; pres. W.Va. Broadcasting Corp., 1980—. Bd. dirs. Rahall Comm. Corp.; mem. US Constn. Bicentennial Commn., Mo. Mem. profl. adv. bd. Alsac-St. Jude Children's Rsch. Hosp.; chmn. March of Dimes, W.Va., 1979; del. Dem. Nat. Conv., 1972, 1974, 1978, 1980, 1984, 1988, 1992, 1996. Recipient Achievement award, Logan Cripple Children Soc., 1978, Citizenship award, KC, 1978, Disting. Svc. award, Am. Fedn. Govt. Employees W.Va., 1984, Seneca award, Sierra Club, 1988, River Conservation award, Am. River Assn., 1988; named Young Man of Yr., Beckley Jaycees, 1972, Coal Man of Yr., Coal Industry News, 1979, Young Dem. of Yr., Dem. Nat. Conv., 1980, Outfitter of Yr., Profl. Outfitters, 1987, Son of Yr., W.Va. Soc. of Washington, 1996; named an Outstanding Young Man in W.Va., W.Va. Jaycees, 1977. Mem.: NAACP, NRA (life), Blue Dog Coalition, Shriners, Elks, Masons (33rd degree), Moose. Democrat. Presbyterian. Office: US House of Representatives 2307 Rayburn House Office Bldg Washington DC 20515 also: 220 Dingess St Logan WV 25601 Office Phone: 202-225-3452. Business E-Mail: nrahall@mail.house.gov.*

RAI, ARTI K., law educator; b. Kanpur, India, Nov. 17, 1966; came to U.S., 1973; d. J.P.Srivastava and Jagdish Bains. BA magna cum laude, in biochemistry and hist., Harvard U., 1983-87; student, Harvard Med. Sch., 1987-88; JD cum laude, Harvard U., 1991. Bar: Pa. 1993, D.C. 1994. Law clk. to Hon. Marilyn Hall Patel US Dist. Ct. (northern dist.) Calif., San Francisco, 1991-92; atty. Jenner & Block LLP, Washington, 1992-94, US Dept. Justice, Washington, 1994-95; lectr. law & medicine U. Chgo., 1995-96; faculty fellow Harvard U., Cambridge, Mass., 1996-97; assoc. prof. law U. San Diego Law Sci., 1997—2001, U. Pa. Law Sch., Phila., 2001—03; prof. law Duke Law Sch., Durham, NC, 2003—08, Elvin R. Larry prof. law, 2008—; adminstr. external affairs US Patent & Trademark Office, US Dept. Commerce, Washington, 2009—10. Vis. prof. law sch. Yale U., 2004, Harvard U., 2007; chair Duke U. Patent Policy Com., 2008-09 Co-author: Law and Mental Health System, 2009, editor, Intellectual Property & Biotechnology: Clinical Concepts; contbr. articles to profl. jours. John Harvard scholar, 1986, 87; Nat. Merit scholar. Mem. ABA (chair intellectual property com. of adminstrv. law sect., 2007-). Office: Duke Law Rm 3022 Box 90360 Durham NC 27708 Business E-Mail: rai@law.duke.edu.

RAIJMAN, ISAAC, gastroenterologist, educator; b. Empalme, Sonora, Mex., July 6, 1959; arrived in US, 1985, naturalized, 2000; s. Jose and Amalia (Langsam) R. MD, Nat. Autonomous U., Mexico City, 1985; postgrad., U. Wis., Milw., 1985—89, U. Tex., Houston, 1989—92. Diplomate Am. Bd. Internal Medicine, Am. Bd. Gastroenterology. Resident in medicine Mt. Sinai Hosp., Milw., 1986-88, chief resident, 1989; fellow in therapeutic endoscopy Wellesley Hosp., U. Toronto, 1992—93; rsch. fellow in gastroenterology U. Tex., Houston, 1989-90, clin. fellow, 1990-92, asst. prof. medicine, 1993-97, dir. therapeutic endoscopy, 1993-97, asst. prof. M.D. Anderson Cancer Ctr., 1993—2000, dir. ann. therapeutic endoscopy course, 1995-97, dir. therapeutic endoscopy, 2002—, assoc. prof. Houston, 2002—, Baylor Coll. Medicine, Houston, 2005—, U. Houston, 2005—. Chair Ann. Therapeutic Endoscopy Meeting; chair gastroenterology and endoscopy sub. com., GI subcom. on endoscopic credentialing and quality assurance Hermann Hosp., Houston, co-chief dept. gastroenterology St. Luke's Hosp., Houston. Author: Pancreas, 1993, Bockus Textbook of Gastroenterology, 1993; also numerous articles; reviewer jours. in field. Fellow Am. Gastroenterology Assn.; mem. Am. Coll. Gastroenterology, Internat. Assn. Pancreatology, Am. Soc. Gastrointestinal Endoscopy, Am. Soc. Internal Medicine. Jewish. Avocation: painting. Office: 6620 Main Ste 1510 Houston TX 77030 Office Phone: 713-795-4444. Personal E-mail: raijman.i@gmail.com.

RAIMER, BEN G., pediatrician, public health service officer; b. Woodville, Tex., Dec. 23, 1946; s. Abner Martin and Ollie Odom Raimer; m. Sharon Smith Smith, May 22, 1976; children: Anna Elizabeth, David William, Lauren Allison. BS, East Tex. Bapt. Coll., Marshall, 1969; MA in Human Genetics, U. Tex., Galveston, 1970, MD, 1974. Cert. Am. Bd. Pediat., 1979. Pediatrician, mng. ptnr. Galveston County Pediat. Assocs., Tex. City, 1977—93; v.p. and CEO cmty. health svcs. U. Tex. Med. Br., Galveston, 1993—2007. Chmn. Tex. Statewide Health Coordinating Coun., Austin, 1997—2007, Tex. Correctional Manage Health Care Com., Huntsville, 1998—2003; mem. Tex. Health Inst., Austin, 1998—2007; vice chmn. Galveston Bd. Health. Author: (medicine) Various. Dir. emeritus Communities Joined in Action, Tampa, Fla., 2007; presdl. elector Rep. Party, Austin, 1988; chmn. Rep. Party Galveston County, 1984—94; chmn. bd. dirs. Galveston C. of C., 2007—. Recipient Ray Helfer Award (Child Abuse Prevention), Am. Acad. of Pediat., 1998, Martin Luther King Jr Humanitarian Award, Kingfest Galveston Com., 2007, Disting. Alumnus Award, Grad. Sch. of Biomedical Sciences, UTMB, 2004, J. Wesley Smith Achievement Award, East Tex. Bapt. U., 1999, Ashbel Smith Disting. Alumnus Award, UTMB Sch. of Medicine, 2004, Best Doctors in Am., Best Doctors in Am., 2003-2004, 2005-2006, 2007-2008, Nicholas and Katherine Leone Award, Adminstrv. Excellence, U. of Tex. Med. Br., 1998, Sealy Soc. Mustard Seed Award, UTMB Sealy Soc., 1996, Thinking Positively for Health, Tex. Pub. Health Assn., 2006. Fellow: Am. Acad. Pediat.; mem.: AMA, Am. Correctional Health Profls., Am. Telemedicine Assn., Tex. Pediat. Soc. (life), Tex. Rural Health Assn., Soc. for Pediat. Dermatology, Arty. Club (life; pres. 1997—98). Conservative. Baptist. Avocations: travel, photography, reading, hiking, camping. Office: U Tex Med Br 301 University Blvd Adminstrn Ste 5118 Galveston TX 77550 Office Fax: 409-772-9935. Business E-Mail: bgraimer@utmb.edu.

RAIMI, BURTON LOUIS, lawyer; b. Detroit, May 5, 1938; s. Irving and Rae (Abel) Raimi; m. Judith Morse, Mar. 31, 1963 (div. Mar. 1985); children: Diane L., and Matthew D. BA, Brandeis U., 1960; JD, U. Mich., 1963; LLM, George Washington U., 1964. Bar: Mich. 1963, D.C. 1964, Fla. 1991, U.S. Ct. Appeals (4th, 7th, 8th, 9th, 10th, 11th and DC cirs.), U.S. Ct. of Fed. Claims, U.S. Supreme Ct. Atty. appelate ct. sect. NLRB, Washington, 1964-69; assoc. Morgan, Lewis & Bockius, Washington, 1969-71; dep. gen. counsel FDIC, Washington, 1971-78; ptnr. Rosenman and Colin, Washington, 1978-86, Dechert Price & Rhoads, Washington, 1986-93; shareholder McCaffrey & Raimi, P.A., Naples and Sarasota, Fla., 1994—2002, Law Offices of Burton L. Raimi PA, Sarasota, Fla., 2003—05; gen. counsel Washington Mgmt. Corp., 2005—07, Law Offices Burtow L. Raimi, 2007—. Spkr. various insts. Mem. ABA (past chmn. bank receiverships subcom. of banking com.), D.C. Bar Assn. (past chmn. banking law com., com. on interest on lawyers trust accounts), Fla. Bar (bus. law com.), Am. Arbitration Assn. (panel of arbitrators), Nat. Arbitration Forum (arbitrator). Avocations: travel, golf, fishing. Office: 8499 S Tamiami Trail No 266 Sarasota FL 34238 Office Phone: 941-927-1603. Office Fax: 941-927-1703. Business E-Mail: burt@moneylaw.com.

RAINA, ROBIN, information technology executive; Degree in Indsl. Engring., Thapar U., Punjab, India. Sr. mgmt. positions Mindware and BPR Inc., 1990—97; v.p., profl. svcs. Ebix, Inc., 1997, sr. v.p., sales & mktg., 1998, exec. v.p., COO, 1998, pres., CEO, 1999—, chmn., 2002—; pres., CEO EbixExchange (subs. of Ebix, Inc.), 1999—, chmn., 2002—. Bd. dirs. EbixExchange (subs. Ebix, Inc.), 2000—, Ebix, Inc., 2000—. Recipient South Asian Personality of the Yr. award, Sony TV, 2008. Office: Ebix Inc 5 Concourse Pkwy Ste 3200 Atlanta GA 30328 Office Phone: 678-281-2020. Office Fax: 678-281-2019. Business E-Mail: rraina@ebix.com.

RAINES, DEBORAH A., neonatal/perinatal nurse specialist, educator, nursing researcher, consultant; BSN, Syracuse U., NY, 1978; MSN, U. Pa., Phila., 1982; PhD, Med. Coll. Va. at Va. Commonwealth U., Richmond, 1992. Disting. practitioner, Nat. Acads. Practice, 2004. Nursing edn. coord., perinatal nurse specialist George Wash. U. Med. Ctr., Washington, 1984—89; nurse, maternal infant nurse Med. Coll. Va. Hosps., Richmond, 1992—98; asst. to assoc. prof. Va. Commonwealth U., Richmond, 1992—2000; prof. Fla. Atlantic U., Boca Raton, Fla., 2000—10. Cmty. svc. assoc. Va. Commonwealth U., 1997—99; online tchg. liaision Fla. Atlantic U., 2001—04, dir., principle investigator, 2003—06, dir. accelerated second degree program, 2003—06, freshman reading program leader, 2007—, dir. scholarship tchg., 2009—; cons. Palm Healthcare Found., West Palm Beach, Fla., 2004—12; grad. faculty Maryville U., 2012—13; faculty U. Buffalo, 2013—; visionary leader VCU, 2013. Editor: (book) Perinatal Secrets, 2004; author: The Quick Study for Nursing, 2007; contbr. articles to profl. jours. Bd. mem. Karen Slattery Early Edn. Devel. Rsch. Ctr., Boca Raton, Fla., 2003—07. Recipient Excellence in Edn. award, Soc. Pediat. Nurses, 2002, Disting. Tchr. the Yr., Fla. Atlantic U., 2004, Excellence in Undergraduate Tchg. award, 2005, Cmty. Ptnr. award, Palm Health Care Found., 2006, Excellence in Online Tchg. award, e-College Internat., 2007, Faculty Svc. award, TIAA/CREF, 2007, Outstanding Alumni award, Med. Coll. Va., 2007. Mem.: Nat. League for Nursing, Assn. Women's Health Obstet. and Neonatal Nurses (Mediallion of Excellence 2000), Sigma Theta Tau (Evidence Based Practice award 2007). Avocations: travel, reading, theater, music. E-mail: deborah.raines.phd@gmail.com.

RAINES, J. PAUL, computer company executive; Staff consumer products group Kurt Salmon Associates, 1986—96; global sourcing positions L.L. Bean, 1996—2000; various retail ops. mgmt. positions including exec. v.p. US stores and pres. Southern divsn, Home Depot Inc., 2000—08; COO GameStop Corp., Grapevine, Tex., 2008—10, CEO, 2010—. Office: GameStop Corp 625 Westport Pky Grapevine TX 76051 Office Phone: 817-424-2000. Office Fax: 817-424-2002. Business E-Mail: paulraines@gamestop.com.

RAINES, JEFF, biomedical scientist, medical research director; b. NYC, Sept. 5, 1943; s. Otis J. and Mildred C. (Wetzler) Raines; children: Gretchen Christena, Victoria Jean. BSME, Clemson U., 1965; MME, U. Fla., 1967; PhD in Biomed. Engring., MIT, 1972. Mem. staff MIT, Cambridge, 1968—70; biophysicist dept. surgery Mass. Gen. Hosp., Boston, 1972—77, dir. Vascular Lab., 1972—77; instr. surgery Harvard Med. Sch., Boston, 1973—77; preceptor Harvard/MIT Sch. Health Scis., 1976—77; rsch. dir., dir. Vascular Lab. Miami (Fla.) Heart Inst., Miami Beach, 1977—88; adj. prof. bioengring. U. Miami, Coral Gables, 1977—; prof. surgery U. Miami (Fla.) Sch. Medicine, 1977—; with Miami Vein Ctr., 2004—. Prin. investigator series NIH programs and pharm. firms, 1977—; Harvard Travelling fellow lectr. in Europe, 1975. Contbr. numerous articles on biomechanics, cardiovasc. diagnosis, dynamics and instrumentation to sci. jours. Recipient Apollo Achievement award, NASA, 1969; fellow, NIH, 1972. Fellow: Am. Assn. Physicists in Medicine, Am. Coll. Radiology, Am. Coll. Cardiology; mem.: ASME, AAAS, Cardiovasc. Sys. Dynamics Soc. (founding mem., editor 1976—, pres. 1980—82), Internat. Cardiovasc. Soc., Instrument Soc. Am., Biomed. Engring. Soc., New Eng. Cardiovasc. Soc., Am. Heart Assn., MIT Club, Harvard Club, Coral Gables Club, Kiwanis, Sigma Xi, Tau Beta Pi. Republican. Presbyterian. Achievements include patents for medical devices; development of mathematical models of arterial hemodynamics and clinical use of autotransfusion. Home Phone: 305-246-0333; Office Phone: 305-987-0922, 305-668-3221. Personal E-mail: drjraines@yahoo.com.

RAINES, STEPHEN SAMUEL, franchising, consulting and development firm executive, lawyer; b. LA, Aug. 2, 1945; s. Harold Charles and Florence (Pynoos) S.; m. Judith Amanda Masterson, July 18, 1981; children: Jennifer, Jeffrey. BA, UCLA, 1967; JD, Loyola U., Los Angeles, 1971. Bar: Calif. Assoc. Thorpe, Sullivan, Clinnin & Workman, Los Angeles, 1971-75; v.p., gen. counsel United Rent-All, Inc., Los Angeles, 1975-80; pres. UDC Properties, Inc., LA, 1977-80, Nat. Franchise Assocs., Inc., Atlanta, 1980—. V.p. and bd. dirs. M&R Advt., Inc., Atlanta; franchising cons. U.S. SBA, Atlanta, 1982—, Ga. Bus. Devel. Ctrs., Atlanta, 1982—; instr. Loyola U., L.A., 1971-72, L.A. Community Colls., 1972-75, U.S. Sml. Bus. Devel., Atlanta, 1982—, Ga. State U., Atlanta, 1982—; instr. leadership program Ga. Vietnam Vets., Atlanta, 1982—. Contbr. numerous articles regarding franchising to newspapers and profl. jours. Bd. dirs., sec. Vets. Resource Bus. Council, Atlanta, 1986. Served with USAR, 1968-74. Law fellow Loyola Law Sch. of L.A., 1970-71; recipient State of Ga. Bus. Adv. of Yr. award, 1987, Ga. Outstanding Citizen award, 1987. Mem. ABA, Calif. Bar Assn., Internat. Bar Assn., U.S. Supreme Ct. Bar Assn., Atlanta C. of C., Atlanta Venture Capital Forum (charter), Am. Mgmt. Assn., Gwinnett County C. of C. Office: Nat Franchise Assocs Inc 240 Lake View Ct Lavonia GA 30553-2018

RAINEY, GORDON FRYER, JR., lawyer; b. Oklahoma City, Apr. 26, 1940; s. Gordon F. and Esther (Bliss) R.; m. Selina Norman, Aug. 3, 1968; children: Kate, Melissa, Gordon III. BA in English, U. Va., 1962, LLB, 1967. Bar: Okla. 1967, Va. 1968. Assoc. Rainey, Flynn, Wallace, Ross & Cooper, Oklahoma City, 1967-68, Hunton & Williams LLP, Richmond, Va., 1968-75, ptnr., 1975—, chmn. exec. com., 1994—2006. Chmn. emeritus Hunton & Williams; sr. trustee, Colonial Williamberg Found.; dir., Brown Adv. Holdings Inc., Brown Investment Adv. & Trust Co., Brown Adv. Funds PLC; bd. visitors, past rector U. Va. Past pres. U. Va. Alumni Assn., chair, UVA Capital Campaign; trustee, Va. Found. Ind. Colls.; mem. Gov.'s Blue Ribbon Commn. on Higher Edn.; campaign chmn. United Way of Greater Richmond, 1982, trustee, 1981-84; bd. dirs., past pres. Sheltering Arms Hosp., 1984; trustee Sheltering Arms Found.; chmn. Gov.'s Econ. Devel. Adv. Coun. Dist. 12; mem. Gov.'s Adv. Com. for Va. Strategy on Econ. Devel.; mem. Bd. Housing and Cmty. Devel.; past mem. bd. govs. St. Catherine's Sch.; past chmn. bd. dirs. Leadership Met. Richmond.; past pres., bd. dirs. Met. Bus. Found. 1st lt. U.S. Army, 1962-64, Korea. Recipient Disting. Grad. award Casady Sch., Humanitarian award Nat. Conf. Cmty. and Justice, 2003, Disting. Alumni award U. Va. Coll. Found., 2005, Ukrop Cmty. Vision award, 2006, Samuel Crockett award, U. Va. Coll., Wise, Svc. award Young Alumni Coun. U. VA. Mem. ABA (sect. on bus. law, banking law com., com. on devel. in investment svcs.), Richmond Metro C. of C. (bd. dirs., past chmn.), Commonwealth Club, Country Club of Va., The Brook (NYC), Forum Club (Richmond), 3 Creek Golf Club, Jackson Republican. Episcopalian. Office: Hunton & Williams Riverfront Plz East Tower PO Box 1535 Richmond VA 23219-4074 Home Phone: 804-353-3004; Office Phone: 804-788-8275. Office Fax: 804-788-8218. Business E-Mail: grainey@hunton.com.

RAINEY, JOHN DAVID, federal judge; b. Freeport, Tex., Feb. 10, 1945; s. Frank Anson and Jewel Lorene (Hortman) R.; m. Judy Davis, Aug. 17, 1968; children: John David Jr., Jacob Matthew, Craig Thomas. BBA, So. Meth. U., 1967, JD, 1972. Bar: Tex. 1972, US Dist. Ct. (northern dist.) Tex. 1974, US Tax Ct. 1974, US Ct. Appeals (5th cir.) 1981, US Supreme Ct. 1981, US Dist. Ct. (southern dist.) Tex. 1986. Assoc. Taylor, Mizell, Price, Corrigan & Smith, Dallas, 1973-79; ptnr. Gilbert, Gilbert & Rainey, Angleton, Tex., 1979-82, Rainey & LeBoeuf, Angleton, 1982-86; judge 149th Dist. Ct., Brazoria County, Tex., 1987-90, US Dist. Ct. (southern dist.) Tex., 1990—2010, sr. judge, 2010—. Bd. dirs. Angleton Bank of Commerce. Mem. City of Angleton Planning & Zoning Commn., 1981-84; mem. Angleton Charter Rev. Commn., 1984, chmn. 1982. Served with US Army, 1969-70. Mem. State Bar Tex., Brazoria County Bar Assn. (pres. 1983-84). Lodges: Lions (pres. Angleton 1986-87). Methodist. Avocations: hunting, fishing, woodworking. Office: US Dist Ct 312 S Main St Rm 406 Victoria TX 77901

RAINS, JOHN W., food service executive; BS in Ins. & Risk Mgmt., Ohio State U., 1979. Corp. mgr. human resources, corp. risk mgr. Coca-Cola Enterprises, Inc., 1983—95; dir. corp. benefits & ins. CIBA Vision, 1995—97; v.p. compensation and benefits Cracker Barrel Old Country Store, Inc., 1999—. Office: Cracker Barrel Old Country Store Inc 307 Hartmann Dr Lebanon TN 37087 Office Phone: 615-444-5533. Office Fax: 615-443-9818.

RAINS, MARY JO, banker; b. Konawa, Okla., Oct. 27, 1935; d. Albert Wood and Mary Leona (Winfield) Starns; m. Billy Z. Rains, June 17, 1956; one child, Nicky Z. Student, Okla. Sch. Banking, 1969, Seminole Jr. Coll., 1970—72, East Ctrl. State U., 1978—79; diploma, Am. Inst. Banking, 1981—83; student, Okla. State U., 1987, Adult Vocat. Tech. Ctr., Pontotoc County, 1987. With acctg. divsn. Universal C.I.T., Okla. City, 1953—56; cashier Okla. State Bank (now Bancfirst), Konawa, 1957—89, sr. v.p., 1989—95; sr. v.p., br. mgr. Bancfirst, Konawa, 1995—2002; bd. sec. Seminole County Election Bd., Okla., 2003—. Mem. cmty. bd. dirs. Bancfist, Konawa, 2006—. Sec. First Bapt. Ch., Konawa, Okla. 1969-79, budgeting com., 1982-92, 2006-, chmn. fin. com., 1994-2004, 06-, lectureship adminstr.; fin. bd. Kennedy Libr., 1997—; bd. dir. Sacred Heart Mission Hist. Soc.; mem. exec. bd. Ctrl. Okla. Family Med. Ctr., 2004-2008, fin. com., 2004-. Mem. Okla. Bankers Assn. (dir. women's divsn. 1974-76), Konawa C. of C., Am. Legion, Wewoka C. of C. Office: Courthouse Ste 101 Wewoka OK 74884 Home: 35204 EW 1410 Rd Konawa OK 74849-5508 Office Phone: 405-257-2786.

RAINWATER, RICHARD EDWARD, retired investor; b. Ft. Worth, June 15, 1944; m. Karen Rainwater, 1975 (div. 1991); children: Courtney, Todd, Matthew; m. Darla Dee Moore, Dec. 13, 1991. BA in Math., U. Tex., 1966; MBA in Finance & Mktg., Stanford U., 1968. With Goldman, Sachs & Co., NYC, Dallas; chief financial arch. Bass Orgn., Ft. Worth, 1970-86; ind. investor Ft. Worth, 1986-94; founder ENSCO Internat. Inc., 1986; co-founder Columbia Hosp. Corp. (now Columbia/HCA Healthcare Corp.), 1988, Mid Ocean Ltd.; founder, chmn. Crescent Real Estate Equities, Inc., Ft. Worth, 1994. Spkr. Harvard Bus. Sch., Stanford U., U. Tex. Bus. Sch. Appeared on cover of Bus. Week mag., Oct. 1986; recipient Man of Yr. award, 1989, Kupfer Disting. Exec. award Tex. A&M U., 1991, Golden Plate award American Acad. Achievement, 1992, Ernest C. Arbuckle award Stanford Bus. Sch. Allumni Assn., 2010; named one of The Forbes 400: Richest Americans, 2006-. Office: Crescent Real Estate Equities Co 777 Main St Fort Worth TX 76102-5304

RAISIG, PAUL JONES, JR., lawyer; b. Jamestown, NY, June 21, 1932; s. Paul Jones and Marian Elizabeth (Christian) R.; m. Carolyn Virginia Sides, June 12, 1955; children: Dawn Virginia, Paul Christian, Anne Sibley. B.G.E., U. Nebr., 1961; MBA, U. Ala., 1965; JD, Campbell U., 1989. Bar: NC, 1989, US Supreme Ct. 1992. Commd. 2d lt. U.S. Army, 1953, advanced through grades to col., 1973, ret., 1977, served in Vietnam, 1963, btn. comdr., Vietnam, 1968; dep. dir. U.S. Army Reorganization, 1973; v.p. Armed Forces Relief and Benefit Assn., Washington, 1977-79; sr. cons. Dept. Def., Washington, 1979-80; exec. dir. Am. Fedn. Info. Processing Socs., Arlington, Va., 1980-84; v.p., dir. Designs, Ltd., Alexandria, Va., 1985-86; ptnr.

Barrington, Herndon & Raisig, P.A., Fayetteville, NC, 1989-92. Adj. prof. bus. law and bus. mgmt. Campbell U., 1992-2004; cons. in field; mediator for Superior Ct. and arbitrator for Dist. Ct. Decorated Legion of Merit (3), Bronze Star medal (2), Air medal (5), Purple Heart (2), Meritorious Service medal, Army Commendation medal with V Device (3), Combat Inf. badge. Mem. U.S. Coun. for World Comms., Beta Gamma Sigma. Home and Office: Carolina House Carry 111 MacArthur Dr Apt #201 Cary NC 27513

RAJKOWSKI, E. MARK, corporate financial executive; BS, Lehigh Univ. CPA NY, NJ, Pa. Positions through mng. ptnr. Pricewaterhouse Coopers LLP, 1981—98; corp. contr. Eastman Kodak Co., 1998—2001, v.p. fin., 2001—03, COO consumer digital bus., 2003, v.p., gen. mgr. worldwide ops imaging systems, 2004; sr. v.p., CFO MeadWestvaco Corp., Glen Allen, Va., 2004—. Bd. dir. Performance Technologies Inc. Mem.: Fin. Executives Inst., Am. Inst. CPAs. Office: MeadWestvaco Corp 501 S 5th St Richmond VA 23219-0501

RAJU, DAN, brokerage house executive; MS in Computer Sci., U. Miss.; BSChemE, JN Tech. U., India. Sr. info. tech. position NCR Corp., Safety-Kleen, Charming Shoppes; sr. dir. tech. infrastructure and ops. Borders Group Inc.; assoc. v.p. global tech. infrastructure & ops. AP; chief info. officer TradeKing, Charlotte, NC. Office: TradeKing PO Box 49050 Charlotte NC 28277-3432

RALEY, JOHN WESLEY, JR., lawyer; b. May 23, 1932; s. John Wesley and Helen Thames; children: John Wesley III, Robert Thames. AB, Okla. Baptist U., 1954, HHD (hon.), 2012; JD, U. Okla., 1959. Bar: Okla. 1959, U.S. Supreme Ct. 1973, U.S. Ct. Appeals (10th cir.), 1962, U.S. Dist. Ct. (we. dist.) Okla. 1961, U.S. Dist. Ct. (no. dist.) Okla. 1988, U.S. Dist. Ct. (ea. dist.) Okla. 1989. Asst. U.S. atty. We. Dist. Okla. U.S. Dept. Justice, 1961-69; ptnr. Northcutt, Raley, Clark and Gardner, Ponca City, Okla., 1969-90; U.S. atty. Ea. Dist. Okla. U.S. Dept. Justice, 1990-97; of counsel Northcutt, Clark, Gardner & Hron, Ponca City, 1997—; mcpl. ct. judge Ponca City, 2001—05. Mayor of Ponca City, Okla., 1980-83; mem. Okla. Ethics Commn., 2002—12, chmn., 2005-06, 2008-09. Capt. USNR, 1950-84, ret., Surface Warfare Officer. Recipient George Washington Honor medal Freedoms Found. at Valley Forge, 1971, Meritorious Achievement award, U.S. Dept. Justice, 1993, Spl. Initiative award, 1994, Outstanding Alumni Achievement award Okla. Bapt. U., 1981, Outstanding Citizen award Ponca City, 1984. Fellow Am. Coll. Trial Lawyers; mem. ABA, Am. Bd. Trial Advs. (pres. Okla. chpt. 2005), Okla. Bar Assn. (bd. govs. 1988-90), Kay County Bar Assn. (pres. 1980), Am. Legion, Masons, Res. Officers Assn., VFW. Republican. Southern Baptist. Office: 400 E Central Ave Ste 401 Ponca City OK 74601-5428 Address: PO Box 1412 Ponca City OK 74602-1412 Office Phone: 580-762-1655.

RALL, WILFRID, neuroscientist, researcher, artist; b. LA, Aug. 29, 1922; s. Udo and Doris (Keiser) R.; m. Ava Lou Freed, 1946 (dec.); children: Sarah E., Madelyn Rall Badger; m. Mary Ellen Condon, 1983. BS summa cum laude, Yale U., 1943; MS, U. Chgo., 1948; PhD, U. N.Z., 1953. Jr. physicist Manhattan Project U. Chgo., 1943-46, biophysics fellow, 1946-48; lectr., sr. lectr. physiology, biophysics U. Otago, Dunedin, N.Z., 1949-56; head biophysics divsn. Naval Med. Rsch. Inst., Bethesda, Md., 1956-57; biophysicist, office math. rsch. Nat. Inst. Arthritis and Metabolic Diseases, Bethesda, 1957-67; sr. rsch. physicist math. rsch. br. Nat. Inst. Diabetes and Digestive and Kidney Diseases, 1967-94; scientist emeritus Nat. Insts. Health, 1994—. Mem. NRC Com. on Brain Scis., 1968-73. Contbr. articles to profl. jours. Fellow: Am. Acad. Arts and Sciences; mem.: Soc. Neurosci. (Swartz prize 2008). Achievements include being an amateur sculptor.

RALLS, W. MATTHEW, energy executive; BME, MBA, U. Tex., Austin. Various positiions including exec. v.p. Nations Bank, San Antonio; exec. v.p., CFO, dir. Kelley Oil Corp., 1990-96; v.p., calital markets & corp. devel. Meridian Resource Corp., 1996-97; v.p., treas. Global Marine, Inc., 1997—2001, CFO, 1997—2005, sr. v.p., 1999—2005; sr. v.p., CFO GlobalSantaFe Corp., 2001—05, exec. v.p., COO, 2005—07; CEO, pres., bd. dirs. Rowan Companies, Inc., 2009—. Former bd. dirs. El Paso Ptnrs., Enterprise Products Ptnrs. LP, Enterprise Products, GP; bd. dirs. Complete Prodn. Svcs., Inc., 2005—. Office: Rowan Companies Inc 2800 Post Oak Blvd Ste 5450 Houston TX 77056 Office Phone: 713-621-7800. Office Fax: 713-960-7560. Business E-Mail: w.ralls@rowancompanies.com.

RALSTON, DAVID EDMUND, state legislator; b. Ellijay, Ga., Mar. 14, 1954; s. David Willard Ralston and Ernestine Pettit Ralaston; m. Jane Burt. Former State Senator, Dist 51, Ga.; former dir. 9th Dist. Young Repub., Ga.; former mem. State Repub. Ctrl. Com., Ga., Appropriations Com.; former sec. Judiciary & Agr. Com.; former mem. Edn Com., Transp. & Youth com., Aging & Human Ecol Com.; alt. del. Repub. Nat Conv., 1972; staff aid John Savage for Lieutenant Gov. Campaign, 1974; atty. David Ralston; state senate Ga.; state rep.Dist 6 Ga., 2003—04; state rep.Dist 7 Ga., 2004—; spkr. of house Ga., 2010—. Recipient Georgia Del. to US Senate Youth Prog., William Randolph Hearst Found., 1972. Mem.: Georgia Conservency. Republican. Baptist. Mailing: 404 Legis Office Bldg Atlanta GA 30334 Office: PO Box 1196 Blue Ridge GA 30513

RAM, ANDY, professional tennis player; b. Montevideo, Uruguay, Apr. 10, 1980; s. Ami and Diana Ram; m. Shiri Ram, Sept. 12, 2006. Profl. tennis player ATP, 1998—. Co-founder Jewish Sports Found., 2007—. Achievements include winning 13 career doubles titles, ATP; winning Australian Open to become first Israeli doubles tennis team (with Jonathan Erlich) to win a Grand Slam title, 2008. Avocation: soccer. Office: Renaissance Tennis Mgmt 3111 University Dr Ste 601 Coral Springs FL 33065

RAM, CHITTA VENKATA, physician; b. Machilipatnam, India, Oct. 24, 1948; s. Chitta M. Row and Chitta (Cheruvu) Sarojini; m. Ashalata Ram, Feb. 17, 1979; children: Gita, Radha. B.Sci, Marathwada U., Aurangabad, India, 1966; MD, Osmania U., Hyderabad, India, 1972. Diplomate Am. Bd. Internal Medicine. Resident in internal medicine Brown U., R.I. Hosp., Providence, 1974-76; fellow in hypertension Hosp. U. Pa., Phila., 1976-77; faculty assoc. U. Tex. Southwestern Med. Ctr., Dallas, 1977-78, asst. prof., 1978-83, assoc. prof., 1983-89, prof. internal medicine, 1989—. Dir. Tex. Blood Pressure Inst., Dallas; dir. rsch. and edn. Dallas Nephrology Assocs.; hypertension unit St. Paul Med. Ctr., Dallas, dir. continuing med. edn. dept., 1996-98, chmn. instnl. rev. com., 1996-98, pres. med. staff, 1997-98; dir. Tex. Blood Pressure Inst., Dallas. Contbr. numerous articles to profl. jours. and chpts. to textbooks; editl. cons., reviewer numerous nat. and internat. jours. and pubs. Pres. Tex. IndoAm. Physician Soc., Dallas, 1988; trustee Dallas/Ft. Worth Hindu Temple Soc., Dallas, 1988. Named Outstanding Tchr. St. Paul Med. Ctr., 1982; recipient Mother of India award, 1992. Master ACP; fellow Am. Coll. Cardiology, Am. Coll. Chest Physicians (regent), Am. Coll. Clin. Pharmacology; mem. Am. Assn. Physicians from India (pres.-elect 1994-95, pres. 1995-96), Tex. Indo-Am. Physicians Soc. Home: 1420 Viceroy Dr Dallas TX 75235 Office Phone: 214-358-2300. E-mail: ramv@dneph.com.

RAMADAN, DAVID I., state legislator; b. Beirut, Lenanon, May 31, 1970; m. Christie K. Wray. BA in Govt. and Politics, George Mason U., 1993, MA in Internat. Transactions, 1995. Mem. Dist. 87 Va. House of Delegates, 2012—, mem. Privileges and Elections Com. & Sci. and Tech. Com. Mem.: NRA, Va. Citizens Def. League, Loudoun County C. of C., Internat. Franchise Assn. Republican. Office: General Assembly Building PO Box 406 Richmond VA 23218 also: 25050 Riding Plaza, #130-650 South Riding VA 20152 Office Phone: 804-698-1087. Office Fax: 804-698-6787. E-mail: DelDRamadan@house.virginia.gov.

RAMADAN, HASSAN H., medical educator; b. Beirut, Feb. 21, 1956; s. Husni Ramadan and Kawkab Masri; children: Jad, Rayya. MD, Am. U. Beirut, Lebanon, 1982. Cert. in otolaryngology Am. Bd. Otolaryngology, 2001. Prof. W.Va. U., Morgantown, 1991—. Recipient Tchg. and Achievement award, Am. Acad. Otolaryngology. Fellow: Am. Rhinology Assn. Office: WVa Univ PO Box 9200 Morgantown WV 26506

RAMAGE, JAMES ALFRED, history professor; b. Paducah, Ky., May 6, 1940; s. Willis Newman and Lora Helen Ramage; m. Judith Ann Winstead, June 6, 1964; 1 child, Andrea Susanne Watkins. BS, Murray State U., Ky., 1965, MA, 1968; PhD, U. Ky., Lexington, 1972. Tchr. history Mehlville H.S., St. Louis, 1965—67; prof. history No. Ky. U., Highland Heights, Ky., 1972—. Author: John Wesley Hunt, 1974, Rebel Raider, 1986 (Freeman award, 1986), Gray Ghost, 1999 (History Book Club selection), Morgan's Great Raid, 2013; co-author (with Andrea Watkins): Kentucky Rising, 2011. Chair Recreation Commn. City of Highland Heights, Ky., 1975—81. With USAF, 1958—62. Recipient Ky. Gov.s Vol. Activist award, 1978, Regents Prof. award, No. Ky. U., 1994, Acorn award, Ky. Advocates Higher Edn., 2003; named Outstanding Prof., No. Ky. U., 1988. Mem.: Ky. Hist. Soc. (Frank R. Levstik Profl. Svc. award 2012), So. Hist. Assn., Phi Alpha Theta (faculty advisor (No. Ky. U. chpt.) 1985—2004, nat. coun. mem. 2002—03, nat. v.p. 2006—08, nat. pres. 2008—10, chair nat. adv. com. 2010—12). Baptist. Achievements include preservation work on Civil War Battery Hooper honored in James A Ramage Civil War Museum. Avocation: reading. Office: History Dept No Ky Univ One Nunn Dr Highland Heights KY 41099*

RAMEE, STEPHEN R., cardiologist; MD, George Wash. U., 1980. Diplomate Am. Bd. Internal Medicine, 1983, Am. Bd. Internal Medicine-cardiovasc. disease, 1985, Am. Bd. Internal Medicine-interventional cardiology, 1999. Resident internal medicine Letterman Army Med. Ctr., San Francisco, 1981—83, fellow cardiovasc. disease, 1983—85; med. dir. Structural and Valvular Heart Ctr. Ochsner Heath Ctr. Office: Ochsner Heath Center-Luling 1057 Paul Maillard Rd Luling LA 70070 Office Phone: 958-785-3740.

RAMIL, JOHN B., energy executive; married; 2 children. BS in Engring., MS in Engring., U. South Fla. Joined Tampa Electric Co., 1976, pres., 1998—2003; exec. v.p. TECO Energy, Inc., 2002—03, exec. v.p., COO, 2003—04, pres., COO, 2004—10, pres., CEO, 2010—. Bd. dirs. Blue Cross Blue Shield of Fla., Inc., Edison Electric Inst., 2010—. Charter bd. trustees Univ. So. Fla., 2001—, chmn. bd. trustees, 2010—; bd. dirs. Fla. C. of C., Tampa Bay Performing Arts Ctr.; past chmn. Greater Tampa C. of C. Mem.: Tau Beta Pi. Office: TECO Energy Inc 702 N Franklin St TECO Plz Tampa FL 33602 Office Phone: 813-228-4111. Office Fax: 813-228-1670. Business E-Mail: jbramil@tecoenergy.com.

RAMILO, OCTAVIO, pediatrician, educator; b. Vigo, Spain; MD, U. Complutense, Madrid, 1981. Prof. pediat. U. Tex. Southwestern Med. Ctr., Dallas, 1993—.

RAMIREZ-RIVERA, JOSE, physician; b. Mayaguez, PR, June 26, 1929; s. Jesus Ramirez and Nieves Rivera; m. Sally P. Wheeler, June 20, 1952; children: Frederico, Steven, Sally, Juliette, Natasha, Leila. BA, Johns Hopkins U., 1949; MD, Yale U., 1953. Diplomate Am Bd Internal Med, re-certified 1974. Intern U. Md. Hosp., 1953-54; resident in medicine Univ. Hosp., Balt., 1954-55, fellow in hematology, 1958-59, resident, 1959; staff physician VA Hosp., Balt., 1960-67, assoc. chief of staff, 1962-68; asst. in medicine Johns Hopkins U., 1960-67, instr. in medicine, 1967-68; asst. prof. medicine U. Md., 1961-68; assoc. prof. Duke U., Durham, NC, 1968-70; dir. med. edn. and clin. investigation Western Region P.R., 1970-80; chief medicine Mayaguez (P.R.) Med. Ctr., 1971-82; chief Pulmonary Disease Sect., Va. Hosp., Durham, 1968—70. Prof med Univ PR, San Juan, 1974—, dir univ med servs Med Sci Campus, 1982—86; prof med Univ Cent del Caribe, 1998—; dir Rincon Rural Health Project, 1975—82; assoc chief staff educ VA Med Ctr, San Juan, 1990—92; dir clin investigation La Concepcion Hosp, San German, 1996—. Contbr. articles to med. jours.;, author books of Puerto Rican Legends. Bd dirs Soc Educ Suroeste. With USPHS, 1955—57. Decorated Comendador Imperial Orden Hispanica de Carlos V; named Man of Yr., PR Med. Soc. Western Sect., 1975, 1981. Master: ACP (pres. PR chpt. 1986—88, Blaine Brower Traveling Scholar 1967, Laureate award 2005); fellow: Coll. Chest Physicians, Royal Soc. Med (London); mem.: Imperial Orden Hispanica de Carlos V (Abelardo Diaz Alfaro prize 2010), Puerto Rican Fedn. Bioethics (bd. dirs. 1999—2002, pres. 2002—10), Soc. Autores Puertorriguenos, PR Lung Assn. (bd. dirs. 1975—80), Casa Espanã (bd. dirs. 1998—2009), Alliance Francaise PR (v.p. 1995—96, pres. 1996—2000, bd. dirs. 2006—09), PEN Club. Roman Catholic. Achievements include creating a technique of lung lavage for alveolar proteinosis. Avocations: classical music, literature. Home and Office: Cond Acqualina # 186 Carr #2 Apt 703 Guaynabo PR 00966-1814 Office Phone: 787-249-7441. Personal E-mail: ramirez.r629@gmail.com.

RAMOS, NELVA GONZALES, federal judge; b. Port Lavaca, Tex., 1965; BS summa cum laude, Southwestern Tex. State U., 1987; JD, U. Tex., 1991. Civil litig. assoc. Meredith, Donnell & Abernethy, Corpus Christi, Tex., 1991—97; mcpl. ct. judge City of Corpus Christi, 1997—99; pvt. practice, 1999—2000; dist. judge 347th Judicial Dist., State of Tex., 2001—11; judge US Dist. Ct. (southern dist.) Tex., 2011—. Office: United States Courthouse 1133 N Shoreline Blvd Corpus Christi TX 78401

RAMOS PEÑA, JORGE L., territorial legislator; b. Sept. 22; s. Pablo Ramos and Doris Pena. Rep., Dist. 30 PR House of Reps., San Juan, 2005—, chmn. transp. and infrastructure com. New Progressive Party Of Puerto Rico. Office: PR Legis PO Box 9022228 San Juan PR 00902 also: Dist Off Calle Francisco G Bruno 23 W Guayama PR 00784 Office Phone: 787-723-5973, 787-725-2535. Fax: 787-725-6669. Business E-Mail: jramos@camaraderepresentantes.org.

RAMPACEK, CHARLES M., manufacturing executive; b. Tuscaloosa, Ala., Apr. 25, 1943; s. Carl and Mary (Kull) R.; m. Lois Ann Klaus; children— Susan, Kristi BSChemE, U. Ala., 1965; MSChemE, U. Tex., 1967. Ops. mgr. Exxon USA, Benicia, Calif., 1978-79, mgr., synthetics planning, 1979-82, mgr., refining planning, 1981-82; pres. Tenneco Gas Transp. Co. (subs. Tenneco Inc.); sr. v.p., refining Tenneco Oil Co. (subs. Tenneco Inc.), 1982-89; various exec. positions Tenneco, Inc. (formerly Tenneco Automotive, Inc.), 1982—95; exec. v.p. Tenneco Gas Co. (subs. Tenneco Inc.), 1989; pres., CEO Lyondell-Citgo Refining, L.P., 1996—2000; chmn., pres. & CEO Probex Corp., 2000—03. Bd. dirs. Enterprise Products GP, LLC, Flowserve Corp., 1998—, Cenovus Energy Inc., 2009—. Mem. Am. Inst. Chem. Engrs. Methodist. Avocations: golf; running; hunting; skiing; softball. Office: Flowserve Corp Bd Directors 5215 N OConnor Blvd Ste 2300 Irving TX 75039 Office Phone: 972-443-6500. Office Fax: 972-443-6800. Business E-Mail: crampacek@flowserve.com.

RAMPERSAD, PEGGY A. SNELLINGS, sociologist, consultant; b. Fredericksburg, Va., Jan. 12, 1933; d. George Daniel and Virginia Riley (Bowler) Snellings; m. Oliver Ronald Rampersad, Mar. 19, 1955; 1 child, Gita. BA, Mary Washington Coll., Fredericksburg, 1953; student, Sch. Art Inst. Chgo., 1953—55; MA, U. Chgo., 1965, PhD, 1978. Grad. admissions counselor U. Chgo., 1954—57, adviser fgn. students, 1958, dir. admissions Grad. Sch. Bus., 1958—63, rsch. project specialist, 1970—78, pers. mgr., 1979—80, mgr. orgnl. devel., 1980—82, adminstr. dept. econs., 1983—95; cons. PSR Consulting, Chgo., 1995—. Cons. North Ctrl. Assn. Colls. and Secondary Schs., Chgo., 1964—70, Orchestral Assn. Chgo. Symphony Orch., 1982, Chgo. Ctr. Decision Rsch., 1982, Harvard U., 1993—97. Exhibitions include Va. Mus. Fine Arts, Art Inst. Chgo., others; editor: North Ctrl. Assn. Quar., 1972; contbr. articles to profl. jours. Grad. fellow, U. Chgo., 1963—67. Mem.: AAUW, Am. Acad. Polit. and Social Sci., Am. Econ. Assn., Art Inst. Chgo. (assoc.), Pi Lambda Theta (past pres.). Episcopalian. Avocations: painting, drawing, opera, reading, walking. Home and Office: 28 Seneca Ter Fredericksburg VA 22401-1115

RAMSAY, CRAIG, professional hockey coach, retired professional hockey player; b. Weston, Ont., Canada, Mar. 17, 1951; m. Susan Ramsay; children: Travis, Jad, Brendon, Summer. Left wing Peterborough Petes, 1971, Buffalo Sabres, 1971—85, asst. coach to head coach, 1986—87; asst. coach Fla. Panthers, 1993—94, 2011—, assoc. coach, 1994—95; scout Dallas Stars, 1995—96; asst. coach Ottawa Senators, 1996—98, Phila. Flyers, 1998—2000, head coach, 2000—01; asst. coach Tampa Bay Lightening, 2001—02, assoc. coach, 2002—07; asst. coach Boston Bruins, 2007—10; head coach Atlanta Thrashers, 2010—11. Recipient Frank J. Selke Trophy, 1985. Office: Florida Panthers BankAtlantic Center One Panther Parkway Sunrise FL 33323

RAMSAY, RICHARD L., lawyer; b. Pine Bluff, Ark., Apr. 30, 1952; BA, U. Ark., 1974, JD, 1977. Bar: Ark. 1977, US Dist. Ct. (Ea. Dist. Ark.) 1977, US Dist. Ct. (We. Dist. Ark.) 1977, US Ct. Appeals (8th Cir.) 1980, US Supreme Ct. 2008. Ptnr. Eichenbaum, Liles & Hester PA, Little Rock. Mem.: Debtor-Creditor Bar Ctl. Ark., ABA (exec. coun. mem. 1987), Ark. Bar Assn. (pres. young lawyers divsn. 1986, pres.-elect 2006—07, pres. 2007—08). Office: Eichenbaum Liles Heister Pa 124 W Capitol Ave Ste 1900 Little Rock AR 72201-3717 Office Phone: 501-376-4531. Office Fax: 501-376-8433.

RAMSEY, BOB (ROBERT L. RAMSEY), state legislator; b. Mar. 13, 1947; m. Margaret Ramsey; children: Heather, Haley. BS in Biology, U. Tenn., Knoxville; DDS, U. Tenn., Memphis. Dentist; mem. Blount Co. Bd. Health, Regional Solid Waste Authority, Agrl. Ext. Com., Cmty. Action Agy., Regional Planning Commn.; mem. Dist. 20 Tenn. House of Reps., 2008—. Republican. Baptist. Mailing: 2120 Middlewood Dr Maryville TN 37803 Office: 207 War Memorial Bldg Nashville TN 37243 Office Phone: 615-741-3560. Business E-Mail: rep.bob.ramsey@capitol.tn.gov.

RAMSEY, CHARLES EUGENE, sociologist, educator; b. Paragon, Ind., Apr. 24, 1923; s. Sarcefield Dodson and Stella (Goss) R.; m. Alberta Mae Jordan, July 19, 1943; children— James D., Charles W., Jane E., Suzanne. BS, Ind. State Tchrs. Coll., 1947; MS, U. Wis., 1950, PhD, 1952. Faculty U. Wis., 1951-52, U. Minn., 1952-54, Cornell U., 1954-62, Colo. State U., 1962-65; prof. sociology U. Minn., Mpls., 1965-77; chmn. dept. sociology U. Tex., Arlington, 1977-83. Vis. prof. Inter-Am. Instn. Agrl. Sci., Costa Rica, 1961, Exptl. Sta., U. P.R., 1961-62; research cons. to various univs., agys. Author: (with Lowry Nelson and Cooley Verner) Community Structure and Change, 1960, (with David Gottlieb) The American Adolescent, 1965, Understanding the Deprived Child, S.R.A, 1967, Problems of Youth, 1967, (with D.J. McCarty) The School Managers: Power and Conflict in American Public Education, 1971; also articles. Achievements include developing and testing theory of variations in community power structure, types of sch. bds., and roles of sch. supt., developed method of comparative measurement of level of living for different countries. Home: 1102 De Pauw Dr Arlington TX 76012-5339 Office: U Tex Dept Sociology Arlington TX 76004

RAMSEY, FORREST GLADSTONE, JR., retired engineering company executive; b. Wichita, Kans., Oct. 25, 1930; s. Forrest Gladstone and Anastasia Ruth (Linot) R.; m. Gwendolyn Moreton, June 22, 1953 (div. Jan. 1982); children: Deborah Jenkins, Rebecca Johnson, Susan Klopp, Diane Hayes, Forrest G. III, Mark, Kenneth; m. Carmen Bergen, Apr. 30, 1988. BS in Engring., U.S. Naval Acad., 1952; postgrad., Wichita State U., 1957-58, U. Colo., 1958-64. Commd. ensign USN, 1952, res., 1957; planner, engr. Boeing Corp., Wichita, Kans., 1957-58; engr., logistician Martin-Marietta, Denver, 1959-65; div. dir. Computer Scis., Washington, 1965-73; program dir. Systems Cons., Washington, 1973-76; CEO Am. Sys. Corp., Washington, 1976-92, chmn., bd. dirs., 1992-97; ret., 1997. Mem. Profl. Svcs. Coun. (vice chmn. 1990), Naval Submarine League (bd. dirs. 1982-90). Roman Catholic. Home: 21105 Cardinal Pond Ter Apt 216 Ashburn VA 20147-6155 Personal E-mail: forrest.ramsey@1952.usna.com.

RAMSEY, FRANK ALLEN, veterinarian, retired army officer; b. Rocksprings, Tex., May 1, 1929; s. Reynolds Allen and June (Burdette) R.; m. Lucette C. Reboul, Jan. 1958; children: Randal R., Ramsay A.; m. 2d, Mary Lou Cain, June 1991. D.V.M., Tex. A & M U., 1954; grad., U.S. Army Command and Gen. Staff Coll., 1965, U.S. Army War Coll., 1972. Commd. 1st lt. U.S. Army Vet. Corps, 1955, advanced through grades to brig. gen., 1980; chief vet. service Ft. Leonard Wood, Mo., 1958-61; acad. vet. U.S. Mil. Acad., West Point, NY, 1962-64; vet. staff officer U.S. Army Combat Devel. Command Med. Service, Ft. Sam Houston, Tex., 1965-67; asst. chief profl. programming and planning br. Office Surgeon Gen., Washington, 1967-68, chief profl. programming and planning br., 1968-71, chief food inspection policy office, 1972-73, sr. vet. staff officer, 1973-77; asst. chief of staff Vet. Service, 7th Med. Command, Army Europe and 7th Army, Heidelberg, W. Ger., 1977-80; asst. for vet. services to surgeon gen. and chief U.S. Army Vet. Corps, Hdqrs. Dept. Army, Washington, 1980-85; ret., 1985. Decorated Army Commendation medal, Legion of Merit with oak leaf cluster, D.S.M. Mem. AVMA, Assn. Fed. Veterinarians, Assn. Mil. Surgeons U.S., Assn. Equine Practitioners, Am. Assn. Food Hygiene Veterinarians, Conf. Pub. Health Veterinarians, Tex. Vet. Med. Assn. Lodges: Masons (32 degree). Presbyterian. Home: 8 El Norte Cir Uvalde TX 78801-4021 Office Phone: 830-591-3736.

RAMSEY, MATT, state legislator; b. Atlanta, Ga., July 08; m. Missy Ramsey; children: Anna Lynne, Jacob. Degree in Polit. Sci., Georgia Southern U.; JD, Georgia State Uni. Coll. Law, 2005. Legis. aide for Representative Mark Burkhalter, 1999; legis. aide Congressman Mac

Collins US Capitol Hill, Washington; atty., ptnr. Warner, Hooper & Ramsey, P.C., Peachtree City, Ga.; mem. Dist. 72 Ga. House of Reps., 2007—. Republican. Methodist. Office: 504 Coverdell Legislative Office Bldg Atlanta GA 30334 also: 200 Terrane Ridge Peachtree City GA 30269 Office Phone: 404-656-0188.

RAMSEY, MICHAEL W., lawyer; b. Galveston, Tex., Feb. 18, 1940; s. V.V. Ramsey; married; 2 children. BA, So. Meth. U., 1962, JD, 1965. Bar: 1965. Atty. Richard Haynes & Assoc., 1965—72; ptnr. Ramsey & Tyson, 1972—85; pvt. practice Houston, 1985—. Named Criminal Def. Lawyer of the Year, Tex. State Bar Assn., 1999. Office: Law Office of Michael Ramsey 2120 Welch St Houston TX 77019

RAMSEY, RONALD B., SR., state legislator; b. Aug. 14; m. Doris Ramsey; children: Ronald Jr., Christyn. BA, 1981, JD, 1992. Mcpl. ct. judge, Stone Mountain, Ga.; mem. Dist. 43 Ga. State Senate, 2007—. Democrat. Office: 5271 Snapfinger Woods Dr Decatur GA 30035 Office Phone: 404-281-9948. Office Fax: 770-591-1253. Business E-Mail: ronald.ramsey@senate.ga.gov.

RAMSEY, RONALD LYNN, Lieutenant Governor of Tennessee; b. Johnson City, Tenn., Nov. 20, 1955; m. Sindy Ramsey; children: Tiffany, Sheena, Madison. BS in Indsl. Tech., East Tenn. State U., Johnson City, 1978. Surveyor, 1981—86; real estate broker/auctioneer, 1986—90; owner Ron Ramsey and Associates, 1990; mem. Dist. 1 Tenn. House of Representatives, 1992—96; mem. Tenn. State Senate, 1996—, asst. Republican floor leader, 1996—98, spkr., 2007—; lt. gov. State of Tenn., Nashville, 2007—. Former mem. adv. bd. Farm Credit Assn. Mem. Elizabeth Chapel United Meth. Ch., Sunday sch. teacher; mem. Blountville Ruritan Elizabeth Chapel United Methodist Church. Recipient Lifetime Achievement award, Bristol C. of C., 2013; named The Best Lawmaker for Business in Tenn., Business Tenn. Magazine; named to Tenn. Auctioneer Hall of Fame. Mem.: Bristol Assn. of Realtors (pres.), Farm Credit Assn. (adv. bd. mem.), Blountville Bus. Assn. (past pres.), Bristol TN-VA Assn. Realtors (past pres.), Blountville Ruritan, Indian Springs Optimist Club. Republican. Methodist. Office: Office of the Lieutenant Governor Suite 1 Legislative Plaza 301 6th Avenue North Nashville TN 37243-0219 also: Dist Address 3311 Hwy 126 Blountville TN 37617 Office Phone: 615-741-4524, 423-323-8700. Office Fax: 615-253-0197. E-mail: lt.gov.ron.ramsey@capitol.tn.gov.*

RANCK, BRUCE E., investment company executive; Chmn. Venturi Techs, Commerce City, Colo.; various positions Browning-Ferris Industries, Inc., 1970—95, pres., CEO, 1995-99; ptnr. Bayou City Partners, 1999—; CEO Tartan Textile Svcs., Inc., 2003—06. Bd. dirs. Dynamex Inc., Quanta Svcs., Inc., 2005—. Office: Bayou City Partners 2500 Citywest Blvd Houston TX 77042 Office Phone: 713-532-0090. Business E-Mail: branck@quantaservices.com.

RAND, ANTHONY EDEN, former state commissioner, former state legislator, lawyer; b. Panther Branch, NC, Sept. 1, 1939; s. Walter and Geneva; m. Karen Rand; 2 children. BA in Polit. Sci., UNC, 1961; LLD (hon.), UNC, Chapel Hill, 2008; JD, UNC Law Sch., Chapel Hill, 1964; LLD (hon.), Fayetteville State U., 2000; HHD (hon.), Meth. U., 2008. Ptnr. Mitchiner, Andrews, Rand, Raleigh, NC, 1965-68, Rose, Thorp, Rand & Ray, Fayetteville, NC, 1968-81, Rose, Rand, Winfrey & Gregory, Fayetteville, 1982-89, Rand, Finch & Gregory, Fayetteville, 1989-93, Rand and Gregory, Fayetteville, 1993—; mem. Dist. 12 NC State Senate, Raleigh, 1982—88, mem. Dist. 24, 1995—2002, mem. Dist. 19, 2003—09, majority leader, 1987—88, 2001—09; chmn. NC Post Release Supervision and Parole Commn., 2010—; assoc. v.p., Cancer Ctr. mgr. Fayetteville Tech. CC. Sec., legal counsel, cons. Lithotripters, Inc.1989-96; cons. Prime Med. Svcs., 1996-2000, Sonorex, Inc., 2001—. Mem. N.C. State Dem. Exec. Com., 1975-77; chmn. exec. com. Cumberland County Dem. party (N.C.), 1977-81; bd. visitors U. N.C.-Chapel Hill, Meth. Coll.; bd. dirs., founding mem. Pub. Sch. Forum; bd. dirs. Fayetteville Area Sentencing, 1985; mem. adv. bd. Mus. Cape Fear, 1989-95; mem. nat. adv. panel Child Care Action Com., 1989; pres. Med-Tech Investments, 1989-97. Recipient William Davie award, U. N.C. Chapel Hill, 1995, DSM, U. N.C. Chapel Hill Gen. Alumni Assn., 1998, Disting. Alumnus award, U. N.C. Chapel Hill, 2001, Legis. Leadership award, N.C. Coun. Cmty. Programs, 2000, Fayetteville C. of C. Realtors Cup, 2000, Chancellor's medallion, Fayetteville State U., 2001, Law Disting. Alumni award, U. N.C. Chapel Hill, 2001, Disting. Svc. award, N.C. State, 2002, Hon. Trustee award, Fayetteville Tech. C.C., 2003, N.C. Gun Violence Prevention Citizen of Yr. award, 2003, Legis. award, ARC of N.C., 2003, William N. Martin award, Covenant with N.C. Children, 2005, Pub. Leadership in Tech. award, N.C. Tech. Assn., 2005, 2007, MOVE award, Nat. MS Soc. NC, 2007, Leadership award, NC Housing Trust Fund, 2007, Dir. award, NC Alcohol Law Enforcement, Charles Dick medal of Merit, NC Nat. Guard, 2007, NC Pub. Lib. Champion award, 2008, Legislative Supporters of Foster and Adoptive Parents award, Childrens & Family Svcs. Assn., 2008, Disting. Svc. award, U. NC Sch. Medicine, 2012; named Legis. of Yr., N.C. Nurses' Assn., 2003, Autism Soc., 2004, Legislator of Yr., Disabled Am. Vet. NC, 2008. Mem. ABA, ATLA (state commiteeman 1968-72), N.C. Bar Assn., Alpha Tau Omega, Delta Theta Phi, State Legislative Leadership Found. (bd. dirs.), Senate Pres. Forum (bd. dir.), NC Cable Telecom. Assoc. (legis. of Yr. award 2009-), Nat. Assn. Mutual Ins. Cos. (Legis. of Yr. award 2009), Am. Diabetics Assoc. (One Care Committment award 2010). Democrat. Episcopalian. Office: Workforce Devel Board 410 Ray Ave Fayetteville NC 28301 Office Phone: 910-323-3421 ext. 2122. Personal E-mail: tonyrand@aol.com. Business E-Mail: anthony.rand@doc.nc.gov, anthony.rand@ncdps.gov.

RAND, RICK W., state legislator; b. La Grange, Ky., Mar. 10, 1957; s. Reggie and Jean Yeager Rand; m. Vicky Perkinson; 1 child, Beaumont. Pres. Rand Ins. Agy., 1978—; chmn. North Ctrl. Ky. Pvt. Ind. Coun., 1983—90; dir. Shelby Rural Electric Coop. Inc., 1989—; mem. Dist. 26 Ky. State Senate, 1991—94; mem. Dist. 47 Ky. House of Reps., 2003—. Mem.: C. of C., NRA, Ky. Bikers Assn., Cattleman's Assn. Democrat. Disciples Of Christ. Office: Capitol Annex Rm 366B Frankfort KY 40601 Office Phone: 502-564-8100 ext. 619. Fax: 502-255-9911. E-mail: randins@netscape.net.

RAND, RIPLEY EAGLES, federal prosecutor; b. Durham, NC, 1967; s. Tony and Karen Rand; m. Shannon Joseph. BA in Polit. Sci., U. NC, Chapel Hill, 1990, JD with honors, 1995. Bar: NC 1995, US Dist. Ct. (ea., mid., and we. dist.) NC 1996, US Dist. Ct. (ea., mid., and we. dist.) NC 1997, US Ct. Appeals (4th cir.) 1997, US Supreme Ct. 2001. Asst. Lithotripters, Inc., Fayetteville, NC, 1990; rsch. asst. North Atlantic Assembly (now NATO Parliamentary Assembly), Brussels, 1991; summer assoc. Manning Fulton and Skinner, Raleigh, 1994, Womble Carlyle Sandridge and Rice, Winston-Salem, 1993, 1994; rschr. Michaels and Jones (now Martin and Jones), Raleigh, 1994—95; rsch. asst. for Chief Justice Burley B. Mitchell, Jr. NC Supreme Ct., 1995—96; judicial clk. for Judge James A. Beaty, Jr. US Dist. Ct. (middle dist.) NC, Winston-Salem, 1996—97; asst. dist. atty. Cumberland County Dist. Atty.'s Office, Fayetteville, 1997, Wake County Dist. Atty.'s Office, Raleigh, 1997—2002, dir. Domestic Violence Unit, 1999—2000, mem. Dangerous Offenders Task Force, 2001—02; spl. superior ct. judge State of NC, 2002—06, 2006—, resident superior ct. judge, 2006; US atty. (middle dist.) NC US Dept. Justice, Greensboro, 2010—. Polit. organizer, dep. campaign dir. Mike Easley Com. for Atty. Gen., 1992; polit. organizer Mile Easley Com. for Gov., 2000; disk jockey WXDU-Durham, 1994—2000; ptnr. Theophilus Junior JV, 2005—; spkr. in field. Co-author: I Want to Go to UNC, 2005; contbr. articles to profl. jours. Dir., sec. Summit House of NC, 2003—; bd. visitors U. NC, Chapel Hill, 2004—08; bd. dirs. U. NC Sch. Law Alumni Assn., 2007—. Fellow NC Inst. Polit. Leadership, 2003. Mem.: Susie Sharp Inn of Ct., NC Conf. Superior Ct. Judges (mem. Standing Com. on Legislation and Law Reform 2002—, Com. on Judicial Edn. 2006—), NC Bar Assn. (Bench Bar Liaison Com. 2008—), Tenth Judicial Dist. Bar Assn. (bd. dirs. 2006—07), Wake County Bar Assn. (bd. dirs. 2006—07, Pres.'s Award of Excellence 2008). Office: Office of US Attorney 101 S Edgeworth St Ste 400 Greensboro NC 27401-6028 Office Phone: 336-333-5351.*

RANDALL, CLIFFORD WENDELL, civil engineer, educator; b. Somerset, Ky., May 1, 1936; s. William Lesbert and Geneva (James) R.; m. Phyllis Amis, Aug. 15, 1959; children: Andrew Amis, William Otis. BSCE, U. Ky., 1959, MS in Sanitary Engring., 1963; PhD in Environ. Health Engring., U. Tex., 1966. Asst. prof. civil engring. U. Tex., Arlington, 1965-68; mem. faculty Va. Poly. Inst. and State U., 1968—2001, prof. civil engring., 1972-81, Charles Lunsford prof., 1981—2001; vis. prof. U. Cape Town, South Africa, 1983; chmn. environ. engring. and scis. program Va. Poly. Inst. and State U., 1979-97, Charles Lunsford prof. emeritus, 2001—. Lectr. Shanghai Archtl. and Mcpl. Engring. Inst., Wuhan Tech. U., 1987; dir. Occoquan Watershed Monitoring Program, 1971-2001; mem. Occoquan watershed monitoring subcom. Va. State Water Control Bd., 1971—, chair, 1971-85, 2001-, vice chair, 1986-2001; US nat. com. Internat. Water Assn., 1976-88, chair 1986-88, mem. 1992 IAWQ Biennial Conf. Com., chair conf. arrangements, Washington; tng. grant cons. EPA, 1970-71; cons. to industry, 1969—; WHO cons. to Nat. Environ. Engring. Rsch. Inst. India, 1983-84; Va. gov. appointee sci. and tech. adv. com. Chesapeake Bay Program, 1984; mem. sci. and tech. adv. com. Chesapeake Bay Program, 1984-2006, chmn. 1993-97; nitrogen tech. adv. com. NYC Dept. Environ. Protection, 1994-2006; blue ribbon panel wastewater treatment City of Atlanta, 1997-2001; nitrogen removal tech. adv. com. mem., Water and Sewage Authority, Washington, DC, 2006-2008. Author tech. papers in field; co-author: Biological Process Design for Wastewater Treatment, 1980, Stormwater Management in Urbanizing Areas, 1983, Design and Retrofit of Wastewater Treatment Plants for Biological Nutrient Removal, 1992. Troop com. chmn. Boy Scouts Am., 1978-82, chmn. dist. Camporee com., 1977; camp pres. Gideons Internat., 1976-78, 80, 95-97, 2008-11, v.p., 2005-2008, 2011-, state cabinet mem., 1985-88; vice moderator Highlands Bapt. Assn., 1980-81, moderator, 1982-83; bd. deacons Blacksburg Bapt. Ch., 1971-74, 79-82, chmn., 1974. (j.g.) US Coast and Godetic Survey, 1959-62. Ford Found. fellow, 1964-65; recipient citation Engring. News-Record, 1988, Disting. Svc. award US nat. com. Internat. Assn. Water Quality, 1989, Salute to Excellence Gov. of Md., 1994, Alumni Pub. Svc. award Va. Tech., 1996, Mathias medal for sci. excellence Chesapeake Rsch. Consortium and the Sea Grant Offices of Md. and Va., 1996, Dean's award Excellence Pub. Svc., Va. Tech. Engring., 1997, Disting. Svc. award Assn. Environ. Engrs. and Scientists Profs., 1997; Lifetime Achievement award Va. Water Resources Ctr., 2006, Leadership award Va. Water Rsch. Ctr., 2006; named Conservationist of Yr. Chesapeake Bay Found., 1986; AEC trainee U. Tex., 1963-65, Joan Hodges Queneau Palladium medal Am. Assn. Engring. Soc., 2009, Audubon Soc., 2010, Named to Hall Distinction, Coll. Engring., U. Ky., 2011 Mem. ASCE (elected disting. mem. 2008,; chmn. water resources mgmt. com. 1977, chmn. environ. engring. rsch. coun. 1989-90, svc. award 1978, 80, meritorious tech. paper award 1969), Am. Acad. Environ. Engrs. (hon.), Am. Water Works Assn. (cert. recognition for acad. excellence 1980, 89), Water Environ. Fedn. (bd. dirs. 1981-84, Morgan cert. of merit for full scale rsch. 1982, Bedell award 1983, svc. award 1984, Gordon M. Fair medal for excellence in engring. edn. 1998), Internat. Water Assn. (nat. com., 1978-88, chair, 1986-88, governing bd. 1986-88, USA rep. on sci. and tech. com. 1994-98, mem. nutrient removal specialist group mgmt. com. 1990-2002, chmn. 1994-98), Va. Water Environment Assn. (v.p. 1974-75, pres. 1975-76), Assn. Environ. Engring. and Scis. Profs. (sec.-treas. 1979-80, bd. dirs. 1978-80, 93-97, v.p. 1994-95, pres. 1995-96, past pres. 1996-97, Founders award, 2008, Lifetime Achievement award 2005, AEESP, WEF lectr., 2009). Home: 1302 Crestview Dr Blacksburg VA 24060-5609 Office: Va Tech Dept Civil and Environ Engring 418 Durham Hall Blacksburg VA 24061-0246 Office Phone: 540-231-6018. Business E-Mail: cliff@vt.edu.

RANDALL, DALE BERTRAND JONAS, English language educator; b. Cleveland Heights, Ohio, Mar. 18, 1929; s. Myron Welcome and Lettie Jane (Perrin) R.; m. Phyllis Rosanna Link, June 25, 1955; children: Lettie Rosanna, Kenneth Dale. BA, Western Res. U., 1951; MA, Rutgers U., 1953; PhD, U. Pa., 1958. Teaching asst. Rutgers U., New Brunswick, NJ, 1951-53, U. Pa., Phila., 1953-57; instr. Duke U., Durham, NC, 1957-60, asst. prof. of English, 1960-65, assoc. prof., 1965-70, asst. grad. dean., 1967—70, assoc. grad. dean, 1970—74, prof., 1970—99, prof. dramatic lit., 1991-94, prof. practice theater arts, 1994—99, prof. emeritus English, theater studies, 1999—; interim dir. Duke Drama, 1991-92. Chmn. Southeastern Inst. of Medieval and Renaissance Studies, 1969-74, 75-76; chmn. Duke Ctr. for Medieval and Renaissance Studies, Durham, 1971-72, governing com., 1969-89, 93-97; mem. ctrl. exec. com. Folger Inst., Washington, 1983-92; assoc. trustee Chi Psi Ednl. Trust, 1994-96, trustee, 1996-2002. Author: The Golden Tapestry: A Critical Survey of Non-Chivalric Spanish Fiction in English Translation, 1963, Gentle Flame: The Life and Verse of Dudley, Fourth Lord North, 1983, Joseph Conrad and Warrington Dawson, 1968, Jonson's Gypsies Unmasked, 1975, Theatres of Greatness, 1986, Winter Fruit: English Drama 1642-1660, 1995, Soliloquy of a Farmer's Wife, 1999, (with J. C. Boswell) Cervantes in Seventeenth-Century England, 2009; editor: Studies in the Continental Background of Renaissance English Literature, 1977, Medieval and Renaissance Studies, 1976-79, Renaissance Papers, 1984-91; also articles. Active Friends of Duke U. Libr., Friends of the Bodleian Libr. Recipient award Am. Philos. Soc., 1986, Alumni award Chi Psi, 1993; Guggenheim fellow, 1970-71, sr. fellow Folger Libr., 1978, 86, Southeastern Inst., 1978. Mem. MLA, Gypsy Lore Soc., Southeastern Renaissance Conf. (adv. coun. 1984-95, v.p. 1992-93, pres. 1993-94, chair adv. coun. 1994-95), Cervantes Soc. Am., Sixteenth Century Soc, Am. Culture Assn., Chi Psi (Disting. Svc. award, 2009), Dale B. J. Randall Ednl. Found. Avocations: gardening, playreaders, antiques. Office: Duke U Dept English Box 90015 Durham NC 27708-0015 Home: 15 Barratts Chapel Ct Durham NC 27705 Business E-Mail: dbjandpr@duke.edu.

RANDALL, DAVID CLARK, medical educator, researcher; b. St. Louis, Apr. 23, 1945; s. Walter Clark and Gwendolyn Ruth (Niebel) R.; m. Lea Carol Wylder, Sept. 1, 1985; children: Christopher C., Matthew F., Benjamin W. BA, Taylor U., 1967; PhD, U. Wash., 1971. Asst. prof. divsn. behavioral biology Johns Hopkins U. Sch. Medicine, Balt., 1972-75; asst. prof. dept. physiology U. Ky., Lexington, 1975-78, assoc. prof., 1978-85, prof., 1985—2007, Donald T. Frazier endowed prof., 2007—. Instr. Asbury Coll., Wilmore, Ky., 1979—; vis. assoc. prof. dept. neurobiology and behavior SUNY, Stony Brook, 1981; dir. grad. studies dept. physiology and biophysics U. Ky., 1981-84, joint prof. grad. ctr. biomed. engring. 1987—, exec. com., 1990-92, chair faculty senate coun., 2008—10; mem. editl. bd. Frontiers in Integrative Physiology, 2010-; master tchr. U. Ky. Coll. Medicine, 1994-. Co-author: Cardiopulmonary Physiology, 1998, 2005, Quick Look Cardiopulmonary System, 1999, ECG Interpretation, 2004; contbr. articles to profl. jours. Mem., bd. dirs. Trinity Christian Acad., Lexington, KY 2008-. Mem. Am. Heart Assn. (various coms., bd. chmn. Ky. affiliate 1994-96), Am. Physiol. Soc., Fedn. Am. Socs. Exptl. Biology, Christian Med. Dental Soc., Pavlovian Soc. Am. (pres. 1983). Avocations: amateur radio, orchard and bee keeping, regional history, horseback riding. Office: U Ky Coll Medicine Dept Physiology Lexington KY 40536-0298

RANDALL, KENNETH C., retired dean, retired law educator; JD, Hofstra U., 1981; MA, Yale U., 1982, Columbia U., 1985, PhD, 1988. Practice law Simpson Thacher & Bartlett, NYC, 1982-84; faculty mem. U. Ala. Sch. Law, Tuscaloosa, 1985—, vice dean, 1989-93, dean, 1993—2013, dean emeritus, 2013—, Thomas E. McMillan prof. law, Thomas E. McMillan prof. law emeritas, 2013—; spl. counsel to the pres. U. Ala. Author: Federal Courts and the International Human Rights Paradigm, 1990; contbr. articles to law jours. and revs. W. Bayard Cutting Jr. fellow internat. law, Columbia U. Sch. Law, 1984—85. Office: University of Alabama School of Law PO Box 870382 101 Paul W Bryant Dr E Tuscaloosa AL 35487-0001 Office Phone: 205-348-5117. E-mail: krandall@law.ua.edu.*

RANDALL, NEIL WARREN, gastroenterologist; b. White Plains, NY, Mar. 24, 1957; s. Leroy Bruce and Libby Cynthia (Brandt) R.; m. Linda Ilene Zell, Oct. 31, 1992. BA, U. Va., 1978; MD, U. Md., 1983. Diplomate Am. Bd. Internal Medicine with subspecialty in gastroenterology, geriat. Resident in internal medicine Ochsner Clinic, New Orleans, 1983-86; fellow in gastroenterology Tufts U., Boston, 1986-88; staff gastroenterologist Cleve. Clinic Fla., Fort Lauderdale, 1988-92, Geisinger Clinic, Danville, Pa., 1992-97, Pa. State Geisinger Health Sys., Danville, 1997-98; med. dir. gastrointestinal endoscopy Geisinger Health Sys., 1999-2000; gastroenterologist Gastroenterology Group of Naples, 2001—. Fellow ACP, Am. Coll. Gastroenterology; mem. Am. Soc for Gastroent. Endoscopy. Avocations: theater, travel, wine. Office: Gasterenterology Group of Naples 1064 Goodlette-Frank Rd Naples FL 34102-5449 Office Phone: 239-649-1186.

RANDALL, NIKKI, state legislator; State rep. Dist. 138, Ga., 1999—; mrm. Health & Ecology Com., Special Judiciary Com., State Planning & Cmty. Affairs Com. Democrat. Mailing: 404 Legis Off Bldg Atlanta GA 30334 Office: PO Box 121 Macon GA 31202 also: 441 Simbury Ridge Macon GA 31220 Office Phone: 404-656-0109. E-mail: nrandall@legis.state.ga.us.

RANDALL, RICHARD D., medical products executive; BS in Biology & Sci. Edn., SUNY, Buffalo, 1975. Pres., CEO Target Therapeutics, Inc.(acquired by Boston Scientific Corp.), 1988—93, chmn., 1989—97; CFO Conceptus, Inc., 1992—95, pres., CEO and bd. dirs., 1992—93, Innovasive Devices, Inc. (acquired by the Ethicon Divsn. of Johnson & Johnson), 1994—2000; pres., CEO Incumed, Inc., 2000—02; pres. TranS1, Inc., 2002—, CEO, bd. dirs., 2002—. Bd. dirs. AbbeyMoor Med. and Urologix Inc., MicroVention, Inc., Neuro Navigational Corp., St. Jude Med. Endocardial Solutions (Endocardial Solutions Inc.), 2000—, Micro Therapeutics Inc., 2002—, Salient Surgical Technologies, Inc., 2005—. Office: TranS1 Inc 301 Govt Ctr Dr Wilmington NC 28403 Office Phone: 910-332-1700. Office Fax: 910-332-1701. Business E-Mail: rrandall@trans1.com.

RANDAZZO, MARISA R., psychologist; d. Hilary Phillip and Susan Hilborn Reddy; m. Robert Salvatore Randazzo, May 15, 2004. BA in Psychology and Religion, Williams Coll., 1989; MA in Psychology, Princeton U., 1993, PhD in Psychology, 1995. Chief rsch. psychologist US Secret Svc., Washington, 1996—2004; sr. expert Bus. Intelligence Advisors, Boston, 2004—06; pres. Threat Assessment Resources Internat., Reno, 2006—; mng. ptnr. Sigma Threat Mgmt. Assoc., 2010—. Editl. bd. Jour. Threat Assessment, 2001—. Contbr. articles. Recipient Recognition award, US Secret Svc., 1998—2004, Bicentennial Medal Recipient, Williams Coll., 2005; fellow, Soc. Psychol. Study Social Issues, Washington, 1995—96. Mem.: APA, Am. Psychology-Law Soc. (program chair 1998—2000). Achievements include research in American school shooters; preventing violence in schools; co-authoring a federal model of school threat assessment credited in the media and law enforcement with preventing school attacks. Office Fax: 775-424-6687. Business E-Mail: mrr@threatresources.com.

RANDELL, CORTES W., news service executive; b. Washington, 1935; m. Joan. V. (Wirz) 1968; children: Cortes John, Christina Alexis. BSME, U. Va., 1959; student, Darden Sch., U. Va., 1962. Engr. Gen. Electric, N.Y., 1959-61, Internat. Telephone & Telegraph, Chgo., 1962-64; pres. Nat. Student Mktg., N.Y., 1964-71; cons. and trustee Washington Trust, 1972-84; pres. Federal News Svc., Washington, 1985—2002; mcht. banker, 2002—. Author: Taking the Stand, Testimony of Oliver North, 1987, The National Press Club's Best Contemporary Speakers, 1995. Mem. Nat. Press Club. Avocations: boating, ballooning. Office: 9017 Swift Creek Rd Fairfax Station VA 22039-2815 E-mail: cort.randell@cox.net.*

RANDI, JAMES (RANDALL JAMES HAMILTON ZWINGE), magician, educator; b. Toronto, Aug. 7, 1928; naturalized U.S. citizen, 1987; s. George Randall and Marie Alice (Paradis) Zwinge. Student, Oakwood Collegiate Inst., Toronto, 1940-45; LittD (hon.), U. Indpls., 1995. Internationally known conjuror, lectr., author, investigator. Regent's lectr. UCLA, 1984; skeptical lectr. on paranormal subjects. Author: The Magic of Uri Geller, 1975 (with Bert Sugar) Houdini, His Life and Art, 1978, Flim-Flam, 1982, Test Your ESP Potential, 1983, The Faith Healers, 1987, The Magic World of the Amazing Randi, 1989, The Mask of Nostradamus, 1990, James Randi: Psychic Investigator, 1991, Conjuring, 1992, An Encyclopedia of Claims, Frauds, and Hoaxes of the Occult and Supernatural, 1995 (English, Chinese, French, Italian, German, Japanese, Korean, Norwegian, Punjabi, Polish and Spanish edits.); host TV spls. Japan, Korea, UK. Recipient Blackstone award Internat. Platform Assn., 1983, 87, Forum award Am. Phys. Soc., 1988, Nat. Consumer Svc. award Nat. Coun. Against Health Fraud, 1988, Gold medal U. Ghent, Belgium, 1989, Humanist Disting. Svc. award Am. Humanist Assn., 1990, medal with golden wreath Hungarian Soc. for Dissemination of Scientific Knowledge, 1992; MacArthur Found. fellow Inner Magic Cir., London 1986, Spl. fellow Acad. Magical Arts and Scis., 1987; inducted into Soc. Am. Magicians Hall of Fame, 1988. Founding fellow Com. for Scientific Investigation of Claims of the Paranormal (exec. bd. dirs. 1973-91). Achievements include performing at White House, 1974. Home: 12000 NW 8th St Fort Lauderdale FL 33325-1406 Office: James Randi Ednl Found 201 SE 12th St Fort Lauderdale FL 33316-1815 Office Phone: 954-467-1112. Personal E-mail: randi@randi.org.

RANDLEMAN, SHIRLEY B., state legislator; b. North Wilkesboro, NC, Oct. 14, 1950; m. Ronnie Randleman; children: Brian, Brad. Grad., Wilkes Cmty. Coll. Clerk Superior Ct. Wilkes County, NC, 1971—2005; mem. Dist. 94 NC House of Reps., 2009—. Republican.

Baptist. Office: North Carolina House of Representatives 300 N Salisbury St Room 531 Raleigh NC 27603-5925 Home: 487 Triple Cove Dr Wilkesboro NC 28697 Home Phone: 336-921-2043; Office Phone: 919-733-5935. Business E-Mail: Shirley.Randleman@ncleg.net.

RANDOLPH, MICHAEL K., state supreme court justice; b. 1946; m. Kathy Webb; 3 children. BA in Bus. Administration, Rollins Coll., Winter Park, Fla., 1972; JD, U. Miss. Sch. of Law, 1974. Atty. Ross, King and Randolph, Biloxi, 1975—76, Bryan, Nelson, Allen, Schroder and Randolph, Hattiesburg, 1976—2004; justice Miss. Supreme Ct., 2004—, presiding justice, 2013—. Mem. Nat. Coal Coun. Former mem. adv. bd. Hattiesburg Salvation Army; former pres. Hattiesburg Civic Assn.; former mem. Hattiesburg Area Devel. Partnership; former mem. bd. dirs. William Carey Coll., Boys and Girls Club Hattiesburg, Hattiesburg Girls Shelter. Air traffic controller US Army, atty., Judge Advocate General Corps USN. Mem.: ABA, Miss. Bar Assn. (Com. on Continuing Legal Ed. 1975—76), S. Central Miss. Bar Assn. (pres. 1986). Office: Miss Supreme Ct 450 High St Jackson MS 39201*

RANDOLPH, SCOTT, state legislator; b. Johnson City, Tenn., Oct. 17, 1973; m. Susannah Lindberg. BS, Bradley U., Peoria, Ill., 1995; JD, U. Ga., 1999. Atty.; mem. Dist. 36 Fla. House of Reps., Tallahassee, 2006—, ranking mem. govt. accountability act coun., mem. governmental affairs policy com., health care svcs. policy com. Democrat. Baptist. Office: 701 E South St Orlando FL 32801-2953 also: 400 House Office Bldg 402 S Monroe St Tallahassee FL 32399-1300 Office Phone: 407-893-3084, 850-488-0660.

RANDOLPH, ZACH, professional basketball player; b. Marion, Ind., July 16, 1981; Attended, Mich. State U., East Lansing, 2000—01. Forward Portland Trailblazers, 2001—07, NY Knicks, 2007—08, LA Clippers, 2008—09, Memphis Grizzlies, 2009—. Named Most Improved Player, NBA, 2004; named to Western Conf. All-Star Team, 2010, 2013. Office: Memphis Grizzlies 191 Beale St Memphis TN 38103

RANEY, JOHN, state legislator; m. Elizabeth Raney; 2 children. BBA, Tex. A&M U., 1969. Founder Tex. Aggieland Bookstore, 1969—; chmn. Republican Party of Brazos County, 1971—78; mem. Dist. 14 Tex. House of Representatives, 2011—. Mem.: Tex. Retailers Assn. Office: Room CAP 1N.09 Capital PO Box 2910 Austin TX 78768 also: 4103 S Texas Ave Ste 103 Bryan TX 77802-4043 Office Phone: 979-822-9797, 512-463-0698.

RANEY, STEVEN M., investment company executive; b. Tampa; m. Natalie Raney; 2 children. Grad., Chamberlain High Sch., 1983; BS in Fin., U. Fla., 1988, MBA, 1999. Tampa pres., comml. banking exec., Ctrl. Fla. Bank of America Corp., various exec. positions, Tampa Bay area, 1988—2005; ptnr., dir., bus. devel. LCM Group, 2005—06; exec. coun. Raymond James & Assocs.; pres., CEO Raymond James Bank, FSB, 2006—. Bd. dirs. Raymond James Trust Co. Elder Palma Ceia Presbyterian Church; mem., govt. rels. com. Florida Banker's Assn.; bd. trustee Tampa Bay History Ctr.; rep. Fin. Svcs. Roundtable; bd. governance Tampa Metro YMCA. Office: Raymond James Bank FSB 710 Carillon Pky Saint Petersburg FL 33716 Office Phone: 727-567-8000. Office Fax: 727-567-8618.

RANKIN, LUKE A., state legislator; b. Horry County, SC, Apr. 9, 1962; s. O. A. and Dorothy S. Rankin; m. Christy Hollingsworth, 1993. BA, U. SC, 1984, JD, 1987. Atty.; mem. Dist. 33 SC State Senate, 1993—; mem. Banking & Ins. Com., Edn. Com., Judiciary Com., Rules Com., Transp. Com. Republican. Mailing: 201 Beaty St Conway SC 29526 Office: 508 Gressette Bldg Columbia SC 29201 Office Phone: 803-248-2405, 803-212-6132. Business E-Mail: lr@legis.lpitr.state.sc.us.

RANKIN, MARY ANN, provost, zoologist; b. 1945; BS in Biology & Chemistry, La. State U., 1966; PhD in Physiology & Behavior of Insects, U. Iowa, 1972. NSF pre-doctoral fellow U. Iowa, Imperial Coll. Field Station, Ascot, England; NIH post-doctoral fellow Harvard U., 1972—74; asst. prof. zoology U. Tex., 1975—81, assoc. prof. zoology, 1981—86, prof. zoology Austin, 1986—2011, dean Coll. Natural Sciences, 1994—2011, chmn. divsn. biological sci., 1989—94; pres., CEO Nat. Math & Sci. Initiative (NMSI), Dallas, 2011—12; sr. v.p., provost U. Md., College Park, 2012—. Vice-chmn. bd. dirs. Southwest Rsch. Inst., San Antonio; bd. mem. Nat. Math & Sci. Initiative (NMSI), 2012—. Named one of The 100 Women Leaders in STEM, STEMconnector, 2012. Mem.: AAAS, Royal Entomological Soc., American Entomological Soc. Office: University of Maryland Office of the Senior VP & Provost 119 Main Administration Bldg College Park MD 20742-5031

RANKIN, ROBERT ARTHUR, retired journalist; b. Richmond, Va., May 31, 1949; s. Arthur Norton and Martha Louise (Rountree) Rankin; m. Janis Johnson, May 11, 1979 (div. May 2001); 1 child, Benjamin John; m. Judy A. Stromberg, Apr. 9, 2005. BA in Polit. Sci., Randolph Macon Coll., 1971; MA in Govt., U. Va., 1974. Cert. in Economics and Bus. Journalism Columbia U., 1979. Reporter Richmond News Leader, Va., 1972-75; reporter Congl. Quar., Washington, 1975-78; editorial writer Miami Herald, Fla., 1980-85, Phila. Inquirer, 1985-87; nat. corr. Washington bur. Knight Ridder Newspapers, Washington, 1987—99, politics and economics editor, 2000—06, McClatchy Newspapers, Washington, 2006—12; adj. prof., media & politics Randolph-Macon Coll., 2009, 2013. V.p. Civic Assn. Hollin Hills, Alexandria, Va., 1991—92. Recipient Olive Br. award, NYU Ctr. War, Peace and News Media, 1990, 1st prize, Va. Press Assn., 1974, Best Editl. award, Phila. chpt. Sigma Delta Chi, 1987; co-recipient Pulitzer prize for editl. writing, 1983. Episcopalian.

RANNEY, CARLETON DAVID, retired plant pathologist; b. Jackson, Minn., Jan. 23, 1928; s. Carleton Oran and Ada Elizabeth (Harriman) R.; m. Mary Kathryn Ransleben, July 16, 1949; children: David Clayton, Mary Elizabeth. AA, Chaffey Jr. Coll., Ontario, Calif., 1952; BS, Tex. A&M U., 1954, MS, 1955, PhD, 1959. Plant pathologist Crops Rsch. Divsn. Agrl. Rsch. Svc. USDA, College Station, Tex., 1955-58, Stoneville, Miss., 1958-70, investigations leader Beltsville, Md., 1970-72; area dir. Ala. No. Miss. area Agrl. Rsch. Svc. USDA, Starkville, Miss., 1973-78, area dir. Delta States area Stoneville, Miss., 1978-84, area dir. Mid-South area, 1984-87; asst. dir. Miss. Agrl. and Forestry Exptl. Stas., Stoneville, 1987-94, head Delta Rsch. and Ext. Ctr., 1987-94, emeritus plant pathologist, 1994—. Adj. prof. agronomy Miss. State U., 1972—94; sr. exec. svc. USDA, Stoneville, 1984—87; adv. bd. belt wide meetings Nat. Cotton Coun., Memphis, 1987—96. Contbr. articles to profl. jours. Sect. advisor SE2 Order of Arrow, Boy Scouts Am., Miss. and West Tenn., 1973-83; pres. Delta Area coun. Boy Scouts Am., Clarksdale, Miss., 1990-91, Eagle Scout; v.p. Leland Habitat for Humanity, 1995-2000, bd. dirs. 2000-06. Served with USAAC, 1946-49. Recipient Silver Beaver Boy Scouts Am., 1981, Disting. Svc. Order of Arrow Boy Scouts Am., 1983, Superior Svc. award USDA, 1981, Cert. of Merit USDA, 1983. Mem. Agron. Soc. Am., Nat. Cotton Disease Coun. (sec. 1959-60, chmn. 1961-62), Lions (pres. Leland club 1995-96), Sigma Xi, Alpha Zeta, Phi Kappa Phi. Methodist. Achievements include development of fungicide control seedling diseases; definition of relationship of microclimate to boll rot of cotton; development of non-mercurial seed treatments. Office: Delta Rsch & Ext Ctr PO Box 226 Stoneville MS 38776-0226 Office Phone: 662-686-9311. E-mail: rs2dk49@tecinfo.net.

RANSONE, MARGARET B., state legislator; b. Richmond, Va., Apr. 24, 1973; m. Christopher Todd; children: Ann Morgan, Christopher Bevan. BA, Randolph-Macon Coll., 2002. Mem. Dist. 99 Va. House of Delegates, 2012—, mem. Privileges and Elections Com., Health Welfare and Institutions Com. & Agr. Chesapeake and Natural Resources Com. Mem.: Va. Bait Assn., Va. Seafood Coun. Republican. Office: General Assembly Building PO Box 406 Richmond VA 23218 also: PO Box 358 Kinsale VA 22488 Office Phone: 804-698-1099. Office Fax: 804-786-6310. E-mail: DelMRansone@house.virginia.gov.

RANTA, RICHARD ROBERT, university dean; b. Virginia, Minn., Nov. 18, 1943; s. V. Robert and Bernice (Smith) R.; 1 child, Erick H.; m. Carol Crown. AS, Hibbing Community Coll., Minn., 1963; BS, U. Minn., 1965; MA, Cornell U., 1967; PhD, U. Iowa, 1974. Floor dir. Sta. KDAL-TV, Duluth, Minn., 1964-65; asst. prof. U. Va., Charlottesville, 1969-72, U. Memphis, 1972-75, assoc. prof., 1975-91, prof., 1991—, interim dean Univ. Coll., 1975, asst. v.p. academic affairs, 1976-78, dean Coll. Comm. and Fine Arts, 1977—; gen. mgr. High Water Records, Memphis, 1980—. Bd. dirs. Concerts Internat., Memphis, pres., 1988-90; TV cons., free-lance producer, 1973—; mem. Rec. Hall of Fame selection panel Nat. Rec. Acad., L.A., 1986-2000; vice-chmn. Gilliam Comm., 1992-. Assoc. prodr.: (TV program) Nat. Arthritis Telethon, 1985-90; Rec. Acad. graphics and prodn. coord. Grammy Awards TV program, 1983—, writer and judge Knowledge Bowl TV Show, 1986-; author articles in Communication Adminstrn. Bull., 1977-2001, editl. bd., 1991-2001, exec. com., 1996-2000. Chmn., v.p. Tenn. Humanities Coun., Nashville, 1980-82; v.p. Memphis Devel. Found., 1983-86; bd. dirs. Leadership Memphis, 1987-90, 94-97, chmn. mktg. com., 1987-90, chmn. selection com., 1994-95; bd. dirs. Life Blood, Memphis, 1984-92; treas. Memphis-Shelby County Film and TV Commn., 1986-98, chair, 1999-2002, bd. dirs., 2002--; mem. Tenn. Film, Entertainment and Music Commn., Nashville, 1987-97, chmn., 1993-95; chmn. bd. dirs. Crime Stoppers Memphis Assn., 1993-95; chmn. Memphis Arts Festival, 1992-94;bd. dirs. Tenn. Arts Commn., 2000-06. Recipient Edn. Operational Models grant Ednl. Testing Svc., 1975, Communication Lab. grant HEW, 1976, Disting. Alumnus award Minn. Cmty. Coll. System, 1984, Alumni Cmty. Svc. award Leadership Memphis, 1997. Mem. NARAS (v.p. 1986-88, 92-93, chmn. edn. com. 1983—2001, trustee 1982-86, 88-92, 93-97, pres. Memphis chpt. 1984-86, bd. govs. 1978-98), So. States Comm. Assn. (pres. 1987-88, fin. bd. 1985-87, 93-95, exec. dir. 1995—2000, publs. bd. mem. 2011-), Tenn. Speech Comm. Assn. (pres. 1986-87, editor Communicator 1993—), Nat. Comm. Assn. (vice chmn., then chmn. exptl. learning com. 1979-83, mem. fin. and adminstrn. coms. 1989-93, chmn. fin. com. 1991-93), Am. Comm. Jour. (edtl. bd. mem. 1997-2003), Southern Arts Fedn. (bd. dirs. 1994-2000, 2003-10, treas.), Internat. Coun. Fine Arts Deans (parliamentarian 1996-2000), Tenn. Arts and Scis. Deans Assn. (chair 1997-98), Advt. Fedn. (bd. dirs. 2001-03, Silver medal 2011), Delta Sailing Assn. Club (sec. 1984-2000), Memphis Rotary Internat. Club (pres.-elect, asst. dist. govs. 2008-), Nat. Metal Mus. (bd. dirs. 2004-, greater memphis greenways bd. mem., 2009-), Memphis Art Pk. Comm., Historic Beale & Street Brass Note (selection com. mem. 2009-), Memphis Light, Gas & Water (citizens adv. bd. mem. 2008-). Avocations: sailing, tennis, photography, fishing. Office: U Memphis Coll Communication & Fine Ar Memphis TN 38152-0001 E-mail: rranta@memphis.edu.

RANU, HARCHARAN SINGH, biomedical scientist, administrator, orthopaedic biomechanics educator; b. Lyallpur, India; came to U.S., 1976; s. Jodh Singh and Harnam Kaur R. BSc, De Montfort U., Eng., 1963; MSc, U. Surrey, Guilford, Eng., 1967, Cambridge U., Eng., 1972; PhD, Middlesex Hosp. Med. Sch. and U. Westminster, London, 1975; diploma, MIT, 1984. Chartered engr., scientist, Eng. Med. scientist Nat. Inst. Med. Rsch. of the Med. Rsch. Coun., London, 1967-70; rsch. fellow Middlesex Hosp. Med. Sch. and Poly. of Cen. London, 1971-76; rsch. scientist Plastics Rsch. Assn. of Great Britain, Shawbury, Eng., 1977; asst. prof. Wayne State U., Detroit, 1977-81; prof. biomed. engring./orthopaedic biomechanics biomaterials La. Tech. U., Ruston, 1982—; prof., chmn. dept. biomechanics N.Y. Coll. Osteo. Medicine, Old Westbury, 1989-93; dir. tng. Rehab. R&D Ctr., 1983-85; mem. La. Tech. U. Libr. Com., 1983-85; chmn. design competition Assn. Biomed. Engrs.; mem. steering com. So. Biomed. Engring. Confs., 1983—; chmn. tech. in health care conf. U. Cambridge, 1985; chmn. Internat. Symposium on Bioengring., Calcutta, India, 1985; dir. orthopaedic biomechanics rsch. labs., staff Nassau County Med. Ctr., Long Island, 1989—; prof., exec. asst. to pres., and dir. doctoral program Life U., Marietta, Ga., 1993—; pres. Am. Orthop. Biomechanics Rsch. Inst., Atlanta, 1997—; prof. Coll. Applied Med. Scis., King Saud U., Riyadh; cons. orthop. dept. Coll. Medicine. Biomed. engring. faculty com. La. Tech. U., faculty com., rsch. awards com., grad. studies com., grad. faculty, acad. bd. dirs; vis. scientist Dryburn Hosp., Durham, Eng., 1985-87, cons., 1988—; vis. prof. U. Istanbul, 1982, Lab. de Recherch Orthopediques, Paris, 1985—, Kings Coll. Med. Sch. U. London, 1989—, Indian Inst. Tech., New Delhi, Postgrad Inst. Med. Edn. and Rsch., Chandigarh, India, 1989—, Polytech. Ctrl. London, 1991—, U. Buenos Aires, Pontific Cath. U. Chile, Fed. U. Rio de Janeiro; adj. prof. Coll. Physicians and Surgeons Columbia U., NYC, 1988—, Inst. Biol. Physics USSR Acad. Sci., Moscow, 1990, NY Coll. Podiatric Medicine, 1991—, CUNY, 1992—; cons. Lincoln Gen. Hosp., Ruston, La., 1982-85, La. State U. Med. Ctr., Shreveport, 1982—, St. Luke's and Roosevelt Hosp. Ctr., NY, 1988—, Foot Clinics N., 1991—, Vets. Affairs Med. Ctr., NY, 1992—, others; media resource svc. Inst. Pub. Info., NY, 1989—; med. scientist, cons. NATO, 1982—; presenter, lectr. in field; external examiner for doctoral candidates All India Inst. Med. Scis., New Delhi, Indian Inst. Tech., New Delhi, Banaras Hindu U., Varanasi, India, 1994; prof. U. Surrey, 2009; pres. Am. Orthop. Biomechanics Rsch. Inst., Atlanta, 1997; rsch. award com. mem. Am. Coll. Sports Medicine. Author: Rheological Behavior of Articular Cartiliage Under Tensile Loads, 1967, Effects of Ionizing Radiation on the Mechanical Properties of Skin, 1975, Effects of Fractionated Doses of X-irradiation on the Mechanical Properties of Skin--A Long Term Study, 1980, Effects of Ionizing Radiation on the Structure & Physical Properties of the Skin, 1983, 3-D Model of Vertebra for Spinal Surgery, 1985, Application of Carbon Fibers in Orthopaedic Surgery, 1985, Relation Between Metal Corrision & Electrical Polarization, 1989, The Distribution of Stresses in the Human Lumbar Spine, 1989, Medical Devices & Orthopaedic Implants in the United States, 1989, Spinal Surgery by Modeling, 1989, Multipoint Determination of Pressure-Volume Curves in Human Intervertebral Discs, 1993, Evaluation of Volume-Pressure Relationship in Lumbar Discs Using Model and Experimental Studies, 1994, A Mechanism of Laser Nuclectomy, 1994, Microminiaturization in Laser Surgery in Vivo Intradiscal Pressure Measurements in Lumbar Intervertebral Discs, 1994, An Experimental and Mathematical Simulation of Fracture of Human Bone Due to Jumping, 1994; editor The Lower Extremity, 1993—; guest editor IEEE Engring. in Medicine & Biology, 1991; mem. editl. bd. Med. Instrumentation, 1988—, Jour. Biomed. Instrumentation & Tech., 1988—, Jour. Med. Engring. & Tech., 1989—, Jour. Med. Design & Material, 1990—, Jour. Long-Term Effects Med. Implants, 1991—, Biomed. Sci. & Tech., 1991—, Health & Fitness, 2007, rsch. award com. Am. Coll. Sports Medicine, 2009; reviewer Jour. Biomechanics, 1981—, Clin. Biomechanics, 1984—, Jour. Biomed. Engring., 1981, Phys. Therapy, 1990—, IEEE Biomed. Transactions, 1991—, Jour. Engring. in Medicine, 1989—; contbr. articles to profl. jours. Faculty advisor India Students Assn. Wayne State U., 1980. Recipient Edwin Tate award U. Surrey, 1968, Third Internat. Olympic Com. World Congress On Sprots Scis. award, Atlanta, 1995; numerous rsch. grants. Fellow ASME (bioengring. com. 1990—, award L.I. chpt. 1991, peer reviewer 2010), Biol. Engring. Soc. (London, President's prize 1984), Instn. Mech. Engrs. (chmn. revv. bd. for corp. memberships, James Clayton awards 1974-76), Inst. Physics and Engring. in Medicine; mem. AAAS, Am. Soc. Biomechanics (edn. com. 1990—), Orthopaedic Rsch. Soc., Am. Coll. Sports Medicine, Biomed. Engring. Soc., India Assn., India Assn. North La., Sci. Coun. Eng. (chartered scientist). Sikh. Achievements include research in microfracture simulation of human vertebrae under compressive loading, laserectomy of the human nucleus pulposus and its effect on the intradiscal pressure, pressure-volume relation in human intervertebral discs, in vitro and in vivo intradiscal pressure measurements before and after laserectomy of the human nucleus pulposus, gait analysis of a diabetic foot, bioengineering in the millennium, bioengineering-building the future of biology and medicine, bioengineering the cutting edge of biology and medicine in the millennium, in vivo micro-fracture simulation in Indian Olympic field hockey players, relief from low-back pain in sports by infusion of saline into the human nucleus pulposus and establishing the pressure-volume relationship, clinical applications of bioinstrumentation for better health, fifth IOC World Congress on sports sciences, micro-fracture simulation in tennis players, human gait analysis normal and pathological, simulation of micro-fracture injury in female gymnasts-an in vivo study, pattern recognition in human gait, identification of ethnicity from human gait; micro-fracture injury simulation in pole-vaulting and female gymnasts; 3-D simulation of drop in intradiscal pressure in spinal discs due to laserectomy; Ranu's principle and laserectomy to relieve low back pain; Ranu's cumulative gait effect phenomenon, invivo micro-fracture simulation in skiers; 3-D foot pressure measurements in normal and diabetic persons; normal and abnormal gait of successive steps with miniature triaxial load cells; gait analysis of amputees initally and one month later for successive steps; stress-fracture simulationi n ski jumpers, the effect of ovariectomy on antioxidant system of bone, micro-fracture simulation in vivo in human bone, amputees gait analyses for sucssessive steps, viscoelastic properties of the human spinal disc, normal and prevention of pedal sequelae in diabetic patients a 3D pattern analysis, ovariec tomy and its antioxidative effects on bone, Use of Ranus Technology in Prevention of High Forefoot Pressures & Amputations in Diabetics, Micro Fracture Injury Simulation in Diabetic Foot An In Vivo Study, Biomedical Engineering Design Education at King Saud University A First of Its Kind Approach, Simulation of Stress Fracture in Human Vertebral Body Due to Extreme Weight Lifting, Amputees Gait Analysis with Miniature Triaxial Load Cells for Successive Steps, Time Dependent Properties of the Human Spinal Column to Loading, Development of An Innovative Masters Programme in Bioinstrumentation King Saud U., micro fracture simulation of Vertebral body due to extreme weight lifting an In vivo study, in vivo injury simulation in female gymnasts, response of the Human spinal Column to loading and its Time Dependent Characteristics. Office: Life Univ Sch Grad Studies Marietta GA 30060 Personal E-mail: profranu@yahoo.com.

RAPER, CHARLES ALBERT, retired management consultant; b. Charleston, W.Va., Aug. 18, 1926; s. Kenneth B. and Louise (Williams) R.; m. Margaret Ann Weers, Dec. 26, 1947; children: Kathleen, Josephine, Charles. Student, Okla. State U., 1945; BS, U. Ill., 1949. Sales mgr. Meyer Furnace Co., Peoria, Ill., 1949-54; v.p. mktg. Master Consol., Inc., Dayton, Ohio, 1954-61; mgmt. cons. McKinsey & Co., Inc., Chgo., 1961-67; v.p. mktg. Gen. Portland Inc., Dallas, 1967-69, pres., also dir., 1969-75; v.p., gen. mgr. Scholl Inc., Chgo., 1975-81; pres. Oxford Group of Sara Lee, 1981-84; mgmt. cons. McKinsey & Co., 1984—. Vice-chmn. devel. bd. U. Tex., Dallas; exec. bd. Circle 10 coun. Boy Scouts Am.; counselor Svc. Corp. of Ret. Execs., 1998-2010. With USN, 1944-46. Mem. Dallas C. of C. (chmn. bd. dirs. 1974—), Sales Execs. Club, Cherokee Country Club, Chattooga Club, Atlanta Mallet Club (pres.), Phi Gamma Delta. Methodist. Home: 3750 Peachtree Rd Apt 482 Atlanta GA 30319

RAPER, WILLIAM BURKETTE, retired college president; b. nr. Wilson, NC, Sept. 10, 1927; s. William Cecil and Beulah Maybelle (Davis) R.; m. Rose Mallard, Aug. 19, 1951; children: Olivia, Kristie, Burkette, Elizabeth, Stephen (dec.), Laura. AB, Duke U., 1947, MDiv, 1951; MS (Kellogg fellow), Fla. State U., 1962; LLD, Atlantic Christian Coll. (now Barton Coll.), 1960. Ordained to ministry Free Will Baptist Ch., 1946; pastor Hull Rd. Free Will Bapt. Ch., Snow Hill, NC, 1951-55; pres. Mt. Olive (N.C.) Coll., 1954-95, ret. pres. emeritus, 1995. Dir. Wachovia Bank and Trust Co., 1979-97; promotional dir. Free Will Bapt. State Conv. N.C., 1953-54; pres. council Ch.-Related Colls. N.C., 1966-67; mem. N.C. Edn. Assistance Authority, 1972-76; sec. Ind. Coll. Fund of N.C., 1976-78; Mem. N.C. Gov.'s Com. on Hwy. Traffic Safety, 1968; regional coordinator U.S. Office Edn. Program with Developing Instns., 1968-70; dir. Edn. Professions Devel. Act Grant for Strengthening Devel. in Pvt. Two-Year Colls., 1970-72; trustee N.C. Coll. Found., 1977-94; adv. com. Ind. Coll. Presidents, U. N.C. Pres. N.C. Found. Christian Ministries, 2005. Recipient Disting. Service award Mt. Olive Jr. C. of C., 1961; named N.C. Young Man of Year, 1961 Mem. Am. Assn. Community and Jr. Colls. (commn. on legislation 1963-66, cons. 1968-71, chmn. commn. on student personnel 1970-71), N.C. Assn. Ind. Colls. and Univs. (exec. com. 1967-70, 76-77, 83-85), N.C. Assn. Colls. and Univs. (pres. 1969-70), Masons. Democrat. Office: Mt Olive Coll Office of Pres Emeritus Mount Olive NC 28365 Home Phone: 919-658-3855; Office Phone: 919-658-5250. E-mail: wraper@moc.edu.

RAPINI, RONALD PETER, dermatology educator; b. Akron, Ohio, Feb. 15, 1954; s. Vincent Thomas and Joann Irene (Tufexis) R.; m. Mary Jo Beigel, June 16, 1979; children: Brianna Marie, Sarina Elizabeth. BS in Biology, U. Akron, 1975; MD, Ohio State U., 1978. Diplomate Am. Bd. Dermatology (bd. dirs. 1996-2004, pres. 2004), Am. Bd. Dermatopathology. Assoc. prof. U. Tex. Med. Sch., Houston, 1983-93; prof. and chair dermatology dept. Tex. Tech. U., Lubbock, 1994—2002; prof., chair dept. dermatology U. Tex. Med. Sch., 2002—, MD Anderson Cancer Ctr., Houston, 2002—. Author (with K.G. Gross and H.K. Steinman): Mohs Surgery, 1999; author: (with J. Bolognia and J. Jorizzo) Dermatology, 2007; author: Practical Dermatopathology, 2005, of over 150 other publications. Fellow Am. Acad. Dermatology (bd. dir. 2010-), Am. Soc. Dermatol. Surgery (bd. dir. 1995-98), Soc. Investigative Dermatology; mem. AMA, Am. Soc. Dermatopathology (pres. 1998-99), Am. Soc. Mohs Surgery (pres. 2003), Internat. Soc. Dermatopathology, Tex. Dermatol. Soc. (pres. 2006—07). Avocations: tennis, entomology, piano. Office: U TEx Med Sch 6655 Travis St 980 Houston TX 77030-0001 Office Phone: 713-745-1113.

RAPP, RAYMOND C., state legislator; State rep. Dist. 118, NC, 2002—; dean Adult Access, Mars Hill Coll. Mem. Commerce, Small Bus. and Entrepreneurship com., Edn. com., Edn. Subcom. on Presch., Elem., and Secondary Edn., Transp. com., Univ. Bd. Govs. Nominating com.; vice chmn. Health com., Appropriations com.; chmn. Appropriations Subcom. on Edn., House Select Com. on Comprehensive Rail Svc. Plan for NC. Democrat. Office: North Carolina House of Representatives 16 W Jones St Rm 1013 Raleigh NC 27601-1096 Office Phone: 919-733-5732. E-mail: Ray.Rapp@ncleg.net.

RAPPAPORT, MARTIN PAUL, internist, nephrologist, educator; b. Bronx, NY, Apr. 25, 1935; s. Joseph and Anne (Kramer) R.; m. Bethany Ann Mitchell; children: Karen, Steven; stepchildren: Aaron Cole, Kevin Cole. BS, Tulane U., 1957, MD, 1960; diploma, Tulane Med. Sch., New Orleans, 2010. Diplomate Am. Bd. Internal Medicine, Nat. Bd. Med. Examiners. Intern Charity Hosp. of La., New Orleans, 1960-61, resident in internal medicine, 1961-64; pvt. practice internal medicine and nephrology, Seabrook, Tex., 1968-72, Webster, Tex., 1972-98; internist Univ. Med. Group, Houston, 1998; mem. courtesy staff Mainland Ctr. Hosp. (formerly Galveston County Meml. Hosp.), Texas City, 1968-96, Bapt. Meml. System, 1969-72, 88-98; mem. staff Clear Lake Regional Med. Ctr., 1972-98; cons. staff St. Mary's Hosp., 1973-79; cons. nephrology St. John's Hosp., Nassau Bay, Tex.; fellow in nephrology Northwestern U. Med. Sch., Chgo., 1967—68; clin. asst. prof. in medicine and nephrology U. Tex., Galveston, 1969—2009; part-time physician dept. family medicine outpatient clinics U. Tex. Med. Br., Galveston, 2000; locum tenens, 2000—06; ret., 2005. Lectr. emergency med. technician cours e, 1974-76; adviser on respiratory therapy program Alvin (Tex.) Jr. Coll., 1976-82; cons. nephrology USPHS, 1979-80. Served to capt. M.C. U.S. Army, 1961-67. Fellow ACP, Am. Coll. Chest Physicians; mem. Internat., Am. Socs. Nephrology, So. Med. Assn., Tex. Med. Assn., Tex. Soc. Internal Medicine (bd. govs. 1994-96), Am. Soc. Artificial Internal Organs, Tex. Acad. Internal Medicine, Harris County Med. Soc., Am. Geriatrics Soc., Bay Area Heart Assn. (bd. govs. 1969-75), Clear Lake C. of C., Conroe Rotary Club, Rotary, Phi Delta Epsilon, Alpha Epsilon Pi, Tulane Alumni Assn. (50 Yr. diploma 1960-2010), Tex. Med. Assn. Home: 15913 Malibu W Willis TX 77318-6784

RAPPAPORT, NORMAN HARVEY, plastic surgeon; b. Phila., Apr. 23, 1947; s. Herbert and Ruth Rappaport; m. Deborah Ann Finn, Oct. 2, 1982; children: Jonathan David, Betsy, William. BA, LaSalle Coll., 1969; DDS, Temple U., 1972; MD, Hahnemann Med. Coll., 1975. Diplomate Am. Bd. Plastic Surgery. Resident in gen. surgery Abington (Pa.) Meml. Hosp., 1975-78; fellow in hand surgery U. Pa., Phila., 1978; resident in plastic surgery Baylor Coll. Medicine, Houston, 1978-80; clin. assoc. prof. surgery Baylor Coll. Surgery, Houston, 1994—. Contbr. articles to profl. jours. Fellow: ACS; mem.: AMA, Houston Surg. Soc. (pres. 2001), Tex. Soc. Plastic Surgeons, Tex. Med. Assn., N.Am. Burn Soc., Houston Soc. Plastic Surgeons (pres. 2002), Harris County Med. Soc., Am. Assn. Hand Surgeons, Am. Assn. Plastic Surgeons, Am. Soc. for Aesthetic Plastic Surgery, Am. Soc. Plastic Surgeons (bd. dirs. 1998—2000), Plastic Surgery Edn. Found. (bd. dirs. 1994—2000), Am. Soc. Maxillofacial Surgeons (pres. 2000), Omicron Kappa Upsilon. Office: 6560 Fannin St Ste 1812 Houston TX 77030-2775 Office Phone: 713-790-4500. E-mail: nhr@hcps.cc.

RAPPAPORT, YVONNE KINDINGER, educator; b. Crestline, Ohio, Feb. 15, 1928; d. Paul Theodore and Florence Iona (Cover) Kindinger; m. Norman Lewis Rappaport; children: Michael, Laura, Hilary, Stephen, Jocelyn Pers. BS summa cum laude, Northwestern U., 1949; MA, Va. Poly. Inst. & State U., 1973, PhD, 1980. Officer, cons. & mgmt. analyst USAF, 1953—63, cons. mgmt. analysis, pers. & pub. rels., 1963—67; cons. program devel., instr. U. Va., 1967—70, dir. continuing edn. women, 1970—75, dir. & faculty continuing edn. adult, 1975—85, dir. continuing edn., 1986—93, cons. human resources, 1993—; dir., performer theatre, children's theatre, radio & TV, 1953—; bd. dirs. Coalition Adult Edn. Orgns. US, 1979—, sec.-treas., 1981—83, v.p., 1983—84, pres.-elect, 1984—85, pres., 1985—87, chair internat. assocs. adult edn., 1987—89; US rep. UNESCO conf. Hamburg, Germany, 1983, 1997; del. Buenos Aires World Assembly, 1985, Helsinki Peace Conf., 1986, Bangkok World Assembly, 1990; cons. in field. Mem. Va. Legis. Adv. Com. Continuing Edn., 1970—71, Northern Va. Adv. Com. Ednl. Telecomm., 1971—; bd. dirs. Home & Sch. Inst., Washington, 1971—; adv. bd. Svc. League Va., 1976—78. Recipient Meritorious Svc. award, USAF, 1959, Career Devel. award, ASTD-TOC, 1980, Outstanding Eucator award, Va. Tech., 1998. Mem.: LWV (state dir. 1968—73, nat. pub. rels. com. 1970—75), PTA, AAUW, Va. C. of C. (mem. edn. com. 1987—), Fairfax C. of C., Am. Bus. Women Assn. (award 1960), World Affairs Coun. (bd. dirs. 1987—), Assn. Continuing Higher Edn., Nat. U. Ext. Assn., Pers. & Guidance Assn., Adult Edn. Assn. Va. (pres. 1971—73, Merit award 1971—73), Adult Edn. Assn. US (v.p. 1978—79, chmn. commn. status women in edn. 1972—74, dir. 1973—83, chmn. coun. affiliate orgns. 1974—75, chmn. pub. affairs 1975—78, chair program gen. session 1987, Nat. Leadership award 1973—74, 1976, 1978—79, 1982—83, 1986, 1988), Nat. Assn. Women Deans, Adminstrs. & Counselors (SE regional coord. 1973—76), Phi Delta Theta, Phi Delta Kappa (v.p. programs 1994, pres.-elect 1994), Order Ea. Star. Home: 3225 Atlanta St Fairfax VA 22030-2127 Office: Sch Continuing Edn U Va Charlottesville VA 22903

RARIDON, RICHARD JAY, retired computer scientist; b. Newton, Iowa, Oct. 25, 1931; s. Jack Allison and Letha Helen (Woods) R.; m. Mona Marie Herndon, May 28, 1956; children— Susan Gayle, Ann Chaney. BA, Grinnell Coll., 1953; MA, Vanderbilt U., 1955, PhD, 1959. Assoc. prof. phys. sci. Memphis State U., 1958-62; rsch. scientist Oak Ridge Nat. Lab., 1962-92; cons. ORNL, 1992—2004. Environ. specialist Coop. Sci. Edn. Center, Oak Ridge, 1971-72 Contbr. articles to profl. jours. Radiol. Physics fellow AEC, 1953-55 Fellow AAAS, Tenn. Acad. Sci. (pres. 1971); mem. Assn. Acads. Sci. (sec.-treas. 1972-76, pres. 1977) Home: 111 Columbia Dr Oak Ridge TN 37830-7720 Personal E-mail: raridon@hotmail.com.

RASH, MARTIN S., healthcare company executive; B, MBA, Mid. Tenn. State U. Exec. v.p., COO Cmty. Health Sys., Inc.; CEO, bd. dirs. Principal Hosp. Co., 1996; co-founder, CEO Province Healthcare Co. (acquired by LifePoint Hospitals, Inc.), 1996—2005, chmn. Brentwood, Tenn., 1998—2005. Bd. dirs. Healthspring Inc., 2005—. Chmn. Fedn. Am. Hosps.; bd. dirs. Nashville Health Care Coun. Office: HealthSpring Inc Bd Directors 9009 Carothers Pky Bldg B Ste 501 Franklin TN 37067 Office Phone: 615-291-7000. Business E-Mail: martin.rash@healthspring.com.

RASH, RON VINCENT, writer, educator; b. Chester Springs, SC, 1953; BA in English, Gardner-Webb Coll., Boiling Springs, NC; MA in English, Clemson U., SC. Vis. writer U. SC; John A. Parris Jr. & Dorothy Luxton Parris Disting. Prof. Appalachian cultural studies Western Carolina U., Cullowhee, NC, 2003—. Author: (novels) One Foot in Eden, 2002 (Novello Literary award, 2002, Gold medal in Lit. Fiction, ForeWord Mag., 2002, Appalachian Book of Yr., 2002), Saints at the River, 2004 (Southern Book Critics Circle Fiction Book of Yr., 2004, Southeastern Booksellers Assn. Fiction Book of Yr., 2004), The World Made Straight, 2006, Serena, 2008, The Cove, 2012, (short story collections) The Night The New Jesus Fell to Earth and Other Stories from Cliffside, North Carolina, 1994, Casualties, 2000, Chemistry and Other Stories, 2007, Nothing Gold Can Stay, 2013, (poetry) Eureka Mill, 1998, Among the Believers, 2000, Raising the Dead, 2002, (children's books) The Shark's Tooth, 2001; contbr. articles, short stories and poems to numerous publs. Recipient GE Younger Writers award, 1987, Sherwood Anderson prize, 1996, James Still award, Fellowship Southern Writers, 2005, O. Henry prize, 2005; grantee Arts Poetry fellowship, NEA, 1994. Office: Western Carolina University Dept English 402 Coulter Cullowhee NC 28723 Office Phone: 828-227-3917. Business E-Mail: ronrash@email.wcu.edu.

RASKIN, JEFFREY B., medical educator; s. James M. and Devy Raskin; m. Bobbie C. Campbell; children: Scott E., Tracy A., Lori A. MD, U. Miami Sch. Medicine, 1965. Diplomate Am. Bd. Internal Medicine, in gastroenterology Am. Bd. Medicine. Prof. medicine U Miami Sch.Medicine, 2002—; prof., Cye Mandel chair gastroenterology U. Miami Sch. Medicine, 2002—. Contbr. articles to profl. jours. Mem., dist. athletic adv. com. Miami-Dade Sch. Dist., 1989—2005. Capt. USAF, 1966—68, Smyrna, Tenn. Recipient Disting. Svc. award, Fla. Gastroenterologic Soc., 2002, Disting. Alumnus award, U. Miami Sch. Medicine, 2004. Fellow: ACP, AGA, ASGE, Am. Coll. Gastroentology. Office: U Miami Jackson Meml Med Ctr 1611 NW 12 th Ave Rm SW 220 Miami FL 33136 Office Phone: 305-243-8644. Office Fax: 305-243-3762. Business E-Mail: jraskin@med.miami.edu.*

RASKIN, PHILIP, physician, educator; b. Pitts., Dec. 31, 1940; BA, Wash. and Jefferson Coll., 1962; MD, U. Pitts., 1966. Prof., medicine U. Tex. Southwestern Med. Ctr. Dallas, 1970—. USAF, 1968—70 AMRL Wright Patterson AFB, Ohio. Recipient Alumni award, Wash. & Jefferson Coll., 2007, Hench award, U. Pitts., 2011; Owens fellowship. Office: 5323 Harry Hines Blvd Ste G05238 Dallas TX 75390-8858 Office Fax: 214-648-4854. Business E-Mail: philip.raskin@utsouthwestern.edu.*

RASMUSSEN, ROBERT L., museum director, military officer; b. Calif. m. Phyllis Colter; children: Kathryn, Eric. Joined USN, 1951, advanced through ranks to capt., ret., 1983; mem. Naval Aviation Cadet Prog., 1951—53; served aboard USS Philippine Sea, 1953—56; 1st exec. officer, commdg. officer Fighter Squadron 111, 1966; chief of staff, ops. officer Carrier Divsn. Seven; commdg. officer USS Mount Hood, Roosevelt Roads Naval Sta., PR; comdr. Bur. Navy Personnel, Aviation Officer Distbn. Divsn., Washington; commdg. officer Naval Aviation Schools Command, Pensacola, Fla.; dir. devel. Nat. Aviation Mus. Found., Pensacola, Fla., 1983—87; dir. Nat. Mus. Naval Aviation, Pensacola, Fla., 1987—. Avocations: watercolors, aviation art, sculpting. Office: Nat Mus Naval Aviation 1750 Radford Blvd Ste C Pensacola FL 32508-5400 Business E-Mail: bob.rasmussen@cnet.navy.mil.

RASOUL, SAM, entrepreneur; b. Warren, Ohio; s. Ralph and Jenny Rasoul; m. Layaly Rasoul, 2006. BBA, Roanoke Coll., Salem, Va.; MBA in Internat. Bus., Hawaii Pacific U., Honolulu. Founder Sunshine Entertainment 2, LLC, 2003—; gen. mgr. Provita USA LLC, 2004—; owner shopping plaza, 2005—. Democrat. Office: Provita USA LLC 8345 Moneta Rd Bedford VA 24523 also: Sunshine Entertainment 2 LLC 8347 Moneta Rd Bedford VA 24523 Office Phone: 540-297-7400, 540-297-3900.

RASPINO, LOUIS A., energy executive; b. 1953; BS, La. State U.; MBA, Loyola U. CPA. Various positions to sr. v.p. fin., adminstrn., CFO La. Land & Exploration Co. (merged with Burlington), 1978—97; sr. v.p. Burlington Resources, 1997—98; v.p., fin. Halliburton Co., 1999—2000; exec. v.p., CFO and COO JRL Enterprises Inc., 2000—01; sr. v.p., fin., CFO Grant Prideco. Inc., Houston, 2001—03; exec. v.p., CFO Pride International, Inc., Houston, 2003—05, pres., CEO and dir., 2005—11. Bd. dirs. Dresser-Rand Group Inc., 2005—, Forum Energy Technologies. Bd. dirs. Mem. Hermann Healthcare System. Office: Dresser Rand West Tower Ste 1000 10205 Westheimer Rd Houston TX 77042

RASSIN, DAVID KEITH, nutrition educator, researcher; b. Liverpool, Eng., Dec. 1, 1942; arrived in US, 1974, naturalized, 1974; s. Meyer and Ella Rosetta (House) R.; m. Mildred Glennda McConnell, Feb. 5, 1965; children: Meya Glynne, Keith David. AB, Columbia U., NYC, 1965; PhD, CUNY, 1974. Rsch. scientist IV Inst. Basic Rsch. in Mental Retardation, Staten Island, NY, 1977-79, rsch. scientist V, 1979-80; with U. Tex. Med. Br., Galveston, 1980—, dir. devel. nutrition and metabolism, 1980—2009, prof. perinatal pediatrics, 1985—, dir. office faculty devel. and comm., 1991—2009, asst. dean office continuing edn., 1999—2005, assoc. dean, 2005—09; ret. Editor: Basic and Clinical Aspects of Nutrition and Brain Development, 1987, Neural Control of Reproductive Function, 1988; mem. editl. bd. Neurochem. Rsch. Mem. Soc. Pediatric Rsch., Am. Inst. Nutrition, Am. Soc. for Neurochemistry, Soc. for Neurosci., Am. Soc. Pharmacology and Exptl. Therapeutics, Internat. Soc. for Devel. Neuroscis., Am. Soc. for Clin. Nutrition. Avocations: tennis, photography. Home: 2801 Beluche Dr Galveston TX 77551-1509 Office: U Tex Med Br Dept Pediatrics Galveston TX 77555-0344 Office Phone: 409-772-1139. Business E-Mail: drassin@utmb.edu.*

RATCHFORD, JOSEPH THOMAS, science and technology policy educator, consultant; b. Kingstree, SC, Sept. 30, 1935; s. Raymond Howard and Elizabeth Arabella (Senn) R.; m. Joanne Walton Causey, June 18, 1960; children: Joseph Thomas, Laura Leigh, James Raymond, David Andrew. BS, Davidson Coll., NC, 1957; MA, U. Va., 1959, PhD, 1961. Asst. prof. physics Washington and Lee U., Lexington, Va., 1961-64; physicist U.S. Air Force Office of Sci. Rsch., Arlington, Va., 1964-70; sci. cons. Com. on Sci. and Tech., U.S. Ho. of Reps., Washington, 1970-77; assoc. exec. officer AAAS, Washington, 1977-89; assoc. dir. Office of Sci. and Tech. Policy White House Office of Sci. and Tech. Policy, Washington, 1989-93; dir. Ctr. for Sci., Trade and Tech. Policy George Mason U., Arlington, Va., 1994—99, prof. internat. sci. and tech. policy, 1993-98, disting. vis. prof., 1998—2009; dir. sci. and trade policy program George Mason U. Sch. Law, Arlington, Va., 1999—2009. Cons. internat. trade and tech., Davidson, NC, 1993—, Alexandria, Va., 1993-2002; chair Forum on Internat. Phys. Am. Phys. Soc., 1994-96, Am. Phys.; mem. Internat. Affairs Commn., Am. Assn. Engring. Soc., 1993—; mem. tech. task force Coun. on Competitiveness, Washington, 1987-88; chmn. adv. com. for internat. programs NSF, Washington, 1984-87; chmn. adv. panel on energy from bio processes Office Tech. Assessment, 1979-80; chmn. Rsch. Coordination Panel, Gas Rsch. Inst., Chgo., 1976-79; prin. Sci., Trade and Tech. Assocs., 1998—; co-chair U.S.-China Sci. Policy Initiative, 1999—2009; bd. dirs., v.p. Charlotte Area Sci. Network, 2004—; bd. trustees, chair acad. affairs com., Lees-McRae Coll., Banner Elk, NC, 2001—, editl. bd. mem., Tech. Soc. Jours., 2008-, Nanotech. Perceptions, 2009-, founding mem., Euro Mediterranean Acad. Arts & Scis., 2009-. Contbr. chpts. to books, numerous articles to profl. jours. Hon. mem. World Innovation Found., 2005—. Fellow AAAS, Am. Phys. Soc.; mem. Coun. on Fgn. Rels., Phi Beta Kappa, Sigma Xi. Achievements include initiation of academic center to address policy interrelationships among science, trade, legal and technology issues; development of legislation on a variety of science-based issues including establishment of Congl. Office of Technology Assessment, innovative approaches to international technological and business alliances; at the White House developed international science policy and math. and science edn. initiatives. Office: PO Box 458 Davidson NC 28036-0458 Home Phone: 704-892-0970; Office Phone: 704-892-3025. Personal E-mail: tomratchford@bellsouth.net. Business E-Mail: stta@bellsouth.net.

RATH, MANIK K., lawyer; BA, U. Va., 1991, JD, 1994. Admitted: State Bar of Tex., Va. State Bar, DC Bar Assn., US Dist. Ct., US Ct. of Appeals. Atty. Baker & McKenzie LLP, McGuire Woods LLP, Richmond, Va., 1997—99, McKenna Long & Aldridge, LLP, 1999—2002; v.p., dep. gen. counsel, asst. sec. & bd. dirs. Alion Sci. and Tech. Corp., 2002—05; sr. v.p., gen. counsel & corp. sec. LMI, 2005—. Office: LMI 200 Corporate Ridge Mc Lean VA 22102-7805 Office Phone: 703-917-9800. Business E-Mail: mrath@lmi.org.

RATHER, DAN (DANIEL IRVIN RATHER, JR.), news correspondent, former network news anchor; b. Wharton, Tex., Oct. 31, 1931; m. Jean Goebel, 1957; children: Dawn Robin, Daniel Martin. BA in Journalism, Sam Houston State Tchrs. Coll., Huntsville, Tex., 1953; student, U. Houston, South Tex. Sch. Law. Journalism instr. Sam Houston State Coll.; reporter AP, Huntsville, Tex., 1950, UPI, 1950—52, Houston Chronicle, 1954—55; news writer, reporter, news dir. KTRH Radio, Houston, 1956; dir. news & pub. affairs KHOU (CBS TV affiliate), Houston, 1959—61; chief southwestern bur. CBS, Dallas, 1961—64, White House corr., 1963, 1966—74, chief London bur., 1965—66, war corr. Vietnam, 1966; anchor, corr. CBS Reports, 1974—75; corr., co-editor 60 Minutes, 1975—81; anchor Dan Rather Reporting, CBS Radio Network, 1977—2005; anchor, mng. editor CBS Evening News with Dan Rather, 1981—2005; anchor 48 Hours, 1988—2002; corr. 60 Minutes II, 1998—2006; prodr., host, Dan Rather Reports HDNet, 2006—. Co-editor TV show Who's Who, CBS, 1977; anchored numerous CBS News spl. programs. Author (with Gary Gates): The Palace Guard, 1974; author: (with Mickey Herskowitz) The Camera Never Blinks, 1977; author: (with Peter Wyden) Memoirs, I Remember, 1991; author: The Camera Never Blinks Twice: The Further Adventures of a Television Journalist, 1994, The American Dream, 2001. Recipient Peabody award for excellence in TV broadcasting, 1975, 1976, 1994, 1995, 2000, 2001, 2004, Robert F. Kennedy Journalism award for internat. TV, 2011, several News & Documentary Emmy awards, Nat. Acad. TV Arts & Scis. Office: HDNet 320 S Walton St Dallas TX 75226

RATHKE, WADE (STEPHEN WADE RATHKE), social services administrator; b. New Orleans, Aug. 5, 1948; m. Beth Butler. Attended, Williams Coll., 1966—68. Organizer Nat. Welfare Rights Organization (NWRO), Springfield, Mass.; co-founder, chief exec. organizer ACORN (Assn. Cmty. Organizations for Reform Now), New Orleans, 1970—2008; founder, chief organizer Svc. Employees Internat. Union (SEIU), New Orleans, 1980—, Community Organizations Internat. (formerly ACORN Internat.); dir. Ctr. for Cmty. Leadership, Canada, 2004—. Pub., editor Social Policy. Author: Citizen Wealth: Winning the Campaign to Save Working Families, 2009.

RATHORE, KEERTI S., botanist, researcher, science educator; BSc, Rajasthan U.; MSc, Gujarat U.; PhD, Imperial Coll., London U., 1981. Rsch. scientist botany / plant pathology Purdue U., 1991—95; rsch. scientist Crop Biotechnology Ctr. Tex. A&M U., 1995—97; asst. prof. Inst. Plant Genomics and Biotechnology, 1997—2003, assoc. prof., 2003—. Plant biotechnolgist Tex. Agr. Experiment Station. Contbr. articles to profl. jours. Office: Inst for Plant Genomics and Biotechnology 116 Borlaug Ctr 2123 Tamu College Station TX 77843-2123 Office Phone: 979-862-4795. Office Fax: 979-862-4790. E-mail: rathore@tamu.edu.

RATLIFF, JAMES, state legislator; m. Georgia Ratliff; 2 children. B, M, Ark. State U. Ret. HS agrl. tchr.; mem. Dist. 73 Ark. House of Reps., 2011—. Bd. mem. Lawrence County Farm Bur., Ark. Fair Managers Assn. Mem.: Lawrence/Randolph Cattle Assn. Democrat. Baptist. Office: PO Box 791 Imboden AR 72434 Office Phone: 501-454-5200. Business E-Mail: jamesratliff3468@yahoo.com.

RAU, RAVI PRAKASH, physics professor, researcher; b. Kolkata, India, Aug. 9, 1945; arrived in USA, 1973, naturalized, 2006; s. Mysore Anantaswamy and Vijaya Lakshmi (Rao) R.; m. Luba Marie Witer, June 28, 1969 (dec. Jan. 1981); children: Nicholas Naveen, Alexander Vikram; m. Dominique Gabrielle Homberger, May 16, 1985. PhD, U. Chgo., 1970. Vis. fellow Tata Inst. Fundamental Rsch., Mumbai, 1972—73; prof. La. State U., Baton Rouge, 1974—. Vis. assoc. prof. Yale U., New Haven, 1978-79; vis. prof. Raman Rsch. Inst., Bangalore, 1983, Australian Nat. U., Canberra, 1987-88, 2013; vis. fellow Joint Inst. for Lab. Astrophysics, Boulder, Colo., 1984; vis. prof. Technische U., Darmstadt, 2007, 2012-13; Humboldt Presitraeger, U. Bielefeld and Freiburg, 1999; adj. prof. Tata Inst. Fundamental Rsch, Mumbai. Co-author: Atomic Collisions and Spectra, 1986, Symmetimes in Quantum Physics, 1996; contbr. articles to profl. jours. Fellowship, Alexander v Humboldt Assn., 1999—2000. Fellow Am. Phys. Soc. Home: 730 Carriage Way Baton Rouge LA 70808 Office: La State Univ Nicholson Hall-Physics & Astronomy Baton Rouge LA 70803 Office Fax: 225-578-5855. Business E-Mail: arau@phys.lsu.edu.*

RAUF, ZAMIR, energy executive; BA in Bus. & Commerce, U. Houston, MBA. Various acctg. and fin. roles, credit and lending roles Comerica Bank; various acctg. and fin. roles Dynegy Inc., Enron N.Am.; mgr. fin. Calpine Corp., 2000—01, dir. fin., 2001—02, v.p. fin., 2002—05, sr. v.p. fin., 2005—08, treas., 2007—08, interim CFO, 2008, exec. v.p., CFO, 2008—. Office: Calpine Corp Ste 1000 717 Texas Ave Houston TX 77002 Office Phone: 713-830-2000. Office Fax: 713-830-2001. Business E-Mail: zrauf@calpine.com.

RAUSCHENBERG, BRADFORD LEE, retired museum program director; b. Atlanta, Sept. 11, 1940; BS in Archaeology and Biology, Ga. State Coll., 1963; MA in History, Wake Forest U., 1995; PhD (hon.), Kendal Coll. Arts and Design, 2006. Archaeologist Ga. Hist. Commn., 1963-64; site supr., asst. Stanley South, State Archaeologist of N.C., 1964-66; antiquarian, asst. Dir. Restoration Old Salem, Inc., Winston-Salem, NC, 1966-73; asst. to dir. Mus. Early So. Decorative Arts, Winston-Salem, 1973-76, rsch. fellow, 1976-87, dir. rsch., 1987-93, Mus. Early So. Decorative Arts and Old Salem, Inc., Winston-Salem, 1993—, sr. fellow emeritus. Cons., lectr. in field. Author: British Regional Carving (1600-1640), and Furniture (1600-1800), 1984, Wachovia Historical Society: 1895-1995, 1995, Charleston Furniture, 1680-1820, 3 vols., 2003. With USCG, 1964-72. Recipient Halifax Resolves award, 1986; grantee NEH, 1972-81, Kaufman Americana Found., 1981-82. Mem. Am. Ceramic Circle (grantee), Orgn. Am. Historians, No. Ceramic Soc., So. Hist. Assn., Friends of Swiss Ceramic Circle, Regional Furniture Soc., Furniture History Soc., Soc. Hist. Archaeology, Soc. Post-Medieval Archaeology, Soc. Historians Early Am. Republic. Address: 221 Harmon Ct Winston Salem NC 27106-4613 Personal E-mail: k4blr@triad.rr.com.

RAUSHENBUSH, WALTER BRANDEIS, retired law educator; b. Madison, Wis., June 13, 1928; s. Paul A. and Elizabeth (Brandeis) R.; m. Marylu de Watteville, May 3, 1956; children: Lorraine Elizabeth,

Richard Walter, Carla de Watteville, Paul Brandeis. AB magna cum laude in Govt., Harvard U., 1950; JD with high honors, U. Wis., 1953. Bar: Wis. 1953. Ptnr. LaFollette, Sinykin & Doyle, Madison, 1956-58; mem. faculty U. Wis., Madison, 1958—, prof. law, 1966-95, prof. emeritus, 1995—; vis. prof. law U. San Diego, 1992—94, 1996—2009; project dir. real estate transfer study Am. Bar Found., 1967-72. Trustee nat. Law Sch. Admission Coun., 1968-70, 72-95, chmn. pre-law com., 1970-74, chmn. svcs. com., 1976-78, pres., 1980-82; legal advisor Madison Citizens Fair Housing, 1961-63, Wis. Citizens Family Planning, 1965-73; real property drafting com. Multistate Bar Exam., 1986-2002. Author: Wisconsin Construction Lien Law, 1974, (with others) Wisconsin Real Estate Law, 1984, 4th edit., 1994, Brown on Personal Property, 3d edit., 1975, Real Estate Transactions Cases and Materials, 1997. With USAF, 1953-56, col. Res. ret. Mem. ABA, State Bar Wis., Order of Coif, Stage Harbor Yacht Club (Chatham, Mass.), Phi Beta Kappa, Phi Delta Phi (province pres. 1963-75). Presbyterian (Elder). Home: 1364 MacBeth St Mc Lean VA 22102

RAUSHER, DAVID BENJAMIN, internist, gastroenterologist; b. Bklyn., Sept. 15, 1952; s. Herbert and Shirley Ruth R.; m. Judy A. Steinlauf, Aug. 8, 1976; children: Scott, Michael, Steven. BA, Hamilton Coll., 1973; MD, SUNY, Bklyn., 1977. Diplomate Am. Bd. Internal Medicine, Am. Bd. Gastroenterology. Resident Emory U. Hosps., Atlanta, 1977-80, fellow in gastroenterology, 1980-82; pres. Atlanta Ctr. for Gastroenterology, Decatur, Ga., 1982—; med. dir. Atlanta Endoscopy Ctr., Decatur, 1994—. Chmn. diagnostic treatment ctr. DeKalb Med. Ctr., Decatur, Ga., 1985—, co-chief gastroenterology, 1995-97, chief sect. gastroenterology, 1998—. Fellow: Am. Gastroenterology Assn., Am. Coll. Gastroenterology. Office Phone: 404-296-1986.

RAVDIN, PETER MARCUS, internist, educator, oncologist; b. June 3, 1949; MD, U. Miami Sch. Med., 1981; PhD in Neurobiology, Cornell U. Cert. Internal Medicine, Med. Oncology. Resident U. Wis., Madison, 1981—84, fellow, 1984—87; asst. prof. to clin. prof. med. oncology U. Tex. Health Sci. Ctr., San Antonio; rsch. prof. biostatistics U. Tex. MD Anderson Cancer Ctr., San Antonio; exec. officer Southwest Oncology Group. Spkr. in field. Prin. author (computer program) Adjuvant!; contbr. several articles to profl. jours.

RAVENEL, SHANNON, book publishing professional; b. Charlotte, NC, Aug. 13, 1938; d. Elias Prioleau and Harriett Shannon (Steedman) R.; m. Dale Purves, May 25, 1968; children: Sara Blake, Harriett. BA, Hollins Coll., 1960. Mktg. asst., sch. dept. Holt, Rinehart & Winston, Inc., NYC, 1960-61; editl. asst. Houghton Mifflin Co., Boston, 1961-64, editor, 1964—70; editl. cons. pvt. practice, St. Louis, 1973-90; sr. editor, co-founder Algonquin Books of Chapel Hill, NC, 1982-91, editl. dir., 1991—2000; dir. Algonquin imprint Shannon Ravenel Books, 2001—. Series editor: Best American Short Stories, 1978-90; editor: Best American Short Stories of the Eighties, 1990, New Stories From the South, 1986-2005 Recipient Disting. Achievement award Coun. Lit. Mags. & Presses, NYC, 1990, R. Hunt Parker Meml. award for contbns. to the lit. of N.C., 2004. Mem. PEN Am. Ctr., Fellowship Southern Writers. Democrat. Office: Algonquin Books of Chapel Hill PO Box 2225 Chapel Hill NC 27515-2225 Business E-Mail: shannonr@algonquin.com.

RAWL, ARTHUR JULIAN (LORD OF CURSONS), corporate director, retail executive, consultant, accountant, writer; b. Boston, July 6, 1942; s. Philip and Evelyn (Rosoff) R.; m. Karen Lee Werby, June 4, 1967; 1 child, Kristen Alexandra. BBA, Boston U., 1967, postgrad, 1974; DBA in Business (hon.), St. George's U., London, 1995. CPA, Mass., N.Y., La. Audit mgr. Touche Ross & Co., Boston, 1967-77, NYC, 1977-79, ptnr., 1979, Newark, 1980-88, NYC, 1988-89, Deloite & Touche, NYC, 1989-90; exec. v.p., CFO Hanlin Group, Inc., Linden, NJ, 1990-94, United Auto Group, Inc., NYC, 1994-97; pres., CEO, bd. dirs. Brazil Internat. Motors, Brazil Am. Auto Group, São Paulo, Brazil, 1999—2003; chmn., CEO Auto Alliance, Englewood, NJ, 2003—07, Rawl & Assocs., Miami, Fla., 2003—. Bd. dirs. BiakalInterPlast (USSR), Kuperwood Enterprises, Hanlin Group, Inc., Quipp, Inc., Ecolocap Solutions, Inc., Montreal, Can.; chmn. Tiger Ethanol, Inc., Montreal, Can., audit com. chair Mariners BanCorp., 2012-; mem. adj. faculty Boston U., 1971-75, Lectr. Practicing Law Institute, NY 2007, KPMG Audit Committee Institue 2006-. Contbr. articles to profl. journals, mags. and trade publs. Mem. Newton Upper Falls (Mass.) Hist. Dist. Commn., 1977; bd. dirs. Sherburne Scholarship Fund Boston U., 1977-80; mem. Englewood (N.J.) Planning Bd., 1981-83; trustee Englewood Bd. Edn., 1983-85, 89-93, pres., 1991-92; trustee, treas. exec. com. Englewood Econ. Devel. Corp., 1986-89; fin. and compensation com. Dwight Englewood Sch., 1985-90; mem. parent devel. com. Mt. Holyoke Coll., 1991-94; chmn. Brit. Meml. Garden Trust, NY, 2003-09; chmn. British Meml. Garden Trust, London, 2007-. Served to 2d class Petty Officer, Aviation Electronics and Combat Air Crewman (hon. discharge 1967) USN, 1960—63. Decorated Naval Expeditionary medal, Armed Forces Expenditionary Medal, Good Conduct Medal, National Defense medal; named member, Her Majesty's Most Excellent Order of the British Empire. Fellow AICPA, Mass. Soc. CPAs, NY Soc. CPAs; mem. VFW, Am. Legion, Navy League U.S., N.J. Hist. Soc. (bd. govs., exec. com., nominating com., treas. 1987-99), St. George's Soc. NY (treas. exec. com. 1998-2005), Coll. Arms Found. (life dir. 2001—), Brit. Am. Inst., Fin. Execs. Internat. Commander of Her Majesty's Most Venerable Order of Hosp. of St. John of Jerusalem, Pilgrims of the UK and US (life), Univ. Club (NY), Essex Club, Sloane Club (London). Conservative. Home: 1451 South Miami Ave Miami FL 33130 Business E-Mail: a.rawl@att.net.

RAWLINGS, MIKE, mayor, Dallas, Texas; m. Micki Rawlings; children: Michelle, Gunnar. B in Philosophy and Comm., Boston Coll. Advt. profl., Dallas; CEO Tracy-Locke, Pizza Hut; mng. ptnr. CIC Partners; mayor City of Dallas, Tex., 2011—. Adj. prof. So. Meth. U., Dallas. Chmn. Dallas Conv. and Visitors Bur., 2006—07; pres. Dallas Park & Recreation Bd.; bd. trustees Jesuit Coll. Preparatory. Recipient Excellence in Humanities award, Dallas Hist. Soc., Innovation award, US Interagency Coun. on Homelessness, Destiny award, St. Philip's Sch. and Cmty. Ctr., 2011; named Humanitarian of Yr., Anti-Defamation League, 2010. Office: Office of the Mayor Dallas City Hall 1500 Marilla St Rm 5EN Dallas TX 75201 Office Phone: 214-670-4054. Office Fax: 214-670-0646.*

RAWLINS, DONALD RAY, lawyer; b. Dyersburg, Tenn., Apr. 28, 1965; s. Dal M. and Rebecca S. Rawlins. BBA, U. Memphis, 1987; JD, Am. U., 1990. Bar: Tenn., 1990, NC, 2008. V.p., asst. gen. counsel, asst. sec. AutoZone, Inc., Memphis, 1990—2004; asst. gen. counsel Thomas & Betts Corp., Memphis, 2004—05, asst. sec., 2004—05, chief compliance officer, 2004—05, Rawlins Law Firm, PC, 2009—; counsel Alston and Bird LLP, Charlotte, NC, 2007—09. Vice chmn. Memphis Landmarks Commn., 2004—05. Recipient Best Brief award ATLA, 1990. Republican. Methodist. Office: Rawlins Law Firm PC 401 Hawthorne Ln Ste 110-197 Charlotte NC 28204 Office Phone: 704-307-2542.

RAWLINS, V. LANE, academic administrator, economics professor; b. Rigby, Idaho, Nov. 30, 1937; m. Mary Jo Rawlins, three children. BA in Economics, Brigham Young U., 1963; PhD in Economics, U of Calif., Berkeley, 1969. Faculty Wash. State U., Pullman, 1968-86, chair. economics, 1977-82, vice provost, 1982—86; vice chancellor, academic affairs U. of Alabama, 1986-91; pres. Memphis St. U., Memphis, 1991-00, Wash. State U., Pullman, 2000—07, prof. econs.; interim dir. William D. Ruckelshaus Ctr. for Conflict Resolution, 2007—09; pres. U. North Tex., 2010—. Office: University of North Texas Office of President 1155 Union Circle, #311425 Denton TX 76203-5017 E-mail: president@unt.edu.

RAWLINSON, HELEN ANN, librarian; b. Columbia, SC, Mar. 30, 1948; d. Alfred Harris and Mary Taylor (Moon) R. BA, U. S.C., 1970; MLS, Emory U., 1972. Asst. children's librarian Greenville (S.C.) County Library, 1972-74, br. supr., 1974-76, asst. head extension div., 1976-78; children's room librarian Richland County Pub. Library, Columbia, 1978-81, sr. adult services librarian, 1981-82, chief adult services, 1982-85, dep. dir., 1985—. Mem. adv. com. S.C. Pre-White House Conf. on Libr. and Info. Svcs., chmn. program com. Recipient Outstanding S.C. Librarian award by S.C. Library Assn., 1998. Mem. ALA, S.E. Libr. Assn., S.C. Libr. Assn. (2d v.p. 1987-89, editl. com. 1993, chmn. pub. libr. sect. 1995), U. S.C. Thomas Cooper Soc. (bd. dirs., v.p., pres.-elect, pres.). Baptist. Home: 1316 Guignard Ave West Columbia SC 29169-6137 Office Phone: 803-799-9084. Business E-Mail: harawlin@rhycpl.com. E-mail: harawlin@richland.lib.sc.us.

RAWSON, CHARLES A., III, gas industry executive; B in Mech. Engring., Ga. Tech.; MBA, Ga. State U. Engr. Atlanta Gas Light (subs. of AGL Resources Inc.), mng. dir., wholesale svcs., 2004; v.p., gen. mgr. Florida City Gas, 2004—07; v.p., gen. mgr., Southeast Ga., mgr., wholesale svcs. AGL Resources, Inc., mng. dir., rsch. and analysis, 2002—04, v.p., gas ops., 2007—. Office: AGL Resources Inc 10 Peachtree Pl NE Atlanta GA 30309 Office Phone: 404-584-4000. Office Fax: 404-584-3714. Business E-Mail: CRawson@aglresources.com.

RAWSON, HARVE E., psychologist, writer; b. Webb City, Mo., July 25, 1934; s. Paul Charles and Florence Landon Rawson; m. Joyce Elaine Blossom, June 9, 1961; children: Paul Gerald, Reed Harve. BA, Antioch Coll., 1957; MA, Ohio State U., 1959, PhD, 1961. Rsch. specialist N.Am. Aviation Inc., Columbus, Ohio, 1961—63; prof. psychology Hanover (Ind.) Coll., 1963—94, prof. emeritus, 1994—; dir. children's svcs. Englishton Pk., Lexington, Ind., 1969—93; dean faculty Franklin (Ind.) Coll., 1994—96; vis. prof. psychology Miss. State U., Starkville, 1998. Grant reviewer Coun. Internat. Exch. Scholars, Washington, 2000—04. Author: Webb City, 2000, Around the World in 30 Years, 2001, Purposeful Parenting, 2002, A Delightful Ordeal, 2003, Travels of an Iconoclast, 2005, Buried In The Ivy, 2008, Dying in Egypt, 2009, Talking Animals, 2010; contbr. over 40 articles to profl. jours. Pres. Lide White Boys and Girls Club, Madison, Ind., 1969, 1974, 1978, 1999—2001; v.p. Jefferson County Youth Shelter, Madison, 1992. Recipient Sagamore of the Wabash award, Gov. Ind., 1993; scholar, Fulbright Found., Bahrain, 1988—89, Fulbright Found., 1994. Mem.: Gwinnett County Sr. Leadership Coun., Ind. Psychol. Assn. (pres. 1974—76, Cmty. Svc. award 1991, Disting. Acad. Psychologist award 1986—87), Traveler's Century Club. Avocation: travel. Home: 1328 Field Creek Ter Lawrenceville GA 30043-5330

RAY, AMY, vocalist, guitarist; b. Decatur, Ga., Apr. 12, 1964; BA, Emory U., 1986. Vocalist, guitarist Saliers & Ray, 1980-83, Indigo Girls, 1983—; signed to Epic Records, 1988—2006, Hollywood Records, 2006—. Founder, pres. Daemon Records, Decatur, Ga., 1990—. Musician: (albums) Stag, 2001, Prom, 2005, Didn't It Feel Kinder, 2008; musician: (with Emily Saliers) Early 45, 1985, Strange Fire, 1987, Indigo Girls, 1989 (Grammy Award for Best Contemporary Folk Album, 1990), Nomads Indians Saints, 1990, Back On the Bus, Y'All, 1991, Rites of Passage, 1992, Swamp Ophelia, 1994, 1200 Curfews, 1995, Shaming of the Sun, 1997, Come On Now Social, 1999, Retrospective, 2000, Become You, 2002, All That We Let In, 2004, Rarities, 2005, Despite Our Differences, 2006, Poseidon and the Bitter Bug, 2009, (songs) Closer to Fine, 1989, Hammer and Nail, 1990, Galileo, 1992, Least Complicated, 1994, Shame on You, 1997; appears in (films) Boys on the Side, 1995, Join the Resistance: Fall in Love, 2003, (documentaries) Trudell, 2005, Wordplay, 2006. Named one of Greatest Women of Rock'n'Roll, VH1; nominee Best New Artist, Grammy Awards, 1990. Office: Russell Carter Artist Management 567 Ralph Mcgill Blvd Ne Atlanta GA 30312-1110 Office Phone: 404-377-9900. E-mail: igfan@rcam.com.

RAY, CREAD L., JR., retired judge; b. Waskom, Tex., Mar. 10, 1931; s. Cread L. and Antonia (Hardesty) Ray; m. Janet Watson Keller, Aug. 12, 1977; children: Sue Ann(dec.), Robert E., Glenn L., David B., Marcie Lynn, Anne Marie. BBA, Tex. A&M U., 1952; JD, U. Tex., 1957; LHD (hon.), Wiley Coll., Marshall, Tex., 1980. Bar: Tex. 1957. Pvt. practice law, Marshall, 1957-59; judge Harrison County, 1959-61; justice 6th dist. Ct. Civil Appeals, Texarkana, 1970-80, Supreme Ct. Tex., Austin, 1980-90; ret., 1990; prin. C.L Ray, Austin, 1991—. Prin. C. L. Ray, Austin, 1991—; pres., CEO White Oil, Inc. Past pres. Marshall Jaycees, Marshall C. of C.; active Boy Scouts Am.; mem. Tex. Ho. of Reps., 1966—70; trustee Wiley Coll. Lt. col. USAF, 1952—54, Korea. Recipient awards, Boy Scouts Am. Mem.: N.E. Tex. Bar Assn. (past pres.), State Bar Tex., Tex. Aggies, Rotary. Democrat. Methodist. Home and Office: 604 Beardsley Ln Austin TX 78746-4929 Home Phone: 512-327-6137; Office Phone: 512-328-9238. Personal E-mail: clray4523@hotmail.com. E-mail: judgeclray@aol.com, judgeclray@msn.com.

RAY, DOUGLAS ELLSWORTH, dean, law educator; b. Mpls., July 7, 1947; s. Henry E. and Hazel O. (Tollefson) R.; m. Caroline Sue Logan, July 25, 1970; children: Kathleen Susan, Michael David. Ba, U. Minn., 1971; JD, Harvard U., 1975. Bar: Minn. 1975, US Dist. Ct. Minn. 1975. Economist US Dept. Labor, Washington, 1971-72; assoc. Dorsey & Whitney, Mpls., 1975-78; assoc. prof. law U. Richmond, Va., 1978-81; prof. U. Toledo Coll. Law, 1981—98, assoc. dean, 1984—86, 1988—89, dean, 2006—10; v.p., dean Widener U. Sch. Law, 1999—2005; dean, prof. law St. Thomas U. Sch. Law, Miami Gardens, Fla., 2010—. Labor arbitrator Fed. Mediation & Conciliation Svc., Toledo, 1981-, taught & pub. fields of labor law, employment discrimination law, torts and labor arbitration, spkr. in field. Co-author: Labor Management Relations: Strikes, Lockouts and Boycotts, 1992, Understanding Labor Law, 1999, 2d edit., 2005; contbr. articles to profl. jours. Bd. dirs. Luther Home Mercy, Williston, Ohio, 1985-88. Sgt. U.S. Army, 1966-70. With US Army, 1966—70. Mem. ABA (labor law sect.), Am. Arbitration Assn., Assn. of Am. Law Schs. (chmn. labor and employment law sect.), Nat. Acad. Arbitrators (chmn. seminar Labor Law & Labor Arbitration 1999, 2005). Lutheran. Office: St Thomas University School Law 16401 NW 37th Ave Opa Locka FL 33054 Office Phone: 877-788-7526.

RAY, HUGH MASSEY, III, lawyer; b. Houston, June 25, 1970; s. Hugh Massey and Florence Hargrove Ray; m. Katheryn Elaine Shaffer, June 19, 1993; children: James Henry, Mary Carol, John William. BA, Vanderbilt U., Nashville, 1992; MDiv, JD, Vanderbilt U., 1996. Cert.: Tex. Bd. Legal Specialization (bus. bankruptcy law) 2005, bar: Tex. 1998, US Ct. Appeals (5th cir.) 2001, US Ct. Appeals (11th cir.) 2001, US Supreme Ct. 2001. Shareholder Weycer, Kaplan, Pulaski & Zuber, P.C., Houston, 2001—09; prin. McKool & Smith, P.C., 2009—. Master of Moeller-Foltz Inn of Ct. Am. Inns of Ct., Houston, 2004—, master of Garland Walker, 2006—. Patron Houston Symphony, 2004; mem. St. Martin's Episc. Ch., Houston, 1993—. Fellow: Coll. of State Bar Tex. (life); mem.: ABA (editl. bd. young lawyers mag. 2004—05, young lawyer divsn. profl. devel. team 2005—06, life fellow), State Bar Tex. (mem. disciplinary rules com. 2000—), Am. Law Inst., Houston Bar Assn. (disting. faculty 2005—10, chair CLE seminar com. 2008—09, chair CLE Inst. com. 2009—10, CLE chair 2010—11, chair CLE com. 2010—11, CLE com., mem. bankruptcy sect.), Houston Livestock Show and Rodeo (life), Briar Club, Houston Club (fellow), Phi Alpha Delta, Lambda Chi Alpha. Episcopalian. Avocations: running, hunting, triathlon. Office: McKool Smith 600 Travis Ste 7000 Houston TX 77002

RAY, LAKE, III, state legislator; b. Jacksonville, Fla., Oct. 4, 1956; m. Brenda Ray; children: Lake IV, Forrest, Hampton. AA in Forensics, St. Johns River Jr. Coll., 1976; BS in Civil Engring., U. Fla., Gainesville, 1981. Registered profl. engr., Fla. Civil engr.; pres. Harbor Engring. Co., 1999—2003; v.p. Halcrow, Inc.; councilman Dist. 1 Jacksonville City Coun., 1999—2007; mem. Dist. 17 Fla. House of Reps., Tallahassee, 2008—, mem. Fla. legis. com. on intergovernmental rels., govt. accountability act coun., govt. ops. appropriations com., mem. pub. safety and domestic security policy com., roads, bridges and ports policy com. Mem.: ASCE, Nat. Soc. Profl. Engineers, Fla. Engring. Soc., Southside Businessmen's Club, Northside Bus. Leader's Club, Delta Upsilon. Republican. Methodist. Office: 9485 Regency Sq Blvd Ste 109 Jacksonville FL 32225-8111 also: 1101 The Capitol 402 S Monroe St Tallahassee FL 32399-1300 Office Phone: 850-488-4388.

RAY, MICHAEL EDWIN, lawyer; b. Charlotte, NC, Dec. 13, 1949; s. Daniel Shaw Ray and Jane (Horne) Keziah; m. Janet Langston Jones, July 14, 1973; children: John Daniel, Jennifer Marjory. BA, Furman U., 1972; JD, U. S.C., 1978. Bar: N.C. 1978, S.C. 1978, U.S. Dist. Ct. (ea., mid. and we. dists.) N.C. 1978, U.S. Ct. Appeals (4th cir.) 1981, U.S. Ct. Appeals (Fed. cir.) 1989. Legal adminstr. Wyche Burgess Freeman & Parham, Greenville, S.C., 1973-75; assoc. Womble Carlyle Sandridge & Rice, PLLC, Winston-Salem, N.C., 1978-85, mem., 1985—. Editor-in-chief S.C. Law Rev., 1977-78. Bd. dirs. Piedmont Opera Theatre, Inc., 1997-98; S.C. Manpower Planning Coun., Columbia, 1971-72. T.B. Clarkson scholar Furman U., 1971-72. Mem. ABA, Internat. Bar Assn., N.C. Bar Assn., S.C. Bar Assn., Fed. Cir. Bar Assn. (bd. govs. 1994-97), Am. Intellectual Property Law Assn., Forsyth County Bar Assn., Furman U. Alumni Assn. (bd. govs. 1995-2000), Lex Mundi, Inc. (dir. 1995-99, sec. 1996-97, chair-elect 1997-98, chair 1998-99, chair emeritus 1999-2000, Best Lawyers in NC, 2009, NC Legal Elite, 2009). Democrat. Presbyterian. Avocations: sailing, woodworking, music. Office: Womble Carlyle Sandridge & Rice PLLC One W Fourth St Winston Salem NC 27101 Home: 440 Wachovia St Winston Salem NC 27101 E-mail: mray@wcsr.com.

RAY, PAUL RICHARD, JR., executive recruiter, consultant; b. Columbus, Ga., Nov. 6, 1943; s. Paul Richard and Sarah (Campbell) R.; m. Elizabeth Richards, June 29, 1968; children: Paul Richard III, John Ray, Alice Ray. BSBA, U. Ark., 1966; JD, U. Tex., 1969. Bar: Tex. 1970. Dir. mktg., various mktg. positions tobacco divsn. R.J. Reynolds Tobacco Co., Winston-Salem, N.C., 1969-78; cons. Paul R. Ray & Co., Ft. Worth, 1978, v.p., 1978-79, sr. v.p., 1979-83, exec. v.p., 1983-84, pres., 1984—, COO, 1984-86; CEO Ray & Berndtson, Ft. Worth, 1986-98, chmn. bd., CEO, 1998—. Chmn. bd. CEO Rays Beradtson, Ft. Worth, 1998—2002; vice chmn. Keavney Exec. Search, 2002—06; mng. dir. EWKP, 2006—07; with Paul Ray & Co., 2007—. Bd. dirs. Cook-Ft. Worth Children's Med. Ctr., United Way Met. Tarrant County; liberal arts adv. bd. U. Tex.; dean's exec. adv. bd. U. Ark. Recipient Brite Divinity Sch. Exec. Com. Bd. Mem. ABA, Assn. Exec. Search Cons. (chmn. 1995-98), Tex. Bar Assn., Young Pres.' Orgn., World Pres. Orgn., River Crest Country Club, City Club, Ft. Worth club. Personal E-mail: pray@poulrayco.com.

RAY, RAYMOND B., federal judge; b. 1943; BA, U. South Fla., 1965; JD, U. Fla., 1971. Bar: Fla. 1971. Asst. U.S. atty. Dept. Justice, So. Dist. Fla., Miami, 1971-74; bankruptcy judge U.S. Bankruptcy Ct. (so. dist.) Fla., Ft. Lauderdale, 1993—. Comdr. USNR, 1961—85, ret. Office: US Courthouse Rm 306 299 E Broward Blvd Fort Lauderdale FL 33301-1944 Business E-Mail: betty_robaina@flsb.uscourts.gov.

RAY, RICK, men's college basketball coach; m. Breyana Cardwell; children: Katriece, Deacon. B in Applied Math. and Secondary Edn., Grand View Coll., Des Moines, 1994; M in Athletic Adminstrn., U. Nebr., Omaha, 1997. Asst. coach U. Nebr.-Omaha Mavericks, 1996—97, Ind. State U. Sycamores, 1997—2004; asst. coach, recruiting coord. No. Ill. U. Huskies, 2004—06; asst. coach Purdue U. Boilmakers, 2006—10; assoc. head coach Clemson U. Tigers, 2010—12; head basketball coach Miss. State U. Bulldogs, 2012—. Office: Mississippi State University Basketball Program Humphrey Coliseum 55 Coliseum Blvd Mississippi State MS 39762

RAY, ROSABELL HARRIET See BATTIN, R.

RAY, WAYNE ALLEN, epidemiologist, educator; b. Yakima, Wash., July 2, 1949; s. Allen and Patsy (McKay) R.; m. Janine Elise Thorson, June 11, 1972; children: Lily Amelia, Lea Camille. BS, U. Washington, 1971; MS, Vanderbilt U., 1974, PhD, 1981. Research assoc. Vanderbilt U. Sch. Medicine, Nashville, 1974-75, research instr., 1975-78, research asst. prof., 1979-83, asst. prof., 1984-85, dir. div. pharmacoepidemiology, 1984—, assoc. prof., 1985-90, prof., 1991—. Contbr. articles to profl. jours. Recipient Burroughs Wellcome scholar in Pharmacoepidemiology Am. Coll. Preventive Medicine, 1984. Mem. Am. Statis. Assn., Assn. Computing Machinery, Computer Soc. of IEEE, Soc. Epidemiologic Research, Am. Pub. Health Assn., Phi Beta Kappa. Avocation: gardening. Office: Vanderbilt U A-1124 Medical Ctr N 1211 22d Ave S Nashville TN 37232-2637

RAYMENT, CARY, retired pharmaceutical executive; BA in Edn., Univ. Wash.; MBA, Univ. Kans., Lawrence; grad., Harvard Program for Mgmt. Devel. Various sales, mktg. positions Kendall Co., 1974—83; dir., sales, mktg. to v.p. mktg. CooperVision IOL (acquired by Alcon), 1983—89; v.p. mktg., surgical products Alcon Inc., Fort Worth, 1989—91, v.p., gen. mgr. surgical products, 1991—95, v.p., gen. mgr., managed care, 1996—97, v.p., internat. mktg., 1997—2000, v.p., gen. mgr., surgical divsn., 2000—01, sr. v.p., US, 2001—04, CEO, 2004—09, chmn., 2005—09, non-exec. chmn., 2009—10, vice chmn., 2010—. Bd. dir. Am. Soc. Cataract, Refractive Surgery Found., Nat. Alliance Eye Vision Rsch., Found. Am. Acad. Ophthalmology, Adv. Med. Tech. Assn. Bd. dir. United Way Met. Tarrant County. Office: Alcon Inc 6201 S Freeway Fort Worth TX 76134

RAYMOND, LISA, professional tennis player; b. Norristown, Pa., Aug. 10, 1973; d. Ted and Nancy Raymond. Student, U. Fla. Profl. tennis player WTA Tour, 1993—. Mem. US team Fed Cup, 1997, 1998, 2000, 2002—04, 2007, 2008, Summer Olympic Games, Athens, Greece, 2004, London, 2012. Recipient Broderick award, 1992, 1993, Bronze medal, mixed doubles, Summer Olympic Games, 2012; named Collegiate Player of Yr., Tennis Mag., 1992; named to U. Fla.

Athletic Hall of Fame, 2003. Achievements include winner of 4 WTA Tour singles titles and 78 WTA Tour doubles titles; winner Grand Slam mixed doubles titles: US Open, 1996, 2002; Wimbledon, 1999, 2012; French Open, 2003; winner Grand Slam doubles titles: Australian Open, 2000; US Open, 2001, 2005, 2011; Wimbledon, 2001; French Open, 2006. Avocations: shopping, hanging out with friends, watching television, football, volleyball. Office: WTA Corp Hdqs 100 Second Ave S Ste 1100-S Saint Petersburg FL 33701

RAYMUND, STEVEN A., computer company executive; b. Van Nuys, Calif., Nov. 16, 1955; s. Edward C. and Annette Leah Raymund. BS in Economics, U. Oreg., 1978; MA in Internat. Polit., Georgetown U. Sch. Fgn. Svc., 1980. With Manufacturers Hanover Corp., NYC, 1980—81; ops. mgr. Tech Data Corp., 1981—84, COO, 1984—86, CEO, 1986—2006, chmn., 1991—2006, non-exec. chmn., 2006—. Bd. Dir. Jabil Circuit. Named Entrepreneur of the Yr., Arthur Young Entrepreneurial Services, 1988; named one of 25 Most Influential Executives in the PC Industry, Computer Reseller News, 1989—2004; named to Industry Hall of Fame, 1999. Office: Tech Data Corp 5350 Tech Data Dr Clearwater FL 33760-3122

RAYSON, EDWIN HOPE, lawyer; b. Earlville, Ill., Jan. 13, 1923; s. Edwin H. and Lillian (Astley) R.; m. Evelyn Sherry Kirkland, Oct. 1, 1983; children: Jane Rayson Young, Edwin Hope III, G. Scott. AB, U. Tenn., 1944, LL.B., 1948. Bar: Tenn. 1948. Pvt. practice, Knoxville, 1948—; ptnr. Kramer Rayson LLP, 1949—. Lectr. labor law U. Tenn. Coll. Law, 1951-71 Served to lt. (j.g.) USNR, 1944-46. Mem. Order of Coif, Sigma Chi, Omicron Delta Kappa. Home: 501 River Rd Loudon TN 37774-5583 Office: 25th Fl 1st Tennesse Plaza Knoxville TN 37901 Office Phone: 865-525-5134. Business E-Mail: ehrayson@kramer-rayson.com.

RAZDAN, SANJAY, urologist; b. Rugby, Northern Ireland, Apr. 24, 1962; s. Jawahar Lal and Shanti Razdan; m. Shashi Khosa; 1 child, Shirin. MD, Ganesh Shankar Vidyarthi Meml. Med. Coll., Kanpur, India, 1985; MCh (Master of Chirurgical), SMS Med. Sch., Jaipur, India, 1993. Diplomate Am. Bd. Urology. Sr. registrar urology SMS Med. Schools & Hospitals, 1990—93; intern urology Univ. Medicine & Dentistry NJ, Newark, 1995—96; fellow female urology & neurourology Boston U. Med. Ctr., 1996—98; resident surgery U. Miami./Jackson Meml. Hosp., Fla., 1996—99, resident urology, 1999—2003; advanced fellowship in endourology & minimally-invasive urologic oncology Thomas Jefferson U. Hosp., Phila., 2003—04; chmn. dept. surgery, dir. Urology Ctr. Excellence Jackson South Cmty. Hosp., Miami, dir. Internat. Robotic Prostatectomy Inst. Dir. Comprehensive Kidney Stone Ctr., Miami. Co-author: Manual of Urology, 1999, Operative Urology/Surgical Skills, 2000, Clinical Urogynecology, 2000; contbr. articles to profl. jours. Physician Doctors Without Boundaries, Miami, 1996—2001. Recipient Pfizer award for outstanding contbn. to field of urology, 2004, Outstanding Laparoscopic Surgeon award, Soc. Laparoscopic Surgeons. Mem.: Endourology Soc., Am. Urol. Assn. Achievements include performing minimally-invasive robotic prostatectomy on patients with prostate cancer in less than 90 minutes resulting with minimal or no blood loss. Avocations: swimming, tennis, golf. Office: Urology Ctr Excellence S Fla Deering Med Plz 9380 SW 150th St Ste 200 Miami FL 33176 Office Phone: 305-251-8650. Personal E-mail: urodoc96@aol.com.

READ, JOHN O., state legislator; b. Bunkie, La., July 8, 1941; m. Patricia A. Yelverton; children: Lynn, Scott, Jason, Rhes. Pharmacist; mem. Dist. 112 Miss. House of Reps., 1993—. Mem.: Miss. Pharmacist Assn., Miss. Mcpl. Assn. Republican. Baptist. Mailing: Capitol PO Box 1018, Rm 201-NC Jackson MS 39215-1018 Home: 2396 Robert Hiram Dr Escatawpa MS 39552 Home Phone: 228-497-9852; Office Phone: 228-497-4090, 601-359-3338. Business E-Mail: jread@house.ms.gov.

READ, KENNETH FRANCIS, JR., physics professor, researcher; married. BS, Stanford U., Calif., 1981; MS, Cornell U., Ithaca, NY, 1984, PhD, 1987. Rsch. assoc. Princeton U., NJ, 1987—90, rsch. staff mem., 1990, Oak Ridge Nat. Lab., Tenn., 1991—2003, sr. rsch. staff mem., 2003—13; joint faculty mem. Oak Ridge Nat. Lab. U. Tenn., Knoxville, 1993—, disting. rsch. staff, 2013—; asst. prof. U. Tenn., 1991—99, assoc. prof., 1999—2005, prof., 2005—. Contbr. articles to profl. jours. Recipient David Levine award, Stanford U., 1980;, NSF, 1981, Andrew D. White fellowship, Cornell U., 1981. Mem.: Am. Phys. Soc., Phi Beta Kappa, Sigma Xi. Office: Oak Ridge Nat Lab Bldg 6025 MS 6373 Oak Ridge TN 37831-2008 Office Fax: 865-574-1118. Business E-Mail: kfread@utk.edu.

READ, MICHAEL OSCAR, editor, consultant; b. Amarillo, Tex., July 11, 1942; s. Harold Eugene and Madeline (Welch) R.; m. Jill Kay Vanderby, July 6, 1963 (div. Apr. 1967); 1 child, Rebecca Anne; m. Fawn Dale Barby, Apr. 10, 1977; 1 child, Nathan Michael. AA in Chemistry, Amarillo Coll., 1962; BA in Journalism, Tex. Tech. U., 1965. News editor Olton Enterprise, Tex., 1963—64; reporter, photographer Lubbock Avalanche-Jour., Tex., 1964—67, copy editor, 1967—70, city editor, 1970—72; copy editor Houston Post, 1972—74, sys. editor, 1974—89, dir. news tech., 1989—95; coord. electronic media content Houston Chronicle, 1995—2000, editor web ops. and devel., 2000—07; dir. online devel. ASP Westward LP, 2008—. Bd. dirs. People's Trust Fed. Credit Union, Houston, 2002—, chmn., 2010-; supervisory com., 1996-2001; tchr. Let's Compute!, Stafford, Tex., 1985—; cons. Newspaper Pub. Sys., Stafford, 1989—; mem. joint Newspaper Assn. Am.-Internat. Press, Telecomm. Coun. Com. Wire Svc. Stds.; mem. adv. bd. Found. for Am. Comms. FACSNET; mem. adv. com. Sch. of Mass Comm., Tex. Tech U., chmn., 2001-04 Author weekly newspaper column, 1977—. Vol. United Way, Houston, 1973—; bd. dirs. Meadows (Tex.) Cmty. Improvement Assn., 1985-95, Meadows Utility Dist., 1988-93, Meadows Econ. Devel. Corp., 1994-99. Named among Outstanding Alumni, Tex. Tech U. Sch. Mass Comms., 2001; Eldon Durrett scholar, 1961-65. Mem. Am. MENSA, Am. Philatelic Soc., Am. 1st Day Cov. Soc. (life), U.S. Chess Fedn. (life), Soc. Profl. Journalists (conv. com. 1989-90), Press Club of Houston. Avocations: stamp collecting/philately, photography, gardening. Office: ASP Westward LP 9833 Flamingo Ln Conroe TX 77385-8501 Business E-Mail: mread@aspwestward.com.

READ, RORY PATRICK, electronics company executive; b. 1961; m. Mary Read. BS in Info. Sys. magna cum laude, Hartwick Coll., 1983. Joined IBM Corp., 1983, gen. mgr. bus. consulting services Asia Pacific, exec. v.p. global bus. transformation IBM Global Services, mng. ptnr. Global Industrial Sector, Bus. Consulting Services Divsn.; sr. v.p. ops. Lenovo Group Ltd., 2006—09, pres., COO, 2009—11; pres, CEO AMD (Advanced Micro Devices, Inc.), 2011—. Office: AMD Austin, Lone Star Advanced Micro Devices 7171 Southwest Parkway Austin TX 78735 Office Phone: 512-602-1000.

READING, ANTHONY JOHN, retired psychiatrist, educator; b. Sydney, Sept. 10, 1933; s. Abe Stanley and Esma Daisy R.; m. Elisabeth Ann Hoffman, July 27, 1975; children— Wendy Virginia Elisabeth, Sarah Alexandra Jane. MBBS, U. Sydney, 1956; MPH, Johns Hopkins U., Balt., 1961, DSc, 1964. Intern Sydney Hosp., 1957-58; resident in psychiatry Johns Hopkins Hosp., Balt., 1965-68; asst. prof. psychiatry and medicine Johns Hopkins U. Sch. Medicine, Balt., 1968-73, assoc. prof. psychiatry, 1973-75, dir. psychiat. liaison service, 1974-75; dir. comprehensive alcoholism program Johns Hopkins Hosp., 1972-75; prof. U. South Fla. Coll. Medicine, 1975—2006, chmn. dept. psychiatry and behavioral medicine, 1975—2002, assoc. dean, 1993-96; med. dir. Bay Med. Behavioral Health Ctr., Panama City, Fla., 2004—05; ret., 2006. Mem.: AAAS.

REAM, JAMES B. (JIM REAM), air transportation executive; married; 1 child. MBA, Northwestern Univ. Mng. dir. fin. planning Am. Airlines Inc.; v.p. fin. Continental Airlines, 1994—96; exec. v.p., COO Continental Micronesia Inc., Guam, 1996, pres., COO Guam, 1996—98; sr. v.p. Asia Continental Airlines, 1998—99; pres. ExpressJet Holdings, Houston, 1999—, CEO, 2002—. Office: ExpressJet Holdings Ste 200 700 N Sam Houston Pkwy W Houston TX 77067 Office Phone: 713-324-4722. Office Fax: 713-324-4716.

REAMS, BERNARD DINSMORE, JR., law educator; b. Lynchburg, Va., Aug. 17, 1943; s. Bernard Dinsmore and Martha Eloise (Hickman) Reams; m. Rosemarie Bridget Boyle, Oct. 26, 1968 (dec. Oct. 1996); children: Andrew Dennet, Adriane Bevin; m. Lee Anne Oberhofer, Apr. 19, 2003. BA, Lynchburg Coll., 1965; MS, Drexel U., 1966; JD, U. Kans., 1972; PhD, St. Louis U., 1983. Bar: Kans. 1973, Mo. 1986, N.Y. 1996, Tex. 2002. Instr., asst. libr. Rutgers U., 1966—69; asst. prof. law, libr. U. Kans., Lawrence, 1969—74; mem. faculty law sch. Washington U., St. Louis, 1974—95, prof. law, 1976—95, prof. tech. mgmt., 1990—95, libr., 1974—76, acting dean univ. libraries, 1987—88; prof. law, assoc. dean, dir. Law Libr. St. John's U. Sch. Law, Jamaica, NY, 1995—97, assoc. dean acad. affairs, 1997—98; prof., dir. law libr. and info. tech. St. Mary's U., San Antonio, 2000—03, prof. law, 2000, disting. prof., 2014, 2014. Vis. fellow Max-Planck Inst., Hamburg, 1995, 97-98, 2001; vis. prof. law Seton Hall U., 1998-2000, Inst. World Legal Problems, Innsbruck, Austria, 2002, 05-07, co-dir. 2008-; guest prof. Leopold-Franzens U. Innsbruck, 2008-09. Author: Law For The Businessman, 1974, Reader in Law Librarianship, 1976, Federal Price and Wage Control Programs 1917-1979: Legis. Histories and Laws, 1980, Education of the Handicapped: Laws, Legislative Histories, and Administrative Documents, 1983, Internal Revenue Acts of the United States: The Revenue Act of 1954 with Legislative Histories and Congressional Documents, 1983, Congress and the Courts: A Legislative History 1978-1984, 1984, University-Industry Research Partnerships: The Major Issues in Research and Development Agreements, 1986, Deficit Control and the Gramm-Rudman-Hollings Act, 1986, The Semiconductor Chip and the Law: A Legislative History of the Semiconductor Chip Protection Act of 1984, 1986, American International Law Cases, 2d series, 1986, Technology Transfer Law: The Export Administration Acts of the U.S., 1987, Insider Trading and the Law: A Legislative History of the Insider Trading Sanctions Act, 1989, Insider Trading and Securities Fraud, 1989, The Health Care Quality Improvement Act of 1989: A Legislative History of P.L. No. 99-660, 1990, The National Organ Transplant Act of 1984: A Legislative History of P.L. No. 98-507, 1990, A Legislative History of Individuals with Disabilities Education Act, 1994, Federal Legislative Histories: An Annotated Bibliography and Index to Officially Published Sources, 1994, Electronic Contracting Law, 1996, Health Care Reform, 1994, The American Experience: Clinton and Congress, 1997, The Omnibus Anti-Crime Act, 1997, The Law of E-SIGN: A Legislative History of the Electronic Signature in Global and National Commerce Act, 2001; co-author: Segregation and the Fourteenth Amendment in the States, 1975, Historic Preservation Law: An Annotated Bibliography, 1976, Congress and the Courts: A Legislative History 1787-1977, 1978, Federal Consumer Protection Laws, Rules and Regulations, 1979, A Guide and Analytical Index to the Internal Revenue Acts of the U.S., 1909-1950, 1979, The Numerical Lists and Schedule of Volumes of the U.S. Congressional Serial Set: 73d Congress through the 96th Congress, 1984, Human Experimentation: Federal Laws, Legislative Histories, Regulations and Related Documents, 1985, American Legal Literature: A Guide to Selected Legal Resources, 1985, U.S.A. Patriot Act: A Legislative History, 2002, Supplement, 2005, 2007, Intelligence Reform: A Legislative History of the Intelligence Reform and Terrorism Prevention Act, 2006, Serve America Act: A Legislative History, 2010, Financial Reform: A Legislative History of the Dodd-Frank Wall Street Reform And Consumer Protection Act, 2011, Health Care Reform: A Legislative History of the Patient Protection and Affordable Care Act, 2011, Texas Community Property & Matrimonial Law, 2013. Trustees Quincy Found. for Med. Rsch. Charitable Trust, San Francisco; bd. dirs. San Antonio Lighthouse for Blind Recipient Thornton award for excellence Lynchburg Coll., 1986, Disting. Alumni award, 1989, Joseph L. Andrews Bibliog. award, 1995,; named to Hon. Order Ky. Cols., 1992; named Admiral Tex. Navy, 2005. Mem. ABA, ALA, Am. Bar Found. (life), Am. Law Inst., Am. Soc. Law and Medicine, Nat. Health Lawyers Assn., Am. Assn. Higher Edn., Spl. Librs. Assn., Internat. Assn. Law Libr. Coll. and Univ. Attys., Order of Coif, Tex. Bar Found., Phi Beta Kappa, Sigma Xi, Beta Phi Mu, Phi Delta Phi, Phi Delta Epsilon, Kappa Delta Pi, Pi Lambda Theta. Office: St Marys U Sch Law One Camino Santa Maria San Antonio TX 78228 Home Phone: 210-479-1316; Office Phone: 210-431-5030. E-mail: breams@stmarytx.edu.

REASONER, HARRY MAX, lawyer; b. San Marcos, Tex., July 15, 1939; s. Harry Edward and Joyce Marjorie (Barrett) Reasoner; m. Elizabeth Macey Hodges, Apr. 15, 1963; 1 child, Barrett Hodges; 1 child, Elizabeth Macey Reasoner Stokes. BA summa cum laude in Philosophy, Rice U., 1960; JD with hons., U. Tex., 1962; postgrad., London Sch. Economics, 1963. Bar: Tex., DC, NY. Law clk. US Ct. Appeals (2nd cir.), 1963—64; assoc. Vinson & Elkins, Houston, 1964—69, ptnr., 1970—, mng. ptnr., 1992—2001. Vis. prof. U. Tex. Sch. Law, 1971, adj. prof., 2002; vis. prof. Rice U., 1976, U. Houston Sch. Law, 1977; mem., adv. com. Supreme Ct. Tex., 1984—90; chair, adv. group US Dist. Ct. (so. dist.) Tex., 1990; at-large rep. Supreme Ct. Tex. Access Justice Commn., 2006—, chair, 2009—. Co-author (with Charles Alan Wright): Procedure: The Handmaid of Justice, 1965. Trustee U. Tex. Law Sch. Found., 1980—, pres., 1998—2001; trustee Baylor Coll. Medicine, 1992—; trustee emeritus Ctr. Am. and Internat. Law, 2008—; chair Tex. Higher Edn. Coordinating Bd., 1991; bd. dirs. Houston A+ Challenge, 1997—2009, Supreme Ct. US Bd. Hist. Soc., 2000—; bd. advs. Rice U. James A. Baker III Inst. Pub. Policy, 2011—. Recipient Professionalism award, US Ct. Appeals 5th Cir., Am. Inns Ct. Found., 2004, Lifetime Achievement award, The American Lawyer mag., 2009, Lola Wright Found. award, Texas Bar Found., 2011, Outstanding 50 Year Lawyer award, 2012; named Disting. Alumnus, U. Tex., 1997, U. Tex. Sch. Law, 1998, Rice U., 2003; named one of 25 Greatest Lawyers of Past Quarter-Century, Texas Lawyer, 2010. Fellow: Tex. Bar Found. (Lola Wright Foundation Award 2011), ABA Found., Internat. Soc. Barristers, Am. Coll. Trial Lawyers, Internat. Acad. Trial Lawyers (bd. dirs. 2005—13); mem.: ABA (chmn., antitrust sect. 1989—90), Am. Law Inst., DC Bar Assn., Am. Bd. Trial Advs., Philos. Soc. Tex., Houston Philos. Soc., Assn. Bar City NY, Houston Bar Assn., Century Assn. NYC, Cosmos Club DC, Phi Delta Phi, Phi Beta Kappa. Office: Vinson & Elkins LLP 1001 Fannin St Ste 2500 Houston TX 77002-6760 Office Phone: 713-758-2358. Business E-Mail: hreasoner@velaw.com.

REASOR, C.C. (CRAIG CLAYTON REASOR, CLAYTON REASOR), oil industry executive; b. 1956; m. Janet Reasor. BS in Finance, U. Richmond, Va., 1978; MBA, Calif. Polytechnic State U. Joined Phillips Petroleum, 1979, various position with petrochemicals divsn., 1979—87, comml. services resource area mgr., Norway divsn., dir. investor rels., 2001—02; gen. mgr. investor rels. ConocoPhillips, 2002—05, pres. US mktg., 2005—09, v.p. corporate & investor affairs, 2009—12; sr. v.p. investor rels., strategy & corporate affairs Phillips 66, Houston, 2012—. Office: Phillips 66 3010 Briarpark Dr Houston TX 77042*

REAVLEY, THOMAS MORROW, federal judge; b. Quitman, Tex., June 21, 1921; s. Thomas Mark and Mattie (Morrow) Reavley; m. Florence Montgomery Wilson, July 24, 1943 (dec.); children: Thomas Wilson, Marian, Paul Stewart, Margaret; m. Carolyn Dineen King, Aug. 27, 2004. BA, U. Tex., 1942; JD, Harvard U., 1948; LLD, Austin Coll., 1974, Southwestern U., 1977, Tex. Wesleyan, 1982; LLM, U. Va., 1983; LLD, Pepperdine U., 1993. Bar: Tex. 1948. Asst. dist. atty., Dallas, 1948—49; mem. Bell & Reavley, Nacogdoches, Tex., 1949—51; county atty. Nacogdoches, Tex., 1951; with Collins, Garrison, Renfro & Zeleskey, 1951—52; mem. Fisher, Tonahill & Reavley, Jasper, Tex., 1952—55; sec. state Tex., 1955—57; mem. Powell, Rauhut, McGinnis & Reavley, Austin, Tex., 1957—64; dist. judge Austin, Tex., 1964—68; justice Tex. Supreme Ct., Tex., 1968—77; counsel Scott & Douglass, 1977—79; judge US Ct. Appeals (5th cir.), Austin, Tex., 1979—90, sr. judge, 1990—. Lectr. Baylor U. Law Sch., 1976—94; adj. prof. U. Tex. Law Sch., 1958—59, 1978—79, 1988—95, South Tex. Sch. Law, Pepperdine Law Sch., 1990, Tex. Tech. Law Sch., 1998; mem. Am. Bar Assn., Am Bar Found., Tex. Bar Assn, Am. Law Inst., Am. Judicature Soc. Chancellor S.W. Tex. conf. United Meth. Ch., 1972—93. Lt. USNR, 1943—45. Mem.: Masons (33 degree). Office: US Ct Appeals Rm 11009 515 Rusk St Houston TX 77002-2605 Home Phone: 713-960-9512; Office Phone: 713-250-5185.

REBELL, ARTHUR LESLIE, energy executive; Various positions Schroder Wertheim & Co., NYC; mng. dir. High View Capital Corp.; assoc. prof., mergers & acquisitions, Stern Grad. Sch. Bus. NYU, 1997—98; mng. dir. Strategic Mgmt. Co., LLC, 1997—98; bd. dirs. Diamond Offshore Drilling, Inc., 1996—; sr. v.p., chief investment officer Loews Corp., 1998—2009; chmn. Boardwalk Pipeline Partners, LP, 2005—. Office: Boardwalk Pipeline Partners LP 9 Greenway Plz Ste 2800 Houston TX 77046 Office Phone: 713-479-8000. Business E-Mail: arthur.rebell@boardwalkpipelines.com.

RECK, ANDREW JOSEPH, philosopher; b. New Orleans, Oct. 29, 1927; s. Andrew Gervais and Katie (Mangiaracina) R.; m. Elizabeth Lassiter Torre, June 17, 1987. BA, Tulane U., 1947, MA, 1949; PhD, Yale U., 1954; student, U. Paris, 1962, student, 1964. Instr. English U. Conn., 1949-50; instr. philosophy Yale U., 1951-52, 55-58; faculty Tulane U., 1958—2003, prof. philosophy, 1964—2003, chmn. dept., 1969-89, dir. Master Liberal Arts program, 1984—2003, emeritus prof. philosophy, 2003—. Thomasfest lectr. Xavier U., Cin., 1970; Suarez Lectr. Spring Hill Coll., 1971; Niebuhr lectr. Elmhurst Coll., Ill., 1976; vis. prof. Fordham U., 1979; vis. scholar Hastings Ctr., NY, 1981; Woodruff lectr. Emory U., 1982; Fairchild lectr. U. So. Miss., 1982, 87; Matchette Found. lectr. Cath. U. Am., 1991, 95; sr. scholar Inst. Humane Studies, Menlo Park, Calif., 1982; vis. scholar Poynter Ctr., Ind. U., Bloomington, 1983; faculty rep. to bd. adminstrs. Tulane Ednl. Fund., 1988-91; bd. dirs. Internat. Soc. for Study of Human Ideas of Ultimate Reality and Meaning, 1989-2005, La. Endowment for Humanities, 1990-96; mem. philosophy screening com. Coun. Internat. Rsch. Scholars, 1974-76; mem. am. studies adv. com. Am. Coun. Learned Socs., 1972-76. Author: Recent American Philosophy, 1964, Introduction to William James, 1967, New American Philosophers, 1968, Speculative Philosophy, 1972; co-author: Die Philosophie des 18. Jahrhunderts 1, 2004; editor: George Herbert Mead Selected Writings, 1964, 2d edit., 1981, Knowledge and Value, 1972, (with T. Horvath, T. Krittek and S. Grean) American Philosophers' Ideas of Ultimate Reality and Meaning, 1993; co-editor Ultimate Reality and Meaning, Interdisciplinary Studies in the Philosophy of Understanding, 1990-2005; editor History of Philosophy Quar., 1993-98. Soldier US Army, 1953—55. Howard fellow, 1962-63, Liberty Fund grantee, 1982, Newcomb fellow, 1991-93; Fulbright scholar, U. St. Andrews, Scotland, 1952-53; Am. Coun. Learned Socs. grantee, 1961-62, Am. Philos. Soc. grantee, 1972, Huntington Libr. grantee, 1973, La. Ednl. Quality State Found. grantee, 1994-96, U.S. Info. Agy. grantee, Brazil, 1993. Mem.: Internat. Soc. for Study of Human Ideas of Ultimate Reality and Meaning (treas. 2001—03, sec., treas. 2003—05), Charles S. Peirce Soc. (sec., treas. 1985—86, v.p. 1986—87, pres. 1987—88), Soc. Advancement Am. Philosophy (exec. com. 1980—82, pres.-elect 1997—98, pres. 1998—2000, exec. com. 2001—03, chair nominating com. 2002—04), Metaphys. Soc. Am. (councillor 1971—75, pres. 1977—78, program com. 1989—90, chair program com. 1995—96), So. Soc. Philosophy and Psychology (treas. 1968—71, pres. 1976—77), Southwestern Philos. Soc. (exec. com. 1965—69, v.p. 1971—72, pres. 1972—73), Am. Philos. Assn. (program com. ea. divsn. 1969, nominating com. western divsn. 1975—76, 1981—82, adv. com. to program com. ea. divsn. 1994—97, chair ad hoc com. on history 1996—2004, La. Endowment Humanities Svc. award 1996), Tulane U. Emeritus Club (Outstanding Grad. of Class of 1947 award 1997), Omicron Delta Kappa, Alpha Sigma Lambda (hon. Theta chpt. of La.), Phi Beta Kappa (pres. Alpha of La. 1966—67). Home: 6125 Patton St New Orleans LA 70118-5832 Home Phone: 504-895-5629. Personal E-mail: ereck@cox.net.

RECORD, PHILLIP JULIUS, journalist; b. Ft. Worth, Jan. 12, 1929; s. Phillip Cross and Frances Virginia (McElwee) R.; m. Patricia Ann Edwards, Sept. 29, 1954; children: Christopher Phillip, Gregory Edwards, Timothy James. BA in Journalism, U. Notre Dame, Ind., 1950. Gen. reporter Lubbock Avalanche-Jour., Tex., 1950-54; copy editor, reporter Fort Worth Star-Telegram, 1954-67, asst. city editor, 1967-68, city editor evening edit., 1968-76, mng. editor, 1976-80, assoc. exec. editor, 1980-91, spl. asst. to pub., ombudsman, 1991-97, columnist, 1997—2001. Mem. mass comms. com. Tex. Tech. U., 1971—2000, chmn., 1990—92, bd. dirs., 1992—; journalism profl. in residence Tex. Christian U., 1999—. Mem. Friends of Ft. Worth Pub. Libr., 2004—08; bd. visitors Tex. Christian U.; conciliation-arbitration bd. Cath. Diocese Ft. Worth, 1994—2009, chair, 1996—2009, publs. adv. com., 1982—; bd. dirs. Tarrant County Mental Health Assn., 1990—95; dir. Freedom Info. Found., Tex., 1987—93; bd. dirs. Depression Connection Team, 1999—, Cassata H.S., 2006—; founding mem. Ft. Worth Theatre. With US Army, 1950—52. Recipient Ethics award Tex. Christian U., 1991, others for reporting, photography and headline writing; named to Tex. Tech U. Mass Comms. Hall of Fame. Mem. ABA (nat. commn. on pub. understanding about law 1984-90, commn. on partnership programs 1990-93), Investigative Reporters and Editors Inc., Soc. Profl. Journalists (pres. 1983-84, bd. dirs. Found. 1980-2001, v.p. Found., 1991-94, bd. chair 1994-01, Wells Key 1991), Creative Thinking Assn., Orgn. News Ombudsmen (dir. 1994-98, v.p. 1995-96, pres. 1996-97). Avocation: tennis. Home and Office: 6144 Walla Ave Fort Worth TX 76133 Business E-Mail: precord@star-telegram.com.

RECTOR, JOHN MICHAEL, pharmaceutical association executive, lawyer; b. Seattle, Aug. 15, 1943; s. Michael Robert and Bernice Jane (Allison) R.; m. Carmen De Ortiz; children: Christian Phillip, Ciera Rose, Zachary Ryan BA, U. Calif., Berkeley, 1966; JD, U. Calif., Hastings, 1969; PharmD (hon.), Ark. State Bd. Pharmacy,

1991. Bar: Calif. 1970, U.S. Supreme Ct. 1974; registered corp. counsel Va. Bar, 2006. Hons. program trial atty. civil rights divsn. Dept. Justice, 1969-71; dep. chief counsel judiciary com. U.S. Senate, 1971-73, counsel to Sen. Birch Bayh, 1971-77, chief counsel, staff dir., 1973-77; confirmed by U.S. Senate as assoc. adminstr. to Law Enforcement Assistance Adminstrn. and adminstr. of Office Juvenile Justice Dept. Justice, 1977-79; spl. counsel to U.S. Atty. Gen., 1979-80; dir. govt. affairs Nat. Assn. Retail Druggists, Washington, 1980-85; sr. v.p. govt. affairs, gen. counsel Nat. Cmty. Pharmacists Assn., Alexandria, Va., 1986—2005, sr. v.p., gen. counsel, 2006—09, sr. v.p., spl. counsel, 2009; advisor Assn. Cmty. Pharm. Congressional Network, 2010—. Chmn. adv. bd. Nat. Juvenile Law Ctr., 1973-77; mem. HEW panel Drug Use and Criminal Behavior, 1974-77; cons. panel Nat. Commn. Protection Human Subjects Biomed. and Behavioral Rsch., 1975-76; chmn. US Interdepartmental Coun. Juvenile Justice, 1977-79; mem. bd. com. civil rights and liberties Am. Dem. Action, 1976-80, Pres.'s Com. Mental Health-Justice Group, 1978; mem. Pharm. Industry Adv. Com.; treas. polit. action com. NARD NCPA, 1981-2006; exec. dir. Retail Druggist Legal Legis. Def. Fund, 1985-2005, founder, chmn. Washington Pharmacy Industry Forum; owner Second Genesis. Mem. editl. bd. Managed Care Law; mem. Hastings Law Jour. 1967-9; contbr. articles to profl. jours. Mem. exec. com. small bus. and fin. couns. Dem. Nat. Com., 1988-92; dir. Dem. Leadership Coun.'s Network, 1989-92, bd. advisers, 1992-94, Clinton-Gore Washington Bus. adv. com.; bd. dirs. Small Bus. Legis. Coun., 1987—, sec., 1999, treas., 2000, chmn. elect, 2001, chmn., 2002; bd. dirs. Nat. Bus. Coalition for Fair Competition, 1984—; policy advisor Presdl. campaigns, 1972-2000; active Reagan for Pres. Task Force on Criminal Justice. Perry E. Towne scholar, 1966-67; recipient Children's Express Birch Bayh Juvenile Justice award, 1981, John W. Dargavel medal Nat. Assn. Retail Drug Assn. 2003, J. Leon Lascoff Meml. award Am. Coll. Apothecares, 2004. Mem. ABA (mem. com. youth citizenship 1978-84), ATLA, Calif. Bar Assn., Nat. Health Lawyers Assn., Am. Soc. Assn. Execs. (mem. govt. affairs sect.), Washington Coun. Lawyers, Assn. Former Sr. Senate Aides (EX-SOBs), Vinifera Wine Growers Assn. Va. (life), Health R Us, Am. League Lobbyists, Theta Chi, Germanna Found. Libertarian. Avocations: antiques, reading. Office: Advice By JMR 11729 Crest Maple Dr Lake Ridge VA 22192-6624 Office Phone: 703-835-1981.

REDD, L. HUGH, manufacturing executive; B in Acctg., Brigham Young U., Provo, Utah; M of Profl. Accountancy in Tax Acctg., U. Tex. With tax dept. Arthur Andersen, 1983—86; sr. fin. analyst General Dynamics, 1986—89, sr. tax adminstr. Falls Church, Va., 1989—94, dir. treasury planning and analysis, 1994—98, staff v.p., asst. treas., 1998—2000, v.p., contr. Land Systems Sterling Heights, Mich., 2000—06, sr. v.p., CFO, 2006—. Office: Gen Dynamics 2941 Fairview Park Dr Ste 100 Falls Church VA 22042-4513 Office Phone: 703-876-3000. Office Fax: 703-876-3125.

REDDEN, SHELTON DENNIS, telecommunications industry executive; b. Cleve., Ohio; s. John Redden and Marian E. Jackson; married; 5 children. AA in Info. Svcs., Cmty. Coll. Air Force; BA in Digital Processing, Golden Gate U., 1976. Prin. computer specialist, chief ARTEL/FEMA Ops., ARTEL Telecom., Reston, Va. Served in USAF, Korea, Japan, Philippines, Thailand, England, served in USAF, 1967—68, TET offensive, Vietnam. Decorated Bronze Star for Valor USAF; named to Power 150, Ebony mag., 2008. Mem.: Prince Hall Masons (maston mason, Lodge 103, Lancaster, Calif. 1970, dep. supreme coun, orient, State of Md. 1988, grand min. state 1991, grand jr. warden, Md. 1993, dist. dep. grand master 13th Masonic Dist., UK 1996, grand master, Md. 1998—, 1st lt. grand comdr., worshipful master Donald E. Jones Lodge 121, mem. King Solomon Lodge 7, former comdr.-in-chief James A. Mingo Consistory 334, former potentate MISR Temple 213, Gold Medal Achievement award 1997). Office: ARTEL Inc 1883 Preston White Dr Reston VA 20191 Office Phone: 703-620-1700. Office Fax: 703-620-4262.

REDDY, J. PATRICK, energy executive; Grad., UCLA; MBA, Univ. So. Calif. Mgmt. positions through v.p. planning & adv. services Pacific Enterprises, 1980—98; v.p. corp. develop Atmos Energy Corp., Dallas, 1998, v.p., treas., 1998—2000, sr. v.p., CFO, 2000—08; CFO Spectra Energy Corp., Houston, 2009—. Office: Spectra Energy 5400 Westheimer Ct Houston TX 77056-5310

REDDY, KAMBHAM RAJA, botanist, educator; b. Ambuvari Palli, India, July 1, 1953; s. Kambi Kambham and Ammannamma (Reddy) R.; m. Anasuya Reddy; 1 son, Sasank. BSc in Biology, S.V. U., Tirupati, India, 1975, MSc in Botany, 1977, PhD in Botany, 1984. Curator in botany S.V. U., 1977-88; prof. plant physiology Miss. State U., 1991—. Editor: Climate Change and Global Crop Productivity, 2000; contbg. author: Climate Change and Agriculture: Analysis of Potential International Impacts, 1995; contbr. articles to profl. jour., chpt. to books. Recipient Career Rsch. award, So. Br. Am. Soc. Agronomy and Assn. Agrl. Scientists Indian Origin, 2004. Fellow Am. Soc. Agronomy, Crop Sci. Soc. Am.; mem. Biol. Sys. Simulation Work Group, Gamma Sigma Delta (Rsch. award of merit 1995). Achievements include development of new theories and concepts in plant growth regulation and incorporated into a cotton simulation model GOSSYM, used by cotton producers, consultants and rschr. across the cotton belt; extensive contributions to the field of climate change, environmental plant physiology, ethnobotany, remote sensing and crop simulation modeling. Home: 505 Banyan Rd Starkville MS 39759-4348 Office: Mississippi State U Box 9555 Mississippi State MS 39762-9555 Home Phone: 662-324-5323; Office Phone: 662-325-9463.

REDINBO, MATTHEW ROBERT, chemistry professor; b. Lafayette, Ind., Oct. 14, 1966; m. Liz Redinbo; 1 child. BS in Biochemistry, Minor in English Literature, U. Calif., Davis, 1990; PhD in Biochemistry, U. Calif., Los Angeles, 1995; postdoctoral fellow, Lab. of Wim G. J. Hol, Biomolecular Structure Ctr., U. Wash., 1995—99. Assoc. prof. chemistry U. NC, Chapel Hill, 1999—2002, assoc. prof., dept. biochemistry and biophysics, sch. of medicine, 2002—, chmn., dept. chemistry, 2007—. U. Calif. Lineberger Comprehensive Cancer Ctr. Recipient Outstanding Dissertation award, UCLA, 1995, Career award in Biomedical Sciences, Burroughs Wellcome Fund, 1999, Phillip & Ruth Hettleman prize for Artistic & Scholarly Achievement, 2004. Office: Dept Chemistry/Dept Biochemistry & Biophysics Univ NC at Chapel Hill Kenan B929 Chapel Hill NC 27599-3290 Office Phone: 919-843-8910. Office Fax: 919-962-2388. Business E-Mail: redinbo@unc.edu.

REDING, ROBERT W., air transportation executive; m. Sherrill Reding. BS in Aero. Engring., Calif. State Poly. U.; MBA, So. Ill. U. Various positions Air Fla.; v.p., flight opers. Midways Airlines, Chgo.; pres., CEO Reno Air, Canadian Regional Airlines; COO Am. Eagle Airlines; sr. v.p., tech. ops. AMR Corp., 2003—07, exec. v.p. ops., 2007—. Mem. Pres.'s Coun., Calif. State Poly. U. With USAF, 1972—79. Office: AMR Corp 4333 Amon Carter Blvd Fort Worth TX 76155

REDMAN, DON, councilman; m. Debbie Redman; 5 children. Bus. ptnr. Safe Place; councilman, Dist. 4 Jacksonville City Coun., Fla. Chmn. Mayor's Coun. on Fitness & Well-Being; mem. Land Use & Zoning, Transp., Energy & Utilities Coms., Courthouse Architectural Rev. Com.; ex-officio mem. Downtown Devel. Rev. Bd.; mem. Downtown Vision, Inc.; coun. liaison Jacksonville Housing Authority. Chmn. Englewood High Sch. Adv. Com., Greenfield Elem. Sch. Adv. Com., Englewood Resource Ctr. Full Svc. Sch.; mem. Full Svc. Schs. Leadership Coun., Youth Crisis Ctr. Adv. Bd.; usher Bapt. Ch. Jacksonville. Republican. Avocation: race dir. Office: 117 W Duval St Ste 425 Jacksonville FL 32202 Office Phone: 904-630-1386, 904-630-1394. Business E-Mail: redman@coj.net.

REDMAN, TIMOTHY PAUL, language educator, writer; b. Elmhurst, Ill., June 26, 1950; s. William Charles and Eileen Marie (Keenan) Redman. BA, Loyola U., Chgo., 1973; MA, U. Chgo., 1974, PhD, 1987. Instr. Loyola U., Rome, 1977, Ill. Inst. Tech., Chgo., 1980-84; lectr. English dept. Loyola U., Chgo., 1982-84, DePaul U., 1982—84; lectr. U. Wis., Parkside, 1984-85; instr. Ohio State U., Lima, 1985-87, asst. prof., 1987-89, U. Tex., Dallas, 1989-91, assoc. prof., 1991-98, prof., 1998—, assoc. dean, coll. master, 1991-92. Author: Ezra Pound and Italian Fascism, 1991; editor: Official Rules of Chess, 3d edit., 1987. Whiting fellow, 1981—82, NEH fellow, 1992—93. Mem.: MLA, U.S. Chess Trust (v.p.), PEN U.S.A. (pres. Tex. chpt.), Nat. Coun. Tchrs. English, U.S. Chess Fedn. (past pres.), World Chess Fedn. (Chess schs. com.). Roman Catholic. Office: U Tex Dallas Sch Arts & Humanities JO31 PO Box 830688 Richardson TX 75083-0688: US Chess Fedn PO Box 3967 Crossville TN 38557 Office Phone: 972-883-2775. Business E-Mail: redman@utdallas.edu.

REDMOND, DAVID DUDLEY, lawyer; m. Eugenia Blount Scott, Aug. 24, 1968; children: R. Scott, Sarah D. BA, Washington and Lee U., 1966, LLB, 1969. Bar: Va. 1970, U.S. Dist. Ct. (ea. dist.) Va. 1972, U.S. Ct. Appeals (4th cir.) 1972. Ptnr. Christisn & Barton LLP, Richmond, Va., 1972—. Mem. editl. bd. Washington and Lee U. Law Rev., 1968—69. Chmn. St. Joseph's Villa Foundation, 2013—; trustee St. Joseph's Villa, 1998—2012, chmn. bd. trustees, 2004—06; chmn. Capital Campaign, 2007—12. Capt. US Army, 1970—71. Decorated Bronze Star; named to Washington and Lee U. Athletic Hall of Fame. Mem.: George Washington Soc. (bd. dirs. 2002—06, 2011—), Richmond Bar Assn. (exec. com. 1980), Va. Bar Assn., Va. State Bar, Washington and Lee Law Alumni Assn. (bd. dirs. 1993—2002, pres. 1995—96), Washington and Lee U. Alumni Assn. (pres. Richmond chpt. 1980—82, bd. dirs. 1997—99, 2003—07, exec. com. 2005—07), Matindale-Hubbell AV (peer rev. mem. 1986—), Legal Elite (Va. bus. exec. 2001—11), Va. Super Lawyers (Chambers Recognition award 2009—11), Omicron Delta Kappa. Office: Christisn & Barton LLP Mutual Bldg Ste 1200 Richmond VA 23219 Office Phone: 804-697-4102. Business E-Mail: dredmond@cblaw.com.

REDMOND, MIKE, professional baseball coach, retired professional baseball player; b. Seattle, Wash., May 5, 1971; m. Michele Redmond; children: Ryan, Michael. Attended, Gonzaga U., Spokane, Wash. Catcher Fla. Marlins, 1998—2004, Minn. Twins, 2005—09, Cleve. Indians, 2010; mgr. Lansing Lugnuts, Midwest League, 2011, Dunedin Blue Jays, Fla. State League, 2012, Miami Marlins, 2012—. Named Midwest League Mgr. of Yr., 2011. Achievements include member of the World Series championship winning Florida Marlins, 2003. Office: Miami Marlins 501 Marlins Way Miami FL 33125*

REDWINE, JOHN NEWLAND, state legislator, physician; b. Pratt, Kans., Oct. 28, 1950; s. Albert Herold and Joyce Nadean (Durall R.; m. Barbara Ann Bomgaars, Dec. 27, 1975; children: John Newland II, William Merritt, Adam Boone. BA with honors, U. Kans., 1972; cert. med. technology, U. Tex. at Houston, 1974; DO, U. Medicine and Bioscis., Kansas City, Mo., 1978. Diplomate Am. Bd. Family Medicine. Intern U. Hosp., Ctr. for Health Scis., Kansas City, Mo., 1978-79; family practice resident Siouxland Med. Edn. Found., Sioux City, Iowa, 1979-81; med. dir. Morningside Family Practice, Sioux City, 1981-95; sr. v.p. St. Luke's Health Sys., Inc., Sioux City, Iowa, 1995-2001; primary care physician Cmty. Based Outpatient Clinic Dept. Veterans Affairs, 2001—04; mem. Iowa Senate from 2nd dist., 1996—2003; mem. med. staff Sioux Falls VA Med. Ctr., SD, 2002—04, Fayetteville VA Med. Ctr., Ark., 2004—07; chmn. Siouxland Instnl. Rev. Bd., 2002—04. Sr. aviation med. examiner FAA, 1979—95; clin. lectr. Iowa U. Coll. Medicine, Iowa City, 1983—95; pres. Siouxland Med. Edn. Found., 1982—2001; past chmn. family practice St. Luke's Regional Med. Ctr., Sioux City, Iowa, pres.-elect, 1993—95. Contbr. articles to profl. jours. Past v.p. Prairie Gold Area coun. Boy Scouts Am., Sioux City, bd. dirs. Mid.Am. coun., 1984-2004; bd. dirs. New Perspectives, Inc., 1996-2002, Sioux City Cmty. Sch. Dist., 1994-97, Crittenton Ctr., 2000-04, Morningside Coll., 2000-04; elected 2d dist. Iowa Senate, 1996-2003, asst. majority leader, 1998-2002, deacon Covenant Presbyn. Ch., PCA, 2009-11, elder, 2011-13; pres. Runnymede Property Owners Assn., 2011-13. Recipient achievement award Upjohn Pharm. Co., Kansas City, 1978, Silver Beaver award Prairie Gold Area Coun., Boy Scouts Am., 1997, Pub. Ofcl. award Siouxland Dist. Health Dept., 1998, Leadership award Iowans for LIFE, 2000, Guardian of Small Bus. award Nat. Fedn. Ind. Bus., 2001, Iowa Friend of the Family award Christian Coalition Iowa, 2001, 02, Legis. award Iowa Acad. Family Practice, 2002. Fellow Am. Acad. Family Physicians; mem. AMA, Am. Osteo. Assn., Iowa Med. Soc., Woodbury Med. Soc. (past pres.), Flying Physicians Assn., Christian Med. & Dental Assn. Republican. Avocation: politics. Personal E-mail: john@redwine.org.

REECE, BARBARA MASSEY, state legislator; State rep. Dist. 11, Ga., 1999—; mem. Edn. Coms., Legislature & Congressional Reapportionment Com., State Inst. & Property Com., 1999—; house rep. Ga.; ret. Democrat. Mailing: 609 Legislative Office Bldg Atlanta GA 30334 Office: 693 Massey Rd Menlo GA 30731 Office Phone: 404-656-0305. Business E-Mail: breece@legis.state.ga.us.

REECE, RICHARD KENT, corporate financial executive; b. Feb. 13, 1956; s. Robert Keith and Shirley (Fly) R.; m. Sonya Rebecca Branum, July 29, 1978; children: Emily, Eric, Ellen. BS in Acctg., Auburn U., 1978. CPA, Tex. Ptnr. Ernst & Young LLP, Houston, 1978—93; v.p., fin., treas. & CFO Belden, Inc., St. Louis, 1993—2005; sr. v.p. Acuity Brands, Inc., Atlanta, 2005, exec. v.p., CFO, 2005—. Bd. dirs. Tex. Accts. & Lawyers for Arts, Houston, 1990-93, North Harriss County YMCA, Houston, 1991-93. Mem. AICPA, Nat. Investors Rels. Assn., Tex. Soc. CPAs. Office: Acuity Brands Inc 1170 Peachtree St NE Ste 2300 Atlanta GA 30309-7676 Office Phone: 404-853-1400. E-mail: richard.reece@acuitybrands.com.

REED, ADAM V., finance professor; BA with honors, U. Calif., Berkeley, 1994; MA, U. Pa., 1998, PhD, 2002. Asst. prof. finance Kenan-Flagler Bus. Sch., U. NC, Chapel Hill, 2001—08, assoc. prof., Julian Price scholar, 2008—. Spkr. in field. Mem.: Financial Mgmt. Assn., European Finance Assn., Western Finance Assn., American Finance Assn. Office: Kenan-Flagler Business School University of North Carolina Chapel Hill Campus Box 3490, McColl Building Chapel Hill NC 27599-3490 Office Phone: 919-962-9785. Office Fax: 919-962-2068. E-mail: adam_reed@unc.edu.

REED, BETTY, state legislator; m. James Reed; children: Levetta, James, Michael, Lorenzo, Cametra. BS, Nat.-Louis U., Evanston, Ill. Ret. educator; mem. Dist. 59 Fla. House of Reps., Tallahassee, 2006—, ranking mem. econ. devel. policy com., mem. health care svcs. policy com., joint legis. auditing com., state univs. and pvt. colls. appropriations com. Mem. citizen's adv. bd. Hillsborough County Commn.; mem. adv. com. Hillsborough County Sch. Bd.; mem. Hillsborough City-County Planning Bd. Bd. mem. Fla. State PTA; pres. Lucy Dell Civic; chair NAACP Polit. Action; assoc. dir. North Tampa Chamber Assn. Democrat. Office: 2109 Palm Ave Ste 204 Tampa FL 33605-3907 also: 1402 The Capitol 402 S Monroe St Tallahassee FL 32399-1300 Office Phone: 813-241-8024, 850-488-5432.

REED, CRAIG, business services company executive; BA in Polit. Sci. & Psychology, SUNY, Albany, 1977; M Internat. Affairs in Internat. security Policy & Internat. Bus., Columbia U., 1981; PhD in Pub. Policy, George Washi. U., 1990. Exec. dir. Energy Adv. Bd. Sec.; sr. policy advisor Sec. Office; presdl. appointee US Dept. Energy; mng. dir. CSP Assocs., Inc., 2003—05; v.p., strategy, Corp. Cyber Campaign Northrop Grumman, v.p., strategy & planning, Intelligence, Surveillance & Reconnaissance Systems divsn., v.p., Bus. Devel., Strategy & Planning, Mission Sys., 2005—08; sr. v.p., Strategy & Corp. Devel. DynCorp International, Inc., 2008—. Chmn. DoE's Counterterrorism, Homeland Security Coun.; rep. White House Nat. Space Policy Coordinating Coun. Office: DynCorp International Inc 3190 Fairview Park Dr Ste 700 Falls Church VA 22042 Office Phone: 571-722-0210. Office Fax: 571-722-0252.

REED, GLEN ALFRED, lawyer; b. Memphis, Sept. 24, 1951; s. Thomas Henry and Evelyn Merle (Roddy) Reed; m. Edith Jean Renick, June 17, 1972; children: Adam Christopher, Alec Benjamin. BA, U. Tenn., 1972; JD, Yale U., 1976. Bar: Ga. 1976. Project dir. Tenn. Rsch. Coordinating Unit, Knoxville, 1972-73; assoc. Alston Miller & Gaines, Atlanta, 1976-77, Bordurant Miller Hishon & Stephenson, Atlanta, 1978-81, ptnr., 1981-85, King & Spalding, Atlanta, 1985—. Author: (book) Practical Hospital Law, 1979. Mem. adv. bd. CARE Atlanta, 1992—2007, chmn., 1994—99; v.p. Ga. Network People with Devel. Disabilities, 1991—92; legal advisor Ga. Gov.'s Commn. on Healthcare, 1994; bd. dirs. Ga. Partnership for Caring, 1999—2002, Ga. Comm. Support and Solutions, 2000—09, vice chmn., 2005—07, chmn., 2008—09; bd. dirs. Healthcare Ethics Consortium Ga., 2002—04, MedShare Internat., 1999—2007, chmn., 2005—06; bd. dirs. Ctrl. Health Ctr., 1989—95, Vis. Nurse Health Sys., 1992—2006, chmn., 1996—99; bd. dirs. MedShare Internat., 2010—; mem. dean's coun. Sch. Pub. Health Emory U., Atlanta, 1998—. Mem.: ABA, Metro Atlanta C. of C., Health Svc. Task Force, Ga. Acad. Hosp. Attys. (pres. 1991—92), Am. Health Lawyers Assn. (bd. dirs. 1997—2000, pres. 1998—99, David J. Greenburg Svc. award 2003, Listed Legal Media Group Best of Best USA 2007, 2009, 2011), Am. Acad. Hosp. Attys. (bd. dirs. 1991—97, pres.-elect 1997), Ga. Bar Assn., Assn. Retarded Citizens (gen. counsel 1979—, bd. dirs. 1986—2006, pres. 1992—96), Phi Beta Kappa. Methodist. Office: King & Spalding 1180 Peachtree St NE Atlanta GA 30309-1740 Home Phone: 404-266-3461; Office Phone: 404-572-3393. Business E-Mail: gareed@kslaw.com.

REED, GLENN W., lawyer; b. Melrose Park, Ill., Jan. 18, 1953; AB summa cum laude, Dartmouth Coll., 1975; JD cum laude, Harvard U., 1978. Bar: Ill. 1978, U.S. Dist. Ct. Ill. (No. dist.). V.p., bd. dirs. Chesapeake Life Ins. Co., Fidelity First Ins. Co., MEGA Life and Health Ins. Co., Mid-West Nat. Life Ins. Co.; with Gardner, Carton & Douglas, 1978—99, ptnr., 1985—99; exec. v.p., gen. counsel HealthMarkets, Inc., North Richland Hills, Tex., 1999—, bd. dirs., 2001—. Bd. dirs. Pepper Companies, Inc., 1990—, Peoples Bankcorp, Inc., Arlington Heights, Ill., 1999—. Mem.: Ill. State Bar Assn. Office: UICI 9151 Grapevine Hwy North Richland Hills TX 76180 Office Phone: 817-255-5200. Office Fax: 817-255-5394.

REED, GREG J., state legislator; b. Jasper, Ala. s. Rufus and Patsy Collier Reed; m. Misty Reed; children: Andrew Reed, James Reed, John Michael Reed. Grad., Bevill State CC, Ala.; BS in Bus. and Mktg., U. Ala. V.p. Preferred Med. Sys. Inc., 2004—; mem. Dist. 5 Ala. State Senate, 2011—. Mem. First Bapt. Ch., Japer, Ala. Mem.: Jasper Rotary Club. Republican. Baptist. Avocations: hunting, sports. Office: Ala State Senate State House Rm 734 11 S Union St Montgomery AL 36130 Office Phone: 334-242-7894. Business E-Mail: greg.reed@alsenate.gov.

REED, JAMES WHITFIELD, internist, educator, endocrinologist; b. Pahokee, Fla., Nov. 1, 1935; s. Thomas Reed and Chineater (Grey) Whitfield; married; children: David M., Robert A., Mary I., Katherine E. BS summa cum laude, W.Va. State Coll., Institute, 1954; MD, Howard U., Washington, DC, 1963. Diplomate Am. Bd. Internal Medicine, Am. Bd. Endocrinology and Metabolism; cert. specialist in clin hypertension, Am. Soc. Hypertension. Commd. US Army, 1963, advanced through grades to col., 1981; postdoctoral rsch. fellow U. Calif. Med. Ctr., San Francisco, 1969—71; resident in internal medicine Madigan Army Med. Ctr., Tacoma, 1966—69, chief endocrinology and metabolism, 1971—76, chief dept. clin. rsch., 1976—78; chief dept. medicine Eisenhower Army Med. Ctr., Augusta, Ga., 1978-81; assoc. prof. internal medicine edn. for FP program U. Tex., Dallas, 1981—84; prof. medicine Morehouse Sch. Medicine, Atlanta, 1985—, chmn. dept., 1985—92, chmn. grad. med. edn., 1992—96, activity chmn., 1986—88, dir. internal medicine residency, 1992—98, dir. Clin. Rsch. Ctr., 1998—2000, assoc. chair and prof. medicine, 1992—, chief endocrinology, 1992—, chief of medicine svc. at Grady. Dir. endocrinology, fellowship Madigan Army Med. Ctr., 1976-78; dir., chief medicine and program dir. internal medicine residency program Eisenhower Army Med. Ctr., 1978-81, chmn. directorate of clin. investigation, 1978-81, dir. endocrinology fellowship program; med. cons. Tuskegee VA Hosp., Ala., 1985—; mem. nat. high blood pressure edn. com. NHLBI/NIH, Nat. Diabetes Mellitus Adv. Coun., Nat. Diabetes Adv. Bd., NHLBI working Com. on Hypertension and Diabetes; chmn. Sub Com. Special Population and Situations, chmn. subcom., exec. com. Joint Nat. Commn. Detection Evaluation and Treatment of High Blood Pressure; diabetes epidemic action coun. Am. Diabetes Assn; mem. IOM/NAS Com. Med. Evaluation Vets. Disability Compensation, 2006-08. Author: Black Man's Guide to Good Health, 1994, rev. edit., 2011, High Blood Pressure: The Black Man and Woman's Guide to Living with Hypertension, 2002, Living with Diabetes: A Guide for Patients and Parents, 2005, 2nd edit., 2011; contbr. articles to profl. jours. Med. advisor, chmn. March of Dimes, Pierce County, Tacoma, 1976-78; pres. Charles Drew Sickle Cell and Health Bd., Tacoma, 1976-78; task force on cardiovascular risk reduction Am. Heart Assn. Decorated Legion of Merit, Meritorious Svc. medal; recipient Disting. Alumni award Nat. Assn. for Equal Opportunity in Higher Edn., 1988, Nat. Alumnus of Yr. award W.Va. State Coll., 1987; named to ROTC Hall of Fame, W.Va. State Coll., 1987. Master ACP; fellow Am. Coll. Clin. Endocrinologists; mem. Assn. Profs. Medicine, Endocrine Soc., Internat. Soc. Hypertension in Blacks (v.p. 1986-92, pres. 1992—2001, Lifetime Achievement award), Assn. Program Dirs. in Internal Medicine, Am. Heart Assn. (task force on cardiovasc. risk), Alpha Phi Alpha, Alpha Omega Alpha Med. Honor Soc. Democrat. Avocations: bowling, skiing. Office: Morehouse Sch Medicine 720 Westview Dr SW Atlanta GA 30310-1495 Office Phone: 404-756-5788. Business E-Mail: jreed@msm.edu.

REED, JOHN BOYD, tax specialist; b. Lubbock, Tex., June 3, 1950; s. Boyd O'Dell and Mildred A. (Musgrove) R.; m. Linda A. Hollingsworth, June 26, 1970; children: Jennifer C., Joshua B. BBA, Tex. Tech U., 1973; MS in Accountancy, U. Houston, 1974. Tax mgr. Arthur Andersen LLP, Houston, 1974-79; tax dir. Union Tex. Petroleum, Houston, 1981-85; ptnr. Deloitte & Touche, NYC, 1985-88, KPMG Peat Marwick, St. Louis, 1988-91; v.p., tax Rubbermaid, Wooster, Ohio, 1991—94, ALLTEL Corp., Little Rock, 1994, Cooper Industries Plc. Mem. Internat. Fiscal Assn., Tax Exec. Inst., Fellowship Bible Ch., Nat. Fgn. Trade Coun. Office: Cooper Industries Plc 600 Travis St Ste 5400 Houston TX 77002-2909 Office Phone: 713-209-8400. Office Fax: 713-209-8996. Personal E-mail: john.reed@cooperindustries.com.

REED, KASIM (MOHAMMED KASIM REED), Mayor, Atlanta, former state legislator; b. Plainfield, NJ, June 10, 1969; BA, Howard Univ., 1991, JD, 1995. Bar: Ga. 1995. Ptnr. Holland & Knight LLP, Atlanta; mem. Dist. 52 Ga. House of Reps., 1999—2003; mem. Dist. 35 Ga. State Senate, 2003—09; mayor City of Atlanta, 2010—. Co-chair Mayor Shirley Franklin Transition Team, 2001. Bd. trustees Howard U., 2002—; bd. mem. Metropolitan Atlanta Arts Fund, Nat. Black Artists Festival; bd. dirs. Sunrise Bank of Atlanta. Named a Lawyer on the Rise, Fulton County Daily Report, Rodel Fellow, Aspen Inst.; named one of 40 Under 40 Rising Stars, Ga. Trend mag., 2001. Democrat. Methodist. Office: City Hall 55 Trinity Ave SW Atlanta GA 30303 Office Phone: 404-330-6100. Office Fax: 404-658-6893. E-mail: mayorreed@atlantaga.gov.*

REED, KATHLYN LOUISE, occupational therapist, retired educator; b. Detroit, June 2, 1940; d. Herbert C. and Jessie R. (Krehbiel) R. BS in Occupl. Therapy, U. Kans., 1964; MA, Western Mich. U., 1966; PhD, U. Wash., 1973; MLIS, U. Okla., 1987. Occupl. therapist in psychiatry Kans. U. Med. Ctr., Kansas City, 1964-65; instr. occupl. therapy U. Wash., Seattle, 1967-70; assoc. prof. dept. occupl. therapy U. Okla. Health Scis. Ctr., Oklahoma City, 1973-77, prof., 1978-85, chmn. dept. occupl. therapy, 1973-85; libr. edn. info. svcs. Houston Acad. Medicine Tex. Med. Ctr. Libr., 1988-97; assoc. prof. Texas Woman's U., Houston, 2006—10, assoc. prof. emeritus, 2010—. Cons. Okla. State Dept. Health, 1976-77, Children's Convalescent Ctr., Oklahoma City, 1977-80, Oklahoma City Pub. Schs., 1980-81; vis. scholars program Tex. Woman's U., 1991-94, adj. prof. Sch. Occupl. Therapy, 1992-97, vis. prof., 1997-2006. Author: (with Sharon Sanderson) Concepts of Occupational Therapy, 1980, 4th edit., 1999, Models of Practice in Occupational Therapy, 1983, Quick Reference to Occupational Therapy, 1991, 2d edit., 2000, 3d edit., 2014 (with Julie Pauls) Quick Reference to Physical Therapy, 1996, 2d edit., 2004; (with S. Cunningham) Internet Guide for Rehabilitation Professionals, 1997; (with Sally Pore) Quick Reference to Speech-Language Pathology, 1999. Vol. crisis counselor Open Door Clinic, Seattle, 1968-72; mem. exec. bd. Seattle Mental Health Inst., 1971-72; Mem. Citizen Participation Liaison Coun., Seattle, 1970-72. Recipient Award of Merit, Can. Assn. Occupl. Therapists, 1988, Svc. award 2010. Fellow: Am. Occupl. Therapy Assn. (chmn. ethics commn. 2008—10, Merit award 1983, Slagle lectr. award 1985, Svc. award 1985, 2001); mem.: Am. Hippotherapy Assn., Soc. for the Study of Occupations, Am. Occupl. Therapy Found., Med. Libr. Assn. (Rittenhouse award 1987, Acad. Health Info. Professions), Tex. Occupl. Therapy Assn. (Roster of Merit award 2002, Disting. Svc. award 2004), Tex. Occupl. Therapy Found. (hon.; pres. 1999—2010), Okla. Occupl. Therapy Assn. (pres. 1974—76), Coun. Exceptional Children, World Fedn. Occupl. Therapists, N.Am. Riding for Handicapped Assn., Sigma Kappa (Colby award 1994), Pi Theta Epsilon. Democrat. Home: 6699 De Moss Dr Houston TX 77074-5003 Personal E-mail: klreed3@juno.com.

REED, LEON SAMUEL, secondary school educator, photographer; b. Warren, Ohio, July 6, 1949; s. Walter Charles and Lois Avalene (Botroff) R.; m. Margaret Smith, Dec. 27, 1975 (div.); m. Lois S. Lembo, Aug. 5, 1997; children: Samuel, Stephen, Catherine. BA in Econs. and Journalism, Antioch Coll., Yellow Springs, Ohio, 1971. Project dir. Coun. on Econ. Priorities, NYC and Washington, 1970-75; sr. mem. profl. staff Joint Com. on Def. Prodn., U.S. Congress, Washington, 1975-77; mem. profl. staff Com. on Banking, Housing and Urban Affairs, U.S. Senate, Washington, 1977-81; analyst TASC, 1981-82, mgr. contingency planning, 1982-85, mgr. instl. resources dept., 1985-91, dir. indsl. and mfg. scis. divsn., 1991-97; freelance writer, photographer, 1996—; rsch. staff Inst. Def. Analyses, 1998—2003; rsch. asst. George Mason U., 2004—; tchr. Woodbridge H.S., 2005—. Contbr. Strategic Survey, 1981-82, The American Defense Mobilization Infrastructure, 1983; author numerous congressional and exec. br. reports, also mag. and jour. articles. Del. White House Conf. on Youth, 1971; pres. Randolph Civic Assn., 1978—80; v.p. North Bethesda Congress of Citizens Assns., 1983—84, pres., 1984—86; v.p. Md. State Youth Soccer Assn., 1998—2005; bd. dirs. Coun. on Econ. Priorities, 1971—73, Montgomery Soccer, Inc., 1994—, pres., 2001—06.

REED, LINDA L., real estate company executive; Exec. v.p. Lennar Fin. Svcs., LLC; pres. North Am. Title Group, Inc.; chmn. Real Estate Services Providers Council, Inc., 2006—. Mem.: Calif. Land Title Assn. (life), Tex. Land Title Assn. (life), Am. Land Title Assn. (life). Office: North American Title Group Inc 3rd Fl 700 NW 107th Ave Miami FL 33172 Office Phone: 305-552-1102. Office Fax: 305-227-1790.

REED, MARK LAFAYETTE, III, retired humanities educator; b. Asheville, NC, Sept. 26, 1935; s. Mark Lafayette Jr. and Edith (Murphy) Fisher; m. Martha Balch Sibley, Aug. 30, 1958; children: Victoria Fisher Reed Gless, Christina Pickering Reed Dowdy. BA, Yale Coll., 1957; MA, Harvard U., 1958, PhD, 1962. From asst. prof. to prof. U. NC, Chapel Hill, 1963—71, Lineberger prof. in the humanities, 1986—2000, prof. emeritus, 2000—. Author: Wordsworth: Chronology of Early Years, 1967, Wordsworth: Chronology of Middle Years, 1975, Bibliography of Wordsworth 1787-1930, 2013; editor: Wordsworth: Thirteen-Book Prelude, 2 vols., 1991; assoc. editor Cornell Wordsworth Series, 1971—; contbr. articles to profl. jours. Bd. advisors Warren Wilson Coll., Swannanoa, N.C., 1976-86; assoc. trustee Wordsworth Trust, Grasmere, Eng., 1975—. Recipient merit award The Asheville Sch., 1985. Mem. MLA, Wordsworth-Coleridge Assn., Elizabethan Club (New Haven, Conn.), Harvard Club (N.Y.C.), Grolier Club (N.Y.C.), Biltmore Forest Country Club. Personal E-mail: mlr@email.unc.edu.

REED, MICHAEL ROBERT, agricultural economist; b. Lawrence, Kans., July 11, 1953; s. Robert Stanley and Marian Lucille (Karr) R.; m. Patricia Gail Gurtler, Mar. 16, 1973; children: Laura Gail, Brian Michael. BS, Kans. State U., 1974; MS, Iowa State U., 1976, PhD, 1979. Asst. prof. U. Ky., Lexington, 1978-83, assoc. prof., 1983-89; prof., 1989—; exec. dir. Ctr. for Export Devel., 1988-95; dir. office of internat. affairs U. Ky., Lexington, 1994-98, dir. office of internat. programs for agr., 1998—. Cons. USDA, 1994-97, 02—, US AID, Washington, 1983-86, 99-01, 04-. Author: (textbook) International Trade in Agricultural Products, 2000; mem. editl. bd. So. Jour. of Agrl. Econs., 1983-86; contbr. articles to profl. jours. Grantee Farmer Coop. Svcs., 1982-84, 87-88, TVA, 1982-85, Fed. Crop Ins. Corp., 1985-87, USDA, 1986-2003, 2005—; recipient Outstanding Jour. Article award Soc. Farm Mgrs. and Rural Appraisers, 1986, Jour. Agrl. and Applied Econs., 2002 Mem. Am. Agrl. Econs. Assn., So. Agrl. Econs. Assn., Gamma Sigma Delta. Home: 2216 Bonhaven Rd Lexington KY 40515-1150 Office: U Ky Dept Agrl Econs 308 Barnhart Bldg Lexington KY 40546-0001 Office Phone: 859-257-7259. Business E-Mail: mrreed@uky.edu.

REED, RALPH EUGENE, JR., political consultant, former political organization administrator; b. Portsmouth, Va., June 24, 1961; s. Ralph Sr. and Marcy R.; m. Jo Anne Young, 1987; children: Brittany, Ralph III, Christopher, Nicole. BA in History, U. Ga., 1985; Ph.D in American History, Emory U., 1991. Exec. dir. Coll. Republican Nat. Com., 1983—85, Christian Coalition, Chesapeake, Va., 1989-97; founder, pres. Century Strategies, Strategies Cons. Co., Duluth, Ga., 1997—; chmn. Ga. Republican Party, 2001—03; southeast regional campaign chmn. George Bush re-election campaign, 2003—04; founder Faith & Freedom Coalition, 2009—. Founder Students for Am., Raleigh, NC, 1984; lobbyist; spkr. in field. Author: (nonfiction) Politically Incorrect: The Emerging Faith Factor in American Politics, 1994, After the Revolution: How the Christian Coalition is Impacting America, 1995, Active Faith: How Christians Are Changing the Face of American Politics, 1996, (novels) Dark Horse: A Political Thriller, 2008, The Confirmation, 2010. Named one of The 25 Most Influential Republicans, Newsmax mag., 2008. Republican. Evangelical Christian. Office: Century Strategies 3235 Satellite Blvd Ste 575 Duluth GA 30096-9017

REED, SHERMAN KENNEDY, chemicals executive, consultant; b. Chgo., Apr. 11, 1919; s. Frank Hynes and Helen Louise (Kennedy) R.; m. Octavia Bailey, Oct. 11, 1943; children: Martin Bailey, Holly Anne Johnson, Julie Marie Reed. BS with honors, U. Ill., 1940; PhD, Cornell U., 1949. Asst. instr. chemistry Cornell U., 1940-43; rsch. scientist Manhattan Project, NYC, 1942-46; asst. prof. Bucknell U., Lewisburg, Pa., 1946-50; with FMC Corp., 1950—, mgr., asst. dir. rsch., 1950-60, divisional dir. rsch. and devel., ctrl. rsch. dir., 1960-76, v.p., 1976-82, cons. Chgo., 1983—; dir. Avicon, Inc., 1970-82; pres., dir. FMC Gold Corp.; mng. dir. COGAS Devel. Co., 1975—; dir. Indsl. Rsch. Inst., NYC, Franklin Inst., Phila., 1976-83; chmn. bd. Franklin Rsch. Ctr., Phila., 1976-83. Fellow Am. Inst. Chemists; mem. AAAS, Am. Chem. Soc., Assn. Rsch. Dirs. (pres. 1973). Republican. Home and Office: 2300 Indian Creek Blvd W #C211 Vero Beach FL 32966-2400 Office Phone: 772-321-3654. Personal E-mail: shermankreed@bellsouth.net.

REED, SUSAN D., prosecutor; m. Robert D. Reed (dec.); 1 child. BA in Econs., Univ. Tex., Austin, JD, 1974. Bar: Tex. 1974, U.S. Dist. Ct. (we. dist.) Tex., U.S. Supreme Ct., bd. cert. criminal law: Tex. Bd. Legal Specialization. Asst. dist. atty., chief pros. 144th & 187th districts Office of Bexar County Dist. Atty., San Antonio, 1974—82; atty., bus. litigation Souls and Reed; adminstrv. judge Dist. Cts. Bexar County, 1996—97; judge 144th Dist. Ct.; criminal dist. atty. Bexar County, San Antonio, 1999—. Mem. Criminal Justice Policy Coun., Govs. Juvenile Justice Adv. Bd., Bush-Cheney Transition Team for Dept. Justice, Nat. Adv. Coun. on Violence Against Women. Mem. Regional Anti-Terrorism Task Force; co-chair Anti-Crime Commn., 2002. Recipient Judge of Yr. award, Tex. Gang Investigators Assn.; named Elected Official of the Yr., San Antonio branch, Nat. Assn. Social Workers, 2010; named to, San Antonio Women's Hall of Fame, 2004. Mem.: Nat. Dist. Attys. Assn., Tex. Dist. and County Attys. Assn. (pres. 2005—). Office: Bexar County Criminal Dist Atty 5th Fl 300 Dolorosa San Antonio TX 78205-3630 Office Phone: 210-335-2342. E-mail: sreed@bexar.org.

REED, TRAVIS DEAN, public relations executive; b. Trinity, Tex., Sept. 27, 1930; s. Travis and Alma (Rains) R.; m. Caroline M. McDonald, June 15, 1957; children: Anne Reed Adams, Lisa Reed Lettau. Student, Tex. A&M U., 1948-51, U. Houston, 1951-53. Reporter Houston Post, 1951-53; Washington Bur. corr. McGraw-Hill Pub. Co., 1955-61, Boston Herald-Traveler, 1961-62; with Newhouse News Svc., Washington, 1962-79, chief corr., 1964-67, editor, 1967-79; pub. rels. cons. Washington, 1979—. 1st lt. U.S. Army, 1953-55. Mem. Nat. Press Club, Gridiron Club, Army and Navy Club. Home: 37277 Branchriver Rd Purcellville VA 20132-1922 Office: T Dean Reed Co PO Box 65276 Washington DC 20035

REED, WENDY, management consultant company and information technology executive; BS in Computer-Based Mgmt., minor in comm., Clarkson U., 1984. Mem. info. tech. dept. Accenture; with MSA (now Dun & Bradstreet Software), Viasoft, Clarus, Hayes Microcomputer Products. Spkr. in field. Bd. dir. AEA, Revegy, Inc., Milton HS Athletic Assn. Recipient Entrepreneurial Success award, Clarkson U., 2001, Entrepreneur of Yr. award, Ernest & Young, 2006; named Woman of Yr. Tech. (small/medium bus.), (WIT) Women in Tech., 2006; named one of 40 Under 40 Georgia's Brightest Stars, Ga. Trend Mag., 2002, Top 50 Entrepreneurs, Catalyst Mag., 2004, 2005. Office: InfoMentis Inc Ste 160 1750 Founders Parkway Alpharetta GA 30004 Office Phone: 770-667-5352. Office Fax: 770-752-9143.

REEDER, GINGER, apparel executive; Attended, Hollins U., 1977. Media buyer, project mgr. Robert A. Wilson Assocs., 1981—86; buyer Horchow, 1986—90; v.p. Neiman Marcus, Inc., 1996—; v.p., corp. comm. Neiman Marcus Group, Inc., 1996—; v.p., pub. rels. Neiman Marcus, Inc., 2004—. Dir., mktg., external svcs. Dallas Mus. of Art, 1992-96. Office: The Neiman Marcus Group Inc 1618 Main St Dallas TX 75201 Office Phone: 972-969-3213. Office Fax: 214-573-5320. Business E-Mail: Ginger_Reeder@neimanmarcus.com.

REEDY, THOMAS W., JR., corporate financial executive; BA, UCLA; MBA, Colgate Darden Sch. Bus. Univ. Va. Fin. mgmt. positions American Airlines, Inc.; asst. treas. corp. fin. GATX Corp., 1996—98, treas., 1998—99; v.p. corp. develop., treas. Gateway Inc., 1999—2003; v.p., treas. CarMax, Inc., 2003—10, sr. v.p. fin., 2010, sr. v.p., CFO, 2010—. Office: CarMax Inc 12800 Tuckahoe Creek Pkwy Richmond VA 23238 Office Phone: 804-747-0422.

REEL, JEROME VINCENT, JR., academic administrator, historian; b. New Orleans, Oct. 16, 1937; s. Jerome Vincent Sr. and Ruby Ella (DeLee) R.; m. Edmee Jane Franklin, Sept. 2, 1961; children: Jerome III, Helen Austin, Elizabeth Whidden. Student, Tulane U., 1955-58; BS, U. So. Miss., 1960, MA, 1961; PhD, Emory U., 1967. Instr. Clemson (S.C.) U., 1963-65, asst. prof., 1965-71, assoc. prof., 1971-75, prof., 1975—, dean undergrad. studies, 1979-80, vice provost, 1980—; sr. vice provost, 1992—2004; univ. historian, 2001—. Vis. scholar Emory U., Atlanta, 1973; cons. Pa. State U., University Park, 1986; chmn. Tri-county Tech. Coll. Adv. Bd., Pendleton, S.C., 1987-88. Author: Index to British Biographies, 1975, A History of American Fraternities, 1976, The Oak, 1980, Integration with Dignity, 2003, Women and Clemson, 2005, Thomas Green Clemson, 2007, The High Seminary Clemson College, 1889-1964, vol. 2, 1964-2000; contbr. articles on Brit. history, intellectual history and opera history to profl. jours. Elder Ft. Hill Presbyn. Ch., Clemson, 1977—; cons. Opera for Youth-Kennedy Ctr., Washington, 1978, Ill. Endowment for Humanities, Chgo., 1983. Grantee NEH, 1977, Named Clemson Alumni Master Tchr.,1975, Thomas Green Clemson award, 2005, SC Gov. award, 2011. Mem. Medieval Acad. Am., Nat. Opera Assn. (v.p. 1983-85, pres. 1985-87), Assn. Univ. Summer Schs., Blue Key, Golden Key, Phi Kappa Phi, Pi Kappa Alpha (Loyalty award 1986), Omicron Delta Kappa. Clubs: Torch (pres. 1985-86) (Greenville, S.C.), Assn. U. Summer Sch.(pres. 1992), Order of West Range Avocations: reading, travel, gardening, music. Office: Clemson University Special Collections Strom Thurmond Inst Clemson SC 29634 Home: 331 Kendra Place Clemson SC 29631 Business E-Mail: jvreel@clemson.edu.

REEN, CHRISTOPHER P., publishing executive; B, SUNY, Buffalo. Intern, various positions in sales & mgmt. The Buffalo News; retail advt. mgr. Daytona Beach News-Jour.; dir. classified advt. Pitts. Post-Gazette; v.p. advt. Rochester Democrat and Chronicle; v.p. sales & mktg. The Oklahoman, pub., 2011—; exec. v.p. OPUBCO Comm. Group, pres., 2011—; pres., chief mktg. officer Wimgo.com LLC. Office: The Oklahoman 9000 N Broadway PO Box 25125 Oklahoma City OK 73125*

REES, CLIFFORD HARCOURT, JR., (TED REES), consulting company executive, retired trade association administrator, military officer; b. Newport News, Va., Dec. 11, 1936; s. Clifford Harcourt Sr. and Mary Evelyn (Brooks) R.; m. Joan Elizabeth Mittong, July 26, 1958; children— Clifford Harcourt III, Steven M., Daniel B., William B. BS in Fgn. Svc., Georgetown U., 1958; MS in Polit. Sci., Auburn U., 1969; grad., Air War Coll., Montgomery, Ala., 1978; grad. program for sr. exec. in nat. and internat. security, JFK Sch. Govt., Harvard U. Commd. 2d lt. U.S. Air Force, 1958; advanced through grades to lt. gen., 1988; comdr. 421st Tactical Fighter Squadron, Udorn Royal Thai AFB, 1974-75; chief, house liaison office US House of Representatives, Washington, 1978-80; asst. col. assignments Randolph AFB, 1980-82; vice-comdr. Air Force Manpower and Personnel Ctr., 1982; dep. dir. legis. liaison Office Sec. Air Force, 1982-84, dir. legis. liaison, 1984-86; comdr. USAF Air Defense Weapons Ctr., Tyndall AFB, Fla., 1986-88; vice comdr. in chief USAF in Europe, Ramstein AB, Federal Republic of Germany, 1988-92, ret., 1992; founder, pres. Rees Group Cons., 1992—; pres. Air Conditioning and Refrigeration Inst., Arlington, Va., 1993—2002. U.S. rep. to v.p. Internat. Coun. Mil. Sports, Brussels, 1982-94; dir. bd. dirs. Armed Forces Benefit Assn. Investment Mgmt. Co., 1996—2010. Decorated D.S.M. with one oak leaf cluster, DFC with one oak leaf cluster, Legion of Merit with one oak leaf cluster, Meritorious Svc. medal with one oak leaf cluster, Air medal with 11 oak leaf clusters, Das Grosse Verdienstkreuz Mit Stern, Fed. Republic Germany; named comdr. Order of Meritorious Svc. Internat. Mil. Sports Coun., 1993, Order of the Sword, US Air Forces in Europe, 1992. Mem. Delta Phi Epsilon (v.p. membership 1957-58, nat. pres. 1984-86) Methodist. Home: 20 Spring Valley Ct Pinehurst NC 28374 E-mail: ted@thereesgroup.com.

REES, FRANK WILLIAM, JR., architect; b. Rochester, NY, June 5, 1943; s. Frank William and Elizabeth R. (Miller) R.; m. Joan Mary Keevers, Apr. 1, 1967; children: Michelle, Christopher. BS in Architecture, U. Okla., 1970; postgrad., Harvard U., Boston, 1979-90; OPM, Harvard U., 1990; DArch, U. Hawaii, 2001. Registered architect, 39 states & D.C.; cert. Nat. Coun. Archtl. Registration Bds.; registered interior designer. Sales mgr. Sta. KFOM, Oklahoma City, 1967-70; project architect Benham-Blair & Affiliates, Oklahoma City, 1970-75; pres., CEO, founder Rees Assocs., Inc., Oklahoma City, 1975—. Pres., chmn. bd. Weatherscan Radio Network, Oklahoma City, 1973-78; chmn. bd. Weatherscan Internat., Oklahoma City, 1972-78; pres. Frontier Communications, Oklahoma City, 1980-84; chmn. architecture bd. U. Okla., Norman, 1988-91; bd. dirs. Century, Inc., Oklahoma City. Past pres. Lake Hefner Trails, Oklahoma City, Hosp. Hospitality House, Oklahoma City, Oklahoma City Beautiful; mem. Leadership Oklahoma City. Mem. AIA, Am. Assn. Hosp. Architects, Am. Healthcare Assn., Tex. Hosp. Assn., World Pres. Orgn. (chmn. 1997-98), Assisted Living Fedn. of Am., Am. Assn. Homes and Svcs. for the Agig. Home: 1104 Stone Gate Dr Irving TX 75063-4676 also: 1801 N Lamar St Ste 600 Dallas TX 75202-1711 Office Phone: 214-522-7337.

REESE, CLARA COOK, retired educator; b. Burke County, NC, Nov. 11, 1931; m. Ned Ervin Reese, Aug. 25, 1950 (dec. Sept. 9, 1993); children: Jerry Alan, Susan Clarice. AB, Lenoir Rhyne Coll., 1969; MA, NC State U., 1972, EdD, 1980. With finishing dept., supr. irregular dept. Ellis Hosiery Co., Inc., Hickory, NC, 1952—62, payroll clk., receptionist, 1962—64; sales staff J.C. Penney Co., Hickory, NC, 1968—69; tchr. Catawba Valley Tech. Inst., 1972—77, Newton-Conover City Schs., NC, 1969—77; prof. dept. vocat. and adult tech. edn. Marshall U., Huntington, W.Va., 1980—2010. Author (co-author) 12 occupational curricula. Chmn. bd. dirs. Career Exploration Clubs NC, 1974—76; state advisor Career Exploration Clubs W.Va., 1982—92; bd. dirs. Huntington Boys and Girls Clubs, 1986—. Mem.: W.Va. Vocat. Assn., Am. Vocat. Assn., Epsilon Pi Tau, Phi Delta Kappa. Democrat. Methodist.

REESE, ELIZABETH W., gas industry executive; married; 1 children. B in Bus. Adminstrn. and Economics, U. NC; M in Acctg., U. Ga. Sr. mgr. Deloitte LLP; v.p., fin. and bus. innovation Atlanta Gas Light (subs. of AGL Resources Inc.), 2004; v.p., fin. and bus. innovation, contr. AGL Resources, 2000; v.p., customer svc. AGL Resources, Inc., 2004—07, v.p., fin., 2007—. Bd. dirs. CHRIS Kids. Office: AGL Resources Inc 10 Peachtree Pl NE Atlanta GA 30309 Office Phone: 404-584-4000. Office Fax: 404-584-3714. Business E-Mail: ereese@aglresources.com.

REESE, GLENN G., state legislator; b. Greenville, SC, Jan. 6, 1942; s. Wilford William Reese and Geneva Margaret; m. Janis Elizabeth Dearybury; children: Glenn, John David, Kathryn, Michael. AA, Mars Hill Coll., 1961; BA, Auburn U., 1963; MA, Converse Coll., 1967. Mem. Dist. 11 SC State Senate, 1991—; mem. Agr. & Natural Resources Com., Banking & Inst. Com., Finance Com., Invitations Com., Labor Com. Deacon Boiling Springs First Baptist Ch. Democrat. Baptist. Mailing: 507 Fagan Dr, Lake Bowen Inman SC 29349 Office: 502 Gressette Bldg Columbia SC 29201 Home Phone: 864-592-2984; Office Phone: 803-212-6108, 864-585-1956. Business E-Mail: gr@legis.lpitr.state.sc.us.

REESE, HAYNE WARING, psychologist, educator; b. Comanche, Tex., Jan. 14, 1931; s. Tom F. and Marion (Waring) R.; m. Patsy Atwood, Aug. 24, 1957 (div. Apr. 1967); children: Anne, William, Margaret; m. Nancy Mann, Dec. 16, 1967; 1 child, Bradley. Student, So. Meth. U., 1949-50; BA, U. Tex., 1953, MA, 1955; PhD, U. Iowa, 1958. Asst. prof. U. Buffalo, 1958-62; assoc. prof. SUNY-Buffalo, 1962-66, prof., 1966-67, U. Kans., Lawrence, 1967-70; Centennial prof. psychology W.Va. U., Morgantown, 1970-2000, dir. grad. tng. in life-span devel. psychology, 1973-2000, Centennial prof. emeritus, 2000—. Mem. initial rev. groups div. research grants NIH, Washington, 1969-71, 74-78, 79-84; vis. prof. SUNY, Buffalo, 1970, U. Iowa, 1972, U. Hawaii, 1975, S.W. China Normal U., 1997, 2000. Author: Perception of Stimulus Relations, 1968, Basic Learning Processes in Childhood, 1976; co-author: Experimental Child Psychology, 1970, Life-Span Developmental Psychology, 1977, 1988, Child Development, 1979; editor: Advances in Child Development and Behavior, 26 vols., 1969-2001; co-editor: Life-Span Developmental Psychology, 8 vols., 1973-97, Behaviour Science, 1986, Varieties of Scientific Contextualism, 1993; assoc. editor: Jour. Exptl. Child Psychology,

1975-83, editor, 1983-97, mem. editl. bd. 1965-74, 98-2000. Served with U.S. Army, 1954. Mem. Soc. for Rsch. in Child Devel., Assn. for Behavior Analysis Home Phone: 817-346-2865. Personal E-mail: haynereese@aol.com.

REES-JONES, TREVOR D., oil industry executive; b. Dallas, Tex., 1950; married; 2 children. BA, Darmouth Coll.; JD, So. Methodist U. Sch. Law, 1978. Atty. Thompson & Knight, Dallas, 1978—84; oil & gas investor, 1984—93; founder Chief Oil & Gas LLC (sold to Devon Energy), 1994—2006; founder, pres. & CEO Chief Operating LLC, Dallas, 2006—. Named one of Forbes 400: Richest Americans, 2006—. Office: Chief Operating Llc 5956 Sherry Ln Ste 1500 Dallas TX 75225-8026 Office Phone: 214-265-9590. Office Fax: 214-265-9593.

REEVE, DEBORAH B., art association administrator, educator; Art teacher; adj. prof. Lesley Coll., Cambridge, Mass.; with US Dept. Edn.; assoc. exec. dir. develop. and special projects Nat. Assn. Elementary Sch. Principals, dep. exec. dir., advocacy and prof. develop., 2001—07; exec. dir. Nat. Art Ed. Assn., Reston, Va., 2007—. Paintings exhibited Gallery West, Alexandria, Va., Cranbury Gallery, Princeton, NJ; mem. curriculum develop. advisory team 100 People: A World Portrait. Office: Nat Art Ed Assn 1916 Association Dr Reston VA 20191

REEVE, THOMAS GILMOUR, physical education educator; b. Memphis, Sept. 23, 1946; s. Paul Goodwin and Dorothy (Bourke) R.; children: Bourke, Spencer. BS in Phys. Edn., Tex. Tech. U., 1969, MEd, 1972; PhD, Tex. A&M U., 1976. Asst. prof. Auburn (Ala.) U., 1977-82, assoc. prof., 1982-87, prof., 1987-91, asst. v.p. for acad. affairs, 1992-93, alumni prof., 1991-95, prof. phys. edn., 1995-98, W.T. Smith Disting. prof., 1998-99; prof., chair Tex. Tech. U., Lubbock, 1999—2004, dir. strategic planning, 2002—08; HS Pliner prof. La. State U., 2008—10, vice provost Fox Academic Affairs, 2010—. Vis. asst. prof. Tex. A&M U., College Station, 1976-77. Co-editor: Stimulus-Response Compatibility, 1990; sect. editor Rsch. Quar. for Exercise and Sport, 1990-92, editor, 1999-2002; assoc. editor Jour. Sport Behavior, 1983—2008. Fellow AAHPERD, Rsch. Consortium (pres. 2008-09), Am. Acad. Kinesiology and Phys. Edn. (pres. 2004-05); mem. N.Am. Soc. Psychology Sport and Phys. Activity (publ. dir. 1985-87, pres. 1991-92), Am. Kinesiology Assn. (pres. 2010-12). Avocation: masters swimming. Office: La State Univ 112 H P Long Fieldhouse Baton Rouge LA 70803 Office Phone: 225-578-6610. Business E-Mail: tgreeve@lsu.edu.

REEVES, BRYCE E., state legislator; b. Calif., Nov. 28, 1966; BS, Tex. A&M U.; MPA in Pub. Adminstrn., George Mason U. Mem. Dist. 17 Va. State Senate, 2012—, mem. Gen. Laws and Tech. Com., Courts of Justice Com., Privileges and Elections Com. & Rehab. and Social Services Com. Republican. Office: Senate of Virginia PO Box 396 Richmond VA 23218 also: PO Box 7021 Fredericksburg VA 22404-7021 Office Phone: 804-698-7517, 804-698-7651. E-mail: district17@senate.virginia.gov.

REEVES, CARLTON WAYNE, federal judge; b. Fort Hood, Tex., 1964; BA magna cum laude, Jackson State U., 1986; JD, U. Va., 1989. Bar: Miss. 1989, US Dist. Ct. (southern dist.) Miss. 1989, US Dist. Ct. (northern dist.) Miss. 1989, US Ct. Appeals (5th cir.) 1989, Supreme Ct. of US 2002. Summer law clk. ACLU of Miss., Jackson, Miss., 1987; summer assoc., law clk. Ferguson Stein Chambers Gresham & Sumter, Charlotte, NC, 1988; rschr. Hinds County Bd. Supervisors, Jackson, Miss., 1989; law clk. to Hon. Reuben V. Anderson Miss. Supreme Ct., 1989—90, staff atty., 1991; atty. Phelps Dunbar, L.L.P., Jackson, Miss., 1991—95; asst. US atty. (southern dist.) Miss., chief Civil Divsn. US Dept. Justice, 1995—2001, dist. election officer, 1998—2001; shareholder Pigott Reeves Johnson & Minor, P.A., 2001—06, Pigott Reeves Johnson, P.A., Miss., 2006—10; Hinds County family master Fifth Chancery Ct. Dist. Miss., Jackson, Miss., 2007—10; judge US Dist. Ct. (southern dist.) Miss., 2010—. Adj. faculty Jackson State U., 1992, Miss. Coll. Sch. Law, 1994; ptnr. North Congress Properties, LLC, 2001—; bd. mem. Miss. Ctr. for Justice, 2003—. Contbr. articles to law jours. Trustee Cmty Found. Greater Jackson, 2005—; bd. mem. Miss. Workers Ctr. for Human Rights, 2006—10, treas., 2008—10; trustee Coll. Hill Missionary Baptist Ch., 2004—; mem. Jackson State U. Investment Mgmt. Com., 2009—; bd. mem. Coll. Savings Plans of Miss., Miss. Treasury Dept., 2008—. Recipient Silver Life Mem., NAACP; named one of Top 40 Under 40, Miss. Bus. Jour.; grantee Mary Claiborne and Roy H. Ritter Fellowship in Recognition of Outstanding Honor, Character, and Integrity. Mem.: ABA, Nat. Bar Assn., Miss. Trial Lawyers Assn., Miss. Bd. Bar Commrs., Miss. State Bar Assn. (Curtis E. Coker Access to Justice Award), Miss. Access to Justice Commn., Magnolia Bar Found., Inc., Magnolia Bar Assn. (R. Jess Brown Award, Alfred E. Rhodes Svc. Award), Hinds County Bar Assn. (Pro Bono Award), Fifth Cir. Bar Assn., Fed. Bar Assn., Charles Clark Inn of Ct., Ctrl. Miss. Legal Svc., American Trial Lawyers Assn., Jackson State U. Alumni Assn. (life). Office: US District Court PO Box 23552 Jackson MS 39225-3552 Office Phone: 601-965-4292.

REEVES, DANNY C., federal judge; b. Corbin, Ky., 1957; BA, Eastern Ky. U., 1978; JD, Northern Ky. U., 1981. Law clk. to Hon. Eugene E. Siler Jr. US Dist. Ct. (ea. and we. dists.) Ky., 1981—83; pvt. practice atty. Ky., 1983—2001; judge US Dist. Ct. (ea. dist.) Ky., Frankfort, 2001—. Office: US Dist Ct Ste 354 330 W Broadway Frankfort KY 40601 Office Phone: 502-875-4777.

REEVES, GENE, retired judge; b. Meridian, Miss., Feb. 27, 1930; s. Clarence Eugene and May (Philyaw) R.; m. Brenda Wages, Sept. 26, 1980. JD, John Marshall U., 1964; cert. judge spl. ct. jurisdiction; postgrad., U. Nev., 1995. Bar: Ga. 1964, U.S. Ct. Appeals (11th cir.) 1965, U.S. Supreme Ct. 1969. Ptnr. Craig & Reeves, Lawrenceville, Ga., 1964-71; sole practice Lawrenceville, 1971-85; prin. Reeves Law Firm, 1985-94; judge City Ct., Lawrenceville, 1969-70, Magistrate Ct. of Gwinnett County, Ga., 1994—; sr. judge Gwinnett Co., 2005. Sgt. USAF, 1951-54. Mem. ABA, ATLA, GTLA, Am. Jud. Soc., Gwinnett County Bar Assn. (pres. 1970-72), Criminal Def. Lawyers Assn., Atlanta Bar Assn. Baptist. Home: 221 Pineview Dr Lawrenceville GA 30046-6035 Office: 75 Langley Dr Lawrenceville GA 30046-6035

REEVES, PAMELA LYNN, federal judge, lawyer; b. Marion, Va., July 21, 1954; BA, U. Tenn., 9176; JD, U. Tenn. George C. Taylor Coll. Law, 1979. Bar: Tenn. 1979, US Dist. Ct. (eastern & middle disricts) Tenn. 1979, US Ct. Appeals (6th cir.), US Supreme Ct. Assoc. Griffin, Burkhalter, Cooper & Reeves, 1979—85, Morrison, Morrison, Tyree & Dickenson, 1985—87; ptnr. Watson Hollow & Reeves, PLC, Knoxville, 1987—2002; founding ptnr. Reeves, Herbert & Anderson P.C., 2002—14; judge US Dist. Ct. (eastern dist.) Tenn., 2014—. Lectr. employment related issues, ethics, and professionalism and civil procedure Knoxville Bar Assn., Tenn. Bar Assn., 1991—. Mem. U. Tenn. Law Rev., 1976; contbr. articles to profl. jours. Mem. ABA, Tenn. Bar Found., Tenn. Bar Assn. (pres. 1998-99, pres. young lawyers cons. 1989-90, house dels. 1987-92), Knoxville Bar Assn. (pres. Knoxville barristers 1983, sec. 1994-96, Governor's award, 2008), American Inns of Ct. (master of the bench, adminstr. 1994), American Coll. Civil Trial Mediators Phi Beta Kappa. Office: US District Court 800 Market St Ste 130 Knoxville TN 37902 Office Phone: 865-545-4228.*

REEVES, RALPH BERNARD, III, publishing executive; b. Raleigh, NC, Apr. 2, 1947; s. Ralph Bernard Reeves Jr. and Frances Rhoda (Campbell) M.; m. Caroline Holton Green, Apr. 24, 1971 (div. 1986); children: Ralph B. IV, Daniel MacQuarrie; m. Katherine Drewry Reid, June 20, 1998. AB in History, U. NC, 1970. Field coord. FMI Mgmt. Group, Raleigh, NC, 1972-76; gen. mgr., v.p. The Leader Newspaper, Rsch. Triangle Pk., NC, 1976-78; pres., pub., founder Spectator Pubs. Inc., Raleigh, 1978-98, Triad Bus., Greensboro, NC, 1986-88, Triangle Bus., Raleigh, 1985-91, Spectator Pub., NC Architect, 1981-84; pres. Reeves Media, 1998—; pub., editor Raleigh Metro Mag., 1999—. Editor: Mr. Spectator, 1978—98; author: (monthly column) My Usual Charming Self in Metro Mag. 1st v.p. Mordecai Square Hist. Soc., Raleigh, 1980—83; pres. Hilltop Home, 1982—84; coun. mem. NC Mus. Art; founder Raleigh Internat. Spy Conf.; chmn. Downtown Adv. Com., 1983—85; bus. adv. com. NC Sec. of State, Raleigh, 1992—; bd. dirs. NC State U. Friends of Libr., Carolina Ballet. Gov's. Bus. award in the Arts and Humanities, Adv. Bd. Raleigh Hall of Fame, 1986, Benjamin Fine award, 1991, AABP award Triangle Bus., 1st place award Feature Writing, 1991; Isocules award AIA NC. Mem. Assn. of Intelligence Officers (assoc.), Pumpkin Papers Irregulars, Fifty Group, English Speaking Union (past pres. RTP br. 1988—), Carolina Co. Club, Sphinx Club, Nat. Press Club. Episcopalian. Avocations: golf, history, travel. Home: 3066 Granville Dr Raleigh NC 27609 Office Phone: 919-831-0999. E-mail: reevesmedia@ncllbiz.com.

REEVES, ROBERT K., lawyer, oil industry executive; BSBA, JD, La. State U., Baton Rouge. Ptnr. energy sect. Onebane Law Firm, Lafayette, La., 1983—93; sr. v.p., gen. counsel, sec. Flores & Rucks, Inc., 1993—97; exec. v.p., gen. counsel, sec. Ocean Energy, Inc., 1997—2003; sr. v.p., corp. affairs and law, chief governance officer Anadarko Petroleum Corp., The Woodlands, Tex., 2004—07, sr. v.p. to exec. v.p., gen. counsel, chief adminstrv. officer, 2007—; exec. v.p., adminstrn., gen. counsel North Sea New Ventures, 2003—04. Bd. dirs. Key Energy Svcs., Inc., 2007. Trustee Episcopal HS; mem. vestry St. Martin's Episcopal Ch.; bd. dirs. Family Svcs. Greater Houston. Mem.: ABA, Am. Corp. Counsel Assn., La. Bar Assn., Tex. Bar Assn. Office: Anadarko Petroleum Corp 1201 Lake Robbins Dr The Woodlands TX 77380-1046 Office Phone: 832-636-1000. Office Fax: 832-636-8220. Business E-Mail: robert_reeves@anadarko.com.*

REEVES, TATE (JONATHON TATE REEVES), Lieutenant Governor of Mississippi, former state treasurer; b. Rankin County, Miss., June 5, 1974; m. Elizabeth Lee Williams; children: Sarah Tyler, Elizabeth Magee. BS in Economics, Millsaps Coll., 1996. CFA. Investment officer Trustmark, 2000; asst. v.p. AmSouth (formerly Deposit Guaranty Nat. Bank); treas. State of Miss., Jackson, 2003—12, lt. gov., 2012—. Bd. dir. Public Employees' Retirement Sys., Miss.; chmn. bd. College Savings Plans of Miss. Named one of The 42 Rising Stars in the Republican Party, Rising Tide mag., 2007. Mem.: Miss. Republican Elected Officials Assn., Nat. Assn. State Treas. (pres. 2006—07, pres. southern region, sr. v.p.), CFA Inst., CFA Soc. of Miss. (Miss. Soc. Financial Analysts award 1996). Republican. Methodist. Office: Office of the Lieutenant Governor New Capitol Room 315 PO Box 1018 Jackson MS 39215-1018 Office Phone: 601-359-3200. Office Fax: 601-359-4054.*

REEVES, W. BOYD, lawyer; b. Easley, SC, Mar. 24, 1932; s. William C. and Lona Elise Reeves; m. Gladys Frances Brown, Nov. 24, 1978; children: Gabrielle Elaine, Stephanie Clair, William Gordon. BA in Bus. Adminstrn., Furman U., 1954; JD, Tulane U., 1959. Bar: La. 1959, Ala. 1960, US Dist. Ct. (so. dist.), Ala. 1961, US Ct. Appeals (5th cir.) 1962, US Ct. Appeals (11th cir.) 1970, US Supreme Ct. 1971, cert.: Nat. Bd. Trial Advocacy (civil trial lawyer). Law clk. U.S. Dist. Ct. Judge Daniel Thomas, Mobile, Ala., 1959—61; practicing atty. Armbrecht, Jackson LLP, Mobile, Ala., 1961—; mem. Kappa Alpha Order. Atty. Sheriff of Mobile City, Ala., 1980; v.p. Talane Law Sch., Eagle Scout. Past chmn. Southeastern Admiralty Inst.; past pres. Ala. Am. Bd. Trial Advocates; chancellor St. Luke's Episcopal Ch., Mobile, 1970—. Capt. US Army, 1954—56, Alaska. Fellow, Am. Coll. Trial Lawyers. Fellow: Ala. Law Found., Internat. Soc. Barristers; mem.: ABA, Baldwin County Bar Assn., Am. Coll. Legal Medicine, Maritime Law Assn. (exec. com. 1987—90), Internat. Assn. of Defense Counsel, Ala. Def. Lawyers Assn. (past pres.), Mobile Bar Assn. (past pres.). Episcopalian. Home: 3755 Rhonda Dr S Mobile AL 36608 Office: Armbrecht Jackson LLP PO Box 290 Mobile AL 36601 Office Fax: 251-432-6843.*

REGALADO, TOMAS PEDRO, mayor, Miami; b. Havana, Cuba, May 24, 1947; s. Tomas Regalado Molina and Carmen Rita Valdez de Regalado; m. Raquel Ferreiro, 1972 (dec. 2008); children: Tomas, Raquel, Jose Francisco. Reporter, asst. prodr., than news prodr., anchor WFAB, La Fabulosa, news dir., 1977, internat. news corr.; reporter WLTV Channel 23, 1974; L.Am. news editor, host Tele-Amigo WCKT; mem. White House Press Corps, Washington, 1983; weekly columnist El Miami Herald; news dir. Spanish Broadcasting Sys.; host Cable Network TeleMiami; host, commentator WWFE la Ponderosa; commr. Dist. 4 City of Miami, Fla., 1996—2009, mayor, 2009—. Republican. Roman Catholic. Office: Office of Mayor City of Miami City Hall 3500 Pan American Dr Miami FL 33133 Office Phone: 305-250-5300. Office Fax: 305-854-4001.*

REGAN, WILLIAM JOSEPH, JR., retired energy company executive; b. Bronx, NY, Mar. 7, 1946; s. William Joseph and Eleanor F. (Malone) R.; m. Mary Lee Wynn; children— Katrina Lee, Thomas Wynn, James William BS, U.S. Air Force Acad., 1967; MBA, U. Wis.-Madison, 1969, PhD, 1972. Asst. prof. Wayne State U., Detroit, 1971-75; with Nat. Bank Detroit, 1975-77; sr. bus. planner Am. Natural Resources Co., Detroit, 1977-78, dir. fin. planning, 1978-82, v.p., treas., 1982-85; v.p. corp. fin. United Svcs. Automobile Assn., San Antonio, 1986-88, sr. v.p., treas., 1988-95; v.p., treas. Entergy Corp., New Orleans, 1995-99; CFO Calif. Ind. Sys. Operator Corp., Folsom, Calif., 1999—2008; mem. bd. dirs. Biglari Holdings Inc., San Antonio, 2008—11, Consumer Credit Consulting Svcs., San Antonio, 2008—. Home: 8624 Fairway Green Dr Fair Oaks TX 78015-4480 Office Phone: 830-755-4368. Personal E-mail: wregan37@earthlink.net.

REGINI, JUDITH L., insurance company executive; b. La Marque, Tex., Nov. 13, 1953; d. Henry Thomas and Nell Beatrice (McNary) Shields; m. Alvine H. Regini, June 29, 1973. ABA, Coll. of the Mainland, Texas City, Tex., 1989; BBA in Mgmt., U. Houston, Clear Lake, 1992, postgrad. Corp. compliance coord. Am. Nat. Ins. Co., Galveston, Tex., asst. v.p., Corp. Compliance. Contbr. articles to profl. jours. Choir dir. Our Lady of Lourdes Ch., Hitchcock, Tex., 1986—; bd. dirs. Cath. Charities, Galveston County, 1994-98, chair, 1996-98. Fellow Life Office Mgmt. Assn. (assoc. customer svc. designation 1992); Phi Theta Kappa, Alpha Chi. Roman Catholic. Home: PO Box 532 Hitchcock TX 77563-0532 Office: American National Insurance Co 1 Moody Plz Galveston TX 77550-7999 Office Phone: 409-763-4661. Office Fax: 409-766-2912. Personal E-mail: judith.regini@anico.com.

REGISTER, JESSE, school system administrator; BA in English, U. NC, Charlotte, EdM; D in Edn. Adminstrn., Duke U., Durham, NC; grad. supt.'s exec. program, U. NC; attended Change Leadership Program, Harvard U. Cert. advanced sch. adminstr. U. NC, Chapel Hill. Supt. Iredell-Statesville Schs., NC; prin. Cabarrus County Schs., NC, asst. supt. curriculum and instrn., asst. supt. adminstrn., supt., Hamilton County Schs., Tenn., 1997—2006; sr. advisor dist. leadership Brown U. Annenberg Inst. Sch. Reform, Providence; vis. assoc. prof. urban edn. U. Tenn., Chattanooga, 2007—09; dir. schs. Met. Nashville Pub. Schs., 2009—. Nat. facilitator Superintendent's Leadership Acad. Ark.; adv. faculty Aspen Inst. Sr. Congl. Edn. Staff. Mem. Gov.'s Task Force on Salary Equity, Gov.'s Basic Edn. Plan Rev. Com. Named Outstanding Supt. of Yr., Tenn. PTA, 2001, Supt. of Yr., Tenn. Sch. Plant Mgmt. Assn. Office: Metropolitan Nashville Public Schools 2601 Bransford Ave Nashville TN 37204*

REGNERY, ALFRED SCATTERGOOD, publishing executive; b. Chgo., Nov. 21, 1942; s. Henry and Eleanor (Scattergood) R.; m. Christina Sparrow, Nov. 29, 1969 (dec.); children: George M., Louise S., Alfred W., Charles H; m. Audrey Garrett, sep. 6, 2008. BA, Beloit Coll., 1965; JD, U. Wis., 1971. Bar: Wis. 1971, D.C. 1987. Pvt. practice law, Madison, Wis., 1971-78; minority counsel Senate Judiciary Com., Washington, 1978-81; dep. asst. atty. gen. for land & nat. resources US Dept. Justice, Washington, 1981-82; adminstr. Office of Juvenile Justice and Delinquency Prevention, 1982-86; pres., CEO Regnery Pub. Inc., Washington, 1986—2003; pres. & pub. The Am. Spectator, Arlington, Va., 2003—. Bd. dirs. Eagle Pub., Inc., Washington. Author (Simon S. Schuster): Upstream: The Ascendance of American Conservatism, 2008. Chmn. Intercollegiate Studies Inst., Wilmington, Del.; bd. dirs. Found. for Am. Studies, Washington, Am. Fgn. Policy Coun., Washington, Jamestown Found. Served with USCG, 1966—67. Office: The American Spectator 1611 N Kent St Arlington VA 22209 Office Phone: 703-807-2011.

REHEARD, DEBORAH ANN, lawyer; m. Dale Gill. BA in Journalism and Criminal Justice, Northeastern Okla. State U.; JD, U. Tulsa. Bar: Okla. 1987. Mcpl. prosecutor City of Tulsa, Okla.; asst. dist. atty. Craig, Mayes, Rogers, Ottawa and Delaware Counties, Okla.; pvt. practice Eufaula, Okla., 1991—. Mem. Judicial Nominating Commn. Recipient Mona S. Lambird Spotlight Award, 2002. Mem.: Okla. Bar Found. (bd. trustees), Okla. Bar Assn. (chair Women in Law Com. 2002, co-chair 2003, mem.-at-large, pres. 2010—11). Office: PO Box 636 Eufaula OK 74432 Office Phone: 918-689-9281. E-mail: dreheard@ReheardLaw.com.

REHM, PATRICE KOCH, radiologist, educator; b. DeSoto, Mo., Nov. 23, 1954; d. James Clarence and Eleanor (Koch) R. BA in Chemistry, U. Mo., 1977; MD, Yale U., 1981. Diplomate Am. Bd. Radiology, Am. Bd. Nuc. Medicine. Intern in medicine Waterbury (Conn.) Hosp., 1981-82; resident in radiology Yale New Haven Hosp., 1982-83, 84-85, fellow in neuroradiology, 1985-86, fellow in nuclear medicine, 1986-87; resident in radiology SUNY Upstate Med. Ctr., Syracuse, 1983-84; clin. assoc. Cleve. Clinic, 1987-88, staff physician, 1988-89, Presbyn. Hosp., Charlotte, N.C., 1989-91, Georgetown U. Med. Ctr., Washington, 1992—2000; assoc. prof. radiology, dir. nuc. medicine U. Va. Health Sys., Charlottesville, Va., 2000—10, dir. nuc. medicine, program dir. nuc. radiology, 2000—, prof. radiology, 2010—. Fellow Am. Coll. Radiology, Radiologic Soc. N.Am., Soc. Nuc. Medicine. Office: U Va Health Sys PO Box 800170 Charlottesville VA 22908

REHWINKLE VASILINDA, MICHELLE, state legislator; b. Rochester, NY, July 9, 1960; m. Michael D. Vasilinda; children: Anna Laura, Catherine. BA in Social & Behavior Sci., U. South Fla., 1982; JD, U. Fla. Coll. Law, 1985. Atty. pvt. practice; instr. Tallahassee Cmty. Coll.; mem. Dist. 9 Fla. House of Reps., 2008—, mem. health and family svcs. policy coun., health care regulation policy com., rules and calendar coun. Mem. Leon County Dem. Exec. Com., 2004; mod. Mayor's Race Rels. Summit Panel. DER key coord. United Way Campaign, 1986—88; mem. Montessori Cooperative Early Sch. Personnel Com., 1988—89; asst. leader Girl Scouts, 1991—2000; mem. Gentiva Corp. Adv. Bd. Advanced Home Health Care, 1994—; bd. dirs. P.A.C.E. Sch. for Girls, 1994—98; mem. North Fla. for Democracy Charter Revision & Mem. Outreach, 2003—04, Kerry Legal Team, 2004. Mem.: Tallahassee Woman Lawyers (bd. mem.), United Faculty Fla. Union, Am. Assn. U. Women (bd. mem. 2006—07), United Way Big Bend, Zonta Internat. Women's Svc. Org. Tallahassee Chpt., Leon High Sch. Found. (bd. dirs.), NAACP Tallahassee Branch, Dem. Club North Fla., Capital Tiger Bay Club Tallahassee, Capital City Dem. Women's Club (legis. liaison). Democrat. Catholic. Avocations: films, movies, gardening, reading, tennis. Office: The Capitol 402 S Monroe St Rm 1001 Tallahassee FL 32399-1300 Office Phone: 850-488-0965. Business E-Mail: michelle.rehwinkel@myfloridahouse.gov.

REIBLE, DANNY DAVID, environmental chemical engineer, educator; b. Rantoul, Ill., Dec. 21, 1954; s. George Anthony and Mavis Otilla (Prause) R.; m. Susanne Cecilia Schulte, Mar. 17, 1979; children: Kristin Nicole, Monica Lynn. BS, Lamar U., 1977; MS, Calif. Inst. Tech., 1979, PhD, 1982. Registered profl. engr., La.; diplomate environ. engr., 2004. Asst. prof. La. State U., Baton Rouge, 1981-86, assoc. prof., 1986-92, prof. chem. engring., 1992—2004, Chevron prof. chem. engring., 1998—2004, dir. Hazardous Substance Rsch. Ctr., 1995—2007; Shell prof. environ. engring. U. Sydney, Australia, 1993-95; Bettie Margaret Smith chair environ. health engring. U. Tex., Austin, 2004—13; dir. Ctr. Rsch. Water Resources, 2011—13; Donoran Maddox disting. engring. chair Tex. Tech. U., 2013—. Vis. rschr. US Army Engr. Waterways Experiment Sta., Vicksburg, Miss., 1990; sr. visitor Cambridge U., Eng., 1992; mem. bd. environ. studies and toxicology Nat. Rsch. Coun.; cons. in field. Author: Fundamentals of Environmental Engineering, 1999, Diffusion Models of Environmental Transport, 2000; contbr. articles to profl. publs. Environ. Sci. and Engring. fellow AAAS, 1987, 2009. Fellow AIChE (exec. bd. 1990-95, LK Cecil award 1992); mem. NAE, Am. Chem. Soc., Am. Geophys. Union, Am. Soc. Engring. Edn. (New Engring. Educator Excellence award 1985), Am. Soc. Civil Engring., Assn. Environ. Engring. Sci. Profs. (Frontier Rsch. award, 2011), Coms. Nat. Rsch. Coun., Sigma Xi. Achievements include identification and evaluation of new mechanisms for contaminant release in the environment; advances in sediment management techniques; development of widely used methods of managing contaminated sediments. Home: 10300 Indigo Broom Loop Austin TX 78733 Office: U Tex 1 University Station C1786 Austin TX 78712 Office Phone: 512-471-4642. Business E-Mail: reible@mail.utexas.edu.

REICH, DAVID LEE, library director; b. Orlando, Fla., Nov. 25, 1930; s. P.F. and Opal Katherine (Wood) Reichelderfer; m. Kathleen Johanna Weichel, Aug. 2, 1954 (div. Sept. 1964); 1 son, Robert Weichel. PhB magna cum laude, U. Detroit, 1961; AM in LS, U. Mich., 1963. Tchr. English Jefferson Davis Jr. Sch., San Antonio, 1961-62; dir. engring. library Radiation Inc., Melbourne, Fla., 1963-

64; asst. to dir. libraries Miami-Dade Jr. Coll., Miami, Fla., 1964-65; dir. learning resources Monroe County C.C., Monroe, Mich., 1965-68; dep. dir. Dallas Pub. Library, 1968-73; dep. chief librarian Chgo. Pub. Library, 1973-74, commr., 1975-78; dir. Bd. Libr. Commrs., Commonwealth of Mass., Boston, 1978-80; exec. sec. New Eng. Libr. Bd., Augusta, Maine, 1980-82, vice chmn., 1979-80; dir. Lakeland (Fla.) Pub. Libr., 1983-99, ret., 1999; exec. sec. Soc. Fla. Archivists, 1999—2001, ret., 2001. Libr. cons. Macomb County C.C., Warren, Mich., 1967; chmn. adv. com. to libr. tech. asst. program El Centro Coll., Dallas, 1969-71; mem. inter-task working group Goals for Dallas, 1968-70, mem. Dallas Area Libr. planning coun., 1970-73; mem. adv. coun. dept. libr. sci. No. Ill. U., 1975-78; v.p., pres.-elect Tampa Bay Libr. Consortium, 1985-86, pres., 1986-87. Co-author: The Public Library in Non-traditional Education, 1974; editor The Villas II News, 1999-2007; contbr. articles to libr. jours. Bd. dirs. The Villas II Homeowners Assn., 1994-96, 98-2001; mem. steering com. Friends of Tampa Bay Libr. Consortium, 2000—. Sgt. U.S. Army, 1952-55. Recipient Disting. Alumnus award U. Mich., 1978; William B. Calkins Found. scholar Orlando, 1963; Carnegie L.S. Endowment scholar, 1963. Mem. ALA (coun.-at-large 1968-72, 75-79), S.E. Libr. Assn., Fla. Libr. Assn. (sec.-treas. coll. and spl. librs. divsn. 1965, steering com. mcpl. librs. caucus 1983-84, chmn. 1984-85, exec. bd. 1984-87), Soc. Fla. Archivists (exec. bd. 1994-96, sec. 1996-97, exec. sec. 1999-2001, treas. 2000-01), Fla. Pub. Libr. Assn. (pres. 1987-88, exec. bd. 1988-89, 94-95, pres. emeritus 1996-98, editor newsletter 1992-93, 96-97, chmn. libr. adminstrn. divsn. 1992, friends and trustees divsn. 1993, 95), Soc. Automotive Historians, Alumni Assn. U. Mich. (pres. Libr. Sch. alumni 1973), Nat. Soc. SAR, Polk Sr. Games (bd. dirs., 2004—09, sec. 2007—09). Home: 4011 Heron Ave Lakeland FL 33813-1123 E-mail: dreich@tampabay.rr.com.

REICH, JONI (JOHNSINE J. REICH), finance company executive; b. 1956; BA in Govt. & Economics summa cum laude, Georgetown U., 1978. Mgr., pub. affairs & pers. Drug Fair, Inc. (subs. Sherwin-Williams.); compensation analyst SLM Corp. (Sallie Mae), asst. v.p., human resources, 1992, v.p., sr. v.p., adminstrn., exec. v.p. adminstrn., 2012—. Mem. George Mason U.; bd. dirs. Sallie Mae Fund, Greater Reston Arts Ctr., Reston C. of C. Office: SLM Corp 12061 Bluemont Way Reston VA 20190 Office Phone: 703-810-3000. Office Fax: 703-984-5042. Business E-Mail: joni.reich@slma.com.

REICH, RICHARD ALLEN, bank executive; b. Rhinelander, Wis., Mar. 12, 1962; s. John E. and Alma Louise (Post) R. BBA, U. Wis., Madison, 1984; MBA, NYU, NYC, 1989. CPA, Okla. Staff acct., cons. Deloitte, Haskins and Sells, NYC, 1984-86; fin. analyst Salomon Bros., Inc., NYC, 1986-89; treasury mgr. Citibank-US Card Products Group, NYC, 1989-92; with Bankers Trust Corp., NYC, 1992-93; v.p., dir. risk mgmt. Nikko Securities Internat., Inc., NYC, 1993-95, CDC Capital, Inc., NYC, 1995-99; dir. risk mgmt. and control OGE Energy Corp., Oklahoma City, 1999—2005, treas.; sr. v.p. corp. fin. BancFirst Corp., Oklahoma City, 2005—. Investment mgr. Wis. Eastern Scholarship Fund, 1996-2001. Mem. AICPA, Okla. Soc. CPA, Okla. Soc. Security Analysts, CFA Inst., U. Wis. Alumni Assn. NY (sec. 1989-91, v.p. 1991-92, pres. 1992-95). Avocations: golf, skiing. Office: BancFirst Corp 101 N Broadway Ste 900 Oklahoma City OK 73102-8405 Home: 100 N Cedar Mountain Rd Edmond OK 73034-7566 Office Phone: 405-218-4126. Personal E-mail: richard_a_reich@yahoo.com.

REICHENTAL, ABRAHAM N., information technology executive; Project mgr. Sealed Air Corp., 1981, project mgr. customer applications engineered products divsn., 1981—85, mgr. sales & mktg. engineered products divsn., Europe, 1985—88, dir. new product devel. engineered products divsn., 1988—93, corp. v.p. tech., 1993—96, v.p., gen. mgr. engineered products divsn., Europe, 1997—99, v.p. Asia-Pacific, 1999—2001, corp. officer, v.p. & gen. mgr. shrink packaging divsn., 2001—03; pres., CEO, bd. dirs. 3D Systems Corp., 2003—. Bd. dirs. Cryovac Inc., Finetooth Enterprises, Inc. Office: 3D Systems Corp 333 Three D Systems Cir Rock Hill SC 29730 Office Phone: 803-326-3900. Office Fax: 803-324-8810. Business E-Mail: areichental@3dsystems.com.

REICHERT, LEO EDMUND, JR., biochemist, department chairman, endocrinologist; b. NYC, Jan. 9, 1932; s. Leo and Anne (Holsten) R.; m. Gerda Sihler, July 20, 1957; children: Leo, Christine, Linda, Andrew. BS, Manhattan Coll., NYC, 1955; PhD, Loyola U., Chgo., 1960. Asst. prof. biochemistry Emory U. Med. Sch., Atlanta, 1960-66, assoc. prof., 1966-72, prof., 1972-79; prof., chmn. dept. biochemistry Albany (N.Y.) Med. Coll., 1979-88, prof. biochemistry and molecular biology, 1988-99; dir. Tucker Endocrine Rsch. Inst., LLC, Atlanta, 2000—12. Dir. human and animal hormone isolation lab. (NIH), Emory U. Med. Sch., 1960-75; mem. med. adv. bd. Nat. Pituitary Agy., 1971-74; com. on glycoprotein hormones Nat. Hormone and Pituitary Program, 1968-86; mem. reproductive biology study sect. NIH, 1971-75; mem. adv. panel on cellular physiology NSF, 1983-86, divsn. of integrative and neuro biology, 1992; mem. WHO Expert Adv. Panel on Biol. Standardization, 1984-2006, Nat. Bd. Med. Examiners, Part I, 1989-91. Mem. editl. bd. Endocrinology, 1967-75, Molecular and Cellular Endocrinology, 1977-83, 90-94, charter mem. Biology of Reproduction, 1968-70, 86-90, Andrology, 1983-86, Molecular Andrology, 1989-99; contbr. more than 275 articles to profl. jours.; patentee in field. With USMC, 1949—52. Listed among 75 endocrinologists, 1000 scientists most cited, 1965-78. Mem.: Soc. for Study of Reprodn., Andrology Soc. (coun. 1983—87), Endocrine Soc. (ethics adv. com. 2000—01, Ayerst award 1970), Am. Soc. Biol. Chemists. Home: 1974 Mountain Creek Dr Stone Mountain GA 30087-1018 Personal E-mail: lerjr@aol.com.

REID, BENJAMINE, lawyer; b. Concord, NC, Jan. 11, 1950; s. Fred Herndon and Frances Barnhardt Reid; m. Jennie Lou Divine, Dec. 19, 1970; children: Elisabeth Divine, Margaret Hethcox, Benjamine Joseph. AB, U. N.C., 1971; JD cum laude, U. Ga., 1974. Bar: Fla., Ga., Fla. State Cts., US Ct. Appeals (3rd, 5th and 11th cirs.), US Dist. Ct. (mid., no., so. dists.) Fla., US Supreme Ct. Atty., shareholder Kimbrell & Hamann, Miami, Fla., 1974-90; shareholder Popham Haik, Miami, 1990-97, Carlton Fields, Miami, 1997—, bd. dirs., mem. exec. com., chmn. of bd., 2006—. Bd. dirs. Fla. Justice Inst., Product Liability Adv. Coun., Washington, co-chmn. action group; faculty mem. Wadham Coll. in Oxford U., DePaul U. Coll. Law, ABA Nat. Inst. Sr. editor U. Ga. Law Rev.; contbr. articles to profl. jours. Vice-chair, exec. com. mem. Greater Miami Chamber; pres. Dade Pub. Edn. Fund; chair Leadership Miami; mem. nat. devel. coun. U. NC, mem. bd. visitors, dir. Arts and Sciences Found. & Gen. Alumni Assn., mem. bd. advisors Ednl. Found., mem. chancellor's club; mem. exec. com., bd. dirs. Governor's Coun. Sustainable Fla.; founder, bd. dirs., pres. Fla. Internat. U. Coun. of 100; mem. WLRN Cir. of Friends; mem. standing com., exec. bd., vice chancellor Episcopal Diocese of SE Fla.; mem. vestry, sr. warden St. Philip's Episcopal Ch.; mem. & chmn. exec. com. Episcopal Charities. Recipient Thomas W. Watkins Humanitarian award, Pinnacle award, Ch. of Incarnation, Miami, Salute to Miami Leaders award, Greater Miami C. of C., 2010, Hon. Theodore Klein award for Advancement Women in the Legal Profession, Fla. Assn. Women, 2011, Pres. Pro Bono Svc. award for 11th Jud. Cir., The Fla. Bar, 2011; named one of The Most Effective Lawyers, Miami-Dade, Broward & Palm Beach Counties, Daily Bus. Rev., America's Leading Bus. Lawyers, Comml. and Appellate Litig., Chambers USA, The Best Lawyers in America, Bet-the Co., Comml., Mass Tort, Personal Injury and Product Liability Litig. and Med. Malpractice Law, Fla. Legal Elite, Fla. Trend, 2004—06, 2008, 2010; named to Fla. Super Lawyers, 2010. Fellow: American Bar Found.; mem.: ABA (co-mng. dir., chmn. task force on the judiciary, chmn. products liability com., co-chmn. Miami ann. meeting, co-chmn. civil justice inst., co-chmn. legal services tng. com.), American Bd. Trial Advocates, Phi Kappa Phi. Democrat. Avocations: golf, history, travel. Office: Carlton Fields PA 100 SE 2nd St Ste 4200 Miami FL 33131-2113 Office Phone: 305-539-7222. Office Fax: 305-530-0055. Business E-Mail: breid@carltonfields.com.

REID, HELEN VERONICA, provost; b. Reading, Eng., Sept. 25, 1956; d. Alan A. and Teresa H. (Thatcher) Ware; m. Gary B. Reid, May 29, 1976; children: Robert, Jennifer, Kristen. BA in Biology, U. Tex., 1976; BSN, U. Tex., Arlington, 1978; MSN, Tex. Women's U., 1983; EdD, U. North Tex., 2000. CCRN, 1980, cert. CPR instr. Asst. nurse coord., staff nurse, float pool nurse Parkland Meml. Hosp., Dallas, 1979—83, float pool nurse, 1987—93; instr. Trinity Valley CC, Kaufman, Tex., 1983—86, leader freshman team, 1986—90, dean health occupations, 1990—2006; provost Health Sci. Ctr., 2007—. Mem.: Tex. Assn. Deans and Dirs. for Profl. Nursing Programs (treas. 2005—), Tex. C.C. Tchrs. Assn., Nat. Orgn. ADN (pub. rels. dir. 1998—2002, treas. 2006—), Tex. Orgn. for ADN (sec. 1988—92, nominating com. chair 1995—96, pres.-elect 2002—03, pres. 2003—05, past pres. 2005—06), Tex. Assn. Vocat. Nurse Educators, Phi Kappa Phi, Sigma Theta Tau. Office Phone: 972-932-4309. Business E-Mail: reid@tvcc.edu.

REID, KATHERINE LOUISE, artist, educator, writer; b. Port Arthur, Tex., Mar. 25, 1941; d. Clifton Commodore and Helen Ross (Moore) Reid. BA, Baylor U., 1963; postgrad. in design and illustration, Kans. City Art Inst., 1964; MEd, U. Houston, 1973; cert. supervision, U. Houston-Clear Lake City, 1980; postgrad., San Jacinto Coll., 1982. Litho reprodn. artist Hallmark Cards, Kansas City, Mo., 1963-64; tchr. art high sch. Pasadena (Tex.) Ind. Sch. Dist., 1964-77, supr. art, gifted and talented and photography, 1977-85, supr. art and photography InterAct, 1985-90, instrnl. specialist, 1990-2000, photography and art, 1990-93, instrnl. specialist in art and spl. programs, 1993-96, rsch. planning, data disaggregation, 1996-2000; internet tchr. recruiter, 2001—02; mural artist Old Car Barn, Edna, Tex., 2000—. 4 MAT learning styles trainer DuPont Leadership Devel. Process Trainer, Selective Rsch., Inst., tchr. perceiver specialist, performance quality sys. trainer, coop. learning trainer, outcome based edn. trainer, integrated unit devel. and authentic assessment trainer Greater Gulf Coast Adminstr. Assessment Project, Assessor, 1990-2000; head crafts, asst. dir., dir. summer, winter discovery program-ski camp Cheley Colo. Camps, Denver, Estes Park, 1967-75; awards com. John Austin Cheley Found., 1990-92; staff artist, media workshop Tex. Edn. Agy., Austin, 1961; art enrichment tchr. Port Arthur Ind. Sch. Dist. (Tex.), 1961; head crafts Camp Waluta, Silsbee, Tex., 1960; mem. Tex. Edn. Agy., Art Leadership Inst., 1989-90, Tracking Rsch. Com., 1991, Core Strategic Planning Team, 1992-2000, Outcome Based Edn. Dist. Planning Com., 1991-92, Quality Sys. Improvement Team, 1991-92, Outcome Based Edn. Com. Exit Outcomes, 1991; Region IV data disk trainer, 1998-2000, target teach coord., 1993-2000, multiple intelligence trainer, 1997-2000, data disaggregation trainer, 1997-2000, supt.'s rsch. com., 1999. Author: Through Their Eyes, 1989. Mem. Friends of Fine Arts-Baylor U., Waco, Tex., 1981—, Scholastic Art awards Regional Bd., Houston, 1978-84; bd. dirs. Houston Coun. Student Art Awards, Inc., 1984-90, Pasadena Ind. Sch. Dist. Edn. Found., 2005-08; mem. Baylor U. Endowed Scholarship Soc., Baylor U. Old Main Scholarship Soc., 2003—. Named Outstanding Secondary Educator of Am., 1975, Tex. Art Educator of Yr., 1985, Outstanding Vol., City of Pasadena, 2004. Mem.: ASCD, Tex. ASCD, Tex. Art Edn. Assn. (rep. editor newsletter 1982-85, chmn. supervision divsn. 1982-83, v.p. membership 1978-80, chmn. pub. info. com., regional chmn. youth art month 1980-82; regional chmn. membership com. 1976-78, pres. elect 1986, sec. 1991-93, Disting. Fellows award 2004), Tex. Alliance for Arts Edn. (bd. vice chmn. 1984-86, treas. 1988-90), Nat. Art Edn. Assn. (conv. com. 1977, 85), Tex. Assn. Sch. Adminstrs., Houston Art Edn. Assn. (sec. 1969), Tex. Ret. Tchrs. Assn. (Dist. IV historian 2001-03, mem. state local unit support com., 2013-), Pasadena Area Ret. Sch. Employees (parliamentarian 2002-04, 1st v.p. 2009-), Delta Kappa Gamma (2d v.p. 1984-86, pres. 2002-2004, state leadership devel. chpt. pres. com., 2003-2005, state banner com., 2004, State Leadership Seminar 2005, area III coord. 2005-07, Internat. Golden Gift Leadership Seminar 2006, state rsch. com. 2007-09, state rsch. com. chairperson 2009-11, state 2nd pres., 2011-13, leadership, Orientation State Pers. Com. 2013-, dir., Alpha State Tex. Ednl. Found., 2013-). Baptist. Achievements include patents for pet car seat. Home: 106 Ravenhead Dr Houston TX 77034-1520 Personal E-mail: klreid2@comcast.net.

REID, LANGHORNE, III, merchant banker; b. Dallas, Apr. 3, 1950; s. Langhorne Jr. and Mary Anne (Beasley) R.; m. Sally Wolf, Dec. 26, 1972 (div. Aug. 1977); m. Eve Catherine Murphy, Sept. 6, 1986 (div. 1996); 1 child, Claire Hart Reid; m. Vera Anderson Reid, 1999. BA in Psychology, U. Tex., 1972, JD, 1975; MBA, U. Pa., 1977. Bar: Tex. 1975. V.p. Dillon, Read & Co., Inc., NYC, 1977-82; mng. dir. Drexel Burnham Lambert Inc., NYC, 1982-87; co-dir. mergers and acquisitions Paine Webber Group, NYC, 1987-89; ptnr. Gordon Investment Inc., NYC, 1989-93; pres. Beacon Advisors, Inc., Dallas, 1993-99; dir. Tex. Security Bank, 2008—. Bd. dirs. Windmill Holdings; pres. Partnership Svcs., 1992-93; chmn. Cedco Sys., Inc., 1997—, Amtex Holdings, Inc., 1996—, Garland Broadcast Investors, Inc., 1997—2004, Pogesa SA, 2002-; dir. Tex. Security Bank, 2008-. Trustee, treas. Animal Med. Ctr., N.Y.C., 1981—; trustee St. Mark's Sch. of Tex., 2002-09. Mem. Tex. Bar Assn., Dallas Country Club. Home: 4109 Windsor Pkwy Dallas TX 75205-1670 Office: Arcady Capital Inc Ste 330 100 Highland Park Village Dallas TX 75205-2726

REID, RUST ENDICOTT, lawyer; b. NYC, Dec. 31, 1931; s. Thorburn and Mary (Newhall) Reid; m. Jeanne Inge, Aug. 5, 1955 (dec. Aug. 31, 2007); children: Dorothy, Elizabeth, Margaret, Mary; m. Margot Hundley, June 16, 2011. BA, U. Va., 1954, JD, 1960. Bar: Tex. 1960, Va. 1960, bd. cert. in estate planning, probate:. Assoc. firm Thompson & Knight, Dallas, 1960—65, ptnr., 1965—2000, of counsel, 2000—. Lectr. SW Grad. Sch. Banking, Dallas, 1978—88; adj. prof. So. Meth. U., Dallas, 1980—86, Dallas, 2002—06, So. Meth. U. Law Sch., 2004—. Co-author: Texas Estate Administration, 1975. Trustee Child Care, Dallas, 1968—72; pres., 1970—72, Hockaday Sch., Dallas, 1972—82; chmn., 1976—78; Texas coun. Girl Scouts US, 1982—83; trustee Vis. Nurse Assn., Dallas, 1984—92; pres., 1990—92; v.p., 1989—91; pres., 1991—93; trustee & v.p. Dallas Children's Advocacy Ctr., 1993—; trustee Bryan's House, 2002—12, pres., 2008—10. Lt. (j.g.) USNR, 1954—57. Fellow: Tex. Bar Found; mem.: Am. Trust and Estate Counsel. Office: Thompson & Knight 1700 Pacific 1700 Pacific 3300 Dallas TX 75201 Home: 4032 Glenwick Ln Dallas TX 75205-1147 Home Phone: 214-522-0692.

REID, SUE TITUS, law educator; b. Bryan, Tex., Nov. 13, 1939; d. Andrew Jackson Jr. and Lorraine (Wylie) Titus. BS with honors, Tex. Woman's U., 1960; MA, U. Mo., 1962, PhD, 1965; JD with distinction, U. Iowa, 1972. Bar: Iowa 1972, US Ct. Appeals (DC Cir.) 1978, US Supreme Ct. 1978. From instr. to assoc. prof. sociology Cornell Coll., Mt. Vernon, Iowa, 1963-72; assoc. prof., chmn. dept. sociology Coe Coll., Cedar Rapids, 1972-74; assoc. prof. law U. Wash., Seattle, 1974-76; exec. assoc. American Sociol. Assn., Washington, 1976-77; prof. law U. Tulsa, 1978—88; dean, prof. Sch. Criminology, Fla. State U., Tallahassee, 1988-90; prof. pub. adminstrn. and policy Fla. State U., 1990—. Acting chmn. dept. sociology Cornell Coll., 1965-66; vis. assoc. prof. sociology U. Nebr., Lincoln, 1970; vis. disting. prof. law and sociology U. Tulsa, 1977-78, assoc. dean 1979-81; vis. prof. law U. San Diego, 1981-82; mem. People-to-People Crime Prevention Del. to People's Republic of China, 1982; George Beto Vis. Disting. Prof. criminal justice Sam Houston U., Huntsville, Tex., 1984-85; lecture/study tour of Criminal Justice systems of 10 European countries, 1985; cons. Evaluation Policy Rsch. Assocs., Inc., Milw., 1976-77, Nat. Inst. Corrections, Idaho Dept. Corrections, 1984, American Correctional Inst., Price-Waterhouse. Author (with others): Bibliographies on Role Methodology and Propositions Volume D - Studies in the Role of the Pub. Sch. Tchr., 1962, The Correctional System: An Introduction, 1981; author: Criminal Law: The Essentials, 2nd edit., 2013, Criminal Law, 9th edit., 2013, Crime and Criminology, 13th edit., 2012, Criminal Justice, 9th edit., 2012; editor (with David Lyon): Population Crisis: An Interdisciplinary Perspective, 1972; contbr. articles to profl. jours. Recipient Disting. Alumni award, Tex. Woman's U., 1979; named One of Okla. Young Leaders of 80's Okla. Monthly, 1980; named Outstanding Tchr., Fla. State U., 1999-2000. Mem. ABA, Am. Soc. Criminology, Acad. Criminal Justice Scis., Am. Bar Assn., Soc. Criminal Jus. Assn. Avocations: walking, reading, cooking, skiing. Office: Fla State Univ Askew Sch Pub Adminstrn & Policy Tallahassee FL 32306 Personal E-mail: suetreid@verizon.net.

REID, WILLIAM HILL, mathematics professor; b. Oakland, Calif., Sept. 10, 1926; s. William Macdonald and Edna Caroline (Hill) R.; m. Elizabeth Mary Kidner, May 26, 1962; 1 child, Margaret Frances. BS, U. Calif., Berkeley, 1949, MS, 1951; PhD, Cambridge U., Eng., 1955, ScD (hon.), 1968; AM (hon.), Brown U., 1961. Lectr. Johns Hopkins U., Balt., 1955-56; NSF fellow Yerkes Observatory, Williams Bay, Wis., 1957-58; asst. prof. Brown U., Providence, 1958-61, assoc. prof., 1961-63, U. Chgo., 1963-65, prof., 1965-89, prof. emeritus, 1989—; prof. Ind. U.-Purdue U., Indianapolis, 1989—2007. Cons. research labs. Gen. Motors Corp., Warren, Mich., 1960-73. Author (with P.G. Drazin): Hydrodynamic Stability, 1981; author: 2d edit., 2004; contbr. articles to profl. jours. Served with U.S. Mcht. Marine, 1945-47, with AUS, 1954-56. Fulbright Rsch. scholar, Australian Nat. U., 1964—65. Fellow Am. Phys. Soc., Cambridge Philos. Soc.; mem. Am. Math. Soc., Am. Meteorol. Soc., Sigma Xi. Home: 30 A Tulipwood Ct Jacksonville FL 32259 Business E-Mail: wreid@math.iupui.edu.

REID-ANDERSON, JAMES, amusement park company executive; BS in Commerce with honors, U. Birmingham, Eng.; MBA, Rutgers U. Exec. level positions with Pepsico Inc., Grand Met. PLC, Mobil Oil Corp.; COO, chief adminstrv. officer Wilson Sporting Goods, Chgo., 1994-96; exec. v.p., CFO Dade Behring, Deerfield, Ill., 1996-97, exec. v.p., CFO, chief adminstrv. officer, 1997-99, pres., COO, 1999—2000, pres., CEO, 2000—02, chmn., pres., CEO, 2002—07; CEO Siemens Healthcare Diagnostics, 2007—08; mem. mng. bd. Siemens AG, 2008, CEO, healthcare sector, 2008, adv. to mng. bd., 2008—10; adv. Apollo Mgmt. L.P., 2008—10; chmn., pres., CEO Six Flags Entertainment Corp., Dallas, 2010—. Bd. dirs. Stericycle Inc., 2009—, Brightpoint, Inc., 2010—, Six Flags Entertainment Corp, 2010—. Fellow Chartered Assn. Cert. Accts. Office: Six Flags Entertainment Corp 924 Ave J East Grand Prairie TX 75050

REIDINGER, MARTIN KARL, federal judge; b. New Haven, Conn., Dec. 18, 1958; BA, U. NC, 1981, JD with honors, 1984. Bar: NC 1984, US Dist. Ct. (we. dist.) NC 1984, US Ct. Appeals (4th cir.) 1985, US Supreme Ct. 1994. Assoc. Adams Hendon Carson Crow & Saenger, PA, Asheville, NC, 1984—89, shareholder, 1989—2007; judge US Dist. Ct. (we. dist.) NC, 2007—. Mem.: NC Bar Assn., Buncombe County Bar Assn. (sec., treas. 1989—92, pres. 2003—04). Office: 200 US Courthouse Bldg 100 Otis St Asheville NC 28801 Office Phone: 828-771-7260.

REIF, JOHN F., state supreme court justice; b. June 19, 1951; married. BA, U. Tulsa, Okla., 1973, JD, 1977. Faculty mem. Nat. Tribal Jud. Ctr., Nat. Jud. Coll., Reno; police officer City of Owasso, Okla., 1973—75; planner and grants specialist, law enforcement assistance adminstrn. Indian Nations Coun. Govt., 1974—77; asst. dist. atty. Tulsa County, 1978—81; spl. dist. judge Okla. 14th Jud. Dist., 1981—84; judge Okla. Ct. Civil Appeals, 1984—2002, vice chief judge, 1993, 2001, chief judge, 1994, 2002; justice Okla. Supreme Ct., 2007—, vice chief justice, 2013—. Bus. law adj. prof. Oral Roberts U., Tulsa, 1983—2007. Recipient Pres.'s Disting. Svc. award, Oral Roberts U., 1995. Mem.: Okla. Bar Assn. Office: Oklahoma Supreme Ct Okla Judicial Ctr 2100 N Lincoln Blvd Ste 4 Oklahoma City OK 73105-4907*

REIFF, PATRICIA HOFER, space physicist, educator, entrepreneur; b. Oklahoma City, Mar. 14, 1950; d. William Henry and Maxine Ruth (Hoffer) R.; m. Thomas Westfall Hill, July 4, 1976; children: Andrea Hofer Hill Palermo, Adam Reiff Hill, Amelia Reiff Hill. Student, Wellesley Coll., 1967-68; BS, Okla. State U., 1971; MS, Rice U., 1974, PhD, 1975. Cert. secondary tchr., Okla., Tex. Resident rsch. assoc. Marshall Space Flight Ctr., Huntsville, Ala., 1975-76; rsch. assoc. space physics and astronomy dept. Rice U., Houston, 1975, asst. prof. space physics and astronomy dept., 1978-81, asst. chmn. space physics and astronomy dept., 1979-85, assoc. rsch. sci., 1981-87, sr. rsch. scientist, 1987-90. Adj. asst. prof. Rice U., 1976-78, disting. faculty fellow, 1990-92, prof. 1992—, chmn. dept. space physics and astronomy, 1996-99, dir. Rice Space Inst., 1999—2012, assoc. dir., 2012-; mem. sci. team Atmosphere Explorer Mission, Dynamics Explorer Mission; co-investigator Global Geospace Sci. Mission, ESA/Cluster Mission, IMAGE Mission, Magnetospheric Multiscale Mission; prin. investigator The Public Connection NASA, Mus. Tchg. Planet Earth Immersive Earth; cons. Houston Mus. Natural Sci., 1986—; adv. com. on atmospheric scis. NSF, Washington, 1988-92; mem. stategic implementation study panel NASA, Washington, 1989-91; mem. space sci. adv. com. NASA, 1993-98, mem. space sta. utilization subcom., 1995-98; mem. adv. com. Los Alamos Non-Proliferation Divsn., 1998-2001; univ. rep. U. Space Rsch. Assn., Washington, 1993—, chair Coun. of Instns., 2001-04; founding mem. ESIP Fedn., bd. trustees, 2007-; exec. com. George Observatory, Houston, 1989-92, CEO pres., MTPE Inc., Space Update Inc., others. Designer Cockrell Sundial/Solar Telescope, 1989; editor EOS (sci. newspaper), 1986-89; contbr. articles to profl. jours. Trustee, Citizens' Environ. Coalition, Houston, 1978-98, pres. 1980-85, adv. com. 1998-2000; mem. air quality com. Houston/Galveston Area Coun., 1980-83, Green Ribbon Com., City of Houston, 1981-83; active coms. Macedonia United Meth. Ch., 1988—. Named rsch. fellow NAS/NRC., 1975, an Outstanding Young Woman Am., 1977, '80, to Houston's Women on the Move, 1990; named Outstanding Aerospace Educator, Women in Aerospace, 1999; NASA grantee 1993-95, 98, 99, 2001-06; recipient NASA Group Achievement award 2001, 04. Fellow Am. Geophys. Union (fin. com. 1980-82, editor search com. 1992, pub. edn. com., Athelstan Spilhaus award, 2009.);

mem. Cosmos Club, Wellesley Club, Internat. Union of Geodesy and Geophysics (del. 1975, 81, 83, 89, 91, 93, 95, chair working group 2F, 1991-95), MTPE, Inc. (pres.), Space Update (pres.). Avocations: organic gardening, beef ranching, scouting. Office: Rice U Dept Physics and Astronomy M S 108 6100 S Main St Houston TX 77251 Business E-Mail: reiff@rice.edu.

REIGEL, ERNEST W., lawyer; AB, Davidson Coll., NC, 1980; JD, Coll. William and Mary, Williamsburg, Va., 1983. Bar: NC 1983. Mem. Moore & Van Allen PLLC, Charlotte, NC, chmn. mgmt. com. Commr. NC Med. Care Comm.; chmn. Charlotte Heartwalk, 2006, 2007; mem. Charlotte area bd. dirs. Teach for America, 2006—10; bd. dirs. Charlotte Ctr. City Partners, 2007—10; chmn. adv. bd. McColl Sch. Bus., 2009—10; chmn. bd. trustees Charlotte Latin Sch., 2009—10. Named one of The Best Lawyers in America, Internat. Trade and Fin. Law, 2003—11; named to NC Super Lawyers, Bus./Corp. Law, 2006—11. Mem.: ABA, NC Bar Assn., Internat. Bar Assn. Office: Moore & Van Allen PLLC 100 N Tryon St Ste 4700 Charlotte NC 28202-4003 Office Phone: 704-331-1093. Office Fax: 704-378-2093. Business E-Mail: erniereigel@mvalaw.com.

REILING, RICHARD BERNARD, physician; b. Dayton, Ohio, June 29, 1941; s. Walter Anthony Sr. and E. Dorothy (Unger) R.; m. Elizabeth Castellini, June 20, 1964; children: Maureen Elizabeth, Richard Bernard Jr. BS, U. Dayton, 1963; MD cum laude, Harvard U., 1967. Diplomate Nat. Bd. Med. Examiners. Intern, then residentin surgery Boston City Hosp., 1967-73; fellow in surgery Lahey Clinic Found., Boston, 1970; practice medicine specializing in surgery Kettering, Ohio, 1975; v.p. cancer svcs. OhioHealth, Columbus, 2000—02; med. dir. Presbyn. Cancer Ctr., Charlotte, NC, 2003—; staff mem. Presbyn. Hosp., Presbyn. Matthews Hosp.; v.p. Presbyn. Healthcare Found. Instr. surgery Harvard Med. Sch., 1968-73; assoc. clin. prof. surgery Wright State U., 1979-81, assoc. prof. surgery, 1991-2000, clin. prof. surgery, 2000—; chief of staff Kettering Med. Ctr., Ohio, 1982-83. Contbr. articles to profl. jours. Scoutmaster Boy Scouts Am., Kettering, 1982-85; past pres. Assn. Cmty. Cancer Ctrs., 2006. Served to maj. USAF, 1973-75, v.p., vice-chair The Am. Coll. of Surgeons, 2008-09, chair, ACCME, 2011. Fellow ACS (past pres. Ohio chpt. 1986-87, Disting. Svc. award 2004, v.p. 2008-09, vice chair 2006-); mem. AMA (mem. Coun. Med. Edn.), Mecklenburg County Med. Soc., Ohio Med. Assn., Montgomery County Med. Soc., Societe Internationale de Churgerie, Assn. Cmty. Cancer Ctrs. (past pres. 2007). Avocations: sailing, golf. Home Phone: 704-373-0133; Office Phone: 704-384-9955. Office Fax: 704-385-5679. E-mail: rbreiling@novanthealth.org.

REILLEY, DENNIS H., oil industry executive; b. Feb. 25, 1953; m. Cindy Reilley; children: Jason, Michael. BS in Finance, Okla. State U., 1975. With Conoco, 1974-80, mgr. adminstrn. surface transp. Houston, 1980-81, exec. asst. to pres. petroleum ops., 1981-83, gen. mgr. planning and adminstrn. North American mktg., 1983-84; v.p. ops. Kayo Oil Co., Chattanooga, 1984-87; pres., mng. dir. Conoco, 1987-89; dir. ops. white pigment and mineral products divsn. DuPont Co., 1989-91, v.p., gen. mgr. white pigment and mineral products, 1991-95, v.p., gen. mgr. specialty chems., 1995-96, v.p., gen. mgr. Lycra/Terathane, 1996-97, sr. v.p., 1997-99, exec. v.p., COO, 1999-2000; pres. Praxair, Inc., Danbury, Conn., 2000—06, CEO, 2006, chmn., 2006—07; non-exec. chmn. Covidien, Ltd., 2007—08, Marathon Oil Corp., Houston, 2013—. Bd. dirs. Entergy Corp., 1999—2005, Marathon Oil Corp., 2002—, H. J. Heinz Co., 2005—13, The Dow Chemical Co., 2007—, Covidien Ltd., 2007—. Office: Marathon Oil Corp 5555 San Felipe Rd Houston TX 77056*

REILLY, JOHN PAUL, manufacturing executive; b. Phila., Aug. 18, 1943; m. Lynda J. Shepley; children: John P., Colleen K., Timothy S. BS, Xavier U., 1965; MBA, U. Detroit, 1967. Various leadership positions Navistar; pres. Brunswick Corp.; pres., CEO Stant Corp.; chmn., pres. & CEO Figgie Internat.; chmn. Exide Technologies; mfg. mgr. Chrysler Corp., 1965-79; pres., Mark Divsn. Core Industries, 1979-80; sr. v.p. Internat. Harvester, 1980-83; sr. v.p., gen. mgr., Walker Mfg. Co. Divsn. Tenneco Automotive, Racine, Wis., 1984-87, pres., chief exec. officer Lincolnshire, Ill., 1987. Bd. dirs. Material Sciences Corp., Marshfield Door Sys., Inc., Timken Co. Dir. Arden Shore Home for Boys, Lake Forest, Ill.; Racine Area Mfrs. and Commerce, 1984—. Mem. Motor and Equipment Mfrs. Assn. (bd. dirs.). Avocations: jogging, golf. Office: Exide Technologies 13000 Deerfield Pky Bldg 200 Milton GA 30004 Office Phone: 678-566-9000. Office Fax: 678-566-9188. Business E-Mail: john.reilly@exide.com.

REILLY, PAUL C., investment company executive; b. St. Petersburg, 1954; 3 children. BS in Profl. Studies, U. Notre Dame, MBA in Fin. CPA. Vice chmn., fin. svcs. KPMG LLP, 1998, pntr., 1987—2001; CEO KPMG Internat., 1998—2001; chmn., CEO Korn Ferry Internat., 2001—07, exec. chmn., 2007—09; pres. Raymond James Financial, Inc., St. Petersburg, Fla., 2009—10, CEO, 2010—. Bd. dirs. Raymond James Fin., Inc., 2005—. Avocation: tennis. Office: Raymond James Financial Inc 880 Carillon Pky Saint Petersburg FL 33716 Office Phone: 727-567-1000. Office Fax: 727-567-8915. Business E-Mail: paul.reilly@raymondjames.com.

REILLY, TRACY LYNN, language educator; b. Alton, Ill., June 10, 1959; d. Jerry John and Deanne Jean (McDonald) Lavick; m. James Edward Harte, July 26, 1980 (div. Dec. 12, 1988); 1 child, Kateland Jean; m. Kenneth Patrick Reilly, Nov. 26, 1994; 1 child, Joseph Patrick. BA in English Lit. cum laude, U. S.Fla., 1981; MA in English Lit., St. Louis U., 1989. Cert. tchr., Fla. Tchr. English, dept. chair Mary Help of Christian Sch., Tampa, Fla., 1981-85; instr. English St. Louis U., 1988-89, Hillsborough C.C., Tampa, Brandon, Fla., 1989-92, St. Petersburg (Fla.) Jr. Coll., 1989—; sr. English tchr. Admiral Farragut Acad., St. Petersburg, 1992—; tchr. English for fgn. students ELS Ednl. Svcs. Eckerd Coll., St. Petersburg, 1997; English dept. chmn. Admiral Farragut, St. Petersburg, 1999. Coord. beginning tchrs. program Mary Help of Christians, Tampa, 1982; selection com. Pinellas County Mid. Sch. and Speech Contest, St. Petersburg, 1992-93, 97-98; bd. dirs. Admiral Farragut Discipline Bd., St. Petersburg, head judge Scripps Regional Spelling Bee, 2009-10 Author: (essay) Quincy Coll. Stylus, 1979; co-author, dir.: (play) Farragut Christmas, 1995, Taming of Shrew, 1996, The Mousetrap, 1998, Grease, 1999; stage dir. Fiddler on the Roof, 2002; asst. dir. Once Upon A Mattress, 2008, Cinderella and the 7 Dwarves, 2009, Little Shop of Horrors, 2010, The Wedding Singer, 2011 Vol. John Anderson Presdl. Campaign, Tampa, St. Petersburg, 1980, Habitat for Humanities. Ill. State scholar, 1977, Acad. scholar Quincy Coll., 1977, St. Louis U., 1988. Mem. Nat. Coun. Tchrs. English, Fla. Fiction Writers Assn., Nat. Cath. Educators Assn., Historic Pk. Neighborhood Assn., Sigma Tau Delta. Avocations: writing, gardening, music. Office: Admiral Farragut Naval Acad 501 Park St N Saint Petersburg FL 33710-6743

REIMAN, SCOTT J., investment company executive; m. Virginia Reiman. BSBA in Fin., U. Denver, 1987. Founder, pres. Hexagon Investments, 1992—. Bd. dirs. Pioneer Natural Resources Co., 2009—. Mem. Mayor's Fin. Mgmt. Task Force City of Denver; bd. trustees U. Denver, 1999—, chair Investment Com. Recipient Josef Korbel Humanitarian Award, 2006. Office: Hexagon Investments 730 17th St # 800 Denver CO 80202-3541 also: Pioneer Natural Resources Co Ste 200 5205 N O Connor Blvd Irving TX 75039 Office Phone: 972-444-9001, 303-571-1010. Office Fax: 972-969-3576.

REINBOLT, PAUL C., oil industry executive; b. Chapel Hill, NC; B in Acctg., Miami U., Oxford, Ohio, MBA. Sr. fin. analyst Marathon Oil Corp., Pitts., 1984—86, short-term investment mgr. New York, 1986—87, mgr. treasury, 1987—91, dir. corp. fin. analysis Pitts., 1991—94, asst. treas., corp. fin., 1994—98, mgr. fin. and adminstrn. prodn., UK London, 1998—2000; comptr. US Steel Corp., Pitts., 2000—01; v.p. fin. and treas. Marathon Oil Corp., Houston, 2001—. Office: Marathon Oil Corp Corp Headquarters 5555 San Felipe Rd Houston TX 77056-2723

REINECKE, MANFRED G., chemistry professor; b. Milw., May 19, 1935; s. Fritz Wilhelm and Erna (Rittmeyer) R.; m. Marlene Zwisler, June 15, 1957; children: Kurt, Kryn, Claire. BS in Chemistry, U. Wis., 1956; PhD in Organic Chemistry, U. Calif., 1960. Asst. prof. U. Calif., Riverside, 1959-64, Tex. Christian U., Ft. Worth, 1964-68, assoc. prof., 1968-73, prof., 1973—2006, Cecil and Ida Green disting. emeritus tutor, 2006—; editl. bd. mem. Jour. Sci. & Tech., 2012—. Chmn. health professions adv. com. Tex. Christian U., 1974-91; mem. sci. adv. bd. Univera Pharm., Inc., 1996-2002; vis. prof. U. Tubingen, Germany, 1971-72, U. B.C., Vancouver, Can., 1987; cons. in field; editl. bd. mem. Natural Product Comm., 2005-, editl. adv. bd. mem. Natural Products Jour., 2011-, hon. editl. bd. mem. Botanics: Targets of Therapy, 2011-. Contbr. more than 85 articles on natural product, organic chemistry and chem. edn. to profl. jours. Recipient W.T. Doherty award Ft. Worth, Dallas sect. Am. Chem. Soc., 1984; NSF Tchg.fellow, 1971-72, NAS fellow, 1979, 90. Mem. Am. Chem. Soc. (chmn. Ft. Worth, Dallas sect. 1976), So. Assn. Advisors Health Professions (bd. dirs. 1986-89), Alpha Epsilon Delta (dir. SW region 1985-2002). Office: Tex Christian Univ Dept of Chemistry PO Box 298860 Fort Worth TX 76129-0001 Business E-Mail: m.reinecke@tcu.edu.

REINEMUND, STEVEN S., dean, educator, retired food products executive; b. Queens, NY, Apr. 6, 1948; s. Ott and Dora (Kramer) R.; m. Gail Timbers, Dec. 14, 1974; children: Steven S. Jr., Jonathan Craig. BS in Naval Sci., U.S. Naval Acad., 1970; MBA, U. Va., 1978. Commd. 2d lt. USMC, 1970, advanced through grades to capt., 1974, resigned, 1975; mktg. rep. IBM Corp., 1975-76; v.p., gen. mgr. Marriott-Roy Rogers, 1978-84; sr. v.p., field operator Pizza Hut, Inc., Wichita, Kans., 1984-86, exec. v.p., 1986, pres., CEO, 1986—92, Frito-Lay North America, 1992—96; chmn., CEO Frito-Lay, 1996—99; pres., COO PepsiCo, Inc., 1999—2001, chmn., CEO, 2001—07; dean, prof. leadership & strategy Calloway School Business & Accountancy & Babcock Graduate School Management, Wake Forest University, Winston-Salem, NC, 2008—. Bd. dirs. Johnson & Johnson, 2003—08, Marriott Internat., Inc., 2007—, American Express Co., 2007—, ExxonMobil Corp., 2007—, Wal-Mart Stores, Inc., 2010—. Chmn. Nat. Minority Supplier Develop. Council; trustee U.S. Naval Acad. Found.; bd. dir. U. Va., Darden Sch. Alumni Assn. Named one of Outstanding Young Men Am. Republican Presbyterian. Avocations: tennis, running. Office: Wake Forest U Calloway School Business & Accountancy 7285 Reynolda Station Winston Salem NC 27109-7285 E-mail: steve@wfu.edu.

REINERT, JAMES A., entomology educator; s. Andrew J. and Emma Reinert; m. Anita Irwin; children: Travis J., Gina N., Mindy K., Melanie B., Gregory W., Teresa J. BS in Entomology, Okla. State U., Stillwater, 1966; MS in Entomology, Clemson U., SC, 1968, PhD in Entomology, 1970. Asst. state entomologist U. Md., College Park, 1970; asst. prof. entomology to prof. entomology Ft. Lauderdale Rsch. and Edn. Ctr., U. Fla., 1970-84; resident dir., prof. entomology Tex. A&M Univ. Sys., Dallas, 1984-94, prof. entomology, 1994—2003; prof., entomology, Tex. agrilife rsch. faculty fellow Tex. A&M U. Sys., Dallas, 2004—, regents fellow, 2005—, regents fellow, prof. emeritus, 2011—. Contbr. more than 500 articles to profl. jours. Recipient Porter Henegar Meml. award, Fla. Entomol. Soc., 1982, TAES Recognition award, 2002, Vice-Chancellor's award, 2003, 2004; NDEA fellowship, 1967—70. Mem.: Inter-Turfgrass Soc., Entomol. Soc. America (S.W. br. sec.-treas. 1998, pres. elect, 1999, pres. 2000, chair, sec. sect. F 2003, vice chair, 2004, chair, 2005, SW Br. Entomologist of Yr., 1985, Recognition award, 2002, 2003, award, urban entomology 2002), Southern Nurserymen's Assn. (Porter Henegar Meml. award 1982), Fla. Entomol. Soc. (v.p. 1983, pres. 1984, Entomologist of Yr. 1985), Fla. State Hort. Soc. (v.p. 1982), S.C. Entomol. Soc. (J.H. Cochran award 2002, Rsch. Ctr. Adminstrs. Soc. (v.p. 1994, state rep. 1991-92, sec. 1993), Dallas Agr. Club (bd. dirs. 1989, v.p. 1990, pres. 1991), Alpha Zeta Fraternity, Phi Sigma, Phi Kappa Phi, Sigma Xi. Roman Catholic. Avocations: gardening, woodworking, reading. Home: 3805 Covinton Ln Plano TX 75023-7731 Office: Tex A&M Agri Life Rsch and Ext Ctr 17360 Coit Rd Dallas TX 75252-6599 Personal E-mail: jim.reinert@yahoo.com. Business E-Mail: j-reinert@tamu.edu.

REINHARDT, DANIEL SARGENT, lawyer; b. Orange, NJ, Jan. 27, 1949; s. Warren Irwin and Winifred Ruth (Sargent) R.; m. Elizabeth Ann Johnson, June 11, 1982; 1 child, Meredith Alexandra. BA, Duke U., 1971; JD, Georgetown U., 1974. Bar: Ga. 1975, U.S. Dist. Ct. (no. dist.) Ga. 1975, U.S. Ct. Appeals (5th and 11th cirs.) 1981, U.S. Dist. Ct. (so. dist.) Ga. 1984, U.S. Dist. Ct. (mid. dist.) Ga. 1985, U.S. Ct. Appeals (4th cir.) 1985. Assoc. Troutman Sanders LLP, Atlanta, 1974—79, ptnr., 1980—, mem. exec. com. Dep. asst. atty. gen. State of Ga., 1975-79. Named a Super Lawyer, Atlanta Mag., 2004. Mem. ABA, Ga. Bar Assn., Atlanta Bar Assn., fellow, Am. Coll. Trial Lawyers, Lawyers Club. Avocation: sports. Office: Troutman Sanders LLP 600 Peachtree St Atlanta GA 30308-2265 Office Phone: 404-885-3206. Office Fax: 404-885-3900. Business E-Mail: daniel.reinhardt@troutmansanders.com.

REINHARDT, THOMAS T., information technology executive; B in Gen. Engring., US Mil. Acad., West Point, 1993; MS in Bus. Adminstrn., Boston U. Assoc. dep. atty. Gen., chief staff Dep. Atty. Gen.; exec. sec. Presidential Commn. on Space Shuttle Challenger Accident; chief staff, DHS Office Under Secretary for Mgmt.; dep. asst. atty gen., dir., Congressional Rels. US Dept. of Justice, 1989—2002; v.p., homeland security bus. devel. NCI Info. Sys. Inc., 2002; joined Computer Sciences Corp., 2005, account mgr., Am. Red Cross, pres., Bus. Devel., v.p., customer relationship exec., Dept. of Homeland Security, N.Am. Pub. Sector, 2008—. Mil. asst., US Ambassador NATO; with Dept. of Army Staff. Recipient Edmund J. Randolph award, US Atty. Gen.'s Office. Office: Computer Sciences Corp 3170 Fairview Park Dr Falls Church VA 22042 Office Phone: 703-876-1000. Business E-Mail: treinhardt@csc.com.

REINHARDT, UWE ERNST, economist, educator; b. Osnabrueck, Germany, Sept. 24, 1937; came to U.S., 1964; s. Wilhelm and Edeltraut (Kehne) R.; m. Tsung-mei Cheng, May 25, 1968; children—Dirk, Kara, Mark B.Commerce with honors, U. Sask., Saskatoon, Can., 1964; MA in Economics, Yale U., 1965, M.Ph. in Economics, 1967, PhD, 1970; DSc (hon.), Med. Coll. of Pa., 1987, CUNY, 1994, SUNY, 1998. Asst. prof., economics and pub. affairs Princeton University, NJ, 1968—74, assoc. prof., 1974-79, prof., 1979, James Madison prof., polit. economy, prof., economics NJ, 1984—. Bd. dirs. McAllister Holdings, Amerigroup Corp.; trustee Tchrs. Ins. and Annuity Assn., 1978-93, H&Q Health Fund; cons. Urban Inst., Washington, 1971-75, HEW, 1974—, HHS, Math., Inc., Princeton, 1970-80, AT&T, Basking Ridge, N.J., 1976-82, Nat. Westminster Bank USA, N.Y.C., 1979—, mem. Nat. Leadership Commn. Health Care, 1986—; mem. spl. adv. bd. VA, 1981-85; mem. U.S. Physicians' Payment Rev. Commn., U.S. Congress, 1986—; pres. Assn. for Health Svcs. Rsch., 1989-90, Found. Health Svcs. Rsch., 1990-91; mem. bd. advisors Nat. Inst. Healthcare Mgmt., 1993—, Pew Health Professions Commn., 1997—; mem. Coun. Econ. Impact Health Reform, 1994—; mem. external adv. panel health and nutrition World Bank, 1997—; chair coordinating com. Commonwealth Fund Internat. Program Health Policy, 1998—; commr. Kaiser Commn. Medicaid and Uninsured; trustee Duke U. Health Sys., Triad Hosps., Inc., Medcast/WebMD. Author: Physician Productivity and the Demand for Health Manpower, 1975; mem. editorial bd. Health Affairs, 1982—, New Eng. Jour. Medicine, 1989-92, Health Mgmt. Quar., Health Policy and Edn., Milbank Meml. Quar., Jour. AMA, 1991—; assoc. editor Jour. Health Econs., 1980-85, mem. editorial bd., 1981-83; contbr. articles to profl. jours. Bd. dirs. Nat. Acad. Aging, 1993—. Mem. Nat. Inst. Health Care Mgmt., Inst. Medicine Nat. Acad. Scis. (gov. council 1979-82) Office: Amerigroup Corp Bd Directors 4425 Corporation Ln Virginia Beach VA 23462 also: Princeton U 351 Wallace Hall Princeton NJ 08544 Office Phone: 757-490-6900, 609-258-4781. Office Fax: 757-518-3600, 609-258-5974. Business E-Mail: reinhard@princeton.edu.

REINHART, JOHN BELVIN, retired child and adolescent psychiatrist, educator; b. Merrill, Wis., Dec. 22, 1917; s. Dabney Belvin and Ann (Toomey) R.; m. Helen Elsen Reinhart, Jan. 3, 1949; children: Peter, Catherine, Ann, John, Frederick, Andrew. BA, Duke U., 1939; MD, Bowman Gray Sch. Medicine, Winston-Salem, NC, 1943. Diplomate Am. Bd. Pediatrics, Am. Bd. Psychiatry in child and adolescent psychiatry. Instr. pediatrics Bowman Gray Sch. Medicine, Winston-Salem, 1950-52; asst. prof., assoc. prof., prof. pediatrics and psychiatry U. Pitts. Sch. Medicine, 1956-83, emeritus prof. pediatrics, 1983—; clin. prof. psychiatry Bowman Gray Sch. Medicine, Winston-Salem, 1986-99, ret., 1999—. Co-Author: A Baby's First Year, 1956. Capt. M.C. AUS, 1946-48. Roman Catholic. Avocations: reading, golf, tennis, travel. Home: 600 Carolina Village Rd Apt 1415 Hendersonville NC 28792-2803

REINICHE, DOMINIQUE, food products executive; b. July 13, 1955; MBA, ESSEC Bus. Sch. Asst. prod. mgr. Procter & Gamble Co., 1978—81, prod. mgr., 1981—83, assoc. advt. mgr., 1983—86; mktg., strategy mgr. Kraft Jacobs Suchard, 1986—92; mktg. mgr. Coca-Cola Enterprises, Inc., 1992—94, comml., operational mktg. mgr., 1994—97, asst. CEO, 1997—98, gen. mgr. France, 1998, chmn., CEO, 1998—2002; pres. Coca-Cola Enterprises, Inc.-Europe, 2003; vice chmn. Coca-Cola Enterprises-Europe Group, 2002—03, pres., 2005—13, chmn., 2013—. Exec. bd. Medef; adv. bd. ING Direct; bd. dir. ECR Europe, Confedn. the Food and Drink Industries, EU; chmn. Union des Annonceurs; first vice chmn. UNESDA (Union of European Soft Drinks Associations), pres., 2005—07, 2013—; supervisory bd. AXA Group. Decorated Legion d'Honneur; named one of The Internat. Power 50, Fortune mag., 2008—12. Address: c/o The Coca-Cola Co PO Box 1734 Atlanta GA 30301*

REINSTEIN, JOEL, lawyer; b. NYC, July 23, 1946; s. Louis and Ruth Reinstein; children: Lesli, Louis, Mindy. BSE, U. Pa., 1968; JD cum laude, U. Fla., 1971; LLM in Taxation, NYU, 1974. Bar: Fla. 1971, U.S. Tax Ct. 1973, U.S. Dist. Ct. (so. dist.) Fla. 1976. Atty., office of chief counsel IRS, 1971-74; ptnr. Capp, Reinstein, Kopelowitz and Atlas, P.A., Ft. Lauderdale, Fla., 1975-85; dir., ptnr. Greenberg, Traurig, Hoffman, Lipoff, Rosen & Quentel, P.A., Ft. Lauderdale, 1985-92; gen. counsel Internat. Magnetic Imaging, Inc., Boca Raton, Fla., 1992-94; prin. Law Offices of Joel Reinstein P.A., Boca Raton, 1993—. Lectr. Advanced Pension Planning, Am. Soc. C.L.U.s; lectr. in field. Mem. editl. bd. U. Fla. Law Rev. 1970-71; contbr. articles to profl. jours. Mem. Fla. Bar Assn. (tax sect.), ABA (tax sect.), Order of Coif, Phi Kappa Phi, Phi Delta Pi. Office: 1200 N Federal Hwy Ste 301 Boca Raton FL 33432-2846 Office Phone: 561-393-6714. E-mail: joel@reinsteinlaw.com.

REIS, DON, publishing executive; b. NYC, Nov. 19, 1927; m. Barbara Weinberg, 1949; children: Robert, Richard. AB, Princeton U., 1947; MA, NYU, 1955. Rsch. editor Bantam Books, 1952-55, edn. editor, 1955-66; editor-in-chief Washington Square Press Divsn. Simon & Schuster, 1966-68; v.p., editorial dir. Ednl. Directions Inc., Westport, Conn., 1968-85; mng. editor Barron's Ednl. Series, 1985-87; gen. and ednl. editor Barron's, 1987-93, sr. cons. editor, 1993-99; editorial dir. Reis Assocs., Raleigh, NC, 1999—. Author (with A. Butman and D. Sohn) Paperback Books in the Schools, 1962; editor The Collected Essays of Aldous Huxley, 1958. Home and Office: Reis Associates 1543 Laureldale Dr Raleigh NC 27609-3572 Personal E-mail: donjreis@yahoo.com.

REISIN, EFRAIN, nephrologist, researcher, educator; b. Cordoba, Argentina, Feb. 25, 1943; came to U.S., 1979; s. Maximo and Elisa Reisin; m. Ilana Hershkovitz, Sept. 6, 1971; children: Eyal, Thalia Alexis. MD, Nat. U., Cordoba, 1966. Intern internal medicine Nat. U. Cordoba-Clinicas Hosp., 1966; resident Jimenes Diaz Found., Madrid, 1966-68, Chaim Sheba Med. Ctr., Tel Hashomer, Israel, 1968-71, fellow in nephrology, 1971-74, staff physician nephrology, 1974-77; rsch. fellow in hypertension Health Sci. Ctr., Winnipeg, Man., Can., 1977-78; vis. scientist in hypertension Nat. Health Welfare Can., Winnipeg, Man., 1978-79; Ochsner vis. scientist in hypertension Ochsner Found. Hosp., New Orleans, 1979-82; from asst. prof. to assoc. prof. medicine La. State U., New Orleans, 1982-89, prof. medicine, 1985—, chief sect. nephrology, 1999—. Panelist Consensus Conf., NIH, Bethesda, Md., 1991. Contbr. chapters to books, over 120 articles to profl. jours. 1st lt. Israel Army, 1971-72. Grantee Nat. Health and Welfare Can., 1978-79, Am. Heart Assn., 1980-81, also several pharm. cos., 1984—. Fellow ACP, Am. Coun. High Blood Pressure Rsch., Am. Heart Fund, Am. Coll. Clin. Pharmacology (counselor south ctrl. regional chpt. 1991-92), Am. Fedn. Clin. Rsch., So. Soc. for Clin. Investigation; mem. Internat. Soc. Nephrology, Internat. Soc. Hypertension, Am. Soc. Nephrology, Am. Soc. Hypertension, Coun. Nephrology, Am. Heart Assn., Inter-Am. Soc. Hypertension, Orleans Parish Med. Soc. Achievements include research in documenting positive effects of weight reduction in treatment of hypertension. Avocations: tennis, reading, movies. Office: La State U Sch Medicine 1542 Tulane Ave New Orleans LA 70112-2825 Business E-Mail: ereisin@lsuhsc.edu.

REISING, RONALD, utilities executive; BA in Economics, Lawrence U.; MA in Mgmt., Northwestern U. CPA. Sr. dir. Deloitte & Touche LLP, 1985—88; v.p. North Am. Venture Group Ltd., 1988—91; various sr. mgmt. positions Ameritech Corp., 1991—99; CFO Bell Can., 1999—2000, Derivon, 2000—01, Focal Comm., 2001—02; v.p., fin. Cinergy Corp. (subs. Duke Energy Corp.), 2002—04, v.p., 2004—09; chief procurement officer Cinergy Corp., 2004—, sr. v.p., 2009—. Office: Duke Energy Corp 526 S Church St Charlotte NC 28202-1803 Office Phone: 704-594-6200. Office Fax: 704-382-3814. Business E-Mail: RReising@duke-energy.com.

REISMAN, JUDITH ANN GELERNTER, media communications executive, educator; b. Hillside, NJ, Apr. 11, 1935; MA in Speech Comm., Case Western Res. U., 1976, PhD in Speech Comm., 1980. Faculty dept. anthropology and sociology Haifa U., Israel, 1981—83; rsch. prof. sch. edn. Am. U., Washington, 1983—85; vis. prof. law Liberty U., Sch. Law, Lynchburg, Va., 2011; founder, pres. Inst. Media Edn., 1985—; founder Internat. Inst. Cultural Renewal, 2012—. Cons., reviewer grant proposals audio-visual drug programs for youth Dept. Edn., 1987; rsch. design cons. Alcohol and Tobacco Media Analysis in Mainstream Mags., Dept. HHS, 1987—90; cons., field reviewer Drug Free Youth Sch. Candidates Dept. Edn., 1988; lectr., adj. prof. George Mason U., Va., 1990; expert witness Pres.'s Commn. on Assignment of Women in Armed Forces, 1992, U.S. Atty. Gen. Commn. on Pornography, 1985—86, U.S. Atty. Gen. Task Force on Domestic Violence, Washington, 1985, Mapplethorpe Trial, Cin., 1990, Australian Parliament, 1992, Ga. State Senate, 1992; nominated to panel on sex harassment in the Air Force U.S. Inspector Gen., 2003; sci. advisor Protective Parents Assn.; subcom. junk sci. Am. Legis. Exchange Coun. Edn. Task Force, 1999—2004. Author: Images of Children, Crime and Violence in Playboy, Penthouse and Hustler, 1989, Kinsey, Sex and Fraud, 1990, Softport Plays Hardball, 1991, Kinsey, Crimes and Consequences, 1998, 2003, Sexual Sabotage, 2010, Stolen Honor, 2013; contbr. preme Ct. cases to profl. jours. Recipient Gold Camera award, 1982, Silver Screen award, 1982, Filmstrip of Yr. award, 1981—82, Silver Plaque award, 1982, Family Svc. Assn. Am. 1st pl. award local TV series, 1974, Best of 1965 award, 1965, Scientist of Yr. for Children award, 1993; co-recipient Scholastic Mag. awards, Dukane award, 1982; U.S. Dept. Justice grantee. Mem.: AAAS, World Net Daily.Com (columnist 1998—), Women in Neurosci., Nat. Black Child Devel. Inst., Soc. Sci. Study Sex, N.Y. Acad. Scis., Internat. Comm. Assn., Am. Statis. Assn., Am. Assn. Composers, Authors and Pubs., Nat. Assn. Scholars. Personal E-mail: jareisman@gmail.com. Business E-Mail: jareisman@cox.net.

REISS, DALE ANNE, corporate financial executive; b. Sept. 3, 1947; d. Max and Nan (Hart) R.; m. Jerome L. King, Mar. 5, 1978; children: Matthew Reiss, Mitchell, Stacey King BS, Ill. Inst. Tech., 1967; MBA, U. Chgo., 1970. CPA, Fla., Ill. Cost acct. First Nat. Bank, Chgo., 1967; asst. contr. City Colls. of Chgo., 1967-71; dir. fin. Chgo. Dept. Pub. Works, 1971-73; prin. Arthur Young & Co., Chgo., 1973-80; sr. v.p., contr. Urban Investment & Devel. Co., Chgo., 1980-85; mng. ptnr. Ernst & Young LLP, Chgo., 1985-98, Ernst & Young, NYC, 1998-99; global dir. real estate, hospitality and constrn. Ernst & Young LLP, NYC, 1999—2008; mng. dir., Artemis Advisor LLC, 2008—; sr. mng. dir. Brock Capital Mgmt. LLC, 2009—; bd. dir. iStar-Fin. Post Properties NYSE. Bd. dirs. Urban Land Inst.; Pension Real Estate Assn., Gutmacher Inst. Mem. AICPA, Fin. Execs. Inst., NAREIT, Columbia U. Real Estate Adv. Group, Econ. Club, NY Athletic Club, Real Estate Roundtable. Personal E-mail: artemisadvisors@gmail.com, daler13@hotmail.com.

REISS, JEROME, retired lawyer; b. Bklyn., Dec. 7, 1924; s. William and Eva (Marenstein) Reiss; m. Naomi Betty Plutzik, June 15, 1947; children: Robert Scott, Harlan Morgan, Andrea Ellen, Samantha Glynis. BA, Bklyn. Coll., 1948; JD, Harvard U., Cambridge, Mass., 1951. Bar: NY 1951, US Dist. Ct. (so. dist.) NY 1954, US Ct. Claims 1960, US Dist. Ct. (ea. dist.) NY 1964, DC 1967, US Dist. Ct. (we. dist.) NY 1979, US Supreme Ct. 1989. Staff atty. civil br. Legal Aid Soc., NYC, 1951—54; asst. corp. counsel City of N.Y., 1954—58; assoc. Max E. Greenberg, 1958-67; sr. ptnr. Max E. Greenberg, Trayman, Cantor, Reiss & Blasky, 1967-80, Max E. Greenberg, Cantor & Reiss, NYC, 1980-88, Thelen, Marrin, Johnson & Bridges, NYC, 1989-97, Thelen, Reid & Priest, 1997-2000, ret., 2000; gen. counsel Kiska Constrn. Co.-USA, Inc., 2004—. Arbitrator Small Claims Ct., 1960—88; bd. adv. Fed. Pub., Inc.; chmn. bd. AMT-Pacific, Israel, 2000—02; former mem. Am. Judges Assn.; rep. various Japanese, British, Turkish, Israeli internat. contractors; lectr. in constrn. field Am. Mgmt. Assoc., AAA, GSA, Turkish Constrn. Assn., Medgar Evers CC, Prac Law Inst. Fla. Atlantic U.; drafter renovation contracts Statue of Liberty; drafter expansion contracts Met. Mus. of Art; drafter construction contract NYC Conv. Ctr., Rockefeller U., New Lab. Bldg.; completed constn. FDR Lib., Hyde Pk., NY; lectr. Am. Mgmt. Assoc., ARA Fed. Pub. Inc., MedgenEK CC. Contbr. articles to profl. jours., chapters to books. Trustee Brownsville Boys Club Alumni Assn., gen. counsel, Artist Fellowship, Inc. With USAAF, 1943—46. Fellow: Am. Coll. Constrn. Lawyers (founding mem.); mem.: Wash. (DC) Bar Assn., NY Bar Assn., Internat. Bar Assn., Jacob K. Javits Conv. Ctr. Oper. Corp. (bd. dirs.), Mcpl. Assist. Corp. City NY (bd. dirs.).

REISS, SUSAN MARIE, editor, writer; b. Washington, Sept. 14, 1963; m. Paul L. Roney Jr., May 25, 1991. BA in English Lit., U. Va., 1985; MA in English, George Mason U., 1989. Editl. asst. Water Pollution Control Fedn., Alexandria, Va., 1985-87; freelance writer, editor Arlington, Va., 1987-90; staff writer George Mason U., Fairfax, Va., 1988-90, Optical Soc. Am., Washington, 1990-91, news editor, 1991-93, mng. editor, 1993-96; editor On Campus With Women Assn. Am. Colls. and Univs., 1996—2000; freelance writer, editor Arlington, 1996—. Newsletter editor: Arlington County Tennis Assn., 1990-91; contbr. articles to profl. jours. and mags. Mem. Am. Soc. Laser Medicine and Surgery, Nat. Assn. Science Writers, Nat. Press Club, Am. Ind. Writers, D.C. Sci. Writers Assn., Sigma Tau Delta (founding mem. U. Va. chpt.). Avocations: tennis, piano, cross country skiing. Home and Office: 6814 30th Rd N Arlington VA 22213-1602

REITAN, BERNT, retired metal products executive; b. Norway, Apr. 11, 1948; married; 2 children. M in Civil Engring., Tech. U. Trondheim, Norway. Various civil engring. project positions, Stavanger and Lillehammer, Norway, 1972—79; plant mgr. Rodsand magnetite mine Elkem, Norway, 1980—83, gen. mgr. Elkem Chems. Ltd. England, 1983—84, plant mgr. Fiskaa silicon plant Norway, 1985—87, bus. unit mgr. ferro alloys divsn., 1987, sr. v.p. materials and tech., mng. dir. Elkem Aluminium ANS, 1988—2000; gen. mgr. World Alumina Chems. Alcoa, Inc., 2000, pres. World Chems., 2000—01, pres. Alcoa World Alumina and Chems., v.p., 2001—03, pres. Primary Metals, 2003, group pres. Global Primary Products, exec. v.p. NYC, 2004—10. Bd. mem. Internat. Primary Aluminium Inst., European Aluminium Assn., Norwegian Employers Fedn., Norwegian Process and Mfg. Assn.; chmn. bd. Norwegian Metall. Industry Assn., 1990—92; bd. dirs. Royal Caribbean Cruise Lines. Office Phone: 212-836-2600.

REITER, DAVID S., engineering company executive, lawyer; b. St. Louis, 1967; m. Susie Reiter; children: Garrett, Audrey. BA, U. Notre Dame, 1989; JD, U. Southern Calif., 1993, M in Internat. Rels.; MBA, U. Sheffield, UK. V.p., gen. counsel 724 Solutions Inc.; sr. counsel Compaq Computer Corp., 1994—2000; founder Phillips & Reiter, PLLC, 2002—09, co-founder, ptnr., 2003—; v.p., gen. counsel, corp. sec. Luminex Corp., Austin, Tex., 2003—. Mem.: Tex. Bar Assn., ABA (chair, Law Dept. Mgmt. subcommittee). Avocations: tennis, bicycling. Office: Luminex Corp 12212 Technology Blvd Austin TX 78727 Office Phone: 512-219-8020. Office Fax: 512-219-5195.

REITZ, DOUGLAS JOHN FRANK, airline captain, computer consultant; b. Salisbury, Rhodesia, May 7, 1955; came to U.S., 1980; s. Francis Charles Deneys and Zeta Ann (Runham) R.; m. Judy Ann White, Mar. 31, 1978 (div. May 1996); child, David Douglas; m. Gala Judith Ruzic, Dec. 12, 1998. Dir. ops. Aviex Jet, Inc., Houston, 1980-84; capt. Am. Airlines, Dallas, 1984—; pres. A Travel Crew-Internet. Travel Agy., 2007, The Reitz Cos., Inc., 1999—2007; v.p. Sterling Travel Group, 2012—. Computer cons., 1983—. Flight lt. Rhodesian Air Force, 1973-80. Recipient Sword of Honor, Rhodesian Air Force, 1974. Mem. Allied Pilots Assn. Business E-Mail: info@atravelcrew.com.

RELLING, MARY V., pharmaceutical researcher, professor; BS, U. Ariz. Coll. Pharmacy, Tucson, 1982; PharmD, U. Utah Coll. Pharmacy, Salt Lake City, 1985. Lic. Nat. Assn. Boards Pharmacy, cert. in pharmacotherapy. Pharmacist, internal medicine/coronary care unit Vets. Adminstrn. Med. Ctr., Tuscon, 1982—83; resident clin. pharmacy U. Utah Health Scis. Ctr., 1983—85; rsch. fellowship pharm. divsn. St. Jude Children's Rsch. Hosp., Memphis, 1985—87; rsch. fellowship dept. pharmacology U. Basel, Switzerland, 1987—88; asst. prof. U. Tenn. Coll. Pharmacy, Memphis, 1988—94, assoc. prof. dept. clin. pharmacy & pharm scis., 1994—99, prof. dept. clin. pharmacy & pharm scis., 1999—. Asst. mem. pharm. dept. St. Jude Children's Rsch. Hosp., 1988—95, assoc. mem., 1995—2001, mem., 2001—, chair pharm. dept., 2003—; dir. pharmacokinetics shared resource St. Jude Children's Rsch. Hosp. Cancer Ctr., 1990—2006; Gerhard Levy disting. lectr. SUNY Buffalo, 2002; mem. clin. pharmacology subcom. FDA Ctr. Drug Evaluation & Rsch., 2002—; prof. dept. pediat. U. Tenn., 2002—. Mem. editl. bd. Pharmacotherapy, 1993—2007, Clin. Pharmacology & Therapeutics, 1996—2008, Leukemia, 1999—, Pharmacogenetics, 2001—, Pharm. Rsch., 2001—, Jour. Clin. Oncology, 2004—06, Blood, 2004—09; contbr. articles to profl. jours. Recipient Roland T. Lakey award, Wayne State U., Detroit, 2006, Jack R. Cole Disting. Alumnus award, U. Ariz., 2007. Mem.: Am. Soc. Human Genetics, Am. Soc. Hematology, Am. Soc. Clin. Oncology (Pediatric Oncology award 2009), Am. Assn. Cancer Rsch., Am. Coll. Clin. Pharmacy (Russell R. Miller award 2002), Am. Soc. Clin. Pharmacology & Therapeutics (bd. dirs. 1999—2002, v.p. 2000—01, Leon I. Goldberg Young Investigator award 1998), Am. Assn. Colleges of Pharmacy. Office: St Jude Childrens Rsch Hosp Pharm Dept 262 Danny Thomas Pl MS 313 Memphis TN 38105 Office Phone: 901-595-3663. Office Fax: 901-595-8869. E-mail: mary.relling@stjude.org.

REMAR, ROBERT BOYLE, lawyer; b. Boston, Nov. 19, 1948; s. Samuel Roy and Elizabeth Mary (Boyle) R.; m. Victoria A. Greenhood, Nov. 11, 1979; children: Daniel A.G., William B.G. BA, U. Mass., 1970; JD, Boston Coll., 1974. Bar: Ga. 1974, Mass. 1975, US Ct. Appeals (5th cir.) 1978, US Ct. Appeals (11th cir.) 1981, US Ct. Appeals (2d cir.) 1995, US Supreme Ct. 1981. Staff atty. Ga. Legal Svcs. Program, Savannah, 1974-76, Western Mass. Legal Svcs., Greenfield, 1976-77; sr. staff atty. Ga. Legal Svcs. Program, Atlanta, 1977-82; ptnr. Remar & Graettinger, Atlanta, 1983-95, Kirwan, Parks, Chesin & Remar PC, Atlanta, 1993-96, Rogers & Hardin, Atlanta, 1996—. V.p. & treas., mem. exec. com., bd. dirs. ACLU, NYC, pres. Ga. chpt., 1985-87, gen. counsel, 1980-83; hearing officer Ga. Pub. Svc. Commn., Atlanta, 1985-98; adj. prof. Ga. State U., Atlanta, 1984-98, spl. asst. atty. gen., 1990-2003; bd. experts Lawyers Alert, Boston, 1985-94; pres. bd. dirs. Fed. Defender Program. Mem. Ga. Energy Regulatory Reform Commn., Gov. of Ga., 1980-82, Ga. Consumer Adv. Bd., 1981-82, City Atl. Bd. Ethics, AAA Comml. Panel; pres. Ga. Consumer Ctr. Inc., 1988-91, pres.; bd. dirs., Ga. Resource Ctr.; v.p. Ga Ctr. Law Pub. Inst., 1991-94; bar coun. U.S.D.C. N.D.G., 1996-99. Fellow Am. Coll. Trial Lawyers; mem. ABA (chmn. individual rights access to civil justice com. 1988-99), Ga. Bar Assn. (chmn. individual rights sect. 1981-83, co-chmn. consumer rights and remedies com. 1979-83, chmn. death penalty re. com. 1993—, mem. legis. adv. com. 1994-97, mem. indigent def. com. 2000—), Atlanta Bar Assn., Lawyers Club Atlanta, Lamar Inn of Ct. (master of the bench). Democrat. Avocations: golf, gardening. Home: 1714 Meadowdale Ave NE Atlanta GA 30306-3114 Office: Rogers & Hardin Internat Tower Peachtree Ctr 229 Peachtree St NE Ste 2700 Atlanta GA 30303-1638 Office Phone: 404-420-4631. Business E-Mail: rremar@rh-law.com.

REMICK, SCOT CLIFTON, oncologist, clinical investigator, educator; b. New Rochelle, NY, Oct. 16, 1956; s. Robert Merrick and Marjorie Allis (Stamm) R. BA, SUNY, Oswego, 1978; MD, N.Y. Med. Coll., Valhalla, 1982. Resident Johns Hopkins Hosp., Balt., 1982-85; fellow Clin. Cancer Ctr. U. Wis. Clin. Cancer Ctr., Madison, 1985-88; assoc. prof. Dept. Medicine Albany (N.Y.) Med. Coll., 1988-96; with Case Western Res. U., Cleve., 1996—, assoc. prof. dept. medicine, dir. devel. therapeutics divsn. hematology/oncology, prof. medicine. Prin. investigator numerous oncology and HIV/AIDS clin. trials, Albany, 1988—, dir., prof. Medicine Mary Babb Randolph Cancer Ctr., W.Va. U. Sch. Medicine, 07-. Contbr. over 130 papers, textbook chpts. and abstracts. Active Am. Cancer Soc. (Career Devel. award 1991), Albany. Fellow Am. Coll. Physicians; mem. Am. Assn. for Cancer Rsch., Am. Soc. Clin. Oncology, Alpha Omega Alpha. Office: West Virginia Unviersity MBR Cancer Ctr 1801 RCB HSC South PO Box 9300 Morgantown WV 26506 Business E-Mail: sremick@hsc.wvu.edu.

REMLEY, AUDREY WRIGHT, retired academic administrator, psychologist; b. Dec. 26, 1931; d. Leslie Frank and Irene Lesetta (Graue) Wright; m. Alvin Remley, Mar. 25, 1951 (dec. Mar. 1986); children: Steven Leslie, David Mark. AA, Hannibal-LaGrange Coll., 1951; BS in Edn. cum laude, U. Mo., 1963, MA, 1969, PhD, 1974; LHD (hon.), Westminster Coll., 1996. Lic. psychologist, Mo.; cert. health svc. provider, Mo. From asst. prof. psychology to assoc. prof. to prof. Westminster Coll., Fulton, Mo., 1969-95, prof., assoc. dean faculty, 1989-95; emeritus prof., 1996; chmn. dept. psychology Westminster Coll., Fulton, Mo., 1975-78, dir. counseling svcs., 1975-79, dir. student devel., 1979-80, dir. advising and counseling svcs., 1980-88; dir. chapel singers Westminster Presbyterian Church, 2002—. Owner It's A Crock Antiques; cons. OVID Bell Press, 1988-89. Mem. adv. bd. Callaway Comty. Hosp., 1988-95, pres., 1992-95; bd. dirs. Serve, Inc., Fulton, 1989-95, pres., 1991-93; mem. adv. bd. social learning program Fulton State Hosp., chair, 1992-94, mng. county govt. task force fin. mgmt. chair; bd. dirs. Cen. Mo. Food Bank, 1995-96, Ft. Worth Symphony League Bd., 1998-2004, pres., 2002-04, v.p. for projects, 2005, exec. advisor, 2005-; bd. dirs. Jubilee Theatre, 2006—,treasurer, 2007-11. Recipient Outstanding Young Woman of Am. award Jaycettes, 1965, Athena award, 1991, Remley Center award (1st recipient) Westminster Coll., 2001; NDEA fellow, 1968; bldg. Remley Women's Resource Ctr. Westminster Coll. named in her honor, 2001 Mem. APA, AACD, Am. Coll. Pers. Assn. (exec. coun. 1982-85, co-editor ACPA Developments 1984-87, v.p. state divns. 1987-89, treas.-elect 1990-91, treas. 1991-93, treas. ednl. found. bd. 1994-96, Outstanding State Divsn. Leader 1982, profl. svc. award 1991, Annuit Coeptis award 1994), Mo. Coll. Pers. Assn. (pres. 1981-82, profl. svc. award 1987), Mo. Psychol. Assn. (lic.), Ft. Worth Newcomers Club (pres. 1998-99), Kiwanis (exec. bd. 1989-92, v.p. 1992, pres.-elect 1992-93, pres. 1993-94, disting. 1995). Presbyterian. Avocations: singing, antiques, knitting.

REMONDI, JOHN F. (JACK REMONDI), finance company executive; b. 1962; s. John J. Remondi; m. Judith Barbara Dickstein, Mar. 20, 1993. BA in Economics, Conn. Coll., 1984. Sr. v.p. corporate finance & adminstrn., CFO New England Edn. Loan Mktg. Corp.; sr. v.p., treas. Nellie Mae, Inc., Braintree, Mass., 1999—2001; exec. v.p. finnace SLM Corp. (Sallie Mae), Reston, Va., 2001—05, vice chmn., CFO, 2008—11, pres., COO, 2011—13, CEO, 2013—; portfolio mgr. PAR Capital Mgmt., Boston, 2005—08. Chmn. Reading is Fundamental, Inc. Office: Sallie Mae 12061 Bluemont Way Reston VA 20190*

REN, CHIANG H., aerospace engineer, senior executive; b. Taipei, Taiwan, Aug. 3, 1965; arrived in U.S., 1972; m. Kelly Yoon, May 20, 1995; children: Heather Victoria, Gloria Isabel. BSE magna cum laude in Mech. Engring., U. Pa., 1987; MS in Aeronautics and Astronautics, MIT, 1989; PhD in Sys. Analysis, U. Bolton, 2012. Sr. aerospace engr. ANSER, Arlington, Va., 1989—2001; chief tech. officer, v.p. Kepler Rsch., Inc., Arlington, 2002—. Contbr. numerous articles to profl. jours.; author: (3 books) Christian Mission Series, 2000. Deacon Presbyn. Ch.; dir. Inst. for Christianity. Recipient Letter of Recognition, Sec. of the Air Force, 2001, Air Force Space Commn. Task Force, 2001. Fellow: AIAA (assoc.); mem.: Six Sigma (Black Belt), Pi Tau Sigma, Tau Beta Pi. Office: Kepler Research Inc 13663 Office Pl Ste 202 Woodbridge VA 22192 Office Phone: 703-465-4035. Business E-Mail: chiangren@keplerresearch.com.

RENEGAR, BRIAN, state legislator, veterinarian; b. Okla. City, Sept. 16, 1950; s. Raymond and Malinda Payne Renegar; m. Theresa Pallan; 4 children. BS, Northeastern Okla. State Univ., 1972; DVM, Okla. State Univ., 1976. Veterinarian Renegar Animal Hosp., McAlester, Okla.; mem. Dist. 17 Okla. House of Representatives, 2007—. Mem.: Okla. Vet. Med. Assn., Okla. State Bd. Vet. Med. Examiners (former v.p.), Am. Vet. Med. Assn., McAlester Rotary Club (former pres.), Pitts. County Cattleman's Assn., McAlester South #96 Masonic Lodge. Democrat. Baptist. Address: 1550 S Main Mcalester OK 74501 Office: Okla House of Representatives 2300 N Lincoln Blvd Rm 504 Oklahoma City OK 73105 Office Phone: 405-557-7381. E-mail: brian.renegar@okhouse.gov.

RENKA, ROBERT JOSEPH, computer science educator, consultant; b. Summit, NJ, Dec. 28, 1947; s. John and Elizabeth (Pierce) R. BA in Computer Sci., BS in Math., U. Tex., 1976, MA in Math., 1979, PhD in Computer Sci., 1981. Numerical analyst Oak Ridge (Tenn.) Nat. Lab., 1981-84; asst. prof. computer sci. U. North Tex., Denton, 1984-89, assoc. prof. computer sci., 1989-99, prof. computer sci., 1999—. Cons. in field. Contbr. articles to profl. jours. With USN, 1967-69, Vietnam. Rsch. grantee U. North Tex., 1984-89, NSF, 1990-93, Nat. Security Agy., 1999—. Mem. Assn. for Computing Machinery (algorithms editor 1988-94, editor-in-chief 1989-94), Soc. Indsl. and Applied Math. Avocations: racquetball, rock climbing. Home: 1700 Kendolph Dr Denton TX 76205-6931 Office: U North Tex Dept Computer Sci and Engring PO Box 311366 Denton TX 76203-1366 Home Phone: 940-566-5487; Office Phone: 940-565-2767.

RENNER, GLENN DELMAR, retired agricultural products executive; b. Greeneville, Tenn., Nov. 18, 1925; s. Charles Dana and Lula Lucille (Hilton) R.; m. Gladys June Brooks, June 30, 1945; children: Glenna June, Joan Phyllis. BA, Tusculum Coll., 1948; MS, U. Tenn., 1950. Sales trainee Parks Belk Co., Greeneville, 1946—47; tchr., coach Greene County Schs., Greeneville, 1947—48; tchr. City of Greeneville Schs., 1950—54; salesman personal ins. co., Greeneville, 1954—76; real estate owner, pres. Brook Glen Farm Supply, Inc., Greeneville, 1976—98, ret., 1998; farmer, 1998—. Rep. Tenn. Legis., Greeneville, 1965-66; elected commr. Greene County, 1990, 94; participant People to People tour, Russia, Germany, Poland, Austria, Belgium, Switzerland, 1966. Mem. Greeneville Bd. Realtors (bd. dirs., pres. 1964, 71), Greeneville C. of C. (pres. 1986), Kiwanis (pres. Greeneville chpt. 1989—), Shriners (v.p. 1989, pres. 1991). Republican. Methodist. Achievements include 23 day tour sanctioned by USA, Austria, Belgium, Switzerland. Avocation: hunting. Home: 104 Reed Ave Greeneville TN 37743-4529

RENNINGER, RICHARD L., food service executive; Grad. in Economics, Harvard U. Various positions, real estate rep., asst. v.p., dir., Franchise Devel., v.p., dir., Real Estate & v.p., constrn. Waffle House, Inc., 1992—2002; v.p., Real Estate RARE Hospitality, 2002—05; sr. v.p., Real Estate & Devel. OSI Restaurant Partners, LLC, 2005—08, exec. v.p., chief devel. officer, 2008—. Office: OSI Restaurant Partners LLC 2202 N West Shore Blvd Ste 500 Tampa FL 33607 Office Phone: 813-282-1225. Business E-Mail: rrenninger@osirestaurantpartners.com.

RENO, JANET, former United States Attorney General; b. Miami, Fla., July 21, 1938; d. Henry Olaf & Jane Wallace (Wood) R. AB in Chemistry, Cornell U., 1960; LL.B., Harvard U., 1963. Bar: Fla. 1963. Assoc. Brigham & Brigham, 1963-67; ptnr. Lewis & Reno, 1967-71; staff dir. Fla. House Judiciary Com., Tallahassee, 1971-72; cons. Fla. Senate Criminal Justice Com. for Revision Florida's Criminal Code, spring 1973; adminstrv. asst. state atty. 11th Jud. Circuit Fla., Miami, 1973-76, state atty., 1978-93; ptnr. Steel Hector & Davis, Miami, 1976-78; atty. gen. US Dept. Justice, Washington, 1993-2001. Mem. jud. nominating commn. 11th Jud. Circuit Fla., 1976-78; chmn. Fla. Governor's Council for Prosecution Organized Crime, 1979-80; bd. dirs. The Innocence Project, 2004-10, dir. emeritus, 2010- Exec. prodr.: (albums) Song of America, 2007. Recipient Women First award YWCA, 1993, Harvard Law Sch. Assn. award, 2001, Coun. on Litigation Management's Professionalism award, 2008; named to The Nat. Women's Hall of Fame, 2000. Mem. ABA (Inst. Jud. Adminstrn. Juvenile Justice Standards Commn. 1973-76), American Law Inst., American Judicature Soc. (Herbert Harley award 1981, Justice award, 2009), Dade County Bar Assn., Fla. Prosecuting Attorney's Assn. (pres. 1984-86). Democrat.*

RENUART, RONALD JOSEPH, state legislator, osteopath; b. Coral Gables, Fla., Jan. 5, 1964; s. Gerald Joseph and Maureen Roberta (Geller) R.; m. Jacqueline Rose Garcia, Dec. 26, 1987; children: Jennifer Lynn, Scarlett Rose, Ronald Joseph Jr. AA, U. Fla., 1984, BS, 1986; DO, Southeastern U. Health Scis., 1990. Diplomate Am. Bd. Internal Medicine. Phlebotomist Alachua Gen. Hosp., Gainesville, Fla., 1983-86; emergency med. technician Alachua County EMS, Gainesville, 1985-86; firefighter/EMT Micanopy Fire Dept., Fla., 1985-86; emergency med. technician Atlantic Ambulance, Ft. Lauderdale, Fla., 1986; intern in osteopath Met. Gov. Hosp., Pinellas Park, Fla., 1990-91; resident in internal medicine U. Fla., Jacksonville, 1991-94; internist Lynch, Vetere & Renuart, Jacksonville, 1994-96, Bapt./St. Vincents Primary Care Network, 1996-2000, Bapt. Primary Care, 2000—; chief of dept. medicine Bapt. Med. Ctr. Beaches, Jacksonville Beach, Fla., 1998—2001, chief of staff, 2004—05; mem. Dist. 18 Fla. House of Reps., Tallahassee, 2008—, mem. health and family svcs. policy coun., health care regulation policy com., mil. and local affairs policy com., preK-12 appropriations com. Asst. med. dir. Fleet Landing Health Ctr., Atlantic Beach, 1994-2000. Co-editor, co-author: Directory of Florida Rural Practice Sites for Health Care Professionals, 1989. Mem. Rep. Nat. Com., 2001—. Lt. col. Fla. Army Nat. Guard, 1990—. Recipient Eagle Scout Boy Scouts of Am., 1977, Fla. Meritorious Svc. ribbon State of Fla., 1992, Army Achievement medal, 1999. Mem. KC, VFW, Fla. Med. Assn., Am. Osteopathic Assn. (del. 2001-08), Fla. Osteopathic Med.

Assn. (exec. bd. mem. 2004-09, v.p. 2008-09, Physician of Yr. 2006), Gator Boosters, U. Fla. Nat. Alumni Assn. (charter life mem.), Ponte Vedra Beach Rotary, Kappa Alpha. Republican. Roman Catholic. Office: 50 A1A North Ste 105 Ponte Vedra Beach FL 32082-1344 also: 317 House Office Bldg 402 S Monroe St Tallahassee FL 32399-1300 Office Phone: 904-270-2550, 850-488-0001.

RENZI, ANTHONY, mortgage company executive; BBA, Holy Family U., Phila., Pa.; MBA in Fin., Phila. U. COO Residential Capital, LLC (known as Res Cap); various exec. positions, exec. v.p., sr. v.p., client branded solutions, v.p., loan adminstrn. and sr. loan counselor GMAC Mortgage, COO, Residential Fin. Group, 2006—08, pres., 2008; exec. v.p., single-family portfolio mgmt. Freddie Mac - Federal Home Loan Mortgage Corp., 2010—. Office: Freddie Mac 8200 Jones Branch Dr Mc Lean VA 22102 Office Phone: 703-903-2000. Office Fax: 703-903-4045. Business E-Mail: Anthony_Renzi@freddiemac.com.

REPHAN, JACK, lawyer; b. Little Rock, Mar. 16, 1932; s. Henry and Mildred (Frank) R.; m. Arlene Clark, June 23, 1957; children: Amy Carol, James Clark. BS in Commerce, 1954; LLB, U. Va., 1959. Bar: Va. 1959, D.C. 1961. Assoc. Kanter & Kanter, Norfolk, Va., 1959-60; law clk. to Judge Sam E. Whitaker, U.S. Ct. Claims, Washington, 1960-62; assoc. Pierson, Ball & Dowd, Washington, 1962-64; ptnr. Danzansky, Dickey, Tydings, Quint & Gordon, Washington, 1964-77; mem. Braude, Margulies, Sacks & Rephan, Washington, 1977-87; ptnr. Porter, Wright, Morris & Arthur, Washington, 1987-88, Sadur, Pelland & Rubinstein, Washington, 1988-93; counsel Hofheimer Nusbaum P.C., Norfolk, Va., 1993-00; principal Rephan Lassiter PLC, Norfolk, 2001—07; shareholder Pender and Coward, P.C., Virginia Beach, 2007—. Mem. Nat. Panel Arbitrators Am. Arbitration Assn., Nat. Panel Mediators Am. Arbitration Assn., FINRA Bd. Arbitrators; lectr. joint com. continuing legal edn. State Bar Va. Contbr. articles to legal jours. Pres. Patrick Henry PTA, Alexandria, Va., 1968-69, Linkhorn Bay Condominium Assn., 2000—02; treas. John Adams Mid. Sch. PTA, Alexandria, 1970-71; pres. Seminary Ridge Citizens Assn., 1976-77; Dem. candidate for Alexandria City Com., 1969. 1st lt. AUS, 1955-57. Mem. ABA (chmn. subcom. on procurement of jud. remedies pub. contract sect. 1973-74), Va. Bar Assn. (govt. sect. constrn. law 1979-81, 99—, vice chmn. 1980-81, 2006-07, chmn. 1981-82, 2007—08), DC Bar Assn., Assoc. Gen. Contractors, Hampton Roads Utility and Heavy Contractors Assn. (gen. counsel), Kiwanis (pres. Landmark Club 1969). Jewish. Home: 1276 Laskin Rd Ste 402 Virginia Beach VA 23451-5272 Office: Pender & Coward PC 222 Central Park Ave Town Ctr Ste 400 Virginia Beach VA 23462 Home Phone: 757-491-5599.

REPPUCCI, NICHOLAS DICKON, psychologist, educator; b. Boston, May 1, 1941; s. Nicholas Ralph and Bertha Elizabeth (Williams) R.; m. Christine Marlow Onufrock, Sept. 10, 1967; children: Nicholas Jason, Jonathan Dickon, Anna Jin Marlow Chapman. BA with honors, U. N.C., 1962; MA, Harvard U., 1964, PhD, 1968. Lectr., rsch. assoc. Harvard U., Cambridge, Mass., 1967-68; from asst. prof. to assoc prof. Yale U., New Haven, 1968-76; prof. psychology U. Va., Charlottesville, 1976—, dir. cmty. psychology tng. program, 1976—, dir. grad. studies in psychology, 1984-95, 97-98. Originator biennial conf. on community rsch. and action, 1986. Author: (with J. Haugaard) Sexual Abuse of Children, 1988; (with P. Britner and J. Woolard) Preventing Child Abuse and Neglect Through Parent Education, 1997; editor: (with J. Haugaard) Prevention in Community Mental Health Practice; (with E. Mulvey, L. Weithorn and J. Monahan) Mental Health, Law and Children, 1984; assoc. editor Law and Human Behavior, 1986-96, mem. editl. bd., 1996-2005; mem. editl. bd. Am. Jour. Cmty. Psychology, 1974-83, 88-91, New Psychology & Pub. Policy, 2008-; contbr. articles to profl. jours., chpts. in books. Adv. bd. on prevention Va. Dept. Mental Health, Mental Retardation and Substance Abuse Svcs., Richmond, 1986-92. Recipient Disting. Scholar in psychology award Va. Assn. Social Sci., 1991, Outstanding Psychology Tchg. award, U. Va., 2005, Mentoring and Tchg. award Am. Psychology and Law Soc., 2007. Fellow APA (chmn. task force on pub. policy 1980-84), Am. Psychol. Soc., Soc. for Cmty. Rsch. and Action (pres. 1986, Disting. Contbn. award in theory and rsch. 1998, Inaugural award for ednl. mentoring 1999), Phi Beta Kappa. Office: U Va Dept Psychology PO Box 400400 Charlottesville VA 22904-4400 Office Phone: 434-924-0662. E-mail: ndr@virginia.edu.

RESIDANTE, EL (RENÉ PÉREZ), singer, composer; b. Hato Rey, PR, Feb. 23, 1978; Co-founder & lead singer Calle 13; signed to White Lion records. Singer: (albums) Calle 13, 2005 (Latin Grammy award for Best Urban Music Album, 2006), Residante O Visitante, 2007 (Best Urban Music album, Latin Grammy Awards, 2007, Grammy award, Best Latin Urban Album, 2008), Los de Atrás Vienen Conmigo, 2008, (songs) Atrévete Te, Te!, 2005 (Latin Grammy award for Best Short Form Music Video, 2006), (with Nelly Furtado) No Hay Igual, 2006, Pal Norte, 2007 (Best Urban song, Latin Grammy Awards, 2007). Recipient Best New Artist award, Best Urban Album & Best Short Music Video, Latin Grammy Awards, 2006. Office: White Lion Records Inc Urb Ocean Park 2072 Cacique Santurce PR 00911-1514

RESMAN-TARGOFF, BETH HOLLY, pharmacist, educator; d. Norman M. and Rowena Resman; m. Ira N. Targoff, June 14, 1981; 1 child, Deborah Judith Targoff. BS in Pharmacy, SUNY, Buffalo, 1973, PharmD, 1976. Registered pharmacist NY, 1974, Okla., 1991. Clin. coord., asst. dir. pharmacy The Buffalo Gen. Hosp., 1976—81; clin. instr. SUNY, 1976—81; clin. prof. U. Okla., Oklahoma City, 1981—. Mem. adv. bd. Annals Pharmacotherapy, 1989—. Contbr. chapters to books. Fellow: Am. Coll. Clin. Pharmacy; mem.: Okla. Soc. Health-Sys. Pharmacists (Pharmacist of Yr. 2011), Am. Assn. Colls. Pharmacy, Am. Pharmacists Assn., Phi Kappa Phi, Rho Chi (region VI councilor 2008—12, Outstanding Faculty Mem., U. Okla. Chpt. 1992—2006, 2008—11). Avocations: travel, photography. Office: University Okla Coll Pharm 1122 NE 13th St Ste 4412 Oklahoma City OK 73117-1039

RESNICK, HEIDI, psychologist, educator; d. Nancy Karasov and Harvey Resnick. PhD, Ind. U., Bloomington, 1987. Cert. clin. psychologist SC, 1989. Prof. Nat. Crime Victims Rsch. and Treatment Ctr., Charleston, SC, 1988—. Assoc. editor Jour. Traumatic Stress, 1997—2005. Contbr. articles to profl. jours. Sec., bd. mem. PAR, Charleston, SC, 1989—2007. Grantee, Ctrs. Disease Ctrl. Prevention, Nat. Inst. Drug Abuse, Nat. Inst. Mental Health.

RESNICK, IRVEN MICHAEL, philosophy educator; b. Rochester, NY, Nov. 22, 1952; m. Elizabeth Anne Scofield, May 28, 1989; children: Austin Scofield, Matthew Scofield, Ariel Resnick. BA, Tulane U., 1974; MA, Cath. U. Am., 1980; PhD, U. Va., 1983. Asst. prof. La. State U., Baton Rouge, 1987-90; prof. Dept. Philosophy and Religion U. Tenn., Chattanooga, 1990—. Chair of excellence in Judaic studies; sr. assoc. Oxford Ctr. for Hebrew and Jewish Studies, 2003—. Author: Divine Power and Possibility in St. Peter Damian's De Divina Omnipotentia, 1992, Two Theological Treatises of Odo of Tournai, 1994; co-author, translator: Albertus Magnus On Animals, 1999, An Annotated Bibliography of Albert the Great (1900-2000), 2004, The Letters of Peter Damian, 121-150, 2004, The Letters of Peter Damian, 151-180, 2005, Petrus Alfonsi's Dialogue against the Jews, 2006, Albert the Great's Questions Concerning Aristotle's 'On Animals', 2008, Albert the Great's On the Causes of the Properties of the Elements, 2010, Marks of Distinction: Christian Perceptions of Jews in the High Middle Ages, 2012; editor: A Companion to Albert the Great. Theology, Philosophy, and the Sciences, 2012; translator: Peter the Venerable's Against the Inveterate Obduracy of the Jews, 2013. Jerusalem Trust fellow Oxford Ctr. for Hebrew Std., Yarnton, Eng., 1995, corr. fellow Ingeborg Rennert Ctr., Bar-Ilan U., Israel, 1996, C.G. Found. Jerusalem Project, Bar-Ilan U., 1996; named disting. vis. fellow Queen Mary, U. London, 2006. Mem.: Medieval Acad. Am., Assn. for Jewish Studies, Soc. for Medieval and Renaissance Philosophy, Oxford Ctr. for Hebrew and Jewish Studies (sr.). Office: U Tenn Chattanooga 615 Mccallie Ave Chattanooga TN 37403-2504 Home: 711 Battery Pl Chattanooga TN 37403 Office Phone: 423-425-4446. Office Fax: 423-425-4153. Business E-Mail: Irven-Resnick@utc.edu.

RESO, ANTHONY, geologist, educator, earth resources economist; b. London, Eng., Aug. 10, 1931; arrived in US, 1940, naturalized, 1952; AB, Columbia Coll., 1954; MA, Columbia U., 1955; postgrad., U. Cin., 1956—57; PhD, Rice U., 1960; postgrad., Grad. Sch. Bus. U. Houston, 1964—68. Instr. geology Queens Coll., Flushing, NY, 1954; geologist Atlantic Richfield Corp., Midland, Tex., 1955—56; asst. prof. geology and curator invertebrate paleontology Beneski Mus. (formerly Pratt Mus.), Amherst Coll., Mass., 1959—62; staff rsch. geologist Tenneco Oil Co., Houston, 1962—86; mgr. geol. Peak Prodn. Co., Houston, 1986—, v.p., 1988—, bd. dirs., 2000—. Cons. in geol. rsch. Tenn. Gas and Oil Co., 1960—61; lectr. U. Houston, 1962—65; vis. prof. Rice U., 1980; mem. bd. advisers Gulf Univs. Rsch. Corp., Galveston, Tex., 1967—75, chmn., 1968—69. Contbr. articles to profl. jours. Recipient Honor award, 2008; named to Hall of Fame, Varsity Basketball Team, Columbia U., 1950—51; Grantee Rsch., Eastman Fund, 1962, NSF fellow, 1958—59. Fellow: AAAS, Geol. Soc. Am. (com. investments 1984—95, chmn. 1985—92, budget com. 1993—95, found. trustee 1999—2004, Rsch. grantee 1958, Disting. Svc. award 1996); mem.: English-Speaking Union US (dir. Houston br. 1978—, v.p. 1982—88, pres. 1997—98), Houston Geol. Soc. (v.p. 1973—75, pres. 1975—76, chmn. constn. revision com. 1981, Disting. Svc. award 1985), Paleontol. Rsch. Instn., Am. Assn. Petroleum Geologists (life; com. convs. 1977—83, gen. chmn. nat. conv. 1979, chmn. 1980—83, com. investments 1982—88, chmn. com. group ins. 1986—88, treas. 1986—88, found. trustee assoc. 1991, Rsch. grantee 1958, 1959, Disting. Svc. award 1985), SEPM Soc. for Sedimentary Geology (com. investments 1990—2004, chmn. 1992—95, treas. SEPM Found. 1997—2003, Disting. Svc. award 2003), Paleontol. Soc., Varsity C Club, Beta Theta Pi, Sigma Gamma Epsilon, Sigma Xi. Episcopalian. Home: 1805 Brun St Houston TX 77019-5712 Office: care Peak Prodn Co PO Box 130785 Houston TX 77219-0785 Personal E-mail: aresogeo@swbell.net.

RESOR, BILL, information technology executive; Mng. ptnr. SRA Internat. Office: SRA International 4300 Fair Lakes Ct Fairfax VA 22033 Office Phone: 703-803-1500. Office Fax: 703-803-1509. Business E-Mail: bill_resor@sra.com.

RESTREPO, WILLIAM J., offshore drilling company executive; BA in Economics, Cornell U., 1980; BS in Civil Engring., U. Miami, 1982; MBA, Cornell U. Johnson Graduate Sch. Mgmt., 1985. Internal auditor Schlumberger Ltd., 1985—87, finance dir., 1987—90, corporate asst. treas. Latin America/Southern Europe, 1990—93, region contr. pressure pumping Latin America, 1993—95, divsn. gen. mgr. pressure pumping Argentina/Bolivia, 1996—98, v.p. finance pressure pumping & directional drilling, 1998—2000, region gen. mgr. Continental Europe, 2000—02, region gen. mgr. Arabian Gulf, 2002—03, corporate treas. Western Hemisphere, 2003—04, v.p. finance North & South America, 2004—05; exec. v.p., CFO, sec. Seitel, Inc., 2005—09; sr. v.p., CFO, treas. Smith International, Inc., 2009—10; CFO Pacific Drilling Services, Inc., Houston, 2011—. Bd. dirs. Probe, Inc., 2008—. Office: Pacific Drilling Services Inc 3050 Post Oak Blvd Ste 1500 Houston TX 77056 Office Phone: 713-334-6662. Office Fax: 713-583-5777.

RETSCH-BOGART, GEORGE Z., pediatric pulmonologist, surgeon; b. 1952; MD, U. Cin., 1978. Diplomate Am. Bd. Pediat., cert. in Pediat. Pulmonology. Resident pediat. U. Minn., Mpls., 1978—81; fellowship pediat. pulmonary U. NC Sch. Medicine, Chapel Hill, 1986—89, assoc. prof. divsn. pediat. pulmonology, dir. Cystic Fibrosis Ctr.; clin. staff NC Children's Hosp. Contbr. articles to profl. jours. Mem.: Cystic Fibrosis Found., Am. Acad. Pediat. Achievements include research in complex airway disorders in children. Mailing: UNC Dept Pediat, CB #7217 130 Mason Farm Rd Chapel Hill NC 27516 Office Phone: 919-966-4131. Office Fax: 919-966-6049.

RETTIG, DWIGHT WILLIAM, lawyer; b. July 6, 1960; BA, Ind. U., 1982; JD, U. Houston, 1986, MBA, 1993. Bar: Tex. 1986. Chief legal officer NATCO Group, Inc., 1997—98; gen. counsel Distbn. Svcs. Group National Oilwell Varco, Inc., Houston, 1998—99, v.p., gen. counsel, 1999—. Mem.: Houston Bar Assn., ABA, State Bar Tex. (mem. Corp., Internat., Banking and Bus. Law Sect.). Office: National Oilwell Varco 10000 Richmond Ave Houston TX 77042 Office Phone: 713-346-7550. E-mail: dwight.rettig@natoil.com.*

RETTIG, JAMES R., university librarian, library association executive; b. Chgo., Nov. 11, 1950; m. Monica Rettig; children: Chris, Tony, Katie. BA cum laude, Marquette U., 1972, MA, 1974; MLS, U. Wis., Madison, 1975. Asst. reference libr. Murray State U. Libr., Ky., 1976—77, head reference libr. Ky., 1977—78; reference libr. Roesch Libr., U. Dayton, Ohio, 1978—83; head reference libr. U. Ill., Chgo., 1983—87; asst. dean univ. librs. for reference & info. svcs. Earl Gregg Swem Libr., Coll. William & Mary, Williamsburg, Va., 1988—98; univ. libr. Boatwright Meml. Libr., U. Richmond, Va., 1998—. Mem. reference svcs. adv. com. Online Computer Libr. Ctr. (OCLC), 1992—95. Author: (columns) Current Reference Books, for Wilson Libr. Bull., Rettig on Reference; editor: (book) Distinguished Classics of Reference Publishing, 1992. Recipient Info. Authorship award, Info. Access Corp., 1997, Faculty Recognition award, Earl Gregg Swem Libr., 1998, Richard A. Mateer Quality of Life award, U. Richmond Student Govt., 2005, Disting. Alumnus award, U. Wis.-Madison Sch. Libr. & Info. Studies, 2006; sr. fellow, UCLA Dept. Info. Studies, 2001. Mem.: ALA (chair pub. com. 1997—99, chair orgn. com. 2000—03, exec. bd. 2003—06, pres. elect 2007—08, pres. 2008—, G.K. Hall award for Libr. Literature 1993), Assn. Coll. Rsch. Librs. (chair news editl. bd. 1986—88), Reference & User Svcs. Assn. (past pres., Mudge Citation 1988, Louis Shores-Oryx Press award 1995). Office: Univ Libr Boatwright Meml Libr U Richmond Richmond VA 23173 Office Phone: 804-289-8456. Office Fax: 804-289-8757. E-mail: jrettig@richmond.edu.

RETTIG, PHILIP J., pediatrician, adolescent medicine, educator; MD, Harvard U., 1972. Diplomate Am. Bd. Pediatrics, 1978, Am. Bd. Pediatrics-infectious disease, 2005, Am. Bd. Pediatrics-adolescent medicine, 2009. Resident pediat. Yale-New Haven Hosp., New Haven, 1973—74, Children's Hosp. Med. Ctr., Boston, 1974—75; fellow pediatric infectious disease Univ. Tex. Southwestern Med. Ctr.; prof. pediat. Univ. Okla. Coll. of Medicine; physician Children's Hosp. Okla. Univ. Med. Ctr. Office: Oklahoma University Medical Center Children's Physicians Bldg 1200 N Phillips Ave 7th Fl Ste 7500 Oklahoma City OK 73104 Office Phone: 405-271-6208.

RETTIG, TERRY, veterinarian, construction executive; b. Houston, Jan. 30, 1947; s. William E. and Rose (Munves) R.; m. Helen Rettig, Mar. 12, 1996; 1 child, Bill; children from previous marriage: Michael Thomas, Jennifer Suzanne. BS in Zoology, Duke U., 1969, MAT in Sci., 1970; DVM, U. Ga., 1975; MBA honors in Constrn. Mgmt., Keller Grad. Sch., 2003. Resident veterinarian, mgr. animal health Wildlife Preserve, Largo, Md., 1975—76; wildlife veterinarian dept. environ. conservation State of N.Y., Delmar, 1976—77; owner Atlanta Animal Hosp., 1976—2001; CEO Quality Home Builders Atlanta Svcs., P.C., 1977—2002; COO, pres. Am. Dream Constrn., Inc., Alpharetta, Ga., 2002—; prof. Brown Mackie Coll., Atlanta, 2007—, Keller DeVry U., 2007—, St. Leo U., 2008—. Sec., dir. Atlanta Pet Supply, Inc., 1983-89; cons. Six Flags Over Ga., Yellow River Game Ranch, Stone Mountain Park Animal Forest, Atlanta Zoo. Author: (with Murray Fowler) Zoo and Wild Animal Medicine (Aardvark award 1978), 1978, 2d edit., 1986 (Order of Kukukifuku award 1986); contbr. articles to profl. jours. Del. Dekalb County Republican Conv., 1983; mem. Roswell United Meth. Ch., Boy Scouts Am., 1954—, mem. troop coun., asst. scoutmaster, scout master, Philmont expedition leader, 1988, 89. Spl. scholar Cambridge U. Coll. Vet. Medicine, 1973-74, Honor Medal with Crossed Palms, 1995. Mem.: AVMA, Sys. Homebuilders Assn. Ga. (Builder of Yr. award 2004), Greater Atlanta Homebuilders Assn., Nat. Assn. Homebuilders, Am. Buffalo Assn., Soc. Aquatic Vet. Medicine, Internat. Wildlife Assn., Am. Animal Hosp. Assn., Am. Assn. Avian Vets., Am. Fedn. Aviculturists, Atlanta Zool. Soc., Nat. Wildlife Assn., Nat. Wildlife Health Found., Am. Assn. Zool. Parks and Aquaria, Am. Assn. Zoo Vets., Acad. Vet. Medicine, Dekalb Vet. Soc., Greater Atlanta Vet. Med. Assn., Ga. Vet. Med. Assn., Cousteau Soc. Methodist. Office: Am Dream Constrn Inc 5005 Kimball Bridge Rd Alpharetta GA 30005-5649 Office Phone: 770-664-5883. Personal E-mail: terryrettig@comcast.net.

RETZ, WILLIAM ANDREW, consultant, retired naval officer; b. Blauvelt, NY, June 3, 1940; s. Andrew Macmillan and Katherine R.; m. Julia Irene, Sept. 23, 1989; children: Andrew, Gregory, Mark, Alyse Reavis, Mark Rogers. Student, Tex. A&M U., Coll. Sta., 1957; BS in Mech. Engring., U. N.Mex., Albuquerque, 1963; MS, George Wash. U., Washington, DC, 1971; grad., Naval War Coll., Newport, RI, 1972. Commd. ensign USN, 1963, advanced through grades to rear adm., 1991, patrol officer river div. 511 Vietnam, 1968-69, flag sec. to comdr. Amphibious Group Two Norfolk, Va., 1972-74, exec. officer USS Ainsworth, 1974-76, commanding officer USS Stump, 1980-82, commodore Destroyer Squadron 22, 1985-87, dep. for ops. US Ctrl. Command Tampa, Fla., 1987—90; comdr. Naval Base Pearl Harbor, 1992-94, Naval Surface Group Mid. Pacific, 1992-94; commanded and closed Naval Base Phila., 1994-95; ret. USN, 1995; v.p. govt. svcs. Aramark Corp., Phila., 1996-99; ind. cons., 1999; CEO Nofire Techs., Inc., 2000—03; exec. dir. Am. Competitiveness Inst., Phila., 2003—05; ind. cons. Retz & Assoc., 2005—; with Def. Solutions, Washington, 2005—. Active Episcopal Ch.; bd. dirs. Indus, Denison Devel. Found., St. Luke's Sch.; adv. bd. U. Tex., Dallas; chmn. Texoma Tech. Enterprise Coun., Denison, Tex. Decorated Disting. Svc. medal, Legion of Merit, Def. Disting. Svc. medal, Meritorious Svc. medal, Bronze Star, Purple Heart. Mem. Surface Navy Assn., Nat. Def. Indsl. Assn. (bd. dirs.). Avocations: gardening, sailing. Personal E-mail: retzw@comcast.net.

REUSSER, CURTIS C., aerospace and defense manufacturing company executive; B in Indsl. Engring., U. Wash., 1983. Cert. bus. mgmt., U. San Diego. Various engring. positions General Dynamics Corp., Heath Tecna, Inc.; mgr., engring. Goodrich Corp., 1988, gen. mgr. England, 1996—99, v.p., gen. mgr., product & process definition, aerostructures divn., 1999—2002, pres., aerostructures divsn., 2002—07, segment pres., electronic sys., 2007—; dir., aero engine controls Rolls-Royce plc., 2009—. Office: Goodrich Corp Four Coliseum Ctr 2730 W Tyvola Rd Charlotte NC 28217-4578 Office Phone: 704-423-7000. Office Fax: 704-423-7002. Business E-Mail: curtis.reusser@goodrich.com.

REUTER, FRANK THEODORE, historian, educator; b. Kankakee, Ill., Mar. 18, 1926; s. Frank Theodore and Evelyn Marie (Scott) R.; m. Kathleen Ann Pester, June 16, 1951; children: Mark, Stephen, Christopher, Ann, Katherine. BS, U. Ill., 1950, MA, 1959, PhD, 1960. Instr. West Liberty (W. Va.) State Coll., 1960-62; asst. prof. Texas Christian U., Fort Worth, 1962-66, assoc. prof., 1966-71; prof. history Tex. Christian U., 1971-92, dean Grad. Sch., 1970-75, chmn. dept. history, 1980-83, prof. emeritus, 1992—. Vis. prof. Pázmány Péter Cath. U., Budapest, Hungary, 1999. Author: West Liberty State College: The First 125 Years, 1963, Catholic Influence on American Colonial Policies, 1898-1904, 1967, Trials and Triumphs: George Washington's Foreign Policy, 1983; co-author: Injured Honor: The Chesapeake-Leopard Affair, 1996. Served with USNR, 1944-46. U. Durham Rsch. fellow, 1991. Mem. Orgn. Am. Historians, Am. Hist. Assn., Soc. Historians Early Republic, Soc. Historians Am. Fgn. Relations, Phi Beta Kappa, Phi Alpha Theta. Roman Catholic. Home: 3617 Winifred Dr Fort Worth TX 76133-2126 Office: Tex Christian U Dept History Fort Worth TX 76129-0001 Office Phone: 817-257-7288. E-mail: rfkreuter@sbcglobal.net.

REVELEY, TAYLOR (WALTER TAYLOR REVELEY III), academic administrator, former dean, law educator; b. Churchville, Va., Jan. 6, 1943; s. Walter Taylor and Marie (Eason) R.; m. Helen Bond, Dec. 18, 1971; children: Walter Taylor IV, George Everett Bond, Nelson Martin Eason, Helen Lanier. AB, Princeton U., 1965; JD, U. Va., 1968. Bar: Va. 1970, D.C. 1976. Asst. prof. law U. Ala., 1968-69; law clk. to Justice Brennan US Supreme Ct., Washington, 1969-70; fellow Woodrow Wilson Internat. Ctr. for Scholars, 1972-73; internat. affairs fellow Coun. on Fgn. Rels., NYC, 1972-73; assoc. Hunton & Williams, Richmond, Va., 1970-76, ptnr., 1976-98, mng. ptnr., 1982-91, cons., 1998—2008; dean William & Mary Sch. Law, 1998—2008, law prof.; interim pres. Coll. William Mary, 2008, pres., 2008—. Lectr. Coll. William and Mary Law Sch., 1978—80; cons. in field. Author: War Powers of the President and Congress: Who Holds the Arrows and Olive Branch, 1981; mem. editl. bd. Va. Law Rev., 1966-68; contbr. articles to profl. jours. Trustee Princeton U., 1986-90, 91-2001, Presbyn. Ch. (U.S.A.) Found., 1991-97, Va. Hist. Soc., 1991-96, 2003—, bd. chair, 2010-, Union Theol. Sem., 1992-2000, Andrew W. Mellon Found., 1994—, JSTOR, 1995—2008, Va. Mus. Fine Arts, 1995-2005, pres. 1996-99, St. Christopher's Sch., 1996-01, 2004—10, Carnegie Endowment for Internat. Peace, 1999—2011; bd. dirs. Fan Dist. Assn., Richmond, Inc., 1976-80, pres., 1979-80; bd. dirs. Richmond Symphony, 1980-92, pres., 1988-90, pres. symphony coun., 1994-99; bd. dirs. Presbyn. Outlook Found., 1985-2003, 2004-09, pres., 1992-95; bd. dirs. Va. Mus. Found., 1990-99; bd. dirs. New Covenant Trust Co., 1997-99, Va. Found. Humanities, 2001-2007. Mem. ABA, Va. Bar Assn.(assoc.), D.C. Bar Assn., Am. Bar Found., Va. Bar Found., Princeton Assn. Va. (bd. dirs. 1981—, pres. 1983-85), Va. State Bar (Edn. Lawyers sect. bd. govs. 1992—2008, chmn. 1992-95), Raven Soc., Phi Beta Kappa, Omicron Delta Kappa.

Home: 2314 Monument Ave Richmond VA 23220-2604 Office: College William & Mary Office of President PO Box 8795 Williamsburg VA 23187-8795 Office Phone: 757-221-7891. Business E-Mail: taylor@wm.edu.*

REVELLE, DONALD GENE, manufacturing and health care company executive, consultant; b. Cape Girardeau, Mo., July 16, 1930; s. Lewis W. and Dorothy R.; m. Jo M. Revelle, Aug. 1, 1954; children—Douglas, David, Daniel, Dianne BA, U. Mo., 1952; JD, U. Colo., 1957; grad., Harvard U. Bus. Sch., 1971. Dir. employee relations Westinghouse Corp., Pitts., 1957-65; asst. to v.p. Diebold Corp., 1966; v.p. human resources TRW Corp., Cleve., 1967-84; sr. v.p. human resources Black and Decker Co., Towson, Md., 1984-86; exec. v.p. corp. rels. Montefiore Acad. Med. Ctr., Bronx, 1987-98; pres., CEO Syzygy, Inc., 1998—. Univ. lectr.; cons. Duerba Ship, Blue Cross N.Y., Windsor Hosp., Salvation Army Contbr. articles to profl. jours. Mem. sch. bd. State of N.Y. Lt. USNR, 1952-54 Mem.: ABA (labor law com.), Human Resource Planning Soc., Fed. Bar Assn., Colo. Bar Assn., MBA Assn., Rotary. Methodist. Home and Office: Syzygy Inc 29903 Baywood Ln Wesley Chapel FL 33543-9744 Office Phone: 813-994-3403.

REVES, JOSEPH GERALD (JERRY REVES), anesthesiology educator, dean; b. Charleston, SC, Aug. 14, 1943; s. George Everett and Frances (Masterson) R.; m. Virginia Cathcart, Jan. 05, 1945; children: Virginia Masterson, Christine Frances, Elizabeth Cathcart. BA, Vanderbilt U., 1965; MD, Medical Coll. S.C., 1969; MS, U. Ala., Birmingham, 1973. Lic. anesthesiologist S.C., Ala., Md., N.C.; Diplomate Am. Coll. Anesthesiology, Am. Bd. Anesthesiology. Rsch. asst., dept. pharmacology Med. Coll. SC, 1965, 1966; intern U. Ala. Hosp. and Clinics, Birmingham, Ala., 1969-70, resident in anesthesiology, 1970-72; post-doctoral, dept. anesthesia and physiology U. Ala. Med. Sch., 1972; instr., dept anesthesiology U. Ala. Hosp. and Clinics, 1973; dept. tng. staff, anesthesiology Nat. Naval Med. Ctr., Bethesda, Md., 1973-75; clin. instr., dept. anesthesiology George Washington U. Sch. Med., Washington, 1973-75; assoc. prof., dept. anesthesiology U. Ala. Hosp. and Clinics, 1975-78; dir., div. anesthesiology rsch. U. Ala., 1977-84, prof. anesthesiology, 1978-84; clin. anesthesia coord. UAB Cardiac Transplant Program, Birmingham, 1982-84; prof. anesthesiology, dir. cardiothoracic anesthesia Duke U. Med. Ctr., Durham, NC, 1984-1991; dir. Duke Heart Ctr., Duke Med. Ctr., Durham, NC, 1987-97; interim chmn., dept. anesthesiology Duke U. Med. Ctr., 1990-91, prof. and chmn., dept. anesthesiology, 1991—2001; dean, v.p. for med. affairs Med. U. SC Coll. Medicine, Charleston, 2001—. Cons. Hoffman-LaRoche, Somatogen, Abbott/Oximetric. Contbr. to numerous profl. jours., refereed jours., chpts. in books, published scientific reviews, selected abstracts, editorials, films, audio visual presentations, letters, positions and background papers; author: Acute Revascularization of the Infracted Heart, 1987, Common Problems in Cardiac Anesthesia, 1987, Intravenous Anesthesia and Analgesia, 1988, Anesthesiology Clinics of North America, 1988, Anesthesia, 1990, International Anesthesiology Clinics, 1991; Cardiac Anesthesia, Privileges and Practice, 1994; editor: Anesthesia and Analgesia, 1984—, cardiovascular sect. editor 1991—; editorial bd. Society Cardiovascular Anesthesia Monograph Series (chmn. 1986-89), Current Opinion in Anaesthesia 1987—, American Antec Newsletter 1989—; co-editor in chief: Current Opinion in Anaesthesiology 1990—. Dir. Clairmont Ave Hist. Preservation Com. 1976-78; Am. Heart Assn. (Durham chpt. pres. 1988-90, com. mem. anesthesiology, radiology and surgery rsch. study com. 1988-91). Grantee NIH 1991—, Janssen Pharmaceutica 1991-93, Anaquest 1989-92, Diprivan Ednl. grant ICI Pharmaceuticals Group 1991-92. Fellow Am. Coll. Cardiology; mem. AMA, Durham County Medical Soc., Internat. Soc. on Oxygen Transport to Tissue, N.C. Soc. Anesthesiologist (edn. com. 1992—), N.C. State Medical Soc., Birmingham Vanderbilt Club (bd. dirs. 1975-80, 1st v.p. 1979, pres. 1980), Southern Med. Assn. (chmn. elect. anesthesiology sect. 1976-77, chmn. 1977-78, chmn. 1988-89), Southern Soc. Anesthesiologists (v.p. 1978-79, pres. elect 1979-80, pres. 1980-81), Soc. Cardiovascular Anesthesiologists (pres. 1979-80), Assn. Univ. Anesthetists (elected to mem. 1980), Assn. Cardiac Anesthesiologists (elected to mem. 1982, pres. 1990), Soc. for Neuroleptanalgesia (bd. dirs. 1988), U. Ala. Birmingham Nat. Alumni Soc. (dist. dir., bd. dirs. 1991-93), Internat. Anesthesia Rsch. Soc. (bd. Trustees 1992—), Am. Soc. Anesthesiologists (com. sub-specialty representation 1980—, subcommittee on clin. circulation 1992—, com. geriatric anesthesia 1992—), Sigma Xi, Alpha Omega Alpha. Achievements include research on effects of age on neurologic response to cardiopulmonary bypass; cerebral blood flow and metabolism during cardiac surgery; automated delivery system of intravenous anesthetic drugs; pathophysiology of cardiopulmonary bypass; redesign of medical education. Office: Med U SC PO Box 250617 96 Jonathan Lucas St Ste 601 Charleston SC 29425 Office Phone: 843-792-2842. Business E-Mail: revesj@musc.edu.

REXFORD, JOHN H., information technology company executive; BBA, MBA, Southern Meth. U. V.p. Citibank, Continental Ill. Corp.; sr. v.p. Affiliated Computer Svcs., Inc. (ACS), Dallas, 1996—2001; exec. v.p. Affiliated Computer Services, Inc. (ACS) (acquired by Xerox Corp.), Dallas, 2001—, CFO, bd. dirs., 2006—. Office: Affiliated Computer Services Inc 2828 N Haskell Dallas TX 75204 Office Phone: 214-841-6111. Business E-Mail: John.Rexford@acs-inc.com.

REYNOLDS, C. LEWIS, JR., materials scientist, educator; b. Roanoke, Va., Dec. 16, 1948; s. Claude Lewis and Lois Anne Reynolds; m. Judith Ann Grenko, May 11, 2002; children: Karen Marie, Brian Lewis, Kristin Marie. BS in Physics, Va. Mil. Inst., Lexington, 1970; MS in Materials Sci., U. Va., Charlottesville, 1972, PhD in Materials Sci., 1974. Sr. scientist U. Va., Charlottesville, 1974—75; rsch. assoc. physics U. Ill., Urbana, Ill., 1975—77; sr. project engr. Union Carbide Corp., Indpls., 1977—80; mem. tech. staff AT&T Bell Labs., Reading, Pa., 1980—88, disting. mem. tech. staff, 1988—92, AT&T/Lucent/Agere Bell Labs., Breinigsville, Pa., 1992—2002; rsch. prof. NC State U., Raleigh, 2003—, tchg. asst. prof., 2004—, tchg. assoc. prof., 2012, dir. Grad. Programs Nanoengring., 2013—. Contbr. more than 150 articles to profl. jours. Mem.: IEEE, Metall. Soc., Am. Assn. Physics Tchrs., Materials Rsch. Soc., Am. Phys. Soc., Sigma Xi. Independent. Methodist. Achievements include 8 patents in field. Avocations: reading, running, hiking. Office: NC State Univ Dept Materials Sci Engring 911 Partners Way Raleigh NC 27695-7907 Office Phone: 919-515-7622. Office Fax: 919-515-7724. Business E-Mail: lew_reynolds@ncsu.edu.

REYNOLDS, CATHERINE BRESCIA, entrepreneur, philanthropist; b. Jacksonville, Fla., Sept. 16, 1957; m. Timothy Dunlevy, 1984 (div. 1999); 1 child, Megan; m. Wayne Reynolds, 1999. BS in Economics, Vanderbilt U., Nashville, 1979; LHD (hon.), Willamette U., Salem, Oreg., 2006, Georgetown U., 2007, Morehouse Coll., Atlanta. Joined as comptr., now CEO & chair EduCap Inc., 1986—; founder, chair Servus Fin. Corp., 1986—2000; chair, CEO Catherine B. Reynolds Found., 2000—. Bd. dirs. CoStar Group, Inc., 2004—, Zenith Nat. Ins., 2004—; mem. US Sec. Edn.'s Commn. on Future of Higher Edn. Vice chair Am. Acad. Achievement, host chair, ann. Internat. Achievement Summit Budapest, Hungary, 1999—; bd. trustees Vanderbilt U., 2004—; chair bd. trustees Dance Theatre Harlem, NYC, 2005—. Recipient Spl. Achievement award in Edn. & Cultural Affairs, Nat. Italian-Am. Found., 2006, Woodrow Wilson award for Corp. Citizenship; named one of 50 Most Philanthropic Living Americans, BusinessWeek Mag., 2004, The 100 Most Powerful Women in DC, Washingtonian mag., 2009. Office: EduCap Inc PO Box 651210 Sterling VA 20165 Business E-Mail: contact@cbrf.org.

REYNOLDS, DOUGLAS R., history professor; b. Detroit, Oct. 2, 1944; s. Ira Hubert and Harriet Robertson Reynolds; m. Aizhen Sun, June 15, 2006; children: Sara Elizabeth Davis, Emily Kathryn; m. Carol Tyson (div. May 2006). PhD, Columbia U., NYC, 1976. Prof., dept. history Ga. State U., Atlanta, 1980—, dir., Asian Studies Ctr., 2006—10. Author: (book) East Meets East: Chinese Discover the Modern World - in Japan, 1854-98, 2013, China, 1898-1912: The Xinzheng Revolution and Japan, 1993, Chinese Edit., 1998, (book) 2nd edit., 2006; translator (editor): China, 1895-1912: State-Sponsored Reforms and China's Late-Qing Revolution, 1995; contbr. articles to numerous profl. jours. (Modern Sino-Japanese Rels. prize, 1988, 1991). Co-pres. US China Peoples Friendship Assn., Atlanta chpt., 2006—. Recipient Meml. prize, To-A Dobun Shoin Meml. Prize Com., Tokyo, 1996; Rsch. fellowship, Social Sci. Rsch. Coun., 1986—87, Luce Found., History Christianity China project, 1987—88. Mem.: World History Assn., Assn. Asian Studies. Achievements include pioneering scholarship on modern Japan-China cultural interactions, 1850-1912. Home: 613 Clairmont Cir Decatur GA 30033-5316 Office: Ga State Univ Dept History 34 Peachtree St Ste 2050 Atlanta GA 30302-4117*

REYNOLDS, GLENN HARLAN, law educator, blogger; b. Birmingham, Ala., Aug. 27, 1960; s. Charles Harlan Reynolds and Glenda Lorraine (Teal) Childress; m. Helen Smith; one child. BA, U. Tenn., 1982; JD, Yale U., 1985. Bar: Tenn. 1985, D.C. 1986. Law clk. U.S. Ct. Appeals, Nashville, 1985-86; assoc. Dewey, Ballantine, Bushby, Palmer & Wood, Washington, 1986-89; assoc. prof. law U. Tenn., Knoxville, 1989-96; Beauchamp Brogan Disting. prof. law U. Tenn. Coll. Law, Knoxville, Tenn., 1996—. Author: An Army of Davids:How Markets and Technology Empower Ordinary People to Beat Big Media, Big Government, Business and Society, 2006; co-author Outer Space: Problems of Law and Policy, 1989, 97, (with Peter W. Morgan) The Appearance of Impropriety: How the Ethics Wars Have Undermined American Government, Business and Society, 1997; supervising exec. editor, Pajamas Media; contbg. editor, TechCentralStation.com; maintains blog site, Instapundit.com.; co-founder, record prodr. (record co.) WonderDog Records; contbr. of articles to Popular Mechanics, Forbes, The Atlantic Monthly, New York Times, Washington Post, The Examiner, Washington Times, Los Angeles Times, and Wall Street Journal; written for TCSDaily.com, and MSNBC websites; writer of regular column, FoxNews website; host with wife (podcast) The Glenn & Helen Show, 2006-10. Recipient Outstanding Svc. award Space Cause, Wash., 1990, Harold C. Warner Outstanding Faculty award, Space Pioneer award by Nat. Space Soc., 1991, W. Allen Separk Outstanding Faculty Scholarship award, 1998; nominee WIRED mag. RAVE award, 2005; named one of Top 25 Web Celebs, Forbes mag. 2006, 2007. Mem. AAAS, Nat. Space Soc. (exec. chair legis. com. 1989-93, CEO 1994-95), Gov. Juvenile Justice Reform Commn., 1997-99, White House Adv. Panel on Space Policy). Avocation: music. Office: U Tennessee College of Law 1505 W Cumberland Ave Knoxville TN 37996-1810 Office Phone: 865-974-2521. Office Fax: 865-974-6595. Business E-Mail: reynolds@libra.law.utk.edu, greynold@utk.edu.

REYNOLDS, H. EUGENE (GENE REYNOLDS), state legislator; BA, MA, La. Tech U., Ruston. Ret. educator, La.; mem. Dist. 10 La. House of Reps., Baton Rogue, 2012—. Democrat. Office: 732 Main St Minden LA 71055 also: La House of Reps 900 N 3rd St Baton Rouge LA 70804 Business E-Mail: reynoldsg@legis.la.gov.

REYNOLDS, JIM, county official, former state legislator; b. Okla. City, Sept. 18, 1960; BA, So. Nazarene Univ. Mem. Dist. 43 Okla. State Senate, 2001—11; treas. Cleveland County, Okla., 2011—. Republican. Assembly Of God. Office: Cleveland County Treasurers Office 201 S Jones Ave Norman OK 73069 Office Phone: 405-366-0217. Office Fax: 405-366-0220. Business E-Mail: countytreasurer@okco14.org.

REYNOLDS, MIKE, state legislator; b. Quantico, Va., Mar. 19, 1951; s. Jack D. and Earlene Lightfoot Reynolds; m. Nancy Smith Reynolds; children: Sarah, Daniel, David. BS, Univ. Okla. Ordained deacon; pres. New Creations Software, Inc., Vote Inc.; info. sys. dir. Vision America; computer cons.; mem. Dist. 91 Okla. House of Representatives, 2003—. Served USAF. Republican. Baptist. Office: 2300 N Lincoln Blvd Rm 301-B Oklahoma City OK 73105-4808 Mailing: 2609 S W 107th Oklahoma City OK 73170 Office Phone: 405-557-7337, 405-691-1650, 405-748-0323. Business E-Mail: mikereynolds@okhouse.gov.

REYNOLDS, PATRICK A., diversified financial services company executive; b. Lebanon, Tenn., 1949; BS in Bus. Adminstrn., Tenn. Technol. U, 1971; MBA, Austin Peay State U., Clarksville, Tenn., 1982. Fin. cons. Merrill Lynch & Co., Inc., 1986—91; dir. benefits Total Sys. Svcs., Inc.; various positions including group v.p., dir. benefits & human resources affiliate bank rels. Synovus Fin. Corp.; v.p., dir. investor rels. Synovus Financial Corp., 1995—. Office: Synovus Financial Corp 1111 Bay Ave Ste 500 Columbus GA 31901 Office Phone: 706-649-2311. Office Fax: 706-641-6555.

REYNOLDS, PETER JAMES, physicist; b. NYC, Nov. 19, 1949; s. Rudolph and Lydia Mary (Schanzer) R.; m. Louise Perini, Aug. 7, 1982. AB in Physics, U. Calif., Berkeley, 1971; PhD, MIT, 1979. Rsch. assoc., lectr. Boston U., 1978, asst. rsch. prof., 1979-83; mem. sci. staff Nat. Resource for Computation in Chemistry Lawrence Berkeley Lab., U. Calif., 1980-81, mem. rsch. staff materials and chem. scis. divsn., 1982-88; program mgr. Office Naval Rsch., 1988—2003, Army Rsch. Office, 2003—09, assoc. dir. phys. scis., 2004—06, divsn. chief, 2006—07, chief scientist phys. scis., 2007—. Vis. scientist NEC Fundamental Rsch. Lab., Kawasaki, Japan, 1986, vis. rsch. chemist U. Calif., Berkeley, 1988; adj. assoc. prof. dept. chemistry San Francisco State U., 1988-91; vis. scientist Inst. Theoretical Physics, Santa Barbara, 1994, U. Insubria, Como, Italy, 2001-02; rsch. prof. Georgetown U., Washington, 1996-2005; adj. prof. physics NC State U., 2008-; lectr. and rschr. in field of statis., chem. and computational physics and Monte Carlo Methods; program mgr. atomic and molecular physics, laser cooling and trapping, Bose-Einstein condensates, quantum degeneracy, optical lattices, quantum coherence and control, atom lasers, quantum computing. Editor: On Clusters and Clustering: From Atoms to Fractals, 1993; co-author: Monte Carlo Methods in Ab Initio Quantum Chemistry, 1994; mem., editl. bd. Am. Jour. Physics, 2002-04; contbr. articles to profl. jours., also rev. articles, book chpts. NATO lectr., NSF predoctoral fellowship, 1971-74, IBM Predoc. fellow, 1976; Winner ARL Hon. award, 2012. Fellow Am. Phys. Soc. (chmn. membership com. 1998, nominating com. Divsn. Computational Physics and Forum on Physics and Soc. 1996-97, 2008-2010, exec. com. Divsn. Computational Physics 1992-96, 2002-04), Army ST and ARL. Office: Army Research Office Physics Divsn PO Box 12211 Research Triangle Park NC 27709

REYNOLDS, RANDOLPH NICKLAS, aluminum company executive; b. Louisville, Nov. 22, 1941; s. William Gray and Mary (Nicklas) R.; m. Susan Van Reypen, Aug. 6, 1964; children: Randolph Nicklas, Ralph Seymour, Robert Gray. BA in Bus., Bellarmine Coll., 1966; postgrad., U. Louisville, 1967-68. With Reynolds Metals Co., Richmond, Va., 1969—2000, market dir. chems., 1975-77, gen. mgr. chem., 1977-78, pres. Reynolds Aluminum Internat. Svcs. divsn., 1978-85, v.p., exec. v.p. info., 1985-94, vice chmn., 1994—2000; v.p. Reynolds Internat., Inc., Richmond, 1978-79, pres., 1979—2000, Reynolds Internat. Svc. Co., Southfield, Mich., 1987—2000. Pres. Malakoff (Tex.) Industries, 1981—; bd. dirs. Reynolds Metals Co. and 36 subs. Bd. sponsors Coll. William and Mary. Democrat. Episcopalian.

REYNOLDS, THOMAS UPTON, II, state legislator; b. Charleston, Miss., Nov. 15, 1954; m. Elizabeth Fedric; children: Rebecca Elaine, Thomas Upton III; 1 child, Daniel Safley. Mem. Dist. 32 Miss. House of Reps., 1980—94, mem. Dist. 33, 1995—; atty; deacon. Mem.: Gideons, Woodmen World, Miss Bar Assn., Farm Bur., Rotary. Democrat. Baptist. Mailing: PO Drawer 220 Charleston MS 38921 Office Phone: 601-647-3203. E-mail: treynolds@house.ms.gov.

REYNOLDS, WILLIAM BRADFORD, lawyer; b. Bridgeport, Conn., June 21, 1942; s. William Glasgow and Nancy Bradford (DuPont) R.; m. Marguerite Lynn Morgan, June 27, 1964 (div. Feb. 1987); children: William Bradford Jr., Melissa Morgan, Kristina DuPont, Wendy Riker; m. Clare Alice Conroy, Aug. 29, 1987 (div. June 2000); 1 child, Linda Matisan; m. Barbara Lynn Wooster, July 15, 2000; children: Courtney Enright, Brooke Ashley. BA, Yale U., 1964; LLB, Vanderbilt U., 1967. Bar: N.Y. 1968, D.C. 1973, U.S. Supreme Ct. 1971. Assoc. Sullivan and Cromwell, NYC, 1967-70; asst. to Solicitor Gen. U.S. Dept. Justice, Washington, 1970-73; ptnr. Shaw, Pittman, Potts & Trowbridge, Washington, 1973-81; asst. atty. gen. Civil Rights div. U.S. Dept. Justice, Washington, 1981-88, counselor to Atty. Gen., 1987-88; ptnr. Ross & Hardies, 1989-91, Dickstein, Shapiro & Morin, 1991-94, Collier, Shannon, Rill & Scott, 1994-2000, Howrey LLP, Washington, 2000—. Chmn. Archtl. Transp. Barriers Compliance Bd., 1982-84. Editor-in-chief Vanderbilt Law Rev., 1966. Disting. scholar Free Congress Found., 1989-93, Disting. fellow Nat. Legal Ctr. for Pub. Interest, Washington, 1989-90. Mem. ABA, Fed. Bar Assn., D.C. Bar Assn., Order of Coif. Republican. Episcopalian. Home Phone: 703-731-8373; Office Phone: 202-383-6912. Business E-Mail: reynoldsw@howrey.com.

RHETT, HASKELL EMERY SMITH, educational association administrator; b. Evanston, Ill., Aug. 29, 1936; s. Haskell Smith and Eunice Campbell (Emery) R.; m. Roberta Teel Oliver, Sept. 9, 1961 (div. 1973); children: Kathryn Emery, Cecily Coffin; m. Anita Leone, May 30, 1983 (div. 1993); m. Janet Lee Rollings, Nov. 15, 1997. Diploma, Gov. Dummer Acad., 1954; AB, Hamilton Coll., 1958; MA, Cornell U., 1967, PhD, 1968. Asst. to the pres. Hamilton Coll., Clinton, NY, 1961-64; rsch. asst. Cornell U., Ithaca, NY, 1964-66; rsch. assoc. U. London, 1966-67; dir. program devel. Ednl. Testing Svc., Princeton, NJ, 1967-73; asst. chancellor NJ Dept. Higher Edn., Trenton, 1973—85; v.p. The Coll. Bd., NYC, 1985-90; pres. The Woodrow Wilson Nat. Fellowship Found., Princeton, NJ, 1990—97, pres. emeritus, 1997—. Author: Going to College in New Jersey, 1978; contbg. author: Government's Role in Supporting College Savings, 1990. Commr. NJ Pub. Broadcasting Authority, Trenton, 1983—85; mem. Nat. Task Force on Student Aid Problems, Washington, 1974—75, Gov.'s Adv. Panel on Higher Edn. Restructuring, State of NJ, 1994; trustee Dominican U. of Calif., San Rafael, 1990—99, 2001—07, William Alexander Procter Found., 1998—2002, The Coll. of NJ, 1992—97, vice-chmn., 1995—97, chmn., 1997; trustee emeritus The Gov.'s Acad., Mass., 1993—2010; trustee Heartland Edn. Cmty., Ohio, 1992—97, Forums Inst. for Pub. Policy, NJ, 1999—2009, treas., 2000—05, chmn., 2005—09, Woodrow Wilson Presdl. Libr. Found., 2009—, The Am. Shakespeare Ctr., 2009—11; del. Dem. Nat. Conv., Miami, 1972; sr. warden Trinity Episcopal Ch., Princeton, 1988—92, vestryman, 1979—82, 1987—88, 2001—04; dep. Gen. Conv., Detroit, 1988, Phoenix, 1991; mem. standing com. Episcopal Diocese of NJ, 1992—97; bd. dirs. Reach the World, Inc., NYC, 1998—2001, Trenton After Sch. Program, 1989—93, 2001—04. Lt. USNR, 1958—61, Heavy Attack Squadron 5 (VAH-5), USS Forrestal, comdr., 2014. Nat. Def. fellow US Govt., 1966-67, Eliot-Winant fellow Brit.-Am. Assocs., 1982, fellow Kennedy Sch. Harvard U., 1985, Wilson Coll., Princeton U., 1993-97. Mem. Nat. Assn. State Scholarship and Grant Programs (pres. 1976-78), Princeton Officers Soc., Waynesboro Country Club (Va.). Avocations: travel, tennis, golf, sailing, classic automobiles. Home (Summer): 615 Elk Mountain Rd Afton VA 22920 Home (Winter): 106 W Bonefish Cir Jupiter FL 33477

RHOADES, ALAN, corporate financial executive; CPA. Mgr., acctg. KPMG LLP; asst. contr. Triton Energy Ltd. (acquired by Amerada Hess Corp.), 1996—2001, Amerada Hess Corp., 2001—03, Denbury Resources, Inc., 2003, contr., fin. reporting, chief acctg. officer, v.p., acctg., 2009—, Encore Energy Partners GP, LLC, 2010—. Office: Denbury Resources Inc 5320 Legacy Dr Plano TX 75024-3127 Office Phone: 972-673-2000. Office Fax: 972-673-2150. Business E-Mail: alan.rhoades@denbury.com.

RHOADES, EVERETT RONALD, retired medical educator; b. Lawton, Okla., Oct. 24, 1931; s. Lee Joseph and Dorothy Apasha Rhoades; m. Bernadine Herwona Toyebo, Oct. 22, 1931; children: Lee Charles, Melanie Cheryl Campos, Melinda Sue Yoder, Dorothy Alison, Lisa Patricia. MD, U. Okla., 1956. Diplomate Am. Bd. Internal Medicine, 1963. Chief infectious diseases sect. USAF Hosp., Lackland Air Force Base, Tex., 1961—66; prof. medicine U. Okla. Health Scis. Ctr., Oklahoma City, 1966—92, chief infectious diseases sect., 1966—82; asst. surgeon gen. USPHS, Rockville, Md., 1982—93; dir. Indian Health Svc., 1982—93; assoc. dean cmty. affairs U. Okla. Health Scis. Ctr., 1993—2000; dir. of edn. initiatives Ctr. Am. Indian and Alaska Native Rsch., Balt., 1993—2000; sr. cons. Ctr. Am. Indian Health Rsch., 2000—; dir. Native Am. Prevention Rsch. Ctr., 2000—03; prof. emeritus of medicine U. Okla. Health Scis. Ctr., 2005—. Coun. Nat. Inst. Allergy and Infectious Diseases, Bethesda, Md., 1971—75, Nat. Inst. Deafness and Other Comm. Disorders, 1996—2000, Nat. Ctr. Complementary and Alt. Medicine, 1997—2001; adv. com. Nat. Ctr. Vital and Health Stats., Washington, 1978—82; cons. Nat. Libr. Medicine, Bethesda, 1974, U. Saigon Sch. Medicine, Saigon, Vietnam, 1970—72; adj. prof. internat. health Johns Hopkins Sch. Pub. Health, Balt., 1993—2000. Editor: (text book) American Indian Health - Innovations in Health Care, Promotion and Policy; contbr. scientific papers. Founder, mem., pres. Assn. Am. Indian Physicians, Oklahoma City, 1972—2005. Maj. USAF, 1957—66. Decorated Commendation medal USPHS, Meritorious Svc. medal, DSM, Commendation medal, Surgeon General's Exemplary Svc. award; recipient Recognition Achievement award, Kiowa Tribe Okla., 1988, St. Martin-Beaumont Rsch. award, Indian Health Svc., 1993, Establishment of Everett R. Rhoades prize, U. Okla. Coll. Medicine, 1995, Child Advocacy award, Am. Acad. Pediat., 1995, Jack B. McConnell, MD Excellence in Volunteerism award, AMA, 2011; named Outstanding Am. Indian, Am. Indian Expn., 1996; named to Kiowa Tribal Hall Fame, Kiowa Tribe Okla., 1997; fellow, John Hay Whitney Found., 1952—56; scholar, Zeta Psi Frat., Lafayette Coll., 1949—52, John and Mary Markle Found., 1967—72; Sequoyah fellow, Am. Indian Sci. and Engring. Soc., 1992. Fellow: Infectious Diseases Soc. Am., Am. Coll. Physicians; mem.: Assn. Am. Indian Affairs (bd. dirs.), Am. Fedn. Clin. Rsch., Kiowa Tribal Bus. Com. (vice chmn. 1978—80), Nat. Congress Am. Indians, Assn. Am. Indian Physicians (pres. 2004—05, Excellence award 1980), Commd. Officers Assn., Assn. Mil. Surgeons US, Kiowa Gourd Clan (life), Kiowa Blacklegging Soc. (life; sr. counsellor 1970—2005), Alpha Omega Alpha, Phi Beta Kappa. Methodist. Avocations: hunting, fishing, cave exploring. Home: 1808 Dorchester Dr Oklahoma City OK 73120 Office: University Okla Health Scis Ctr 801 NE 13th St Oklahoma City OK 73104

RHOADS, JERRY P., state legislator, lawyer; b. Apr. 5, 1941; BA, Murray State U.; JD, U. Ky. Atty. Rhoads & Rhoads, PSC; minority whip; state senate Dist. 6 Ky., 2003—. Democrat. Baptist. Office: 702 Capitol Ave Annex Rm 254 Frankfort KY 40601 also: 700 Capitol Ave Capitol Rm 330 Frankfort KY 40601 Home: 9 E Center St Madisonville KY 42431-2037 Home Phone: 270-825-2949; Office Phone: 270-825-1490, 502-564-2470.

RHOADS, MARK B., lawyer; b. Mar. 1, 1959; BA, Coll. William and Mary, 1981; JD, U. Richmond, 1985. Bar: Pa. 1985, Va. 1988, US Dist. Ct. Ea. Dist. Pa. 1985, US Dist. Ct. Ea. Dist. Va. 1988. With Montgomery McCracken Walker & Rhoads, Pa., 1985—88, McCandlish Holton (formerly Mezzullo McCandlish), Richmond, Va., 1988—2003; ptnr., practice group leader bus. immigration group Reed Smith LLP, Richmond, Va., 2003—05; ptnr., Bus. Immigration Group McCandlish Holton, 2005—. Editor: US Immigration Law Handbook, A Guide for Foreign Business. Office: 1111 E Main St Suite 1500 Richmond VA 23219 Office Phone: 804-775-3824.

RHOADS, STEVEN ERIC, political science professor; b. Abington, Pa., May 12, 1939; s. John Reginald and Barbara Ann (Dugan) Rhoads; m. Diana Cabanis Akers, May 17, 1944; children: Christopher, Nicholas, John. BA, Princeton U., 1961; MPA, Cornell U., 1965, PhD, 1972. Mem. staff Office Mgmt. and Budget, Washington, 1965—66; asst. prof. dept. politics U. Va., Charlottesville, 1970—76, assoc. prof., 1977—86, prof., 1986—. Author: Policy Analysis in the Federal Aviation Administration, 1974, Valuing Life: Public Policy Dilemmas, 1980, The Economist's View of the World: Government, Markets and Public Policy, 1985, Incomparable Worth: Pay Equity Meets the Market, 1993, Taking Sex Differences Seriously, 2004; contbr. articles to profl. jours. Lt. (j.g.) USN, 1961—63. Fellow, Sloan NEH, Inst. Ednl. Affairs, Bradley Found., Olin Found. Mem.: Assn. Pub. Policy and Mgmt., Am. Polit. Sci. Assn. Office: U Va Dept Politics Cabell Hall 232 Charlottesville VA 22903 Home: 341 Claymont Dr Earlysville VA 22936-1638 Office Phone: 434-924-7866. Business E-Mail: sw6f@virginia.edu.

RHODES, ARTHUR DELANO, benefits administrator; b. Philadelphia, Miss., Nov. 26, 1960; s. A.D. and Mary (McNair) R.; m. Angela Marie Jolly, May 21, 1988. AA, Miss. Delta Jr. Coll., Moorhead, 1980; BA in Polit. Sci., Millsaps Coll., 1982; JD, U. Miss., 1985. Bar: Miss. 1985, U.S. Dist. Ct. (no. and so. dist.) Miss. 1985. Intern asst. dist. atty. Dist. Atty's Office, Hernando, Miss., 1985; counsel Child Support Unit, Dept. of Human Svcs., Brookhaven, Miss., 1985-87; assoc. Prewitt & Bradley, Jackson, Miss., 1987-88; chief of staff Congressman Mike Parker, Washington, 1988-98; pres., CEO The Benefits Bd., Inc., Cleveland, Tenn., 1999—. Republican. Mem. Ch. Of God. Avocations: travel, reading. Home: 2014 Woodchase Way NE Cleveland TN 37311-1461 Office: The Benefits Bd PO Box 4608 Cleveland TN 37320-4608 Office Phone: 423-478-7131, 423-478-7191. Business E-Mail: artrhodes@benefitsboard.com.

RHODES, DONALD ROBERT, musicologist, educator, retired electrical engineer; b. Detroit, Dec. 31, 1923; s. Donald Eber and Edna Mae (Fulmer) R.; children: Joyce R. Holbert, Jane E., Roger C., Diane R. Herran. BEE, Ohio State U., 1945, MEE, 1948, PhD, 1953. Research assoc. Ohio State U., Columbus, 1945-54; research engr. Cornell Aero. Lab., Buffalo, 1954-57; head basic research dept. Radiation, Inc., Orlando, Fla., 1957-61, sr. scientist Melbourne, Fla., 1961-66; Univ. prof. N.C. State U., Raleigh, 1966-94, univ. prof. emeritus, 1994—. Author: Introduction to Monopulse, 1959, 2d edit., 1980, Synthesis of Planar Antenna Sources, 1974, A Reactance Theorem, 1977. Co-founder Central Fla. Community Orch., Winter Park, 1961, pres., 1961-62. Recipient Benjamin G. Lamme medal Ohio State U., 1975; Eminent Engr. award Tau Beta Pi, 1976; named to N.C. State U. Acad. Outstanding Tchrs., 1980. Fellow AAAS, IEEE (John T. Bolljahn award 1963, pres. Antennas and Propagation Soc. 1969); mem. Am. Musicological Soc. Home: 625 Centennial Pkwy Apt 101 Raleigh NC 27606-3255 Office: PO Box 7911 Raleigh NC 27695-7911

RHODES, GENE PAUL, small business owner; b. Houma, La., Feb. 2, 1955; s. Kirby Francis and Jenny (Kraemer) R.; m. Sally Ann Romano, June 7, 1975; children: Chris Michael, Corey Francis, Cade Anthony. AS, Nicholls State U., 1975; cert. in banking, La. State U., 1984, degree in banking, 1987. Sr. computer operator Terrebonne Bank and Trust, Houma, La., 1975-78; mgr. computer ops. First Nat. Bank of Jefferson, Gretna, La., 1979-80, v.p., mgr. info. systems, 1980-86, v.p. info. systems and ops., 1986-87; v.p. info. systems, ops. and adminstrn. South Savs. and Loan, Slidell, 1987-90; owner Svc. Master Quality Svcs., Houma, 1990—, Automation Cons. La., Houma, 1991-97, Servicemaster Action Cleaning, Baton Rouge, 1995-99, Gene Rhodes Properties, LLC, 2003—. Pres. Greenacres Subdiv. Civic Assn., Bourg, La., 1986-87. Mem. Am. Mgmt. Assn., Bank Adminstrn. Inst., Data Processing Mgmt. Assn. (bd. dirs. New Orleans chpt. 1983-89, pres. chpt. 1987-88). Republican. Roman Catholic. Avocations: sports, bass fishing, reading. Home: 4015 Kerr Dr Bourg LA 70343-3637 Office: PO Box 766 Houma LA 70361-0766 Home Phone: 985-872-1029; Office Phone: 985-872-1029. E-mail: gene@s-mgs.com.

RHODES, OLIN EUGENE, JR., science administrator, educator; b. Dec. 5, 1960; BS in Biology, Furman U., 1983; MS in Wildlife Biology, Clemson U., 1986; PhD in Wildlife Science, Tex. Tech. U., 1991. Asst. rsch. ecologist U. Ga., Aiken, 1991-95; asst. prof. forestry and natural resources Purdue U., West Lafayette, Ind., 1995—98, assoc. prof. forestry and natural resources, 1999—2002, prof. forestry and natural resources, 2003—10; dir. Purdue Interdisciplinary Ctr. for Ecological Sustainability, 2004—10; asst. dir. USDA-APHIS-WS Nat. Wildlife Rsch. Ctr., 2010—11; dir. Savannah River Ecology Lab, 2011—; prof. U. Ga., 2011—. Presenter in the field; adj. grad. faculty Clemson U. Dept. of Aquaculture, Fisheries and Wildlife, 1991—2001, Tex. Tech. U. Dept. of Range and Wildlife Management, 1991—, Frostburg State U., Dept. of Biology, 2000—, U. of Vermont, Dept. of Biology, 2002—; affiliate assoc. prof. U. Idaho Dept. of Fish and Wildlife Resources, 2002—. Co-author: Molecular Approaches to Natural Resource Conservation, 2010; contbr. several articles to profl. publications; assoc. editor Genetics, Journal of Wildlife Management, 2007—09, reviewer for several profl. journals. Purdue U. Faculty Scholar, 2006—10. Mem.: Indiana Acad. of Science, Nat. Wild Turkey Federation, Arizona Mule Deer Assn., Arizona Antelope Found., American Genetic Assn., Cooper Ornithological Soc., Assn. of Field Ornithologists, Wilson Ornithological Soc., American Ornithologists' Union, American Soc. of Mammalogists, The Wildlife Soc. (pres. elect, pres., & past pres., Ind. Chapter 2001—03, cert. wildlife biologist 2007, SC Outstanding Wildlife Researcher 1995, Ind. Chapter Best Paper award 1998, 2000, Hoosier Wildlife award 2007, North Central Sect. Profl. Award of Merit 2008), Nat. Honor Soc. of Agriculture-Gamma Sigma Delta. Office: Savannah River Ecology Laboratory PO Box Drawer E Aiken SC 29802 Office Phone: 803-725-8191. Office Fax: 803-725-3309. Business E-Mail: rhodes@srel.edu.

RHODES, THOMAS WILLARD, lawyer; b. Lynchburg, Va., Mar. 9, 1946; s. Howard W. and Ruth R.; m. Ann Bloodworth, May 31, 1975; children: Mildred, Andrew. AB, Davidson Coll., NC, 1968; JD, U. Va., 1971. Bar: Ga. 1971. Assoc. Smith, Gambrell & Russell and predecessor firms, Atlanta, 1971-76, ptnr., 1976—. Dir., pres. Atlanta Vol. Lawyers Found., 1984-89; dir. Fed. Defender Program, Atlanta, 1988-92, 2003—07, pres., 1991-92. Contbr. profl. jours. and textbooks; editor: Nonprofit News. Capt. USAR, 1968—72. Recipient Heiner award Atlanta Vol. Lawyers Found., 1989, Anderson Lecture award Am. Acad. Facial Plastic and Reconstructive Surgery, 2004. Fellow Am. Law Inst. (life); mem. Ga. Bar Assn. (past chmn. antitrust law sect.). Office: Smith Gambrell & Russell Promenade II 1230 Peachtree St NE Ste 3100 Atlanta GA 30309-3592

RHODES, WILLIAM C., III, automotive executive; B in Acctg., U. Tenn.; MBA, U. Memphis. CPA. With Ernst & Young LLP, 1988—94; Joined AutoZone, Inc., Memphis, 1994; v.p. Autozone Inc., Memphis, 1997—99, sr. v.p., 1999—2002, exec. v.p., 2002—05, pres., CEO, 2005—07; chmn., pres., CEO AutoZone, Inc., Memphis, 2007—. Bd. mem. Memphis Tomorrow; treas. Nat. Civil Rights Mus.; mem. partners bd. FedEx Inst. Tech. Mem.: Retail Industry Leaders Assn. (chmn.). Office: Autozone Inc 123 S Front St Memphis TN 38103

RHODY, RONALD EDWARD, bank executive, communications executive; b. Frankfort, Ky., Jan. 27, 1932; s. James B. and Mary M. (Clark) R.; m. Patricia Schupp, Apr. 23, 1955; children: Leslie K., Mary M., Virginia K., Ronald C. Student, Georgetown Coll., Ky., 1950-52, U. Ky., 1953-55. Pub. rels. dir. Kaiser Aluminum & Chem. Corp., Ravenswood, W.Va., 1959-62, NYC, 1962-67, corp. v.p. Oakland, Calif., 1967-83; sr. v.p. corp comm. Bank of Am. NT&SA, San Francisco, 1983—, exec. v.p., 1992-94; CEO Rhody, Inc., 1994—; prin. The Rhody Consultancy, 1998—. Author: The CEO's Playbook, 1999, Wordsmithing, 2006, Theos Story, 2009; contbr. articles to profl. jours. Founding chmn. San Francisco Acad. Named Pub. Rels. Profl. of Yr., Pub. Rels. News, 1981; recipient Hall of Fame award Page Soc., 1997, Ferquson award PR S A, 2009. Fellow Pub. Rels. Soc. Am.; mem. Pub. Rels. Soc. Am. (accredited, pres.'s adv. coun. Rex Harlow award), Internat. Assn. Bus. Communicators (Gold Quill award 1980), Pub. Rels. Roundtable San Francisco (mem. bd. govs., awards 1980, 85). Home: 187 Juniper Creek Blvd Pinehurst NC 28374-6993 Personal E-mail: ron.rhody@yahoo.com.

RHOTON, ALBERT LOREN, JR., neurosurgeon, educator; b. Nov. 18, 1932; s. Albert Loren and Hazel Arnette (Van Cleve) R.; m. Joyce L. Moldenhauer, June 23, 1957; children: Eric L., Albert J., Alice S., Laural A. BS, Ohio State U., 1954; MD cum laude, Washington U., St. Louis, 1959. Diplomate Am. Bd. Neurol. Surgery (bd dirs. 1985-91, vice-chmn. 1991). Intern Columbia Presbyn. Med. Ctr., NYC, 1959; resident in neurol. surgery Barnes Hosp., St. Louis, 1961-65; cons. neurol. surgery Mayo Clinic, Rochester, Minn., 1965-72; chief divsn. neurol. surgery U. Fla., Gainesville, 1972-80, R.D. Keene prof., 1980—, chmn. dept. neurol. surgery, 1980-2000, chmn. emeritus, 2000—. Developer microsurg. tng. ctr.; hon. v.p. World Congress of Neurosurgery, 2005-; hon. prof. Beijing (China) Capital U., 2005—; lectr. in field. Author: The Orbit and Sellar Region: Microsurgical Anatomy and Operative Approaches, 1996, Anatomy and Surgical Approaches to the Temporal Bone, Cranial Anatomy and Surgical Approaches, Chinese and English edits., 2003, Anatomy and Surgery Approaches to the Temporal Bone; mem. editl. bd. Neurosurgery, Jour. Microsurgery, Surg. Neurology, Jour. Fla. Med. Assn., Am. Jour. Otology, Skull Base Surgery; contbr. articles to profl. jours. Hon. pres. World Congress Endoscopic Skull Base Surgery, 2009; bd. dirs. Neurosurgery Edn. and Rsch. Found. Recipient Disting. Faculty award, U. Fla., 1981, Alumni Achievement award, Washington U. Sch. Medicine, 1985, Jones award for outstanding spl. med. exhibit of yr., Am. Assn. med. Illustrators, 1969, Jameison medal, Neurosurg. soc. Australasia, 1997, Outstanding Achievement award, World Congress of Skull Base Surgery, 2000, medal of honor, World Fedn. Neurosurg. Socs., 2001, medal, Neurosurg. Soc. Am., 2001, endowed professorship named in his honor, U. Fla., Lifetime Achievement award, Wall of Fame Honoree, Honorary Alumnus award, 2001, medal of honor, Neurosurg. Soc. of Am., 2001, Bucy award, U. Chgo., 2002, Golden Neuron award, World Acad. Neurosurgery, 2009, Disting. Svc. award, Southern Surg. Soc., 2010; named Neurosurgeon of Yr., World Neurosurgery Jour., 2011; grantee NIH, VA, Am. Heart Assn. Mem. ACS (bd. govs. 1978-84), AMA (Billings Bronze medal 1969), Fla. Brain Tumor Assn. and Moffitt Cancer Ctr. (Lifetime Achievement award, 2008), Congress Neurol. Surgeons (pres. 1978, Exceptional and Disting. Svc. award 2004, honored guest 1993, Founders Laurel award 2006), Nat. Found. Brain Rsch. (bd. dirs. 1990-94), Nat. Coalition for Rsch. in Neurol. Disorders (bd. dirs. 1990-94), Neurol. Soc. Am. (medal 2001), Internat. Congress Meningiomas (hon. pres. 2000), Neurosurg. Soc. Brazil (hon., honored guest 2004), Neurosurg. Soc. Japan (hon., Honored guest 2002), Neurosurg. Soc. Mex. (hon.), Neurosurg. Soc. Can. (hon.), Neurosurg. Soc. Uruguay (hon.), Neurosurg. Soc. Venezuela (hon.), Neurosurg. Soc. Turkey (hon.), Korean Neurol. Soc. (hon.), Neurosurg. Soc. Tex. (hon.), Neurosurg. Soc. Okla. (hon.), Neurosurg. Soc. Wis. (hon.), Neurosurg. Soc. Ga. (hon.), Neurosurg. Soc. Rocky Mountain (hon.), Neurosurg. Soc. China (hon.), Neurosurg Soc. Argentina (hon.), Latin Am. Neurosurg. Soc. (hon.), Neurosurg. Soc. Chili (hon.), Fla. Neurosurg. Soc. (pres. 1978), Am. Assn. Neurol. Surgeons (chmn. vascular sect., treas. 1983-86, v.p. 1987-88, pres. 1989-90, exec. com. 1993, Cushing medal 1998), Soc. Neurol. Surgeons (treas. 1975-81, pres. 1993), So. Neurol. Soc. (v.p. 1976), Alachua County Med. Soc. (exec. com. 1978), Fla. Med. Assn., Am. Surg. Assn., Soc. Univ. Neurosurgeons, Am. Heart Assn. (stroke coun., Outstanding Achievement award 1971), N.Am. Skull Base Soc. (pres. 1993-94, honored guest 2001, Lifetime Achievement award 2005), Am. Acad. Neurol. Surgery, Acoustic Neuroma Assn. (med. adv. bd. 1983-2000, chmn. 1992-2001, chmn. emeritus 2001—), Trigeminal Neurol. Assn. (med. advisor bd. 1992—), Hemifacial Spasm Assn. (med. adv. bd. 2002—), Internat. Interdisciplinary Congress on Craniofacial and Skull Base Surgery (pres. 1996-97), Internat. Soc. Neurosurg. Tech. and Instrument Invention (pres. 1997—), Japanese Skull Base Soc. (hon. pres. 2000), Internat. Soc. for Microsurgery Anatomy (hon. pres. 2002, 2004-), World Fedn. Neurosurg. Soc. (hon. v.p. 2005—), World Congress Endoscopic Surgery Brain, Skull Base & Spine (hon. guest), Internat. Levantine Forum, (Turkey) (hon. pres., 2008-), Congress World Fed. SROH Base Socs., Vancouver, BC (honored guest 2008), European Skull Base Soc.(Rotterdam)(hon. mem.), Columbian Neurosurg. Soc., European Skull Base Soc.(hon.) Achievements include design of more than 200 microsurgery instruments; fundraising for 11 endowed chairs at University of Florida. Home: 2505 NW 22d Ave Gainesville FL 32605-3819 Office: U Fla Dept Neurosurgery PO Box 100265 100 S Newell Dr Gainesville FL 32610 Office Phone: 352-273-7788, 352-273-9000, 352-273-6960. Business E-Mail: rhoton@neurosurgery.ufl.edu.

RHYNE, JOHNATHAN, JR., former state legislator; Atty. pvt. practice; mem. Dist. 97 NC House of Reps., 2009—11. Mem. Edn. com., Edn. Subcom. on Universities, Ethics com., Fin. com., Fin. Instns. com., Judiciary II com., Wildlife Resources com. Republican.

RIBBLE, JOHN CHARLES, medical educator; b. Paris, Tex., July 26, 1931; s. Elbert Alfred and Dorothy (Pyeatt) R.; m. Anne Blythe Hoerner; 1 stepchild Helen Blythe Strate Kielty. MD, U. Tex., 1955. Diplomate Am. Bd. Internal Medicine. Asst. prof. medicine Cornell U., NYC, 1962-66, assoc. prof. pediatrics, 1966-78, assoc. dean, 1974-78, Med. Sch., U. Tex., Houston, 1978-86, dean, 1986-95; vis. scholar The Health Inst. New Eng. Med. Ctr., Boston, 1995-96; prof. medicine U. Tex., Houston, 1996—. Mem. Nat. Adv. Coun. Gen. Med. Scis. NIH, Bethesda, Md., 1988-91. Episcopalian. Home: 6200 Willers Way Houston TX 77057-2808 Office: U Tex Med Sch 6431 Fannin St Houston TX 77030-1501 Office Phone: 713-500-6709. E-mail: johnribble@comcast.net.

RIBES, JULIE A., physician; MD, U. Rochester, PhD, 1990. Cert. specialist in parasitology, mycology, Am. Bd. Pathologists in Clin. Pathology, Med. Microbiology and Hematopathology, specialist in parasitology and mycology. Dir., clin. microbiology U. Ky., 1997—, assoc. dir. Clin. Labs., UK HealthCare, 2007—12, prof. pathology and lab. medicine, 2009—; interim dir. Hosp. Labs., 2012—. Bd. dirs. South Ctrl. Assn. Clin. Microbiology, 1999—; com. mem. Coll. Am. Pathologists Microbiology Resource, 2008—; planning mem. Am. Soc. Microbiology, 2011—. Contbr. scientific papers to rsch. publs. Fellow: Coll. Am. Pathologists; mem.: South Ctrl. Assn. Clin. Microbiology (dir. at large), Am. Soc. Microbiology. Office: University Ky UK HealthCare HA 603 Critical Care Tower MS-117 Med Ctr 800 Rose St Lexington KY 40536-0298 Business E-Mail: jaribes@email.uky.edu.*

RICAPITO, JOSEPH VIRGIL (GIUSEPPE RICAPITO), literature educator; b. Giovinazzo, Bari, Italy, Oct. 30, 1933; came to U.S., 1935; s. Frank and Filomena (Cervone) R.; m. Carolyn Sue Kitchen, Apr. 7, 1958; children: Frank Peyton, Maria Avadna. BA, CUNY, Bklyn., 1955; MA, U. Iowa, Iowa City, 1956; PhD in Romance Langs., U. Calif., LA, 1966. From instr. to asst. prof. Pomona Coll., Claremont, Calif., 1962-70; from assoc. prof. to prof. Ind. U., Bloomington, Ind., 1970-80; prof. La. State U., Baton Rouge, 1980—, chmn. dept., 1980-85, Joseph Yenni disting. prof. Italian studies, 1999. Author: Bibliografia Razonada y anotada, 1980; editor: La Vida de Laz de Tormes, 1976; translator: Dialogue of Mercury and Charon, 1986, Cervantes's Novelas ejemplares: Between History and Creativity, 1996, Consciousness and Truth in Don Quijote (Juan de la Cuesta Hispanic Series), 2007, Fratelli: A Novel, 2007. Pres. Greater Baton Rouge Am.-Italian Assn., 1984-85. With U.S. Army, 1957-59. Grantee NEH, 1981; named Knight Order of Merit, Republic of Italy, 1988, Knight Order of Queen Isabel, Govt. of Spain, 1990; named Disting. Rsch. Master La. State U., 2001, Cervantes Lectr., Fordham U., 2004. Mem. MLA, Renaissance Soc. Am., Am. Comparative Lit. Assn., Am. Assn. Tchrs. Spanish and Portuguese, Cervantes Soc. Am. Avocations: music, photography, films. Office: La State U 309 Hodges Hall Baton Rouge LA 70803-0001 Home Phone: 225-769-2762; Office Phone: 225-578-6616. Business E-Mail: ricapito@lsu.edu.

RICARD, JOHN HUSTON, bishop, religious studies educator; b. Baton Rouge, Feb. 29, 1940; s. Maceo and Albanie (St. Amant) Ricard. BA, St. Joseph Sem., 1962, MA, 1968; MS, Tulane U., 1970; D, Cath. U. Am., Washington, DC, 1984. Ordained priest St. Joseph's Soc. of the Sacred Heart, 1968; pastor Holy Redeemer Ch., Washington, 1972—75, Holy Comforter Ch., Washington, 1975—84; ordained bishop, 1984; aux. bishop Archdiocese of Balt., 1984—97; assoc. prof. Cath. U. Am., Washington, 1973—; bishop Diocese of Pensacola-Tallahassee, Fla., 1997—2011, bishop emeritus, 2011—. Mem. priest's senate Archdiocese of Washington, 1974—, mem. sch. bd., 1976—. Pres. Cath. Relief Svcs. USCC, 1995—, chair, 1995—2002; mem. Pontifical Coun., COR UNUM, 1996—; Chmn. Com. on Social Devel. and World Peace, Domestic Social Devel., 1992—95. Mem.: Secretariat of Black Caths. Roman Catholic. Office: 11 N B St Pensacola FL 32501

RICCIO, CINDY, consumer products company executive; Attended, NYU. V.p., product pub. rel. Hanesbrands, Inc. Office: Hanesbrands Inc 1000 E Hanes Mill Rd Winston Salem NC 27105 Office Phone: 336-519-4400. Business E-Mail: cindy.riccio@hanesbrands.com.

RICE, ANDREW, former state legislator; b. Okla. City, Apr. 23, 1973; s. Hugh and Cindy Rice; m. Apple Newman Rice; children: Noah David, Parker Harrison. BA in Religious Studies, Colby Coll., 1996; MA in Theol. Studies, Harvard U., 1999. Staff Texas Faith Network, Austin, 2001; freelance doc. prodr. and editor; mem. Dist. 46 Okla. State Senate, 2006—11. Founder Hunger Task Force; co-chair Senate Health and Human Resources Com.; mem. Senate Bus. and Labor Com., Senate Criminal Jurisprudence and Pub. Safety Com., Senate Homeland Security Com.; founder Prog. Alliance Found., Red River Democracy Project. Mem. Sept. 11th Families for Peaceful Tomorrows, Fundamentalism Edn. Project; bd. mem. People's Opinion Project; mem. Mayflower Congl. Ch. Democrat. Office: PO Box 61333 Oklahoma City OK 73146-1333 Office Phone: 405-521-5610. Business E-Mail: rice@oksenate.gov.

RICE, EDWARD A., JR., career military officer; b. 1956; BS in Engring. Scis., USAF Acad., Colorado Springs, 1978; M in Aero. Sci. and Tech., Embry-Riddle U., 1986; M in Nat. Security and Strategic Studies, Naval War Coll., Newport, RI, 1989; Disting. Graduate, Squadron Officer Sch., Maxwell AFB, 1983; Nat. Security Fellow, Harvard U., 1994; Grad., Program for Sr. Officials in Nat. Security, Harvard U., 2001, Joint Force Air Component Comdr. Course, Maxwell AFB, 2004, Joint Flag Officer Warfighting Course, 2005, Joint Force Maritime Component Comdr. Course, Naval War Coll. Advanced through ranks to gen. USAF, 2010, undergraduate pilot tng. Williams AFB, 1978—80, B-52G co-pilot, aircraft comdr., 69th Bombardment Squadron Loring AFB, Maine, 1980—84, air staff program tng. asst. dep. chief exec. services divsn., directorate adminstrn. Washington, 1984—85, B-52G instr. pilot, chief standardization & evauation flight, flight comdr. 41st Bombardment Squadron Mather AFB, Calif., 1985—88, programmer air crew mgmt. br., dep. chief of staff air and space ops. Washington, 1989—90, dep. dir. expeditionary aerospace force implementation, dep. chief staff space ops., 1999—2000; White House fellow US Dept. Health & Human Services (HHS), Washington, 1990—91; chief standardization and evaluation divsn., 410 ops. group USAF, K.I. Sawyer AFB, Mich., 1991—92, comdr. 34th Bomb Squadron Castle AFB, Calif., 1992—93; nat. security fellow, John F. Kennedy Sch. Govt. Harvard U., Cambridge, 1993—94; profl. staff mem. Comm. on Roles & Missions of Armed Forces Office Sec. of Def., Washington, 1994—95; dep. comdr. 509th Ops. Group USAF, Whiteman AFB, Mo., 1995—96, comdr. 552 Ops. Group Tinker AFB, Okla., 1996—97; dep. exec. sec. NSC, Washington, 1997—99; dep. dir. for expeditionary aerospace force implementation, dep. chief of staff for air & space ops. USAF, Washingtoin, DC, 1999—2000, comdr. 28th Bomb Wing Ellsworth AFB, SD, 2000—02; comdr. Air Force Recruiting Svc. Air. Edn. & Tng. Command (AETC), Randolph AFB, Tex., 2002—04; chief of staff Office Rep. & Exec. Dir., Coalition Provisional Authority Office Sec. of Def., Washington, 2004; dir. air, space & info. ops., plans and requirements Pacific Air Forces, Hickam AFB, Hawaii, 2005—06, vice comdr., 2006—08; comdr. 13th Air Force USAF, Anderson AFB, Guam, 2005, comdr. 13th Air Force & Kenney Hdqs. Hickam AFB, Hawaii, 2006; comdr. US Forces Japan, 5th Air Force, Yokota AFB, Japan, 2008—10, Air. Edn. & Tng. Command (AETC), Randolph AFB, Tex., 2010—. Decorated Legion of Merit with two oak leaf clusters, Disting. Svc. medal, Def. Superior Svc. medal with oak leaf cluster, Meritorious Svc. medal with three oak leaf clusters, Aerial Achievement medal, Air Force Commendation medal; recipient Moller trophy for Outstanding Wing Comdr., Air Combat Command (ACC), 2002; named to The Power 150, Ebony mag., 2008. Office: HQ AETC/PA 100 H St Ste 4 Randolph AFB TX 78150

RICE, MARY ESTHER, biologist; b. Washington, Aug. 3, 1926; d. Daniel Gibbons and Florence Catharine (Pyles) R. AB, Drew U., 1947; MA, Oberlin Coll., 1949; PhD, U. Wash., 1966. Instr. biology Drew U., Madison, NJ, 1949-50; rsch. assoc. Columbia U., NYC, 1950-53; rsch. asst. NIH, Bethesda, Md., 1953-61; curator invertebrate zoology and dir. Smithsonian Marine Sta., Smithsonian Instn., Washington, 1966—2002, sr. rsch. scientist emeritus, 2002—. Mem. adv. panel on systematic biology NSF, Washington, 1977-78; mem. com. on marine invertebrates Nat. Acad. Sci., 1976-81; mem. overseers com. on biology Harvard U., Cambridge, Mass., 1982-88. Assoc. editor Jour. Morphology, Ann Arbor, Mich., 1985-91, Invertebrate Biology, 1995—; editor: (with M. Todorovic) Biology of Sipuncula and Echiura, 1975, 2nd vol., 1976, (with F.S. Chia) Settlement and Metamorphosis of Marine Invertebrate Larvae, 1978, (with F.W. Harrison) Microscopic Anatomy of Invertebrates, Vol. 12, 1993; contbr. articles to profl. jours. Recipient Drew U. Alumni Achievement award in sci., 1980. Fellow AAAS; mem. Am. Soc. Zoologists (pres. 1979), Am. Microscopical Soc. (pres. 1999), Phi Beta Kappa. Office: Smithsonian Marine Sta 701 Seaway Dr Fort Pierce FL 34949-3140

RICE, RONALD JAMES, retired hospital administrator; b. Springfield, Mo., Feb. 5, 1944; s. Glen Elwood and Alice Jeanett (Robinson) R. BSBA, Cen. Mo. State U., 1966, MABA, 1969, Specialist, 1972. Lic. nursing home adminstr.; lic. risk mgr. Unit mgr. Bapt. Med. Ctr., Kansas City, Mo., 1970-71; dir. unit mgmt. Ind. Health Ctr., Independence, Mo., 1971-72; adminstrv. officer Meth. Hosp., Jacksonville, Fla., 1972-73, dir. personnel, 1973-74; assoc. adminstr. Humana Hosp. Orange Park (Fla.), 1974-77; adminstr. Cathedral Rehab. Hosp., Jacksonville, 1977-79, Marion County Gen. Hosp., Hamilton, Ala., 1979-80, Nassau Gen. Hosp., Fernandina Beach, Fla., 1980-85, Reception Med. Ctr., Lake Butler, Fla., 1985-91; regional adminstr. health svcs. Dept. Corrections, Gainesville, Fla., 1991—; sr. health svc. adminstr. Columbia Correctional Instn., 1999—2006; ret., 2010. Cons. Clay Meml. Hosp., Green Cove Springs, Fla., 1976-77, Allied Health Care, Jacksonville, 1989. Mem. Polit. Action Com., Fla. Hosp. Assn., 1990, Coun. on Crime and Delinquency, Gainesville, 1990, Human Resources Com., Orlando, 1991; active Orange Park Presbyn. Ch. With U.S. Army, 1967-69. Decorated Army Commendation medal. Fellow Am. Coll. Health Care Execs.; mem. Am. acad. Med. Adminstrs., Am. Coll. Health Care Adminstrs., Am. Soc. Personnel Adminstrs., Fla. Hosp. Assn., Rotary (pres. 1984-86). Democrat. Avocations: boating, collecting model cars, reading. Home: 1744 Horton Dr Orange Park FL 32073-2757 Personal E-mail: ricerjq45@aol.com

RICE, STANLEY ARTHUR, biology professor, writer; b. Cushing, Okla., May 30, 1957; s. Arthur John and Nina Irene (Hicks) R.; m. Althea Lisette Clarkston, June 9, 1984; 1 child, Anita. BA, U. Calif., Santa Barbara, 1979; PhD, U. Ill., 1987. Vis. teaching specialist U. Ill., Urbana, 1986-87; asst. prof. The King's Coll., Briarcliff Manor, NY, 1987-90; vis. faculty Sarah Lawrence Coll., Bronxville, NY, 1989-90; asst. prof. Huntington (Ind.) Coll., 1990-93, S.W. State U., Marshall, Minn., 1993-98, S.E. Okla. State U., Durant, 1998—2003, assoc. prof., 2003—09, prof., 2009—; pres. elect. Okla. Excellence in Sci. Edn., 2012—. Vis. faculty mem. Wheaton (Ill.) Coll. Sci. Sta., 1993—2005, Taylor U., Upland, Ind., 1993; pres. Okla. Acad. Scis., 2012-. Author: Encyclopedia of Evolution, 2006, Green Planet, 2008, Life of Earth, 2011, Encyclopedia of Biodiversity, 2012; contbr. articles to profl. jours. including Internat. Jour. Plant Sci., Am. Jour. Botany, Am. Biol. Tchr., Okla. Native Plant Record, Oecologia, Nat. Ctr. for Sci. Edn. Reports. Predoctoral fellow NSF, U. Ill., 1980. Mem. Ecol. Soc. Am., Bot. Soc. America, Okla. Native Plant Soc. Office: SE Okla State University Dept Biol Sci 1405 N 4th Ave PO Box 4027 Durant OK 74701 Office Phone: 580-745-2688. Business E-Mail: srice@se.edu.

RICE, SUE ANN, retired dean, psychologist; b. Ponca City, Okla., Sept. 17, 1934; d. Allred and Helen (Revard) R. BS in Edn., U. Okla., 1956; MA, Cath. U., 1979, PhD, 1988. Ensign USN, 1956, advanced through grades to comdr., 1973; ednl. svcs. officer 9th Naval Dist., Great Lakes, Ill., 1956-58; adminstr., asst. staff, comdr. in-chief Pacific Fleet, Honolulu, 1958-61; head edn. div. Naval Air Sta., Lemoore, Calif., 1961-63; instr., acad. dir. Women Officers' Sch., Newport, R.I., 1963-66; head. tng. div. Naval Command Systems Support Activity, Washington, 1966-70; head, ops. support sec. staff, comdr.-in-chief Lant FLT, Norfolk, Va., 1970-74; sr. U.S. rep. NATO, subgroup 5 orgn. JCS, Washington, 1974-77; ret. USN, 1977; coord. vocation program Archdiocese of Washington, 1977-78; cons. Notre Dame Inst., Arlington, Va., 1989-97, dean of students, 1990-95; ret., 1995. Lectr. Cath. U. Am., Washington, 1983-84; bd. dirs. Villa Cortona Apostolic Ctr., Bethesda, 1984-94. Tech. reviewer Personnel Administration, 1964; editor (newsletter) Vocation News, 1978. Conoco scholarship Continental Oil Co., 1952-56; recipient Meritorious Svc. medal Sec. Navy, 1977, rsch. grant Cath. U., Sigma Xi, 1986. Mem.: Cath. War Vet. (nat. standard com.), Secular Franciscan Order Ponca City (formation dir.), Lay Women's Assn. (nat. bd. dirs.), Gamma Phi Beta, Kappa Delta Pi. Roman Catholic. Avocations: travel, music, gardening, woodworking. Home: PO Box 2742 Ponca City OK 74602-2742

RICE, TERRY, state legislator; m. JoAnn Rice; children: Paul, Jeremy. Co-owner Rice Furniture & Appliance; mem. Dist. 62 Ark. House of Reps., 2009—. Former pres. State Line Vol. Fire Dept.; southeast regional bd. mem. Associated Volume Buyers & Brand Source. Mem.: Ark. Home Furnishings Assn. (pres.). Republican. Baptist. Office: State Capitol Rm 350 Little Rock AR 72201 also: PO Box 2195 Waldron AR 72958 Office Phone: 501-682-6211, 501-682-7771, 479-637-3100. Business E-Mail: ricet@arkleg.state.ar.us.

RICE, THOMAS P., health products executive; MS in Fin., Loyola Coll.; BS, U. Md. CPA. CEO Andrx Corp. (sold to Watson Pharmaceuticals), Fort Lauderdale, Fla., 2004—06; prin., co-founder Columbia Investments LLC; owner Roto-Rooter, VITAS Healthcare Corp. Bd. dirs. Andrx Corp., 2003—06, Par Pharmaceutical Companies Inc., 2009—, Chemed Corp. Office: VITAS Healthcare Corp Ste 1500 100 S Biscayne Blvd Miami FL 33131 Office Phone: 305-374-4143. Office Fax: 305-350-6797. Business E-Mail: Thomas.Rice@parpharm.com.

RICE, THOMAS (TOM) R., state legislator; m. Ann Rice; children: Janet, Jennifer, Daniel. Former state rep. Dist. 79, Ga.; former US industry edn. mgr. IBM; house rep. Ga.; state rep. Dist. 64 Ga., 2003—04; state rep. Dist. 51 Ga., 2004—; mem. Banks Com., Banking Com., Edn. Com., Motor Vehicles Com.; deacon Peachtree Corners Bapt. Ch.; ptnr., CEO Quality Group. Mem. United Peachtree Corners Civic Assn. Republican. Baptist. Office: 6100 Lockland Court Norcross GA 30072 Mailing: 612 Legis Office Bldg Atlanta GA 30334 Office Phone: 770-447-1438. Fax: 770-447-8738. E-mail: tqgrice@aol.com.

RICE, TOM (HUGH THOMPSON RICE JR.), United States Representative from South Carolina, lawyer; b. Charleston, SC, Aug. 4, 1957; s. Hugh Thompson and Katherine Louise (Miller) R.; m. Wrenzie Lee Calhoun, Aug. 7, 1982; children: Hugh Thompson III, Jacob Calhoun, James Lucas. BS in Acctg., U. S.C., 1979, MS, JD, U. S.C., 1982. Bar: S.C. 1982; CPA, S.C.; cert. tax specialist. Sr. tax cons. Deloitte Haskins & Sells, Charlotte, N.C., 1982-84; ptnr. Van Osdell, Lester, Howe & Rice, P.A., Myrtle Beach, S.C., 1984-97; founding ptnr. Rice & MacDonald Law Firm, 1997—2012; chmn. Horry County Council, 2010—12; mem. US Congress from 7th SC Dist., Washington, 2013—, US House Budget Com., 2013—, US House Small Bus. Com., 2013—, US House Transp. & Infrastructure Com., 2013—. Adj. prof. acctg. U. S.C., Myrtle Beach, 1985-86. Vol. Bros. and Sisters Community Action, Columbia, S.C., 1978-82; mem. Probate Adv. Bd. Horry County, 1989—; mem. vestry Episcopalian Ch., 1989-92, treas. capital bldg. fund, 1989-92, finance chmn., 1990-92; bd. dirs. YMCA, Myrtle Beach Haven, 1989—, pres. 1994—. Recipient Outstanding Svc. award Brothers & Sisters Community Action, 1980, 81. Mem. S.C. Bar Assn. (cert. specialist in taxation and estate planning), S.C. Assn. CPAs, Sertoma (Gem award 1987, Centurion award 1988, sec. 1988-89, pres. 1989-90, chmn. bd. dirs. 1990-91). Republican. Episcopalian. Office: US House of Representatives 325 Cannon House Office Bldg Washington DC 20515 also: 2411 N Oak St Myrtle Beach SC 29577 Office Phone: 202-225-9895, 843-445-6459. Office Fax: 202-225-9690, 843-445-6418.*

RICE, WINSTON EDWARD, lawyer, priest; b. Shreveport, La., Feb. 22, 1946; s. Winston Churchill and Margaret (Coughlin) R.; m. Barbara Reily Gay, Apr. 16, 1977; 1 child, Andrew Hynes; children by previous marriage: Winston Hobson, Christian MacTaggart. Student, Centenary Coll. La., 1967; JD, La. State U., 1971. Bar: La. 1971, Colo. 1990, Tex. 1992; ordained to priesthood Episcopal Ch., 2005. Cons. geologist, Gulfport, Miss., 1968-70; ptnr. Phelps, Dunbar, New Orleans, 1971-88; sr. ptnr. Rice, Fowler, New Orleans, Houston, Miami, Fla., London and Bogota, 1988-2000; gen. mgr. Winston Edw. Rice LLC, Covington, La., 2000—. Instr. law La. State U., Baton Rouge, 1970-71. Assoc. editor La. Law Rev., 1970-71. Chaplain Gulf Mexico Region Seamens Ch. Inst., NY, NJ, 2011—; asst. rector Christ Ch., Covington, La., 2005—. Mem.: Trucking Industry Def. Assn., Ctr. Transp. Law and Policy, Soc. Ins. Trainers and Educators, Assn. Average Adjusters (U.K.), Assn. Average Adjusters U.S., Maritime Law Assn. U.S. (chmn. subcom. on offshore exploration and devel. 1985—88, vice chmn. com. internat. law of the sea 1988—91, chmn. 1991—95, membership sec. 1998—2002), Com. Maritime Internat. (titulary mem.), La. Assn. Def. Counsel, New Orleans Assn. Def. Counsel, New Orleans Bar Assn., Tex. State Bar, Colo. State Bar Assn., La. Bar Assn., Stratford Club, Mariners Club (treas. 1974—75, 1978—79, sec. 1975—76, v.p. 1976—77, pres. 1977—78), Boston Club, Kappa Alpha, Phi Kappa Phi, Phi Delta Phi, Order of Coif. Republican. Episcopalian. Office: 512 E Boston Ave Covington LA 70433-2943 Home: 1008 So New hampshire St Covington LA 70433 Home Phone: 985-893-8934; Office Phone: 985-893-8949. Business E-Mail: rice@ricellc.com.

RICH, BARRETT, state legislator; b. Somerville, Tenn., June 14, 1977; m. Stacey Rich. BS in Mgmt., Bethel Coll.; graduate, Tenn. Law Enforcement Tng. Acad., Tenn. Hwy. Patrol Trooper Sch. Former sheriff's dep. Fayette Co.; former police officer; former Tenn. State Trooper Fayette, Hardeman, & Shelby Counties; former security detail for Gov. Don Sundquist & Gov. Phil Bredesen Tenn. Hwy. Patrol; agt. Tenn. Farm Bur. Ins.; mem. Dist. 94 Tenn. House of Reps., 2008—. Republican. Methodist. Mailing: PO Box 505 Somerville TN 38068 Office: 204 War Memorial Bldg Nashville TN 37243 Office Phone: 615-741-6890. Business E-Mail: rep.barrett.rich@capitol.tn.gov.

RICH, JOHN, musician, songwriter; b. Amarillo, Tex., Jan. 7, 1974; m. Joan Bush, Dec. 6, 2008; 1 child, Cash. Base guitarist, singer Lonestar, 1992—98, Big & Rich, 2002—. Musician: (albums) (with Lonestar) Lonestar, 1995, Crazy Nights, 1997, (with Big & Rich) Horse of a Different Color, 2004, Comin' to Your City, 2005, Between Raising Hell and Amazing Grace, 2007, Underneath the Same Moon, 2006, Son of a Preacher Man, 2009; host (TV series) Gone Country, Country Music TV, 2007, judge Nashville Star, NBC, 2008, candidate The Celebrity Apprentice, 2011 (winner, 2011). Office: c/o Warner Music Nashville 20 Music Square E Nashville TN 37203

RICH, JOHN MARTIN, humanities educator, researcher; b. Tuscaloosa, Ala., Dec. 14, 1931; s. Emanuel Morris and Bertha (Rose) R.; m. Martha Elaine Schur, June 6, 1955 (div. June 1966); children—Jeffrey Brian, Suzanne Elon; m. Joyce Ann Stegemoller, Aug. 28, 1967 (div. Mar. 1985); m. Audrey Faye Arnold, Aug. 1, 1987. BA, U. Ala., 1954, MA, 1955; PhD, Ohio State U., 1958. Grad. asst. Ohio State U., Columbus, 1955, asst. instr. edn., 1956-58; asst. prof. edn. U. Tenn.-Martin, 1958-60; assoc. prof. edn. Coll. SUNY-Oneonta, 1960-61; from asst. prof. to assoc. prof. Iowa State U., Ames, 1961-66; assoc. prof. social and philos. studies U. Ky., Lexington, 1966-69; prof. cultural founds. edn. U. Tex., Austin, 1969-96, prof. emeritus, 1996—, chmn. dept. cultural founds. edn., 1969-75. Vis. lectr. Nat. Kaohsiung (Taiwan) Normal U., 1993. Author: (books) Education and Human Values, 1968, Humanistic Foundations of Education, 1971, Portuguese translation, 1975, Korean translation, 1985, Challenge and Response, 1974, New Directions in Educational Policy, 1974, Discipline and Authority in School and Family, 1982, Professional Ethics in Education, 1984, Innovative School Discipline, 1985, Foundations of Education, 1992; co-author: Theories of Moral Development, 1985 (named an Outstanding Book of 1985-86 Choice mag.), 2d edit., 1994, Korean translation, 1999, Helping and Intervention, 1988, Competition in Education, 1992, The Success Ethic, Education, and the American Dream, 1996, Korean translation, 1998; editor: Readings in the Philosophy of Education, 1966, 2d edit., 1972, Conflict and Decision, 1972, Innovations in Education, 6th edit., 1992; co-editor, editl. adv. bd. Ednl. Studies, 1970-74, 77-80, 89-91; bd. contbg. editors Rev. Edn., 1977-85; editl. bd. Focus on Learning, 1980-84, Educational Foundations, 1985-91; bd. cons. Jour. Rsch. and Devel. in Edn., 1982-96, Ednl. Theory, 1991-95; contbr. articles to profl. jours., U.S., Can., Eng., Australia. Recipient Faculty Research Assignment award Univ. Research Inst., Austin, Tex., 1983-84; vis. scholar U. London, 1977; Univ. Research Inst. grantee, 1981-82, 84-85 Mem. North Central Philosophy of Edn. Soc. (pres. 1966-67), Ohio Valley Philosophy of Edn. Soc. (pres. 1967-68), Philosophy of Edn. Soc. (exec. bd. 1967-68, 80-82, Cert. Significant Svc.), Am. Ednl. Studies Assn. (exec. council 1972-74, pres. 1975-76) Home: 1801 Lavaca St Apt 8M Austin TX 78701-1312 Office: U Tex Edn Bldg 406 Austin TX 78712 E-mail: jmr1801@hotmail.com.

RICH, KERRY, state legislator; Mem. Ala. House of Representatives, 1974—78, 1990—98, mem. Dist. 26, 2011—; legis. dir. to Fob James Office of Gov., Ala., 1996—98; mgr. WJIA 88.5 FM, Guntersville. Mem. Hewett Meml. Meth. Ch., Albertville, Ala. Mem.: Ala. Broadcasters Assn. (past pres.), Kiwanis, Guntersville Rotary Club. Republican. Office: Ala House of Reps Rm 527-D 11 S Union St Montgomery AL 36130 Office Phone: 334-242-7538. Personal E-mail: kerryrich@bellsouth.net.

RICH, MICHAEL JOSEPH, lawyer; b. NYC, June 19, 1945; s. Jesse and Phyllis (Sternfeld) R.; m. Linda Christine Kubis, July 19, 1969; children: David Lawrence, Lisa Diane. BA, Gettysburg Coll., 1967; JD, Am. U., 1972. Bar: Del. 1973, U.S. Dist. Ct. Del. 1973, U.S. Supreme Ct., 1976, Pa., 1981. Law clk. Del. Supreme Ct., Georgetown, 1972-73; assoc. Tunnell & Raysor, Georgetown, 1973-76; ptnr. Dunlap, Holland & Rich, P.A., Georgetown, 1976-80; gen. counsel Pearlette Fashions, Inc., Lebanon, Pa., 1981-83; assoc. Morris, Nichols, Arsht & Tunnell, Georgetown, 1983-86; ptnr., 1987-91, Twilley, Street, Rich Braverman & Hindman, P.A., Dover, Del., 1991-95; state solicitor, 1995-2001; dep. atty. gen., 2001—07; v.p., regulatory counsel Fidelity Nat. Fin. Inc., 2007—. Mem. Bd. Bar Examiners, Del., 1986-97, chmn., 1996-97;minority counsel Del. Ho. of Reps., Dover, 1977-79; mem. Del. Gov's Magistrate Commn., 1980, 83-86; sec. Del. Gov's. Jud. Nominating Commn., 1986-89. Bd. dirs. People's Place II, Inc., Milford, Del., 1973-77; pres. Bi-County United Way, Inc., Milford, 1977-78; mem. Partnership Greater Milford Commn., 1987-89, Friends Milford Library. Served to 1st lt. U.S. Army, 1967-69, Vietnam. Dean's fellow Am. U., 1971-72. Mem. Del. Bar Assn. (pres. 1990-91), Sussex County Bar Assn. (pres. 1987-89). Office Phone: 904-854-3558. Business E-Mail: michael.rich@fnf.com.

RICH, NAN H., state legislator; b. NYC, Feb. 9, 1942; m. David Rich; children: Laurie Rich Levinson, Larry, Marcie, Jennifer. Attended, U. Fla., 1959—61. Mem. Dist. 97 Fla. House of Reps., Tallahassee, 2000—04; mem. Dist. 34 Fla. State Senate, Tallahassee, 2004—, minority policy chair, 2006—08, vice chair policy & steering com. energy, environment & land use, children, families & elder affairs com., health and human svcs. appropriations com., mem. policy and steering com. on ways and means, commerce com., environ. preservation and conservation com., ethics and elections com., mem. joint legis. sunset com. Bd. dirs. US Holocaust Meml. Coun., 1999-2003; pres. Charlee, 1985-87, Resourcemobile, 1990-92, Home Instruction Program Preschool Youngsters-USA, 1991-94; vice chmn. Jewish Coun. Pub. Affairs, 2000-01. Mem. Fla. Assn. Jewish Fedns. (chmn. govt. affairs com. 1989-99), Nat. Coun. Jewish Women (nat. pres. 1996-2000). Democrat. Jewish. Office: 777 Sawgrass Corp Pky Sunrise FL 33325-6256 also: 214 Senate Office Bldg 404 S Monroe St Tallahassee FL 32399-1100 Office Phone: 954-747-7933, 850-487-5103. Business E-Mail: rich.nan.web@flsenate.gov.

RICH, TYVIN ANDREW, radiation therapist; b. Trenton, NJ, Feb. 6, 1948; s. Joseph Anthony and Mary Virginia R.; m. Christine Schmiel, June 5, 1977; children: Andrew, Karina, Alexander, Austin. BA, Rutgers U., 1969; MD, U. Va., 1973. Instr. Joint Ctr., Boston, 1979-82; asst. prof. Harvard Med. Sch., Boston, 1982-84, M.D. Anderson Cancer Ctr., Houston, 1984-85, assoc. prof., 1986-92, dir. clinics, 1988-90, prof., 1992—; chmn. dept. radiation oncology U. Va. Health Scis. Ctr., prof. dept. radiation oncology. Chmn. GI com. Radiation Therapy Oncology Group, Phila., 1990—; mem. editl. bd. Jour. Infusional Chemotherapy, Ontario, Can., 1991—, M.D. Anderson Cancer Ctr., Oncology, Houston, 1990—, Internat. Jour. GI Cancer, London, 1991—. Recipient Nat. Rsch. Svc. award Nat. Cancer Inst., 1978. Mem. AMA, Am. Coll. Radiology, Am. Soc. Clin. Oncology, Soc. for Surgical Oncology, Am. Radium Soc., Am. Soc. for Therapeutic Radiology and Oncology, New Eng. Cancer Soc., Tex. Radiol. Soc. Office: U Va Health Cancer Ctr Dept Radiation Oncology Box 800383 Jefferson Park Ave Charlottesville VA 22908

RICHARD, DEBRA LYNN, school librarian; d. Louis A. and Bettye J. Daniel; children: Erin, Ryan. BME, U. North Tex., Denton, 1979; MLS, Tex. Woman's U., Denton, 1999. Sch. libr., sch. music specialist Richardson Ind. Sch. Dist., Dallas, 1985—2000; sec., qep steering com. Dallas Bapt. U., 2003—08, sec., NCATE/CAEP coun., 2009—14, chair, fin. aid com., 2010—12, chair, curriculum com., 2013, prof. libr. sci., dir. distance learning libr. svcs., 2000—, Adj. prof., Coll. Fine Arts, 2004—. Dir.: (film) Library Anxiety; contbr. articles to profl. jours. Sunday sch. tchr., small group leader Big Springs Bapt. Ch., Garland, Tex., 1995—2012, organist, 1998—2014. Mem.: Tex. Libr. Assn. Baptist. Avocations: reading, Scrabble, music. Office: Dallas Baptist University 3000 Mountain Creek Pky Dallas TX 75211 Office Fax: 214-333-5323. Business E-Mail: debbi@dbu.edu.*

RICHARD, JEROME, state legislator; BS, La. State U., 1978. Ter. sales mgr. Curtiss Wright Flow Controls; mem. Dist. 55 La. House of Reps., 2008—, mem. house and govtl. affairs com., ways and means com., joint legis. com. on capital outlay. Independent. Office: 907 Jackson St Thibodaux LA 70301 also: Capitol Office PO Box 44486 Baton Rouge LA 70804 Office Phone: 985-447-0999, 225-342-6945. Office Fax: 985-447-0998. E-mail: richardj@legis.state.la.us.

RICHARD, OLIVER G., III, (RICK RICHARD), energy and management consultant, board member; b. Lake Charles, La., Oct. 11, 1952; s. Oliver Gonzard and Mary Jean (Turvey) Richard; m. Donna Margaret Guzman, July 6, 1974; 1 child, David Turvey. BA in Journalism, La. State U., 1974; JD, Paul M. Hebert Law Ctr., Baton Rouge, 1977; ML in Taxation, Georgetown U., Washington, 1981. Bar: La. 1977, US Dist. Ct. (ea., we. and mid. dists.) La. 1977, US Supreme Ct. 1981. Assoc. Sanders, Downing, Kean & Cazedessus, Baton Rouge, 1977; legis. asst. energy issues US Senate, Washington, 1978—81; ptnr. Hayes Durio & Richard, Lafayette, La., 1981—82; commr. FERC, Washington, 1982—85; v.p., gen. counsel Tenngasco Corp., 1985—87; v.p. regulatory & competitive analysis, gas pipeline group Enron Corp., 1987—88; pres., CEO Northern Natural Gas Co., 1989—91, New Jersey Resources Corp., 1991—95, chmn., 1992—95; chmn., pres. & CEO Columbia Energy Group, Inc. (acquired by NiSource), Reston, Va., 1995—2000; owner, pres. Empire of the Seed LLC, Lake Charles, 2004—. Bd. dirs. Buckeye GP Holdings L.P., 2008—09, Buckeye Ptnrs., L.P., 2009—; chmn. bd. dirs. CleanFuel USA. Mem.: Interstate Natural Gas Assn. America (chmn.), Nat. Petroleum Coun., American Gas Assn. (bd. dirs.), Interstate Pipeline Assn. Democrat. Roman Catholic. Mailing: Buckeye Partners LP Bd Directors 1 Greenway Plz Ste 600 Houston TX 77046 Office: Empire of the Seed 949 Ryan St # 200 Lake Charles LA 70601-5247 Office Phone: 832-615-8600. E-mail: orichard@buckeye.com.

RICHARDS, CHRISTINE P., delivery service executive, lawyer; b. Amityville, NY, Jan. 8, 1955; BA magna cum laude, Bucknell U., 1976; JD, Duke U., 1979. Bar: Tenn. 1987, NC 1980. Joined FedEx Corp., 1984, corp. v.p. customer and bus. transactions & gen. counsel

FedEx Corp. Services, exec. v.p., gen. counsel, sec., 2005—. Office: FedEx Corp 942 S Shady Grove Rd Memphis TN 38120 Office Phone: 901-818-7500. Office Fax: 901-395-2000.*

RICHARDS, CLIFTON MARC, personal care industry executive; b. Alexandria, Va., Feb. 6, 1971; s. Douglas Arthur and Carla (Bean) R. BS, George Mason U., 1993; MS, Strayer Coll., 1995. Contr. JER Investors Trust; head instr. U.S. Tae Kwon Do Ctr., Woodbridge, Va., 1987—94; tchr. Fairfax (Va.) County Pub. Schs., 1994—95; acctg. contr. Crisak Inc., McLean, Va., 1995; group v.p., corp. acct. Mills Corp., property contr., 1999—2001, dir., property acctg., 2001—03, dir., corp. acctg., 2003—04; v.p., corp. contr. Rep. Property Trust, 2006—07; v.p. JE Robert Companies, 2007—09; chief acctg. officer Sunrise Senior Living, Inc., 2009—. Mem. Inst. Mgmt. Accts. Avocations: golf, martial arts, fishing. Office: Sunrise Senior Living Inc 7900 Westpark Dr Ste T900 Mc Lean VA 22102-4217 Office Phone: 703-273-7500. Office Fax: 703-744-1601. Business E-Mail: clifton.richards@sunrise-al.com.

RICHARDS, DAVID GLEYRE, German language educator; b. July 27, 1935; s. Oliver L. and Lilian Marie (Powell) R.; m. Annegret Horn, Sept. 3, 1959 (div. 1992); 1 child, Stephanie Suzanne; m. Friederike Hensler, Oct. 11, 1997. BA, U. Utah, 1960, MA, 1961; PhD, U. Calif., Berkeley, 1968. Asst. prof. German SUNY, Buffalo, 1968, assoc. prof., 1974—84, prof., 1984—99, chair dept., 1986—92, prof. emeritus, 1999—. Author: Georg Buchners Woyzeck, 1975, George Buchner and the Birth of the Modern Drama, 1976, The Hero's Quest for the Self: An Archetypal Approach to Hesse's Demian and other Novels, 1987; editor: (with H. Schulte) Crisis and Culture in Post-Enlightenment Germany: Essays in Honor of Peter Heller, 1993, Exploring the Divided Self: Hermann Hesse's Steppenwolf and its Critics, 1996, Georg Buchner's Woyzeck: A History of Its Criticism, 2001. SUNY grantee, 1973; NEH grantee, 1977-78, Fulbright Commn. grantee, 1980. Rsch. Found. of SUNY fellow, 1982. Democrat. Avocations: photography, painting. Personal E-mail: dgrich@nc.rr.com.

RICHARDS, FREDERICK FRANCIS, JR., investment company executive; b. Payette, Idaho, Jan. 28, 1936; s. Frederick Francis and Dorothy Lucille (Taylor) R.; m. DeAnne Aden, Aug. 10, 1958; children: Frederick Francis III, Craig, Jeffrey. BS in Indsl. Engring., So. Meth. U., 1959; MBA, Harvard U., 1961. Indsl. engr. Collins Radio Inc., 1955—59; rsch. asst. Harvard U., 1961—62; fin. analyst H.F. Linder & William T. Golden, NYC, 1962—65; pres., CEO Adrich Corp. and subs., Dallas, 1965—; pres. Resource Locators Inc., Dallas, 1992—95; editor, publisher Strategic Investing, Dallas, 1996—. Exec. v.p. FSE Corp., Plano, Tex., 1990-92; v.p. and prin. Capital Alliance Corp., Dallas, 1985-91; v.p. GTex., Inc., Dallas, 1986-87; pres. Work Lite Dist., Dallas, 1990-95, AR Assocs., internat. mgmt. cons., Dallas, 1972—2002; dir. Dallas Pub. Inc., 1982-84, Aden-Richards Inc., 1979—, pres., Tech. Club Dallas, 2001; founder, Arlington Tech. Club, 2001; pres., AAII-DFW Chapter 2012-; director, Dallas Investors Forum 1997-. Author papers in field; bus. and fin. columnist. Mem. ASTM, Am. Inst. Indsl. Engrs. (sr.), Assn. for Tech. Analysis, Airplane Owners and Pilots Assn., Am. Soc. Indsl. Security, Internat. Assn. Chiefs Police, Nat. Pilots Assn., Exptl. Aircraft Assn., Harvard Club (N.Y.C.), The Tech. Club of Dallas, Am. Assn. Ind. Investors; Tau Beta Pi. Home and Office: 3 Cumberland Pl Richardson TX 75080-4926 Office Phone: 972-783-8625. Business E-Mail: ffr@adrich.com.

RICHARDS, JODY, state legislator, communications educator, small business owner; b. Columbia, Ky., Feb. 20, 1938; m. Neva Richards; 1 child, Roger. BA in English, Ky. Wesleyan Coll., Owensboro; MA in Journalism, U. Mo., 1962. Mem. faculty in journalism Western Ky. U., from 1962; owner Superior Books, Bowling Green, Ky.; speaker Ky. House of Reps., 1995—, mem. Dist 20, 2006—; vice chair So. Legislative Conf., 1998—. Mem. adv. bd. dirs. Republic Savs. Bank. Pres. bd. dirs. So. Ky. Fair; bd. dirs. Bowling Green Girls Club, United Way, Warren County (Ky.) Drug Abuse Task Force. Recipient Disting. Svc. award Nat. Art Edn. Assn., 1992. Mem. Bowling Green C. of C., Bowling Green Noon Rotary Club. Democrat. Christ Of Church. Office: Ky Ho of Reps State Capitol Rm 309 Frankfort KY 40601 also: Annex Rm 324D 702 Capitol Ave Frankfort KY 40601 Office Phone: 270-781-9946. Fax: 270-781-9963. E-mail: Jody.Richards@lrc.ky.gov.

RICHARDS, LEONARD MARTIN, investment executive, consultant, coach; b. Phila., June 4, 1935; s. Leonard Martin and Marion Clara (Lang) R.; m. Phyllis Janelle Mowrey, Aug. 26, 1961 (div. Aug. 1978); children: Lisa, David Reed. BS, Pa. State U., 1957; MBA, U. Pa., 1963; MTh, Universal Sem., 1996, ThD, 2000. Asst. to sr. ptnr. Van Cleef, Jordan & Wood, NYC, 1963-68; v.p., portfolio mgr. Bernstein-Macaulay, Inc., NYC, 1968-72; ptnr. G. H. Walker, Laird Co., NYC, 1972-74; v.p., trust officer, mgr. instnl. funds group Republic Bank N.A., Dallas, 1974-77; v.p., sr. investment officer, mem. exec. com. Variable Annuity Life Ins. Co., Houston, 1977-88; v.p., sr. investment officer Am. Gen. Series Portfolio Co., 1985-88; pres. L.M. Richards & Co., Houston, 1982—2009, also bd. dirs.; mem. adv. bd. Trinity Life Ctr., Houston, 1996-2000; mng. dir. The Enhancement Inst., Houston, 2003—11; pres. Lenan Holdings, Inc., Houston, 2005—09; prin. Lenan Ptnrs., 2010—; clin. assoc. Unique Mindcare Houston, 2011—. Pres., bd. dirs. Sand Dollar, Inc., Houston, 1985—96; trustee Post Oak Sch., Houston, 1997—99, Universal Sem., 1997—2000, pres., 2001—; mem., bd. dir. Capital Institutional Services, Dallas, 1991—99; trustee PAIRS Found., Weston, Fla., 2004—06; bd. dirs. Houston Chorale, 1988—90. Capt. US Army, 1957—65. Mem. ACFA Inst., Houston Soc. Fin. Analysts, Wharton Club (Houston), Houstonian Club Independent. Avocations: skiing, travel, scuba. Home: 9023 Briar Forest Dr Houston TX 77024-7220 Office: Lenan Partners 1776 Yorktown Ste 550 Houston TX 77056 Office Phone: 713-337-2400. Business E-Mail: leonard@uniquemindcare.com.

RICHARDS, MARTA ALISON, lawyer; b. Mar. 15, 1952; d. Howard Jay and Mary Dean (Nix) Richards; m. Richard Peter Massony, June 16, 1979 (div. Apr. 1988); 1 child, Richard Peter Massony Jr. Student, Vassar Coll., 1969-70; AB cum laude, Princeton U., 1973; JD, George Washington U., 1976. Bar: La. 1976, U.S. Dist. Ct. (ea. dist.) La. 1976, U.S. Ct. Appeals (5th cir.) 1981, U.S. Supreme Ct. 1988, U.S. Dist. Ct. (mid. dist.) La. 1991. Assoc. Phelps, Dunbar, Marks, Claverie & Sims, New Orleans, 1976-77; assoc. counsel Hibernia Nat. Bank, New Orleans, 1978; assoc. Singer, Hutner, Levine, Seeman & Stuart, New Orleans, 1978-80, Jones, Walker, Waechter, Poitevent, Carrere & Denegre, New Orleans, 1980-84; ptnr. Montgomery, Barnett, Brown, Read, Hammond & Mintz, 1984-86, Montgomery, Richards & Ballin, 1986-89, Gelpi, Sullivan, Carroll and Laborde, 1989; gen. counsel Maison Blanche Inc., Baton Rouge, 1990-92, La. State Bond Commn., 1992-97; pvt. practice, cons., 1998—. Lectr. paralegal inst. U. New Orleans, 1984-89, adj. prof., 1989; of counsel Sanford & Assocs. Law Firm, 2004—09, pvt. practice, 2009-, lectr in fields Contbr. articles to legal jours. Treas. alumni coun. Princeton U., 1979-81, bd. mem., Baton Rouge Friends of the Animals, 2012-. Mem. ABA, La. State Bar Assn., New Orleans Bar Assn., Baton Rouge Bar Assn., Nat. Assn. Bond Lawyers, Princeton Alumni Assn. New Orleans (pres. 1982-86), Princeton Alumni Assn. Baton Rouge (pres. 2002—), Lawyers Divsn. Animal Legal Def. Fund Episcopalian. Home and Office: 4075 S Ramsey Dr Baton Rouge LA 70808-1653 Home Phone: 225-344-2746; Office Phone: 225-726-9700. Personal E-mail: marta73@alumni.princeton.edu.

RICHARDS, ROY, JR., wire and cable manufacturing company executive; b. Dec. 19, 1958; Co-pres. Southwire Co., Carrollton, Ga., 1985—89, CEO, dir., 1989—2002, chmn., 1989—. Office: Southwire Co Inc PO Box 1000 Carrollton GA 30119-1000

RICHARDS, STEPHEN HAROLD, engineering educator; b. Austin, Tex., July 19, 1952; s. Harold Richards Jr. and Janice Valerie (Mahone) Jackson; m. Mary Kathryn King Coleman, Aug. 15, 1974 (div. July 1981); 1 child, Adam King; m. Elizabeth "Jeannie" Stevens, Apr. 5, 2006. BSCE, U. Tex., 1976; MCE, Tex. A&M U., 1977; PhDCE, U. Tenn., 1989. Registered profl. engr., Tenn., Tex. Rsch. asst. Tex. Transp. Inst., Tex. A&M U., 1976-77, engring. rsch. assoc., 1977-81, asst. rsch. engr., 1982-84; asst. dir. transp. ctr. U. Tenn., Knoxville, 1984-87, acting dir. transp. ctr., 1987-89, dir. transp., 1989—, assoc. prof. civil engring., 1989—; traffic engring. cons. Ctr. Transp. Rsch., 1976—. Engr., mgr. Walton & Assocs./Cons. Engrs., Inc., Houston, 1981-82; lectr. in civl engring. U. Houston, 1982, Tex. A&M U., 1978-81, 83-84; instr. Tex. Engring. Extension Svc., Tex. A&M U., 1978-84; Dwight D. Eisenhower Fellowship Rev. Com., Tenn. State U., 1993, N.C. A&T Univ., 1992; Bicentennial planning Com. U. Tenn., 1993, dir. program for minority student recruitment into transp. careers, 1992—, coll. engring. awards com., 1991—, chmn. spl. events traffic planning com., 1985—. Contbr. numerous articles to profl. jours. Mem. Cumberland Gatewaa Com., 1993—; edn. com. Southeastern Transp. Ctr., 1992—; exec. dir. Southeastern Consortium of U. Transp. Ctrs., 1992—; chmn. Knoxville Transp. Authority, 1992-94, vice-chmn., 1990-92, commr., 1989-93; rep. Coun. of Univ. Transp. Ctrs. U. Tenn., 1987—, bd. dirs. 1992—, sec., 1994-95, v.p., 1995-96, pres., 1996—; adv. com. Ga. State U. Transp. Ctr., 1989—; traffic control device subcom. Transp. Rsch. Bd., 1989-91, traffic control devices, 1991—, many other coms. Hwy. Safety fellowship Fed. Hwy. Adminstrn., U.S. Dept. Transp., 1976-77. Mem. ASCE, Inst. of Transp. Engrs. (chmn. tech. com. Tenn. sect. 1988—, area coord. Tex. sect. 1982-84, guidelines for driveway design and location), Transp. Rsch. Bd., Soc. Profl. Engrs., Am. Road and Transp. Builders Assn. (edn. com. 1988—), Phi Kappa Phi, Chi Epsilon. Office: Ctr Transp 600 Henley St Ste 309 Knoxville TN 37996-4133 Home Phone: 865-382-0123; Office Phone: 865-974-5255. Personal E-mail: shrichards@tds.net.

RICHARDSON, CLIFTON R., state legislator; Owner/mgr. Rebel Electric Co.; mem. Dist. 65 La. House of Reps., mem. civil law and procedure com., edn. com., mcpl., parochial and cultural affairs com. Republican. Office: PO Box 78280 Baton Rouge LA 70837 also: Capitol Office PO Box 44486 Baton Rouge LA 70804 Office Phone: 225-261-5739, 225-342-6945. Office Fax: 225-261-5741. E-mail: richardc@legis.state.la.us.

RICHARDSON, CURTIS JOHN, ecology educator; b. Gouverneur, NY, July 27, 1944; s. Nilie John and Rose Marie (LaPierre) R.; m. Carol Bartlett, Aug. 22, 1972; children: John, Suzanne. BS in Biology, SUNY, Cortland, 1966; PhD in Ecology, U. Tenn., 1972. Asst. prof. resource ecology Sch. Natural Resources U. Mich., Ann Arbor, 1972-77, asst. prof. plant ecology Biologican Station, Mich., summer 1973; assoc. prof. resource ecology Sch. Forestry and Environ. Studies Duke U., Durham, N.C., 1977-87, prof. resource ecology, 1988—, dir. Wetland Ctr., 1990—; sr. rsch. fellow in applied ecology and forestry U. Edinburgh, Scotland, 1982. Mem. sci. adv. bd. Nat. Wetland Rsch. Plan, U.S. EPA, Washington, 1991, chmn. Nat. Wetland EMAP rev. panel, 1992; panel mgr. competitive grants program water quality USDA, Washington, 1990-91. Fellow Soil Sci. Soc. Am., AAAS; mem. Am. Inst. Biol. Scis., Am. Soc. Agronomy, Ecol. Soc. Am., Soc. Wetland Scientists (v.p. 1986-87, prs. 1987-88, assoc. editor 1987-93). Avocations: jogging, hiking, fishing. Office: Duke U Wetland Ctr Nichols Sch Environ LSRC Research Dr Durham NC 27708-0333 Home: 717 Anderson St Durham NC 27705-1013

RICHARDSON, DAVID WALTHALL, cardiologist, educator, consultant; b. Nanking, China, Mar. 22, 1925; s. Donald William and Virginia (McIlwaine) R.; m. Frances Lee Wingfield, June 12, 1948; children: Donald, Sarah, David. BS, Davidson Coll., 1947; MD, Harvard U., 1951. Diplomate Am. Bd. Internal Medicine, Am. Bd. Cardiology. Intern, resident Yale New Haven Hosp., 1951-53; resident, fellow Med. Coll. Va., Richmond, 1953-56, assoc. prof. to prof. medicine, 1962-95, prof. emeritus, 1995—2007, prof. medicine, 2007—. Chmn. divsn. cardiology, 1972-87; interim chmn. dept. medicine, 1973-74; chief cardiology, assoc. chief staff for rsch. VA Hosp., Richmond, 1956-61, dir. cardiology tng. program, 1990-95, prof. medicine Health Sci. Disease Va. Commonwealth U., 1995-; vis. scientist Oxford U., Eng., 1961-62; vis. prof. U. Milan, Italy, 1972-73. Contbr. articles to profl. jours. Moderator Hanover Presybery, Presbyn. Ch. U.S., Richmond, 1970; chmn. events com., NHLBI Cardiac Arrhythmia Suppression Trial, 1983-92, NHLBI Anti-Arrhythmics versus Implantable Defibrillators Trial, 1993-97. Served with USN, 1944-46. Fellow Am. Coll. Cardiology (gov. VA 1970-72), Am. Heart Assn. (coun. clin. cardiology and high blood pressure rsch.); mem. Am. Soc. Clin. Investigation, Am. Clin. and Climatol. Assn. Democrat. Presbyterian. Home: 1500 Westbrook Ct CYA 1105 Richmond VA 23227-3366 Office Phone: 804-200-1256. Personal E-mail: davidr1925@gmail.com.

RICHARDSON, DOUGLAS J., career officer; b. New Britain, Conn. m. Denise Richardson; children: Erin, Megan. BS, USAF Acad., 1973; M in Pub. Adminstrn., George Washington U., 1990. Commd. 2d lt. USAF, 1973, advanced through grades to col., 1994; F-4E pilot 526th Tactical Fighter Squadron, Ramstein AB, Germany, 1975-79; F-4E weapons officer 36th TFS, Osan AB, Republic of Korea, 1979-80, wing weapons, flight comdr., 1980-81; F-4 FWIC instr. pilot 414th Fighter Weapons Sch., Nellis AFB, 1981-82; exec. officer 57th Weapons Wing, Nellis AFB, Nev., 1983-84; F-16A test project mgr. Nellis AFB, 1985-86; asst. chief F-16C/LANTIRN test, 1985-86; action officer NATO divsn. Hdqr. USAF Europe, the Pentagon, Washington, 1986-87, action officer TAC divsn., 1987-89; F-16C pilot 612 Tactical Fighter Squadron, 1990-91; chief of safety 401st TFW, Torrejon AB, Spain, 1991; comdr. 613th TFS, Torrejon AB, 1991; asst. dir. of ops. 401st TFW, Torrejon AB, 1991-92; with sr. officer mgmt. divsn. Hdqs. USAFE, Ramstein Air Base, Germany, 1992-93; dep. comdr. 86th Ops. Group, Ramstein Air Base, 1993; comdr. 39th Ops. Group, Incirlik Air Base, Turkey, 1993-94; dep. chief of staff Plans and Ops., 5th ATAF, Vicenza, Italy, 1994-96; comdr. 48th Fighter Wing, Royal Air Force Station, Lakenheath, Eng., 1996-98, 53rd Wing, Eglin AFB, Fla., 1998—. Decorated Legion of Merit, Air medal with two oak cluster, Aerial Achievement medal, Combat Readiness medal with one oak leaf cluster, NATO medal. Office: 53 WG/CC 203 WD Ave Ste 600 Eglin AFB FL 32542-6867

RICHARDSON, EMILIE WHITE, manufacturing, investment company executive, educator; b. Chattanooga, July 08; d. Emmett and Mildred Evelyn (Harbin) White; 1 child, Julie Richardson Milunic. BA, Wheaton Coll. With Christy Mfg. Co., Inc., Fayetteville, N.C., Ft. Lauderdale, Fla., 1952—, sec., 1956-66, v.p., 1967-74, exec. v.p., 1975-79, pres., CEO, 1980—; lectr. aboard cruise ships. V.p. E. White Investment Co., 1968-83, pres., 1983—; cons. Aerostatic Industries, 1979—; v.p. Gannon Corp., 1981—; cons. govt. contacts and offshore mfg., 1981—; lectr., spkr. in field. V.p. pub. rels. Ft. Lauderdale Symphony Soc., 1974-76, v.p. membership, 1976-77, adv. bd., 1978—; active Atlantic Found., Ft. Lauderdale Mus. Art, Beaux Arts, Freedoms Found.; mem. East Broward Women's Rep. Club, 1968—, Americanism chmn., 1971-72. Mem. Internat. Platform Assn., Nat. Spkrs. Assn., Fla. Spkrs. Assn., Toastmasters, Coral Ridge Yacht Club. Methodist. Home: 451 Lakeside Cir Apt 314 Pompano Beach FL 33060 Personal E-mail: emilier@mindspring.com.

RICHARDSON, GLENN, lawyer, former state legislator; b. Douglas County, Ga., Jan. 12; m. Susan Richardson (div.); children: Maggie, Bryn, Will. BA in Polit. Sci., Georgia State U., 1981, JD, 1984. Ptnr. Vinson, Talley, Richardson & Cable (formerly Vinson & Osborne), 1985—; county atty. Paulding County, 1989—2005; minority leader Republican Caucus, 2003; mem. Dist. 19 Ga. House of Reps., 1996—2009, admin. fl. leader, 2003, spkr., 2005—09. Republican. Office: Talley Richardson & Cable PA 367 W Memorial Dr PO Box 197 Dallas GA 30132 Office Phone: 770-445-4438. E-mail: grichardson@trc-lawfirm.com.

RICHARDSON, HERBERT HEATH, retired mechanical engineer, educator, dean, academic administrator; b. Lynn, Mass., Sept. 24, 1930; s. Walter Blake and Isabel Emily (Heath) R.; m. Barbara Ellsworth, Oct. 6, 1973. SB, SM with honors, MIT, 1955, ScD, 1958. Registered profl. engr., Mass., Tex. Rsch. asst., rsch. engr. Dynamic Analysis and Control Lab. MIT, 1953-57, instr. dept. mech. engring., 1957-58, mem. faculty, 1958-84, prof. mech. engring., 1968-85, head dept., 1974-82, assoc. dean engring., 1982-84; disting. prof. engring. Tex. A&M U. Sys., Coll. Sta., 1984—2006, regents prof., 1993—2006, dean, vice chancellor engring., 1984-85, dep. chancellor, dean, dir. Tex. Engring. Expt. Sta., 1985-91, chancellor, 1991-93, assoc. vice chancellor engring., assoc. dean engring., dir. Tex. Transit Inst., 1993—2006, dir. emeritus Tex. Transp. Inst., 2006—, disting. prof. engring. emeritus, chancellor emeritus, 2006—. With Ballistics Rsch. Lab. Abderdeen Proving Ground, Md., 1958; chief scientist U.S. Dept. Transp., 1970-72; chmn. adv. com. for engring. NSF, 1987-89, adv. com. basic energy scis. U.S. Dept. Energy, 1987-91. Author: Introduction to System Dynamics, 1971; contbr. articles to profl. publs. Trustee S.W. Rsch. Inst. Officer U.S. Army, 1968. Recipient medal Am. Ordnance Assn., 1953, Gold medal Pi Tau Sigma, 1963, Meritorious Svc. award and medal Dept. Transp., 1972, Disting. Svc. award Coun. U. Transp. Ctrs., 2006. Fellow AAAS, ASME (Moody award fluid engring. divsn. 1970, Centennial medallion 1983, Rufus Oldenberger medal 1984, Meritorious Svc. medal 1986, Disting. Svc. award 1986, hon. mem. 1987), Transp. Rsch. Bd. (Roy Crumm award 2007, Tex. Transp. Hall of Honor, 2013); mem. NAE (coun. 1986-92, com. on engring. edn.), Am. Soc. Engring. Edn. (Disting. Svc. medal 1993, Lamme award 1997), Nat. Rsch. Coun. (gov. bd. 1986-92, chmn. transp. rsch. bd. 1988-89), Nat. Acads. (nat. assoc., life), Sigma Xi, Tau Beta Pi. Office: Tex A&M U Sys MS 3135 College Station TX 77843-3135 Home Phone: 979-774-9616. E-mail: herbert-richardson@tamu.edu.

RICHARDSON, JAMES DAVID, surgeon; b. Morehead, Ky., 1945; MD, U. Ky., 1970. Diplomate Am. Bd. Surgeons, Am. Bd. Vascular Surgery, Am. Bd. Thoracic Surgery, Am. Bd. SCC. Intern U. Ky. Med. Ctr., Lexington, 1970, resident, 1971-72, U. Tex., San Antonio, 1972-76; surgeon Norton Hosp., Louisville, 1977—; prof. surgery U. Louisville, 1979—; pres. Am. Bd. Surgery, 1998-99. Past pres. So. Surg. Assn., Western Surg. Assn. Editor: (jour.) Am. Surgeon, 2005—. Fellow ACS (bd. regents); mem. AMA, Am. Assn. Surgery of Trauma, Soc. Surgergy Alimentary Tract, Alpha Omega Alpha. Office: U Louisville Dept Surgery 550 S Jackson St Louisville KY 40202-1622 Office Phone: 502-583-8303, 502-852-5452.

RICHARDSON, JEANNE D., state legislator; b. Memphis, Tenn. children: Robert, Ellyn, Danielle. BA in Social Work, Memphis State U., 1971, MPA in Health Svcs. Admin., 1980; attended, U. Tenn. Sch. Social Work, 1977. Health & Human Svcs. Program Developer; welfare worker/ protection svcs. Tenn. Dept. Human Svcs., 1972—73; mental health worker Northeast Cmty. Mental Health Ctr., 1973—74, inpatient supr., 1974—75, coord. psychiatric svcs., 1975—77, coord. cmty. svcs., 1977—82; dir. Planning & Devel. Midtown Mental Health Ctr. Inc., 1982—97, dir. Admin. Svcs., 1982—97, exec. dir., 1982—97; consultant, 2001—; del. Dem. Nat. Conv., 2004; mng. dir. XMI Memphis, 2006—07; mem. Dist. 89 Tenn. House of Reps., 2008—, vice chmn. Family Justice Subcommittee. Democrat. Catholic. Mailing: 797 N Evergreen Memphis TN 38107 Office: 26 Legislative Plaza Nashville TN 37243-0189 Office Phone: 615-741-2010. Office Fax: 615-253-0195. Business E-Mail: rep.jeanne.richardson@capitol.tn.gov.

RICHARDSON, JERRY, professional sports team executive; b. Spring Hope, NC, July 18, 1936; s. George and Mary Richardson; m. Rosalind Sallenger; children: Jon, Mark, Ashley. Attended, Wofford Coll., Spartanburg, SC. Wide receiver Balt. Colts, 1959—60; cofounder Spartan Foods; exec. positions including pres. and CEO Flagstar Corp. (formerly Transworld Corp. and TW Services), 1979—95; founder, owner Carolina Panthers, Charlotte, NC, 1993—. Recipient Order of Palmetto, State of SC; named one of 50 Most Influential People in Sports Bus., Street & Smith's SportsBus. Jour., 2007, 2008; named to NC Sports Hall of Fame, SC Sports Hall of Fame, 2006. Achievements include member of National Football League championship winning Baltimore Colts, 1959. Office: Carolina Panthers 800 S Mint St Charlotte NC 28202

RICHARDSON, PHIL, state legislator, veterinarian; m. Janalee Richardson; children: Steve, Stan, Shannon. BS in Agriculture, Okla.State Univ.; DVM, Okla. State Univ. Veterinarian, farmer; deacon Hazel/Dell Baptist Church; mem. Dist. 56 Okla. House of Representatives, 2005—. Capt. US Army, 1967—70. Decorated Bronze Star. Mem.: Okla. Veterinarian Med. Assn., Okla. Cattleman's Assn., Bingo Lions Club, Minco American Legion, Pocasset Masonic Lodge. Republican. Office: 2300 N Lincoln Blvd Rm 438 Oklahoma City OK 73105 Mailing: 289 C.S. 2760 Minco OK 73059 Office Phone: 405-557-7401, 405-779-0270. E-mail: philrichardson@okhouse.gov.

RICHARDSON, REY, JR., dancer; b. Scotland; m. Carmen Francis Richardson; 3 children. Studied with Roger Fitzwilliam, 1996—98; student, Professional Children's Sch., NYC, 1999. Principal England Nat. Ballet; dancer Royal Ballet London, 2002—04; artistic dir. Meriks Dance World, Sandy Springs, Ga., 2004—, ballet master. Founder, instr. Bring a Smile Through Dance, Alpharetta, Ga., 2010—. Recipient Gold medal, 6th Ann. Ballet Competition, Paris, 1993, Silver medal, 8th Ann. Ballet Competition, 1995. Avocations: winemaking, album collecting, pottery. Studio: Meriks Dance World 6065 Roswell Rd NE #2227 Sandy Springs GA 30328-4044

RICHARDSON, RICHARD JUDSON, retired political science professor; b. Poplar Bluff, Mo., Feb. 16, 1935; s. Jewel Judson and Naomi Fern (Watson) R.; m. Sammie Sue Cullum, Dec. 29, 1961;

children: Jon Mark, Anna Cecile, Ellen Elizabeth, Megan Leigh. BS, Harding Coll., Searcy, Ark., 1957; cert., U. Dublin, Trinity Coll., Ireland, 1958; MA, Tulane U., New Orleans, 1961, PhD, 1967. Instr. Tulane U., 1962—65; asst. prof. polit. sci. Western Mich. U., Kalamazoo, 1965, assoc. prof., 1967—69; vis. assoc. prof. U. Hawaii, 1967—68; Burton Craige prof. UNC, Chapel Hill, 1985—90, assoc. v.p. acad. affairs univ. gen. adminstrn., 1991—92, chmn. dept. Adj. prof. Duke U., Durham, 1972-74; provost, vice chancellor acad. affairs U. N.C., 1995-2000; cons. in field. Author: (with Kenneth Vines) The Politics of Federal Courts, 1971, (with Darlene Walker) People and the Police, 1973, (with Marian Irish, James Prothro) The Politics of American Democracy, 1981. Del. County Dem. Conv., 1972, 83; vice chmn. Dem. Party Precinct, 1983-85; chmn. bldg. fund YMCA, 1976; chmn. Carolina Challenge for endowment U. N.C., Chapel Hill, 1979-80; chmn. U. N.C. Bicentennial Observance, 1991-94; chmn. United Way, 1983, pres., 1985; pres. PTA County Coun., 1984. Recipient Edward S. Corwin award Am. Polit. Sci. Assn., 1967, Tanner Disting. Teaching award U. N.C., 1972, Univ. award for Outstanding Teaching, 1981, Thomas Jefferson award, 1987, James Johnston Disting. Tchg. award, 1993, Alumni Faculty Disting. Svc. award, 1994, Disting. Eagle Scout award Boy Scouts Am., 1998, Laura Thomas award, 1999, C. Knox Massey award, 2000, Disting. Svc. medal U. N.C. Alumni Assn., 2001, William Richardson Davie award, 2005; named life regent Boy Scouts Am., 1998; Edgar Stern fellow, 1959-61; Paul Harris fellow, Rotary Internat. Found. 2008, Humanity award Rotary Internat. Global Svc., 2009; NEH grantee, 1970 Mem. N.C. Polit. Sci. Assn. (pres. 1978-79), Am. Polit. Sci. Assn., So. Polit. Sci. Assn., ACLU (bd. dirs. local chpt. 1985-88, state bd. dirs. 1988-89), Order of Janus, Order of the Long Leaf Pine, Order of Golden Fleece, Order of the Grail. Home: 220 Carolina Meadows Villa Chapel Hill NC 27516

RICHARDSON, ROBERT DALE, JR., language educator; b. Milw., June 14, 1934; s. Robert Dale and Lucy Baldwin (Marsh) R.; m. Elizabeth Hall, Nov. 7, 1959 (div. 1987); m. Annie Dillard, Dec. 10, 1988; children: Elisabeth, Anne, Cody Rose. AB magna cum laude in English, Harvard U., 1956, PhD in English Lit., 1961; DHL (hon.), Meadville-Lombard Theol. Sch., 2003, U. Denver, 2008. Instr. English Harvard U., Cambridge, Mass., 1961-63; asst. prof. English U. Denver, 1963-68, assoc. prof., 1968-72, prof., 1972-87, Lawrence C. Phipps prof. humanities, 1979-82, chmn. dept., 1968-73, pres. Univ. senate, 1972-73, assoc. dean grad. studies, 1975-76; prof. English, U. Colo., Boulder, 1987; vis. prof. letters Wesleyan U., Middletown, Conn., 1989-94. Vis. prof. Harvard U., summer 1976, CUNY, 1978, Sichuan U., 1983, U. N.C., Chapel Hill, 2002, 05; vis. fellow Huntington Libr., 1973-74; vis. instr. Yale U., 1988; bd. dirs. David R. Godine Pub., R. W. Emerson Inst.; mem. editl. bd. New Eng. Quar. Author: Literature and Film, 1969, Henry Thoreau: A Life of the Mind, 1986 (Melcher award, 1986), Emerson: The Mind on Fire, 1995 (Parkman prize, 1995, Melcher award, 1995, Washington Irving award, 1995), Myth and Literature in the American Renaissance, 1978; author: (with Burton Feldman) The Rise of Modern Mythology 1680-1860, 1972; author: (with Allen Mandelbaum) Three Centuries of American Poetry, 1999; author: William James: In the Maelstrom of American Modernism, 2006 (Bancroft prize, 2006), First We Read, Then We Write: Emerson on the Creative Process, 2009; editor: The Heart of Williams James, 2010; author (with Lincoln Perry): October, or Autumnal Tints, 2012; author: (with John Paul Russo) Splendor of Heart: Walter Jackson Bate and the Teaching of Literature, 2013. Trustee Meadville-Lombard Theol. Sch., 1981-87 Fellow Guggenheim Found., 1990, Nat. Humanities Ctr., 1999-00; recipient Acad. award in lit. Am. Acad. Arts and Letters, 1998. Mem. Soc. Am. Hist., Author's Guild, Thoreau Soc., Emerson Soc., Assn. Lit. Scholars and Critics, William James Soc. Democrat. Unitarian Universalist. Personal E-mail: rrchardson@gmail.com.

RICHARDSON, R(OSS) FRED(ERICK), insurance company executive, consultant; b. Renfrew, Ont., Can., Feb. 4, 1928; came to U.S., 1980; s. Garfield Newton and Grace Mary (MacLean) R.; m. Betty Blanche Betts, Feb. 4, 1972; children by previous marriage: Sheri Joan, Robert John, Paul Frederick. BA in Math. and Physics with honors, Queens U., 1950. Actuarial asst. Empire Life Ins. Co., Kingston, Ont., Canada, 1950-55; sec. Maritime Life Ins. Co., Halifax, N.S., Canada, 1955-59, dir. sales, 1959-65, chief exec. officer, 1967-72; mng. dir., chief exec. officer Abbey Life Ins. Co., England, 1972-80; group gen. mgr. Hartford Europe Group, 1975-80; sr. v.p., dir. worldwide life ins. ops. Hartford Ins. Group, Conn., 1980-83, dir. worldwide life ins. ops. Conn., 1983-88; pres., COO, Hartford Life Cos., 1983-88; pvt. ins. cons., Boca Raton, Fla., 1988; pres., CEO, Crown Life Ins. Co., 1988-93; cons. INSCE, Boca Raton, 1993—. Fellow Soc. Actuaries, Can. Inst. Actuaries. Home: 401 E Linton Blvd Apt 263 Delray Beach FL 33483-5083 Personal E-mail: rfredr@gmail.com.

RICHARDSON, SALLY KEADLE, academic administrator; b. Mar. 2, 1933; d. Okey P. and Viola Miriam (Graybeal) Keadle; m. Don Rule Richardson, Dec. 15, 1961; children: Miriam Paige, Ruth Evan. AB, Vassar Coll., 1954. Regional pub. info. rep. Columbia Gas Sys., Charleston, W.Va., 1958-62; dir. Children's Mus., Charleston, 1963; coord. space-related sci. project Kanawha County Schs., Charleston, 1967-68; vol. dir. Rockefeller for Gov. Campaign, Charleston, 1972, program dir., 1976, 80; dir. admissions W.Va. Wesleyan Coll., Buckhannon, 1974-75; spl. asst. Office of Gov. State of W.Va., 1977, dep. commr. dept. welfare, 1978-79, dep. dir. dept. health, 1979-83; chmn. W.Va. Health Care Cost Rev. Authority, Charleston, 1983-85. Health care cons., Charleston, 1985-89; dir. W.Va. Pub. Employees Ins. Agy., Charleston, 1989-93; vice-chmn. W.Va. Health Care Planning Task Force, 1992-93; mem. White House Health Care Reform Task Force, Washington, 1993; dir. Medicaid Bur., Health Care Financing Adminstrn., U.S. DHHS, Balt., 1993-96; acting dep. adminstr. HCFA, U.S. DHHS, Washington, 1996-97; dir. HCFA Ctr. for Medicaid and State Ops., 1997-99; mem. U.S. DHHS Governing Coun. on Children and Youth, 1993-97, co-chmn. U.S. DHHS Children's Health Initiative, 1997-99; co-chmn. U.S. DHHS Home and Cmty. Based Svcs. Task Force, 1996-99; mem. U.S. DHHS Pub. Health Coun.'s D.C. Task Force, 1994-99; mem. Nat. Adv. Com. on Rural Health, DHHS, 2000-04; bd. dirs. Molina Healthcare, Inc. W.Va. rep. Task Force on So. Children, So. Growth Policies Bd., 1978-79; co-chmn. exec. com. W.Va. Internat. Yr. of Child, 1979; staff mem. Com. on Human Resources Nat. Gov. Assn., 1983-85; trustee U. Charleston, 1994-; bd. dirs. Children's Home Soc., Charleston, 1999—. Mem. Acad. Health, Nat. Rural Health Assn. Democrat. Office: WVa U Inst Health Policy Rsch 3110 Maccorkle Ave SE Rm 3015 Charleston WV 25304-1210

RICHARDSON, WILLIE LEE, JR., federal marshal; AS, Cmty. Coll. of Air Force, 1984. Dep./investigator Lowndes County Sheriff's Office, Valdosta, Ga., 1986—89; numerous positions of increasing responsibility to supervisory criminal investigator US Marshals Svc., US Dept. Justice, 1989—2009, US Marshal (mid. dist.) Ga., 2010—. Svc. with USAF, 1981—85. Office: US Courthouse 3rd & Mulberry St Rm 101 Macon GA 31201 Office Phone: 912-752-8280.

RICHARDS-PERSON, MELISSA, marketing executive; Promotions & mktg. dir. Sta. Cool 105.9, WOCL-FM, Orlando, Fla., 1991—94; account exec. Todd Persons Comm., Orlando, 1994—96; sr. account exec. Fahlgren Advt., 1996—99; dir. mktg. Jacor Comm., Inc. (merged with Clear Channel), 1999—2000; field/brand mktg. mgr. Olive Garden divsn., Darden Restaurants, Inc., 2000—01; regional mktg. mgr. Starbucks Corp., 2001—02; various mktg. positions Yum! Brands, Inc., 2002—04, dir. family meals mktg. KFC, 2004—07; prin. Third Arm Consulting, 2007—08; dir. mktg. enterprise-wide intitatives Humana Inc., 2008—09; sr. dir. advt. & promotions Papa John's Pizza, 2009—. Office: Papa Johns Internat Inc 2002 Papa Johns Blvd PO Box 99900 Louisville KY 40299

RICHELS, JOHN, energy executive, lawyer; BA, York Univ.; LLB, Univ. Windsor, 1978. Mng. ptnr., COO, mem. exec. com. Bennett Jones; bd. dir. Northstar Energy Corp., 1993—96, exec. v.p., CFO, 1996—98; pres., CEO Devon Canada, 1998—2001; sr. v.p. Canadian div. Devon Energy Corp., Oklahoma City, 2001—04, pres., 2004—10, pres., CEO, 2010—. Gen. counsel XV Olympic Winter Games, Calgary, 1986—88. Office: Devon Energy Corp 333 W Sheridan Ave Oklahoma City OK 73102-5010

RICHELSON, PAUL WILLIAM, curator; b. Montpelier, Idaho, Sept. 27, 1939; s. Paul Newton and June (Quayle) R. BA, Yale U., 1961; MFA, Princeton U., 1967, PhD, 1974. Asst. prof. Lawrence U., Appleton, Wis., 1970-77, U. Denver, 1977-84; asst. dir., curator Trisolini Gallery of Ohio U., Athens, 1984-87; chief curator Grand Rapids (Mich.) Mus., 1987-91; curator of Am. art Mobile Mus. Art, Mobile, Ala., 1991-97, asst. dir., chief curator, 1997—. Author: (book) Studies in the Personal Imagery Collection of 20th Prints Ohio University, 1985, (catalogue) The Golden Age 19th Century Prints by David Roberts, 1988, Lee Loring: A Southern Sophisticate, 1992, Modernism and American Painting of the 1930s, 1993, ThirtySomething, 1994, Alabama Impact: Contemporary Artists with Alabama Ties, 1995, Louise Lyons Heustis (1865-1951): A Retrospective, 1995, The French Connection: Jean Simon Chaudron Returns To Mobile, 1996, John Roderick Dempster MacKenzie (1865-1941): A Retrospective, 1997, Celebrating the Creative Spirit, 1998, Contemporary Southeastern Furniture, 1998, Coming Home: American Paintings, 1930-1950, from the Schoen Collection, 2003, Craig Nutt: Certified Organic, 2008; A Perfect Marriage: Wood and Color, 2008; Alabama Masters: Artists and Their Work, 2008, The Silent Cities of Peru Archeological Photography/Fernando LaKosa, 2013, Opulent Object: Tapestries by Jon Eric Riis with Sculpture by Richard Mayfong and Mike Harrison, 2013, Burroughs-Chapin Art Ctr., Myrtle Beach, SC. Lt. (j.g.) USN, 1961-63. Recipient Elizabeth B. Gould Rsch. award Mobile Hist. Devel. Commn., 1997; Fulbright-Hays fellow to Italy, 1967-69; Mus. Purchase Plan grantee Nat. Endowment for the Arts, 1991; grantee Mus. Loan Network, 2002. Mem. Southeastern Museums Conf. Home: 6427 Grelot Rd Apt 405 Mobile AL 36695-2630 Office: Mobile Museum of Art 4850 Museum Dr Mobile AL 36608-1917 Home Phone: 251-633-8596; Office Phone: 251-208-5215. Fax: 251-208-5201. E-mail: prichelson@mobilemuseumofart.com.

RICHENHAGEN, MARTIN H., manufacturing executive; b. July 1, 1952; married; 3 children. Grad., Univ. Bonn, Germany, 1975. Vice-pres. field ops. Schindler Aufzugefabrik GmbH, Germany, 1995—98; group pres. GLAAS KgaA mbH, Germany, 1995—2003; group exec. vice-pres. Forbo Internat. SA, 2003—04; pres., CEO AGCO Corp., Duluth, Ga., 2004—, chmn., 2006—. Bd. dir. PPG Industries, 2007—. Office: AGCO Corp 4205 River Green Pkwy Duluth GA 30096 Office Phone: 770-813-9200.

RICHIE, RODNEY CHARLES, critical care and pulmonary medicine physician; b. Big Springs, Tex., Aug. 17, 1946; s. Howard Mouzon and Gloria (Hollingshead) R.; m. Sara Lee Dilley, July 13, 1968; children: Megan Kathryn, Paul Nathan. BA in Chemistry, So. Meth. U., 1968; MD cum laude, Baylor Coll., 1972. Diplomate in Internal Medicine, Pulmonary, Ins. Medicine. Resident in medicine Baylor Affiliated Hosps., Houston, 1973-75, chief med. resident, 1975, fellow in pulmonary medicine, 1976-77; pres. Waco Lung Assocs., Tex., 1977—2007; assoc. clin. prof. cmty. medicine Heart of Tex. Cmty. Health Ctr./U. Tex. SW Med. Sch., 2004—. Med. dir. Tex. Life Ins., Waco, 1985—, Cmty. Hospice of Waco, 1996—, EMSI, Waco, Tex., 1997—. Chmn. med. staff Hillcrest Bapt. Med. Ctr., Waco, 1993; chmn. bd. dirs. GH Pape Found., Waco, 1993. Fellow: ACP, Am. Coll. Chest Physicians; mem.: AMA, Am. Thoracic Soc., Am. Acad. Internal Medicine (del. to AMA), Tex. Club Internists. Episcopalian. Avocations: skiing, writing, reading. Home: 3509 Lake Heights Dr Waco TX 76708-1005 Office: 7003 Woodway Dr Ste 311 Waco TX 76712 Office Phone: 254-741-1688. Personal E-mail: rodney.richie@gmail.com.

RICHMOND, C. BRADFORD (C. BRADFORD RICHMOND), food service executive; married. Food beverage analyst, Casa Gallardo Darden Restaurants, Inc., Orlando, Fla., 1982—85, fin. & mktg. positions with York Steak House, Red Lobster and Olive Garden, 1985—98, sr. v.p. fin. & contr. Olive Garden, 1998—2003, sr. v.p. fin., strategic planning & contr. Red Lobster, 2003—05, sr. v.p., corp. contr., 2005—06, sr. v.p., CFO, 2006—. Office: Darden Restaurants Inc 5900 Lake Ellenor Dr PO Box 593330 Orlando FL 32859-3330 Office Phone: 407-245-4000.

RICHMOND, CEDRIC LEVON, United States Representative from Louisiana, former state legislator; b. New Orleans, Sept. 13, 1973; BA, Morehouse Coll., 1995; JD, Tulane U., 1998; Grad. Exec. Program, John F. Kennedy Sch. Govt. Harvard U. Mem. Dist. 101 La. House of Reps., 2000—10; mem. US Congress from 2nd La. Dist., 2011—, US House Small Bus. Com., 2011—. Named one of The Politics 40 Under 40, TIME Mag., 2010. Mem.: La. Bar Assn. Democrat. Baptist. Office: US House of Representatives 240 Cannon House Office Bldg Washington DC 20515 Office Phone: 202-225-6636. Office Fax: 202-225-1988.*

RICHMOND, GAIL LEVIN, law educator; b. Gary, Ind., Jan. 9, 1946; d. Herbert Irving and Sylvia Esther (Given) Levin; children: Henry, Amy. AB, U. Mich., 1966, MBA, 1967; JD, Duke U., 1971. Bar: Ohio 1971, U.S. Claims Ct. 1986, U.S. Ct. Mil. Appeals, 1994; CPA, Ill. Acct. Arthur Andersen & Co., Chgo., 1967-68; assoc. Jones, Day, Cleve., 1971-72; asst. prof. Capital U. Law Sch., Columbus, Ohio, 1972-73, U. N.C. Law Sch., Chapel Hill, 1973-78; vis. asst. prof. U. Tex. Law Sch., Austin, 1977-78, Nova U. Law Ctr., Ft. Lauderdale, Fla., 1979-80, assoc. prof., 1980-81, assoc. prof., assoc. dean, 1981-85, prof., assoc. dean., 1985—93, 1995—2009, prof., acting dean, 1993-95, prof., 2009—. Author: Federal Tax Research, 8th edit., 2010; co-author: Mastering Corporate Tax, 2009, Tax Planning for Lifetime and Testamentary Dispositions, 1997, A Complete Introduction to Corporate Taxation, 2006, Florida Wills, Trusts and Estates: Cases and Materials, 2007; contbr. articles to profl. jours. Pres. Greater Ft. Lauderdale Tax Coun., 1987-88; trustee Law Sch. Admission Coun., 1994-99, chair audit com., 1991-93, chair svcs. and programs com., 1997-99. Mem. ABA (chair commn. on individual income, tax sect. 2001-03, supervising editor News Quar. 2006—, chair AMT task force 2003-2004, chair adj. com., legal edn. sect. 2002-05), Am. Assn. Atty.-CPAs (dir. Fla. chpt. 1992-98), Assn. Am. Law Schs. (chmn. audit com. 1992, chair sect. adminstrn. of law schs. 1996, pres. S.E. chpt. 1993-94, sec. S.E. chpt. 1995-2002), S.E. Assn. Law Schs. (pres. 2002-03, sec. 2004—). Office: Nova Southeastern Univ Shepard Bd Law Ctr 3305 College Ave Davie FL 33314-7721

RICHTER, GARRETT S., state legislator; b. Pitts., Aug. 1, 1950; s. F. Garrett Richter; m. Diana Richter; children: Melissa, Elizabeth, Robert. BS, U. Pitts., 1981; attended, Grad. Sch. Banking, Madison, Wis., 1985. Founder, CEO First Nat. Bank of Fla.; mem. Dist. 76 Fla. House of Reps., Tallahassee, 2006—08; mem. Dist. 37 Fla. State Senate, Tallahassee, 2008—, chair banking and ins. com., mem. policy and steering com. on commerce and industry, comm., energy and pub. utilities com., edn. preK-12 appropriations com., mem. ethics and elections com., judiciary com., select com. on Fla.'s economy, joint legis. com. on Everglades oversight. Emeritus bd. mem. Collier County Edn. Found.; trustee Quest for Kids. Served with US Army, 1969—71, served with USAFR, 1979—81. Decorated Vietnam Bronze Star, Combat Infantry Badge. Republican. Presbyterian. Office: 3301 E Tamiami Trail Bldg F Ste 203 Naples FL 34112-3972 also: 310 Senate Office Bldg 404 S Monroe St Tallahassee FL 32399-1100 Office Phone: 239-417-6205, 850-487-5124. Business E-Mail: richter.garrett.web@flsenate.gov.

RICHTER, JOHN CHARLES, lawyer, former prosecutor; b. 1963; Grad., Emory U.; JD, U. Va., 1992. Law clk. to Hon. J. Owen Forrester US Dist. Ct. (no. dist.) Ga.; asst. dist. atty. Cobb County, Ga., 1998; chief of staff, criminal divsn. US Dept. Justice, 1998, acting asst. atty. gen. criminal divsn., acting US atty. (we. dist.) Okla., 2005—06, US atty. (we. dist.) Okla., 2006—09; v.p., chief litigation counsel WellCare Health Plans, Inc., 2010—. Mem.: State Bar Ga., Okla. Bar Assn. Office: WellCare Health Plans Inc 8735 Henderson Rd Tampa FL 33634 Office Phone: 813-290-6200.

RICHTON, SAMUEL M., pediatric endocrinologist; b. Pittsfield, Mass., Aug. 17, 1948; m. Marsha Lee Richton, May 25, 1975; children: Jonathan, Joshua, Jeanette, Simcha, Jesse. BS, U. Mass., 1970; MS, Yale U., New Haven, 1972; MD, Albert Einstein Coll. Medicine, Bronx, NY, 1975. Diplomate Am. Bd. Pediat., Am. Bd. Pediat. Endocrinology. Resident pediat. Rainbow Babies & Children's Hosp., Cleve., 1975-77; fellow pediat. endocrinology and metabolism U. Md., Balt., 1977-78; fellow pediat. Harvard Med. Sch., Boston; rsch. fellow Juvenile Diabetes Found. Children's Hosp., Boston, 1978-80; physician Diabetes Med. Group, LA, 1980-81; asst. prof. U. Ill. Coll. Medicine, Chgo., 1981-84, Chgo. Med. Sch., 1984-87; dir. endocrinology Cook County Children's Hosp., Chgo., 1984-87; dir. divsn. pediat. endocrinology Miami Children's Hosp., 1987—. Med. dir. South Fla. Diabetes Camp, Miami, 1987—. Contbr. articles to profl jours. Fellow: Am. Acad. Pediat.; mem.: Lawson Wilkens Pediat. Endocrine Soc., Internat. Diabetes Fedn., Am. Diabetes Assn. Office: Miami Childrens Hosp 3100 SW 62nd Ave # 122 Miami FL 33155-3009 Office Phone: 305-662-8398. Office Fax: 305-663-8581.

RICKARD, MARGARET LYNN, library director, consultant; b. Detroit, July 31, 1944; d. Frank Mathias and Betty Louise (Lee) Sieger; m. Cyriac Thannikary, Nov. 13, 1965 (div. Feb. 1973); 1 child, Luke Anthony Thannikary; m. Marcos T. Perez, Mar. 1973 (dec. Oct. 1973); m. Lui Gotti, Dec. 23, 1984 (dec. Aug. 1997); m. William A. Rickard, Aug. 22, 1998 (dec. Aug. 21, 2005). AB, U. Detroit, Mich., 1968; MLS, Pratt Inst., Bklyn., 1969; postgrad., NYU, 1976—77. Cert. libr. N.Y. Sr. libr. Queens Pub. Libr., Jamaica, NY, 1969-77; libr. dir. El Centro (Calif.) Pub. Libr., 1977-99; ret., 1999. Vice chmn., chmn. Serra Coop. Libr. Sys., San Diego, 1980—82, libr. cons., 1998—; county libr./cons. Imperial County Free Libr., 1993—99. Pres. Hist. Site Found., El Centro, 1988—99, 1992, sec., 1989, trustee, 1989—99, v.p., 1991—92; mem. Downton El Centro Assn., mem. arches bus. improvement dist.; mem. comm. and arts task force Imperial County Arts Coun.; coord. arts and culture com. City of El Centro Strategic Plan; fin. sec. St. Elizabeth Luth. Ch., El Centro, 1988. Recipient Disting. Svc. award, El Dorado County ACSA, 2004, El Dorado County Disting. Employee Svc. award, ACSA, 2004; Title IIB fellow, Pratt Inst., 1968—69. Mem.: AAUW (v.p. El Centro 1988), ALA, Calif. County Librs. Assn., Calif. Libr. Assn., Toastmasters, El Centro C. of C., Women of Moose (sr. regent El Centro 1988—89, ednl. advancment chmn. 1999—2000), Soroptomists (life; v.p. El Centro 1978, corr. sec. 1990—91, 1st v.p. 1991—92, pres. 1992—93, 2d v.p. 1995—96, 1998—99, rec. sec. 1997—98). Democrat. Lutheran.

RICKEL, JOHN C., automotive executive; b. 1961; B in Finance, Ohio State U., MBA. Various exec. and managerial positions including contr. Ford Americas and CFO Ford Europe Ford Motor Co., 1984—2005, mem. audit com., bd. dirs. Ford Otosan Turkey, chmn. bd. dirs. Ford Russia, 2002—04; sr. v.p., CFO Group 1 Automotive, Inc., Houston, 2005—. Office: Group 1 Automotive Inc 800 Gessner Ste 500 Houston TX 77024 Office Phone: 713-647-5700.

RICKETSON, GEORGE MANNING, III, retired surgeon; b. Atlanta, Ga., 1937; MD, U. Fla., 1966. Diplomate Am. Bd. Surgery. Intern Bethesda Naval Hosp, Md., 1966-67; resident in surgery USN Hosp., Portsmouth, Va., 1967-71; pvt. practice Sacred Heart Hosp., Pensacola, Fla.; pvt. practice, group partnership McMahon Ricketson Stockamp, Pensacola, Fla.; ret., 2002. Fellow: ACS; mem.: Southeastern Surg. Congress. Office: McMahon Ricketson Stockamp 5014 Barranca Lora Pensacola FL 32514 Home Phone: 850-477-5146. Personal E-mail: pricketson@cox.net.

RICKLEFS, DALE LYNNE, retired library director; b. Chgo., July 29, 1953; d. Glenn Harley and Eleanor Clara Rogers; 1 child, Reyhan. BA, Ill. Wesleyan U., 1974; MLS, U. Tex., 1977; PhD in Bus., Capella U., 2014. Libr. Radian Corp., Austin, Tex., 1975—80; libr. dir. City of Round Rock, Tex., 1980—2010; mem. adv. coun. U. Tex., Sch. Info., 2010—. Vol. Round Rock Pub. Libr., Round Rock Area Arts Coun., 2009—, VITA2014; mem. Friends Round Rock Pub. Libr., 1983—; past pres.,past. dist. gov. Round Rock Rotary, 1992—2006; mem. ex officio Round Rock Cmty. Choir, 1998—2014; past pres. United Way Greater Williamson Co., Round Rock, 2005—12, Williamson County Hist. Mus., 2005—12; boy scout dist. cub trainer Boy Scouts American Tomahawk Dist., Austin-Georgetown, Tex., 1991—92; pres. Main St. Quilt Guild, 2002—03, 2012—13. Recipient Dist. Cubscouter of Yr., Boy Scouts Am. Tomahawk Dist., Texas, 1992. Mem.: ALA, Texas Mcpl. League Libr. Dir.'s Divsn. (pres. 1988—89), Tex. Libr. Assn. (chmn. dist. 3 1984—85). Avocations: machine embroidery, quilting, art.

RICKMAN, ELLEN ERWIN, museum administrator; BA in Lit., U. NC, Asheville. Cert. in mgmt. U. SC. Various positions including curator, collections mgr. and registrar Biltmore Estate, Asheville, NC, 1977—2000, dir., mus. svcs., 2000—. Mem. pub. art bd. City of Asheville. Mem.: NC Mus. Conf., Southeastern Mus. Conf., Am. Assn. Mus. Office: Biltmore Estate 1 Approach Rd Asheville NC 28803 Office Phone: 828-225-1333.

RICKMERS, BRIAN L., corporate financial executive; BBA in Acctg., Tex. A&M U. CPA. Joined Newfield Exploration Co., 1993, various postions, including acct., fin. analyst, asst. contr., 2000—01, contr., asst. sec., 2001—. Mem.: Tex. Soc. of CPAs. Office: Newfield Exploration Co 363 N Sam Houston Pky E Ste 100 Houston TX 77060 Office Phone: 281-847-6000. Office Fax: 281-405-4242.

RICKS, RON, air transportation executive, lawyer; b. Del Rio, Tex., Sept. 25, 1949; s. Philip A. and Leota B. (Petty) R.; m. Eileen Susan Townley, Jan. 8, 1972; 1 child: Alan A. BA in History, U. Tex., 1972; JD, George Washington U., 1977. Bar: N.M. 1977, Tex. 1981. Legislative aide to Rep. O.C. Fisher US Congress, Washington, 1972-74; ptnr. Zinn & Donnell, Santa Fe, 1977-81, Oppenheimer, Rosenberg, Kelleher & Wheatley Inc., San Antonio, 1981-86; v.p. govt. affairs Southwest Airlines Co., Dallas, sr. v.p. for law airports & pub. affairs, 2004—06, exec. v.p. for law, airports & public affairs, 2006—08, exec. v.p. for corporate services, corporate sec., 2008—11, exec. v.p., chief legal & regulatory officer, 2011—. Recipient Graduate award, Leadership Dallas, 1987. Mem. N.Mex. Bar Assn., Tex. Bar Assn., Air Transport Assn., North Dallas Chamber of Commerce (bd. dirs.), North Dallas Chamber Aviation Com. (co-chmn.), Dallas Chamber of Commerce Aviation Com. (exec. com.). Clubs: Dallas Friday Group. Democrat. Office: Southwest Airlines Co PO Box 36611- 4GA Dallas TX 75235*

RICKS, THOMAS G., investment company executive; BA in Economics, Trinity Coll.; MBA, U. Chgo. CPA. Exec. dir, fin. & pvt. investments U. Tex. Sys., 1988—92, vice chancellor asset mgmt., 1992—96; pres., CEO U. Tex. Investment Mgmt. Co., 1996—2001; chmn. DTM Corp., 1991—96; chief investment officer H&S Ventures, LLC, 2001—. Former bd. dirs. Argus Pharmaceuticals. Inc., LifeCell Corp., BDM Internat., Inc., 1992; bd. adv. Miramar Venture Ptnrs.; bd. dirs. Newfield Exploration Co., 1992—. Bd. dirs. Ocean Inst., Dana Point, Calif. Office: H&S Ventures LLC 2101 E Coast Hwy Ste 220 Corona Del Mar CA 92625 also: Newfield Exploration Co Bd Directors 363 N Sam Houston Pky E Ste 100 Houston TX 77060 Office Phone: 281-847-6000. Office Fax: 281-405-4242.

RICORDI, CAMILLO, surgeon, researcher; b. NYC, Apr. 1, 1957; m. Valerie A. Grace, Aug. 8, 1986; children: M. Caterina, Eliana G., Carlo A. MD, Milan U., Italy, 1982. Trainee in gen. surgery San Raffaele Inst., Milan, 1982-85; NIH trainee Washington U. Sch. Medicine, St. Louis, 1985-88; attending surgeon San Raffaele Inst., Milan, 1988-89; asst. prof. to assoc. prof. surgery U. Pitts., Pa., 1989-93; disting. prof. medicine, prof. biomed. engring., microbiology and immunology, chief divsn. cellular transpl., dir. cell transplantation ctr. Diabetes Rsch. Inst., U. Miami, Fla., 1993—, sci. dir., chief acad. officer Fla., 1996—, Stacy Joy Goodman chair in Diabetes Rsch., 1998—. Reviewer of applications for grants Can. and Am. Diabetes Assns., Juvenile Diabetes Found., NIH; chmn. First and Third Internat. Congresses of Cell Transplant Soc., Pitts., 1992, Miami, 1996, 5th Internat. Congress on Pancreas and Islet Transplantation, Miami, 1995, others; mem. editl. bd. Transplantation, Cell Transplantation, Transplantation Procs., Jour. Tissue Engring. Editor: Pancreatic Islet Cell Transplantation, 1992, Methods in Cell Transplantaion, 1995; co-editor-in-chief Cell Transplantation, Graft; assoc. editor Am. Jour. Transplantation, 2003—; contbr. numerous chpts. to books and articles to jours. including Immunology Today, Jour. Clin. Investigation, New Eng. Jour. Medicine, Hepatology, Diabetes, Transplantation, Endocrinology, Procs. NAS, USA, Am. Jour. Physiology, Surgery, Nature, Nature Genetics, Lancet, Nature Immunology Rev. Grantee Juvenile Diabetes Found. Internat., 1988—, NIH, 1993—, Galileo Lectr., EASD, Rome, 2008; recipient Nessim Habif World prize of surgery, 2001. Mem. AAAS, Cell Transplant Soc. (founder, pres. 1992-94), Am. Soc. Transplant Surgeons, Internat. Pancreas and Islet Transplant Assn. (v.p. 1979-99, pres. 1999-2001), The Transplantation Soc., Am. Diabetes Assn. (councillor, 2003-, Outstanding Sci. Achievement award 2002). Achievements include patents in cellular biotechnologies. Office: U Miami Diabetes Rsch Inst PO Box 016960 Miami FL 33101 Business E-Mail: ricordi@miami.edu.

RIDDICK, FRANK ADAMS, JR., physician, healthcare administrator; b. Memphis, June 14, 1929; s. Frank Adams and Falba (Crawford) Riddick; m. Mary Belle Alston, June 15, 1952; children: Laura Elizabeth Dufresne, Frank Adams III, John Alston. BA cum laude, Vanderbilt U., 1951, MD, 1954. Diplomate Am. Bd. Internal Medicine. Intern Barnes Hosp., St. Louis, 1954—55, resident in medicine, 1957—60; fellow in metabolic diseases Washington U., St. Louis, 1960—61; staff Ochsner Clinic (Ochsner Found. Hosp.), New Orleans, 1961—, head sect. endocrinology and metabolic disease, 1976—83, asst. med. dir., 1968—72, assoc. med. dir., 1972—75, med. dir., 1975—92; CEO Alton Ochsner Med. Found., New Orleans, 1992—2001; CEO emeritus Ochsner Clinic Found., 2001—. Bd. govs. Am. Bd. Internal Medicine, 1973—80; clin. prof. Tulane U., New Orleans, 1977—; trustee Alton Ochsner Med. Found., 1973—, CEO, 1991—; chmn. bd. Ochsner Health Plan, 1983—92; pres. Orleans Svc. Corp., 1976—80, South La. Med. Assocs., New Orleans, 1978—; dir. Brent House Corp., New Orleans, 1980—; chmn. Accreditation Coun. on Grad. Med. Edn., 1986—87, v.p. nat. resident matching program, 1986—90, mem. accreditation coun. on med. edn., 1988—90. Bd. govs. Isidore Newman Sch., New Orleans, 1987—93; trustee St. Martin's Protestant Episc. Sch., Metairie, La., 1970—84. Recipient Tchg. award, Alton Ochsner Med. Found., 1969, Disting. Alumnus award, Castle Heights Mil. Acad., 1979, Physician Exec. award, Am. Coll. Med. Group Adminstrs., 1984, Disting. Alumnus award, Vanderbilt U. Sch. Medicine, 1988. Master: ACP; fellow: Am. Coll. Physician Execs. (pres. 1987—88); mem.: NAS Inst. Medicine, AMA (ho. dels. 1971—92, chmn. coun. on med. edn. 1983—85, coun. on jud. and ethical affairs 1995—2002, chair 2001—02, Disting. Service award 2003), Am. Group Practice Assn. (pres. 1992—94), Soc. Med. Adminstrs. (pres. 1995—), Am. Diabetes Assn., Endocrine Soc., Am. Soc. Internal Medicine (trustee 1970—76, Disting. Internist award), Cosmos Club, New Orleans Country Club, Boston Club. Office: Ochsner Clinic 1516 Jefferson Hwy New Orleans LA 70121-2429 Home: 150 Broadway 709 New Orleans LA 70118-7610 Office Phone: 504-842-4019. Business E-Mail: friddick@ochsner.org.

RIDDIFORD, LYNN MOORHEAD, biologist, educator; b. Knoxville, Tenn., Oct. 18, 1936; d. James Eli and Virginia Amalia (Berry) Moorhead; m. Alan W. Riddiford, June 20, 1959 (div. Jan. 1966); m. James William Truman, July 28, 1970. AB magna cum laude, Radcliffe Coll., 1958; PhD, Cornell U., 1961. Rsch. fellow in biology Harvard U., Cambridge, Mass., 1961-63, 65-66, asst. prof. biology, 1966—71, assoc. prof., 1971—73; instr. biology Wellesley Coll., Mass., 1963—65; from assoc. prof. to prof. zoology U. Wash., Seattle, 1973—2003, prof. biology, 2003—07, prof. biology emeritus, 2007—, Va. and Prentice Bloedel prof., 2000—05, assoc. chmn., 2003—04; sr. fellow Janelia Farm Howard Hughes Med. Inst., Ashburn, Va., 2007—. Mem. study sect. tropical medicine and parasitology NIH, Bethesda, Md., 1974—78, 1997; mem. Competitive Grants panel USDA, 1979, 1989, 1995; mem. regulatory biology panel NSF, 1984—88, 2001, 2005, 2007, mem. biol. adv. com., 1992—95; mem. governing coun. Internat. Ctr. for Insect Physiology and Ecology, 1985—91, chmn. program com., 1989—91; chmn. adv. com. SeriBiotech, Bangalore, India, 1989; mem. coun. Internat. Cong. Entomology, 1988—2008, pres., 2000—04; mem. coun. Internat. Fedn. Comparative Endocrine Socs., 1996—2009, pres., 2001—05. Mem. editl. bd. profl. jours.; contbr. articles to profl. jours. Bd. dirs. Entomol. Found., 1998—2001, chmn., 2001; bd. dirs. Whitney Lab., 2000—04, chmn., 2004. Recipient Gregor J. Mendel award, Czech Republic Acad. Scis., 1998, Ann. Dinner honoree, Entomol. Found., 2006, Vollum award, Reed Coll., 2011; grantee, NSF, 1964—65, 1967—2010, Rockefeller Found., 1970—79, USDA, 1978—82, 1989—2006, NIH, 1975—2009; fellowship, NSF, 1958—60, 1961—63, NIH, 1960—61, 1986—87, John S. Guggenheim Found., 1979—80. Fellow: AAAS, Entomol. Soc. America (Recognition award in insect physiology, biochemistry and toxicology 1997), Royal Entomol. Soc., Am. Acad. Arts and Sci.; mem.: NAS, Genetics Soc. America, Soc. Exptl. Biology, Soc. Devel. Biology, Am. Soc. Biochem. and Molecular Biology, Soc. Integrative and Comparative Biology. Methodist. Achievements include research in endocrinology of larval molting and metamorphosis of insects, especially the cellular and molecular basis of juvenile hormone action. Office: Janelia Farm Howard Hughes Med Inst 19700 Helix Dr Ashburn VA 20147 Home: 40733 Manor House Rd Leesburg VA 20175 Business E-Mail: riddifordl@janelia.hhmi.org.

RIDDLE, CHARLES ADDISON, III, district attorney, former state legislator; b. Marksville, La., June 8, 1955; s. Charles Addison Jr. and Alma Rita (Gremillion) R.; m. Margaret Susan Noone, Mar. 24, 1978; children: Charles Addison IV, John H., Michael J. BA, La. State U., 1976, JD, 1980. Bar: La. 1980, U.S. Dist. Ct. (mid. and we. dists.) La. 1983, U.S. Ct. Appeals (5th cir.) 1988, U.S. Supreme Ct. 1991, U.S. Ct. Vets. Appeals 1994. Ptnr. Riddle & Bennett LLC, Marksville, 1980; pvt. practice Marksville, 1981—2004; mem. La. Ho. of Reps., Baton Rouge, 1992—2003; reelected La. House of Reps., Baton Rouge, 1995—99, 1999—2003; dist. atty. Avoyelles Parish 12th Jud. Dist., 2003—. Elected La. State Dem. Cen. com., Avoyelles Parish, 1983-87, Parish Exec. Demo. Com. 1987-91. Mem. Avoyelles Bar Assn. (pres. 1987-88), Bunkie Rotary (bd. dirs.), Marksville Lions, Marksville C. of C. (pres. 1988-92). Office: PO Box 608 208 E Mark St Marksville LA 71351-2416 Office Phone: 318-253-4551. Personal E-mail: criddle777@aol.com.

RIDDLE, DEBBIE, state legislator; b. Oct. 15, 1948; m. Mike Riddle; 3 children. Mem. Dist. 150 Tex. House of Representatives, 2002—. Recipient of several honors and awards. Republican. Office: 3648 F.M. 1960 West Ste 106 Houston TX 77068 also: Room E2.306 Capitol Extension PO Box 2910 Austin TX 78768 Office Phone: 281-537-5252, 512-463-0572.

RIDDLE, W. CURTIS, publisher; b. 1951; BA in English and Journalism, Southern Ill. U., Edwardsville, 1972. Deputy mng. editor,sports Gannett Co., Inc., 1982; mng. editor Cincinnati Enquirer, 1985; pres., pub. and sr. group pres., News Journal Gannett Co., Inc., New Castle, Del., 1991—. Chmn. adv. group Gannett's Newspaper Tech.; founding mem. Nat. Assn. Black Journalists. Office: 950 W Basin Rd New Castle DE 19720-1008 also: Gannett Co Inc 7950 Jones Branch Dr Mc Lean VA 22107 Office Phone: 703-854-6000. Office Fax: 703-854-2053. Business E-Mail: wriddle@gannett.com.

RIDER, BRIAN CLAYTON, lawyer; b. San Antonio, Oct. 8, 1948; s. Ralph W. and Emmie(Rider); m. Patsy Anne (Ruppert), Dec. 27, 1970; children: Christopher, David, James, Andrew. BA, Rice U., 1969; JD, U. Tex., 1972. Bar: Tex., 1972. Assoc. then ptnr. Dow, Cogburn, and Friedman, Houston, 1972-83; ptnr. Brown, McCarroll, Oaks, and Hartline, Austin, Tex., 1983-96. Adj. prof. U. Tex., 1997—; lectr. in field. Contbr. articles to profl. journal Mem. Am. Coll. Real Estate Lawyers; Travis County Bar Assn. (bd. dirs. 1986-88, chmn. Travis County real estate sect. 1986-88); State Bar of Tex. (coun. real estate and probate sect. 1992-96),; Tex. Coll. Real Estate Lawyers (chair 1999-2002, sec. treas. 2003—). Home: 2906 Hatley Dr Austin TX 78746-4613 Office: 6300 Bee Caxe Rd Bldg Two Ste 500 Austin TX 78746 Office Phone: 512-433-5248. Personal E-mail: brider@sbcglobal.net. Business E-Mail: brianrider@forestargroup.com.

RIDGWAY, ROZANNE LEJEANNE, corporate director, retired ambassador; b. St. Paul, Aug. 22, 1935; d. H. Clay and Ethel Rozanne (Cote) R.; m. Theodore E. Deming. BA, Hamline U., 1957, LLD (hon.), 1978, George Washington U., 1986, Elizabethtown Coll., 1990, U. Helsinki, 1992; LLD in Pub. Svc. (hon.), Coll. of William and Mary, 1994; DHL (hon.), Hood Coll., 1994; LLD (hon.), Albright Coll.; DHL in Pub. Adminstrn. (hon.), The Citadel, 2003; DHL (hon.), Ill. Coll., 2003. Career diplomat U.S. Fgn. Svc., 1957-89, amb. at large for oceans and fisheries, 1975-77, US amb. to Finland Helsinki, 1977—80; counselor State Dept., 1980—81, spl. asst. to sec., 1981, amb. to German Dem. Republic, 1982-85, asst. sec. Europe and Can., 1985-89; pres. Atlantic Coun. US, 1989-92, co-chmn., 1993-96; chmn. Baltic-Am. Enterprise Fund, Washington, 1994—2011, Baltic-Am. Freedom Found., Ctr. Naval Analyses, 2009—. Bd. dirs., Emerson Electric Co., New Perspective Fund, Europacific Fund, New World Fund. Life trustee Hamline U.; dir. Washington Inst. Fgn. Affairs; trustee Sri Living Found. Decorated Grand Cross Order of the Lion (Finland); recipient Profl. awards Dept. State, Presdl. Disting. Performance awards, Joseph C. Wilson Internat. Rels. Achievement award, 1982, Sharansky award Union Couns. Soviet Jewry, 1989, U.S. Presdl. Citizens medal, 1989; named Person of Yr. Nat. Fisheries Inst., 1977, Knight Comdr., Order of Merit, Germany; inducted into Nat. Women's Hall of Fame, 1998. Fellow Nat. Acad. Pub. Adminstrn.; mem. Am. Acad. Diplomacy, Army-Navy Country Club. Office Phone: 703-527-3611.

RIDLEY, BETTY ANN, theology studies educator; b. St. Louis, Oct. 19, 1926; d. Rupert Alexis and Virginia Regina (Weikel) Steber; m. Fred A. Ridley, Jr., Sept. 8, 1948; children: Drue Alexis, Clay Kent. BA, Scripps Coll., Claremont, Calif., 1948. Christian Sci. practitioner, Oklahoma City, 1973—. Tchr. Christian Sci., 1983—; mem. Christian Sci. Bd. Lectureship, 1980-85. Trustee Daystar Found., 1990-; mem. First Ch. of Christ Scientist, Boston, 1956-2005, Fifth Ch. of Christ Scientist, Oklahoma City. Mem. Jr. League Am. Home: 2933 Lansdowne Ln Oklahoma City OK 73120-4343 Office: 3007 United Founders Blvd Oklahoma City OK 73112 Office Phone: 405-848-7565. Personal E-mail: baridley@bettyannridley.csb.org. Business E-Mail: baridley@aol.com.

RIDLEY, CLARENCE HAVERTY, retail executive; b. Atlanta, June 3, 1942; s. Frank Morris Jr. and Clare (Haverty) R.; m. Eleanor Horsey, Aug. 22, 1969; children: Augusta Morgan, Clare Haverty. BA, Yale U., 1964; MBA, Harvard U., 1966; JD, U. Va., 1971. Bar: Ga. 1971. Ptnr. King & Spalding, Atlanta, 1977—2000, chmn., policy com., 1995—97; chmn. bd. Haverty Furniture Cos., Inc., 2001—. Bd. dirs. Crawford & Co., Inc.; bd. trustees STI Classic Funds and Variable Trusts, 2001—. Co-author: Computer Software Agreements, 1987, 3d edit., 2003; exec. editor Va. Law Rev., 1970-71. Chmn., bd. trustees St. Joseph's Health Sys., 2003-04; founding trustee Atlanta Girls Sch., 2000-2003; chmn., bd. visitors Emory U., 1999-2000; bd. councilors Carter Ctr., 2000-. Lt. US Army, 1967—68, Korea. Mem.: Atlanta Rotary Club. Roman Catholic. Home: 2982 Habersham Rd NW Atlanta GA 30305-2854 Office: Haverty Furniture Companies Inc 780 Johnson Ferry Rd Atlanta GA 30342

RIDLEY, DAVID A., investment company executive; BBA in Fin., U. Tex., Austin. CEO Invesco Real Estate (subs. of Invesco Ltd.), 2004—. Mem. Nat. Assn. Real Estate Investment Mgrs., Pension Real Estate Assn., Urban Land Inst. Office: Invesco Ltd 1555 Peachtree St NE Ste 1800 Atlanta GA 30309 Office Phone: 404-479-1095. Office Fax: 404-439-4911. Business E-Mail: david_ridley@invesco.com.

RIDLEY, DAVIS S., air transportation company executive; V.p., ground ops. Southwest Airlines Co., 1998—2004, sr. v.p., people & leadership devel., 2004—06, cons., 2006—07, sr. v.p., mktg., 2007—08, sr. v.p., mktg. & revenue mgmt., 2008—. Office: Southwest Airlines Co 2702 Love Field Drive Dallas TX 75235 Office Phone: 214-792-5015. Office Fax: 214-792-4000. Business E-Mail: davis.ridley@southwest.com.

RIDLEY, J. DORSEY, state legislator; b. Nov. 26, 1953; Bank pres.; state rep. Dist. 12 Ky., 1987—94; state senator Dist. 4, 2004—. Named Outstanding Young Man of America, 1977, 1988. Mem.: Rotary Club, Masonic Lodge. Democrat. Presbyterian. Office: Capitol Annex Rm 251 Frankfort KY 40601 Home Phone: 270-826-5402; Office Phone: 270-869-8400, 502-564-8100 655.

RIED, STEPHANIE, physiatrist, educator; BS in Speech Pathology and Audiology, Howard U., Washington, 1973; MA in Speech Pathology, Western Mich. U., Kalamazoo, 1974; postgrad in Phys. Medicine and Rehab., U. Mich., Ann Arbor, 1989—92, MD, 1986. Diplomate Am. Bd. Physical Medicine and Rehab., Am. Bd. Pediatrics, Nat. Bd. Medical Examiners, cert. clin. competence in speech pathology. Resident Baylor Coll. of Medicine, Houston, 1986—89; chief resident dept. of phys. medicine and rehab. Univ. of Mich. Med. Ctr., Ann Arbor, 1991—92; pediatric physiatrist Children's Seashore House, Phila., 1992—97; med. staff. mem. Children's Hospital of Phila., 1992—97; pediatric physiatrist Driscoll Children's Hosp., Corpus Christi, Tex., 1997—2002; clin. dir. nat. ctr. for children's rehab. Nat. Rehab. Hosp., Washington, 2003—04; asst. prof. sch. of medicine Temple Univ., Phila.; med. dir. Spina Bifida program Children's Nat. Med. Ctr., Washington; pediatric physiatrist Shriners Hosps. for Children, Phila., 2002—04, med. dir. for rehab., 2004—. Office: Shriners Hospitals for Children 2900 Rocky Point Dr Tampa FL 33607 Office Phone: 813-281-0300.

RIEDEL, ALAN ELLIS, manufacturing executive, lawyer; b. Bellaire, Ohio, June 28, 1930; s. Emil George and Alberta (Shafer) R.; m. Ruby P. Tignor, June 21, 1953; children: Ralph A., Amy L., John T. AB magna cum laude, Ohio U., 1952, LLD (hon.), 1994; JD, Case Western Res. U., 1955; grad., Advanced Mgmt. Program, Harvard, 1971. Bar: Ohio 1955, Tex. 1968. Assoc. Squire, Sanders & Dempsey, Cleve., 1955-60; from gen. counsel to sec. Cooper Industries Inc. (formerly Cooper Bessemer Co.), Mt. Vernon, Ohio, 1960-68; from sec. to v.p. indsl. rels. Cooper Industries Inc., Mt. Vernon, Ohio, 1963-73; from sr. v.p. adminstrn. to vice chmn. Cooper Industries, Inc., Houston, 1973-94. Dir. Factory Mut. Ins., 1999-2000; bd. dirs. Belden Inc., St. Louis, 1993-2000, Gardner Denver Inc., Quincy, Ill., 1994-2000, chmn. bd. dirs., 1994-98; of counsel Squire, Sanders & Dempsey, Houston, 1994-2000. Past chmn. bd. dirs. Jr. Achievement of S.E. Tex.; trustee, past chmn. bd. trustees Ohio U. Endowment Found. Mem. Order of Coif, Phi Beta Kappa, Omicron Delta Kappa, Delta Tau Delta. Home: Bunker Hill Village 4 Heritage Ct Houston TX 77024 Personal E-mail: aeriedel@swbell.net.

RIEDLINGER, STEPHEN C., federal judge; b. 1950; BA, La. State U., 1971, JD, 1977. Bar: La. 1977, U.S. Dist. Ct. (ea. dist.) La. 1979, U.S. Dist. Ct. (mid. dist.) 1978, U.S. Ct. Appeals (5th cir.) 1983. Law clk. U.S. Dist. Ct. La., 1977-78; pvt. practice Baton Rouge, 1978-86; magistrate judge U.S. Dist. Ct. (mid. dist.) La., Baton Rouge, 1986—. With USNR, 1971-77. Office: Russell B Long Fed Bldg & Courthouse 777 Florida St Ste 260 Baton Rouge LA 70801-1717 Office Phone: 225-389-3584. Office Fax: 225-389-3585.

RIEDMAN, MARY SUZANNE, lawyer; b. June 1951; JD, Yale U., 1979. Bar: Wash. 1980, DC 1983, Calif. 1988. Assoc. Riddell, Williams, Bullitt & Walkinshaw, 1979—82; ptnr. Casson & Harkins, 1982—90; dep. gen. counsel Beverly Enterprises, Inc., Ft. Smith, Ark., 1990—95; counsel Kindred Healthcare Inc. (formerly Vencor Inc.), 1995—96, assoc. gen. counsel, 1996—98, v.p., assoc. gen. counsel, 1998—99, sr. v.p., gen. counsel, 1999—2010; sr. v.p., gen. counsel, chief diversity officer Kindred Healthcare, Inc., Louisville, 2010—. Office: Kindred Healthcare Inc 680 S 4th St Louisville KY 40202-2412 Office Phone: 502-596-7300. Office Fax: 502-596-4170. Business E-Mail: suzanne_riedman@kindredhealthcare.com.

RIEFLER, DONALD BROWN, financial consultant; b. Washington, Nov. 10, 1927; s. Winfield W. and Dorothy (Brown) R.; m. Patricia Hawley, Oct. 12, 1957; children: Duncan, Linda, Barbara. BA, Amherst Coll., 1949. With J.P. Morgan & Co. Inc., NYC, 1952-91; v.p. Morgan Guaranty Trust Co. of N.Y., 1962-68, sr. v.p., 1968-77, chmn. sources and uses of funds com., 1977—88, chmn. market risk com., 1989—91; fin. mkts. cons., 1991—. With U.S. Army, 1950-52. Mem. John's Island Club, Riomar Country Club, Quail Valley River Club, Birchwood Farms Club, Harbor Point Club, Creek Club. Home: 512 Bay Dr Vero Beach FL 32963-2107

RIEMAN, DEBORAH D., investment company executive; BA in Math., Sarah Lawrence Coll., 1973; Ph.D in Math., Columbia U., 1978. Asst. prof. math. University of California, Santa Cruz; with MITRE Corp., Xerox Corp.; pres., CEO Sitka Corp. (subs. of Sun Microsystems); entrepreneur-in-residence US Venture Ptnrs.; joined Adobe Sys. Inc., 1993, v.p. mktg., 1995; pres., CEO Check Point Software Technologies, Inc., 1995—99; mng. dir. Equus Mgmt. Corp. Bd. dirs. Switch and Data Facilities Corp., Arbinet, Altera, 1996—99, Keynote Systems, Tumbleweed Comm., 2001—, Kintera, 2003—, Corning Inc., 1999—. Office: Equus Capital Management Corp 2727 Allen Pky Ste 1350 Houston TX 77019-2100 Office Phone: 713-529-0900.

RIEMANN, STANLEY A., oil industry executive; BS, Univ. Nebr., 1973; MBA, Rockhurst Univ., 1992. Various mgmt. positions Farmland Industries Inc., 1974—99, exec. v.p., pres. energy & crop nutrient divsn., 1999—2004; COO Coffeyville Resources LLC, 2004—06, CVR Energy, Inc., Sugar Land, Tex., 2006—. Bd. mem. The Fertilizer Inst.; past bd. mem. Phosphate Potash Inst., Fla. Phosphate Coun., Internat. Fertilizer Assn. Office: CVR Energy Inc Ste 500 2277 Plaza Dr Sugar Land TX 77479

RIEPE, JAMES SELLERS, investment company executive; b. Bryn Mawr, Pa., June 25, 1943; s. Henry Brunt and Marjorie (Sellers) R.; m. Gail Nelms Petty, Sept. 14, 1968; children: Christina, James, Jr. BS, Wharton Sch., U. Pa., 1965, MBA, 1967. Mem. audit staff Coopers & Lybrand, C.P.A.s, Phila., 1967-69; asst. pres. Wellington Mgmt. Co., Phila., 1969-72, v.p., 1972-75; exec. v.p. Vanguard Group, Inc., Valley Forge, Pa., 1975-82, dir., 1979-82; chmn. T. Rowe Price Investment Services, TRP Trust Co., TRP Retirement Plan Svcs., 1982—97; vice chmn., mem. mgmt. com. T. Rowe Price Group, Inc., Balt., 1997—2005; chmn., dir. T. Rowe Price Funds, 2006; non-exec. chmn. Genworth Financial, 2012—. Bd. dirs. Balt. Equitable Soc., NASDAQ Stock Market, Inc., T. Rowe Price Group, Inc., PL Investment Holdings, Inc., Genworth Financial, Inc., 2009-. Trustee, former chmn. Balt. Mus. Art; trustee U. Pa., chmn. bd. trustees, 1999-. Mem. Investment Co. Inst. (gov.), Greenspring Valley Hunt Club, Caves Valley Golf Club. Office: Genworth Financial Inc Bd Directors 6620 W Broad St Richmond VA 23230 Office Phone: 804-281-6000. Office Fax: 804-662-2414. Business E-Mail: james.riepe@genworth.com.

RIESS, RICHARD K., finance company executive; BA in Bus. with honors, U. South Fla., 1971; MBA, Harvard U., 1975. Joined Eagle Asset Management, Inc., 1987, pres., 1995—96, COO, 1988—95; CFO Raymond James Financial, Inc., 1983, exec. v.p., Asset Mgmt. Group; CEO Eagle Asset Management, Inc., 1996—. Former bd. dirs. Eagle Family of Funds (formerly Heritage Family of Funds); bd. dirs. Eagle Asset Mgmt., Inc. Office: Raymond James Financial Inc 880 Carillon Pky Saint Petersburg FL 33716 Office Phone: 727-567-1000. Office Fax: 727-567-8915. Business E-Mail: richard.riess@eagleasset.com.

RIFENBURGH, RICHARD PHILIP, retired investment company executive; b. Syracuse, NY, Mar. 3, 1932; s. Russell D. and Edna (MacKenzie) R.; m. Doris Anita Hohn, June 24, 1950 (dec. July 2, 2011); children: David, Susan, Robert, m. Louise E. Vanpelt, April 9, 2012; 1 child: Craig Vanpelt. Student, Wayne State U. With Mohawk Data Scis. Corp., Herkimer, NY, 1964-74, pres., 1970-74, chmn., 1974, Moval Mgmt. Corp., Herkimer, 1968—; CEO, GCA Corp., Andover, Mass., 1986-87; gen. ptnr. Hambrecht and Quist Venture Ptnrs., 1987-90; chmn. Miniscribe Corp., Longmont, Colo., 1988-91, Ironstone Group Inc., 1988-91, St. G Crystal Ltd., Jeannette, Pa., 1985—2008. Chmn. Tristar Corp., 1992—2002. With USAF, 1951-55. Address: Moval Mgmt Corp 133 2637 E Atlantic Blvd Pompano Beach FL 33062-4939 Personal E-mail: dickrif@gmail.com.

RIFKIN, NED, former museum director; b. Florence, Ala., Nov. 10, 1949; s. Arthur Robert and Ina Blanche (Steinberg) R.; children: Moses Kleinman, Amos Kleinman. BA, Syracuse U., 1972; MA in Art History, U. Mich., 1973, PhD in Art History, 1976. Asst. prof. dept. art U. Tex., Arlington, 1977-80; curator, asst. dir. New Mus. Contemporary Art, NYC, 1980-84; curator contemporary art Corcoran Gallery Art, Washington, 1984-86; chief curator exhbns. Hirshhorn Mus. and Sculpture Garden, Washington, DC, 1986-90, chief curator, 1990-91, dir., 2002—05; Nancy and Holcombe T. Green Jr. dir. High Mus. Art, Atlanta, 1991—99; dir. Menil Collection and Found., Houston, 2000—01; under sec. for art Smithsonian Inst., Washington, 2004—08.

RIGBY, WELDON, realtor; Cert. Residential Specialist, Accredited Buyer Rep. Owner, realtor Weldon Rigby Inc. Realtors, Houston; realtor Keller Williams Realty, Houston. Named #1 GCI, Keller Williams Realty Houston Region, 2007, #4 GCI, Keller Williams North America and Can., 2007. Office: Keller Williams Realty 5050 Westheimer Rd Houston TX 77056-5835 Office Phone: 713-621-2555. Office Fax: 713-621-2550.

RIGELL, SCOTT (EDWARD SCOTT RIGELL), United States Representative from Virginia; b. Titusville, Fla., May 28, 1960; m. Terri Rigell; 4 children. AA, Brevard Cmty. Coll., Fla.; BBA, Mercer U., Macon, Ga., 1983; MBA, Regent U., Virginia Beach, Va., 1990. V.p., gen. mgr. Conoly Phillips Lincoln Mercury, Norfolk, Va., 1986—90; founder, chmn. Freedom Automotive, Virginia Beach, 1991—; mem. US Congress from 2nd Va. Dist., Washington, 2011—, US House Armed Services Com., Washington, 2011—, US House Homeland Security Com., Washington, 2011—, US House Science, Space & Tech., Washington, 2011—. Apptd. mem. Motor Vehicle Dealer Bd.; past pres. Hampton Roads Automobile Dealers Assn. Svc. with USMCR, 1978—84. Mem.: NRA (life). Republican. Christian. Office: US House of Representatives 1201 Longworth House Office Bldg Washington DC 20515 Office Phone: 202-225-4215.*

RIGGENBACH, JEFF, journalist, broadcaster; b. Highland Pk., Mich., Jan. 12, 1947; s. Frank Riggenbach and Dorothy Jane Miller; m. Suzanne Hoy Riggenbach, Mar. 10, 1996; m. Leslee J. Newman, Sept. 5, 1976 (div. 1989); m. Patricia Streeter, Mar. 29, 1967 (div. 1973); children: Max Rigman, Blaine Streeter. BS in Liberal Studies, Excelsior Coll. (formerly Regents Coll.); MA in Humanities, Calif. State U., 2004. Anchor/newswriter KNUZ, KQUE Radio, Houston, 1967—72; anchor/book critic/cultural affairs reporter KFWB All News Radio, LA, 1972—78; editor The Castalian (mag.), LA, 1972—74; instr. (journalism) Pierce Coll., LA, 1977—78; freelance writer L.A. Times, 1977—86; reporter, prod. Pub. Affairs Broadcast Group, Los Angeles, 1977—79; exec. editor The Libertarian Rev., San Francisco, 1978—82; exec. prodr., Byline Cato Inst., Washington, 1979—90; contbg. editor Inquiry mag., Washington, 1982—85; freelance writer San Jose (Calif.) Mercury News, 1983—88, U.S.A. Today, 1983—95; editl. writer Oakland Tribune, Calif., 1984—85; contbg editor Reason mag., LA, 1984—90; editl. writer/columnist Orange County Register, Santa Ana, Calif., 1985—87; daily economics commentator CNN Radio, Atlanta, 1985—87; prodr./program host KFAC Classical Radio, LA, 1987—89; mng. editor Pacific Bus. Rev., San Francisco, 1992—93; prodr./program host KKHI Classical Radio, San Francisco, 1993—94; instr. (liberal arts) Acad. of Art Coll., San Francisco, 1996—2000; contbg. editor Liberty mag., Port Townsend, Wash., 2001—08. Co-founder, vice chair Free Press Assn., Columbus, Ohio, 1983—87; sr. fellow Randolph Bourne Inst., Redwood City, Calif., 2005—; adj. scholar Ludwig von Mises Inst., Auburn, Ala., 2010—. Author: (books) In Praise of Decadence, 1998, Why American History Is Not What They Say, 2009; books columnist: Rational Review.com, 2005—. Mem.: Orgn. of Am. Historians. Home: 5622 Allendale Rd Houston TX 77017 Personal E-mail: jriggenbach@bigfoot.com.

RIGGLEMAN, JIM (JAMES DAVID RIGGLEMAN), professional baseball coach; b. Fort Dix, NJ, Nov. 9, 1952; 1 child. B in Phys. Edn., Frostburg State U., Md., 1974. Minor league player Waterbury, Ark., New Orleans, Springfield, 1974—81; minor league mgr. St. Louis Cardinals, 1982—88, dir. player devel., 1988—89, first base coach, 1989—91, minor league field coord., 2005—07; minor league mgr. AAA Las Vegas, 1991—92; mgr. San Diego Padres, 1992—94, Chgo. Cubs, 1995—99; bench coach LA Dodgers, 2001—04, Seattle Mariners, 2008, mgr., 2008; bench coach Washington Nationals, 2008—09, mgr., 2009—11, Pensacola Blue Wahoos, So. League Prof. Baseball, 2012, Louisville Bats, Internat. League, 2013—. Office: Louisville Bats 401 E Main St Louisville KY 40202*

RIGGS, STEVEN RAY, state legislator; b. Louisville, Ky., June 8, 1959; s. Raymond Leroy Riggs and Shirley Toll R.; m. Virginia Lynn Craft, 1987. Ins. sales rep. & cons.; mem. Dist. 31 Ky. House of Reps., 1991—; chmn. Counties & Local Govt., Seniors Com., Mil. Affairs & Pub. Safety & Vet. Affairs Com.; bd. dir. Hikes Point Neighborhood & Bus. Coun., 1989—; mem. Cmty. Coord. Child Care Bd. Named Outstanding Young America, 1987. Mem.: Jeffersontown Optimist Club, Sierra Club, Jeffersontown C. of C. Democrat. Methodist. Mailing: 8108 Thornwood Rd Louisville KY 40220 Office: Capitol Annex Rm 329C Frankfort KY 40601 Home Phone: 502-499-6050; Office Phone: 502-564-8100 ext. 674. Fax: 502-564-6543. E-mail: steve.riggs@lrc.state.ky.us.

RIGGS, SUSAN G., oil and gas company executive; BBA in Acctg., U. Tex., MS in Profl. Acctg. CPA. Treas., contr. The Huffco Group, 1995—97; fin. analyst Newfield Exploration Co., 1997—99, treas., 1999—. Mem.: Assn. for Fin. Profls., Tex. Soc. CPA. Office: Newfield Exploration Co Ste 2020 363 N Sam Houston Pkwy E Houston TX 77060 Office Phone: 281-847-6000. Office Fax: 281-405-4242.

RIGGSBY, DUTCHIE SELLERS, retired education educator; b. Montgomery, Ala., Oct. 26, 1940; d. Malcolm Sellers and Marcelia Sellers Dickman; m. Ernest Duward Riggsby, Aug. 25, 1962; 1 child, Lyn. BS, Troy State Coll., 1962, MS, 1965; postgrad., George Peabody Coll., 1963; EdD, Auburn U., 1972. Cert. tchr., Ala., Ga.; cert. libr., Ga. Tchr. Montgomery Pub. Schs., 1962—63, Troy City Schs., 1963—67; instr. Auburn U., Ala., 1968—69, dir. media svcs., 1972—77; asst. prof. Columbus Coll., Ga., 1972—77, assoc. prof., 1978—83, prof., 1983—2009, parttime prof., 2009—. Vis. prof. U. P.R., Rio Piedras, 1972—73; leader various workshops, 1989, 1993—; sorfware reviewer NSTA, 2000—; chmn. publicity Ga. Edni. Tech. Conf., 1997—, bd. dirs.; bridal cons. Hist. Moments, Inc., v.p., 1998—2001; coord. instrnl. Tech. Sch. Edn., 1996—97; coord. program Ednl. Founds., 2001—04; bd. dirs. Ga. Ednl. Tech. Consortium, 2002—. Contbr. more than 90 articles on state, regional, nat., and internat. programs to profl. jours., 1968—. Active Internal Aerospace Edn. CAP, Maxwell AFB, 1980-90; dir. Air and Space Camp for Kids, 1990-98; apptd. selection com. Coll. Edn. Columbus State U. Hall of Fame, 2005—09 Recipient STAR Tchr. award NSTA, 1968; named to Lee H.S. Hall of Fame, Montgomery, 1997. Mem.: Ga. Assn. Instrnl. Tech. (bd. dirs. 1982—84), World Aerospace Edn. Orgn. (v.p. for Ams. 1996—98, pres. for Ams. 1998—2008), Nat. Congress on Aviation and Space Edn. (dir. spl. promotions 1986—90), Assn. for Ednl. Commn. and Tech. (awards com. 1994—96, non-periodical publs. com. 1994—99, chair meml. awards com. 1996—99), Phi Delta Kappa (pres. Chattahoochee Valley chpt. 1986—87, membership v.p. 2005—06, pres. Chattahoochee Valley chpt. 2006—07, v.p. 2008—09, membership v.p. 2008—, faculty sponsor student chpt. 2010—, Svc. award 1989, Svc. Key award 1993). Baptist. Avocations: photography, mining for gemstones. Office Phone: 706-565-7802.

RIGHTS, GRAHAM HENRY, retired minister; b. Winston-Salem, NC, Jan. 14, 1935; s. Douglas LeTell and Cecil Leona (Burton) R.; m. Sybil Critz Strupe, Sept. 7, 1963; children: Susan Elizabeth, John Graham. BA, U. N.C., 1956; BD, Yale U., 1959; postgrad., Moravian Theol. Sem., 1959-60, DHL (hon.), 1997; postgrad., U. Edinburgh, Scotland, 1965-66; DD (hon.), Wofford Coll., 1989. Ordained to ministry Moravian Ch., 1960. Pastor Union Ch., Managua, Nicaragua, 1960-63, Managua Moravian Ch., 1960-65, Mayodan (N.C.) Moravian Ch., 1966-72, Messiah Moravian Ch., Winston-Salem, 1972-81; exec. dir. Bd. World Mission Moravian Ch., Bethlehem, Pa., 1981-83, pres. exec. bd. so. province Winston-Salem, 1983-95, pres. exec. bd. world-wide, 1991-94; pastor First Moravian Ch., Greensboro, NC, 1995-2000; ret. Bd. dirs. Crisis Control Ministry, Forsyth County, 1976-, Wachovia Hist. Soc., 2004-, Cherokee-Moravian Hist. Assn., 2004-. Mem. N.C. Soc. Mayflower Descendants (elder 2000—). Mem. Moravian Ch. Home: 553 Steeple View Ct Winston Salem NC 27101-5850

RIGSBY, LINDA FLORY, lawyer, director; b. Topeka, Dec. 16, 1946; d. Alden E. and Lolita M. Flory; m. Michael L. Rigsby, Aug. 14, 1963; children: Michael L. Jr., Elisabeth A. MusB, Va. Commonwealth U., 1969; JD, U. Richmond, 1981. Bar: Va. 1981, D.C. 1988. Assoc. McGuire, Woods, Battle & Boothe, Richmond, Va., 1981-85; dep. gen. counsel and corp. sec. Crestar Fin. Corp., Richmond, 1985-99, gen. counsel, 1999-2000; mng. atty. Sun Trust Banks Inc., 2000—05, deputy gen. coun., 2006; ret., 2007; of counsel Williams Mullen law, 2007—. Mem. audit com. Bon Secours Health Systems, Richmond, 1999—. Bd. dirs. Commonwealth Cath. Charities, 2004-, vice chmn., 2008; mem. Bar Secours Foundation Bd, 2008- Recipient Disting. Svc. award U. Richmond, 1987; named Vol. of Yr. U. Richmond, 1986, Woman of Achievement, Met. Richmond Women's Bar, 1995. Mem. Va. Bar Assn. (exec. com. 1993-96), Richmond Bar Assn. (bd. dirs. 1992-95), Va. Bankers Assn. (chair legal affairs 1992-95), U. Richmond Estate Planning Coun. (chmn. 1990-92), Va. Bar Assn. (elected fellow 2008). Roman Catholic. Avocations: music, gardening. Home: 163 W Square Pl Richmond VA 23238-6157 Office: Williams Mullen Law Firm PO Box 1320 Richmond VA 23218-1320 Home Phone: 804-784-7479; Office Phone: 804-783-6404. Personal E-mail: mlrigsby163@comcast.net.

RIKVOLD, PER ARNE, physicist, educator; b. Hadsel, Norway, Oct. 4, 1948; arrived in U.S., 1980; s. Per and Inger-Johanne (Corneliussen) Rikvold. BS, U. Oslo, 1971, MS in Physics, 1976; cert. Japanese lang., Osaka U., Japan, 1977; PhD in Physics, Temple U., 1983. Rsch. assoc. dept. physics U. Oslo, 1978-81; rsch. assoc. dept. mech. engring. SUNY, Stony Brook, N.Y., 1983-85; sr. rsch. chemist ARCO Chem. Co., Newtown Square, Pa., 1985-87; assoc. prof. physics Fla. State U., Tallahassee, 1987-92, prof. physics, 1992—2004, James G. Skofronick prof. physics, 2004—, prof. Sch. Computational Sci., 2005—08, disting. rsch. prof., 2010—. Vis. scientist Kyushu U., Fukuoka, Japan, 1979, U. Geneva, 1981—82, Inst. Solid State Physics, Jülich, Germany, 1982; vis. scholar Temple U., Phila., 1986—87; vis. rschr. IBM, Bergen, Norway, 1987, 1988; vis. scholar Tohwa Inst. Sci., Japan, 1991, Kyushu (Japan) U., 1991, Kyoto (Japan) U., 1993, 1996, 1998, 2001, 2005, McGill U., Montreal, Que., Canada, 1995; vis. rschr. U. Colo., Boulder, 1997, U. Tex., Austin, 1999, Va. Poly. Inst. and State U., 2002—03, U. Tokyo, 2007, 2008, 2009, 2010—13; vis. rsch. prof. Miss. State U., 2003. Contbr. numerous articles to profl. jours. and books. Grantee, Petroleum Rsch. Fund, 1988—91, NSF, 1991—; fellow, Japanese Ministry Edn., 1976—78, Norwegian Rsch. Coun., 1981—83, Japan Found. Ctr. Global Partnership, 1996. Fellow: AAAS, Am. Phys. Soc.; mem.: European Phys. Soc., Norwegian Acad. Sci. and Letters, Norwegian Phys. Soc., Electrochem. Soc., Materials Rsch. Soc., Sigma Xi. Democrat. Achievements include research in statistical and condensed-matter physics and complex systems theory with applications to materials science, electrochemistry, engineering, computer science and ecology and evolutionary biology. Office: Fla State U Physics Dept Tallahassee FL 32306 Business E-Mail: prikvold@fsu.edu.

RILEY, HAROLD EUGENE, insurance company executive; b. Grandfield, Okla., July 23, 1928; s. Raymon I. and Ruby Emma (Short) R.; m. Marjorie Denson, Dec. 21, 1950; children: Rick Denson, Randall Harold, Jana Lynn, Ray Allen; m. Dottie S. Riley, Oct. 28, 1991. BBA, Baylor U., 1951. Tchr., coach Crane-Plainview (Tex.) High Schs., 1952-54; v.p. Profl. & Businessmen's Ins. Co., Houston, 1954-61; pres. Nat. Western Life, Austin, Tex., 1962-68; chmn., pres. Citizens Ins. Co. Am., Austin, 1969; chmn., CEO Citizens, Inc., 1969—, pres. Austin, 1988; chmn., pres. HERMAR Corp., Austin, 1982, HERMAR Oil Co., Inc., Austin, 1983-88, Continental Leasing Corp., Austin, 1987, Continental investors Life Ins. Co., Birmingham, Ala., 1988. Adv. trustee, chmn. Southwestern Bapt. Sem., 1967; chn. athletic com. Baylor U. Operation Second Century, 1959; mem. exec. bd. Bapt. Gen. Conv.-Tex., 1979-87; with Harold E. Riley Found. Recipient Oustanding Alumni award Hankamer Bus. Sch., Baylor, 1977, inducted into Baylor U. Hall of Fame, 1978. Mem. Nat. Assn. Underwriters Assn., Nat. Assn. Life Cos., Life Ins. Polit. Assn. (chmn. Austin 1987), Tex. Legal Res. Ofcls. Assn. (pres. 1981), Colo. Life Conv., Austin Life Underwriters Assn., Austin C. of C., Rotary. Republican. Avocations: golf, flying, travel, hunting. Office: Citizens Inc 400 E Anderson Ln Austin TX 78752-1224 Office Phone: 512-837-7100. Office Fax: 512-836-9785. Business E-Mail: harold.riley@citizensinc.com.

RILEY, HAROLD JOHN, JR., chemicals executive; b. Syracuse, NY, Nov. 13, 1940; s. Harold John and Esther Emma (Denmark) R.; m. Diane Marie Slattery, June 15, 1963; children— Beth Ann, Thomas, Patrick BS in Indsl. Engring., Syracuse U., 1961; postgrad., Harvard U., 1985. Mfg. tng. program Gen. Elec. Co., 1961—63; various positions Crouse-Hinds Co., Syracuse, 1963—74; gen. mgr. Midwest Elec., 1974—77; v.p. Crouse-Hinds Co., Syracuse, 1979—82; v.p., gen. mgr. Crouse Hinds Distbn. Equipment Div., Earlysville, 1977—79; associated Cooper Industries, Ltd; exec. v.p. Cooper Industries, Inc., 1982—92, COO, 1992—95, pres., 1992—2004, CEO, 1995—2005, chmn., 1996—2006. Bd. dirs. Allstate Corp., Post Oak Bank, N.A.; trustee Mus. of Fine Arts, Syracuse U.; bd. dirs. Westlake Chemical Corp., 2007—. Bd. dirs. Jr. Achievement Southeast Tex., Houston Ctrl., Houston Symphony, The Greater Houston Partnership, The Houston Forum, The Mus. Fine Arts, Houston, Jr. Achievement, Inc. Mem. Mfrs. Alliance for Productivity Improvement, The Bus. Roundtable, Houston Club, Lakeside Country Club, Farmington Country Club. Republican. Roman Catholic. Home: 3669 Chevy Chase Dr Houston TX 77019-3009 Office: Westlake Chemical Corp 2801 Post Oak Blvd Ste 600 Houston TX 77056 Office Phone: 713-960-9111. Office Fax: 713-963-1590. Business E-Mail: hriley@westlake.com.

RILEY, HENRY CHARLES, banker; b. Newton, Massachusetts, Mar. 23, 1932; s. Charles Matthew and Marion Anna (Armstrong) R.; m. Patricia Ann (Buchanan), Mar. 3, 1962; children: Lauren Elizabeth, Carolyn Ann, Julie Louise. BA, Yale U., 1954; MBA, Boston Coll., 1965. With BayBank Harvard Trust Co., Cambridge, Mass., 1958—89, treas., sec., 1967—70, sr. v.p., sec., 1972—82, exec. v.p., 1982—87; mng. dir. cmty. banking BayBank Systems Inc., Waltham, Mass., 1987—90; exec. v.p., dir. cmty. banking BayBank Boston, 1990—92; exec. v.p. BayBank Systems, Inc., Waltham, Mass., 1992—97; bd. dir. BayBank F.S.B., BayBank N.A., NH, 1995—96. Mem. pvt. banking adv. com. Fleet Boston, Sarasota, Fla., 2000-04. Trustee, treas. Longy Sch. Music, 1970-92; bd. dir. Richard Warren Surg. Rsch. and Ednl. Fund Inc., 1984-2009; bd. dir., pres. Cambridge Econ. Devel. Corp., 1982-87; corporator, past asst. treas. Mt. Auburn Hosp.; mem. exec. bd. Gettysburg Coll. Parents Assn.; treas. St. John's Episcopal Ch., sr. warden, Westwood, Mass., 1982-85; mem. St. Paul's Cathedral chpt., Boston, 1990-93. Served in USNR, 1956-57. Mem. Am. Bankers Assn. (chmn. 1991-92, exec. com. br. adminstrv. divsn. 1992, chmn. nat. retail banking conf. 1990), Nat. Br. Adminstr. Roundtable, Boston Coll. Sch. Mgmt. Alumni Assn. (past dir., pres.), Harvard Sq. Bus. Assn. (past dir.), Cambridge C. of C. 1975-87 (past dir., past treas., v.p.) Rotary (club dir. 1976-80, pres. 1979-80), Yale Club, Boston, Yale Club of the Suncoast (bd. dir. 2001-11, v.p., 2004), Harvard Club, Dennis Yacht Club (mem. bd. govs., treas. 1993-94), The Meadows Country Club, Ivy League Club, The Club at Yarmouthport. Episcopalian. Home: 33 York Way Westwood MA 02090-2633 also: PO Box 1192 240 New Boston Rd Dennis MA 02638-2121 also: 5284 Huntingwood Ct Sarasota FL 34235-5600 Personal E-mail: Marshwind@aol.com.

RILEY, JOSEPH P., JR., mayor; married; 2 children. Grad., The Citadel, 1964; JD, U. S. Calif. Sch. Law, 1967. Mem. SC House of Reps.; mayor Charleston, SC, 1975—. Founder Mayors' Inst. on City Design, 1986; pres. US Conf. Mayors, 1986—87. Recipient Thomas Jefferson award, Architectural Inst. Am., 1994, JC Nichols Prize for Visionary Urban Devel., Urban Land Inst., 2000, Keystone award, Am. Architectural Found., 2002, Nat. Medal of Arts award, Nat. Endowment for the Arts, 2010. Office: Office of the Mayor PO Box 304 Charleston SC 29402-0304 also: Office of Mayor 80 Broad St Charleston SC 29401-2901

RILEY, LYNNE, state legislator; b. Sept. 08; m. Mike Riley; children:Greg, Katie, Eileen. Attended, Bentley Coll., Waltham, Mass., Northeastern U., Boston, Mass., Am. Inst. Banking, Boston. Prin. Riley Acctg. Svcs.; mem. Dist. 50 Ga. House of Representatives, 2011—. Office: 10605 Wren Ridge Rd Johns Creek GA 30022 also: Georgia House of Reps 504 Coverdell Legis Office Bldg Atlanta GA 30334 Office Phone: 770-664-0436, 404-656-0188. Business E-Mail: lynnerileyforgeorgia@gmail.com, lynne.riley@house.ga.gov.

RILEY, PATRICK JAMES, professional sports team executive; b. Rome, NY, Mar. 20, 1945; s. Leon R.; m. Chris Riley; children: James Patrick, Elisabeth Marie. Grad., U. Ky., 1967. Guard San Diego Rockets, 1967-70, Phoenix Suns, 1975-76, LA Lakers, 1970-75, asst. coach, 1979-81, head coach, 1981-90, NY Knicks, 1991-95, Miami Heat, 1995—2003, 2005—08, pres. basketball ops., 2003—. Broadcaster LA Lakers games Sta. KLAC and Sta. KHJ-TV, 1977—79; broadcaster NBC Sports, 1990—91. Author: Show Time: Inside the Laker's Breakthrough Season, 1988, The Winner Within: A Life Plan for Team Players, 1993. Co-recipient NBA Exec. of Yr. award, NBA, 2011; recipient Chuck Daly Lifetime Achievement award Nat. Basketball Coaches Assn., 2012; named NBA Coach of Yr., 1990, 93, 97, NBA Exec. of Yr. The Sporting News, 2011; named to Naismith Meml. Basketball Hall of Fame, 2008. Achievements include head coach of the NBA Finals Championship winning: Los Angeles Lakers, 1982, 85, 87, 88; Miami Heat, 2006. Office: Miami Heat Am Airlines Arena 601 Biscayne Blvd Miami FL 33132

RILEY, RICHARD WILSON, lawyer, former United States Secretary of Education; b. Greenville, SC, Jan. 2, 1933; s. Edward Patterson and Martha Elizabeth (Dixon) Riley; m. Ann Osteen Yarborough, Aug. 23, 1957; children: Richard Wilson, Anne Y., Hubert D., Theodore D. BA, Furman U., 1954; JD, U. S.C., 1959. Bar: S.C. 1960. Ptnr. Riley & Riley, Greenville, 1959—78, Nelson, Mullins, Riley & Scarborough, Greenville and Columbia, 1987—93, Greenville, 2001—; gov. State of S.C., 1979—87; sec. US Dept. Edn., Washington, 1993—2001; disting. univ. prof. U. S.C., Columbia, 2001—; disting. prof. govt., politics, and pub. policy Furman U., 2001—. Spl. asst. to subcom. U.S. Senate Jud. Com., 1960; mem. S.C. Ho. of Reps., 1963—66, S.C. Senate from Greenville-Laurens Dist., 1966—76; sr. adv. and chair Richard W. Riley Inst. Govt., Politics and Pub. Leadership, Furman U., 2001—; bd. dirs. ACT (Am. Coll. Testing Program); bd. trustees Knowledge Works Found., 2001—; trustee Carnegie Corp. N.Y., 2004—, Furman U., 2001—; former bd. dirs. Pub. Broadcasting Svc. (PBS). Lt. (j.g.) USNR, 1954—56. Recipient Dist. Svc. award, Coun. Chief State Sch. Officers, 1994, James Bryant Conant award, Edn. Comm. of the States, 1995, T.H. Bell award for outstanding edn. advocacy, Com. for Edn. Funding, 1996, Dist. Svc. award, Am. Coun. on Edn., 1998; disting. sr. fellow, NAFSA: Assn. Internat. Educators, Wash., D.C. Mem.: Greenville Bar Assn., S.C. Bar Assn., Rotary, Phi Beta Kappa. Office: Nelson Mullins Riley & Scarborough Poinsett Plaza Ste 900 104 S Main St Greenville SC 29601 Office Phone: 864-250-2300. Business E-Mail: dick.riley@nelsonmullins.com.

RILEY, WILLIAM JOHN, neurologist; b. Seattle, Oct. 24, 1930; s. William John and Virginia (McCarthy) R.; m. Joan Marie Weismann, 1956 (div. 1976); children: Sean, Kevan, Megan, Janeen, Michael; m. Margit Mary Winstrom, 1976; children: Britta, Shane, Timothy. MS in Anatomy, U. Chgo., 1958, MD, 1960; PhD, U. Minn., 1965. Intern Mpls. Gen. Hosp., 1961-62; resident U. Minn. Hosps., 1962-65; asst. chief neurology Mpls. Gen. Hosp., 1965-69; chief neurology St. Luke's Episcopal Hosp., Houston, 1970-85; pres., CEO Tex. Neurol.

Clinic Assn., Houston, 1969—. Staff sgt. USAF, 1951-55. Recipient Disting. Tchg. award Minn. Med. Found., Mpls., 1969. Fellow: ACP, Tex. Neurol. Soc. (pres. 2002—, Lifetime Achievement award 2005), Am. Acad. Neurology; mem.: Alpha Omega Alpha, Tex. Med. Assn. (pres. 9th dist. 1991), Sigma Xi. Roman Catholic. Avocation: ranching. Office: Tex Neurological Clinic Assn 4126 SW Freeway # 1030 Houston TX 77027-7306 Office Phone: 713-621-9291. Personal E-mail: wjrileymd@aol.com.

RILLING, JOHN ROBERT, history professor; b. Wausau, Wis., Apr. 28, 1932; s. John Peter and Esther Laura (Wittig) R.; m. Joanne Marilyn McCrory, Dec. 21, 1953; children: Geoffrey Alan, Andrew Peter. BA summa cum laude, U. Minn., 1953; AM, Harvard U., 1957, PhD, 1959. Asst. prof. history U. Richmond, Va., 1959-62, assoc. prof. history, 1962-68, prof. history, 1968-99, prof. English history emeritus, 1999—, chmn. dept. history, 1977-83, Westhampton Coll., 1965-71. Pres. Faculty Senate of Va., 1975—77, Shepherd's Ctr., Richmond, Va., 2008—10. Contbr. articles to profl. jours. Elder, Ginter Park Presbyn. Ch., 1973-83. Served with U.S. Army, 1953-55. Recipient U. Richmond Disting. Educator award, 1975, 76, 77, 80, 87, Prof. of Yr. finalist Coun. for Advancement and Support of Edn., 1981. Woodrow Wilson fellow, 1955-59; Harvard U. travelling fellow, 1958; Coolidge fellow, 1955-56; Folger Libr. fellow, 1960. Mem.: Agecroft Assn. (bd. dir.), Am. Hist. Assn., Omicron Delta Kappa (Prof. of Yr. 1995), Phi Beta Kappa. Avocation: hiking. Home: 1507 Wilmington Ave Richmond VA 23227-4429 Office: U Richmond Dept History Richmond VA 23173 Business E-Mail: jrilling@richmond.edu.

RIMER, BARBARA K., dean, healthcare educator; b. Wilkes Barre, Pa., Jan. 14, 1949; BA in English, U. Mich., 1970, MPH in Med. Care Adminstrn. and Health Edn., 1973; PhD in Health Edn., Johns Hopkins Sch. of Hygiene and Public Health, 1981. Instr. Wayne State U. Sch. Medicine, Detroit, 1973-75; program dir. Nat. Cancer Inst., Bethesda, Md., 1975-77; intervention coord. Johns Hopkins Oncology Ctr., Balt., 1977-79; rsch. assoc. Johns Hopkins Sch. Hygiene and Public Health, Balt., 1977-79; sr. health educator Fox Chase Cancer Ctr., Phila., 1981-87, dir. health comms. rsch., 1981-87, dir. behavioral rsch., 1987-91, dir. population sci. for behavioral rsch., 1990-91; dir. cancer prevention, detection and ctrl. rsch. Duke Comprehensive Cancer Ctr., Durham, NC, 1991-97; sr. fellow Aging Ctr. Duke U. Med. Ctr., Durham, NC, 1991-97, assoc. prof. in cmty. and family medicine, 1991-93, prof. cmty. and family medicine, 1993-97; acting dep. dir. Duke Comprehensive Cancer Ctr., Durham, NC, 1995-96; dir. cancer ctrl. and population scis. Nat. Cancer Inst., Rockville, Md., 1997—2002; dep. dir. population scis. Lineberger Cancer Ctr. University of North Carolina, Chapel Hill, 2003—05, alumni disting. prof. Dept. Health Behavior & Health Edn., 2003—, dean Sch. Pub. Health, 2005—. Adj. assoc. prof. dept. health behavior and health edn. U. N.C. Sch. of Public Health, Chapel Hill, NC, 1992-97; adj. mem. Fox Chase Cancer Ctr., Phila., 1992-97; preceptor, lectr. Temple U., 1983-91; guest lectr. Duke U. Med. Ctr., 1991-97, U. N.C. Sch. Public Health, 1991-93; Judith P. Schlager vis. prof. Dana-Farber Cancer Inst., 1995; disting. vis. lectr. Harvard U., 1998; mem. institutional review bd. Fox Chase Cancer Ctr., 1983-88, vice chair, 1988-91; proposal review, site visitor Nat. Cancer Inst., 1985-95; chairperson tech. advisory com. Am. Lung Assn., 1987; external advisory com. Vermont Regional Cancer Ctr., 1988-89; advisory com. Brown U., U. R.I. Cancer Prevention Rsch. unit, 1988-95; mem. Am. Assn. Retired Persons task force on smoking, 1989-91, Health Promotion adv. bd. Wesley Found., 1990-91, program com. annual mtg. Am. Soc. Preventive Oncology, 1990-93, chair, 1993 mtg., expert adv. com. AMC Cancer Rsch. Ctr./Ctrs. for Disease Ctrl. Coop. Agreement, 1991, adult edn. subcom. and tobacco materials review group Am. Cancer Soc., 1991; mem. Nat. Task Force on Breast Cancer Ctrl. Am. Cancer Soc., 1992, chair Nat. and State (NC) Task Force on Breast Cancer Ctrl., 1992; mem. Pub. Edn. subcom. on Adult Edn. Am. Cancer Soc., 1992; mem. adv. bd. Office of Cancer Comms., NCI, 1992; mem. Clin. Cancer com. Duke U. Med. Ctr., 1992-95; mem. Cancer Ctrs.' Support com. NCI, 1993-94, Recruitment and Adherence com. Office of Women's Health NIH, 1993, Report com. Internat. Workshop on Screening for breast cancer NCI, 1993, Detection and Treatment subcom. on Breast Cancer Am. Cancer Soc., 1993, 94, Nominating com. Soc. Behavioral Medicine, 1993-96, adv. com. on cancer coordination and ctrl. State of NC, 1993-97; invited participant and com. chair Frontiers of Behavioral Medicine mtg., Chantilly, Va., 1993; invited co-chair Sec. Shalala's Mtg. to develop nat. strategic plan for breast cancer, Bethesda, Md., 1993; chair, mem. Nat. Cancer Adv. Bd. (presdl. appointment), 1994-97; bd. dirs. Am. Family Life Assurance Corp., 1995—; fellowship selection com. Am. Assn. Cancer Rsch., 1996; mem. exec. com. Acad. Behavioral Medicine Rsch., 1998, Charles S. Mott Selection com. of Gen. Motors Cancer Rsch. Found., 1999, Inst. Medicine com. effective health comm. and behavior change strategies for diverse populations, 2000. Editor: special cancer issue Health Education Research, 1998-89; editl. bd. Health Education Quarterly, 1985-87, guest editl. bd. 1983; editl. bd. Jour. of Compliance in Health Care, 1989-90, Health Edn. Rsch., 1990-98, Cancer Prevention, Epidemiology and Biomarkers, 1990—, Patient Edn. and Counseling, 1994—, Breast Diseases, 1998—, Cancer Causes and Control, 1998—, Effective Clin. Practice, 2000—; assoc. editor: Preventive Medicine, 1990—; reviewer Am. Jour. Preventive Medicine, Am. Jour. Public Health, Annals of Internal Medicine, Health Edn. Quarterly, Health Services Research, Jour. of Am. Med. Assn., Jour. Nat. Cancer Inst., Milbank Quarterly, Women's Health, 1986—; contbr. numerous articles, papers to profl. pubs. Fellow Johns Hopkins Sch. of Hygiene and Public Health, 1979-81, Soc. of Behavioral Medicine, 1997; recipient Mayhew Derryberry award Am. Public Health Assn., 1992, Best Visual Presentation of Session award Soc. of Behavioral Medicine, San Diego, 1995, Citation award Soc. Behavioral Medicine, 1996, Disting. Achievement award Am. Soc. Preventive Oncology, 1997, Herbert J. Block Leadership award Ohio State U., 1997, John P. McGovern award in Health Promotion U. Tex. Sch. Public Health, 1999. Mem.: Inst. Medicine. Office: Sch Public Health Univ North Carolina 170 Rosenau Hall Campus Box 7400 Chapel Hill NC 27599-7400 Office Phone: 919-966-3215. Office Fax: 919-966-7678. E-mail: brimer@unc.edu.

RIMMER, TODD, gas industry executive; m. Donna Rimmer; 1 children. BBA in Acctg. summa cum laude, Stephen F. Austin State U. CPA Tex. Sr. mgr. Deloitte & Touche LLP; dir. fin. reporting Am. Electric Power, Columbus, Ohio; v.p., contr. Sequent Energy Management, LP, 2004, sr. v.p., CFO, 2008—. Mem. AICPA, Tex. Soc. Cert. Pub. Accountants. Office: AGL Resources Inc Ten Peachtree Pl NE Atlanta GA 30309 Office Phone: 404-584-4000. Office Fax: 404-584-3714. Business E-Mail: trimmer@sequentenergy.com.

RINAMAN, JAMES CURTIS, JR., lawyer; b. Miami, Fla., Feb. 8, 1935; s. James Curtis and Ruth Marie (Rader) R.; m. Gloria Margaret Kaspar; children: James, Mark, Christine, Karen BA, U. Fla., 1955, JD, 1960. Bar: Fla. 1960, U.S. Dist. Ct. (so. dist.) Fla. 1960, U.S. Ct. Appeals (5th cir.) 1960, U.S. Supreme Ct. 1963, U.S. Dist. Ct. (mid. dist.) Fla. 1967, U.S. Dist. Ct. (no. dist.) Fla. 1981, U.S. Ct. Appeals (11th cir.) 1981, U.S. Ct. Claims 1991, U.S. Ct. Mil. Appeals 1994; cert. civil trial lawyer Fla. Bar. With Marks, Gray, Conroy & Gibbs, P.A., Jacksonville, Fla., 1960—. Gen. counsel Fla. Bd. Architecture, 1965-79, City of Jacksonville, 1970-71, Jacksonville C. of C., 1973-76, 90; adj. prof. Coll. Architecture, U. Fla., 1975-90; dir. gen. The Southern Acad. Letters, Arts and Scis., 1997—; chmn. adv. com. constrns. Jacksonville Ct. house, 2004-. Pres. Jacksonville Cmty. Coun. Inc., 1985. Leadership Jacksonville, Inc., 1987; mem. Jacksonville Transp. Authority, 1971-80, Jacksonville Base Realignment and Closure Commn., 1993-95. Jacksonville Cecil Field Devel. Commn., 1994-96; chmn. N.E. Fla. chpt. ARC, 1996; chmn. JCCI Elections, 2001; trustee US 11th Cir. Ct. of Appeals Hist. Soc., 2005-. With U.S. Army, 1955-57, Fla. NG, 1957-92. ret. brig. gen., 1992. Named to U. Fla. Hall of Fame. Fellow Am. Coll. Trial Lawyers, Am. Bar Found., Fla. Bar Found. (bd. dirs. 1982-87, 88, Disting. Svc. award 1983, 86, Medal of Honor 1988); mem. ABA (ho. of dels. 1982-86), Jacksonville Bar Assn. (pres. 1972-73, Lawyer of Yr. 1994), The Fla. Bar (pres. 1982-83), Def. Rsch. Inst. (so. regional v.p. 1980-83, bd. dirs. 1976-78, 83-87), Am. Judicature Soc. (Herbert Harley award 1987), Fla. Coun. Bar Pres. (Outstanding Past Pres. award 1989), Lawyers for Civil Justice (pres. 1989-91, chmn. bd. dirs. 1991-94), Vol. Lawyers Resource Ctr. of Fla., (pres. 1984-89, chmn. bd. dirs. 1989-93), So. Conf. of Bar, Nat. Conf. of Bar, Assn. Def. Trial Attys. (internat. pres. 1976-77), Internat. Assn. Def. Counsel, Jacksonville Assn. Def. Counsel, Fla. Defense Lawyers Assn. (pres. 1973), Fla. C. of C., Jacksonville C. of C. (chmn. 1994), Meninak Civic Club (pres. 1986), Jacksonville Commodores League (Flag Commodores 2008-09), The Army War Coll. Alumni Assn. (life), Fla. Blue Key, Jacksonville Courthouse Archtl. Rev. Com. (chmn. 2003-), Camp Blanding Mil. Mus. (bd. dirs 2001-, pres. 2010-2012), San. Jose Country Club, Phi Gamma Delta (bd. trustees ednl. found. 1995-2003), Phi Alpha Delta. Republican. Methodist. Office: Marks Gray Conroy & Gibbs 1200 Riverplace Blvd Ste 800 Jacksonville FL 32207-1805 also: PO Box 447 Jacksonville FL 32201-0447 Office Phone: 904-398-0900. E-mail: jrinaman@marksgray.com.

RINER, RONALD NATHAN, healthcare company executive; b. Mar. 7, 1949; AB, Princeton U., 1970; MD, Cornell U., NYC, 1974. Diplomate Am. Bd. Internal Medicine, Am. Bd. Cardiovasc. Disease. Resident in internal medicine NY Hosp., Meml. Sloan-Kettering, Hosp. for Spl. Surgery, NYC, 1974-76; resident in cardiology Mayo Grad. Sch. Medicine, Rochester, Minn., 1976-79; with, 1979—95; program dir., internal medicine St. Mary's Health Ctr., 1979—82, chmn., dept. internal medicine, 1980—82; chief med. officer Health Mgmt. Assocs., Inc. Asst. prof. medicine, Washington U. Med. Ctr., 1985-88, pres. Riner Group, Inc., 1980—, Riner Heart Group, Inc., 1980-95; sr. sci. advisor pharm. divsn. BioMed Sys., St. Louis, 1984-95; prof. St. Louis U.; corp. dir. quality affairs SSM Health Care Sys., 1989-91; chmn. Mo. State Med. Assn. Commn. on Med. Econs., 3rd Party Medicine and Govt. Rels., 1990-92; v.p. clin. svcs. Daus. Charity Nat. Health Sys., 1991-95; bd. dirs. Alleghany Health Sys., Tampa, Fla., 1991-96, chmn. bd. dirs., 1994-96; bd. dirs. Horizon/CMS Healthcare, 1996-98, Seton Inst. for Internat. Devel., San Francisco, 1995-97, Seton Inst. for Internat. Devel., San Francisco, 1995-97, Liferate Sys., Inc., 1997-99, Assn. for Corp. Growth, 1998-2001, Mathew Dickey Acad., St. Louis, 1998-2001, Angelica, also mem. nominating and audit coms., 2005—. Editor practice mgmt. and econs. sect. Jour. Invasive Cardiology, 1996—. Adv. bd. Washington U. Health Policy Inst., 2004—. Fellow Inst. for Advanced Study in Internat. Bus., Washington U., 1991. Fellow ACP, Am. Coll. Cardiology, Am. Acad. Med. Dirs.; mem. AAAS, NY Acad. Scis. (life), Mo. Soc. Internal Medicine (coun.), Gov. Rel. Com., Am. Acad. Physician Execs., Mayo Alumni Assns., Am. Cons. League, Am. Mgmt. Assn., Cornell U. Alumni Assn., Princeton Alumni Assn., Princeton U. Club (bd. dirs. 2000—). Office: Health Management Associates Inc 5811 Pelican Bay Blvd Ste 500 Naples FL 34108-2710 Office Phone: 239-598-3131. Office Fax: 239-598-2705. Business E-Mail: rriner@rinergroup.com.

RINER, TOM, state legislator; b. Oct. 7, 1946; married. Pastor; mem. Dist. 41 Ky. House of Reps., 1982—. Author: (book) The Riner Report, 1989. Mem.: SAR, Exec. Club Louisville, Ky. Hist. Soc., Jefferson Club, Filson Club, Am. Legion, Kiwani. Democrat. Baptist. Mailing: 1143 E Broadway Louisville KY 40204 Office: Capitol Annex Rm 457C Frankfort KY 40601 Home Phone: 502-584-3639; Office Phone: 502-564-8100 ext 606. Business E-Mail: tom.riner@lrc.ky.gov.

RING, JEREMY, state legislator; b. New Haven, Aug. 10, 1970; m. Sharon Ring; children: Elijah, Levi, Eliana, Galit. Attended, Syracuse U., NY, 1992. Entrepreneur; mem. Dist. 31 Fla. State Senate, 2006—, vice chair policy and steering com. on commerce and industry, select com. on Fla.'s economy, chair govtl. oversight and accountability, co-chair joint select com. on collective bargaining, mem. policy and steering com. on govtl. ops., banking and ins. com., cmty. affairs com., fin. and tax com., judiciary com., reapportionment com., mem. joint legis. auditing com., joint legis. budget commn. Co-founder Students United with Parents and Educators to Resolve Bullying; bd. dirs. Fla. Ocean Scis Inst., Daniel Cantor Sr. Ctr., Nat. Jewish Dem. Com. Mem.: Knights of Pythias. Democrat. Office: 5790 Margate Blvd Margate FL 33063 also: 326 Senate Office Bldg 404 S Monroe St Tallahassee FL 32399-1100 Office Phone: 954-917-1392, 850-487-5094. Business E-Mail: ring.jeremy.web@flsenate.gov.

RING, JUDITH A., state librarian; BS in Elem. Edn., Edinboro Coll., Pa., BLS; MLS, Clarion U., Pa. Exec. dir. Erie County Libr. System, Pa.; dep. divsn. dir. Lee County Libr. System, interim libr. dir.; asst. divsn. dir. Divsn. Libr. and Info. Services, Tallahassee, 2001—03, state libr., 2003—. Mem. adv. com. Fla. Book Awards, 2007. Mem.: Chief Officers of State Libr. Agys., Fla. Libr. Assn. (mem. exec. bd. 2007—08). Office: Fla State Libr RA Gray Bldg 500 South Bronough St Tallahassee FL 32399-0250 Office Phone: 850-245-6600. Office Fax: 850-245-6735. Business E-Mail: jring@dos.state.fl.us.

RING, SUSAN, medical insurance company executive; Grad. in English & German, Warwick U. Head, customer svcs. Private Patients Plan; dir., risk mgmt. Unum Ltd., dir., customer svcs., 1995, ops. dir., 1999—2002, chmn., mng. dir., 2002—06, exec. v.p., CEO, 2006; joined Unum Group, 1995, pres., CEO, Unum UK, 2002—, exec. v.p., Unum UK, 2007—. Mem. Surrey Chpt. Phab. Office: Unum Group 1 Fountain Square Chattanooga TN 37402 Office Phone: 423-294-1011. Business E-Mail: sring@unum.com.

RING, W(ILLIAM) STEVES, thoracic and cardiovascular surgeon; b. Patterson, NJ, Aug. 12, 1945; s. William Steves and Nancy J. (Gettings) R.; m. Denise B. Passmore, 1969; children: William Steves III, Ashley Brinton. BA, Brown U., 1967, MMS, 1969; MD, Harvard U., 1971. Diplomate Am. Bd. Surgery, 2001, Am. Bd. Thoracic Surgery, 2004; cert. Nat. Bd. Med. Examiners, 1972, Tex. State Bd. Med. Examiners. Intern, then resident in surgery, fellow Duke U., Durham, NC, 1971-73, 75-77, resident in surgery, fellow, 1977-82; instr. surgery U. Minn., Mpls., 1983-85, asst. prof., 1985-87, dir. cardiac transplantation, 1984-87; prof., chmn. divsn. thoracic surgery U. Tex. Southwestern Med. Ctr., Dallas, 1988—2000, Frank M. Ryburn, Jr. disting. chair cardiothoracic surgery, 1989—, chmn. dept. cardiovascular thoracic surgery, 2000—; chief thoracic and cardiovascular surgery Parkland Meml. Hosp., Dallas, 1988—, Zale Lipshy Univ. Hosp., Dallas, 1988—; dir. cardiac transplantation St. Paul Med. Ctr., Dallas, 1988—. William D. Seybold lectr. in surgery U. Tex. Southwestern Med. Ctr., 1988, presenter, president's lecture series, 2007. Mem. editl. bd. Clin. Transplantation; contbr. articles to profl. jours. Mem. exec. com. Dallas affiliate Am. Heart Assn., 1988—, pres., 1992-93; mem. exec. com. S.W. Organ Bank, 1988—. Maj. USAF, 1973-75. Recipient Nat. Rsch. Svc. award NIH, 1978-79, Gladys Faschena award Dallas affiliate Am. Heart Assn., 1990. Fellow ACS, Am. Coll. Cardiology, Am. Coll. Chest Physicians; mem. Am. Soc. Transplant Surgeons (mem. membership com. 1991—), Internat. Soc. Heart and Lung Transplantation, Am. Assn. Thoracic Surgery, Transplant Soc, World Soc. Pediatric and Congenital Heart Surgery, Southern Thoracic Surg. Assn. (councilor 2004, Kent Trinkle edn. lectr. 2002) Office: U Tex Southwestern Med Ctr 5323 Harry Hines Blvd Dallas TX 75390-7208 Home: 3368 Blackburn St Dallas TX 75204-1531

RINGLE, BRETT ADELBERT, lawyer, oil and gas industry executive, trustee; b. Berkeley, Calif., Mar. 17, 1951; s. Forrest A. and Elizabeth V. (Darnall) R.; m. Sue Kinslow, May 26, 1973. BA, U. Tex., 1973, JD, 1976. Bar: Tex. 1976, US Dist. Ct. (no. dist.) Tex. 1976, US Supreme Ct. 1980, US Ct. Appeals (5th cir.) 1984. Ptnr. Shank, Irwin & Conant, Dallas, 1976-86, Jones, Day, Reavis & Pogue, Dallas, 1986-96; v.p. Hunt Petroleum Corp., Dallas, 1996—2008; trustee Margaret Hunt Trust Estate, 2008—. Adj. prof. law So. Meth. U., Dallas, 1983. Author: (with J.W. Moore and H.I. Bendix) Moore's Federal Practice, 2d edit., Vol. 12, 1980, Vol. 13, 1981, (with J.W. Moore) Vol. 1A, 1982, Vol. 1A Part 2, 1989. Mem. Dallas Bar Assn. Home: 3514 Gillon Ave Dallas TX 75205-3220 Office: Margaret Hunt Trust Estate Ste 4900 1601 Elm St Dallas TX 75201 Office Phone: 214-922-1004. Business E-Mail: bringle@hh-services.com.

RINKS, RANDY (BEAR) S., state legislator; b. Houston, Jan. 1, 1954; married; 2 children. Former commr., Savannah, Tenn.; former mayor; state rep. Dist. 71 Tenn., 1991—; majority caucus chmn.; bd. dir. Tenn.-Tom Devel. Authority; bldg. supply dealer. Elder 1st Cumberland Presbyn. Ch. Mem.: Carolina-Tenn. Bldg. Material Assn. Democrat. Presbyterian. Mailing: PO Box 58 Pickwick Dam TN 38365-0058 Office Phone: 901-925-3985. Fax: 901-925-3351. E-mail: rep.randy.rinks@legislature.state.tn.us.

RINNE, KRISTIN, telecommunications industry executive; V.p., Tech. Strategy SBC Wireless; mng. dir., ops. Southwestern Bell Mobile Sys.; v.p., tech., product realization Cingular Wireless, chief tech. officer, AT&T Mobility, LLC, sr. v.p., architecture & planning, 2006—. Chmn. 3G Americas, 2004—. Office: AT&T Mobility LLC Glenridge Highlands Two 5565 Glenridge Connector Atlanta GA 30342 Office Phone: 404-236-6000. Office Fax: 404-236-6005. Business E-Mail: kristin.rinne@att.com.

RINNE, PEKKA, professional hockey player; b. Kempele, Finland, Nov. 3, 1982; Goaltender Milw. Admirals (American Hockey League), 2005—08, Nashville Predators, 2008—. Named to Second All-Star Team, NHL, 2011; finalist Vezina Trophy, 2011. Avocations: tennis, reading. Office: Nashville Predators Bridgestone Arena 501 Broadway Nashville TN 37203

RIORDAN, DEBORAH TRUBY, lawyer; b. Georgetown, SC, May 29, 1968; d. David Charles and Vickie (Turner) Truby; m. Gary Ray Riordan, Aug. 26, 1995; children: Katherine Spencer, Neely McAdams. BA in polit. sci., U. Ark., 1990; JD, Vanderbilt U., 1993. Bar: Ark. 1993, Tenn. 2005, Pa. 2006, Ky. 2007, U.S. Dist. Ct. (ea. and we. dists.) Ark. 1993. Law clk. various law firms, Little Rock, 1991-92; assoc. Shults Ray & Kurrus LLP, Little Rock, 1993-99; dir. Hill, Gilstrap, Perkins & Trotter, Little Rock, 1999—2004; atty. Wilkes & Mchugh, P.A., Little Rock, 2004—. Staff writer Interaction mag., 1997-98; co-editor League mag., 2000-01; editor Interaction mag., 2002-. Vol. Ctrl. Ark. Legal Svcs., Little Rock, 1993-97, St. Vincents Hosp. Aux.; vol. coord. Ark. Arts Ctr., Little Rock, 1993-95; tng. com., sec., yearbook editor, mktg. v.p., chair devel. task force Jr. League, Little Rock, 1996—2005; chair pastor parish rev. com. Trinity United Meth. Ch., Little Rock, 1998—; mem. presch. com. Immanuel Bapt. Ch., 2002—. Mem. ABA, Arkansas County Bar Assn., Pulaski County Bar Assn. Avocations: tennis, walking, reading, arkansas razorbacks football, spending time with daughters. Home: 85 Pebble Beach Dr Little Rock AR 72212 Office Phone: 888-777-9424.

RIORDAN, JAMES QUENTIN, retired oil industry executive, lawyer; b. Bklyn., June 17, 1927; s. James A. and Ruth M. (Boomer) R.; m. Gloria H. Carlson, June 23, 1951; children: Harris, Susan, James, Ruth. BA, Bklyn. Coll., 1945; LLB, Columbia U., 1949. Bar: N.Y. 1951, U.S. Supreme Ct. 1954. Atty. Winthrop, Stimson, Putnam & Roberts, NYC, 1949-51; mem. staff Ways and Means sub-com., Washington, 1951-52; atty. tax div. Justice Dept., Washington, 1952-55; atty. Chadbourne, Parke, Whiteside & Wolff, NYC, 1955-57; various positions to vice chmn., chief fin. officer Mobil Corp., 1957-89; pres. Bekaert Corp., 1989-92; chmn. Quentin Ptnrs. Co., 1996—. Bd. dirs. Com. Econ. Devel., Tax Found., Inc.; trustee Bklyn. Mus. Mem. Rembrandt Club (N.Y.C.), Blind Brook Club, Sailfish Point (Fla.), Stockbridge Club. Office: 851 Johnson Ave Ste 100 Stuart FL 34994 Office Phone: 772-220-4127.

RIORDAN, KEVIN, healthcare company executive; Attended, U. Mass., Amherst. V.p., state govt. rels. Amerigroup Corp. Office: Amerigroup Corp 4425 Corporation Ln Virginia Beach VA 23462 Office Phone: 757-490-6900. Office Fax: 757-518-3600. Business E-Mail: kriordan@amerigroupcorp.com.

RIORDAN, MICHAEL C., hospital administrator; b. NJ, 1959; BA in Liberal Arts and English, Columbia U., 1980, MA in Edn. and Psychology, 1981; M in Health Sys., Ga. Inst. Tech., 1986. Various positions Crawford Long Hosp., Atlanta; COO, sr. assoc. adminstr. Emory U. Hosp. Sys., Atlanta, 1995—2000; exec. v.p. and COO U. Chgo. Hospitals, 2000—01, pres. and CEO, 2001—06; pres., CEO Greenville Hosp. Sys., 2006—. With USMC, 1981—85. Office: Greenville Hosp Sys 701 Grove Rd Greenville SC 29605

RIORDAN, STEPHEN A., corporate financial executive; BS in Accountancy, Bentley Coll.; MBA, Lehigh U. CPA; cert. mgmt. acct. Joined Ingersoll-Rand Co. Ltd., 1981, worldwide divsn. contr., European paving equipment bus. unit Germany, 1993—97, ind. cons., 1998—2002; v.p., fin. Dresser-Rand Group, Inc., 2003—04, CFO, 2004—05, v.p., fin., 2005—. Office: Dresser-Rand Group Inc 10205 Westheimer Rd W 8 Tower Ste 1000 Houston TX 77042 Office Phone: 713-354-6100. Office Fax: 713-354-6110.

RISCASSI, ROBERT W., communications systems company executive, retired military officer; Comdr. Combined Arms Ctr. US Army, dep. chief of staff Ops. and Plans, dir. joint staff Joint Chief of Staff, vice chief of staff, comdr. in chief UN Command/Korea; positions up to v.p. land systems Washington ops. Loral Corp., 1993—96; v.p. land systems C3I and Systems Integration Sector Lockheed Martin; sr. v.p. Washington ops. L-3 Communications Holdings, Inc. Office: L-3 Comm Holdings Inc 1215 S Clark St Ste 1205 Arlington VA 22202 Office Phone: 703-412-7190.

RISCH, FRANK A., oil industry executive; BBA, Pa. State U., 1964; M in Indusl. Adminstrn., Carnegie Mellon U. Treas. Exxon Chem. Co., 1984, v.p. fin. and corp. affairs, mem. exec. com., 1986; various positions fin., planning and mktg. ExxonMobil Corp., London, Athens, Seattle, fin. analyst dept. treas., 1966, mgr., corp. fin. NY, 1980, exec. asst. to chmn., 1990, asst. controller, 1992, v.p., treas., 1999—2004, asst. treas., 2002—; treas. Dallas Theater Ctr. Bd. dirs. Pioneer Natural Resources Co., Irving, Tex., 2005—; vice chmn. Dallas Zoological Soc. Mem. bd. dirs., exec. com. Dallas-CASA; mem. exec. com. Dallas Meml. Ctr. Holocaust Studies. Mem.: Carnegie Mellon U. Grad. Sch. Indusl. Adminstrn. (co-chmn. coun. on fin.), Am. Petroleum Inst., Fin. Execs. Inst. Office: Dallas Theater Center 2400 Flora St Dallas TX 75201 Office Phone: 214-526-8210. Office Fax: 214-521-7666.

RISER, NEIL, state legislator; b. Apr. 25, 1962; m. Vicki Riser; 2 children. BA of Sci. in Bus. Mgmt., U. La. at Monroe & NE La. U. Bd. mem. Caldwell Bank & Trust, Columbia; pres., owner Riser Funeral Homes Caldwell & La Salle parishes; former pres. Pelican State Life Ins. Co.; former mem. Rep. State Ctrl. Com., 1996—2000; mem. Dist. 32 La. State Senate, 2008—, chair labor and indsl. rels. com., mem. agr., forestry, aquaculture and rural devel. com., revenue & fiscal affairs com., select com. on homeland security, select com. on vets. affairs. Republican. Mailing: District Office 216 Main St Columbia LA 71418 Address: Capitol Office PO Box 94183 Baton Rouge LA 70804 also: PO Box 117 Columbia LA 71418 Office Phone: 318-649-0977. E-mail: risern@legis.state.la.us.

RISHER, WILLIAM HENRY, cardiothoracic surgeon, educator; b. New Orleans, Oct. 3, 1958; m. Michele Helene Van Kuren, July 11, 1981; children: Amelia Alexandra, Jordan Prescott, Olivia Leigh. Student, U. New Orleans, 1981; BS in Biomed. Engring., Tulane U., 1981; MD, La. State U., 1985. Diplomate Am. Bd. Surgery, Am. Bd. Thoracic Surgery; lic. surgeon, NY, Pa., Ga., La.; cert. ACLS, advanced trauma life support, pediatric advanced life support provider, basic life support provider. Resident in gen. surgery Alton Ochsner Med. Found., New Orleans, 1985-90, chief resident, 1989-90, resident and fellow in cardiovascular surgery, 1990-92, chief resident, 1991-92; flight care physician Ochsner Flight Care, 1986-92; assoc. prof. cardiothoracic surgery Med. Ctr. U. Rochester, NY, 1992—2002; chief St. Luke's Regional Heart Program, Bethlehem, Pa., 2002—10; chief cardiothoracic surgery La. State U. Med. Ctr., New Orleans, 2010—. Presenter in field. Contbr. over 20 articles to med. and sci. jours. T.H. Harris scholar Tulane U, 1977-79, full scholar, 1979-81. Fellow ACS, Am. Coll. Cardiology (assoc.); mem. AMA, Am. Coll. Chest Physicians, Soc. Thoracic Surgeons, Internat. Soc. Heart and Lung Transplantation, S.E. Surg. Congress, So. Med. Assn., Med. Soc. County Monroe, Rochester Acad. Medicine, Rochester Cardiovascular Soc., Upstate Soc. Thoracic Surgeons, Rochester Surg. Soc., Assn. for Advancement of Med. Instrumentation, Alton Ochsner Med. Soc., Tau Beta Pi, Alpha Omega Alpha. Office: La State University Health Scis Ctr Dept Surgery 1542 Tulane Ave New Orleans LA 70112 Office Phone: 504-568-4752. Personal E-mail: mbajo5@aol.com. Business E-Mail: wrishe@lsuhsc.edu.

RISIN, SEMYON AARON, pathologist, educator; b. Belarus; m. Diana Risin; 1 child, Michael. MD, PhD, Minsk State Med. Inst., Belarus, 1964. Diplomate Am. Bd. of Pathology, 2003. Physician, physician-in-chief Village Hosp., Khominka, Belarus, 1964—66; rschr. Minsk State Med. Inst., 1971—79, prof., 1979—89; rsch. prof. U. Tex. M. D. Anderson Cancer Ctr., Houston, 1990—97; resident physician dept. pathology & lab. medicine U. Tex.-Houston Med. Sch., 1997—2001, prof. dept. pathology & lab. medicine, 2001—. Med. cons. Am. Biomed, Houston, 1990—91; med. interpretor and cons. Johnson Space Ctr., NASA, Houston, 1996—97. Avocation: travel. Office: UT-Houston Medical School 6431 Fannin Street MSB 2290 Houston TX 77030 Office Fax: 713-500-0730.

RISLEY, ROD ALAN, educational association administrator; b. Hutchinson, Kans., Oct. 17, 1954; s. Ralph Edward and Patricia Ann (Gaulding) R. AA, San Jacinto Coll., Tex., 1975; BBA, Sam Houston State U., Huntsville, Tex., 1982; AA (hon.), Austin Community Coll., Tex., 1991; MBA, Millsap Coll., 1995; PhD (hon.), Highpoint U., 1996, Mt. Ida Coll., Newton Centre, Mass., 1996, Landmark Coll., Putney, Vt., 2003; ABD, Miss. State U., 2003. Dir. alumni affairs Phi Theta Kappa, 1976-82; assoc. dir. Phi Theta Kappa Internat. Hdqrs., Jackson, Miss., 1982-85, exec. dir., 1985—. Chmn. bd. dirs. Miss. Humanities Coun.; bd. dirs. Jack Kent Cooke Found., CC Transfer Initiative; chmn. bd. devel. com. Miss. Ctr. Non-Profit Orgns., Am. Soc. Assn. Execs.; grant reviewer NSF, CC Humanities Assn., NEH; mem. adv. bd. Horne CPA Group. Judge Truman Scholarship Found., 1993, 94, Coca-Cola Scholars Found., 2001-04, USA Today's All-USA Acad. Team HS, 2003-04, Jack Kent Cooke Found., 2004-06, Nat. Assn. C.C. Tchr. Edn. Program, 2004-07. Named one of Outstanding Young Men Am., 1982, 83, 84, 85, 86, 87, 88, 89, Top Bus. Leaders Miss., 1994, Disting. Alumnus, San Jacinto Coll., 1997; Mid South Found. C.C. fellow, 2001, Am. Assoc. Comm. Coll. Leadership award, 2008. Mem. Am. Assn. of Cmty. Colls. (commr. coun. for acad., student and cmty. devel., grant reviewer, Disting. Alumnus award 1996), Am. Soc. Assn. Execs., Phi Theta Kappa (sec., pub. jour.), Phi Kappa Phi. Episcopalian. Office: Phi Theta Kappa Soc PO Box 13729 Jackson MS 39236-3729 Office Phone: 601-984-3518. Business E-Mail: rod.risley@ptk.org.

RISTOW, GEORGE EDWARD, neurologist, educator; b. Albion, Mich., Dec. 15, 1943; s. George Julius and Margaret (Beattie) R.; 1 child, George Andrew Martin. BA, Albion Coll., 1965; DO, Coll. Osteo. Medicine/Surgery, Des Moines, 1969. Diplomate Am. Bd. Psychiatry and Neurology. Intern Garden City Hosp., 1969-70; resident Wayne State U., 1970-74; fellow U. Newcastle Upon Tyne, 1974-75; asst. prof. dept. neurology Wayne State U., Detroit, 1975-77; assoc. prof. Mich. State U., East Lansing, 1977-83, prof., 1983-84, 95—, prof., chmn., 1984-95, prof. emeritus, 2001—. Fellow Am. Acad. Neurology, Royal Soc. Medicine; mem. AMA, Am. Osteo. Assn., Pan Am. Med. Assn., World Fedn. Neurology, Am. Coll. Neuropsychiatrists (sr.). Home: 13211 Lost Key Pl Lakewood Ranch FL 34202 Personal E-mail: ristowge@aol.com.

RITCHEY, LORI A., corporate financial executive; Attended, Wright State U. Audit mgr. Deloitte; fin. analysis Ethicon Endo Surgery, Inc.; mgr., external reporting MeadWestvaco Corp., 2003—06, dir., internal audit dept., 2006—08; v.p., internal audit Chiquita Brands International, Inc., 2008—09, v.p., contr., chief acctg. officer, 2009—. Office: Chiquita Brands International Inc 550 S Caldwell St Ste 1010 Charlotte NC 28202-2681 Office Phone: 513-784-8000. Office Fax: 513-784-8030. Business E-Mail: lritchey@chiquita.com.

RITCHIE, HAROLD L., state legislator; b. Bogalusa, La., May 24, 1949; m. Patsy Terrell Ritchie; children: Bill, Tara, Kristen, Lewis, Rob. Former councilman-at-lg, Bogalusa; pres. Poole-Ritchie Funeral Home, 1980—; mem. Dist. 75 La. House of Reps., 2004—, vice chair agr., forestry, aquaculture and rural devel. com., mem. edn. com., ways and means com., joint legis. com. on capital outlay. Democrat. Baptist. Address: 302 Louisiana Ave Bogalusa LA 70427 Office: PO Box 94062 Baton Rouge LA 70804 Fax: 985-730-2149. E-mail: larep075@legis.state.la.us.

RITCHIE, JAMES H., state legislator; b. Morgantown, W.Va., Aug. 12, 1961; s. James H. and Barbara R. Ritchie; m. Evelyn Dupre Cribb, 1984; children: Caroline Johnston, James H. III, Anna Grace Hamilton. State senator Dist. 13, SC, 2000—; mem. Banking & Ins. Com., Med. Affairs Com., Judiciary Com., Rules Com., Transp. Com. Mem.: Spartanburg County Young Lawyers Assn. (former pres.), Leadership Spartanburg, Leadership SC, Spartanburg Area C. of C. (exec. com. mem. 1996—98, gen. counsel 1996—98), Masters Internat. Bus. Degree, U. SC Bd. Adv.Joint Law, Athletic Booster Club (Spartanburg) (former chmn.). Republican. Methodist. Mailing: 602 Gressette Bldg PO Box 142 Columbia SC 29202-0142 Office Phone: 803-212-6008. Fax: 803-212-6299. E-mail: JHR@scsenate.org.

RITCHIE, KEVIN, electronics executive; BSEE, U. Dayton, Ohio, 1978. Product engr. def. bus. Texas Instruments, Inc., 1978—80, with semiconductor group, 1980—90, wafer fab mgr., 1990—96, mgr. worldwide application-specific products mfg. ops., 1996—2000, sr. v.p. worldwide mfg. ops., tech. and mfg. group Dallas, 2000—. Office: Tex Instruments Inc PO Box 660199 Dallas TX 75266-0199 Office Phone: 972-995-2011. Office Fax: 972-995-4360.

RITTER, ALLAN B., state legislator; b. Beaumont, Tex., May 6, 1954; m. Peggy Ritter; 4 children. Mem. sales & mgmt. Ritter Lumber Co., 1972—88, pres., 1988—98, Triple R Brothers, Ltd.; vice chmn. Allied Bldg. Stores, 1996—98; mem. Dist. 21 Tex. House of Representatives, 1999—. Bd. mem. Nederland Sr. Citizens Trust Fund, Gov.'s Small Bus. Coun., Tex. Constrn. Coun., Nederland Econ. & Devel. Coun. Mem.: NRA, Lumbermen's Assn. Tex., Southwestern Cattle Assn., C. of C., Crimestoppers. Democrat. Baptist. Office: PO Box 1265 Nederland TX 77627 also: Room 1W.03 Capitol Extension PO Box 2910 Austin TX 78768 Office Phone: 409-729-3228, 512-463-0706.

RITTER, JAY RIAL, finance educator; b. Milw., Apr. 29, 1954; s. Jack R. and June E. (Sebastian) R. BA in Econs., MA in Econs., U. Chgo., 1976, PhD in Econs., 1981. Asst. prof. U. Pa., Phila., 1981-85, U. Mich., Ann Arbor, 1985-89; assoc. prof. U. Ill., Champaign, 1989-92, prof., 1992-94, Bailey Meml. prof., 1994-96. Vis. prof. MIT, Cambridge, 1995-96, U. of Florida, Gainesville, 1996—, Cordell prof. Assoc. editor Fin. Mgmt., 1990-93, 2000—, Jour. Fin., 1991-2000, Jour. Fin. Econs., 1993—, Jour. Fin. Quantitative Analysis, 2001-. Recipient Smith Breeden award Am. Fin. Assn., 1991; named MBA Prof. of Yr. U. Ill., 1992. Mem. Am. Fin. Assn. (bd. dirs. 1993-96), Fin. Mgmt. Assn. (v.p. program 2012), Vericimetry US Small Cap Value Mutual Fund (bd. trustees, 2011-). Office: University Fla Dept Fin PO Box 117168 Gainesville FL 32611-7168 Office Phone: 352-846-2837. Business E-Mail: jay.ritter@warrington.ufl.edu.*

RITVO, ROGER ALAN, research management professor, health management-policy educator; b. Cambridge, Mass., Aug. 12, 1944; s. Meyer and Miriam R.S. (Meyers) R.; m. Lynn Lieberman; children: Roberta, Eric. BA, Western Res. U., 1967; MBA, George Washington U., 1970; PhD, Case Western Res. U., 1976. Asst. adminstr. N.Y. Mental Health System, 1968-70; asst. prof., asst. dean Sch. Applied Social Scis. Case Western Res. U., Cleve., 1976-79, assoc. prof., 1981-83; assoc. prof., founding dir. Grad. Program in Health Adminstrn. Cleve. State U., 1983-87; prof. health mgmt. and policy, dean Sch. Health and Human Svcs. U. N.H., Durham, 1987-97; sr. health policy analyst to sec. DHHS, Washington, 1980-81; vice chancellor acad. and student affairs Auburn U. Montgomery, Ala., 1997—2005. Vis. rsch. scholar WHO, Copenhagen, 1978; vis. prof. Am. U., Washington, 1980-81, U. W.I., 1993; chair Ala. Coun. Chief Acad. Officers, 1998-2000; vis. scholar U. Sheffield, Eng., 1985; cons. to numerous orgns. on profit and non-profit strategic planning. Editor, author 8 books, including Managing in the Age of Change, 1994, Improving Governing Board Effectiveness, 1996, Sisters in Sorrow Voices of Care in the Holocaust, 1998, Ethical Governance in Health Care, 2004, Nonprofit Organizations: Principles and Practices, 2008; mem. cmty. editl. bd. Montgomery Advertiser newspaper, 1999; contbr. articles to profl. jours. Trustee Hosp. Sisters of Charity, Cleve., 1980-85, Greater Seacoast United Way, 1991-93; chmn. health care adv. com. Ohio Senate, 1983-85; bd. mem. Fairmount Temple, Beachwood, Ohio, 1980-85; trustee Leadership Seacoast, 1991-93, bd. dirs., 1992-95; bd. dirs. N.H. chpt. United Way, 1992-95, Higher Edn. Leadership Partnership, 1998-2000; chair higher edn. divsn. United Way, Montgomery, Ala., 2004. Recipient Outstanding Adminstr. award, 1992, Cert. of Merit U. N.H. Pres.'s Commn. on Women, 1994; Govt. fellow Am. Coun. Edn., 1980-81; Fulbright scholar Azerbaijan, 2006. Mem. Nat. Tng. Labs. Inst. (bd. dirs. 1981-85, 92-96), Cert. Cons. Internat., Jewish Philatelic, Hist. Soc. N.Y.C. Avocations: collecting flat irons and masks, philatelist, white water rafting. Office Phone: 334-244-3603.

RITZE, MIKE, state legislator; b. Trenton, Mo. m. Connie Ritze; 4 children. BS in Zoology, Northeast Mo. State U.; DO, Kirksville Coll. Osteopathic Medicine; residency in Family Practice, OSUMC; M in Forensic Sci. Admin., Okla. State U., Christiansborg. Physician & surgeon; former police physician Broken Arrow; former med. staff sec./treas. Broken Arrow Med. Ctr.; former adj. prof. Okla. State U. Coll. Osteopathic Medicine, Northeastern State U., Broken Arrow, Coun. Law Enforcement Ed. Tng.; med. & child abuse examiner Okla.; sr. med. examiner Fed. Aviation Admin.; private helicopter pilot; mem. Dist. 80 Okla. House of Representatives, 2008—. Deacon Bapt. Ch., Arrow Heights, Sunday Sch. tchr. Capt. Med. Corps. US Army. Mem.: Tulsa County Osteopathic Med. Soc. (past pres.), Disabled American Veterans (life). Republican. Baptist. Office: 2300 N Lincoln Blvd Rm 300-A Oklahoma City OK 73105 Mailing: 18574 E 101st St S Broken Arrow OK 74011 Office Phone: 405-557-7338. Business E-Mail: mike.ritze@okhouse.gov.

RIVER, SANDRA A., university librarian; BA in Polit. Sci., Minn. State U., Mankato, 1972; MSLS, U. North Tex., 1990; MA in Philosophy, Tex. Tech. U., Lubbock, 1993. Current periodicals/microforms libr. Tex. Tech. U. Librs., Lubbock, Tex., architecture & humanities libr., 2003—; pres. Tex. Tech Faculty Senate, 2008—09, Tex. Tech Women's Studies Affiliated Faculty; sec. Tex. Tech Chpt., AAUP, 2009—. Mem.: Tex. Libr. Assn. (Continuing Edn. & Devel. com.), Assn. Coll. & Rsch. Librs. (Women's Studies Sect., Career Achievement award 2007). Office: Tex Tech University Arch Libr PO Box 42091 Lubbock TX 79409-2091 Office Phone: 806-742-8058. Office Fax: 806-742-2855. Business E-Mail: sandy.river@ttu.edu.

RIVERA, RON (RONALD EUGENE RIVERA), professional football coach; b. Fort Ord, Calif., Jan. 7, 1962; m. Stephanie Rivera; children: Christopher, Courtney. Attended, U. Calif., Berkeley. Linebacker Chgo. Bears, 1984—92, defensive quality coach, 1997—98, defensive coord., 2004—06; football analyst Sta. WGN-TV, Chgo., 1993—96; linebackers coach Phila. Eagles, 1999—2003; inside linebackers coach San Diego Chargers, 2007—08, defensive coord., 2008—10; head coach Carolina Panthers, 2011—. Named NFL Coach of Yr., AP, 2013; named to The U. Calif. Berkeley Sports Hall of Fame, 1994, The Coll. Football Hall of Fame, 2003. Achievements include member of Super Bowl XX championship winning Chicago Bears, 1986. Office: Carolina Panthers 800 S Mint St Charlotte NC 28202*

RIVERA CRUZ, RAMON LUIS, JR., (RAMON LUIS RIVERA JR), Mayor, Bayamon, Puerto Rico; b. Feb. 3, 1956; s. Ramon Luis Rivera. Attended, U. PR, 2001—, Bayamón Regional Coll.; BA with highest honors, America U. Real estate broker; campaign dir. Mayor Ramon Luis Rivera, 1980; former senator Dist. 2 PR Legis.; former vice chmn. Fin. Com.; mayor City of Bayamon, PR, 2000—. Former mem. Health & Social Welfare, Pub. Safety & Govt. & Fed. Affairs coms.; former chmn. Youth, Recreation & Sports, Ethics & Urban & Infrastructure Affairs coms. Mailing: Municipio de Bayamon Casa Alcaldia Bayamon Box 1588 Bayamon PR 00960 Fax: 787-780-5552. E-mail: rrivera@senado.gvmt.pr.us.*

RIVERA GARCÍA, EDGARDO, territorial supreme court justice; b. San Juan, Jan. 3, 1955; 3 children. BA, U. PR, 1977, MPA, 1983, JD, 1988. Dist. atty. Dist of PR, 1994—97; legis. dir. to Charlie Rodriguez Senate of PR, 1997—2000; judge PR Superior Ct., 2000—09, PR Ct. Appeals, 2009—10; assoc. justice Supreme Ct. of PR, 2010—. Office: Supreme Court of Puerto Rico PO Box 9022392 San Juan PR 00902-2392 Office Phone: 787-723-6033. Office Fax: 787-722-9177.*

RIVERA PÉREZ, EFRAÍN E., former territorial supreme court justice; b. Mayaguez, PR, July 15, 1951; s. Efrain Rivera Padilla and Irene Perez Camacho; 1 child, Mariela. BBA, U. PR, 1971; JD, Pontifica Cath. U., PR, 1975. Pvt. practice, 1976—82, 1985—92; dist. judge, 1983—84; superior ct. judge Judicial Region Mayaguez, 1984—85; prof. U. PR, 1986—92; atty. general PR, 1993; dir. Comml. Jud. Reform, 1993—95, Jud. Nominations, 1993—95; judge Cir. Ct. Appeals Judge, 1995—2000; assoc. justice PR Supreme Ct., 2000—10; spl. monitor PR Police Dept., 2010—. Office: Puerto Rico Police Department PO Box 70166 San Juan PR 00936 Personal E-mail: efrain.erp@hotmail.com. E-mail: efrain.rivera@ramajudicial.pr.

RIVIERE, JIM EDMOND, pharmacologist, toxicologist, educator; b. New Bedford, Mass., Mar. 3, 1953; s. Raymond R. Riviere and Gertrude E. Pelletier-Riviere; m. Nancy Ann Monteiro-Riviere, May 31, 1976; children: Christopher, Brian, Jessica. BS, MS, Boston Coll., 1976; DVM, PhD, Purdue U., 1980, DSc (hon.), 2007. Lic. vet. medicine; diplomate Am. Bd. Forensic Medicine, Acad. Toxicological Sci. From asst. prof. to assoc. prof. NC State U., Raleigh, 1981-88, prof., 1988-92, Burroughs-Wellcome disting. prof. pharmacology, 1992—2012, dir. Ctr. Chem. Toxicology Rsch. and Pharmacokinetics, 1989—2012, dir. Biomath. Prog., 2005—07, alumni disting. grad. prof., 2010—; dir. Inst. Computaional Comparative Medicine; Mcdonal chair vet. medicine Kans. State U. Cons. for govt. and pharm. cos.; mem. sci. bd. FDA. Author, editor 10 books, author over 477 rsch. manuscripts. Recipient Ebert prize Am. Pharm. Assn., 1991, Disting. Alumni award Purdue U., 1991, Outstanding Rsch. award NC State U. Alumni Assn., 1993, Harvey Wiley medal, 1997, LE Davis award, 2011, FDA Commrs. Spl. citation, 1997, O. Max Gardner award U. NC Sys., 1999; numerous rsch. grants. Fellow Am. Acad. Vet. Pharmacology and Therapeutics (editor 1989-92, 99—, First Rsch. award 1998, Disting. fellow), Inst. Medicine Nat. Academies (elected); mem. Am. Assn. Pharm. Scientist, Soc. Toxicology, Am. Vet. Med. Assn., Am. Coll. Forensic Examiners, Bd. of Sci. Coun. Nat. Toxicology Prog. Achievements include 6 patents in field. Avocations: baseball, boating, beachcombing. Office: Kans State University Manhattan KS 66506-5802 Home Phone: 919-881-9219. Business E-Mail: Jim_Riviere@ksu.edu.

RIVO, SHIRLEY WINTHROPE, artist; arrived in U.S., 1953, naturalized, 1960; m. Julian David Rivo, Mar. 22, 1953; children: Morissa, Sandra, Philip. BA, Kean U., 1977, MA, 1980. Cert. arts tchr. K-12. Window display designer Belgium Stores, Toronto, 1945-53; needlepoint design Creative Kits, Inc., N.J., N.Y., 1965-72. Chair person exhbn. We Love New York, Lever House, N.Y., 1996; guest spkr. Old Guard of Summit, 2004; spkr. in field, substitute tchr., regional neighborhood tchr. Union County HS Dist., 1977-90. One-woman shows include New Hampshire House, Summit, N.J., 1970, Chemical Bank, N.Y.C., 1977, New Providence Libr., 2008-09, St. Barnabas Med. Ctr., Livingston, N.J., 1978, N.J. Ctr. for Visual Arts, Summit, 1979, 85, Ciba-Geigy, Summit, 1979, AT&T, Basking Ridge, N.J., 1982, Exxon, Warren, N.J., 1985, Chubb Corp. World HQ, Warren, N.J., 1985, Summit Art Ctr., 1985, B'nai Jeshurun, Short Hills, N.J., 1987, John Trapp Gallery, Summit, 1988, Johnson & Johnson, New Brunswick, N.J., 1994, 2004, Schering-Plough, Kenilworth, N.J., 1994, photography, Johnson & Johnson Health Care Systems, Piscataway, N.J., 2004, Summit Free Pub. Libr. Gallery, N.J., 2006, NJ Libr., New Providence, 2008-09, Morris Mus., Morristown, NJ, 2010-11, Met. Life Ins. Co., Misner Pk., Boca Raton, Fla., 2013; two-person exhbn. Overlook Hosp., Summit, N.J., 2003; group shows include N.J. Ctr. for Visual Arts, N.Y.C., 1970, 72, 76, 81, 2008, Kean Coll., Union, N.J., 1972, 80, Visual Arts, Merck & Co., 1990, Papermill Playhouse, N.J., 1972-2010, Somerset Art Assn., 1973, 74, 77, 08, Drew U., Madison, N.J., 1978, Allied Arts of Am., Nat. Arts Club, 1982, Morris County Cultural Ctr., 1983, Morris Mus., Morristown, N.J., 1984, 2010, Nat. Soc. NYC, 2010, Hunterdon Art Ctr., 1987, Visual Spectrum, Schering-Plough, 1993, 2000, numerous others; permanent collections include Morris Mus., Morristown, Johnson & Johnson, New Brunswick, Nabisco Hdqs., Hanover, N.J., Deloitte and Touche LLP, Parsippany N.J., Nat. Baseball Hall of Fame, Cooperstown, N.Y., 1998, Yankee Stadium, Bronx, N.Y., Bklyn. Bot. Garden, Statue of Liberty, N.J., N.Y. Bot. Garden, Bronx, Baseball Hall of Fame, Cooperstown, 2007, Kean U., 2008, Summit Pub. Libr. Partnership Visual Arts Ctr. NJ, 2006, Morris Mus. Morristown NJ, 2010-11. Recipient Best in Show, Millburn Short Hills Art Ctr. 1985, other awards, 1972, 74, 86, 88, 89, 90, 91, 92, 97, 99, 1st prize Papermill Playhouse and in 1995, award of excellence, Pauline Wick award Am. Artists Profl. League Mems. Show, 1990, award for photography Papermill Playhouse, 2003, Merit award, Photography Millburn Shorthills Art Ctr., 2008-, Outstanding Achievement Amateur Photography award Internat. Soc. Photographers, 2004, numerous others, named to Nat. Baseball Hall of Fame, 2012. Mem. N.J. Ctr. Visual Arts (program chair 1979-84, chair spl. events, 1982-84, chair classes 1990-98), Millburn Shorthills Arts Ctr. (trustee, 1990-2006, chmn. pub. rels. 1986-92, chmn. corp. exhibits, 1986-96, 1st v.p. 2006). Avocations: writing, painting, photography.

RIVOLI, GARY JOSEPH, academic administrator, consultant; b. Rochester, NY, Mar. 22, 1947; s. George and Marian (Kahler) R.; m. Shirley Ann Fletcher, Oct. 5, 1973; 1 child, Rachel Anna. AAS, Monroe Community Coll., 1966; BS, U. Louisville, 1969, MS, 1981. Draftsman, designer Xerox Corp., Rochester, 1970-72, Eastman Kodak Co., Rochester, 1973-74, Diebold/Porta-Branch Systems, Clearwater, Fla., 1974-76; sales engr., designer Ryan Industries, Louisville, 1976-78; dir. continuing edn. J.B. Speed Sci. Sch. U. Fla., 1981-82; asst. prof. engring. graphics civil engring. dept. U. Louisville Speed Scientific Sch., 1978-82; pres. Ky. Polytech. Inst., Louisville, 1982—. Dir. continuing edn. J.B. Speed Scientific Sch. U. Louisville, 1978-82. Big brother Met. Big Bros./Big Sisters, Louisville, 1976—; mem. Ky. Derby Festival Com., Louisville, 1980; chmn. profl. tech. com. Increasing the Number of Career Opportunities for Minorities in Engring., Louisville, 1980-82; capt. Mayor's Commn. Bell of Louisville; mem. engring. tech. adv. bd. Jefferson Community Coll., 1987—; bd. dirs. St. Agnes Sch. Bd., Louisville, 1987—. N.Y. Regents scholar N.Y. State Bd. of Regents, 1964; named to Hon. Order Ky. Cols., 1984; recipient Key to City, Owensboro, Ky., 1987. Mem. So. Assn. Colls. and Schs., Ky. Assn. of Career Colls. and Schs. (pres. 1986-87), Council on Non-Collegiate Continuing Edn., Ky. State Bd. for Proprietary Edn. (bd. dirs. 1984—), Louisville Area C. of C., Ky. Occupational Info. Coordinating Com., U. Louisville Alumni Assn., Gamma Chi. Clubs: Derby City Met. (sec. 1982, pres. 1984), Audubon Country (Louisville). Roman Catholic. Avocations: golf, antique cars, collectables, baseball cards. Home: 962 Eastern Pky Louisville KY 40217-1548 Office: Ky Polytech Inst 7410 La Grange Rd Ste 100 Louisville KY 40222-8837*

RIZZETTA, CAROLYN TERESA, sound recording entrepreneur; b. Chgo., June 22, 1942; d. Frank Thomas and Teresa Margaret (Sylvester) Peter; m. Samuel Charles Rizzetta, Apr. 23, 1966. Student, Art Inst. Chgo., 1961-63; BA, Dominican U., 1964, MLS, 1965. Reference librarian Art Dept. Chgo. Pub. Library, 1965; freelance illustrator Macmillan Pub. Co., NYC, 1966; registrar, cataloger Kalamazoo (Mich.) Pub. Mus., 1967; asst. librarian Def. Nuclear Agy., Washington, 1968-69; serials cataloger Library of Congress, Washington, 1970-73, with intern, 1971-72; head of serials U. Va., Charlottesville, 1974-77; musical instrument maker Valley Head, W.Va., 1978-83; bus. mgr. Rizzetta Music, Inwood, W.Va., 1984—. Illustrator Invertebrate Zoology, 1969. Mem. Am. Craft Council, Guild of Am. Luthiers. Avocations: photography, gardening, hiking. Home and Office: Rizzetta Music PO Box 530 Inwood WV 25428-0530

RIZZIERI, L. STEPHEN, lawyer; b. Seneca Falls, NY, June 27, 1955; s. Louis Roy and Barbara Joan (Yates) R.; m. Robin Sue Ray, Aug. 14, 1982; children: Stephen Adam, Sean, Rachel BA, SUNY, Geneseo, 1977; JD, U. Okla., 1980. Bar: Okla. 1980, U.S. Dist. Ct. (we. dist.) Okla. 1981. Assoc. gen. counsel enforcement div. Okla. Securities Commn., Oklahoma City, 1980; counsel Woods Petroleum Corp., Oklahoma City, 1981-85, asst. sec., 1985-87; asst. gen. counsel Sunshine Mining Co., Dallas, 1987—93, Enserch Development Corp., 1993—96; dep. gen. counsel Panda Energy Internat., Inc., Dallas, 1996, sr. v.p., gen. counsel, 1997—2000, chief legal officer, gen. counsel, 2000—. Mem. ABA, Okla. Bar Assn. Democrat. Roman Catholic. Avocations: investments, travel, racquetball. Office: Panda Energy International Inc 4100 Spring Valley Rd Ste 1001 Dallas TX 75244 Office Phone: 972-980-7159. Office Fax: 972-980-6815. E-mail: stever@pandaenergy.com.

RIZZOTTO, VINCENT MICHAEL, bishop emeritus; b. Houston, Tex., Sept. 9, 1931; Attended, St. Mary's Sem.; degree in Canon Law, Cath. U. Am., 1963. Ordained priest Archdiocese Galveston-Houston, 1956, officialis Marriage Tribunal, 1967—72, consultor to bishop, pres. senate of priests, coord. liturgical commn., dir. secretariat chaplaincy svcs. clergy formation, vicar ethnic ministries, vicar African Am. catholics; pastor All Saints Parish, Houston, 1969—72, St. Francis de Sales, Houston, 1972—82, St. Cecilia Cath. Cmty., Houston, 1982—2002; ordained bishop, 2001; aux. bishop Archdiocese Galveston-Houston, 2001—06, aux. bishop emeritus, 2006—. Recipient Monsignor John J. Roach Recognition award, Associated Catholic Charities. Roman Catholic. Office: Archdiocese 1700 San Jacinto PO Box 907 Houston TX 77002

ROACH, DENNIS E., state legislator; m. Glenda Roach; children: Willie, Candace, Julia. State rep. Dist. 35, Tenn., 1995—; tchr.; coach; farm owner. Mem.: Tenn. Coaches Assn., Gideon's Internat. Republican. Baptist. Office: 4519 Hwy 92 Rutledge TN 37861 also: 217 War Memorial Bldg Nashville TN 37243-0135 Office Phone: 615-741-2534, 865-828-4356. Office Fax: 615-532-8221. Business E-Mail: rep.dennis.roach@capitol.tn.gov.

ROACH, JOHN D., building products company executive; b. West Palm Beach, Fla., Dec. 3, 1943; s. Benjamin Browning and Margaret (York) Roach; divorced; children: Vanessa, Alexandra; m. Betty Lou Phillips, Aug. 28, 1982; children: Bruce, Bryce, Brian. BS in Indsl. Mgmt., MIT, 1965; MBA, Stanford U., 1967. Dir. mgmt. acctg. and info. sys. Ventura divsn. Northrop Corp., Thousand Oaks, Calif., 1967—70; co-founder, mgr. Northrop Venture Capital, Century City, Calif., 1970—71; v.p., dir. Boston Consulting Group, Boston and Menlo Park, Calif., 1971—80; v.p., world-wide strategic mgmt. practice mng. officer Booz, Allen, Hamilton, San Francisco, 1980—82, Houston, 1982—83; vice chmn., mng. dir. Braxton Associates, Houston, 1983—87; sr. v.p., CFO Manville Corp., Denver, 1987—88, exec. v.p. ops., 1988-91; pres. Manville Bldg. Products Group, Denver, 1988-90, Manville Mining and Minerals Group, Denver, 1990-91, Celite Corp., Denver, 1990-91; chmn., pres., CEO Fibreboard Corp., Walnut Creek, Calif., 1991—97, Stonegate Resources, Dallas, 1997—2001; founder, chmn., pres., CEO Builders FirstSource, Inc., Dallas, 1998—2001; chmn., CEO, pres. Stonegate Internat., Dallas, 2001—; chmn. Unidare U.S., Muskogee, Okla., 2002—06. Bd. dirs. PMI Group, URS Corp., VeriSign, Mat. Scis., NCI Bldg. Systems, Wash. Group Internat., Am. Stock Exch., Thompson PBE, Magma Power, Fibreboard Corp., Builders First Source, Ply Gem Industries Build Direct. Author: Strategic Management Handbook, 1983. Bd. dirs. Opera Colo., Denver, 1987—91, Bay Area Coun., San Francisco, 1991—96; bd. dirs., mem. exec. com. Dallas Symphony, 1996—2003; mem. exec. com. San Francisco Opera Assn.; trustee Alta Bates Med. Ctr. Mem.: MIT Alumni Club, Stanford Grad. Sch. Bus. Club, Dallas Country Club, Cordillera Country Club (Colo.), Beaver Creek (Colo.) Country Club, Red Sky Golf Club (Wolcott, Colo.), Preston Trail Golf Club (Dallas), Cherry Hills Country Club (Englewood, Colo.). Avocations: golf, skiing, hunting. Office: Stonegate Internat 100 Crescent Ct 7th Fl Dallas TX 75201 Home: 4200 St Johns Ave Dallas TX 75205-3718 Office Phone: 214-459-3460. Personal E-mail: johndcroach@aol.com.

ROACH, MICHAEL, food service executive; Attended, U. Houston. Joined Ben E. Keith Co., 1980, v.p., sales & mktg., 1983, sr. v.p., ops., 1986, prres., 1998, pres., Food Divsn., 1998—, exec. v.p. Office: Ben E Keith Co 601 E 7th St Fort Worth TX 76102-5501 Office Phone: 817-877-5700. Office Fax: 817-338-1701. Business E-Mail: michaelroach@benekeith.com.

ROACH, WESLEY LINVILLE, lawyer, insurance executive; b. Norlina, NC, Oct. 8, 1931; s. Joseph Franklin and Florence G. (Sink) R.; m. Mary Jon Gerald, Aug. 13, 1955; children: Gerald, Mary Virginia. BS, Wake Forest U., 1953, JD, 1955. Bar: N.C. 1955. With Pilot Life Ins. Co., Greensboro, NC, 1958-86, also bd. dirs.; sr. v.p., gen. counsel Jefferson-Pilot Life Ins. Co., Greensboro, 1986-88; sec. Great Ea. Lif. Ins. Co., 1975-85; of counsel Smith, Anderson, Blount, Dorsett, Mitchell & Jernigan, Attys. at Law, Raleigh, NC, 1988—. Former chmn. bd. dirs. N.C. Life and Accident and Health Ins. Guaranty Assn., Va. Life, Accident and Health Guaranty Assn., S.C. Life, Accident and Health Guaranty Assn.; sec. JP Investment Mgmt. Co., Jefferson-Pilot Equity Sales, Inc., Spl. Services Agy., Inc., 1974-84; mem. exec. com., bd. dirs. N.C. Ins. Edn. Found., 1978—; trustee In-Home Care, Inc., 1999—, chmn., 2001. Mem. fin. com. Greensboro United Fund, 1964-65; mem. fin. com. Greensboro 1st Bapt. Ch., 1963-66, 83-86, chmn., 1983-85, chmn. bd. deacons, 1974-76, 80-81; nat. chmn. alumni coun. coll. fund Wake Forest U., 1971-76, pres. nat. alumni coun., 1975-76, trustee univ., 1978-82, emeritus trustee, 1999—; trustee So. Bapt. Theol. Sem., Louisville, 1973-84; trustee Bapt. Retirement Homes N.C., Inc., 1992-2000, chmn., 1993-94, emeritus trustee, 2001-; trustee In Home Care, Inc., 1997—, chmn., 2001; trustee Bapt. Retirement Homes Found. 2001-. With USNR, 1955-58. Mem. ABA, N.C. Bar Assn., Raleigh Bar Assn., Assn. Life Ins. Counsel (bd. govs. 1984-88), Greensboro C. of C. (chmn. nat. legis. com. 1973—), Nat. Orgn. Life Guaranty Assn. (bd. dirs. 1982-87). Democrat. Home: PO Box 1690 601 Selma Rd Wendell NC 27591-8648 Office: 2500 Wells Fargo Capitol Ctr PO Box 2611 Raleigh NC 27602-2611 Office Phone: 919-821-6630.

ROACH, WILLIAM HENRY, JR., investment company executive; BS in Chem. Engring., Purdue U., Ind.; MBA, Columbia U., NYC. Formerly with Security Pacific Merchant Bank; v.p. instl. fixed income svcs. Goldman Sachs Group Inc.; v.p. mktg. & client svcs. Western Asset Mgmt.; various positions including sr. v.p. & prin. GLOBALT Investments, Atlanta, 1991—; now pres., CEO Globalt Investments, Atlanta. Grad. Leadership Atlanta, 1998; mem. adv. bd. Emory U. Goizueta Bus. Sch., Atlanta; bd. dirs. Girls, Inc., Cobb County, Ga. Mem.: Nat. Assn. Securities Professionals, Assn. Investment Mgmt. Sales Execs., Internat. Found. Employee Benefit Plans, Nat. Conf. Pub. Employee Retirement Systems, Mich. Assn. Pub. Retirement Systems. Office: Globalt Investments 3280 Peachtree Rd Ste 500 Atlanta GA 30305 Office Phone: 404-364-2188. Office Fax: 404-364-2189.

ROAN, FORREST CALVIN, JR., lawyer; b. Waco, Tex., Dec. 18, 1944; s. Forrest Calvin and Lucille Elizabeth (McKinney) Roan; m. Vickie Joan Howard, Feb. 15, 1969 (div. Dec. 1983); children: Amy Katherine, Jennifer Louise; m. Leslie D. Hampton, Jan. 2, 1999. BBA, U. Tex., Austin, 1973, JD, 1976. Bar: Tex. 1976, US Dist. Ct. (we. dist.) Tex. 1977, US Dist. Ct. (so. dist.) Tex. 1998, US Ct. Appeals (5th cir.) 1977, US Supreme Ct. 1979, US Ct. Appeals (11th cir.) 1981, US Ct. Appeals (fed. cir.) 1998, US Ct. Internat. Trade 1998. Prin. Roan & Assocs., Austin, 1969-71; counsel, com. dir. Tex. Ho. of Reps., 1972-75; assoc. Heath, Davis & McCalla, Austin, 1975-78; prin. Roan & Gullahorn, P.C., Austin, 1978-85, Roan & Autrey (formerly Roan & Simpson), P.C., 1986-99; sr. ptnr. Cantey, Hanger, Roan & Autrey, 1999—2003; shareholder & chair pub. regulatory law practice group Winstead, P.C. (formerly Winstead, Sechrest & Minick, P.C.), Austin, 2003—11; owner Roan Law PLLC, 2011—; dir., gen. counsel 1st Nat. Title Ins. Co. Chair leadership coun. Am. Lung Assn., 2009—11, bd. dirs. PGR, 2011—12; bd. dirs. Lawyers Credit Union, chmn., 1982—83; bd. dirs. pub. law sect. State Bar Tex., 1980—84; mem. 1881 Soc., Littlefield Soc., Chancellor's Coun. U. Tex. With Tex. N.G. US Army, 1966—74. Fellow: Am. Bar Found. (life), Austin Bar Found. (life; founding fellow), Tex. Bar Found. (life); mem.: ABA, Austin Assembly (treas. 2010), Fed. Regulatory Counsel, Assn. Life Ins. Counsel, Austin Bar Assn., Tex. Assn. Def. Counsel, Tex. Lyceum Assn. (v.p., bd. dirs. 1980—87), Mensa (life), Headliners Club, Shriners Masons (Parsons Masonic master 1976—77), Knights of the Symphony (Lord Chancellor 2003—04). Methodist. Office: RoanLaw PLLC 6805 N Capital Tex Hwy Ste 268 Austin TX 78731 Office Phone: 512-372-0000. Business E-Mail: roan@roanlaw.com.*

ROAN, PAUL D., state legislator; b. Ada, Okla., Jan. 11, 1943; s. Jess Nunn and Pauline Ellis Roan; m. Betty L. Melton; children: Chris W., Brad M., Angela L. BA, Ea. Ctrl. Univ., 1968, MEd, 1971. Educator Tipton Pub. Schs., 1968—70; police officer Ea. Ctrl. Univ., 1970—72; dep. sheriff Pontotoc County, 1972—75; state trooper Okla. Hwy. Patrol, 1975—2000; mem. Dist. 20 Okla. House of Representatives, 2001—. Served USAF, 1961—65. Master: Tishomingo Lodge; mem.: Okla. State Troopers Assn. (1st vice pres. 1998—2000), Johnson County C. of C., Am. Legion, Tishomingo Club (pres. 1980), Mason Club, Lions Club (pres.). Democrat. Office: oklahoma House of Representatives 2300 N Lincoln Blvd Rm 540 Oklahoma City OK 73105 Mailing: 3300 Deer Pond Ln Tishomingo OK 73460-4405 Office Phone: 405-557-7308, 580-371-3526. Fax: 580-371-9526. Business E-Mail: paulroan@okhouse.gov.

ROBB, GEOFFREY LAWRENCE, plastic surgeon; b. El Paso, Tex., May 28, 1946; s. Giles Anthony and Mary Jo (Lawrence) R.; m. Cathy Jean Cross, May 31, 1974; children: Tiffany, Kimberly, Courtney, Carly, Melaney, Mary. BS, U. Miami, 1969, MD, 1974. Diplomate Am. Bd. Otolaryngology. Commd. ensign USNR, 1970-92; advanced through grades to capt., 1989; resident in otalaryngology, mem. staff US Naval Hosp., San Diego, 1974-79, otolaryngologist Orlando, Fla., 1979-83; plastic surgeon USN Sponsorship at U. Pitts., 1983-85, microvascular surgeon, 1985; plastic surgeon U.S. Naval Hosp., Portsmouth, Va., 1985-88; ret., 1992; chief plastic surgery U.S. Naval Hosp., Portsmouth, Va., 1988-92; vice chmn. plastic surgery M.D. Anderson Cancer Ctr., Houston, 1992-97, chmn. plastic surgery, 1997—, dep. chmn. divsn. surgery, 1994—, dir. postgrad. med. edn., 1992—, med. dir. plastic surgery clinic, 1992—, assoc. med. dir. skin cancer ctr., 1996. Contbg. author: Reconstructive Plastic Surgery for Cancer, 1995, Endoscopic Plastic Surgery, 1995, Advanced Skin Cancer of Head and Neck, 1995; contbr. articles to profl. jours. Fellow ACS, Am. Soc. Plastic Reconstructive Surgeons, Am. Soc. Reconstructive Microsurgeons, Am. Assn. Plastic Surgeons; mem. Internat. Soc. Reconstructive Microsurgery, Tex. Soc. Plastic Surgeons, Houston Soc. Plastic Surgeons, KC. Avocations: physical fitness, weightlifting, tennis, running. Office: MD Anderson Cancer Ctr 1515 Holcombe Blvd # 443 Houston TX 77030-4009 E-mail: grobb@mdanderson.org.

ROBBINS, FRANKIE, civil engineer; b. Enid, Okla., Dec. 7, 1945; children: Christian, Joshua. BS in Civil Engring., Okla. State U., 1969. Registered profl. engr., Kans., 1973. Forest transp. program mgr. USDA Forest Svc., 1990—99, regional transp. planner, 1999—2005. Chmn. bd. dirs. Ptnrs.-Mentoring Kids at Risk, 1989—90; mem. Medford C. of C., 2007—10; dem. candidate US House Rep., 3rd Congretional Dist., 2008; past mem. Wakita First Bapt. Ch.; mem., choir mem. Medford United Meth. Ch. Democrat. Office: 118 Fir Dr Medford OK 73759 Office Phone: 580-395-2500. Office Fax: 580-395-2510. Business E-Mail: campaign@robbinsforcongress2008.com, robbinsforcongress@att.net.

ROBBINS, MARY, concert pianist, mozart specialist; b. Shelby, NC, Feb. 14, 1950; d. Clyde Hugh and Hazel Marguerite (Lovett) Robbins; m. Carl Brockman, Jan. 16, 1983. Student, Converse Coll., Spartanburg, SC, 1968-71; BMusic, U. Tex., 1973, MMusic, 1975, D Musical Arts, 1992. Concert coord. Austin (Tex.) Virtuosi, 1980-82; piano clinician Alfred Music Pub., Van Nuys, Calif., 1991-94; pianist various chamber org., Austin, 1976-91; pvt. piano instr. Austin, 1971—; tchg. asst., instr. piano U. Tex., Austin, 1971-75; founder, prin. pianist A. Mozart Fest, Austin, 1991—2008, artistic dir., 1991—2008; founder, prin. pianist A. Mozart Fest Kidskonzerts, Austin. Invited lectr. Mozart Internat. Bicentennial Congress, Salzburg, Austria, 1991. Composer music and cadenzas following Mozart's style for his piano concertos, 1989—2009; performer CD, A. Mozart Fest, 1998, CD with Austrian pianist Paul Badura-Skoda, 2002, CD with pianist Anton Nel, 2005. Presenter, Music Tchr. Nat. Assoc. Conf., 2003. (Presenter of session on stylistic issues of interpretation in Mozart), soloist Mozart Concert Katrineholm Sweden, 2008, Juror Swedish Internat. Duo Competition, Katrineholn, 2008, Mozart Soc. America Presenter Tchg. Mozart award, 2010, Mozart Soc. America Newsletter Vol. XV, 2011, Mozart Concerto K495, 2014. Founding mem. combined groups Classical Music Consortium, Austin, 1997, 2008. Grantee Tex. Commn. on Arts, 1991, 93, 2004—08, City of Austin, 1992—2008. Mem. Austin Dist. Music Tchrs. Assn. (v.p. 1997-98, chair adult programs 1997—2008, 13-14, chair festivals 1997-98, judge ADMTA, 2012, Pre-Coll. Tchr. of Yr. 1998), Mu Phi Epsilon. Lutheran. Avocations: cooking, dance. Home: 2600 La Ronde St Austin TX 78731-5924 Personal E-mail: mozart4@peoplepc.com.

ROBBINS, RICHARD JAMES, endocrinologist, researcher; b. Danbury, Conn., Sept. 21, 1948; s. James Bernard and Ann Patricia Robbins; m. Anne Kathleen Schmiesing, Aug. 29, 1970; children: Andrew Richard, Heather Kathleen Kollar. MD, Creighton U., Omaha, Nebr., 1975. Cert. internal medicine and endocrinology Am. Bd. Internal Medicine, 1978. Dir. neuroendocrine unit Yale Med. Sch., New Haven, 1985—94; chief, endocrine svc. Meml. Sloan-Kettering Cancer Ctr., NYC, 1994—2005; prof., chmn. dept. medicine Meth. Hosp., Houston, 2005—. Recipient Alpha Omega Alpha, Creighton U., 1975, Henry Christian award, Am. Fedn. Clin. Rsch., 1993, Disting. Svc. award, Pituitary Soc., 1995, William Lees Lectureship, Johns Hopkins U., 2004, Best Doctors in NYC, 2005, Top Doctors in Cancer, Castel Connolly Med., Ltd., 2005—07, Charles and Anne Duncan Disting. Chair, Meth. Hosp., 2006, Best Doctors in Am., 2007. Fellow: ACP. Achievements include research in the synthesis of neuropeptides in mammalian cerebral cortex; first human to human neural transplantation for Parkinson's Disease; discovery of selective loss of inhibitory somatostatin interneurons in human epilepsy; use of recombinant human TSH for treatment of thyroid cancer; prognostic value of PET scanning in metastatic thyroid cancer.

ROBBINS, ROBERT CLAYTON (BOBBY ROBBINS), hospital administrator, surgeon; b. Laurel, Miss., Nov. 20, 1957; m. Debbie Robbins; children: Craig, Clay. AA in Chemistry, Jones Jr. Coll., Ellisville, Miss., 1977; BS in Chemistry, Millsaps Coll., Jackson, Miss., 1979; MD, U. Miss. Med. Ctr., Jackson, Miss., 1983. Cert. cardiothoracic surgery American Bd. Thoracic Surgery, gen. surgery American Bd. Surgery. Intern, gen. surgery U. Miss. Med. Ctr., Jackson, 1983—84, resident, gen. surgery, 1984—85, chief resident, gen. surgery, 1988—89; postdoctoral fellow, cardiothoracic transplantation, dept. surgery Columbia-Presbyn. Med. Ctr., 1986; clin. assoc., cardiothoracic surgery, surgery br., Nat. Heart Lung Blood Inst. NIH, Bethesda, Md., 1986—88; resident, cardiothoracic surgery Stanford U. Hosp., Calif., 1989—91, chief resident, cardiothoracic surgery Calif., 1991—92, co-dir., Cardiac Clin. Ctr. Calif., 2002—, dir., Stanford Inst. for Cardiovascular Medicine Calif., 2004; pediat. fellow, congenital heart surgery Emory U. Sch. Medicine, Atlanta, 1992, Royal Children's Hosp., Melbourne, Australia, 1993; dir., cardiothoracic transplantation lab. Stanford U. Sch. Medicine, 1993—2012, acting asst. prof., cardiothoracic surgery, 1993—95, asst. prof., cardiothoracic surgery, 1995—2001, dir., heart, heart-lung, and lung transplant program, 1998—2012, assoc. prof., cardiothoracic surgery, 2001—05, chmn., dept. cardiothoracic surgery, 2005—12, prof., cardiothoracic surgery, 2005—12; pres., CEO Tex. Medical Ctr., Houston, 2012—. Dir., clin. cardiothoracic surgery tchg. conf., 1993—2006; mem. expert panel on minimally invasive surgery Health Tech. Ctr., 2001; bd. dirs. Calif. Transplant Donor Network, 1997—2005, Cohesion Technologies, Palo Alto, 2000—; mem. scientific adv. bd. Cardica, Inc., Menlo Park, Calif., 1997—, bd. dirs., 2000—; mem. scientific adv. bd. Cytograft Tissue Engring. Inc., Novato, Calif., 2000—, bd. dirs., 2003—; mem. scientific adv. bd. Transvascular, Inc., Menlo Park, Calif., 1995—2000, Embol-X, Inc., Sunnyvale, Calif., 1995—98, ArthroCare, Corp., Sunnyvale, Calif., 1997—2000, Cardio Vention, Inc., Palo Alto, 1997—99, A-med, Inc., Sacramento, 1997—2000, Microheart, Inc., Sunnyvale, Calif., 1999—2001, Radiant Med., Redwood City, Calif., 2000—, Curis, Inc., Cambridge, Mass., 2001—, Paracor Surgical, Inc., Sunnyvale, Calif., 2001—; mem. clin. adv. bd. Xoma, LLC, Berkeley, Calif., 2002—, Afmedica, Inc., Kalamazoo, 2005, Theregen, Corp., San Francisco, 2005—; mem. physician adv. panel Cardiac Surgery Technologies, Medtronic, Inc., Mpls., 2001—. Ad hoc reviewer Nat. Inst. Neurological Disorders and Stroke Study Sect., NIH, 1996, manuscript reviewer Jour. Thoracic and Cardiovascular Surgery, 1996—, mem. editl. bd., 2001—, manuscript reviewer Annals Thoracic Surgery, 1995—, New Eng. Jour. Medicine, 1996—, abstract reviewer Internat. Soc. Heart and Lung Transplantation, 1996—, mem. editl. bd. Cardiac Surgery Digest, 2001—, Jour. Heart and Lung Transplantation, 2003—, Innovations, 2005—, guest editor, surgical supplement Circulation, 2002—05; contbr. several articles to peer-reviewed jours. Mem. Thoracic Organ Transplantation Com. United Network for Organ Sharing, 1999—2002, Region 5 Thoracic Organ Rep. and Review Bd. Chamn., 1999—2002; rsch. com. mem. Thoracic Surgery Found. for Rsch. and Edn., 2000—; mem. Calif. Transplant Donor Network-Med. Affairs Com., 1996—. Fellow: American Coll. Cardiology, American Heart Assn. (Vivien Thomas Young Investigator award selection com. 1997—, mem. exec. com., coun. on cardiothoracic and vascular surgery 1997—, mem. program com. 1999—), ACS; mem.: Bay Area Soc. Thoracic Surgeons (founding mem.) (pres. 2006, bd. dirs. 2000—), Soc. U. Surgeons, American Soc. Transplantation, American Soc. Transplant Surgeons, 21st Century Cardiac Surgical Soc., Transplantation Soc., AAAS, Internat. Soc. Heart and Lung Transplantation (co-chair, ventricular assist device coun. 2000—02, bd. dirs. 2000—, program chair 2001—02, mem. program com. 2003, pres. 2006), San Francisco Surgical Soc., Assn. Academic Surgeons (vice-chair, cardiovascular surgery and anesthesia coun. 2005—, mem. strategic planning com. 2006), Soc. Thoracic Surgeons (mem. workforce on clin. edn. 2004—, workforce on surgical treatment end-stage cardiopulmonary disease 2004—), Western Thoracic Surgical Assn., American Assn. Thoracic Surgery (membership com. 2003—06, mem. edn. com. 2003—, chair. membership com. 2005—06), Cardiothoracic Surgery Network, James D. Hardy Soc., Andrew G. Morrow Soc., Alpha Omega Alpha (Resident award 1989). Achievements include patents in field. Office: Texas Medical Center 2450 Holcombe Blvd Houston TX 77021 Office Phone: 713-791-6454.*

ROBBOY, STANLEY J., pathologist, educator; s. John and Sarah (Shapiro) R.; m. Anita Wyzanski, July 21, 1968 (div. 1981); children: Elizabeth, Caroline; m. Marion Meyer, June 14, 1990. Student, U. Mich., 1958-61, MD, 1965. Diplomate Am. Bd. Pathology, Am. Bd. Med. Mgmt. Intern Mt. Sinai Hosp, Cleve., 1965-66; resident to chief in pathology Mass. Gen. Hosp., 1966-70, asst. in pathology, 1972-73, asst. pathologist, 1973-76, assoc. pathologist, 1976-84; resident in pathology Boston Hosp. for Women, 1970; instr. Tufts Med. Sch., 1968-69; asst. prof. pathology Harvard Med. Sch., Boston, 1972-76, assoc. prof., 1976-84; prof. pathology U. Medicine and Dentistry N.J.-N.J. Med. Sch., Newark, 1984—92, chmn. dept., 1984-89, prof. ob-gyn, 1990—92, pathologist-in-chief, 1984-89, dir. faculty practice service, 1985-89; prof., vice chmn. dept. pathology Duke U., 1992—, prof. ob-gyn., 1993—. Cons. pathologist St. Joseph Hosp., Paterson,

NJ, 1985—92, St. Barnabas Hosp., Livingston, NJ, 1985—92, Beth Israel Hosp., Newark, 1985—92, VA Med. Ctr., Durham, 1992-2011, Durham Reg. Hosp., 2003-11, Raleigh Com. Hosp., 2003-11; pathologist (DES) Registry Rsch. Transplacental Hormonal Carcinogenesis (formerly Clear-Cell Adenocarcinoma Registry), 1972-83; pathologist, prin. investigator Nat. Collaborative Diethylstilbestrol project, 1974-82; vis. scientist New Eng. Primate Ctr., 1973-84; vis. prof. U. Shiraz Med. Sch., Iran, 1976; commr. NJ Commn. on Cancer Rsch., 1987-92; sr. advisor East Asia Cons. Group, Boston, LA and Tokyo, 1984-85; reference panel for diagnostic and therapeutic tech. AMA, 1982—99; mem. nat. med. com. Planned Parenthood Fedn. Am., 1990-93, vice chmn. com. on oncology, 1993; mem. DES steering com. Nat. Cancer Inst., 1995—; mem. exec. editl. bd. Arch Path Lab Med, 2005-; bd. dir. Pamet Sys. Inc., 1991-09. Mem. editl. bd. Human Pathology, 1980-90, Cervix and the Low Female Genital Tract, 1983-94, Internat. Jour. Gynecologic Pathology, 1985-; editor: Informatics in Pathology, 1985-88, Pathology Rsch. and Practice, 1990-2000, Gynecologic Oncology, 1997-2004, InsScight, 1998-; sect. editor Functional Biomarkers in Disease, 2005-; editor-in-chief, Pathology the Female Reproductive Tract, edits. 1 & 2; contbr. articles to profl. jours. Trustee Am. Pathology Found., 1984—86; NJ commn. Cancer Rsch., 1987—92; co-pres. Chapel Hill Kehillah, 2005—08, Triangle Jewish Film Festival, 2007—08; pres. Coll. Am. Pathologists, 2011—; chair Triangle Jewish Film Festival, 2007—08. Maj. US Army, 1970—72. Recipient Jr. Faculty award Am. Cancer Soc., 1972-75, Found. prize Am. Coll. Ob-Gyn, 1975, Coll. Am. Pathologist Pres. award, 2005; Sara & Mutt Evans Outstanding Cmty. Svc. award, Durham-Chapel Hill, 2005, Americas Top Physician award, 2007; Pardee fellow U. Mich., 1961, Lederle Lab. fellow, 1962, Eliza Howell fellow, 1964, Ford Found. fellow, 1964-65; clin. fellow Am. Cancer Soc., 1967-68, Hon. fellow, Assn. Affiliated Pathologists New Delhi, India, 2011, Hon. Faculty Pathology Royal Colls. Physicians Ireland, 2012, Paul harris fellow, Rotary Internat., 2009, Pathologists Royal Coll. United Kingston, 2012, Hon. Order award, Ky. Cols., 2013. Fellow Am. Soc. Clin. Pathologists (chmn. pathology telecommunications network com. 1983, task force on computers 1980-83, council on med. informatics 1983-84, planning and scope com. 1983-84, co-chmn. pathology communication network 1983-87, coun. anat. pathology, 1995-2001, future directions, 1995-98), Coll. Am. Pathologists (alt. Mass. del. to house dels. 1981-84, co-chmn. pathology comm. network 1983-85, alt. NJ del. to house dels. 1985-92, exec. com. and advisor nomenclature and classification of disease 1975-80, editl. bd. Systematized Nomenclature Medicine 1976-80, gov. 1999-2005, mem. reimbursement com., 1992-94, profl. and econ. affairs com., 1995-97, outcomes com., 1999-2000, vice chmn. coun. on pub. affairs 1999-2005, coun. of govt. prof. affairs, 2000-2004, credentials com., 2000-04, spokesperson, 2001—, performance measurement com. 2000, nat. meeting planning com. 2003—08, vice chmn. election oversight com. 2006-09, leadership devel. com. 2006-08; strategic planning com., 2008-11, pres. elect 2009-11, pres. 2011-13, chair transformation program office steering com.), Soc. Gynecologic Oncologists Assocs.; mem. Arthur Purdy Stout Soc. Surg. Pathology (membership com. 1980-86, treas. 1993-2001, pres.-elect 2001-03, pres. 2003-05), Internat. Acad. Cytology, Internat. Acad. Pathology (edn. com. 1979-83), Internat. Soc. Gynecologic Pathologists (chmn. membership com. 1982-84), Mass. Soc. Pathology (3d party relations 1978-84, chmn. computer com. 1981-84), NC Med. Soc., NC Soc. Pathology, NJ Med. Soc., NJ Soc. Pathology (edn. and profl. rels. coms. 1984-92, exec. com. 1985-92), Chapel Hill Kehillah (co-pres. 2004—08). Jewish. Office: Duke U Med Ctr PO Box 3712 Durham NC 27710-0001 Office Phone: 919-684-3656. Business E-Mail: stanley.robboy@duke.edu.

ROBE, THURLOW RICHARD, retired engineering educator, dean; s. Thrulow Scott and Mary Alice (McKibben) R.; m. Eleanora C. Komyati, Aug. 27, 1955; children: Julia, Kevin, Stephen, Edward. BSC.E., Ohio U., 1955, MS in Mech. Engring., 1962; PhD in Applied Mechanics, Stanford U., 1966. Engr. Gen. Electric Co., Niles, Ohio, Cleve., Erie, Pa., Evendale,Ohio, 1954-60; acting instr. to instr. Ohio U., Athens, 1960-63, dean Russ Coll. Engring. and Tech., 1980-96, Cruse W. Moss prof. Engring. Edn., 1992-96, founding dir. T. Richard and Eleanora K. Robe Leadership Inst., 1997—2005, dir. Innovation Ctr. Authority, 1983-96; asst. prof to prof., assoc. dean, spl. asst. to pres. U. Ky., Lexington, 1965-80; rsch. fellow Postgrad. Sch. Applied Dynamics U. Edinburgh, Scotland, 1973; dean emeritus, Moss prof. emeritus Russ Coll. Engring. and Tech., Ohio U., Athens, 1996—; pres., chmn. bd. Q.E.D. Assocs., Inc., Lexington, 1975-83. Trustee Engring. Found. Ohio, 1988-94; bd. trustees Ohio Aerospace Inst. 1990-96, bd. govs. Edison Materials Tech. Ctr., 1987-96; mem. adv. bd. Robe Leadership Inst., 2005—; liaison engring. accreditation commn. Accreditation Bd. Engring. and Tech., 1989-91; mem. Russ Prize Selection Com., NAE, 2000—, adv. bd. mem., Salvation Army Oconee Co, 2011-. Contbr. articles to profl. jours.; patentee trailer hitch. Bd. dirs. Athens County Cmty. Redevel. Corp., 1980-86; treas. South Lexington Little League, 1976-80; vice chmn. Thoroughbred dist., Boy Scouts Am., 1975-77; mem.-at-large Oconee Dist. Boy Scouts Am., 2007—09; pres. Tates Creek H.S. PTA, Lexington, 1975-76; bd. dirs. U. Ky. Athletics Ass.n, 1975-80; bd. trustees Assn. Ohio Commodores, 1995-97; trustee Ohio U. Found., 1998-2007, trustee emeritus, 2007—, Nat. Acad. Engring.Russ Prize Selection Com. Advisor, 2000-, Salvation Army Oconee Co Adv. Bd., 2011-. Maj. USAFR, 1955—85, officer, jet fighter pilot USAF, 1956—59, liaison officer US Air Force Acad., 1975—80, Kty. Recipient Alumni medal of merit Ohio U., 1993, Match Play Champion Keowee Key,SC, 2010; named Am. Coun. on Edn. Adminstrn. fellow, 1970-71, Ohio U. Alumnus of Yr., 1996, inductee Acad. Disting. Grads., Russ Coll. Engring. & Tech., 2001. Mem. ASME, NSPE (profl. engring. in edn. exec. bd., ctrl. region vice-chmn. 1987-89), Am. Soc. Engring. Edn. (Outstanding Contbn. in Rsch. award 1966), Athens Reading Club, Athens Symposiarchs, Rotary, Sigma Xi, Tau Beta Pi, Omicron Delta Kappa, Alpha Lambda Delta,, Am. Legion Avocations: reading, tennis, golf. Personal E-mail: robe@ohio.edu.

ROBERSON, ERIC N., lawyer; b. Dallas, Jan. 26, 1965; m. Kristina Roberson; children: Tori, Ali, Luke, Julia. BA in Fgn. Svc., Baylor U., Waco, Tex., 1986; JD cum laude, Baylor U. Sch. Law, 1995. Employment litig. atty. Haynes and Boone, L.L.P., Dallas, 1995—97, Hughes & Luce, L.L.P., Dallas, 1995—97; atty., trainer Trinity Legal Found., Roberson Law Firm, 2000—02; briefing atty. The Mulligan Law Firm, Dallas, 2002—. Vol. Plano Ind. Sch. Dist.; citizens' rev. com. Tex. Bd. Edn.; employment law trainer Meth. Ch. North Tex., bishop's com. for ins. issues; mem. St. Andrew United Meth. Ch., Plano, Tex., 1995—, adult Sunday sch. tchr., discipleship com., mem. governing bd., adult ministries com., stewardship campaign com.; bd. mem. Home Owners Assn., pres., v.p. Naval flight officer, lt. USN, 1987—92, USS Independence, USS Constellation. Democrat. Office: The Mulligan Law Firm 4514 Cole Ave # 300 Dallas TX 75205 Office Phone: 214-219-9779.

ROBERSON, JAMES O., foundation executive; m. Rita Quinn; children: Melanie Merrill, Sharyl, James Jr., Trisha, Joel. AB in Journalism, Baylor U., 1956; student Indsl. Devel. Inst., U. Okla.; student Inst. Orgnl. Mgmt., U. Houston. Cert. econ. developer. Dir. info. West Tex. C. of C., Abilene, 1956-59; area devel. mgr. Mo.-Kans.-Tex. R.R., 1959-63; exec. dir. Albuquerque Indsl. Devel. Svc., 1963-65; dir. N.Mex. Dept. Devel., Santa Fe, 1965-69; mgr. Forward Metro Denver, 1969-72; dir. R.I. Dept. Econ. Devel., Providence, 1972-77; v.p., dir. new bus. devel. Howard Rsch. and Devel. Corp. subs. Rouse Co., Columbia, Md., 1977-79; sec. Md. Dept. Econ. and Community Devel., Annapolis, 1979-83; pres. Louisville C. of C., 1983-88; pres., CEO Rsch. Triangle Found. N.C., 1988—. Chmn. bd. dirs. Charlotte br. Fed. Res. Bank Richmond; cons., speaker in field. Editor West Tex. Today mag., 1956-59. Trustee, vice chmn. Wake Tech. C.C.; bd. dirs. N.C. Biotech. Ctr. Fellow Am. Econ. Devel. Coun. (past chmn.); mem. Indsl. Devel. Rsch. Coun., Nat. Assn. State Devel. Agys. (past pres.), Assn. Univ. Related Rsch. Parks (pres.).

ROBERSON, KENNETH L., state legislator; b. Bradenton, Fla., Nov. 5, 1943; children: James, Mark. AA, Manatee Junior Coll., 1963; AS, Dallas Inst. Mortuary Sci., 1965; grad., U. South Fla., 1969. Pres. Roberson Funeral Home & Crematory, 1976—2008, Restlawn Meml. Park & Mausoleum, 1986—2008; precinct committeeman Charlotte County Rep. Party, 2007—08; mem. Dist. 71 Fla. House of Reps., 2008—, vice chair govtl. affairs policy com., mem. elder and family svcs. policy com., health care appropriations com. Pres. & bd. trustees Cultural Ctr. Charlotte County; former mem. Charlotte County Cemetery Adv. Com., Charlotte County Emergency Med. Svcs. Adv. Com.; former mem. & pres. Fla. Funeral Dirs. Polit. Action Com.; former non-lawyer mem. 20th Jud. Circuit Grievance Com."C"; vol. Jeb Bush Campaign for Gov., 1998—2002; charter mem. Sahib Temple of Shrine, Sarasota; bd. mem. & chmn. Bd. Funeral Dirs. & Embalmers, 1998—2004. Mem.: NRA, Republican Nat. Com., Nat. Funeral Dirs. Assn., Internat. Funeral & Cemetery Assn., Fla. Funeral Dirs. Assn. (former pres.), Fla. Funeral & Cemetery Alliance, Cremation Assn. North America, Am. Assn. Retired Persons, Scottish Rite-Valley of Fort Myers, Port Charlotte Rotary Found. (trustee), Charlotte County Rep. Club, Rotary Internat. (Paul Harris Fellow), Port Charlotte Lions Club, Port Charlotte Rotary Club (former pres.), Peace River Federated Rep. Women's Club (assoc.), Punta Gorda Lodge Number 115, Port Charlotte Elks Lodge Number 2153. Republican. Methodist. Office: House Office Bldg 402 S Monroe St Rm 308 Tallahassee FL 32399-1300 also: 992 Tamiami Tr Unit E-2 Port Charlotte FL 33953-3868 Office Phone: 850-488-0060, 941-613-0914. Business E-Mail: ken.roberson@myfloridahouse.gov.

ROBERTS, BILL, state legislator; 1 child, David. Asst. state commr. labor State of Ala., 1972—76; v.p. human resources CMI Internat. Inc., Southfield, Minn.; mem. Dist. 13 Ala. House of Representatives, 2011—. Vol. Meals on Wheels. Mem.: American Foundrymans Edn. Assn. (bd. dirs.). Republican. Methodist. Office: Ala House of Reps Rm 522-A 11 S Union St Montgomery AL 36130 Office Phone: 334-242-7694.

ROBERTS, BILL GLEN, retired protective services official; b. Deport, Tex., June 2, 1938; s. Samuel Westbrook and Ann Lee (Rhodes) R.; m. Ramona Ryall, June 1, 1963 (dec. Nov. 1988); 1 child, Renee Ann; m. Johana R. Caines, Oct. 14, 2000. Student, So. Meth. U., 1968, North Tex. State U., 1974; grad. paramedic course, U. Tex. Southwestern Med. Sch., 1974; grad. Exec. Program for Fire Service, Tex. A&M U., 1978; AAS, El Centro Jr. Coll., Dallas, 1980; grad. exec. fire officer program, Nat. Fire Acad., 1989. With Dallas Fire Dept., 1958-82, lt., 1964-67, capt., 1967-71, div. fire chief, 1971-79, asst. fire chief, 1979-83; fire chief Austin (Tex.) Fire Dept., 1983-94. Tech. bd. dirs. Found. Fire Safety, Washington, 1982-85; adj. faculty Nat. Fire Acad., 1981-86; aft. State Life of Indpls., Dallas, 1962; owner Personnel Testing Lab., Dallas, 1963; real estate salesman Dale Copus Realtor, Dallas, 1963-66; salesman intercommunications equipment Chandler Sound, Dallas, 1966-67; field engr. IBM Corp., Dallas, 1968; cons. U. Tenn., 1974, Ga. Inst. Tech., 1974, Tex. Dept. Health Resources, 1973-78, Rand Corp., Washington, Mission Rsch., Santa Barbara, Calif., Macro Author: EMS Dallas, 1978; (with others) Anesthesia for Surgery Trauma, 1976, EMS Measures to Improve Care, 1980; contbr. articles to periodicals. Com. chmn. Dallas Jaycees, 1962-65; mem. task force Am. Heart Assn., Austin, 1973-83; bd. dirs. Brackenridge Hosp., 1989, Rehab. Hosp. Austin, 1992-94, Austin Police Pensions Bd., 1989, Capitol Area coun. Boy Scouts Am., 1989-92. Recipient John Stemmons Service award Dallas Fire Dept., 1979; Internat. Assn. Fire Chiefs scholar, 1967. Mem. Internat. Assn. Fire Chiefs, Am. Heart Assn., North Tex. Coun. of Govts. (regional emergency svc. adv. coun. 1973-79), Found. Fire Safety (tech. bd. dirs. 1982-85), Tex. Assn. Realtors, Rotary. Methodist. Home: 192 Hunter's Ridge Rd Canton NC 28716 Office Phone: 828-648-4345. E-mail: bglenrob@aol.com.

ROBERTS, CAROL, paper company executive; married; 2 children. B in Mech. Engring., Yale U., New Haven, 1981. Joined as an assoc. engr. International Paper, Mobile, Ala., 1981, mill mgr. Oswego, NY, 1991—93, gen. mgr. Kraft packaging, 1993—96, gen. mgr. Kraft paper & packaging, 1996—97, v.p. people devel. Memphis, 1997—2000, v.p. indsl. packaging, 2000—05, sr. v.p. indsl. packaging, 2005—11, CFO, 2011—. Office: International Paper 6400 Poplar Ave Memphis TN 38197

ROBERTS, CECIL EDWARD, JR., labor union administrator; b. Oct. 31, 1946; s. Cecil Edward and Evelyn Roberts; m. Carolyn Sue Stewart; children: Kyle Edward, Melissa Dawn. Grad., W.Va. Tech. Coll., 1987; HD (hon.), W.Va. U. Tech., 1997. Gen. inside laborer, shuttle car operator, unitrack operator, greaser, beltman & mechanic Carbon Fuels Mine, Winifred, W.Va., 1971—77; v.p. Dist. 17 United Mine Workers of America (UMWA), 1977—82, v.p. UMWA, 1982—95, pres., 1995—. Mem. Com. Employer Support Vet. Employment, 1985—86; pres. Nat. Coun. Holmes Safety Assn., 1985; mem. W. Va. Employment Opportunities & Econ. Devel. Commn.; mem. exec. coun. AFL-CIO, 2001—, apptd. exec. com., 2005. Gen. v.p. Nat. Coun. Sr. Citizens; mem. adv. bd. W.Va. U. Inst. Labor Studies & Rsch., 1996; mem. adv. com. Black Lung Prog.; bd. dirs. Am. Income Life Ins. Co., Cabin Creek Clinic, W.Va., Blue Cross Blue Shield So. W.Va. Served with US Army, 1966—67, Vietnam. Recipient Martin Luther King award, Rainbow Coalition. Mem.: Vietnam Vets. of America, Am. Legion, VFW (life). Office: UMWA 18354 Quantico Gateway Dr Ste 200 Triangle VA 22172-1779 Office Phone: 703-208-7200.*

ROBERTS, DAVID A., manufacturing executive; b. Dec. 8, 1947; m. Susan Roberts; 2 children. BS, Purdue Univ., 1974; MBA, Indiana Univ., 1978. Mgmt. positions Budd Co., Detroit, 1969—83; v.p., gen. mgr. Pitney Bowes, Stamford, Conn., 1983—93; div. gen. mgr. FMC Corp., Chgo., 1993—95; pres. AM Internat., Mt. Prospect, Ill., 1995—96; group v.p. Marmon Group, Chgo., 1996—2001; pres., CEO Graco Inc., Mpls., 2001—07, chmn., 2006—07; chmn., pres., CEO Carlisle Companies Inc., Charlotte, NC, 2007—. Bd. dir. Franklin Elec. Co., Arctic Cat Inc. Served USMC, 1967—69. Office: Carlisle Companies Inc Ste 400 13925 Ballantyne Corp Pl Charlotte NC 28277

ROBERTS, DAVID E., JR., oil industry executive; BS in Min. Engring., Univ. Alabama, Tuscaloosa, Ala. Engr., oil and gas ops. Texaco No. Am., 1983—96, regional mgr., 1997, dir. strategic mgmt., worldwide ops., 1999—2001; adv. to vice-chmn. Chevron Texaco Corp., 2001—03; exec. v.p., mng. dir. BG Group, 2003—06; sr. v.p. bus. devel. Marathon Oil Corp., Houston, exec. v.p. upstream, 2008—. Office: Marathon Oil Co 5555 San Felipe St Houston TX 77056

ROBERTS, DELMAR LEE, editor; b. Raleigh, NC, Apr. 9, 1933; s. James Delmer and Nellie Brockelbank (Tyson) R. BS in Textile Mgmt., NC State U., 1956; postgrad., Inst. Polit. Studies, U. Paris, 1963; MA in Journalism, U. SC, 1974. Product devel. engr. U.S. Rubber Co. (Uniroyal), Winnsboro, SC, 1959—63; process improvement engr. Allied Chem. Co., Irmo, SC, 1965-67; assoc. editor S.C. History Illustrated Mag., Columbia, 1970; editor-in-chief, editl. v.p. Sandlapper-The Mag. of S.C., Columbia, 1968-74; mng. editor, art dir. Legal Econs. mag. of the ABA, Chgo., 1975-89, Law Practice Mgmt. mag. of the ABA, Chgo., 1990-2000, editor emeritus, 2000—. Editor: The Best of Legal Economics, 1979; freelance editor and/or designer of over 35 books. Active World Affairs Coun. Columbia, 1997-; 1st v.p. English-Speaking Union, 1996, 2013, pres. 1997-2012, bd. dirs. 2003—. With U.S. Army, 1956-58. Hon. fellow Coll. of Law Practice Mgmt., Golden, Colo., 1995—. Mem. Soc. Profl. Journalists, U. SC Horseshoe Soc., U SC Guardian Soc., charter mem. Capital City Club (Columbia), Columbia Drama Club, Phi Kappa Tau, Kappa Tau Alpha. Avocations: travel, turkish carpet/kilim collecting, antiques.

ROBERTS, EDWIN ALBERT, JR., editor, journalist; b. Weehawken, NJ, Nov. 14, 1932; s. Edwin Albert and Agnes Rita (Seuferling) R.; m. Barbara Anne Collins, June 14, 1958; children: Elizabeth Adams, Leslie Carol, Amy Barbara, Jacqueline Harding. Student, Coll. William and Mary, 1952-53, NYU, evenings 1955-58; AA in Coll. & Cmty. Svc., St. Petersburg Jr. Coll., 1994. Reporter N.J. Courier, Toms River, 1953-54, Asbury Park (N.J.) Press, 1954-57; reporter Wall Street Jour., NYC, 1957, editorial writer, 1957-63; news editor Nat. Observer, Silver Spring, Md., 1963-68, columnist, 1968-77; editorial writer, columnist Detroit News, 1977-78, editorial page editor, 1978-83; editor editorial page Tampa Tribune, 1983—2003, ret., 2003. Author: Elections, 1964, 1964, Latin America, 1965, The Smut Rakers, 1966, Russia Today, 1967; Editor anthology: America Outdoors, 1965. Recipient Disting. Reporting Bus. award U. Mo., 1969; Pulitzer prize for distinguished commentary, 1974 Business E-Mail: ededitor@tampabay.rr.com.

ROBERTS, ERNST EDWARD, marketing consultant; b. Wheeling, W.Va., Dec. 19, 1926; s. Charles Emmitt and Virginia Mae (Stephenson) R.; m. Donna Clare Davis, Dec. 27, 1949; children: Ernst Edward II, Carol Lee Roberts Gaydac. BS, U.S. Mil. Acad., 1949; MBA, Xavier U., Cin., 1954; MS in Mech. Engring., U. So. Calif., 1957; grad. with distinction, Air War Coll., 1970. Commd. 2nd lt. U.S. Army, 1949, advanced through grades to brig. gen., 1971, served as officer in combat Korea, 1950-52; prof. mil. sci. Xavier U., 1952-54; mgmt. asst. to asst. comdt. U.S. Army Air Def. Sch., Fort Bliss, Tex., 1957-60; admissions officer U.S. Mil. Acad., West Point, NY, 1961-62, asst. to supt. (pres.), 1962-64, dir. admissions, 1964-65; comdg. officer 3d Missile Bn., 71st Arty., Fed. Republic of Germany, 1965-67; staff officer Gen. Staff U.S. Army, Washington, 1968-70; commdg. officer NATO Air Def. Arty. Group, Germany, 1970-71; commdg. gen. 38th Air Def. Arty. Brigade, Korea, 1971-72; dep. commanding gen. U.S. Army Air Def. Sch. and Ctr., Fort Bliss, 1972-74; ret. U.S. Army, 1974; v.p. bldg. and property mgr. El Paso (Tex.) Nat. Bank and Corp., 1974-79, sr. v.p., dir. pers. and tng., 1979-83, exec. v.p., dir. mktg., 1983-92; mktg. cons., 1992—. Mem. exec. mgmt. com. Tex. Commerce Bank, El Paso, 1983-92; vis. lectr. mktg. Webster U. Mem. bd. advisors SBA; mem. mayor's Citizens Com. on Police Dept. Matters, El Paso; mem. Task Force to Evaluate Mgmt. of Sheriff's Dept.; head bond-issue campaign, El Paso; adv. dir. Armed Svcs. YMCA, past pres.; adv. dir. nat. bd. dirs. Armed Svcs. YMCA, El Paso Cmty. Found.; past pres. U. Tex.-El Paso Eldorados; mem. bd. dirs., trustee Found. Lighthouse for Blind; chmn. adv. bd. dirs. El Paso Bus. Com. for Arts; chmn. capital fund drive com. Rio Grande Girl Scouts Am., Plz. Theatre-Plz. Park Restoration bd.; past mem. campaign cabinet United Way El Paso County; chmn. Capital Fund Drive, Air Def. Arty. Mus., Ft. Bliss; bd. dirs. City of El Paso, mem. steering com. Safe 2000; bd. dirs. Crimestoppers of El Paso. Decorated D.S.M., Legion of Merit, Silver Star, Meritorious Svc. medal; recipient Pro Eclesio Et Pontifice, Vatican, 1971; Conquistator award City of El Paso, Liberty Bell award Legal Cmty. El Paso, 1988. Mem. Am. Inst. Banking, Assn. U.S. Army (Gen. Army Omar N. Bradley chpt.), El Paso C. of C. (mem. armed forces com., chmn. spl. task force to evaluate chamber mgmt.), Mil. Order World Wars (chpt. chmn. citizen of yr. award 1996-2001), U.S. Army Air Def. Arty. Assn. (past pres., named Disting. Korean War Vet. 2004), El Paso Club (past pres., bd. dirs.), Rotary (past pres.). Republican. Roman Catholic. Home: 8212 Antero Pl El Paso TX 79904-2401

ROBERTS, GARY, retired professional hockey player; b. North York, Ont., Canada, May 23, 1966; Left wing Calgary Flames, 1987—97, Carolina Hurricanes, 1997—2000, Toronto Maple Leafs, 2000—05, Fla. Panthers, 2005—07, Pitts. Penguins, 2007—08, Tampa Bay Lightning, 2008—09; ret., 2009; player devel. cons. Dallas Stars, 2010—. Player NHL All-Star Game, 1992, 1993, 2004. Recipient Bill Masterton Trophy, NHL, 1996; named to NHL All-Star team, 1992, 1993, 2004. Achievements include being a member of Stanley Cup Champion Calgary Flames, 1989. Office: Dallas Stars 2601 Avenue of the Stars Frisco TX 75034

ROBERTS, HARRY MORRIS, JR., lawyer; b. Dallas, June 10, 1938; s. Harry Morris and La Frances (Reilly) R.; m. Nancy Beth Johnson, Mar. 7, 1964; children: Richard Whitfield, Elizabeth Lee. BBA, So. Meth. U., 1960; LLB, Harvard U., 1963. Bar: Tex. 1963, U.S. Dist. Ct. (no. dist.) Tex. 1964, U.S. Ct. Appeals (5th cir.) 1972. Assoc. Thompson & Knight, Dallas, 1963-69, ptnr., 1970-75, sr. ptnr., 1975—2008, of counsel, 2009—. Chmn. real estate, probate and trust law sect. State Bar Tex., 1984-85; vis. scholar U. Tex. Law Sch., 1986; adj. prof. Southern Meth. U. Law Sch., 2007-11. Contbr. articles to profl. jours. Trustee Shelter Ministries of Dallas, 1982—, chmn. bd. trustees, 1992-95, 2004-05; trustee Conf. Crimes Against Women, Inc., 2006-, U. Tex. Liberal Arts Adv. Coun., 2010-; bd. trustees Episcopal Found. Dallas, 2012-. Mem. Dallas Bar Assn. (chmn. real estate sect. 1981), Am. Bar Found., Tex. Bar Found., Dallas Bar Found., Am. Coll. Real Estate Lawyers, Salesmanship Club (Dallas), Dallas Country Club. Episcopalian. Office: Thompson & Knight 1722 Routh St Ste 1500 Dallas TX 75201-2533 Home: 6404 Williams Pky Dallas TX 75205 Office Phone: 214-969-1616. Business E-Mail: harry.roberts@tklaw.com.

ROBERTS, JAMES ALLEN, retired urologist, educator; b. Beach, ND, May 31, 1934; s. Earl Fernando and Maria Ellen Roberts; m. Hilda Peachy Roberts, Nov. 29, 1986; children from previous marriage: Jennifer Lou Roberts Walsh, Mary Ellen Roberts Wargo, Thomas Jay. MD, U. Chgo., 1959. Diplomate: Am. Bd. Urology. Intern U. Chgo. Sch. Medicine, 1959-60, resident in urology, 1961-65; from mem. faculty to prof. Tulane U. Med. Sch., New Orleans, 1971-99, prof. urology, 1999—, assoc. chmn., 1986—99; sr. research scientist, head dept. urology Tulane Regional Primate Research Center, Covington, 1972-99; prof. emeritus, 1999—; fellow Fogarty Sr. Internat. NIH, 1984; ret., 2005. Mem. editorial bd. Am. Jour. Kidney Diseases and Urol. Rsch.; contbr. articles to profl. jours. Bd.

dirs. Highland Park Hosp., 1985-87. With USN, 1965—67. Recipient grants NIH, Original Rsch. award Southern Med. Assn., 1990, Cert. Achievement Am. Urological Assn., 1997; Fulbright Sr. scholar, 1999-2000. Fellow ACS; mem. St. Tammany Parish Med. Soc. (pres. 1979), Soc. Rsch. on Calculous Kinetics, La. Urol. Soc., Am. Urol. Assn., Soc. Univ. Urologists, Nat. Kidney Found., Soc. Exptl. Biology and Medicine, Nat. Inst. Health (SAT study sect. 1995-99), Sigma Xi. Office: 83 Towne Place Dr Hendersonville NC 28792 Personal E-mail: jamroberts83@gmail.com.

ROBERTS, JAY, state legislator; House rep., Ga.; mem. Agr. Com., Consumer Affairs Com., Children & Youth Com., State Planning & Cmty. Affairs Com.; mgr. Cotton Gin; state rep. Dist. 131 Ga., 2003—04; state rep. Dist. 154 Ga., 2004—; majority caucus vice chmn. Republican. Mailing: 767 Brushy Creek Rd Ocilla GA 31774 Office: 609 Legislative Office Bldg Atlanta GA 30334 Office Phone: 229-387-0061. Fax: 229-386-5400. E-mail: gacotton@surfsouth.com.

ROBERTS, JOHN N., III, transportation executive; Mgmt. trainee J.B. Hunt Transport Services, Inc., 1989, exec. v.p., pres., dedicated contract services, 1997—2010, pres., CEO, 2011—. Office: J B Hunt Transport Services Inc 615 J B Hunt Corporate Dr Lowell AR 72745-0130 Office Phone: 479-820-0000. Office Fax: 479-659-6297. Business E-Mail: john_roberts@jbhunt.com.

ROBERTS, KAREN L., retail executive, lawyer; b. 1970; BS in Public Adminstration, Harding U.; JD, U. Arkansas. With Wal-Mart Stores, Inc., 1995—, real estate mgr., 1995, various positions within the company, including v.p., gen. counsel for real estate and construction, exec. v.p., general counsel, 2013—; sr. v.p., chief compliance officer Walmart US, exec. v.p., pres., Walmart Realty. Mem.: Internat. Assn. of Attorneys and Executives in Corp. Real Estate, Internat. Council Shopping Centers, ABA, Arkansas Bar Assn. Office: Wal-Mart Stores Inc 702 SW 8th St Bentonville AR 72716-8611*

ROBERTS, KENNETH BARRY, pediatrician; b. Macon, Ga., Feb. 27, 1944; MD, Johns Hopkins U., Baltimore, 1969. Cert. in pediat. Am. Bd. Med. Specialties. Intern in pediat. Johns Hopkins Hosp., 1969—70, resident in pediat., 1970—71, resident, 1973—76; dir. pediat. tchg. programs Moses H. Cone Meml. Hosp., Greensboro, NC; prof. pediat. U. NC, Chapel Hill. Mem.: Fedn. Pediat. Orgns. Office: Moses H Cone Meml Hosp 1200 N Elm St Greensboro NC 27401 Office Phone: 336-832-8064. Office Fax: 336-832-7893. Business E-Mail: kenneth.roberts@mosescone.com.

ROBERTS, KENNETH BOYETT, pharmacy educator, former dean; b. Sharon, Tenn., Nov. 7, 1944; s. James Russell and Blanche (Boyett) Roberts; m. Kittye Louise Rice, Oct. 20, 1968; children: Millicent Boyett, LouAnne Rice. BS in Pharmacy, U. Tenn., Memphis, 1964-67; MBA in Mktg., U. Tenn., Knoxville, 1973; PhD in Health Care Adminstrn., U. Miss., Oxford, 1975. Tchg. asst. U. Miss. Sch. Pharmacy, Oxford, 1973-75, prof., dean, 1989—2000; asst. prof. U. Tex., Austin, 1975-77; exec. dir. Mo. Found. Pharm. Care, St. Louis, 1977-79; prof. pharmacy U. Tenn., Memphis, 1979-89, assoc. dean, 1984-89; exec. dir. Am. Coll. Apothecaries, Memphis, 1981-85; dean U. Ky. Coll. Pharmacy, 2000—09, dean emeritus, 2009—. Cons. Chapman Drug Co., 1985—92, Cardinal Health, 1992—96; pres. West Tenn. Health Edn. Ctr., Memphis, 1987—88. Author: Establishing a Professional Pharmacy Practice, 1980, Managing Support Personnel in Community Pharmacy, 1982, Guidelines for Marketing a Pharmacy Practice, 1983, Guidelines for Pharmacy Management by Self Study, 1984, Guidelines for Establishing Pharmacy Services for Hospice, 1987. Asst. dir. pharmacy US Naval Hosp., Great Lakes, Ill., dir. pharmacy Taipei, Taiwan; mem. Ky. Pharmacy Leadership Coun.; appt. mem. Ky. Innovations Commn., 2000. Recipient Profl. Promotions award, Ky. Pharmacists Assn., 2002, Disting. Svc. award, 2011, Pres.'s award, Ky. Soc. Hosp. Pharmacists, 2003, Outstanding Dean award, Am. Pharmacists Assn. Student Acad., 2009; named a Charles R. Walgreen Meml. fellow, Am. Found. Pharm. Edn., 1974—75. Fellow: Am. Coll. Apothecaries (Dean's Recognition award 1998); mem.: Am. Soc. Health Sys. Pharmacists., Kty. Pharm. Assn., Rsch. & Edn. Found. (bd. dirs.), Profl. Pharma. Fraternity Rsch. & Edn. Found. (bd. dirs.), Tenn. Pharmacists Assn., Am. Assn. Colleges of Pharmacy (bd. dirs. 1997—99), Am. Soc. Hosp. Pharmacists, Am. Pharm. Assn., Internat. Fedn. Pharmacists, Am. Assn. Pharm. Scientists, Phi Lambda Sigma, Phi Kappa Phi, Rho Chi, Kappa Psi (nat. pres. 1987—89, Citation of Appreciation 1989), Pi Kappa Alpha, Sigma Xi, Kappa Psi (dir.). Address: 701 The Grange Ln Lexington KY 40511-9577 Office: University Ky Coll Pharmacy 789 South Limestone St Rm 251 Lexington KY 40536-0596 Office Phone: 859-323-7148. E-mail: krobe2@email.uky.edu.

ROBERTS, LARRY J., construction executive; m. Laura Roberts; children: Phillip, Joel. BBA in Acctg., St. Mary's U. V.p. transp. Redland Stone Products (acquired by Martin Marietta Materials, Inc.); v.p., gen. mgr. San Antonio Dist., S.W. Divsn. Martin Marietta Materials, Inc., v.p., gen. mgr. So. Region, S.W. Divsn., pres. S.W. Divsn. San Antonio, 2006—. Office: Martin Marietta Materials Southwest 5710 Hausman Rd W #121 San Antonio TX 78249-1646

ROBERTS, LEONARD H., board member; b. Chgo., Feb. 19, 1949; s. Jack and Goldie (Solomon) R.; m. Laurie Susan Osser, Aug. 20, 1967; children: Dawn, Adina, Melissa. BS in Chemistry & Mktg., U. Ill., 1971; JD, DePaul U., Chgo., 1974. Food scientist Armour Foods, 1968-71, Cen. Soya, 1971-74; govt. lobbyist Ralston Purina Co., 1974-76, dir., mktg., 1976-78, mng. dir., Raltech Madison, Wis., 1978-81, v.p., food service ops., 1981-85; pres., CEO Arby's Inc., 1985—90; chmn., CEO Shoney's Inc., 1989-93; pres. Tandy Corp., Fort Worth, Tex., 1996—99, RadioShack Corp., Fort Worth, Tex., 1993—99, chmn., CEO, 1999—2005, exec. chmn., 2005—06. Bd. dirs. Ghirardelli Chocolate Co., Tandy Corp. Holder numerous patents on Soya protein research. Active United Way Met. Tarrant County, 1994, Nat. Crime Prevention Coun., 1994, Clark U. Students in Free Enterprise, Girl Scouts U.S., Harris Meth. Bd.; mem. exec. com. Fort Worth Symphony; exec. dir. Nat. Ctr. For Missing and Exploited Children; vice chmn. Tex. Health Resources. Recipient Pvt. Sector Initiative award Office Pres. of U.S., Washington, 1987, Disting. Achievement award B'nai B'rith, Restaurant Bus. Leadership award, 1991, Golden Plate award Nations Restaurant News, 1991, Wall St. Bronze Critics award, 1992. Mem. ABA, Ill. Bar Assn. Home: 3516 Briarhaven Rd Fort Worth TX 76109-3128 Office: Rent-A-Center Inc Bd Directors 5501 Headquarters Dr Plano TX 75024-3556 Office Phone: 972-801-1100. Business E-Mail: leonard.roberts@rentacenter.com.

ROBERTS, MARGARET HAROLD, editor, publisher; b. Aug. 18, 1925; Editor, pub. series Award Winning Art, 1960-70, New Woman mag., Palm Beach, Fla., 1971-84; editor, pub. BONKERS mag., 1992—2001. Author: juvenile book series Daddy is a Doctor, 1965.

ROBERTS, MARILYN GOTTLIEB, artist, educator; b. Rome, Ga., Apr. 18, 1939; d. John Treadwell and Mary Georgina (Crichton) Roberts; m. Norman Lee Gottlieb, May 6, 1964 (div. Sept. 1975); children: Eric Inness, Karla Lewis. AB in Painting and Lit., Goddard Coll., 1975; MFA, U. Miami, 1977. Prof. Miami Dade Coll., Fla., 1980—2006, R.W. Greenfield Endowed chair, 1993—96, 1996—99. Exhibns. include Carpenter Ctr. Arts Harvard U., Mass., Currier Gallery Art, NH, Clocktower, NYC, Exit Art, NYC, Fleming Mus. U. Vt., New Gallery U. Miami, Birmingham Mus. Art, Ala., Columbus Mus. Art, Ga., Mus. Contemporary Art, Fla., others. Trustee Miami Beach Devel. Corp., 1992—. Fulbright scholar U. Jos, Nigeria, 2000-02. Business E-Mail: m427@bellsouth.net.

ROBERTS, NORM, men's college basketball coach; b. Queens, NY, July 21, 1965; m. Pascale Roberts; children: Nicholas, Justin. BS in Health and Phys. Edn., CUNY: Queens Coll., Flushing, 1987. Freshman team head basketball coach, varsity team asst. Archbishop Molloy HS, Queens, 1987—90; head basketball coach Queens Coll. Knights, 1991—95; team asst., men's basketball Oral Roberts U. Golden Eagles, 1995—97, U. Tulsa Golden Hurricane, 1997—2000; asst. coach U. Ill. Fighting Illini, 2000—02, assoc. head coach, 2002—03, U. Kans. Jayhawks, 2003—04; head basketball coach St. John's U. Red Storm, Queens, 2004—10; asst. coach U. Fla. Gators, 2011—. Active Coaches vs. Cancer. Mem.: Black Coaches Assn., Nat. Assn. Basketball Coaches. Office: University Fla Basketball Program c/o Univ Athletic Assn PO Box 14485 Gainesville FL 32604 Office Phone: 352-375-4683 ext. 4200.

ROBERTS, PAUL CRAIG, III, economics professor, writer, columnist; b. Atlanta, Apr. 3, 1939; s. Paul Craig and Ellen Lamar (Dryman) R.; m. Becky B. Bickerstaff, 1959 (div. 1968); m. Linda Jane Fisher, July 3, 1969 (div. 1994); children: Becky Ellen, Stephanie Bradford, Pendaran Struan Sherman. BS, Ga. Inst. Tech., 1961; postgrad., U. Calif., Berkeley, 1962—63, Merton Coll., Oxford U., Eng., 1964—65; PhD, U. Va., 1967. Asst. prof. econs. Va. Poly. Inst., 1965-69; assoc. prof. U. N.Mex., 1969-71; rsch. fellow Hoover Instn., Stanford U., 1971-77, sr. rsch. fellow, 1978—2004; mem. U.S. Congl. Staff, 1975-78; asst. sec. of treasury for econ. policy Dept. Treasury, Washington, 1981-82; William E. Simon prof. polit. economy Georgetown U. Ctr. for Strategic and Internat. Studies, Washington, 1982-93; chmn. Inst. for Polit. Economy, 1985—, John M. Olin fellow, 1994—2004; rsch. fellow Ind. Inst., 1990—. Disting. adj. scholar Ctr. Strategic and Internat. Studies, Washington, 1993-96; adj. scholar Cato Inst., 1987-93, disting. fellow, 1993-96; assoc. editor, columnist Wall St. Jour., N.Y.C., 1978-80; columnist Bus. Week, 1983-98, Fin. Post, Can., 1988-89, Liberation, Paris, 1988-89, Erfolg, Fed. Rep. of Germany, 1988, Washington Times, 1988—2002, San Diego Union, 1988-92, Le Figaro, Paris, 1992-96, Investors Bus. Daily, 1998-2005; nationally syndicated columnist Scripps Howard News Svc., 1989-97, Creators Syndicate, 1997—2010; contbr. editor: Nat. Rev., 1993-2003, Reason Mag., 1993-95, World Trade mag., 1997-98, Trends Jour., 2011-; mem. Pres.-elect Reagan's Task Force on Tax Policy, 1980; dir. Value Line Investment Funds, N.Y.C., A. Schulman, Akron, Ohio; cons. Morgan Guaranty Trust Co., Lazard Freres Asset Mgmt., 1983-97; pres. Econ. & Communication Svcs. Inc.; cons. Dept. Commerce, 1983, Dept. Def., 1983-84; mem. adv. bd. Marvin and Palmer, 1986-96, Am. studies program Harding U.; mem. ad. com. Ctr. for the Am. Founding; mem. Wright Investors' Svc. Internat. Bd. Econ. and Invesmtent Advisors; bd. dirs. Com. on Present Danger; trustee Intercollegiate Studies Inst., Com. on Developing Am. Capitalism; mem. selection com. Frank E. Seidman disting. award in Polit. Economy; pres. Inlet Beach Water Co., 2000-06. Author: Alienation and the Soviet Economy, 1971, new edit., 1990, Marx's Theory of Exchange, 1973, new edit., 1983, The Supply-Side Revolution: An Insider's Account of Policymaking in Washington, 1984, Chinese edit., 2012, The Cost of Corporate Capital in the U.S. and Japan, 1985, Meltdown: Inside the Soviet Economy, 1990, The New Color Line: How Quotas and Privilege Destroy Democracy, 1995; The Capitalist Revolution in Latin America, Oxford U. Press, 1997, The Tyranny of Good Intentions, 2000, new edit., 2008, Chile: Dos Visiones-la Era Allende-Pinochet, 2000, How The Economy Was Lost, 2010, Wirtschaft Am Abgrund, 2012, The Failure of Laissez Faire Capitalism, 2013, Chinese edit., 2014, Amerikas Kriege, 2013, How America Was Lost, 2014; mem. editl. bd. Modern Age, Intercollegiate Rev.; contbg. editor Harper's Mag. Drafted original Kemp-Roth Bill, 1976. Recipient Meritorious Svc. award Dept. Treasury, 1982, Pub. Svc. award GSA, 1991, Warren Brookes award for Excellence in Journalism, 1992; Am. Philos. Soc. grantee, 1968; named to Chevalier de la Légion d'Honneur, 1987, Gridiron Secret Soc., U. Ga.; Earhart fellow U. Va., 1966-67, Nat. Chamber Found. fellow, 1984-85. Mem. Beethoven Soc., Am. Soc. French Legion of Honor, U.S. C. of C. (taxation com.), Polanyi Soc., Sierra Club, Fla. Wildlife Fedn., Am. Civil Liberties Union, Union Concerned Scientists, Audubon Soc., Wilderness Soc., Environ. Def. Fund. Home and Office: 169 Pompano St Panama City FL 32413-7245

ROBERTS, PAUL FRANKLIN, II, financial executive; b. Laredo, Tex., Apr. 16, 1949; s. Paul Franklin and Bernice Clevenger (Alworth) R.; m. Martha Diane Dow, Dec. 19, 1970; children: Averi Alison, Briana Alane, Paul Franklin III. BS in Math. cum laude, S.W. Tex. State U., 1970; M of Pub. Fin. Mgmt., The Am. U., 1983; postgrad., George Mason U., 1989-95. Team leader U.S. Army Communications Command, Fort Huachuca, Ariz., 1975-77; dep. comptroller U.S. Army Combined Arms Ctr., Fort Leavenworth, Kans., 1977-79; tech. dir. Comptroller of Army, Pentagon, Washington, 1981-82, dir. mgmt.engring., 1982-84; supr. program analyst U.S. Army Material Command, Alexandria, 1982-84, chief productivity mgmt. div., 1985-89; dir. resource mgmt. U.S. Army Devel. & Employment Agy., Fort Lewis, Wash., 1984-85; chief productivity improvement div. Asst. Sec. of Def., Pentagon, Washington, 1989-90; dir. investment Asst. Sec. of Army, Pentagon, Washington, 1990-95, dir. bus. resources, 1995-98; CFO, chief adminstrv. officer NOAA, Dept. Commerce, Washington, 1998—2000, Nat. Tech. Info. Svc., Dept. Commerce, Washington, 2000—. Mem. sr. exec. svc. Fed. Civil Svc., 1990—. Author: (study) Functional Army Manpower Evaluation, 1981. Dist. scout commr. Cochise dist. Boy Scouts Am., 1975—77, asst. scoutmaster George Washington dist., 1998—2000, asst. dist. commr. Tomahawk dist., cubmaster George Washington Dist., 1995—98; bd. dirs. Marriage Encounter/United Meth. Ch., 1986—88, jurisdictional exec. couple, 1986—88, state exec. couple Va., Md., and DC, 1981—84. Recipient Eagle Scout award, 1962. Mem.: Ctr. for Study of Presidency, Am. Assn. Program and Budget Analysts, Am. Soc. for Pub. Adminstrn., Sr. Exec. Assn., Delta Tau Delta. Methodist. Avocations: golf, basketball, baseball card collecting. Office: 5285 Port Royal Rd Springfield VA 22161-0001 Home: 6948 Vernon Hall Williamsburg VA 23188-7298 E-mail: proberts@ntis.gov.

ROBERTS, RICHARD CHARLTON, III, lawyer; b. Jackson, Miss., Mar. 18, 1951; BA, U. Miss., 1973, JD with distinction, 1976. Bar: Miss. 1976, U.S. Dist. Ct. (no. and so. dists.) Miss. 1976, U.S. Ct. Appeals (5th cir.) 1976, U.S. Ct. Appeals (11th cir.) 1981, U.S. Supreme Ct. 1989. Pvt. practice, Jackson, Miss. Assoc. editor Miss. Law Jour., 1976. Named Best Lawyers in America, Middle South Super Lawyers, 2006—; named one of Outstanding Lawyers Am. Fellow: Nat. Conf. Bar Pres., Miss. Bar Found.; mem.: ABA (sect. on family law, gen. practice, solo and small firm practice), Nat. Lawyer's Assn., Bar Assn. 5th Fed. Cir., Miss. Bar (chmn. solo and small firm practitioner's task force 1993—94, exec. com. family law sect. 1994—95, chmn. 1996, bd. bar commrs. 1996—99, nominating com. 1998—99, bench-bar liaison standing com. 2001—10, bd. bar commrs. 2002—05, pres. 2003—04), Hinds County Bar Assn. (bd. dirs. 1990—96, sec.-treas. 1992—93, pres. 1994—95, chmn. long range planning com. 1995—97), Fed. Bar Assn. (pres. Miss. chpt. 1987—88, nat. coun. 1988, jud. liaison for U.S. Dist. Cts.-So. Dist. Miss. 1989), Am. Inns of Ct., Phi Kappa Phi. Office: PO Box 55882 Jackson MS 39296-5882 Office Phone: 601-607-4144.

ROBERTS, RUSTY (RUSSELL LEON ROBERTS), transportation executive, former legislative staff member; b. 1953; Attended, Western Carolina U., Cullowhee, NC, 1972, St. Petersburg Jr. Coll., Fla., 1973—75, U. South Fla., Tampa, 1976—77. Adminstrv. asst. Fla. House of Reps., Tallahassee, 1976—79; dist. rep. to Senator Paula Hawkins US Senate, Washington, 1981—86; fed. liaison Metro-Dade County, Fla., 1987—88; public affairs dir. Capital Bank, Miami, Fla., 1988—89; adminstrv. asst. to Rep. Ileana Ros-Lehtinen US House of Representatives, 1989—93, chief of staff to Rep. John L. Mica, 1993—2011; mng. dir. transp. practice BGR Govt. Affairs, Washington, 2011—13; v.p. govt. & corporate rels. Fla. East Coast Industries, Inc. (FECI), Orlando, 2013—. Republican. Office: Florida East Coast Industries Inc (FECI) 2855 Le Jeune Rd 4th Fl Miami FL 33134 Office Phone: 305-520-2300.

ROBERTS, SAMUEL SMITH, television news executive; b. Port Chester, NY, Feb. 8, 1936; s. Robert M. and Lillian (Smith) R.; m. Harriet Rubin, 1975; children: Rachel, David; children by previous marriage: Nancy, Pamela. BS, Northwestern U., 1957. With UPI, NYC, 1961, Capital Cities Broadcasting, Providence, 1962, CBS News, 1962-95; sr. prodr. CBS Evening News, NYC, 1978-81, nat. editor, 1982-84, fgn. editor, 1984-87; exec. prodr. CBS News Prodns., 1992-95; pres. Roberts Media Internat., NYC, 1995-96; v.p., gen. mgr. TV programming Electronic Media Co., N.Y. Times, 1996-99; Frances L. Wolfson chair U. Miami, Coral Gables, Fla., 1999—2008. Served to lt. USN, 1957-61.

ROBERTS, SEAN, state legislator; Mem. Dist. 36 Okla. House of Representatives, 2011—. Office: 2300 N Lincoln Blvd Room 322 Oklahoma City OK 73105 Office Phone: 405-557-7322. Business E-Mail: sean.roberts@okhouse.gov.

ROBERTS, THOMAS GEORGE, retired physicist; b. Ft. Smith, Ark., Apr. 27, 1929; s. Thomas Lawrence and Emma Lee (Stanley) R.; m. Alice Anne Harbin, Nov. 14, 1958 (dec. 1994); children: Lawrence Dewey, Regina Anne; foster child, Marcia Roberts Dale Harmon; m. Betty Howard McElyea, July 28, 1995. AA, Armstrong Coll., 1953; BS, U. Ga., 1956, MS, 1957; PhD, NC State U., 1967. Rsch. physicist U.S. Army Missile Command, Huntsville, Ala., 1958-85; cons. industry and govt. agys., 1970—, SAIC, Huntsville, Ala., 1997-2001; owner Technoco, Huntsville, 1985-96. Contbr. articles to profl. jours.; patentee in field. Sgt. USAF, 1948-52. Fellow Am. Optical Soc.; mem. Am. Phys. Soc., IEEE, Huntsville Optical Soc. Am. (pres. 1980, 92), Toastmaster Internat. (pres. 1963), Phi Beta Kappa, Phi Kappa Phi (Wheatly Physics award). Episcopalian. Achivements include research in laser physics, optics, particle beams and instrumentation; diagnostic devices and techniques development; 70 patents. Personal E-mail: robertsbetty@bellsouth.net.

ROBERTS, WILLIAM A., relief organization administrator; b. Feb. 26, 1946; m. Nancy Overly, 1968; children: William, Rebecca, Barbara, Bramwell. BSBA, Wayne State U., Detroit; MA in Religious Studies, U. Detroit; attended, U. Minn., Nazarene Theol. Sem., North Pk. Sem., Internat. Coll. Officers, London, 1982. Commd. officer The Salvation Army, 1971, corps appointment, USA ctrl. territory, 1971—76, fin. sec., divisional sec. & gen. sec., USA ctrl. territory, 1976—93, divisional comdr., USA ctrl. territory, 1993—2001, territorial comdr., South America east, 2001—05, internat. sec. bus. adminstrn., internat. hdqs., 2005—08, territorial comdr., Kenya west territory, 2008—10, nat. comdr., USA nat. hdqs., 2010—. Mem. tchg. staff officer continuing edn. program and Asbury theol. sem. preaching seminar The Salvation Army USA Ctrl. Territory. Office: Salvation Army USA Nat Hdqs 615 Slaters Ln PO Box 269 Alexandria VA 22313

ROBERTS, WILLIAM B., lawyer; b. Detroit, Aug. 23, 1939; s. Edwin Stuart and Marjorie Jean (Wardle) R.; m. Cathleen Anne Thompson, Sept. 1, 1962; children: Bradford William, Brent William, Katrina Marjorie. BA, Mich. State U., East Lansing, 1961; JD with distinction, U. Mich., Ann Arbor, 1963; China law diploma, U. East Asia, Macau, 1989. Bar: Mo. 1964, Fla. 1983, US Dist. Ct. (ea. dist.) Mo. 1964, US Dist. Ct. (mid. dist.) Fla. 1993. Mem. firm Thompson & Mitchell, St. Louis, 1963-67; atty. Monsanto Co., 1967-70; sr. exec. v.p. adminstrn., sec., gen. counsel Chromalloy Am. Corp. (successor Segua Corp. NY), St. Louis, 1970—78, exec. v.p.-adminstrn., gen. counsel, sec. Clayton, Mo., 1978—82; pvt. practice, 1983-87, St. Louis and Naples, 1989-90, Naples, 1994—, Kansas City, Mo., 1999—; mng. ptnr., corp. bus. counselor and broker Fairborne Group, Ltd., 1986—89; mng. ptnr. Roberts and Nordahl, St. Louis and Naples, Fla., 1988-89, Darrow & Roberts, P.A., Naples, 1992-93. Pres., mng. dir. The Fairborne Group, Ltd., St. Louis and Naples, 1988-91, Kansas City, 1999-2007, William B. Roberts & Assocs. Co., Merger and Acquisitions Specialists, 1982—; mem. exam. com. of policyowners Northwestern Mut. Life Ins. Co., Milw., 1978; del. to US-China Joint Session on Trade Investment and Econ. Law, Beijing, 1987; sports rep. Steve Carlton, St. Louis Cardinals, Phila. Phillies baseball clubs, 1987-89; pres., BBB Arbitration, 2004-; internat. bus. and legal adviser, 1982-. Named Halls of Excellence, Bellevue HS, 2013. Mem. ABA, Fed. Bar Assn. (Mid. Dist. Fla.), Mo. Bar Assn., St. Louis Bar Assn. (chmn. antitrust sect. 1973, spl. assignments law & counsel corp. and internat.), Fla. Bar Assn., Collier County Bar Assn., Delta Theta Phi. Methodist.

ROBERTSON, DARYL BRUCE, lawyer; b. Ft. Wayne, Ind., Mar. 16, 1954; s. Harold Clifford and Jean Marilyn (Fackler) R.; m. Darleen Marie Munsch, Dec. 12, 1981; children: Brennan Hogan, Daryl Bruce II, Cameron Maureen. AB summa cum laude, Duke U., 1976; JD cum laude, Harvard U., 1979. Bar: Tex. 1979. Assoc. Jenkens & Gilchrist, Dallas, 1979-81, Rentzel, Wise & Robertson, Dallas, 1981-85, Stinson, Mag & Fizzell, Dallas, 1985—89; ptnr. Bracewell & Patterson, L.L.P., Dallas, 1989—97; shareholder Jenkens & Gilchrist, Dallas, 1997—2007; ptnr. Hunton & Willions LLP, Dallas, 2007—. Mem. ABA, Tex. Bar Assn., Dallas Bar Assn., Tex. Bus. Law Found., Tex. Bar Found., Dallas Bar Found., Phi Beta Kappa, Phi Eta Sigma, Phi Lambda Upsilon. Office: Hunton & Williams LLP 1445 Ross Ave Ste 3700 Dallas TX 75202 Office Phone: 214-468-3371. Office Fax: 214-880-0011. Business E-Mail: drobertson@hunton.com.

ROBERTSON, DAVID, physician, pharmacologist, educator; b. Sylvia, Tenn., May 23, 1947; s. David Herlie and Lucille Luther (Bowen) R.; m. Rose Marie Stevens, Oct. 30, 1976; 1 child, Rose. BA, Vanderbilt U., 1969, MD, 1973. Diplomate Am. Bd. Internal. Medicine, Am. Bd. Clin. Pharmacology. Intern Johns Hopkins U., Balt., 1973-74, asst. resident, 1974-75, asst. chief svc. in medicine, 1977-78; fellow in clin. pharmacology Vanderbilt U., Nashville, 1975-77, asst. prof. medicine and pharmacology, 1978-82, assoc. prof., 1982-86, prof., 1986—, prof. neurology, 1991—, Elton Yates prof. autonomic disorders, 1998—, dir. clin. rsch. ctr., 1987—; dir. Ctr. Space Physiology and Medicine, 1989—, Med. Sci. Tng. Program, 1993—2003; mem. staff Vanderbilt Hosp., Burroughs Wellcome scholar in clin. pharmacology, 1985-91; prin. investigator Autonomic Rare Diseases Clin. Rsch. Consortium, 2009—. Author: (with B.M. Greene and G.J. Taylor) Problems in Internal Medicine, 1980, (with C.R. Smith) Manual of Clinical Pharmacology, 1981, (with Italo Biaggioni) Disorders of the Autonomic Nervous System, 1995, (with Italo Biaggioni, Geoffrey Burnstock, Phillip A. Low and Julian F.R. Paton) Primer on the Autonomic Nervous System, 1996, 3rd edit., 2011, Robertson's Autonomic Neuroscience, Japanese, 2007, (with Gordon H. Williams) Clinical and Translational Science: Principles of Human Research, 2009; editor: APOR Newsletter, 2004-08, Spotlight on Rare Diseases, 2010-; editor-in-chief: Drug Therapy, 1991-94; assoc. editor, Jour. Pharmacol. Exptl. Therapy, 1998—; assoc. editor: Jour. Chinese Med. Assn., 1995-; mem. editl. bd. Am. Jour. Medicine, Autonomic Neuroscience, Clin. Pharm. and Therapeutics, Clin. Autonomic Rsch., Am. Jour. Med. Sci., Current Topics in Pharmacology, Rambam-Maimonides Med. Jour., 2009-. Logan Clendening fellow, Reykjavik, Iceland, 1969; Adolph-Morsbach grantee Bonn, Germany, 1968; recipient Rsch. Career Devel. award NIH, 1981, Grant W. Liddle award for leadership in rsch., 1991, 1995-99 NASA Neurolab prin. investigator, Tchg. award Nat. Program Dir.'s Assn., 2003, Rschr. of Yr. award Nat. Dysautomia Rsch. Found., 2001, PhRMA award for Excellence in Pharmacology, Earl Sutherland prize, 2007. Fellow Am. Heart Assn. Coun. Hypertension and Circulation, ACP (tchg. and rsch. scholar 1978-81), Am. Autonomic Soc. (founding pres. 1992-94); mem. Am. Acad. Neurology, Soc. Neurosci., Am. Inst. Aeronautics and Astronautics, U.S. Pharmacopeial Conv., Nat. Bd. Med. Examiners, Aerospace Med. Assn. (space sta. sci. and applications com.), NASA (microgravity human rsch. com.), FDA Com. on Rare Disorders, Am. Fedn. Med. Rsch., Am. Soc. Clin. Investigation, Assn. Am. Physicians, Assn. Patient-Oriented Rsch. (bd. dirs., founding pres. 1998-99), So. Soc. Clin. Investigation, Am. Soc. Clin. Pharmacology and Therapeutics, Automatic Disorders Clin. Rsch. Consortium (prin. investigator, 2009-), Phi Beta Kappa, Alpha Omega Alpha (hon., bd. dirs. 1995-2004. William Darby award 2000). Baptist. Home: 4003 Newman Pl Nashville TN 37204-4308 Office: Vanderbilt U Clin Rsch Ctr 21st Ave S Nashville TN 37232-2195 Business E-Mail: david.robertson@vanderbilt.edu.

ROBERTSON, GLEN, mayor, Lubbock, Texas; b. Lubbock, Tex. m. Karen Robertson; children: Jason, Jeremy, Jared 1 stepchild, Kirby Phillips. Attended, Tex. Tech U., Lubbock, 1976—78. Owner, operator Burger House, Lubbock, 1978—86; pres. Robertson Bonded Warehouse, Inc., Lubbock, 1987—; sole proprietor Robertson Investments, Lubbock, 1988—; owner Hillcrest Golf & Country Club, Lubbock, 2003—; mayor City of Lubbock, 2012—. Alderman Ransom Canyon City Coun., 2002—03, mayor pro-tem, 2004—05; trustee Cooper I.S.D., 1994—96, Southland I.S.D., 1998—2000; bd. mem. Garza County Tax Appraisal Bd., 1999—2000, City of Lubbock Zoning Bd. Adjustments, 2005—10, City of Lubbock Utility Bd., 2010—. Office: City of Lubbock Office of the Mayor PO Box 2000 Lubbock TX 79457 Office Phone: 806-775-3000. Business E-Mail: grobertson@mylubbock.us.*

ROBERTSON, GREGORY B., lawyer; b. Sandusky, Ohio, Apr. 2, 1951; BA, Washington & Lee Univ., 1973; JD, Univ. Richmond, 1976. Bar: Va. 1976. Ptnr., co-chmn. labor, employment practice group Hunton & Williams LLP, Richmond, Va. Mem.: ABA, Va. Bar Assn., Energy and Mineral Law Found. (past pres.), Va. CofC (bd. dir., counsel), Phi Delta Phi, Pi Sigma Alpha. Office: Hunton & Williams LLP Riverfront Plz East Tower 951 E Byrd St Richmond VA 23219-4074 Office Phone: 804-788-8526. Office Fax: 804-788-8218. Business E-Mail: grobertson@hunton.com.

ROBERTSON, HORACE BASCOMB, JR., retired law educator; b. Charlotte, NC, Nov. 13, 1923; s. Horace Bascomb and Ruth (Montgomery) R.; m. Patricia Lavell, Aug. 11, 1947; children— Mark L., James D. BS, U.S. Naval Acad., 1945; JD, Georgetown U., 1953; MS, George Washington U., 1968. Commd. ensign U.S. Navy, 1945, advanced through grades to rear adm., 1972; line officer, 1945-55; law specialist, 1955-68; spl. counsel to sec. Navy, Washington, 1964-67, judge adv., 1968-76; spl. counsel to chief naval ops. Washington, 1970-72; dep. judge adv. gen. Navy Dept., Washington, 1972-75, judge adv. gen., 1975-76; prof. law Duke U., 1976-89, sr. assoc. dean, 1986-89, ret., 1990; Chas H. Stockton chair of internat. law Naval War Coll., Newport, R.I., 1991-92. Decorated D.S.M. Mem. ABA, Am. Soc. Internat. Law. Office: Duke U Sch Law Durham NC 27708 Home: 2701 Pickett Rd Apt 4049 Durham NC 27705-5653 Business E-Mail: hbr@law.duke.edu.

ROBERTSON, JACK CLARK, accounting educator; b. Marlin, Tex., Apr. 27, 1943; s. Rupert Cook and Lois Lucille (Rose) R.; m. Caroline Susan Hughes, Oct. 23, 1965; children: Sara Ellen, Elizabeth Hughes. Student, Rice U., 1961-63; BBA with honors, U. Tex., Austin, 1965, M in Profl. Acctg., 1967; PhD, U. N.C., 1970. CPA, Tex. Tax acct. Humble Oil and Refining Co., Houston, 1964-65; auditor Peat, Marwick, Mitchell & Co., Houston, 1965-66; acct. Wade, Barton, Marsh CPAs, Austin, Tex., 1966-67; from asst. prof. to prof. emeritus U. Tex., Austin, 1970—2003, C.T. Zlatkovich Centennial prof. emeritus, 2003—. Acad. assoc. Coopers & Lybrand, N.Y.C., 1975-76; acad. fellow U.S. Securities and Exchange Commn. Office of the Chief Acct., Washington, 1982-83; Erskine fellow U. Canterbury, Christchurch, New Zealand, 1988; tng. the trainers instr. Vilnius, Lithuania, 1993; lectr. in field. Contbr. articles to profl. jours. Lay reader St. Matthews Episcopal Ch., Austin, 1972-75, mem. vestry, 1973-75, 77-79, 84-86, treas., 1974-75, 77-96, chmn. bldg. fund, 1976-87, chmn. everymen. canvass, 1980, sr. warden, 1986; del. Diocese of Tex. Coun., 1993-95, Usher Guild, 2006-; Trompetista El Grupo Chinampa, 2000—, lector laico, 2000-03, Miembro comite del obispo Iglesia San Francisco de Asis, 2000-03, treas., 2002-03; dir., treas. Austin Chamber Music Ctr., 2003-07; mem. New Horizons Band & Austine Wonder Brass, 2006-; ofcl. U.S.A Track and Field, 1996—2010; bd. dirs. Episcopal Province VII Ctr. for Hispanic Ministries, 2006—2010; mem. Austin Fine Woodworkers Assn., 2003-; adminstr. Jovences Episcopales Coll. Scholarship Fund, 2001-. Mem. AICPA, Am. Acctg. Assn. (sec.-treas. auditing sect. 1976-77, v.p. auditing sect. 1977-78, pres. auditing sect. 1978-79, chmn. auditing stds. com. 1980-81, chmn. SEC liaison com. 1983-84, historian auditing sect. 1999-2001), Tex. Soc. CPAs (vice-chmn., profl. ethics com. 1986-94, 95-97, Presdl. citation 1994), Assn. Cert. Fraud Examiners (regent emeritus, cert.), Kosse Heritage Soc. (Tex.) (dir. devel. 2008-), Phi Kappa Phi, Beta Gamma Sigma, Beta Alpha Psi, VITA (vol. 2010-).

ROBERTSON, MARK WAYNE, investment specialist; b. St. Louis, June 28, 1929; s. Harold LaGrand and Mabel Margaret (Mangels) R.; 1 child, A. Rafael Nuncio. Student, U. Houston, 1949-51. Cost acct. Mo. Pacific Railroad, Houston, 1951-55; contract adminstr. Air Cruisers Co., Belmar, N.J., 1955-57; right of way cons. Tex. Hwy. Dept., Houston, 1957; land mgr. Houston Natural Gas Co., 1957-71; adminstrv. asst. Houston Pile Line Co., 1971-84; real estate broker, investor, 1975—; pvt. practice as investor Kerrville, Tex., 1984—. Co-owner several small businesses and distributorships. Profl. artist. Fundraiser John Tower for Senator, Houston, Am. Heart Assn., Houston, 1971-81; officer Mended Hearts Assn., Houston, 1971-81; 2d v.p. Hill County Art Foun., Kerrville, 1989-92, treas., 1990-91, adv. bd. 1996—; sr. mem. Soc. Ambs. St. Joseph Hosp., 1989—; adv. Butt Holdworth Libr., 1991, 96; cultural adviser to mayor, 1991-97; mem. adv. bd. Kerr Arts and Cultural Ctr., 2001. Cpl. U.S. Army, 1951-53. Mem. Internat. Right of Way Assn. (officer 1958-83), Kerrville Art Club (pres. 1990), Art League of Houston, Nat. Soc. Painters in Casein and Acrylic, Allied Artists in Am., River Art Group. Roman Catholic. Avocation: owner of a small ranch resort. E-mail: marcos@ktc.com.

ROBERTSON, NAT, Mayor, Fayetteville, North Carolina; m. Kim Robertson; children: Cameron, Carlin. Student, Fayetteville State U.; BA in pub. adminstrn., Elon U., NC. Ptnr. Robertson Jewelers; owner GNC stores, Fayetteville and Spring Lake, NC; physician rep. LabCorp; mem. Fayetteville City Coun.; mayor City of Fayetteville, 2013—. Mem. Highland Presbyn. Ch. Office: Office of the Mayor 433 Hay St Fayetteville NC 28301 Office Phone: 910-433-1992. Office Fax: 910-433-1948. E-mail: mayor@ci.fay.nc.us.

ROBERTSON, PAT (MARION GORDON ROBERTSON), religious broadcasting executive, university president and chancellor; b. Lexington, Va., Mar. 22, 1930; s. A. Willis and Gladys (Churchill) R.; m. Adelia Elmer; children: Timothy, Elizabeth, Gordon, Ann. BA, Washington and Lee U., 1950; JD, Yale U., New Haven, 1955; MDiv, NY Theol. Sem., 1959; ThD (hon.), Oral Roberts U., Tulsa, Okla., 1983. Ordained minister So. Bapt. Conv., 1961-87. Founder, CEO, chmn. Christian Broadcasting Network, Virginia Beach, Va., 1960—; host 700 Club, 1968—; founder, chancellor, pres. Regent U. (formerly CBN U.), 1977—; founder, chmn. Operation Blessing Internat. Relief and Devel. Inc., 1978—; founder, pres. The Christian Coalition, 1989—; founder, pres., chmn. The Am. Ctr. for Law and Justice, 1990—; founder, chmn. Internat. Family Entertainment, Inc., 1990-97, Asia Pacific Media Corp., 1993—; chmn. Starguide Digital Networks, Inc., 1995—, Porchlight Entertainment, Inc., 1995—. Bd. dirs. United Va. Bank, Norfolk; mem. Pres. Task Force on Victims of Crime, Washington, 1982. Author: (with Jamie Buckingham) Shout It From the Housetops: The Story of the Founder of the Christian Broadcasting Network, 1972, My Prayer for You, 1977, The Secret Kingdom, 1982, Answers to 200 of Life's Most Probing Questions, 1984, (with William Proctor) Beyond Reason: How Miracles Can Change Your Life, 1984, America's Dates with Destiny, 1986, The Plan, 1989, The New Millennium: 10 Trends that Will Impact Your Family by the Year 2000, 1990, The New World Order, 1991, The Turning Tide: The Fall of Liberalism and the Rise of Common Sense, 1993, The End of the Age, 1995, Six Steps to Spiritual Revival: God's Awesome Power in Your Life, 2002, Bring It On: Tough Questions. Candid Answers, 2002, The Ten Offenses: Reclaim the Blessings of God's Eternal Truth, 2003, Courting Disaster: How the Supreme Court Is Usurping the Power of Congress and the People, 2004, Miracles Can Be Yours Today, 2005 Candidate for Rep. nomination for Pres. U.S., 1988. Served in USMC, 1950—52. Recipient Disting. Merit citation NCCJ, Knesset medallion Israel Pilgrimage Com., Faith and Freedom award Religious Heritage Am., Bronze Halo award So. Calif. Motion Picture Council, Humanitarian award Food for the Hungry, 1982, George Washington Honor medal Freedoms Found. at Valley Forge, 1983, Defender of Israel award Christians Israel Pub. Action Campaign, 1994, John Connor Humanitarian Svc. award Operation Smile Internat., 1994, Cross of Nails award, 2000, The State of Israel Friendship award, Zionist Org. of Am., 2002; named Internat. Clergyman of Yr. Religion in Media, 1981, Man of Yr. Internat. Com. for Goodwill, 1981. Mem. Nat. Religous Broadcasters (bd. dirs. 1973—2006), Kentucky Colonels. Office: The Christian Broadcasting Network 977 Centerville Tpke Virginia Beach VA 23463-7701 also: Regent U 1000 Regent U Dr Virginia Beach VA 23464

ROBERTSON, PAULINE DURRETT, publishing executive, writer, poet; b. Amarillo, Tex., Apr. 17, 1922; d. Walter Lucius and Mary Eddie (Jones) Durrett; m. Roy Lewis Robertson, Dec. 18, 1940; children: Kay Linda Robertson Savage, Kent Lewis, Robyn M. Robertson Turner, Paula Jo Robertson Pierce, Roy Durrett, Laurel Annette Robertson Gibson, Virginia Lee Robertson-Baker, Ellen Teresa Robertson Green, Neil Thomas, Carrie Beth Robertson Meyer. AA, Amarillo Coll., 1969; BA in English Writing, St. Edward's U., Austin, Tex., 1992. Editor project history U.S. Reclamation Bur., Amarillo, 1942-43; editor post newspaper U.S. Army Air Force, Amarillo, 1943-44; freelance writer, 1944-73; writer books of history Staked Plains Press, Canyon, Tex., 1973-77; writer books of history and poetry Paramount Pub. Co., Amarillo, 1977—, pub. house pres., editor, 1977—; tchr. poetry writing and history Amarillo Coll., 1971—2002. Tchr. poetry writing Elderhostel, U. Tex., Austin, 1988-89; writer book revs. Amarillo Globe News, 1968-2005; editor books, articles, newspapers, 1985-; spkr. in field. Author: (with R.L. Robertson) Panhandle Pilgrimage: Illustrated Tales Tracing History in the Texas Panhandle, 1976, 77, 81, 85, 90, Tascosa: Historic Site in the Texas Panhandle, 1978, 2d edit., 1995, Mystery Woman of Old Tascosa: The Legend of Frenchy McCormick, 1979, 2d edit., 1995, Cowman's Country: Fifty Frontier Ranches in the Texas Panhandle 1876-1887, 1981, 2d edit., 1995, (poetry) Fringe Benefits: Light Verse From Living, 1985, Borrowed Moccasins: Poems From Other Viewpoints, 1986, Field Notes: Poems on Late Light, 1987; editor and designer: Austin Originals: Chats With Colorful Characters by Robyn Turner, 1982, Long Shadows: Indian Leaders Standing in the Path of Manifest Destiny 1600-1900 (by Jack Jackson), 1985; designer, editor: (poetry) Bootsteps: Poems of the West-Then and Now (by Mildred C. Speer), 1978, 83, coauthor, editor: Eve's Version: 150 Women of the Bible, 1983; featured in documentary Story Of A Family on NBC-TV, 1960; mem. writing team Ch. Women United U.S.A., 2001—09, PBS Documentary on Droughts Worldwide, Documentary on Palo Duro Canyon, PBS TV Specials, 2009-, history documentaries interviews on Ken Burns projects, 2009-. Co-founder, sec. Cerebral Palsy Treatment Ctr., Amarillo, 1948-60, Opportunity House, Amarillo, 1970-87; founder, pres. Children's Cottage, Amarillo, 1964-84, Women's Coalition for Change: Focus on Poverty, Amarillo, 1989-95; co-founder, dir. for underprivileged children Camp Friendship, Ceta Glen, Tex., 1971-74; vol. tutor neighborhood pub. schs., 1992-2006; chair of elders First Christian Ch., 1979-81; host family Internat. Christian Youth Exch., 1963-64, sending family, 1968, 78; active Potter County Hist. Commn., Tex., 1988-96; pres.-elect Ch. Women United of Tex., 1996-98, pres., 1998-2000; chair Amarillo Mayor's Commn. on Early Childhood Nurture/Neglect, 1997—2005; nat. del. Christian Ch. Named Amarillo's Family of the Yr., Amarillo Globe-News, 1957, Tex. Merit Mother, Am. Mothers Assn., Boston, 1991, 1995 Woman of the Yr. in Amarillo, Beta Sigma Phi, Amarillo, 1995, Yellow Rose Tex., Gov. Anne Richards, 1991, Mayor's Friend of Young Children, 1999, Tex. Mother of Yr., Am. Mothers Assn., Boston, 2003; named to Amarillo HS Hall Fame, 1998; recipient Tex. Panhandle Disting. Svc. award West Tex. A&M U., Canyon, 1977, Lifetime Career Achievement award Amarillo Women's Network, 1996, Woman of Distinction award Girl Scouts Tex. Plains Coun., 2002. Mem. AAUW, LWV (v.p., Amarillo program chair), Western Writers Am., Acad. Am. Poets, Amarillo Photog. Soc. (Salon awards 1961-), Panhandle Profl. Writers (pres. 1978-80, bd. mem.), Poetry Soc. Tex. (founder. area chpt. 1972, pres. area chpt. 1979-81, Tex. state councilor 1973—), Tex. Tchrs. of Creative Writing, Common Cause (area rep. 1971—). Democrat. Avocations: photography, travel, reading, walking. Home: 6811 Glen Ridge Dr Austin TX 78731-2909 E-mail: pdr-rlr@suddenlink.net.

ROBERTSON, ROSE MARIE, cardiologist, educator; b. Detroit, May 15, 1945; d. Joseph Michael and Rose Marie (Pink) Stevens; m. David Robertson, Oct. 31, 1978; 1 child, Rose Marie. BA, Manhattanville Coll., 1966; MD, Harvard Med. Sch., 1970. Diplomate Nat. Bd. Medicine, 1971, Am. Bd. Internal Medicine, 1974, Cardiovascular Medicine, 1975. Intern in medicine Mass. Gen. Hosp., Boston, 1970-71, resident in medicine, 1970-72; fellow in cardiovasc. medicine Johns Hopkins Med. Sch., Balt., 1973-75, asst. prof. medicine, 1976—77, Vanderbilt U. Med. Ctr., Nashville, 1975-82, assoc. prof. medicine, 1982-89, dir. cardiovasc. tng. program, 1990—2000, assoc. dir. cardiology, 1987—2000, prof. medicine, 1989—. Mem. adv. bd. Robert Wood Johnson Found., AMFDP, 1990-, chair, 2003-; mem. bd. Assn. for Patient-Oriented Rsch., pres. 2008-09; mem. cardiovasc. study sect. NIH, Bethesda, Md., 1993-97; invited spkr., lectr. Contbr. articles to profl. jours., chpts. to books. Fellow Am. Coll. Cardiology, Am. Heart Assn. (pres. 2000-01, chief sci. officer 2003-), Am. Autonomic Soc., Am. Fedn. for Clin. Rsch., Am. Soc. Clin. Investigation, Am. Clin. and Climatol. Assn., Assn. Univ. Cardiologists. Home: 4003 Newman Pl Nashville TN 37204-4308 Office: 7272 Greenville Ave Dallas TX 75231 Office Phone: 214-706-1295. E-mail: rosemarie.robertson@heart.org.

ROBERTSON, STEVE, political organization administrator; Attended, U. Ky. Polit. dir. Rep. Party of Ky., 1994—2000, dir. ops., 2002—03, chmn., 2007—; dir. ops. Ga. Rep. Party, 2000; legis. aide/analyst to senate pres. David Williams Ky. Senate, 2000—01; pres., CEO Robertson Group, 2004—05; commr. Gov.'s Office for Local Devel., Commonwealth of Ky., 2005—07. Legis. polit. dir. Rep. Nat. Com., 2001—02. Republican. Office: Rep Party of Ky 105 W Third St PO Box 1068 Frankfort KY 40602 Office Phone: 502-875-5130. Office Fax: 502-223-5625. E-mail: steve@rpk.org.*

ROBERTSON, WALTER S., III, bank executive; b. Richmond; B, Washington & Lee U. Pres. DeJarnette & Paul Ins., Richmond; COO Scott & Stringfellow, Inc. (subs. of BB&T Corp.), pres., CEO, 2009—; exec. officer, sales devel. and mktg. BB&T Insurance Svcs., Inc. (subs. of BB&T Corp.), 1998—2001; sr. mng. dir. BB&T Corp. (Branch Banking and Trust Co.), 2009—. Bd. dirs. St. Christopher's Sch., VCU Sch. Engring. Office: BB&T Corp 200 W Second St Winston Salem NC 27101 Office Phone: 336-733-2000. Office Fax: 336-733-2470. Business E-Mail: wrobertson@bbandt.com.

ROBIDAS, STEPHANE, professional hockey player; b. Sherbrooke, Que., Can., Mar. 3, 1977; m. Marie-Eve Robidas; children: Justin, Lexie. Defenseman Montreal Canadiens, 2000—02, Dallas Stars, 2002—03, 2005—, Chgo. Blackhawks, 2003—04. Named to NHL All-Star Game, 2009. Office: Dallas Stars 2601 Avenue of the Stars Frisco TX 75034 also: Am Airlines Ctr 2500 Victory Ave Dallas TX 75201

ROBIDEAUX, JOEL C., state legislator; Mem. Dist. 45 La. House of Reps., 2004—, chair retirement com., mem. ways and means com., joint legis. com. on capital outlay. Independent. Office: Dist Off 102 Woodvale Ave Ste B Lafayette LA 70503 also: PO Box 94062 Baton Rouge LA 70804-9062 Office Phone: 225-342-7263, 337-984-1091. Office Fax: 225-342-8336, 337-984-8987. Business E-Mail: larep045@legis.state.la.us.

ROBINS, CRAIG, construction executive; b. Miami Beach, Fla., 1963; BA, U. Mich., 1984; JD, U. Miami Law Sch., 1987. Founder Bridge House, 1994; founder, pres. Dacra Devel., 1987—. Founder, chmn. Anaphiel Found.; vice-chmn. mus. adv. bd. Wolfsonian-Florida Internat. U.; bd. trustees Hirshhorn Mus. and Sculpture Garden, Miami Art Mus.; mem. trustee com. architecture/design Mus. of Modern Art; bd. dirs. Colonial Bank; investor Thorium Power, Inc.; mem. dean's coun. Yale Sch. Architecture; mem. inaugural nat. adv. coun. Inst. City Design, Miami. Recipient Design Patron award, Smithsonian Inst. Cooper-Hewitt Nat. Design Mus., 2006; named a Maverick, Details mag., 2007. Office: Dacra Devel 3841 NE 2nd Ave Ste 400 Miami FL 33137 Office Phone: 305-531-8700. E-mail: info@craigrobins.com.

ROBINSON, ARMSTRONG MATTHEWS, former legislative staff member; b. 1978; BA in Internat. Affairs, George Washington U., 2000; JD, Cath. U. America, 2004. Rsch. asst. The Coca-Cola Co., 1999; ski instructor Vail Associates, 2000—01; judicial intern to Hon. Mary Ellen Albrecht DC Superior Ct., 2002; volunteer Geoff David for Congress, 2004, policy dir., 2006; legis. asst. to Rep. Geoff Davis, US House of Reps., Washington, 2005, legis. dir., counsel, 2005—07, chief of staff, counsel, 2008—12. Republican. Office Phone: 202-225-3465. E-mail: armstrong.robinson@mail.house.gov.

ROBINSON, BRIAN J., corporate financial executive; BS in Acctg., U. Dayton. CPA 1993. Various postions. Deloitte and Touche LLP, 1991—97, audit mgr., 1997—99; asst. contr. General Cable Corp., 1999—2000, contr., 2000—06, sr. v.p., 2006—08, treas., 2006—, CFO, 2007—, exec. v.p., 2008—. Bd. dirs. GK Technologies Inc. Office: General Cable Corp 4 Tesseneer Dr Highland Heights KY 41076-9753 Office Phone: 859-572-8000. Office Fax: 859-572-8458. Business E-Mail: brobinson@generalcable.com.

ROBINSON, CHESTER HERSEY, retired dean; b. Yonkers, NY, Nov. 8, 1918; s. Sherman Alexander and Alice (Hersey) R.; m. Marguerite Davis, Dec. 14, 1945 (div. Oct. 1976); children— Barry, Roslyn; m. Heidemarie Höfler, Dec. 30, 1976. AB, Union Coll., Schenectady, 1940; PhD, Stanford U., 1950. Asst. registrar Stanford U., 1949-50; dir. div. extension and summer session Miami U., Oxford, Ohio, 1950-54; assoc. dir. Sch. Gen. Studies, Hunter Coll., 1954-60; dir. Sch. Gen. Studies, Bronx campus, 1960-66, dean, 1966-68; dean Sch. Gen. Studies, Herbert H. Lehman Coll. CUNY, 1968-82, dean Continuing Edn., 1982-86; prof. emeritus, 1986—. Served to lt. USNR, 1942-46. Mem. NEA, Beta Theta Pi, Phi Delta Kappa. Lodges: Elks, Am. Legion. Presbyterian. Home: Bldg 500 Apt 216 4920 Locust St NE Saint Petersburg FL 33703 Home Phone: 727-528-9116.

ROBINSON, DAVID BROOKS, retired naval officer; b. Alexandria, La., Oct. 26, 1939; s. Donald and Marion (Holloman) R.; m. Gene Kirkpatrick, Aug. 1, 1964; children: Kirk, David. Student, Tex. A&M U., 1958—59; BS, U.S. Naval Acad., 1963; MS in Physics, Naval Postgrad. Sch., Monterey, Calif., 1969. Commd. ensign USN, 1963, advanced through grades to vice adm., 1993; commdg. officer USS Canon and USS Ready, Guam, 1969-71; adminstrv. aide to Chmn. Joint Chiefs Staff, Washington, 1971-74; commdg. officer USS Luce, Mayport, Fla., 1976-78; surface comdr. assignment officer. and dir. fiscal mgmt. and procedural control divsn. Naval Mil. Pers. Command, 1979-81; mem. Fgn. Svc. Inst. Exec. Seminar, Washington, 1982; commdg. officer USS Richmond K. Turner, Charleston, SC, 1983-84; chief of staff, comdr. Naval Surface Force, Atlantic Fleet, Norfolk, Va., 1984; exec. asst. and sr. aide to vice chief Naval Ops., Washington, 1985, dir. Manpower and Tng. divsn., 1986, dir. Surface Warfare divsn., 1987-88; comdr. cruiser destroyer group 8, 1988-89; vice dir. and subsequently dir. operational plans and inter-operability directorate Joint Staff, Washington, 1989-91; dep., chief of staff to comdr. U.S. Pacific Fleet, 1991-93, comdr. naval surface force, 1993-96; ret. USN, 1996. Decorated Navy Cross, Def. D.S.M.,

D.S.M., Legion of Merit with 4 gold stars, Bronze Star, Purple Heart. Mem. Optimists (pres. Oakton, Va. 1986-87). Methodist. Avocations: golf, bicycling, stamp collecting/philately, reading. Home Phone: 972-763-0760; Office Phone: 703-902-5001, 214-800-2681. Personal E-mail: drobinson022@tx.rr.com. Business E-Mail: drobinson1963@tx.rr.com.

ROBINSON, DAVID MAURICE, philanthropist, retired professional basketball player; b. Key West, Fla., Aug. 6, 1965; m. Valerie Robinson. BS in Math., US Naval Acad., Annapolis, Md., 1987. Commd. ensign USN, 1987—89; ctr. San Antonio Spurs, 1989—2003; ret. NBA, 2003. Mem. US Olympic Basketball Team, 1988, 1992, 1996. Founder David Robinson Found., San Antonio, 1992—; founder, patron The Carver Acad., San Antonio, 1997—. Recipient Naismith award, 1987, Wooden award, 1987, Bronze medal, men's basketball, Seoul Olympic Games, 1988, Gold medal, men's basketball, Barcelona Olympic Games, 1992, Atlanta Olympic Games, 1996; named 1st Team All-Am., Sporting News, 1986, 1987, Coll. Player of Yr., 1987, NBA Rookie of Yr., 1990, 1st Team All-NBA, 1991, 1992, 1995, 1996, NBA Defensive Player of Yr., 1992, NBA Most Valuable Player, 1995; named one of America's Best Leaders, US News & World Report, 2009; named to Western Conf. All-Star Team, NBA, 1990—96, 1998, 2000, 2001, Naismith Meml. Basketball Hall of Fame, 2009. Achievements include leading the NBA in: rebounds, 1991, 1996; blocks, 1991, 1992; free throws, 1994-96; scoring, 1994; member of the NBA Championship winning San Antonio Spurs, 1999, 2003. Office: c/o The Carver Acad 217 Robinson Pl San Antonio TX 78202-8885 Office Phone: 210-223-8885. Office Fax: 210-223-8970.

ROBINSON, DONALD R., death care product and service company executive; BSBA in Computer Svc., Taylor U., Upland, Ind. Various procurement, logistics and info. tech. positions Marathon Oil Corp.; dir., procurement Svc. Corp. Internat., 1996, mng. dir., bus. support svcs., 2003—05; v.p., supply chain mgmt. Service Corp. International, 2005—. Office: Service Corporation International 1929 Allen Pky Houston TX 77019 Office Phone: 713-522-5141. Office Fax: 713-525-5586.

ROBINSON, GLADYS, state legislator; 2 children. B, Bennett Coll. for Women; PhD in Leadership Studies, NC Agrl. & Tech. State U. Trustee Bennett Coll.; mem. Dem. Women of Guilford County, Greensboro Conv. and Visitors Bureau-Setrac Com.; chmn. Health-serve Med. Ctr.; mem. NC Minority Health Coun.; life mem. Nat. Assn. Advancement of Colored; mem. NC Commn. on Edn. Minority and At-Risk Students; exec. dir. Piedmont Health Svcs., Sickle Cell Agy.; mem. U. NC Bd. of Governers, Women's Profl. Forum, Greensboro, 1993; co chmn. Piedmont Triad Leadership Network, 2003—04; mem. Dist. 28 NC State Senate, 2011—. V.p., bd. dirs. Guilford Cmty. AIDS; bd. dirs. NC Tchr. Acad., NC Black Caucus Found. Democrat. Baptist. Office: 2107 Hunters Ridge Dr Pleasant Garden NC 27313 Address: NC Senate 16 W Jones St Room 1120 Raleigh NC 27601-2808 Office Phone: 919-715-3042. Business E-Mail: Gladys.Robinson@ncleg.net.

ROBINSON, HOBART KRUM, management consulting company executive; b. Quincy, Mass., Oct. 8, 1937; s. Hobart Krum and Charlotte Elizabeth (Hall) R.; m. Gerd Ingela Janhede, Oct. 17, 1964; children: Steven Whitney, Karina Jill, Peter Danforth. BA, Williams Coll., 1959; MBA, Columbia U., 1964. Market analyst Mobil Chem. Co., Richmond, Va., 1964-67; mgr. program analysis and control Polaroid Corp., Cambridge, Mass., 1967-69; exec. v.p., dir. Simplex Wire and Cable, Inc., North Berwick, Maine, 1969-73; sr. engagement mgr. McKinsey and Co., Inc., NYC, 1973-76, prin. Copenhagen, 1977-81, NYC, 1985-89, Stockholm, 1989-95, dir. adminstrn. Eastern Europe, 1993-95, dir. adminstrn. NYC, 1995-98; pres., CEO Brink's Inc., Darien, Conn., 1981-84; ret., 1998. Dir. Burlington No. Air Freight, Inc., Newport Beach, Calif., 1982-84. Pres. Am. Club in Copenhagen, 1980-81; dir. Fulbright Commn., Copenhagen, 1980-81; vice chair Williams Coll. Alumni Fund, 1999-2004; class agt. Williams Coll. Alumni Fund, 1998-. Lt. USNR, 1959-62. Mem. Tournament Players Club (Ponte Vedra, Fla.), Sawgrass Country Club (Ponte Vedra), Taconic Golf Club. Republican. Episcopalian. Avocations: golf, singing. Personal E-mail: hkrobinson59@gmail.com.

ROBINSON, JAMES ARTHUR, political scientist; b. Blackwell, Okla., June 9, 1932; s. William L. and Ethel Bell (Hicks) R.; children: Adelaide, Luke; m. Andrea C. Hatcher, Jan. 20, 2006 AB, George Washington U., 1954, DPS (hon.), 1977; MA, U. Okla., 1955; PhD, Northwestern U., 1957. Congl. fellow Am. Polit. Sci. Assn., 1957-58; Instr. polit. sci. Northwestern U., 1958-59, asst. prof., 1959-62, assoc. prof., 1962-64; prof. polit. sci. Ohio State U., Columbus, 1964-71; dir. Mershon Center, 1967-70, v.p. acad. affairs, provost, 1969-71; pres., prof. polit. sci. Macalester Coll., St. Paul, 1971-74; pres. U. West Fla., Pensacola, 1974-88, pres. emeritus, 1988—, Regents prof., 1988—2002. Author: (with R.C. Snyder) National and International Decision Making, 1961, Congress and Foreign Policy Making, rev. edit, 1967, House Rules Committee, 1963, (with J. Baum) Party Primaries in Taiwan, 1999, (with D. Brown and E. Moon) Appraising Steps in Democratization: Elections in Taiwan, 1986-2000, 2000. Mem.: Cosmos (Washington).

ROBINSON, JAMES WILLIAM, chemistry professor; b. Kidderminster, Eng., July 12, 1923; arrived in U.S., 1955, naturalized, 1958; s. James William and Eva Robinson; m. Winifred Gladys Nixon, Jan. 8, 1946; children: James William, Linda Juanita, Sandra Jacqueline. BSc with hons., U. Birmingham, England, 1949, PhD, 1952, DSc, 1978. Sr. sci. officer Brit. Civl Svc., Birmingham, England, 1952—55; from rsch. assoc. to prof. La. State U., Baton Rouge, 1955—93, prof. emeritus, 1993—; sr. chemist Esso Rsch. Labs., Baton Rouge, 1956—63; tech. advisor Ethyl Corp., Baton Rouge, 1963—64, Nat. U. Accreditation Com., 1970—71. Mem. rsch. grants adv. com. EPA, 1969—75; vis. prof. U. Colo., 1970, U. Sydney, 1983; lectr. in spectroscopy. Author: Atomic Absorption Spectroscopy, 1966, 2d edit., 1975, Undergraduate Instrumental Analysis, 1970, 6th edit., 2005, Atomic Spectroscopy, 1990, 2d edit., 1996; editor: Analytica Chemica Acta, 1956—80, Spectroscopy Letters, 1966—98, Environl. Sci. and Health, 1971—97, Monograph Series Analysis Environ. Control, 1977—85, Applied Spectroscopy Revs., 1977—90, Jour. Applied Spectroscopy, 2003, Handbook of Spectroscopy, Vol. I, 1974, Vol. II, 1974, Vol. III, 1981, Practical Handbook of Spectroscopy, 1991; contbr. 220 articles to profl. jours., 10 chapters to books. Recipient Gold medal, N.Y. Soc. Applied Spectroscopy, 2000; named to Hall of Distinction, La. State U., 2011; fellow, Guggenheim Found., 1975. Fellow: Royal Chem. Soc. Avocations: gardening, travel, snorkeling. Home: 375 Amherst Ave Baton Rouge LA 70808 Business E-Mail: jrobi24@lsu.edu.*

ROBINSON, JOE SAM, neurosurgeon, educator; b. Atlanta, July 21, 1945; s. Joe Sam and Nell (Mixon) R.; m. Elizabeth Ann Moate, Apr. 3, 1982; children: Joe Sam III, Edward Richard, Thomas McRae. AB cum laude, Harvard Coll., 1967; MD, U. Va., 1971; MS, Northwestern U., 1975. Surg. intern Emory U., 1971-72, resident in surgery, 1972-73; resident in neurosurgery Northwestern U., 1973-78; instr. U. Ill., 1978-79, Yale U., 1979-81; pres. Ga. Neurosurg. Inst. P.A., Macon, 1981—. Prof., chief neurosurgery Mercer U. Sch. Medicine, Macon, 1986; chief surgery Med. Ctr. Ctrl. Ga., Macon, 1989—, vice chmn. surgery, 1991-97, chmn. dept. surgery, 1996—; vis. neurosurgeon China, 1992, Konaus Acad. Neurosurgery Inst., Lithuania, 1992; clin. prof. Med. Coll. Ga., 2002; chmn. Ga. Bd. Physicians Workforce, 2007, physician Trauma Rep. Ga. Trauma Commn. Lt. col. USANG, 1972-95. Fellow Internat. Coll. Surgeons (vice regent 1983-93); mem. Am. Assn. Neurol. Surgeons, Congress Neurol. Surgeons, AAAS, Ga. Neurosurg. Soc., Alpha Omega Alpha. Republican. Methodist. Office: Ga Neurosurg Inst PA 840 Pine St Ste 880 Macon GA 31201-7525

ROBINSON, JOHN, state legislator; b. Mar. 22, 1950; 1 child, Lawson. Attended, Jacksonville State U., Ala.; JD, Birmingham Sch. Law. Ret. trial coord. Jackson County Dist. Attorney's Office; mem. Dist. 23 Ala. House of Reps., Montgomery, 1994—. Mem. St. Luke's Episc. Ch. Democrat. Episcopalian. Office: 100 E Peachtree St Scottsboro AL 35768 also: Ala House of Reps Ala State House 11 S Union St Rm 534-D Montgomery AL 36130 Office Phone: 334-242-7728. Business E-Mail: john.robinson@alhouse.gov.

ROBINSON, JOHN WILLIAM, IV, lawyer; b. Atlanta, Apr. 29, 1950; s. J. William III and Elizabeth (Smith) R.; m. Ellen Showalter, Dec. 28, 1976; children: William, Anna. BA with honors, Washington & Lee U., 1972; JD, U. Ga., 1975. Bar: Fla., Ga., U.S. Dist. Ct. (no., so. and mid. dists.) Fla., U.S. Ct. Mil. Appeals, U.S. Ct. Appeals (5th and 11th cirs.), U.S. Supreme Ct.; cert. labor & employment law, civil trial and bus. litigation lawyer, Fla. Trial atty. Nat. Labor Rels. Bd., New Orleans, 1975—76; trial def. counsel 8th infantry U.S. Army, Mainz, Germany, 1977—78, trial counsel 8th infantry, 1979; law clk., commr. Ct. Mil. Rev., Washington, 1980; atty. Fowler, White, Boggs, PA, Tampa, Fla., 1980—, head labor and employment law dept., 1993—, dir., 1998—, sec./treas., 2001—. Mem. faculty U. Md., 1977-79; arbitrator U.S. Dist. Ct. (mid. dist.) Fla.; mem. Leadership Fla., 2004— Editor-in-chief: Employment & Labor Relations Law, 1991-95; editor: Developing Labor Law, 1982—, Model Jury Instructions for Employment Litigation, 1994—; editor: Employment Litigation Handbooks, 1998, 2010. Chmn. Tampa Bay Internat. Trade Coun., 1990-91, Rough Riders Dist. Boy Scouts Am., 1990; legal counsel, chair Drug Free Workplace Task Force, 1999-00; legal counsel, chair, gen. counsel, bd. dirs., 1996, 04-, Greater Tampa C. of C., 1996, 05-; trustee U. Tampa, bd. fellows, chair bus. symposia, 2006-. Capt. U.S. Army, 1976-80. Named one of Best Lawyers in Am. for labor and employment law, Top Ten Super Lawyers in Fla., Fla. Legal Elite. Fellow: Am. Bar Found., Coll. Labor and Employment Lawyers (Founding fellow); mem.: ABA (chmn. employment and labor rels. com. 1993—96, divsn. dir. 1996—2000, mem. coun. 2000—03, chmn. com. on multijurisdictional practice 2000—, task force on electronic discovery 2003—04, litigation sect.), Acad. Fla. Mgmt. Attys. (pres., founding mem. 1993—, chair 2008, charter mem.), Leadership Tampa (chmn. 2006), Hillsborough County Bar Assn. Trial Lawyers (bd. dirs. 1996—, chmn. 2003—), Comml. Bar Assn.(London) (hon.), Am. Inn of Ct. (pres., dir. and master barrister, trustee Am. Inns of Ct. Found., exec. com. Am. Inns of Ct. Found.), Washington & Lee U. Bd. (pres. nat. alumni bd. 1990—91, trustee 1995—2005), Fla. Bar Assn. (chmn. labor and employment law sect. 1992—93), Rotary (past pres.). Avocation: history. Office: Fowler White Boggs PA 501 E Kennedy Blvd Tampa FL 33602-5237

ROBINSON, KAYNE B., lobbyist, former political organization officer; m. Donna R. Robinson. B, Drake U. With Des Moines Police Dept., 1968—99; dep. Iowa chmn. Dole Presdl. campaign, 1988; Iowa chmn. Gramm Presdl. campaign, 1996; chmn. Iowa Rep. Party, 1999—2001; 1st v.p. NRA, Fairfax, Va., 1997—2003, pres., 2003—. With USMC. Named Police Officer of the Yr. Iowa Assn. Women Police. Office: NRA 11250 Waples Mill Rd Fairfax VA 22030

ROBINSON, KENNETH LARRY, insurance company executive; b. Carrollton, Ga., Sept. 20, 1944; s. Tommy Esper and Annie Eunie (Bowie) R.; m. Peggy Marie Tally, Jan. 20, 1967 (div. Feb. 1974); 1 child, Toni Marie; m. Malinda Gayle York, Jan. 11, 1975; 1 child, Tommy Eric. Student, U.S. Armed Forces Inst., Quantico, Va., 1964; cert., Life Ins. Mktg./Rsch. Assn., Atlanta, 1982, Life Underwriters Tng. Coun., Montgomery, Ala., 1987. Dist. mgr. United Family Life Ins. Co., Atlanta, 1967-77, Mut. Savs. Life Ins. Co., Decatur, Ala., 1978-88; agy. mgr. Robinson Ins. Agy., Montgomery, Ala., 1989; regional mgr. Nat. Security Ins. Co., Elba, Ala., 1989-97, agy. devel., 1997—, pres. coastal mktg., 2003—. Master mgr., United Family Life Ins. Co., Atlanta, 1975-77; president's advisory coun., Mut. Savs. Life Ins. Co., Decatur, 1985-87, pres.' club, 1987. Recipient Cert. Achievement Cotton States Ins. Co., 1989. Mem. Nat. Assn. Life Underwriters, Lions. Republican. Baptist. Avocations: golf, fishing. Home: 3364 W Mildred St Mobile AL 36605-4124

ROBINSON, LARRY CLARK, professional hockey coach, retired professional hockey player; b. Winchester, Ont., Can., June 2, 1951; m. Jeannette Robinson; children: Jeffery, Rachelle. Defenseman Montreal Canadians, 1971—89, LA Kings, 1989—92; asst. coach NJ Devils, 1993—95, 1999—2000, 2007—08, 2010—, head coach, 2000—02, 2005, spl. assignment coach, 2002—05, 2006—07, 2008—10; head coach LA Kings, 1995—99. Mem. Team Can., Can. Cup, 1976, 1981, 1984. Recipient James Norris Meml. Trophy, 1977, 1980, Conn Smythe Trophy, 1978; named to NHL All-Star game, 1974, 1976—78, 1980, 1982, 1986, 1988, 1989, 1992. Achievements include being a member of Stanley Cup Champion Montreal Canadians, 1971, 1973, 1976, 1977, 1978, 1979; being inducted into the Hockey Hall of Fame, 1995; being the head coach of Stanley Cup Champion New Jersey Devils, 2000; having his number, 19, retired by Montreal Canadians, 2007. Avocations: polo, boating. Office: NJ Devils Prudential Ctr 165 Mulberry St Newark NJ 07102

ROBINSON, MARY LOU, federal judge; b. Dodge City, Kans., Aug. 25, 1926; d. Gerald J. and Frances Strueber; m. A.J. Robinson, Aug. 28, 1949; 3 children. BA, U. Tex., 1948, LL.B., 1950. Bar: Tex. 1949. Ptnr. Robinson & Robinson, Amarillo, 1950-55; judge County Ct. at Law, Potter County, Tex., 1955-59, (108th Dist. Ct.), Amarillo, 1961-73; assoc. justice Ct. of Civil Appeals for 7th Supreme Jud. Dist. of Tex., Amarillo, 1973-77, chief justice, 1977-79; judge US Dist. Ct. (no. dist.) Tex., Amarillo, 1979—. Named Woman of Year Tex. Fedn. Bus. and Profl. Women, 1973; recipient Sandra Day O'Connor award profl. excellence, 2005, judicial Recognition award Nat. Assn. Criminal Defence Lawyers, 2010 Mem. Nat. Assn. Women Lawyers, ABA, Tex. Bar Assn. (Outstanding 50-Yr. Lawyer award 2002), Tex. Bar Found. (Samuel Pessara Outstanding Judge award), Amarillo Bar Assn., Delta Kappa Gamma. Presbyterian. Office: US Dist Ct Rm 226 205 E 5th Ave # F13248 Amarillo TX 79101-1559 Office Phone: 806-468-3822.

ROBINSON, OLIVER, state legislator; b. Mar. 14, 1960; m. Sakina; children: Amanda, Adriana, Oliver, III. BS in Urban Affairs, U. Ala. Birmingham. Profl. basketball player San Antonio Spurs; mem. Dist. 58 Ala. House of Reps., 1999—. Treas. Keep Birmingham Beautiful Commn.; mem. Birmingham Pub. Pk. & Recreation Bd., Bethel Bapt. Ch., West End, Ala. Named one of Top 40 Under 40 Birmingham Bus. Jour., 1996. Mem.: Phi Beta Sigma. Democrat. Baptist. Office: 9640 Eastpoint Cir Birmingham AL 35217 also: Ala House of Reps Ala State House 11 S Union St Rm 534-B Montgomery AL 36130 Office Phone: 334-242-7769.

ROBINSON, RAYMOND EDWIN, conductor, music educator, writer; b. San Jose, Calif., Dec. 26, 1932; s. Elam Edwin and Zula Mai (Hatley) R.; m. Ruth Aleen Chamberlain, Mar. 12, 1954; children: Cynthia Rae, Greg Edwin, David L., Brent Steven, Jeffrey Vernon. BA, San Jose State U., 1956; MMus, Ind. U., 1958, D in Mus. Edn., 1969; LHD, Westminster Choir Coll., 1987; postdoctoral study, Jagiellonian U., Poland, 1995, Cambridge U., 1987—89, postdoctoral study, 2002—03. Instr. music Ind. U., Bloomington, 1958-59; music critic Portland Reporter, 1962-63, Balt. Evening Sun, 1964-68, Palm Beach (Fla.) Post, 1991—, Palm Beach Daily News, 2003—04; founder, tchr. seminar for music adminstrs., 1972—; chmn. divsn. fine arts Cascade Coll., Portland, Oreg., 1959-63; dean Peabody Inst., Balt., 1963-69; pres. Westminster Choir Coll., Princeton, NJ, 1969-87; vis. fellow Wolfson Coll. U. Cambridge, England, 1987—89, 2002—03; disting. prof. choral studies, choral condr. Palm Beach Atlantic U., West Palm Beach, Fla., 1989—; pres. Prestige Publs., Inc., 1978—; prof. Sch. Ch. Music Knox Theol. Sem., Ft. Lauderdale, Fla., 1989—; vis. prof. U. Miami, 2001—02. Choral condr. Palm Beach CC, Lake Worth, Fla., 1992-93; condr.-in-residence, dir. music First Presbyn. Ch., West Palm Beach, 1989-97; dir. music Coral Ridge Presbyn. Ch., Ft. Lauderdale, Fla., 1997, music dir., conductor Palm Beach Symphony Orch., 2004—; spl. guest choral condr. Palm Beach Opera, 1990—; interim condr. Choral Soc. Palm Beaches, 1992; condr. Ray Robinson Chorale, 1994—, Cambridge (Eng.) U., Cambridge, Eng., 1987-89, 2002-03, Kiev, Ukraine, 1997, Budapest, 1997, Cracow, 2002, Coral Ridge Presbyn. Ch., 1997; vis. prof. U. Miami, Fla., 2001-2002. Author: The Choral Experience, 1976, Choral Music, 1978; Krzysztof Penderecki, A Guide to His Works, 1983, A Study of the Penderecki St. Luke Passion, 1983, John Finley Williamson: A Centennial Appreciation, 1987, Postcards from Cambridge, 2005, A Bach Tribute: Bach Essays in Honor of William H. Scheide, 1993; co-author, editor: Studies in Penderecki, 1998, 2003; editor: Labyrinth of Time: Five Addresses for the End of the Millenium, 1998; The Choral Tradition Series, Hinshaw Music Inc., 1978—. Bd. dirs. Balt. Symphony Orch., 1967-69, Am. Boy Choir Sch., 1970-73, N.Y. Choral Soc., 1972—, Palm Beach Atlantic U. choral series Hinshaw Music Inc., 1990—; bd. dirs. Palm Beach County Coun. Arts, chmn. profl. artists com., mem. task force for master plan, 1990-92; mem. cultural plan com. Palm Beach County Cultural Coun., 1992; mem. task force for edn. Fla. Philharm. Orch., 1994-95; mem. art in pub. places com. West Palm Beach, Fla. 2004—. Recipient Disting. Alumni Merit award Ind. U., 1975, Disting. Alumni award Sch. Music Ind. U., 1973, Disting. Alumni award San Jose State U., 1990. Mem. Coll. Music Soc. (life), Am. Choral Dirs. Assn. (life, chmn. rsch. and publs. com. 1986—), Internat. Heinrich Schütz Soc. (chmn. Am. sect. 1984-87), Univ. Club N.Y., Nassau Club Princeton, Govs. Club West Palm Beach. Presbyterian. Home: 349 Palmer Dr Lexington SC 29072-7476 Business E-Mail: ray_robinson@pba.edu.

ROBINSON, RONALD ALAN, manufacturing executive; b. Louisville, Mar. 23, 1952; s. J. Kenneth and Juanita M. (Crosier) R.; m. Joan Parker, 1986; children: Rex, Jay. BS, GA Inst. Tech., 1974; MBA, Harvard U., 1978. Staff engr., asst. to exec. v.p. ops. Dual Drilling Co., Wichita Falls, Tex., 1978-80; v.p. Dreco, Inc., Houston, 1980-84, pres., dir. subs. Triflo Industries Internat., Inc.; pres., COO Ramteck Sys., Inc., 1984-87; chmn., CEO Denver Techs. Inc., 1988-95; pres. Svedala Industries, Inc., 1996-99; pres., CEO Alamo Group, Inc., Seguin, Tex., 1999—. Recipient Optimist Internat. Citizenship award, 1970; Gardiner Symonds fellow, 1977. Mem. Harvard Alumni Assn. Home: 18 Pourtales Colorado Springs CO 80906 Office: Alamo Group Inc 1627 E Walnut St Seguin TX 78155-5202

ROBINSON, SALLY WINSTON, artist; b. Detroit, Nov. 2, 1924; d. Harry Lewis and Lydia (Kahn) Winston; m. Eliot F. Robinson, June 28, 1949; children: Peter Eliot, Lydia Winston, Sarah Mitchell, Suzanne Finley. BA, Bennington Coll., 1947; postgrad., Cranbrook Acad. Art, 1949; grad., Sch. Social Work, Wayne U., 1948, MA, 1972; MFA, Wayne State U., 1973. Psychol. tester Detroit Bd. Edn., 1944; psychol. counselor and tester YMCA, NYC, 1946; social caseworker Family Svc., Pontiac, Mich., 1947; instr. printmaking Wayne State U., Detroit, 1973—; rschr. Selby Gardens Assoc., Selby Gardens Rsch. Tchr. children's art Detroit Inst. Art, 1949-50, now artistic advisor, bd. dirs. drawing and pring orgn. One-woman shows include, U. Mich., 1973, Wayne State U., 1974, Klein-Vogel Gallery, 1974, Rina Gallery, 1976, Park McCullough House, Vt., 1976, Williams Coll., 1976, Arnold Klein Gallery, 1977, exhibited in group shows, Bennington Coll., Cranbrook Mus., Detroit Inst. Art, Detroit Artists Market, Soc. Women Painters, Soc. Arts and Crafts, Bloomfield Art Assn., Flint Left Bank Gallery, Balough Gallery, Detroit Soc. Woman Painters, U. Mich., U. Ind., U. Wis., U. Pitts., Toledo Mus., Krannert Mus., Represented in permanent collections. Bd. dirs. Planned Parenthood, 1951—, mem. exec. bd., 1963—; bd. dirs. PTA, 1956-60, Roeper City and Country Sch., U. Mich. Mus. Art, 1978; trustee Putnam Hosp. Med. Rsch. Inst., 1978; mem. Gov.'s Commn. Art in State Bldgs., 1978-79; mem. art and devel. coms. So. Vt. Art Ctr., 1987-88; mem. vol. com. Marie Selby Gardens; patron Graphic Art Studio, U. So. Fla., Tampa; patron, benefactor Clark Mus., Williamstown, Mass.; vol. Shelburne Art Ctr., Vt. Fellow: Williams Coll. Mus. Art (mem. visiting com.); mem.: Sarasota Selby Gardens Rsch. Com., Selby Gardens Assoc. (Sarasota), Town Hall Sarasota Bd., Bloomfield Art Assn. (program co-chmn. 1956), Birmingham Soc. Women Painters (pres. 1974—76), Detroit Soc. Women Painters, Detroit Artists Market (dir. 1956—, hon. bd. mem.), Founders Soc. Detroit Inst. Art, Bennington Coll. Alumnae Assn. (regional co-chmn. 1954), Vt. Tennis Club, Burlington Tennis Club, Harvard Club (Sarasota, Fla.), Williams College Club (NYC), Cosmopolitan Club (NYC), Founders Garden Club (Sarasota), Garden Club Am. (selby gardens herbarium vol. 2006—), Oaks Club (Fla.), Women's City Club (coord. art shows Detroit 1950), Village Women's Club (Birmingham, Mich.). Unitarian Universalist. Home: 209 Hills Point Rd Charlotte VT 05445-9698 also: 639 Eagle Watch Ln Osprey FL 34229 Personal E-mail: sallyrobinsonflorida@msn.com.

ROBINSON, THOMAS CHRISTOPHER, health science educator; b. Buffalo, Oct. 16, 1944; s. Christopher Sidney and Eleanor Florence (Martin) R.; m. Rena H. Robinson; children: Diane Robinson Dunn, Kristen O'Melia. BA, SUNY, Buffalo, 1966, EdM, 1968, PhD, 1971; grad. mgmt. devel. program, Harvard U., Cambridge, Mass., 1989. Admissions officer, office of admissions and records SUNY, Buffalo, 1966-72, assoc. dean Sch. Health Related Professions, 1975-78; asst. dir. Erie County Lab., Buffalo, 1972-75; assoc. dean Coll. Allied Health Professions, U. Ky., Lexington, 1978-84, dean Coll. Health Scis., 1984—2004, prof., 1984—2008, dean emeritus, 2005—, prof. emeritus, 2008—; wine educator Tamber Bey Vineyards, Oakville, Calif. Cons. MDS Labs., Hamilton, Ont., Can., 1973-75, Joint US-Arabian Commn. on Econ. Cooperation, 1986-87, West Sussex Inst. Higher Edn., Bogner Regis, U.K., 1987, U. Wis. Sys. Ctrs. of Excellence Program, 1988, Pub. Health Svc. Health Resources Adminstrn., 1983, 90-91; mem. exec. com. Nat. Practitioner Data Bank, 1992-94, cons. 1994-95; hon. mem. faculty Khabarovsk (Russia) Med. Inst., 1996; bd. dirs. Health Ky. Contbr. articles to profl. jours. Mem. Health Sys. Agy. Coun., Buffalo, 1977-78, Western NY Hemophilia Soc. Bd. Buffalo, 1977-78, Lexington-Fayette County Bd. Health, Lexington, 1987-91, program excellence project Ohio Bd. Regents, United Way of Bluegrass Healthcare Devel. Bd., 1991; cons.

La. Bd. Regents, 1995, 98, 2001, 04, 06, 07, 10, Univ. Wolverhampton fellow, UK, 1991; bd. dirs. Ky. HealthCare Improvement Authority, 2006—; mem. leadership coun. Am. Diabetes Assn., Lexington, 2007-09. Sgt. NY Army N.G., 1968-74. Guard Staff Sgt. New York State US Army, 1968—74. Recipient Svc. award, Jour. Allied Health, 1986; Internat fellow, Hatfield Coll., Un. Durham, Eng., 2005. Mem. Assn. Schs. Allied Health Professions (bd. dirs. 1985-87, Svc. award 1987, Fellow award 1988, pres. 1991-94, past pres. 1994-95, Outstanding Mem. award 1995), Ky. Allied Health Consortium (bd. dirs. 1985-93, chair 1995-96), So. Assn. Allied Health Deans (sec. 1986-88, chmn. 1988-90), Assn. Schs. Allied Health Professions (pres. 1991-94), Ky. Hosp. Assn., Ky. Assn. Healthcare Facilities, So. Assn. Colls. and Schs. (chair and accreditation evaluator), Sigma Phi Epsilon. Avocations: travel, genealogy, gardening. Business E-Mail: tcrobi01@uky.edu.

ROBINSON, W. LEE, lawyer; b. Rome, Ga., Sept. 24, 1943; m. Irene Scales, 1966; children: Christine, Jacquelyn. BS, Ga. Inst. Tech.; MBA, JD, Mercer U., 1985. With Robinson Hardware Store, Macon, Ga., 1954-86; mem. Ga. Senate, Atlanta, 1975-83; mayor City of Macon, Macon, 1987—91; pvt. practice Macon, 1985—2004; circuit pub. defender Macon Jud. Circuit, 2005—. Judge mcpl. ct. (part time), Macon. Bd. dirs. Cherry Blossom Festival, 2006—, chmn., 2008—, bd. chmn., 2009, festival chmn., 2010. 2d lt. US Army, col. USAR. Decorated Bronze Star with two oak leaf clusters, Legion of Merit with oak leaf cluster; recipient Justice Robert Benham award for Cmty. Svc., 2007; named to U.S. Army Officer Candidate Sch. Hall of Fame. Mem. Ga. Assn. Criminal Def. Lawyers, Macon C. of C. (former bd. dirs.), Macon Bar Assn, Alzheimer's Assn. (chmn., bd. govs. Ga. chpt. 2005-07) Address: 3824 Overlook Ave Macon GA 31204-1325 Office: 201 2nd St Ste 550 Macon GA 31201-8282 E-mail: wlrmcnlaw@aol.com.

ROBINSON, WILLIAM T., III, lawyer; b. Covington, Ky., Jan. 6, 1945; s. William T. Jr. and Hilda C. (Tatermann) R.; m. Joan Mary Wernersbach, Aug. 2, 1969; children: William Taylor IV, Todd Arthur. AB, Thomas More Coll., 1967; JD, U. Ky., 1971. Bar: Ohio 1971, Ky. 1972, Tenn. 1999, U.S. Dist. Ct. (ea. dist.) Ky. 1972, U.S. Dist. Ct. (so. dist.) Ohio 1971, U.S. Dist. Ct. (we. dist.) Ky. 1993, U.S. Dist. Ct. (so. dist.) Ind. 1996, U.S. Ct. Appeals (6th cir.) 1972, U.S. Supreme Ct 1978. Ptnr. Robinson, Arnzen, Parry & Wentz, P.S.C., Covington, Ky., 1971—; mem. in charge, Greater Cincinnati & No. Ky., exec. comm. Greenebaum Doll & McDonald, Covington, Ky.; mem.-in-charge Florence office Frost Brown Todd, Florence. Found. bd. mem. Appellate Judges Edn. Inst., 2003; adj. prof. No. Ky. U., 1977—; lectr. numerous seminars. Bd. of trustees Redwood Sch. and Rehabilitation Ctr., 1971-81, 83—, sec., 1972-73, 1st v.p., 1973-75, pres., 1975-78, bd. of overseers, 1981-83; bd. of trustees, chmn. Dorothy Wood Found., 1980—, bd. mem. emeritus 2003-; bd. dirs. Cin. chpt. ARC, 1979-85; sust. atty. mem. Product Liability Adv. Council 1997-; Coll. Law Univ. Ky. Lafferty Soc. 1981-, mem. visiting comm. 1988- (chmn. 1995 & 1998), commencement speaker 1988, Hall of Fame 2004; bd. mem. Boy Scouts Am. Powder Horn dist. 1994-; bd. mem. Cincinnati Inst. Fine Arts 1999-2004; bd. dir. Cincinnati/No. Ky. Internat. Airport 1998-, vice chmn. 2004-; bd. trustees Cincinnati Symphony 1998-2004; found. bd. mem. Cincy-Tech USA, 2002-; found. bd. mem. Forward Quest 1997-; policy bd. mem. Partnership for Greater Cincinnati 1999-, chmn. 1999-2003; bd. mem. Greater Cincinnati C. of C. 1994-, exec. comm. 1999-2003; bd. mem. Greater Cincinnati Scholrship Assn. 1994-; bd. mem. Kentuckians for Better Transp. 1996-2004; bd. mem. Ky. C. of C. 1987-93, chmn. 1992-92, Dunlevy frontiersman Comm. Svc. award 1991; mem. Legatus Cincinnati chptr. 1996-2004; bd. trustees Mt. St. Joseph Coll. 1997-; bd. mem. Nat. Conf. Community & Justice 1986-97, treas. 1990-97, co-chmn. 1995-97, emeritus bd. 1997-, Disting. Svc. Citation 2004; adv. trustee Nat. Underground Railroad Freedom Ctr. 2001-; found. bd. mem. & sec./treas. Tri-County Econ. Dev. Corp. 1987-; co-found. & charter bd. mem. Tri-County Econ. Devel. Found. 1996-, charter sec./treas. 1996-2000, treas. 2000-; life mem. Univ. Ky. Alum. Assn., fellow 1981-. Recipient Covington award, Friends of Covington, 1998, Judge Learned Hand Human Rels. award, Am. Jewish Comm., 1998, Governor's Econ. Devel. Leadership award, Ky., 1997, Knight of Malta, 1992. Fellow Am. Acad. Appellate Lawyers 1998, Internat. Soc. Barristers 1988; Mem. ABA (bd. govs. 2000-, exec. com. 2002-03, treas.-elect 2004-2005, treas. 2005-2008, chmn. fin. comm. 2002-03, pres.-elect, 2010-11), Ohio Bar Assn., Fed. Bar Assn. (mem. steering comm. 2002-), Ky. Bar Assn. (past pres., Outstanding Lawyer award, 1989), Am. Bar Found. (life fellow, fellows chmn Ky. 2000-2004), Am. Law Inst., Sixth Cir. Jud. Conf. (life mem.), Ky. Bar Found. (pres. 1988-89, charter life fellow 1986-), No. Ky. Bar Assn., Louisville bar Assn., Cincinnati Bar Assn. (Themis award 2003), Kenton County Bar Assn. (mem. exec. com. 1973-75, chmn. legal-med. com. 1978-83, Ann. Merit award 1973), Ky. Def. Counsel Assn., Internat. Assn. Ins. Counsel, Internat. Assn. Def. Counsel, Salmon P. Chase Am. Inn Ct. (co-founder & pres. 1993-94, master 1993-), Acad. Trial Lawyers Am., So. Conf. Bar Pres., Nat. Conf. Bar Pres.s', U. Ky. Alumni Assn. (bd. dirs. 1981—), No. Ky. C. of C. (vice chmn. 1985-86, bd. dirs. 1980—, Profl. of Yr. 1980), Thomas More Coll. Alumni Assn. (bd. dirs. 1972—, pres. 1974-75, chmn. alumni fund drive 1974-75, Disting. Alum. award 1982), Phi Alpha Theta, Alpha Delta Gamma, Phi Delta Phi. Office: Frost Brown Todd 7310 Turfway Rd Ste 210 Florence KY 41042 Office Phone: 859-817-5901. Office Fax: 859-283-5902. E-mail: wrobinson@fbtlaw.com.

ROBISON, EMILY BURNS, musician; b. Pittsfield, Mass., Aug. 16, 1972; d. Paul and Barbara Burns; m. Charlie Robison, May 1, 1999 (div. Aug. 6, 2008); children: Charles Augustus, Julianna Tex, Henry Benjamin; 1 child (with Martin Strayer), Violet Isabel Strayer. Performer Blue Night Express, 1984—89; musician and vocalist Dixie Chicks, 1989—, Court Yard Hounds, 2010—. Musician: (albums) (with The Dixie Chicks) Thank Heavens for Dale Evans, 1990, Little Ol' Cowgirl, 1992, Shouldn't a Told You That, 1993, Wide Open Spaces, 1998 (Maximum Vision Clip of Yr., Billboard, 1998, Best New Country Artist Clip of Yr., Billboard, 1998, Best Country Album, Grammy Awards, 1998, Album of Yr., Acad. Country Music, 1998, Best Selling Album, Can. Country Music Awards, 1999, Song of Yr., WB Radio Music Award, 1999, Album of Yr., ACM, 1999), Fly, 1999 (Best Country Album, Grammy Awards, 1999, Best Selling Album, Can. Country Musc Awards, 2000, Internat. Album, British Country Music Award, 2000, Country Album of Yr., Billboard Awards, 2000, Album of Yr., ACM, 2000, Album of Yr., CMA, 2000), Home, 2002 (Favorite Country Album, Am. Music Awards, 2002, Best Recording Package, Grammy Awards, 2002, Best Country Album, Grammy Awards, 2002), Top of the World Tour: Live, 2003 (Best Country Group Vocal Performance, Grammy Awards, 2005), Taking the Long Way, 2006 (Album of Yr. and Best Country Album, Grammy Awards, 2007), (with Court Yard Hounds) Court Yard Hounds, 2010, (songs) Not Ready to Make Nice, 2006 (Record of Yr., Song of Yr., Best Performance by a Duo or Group with Vocal, Grammy Awards, 2007); performer: (documentary) Dixie Chicks: Shut Up and Sing, 2006. Recipient Horizon award, CMA, 1998; named Most Significant New Country Act, Country Monitor, 1998, Top New Country Artist, Billboard, 1998, Top Vocal Group, Acad. Country Music, 1998, Country Artist of Yr., Rolling Stone, 1999, Top Country Artist, Billboard, 1999, Internat. Rising Star, British Country Music Awards, 1999, Artist of Yr. (Country), WB Radio Music Award, 1999, Favorite New Artist (Country), AMA, 1999, Vocal Group of Yr., CMA, 1999, Country Artist of Yr., Billboard, 1999, 2000, Entertainer of Yr., CMA, 2000, ACM, 2000, Vocal Group of Yr., 2001, Entertainer of Yr., 2001, Favorite Musical Group or Band, People's Choice Award, 2002, Vocal Group of Yr., Country Music Assn., 2002, others; named one of 100 Most Influential People, Time Mag., 2006. Office: c/o Sony BMG Music 1400 18th Ave S Nashville TN 37212-2809

ROBLES, JOSUE, JR., insurance company executive; b. Rio Piedras, PR, Jan. 24, 1946; B in Acctg., Kent State U., Ohio, 1972; MBA, Ind. State U., Terre Haute, 1979. Exec. v.p., chief adminstrv. officer, CFO, corp. treas. USAA (United Services Automobile Association), San Antonino, Tex., 1994—2007, pres., CEO San Antonio, 2007—. Mem. Def. Base Closure and Realignment Commn., 1995; bd. dirs. DTE Energy Co., 2003—. Advanced through grades to maj. gen., comdr. 1st Infantry Div. US Army, 1966—94, ret. US Army, 1994. Office: USAA 9800 Fredericksburg Rd San Antonio TX 78288-0002 Office Phone: 210-498-2211.

ROBO, JAMES L., utilities executive; BA summa cum laude, Harvard Coll.; MBA, Harvard Bus. Sch. V.p. Strategic Planning Assocs.; various positions including gen. mgr. distbn. ops. GE Lighting, gen. mgr. Six Sigma GE Lighting, pres. and CEO GE Mex. General Electric Co., pres., CEO Capital TIP/Modular Space; pres. FPL Energy, LLC, 2002—06; v.p. corp. devel. and strategy FPL Group, Inc., Juno Beach, Fla., 2002—06, pres., COO, 2006—08, NextEra Energy, Inc. (formerly FPL Group, Inc.), Juno Beach, Fla., 2010—. Bd. dirs. J.B. Hunt Transport Svcs., Inc., Lowell, Ark., 2003—. Mem.: Phi Beta Kappa. Office: NextEra Energy Inc 700 Universe Blvd Juno Beach FL 33408-0420

ROBREDO, TOMMY, professional tennis player; b. Hostalric, Spain, May 1, 1982; s. Angel and Dolores. Profl. tennis player ATP, 1998—. Achievements include winner 9 career singles titles, 2 career doubles title, ATP; winner (singles) Sopot, 2001, Barcelona, 2004, Masters Series Hamburg, 2006, Swedish Open, 2006, 2008 Orange Prokom Open, 2007, Open de Moselle, 2007, Brasil Open, 2009, Copa Telmex, 2009; winner (doubles) Chennai, 2004, Monte-Carlo, 2008; Number 1 junior tennis player in Spain, 2000.

ROBSON, DONALD, physics professor; b. Leeds, Eng., Mar. 19, 1937; came to U.S., 1963; s. Albert and Rose Hannah (Parbutt) Robson; m. Joy Olivia Burkitt Findlay, Aug. 1960 (div. May 1971); children: Donald Peter, David Ian, Karen Joy; m. Martha Breitenlohner, Aug. 26, 1971 (div. Sept. 1999); m. Kimberly G. Kitchen, Dec. 18, 1999; 1 child, Nadirah Berge. BSc, U. Melbourne, Australia, 1959, MSc, 1961, PhD, 1963. Rsch. assoc. Fla. State U., Tallahassee, 1963-64, asst. prof. physics, 1964-65, assoc. prof., 1965-67, prof., 1967—, chmn. dept. physics, 1985-91, Disting. prof., 1990—2003, emeritus prof., 2003—. Editor: (with J.D. Fox) Isobaric Spin in Nuclear Physics, 1966, Nuclear Analogue States, 1976; assoc. editor Nuclear Physics A., 1972-96; contbr. more than 100 articles to profl. jours. Chmn. bd. trustees Southeastern Univ. Rsch. Assn., 1996-98. Fulbright scholar, 1963-64; A.P. Sloan fellow, 1966-67; Alexander Von Humboldt sr. scientist, 1976-77. Fellow Am. Phys. Soc. (co-recipient Tom W. Bonner prize 1972). Avocations: chess, golf, running. Office: Fla State U Dept Physics Tallahassee FL 32306 Office Phone: 850-644-1767. Business E-Mail: robson@csit.fsu.edu.

ROBY, MARTHA D., United States Representative from Alabama; b. Montgomery, Ala., July 26, 1976; m. Riley Roby; children: Margaret, George. BA in Music, NYU, NYC, 1988; JD, Samford U., Birmingham, Ala., 2001. Atty. Copeland, Franco, Screws & Gill; mem., Dist. 7 Montgomery City Coun., 2003—10; mem. US Congress from 2nd Ala. Dist., 2011—, US House Agrl. Com., 2011—, US House Edn. & Workforce Com., 2011—, US House Armed Services Com., 2011—. Mem. Montgomery Area Bus. Com. for the Arts; mem. exec. bd. Montgomery Weed & Seed; bd. dir. Sav-A-Life Montgomery. Mem.: Ala. Bar Assn., Miss. Bar Assn., Cleveland Ave. YMCA, Britton YMCA. Republican. Presbyterian. Office: US House of Representatives 428 Cannon House Office Bldg Washington DC 20515 Office Phone: 202-225-2901. Office Fax: 202-225-8913.*

ROCHE, CATHY, energy executive; m. Terry Roche; 2 children. BA in Journalism, U. NC, Chapel Hill. Reporter AP, Charlotte News; self-employed pub. rels. cons., 1980—83; dir. publs. Duke Power Co., 1983—89; v.p. pub. and industry comm. Nuc. Energy Inst., Washington, 1989—96; v.p. corp. comm. Entergy Corp., New Orleans, 1996—99; dir. external rels. pub. affairs dept. Duke Energy, Charlotte, NC, 2000—03, v.p. corp. comm., 2003—06, sr. v.p., chief comm. officer, 2006—. Bd. visitors U. NC Sch. Journalism; bd. visitors Carolina Environ. Prog. U. NC, Chapel Hill. Office: Duke Energy 526 S Church St Charlotte NC 28202-1904 Office Phone: 704-594-6200.

ROCK, DOUGLAS LAWRENCE, former manufacturing executive; b. Glen Cove, NY, Jan. 25, 1947; s. Herb and Beatrice (Vyse) R.; m. Cindy Pegoraro, May 11, 1967 (div. Apr. 1973); 1 child, Jason; m. Mary Sue Bell, Mar. 23, 1991 (div. Jan. 1996); m. Julie Rock BS in Psychology and Chemistry, Pa. State U., 1968; postgrad., U. Chgo., 1971-73. Rsch. chemist FMC Corp., Princeton, NJ, 1968-69; mfg. system project leader A.O. Smith Corp., Erie, Pa., 1969-71; dir. materials & info. systems Joy Mfg., Michigan City, Ind., 1971-74; dir. info. systems Smith Tool div. Smith Internat. Inc., Irvine, Calif., 1974-75, dir. materials, 1975-77, v.p. mfg., 1977-80, sr. v.p. ops., 1980-82, pres., 1985-87, Drilco div. Smith Internat. Inc., Houston, 1982-85; pres., CEO Smith International, Inc., Houston, 1987—91, chmn., pres., CEO, 1991—2008, chmn., pres., CEO, COO, 2008, chmn., 2009—10. Bd. dirs. CE Franklin Ltd, 1999-2008, Trinity Industries Inc., 2010-; co-founder Pa. State U. Rock Ethics Inst., 2002- Named Golden Knight, Nat. Mgmt. Assn., 1983. Mem. Internat. Assn. Drilling Contractors, American Petroleum Inst., Petroleum Equipment Suppliers Assn. (bd. dirs. Houston chpt. 1987—, 1st v.p. 1996), Nat. Offshore Industries Assn. (finance com. 1988, audit com. 1989), Greenspoint Club. Avocations: golf, racquetball, reading.

ROCK, JOHN AUBREY, gynecologist, obstetrician, educator, administrator, emeritus chancellor; b. Corpus Christi, Tex., Oct. 21, 1946; s. William A. and Burta (Wheeler) R.; children: John Aubrey Jr., Deborah Ellen, Daniel Authur; m. Martha Miller. BS in Zoology, La. State U., Baton Rouge, 1968; MD, La. State U., New Orleans, 1972; MS in Healthcare Mgmt., Harvard U., 2003. From asst. prof. to prof. ob-gyn. Sch. Medicine Johns Hopkins U., Balt., 1978-80, prof. pediatrics Sch. Medicine, 1988-92, dir. reproductive endocrinology Sch. Medicine, 1979-91, dep. dir. Sch. Medicine, 1985-88; chmn. Union Meml. Hosp., Balt., 1991-92; James Robert McCord prof., chmn. dept. ob-gyn. Emory U. Sch. Medicine, Atlanta, 1992—2002; chancellor La. State U. Health Scis. Ctr., New Orleans, 2002—06, chancellor emeritus, prof. ob-gyn., pediat. and pub. health, 2002—07; sr. v.p. health affairs Fla. Internat. U., Miami, 2007—. Cons. Dept. Army, Washington, 1982-93, NASA, Houston, 1988—; chmn. ad hoc com. on in vitro fertilization State of Md., 1985. Author: Reparative and Constructive Surgery of the Female Generative Tract, 1983, Endometriosis, 1988, TeLinde's Operative Gynecology, 1991, 9th edit., 2003, Reproductive Endocrinology, Surgery and Technology, 1995; mem. editl. bd. Fertility and Sterility jour., 1986-94, Gynecology Surgery, 1989—. Fellow ACOG; mem. Am. Gynecol. and Obstet. Soc., Soc. Gynecol. Surgeons (pres. 1998-99), Am. Soc. for Reproductive Medicine (pres. 1996-97), Soc. Gynecologic Investigation, Soc. Reproductive Surgeons (pres. 1986), World Endometriosis Soc. (pres. 2000-02), Rotary, Phi Kappa Phi, Alpha Omega Alpha. Methodist. Office Phone: 305-348-0570. Business E-Mail: rockj@fiu.edu.

ROCK, MEGAN, broadcast executive; B in Bus. Psychology, Miami U., Oxford, Ohio; Exec. Mgmt. Program, Harvard U., 2007. Various sales & mktg. positions Alvarez & Marsal Bus. Consulting, LLC, MediaOne; regional dir. Fox Family Channel; dir. sales & mktg. Turner Broadcasting Systems, Inc.; mktg. & promotions mgr. Comcast Spotlight (formerly Cable Adv. Metro Atlanta); various positionsincluding dir. local ad sales and dir. domestic distbn. Discovery Communications, Inc., Atlanta, v.p. domestic distbn., 2009—10; v.p. partnership mktg. & ops. Weather Channel Companies, Atlanta, 2010—. Mem.: Cable & Telecomm. Assn. Mktg., Women in Cable Telecomm. Office: TWCC 300 Interstate N Pkwy Atlanta GA 30339 Office Phone: 240-662-2000. Office Fax: 240-662-1868. Business E-Mail: megan_rock@discovery.com.

ROCKEFELLER, JAY (JOHN DAVISON ROCKEFELLER IV), United States Senator from West Virginia; b. NYC, June 18, 1937; s. John Davison III and Blanchette Ferry (Hooker) R.; m. Sharon Percy, Apr. 1, 1967; children: John, Valerie, Charles, Justin. Student, Japanese lang. Internat. Christian U., Tokyo, 1957-60; BA in Far Eastern Languages and History, Harvard U., 1961, MA, 1954—57; postgrad. in Chinese, Yale U., 1961-62. Mem. nat. adv. council Peace Corps, 1961, spl. asst. to dir. corps, 1962, ops. officer in charge work in Philippines, until 1963; desk officer for Indonesian affairs, Bur. Ea. Affairs US Dept. State, 1963; cons. Pres.'s Commn. on Juvenile Delinquency and Youth Crime, 1964; mem. W.Va. Ho. of Delegates, 1966-68; sec. state State of W.Va., Charleston, W.Va., 1968-72, gov., 1977—85; pres. W.Va. Wesleyan Coll., Buckhannon, 1973-75; US Senator from W.Va., 1985—; mem. US Senate Finance Com., Joint Com. on Taxation, US Senate Veterans Affairs Com., chmn., 1993—95, 2001, 2001—03, US Senate Select Com. on Intelligence, 2007—09, US Senate Commerce, Sci. & Transp. Com., 2009—. Contbr. articles to mags. including N.Y. Times Sunday mag. Trustee U. Chgo., 1967—; chmn. The White House Conf. Balanced Nat. Growth & Econ. Devel., 1978, Pres.'s Commn. on Coal, 1978-80, White House Adv. Com. on Coal., 1980 Recipient Excellence in Public Svc. award, American Acad. Pediatrics, 1990, Congressional Adv. of Yr. award, Child Welfare League of America, 1997, Langer Chip award, Sci. Coalition, 1999, Award Excellence in Public Svc., Consortium Sch. Networking, 2002, Wellstone award, United Steelworkers of America, 2003; named one of Top 200 Collectors, ARTnews Mag., 2004—08. Mem.: Nat. Gov. Assn. Democrat. Presbyn. Avocation: collecting 19th-century Am. art and Am. impressionism. Office: US Senate 531 Hart Senate Bldg Washington DC 20510-0001 also: District Office Ste 308 405 Capitol St Charleston WV 25301-1786 Office Phone: 202-224-6472, 304-347-5372. Office Fax: 202-224-7665, 202-228-4656, 304-347-5371. Business E-Mail: senator@rockefeller.senate.gov.*

ROCKEFELLER, SHARON PERCY, broadcast executive; b. Oakland, Calif., Dec. 10, 1944; d. Charles H. and Jeanne (Dickerson) Percy; m. John D. (Jay) Rockefeller IV; children: John, Valerie, Charles, Justin. BA cum laude, Stanford U., 1966; DPS (hon.), Alderson-Broaddus Coll., 1977; LLD (hon.), U. Charleston, 1977, Beloit Coll., 1978; LHD (hon.), West Liberty State Coll., 1980, Hamilton Coll., 1982, Wheeling Coll., 1984. Founder, chmn. Mountain Artisans, 1968—78; teacher's asst., Head Start Head Start program, Coal Branch Heights, W.Va.; chmn. Corp. Pub. Broadcasting, Washington, 1981—84; bd. dirs. Stas. WETA-TV-FM, Washington, 1987—89, pres., CEO, 1989—. Former chmn. Va. Assn. Pub. TV Stas.; bd. dirs. Pub. Broadcasting Svc., W.Va. Edn. Broadcasting Authority, Corp. for Pub. Broadcasting, PepsiCo, Smithsonian Instn., Nat. Gallery of Art, Nat. Cathedral, Stanford Univ., Chgo. Univ., George Washington Univ., Phillips Collection, Colonial Williamsburg Found., Rockefeller Bros. Fund, Rockefeller Family Office, NYC; trustees coun. Nat. Gallery of Art. Adv. bd. Nat. Women's Polit. Caucus, 1975—; adv. bd., bd. dirs. Women's Campaign Fund, 1975—81; co-chairwoman ERAmerica, 1972—82; mem.-at-large Dem. Nat. Conv., del., 1976, 1980, 1984; mem.-at-large Dem. Nat. Com., 1980—; trustee Fed. City Coun.; bd. mem. Day Care and Child Devel. Coun. America, 1969—72; former mem. bd. dir. Sunrise Mus., W.Va.; bd. mem. Sotheby's, NYC, Colonial Williamsburg Found; mem. internat. coun. Mus. Modern Art, NYC, 1973—81; former chmn. Va. Assn. Pub. TV Stas. Recipient Charles Frankel Prize, Nat. Endowment for the Humanities, 1994, Distinguished Broadcaster Award, 1994, Woman of Vision Award, Women in Film & Video, CINE Lifetime Achievement Award; named Washingtonian of Yr., Washingtonian Mag., 1994; named one of Top 200 Collectors, ARTnews Mag., 2004—08. Fellow: Am. Acad. Arts & Sciences, Smithsonian Am. Art Commn. (bd. mem.); mem.: Stanford-in-Washigngton Coun. (former chmn.). Avocation: collecting 19th-century Am. art and Am. impressionism. Office: Sta WETA-FM 2775 S Quincy St Arlington VA 22206-2236

ROCKETT, D. JOE, lawyer, director; b. Drumright, Okla., May 3, 1942; s. Gordon Richard and Hazel Peggy (Rigsby) R.; m. Mary Montgomery, Aug. 31, 1963; children: David Montgomery, Ann Morley. BA, U. Okla., 1964, JD, 1967. Bar: Okla. 1967, U.S. Dist. Ct. (we. dist.) Okla. 1968. Assoc. Kerr, Davis, Irvine & Burbage, Oklahoma City, 1967-69, Andrews Davis Legg Bixler Milsten & Price, Oklahoma City, 1969—, mem., 1973—, also bd. dirs., pres., 1986-90, 96-00. Securities law advisor Oil Investment Inst., Washington, 1984-87. Bd. dirs. Myriad Gardens Found., Oklahoma City, 1987—, chmn., 1991-92. Mem. ABA (fed. regulation of securities and partnership coms. of bus. law sect. 1984), Okla. Bar Assn. (securities liaison com. 1983, chmn. bus. assocs. sect. 1985, securities adminstr.'s select com. 1986—), Meritas Law Firms Worldwide (bd. dirs. 2006-09). Avocations: sailing, fishing, skiing. Office: Andrews Davis 100 N Broadway Ste 3300 Oklahoma City OK 73102-8812 Business E-Mail: djrockett@andrewsdavis.com.

ROCKINGHAM, P.Y., consumer products company executive; m. Darrel Rockingham. BA in Pub. Rels. & Journalism, McKendree Coll.; MA in Orgnl. Communication, Western Mich. U. V.p., cmty. rels. & comm. Jarden Consumer Solutions (subs. Jarden Corp.). Mem. Nat. Coun. of Negro Women, Nat. Urban League, Exec. Leadership Coun., INROADS, Nat. Assn. of Black/Hispanic Journalists, Boca Raton C. of C., Am. Heart Assn., Am. Cancer Soc., Gilda's Club, OS Children's Villages, Fla.; bd. dirs., Broward County Chapter Am. Red Cross; vice chmn. March of Dimes, Palm Beach; chmn. Cooperative Feeding Program; bd. advisor Women that Win. Office: Jarden Consumer Solutions 2381 Northwest Executive Ctr Dr Boca Raton FL 33431 Office Phone: 561-912-4100. Business E-Mail: rrockingham@jardencs.com.

RODAY, LEON E., lawyer, finance company executive; b. 1954; BA, U. Calif., Santa Barbara; JD, Brooklyn Law Sch. Assoc. LeBoeuf, Lamb, Greene & MacRae, LLP, 1982—91, ptnr., 1991—96; sr. v.p., gen. counsel, sec. GE Financial, 1996—2004, Genworth

Financial, Inc., Richmond, Va., 2004—. Chmn. Ins. Marketplace Standards Assn., 2005. Mem.: NY Bar Assn. Office: Genworth Financial, Inc 6620 W Broad St Richmond VA 23230 Office Fax: 804-281-6000.*

RODBELL, CLYDE ARMAND, retired distribution executive; b. Atlanta, Aug. 16, 1927; s. Joseph Hirsch and Fannie (Turetzky) R.; m. Cecile Rosenson, Mar. 27, 1949 (div.); children: Marsha, Jeffrey, Keith, Kim; m. Robin Graham McKenzie Rodbell, Dec. 15, 1974; 1 child, Lindsey. BBA, Emory U., 1949. Chmn. Apex Supply Co. Inc., Atlanta, 1949—2002. Co-chmn. George Bush Presdl. Fund Raising, Ga., 1988-89; mem. State of Ga. Electoral Coll., 1989, exec. commr. Am. Bicentenial Pres. Inaugural Bus. Adv., 1989, Pres' Commn. on White House Fellowships, 1989-92. With U.S. Army, 1945. Mem. Wholesale Assn. Ga., Southern Wholesalers Assn., Am. Supply Assn., Standard Club, Rotary Club. Republican. Jewish. Avocations: reading, gardening, antiques, politics. Personal E-mail: rrodbell@aol.com.

RODDICK, ANDY STEPHEN, retired professional tennis player; b. Omaha, Aug. 30, 1982; s. Jerry and Blanche Roddick; m. Brooklyn Decker, Apr. 17, 2009. Profl. tennis player ATP, 2000—12. Mem. US nat. tennis team Summer Olympic Games, Athens, 2004, London, 2012; spokesman Lacoste for Men, 2010. Host: Saturday Night Live, 2003. Founder The Andy Roddick Found. Recipient Arthur Ashe Humanitarian award, ATP, 2004; named to President's Coun. of Sports and Fitness, Pres. George W. Bush, 2006. Achievements include winner of 32 ATP singles titles; winner of 4 ATP doubles titles; winner of Grand Slam title: US Open, 2003. Avocations: movies, music, skydiving. Office: Andy Roddick Foundation 5458 Town Center Rd Ste 8 Boca Raton FL 33486-1026

RODENBERGER, CHARLES ALVARD, aerospace engineer, consultant; b. Muskogee, Okla., Sept. 11, 1926; s. Darcy Owen and Kathryn Martha (Percival) R.; m. Molcie Lou Halsell, Sept. 3, 1949 (dec. April 9, 2009); children: Kathryn Sue Wilcox, Charles Mark; m. Nancy Johnston, April 17, 2011. Student, U. Ark., 1944—45; BS in Gen. Engring., Okla. State U., 1948; MSM.E., So. Meth. U., 1959; PhD in Aero. Engring., U. Tex.-Austin, 1968. Registered profl. engr., Tex. Petroleum engr. Amoco Oil Co., Levelland, Tex., 1948-51; chief engr. McGregor Bros., Odessa, Tex., 1953; petroleum engr. Gen. Crude Oil Co., Hamlin, Tex., 1954; sr. design engr. Gen. Dynamics, Ft. Worth, 1954-60; aerospace engr. NASA, Houston, summer 1962; prof. aerospace engring. Tex. A&M U., College Station, 1960-82, prof. emeritus, 1982—; chmn. bd. Meiller Research, Inc., College Station, 1967-82; pres. JETS, Inc., NYC, 1977-79; cons. Southwest Research Inst., Gen. Motors Corp., Gen. Dynamics. Patentee hypervelocity gun and orthotic device; newspaper columnist: Livestock Weekly, 1986—; mag. columnist, Santa Gertrudis, Tex., 2002. Bd. dirs. Cross Plains Pub. Libr., 1986—2011, pres., treas.; meth. Sunday sch. tchr., 1984—2012. Served with USAAF, 1945, served with USAF, 1951—53. NSF fellow, 1964-65; recipient Disting. Teaching award Tex. A&M U., 1962 Fellow AIAA (assoc.); mem. ASME, NSPE (v.p. 1980-81), Tex. Soc. Profl. Engrs., Am. Soc. for Engring. Edn., Creation Rsch. Soc., Sigma Xi, Kiwanis Club (pres. Cross Plains chpt. 2002-03, 2010-11). Methodist. Home: PO Box 5464 Granbury TX 76049-0464 Office Phone: 254-653-7551. Personal E-mail: crodenberg@aol.com. Business E-Mail: car926@aol.com.

RODGERS, JOHN HUNTER, lawyer; b. Lubbock, Tex., Jan. 18, 1944; s. James O'Donnell Rodgers and Dorothy (Ulin) Carpenter; m. Anne C. Smith, Nov. 29, 1969; children: Anne Elizabeth, Catherine Hunter Rodgers Flaming. BA, Tex. A&M, 1966; JD, U. Tex., 1969. Bar: Tex. 1969, U.S. Supreme Ct. 1973. Atty. The Southland Corp., Dallas, 1973-79, gen. counsel, 1979-91, sec., 1987-95, sr. v.p., chief adminstrv. officer, 1991-93, exec. v.p., chief adminstrv. officer, 1993-95; pres. Clairemead Corp., Dallas, 1996-2000; sr. v.p., gen. counsel, sec. Am. Pad & Paper Co., Dallas, 1998-2000, pres., 2000—04; prin. J. Hunter & Assocs., Dallas, 2003—; bd. dirs. Promising Youth Alliance, 2009—, chmn., 2009—10, pres., CEO, 2010. Mem. visual arts com. Tex. A&M U., 1985-94, bd. dirs. student fund enrichment bd., 1986-94; mem. exec. com. Jr. Achievement Dallas, 1988-93; mem. Dallas Citizens Coun., 1992-95; bd. dirs. Boys and Girls Clubs of Greater Dallas, 1998—, vice chmn., 2003-04, chmn., 2005—07; nat. chair Tulane U. Parents Coun., 1997-98; trustee Goals for Dallas, 1991-92; bd. trustees The Sci. Pl. Mus., 2004-06, Dallas Mus. Nature and Sci., 2006-07, Perot Mus. Nature and Sci., 2008-; nat. bd. dirs. Boys and Girls Clubs Am., 1993-98; mem. mktg. com. Dallas Mus. Art, 1994-97; bd. mem. Friends of War, 2012-, pres., 2014. Capt. JAGC, US Army, 1969-73, Vietnam. Mem. ABA, Tex. Bar Assn. (coun. mem. corp. counsel sect. 1988), Dallas Bar Assn., Southwestern Legal Found. (adv. bd. Internat. and Comparative Law Ctr., rsch. fellow 1986-94), Nat. Assn. Convenience Stores (bd. dirs. 1993-95). Roman Catholic. Office: 4144 North Central Express Way Ste 518 Dallas TX 75204 Office Phone: 214-219-7771. E-mail: Jhunterlp@sbcglobal.net.

RODGERS, MARGARET CATHARINE, federal judge; b. Pensacola, Fla., 1964; BA, U. West Fla., 1989; JD, Calif. Western Sch. Law, 1992. Law clk. to Hon. Lacey A. Collier US Dist. Ct. (northern dist.) Fla., 1992—94; pvt. practice atty. Pensacola, Fla., 1994—98, 1999—2002; gen. counsel West Fla. Med. Ctr., Pensacola, 1998—99; magistrate judge US Dist. Ct. (northern dist.) Fla., 2002—03, judge, 2003—, chief judge, 2011—. Served in US Army, 1985—87. Office: US Dist Ct US Courthouse 1 N Palafox St Pensacola FL 32502 Office Phone: 850-435-8448. Office Fax: 850-437-7897.

RODGMAN, ALAN, chemist, consultant; b. Aberdare, Wales, Feb. 7, 1924; came to U.S. from Canada, 1954, naturalized, 1961; s. Arch and Margaret (Llewellyn) R.; m. Doris Curley, June 7, 1947; children: Eric, Paul, Mark. BA in Chemistry, U. Toronto, 1949, MA in Organic Chemistry, 1951, PhD in Organic Chemistry, 1953. Rsch. asst. med. rsch. dept. U. Toronto, 1947-51, rsch. assoc., 1951-54; tchr., courses in organic chemistry, phys. chemistry, math. Chem. Inst. Can., 1951-54; sr. rsch. chemist R.J. Reynolds Tobacco Co., Winston-Salem, N.C., 1954-65, head smoke rsch. sect., 1965-75, mgr. analytical rsch., 1975-76, dir. rsch., 1976-80, dir. fundamental rsch. and devel., 1980-87; cons. in field, 1987—. Co-author: (T. A. Perfetti) The Chemical Components of Tobacco and Tobacco Smoke, 2008, The Chemical Components of Tobacco and Tobacco Smoke 2nd Edit., 2013; mem. editl. bd. Tobacco Sci., 1963-67 (Vol. 31 Tobacco Sci. dedicated in his name 1987), Beitrage zur Tabakforschung Internat., 1978-87. Mem. Tobacco Working Group, Nat. Cancer Inst., 1976-77, Tech. Study Group on Cigarette and Little Cigar Fire Safety, 1984-87, Sci. Commn. Cooperation Ctr. for Sci. Rsch. Relative to Tobacco, 1982-84. With Royal Can. Navy, 1942-45. Recipient Tobacco Sci. Rsch. Conf. Inaugural Lifetime Achievement award, 2003; co-recipient prize, CORESTA, 2010. Mem. Coun. Tobacco Rsch. (industry tech. com. 1956-62), Chem. Inst. Can., Can. Chem. Soc., Am. Chem. Soc. Episcopalian. Home: 2828 Birchwood Dr Winston Salem NC 27103-3410 E-mail: arodgman@triad.rr.com.

RODI, THOMAS JOHN, archbishop; b. New Orleans, Mar. 27, 1949; BA, Georgetown U., 1971; JD, Tulane U. Law Sch., 1974; MDiv, Notre Dame Sem., 1978; JCL in Canon Law, Cath. Am. U., Washington, 1986. Ordained priest Archdiocese of New Orleans, 1978; assoc. pastor St. Ann, Metairie, Miss., St. Christopher, Metairie, St. Agnes, Jefferson, Miss.; judge Met. Tribunal; prof. canon law Notre Dame Sem., 1986—95; ordained bishop, 2001; bishop Diocese of Biloxi, Miss., 2001—08; archbishop Archdiocese of Mobile, Ala., 2008—. Dir., Office Religious Edn. Notre Dame Sem., 1988—89, exec. dir., dept. pastoral svcs., 1989—96. Named a Prelate of Honor, 1992. Office: Archdiocese of Mobile PO Box 1966 400 Government St Mobile AL 36633 Office Phone: 334-434-1585. Office Fax: 334-434-1588.

RODMAN, LEIBA, mathematician; b. Riga, Latvia, June 9, 1949; arrived in U.S., 1985; s. Zalman and Haya Rodman; m. Ella Levitan, Feb. 2, 1983; children: Daniel, Ruth, Benjamin, Naomi. Diploma in maths., Latvian State U., 1971; MA in Statis., Tel Aviv U., 1976, PhD in Maths., 1978. Instr. Tel Aviv U., 1976-78, sr. lectr., 1981-83, assoc. prof., 1983-85; postdoctoral fellow U. Calgary, Can., 1978-80; from assoc. to full prof. Ariz. State U., Tempe, 1985-87; prof. math. Coll. William and Mary, Williamsburg, Va., 1987—. Author: Introduction to Operator Polynomials, 1989, (with others) Matrix Polynomials, 1982, Matrices and Indefinite Scalar Products, 1983, Invariant Subspaces of Matrices with Applications, 1986, Interpolation of Rational Matrix Functions, 1990, Algebraic Riccati Equations, 1995, Indefinite Linear Algebra and Applications, 2005; co-editor: Contributions to Operator Theory and Its Applications, 1988, Current Trends in Operator Theory and its Applications, 2004, Topics in Operator Theory, Vols. I And II, 2010. Mem. Am. Math. Soc., Internat. Linear-Algebra Soc., Soc. Indsl. and Applied Math. Office: Coll of William & Mary Dept Math PO Box 8795 Williamsburg VA 23187-8795 Office Phone: 757-221-2027. E-mail: lxrodm@math.wm.edu.

RODNING, CHARLES BERNARD, surgeon; b. Pipestone, Minn., Aug. 4, 1943; s. Selmer Bernard and Ida Amanda (Selness) R.; m. Mary Elizabeth Lipke, June 15, 1968; children: Christopher Bernard, Soren Piers, Kai Johannes. BS, Gustavus Adolphus Coll., St. Peter, Minn., 1965; MD, U. Rochester, 1970; PhD, U. Minn., 1979. Diplomate Am. Bd. Med. Examiners, Am. Bd. Surgery. Intern, asst. resident dept. surgery U. Rochester Sch. Medicine and Dentistry, 1970-72; assoc. resident to chief resident, med. fellow dept. surgery U. Minn. Health Scis. Ctr., Mpls., 1972-79; prof. dept cell biology and neurosci. U. South Ala., Mobile, 1981—, prof. dept. surgery, 1981—, vice chmn. dept. surgery, 1981—2006, chmn. dept. surgery, 2006—, dir. gen. surgery, 1996—; pres. Med. Soc., County Mobile, 2010—; pres. ala. chpt. ACS, 2010—. Field liaison physician Commn. on Cancer-ACS, Chgo., 1984—; mem. med. adv. bd. Ala. Organ & Tissue Ctr., Birmingham, 1988—; mem. Bd. Health County of Mobile, pres., 2007, counsellor, Med. Assn. State Ala., 2011. Author: Elan Vital, 1988, Wode and Ston, 1988, Sorrowful Wheel, 1989, Ponderings, 1990, The Sea Rises in the West, 1991, Stepping Stones, 1991, Snowbound Below the Firn Line, 1991, Love Knot, 1994, Papering Dreams, 1994, Carry Onward, 1996, Swaying Grass, 1998, Tradition of Excellence: Pictorial History of Surgical Education at the Mobile General Hospital and University of South Alabama College of Medicine and Medical Center, 1999; reviewer: Jour. Histochem. Cytochem., 1988—; contbr. (articles) Clin. Anatomy, Surg. Endoscopy, Pharos, Jours. Thoracic Cardiovasc. Surgery, So. Med. Jour., others. Bd. dirs. Mobile Mental Health Ctr., Mental Health Found. of South Ala., Mobile Med. Mus., Christian Med. Ministry of South Ala., bd. trustees; sec.-treas. bd. censors Med. Soc. Mobile County, 2006. Comdr. USN, 1974-81. Recipient Physicians Recognition award AMA, 1980, 85, 88, 91, 95, 99, 02, Bacaner Rsch. award Minn. Med. Found., 1979, Humanism in Medicine award Arnold P. Gold Found., Healthcare Found. N.J., 2002, Howard L. Holley award Med. Assn. State Ala., 2002, Disting. Svc. award Alumni Assn., South Ala., 2010 Fellow ACS (mem, exec. coun.), Internat. Coll. Surgeons (vice regent Ala. chpt. 1989—); mem. Iota Delta Gamma, Alpha Omega Alpha, Phi Kappa Phi, Gold Humanism Honor Soc, Med. Soc. County Mobile, (sec.-treas. 2007, mem. bd. censors, 2006, 08, v.p. 2008, pres.-elect 2009, pres. 2010), Ala. Chapter Am. Coll. Surgeons (sec., treas., 2008, pres.-elect 2009, pres. 2010). Office: U South Ala Coll Med Allied Health Professions Mobile AL 36617-2293 Office Phone: 251-471-7034. Business E-Mail: crodning@usouthal.edu.

RODRIGUEZ, ANNABELLE, territorial supreme court justice, former attorney general; b. Santurce, PR, 1953; m. Francisco de Jesus-Schuck; children: Ricardo Enrique Candle, Fernando Manuel Vela. BA in history magna cum laude, U. PR, JD, 1985. From asst. solicitor gen. to solicitor gen. PR Dept. Justice, 1986—93; ptnr. Martino, Odell & Calabria, Hato Rey, PR, 1993—96; judge US Dist Ct. (PR dist.), 1996; sec. justice PR, 2001—04; assoc. judge PR Supreme Ct., 2004—. Democrat. Office: Tribunal Supremo de PR PO Box 2392 San Juan PR 00902*

RODRIGUEZ, EDDIE, state legislator; b. McAllen, July 1, 1971; Studied, St. Mary's U., San Antonio; BA in Govt., U. Tex., 1995; JD, U. Tex. Sch. Law, 2008. Mem. Dist. 51 Tex. House of Representatives, 2002—. Bd. pres. Austin Pets Alive!. Democrat. Office: Room E2.408 Capitol Extension PO Box 2910 Austin TX 78768 Office Fax: 512-463-0314.

RODRIGUEZ, EDUARDO ROBERTO, lawyer; b. Edinburg, Tex., 1943; BA, George Wash. U., 1965; JD, U. Tex., 1968. Bar: Tex. 1968, U.S. Dist. Ct. (so. dist. Tex.) 1969, U.S. Ct. Appeals (5th Cir.) 1969, U.S. Supreme Ct. 1971. Sr. ptnr. Rodriguez & Nicolas LLP, Brownsville, Tex. Lectr. in field; v.p. Tex. adv. coun. Nat. Legal Svcs. Corp., 1976—78; mem. bd. disciplinary appeals Supreme Ct. Tex., 1991, mem. task for on discovery, 1991; bd. advisors Tex. Jour. Law and Pub. Policy U. Tex. Sch. Law, 2001—02, pres. law alumni com., 2001, mem. dean's roundtable, 1992. Chmn. Greater Brownsville Incentives Corp., 1997—98; bd. dirs. Brownsville Pub. Libr. Found., Inc., 1992; dir. Brownsville Boys' Club, 1973, basketball coach, Brownsville Girls' Club; mem. Downtown Devel. Corp. Brownsville, 1991; dir. Driscoll Found. Children's Hosp. Corpus Christi, 1969—77. Fellow: Tex. Bar Found. (mem. adv. bd. 1994); mem.: ABA (standing com. fed. jud. improvements 1991, ho. of delegates 1991—95, mem. nom. com. 1996—97, presdl. adv. coun. diversity in the profession 2002, chmn. Hispanic-Am. lawyers com., mem. drug and alcohol abuse com. criminal justice sect.), Mex. Am. Assn. Houston, Hispanic Nat. Bar Assn., Tex. Criminal Def. Lawyers Assn. (dir.), State Bar Tex. (dir. 1987—90, exec. com. 1988—90, pres.-elect 2004—), Cameron County Bar Assn. (law day chmn. 1970—71, dir. 1972—74, v.p. 1974—75, pres. 1975), Internat. Assn. Def. Counsel (mem. gen. convention com. 1994—95), Philosophical Soc. Tex., Am. Law Inst., Tex. Assn. Def. Counsel (v.p. 1992—96, mem. political action com. 2000—), Product Liability Advisory Coun., Inc., Kiwanis Club (v.p. 1971—72, pres. 1972—73). Office: Rodriguez & Nicolas LLP 50 W Morrison Rd Ste A Brownsville TX 78520 Office Phone: 956-574-9333. Office Fax: 956-574-9337. Business E-Mail: errodriguez@rodrigueznicolas.com.

RODRÍGUEZ, FÉLIX M., oil industry executive; Grad. in Petroleum Engring., U. Oriente, Venezuela; student in Sys. Analysis, Harvard U., Columbia U. With Corporación Venezolana de Petróleo, Exxon Rsch., ELF Aquitaine; dir. Nynas AB (Formerly known as Nynas Petroleum AB); v.p. Petróleos de Venezuela, S.A. (CITGO's ultimate parent co.), 2003; prin. dir. PDVSDA Fin. Ltd., 2003; dep. pres. CITGO Petroleum Corp., 2004—05, pres., CEO, 2005—. Prof., math. and stats. Ctrl. U. of Venezuela Sch. Geography; bd. dirs. Citgo Petroleum Corp. Office: CITGO Petroleum Corp 1293 Eldridge Pky Houston TX 77077 Office Phone: 832-486-4000. Office Fax: 832-486-1814.

RODRIGUEZ, JAMES G., councilman; m. Wendy Montoya, June 30, 2007. B in Bus. Adminstrn., U. Houston, 1998. Former staff mem. PaperCity Mag., Houston; mktg. dir. Entech Civil Engrs., Inc., Houston; councilman, Dist. I Houston City Coun., 2007—. Campaign mgr., chief of staff to councilwoman Carol Alvarado Houston City Coun., 2002—06; cons. Tony Sanchez for Gov. Campaign, Mayor Lee P. Brown Campaign. Vol. Al Gore Presdl. Campaign, Houston, 2000; coord. Houston Ind. Sch. Dist.'s Rebuild 2002 Bond Campaign; active Our Lady of Mt. Carmel Ch.; bd. dirs. El Centro de Corazon, Houston. Mem.: Tejano Assoc. Cmty. Concerns (bd. dirs.), Houston Hispanic Architects & Engrs., Harris County Tejano Dems., Greater East End C. of C., U. Houston Young Alumni Connection (adv, bd. mem.), Houston Alumni Orgn., Garden Villas Civic Club. Democrat. Office: City Hall Annex 900 Bagby 1st Fl Houston TX 77002 Office Phone: 832-393-3011. Office Fax: 713-247-3067. Business E-Mail: districti@cityofhouston.net.

RODRIGUEZ, MANUEL, JR., food products executive, lawyer; BS in Psychology, St. Joseph's Coll., cert. Latin Am. Studies; JD, U. Puerto Rico; LLM, Columbia U. Legal counsel, migration divsn. Govt. of Puerto Rico, dep. nat. dir. & dir. agrl. program, dir. medical plan for agrl. workers; various legal, govt., affairs, labor rels. positions Chiquita Brands International, Inc., 1980, v.p., govt. affairs, assoc., gen. counsel, 2003—04, sr. v.p., govt., internat. affairs, 2004—, corp. responsibility officer, 2005—. Recipient Protection of Puerto Rican Agrl. Workers, Bd. of Trustees of Group Ins. Fund, 1982, Recognition for Welfare in award, 1982, Outstanding Hispanic Achiever award, Internat. Hispanic Corp. Achiever's Scholarship Funds, Inc., 1988, Outstanding Individual Contribution, Chiquita Brands Internat., 1992, Outstanding Svc. in Connecting Cultures, Ohio commission on Hispanic and Latino Affairs, 2006, Resolution for Support and Dedication to Human and Civil Rights of Hispanic workers throughout L.Am., Ohio Civil Rights Commn., 2006. Office: Chiquita Brands International Inc 550 S Caldwell St Ste 1010 Charlotte NC 28202-2681 Office Phone: 513-784-8000. Business E-Mail: mrodriguez@chiquita.com.

RODRIGUEZ, PLACIDO, bishop; b. Celaya, Mex., Oct. 11, 1940; came to US, 1953; s. Eutimio and Maria Concepcion (Rosiles) Rodriguez. STB, STL, Cath. U., Washington, 1968; MA, Loyola U., 1971. Ordained priest Missionary Sons of the Immaculate Heart of Mary, 1968; pastor Our Lady Guadalupe Ch., Chgo., 1972-75, Our Lady of Fatima Ch., Perth Amboy, N.J., 1981-83; vocat. dir. Claretians, Chgo., 1975-81; ordained bishop, 1983; bishop aux. Archdiocese of Chgo., 1983-94; bishop Diocese of Lubbock, Tex., 1994—. Roman Catholic. Office: The Catholic Ctr PO Box 98700 Lubbock TX 79499-8700

RODRIGUEZ, RAY, retired broadcast executive; b. Camaguey, Cuba, Jan. 31, 1951; s. Ray and Maria (Tobin) Rodriguez; m. Liana Silvia Garcia, July 27, 1975; children: Liana Marie, Rainaldo Gabriel, Claudia Marie. BBA, U. Miami, 1973. Mgr. Deloitte Haskins & Sells CPAs, Miami, Fla., 1973-83; mgr., chief exec. officer Julio Iglesias, Miami, Fla., 1983-88; pres. Ray Rodriguez Co., Miami, Fla., 1988-90; v.p. and dir. of Talent Rels. Univision Holdings, Miami, 1990—91; sr. v.p. & operating mgr. Univision Networks, Miami, 1991—92, pres., 1992—2005, Univision's TeleFutura and Galavision Cable Network, Miami, 2001—05; pres. & COO Univision Comm. Inc., Miami, 2005—09. Mem. rep. bd. govs. Dade County, Fla., 1989—. Mem.: Kiwanis Little Havana Found. (chap. pres. 1987—, trustee, bd. dirs. 1974—88). Roman Catholic. Avocations: golf, boating, tennis.

RODRIGUEZ, XAVIER, federal judge; b. San Antonio, 1961; BA, Harvard U., 1983; MPA, JD, U. Tex., 1987. Cert.: Tex. Bd. Legal Specialization (labor and employment law). Ptnr. Fulbright & Jaworski; justice Supreme Ct. State of Tex., 2001—02; atty. pvt. practice, San Antonio, 2002—; judge US Dist. Ct. (we. dist.) Tex., 2003—. Served Judge Advs. Gen's. Corps.; lectr. continuing legal edn. courses. Contbr. chapters to books. Past pres. Respite Care San Antonio; San Antonio C. of C.; vice chmn. State Bd. Educator Certification; mem. bd. dirs. San Antonio Area Found.; mem. adv. bd. to dean St. Mary's U. Sch. Law, U. Tex. at San Antonio Coll. Social and Behavioral Scis. Officer USAR, 1983. Named 40 under 40 Rising Stars, San Antonio Bus. Jour. Fellow: Tex. Bar Found.; mem.: ABA, State Bar of Tex. (immediate past. chmn. labor and employment law sect., standing com. on legal assts.). Office: 300 Convent Ste 2200 San Antonio TX 78205 also: 655 E Durango Blvd San Antonio TX 78206

RODRIGUEZ-CAMILLONI, HUMBERTO LEONARDO, architect, historian, educator; b. Lima, Peru, May 30, 1945; came to U.S., 1963; s. Alfonso and Elda (Camilloni) R.; m. Mary Ann Alexanderson, July 1, 1972; children: Elizabeth Marie, William Howard. BA magna cum laude, Yale U., 1967, MArch, 1971, MPhil, 1973, PhD, 1981. Rsch. asst. Sch. Architecture Yale U., 1964-70, teaching fellow dept. history art, 1971-72, 74-75; chmn. research dept. Centro de Investigacion y Restauracion de Bienes Monumentales Instituto Nacional de Cultura, Lima, 1973; restoration architect OAS, Washington, 1976—; prof. Sch. Architecture Tulane U., New Orleans, 1975-82; prof., dir. Henry H. Wiss Ctr. Theory and History of Art and Architecture, Coll. Architecture and Urban Studies Va. Poly. Inst. and State U., Blacksburg, 1983—, dir. Ctr. for Preservation and Rehab. Tech., Coll. Architecture, 1986—. Vis. prof. U. Ill., Chgo., 1982-83; reviewer, cons. Choice, 1975—; interim bd. dirs. Ctr. Planning Handbook Latin-Am. Art, 1978-87; cons., adviser Internat. Exhbn. and Symposium Latin-Am. Baroque Art and Architecture, 1980; adv. bd. Mountain Lake Symposium on Art and Architecture Criticism, 1985—, Internat. Symposium Luis Barragan, 1990; coord., advisor exhbn. Tradition and Innovation: Painting, Architecture and Music in Brazil, Mex. and Venezuela between 1950-80, 1991, Internat. Art History Colloquium, 1993, Internat. Congress of Americanists, 1994, 97, 2006, 09, Frank Lloyd Wright: An Architect in America, 1995, Congress Internat. Union Architects, 1996, European Assn. for Archtl. Edn./Archtl. Rsch. Ctrs. Consortium Conf., 2000, The Jesuits, Conf. II: Cultures, Scis. and the Arts, 1540-1773, 2002, Internat. Congress on Constrn. History, 2003, 06-09, III Internat. Copan Maya Congress, 2007, 5th Internat. Congress ICOMOS Sci. Coun. 20th Architecture, 2008. Author: (with Walter D. Harris) The Growth of Latin American Cities, 1971; (with Charles Seymour, Jr.) Italian Primitives, The Case History of a Collection and its Conservation, 1972, Religious Architecture in Lima of the Seventeenth and Eighteenth Centuries: The Monastic Complex of San Francisco el Grande, 1984; contbg. editor Handbook of Latin American Studies, 1987—, The Retablo Facade as Transparency: A Study of the Frontispiece of San Francisco, Lima, 1991, Tradición e Innovación en la Arquitectura del Virreinato del Perú, Constantino de Vasconcelos y la Invención de la Arquitectura de Quincha en Lima Durante el Siglo XVII, 1994, (with Graziano Gasparini) Arquitectura Iberoamericana, 1997, Manuel de Amat y Junyent y la Navona de Lima: un ejemplo de diseño urbano barroco del siglo XVIII en el virreinato del Perú, 1999, (with Michael Setareh) Monticello's Dome: Development of an Integrated Resource for the Study of Thomas Jefferson's Architecture, 2000, Quincha Architecture: The Development of an Antiseismic Structural System in Seventeenth Century Lima, 2003, The Rural Churches of the Jesuit Haciendas in the Southern Peruvian Coast, 2004, The Survival of Gothic Rib Vaulting in the Viceroyalty of Peru, 2006, Rethinking Bamboo Architecture as a Sustainable alternative for Developing Countries: Juvenal Baracco and Velez, 2009; contbg. editor: The Dictionary of Art, 1991-96, Encyclopedia of Twentieth Century Architecture, 1999. Named Ellen Battell Eldridge fellow, 1970-72, Robert C. Bates Jr. fellow Jonathan Edwards Coll., Yale U., 1970-71, Social Sci. Rsch. Coun. fellow, 1972-74, Yale Concilium Internat. Studies fellow, 1972-73, Giles Whiting fellow, 1974-75, NEH fellow Columbia U., 1983, Hobart and William Smith Colls. fellow, 1987, U. Ill. fellow, 1990, Edilia De Montequin fellow, 1991, NEH fellow U. N.Mex., 1992. Mem.: KC, Ctr. Palladian Studies America, Construction Hist. Soc. America, Constrn. His. Soc. Am., Ctr. Palladian Studies in Am., Preservation Resource Ctr. (past bd. dirs.), Inter-Am. Inst. Advanced Studies in Cultural History (bd. dirs. 1998—), Blacksburg Regional Art Assn., Assn. for Preservation Tech., Save Our Cemeteries (past bd.dirs.), Nat. Trust Hist. Preservation, New River Valley Preservation League (bd. dirs. 1987—), Assn. Preservation Va. Antiquities, Coll. Art Assn. Am., S.E. section Soc. Archtl. Historians, Soc. Archtl. Historians (bd. dirs. 1977—80, past pres., past sec. South Gulf chpt.), Internat.Archive of Women in Architecture (treas. 1999—2002), Assn. Latin Am. Art, S.E. Coll. Art Conf., Latin Am. Studies Assn., Phi Beta Delta, Sigma Delta Pi, Tau Sigma Delta. Roman Catholic. Office: Va Poly Inst and State U Coll Architecture & Urban Studies Blacksburg VA 24061-0205 Home Phone: 540-961-1296; Office Phone: 540-231-5324. E-mail: hcami@vt.edu.

RODRIGUEZ-VELEZ, ROSA EMILIA, federal prosecutor; Grad., U. Sacred Heart, 1973; M in Criminal Justice, Interamerican U., PR, JD, 1977. Bar: PR 1977. Asst. dist. atty. PR Dept. Justice, San Juan, 1979—88; asst. US atty. Dist. PR US Dept. Justice, 1988—94, violent crime coord., 1994—2002, exec. asst., 1994—2992, acting chief civil divsn., 1995—97, 1st asst. US atty., 2002, US atty., 2006—. Coord. High Intensity Drug Trafficking Area, 1994—96, chair, 2006. Recipient Dir. Commendation Letter, FBI, 1987. Office: US Attorneys Office Torre Chardon Ste 1201 350 Carlos Chardon Ave San Juan PR 00918 Office Phone: 787-766-5656. Office Fax: 787-766-6219.*

ROE, LESA B., federal agency administrator; b. 1963; m. Ralph Roe. B. in elec. engring., U. Fla., Gainesville; M. in elec. engring., U. Ctrl. Fla., Orlando. Satellite comm. analyst Hughes Space & Comm., El Segundo, Calif.; with NASA, 1987—, comm. engr. Space Shuttle Engring. Directorate Kennedy Space Ctr., Fla., 1987, payloads office mgr. Internat. Space Sta. (ISS) Program Office, Johnson Space Ctr. Houston; assoc. dir. bus. mgmt. Langley Rsch. Ctr., NASA, Hampton, Va., 2003—04, dep. dir., 2004—05, dir., 2005—. Office: Bldg 1219 Rm 213 Mail Stop 106 Hampton VA 23681-2199 also: Langley Rsch Ctr 100 NASA Rd Hampton VA 23681 Office Phone: 757-864-4111. E-mail: lesa.b.roe@nasa.gov.

ROE, PHIL (DAVID PHILLIP ROE), United States Representative from Tennessee; b. Clarksville, Tenn., July 21, 1945; m. Pam Roe; children: David, Whitney, John. BS in Biology, Austin Peay State U., Clarksville, 1967; MD, U. Tenn. Coll. Medicine, Memphis, 1970. Pvt. practice ob-gyn., Johnson City, Tenn., 1974—2005; commr. Johnson City Bd. Commissioners, 2003—08; vice-mayor Johnson City, 2003—07; mayor, 2007—09; mem. US Congress from 1st Tenn. dist., 2009—. Past pres. Tri-County Med. Soc.; del. Tenn. Med. Assn. Mem. Munsey United Meth. Ch.; bd. dirs. East Tenn. U. Found., 2006—. Maj. US Army Med. Corps, 1973—74. Recipient Excellence in Philanthropy award, Tenn. Bd. Regents. Republican. Methodist. Office: US House of Representatives 407 Cannon House Office Bldg Washington DC 20515 also: 1609 College Park Dr Ste 4 Morristown TN 37813 Office Phone: 202-225-6356, 423-317-7459. Office Fax: 202-225-5714, 423-317-7562.*

ROE, PHILLIP W., surgical hospital company executive; Attended, Okla. Christian U., 1979. Assoc. Ernst & Young LLP; contr., chief acctg. officer OrNda HealthCorp, 1994—97, v.p., 1994—96, sr. v.p., 1996—97; sr. v.p., contr. & chief acctg. officer Vanguard Health Sys., Inc., 1997—2007, exec. v.p., CFO, treas., 2007—. Office: Vanguard Health Systems Inc Ste 100 20 Burton Hills Blvd Nashville TN 37215 Office Phone: 615-665-6000. Office Fax: 615-665-6099. Business E-Mail: proe@vanguardhealth.com.

ROEDDER, WILLIAM CHAPMAN, JR., lawyer; b. St. Louis, June 21, 1946; s. William Chapman and Dorothy (Reifeiss) R.; m. Gwendolyn Arnold, Sept. 13, 1968; children: William Chapman, Barcley Shane. BS, U. Ala., 1968; JD cum laude, Cumberland U., 1972. Bar: Ala. Law clk. to chief justice Ala. Supreme Ct., Montgomery, 1972; ptnr. McDowell Knight Roedder & Sledge, L.L.C., Mobile, Ala., 1997—. Comments editor Cumberland-Samford Law Rev.; contbr. articles to legal publs. Bd. dirs. Def. Rsch. Inst., 1999—2002; mem. Bd. Lawyers for Civil Justice. Named to Best Lawyers in Am. Mem.: ABA (vice chair com. trial tactics, torts and ins. practice 1995—96), Lawyers for Civil Justice (pres. 2006—07, bd. dirs), Def. Rsch. Inst. (bd. dirs. 1999—2002), Ala. Def. Lawyers Assn., Fedn. Def. and Corp. Counsel (chmn. products liability sect. 1990—93, bd. dirs. 1993—2000, regional v.p. 1994—96, exec. com. 1997—, sec.-treas. 1999—2000, pres.-elect 2000—01, pres. 2001—02, chmn. bd. dirs. 2002—03), Mobile County Bar Assn. (sec., chmn. ethics com. 1988—90, grievance com. 1994—96), Ala. State Bar Assn., Order of Barristers, Curia Honoris, Phi Alpha Delta (pres. 1971—72). Home: 211 Levert Ave Mobile AL 36607-3219 Office: McDowell Knight Roedder & Sledge LLC PO Box 350 Mobile AL 36601-0350 E-mail: broedder@mcdowellknight.com.

ROEDER, ELIZABETH ROSE, clinical geneticist, educator; Attended, Tex. A&M U., 1989. Lic. Tex., 2004, cert. Am. Bd. Med. Genetics-clin. genetics, 2009. Resident pediat. Univ. Ariz. Health Sci. Ctr., 1989—92; fellow med. genetics Univ. Calif., San Francisco, 1992—95; assoc. prof. pediat. Univ. Tex.; hosp. affiliation includes Univ. Hosp., Christus Santa Rosa Hosp. Office: Christus Santa Rosa Hospital Ste F1663 333 N Santa Rosa St San Antonio TX 78207 Office Phone: 210-704-2795.

ROEHLK, THOMAS M., consumer products company executive; Sr. v.p., gen. counsel Tupperware Brands Corp., 1995—2005, sec., 1995—, exec. v.p., chief legal officer, 2005—. Office: Tupperware Brands Corp 14901 S Orange Blossom Trail Orlando FL 32837 Office Phone: 407-826-5050. Office Fax: 407-826-8874.

ROELLER, HERBERT ALFRED, biology professor; b. Magdeburg, Germany, Aug. 2, 1927; came to U.S., 1962; s. Alfred H. and Elfriede (Wartner) R.; m. Manuela R. Buresch, Dec. 20, 1957. Abiturium, Christian Thomasius Schule, Halle/Saale, 1946; PhD, Georg August U., Goettingen, 1962; MD, U. Muenster, 1955. Project assoc. zoology U. Wis., Madison, 1962-65, asst. prof. pharmacology, 1965-66, rsch. assoc. zoology, 1966-67, assoc. prof. zoology, 1967-68; prof. biology Tex. A&M U., 1968-83, prof. biochemistry and biophysics, 1974-83, dir. Inst. Devel. Biology, 1973-83, Disting. prof., 1977—, Alumni prof., 1980-85. V.p. and dir. rsch. Zoecon Corp., Palo Alto, Calif., 1968-72, sci. adv., 1972-85, chief scientist, Zoecon Rsch. Inst., Palo Alto, 1985-88; sci. advisor Syntex Rsch., Palo Alto, 1966-68, European Cmty., 1988—, Affymax Rsch. Inst., Palo Alto, 1989-96; corp. advisor Symyx Techs., Sunnyvale, Calif., 1996—2010; mem. adv. panel regulatory biology, divsn. biol. and med. scis. NSF, 1969-72; mem. Internat. Centre Insect Physiology and Ecology, Nairobi, Kenya, 1970—, dir. rsch., 1970-75. Mem. editl. bd. Jour. Chem. Ecology, 1974—; Contbr. articles to profl. jours. Recipient Disting. Achievement award for research Tex. A&M U., 1976. Fellow Tex. Acad. Sci.; mem. German Acad. Naturforscher Leopoldina, Sigma Xi.

ROELOFS, LYLE DEAN, academic administrator, physics professor; b. Grand Rapids, Mich., Dec. 19, 1953; s. Harlan Ray and Cynthia Clara (Van Dyke) Roelofs; m. Lauren Beth Mulder, June 14, 1975; children: Christopher Dean, Brian Alexander. BS with honors in Physics and Math., Calvin Coll., 1975; MS in Physics, U. Md., 1978, PhD in Physics, 1980. Instr. Calvin Coll., Grand Rapids, 1977; rsch. asst., instr. U. Md., College Park, 1977-80; rsch. assoc. Brown U., Providence, 1980-82; asst. prof. physics Haverford Coll., Pa., 1982-87, assoc. prof. physics Pa., 1987-93, prof. physics Pa., 1993—2004, assoc. provost Pa., 2001—04; provost and dean faculty, prof. physics Colgate U., NY, 2004—12, interim pres. NY, 2009—10; pres. Berea Coll., Ky., 2012—. Author: Electricity and Magnetism Simulations, 1995, Handbook of Surface Science; contbr. articles to profl. jours. Democrat. Office: Office of the President Lincoln Rm 211 CPO 2182 Berea College Berea KY 40404 Office Phone: 859-985-3520. Office Fax: 859-985-3915. Business E-Mail: lyle_roelofs@berea.edu.*

ROESLER, ROBERT HARRY, media consultant; b. Hammond, La., Oct. 5, 1927; s. Albert N. and Hilda (Schwartz) R.; m. Cloe Alferez, May 7, 1955; children: Kim, Bob, Toby. Student, Tulane U. Mem. sports staff Times Picayune, New Orleans, 1949-94, sports editor, 1964-80; exec. sports editor Times Picayune and States-Item, 1980-94; sports coord. New Orleans Met. Conv. and Visitors Bur., 1994—99; CEO Roesler Media Cons. Chmn. faculty coun., Student Publs. Bd., U. New Orleans, 1998-2001. Author: Fair Grounds: Big Shots and Long Shots, 1998. Vice-chmn. Navy Recruiting Dist.; mem. assistance coun., New Orleans, 1992-96. With USN, WWII, Korean conflict. Mem. Profl. Football Writers Assn. Am. (pres. 1976-77, PFWA McCAnn Meml. award NFL Hall of Fame, 1997), Nat. Turf Writers Assn., Football Writers Am., Am. Legion, Navy League U.S., New Orleans Press Club (pres. 1959-60, sports writing awards). Home and Office: 982 Robert E Lee Blvd New Orleans LA 70124 Home Phone: 504-304-9266. Personal E-mail: bobroesler@gmail.com.

ROFF, J(OHN) HUGH, JR., energy executive; b. Wewoka, Okla., Oct. 27, 1931; s. Hugh and Louise Roff; m. Ann Green, Dec. 23, 1956; children— John, Charles, Andrew, Elizabeth, Jennifer AB, U. Okla., 1954, LL.B., 1955. Bar: Okla., Mo., N.Y. Law clk. to presiding justice U.S. Ct. Appeals (10th cir.), 1958; atty. Southwestern Bell Telephone Co., St. Louis, 1959-63, AT&T, NYC, 1964-68; v.p., gen. atty. Long Lines, NYC, 1969-73, gen. atty., 1973-74; chmn., pres., chief exec. officer United Energy Resources, Houston, 1974-86; chmn. PetroUnited Terminals Inc., Houston, 1986-98, Roff Resources LLC, Houston, 1998—. Past chmn. Cen. Houston Inc.; mem. adv. bd. Ctr. for Strategic and Internat. Studies, Washington; trustee Baylor Coll. Medicine; past chmn. adv. bd. The Salvation Army, Houston; dir., Inasmuch Found., Ethics and Excellence in journalism Found.; 1st lt. U.S. Army, 1955-58. Mem. Order of Coif, Phi Beta Kappa, Beta Theta Pi. Clubs: Houston Country, Coronado, Houstonian. Office: 600 Travis St Ste 7070 Houston TX 77002-3012 Office Phone: 713-655-5310. Business E-Mail: hughroff@roffresources.com.

ROGERO, MADELINE, mayor, Knoxville, Tennessee; b. Jacksonville, Fla., 1952; m. Gene Monaco; 5 children. BA in Polit. Sci., Furman U., Greenville, SC; MA in Urban and Regional Planning, U. Tenn., 1987. Cmty. & econ. devel. planner East Tenn. Cmty. Design Ctr., Tenn. Valley Authority; grants cons. Levi Strauss Found.; exec. dir. Coal Empowerment Project, U. Tenn. Cmty. Partnership Ctr., Dolly Parton's Dollywood Found., Knoxville's Promise-The Alliance for Youth; cons. America's Promise-The Alliance for Youth, Capital One Fin. Corp. Cmty. Affairs Office; mem. Dist. 2 Knox County Commn., Tenn., 1990—98; commr. Knoxville Transp. Authority, 2003—07; dir. cmty. devel. City of Knoxville, 2007—10, mayor, 2011—. Office: City of Knoxville Mayors Office City County Bldg Rm 691 PO Box 1631 Knoxville TN 37901 Office Phone: 865-215-2040. Office Fax: 865-215-2085. Business E-Mail: mayor@cityofknoxville.org.*

ROGERS, ALAN T., lawyer; BA, Birmingham-So. Coll., Ala., 1977; JD cum laude, Tulane U. Law Sch., New Orleans, 1980. Bar: La. 1980, Ala. 1983, cert.: American Arbitration Assn. (mediator). Ptnr. Balch & Bingham, LLP, Birmingham, former chmn. litig. com., chmn. exec. com. Adj. prof. product liability U. Ala. Sch. Law; spkr., mem. planning com. Cumberland Law Inst. Past mem. editl. bd. The Ala. Lawyer. Mem. class XX Leadership Ala.; past mem. bd. dirs. Birmingham YMCA; mem. Norton bd. advisors mgmt. & profl. edn. Birmingham-So. Coll.; past pres. bd. dirs., mem. adv. bd. The Exceptional Found.; bd. dirs., mem. Tocqueville Coun. United Way Ctrl. Ala.; mem. chmn. cir. Birmingham Bus. Alliance; mem. members coun. Leadership Birmingham, 2009 Class. Named Lawyer of Yr., Birmingham Ins. Law, Best Lawyers, 2011; named a Local Star, Benchmark Litig.; named one of America's Leading Bus. Lawyers, Comml. Litig., Chambers USA, The Best Lawyers in America, 2005—; named to Ala. Super Lawyers, 2008, 2009. Fellow: American Coll. Trial Lawyers; mem.: Ala. State Bar (past chmn. bus. torts and antitrust sect., chmn. legal services Ala. task force), Ala. Def. Lawyers Assn. (past mem. bd. dirs., chmn. task force long range planning, faculty mem. ADLA Trial Acad.), Birmingham Bar Assn. (chmn. grievance com. 2009), La. State Bar, American Inns of Ct., Fedn. Ins. and Corp. Counsel, Newcomen Soc., Rotary Internat. Office: Balch & Bingham LLP 1901 6th Ave N Ste 1500 Birmingham AL 35203-4642 Office Phone: 205-226-3486. Office Fax: 205-488-5819. Business E-Mail: arogers@balch.com.

ROGERS, ALAN VICTOR, former CEO, air force major general; b. Hannibal, Mo., Nov. 13, 1942; s. Julian Alan and Gladys Cuneo R.; m. Linda Rae Peterson, May 7, 1966; children: Kimberly Rae, Krista Anne, Peter Alan. BS in Mil. Sci., USAF Acad., 1964; MBA with distinction, Harvard Bus. Sch., 1972; grad. with distinction, Air War Coll., 1980. Commd. 2d lt. USAF, 1964, advanced through grades to maj. gen., 1989, ret., 1993; combat fighter pilot 355th Tactical Fighter Wing, Takhli, Thailand, 1966-67; jet pilot instr. Flying Tng. Wing, Williams AFB, Ariz., 1967-69; student Harvard Bus. Sch., Cambridge, Mass., 1970-72; pers. officer Cols. Group USAF Pentagon, Washington, 1972-75; student Air War Coll., Maxwell AFB, Ariz., 1980; wing comdr. 5th Bomb Wing, Minot AFB, ND, 1982-84, 96th Bomb Wing (1st B-1 Wing), Dyess AFB, Tex., 1984-86; dir. ops. SAC, Offutt AFB, Nebr., 1986-89; asst. chief of staff ops. Supreme HQ Allied Powers Europe NATO, Mons, Belgium, 1989-91; dir. J-7 Joint Staff, Pentagon, Washington, 1991-93; assoc. Burdeshaw Assocs., Ltd., Bethesda, Md., 1993-94; prin. Gemini Consulting, Morristown, NJ, 1994-97; sr. v.p., gen. mgr. Fed. Defense Group, Am. Mgmt. Sys., Inc., Fairfax, Va., 1997—2002; exec. v.p. CACI Internat., 2003—07; CEO Command Info., 2009—11; dirs. on bds. A.V. Rogers & Assoc., LLC, 2011—. Mem. Active Angel Investors, Vienna, 2003—; mem. adv. bd. Infodata, Inc., 2003—06, Our Military Kids, 2008—; dir. Command Info., Inc., 2009—11, XEDAR, Inc., 2009—12, GeoTree Techs., Inc., 2010—12, DCS Corp Inc., 2010—, Glimmerglass Networks, Inc., 2011—. Mem., mil. adviser C. of C., Minot, N.D., 1982-84, Abilene, Tex. 1984-86; trustee The Falcon Found., Colorado Springs, 2003-; mem. bd. advisors Our Mil. Kids, 2006-. Decorated Defense Disting. Svc. Medal, Legion of Merit, D.F.C. with two oak leaf clusters, Purple Heart, Def. Superior Svc. medal, Disting. Svc. medal, Def. Disting. Svc. medal; recipient Am. U. Leadership award, 2000. Mem.: Nat. Assn. Corp. Dirs., Daedalians (chpt. pres. 1986), Nat. Eagle Scout Assn., Red River Valley Fighter Pilots Assn., Sabre Soc., USAF Acad. Assn. Grads. (bd. dirs. 1999—2007), Air Force Assn. Republican. Lutheran. Avocations: skiing, travel, antiques, Fitness. Home: 1492 Evans Farm Dr Mc Lean VA 22101-5653 Office Phone: 703-795-3802.

ROGERS, BETSY, elementary school educator; b. Birmingham, Ala., Mar. 2, 1952; children: Alan, Rick. BA in Elem. Edn., Samford Univ., 1974, MA, 1998, PhD, 2002. Cert. generalist/early childhood Nat. Bd. Profl. Tchg. Standards, 2000. Tchr. Hewitt Elem. Sch., 1974—76; kindergarten tchr. Leeds First Baptist Church, 1982—85; first grade tchr. Leeds Elem. Sch., Ala., 1985—2004; tchr., curriculum coord. Brighton Sch., Ala., 2004—. Chair Governor's Task Force on Tchr. Quality. Named Nat. Tchr. of Yr., 2003. Mem.: Ala. Conf. of Educators (past pres.). Office: Gov Commission on Quality Teaching 3323 Gordon Persons Bldg PO Box 302101 Montgomery AL 36130-2101

ROGERS, C. B., lawyer; b. Birmingham, Ala., July 10, 1930; s. Claude B. Rogers and Doris (Hinkley) Rogers Lockerman; m. Patricia Maxwell DeVoe, Dec. 22, 1962; children: Bruce Lockerman, Evelyn Best, Brian DeVoe. AB, Emory U., 1951, LL.B., 1953. Bar: Ga. 1953. Adj. prof. litigation Emory U., 1968-70; assoc., then partner firm Powell, Goldstein, Frazer & Murphy, 1954-76; founding partner Rogers & Hardin, Atlanta, 1976—. Recipient A. Sherman Christensen award, Am. Inns of Ct., 2005. Fellow Am. Coll. Trial Lawyers; mem. Am. Law Inst., Atlanta Bar Assn., State Bar Ga., Capital City Club (Atlanta). Democrat. Episcopalian. Home: 1829 W Wesley Rd NW Atlanta GA 30327-2019 Office: Rogers & Hardin 2700 International Tower 229 Peachtree St NE Atlanta GA 30303-1638 Office Phone: 404-520-4606. Office Fax: 404-525-2224. E-mail: cbr@rh-law.com.

ROGERS, CARL, state legislator; b. Feb. 9, 1948; m. Linda B. Rogers. Former state rep. Dist. 20; former mem. Natural Resources Com., Legislature Com., Congl. Reapportionment Com., Appropriations Com.; house rep. Ga.; state rep. Dist. 26 Ga., 2004—; ins. agent. Mem.: Gainesville Kiwanis Club. Democrat. Methodist. Address: PO Box 1058 Gainesville GA 30503 Mailing: State Capitol 507 Legis Off Bldg Atlanta GA 30334 Office Phone: 404-656-0202. Business E-Mail: crogers@legis.state.ga.us.

ROGERS, CHIP, state legislator; b. May 03; m. Amy Rogers; children: Emma, Quinn, Reagan, Sarah. BS, Ga. Inst. Tech.; MBA, Ga. State U. Radio station owner; mem. Dist. 15 Ga. House Reps., 2003—04; mem. Dist. 21 Ga. State Senate, 2005—, majority leader, 2009—. Republican. Mailing: PO Box 813 Woodstock GA 30188 Office Phone: 770-516-0543. Business E-Mail: chip.rogers@senate.ga.gov.

ROGERS, DALE CRAIG, finance company executive; b. Wichita Falls, TX, Jan. 21, 1945; s. Moral W. and Opal Davlin Rogers; m. Judy Carole Coburn, Sept. 11, 1965; children: Lori Alyssa Rogers-Williams, Craig Coburn. Cert. pension cons. Am. Soc. Pension Cons. & Actuaries Wash., DC, 1989. Ins. & securities agt. Penn Mut. Life Ins. Co., Wichita Falls, Tex., 1966—68; divsn. mgr. Jefferson-Pilot Equity Co., Fort Worth, Tex., 1968—73; chmn., CEO Rogers Co., Fort Worth, 1973—, Rogers & Associates- Pension Cons., Fort Worth, 1973—, Rogers Capital Mgmt., Inc., Fort Worth, 1990—. Author: The First Time Investor, How to Build, Protect & Maintain Your 401(k) Plan. Pres., bd. trustees Keller Ind. Sch. Dist., Tex., 1983—89; bd. dirs. Keller Youth Assn., 1980—88. Mem.: Am. Soc. Pension Actuaries & Cons. (licentiate). Republican. Baptist. Avocations: travel, boating. Home: 6905 Old Homestead Rd Fort Worth TX 76132 Office: Rogers Co 1330 Summit Ave Fort Worth TX 76102 Business E-Mail: dcrogers@rogersco.com.

ROGERS, DEWITT RALPH, lawyer; b. Durham, NC, Sept. 26, 1952; s. Ralph P. and Elizabeth (Stutts) R.; m. Claire Hamby, Sept. 25, 1982; children: DeWitt Ralph Jr., Elizabeth Lee, Laura Alice. BA, Emory U., 1974, JD with distinction, 1986; MS in Journalism, Columbia U., 1975. Bar: Ga. 1986. Staff writer The Atlanta Constn., 1975-77, bus. editor, 1977-79, city editor, 1979-82; asst. mng. editor The Atlanta Jour. & Constn., 1982-83; assoc. Troutman Sanders LLP, Atlanta, 1986-93, ptnr., regulatory grp., 1994—. Bd. dirs. So. Inst. Bus. and Profl. Ethics, 1998-2006, bd. govs. Ga. State U. Ctr. Ethics & Corp. Responsibility, 2007-. Editor-in-chief Emory Law Jour. Mem.: Order of Coif. Office: Troutman Sanders LLP 600 Peachtree St NE Ste 5200 Atlanta GA 30308-2216 Office Phone: 404-885-3412. Office Fax: 404-962-6671. Business E-Mail: dewitt.rogers@troutmansanders.com.

ROGERS, ERNEST MABRY, lawyer; b. Demopolis, Ala., Sept. 22, 1947; s. James B. and Ernestine B. (Brewer) R.; m. Jeanne Edwards, Dec. 15, 1979; children: Gilbert B., Katherine B., Mary C. BA, Yale U., New Haven, Conn., 1969; JD, Harvard U., Cambridge, Mass., 1974. Bar: Ala. 1974, US Dist. Ct. (no. dist.) Ala. 1975, US Ct. Appeals (5th cir.) 1976, US Ct. Appeals (11th cir.) 1981, US Supreme Ct. 1981, US Ct. Claims 1983, US Ct. Appeals (6th cir.) 1987. Law clk. to judge U.S. Dist. Ct. (no. dist.) Ala., 1974—75; ptnr. Bradley Arant Rose & White LLP, Birmingham, Ala., 1981—2008, Bradley Arant Boult Cummings LLP, 2009—. Contbr. articles to profl. jours. Mem. Jefferson County Bd. of Code Appeals, Ala., 2001—, City of Birmingham Bd. of Code Appeals. Fellow: Am. Coll. Constrn. Lawyers; mem.: Am. Arbitration Assn. (bd. dirs. 2001—05), Kiwanis. Episcopalian. Office: One Federal Pl 1819 5th Ave N Birmingham AL 35203-2104 Office Phone: 205-521-8225. Business E-Mail: emr@babc.com.

ROGERS, HAROLD DALLAS (HAL ROGERS), United States Representative from Kentucky; b. Barrier, KY, Dec. 31, 1937; m. Shirley Rogers (dec.); 3 children; m. Cynthia Doyle Stewart, 1999. BA, U. Ky., 1962, LLB, 1964. Bar: La. 1964. Assoc. Smith & Blackburn, 1964—67; pvt. law practice Somerset, Ky., 1967-69; Commonwealth atty. Pulaski and Rockcastle counties, Ky., 1969-80; mem. US Congress from 5th Ky. Dist., Washington, 1981—; chmn. US House Appropriations Com., Washington, 2011—. Mem. Congressional Horse Caucus, Tenn. Valley Authority Caucus. Founder Southern. Ky. Economic Council. With KY and NC Nat. Guard, 1957—64. Mem.: Ky. Commonwealth Atty. Assn. (past pres.). Republican. Office: US House of Representatives 2406 Rayburn Ho Office Bldg Washington DC 20515-1705 Office Phone: 202-225-4601. Business E-Mail: talk2hal@mail.house.gov.*

ROGERS, HAZELLE, state legislator; b. Jamaica, Sept. 28, 1952; m. Clifton Rogers. AAS, NYC Cmty. Coll., 1976; attended, Pace U., 1980; BS, U. Phoenix, 2003. Mem. Dist 94 Fla. House of Reps., 2008—, mem. health care svcs. policy com., roads, bridges and ports policy com., transp. and econ. devel. appropriations com. Commr. City of Lauderdale Lakes. Bd. mem. Greater Caribbean Am. Chamber, 2005—08, Fla. Med. Ctr., 2006—08; mem. Broward County Charter Rev. Commn., 2006—08, Broward County Land Preservation Adv. Bd., Broward Mgmt. & Efficiency Study Commn., Fla. Consumer Adv. Bd. Mem.: Broward League of Cities (pres.), Broward UNCF (vice chmn. 2001—07), State Rd 7 Collaborative (vice chmn.), One Cmty., Saints Netball Club, Kiwanis Club Lauderdale Lakes, Caribbean Am. Dem. Club (founding mem.). Democrat. Office: 402 S Monroe St Rm 1402 Tallahassee FL 32399-1300 also: Inverrary Corporate Park 3800 Inverrary Blvd Ste 307 Lauderhill FL 33319-4359 Office Phone: 850-488-8234, 954-497-3367. Business E-Mail: hazelle.rogers@myfloridahouse.gov.

ROGERS, JAMES EUGENE, JR., (JIM ROGERS), energy executive; b. Birmingham, Ala., Sept. 20, 1947; s. James E. and Margaret (Whatley) R.; m. Robyn McGill (div.); children: Chrissi, Kara, Ben; m. Mary Anne Boldrick, Oct. 28, 1977. BBA, U. Ky., 1970, JD, 1974; LLD (hon.), Ind. State U.; DHL (hon.), Queens Univ., Charlotte NC. Reporter Lexington (Ky.) Herald Leader, 1967—70; asst. atty. gen. Commonwealth of Ky., Louisville; asst. chief trial atty. Fed. Energy Regulation Commn. (FERC), Washington, dep. gen. counsel for litigation & enforcement; law clk. to presiding justice Supreme Ct Ky., Louisville; ptnr. Akin, Gump, Strauss, Hauer & Feld LLP, Dallas, Akin Gump Strauss Hauer & Feld, LLP, Houston, 1985-86; exec. v.p. Enron Gas Pipeline Group, 1986—88; pres., CEO, chmn. PSI Resources, Inc, 1988—94, Cinergy Corp. (formerly PSI Resources, Inc.), Cin., 1994—2006; pres., CEO Duke Energy Corp., Charlotte, NC, 2006—07, chmn., pres., CEO, 2007—12, 2012—13, chmn., 2012, 2013—. 2nd vice chmn. Edison Electric Inst., 2004—05, vice chmn., 2005—06, chmn., 2006—; bd. dirs. Chesapeake Corp., 1999—2004, Duke Energy Corp., 2006—, Cigna Corp., 2007—, Applied Materials Inc., 2008—, Advanced Energy Economy, 2012—. Trustee Nat. Symphony Orch.; bd. dirs. Cin. Mus. Assn., The Nature Conservancy-Ind. chpt., U. Ky. Bus. Partnership Found. Recipient Disting. Svc. Citation, NCCJ, 2004, Keystone Ctr. in Leadership in Industry award, 2005, Ronald McDonald House Lifetime Achievement award, 2005, Human Rels. award, American Jewish Com., 2006, Ellis Island Medal of Honor, Nat. Ethnic Coalition of Org., 2007; named CEO of Yr., Platts Global Energy awards, 2007; named one of The Global Elite, Newsweek mag., 2008. Mem. Ky. Bar Assn., D.C. Bar Assn., Meridian Hills Country Club, Crooked Stick Golf Club, Queen City Club, Met. Club. Baptist. Avocations: tennis, bicycling, skiing, golf. Office: Duke Energy Corp 526 S Church St Charlotte NC 28202*

ROGERS, JAMES FREDERICK, banker, management consultant; b. Centerville, Iowa, June 27, 1935; s. John W. and Mildred Holly (Morris) R.; m. Janet L. Marsden, July 27, 1957; children: Jennifer Burke, John William. AB, U. Mo., 1957; postgrad., Rutgers U. Grad. Sch. Banking, 1970-72. With Am. Security and Trust Co., Washington, 1959-85, exec. v.p., 1980-83. Bd. dirs., 1972-85, pres. Am. Security Corp., 1983-85; cons. B.E.I.-Golembe Assoc., 1985-93; chmn. Nat. Bank of No. Va., 1988-89. Commr. Arlington County Planning Commn., 1979-80; asst. treas. Kennedy Ctr. Performing Arts; pres., trustee Leonard Wood Found.; trustee Friends of Nat. Zoo; mem. Greater Washington Rsch. Ctr., Washington Dulles Task Force; trustee Arena Stage; adv. bd. mem., Sch. Commerce U. Va., Officer AUS, 1958-59; dir. Conococheague Inst. Mem. D.C. Bankers Assn. (pres. 1984-85), Davenport Soc., U. Mo., Met. Club (Washington), Chevy Chase Club, NY Ave. Presbyn. Ch. (trustee). Presbyterian. Home: 4201 38th Rd N Arlington VA 22207-4554 Personal E-mail: jroger@comcast.net.

ROGERS, JAMES GORDON, JR., retired art educator; b. Dec. 16, 1944; AB in English, U. Mo., 1967, MA in Art History and Archaeology, 1983, PhD, 1989. Asst. prof. art history William Woods Coll., Fulton, Mo., 1989-90; prof. art history Savannah Coll. Art & Design, Ga., 1990-92, Fla. So. Coll., Lakeland, Fla., 1992—2014; ret., 2014. Adj. prof. Sch. Arch. and Cmty. Design, U. S. Fla., 1995—2002; pres. Design Ctr., 1977—84, chair dept. art and art history; dir. Melvin Art Gallery, 1999—2006; chair, divsn. fine and performing arts Fla. Southern Coll., 2007—12; lectr. in field. Contbr. articles to profl. jours. Active Nat. Holocaust Meml. Mus.; past bd. dirs. Mid-Mo. chpt. Am. Heart Assn.; past bd. dirs. Sta. KBIA Pub. Radio, Columbia, Mo., Columbia Art League, co-chmn. fin. com.; mem. bd. trustees Polk Mus. Art, 2010—14; mem. bd. dirs. Imperial Symphony Orch., Lakeland, Fla., 2011—14; past mem. peer rev. com. Fla. Arts Coun. Mem.: AAUP, Hist. Lakeland Inc. (bd. dirs.), Coll. Art Assn., Soc. Archtl. Historians, Am. Soc. Hispanic Art Hist. Studies. Personal E-mail: jas_rogers@msn.com.

ROGERS, JAMES N., anesthesiologist, educator; MD, U. Ariz., 1987. Diplomate Am. bd. Anesthesiology, 1993, Am. bd. Anesthesiology-pain medicine, 1994. Intern Tucson Med. Ctr., 1988; resident Bexar County Hosp., 1991, fellow, 1992; attending physician Audie L. Murphy Veterans Hosp., 1991—, chief anesthesia svcs, 2009—; attending physician faculty Univ. Hosp., San Antonio, 1991—; active med. staff dept. of anesthesiology St. Luke's Baptist Hosp., Houston, 1995—; assoc. prof. orthopaedics Univ. Tex. Health Sci. Ctr., San Antonio, 1995—, assoc. prof. anesthesiology, 2000—, dir. of residency program, 2009—. Office: University Tex Health Sci Ctr 7703 Floyd Cuil Dr San Antonio TX 78229-4493 Office Phone: 210-358-4000. E-mail: rogersjn@uthscsa.edu.

ROGERS, JAMES P., chemicals executive; b. Bethesda, Md., Mar. 23, 1951; BA in Psychology, U. Va., 1973; MBA, U. Pa., 1983. Corp. fin. calling officer Morgan guaranty Trust Co., 1983-87; treas. LPL Techs., Inc., 1987-92, GAF Corp./INternat. Specialty Products, Inc.; exec. v.p., CFO GAF, 1992-99; exec. v.p. fin. Internat. Specialty Products, Inc., 1992-99; sr. v.p., CFO & COO Eastman div. Eastman Chemical Co., Kingsport, Tenn., 1999—2003, exec. v.p., 2003—06, pres., head chemicals & fibers bus. group, 2006—09, pres., CEO, 2009—10, chmn., CEO, 2011—. Lt. USN, 1973-80. Office: Eastman Chem Co 100 N Eastman Rd Kingsport TN 37660

ROGERS, JOHN MARSHALL, federal judge; b. Rochester, NY, June 26, 1948; s. Harry Lovejoy III and Virginia Kathryn (Meyers) R.; m. Ying Juan Xiong, 1990. BA, Stanford U., 1970; JD, U. Mich., 1974. Bar: DC 1975, Ky. 1980, US Ct. Appeals, US Supreme Ct. Commd. USAR, 1970; appellate atty. civil div. US Dept. Justice, Washington, 1974-78; asst. prof. U. Ky., Lexington, 1978-81, assoc. prof., 1981-86, prof., 1986—2002, prof. emeritus, 2002—; cir. judge US Ct. Appeals (6th cir.), 2002—. Vis. prof. Civil Divsn. US Dept. Justice, Washington, 1983-85; Fulbright lectr. Fgn. Affairs Coll., Beijing, 1987-88, Zhongshan U., Guangzhou, People's Republic of China, 1994-95; spl. counsel impeachment com. Ky. Ho. of Reps., 1991. Author: Internat. Law and U.S. Law, 1999; contbr. articles to profl. jours. Mem. Coun. on Fgn. Rels., Am. Law Inst., Order of Coif, Phi Beta Kappa. Office: 532 Potter Stewart US Courthouse 100 E 5th St Cincinnati OH 45202-3988 also: Cmty Trust Bank Bldg 100 E Vine St Lexington KY 40507

ROGERS, JOHN W., state legislator; b. Birmingham, Ala., Dec. 16, 1940; m. Jennie Rogers; children: Jerena, Tammy, John III. BS, Tenn State U.; MS, U. Ala.; AA in Vocat. Edn., U. Ala. Birmingham. Pres. Rogers & Rogers, Inc.; photographer, pub. rels. counselor, coll. adminstr., dir. minority affairs U. Ala. Birmingham; mem. Dist. 52 Ala. House of Reps., Montgomery, 1982—. Mem. St. Mary's Cath. Ch.; bd. mem. St. Andrews Found., Sickle Cell Found., Fourth Ave. YMCA, 1985—, Birmingham Convention & Tourism Bur., 1991—. Mem. Associated Photographers Inst. Am., Boy Scouts America, Nat. Conf. Christians & Jews, Century Club, Alpha Phi Alpha. Democrat. Roman Catholic. Office: 1424 18th St SW Birmingham AL 35211 also: Ala House of Reps Ala State House 11 S Union St Rm 541-D Montgomery AL 36130 Office Phone: 205-934-0364, 334-242-7761. Business E-Mail: yke@cec.conteduc.uab.edu.

ROGERS, JOSEPH GORDON, cardiologist, educator; MD, U. Nebr., 1988. Diplomate Am. Bd. Internal Medicine-cardiovasc. disease, 2005. Resident internal medicine Univ. of Nebr. Med. Ctr., Omaha, 1989—91; fellow cardiovasc. disease Wash. Univ. Med. Ctr., St. Louis, 1991—95; assoc. prof. medicine Duke Univ., Durham, NC; hosp. affiliation includes Duke Univ. Med. Ctr., Durham, NC. Office: Duke University Medical Center PO Box 3034 Durham NC 27710 Office Phone: 919-681-3398. Office Fax: 919-681-6833.

ROGERS, KENNY (KENNETH DONALD ROGERS), entertainer, recording artist; b. Houston, Aug. 21, 1938; s. Edward Floyd and Lucille (Hester) R.; m. Janice Gordon, May 15, 1958 (div. Apr. 1960), 1 child: Carol; m. Jean Rogers, Oct. 1960 (div. 1963); m. Margo Anderson, Oct. 1964 (div. 1976), 1 child: Kenneth; m. Marianne Gordon, Oct. 1, (div. 1993), 1 child: Christopher Cody; m. Wanda Miller, June 1, 1997; children: Justin Charles, Jordan Edward. Student, U. Houston. Founder Kenny Roger's Roasters. Recording artist, Liberty Records, 1976-82, RCA Records, 1983-88, Warner Records, 1988-93, Atlantic Records, 1993-94, Magnatone Records, 1996-97, co-founder and rec. artist, Dreamcatcher Entertainment, 1998-2000. Appeared on American Bandstand, 1958; mem. Bobby Doyle Trio, 1959-66, Christy Minstrels, 1966-67, The First Edition, 1967-69, Kenny Rogers and The First Edition, 1969-75, solo career, 1975—; hosted TV spls. Kenny Rogers Classic Weekend, 1988-90, Kenny, Dolly & Willie, 1989, Kenny Rogers in Concert, 1989, Goodwill Games, 1990; starred in TV series Rollin' with The First Edition, 1972; appeared in movies Six Pack, 1982; actor: (TV appearances) The Muppet Show, 1979, Evening Shade, 1991, A&E The Real West, 1993, MacShayne, 1994, Touched by an Angel, 2000, Reno 911, 2004, (TV films) Saga of Sonora, 1973, Kenny Rogers as the Gambler, 1980, Coward of the County, 1981, Gambler, Part II, 1983, Wild Horses, 1985, Gambler III: The Adventure Continues, 1987, Christmas in America, 1989, The Gambler Returns, Gambler IV: The Luck of the Draw, 1991, Rio Diablo, 1993, Gambler V: Playing for Keeps, 1994, Big Dreams & Broken Hearts: The Dottie West Story, 1995; recordings include: That Crazy Feeling (Gold single), I Don't Need You (Brit. Country Music Assn. award, Acad. Country Music award), Love is What We Make It, 1985, The Heart of the Matter, 1985, They Don't Make Them Like They Used To, What About Me, I Prefer the Moonlight, 1987, When You Put Your Heart in It, 1988 (ofcl. theme song US Gymnastics Fedn.), Christmas in America, 1989, Love Is Strange, 1990, Greatest Country Hits, 1990, If Only My Heart Had a Voice, 1993, Greatest Hits, 1994; (albums): Kenny Rogers-Lucille, 1976, Love or Something Like It, 1978, The Gambler, 1978, Kenny, 1979, Gideon, 1980, Share Your Love, 1981, Eyes That See in the Dark, 1983, Something Inside So Strong, 1989, Timepiece, 1994, The Gift, 1996, Across My Heart, 1997, Christmas From the Heart, 1998, She Rides Wild Horses, 1999, Christmas Greetings, 2000, There You Go Again, 2000, The Way It Used to Be, 2001, Calico Silver, 2002, Heart of the Matter, 2003, Back to the Well, 2003, Christmas with Kenny, 2004, Water & Bridges, 2006, After Dark, 2006, 50 Years, 2008, The Love of God, 2011, Amazing Grace, 2012, You Can't Make Old Friends, 2013; author: Kenny Roger's America, 1986, Your Friends and Mine, 1987, Christmas in Canaan, 2002, Luck or Something Like It: A Memoir, 2012. Hon. capt. 1988 US Gymnastics Team. Named Cross-Over Artist of Year Billboard mag., 1977, named Top Male vocalist People mag., 1979, 80; recipient Country Music Assn. award, 1978, 79, Star, Hollywood Walk of Fame, 1979, Am. Music award, Best Male Vocalist, Best Album, 1984, Am. Music award, Best Male Country Vocalist, Best Album, 1985, Country Music Found. Roy Acuff award, 1985, UN Peace award, 1984, Rec. Industry Assn. Am. Most Awarded Artist award, 1984 (11 platinum, 18 gold albums), Grammy award for Best Male Country Vocal, 1977, 79, co-recipient (with Ronnie Milsap) for Best Country Vocal Duet, 1987, 1st Harry Chapin award for Humanitarianism ASCAP, 1988, Horatio Alger award, 1990, Awd. for sales in excess of ten million copies for "Greatest Hits", Lifetime Achievement Awd., Songwriters Hall of Fame, N.A.R.M. Chmns. Awd. for Sustained Achievement, 1999, American Eagle award, Nat. Music Coun., 2010; numerous other music awards. Home: 103 Paradise Dr Hendersonville TN 37075-4201*

ROGERS, MARGARET ELLIS, state legislator; b. Oxford, Miss., Jan. 22, 1949; Mem. Dist. 14 Miss. House of Reps., 2004—, vice chair oil, gas and other minerals com., mem. banking and fin. svcs. com., ethics com., judiciary A com., judiciary en banc com., juvenile justice com., mgmt. com., transp. com., mem. univs. and colls. com. Democrat. Methodist. Address: 619 Owen Rd New Albany MS 38652 Office Phone: 601-359-3353. E-mail: mrogers@house.ms.gov.

ROGERS, MICHAEL BRUCE, orthodontist; b. Augusta, Ga., Oct. 25, 1945; s. Bruce Latimer and Dorothy (Baird) R.; m. Elizabeth Bennett, Dec. 21, 1968; children: Bruce, Kay, Alison, Lisa. Student, Emory U., 1963-65, DDS, 1969; cert. in orthodontics, Med. Coll. Ga., 1973. Diplomate Am. Bd. Orthodontists, 1980. Pvt. practice orthodontics, Augusta, 1973—; orthodontic resident Ga. Regents U., asst. clin. prof. Sch. Dentistry, 1973—, New Dental Sch. Search Com., 2013. Decorated Army Commendation medal; named John F. Mac Meritorous Svc. award, Emory Dental Alumni Assn., 2009. Fellow: Ga. Acad. Dental Practice, Internat. Coll. Dentists, Pierre Fauchard Acad., Am. Coll. Dentists, Ga. Dental Assn. (hon.; spkr. ho. of dels. 1999—2004, v.p. 2004—05, pres.-elect 2005—06, pres. 2006—07, gen. chn. 1993 ann. meeting, Merit award 2012); mem.: Augusta Dental Soc. (pres. 1985—86), Med. Coll. Ga. New Dental Sch. (mem. dental sch. steering. com., dean search com.), Ea. Dist. Dental Soc. (pres. 1982—83), Med. Coll. Ga. Orthodontic Alumni Assn. (pres. 1981—83), Ga. Assn. Orthodontists (v.p. 1983—84, pres. 1984—85, Exemplary Svc. award 1991, 2006), So. Assn. Orthodontists (spokesperson, sec.-treas. 1993—95, dir. 1995—97, pres. 1999—2000, Disting. Svc. award 2002), Am. Assn. Orthodontists (Ga. del., chmn. mem., ethics and jud. concerns, spkr. of house 1995—97, trustee 2002—10, chmn. investment com. 2008—09, chmn. budget adv. com. 2008—09, mem. exec. com. 2008—12, sec., treas. 2009—10, pres. 2011—12, found. bd. dirs. 2008—10, course coord. 1981—94, mem. strategic planning com. 1997—2000), ADA (del. 1992—99, 2003—06), Omicron Kappa Upsilon, Psi Omega (pres. 1967—68, Fraternal Achievement award 1969). Roman Catholic. Home: 3214 Candace Dr Augusta GA 30909-3259 Office: 3545 Wheeler Rd Augusta GA 30909-6517

ROGERS, MIKE D., United States Representative from Alabama; b. Hammond, Ind., July 16, 1958; m. Beth Rogers; children: Emily, Evan, Elliot. BA in Polit. Sci., Jacksonville State U., 1981, MPA, 1985; JD, U. Birmingham, 1991. Dir., dislocated worker's project United Way of Etowah County; community rep., psychiatric counselor Northeast Ala. Regional Med. Ctr.; atty. Bolt, Isom, Jackson and Bailey; assoc. then ptnr. Rogers, Young, Wollstein and Hughes; mem. Ala. House of Representatives, 1994—2002, US Congress from 3rd Ala. Dist., 2003—. Mem. Calhoun County Commn., 1987—91; active State Rep. Exec. Com., 1990—. Republican. Baptist. Office: US House of Representatives 324 Cannon House Office Bldg Washington DC 20515-0103 Office Phone: 202-225-3261.*

ROGERS, RALPH A., JR., insurance company executive; BBA in acctg., Tenn. Technol. U., Cookeville. CPA. Sr. v.p. fin. resources UnumProvident Corp.; sr. v.p. fin. svcs. AFLAC, Inc., Columbus, Ga., 2000—, chief acctg. officer, 2002—. Mem.: AICPA, Inst. Mgmt. Accts., Fin. Execs. Internat., Tenn. Soc. CPAs. Office: AFLAC Inc 1932 Wynnton Rd Columbus GA 31999 Office Phone: 706-323-3431. Office Fax: 706-324-6330.

ROGERS, RAY (NOLAN RAY ROGERS), state legislator; b. Rankin County, Miss., Nov. 3, 1931; m. Shirley Greer; children: Sherry Downs, Pamela, Kimberly Prestel. Former justice of peace; mem. Dist. 61 Miss. House of Reps., 1984—. Mem.: Rankin First, Shriner, Pearl C. of C., Riverchase Theatre, Pearl Athletic Alumni Assn., Mason, Exchange, Kiwanis. Republican. Methodist. Mailing: 3403 Lanell Lane Pearl MS 39208-5425 Home Phone: 601-939-9633. Fax: 601-932-1060. E-mail: rrogers@house.ms.gov.

ROGERS, RAYMOND JESSE, retired federal railroad associate administrator; b. Eugene, Oreg., Mar. 1, 1941; s. Raymond Everett and Virginia Elaine (Simpkins) R.; m. Joan Katherine Peterson, June 6, 1964 (div. Aug. 1974); 1 child, Virginia Arlene; m. Kim Lien Nguyen, Dec. 26, 1974; children: Kim Lan, Vincent Minh. Student, Santa Rosa Jr. Coll., Calif., 1960-61, U.S. Army Non-commd. Officer Acad., Anchorage, Alaska, 1963, U. Md., 1967-74, Fed. Exec. Inst., Charlottsville, Va., 1981. Sr. asst. mgr. Household Fin. Corp., Md., 1964-67; contract specialist Dept. Navy, Washington, 1967-71; contract svcs. officer AID, Saigon, Vietnam, 1971-76; contracting officer Dept. Transp., Fed. R.R. Adminstrn., Washington, 1976-80, dir. fin. svcs., 1980-84, assoc. adminstr. for adminstrn., 1984—2002, CFO, CIO, 1994—2002, ret., 2002. Leader local group Boy Scouts Am., Vienna, Va., 1987-92, Izaac Walton League of Am., Am. Legion, Am. Assn. of Retired Persons. Sgt. U.S. Army, 1961-64. With US Army, 1961—64, sgt. US Army Security Agy. Decorated Vietnam Civilian Svc. medal. Mem. U.S. Sr. Exec. Svc., Fed. Exec. Inst. Alumni Assn. Avocations: fishing, hiking, camping, house remodeling. Home: 102 Yeonas Dr SW Vienna VA 22180-6557 Personal E-mail: Rayvin78@aol.com.

ROGERS, RICHARD HILTON, hotel executive; b. Florence, SC, May 26, 1935; s. Leslie Lawton and Bessie (Holloway) R.; m. Evelyn Pasciuto; children: Richard Shannon, Leslie Anne. Student, U. N.C., 1953-55; BA in Bus. Adminstrn. cum laude, Bryant U., 1961; postgrad., Memphis State U., 1964; DHL (hon.), Schiller Internat. U., Dunedin, Fla., 2003. Innkeeper Helmsley Spear, NYC, 1961—62; v.p. Holiday Inns of Am., Memphis, 1963—73; exec. v.p. First Hospitality Corp., Hackensack, NJ, 1974—77; v.p., chief oper. officer Cindy's Inc., Atlanta, 1978—82; v.p. Mktg. Dept. World's Fair, Knoxville, Tenn., 1982; pres., chief exec. officer Hospitality Internat., Atlanta, 1982—92; dir. franchise devel. Baymont Inns, 1992, 2000. Developer, operator The Warehouse Restaurant, Oxford, Miss., 1973-75, Beauregard's Restaurant, Hattiesburg, Miss., 1975-78. Contbr. to profl. jours. Mem. adv. bd. U. South Fla. With USN, 1954-58, Korea. Mem. Am. Hotel/Motel Assn. (mktg. com. 1986-92, adv. coun. 1987-92, industry adv. bd., chmn.), Economy Lodging Coun. Avocations: sailing, photography. Home and Office: 8525 Hope Vine Roswell GA 30076 Personal E-mail: innkpr@charter.net.

ROGERS, RUTHERFORD DAVID, librarian; b. Jesup, Iowa, June 22, 1915; s. David Earl and Carrie Zoe (Beckel) R.; m. E. Margaret Stoddard, June 4, 1937; 1 child, Jane Shelley; m. Bernette W. Barton, Feb. 28, 2002. BA, U. No. Iowa, 1936, Litt.D., 1977; MA, Columbia, 1937, BS (Lydia Roberts fellow), 1938; D.Library Adminstrn. (hon.), U. Dayton, 1971. Asst. N.Y. Pub. Library, 1937-38; reference librarian Columbia Coll. Library, Columbia U., 1938- 41, acting librarian, 1941-42, librarian, 1942-45; research analyst Smith, Barney & Co., NYC, 1946-48; dir. Grosvenor Library, Buffalo, 1948-52, Rochester Pub. Library, 1952-54; chief pers. office N.Y. Pub. Libr., 1954-55; chief reference dept., 1955-57; chief asst. librarian of Congress, Washington, 1957-62, dep. librarian of, 1962-64; dir. univ. libraries Stanford U., 1964-69; univ. librarian Yale U., 1969-85, univ. librarian emeritus, 1985—. Founder, chmn. bd. dirs. Rsch. Librs. Group, Inc.; mem. Exam. Com. for Pub. Librarians' Certs., N.Y. State, 1951-54; mem. U.S. Adv. Coun. Coll. Libr. Resources; bd. govs. Yale U. Press; bd. dirs., v.p. H.W. Wilson Found., 1969-98; chmn. program mgmt. com. Internat. Fedn. Libr. Assns. Author: Columbia Coll. Library Handbook, 1941, (with David C. Weber) University Library Administration, 1971; also articles in profl. jours. Served from pvt. to 1st sgt. Air Transp. Command USAAF, 1942-43; from 2d lt. to capt., planning officer, chief, spl. Planning Div., Office Asst. Chief Staff, Plans, Air Transport Command 1943-46. Decorated officier de L'Ordre de la Couronne Belge; recipient U. No. Iowa Alumni Achievement award, 1958, Disting. Alumni award Columbia U. Sch. Libr. Svc., 1992, medal Internat. Fedn. of Libr. Assns., 1977. Fellow Nat. Acad. Arts and Scis.; mem. A.L.A. (chmn. com. Intellectual Freedom 1950-51), (1950-60), (2d v.p. 1965-66), (mem. exec. bd. 1961-66), (trustee endowment fund), Assn. Research Libraries (dir., pres. 1967-68), N.Y. Library Assn., AAUP, Bibliog. Soc. Am., Assn. Coll. and Reference Libraries, Blue Key, Kappa Delta Pi, Sigma Tau Delta, Theta Alpha Phi. Clubs: Grolier; N.Y. Library (N.Y.C.), Columbia U. (N.Y.C.), Yale (N.Y.C.); Cosmos (Washington), Kenwood Country (Washington); Roxburghe (San Francisco); Book of Calif. Home: 1111 S Lakemont Ave Apt 510 Winter Park FL 32792-5400

ROGERS, STEPHEN HITCHCOCK, retired ambassador; b. Flushing, NY, June 21, 1930; s. Francis Walker and Julia (Wheeler) R.; m. Kent Brain, June 23, 1956; children: Kryston R. Fischer, F. Halsey, Julia L., John H. BA, Princeton U., 1952; MA, Columbia U., 1956; MPA, Harvard U., 1962. Fgn. svc. officer Dept. of State, 1956-93; econ. counselor Am. Embassy, London, 1970-72; counselor U.S. Mission to OECD, Paris, 1972-75; office dir. Bur. Inter.-Am. Affairs Dept. of State, Washington, 1975-78; econ. counselor Am. Embassy, Mexico City, 1978-82; prof. Nat. Def. U., Washington, 1982-85; econ. counselor Am. Embassy, Pretoria, South Africa, 1986-90, amb. Mbabane, Swaziland, 1990-93; ret., 1993. Bd. dirs. Cen. Atlantic Conf., United Ch. of Christ, 2000-03; v.p. Princeton U. Class 1952, 2002-07, pres., 2007—12. Lt. (jg) USN, 1952-55. Recipient Outstanding Civilian Svc. award Dept. of Army, 1985. Mem. Am. Fgn. Svc. Assn., Diplomatic and Consular Officers Ret., Nassau Club (Princeton, N.J.). Mem. United Ch. Of Christ. Home: 3803 Ivydale Dr Annandale VA 22003-2006

ROGERS, STEVEN A., energy executive; B in Economics & Acctg., Coll. Holy Cross, Worcester, Mass., 1983. With Deloitte & Touche; contr., treas. Rehab Mgmt. Inc.; mgr., internal audit Dominion Resources, Inc., Richmond, Va., 1996—97, v.p., contr., OptaCor Fin. Svcs. Co. subs. of Dominion Capital Inc., 1997—98, corp. contr., Dominion Energy Inc., 1998—2000, v.p., contr., 2000—06; v.p., prin.

acctg. officer Va. Power Co. (subs. Dominion Resources, Inc.), 2000—06; sr. v.p., contr. Consol. Natural Gas Co. (subs. Dominion Resources, Inc.), 2006; sr. v.p. Dominion Resources, Inc., 2006—, chief acctg. officer, 2007; sr. v.p., chief acctg. officer Va. Power Co. (subs. Dominion Resources, Inc.), 2007, Consol. Natural Gas Co. (subs. Dominion Resources, Inc.), 2007; chief adminstrv. officer Dominion Resources, Inc., 2007—; pres., chief adminstrv. officer Dominion Resources Services, Inc., 2007—. Mem. acctg. exec. adv. com. Edison Electric Inst., 2002—, chmn. acctg. exec. adv. com., 2005—06. Bd. mem. Crisis Pregnancy Ctr. Met. Richmond, 2003—, chmn. bd. Office: Dominion Resources Inc 120 Tredegar St Richmond VA 23219 Office Phone: 804-819-2000. Office Fax: 804-819-2233. Business E-Mail: steven.rogers@dom.com.

ROGERS, TERRY, state legislator; b. Nov. 04; m. Laura Rogers; 5 children. B, Berry Coll., Mount Berry, Ga., 1977. Sales, mktg. and banking profl.; founder, mng. ptnr. Diversified Technologies, 2001—; mem. Dist. 10 Ga. House of Reps., Atlanta, 2011—. Chmn. Banks, Rabun and Habersham County Joint Devel. Authority; vice chmn. Habersham Devel. Authority. Mem., elder First Presbyn Ch. Clarkesville, Ga.; mem. exec. bd. NE Coun. of Boy Scouts America. Republican. Office: 2403 New Liberty Rd Clarkesville GA 30523 also: Ga House of Reps 612-B coverdell Legis Office Bldg Atlanta GA 30334 Office Phone: 706-754-8322, 404-656-0325. Business E-Mail: terry.rogers@house.ga.gov.

ROGERS, WILLIAM H., JR., bank executive; Exec. v.p. SunTrust Securities, Inc., Atlanta; sr. v.p. fin. SunTrust Banks, Inc., Atlanta, corp. exec. v.p. wealth and investment mgmt., mortgage, comml. and corp. and investment banking lines of bus., pres., 2008—11, pres., CEO, 2011—, chmn., 2012—. Office: SunTrust Banks Inc PO Box 4418 Atlanta GA 30302-4418 Office Phone: 404-588-7711. Office Fax: 404-827-6173.

ROGOVIN, LAWRENCE H., lawyer; b. NYC, June 10, 1932; s. Abraham and Laura R.; m. Saundra Schwartz, Aug. 11, 1957; children: Jayne Lina, Wendy Renee, Evan Lewis. BS in Econ., Wharton Sch. U. Pa., 1953; LLB cum laude, NYU Law Sch., 1956. Bar: NY 1956, Fla. 1971. Dep. asst. atty. gen. State of N.Y., 1956-57, asst. atty. gen., 1960-61; assoc. Squadron, Gartenberg, Ellenoff & Plesent and predecessors, NYC, 1962-67, ptnr., 1967-72; pvt. practice Miami, Fla., 1972—74, Lawrence H. Rogovin, P.A., Miami, 1983—98, 2002—; ptnr. Squadron, Ellenoff, Plesent & Lehrer, NYC, 1974-75, Cohen, Angel & Rogovin, North Miami, Fla., 1978-82, Cohen, Rogovin, Reed & Ivans, Miami, 1982-83; v.p., gen. counsel Rarc, Inc., Miami, 1998—2002. 1st lt. JAGC, USAFR, 1957-60. Recipient NYU Founders Day award, 1956. Mem.: ABA, Fla. Bar Assn. Office: 20281 E Country Club Dr Ste 1901 Miami FL 33180 Business E-Mail: lrogovin@bellsouth.net.

ROGOWSKI, GREGORY S., manufacturing executive; BS in Chemistry, Va. Tech.; MS in Polymer Chemistry, U. Akron, Ohio; MBA in Mktg., U. Richmond, Va. Worked Atlantic Rsch. Corp., Goodyear Tire and Rubber Co.; joined AlliedSignal, 1986, global mktg. dir.; pres., CEO Performance Fibers, 2004—09; pres., Mueller Co. Ltd Mueller Water Products, Inc., 2009—. Office: Mueller Water Products Inc Ste 1200 1200 Albernathy Rd NE Atlanta GA 30328 Office Phone: 770-206-4200. Business E-Mail: grogowski@muellerwp.com.

ROGSTAD, BARRY KENT, electric power industry executive; b. Winchendon, Mass., Sept. 14, 1940; s. Harry Nelson and Harriet Atherton (Cross) H.; m. Lorraine Ann Arsenault, June 13, 1964; children: Aimee Grace, Erik Nils. AB in History, Clark U., 1962, MA in Economics, 1963; PhD in Economics, Brown U., 1968. Instr., economics Brown University, Providence, 1965—68; mgr., economics divsn. Planning Rsch. Corp., McLean, Va., 1968—71; v.p., bd. dirs. Systan, Inc., Washington, 1971—75; chief economist Coopers & Lybrand, ptnr., bd. dirs. Washington, 1975—88; pres. Am. Bus. Conf., Washington, 1988. Bd. dirs. Baldor Electric Co., 2001—. Home: 11610 Beall Mountain Rd Potomac MD 20854-1126 Office: Baldor Electric Co 5711 R S Boreham Jr St Fort Smith AR 72901 Office Phone: 479-646-4711. Office Fax: 479-648-5792. Business E-Mail: brogstad@baldor.com.

ROHACK, JOHN JAMES, cardiologist; b. Rochester, NY, Aug. 22, 1954; s. John Joseph and Margaret Elizabeth (McLaughlin) R.; m. Charlotte (Charli)McCown, Dec. 7, 1980; 1 child, Elisha Monique Feigle. BS with highest honors, U. Tex., El Paso, 1976; MD with honors, U. Tex. Med. Branch, Galveston, 1980. Diplomate Am. Bd. Internal Medicine. Intern U. Tex. Med. Br. Hosps., Galveston, 1980—81, resident internal medicine, 1981-83, chief resident internal medicine, 1983-84, fellow cardiology, 1984-86; instr. medicine U. Tex. Med. Br., Galveston, 1983-86; asst. prof. medicine to assoc. prof. Tex. A&M Coll. Medicine, College Station, 1986—2002, prof., 2002—, sect. chief cardiology, 1989-97, prof., 2002—. Assoc. med. dir. Scott and White Health Plan Bryan Coll. Sta., 1995-97; assoc. med. dir. for med. ops. Scott and White Clinic, Temple, Tex., 1997-2000, med. dir. Health Plan, 2000-04, med. dir. sys. improvement, 2004-, dir. healthcare policy, 2004-, sr. staff cardiologist; bd. dirs. Health for All Clinic, v.p., 1994-96; mem. Accreditation Coun. on Continuing Med. Edn., 1995-99, Liaison Com. on Med. Edn., 1999-2001; med. dir. Fitlife Ctr. Tex. A&M U., College Station, 1990-97; mem. bd. commrs. Joint Commn. on Accreditation of Healthcare Orgns., 2002—2008. Bd. dirs. Am. Heart Assn., Brazos Valley College Station, 1987-97, Tex. affiliate Austin, 1991-98, 1st v.p., 1994-95, pres.-elect, 1995-96, pres., 1996-97. Named Disting. Alumnus, U. Tex., El Paso, U. Tex., Galveston; named one of 50 Most Powerful Physician Executives in Healthcare, Modern Healthcare and Modern Physician, 2009. Fellow ACP, Am. Coll. Cardiology (bd. dirs. Tex. chpt. 1992-97); mem. AMA (alt. del. house of dels. 1984-93, del. 1993-2001, coun. on med. edn. 1995-2001, chair elect 1996-97, chair 1997-98, bd. trustee 2001-11, pres.-elect 2008-, exec. com. 2003-06, chair 2004-05, pres.-elect 2008-2009, pres. 2009-10, immediate past. pres., 2010-11), Tex. Med. Assn. (exec. coun. med. student sect. 1981-82, chair, coun. on med. edn., house of dels. 1982—, trustee 1994-2002, pres.-elect 1999-2000, pres. 2000-2001). Avocations: golf, gardening, reading, ranching. Office: Scott and White Clinic 2401 S 31st St Temple TX 76508-0001

ROHMAN, THOMAS P., lawyer; b. Portsmouth, Va., 1955; BBA in acctg., Notre Dame U., 1977; JD summa cum laude, Mich. State U., 1982; LLM in Taxation, NYU, 1983. CPA Va., 1980; bar: Va. 1983, US Tax Ct. 1986. With KPMG Peat Marwick, 1977—80; ptnr. McGuireWoods LLP, Richmond, Va., 1991—, chmn. firm taxation & employee benefits dept., 1999—2005. Adj. prof. corp. reorganization Va. Commonwealth U. Grad. Tax Program, 1986—92; adj. prof. partnership taxation & corp. taxation TC Williams Sch. Law, U. Richmond, 1989—; mem. adv. coun. William and Mary Tax Conf., 1994—. Co-author: S Corporations: Federal Taxation, 1989. Mem. adv. bd. Meml. Found. for Children, 1987—; me. bd. dirs. Va. Commonwealth U. Found., 2008—, Feed More, 2009—; mem. U. Va. Tax Conf. Bd. Advisors. Fellow: Am. Coll. Tax Counsel; mem.: ABA (mem. com. on S corporations, com. on corp. tax, com. on partnerships), Va. Soc. Cert. Pub. Accountants, Am. Inst. Cert. Pub. Accountants. Office: McGuireWoods LLP One James Ctr 901 E Cary St Richmond VA 23219-4030 Office Phone: 804-775-1032. Office Fax: 804-698-2154. Business E-Mail: trohman@mcguirewoods.com.

ROHR, DAVIS CHARLES, aerospace consultant, retired military officer; b. Burlington, Wis., Oct. 29, 1929; s. Charles Davis Rohr and Dorothy Elizabeth (Hahn) Rohr Larson; m. Gayle Lynn White, Aug. 22, 1959; children— Ellen Louise, Jean Elizabeth Student, Northwestern U., 1947-48; B.Sc., U.S. Mil. Acad., 1952; MA, U. Wash., 1960. Commd. 2d lt. USAF, 1952, advanced through grades to maj. gen, 1980, fighter pilot Ohio, Korea, Japan, 1954-58; asst. prof. history USAF Acad., Colo., 1960-64; fighter pilot, squadron ops. officer Idaho and, Fed. Republic Germany, 1965-69; fighter squadron comdr. Vietnam, 1969-70; country dir. S.Am. Office of Sec. of Def., Washington, 1970-73; exec. officer, dep. dir. maintenance Hdqrs. Tactical Air Command, 1973-75; tactical fighter wing comdr. Tex., Utah, 1976-79; chief Office of Mil. Coop., Cairo, 1979—81; dir. plans and policy U.S. European Command, Stuttgart, Fed. Republic Germany, 1981-84; dep. comdr. in chief U.S. Cen. Command, MacDill AFB, Fla., 1984-87, ret.; aerospace cons., 1988—. Adj. prof. history Paradise Valley C.C., 1991-94; real estate broker, 1991—; mem., chmn. Scottsdale Airport Commn., 1995-2001. Decorated Def. Dist. Svc. medal, 2 Def. Superior Service medals, Legion of Merit with cluster, Dist.Flying Cross, Meritorious Service medal, Air medal with 14 clusters, Air Force Commendation medal, Purple Heart

ROHR, MARK C., chemicals executive; BS in Chemistry and Chem. Engring., Miss. State U. Exec. leadership positions including sr. v.p. Occidental Chem. Corp.; exec v.p. ops. Albemarle Corp., Richmond, Va., 1999, pres., COO, 2000—02, pres., CEO, 2002—08, chmn., pres., CEO, 2008—11, exec. chmn., 2011—12; chmn., CEO Celanese Corp., Irving, Tex., 2012—. Bd. dirs. Ashland Corp., American Chem. Coun., Celanese Corp., 2007—; sec. Synthetic Organic Chem. Mfr. Assn.; mem. exec. com. NAM. Mem. adv. bd. Miss. State U. Coll. Arts & Sciences. Office: Celanese Corporation 222 W Las Colinas Blvd Ste 900N Irving TX 75039 Office Phone: 804-788-6000. Office Fax: 804-788-5688. Business E-Mail: mark_rohr@albemarle.com.

ROHRICH, ROD(NEY) JAMES, plastic surgeon, educator; b. Eureka, SD, Aug. 5, 1953; s. Claude and Katie (Schumacher) R.; m. Diane Louise Gibby, July 3, 1990; children: Taylor Rodney, Rachel Nicole. BA summa cum laude, ND State U., 1975; MD with honors, Baylor Coll., 1979; LittD (hon.), U. ND, 2006. FLEX 1979; diplomate Am. Bd. Plastic Surgery, 1987, Nat. Bd. Med. Examiners, 1980; cert. in hand surgery, 1990. Resident U. Mich. Med. Ctr.; pediatric plastic surgery Oxford U., England; chief plastic surgery Parkland/Zale U. Med. Ctr., Dallas, 1989—99; prof., chmn. dept. plastic surgery U. Tex. Southwestern Med. Ctr., 1991—. Pres., faculty senate U. Tex., chair in plastic surgery; pres. ASPS Mem. editl. bd. Selected Readings in Plastic Surgery, The Cleft Palate and Craniofacial Jour.; editor Plastic and Reconstructive Surgery, 2005—; contbr. more than 500 articles to med. jours. Bd. dirs. March of Dimes, Dallas, Save-the-Children Dallas, Am. Cancer Soc.; adv. bd. Evergreen Gala, ACS; founding mem. Dallas for Children Found., co-chair; vol. East Dallas Mobile Health Unit. Grantee Urban Rsch. Fund, 1982, United Kingdom Ltd. Ednl. Rsch. Fund, 1983, Oxford Cleft Palate Found., 1983, Am. Assn. Plastic Surgeons, 1985, Plastic Surgery Ednl. Found., 1985, 89, 90, U. Tex. Health Sci. Ctr. Dept. Surgery, 1986, Howmedica, 1989, ConvaTec-Squibb, 1989, 91, ConvaTec, 1991; recipient Disting Svc. award Plastic Surg. Ednl. Found., 1997, Alumni Achievement award, N.D. State U., 1997; named one of Best Drs. in Dallas, 2000-, Super Drs. in Tex., 2005-, Best Drs. in America, 1996-, Good Housekeeping Mag., 1998. Mem. AAAS, AMA (Thomas Cronin award 1988, 90, Clifford C. Snyder award 1990), fellow, ACS, Am. Assn. Hand Surgery, Am. Burn Assn., Am. Cleft Palate Assn., Am. Soc. Law and Medicine, Am. Soc. Maxillofacial Surgeons, Am. Soc. for Surgery the Hand, Am. Soc. Plastic and Reconstructive Surgeons, Am. Trauma Soc., British Med. Assn., Nat. Vascular Malformations Found. Inc. (med. and sci. adv. bd.) Tex. Med. Assn., Tex. Soc. Plastic Surgeons, Mass. Gen. Hosp. Hand Club, Dallas County Med. Soc., Assn. Acad. Chmn. Plastic Surgery (pres.), Dallas Soc. Plastic Surgeons, Harvard Med. Sch. Alumni Assn., Inst. for Study of Profl. Risk, Plastic Surgery Rsch. Coun., Reed O. Dingman Soc. Plastic Surgeons, So. Med. Assn., Am. Soc. Plastic Surgeons (pres. 2004), Assn. Academic Chairmen Plastic Surgery (pres. 2008). Republican. Roman Catholic. Office: UT Southwestern Med Ctr Dept Plastic Surgery 1801 Inwood Rd WA4 212 Dallas TX 75390-9132 Office Phone: 214-645-3119. Office Fax: 214-645-3105. Business E-Mail: rod.rohrich@utsouthwestern.edu.

ROJAS, CARLOS, literature and language educator; b. Barcelona, Aug. 12, 1928; s. Carlos and Luisa (Vila) R.; m. Eunice Anne Mitcham, Mar. 19, 1966; children: Carlos, Eunice Anne. MA, U. Barcelona, 1951; PhD, U. Cen., Madrid, 1955; PhD (hon.), U. Simón Bólivar, Barranquilla, Colombia, 1985. Teaching asst. U. Barcelona, 1951-52; fgn. asst. U. Glasgow, Scotland, 1952-54; asst. prof. Rollins Coll., Winter Park, Fla., 1957-60, Emory U., Atlanta, 1960-63, assoc. prof., 1963-68, prof., 1968-80, Charles Howard Candler prof. Spanish lit., 1980-96, Charles Howard Candler prof. emeritus, 1996. Author: Auto de fe, 1968 (Premio Nacional de Literatura 1968), Azana, 1973 (Planeta award 1973), El Igenioso Hidalgo y Poeta F.G. asciende a los infiernos, 1980 (Nadal award 1980), El Sueno de Sarajevo, 1982, El Jardin de las Hespèrides, 1988, El Jardin de Atocha, 1990, Yo, Goya, 1990, Proceso A Godoy, 1992, Salvador Dali, or the Art of Spitting on Your Mother's Portrait, 1993, Alfonso de Borbón Habla Con El Demonio, 1995, !Muera La Inteligencia! !Viva La Muerte! Salamanca, 1995, The Garden of Janus, 1996, Crónica de la Guerra Civil Española, 1996; co-author, contbg. editor Spanish Civil War documents, Momentos estelares de la guerra de España, 1996, La Vida y la Época de Carlos IV, 1997, Los Borbones Destronados, 1997, El bastardo del Rey, 1999, The Garden of the Hesperides, 1999, Puneta La Espaneta, 2000, Despiada Memoria: Memorias, 2002, Diez Crisis del Franquismo, 2003, Por Que Perdimos la Guerra, 2006, El Enigma de la Vie, 2007, The Ingenious Gentleman and Poet Federico Garcia Lorca Ascands to Hall, New Haven & London, 2013. Recipient Premio Espejo de España award, Madrid, 1984, Encomienda al Mérito Civil, King of Spain, 1986, Univ. Scholar/Tchr. award Emory U., 1987, Arts and Scis. award of Distinction, Emory U., 2001; honoree of yr. Philol. Assn. of Carolinas, 1987, Llave de Barcelona, 2003. Mem. MLA, Am. Assn. Tchrs. Spanish and Portuguese (Premio a la Lealtad Republicana Madrid 2004), Assn. Doctores y Licenciados Españoles en los Estados Unidos (bd. dirs.), South Atlantic MLA (hon.). Avocation: painting. Home: 1378 Harvard Rd NE Atlanta GA 30306-2413 Home Phone: 404-378-0678. Personal E-mail: crojas49@gmail.com.

ROJIANI, AMYN M., pathologist, educator; MD, U. Karachi, 1982; PhD, UMDNJ, 1988. Diplomate Am. Bd. Pathology, 1992; cert. in neuropathology 1992, physician exec. 2012. Instr. dept. pathology, immunology and lab. medicine U. Fla. Coll. Medicine, 1992—94; asst. prof. U. Fla., Gainesville, 1994—98; mem. Graduate Faculty, UF, USF, 1997—2010; assoc. prof. pathology and interdisciplinary oncology USF, 2003, prof. dept. oncologic scis. and pathology, 2003—10; Edgar R. Pund disting. prof. chmn., dept. pathology Med. Coll. Ga., 2010—; course dir. MGI Faculty Regional Adv. Panels, San Antonio, 2006—07, Osler Bd. Review Course Neuropathology Sect., Am. Soc. Clin. Pathologists, 2004; dir. Nat. Meeting Workshop, Am. Soc. Clin. Pathologists, 1999. Chair program com. AANP, 2008—09; v.p. Am. Assn. Neuropathologists, 2008—09, exec. coun. mem., 2007—09; editl. bd. mem. Jour. Neuropathology & Experimental Neurology, 1999—2004, 2006—, Int J Clin. & Experimental Pathology, 2009—. Contbr. articles to profl. publs. Recipient Bronze Leadership award, USF Leadership Inst., 2006, Tchg. Excellence award, Osler Bd. Review Course Neuropathology Section, 2008, Faculty Recognition award, Resident Tng. Program, U. Fla., 1995, 1997, Ga. Disting. Cancer award, 2010—; named Guide to America's Top Physicians, CRCA, 2004—09. Mem.: Am. Assn. Cancer Rsch., Metastasis Rsch. Soc., Am. Coll. Physician Execs., Internat. Soc. Neuropathologists, Am. Assn. Neuropathologists, Assn. Pathology Chairs. Office: 1120 Fifteenth St BF 104 Augusta GA 30912 Office Phone: 706-721-2923. Business E-Mail: arojiani@georgiahealth.edu, argian@gru.edu.*

ROLF, HOWARD LEROY, mathematician, educator; b. Laverne, Okla., Nov. 25, 1928; s. James Walter and Edith (Yoho) R.; m. Anita Jane Ward, June 24, 1961; children: James Scott, Jennifer Jane, Stephanie Kaye, Rhonda Mary. BS, Okla. Baptist U., 1951; MA, Vanderbilt U., 1953, PhD, 1956. Instr. math. Vanderbilt U., 1954-56, asst. prof., dir. computer ctr., 1959-64; asst. prof. Baylor U., 1956-57, prof., 1964-98, dir. acad. computing, 1968-70, chmn. dept. math., 1971-97. Assoc. prof. Georgetown Coll., Ky., 1957—59. Author: (with William C. Brown) Mathematics, 1982, Finite Mathematics, 1988, 91, 94, 99, 02, 05, 08, (with Brooks-Cole) Mathematics for Management, Social and Life Sciences, 1991. Mem. Math. Assn. Am. (chmn. Tex. sect. 1977), Sigma Xi, Pi Mu Epsilon, Golden Key. Baptist. Home: 4096 Speegleville Rd Waco TX 76712-4033 Business E-Mail: howard_rolf@baylor.edu.

ROLFE, CHRISTOPHER C., energy executive; BS in Mech. Engring., NC State U. Registered profl. engr., NC, SC. Engring. asst. design engring. dept. Duke Energy (formerly Duke Power Co.), 1972, v.p. corp. performance, 1992—97, v.p. corp. human resources, 1997—2000, v.p. human resources, 2000, group exec., chief human resources officer, group exec., chief adminstrv. officer, 2006—. Chmn. NC Commn. Workforce Devel. Recipient Jack Callahan Cornerstone award, Goodwill Industries of So. Piedmont of NC, 2007. Office: Duke Energy 526 S Church St Charlotte NC 28202-1904 Office Phone: 704-594-6200.

ROLFE, ROBERT MARTIN, lawyer; b. Richmond, Va., May 16, 1951; s. Norman and Bertha (Cohen) R.; children: P. Alexander, Asher B., Joel A., Zachary A. BA, U. Va., 1973, JD, 1976. Bar: Va. 1976, NY 1985, US Dist. Ct. (ea. and we. dists.) Va. 1976, US Ct. Appeals (4th cir.) 1976, US Ct. Appeals (2d cir.) 1979, US Dist. Ct. (ea. dist.) Mich. 1985, US Ct. Appeals (DC cir.) 1985, US Dist. Ct. (so. and ea. dists.) NY 1985, US Ct. Appeals (7th cir.) 1995, US Ct. Fed. Claims, 1997, US Supreme Ct. 1979, US Dist. Ct. DC, 2010. Assoc. Hunton & Williams LLP, Richmond, 1976—83, ptnr., 1983—, co-head litig., intellectual property and antitrust team, 1995—2007, gen. counsel, 1995—, exec. com., 1998—2004. Editorial bd. Va. Law Rev., 1976; contbr. articles to profl. jours. Trustee, pres. bd. trustees Jewish Family Supporting Found., chmn. of bd. trustees, 2005-; bd. dirs. Jewish Family Svcs., Richmond, pres., 1993-95; bd. mgrs., 2d v.p. Congregation Beth Ahabah, 1995-97, 1st v.p., 1997-99, United Way of Greater Richmond Action Coun. Children Youth and Families, 2008-. Fellow Am. Bar Found.; mem. ABA (litig. sect.), Va. Bar Assn., Va. State Bar, Richmond Bar Assn., Order of Coif (Alumni award for acad. excellence U. Va. 1976), Youth and Families Action Coun. Home: 18 Greenway Ln Richmond VA 23226-1630 Office: Hunton & Williams Riverfront Plz East Tower 951 E Byrd St Richmond VA 23219-4074 also: 200 Park Ave New York NY 10166-0005 Office Phone: 804-788-8466. Office Fax: 804-343-4568. Business E-Mail: rrolfe@hunton.com.

ROLLING, LINCOLN CURTIS, history professor; b. Houston, Sept. 12, 1950; s. Lincoln Curtis and Laurel Rolling; m. Jacquelyne Jones, Feb. 26, 1972; children: Jacquelyn Michelle, Lincoln Curtis III. BA, Sam Houston State, 1971, MA, 1975; PhD, U. Tex., Austin, 1992. Prof. history Cedar Valley Coll., Lancaster, Tex., 1977—; tchr. Windham Sch. Dist., Huntsville, Tex. Fulbright curriculum specialist Eastfield Coll., Mesquite, Tex. Pres. So. Hills Assn., Dallas. Home: 942 Brookwood Dallas TX Office: Cedar Valley Coll 3030 N Dallas Ave Lancaster TX 75134 Office Fax: 972-860-2988. Personal E-mail: aka1808@aol.com. Business E-Mail: linc@dcccd.edu.

ROLLINS, CARL P., II, state legislator; b. Aug. 4, 1947; Former mem. Midway City Coun.; former mayor. Midway, Ky.; mkt. mgr. The Student Loan People; mem. Woodford County Bd. of Health, Midway Nursing Home Task Force, Woodford Fiscal Ct.; mem. Dist. 56 Ky. House of Reps., 2007—. Mem.: KCEA, KCEA, KASFAA, Midway Lions Club. Democrat. Disciples Of Christ. Office: Ky Legislature Rm 367 702 Capitol Ave Frankfort KY 40601 Mailing: PO Box 424 Midway KY 40347 Office Phone: 502-564-8100 ext. 736. E-mail: Carl.Rollins@lrc.ky.gov.

ROLLINS, GARY WAYNE, landscape company executive; b. Chattanooga, Aug. 30, 1944; s. Orville Wayne and Grace (Crum) R.; m. Ruth Magness; children: Glen William, Ruth Ellen, Nancy Louise, Orville Wayne. BSBA, U. Tenn., 1967. Sales mgmt. Orkin Exterminating Co., 1967-72, v.p., ops., 1975-78, pres., 1978; chmn. Orkin, LLC, 2004; v.p., gen. mgr. Dwoskin, 1972-75; v.p. LOR, Inc., 1978; pres. Rollins Supply, Inc., Atlanta; with Rollins, Inc., 1959, v.p., 1972-84, bd. dirs., 1981—, pres., COO, 1984—, CEO, 2001—. Bd. dirs. Rollins Leasing Co., Wilmington, Del., Rollins Energy Services, Atlanta, RPC Energy Svcs., Inc. Mem. Atlanta Symphony, 1970—, Atlanta Humane Soc., 1970—, Atlanta High Mus. Art, 1970—, Ga. Structural Pest Control Commn., 1967; founding dir. Tuxedo Park Civic Assn., Atlanta, 1984—. Recipient de Tocqueville Soc. award United Way, 1987. Mem. PADI Open Water Diving, Piedmont Driving Club. Clubs: Cherokee (Atlanta). Methodist. Avocations: hunting, camping, scuba diving, family activities. Office: Rollins Inc 2170 Piedmont Rd NE Atlanta GA 30324-4196 Office Phone: 404-888-2000. Office Fax: 404-888-2662. Business E-Mail: grollins@rollinscorp.com.

ROLOSON, DWAYNE, professional hockey player; b. Simcoe, Ont., Canada, Oct. 12, 1969; m. Melissa Roloson; children: Brett, Ross. Grad., U. Mass., Lowell, 1994. Goaltender Calgary Flames, 1996—98, Buffalo Sabres, 1998—2000, Minn. Wild, 2001—06, Edmonton Oilers, 2006—09, NY Islanders, 2009—11, Tampa Bay Lightning, 2011—. Recipient Roger Crozier Saving Grace Award, NHL, 2004; named to NHL All-Star Game, 2004; finalist Hobey Baker Award, 1994. Office: Tampa Bay Lightning Hockey Club St Pete Times Forum 401 Channelside Dr Tampa FL 33602

ROMAN, GREGORY A., information technology executive; BS in Polit. Sci., U.S. Air Force Acad.; MS in Mgmt., Troy State U., Ala.; MBA in Info. Tech., Colo. Tech. U. Air staff tactical cryptologic program element monitor US Air Force, comdr., 390th Intelligence Squadron, Kadena AB Japan, chief, Intelligence Ops. Divsn., North Am. Def. Command and US Space Command, various positions including comdr., 544th Info. Ops. Group, Peterson AFB Colo.; air force legis. liaison US Armed Svcs. Com., US Senate Intelligence Com., House Intelligence Com.; v.p., dir., remote sensing programs SRA Internat., Inc., Colorado Springs; sr. v.p., space and intelligence, surveillance and reconnaissance svcs. ManTech International Corp., 2010—. Office: ManTech Internat Corp 12015 Lee Jackson Hwy Fairfax VA 22033 Home: 2910 Bonne Vista Dr Colorado Springs CO 80906 Office Phone: 719-229-7464. Office Fax: 703-218-8296. Business E-Mail: gregory.roman@mantech.com.

ROMAN, JUAN JOSE, corporate financial executive; BA in Bus. Adminstrn., U. Puerto Rico, Rio Piedras. CPA, 1989. With KPMG LLP, 1987—95; v.p., fin. Triple-C, Inc., 1996—99, exec. v.p., 1999—2002; v.p., fin., CFO Triple-S Management Corp., 2002—. Mem.: The Puerto Rico Society of Cert. Public Accountants. Office: Triple-S Management Corp 1441 FD Roosevelt Ave San Juan PR 00920 Office Phone: 787-749-4949. Office Fax: 787-749-4191. Business E-Mail: jroman@ssspr.com.

ROMAN, RAY, information technology executive; BS in Fin., U. Ill., Chgo.; MBA in Fin. & Mktg., U. Chgo., 1992. Gen. mgr., sales and service Ameritech Small Bus. Svcs.; pres. NE divsn., corp. controller, v.p., fin. planning & analysis Alliant Foodservice; v.p., sales AT&T Wireless, 2001—03; corp v.p., gen. mgr., North Am., mobile devices Motorola, Inc., 2003—05; sr. v.p., worldwide sales, mobile devices Motorola Inc, 2005—07; v.p., Global Consumer Ops., Svc., Software & Peripherals Dell, Inc. Coach youth soccer team, youth basketball team. Named one of the best 40 under 40 in business, Crain's Chicago Business, 2005. Office: Dell Inc One Dell Way Round Rock TX 78682 Office Phone: 512-338-4400. Office Fax: 512-728-3653. Business E-Mail: ray_roman@dell.com.

ROMANKO, MARK W., food service executive; Regional v.p. restaurant ops. Cracker Barrel Old Country Store, Inc. Office: Cracker Barrel Old Country Store Inc 305 Hartmann Dr Lebanon TN 37088-0787 Office Phone: 615-444-5533. Office Fax: 615-443-9476.

ROMANO, EMILIO, broadcast executive; married; 2 children. Grad. in Law cum laude, Escuela Libre De Derecho, Mexico City, Mexico; grad. in Internat. Law, City of London Polytechnic, London, Eng. With Mexican Ministry Fin., 1989—94, gen. dir. revenue policy, fed. fiscal atty.; dir. mergers & acquisitions then v.p. internat. ops. Grupo Televisa; co-founder, mng. ptnr. Border Group, LLC, 2001; CEO Grupo Mexicana de Aviacion, 2004—07; pres., CEO Grupo Puerta Alameda, Telemundo Network, Hialeah, Fla., 2011—. Prof. tax law Escuela Libre de Derecho, 1994; bd. dirs. Univision Comm., 1995—98, Claxson Interactive, Tam Linhas Aereas, 2009—. Mem.: Internat. Air Transport Assn. (pres. Internat. Airline Training Fund Coun.). Office: Telemundo Network 2290 W 8th Ave Hialeah FL 33010-2017*

ROMANO, RAYMOND G., mortgage company executive; married, May 17, 1986. BS in Fin., Long Island U. Cert. IMC. Asst. mortgage fin. mgr. Citicorp N. Am. Investment Bank; v.p. underwriting ops. Dime Savs. Bank; sr. v.p., chief credit risk officer and exec. positions N.Am. Mortgage Co., Tampa, 1997—2001; sr. v.p. chief credit & risk mgmt. officer home loan divsn. Washington Mutual, 2001—04; sr. v.p., chief credit officer, credit risk oversight Freddie Mac, 2004—09; exec. v.p., chief credit officer Freddie Mac - Federal Home Loan Mortgage Corp., 2009—. Office: Freddie Mac 8200 Jones Branch Dr Mc Lean VA 22102 Office Phone: 703-903-2000. Office Fax: 703-903-2759. Business E-Mail: raymond.romano@freddiemac.com.

ROMANOWITZ, BYRON FOSTER, architect, engineer; b. Covington, Ky., Nov. 14, 1929; s. Harry Alex and Mildred (Foster) R.; m. Mildred Elaine Gize, June 15, 1957; children: Laura Ann, Mark Walter, Cynthia Ellen. BS in Civil Engring, U. Ky., 1951; M.F.A. in Architecture, Princeton, 1953. Instr. sch. architecture Princeton U., 1954; architect Brock & Johnson, Lexington, 1958-59, Johnson & Romanowitz, Architects, Lexington and Louisville, 1960-2000; ret., 2000. Pres. Ky. Bd. examiners and Registration of Archs., 1975-91; instr. U. Ky. Sch. Architecture, 1996, 2000; mem. Ky. Archtl. Svcs. Selection Com., 2006, 2007, 2008, 2009, 2010, 2011. asst. resident officer in Charge of Constrn., Naval Air Sta. Denver, Grissom Air Force Base Peru, Ind. Artist. Voice of Practice U. Cin. Coll. Design, Arch. Art & Planning, 2001-02, prin. works include U. Ky. campus bldgs., 1959-96, Ea. Ky. U. campus bldgs., 1959-77, Centre Coll., Danville, Ky., campus bldgs., 1967-89, Georgetown (Ky.) Coll. campus bldgs., 1964-84, Asbury Coll., Wilmore, Ky., 1972-78, Asbury Theol. Sem., 1978-93, Berea Coll. bldgs., 1978-91, Transylvania U. bldgs., 1974-98, U. Louisville, 1990-98, 11 downtown Lexington office bldgs.; leader Men of Note Orch., 1986—, Jazzberry Jam Combo, 1993—; author: Jazz in Lexington, A Personal View, 2006, Issues & Images-Fifty Years as a Kentucky Architect, 2007. Mem. Lexington Urban Renewal Commn., 1963-69; chmn. adv. bd. Salvation Army, 1971-72; trustee Midway (Ky.) Coll., 1986-95; appt. architect svcs. sel. com. Commonwealth Ky., 20050172. lt. comdr. USNR. Lt. comdr. Civil Engineer Corps USNR. Recipient award of merit nat. archtl. competition AIA/Ednl. Facilities Lab., 1966 Fellow AIA (1st honor awards Ky. archtl. competition 1959, 61, 68, 70, 73, 78, 80, 81, pres. East Ky. chpt. 1965); mem. Ky. Soc. Architects (pres. 1966), Masons, Rotary, Lexington Club, Navy League, Tau Beta Pi, Phi Mu Alpha, Phi Sigma Kappa. Avocation: jazz. Home: 2057 Lakeside Dr Lexington KY 40502-3016 Business E-Mail: mbromano@insightbb.com.

ROMANS, DONALD BISHOP, retired manufacturing executive; b. Louisville, Apr. 22, 1931; s. Albert D. and Moneta (Bishop) R.; m. Marilyn Yvonne Neff, June 13, 1953 (dec. Aug. 2000); children: Rebecca Ann, Jennifer. BS, U. Louisville, 1953; MBA, Harvard U., 1958. Mgr. internal auditing and data processing, mem. contr. staff Container Corp. Am., Chgo., 1958-62; successively asst. to pres., asst. treas., treas., v.p. fin., sr. v.p. fin., exec. v.p. Trans Union Corp., Chgo., 1962-81; exec. v.p., chief fin. officer Sunbeam Corp., Chgo., 1981-82, Bally Mfg. Corp., Chgo., 1982-87; fin. cons. Chgo., 1987; pres. Romans and Co., Chgo., 1987—. Cantor Op. Alt. Inv. Fund; life trustee St. Mary of Nazareth Hosp. Capt. USMCR, 1953-56. Republican. Avocation: tennis. Home: 3234 Golfside Dr Naples FL 34110-7006

ROMANS, JAY, waste management executive; BS, Kent State U., Ohio; MS, Tex. A&M U., College Station. Corp. orgn. devel. specialist Firestone Tire & Rubber Co., 1974; mgr. orgnl. devel. Clark Equipment, 1979—81; mgr. tng. and devel. Union Pacific/Champlin Petroleum Co., 1981—88; supr. orgnl. devel. Amoco Pipeline Co., 1988—89; dir. orgn. devel. and staffing Ecolab/Chemlawn Svc. Corp.; mgr. tng. and devel. to dir. employee and orgn. devel. Amoco Oil Co., 1990—93; sr. ptnr. STS Internat., 1993—95; dir. orgn. effectiveness and learning to worldwide v.p. human resources for pre-analytical solutions bus. Becton Dickinson; founder, pres. Romans & Assocs.; sr. v.p. Std. Register Co., Dayton, Ohio, 2001—04; sr. v.p. human resources Hughes Supply, 2004; with St. Joe Co.; sr. v.p. people Waste Management, Inc. Office: Waste Mgmt Inc 1001 Fannin Ste 4000 Houston TX 77002 Office Phone: 713-512-6200.

ROMASKO, DAN, marketing executive; BS in Chem. Engring., Montana State U. With ConocoPhillips; gen. mgr. forts hill syncrude ops. Petro-Canada; v.p. ops. integrity Suncor Energy, v.p. tech. ops. and competence; exec. v.p. ops. Tesoro Corp., 2011—. Office: Tesoro Corporation 19100 Ridgewood Pky San Antonio TX 78259 Office Phone: 210-626-6000. Office Fax: 210-579-4574.

ROMERE, SHARON, human resources specialist; B in Mgmt. Cert. sr. profl. human resources. Dir., human resources Maxxam, Inc., 1990—96; dir., human resources for mergers & acquisitions Aqua-Source, Inc., 1996—2003; dir., human resources Metals USA Holdings Corp., 2003—05, v.p., human resources, 2005—. Office: Metals USA Holdings Corp 2400 E Commercial Blvd Ste 905 Fort Lauderdale FL 33308-4059 Office Phone: 713-965-0990. Office Fax: 713-965-0067.

ROMERO, CRAIG F., state legislator; b. Sept. 25, 1954; m. Pamela Hulin. Parish pres., 1984—92; state senator Dist. 22 La., 1992—; Oilfield Corp. Sales & Cattle farmer. Mem.: La Charolais Breeders Assn., Iberia Cattlemen's Assn. (former pres.). Republican. Mailing: 300 Iberia St Suite B-150 New Iberia LA 70560 Fax: 318-364-7355.

ROMERO, JOYCE E., aerospace and defense manufacturing company executive; Grad. in Advance Program Mgmt., Dept. of Defense Sys. Mgmt. Coll.; B in Bus. Mgmt., Pepperdine U.; M in Sys. Mgmt., U. Southern Calif. Project, design engr. Rockwell Internat., 1982; pres. Boeing Can. Ops. Ltd.; dir., components mfg. site Boeing Co., Salt Lake City, 2005—06; gen. mgr., Boeing Winnipeg Boeing Can. Ops. Ltd., 2006—07; dir., 787 North Am. supply chain integration Boeing Commercial Airplanes, 2007; v.p., advanced aero-solutions Vought Aircraft Industries, Inc., 2007—. Office: Vought Aircraft Industries Inc Tower 1 Ste 900 201 E John Carpenter Freeway Irving TX 75062 Office Phone: 972-946-2011. Business E-Mail: joyce_romero@voughtaircraft.com.

ROMNEY, CARL F., seismologist; b. Salt Lake City, June 5, 1924; m. Barbara Doughty; children: Carolyn Ann, Kim. BS in Meteorology, Calif. Inst. Tech., 1945; PhD, U. Calif., Berkeley, 1956. Seismologist U.S. Dept. Air Force, 1955-58; asst. tech. dir. Air Force Tech. Applications Center, 1958-73; dep. dir. Nuclear Monitoring Research Office, Def. Advanced Research Projects Agy., 1973-75, dir., 1975-79; dep. dir. Def. Advanced Research Projects Agy., 1979-83; dir. Ctr. Seismic Studies, 1983-91; v.p. Sci. Applications Internat. Corp., 1987—2001. Tech. adviser U.S. reps. in negotiations Test Ban Treaty; mem. U.S. del. Geneva Conf. Experts, 1958, Conf. on Discontinuance Nuclear Weapons Tests, 1959, 60; negotiations on threshold Test Ban Treaty, Moscow, 1974; mem. U.S. del. Peaceful Nuclear Explosions Treaty, Moscow, 1974-75 Contbr. articles to tech. jours. Recipient Exceptional Civilian Service awards Air Force, 1959, Exceptional Civilian Service awards Dept. Def., 1964, 79; Pres.'s award for Distinguished Fed. Civilian Service, for outstanding contbns. to devel. of control system for underground nuclear tests, 1967; Presdl. Rank of Meritorious Exec., 1980; inducted in Hall of Honor, Air Intelligence Agy., 1996. Achievements include research on earthquake mechanism, seismic noise; generation, propagation, detection seismic waves from underground explosions. Home: 6739 Stream View Ln Warrenton VA 20187 E-mail: cromney@earthlink.net.

ROMO, LAWRENCE G., federal agency administrator; b. 1956; BS, USAF Acad.; MEd, Mont. State U.-No. Item mgr. Directorate of Spl. Weapons, 1987—92; transition assistance program specialist Kelly AFB, San Antonio, 1992—99; soldier and family assistance program mgr. US Army 5th Recruiting Brigade, San Antonio; dir. Selective Svc. Sys., Arlington, Va., 2009—. Admissions liaison officer dir. South Tex. USAF Acad. Chmn. Bexar County Vets. Com., San Antonio Commn. for Children and Families, Tex. Lt. col. USAFR. Mem.: Mil. Officers Assn. of America, Assn. of US Army, Am. GI Forum, Am. Legion. Office: Selective Service System 1515 N Wilson Blvd Arlington VA 22209-2461*

ROMO, RICARDO, academic administrator, history educator; b. San Antonio, June 23, 1943; s. Henry and Alice (Saenz) R.; m. Harriett Durr, July 1, 1967; children: Anadelia, Carlos. BS, U. Tex., 1967; MA in History, Loyola U., LA, 1970; PhD in History, UCLA, 1975. Tchr. Franklin H.S., LA, 1967-70; asst. prof. Chicano studies Calif. State U., Northridge, 1970-73; asst. prof. history U. Calif., San Diego, 1974-80; assoc. prof. history U. Tex., Austin, 1980-99, vice provost, 1993-99, pres. San Antonio, 1999—; v.p., dir. Tomas Rivera Ctr., San Antonio, 1987-93. Expert witness in field; Chancellor's disting. lectr. U. Calif., Berkeley, 1985; bd. dirs. San Antonio Br. Fed. Res. Bank, Dallas; pres. U. Tex., San Antonio, 2002. Author: East Los Angeles: History of A Barrio, 1983; co-author: The Mexican American Experience: An Interdisciplinary Anthology, 1985; editl. bd. Social Sci. Quar. Mem. Men's Athletic Coun., Nat. Coun. of La Raza, 1999—; bd. dirs. Smithsonian Nat. Bd.for Latino Initiatives, 1999—, Greater San Antonio C. of C., 1999—; mem. com. edn. UN Ednl. Scientific and Cultural Orgn.; apptd. pres. bd. Historically Black Colls. and Univs.; bd. advisors Historially Black Colls. and Univs., 2004; bd. dirs. Fed. Res. Bank of Dallas, San Antonio Br., 2005. Fellow Ctr. for Advanced Studies in Behavioral Studies, Stanford U., 1989-90; named to Longhorn Hall of Honor. Mem. San Antonio Med. Found. (trustee 1999—), Tex. Rsch. Park Found. (bd. trustees 1999—). Roman Catholic. Avocations: hiking, photography. Office: University of Texas Office of President One UTSA Cir San Antonio TX 78249-1130 Office Phone: 210-458-4101. E-mail: president@utsa.edu.

ROMO, TONY (ANTONIO RAMIRO ROMO), professional football player; b. San Diego, Apr. 21, 1980; m. Candice Crawford, May 28, 2011; 1 child, Hawkins Crawford. BBA, Ea. Ill. U., Charlston, 2003. Quarterback Dallas Cowboys, 2003—. Co-host (radio show) Inside the Huddle, 2006. Recipient Walter Payton award, 2002; named Player of Yr., Ohio Valley Conf., 2000—02, 1st Team All-Conf., 2000—02; named to Nat. Football Conf. Pro Bowl Team, NFL, 2006, 2007. Mem.: Sigma Pi. Achievements include leading the NFL in: yards per pass attempt, 2006. Avocation: golf. Office: Dallas Cowboys 1 Cowboys Pky Irving TX 75063-4999

ROMOND, EDWARD H., medical oncologist, educator; MD, U. Ky., Lexington, 1977. Diplomate American Bd. Internal Medicine, 1980, American Bd. Internal Medicine-med. oncology, 1983, American Bd. Internal Medicine-hematology, 1984. Resident internal medicine Mich. State Univ. Associated Hosps., Lansing, 1978—80; fellow hematology and oncology Mich. State Univ., Lansing, 1980—83; clin. fellow Children's Leukemia Found.; prof. Coll. Medicine Univ. Ky.; hosp. affiliation includes Univ. Ky. Albert B. Chandler Hosp. Recipient The Leonard Tow Humanism in Medicine award, 2003. Fellow: American Cancer Soc. Office: University of Kentucky Albert B Chandler Hospital 800 Rose St 1000 S Limestone Lexington KY 40536-0293 Office Phone: 859-257-4488.*

RONALD, PETER, utilities executive; b. Duluth, Minn., Aug. 26, 1926; s. George W. and Florence (Jones) R.; m. Mary Locke Boyd, Nov. 25, 1950 (dec. 2003); children: Peter Webb, Pauline Morton, Samuel Herschel; m. Anne H. Moore, Dec. 28, 2005. BA, U. Va., 1950. With Louisville Gas & Electric Co., 1950-88, treas., 1962—, v.p., 1969-82, sr. v.p., 1982-88, dir., 1979-89. Bd. dirs., mem. exec. com. Bus. Devel. Corp. Ky., 1967-75, pres., 1971-72; bd. dirs. Louisville Community Chest, 1967-72, v.p., 1969-72; bd. dirs., v.p. Louisville Rehab. Ctr., 1964-82, pres., 1970-71; bd. overseers Louisville Country Day Sch., 1967-70; trustee Children's Hosp. Found., 1978-81, sec.-treas., 1978-81; bd. govs. Captiva (Fla.) Civic Assn., 1990-94, v.p., 1992; commr. Captiva, Fla. Erosion Prevention Dist., 1996-98. With USNR, 1945-46. Mem. Louisville Country Club, Captiva Yacht Club, Zeta Psi. Home: 4710 Indian Hills Green Louisville KY 40207-1366

RONON, BARBARA LYNNE, retail executive; Attended, Harcum Coll. Various positions Gimbels; buyer, petites Saks Fifth Ave., 1986—87, v.p., divisional mdse. mgr., 1987—95, sr. v.p., gen. mdse. mgr., 1995—2000, sr. v.p., chief merchant, 2000—01; cons. Lane Crawford, Hong Kong, 2001—02, sr. v.p., comml., 2002—03; sr. v.p., North Asia Burberry, 2003—07; exec. v.p., merchandising HSN, Inc., 2007—. Office: HSN Inc 1 HSN Dr Saint Petersburg FL 33729 Office Phone: 727-872-1000. Office Fax: 727-872-6615. Business E-Mail: barbara.ronon@hsn.net.

ROOD, JOHN DARRELL, real estate developer, former ambassador; b. 1954; m. Jamie A. Rood; children: Jennifer, Christopher; 1 child, Holly. Founder, mng. ptnr. Vestcor Companies, Inc., Jacksonville, Fla., 1983—2004, chmn., 2007—, JDR Cos., Inc., 2007—; US amb. to Bahamas US Dept. State, Nassau, 2004—07. Housing/edn. com. chmn. Jacksonville Downtown Master Plan; vis. prof. U. North Fla.; founding bd. mem. First Coast Family & Housing Found.; apptd. adv. coun. on renewal communities US Dept. Housing & Urban Devel.; apptd. commr., chmn. Fla. Fish & Wildlife Conservation Commn., 2002—04. Former vol. Kesler Mentoring Connection, Jacksonville; hon. bd. dirs. Fla. Apartment Polit. Action Com.; bd. trustees Fresh Ministries; past bd. dirs. James Madison Inst., Jacksonville Symphony Assn., Jacksonville Housing Partnership. Named Entrepreneur of Yr., Ernst & Young, 2001. Mem.: Jacksonville C. of C., Rotary Club of Mandarin (past pres.). Office: Vestcor Companies Inc 3030 Hartley Rd Ste 310 Jacksonville FL 32257-8213 Office Phone: 904-260-3030.

ROOKE, PAUL A., electronics executive; B in Mech Engring., U. Mich.; MBA, U. Ky. Various positions, including mgr., cost engring., product planning, asst. to the v.p., Sys. Printer Divsn. IBM Corp., mfg. engr., 1980—84, mgr., wheelprinter automation Lexington, Ky., 1984; joined Lexmark International, Inc., 1991, various mgmt. positions, including v.p., worldwide mktg., US sales, Consumer Printer Divsn., pres., Lexmark's former Imaging Solutions Divsn., pres., Lexmark's Printing Solutions, Svcs. Divsn., 1999—2007, pres., Consumer Printer Divsn., 2007—09, exec. v.p., 2002—10, pres., Imaging Solutions Divsn., 2009—10, pres., CEO, 2010—11, chmn., CEO, 2011—. Office: Lexmark International Inc 1 Lexmark Cir Dr 740 W New Cir Rd Lexington KY 40550 Office Phone: 859-232-2000. Office Fax: 859-232-2403. Business E-Mail: prooke@lexmark.com.

ROOMSBURG, MARGARET M., corporate financial executive; CPA. Dir., fin. ValueOptions, Inc. (formerly Options Mental Health); joined Amerigroup Corp., 1996, contr., 1999—, sr. v.p., chief acctg. officer, 2007—. Office: Amerigroup Corp 4425 Corporation Ln Virginia Beach VA 23462 Office Phone: 757-490-6900. Office Fax: 757-222-2330. Business E-Mail: mroomsburg@amerigroupcorp.com.

ROONEY, FRANCIS (LAURENCE FRANCIS ROONEY III), construction executive, former ambassador; b. Dec. 4, 1953; m. Kathleen Rooney; 3 children. AB, Georgetown U., 1975, JD, 1978; PhD (hon.), U. Notre Dame, 2006. Bar: DC, Tex.; 100-Ton Master's Lic. U.S. Coast Guard. Chmn., pres., CEO Rooney Holdings, Inc., Naples, Fla., 1984—; US amb. to The Holy See US Dept. State, 2005—08. Dir. Wash. Adv. Coun. Ctr. for Strategic and Internat. Studies, 20/20 com.; transition team for gov. elect Brad Henry State of Okla.; vice chmn. Okla. Turnpike Authority; bd. dirs. NASDAQ, NY Stock Exch., Okla. Capital Investment Bd., BOL Fin. Corp., BOK Fin. Corp., 1995—2005, Cimarex Energy Co., 2002—05, Fla. Corp., 2008—09, Helmerich and Payne, Inc., 2008—, Vetra Energy Group, LLC, 2009—, Laredo Petroleum, Inc., 2010—. Mem. Sch. of Architecture Coun. U. of Notre Dame; trustee Ctr. for the Study of the Presidency and Congress; bd. advisor Panama Canal Authority; mem. Sovereign Military Order of Malta (Fed. Assn.), Washington. Mem.: Young President's Org. (dir. 1992—98, internat. pres. 1997—98). Republican. Roman Catholic. Office: Rooney Holdings Inc 5601 S 122nd E Ave Tulsa OK 74146 Office Phone: 918-583-6900. Office Fax: 918-585-5961. Business E-Mail: frooney@rooneyholdings.com.

ROONEY, PATRICK, JR., state legislator; b. Pitts., Feb. 9, 1964; m. Patti Rooney; children: Mary, Frannie, Patrick, Anthony. BA in Polit. Sci., Clemson U., SC, 1986; JD, Villanova U., Phila., 1989; MBA, Lehigh U., Bethlehem, Pa., 1992. Pres. Palm Beach Kennel Club; mem. Dist. 83 Fla. House Of Representatives, 2011—. Republican. Office: 3970 RCA Blvd Ste 7001 Palm Beach Gardens FL 33410-4231 also: Fla House of Reps 324 The Capitol 402 S Monroe St Tallahassee FL 32399-1300 Office Phone: 561-625-5176, 850-488-0322.

ROONEY, TOM (THOMAS J. ROONEY), United States Representative from Florida, lawyer; b. Phila., Nov. 21, 1970; s. Patrick J. Rooney; m. Tara Rooney; children: Tom Jr., Sean, Seamus. Student, Syracuse U., NY; BS in English Lit., Washington and Jefferson Coll., Pitts.; MA in Polit. Sci., U. Fla.; JD, U. Miami Sch. Law. Bar: Fla. 1999. Commd. officer JAG Corps, spl. asst. US atty. US Army, Fort Hood, Tex., 1999—2004; asst. atty. gen. State of Fla., 2004—06; bd. dirs. Children's Services Coun. Palm Beach County, 2006—08; atty. Kramer, Sopko & Levenstein, P.A., Stuart, Fla., 2008—09; mem. US Congress from 16th Fla. Dist., Washington, 2009—13, US Congress from 17th Fla. Dist., 2013—. Bd. dirs. Children's Place at Home Safe, South Lake Worth, Fla. Serves US Army Inactive Ready Reserves. Republican. Roman Catholic. Office: US House of Representatives 221 Cannon House Office Bldg Washington DC 20515-0916 also: 226 Taylor St Ste 600 Punta Gorda FL 33950 Office Phone: 202-225-5792, 941-575-9101. Office Fax: 202-225-3132, 941-575-9103.*

ROORDA, JOHN FRANCIS, JR., manufacturing executive, consultant; b. Evanston, Ill., Jan. 16, 1923; s. John Francis and Sadie M. (Daley) R.; m. Elizabeth Mulcahy, July 2, 1949; children: Elizabeth Roorda Barker, John F., Ann Roorda Hollis. BSChemE, Purdue U., 1943, PhD, 1949. With Shell Oil Co., 1949-83; gen. mgr. combined oil products/chem. econs. dept., 1973-74; v.p. planning and econs., 1974-77; v.p. Shell Devel. Co., Houston, 1977-78; v.p. corp. planning Shell Oil Co., 1978-83; pres. John Roorda, 1983—. Coordinator Exec. Service Corps, Houston, 1985— Served to lt. (j.g.) USNR, 1943-46. Recipient Disting. Engring. Alumnus award Purdue U., 1976, Outstanding Chem. Engr. award Purdue U., 1993. Mem. Sigma Xi. Roman Catholic.

ROOS, JEFF, construction executive; With Lennar Corp. (Orange County divsn.); regional pres., Lennar Land And Homebuilding, South-West region Lennar Corp.; sec. Lennar Charitable Housing Found. Bd. dirs. HomeAid America, The Boys and Girls Club of the South Coast, The Chimbote Found.; active, internat. relief team

Orangewood Found. Recipient The Rainbow of Hope Builder award, 2003. Office: Lennar Corp 700 NW 107th Ave Miami FL 33172 Office Phone: 305-559-4000. Office Fax: 305-226-4158. Business E-Mail: jeff.roos@lennar.com.

ROOT, ALLEN WILLIAM, pediatrician, educator; b. Phila., Sept. 24, 1933; s. Morris Jacob and Priscilla R.; m. Janet Greenberg, June 15, 1958; children: Jonathan, Jennifer, Michael. AB, Dartmouth Coll., 1955, postgrad. Med. Sch., 1954-56; MD, Harvard U., 1958. Diplomate Am. Bd. Pediatrics & Subboard Pediatric Endocrinology, Am. Bd. Pediatric Endocrinology. Intern Strong Meml. Hosp., Rochester, NY, 1958-60; resident in pediatrics Hosp. U. Pa., Phila., 1960-62; fellow in pediatric endocrinology Children's Hosp. of Phila., 1962-65; assoc. physician in pediatrics U. Pa. Sch. Medicine, 1964-66, asst. prof. pediatrics, 1966-69; assoc. prof. pediatrics Temple U. Sch. Medicine, Phila., 1969-73, prof., 1973; asst. physician in endocrinology Children's Hosp. Phila., 1965-69; chmn. divsn. pediatrics Albert Einstein Med. Center., Phila., 1969-73; prof. pediatrics U. South Fla. Coll. Medicine, Tampa, 1973—2012, emeritus prof., 2012—, prof. biochemistry, 1987—2007, assoc. chmn. dept. pediatrics, 1974-99, dir. sect. pediatric endocrinology, 1973-96; pediat. emeritus prof., 2012; pediatric endocrinologist All Children's Hosp., Johns Hopkins Medicine, 2012—. Dir. univ. tchg. svcs. All Children's Hosp., St. Petersburg, 1973-89, staff pediatric endocrinologist All Childrens Hosp., John Hopkins medicine, 2012-; mem. Fla. Infant Screening Adv. Coun., 1979-06, chmn., 1994-06; mem. Hillsborough County Thyroid Adv. Com., 1980; mem. med. adv. com. Nat. Pituitary Agy., 1974-78, mem. growth hormone subcom., 1972-79, 81-85; chmn. Fla. Legis. Infant Screening Task Force, 2002. Author: Human Pituitary Growth Hormone, 1972; co-editor: (with C. La Cauza) Problems in Pediatric Endocrinology, 1980; mem. editl. bd. Jour. Pediats., 1973-81, Jour. Adolescent Health Care, 1979-95, Jour. Pediat. Endocrinology and Metabolism, 1985-, Jour. Clin. Endocrinology and Metabolism, 1993-96, 2001-04, Growth, Genetics and Hormones, 1993-2011, Pediat. in Rev., 1995-2001; assoc. editor Adolescent and Pediat. Gynecology, 1992-95, Current Opinion in Pediats., sect. editor, Endocrine and Metabolism, 1993-, mem. editl. bd. 2006-, Internat. Jour. Pediatric Endocrinology, 2009-. USPHS grantee; Birth Defects Found. grantee. Mem. AAAS, Am. Pediatric Soc., Soc. Pediatric Rsch., Lawson Wilkins Pediatric Endocrine Soc. (treas. 1979-88, pres. 1988-89), Endocrine Soc., Am. Acad. Pediatrics, Am. Fedn. Clin. Rsch., Soc. Exptl. Biology and Medicine, Soc. Nuclear Medicine, N.Y. Acad. Sci., Phila. Coll. Physicians, Phila. Endocrine Soc. (bd. dirs. 1971-72, treas. 1973), Dartmouth Coll. Alumni Coun., Dartmouth Club. Office: 501 6th Avenue South Saint Petersburg FL 33701-4816 Business E-Mail: roota@allkids.org.

ROOT, JAMES BENJAMIN, landscape architect; b. Detroit, Jan. 26, 1934; s. William Jehial and Helen Elizabeth (English) R. BBA, Memphis State U., 1960; B Landscape Architecture, U. Ga., 1966. Registered landscape architect; lic. real estate agt., Va. Asst. prof. W.Va. U., Morgantown, 1973-75, 93; pvt. practice Charlottesville, Va., 1976-85, 91—; site planner LBA, PH&R, Charles P. Johnson & Assocs., Fairfax, Va., 1986-90. Pvt. practice as golf course architect, Charlottesville, 1976—; instr. Parkersburg C.C., 1975, Piedmont Va. C.C., 1981. Author: Fundamentals of Landscaping and Site Planning, 1985, From Stardust to Insanity: The Moral Demise of a Troubled Nation, 2007; contbr. articles to profl. jours., also poetry. Mem. Planning Commn., Marietta, Ohio, 1972. Mem. Nat. Golf Found., Golf Course Builders Assn. Am. (assoc.), Va. Writers Club. Avocations: piano, drums. Office: PO Box 7017 Charlottesville VA 22906-7017 Office Phone: 434-971-4000. E-mail: jamesbroot@aol.com.

ROOT, LEON A., JR., healthcare company executive; BBA, Pa. State U., MS in Bus. Adminstrn. Sys. arch. Eastman Kodak; sr. v.p., gen. mgr., bus. sys. divsn. McKesson HBOC; chief info. officer Medunite, Inc.; sr. v.p., chief tech. officer Amerigroup Corp., 2002—03, exec. v.p., chief info. officer, 2003—. Office: Amerigroup Corp 1330 Amerigroup Way Virginia Beach VA 23462 Office Phone: 757-490-6900. Office Fax: 757-518-3600.

ROOT, MARK A., communications executive; Exec. dir., corp. comm. ManTech Internat., Inc., ManTech SRS Technologies, Inc. Office: ManTech International Corp 12015 Lee Jackson Hwy Fairfax VA 22033 Office Phone: 703-218-6000. Office Fax: 703-218-8296. Business E-Mail: mark.root@mantech.com.

ROPER, RICHARD B., III, lawyer, former prosecutor; b. 1957; BA cum laude, U. Tex., Arlington, 1979; JD, Tex. Tech. U., 1982. Asst. dist. atty. Tarrant County, Tex., 1982—87; asst. US atty. (no. dist.) Tex. US Dept. Justice, Dallas, 1987—2004, interim US atty. (no. dist.) Tex., 2004, US atty. (no. dist.) Tex., 2004—08; ptnr. Thompson & Knight LLP, Dallas, 2009—. Recipient Jane Doe award, Dallas Genesis Women's Shelter; named a Disting. Alumnus, Tex. Tech. U. Sch. Law, 2007. Fellow: Tex. Bar Found.; mem.: State Bar of Tex. Office: Thompson & Knight LLP One Arts Plz 1722 Routh St Ste 1500 Dallas TX 75201 Office Phone: 214-969-1210. Office Fax: 214-880-3357. E-mail: Richard.Roper@tklaw.com.

ROPER, WILLIAM LEE, dean, preventive medicine physician, administrator; b. Birmingham, Ala., July 6, 1948; s. Richard Barnard and Jean (Fyfe) R.; m. Maryann Roper, Jan. 14, 1978 AA, Fla. Coll., 1968; BS, U. Ala, 1970, MD, 1974, M.P.H., 1981. Diplomate Am. Bd. Pediatrics, Am. Bd. Preventive Medicine. Intern, resident in pediatrics U. Colo. Med. Ctr., Denver, 1974-77; health officer Jefferson County Dept. Health, Birmingham, 1977-82, 83; White House fellow Washington, 1982-83; spl. asst. to Pres. for health policy, 1983-86; adminstr., Health Care Finance Adminstrn. HHS, Washington, 1986-89; dep. asst. to pres. for domestic policy The White House, Washington, 1989-90; adminstr. Agy. for Toxic Substances and Disease Registry and dir. Ctrs. for Disease Control and Prevention, Atlanta, 1990-93; sr. v.p. Prudential Health Care, Roseland, NJ, 1994-97; pres. Prudential Ctr. for Health Care Rsch., Atlanta, 1993-95; dean, sch. pub. health, prof. medicine and health policy U. NC, Chapel Hill, 1997—2004, dean Sch. Medicine, 2004—, vice chancellor med. affairs, 2004—, CEO U. NC Health Care, 2004—. Mem. Inst. Medicine, Phi Beta Kappa, Alpha Omega Alpha Republican. Office: Office of Dean U NC Med School 125 MacNider Bldg CB #7000 Chapel Hill NC 27599 Office Phone: 919-966-4161.

ROQUEMORE, JAMES W., consumer products company executive; b. 1954; s. W. A. Roquemore. Gen. mgr. Super-Sod Carolina; CEO, chmn. Patten Seed Co., Inc., Lakeland, Ga. Bd. dirs. SC Bank and Trust, N.A, SCBT Fin. Corp., 2007—, SCANA Corp., 2007—, SC Electric & Gas Co., 2007—. Pres. Palmetto Agribusiness Coun., bd. dirs.; co-chmn., agribusiness New Carolina; bd. dirs. Boy Scouts of America. Recipient Order of the Palmetto, Orangeburg Citizen of the Yr., Silver Beaver award, SC Ambassador, 2001. Office: Patten Seed Co Inc 119 E Murrell Ave Lakeland GA 31635-1520 Office Phone: 229-482-3231. Business E-Mail: James.Roquemore@scbandt.com.

RORIE, NANCY CATHERINE, retired secondary school educator; d. Carl and Mildred Rorie. BA, U. NC, 1962, MEd, 1967; EdD, Duke U., 1977. Cert. curriculum and instrnl. specialist, social studies tchr. for middle and secondary levels, English tchr., N.C. Tchr. social studies and English Guilford County Schs., Greensboro, NC, 1962—67; instr. social studies Lees-McRae Coll., Banner Elk, NC, 1967—76; tchr. social studies and English Monroe City Schs., NC, 1977—93, Union County Schs., Monroe, 1993—2002; ret., 2002. Bd. mem. Wingate U. Friends Arts, NC, 2006—07; mem. Mountain Springs Baptist Ch. Mem.: Monroe Aquatics And Fitness Ctr.

RORISON, MARGARET LIPPITT, reading consultant; b. Wilmington, NC, Feb. 6, 1925; d. Harmon Chadbourn and Margaret Devereux (Lippitt) Rorison. AB, Hollins Coll., 1946; MA, Columbia U., 1956; diploma, L'Alliance Française, Paris, 1966; postgrad., U. S.C., 1967—70, postgrad., 1981—. Market and editl. rschr. Time, Inc., NYC, 1949—55; tchr. classroom and corrective reading N.Y.C. Pub. Schs., 1956—65; TV instr. ETV-WNDT, Channel 13, NYC, 1962—63; grad. asst., TV instr. U. S.C., Columbia, 1967—70; instrnl. specialist in reading S.C. Office Instrnl. TV and Radio, S.C. Dept. Edn., Columbia, 1971—81; reading cons. S.C. Office Instrnl. Tech., Columbia, 1982—. Author instrnl. TV series: Getting the Word (So. Ednl. Communications Assn. award 1972, Ohio State award 1973, S.C. Scholastic Broadcasters award 1973), Getting the Message, 1981. Episcopalian. Home: 460 S 23rd St Wilmington NC 28403-0200

RORSCHACH, RICHARD GORDON, lawyer; b. Tulsa, Aug. 9, 1928; s. Harold Emil and Margaret (Hermes) R.; m. Martha Kay King, Dec. 23, 1979; children by previous marriage: Richard Helm, Reagan Cartwright, Andrew Maxwell. BS, MIT, 1950; MS, U. Okla., 1952; JD, U. Houston, 1961. Bar: Tex. 1961; lic. prof. engr., Tex. Cons. civil engr. Freese & Nichols, Ft. Worth, 1955; cons. engr. Freese, Nichols & Turner, Houston, 1955-56; petroleum engr. Marathon Oil Co., Bay City, Tex., 1956-57, Houston, 1957-61, atty., 1961-64; ptnr. Broady, Kells & Rorschach, Houston, 1964-68, Ragan, Russell & Rorschach, Houston, 1968-80, R.G. Rorschach & Assocs., Kilgore, Tex., 1980—. Mem. exec. com. Colonial Royalties Co., Tulsa, 1970-77; officer Little River Oil & Gas Co., 1980-88; mng. ptnr. Pentagon Oil Co., 1988—; pres. Nat. Assn. Royalty Owners-Tex., 1993-96, trustee, 2004-05; chmn. Nat. Assn. Royalty Owners, Inc., 1996-99, bd. dirs., 1999-2000, adv. bd. dirs., 2004-05; mem. exec. com. Nat. Assn. Royalty Owners, Inc., v.p. gen. counsel Bldg. Innovations LLC, Hilton Head Island, SC, 2011; owner, breeder, exhibitor Arabian Horses Shadowbrook Farm, Kilgore, Tex., 1980—. Author: How to Protect Your Royalty Interests: Texas Perspectives, Vols. 1 & 2, 2002, The Ultimate Royalty Owner's Guide: A Manual of Procedure and Operation. 1st lt. CE US Army, 1952—54, Korea. Mem. ASCE, Soc. Petroleum Engring., Legion of Hon., Tex. Bar Assn., Rotary Club (pres. Kilgore chpt. 1984-85), Sigma Xi, Sigma Alpha Epsilon. Republican. Presbyterian. Avocations: fly fishing, fly tying, golf, tennis. Home: 1893 CR 186 East Kilgore TX 75662-9023 Office: 1100 Stone Rd PO Box 1934 Kilgore TX 75663-1934 Office Phone: 903-984-0589.

ROSA, JOHN WILLIAM, academic administrator, career military officer; m. Donna Kangeter; children: Jonathan, Brad. BA in Bus. Adminstrn., The Citadel, 1973; M in Pub. Adminstrn., Golden Gate U., 1985. Commd. 2d. lt. USAF, 1973, advanced through grades to lt. gen., 2003; A-7D pilot, scheduler, weapons officer 353rd Tactical Fighter Fighter Squadron, Myrtle Beach AFB, SC, 1975-77; A-10 pilot 356th Tactical Fighter Squadron, Myrtle Beach AFB, 1977—78; weapons officer 353rd Tactical Figher Squadron, Myrtle Beach AFB, 1979—80; pilot Hunter and Jaguar Aircraft, RAF Lossiemouth, Scotland, 1980-81; weapons instr. RAF Lossiemouth, 1981-83; instr. pilot, weapons officer, flight comdr. 61st Tactical Fighter Tng. Squadron, MacDill AFB, Fla., 1983-86; programmer, dir. of programs and resources Hdqrs. USAF, Washington, 1987-90; comdr. 35th Tactical Fighter Squadron, Kunsan AB, Korea, 1991-92, 366th Ops. Support Squadron, Mountain Home AFB, Idaho, 1992, dep. comdr., 1992-93; dep. comdr. to comdr. 49th Ops. Group, Holloman AFB, N.Mex., 1994-95; comdr. 20th Fighter Wing, Shaw AFB, SC, 1995-97; inspector gen. Hdqrs. Pacific Air Forces, Hickman AFB, Hawaii, 1997-98; comdt. Air Command and State Coll., Air U., Maxwell AFB, Ala., 1998—2000; comdr. 347th Wing, Moody AFB, Ga., 2000—01, 347th Rescue Wing, Moody AFB, 2001; dep. dir. ops. Ops. Directorate, the Joint Staff, Washington, DC, 2001—03; supt. USAF Acad., Colorado Springs, 2003—05; pres. The Citadel, Mil. Coll. of SC, Charleston, 2005—. Decorated Def. Superior Svc. award, Meritorious Svc. medal with four oak leaf clusters, Air Force Commendation medal, Legion of Merit with oak leaf cluster, Combat Readiness medal with two oak clusters. Office: The Citadel Office of Pres 171 Moultrie St Charleston SC 29409 Office Phone: 843-225-3294.

ROSA, ROBERT H., JR., ophthalmologist, medical educator, researcher; b. San Antonio, Oct. 27, 1964; s. Robert H. and Rosita L. Rosa; m. Maria B. Uryga; children: Zachary A., Matthew L., Cara Beth. BS, Tex. A&M U., College Station, 1986; MD, Tex. A&M Health Sci. Ctr., College Station, 1990. Diplomate Am. Bd. Ophthalmology, 1996. Intern internal medicine Scott & White Meml. Hosp., Tex. A&M Health Sci. Ctr., Temple, 1990—91; resident ophthalmology Bascom Palmer Eye Inst., U. Miami Sch. Medicine, Fla., 1991—94, asst. prof., clin. ophthalmology, 1996—2000, dir., ocular pathology lab., 1996—2000, dir., rsch. histology lab., 1997—99; fellow, ophthalmic pathology Wilmer Eye Inst., Johns Hopkins U., Balt., 1994—95; fellow, med. retina Moorfields Eye Hosp., U. London, 1995—96; assoc. prof., ophthalmology and surgery, Tex. A&M Health Sci. Ctr. Scott & White Eye Inst., Temple, 2000—08, dir., divsn. ophthalmic pathology, 2000—, asst. dir., ophthalmology residency program, 2002—13, vice-chair rsch., dept. ophthalmology, 2008—; prof. ophthalmology and surgery Tex. A&M Health Sci. Ctr., 2008—. Med. dir. Fla. Lions Eye Bank, Miami, 1996—2000. Com. chair, BCSC sect. 4, ophthalmic pathology and intra-ocular tumors Am. Acad. Ophthalmology, 2008—. Recipient First Yr. Resident Tchg. award, Bascom Palmer Eye Inst., U. Miami Sch. Medicine, 1998—99, Ross Carr Meml. award, Fla. Lions Eye Bank, 1999—2000, Chief's award, Scott & White Eye Inst., Tex. A&M Health Sci. Ctr., 2003—04, Physician FOCUS award, Scott & White Bd. Dirs., 2004—06, K08 award, Nat. Eye Inst., Nat. Insts. Health, 2004—12, Achievement award, Am. Acad. Opthalmology, 2008; named Tex. Super Drs., 2008—13; named one of America's Top Ophthalmologists, Consumers' Rsch. Coun. America, 2006—12. Fellow: Am. Acad. Ophthalmology; mem.: AMA, Tex. Ophthal. Assn., Tex. Med. Assn., Am. Assn. Ophthalmic Pathologists, Verhoeff Zimmerman Soc., Assn. Rsch. Vision and Ophthalmology. Achievements include research in retinal vasoregulation; macular degeneration; diabetic retinopathy. Office: Scott & White Eye Inst 2401 S 31st St Temple TX 76508*

ROSALES, OSCAR R., cardiologist; b. Barranquilla, Colombia, Mar. 17, 1959; s. Oscar and Grace (Cepeda) R.; m. Marguerite F. Miranne, Jan. 11, 1960; children: Andrew Daniel, Sophie Marguerite. MD, Javeriana U., Bogota, Colombia, 1982. Diplomate in cardiovasc. medicine, Am. Bd. Internal Medicine, Interventional Cardiology and Internal Medicine. Intern, chief med. resident Tulane U., New Orleans, 1984-88; fellow in cardiology Yale U., New Haven, 1988-91, asst. prof. medicine, 1993-96; fellow in interventional cardiology U. Tex., Houston, 1991-92, assoc. prof. medicine; dir. critical care quality assurance program West Haven VA Med. Ctr., 1993-96; dir. coronary care unit Ochsner Clinic, New Orleans, 1996-97; dir. cath lab., pres. med. staff Meml. Hermann Hosp., Houston; co-dir. cardiology U. Tex. Med. Sch. Houston, 2002; pres. med. staff Meml. Hermann Hosp. Tex. Med. Ctr. Houston, 2008—10; founder Houston Ctr. Vascular Health. Author: Hemodynamic Forces and Vascular Cell Biology, 1993; contbr. articles to profl. jours. Recipient Humanism in Medicine award, Arnold P. Gold Found., NJ, 2002, Tchg. award, Alpha Omega Alpha, 2006, Tulane U., Ochsner Clinic and U. Tex. Med. Sch., Houston, Multiple Tchg. awards, Tulane U. Sch. Medicine, Ochsner Clinic New Orleans, U. Tex. Med. Sch. Houston. Fellow Am. Coll. Cardiology, Soc. Cardiovas. Angiography and Interventions; mem. Am. Heart Assn. Roman Catholic. Avocations: tennis, reading, jogging. Office: Houston Cardiovascular Assoc 6400 Fannin St Ste 3000 Houston TX 77030 Home Phone: 713-838-0224; Office Phone: 713-790-0841. E-mail: orosales@houstoncardiovascular.com.*

ROSATO, CRAIG RICHARD, bank executive; b. 1964; V.p., fin. group Bank of America Corp., 1996—2000, v.p. consumer fin. group, 2000—04, comml. credit risk exec., Enterprise Credit Risk, 2004—07, contr., Global Consumer & Small Bus. Banking Group (GCSBB), 2007—08, sr. v.p., chief acctg. officer, 2008—09, credit consumer risk exec., 2009—. Office: Bank of America Corp 100 N Tryon St Charlotte NC 28255 Office Phone: 704-386-5681. Office Fax: 704-386-6699. Business E-Mail: craig.rosato@bankofamerica.com.

ROSCOPF, CHARLES BUFORD, lawyer; b. Marvell, Ark., Apr. 21, 1928; s. Emmett Lee and Sally Virginia (King) R.; m. Mary Anne Maddox, Aug. 22, 1954; children— Charles David; Ann Karen. Student, Hendrix Coll., 1948-50; JD, U. Ark., 1954. Bar: Ark. bar 1954, U.S. Dist. Cts 1955, 64, U.S. Supreme Ct. bar 1965. Pvt. practice, Helena, Ark., 1954—; assoc. firm Burke, Moore & Burke, 1954-58; ptnr. firm Burke & Roscopf, 1958-64; sr. ptnr. Roscopf and Roscopf, P.A., 1964—. Mem. Ark. Ho. of Reps., 1953-58; del. Ark. Constl. Conv., 1968; mem. Ark. Probate Drafting Com.; mem. Ark. State Bd. Law Examiners, 1973-79; spl. justice Ark. Supreme Ct. Served with USN, 1946-48; served with USAFR, 1962-68. Fellow Am. Bar Found., Ark. Bar Found. (pres. 1995-96); mem. ABA, Ark. Bar Assn. (pres. 1990-91), Am. Law Inst., Rotary (Paul Harris fellow), Masons, Shriners, Kappa Sigma. Methodist. Home: 117 Avalon Pl Helena AR 72342-1715 Office: Helena Nat Bank Bldg PO Box 610 Helena AR 72342-0610

ROSE, EDWARD W., III, (RUSTY ROSE), investment company executive, former professional sports team executive; b. Dallas; m. Deedie Potter. MBA, Harvard Bus. Sch. Founder, prin. Cardinal Investment Co., Inc., Dallas, 1974—; co-gen. partner (with George W. Bush) Texas Rangers, Arlington, Tex., 1989—98. Named one of Top 200 Art Collectors, ARTnews mag., 2007—12. Republican. Avocation: collecting contemporary German, American, and South American art. Office: Cardinal Investments 500 Crescent Court Ste 250 Dallas TX 75201 Office Phone: 214-871-6800. Office Fax: 214-871-6801.

ROSE, ERNST, dentist; b. Oldenburg, Germany, July 22, 1932; came to U.S., 1940, naturalized, 1946; s. William and Elsie (Lowenbach) R.; m. Shirley Mae Glassman, Dec. 24, 1960 (div. Dec. 1997); children: Ruth Ellen, Michele Ann, Daniel Scot, Seth Joseph; m. Sally Rayen Dunn, Mar. 14, 1998; 1 stepchild, Toby Jugenheimer. BS, Georgetown U., DC, 1955; DDS, Case Western Res. U., Cleve., 1963. Intern Waterbury Hosp., Conn., 1964; pvt. practice dentistry Hubbard, Ohio, 1964-96. Pres., treas. Dr. Ernst Rose, Inc.; lab. instr. Ohio State U., Columbus, 1956-57; dental adviser Assoc. Neighborhood Ctr. Active Liberty Twp. Zoning Commn., 1967-74, 88-92, vice chmn., chmn., 1970-74, 90; chmn. Hubbard Urban Renewal Com., Ohio, 1968-74; mem. Brotherhood Bd., 1967—, treas., 1971-73, 88-90, pres. 1975-77, 90-92, 97-99, temple bd. dirs., 1975-84, 89-95, 1997-2003; bd. dirs. The Playhouse, 2000-01, Victorian Players, 2000-2003, Beth Israel SCC Men's Club. With AUS US Army, 1957—59, Eniwitok nuclear testing. Mem. ADA (life), Ohio Dental Assn. (life), Corydon Palmer Dental Soc. (life, mem. coun. 1983-87), Warren Dental Soc., Hubbard C. of C. (bd. dirs. 1967-97, v.p. 1995-97), Jewish Chataugua Soc. (life), German Am. Club of Sun City Center, Mil. Officers World Wars, Alpha Omega (coun. mem. 1968—2002, sec. 1970-71, v.p. 1971-72, pres. 1972-73, pres. 1989-90, 99-2000), B'nai B'rith (pres. 1970-71, trustee 1971—), Rotary (life, Paul Harris fellow, sec. 1999-2001, vice chmn. Kashrut com. 1983-85, Mikvah com. 1983-93, chmn. Kashrut com. 1985-94), Freedom Plaza Wood Worker Club (v.p. 2008-). Personal E-mail: dresrose@webtv.net.

ROSE, JAMES TURNER, aerospace engineer, consultant; b. Louisburg, NC, Sept. 21, 1935; s. Frank Rogers and Mary Burt (Turner) R.; m. Daniele Raymond, Sept. 15, 1984. BS with high honors, N.C. State U., 1957. Aero. rsch. engr. NASA, Langley Field, Va., 1957-59; project engr. NASA (Mercury and Gemini), Langley Field, Va. and Houston, 1959-64; program sys. mgr. McDonnell Douglas Astronautics Co (MDAC), St. Louis, 1964-69; mgr. shuttle ops. and implementation (MDAC) McDonnell Douglas Astronautics Co., St. Louis, 1969-72, mgr. shuttle support (MDAC), 1972-74, mgr. space processing programs, 1976-83; dir. electrophoresis ops. in space McDonnell Douglas Astronautics Co (MDAC), St. Louis, 1983-86; dir. space shuttle engring. NASA, Washington, 1974-76, asst. adminstr. comml. programs, 1987-91; aerospace cons., 1992—. Chmn. Fla. Space Bus. Roundtable, 1995-98. Recipient Lindberg award for mgmt. leadership AIAA, 1983, Presdl. Meritorious Rank award, 1989, NASA Exceptional Svc. medal, 1990, Laurels award Aviation Week, 1990, Aerospace Contribution to Soc. award AIAA, 1993. Mem. Phi Kappa Phi. Episcopalian. Personal E-mail: jrose935@aol.com.

ROSE, JOHN THOMAS, finance educator; b. Ft. Worth, Aug. 20, 1943; s. Paul Pittman and Francis Nan (White) R.; m. Sandra Kaye Rolen, Sept. 5, 1969; children: Melanie Ann, Leah Nan, Lynnelle Renee. BA with honors, Tex. A&M U., 1965; MA, Washington U., St. Louis, 1968, PhD, 1976. Economist Bd. Govs. of FRS, Washington, 1972-82, sr. economist, 1982-84; prof. fin., Harriette L. & Walter G. Lacy, Jr. chair banking and fin. Baylor U., Waco, Tex., 1984—2014, acting chmn. dept. fin. ins. and real estate, 1996-97, chmn. dept., 1997—2006. Contbr. articles to profl. jours. Bd. visitors, coll. bus. Abilene Christian U., Tex., 1989-92; acad. adv. bd., coll. bus., Harding U., Arkansas, 2013- Capt. US Army, 1969—71. Decorated Bronze Star; recipient Disting. Bus. Prof. award Baylor U., 1988, Alpha Kappa Psi Favorite Prof. award Hankamer Sch. Bus. Baylor U., 2004; Econ. Devel. Adminstrn. US Dept. Commerce fellow, 1968-69; Ernst & Young Found. Rsch. grantee, 1991. Mem. So. Fin. Assn., Southwestern Fin. Assn., Fin. Mgmt. Assn., Omicron Delta Epsilon, Beta Gamma Sigma. Mem. Ch. of Christ. Office: Baylor U Hankamer Sch of Bus Dept Fin Ins and Real Estate One Bear Pl # 98004 Waco TX 76798-8004 Business E-Mail: jt_rose@baylor.edu.

ROSE, KENNETH L., food products executive; BS, U. San Diego. Contr., Teledyne Micronetics Divsn. Teledyne Components, 1982—85, v.p., fin. & adminstrn., Teledyne CME Divsn., 1985—90, v.p., fin. & adminstrn., 1990—93; corp. contr. Tyson Foods, Inc., Springdale, Ark., 1993—, sr. v.p., indirect purchasing, aviation &

travel, chief acctg. officer, 1995—. Office: Tyson Foods Inc 2200 Don Tyson Pky Springdale AR 72762-6999 Office Phone: 479-290-4000. Office Fax: 479-290-4061. Business E-Mail: kenneth.rose@tyson.com.

ROSE, MATT (MATTHEW K. ROSE), rail transportation executive; b. Salina, Kans., 1959; m. Lisa Rose; 3 children. BS in Mktg. & Logistics, U. Mo., 1981. With Mo. Pacific RR; various positions Schneider Nat., Internat. Utilities; v.p. transp. Triple Crown Services (Norfolk Southern RR subs.); v.p. vehicles & machinery Burlington Northern Santa Fe Corp., Fort Worth, Tex., 1994—95, v.p. chemicals, 1995—96, sr. v.p. mdse. bus. unit, 1996—97, sr. v.p., COO, 1997—99, pres., COO, 1999—2000, pres., CEO, 2000—02, chmn., pres., CEO, 2002—10; chmn., CEO Burlington Northern Santa Fe LLC (subs. Berkshire Hathaway), 2010—13, exec. chmn., 2014—. Bd. dirs. Burlington Northern Santa Fe Corp., 2000—, AMR Corp., 2004—13, Centex Corp., 2006—09, AT&T Inc., 2010—, Fed. Reserve Bank Dallas, 2014—; mem. President's Coun. on Jobs & Competitiveness, 2009—, The Bus. Roundtable, The Bus. Coun., Nat. Surface Transp. Policy & Revenue Study Commn., Tex. Governor's Bus. Coun. Trustee Tex. Christian U.; mem. exec. bd. Boy Scouts of America. Mem.: US Chamber of Commerce, Assn. American Railroads (bd. dirs.). Republican. Office: Burlington Northern Santa Fe LLC PO Box 961056 Fort Worth TX 76161-0056 Office Phone: 817-867-6100.*

ROSE, MICHAEL DAVID, bank executive, lawyer; b. Akron, Ohio, Mar. 2, 1942; s. William H. and Annabel L. (Kennedy) R.; children: Matthew Derek Franco, Gabrielle Elaine Franco, Morgan Douglas BBA, U. Cin., 1963; LLB, Harvard U., 1966. Bar: Ohio 1966. Lectr. University of Cincinnati, 1966-67; atty. Strauss, Troy & Ruehlmann, Cin., 1966-72; exec. v.p. Winegardner Internat., Cin., 1972-74; v.p. hotel group Holiday Inns, Inc., Memphis, 1974-76, pres. hotel group, 1976-78, corp. exec. v.p., 1978-79, pres., 1979, CEO, 1981, chmn. bd. dirs., 1984; chmn., CEO Promus Cos. Inc., 1990—95; chmn. Promus Hotel Corp., 1995—97, Harrah's Entertainment Inc., 1995—96, First Horizon National Corp., 2007—, First Tennessee Bank, 2007—. Bd. dirs. Darden Restaurants Inc., FelCor Lodging Trust, First Tenn. Nat. Corp., SteinMart, Gaylord Entertainment Co., Gen. Mills, Inc.; chmn. Gaylord Entertainment Co., 2001—05. Bd. dirs. Memphis Arts Coun., from 1979; mem. Future Memphis, from 1979; mem. bd. advisors U. Cin., from 1979; hon. chmn. bd. trustees Jr. Achievement, Memphis. Named one of Corp. Am.'s Ten Outstanding Dirs. for 2000, Dir.'s Alert. Mem. Ohio Bar Assn., Young Pres.' Orgn. Office: First Horizon National Corp 165 Madison Memphis TN 38103 Office Phone: 901-523-4444. Business E-Mail: mrose@fhnc.com.

ROSE, MICHAEL THOMAS, state legislator, lawyer; b. Charleston, SC, Oct. 13, 1947; s. Artman Alvin Rose and Lynnette Marguerite (Davis) Pullen; m. Vivian Osborn, May 25, 1985. BS, USAF Acad., 1969; JD, NYU, 1973; MBA, Harvard U., 1981. Bar: Pa., 1973, Calif. 1975, Minn., 1978, Colo. 1981, S.C. 1983, U.S. Dist. Cts., U.S. Ct. Claims, U.S. Ct. Mil. Appeals, U.S. Supreme Ct. Atty. Robins, Davis & Lyons, St. Paul, 1977-79; exec. dir. Farmers Assistance Relief Mission Inc., Summerville, S.C., 1986-94; mem. Dist. 38 SC State Senate, 1988—. Vice chmn. Rep. Forum, 1989-91; S.C. chmn. Am. Legis. Exch. Coun., 1990-91. Editor NYU Law Rev., 1971-73; contbr. articles to profl. jours. Founder Save the Yorktown, Inc.; founder, dir. Adopt-A-Cow Program; chmn. Dorchester County Legis. Delegation, 1989-90, 94-95; active Bethany United Meth. Ch.; project dir. Entrepreneurship Ctr. U. Charleston, 1994-95. Capt. USAF, 1969-74. Decorated Order of Palmetto, Gov. S.C., 1987; named Outstanding State Legislator, Am. Legis. Exchange Coun., 1990. Mem. Summerville Noon Lions Club, Goose Creek Rotary Club, Summerville Lodge, Elks. Republican. Methodist. Avocations: travel, sports, genealogy. Home: 409 Central Ave Summerville SC 29483-5903 Office: Mortimer Leiendecker & Rose 1410 Trolley Rd Summerville SC 29485-5210 also: 613 Gressette Bldg Columbia SC 29201 Office Phone: 803-212-6056. Business E-Mail: MikeRose@scsenate.org.

ROSE, MITCH (MITCHELL FRANKLIN ROSE), lobbyist; b. 1963; BA in Polit. Sci., U. Wash., 1985; JD, Washington Coll. Law, 1992. Press asst. to Senator Bob Dole US Senate, 1985—87; legis. asst. to Rep. Don Young US House of Representatives, 1988—91; press sec. to Senator Ted Stevens US Senate, 1991—96, chief of staff, 1996—2000; v.p. govt. rels. The Walt Disney Co., 2000—06; pres. Mitch Rose Strategic Consulting, Washington, 2006—. Democrat. Office: Mitch Rose Strategic Cons 1431 Cola Dr Mc Lean VA 22101

ROSE, RONALD V., computer company executive; BS, Tulane U., U. Aberdeen Scotland; MS in Info. Tech., Ga. Inst. Tech. Tech. cons. CNBC; mgr. Delta Air Lines, Inc.; with Standard & Poor's (ComStock Tech. divsn.); various positions, including chief tech. officer, retail markets Std. & Poor's, 1995—99; chief info. officer Priceline.com, Inc., 1999—2010; sr. v.p. Dell.com Dell, Inc., Round Rock, Tex., 2010—. Former bd. dirs. Monitor110, Inc. Office: Dell Inc 1 Dell Way Round Rock TX 78682 Business E-Mail: ronald_rose@dell.com.

ROSE, WILLIAM SHEPARD, JR., lawyer; b. Columbia, SC, Mar. 9, 1948; s. William Shepard and Meta Cantey (Boykin) R.; m. Frances John Hobbs, Aug. 11, 1973; children: Katherine Cummings, William Shepard, III, Whitaker Boykin. BA in English, U. South, 1970; JD, U. S.C., 1973; LLM in Taxation, Georgetown U., 1976. Bar: S.C. 1973, Ohio 1977, D.C. 1974, U.S. Dist. Ct. D.C. 1976, U.S. Tax Ct. 1976, U.S. Supreme Ct. 1976, U.S. Ct. Claims Ct. 1978, U.S. Ct. Appeals (10th cir., 5th cir., 4th cir.) 1987, U.S. Ct. Appeals (3d, 6th, 7th, 8th, 9th and 11th cirs.) 1988. Trial atty. Office of Chief Counsel IRS, Washington, 1973-77; assoc. Frost & Jacobs Cin., 1977-80, McNair Law Firm PA, Hilton Head Island, SC, 1981—83, ptnr., 1983—87, 1989—2008, of counsel, 2008—. Asst. atty. gen., tax divsn. U.S. Dept. Justice, Washington, 1987-89; chmn., dir. Sea Pines Montessori Sch., 1983-86, Hilton Head Broadcasting, 1983-87, MBR Corp., Adwell Corp., and subsidiaries, Links Group, Inc., 1989-2000, The Dye Preserve, LLC, Hilton Head Prep. Sch., 1986-87, 89-93; bd. dir. Contbr. articles to profl. jours. Asst to chmn. bus. fundraising Beaufort County United Way, Hilton Head Island, 1984; vice chmn. Beaufort County Rep. Party, 1991-92, 93, chmn., 1992-93, vice chmn., 1993-95; mem. Beaufort County Transp. Com., 1994-95; commr. Sea Pines Pub. Svc. Dist., 2003-06, South Island Pub. Svc. Dist., 1995-2006; S.C. aquarium dir. Carolinian Ball, 2004-2007. Fellow Am. Coll. Tax Counsel; mem. ABA (past co-chmn. subcom. tax sect.), Beaufort County Bar Assn., S.C. Yacht Club (bd. govs. 1989-94, exec. com. 1993-94, rear commodore 1993-94), Low Country Citizens Com. Jud. Qualifications (dir. vols. medicine clinic 2009-). Republican. Episcopalian. Office: PO Drawer 3 23-B Shelter Cove Ln Ste 400 Hilton Head Island SC 29928-3588 E-mail: rrose@mcnair.net.

ROSEBOROUGH, TERESA WYNN, lawyer; b. Iowa City, Nov. 28, 1958; d. Robert Larry Wynn Jr. and Ethel (Crawford) Wynn; m. Joseph Anthony Roseborough, May 24, 1980. BA, U. Va., 1980; MEd, Boston U., 1983; JD with high honors, U. N.C., 1986. Bar: Ga. 1987, US Ct. Appeals (4th cir.) 1987, U.S. Dist. Ct. (northern dist.) Ga. 1989, US Ct. Appeals (11th cir.) 1989, US Ct Appeals (5th, 6th and 7th cir.), US Supreme Ct. Counselor Dept. Army, US Dept. Def., Giebelstadt, Germany, 1980-83; law clk. to Hon. J. Dickson Phillips US Ct. Appeals (4th cir.), 1986-87; law clk. to Justice John Paul Stevens US Supreme Ct., Washington, 1987-88; assoc. Sutherland, Asbill & Brennan, Atlanta, 1988-93; ptnr. Sutherland, Asbill & Brennan LLP, Atlanta, 1996—2006; dep. asst. atty. gen. Office Legal Counsel US Dept. Justice, Washington, 1994—96; chief litigation counsel MetLife, Inc., NYC, 2006—11; exec. v.p., gen. counsel, corporate sec. The Home Depot, Inc., Atlanta, 2011—. Adj. prof. litig. Emory U. Sch. Law, 1996—98. Editor in chief U. N.C. Law Rev., 1985-86. Bd. dirs. Howard Schs., Atlanta, 1990—, Neighborhood Justice Ctr., 1993—, Nat. Assn. for Pub. Interest Law, The Children's Sch.; chair pro bono com. Atlanta Coun. Younger Lawyers, 1990-92, bd. dirs., 1990-93. Named one of America's Top Black Lawyers, Black Enterprise mag., 2003, The 45 Under 45, The American Lawyer mag., 2003, The 25 Most Influential Black Women in Bus., The Network Journal, 2009. Mem. ABA (vice chair young lawyers sect. pro bono com. 1990-92, vice chair water quality com. sect. on natural resources energy and environment 1992—), American Constn. Soc. (chair, 2004-), State Bar Ga., Gate City Bar Assn., Ga. Assn. Black Women Attys., American Acad. Appellate Lawyers, Order of Coif Democrat. Avocations: skiing, golf. Office: The Home Depot Inc 2455 Paces Ferry Rd NW Atlanta GA 30339*

ROSELLI, RICHARD JOSEPH, lawyer; b. Chgo., Ill., Mar. 2, 1954; s. H. Joseph and Dolores Roselli; m. Lisa McNelis; children: Nicholas Joseph, Christiana Elise, Alexandra Grace, Michaela Luciana, Anthony Santino. BA, Tulane U., 1976, JD, 1980. Bar: Fla. 1981, U.S. Dist. Ct. (so. dist.) Fla. 1981, U.S. Ct. Appeals (5th and 11th cirs.); Bd. Cert. Civil Trial Lawyer. Ptnr. Krupnick, Campbell, Malone, Roselli et al, Ft. Lauderdale, 1981—2002, Roselli & Roselli Trial Lawyers, Boca Raton, Fla., 2002—05, Roselli & McNelis, PA, Boca Raton, Fla., 2005—. Adj. asst. prof., mem. bd. advisors Physician Asst. Program, Nova Southeastern U., 2005. Trustee Fla. Dem. Party. Mem. Am. Assn. Justice (pres.' coun. 1996-97), Am. Bd. Trial Advocates, Am. Soc. Law and Medicine, So. Trial Lawyers Assn. (founder), Fla. Justice Assn., Acad. Fla. Trial Lawyers (bd. dirs. 1987—, exec. com. 1990-97, sec. 1993, treas. 1994, pres. elect. 1995, pres. 1996, chmn., Fla. Lawyers Action Group-PAC 1996, Golden Eagle award, 1989, 1996, 98, Silver Eagle award, 1990, Crystal Eagle award 1995, named one of Best Lawyers in America, Top 100 Lawyers in Fla., Fla. Super Lawyers), Broward County Trial Lawyers (bd. dirs.), Trial Lawyers for Pub. Justice, Lawyer Pilots Bar Assn., Am. Assn. for Justice, Fla. Justice Assn., Palm Beach Trial Lawyers Assn, Fla. Grand Opera. Democrat. Roman Catholic. Office: 4800 N Federal Hwy Ste 202E Boca Raton FL 33431 Office Phone: 561-826-0826. Business E-Mail: rroselli@rosellimcnelis.com.*

ROSEN, CHARLES, II, retired lawyer; b. New Orleans, Jan. 29, 1925; s. Louis Leucht and Nita (Silverstein) R.; m. Mary Alice Waldauer (div. 1976); children: Charles III, Virginia, Jane, James Louis; m. Sandra Reed (div. 1995); m. Emily Hart, 1995. BA, Tulane U., 1948, LLB, 1951. Bar: La. 1951. Assoc. Rosen, Kammer, Wolff, Hopkins & Burke, New Orleans, 1951-55, Jones, Walker, Waechter, Poitevent, Carrere & Denegre, New Orleans, 1955-58, ptnr., 1958-90; spl. counsel Locke, Purnell, Rain, Harrell (now Locke Liddell & Sapp), New Orleans, 1990-97; of counsel Sullivan Stolier & Resor, New Orleans, 1997—2005; ret. Past chmn. and mem. exec. com. Golf & Sports Attractions, Inc., ret. mem. fore kids Found. Past trustee Touro Synagogue; hon. trustee Touro Infirmary; chmn. lawyers div. Jewish Fedn. Greater New Orleans, 1969; past chmn. lawyers div. United Fund. 1st lt. U.S. Army, 1944-46, PTO. Mem. ABA, La. Bar Assn., New Orleans Bar Assn., Am. Coll. Real Estate Attys., Anglo Am. Real Property Inst., So. Golf Assn. (past bd. dirs.), New Orleans Golf Assn. (past pres., past bd. dirs.), Tulane Green Wave Club (past bd. dirs.), Lakewood Country Club (past pres., bd. dirs.). Republican. Avocation: golf. Home: 140 E Oakridge Park Metairie LA 70005 Personal E-mail: crosen1975@aol.com.

ROSEN, MIKE, legislative staff member; Polit. reporter Fox Broadcasting, 1995—2008; comm. dir. to Rep. Michael McCaul US House of Representatives, Washington, 2008—. Office: Office of Rep Michel McCaul 131 Cannon House Office Bldg Washington DC 20515-4310 also: 5929 Balcones Dr Ste 305 Austin TX 78731-4286 Office Phone: 202-225-2401, 512-473-2357. Office Fax: 202-225-5955, 512-473-0514. E-mail: mike.rosen@mail.house.gov.

ROSEN, WILLIAM WARREN, lawyer; b. New Orleans, July 22, 1936; s. Warren Leucht and Erma (Stich) R.; m. Eddy Kahn, Nov. 26, 1965; children: Elizabeth K., Victoria A. BA, Tulane U., 1958, JD, 1964. Bar: La. 1964, US Dist. Ct. (ea. dist.) La. 1965, US Ct. Appeals (5th cir.) 1965, US Supreme Ct. 1984, US Dist. Ct. (mid. dist.) La. 1985, Colo. 1989. Assoc. Dodge & Friend, New Orleans, 1965-68, Law Office of J.R. Martzell, New Orleans, 1968-70; pvt. practice New Orleans, 1970-79, 89-90; ptnr. Lucas & Rosen (and predecessor firm), New Orleans, 1979-87, Herman, Herman, Katz & Cotlar, New Orleans, 1987-88, Rosen and Samuel, New Orleans, 1990-95; of counsel Rittenberg & Samuel, New Orleans, 1996-99; ptnr. Rosen & Lundeen, LLP, New Orleans, 1999—2002; pvt. practice New Orleans, 2002—05; founder & dir. Litigation Consultation Svcs., New Orleans, 1996—. Adj. prof. trial advocacy Law Sch. Tulane U., 1988-2006, mem. adv. com. paralegal studies program, 1977-86, instr. bus. orgns., 1978, instr. legal interviewing, 1980-81; mem. adv. com. Paralegal Inst. U. New Orleans, 1990-2006, instr. legal interviewing and investigations, 1986-87; lectr. legal and paralegal fields; lectr. real and demonstrative evidence Nat. Edn. Network, 1993; lectr. new judges seminar La. Jud. Coll., 2000, 01, 02, 03. Author: (with others) Trial Techniques publ. La. Trial Lawyers Assn., 1981; columnist Briefly Speaking publ. New Orleans Bar Assn., 1993-2000; Photographer: Immersion: A Katrina Rm. Photo Instalation, Parthenon Mus., Nashville, Tn., 2009. Mem. budget and planning com. Jewish Welfare Fedn., 1970-73; mem. adv. coun. on drug edn. La. Dept. Edn., 1973; mem. profl. adv. com. Jewish Endowment Found., 1982—2006; mem. exec. com. US Olympic Com., La., 1982-84; bd. dirs. Planned Parenthood La., 1994-2001, Hillel Found. New Orleans, 2003-05, Dad's Club, Isidore Newman Sch., 1984-85, Uptown Flood Assn., 1982-85; bd. dirs. Jewish Children's Home Svc., 1973-76, Met. Crime Commn. New Orleans, 1976-82. Spl. agt. Office Spl. Investigations USAF, 1958—61. Fellow, Inst. of Politics. Loyola U. Mem. ABA, ATLA (keyperson com. 1986-89, vice chmn. paralegal com. 1986-89, mem. family law adv. com. 1989-90, sec. family law sect. 1990-91, lectr. legal edn. 1979, 81, 83, 86, 88); mem. La. Bar Assn. (vice chmn. pub. rels. com. 1970-73, 88-89, past chmn. state youth drug abuse edn. program, vol. lawyers for arts 1986-96, chmn. sr. counsel com. 1995-96), Am. Arbitration Assn., Nat. Fedn. Paralegal Assn. (adv. coun. 1989-1998), Assn. Atty. Mediators (pres. La. chpt. 1995), Nat. Choice in Dying (legal adv. com. 1992-96), Nat. Edn. Network (lectr. legal edn. 1993), New Orleans Bar Assn. (CLE com. 1990-91, chmn. 1991-92, mem. alternative dispute resolution com. 1996-2000, panel moderator 1997), Inn of Ct. (master 1992-2004), Tenn. Assoc. Justice, Rotary Club New Orleans (bd. dirs. 1996-98, 2003-05, chmn. legal com. 1996—2005), Franklin Noon Rotary Club, Audubon Park Tennis Club (pres. 2004-06), Audubon Pub. Tennis Assn., Inc. (v.p. 2006-2011), Nashville Pub. Television (pub. adv. comm. 2009-), Miss Rodeo Tenn. Pageant (pres., 2012-2013). Avocation: photography. Office: 704 Wild Timber Ct Franklin TN 37064 Personal E-mail: lcsno@aol.com.

ROSENBAUM, DAVID MARK, engineering executive, consultant, educator; b. Boston, Feb. 11, 1935; s. Frederick and Elizabeth (Gelman) R.; m. Karen Jeanne Smith, Dec. 27, 1964; children: Benjamin Micah, Shoshana Elizabeth. BSc, Brown U., 1956; MS, Renessaler Poly. Inst., 1958; PhD, Brandeis U., 1964. Asst. rsch. prof. Boston U., 1964-65; assoc. prof. Poly. U., Bklyn., 1969-70; pres. Network Analysis Corp., Glen Cove, NY, 1970-72; asst. dir. Office of Nat. Narcotics Intelligence, Washington, 1973-74; cons. to comptr. gen. GAO, Washington, 1975-78; dir. Office of Radiation Programs EPA, Washington, 1978-81; pres. Tech. Analysis Corp., McLean, Va., 1981—. Cons. Dir. of Licensing, AEC, Washington, 1972-73. Author: Super Hilbert Space and the Quantum Time Operator, 1969, Liquefield Energy Gases Safety, 1978, A Statistical Procedure for Testing Pacemakers, 1978, Health Effects of Low-Level Radiation, 1981, A Statistical Procedure for Cluster Recognition with Application to Atlanta Leukemia Data, 1983. Mem. IEEE (sr.), Am. Phys. Soc. Office: Tech Analysts Corp # 202 6723 Whittier Ave Mc Lean VA 22101-4533 Personal E-mail: dmrose@radix.net.

ROSENBAUM, ROBIN STACIE, federal judge; b. Chapel Hill, NC, 1966; BA, Cornell U., 1988; JD, U. Miami Sch. Law, 1991. Trial atty. Fed. Programs Bench US Dept. Justice, 1991—95; staff counsel Office Ind. Counsel Dan Pearson, 1995—96; assoc. Holland & Knight LLP, 1996—97; law clk. to Hon. Stanley Marcus US Ct. Appeals (11th Cir.), 1998; asst. US atty. (southern dist.) US Dept. Justice, 1998—2007, chief economics crime section, 2002; magistrate judge US Dist. Ct. (southern dist.) Fla., 2007—12, judge, 2012—. Adj. prof. U. Miami Sch. Law, 2009—. Office: US District Court 400 N Miami Ave Miami FL 33128 E-mail: Robin_S_Rosenbaum@flsd.uscourts.gov.*

ROSENBERG, DAVID ALAN, military historian, strategic analyst; b. NYC, Aug. 30, 1948; s. Sidney and Fay (Breitman) R.; m. Deborah Lee Haines, July 1, 1973; 1 child, Rebecca Haines. BA in History, Am. U., 1970; MA in History, U. Chgo., 1971, PhD in History, 1983. Asst. historian, cons. Lulejian & Assocs., Inc., Falls Church, Va., 1974-75; instr. history U. Wis., Milw., 1976-78; pvt. practice cons., rschr. Chgo., Washington, 1978-82; asst. prof. history U. Houston, University Park, 1982-83; sr. fellow Strategic Concepts Devel. Ctr., Nat. Def. U., Washington, 1983-85; prof. strategy and ops. U.S. Naval War Coll., Newport, RI, 1985-90; assoc. prof. history Temple U., Phila., 1990-2000, professorial lectr., 2001—; Adm. Harry W. Hill prof. maritime strategy Nat. War Coll., Washington, 1996—2003; sr. prof. U.S. Naval War Coll., 1998—2006, asst. to vice chief naval ops., 1996—2004; dir. Task Force History for chief naval ops. Operation Iraqi Freedom, Global War on Terror, 2003—04; rsch. staff mem. and project dir. intelligence studies Inst. for Defense Analyses, 2006—. US exec. com. four Nation Nuc. History Program, project dir. Berlin Crisis, 1989-95; cons. Office of Sec. Def., 1991-93, Office Chief of Naval Ops., 1991-2005, Office Sec. of Navy, 1992-2003; chair Sec. Navy's Adv. Subcom. Naval History, 1995-2005; ret. capt. USNR, 1982-2010. Co-author: The Admiral's Advantage U.S. Navy Operational Intelligence in World War II and the Cold War, 2005, paperback edit., 2014; co-editor: (15 vol.) U.S. Plans for War, 1945-1950, 1990; contbr. articles to profl. jours., chpts. to books. Command USNR, 2003—05, command USNR, 2007—09. Recipient Meritorious Pub. Svc. award Dept. of Navy, 1995, Superior Civilian Svc. medal, 2000; Advanced rsch. scholar U.S. Naval War Coll., 1974-79; Ford Found grantee, 1985-86, MacArthur rsch. grantee 1987-88; MacArthur fellow 1988-93, 3 Meritorious Svc. medals, USNR, Legion of Merit, USNR. Mem. Orgn. Am. Historians (Binkley-Stephenson article prize), Soc. for Historians of Am. Fgn. Rels. (Bernath article prize), Soc. for Mil. History, U.S. Naval Inst., Internat. Inst. for Strategic Studies. Jewish.

ROSENBERG, MARK B., academic administrator; b. Athens, Ohio, Aug. 15, 1949; married; 2 children. BA, Miami U., Oxford, Ohio, 1971; PhD in Polit. Sci., U. Pitts., 1976. Prof. polit. sci. Fla. Internat. U., Miami, 1976—, chmn. Caribbean L.Am. studies coun., 1977-79, founding dir. L.Am. and Caribbean Ctr., 1979—, founding/acting dean Coll. Urban and Pub. Affairs, 1994-97, vice provost for internat. studies, 1996-98, provost, acting pres., 1998—, acting pres., 1999-2000, provost, exec. v.p. acad. affairs, 2000—05, pres., 2009—; chancellor State Univ. Sys. of Fla., Tallahassee, 2005—09; vis. rsch. prof. Vanderbilt U., 2009. Mem. exec. com. OLAM; mem. articulation coordination com. Fla. Bd. Edn.; mem. Coun. of Fgn. Relations, Pacific Coun. on Internat. Realtions. Author, editor, co-editor 6 books; former bd. editors Fla. Trend, Latin Trade; contbr. articles to profl. jours. Presdl. appointee U.S. Customs Dist. Export Coun.; mem. exec. com. OLAM, the Jewish Leadership Inst./Jewish Fedn. Miami; mem. statewide articulation coordination com. Fla. Bd. Edn. Mem. Greater Miami C. of C. (vice chair exec. com. for internat. econ. devel. 1992-94), Coun. Fgn. Rels., Pacific Coun. in Internat. Rels. Office: Fla Internat U Office of Pres University Park Pc 526 Miami FL 33199-0001 Office Phone: 850-245-0466. Office Fax: 850-245-9685. E-mail: Chancellor@flbog.org.

ROSENBERG, MICHAEL, lawyer; b. NYC, Oct. 13, 1937; s. Walter and Eva (Bernstein) Rosenberg; m. Jacqueline Raymonde Combe, Apr. 29, 1966; children: Andrew James, Suzanne Jennifer. AB in Econs. with honors, Ind. U., 1959; LLB, Columbia U., 1962. Bar: NY 1963, US Ct Appeals (2d cir) 1975, US Dist Ct (ea dist so div) Mich 1989. From. dep. asst. atty. gen. to asst. atty. gen. N.Y. State Dept. Law, NYC, 1963-66; assoc. Hellerstein, Rosier & Rembar, NYC, 1966-73; assoc. gen. counsel Gen. Instrument Corp., NYC, 1973-78; from assoc. gen. counsel to dep. gen. counsel U.S. Filter Corp., NYC, 1978-82; v.p., gen. counsel, sec. Alfa-Laval Inc., Ft. Lee, NJ, 1982-88; counsel Becker Ross Stone De Stefano & Klein, NYC, 1988-89; ptnr. Rosenberg & Rich, White Plains, NY, 1989-95, Quinn, Marantis & Rosenberg, LLP, White Plains, NY, 1995-97, Marantis, Rosenberg & van Nes, LLP, 1997-2001; atty. Law Offices of Michael Rosenberg, Armonk, 2001—. Mem Zoning Bd. Appeals Town of North Castle, NY, 1995—2006. Home and Office: Law Offices 2135 Arielle Dr 2410 Naples FL 34109

ROSENBERG, ROGER NEWMAN, neurologist, educator, department chair; b. Milw., Mar. 3, 1939; s. Sol J. and Cora D. (Newman) R.; m. Adrienne Turick, June 24, 1962; children: Jennifer, Lara Degree, Tufts U., 1957-60; BS, Northwestern U., 1961, MD with distinction, 1964. Diplomate Am. Bd. Psychiatry and Neurology. Intern Harvard Med. Service, Beth Israel Hosp., Boston, 1964-65; resident in neurology Neurol. Inst., Columbia U., NYC, 1965-67, instr. neurology, 1967-68; research assoc. Lab. of Biochem. Genetics, NIH, Bethesda, Md., 1968-70; clin. instr. Howard U. Med. Sch., Washington, 1969-70; asst. prof. neuroscis. Sch. Medicine, U. Calif.-San Diego, 1970-71; assoc. prof. neuroscis. and pediatrics, attending neurologist Univ. Hosp., U. Calif.-La Jolla, 1971-74; prof., chmn. dept. neurology U. Tex. Southwestern Med. Ctr., Dallas, 1973-91, prof. physiology, 1976—, Zale Disting. chair, prof. neurology, 1990—, dir. Alzheimer's Disease Rsch. Ctr., 1989—. Attending neurologist Parkland Meml. Hosp. and Children's Med. Ctr., Dallas, 1974—, Zale Lipshy Univ. Hosp., 1990—; mem. staff Presbyn. Hosp., Dallas, 1974—, St. Paul's Hosp., Dallas, 1974—; cons. staff VA Hosp., Dallas, 1974—; mem. nat. med. adv. bd. Nat. Ataxia Found., Mpls., 1971—, Myasthenia Gravis Found., 1973; chmn. med. adv. bd., dir. med. sci. research Internat. Joseph Diseases Found., Livermore, Calif., 1977—; lectr. Japanese Soc. Neurology, 1987, 94, 2010, Chinese Neurol. Soc., 1987, Spanish Neurol. Soc., 1992; chmn. bd. sci. councilors NINDS/NIH, 1984-86; pres. (hon.), Intl. French Soc. of Neurology Charcot Centenary Symposium, 1993. Editor Jour. Neurogenetics; mem. editl. bd. Neurology, 1977-82, 91-97, Trends in Neurosci., 1980-86, Current Opinion in Neurology & Neurosurgery, 1990—, Jour. of AMA, 1997—; chief editor Archives of Neurology, 1997—; contbr. articles to profl. jours. Bd. dirs. Winston Sch., Dallas, 1974-80; trustee World Fedn. Neurology, 2005. 1st Woody Guthrie scholar, 1971; USPHS grantee; recipient Disting. Alumnus award Neurol. Inst., N.Y., 1994, Nancy R. McCune Alzheimer's Rsch. award Alzheimer's Ass., 2005, Lifetime Achievement award Tex. Neurol. Soc., 2005, 1st Sci. medal World Congress Neurology, Bangkok, 2009. Fellow AAAS; mem. Am. Neurol. Assn. (hon.), Am. Acad. Neurology (chmn. sci. program com. nat. meetings 1979-84, elected councillor exec. bd. 1984-89, pres. 1991-93), Am. Neurochem. Soc., Tissue Culture Soc., Soc. Neurosci., Am. Fedn. Clin. Rsch., Soc. Pediat. Rsch., Internat. Child Neurology Assn., Am. Neurol. Assn. (hon., 1st v.p. 1987), Ctrl. Soc. Neurol. Rsch., Can. Congress Neurol. Scis. (hon.), Spanish Neurol. Soc. (hon.), Sigma Xi, Alpha Omega Alpha (Merit award Northwestern U. Alumni Assn. 1986). Home: 4425 Wildwood Rd Dallas TX 75209-2801 Office: U Tex Southwestern Med Ctr Dallas TX 75235 Business E-Mail: roger.rosenberg@utsouthwestern.edu.

ROSENBERG, STEVEN P., food products executive; BS in Fin., NY U. Founding investor Packaged Ice, Consumer Ice, 1992; pres., Arrow divsn. ConAgra, Inc., 1992—97; founder SPR Ventures Inc., 1997, pres., SPR Packaging, LLC. Bd. dirs. Tex. Capital Bank, 1999—2001, PRG-Schultz Internat., Inc., Tex. Capital Bancshares, Inc., 2001—, Cinemark Holdings, Inc., 2008—. Office: SPR Packaging LLC 1480 Justin Rd Rockwall TX 75087 Office Phone: 469-252-1070. Office Fax: 469-252-1069. Business E-Mail: steven.rosenberg@texascapitalbank.com.

ROSENBLOOM, ARLAN LEE, pediatrician, educator; s. Harris Phillip and Esther (Schneider) R.; m. Edith Kathleen Peterson, Sept. 14, 1958; children: Eric David, Maliah Jo, Disa Lynn, Harris Phillip. BA, U. Wis., 1955, MD, 1958. Diplomate Am. Bd. Pediatrics, Am. Bd. Pediatric Endocrinology, Am. Coll. Epidemiology. Intern Los Angeles County Gen. Hosp., 1958-59; resident in gen. practice Ventura County Hosp., Ventura, Calif., 1959-60; physician-in-chief Medico Hosp., Kratie, Cambodia, 1960-61; med. officer Pahang, Malaysia, 1961-62; resident in pediatrics U. Wis. Hosp., Madison, 1962-63, 64-65, fellow in pediatric endocrinology, 1963-64, 65-66; asst. prof. pediatrics U. Fla., Gainesville, 1968-71, assoc. prof., 1971-74, prof., 1974-96, disting. svc. prof., 1996—99, adj. disting. svc. prof. emeritus, 1999—, founder, chief div. endocrinology, 1977-94, dir. Office for Internat. Health Programs, 1995-99, mem. Ctr. for African Studies, mem. Ctr. for Latin Am. Studies. Assoc. dir. Clin. Rsch. Ctr., 1969-74, dir., 1974-80; dir. Nat. Found. March of Dimes Birth Defects Ctr., 1969-73; med. dir. Gainesville Youth Clinic, 1972-74; mem. adv. com. Nat. Disease and Therapy Index; mem. Fla. Com. Children and Youth, 1972; data work group chmn. Nat. Diabetes Commn., 1975; mem. epidemiology and disease control study sect. NIH, 1978-82; vis. prof. McMaster U. Med. Centre, 1974-75; cons. epidemiologist Boston U. Health Policy Inst., West Africa, 1983-84; mem. affiliate faculty dept. clin. psychology U. Fla., 1984—; pres., dir. Fla. Camp for Children and Youth with Diabetes, 1970-90; dir. N. Fla. Regional Diabetes Program Children and Youth, 1974-88; dir. U. Fla. Diabetes Rsch. Edn. and Treatment Ctr., 1977-90; clin. and sci. adv. bd. Children's Diabetes Found., Denver, 1978-86; dir. N. Fla. Regional Diabetes and Endocrine Program for Children and Youth, 1988-96; asst. med. dir. Children's Med. Svcs., Dist. 3/13, 1986-2000, med. dir., 2001-04; med. dir. Med. Foster Care Prgm., 1995-2000; mem. nat. diabetes adv. bd. NIH, 1990-94; internat. dir. Inst. for Endocrinology, Metabolism and Reprodn., Quito, 1989-; mem. panel on devices FDA, 1999—2003, mem. editl. bd. Internat. Jour. Pediat. Endocrinology 2009-, eMedicine 2002-, UpToDate 2006-. Editor Acta Paediatrica Belgica, 1979-82, Today in Medicine (Diabetes), 1989—; mem. editl. bd. European Jour. Pediat., 1982-02, Jour. Pediat. Endocrinology and Metabolism, 1983-09, Clin. Pediat., 1989-2002, Diabetes Care, 1992-95, Jour. Clin. Endocrinology and Metabolism, 1995-2000, Clin. Diabetes, 1996-99, Pediatric Diabetes, 1999—; contbr. over 460 articles to profl. jours. & chpts. to books. Sr. surgeon, comdr. med. epidemiologist, advisor West African Smallpox Eradication, Measles Control Program, Yaounde, Cameroon, 1966, 68, Inactive Res., 1969, 79; capt. Inactive Res. 1979, 2010; assoc. recruiter 2005-10; active duty, St Bernard Parish LA, USPHS Clinic, 2006. Recipient Faculty Rsch. prize U. Fla. Coll. Medicine, 1994, U. Wis. Med. Alumni Citation, 1995, U. Fla. Blue Key Disting. Faculty award, 1995, Hon. Prof. Ctrl. U. Quito Ecuador 2001, Disting. Physician award Endocrine Soc., 2003, Internat. Soc. Pediat. and Adolescent Diabetes, Prize for Achievement in Sci., Edn., & Advocacy on Behalf of Young People with Diabetes, 2004, Lilly Life Profl. hero award, 2006, Crisis Response Svc. award. Dept. Health & Human Svcs., Pub. Health Svc., 2006, Qforma's Most Influential Dtrs. award USA TODAY 2009, U. Fla. Outstanding Achievement award, 2013. Mem. Am. Acad. Pediatrics (sect. on endocrinology, sr. sect.), Am. Diabetes Assn. (bd. dirs. 1986-90), Fla. Diabetes Assn. (dir.), Alachua County Med. Soc., Internat. Soc. Pediatric Adolescent Diabetes, Endocrine Soc., Pediatric Endocrine Soc., Am. Pediatric Soc., Soc. Pediatric Rsch., Commissioned Officers Assn. Democrat. Avocations: photography, art. Home: 2902 SW 1st Ave Gainesville FL 32607-3002 Office: Children's Med Svcs Ctr 1701 SW 16th Ave Gainesville FL 32608-1153 Home: 9333 Old A1A St Saint Augustine FL 32086-8580 Office Phone: 352-393-2763. Business E-Mail: rosenal@peds.ufl.edu.

ROSENBLOOM, BRUCE S., corporate financial executive; BA in Economics, U. Tex., Austin, 1992; BS in Acctg., Fla. Atlantic U., Boca Raton, Fla., 1996. CPA. Account exec. MCI Telecom., 1992—95; sr. audit acct. Deloitte & Touche LLP, West Palm Beach, Fla., 1996—2000; mgr., fin. and fin. reporting Cooker Restaurant Corp., West Palm Beach, Fla., 2000—01; CFO PetMed Express, Inc., 2001—. Office: PetMed Express Inc 1441 SW 29th Ave Pompano Beach FL 33069 Office Phone: 954-979-5995. Business E-Mail: brosenbloom@1800petmeds.com.

ROSENBLUM, MARTIN JEROME, ophthalmologist; b. NYC, Apr. 7, 1948; s. Philip and Rita (Steppel) R.; m. Zina Zarin, May 31, 1975; children: Steven David, Richard James. BS, Bklyn. Coll., 1968; MD, U. Ariz., 1973; postgrad., Columbia U., 1977. Diplomate Am. Bd. Ophthalmology, Nat. Bd. Med. Examiners. Intern Cornell U., NYC, 1973-74; resident N.Y. Med. Coll., 1975-78, instr., 1978-79; practice medicine specializing in eye surgery St. Petersburg, Fla., 1979—. Asst. clin. prof. ophthalmology, U. So. Fla.; attending surgeon St. Anthony's Bayfront Med. Ctr., Am. Soc. for Cataract and Refractive Surgery, Ctr. Spl. Surgery; med. dir. Suncoast Eye Clinic, Pa. Fellow ACS, Am. Acad. Ophthalmology; mem. AMA, Am. Soc. Ophthalmic Plastic and Reconstructive Surgery, Fla. Med. Assn., Fla. Soc. Ophthalmology, Pinellas County Med. Soc., Bayou Country Club. Republican. Jewish. Avocations: tennis, golf, travel, skiing. Office: 2200 16th St N Saint Petersburg FL 33704-3106 Home: 7676 Hunter Lane Pinellas Park FL 33782 Office Phone: 727-822-4729. E-mail: mjreye@aol.com.

ROSENBLUM, ZINA MICHELLE ZARIN, psychology professor, marketing professional, researcher; b. NYC, Mar. 4, 1949; d. Harry and Miriam (Bachrach) Zarin; m. Martin Jerome Rosenblum, May 31, 1975; children: Steven David, Richard James. BA magna cum laude, Queens Coll., 1971; MEd, Columbia U., 1973, MEd Counseling Psychology, 1973. Prof. psychology Marymount Manhattan Coll., NYC, 1971—73; addictions counselor Manhattan Vets. Hosp., NYC, 1971—73; project dir. BBD&O Advt., NYC, 1973—74, Grey Advt., NYC, 1974—75; supr. market rsch. Doyle Dane & Bernbach, NYC, 1975—77, SSC& B, NYC, 1977—78; dir. rsch. Hershey Co., Pa., 1978—79; adminstr. Suncoast Eye Clinic, St. Petersburg, Fla., 1979—97; prof. psychology St. Petersburg Coll., Seminole, Fla., 1997—. Sec. Nat. Coun. Jewish Women, Fla., 1980—81; docent Fla. Holocaust Mus., 2005—. Scholar, Columbia U., 1971; Nat. Merit acholar, Coll. Bd., 1970. Mem.: APA, Phi Beta Kappa. Office: Suncoast Eye Clinic Martin Rosenblum 2200 16th St North Saint Petersburg FL 33704 Personal E-mail: zcurl@aol.com.

ROSENBLUTH, MORTON, retired periodontist educator; b. NYC, Sept. 28, 1924; s. Jacob and Eva (Bigeleissen) R.; m. Sylvia Fradin, July 2, 1946; children: Cheryl Bonnie, Hal Glen. BA, NYU, 1943, grad. program in periodontia, oral medicine, 1946, DDS, 1946. Diplomate Am. Bd. Periodontology. Intern Bellevue Hosp., NYC, 1946-47, resident, 1947; individual practice dentistry NYC, 1947-59; individual practice periodontia North Miami Beach, Fla., 1960—; individual practice periodontia, TMJ, implantology Bay Harbor Islands, Fla., 1995—2010. Periodontist Mt. Sinai Hosp., N.Y., Polyclinic Hosp. and Med. Sch. N.Y., Mt. Sinai Hosp., Miami Beach, Fla., Parkway Gen. Hosp.; chief dental dept. North Miami Gen. Hosp.; chmn. periodontia sect. Dade County Rsch. Ctr.; clin. assoc. prof. divsn. oral and maxillofacial surgery U. Miami Sch. Medicine; assoc. clin. prof. Southeastern U. Health Scis.; assoc. prof. Nova Southeastern U. Coll. Dental Medicine; lectr. throughout U.S.A., Israel, Mexico, Rome, Teheran, Bangkok, Hong Kong, Tokyo, Honolulu, Jamaica, Paris, London, Sicily, Budapest, Berlin, Luxembourg, South Africa and others; vis. lectr. U. Tenn. Dental Coll., NYU Dental Coll.; cons. VA Hosp., Miami. Contbr. articles to profl. jours. Mem. adv. bd. U. Fla. Coll. Dentistry; mem. profl. adv. bd. North Dade Children's Ctr., Hope Sch. Mentally Retarded Children; mem. sci. adv. com. United Health Found.; chmn. Dental divsn. United Fund of Dade County, Combined Jewish Appeal; nat. chmn. Hebrew U. Sch. Dental Medicine; bd. dirs. Health Planning Coun. South Fla.; pres. Condominium Assn.; bd. dirs. and bd. overseers Am. Friends of Hebrew U.; mem. med. adv. bd. Dade-Broward Lupus Found.; trustee Jewish Congregation, 1961-64. With AUS, 1943-44, as capt. USAF, 1951-52. Recipient Maimonides award State of Israel, 1979. Fellow Am. Coll. Dentists, Internat. Coll. Dentists; mem. ADA, Am. Acad. Periodontology, Am. Assn. Hosp. Dental Chiefs, Am. Acad. Dental Medicine, Am. Soc. Advancement Gen. Anesthesia in Dentistry, Am. Soc. Periodontists, Fla. Soc. Periodontists, Northeastern Soc. Periodontists, Fla. Dental Soc. (chmn. coun. on legislation), Miami Dental Soc., Miami Beach Dental Soc., East Coast Dental Soc. (sec.-treas. 1968, pres. 1971-72), North Dade Dental Soc. (pres. 1963-64), Fedn. Dentaire Internat., Fla. Acad. Dental Practice Adminstrn., Alpha Omega (pres. 1978-78, internat. regent 1973-75, internat. editor 1975-77, internat. pres.-elect 1977-78, internat. pres. 1979, chmn. bd. Alpha Omega Found. 1985-90), Am. Dental Interfrat. Coun. (pres. 1981-82), Nocoma Club (pres. 1958-60), NYU Century Club (local chmn.), Jockey Club (bd. govs.), KP, Masons, Kiwanis (bd. dirs. 1965), Chaine Des Rotisseurs (Miami Beach charge de missions). Home: 20281 E Country Club Dr Apt # 1001 Aventura FL 33180 Personal E-mail: periomort@aol.com.

ROSENE, PAUL EARL, music educator; b. Chgo., Ill., Mar. 26, 1930; s. Earl Nile and Dorothy Mae Rosene; m. Doris J. Mehrkens, Nov. 18, 1951; children: Richard, Cindy Mann. MusD Edn., U. of Ill., Champaign-Urbana, Illinois, 1968—76; Master degree in Edn. -Psychology and Music, Ill. State U., Normal, IL, 1955—57; BS in Music Edn., Ill. State Normal U., Normal, Illinois, 1951. Cert. master tchr. Ill., supr. student tchg. in music Ill., master tchr. Music Educators Nat. Conf. Dir. music edn. Saybrook Pub. Sch., Ill., 1951—52; supr. music, dir. bands Chenoa Pub. Schs., Ill., 1952—53; instructor band sch. USAF, Geneva, NY, 1953—54, bandsman French horn Dayton, Ohio, 1954—55, dir. men's glee club, 1954—55; dir. instrumental music Avon Pub. Schs., Ill., 1955—57; supr. music and dir. HS bands Pittsfield Pub. Schs., Ill., 1957—67; prof. music edn., supr. student tchg. music Ill. State U., Normal, 1967—90; music cons. handbells and choirchimes Malmark, Inc., Orlando, Fla., 1990—. USA pers. dir. Sch. Band/Chorus of Am., Bloomington, Ill., 1967—79. Author: (music book) Making Music With Choirchimes Instruments, 1982; author: (composer) (music techniques book) Making Music with Choirchimes Instruments - Advanced Method, 1986; composer (music for choirchimes): (music publ.) Pontifest, 1988; author: (techniques book) Special Effects for Choirchimes, 2003, Special Effects For Handchimes, 2010. Dir. of handbells Bethany Luth. Ch., Leesburg, Fla., 1990—2006; dir. Ctrl. Ill. Cmty. Band, Bloomington-Normal, 1979—90; dir. and founder Ill. State U. Handbells and Choirchime Ensembles, Normal, 1974—90. Staff sgt. band dir., instr. band sch. USAF, 1953—55. Recipient Disting. Tchg. award, Sch. Music, Ill. State U., 1981, Outstanding Alumnus award, 2001, Disting. Svc. award, Tchrs. Coll., Ill. State U., 1990, Svc. Appreciation award, Malmark Inc., 1999; named to Hall of Fame, Ill. State U., 2010. Mem.: Pittsfield Tchrs. Assn. (pres. 1960—67), Ill. Music Edn. Assn. (v.p. 1972—80, pres. dist. III 1972—84, Disting. Svc. Award 1991), Fla. Music Educators Assn., Nat. Assn. for Music Therapy (editor Gt. Lakes newsletter 1967—90), Music Educators Nat. Conf. (univ. contact Gt. Lakes divsn. 1979—84), Fla. Band Assn. (adjudicator 1994—). Republican. Lutheran. Avocations: walking, reading, computers, calligraphy. Home: 822 Pinar Dr Orlando FL 32825-7822 Office: Music Edn Cons 822 Pinar Dr Orlando FL 32825-7822 Office Phone: 407-803-7861. Personal E-mail: rosenebell@aol.com.

ROSENFELD, STEVEN IRA, ophthalmologist; b. NYC, Nov. 18, 1954; s. Frederick and Pearl (Stern) R.; m. Lisa Allyson Klar, June 24, 1978; children: Michael, Julie. BA, Johns Hopkins U., 1976; MD, Yale U., 1980. Diplomate Am. Bd. Ophthalmology, Nat. Bd. Med. Examiners. Intern Yale-New Haven Hosp., 1980-81; resident Barnes Hosp., St. Louis, 1981-84; fellow Bascom Palmer Eye Inst., Miami, Fla., 1984-85; ptnr. in pvt. practice Delray Eye Assocs., Delray Beach, Fla., 1985—. Clin. instr. Bascom Palmer Eye Inst., 1985-90, asst. clin. prof., 1990-96, assoc. clin. prof., 1996—2009, clin. prof., 2010-; assoc. examiner Am. Bd. Ophthalmology, Phila., 1993—. Author: The Eye in Systemic Disease, 1990, Lens and Cataract, 1996, Refractive Surgery, 2010; contbr. articles to profl. jours. Recipient Harry Rosenbaum Rsch. award Washington U. Sch. Medicine, 1984; named one of Best Doctors in Am., 1996—; Heed Ophthalmic Found. fellow, 1984. Fellow ACS, Am. Acad. Ophthalmology (chmn. B.C.S.C. section Lens and Cataract Surgery 2002-06, BCSC sect. Refractive Surgery 2006-, Honor award 1999, Sr. Achievement award 2007, Secretariat award 2007, 2012), Soc. Heed Fellows; mem. Castroviejo Corneal Soc., Eye Bank Assn. Am., Fla. Med. Assn., Fla. Soc. Ophthalmology, Assn. for Rsch. in Vision and Ophthalmology, Ocular Microbiology and Immunology Group, Phi Beta Kappa, Alpha Omega Alpha. Avocations: tennis, golf, fly fishing, lacrosse. Office: Delray Eye Assocs 16201 South Military Trail Delray Beach FL 33484-6503 Office Phone: 561-498-8100.

ROSENHAUS, DREW, professional sports agent; b. Oct. 29, 1965; BA, U. Miami, 1987; JD, Duke U., 1990. CEO Rosenhaus Sports Representation, Miami Beach, Fla. Co-author (with Don Yaeger): A Shark Never Sleeps: Wheeling and Dealing with the NFL's Most Ruthless Agent, 1988; film appearances include Jerry Maguire, 1996, Any Given Sunday, 1999. Office: Rosenhaus Sports Representation 6400 Allison Rd Miami Beach FL 33141 Office Phone: 305-936-1093. Fax: 305-864-3731.

ROSENKRANZ, ROBERT BERNARD, aerospace transportation executive; b. Paterson, NJ, Sept. 26, 1939; s. Irving Morton and Lucille (Kane) R.; m. Barbara Jean Larson, May 17, 1970; children: Stephen Robert, Deborah Anne, Diana Rebecca, Susan Leslie. BS, U.S. Mil. Acad., 1961; MA, U. Pa., 1969. Commd. 2d. lt. U.S. Army, 1961, advanced through grades to maj. gen., 1962, officer Germany, 1962—65, battery comdr. Vietnam, 1966—67, bn. exec. officer Republic of Korea, 1973—74, bn. and brigade comdr. Germany, 1977—79; assoc. prof. U.S. Mil. Acad., West Point, NY, 1969—72; dir., soviet studies U.S. Army War Coll., Carlisle, Pa., 1981—83; sr. mil. asst. under sec. of def. Pentagon, 1986—88; dep. dir., Army Ops., Readiness and Mobilization U.S. Army Pentagon, 1988—89, dir., force programs, 1989—92; comdr. U.S. Army Optec, 1992—95; sr. v.p., range and logistics svcs. Dyncorp, Reston, Va., also Ft. Worth, 1995—2001; v.p., bus. devel. MPRI/L-3, Alexandria, Va., 2001—03, gen. mgr. Columbia, Md., 2003—04; v.p., bus. devel. KEI Pearson Inc., Arlington, Va., 2005; pres. DynCorp International Tech. Svc., Falls Church, Va., 2005—08; exec. v.p., chief of staff DynCorp International, Inc., 2008—. Decorated Bronze Star, Air medal; recipient Superior Svc. medal U.S. Dept. Def., 1988, Disting. Svc. medal., 1992, 95. Mem.: Nat. Def. Indsl. Assn., Internat. Test and Evaluation Assn., Assn. of the U.S. Army, Internat. Inst. Strategic Studies. Republican. Jewish. Avocations: jogging, reading, woodworking, golf, racquetball. Home: 3222 Wynford Dr Fairfax VA 22031-2828 Office: DynCorp International Inc 3190 Fairview Park Dr Ste 700 Falls Church VA 22042 Office Phone: 571-722-0238, 571-722-0210. Office Fax: 571-722-0252. Business E-Mail: bob.rosenkranz@dyn-intl.com.

ROSENN, KEITH SAMUEL, lawyer, educator; b. Wilkes-Barre, Pa., Dec. 9, 1938; s. Max and Tillie R. (Hershkowitz) R.; m. Nan Raker, June 21, 1960; 1 child, Eva; m. Silvia R. Rudge, Mar. 21, 1968; children: Jonathan, Marcia AB, Amherst Coll., 1960; LLB, Yale U., 1963. Bar: Pa. 1964, U.S. Ct. Appeals (3rd cir.) 1979, Fla. 1981, U.S. Ct. Appeals (11th cir.) 1982. Law clk. to Judge Smith U.S. Ct. Appeals (2nd cir.), 1963-64; asst. prof. law Ohio State U. Coll. Law, 1965-68, assoc. prof., 1968-70, prof., 1970-79; project assoc. Ford Found., Rio de Janeiro, 1966-68; assoc. Escritorio Augusto Nobre, Rio de Janeiro, 1979-80; prof. law U. Miami, Fla., 1979—; project coord. Olin Fellowship Program Law and Econs. Ctr., U. Miami, Fla., 1980-81, assoc. dean Law Sch. Fla., 1982-83, chmn. fgn. grad. law program Fla., 1985—. Cons. Hudson Inst., 1977, U.S. State Dept, 1981-82, World Bank, 1988-90; Fulbright lectr. Argentina, 1987, 88. Author: (with Karst) Law and Development in Latin America, 1975; Law and Inflation, 1982, Foreign Investment in Brazil, 1991; co-editor: A Panorama of Brazilian Law, 1992, Corruption and Political Reform in Brazil, 1999; advisor InterAm. Law Rev.; contbr. articles to law jours. Recipient Order of Democracy award Congress of Republic of Colombia, 1987, Lawyer of the Ams. award, 1989, Inter-Am. Jurisprudence prize, 1998, Order of Congress award Republic of Colombia, 2000; grantee Social Sci. Rsch. Coun., 1970, Dana Found., 1982. Mem. ABA, Am. Law Inst., Inter-Am. Bar Assn., Fla. Bar, Am. Soc. Comparative Law (bd. dirs.). Jewish. Office: U Miami Law Sch PO Box 248087 Coral Gables FL 33124-8087

ROSENSTEEL, GEORGE THOMAS, nuclear physicist, professor; b. Balt., Sept. 30, 1947; s. Walter St. George and Marie Emily (White) R.; m. Tsetsa Dankova. BSc, U. Toronto, Ont., Can., 1973, PhD, 1975. Can. fellow NRC, 1976-78; prof. physics Tulane U., New Orleans, 1978—, chmn. dept., 1985-91. Vis. fellow Brit. Sci. and Engring. Coun., U. Sussex, Eng., 1986; vis. prof. Nat. Inst. Nuclear Theory, U. Washington, 1992, Inst. Theoretical Physics U. Gent, Belgium, 1999. Contbr. numerous articles to profl. jours. Delivered grad. sch. commencement address Tulane U., 1987; recipient 7 grants NSF, 1979—. Mem. Am. Phys. Soc., Am. Math. Soc., Sigma Xi (young scientist award 1987). Office: Tulane U Dept of Physics New Orleans LA 70118 Office Phone: 504-862-3174. Business E-Mail: george.rosensteel@tulane.edu.

ROSENTHAL, LEE HYMAN, federal judge; b. Richmond, Ind., Nov. 30, 1952; m. Gary L. Rosenthal; children: Rebecca, Hannah, Jessica, Rachel. BA in Philosophy with honors, U. Chgo., 1974, JD with honors, 1977. Bar: Tex. 1979. Law clk. to Hon. John R. Brown U.S. Ct. Appeals (5th cir.), 1977-78; assoc. Baker & Botts, 1978-86, ptnr., 1986-92; judge US Dist. Ct. (so. dist.) Tex., 1992—. Chair Fed. Jud. Conf. Standing Com. on Rules of Practice and Procedure, 2007-, Adv. Com. for Fed. Rules of Civil Procedure, 1996-2003, mem. Am. Law Inst. & Coun., advisor transactional rules of civil procedure, adviser aggregate litigation project, adviser employment law project. Mem. bd. editors Manual for Complex Litigation, 1999—. Mem. vis. com. Law Sch. U. Chgo., 1983-86, 94-97, 99-2001; pres. Epilepsy Assn. Houston/Gulf Coast, 1989-91; trustee Briarwood Sch. Endowment Found., 1991-92; bd. dirs. Epilepsy Found. Am., 1993-98, DePelchin Children's Ctr., 2000-; bd. trustees Kinkaid Sch., Rice U., 2009-. Fellow Tex. Bar Found.; Mem. ABA, Texas Bar Assn., Houston Bar Assn. Office: US Dist Ct US Courthouse Rm 11535 515 Rusk Ave Houston TX 77002-2600

ROSENTHAL, SUSAN BARBARA, retired librarian; b. Elberon Park, NJ, Apr. 7, 1946; d. Joseph and Anna (Warar) Rosenthal. BA, Montclair State Coll., NJ, 1967; MEd in Libr. Sci., U. Miami, 1973. Cert. media specialist, tchr., Fla., NJ. Tchr. Manasquan Bd. Edn., NJ, 1967-71; tech. svcs. libr. Oakland Park Libr., Fla., 1978-92, asst. dir., 1992—93, acting dir., 1993, ret. Author: (mag.) Galumph, 1965-67; contbr. A Micro Handbook for Small Libraries and Media Centers, 1983, 2d edit., 1986, 3d edit., 1991. Mem. Humane Soc., Broward County, Fla., 1981, WPBT-TV PBS sta., 1975-2000, So. Mus. Flight, 1997—, Friends of the Oakland Park Libr., 1998—, mem. luncheon com., 1999, mem. planning com., 1999, book sales vol., 1998-; charter mem. Mus. of Discovery and Sci., 1989-96, US Holocaust Meml. Mus., 1994—; donor Miami Book Fair Internat., 1990—, Boca Raton Mus. Art, Fla., So. Poverty Law Ctr. Wall of Tolerance, Survivors of the Shoah Visual History Found., Martin Luther King Jr. Meml. Found., Poverello Ctr., thehungersite.com, freerice.com, Friends of the Oakland Park Libr., Sierra Club, WPBT-TV PBS Sta. Recipient St. Cloud Tchg. award Société d'Enseignement, St. Cloud, France, 1966, 2 awards Libr. Pub. Rels. Coun., winner, 1983, hon. mention, 1985, cert. appreciation U.S. Holocaust Meml. Mus., 1996, 2000. Mem. ACLU, AARP, Pub. Concern Found., Friends Smithsonian, Internat. Solidarity Human Rights, History Channel Club, Mensa, act-forchange.org, moveon.org, Twitter, YouTube, Procrastinators Club Am., Pi Delta Phi.

ROSETTE, ASHLEIGH SHELBY, management professor; BA, U. Tex., Austin, MA in Acctg.; PhD in Mgmt. and Organizations, Northwestern U. Assoc. prof. mgmt. Fuqua Sch. Bus., Duke U., Ctr. of Leadership and Ethics scholar, fellow Ctr. for Study of Race,

Ethnicity and Gender in Social Sciences; mem. Duke Corp. Edn. Global Learning Resource Network. Contbr. articles to profl. jours. Office: Duke University Fuqua School of Business 100 Fuqua Dr Durham NC 27708 Office Phone: 919-660-8021. E-mail: arosette@duke.edu.

ROSKOSKI, ROBERT, JR., biochemist, educator, author; b. Elyria, Ohio, Dec. 10, 1939; s. Robert and Mary R.; m. Laura Martinsek, Aug. 27, 1974. BS, Bowling Green State U., 1961; MD, U. Chgo., 1964, PhD, 1968. Asst. prof. U. Iowa, Iowa City, 1972-75, assoc. prof., 1975-79, vis. prof. Iowa City, 1993; prof. dept. biochemistry and molecular biology Health Scis. Ctr., La. State U., New Orleans, 1979—2006; Fred G. Brazda prof. Med. Ctr., La. State U., New Orleans, 1991—2006; founder, sci. dir. Blue Ridge Inst. for Med. Rsch., 2006—. Sr. investigator USAF Sch. Aerospace Medicine, 1967-69; assoc. dir. Med. Sci. Tng. Program, 1978-79; cons. biochemistry test com. Nat. Bd. Med. Examiners, 1981-84, 2003-06, Assn. Internat. Cancer Rsch., Royal Soc. New Zealand; mem. merit rev. bd. for basic scis. VA, 1992-95; mem. rev. com. biol. scis. U. South Fla., 1992, biochemistry St. George's U. Sch. Medicine, 1997, Kuwait U. Health Scis. Ctr., 2002, editl. bd. mem. Pharmacological rsch., 2014-With USAF, 1966—69. NIH postdoctoral fellow U. Chgo., 1964-66; NIH spl. fellow Rockefeller U., 1969-71 Mem. Am. Chem. Soc., Am. Soc. Neurochemistry, Soc. for Neurosci., Am. Soc. Biol. Chemists, Am. Soc. Pharmacology and Exptl. Therapeutics, Internat. Soc. Neurochemistry, Assn. Med. and Grad. Depts. Biochemistry (sec. 1994-96, pres. 1997), Am. Assn. Med. Colleges (coun. Acad. socs., 1998-01), Greater New Orleans Soc. for Neurosci. (pres. 1982-83, editl. bd. mem. pharmacological rsch., 2014-), Am. Med. Writers Assn., Am. Soc. Clin. Oncology. Achievements include research in signal transduction and cancer therapy. Home: 221 Haywood Knolls Dr Hendersonville NC 28791-8717 Office: 3754 Brevard Rd Ste 116 Box 19 Horse Shoe NC 28742-8814 Office Phone: 828-891-5637. Office Fax: 828-890-8130. Business E-Mail: rrj@brimr.org.

ROSKY, THEODORE SAMUEL, insurance company executive; b. Chgo., Apr. 14, 1937; s. Theodore and Lora Marie (O'Connell) R.; m. Jacqueline Reed, Apr. 19, 1958; 1 child, Laura Marie. BA, State U. Iowa, 1959. Various actuarial positions Conn. Gen. Life Ins. Co., Hartford, 1959-66, assoc. actuary, 1967-70, controller, 1970-73, 2d v.p., actuary, 1973, v.p., 1973-78; exec. v.p. Capital Holding Corp., 1978-84, exec. v.p., CFO, 1984-91, exec. v.p., 1991-92; bd. dirs. Legend Funds, 1993-98, SBM Mut. Funds, 1995-97, SBM Certificate Co., 1996-98; fin. svcs. Dory L.P., 1998-99. Instr. State U. Iowa, 1958-59, U. Hartford, 1964-66, U. Conn., 1967-68. Active Mayor's Adv. Com. on Pub. Art, 1990—2005; mem. bd. pensions Evang. Luth. Ch. Am., 1974—82, 1984—87, 1989—95; bd. dirs. Hartford Coll. for Women, 1974—78, Macauley Theater, 1983—85, Louisville Fund for the Arts, 1980—97, Louisville Luth. Home, 1983—97, Louisville Orch., 1982—88, 1989—95, Ky. Opera, 1992—2001, Lincoln Found., 1992—2002, Actors Theatre of Louisville, 1995—, New Performing Arts, 1996—98, Oak and Acorn, 1995—2001, Glassworks Found., 2002—03, Pub. Radio Partnership, 2003—04, YMCA Safe Place, 2003—11, Sch. Choice Scholarships, 2004—05. Recipient award Soc. Actuaries, 1958 Fellow Soc. Actuaries; mem. Am. Acad. Actuaries, Southeastern Actuaries Club. Independent. Lutheran. Home and Office: 2304 Speed Ave Louisville KY 40205-1642

ROS-LEHTINEN, ILEANA CARMEN, United States Representative from Florida; b. Havana, Cuba, July 15, 1952; arrived in US, 1959; d. Enrique Emilio and Amanda (Adato) Ros; m. Dexter Lehtinen, June 9, 1984; children: Amanda, Patricia stepchildren: Douglas, Katherine. AA, Miami-Dade Cmty. Coll., Fla., 1972; BA in Edn., Fla. Internat. U., Miami, 1975, MS in Ednl. Leadership, 1986; PhD in Higher Edn., U. Miami, 2004. Founder, chief adminstr. Eastern Acad., Miami-Dade County, 1978—; mem. Dist. 110 Fla. House of Reps., Tallahassee, 1983—86; mem. Dist. 34 Fla. State Senate, Tallahassee, 1987—89; mem. US Congress from 18th Fla. Dist., Washington, 1989—2013, US Congress from 27th Fla. Dist., Washington, 2013—; chairwoman US House Fgn. Affairs Com., Washington, 2011—13. Co-chair Nat. Marine Sanctuary Caucus, 2008—, Congressional Vision Caucus, 2008—. Recipient Nat. Legis. award, LULACH, 1999, Edn. award, Hispanic Heritage Found., 2007; named Ofcl. of Yr., Youth Crime Watch America, 2001. Mem.: Bi-lingual Pvt. Sch. Assn. Republican. Episcopalian. Office: US House of Representatives 2206 Rayburn House Office Bldg Washington DC 20515-0918 also: Ileana Ros Lehtinen Congress Woman 8660 W Flagler St Ste 131 Miami FL 33144-2035 Office Phone: 202-225-3931, 305-275-1800. Office Fax: 202-225-5620, 305-275-1801.*

ROSS, DAVID EDMOND, church official; b. Lewiston, Maine, Oct. 1, 1950; s. Rev. and Mrs. Lorne Arla Collins R.; m. Shirley Evelyn Godin, Aug. 19, 1972. BA in Theology cum laude, Berkshire Coll., 1973; MPA, U. Maine, 1989. Ordained to ministry Advent Christian Ch., 1975. Pastor State Road Advent Christian Ch., Presque Isle, Maine, 1973-91; exec. dir. Advent Christian Ch. Gen. Conf., Charlotte, NC, 1991—2003; sr. pastor Fellowship Advent Christian ch., Bethlehem, NC, 2003—. V.p. Maine State Conf. Advent Christian Chs., 1975-76, pres., 1976-81, 86-91; mem. exec. coun. Advent Christian Ch., 1981-90, long range strategy com., 1986—96; seminar leader Am. Festival of Evangelism, Kansas City, 1981; dir. Northern Lights Youth Choir, 1974-90. Pres. Piedment Conf. Advent Christian Chs., 2007—. Office: Fellowship Advent Christian Church 885 Icard Ridge Rd Taylorsville NC 28681 Office Phone: 828-495-8086. Personal E-mail: bethlehemshepherd@hotmail.com.

ROSS, DEBORAH K., state legislator; Atty.; sr. lecturing fellow; cons.; state rep. Dist. 38 NC, 2002—. Mem. Appropriations com., Appropriations Subcom. on Capital, Edn. com., Edn. Subcom. on Universities, Pensions and Retirement com., Fin. com.; vice chmn. Election Law and Campaign Fin. Reform com., Rules, Calendar and Ops of the House com.; chmn. Judiciary I com., Ethics com. Democrat. Mailing: Dist Off 425 S Boylan Ave Raleigh NC 27603 Office: NC House of Reps 16 W Jones St Rm 1023 Raleigh NC 27601-1096 Office Phone: 919-733-5773. E-mail: Deborah.Ross@ncleg.net.

ROSS, DENNIS ALAN, United States Representative from Florida, former state legislator; b. Lakeland, Fla., Oct. 18, 1959; s. William A. and Loyola Ross; m. Cindy Hartley, Aug. 6, 1983; children: Shane, Travis. BS in Bus., Auburn U., 1981; JD, Samford U., 1987. Bar: Fla. 1987, US Dist. Ct. (middle dist.) Fla. 1987. Assoc. Holland & Knight, Lakeland, 1987-89; staff counsel Walt Disney World Co., Lake Buena Vista, Fla., 1989; ptnr. Ross Vecchio P.A. (formerly Ross Williams & Deal PA), Lakeland, 1989—; mem. Dist. 63 Fla. House of Reps., Tallahassee, 2000—08; mem. US Congress from 12th Fla. Dist., Washington, 2011—13, US Congress from 15th Fla. Dist., 2013—, US House Edn. & Workforce Com., 2011—13, US House Ethics Com., 2011—13, US House Judiciary Com., 2011—13, US House Financial Services Com., 2013—. Chmn. Polk County Republican Party, Lakeland, 1992-95. Recipient Legis. Leadership award The Trust for Public Lands, 2001, Fla. Workers Adv. Outstanding Freshman award, 2001, AIF Champion Bus. award, 2006; named Legis. of Yr. Fla. Bldg. Material Assn., 2001, Fla. Automobile Dealers, 2003, Trucking Assn., 2005, Fla. League Cities, 2006, Fla. Assn. Ins. Agents, 2006. Mem. Lakeland Bar Assn. (past pres.), Lakeland Kiwanis Club (bd. mem. 1987). Republican. Presbyterian. Office: US House of Representatives 229 Cannon House Office Bldg Washington DC 20515 also: 170 Fitzgerald Rd Ste 1 Lakeland FL 33813 Office Phone: 202-225-1252, 863-644-8215. Office Fax: 202-225-0585, 863-648-0749.*

ROSS, EDWARD JOSEPH, architect; b. Dec. 13, 1934; s. Miriam Ross; children: Linda Joy, Melissa Carol. Student, Boston Archtl. Ctr., 1952-55, 61-62, USAF Surveying Sch., 1955-56, Boston Soc. Civil Engrs., 1956-57, Carl Bolivar Structural Engr., 1962-63. Registered arch., Mass., Calif., NY, Fla., NH, Vt., cert. Nat. Coun. Archtl. Registration Bds.; lic. constrn. supr. Mass., expert witness constrn. law. Draftsman, assoc. William W. Drummey, Architect, Boston, 1952-59; job capt., designer Drummey-Rosane-Anderson, Boston, 1959-64; projects arch. Maginnis & Walsh & Kennedy, Boston, 1964-69; v.p. William Nelson Jacobs Assocs., Inc., Boston, 1969-73; staff arch. Robert Charles Assocs., Inc. Archs., Boston, 1973-74; office mgr. Charles F. Jacobs Assocs., Inc., Cambridge, Mass., 1974-76; cons. arch. Linenthal, Eisenberg & Anderson, Boston, 1976-77; staff arch. Eisenberg Haven Assocs., Inc., Boston, 1977-78; chief arch., chief insp. Boston Housing Authority, 1978-83; prin. Edward J. Ross, AIA/FARA, Randolph, Mass., 1983-84; arch., sr. assoc., dir. constrn. adminstrn. Stull and Lee, Inc., Boston, 1984-91; pvt. practice Randolph, Stoughton, Mass., West Palm Beach, Fla., 1963—2000; consulting arch., contrn. adminstr., expert witness, 2000—06. Mem. FCC Tech Plus. Mem. exec. bd. and ops. com. United Civic Orgn.; bd. dir. Linderhof Property Owners Assn., Knollsbrook Condominium Complex. Staff sgt. USAF, maj. Mass. Mil. Res. Fellow: Soc. Am. Registered Archs.; mem.: USO (New Eng. coun.), AIA, Boston Soc. Archs. (mem. housing com. 1982—86), Constrn. Specifications Inst., Mass. State Assn. Archs., Am. Arbitration Assn. (nat. panel 1965—2005), United Civic Orgn. (mem. exec. bd. and ops. com.), Assn. First Corps Cadets, Am. Assn. Ret. Persons, Air Force Assn. (pres. Boston chpt.), Mass. Air N.G. Hist. Assn., Mil. Hist. Soc. Mass., Oxford 100 Condominium Assn. (pres.), Linderhof Golf Course Site One Assn. (pres. 1980—86), Ancient and Hon. Arty. Co. Mass., Oxford Colony Club Century Village (v.p.), Ten of Us Club, Am. Legion, KP, Elks. Address: 5298 Tiffany Anne Cir West Palm Beach FL 33417 Home Phone: 561-512-2273; Office Phone: 561-615-6680. Office Fax: 561-686-6345. Business E-Mail: edwardjross34@att.net.

ROSS, JOSEPH COMER, pulmonologist, educator, academic administrator; b. Tompkinsville, Ky., June 16, 1927; s. Joseph M. and Annie (Pinckley) R.; m. Isabelle Nevins, June 15, 1952; children: Laura Ann, Sharon Lynn, Jennifer Jo, Mary Martha, Jefferson Arthur. BS, U. Ky., 1950; MD, Vanderbilt U., 1954. Diplomate Am. Bd. Internal Medicine (bd. govs. 1975-81), with added qualifications in pulmonary disease. Intern Vanderbilt U. Hosp., Nashville, 1954-55; resident Duke U. Hosp., Durham, NC, 1955-57, rsch. fellow, 1957-58; from instr. medicine to prof. Ind. U. Sch. Medicine, Indpls., 1958-70; prof., chmn. dept. medicine Med. U. of S.C., Charleston, 1970-80; vis. prof. Vanderbilt U. Sch. Medicine, Nashville, 1979-80, prof. medicine, 1981-99, prof. medicine emeritus, 1999—, assoc. vice chancellor for health affairs, 1982-99, assoc. vice chancellor for health affairs emeritus, 1999—. Mem. cardiovascular study sect. NIH, 1966-70, program project com., 1971-75; mem. adv. coun. Nat. Heart, Lung and Blood Inst., 1982-86; mem. ad hoc coms. NAS, 1966, 67; mem. Pres.'s Nat. Adv. Panel on Heart Disease, 1972; mem. merit rev. bd. in respiration VA Rsch. Svc., 1972-76, chmn., 1974-76. Mem. editorial bd. Jour. Lab. and Clin. Medicine, 1964-70, Chest, 1968-73, Jour. Applied Physiology,1968-73, Archives of Internal Medicine, 1976-82, Heart and Lung, 1977-86; contbr. articles to profl. jours. Bd. dirs. Nashville Ronald McDonald Ho., past pres.; bd. dirs. Agape, Leadership Nashville, v.p.; mem. adv. com. Davidson County Cmty. Health Agy.; active Tenn. Lung Assn.; elder Ch. of Christ. With US Army, 1945—47. Fellow: ACP, Am. Coll. Cardiology, Am. Coll. Chest Physicians (gov. S.C. 1970—76, chmn. sci. program com. 1973, vice chmn. bd. govs. 1974—75, exec. coun. 1974—80, chmn. bd. govs. 1975—76, pres.-elect 1976—77, pres. 1977—78, chmn. bylaws com. 2002—04, bd. regents 2002—04); mem.: AMA (sect. on med. schs.), Am. Soc. Internal Medicine, So. Soc. Clin. Rsch., Am. Thoracic Soc. (nat. councillor 1972—76), S.C. Med. Soc., Ctr. Social Clin. Rsch., Assn. Profs. Medicine, Assn. Am. Physicians, Am. Soc. Clin. Investigatrion, Am. Physiol. Soc., Am. Fedn. Clin. Rsch. (chmn. Midwest sect.), S.C. Lung Assn. (v.p. 1974—75), Phi Beta Kappa, Alpha Omega Alpha. Office: Vanderbilt U Med Ctr Oxford House Ste 212 Nashville TN 37232-0001 Personal E-mail: joseph.ross@comcast.net.

ROSS, PATTI JAYNE, obstetrics and gynecology educator; b. Nov. 17, 1946; d. James J. and Mary N. Ross; m. Allan Robert Katz, May 23, 1976. BS, DePauw U., 1968; MD, Tulane U., 1972. Diplomate Am. Bd. Ob-Gyn. Asst. prof. U. Tex. Med. Sch., Houston, 1976—82, assoc. prof., 1982—98, prof., 1998—2004, dir. adolescent ob-gyn., 1976—, dir. student edn., dir. devel. dept. ob-gyn.; adv. bd. Teva Bayer, Meck Pharm. Cons. in field; spkr. in field; appeared on Lifetime TV network. Contbr. articles to profl. jours. Mem. Rape Coun.; vol. Children's Miracle Network/Hermann's Children's Hosp.; Olympic torch relay carrier, 1996; founder Women's Med. Rsch. Fund, U. Tex. Med. Sch., Houston; bd. dirs. Am. Diabetes Assn., 1982—, Susan Komen Found. Recipient Patti Jayne Ross Professorship, 2004. Mem.: Profl. Women Execs., Orgn. Women in Sci., Am. Women's Med. Assn., AAAS, Soc. Adolescent Medicine, Assn. Profs. Ob-Gyn., Houston Ob-Gyn. Soc., Harris County Med. Soc., Tex. Med. Assn., River Oak Breakfast Club, Sigma Xi. Roman Catholic. Office: 6431 Fannin St 3278 Houston TX 77030-1501 Office Phone: 713-500-6431. Business E-Mail: patti.j.ross@uth.tmc.edu.

ROSS, QUINTON T., state legislator; b. Mobile, Ala., Oct. 30, 1968; m. J. Kelley Ross; 1 child, Quinmari T. BS in Polit. Sci., Ala. State U., Montgomery, MA in Edn. Prin. Booker T. Washington Magnet HS, Ala.; dir. adult edn. consortium H. Trenholm State Tech. Coll.; mem. Dist. 26 Ala. State Senate, Ala., 2003—. Mem. Hutchinson Missionary Bapt. Ch. Mem. Nat. Assn. Secondary Sch. Prins., County Leaders in Ala. Schs., Omega Psi Phi. Democrat. Baptist. Office: PO Box 6183 Montgomery AL 36106 also: Ala State Senate Ala State House 11 S Union St Rm 731 Montgomery AL 36130 Office Phone: 334-242-7880. Business E-Mail: qtross2002@hotmail.com.

ROSS, SHARONA B., surgeon; MD, George Washington U., Washington, 2001. Cert. in surgery ABS, 2008. Surgeon, med. dir. surg. endoscopy Fla. Hosp. Physician Group, Tampa, 2012—. Dir., founder Fla. Hosp. Tampa Women in Surgery, 2008. Recipient award, SLS, 2008—13, Disting. Svc. award, Am. Soc. Abdominal Surgeons, 2011, Rep. Nat. Conv. Disting. Surgeon, 2012. Mem.: AHPBA (mem. program com. 2012), SAGES (mem. program com. 2011), Am. Bd. Surgery (mem. exam. cons. com.). Achievements include development of laparoscopic cameras. Office: Fla Hosp Tampa Physician Group 3000 Medical Park Dr Ste 310 Tampa FL 33611 Office Fax: 813-615-8350. Personal E-mail: sharona.ross@yahoo.com.*

ROSS, STEPHEN MICHAEL, real estate company executive, professional sports team owner; b. Detroit, May 10, 1940; m. Kara Ross. BS, U. Mich., 1962; JD, Wayne State U., 1965; LLM in Taxation, NYU, 1966. Tax atty. Coopers & Lybrand, Detroit; dir. Insignia Fin. Group, Inc.; founder, dir. Charter Mcpl. Mortgage Acceptance Co.; founder, chmn., CEO The Related Comapnies L.P., NYC, 1972—; co-owner Miami Dolphins, 2008—09, majority owner, 2009—. Chmn. Equinox Fitness Clubs, Real Estate Bd. NY. Trustee Juvenile Diabetes Rsch. Found., Solomon R. Guggenheim Mus., Jackie Robinson Found., Jewish Assn. for Svcs. for Aged, Lincoln Ctr., NY Presbyterian Hosp., Urban Land Inst., Levin Inst., Nat. Bldg. Mus.; chmn. bd. trustees Centerline Holding Co. Recipient Tree of Life award, 1998, "What NY Needs" award, The Dow Fund, 1999, Henry Pearce award, Jewish Assn. for Services for the Aged, 2001, Leadership in Tourism award, NYC & Co., 2002, Jack D. Weiler award, United Jewish Appeal, 2003, The Harry B. Helmsley Disting. New Yorker award, The Real Estate Bd. NY, 2005; named Housing Person of Yr., Nat. Housing Conf., Owner & Developer of the Yr., NY Construction News, 2000; named one of The 100 Most Influential Leaders in Bus., Crain's NY Bus., 2002, Forbes 400: Richest Americans, 2006—. Mem.: Real Estate Board of NY (dir.). Office: The Related Cos LP 60 Columbus Cir New York NY 10023 also: Miami Dolphins 7500 SW 30th St Davie FL 33314 Office Phone: 212-421-5333.

ROSS, THOMAS WARREN, SR., academic administrator, former judge; b. Greensboro, NC, June 5, 1950; s. Charles Burdette and Mary Brownie (Franklin) R.; m. Susan Donaldson, June 17, 1972; children: Thomas Warren Jr., Mary Kathryn. BA in Polit. Sci., Davidson Coll., 1972; JD with honors, U. N.C., 1975; grad., Nat. Jud. Coll., 1985. Bar: N.C. 1975, U.S. Ct. Appeals (4th cir.) 1979, U.S. Supreme Ct. 1979. Asst. prof. pub. law Inst. Govt., U. NC, Chapel Hill, 1975-76; ptnr. Smith, Patterson, Follin, Curtis, James & Harkavy, 1976-82; adminstrv. asst. to Rep. Robin Britt US Congress, NC, 1983-84; judge NC Superior Ct., 1984—2000; dir. Adminstrv. Office of the Cts., 1999—2000; exec. dir. Z. Smith Reynolds Found., 2001—07; pres. Davidson Coll., NC, 2007—10, U. NC, 2011—. Pres. Ctrl. Carolina Legal Svcs., Inc., 1981-82; mem. com. on sentencing and corrections Nat. Conf. State Trial Judges; chmn. N.C. Sentencing and Policy Adv. Commn., 1990-99, com. on probation and parole Conf. Superior Ct. Judges, 1988-94; mem. com. on professionalism N.C. State Bar, 1990-91. Deacon, elder 1st Presbyn. Ch., Greensboro; chmn. Guilford County Dem. Party, 1981-83, Ctr. for Creative Leadership Bd. Assocs., 1995—, Guilford County Substance Abuse Study Commn., 1987-88, Guilford County Corrections Commn., 1988-94; active campaign United Way, 1979-82, Greensboro Heart Fund, 1980-82, Greensboro Sports Coun., 1989-2000; trustee U. NC, Greensboro, 2001—07, chair, 2005—07; trustee Davidson Coll., 2003—; mem. N.C. Gov.'s Statewide Comprehensive Recreation Plan Policy, 1982-83; mem. exec. coun. Gen. Green coun. Boy Scouts Am., 1988-91, chmn. Eagle scout bd. rev., 1990-91, mem. exec. bd. Old North State coun., 1992-2000, chmn. Eagle scout bd. rev., 1992-2000; bd. dirs. Women's Residential Ctr., 1986-89; mem. steering com. Greensboro Coalition Substance Abuse, 1986-87, N.C. Open Govt. Coalition, 2004-06, Hispanics in Philanthropy, 2004-07, Southeastern Coun. Founds., 2005-07; chmn. bd. govs. Summit House, Inc., 1994-95. Recipient Silver Beaver award Boy Scouts Am., 1993, Pub. Ofcl. of Yr. Gov. Mag., 1994, Found. for the Improvement of Justice award, 1995, Disting. Alumni award, Davidson Coll., 2001, Disting. Alumni award, UNC-Chapel Hill Sch. Law, 2005, Chief Justice William H. Rehnquist award for Judicial Excellence, 2000; named Boss of Yr., Greensboro Legal Secs. Assn., 1981, Outstanding Young Man in Am., Greensboro Jaycees, 1984, N.C. Trial Judge of Yr., N.C. Acad. Trial Lawyers, 1996. Mem. ABA (jud. adminstrn. sect.), N.C. Bar Assn. (dispute resolution com. 1991-92, nominating com. 1991-92, v.p. 1997-98), Greensboro Bar Assn., U. N.C-Chapel Hill Law Alumni Assn. (bd. dirs. 2003-06). Office: University of North Carolina / Office of President 910 Raleigh Rd PO Box 2688 Chapel Hill NC 27514 E-mail: tomross@northcarolina.edu.

ROSS, WILLIAM JARBOE, lawyer; b. Okla. City, May 9, 1930; s. Walter John and Bertha (Jarboe) R.; m. Mary Lillian Ryan, May 19, 1962; children: Rebecca Anne Roten, Robert Joseph Ross, Molly Kathleen Ross. BBA, U. Okla., 1952, LLB, 1954, LHD (hon.), 2012, Okla. City U., 2005. Bar: Okla. 1954. Since practiced in, Oklahoma City; asst. mcpl. counselor, 1955-60; mem. firm Rainey, Ross, Rice & Binns, 1960—2010; chmn. bd. Ethics and Excellence in Journalism Found., Inasmuch Found. Mem., co-chmn., bd. visitors U. Okla. Coll. Law; bd. dirs. Ethics and Excellence in Journalism Found., Inasmuch Found. Named to Hall of Fame, Order of the Owl-U. Okla., Coll. Law, 2011. Mem. Okla. Bar Assn., Okla. City Golf and Country Club, Econ. Club (Okla.), Fortune Club, Phi Alpha Delta, Beta Theta Pi. Home: 6923 Avondale Ct Nichols Hills OK 73116-5008

ROSSBACHER, LISA ANN, academic administrator; b. Fredericksburg, Va., Oct. 10, 1952; d. Richard Irwin and Jean Mary (Dearing) R.; m. Dallas D. Rhodes, Aug. 4, 1978. BS, Dickinson Coll., 1975; MA, SUNY, Binghamton, 1978, Princeton U., 1979, PhD, 1983. Cons. Republic Geothermal, Santa Fe Springs, Calif., 1979-81; asst. prof. geology Whittier (Calif.) Coll., 1982-84, Calif. State Poly. U., Pomona, 1984-86, assoc. prof. geol. sci., 1986-91, assoc. v.p. acad. affairs, 1987-93, prof. geol. sci., 1991-93; v.p. acad. affairs, dean faculty Whittier (Calif.) Coll., 1993-95; dean of coll., prof. geology Dickinson Coll., Carlisle, Pa., 1995-98; pres. So. Poly. State U., Marietta, Ga., 1998—. Vis. rschr. U. Uppsala, Sweden, 1984. Author: Career Opportunities in Geology and the Earth Sciences, 1983, Recent Revolutions in Geology, 1986; (with Rex Buchanan) Geomedia, 1988; columnist Geotimes, 1988—; contbr. articles to profl. jours. Recipient scholarship Ministry Edn. of Finland, Helsinki, 1984; grantee Sigma Xi, 1976, NASA, 1983-94. Fellow AAAS (geol. nominating com. 1984-87, chair-elect geology and geography sect. 1997-98, chair 1998-99, past chair 1999-00); mem. Geol. Soc. Am., Ga. Assn. Colls. (pres. 2005-06). Office: So Poly State U 1100 S Marietta Pkwy SE Marietta GA 30060-2855

ROSSEL, CARY, corporate financial executive; Attended, Hebrew U., Jerusalem, So. Meth. U., 1969. Sr. v.p. Sporting Goods; various positions Zale Corp., 1969—80; CFO Bus. Marketplace, Inc., 1980—86; v.p. Glazer's Wholesale Drug Co. Inc., 1986—2006, CFO, 1986—, exec. v.p., 2006—. Chmn. Alcoholic Beverage Industry Electronic Commerce Coun. Mem.: Alcoholic Beverage Industry Elec. Data Inerchange Coun. (retail subcom. chair). Office: Glazers Wholesale Drug Co Inc 14911 Quorum Dr Ste 400 Dallas TX 75254 Office Phone: 972-392-8200. Office Fax: 972-702-8508. Business E-Mail: crossel@glazers.com.

ROSSI, CHRISTOPHER, manufacturing executive; m. Georgia Rossi; 2 children. BS in Mech. Engring., Va. Tech.; MBA in Corp. Fin. & Ops. Mgmt., U. Rochester. Various positions, engring., prodn., materials mgmt. & supply chain mgmt. Dresser-Rand Group, Inc., 1977—98, v.p., supply chain mgmt worldwide, 1998—2001, v.p., gen. mgr., Painted Post ops., 2001—03, v.p., gen. mgr., North Am. ops., 2003—07, exec. v.p., worldwide product svcs., 2007—08, v.p., tech. & bus. devel., 2009—. Office: Dresser-Rand Group Inc West8 Tower 10205 Westheimer Rd Ste 1000 Houston TX 77042 Office Phone: 713-354-6100. Office Fax: 713-354-6110. Business E-Mail: crossi@dresser-rand.com.

ROSSKY, PETER JACOB, chemistry professor, chemical engineer, researcher; BA, Cornell U., Ithaca, NY, 1971, MA, 1972; PhD in Chemical Physics, Harvard U., 1978. Postdoc. rschr. SUNY, Stony

Brook, 1978—79; faculty dept. chem. engring. U. Tex., Austin, 1979—, Marvin K. Collie-Welch Regents chair chemistry, 2002—, dir. Inst. Theoretical Chemistry. Mem. editl. bd.: Theoretical Chemistry Accounts, Understanding Chem. Reactivity, Jour. Chem. Theory & Computation; contbr. articles to profl. jours. Recipient Joel Henry Hildebrand award, American Chem. Soc., 2010; fellow John Simon Guggenheim Meml. Found., 1997. Fellow: AAAS, American Phys. Soc., American Acad. Arts & Scis.; mem.: NAS. Office: U Tex Office WEL 3204A Dept Chemistry & Biochemistry 1 University Station A5300 Austin TX 78712 Office Phone: 512-471-3555. Office Fax: 512-471-1624. E-mail: rossky@mail.utexas.edu.

ROSSON, GLENN RICHARD, building products and furniture company executive; b. Galveston, Tex., Aug. 17, 1937; s. John Raymond and Elsie Lee R.; m. Edwina Lucille Hart, June 2, 1956; children— Darrell Richard, Alex Mark. BBA, Tex. Tech U., 1959. C.P.A., Tex. Supr., accountant Axelson div. U.S. Industries Inc., Longview, Tex., 1960-67, controller, 1968, group financial v.p. Dallas, 1969, group chmn., 1969-72, v.p., 1973-74, sr. v.p., 1974, exec. v.p., 1974-80, also dir.; pres. Rosson Investment Co., 1980—; chmn. bd. Yorktowne Inc., 1988—. Chmn. bd. dirs. Quality Product Finishing, Inc., 1998—. Mem. Am. Inst. C.P.A.s, Tex. Soc. C.P.A.s, Nat. Assn. Accts. (past nat. dir., past pres. E. Tex. chpt.), Assn. for Corp. Growth (past pres.). Clubs: Dallas Athletic, TBARM Raquet. Home: 11367 Drummond Dr Dallas TX 75228-1946 Office: 6060 N Central Expy Ste 526 Dallas TX 75206-5142 Office Phone: 214-891-6357. E-mail: rosson@gte.net.

ROTH, GREG, healthcare industry executive; BS Allied Health Professions, Ohio State U.; MHA in Hosp. & Health Adminstrn., Xavier U. CPA; registered respiratory therapist. Hosp. COO, CFO EPIC Healthcare Group, 1988—94; divsn. CFO Ornda Health Corp., 1994—95; CFO, ambulatory surgery divsn. HCA-The Healthcare Co., 1995—97, sr. v.p., ops., western region, 1997—98, pres., ambulatory surgery divsn., 1998—2004; CEO TeamHealth, Inc., pres., 2004—, COO, 2004; pres., CEO, bd. dirs. Health Fin. Corp., 2008—; COO Team Fin., LLC, 2004, pres., 2004—, CEO, bd. dirs., 2008—; COO Team Health Holdings, Inc. (formerly Team Health Holdings, LLC), 2004, pres., 2004—, CEO, bd. dirs., 2008—. Office: Team Health Holdings Inc 265 Brookview Toen Ctr Way Ste 400 Knoxville TN 37919 Office Phone: 865-693-1000. Office Fax: 865-539-3073. Business E-Mail: greg.roth@teamhealth.com.

ROTH, HARVEY PAUL, retired publishing executive; b. NYC, Feb. 20, 1933; s. Lewis Theodore and Harriet (Wallow) R.; m. Tanya Cohen; children by previous marriage: Andrea Warriner, Matthew Jay; stepchildren: Laura Meryl Becker, Matthew Robert Turetzky. AB, Bklyn. Coll., 1954; LL.B., N.Y. U., 1957. Bar: N.Y. bar 1959. Editor West Pub. Co., NYC, 1959-61; pres. BFL Communications, Inc., Plainview, NY, 1961-76, Roth Pub., Inc., Great Neck, NY, 1976—2005, ret., 2005. Chmn. Alcove Press, London, 1970—75, Nash Pub. Corp., LA, 1971—75. With US Army, 1957—58. Personal E-mail: harveyproth@gmail.com.

ROTH, JOHN REECE, electrical engineer, educator, researcher, inventor; b. Washington, Pa., Sept. 19, 1937; s. John Meyer and Ruth Evangeline (Iams) R.; m. Helen Marie DeCrane, Jan. 14, 1972; children: Nancy Ann, John Alexander. BS in Physics, MIT, 1959; PhD, Cornell U., 1963. Engring. aide Aerojet-Gen. Corp., Azusa, Calif., 1957, 1958; aerospace engr. N.Am. Aviation, Canoga Park, Calif., 1959; prin. investigator NASA Lewis Rsch. Ctr., Cleve., 1963—78; prof. U. Tenn., Knoxville, 1978—2004, prof. emeritus, 2004—06; hon. prof. U. Electronic Sci. and Tech. China, Chengdu, 1992—; ret.; prin. investigator Office Naval Rsch., Washington, 1980—89, Air Force Office Sci. Rsch., Washington, 1981—95, 2001—03, Army Rsch. Office, 1988—93, NASA Langley Rsch. Ctr., Hampton, Va., 1995—98, 2001—03, March Instruments, Inc., Concord, Calif., 1996—98, NSF, 2002—03. Cons. TVA, Chattanooga, 1982-84, BDM Corp., 1987-88, Tenn. Eastman, 1989-90, March Instruments, 1995-98, Procter & Gamble, 1996, 2000, Internat. Eco Scis., 1997-98, Environ. Elements Corp., 1997-00, Tetra Pak Suisse, 1998-00, Atmospheric Glow Techs., Inc., 1999-05, YTC-Am., Inc., 2005, Harrick Plasma, 2006; mem. NAS-NRC Com. on Aneutronic Fusion, 1986-87; hon. guest prof. Tsinghua U., Shenzhen campus, 2006-08; spkr. at profl. meetings Author: Industrial Plasma Engineering, Introduction to Fusion Energy; contbr. articles to profl. jours. Sloan scholar, 1955-59; Ford fellow, 1961-62; recipient B. Otto and Katherine Wheeley award for Excellence in Tech. Transfer, 1999, NASA Inventor's award, 2004, Gonzalez Family Lifetime Achievement award, 2006. Fellow IEEE, AIAA (assoc.); mem. Am. Phys. Soc., Am. Chem. Soc., Am. Nuc. Soc. (exec. com. No. Ohio sect. 1975-78), Nuc. and Plasma Scis. Soc., Am. Soc. Engring. Edn., Knoxville Mus. Art, East Tenn. Soc. Archaeol. Inst. Am., Sigma Xi (pres. U. Tenn. Knoxville chpt. 1985-86). Achievements include 11 US patents. Home (Winter): 12359 N Fox Den Dr Knoxville TN 37934-3755 Home (Summer): PO Box 181 Oakland ME 04963-0181 E-mail: jreeceroth@gmail.com.

ROTH, PHILIP R., manufacturing executive; BS in Bus. Adminstrn., U. Mo.; MBA, Washington U. CPA. With Price Waterhouse Co., Valley Industries, Inc.; v.p. fin., CFO, Wiegand Indsl. divsn. Emerson Electric Co., 1980—96; v.p. fin., CFO Gardner Denver, Inc., Quincy, Ill., 1996—2004. Bd. dirs. Dresser-Rand Group Inc., 2005—. Office: Dresser Rand Group Inc Bd Directors 10205 Westheimer Rd Ste 1000 Houston TX 77042 Office Phone: 713-354-6100. Office Fax: 713-354-6110. Business E-Mail: phillip.roth@dresser-rand.com.

ROTHBERG-BLACKMAN, JUNE SIMMONDS, retired nursing educator, psychotherapist; b. Phila., Sept. 4, 1923; d. David and Rose (Protzel) Simmonds; m. Jacob Rothberg, Sept. 7, 1952 (dec. Feb. 2001); children: Robert Rothberg, Alan Rothberg; m. Stanley F Blackman, May 27, 2002 (dec. July 2005). Diploma in nursing, Lenox Hill Hosp., 1944; BS, N.Y. U., 1950, MA, 1959, PhD (NIH fellow), 1965; Diploma in Psychotherapy and Psychoanalysis, Adelphi U., Inst. for Advanced Psychol. Studies, 1987. USPHS traineeship N.Y. U., 1957-59; sr. public health nurse Bklyn. Vis. Nurse Assn., 1951-53; prin. investigator in nursing, homestead study project Goldwater Hosp. and N.Y. U., 1959-61; instr. N.Y. U., 1964-65, asst. prof., 1965-68, assoc. prof., 1968-69, project dir. grad. program rehab. nursing, 1964-69, prof., 1969-87, prof. emeritus, 1987—; dean Adelphi U., Garden City, NY, 1969-85, v.p. acad. adminstrn., 1985-86; pvt. practice West Hempstead, NY, 1993-97. Pres. David Simmonds Co. Inc., Med. Supply Co., 1982-89; dir., chmn. compensation com. Quality Care, Inc.; cons. region 2 Bur. Health Resources Devel., HHS.; audit com. Ipco Corp. (formerly Sterling Optical Corp.), 1991; cons., spkr. in field. Contbr. articles to profl. jours. Mem. pres's coun. N.Y. U. Sch. Edn., 1973-75; treas. Nurses for Polit. Action, 1971-73; trustee Nurses Coalition for Action in Politics, 1974-76; bd. visitors Duke Med. Ctr., 1970-74; mem. governing bd. Nassau-Suffolk Health Systems Agy., 1976-79; leader People-to-People Internat. med. rehab. del. to People's Republic of China, 1981; mem. com. for the study pain disability and chronic illness behavior Inst. Medicine, 1985-86, com. on ethics in rehab. Hastings Ctr., 1985-87; trustee Paget's Disease Found., 1987-89. Recipient Disting. Alumna award NYU, 1974, recognition award Am. Assn. Colls. Nursing, 1976, Achievers award Ctr. for Bus. and Profl. Women, 1980 Fellow Am. Acad. Nursing (governing coun. 1980-82); mem. Nat. League Nursing (exec. com. coun. of baccalaureate and higher degree programs 1969-73), Am. Nurses Assn. (joint liaison com. 1970-72), Commn. Accreditation of Rehab. Facilities, Am. Congress Rehab. Medicine (pres. 1977-78, chmn. continuing edn. com. 1979-86, 34th Ann. John Stanley Coulter Meml. lectr. 1984, Gold Key award 1984, Edward W. Lowman award 1990), Am. Assn. Colls. Nursing (pres. 1974-76), L.I. Women's Network (pres. 1980-81), Kappa Delta Pi, Sigma Theta Tau, Pi Lambda Theta. Achievements include having June S. Rothberg collection in Nursing Archives, Mugar Meml. Library, Boston U. Home and Office: 401 E Linton Blvd Apt 252 Delray Beach FL 33483 Personal E-mail: stanleyb2@aol.com.

ROTHSCHILD, DONALD PHILLIP, retired lawyer, arbitrator; b. Mar. 31, 1927; s. Leo and Anne (Office) R.; m. Ruth Eckstein, July 7, 1950; children: Nancy Lee, Judy Lynn Hoffman, James Alex. AB, U. Mich., 1950; JD summa cum laude, U. Toledo, 1965; LLM, Harvard U., Cambridge, Mass., 1966. Bar: Ohio 1966, DC 1970, US Supreme Ct. 1975, RI 1989. Tchg. fellow Harvard U. Law Sch., Cambridge, Mass., 1965—66; instr. solicitor's office U.S. Dept. Labor, Washington, 1966—67; prof. law George Washington U. Nat. Law Ctr., Washington, 1966—89, prof. emeritus, 1989; prof. law NY Law Sch., 1989—96; ret., 1996. Vis. prof. U. Mich. Law Sch., Ann Arbor, 1976; dir. Consumer Protection Ctr., 1971—, Inst. Law and Aging, Washington, 1973—89, Ctr. for Cmty. Justice, Washington, 1974—78, Nat. Consumers League, Washington, 1981—87; v.p. Regulatory Alternatives Devel. Corp., Washington, 1982—; cons. Washington Met. Coun. Govt., 1979—82; counsel Tillinghast, Collins & Graham, Providence, 1989—95, chair human resource group. Author: From the Cockpit of the Rubaiyat, 2002, Kiosks Keep the Devils Away: A Novel About Mental Health, 2006, Amazon Kindle Books, Recent Strides in Cancer Research Funding the Future, 2009; co-author: Consumer Protection Text and Materials, 1973, Collective Bargaining and Labor Arbitration, 1979, Fundamentals of Administrative Practice and Procedure, 1981; contbr. articles to profl. jours.; exhibitions include Koi Krane Gallery, Fort Heyens, Fla. Chmn. bd. dirs. D.C. Citizens Complaint Ctr., Washington, 1980; mayoral appointee Adv. Com. on Consumer Protection, Washington, 1979—80. Recipient Cmty. Svc. award, Television Acad., Washington, 1981. Mem.: ABA, D.C. Bar Assn., Am. Arbitration Assn., Fed. Mediation and Conciliation Svc., Nat. Acad. Arbitrators, Nat. Assn. Coll. and Univ. Attys. (Brown U.), Fed. Trade Commn. Adv. Coun., Phi Kappa Phi. Jewish. Home: 12823 Waterford Cir Fort Myers FL 33919-8004 Personal E-mail: dpchild@embargmail.com.

ROTHSTEIN, RONALD, professional basketball coach; b. Bronxville, NY, Dec. 27, 1942; m. Olivia Pierorazio; children: David, Dana. B, U. RI, Kingston, 1964; M, CUNY Hunter Coll. Asst. coach Upsala Coll. Vikings, East Orange, NJ, 1974-75; head basketball coach Eastchester HS, NY, 1976-79; northeastern regional scout Atlanta Hawks, 1979-82, asst. coach, 1983-86; scout NY Knicks, 1982-83; asst. coach Detroit Pistons, 1986-88, head coach, 1992-93, Miami Heat, 1988-91, asst. coach, 2005—, interim head coach, 2007; asst. coach Cleve. Cavaliers, 1993-99; head coach Miami Sol, WNBA, 1999—2002; asst. coach Ind. Pacers, 2003—04. Named Westchester County Coach of Yr., 1979; named to U. RI Athletic Hall of Fame, 1989, Miami Sports Hall of Champions, 2005. Office: Miami Heat 601 Biscayne Blvd Miami FL 33132

ROUB, BRYAN R(OGER), electronics executive; b. Berea, Ohio, May 1, 1941; s. Bernard Augustus and Pearl Irene (Koeblitz) R.; m. Judith Elaine Penman, June 19, 1965; children: Paul, Bradley, Michael. Student, Ohio Wesleyan U., 1959-62; BS, Ohio State U., 1966; MBA, U. Pa., 1978. Mem. audit staff Ernst & Ernst, Cleve., 1966-70; asst. contr. Midland-Ross, Cleve., 1970-73, contr., 1973-81, v.p., 1977-81, sr. v.p., 1981-82, exec. v.p. fin., 1982-84; sr. v.p. fin. Harris Corp., Melbourne, Fla., 1984-93, sr. v.p., CFO, 1993—2006. Bd. dirs. Fairchild Semicondr., 2004-; mem. fin. coun. II Machinery and Allied Products Inst., Washington, 1978-84, coun. I, 1984—2004, vice chmn., 1994-95, chmn., 1996-98; mem. conf. bd. coun. CFOs, 1993-96. Mem. adv. coun. Coll. Adminstrv. Scis., Ohio State U., 1978-81; mem. citizen's adv. coun. Westlake (Ohio) Schs., 1981-83; trustee Alcoholism Svcs. Cleve., 1982-84; mem. devel. bd. St. John's Hosp., 1983-84; pres. Westridge Homeowners' Assn., 1977; dir., treas. Tortoise Island Homeowners' Assn., 1988-90; bd. dirs. Easter Seal Soc. of Brevard County, 1993-98. Mem. AICPA, Ohio Soc. CPAs, Fin. Execs. Inst. (treas. N.E. Ohio chpt. 1976-78, bd. dirs. 1980-81, 83-84, v.p. 1981-82, pres. 1982-83, bd. dirs. Orlando chpt. 1984—, v.p. 1985-86, pres. 1986-87, nat. bd. dirs. 1987-90, area v.p. 1990-91, chmn. budget and fin. com. 1988-89, chmn. planning com. 1995-97, v.p. at large 1997-99, vice-chmn. 1999-2000, chmn. 2000-01, office of chmn. 1997-2002), Fin. Execs. Rsch. Found. (trustee 1994-97, 1999-2000, 2009-), Westwood Country Club, Eau Gallie Yacht Club (bd. govs., treas. 1990-92), Suntree Country Club. Address: 10280 S Tropical Trail Merritt Island FL 32952-6919 Personal E-mail: bryan@roub.net.

ROUECHE, JOHN EDWARD, II, education educator, director; b. Sept. 3, 1938; s. John Edward and Mary (Harris) R.; m. Suanne Davis; 1 stepchild, Robin Sue Maca; children by previous marriage: Michelle Renee, John Edward III. BA, Lenoir Rhyne Coll., Hickory, NC, 1960, LittD, 2001; LHD, Lenoir Rhyne Coll., 2001; MA, Appalachian Coll., Boone, NC, 1961; PhD, Fla. State U., 1964. Dean Gaston Coll., Gastonia, NC, 1964-67; assoc. rsch. educator UCLA, 1967-69; dir. jr. coll. divsn. Nat. Lab. Higher Edn., 1968-71; assoc. prof. edn. Duke U.; prof. edn., dir. c.c. leadership program U. Tex., Austin, 1971—, Sid W. Richardson regents chair, 1987—. Chancellor's coun. U. Tex. Sys., 1990—, U. Tex. Littlefield Soc., 1992—; lectr. Earl Pullias lectr. U. So. Calif., 1992, Coll. Bd. Disting. Lectr. NYC, 1993, Frances Crain Cook Disting. Lectr. U. Tex., 1994; chmn. nat. ednl. adv. bd. Gt. Am. Res. Ins. Co., 1988-94; co-chair Nat. Adv. Bd. for C.C.s, Invest Learning Corp., 1993-96; chair nat. adv. com. Kaplan Ednl. Partnerships, 1995-98; La Platica Disting. lectr. Ariz. State U., 1999; chmn. nat. adv. bd. 3-D Internat., 2000-06, chair Nat. CC Adv. Com., Nat. Am. U., 2011-, mem. bd. dirs., Nat. Alliance Cmty. & Tech. Coll., 2009-, mem. 21st century futures, Am. Assoc. CC, 2011-12. C.C. editor Jossey-Bass Publs., 1971-82; editor Creative Teaching Series, Media Systems Corp., 1980-85; mem. editl. bd. C.C. Times, C.C. Jour., 1990-94, others; author 35 books, including Profiles of Excellence in America's Schools, 1986, Access with Excellence, 1987, Shared Vision, 1989, Teaching as Leading, 1990, Underrepresentation: A Question of Diversity, 1991, Between a Rock and a Hard Place, 1993, The Company We Keep, 1995, Strangers in Their Own Land: Part Time Faculty, 1995, Embracing the Tiger: The Effectiveness Debate and the Community College, 1997, High Stakes, High Performance: Making Remedial Education Work, 1999, In Pursuit of Excellence: The Community College of Denver, 2001, Practical Magic: On the Front Lines of Teaching Excellence, 2003, Opting for Opportunity: Entrepreneurship in the Community College, 2005, The Creative CC, 2008, Rising to the Challenge: Lessons From Guilford Tech CC, 2012; contbr. articles to profl. jours. Pres. Doss Sch. PTA, 1974-75; chmn. bd. N.W. Hills United Meth. Ch., 1973-76. Recipient Disting. Svc. award Nat. Coun. Univs. and Colls., 1984, Disting. Rsch. Publ. award, 1990, 93, 95, 97, Outstanding Alumnus award Appalachian State U., 1979, Disting. Grad. award Fla. State U., 1981, Mitchell Coll., 2009, Tchg. Excellence award U. Tex., 1982, Outstanding Rschr. award, 1985, Excellence award for outstanding learned article U.S. Edn. Press Assn., 1983, Disting. Rsch. award Nat. Assn. Devel. Edn., 1984-86, Disting. Rsch. Publ. award Nat. Coun. Student Devel., 1987, Disting. Rsch. award Nat. Coun. Staff, Program, and Orgn. Devel., B. Lamar Johnson Nat. Leadership award League for Innovation in the Cmty. Coll., 1988, Disting. Svc. & Leadership award CCP, INC., 1993, Disting. Faculty award U. Tex., 1994, Disting. Rsch. award Interassn. Student Devel. Orgns., 1995, Chancellor's Leadership award State of Ala., 1995, Career Rsch. Excellence award U. Tex., 1998, Disting. Grad. award Lenoir-Rhyne Coll., 2000; named lifetime amb. for N.C., 1978; Kellogg fellow, 1962-64, Disting. Internat. Leadership award Govt. of South Africa, 2000, 01, Disting. Nat. Svc. award Nat. Coun. Instrnl. Adminstrs., 2001, Disting. Leadership award Tex. Assn. Cmty. Colls., 2003 Star Leadership award Nat. Hispanic Border Inst., 2005, Mirabeau Lamar award Assn. Tex. Colls. and Univs., 2005, Disting. Grad. award., Mitchell CC, 2009, O'Banion Leadership prize, ETS, 2011. Mem. Am. Assn. CCs. (bd. dirs. 1989-94, mem. 21st century futures commn., 2011-; Nat. Leadership award 1986, Disting. Rsch. award coun. colls. and univs. 1990, 94, 96, dist. rsch. sr. scholar award 1994, 96, nat. student devel. inter-assn. rsch. award 1995-96), Am. Assn. Higher Edn., Coun. Univs. and Colls. (past pres., bd. dirs.), Phi Beta Kappa, Phi Delta Kappa. Home: 4700 Lookout Mountain Cv Austin TX 78731-3654 Office: U Tex Austin One University Sta D5600 Austin TX 78712-0378 Office Phone: 512-471-7545. Business E-Mail: roueche@mail.utexas.edu.

ROUGHTON, BILLY G., diversified financial services company executive; m. Mildred H. Roughton. Chmn. Gateway Bank & Trust Co., 2009; pres., CEO BGR Devel. Inc., Southern Shores, NC. Bd. dirs. Gateway, 2005—08, Hampton Roads Bankshares Inc., 2008—. Office: BGR Development Inc Ste A 2522 S Virginia Dare Trl Nags Head NC 27959-9248 Office Phone: 252-441-4988. Business E-Mail: billyroughton@gwfh.com.

ROUHANI, SHAHROKH, civil engineering environmental educator, consultant; b. Tehran, Iran, Mar. 28, 1956; came to U.S., 1974; s. Aboutorab and Parirokh (Garakani) R.; m. Firouzeh Yekta, Aug. 18, 1983; children: Nina, Shiva. BSCE, U. Calif., Berkeley, 1978, BA in Econs., 1978; SM in Engring., Harvard U., 1980, PhD in Environ. Scis., 1983. Registered profl. engr., Ga. Asst. prof. Ga. Inst. Tech., Atlanta, 1983-90, assoc. prof. civil engring., 1990-96; sr. cons. Dames & Moore, Atlanta, 1990-95; pres. New Fields, Inc., Atlanta, 1995—. NSF vis. scientist Ctr. Geostats., Paris Sch. of Mines, 1987-88; expert mem. ASTM, EPA, U.S. Geol. Survey, Dept. Def. Geostats. Standardization Com., 1991-96. Co-author: Ground Water, 1991; contbr. articles to profl. publs., chpts. to books., also numerous reports, papers in field. Mem. ASCE (award 1991, chmn. nat. ground water hydrology 1991, chmn. task com. on geostatis. techniques in geohydrology 1987-89, sec. water resources com. Ga. sect. 1988, spl. session organizer 1989, 90, contact mem. task com. 1988-90, symposium organizer 1991), Am. Geophys. Union (assoc. editor Water Resources Rsch. 1989-94), Internat. Water Resources Assn., Am. Water Resources Assn., N.Am. Coun. on Geostats., Internat. Geostatis. Assn., Phi Beta Kappa, Tau Beta Pi, Chi Epsilon, Sigma Chi. Office: Newfields Inc 1349 W Peachtree St NW Ste 2000 Atlanta GA 30309-2926 Office Phone: 404-347-9050. Business E-Mail: srouhani@newfields.com.

ROUNSAVILLE, KEITH EUGENE, retired lawyer; b. Ancon, Canal Zone, Aug. 6, 1945; s. William Russell Rounsaville and Dorothy Naletta Chambers; m. Linda Ann White, Feb. 14, 1976 (div. Oct. 1, 1994); m. Karla Rae Spaulding, May 24, 2000; children: Keith Chambers, David William. BA with honors, Yale U., 1967; JD cum laude, Columbia U., 1970. Cert.: Fla. Bar (in antitrust and trade regulation), bar: Calif. 1971, DC 1972, Fla. 1974. Assoc. O'Melveny & Myers LLP, LA, 1970; shareholder Trenam, Kemker, Scharf, Barkin, Frye, O'Neill & Mullis, P.A., Tampa, Fla., 1974—2000, Stearns Weaver Miller Alhadeff & Sitterson, P.A., Tampa, 2000—02, Litchford & Christopher, P.A., Orlando, 2007—11; shareholder, chmn. antitrust dept. Akerman Senterfitt, Orlando and Tampa, Fla., 2002—06. Chmn. Rough Riders dist., Gulf Ridge coun. Boy Scouts Am., Tampa, 1991—92, dist. commr., 1990—91; pres. Rotary Club of Tampa Bay, Tampa, 1994—95, sec., 1993—94. Capt. JAGC USMC, 1971—73, Vietnam. Recipient Dist. award of Merit, Boy Scouts Am., 1991; named Rotarian of the Yr., Rotary Club of Tampa Bay, 1992; named one of America's Leading Lawyers Bus., Antitrust Law, Chambers USA, 2003—, The Best Lawyers in Am. Antitrust Law, Fla., 2005—, Fla. Super Lawyers Antitrust Law, 2006—; Harlan Fiske Stone scholar, Columbia U. Sch. of Law. Mem.: ABA (mem. Sherman Act com. sect. antitrust law 1974), Fla. Bar (chmn. and vice chmn. antitrust com. 1984—92, exec. coun., bus. law sect. 1984—92, chair antitrust law and trade cert. com. 2006—08), Am. Law Inst., Am. Bar Found. (life). Avocations: hiking, international travel.

ROUSE, DORIS JANE, physiologist, research scientist; b. Greensboro, NC, Oct. 3, 1948; d. Welby Corbett and Nadia Elizabeth (Grainger) R.; m. Blake Shaw Wilson, Jan. 6, 1974; children: Nadia Jacqueline, Blair Elizabeth. BA in Chemistry, Duke U., Durham, NC, 1970, PhD in Physiology and Pharmacology, 1980. Tchr. sci. Peace Corps, Tugbake, Liberia, 1970-71; rsch scientist Burroughs Wellcome Co., Rsch. Triangle Park, NC, 1971-76; sr. physiologist Rsch. Triangle Inst., Durham, 1976-83, ctr. dir., 1980-2000, also dir. NASA tech. application team, 1980-2000, dir. TB Tech. Transfer Program, 1999—, dir. Global Health, 2001—07, v.p., Global Health, 2007—; portfolio project mgr. Global Alliance for Tb Drug Devel., 2002—. Adminstr. ANSI Tech. Adv. Group for Wheelchairs, NYC, 1982-86; adj. asst. prof. U. NC Sch. Medicine, 1983-92; chair Instl. Rev. Bd., Profl. Devel. Award com., chair salary com. Rsch. Triangle Inst.; mem. adv. bd. Assistive Tech. Rsch. Ctr., 1994-96; mem. global health adv. com., U. NC, Chapel Hill, 2007-, mem. bd. dirs. ImaGYN, 2007-. Mem. adv. bd. Assn. Retarded Citizens, Arlington, Tex., 1981—88, Western Gerontology Soc., San Francisco, 1982—85; bd. dirs. Simon Found., Chgo., 1983—95; mem. spl. rev. com. small bus. applications Nat. Forum on Tech. and Aging; mem. fund steering com. Academy Venture, 2000—04. Recipient Group Achievement award NASA, 1979, 2000, President's award, RTI, 2003, 05, 06. Mem.: Am. Soc. Microbiology, Assn. Fed. Tech. Transfer Execs., Licensing Execs. Soc., Rehab. Engring. Soc. N.Am. (chmn. wheelchair com. 1981—86, Disting. Svc. award 1984). Home: 2410 Wrightwood Ave Durham NC 27705-5802 Office: Research Triangle Inst PO Box 12194 Durham NC 27709-2194 Office Phone: 919-541-6980. Personal E-mail: drouse@nc.rr.com. Business E-Mail: rouse@rti.org.

ROUSE, JOHN WILSON, JR., technology consultant; b. Kansas City, Mo., Dec. 7, 1937; s. John Wilson and Gail Agnes (Palmer) R.; m. Susan Jane Davis, May 3, 1981; 1 son, Jeffrey Scott. A.S., Kansas City Jr. Coll., 1957; BS, Purdue U., 1959; MS, U. Kans., 1965, PhD, 1968. Registered profl. engr., Mo., Tex. Engr. Bendix Corp., Kansas City, Mo., 1959-64; rsch. coord. Ctr. for Rsch., U. Kans., Lawrence, 1964-68; prof. elec. engring., dir. remote sensing ctr. Tex. A&M U., College Station, 1968-78; Logan prof. engr., chmn. elec. engring. U. Mo., Columbia, 1978-81; dean engring. U. Tex., Arlington, 1981-87; pres. So. Rsch. Inst., Birmingham, Ala., 1987-97, The Rouse Group, Hoover, Ala., 1997—. Mgr. microwave program NASA Hdqrs., Washington, 1975-77. Contbr. articles to profl. jours. Recipient

Outstanding Tchr. award Tex. A&M U., 1971; Outstanding Prof. award U. Mo., 1980; Engr. of Yr. Tex. Soc. Profl. Engrs., 1983 Mem. IEEE, Nat. Soc. Profl. Engrs., Am. Soc. Engring. Edn., Internat. Bus. Fellows, Internat. Union Radio Sci., Sigma Xi, Eta Kappa Nu., Tau Beta Pi Home: 39 Camden Cir San Antonio TX 78218 also: 39 Campden Cir San Antonio TX 78218-6055

ROUSE, ROSCOE, JR., retired librarian, educator; b. Valdosta, Ga., Nov. 26, 1919; s. Roscoe and Minnie Estelle (Corbett) R.; m. Charlie Lou Miller, June 23, 1945 (dec. Nov. 06, 2013); children: Charles Richard, Robin Rouse Wells. BA, U. Okla., 1948, MA in Libr. Sci., 1952; student (Grolier Soc. scholar), Rutgers U., 1956; AMLS, U. Mich., 1958, PhD, 1962. Bookkeeper C & S Nat. Bank, Valdosta, Ga., 1937-41; draftsman R.K. Rouse Co. (heating engrs.), Greenville, SC, 1941-42; asst. librarian Northeastern State Coll., Tahlequah, Okla., 1948-49, acting librarian, instr. library sci., 1949-51; circulation librarian Baylor U., 1952-53, acting univ. librarian, 1953-54, univ. librarian, prof., 1954-63, chmn. dept. library sci., 1956-63; dir. libraries State U. NY at Stony Brook, LI, 1963-67; dean libr. svcs., prof. Okla. State U., Stillwater, 1967-87, univ. libr. historian, 1987-92, chmn. dept. libr. edn., 1967-74; ret., 1987. Grolier Soc. scholar, Rutgers U., 1956; vis. prof. U. Okla. Sch. Library Sci., summer 1962, N. Tex. State U., summer 1965; acad. library cons.; pub. dir. Seretean Wellness Ctr., Okla. State U., 2002—07; mem. AIA-Am. Library Assn. Library Bldg. Awards Jury, 1976; bd. dirs. Fellowship Christian Libr. and Info. Specialists; in retirement, volunteers writing and photography for local newspaper. Author: A History of the Baylor University Library, 1845-1919, 1962; editor: Okla. Librarian, 1951-52; co-author: Organization Charts of Selected Libraries, 1973; A History of the Okla. State U. Library, 1992; contbr. articles, book revs., chpts. to publs. in field. Bd. dirs. Okla. Dept. Librs., 1989-92, chmn., 1990-92. 1st lt. USAAF, 1942-45. Sgt. USAF, 1942—45. Decorated Air medal with 4 oak leaf clusters; recipient citation Okla. State Senate, 1987, Rotary Outstanding Achievement award, 1996; named in 150 Prominent Individuals in Baylor's History. Mem. ALA (life, mem. coun. 1971-72, 76-80, 83-84, 84-88, chmn. libr. orgn. and mgmt. sect. 1973-75, planning and budget assembly 1978-79, coun. com. on coms. 1979-80, bldgs. and equipment sect. exec. bd. 1979-80, chmn. bldgs. for coll. and univ. librs. com. 1983-85, chmn. nominating com. libr. history roundtable 1993-94), AARP, (sec. local chpt. 1998-2000), Okla. Libr. Assn. (life, pres. 1971-72, ALA coun. rep. 1976-80, 83-84, OLA Disting. Svc. award 1979, Spl. Merit award 1987), S.W. Libr. Assn. (chmn. coll. and univ. div. 1958-60, chmn. scholarship com. 1968-70), Internat. Fedn. Libr. Assns. (standing com. on libr. bldgs. and equipment 1976-88), Assn. Coll. and Rsch. Librs. (chmn. univ. librs. sect. 1969-70, mem. exec. bd. and rep. to ALA Coun., 1971-72), U. Mich. Sch. Libr. Sci. Alumni Soc. (pres. 1979-80, Alumni Recognition award 1988), mem. Alumni Found. Com., 1992-94, Payne County Ret. Educators Assn. (v.p., pres. elect 1991-92, pres. 1992-93), Okla. State U. Emeriti Assn. (pres. 2000-01), Okla. Hist. Soc. (com. on Okla. Higher Edn. mus. 1985—, pub. dir. 2002—), Stillwater Rotary Club (pres. 1980-81, Rotarian of Yr. 1999, editor Rotary Weekly bulletin, various coms., pub. dir. 1998—), Beta Phi Mu, Archons of Colophon. Baptist (chmn. bd. deacons 1973). Personal E-mail: rouse74074@aol.com.

ROUSH, JOHN A., academic administrator; b. Wis. m. Susie Miller Roush; children: Luke, Mark. B in English, Ohio U.; M, M, D, Miami U., Ohio. Grad. asst. football coach to exec. asst. to pres. Miami U., Ohio; exec. asst. to pres. U. of Richmond, 1982—90, v.p. planning, 1990—98; pres. Centre Coll., Danville, Ky., 1998—. Mem. Coun. of Pres., Assn. of Gov. Bds., Nat. Assn. Independent Coll. & Univ.; treas. Assn. Presbyn. Coll. & Univ., 2002—03. Contbr. articles to profl. jours. Capt. US Army. Office: Centre College Office of President 600 W Walnut St Danville KY 40422 Office Phone: 859-238-5200. E-mail: jroush@centre.edu.*

ROUSH, ROBERT WARREN, electrical engineer, director; b. Tulsa, Oct. 30, 1930; s. Ernest Edwin and Georgiana Roush; m. Emily Sinclair Knoblock, Sept. 2, 1956; children: Kathryn Elizabeth, Robert Mark. BSEE, Okla. A&M Coll., 1957. Lic. profl. engr., Okla., Fla., Colo., Tex., Md. Field engr. Schlumberger Well Surveying Corp., Houston, 1957—65; aerosystems engr. Gen. Dynamics, Inc., Ft. Worth, 1966—69; elec. engr. Persons & Assocs., Oklahoma City, 1969—71; adj. assoc. prof., guest lectr. dept. environn. control, Sch. Arch. Okla. State U., 1978—82; from elec. engr. to sr. corp. v.p. The Benham Group, Oklahoma City, 1971—83; pres. Roush Engring. Co., Inc., Oklahoma City, 1983—87; elec. engring. dept. head Hansen Lind Meyer, Inc., Iowa City, 1987—89; mgr. elec. engring. dept. Gee & Jenson, Inc., West Palm Beach, Fla., 1989—92; chief elec. engr. FSB/Texas, Inc., Ft. Worth, 1992—2001; v.p. Setty & Assocs., Ltd., Fairfax, Va., 2001—06; dir., elec. engring. Calvin-Giordano & Assoc., Inc., 2006—. Lectr. in field. Contbr. articles to profl. jours. 1st lt. USAF, 1951—55. Recipient IES Lighting Design Award of Merit. Mem.: NSPE, IEEE (life; past chmn. ctrl. Okla. chpt., past chmn. bd. dirs. ctrl. Okla. chpt., Engr. of Yr. in mgmt. 1977—78), Am. Consulting Engrs. Coun. (cons. membership com.), Computer Soc., Industry Applications Soc. (past chmn.), Power Engring. Soc. (past chmn.), Okla. Soc. Profl. Engrs. (past state chmn. profl. engrs. in pvt. practice), Illuminating Engring. Soc. N.Am. (past pres. ctrl. Okla. chpt.). Republican. Home: 3422 Sands Harbor Trce Pompano Beach FL 33069-6120 Personal E-mail: r_w_roush@bellsouth.net. E-mail: rroush@calvin-giordano.com.

ROUSON, DARRYL ERVIN, state legislator; b. New Orleans, La., July 20, 1954; m. Angela Rouson; 8 children. Former prosecutor Pinellas County; mem. Dist. 55 Fla. House of Reps., 2008—, ranking mem. criminal and civil justice appropriations com., mem. govt. accountability act coun., pub. safety and domestic security policy com. Former chmn. Nat. Bar Assn. Substance Abuse & Addictions Task Force. Mem.: St. Petersburg NAACP (pres. 2000—05). Democrat. Office: 402 S Monroe St Rm 1003 Tallahassee FL 32399-1300 also: 441 45th Ave S Saint Petersburg FL 33705-4510 also: 302 Manatee Ave E Ste 304 Bradenton FL 34208-1901 Office Phone: 850-488-0925, 727-552-1370, 941-708-8570. Business E-Mail: darryl.rouson@myfloridahouse.gov.

ROUSSEL, LEE DENNISON, economist, federal agency administrator; d. Ethan Allen and Frances Isabel (Ferry) Dennison; m. Andre Homo Roussel, Sept. 6, 1980; children: Cecilia Frances, Stephanie Anne. AB, Wellesley Coll., 1966; MA, Northeastern U., 1974. Mgmt. intern U.S. Dept. HEW, 1966-68; with Planning Office Commonwealth of Mass., 1968-70; exec. dir. Gov.'s Commn. Citizen Participation, Boston, 1973; with Boston area office U.S. Dept. HUD, 1970-78; fgn. svc. officer USAID, 1978-99, with housing and urban devel. office Washington and Tunis, 1978-82, chief housing and urban devel. office for C.Am. Honduras, 1982-87, asst. dir. office housing and urban programs Washington, 1987-91, country rep. for Czech and Slovak Fed. Rep., 1991-92, country rep. for Czech Rep., 1993-94; min. counselor, U.S. rep. to devel. assistance com. OECD, Paris, 1994-99; sr. advisor USAID, Panama, 1999—2002, chief, exec. mgmt. human resources, 2004—05, mgmt. advisor Office of Econ. growth, 2006—07; resident county dir. Millennium Challenge Corp., 2007—12. Decorated Nat. Order of Merit Republic of Benin. Episcopalian. Personal E-mail: leeroussel@hotmail.com.

ROUSSEL, MARTINE F., molecular sciences professor; married. PhD, Université de Lille, France. Fogarty Internat. fellow Nat. Cancer Inst., Bethesda, Md.; full mem. in dept. Genetics and Tumor Cell Biology St. Jude Children's Rsch. Hosp., co-dir., Cancer Ctr. Signal Transduction Program, endowed chair in Molecular Oncogenesis; chair St Jude Exch. Program, Spring/Summer Lab. Tng. for Masters Students; full prof. in dept. Molecular Sciences Univ. of Tenn.; chair Erasmus Univ. of Sciences, Paris; v.p. for US Eurocancer, Paris, 2003—. Author: (publs.) New concepts in organ site research on medulloblastoma: genetics and genomics, 2010, Cerebellum development and medulloblastoma, 2011; co-author: E2-RING expansion of the NEDD8 cascade confers specificity to cullin modification, 2009, Whole body physiologically-based pharmacokinetic model for nutlin-3a after intravenous and oral administration, 2011. Fellow: American Acad. of Arts and Sciences. Office: St Jude Children's Research Hospital 262 Danny Thomas Pl Memphis TN 38105 Office Phone: 901-595-3481. Office Fax: 901-595-2381. E-mail: martine.roussel@stjude.org.

ROUSSELOT, WADE, state legislator; Attended, Northeastern Okla. A&M; BS in Animal Sci., Okla. State Univ., 1981. Mem. Dist. 12 Okla. House of Representatives, 2005—. Mem.: Okmulgee County Cattlemen's Assn., Benevolent Order Elks, Nat. Rifle Assn., Air America Assn., Okla. Farmer's Union, Coweta C. of C., Wagoner C. of C., Wagoner Lions Club, Texas and Southwest Cattlemen's Assn., Okla. Farm Bur., Okla. Cattlemen's Assn., Wagoner County Cattlemen's Assn., Wagoner County Farm Bur. Democrat. Office: Oklahoma House of Representatives 2300 N Lincoln Blvd Rm 314 Oklahoma City OK 73105 also: 5298 E 110th St N Wagoner OK 74467 Office Phone: 405-557-7388. E-mail: waderousselot@okhouse.gov.

ROUTH, DONALD K(ENT), psychologist, historian, educator; b. Oklahoma City, Mar. 3, 1937; s. Ross Holland and Fay (Campbell) R.; m. Marion Starbird Wendler, Sept. 10, 1960(Dec. Sept. 10, 2008); children: Rebecca Ann (dec.), Laura Diane; m. Margaret Gonzalez, June 27, 2010. BA, U. Okla., 1962; PhD, U. Pitts., 1967; BA in History, Fla. Gulf Coast U., 2006, MA in History, 2011. Diplomate Am. Bd. Profl. Psychology. Asst. prof. psychology and pediatrics U. Iowa, Iowa City, 1967-70, prof., 1977-85; assoc. prof. psychology Bowling Green State U., Ohio, 1970-71; assoc. prof. U. N.C., Chapel Hill, 1971-77; prof. psychology and pediat. U. Miami, Coral Gables, Fla., 1985—2002, prof. emeritus, 2002—. Chmn. behavioral medicine study sect. NIH, 1983-85 Editor Jour. Pediatric Psychology, 1976-82, Jour. Clin. Child Psychology, 1987-91, Jour. of Abnormal Child Psychology, 1992-98, Am. Jour. on Mental Retardation, 1998-2002, Internat. Clin. Psychologist, 2001—04; contbr. numerous articles to profl. jours., books Pres. Eno River Unitarian Universalist Fellowship, 1976-77; vol. faculty Fla. Gulf Coast U., 2002—05. Recipient award for disting. contbn. Soc. Pediatric Psychology, 1981, Presdl. award, 1988; Rsch. Psychologist of Yr. award Fla. Psychol. Assn., 1987, Reconocimiento, El Colegio Nacional de Psicologis de Mex., 1999, Disting. Alumni award Okla. Mil. Acad., 2004. Mem. APA (pres. div. child, youth and family svcs., 1984, pres. div. on mental retardation 1987, pres. divsn. clin. psychol. 1998, Wallace Russell lectr. divsn. history of psychology, 2011), Internat. Soc. Clin. Psychology (founder, pres. 1998-99), Disting. Profl. Contbns. to Clin. Psychology (sect. on clin. child psychology 1989, div. clin. psychology, 1992, Nicholas Hobbs award div. child youth and family svcs., 1996, Edgar A. Doll award divsn. mental retardation and devel. disabiities 2001), Assn. Southwest Fla. (founder, 2003),Phi Beta Kappa. Democrat. Home: 4528 Palm Tree Blvd Cape Coral FL 33904 Personal E-mail: donaldrouth@mac.com.

ROWE, LARRY LINWELL, lawyer, former state senator; b. Bluefield, W.Va. m. Julia Beury; 2 children. BA, W.Va. U., 1970, MPA, JD, W.Va. U., 1976. Bar: W.Va. 1976, U.S. Dist. Ct. (so. dist.) W.Va. 1976, U.S. Ct. Appeals (4th cir.) 1978, U.S. Supreme Ct. 1992. Staff counsel W.Va. Housing Devel. Fund, Charleston, 1976-77; sr. law clk. to Hon. K. K. Hall U.S. 4th Cir. Ct. Appeals, Charleston, 1978-79; pvt. practice Charleston, 1980—. Adj. prof. law U. Charleston, 1980—81. Bd. dirs. W.Va. Artists & Craftsmen's Guild, Charleston, 1980—84, Cedar Lakes' Mountain State Arts & Crafts Fair, Ripley, 1981—82; chmn., mem. Legal Aid Soc. Charleston, 1981—84; pres. W.Va. Dance Theatre, Charleston, 1981—82; hearing examiner W.Va. Bd. Regents, Charleston, 1985—89, W.Va. Bd. Medicine, Charleston, 1987—88; bd. gov. W.Va. State U.; mem. W.Va. Ho. of Del., 1997—2000, W.Va. Senate, 2001—05, W.Va. State Ethics Commn., 2005—10. W.Va. Bd. Regents scholar, W.Va. U. Coll. Law, 1974—76, Cato scholar, 1974—76. Mem.: Phi Beta Kappa, Order of Coif. Democrat. Office: 4200A Malden Dr Charleston WV 25306-6442 Home Phone: 304-925-9382; Office Phone: 304-925-1333. Personal E-mail: larrylrowe1@gmail.com.

ROWE, LOUIS E., former councilman; m. Brenda Kelly; 1 stepchild. BS in Elec. Engring., U. Tex, 1971. Registered profl. engr., Tex., 1976. Pres. Goetting & Assocs., 1991—; bd. dirs. Dist. 3 San Antonio River Authority, 1996—2007, chmn., 2005—08; councilman, Dist. 9 San Antonio City Coun., 2008—09. Bd. mem. San Antonio Elec. Examining & Supervising Bd., 1989—90; mem. CPS Adv. Bd., 1998—2003, chmn., 1998—2003; mem. Bexar County Citizens Adv. Com. on Elected Officials Salaries, 2000—02, chmn., 2002. Mem. Greater San Antonio C. of C., 1975—, chmn., Govt. Affairs Coun., 2000, bd. dirs., 2000—07, chmn., 2005—07; mem. North San Antonio C. of C., 1990—, former chmn. Govt. Affairs Com.; mem. UTSA Pres. Coun., 1991—, UTHSC Pres. Coun., 1992—, Real Estate Coun. San Antonio, 1992—, former chmn., Govt. Affairs Com., pres., 1995; mem. UTSA Coll. Engring. Adv. Coun., 1995—2006, chmn., 2006—; mem. Leadership San Antonio XXII, 1996—97, class XXV steering com., 1999—2000; chmn. Christy's Hope for Battered Women & Children Golf Classic, 2000—07, Cystic Fibrosis Twilight Gala, 2003. Mem.: Alamo Area Coun. Govts. (bd. mem. 2006—, vice chmn. 2008—), San Antonio Econ. Devel. Found., Soc. Mktg. Profl. Svcs. (pres. 2005—06), Profl. Engrs. in Pvt. Practice (former pres.), Nat. Soc. Profl. Engrs., Urban Land Inst., Am. Heart Assn.-San Antonio Div. (bd. dirs. 2001—07, AHA Heart Walk chmn. 2002, chmn. 2006), March of Dimes (chmn. 1996—97), Boys Hope/Girls Hope (bd. mem. 1997—2003), Jr. Achievement South Tex. (bd. mem. 2005—06), Tex. Bus. Hall Fame Found. (bd. mem. 2002—), Downtown Rotary. Office: 12042 Blanco Rd, Ste 200 San Antonio TX 78216 Office Phone: 210-207-7325, 210-341-2390. Business E-Mail: district9@sanantonio.gov.

ROWE, THOMAS DUDLEY, JR., law educator; b. Richmond, Va., Feb. 26, 1942; s. Thomas Dudley and Georgia Rosamond (Stripp) R.; m. Susan Fletcher French, Jan. 5, 2001. BA, Yale U., 1964; MPhil, Oxford U., Eng., 1967; JD, Harvard U., 1970. Bar: D.C. 1971, N.C. 1976. Law clk. to assoc. justice Potter Stewart U.S. Supreme Ct., Washington, 1970-71; asst. counsel adminstrv. practice subcom. U.S. Senate, Washington, 1971-73; assoc. Miller, Cassidy, Larroca & Lewin, Washington, 1973-75; assoc. prof. Duke U. Sch. Law, Durham, NC, 1975-79, prof., 1979-96, Elvin R. Latty prof., 1996—2007, Elvin R. Latty prof. emeritus, 2008—, assoc. dean for rsch., 1981-84, sr. assoc. dean acad. affairs, 1995-96. Vis. prof. Georgetown U. Law Ctr., Washington, 1979—80, U. Mich. Law Sch., Ann Arbor, 1985, U. Va. Law Sch., Charlottesville, 1991, UCLA Law Sch., 2002, 2010; Straus Disting. vis. prof. Pepperdine U. Sch. Law, 2006; atty. Munger, Tolles & Olson, LA, 1991; adv. com. on rules of civil procedure U.S. Jud. Conf., 1993—99. Co-author: Constitutional Theory: Arguments and Perspectives, 1993, 2000, 2007, Federal Courts in the 21st Century: Cases and Materials, 1996, 2002, 2007, Civil Procedure, 2004, 2008; contbr. articles to profl. jours. Fellow U.S. Dept. Justice, Washington, 1980-81; Rhodes scholar, 1964-67; recipient Disting. Teaching award Duke Bar Assn., 1985. Mem.: ABA, Am. Law Inst. (life). Democrat. Business E-Mail: trowe@law.duke.edu.

ROWLAND, ARTHUR RAY, librarian; b. Hampton, Ga., Jan. 6, 1930; s. Arthur and Jennie (Goodman) R.; m. Jane Thomas, July 1, 1955; children: Dell Ruth, Anna Jane. AB in History, Mercer U., Macon, Ga., 1951; MA in in Lib., Emory U., Atlanta, 1952; postgrad. in Brit. Libraries and History, Oxford U., Eng., 1989; postgrad., Vanderbuilt U., Nashville, 1970. Circulation asst. Ga. State Coll. Library, 1952, circulation librarian, 1952-53; librarian Armstrong Coll., Savannah, Ga., 1954-56; head circulation dept. Auburn U. Library, 1956-58; librarian, assoc. prof. library sci. Jacksonville U., 1958-61, Augusta Coll., 1961-76, prof., libr., 1976-91, libr. emeritus, 1991—. Lectr. libr. edn. U. Ga., 1962-66; trustee Augusta-Richmond County Pub. Libr., 1980-93, pres. bd. trustees, 1983-85, v.p. bd., 1988-91; trustee Augusta Regional Libr., chmn., 1984-85; trustee East Cen. Ga. Regional Libr., 1987-93, chmn., 1988-91; chmn. Gov.'s Conf. on Ga. Librs. and Info. Svcs., 1977; del. White House Conf. on Librs. and Info. Sci., 1979; cons. on libr. mgmt. to Govt. of Indonesia. Author: Bibliography of the Writings of Georgia History, 1966, A Guide to the Study of Augusta and Richmond County, Georgia, 1967, (with Helen Callahan) Yesterday's Augusta, 1976, (with James E. Dorsey) A Bibliography of the Writings on Georgia History 1900-1970, rev. edit., 1978, (with Marguerite F. Fogleman) Reese Library Genealogical Resources, 1988, supplement, 1990, Goodman Cousins, 1988, Rowland Cousins, 1990, New Guide to the Study of Augusta, 1990, Index to City Directory of Augusta, Georgia, 1841-1879, 1991, More Goodman Cousins, 1993, My Fair Grandmother, 1994, Distant Cousins, The Huguenots Connecting Rowland, Bulloch, de Bourdeaux, DeVeaux and Roosevelt Families of S.C., N.C. and Ga., 1995, The Bessent Family of Georgia, 1995, Reeves Family of Georgia, 1996, Descendants of Wiley Reeves, 1996, Rowland-Huckaby Connections, 1996, Georgia Almanacs, 1996, Rowland Family of Virginia, North Carolina and Georgia and Beyond, 1998, Atkinson Family in Virginia, 1998, Ancestors of David Jackson, 1998, Ancestors of Rachael Hines Lewis, 1998, Ancestors of Elizabeth Proctor in Virginia and England, 1998, Ancestors of Martha Whitehead, 1998, Wiley Reeves, His Descendants and Ancestors, 1999, John Rowland, Immigrant, 2000, Reeves Family in England, Virginia, North Carolina, Georgia and Beyond, 2000, The Mississippi Branch of the Rowland Family, 2000, Ancestors and Connections of Dunbar Rowland, 2000, Printing in Louisville, 2000, Confederate Printing in Augusta, Ga., 2000, Goodman Family of N.C., Ga. and Beyond Their Cherokee Indian Heritage, 2000, Hillhouse Family of Wash., Ga., 2000, Printing in Wash., Ga., 2000, Jacob Martin Hugenot of Charleston, S.C., 2000, John Gensel of Charleston, S.C., 2000, Bessent Family, 2000, Rowland Family in Ga., 2000, Printers of Augusta, Georgia, 1786-1900, 2003, Printing in Milledgeville, Georgia, 2003, Preliminary Checklist of Penfield, Georgia Imprints, 2003, A Preliminary Checklist of Georgia Imprints, 1763-1860, 2003, Civil War Marriages Richmond County, Georgia, 2004, Grocers, Butchers, Baker and Others, 2004, 1890 Census of Augusta and Richmond County Georgia, 2004, 2d edit., 2006, Citizens of Augusta and Richmond County, Georgia During the Civil War, 2005, 2d edit., 2006, Confederate Soldiers From Augusta and Richmond County, Georgia, 2005, Name Index to Augusta Georgia City Directories 1880-1891, 2006, Business Directory of Augusta Georgia 1841-1901, 2006, Brides and Grooms: Marriage Licesnes and Certificates of Richmond County Georgia 1785-1890, 2006, China and Immigrants to Augusta and Richmond County Georgia, 2006, Citizens of North Augusta in Aiken County South Carolina, 2006, Black or Mulatto in Richmond County Georgia, 2006, Women in Business in Augusta Georgia 1841-1901, 2006, Ecclesiastical Index to Augusta Georgia 1736-1901, 2006, Foreign Born Citizens in Augusta and Richmond County Georgia 1850 and 1860, 2006, Hephzibah Georgia in Richmond County Georgia, 2006, Village of Summerville 1880-1910, 2006, Names Changed Legally in Georgia 1800-1856, 2007, List of Prisoners in Penitentiary, Convict Camps, Chain Gangs and Jails in Georgia, 2007, McPherson Barracks, 2007, Brides and grooms, Book, Richmond county, Georgia.,2007, Classified Business Directory August Georgia 1901-1930, 2007, Banker, Cashier, Teller, 2007, Index to Marriage Licences Book, Richmond County, Ga., 2008, Cross References to Personel Names, 2008, Public Buildings in August Georgia, 2008, others; co-author: (with Jane T. Rowland) Index to Marriage 1912-1942, Is This Your Alma Mater? Name Changes for Your College, University, Institute, Seminary or Manual School in Georgia, 2010, Georgia Imprints, 1861-1976, Using the WPA Files and Other Sources, 2010, Tubman High School Graduates, 1874-1950, 2011, Teachers at Tubman High School, 1874-1950, 2012, Schools of Columbia County, Ga., 2013; co-author (with Sarah Mitravich) Reference Services, 1964, Historical Markers of Richmond County, Georgia, rev. edit., 1971, The Catalog and Cataloging, 1969, The Librarian and Reference Service, 1977, Reminiscences of Augusta Marines, 1985; supervising editor (with Heard Robertson) Jour. Archibald Campbell, 1981; contbr.articles to profl. publs. V.p. Ga. Libr. Assn. Trustees and Friends, 1989-91. With USN, 1948-49. Recipient Nix-Jones award for disting. service Ga. Library Assn., 1981, Town and Gown award Augusta Coll. Alumni Assn., 1985. Mem. ALA, Am. Assn. State and Local History, Bibliog. Soc. Am., Southeastern Libr. Assn. (hon. life, exec. bd. 1971-72), Ga. Libr. Assn. (hon. life, 2d v.p. 1965-67, 71-73, 1st v.p., pres.-elect 1973-75, pres. 1975-77, chmn. budget com. 1977-79, adv. to pres. 1979-83, 85-92), Ctrl. Savannah River Area Libr. Assn. (past pres., editor union list of serials 1967, contbn. local history and geneaology, 2007), Duval County Libr. Assn. (past v.p.), Nat. Geneal. Soc., Ga. Geneal. Soc., N.C. Geneal. Soc., Va. Geneal. Soc., Augusta Geneal. Soc., Richmond County Hist. Soc. (curator 1964-91, pres. 1967-69, founder, editor Richmond County History), Huguenot Soc. S.C., Ga. Hist. Soc. (curator emeritus), Ga. Bapt. Hist. Soc., Nat., Young Men's Libr. Assn. (v.p. 1988-91), Ga. Trusts for Hist. Preservation, Hist. Augusta (trustee emeritus), Soc. Ga. Archivists, Kappa Phi Kappa. Baptist. Address: 334 Connor Cir Evans GA 30809 Personal E-mail: rrow999@comcast.net.

ROWLAND, ROBERT ALEXANDER, III, lawyer; b. McAllen, Tex., Apr. 27, 1943; s. Robert Alexander Jr and Marguerite (Gerry) Rowland; m. Victoria Nalle, Apr. 2, 1977; children: Julia Marie, Emily Nalle. BS, Tex. A&M U., 1966; JD, George Washington U., 1972. Bar: Tex. 1972, U.S. Dist. Ct. (so. dist.) Tex. 1973, U.S. Ct. Appeals (5th cir.) 1973, U.S. Supreme Ct. 1976, U.S. Dist. Ct. (no. dist.) Tex. 1979, U.S. Dist. Ct. (we. dist.) Tex. 1982, U.S. Dist. Ct. (ea. dist.) Tex. 1983. Law clk. U.S. Ct. Appeals (5th cir.), Houston, 1973-74; assoc. Vinson & Elkins, Houston, 1975-81; ptnr. Susman, Godfrey & McGowan, Houston, 1982—88; mng. dir. Johnson and Gibbs, Houston, 1988-91; ptnr. Hutcheson & Grundy, LLP, Houston, 1992-94; chmn., CEO Associated Counsel of Am., 1995—; ptnr. Roach & Rowland, Houston, 2003—07, Law Offices Robert A. Rowland III and Assocs., 2008—, Am. Mid. Eastern Group for Investment and

Devel., LLC, 2012—, mem.; sec., dir. Am. Mid. Eastern Connection Inc. Bd. dirs. Vol. Ctr., Houston, 1975—84, pres., 1982—83; founding mem., bd. dirs. Tex. Accts. and Lawyers for Arts, 1979—92, pres., 1989—91; devel. coun. Sch. Liberal Arts Tex. A&M U., 1992—2009, steering com., 1995—2007, devel. coun. George Bush Sch. Govt. and Pub. Svc., 2004—; trustee Houston Pks. Bd. Found., 2002—; chmn. endowment com. Houston Audubon Soc., 2006—09; endowment com. The Beacon, 2006—09; bd. dirs. Tex. Assn. Bus., 2008—09; bd. adv. US Pub. Svc. Acad., 2007—; co-chmn. Mayor's Transition Com. for Parks, City of Houston, 1992—94; candidate for State Rep., Tex. Legis. Dist. 134, Rep. Primary, 2002; fin. com. Harris County Rep. Party, 2003—07, chmn., 2005—07; bd. dirs. United Reps. of Harris County, 2002—09, adv. adj. com., 2010—12; Rep. precinct chmn. Harris County Precinct, 2003—05, 2008—; mission outreach coun. Christ Ch. Cathedral, 2002—05, chmn., 2004—05, co-chmn., grants subcom., 2005—06, chmn. grants subcom., 2006—07, stewardship coun., 2006—10, chmn., 2008—09, vestry, 2011—, bldg. & grounds com. mem., 2011—14, jr. warden, 2013—14; bd. dirs. Camp Allen Retreat for Episcopal Diocese Tex., 2014—, Houston Pks. Bd., 1993—2005, chmn., 2003—05; bd. dirs. Contemporary Art Mus. Houston, 1974—80, 1991—94; bd. dirs. Sarah Campbell Blaffer Gallery of Art U. Houston, 1989—94; bd. dirs. Tex. Opera Theater, 1988—89; bd. trustees Nat. Recreation and Pk. Assn., 1992—95; bd. dirs. Cultural Arts Coun., Houston, 1981—86, Pk. People Inc., 1979—2001, pres., 1991—92, endowment com. chmn., 1994—2004; bd. dirs. Compass, 2006—12, v.p., 2008—09, pres., 2009—10, sec., 2010—11; with parks and open spaces com. Greater Houston Partnership, 2006—09, chair, 2009, quality of life adv. com., 2006—09, culture & tourism com. mem., 2011—; bd. dirs. Houston Bot. Garden, 2007—, vice chmn., 2013—, chmn. bylaws com., 2007—12, sec., 2009—11, chmn., pub. affairs com., 2009—11, chmn. nominations com., 2011—, exec. com. mem., 2009—. Capt. US Army, 1966—69, Vietnam. Fellow: Tex. Bar Found., Houston Bar Found.; mem.: State Bar Tex., Houston Bar Assn. (dir. 1979—88, sec., chmn. law and art com. 1984—85, 2d v.p. 1985—86), C Club (program chmn. 2005, exec. com. 2005—07, membership chmn. 2006, treas. 2007), Coronado Club, River Oaks Country Club, Phi Delta Phi. Republican. Episcopalian. Home: 2010 Chilton Rd Houston TX 77019-1502 Office: Associated Counsel Am Inc Ste 125 4605 Post Oak Pl Houston TX 77027-9744 Office Phone: 713-840-7100 ext. 234. Personal E-mail: rob@robrowland.com.

ROWLANDS, SHARON THERESA, publishing executive; b. England, 1958; BA with honors, Newcastle U.; postgraduate teaching degree, U. London Goldsmiths Coll. Mng. dir. Extel Fin.; head Northern American ops. FT Information; mgmt. positions through mng. dir. database group Thomson Financial, 1996—2000, pres., COO, 2000—05, pres., CEO, 2005—08; CEO Penton Media Inc., NYC, 2008—11; CEO, bd. dirs. Altegrity, Inc., Falls Church, Va., 2011—. Bd. dirs. Automatic Data Processing Inc., Roseland, NJ, 2008—, Constant Contact, Inc., 2010—; mem. advisory bd. Ultimate Resort LLC; mem. global bd. managers Omgeo LLC. Bd. dir. Junior Achievement of NY, 2006—. Recipient Merit award, Women's Bond Club, 2005. Office: Altegrity Inc 7799 Leesburg Pike Ste 1100 N Falls Church VA 22043-2413 Office Phone: 703-448-0178.

ROWLINGSON, JOHN CLYDE, anesthesiologist, physician, educator; b. Syracuse, NY, Aug. 3, 1948; s. John Winthrop and Genevieve Estelle (Mahan) R.; m. Rosemary Colette Laney, Oct. 26, 1974 (div. 1992); children: Kristen, Andrew; m. Karen Wheeler, Aug. 4, 2001; stepchild, Isaac. BS, Allegheny Coll., 1970; MD, SUNY, Buffalo, 1974. Diplomate Am. Bd. Anesthesiology. Intern Millard Fillmore Hosp., Buffalo, 1974-75; resident in anesthesiology U. Va., Charlottesville, 1975-77; fellow in anesthesia pain mgmt. U. Va. Med. Ctr., 1977-78; asst. prof. anesthesiology U. Va. Sch. Medicine, Charlottesville, 1978-82, assoc. prof., 1982-86, prof., 1986—, Cosmo A. DiFazio prof. anesthesiology, 2005. Assoc. dir. Pain Mgmt. Ctr., U. Va. Health Sci. Ctr., 1978-79, dir., 1980-98, dir. acute pain svc., Acad. Disting. Educators, 1987-2007. Author: Regional Anesthesia, 1984; co-editor: Handbook of Critical Care Pain Management, 1993. Recipient Nils Lofgren award ASTRA, 1999; Nat. Inst. Handicapped Rsch. fellow, 1983-87, Pain fellow 1977-78. Fellow Am. Coll. Anesthesiology; mem. Am. Soc. Anesthesiologists, Am. Soc. Regional Anesthesia (rsch. grantee 1977, pres. 1996-97, interim pres. elect, 2012-2013, recipient Disting. Svc. award 2007, Bonica Lectr., 2007), Am. Pain Soc., Internat. Assn. Study of Pain, Am. Acad. Pain Medicine (editl. bd. Anesthesia Analg 1996—, Reg. Anesthesia and Pain Medicine, 1997—), Va. Soc. Anesthesiology (sec, treas. 2005-07, pres. 2009-2011). Methodist. Avocations: running, tennis, skiing, biking. Home: 5006 Lake Tree Ln Crozet VA 22932 Office: U Va Hlth Sys Health Sci Ctr Anesthesiology PO Box 800710 Charlottesville VA 22908-0710 Home Phone: 434-823-9626; Office Phone: 434-924-2283. Business E-Mail: jcr3t@virginia.edu.

ROWSE, DARREN, blogger; married. Creator problogger.net, 2004—; co-founder, v.p. blogger tng. b5media, 2005—; owner, blogger Digital Photography School; blogger TwiTip-Twitter Tips. Co-author: Problogger: Secrets for Blogging Your Way to a Six-Figure Income, 2008, 31 Days to Build a Better Blog Workbook, 2010, Copywriting Scorecard for Bloggers, ProBlogger's Guide to Your First Week of Blogging. Named one of Top 25 Web Celebs, Forbes mag., 2007. Office: b5media Inc 10802 Nunn Jones Rd College Station TX 77845

ROY, LORIENE, library and information scientist, association executive; Student, Coll. St. Benedict, St. Joseph, Minn., 1972; AS, BT, Oreg. Inst. Tech., Klamath Falls, 1977; MLS, U. Ariz., Tucson, 1980; student, Ariz. Western Coll., Yuma, 1979—81; PhD, U. Ill., Urbana-Champaign, 1987. Med. radiologic technologist extern Presbyn. Intercommunity Hosp., Klamath Falls, Oreg., 1976—77; med. radiologic technologist Yuma Regional Med. Ctr., Ariz., 1977—79; oral history coord. Century House Mus., Yuma, Ariz., 1981—82; reference libr. Yuma City-County Libr., 1981—82; instr. U. Ill. Grad. Sch. Libr. & Info. Sci., Urbana, 1985; rsch. assoc. U. Ill. Libr. Rsch. Ctr., Urbana, 1984—86; instr. U. Tex. at Austin Grad. Sch. Libr. & Info. Sci., 1987, asst. prof., 1987—93, assoc. prof., 1993—99, dir. If I Can Read,I Can Do Anything nat. reading club for native children, 1999—; prof. U. Tex at Austin Sch. Info., 1999—, U. Tex at Austin Ctr. for Women's & Gender Studies, 2002—; rsch. assoc. Four Directions, Pueblo of Laguna Dept. Edn., N.Mex., 1997—2001. Mem. steering com. U. Ariz. Sch. Info. Resources & Libr. Sci., 2001—05; mem. nat. envisioning com. Tribal Libr., Archives, and Museums: Preserving our Lang., Memory, and Lifeways: Nat. Conf., 2001—; adv. bd. for Peep & the Big Wide World & We Shall Remain WBGH-Boston, 2006—, adv. bd., We Shall Remain, 2006—; mem. Libr. Leadership Network, 2006—; invited co-presenter in field; cons. in field. Co-editor (with Dr. Brooke Sheldon): Library & Information Studies Education in the United States, 1998; co-editor: (with Antony Cherian) Getting Libraries the Credit They Deserve: A Festschrift in Honor of Marvin H. Scilken, 2002; manuscript reviewer Am. Indian Culture & Rsch. Jour., 1988, Jour. Edn. for Libr. & Info. Sci., 1998, Can. Jour. Native Studies, 2000, asst. editor Native Am. studies Counterpoise, 1996—98, bd. mem. reviews sect. Libr. Acquisitions: Practice & Theory, 1997—, mem. editl. bd. Libr. & Culture, 1987—97, editl. adv. bd. New Advocate: For Those Involved with Young People & Their Literature, 2000—, Electronic Libr., 2002—; contbr. articles and newsletters, chapters to books. Adv. bd. Sequoya Rsch. Ctr., 2001—, Internat. Children's Digital Libr., 2002—, Heart of the Cmty.: The Libraries We Lover, Berkshire Pub. Group, 2005—06; adv. com. El dia de los ninos, 2004—05, El dia de los libros, 2005—06, WebJunction.org, 2002—, Online Computer Libr. Ctr. (OCLC), 2002—, Bill & Melinda Gates Found., 2002—, Pub. Access Computing Portal, 2002—; mem. Freedom to Read Found., 1998—, trustee, 2006—; vol. Am. Diabetes Assn., 1990; vol. trainer Austin Free Net, 1997—98; mem., cultural awareness com. Fulmore Middle Sch., 2002; vol. Fulmore Middle Sch. Libr., 2003. Recipient Squibb award, Oreg. Inst. Tech., 1975, Tex. Excellence in Teaching award, U. Tex. at Austin Grad. Sch. Libr. & Info. Sci., 1988, 1991, James W. Vick Tex. Excellence award, 1992, Joe & Bettie Branson Ward Excellence award, 2001, Outstanding Alumna award, U. Ariz. Sch. Info. Resources & Libr. Sci., 2002, Texas Exes Teaching award, U. Tex. at Austin, 2005; named a Mover & Shaker, Libr. Jour., 2005; named an Hon. Tex. Citizen, 1990. Mem.: ALA (libr. rsch. roundtable 1987—92, libr. history roundtable 1987—92, continuing libr. edn. network and exchange round table 1987—94, reference and adult svcs. divsn. 1987—96, pub. libr. assn. 1987—, assn. for libr. svc. to children 1989—96, libr. rsch. roundtable 1995—, social responsibilities roundtable 1996—, reference and user svcs. assn. 1996—, nominating com. mem. 1999—, assn. for libr. svc. to children 2000—05, internat. rels. roundtable 2001—, ethnic & multicultural info. exch. roundtable 2001—, edn. assembly chair 2004—06, planning and budget assembly mem. 2004—06, pres. elect 2006—07, co-chair 2006—07, Allied Profl. Assn.:Orgn. Advancement Libr. Employees, pres.-elect 2006—07, pres.-elect 2006—07, ALISE liason 2006—, Am. Indian Libr. Assn. liason 2006—, players 2006—, exec. bd. mem. 2006—09, exec. com. mem. 2006—09, pres. 2007—08, and several other positions, Equality award 2006), Tex. State Libr. and Archives Commn. (TexShare Adv. Bd. mem. 2005—), Tex. State Historical Assn., Nat. Assn. Native Am. Studies, Tex. Oral History Assn., Assn. Coll. & Rsch. Librs., Am. Soc. for Info. Sci., Internat. Indigenous Librarians' Coun., Internat. Fedn. Libr. Assn. (mem. presdl. com. on indigenous matters 2006—), Am. Culture Assn., Reference & User Svcs. Assn., Am. Indian Libr. Assn. (v.p./pres. elect 1996—97, exec. bd. 1996—99, pres. 1997—98, and several other positions), Assn. Libr. & Info. Sci. Edn. (convener, libr. history spl. interest group 1988, govt. rels. com. 1988—90, mentor 2002), Libr. Leadership Network, Oral History Assn., REFORMA: Nat. Assn. to Promote Libr. and Info. Svcs. to Latinos and the Spanish Speaking, Tex. Libr. Assn. (pub. relations com. mem. 2001—, mem. cultural diversity com. 2006—, and several other positions), Wordcraft Cir. Native Writers & Storytellers, Tex. Libr. Legis. Hotline, Faculty Women's Orgn., U. Tex. Austin, Austin Songwriters Group (libr. 1995—96), Aboriginal and Torres Strait Islander Libr. Resource Network, Inc., Austin Book Workers, Beta Phi Mu, Phi Kappa Phi. Office: Sch Info U Tex at Austin 1 University Station D7000 Austin TX 78712-0390 Office Phone: 512-471-0390, 512-471-3959. Office Fax: 512-471-3971. E-mail: loriene@ischool.utexas.edu.

ROY, MANIK, lobbyist; BS in Civil Engring., Stanford U., Calif., MS in Environ. Engring.; PhD in Pub. Policy, Harvard U., Cambridge, Mass. Pollution prevention specialist Mass. Dept. Environ. Protection, Environ. Def. Fund; dir. pollution prevention policy US EPA; aide to Henry A. Waxman US House of Representatives, Washington; aide to Frank Lautenberg US Senate, Washington; dir. Congl. affairs Pew Ctr. on Global Climate Change, v.p. fed. govt. outreach. Named one of Washington's Top Lobbyists, The Hill, 2010. Office: Pew Ctr on Global Change 2101 Wilson Blvd Ste 550 Arlington VA 22201 Office Phone: 703-516-4146. Office Fax: 703-841-1422.

ROY, RAYMOND CLYDE, anesthesiologist; b. 1944; PhD in Chemistry, Duke U., 1971; MD, Tulane U., 1974. Resident Hosp. U. Pa.; prof., chair dept. anesthesia & perioperative medicine Med. U. S.C., 1996; prof., chmn. dept. anesthesiology U. Vir. Med. Ctr., Charlottesville, 1996-98. Dir. Am. Bd. Anesthesiology. Office: Wake Forest University Med Ctr Med Ctr Blvd Winston Salem NC 27157-1009 Business E-Mail: rroy@wfubmc.edu.

ROYAL, C. ASHLEY, federal judge; b. Augusta, Ga., 1949; AB, U. Ga., 1971, JD, 1974, MS, 1976. Asst. dist. atty. Dist. Atty.'s Office, Augusta Jud. Cir., 1974—75; pvt. practice atty. Ga., 1976, Ga., 1977—2001; pub. defender Glynn County, Ga., 1976—77; judge US Dist. Ct. (mid. dist.) Ga., Macon, 2001—08, chief judge, 2008—. Office: PO Box 129 Macon GA 31202-0129

ROYAL, FRANK S., physician, board member; b. 1939; Undergraduate, Va. Union U., 1961; MD, Meharry Med. Coll., 1968. Pres., mem. Frank S. Royal, M.D., P.C. Former bd. dirs. Va. Electric and Power Co., Canal Corp.; bd. dirs. Crestar Fin. Corp., 1979, Chesapeake Corp., 1990—2007, HCA Inc., 1994—2006, CSX Corp., 1994—2008, The Healthcare Corp., Crestar Bank, Dominion Resources, Inc., 1994—, SunTrust Banks, Inc., 1998—, Smithfield Foods, Inc., 2002—. Former bd. dirs. Va. Biotechnology Rsch. Park., YMCA of Greater Richmond; pres., chmn. Nat. Med. Assn.; chmn. Richmond Cmty. Hosp. Found., Virginia Union U.; bd. trustees Meharry Med. Coll. Mem.: Meharry Med. Coll. (hon. chmn.). Office: SunTrust Banks Inc Bd Directors 303 Peachtree St NE Atlanta GA 30308 Office Phone: 404-588-7711. Office Fax: 404-332-3875. Business E-Mail: Frank.S.Royal@dom.com.

ROYAL, REY, apparel designer; b. Seattle, Mar. 5, 1976; s. Marco and Betsy (Talarico) Royal; m. Joella Royal, May 2000. BA in Fashion Design, Fashion Inst. Tech., 1998, MA in Fashion Design, 2000. Buyer, merchandiser Bloomingdales, NYC, 1999—2002; salesman, designer Neiman Marcus, NYC, 2000—03; designer, cons. Rock & Republic Jeans, Phila., 2003—08; designer, principal Meriks & Royal, Dover, Ark., 2008—12, owner, 2013—, principal sportswear designer. Named Womenswear Designer of Yr., Coun. Fashion Designers Am., 2001, 2003. Mem.: Cross-Continent Fashion Soc. (pres. 2013—). Democrat. Avocations: architecture, white-water rafting. Office: Meriks & Royal 4504 SR 27 Dover AR 72837-8114

ROYCE, RAYMOND WATSON, lawyer, rancher, investor; b. West Palm Beach, Fla., Mar. 5, 1936; s. Wilbur E. and Veda (Watson) R.; m. Catherine L. Setzer, Apr. 21, 1979; children: Raymond, Steven, Nancy, Kathryn, Ryan. BCE, U. Fla., 1958, JD, 1961. Bar: Fla. 1961, U.S. Dist. Ct. (so. dist.) Fla. 1961, U.S. Ct. Appeals (5th cir.) 1961, U.S. Ct. Appeals (11th cir.) 1981. With Scott, Royce, Harris & Bryan P.A., Palm Beach, Fla., 1962-99; pres. Scott, Royce, Harris, Bryan, Barra and Jorgensen, P.A., Palm Beach Gardens, Fla., 1982-99; ptnr. Holland & Knight LLP, West Palm Beach, 1999—2009, Shutts & Bowen LLP, West Palm Beach, 2009—. Bd. suprs. No. Palm Beach Improvement Dist., 1995-99., pres. Palm Beach Couty Bar Assn., 1973-74 Mem. Fla. Bar (bd. govs. 1974-78), Fla. Blue Key, Phi Delta Phi. Democrat. Presbyterian. Home: 5550 Whirlaway Rd Palm Beach Gardens FL 33418-7735 Office: Shutts & Bowen LLP 525 Okeechobee Blvd Ste 1100 West Palm Beach FL 33401-4027 Office Phone: 561-650-8536.

ROZANSKI, HORACIO DANIEL, business services executive; BBA summa cum laude, U. Wis., Eau Claire, 1990; MBA with high honors, U. Chgo., 1992. Joined Booz Allen Hamilton Holding Corp., 1992, chief personnel officer, 2002—10, exec. v.p., 2009—, chief strategy and talent officer, 2010—. Bd. advisors Catalyst, Inc. Bd. advisors Hidden Brain Drain task force; bd. dirs. Wolftrap Found. For The Performing Arts. Office: Booz Allen Hamilton Holding Corp 8283 Greensboro Dr Mc Lean VA 22102 Office Phone: 703-902-5000. Office Fax: 703-902-3333. Business E-Mail: horacio_rozanski@boozallen.com.

ROZGONYI, EUGENE V., JR., gas industry executive; Degree in Economics, Regis U. Owner NY Merc. Exch., Inc.; dir., risk mgmt. New Century Energies; v.p., chief risk officer AGL Resources, Inc., 2001—. Bd. dirs. NY Merc. Exch. Charitable Found. Com., 1995-96, Sr. Housing Options, Colo., 1999-00. Office: AGL Resources Inc Ten Peachtree Pl NE Atlanta GA 30309 Office Phone: 404-584-4000. Office Fax: 404-584-3714. Business E-Mail: erozgonyi@aglresources.com.

ROZZELL, SCOTT ELLIS, lawyer, energy executive; b. Texarkana, Tex., Apr. 12, 1949; s. George M. and Dora Mae (Boyett) Rozzell; m. Karen Brandstrader Rozzell; children: Stacey Rozzell Murphree, Kimberly Rozzell McVey. BA, So. Meth. U., 1971; JD, U. Tex., 1975. Bar: Tex. 1975, U.S. Dist. Ct. Tex. (so. dist), 1975, U.S. Dist. Ct. Tex. (no. dist.), 1977, U.S. Ct. Appeals (1st, 3d, 9th cirs.) 1977, U.S. Ct. Appeals (5th and D.C. cirs.) 1976. Assoc. BakerBotts, LLP, Houston, 1975-82, ptnr., 1983-94, sr. ptnr., 1995-2000; exec. v.p., gen. counsel, corp. sec. CenterPoint Energy, Inc., Houston, 2001—; exec. v.p., gen. counsel, corp. sec., bd. dir. Tex. Genco Holdings Inc., 2003—04; bd. dirs. Powell Industries Inc., 2011—. Bd. dirs. Houston Young Lawyers Assn. 1979-1982, pres. 1983-1984; mem. Tex. Commn. Lawyer Discipline, 2001-03, chair 2002-03. Bd. dirs. Manned Space Flight Edn. Found., Inc., 1997—2007, vice chair 2000-06, Lone Star Flight Mus., 2001-; vice-chmn., 2006—; mem. so. regional adv. bd. Inst. Internat. Edn., 2002—07; bd. dirs. Assn. Electric Cos. Tex., 2004-13, chmn. 2006-07; bd. dirs. Cancer Counseling, Inc., 1984-88, mem., State Tex. Aircraft Pooling Bd., 1997-2002, Houston Cmty. Coll. Found., 2006-13, Southern Meth. U. Alumni Assn. 2007-11, bd. dirs. March of Dimes, Houston, 2007-10, Alley Theater, 2008-10, commr. Tex. Equal Access to Justice Commn., 2010-13; devel. bd. mem. U. Health Sci. Ctr. Houston, 1992-99, 2002-12, mem. bd. visitors Md. Anderson Cancer Found., 2011- Mem. ABA, Houston Bar Assn. (bd. dirs. 1992-96, pres. 1996-97), Houston Bar Found. (bd. trustees 1990-92, chmn. 1992-93), State Bar Tex. (bd. dirs. 1997-2000, Outstanding Dir. 1999-2000), Texa. Bar Found. (bd. trustees 2007-11, chmn. 2009-2010), Am. Bar Found., Experimental Aircraft Assn., Aircraft Owners and Pilots Assn., Commemorative Air Force, Coronado Club, Houstonian Club. Republican. Presbyterian. Avocation: flying vintage military aircraft. Office: CenterPoint Energy Inc 1111 Louisiana 47th Floor PO Box 457 Houston TX 77210-4567 Home: 8 N West Oak Dr Houston TX 77056 Office Phone: 713-207-1502. Office Fax: 713-207-0894. Business E-Mail: scott.rozzell@centerpointenergy.com.

RTBEILLT, JEAN-CLAUDE, pharmaceutical executive; Chief tech. ops. officer King Pharmaceuticals, Inc. Office: King Pharmaceuticals Inc 501 5th St Bristol TN 37620 Office Phone: 423-989-8000. Office Fax: 423-274-8677. Business E-Mail: jean-claude.rtbeillt@kingpharm.com.

RUBEN, PETER N., broadcast executive; b. Passaic, NJ, June 1, 1960; s. Harris Michael Ruben and Susan Gail (Randolph) Oliveti; m. Karen Hillary Benson, Nov. 22, 1987; 1 child, Jessica. BA in Economics, Rutgers U., 1984; MBA, UCLA. With IAC/InteractiveCorp.; v.p., Nat. Accts. HSN Interactive LLC., sr. v.p., Nat. Accts., exec. v.p., Affiliate Rels.; mktg. analyst TKR Cable, Warren, 1985—86; mgr., Mkt. Planning Warner Cable/BK Cable, Flushing, 1986—87; v.p., Sales & Mktg., Los Angeles Divsn. Paragon Cable, dir., Mktg. NE Divsn. Mahwah, 1987—89, v.p., Mktg. & Programming, Manhattan Divsn., 1989. Recipient CTAM award for Mktg. Excellence Cable TV Adminstrn. and Mktg. Soc., 1990. Mem. So. Calif. Cable TV Mktg. Coun. (bd. dirs. 1984-89). Home: 5120 Broadway # Mktdpt New York NY 10034-1153 Office: HSN Interactive LLC 1 Hsn Dr Saint Petersburg FL 33729-0001 Office Phone: 727-872-1000. E-mail: peter.ruben@hsn.net.

RUBENFELD, STANLEY IRWIN, lawyer, director, mediator, arbitrator; b. NYC, Dec. 7, 1930; s. George and Mildred (Rose) R.; children: Lise Susan, Kenneth Michael, Andrew James, Victoria Louise, Alexandria Elizabeth; m. Madeleine Conway, Nov. 5, 2000. BA, Columbia U., 1952, JD, 1956. Bar: N.Y. 1956. Practice law, NYC, 1956—2002, 1965-68; assoc. Shearman & Sterling, 1956-65, ptnr. Paris, 1965-68, NYC, 1968-93, of counsel, 1994—2002. Arbitrator and mediator NASD; mediator U.S. Fed. Ct., IRS Panel, CPR Panel; arbitrator NYSE, Internat. C. of C.; South Shore Music, Inc. Editor-in-chief Columbia Law Rev., 1955-56; contbr. articles to profl. jours. Past pres. Port Washington (N.Y.) Cmty. Chest; former bd. dirs. Residents for a More Beautiful Port Washington. Lt. (j.g.) USNR, 1952-54. Stone scholar, 1951-52, 54-55, 55-56; Rockefeller Found. grantee, 1955 Mem. ABA, N.Y. State Bar Assn. (tax sec., past chmn. fgn. activities com., reorgn. corp.), Assn. Bar City N.Y. (past chmn. com. on recruitment lawyers), Nat. Assn. Law Placement (past bd. dirs., exec. com.), Columbia U. Law Sch. Alumni Assn. (bd. visitors, adviser, past bd. dirs.), Columbia Coll. Alumni Assn., Tax Club (past chmn.), Phi Delta Phi, Tau Epsilon Phi (past pres.). Office Phone: 203-253-1056, 305-867-9744. Personal E-mail: srubenfeld@optonline.net.

RUBENSTEIN, DAVID AARON, military officer, healthcare executive; b. Rockville Centre, NY, Nov. 23, 1954; s. Robert R. and Mona Sydney (Feder) R.; m. Patricia Barrier, Mar. 18, 1978; children: Sarah Elizabeth, William Robert. BS in Health Edn., Tex. A & M U., 1977; MHA, Baylor U., 1989; M of Mil. Arts and Sci., Command and Gen. Staff Coll., 1990. Commd. 2d lt. U.S. Army, 1977, advanced through grades to maj. gen., 2008, med. platoon leader 3d inf. div. Germany, 1977—79, ops. officer 3d med. battalion, 1979—80, pers. officer 307th med. battalion Ft. Bragg, NC, 1981—82, co. comdr., 1982—83, mil. instr. Acad. of Health Scis. Ft. Sam Houston, Tex., 1984—87, grad. student, 1987—88, adminstrv. resident William Beaumont Army Med. Ctr. Ft. Bliss, Tex., 1988—89, grad. student Command and Gen. Staff Coll. Ft. Leavenworth, Kans., 1989—90; adminstrv. asst. Office of the Army Surgeon Gen. Army Med. Svc. Corps, Washington, 1990—92; chief coordinated care Army Hosp., Ft. Belvoir, Va., 1992—93; hosp. comdr. 18th Mobile Army Surg. Hosp., Ft. Lewis, Wash., 1994—96; grad. student Army War Coll., Carlisle Barracks, Pa., 1996—97; dep. comdr. Eisenhower Army Med. Ctr., Ft. Gordon, Ga., 1997—99; hosp. comdr. 21st Combat Support Hosp., Ft. Hood, Tex., 1999—2001, Bosnia-Herzegovina, 1999—2000; cmdr. Landstuhl Regional Med. Ctr., Germany, 2001—03; chief of staff Europe Regional Med. Commd., 2003—04; cmdr. 30th Med. Brigade, 2004; asst. surgeon gen., 2005—06; commanding gen. Europe Med. Commd., 2006—08; major general, army deputy surgeon general US Army, 2008—10; comdr. Med. Ctr. & Sch., 2010—12. Pres. Health Orgn. Network, El Paso, Tex., 1989, asst. surgeon gen. force sustainment, 2005; pres. Healthcare Execs. Ctrl. Savannah River Area, 1998-99; participant U.S. Army seminar Baylor U., Ft. Sam Houston, 1989. Author leadership seminar; reviewer books Lehigh U. Press, 1990, Mil. Rev. Jour., Mil. Medicine; contbr. articles to profl. jours. Religious lay leader Office of the Jewish Chapel, Ft. Bragg, 1982-83,

Ft. Bliss, 1988-89, Ft. Leavenworth, 1989-90, Bosnia-Herzegovina, 1999-2000; fund drive coord. United Fund, Ft. Leavenworth, 1989; vol. Muscular Dystrophy Assn., Washington, 1990-91. Decorated Legion of Merit; recipient Fed. Healthcare Leadership award, 2003, Ray E. Brown award, Assn. Military Surgeons, US, 2006, Mentor of the Year award, U.S. Army Med. Svc. Corps., Federal Excellence in Healthcare Leadership award, Regent's healthcare Executive award, Am. Coll. Healthcare Executives. Fellow: Am. Coll. Healthcare Execs. (Regent's award 1993, regent 2000—02, gov. 2002—, chmn. 2008, Fed. Excellence in Healthcare Leadership award, Regent's Healthcare Exec. award); mem.: VFW, Assn. of U.S. Army, Am. Hosp. Assn., Assn. Mil. Surgeons of U.S. (Ray E. Brown 2006). Republican. Jewish. Avocations: flying, running, history reading. Home and Office: 310 E Langley Blvd Universal City TX 78148 Office Phone: 210-221-6325. Business E-Mail: david.rubenstein@us.army.mil.

RUBIN, ALLEN, social worker, educator; b. Pitts., Mar. 15, 1943; s. Yetta and Nathan Rubin; m. Christina Marcus, Aug. 4, 1974; children: Anne, Joshua, David. PhD, U. Pitts., 1976. Prof. U. Tex., Austin, 1979—. Author: (scholarly books) Practitioner' Guide to Using Research for Evidence-Based Practice (Significant Lifetime Achievement in Social Work Edn., 2007). Recipient Disting. Alumnus award, U. Pitts., Sch. Social Work, 1993. Home: 8011 Cardin Dr Austin TX 78759 Office: Univ Texas Austin 1925 San Jacinto Blvd Austin TX 78712 Office Fax: 512-471-9600. Business E-Mail: arubin@mail.utexas.edu.

RUBIN, BRUCE KALMAN, medical professor, researcher; b. Miami Beach, Fla., May 8, 1954; s. Arnold and Dorothy Bella (Firtel) Rubin; m. Tomomi Tainaka, July 29, 1990; children: Noah David, Max Aaron, Sam Tainaka. BSc, Tulane U., New Orleans, 1975, MEngr in Biomed. Engring., 1977, MD, 1979; MBA, Wake Forest U. Babcock Sch. Mgmt., Winston-Salem, NC, 2004. Diplomate Am. Bd. Pediat., cert. in Pediatric Pulmonology. Rhodes scholar Oxford U., 1978—80, intern pediat. England, 1979; resident Tulane U., 1980-81; respirology fellow Hosp. for Sick Children, Toronto, Ont., Canada, 1981-83; asst. prof., dir. pediat. ICU Queen's U., Kingston, Ont., 1983-87; asst. prof. pediat. U. Alberta, Edmonton, Canada, 1987-91; prof. pediat., dir. pulmonary medicine St. Louis U., Cardinal Glennon Hosp., 1991-97; prof., vice chair rsch., dept. pediat. Wake Forest U. Sch. Medicine, 1997—2009, chief pediat. pulmonology, 1999—2005; also prof. physiology and pharmacology, biomed. engring. Va. Tech.-Wake Forest U. Sch. Biomed. Engring., 1997—2009; faculty Internat. Course Pediat. Pulmology, 2002—; Jessie Ball duPont prof. & chmn. dept. pediat. Va. Commonwealth U., 2009—, prof., biomed. engring., prof. physiology & biophysics, 2009—; physician-in-chief Children's Hosp. Richmond, Va., 2010—. Pres. Internat. Congress Pediatric Pulmonology, 2004—06; trustee Am. Respiratory Care Found., 2005—; mem. editl. bd. 12 med. jours. Author: Therapy for Mucus Clearance Disorders (Lung Biology in Health and Disease), 2004, Antibiotics as Antiflammatory and Immunomodulatory Agents (Progress in Inflammation Research), 2005; contbr. over 200 articles to profl. jours., over 30 chapters to books. Recipient Achievement award for Excellence in Pulmonary Disease State Mgmt., Am Assn. Respiratory Care, 2007, Donald Egan Meml. Lectr. award, 2009, 27th Philip Kittredge Meml. Lectr. award, 2011, Forrest M. Bird Lifetime Sci. Achievement award, Am. Respiratory Care Found. & Am. Assn. Respiratory Care, 2008, Prix Extraordinaire, CIPP, Jessie Young medal, 2012, Past Pres. award, CIPP, 2012. Fellow: Am. Coll. Chest Physicians (Young Investigator award 1989, Critical Care Rsch. award 1990, Alfred Soffer award 2004), Am. Pediat. Assn., Royal Coll. Physicians Can.; mem.: Soc. Am. Magicians, Internat. Brotherhood Magicians, Assn. Med. Sch. Pediat. (dept. chair), Am. Pediatric Soc., Soc. Pediat. Rsch. Avocation: magic. Business E-Mail: brubin@vcu.edu.

RUBIN, DAVID LEE, humanities educator, critic, editor, book publisher, editorial consultant; b. Indpls., Sept. 30, 1939; s. Ira Bertram and Jeanne Iva (Gamso) R.; m. Carolyn Dettman, June 12, 1965; 1 child, Timothy Craig. BA, U. Tenn., 1962; cert., U. Paris, 1963; MA, U. Ill., 1964, PhD, 1967. Instr. French U. Ill., Urbana, 1966-67; asst. prof. U. Chgo., 1967-69, U. Va., Charlottesville, 1969-74, assoc. prof., 1974-82, prof. French, 1982-2001, mem. Fulbright selection com., 1996—, mem. com. on comparative lit., 1997-2001, prof. emeritus, adj. univ. seminar program, 2001—12; seminar dir. Folger Inst., 1989; academic and profl. writing program U. Va., 2010; cons. Ctr. Undergrad. Excellence, 2001—; facilitator Themis Argumentation Forum, 2011—12. Chair poetry bd. Va. Quar. Rev., 2003—10, Great Books discussion leader Jefferson Inst. Life-long Learning, U. Va., 2001-08, 2014-, Humanities Forum Moderator Charlottesville Sr. Ctr., 2008-14; assoc. ctr. advanced studies U. Va.,1973, 1979, 80-81, 87, 93, 99-2000; pub., editor-in-chief Rookwood Press, 1992—; founder, prin. Fox Hill Editl., 2010-; cons. PMLA, Can. Coun., Etudes littéraires françaises, NEH, numerous univ. presses; editl. adv. Human Impacts Inst., 2010-; lectr., spkr. in field. Author: Higher Hidden Order, 1972, The Knot of Artifice, 1981, A Pact with Silence, 1991; editor: The Selected Poetry and Prose of John T. Napier, 1972, La poésie française du premier 17e siècle, 1986, 2d edit., 2006, Sun King, 1991; co-editor: La Cohérence Intérieure, 1977, Convergences, 1989, The Ladder of High Designs, 1991, The Fulbright Difference, 1993; founding editor Continuum, 1989-93, EMF: Studies in Early Modern France, 1994-2008, EMF Critiques, 1994-, Rookwood Texts, 1997—, Rookwood Reprints, 2002—; mem. editl. bd. Purdue Studies in Romance Literatures, 1975-2001, Oeuvres et Critiques, 1976-2001, French Rev., 1986-94; Am. corr. Cahiers Maynard, 1973-2001, Cahiers Tristan L'Hermite, 1989-2001; contbr. articles to profl. jours., chpts. to books. U.S. State Dept. Fulbright fellow, 1963—64, fellow, Woodrow Wilson Found., 1963—65, Guggenheim Found., 1980—81, Hewlett fellow, summer, 1997, The Shape of Change: Studies in Honor of David Lee Rubin, 2002. Mem. MLA, ACLU, Phi Beta Kappa. Avocations: reading, travel. Home: 520 Rookwood Pl Charlottesville VA 22903-4734 Personal E-mail: dlr93039@yahoo.com.

RUBIN, DAVID STUART, curator, art critic, art historian, artist; b. LA, June 18, 1949; s. Allen Morris and Ruth Elinor (Persky) R. AB in Philosophy, UCLA, 1972; MA in Art History, Harvard U., 1974. Mus. mgmt. Mus. Mgmt. Inst., 1999. Tchg. asst. Harvard U., 1973—75, asst. prof. art history, 1977—82; asst. dir. Galleries of The Claremont Colls., 1977-82; prof. Topical Art Hist. Survey Sch. Visual Arts, 1976—77; art critic Art in America, NYC, 1981-89; adj. curator San Francisco Mus. Modern Art, 1983-85; dir. exhbns. San Francisco Art Inst., 1983-85; dir. Freedman Gallery, Albright Coll., 1986-90; assoc. dir., chief curator Cleve. Ctr. Contemporary Art, 1990-94; curator 20th Century Art Phoenix Art Mus., 1994—99; curator visual arts Contemporary Arts Ctr., New Orleans, 2000—06; Brown Found. curator contemporary art San Antonio Mus. Art, 2006—. Guest curator security Pacific Nat. Bank, LA, 1982; project dir. Artist/Architect collaboration between Mary Miss and Adele Santos, Albright Coll., Reading, Pa., 1988—90, Outside the Frame: Performance and the Object, 1991—93; juror nat. art exhibitions, 1991—; arts peer Art in Architecture Design Excellence Prog., US Gen. Svcs. Adminstrn., 2002—; mem. U.S. Commr. Cuenca Bienal Painting, 1996; peer reviewer Mus. Assessment Program, 2007—. Contbg. editor Arts mag., NYC, 1979-81; author exhbn. catalogues Black and White are Colors, 1979, Contemporary Triptychs, 1982, Jay De Feo, 1984, Wally Hedrick, 1985, Concerning the Spiritual, the 80's, 1985, Contemporary Hispanic Shrines, 1989, Cynthia Carlson, 1989, Donald Lipski, 1990, Cruciformed, 1991, Petah Coyne, 1992, Old Glory, 1994, It's Only Rock and Roll, 1995, Phoenix Triennial, 1998, Photography Now, 2000, 2001 Entergy Louisiana Open, Chelsea Rising, 2001, Expanding Universe: The Recent Paintings of Al Held, 2002, 2003 Louisiana Biennial, Douglas Bourgeois, 2003, Birdspace: A Post-Audubon Artist's Aviary, 2004, The Culture of Queer: A Tribute to J.B. Harter, 2005, Celebrating Freedom: The Art of Willie Birch, 2006, Stuart Allen: Mapping Daylight, 2007, Playing with Time, 2008, Chocolate: A Photography Exhibition, 2008, Marcia Gygli King: Botanical Paintings, 2009, Ry Cooder/Vincent Valdez: El Chavez Ravine, 2009, John Hernandez Zoes Room, 2009, Waterflow, 2009, Culinary Delights: Photographs by David Halliday, 2009, Psychedelic: optical and Visionary Art Since the 1960s, 2010, The Brothers Montiel Klint, 2010, Animal Instinct Photographs of Daniel Lee, 2011, Adad Hannah, 2012, Sylvie Blocher: The Color of Confusion, 2014; contbr. articles to Arts, 1976-80, Art in Am. mag., 1981-89, Artweek, 1978-83; film appearances include Drapeau, 1998, Exhibiting artist solo exhibitions: Blue Star Contemporary Art Center, San Antonio, 2007; Barrister's Gallery, New Orleans, 2010; High Wire Arts, San Antonio, 2012; group exhibitions: Tenri Cultural Center, New York, 2005; Domestic Setting, Los Angeles, 2006; Talento Bilingue de Houston, 2011, Second Site, San Antonio, 2014 Trustee Working Theatre, Cleve., 1993—94. Nat. Endowment Humanities M us. fellow, 1975-76, S.R.Guggenheim Mus. summer fellow, 1976, Northern Ohio LIVE award of Achievement in Visual Arts, 1992, 1994, Hon. Lifetime Docent, Phoenix Art Mus., 1999; named San Antonio Current Best Local Curator, 2011; FotoSeptiembreUSA Choice award, Mus. Curator, 2013 Mem. Internat. Assn. Art Critics, Coll. Art Assn., American Alliance of Museums., Assn. Art Mus. Curators. Democrat. Jewish. Home: 427 Quentin Dr San Antonio TX 78201 Personal E-mail: dsr18@satx.rr.com.

RUBIN, GERALD MAYER, biochemistry researcher, educator; b. Boston, Mar. 31, 1950; s. Benjamin H. and Edith (Weisberg) R.; m. Lynn S. Mastalir, May 7, 1978; 1 child, Alan F. BS, MIT, 1971; PhD in Molecular Biology, Cambridge U., Eng., 1974, ScD, 2002. Helen Hay Whitney Found. fellow Stanford U. Sch. Medicine, Calif., 1974-76; asst. prof. biol. chemistry Sidney Farber Cancer Inst.-Harvard U. Med. Sch., Boston, 1977-80; instructor, embryology Marine Biol. Lab., Woods Hole, Mass.; staff mem., dept. embryology Carnegie Instn. of Washington, Balt., 1980-83; John D. MacArthur prof. genetics, dept. molecular & cell biology U. Calif., Berkeley, 1983—2000, head, divsn. genetics, dept. molecular and cellular biology, 1987—95, HHMI investigator, 1987—2000, dir. Drosophila Genome Ctr., 1992—2006, prof. genetic dept. molecular & cell biology, 2000—09; v.p. biomedical rsch. Howard Hughes Med. Inst., Chevy Chase, Md., 2000—01, v.p., dir. planning Janelia Farm Rsch. Campus, Ashburn, Va., 2002—03, v.p., dir., 2003—10; exec. dir. Janelia Farm Rsch. Campus, Ahsburn, Va., 2010—. Adj. prof. dept. biochemistry and biophysics U. Calif. Sch. Medicine, San Francisco, 1987-; assoc. faculty mem., cell and molecular biology divsn. Lawrence Berkeley Nat. Lab., Calif.; mem. sci. adv. bd. Athena Neurosci., Inc., Tularik, Inc.; co-founder, chair sci. adv. bd. Exelixis Pharm., Inc. Predoctoral fellow, NSF, Helen Hay Whitney Found. Fellow; Recipient Young Scientist award Passano Found., 1983, Eli Lilly award in biol. chemistry, Am. Chem. Soc., 1985; co-recipient Newcomb Cleveland prize, AAAS, 2000, George W. Beadle Medal, Genetics Soc. Am., 2003; named Scientist of Yr., R&D Mag., 2006. Mem. AAAS, NAS (US Steel Found. award in molecular biology, 1985), Inst. Medicine, Genetics Soc. Am. Med., Phi Beta Kappa, Phi Lambda Epsilon, Royal Soc. UK (fgn.); Fellow Am. Acad. Arts & Sciences, Am. Acad. Microbiology. Office: Janelia Farm Rsch Campus Howard Hughes Med Inst 19700 Helix Dr Ashburn VA 20147-2408 Business E-Mail: rubing@janelia.hhmi.org.

RUBIN, LARRY JEROME, retired literature educator; b. Bayonne, NJ, Feb. 14, 1930; s. Abraham Joseph and Lillian (Strongin) R. BA, Emory U., 1951, MA, 1952, PhD, 1956. Instr. English Ga. Inst. Tech., Atlanta, 1955—58, asst. prof., 1958—65, assoc. prof., 1965—73, prof., 1973—99; ret., 1999. Author: The World's Old Way, 1962 (award Ga. Writers Assn. 1963), Lanced in Light, 1967 (award Dixie Coun. 1967), All My Mirrors Lie, 1975 (award Dixie Coun. 1975), Unanswered Calls, 1997; contbr. articles on various authors to profl. jours. Recipient Smith-Mundt lectureship U.S. State Dept., 1961-62; Fulbright lectureship, 1966-67, 69-70, 71-72. Mem. Poetry Soc. Am. (Reynolds lyric award 1961, ann. award 1973), South Atlantic MLA, Coll. English Assn. Democrat. Jewish. Home: PO Box 15014 Atlanta GA 30333-0014

RUBIN, MELVIN LYNNE, ophthalmologist, educator; b. San Francisco, May 10, 1932; s. Morris and May (Gelman) R.; m. Lorna Isen, June 21, 1953; children: Gabrielle, Daniel, Michael. AA, U. Calif., Berkeley, 1951, BS, 1953; MD, U. Calif., San Francisco, 1957; MS, State U. Iowa, 1961. Diplomate Am. Bd. Ophthalmology, 1963. Intern U. Calif. Hosp., San Francisco, 1957-58; resident in ophthalmology State U. Iowa, 1958-61; attending surgeon Georgetown U., Washington, 1961-63; asst. prof. surgery U. Fla. Med. Sch., Gainesville, 1963-66, assoc. prof. ophthalmology, 1966-67, prof. ophthalmology, 1967—97, prof. emeritus, 1997—, chmn. dept. ophthalmology, 1978-95, eminent scholar, 1989-97, eminent scholar emeritus, 1997. Author: Studies in Physiological Optics, 1965, Fundamentals of Visual Science, 1969, Optics for Clinicians, 1971, 2d edit., 1974, 25th ann. edit., 1995, The Fine Art of Prescribing Glasses, 1978, 3d edit., 2004; editor: Dictionary of Eye Terminology, 1984, Eye Care Notes, 1989, revised edit., 2001, Taking Care of Your Eyes, 2003; cons. editl. bd. Survey Ophthalmology; contbr. more than 100 articles to profl. jours. Co-founder Citizens for Pub. Schs., Inc., 1965, ProArteMusica Gainesville, Inc., 1969, pres., 1971-73; mem. Thomas Ctr. Adv. Bd. for the Arts, 1978-84, nat. sci. adv. bd. Helen Keller Eye Rsch. Found., 1989-96; bd. dirs. Hippodrome State Theater, 1981-87, Friends of Photography Ansel Adams Ctr., 1991-97, Friends of Classic 89 public radio, 2002-08, U. Fla. Found., 2005-, Friends of Music; trustee U. Fla. Performing Arts Ctr., 1995—2008; chmn. nat. art coun. U. Fla. Harn Mus. Art, 2005—; With USPHS, 1961-63. Recipient Best Med. Book for 1978 award Am. Med. Writers Assn., 1979, Shaler Richardson award for svc. to medicine Fla. Soc. Ophthalmology, 1995; M.L. Rubin Ann. Lectureship established in his honor by Fla. Soc. of Ophthalmology, 1993. Fellow ACS, Am. Acad. Ophthalmology (sec., dir. 1978-92, pres. 1988, Sr. Honor award 1987. Guest of Honor 1992; Spl. Recognition award 2010), Found. Am. Acad. Ophthalmology (bd. trustees, 1988-95, chmn., 1992-94), Joint Commn. on Allied Health Pers. in Ophthalmology (Statesman of Yr. award 1987); mem. Assn. Rsch. in Vision and Ophthalmology (trustee 1973-78, pres. 1979), Retina Soc., Macula Soc., Club Jules Gonin, NY Acad. Sci., Fla. Soc. Ophthalmology, Am. Ophthal. Soc. (coun. 1998-2002, chmn. 2002), Pan Am. Soc. Ophthalmology, Ophthalmic Photographers Soc., Alachua County Med. Soc., Fla. Med. Assn., AMA (editorial bd. Archives of Ophthalmology 1975-85), Sigma Xi, Alpha Omega Alpha, Phi Kappa Phi, U. Calif. San Francisco Medicine Alumni Assn. (Alumnus of Yr. 2012). Office: U Fla Med Ctr PO Box 100284 Gainesville FL 32610-0284 Office Phone: 352-273-8790. Business E-Mail: melrubin@ufl.edu.

RUBIN, ROSE MOHR, economics professor emeritus; b. Montgomery, Ala., Nov. 20, 1939; d. Michael and Bernice (Solomon) Mohr; m. Richard M. Rubin, June 20, 1963; children: Mark, Debra. BS, Wellesley Coll., 1961; MA, Emory U., 1966; PhD, Kans. State U., 1968. Economist OEA, State of Kans., Manhattan, 1969-70; asst. prof. Miss. State U., Starkville, 1970-77; resident in pub. svc. NSF, Fort Worth, 1980-81; asst. prof. econs. U. North Tex., Denton, 1977-84, assoc. prof., 1984-90, prof., 1990-94; chair dept. econs. U. Memphis, 1994-96, prof. economics, 1996—2009. Robert Woods Johnson fellow Johns Hopkins U., Balt., 1986-87; vis. fellow Brookings Inst., Washington, 1987; rsch. fellow, Urban Child Inst., Memphis, 2007-09; exec. bd. mem. Plough Towers, Tenn. Comm. Aging, 2010-; pres. Memphis Wellesley Coll. Alumnae Club. Bd. dirs. Vis. Nurses Assn., Ft. Worth, 1987-90, Temple Beth El, Ft. Worth, 1988-91, Plough Towers, Memphis, 1998-2004, 08-, exec. bd. mem., 2010-; adv. coun. Mid-South Commn. Aging, 2008-, Tenn. Commn. on Aging and Disability, 2010-. Assoc. Danforth Found., 1981-87; grantee Robert Wood Johnson Found., 1987-88, Andrus Found. grantee Am. Assn. Ret. Persons, 1990-94, Urban Child Inst., 2007-08. Mem.: Mo. Valley Econs. Assn. (bd. dirs. 1998—), Midsouth Acad. Econs. and Fin. (exec. bd. 1983—87, v.p. 1991—92), Assn. for Social Econs. (exec. coun. 1988—90), Southwestern Social Sci. Assn. (treas. 1990—93, v.p. 1998—, pres. 2000—01), Southwestern Econs. Assn. (treas. 1981—89, v.p. 1989—99, pres.-elect 1990—91, pres. 1991—92), Phi Kappa Phi, Omicron Delta Epsilon, Golden Key (hon.), Phi Chi Theta (hon.). Business E-Mail: rmrubin@memphis.edu.

RUBIN, STEVEN D., lawyer; b. June 1, 1960; BA in Economics, Tulane U., 1982; JD with honors, U. Fla., 1986. Bar: Fla. 1986. Assoc. Stearns, Weaver, Miller, Weissler, Alhadeff & Sitterson, 1986—91, shareholder, 1991—2000, bd. dirs., 1998—2000; sr. v.p., gen. counsel Telergy, Inc., 2000—01; sr. v.p., gen. counsel & sec. Ivax Corp., Miami, 2001—. Office: Ivax Corp 4400 Biscayne Blvd Miami FL 33137 Office Phone: 305-575-6000. Office Fax: 305-575-6055. E-mail: steven_rubin@ivax.com.

RUBINSON, HOWARD ALAN, physician; b. Bklyn., Aug. 24, 1949; s. Samuel and Hilda (Cohen) R.; m. Carol Berman, May 16, 1976; children: Roger, Abby. AB, Cornell U., Ithaca, NY, 1971; MD, Hahnemann Med. Coll., Phila., 1975. Diplomate Am. Bd. Radiology. Radiology instr. Sch. Medicine U. Miami, Fla., 1979-81, asst. prof. radiology Fla., 1981-84; mem. attending staff North Beach Hosp., Ft. Lauderdale, Fla., 1984-89, North Ridge Med. Ctr., Ft. Lauderdale, Fla., 1989—2006, Hollywood Med. Ctr., Fla., 1998—2006, Parkway Regional Med. Ctr., 2001—05; attending staff Holy Cross Hosp., Ft. Lauderdale, Fla., 2004—, Mercy Hosp., Miami, Fla., 2005—12. Contbr. articles to profl. jours. Mem. Am. Coll. Radiology, Am. Soc. Emergency Radiology, Soc. Breast Imaging, Radiol. Soc. N.Am., Am. Roentgen Ray Soc., Soc. Thoracic Radiology, South Fla. Radiol. Soc. (pres. 1996-97), Fla. Radiol. Soc., Fla. Med. Assn., Broward County Med. Assn. Office: 2929 E Commercial Blvd Ste 600 Fort Lauderdale FL 33308 Personal E-mail: hrubinson@comcast.net.

RUBIO, EDMUNDO RAUL, physician, educator; b. Santiago, Chile, Mar. 15, 1965; MD, U. Chile, 1990. Chief resident New Hanover Regional Med. Ctr., Wilmington, NC; mem. med. exec. com. Select Splty. Hosp. Gulfport, Miss., 2006—08, dir. critical care program, 2007—08; dir. critical care & respiratory units Garden Pk. Med. Ctr. Gulfport, Miss., 2007—08; CEO, founder Gulf Coast Lung & Sleep Medicine Inst. Gulfport, Miss., 2006—08; dir., interventional pulmonology program, asst. prof. medicine Tulane U. New Orleans, 2006—08; chief, sect. pulmonary, critical care, environ. and sleep medicine, asst. prof. medicine Carilion Clinic Va. Tech Carilion Sch. Medicine, 2008—, preceptor LACE program, 2010—. Mem. computer med. info. sys. implementation com. Meml. Hosp. Gulfport, 2003—05; mem. med. exec. com. Carilion Clinic Roanoke, Va., 2008—, mem. clin. practice com., 2009—10; dir. Gulf Coast Sleep Lab., tenet Healthcare, 2002—06; co-dir. carilion Clinic, Va., 2008—; adv. bd., co-med. dir. Jefferson Coll. Health Scis., 2013—. Recipient Spl. award, New Hanover Regional Med. Ctr. Wilmington; Pulmonary and Critical Care Medicine fellowship, Tulane U. New Orleans, Sleep Medicine fellowship, Tulane U. Hosp. and Clinic New Orleans. Fellow: Am. Coll. Chest Physicians; mem.: Am. Thoracic Soc. Avocations: chess, swimming. Office: 1906 Bellevue Ave Office 320 Roanoke VA 24014 Office Fax: 540-983-1133.*

RUBIO, MARCO ANTONIO, United States Senator from Florida, former state legislator; b. Miami, Fla., May 28, 1971; s. Mario and Oria (Garcia) Rubio; m. Jeanette Dousdebed, 1997; children: Amanda, Daniella, Anthony, Dominic. Student, Tarkio Coll., 1989—90; BS in Political Science, U. Fla., 1993; JD, U. Miami Sch. Law, 1996. City commr., West Miami, Fla., 1998—2000; mem. Dist. 111 Fla. House of Reps., 2000—08, majority leader, 2003—06, spkr., 2006—08; vis. prof. Fla. Internat. U. Met. Ctr., 2008; US Senator from Fla. Washington, 2011—; mem. US Senate Commerce, Sci. & Transp. Com., Washington, 2011—, US Senate Select Com. on Intelligence, Washington, 2011—, US Senate Small Bus. & Entrepreneurship, Washington, 2011—, US Senate Fgn. Rels. Com., Washington, 2011—. Polit. analyst Univision, 2008. Author: 100 Innovative Ideas for Florida's Future: A Plan of Action, 2006, An American Son: A Memoir, 2012. Recipient Freshman Legislator of Yr., Florida Petroleum Marketers Assn.; named one of The 100 Most Influential People in the World, TIME mag., 2012. Republican. Roman Catholic. Office: US Senate 284 Russell Senate Office Bldg Washington DC 20510 also: 8669 NW 36th St Ste 110 Miami FL 33166 Office Phone: 202-224-3041, 305-418-8553. Office Fax: 202-228-5171.*

RUBNER, MICHAEL, international relations educator, university administrator; b. Tel Aviv, Aug. 3, 1940; came to U.S., 1956; s. Maurice and Eva Edith (Katz) R.; m. Audrey Ann Pfingst, Feb. 16, 1969; children: Daniel, Jessica. BA, Rockford Coll., Ill., 1962; MA, Marquette U., 1964; PhD, U. Calif., Berkeley, 1975. Instr. James Madison Coll. Mich. State U., East Lansing, 1970-75, asst. prof., 1975-80, assoc. prof., 1980-85, prof., 1985—2006; ret., 2006. Univ. faculty grievance ofcl. Mich. State U., 1989-2004 Co-author: The Palestinian Problem and U.S. Policy, 1986; contbr. articles to profl. jours. Pres. Jacob Schiff B'nai B'rith Lodge 694, Lansing, 1980-93; pres. Congregation Shaarey Zedek, East Lansing, 2002-04; v.p. Temple Shalom, Naples, Fla., 2010-11. Mem. Acad. Polit. Sci., Internat. Studies Assn. (governing coun. Midwest divsn. 1986-92), U.S. Arms Control Assn., Midwest Consortium for Internat. Security Studies, Phi Beta Kappa (pres. Epsilon of Mich. 1983-84), Alpha Sigma Nu, Phi Beta Delta. Democrat. E-mail: exfgomsu@aol.com.

RUBRIGHT, JAMES ALFRED, manufacturing executive; b. Phila., Dec. 17, 1946; s. James Alfred and Helen Lucille (Evans) R. (deceased); m. Mary Elizabeth Angelich, Dec. 30, 1987; children: Noah Michael, Benjamin James, Jami Anne, Nathaniel Drew, James McCurdy, William Angelich. BA, Yale U., 1969; JD, U. Va., 1972. Bar: Ga. 1972. Ptnr. King & Spalding, Atlanta, 1972-94; sr. v.p., gen. counsel Sonat Inc., Birmingham, 1994-97; pres. So. Natural Gas Co. (subs. Sonat Inc.), Birmingham, 1997-98; exec. v.p. Sonat Inc., Birmingham, 1998-99; chmn., CEO Rock-Tenn Co., Norcross, Ga., 1999—. Bd. dirs. Avondale Inc., AGL Resources Inc., 2001—. Office: Rock-Tenn Co 504 Thrasher St Norcross GA 30071-1914 Office Phone: 770-448-2193. Business E-Mail: jrubright@rocktenn.com.

RUBY, ROY HARRIS, academic administrator; b. Yazoo City, Miss., Jan. 22, 1939; s. Albert Roy and Jennie Louise (Harris) Ruby; m. Patricia Randle, Feb. 11, 1962; children: Mary, Robert Harris. BA in Polit. Sci., Miss. State U., 1961, MA in Polit. Sci., 1966, EdD, 1973. Program dir. univ. union Miss. State U., 1964—66, coord. student activities, 1966—67, asst. dean of men, 1967—69, acting dean of men, 1969—70, acting dean of students, 1970, asst. dean student devel., 1971—74, assoc. dean student devel., 1974, dir. Jackson Br., 1974—78, asst. to v.p. student affairs, 1978—81, dean student adminstrv. svcs., 1981—85, v.p. student affairs, 1985—2002, dean Coll. Edn., 2002—04, interim pres., 2008—. Lectr. in field. Trustee Starkville Separate Mcpl. Sch. Dist., 1980—84, pres., 1983. 2d lt. US Army, 1961—63, maj. USAR. Mem.: Miss. Counselors Assn., So. Assn. Coll. Student Affairs, Nat. Assn. State Univs. and Land Grant Colls., Nat. Assn. Student Pers. Adminstrs., Phi Delta Kappa, Pi Delta Epsilon, Phi Alpha Theta, Phi Kappa Phi. Methodist. Home: 104 Langston Ct Starkville MS 39759-4242 Office: Miss State U PO Box 6018 610 Allen Hall Mississippi State MS 39762 Office Phone: 662-325-3221. E-mail: president@msstate.edu.

RUCHO, ROBERT A., state legislator; b. Dec. 8, 1948; m. Theresa Rucho; 2 children. BA, Northeastern U., 1970; DDS, MCV/VCU Sch. Dentistry, 1974, 1974; advanced degree in Prosthodontics, Boston U., 1977; MBA, U. N.C., Charlotte, 1994. Dentist; mem. Dist. 39 NC State Senate, 1996—. Mem. appropriations on Dept. of Transp., appropriations/base budget, commerce, edn./higher edn., judiciary II, rules and ops. of Senate, transp. coms. N.C. State Senate, ranking minority mem. health care. Republican. Catholic. Office: NC Senate 300 N Salisbury St Room 300 A Raleigh NC 27603-5925 Office Phone: 919-733-5655, 704-847-3461. Fax: 919-733-2599. Business E-Mail: Bob.Rucho@ncleg.net.

RUCKER, DARIUS, musician; b. Charleston, SC, May 13, 1966; s. Carolyn; m. Beth Leonard, 2000; 1 child, Daniella Rose, Jack; 1 child (from a previous relationship) Carolyn Pearl. Musician: (albums) (with Hootie & The Blowfish) Cracked Rear View, 1994, Fairweather Johnson, 1996, Musical Chairs, 1998, Take 2, 2000, Hootie & the Blowfish, 2003, Looking for Lucky, 2005, (solo) Back to Then, 2002, Learn to Live, 2008, Charleston, SC 1966, 2010, True Believers, 2013, (songs) (with Hootie & the Blowfish) Let Her Cry, 1994 (Best Pop Vocal Performance by a Duo or Group, Grammy Awards, 1995), Wagon Wheel, 2013 (Best Country Solo Performance, Grammy Awards, 2014). Recipient Best New Artist award (with Hootie & the Blowfish), Grammy Awards, 1995, New Artist of Yr. award, Country Music Assn., 2009. Office: Essential Broadcast Media LLC 21 Music Sq W Nashville TN 37203*

RUDACILLE, SHARON VICTORIA, retired technologist; b. Ranson, W.Va., Sept. 11, 1950; d. Albert William and Roberta Mae (Anderson) Rudacille. BS cum laude, Shepherd Coll., 1972. Registered med. technologist Am. Soc. Clin. Pathologies, 1972. Med. technologist VA Ctr., Martinsburg, W.Va., 1972—2006. Instr. Sch. Med. Tech., 1972—76, assoc. coord. edn., 1976—77, edn. coord., 1977—78, quality assurance officer clin. chemistry, 1978—80, lab. svc. quality assurance and edn. officer, 1980—84, clin. chemistry sect. leader, 1984—86, staff med. technologist, 1986—94, supervisory med. technologist, 1994—95, sr. med. technologist, 1995—; adj. faculty mem. Shippensburg (Pa.) State Coll., 1977—78, Shepherd Coll., 1977—78. Mem.: Shepherd Coll. Alumni Assn., W.Va. Soc. Med. Technologists, Am. Soc. Clin. Pathologists, Am. Soc. Med. Tech., Sigma Pi Epsilon. Bapt.

RUDDICK, LINDA S., bank executive; V.p. Colonial Bank, Atlanta, 1996—2004, sr. comml. loan officer, 1996—2004; sr. v.p. credit adminstrn. Flag Bank, Atlanta, 2004—06; mgr. comml. policy and procedure RBC Bank, 2006—11; dir. credit adminstrn. State Bank & Trust Co., Macon, Ga., 2011—, exec. v.p., 2011—. Office: State Bank & Trust Company 1535 Bass Rd Macon GA 31210 Office Phone: 478-757-3300.

RUDLEY, JOHN M., academic administrator; m. Docia Rudley. BA, U. Toledo; M.Ed. in Adminstrn. and Supervision, Tenn. State U., ED.D in Adminstrn. CPA Tenn. Accountant Coopers and Lybrand, LA, Seattle; internal auditor Tex. So. U., v.p. fiscal affairs, 1984; adminstr. U. Tenn., Chattanooga; sr. tech. advisor US Dept. Edn.; vice chancellor bus. and fin. Tenn. Bd. Regents, 1995—2002; vice chancellor adminstrn. and fin. U. Houston Sys., 2002—08, interim chancellor, 2007—08; v.p. adminstrn. and fin. U. Houston, 2002—08, interim pres., 2007—08; pres. Tex. So. U., Houston, 2008—. Mem.: Bioltonston Bd., 100 Black Men (Houston), Internat. Edn. Consortium (chmn.), Tex. Med. Ctr. (CEO, group mem.), Houston Tech. Bd., Greater Houston Partnership Bd., Tenn. Soc. of CPAs. Office: Tex So U Hannah Hall, Suite 220 3100 Cleburne St Houston TX 77004 Office Phone: 713-313-7011.

RUDNICK, IRENE KRUGMAN, lawyer, educator, former state legislator; b. Columbia, SC, Dec. 27, 1929; d. Jack and Jean (Getter) Krugman; m. Harold Rudnick, Nov. 7, 1954 (dec.); children: Morris, Helen Gail. AB cum laude, U. SC, 1949, JD, 1952, EdD (hon.), 2012. Bar: (S.C.) 1952. Individual practice law, Aiken, SC, 1954—; now ptnr. Rudnick & Rudnick; instr. bus. law U. S.C., Aiken, 1962—; tchr. Warrenville Elem. Sch., 1965-70; supt. edn. Aiken County, 1970-72; mem. S.C. Ho. of Reps., 1972—78, 1980—84, 1986—94. Pres. emeritus Adath Yeshurun Synagogue, Aiken County Dem. Party, S.C. Dem. Party; hon. mem. Aiken Able-Disabled; life mem. U. SC Alumni Assn. Recipient Citizen of Yr. award, 1976-77, Bus. and Profl. Women's Career Woman of Yr., 1978, 94, Aiken County Friend of Edn. award, 1985, 93, Outstanding Legis. award Disabled Vets., 1991, Citizen of Yr. award Planned Parenthood, 1994, Sertoma Svc. to Mankind award, 1996, Pickens Salley So. Woman of Distinction award, 2005; named Aiken County C. of C. Woman of Yr., 2005. Mem. AAUW (life), Aiken Hist. Soc., Hist. Aiken Found., Aiken Mended Hearts, Aiken Master Gardners, Alpha Delta Kappa, Order Eastern Star, Adath Yeshurun Sisterhood, Hadassah (life), Am. Legion Aux., SC Bar Assn.(former sr. bar. com. mem.) Office: PO Box 544 135 Pendleton St NW Aiken SC 29801

RUDO, MILTON, retired manufacturing executive; b. Balt., Jan. 17, 1919; s. Saul E. and Bertha (Berkowitz) R.; m. Roslind Mandel, Mar. 27, 1943 (dec. Aug. 13, 2010); children: Stephanie Ellen, Neil Dennis. BA, Johns Hopkins U., 1940; AMP, Harvard U., 1964. Various positions Brunswick Corp., Skokie, Ill., 1940-66, corp. v.p., pres. Bowling divsn. Chgo., 1966-74, group v.p. recreation bus., 1974-84, ret., 1984, cons. to the CEO, 1984-87; dir., cons. to the CEO Donlen Leasing Corp., Northbrook Inc., 1986—90. Pres. Nat. Bowling Hall of Fame and Mus., 1979. Capt. AUS, 1942-45, ETO. Recipient ann. award N.Y. Mktg. Club, 1960, Industry Svc. award, 1973; named to Bowling Hall of Fame, 1984; decorated with 3 Battle Star. Mem. Nat. Bowling Coun. (pres. 1972), Briarwood Country Club (Deerfield, Ill., pres. 1965-67), Hamlet Country Club (Delray Beach Fla.). Home (Summer): 1755 Lake Cook Rd Highland Park IL 60035 Home (Winter): 712 Pine Lake Delray Beach FL 33445

RUDOLPH, ANDREW HENRY, retired dermatologist, educator; b. Detroit, Jan. 30, 1943; s. John J. and Mary M. Rudolph; children: Kristen Ann, Kevin Andrew. MD cum laude, U. Mich., 1966. Diplomate Am. Bd. Dermatology. Intern Univ. Hosp., U. Mich. Med. Ctr., Ann Arbor, 1966-67, resident dept. dermatology, 1967-70; pvt. practice medicine specializing in dermatology, 1972—2007; ret., 2007. Asst. prof. dermatology Baylor Coll. Medicine, Houston, 1972-75, assoc. prof., 1975-83, clin. prof., 1983—; chief dermatology svc. VA Hosp., Houston, 1977-82; mem. staff Meth. Hosp. Mem. editl. bd. Jour. Sexually Transmitted Diseases, 1977-85; contbr. to med. publs. Served as surgeon USPHS, 1970-72. Regent's scholar U. Mich., 1966. Fellow Am. Acad. Dermatology; mem. AMA, Am. Dermatol. Assn., Tex. Med. Assn., Harris County Med. Soc., Houston Dermatol. Soc. (past pres.), Tex. Dermatol. Soc., Skin Cancer Found., Am. Venereal Disease Assn. (past pres.), Mich. Alumni Assn. (life), Alpha Omega Alpha, Phi Kappa Phi, Phi Rho Sigma, Theta Xi.

RUDOLPH, GILBERT LAWRENCE, lawyer; b. LA, Aug. 23, 1946; BA, Ariz. State U., 1967; JD, U. Cin., 1973. Bar: D.C. 1973, U.S. Dist. Ct. D.C. 1974, U.S. Ct. Appeals (D.C. cir.) 1974, Ariz. 1975, U.S. Dist. Ct. Ariz. 1975, Calif. 1979. Assoc. Streich, Lang, Weeks & Cardon, P.A., Phoenix, 1975-78; ptnr. Gilbert L. Rudolph, P.C., Phoenix, 1978-87; sr. mem. O'Connor, Cavanagh, Anderson, Killingsworth & Beshears, P.A., 1987—99; shareholder, co-chair fin. regulatory & compliance practice group Greenberg Traurig LLP, 1999—. Lectr. on lending issues; mem., bd. observers Muhlenberg Coll., 2011—. Bd. dirs. Make-A-Wish Found. of Am., 1984—89, Aid to Adoption of Spl. Kids, Ariz., 1995—2003. Fellow Am. Coll. Consumer Fin. Svcs. Lawyers (regent 2011-); mem. ABA (com. on consumer fin. svcs. bus. law sect. 1981—, com. on comml. fin. svcs. 1989—, mem. com. on uniform comml. code 1992—), Conf. on Consumer Fin. Law (governing com. 1986-, pres. 2009-12, chmn. 2012-). Republican. Jewish. Office Phone: 602-445-8206. Business E-Mail: rudolphg@gtlaw.com.*

RUDOLPH, LAWRENCE, lawyer; BA in English, Adelphi U., 1973; JD, Georgetown U. Law Ctr., 1976. Bar: DC, Pa., admitted to: DC Dist. Ct., Cir. Ct. Appeals. Staff atty. Office of Preceedings US Interstate Commerce Commn., 1976—78; assoc. Verner, Liipfert, Bernhard, McPherson and Hand, Washington, 1978—82; sr. atty. then dep. asst. dir. Office of Hearings and Appeals, US Dept. Energy, 1982—88; asst. gen. counsel NSF, Arlington, Va., 1988, dep. gen. counsel, 1988, gen. counsel, 1995—. Bd. trustee Adelphi U. Recipient Presdl. Rank award of Meritious Exec., 1997. Mem.: ABA, Pa. Bar Assn., DC Bar Assn. Office: NSF Rm 1265S 13314 Point Pleasant Dr Fairfax VA 22033-3507 Office Phone: 703-292-8060. Office Fax: 703-292-9041. Business E-Mail: lrudolph@nsf.gov.

RUDY, STEVEN J., state legislator; b. Aug. 9, 1978; Part owner Rudy's Farm Ctr.; state rep. Dist. 1 Ky., 2005—; mem. Judiciary Com., Agr. & Small Bus. Com. Republican. Address: 221 Mt Pleasant La Center KY 42056 Office: 432H Capitol Annex Frankfort KY 40601 Home Phone: 270-224-2471; Office Phone: 270-462-3156, 502-564-8100 ext. 637. Fax: 270-462-3158.

RUFF, FRANK MILLER, state legislator; b. Bedford, Va., Sept. 22, 1949; s. Frank M. Ruff, Sr. and Mildred Thomas Ruff; m. Jessica Bowne, 1982; children: Frank Miller III, Thomas Bowne, David Harrison, Genevieve Elizabeth. Former chmn. Mecklenburg County Rep. Com.; former chmn. Dist. 61 GOP Com.; mgr. W T Grant County, 1975—76; owner Buffalo Springs Inn, 1976—80; with Ruff's Market, 1980—85; gen mgr. Boyd Mecklenburg Inc., 1985—86; pres. Able TS Inc., 1986—; vice chmn. Mecklenburg County Bd. Suprs., 1988—92; candidate, rep. senate Dist. 18 Va., 1991; state del. Dist. 61 Va., 1994—2000; state senate Dist. 15 Va., 2001—. Named Citizen of Yr., Clarksville C. of C., 1984. Mem.: Va. Retail Merchant Assn. (legis. com. mem. 1992—), Kerr Lake Protective Assn. (dir. 1992—), Roanoke River Basin Assn. (vice chmn. 1984—), Clarksville C. of C. (former pres.), Mason Club. Republican. Presbyterian. Address: 237 Old Rock Rd Clarksville VA 23927 Mailing: PO Box 332 Clarksville VA 23927 Office Phone: 804-374-5129. Business E-Mail: district15@sov.state.va.us.

RUFF, GARY KAY, lawyer; b. Lunwood, Calif., Dec. 9, 1959; BBA, Gonzaga Univ., 1981; JD, Pepperdine Univ., 1984; LLM in taxation, Georgetown Univ., 1985; M in mgmt., Northwestern Univ., 1992. Bar: Calif. 1985, Tex. 1995. Tax mgr. Deloitte & Touche; various Legal Dept. positions through v.p. & asst. gen. counsel Tenet Healthcare Corp., Dallas, 1992—2008, sr. v.p., gen. counsel, 2008—. Mem.: ABA, Tex. Bar Assn., State Bar Calif., Am. Health Lawyers Assn. Office: Tenet Healthcare Corp Ste 100 13737 Noel Rd Dallas TX 75240 also: Tenet Healthcare Corp 1445 Ross Ave Ste 1400 Dallas TX 75202-2703

RUFF, LINDY, professional hockey coach; b. Warburg, Alta., Canada, Feb. 17, 1960; m. Gaye Ruff; children: Brett, Eryn, Brian, Madeleine. Defenseman Lethbridge Broncos, 1976—79, Buffalo Sabres, 1979-89, NY Rangers, 1989-91; player, asst. coach Rochester Americans, 1991-92, San Diego Gulls; asst. coach Fla. Panthers, 1993—97; head coach Buffalo Sabres, 1997—2013, Dallas Stars, 2013—. Asst. coach Team Canada, Olympic Games, Vancouver, 2010. Vol. Children's Hosp., Buffalo, Muscular Dystrophy Assn. Recipient Jack Adams Award, 2006; named Buffalo Sabre's Rookie of the Yr., 1980, NHL Coach of Yr., Sporting News, 2006. Achievements include being the NHL's longest active-serving coach with one team. Office: c/o Dallas Stars 2601 Avenue of the Stars Frisco TX 75034*

RUFFIN, RICHARD A., orthopedic surgeon; b. Sept. 29, 1959; BS, U. Norte Dame, South Bend, Ind., 1981; MD, U. Okla., 1985. Cert. Am. Bd. Orthop. Surgery, Am. Bd. Orthop. Hand Surgery. Resident, orthop. U. iowa, Iowa City, 1985—90; fellow, upper extremity and microsurgery Kleinert Inst., Louisville, 1990—91; with Orthop. Assocs., Inc., Okla., 1991—. Named one of Golf Digest 2006 Top Golf Doctors in Am. Mem.: Arthoscopy Assn. N.Am., Am. Soc. for Surgery of the Hand, Am. Acad. Orthop. Surgeons. Office: Orthop Assocs Inc 3301NW 50th St Oklahoma City OK 73112 Office Phone: 405-947-0911. Office Fax: 405-942-5043.

RUFFING, ANNE ELIZABETH, artist; b. Bklyn. d. John Paul and Ruth Elizabeth (Price) Frampton; m. George W. Ruffing, Mar. 29, 1967; 1 dau., Elizabeth Anne. BS, Cornell U., 1964; postgrad., Drexel Inst. Tech., 1966. One-woman exhbns. include, IBM, 1966, Hall of Fame, Goshen, NY, 1971, exhibited in group shows at Internat. Women's Arts Festival, World Trade Center, NYC, 1975-76, Berkshire Mus., Pittsfield, Mass., 1965, 76, Cooperstown Mus., NY, 1969; represented in permanent collections, Met. Mus. Art, Bklyn. Mus., Library of Congress, Harvard U., Smithsonian Instn., NY Hist. Soc. Johnston Hist. Mus., Atwater Kent Mus., Albany Inst. History and Art, Whitney Mus. Am. Art, Boston Public Library. Recipient 1st place Eric Sloane award, 1974, Internat. Women's Year award, Internat. Women's Art Festival, 1976. Address: 1031 Lewis Farm Rd Zebulon NC 27597

RUIZ, BRIAN PATRICK, former radio producer; b. Austin, Tex., Dec. 27, 1975; s. Abel and Gloria Ruiz; m. Rebecca Ruiz; children: Hanna, Christian. BA in Comm., St. Edwards U., Austin. Campaign staffer Lloyd Dogget for Congress, 1994, Abel Ruiz for State Representative, 1996; radio prodr., ESPN The Zone Clear Channel Radio, 2000—04; real estate agent, 2005—07. Del. Tex. Democratic State Convention, 1994. Democrat. Office: c/o Williamson County Democratic Party Coordinated Campaign Hdqs 110 S I-35 Ste 170 Round Rock TX 78681

RUIZ, GISEL A., retail executive; b. 1970; Studied Retail Mgmt. Inst. program, Santa Clara U., BS in Mktg., 1992. Mgmt. trainee Wal-Mart Stores, Inc., 1992, asst. mgr., co-mgr., store mgr. in field ops., labor rels. mgr., dir. personnel & ops. coord., v.p., regional gen. mgr. field ops. divsn., 2006—08, exec. v.p., People, 2008—12, exec. v.p., COO Walmart U.S., 2012—. Recipient Walmart Leadership award, 2008; named Latina Exec. of Yr., Latina Style, 2010; named one of The Top 15 Elite Hispanic Women in Bus., Hispanic Bus. Mag., 2007, The Top 25 Bus. Women, 2009, The Top 25 Powerful Minority Women in Bus., Minority Enterprise Exec. Coun., 2008, The 50 Most Powerful Women in Bus., Fortune mag., 2012—13. Office: Wal-Mart Stores Inc 702 SW 8th St Bentonville AR 72716 Office Phone: 479-273-4000. Office Fax: 479-273-4053.*

RUIZ-COMAS, RAMÓN M., insurance company executive, lawyer; BBA in Acctg., U. PR, JD; completed Advance Mgmt. Program, U. Pa., 2000. CPA. Various positions KPMG LLP, 1978—90; bd. dirs. Triple-S, Inc., v.p., fin., 1990—95, sr. v.p., fin., 1995—99; sr. v.p., CFO Triple-S Mgmt. Corp., 1999—2001, exec. v.p., 2001—02, pres., CEO, bd. dirs., 2002—. Bd. dirs. Interactive Sys., Inc., Signature Ins. Agy., Inc. (subs. of Seguros Triple-S, Inc.), Seguros de Vida Triple-S, Seguros Triple-S, Inc., Triple-S Vida, Inc., Triple-C, Inc. Mem. Puerto Rico Soc. CPAs, AICPA. Office: Triple-S Management Corp 1441 F D Roosevelt Ave San Juan PR 00920 Office Phone: 787-749-4949.

RUKEYSER, M.S., JR., television consultant, writer; b. NYC, Apr. 15, 1931; s. Merryle Stanley and Berenice (Simon) Rukeyser; children: Jill Victoria, Patricia Bern. Student, U. Va., 1948-52. Reporter Albany (N.Y.) Times-Union, 1949, Internat. News Service, NYC, 1951; TV publicist Young & Rubicam, Inc., NYC, 1952-57; with NBC, 1958-80, 81-88, dir. news info. Washington, 1962, v.p. press and publicity NYC, 1963-72, v.p. corp. info., 1972-74, v.p. pub. info., 1974-77, exec. v.p. pub. info., 1977-80, 81-84, exec. v.p. corp. communications, 1984-88; v.p. comm. Newsweek Inc., 1980-81; sr. v.p. GTG Entertainment, 1988-90; pres. Rukeyser Communications, NYC, 1990—. Sr. fellow Freedom Forum Media Ctr., 1991-92. Author (with Grant Tinker): Tinker in Television: From General Sarnoff to General Electric, 1994. With US Army, 1953—54. Office: Ste 1213 616 Clearwater Park Rd West Palm Beach FL 33401-6250 Personal E-mail: budruk@gmail.com.

RUKEYSER, WILLIAM SIMON, journalist; b. NYC, June 8, 1939; s. Merryle Stanley and Berenice (Simon) R.; m. Elisabeth Mary Garnett, Nov. 21, 1963; children: Lisa Rukeyser Burn, James William. AB, Princeton U., 1961; rsch. student, Cambridge U., Eng., 1962—63; LittD (hon.), Maryville Coll., 2002. Copyreader Wall St. Jour., 1961-62, staff reporter Europe, 1963-67; assoc. editor Fortune mag., 1967-71, mem. bd. editors, 1971-72; founding mng. editor Money mag., NYC, 1972-80; mng. editor Fortune mag., 1980-86; dir. internat. bus. devel. Time Inc., 1986-88; editor in chief, exec. v.p. Whittle Communications, Knoxville, Tenn., 1988-91; chmn., CEO, Whittle Books, Knoxville, 1991-94; pres. William Rukeyser, Inc., Knoxville, 1994—; editl. dir. Corporate Board Member mag., 1998—2009; contbg. editor CNN, 1995-97; freelance book editor, 2007—. Commentator Good Morning America, ABC-TV, 1978-85, CBS Radio Stas. News Svc., 1979-86; mem. nat. adv. coun. Maryville Coll., Tenn., 1998-2007, chmn. nat. adv. coun., 2007-09; mem. adv. bd. Ctr. of Inquiry in Liberal Arts Wabash Coll., Crawfordsville, Ind., 2001—10. Editor: The Partnership: The Making of Goldman Sachs, 2008, Winning the Loser's Game, 2009, The Elements of Investing, 2010, What it Takes: Seven Secrets of Success From the World's Greatest Professional Firms, 2013. Jud. com. Union County (NJ) Med. Soc., 1977-80; co-chair capital campaign Nat. Mental Health Assn., 1984-85; liaison com. U. Tenn. Med. Ctr., 1992-99; vice chmn. U. Health Sys. Inc., 1999—2012, chmn. 2012-; chmn. bd. dirs. Knoxville Jazz Orch., 2001—09; mem. 2009-; mem. alumni adv. bd. Univ. Press Club, Princeton, 2005—, vice-chair alumni adv. bd., 2009-; mem. bd. dirs. Overseas Press Club Found., 2009-. Office: 1001 First Tennessee Plz Knoxville TN 37929 Personal E-mail: wsr@finehand.com.

RULIS, RAYMOND JOSEPH, manufacturing executive, consultant; b. New Britain, Conn., June 2, 1924; s. James Alexander and Eva (Ragauskas) R.; m. Thelma Pelchat, June 16, 1949 (dec.); children: Elaine, Jeffery, Catherine, Elizabeth, Amy, Daniel, Jean; m. Virginia Kleene, Oct. 9, 1999. BSME, U. Conn., 1949; postgrad., U. Conn., Ohio State U., Northeastern U., 1949-58; student, Fed. Exec. Inst., Charlottesville, Va., 1976. Devel. engr. Hamilton Standard, U.T.C., Windsorlocks, Conn., 1951-55; mgr. fuel controls Lycoming Textron, Stratford, Conn., 1955-59; mgr. controls and accessories GE, Lynn, Mass., 1959-62; successively program mgr. sert spacecraft, chief spacecraft engr., chief launch vehicle engr., chief engring design, program mgr. QCSEE program NASA Lewis Rsch. Ctr., Cleve., 1962-81; v.p. rsch. and. devel. Textron Turbocomponents Group, Walled Lake, Mich., 1981-92; cons., 1992—. Cons. Joint FAA/NASA Civil Aero Rsch. Document Study, 1972, Cruise Missile PRogram, 1977-78, C-17 Aircraft Source Selection Bd., 1978, Tri-Svcs. Propulsion Group, 1976-78; chmn. Conf. on Short Haul Systems, NASA, 1976; mem. exec. coun. Aerospace Industries Tech. Coun., 1988-89. Contbr. articles to profl. jours.; patentee in field. Chmn. Boy Scouts Am. Fund Drives, Cleve., 1976-78; mem. Coun. on World Affairs, Cleve., 1976-81. With US Army, 1943—46. Decorated Combat Infantryman's badge, Bronze Star medal, Purple Heart. Mem. Am. Helicopter Soc. (chmn. tech. session 1970), AIAA (chmn. tech. session 1965), Detroit Engring Soc., KC. Roman Catholic. Avocation: golf. Office: RJR Cons 9 Outpost Ln Hilton Head Island SC 29928-3820 Home Phone: 843-681-7998. Personal E-mail: pfnnyraymond@aol.com.

RUMBAUGH, JEFFREY ARLIN, neurologist, neuroscientist; b. Lansing, Mich., Jan. 8, 1971; s. Stanley A. and Marcia L. Rumbaugh; 1 child, Jonh J. A. BS, Haverford Coll., Pa., 1993; MS, U. Rochester, NY, 1996, PhD, 1998, MD, 2000. Lic. physician Md., 2004, Ga., 2009, diplomate Am. Bd. Psychiatry and Neurology, 2005. Intern Johns Hopkins U., Balt., 2000—01, resident neurology, 2001—03, chief resident neurology, 2003—04, asst. prof. neurology Divsn. Neuroimmunology and Neuro-Infectious Diseases, 2004—09. Founder, dir. neuroimmunolgy, neuro-infectious disease consult svc. Johns Hopkins U., 2004—09; asst. prof. neurology Emory U., 2009—. Contbr. articles to profl. jours. Mem. humanism in medicine com., Rochester, 1999—2000; vol. outreach for AIDS awarenes Students Rochester, 1993—2000. Recipient Analytical Chemistry award, Am. Chem. Soc., 1993, Travel award, Am. Soc. Clin. Investigation, 2006, S. Weir Mitchell award, Am. Acad. Neurology, 2005; fellow, Elmer Stotz Found., 1995, Louis and Molly Wolk Found., 1996, NIH Genetics, 1996, E. H. Hooker, 1997; scholar, Phi Beta Kappa, 1992, Med. Scientist Tng. Program, 1993. Achievements include discovery of a possible new host defense mechanism involving matrix metalloproteinases and viral proteins; research in several new biochemical mechanisms involved in DNA replication and repair;

a possible biochemical pathway involved in HIV replication. Avocation: running. Office: 1670 Clairmont Rd Decatur GA 30033 Home: 1103 Masons Creek Cir Atlanta GA 30350 Office Fax: 404-238-4715.

RUMBOUGH, ROY ALBERT, JR., manufacturing executive; b. Bethesda, Md., Apr. 19, 1955; s. Roy Albert Sr. and Patsy Ann (Ellinger) R.; m. Kimberly Reyes, Dec. 1, 1989. BA in Acctg., N.C. State U., 1986; MBA, Northwestern U. CPA, N.C.; cert. mgmt. acct. Sr. acct. Touche Ross & Co., NYC, 1986—89; v.p., contr. Blodgett Corp., 1998—2002; sr. auditor Maytag Corp., Newton, Iowa, 1989, v.p., corp. contr., 2002; v.p., contr. & chief acctg. officer Lennox International, Inc., 2006—. Mem. Nat. Assn. Accts. (Cert. Mgmt. Accountant, bd. dirs. 1986-89). Home: 675 Live Oak Trl NE Cleveland TN 37323-5536 Office: Lennox International Inc 2140 Lake Park Blvd Richardson TX 75080 Office Phone: 972-497-5000. Office Fax: 972-497-5292. E-mail: roy.rumbough@lennox.com.

RUMBOUGH, STANLEY MADDOX, JR., industrialist; b. NYC, Apr. 25, 1920; s. Stanley Maddox and Elizabeth (Colgate) R.; m. Nedenia Hutton, Mar. 23, 1946 (div. 1966); children: Stanley H., David P. (dec.), Nedenia Colgate; m. Margaretha Wagstrom, Dec. 21, 1967 (div. 1990); m. Janna Herlow, Mar. 8, 1990. AB, Yale U., 1942; postgrad. in bus. adminstrn., NYU, 1947-51. Vice pres., dir. Willis Air Service, Teterboro, NJ, 1946-47; v.p., dir. White Metal Mfg. Co., Hoboken, NJ, 1945—53, 1956—60, pres., 1960-61; pres., dir. Metal Container Corp., 1950—53, 1956—59; pres. Am. Totalisator, Balt., 1956—58; chmn. bd. Extrusion Devel. Corp., 1959-61; co-founder, chmn. bd. Elec. Engring. Ltd., 1960-69; co-founder, dir. Trinidad Flour Mills, 1961-72; dir. Dart Industries, 1961—83; chmn. bd. Wallace Clark & Co., 1962—69; co-founder, dir. Jamaica Flour Mills, 1963—66. Spl. asst. to sec. Dept. Commerce, 1953; spl. asst. White House charge exec. br. liaison, 1953-55; founder Washington D.C. Tennis Patrons Found.; dir. Health Legacy Partnership, 2009-. Chmn. U.S. Com. for UN, 1957-58; co-founder Citizens for Eisenhower, 1951; founding mem. Young Pres.'s Orgn., 1950; vice chmn. Citizens for Eisenhower-Nixon Com., 1952; bd. dirs. Young Pres. Orgn., 1958-65, 69-80; trustee Young Pres. Found., 1957-70, pres., 1962-65; bd. dirs. N.Y. World's Fair Corp., 1961-70, Nat. Conf. on Citizenship, 1973-2003, Population Resource Ctr., 1978-92, Planned Parenthood of Palm Beach Area, 1979-95, Planned Parenthood Fedn. Am., 1981-84, life trustee Kravis Ctr. Performing Arts; bd. dirs. Palm Beach Civic Assn., chmn. 2005—09, chmn. emeritus 2009-, co-chmn., 1997-2005; trustee Libr. for Presdl. Papers, 1966-70, Fgn. Policy Assn., 1961-70, Am. Health Found., 1972-76; life trustee Internat. House 1959—. Capt. USMCR, 1942-46. Decorated Air medal (8), D.F.C. (2); recipient Ellis Island Medal of Honor, NECO, 2010, Pride of Palm Beach award, C. of C. Palm Beach, 2010, Alexis Tocqueville award United Way Palm Beach, 2012, Harry Edmonds Founders award Internat. House NY, 2012. Mem. Chief Execs. Orgn., World Pres.'s Orgn. (founding), Def. Orientation Conf. Assn., Racquet and Tennis Club, Internat. Lawn Tennis Club, Maidstone Club, Bath and Tennis Club, Everglades Club, Zeta Psi. Republican. Home: 655 Island Dr Palm Beach FL 33480-4744 Office: 44 Cocoanut Row Ste B103 Palm Beach FL 33480-4069

RUNGE, DONALD EDWARD, food wholesale company executive; b. Milw., Mar. 20, 1938; s. Adam and Helen Teresa (Voss) R.; divorced; children: Roland, Richard, Lori. Grad., Spencerian Coll., Milw., 1960. Fin. v.p. Milw. Cheese Co., Waukesha, Wis., 1962-69; dir. Farm House Foods Corp., Milw., 1966-89, pres., 1966-89, CEO, treas., 1984-89, chmn., pres., 1985-89; chmn., CEO Retailing Corp. Am., Milw., 1982-89; CEO, treas. Drug Sys. Inc., Milw., 1984-89; chmn. Drug Sys. Inc. (now Retailing Corp. of Am.), Milw., 1985-89; pres. TDC, 1987-89; chmn., pres. Runge Industries, Gen. Growth, Inc., 1989—. Bd. dirs. Convenient Food Mart, CasaBlanca Industries, Inc., City of Industry, Calif., Palm Beach Opera, 1992—; sec. The Diana Corp., Milw., 1985-86, treas. 1986—, pres. 1987-96; chmn. Economy Dry Goods Co. Inc.; treas. Fairbanks Farms Inc.; chmn., CEO Internat. Diamond Exch., LLC, 2006—. Adventist. Address: 12108 Aviles Cr Palm Beach Gardens FL 33418-4032 Office Phone: 561-625-4844. Personal E-mail: donald.runge@gmail.com.

RUNGE, PAUL EDGAR, ophthalmologist, educator; b. Milw., June 7, 1946; m. Cheryl Maureen Foley; children: Sarah, Megan. AA in Liberal Arts, Orange Coast Coll., Costa Mesa, Calif., 1970; BS in Biology and Immunology, U. Calif., Irvine, 1972, MS in Cellular Immunology, 1974; B Medicine B Surgery, Flinders U., Adelaide, Australia, 1979. Diplomate Am. Bd. Pediat., Am. Bd. Ophthalmology. Rotating intern Flinders Med. Ctr., Adelaide, 1979—80; pediat. resident Hosp. Sick Children, Toronto, Ont., Canada, 1980—82; sr. pediat. resident U. Calif. San Diego Med. Ctr., Children's Hosp., 1982—83; pediat. ophthalmology fellow Hosp. Sick Children and Inst. Ophthalmology, London, 1983—85; resident in ophthalmology Cook County Hosp., Chgo., 1985—88; med. retina fellow U. Calif. Jules Stein Eye Inst., Harbor/UCLA Med. Ctr., LA, 1988—89; surg. retina and vitreous fellow U. Tenn., Charles Retina Inst., Memphis, 1989—90, assoc., 1990—92; clin. instr. U. Tenn. Health Scis. Ctr., Memphis, 1992—93; clin. prof. So. Ill. U., Carbondale, 1993—96; ptnr. Ophthalmic Cons., Sarasota, Fla., 1996—; clin. assoc. prof., dept. ophthalmology U. South Fla., Tampa, 1998—. Presenter in field. Contbr. articles to med. jours. With US Army, 1965—67, Vietnam. Scholar, Given Inst. Pathobiology, 1972; rsch. fellow, NIH, 1973, Brit. Retinitis Pigmentosa Soc., 1984, ARVO traveling fellow, Nat. Eye Inst., 1989. Fellow: ACS, Ont. Coll. Physicians and Surgeons, Am. Acad. Pediat., Am. Acad. Ophthalmology, Am. Ophthal. Soc.; mem.: Royal Coll. Ophthalmology London, Royal Soc. Medicine, Alpha Gamma Sigma. Office: 1700 S Tuttle Ave Sarasota FL 34239 Office Phone: 941-952-0900.*

RUNGE, VAL MURRAY, medical educator; b. Austin, Tex., Aug. 28, 1956; BS in Chemistry with honors, Stanford U., 1978, MD, 1982. Diplomate Am. Bd. Radiology. Chief magnetic resonance svcs. New Eng. Med. Ctr. Hosps., Boston, 1986-90; asst. prof. Tufts U. Sch. Medicine, Boston, 1986-88, assoc. prof., 1988-90; dir. Magnetic Resonance Imaging and Spectroscopy Ctr. U. Ky. Med. Ctr., Lexington, 1990—94; rosenbaum prof. diagnostic radiology U. Ky., Lexington, 1990—2001, prof. biomed. engring., 1992—2001; centennial prof. diagnostic radiology Tex. A&M U., Scott & White Clinic and Hosp., 2002—10; John Sealy disting. chair radiology U. Tex. Med. Branch, Galveston, 2010—12. Editor-in-chief Investigative Radiology, 1994—; vis. prof. radiology Tongji Medical Coll., Wuhan, China, 2012—, U. Hosp. Zurich, Switzerland, 2013—. Editor: (textbooks) Clinical Magnetic Resonance Imaging, 2002, Clinical 3 T Magnetic Resonance, 2007, Essentials of Clinical MR, 2011, The Physics of Clinical MR Taught Through Images, 3rd edit., 2014; contbr. sci. papers; contbr. articles to profl. med. jours. Recipient Harry Fisher award, Contrast Media Rsch. Soc. Fellow Soc. Magnetic Resonance Imaging; mem. Am. Roentgen Ray Soc. (Exec. Coun. award 1984), Am. Soc. Neuroradiology (Dyke Meml. award 1984), Radiol. Soc. N.Am. (Magna Cum Laude award 1984). Office: University Hosp Zurich Dept Radiology Zurich 8091 Switzerland

RUNYON, KEITH LESLIE, lawyer, editor; b. Louisville, Oct. 3, 1950; s. Leslie Thomas and Marjorie Fillmore (Fisher) R.; m. Amelia Payne Sweets, Dec. 29, 1979; children: Amelia Brown Payne, Keith Leslie Jr. Student, U. London, 1971; BA summa cum laude, U. Louisville, 1972, JD, 1982. Staff writer Courier-Jour., Louisville, 1972-77, staff atty., 1984-86; staff atty., assoc. editor Louisville Times and Courier Jour., 1977-86, forum editor, 1986-90; editl. page editor, 1990-92; editor opinion pages, 1992-96; opinion editor, 1996—. Moderator Ky. Author Forum, 1996-. Editor: The Forum and Book Editor, 2001—. Nat. bd. dirs. English-Speaking Union U.S., N.Y., 1976-79, pres. Ky. br., Louisville, 1986-87; pres., dir. U. Louisville Alumni Assn., 1987-93; mem. exec. com. Louisville com. on fgn. rels., 1985-87, Leadership Louisville, 1990-91; clk. Session Calvin Presbyn. Ch., Louisville, 1986-88; mem. St. Francis in the Fields Episcopal Ch., Harrods Creek, Ky.; bd. dirs. Walden Theatre, Louisville, 1999-2001; mem. alumni bd. U. Louisville Brandeis Sch. of Law, 2001—. Recipient William E. Leidt award The Episc. Ch. of U.S., 1975, Roy Howard award (shared) Scripps Howard Journalists Nat. for Pub. Svc., 1976; named Alumnus of Yr., U. Louisville, 1991, disting. alumnus U. Louisville Sch. Law, 1996; Ctr. Fgn. Journalists fellow, 1993, Bingham fellow, 1995-96. Mem. ABA, Ky. Bar Assn., Louisville Bar Assn., Nat. Conf. Edit. Writers (editor The Masthead, 1994-96), Soc. Profl. Jours. (Outstanding Editl. Writing award, 1983, 84, 85, Outstanding Criticism award 1997, 98). Home: Nitta Yuma Harrods Creek KY 40027 Office: Courier-Jour and Louisville Times Co 525 W Broadway Louisville KY 40202-2206 Home Phone: 502-228-5373. Business E-Mail: krunyon@courier-journal.com.

RUNYON, THEODORE HUBERT, JR., religion educator, minister; b. Tomahawk, Wis., Mar. 20, 1930; s. Theodore H. Sr. and Carol Louise (Jett) R.; m. Cynthia Margaret Guild, June 25, 1955; children: Margaret, David, Stephen. BA, Lawrence U., 1952; BD, Drew U., 1955; ThD, U. Goettingen, Germany, 1958. Ordained to ministry United Meth. Ch. as deacon, 1953, as elder, 1955. Min. to youth Hanson Pl. Cen. United Meth. Ch., Bklyn., 1952-54; pastor Christ United Meth. Ch., Phila., 1954-55; prof. systematic theology Candler Sch. Theology Emory U., Atlanta, 1958—98; dir. United Meth. and ecumenical studies, 1980-97. Co-chmn. Oxford (Eng.) Inst. of Meth. Theol. Studies, 1976-80; mem. exec. com. World Meth. Coun., 1976-81; pres. Emory U. Senate, 1983-84; mem. gen. conf. commn. on Our Theol. Task, 1984-88. Author: The New Creation, 1998, John Wesley's Theology Today, Exploring the Range of Theology, 2012; editor: Hope for the Church, 1979, Sanctification and Liberation, 1981, Wesleyan Theology Today, 1985, Theology, Politics and Peace, 1989. Trustee CRISIS INC, Atlanta, 1968-72, Atlanta Assn. for Internat. Edn., 1979-82; ministerial mem. Fla. Conf. United Meth. Ch. Recipient Disting. Alumnus award Lawrence U., 1986; named One of Outstanding Educators Am., 1975; Fulbright grantee, 1955-57, 64-65, Danforth Found. grantee, 1971-72, Assn. Theol. Schs. grantee, 1987-88. Mem. AAUP, Am. Acad. Religion, Bonhoeffer Soc., N.Am. Paul Tillich Soc. (pres. 1989-90), Wesleyan Theol. Sem. Democrat. Office: Emory U Candler Sch Theology Atlanta GA 30322-0001 Home: 1800 Clairmont Lk Apt 628 Decatur GA 30033-4041

RUSCHE, MARK C., lawyer; b. Marietta, Ga., Jan. 19, 1959; BA, Furman Univ., 1981; JD cum laude, Univ. SC, 1985. Bar: Ga. 1986. Ptnr., leader, real estate, fin. and investment group Alston & Bird LLP, Atlanta. Bd. of editors Comml. Leasing Law & Strategy. Mem.: Order of Coif. Office: Alston & Bird LLP One Atlantic Ctr 1201 W Peachtree St NW Atlanta GA 30309-3424 Office Phone: 404-881-7281. Office Fax: 404-253-8798. Business E-Mail: mark.rusche@alston.com.

RUSCIO, KENNETH PATRICK, academic administrator, political science professor; b. Red Bank, NJ; BA, Washington and Lee U., 1976; MPA, Syracuse U., 1979, PhD, 1983. Asst. prof. social sci. and policy studies Worcester Polytechnic Inst., 1985—87; asst. prof. politics Washington and Lee U., 1987—94, dean Freshman, 1987—94, assoc. dean Williams Sch. Commerce, Econs. and Politics, 1991—98, assoc. prof., 1994—2000, prof., 2000—02, acting assoc. dean, 2001—02, pres., 2006—; dean Jepson Sch. Leadership Studies, U. Richmond, 2002—06. Contbr. articles to profl. jours. Mem.: Am. Conf. of Academic Deans, Assn. Am. Colls. and Univs., Internat. Leadership Assn., Am. Polit. Sci. Assn. Office: Washington and Lee University Office of President 204 W Washington St Lexington VA 24450-0303 Office Phone: 540-458-8700. Office Fax: 540-458-8945. E-mail: president@wlu.edu.*

RUSH, JULIA ANN HALLORAN (MRS. RICHARD HENRY RUSH), artist, writer; b. St. Louis, Oct. 25, 1927; d. Edward Roosevelt and Flavia Hadley (Griffin) Halloran; m. Richard Henry Rush, Aug. 15, 1956; 1 child, Sallie Haywood. Student, Washington U., St. Louis, 1945—47; BA, George Washington U., 1949. Model John Robert Powers Agy., 1950; ptnr. Rush and Halloran, Inc., 1954—57, v.p., 1957—58; sec.-treas., dir. N.Am. Acceptance Corp., 1956—58; rsch. asst. bi-weekly newsletter Art/Antiques Investment Report, 1973—. Rsch. asst. Investments You Can Live With and Enjoy, 1974, 2d, edit., 1975, 3rd, edit., 1976. One-woman shows include Fort Amador Officers Club, Panama Canal Zone, El Panama Hotel, George Washington U., Statler Hotel, Roosevelt Hotel, Washington, Newspaper Women's Club, Washington (1st prize, 1953), Waukegan Libr., Ill., Epworth Heights Hotel, Ludington, Mich., exhibited in group shows at Panama Art League (1st prize, 1953), Corcoran Gallery, Represented in permanent collections U. Panama, Watercolors Now Represented at The Richard H. Rush Lib. Edison State Coll., Ft. Myers, Fla., —, pvt. collections; illustrator Antiques As An Investment, 1968, photographer Automobiles as an Investment, 1982, Investing in Classic Cars, 1984; exhibitions include Julia and Richard H. Rush Collection Gallery at Richard H. Rush Libr. Mem.: DAR, Florence Crittenton Circle (rec. sec. 1968—69), Nat. League Am. Penwomen, Royal Palm Yacht Club (No. Ft. Myers, Fla.), Washington Club, Kappa Kappa Gamma.

RUSH, LARRY N., state legislator; b. Christiansburg, Va., Mar. 8, 1968; m. Jennifer Gaye Whitaker; children: Cody, Forrest, Lilly. Attended, New River CC. Mem. Dist. 7 Va. House of Delegates, 2012—, mem. Gen. Laws Com. & Militia Police and Pub. Safety Com. Mem.: New River Econ. Devel. Alliance, Floyd County C. of C., Pulaski County C. of C., Montgomery County C. of C. Republican. Office: General Assembly Building PO Box 406 Richmond VA 23218 also: PO Box 1591 Christiansburg VA 24068 Office Phone: 804-698-1007. Office Fax: 804-698-6707. E-mail: DelNRush@house.virginia.gov.

RUSH, W.M. (RUSTY), trucking executive, board member; children: W.M. (Rusty), Robin. V.p., exec. v.p. Rush Enterprises Inc., New Braunfels, Tex., 1990—95, pres., bd. dirs., 1995—, COO, 2001—06, CEO, 2006—. Office: Rush Enterprises Inc 555 IH-35 S Ste 500 New Braunfels TX 78130 Office Phone: 830-626-5200. Office Fax: 830-626-5310. Business E-Mail: rushr@rush-enterprises.com.

RUSHDIE, SIR SALMAN (AHMED SALMAN RUSHDIE), writer, educator; b. Mumbai, June 19, 1947; s. Anis Ahmed and Negin (Butt) Rushdie; m. Clarissa Luard, 1976 (div. 1987); 1 child, Zafar; m. Marianne Wiggins, 1988 (div. 1993); m. Elizabeth West (div.); 1 child, Milan; m. Padma Parvati Lakshmi, Apr. 17, 2004 (div. 2007). MA in Hist., with honors, King's Coll., Cambridge U., Eng., 1968; PhD (hon.), Chapman U., Orange, Calif. Freelance advt. copywriter Ogilvy & Mather, Ayer Barker; Disting. writer in residence English Dept. Emory U., Atlanta, 2007—. Pres. PEN American Ctr., 2004—06; hon. prof. MIT. Author: Grimus, 1975, Midnight's Children, 1981 (Booker prize for fiction, 1981, English Speaking Union Lit. award, 1981, James Tait Black Meml. prize, 1982, Booker of Bookers prize, 1993, Best of Booker prize, 2008), Shame, 1983 (Prix de Meilleur Livre Etranger, 1984), The Jaguar Smile: A Nicaraguan Journey, 1987, The Satanic Verses, 1988 (Whitbread Novel award, 1988, German Author of Yr. award, 1988), Haroun and the Sea of Stories, 1990 (Writer's Guild prize for children's fiction, 1991), Imaginary Homelands: Essays and Criticism, 1981-1991, 1992, Homeless by Choice (with R. Jhabvala and V. S. Naipaul), 1992, East, West, 1994, The Moor's Last Sigh, 1995 (Whitbread Novel award, 1995, Brit. Book awards Author of Yr., 1995), The Ground Beneath Her Feet, 1999, Fury, 2001, Step Across This Line: Collected Nonfiction 1992 - 2002, 2002, Shalimar the Clown, 2005, The Enchantress of Florence, 2008, Luka and the Fire of Life, 2010, Joseph Anton-A Memoir, 2012; editor: Best American Short Stories, 2008. Recipient Hutch Crossword Fiction prize, India, India Abroad Lifetime Achievement award, Outstanding Lifetime Achievement in cultural humanism, Harvard U., Kurt Tucholsky prize, Sweden, 1992, Prix Colette, Switzerland, 1993, State Prize for European Lit., Austria, 1994, Aristeion Lit. prize, European Union, 1996, Mantova Lit. prize, 1997, Budapest Grand prize lit., 1998, Commandeur de l'Ordre des Arts et des Lettres, 1999, Best of Booker award, 2008; named an Honorary Knight Comdr. Most Excellent Order of the Brit. Empire, Her Majesty Queen Elizabeth II, 2008. Fellow: Royal Soc. Lit.; mem.: AAAL (hon.). Address: Author Mail Random House UK 20 Vauxhall Bridge Rd London SW1V 2SA England Office: Emory U English Dept 1535-003-1AA 201 Dowman Dr Atlanta GA 30322 Business E-Mail: salman.rushdie@emory.edu.

RUSHING, CORETHA M., human resources executive; b. Va. married; 1 child. B in Indsl. Psychology, East Carolina U., 1979; M in Human Resources & Counseling, George Wash. U. Sr. profl. human resources Soc. Human Resource Mgmt. Tng. dir. East River Savings Bank; recruiter, corp. tng. specialist R.H. Macy's & Co.; held human resource mgmt. positions IBM Corp., 1983—94; dir., human resource, midwest divsn., Pizza Hut PepsiCo., 1994—96; joined Coca-Cola Co., 1996, sr. v.p., human resources, 2000—04; exec. coach, human resources cons. Cameron Wesley LLC., 2004—06; chief adminstrv. officer Equifax, Inc., 2006, corp. v.p., chief human resources officer, 2006—. Office: Equifax Inc 1550 Peachtree St NW Atlanta GA 30302 Office Phone: 404-885-8000. Office Fax: 404-885-8682.

RUSHING, RANDY, state legislator; m. Lea Ann Kline. Attended, East Ctrl. CC, Decatur, Miss., CC of Air Force, Maxwell AFB, Ala. Rental property mgr.; mem. Dist. 78 Miss. House of Reps., Jackson, 2012—. Bd. mem. North Decatur Water Assn. Served with USAF, ret. Miss. Air Nat. Guard. Mem.: NRA, Decatur C. of C., American Legion Post 89. Republican. Methodist. Office: Miss House of Reps PO Box 1018 Jackson MS 39215 Business E-Mail: rrushing@house.ms.gov.

RUSS, TODD, state legislator; m. Khristy Russ; children: Ryan, Lacey, Lauren. BS in Internat. Fin., Southwestern Okla. State Univ.; postgraduate studies, Colo. Grad. Sch. Banking, Berean Univ. Sch. Bible. Bank mgmt. positions including pres., CEO, dir. State Bank of Rocky, Washita State Bank; v.p. commerical loans First Nat. Bank & Trust Co.; exec. v.p., dir., interim pres./CEO Frontier State Bank, Okla.; mem. Dist. 55 Okla. House of Representatives, 2010—. Mem.: Okla. Bankers Assn. Republican. Assembly Of God. Mailing: PO Box 98 Cordell OK 73632 Home: 1634 Crestview Dr Cordell OK 73632-1413 Office: 2300 N Lincoln Blvd Room 300 Oklahoma City OK 73105 Office Phone: 580-660-5100. Business E-Mail: todd.russ@okhouse.gov.

RUSSELL, ALLEN STEVENSON, retired metal products executive; b. Bedford, Pa., May 27, 1915; s. Arthur Stainton and Ruth (Stevenson) R.; m. Judith Pauline Sexauer, Apr. 5, 1941. BS, Pa. State U., 1936, MS, 1937, PhD, 1941. With Aluminum Co. Am., 1940-82, assoc. dir. rsch., 1973-74; v.p. Alcoa, Pa., 1974-78; v.p. sci. and tech. Pitts., 1978-81; v.p., chief scientist, 1981-82. Adj. prof. U. Pitts., 1981-86 Contbr. articles to profl. jours.; patentee in field. Named IR-100 Scientist of Yr., 1979; Pa. State U. alumni fellow, 1980; K.J. Bayer medalist, 1981; recipient chem. Pioneer award Am. Inst. Chemists, 1983 Fellow Am. Soc. Metals (Gold medal 1982), AIME (James Douglas gold medal 1987), Am. Inst. Chemists; mem. NAE (coun. 1978-84), Am. Chem. Soc., Sigma Xi. Republican. Presbyterian. Home: 27 Meadowlark Ln Hilton Head Plantation Hilton Head Island SC 29926 Home Phone: 843-682-3455. E-mail: russell2610@roadrunner.com.

RUSSELL, CHARLES STEVENS, retired state supreme court justice; b. Richmond, Va., Feb. 23, 1926; s. Charles Herbert and Nita M. (Stevens) R.; m. Carolyn Elizabeth Abrams, Mar. 18, 1951; children: Charles Stevens Jr., David Tyler. BA, U. Va., 1946, LL.B., 1948. Bar: Va. 1949, U.S. Dist. Ct. (ea. dist.) Va. 1952, U.S. Ct. Appeals (4th cir.) 1955, U.S. Supreme Ct. 1958. Assoc. Jesse, Phillips, Klinge & Kendrick, Arlington, Va., 1951-57, ptnr., 1957-60, Phillips, Kendrick, Gearheart and Aylor, Arlington, 1960-67; judge 17th Jud. Ct. Va., Arlington, 1967-82; justice Supreme Ct. of Va., Richmond, 1982—91, sr. justice, 2004—. Mem. jud. coun. Va., 1977-82; adj. prof. law George Mason U., Arlington, 1977-86, T.C. Williams Sch. Law U. Richmond, 1987-90; mem. exec. com. Va. State Bar, Richmond, 1964-67; mem. faculty Nat. Jud. Coll., Reno, 1980—, Appellate Judges Inst., NYU, 1986—. Mem. Adv. Com. on Youth, Arlington; mem. nat. council of trustees Freedoms Found., Valley Forge, Pa., 1986-91. Served to lt. comdr. USNR, 1944-51. Fellow Am. Bar Found.; mem. ABA, Arlington County Bar Assn., Va. Bar Assn., Richmond Bar Assn., Va. Trial Lawyers Assn., Am. Judicature Soc., Am. Law Inst. (adv. com. on complex litigation 1989-91). Anglican. Office: Supreme Court of Virginia PO Box 1315 Richmond VA 23218-1315*

RUSSELL, DAVID L., federal judge; b. Sapulpa, Okla., July 7, 1942; s. Lynn and Florence E. (Brown) R.; m. Dana J. Wilson, Apr. 16, 1971; 1 child, Sarah Elizabeth BS, Okla. Bapt. U., 1963; JD, Okla. U., 1965. Bar: Okla. 1965. Asst. atty. gen. State of Okla., Oklahoma City, 1968-69, legal adviser to gov., 1969-70; legal adviser Senator Dewey Bartlett, Washington, 1973-75; U.S. atty. for Western dist. Okla. Dept. Justice, 1975-77, 81-82; ptnr. Benefield & Russell, Oklahoma City, 1977-81; judge US Dist. Ct. (we. dist.) Okla., Oklahoma City, 1981—94, 2001—, chief judge, 1994—2001. Lt. comdr. JAGC, USN, 1965-68. Selected Outstanding Fed. Ct. Trial judge Okla. Trial Lawyers Assn., 1988, The Jour. Record award Okla. County Bar Assn., 2005. Mem. Okla. Bar Assn., Fed. Bar Assn. (pres. Oklahoma City chpt. 1981), Order of Coif (alumnus mem.), Jud. Conf. US (mem. exec. com. 2003-06). Republican. Methodist. Office: US Dist Ct US Courthouse 200 NW 4th St Oklahoma City OK 73102-3026 Home Phone: 405-478-1990; Office Phone: 405-609-5100.

RUSSELL, JAMES ALVIN, JR., college administrator; b. Lawrenceville, Va., Dec. 25, 1917; s. Dr. James Alvin and Nellie M. (Pratt) R.; m. Lottye J. Washington, Dec. 25, 1943; children: Charlotte Justyne, James Alvin III. BA, Oberlin Coll., 1940; BS, Bradley U., 1941, MS, 1950, spl. insts.; EdD, U. Md., 1967; spl. insts., Wayne U., U. Mich., U. Ill., NSF. Prof., dir. div. engring., also prof. edn. div. grad. studies Hampton Inst., 1950-71; pres. St. Paul's Coll.,

Lawrenceville, 1971-81; dir. instructional programs and student services Va. C.C. System, 1981-82; chmn. div. profl. studies W.Va. State Coll., 1982-86, acting pres., 1986-87, exec. asst. to pres., 1987-88; pres. So. W.Va. C.C., 1988-89, ret., 1989. Pres. Peninsula Council Human Relations, 1961-65. United Negro Coll. Fund fellow, 1966-67. Mem. IEEE, Am. Soc. Engring. Edn., Am. Assn. Univ. Adminstrs., Am. Vocat. Assn., Am. Tech. Edn. Assn., Nat. Assn. Indsl. Tech., Am. Assn. for Higher Edn., Nat. Assn. for Equal Opportunity in Edn., Brunswick C. of C., Sigma Pi Phi, Alpha Kappa Mu, Iota Lambda Sigma, Omega Psi Phi. Home: 811 Grandview Dr Dunbar WV 25064-1175 E-mail: Drjarusdun@yahoo.com.

RUSSELL, JAMES WEBSTER, JR., retired editor, columnist; b. Shreveport, La., Nov. 30, 1921; s. James Webster and Aline (Faulk) R.; m. Jean Buck, June 29, 1949 (dec. Sept. 2002); children: Nancy Russell Dearr, Eileen Russell Goure; m. Sylvia Swogger Sheldon, Aug. 17, 2004. BA, La. State U., 1942. Fla. mgr. Internat. News Service, 1946-51; bur. chief UPI, Tallahassee, 1951-52; regional editor U.P.I., Atlanta, 1953-57; asst. city editor Miami (Fla.) Herald, 1957-58, bus.-fin. editor, 1958-74, fin.-econ. columnist, 1974—99. Guest lectr. U. Miami, Fla. Internat. U., Miami-Dade Community Coll., La. State U. Contbr. articles to jours. and newspapers; author: (book) Out Of Ouachita. Trustee Fla. So. Coll. Served with USAAF, 1942-45. Recipient Eagle award Invest-in-Am. Nat. Coun., 1976; decorated Air medal with eleven oak leaf clusters; inducted La. State U. Sch. of Mass Comms. Hall of Fame, 1998. Mem. Soc. Am. Bus. Writers, Lambda Chi Alpha, Sigma Delta Chi. Republican. Methodist (chmn. ch. council on ministries 1971-72). Home: 4800 SW 64th Ct Miami FL 33155-6133

RUSSELL, JOHN R., lawyer; b. Apr. 4, 1951; s. Donald S. and Virginia U. Russell; m. Jane McCall, Nov. 13, 1985; children: Richardson Hunt, Aley Elizabeth, Robeson Clay. Bar: S.C. Mem. S.C. Ho. of Reps., Columbia, 1983-87, S.C. Senate, Columbia, 1983. Mem. banking and ins. com., edn. com., gen. com., invitations com., judiciary com., rules com. Republican. Office: 606 Gressette Bldg Columbia SC 29202 also: PO Box 5524 Spartanburg SC 29304-5524

RUSSELL, JUDITH, librarian, dean; BA cum laude, Dunbarton Coll. of Holy Cross; MLS, Cath. U. Am. Dir. Office of Electronic Info. Dissemination Svcs. US Govt. Printing Office, Washington, 1991—96, dir. Fed. Depository Libr. Program, supt. documents, 2003—06; dean univ. librs. U. Fla., Gainesville, 2007—. Former dep. dir. Nat. Commn. on Librs. and Info. Sci. (NCLIS). Mem.: ALA. Office: George A Smathers Librs U Fla PO Box 117001 Gainesville FL 32611-7001 Office Phone: 352-273-2505. E-mail: judruss@uflib.ufl.edu.

RUSSELL, LIANE BRAUCH, retired geneticist; b. Vienna, Aug. 27, 1923; came to U.S., 1941; d. Arthur and Clara (Starer) Brauch; m. William Lawson Russell (dec.), Sept. 23, 1947; children: David Lawson, Evelyn Ruth. AB Summa cum laude, CUNY, NYC, 1945; PhD in Zoology, U. Chgo., 1949; ScD (hon.), Hunter Coll., NYC, 1999; LHD (hon.), Berea Coll., 2005. Fellow U. Chgo., 1945-46, teaching asst., 1946-47; rsch. asst. Jackson Lab., Bar Harbor, Maine, 1945, 46; rsch. staff mem. Oak Ridge (Tenn.) Nat. Lab., 1947-75, sect. head., 1975-95, sr. rsch. fellow, 1988—2001; ret., 2002. Sci. advisor U.S. Del. at 1st Atoms for Peace Conf., Geneva, Switzerland, 1955; mem. numerous sci. bds. including Nat. Research Council com. on energy and environment, 1975-77, com. on biol. effects of ionizing radiation, 1977-80, bd. on environ. studies and toxicology, 1981-90, Nat. Council on Radiation Protection and Measurement Task Group, Washington, 1975-77, Genetox Program EPA, Washington, 1979—, Internat. Com. for Protection Against Environ. Mutagens and Carcinogens, Lausanne, Switzerland, 1977-83, Internat. com. on standardized genetic nomenclature for mice, 1977-91, office of tech. assessment, scientific adv. panel, 1985-86; mem. task group Internat. Agy. for Research on Cancer, Hanover, Fed. Republic of Germany, 1979, EPA review panel on mutagenicity guidelines, 1985-86; adj. faculty U. Tenn., 1980-. Assoc. editor Mutation Rsch., 1976-96, Environ. Mutagenesis, 1980-83; editor TCWP Newsletter, 1966—; editor: (book) Genetic Mosaics and Chimeras, 1979; contbr. more than 170 articles to profl. jours. Founder Tenn. Citizens for Wilderness Planning, Oak Ridge, 1966, pres. 1967-70, 86-87; active numerous environ. groups. Corp. fellow Union Carbide, 1983; corp. fellow Martin Marietta, 1985, sr. corp. fellow, Martin Marietta, 1988; recipient Merit award Mademoiselle, 1955, Roentgen medal City of Remscheid-Lennep, 1973, Disting. Assoc. award U.S. Dept. Energy, 1987; named to Hunter Coll. Hall of Fame, 1979, Sol Feinstone Environ. Achievement award SUNY, 1987, Lifetime Achievement award Tenn. Environ. Coun., 1990, Vocational Svc. award Oak Ridge Rotary, 1992, Marjorie Stoneman Douglas award Nat. Parks Conservation Assn., 1993, Environmental Mutagen Soc. EMS award, Enrico Fermi award U.S. Dept. Energy, 1993, Lifetime Conservation Achievement award So. Appalachian Forest Coalition, 1999, Lifetime Environ. Conservation Achievement award Tenn. Dept. Environment and Conservation, 2000; Tenn. Clean Water Network River Hero, 2008, River Network River Achievement award, 2009, YWCA Lifetime Achievement award, 2009. Fellow AAAS; Fellow Environ. Health Inst.; mem. Nat. Acad. Scis., Environ. Mutagen Soc. (pres. 1984-85), Tenn. Environ. Honor Soc. Achievements include research in findings in basic mammalian genetics in germ-cell mutagenesis and in teratogenesis. In the area of environmental advocacy, and creation of two new units of the National Park System. Avocation: environmental activism. Business E-Mail: russelllb@ornl.gov.

RUSSELL, RALPH TIMOTHY, retired insurance company executive; b. Foley, Ala., May 26, 1948; s. Ralph Joseph and Dorothy Eleanor (Peterson) R.; m. Sandra Earle Schultz, May 30, 1970; children: Karen, Kevin, Kenton. BS in Acctg., U. Ala., 1970; MBA, U. South Ala., 1975. Chartered property casualty underwriter. Pres. Baldwin Mutual Ins. Co., Foley, Ala., 1972—; mayor City of Foley, 1996—2006; commr. revenue Gov.'s cabinet State of Ala.; judge Probate Baldwin Co. Ala. Bd. dirs. Baldwin Mutual Ins. Co., 1976—, Riviera Utilities, Foley, 1976—, Gulf Coast Title Ins. Co., Foley, 1978—, Colonial Bank, Foley, 1991—. Pres. South Baldwin United Way, 1981-82; nat. v.p. U. Ala. Alumni Assn., Tuscaloosa, 1978-79; chmn. Foley Pub. Libr., 1975-84, St. Margaret's Ch. Bd., Foley, 1989-90, Baldwin County Econ. Devel. Alliance, South Ala. Regional Planning Commn.; treas. South Baldwin Hosp.; bd. dirs. Bus. Coun. Ala.; mem. bd. commrs. Ala. Battleship Commn.; trustee US Naval Air Mus. Paul Harris fellow, 1986. Mem. Nat. Assn. Mut. Ins. Cos. (chmn. bd. dirs. 1986-94), Ala. Ins. Planning Com. (bd. dirs.), Ins. Edn. Found. (bd. dirs. 1991-94), Soc. CPCU (pres. 1982), South Baldwin C. of C. (past pres.), Ala. League Municipalities (past mem. exec. com.). Roman Catholic. Home: 117 W Rosetta Ave Foley AL 36535-2223 Office: Baldwin Mutual Ins Co 315 E Laurel Ave Foley AL 36535-2617

RUSSELL, RICHARD OLNEY, JR., retired cardiologist; b. Birmingham, Ala., July 9, 1932; s. Richard Olney and Louise (Taylor) R.; m. Phyllis Hutchinson, June 15, 1963; children: Scott Richard, Katherine Hutchinson, Meredith Cooper, Stephen Wilbon. AB cum laude, Vanderbilt U., Nashville, 1953, MD, 1956. Diplomate Am. Bd. Internal Medicine, 1964, Am. Bd. Cardiovascular Disease, 1967. Intern Peter Bent Brigham Hosp., Boston, 1956-57, resident, 1959-60, 63-64; fellow in cardiology Med. Coll. Ala., Birmingham, 1960-62, instr., 1962-63; instr. medicine U. Ala., Birmingham, 1964-65, asst. prof., 1965-70, assoc. prof., 1970-73, prof., 1973-81, clin. prof., 1981—2006; pvt. practice medicine specializing in cardiology Birmingham, 1981—2006; ret., 2006. Mem. Jefferson County Bd. Health, 1977—81, chmn., 1979. Author: (with Charles Edward Rackley) Hemodynamic Monitoring in a Coronary Intensive Care Unit, 1974, 2d rev. and enlarged edit., 1981, Coronary Artery Disease: Recognition and Management, 1979, (with others) Radiographic Anatomy of the Coronary Arteries: An Atlas, 1976, Acute Ischemic Syndromes in American College of Cardiology Self Assessment Program, 1993; mem. editl. bd. Circulation, 1976-80, Am. Jour. Cardiology, 1977-82, Heart and Lung, 1978-83, Chest, 1978-83, Ala. Jour. Med. Scis, 1977-80, Jour. Am. Coll. Cardiology, 1987-90; sect. editor for Case Studies for Cardiosource for Am. Coll. Cardiology, 2001-06, assoc. editor, 2006-10; contbr. articles to profl. jours. Distbn. com. Greater Birmingham Found., 1984-90; exec. bd. Birmingham area coun. Boy Scouts Am., 1987-1998, v.p., 1990-96, coun. commr., 1996-98; vice chmn. Vulcan dist., 1988-89, chmn., 1989-91, bd. dirs. S.E. region, 1990-92, bd. dirs. southern region, 1992—; bd. dirs. Ctrl. Ala. United Way, 1988-92; mem. Newcomen Soc., 1988—; chmn. exec. com. Birmingham Bapt. Med. Ctr., Montclair, 1995, pres.-elect med. staff, 1998-99, pres. 1999-2000; chmn. Nat. Eagle Scout Assn. Scholarship Com. So. Region, 2001-03, chmn. area nine, 2009-13; asst. coun. cmmr. Greater Ala. coun. Boy Scouts Am., 1998-2000, coun. commr., 2001-04, v.p. bd., 2006, pres., 2007; mem. Am. Bd. Cardiovasc. Disease, 1991-96. Capt. U.S. Army. Decorated Commendation medal; recipient Dist. Award of Merit, Boy Scouts Am., 1991, Silver Beaver award, 1990, Disting. Eagle Scout, 1999, Silver Antelope award 2001, Vigil Honor, 2007; NIH rsch. fellow, 1966-67. Fellow: ACP, Am. Coll. Cardiology (bd. govs. 1979—81, trustee 1984—85, 1989—94, ann. sci. session program chmn. 1994, disting. fellowship 2001, Ala. chpt. named lectureship in honor); mem.: Med. Assn. State Ala. (spkr. house counselors dels. 1989—94, Laureate award 1999), Birmingham Soc. Internists (pres. 2001—03), Birmingham Cardiovascular Soc. (pres. 1981), Jefferson County Med. Soc. (v.p. 1982, pres. 1984), So. Soc. Clin. Investigation, Am. Fedn. Clin. Rsch., Am. Coll. Chest Physicians (bd. regents 1985—91), Am. Heart Assn. (pres. Ala. affiliate 1975—76, v.p. so. region 1986—87, task force on practice guidelines 1998—2000), Royal Soc. Medicine, NY Acad. Scis., Kiwanis (Brimingham sec. 1984—85, disting. pres. 1994—95), Leadership Birmingham, Omicron Delta Kappa, Alpha Omega Alpha, Phi Beta Kappa. Home: 4408 Kennesaw Dr Birmingham AL 35213-1826 Personal E-mail: rorussell@charter.net.

RUSSELL, ROB, academic administrator; b. Knoxville, Tenn., Dec. 8, 1969; m. Tracey Russell; children: Kieran, Lucinda. BA in English/History, East Tenn. State U., 1991; MA in English, U. Tenn., 1993. Dir. Va. Intermont Coll. Writing Ctr., 1995—97, East Tenn. State U. Writing and Communication Ctr., 1997—; instr. NE State Tech. Cmty. Coll., 1993—95. Democrat. Unitarian Universalist. Office Phone: 423-571-2515. Office Fax: 423-283-7600. Business E-Mail: rob@robrussellforcongress.com.

RUSSELL, STEVE, state legislator; m. Cindy Russell; 5 children. BS, Ouachita Bapt. U, 1985. Served 21 years through Lt. Col., with Airborne & Ranger qualification, serving in Kosovo, Kuwait, Afghanistan & in Operation Iraqi Freedom US Army; mem. Dist. 45 Okla. State Senate, 2008—. Featured spkr. Premiere Speaker's Bureau. Author: We Got Him! A Memoir of the Hunt and Capture of Saddam Hussein. Decorated Legion of Merit US Army, Bronze Star with Valor Device & Oak Leaf Cluster, Combat Infantryman Badge, Valorous Unit award. Republican. Office: 2300 N Lincoln Blvd Rm 428B Oklahoma City OK 73105 Office Phone: 405-521-5618. Business E-Mail: russell@oksenate.gov.

RUSSELL, TERRENCE JOSEPH, lawyer; b. Jacksonville, Fla., Sept. 26, 1944; AA, St. Leo Coll., 1964; BA, U. Fla., 1966; JD, Fla. State U., 1968. Bar: Fla. 1969. Law clk. to Hon. W.O. Mehrtens U.S. Dist. Ct. (so. dist.) Fla., 1969; atty. Ruden, McClosky, Smith, Schuster & Russell, P.A., Ft. Lauderdale, Fla. Mem. appellate restructure commn. Fla. Supreme Ct., 1985—86, mem. nominating com., 1994—, chmn. nominating com., 1997, 1998; mem. Fed. Magistrate's merit selection panel, 1985; vice-chmn. 17th Jud. Cir. Nominating Com., 1982—84, chmn., 1985—86; mem. spl. com. representation of death sentenced inmates Fla. Bar, bd. govs., 1987—91, pres., 2001—02. Bd. govs. Nova U. Law Sch., 1981, chmn., 1993—97; bd. dirs. Broward County Legal Aid Svcs., 1985—86. Mem.: ATLA, ABA (ho. of dels. 2000—04, sects. litig., legal edn.), Fla. Jud. Qualifications Commn., Fla. Bar Found. (bd. dirs. 1992—98, pres. 2004—), Fla. State U. Law Sch. Alumni Assn. (pres. 1985), Am. Bd. Trial Advs., Am. Bar Found., Acad. Fla. Trial Lawyers (coll. diplomates), Broward County Trial Lawyers Assn., Broward County Bar Assn. (chmn. spl. com. legal malpractice ins. 1978, bar-bench liaison com. 1978, jud. selection and tenure com. 1978—79, exec. com. 1980, 1981, pres. 1984—85), Gold Key, Delta Theta Phi. Office: Fowler White Boggs PA 1200 E Las Olas Blvd Ste 500 Fort Lauderdale FL 33301-2468 Office Phone: 954-527-2460. Business E-Mail: terrence.russell@fowlerimte.com.

RUSSELL, THEODORE EMERY, diplomat; b. Madras, India, Nov. 21, 1936; s. Paul Farr and Phyllis Hope R.; m. Sara Mather Stedman, Sept. 3, 1960; children: Douglas Richmond, Richard Mather. BA, Yale U., 1958; MA, Fletcher Sch. Law & Diplomacy, 1960, MALD, 1961; sr. tng., Nat. War Coll., 1980—81. Fgn. svc. officer Dept. State, Italy, Czechoslovakia, Washington, 1963-80, dep. office dir. (EUR/RPE) Washington, 1981-83; dep. chief mission Copenhagen, 1983-87, Prague, Czechoslovakia, 1988-91; dep. asst. adminstr. for internat. activities EPA, Washington, 1992-93; amb. to Slovak Republic Bratislava, Slovakia, 1993-96; dep. comdt. internat. affairs Army War Coll., Carlisle, Pa., 1996-99; dir. internat. rels. MHz Networks, 2001—03; internat. security affairs cons., 2001—. Adj. fellow CSIS. Founding chmn. Friends of Slovakia. Mem. Washington Inst. Fgn. Affairs, Fgn. Svc. Assn., Nat. War Coll. Alumni Assn. Avocations: hiking, fishing, history. Home and Office: 1833 Briar Ridge Ct Mc Lean VA 22101-4233

RUSSELL, THOMAS ARTHUR, humanities educator, religious studies educator, researcher; b. Wash., DC, May 10, 1954; s. Donald Earle and Elizabeth Fowler Russell; m. Anne Elizabeth Holmes Russell, June 6, 1981; 1 child, Thomas Donald. BA in History, Furman U., Greenville, SC, 1976; MDiv, Gordon-Conwell Theol. Sem., S.Hamilton, Mass., 1980; MA in Religious Studies, Vanderbilt U., Nashville, 1992; PhD in Religious Studies, Vanderbilt U., 1999. Assoc. pastor 1st United Ch., Swampscott, Mass., 1977—81; min. christian edn. Ch. of Apostles, Fairfax, Va., 1982—85; tchg. asst. world religions and Hebrew bible Vanderbilt U., 1986—88; bibliographer world religions Vanderbilt Div. Sch. Libr., 1986—96; vis. asst. prof. religious studies, lectr. Western Ky. U., Bowling Green, 1988—2003, rsch. dir. so. migrations rsch. project, 2001—04; adj. instr. Belmont U., Nashville, 2003—, Palm Beach Cmty. Coll., Fla., 2003—, U. Md., Coll. Park, 2004—, Excelsior Coll., Albany, NY, 2004—, grad. thesis dir., 2007—; undergrad. and grad. instr. humanities U. Memphis, 2004—; chaplain Just Crumbs Ministry, Franklin, Tenn., 2007—. Cons. Christian edn. Diocese of Va., Richmond, 1982—84, organizer diocesan-wide christian edn. confs., 1982—84; faculty rep. Potter Coll. libr. com. Western Ky. U., 1999—2001, faculty rep. Asian studies minor com., 1999—2001, organizer spl. presentations, 2001—04, organizer spl. events, 2001, grant overseer, 2001—04; cons. various newspapers Bowling Green, Nashville, Owensboro, 2001—; del. to ann. conv. Episcopal Diocese Tenn., Nashville, 2005—07, diocesan christian edn. com. mem., 2008—; cons. Excelsior Coll., 2006; del. Diocese Tenn., 2006—07; spkr. in field. Contbr. articles to profl. jours. and manuscripts. Adult Sunday sch. tchr. St. Paul's Episcopal Ch., Franklin, 1995—2004, Ch. of Apostles, Franklin, 2004—07; guest bible tchr. Ch. of Resurrection, Franklin, 2007. Nominee Pres. Diversity award, Western Ky. U., 2001, Chaney Disting. Prof. award, Belmont U., 2006, Stanley J. Drazek Tchg. Excellence award, U. Md., 2007, Tchg. Recognition award, 2007; Rsch. grant, Pluralism Project of Harvard U., 1999, Louisville Inst., 2001—02, 2002. Mem.: Am. Soc. Missiology (founding mem. 1989—91, student officer 1989—91), Am. Acad. Religion. Avocations: swimming, travel, cooking. Office: Univ Memphis Brister Hall 201 Memphis TN 38152 Home: 2118A Natchez Trce Nashville TN 37212-4125 Personal E-mail: drtomrussell@yahoo.com. Business E-Mail: tarussel@memphis.edu.

RUSSELL, THOMAS B., federal judge; b. 1945; BA, Western Ky. U., 1967; JD, U. Ky., 1970. Ptnr. Whitlow, Roberts, Houston & Russell, Paducah, Ky., 1970—94; judge US Dist. Ct. (we. dist.) Ky., Paducah, Ky., 1994—2008, chief judge Ky., 2008—. Mem. ABA, Ky. Bar Assn., Ky. Bar Found., Am. Bd. of Trial Advocates, Am. Bar Found., McCracken County Bar Assn., Am. Coll. of Trial Lawyers, Rotary. Methodist. Office: US Dist Ct W Ky Federal Bldg 501 Broadway St Rm 121 Paducah KY 42001-6856

RUSSO, JAMES MICHAEL, political consultant; b. Providence, Feb. 22, 1959; BA, Providence Coll., 1981; JD, Suffolk U., 1984. Law clk. RI Superior Ct., Warwick, 1985-86, law clk., chief justice RI, 1986; atty.-at-law Marzilli & Lanni, 1987-89; asst. city solicitor City of East Providence, RI, 1986-92; pvt. practice, 1989-93; legal counsel RI House Corps. Com., 1991-92; chief of staff Lt. Gov. Bob Weygand, 1993-96; campaign mgr. Weygand Com., 1996; chief of staff to Rep. Robert A Weygand US House of Representatives, Warwick, RI, 1997; sr. political assoc. Douglas Fulmer & Associates, Nashville. Campaign mgr. Weygard for Senate, 2000. Office: Douglas Fulmer & Associates 51 Fawn Creek Pass Nashville TN 37214 Office Phone: 615-391-9012.

RUST, ROBERT STANLEY, pediatrician, educator; b. Van Nuys, Calif., Aug. 11, 1948; s. Robert Bonham and Emily Frances Rust; m. Elizabeth Howe Merrill, June 26, 1976; children: James Robert Bonham, Merrill Alexander Campbell, David Armistead Lee, Thomas Ludwell Akers. BA, Kent State U., Ohio, 1970; MA, U. Va., Charlottesville, 1972, MD, 1981. Diplomate Am. Bd. Pediat., 1988, in neurology and child neurology Am. Bd. Psychiatry and Neurology, 1988, cert. in physician and surgeon Mo. State Bd. Medicine, 1984, in medicine and surgery Wis. State Bd. Medicine, 1990, Va. State Bd. Medicine, 1999. Assoc. dir. Internat. Coll., Salzburg, Austria, 1972—76; rsch. assoc. dept. plastic surgery U. Va., 1974—77, Worrell prof. neurology and pediat., 1999—, dir. child neurology, 1999—; resident dept. pediat. Yale U., New Haven, 1981—83; resident dept. neurology Wash. U., St. Louis, 1983—84, fellow dept. neurology and pediat., 1984—87, instr. and rsch. fellow, dept. pediat., neurology, 1987—90; asst. prof. pediat. and neurology U. Wis., Madison, 1990—97, dir. cerebral palsy clinic, 1990—97, dir. child neurology, 1991—97; assoc. prof. neurology and pediat. Harvard Sch. Medicine, Boston, 1997—99. Chair archives com. Child Neurology Soc., St. Paul, 1990—; clinic and tng. dir. child neurology Boston Children's Hosp., Harvard Med. Sch., 1997—99; chair child neurology sect. Am. Acad. Neurology, St. Paul, 2008—. Contbr. articles to profl. jours. Recipient Raven award, U. Va., 1981, Irwin P. Levy award, Wash. U., 1986, Outstanding Clin. Tchr. award, St. Louis Children's Hosp., 1989—90, Med. Alumni Assn. Disting. Tchg. award, U. Wis., 1997, Outstanding Physician award, Wis. Epilepsy Assn., 1998—99, Spl. award, mentorship and child neurology, Harvard Med. Sch., 1999, Hower award, lifetime achievement, Child Neurology Soc., 2008; Woodrow Wilson fellowship, 1970—72, 1974—76, Gov. Va. fellow, Commonwealth Va., 1974—76, Rsch. fellowship, NIH, 1991—96. Mem.: Internat. Child Neurology Assn. (presdl. adv. com. 2007—), Child Neurology Soc. (chair archives com. 1990—2008), Am. Headache Soc., Am. Acad. Neurology (chair sect. child neurology 2008—). Liberal. Presbyterian. Achievements include development of brain chemistry, neonatal brain injury, inflammatory neurologic diseases, headache, epilepsy. Avocations: carpentry, tennis, fishing, golf, horseback riding. Office: Univ Virginia Box 800394 Charlottesville VA 22908-0394

RUST, THOMAS DAVIS, state legislator; b. Front Royal, Va., July 21, 1941; m. Ann Edwards; children: Robin Mullet, Douglas Wharam, James Wharam. Former chmn. Fairfax/Falls Ch. United Way; mem. elected Herndon Town Coun., 1971—76, Northern Va. Regional Com.; elected mayor Herndon, Va., 1976—84; bd. visitor Longwood Coll., 1980—88; state del. Dist 86 Va., 2002—; elected mayor Herndon, Va., 1990—2001; exec. com. mem. Northern Va. Transp. Coord. Coun.; civil engr.; honorey dir. America Red Cross; bd. visitor Va. Recipient Man of Year, Herndon Jaycees, 1979, Vecinos Unidos Recognition, Asst. to Hispanic Youth, 1998, Acad Disting. Alumni Dept. Civil & Environ. Eng., Va. Tech., 2001. Mem.: Com. of 100, America Inst. Cert. Planners, America Planning Assn., Va. Tech. Com. of 100, Northern Va. Cmty. Found, Dulles Area Transp. Assn. Republican. Mailing: District Off 730 Elden St Herndon VA 20170 Office: Gen Assembly Bldg Rm 516, PO Box 406 Richmond VA 23218 Office Phone: 703-437-9400, 804-698-1086. Fax: 703-435-6655, 804-786-6310. E-mail: Del_TRust@house.state.va.us.

RUSTAY, JENNIFER BETH, lawyer; b. Kansas City, Mo., Jan. 30, 1973; m. Allen Harrington Rustay, Sept. 29, 2001. BA, Baylor U., 1995, JD, 1997. Bar: Tex. 1997, U.S. Dist. Ct. (all dists. Tex.), US Dist. Ct. (dist. Colo.), US Ct. Appeals (5th cir.). Law clk. Hon. Sam Johnson US Ct. Appeals (5th cir.), Austin, Tex., 1997—98; atty. Bracewell & Patterson, Houston, 1998—2000, Hagans Burdine Montgomery & Rustay P.C., Houston, 2001—. Notes and comments editor: Baylor Law Rev., 1996—97. Named a Rising Star, Tex. Super Lawyers mag., 2006—09. Fellow: State Bar Tex., Houston Bar Assn. Office: Hagans Burdine Montgomery & Rustay PC 3200 Travis 4th Fl Houston TX 77006 Office Phone: 713-222-2700.

RUTFORD, ROBERT HOXIE, geologist, educator; b. Duluth, Minn., Jan. 26, 1933; s. Skuli and Ruth (Hoxie) R.; m. Marjorie Ann, June 19, 1954; children: Gregory, Kristian, Barbara. BA, U. Minn., 1954, MA, 1963, PhD, 1969; DSc (hon.), St Petersburg State Tech U., Russia, 1994. Football and track coach Hamline U., 1958-62; rsch. fellow U. Minn., 1963-66; asst. prof. geology U. SD, 1967-70, assoc. prof., 1970-72, chmn. dept. geology, 1968-72, chmn. dept. physics, 1971-72; dir. Ross Ice Shelf Project U. Nebr., Lincoln, 1972-75, vice chancellor for research and grad. studies, prof. geology, 1977-82, interim chancellor, 1980-81; dir. divsn. Polar Programs NSF, Washington, 1975-77; pres., prof. geoscis. U. Tex., Dallas, 1982-94, Excellence in Edn. Found. prof. of geoscis., 1994—2007, pres. emeritus, 2007. US del. to Sci. Com. on Antarctic Rsch., 1986-02, v.p., 1996-98, pres., 1998-02, exec. com., 2002-04, hon mem, 2004—;

chmn. NRC Polar Rsch. Bd., 1991-95; bd. trustees Geol. Soc. Am. Found., 2005—, vice chmn., 2006-07, chmn., 2007-; bd. govs. US Corp., 1988—, Arctic Inst. N.Am., Mem. editl. bd. Issues in Sci. and Tech., 1991-94. Trustee Baylor Coll. Dentistry, 1989-96. 1st lt. U.S. Army, 1954-56. Recipient Antarctic Svc. medal, 1964, Disting. Svc. award NSF, 1977, Ernie Gunderson award for svc. to amateur athletics S.D. AAU, 1972, Outstanding Achievement award U. Minn., 1993, "M" Club Lifetime Achievement award, 1995, Commemorative medal Polish Acad. Scis., 2004. Fellow Geol. Soc. Am.; mem. Antarctican Soc. (pres. 1988-90), Arctic Inst. N.Am. (mem. bd. govs. US corp. 1996-), Explorers Club, Am. Polar Soc. (hon.), Philos. Soc. Tex., St. Petersburg Acad. Engring. (Russia), Tex. Acad. Sci., Sigma Xi. Lutheran. Office: Univ Tex Dallas Geosciences Program Richardson TX 75083-0688

RUTHERFORD, JAMES TODD, state legislator; b. Columbia, SC, Oct. 10, 1970; BA, Howard U., 1992; JD, U. SC, 1996. Legis. asst. to Rep. Robin Tallon US House of Representatives, 1992—93; atty. The Rutherford Law Firm, LLC, 1998—2006; asst. solicitor, spl. prosecutor 5th Solicitor's Office, SC, 1996—98; mem. Dist. 74 SC House of Reps., 1999—, mem. Judiciary Com. & Subcommittee on Criminal Laws. Owner 803 Motorsports, 3 Tech. Integrated Sys., 1993. Mem.: NAACP, Columbia Lawyers' Assn. Democrat. Baptist. Office: 530A Blatt Bldg Columbia SC 29201 Mailing: PO Box 1452 Columbia SC 29202 Home Phone: 803-799-8633; Office Phone: 803-734-9441. E-mail: jtr@legis.lpitr.state.sc.us.

RUTHERFORD, JIM, professional sports team executive; b. Beeton, Ont., Can., Feb. 17, 1949; 1 child, Andrea. Goalie Detroit Red Wings, 1970—71, 1973—80, 1982—83, Pitts. Penguins, 1971—73, Toronto Maple Leafs, 1980—81, LA Kings, 1981—82; dir. hockey ops Compuware Sports Corp., 1982-94; gen. mgr. Windsor Spitfires, Ont., 1984-88, head coach Ont., 1986-87; dir. hockey ops. Detroit Ambassadors, 1989-91, coach, dir. hockey ops., 1991-92, Detroit Jr. Red Wings (formerly Ambassadors), 1992-94; COO KTR Hockey Ltd. Partnership, Hartford, Conn., 1984—; pres., gen. mgr., COO Carolina Hurricanes (formerly Hartford Whalers), 1994—. Mem. Team Can. hockey world championships, Vienna, 1977, Moscow, 1979; player rep. 5 seasons Red Wings. Named Exec. of Yr., Can. Hockey League, 1993, Ont. Hockey League, 1994, The Hockey News, 2002, NHL Exec. of Yr., Sporting News, 2006. Achievements include being the general manager of Stanley Cup Champion Carolina Hurricanes, 2006. Office: Carolina Hurricanes 1400 Edwards Mill Rd Raleigh NC 27607-3624

RUTHERFORD, JOHN, sheriff; b. Sept. 2, 1952; m. Patricia Rutherford; children: Michelle, Lee. Grad., Fla. State U., Fla. Nat. Acad., Nat. Exec. Inst. Uniformed patrolman City of Jacksonville, Fla., sergeant, lt. patrol and detective divsn., dir. region five criminal justice tng. ctr., capt., chief svcs., chief traffic and spl. ops., chief patrol, dir. corrections, 1995—2003, sheriff, 2003—. Achievements include created several programs within Jacksonville including Justice and the Revolving Door, Operation Showdown, and Anti-Litter. Office: 501 E Bay St Rm 303 Jacksonville FL 32202 Office Phone: 904-630-2134. Office Fax: 904-630-4741.

RUTHERFORD, JOHN R., energy executive; BBA, Univ. Tex., Austin; MBA, Univ. Pa. Ptnr., CFO Sandefer Offshore; investment banker First Boston, Wasserstein Perella & Co., Houston; sr. M&A banker, nat. resources group Lehman Bros., Houston; ptnr., mng. dir. energy practice Simmons & Co., Houston, 1988—98; mng. dir., head No. Am. energy investment banking Lazard Freres & Co., Houston, 2008—10; exec. v.p. Plains All American Pipeline LP, Houston, 2010—. Office: Plains All American Pipeline 333 Clay St Houston TX 77002 Office Phone: 713-646-4100.

RUTHERFORD, JOHN SHERMAN, III, (JOHNNY RUTHERFORD), retired professional race car driver; b. Coffeyville, Kans., Mar. 12, 1938; s. John Sherman and Mary Henrietta (Brooks) R.; m. Betty Rose Hoyer, July 7, 1963; children: John Sherman Rutherford IV, Angela Ann Rutherford-Price. Student, Tex. Christian U., 1956. Profl. race car driver, 1959-94; ret., 1994; driver super-modified race cars, sprint cars, stock cars, midgets, sports cars, Indy cars, Trans-Am cars and formula 5000. Mem. Indy Car Racing Inc.; dir. spl. events Indy Racing League, 1995—; pace car driver for Championship Auto Racing Teams, 1992-95; auto racing cons. Pennzoil Products-Racing Divsn.; lectr. in field. Author: (autobiography) Lone Star J.R., 2000; host: TV show The Racers; race commentator TV show, NBC, ESPN, CBS, ABC; appeared in numerous TV commercials; art work included in traveling exhbn. Art and Athletes; TV and radio pub. services messages for Nat. Safety Council, Calif. Hwy. Patrol, U.S. Marines, Muscular Dystrophy Assn., Cystic Fibrosis Assn., Boy Scouts, Camp Fire, Jewel Charity, Shriner's Hosp., Tex. Soc. to Prevent Blindness, Air N.G. Hon. state chmn. Am. Cancer Soc., Tex., Tarrant County Soc. to Prevent Blindness, Emergency Medicine Found., Ft. Worth Kidney Assn., Ft. Worth Burn Ctr.; Ind. chmn. Am. Heart Assn.; hon. mem. bd. dirs. Tex. chpt. Speedway Children's Charities, 1998—. CARA Charities, 2000--; bd. dirs. Indy HOF and Oldtimers, 2002—. With USMC Res., 1955—61. Named Ft. Worth Newsmaker of Yr., 1974, Driver of Yr. Sport Mag., 1976, Driver of Yr. Auto Race Writers and Broadcasters Am., 1974, 80, Olsonite Driver of Yr., 1980, Corvette Challenge's Sportsman of Yr., 1988, Motorsports amb., 1993; recipient Jim Clark award, 1969, Extra Mile award, 1973, Jim Malloy award, 1974, Eddie Sachs award, 1975, Louie Meyer award, 1992; chosen for Internat. Race of Champions, 1974, 76-79, 84, chosen Fast Masters, 1993; named to Tex. Sports Hall of Fame, 1981, Indy 500 Hall of Fame, 1987, Boys Clubs Am.'s Celebrity Hall of Fame, 1987, Tex. Auto Racing Hall of Fame, 1988, Nat. Sprint Car Hall of Fame, 1995, Internat. Motorsports Hall of Fame, 1996, Tex. Motorsports Hall of Fame, 2003, Philanthropy Hall of Fame, 2006, USAC Hall of Fame, 2013. Mem. Fedn. Internat. Automobile, Internat. Motors Sports Assn., Exptl. Aircraft Assn., Warbirds of Am., Confederate Air Force, Internat. Aerobatic Club, League Auto Racing (sec., bd. dirs.), Championship Drivers Assn. (bd. dirs.), Nat. Rifle Assn., Air Force Assn., Air Power Coun., Blue Angels Assn., Ft. Worth Boat Club, Shady Oaks Country Club, Speedway Club, Lions. Republican. Disciples Of Christ. Achievements include winning 27 championship car races; winner Indianapolis 500, 1974, 76, 80, second place, 1975; set new world's record for stock cars, Daytona Beach, Fla., 1963; set record at Indpls. 500, 1973; at Mich. Internat. Raceway, 1984; U.S. Auto Club Nat. Sprint Car champion, 1965; Nat. Driving champion USAC and CART, 1980; oldest driver (48) to win a 500 mile Indy Car Race, 1986. Personal E-mail: john.sherir38@hotmail.com.

RUTHERFORD, ROBERT BARRY, vascular surgeon; b. Edmonton, Alta., Can., July 29, 1931; s. Robert Lyon and Kathleen Emily (Gunn) R.; m. Beulah Kay Folk, Aug. 20, 1955; children: Robert Scott, Lori Jayne, Holly Anne, Trudy Kay, Jay Wilson. BA in Biology, Johns Hopkins U., 1952, MD, 1956. Emeritus prof. surgery U. Colo., Denver, 1996—. Editor: (texts) Management of Trauma, 1968, 4 edits., Vascular Surgery, 1978, 6th edition, 2005, An Atlas of Vascular Surgery, Vol. 1, 1993, Vol. 2, 1998, Decision Making in Vascular Surgery, 2001; editor quar. rev. Seminars in Vascular Surgery. Fellow ACS, Royal Coll. Surgeons Glasgow, Soc. for Vascular Surgery (disting. fellow); mem. Phi Beta Kappa, Alpha Omega Alpha. Republican. Unitarian Universalist. Avocations: skiing, biking, wind surfing, sailing. Home (Summer): 345 Small Shore Trl Oakland ME 04963-4317 Home: 136 Village Park Dr Boerne TX 78006-1862

RUTHERFORD, WILLIAM B., corporate financial executive; m. Nancy Rutherford; 2 children. B in Acctg. & Fin., U. Tampa. Various positions, including dir., ops. support HCA Inc., CFO Ga., staff auditor, 1986—, CFO, Eastern Group, 1996—2005, CFO, Outpatient Svcs. Group; COO Psychiatric Solutions, 2006—07. Former bd. dirs. Ctr. for Non-Profit Mgmt., Argyle Accts. Receivable Solutions; bd. dirs. YMCA. Office: HCA Inc 1 Park Plz Nashville TN 37203 Office Phone: 615-344-9551. Business E-Mail: william.rutherford@hcahealthcare.com.

RUTKOWSKI, JOSEPH A., manufacturing executive; Mgr. Cold Finish Nucor Corp., Norfolk, Nebr., 1989-91, mgr. melting & casting steel divsn. Plymouth, Utah, 1991—92, gen. mgr. steel divsn. Darlington, SC, 1992—98, Hertford, NC, 1998, v.p., 1993—98, exec. v.p. steel mills Charlotte, NC, 1998—. Office: Nucor Corp 1915 Rexford Rd Charlotte NC 28211 Office Phone: 704-366-7000. Office Fax: 704-362-4208.

RUTLEDGE, PETER BOWMAN (BO RUTLEDGE), law educator; BA in Govt., magna cum laude, Harvard U., 1992; MLitt in Applied Ethics, U. Aberdeen, Scotland, 1994; JD, U. Chgo. Law Sch., 1997. Bar: Md., DC, US Ct. Appeals (2nd, 7th and 11th cirs.), US Supreme Ct. Law clk. to Judge J. Harvie Wilkinson III US Ct. Appeals (4th cir.), 1997—98; law clk. to Justice Clarence Thomas US Supreme Ct., Washington, 1998—99; assoc. Freshfields Bruckhaus Deringer, Austria, 1999—2001, Wilmer, Cutler & Pickering, 2001—03; assoc. prof. Cath. U. America, Washington, 2003—08, U. Ga. Sch. Law, Athens, 2008—. Fulbright vis. prof. U. Vienna Law Sch., Austria, 2010—11. Co-author: International Civil Litigation in United States Courts, 2006; contbr. articles to profl. jours., chapters to books. Mem. academic coun. Inst. Transnational Arbitration, Plano, Tex., 2009—. Mem.: Supreme Ct. Bar Assn., DC Bar, Md. State Bar Assn., Joseph Henry Lumpkin Inn of Ct., American Law Inst., Order of the Coif. Office: Univ Georgia Sch Law 205 Hirsch Hall 225 Herty Dr Athens GA 30602 Office Phone: 706-542-1328. Office Fax: 706-542-5556. E-mail: borut@uga.edu.

RUTSTEIN, STANLEY HAROLD, apparel retailing company executive; b. Wilkes-Barre, Pa., July 1, 1941; s. Sydney D. and Bessie H. (Cohen) R.; m. Jo Ella Rutstein; children: Wendy Sue, Michael Scott, Lynne Elizabeth. Student, Wilkes Coll., 1959-61; grad., Advanced Mgmt. Program, Harvard U., 1975. Buyer Barbara Lynn Stores, Inc., NYC, 1961-63; buyer, then mdsg. mgr. Casual Corner div. U.S. Shoe Corp., Enfield, Conn., 1963-71, pres., 1971-76; pres., cons., dir. U.S. Shoe Corp., Cin., 1976-79; pres. Commonwealth Trading, Inc., Stoughton, Mass., 1979-85, Chadwick's of Boston Ltd., 1983-85; cons. Commonwealth Trading, Inc., 1985—; pres. Trim Trends, Inc., Boston, 1986-87, chmn., 1987-91; chmn., chief exec. officer, pres. Narragansett Clothing Co., Tiverton, RI, 1987-90, also bd. dirs.; bd. dirs. Reynolds Bros. Inc., 1989-95; pres., CEO S/J Designs Inc., 1989—2002, DBA, Northeast Knitters, Wagner Realty, Bradenton, Fla., 2002—; sales exec. Remax Alliance Realty, Bradenton, Fla., 2007—. Bd. dirs. The Icing, Inc., Sycamore Shops, Inc., Sarasota Econ. Devel. Corp., 2008-; dir. Sarasota Film, 2008-, dir., chmn. Sarasota Season Sculpture, 2009-. Bd. dirs. Ptnrs. for Disabled Youth, 1992. Mem. Young Pres. Orgn. Home: The Water Club 1281 Gulf of Mexico Dr #203 Longboat Key FL 34228 Office: Remax Alliance Realty 3007 Manatee Ave W Bradenton FL 34205 Office Phone: 941-758-7777. Personal E-mail: nextmoveboston@aol.com.

RUTSTROM, DANTE JOSEPH, chemicals executive; b. Beverly, Mass., Nov. 10, 1958; s. Eric and Laura (Grimaldi) R.; m. Melanie Sue Bragdon, June 25, 1983; children: Stephanie Lynne, Kristen Ashley, Daniel Joseph. BA, Gordon Coll., Wenham, Mass., 1980; PhD, Tufts U., 1985. Chemist Bethlehem (Pa.) Steel Corp., 1985-86; analytical chemist Eastman Chemical Co., Kingsport, Tenn., 1986, v.p., gen. mgr., Splty. Plastics Bus. Orgn. Co-author: Analytical Chemistry, vol. 57; contbr. articles to Jour. Electroanalytical Chemistry, Advances in Lab. Automation. Achievements include research in laboratory automation, robotics and cosmetics. Office: Eastman Chemical Co 200 S Wilcox Dr Kingsport TN 37662 Office Phone: 423-229-2000. Office Fax: 423-229-2145. Business E-Mail: rutstrom@eastman.com.

RYAN, HEATHER A., former not-for-profit company executive; b. Des Moines, Apr. 2, 1972; d. Richard and Mary Ryan; m. Carl McNew; children: Heaven, Ireland. Attended, Chapman U.; BA in Polit. Sci., Drake U., 2000. Membership mgr. NARAL Pro-Choice America, 2000—05; campaign mgr. Eric Streit for Congress, 2005—06; exec. dir. Paducah Film Soc., 2007. Leader troop 4077 Girl Scouts US, 2001—05. Petty officer USN. Democrat. Office: PO Box 914 Paducah KY 42002-0914 Office Phone: 270-444-0961. Business E-Mail: info@ryanforkentucky.com.

RYAN, IONE JEAN ALOHILANI RATHBURN, retired education educator, counselor; b. Honolulu, Oct. 18, 1926; d. William Alexander and Lilia (Nainoa) Rathburn; m. Edward Parsons Ryan, June 23, 1962 (dec.); children: Ralph M., Lilia K. BEd, U. Hawaii, 1948; MS in Pub. Health, U. Minn., 1950; EdD, Stanford U., 1960. Lic. marital and family therapist, N.C. Tchr. W.R. Farrington High Sch., Honolulu, 1948; instr. to asst. prof. U. Hawaii, Honolulu, 1950-66; assoc. prof. to prof. East Carolina U., Greenville, 1966-90, prof. emerita, 1990—. Contbr. articles to profl. publs. Recipient first scholarship Honolulu C. of C., 1948-50.

RYAN, J. STUART, investment company executive; BS, Lehigh Univ.; MBA, Harvard Univ. Various mgmt. positions AES Corp., 1986—2000, exec. v.p., 2000—03, COO, 2002—03; founding owner, pres. Rydout LLC, 2003—; ptnr. SPO Partners & Co., 2003—. Bd. dir. Calpine Corp., 2008—, chmn., 2010—; mem. adv. bd. Banyan Energy Inc., 2010—. Mailing: Calpine Corp Ste 1000 717 Texas Ave Houston TX 77002

RYAN, JAMES, insurance company executive; b. Pitts., Jan. 21, 1937; s. Martin Charles and Lucy Elizabeth (Misklow) r.; m. Marlene Sullivan Ryan, Jan. 27, 1973. BA, U. Pitts., U. Louisville. Cert. ins. wholesaler. Chmn. Market Finders Ins. Corp., Louisville, 1972—. Com. chmn. Am. Assn. Mng. Gen. Agts., 1988-89; pres. Ky. Lloyd's Agts. Assn., 1985—; bd. dirs. Nat. Assn. Profl. Surplus Lines Office, Inc., 1983-86; pres. Ky. Surplus Lines Assn., Louisville, 1988-89; mem. adv. coun. Essex Ins. Co., 1991-93, Am. Equity Ins. Co., Scottsdale, Ariz., 1999. Pub. in Best Rev., 1995. Mem. Ky. Thoroughbred Owners & Breeders, Inc., Hon. Order of Blue Goose Internat., Kosair Shrine Temple, Hon. Order of Ky. Col. Named Adv. Coun. Colony Ins. Co., Glen Allen, Va., 1991-93, Hamilton Ins. Co., 1993, Cardinal Ins. Co., 1991-93. Mem. Profl. Ins. Agts., Ind. Ins. Agts. Assn., Am. Assn. Mng. Gen. Agts. (cert., chmn. adv. com. 1991-92, bd. dirs. 1994-96, v.p. zone 2 1995-96, pres.-elect 1996-97, pres. 1997-98), Nat. Assn. Profl. Surplus Lines Offices (chmn. legis. com. 1988-89, Published Best Rev. 1995), Am. Assn. of Gen. Agts. Republican. Roman Catholic. Avocations: breeding and racing thoroughbred horses, golf. Office Phone: 502-423-1800. Business E-Mail: jryan@mfic.com.

RYAN, JAMES WALTER, physician, researcher; s. Lee W. and Emma E. (Haddox) R.; children: James P.A., Alexandra L.E., Amy J.S. AB in Polit. Sci., Dartmouth Coll., 1957; MD, Cornell U., 1961; D.Phil., Oxford U., Eng., 1967. Diplomate Nat. Bd. Med. Examiners. Intern, Montreal (Que.) Gen. Hosp., McGill U., Can., 1961-62, asst. resident in medicine, 1962-63; USPHS research asso. NIMH, NIH, 1963-65; guest investigator Rockefeller U., NYC, 1967-68, asst. prof. biochemistry, 1968; investigator Howard Hughes Med. Inst., 1968—71; assoc. prof. medicine U. Miami (Fla.) Sch. Medicine, 1968-79, prof. medicine, 1979-95, mem. vasc. biology ctr., 1995-00; prof. anesthesiology, pharmacology and toxicology Med. Coll. Ga., Augusta, 1995-00; sr. cons. ntGen, 2000—; chief scientist Ryogen, LLC, 2005—. Sr. scientist Papanicolaou Cancer Rsch. Inst., Miami, 1972-77; hon. med. officer to Regius prof. medicine Oxford U., 1965-67; vis. prof. Clin. Rsch. Inst. Montreal, 1974; mem. vis. faculty thoracic disease divsn., dept. internal medicine Mayo Clinic, 1974; vis. prof. Montreal Gen. Hosp./McGill U., 1985. Contbr. numerous articles on biochem. rsch. and pathology to sci. jours.; patentee in field. Rockefeller Found. travel awardee, 1962; William Waldorf Astor traveling fellow, 1966; USPHS spl. fellow, 1967-68; Pfizer travelling fellow, 1972; recipient USPHS Rsch. Career Devel. award NIH, 1968, Louis and Artur Luciano award for research of circulatory diseases McGill U., 1984-85. Fellow Am. Heart Assn. (mem. coun. cardiopulmonary diseases 1972—, coun. for high blood pressure rsch. 1976—); mem. AAAS, Am. Physiol. Soc., Am. Chem. Soc., Biochem. Soc., Am. Soc. Biochemist and Molecular Biology, Oxford and Cambridge Club (London), Sigma Xi. Baptist. Home: 3047 Lake Forest Dr Augusta GA 30909-3027 Office: ntGen Ryogen LLC 3047 Lake Forest Dr Augusta GA 30909

RYAN, JASON MICHAEL, lawyer; b. Wharton, Tex., Oct. 30, 1975; m. Megan A. Ryan, Dec. 30, 2000. BBA with honors, U. Tex., 1998, JD with honors, 2001. Bar: Tex. 2001, US Dist. Ct. (So. Dist.) Tex., US Ct. Appeals (5th cir.), US Ct. Appeals (11th cir.), US Ct. Appeals (Armed Forces), US Tax Ct. With Baker Botts LLP, Houston, 2001—08, Ryan Glover LLP, Houston, 2008—09, CenterPoint Energy Inc., 2009—; reserve officer USN, 2005—. Editor-in-chief Am. Jour. Criminal Law; contbr. articles to law jours. Decorated Nat. Def. Svc. medal, Global War on Terror Svc. medal, Joint Meritorious Unit award; recipient Pro Bono award, Nat. Law Jour., 2005; named Outstanding Young Houstonian, Houston Jaycees, 2007, Outstanding Young Texan, Tex. Jaycees, 2007, Man of Yr., Leukemia & Lymphoma Soc., 2013; named one of 40 under 40, Houston Business Jour., 2013. Mem.: Leukemia & Lymphoma Soc. (bd. trustees 2013—), Tex. Diabetes Coun. (gov. apptd. 2013—), Houston Urban Delate League (bd. dirs. 2013—), First Response Team of America (bd. dirs. 2008—), Houston Club (bd. dirs. 2012—), Houston Vol. Lawyers Program, Pro Bono Coll. of State Bar Tex., Houston Young Lawyers Assn. (past pres.), Houston Bar Found., Houston Bar Assn., Energy Bar Assn., Alpha Phi Omega. Home and Studio: 6922 Van Etten Houston TX 77021 Office: CenterPoint Energy Inc 1111 Louisiana St Houston TX 77002 Office Phone: 713-207-1111. Office Fax: 713-207-0101. Business E-Mail: jason.ryan@centerpointenergy.com.

RYAN, JOHN D., not-for-profit organization administrator; BA, Fordham U., Bronx, NY; JD, St. John's U., Jamaica, NY. Asst. dist. atty., chief major offenses Office of Dist. Atty., Bronx; dir. investigative affairs AT&T Wireless, NYC; sr. v.p., dep. gen. counsel & head of pub. safety & criminal investigations unit AOL Inc., 1996—2012; pres., CEO Nat. Ctr. Missing & Exploited Children, Alexandria, Va., 2012—. Former industry advisor INTERPOL. Prodr.: (tng. video) Cyber Crime Fighting, 1998. Chmn. law enforcement com. Families Online Summit, 1997; bd. dirs., former chmn. Nat. Ctr. Missing & Exploited Children; bd. dirs. US Internet Svc. Providers Assn., Cal Ripken, Sr. Found. Mem.: Cellular Telecommunications Industry Assn. (former chmn. fraud task force), High Tech Crime & Industry Assn. (former pres.). Office: National Center for Missing & Exploited Children Charles B Wang Internat Children's Bldg 699 Prince St Alexandria VA 22314-3175*

RYAN, JOHN MORGAN, lawyer; b. Glen Ridge, NJ, May 18, 1936; AB, Dartmouth Coll., 1958; LLB, U. Va., 1963. Bar: Va. 1964. Lectr. at law Marshall-Wythe Sch. Law Coll. William and Mary, 1976-86; ptnr. Vandeventer Black LLP, Norfolk, Va.; gen. counsel Va. Internat. Terminals, Inc. Past chair Arts and Humanities Commn., Va. Beach, Va.; bd. dirs. Greater Norfolk Corp. Fellow: Va. Law Found., Am. Bar Found., Am. Coll. Trial Lawyers; mem.: ABA (labor rels., litigation sect.), So. Conf. Bar Pres., Nat. Conf. Bar Pres., Va. State Bar, Norfolk-Portsmouth Bar Assn., Maritime Law Assn. US (bd. dirs. 2005—08), Va. Bar Assn. (pres. 1988), S.E. Admiralty Law Inst., James Kent Am. Inn of Ct. (past pres.), 4th Cir. Jud. Conf., Hampton Rds. Maritime Assn. (legis. com.). Office: Vandeventer Black LLP 500 World Trade Ctr Norfolk VA 23510-1679 Office Phone: 757-446-8605, 757-446-8600. Business E-Mail: jryan@vanblk.com.

RYAN, KEVIN, state legislator; b. Mar. 30, 1988; Gad. in Polit. Sci., Clemson U.; MPA, U. Charleston, 2009. Mem. Agr., Natural Resources, House Sportsmens Caucus, Ducks Unlimited, Coastal Conservation Assn., Georgetown County Rep. Party exec. Com., 2009—; mem. Dist. 108 SC House of Representatives, 2011—. Republican. Address: 320A Blatt Bldg Columbia SC 29201 Home: 502 Center St Walterboro SC 29488-3608 E-mail: kevin@ryanforhouse.com.

RYAN, MARLEIGH GRAYER, language educator; b. NYC, May 1, 1930; d. Harry and Betty (Hurwick) Grayer; m. Edward Ryan, June 4, 1950; 1 child, David Patrick. BA, NYU, 1951; MA, Columbia U., 1956; postgrad., Kyoto U., 1958-59; PhD, Columbia U., 1965, cert. in Japanese Lit., 1968. Research assoc. Columbia U., NYC, 1960-61, lectr. Japanese, 1961-65, asst. prof., 1965-70, assoc. prof., 1970-72; vis. asst. prof. Yale U New Haven, 1966-67; assoc. prof. U. Iowa, Iowa City, 1972-75, prof., 1975-81, chmn. dept., 1972-81; prof. Japanese SUNY, New Paltz, 1981-98, dean liberal arts and scis., 1981-90, prof. emeritus, 1999—; assoc. in rsch. Reischauer Inst. for Japanese Studies Harvard U., Cambridge, Mass., 1999—, chair study group on Asian Am. Lit., 2000—02; study group leader Harvard Inst., 2003—. Vice chmn. seminar on modern Japan, Columbia U., 1984-85, chmn., 1985-86; co-chmn. N.Y. State Conf. on Asian Studies, 1986, editor, 1993-99, mem. exec. com., 1993-96, sec., 1993-99, co-chmn., 1998. Co-author: (with Herschel Webb) Research in Japanese Sources, 1965; author: Japan's First Modern Novel, 1967, The Development of Realism in the Fiction of Tsubouchi Shoyo, 1975; assoc. editor: Jour. Assn. Tchrs. Japanese, 1962-71, editor, 1971-75. East Asian Inst. fellow Columbia U., 1955; Ford Found. fellow, 1958-60; Japan Found. fellow, 1973, Woodrow Wilson Ctr. Internat. Scholars fellow, 1988-89; recipient Van. Am. Disting. Book award Columbia, 1968 Mem. MLA (sec. com. on teaching Japanese Lang. 1962-68, mem. del. assembly 1979-87, mem. exec. com. div. Asian lit. 1981-86), Assn. Tchrs. Japanese (exec. com. 1969-72, 74-77), Assn. Asian Studies (bd. dirs. 1975-78, N.E. asian coun. 1975-78, coun. of confs., 1993-96), Midwest Conf. Asian Studies (pres. 1980-81) Business E-Mail: marleighryan@comcast.net.

RYAN, MATT (MATTHEW THOMAS RYAN), professional football player; b. Exton, Pa., May 17, 1985; s. Michael and Bernice Ryan. BS in Mgmt., Boston Coll., 2007. Quaterback Atlanta Falcons, 2008—. Recipient Johnny Unitas Golden Arm award, 2007, Manning award, Sugar Bowl Com., 2007; named MVP, MPC Computers Bowl, 2005, Player of Yr., Atlantic Coast Conf., 2007, NFL Offensive Rookie of Yr., AP, 2008; named to Nat. Football Conf. Pro Bowl Team, NFL, 2010, 2012. Achievements include being the third overall pick by the Atlanta Falcons in the NFL Draft, 2008. Office: Atlanta Falcons 4400 Falcon Pky Flowery Branch GA 30542

RYAN, NOLAN, professional baseball team executive, former professional baseball player; b. Refugio, Tex., Jan. 31, 1947; s. Lynn Nolan and Martha (Hancock) Ryan; m. Ruth Elsie Holdruff, June 26, 1967; children: Reid, Reese, Wendy. Student, Alvin Jr. Coll., Tex., 1966—69. Pitcher NY Mets, NYC, 1966, 1968—71, Calif. Angels, 1972—79, Houston Astros, 1980—88, Tex. Rangers, 1989—93, pres., 2008—. Cattle rancher, China Grove, Ray and Gonzalvez, Tex.; owner Bass Inn, Waterfront Steakhouse and Grill, Round Rock Express (Pacific Coast League AAA team), Tex., Corpus Christi Hooks (Houston Astros AA team), 2004—; investor, ptnr. Express Bank Tex., 2003—. Co-author (with Steve Jacobson): Nolan Ryan: Strike-Out King, 1975; co-author: (with Bill Libby) Nolan Ryan: The Other Game, 1977; co-author: (with Joe Torre) Pitching and Hitting, 1977; co-author: (with Harvey Frommer) Throwing Heat: The Autobiography of Nolan Ryan, 1988; co-author: (with Tom House) Nolan Ryan's Pitcher's Bible, 1991; co-author: (with Jerry Jenkins) Miracle Man: Nolan Ryan, The Autobiography, 1992; co-author: (with others) Kings of Hill, 1992. Founder, bd. dirs. Nolan Ryan Found.; commr. Tex. Pks. and Wildlife Commn., 1995—2001, vice chmn., 1995—97; bd. dirs. Justin Cowboy Crisis Fund, Tex. Water Found., Natural Resources Found., Tex. With AUS, 1967. Named Am. League Pitcher of Yr., Sporting News, 1977; named to Am. League All-Star Team, 1972—73, 1975, 1977, 1979, Nat. League All-Star Team, 1981, 1985, 1989, Baseball Hall of Fame, 1999. Achievements include holding over 53 Major League records including most seasons pitched (27), most strikeouts (5,714) and most no-hit games (7); being the only Major League Baseball player to have his uniform retired by three different teams, the Angels, Astros and Rangers; holding Guinness Book of World Records for throwing the fastest baseball pitched (100.9 miles per hour). Office: Tex Rangers Rangers Ballpark Arlington 1000 Ballpark Way Arlington TX 76011

RYAN, ROB, professional football coach; b. Ardmore, Okla., Dec. 13, 1962; s. James David and Doris (Ward) Ryan; m. Kristin Ryan; children: Joseph, Matthew, Dimitra. Attended, Southwestern Okla. State U., Weatherford. Grad. asst. Western Ky. U. Hilltoppers, 1987, Ohio State U. Buckeyes, 1988; running backs coach Tenn. State U. Tigers, 1989—91, linebackers coach, 1992, defensive line coach, 1993; defensive backs coach Ariz. Cardinals, 1994—95; defensive coord. Hutchinson CC Blue Dragons, Kans., 1996, Okla. State U. Cowboys, 1997—99; linebackers coach New Eng. Patriots, 2000—03; defensive coord. Oakland Raiders, 2004—08, Cleve. Browns, 2009—10, Dallas Cowboys, 2011—12, New Orleans Saints, 2013—. Named Coord. of Yr., The Sporting News, 1997, All-Joe Coord. of Yr., USA Today, 2006. Achievements include assistant coach of Super Bowl championship winning New England Patriots, 2002, 2004. Office: New Orleans Saints 5800 Airline Dr Metairie LA 70003

RYAN, SHARON R., lawyer; b. Bryn Mawr, Pa., Mar. 15, 1959; BA, George Washington U., 1981; JD, Boston Coll.Law Sch., 1985. Bar: Tex. 1985, Tenn. 2000. Assoc., real estate practice Baker, Smith & Mills, Dallas, 1985—88; atty. Internat. Paper Co., 1988—92; v.p., gen. counsel Masonite Corp. (subs. Internat. Paper), 1992—97; gen. counsel bldg. materials group Internat. Paper Co., Memphis, 1997—2000, gen. counsel, consumer packaging & corp. sales & mktg., 2000—06, assoc. gen. counsel corp. law, 2006—09, assoc. gen. counsel, chief ethics & compliance officer, 2009—11, v.p., acting gen. counsel & corp. sec., 2011, sr. v.p., gen. counsel, corporate sec., 2011—. Mem.: ABA, ACCA, State Bar Tex., Tenn. Bar Assn. Office: International Paper Co 6400 Poplar Ave Memphis TN 38197

RYAN, STEPHEN M., lawyer; s. Alex L. Ryan and Lynda A. Turner; m. Christine M. Ryan, Dec. 31, 1988; children: Travis A., Caroline A., Taylor R. BA, U. Tex., 1988; JD with honors, U. Mich., 1997. Bar: Tex. 1997. B-52 navigator/electronic warfare officer USAF, 1988—94, active duty law student Ann Arbor, Mich., 1994—97, asst. staff judge adv. Barksdale AFB, La., 1997—2002; atty. Nathan Sommers Jacobs & Gorman, Houston, 2002—05, LeBoeuf, Lamb, Greene & MacRae LLP, Houston, 2005—07, Dewey & LeBoeuf LLP, Houston, 2007—10, DLA Piper LLP, 2010—; staff judge adv. 147th Fighter Wing, Tex. ANG, Houston, 2002—08, HQ Tex. ANG, 2008—12; legal advisor to sec. Air Force-Insp. Gen., 2012—. With Boy Scouts of America, Eagle Scout, 1982. Maj. USAF, 1988—2002, lt. col. Tex. ANG, USAFR, 2004—08, col., 2010—. Decorated Meritorious Svc. medal, 2nd oak leaf cluster, Air medal, Air Force Commendation medal, Achievement medal USAF, Oustanding Unit award, V device, 5th oak leaf cluster, Combat Readiness medal, 1st oak leaf ctuster, Nat. Def. Svc. medal, 1 svc. star, SW Asia Svc. medal, 2 svc. stars, Global War on Terrorism Svc. medal, Kuwait Liberation medal Saudi Arabia, Kuwait, Humanitarian Svc. medal; recipient Corpus Juris Secundum award, Torts, 1995, Tex. medal of merit. Mem.: Mil. Officers Assn. America, Am. Legion, MOAA, Res. Officers Assn., VFW, Delta Sigma Phi. Roman Catholic. Avocations: scouting, world travel, aviation. Office: DLA Piper LLP 1000 Louisiana St Suite 2800 Houston TX 77002

RYAN, THOMAS L., funeral company executive; BBA, U. Tex. CPA PricewaterhouseCoopers, 1988—96; fin. mgmt. positions Service Corp. Internat., Houston, 1996—2000, CEO European ops., 2000—02, pres. & COO, 2002—05; pres. & CEO Service Corp. International, Houston, 2005—. Mem.: Young Presidents Org. Office: Service Corporation Internat 1929 Allen Pkwy Houston TX 77019

RYAN, THOMAS MICHAEL (TOM RYAN), retired retail executive; b. Patterson, NJ, Aug. 15, 1952; m. Cathy H. Ryan; 4 children. BS in Pharmacy, U. RI, 1975. Joined CVS Corp., Woonsocket, RI, 1975, numerous managerial positions v.p. pharmacy ops., sr. v.p. pharmacy, 1988—90, exec. v.p. stores, 1990—96; pres., CEO CVS Pharmacy, Inc. (then part of Melville Corp.), Woonsocket, RI, 1993—96; vice chmn., COO CVS Corp., Woonsocket, RI, 1996—98, pres., CEO, 1998—2007, chmn., 1999—2007; pres., CEO CVS Caremark Corp., Woonsocket, RI, 2007, chmn., pres., CEO, 2007—10, chmn., CEO, 2010—11, non-exec. chmn., 2011. Bd. dirs. CVS Corp., 1996-2007, CVS Caremark Corp., 2007-11, Reebok Internat., 1988-2005, FleetBoston Financial Corp., 1997-2004, Bank of America Corp., 2004-10, Yum Brands!, Inc., 2002-

RYAN, VINCE, lawyer; b. Houston, Aug. 12, 1947; m. Teresa Pamela Rodriguez; 3 children. BA in English, U. Houston, 1969, JD, 1974; MA in History, Rice U., 1979. Bar: Tex. 1974. Assoc. James Patrick Smith, 1974—75, Thomas P. Duncan, Houston, 1975—76, Smith and Conner, Houston, 1976—79, Watrous, Joyce and Ryan, Houston, 1980—81; divsn. chief commrs. ct. divsn. Office of Harris County Atty., Houston, 1981—83, first asst., 1984—88, 2009—; of counsel Sinex & Stephenson, Houston, 1988—95; regional mng. atty. Calame Linebarger, Houston, 1996—98; of counsel Linebarger Goggan, Houston, 1998—2004, Travis Law Firm, Houston, 2004—06, Stephenson Snokhous & Fournier, 2007—08; atty. Harris County, 2009—. Dir. legal rsch. svc. U. Houston; adj. faculty U.S. Army Command and Gen. Staff Coll., 1988—. Mem. Dist. C Houston City Coun., 1988—94; alt. City of Houston rep. Houston-Galveston Area Coun., 1989—94; pres. Region 14, Tex. Mcpl. League, 1993—94; bd. dirs. Panama Canal Commn., 1995—99. With US Army, 1969—72, Vietnam, with US Army, 1990, ret. lt. col. USAR. Grad. fellow, 1977—78, Rsch. fellow, 1978—79. Mailing: 3720 Blue Bonnet Houston TX 77025 Office: Office of Harris County Atty 1019 Congress 15th Fl Houston TX 77002 Home Phone: 713-661-1941; Office Phone: 713-755-5101. Personal E-mail: vinceryanlaw@aol.com. Business E-Mail: vince.ryan@cao.hctx.net.

RYAN, WILLIAM J., insurance company executive, retired bank executive; b. 1943; With All Allstate, White Plains, 1964-72, Essex Bank, Peabody, Mass., 1973-82, Bank New Eng. Corp., 1982-89; pres., CEO People's Heritage Bank (now Banknorth), Portland, Maine, 1989—2000; chmn., pres., CEO Banknorth, Portland, Maine, 2000—05; pres., CEO TD Banknorth, Inc., Portland, Maine, 2005—07, chmn., 2005—09, Unum Group, 2011—. Bd. dirs. Unum Group, 2004—. Office: Unum Group Bd Directors 1 Fountain Sq Chattanooga TN 37402

RYBAK, JAMES J., healthcare industry executive; Undergraduate, U. Notre Dame, Ind.; MD cum laude, Ohio State U. CERT. ACLS; Other Advanced Trauma Life Support; Diplomate Am. Bd. of Family Practice; Diplomate Am. Bd. of Emergency Medicine. Residencies Hines Veterans Adminstrn. Hosp., Stanford U. Med. Ctr., Calif.; intenship Chgo. Wesley Meml. Hosp., Ill.; bd. dirs., Cuyahoga County, bd. advisor, regional physician, Region IX Emergency Med. Svcs., Ohio; exec. v.p., TeamHealth Midwest Team Health Holdings, Inc. Mem.: The Am. Coll. of Emergency Physicians (ACEP). Office: Team Health Holdings Inc 265 Brookview Ctr Way Ste 400 Knoxville TN 37919 Office Phone: 865-693-1000. Office Fax: 865-539-3073. Business E-Mail: james.rybak@teamhealth.com.

RYBERG, WALTER GREG, state legislator; b. Eau Claire, Wis., Oct. 5, 1946; s. Walter G. and Patricia C. Ryberg; m. Elizabeth Rose Denkewalter, 1968; children: Amy, Kyle, Shana. BS in Math., Marquette U., 1968. Pres. R & H Maxxon Inc.; CEO REI Inc.; mem. Dist. 24 SC State Senate, 1993—, chair Labor, Commerce and Industry Com. Named Aiken County Bus. Person of Yr., 1993. Mem.: Greater Aiken C. of C. Republican. Roman Catholic. Address: PO Box 1077 Aiken SC 29801 Office: 313 Gressette Bldg Columbia SC 29201 Office Phone: 803-641-4125, 803-212-6320. Business E-Mail: wgr@legis.lpitr.state.sc.us.

RYDER, BARBARA GERSHON, computer science professor; PhD, Rutgers, The State U. NJ, 1982. With Bell Labs., Murray Hill, NJ, Rutgers, The State U. NJ, 1982—, prof. computer sci. Piscataway, NJ. Sabbatical leave IBM T.J. Watson Rsch. Ctr., 2004; disting. prof. Computer Rsch. Assn. Com. on the Status of Women in Computing Rsch. (CRA-W), 2004; invited keynote spkr. Internat. Conf. on Compiler Construction, Warsaw, 2003; invited spkr. 4th Internat. Static Analysis Symposium, Paris, 1997, 3rd Internat. Summer Sch. on Advanced Computer Arch. and Complication for Embedded Sys., L'Aquila, Italy, 2007; gen. chair Internat. Symposium on Software Testing and Analysis, Seattle, 2008; mem. adv. bd. Douglass Project for Rutgers Women in Sci., Math & Engring.; mem. adv. com. Office of Promotion of Women in Sci., Engring. and Math.; co-advisor Women in Computer Sci., Rutgers, The State U. NJ; co-chair NSF workshop, Integrative Computing Edn. & Rsch.: Preparing IT Graduates for 2010 and Beyond, U. Mass., 2005; co-organizer WOWinC (Work Opportunities for Women in Computing, NYU Conf., 2005; panelist, New Software Engring. Faculty Symposia Internat. Conf. on Software Engring., spkr., Setting up a Rsch. Agenda and Mentoring Students, New Software Engring. Faculty Symposium, 2005, 2006, co-chair, doctoral symposium, Univ. Coll., 2007; invited disting. lecture series spkr. Mem. editl. bd. Software, Practice and Experience, 2004, assoc. editor IEEE Transactions on Software Engring., 2003. Recipient NSF Faculty award for Women Scientists and Engineers, 1991—96; named Prof. of Yr. for Excellence in Tchg., Computer Sci. Grad. Students Soc., Rutgers U., 2003. Fellow: Assn. for Computing Machinery (nat. lectr. 1985—88, SIGPLAN 1995—97, coun. mem. 2000—, Transactions on Programming Languages and Sys. 2001—07, gen. chair, Federated Conf. on Rsch. in Computing 2003, served on many programs and conf. com., SIGPLAN and SIGSOFT, SIGPLAN Disting. Svc. award 2001); mem.: Computer Rsch. Assn. (bd. dir. 1998—2001, panelist, Workshops on Academic Careers for Woemn). Office: Head Dept Computer Sci Virginia Tech 1107 Knowledgeworks II 2050 Torgersen -106 Blacksburg VA 24061 Office Phone: 540-231-4260. Office Fax: 540-231-4240. Business E-Mail: ryder@cs.vt.edu.

RYDER, JOHN L., lawyer, political organization worker; b. Chgo., Ill., May 31, 1949; m. Lain Whitaker. BA, Wabash Coll., 1971; JD, Vanderbilt U., 1974. Bar: Tenn. 1974, US Supreme Ct. 1979. Assoc. Canada, Russell & Turner, Memphis, 1974-77; ptnr. Laughlin, Halle, Regan, Clare & Gibsco, Memphis, 1977-85, Apperson, Crump & Maxwell, Memphis, 1985; mem. Harris Shelton, Memphis, 2000—; gen. counsel Rep. Nat. Com. (RNC), Washington, 2013—. Editor: Laws of Shelby County, 1980. Del. Rep. Nat. Conv., 1984, 2004, 2008, 2012; nat. committeeman from Tenn. Rep. Nat. Com. (RNC), 1996—2004, 2008—, mem. rules com.; chair Shelby County Rep. Party, Memphis, 1987—91; chmn. Opera Memphis, 2007—10. Mem.: Am. Boulder Inst., Rep. Nat. Lawyers Assn. (v.p.), Memphis Bar Assn., Tenn. Bar Assn. Republican. Office: Harris Shelton Ste 2700 One Commerce Sq Memphis TN 38103-2555 Office Phone: 901-525-1455. E-mail: jryder@harrisshelton.com.

RYMER, JON THOMAS, federal agency administrator; b. Apr. 2, 1955; m. Debra Rymer; 1 child, Thomson. BA in Economics, U. Tenn., 1981; MBA, U. Ark., 1996. Exec. v.p. First American Nat. Bank (now AmSouth Bank), Knoxville and Nashville, 1981—92, Boatman's Bank Ark. (now Bank of America), Little Rock, 1992—97; dir., practice leader assurance based adv. services KPMG LLP, Chgo. & Cin., 1997—2004; insp. gen. FDIC, Washington, 2006—13, US Dept. Def., Washington, 2013—. Served with US Army, 1975—2007. Decorated Meritorious Svc. medal with oak leaf cluster, Humanitarian Svc. medal. Mem.: Inst. Internal Auditors, American Legion. Office: US Dept Defense 4800 Mark Ctr Dr Alexandria VA 22350*

RYNDERS, ED, state legislator; m. Jane Rynders. State rep. Dist. 137, Ga., 2003—04; state rep. Dist. 152 Ga., 2004—; mem. Children & Youth Coms., Higher Edn. Coms., State Planning & Cmty. Affairs Coms. Republican. Methodist. Mailing: 404 Legislative Office Bldg Atlanta GA 30334 Home Phone: 229-436-7456; Office Phone: 229-888-9928, 404-656-0109. Fax: 229-888-9956. Business E-Mail: erynders@legis.state.ga.us.

RYNESKA, JOHN JOSEPH, government agency employee; b. Lebanon, Tenn., Sept. 13, 1946; m. Judith Ailene Moore; children: Jennifer, Kristine, Ashley, Kimberly, John. BBA, U.S. Mil. Acad., 1968; MA in Bus. Adminstrn., Webster U., 1979; grad., Command and Gen. Staff Coll., Nat. War Coll., 1979. Commd. 2nd lt. U.S. Army, 1988, advanced through grades to maj. gen., 1997, various positions, G3 exercise officer So. European Task Force, with Vicenza, Italy, 1975-78, tactics instr., field artillery br. rep. West Point, N.Y., 1979-82, bn. S3, divsn. asst. fire support coord. 82d Airborne Divsn. Ft. Bragg, N.C., 1982, bn. comdr. 2d Bn. (Airborne), 319th Field Artillery, 1985-88, asst. dep. dir. ops., J3 Joint Staff Washington, 1988-90, comdr. 7th Inf. Divsn. (Light) Artillery Ft. Ord, Calif., 1990, comdr. Battle Command Tng. Program Ft. Leavenworth, Kans., 1992-94, comdr. XVIII Airborne Corps Artillery Ft. Bragg, N.C., 1994, dep. comdr. JTF 190; asst. chief of staff, C3/J3/G3 Combined Forces Command U.S. Forces Korea/Eighth U.S. Army, 1996; dep. commdg. gen. XVIII Airborne Corps and Ft. Bragg U.S. Army, 1998—2001; with nat. security dept. Oak Ridge Nat. Lab., Dept. Def., 2003—. Decorated Def. Disting. Svc. medal, Silver Star, Legion of Merit with oak leaf cluster, Bronze Star with two oak leaf clusters, Def. Meritorious Svc. medal with oak leaf cluster, Meritorious Svc. medal with oak leaf cluster, 23 Air medals. Avocation: golf. Office: Nat Security Oak Ridge Nat Lab PO Box 2008 Oak Ridge TN 37831

RYSKAMP, KENNETH LEE, federal judge; b. Grand Rapids, Mich., 1932; m. Karyl Sonja Ryskamp; 1 child, Cara Leigh. AB, Calvin Coll., 1954; JD, U. Miami, 1956. Bar: Fla. 1956, Mich. 1957, U.S. Supreme Ct. 1970. Law clk. to presiding judge Fla. Ct. Appeals 3rd Dist., 1957-59; pvt. practice Miami, Fla., 1959-61; ptnr. Goodwin, Ryskamp, Welcher & Carrier, Miami, 1961-84; mng. ptnr. Squire, Sanders & Dempsey, Miami, 1984-86; judge US Dist. Ct. (so. dist.) Fla., Miami, 1986—2000, sr. judge, 2000—. Office: US Dist Ct 701 Clematis St Rm 416 West Palm Beach FL 33401-5112

SAALFELD, FRED ERICH, science educator, researcher; s. Eric Arthur and Milla (Kessler) S.; m. Elizabeth Renner, Nov. 22, 1958; 1 child, Fred E. Jr. (dec.). BS cum laude, So. East Mo. State U., 1957; MS in Phys. Chemistry, Iowa State U., 1959, PhD in Phys. Chemistry, 1961. Instr. Iowa State U., Ames, 1961—62; chemist Naval Rsch. Lab, Washington, 1962—63, head mass spectrometry sect., 1963—74, head phys. chem. br., 1974—76, supt. chem. divsn., 1976—82; chief scientist Office Naval Rsch., London, 1979—80, dir. rsch. Arlington, Va., 1982—87, dir., 1987—93, dep. chief naval rsch., tech. dir., 1993—98, exec. dir., tech. dir., 1998—2002; disting. rsch. prof. Ctr. for Tech. and Nat. Security Policy Nat. Def. U., 2003—04; sr. fellow Potomac Inst. for Policy Studies, 2002—, bd. regents, 2007—. Author more than 500 publications, reports, presentations on applications of mass spectrometry to fields of combustion, laser, environ. analysis. Recipient Disting. Rank awards U.S. Pres., Washington, 1989, 96, Meritorious Rank award U.S. Pres., Washington, 1986, Robert Conrad award Sec. USN, Washington, 1988, Disting. Civilian Svc. award Sec. of Def./Dept. Def., 1999; named Fed. Exec. of Yr., Fed. Exec. Inst., Washington, 1991, named Fred E. Saalfed award for lifetime achievement in sci., Chief Naval Rsch., 2001. Fellow AAAS, Potomac Inst. Policy Studies (sr.); mem. Am. Chem. Soc. (councilor 1973-89), Am. Soc. Mass Spectrometry (sec. 1970-74), Combustion Inst., Chem. Soc. Washington (pres. 1972). Achievements include provision for science base for life support systems used in enclosed environments; development of educational programs used by USN for scientist training. Office Phone: 703-887-2197. Personal E-mail: fsaalfeld@verizon.net.

SABAN, NICK (NICHOLAS LOU SABAN), college football coach, former professional football coach; b. Fairmont, W. Va., Oct. 31, 1951; s. Nicholas Lou and Mary Saban; m. Terry Constable, Dec. 18, 1971; children: Nicholas, Kristen. BS in Bus., Kent State U., 1973, MA in Sports Adminstrn., 1975. Grad. asst. Kent State U. Golden Flashes, 1973—74, linebackers coach, 1975—76; outside linebackers coach Syracuse U. Orangemen, 1977; secondary coach W. Va. U. Mountaineers, Morgantown, 1978—79, Ohio State U. Buckeyes, Columbus, 1980—81, US Naval Acad. Midshipmen, Annapolis, 1981; secondary coach & defensive coord. Mich. State U. Spartans, East Lansing, 1983—87, head coach, 1995—2000; secondary coach Houston Oilers, 1988—89; head coach Toledo U. Rockets, 1990; defensive coord. Cleve. Browns, 1991—94; head coach La. State U. Fighting Tigers, Baton Rouge, 2000—05, Miami Dolphins, 2005—07, U. Ala. Crimson Tide, Tuscaloosa, 2007—. Co-author (with Sam King): Tiger Turnaround: LSU's Return to Football Glory, 2001; co-author: How Good Do You Want to Be, 2005. Founder Nick's Kids; active Children's Miracle Network. Recipient Paul "Bear" Bryant award, Nat. Sportscasters & Sportswriters Assn., 2003, Eddie Robinson award, 2003, Coach of Yr. award, Liberty Mutual, 2008, Walter Camp Coach of Yr. award, Walter Camp Football Found., 2008, Bobby Bowden Nat. Collegiate Coach of Yr. award, Over the Mountain Touchdown Club, 2011—13; named Nat. Coach of Yr., AP, 2003, 2008, SEC Coach of Yr., 2003, 2008, The Sporting News, 2008, Nat. Coach of Yr., 2008, Home Depot Coach of Yr., ESPN, ABC Sports, 2008, Coach of Yr., Southeastern Conf., 2009. Achievements include head coach of the BCS National Championship winning Louisiana State University Fighting Tigers, 2003; University of Alabama Crimson Tide, 2009, 2011, 2012. Avocation: golf. Office: University of Alabama Football Program Box 870393 Tuscaloosa AL 35487-0393

SABATINI, SANDRA, physician; b. NYC, Dec. 1, 1940; BS in Chemistry, Millsaps Coll., 1962; MS in Pharmacology, Marquette U., 1966; PhD in Pharmacology, U. Miss., 1968; MD in Internal Medicine, Tex. Med. Sch., 1974. Lic. physician, Ill., Tex. Intern in medicine U. Ill. Hosp., Chgo., 1974-75; asst. prof. U. Tex. Med. Sch., San Antonio, 1968-70; assoc. dir. U. Ill. Hosp., Chgo., 1977-78; asst. prof. U. Ill. Coll. of Medicine, Chgo., 1977-83, assoc. prof. medicine and physiology, 1983-84; attending physician in nephrology VA, Chgo., 1977-84; med. dir. Dialysis Unit U. Ill., Chgo., 1978-84; prof. internal medicine and physiology Tex. Tech. U. Health Sci. Ctr., Lubbock, 1985—, chmn. dept. physiology, 1993-96; attending physician in nephrology U. Med. Ctr., Lubbock, 1985—. Lab. instr. Millsaps Coll., Jackson, Miss., 1961-62; instr. pharmacology Bapt. Hosp. Sch. Nursing, Jackson, 1966-68; merit rev. mem. NSF, 1987, 91, 92; rev. mem. several orgns. including Chgo. Heart Assn., 1984, NIH, 1983, 86, 89-93, 96, Nat. Kidney Found., 1987, 89—, Am. Heart Assn., 1981-84, others; cons. U.S. Med. Licensing Exam/Nat. Bd. Med. Examiners, Step 1 Physiology Test Com., 1996-99. Editl. referee Am. Jour. Kidney Disease, Am. Jour. Physiology, Am. Jour. Nephrology, Annals of Internal Medicine, others; mem. editl. bd. Am. Jour. Nephrology, 1989-93, Seminars in Nephrology, 1984—; co-editor Am. Jour. Kidney Diseases, 1997—; author numerous publs. and abstracts in field; contbr. articles to profl. jours. Bd. dirs. YWCA of Lubbock, 1994-99; mem. Leadership Tex., 1994. Predoctoral fellowship grantee Marquette U., 1963-66; pub. health predoctoral fellow U. Miss. Med. Sch., 1967-69, gen. medicine sci. rsch. grantee U. Tex. Med. Sch., 1968-70, post-grad. fellow Karolinska Inst., Swedish Med. Coun., 1971, 73, NIH grantee, 1979-82, 84-99, Chgo. Heart Assn. grantee-in-aid, 1979-85, 99; grantee Nat. Eye Inst., 1979-80; recipient Banes Charitable trust award U. Ill., 1984-85, U.S. Olympic com. Rsch. Foudn., 1986-87; recipient Outstanding Alumnus award Tex. Med. Sch., 1994, numerous other awards in field. Fellow: ACP; mem.: AAUP, AAAS, ADA (hon.), Lubbock Arts Alliance, Leadership Tex. Alumnae Assn., Nat. Kidney Found. West Tex. (bd. dirs. 1993—99, Outstanding Vol. 1995, 2001, Disting. Svc. award 1996), Nat. Kidney

Found. (numerous offices including chmn. several coms.), Italian-Am. Nephrologists, Inc., Internat. Soc. Nephrology, Ill. Kidney Found., Ctrl. Soc. Clin. Rsch., So. Soc. Clin. Rsch. (councillor 1997—99, pres.-elect 1999, pres. 2000), Assn. Chairs Dept. Physiology (councillor 1995—97), Am. Soc. Renal Biochemistry and Metabolism (pres.-elect 1994), Am. Soc. Pharmacology and Exptl. Therapeutics, Am. Soc. Nephrology, Am. Physiol. Soc., Am. Heart Assn., Am. Fedn. Med. Rsch., Lubbock Women's Club, Rotary Internat. Office: Tex Tech U Health Sci Ctr 3601 4th St Lubbock TX 79430-0001

SABATO, LARRY JOSEPH, political science professor, director; b. Norfolk, Va., Aug. 7, 1952; s. N.J. and Margaret F. (Simmons) S. BA, U. Va., 1974; postgrad., Princeton U., 1974-75; DPhil, Oxford U., 1977. Lectr. politics New Coll. Oxford U., 1977-78; Robert Kent Gooch prof. politics U. Va., Charlottesville, 1978—; founder, dir. U. Va. Ctr. for Politics, 1998—, Larry J. Sabato's Crystal Ball. Guest scholar Brookings Instn., 1980; Thomas Jefferson vis. prof. Downing Coll., Cambridge U., 1982. Author: The Rise of Political Consultants: New Ways of Winning Elections, 1981, Goodbye to Goodtime Charlie: The American Governorship Transformed, 1983, PAC Power: Inside the World of Political Action Committees, 1984, The Party's Just Begun: Shaping Political Parties for America's Future, 1988, Feeding Frenzy: How Attack Journalism Has Transformed American Politics, 1991, American Government: Roots and Reform, 1992, Dirty Little Secrets: The Persistence of Corruption in American Politics, 1996, Midterm Madness: The Elections of 2002, 2002, Toward the Millennium: The Elections of 1996, 1997, Overtime!, 2001, The Election 2002, Thriller, 2001, Get In The Booth: A Citizen's Guide to the 2004 Election, 2004, Divided States of America: The Slash and Burn Politics of the 2004 Presidential Election, 2005, Get in the Booth! A Citizen's Guide to the 2006 Election, 2006, The Sixth Year Itch: The Rise and Fall of the George W. Bush Presidency, 2007, A More Perfect Constitution, 2007. Danforth fellow, 1975; Kellog fellow, 1983; Rhodes scholar; recipient Thomas Jefferson award U. Va., 2001. Mem. Am. Polit. Sci. Assn., Phi Beta Kappa. Office: U Va Dept Politics S183 Gibson Hall 1540 Jefferson Park Ave Charlottesville VA 22904 Office Phone: 434-243-8472. Business E-Mail: sabato@virginia.edu.*

SABB, RONNIE A., state legislator; b. Greeleyville, Sept. 2, 1958; children: Annie Ree Sabb, John Earl. BS, Voorhees Coll., 1980; attended, U. Fla., 1987. Deacon Good Hope Bapt. Ch.; mem. Residing in Williamsburg County; atty.; asst. solicitor, 1990—2010; gen. Counsel Santee Electric Coop., 1997—; bd. govs. Assn. of Justice, 2005—, SC Bar, 2007; mem. Dist. 101 SC House of Representatives, 2011—. Recipient Hall of Fame award, Voorhees Coll., 2008. Democrat. Mailing: South Carolina House of Representatives District 101 PO Box 311 Greeleyville SC 29056 Address: 432A Blatt Bldg Columbia SC 29201 Office Phone: 843-426-4138.

SABBATINI, RORY, professional golfer; b. Durban, South Africa, Apr. 2, 1976; Student, U. Ariz., Tucson. Mem. PGA Tour, 1998—. Mem. South African team World Golf Championships-World Cup, 2002—04, 2006, 2008; mem. internat. team. Presidents Cup, 2007. Named to U. Ariz. Sports Hall of Fame, 2004. Achievements include winning (with Trevor Immelman) the World Golf Championships-World Cup, 2003; winning PGA Tour events: Air Canada Championship, 2000; FBR Capital Open, 2003; Nissan Open, 2006; Crowne Plaza Invitational at Colonial, 2007; Byron Nelson Championship, 2009; The Honda Classic, 2011. Office: PGA Tour 112 PGA TOUR Blvd Ponte Vedra Beach FL 32082

SABIN, JOHN ROGERS, retired physics professor; b. Springfield, Mass., Apr. 29, 1940; s. Henry Bowman and Elizabeth (Rogers) S.; m. Claudia Ball, 1963 (div. 1978); children: Peter Bowman, Amanda Ball; m. Birgit Horn, Aug. 8, 1987; children: Lene Elizabeth Horn, Niels Kristian Horn. AB, Williams Coll., 1962; PhD, U. N.H., 1966. Asst. prof. chemistry U. Mo., Columbia, 1968—71; assoc. prof. physics U. Fla., Gainesville, 1971—77, prof., 1977—, dir. info. tech., Coll. Liberal Arts and Scis., 1998—2008, interim chmn. dept. physics, 2002; adjungeret prof. U. So. Denmark, 1992—; assoc. dean Coll. Liberal Arts and Scis., 2006—08. Guest prof. Odense (Denmark) U., 1980-92, Nordita prof., Odense, 1982-83, Fulbright prof., 1986, 91. Editor Advances in Quantum Chemistry; cons. editor Internat. Jour. Quantum Chemistry; mem. editl. bd. Croatia Chemica Acta, 2000—, The Open Chemical Physics Jour. 2007-. Fellow Am. Phys. Soc., Am. Inst. Chemists; mem. Am. Chem. Soc., Danish Phys. Soc., Danish Chem. Soc. Home: 415 NW 23rd St Gainesville FL 32607-2618 Office: U Florida Dept Physics PO Box 118435 Gainesville FL 32611-8435 Home Phone: 352-336-8635; Office Phone: 352-392-1597. Business E-Mail: sabin@qtp.ufl.edu.

SABOL, STUART J., otolaryngologist; b. Indpls. m. Michele J. Sabol; children: Nicole, Taylor. BA in Biology and Chemistry, Ind. U., Indpls., 1983, MD, 1990. Resident U. Tex., San Antonio, 1990—95; physician Stuart, Fla., 1995—. Fellow: Am. Acad. Otolaryngology, Head and Neck Surgery; mem.: AMA, Martin County Med. Soc. (pres.), Fla. Med. Assn. Office: 2221 E Ocean Bldg Ste 300 Stuart FL 34996

SACHER, STEVEN JAY, lawyer; b. Cleve., Jan. 28, 1942; s. Albert N. and Cecil P. (Chessin) S.; m. Colleen Marie Gibbons, Nov. 28, 1970; children— Alexander Jerome, Barry Elizabeth, William Paul. BS, U. Wis., 1964; JD, U. Chgo., 1967. Bar: D.C. 1968. Assoc. solicitor Employee Retirement Income Security Act U.S. Dept. Labor, Washington, 1974-77; spl. counsel com. on labor and human resources U.S. Senate, Washington, 1977-79, gen. counsel, 1980-81; ptnr. Pepper Hamilton, Washington, 1982-88; shareholder Johnson & Gibbs, Washington, 1988-94; ptnr. Kilpatrick Stockton LLP, Washington, 1994—2007, Jones Day, Washington, 2007—11, ret., 2012; vis. com. mem. U. Chgo. Law Sch., 2009—11. Adj. prof. law Georgetown U. Law Ctr., 1977; co-chair sr. editors Employee Benefits Law and Annual Supplements, Bur. Nat. Affairs, Washington, 1991-2000. Mem. adv. bd. BNA Pension and Benefits Reporter, 1981-, co-chair, 2009-10; mem. editorial bd. Benefits Law Jour., Jour. Pension Planning and Compliance. Founding mem. ERISA Roundtable, Washington. Recipient AV ranking, Martindale-Hubbell, 1984—2012, top-ranking, Chambers USA, 2005—12; named Lawdragon's 100 Most Powerful Employment Attys. in America, Human Resource Exec. Mag., 2009; named one of Washington Super Lawyers, 2007—11, Top 100 Washington Super Lawyers, 2009—11; named to Best Lawyers in Am., 1987—. Fellow Coll. Labor and Employment Lawyers, Am. Coll. Employee Benefits Counsel (charter); mem. ABA (mgmt. co-chmn. com. on employee benefits, sect. on labor and employment law 1988-91, chmn. prohibited trans. subcom., com. on employee benefits, sect. on taxation 1986-91), D.C. Bar Assn. Personal E-mail: homebase307@comcast.net.

SACHS, BENJAMIN PAUL, medical educator, dean; b. London, May 26, 1951; MBBS, Imperial Coll., London, 1975; DPH, U. Toronto, Can., 1977; completed bus. mgmt. program, Harvard U. Bus. Sch., 1987. Residency in ob-gyn. and fellowship in maternal-fetal medicine Brigham & Women's Hosp.; vis. scientist Centers for Disease Control and Prevention; faculty mem. Harvard U.; dept. chmn. ob-gyn. Beth Israel Deaconess Med. Ctr.; Harold Rosenfield prof. ob-gyn. and reproductive biology Harvard U. Med. Ctr.; prof. Harvard U. Sch. Pub. Health; sr. v.p., dean, sch. medicine Tulane U., 2007—. Recipient The Joint Commn. Eisenberg Nat. award, Nat. Quality Forum, 2007, Healthcare Excellence award, Blue Cross Blue Shield, 2007, Spencer Foreman award, Assn. Academic Med. Ctr., 2010. Office: Tulane University Sch Medicine Office of Dean 1430 Tulane Ave New Orleans LA 70112 Business E-Mail: bsachs@tulane.edu.*

SACHS, MARIA LORTS, state legislator; b. Battle Creek, Mich., Mar. 25, 1949; m. Peter Sachs; children: Natasha, Marcello, Taylor. BA cum laude, U. Md.; MA, Boston U.; JD, U. Miami. Atty.; assoc. prof. U. Md.; mem. Dist. 86 Fla. House of Reps., Tallahassee, 2006—10; mem. Dist. 30 Fla. State Senate, 2011—. Mem.: NOW, Statewide Fla. Assn. Women Lawyers, Calif. Bar. Assn., Fla. Bar Assn., Fed. Bar, So. Dist. Fla., Delray Beach C. of C., Boynton Beach C. of C., Boca Raton C. of C. Democrat. Roman Catholic. Office: Fla State Senate 216 Senate Office Bldg 402 S Monroe St Tallahassee FL 32399-1100 also: 100 NW 1st Ave Delray Beach FL 33444-2612 Office Phone: 561-279-1427, 850-487-5091. Business E-Mail: sachs.maria.web@flsenate.gov.

SACHSON, RICHARD A., endocrinologist, educator; BS, CUNY: Bklyn. Coll., 1960—64; MD summa cum laude, SUNY, 1964—68. Diplomate American Bd. Internal Medicine, 1973, American Bd. Internal Medicine-endocrinology, diabetes and metabolism, 1973. Guest investigator Rockefeller Univ., NYC, 1967—68; intern, dept. medicine Univ. of Chgo. Hosps., 1968—69, resident, dept. medicine, 1969—70; clin. assoc. NIH, Bethesda, Md., 1970—72; clin. rsch. fellow, endocrine unit Mass. Gen. Hosp., Boston, 1972—74; investigator/sub-investigator Endocrine Assocs. of Dallas Rsch. Inst. of Dallas, 1974—; clin. endocrinologist Endocrine Assocs. of Dallas, P.A., 1974—; attending physician Presbyn. Hosp., Dallas, 1974—, St. Paul Hosp., Dallas, 1974—, med. dir., diabetes mgmt., 1986—97; clin. asst. prof. medicine Univ. of Tex. Southwestern Med. Ctr., Dallas, 1974—80, clin. assoc. prof. medicine, 1980—81, clin. prof. medicine, 1991—. Recipient Hilger Perry Jenkins award, Univ. Chgo., 1970. Fellow: ACP, American Coll. of Endocrinology; mem.: AMA, Tex. Endocrine and Diabetes Assn. (bd.dirs. 1985—87), Endocrine Soc. (clin. endocrinology initiatives com. 1993—96), American Diabetes Assn. (bd. dirs. Tex. affiliate 1982—89, bd. dirs. Dallas chpt. 1982—98, v.p. Tex. affiliate 1983—86, pres. Tex. affiliate 1986—88, nat. bd. dirs. 1988—91, profl. practice com. 1989—91, vice chmn., profl. membership task force 1991—92), Dallas Acad. of Internal Medicine, Tex. Med. Assn., American Assn. of Clin. Endocrinologists, Dallas Internist Club (pres. 1979—80). Office: Endocrine Associates of Dallas PA Ste 100N 10260 N Central Expy Dallas TX 75231 Office Phone: 214-365-5535.

SACKHEIM, ROBERT LEWIS, aerospace engineer, educator; b. NYC, May 16, 1937; s. A. Frederick and Lillian L. (Emmer) S.; m. Babette Freund, Jan. 12, 1964; children: Karen Holly, Andrew Frederick. BSChemE, U. Va., 1959; MSChemE, Columbia U., 1961; postgrad., UCLA, 1966—72. Project engr. Comsat Corp., El Segundo, Calif., 1969-72; project mgr. TRW, Redondo Beach, Calif., 1964-69, sect. head, 1972-76, dept. mgr., 1976-81, mgr. new bus., 1981-86, lab. mgr., 1986-90, dep. ctr. dir., 1990-93, ctr. dir., 1993-99; asst. dir, chief engr. for space propulsion systems Marshall Space Flight Ctr, NASA, Huntsville, Ala., 1999—2006; adj. prof. mech. and aerospace engring. U. Ala., Huntsville, 2006—; ind. cons. in space and launch vehicles and propulsion sys. and tech. Instr. UCLA engring. ext., 1986, Continuing Engring. Edn., U. Ala., Huntsville, 2001; mem. adv. bds. NASA, Washington, 1989—; mem. peer rev. bd. various univs. and govtl. agys., 1990—; mem. Nat. Rsch. Coun./Aeronautics and Space Engring. Bd., 1994—; mem. NRC com. propulsion evaluation, 2003; mem. various NASA investigation teams; guest lectr. various univs. and AIAA short courses. Author: Space Mission Analysis and Design, 1991, Space Propulsion Analysis and Design, 1994, Space Launch and Transportation Systems, 2004; contbr. chpt. to book, more than 250 articles to profl. jours., confs. Mem. adv. bd. L.A. Bd. Edn., 1990-92; fund raiser March of Dimes, L.A., 1970-90, YMCA, San Pedro, Calif., 1974-86. Capt. USAF Reserve, 1960-63. Recipient 16 Group Achievement awards NASA, 1970, 78, 86, 2000, 2001, 2003, 2005, Sustained Svc. award AIAA, 2000, medal for outstanding tech. leadership NASA, Propulsion Outstanding Contbns. award French Acad. Aero/Astro., 2002, NASA/Dir.'s commendation, 2003, Presdl. Rank award for disting. fed. civil svc., 3rd ann. TRW Chmn. awards, TRW Patent of Yr. award, 1992, Govs. award for disting. svc. state Ala., 2004. Fellow AIAA (chmn. com. 1980-83, chmn. L.A. sect. 1997, chmn. Ala./Miss. sect. 2000, 2001, J.H. Wyld Propulsion award 1992, Shuttle Flag award 1984, Martin Schilling award 2001, Hermann Oberth award 2002, Holgar Toftoy award 2003), Internat. Acad. Astronautics, Nat. Acad. Engring., Sigma Xi. Achievements include 9 patents in field. Office: U Alabama Rm N249 Huntsville AL 35812 Office Phone: 256-824-5121. Business E-Mail: sackheir@uah.edu.

SACKS, JEFFREY D., information technology executive; BS in Mktg., Fla. State U., BS in Mgmt. Info. Sys. & Computer Sciences, 1985. Sr. computer specialist USDOT/VNTSC, 1989—94; mng. assoc., mgmt. consulting Coopers & Lybrand LLP, 1994—95; dir., mgmt. consulting Litton PRC, 1995—98; v.p., mgmt. consulting ADI, 1998—99; v.p., equity ptnr. The Revere Group, 1999—2003; sr. dir., v.p. level H&R Block, 2003—06; v.p., tech. JP Morgan Chase, Columbus, Ohio, 2006—09; chief tech. officer Access Systems, Inc., 2009—. Office: Access Systems Inc Ste 900 12011 Sunset Hills Rd Ste 1200 Reston VA 20190-5922 Office Phone: 703-464-6900. Office Fax: 703-464-6990. Business E-Mail: jsacks@accsys-inc.com.

SACKS, JOEL GERALD, ophthalmologist, educator; b. Chgo., Sept. 14, 1939; s. Louis and Rose S.; m. Cynthia Ann Dana, June 10, 1967; children: Charles, David, Martha. BA, Northwestern U., 1960, MS, 1962, MD, 1963; MBA, U. Cin., 1986. Diplomate, Am. Bd. Ophthalmology. NIH spl. fellow Md. Med. Legal Found., Balt., 1967-68; rsch. fellow Johns Hopkins Sch. Medicine, Balt., 1968-69; asst. prof. to assoc. prof. Northwestern U., Chgo., 1969-77; prof., dir. dept. ophthalmology U. Cin., 1977-94, prof. emeritus ophthalmology, 2005—; pres. Ophthalmic Cons., Inc., Cin., 1977-94; clin. prof. surgery Mich. State U., 1994-97; v.p. med. affairs, dir. med. edn. Butterworth Hosp., Grand Rapids, Mich., 1994-97; v.p., chief med. officer Touro Infirmary, New Orleans, 1998-99; clin. prof. ophthalmology Tulane U., New Orleans, 2000—06, prof. emeritus, 2006—. Pres. Med. Ctr. Fund Cin., 1985-88, Univ. Health Plan, Inc., Cin., 1987-89. Co-author: Neuropathology of Vision: an Atlas, 1973; contbr. articles to sci. jours. Founding mem. Beth Adam: The Cin. Congregation Humanistic Judaism, 1980. Capt. U.S. Army, 1967-74. Fellow Am. Acad. Ophthalmology (Honor award 1982); mem. Phi Beta Kappa, Alpha Omega Alpha. Home: 47 Fairway Oaks Dr New Orleans LA 70131-3339

SADANA, AJIT, chemical engineer, educator; b. Rawalpindi, India, Feb. 14, 1947; arrived in US, 1980; s. Jai Chand and Jinder Sadana; m. Lopa Mudra Sadana, Jan. 16, 1953; children: Neeti, Richa. B, Indian Inst. Tech., 1969; M of Chem. Engring., U. Del., 1972, PhD, 1975. Project engr. Environengineering, Inc., Somerville, NJ, 1974—75; sr. scientific officer Nat. chem. Lab., Pune, India, 1975—80; assoc. prof. chem. engring. U. Miss., University, 1981—90, prof., 1990—. Vis. assoc. prof. Auburn U., Ala., 1980—81; engr. duPont, Inc., Newark, 1989; sr. fellow Naval Rsch. Lab., Washington, 1990, disting. fellow, 1991; cons. in field. Author: Biocatalysis: Fundamentals of Enzyme Deactivation Kinetics, 1991, Bioseparations, 1997, Biosensors, 2002, 6th edit., 2010. Avocations: gardening, tennis. Home: 229 St Andrews Cir Oxford MS 38655 Office: U Miss Chem Engring Dept University MS 38677-1848 Home Phone: 662-513-6266; Office Phone: 662-915-5349. Business E-Mail: cmsadana@olemiss.edu.

SADATI, SAM S., dentist; m. Olivia Sadati; children: Sarah, Nadia. Grad. with honors, Creighton U., Omaha, 1992; postgrad in Esthetic Dentistry, U. Fla.; studied in Periodontal Esthetics, Atlantic Coast Dental Rsch. Clinic, studied in Dental Implantology, studied in Prosthetic Restoration and Dental Implantology; studied in Orthodontic Tng., US Dental Inst. Diplomate Am. Bd. of Cosmetic Dentistry. Fellow Acad. of Gen. Dentistry. Recipient gold medal, Am. Acad. of Cosmetic Dentistry's, 2003—07. Fellow: Internat. Acad. for Dental Facial Esthetics, Am. Acad. of Cosmetic Dentistry; mem.: Palm Beach County Dental Assn., Fla. Dental Assn., Am. Acad. of Implant Dentistry, ADA. Office: The Sadati Center for Aesthetic Dentistry 10140 Forest Hill Blvd 140 West Palm Beach FL 33414 Office Phone: 888-873-3558. Office Fax: 561-753-8585.

SADOSKI, MARK CHRISTIAN, education educator; b. Bristol, Conn., June 2, 1945; s. Waldmyr John Sadoski and Ruth Elaine Strong; m. Carol Ann Bove, June 28, 1969; 1 child, Thomas Christian. BS, So. Conn. State U., 1968, MS, 1973; PhD, U. Conn., 1981. Cert. reading, English, social studies tchr. Tchr., reading cons. Milford (Conn.) Pub. Schs., 1968-81; assoc. faculty So. Conn. State U., New Haven, 1978-81; prof. edn. Tex. A&M U., Coll. Sta., 1981—2010; dir. ednl. r & d, Coll. Medicine Tex. A&M U. Health Sci. Ctr., 2010—13. Author: Conceptual Foundations of Teaching Reading, 2004, (with Allan Paivio) Imagery and Text: A Dual Coding Theory of Reading and Writing, 2001, 2nd edit., 2013; mem. consulting editl. bd. Reading Rsch. Quar., 1989—2007, 2012-, Jour. Reading Behavior, 1990-95, Reading Psychology, 1990—, Jour. Literacy Rsch., 1995-2005, 2013-, Info. Design Jour./Document Design, 1998—, Reading and Writing, 2001—; contbr. over 100 articles to profl. jours. and books. Recipient Disting. Alumnus award So. Conn. State U., 1994. Mem. Internat. Reading Assn. (outstanding dissertation award com. 1983-85, finalist Outstanding Dissertation award 1982), Nat. Reading Conf. (Outstanding Book award com. 1994-99), Am. Ednl. Rsch. Assn. (outstanding book award com. 1994-2000), Soc. for Sci. Study of Reading (chair pubs. com. 1996-97), Phi Kappa Phi. Avocations: reading, photography. Office: Health Professions Edn Bldg 8447 State Hwy 47 MS 1359 Bryan TX 77807 Business E-Mail: mcsadoski@medicine.tamhsc.edu.

SADOWSKI, CAROL JOHNSON, artist; b. Chgo., Mar. 20, 1929; d. Carl Valdamar Johnson and Elizabeth Hilma (Booth) Johnson Chellberg; m. Edmund Sadowski, July 9, 1949; children: Lynn Carol Mahoney, Christie Sadowski Cortez. AAS, Wright Coll., Ill., 1949. Tchr. art Malverne H.S., NY, 1968-69; artist Valley Stream, NY, 1968-76, Hollywood, Fla., 1976—. Guest spkr. Mus. Art, Ft. Lauderdale, Fla., 1991; Libr. League, Oakland Park, 1985; Boca Raton, Fla. Mus., others; TV appearances on WCGB, Gainesville; WSVN, Miami; Storer and Hollywood Cable; Artist Guild, Boca Raton Mus.; Broward C.C., Hollywood, Fla. One woman shows include Mus. Fla. History, Tallahassee, 1984-85, 87; Hist. Mus. South Fla., Miami, 1986; Thomas Ctr. Arts, Gainesville, Fla., 1985, 87; Elliott Mus., Stuart, Fla., 1987; Hemingway Mus. and Home, Key West, Fla., 1986; I.G.F.A. Fishing Hall of Fame Mus., Dania, Fla., 1999, Alliance Francaise de Miami, 1995; commd. painting St. Agustin Antigua Found., St. Augustine, Fla., 1985, Atlantic Bank, Ft. Lauderdale, Fla., Bonnet House Fla. Trust, Ft. Lauderdale, Hollywood Art & Culture Ctr., Hemingway Mus., San Francisco de Paula, Presdl. Palace, Havana, Tropical Art Gallery, Naples, Fla., 1981-83, Tequesta (Fla.) Art Gallery, 1985-89, Gingerbread Square Gallery, Key West, 1990—, Wally Findlay Galleries, Inc., Palm Beach and N.Y.C., DeBruyne Fine Arts Gallery, Naples, 1998—, Patricia Cloutier Gallery, Tequesta, Fla., 1992-. Mem. Ft. Lauderdale Mus. Art; Hollywood Art and Culture Ctr. Recipient Hemingway medal, Ernest Hemingway Mus., Cuba, 1990; appreciation award City of Hollywood; Chgo. Art Inst. scholar; Salmagundi Club N.Y. scholar. Mem. Internat. Platform Assn., Broward Art Guild, Fla. Hist. Assn., Ernest Hemingway Soc., Chopin Found., Am. Inst. for Polish Culture, Alliance Francaise de Miami, Women in the Arts Nat. Mus. (charter mem.), Nat. Women's History Mus. (charter mem.). Avocations: travel, bicycling, swimming, reading. Home and Office: 1480 Sheridan St Apt B 17 Hollywood FL 33020-2295 Office Phone: 954-925-7482. Personal E-mail: carolsadowski@att.net.

SADOWSKI, PETER T., lawyer; b. Warsaw, Oct. 30, 1954; came to U.S., 1968; s. Fryderyk and Maria (Jaklinska) S.; m. Denise A. Decker, Oct. 13, 1979; children: Katherine, Rachel. BA, St. Louis U., 1976; JD, St. Louis U. Law Sch., 1979. Asst. atty. gen. Mo. Atty. Gen.'s Office, Jefferson City, 1979-81; ptnr. The Stolar Partnership, St. Louis, 1981-96; shareholder Goldberg, Katz, Sadowski & Croft, St. Louis, 1996—99; exec. v.p., chief legal officer Fidelity National Financial, Inc., Jacksonville, Fla., 1999—. Chmn. bd. dirs., greater needs com. YMCA, St. Louis, 1995—. Office: Fidelity National Financial 601 Riverside Ave Jacksonville FL 32204 Office Phone: 888-934-3354.

SAENZ, MICHAEL, retired academic administrator; b. Laredo, Tex., Oct. 25, 1925; s. C.A. and Pola R. Saenz; m. Nancy Elizabeth King; children: Michael King, Cynthia Elizabeth. BS in Acctg. with honors, Tex. Christian U., 1949, MEd, 1952; PhD in Econs., U. Pa., 1961. Dep. collector IRS, Ft. Worth, Dallas, 1949-52; adminstr. United Christian Missionary Soc., Bayamon, PR, 1954-57, 59-65, exec. sec. Indpls., 1965-71; acad. dean Laredo (Tex.) Jr. Coll., 1971-74; pres. N.W. campus Tarrant County Coll., Fort Worth, Tex., 1975—2006. Founder Nat. Comm. Coll. Hispanic Coun., 1985, bd. dirs., 1985—, pres., 1989-91; founder, co-dir. Nat. Hispanic Leadership Inst., 1989—; trustee Tex. Christian U., Brite Div. Sch., 1973-2001. Bd. dirs. Civic Ballet of Laredo, Ft. Worth chpt. NCCJ, Juliette Fowler Homes, Dallas; chmn. Aztec dist., dir. Gulf Coast coun. Boy Scouts Am., 1971-75; gov. Career Devel. Ctr., Arlington, Tex.; chmn. Laredo's Bicentennial Com., 1973-76; trustee, bd. dirs. United Way Ft. Worth, 1979-88; mem., vice moderator gen. bd. Christian Ch. (Disciples of Christ), 1991-93. Mem. Am. Assn. Cmty. Colls. (bd. dirs. 1991-94), Commn. Internat. Edn. Am. Coun. Edn., Tex. Jr. Coll. Tchrs. Assn., Tex. Assn. Jr. Coll. Instructional Adminstrs., Am. Acad. Polit. and Social Scis., Urban Ministries in Higher Edn., Civic Music Assn. Laredo, Rotary.

SAFER, JOHN, sculptor; b. Washington, Sept. 6, 1922; m. Joy Scott; children: Janine Whitney, Thomas. AB, George Washington U., 1947; DPhil (hon.), George Washinton U.; DFA (hon.), George Washington U., 2009; LLB, Harvard U., 1949. Chmn. NationsBank/DC, 1980-92; chmn. exec. com. Fin. Gen. Bankshares, 1977-80; bd. dirs. Nat. Air and Space Mus., The Shakespeare Guild, Materia. Represented in permanent collections at Smithsonian Am. Art Mus., Am. Mus. Britan, Balt. Mus. Art, Corocoran Gallery Art, Am. Mus. Britain, Dayton Art Inst., Frederik Meijer Sculpture Gardens, Folger Shakespeare Libr., Johns Hopkins U., Nat. Air and Space Mus., Washington Tennis

Fedn., High Mus. Art, Atlanta, Milw. Mus. Art, Harvard Law Sch., Harvard Bus. Sch., Hofstra U., Mayo Clinic, Kimmel Cancer Ctr. Phila., Mayo Jacksonville, Fla., Pine Manor Coll, Phila. Mus. Art, San Francisco Mus. Art, Duke U. Med. Ctr., Embry-Riddle Aero. U., Georgetown U., George Washington U., Williams Coll., Wilmer Eye Inst., Scripps Rsch. Inst., Am. Hosp., Paris, Embassy of U.S., London, Nassau, Beijing, New Delhi, Nat. Jewish Mus., Nat. Peace Inst., Ponce (PR) Mus. of Art, United Nation, N.Y.C., corporate collections. including General Dynamics Celanese Corp., NY, Crown Equipment Corp., New Bremen, Ohio, First Union Bank of Md., Bank of Am. Ctr., Norfolk, Va., Gen. Mills Corp., Mpls, West Chase Corp., Houston, Nat. Air Traffic Controller, numerous others. 1st lt. USAAF, 1942-46. Mem.: Cosmos, Burning Tree, Harvard, Woodmont (Washington), Lyford Cay (Nassau), Linville Ridge (N.C.). Office: PO Box 6716 Mc Lean VA 22106-6716 Personal E-mail: johnsafer@mac.com.

SAFF, EDWARD BARRY, mathematics professor; b. NYC, Jan. 2, 1944; s. Irving H. and Rose (Koslow) Saff; m. Loretta Singer, July 3, 1966; children: Lisa Jill, Tracy Karen, Alison Michelle. BS with highest honors, Ga. Inst. Tech., 1964; PhD, U. Md., 1968. Asst. prof. U. Md., 1968; post-doctoral rschr. Imperial Coll., London, 1968-69; from asst. prof. to assoc. prof. math. U. S. Fla., 1969—76, prof., 1976-86, disting. rsch. prof., 1986—2001, dir. Ctr. Math. Svcs., 1978-83, dir. Inst. Constructive Math., 1985—2001, dir. Ctr. Constructive Approximation, 2001—; exec. dean Coll. Arts and Sci. Vanderbilt U., Nashville, 2004—07. Sr. vis. fellow Oxford U., 1978; hon. prof. Zhejiang Normal U. Author (with A. D. Snider): Fundamentals of Complex Analysis, 1976, 3d edit., 2003; author: (with A. W. Goodman) Calculus, Concepts and Calculations, 1981; author: (with A. Edrei and R. S. Varga) Zeros of Sections of Power Series; author: (with V. Totik) Logarithmic Potentials with External Fields, 1997; author: (with R. K. Nagle) Fundamentals of Differential Equations, 1993, Fundamentals of Differential Equations and Boundary Value Problems, 1993; author: (with D. S. Lubinsky) Strong Asymptotics for External Polynomials Associated with Weights on R, 1988; editor: Jour. Approximation Theory, 1990—; editor: (with R. S. Varga) Pade and Rational Approximation: Theory and Applications, 1977; editor: Cambridge U. Press, 1995—2001, Founds. Comp. Math., 1999—2004; editor-in-chief: Constructive Approximation Jour., 1983—, Computational Methods and Function Theory Jour., 2001—. Recipient Chancellor's Rsch. award, Vanderbilt U., 2005; named Highly Cited Rschr., ISI, 2000—; grantee, NSF, 1970—72, 1980—; fellow, Fulbright Found., 1968—69, Guggenheim Found., 1978. Fellow: Am. Math. Soc.; mem.: Soc. for Industrial and Applied Math., Bulgarian Acad. Scis. (fgn. mem.), Am. Math. Soc. (Inaugural mem.), Sigma Xi. Office: Ctr Constructive Approximation Vanderbilt U Dept Math Nashville TN 37240 Office Phone: 615-322-2014. Business E-Mail: ed.saff@vanderbilt.edu.

SAFFIR, LEONARD, public relations executive; b. NYC, Apr. 19, 1930; s. Abraham and Getrude Saffir; m. Patricia Roemer (div. 1980); children: Andrew, Michelle; m. Wendy McConaughy (div. 1992); 1 child, Samantha; m. Eleanor Unger, 1997. Student, Syracuse U., 1948-51. Editor, bur. chief Internat. News Service, Dallas, Tokyo, 1953-58; producer Eng., Australia, Asia, 1958-60; bur. chief Internat. News Svc., Tokyo, 1959—60; ptnr. Haft, Saffir, Siegel Pub. Relations & Advt., NYC, 1960-62; asst. pub. N.Y. Standard, 1962-63; cons. Ferdinand Marcos, 1964; pub. Latin Am. Times, NYC, 1965; exec. v.p. Franchises Internat., NYC, 1965-69; press sec., chief of staff to Senator James Buckley U.S. Senate, Washington, 1970-76; pub., editor The Trib, NYC, 1977-78, The Sun, Bridgehampton, NY, 1978-84; exec. v.p. Porter/Novelli, NYC, 1984-90; pres. Jay DeBow & Ptnrs., NYC, Fla., 1989-90, Leonard Saffir & Assocs. Pub. Rels., 2000—; investigative reporter, columnist Lake Worth Herald, 2001—03. CEO Adventures One, 1998—2000, Celebrity Stores.com, 1998—2000; chmn., CEO Fla. Hall of Fame. Author: Power Public Relations, 1992, Power Public Relations: How to Master the New PR, 2000, PR on a Budget, 2007. Campaign mgr. Marchi for Mayor, NYC, 1973, Buckely for Senator, NY, 1976; mgr. Ferdinand Marcos Presdl. Campaign Philippines, 1964. Sgt. USMC, 1951—53. Recipient Silver Anvil award, Pub. Rels. Soc. Am., Big Apple award, Mayor's award, City of NY, others. Mem.: Overseas Press Club (pres. 1988—89). Home: 6137 Rainbow Circle Lake Worth FL 33463 Personal E-mail: lenpr33@comcast.net.

SAFINA, DINARA MIKHAILOVNA, professional tennis player; b. Moscow, Apr. 27, 1986; d. Michail and Raouza Islanova. Profl. tennis player WTA, 2000—. Achievements include winning 12 career singles titles, 8 career doubles titles, WTA; winning 4 career singles titles, 3 career doubles titles, ITF; mem. Russian Fed Cup Team, 2005-06. Avocations: music, movies, reading. Office: c/o WTA Hdqs One Progress Plz Ste 1500 Saint Petersburg FL 33701

SAFIR, HOWARD, security firm executive, former police commissioner; b. NYC, Feb. 24, 1942; s. George and Rose (Weiner) S.; m. Carol Ferrara, Nov. 21, 1965; children: Jennifer, Adam. BA in History and Polit. Sci., Hofstra U., 1963; postgrad., Bklyn. Law Sch., 1963-65; cert., Harvard U., 1988-89. Spl. agent Fed. Bur. Narcotics, US Dept. Treasury, 1965—68; spl. agent. Bur. Narcotics and Dangerous Drugs, US Dept. Justice, 1968—70, dep. chief spl. projects, 1970-72; asst. regional dir. Drug Enforcement Adminstrn. (DEA), 1972-74, spl. asst. for organized crime, 1974-75, chief spl. enforcement programs, 1975-76, dep. regional dir., 1976-77, asst. dir., 1977-79; chief witness security divsn. U.S. Marshals Svc., 1979-81, asst. dir. ops., 1979-84, assoc. dir. ops., 1984-90; pres. Safir Assocs. Ltd., 1990-96; commr. NYC Fire Dept., 1994-96, NYC Police Dept., 1996—2000; founder, CEO SafirRosetti, 2000—; CEO Bode Technology, 2007—. Del. Interpol Gen. Assembly, 1981-88, Nat. Drug Policy Bd., 1986-88, Nat. Office Drug Policy; directed Warrant Apprehension Narcotic Team Program, 1989; dir. security Pres. Task Force on Victims of Crime, 1982; operational dir. security force fgn. delegations UN Gen. Assembly, 1979-89; nat. coord. Spl. Op. Mex. Nat. Heroin Interdiction Program, 1975, Spl. Op. SE Asia Interdiction Program, 1971; rep. Pres. Law Enforcement Com. Domestic Coun. Drug Abuse Task Force, 1975; mem. steering com. Nat. Conf. Organized Crime, 1975; dir. spl. investigations. Co-author (with Ellis Whitman): Security: Policing Your Homeland, Your State, Your City, 2003. Served USMCR, 1960-66. Recipient Ellis I. Medal of Honor, 1996, Pres. Meritorious Exec. award (2), Atty. Gen.'s Achievement award, US Marshals Svc. Meritorious Svc. award. Mem. Internat. Assn. Chiefs of Police (chmn. N.Am. subcom., chmn. internat. adv. com. 1988-90, mem. exec. com. 1996—), Internat. Assn. Intelligence Analysts, Am. Soc. Indsl. Security, Pi Delta Epsilon. Office: The Bode Technology Group Inc 10430 Furnace Rd Ste 107 Lorton VA 22079 also: SafirRosetti 415 Madison Ave 17th Ave New York NY 10017 Office Phone: 212-817-6700. E-mail: hsafir@safirrosetti.com.

SAGAFI-NEJAD, TAGI, business educator; b. Khorasan, Iran, Dec. 19, 1941; arrived in U.S., 1968; m. Nancy Gail Black Nov. 22, 1967; children: Jahan C. R., David J. H. MA, U. Pa., 1971, PhD, 1979. Lectr. U. Pa., Phila., 1974—76; asst. prof. U. Wash., Seattle, 1976—80, U. Tex., Austin, 1980—84; assoc. prof. Loyola Coll., Balt., 1984—93, prof., 1993—2002, dept. chair, 1995—96, prof. emeritus, 2002—; Keating-Crawford chair in internat. bus. Stillman Sch. Bus., Seton Hall U., 2002—03; Killam Disting. prof., dir. PhD program in internat. bus. Tex. A&M Internat. U., 2003—08, dir., Tex. Ctr., Border Entreprise & Econ. Devel., 2008—09, dir., Ctr. Study Western Hemisphere Trade, 2009—, dir., Internat. Trade Inst., 2009—. Cons. UN Indsl. Devel. Orgn., 1982—84, U.S. Congress, 1983—84, UN Ctr. on Transnat. Corp., 1993—; lectr., spkr. in field; editor Internat. Trade Jour., 2007—. Author: The UN and Transational Corporations: From Code of Conduct To Global Compact, 2008, Technology Transfer Trilogy, 1980, 1981; editl. bd. Transnational Corp., 1993—; contbr. to 32 articles, 12 book chapters. Recipient Two Best Paper award Acad. of Mgmt., 1994, Pacific Asia Mgmt. Inst., U. Hawaii, 1988, Anthologized Border Trade Champion award, US Dept. Commerce, 2012. Mem. Acad. of Internat. Bus. (chair N.E. chpt. 1988-93), Acad. Mgmt. Democrat. Avocations: gardening, golf, painting, walking. Office: Tex A&M Internat U 5201 University Blvd Laredo TX 78041-1900 Office Phone: 956-326-2547. Office Fax: 956-326-2544. Business E-Mail: tagi.sagafi@tamiu.edu.

SAGALOWSKY, ARTHUR I., urologist, educator; b. Indpls., Aug. 19, 1948; s. Meyer and Goldie Sagalowsky; m. Hanne Albaek, June 11, 1972; children: Julie, Jordan. BA, Ind. U., 1970; MD, Ind. U. Med. Ctr., 1973; M, U. Tex. Southwestern Med. Sch., 2010—. Intern, resident Ind. U. Med. Ctr., Indpls., 1973—75, resident, 1975—78; clin. asst. prof. surgery and urology U. Tex. Southwestern Med. Ctr., Dallas, 1978—80, asst. prof. urology, 1980—84, assoc. prof. urology and surgery, 1984—89, prof. urology and surgery, 1989—; tchr. Cary Coll. U. Tex. Southwestern Med. Sch., 2011—. Fellow Clin. Pharmacology, U. Tex. Southwestern, 1978—80; surg. dir. renal transplantation U. Tex. Southwestern Med. Ctr., 1983—95, chief urologic oncology, dept. urology, 1995—2011, co-investigator NIH O'Brien Ctr. Urologic Rsch., 1993—2000, prin. investigator urology, 2000—, prin. investigator urology NIH Cancer Inst. Urologic Cancer Outreach Program, 1989—98. Avocations: piano, golf, fly fishing. Home: 4450 Cedarbrush Dallas TX 75346 Office: U Tex Southwestern Med Ctr Dept Urology 5323 Harry Hines Blvd Dallas TX 75390-9110 Office Phone: 214-648-3976. Business E-Mail: arthur.sagalowsky@utsouthwestern.edu.

SAGE, ANDREW PATRICK, systems engineering and management educator; b. Charleston, SC, Aug. 27, 1933; s. Andrew Patrick and Pearl Louise (Britt) S.; m. LaVerne Galhouse, Mar. 3, 1962; children: Theresa Annette, Karen Margaret, Philip Andrew. BS in Elec. Engring, The Citadel, Charleston, SC, 1955; SM, MIT, Cambridge, Mass., 1956; PhD, Purdue U., Lafayette, 1960; DEng (hon.), U. Waterloo, Can., 1987, Dalhousie U., Halifax, Nova Scotia, Can., 1997. Registered profl. engr., Tex. Instr. elec. engring. Purdue U., 1956-60; assoc. prof. U. Ariz., 1960-63; mem. tech. staff Aerospace Corp., Los Angeles, 1963-64; prof. elec. engring. and nuclear engring. scis. U. Fla., 1964-67; prof., dir. Info. and Control Scis. Center, So. Methodist U., Dallas, 1967-74; head elec. engring. dept. So. Meth. U., 1973-74; Quarles prof. engring. sci. and systems U. Va., Charlottesville, 1974-84, chmn. dept. chem. engring., 1974-75, chmn. dept. engring. sci. and systems, 1977-84, assoc. dean, 1974-80; First Am. Bank prof. info. tech. George Mason U., Fairfax, Va., 1984—, assoc. v.p. for acad. affairs, 1984-85, dean Sch. Info. Tech. and Engring., 1985-96, univ. prof., founding dean emeritus, 1996—. Cons. Martin Marietta, Collins Radio, Atlantic Richfield, Tex. Instruments, LTV Aerospace, Battelle Meml. Inst., TRW Sys., NSF, Inst. Def. Analyses, Planning Rsch. Corp., MITRE, Engring. Rsch. Assocs., Software Productivity Consortium; gen. chmn. Internat. Conf. on Sys., Man and Cybernetics, 1974, 87; mem. spl. program panel on sys. sci. NATO, 1981-82; trustee, cons. Ctr. Naval Analysis, 1990-94. Author: Optimum Systems Control, 1968, 2d edit., 1977, Estimation Theory with Applications to Communications and Control, 1971, System Identification, 1971, An Introduction to Probability and Stochastic Processes, 1973, Methodology for Large Scale Systems, 1977, Systems Engineering: Methodology and Applications, 1977, Linear Systems Control, 1978, Economic Systems Analysis, 1983, System Design for Human Interaction, 1987, Information Processing in Systems and Organizations, 1990, Introduction to Computer Systems Analysis, Design, and Applications, 1989, Software Systems Engineering, 1990, Decision Support Systems Engineering, 1991, Systems Engineering, 1992, Systems Management for Information Technology and Software Engineering, 1995, Handbook of Systems Engineering and Management, 1999, 2nd edit., 2009, Introduction to Systems Engineering, 2000, Economic Systems Analysis 2nd Assessment, 2011; assoc. editor IEEE Transactions on Systems Sci. and Cybernetics, 1968-72; editor: IEEE Transactions on Systems, Man and Cybernetics, 1972-98; assoc. editor: Automatica, 1968-81; editor, 1981-96; mem. editl. bd. Systems Engring, 1968-72, IEEE Spectrum, 1972-73, Computers and Elec. Engring., 1972, Jour. Interdisciplinary Modeling and Simulation, 1976-80, Internat. Jour. Intelligent Sys., 1986—, Orgn. Sci., 1994-2002; editor Elsevier North Holland textbook series in sys. sci. and engring., 1970-88, John Wiley textbook series on sys. engring. and mgmt., 1989—; co-editor-in-chief Jour. Large Scale Sys.: Theory and Applications, 1978-88, Info. and Decision Technologies, 1988-94, Info. and Sys. Engring., 1995-96; editor in chief Sys. Engring., 1998—; co-editor in chief Info., Knowledge and Sys. Mgmt., 1999—; contbr. articles to profl. jours. Recipient Norbert Wiener award, 1980, Joseph G. Wohl career award, 1991, Superior Pub. Svc. award Sec. of the Navy, 1994; Case Centennial scholar, 1980, Award Washington Soc. of Engrs., 1996. Fellow: AAAS (chmn. sect. M 1990), IEEE (life M. Barry Carlton award 1970, Centennial medal 1984, Outstanding Contbn. award 1986, Donald G. Fink prize 1994, Simon Ramo medal 2000), Internat. Coun. on Sys. Engring. (Pioneer award 2002); mem.: NAE, Inst. for Ops. Rsch. and Mgmt. Sci., Washington Soc. Engrs. (award 1996), Am. Soc. Engring. Edn. (Frederick Emmonds Terman award 1970, Centennial cert. for exceptional contbn. 1993), Internat. Fedn. Automatic Control (Oustanding Svc. award), IEEE Sys./Man and Cybernetics Soc. (pres. 1984—85), Omega Alpha, Tau Beta Pi, Eta Kappa Nu (eminent mem. award 2002), Sigma Xi. Home: 8011 Woodland Hills Ln Fairfax VA 22039-2433 Office: George Mason U Sch Info Tech Fairfax VA 22030-4444 Office Phone: 703-993-1506. Business E-Mail: asage@gmu.edu.

SAGER, EFTON, state legislator; b. Galena, Mo., June 10, 1933; m. Deloris Sager; children: Debra Ann, David. AB, Wayne Cmty. Coll., 1981. Salesman Wilders Inc., 1971—77; mgr. Comer Equipment Co. & Parts Svc., 1977—81, JW Logging Inc., 1983—2008; commr. Wayne County, 2000—08; state rep. Dist. 11 NC House of Reps., 2009—. 1st sgt USAF, 1950—71. Republican. Methodist. Office: North Carolina House of Representatives 300 N Salisbury St Rm 416B Raleigh NC 27603-5925 Office Phone: 919-733-5755. E-mail: Efton.Sager@ncleg.net.

SAGER, LAWRENCE GENE, law educator; b. 1941; AB, Pomona Coll., 1963; LLB magna cum laude, Columbia Coll., 1966. Bar: Calif. 1967. Asst. prof. U. Calif., LA, 1966—68, acting prof., 1968—71; assoc. prof NYU, NY, 1972—74, prof., 1974—95, Robert B. McKay prof. law, 1995—2002; Alice Jane Drysdale Sheffield Regents Chair in Law U. Tex., Austin, 2002—, dean, 2006—11, John Jeffers rsch. chair law. Vis. prof. law and social planning Woodrow Wilson Sch., Princeton, 1974-76; vis. prof. U. Mich., Harvard U., spring 1981, Boston U., 1986-89. Recipient Disting. Alumni Award, Pomona Coll. Mem. N.Y. CLU. Office: School of Law University of Texas at Austin 727 E Dean Keeton Street Austin TX 78705 Office Phone: 512-232-1322. Office Fax: 512-471-6987. Business E-Mail: lsager@mail.law.utexas.edu.

SAH, CHIH-TANG, electrical and computer engineering and physics educator; b. Beijing, Nov. 10, 1932; s. Adam Peng-tung and Shu-shen Huang; m. Linda Chang, Nov. 29, 1959; children: Dinah W.Y., Robert L.Y. BS Physics, U. Ill., 1953, BSEE, 1953; MSEE, Stanford U., 1954, PhD, 1956; D honoris causa, U. Leuven, Belgium, 1975; Doctorate (hon.), Hsinchu Chao-Tung U., Taiwan, 2004, China Nat., 2010. Research assoc. Stanford Electronics Lab., Palo Alto, Calif., 1956; sr. mem. tech. staff Shockley Transistor Corp., Palo Alto, 1956—59; head, mgr. physics dept. Fairchild Semiconductor Lab., Palo Alto, 1959-64; prof. physics and elec. engring. U. Ill., Urbana, 1962-88, dir. Ill. Solid State Electronics Lab.; Pittman Eminent Scholar chair, grad. rsch. prof., chief scientist Coll. Engring. U. Fla., Gainesville, 1988—2010; academician prof. Sch. Physics & Mech. Electrical Engring. Xiamen U., China, 2010—. Program dir. 1st generation Si VLSI tech. Fairchild Corp., 1959-64; cons. Jet Propulsion Lab. Solar Cells, Dept. Energy, Pasadena, Calif., 1976-85, Harry Diamond Lab. Radiation Effects in MOS Transistors, Washington, 1974-75, IBM Corp. Reliability & Gate Oxide, NY, numerous other electronics firms 1964-88; advisor Intel Corp., Oreg., Calif., other semicondr. mfrs., 1988—; hon. prof. Peking U., 2003, Tsnghua U., 2003, Xiamen U., 2004., mem. CTSAH Assocs., Fla., 2010- Author: Fundamentals of Solid-State Electronics, 1991, Transistor Reliability in Fundamentals of Solid-State Electronics—Solution Manual, 1996; founding editor Internat. Series Advances in Solid-State Electronics and Tech., 1991—; contbr. 300 articles to profl. jours. Recipient first high tech. award Asian Am. Mfg. Assn., 1982, U. Rsch award, US Semiconductors Assn., 1998, Pioneer Recognition award Com. of the 100, 2002, Disting. Lifetime Achievement award Chinese Inst. Engrs. USA, 2003. Fellow IEEE (life, IRE Browder J. Thompson prize 1963, J.J. Ebers award 1980, Jack Morton award 1989, EDS Celebrated mem. 2012), AAAS, Am. Phys. Soc., Franklin Inst. (life, Cert. of Merit award 1975); mem. Nat. Acad. Engring., Academia Sinica Taiwan (academician), Chinese Acad. Scis. (academician). Achievements include development of complementary metal-oxide semiconductor circuit in 1963; Si P-N junction diode phenomena Sah-Noyce-Shockley Theory in 1956; MOS transistor compact models, Sah, Pao, Jie in 1964, 1966, 2005; invention of deep-level transient spectroscopy Sah, Tasch, Yau in 1967, 1971; DCIV diagnosis for deep-submicron transistor design and reliability Sah, Cai, Wang, Jie; development of theory of generation-recombination-trapping and thermal noise noise in transistors in 1964; discovery of theory of bipolar currents in nanometer MOS field-effect transistors Sah, Jie 2007; giant trapping capacitance with spin-orbit degeneracy Sah, Jie 2011. Personal E-mail: tom_sah@msn.com.

SAHAI, HARDEO, medical statistics educator; b. Bahraich, India, Jan. 10, 1942; m. Lillian Sahai, Dec. 28, 1973; 3 children. BS in Math., Stats. and Physics, Lucknow U., India, 1962; MS in Math., Banaras U., Varanasi, India, 1964; MS in Math. Stats., U. Chgo., 1968; PhD in Stats., U. Ky., Lexington, 1971. Lectr. math. and stats. Banaras U., Varanasi, India, 1964—65; asst. stats. officer Durgapur Steel Plant, West Bengal, India, 1965; statistician Rsch. and Planning divsn. Blue Cross Assn., Chgo., 1966; statis. programmer Cleft Palate Ctr. U. Ill., 1967; statis. programmer Chgo. Health Rsch. Found., 1968; mgmt. scientist Mgmt. Sys. Devel. Dept. Burroughs Corp., Detroit, 1971—72; from asst. prof. to prof. dept. math. U. PR, Mayaguez, 1972—82; vis. rsch. prof. Dept. Stats. and Applied Math. U. Ceara, Brazil, 1978—79; sr. rsch. statistician Travenol Labs., Inc., Round Lake, Ill., 1982—83; chief statistician US Army Hqrs., Ft. Sheridan, Ill., 1983—84; sr. math. statistician U.S. Bur. Census Dept. Commerce, Washington, 1984—85; sr. ops. rsch. analyst Def. Logistics Agy. Dept. Def., Chgo., 1985—86; prof. Dept. Biostats. and Epidemiology U. PR Med. Scis., San Juan, 1986—. Cons. PR Univ Cons., PR Driving Safety Evaluation Project, Water Resources Rsch. Inst., Travenol Labs., Campo Rico, PR, US Bur. Census, Washington, Lawrence Livermore Nat. Lab., Calif., others; vis. prof. U. Granada, Spain, U. Veracruzana, Mex., patrimonial prof. stats., 1997—; vis. prof. U. Nacional de Colombia, U. Nacional de Trujillo, Peru, 1993-94, hon. prof. stats., 1994—; adj. prof. dept. math. U. P.R. Natural Scis. Faculty, 1995—; Patrimonial prof. stats U. Veracruzana, 1997—. Author: Statistics and Probability: Learning Module, 1984; author: (with Jose Berrios) A Dictionary of Statistical Scientific and Technical Terms: English-Spanish and Spanish-English, 1981, (with Wilfredo Martinez) Statistical Tables and Formulas for the Biological Social and Physical Sciences, 1996, (with Anwer Khurshid) Statistics in Epidemiology: Methods, Techniques and Applications, 1996, (with Satish C. Misra and Amwer Khurshid) Quotations on Probability and Statistics with Illustrations, 2004, (with Anwer Khurshid) A Pocket Dictionary of Statistics, 2000, (with Mohammad I. Ageel) The Analysis of Variance: Fixed, Random and Mixed Models, 2000, (with Mario M. Ojeda) A Glossary of Statistical, Sciebtfic and Technical Terms: English-Spanish, 2004, (with Lucas López Segovia and Hector W. Colón-Rosa) A Glossary of Medical Epidemiologic and Demographic Statistics: English-Spanish, 2003, (with Mario M. Ojeda) Un Manual de Distribuciones t, x2y F Centrales Y No Centrales, 2000, (with Mario M. Ojeda) A Glossary of Computer and Management Terms: English/Spanish, 2004, (with Mario M. Ojeda) Comparisons of Approximations to the Percentiles of Noncentral t, x2 and F Distributions, 2001, (with A. Khurshid) Pocket Dictionary of Statistics, 2001, (with Mario M. Ojeda) Analysis of Variance for Random Models, Vol. 1: Balanced Data and Vol. 2: Unbalanced Data, 2004; mem. editl. bd. Sociedad Colombiana de Matematicas, P.R. Health Scis. Jour.; contbr. editor Current Index to Stats.; reviewer Collegiate Microcomputer, Comm. in Statistics, Indian Jour. Stats., Jour. Royal Statis. Soc. (series D, The Statistician), New Zealand Statistician, Biometrics, Can. Jour. Stats., Technometrics, Problems, Resources and Issues in Math. Undergrad. Studies; contbr. more than 150 articles and papers to profl. and sci. jours., numerous articles to tech. mags. Active Dept. Consumer Affairs Svcs. Commonwealth of PR, San Juan, Dept. Anti-Addiction Svcs., Commonwealth of P.R., San Juan., Inst. of AIDS, Municipality of San Juan, VA Med. Ctr. of San Juan, Caribbean Primate Rsch. Ctr., Ctr. Addiction Studies Caribbean Ctrl. U. Recipient Dept. Army Cert. Achievement award, 1984, U. Ky. Outstanding Alumnus award, 1993, medal of honor U. Granada, 1994, plaque of honor U. Nacional de Trujillo, 1994; fellow Coun. Sci. and Indsl. Rsch., 1964-65, U. Chgo., 1965-68, Harvard U., 1979, Fulbright Found., 1982; U.P. Bd. Merit scholar, 1957-59, Govt. India Merit scholar, 1959-64; grantee NSF, 1974-77, NIMH, 1987-90, 91—, NIDA, 1991—. Fellow AAAS, Am. Coll. Epidemiology, Inst. Statisticians (charter statistician), Inst. Math. and Its Applications (charter mathematician), N.Y. Acad. Scis., Royal Statis. Soc.; mem. Internat. Statis. Inst., Internat. Assn. Tchg. Stats., Soc. Epidemiol. Rsch., Inst. Math. Stats., Bernouilli Soc. for Math. Stats. and Probability, Internat. Biometric Soc., Am. Soc. for Quality Control, Am. Stats. Assn., Japan Statis. Soc., Can. Statis. Soc., Inter-Am. Statis. Inst., Internat. Assn. Statis. Computing, Sch. Sci. and Math. Assn., Sigma Xi. Avocations: religious studies, philosophy, reading, gardening. Home: Urb Mayaguez Ter 7083 Calle B Gaudier Texidor Mayaguez PR 00682-6617 Personal E-mail: hardeosahai@yahoo.com.

SAHN, STEVEN ALAN, internist, educator, pulmonologist; b. Bklyn., Jan. 25, 1943; s. Irwin H. and Mildred P. Sahn; m. Margaret Hoefer Sahn, June 8, 2002; children: Karen, Stacey, James, Michael, Rachel. BA, Duke U., 1964; MD, U. Louisville, 1968. Diplomate Am. Bd. Internal Medicine, Am. Bd. Pulmonary Medicine, Am. Bd. Critical Care Medicine. Intern in internal medicine U. Iowa Hosp., Iowa City, 1968-69, resident in internal medicine, 1969-71; fellow in pulmonary disease U. Colo. Health Sci. Ctr., Denver, 1971-73, instr. medicine, 1973-74, asst. prof. medicine, 1974-78, assoc. prof. medicine, 1978-83; prof. medicine, dir. divsn. pulmonary and critical care, allergy and sleep medicine Med. Univ. S.C., Charleston, 1983—; dist. prof. medicine, divsn. pulmonary critical care, allergy & sleep medicine, 2012. Vis. prof. U. Calif., San Francisco, 1980, Kans. U. Med. Ctr., Kansas City, 1981, U. Louisville Sch. Medicine, 1982, Wright State U. Med. Sch., Wright-Patterson AFB Hosp., Dayton, Ohio, 1982, Oreg. Health Scis. U., 1982, Vanderbilt U., Nashville, 1984, U. S.C. Sch. Medicine, 1985, U. Ariz. Health Sci. Ctr., Tucson, 1985, 92, 93, Yale U., New Haven, Conn., 1986, Hershey (Pa.) Med. Ctr., 1986, SUNY, Stonybrook, 1987, Dartmouth-Hitchcock Med. Ctr., Hanover, N.H., 1988, Maine Med. Ctr. U. Vt., Portland, Maine, 1988, Fitzsimmons Army Med. Ctr., Denver, 1989, Seton Hall U. Grad. Med. Edn., 1989, Newark, 1989, Loyola U. Med. Ctr., Chgo., 1989, Andrews AFB, Washington, 1990, Keesler AFB, Biloxi, Miss., 1990, U. Rochester, N.Y., U. Ala., Birmingham, 1990, N.Y. Med. Coll., 1990, Temple U. Sch. Medicine, Phila., 1990, U. Milan, Italy, 1990, Georgetown U. Med. Ctr., Washington, 1991, Albert Einstein Sch. Medicine, 1991, Johns Hopkins U. Sch. Medicine, Balt., 1991, Ind. U. Med. Ctr., 1994, Ohio State U. Sch. Medicine, 1994, 33 others; cons. Fitzsimons Army Med. Ctr., 1980-83, 88-90, DHEC of S.C., 1982—, USAF, 1989—93, FDA Office of Orphan Product Devel., 1993—95; presenter numerous seminars; vis. prof., keynote spkr. at numerous state thoracic meetings. Author: (with J.E. Heffner) Pulmonary Pearls, 1988, vol. II, 1994, Critical Care Pearls, 1989; editor: (with L.B. Reller and R.W. Schrier) Clinical Internal Medicine, 1979, Pulmonary Emergencies, 1982, Diseases of the Pleura: Seminars in Respiratory Medicine, 1987, Infections of the Pleural Space: Seminars in Respiratory Infections, Vol. III, 1988, (with J.E. Heffner) Internal Medicine Pearls, 1993, (with J.E. Heffner) Cardiology Pearls, 1993, Tuberculosis Pearls, 1996, Critical Care Pearls, II, 1997, Respiratory Care Pearls, 1997; mem. editorial bd. Chest, 1987—, Pulmonary and Critical Care Update, 1988—, editor 2007-; dept. editor Pulmonary and Critical Care Pearls Chest, 1992—, Pulmonary Pearls Jour. Respiratory Disease, 1990—, Critical Care Pearls Jour. Critical Illness, 1990—; cons. to 53 editorial bd. Am. Jour. Diseases of Children, Am. Jour. Medicine, Am. Jour. Respiratory Critical Care Medicine, Cancer, Cancer Rsch., Annals of Internal Medicine, Chest, Critical Care Medicine, Jour. Am. Acad. Dermatoloty, Jour. Am. Med. Assn., European Respiratory Jour., Jour. Applied Physiology, Jour. Intensive Care Medicine, Jour. Laboratory and Clin. Medicine, Jour. Respiratory Diseases, Lung, Mayo Clinic Proceedings, Med. Toxicology, N.Y. State Jour. Medicine, Tubercle and Lung Diseases, Western Jour. Medicine; contbr. to numerous articles, peer reviewed jours., revs. to profl. jours. & publs., chpts. to books. Recipient Young Investigator Pulmonary Rsch. award NHLBI, 1975-77, Edward Livingston Trudeau Medal for Outstanding Contributions in the Field of Lung Disease, 2011, Disting. Prof. award; grantee 1975-77; named one of Outstanding Med. Specialists in the U.S. Town and Country Mag., 1990, one of Best Med. Specialists in N.Am., 1995, one of 400 Best Doctors in Am., Good Housekeeping Mag., 1991, one of Best Drs. in Am., Am. Health Mag., 1995; grantee Milheim, 1977-78, Beecham, 1977-78, 82-83, Warner-Chilcott, 1978-79, Squibb, 1978, 79-80, Lilly, 1979-80, 81-82, Boehringer-Ingelheim, 1980, 89-90, Med. Coll. S.C., 1985-86, ALASC, 1985-86, 86-87, 87-88, 88-89, Lederle, 1988-92, Hoescht-Roussel, 1988-90, Support Systems Internat., 1990-92, 92-93, Cutter Biological, Miles, Inc., Glaxo, 1991-92, Schering-Plough, 1992-93, Tap Pharmaceuticals, 1993. Fellow Am. Coll. Chest Physicians (annual meeting com. 1986, gov. S.C. 1988-91, 91-94, organizing com. nat. pulmonary bd. review course 1990, 92, 94, membership com. 1992-93, annual internat. sci. program com. 1993-95, reviewer MKSAP 1994), Am. Coll. Physicians, Am. Coll. Critical Care Medicine; mem. Am. Fedn. Clin. Rsch. (so. sect.), Am. Thoracic Soc. (respiratory care com. 1978-80, rsch. coord. com. 1985-87, annual meeting com. 1985-89, chmn. sci. assembly on clin. problems 1986-87, coun. chpt. reps. 1987-90), Am. Lung Assn. (adv. bd. S.C. coastal br. 1985-87, 89-91, 92-94, med. review com. 1985-89), We. Soc. Clin. Investigation, S.C. Thoracic Soc. (sci. planning com. 1985-86), Charleston County Med. Soc. Office: Med University SC Divsn Pulmonary Critical Care Allergy & Sleep Medicine 171 Ashley Ave Charleston SC 29425-0001 Office Phone: 843-792-3167. Business E-Mail: sahnsa@musc.edu.

SAINE, JASON, state legislator; Public relations and social media mgr.; state rep. Dist. 97 NC, 2011—. Republican. Office: North Carolina House of Representatives 16 W Jones St Room 1004 Raleigh NC 27601-1096 Home: 1760 Whispering Pnes Lincolnton NC 28092-0937 Office Phone: 919-733-5782. Office Fax: 704-479-1803. Business E-Mail: Jason.Saine@ncleg.net.

ST. GEME, JOSEPH W., III, pediatric and infectious diseases physician, educator; b. Mpls., Nov. 24, 1957; BS, Stanford U., Calif., 1979; MD, Harvard Med. Sch., 1984. Diplomate American Bd. Pediat., cert. in pediatric infectious diseases. Intern, resident pediat. Children's Hosp. Phila., 1984—87, chief resident pediat., 1987—88; postdoc. fellow dept. microbiology and immunology Stanford U., 1988—92, postdoc. fellow dept. pediat., divsn. infectious diseases, 1991—92; faculty, prof. pediat. and molecular microbiology Washington U. Sch. Medicine, St. Louis, 1992—2005; chair dept. pediat. Duke U. Sch. Medicine, Durham, NC, 2005—, James B. Duke prof. dept. pediat. & dept. molecular genetics and microbiology, 2007—. Contbr. articles to profl. jours. Recipient Calif. Rsch. Fellowship award, American Lung Assn., 1990, Young Investigator award in bacterial vaccine devel., Infectious Diseases Soc. America/Lederle-Praxis Biologics, 1993, Basil O'Connor award, March of Dimes Found., 1994, Established Investigator award, American Heart Assn., 1997, Squibb award, Infectious Diseases Soc. America, 1998; named Clin. Tchr. of Yr., Washington U. Sch. Medicine, 2001—03. Mem.: Assn. American Physicians, Inst. Medicine, Pediatric Infectious Diseases Soc. (Young Investigator award 1996), American Acad. Microbiology, American Soc. Clin. Investigation, Alpha Omega Alpha, Phi Beta Kappa. Achievements include research in pediatric infectious diseases, antibiotic resistance, respiratory tract infections, central nervous system infections, tick-borne infections, vaccine development and microbial pathogenesis. Office: Duke Univ Med Ctr Box 3352 Durham NC 27710 Business E-Mail: j.stgeme@duke.edu.

ST. GERMAIN, KAREN GAUDET, state legislator; Mem. Dist. 60 La. House of Reps., 2003—, vice chair natural resources and environment com., mem. agr., forestry, aquaculture and rural devel. com., transp., hwys. and pub. works com., house com. on homeland security, mem. joint com. on homeland security. Democrat. Office: Dist Off 57835 Plaquemine St Plaquemine LA 70764 also: PO Box 94062 Baton Rouge LA 70804 Fax: 225-687-6272. E-mail: larep060@legis.state.la.us.

ST. JOHN, ANTHONY PAUL, retired manufacturing executive; b. Washington, Jan. 13, 1937; s. Sterling St. John and Beulah Marston; m. Myra Grace Cornfeld, Oct. 30, 1959; children: James Sterling, Ivy Kemp Hurley, Mary Marston. JD, U. Va., Charlottesville, 1960; postgrad., Harvard U., Boston, 1979. Bar: Md. 1961. Atty. Amco Steel Corp., Balt., 1960—61, Nat. Labor Rels. Bd., Balt., 1961—65; asst. G.C., asst. v.p. law, v.p. union rels. Bethlehem Steel Corp., 1965—84; v.p. employee rels. Chrysler Corp., Auburn Hills, Mich., 1985—93. Adj. prof. Lehigh U., Bethlehem, 1993, 1995; bd. dirs. Qualitech Steel Corp., 1999—2000. Bd. dirs. Moravian Acad., Bethlehem, 1978—85; chmn. Greater Detroit Alliance Bus., 1989—90; chmn. indsl. rels. com. Motor Vehicles Mfrs., 1990—92; bd. dirs. Henry Ford Hosp. NE, Bloomfield Hills, Mich., 1991—92, Red Cross of So. Mich., Detroit, 1989—92, Kids Peace Hosp., Bethlehem, 1993—95, Detroit C. of C., 1989—90, Muhlenberg Evening Coll., 1997—98. 1st lt. US Army, 1961—68. Mem.: Sanctuary Golf Club (sec. chmn. legal com.), Saucon Valley Country Club. Republican. Avocation: golf. Home: 1556 Saucon Valley Rd Bethlehem PA 18015 Address: 2957 Wulfert Rd Sanibel FL 33957 Personal E-mail: saintmyty@embarqmail.com.

ST. JOHN, HENRY SEWELL, JR., utility company executive; b. Birmingham, Ala., Aug. 18, 1938; s. H. Sewell and Carrie M. (Bond) St. John; m. J. Ann Morris, Mar. 7, 1959; children: Sherri Ann, Brian Lee, Teresa Lynn, Cynthia Faye. Student, David Lipscomb Coll., 1956—58, U. Tenn., 1958—59, U. Ala., 1962—64. Engring. aide Ala. Power Co., Enterprise, 1960—62, Birmingham, 1962—66; asst. chief engr. Riviera Utilities, Foley, Ala., 1966—71, sec.-treas., gen. mgr., 1972—2001. Chmn. Baldwin County unit Am. Cancer Soc., 1977; treas. Christian Care Ctr. Inc., 1981—; deacon Foley Ch. of Christ, 1975—82, elder, 1983—, bd. trustees, vice chmn., 1986—; bd. dirs. AGAPE of Mobile, 1977—80; bd. dirs., pres. South Baldwin Civic Chorus, 1979—82; bd. dirs. Baldwin County Econ. Devel. Alliance, 1997—2001, exec. com., 1999—2001, sec., 1998—99, treas., 1999—2000, chmn., 2000—01. Mem.: IEEE (life), Chevrolet Nomad Assn. (bd. dirs. 1991—2002, v.p. 1993—2002), South Baldwin C. of C. (dir. 1972—75, pres. 1974, dir. 1981—90, 1992—95, amb. 2002—), Pub. Gas Assn. Ala. (bd. dirs. 1987—88), Am. Pub. Power Assn. (com. legis. and resolutions 1972—2001, chmn. State of Ala. mem. com. 1982—2001, com. on coms. 1997—2000, bd. dirs. 1997—2001, exec. com. 1999—2000, chmn. nat. membership com. 1999—2000, chmn. bylaws com. 2000—01, Kramer-Preston Pub. Svc. award 2002), United Mcpl. Distbrs. Group (bd. dirs. 1972—2001), Electric Cities Ala. (bd. dirs. 1983—2001, exec. com. 1989—2001, vice chmn. 2000—01, chmn. 2001, Heritage award 2005), Ala. Mcpl. Electric Authority (vice chmn. 1981—83, bd. dirs. 1981—2001, chmn. 1984—2001, Pres. award 2012), Mcpl. Electric Utility Assn. Ala. (exec. com., dir. 1971—85), Ala. Consumer-Owned Power Distbrs. Assn. (chmn. 1974—75, sec.-treas. 1980, vice chmn. 1981, chmn. 1982—83), S.E. Electric Reliability Coun. (assoc.), South Ala. Power Distbrs. Assn. (life; chmn. 1973—74), Nat. Corvette Mus., Nat. Corvette Owners Assn., Azalea City Classic Chevy (bd. dirs., exec. com. 1989—99, v.p. 1991—92, 1996—99), Gulf Shores Golf (dir. 1974—75), Foley Quarterback (sec.-treas. 1984—85), Classic Chevy, Internat. (life). Home: PO Box 1817 Foley AL 36536-1817 Personal E-mail: stjohn@gulftel.com.

ST. JOHN, PAIGE, investigative reporter; Grad. in Journalism, Southern Ill. U., Edwardsville. Corr. AP, Traverse City, Mich.; environment reporter Detroit News, 1993—95; statehouse reporter, bur. chief Gannett News Svc., 2001—08; investigative reporter Sarasota Herald-Tribune, Fla., 2008—. Recipient Pulitzer prize for investigative reporting, 2011. Mailing: Sarasota Herald Tribune 801 S Tamiami Trail Sarasota FL 34236

SAIZAN, PAULA THERESA, business consultant; b. New Orleans, Sept. 12, 1947; d. Paul Morine and Hattie Hayes Saizan; m. Paul R. Valteau Jr., Aug. 11, 2007. BS in Acctg. summa cum laude, Xavier U., 1969. CPA Tex. Sys. engr. IBM, New Orleans, 1969—71; acct., then sr. acct. Shell Oil Co., Houston, 1971—76, sr. fin. analyst, 1976—77, fin. rep., 1977—79, corp. auditor, 1979—81, treasury rep., 1981—82, sr. treasury rep., 1982—86; asst. treas. Shell Credit Inc., Shell Leasing Co., Shell Fin. Co., Houston, 1986—88, sr. pub. affairs rep., 1988—89, sr. staff pub. affairs rep., 1990—91, program mgr., 1991—96, sr. program mgr., 1996—97, mgr. constituent rels. and edn. support, 1997—2000, mgr. nat. and cmty. outreach, 2000—03, mgr. stakeholder mgmt., 2003—04, sr. advisor corp. affairs, 2005—. Pres. PTBS, Inc., Houston; chair Signature Arts. Bd. dirs., Xavier U.; governance coun. The Links, Incorporate; bd. dir., exec. com. mem.; del. White House Conf. on Small Bus., 1995; prior bd. svc., treas., sec. Greater Houston Convention & Visitors Bur., Houston Downtown Mgmt. Dist., Nat. Coun. Negro Women, Inc., Houston Chpt., TSCPA and NAACP Special Contbn. Fund, St. Joseph Hosp. Found., Cath. Charities Houston, UNCF SW. Mem. AICPA, NAACP (life mem., prior bd. dirs., trustee spl. contbn. fund), Tex. Soc. CPAs, Assn. Governing Bds. of Univs. and Colls., Leadership Houston, LWV Houston, Xavier U. Alumni Assn., Nat. Coun. Garden Clubs (life), Nat. Congress Black Women, Alpha Kappa Alpha, Phi Gamma Nu, Kappa Gamma Phi. Roman Catholic. Office: PTBS Inc 9211 West Rd Ste 143-146 Houston TX 77064 Business E-Mail: ptbs3@aol.com.

SAJWAN, KENNETH SHANE, science educator; BS in Agr. and Animal Husbandry, Pant U. Agr. and Tech., 1972; MS in Agronomy, J.N. Agr. U., India, 1975; PhD in Post Harvest Tech., Indian Inst. Tech., 1980; PhD in Agronomy and Environ. Quality, Colo. State U., 1985. Rsch. assoc. Dept. Soil Sci. U. Wis., 1986—87; rsch. assoc. Dept. Agronomy U. Ky., 1988—89; asst. prof. Savannah River Ecology Lab., U. Ga., 1989—92; assoc. prof. math. Savannah State U., 1992—96, coord. Environ. Sci. Program, Dept. Natural Scis. and Math., 1992—, prof., 1996—. Adj. prof. U. SC, Aiken, Ala. A & M U.; faculty affiliate Inst. Ecology, U. Ga. Co-author: Trace Elements in the Environment, 2006, Coal Combustion Byproducts and Environmental Issues, 2006; contbr. articles to profl. jours. Recipient Richard Nicholson Excellence in Sci. Tchg. Award, 2005, Outstanding Undergraduate Sci. Tchr. Award, Soc. Coll. Sci. Tchr., 2006, Presdl. Award for Excellence in Sci., Math. and Engring. Mentoring (PAESMEM), 2009; named Ga. Prof. of Yr., Carnegie Found. for Advancement of Tchg. and Coun. for Advancement and Support of Edn., 2009. Fellow: Am. Soc. Agronomy, Soil Sci. Soc. America. Office: Savannah State University Dept Natural Science and Math 3219 College St Savannah GA 31404 Office Phone: 912-356-2315. E-mail: sajwank@savannahstate.edu.

SAKMANN, BERT, physician, cell physiologist; b. Stuttgart, Germany, June 12, 1942; Grad, U. Tübingen, 1967; PhD, U. Göttingen, Munich, 1974; degree (hon.), U. Alicante, Spain, U. Liverpool, U. Bordeaux, France, U. Munich, Germany, U. Colorado, Denver, U. Coll. London, Weizmann Inst., Rehovot, Israel. Research asst. dept. of neurophysiology Max Planck Inst. for Psychiatry, Munich, 1969—70; council fellow dept. of biophysics University Coll., London, 1971—73; research asst. dept. of neurobiology Max Planck Inst. for Biophysical Chem., Göttingen, Germany, 1974—79, research assoc. membrane biology group, 1979—82, dir. membrane biology group, 1983—85, dir. dept. of cell physiology, 1985—89, Max Planck Inst. for Med. Research, Heidelberg, Germany, 1989—2008; sci. dir., rsch. group leader digital neuroanatomy Max Planck Fla. Inst., Jupiter, Fla., 2008—. Fgn. mem. NAS, Royal Society, London. Recipient Nernst prize, German Bunsen Soc. for Physical Chem., 1977, Feldberg prize, Feldberg Found., 1979, Magnes award, Magnes Found., 1981, Spencer prize, Columbia U., 1983, Adolf Fick prize, U. Würzburg, 1984, Zottermann prize, Swedish Physiological Soc., 1984, Gross-Horwitz prize, Columbia U., 1986, Leibniz prize, German Research Found., 1986, Louis Jeantet prize, Louis Jeantet Found., 1988, Gairdner prize, Gairdner Found., 1989, Ernst Hellmut Vits prize, U. Münster, 1990, Harvey prize, Technion, 1991, Gerard prize, Soc. for Neuroscience, 1991, Research prize, Min. of Sci., Research & Art, Baden-Württemberg, 1991, Nobel prize in physiology or medicine, Nobel Found., 1991. Mem.: Orden Pour le Mérite, Heidelberger Acad. of Sciences, Goettinger Acad. of Sciences, Bavarian Acad. of Sciences and Humanities, German Acad. of Natural Scientists Leopoldina (Carus medal 1991). Office: Max Planck Fla Inst 5353 Parkside Dr MC19-RE Jupiter FL 33458-2906 Office Phone: 561-972-9400.

SAKS, JUDITH-ANN, artist; b. Anniston, Ala., Dec. 20, 1943; d. Julien David and Lucy-Jane (Watson) S.; m. Haskell Irvin Rosenthal, Dec. 22, 1974; 1 child, Brian Julien. Student, Tex. Acad. Art, 1957-58, Mus. Fine Arts, Houston, 1962, Rice U., 1962; BFA, Tulane U., 1966; postgrad., U. Houston, 1967. Curator student art collection U. Houston, 1968-72; artist Am. Revolution Bicentennial project Port of Houston Authority, 1975-76. One-woman shows include Alley Gallery, Houston, 1969, 2131 Gallery, Houston, 1969; group shows include Birmingham (Ala.) Mus., 1967, Meinhard Galleries, Houston, 1977, Galeire Barbizon, Houston, 1980, Park Crest Gallery, Austin, 1981, Margolis Gallery, 2005-06; represented in permanent collections at L.B. Johnson Manned Space Mus., Clear Lake City, Tex., Harris County Heritage Mus., Windsor Castle, Smithsonian Instn., Houston Maritime Mus.; commns. include Pin Oak Charity Horse Show Assn., Roberts S.S. Agy., New Orleans, Cruiser Houston Meml. Rm., U. Houston; contbr. popular mags. Recipient art awards including 1st prize for water color Art League Houston, 1969, 1st prize for graphics, 1969, 1st prize for sculpture, 1968, Tex. Women Arts award, 2013, Nat. 2nd Pl. Acrylics award, 2013, Nat. 3rd Pl. Acrylics award, 2012, Nat. 1st place award for original print DAR/Am. Heritage Com., 1987, Nat. 1st place award for acrylic painting, DAR, 2000, Nat. Hon. Mention for Acrylics, 2006, Tex. award for Acrylic, 2003, 06, Nat. 3rd place award for painting, 2003, Nat. 3rd prize for acrylic, 2005, Nat. 3rd Pl. award, Acrylics Am. Heritage, 2012, Nat. 1st prize for acrylic, 2007, Nat. 2nd prize for acrylic, 2013, Tex. State 1st prize for drawing DAR, 2002, Shofar award, 2003, Outstanding Svc. award Boy Scout Troop 806, 2002, Tex. award for art, 2005, Artist Martha Washington Pin, 2008, Nat. 1st prize for Collage, 2009, America's Heritage Remembered Houston, 2010, 1st Pl., South Ctrl. Divsn., 2010, Tex., Nat. 1st Pl., 2010, 2nd Pl., St. Lukes Hosp. Art Project CDA, 2011, Pressbook, 2008, 09, Nat. Ist. Pl., Tex. Woman in Arts award, 2013. Mem. Art League Houston, Houston Mus. Fine Arts, DAR (chpt. curator 1983-85, 93-95, 2007-09, rec. sec. 2001-03, libr. 2003-2005, counselor, 2005-07, chaplain, 2009-11, corr. sec. 2011-13, Recording sec., 2013-, Pineapple award 2009, Tex. Best Chpt. Chmn. award 2003, 06, Tex. award for art 2003, Tex. State 1st prize acrylic 2004, 2005, Tex. Cert. award for acrylic 2006, CDA 85th Ann. Celebration award), Daus. Republic of Tex., Magna Charta Dames, Colonial Dames America (2nd v.p., 2011-, bd. dir., 2013-, Outstanding Svc. award, 2012), Jamestowne Soc., Daus. Am. Colonists.

SALAMA, MAURICE A., dentist; married; 2 children. BA, SUNY, Binghamton, 1985—85; DMD, U. Pa., Phila., 1985—89. Cert. periodontics, orthodontics, implant surg. tng. Tchg. asst. dept. of biology SUNY, Binghamton, 1984—85; dental asst. to Dr. Mitchell Silverman Margate, 1987—89; extern Beth Israel Hosp., 1988, Hadassah Hosp., 1988; resident Maimonides Med. Ctr., Bkly., 1989—90; clin. asst. prof. periodontics and orthodontics shc. of dental medicine Univ. Pa., 1993—96, clin. asst. prof. of periodontics sch. of medicine, 1996—; clin. prof. of periodontics Med. Coll. of Ga., 1996—; vis. prof. of periodontics Nova Univ. Fla., 1996—; vis. prof. dept. of periodontics La. State Univ., 2000—; dentist Goldstein, Garber & Salama LLC. Scholar George Coslet award, Univ. Pa., Richard Chase award. Mem.: ADA, Ga. Dental Assn., Thomas P. Hinman Dental Soc, Alpha Omega Internat. Dental Frat., Acad. of Osseointegration, Am. Acad. of Periodontics, Am. Acad. of Orthodontics. Office: Goldstein, Garber & Salama LLC 300 Galleria Pkwy Atlanta GA 30339 Office Phone: 404-261-4941. Office Fax: 404-261-4946.

SALAMO, GREGORY J., physics professor; b. Sept. 14, 1944; married; 4 children. BS in Physics, Brooklyn Coll., 1996; MS, Purdue U., 1968; PhD in Optics, CUNY, 1973. Asst. prof. physics U. Ark., 1975—81, assoc. prof., 1981—95, dir. Fulbright Coll. Honors Program, 1985—86, prof., 1985—95, assoc. dir. High Density Electronics Ctr., 1991—, univ. prof. physics, 1995—. Vis. scholar Bell Lab., 1970—73; vis. prof. Army Night Vision Electro-Optics Lab., 1987—89. Contbr. articles to profl. jours. Named Ark. Prof. of Yr., Carnegie Found. for Advancement of Tchg. and Coun. for Advancement and Support of Edn., 2009. Fellow: Optical Soc. of America; mem.: IEEE, Electrochemical Soc., Materials Rsch. Soc., Am. Physical Soc., Sigma Xi. Office: University of Arkansas Dept Physics Fayetteville AR 72701 Office Phone: 501-575-2506. E-mail: salamo@uark.edu.

SALAMON, MYRON BEN, physicist, educator, dean; b. Pitts., June 4, 1939; s. Victor William and Helen (Sanders) S.; m. Sonya Maxine Blank, June 12, 1960; children: David, Aaron. BS, Carnegie-Mellon U., 1961; PhD, U. Calif., Berkeley, 1966. Asst. prof. physics U. Ill., Urbana, 1966-72, assoc. prof., 1972-74, prof., 1974—2006, program dir. Materials Research Lab., 1984-91, assoc. dean. Coll. Engring., 2000—06, emeritus prof., 2006—; dean natural sci. and math. U. Tex., Dallas, 2006—11. Vis. scientist U. Tokyo, 1966, 71, Tech. U. Munich, Fed. Republic Germany, 1974-75; cons. NSF; Disting. Vis. Prof. Tsukuba (Japan) U., 1995-96. Editor: Physics of Superionic Conductors, 1979; co-editor: Modulated Structures, 1979; divisional assoc. editor: Phys. Rev. Letters, 1992-96; contbr. sci. papers to profl. jours. Recipient Alexander von Humboldt Sr. US Scientist award, 1974-75; NSF coop. fellow, 1964-66; postdoctoral fellow, 1966; A.P. Sloan fellow, 1972-73; Berndt Matthias scholar Los Alamos Nat. Lab., 1995-96; visiting scientist CNRS and Inst. Laue-Langevin Grenoble, France, 1981-82. Fellow Am. Phys. Soc. Office: Univ Tex Dallas Sch Nat Sci and Math POB 830688 EC36 Richardson TX 75083 Office Phone: 972-883-5237. Business E-Mail: salamon@utdallas.edu.

SALAMONE, JOSEPH CHARLES, polymer chemistry professor; b. Bklyn., Dec. 27, 1939; s. Joseph John and Angela (Barbagallo) S.; children: Alicia, Christopher. BS in Chemistry, Hofstra U., 1961; PhD in Chemistry, Poly. Inst. Bklyn., 1967. NIH postdoctoral fellow U. Liverpool, England, 1966-67; rsch. assoc., Horace H. Rackham postdoctoral fellow U. Mich., Ann Arbor, 1967-70, adminstrv. sec., 1968-70; asst. prof., then assoc. prof. chemistry U. Mass., Lowell, 1970-76, prof., 1976-90, prof. emeritus, 1990—, dean Coll Sci., 1978-84, Disting. Rsch. fellow, 1984-90, chmn. dept. chemistry, 1975-78; adj. prof. biomed. engring. U. Tex., San Antonio, 2010, Austin, 2012. Pres. Optimers Inc., Lowell, 1985-99; bd. dirs. Rochal Industries, Inc., Boca Raton, Fla.; chief sci. officer, Rochal Industries, LLP; cons. editor CRC Press, Inc., Boca Raton, 1992-97; v.p. chem. rsch. Bausch and Lomb, 1997-2000, v.p. rsch., 2000-2005, v.p. and spl. adv., 2006. Author 2 books, 2 encys.; mem. editl. bd. Polymer, 1976-94, Jour. Macromolecular Sci.-Chemistry, 1985-2003, Progress of Polymer Sci., 1987-2002, ChemTech, 1995-99; adv. bd. Jour. Polymer Sci., 1974—2011; editor-in-chief Polymeric Materials Ency., 1993-97; contbr. over 174 articles to profl. jours.; holder 207 US patents and patent applications. With Nat. Acad. Engring., 2011, Acad. Medicine Engring. & Sci. Tex., 2011. Recipient Disting. Alumnus award Poly. Inst. N.Y., 1984, Herman F. Mark award for Recognition of Work in Applied Tech., Poly. U., 2005, 2011. Fellow Am. Inst. Med. and Biol. Engring. (chmn. industry coun. 2006-09), Am. Chem. Soc. (chmn. divsn. polymer chemistry 1982, fellow divsn. polymer chemistry 2010, Indsl. Chemistry award 2004), Biomaterials Sci. & Engring., Nat. Acad. Inventors; mem. NAE, Polymer Sci., Pacific Polymer Fedn. (sec., treas. 1988-90, dep. v.p. 1991-92, v.p., 1993, pres. 1994-95), Soc. Biomaterials (Clemson award for applied rsch.), Biomed. Engring. Soc., Wound Healing Soc., Contact Lens Soc. America. Office Phone: 561-703-4007. Personal E-mail: jcsalamone@yahoo.com.

SALANT, RICHARD FRANK, mechanical engineer, educator; b. NYC, Sept. 4, 1941; s. Joseph and Augusta (Dick) S.; m. Barbel Lang, Sept. 9, 1962; children: Scott M., Stephanie. BS, MS, MIT, 1963, DSc, 1967. Registered profl. engr., Ga. Asst. prof. U. Calif. Berkeley, 1966-68; asst. prof., assoc. prof. MIT, Cambridge, 1968-72; mgr. fluid mech. and heat transfer Borg-Warner Rsch. Ctr., Des Plaines, Ill., 1972-87; prof., chair tribology rsch. group Ga. Inst. Tech., Atlanta, 1987—2013, Ga. Power Disting. prof., 2001—13; prof. emeritus, 2014—. Cons. fluid sealing tech., Atlanta, 1987—. Assoc. editor Jour. Tribology, 1993-99, Jour. Fluids Engring., 1984-87, Tribology Transactions, 2010-; mem. editl. bd. Jour. Engring. Tribology, 2006—, Mechanika, 2006—; contbr. articles to profl. jours. Fellow ASME (Henry R. Worthington medal 1996, Machine Design award 2003, Mayo D. Hersey award, 2009), Soc. Tribologists and Lubrication Engrs. (Edmond E. Bisson award 2000, Frank P. Bussick award 2002, 05, 07, 08). Achievements include patents in field. Home: 1138 Manning Farms Ct Dunwoody GA 30338-2648 Office: Ga Inst Tech Sch Mech Engring Atlanta GA 30332-0405 Business E-Mail: richard.salant@me.gatech.edu.

SALDAÑA, DIANA, federal judge; b. Carizzo Springs, Tex., 1971; BA, U. Tex., Austin, 1993; JD, U. Tex. Sch. Law, 1997. Law clk. to Hon. George P. Kazen US Dist. Ct. (southern dist.) Tex., Laredo, 1997—98; staff atty. Office Gen. Counsel, USDA, Washington, 1998; trial atty., civil rights divsn. US Dept. Justice, Washington, 1998—99, asst. US atty. (southern dist.) Tex. Houston, 2001—06; atty. Beirne, Maynard & Parsons, L.L.P., Houston, 2000—01; magistrate judge US Dist. Ct. (southern dist.) Tex., 2006—11, judge, 2011—. Office: US Courthouse 1300 Victoria St Ste 2317 Laredo TX 78041 Office Phone: 956-790-1381 956-790-1381. Office Fax: 956-794-1027.

SALDAÑA, REY, councilman; s. Reynold and Marisela Saldaña. BA in Polit. Sci. and Comm., Stanford U., MA in Policy Orgn. and Leadership Studies. Councilman Dist. 4 San Antonio City Coun., 2011—. Tchr. urban edn. Trinity U. Coord. Kinds With Dreams. Gates Millennium Scholarship. Office: City Hall PO Box 839966 San Antonio TX 78283 also: 5102 Old Pearsall Rd San Antonio TX 78242 Office Phone: 210-207-7281, 210-207-0884.

SALDAÑA, SARAH RUTH, federal prosecutor; b. Corpus Christi, Tex., 1951; AA, Del Mar Coll., Corpus Christi, 1971; BS summa cum laude, Tex. A&M U., Kingsville, 1973; JD, Southern Meth. U., Dallas, 1984. Bar: Tex. 1984, US Dist. Ct. (northern dist.) Tex. 1984, US Dist. Ct. (eastern dist.) Wis. 1987, US Ct. Appeals (5th cir.) 1987. Lang. arts tchr. Dallas Ind. Sch. Dist., 1973—74; technician Equal Employment Opportunity Commn. (EEOC), Dallas, 1974—76; mgmt. intern US Dept. Housing & Urban Devel. (HUD), Dallas, 1975, investigator, 1975—76; CETA specialist Employment & Tng. Adminstrn. US Dept. Labor, Dallas, 1976—81; summer law clk. Passman Jones Andrews Holly & Co., Dallas, 1982—83, Vial, Hamilton, Koch & Knox, Dallas, 1983—84, Haynes & Boone, LLP, Dallas, 1984, mem., 1985—87; summer law clk. Hughes & Luce, LLP, Dallas, 1984; assoc. trial dept. Baker Botts, LLP, Dallas, 1987—94, ptnr. trial dept., 1994—98; asst. US atty. (northern dist.) Tex. US Dept. Justice, Dallas, 2004—08, asst. US atty., dep. criminal chief for fraud/pub. corruption group, 2009—11, US atty., 2011—. Instr. legal writing & rsch. methods Southern Meth. U., Dallas, 1985—87. Contbr. articles to profl. jours. Alt. mem. City Dallas Zoning Bd. Adjustment, 1989—91; bd. dirs. First Unitarian Ch. Dallas, 2011—, Dallas Ctr. Contemporary Arts, 2002—05. Mem.: State Bar Tex., Dallas Bar Assn., Dallas Hispanic Bar Assn., Nat. Hispanic Bar Assn., William Mac Taylor Inn Ct., Dallas Bar Found., Tex. Bar Found. Office: Office of US Atty for No Dist of Texas Earle Cabell Fed Bldg 1100 Commerce St Ste 300 Dallas TX 75242-1699 Office Phone: 214-659-8600.*

SALDÍVAR, RICARDO E., retail executive; BS in Mech. & Indsl. Engring., Monterrey Inst. Tech., Mex.; MS in Sys. Engring., Ga. Inst. Tech.; diploma in Bus., IPADE Bus. Sch., Mex. Various mgmt. & exec. level positions including chief staff emerging bus. divsn. Grupo Indsl. Alfa, Mexico, 1980—99, pres., CEO Total HOME subs. (acquired by Home Depot), 1999—2001; regional pres., mng. dir. Mex. ops. Home Depot, Inc., 2001—06, pres. Mex. divsn., 2006—. Bd. dirs. FEMSA beverage co. Pres. nonprofit assn. Vida y Salud ABP. Mem.: ANTAD (Mex. Nat. Assn. Retail & Dept. Stores) (bd. dirs., v.p. specialty retail group), Mex. Inst. Fin. Executives. Office: The Home Depot Inc 2455 Paces Ferry Rd NW Atlanta GA 30339-4024 Office Phone: 770-433-8211. Office Fax: 770-384-2356. E-mail: Ricardo_Saldivar@homedepot.com.

SALEH, FARIDA YOUSRY, chemistry professor; b. Cairo, June 17, 1939; came to U.S., 1968; d. Michael Yousry and Fakiha Yousef (Badawy) Wassif; m. Hosny Gabra Saleh, Oct. 8, 1959; children: Magda, Nagwa. BS, Ain Shams U., 1959; MS, Alexandria U., Egypt, 1967; PhD, U. Tex., Dallas, 1976. Postdoctoral rsch. assoc. Tex. A&M U., College Station, 1977-78; rsch. scientist II U. North Tex., Denton, 1978-83, asst. prof. chemistry, 1980-83, assoc. prof., 1985-94, prof., 1994—2005; ret., 2005. Cons. Stanford Rsch. Inst., Menlo Park, Calif., 1983-84, Allied Chems. Co., Hackettstown, N.J., 1985-86, Am. Chrome Chems., Corpus Christi, Tex., 1988-89, USEPA Rev. Panel, Washington, 1986—. Contbg. author book chpts. in field; contbr. more than 60 articles to profl. jours. Recipient Svc. award U.S. EPA, Washington, 1993; recipient numerous grants in field. Mem. Am. Chem. Soc., Internat. Union of Pure and Applied Chemistry, Internat. Humic Substances Soc., Assn. Women in Sci. Avocations: music, swimming, tennis. Home: 9521 Rivercrest Dr Denton TX 76207 Personal E-mail: alex4y@aol.com.

SALEH, PAUL N., information technology company executive; b. 1956; BSEE, MSEE, U. Mich., MBA in Finance with distinction, 1985. Various leadership positions to treas. Honeywell Inc., 1985—96; sr. v.p., treas. Walt Disney Co., 1997—99; sr. v.p., CFO Walt Disney International, 1999—2001; exec. v.p., CFO Nextel Communications, Inc. (merged with Sprint Corp.), 2001—05; CFO Sprint Nextel Corp., Reston, Va., 2005—08, acting CEO, 2007; mng. ptnr. Menza Partners LLC, 2008—10; sr. v.p., CFO Gannett Co., Inc., McLean, Va., 2010—12; v.p., CFO Computer Sciences Corp., 2012—. Bd. dir. Wolf Trap Found. Named The Best CFO in Telecom Services/Wireless Sector, Institutional Investor mag., 2004, 2005; named one of The 100 Most Influential People in Finance, Treasury & Risk Mgmt. mag., 2005. Office: Computer Sciences Corp 3170 Fairview Park Dr Falls Church VA 22042

SALEMI, MICHAEL KERRY, economist, educator; b. Chgo., Mar. 30, 1946; s. Michael and Helen Hill S.; m. Carrie Frances Benoit, Dec. 27, 1967 (div. July 1989); children: Benjamin, Caitlin; m. Ariana Pancaldo, Aug. 18, 1990; 1 child, Chiara. BA, St. Mary's Coll., 1968; MS, Purdue U., 1969; PhD, U. Minn., 1976. Asst. dir. Ctr. for Econ. Edn. U. Minn., Mpls., 1973—76; asst. prof. econs. U. NC, Chapel Hill, 1976—82, assoc. prof. econs., 1982—87, prof. economics, 1987—, dept. economics chairperson, 2010—12; rsch. assoc./vis. prof. Grad. Inst. Internat. Studies, Geneva, 1982—83. Bd. editors Jour. of Econ. Edn., 1995—; contbr. articles to profl. jours. Adv. bd. The Econ. Literacy Project of Fed. Res. Bank, Mpls., 1999; bd. dirs. NC Coun. Econ. Edn., Raleigh, NC, 1999-2000; chair rev. com. Vol. Nat. Content Stds. in Econs. Project, NY, 1996-97; bd. founders Nat. Coun. on Econ. Edn., NY, 1995—. Recipient Bower medal Nat. Coun. Econ. Edn., NY, 1998, Erskine fellow Canterbury U., Christchurch, New Zealand, 1998, Zachary Smith Professorship U. NC, Chapel Hill, 1993-96, Bowman and Gordon Gray Professorship for Excellence in Undergrad. Tchg., 1987-90, 2005-10, Villard award, Am. Assn. Econ. Educators, 2001, Great Tchr. award, Stavros Ctr., 2007, Disting. Tchg. award Southern Economic Assn., 2012; finalist Cherry award Baylor U., 2013. Mem. Am. Econ. Assn. (chair com. econ. edn. 1995-2000), Econometric Soc., Soc. Econ. Educators. Avocations: squash, photography, fishing. Office: Dept Econs Cb 3305 Gardner Hl Chapel Hill NC 27599-3305 Business E-Mail: michael_salemi@unc.edu.*

SALENTINE, THOMAS JAMES, pharmaceutical executive; b. Milw., Aug. 8, 1939; s. James Edward and Loretta Marie S.; m. Susan Anne Sisk, Apr. 16, 1966; children: Anne Elizabeth, Thomas James Jr. BS in Acctg., Marquette U., Milw., 1961. CPA, Ind., Wis. Sr. audit mgr. Price Waterhouse, Milw., 1961-74; dir. corp. acctg. Ward Foods Inc., Wilmette, Ill., 1974-78; corp. contr. Johnson Controls Inc., Milw., 1984-85; v.p., contr. Stokely Van Camp Inc., Indpls., 1978-87; exec. v.p., CFO Bindley Western Industries Inc., Indpls., 1987—2001, also bd. dirs.; ptnr. Bindley Capital Ptnrs., LLC, 2001—. Bd. dirs. Priority Healthcare Corp., Nat. Refrigeration Svcs. Inc. Chmn. com. United Way, Indpls., 1989-90. Lt. USN, 1962-65. Mem. AICPA, Fin. Execs. Inst. Republican. Roman Catholic. Home: 3991 Gulf Shore Blvd Naples FL 34103 Office Phone: 317-704-4154.

SALERNO, JUDITH ALYCE, foundation administrator, former health science association administrator; b. Mar. 2, 1952; MSc in Health Policy, Harvard Sch. Public Health, 1976; MD, Harvard Medical Sch., 1985. Cert. Internal Medicine, Geriatric Medicine. Clin. and fellowship tng., internal medicine Georgetown U., George Washington U., NIH; assoc. chief staff Veterans Affairs Med. Ctr., Washington; chief cons., geriatrics and extended care US Dept. Veterans' Affairs, Washington; assoc. clin. prof., healthcare sciences and medicine George Washington U.; sr. clin. investigator, Nat. Inst. Aging NIH, US Dept. Health & Human Services, Bethesda, Md., 1989—92, guest researcher, Nat. Inst. Aging, 1992—95, dep. dir., Nat. Inst. Aging, 2001—08; exec. officer, COO Inst. of Medicine (IOM) Nat. Acad. Sciences, 2008—13; pres., CEO Susan G. Komen Breast Cancer Found., Dallas, 2013—. Co-founder Geriatric Edn. Ctr. Consortium, Washington; commr. Nat. Comm. for Quality Long-Term Care, Washington. Contbr. several articles to prof. jours. Recipient NIH Director's award for Outstanding Leadership & Svc., Secretary's Meritorious Svc. award. Office: Susan G Komen Breast Cancer Foundation PO Box 650309 Dallas TX 75265*

SALES, JAMES BOHUS, lawyer; b. Weimar, Tex., Aug. 24, 1934; s. Henry B. and Agnes Mary (Pesek) Sales; m. Beuna M. Vornsand, June 3, 1956; children: Mark Keith, Debra Lynn, Travis James. BS, U. Tex., 1956, LLB with honors, 1960. Bar: Tex. 1960. Practiced in, Houston, 1960—; head litig. dept. Fulbright & Jaworski, 1979—2000, sr. ptnr., 1980—2000, of counsel, 2000—. Author: Products Liability in Texas, 1985; co-author: Texas Torts and Remedies, 6 vols., 1986; assoc. editor: Tex. Law Rev., 1960; contbr. articles to profl. jours. Trustee South Tex. Coll. Law, 1982—88, 1990—2005, A.A. White Dispute Resolution Ctr., 1991—94; cir. chair membership Supreme Ct. Hist. Soc., 1998—2001; trustee Tex. Supreme Ct. Hist. Soc., 2003—; chair commrs. Tex. Access Justice Commn., 2004—09, emeritus chair, 2009—; bd. dirs. Tex. Resource Ctr., 1990—97, Tex. Bar Hist. Found., 1990—2001. Recipient Lifetime Achievement award, U. Tex. Law Sch. Alumni, 2005, Interface Samaritan Counselling award, 2013; named among Best Lawyers in Am., 1989—. Fellow: Nat. Conf. Bar Pres. (coun. 1989—92, Outstanding Svc. award 2007), Houston Bar Found. (chmn. bd. 1982—83, sustaining life, James B. Sales Pro Bono Leadership award 2010), Am. Bar Found. (state chmn. 1993—98, sustaining life, Outstanding Svc. award 2009), Tex. Bar Found. (trustee 1991—95, vice-chmn. 1992—93, chmn. 1993—94, chair adv. bd. planned giving 1994—2004, sustaining life mem.), Am. Bd. Trial Advocates, Internat. Acad. Trial Lawyers, Am. Coll. Trial Lawyers (state chmn. 1993—96, Samuel E. Gates Litig. award 2011, Tex. Bar Found. Outstanding 50 Yrs. Lawyer award 2011); mem.: FBA, ABA (ho. of dels. 1984—2003, mem. Commn. on IOLTA 1995—97), Anti Defamation League (Karen H. Susman Jurisprudence award 2010), Tex. Assn. Civil Trial and Appellate Specialists (Lifetime of Excellence in Advocacy award 2009), Bar Assn. 5th Fed. Cir., Gulf Coast Legal Found. (bd. dirs. 1982—85), Houston Bar Assn. (bd. dirs. 1970—79, pres.-elect 1979—80, pres. 1980—81), Tex. Law Rev. Assn. (bd. dirs. 1996—2002, pres. 1999—2000, Dean Leon Green award), Tex. Assn. Def. Counsel (v.p. 1977—79), State Bar Tex. (bd. dirs. 1983—88, chmn. bd. 1985—86, pres. 1988—89, Pres.'s award 2006), So. Tex. Coll. Trial Advocacy (dir. 1983—87), So. Conf. Bar, Internat. Assn. Def. Counsel, The Forum, Order of Coif, Inns of Ct. (bd. dirs. 1981—84), Westlake Club (bd. govs. 1980—85). Roman Catholic. Home: 10803 Oak Creek St Houston TX 77024-3016 Office: Fulbright & Jaworski 1301 McKinney St Houston TX 77010-3095 E-mail: jsales@fulbright.com.

SALIERS, EMILY, singer, musician; b. New Haven, July 22, 1963; d. Don Saliers; life ptnr. Leslie Zweben. Student, Vanderbilt U.; BA, Emory U., 1985. Mem. folk rock duo Indigo Girls, 1983—; represented by Epic Records, 1988—2006, Hollywood Records, 2006—. Co-owner Watershed Restaurant, Decatur, Ga.; co-founder Flying Biscuit Cafe, Atlanta. Singer (with Amy Ray): (albums) Early 45, 1985, Strange Fire, 1987, Indigo Girls, 1989 (Grammy award for Best Contemporary Folk Album, 1990), Nomads Indians Saints, 1990, Rites of Passage, 1992, Swamp Ophelia, 1994, Touch Me Fall, 1995, 1200 Curfews, 1995, Shaming of the Sun, 1997, Come on Now Social, 1999, Retrospective, 2000, Become You, 2002, All That We Let In, 2004, Rarities, 2005, Despite Our Differences, 2006, Poseidon and the Bitter Bug, 2009, (songs) Closer to Fine, 1989, Hammer and Nail, 1990, Galileo, 1992, Least Complicated, 1994, Shame on You, 1997; composer: (films) One Weekend a Month, 2004; co-author (with Don Saliers): A Song to Sing, A Life to Live: Reflections on Music as Spiritual Practice, 2004; appearances include (films) Boys on the Side, 1995, (documentaries) Wordplay, 2006. Mem.: Phi Beta Kappa. Office: Russell Carter Artist Management 567 Ralph Mcgill Blvd Ne Atlanta GA 30312-1110 Office Phone: 404-377-9900. E-mail: igfan@rcam.com.

SALINAS, MARTIN, energy executive; Acctg. positions through sr. audit mgr. KPMG, San Antonio, 1994—2004; joined Energy Transfer Partners, LP, Dallas, 2004, controller, treas., 2004—08, CFO, 2008—. Office: Energy Transfer Company 3738 Oak Lawn Ave Dallas TX 75219-4333 Office Phone: 214-981-0700. Office Fax: 214-981-0703.

SALINAS, RAUL G., mayor, Laredo, Texas; BA in Law Enforcement & Criminology, U. Md. Former police officer US Capitol, Wash., DC; ret. agent FBI; former aide to Hon. Eligio (Kika) De La Garza; asst. legal attache US Embassy, Mexico City; mayor City of Laredo, Tex., 2006—. Office: City Hall 1110 Houston St Laredo TX 78040 Office Phone: 956-791-7389. Fax: 956-791-7314. E-mail: rgsalinas@ci.laredo.tx.us.*

SALINAS, RODNEY JAY C., media company executive; b. Philippines; s. Dannie and Trinidad; m. Taryn Costanzo. BA in Internat. Affairs, George Washington U., MA in Polit. Mgmt. Corr. Balitang Am.; contr. editor NetPulse; nat. fin. dir. Jon Amores for Congress Campaign, W.Va.; comm. coord. Assoc. of Fundraising Professionals; exec. dir. Asian Pacific Am. Inst. for Congl. Studies; founder, pub. PoliticalCircus.com, 2001—; founder, pres. Rainmaker Political Group, LLC, 2001—. Mem. Human Rights Commn., Alexandria, Va., 2001—. Named Rising Star of Polit., Campaigns & Elections Mag., 2002.

SALISBURY, ALAN BLANCHARD, information technology officer; b. Newark, Jan. 21, 1937; s. Lloyd Wade and Elizabeth Barry (Blanchard) S.; m. Florence Dorothy Conrad, May 21, 1971; children: Katherine Anne, Barbara Lynn. BS with distinction, U.S. Mil. Acad., 1958; MSEE, Stanford U., 1964, PhD, 1973; postgrad., Indsl. Coll. of Armed Forces, Washington, 1978. Commd. 2d lt. Signal Corps U.S. Army, 1958, advanced through grades to Maj. Gen., ret., 1987; asst. prof. U.S. Mil. Acad., West Point, N.Y., 1964-67; chief of data communications 1st Signal Brigade, Republic of Vietnam, 1968-69; tech. adv. Directorate of Mgmt. Info., Washington, 1970-71; dir. U.S. Army Ctr. for Tactical Computer Sci., Ft. Monmouth, N.J., 1975-77; project mgr. Operations Tactical Data Systems, Ft. Monmouth, N.J., 1978-82; program mgr. Joint Tactical Fusion Program, Washington, 1982-84; comdr. U.S. Army Info. Systems Engring., Ft. Belvoir, Va., 1984-87; pres. Contel Technology Ctr., Fairfax, Va., 1987-91; exec. v.p. Microelectronics & Computer Tech. Corp., Austin, Tex., 1991-93; pres. Learning Tree Internat. USA, Inc., Reston, Va., 1993-99; ind. cons., 1999—; chmn., CEO Code of Support Found., 2010—. Bd. dirs. Sybase, Dublin, Calif., 1994-2010, Challenger Ctr. for Space Sci. Edn., Alexandria, Va., 1990-2008; dir. Noblis, Inc., Fairfax, Va., 1996-2009, Assn. Grads. U.S. Mil. Acad. 1999-2009; chmn. Ctr. for Nat. Software Studies, 1996-2009; bd. visitors Software Engring. Inst. Carnegie Mellon U., 1988-2002, Coll. of Engring. U. Md., 1993-2001, chmn., Code of Support Found., 2010-. Author: Microprogrammable Computer Architectures 1976, numerous articles in profl. jours.; founding editor Journal of Systems & Software, 1979-85. Decorated Bronze Star (2), 1969, D.S.M., 1987. Mem. Inst. for Elec. & Electronic Engrs. (sr.), Assn. for Computing Machinery, Armed Forces Communications & Electronics Assn. (chpt. pres. 1981-82), Phi Kappa Phi, Soc. of the Sigma Xi. Office Phone: 703-821-2215. Business E-Mail: abslsbry@aol.com.

SALL, JOHN, information technology executive; married; 4 children. BS, Beloit Coll.; MS, No. Ill. U. Co-founder, exec. v.p. SAS Inst., Cary, NC; leader JMP Bus. Divsn. Named one of Forbes 400: Richest Americans, 2006—. Office: SAS Inst 100 SAS Campus Dr Cary NC 27513-2414

SALMON, MARY ANNE, state legislator; b. Fort Smith, Ark., Apr. 9, 1939; m. Don Salmon; children: Dona, Karen. BA, Ark. Tech. Univ., 1961. Tchr. & cons.; appointment coord. for Ark. Gov. Bill Clinton; commr. Lakewood Improvement Dist.; mem. Dist. 61 Ark. House of Reps., 1999—2002; mem. Dist. 31 Ark. State Senate, 2003—. Bd. mem. United Cerebral Palsy, 1997—, Metro YMCA, 1998—, Baptist Health Sys., 1999—, Twin City Bank, 2001—, Carti Found., 2002. Democrat. Southern Baptist. Office: 29 Heritage Park Cir North Little Rock AR 72116 also: Ark Senate State Capitol, Rm 320 Little Rock AR 72201 Office Phone: 501-753-4521. Office Fax: 501-753-2492. Business E-Mail: msalmon@arkleg.state.ar.us.

SALMON, ROBIN ROBERTSON, museum curator, editor; b. Columbia, SC, Mar. 18, 1952; d. Homer Hoyt and Elsie Rose (Garvin) Robertson; m. Timothy Dane Salmon, Dec. 1, 1979 (div. 1990); 1 child, Alexander Robertson; m. J. Grover Shuler, Mar. 8, 1997. BA, MA, U. SC, 1973; postgrad., U. SC, Conway, 1981-82; grad. Mus. Mgmt. Inst., U. Calif., Berkeley, 1992. Cert. Am. Soc. Appraisers, 1999. Historian & archivist Brookgreen Gardens, Murrells Inlet, SC, 1975—97, editor publ., 1978—96, v.p. academic affairs, cur. collections, 1990—95, v.p. collections, curator of sculpture, 1995—. Sculpture cons. SC State Mus., Columbia, 1984; mem. founding com. Georgetown (SC) County Arts Coun., 1987-88; regional advisor SC Arts Commn., Columbia, 1987; developer mus. edn. programs, 1981; advisor US Mint, State Quarters Project & medallic art projects, 2002-; advisor SC ETV Art Website for Schools, 2002-; bd. dirs. SC Arts Alliance, 2006-. Contbr.: Paul Manship: Changing Taste in America, 1985, A Century of American Sculpture Treasures from Brookgreen Gardens, 1981, rev., 1988, Spirit of the Wild Things: The Art of Sandy Scott, 1998, The Sculpture of Grainger McKoy, 1999, Marshall M. Fredericks: Sculptor, 2003, Language of Art: Rosie Sandifer, 2007; author: Brookgreen Gardens Sculpture, Vol. II, 1993, American Masters: Sculpture from Brookgreen Gardens, 1996, Images of America: Brookgreen Gardens, 2006; co-author: Masterworks of American Sculpture, 1999; contbr. articles to manuscripts, booklets, guide and scripts. Mem. SC Abandoned Cultural Property Bd., 1992, SC Save Outdoor Sculpture Project adv. bd., 1993. Named Young Career Woman Bus. & Profl. Women, 1977-78, Career Woman of Yr., 1989-90; recipient Inaugural Brookgreen Culture award, Brookgreen Gardens, 2005; rsch. fellow Waccamaw Ctr. Hist. & Cultural Studies, Coastal Carolina U., 1993-. Mem. Am. Assn. Mus. (S.E. mus. conf., edn. com., chair SEMC curators com. 1993-), Nat. Sculpture Soc. (bd. dirs. 1996-2006, editl. bd. Sculpture Rev. mag., 1996-, mem. exhbns. com., 1997-, chair exhbns. com., 1997-2004, 2006-, adv. bd. dirs., 2006-, Allied Profl. mem., 1991, Sculpture House Am. award, 2007), SC Fedn. Mus. Republican. Office: Brookgreen Gardens PO Box 3368 Pawleys Island SC 29585 Office Phone: 843-235-6012. E-mail: rsalmon@brookgreen.org.

SALO, ANN SEXTON DISTLER, lawyer; b. Indpls., Sept. 2, 1947; d. Harry W. and Ann (Malloy) Distler; m. Donald R. Salo, June 3, 1972 (div. Feb. 1983); 1 child, Eric V.; m. Phillip G. Clark, May 5, 1990; children: Ann Potter Clark, Phillip Gray Clark. BA, Purdue U., 1969; JD, George Washington U., 1972; LLM in Taxation, Emory U., 1976. Bar: Ga. 1973, U.S. Dist. Ct. (no. dist.) Ga. 1974. Assoc. Hansell & Post, Atlanta, 1972-78, mng. ptnr., 1978-89; ptnr. Grenwald and Salo, Atlanta, 1989-92, Long, Aldridge & Norman, Atlanta, 1992-95, Salo & Walker, Atlanta, 1995—. Adj. prof. law Emory U., 1983—86; mem. fin. planning adv. bd. Warren Gorham & Lamont, 1988—2000. Author: Estate Planning, 1988. Bd. dirs. Auditory Edn. Ctr., Atlanta, 1987—93, 1998—2001; pres. Planned Parenthood, Atlanta, 1984—88, Atlanta Humane Soc., 1990—93. Fellow: Am.

Coll. Trust and Estate Counsel (state chair 2001—); mem.: Atlanta Estate Planning Coun. Office: Salo Walker 3235 Roswell Rd NE Unit 400 Atlanta GA 30305-1887 Office Phone: 404-264-4555. Personal E-mail: adsalo@bellsouth.net.

SALOMON, DALAL MARIA, financial consultant; b. Tela, Honduras, Sept. 22, 1955; came to the US, 1956; d. John and Widad (Isaac) S. BS in Bus., Mich. State U., 1977; grad., Fin. Planning Inst., Richmond, Va., 1994. V.p. sales and mktg. New Dawn, Inc., Lansing, Mich., 1977-81; pvt. practice bus. cons. Washington, 1981-82; fin. planner Wallace Fin. Group, Bethesda, Md., 1982-84; fin. advisor Wachovia Securities (formerly Wheat First Securities), 1984, founder, mng. dir., investment officer Salomon & Ludwin Fin. Consulting. Mem. premier advisor program Wachovia Securities, mem. dirs. adv. coun., mem. sr. leadership coun., mem. pres.'s club, mem. chmn.'s cir. excellence. Mem. bd. dirs. Va. Birth-Related Neurological Injury Compensation Program, 2006—. Named one of The 30 Top Fin. Advisors for Va., R.J. Shook, 2005—08, The Top 100 Women Fin. Advisors, Barron's, 2006, 2007, 2008. Avocations: sports, travel. Office: Salomon & Ludwin Group Wachovia Securities 901 E Byrd St Richmond VA 23219-4047

SALOMON, ROBERT L., homebuilding company executive, accountant; BBA, U. Iowa. CPA. Formerly with MDC Holdings, Inc.; various positions including v.p. fin. Ashton Woods Homes, Roswell, Ga., 1989—98, CFO, treas., 1998—2008; sr. v.p., chief acctg. officer, contr. Beazer Homes USA, Inc., Atlanta, 2008—. Mem. AICPA. Office: Beazer Homes USA Inc 1000 Abernathy Rd NE Ste 260 Atlanta GA 30328-5648 Office Phone: 770-829-3700. Office Fax: 770-481-2808. Business E-Mail: rsalomon@beazer.com.

SALSBURY, FREDDIE R., JR., physics professor, educator; b. Berlin, Feb. 18, 1974; (parents Am. citizens); s. Freddie and Margaret Salsbury; m. Rebecca Jane Free, July 7, 2006. BS, U. Chgo., 1991—95; PhD, U. Calif., Berkeley, 1995—99. Rsch. assoc. Scripps Rsch. Inst., La Jolla, Calif., 1999—2002; asst. prof. Wake Forest U., Winston-Salem, NC, 2002—08, assoc. prof., 2008—, mem., 2004—, dir., Interdisciplinary Program Computational & Structural Biophysics, 2009—; mem. Ctr. Structural Biology at Wake Forest U., 2003—, WFU Comprehensive Cancer Ctr., 2009—; co-dir. crystallography and computational bioscis. core Comprehensive Cancer Ctr., 2011—; cross-appointment WFU Cancer Biology, 2009—. Mem. Com. Internat. Rels., BioPhys. Soc., 2007—, Com. Mem. Svcs., BioPhys. Soc., 2009—12, NIH Study Sect., 2008, 2012; panel mem. NSF GRFP, 2010—, DOD NDSEG, 2013. Fellow Nat. Svc. Rsch. award, NIH, Inst. Gen. Med. Scis., 1999—2002. Mem.: Protein Soc., Biophysical Soc., Am. Phys. Soc. Achievements include research in method development in density functional theory and molecular dynamics; application of computational methods to biomedical research, especially relating to cancer biology; patents pending for novel therapeutics designed, at least in part, computationally. Office: Wake Forest Univ Dept Physics PO Box 7507 Winston Salem NC 27109 Business E-Mail: salsbufr@wfu.edu.*

SALTARELLI, ROBERT J., corporate financial executive; BA in Acctg., Seattle U.; MBA, Columbia U., NY. CPA. Various fin. audit, planning & treasury positions JCPenney Co., Inc., 1976—90; various fin. leadership positions, including asst. treas. Melville Corp., 1990—92; various fin. leadership positions, including dir., capital markets, dir., internat. fin. W.R. Grace & Co., 1992—95; various fin. leadership positions, including dir., internat. & corp. fin. Tupperware Corp., 1996—97; treas. Breed Technologies, Inc., 1997—99; various fin. leadership positions, including v.p., treas. Sunterra Corp., 1999—2000; various fin. leadership positions, including treas. Breed Technologies, Inc., 2000—03; v.p., treas. Am. Household, Inc. (formerly the Sunbeam & Coleman companies), 2003—05, Dresser-Rand Group, Inc., 2005—09, v.p., gen. mgr., worldwide field ops., 2009—. Office: Dresser-Rand Group Inc West8 Tower 10205 Westheimer Rd Ste 1000 Houston TX 77042 Office Phone: 713-354-6100. Office Fax: 713-354-6110.

SALTER, MARK, speechwriter; b. Davenport, Iowa, 1955; s. Pete Salter; m. Diane M. Salter; 2 children. JD, Georgetown U.Law Ctr., Washington, DC, 1981. Press officer US Mission to the UN US Dept State, NYC, 1982—86; speechwriter to UN amb. Jeanne Kirkpatrick US Dept. State, NYC, 1986—89; position incuding chief speechwriter & chief of staff to Senator John McCain US Senate, 1989—2008; sr. advisor Senator John McCain's Presdl. Campaign, 2008—09. Co-author (with John McCain): Faith of My Fathers: A Family Memoir, 2000, Worth the Fighting For: A Memoir, 2002, Why Courage Matters: The Way to a Braver Life, 2004, Character is Destiny: Inspiring Stories Every Young Person Should Know and Every Adult Should Remember, 2005, Hard Call: Great Decisions and the Extraordinary People Who Made Them, 2007. Named one of 25 Most Influential Republicans, Newsmax Mag., 2008. Republican.

SALTZ, HOWARD JOEL, newspaper editor; b. Bronx, NY, Apr. 11, 1960; s. Fred Raymond and Sheila Lois (Goldberg) S. BA in Liberal Arts, SUNY, Stony Brook, 1983. Reporter Greenwich Time, So. Conn. Newspapers divsn. Times Mirror, 1983-85; with MediaNews Group, 1985—2011, N.J. Advance, Dover, 1985-87, editor, 1987-88, Hamilton (Ohio) Jour.-News, 1988-89, Fremont (Calif.) Argus, 1989-91, Johnstown Tribune-Democrat, 1991; dep. bus. editor Denver Post, 1996-98, dep. mng. editor features, 1998-2000, multimedia editor, 2000—02, assoc. editor/new media & strategic devel., 2002—06; v.p. content devel. MediaNews Group Interactive, 2006—11; editor Sun Sentinel, Ft. Lauderdale, Fla., 2011—. Adv. com. dept. journalism Ohlone Coll., Fremont, Calif., 1990-91. Bd. dirs. YMCA, Fremont-Newark, Calif., 1990-91, Johnstown Area Heritage Assn., 1991-93. Mem. Greater Johnstown C. of C. (bd. dirs. 1991-96), Soc. Profl. Journalists (bd. dirs. Northern Calif. chpt. 1990-91). Avocations: skiing, travel, scuba. Office: Sun Sentinel 500 E Broward Blvd Fort Lauderdale FL 33394

SALTZMAN, ROBERT PAUL, retired diversified financial services company executive; b. Chgo., Oct. 25, 1942; s. Al and Viola (Grossman) S.; m. Diane Maureen Schulman, Apr. 10, 1964; children: Amy, Adam, Suzanne. BA in Math., Northwestern U., 1964. Mgr. Continental Casualty Co., 1964-69; sr. v.p. Colonial Penn Group, 1969-83; pres., CEO Sun Life Ins. of Am. and Anchor Nat. Life Ins. Co., 1985-93; exec. v.p., mktg. Kaufman & Broad (now Broad, Inc.), 1987-93; pres., CEO Jackson Nat. Life Ins. Co., Lansing, Mich., 1994—2001. Bd. dirs. Raymond James Fin., Inc., 2007—. Office: Raymond James Financial Inc 880 Carillon Pky Saint Petersburg FL 33716 Office Phone: 727-567-1000. Office Fax: 727-567-8915. Business E-Mail: rsaltzman@rjf.com.

SALVUCCI, LINDA, history professor; b. Pittston, Pa., Mar. 28, 1951; d. Joseph A. and Helen Shegelski Kerrigan; m. Richard Salvucci, Aug. 25, 1973; children: Martin J., Rosemary C. AB in History, Villanova U., 1973; AM in History, Princeton U., 1979, PhD in History, 1985. Asst. prof. history Trinity U., San Antonio, 1985—91, assoc. prof. history, 1991—. Chmn., mem. coms. various confs. in field. Co-author: (textbook) Call to Freedom, various edits., 2000—05; contbr. articles to profl. publs. Trustee St. Luke's Episc. Sch., 1998—2005, vice chmn., 2002—04; bd. editors The Americas, 2002—06; bd. dirs. Youth Orchs. San Antonio, 2005—06. Recipient Hubert Herring award for best article, Pacific Coast Coun. on L.Am. Studies, 1985, Coll. Tchrs. award, NEH, 1988—89, prize, Conf. on L.Am. History, 2001. Mem.: Hist. Soc. (bd. govs. 2006—), Nat. Coun. History Edn. (trustee 2005—, vice chair 2009—, chair 2012—), Omohundro Inst. Early Am. History and Culture, Am. Hist. Assn. Office: Trinity U Dept History 1 Trinity Pl San Antonio TX 78212 Office Phone: 210-999-7628. Business E-Mail: lsalvucc@trinity.edu.

SALYER, KENNETH E., surgeon; b. Kansas City, Kans., Aug. 18, 1936; s. Everett A. and Laurene S.; m. Luci Lara-Salyer; children: Kenneth E. Jr., Leigh Green-Salyer. BS, U. Mo., 1958; MD, U. Kans., 1962. Intern Parkland Meml. Hosp., Dallas, 1962-63, resident in gen. surgery, 1963-67; fellow in surgery U. Tex. SW Sch. Med., Dallas, 1965-67, founder, dir. residency tng. program, 1969-78; prof. surgery, chair plastic surgery, 1969-78; resident in plastic surgery U. Kans. Sch. Med., Kansas City, 1967-69; founder, dir. Internat. Craniofacial Inst., Dallas, 1986—. Editl. bd. mem. Annals of Plastic Surgery, 1977-79, Jour. of Speech and Hearing Disorders (editl. cons.) 1982, Tex. Medicine (editl. cons.) 1981-85, Jour. of Craniofacial Surgery, 1990—, Italian Jour. Craniomaxillofacial Surgery, 1990—, Argentinian Jour. Plastic Surgery (internat. consultative coun. 1995—). Author: Techniques in Aesthetic Craniofacial Surgery, 1989, Cleft Lip and Palate Treatment Center: A Booklet for Parents, 1994, (with J. Bardach) Surgical Techniques in Cleft Lip and Palate, 1987, 2d edit. 1991, (with others) The Atlas of Craniomaxillofacial Surgery, 1982; editor: Symposium on Plastic Surgery in the Orbital Region, 1976; author various book chpts. Recipient Nat. Inst. Health award public health svc., sr. clin. traineeship Cancer Control Program 1967-69, Plastic Surgery Resident Program Participation award 2nd place 1967-69, scholar. competition (hon. mention) Edn. Found. Am. Soc. Plastic and Reconstructive Surgeons, 1972, Rsch. Grant award Ednl. Found. Am. Soc. Plastic and Reconstructive Surgeons 1975-76, Hektoen Gold medal for original investigation "Spectrum of Rsch. and Clin. Mgmt. of Craniofacial Anomalies" exhibit at AMA, San Francisco 1977, selected hon. mem. Japanese Soc. Craniofacial Surgery 1993, selected chmn. med. adv. bd. Children's Craniofacial Assn. 1993; grantee Internat. NIH Microvascular Surg. Rsch. 1969, Vets. Admin. Hosp. Maxillofacial Rsch. 1972-78, Sid Richardson Found. med. rsch. 1975-76, Gen. Electric Found. for Craniofacial Deformities 1985-87; recipient various awards for videos. Mem. AMA (mem. various coms.), Am. Acad. Pediat. (exec. com. section on plastic surgery, founding mem., sec.-treas. 1987-90, chmn. 1991—), Am. Assn. of Pediat. Plastic Surgery (founding mem., chmn. 1991—), Am. Assn. Plastic Surgery (mem. various coms.), Am. Burn Assn., Am. Cleft Palate Assn. (mem. various coms.), Am. Coll. Surgeons, Am. Soc. for Aesthetic Plastic Surgery, Am. Soc. Maxiofacial Surgery (pres. 2003-04), Am. Soc. Plastic and Reconstructive Surgery (mem. various coms.), Am. Soc. for Reconstructive Microsurgery, Argentine Soc. of Plastic Surgery, Children's Craniofacial Assn. (chmn. med. adv. bd.), Chirugio Soc., Craniofacial Biology Group, Dallas County Med. Soc., Dallas Soc. Plastic Surgery, Euro. Assn. for Craniomaxillofacial Surgery, Internat. Coll. Surgeons, Internat. Confederation for Plastic Reconstructive Surgery (founding mem.), Internat. Craniofacial Club, Internat. Craniofacial Travel Club, Internat. Soc. Clin. Plastic Surgery, Internat. Soc. Cranofacial Surgery (pres. 2001-03), Lipoplasty Soc. of N.A., Inc., Plastic Surgery Rsch. Coun. (chmn. 1978), Soc. for Biomaterials, Soc. Craniofacial Genetics, Soc. Head and Neck Surgery, So. Med. Assn., Southwestern Med. Found., Tex. Soc. Plastic Surgery (mem. various coms., pres.-elect 1982-83, pres. 1983-84), Tex. State Med. Assn., Wound Healing Soc, Craniofacial Surgery Fellowship (founder and dir. 1979-2006), Japanese Soc. Craniofacial Surgery, World craniofacial Found. (founder and chmn. 1990-), Am. Soc. Craniofacial Surgery (pres. 1996-99). Avocations: skiing, running, travel. Office Phone: 972-566-6669.

SAMBURG, A. GENE, security company executive; b. Indpls., Apr. 25, 1941; s. A. George and Hermine (Wittgenstein) S.; m. Lorrie Silverman, June 26, 1966; children: Kimberly Jill, Thomas Blair. BEE, Cornell U., 1964; OPM, Harvard U., 1985. Engr. Westinghouse Corp., 1964-72; founder, pres. and CEO Kastle Systems, Inc., 1972—2007. Adv. on bus. programs Cornell U.; lectr. on entrepreneurship Georgetown U.; spl. lectr. for numerous profl. and ednl. courses in field. Patentee in field. Bd. dirs. Arena Stage. Named E&Y Master Entrepreneur of Yr., Washington, 1999, Top Entrepreneurs of Yr. Security Sales and Integration, 2006. Mem. IEEE, ASME, CPP, Am. Soc. Indsl. Security, Woodmont Country Club, City Club (Washington), Tower Club (McLean, Va.), Gridiron Club and Found. Avocations: writing, travel. Home and Office: Unit 912 1401 N Oak St Arlington VA 22209 Office Phone: 703-528-8800. Business E-Mail: gene@kastle.com.

SAMFORD, KAREN ELAINE, small business owner, consultant; d. George C. and Agnes M. (Phillips) Sanford; m. Jeff E. Samford, Aug. 18; children: Jeffrey Barton, Keri Lynn. BA in English, History, Tex. Christian U. Cert. secondary tchr., Tex. Tchr. secondary schs., Tex., La., Mo., 1964-74; saleswoman, 1974-83; corp. trainer, 1983-86; owner Karen E. Samford Tng. Cons., Plano, 1986—. Republican. Home and Office: 3409 Haversham Dr Plano TX 75023-6109 Personal E-mail: kesam8@gmail.com.

SAMFORD, YETTA GLENN, JR., lawyer, director; b. Opelika, Ala., June 8, 1923; s. Yetta Glenn and Mary Elizabeth (Denson) S.; m. Mary Austill, Sept. 6, 1949; children: Mary Austill Lott, Katherine Park Alford, Yetta Glenn III (dec.). BS, Auburn U., Ala., 1947; LLB, U. Ala., Tuscaloosa, 1949, LLD (hon.), 1995; DHL (hon.), U. Mobile, Ala., 2001. Bar: Ala. 1949, U.S. Dist. Ct. (mid. dist.) Ala. 1950, U.S. Ct. Appeals (5th cir.) 1961, U.S. Ct. Appeals (11th cir.) 1981. Pvt. practice, Opelika, Ala.; ptnr. Samford & Denson LLP and Predessors, 1949—. Mem. Ala. Senate from Lee and Russell counties, 1958-62; mem. bd. edn.Opelika City, 1963-75, pres. 1966-74; mem. State of Ala. Bd. of Corrections, 1969-75; mem. adv. bd. State Docks, 1987-2000. Trustee U. Mobile, 1963-92, life trustee, 1992—, trustee U. Ala., 1972-93, trustee emeritus, 1993— Mem. Ala. Law Inst. (exec. com.), Ala. Acad. Honor (exec. com. mem.), Masons, Phi Delta Phi, Omicron Delta Kappa, Alpha Tau Omega. Republican. Baptist. Home: 615 Terracewood Dr Opelika AL 36801-3850 Office: Samford & Denson LLP 709 Ave A PO Box 2345 Opelika AL 36801-2345 Office Phone: 334-745-3504. Office Fax: 334-745-3506. Personal E-mail: maryann@samfordlaw.com.

SAMMARCO, PAUL WILLIAM, ecologist, researcher; b. Hackensack, NJ, Oct. 18, 1948; s. Giacomo and Esther (Galanti) S.; m. Jean Sogioka, May 29, 1971 (div. 1996); children: Mimi Cecile, Dustin Paul, Jack Isao; m. Donna M. Melancon, Aug. 12, 1998; stepchildren: Lindsay Claire, Ben Charles. BA, Syracuse U., 1970, postgrad., 1970—71; cert., Marine Biology Lab., Woods Hole, Mass., 1971, Fairleigh Dickinson U., 1972; PhD, SUNY Stony Brook, 1977. Tchg. asst. Syracuse U., NY, 1970—71; tchg. asst. Discovery Bay Marine Lab. SUNY-Stony Brook Overseas Acad. Program, Jamaica, 1974; tchg. asst. SUNY, Stony Brook, 1971—77; asst. prof. Clarkson U., Potsdam, NY, 1977—79; vis. asst. prof. tropical ecology SUNY Potsdam, St. Croix, V.I., 1979; sr. rsch. scientist Australian Inst. Marine Sci., Townsville, Queensland, 1979—89; coord. Shelf Seas Rsch. Program, 1985—86; dir. environ. rsch. Resource Assessment Commn. Prime Minister's commn. on natural resources, Canberra, Australia, 1989—91; exec. dir. La. Univs. Marine Consortium, Chauvin, 1991—95, prof., 1995—. Adj. prof. La. State U., U. La. at Lafayette, 1992-2008, U. New Orleans, Nicholls State U., 1992-, U. Campinas-Brazil, 1997-99, Ctrl. Queensland U., Australia, 1997-2002, U. Maine at Orono, 2001—03; pres. Endless Shores Music Pubs.; pres. P&J Records, LLC. Composer, arranger, prodr. popular and sacred music; former mem. Australian Chamber Choir, Wesley Choir, Canberra; co-author: (with S. Kolian) Mariculture and Other Uses for Offshore Oil and Gas Platforms: Rationale for Retaining Infrastructure, 2005; editor: (with M.L. Heron) The Bio-Physics of Marine Larval Dispersal, 1994, Marine Biology (Berlin), 2000—08, Aquatic Biology, 2007—; contbr. numerous articles to profl. jours.; editl. advisor Marine Ecology Progress Series, 1985-93; co-editor: Procs. 6th Internat. Coral Reef Symposium, 1988, Procs. 8th Internat. Coral Reef Symposium, Procs. Internat. BioIndicators Conf., Jour. Environ. Bioindicators, 2007. Mem. La. State Gov.'s Platform for Mariculture Task Force, 2004-05; mem. chancel choir First United Meth. Ch., Houma, La. Recipient Internat. Sci. Exch. award, 1988-89, Me Master U., Can. Mem. ASCAP (exec. dir.), Assn. Marine Labs. Caribbean (exec. dir.-elect), Australian Marine Scis. Assn. (keynote spkr. 1981, counselor 1984-89, chmn., organizer nat. conf. 1987, chmn. Australia Acad. Sci. Boden Conf. 1990), Internat. Soc. Reef Studies (counselor 1997-2000), Australian Coral Reef Soc., South LA Wetlands Discovery Ctr. State Commn. (chairperson 2009-), Sigma Xi. Office: La Univs Marine Consortium 8124 Highway 56 Chauvin LA 70344-2110 Office Phone: 985-851-2876.

SAMPLE, BILL, state legislator; b. Hazen, Ark., Apr. 16, 1946; m. Betty Ann Sample; children: Cleta, Brandi. Attended, Little Rock U. Owner Pestco Inc., 1977—; mem. Dist. 30 Ark. House of Reps., 2004—11; mem. Dist. 19 Ark. State Senate, 2011—. Mem.: Ark. Pest Mgmt. Assn. (regional dir. 2002, v.p. 2004). Republican. Methodist. Mailing: Dist Address 2340 N Hwy 7 Hot Springs AR 71909 Office Phone: 501-321-0040. Office Fax: 501-321-4249. Business E-Mail: bsample@cablelynx.com.

SAMPSON, KELVIN DALE, professional basketball coach, former college basketball coach; b. Laurinburg, NC, Oct. 5, 1955; s. John W. and Eva (Brewington) S.; m. Karen Sue Lowry, June 16, 1979; children: Lauren Elizabeth, Kellen Matthew. BS, Pembroke State U., 1978; MS, Mich. State U., 1980. Asst. coach Mont. Tech. U., 1979—80, head coach, 1981—85; asst. coach Wash. State U. Cougars, 1985—87, head coach, 1987—94, U. Okla. Sooners, Norman, Okla., 1994—2006, Ind. U. Hoosiers, Bloomington, 2006—08; asst. coach Milw. Bucks, 2008—11, Houston Rockets, 2011—. Contbr. articles to profl. jours. Named Big Eight Coach of Yr., 1995, Nat. Coach of Yr., AP, 1995. Mem. Nat. Assn. Basketball Coaches (Dist. Coach of Yr. 1991, PAC 10 Coach of Yr. 1991, Nat. Coach of Yr., 2002) Avocations: golf, reading, exercise. Office: Houston Rockets 1510 Polk St Houston TX 77002

SAMPSON, ROBERT NEIL, professional society administrator, consultant; b. Spokane, Wash., Nov. 29, 1938; s. Robert Jay and Juanita Cleone (Hickman) S.; m. Jeanne Louise Stokes, June 7, 1960; children— Robert W., Eric S., Christopher B., Heidi L. BS in Agr, U. Idaho, 1960; M.Public Adminstrn., Harvard U., 1974. Soil conservationist Soil Conservation Service, Burley, Idaho, 1960-61, work unit conservationist Orofino, Idaho, 1962-65, agronomist Idaho Falls, Idaho, 1967-68, info. specialist Boise, 1968-70, area conservationist, 1970-72, land use specialist Washington, 1974-77, dir. environ. services div., 1977; land use program mgr. Idaho Planning and Community Affairs Agy., Boise, 1972-73; exec. v.p. Nat. Assn. Conservation Dists., Washington, 1978-84, Am. Forestry Assn., Washington, 1984-95; sr. fellow Am. Forests, Washington, 1995-2000; affiliate prof. Dept. Forest Resources U. Idaho, 1997—2000; pres. Vision Forestry LLC, 2000—. Instr. soils and land use Boise State U., 1972; F.K. Weyerhaeuser vis. fellow in comml. forestry Yale Sch. Forestry and Environ. Studies, 2001; pres., The Sampson Group, Inc., 1996—, Vision Forestry LLC, 2000—; rsch. scientist, Yale Sch. Forestry and Environ. Studies, 2001—; land use and forestry cons. Author: Farmland or Wasteland: A Time To Choose, 1981, For Love of the Land, 1985, With One Voice, 2008; contbr. articles to profl. and popular publs. Pres. Orofino Golf Assn., 1966, Clearwater County Search and Rescue Unit, 1966-67; chmn. Nat. Commn. on Wildfire Disasters, 1992-94. Recipient President's citation Soil Conservation Soc. Am., 1978; named Boise Fed. Civil Servant of Year Boise Fed. Bus. Assn., 1972 Fellow Soil and Water Conservation Soc. (Hugh Hammond Bennett award 1992); mem. Soc. Am. Foresters. Presbyterian. Personal E-mail: neil@visionforestry.com.

SAMS, LOUISE S., broadcast executive, lawyer; b. Atlanta, 1957; BA magna cum laude, Princeton U., 1979; JD, U. Va. Sch. Law, 1985. Bar: NY 1986, Ga. 1995. Corp. assoc. White & Case, NYC, 1986—93; Joined Turner Broadcasting Systems, Inc., Atlanta, 1993, exec. v.p., gen. counsel, 2000—; pres. Turner Broadcasting Systems International, Atlanta, 2003—. Mem. editl. bd. U. Va. Jour. Internat. Law, 1983—84, exec. editor, 1984—85. Mem. bd. dirs. Princeton U. Named one of The 50 Most Influential Women Lawyers in America, Nat. Law Jour., 2007. Mem.: ABA, State Bar Ga., NY State Bar Assn. Office: Turner Broadcasting System Inc 1 CNN Ctr 100 Internat Blvd Atlanta GA 30303 Office Phone: 404-827-1700. Office Fax: 404-827-2437. E-mail: louise.sams@turner.com.

SAMUELS, WILLIAM MASON, physiology association executive; b. Dover, Ohio, Jan. 17, 1929; s. William Mason and Anne Frieda (Fankhauser) S.; m. Joanne Gorenflo, Oct. 2, 1971; children: Robert Lee(dec.), Ann Frances. AB, U. Ky., 1951; postgrad., Georgetown U., 1952. Mng. editor for Ind., Courier-Jour. & Times, Louisville, 1955-65; dir. office of v.p. U. Ky. Med. Center, Lexington, 1965-70; exec. dir. Am. Soc. Allied Health Professions, Washington, 1973—78; assoc. Schs. Allied Health Professions, 1970—73; exec. dir. Am. Assn. Blood Banks, Washington, 1978-80, Nat. Soc. Med. Research Washington, 1980-84, Am. Physiol. Soc., Bethesda, Md., 1984-92; retired, 1992—. Contbr. articles to profl. jours. Mem. secretarist Nat. Commn. Health Certifying Agys.; v.p. Coalition Health Funding; cons. to fed. agys.; vol. Habitat for Humanity, Boca Raton; elder Presbyn. Ch., corp. dir. With USAF, 1951-53, USAFR, 1954-76, lt. col. ret. Named Ky. Man of Yr. Sigma Phi Epsilon, 1968 Mem.: AMA (coun. on allied health edn. accreditation), Washington Soc. Assn. Execs., Health Staff Soc., Am. Hosp. Assn. (coun. on edn.), Am. Optometric Assn. (coun. on edn., coun. on optimetric clin. care, nat. commn. on paraoptometric cert.), Am. Soc. Assn. Execs., Pinehurst (NC) Country Club, Lions. Presbyterian. Home: 6055 S Verde Trail H-120 Boca Raton FL 33433-4450

SAMUELSON, RUTH, state legislator; b. Charleston, SC, Nov. 4, 1959; m. Ken Samuelson; children: Bobby, David, Joy, Alex. BA, U NC., 1981. Bd. commr. Dist. 5, Mecklenburg County, 2000—04; pres. Philanthropy in Motion, 2004—; mem. Dist. 104 NC House of Reps., 2007—. Bd. dirs. Peacemaker Ministries, Inc.; pres. ruth: Philanthropy in Motion. Recipient Environ. award, Charlotte Bus. Jour., 2008; named one of 50 Most Influential Women in Bus., Mecklenburg Times, 2009. Republican. Office: North Carolina House of Representatives 300 N Salisbury St Rm 419B Raleigh NC 27603-5925 Office Phone: 919-715-3009. E-mail: Ruth.Samuelson@ncleg.net.

SANBERG, PAUL RONALD, medical educator, research scientist, administrator; b. Coral Gables, Fla., Jan. 4, 1955; s. Bernard and Molly (Spector) Sanberg BS with honors, York U., 1976; MS, U. B.C., 1979; PhD, Australian Nat. U., 1981, DSc, 1998; grad. diploma sci. edn., West Australia Inst. Tech., 1986; MD, St. James Sch. Med., 2008. Postdoctoral fellow Johns Hopkins Med. Sch., Balt., 1981—83; asst. prof. Ohio U., Athens, 1983—86; assoc. prof. U. Cin., 1986—89; prof. Brown U., Providence, 1990—92, U. South Fla., Tampa, 1992—2003, assoc. v.p., 2003—10, disting. prof., 2003—, assoc. dean, 2003—06, sr. assoc. v.p., 2010—11, spl. asst. to the pres., 2011—12, chair neurosci., 1997—2005, exec. dir. Ctr. of Excellence for Aging and Brain Repair, 2000—, v.p., 2012—13, sr. v.p., 2013—. Co-founder Saneron CCEL Therapeutics, Inc., 2000—. Recipient award Am. Coll. Neuropsychopharmacology, Tourette Syndrome Assn., Sir. J.G. Crawford medal, Ove Ferno prize Coll. Internat. Neuropsychopharmacology; grantee NIH, Am. Heart Assn., Childrens Med. Rsch. Found., Hereditary Disease Found., Huntington's Disease Found., Outstanding Rschr. award Sigma Xi; named Healthcare Hero, Tampa Bay Bus. Jour., 2006, Everfront award, Taiwan, 2011. Fellow AAAS, ACNP, APA, APS, ASNTR, IBNS, NAI, Royal Soc. Chemistry, Royal Soc. Medicine, Royal Soc. Pub. Health; mem. Soc. for Neurosci., Internat. Brain Rsch. Orgn., Internat. Behavioral Neurosci. Soc. (pres. 1994, Outstanding Rschr. award 2004), Am. Soc. for Neural Transplant (pres. 1995), Cell Transplant Soc. (pres. 1996, editor), Nat. Acad. Inventors.(pres., 2010-, Evaluation Com. Presdl. medal for technol. innovation 2012-). Home: 11751 Pilot Country Dr Spring Hill FL 34610-7912 Office: University South Fla Office SVP Rsch and Innovation 3702 Spectrum Blvd Ste 165 Tampa FL 33612-9444 Business E-Mail: psanberg@usf.edu.*

SANCHEZ, ANTONIO RODOLFO, JR., oil industry executive; b. Laredo, Tex., Feb. 3, 1943; s. Antonio Rodolfo and Alicia M. Sanchez; m. Maria Josefina Guajardo, 1972; children: Antonio III, Ana Lee, Eduardo, Patricio. BBA, St. Mary's U., San Antonio, 1965, JD, 1969. Aide to lt. gov., Tex.; co-founder, chmn., CEO Sanchez Oil and Gas Corp. (formerly Sanchez-O'Brien Oil & Gas), Laredo, Tex., 1973—; majority owner Internat. Bancshares Corp., Laredo, Tex. Mem. Tex. Parks and Wildlife Commn., 1985—91; bd. regents U. Tex., 1997—2003. Dem. candidate for gov., Tex., 2002. Office Phone: 952-722-7611. Office Fax: 956-726-6637. Business E-Mail: tony@sanchezog.com.

SANCHEZ, FABIAN, dancer; m. Jacqueline Sanchez. Profl. & competitive dancer, 1992—; three-time finalist US Open Am. Rhythm Championship; four-time winner Fred Astaire Nat. Championship; winner US Rising Star Championship, Am. Rhythm divsn., 1999, World Mambo Championship, 2006—; profl. dancer Dancing with the Stars, ABC, 2008—. Co-owner Fred Astaire Dance Studio, Birmingham, Ala.; nat. dance bd. Fred Astaire Dance Studios. Office: Fred Astaire Dance Studio Ste J 1941 Hoover Ct Birmingham AL 35226 Office Phone: 205-979-4777. E-mail: fadshoover@bellsouth.net.

SANCHEZ, ROBERT E., corporate financial executive; BS in Elec. Engring., U. Miami; MBA, Wharton Sch. U. Pa. Former controls engr. Pratt & Whitney Aircraft; former applications engr. Fla. Power & Light; regional finance dir., group dir. fin. analysis, mgr. strategic planning, v.p. asset mgmt., sr. v.p. global transp. mgmt. Ryder System, Inc., 1993—2003, sr. v.p. & CIO, 2003—05, exec. v.p. ops. US Fleet Mgmt., 2005—07, exec. v.p. & CFO, 2007—10, pres. global fleet mgmt. solutions, 2010—. Chmn. Ryder United Way Campaign. Recipient Engr. of Yr. award, ACE, 2001, Young Hispanic Leadership award, 2002. Mem.: Assn. Cuban Engrs. (bd. mem.), Miami-Dade Beacon Coun. (bd. mem.), United Way Leadership Circle, Wharton Alumni Assn. Office: 11690 NW 105th St Miami FL 33178 Office Phone: 305-500-3726.

SANCHEZ, ROBERT FRANCIS, journalist; b. Bradenton, Fla., Jan. 1, 1938; s. Robert and Frances Alice (Thompson) S. BS in English Edn., Fla. State U., 1959, MS, 1962, postgrad., 1971-74. Mem. faculty Fla. State U., Tallahassee, 1962-67; mem. faculty Fla. A&M U., Tallahassee, 1968-71; writer, editor Tallahassee Democrat, 1965-74; editl. writer Miami Herald, 1974-2000; dir. pub. policy James Madison Inst., Tallahassee. Co-recipient Pulitzer Prize, 1983 Republican. Methodist. Home: 2324 Williams Rd Tallahassee FL 32311 Office: James Madison Inst 2017 Delta Blvd Tallahassee FL 32315

SÁNCHEZ-BETANCES, LUIS, lawyer, former attorney general; b. June 21, 1947; BBA, U. Puerto Rico, 1969, LLB cum laude, 1972; Administrative and International Law Courses, NYU, 1971. Bar: Supreme Court, Commonwealth of Puerto Rico, US District Court for the District of Puerto Rico and US Court of Appeals, First Circuit 1973, Washington, DC, Court of Appeals 1984, US Supreme Court 2001. Counsel Environmental Quality Bd., 1973, hearing examiner, 1974—75; instructor dept. mgmt. and business U. Puerto Rico, Sch. of Business, 1973—76, dir., Business Research Ctr., 1974—76; assoc. Bauza & Dávila, San Juan, 1976—81; ptnr. Sánchez-Betances & Sifre, 1981—2004, Sánchez-Betances, Sifre & Muñoz-Noya, 2004—; sec. justice Commonwealth of Puerto Rico, 2013. Pres. Commission for Legal Edn. to the Community, 1976; pres., Hearing Panel for State Implementation Plan Environmental Quality Bd., 1979, pres., Hearing Panel for Atmospheric Pollution Control Regulation, 1979; mem. Defense Research Inst., Interamerican U. Sch. of Law Com. on Health Law Conference, Permanent Com. on Rules of Civil Procedure, Judicial Conf., Supreme Court of the Commonwealth of Puerto Rico, 1988—; spkr. Biannual Health Law Conf. on related topics. Mem. editl. bd. Law Journal, 1976. Mem.: International Soc. of Barristers, American Health Lawyers Assn., ABA, Puerto Rico Bar Assn. (commissioner, profl. ethics commission 1983—86). Office: Sanchez-Betances Sifre & Munoz-Noya 33 Bolivia Fifth Flo San Juan PR 00917*

SANDBERG, IRWIN WALTER, retired electrical and computer engineering educator; b. NYC, Jan. 23, 1934; s. Ben and Estelle S.; m. Barbara A. Zimmerman, June 15, 1958; 1 dau. Heidi L. B.E.E., Poly. Inst. Bklyn., 1955, M.E.E., 1956, D.E.E., 1958. Tech. aid Bell Telephone Labs., Inc., Murray Hill, NJ, summer 1954, mem. tech. staff, 1958-67, head systems theory research dept., 1967-72, mem. math. and statis. research ctr., 1972-86; prof. elec. and computer engring. U. Tex., Austin, 1986—2005, Cockrell Family Regents chair in engring. emeritus; engr. Wheeler Labs., Great Neck, NY, summer 1955. Vis. prof. U. Calif.-Berkeley, 1965; U.S. del. Union Radio Scientifique Internationale, Munich, Germany, 1966; U.S. nat. inst. rep. Advanced Study Inst. on Network and Signal Theory, NATO, Bournemouth, Eng., 1972; lectr. study inst. NATO (Knokke), Belgium, 1966, Copenhagen, 1970; disting. invited spkr. Asilomar Conf., 1973-74; main lectr. European Conf. on Circuit Theory and Design, The Hague, 1981; advisor Inst. Electronics, Info. and Comm. Engrs., Tokyo; advisor Am. Men and Women of Sci., 1993. Patentee (in field). Recipient Best Paper award Asilomar Conf., 1970, Achievement award IEEE Circuits and Systems Soc., 1986, Classic Paper citation ISI press, 1984, Outstanding Alumnus award Poly. U., 1993. Fellow IEEE (life, adminstrv. com. group circuit theory 1969-70, vice chmn. group circuit theory 1971-72, Centennial medal, Millennial medal, Cirs. and Sys. Soc. Golden Jubilee medal, Cirs. and Sys. Soc. disting. lectr.), AAAS; mem. NAE, Soc. for Indsl. and Applied Math., Acad. Medicine, Engring. and Sci. Tex., Eta Kappa Nu, Sigma Xi, Tau Beta Pi. Home: 8505 Hickory Creek Dr Austin TX 78735-1527 Home Phone: 512-328-1004. E-mail: sandberg@ece.utexas.edu.

SANDBERG, JOEL S., ophthalmologist; s. Emanuel and Sadie Sandberg; m. Adele Einhorn Sandberg, June 26, 1965; children: Sheryl, David, Michelle. BA, Johns Hopkins U., Balt., 1964, MD, 1967. Intern NY Hosp.-Sloan Kettering Meml. Hosp., Cornell U. Sch. Medicine, NYC, 1967—68; staff assoc. Cancer Chemotherapy Rsch. Nat. Cancer Inst., NIH, Bethesda, Md., 1968—70; cancer chemotherapy fellow Tel Hashomer Hosp., U. Tel Aviv Med. Ctr., 1970—71; ophthalmology resident Bascom Palmer Eye Inst., U. Miami Sch. Medicine, 1971—74; ophthalmologist Eye Surgery Assocs., Hollywood, Fla., 1974—. Vol. prof. ophthalmology Bascom Palmer Eye Inst., U. Miami Sch. Medicine, Fla., 1974—; chmn. dept. ophthalmology Meml. Regional Hosp., Hollywood, 1986—88. Lt. comdr. USPHS, 1968—70. Scholar, Am. Cancer Soc., 1963—67. Fellow: Am. Acad. Opthalmology; mem.: Miami Ophthal. Soc. (pres. 1996), Alpha Omega Alpha. Office: 2740 Hollywood Blvd Hollywood FL 33020

SANDERFORD, HOWARD, state legislator; b. Meridian, Miss., Oct. 18, 1935; m. Dot Sanderford, 1958; children: Mary Ann, Peggy, Betty. BS in Acctg., Miss. State U. Exec. IBM, 1957—87; pres. Computer Leasing Co., Inc.; mem. Dist. 20 Ala. House of Reps., Montgomery, 1989—. Mem. Ala. Commn. on Aerospace Sciences, Ala. Mgmt. Improvement Program, Ala. Bd. Med. Scholarship Awards, Ala. State Rep. Exec. Com.; past chmn. Madison County Rep. Com., Ala.; deacon First Bapt. Ch.; past v.p. Met. YMCA Bd. Officer USMC. Recipient IBM Golden Cir., 1980. Mem.: Huntsville C. of C., Huntsville Rotary (past pres.). Republican. Baptist. Office: 908 Tannahill Dr SE Huntsville AL 35802-1971 also: Ala House of Reps Ala State House 11 S Union St Rm 528-B Montgomery AL 36130 Office Phone: 256-533-1989, 334-242-4368. Business E-Mail: hs1989@aol.com.

SANDERFORD, ROBIN, retail executive; Grad., U. South Ala., Mobile. Dir. real estate & long range planning Mercantile Stores Co., Inc., Fairfield, Ohio, 1993—95, pres. Montgomery Gayfers/J.B. White divsn. Montgomery, Ala., 1995—98; v.p. Dillard's, Inc., 1998—. Office: Dillard s Inc 1600 Cantrell Rd Little Rock AR 72201 Office Phone: 501-376-5200. Office Fax: 501-399-7831. E-mail: robin.sanderford@dillards.com.

SANDERLIN, JAMES L., energy executive, lawyer; s. Linwood and Elsie R. Sanderlin; m. Ginger Sanderlin; children: Meredith, Elaine, Barry. B, Randolph-Macon Coll., Ashland, Va.; degree in Law, U. Va., 1966. With McGuireWoods, Richmond, Va.; sr. v.p. law, DRI & CNG Dominion Resources, Inc., 2000—. Bd. dirs. Tredegar Nat. Civil War Ctr. Found., Richmond, Richmond Pub. Libr.; co-chair VCU/MCV Heart Ctr. Fund. Office: Dominion 120 Tredegar St Richmond VA 23219-4306 Office Phone: 804-819-2000. Office Fax: 804-819-2233. Business E-Mail: james_sanderlin@dom.com.

SANDERS, BARRY, retired professional football player; b. Wichita, July 16, 1968; s. William and Shirley Sanders; m. Lauren Campbell, 2000 (separated 2012); 3 children. Student, Okla. State U., 1986—89. Running back Detroit Lions, 1989—99. Co-author (with Mark E. McCormick): Now You See Him: The Barry Sanders Story, 2003. Recipient Heisman Meml. Trophy award, Heisman Trophy Trust, 1988, Bert Bell award, 1991, 1997; named 1st Team NFL All-Pro, 1989—91, 1994, 1995, 1997, NFL Rookie of Yr., 1990, NFL Offensive Player of Yr., 1994, 1997, NFL MVP, AP, 1997; named to The Sporting News Coll. All-American team, 1987, 1988, The Nat. Football Conf. Pro Bowl Team, NFL, 1989—98, The NFL All-Decade Team, 1990s, The Coll. Football Hall of Fame, 2003, The Pro Football Hall of Fame, 2004. Achievements include setting the NCAA single-season record in rushing yards (2,628 yards), 1988; leading the NFL in: rushing, 1990, 1994, 1996, 1997; touchdowns, 1990, 1991; yards from scrimmage, 1994, 1997; all-purpose yards, 1997; being the NFL's third all-time leader in rushing yards, (15,269 yards). Business E-Mail: jb@barry.sanders.com.

SANDERS, DAVID J., state legislator; m. Rebecca Sanders; children: Abigail Sanders, Noah Sanders, Isaac Sanders, Elijah Sanders, Levi Sanders. Grad. in Polit. Sci. & Mass Comm., Ouachita Bapt. U., 1997. Mem., deacon Little Rock First Bapt. Ch.; columnist Stephens Media; mem. Office of Gov.r, State of Ark., 1997—98, Policy and Comm. Aide, 1997—98; comm. dir. Fay Boozman for US Senate, 1998; mem. Johnson Controls, Inc., 1999—2005, Ark. Health Care Svcs., 1999—2005; dir., devel. Arkansas Bapt. Sch. System, 2006—; creator, prodr., Host Ark. Ednl. TV Network, 2006—09; columnist Associated Bapt. Press, 2009; mem. Dist. 31 Ark. House of Representatives, 2011—. Republican. Office: PO Box 25847 Little Rock AR 72221 Office Phone: 501-766-8703. Personal E-mail: davidjamessanders@gmail.com.

SANDERS, GEORGIA ELIZABETH, secondary school educator; b. Holmwood, La., July 14, 1933; d. Frederick Rudolph and Susie W. (Hackett) S. Student, La. Coll., Pineville, 1951-53, La. State U., Baton Rouge, 1959-60; BS, then MS in Microbiology, U. Southwestern La., Lafayette, 1970; MS in Math., U. So. Miss., Hattiesburg, 1983. Instr. dept. biology U. New Orleans, 1976-79, instr. dept. math., 1983-86; tchr. East Baton Rouge Parish Schs., 1988-89; tchr. math. St. Tammany Parish, La., 1990—98. Instr. Degado CC, 2003—. Mem. NEA, Am. Math. Soc., Math. Assn. Am., Nat. Coun. Tchrs. Math. Home: PO Box 968 Slidell LA 70459-0968 Personal E-mail: gsan863722@charter.net.

SANDERS, HANK, state legislator; b. Baldwin County, Ala., Oct. 18, 1942; m. Rose M.; children: Malika, Kindaka, Ainka, Maurice, Charles, Rosie, Jennifer. Grad., Talladega Coll.; JD, Harvard U. Law Sch. Pvt. practice atty.; mem. Dist. 23 Ala. State Senate, Montgomery, 1983—. Recipient Nat. Svc. award Emergencies Land Fund, Nat. Assn. Landowners; named Senator of Yr. Ala. Legislature Black Caucus, 1986, Legislator of Yr. Nat. Assn. Social Workers, West Ala. Unit. Mem. ABA, Nat. Bar Assn., Ala. New South Coalition, Ala. Lawyer's Assn. (pres.), Ala. Trial Lawyer's Assn., Nat. Voting Rights Mus. Inst. (bd. chmn.), Nat. Conf. Black Lawyers (Lawyer of Yr. 1990). Democrat. Baptist. Office: PO Box 1305 Selma AL 36702 also: Ala State Senate Ala State House 11 S Union St Rm 730 Montgomery AL 36130 Office Phone: 334-875-9264, 334-242-7860.

SANDERS, HARVEY GIBERT, JR., lawyer; s. Harvey Gibert and Sue Lee Sanders; m. Barbara Langley, June 10, 1956 (dec.); children: Suzanne Sanders Putnam, Harvey G. Sanders, III, Barry L.; m. Nancy Anne Sanders, Dec. 2, 2002. BS, U. SC, Columbia, 1957, LLB, 1960. Bar: SC, US Dist. Ct. SC 1960, US Ct. Appeals (4th cir.) 1960. Mem. plaintiff's exec. com. Am. Honda MDL Dealerships Litig., Baltimore, 1995—2000; co-class counsel Borman v. Am. Honda MDL Litig., Baltimore, 2000—02; assoc. Leatherwood Walker Todd & Mann, P.C., Greenville, SC, 1960—64, shareholder, 1974—. Instr. accounting Palmer Bus. Coll., Columbia, 1960—62; bd. dirs. Greenville Symphony Orch., 2000—08. Editor (assoc.): U. SC Law Rev., 1958—59. Aide SC State Senate, Columbia, 1955—59; mem., exec. com. Miss SC Pageant, Columbia, 1965—95, legal counsel, All Am. City Com., Greenville, SC, 1965; pres. Greenville Jaycees, 1966—67, Greenville Literacy Assn., 1969—70, Greenville County Commn. on Alcoholism, 1970—73; mem. senate Jaycees Internat.; v.p. USC Alumni Assn., Carolina Scholars Scholarship Selection Com., Columbia, SC; bd. dirs. Greenville C. of C., 1967, v.p. govt. affairs, 1972, gen. counsel, 1976—78, Cmty. Found. of Greater Greenville, 1987; bd. dir. Greenville Art Mus., 1968, Greenville Symphony Orch. Named to Hall of Fame, Greenville-Jaycee. Mem.: ABA (assoc.), SC. Bar (assoc.; mem. exec. com. Young Lawyers Sect.), Greenville County Bar (assoc.; exec. com. mem. 1986—88, pres. 1987), Order of Wig and Robe, Greenville Touchdown Club, J.L. Mann Booster Club (pres. 1982—83), Greenville Country Club (pres. 1979), DeBordieu Club, The Res. Club, Colonial Club (pres. 1974), Greenville Young Lawyers Club (v.p. 1976), Greenville-Pickens Gamecock Club (v.p. 1965, pres. 1966), The Commerce Club, Kiwanis Club of Greenville (bd. dir. 1976—77), Phi Alpha Delta (Chief Justice 1959). Baptist. Avocations: golf, boating, travel, reading. Office: Smith Moore Leatherwood LLP 300 E McBee Ave Ste 500 Greenville SC 29601 Office Phone: 864-240-2401. Office Fax: 864-240-2498. Business E-Mail: harvey.sanders@smithmoore.com.

SANDERS, JAMES GRADY, biogeochemist; b. Norfolk, Va., June 10, 1951; s. Allen Buford and Maple Seretha (Myers) S.; m. Dorothea L. Palmer, 2001. BS in Zoology, Duke U., 1973; MS in Marine Scis., U. N.C., 1975, PhD in Marine Scis., 1978. Postdoctoral investigator Woods Hole (Mass.) Oceanog. Instn., 1978-80; vis. scientist Chesapeake Biol. Lab. U. Md., Solomons, 1980-81; asst. curator Estuarine Rsch. Ctr., Md. Acad. Natural Scis., 1981-85, assoc. curator, 1985-89, curator, 1989-99, dir., 1983-99, v.p., 1999; chair dept. ocean, earth and atmospheric scis. Old Dominion U., Norfolk, 1999-2001; dir. Skidaway Inst. Oceanography, Savannah, Ga., 2001—13; exec. dir. U. Ga., Skidaway Inst. Oceanography, 2013—. Cons. EPA Sweden, Stockholm, 1985-90; mem. Md. Sea Grant Adv. Com., College Park, 1983-90, Environ. Commn., Calvert County, Md., 1981-88; mem. environ. biology panel Office R&D EPA, Washington, 1986-95, sci. adv. bd., ecol. processes and effects com., 2003-09; EPA Sci. Adv. Bd., 2007-; bd. dirs., SE Coastal Ocean Observing Regional Assn., 2007-09, bd. dirs. Am. Chestnut Land Trust, 1997-99; mem. bd. govs. Consortium for Oceanog. Rsch. and Edn., 1999-07, exec. com., 2003-07; mem. adv. bd. SC Sea Grant Program, 2005-; mem. bd. trustees Consortium for Ocean Leadership, 2008-14, exec. com. mem., 2009-14, treas., 2012-14. Assoc. editor Estuaries, 1996-99; mem. editl. bd. Environ. Toxicology and Chemistry, 2000-03; contbr. more than 75 articles to sci. jours. Grantee NOAA, EPA, NSF. Mem. AAAS, Am. Geophys. Union, Am. Soc. Limnology and Oceanography, Coastal and Estuarine Rsch. Fedn. (treas. 1993-97), Southern Assn. Marine Labs. (pres. 2004-05), Nat. Assn. Marine Labs. (pres., 2008-09), Oceanography Soc. Achievements include first identification of relationships between algal growth and chemical transformations of arsenic in aquatic systems. Office: Skidaway Inst Oceanography 10 Ocean Science Cir Savannah GA 31411 Home: 11 Wesley Crossing Savannah GA 31411 Office Phone: 912-598-2400. Business E-Mail: sandersj@uga.edu.

SANDERS, M. JACK, consumer products company executive; BS in Fin., La. State U., 1976. Divsn. v.p. Protective Packaging Corp., 1998—2001, gen. mgr., 1991—2001; joined Sonoco Products Co., 1987, v.p., indsl. products, N.Am., 2001—06, v.p., global indsl. products, 2006—07, sr. v.p., global indsl. products and converting bus., 2007—08, exec. v.p., indsl., 2008—09, exec. v.p. global consumer, 2010, pres., COO, 2010—. Office: Sonoco Products Co 1 N Second St Hartsville SC 29550 Office Phone: 843-383-7000. Office Fax: 843-383-7008. Business E-Mail: mjack.sanders@sonoco.com.

SANDERS, MARC ANDREW, computer technical consultant; s. Edward and Elizabeth Sanders. BA, Roosevelt U., 1973; MAS, Fla. Atlantic U., 1987. Computer programmer Market Facts, Inc., Chgo., 1973-76, N.E. Ill. Planning Commn., Chgo., 1977; salesman Radio Shack, Tamarac, Fla., 1982-83; sr. analyst/tech. cons. Birch/Scarborough Rsch., Coral Springs, Fla., 1984-91; programmer/analyst Datateam, Inc., Margate, Fla., 1992-93, SIRS, Inc., Boca Raton, Fla., 1994-99, Bristol West Ins. Group, 2000—01, Spraymation, Inc., 2001—. Mem. ACM, IEEE Computer Soc., Phi Kappa Phi, Beta Gamma Sigma, Upsilon Pi Epsilon. Democrat. Jewish. Avocations: golf, working-out, walking, writing. Office: PO Box 9742 Coral Springs FL 33075-9742

SANDERS, MIKE, state legislator; b. Kingfisher, Okla. m. Nellie Tayloe; children: David Lee, Walker Tayloe. Degree in History & Pre-law, Okla. Christian U., 1997; attended, Georgetown U. Dir. interns Bush Admin.; dep. chief staff for Rural Devel. USDA; sr. adv. to Chief Natural Resources Conservation Svc.; chmn. Kingfisher Co. Rep. Party, 1999—2001; mem. Coun. for Small Bus. for Gov. Frank Keating & Lt. Gov. Mary Fallin, 1999—2003; with Sanders Funeral Svc.; mem. Dist. 59 Okla House of Representatives, 2008—. Recipient Distinguished Honor Service Award, bestowed by President George W. Bush. Mem.: NRA, American Coun. of Young Political Leaders (life), Kingfisher Rotary Club, Knights of Columbus. Republican. Address: 2300 N Lincoln Blvd Rm 536 Oklahoma City OK 73105 Office: PO Box 861 Kingfisher OK 73750 Office Phone: 405-557-7407. Business E-Mail: mike.sanders@okhouse.gov.

SANDERS, RICHARD (RICHIE) A., state legislator; b. Aug. 6, 1963; s. Richard A. Sanders and Sue Alexander S.; m. Leslie Sanders. State rep. Dist.19, Ky., 1991—96; state senator Dist. 9 Ky., 1996—; mem. Appropriations & Revenue Com., Banking & Ins. Com.; state senator Ky.; chmn. Majority Caucus; farmer, restaurant owne; specialist Econ. Devel. Named Outstanding Young Kentukian, KY Jaycees, 2003, Legislator of Yr., Ky. League Cities, 2003. Mem.: Franklin Rotary Club, C. of C., Lions, Edmonson Co. Saddle Club. Republican. Baptist. Office: Capitol Annex Rm 203 Frankfort KY 40601 Home: 906 Dinwiddie Rd Franklin KY 42134-7442 Office Phone: 270-781-2381. Fax: 270-842-0768. E-mail: richard.sanders@lrc.state.ky.us.

SANDERS, WAYNE R., board member, retired paper products manufacturing executive; b. Chgo., July 6, 1947; s. Ralph G. and Bernice F. (Swanson) S.; m. Kathleen E. Lessard, Aug. 22, 1970; children: Tracy, Amy, Megan. BCE, Ill. Inst. Tech., 1969; MBA, Marquette U., 1972. Fin. analyst Ford Motor Co., Dearborn, Mich., 1972-75; sr. fin. analyst Kimberly-Clark Corp., Neenah, Wis., 1975, dir. bus. planning internat., 1976-80, dir. bus. planning U.S. consumer bus., 1980-81; v.p. strategic planning Kimberly-Clark of Can., Toronto, Ont., 1981-82, pres., 1982-85; sr. v.p. Kimberly-Clark Corp., Dallas, 1986, pres. infant care sector Neenah, Wis., from 1987, former pres. personal care div., pres., COO world consumer, nonwovens and svc. and indsl. ops., 1990, pres., CEO Dallas, 1990-91, CEO, 1991—2002, chmn., 1991—2003; bd. dirs., non-exec. chmn. Dr. Pepper Snapple Group, 2008—. Bd. dirs. Belo Corp., Tex. Instruments Inc. Nat. trustee and gov. Boys and Girls Clubs Am., 1994—; trustee Marquette U., Milw., 1992—2007, vice-chmn. bd., 1997—2001, 2003—05, chmn. bd., 2001—03; elected mem. Neenah Sch. Bd., 1980—81. Recipient Disting. Alumnus award, Marquette U. Coll. Bus. Adminstrn., 1994; named Alumnus of Yr., Marquette U.,

2001. Mem.: Marquette U. Archbishop Henni Soc. Roman Catholic. Office: Dr Pepper Snapple Group Inc 5301 Legacy Dr Plano TX 75024 Office Phone: 972-673-7000.

SANDERS, W(ILLIAM) EUGENE, JR., retired internist; b. Frederick, Md., June 25, 1934; s. W(illiam) Eugene and E. Gertrude (Wilburn) Sanders; m. Christine Culp, Feb. 22, 1974. AB, Cornell U., 1956, MD, 1960. Diplomate Am. Bd. Internal Medicine. Intern Johns Hopkins Hosp., Balt., 1960-61, resident, 1961-62; instr. medicine Emory U. Sch. Medicine, Atlanta, 1962-64; chief med. resident, instr. U. Fla. Coll. Medicine, Gainesville, 1964-65, asst. prof. medicine and microbiology, 1965-69, assoc. prof., 1969-72; prof., chmn. dept. med. microbiology, prof. medicine Creighton U. Sch. Medicine, Omaha, 1972-95, prof. emeritus, 1995—. Cons-in-rsch. Fla. Dept. Health and Rehab. Svcs., 1966—. Editor: Am. Jour. Epidemiology, 1974—95; contbr. scientific papers to profl. jours. Med. officer USPHS, 1962—64. Recipient Rsch. Career Devel. award, NIH, 1968—72; John and Mary R. Markle scholar in acad. medicine, 1968—73. Mem.: N.Y. Acad. Scis., Thoracic Soc., Am. Lung Assn., Soc. Epidemiol. Rsch., Infectious Diseases Soc. Am., Am. Soc. Microbiology, Sigma Xi, Phi Beta Kappa, Phi Kappa Phi. Achievements include patents for enocin antibiotic and RBE limonene and perrilyl alcohol. Home: 1901 Pennsylvania Ave Englewood FL 34224-5530 E-mail: ecsanders@mac.com.

SANDERSON, JOE F., JR., food products executive; Grad., Millsaps Coll. V.p., processing & mktg. Sanderson Farms, Inc., 1984—89, pres., 1989—2004, CEO, 1989—, chmn., 1998—. Office: Sanderson Farms Inc 127 Flynt Rd Laurel MS 39441-0988 Office Phone: 601-649-4030. Office Fax: 601-426-1461. Business E-Mail: jsanderson@sandersonfarms.com.

SANDERSON, MARY LOUISE, medical association administrator; b. Fairmont, W.Va., Oct. 29, 1942; d. Lawrence Oliver and Frances Evelyn (Shuttleworth) Shingleton; m. William W. Olmstead III, Dec. 1966 (div. June 1974); children: William W. IV, Happy; m. Lester F. Davis, III, Oct. 1979 (div. Dec. 1986); m. David S. Sanderson, Sept. 1992. Student, Vassar Coll., 1960-62, Carnegie Mellon, 1962-63. Real estate broker, N.C. Exec. sec. Creative Dining, Raleigh, NC, 1980-83, Sea Pines Plantation Co., Hilton Head, SC, 1973-79; from adminstr. to exec. dir. Am. Bd. Neurol. Surgery, Houston, 1983—. Vol. Interact, Raleigh, 1984-86, M.D. Anderson Cancer Ctr./Camp Star Trails, 1994-96; docent Mordecai House Hist. Preservation, Raleigh, 1981-83; mem./vol. Reach to Recovery, 1995-2001, Houston Symphony, 2002-, Mus. of Fine Arts, Houston, 1999-. Recipient Vol. award N.C. State Gov., 1986. Mem. Am. Soc. Assn. Execs. Democrat. Episcopalian. Office: Am Bd Neurol Surgery 245 Amity Rd Ste 208 Woodbridge CT 06525-2256

SANDERSON, NORMAN WESLEY, JR., state legislator; b. July 7, 1951; m. Linda Sanderson; children: Jennifer, Lee. Child care owner; state rep. Dist. 3 NC, 2010—. Republican. Office: 269 Bennett Rd #4 Arapahoe NC 28510 Address: North Carolina House of Representatives 300 N Salisbury St Rm 306A2 Raleigh NC 27603 Office Phone: 919-733-5853. Business E-Mail: Norman.Sanderson@ncleg.net.

SANDIFER, WILLIAM EDWARD, III, state legislator; b. Aiken, SC, Feb. 21, 1945; s. William E. and Frances Harley Sandifer; m. Sandra Prater Sandifer, 1981; children: Lori, Will, Jennifer Rae Collins, Wes Edward. V.p. Seneca Mortuary Inc., 1967—75, pres., 1975—98, Seneca C. of C., 1978, Oconee Mem. Hosp. Bd. Dirs., 1986—88; chmn. bd. dir. Ft. Hill Natural Gas Authority, 1992—94; mem. Dist. 2 SC House of Reps., 1995—. Recipient Hammer & Trowel award, SC Home Builders Assn.; Paul Harris fellow, 1994. Mem.: America Legion, SC Funeral Dir. Assn. (pres. 1986—87), Seneca Rotary Club (G. W. Ballenger award), Seneca Lodge 185 AFM. Republican. Methodist. Mailing: 112 Cardinal Dr Seneca SC 29672 Office: 407 Blatt Bldg Columbia SC 29201 Home Phone: 864-882-1225; Office Phone: 803-734-3015. Fax: 864-882-3125. E-mail: sandifer@carol.net, HLC@schouse.org.

SANDLER, BETTY MOORE, lawyer; b. Martin, Ky., Dec. 10, 1947; BA, U. Ky., 1969; JD, U. Ky. Coll. Law, 1981. Bar: Ky. 1981, US Dist. Ct. (ea. dist.) Ky. 1981, US Supreme Ct. 1985, Va. 1986, US Bankruptcy Ct. (ea. dist.) Va. 1990. Lobbyist, fed. legis. analyst US House of Representatives; founding ptnr. Nichols Zauzig Sandler P.C., Woodbridge, Va., 1989—. Founding pres. Prince William County Bar Found. Contbr. articles to profl. law publs. Named a Va. Super Lawyer, Law & Politics mag., 2006—07, DC Super Lawyer, 2007—11; named one of Top 20 Divorce Attorneys, Washingtonian mag., Top 25 Va. Female Attorneys, Law & Politics mag. Fellow: American Acad. Matrimonial Lawyers (past pres. Va. chpt.), Internat. Acad. Matrimonial Lawyers (bd. dirs. US chpt.); mem.: Prince William County Bar Found. (founding pres.), Va. Trial Lawyers Assn., McLean Bar Assn., Va. State Bar. Office: Nichols Zauzig Sandler PC 12660 Lake Ridge Dr Woodbridge VA 22192-2335 Office Phone: 703-492-4200. Office Fax: 703-492-4201.

SANDLER, TODD MICHAEL, economist, political scientist, educator; b. Mt. Kisco, NY, Dec. 16, 1946; s. Louis and Susie Sandler; m. Jean Marie Murdock, June 28, 1985; 1 child, Tristan Jon. BA, SUNY, Binghamton, 1968, MA, 1969, PhD, 1971. Asst. prof. Ariz. State U., Tempe, 1971-76; assoc. prof. U. Wyo., Laramie, 1976-79, prof., 1979-85, U. S.C., Columbia, 1985-86; prof. econs. and polit. sci. Iowa State U., Ames, 1986-2000, Disting. prof., 1995—2001; Dockson prof. U. So. Calif., LA, 2000—07; Shukla prof. U. Tex., Dallas, 2006—. Author: Collective Action: Theory and Applications, 1992, Global Challenges, 1997, Economic Concepts for the Social Sciences, 2001, Global Collective Action, 2004; co-author: The Theory of Externalities, Public Goods and Club Goods, 1986, The Economics of Defense, 1995, (book) The Theory of Externalities, Public Goods and Club Goods, 2d edit., 1996, International Terrorism in 1980s, 1989, The Political Economy of NATO, 1999, The Future of Development Assistance: Common Pools and International Public Goods, 1999, Regional Public Goods: Typologies, Provision, Financing, and Development Assistance, 2002, The Political Economy of Terrorism, 2006, 2012; co-editor: Defense Economics, 1989—94, Handbook of Defense Economics, 1995;: Handbook of Defense Economics, 2007, Economics of Defense, 2001, Economics of Conflict, 2003; assoc. editor: Jour. Environ. Econs. and Mgmt., 1988—89, Jour. Pub. Econ. Theory, 1999—2005; assoc. editor Rev. Internat. Organizations; mem. editl. bd.: Pub. Fin. Rev., Fiscal Studies, Bull. Econ. Rsch., Internat. Studies Quar., Terrorism and Political Violence; mem. editl. bd. Fiscal Studies, Bull. Econ. Rsch., Global Policy, Internat. Studies Quar., chmn. editl. bd. Jour. Conflict Resolution, 2004—; spl. adv. editor: Def. and Peace Econs., 2000—, Am. Polit. Sci. Rev., 2011—, reviewer: numerous internat. orgns. Recipient Duncan Black award, Pub. Choice Soc., 2005; co-recipient Rsch. Related to Prevention of Nuc. War award, Nat. Acad. of Scis., 2003; grantee NSF, 1989, 1993; fellow NATO postdoctoral, 1977, 1998—2000, Australian Nat. U., 1981, 1994, Sr., Inst. Policy Reform, 1990—91, 1992—94, Hon., U. Wis.-Madison, 1990; grant, CREATE, Dept. Home Land Security, 2006—13. Mem.: Pub. Choice Soc., So. Econ. Assn., Assn. Environ. and Resource Econs., Royal Econ. Soc., Am. Econ. Assn., Internat. Def. Econs. Assn. (exec. bd.). Office: U Tex Dallas Sch Econ Polit and Policy Scis 800 W Campbell Rd Richardson TX 75080 Business E-Mail: tsandler@utdallas.edu.

SANDOVAL, ARTURO, jazz musician; b. Havana, Cuba, Nov. 6, 1949; arrived in US, 1990, naturalized, 1999; s. Arturo and Cira (Arocha) S.; m. Carmen Marianela, Oct. 17, 1975; 1 child, Arturo Jr. Prof. Fla. Internat. U., 1990—. Lectr. in field; bd. dirs., ednl. com. Chgo. Symphony Orch., 1994; featured artist Dizzy Gillespie UN Orch., Live at Royal Festival Hall album (Grammy 1991); owner The Arturo Sandoval Jazz Club, Miami Beach, 2006-08. Performed with Cuban Orch. Modern Music; guest artist BBC Symphony, London, Leningrad Symphony; founding mem. Irakere mus. group; albums include Irakere I, 1978, (Grammy award, Best Latin Album), Irakere II, 1980, To a Finland Station, 1982, Breaking the Sound Barrier, 1983, Tumbaito, 1986, No Problem, 1986, Straight Ahead, 1988, Flight to Freedom, 1991, I Remember Clifford, 1992, Dream Come True, 1993, Danzon (Dance On), 1993 (Grammy award, Best Latin Jazz Peformance, 1995, Billboard award for Best Latin Jazz Album, 1995), Cubano, 1994, Arturo Sandoval & The Latin Train, 1995 (Billboard award, Best Latin Jazz Album, 1996), Latin Train, 1995, Tren Latino, 1995, Concerto, 1995, Swingin, 1996, Just Music, 1996, Hot House, 1998 (Grammy award, Best Latin Jazz Performance, 1998, Billboard award, Best Latin Jazz Album, 1998), Americana, 1999, Ronnie Scott's Jazz House, 2000, For Love or Country, 2001, LA Meetings, 2001, My Passion for the Piano, 2001, From Havana with Love, 2003, Trumpet Evolution, 2003 (Latin Billboard award, 2004), Live at the Blue Note, 2005, Arturo Sandoval & the Latin Jazz Orchestra, 2007, Arturo Sandoval & His Group, 2007, Rumba Palace, 2007 (Latin Grammy award, Best Latin Jazz Album, 2007), A Time for Love, 2010, Arturo Sandoval & WDR Big Band Mambo Nights, 2011, Dear Diz (Every Day I Think of You), 2013 (Grammy award, Best Large Jazz Ensemble Album, 2013); composer (films) The Perez Family, 1995, Sacred Waters, 2006, (TV films) For Love or Country: The Arturo Sandoval Story, 2000 (Emmy award for Outstnading Music Composition, 2001). Named Cuba's Best Instrumentalist, 1982-1990; named to Walt Disney World Jazz Hall of Fame, 1994; recipient Gold Tucan award, Brazil, 1988, Golden Feather award for Artist of Yr., LA Times, 1991, Internat. Jazz award, Clearwater Jazz Holliday, 1993, Hispanic Achievement award, 1994, Nat. Assn. Rec. Arts & Sciences Found. award for Excellence in Music Edn., 1994, American Jazz award, 1997, ASCAP Founder's award, 2001, Heroes award, Nat. Assn. Rec. Arts & Sciences, 2002, Presdl. Medal of Freedom, The White House, 2013 Roman Catholic. Home: PO Box 143936 Coral Gables FL 33114-3936*

SANDOVAL, ARTURO ALONZO, artist, educator; b. Espanola/Cordova, N.Mex., Feb. 1, 1942; s. Lorenzo Sandoval and Cecilia Eulalia (Archuleta) Harrison; (div. Sept. 1982); 1 child, Avalon Valentine Galaglorial. Student, U. Portland, 1959; BA, Calif. State Coll., LA, 1964, MA, 1969; MFA, Cranbrook Acad. Art, Bloomfield Hills, Mich., 1971. Designer, illustrator Western Lighting Corp., LA, 1964-66; advt. designer, adult edn. instr. spl. svcs. USN, Yokosuka, Japan, 1966; interior design asst. Walter B. Broderick & Assocs., La Mesa, Calif., 1967; asst. prof. art dept. U. Ky., Lexington, 1974—76, assoc. prof., 1976—86, prof., 1986—, dir. art dept. Barnhart Gallery, 1976—, curator, 1979—. Teaching asst. Calif. State Coll., L.A., 1969, Cranbrook Acad. Art, Bloomfield Hills, 1969-71; fiber art demonstrator Mus. Art, Grand Rapids, Mich., 1970; batik and tie-dye demonstrator Gwynn's Fabric Shop, Birmingham, Mich., 1970; instr. Calif. State Coll., L.A., 1970, So. Ill. U., Carbondale, 1971, Edwardsville, 1971, 72, 73, asst. prof., 1971-73; presenter various lectures and workshops throughout the U.S., 1973—; juror Mo. Women Festival Arts, St. Louis, So. Ill. U., East St. Louis, 1974, Paramount Arts Assn., Ashland, Ky., 1975, Ind. Weavers Guild, Indpls., 1979, Fed. Corrections Inst., Lexington, 1979, Hawaii Craftsman Hui and Art Dept. U. Hawaii, Manoa, Honolulu, 1982, art dept. Va. Intermont Coll., Bristol, 1982, Arrowmont Sch. Arts and Crafts, Gatlinburg, Tenn., 1984, Ctr. Contemporary Art, U. Ky., Lexington, 1984, Guild Greater Cin., Carnegie Art Ctr., Covington, Ky., 1989, S.C. Arts Commn., Charleston, 1990, Adams Art Gallery, Dunkirk, N.Y., 1994; visual arts cons. Ky. Arts Commn., Frankfort, 1977; curator Visual Arts Ctr. Alaska, Anchorage, 1982, Ky. Art and Crafts Found., Inc., Louisville, 1985; mem. artist adv. panel Ky. Art and Crafts Found., Louisville, 1986, 87, 92-2000; visual arts cons. Arts Midwest, 1987; artistic advisor Ky. Guild Mktg. Bd., Berea, 1988, 91, 92, 93; bd. trustees Ky. Guild 1995-98, Am. Craft Coun., N.Y.C., 1996—; vis. artist/critic Allen R. Hite Inst., U. Louisville, 1992; vis. artist Coll. Human Environ. Scis., U. Ky., Lexington, 1993; vis. artist/lectr. fiber dept. Cranbrook Acad. Art, Bloomfield Hills, Mich., 1994, Art. Dept. St. Louis Comm. Coll.-Florissant Valley, 2001, U. Ariz., 2001; curator Art Quilts 2001, River Oaks Square Art Ctr., Louisiana, 2001; alumni-endowed rsch. prof. U. Ky., 2007-. Exhibited in group shows at Yeiser Art Ctr., Paducah/Paramount Arts Ctr., Ashland/S.E. Cmty. Coll., Cumberland, 1994, Textile Arts Centre, Chgo., 1994, Winnipeg (Man., Can.) Art Gallery, 1994, Riffe Gallery, Ohio Arts Coun., Columbus, 1994, Royal Hiberian Acad., Gallagher Gallery, Dublin, Ireland, Cooper Gallery, Barnsley, South Yorks, Gt. Britain, Shipley Art Gallery, Gateshead, Gt. Britain, 1994, Grand Rapids (Mich.) Art Mus., 1994, Whatcom Mus. History and Art, Bellingham, Wash., The Rockwell Mus., Corning, N.Y., Mus. Art, Washington State U., Pullman, The Hyde Collection, Glen Falls, N.Y., 1994, U. Art Galleries, U. S.D., Vermillion, 1994, Barnhart Gallery, U. Ky., Lexington, 1994, Sawtooth Ctr. Visual Art, 1994, Santa Fe Gallery, Santa Fe Cmty. Coll., Gainesville, Fla., 1994, Liberty Gallery, Louisville, 1994, Asahi Shimbun Gallery, Tokyo, Takashimaya Gallery, Osaka, 1994, Minn. Mus. Art, Landmark Ctr., St. Paul, 1994, S.C. State Mus., Columbia, 1994, Galbreath Gallery, Lexington, 1994, U.K. Art Mus., 1998, Giles Gallery, Richmond, Ky., 2004, Ky. Mus. of Art and Design, 2004, Ronald Barr Gallery, New Albany, Ind., 2004, City Gallery, S.C., 2004, Tuska Gallery, Ky., 2004, Pres. Room. Ky., 2004, numerous others; represented in permanent collections at Wabash Coll., Crawfordsville, Ind., Greenville County Mus. Art, Greenville, S.C., Mus. Modern Art, N.Y.C., St. Mary's Coll., Notre Dame, Ind., Coll. St. Rose, Albany, N.Y., Bowling Green (Ohio) StateU., U. Notre Dame, Transylvania U., Lexington, U. Ky. Mus. Art, Lexington, Mid-Am. Rare Coin Auction Galleries, Lexington, Henry Luce Found., N.Y.C., Lexington Ctrl. Libr., UK Art Mus., Nat. Mus. Am. Art, Renwick Gallery, J.B. Speed Art Mus., Louisville, Linda Schwartz Gallery, Tuska Gallery, Pres.'s Room, KY, Shands Gallery, Friedman Gallery, KGAG Offices, Actor's Theater, Ronald Barr Gallery, Opera House Gallery, Waltron Ltd., Whitehouse, N.J., Nat. Hispanic Cultural Arts Ctr., Albuquerque, N.Mex., Rocky Mt. Quilt Mus., Golden, Colo., Mus. Art and Design, N.Y. Recipient Alexandra Korsakoff Galston Meml. prize St. Louis Artist's Guild, 1971, Mus. Merit award Mus. Arts and Scis., Evansville, 1972, Creative Rsch. Grant So. Ill. U.-Edwardsville Rsch. Found., 1972, Craftsman fellowship Nat. Endowment Arts, Washington, 1973, Friend of Mus. award Mus. Arts and Scis., Evansville, 1973, Clay Eugene Jordan ann. bequest prize crafts St. Louis Artist's Guild, 1973, Teaching Improvement grant U. Ky. Rsch. Found., 1974, Travel grant U. Ky. Rsch. Found., 1977, Judges Choice award Berea (Ky.) Coll., 1978, Handweaver's Guild Am. award, 1978, Fiber award LeMoyne Art Found., Tallahassee, 1981, Elise Strout Merit award Mus. Arts and Scis., Evansville, 1981, Handweavers Guild Am. award, 1983, Martha Ryan Merit award Mus. Arts and Scis., Evansville, 1984, Best of Show award Gayle Willson Galleries, Southampton, 1984, Juror's merit award Brenau Coll., Gainesville, Ga., 1985, Installation Grant Ind. Arts Commn., Ft. Wayne, 1985, All Smith fellowship Ky. Arts Coun., Frankfort, 1987, 2006, Merit award Spotlight '88 Am. Craft Coun., fellow, 2008, Southeast Conf., Tuscaloosa, Ala., 1988, Merit award Mus. Arts and Scis., Evansville, 1989, Design Grant, Arts and Cultural Coun. for O.A. Singletary Ctr. Arts, Lexington, 1990, Visual Arts fellowship Nat. Endowment for Arts, Washington, 1992, Hon. award Ky. Crafts Mktg. Bd., Frankfort, 1994, Rude Osolnik Craftsman award Ky. Crafts Mktg. & KAC Fund, 1998, 1st pl. Lexington Art League, Reverse Raffle, Lexington, 1999, Art-in-Arch. Program commn. Gen. Svcs. Adminstrn., London, Ky., 2002; Artist award Ky. Gov.'s award in the arts, 2003, Merit award ACCSE, 2006, Kirwan Meml. prize U. Ky., 2007; grantee NEA, Pyramid Atlantic Press, Riverdale, Md., 1996; Gen. Svcs. Adminstrn.; Kirwan prize, U. Ky, 2007, Alumni professorship, 2007—. Mem. Lexington Fiber Guild Inc., Louisville Visual Arts Assn., Ky. Art and Craft Found., Inc., Ky. Guild Artists and Crafstmen, Am. Craft Coun., Friends of U. Ky. Mus. Art, Friends of Fiber Art, Surface Design Assn. Home: PO Box 25153 Lexington KY 40524-5153 Office: Univ Ky Dept Art Coll Fine Arts 207 Fine Arts Bldg Lexington KY 40506-0022 Office Phone: 859-230-9635.

SANDOVAL, JUAN, municipal official, commissioner; Coach, tchr. El Paso Ind. Sch. Dist., Tex.; tax assessor, collector City of El Paso; commr. Tex. Hist. Commn., Austin, 1999—. Bd. dirs. El Paso Hist. Soc., El Paso United Way. Office: City of El Paso 2 Civic Center Plz El Paso TX 79901 also: Tex Hist Commn PO Box 12276 Austin TX 78711-2276

SANDOVAL, MATHIAS F., electronics executive; Grad. in Indsl. Electronics, Montani Inst., Italy; BSEE, U. Costa Rica. Various positions gen. mgr., pres., Venezuelan ops., v.p., Global Aluminum Bus. Segment and v.p., Global Energy Segment Phelps Dodge Internat. Corp., process engr. Costa Rica, pres., 2001, CEO, 2007—; exec. v.p., CEO, L.Am., Sub-Saharan Africa, and the Mid. East and Asia Pacific General Cable Corp., 2007, exec. v.p., General Cable Rest of World, 2007—. Office: General Cable Corp 4 Tesseneer Dr Highland Heights KY 41076 Office Phone: 859-572-8000. Office Fax: 859-572-8458. Business E-Mail: mathias_sandoval@pdic.com.

SANDRIDGE, WILLIAM PENDLETON, JR., lawyer; b. Winston-Salem, NC, Jan. 27, 1934; m. Jane Carolyn Yeager, Dec. 10, 1966; children: Jane, William. AB, U. N.C., 1956; LLB, U. Va., 1961. Bar: N.C. 1961. Mem. Womble Carlyle Sandridge & Rice, PLLC, Winston-Salem, 1962—. Chmn., bd. dirs. Horizons Residential Care Ctr., 1980, Food Bank N.W. N.C., Inc., 1988-89, Data Max Corp., 1996. Office: Womble Carlyle Et Al One W Fourth St Winston Salem NC 27101

SANDS, ARTHUR T., biopharmaceutical executive, medical geneticist; BA in Econ. & Polit. Sci., Yale U.; MA, Baylor Coll. of Medicine, PhD, 1992. Former Am. Cancer Soc. postdoctoral fellow, dept. of human and molecular genetics Baylor Coll. of Medicine, 1992—95; co-founder (with Allan Bradley), pres., CEO Lexicon Pharmaceuticals (formerly Lexicon Genetics), The Woodlands, Tex., 1995—. Bd. mem. Tex. Inst. for Genomic Medicine. Recipient BioHouston Life Sci. award, 2004. Achievements include developing large-scale gene knockout technology for use in drug discovery. Office: Lexicon Pharms 8800 Technology Forest Pl The Woodlands TX 77381-1160 Office Phone: 281-863-3000. Office Fax: 281-863-8088.

SANDS, FRANKLIN, state legislator; b. NYC, July 12, 1940; m. Leslie Sands; children: Rob, Roger, Stephanie, David, Dana, Charlie, Alexander, Jacqueline. Grad., Bklyn. Coll., 1961. Ind. NIKKEN wellness cons.; mem. Dist. 98 Fla. House of Reps., Tallahassee, 2004—, Dem. whip, 2004—06, minority leader, 2008—10. Mem. Broward County Children's Services Bd., Broward County Coordinating Bd. for Transp. Disadvantaged Services, Broward County Sch. Bd. Facilities Task Force, City of Weston Charter Rev. Bd. Democrat. Jewish. Office: IMACS Office Ctr 7487 NW 4th St Plantation FL 33317-2227 also: 316 The Capitol 402 S Monroe St Tallahassee FL 32399 Office Phone: 954-424-6800, 850-488-9622.

SANDS, JEFF MICHAEL, medical educator; s. Joseph and Jean Lillian Sands; m. Abbe Maureen Zorn, Nov. 23, 1986; children: Jared Samuel, Jenna Shari. BA summa cum laude, Harvard Coll., Cambridge, 1977; MD, Boston U., Mass., 1981. Diplomate internal medicine Am. Bd. Internal Medicine, 1984, nephrology Am. Bd. Internal Medicine, 1992. Asst. prof. medicine Emory U., Atlanta, 1989—93, assoc. prof. medicine, 1993—98, prof. medicine and physiology, 1998—, assoc. dean clinical and translational rsch., 2006—10. Renal divsn. dir. Emory U., 2002—; exec. vice chair dept. medicine emory, 2009—. Editor-in-chief Am. Jour. Physiology, Bethesda, 2001—07. Rsch. grants, NIH, 1989—. Mem.: Am. Physiol. Soc. (councillor 2003—06), Am. Soc. Nephrology (program com. chmn. 2003—04), Am. Soc. Clin. Investigation, Am. Assn. Physicians. Achievements include research in renal physiology. Office: Emory U Renal Divsn WMB Rm 338 1639 Pierce Drive Atlanta GA 30322 Business E-Mail: jeff.sands@emory.edu.

SANDS, WILLIE LOUIS, federal judge; b. Bradley, Ga., Apr. 12, 1949; BA, Mercer U., 1971, JD, 1974. Chief legal asst. to dist. atty. Macon Jud. Cir., 1974, asst. dist. atty., 1975-78; asst. US atty. US Dist. Ct. (mid. dist.) Ga., 1978-87; with Mathis, Sands, Jordan & Adams, Macon, 1987-91; judge superior ct. Macon Jud. Cir., 1991-93; judge US Dist. Ct. (mid. dist.) Ga., Albany, 1994—2001, 2006—, chief judge, 2001—06. Ptnr. Investors Ltd., 1984-91; mem. task force substance abuse Ga. Supreme Ct., 1991—, mem. com. gender equality, 1993—; bd. dirs. Bank Corp. Ga./1st South Bank, N.A. Organist/min. music, officer Steward Chapel AME Ch., 1976—; active Cmty. Found. Ga., Inc.; mem. 30th anniversary planning com. Mercer U., mem. bd. visitors Walter F. George sch. law, 1994—; v.p. Ga. Commn. Family Violence, 1992—; bd. dirs. Macon Symphony, 1992—. 2d lt. Signal Corps, U.S. Army, 1971, res. Acad. scholar Mercer U.; grad. Leadership Macon, 1985, Leadership Ga., 1986. Mem. ABA, Am. Judicature Soc., State Bar Ga. (mem. bench and bar com. 1991—), Macon Bar Assn. (pres. 1991-92), Coun. Superior Ct. Judges (mem. bench and bar com. 1991—), Walter F. George Sch. Law Alumni Assn. (bd. dirs.), Scabbard and Blade Mil. Honor Soc., Alpha Phi Alpha, Sigma Pi Phi, Homosophian Club. Office: 201 W Broad St Albany GA 31701-2566

SANDSTEAD, HAROLD HILTON, physician, researcher, educator, director; b. Omaha, May 25, 1932; s. Harold Russel and Lula Florence (Hilton) S.; m. Kathryn Gordon Brownlee, June 6, 1959 (dec. May 13, 1989); m. Victoria Regan Liddle, Feb. 14, 1990 (div. Oct. 1993); m. Wilma Helen Carter Streaker, Sept. 25, 2004 (div. July 2008); children: Eleanor McDonald, James Brownlee, William Harold. BA in Pre-Medicine, Ohio Wesleyan U., 1954; MD, Vanderbilt U., 1958. Cert. Am. Bd. Internal Medicine, 1967, Am. Bd. Nutrition, 1967, Am. Bd. Physician Nutrition Specialists, 2001. Intern, internal medicine Barnes Hosp. Washington U., St. Louis, 1958—59, asst. resident, internal medicine, 1959—60; asst. resident, pathology Vanderbilt U.

Hosp., Nashville, 1960-61; asst. surgeon USPHS U.S. NAMRU 3, Cairo, 1961-63; rsch. resident, internal medicine Thayer VA Hosp., Vanderbilt U., Nashville, 1963-64; chief med. resident, internal medicine Vanderbilt U. Hosp., Nashville, 1964-65; instr. internal medicine, asst. prof. biochemistry Med. Sch. Vanderbilt U., Nashville, 1965-70, asst. prof. internal medicine, assoc. prof. biochemistry in nutrition, 1970-71; dir. USDA-ARS Human Nutrition Rsch. Ctr., Grand Forks, ND, 1971-84; adj. prof. biochemistry and internal medicine Sch. Medicine U. ND, Grand Forks, 1971-84; dir. USDA-ARS Human Nutrition Rsch. Ctr. on Aging at Tufts U., Boston, 1984-85; prof. nutrition Tufts U., Medford, Mass., 1984-85; prof. preventive medicine and community health U. Tex. Med. Br., Galveston, 1985—2006; chmn. preventive medicine and community health Med. Br. U. Tex., Galveston, 1985-90, prof. internal medicine, biochem. and molecular biology, 1986—2006, prof. emeritus preventative medicine and cmty. health and internal medicine, 2006—. Cons. IAEA, FAO, WHO, Internat. Programme on Chem. Safety, UN Environment Programme, Agency Internat. Devel., Nat. Cancer Inst., Nat. Inst. Child Health and Human Devel., Nat. Eye Inst., Nat. Heart, Lung, and Blood Inst., Officer Internat. Rsch., NIH, FDA, EPA, USDA, Food Nutrition Bd., NRC, Inst. Medicine, NAS, Life Sciences Rsch. Office, Fedn. Am. Societies Exptl. Biology, US Pharmacopeia, Am.Acad.Pediat., ACS, Am. Soc. Parenteral and Enteral Nutrition, Am. Health Found., Mead Johnson Co., Internat. Lead Zinc Rsch. Org., Nat. Cattlemen's Beef Assn., NeuroBioTex; clinician, Nutrition Survey Panama, Interdepartmental Com. Nutrition & Nat. Devel., NIH, 1967; field team dir., Texas Nutrition Survey, 10 State Nutrition Survey, US Nutrition Program, NIH, 1968; clinician, Kentucky Nutrition Survey, 10 State Nutrition Survey, US Nutrition Program, NIH, 1969; panel mem., White House Conf. on Food, Nutrition & Health, 1969, Am. Bd. Nutrition, 1975-81, USDA, ARS, human studies rev. com. (chmn., 83-85), 1976-85; rsch. adv. com., NSLS X-Ray Microprobe, Brookhaven Nat. Lab., 1984-90; advisor, Am. Coun. on Sci. & Health, 1988-; FASEB Wellcome vis. prof. in Basic Med. Sci., Pa. State U., 1988; zinc information nutrition ctr. adv. bd. Am. Zinc Assn., 1999-, Permanent Commn. on Occupl. Health, 2004-07. Mem. editl. bd. Jour. Nutrition, 1972-76, 81-85, 2011-, Am. Jour. Clin. Nutrition, 1975-78, Annual Rev. Nutritional Rsch., 1975-1991, Jour. Lab. Clin. Medicine, 1978-1983, Biol. Trace Element Rsch., 1979—, Nutrition Rsch., 1981-85, Nutritional Reports Internat., 1981-88, Trace Elements Medicine Biology, 1983-98, Jour. Trace Elements Exptl. Medicine, 1982-2004, Jour. Am. Coll. Nutrition, 1987-88, Nutrition Rsch. Newsletter, 1989-98, Cancer Prevention, 1990-1994, assoc. editor history & biography; contbr. over 300 articles to profl. jours., chapters to books. 4 ISI Citation Classics. Recipient Future Leader award, Nutrition Found., 1968—71, Hull Gold medal, with HC Meng, AMA, 1970, Special Recognition award, Vanderbilt U. Sch. Medicine, 1971, Mead Johnson award, Am. Inst. Nutrition, 1971, WO Atwater award medal and lecture, US Dept. Agr., 1984, Ellen Swallow Richard Meml. Lecture, U. NC Inst. Nutrition, 1985, Sam & Mary Roberts Nutrition medal and Lecture, U. Kans. Sch. Medicine, 1985, Raymond Ewell Meml. lecture, U. Buffalo, SUNY Sch. Medicine, 1985, Special Recognition award, USDA Agrl. Rsch. Svc., 2004. Fellow ACP, Am. Soc. Nutrition (Mead Johson award 1972, fellow 1998); mem. Am. Soc. Clin. Nutrition (pres. 1982-83), Internat. Soc. for Trace Element Rsch. in Humans (pres. 2002-04, Raulin award 2007), Cosmos Club, Sigma Xi, Alpha Omega Alpha. Achievements include description of adverse effects of lead poisoning on renin-aldoserone function, pituitary-adrenal function, and pituitary-thyroid function; description of zinc deficiency in Egyptian adolescents, endocrine functions, and effects of zinc treatment; confirmation in rat of essentiality of zinc for nucleic acid and protein synthesis; confirmation in rats of the essentiality of zinc for wound healing; demonstration of some effects of zinc deficiency on development and function of rat on brain and on function later in life; demonstration of essentiality of zinc for neuropsychological functions of children and premenopausal women; demonstration of inhibition of zinc absorption by folic acid, demonstration by zinc kinetics of associations between iron status by serum ferritin and zinc status by zinc kinetics and plasma zinc concentration in premenopausal women; demonstration of zinc deficiency among low-income pregnant black US teenagers, Mexican-American children and premenopausal US women. Office: U Tex Med Br Ewing Bldg Galveston TX 77555-1109 Home: 77005 Seawall Blvd 407 Galveston TX 77551 Office Phone: 409-772-4661. Personal E-mail: hsandste@mac.com. Business E-Mail: hsandste@utmb.edu.

SANDY, WILLIAM HASKELL, training and communication systems executive; b. NYC, Apr. 28, 1929; s. Fred and Rose S.; m. Marjorie Mazor, June 15, 1952; children: Alan, Lewis, Barbara. AB, U. Md., 1950, JD, 1953; postgrad. Advanced Mgmt. program, Harvard Bus. Sch., 1970—71. Bar: Md. 1953. From planner-writer to acct. supr. Jam-Handy Orgn., Detroit, 1953—64, v.p., 1964—69, sr. v.p., 1969—71; pres. Sandy Corp., Troy, Mich., 1971—88, chmn., 1988—96; pres. Rudgate Corp., Bloomfield Hills, Mich., 1996—. Bd. dirs. U. Mich. Press, Asolo Repertory Theatre. Author: Forging the Productivity Partnership, 1990, Learning From Upheaval, 2012. Bd. govs. Northwood Inst., 1976-80; bd. dirs. Cranbrook Sci. Inst., Met. Ctr. High Tech., 1993, Birmingham (Mich.) Cmty. House, 1997-2003, Mich. Opera Theatre, 1990-2011; pres. Graphic Arts Coun., 1992-93; trustee Detroit Inst. Arts, 1992-93; v.p. internat. exec. coun. Harvard Bus. Sch., 1985-89; mem. Bloomfield Hills Zoning Bd., Walsh Coll. Leader in Residence, Pres.'s Adv. Coun.; mayor City of Bloomfield Hills, 1996-97; mem. Troy Downtown Devel. Authority, 1996-99; Inst. for Humanities trustee U. Mich. Mem. Am. Mktg. Assn. (pres. Detroit chpt. 1975), Nat. Found. Am. Mktg. Assn (bd. dirs. 1998), S.E. Mich. BBB (bd. dirs. 1999), Adcraft Club, Harvard Bus. Sch. Club (pres. Detroit chpt. 1983-85). Home: 535 Sanctuary Dr Apt B404 Longboat Key FL 34228 Home Phone: 248-540-2001. Personal E-mail: sandyfamily@aol.com.

SANFELICI, ARTHUR H(UGO), editor, writer; b. Haledon, NJ, May 23, 1934; s. Hugo and Anna (Schilder) S.; m. Betty Louise Van Riper, Aug. 10, 1957; children: Brian Arthur, Amy Elizabeth, Gary Hugh, Bruce Richard. Attended, Lehigh U., 1952-55. Assoc. editor Flying Mag., NYC, 1961-64; mng. editor Am. Aviation Mag., Washington, 1964-68; dist. sales mgr. Gates Learjet Co., NYC, 1969-71; exec. editor Airport World Mag., Westport, Conn., 1971-74; spl. project editor Aircraft Owners & Pilots Assn., Washington, 1974-75, mng. editor Pilot mag., 1975-79, editor AOPA Newsletter, AOPAirport Report, Gen. Aviation Nat. Report, 1979-88; pub. cons., 1989-90; sr. editor Flight Safety Found., Washington, 1989-92; editor S-Cubed divsn. Maxwell Labs., Alexandria, Va., 1992-95; comms. dir. Helicopter Assn. Internat., Alexandria, 1996-97; editor Shooting Sports USA, 1997-98. Editor, compiler: Yesterday's Wings; editor emeritus Aviation History Mag., Leesburg, Va., 1990—; author: 135 Ways to Get Even With Your Kids, 2003. Pilot USAF, 1955—60. Mem. Nat. Aeronautic Assn., Aero Club of Washington, Soc. Aerospace Comms. Home: 44476 Oakmont Manor Sq Ashburn VA 20147

SANFILIPPO, FRED PAUL, academic administrator, medical educator, pathologist; b. Racine, Wis., Aug. 30, 1949; s. Paul Joseph and Therese (Rhode) Sanfilippo; m. Janet Lee Thompson, 1973; children: Lisa, Joseph. Student, Max Planck Inst. Exptl. Medicine, Gottingen, Germany, 1966—68; BA in Physics, MS in Physics, U. Pa., 1970; PhD in immunology, Duke U., 1975, MD, 1976. Diplomate Am. Bd. Pathology, lic. physician NC, Md. Intern in anatomic pathology Duke U. Hosp., 1976—77, resident in anatomic and clin. pathology, 1977—79, postdoctoral rschr. divsn. tumor virology dept. surgery, 1976—79; asst. prof. pathology and exptl. surgery, lectr. immunology Duke U., 1979—84, from assoc. prof. to prof. pathology, 1984—93, from assoc. prof. to prof. exptl. surgery, 1985—93, prof. immunology, 1990—93; attending pathologist Duke U. and Durham VA Hosps., 1979—93; staff mem. Duke Surg. Pvt. Diagnostic Clinic, 1979—93; dir. Transplantation Lab Durham VA Hosp., 1979—93; dir. immunopathology Duke U. Med. Ctr., 1982—93, exec. com. dept. pathology, 1989—91; Baxley Prof. and chair pathology dept. John's Hopkins U., Balt., 1993—2000; pathologist-in-chief Johns Hopkins Hosp., Balt., 1993—2000; sr. v.p. health scis. Ohio State U., Columbus, 2000—07, exec. dean health scis., 2004—07, dean. coll. medicine, 2000—06; CEO Ohio State U. Med. Ctr., 2000—07; exec. v.p. health affairs, CEO Woodruff Health Scis. Ctr., chmn. Emory Healthcare Emory U., 2007—10; dir. Emory-Georgia Tech. Healthcare Innovation Program, 2010—. Mem. Duke Comprehensive Cancer Ctr., 1979—93; dir. rsch. Johns Hopkins Comprehensive Transplant Ctr.; mem. Third Frontier Commn. Adv. Bd., Ohio, 2004—; cons. Battelle Human Affairs Rsch. Ctrs., Seattle, 1985—93, NSF of Switzerland, 1992—93, numerous US govt. adv. coms.; mem. editl. bd. Transplantation, 1985—2001, Pathobiology, 1989—2001, Transplantation Now, Japan, 1989—2001, Pathology, Rsch. and Practice, 1990—2001, Human Immunology, 1992—2001, Lab. Investigation, 1993—2005, Xeno, 1994—2002, Virchows Archiv, 1998—2002, Transplant Immunology, 1998—2002; reviewer Am. Jour. Kidney Diseases, Am. Jour. Ophthalmology, Am. Jour. Pathology, New Eng. Jour. Medicine, Jour. of AMA, Jour. Am. Soc. Nephrology, Jour. Clin. Investigation, Jour. Leukocyte Biology, Kidney Internat., others; contbr. numerous articles to prof. jours.; speaker and presenter in field. Bd. trustees Omeris, Columbus, Ohio, 2004—07; trustee Marcus Found., 2012—. Recipient Kermit G. Osserman Award, Myasthenia Gravis Found., 1976, Wiley D. Forbus Award, NC Soc. Pathologists, 1979, Reach for Sight Physician Investigator Award, 1990; grantee numerous, NIH. Fellow: Am. Soc. Clin. Pathologists (coun. on edn. and rsch. 1994—96); mem.: Southeastern Organ Procurement Found. (exec. com 1992—97, sec. 1992—93, treas. 1993—94, v.p. 1994—95, pres. 1995—96), Assn. for Rsch. in Vision and Ophthalmology, Am. Soc. Nephrology, Am. Soc. Transplant Physicians (pres. 1985—86), Am. Soc. Histocompatibility and Immunogenetics, Transplantation Soc., US-Can. Acad. Pathology, Am. Assn. Med. Colls., Am. Assn. Immunologists, AMA, Am. Soc. Investigative Pathology (pres. 2002—03), Intersociety Pathology Coun., Assn. Pathology Chairs (sr. fellow), Am. Soc. Transplantation (past pres.), Alpha Omega Alpha. Office: Emory U 730 GCR 1518 Clifton Rd Atlanta GA 30322 Office Phone: 404-778-0234. Office Fax: 404-778-3100. Business E-Mail: fred.sanfilippo@emory.edu.

SANFORD, BEVERLY SHAW, museum director; m. Don Sanford; 3 children. BS in Health and Phys. Edn., Wake Forest U., Winston-Salem, NC, 1970; MH in Human Devel. and Learning, U. NC, Charlotte, 1980; PhD in Edn., Pacific Western U., LA, 1997. Tchr. Charlotte-Mecklenburg Schs., 1970—81; life ctr. coord., 1981—84; dir., programs and edn. Sci. Mus. of Charlotte, Inc., 1984—91; v.p., programs and edn. Discovery Pl., Inc., 1991—95; exec. dir. SciWorks, 1996—. Adj. instr. Gardner-Webb Coll., 1988, U. NC, Charlotte, 1995. Bd. dirs. YMCA of Northwest NC; mem. bd. advisors Wake Forest U. Sch. Medicine Ctr. Excellence Rsch., Tchg. and Learning; bd. dirs. Forsyth County Tourism Devel. Authority. Mem.: NC Grassroots Sci. Mus. (pres. 1999—2001, bd. dirs.), Assn. Sci. Tech. Ctrs. (bd. dirs.), NC Mus. Coun. (pres. 1996—98, bd. dirs.), Southeastern Mus. Coun. (bd. dirs.), Winston-Salem Rotary Club. Office: SciWorks Sci Ctr and Environ Pk 400 W Hanes Mill Rd Winston Salem NC 27105 Office Phone: 336-767-6730. Office Fax: 336-661-1777. Business E-Mail: bssanford@sciworks.org.

SANFORD, JENNY (JENNIFER SULLIVAN SANFORD), not-for-profit fundraiser, former investment banker; b. Winnetka, Ill., Sept. 11, 1962; m. Mark Sanford, Nov. 4, 1989 (div. Mar. 19, 2010); children: Marshall, Landon, Bolton, Blake. BA in Fin. magna cum laude, Georgetown U., 1984. Investment banker Lazard Freres & Co., NYC, 1984—90, v.p. mergers and acquisitions; campaign mgr. Mark Sanford for House of Reps., 1994, 1996, Mark Sanford for Gov., SC, 2002, co-mgr. re-election campaign, 2006; First Lady of SC, 2002—. Author: Staying True, 2010. Founder Healthy SC Challenge, 2005; bd. mem. Children's Hosp. Adv. Fund, Coastal Cmty. Found.; mem. site adv. coun. Drayton Hall, Charleston; mem. adv. com. Hollings Cancer Ctr. Republican. Office Phone: 803-737-4772. Office Fax: 803-737-3860.

SANFORD, MARK (MARSHALL CLEMENT SANFORD JR.), United States Representative from South Carolina, former Governor of South Carolina; b. Ft. Lauderdale, Fla., May 28, 1960; s. Marshall Clement and Peggy (Pitts) Sanford; m. Jennifer Sullivan, Nov. 4, 1989 (div. Mar. 19, 2010); children: Marshall, Landon, Bolton, Blake. BBA, Furman U., Greenville, SC, 1983; MBA, U. Va. Darden Grad. Sch. Bus. Adminstrn., 1988. Assoc. Coldwell Banker, 1983; project supr. Beachside Real Estate, Isle of Palms, Charleston County, 1984—86; training positions Goldman Sachs; financial analyst Chem. Realty Corp., 1988—90; prin. Southeastern Ptnrs., 1989—93; real estate broker Brumley Co., Charleston, SC, 1990—91; prin. Norton & Sanford Real Estate Investment, 1993—95, 2001—02; mem. US Congress from 1st SC Dist., Washington, 1995-2001, 2013—, US House Transportation Com., 2013—; gov. State of SC, Columbia, 2003—11. Chmn. Republic Governors Assn., 2008—09. Author: The Trust Committed to Me, 2000. Mem. USAF. Mem.: Preservation Soc. Charleston. Republican. Episcopalian. Avocations: windsurfing, running. Office: US House of Representatives 322 Cannon House Office Bldg Washington DC 20515 Office Phone: 202-225-3176.*

SANFORD, PAUL, state legislator; b. Huntsville, Ala. s. Jess and Louise Sanford; m. Danielle Sanford; children: Chase, Ryan. AOS in Culinary Arts, Culinary Inst. America, NYC. Restaurant owner Little Paul's Barbecue, Huntsville, 2002—; mem. Dist. 7 Ala. State Senate, Montgomery, Ala., 2009—. Vol. coach Upward Basketball Program; vol. youth soccer coach Am. Youth Soccer Orgn., Huntsville. Republican. Office: 100 St Clair Ave Ste A Huntsville AL 35801 also: Ala State Senate Rm 731 11 S Union St Montgomery AL 36130 Office Phone: 256-539-5441, 334-242-7867. Business E-Mail: paul.sanford@alsenate.gov.

SANSOM, WILLIAM B., wholesale distribution executive; BS in Civil Engring., The Citadel, 1964. With Am. Limestone Co., 1964—74, pres., 1974—79; commr. transp. State of Tenn., 1979—81, commr. finance & adminstrn., 1981—83; chmn. H.T. Hackney Co., Knoxville, Tenn., CEO, 1983—. Bd. dirs. Mid-America Apt. Cmtys., Inc., Astec Industries Inc., First Horizon Nat. Corp., 1984—, Martin Marietta Materials, NC, 1994—; chmn. Tenn. Valley Authority, 2006—09, bd. dirs., 2006—. Republican. Mailing: The HT Hackney Co PO Box 238 Knoxville TN 37901-0238 Office: The HT Hackney Co 502 S Gay St Knoxville TN 37901 also: First Horizon National Corp Bd Directors 165 Madison Memphis TN 38103 Office Phone: 865-546-1291, 901-523-4444. Business E-Mail: william.sansom@hthackney.com.

SANTIAGO, RAYMOND, library director, educator; b. NYC, July 13, 1949; s. Raymond and Livia Santiago; m. Crystal C. Capelis, May 15, 1979; 1 child, Jason Esrael. BFA, Rochester Inst. Tech., NY, 1974; MLS, SUNY, Buffalo, 1975. Co-chair, head non-print svcs. World U., San Juan, 1978—84; libr. Tampa-Hillsborough Pub. Libr. Sys., Fla., 1984—88, sect. mgr. Fla., 1988—90; supr. libr. svcs. Miami-Dade Pub. Libr. Sys., Fla., 1990—91, asst. dir. Fla., 1991—98, dir. Fla., 1998—. Adj. faculty Sch. Libr. and Info. Sci., U. South Fla., 1994—. Named Libr. of Yr., Libr. Jour., 2003. Mem. ALA, Pub. Libr. Assn., Fla. Libr. Assn. Office: Miami-Dade Pub Libr Sys 101 W Flagler St Miami FL 33130-1504 Office Phone: 305-375-5184. Business E-Mail: santiagor@miamidade.gov.

SANTIAGO-BORRERO, PEDRO J., dean, pediatrician, educator; MD, U. PR, San Juan, 1960. Cert. American Bd. Pediat. Residency in pediat. U. PR Med. Sciences Campus, fellowship in pediatric hematology-oncology, dean sch. medicine, 1978—85, prof. pediat., 1983—, dir. hematology-oncology sect. and pediatric hematology svc., chancellor, acting dean sch. medicine. Coord. human molecular genetics unit, prin. investigator U. PR Med. Sciences Campus Rsch. Centers in Minority Institutions. Mem.: American Acad. Pediat., Internat. Soc. Hematology, American Soc. Hematology, American Fedn. Clin. Rsch. Office: University PR A-878 Main Bldg Med Scis Campus PO Box 365067 San Juan PR 00936-5067 Office Phone: 787-765-2363. Office Fax: 787-756-8475. Business E-Mail: pedro.santiago@upr.edu.*

SANTILLAN, LAURA, corporate financial executive; BA, Southern Methodist U. CPA Tex. With Ernst & Young LLP, 1993—97; dir., fin. reporting Wyndham Internat., Inc., 1997—2002; sr. mgr., reporting Dresser, Inc., 2002—04; v.p., fin. Alliance Data Sys. Corp., 2007—09, sr. v.p., fin., 2009—10; sr. v.p., chief acctg. officer Alliance Data Systems Corp., 2010—. Office: Alliance Data Systems Corp 7500 Dallas Pkwy Ste 700 Plano TX 75024-4006 Office Phone: 972-348-5100. Office Fax: 972-348-5335.

SANTORA, KATHLEEN CURRY, lobbyist, lawyer; b. Hazelton, Pa., Sept. 14, 1958; d. Joseph Anthony and Irene Mary C.; m. Hugo Gary Santora, Jan. 6, 1990. BS in Polit. Sci., U. Scranton, 1980; JD, Cath. U. Am., 1983. Bar: Pa. 1984; lic. emergency med. technician. Assoc. dir. govt. rels., assoc. gen. counsel Nat. Assn. Ind. Colls. and Univs., Washington, 1984—86, exec. dir., counsel for state rels., 1987—89, v.p. ops., counsel, 1989; dir. pub. policy Assn. Governing Bds. Colls. and Univs., Washington, 1986—87; v.p., COO Am. Assn. Higher Edn., Washington; pres., CEO Nat. Assn. Coll. and Univ. Attys., Washington, 2001—. Mem. nat. adv. bd. Ctr. Constl. Studies Baylor U., Waco, Tex., 1987—; various positions, Georgetown U. Trustee Western New Eng. Coll., Springfield, Mass., 1986—; emergency med. technician Fairfax County, Annondale, Va., 1991; bd. mem. U. Scanton, Coun. for Advancement and Support of Edn., EDUCAUSE, American Coun. on Edn., Academic Search Consultation Service, Western New Engalnd Coll. Boards; chair Washington Higher Edn. Secretariat Steering Com. Mem. ABA, Pa. Bar Assn., Coun. of Higher Edn. Management Assn. (mem. steering com.), Assn. Mutual Health Ins. Co. Democrat. Roman Catholic. Avocation: skiing. Office: National Association College & University Attorneys One Dupont Cir Ste 620 Washington DC 20036 Office Phone: 202-833-8390. Office Fax: 202-296-8379. E-mail: ksantora@nacua.org.*

SANTORO, SAL, state legislator; b. July 14, 1951; BA, U. Cin.; MA, Xavier U. Former state trooper, Ky.; pres. Santoro Electric Co. Inc.; mem. Dist 60 Ky. House of Reps., 2007—. Mem.: St. Paul Ch., fin. mem., Florence Fire Protection Dist. (chmn.), Assoc. Builders & Contractors, KofC. Republican. Catholic. Office: Ky Legislature Rm 413D 702 Capitol Ave Frankfort KY 40601 Mailing: 596 Walterlot Court Florence KY 41042 Office Phone: 502-564-8100 ext. 691. Business E-Mail: sal.santoro@lrc.ky.gov.

SANTOROSKI, RICHARD, electric power industry executive; BSEE, Pa. State U.; MSEE, MBA, Syracuse U. Lic. profl. engr., NY. Various engring., trading & risk mgmt. positions NY State Electric & Gas; v.p., Risk Mgmt., v.p., Energy & Natural Resources AES Corp., mgmt. position, Eastern Energy's commodity, 1999, v.p., Non-Power Devel., 2007, v.p., Global Risk & Commodity Orgn., 2008—10, exec. v.p., chief risk officer, 2010—. Office: The AES Corp 11th Fl 4300 Wilson Blvd Arlington VA 22203 Office Phone: 703-522-1315. Office Fax: 703-528-4510. Business E-Mail: richard.santoroski@aes.com.

SANTORUM, RICK (RICHARD JOHN SANTORUM), lawyer, former United States Senator from Pennsylvania; b. Winchester, Va., May 10, 1958; s. Aldo and Catherine (Dughi) S.; m. Karen Garver, June 2, 1990; children: Elizabeth Anne, Richard John Jr., Daniel James, Sarah Maria, Peter Kenneth, Patrick Francis, Bella BA in Polit. Sci., Pa. State U., 1980; MBA, U. Pitts., 1981; JD, Dickinson Sch. Law, 1986. Bar: Pa. 1986. Adminstrv. asst. to Senator Doyle Corman Pa. State Senate, Harrisburg, 1981-86, exec. dir. local govt. com., 1981-84, exec. dir. transp. com., 1984-86; assoc. Kirkpatrick & Lockhart LLP, Pitts., 1986-90; mem. US Congress from 18th Pa. Dist., Washington, 1991-95; US Senator from Pa., 1995—2007; chmn. US Senate Republican Conf., 2001—07; cons. Eckert Seamans Cherin & Mellott, LLC, Washington, 2007—08; CEO EchoLight Studios, Dallas, 2013—. Sr. fellow The Ethics & Pub. Policy Ctr., 2007—11; polit. contr. Fox News Channel, 2007—11; bd. dirs. Universal Health Services, Inc., 2007—11; candidate for Republican nomination 2012 US Presdl. Election. Author: Rick Santorum: A Senator Speaks Out on Life, Freedom and Responsibility, 2005, It Takes A Family: Conservatism and the Common Good, 2005, Blue Collar Conservatives: Recommitting to an America That Works, 2014. Bd. dirs. Mt. Lebanon Extended Day Program, 1987-91; mem. Child Advocacy Project, 1987-91. Recipient Award for Legis. Excellence, American Soc. Consultant Pharmacists, 1997, Award for Mfg. Legis. Excellence, Nat. Assn. Mfrs., 1999, Disting. Svc. award, Brent Soc. of Arlington, Va. Diocese, 1999, Med. Miracle award, Healthcare Leadership Coun., 2000, John Paul II award, Inst. Psychol. Sciences, 2003, Legis. of the Yr., Nat. Multiple Sclerosis Soc., 2003, Friend of Seniors award, Bucks County, Pa. Area Agy. on Aging, 2004, Higher Edn. Leadership award, Washington Ctr. Internships & Academic Studies, 2005. Mem. KC, Italian Sons & Daughters Assn., Allegheny County Bar Assn. Child Advocacy Program. Republican. Roman Catholic. Avocations: golf, racquetball.*

SANTOS, ISABEL RODRIGUEZ, marketing educator; Mktg. tchr. Lorenzo Coballes Gandia HS, Hatillo, PR. Named PR Tchr. of Yr., 2007. Office: Lorenzo Coballes Gandia HS PO Box 1357 Hatillo PR 00659 E-mail: isaymario99@yahoo.com.

SANTOS DE ALVAREZ, BRUNILDA, lawyer, retired bank executive; b. 1958; BS in Fgn. Svc., Georgetown U.; JD, Boston Coll. Bar: P.R. 1983. Sr. v.p. Popular, Inc., San Juan, 1996—2001, chief legal officer, 1997—2010, exec. v.p., 2001—10. Sec. of bd. Popular Internat. Bank, Inc., Banco Popular N. Am., Popular Cash Express, Inc., Banco Popular, Popular Insurance, Inc., Popular Securities, Inc., Levitt Mortgage Corp., Popular Insurance Agy. USA, Inc., Popular Mortgage, Inc., P.R. Investor Tax Free Fund, Inc., P.R. Tax Free Target Maturity Fund, Inc., P.R. Investors Flexible Allocation Fund, Inc., Popular Fin. Holdings; asst. sec. of bd. Popular Auto, Inc., Popular

Finance, Inc.; mem. bd. of regents Colegio Puertorriqueno de Ninas, 2002—. Office: Colegio Puertorriqueno de Ninas Urb Golden Gate Calle Turquesa Guaynabo PR 00968-3401 Office Phone: 787-787-2618. Office Fax: 787-782-8370.

SANZ, LUIS E., gynecologist, educator; b. Camaguey, Cuba; m. Miriam D. Sanz; 1 child, Monica G. MD, Georgetown U., 1976. Uro-gynecology and vaginal reconstruction surgery dept. ob-gyn. Va. Hosp. Ctr., Washington, 1980. Author: Gynecologic Surgery, 1995; contbr. over 40 articles to profl. jours., chapters to books. With US Army, 1966—68, Vietnam. Decorated Vietnam Campaign medal U.S. Army. Fellow: ACOG (assoc.; memberr). Roman Catholic. Avocations: biking, reading, travel, weightlifting. Office: 1625 N George Mason Dr #475 Arlington VA 22101 E-mail: lsanz@virginiahospitalcenter.com.

SAPOFF, MEYER, retired electronics executive; b. NYC, June 2, 1927; s. Benjamin and Mary (Charney) Sapoff; m. Lynn Joy Sapoff; children: Robert J., Judy B. Finazzo. Student, Mohawk Coll., 1946—48; BSEE magna cum laude, Poly. Inst. Bklyn., 1950, postgrad., 1952—53, MIT, 1951, U. Pa., 1951—52; MSEE, Drexel Inst. Tech., 1952. Rsch. engr. Franklin Inst. Labs., Phila., 1950-52; rsch. fellow sr. grade Poly. Inst. Bklyn., 1952-53; dir. rsch. Victory Engring. Corp., Springfield, NJ, 1953-57, dir. engring., 1957-63, v.p., 1963-69; cons., sr. staff scientist Keystone Carbon Co., St. Mary's, Pa., 1969-70; pres. Thermometrics, Inc., Edison, NJ, 1970-86, chmn. bd. dirs., 1986-93, sr. staff cons., 1993-96; pres. MS Cons., Princeton, NJ, 1993—96; ret., 1996. Chmn. E20 temperature com. 6th Symposium Temperature, Measurement and Control in Sci. and Industry; U.S. del. to tech. com. 65th Internat. Electrotech. Commn.; cons. in field. Contbr. articles to profl. jours.; patentee in field. Active West Orange (NJ) PTA, 1960—76, Citizens League West Orange, 1962—75; trustee George St. Playhouse, New Brunswick, NJ, 1993—2001; bd. dirs. Jewish Ctr., Princeton, 1995—98, fin. chmn., 1995—96, v.p. fin., 1996—98; bd. dirs. United Jewish Fedn. Princeton Mercer Bucks, 1998—2008, treas., 2001—03. Recipient Indsl. Rsch. IR-100 award, 1974; fellow, Poly. Inst. Bklyn., 1953; scholar, NYU, 1948—50. Mem.: AAAS, ASTM (1st vice-chmn. E20 com. temperature measurement 2000—05, award of merit 1998), IEEE, Am. Ceramic Soc., Poly. Inst. Bklyn. Alumni Assn., Tau Beta Pi, Eta Kappa Nu.

SAPP, BETTY JEAN, federal agency administrator; b. 1955; BA, U. Mo., Columbia, MBA in Mgmt. Officer acquisition and fin. mgmt. positions USAF; program element monitor MILSTAR Sys., Washington; program mgr. FLTSATCOM program Space and Missile Sys. Ctr., LA; mng. joint-svc. devel. effort for A-10 Engine, Wright-Patterson AFB, Ohio; joined CIA, 1997; dep. dir. bus. plans & ops. Nat. Reconnaissance Office (NRO), Chantilly, Va., 2005—07, prin. dep. dir., 2009—12, dir., 2012—; dep. under sec. (portfolio, programs and resources) US Dept. Def., 2007—09. Office: Nat Reconnaissance Office Office of Prin Dep Dir 14675 Lee Rd Chantilly VA 20151-1715*

SAPP, ERIC, religious organization executive; m. Julie Sapp. Grad., Davidson Coll., NC; MDiv, Duke U., NC, MA Pub. Policy. Youth pastor First Presbyn. Ch., Durham; part-time dir. Christian Edn. at Heritage Presbyn. Ch., Alexandria, Va.; aide Senate Health, Edn., Labor, and Pensions Com., Rep. David Price's (NC-04) Washington D.C. office, 2004; sr. ptnr. Common Good Strategies. Named a Maverick, Details mag., 2007. Mem.: Heritage Presbyn. Ch. Home: 422 River Bend Rd Great Falls VA 22066-4017 Office Phone: 703-863-6403. E-mail: eric@cg-strategies.com.

SAPP, JOHN RAYMOND, lawyer; b. Lawrence, Kans., June 18, 1944; s. Raymond Olen and Amy (Kerr) S.; m. Linda Lee Tebbe, July 3, 1965; children: Jeffrey, Jennifer, John. BA, U. Kans., 1966; JD, Duke U., 1969. Bar: Wis. 1969, U.S. Dist. Ct. (ea. dist.) Wis. 1969, U.S. Ct. Appeals (7th cir.) 1974, U.S. Ct. Appeals (4th cir.) 1984, U.S. Supreme Ct. 1974. Assoc. Michael, Best & Friedrich, Milw., 1969-76, ptnr., 1976-90, mng. ptnr., 1990—2004, sr. ptnr., 2004—. Dir. Roadrunner Freight Sys., Milw., 1992-2004, J.J. Keller Co., 2003-. Author: (book) Making Partner, A Guide for Law Firm Associates, 2005. Bd. dirs. Milw. Symphony, 1981-95, mem. exec. com., 1993-95; bd. dirs. Boy Scouts Am., Milw., 1986—95, pres. 1990-92; mem. Milw. Arts Bd., 1990, Greater Milw. Com.; bd. dirs. Zool. Soc., 1995-, v.p., 2000-05, chmn., 2005-07; bd. dirs. Lex Mundi, 1997-2001, mem. exec. com., 1997-2001; bd. dirs. Jr. Achievement Greater Milw., 2001—04; pres. Pinehurst Consulting LLC, 2010-. Avocations: golf, curling, print collecting. Office Phone: 414-271-6560. Business E-Mail: jrsapp@michaelbest.com.

SAPPENFIELD, CHARLES MADISON, architect, educator; b. Columbia, SC, Mar. 17, 1930; s. Charles Madison and Elizabeth Olive (Moss) S.; m. Mary Frances McGowan Dec. 14, 1963 (div. June 1990); children— Charles Ross, Sarah Kathleen B.Arch., N.C. State U., 1956; Cert., Denmark's Royal Acad., Copenhagen, 1961. Asst. prof. N.C. State U., Raleigh, 1956-57, asst. prof., 1961-63; head archtl. firm C.M. Sappenfield, Asheville, N.C. and Muncie, Ind., 1961—; assoc. prof. Clemson U., SC, 1963-65; prof. architecture Ball State U., Muncie, Ind., 1965-94, prof. emeritus, 1994—, dean, 1965-81, dean emeritus, 1994—, dir. Design Indiana, 1983-88. Awards juror Interfaith Forum on Religious Art and Architecture, 1981, Am. Cons. Engrs. Council, 1982; mem. accreditation teams Nat. Archtl. Accrediting Bd., 1967-82. Archtl. works include: Dormitories, U. N.C., Gumpert residence, Dave residence. Pres. Asheville Art Mus., N.C., 1964-65; chmn. Ind. Commn. on Aging, Indpls., 1983-85; pres. Alpha Day Care Ctr. for Elderly, Muncie, 1985; mem. State Planning Adv. Commn., Indpls., 1974-82. Served with U.S. Army. Recipient Gold medal for svc. Ball State U., 1983; named Sagamore of the Wabash, Gov. of Ind., 1982 Fellow AIA (dir. nat. bd. dirs. 1989-92); mem. Ind. Soc. Archs. (pres. 1976), Ind. Archtl. Found. (chmn. 1975), Am. Soc. Landscape Archs. (awards juror 1983), Danish Fedn. Archs. (hon., Aeresmedallion 1987), Fulbright Alumni Assn., Alpha Rho Chi. Lodges: Rotary, Civitan. Democrat. Episcopalian. Avocations: bicycling, photography. Home and Office: 11607 Oakmont Ct Fort Myers FL 33908

SARAZIN, CRAIG LEIGH, astronomer; b. Milw., Aug. 11, 1950; s. Valley V. and Martha V. (Gustafson) Sarazin; children: Stephen N., Andrew T. BS in Physics, Calif. Inst. Tech., 1972; MA in Physics, Princeton U., 1973, PhD in Physics, 1975. Millikan fellow Calif. Inst. Tech., Pasadena, 1975; mem. Inst. Advanced Study, Princeton, NJ, 1975-77; asst. prof. U. Va., Charlottesville, 1977-79, assoc. prof. dept. astronomy, 1979-86, prof., 1986-96, W.H. Vanderbilt prof. astronomy, 1996—, chmn. dept., 1992-95. Vis. asst. prof. U. Calif., Berkeley, 1979; vis. scientist Nat. Radio Astronomy Obs., Charlottesville, 1977-82; vis. prof. physics Inst. Advanced Study, 1981-82, Joint Inst. Lab. Astrophysics vis. fellow U. Colo., Boulder, 1985-86, Erasmus Mundus vis. prof., U. Innsbruck, 2011; mem. com. on Space Astronomy Astrophysics, Washington, 1984-86, mem. x-ray astronomy working group, 1989-99, mem. Heineman prize com., 1995-98; chmn. Chandra users com., 1993-01, Advanced Satellite for Cosmology and Astrophysics users com., 1995-2000; mem. High Energy Astrophysics from Space Panel, 1999-2000; chmn. USRA Sci. Coun., 2000-06; mem. program assessment com. Beyond Einstein, 2006-07; chmn. NASA XMM Newton Users Com. 2009-, mem., ESA XMM Newton Users Group, 2011-. Author: X-ray Emission from Clusters of Galaxies; contbr. numerous articles to profl. jours. NSF grantee, 1981-86, NASA grantee, 1979-82, 86—; recipient Haren Fischer Physics prize Calif. Inst. Tech., 1971. Mem. Am. Astron. Soc., Internat. Astron. Union. Home: 664 Courtyard Ct Charlottesville VA 22903-7876 Office: U Va Dept Astronomy PO Box 400325 Charlottesville VA 22904-4325 Office Phone: 434-924-4903. Business E-Mail: sarazin@virginia.edu.

SARGENT, CHARLES LEE, manufacturing executive; b. Flint, Mich., Mar. 22, 1937; s. Frank T. and Evelyn M. (Martinson) S.; m. Nancy Cook, June 9, 1962; children: Wendy L., Joy A., Candace L. B ME, GM Inst., 1960; MBA, Harvard U., 1962; D in Engring. (hon.), Kettering U., 2004. Reliability engr. AC Spark Plug div. GM, Flint, 1962-63; with Thetford Corp., Ann Arbor, Mich., 1962-95, pres., chmn. bd. dirs., 1974-95, Thermassan Corp., 1969-72; pres., owner Quality Boat Lifts, Inc., Fort Myers, Fla., 1996—2007. Trustee Lincoln Cons. Schs., 1973-77, Ketterine U., 1989-2004, chmn. 1995-97. Sch. bd. Lincoln Consolidated Schs., Ypsilanti, Mich.; elder Presbyn. Ch. Recipient Entrepreneurial Achievement award GMI, 1989; named Entrepreneur of the Yr., Harvard Bus. Sch. Club of Detroit, 1981, Engring. Achievement award Kettering U., 1999. Mem. Barton Hills Country Club (bd. dirs. 1985-87, pres. 1987), Harvard Bus. Sch. Club of Detroit (bd. dirs. 1983-93). Achievements include patents in field. Avocations: travel, golf.

SARGENT, CHARLES M., state legislator; b. NYC, Feb. 3, 1945; s. Charles Michael and Marion Geagan Sargent; m. Nancy Willis Sargent, 1977; children: Margaret, Robert Gurley, David Shawn. House rep., Tenn.; ins. agt. CM Sargent Ins Agy., Nashville, 1975—; mem. Williamson County Regional Planning Commn., 1989—; co. commr. Williamson County, 1990—96; state rep. Dist. 61 Tenn., 1997—; rep. chmn.; mem. Williamson County Rep. Com. Mem.: Grassland Athletic Assn. (co-founder, pres.), Williamson County C. of C., Nat. Rifle Assn., Ct. Apptd. Spl. Advisor (bd. mem. 1995—), Williamson County Heritage Found., Nat. Assn. Life Underwriters. Republican. Presbyterian. Office: 117 Ashton Park Blvd Franklin TN 37067 also: 206 War Memorial Bldg Nashville TN 37243-0161 Office Phone: 615-741-6808, 615-771-7222. Office Fax: 615-253-0217. Business E-Mail: rep.charles.sargent@capitol.tn.gov.

SARGON, SIMON A., composer, music educator; b. Mumbai, Apr. 6, 1938; s. Benjamin Isaac Sargon and Esther Cottin; m. Bonnie Glasgow, Nov. 17, 1961; 1 child Olivia Sargon Glasgow BA in Music, Brandeis U., 1959; MS in Composition, Juilliard Sch. Music, NY, 1962. Instr. Julliard Sch., NYC, 1967—68, Sarah Lawrence Coll., Bronxville, NY, 1968—71; chmn. dept. voice Rubin Acad. Music, Jerusalem, 1970—74; dir. music Temple Emanu-El, Dallas, 1974—2001, condr. choir; prof. music Southwestern Meth. U., Dallas, 1983—. Assisting artist South Meth. U., Dallas, 1983—, Cin. Cll. Music, Ohio, 2003—05, U. Ill., 2003—05, U. Nevada, Las Vegas, 2003—05, U. Ohio, 2003—05; composer in residence Bradley U., Peoria, Ill., 1998, Susquehanna U., Pa., 2000, U. Mo., Columbia, 2001. Composer: El Nora, 2004, Questings (horn concerto), 2005; composer and pianist: Shema, Gasparo, 1998, A Clear Midnight, 2001, Flame of the Lord, 2004, Homage to Hafiz, 2007, numerous others; pianist: Songs of Alma Mahler, 2002; narrator: Town Music of Bremen; Performance at Music in the Mountains, 2006. Condr. Festival Jewish Choirs, Indpls., 2002—04, Washington, 2007. Recipient Sigma Iota award, 1988, Honors Commd. Composer Tex. Music Assn., 1993, 2003, finalist Nat. Opera Assn. Composition Competition, 1997, Honors Adjudicator Guild Temple Musician's Young Composer, 1998, 2001, 03, 04, Music Tchr.'s Nat. Assn., 2007; grantee Meadows Found., 1986, Meadows Wind Ensemble, 2003, Voices Change Coomn., 1988, 2007. Mem. Phi Beta Kappa, Phi Kappa Lambda, Dallas Symphony Assn. (bd. dirs. 1978-79), Am. Soc. Composers Authors Pubs. (award) Office: South Methodist Univ Dallas TX 75223

SARIC, WILLIAM SAMUEL, aerospace engineering educator; b. Chgo., Sept. 28, 1940; s. Sam and Antonia (Cerovac) S.; m. Carol Powlick, Aug. 25, 1962 (div. Aug. 1987); 1 child, William George; m. Helen L. Reed, Mar. 17, 1990. BSME, Ill. Inst. Tech., 1963, PhD in Mechanics, 1968; MSME, U. N.Mex., 1965. Registered profl. engr., Va. Instr. Ill. Inst. Tech., Chgo., 1966-68; assoc. prof. Va. Poly. Inst. and State U., Blacksburg, 1975-79, prof., 1979-84, Tohoku U., Sendai, Japan, 1991-92; prof. mech. engring. Ariz. State U., Tempe, 1984—2005, prof. emeritus, 2005—; prof. aerospace engring. Tex. A&M U., College Station, 2005—. Mem. fluid dynamics panel AGARD/NATO, 1989-95. Contbr. over 100 articles to profl. jours., chpts. to books. Recipient Sci. Achievement award AGARD/NATO, 1996, G.I. Taylor medal Soc. Engring. Sci., 1993, Alumni award for rsch. excellence Va. Poly. Inst. and State U., 1984. Fellow AIAA (assoc., mem. tech. com. fluid dynamics 1975-78), AMSE (chmn. applied mech. divsn. 1991-92), Am. Phys. Soc. (exec. com. divsn. fluid dynamics 1985-86); mem. NAE. Office: Tex A&M U Engring 3126 TAMU College Station TX 77843 Office Phone: 979-862-1749. E-mail: saric@tamu.edu.

SARKIS, ELIAS, aerospace and defense parts manufacturing company executive; b. France; M in Indsl. Engring., Ecole Centrale Lille, France, 1989. Worked Kvaerner Metals Davy Clecim, France; sr. project mgr., internat. devel., Mass Market Rolled Products Divsn. Pechiney, France, 1999—2002; v.p., supply chain mgmt., v.p., strategy bus. devel. Alcan Rolled Products, v.p., sales and mktg., 2004—07; v.p., strategy bus. devel. Vought Aircraft Industries, Inc., 2007—. Office: Vought Aircraft Industries Inc Ste 900 201 E John Carpenter Freeway Tower 1 Irving TX 75062 Office Phone: 972-946-2011. Business E-Mail: elias_sarkis@voughtaircraft.com.

SAROFIM, FAYEZ SHALABY, investment company executive; b. Nov. 19, 1928; m. Louisa Stude (div. 1990); m. Linda Hicks (div. 1996); 5 children. BS in Food Tech., U. Calif., Berkley, 1949; MBA, Harvard, 1951. Founder, chmn., pres. Fayez Sarofim & Co., 1958—. Bd. dirs. Argo Group Internat. Holdings, Ltd., Kinder Morgan, Inc., Unitrin, Inc., 1990—. Bd. mgr. Meml. Sloan-Kettering Cancer Ctr.; coun. mem. Rockefeller Univ.; bd. dir. Alley Theatre, Houston Ballet Found., Mus. Fine Arts, Houston; dir. Tex. Heart Inst. Named one of Top 200 Collectors, ARTnews, 2004—12, 400 Richest Americans, Forbes, 2006. Mem.: Houston Symphony Soc. (former vice chmn. bd. dirs.). Avocation: collector of Coptic sculpture, Old Masters, 19th century art, Am. Impressionism, modern & contemporary art. Office: Fayez Sarofim & Co 909 Fannin St Ste 2907 Houston TX 77010-1024 Office Phone: 713-654-4484. Business E-Mail: fsarofim@sarofim.com.

SARROS, P. PETER, diplomat, consultant; b. Greece, Aug. 20, 1935; (parents Am. citizens); s. Basil and Helen Sarros BA summa cum laude, Hobart Coll., 1957; M Pub. and Internat. Affairs, Princeton U., 1959, PhD, 1964. US fgn. svc. officer Dept. of State, Washington, 1960—92, sr. cons. fgn. affairs, 1993—. Spl. amb. to the Vatican, 1978; charge U.S. Mission to The Vatican, 1975—80; acting dep. asst. sec. for Human Rights, 1980—82; dir. Regional Polit. Affairs for Latin Am., 1985—92; adj. prof. diplomacy George Mason U., 1992—93; diplomatic assignments in Vatican, Venezuela, Dominican Republic and Iceland, 1961—67; diplomat in residence Sch. Advanced Internat. Studies Johns Hopkins U., 1972—73. W. Wilson fellow Princeton U., 1957-60; recipient Superior Honor award Dept. State. Mem. Am. Fgn. Svc. Assn., Phi Beta Kappa Avocation: bibliophile. Home: 1200 N Nash St Apt 249 Arlington VA 22209-3616 Office Phone: 202-634-3684.

SARVADI, PAUL J., professional employer organization executive; Attended, Rice U., Houston, U. Houston. Owner and operator of various small businesses; co-founder, dir., chmn. Insperity Inc. (formerly Administaff, Inc.), Kingwood, Tex., 1986—, treas., 1986—87, v.p., 1986—89, pres., 1989—2003, CEO, 1989—. Bd. trustees De-Pelchin Children's Ctr., Houston. Recipient Conn Family Disting. New Venture Leader award, Mays Bus. Sch., Texas A&M U., 2004; named Nat. Entrepreneur of Yr., svc. industries, Ernst & Young, 2001; named to Tex. Bus. Hall of Fame, 2007. Mem.: Nat. Assn. Profl. Employer Organizations (past. pres., bd. dirs.). Office: Insperity Inc 19001 Crescent Springs Dr Kingwood TX 77339 Office Phone: 281-358-8986.

SARVARY, MARK A., consumer products company executive; BS in Physics, Kent U., Eng.; MBA, INSEAD, France. Mktg. mgr. IBM Corp., England, account mgr., various positions in sales and mktg., Europe; indsl. ptnr. CVC Capital Ptnrs.; cons. Bain & Co., Inc., 1988—93; v.p., bus. devel., food divsn. and retail confections, chocolate divsn. Nestle, pres., stouffer's frozen food divsn., with NY, 1993—99, v.p., mktg., frozen food divsn., 1995—96, pres., gen. mgr., frozen food divsn., 1996—99; bd. dirs. J. Crew Group, Inc., 1999—, CEO, 1999—2002; pres., pepperidge farms divsn. Campbell Soup Co., 2002—04, pres., North American divsn., 2004—07; pres., CEO Tempur-Pedic International, Inc., 2008—. Office: Tempur Pedic International Inc 1713 Jaggie Fox Way Lexington KY 40511-2512 Office Phone: 859-259-0754. Office Fax: 859-514-5852. Business E-Mail: mark.sarvary@tempurpedic.com.

SARVIS, MICHAEL M., bank executive; BS, MBA, Clemson U., SC; diploma, Georgetown U. Stonier Grad. Sch. Banking. V.p., comml. lender First Citizens Bank & Trust of SC, Greenville; comml. banking mgr., then exec. v.p. banking Cohutta Banking Co., Chatsworth, Ga., 2001—04, pres., CEO, Chatsworth Ga., 2004—, pres., CEO, Chattanooga, 2008—. Deacon First Presbyn. Ch.; bd. dirs., treas. Whitfield County/Dalton Day Care Ctr., Ga. Mem.: Carpet City Rotary Club (past pres.). Office: Cohutta Banking Co 211 S 3rd Ave PO Box 10 Chatsworth GA 30705-2945 Office Phone: 706-695-9431.

SARWAR, SEHBA, writer; b. Karachi, Pakistan; d. Zakia Sarwar; married. Founding dir. Voices Breaking Boundaries (VBB), Houston; radio prodr. KPFT Pacifica Radio 90.1 FM. Author: (novels) Black Wings, 2004, (blogs) Daily Noise; dir.: (series) Living Room Art: Women's Voices, Living Room Art: Art Car Sprawl in the First Ward (First prize in the Free Speech Category, 2011), Living Room Art: Honoring Dissent / Descent. Recipient Creative Writing award, Cultural Arts Council of Houston, 1996, 2002, Houston Arts Alliance's Creative Artist award for excellence, USA, 2007; named hon. poet, Houston Poetry Fest Univ. of Houston-Downtown, 2003, conversationalist at Table-Talk, Women's Studies Univ. of Houston, 2005, honoree for cmty. svc. and writing, Living Smart's Annual conf. Channel 8, 2007, featured poet, Border Senses, 2007, honored, Houston's First Lady Andrea White, 2008, Fatima Jinnah Women Univ., 2009. Mem.: Texas Commn. on the Arts' Traveling Artist Roster, Sandra Cisneros' Macondo Writers' Workshop (life). Office: Voices Breaking Boundaries PO Box 541247 Houston TX 77254-1247 Office Phone: 713-524-7821.

SASLAW, RICHARD LAWRENCE, state legislator; b. Washington, Feb. 5, 1940; s. Isreal and Goldie Feldman Saslaw; m. Eleanor Barbara Berman, 1968; 1 child, Jennifer. Mem. Va. House of Reps., 1976—80; state senate Dist. 35 Va., 1980—; minority leader, 1996—98; mem. commerce com.; mem. labor com.; mem. edn. com.; mem. health com.; mem. fin. com.; mem. rules com.; mem. cts. justice com. Democrat. Jewish. Mailing: PO Box 1856 Springfield VA 22151-0856 Office: Capitol Office Senate of Virginia Rm 613 PO Box 396 Richmond VA 23218 Office Phone: 703-978-0200, 804-698-7535. Office Fax: 703-978-1221, 804-698-7651. E-mail: district35@senate.virginia.gov.

SASLOW, DEBBIE L., cancer control specialist, director; d. H. Arnold and Ann E. Weinstat; children: Kayla M., Rianna N. BS, Brown U., 1983—87; PhD, Yale U., 1987—92. Coord., president's nat. action plan on breast cancer PHS Office on Women's Health, Washington, 1995—97; dir., breast and gynecologic cancers Am. Cancer Soc., Atlanta, 1997—. Spkr. in field. Office: 250 Williams St 6th Floor Atlanta GA 30303

SASS, ARTHUR HAROLD, educational training administrator; b. NYC, Nov. 22, 1928; s. Maxwell Sigmund and Alice May (McGillick) S.; m. Eleanore G. Schmidt, Dec. 31, 1949; children: Nancy, Arlene, Susan, Eric. BS, SUNY Oswego, 1949; EdM, Rutgers U., 1959, postgrad., 1960—68. Cert. chief sch. adminstr. Tchr. Millsboro Pub. Sch. Sys., Del., 1949—51, Eatontown (N.J.) Pub. Sch. System, NJ, 1955—66; coord. coop. indsl. edn. Monmouth Regional H.S., Tinton Falls, NJ, 1966—68; prin. Mt. Holly Pub. Sch. Sys., NJ, 1968—71; supt. Lumberton Twp. Pub. Sch. Sys., NJ, 1971—72, Lacey Twp. Pub. Sch. Sys., NJ, 1973—74; analyst mil. pers. Naval Sea Sys. Command, Washington, 1975—79; head employee devel. Naval Rsch. Lab., Washington, 1979—83, 1985—90; acad. dir. Naval Res. Engring. Duty Officer Sch., Leesburg, Va., 1983—85. Pres. DEVPRO, Inc., Warrenton, Va., 1985—; prin. founder Dept. Def. Sci. and Engring. Apprentice Program; established nation's first fed. svc. high sch. coop. indsl. edn. program, 1967. Author: Guide to the Naval Ammunition Depot, 1967; editor: (brochure) Commodore John Barry-Father of the U.S. Navy, 1976. Chmn. Shade Tree Commn., Little Silver, NJ, 1968—75, Rapidan/Rappahannock (Va.) Cmty. Mental Health Ctrs., 1980—81; mem. Va. Gov.'s Adv. Bd. for Emergency Med. Svcs., 1994—96, Shade Tree Commn., Monmouth County, NJ, 1969—75; dir. Peninsula Agy. on Aging, Williamsburg, Va., 2004; deacon Warrenton Ch. of Christ, 1985, elder, 1995—99; deacon Williamsburg Ch. of Christ, 2005. Recipient Tng. Officers' Conf. Disting. Svc. award, 1988, Outstanding Contbn. to Engring. Edn. and Rsch award George Washington U., 1991. Mem. ASTD, SAR, Res. Officers Assn. (v.p. Va. chpt. 1982-83), Naval Res. Assn. (Plimsoll Mark award 1975), Am. Soc. Naval Engrs., Navy League, Wash. Acad. Scis., Tng. Dirs. Forum. Republican. Avocation: outdoor activities. Home: 120 Dogwood Ln Orange VA 22960-1058

SASS, NEIL LESLIE, toxicologist; b. Balt., Oct. 24, 1944; s. Samuel and Blanche (Radoon) S.; m. Anita Paige Hoswell, June 29, 1984. BS, Wake Forest Coll., 1966; MS, W.Va. U., 1969, PhD, 1971; MS, Johns Hopkins U., 1984. Commd. officer US Army, 1966, advanced through grades to capt. served as rsch. toxicologist, med. labs, 1988; served as rsch. toxicologist med. labs. U.S. Army, Edgewood Arsenal, Md., 1971-74; chief clin. investigations William Beaumont Army Med. Ctr., El Paso, Tex., 1974-77; toxicologist Bur. of Foods FDA, Washington, 1977-82; spl. asst. to dir. Ctr. for Food Safety and Applied Nutrition, FDA, Washington, 1982-99; dir. divsn. toxicological rsch. Ctr. for Food Safety and Applied Nutrition, Washington, 1996-99; state toxicologist State Counterterrorism Coordinator, and

Director, Chemical Lab., Ala. Dept. Pub. Health, Montgomery, 1999—2010; comdr. USPHS Preventive Medicine Unit. Dir. Divsn. Toxicological Rsch. Mem. Dauphin Island Planning & Zoning Commn., Dauphin Island Industrial Authority, Docent, Dauphin Island Sea Lab Estuarium, Marine Mamma. Jewish. Office: Ala Dept Pub Health The RSA Tower 201 Monroe St Ste 1450 Montgomery AL 36104-3735 Home: 904 Longfellow Pl Dauphin Island AL 36528-4432 Business E-Mail: nsass@adph.state.al.us.

SASSE, BENJAMIN ERIC, public policy educator, former federal agency administrator; b. Nebr., Feb. 22, 1972; s. Gary and Jean Sasse; m. Melissa McLeod; children: Elizabeth, Katherine. AB, Harvard U., Cambridge, Mass., 1994; MA in Liberal Arts, St. John's Coll.; PhD in Am. History, Yale U., New Haven. Chief staff Office Legal Policy US Dept. Justice, 2003—05; chief staff to Rep. Jeff Fortenberry US Congress; asst. prof. pub. affairs Lyndon B. Johnson Sch. Pub. Affairs, U. Tex., Austin; counselor to sec. US Dept. Health & Human Svcs., asst. sec. for planning & evaluation, 2007—09. Co-editor: Here We Stand!: A Call From Confessing Evangelicals For A Modern Reformation, 1996. Recipient Theron Rockwell Field Prize, George Washington Egleston Prize. Republican. Office: LBJ School Public Affairs U Texas PO Box Y Austin TX 78713 Office Phone: 512-471-3033. Business E-Mail: sasse@mail.utexas.edu.

SASSER, GARY, trucking executive; Attended, U. Tenn. Pres., CEO Averitt Express Inc., Cookeville, Tenn., 1971—. With USMCR. Office: Averitt Express Inc PO Box 3145 Cookeville TN 38502-3145 Office Phone: 931-526-3306. Office Fax: 931-520-5603. Business E-Mail: gsasser@averittexpress.com.

SASSER, ROBERT, retail executive; Various positions to sr. v.p. Roses Stores, Inc., sr. v.p. merchandise and mktg., 1997—99; v.p., gen. merchandise mgr. Michaels Stores, Inc., 1994—96; sr. v.p., COO Dollar Tree Stores, Inc., Chesapeake, Va., 1999—2004, pres., COO, 2001—04, pres., CEO, 2004—. Named one of Bus. People of Yr., Fortune mag., 2010. Office: Dollar Tree Stores Inc 500 Volvo Pkwy Chesapeake VA 23320

SATCHER, DARAKA E., management consultant, former federal agency administrator; b. L.A., Sept. 13, 1974; BA, Morehouse Coll, Atlanta, 1996; JD, Emory U., Decatur, Ga., 1999. Legis. asst. to Rep. John Spratt, US House of Representatives, Washington, 2000—01, legis. dir. to Rep. Harold Ford, 2005—07, chief of staff to Rep. Hank Johnson, 2007—09; legis. asst. to Senator Debbie Stabenow, US Senate, 2002—03; dep. asst. sec. for legislative & intergovernmental affairs US Dept. Commerce, Washington, 2009—11; ptnr., COO Pendleton Consulting Group, LLC, Atlanta, 2011—. Democrat. Office: Pendleton Consulting Group 2526 Mount Vernon Rd Ste B #159 Atlanta GA 30338 Office Phone: 404-337-3144. Business E-Mail: dsatcher@pendletonatlanta.com.

SATCHER, DAVID, public health service officer, former Surgeon General of the United States; b. Anniston, Ala., Mar. 2, 1941; s. Wilmer and Anna Satcher; m. Nola Satcher; children: Gretchen, David, Daraka, Daryl. BS, Morehouse Coll., 1963; MD, PhD, Case Western Reserve U., 1970; DSc, Harvard U., 2011. Resident and fellow Strong Mem. Hosp., U. Rochester, UCLA, and King Drew; former faculty UCLA Sch. Medicine and Pub. Health; faculty, chair dept. family medicine King-Drew Med. Ctr., LA, interim dean, 1977—79; dir. King-Drew Sickle Cell Rsch. Ctr.; prof., chmn. dept. cmty. and family medicine Morehouse Sch. Medicine, Atlanta, 1979—82; pres. Meharry Med. Coll., Nashville, 1982—93; dir. Ctrs. for Disease Control and Prevention, Atlanta, 1993—98; adminstr. Agy. for Toxic Substances and Disease Registry, 1993—98; surgeon gen. US Dept. Health & Human Services, Washington, 1998—2002, asst. sec. health, 1998—2001; sr. vis. fellow Kaiser Family Found., Washington, 2002—; dir. Nat. Ctr. for Primary Care Morehouse Sch. Medicine, Atlanta, 2002—, interim pres., 2005—06, founder, dir. Satcher Health Leadership Inst., 2006—. Mem. Coun. of Grad. Med. Edn., 1986; bd. dir. Johnson & Johnson, 2002—13, MetLife Inc., 2007—. Recipient Watts Grassroots award for cmty. leadership, 1979, Nat. Conf. Christians and Jews awards, 1985, Black Achievment award, Ebony Mag., 1994, Breslow award in pub. health, 1995, Dr. Nathan B. Davis award, AMA, 1996, Lifetime Achievement award, NY Acad. Medicine, 1997, Benjamin E. Mays Trailblazer award, Nat. Found. for Infectious Diseases, 2004, Jimmy & Roslyn Carter award for Humanitarian Contribution to the Health of Mankind, 2004, Discovery Health Channel Med. Honors, 2004, Public Health Heroes award, U. Calif. Berkeley Sch. Public Health, 2013; named Nashvillian of Yr., 1992. Fellow: Am. Acad. of Family Physicians; mem.: Inst. Medicine NAS, Alpha Omega Alpha, Phi Beta Kappa. Focuses on promoting healthly lifestyles and ending disparities in health; as director of the CDC, he raised childhood immunization rates to 78% in 1996 from 55% in 1992. Office: Nat Ctr for Primary Care at Morehouse Sch Medicine 720 Westview Dr SW Atlanta GA 30310 Office Fax: 404-756-5767.*

SATHYAMOORTHY, MUTHUKRISHNAN, engineering educator, associate provost; b. Sathanur, Tamil Nadu, India, Feb. 21, 1946; s. Kuppusamy and Visalakshi Muthukrishnan; m. Chitra Subbiah, May 26, 1971; children: Mohanakrishnan, Kumaran. B in Civil Engring., U. Madras, India, 1967; M in Engring. Mechanics, Indian Inst. of Tech., Madras, India, 1969, PhD in Aero. Engring., 1973. Lectr. Indian Inst. of Tech., Madras, India, 1969-74; rsch. fellow U. Birmingham, Eng., 1974-76; asst. prof. Clarkson U., Potsdam, NY, 1979-82, assoc. prof., 1982-92, assoc. prof., exec. officer, 1992-94, prof., exec. officer, 1994-97, prof., chair, 1997-2001; dean engring. W.Va. U. Inst. Tech., 2001—06; assoc. provost U. Tex., Tyler, 2006—. Vis. rsch. faculty U. Calgary, Can., 1977-79. Contbn. author: Handbook of Civil Engineering Practice, 1988; editor: Material Nonlinearity in Vibrations, 1985; author: Nonlinear Analysis of Structures, 1998. Recipient Appreciation cert. U.S. Army, 1990, Outstanding Advisor award Clarkson U., 1993, Tau Beta Pi Faculty award, 1997, Disting. Tchg. award Clarkson Univ., 2001. Fellow ASME (mem. nat. student sect. com. 1992-94, mem. gen. awards com. 1994-99, Nat. Faculty Advisor award 1993, Dedicated Svc. award 1999); AIAA (assoc.), Aero. Soc. India. Avocations: overseas travel, camping, photography, fishing. Office: Office Assoc Provost U Tex at Tyler 3900 University Blvd Tyler TX 75799 Home: 13325 White Tail Dr Tyler TX 75707 Office Phone: 903-565-5939. Business E-Mail: msathy@uttyler.edu.

SATRUM, JERRY R., chemicals company executive; b. 1933; BS, Oreg. State U., 1967. With Georgia-Pacific Corp., Atlanta, 1968-84; v.p., treas. fin. and adminstr. Georgia Gulf Corp., 1984-89, pres., 1989—97, CEO, 1991—98. Bd. dirs. Cytec Industries Inc., 1996—, Ga. Gulf Corp., 1998. Office: Georgia Gulf Corp Ste 460 115 Perimeter Ctr Pl Atlanta GA 30346 also: Cytec Industries Inc Bd Directors 5 Garret Mountain Plz West Paterson NJ 07424 Office Phone: 973-357-3100. Office Fax: 973-357-3065. Business E-Mail: satrumj@ggc.com.

SATTERLEE, WARREN SANFORD, II, retired retail management professional, writer; b. Harlingen, Tex., Dec. 8, 1946; s. Ralph Pickard and Diane (Royall-Mann) S.; m. Virginia Lou Schumacher, July 17, 1971 (dec. May 24, 2011); 1 child, Heather Irene. AA, Cayuga C.C., Auburn, NY, 1972; BA, St. Cloud State U., 1974. Grad. cert. in Theol. Studies Tex. Christian U., 1991. Supr. and bakery support staff Schlotzsky's, Arlington, Tex., 1989-93, Schlotzsky's Deli Sandwich Shop, Arlington, 1993-96; retail mgmt. Eckerd Drug #3156, Arlington, 1995-2000; mem. customer svc. staff Office Depot, Arlington, 1998; mem. mgmt. tng. program retail mgmt. practices Eckerd Drug, 1999, mem. supervisory tng. program, 1999; retail mgmt. staff Ross Dress For Less, Ft. Worth, 2000—06, AARP Southwest Chapt; ret., 2006. Author: Meditation, 1997, Meditation III, 1997, numerous poems; contbr. articles to profl. jours Mem. Rite I, Ch. of Sts. Peter and Paul Anglican Ch. Choir, Arlington, Tex., 1999-2006, mem. ch. choir, 1999-2001, mem. Rite I Choir, 2012-; vol. Cowtown Marathon, Fort Worth, Tex., 1991—2011, Monthly Refreshment Com. AARP Chpt. 4116, Ft. Worth, Tex., 2009-11; past mem. Ft. Worth Geneal. Soc., Crowley Art Guild, Hereditary Register of the USA, contbr. With USAF, 1966-70. Mem. Internat. Order of St. Luke the Physician. Anglican. Avocations: creative writing, making church worship banners and visuals, music, crafts. Home: 4004 Bradley Ln Arlington TX 76017-4148 Personal E-mail: wss2osl@gmail.com.

SAUCIER, GENE DUANE, state legislator, import/export company executive; b. Dallas, Sept. 25, 1931; s. Albert L. and Myrtle Irene (West) S.; m. Marilyn Emmy Cox, Dec. 27, 1952 (div. Sept. 1980); children: Alan, Steve, Renee; m. Giulia Riga LaCagnina, Nov. 28, 1981. BS in Agronomy Soils, Miss. State U., 1953; MS in Counseling, U. So. Miss., 1970, EdD in Adult Edn., 1978. Builder, developer Saucier Co., Hattiesburg, Miss., 1957-70; dir. admissions U. So. Miss., Hattiesburg, 1970-74, dean spl. acad. svcs., 1974-84, asst. v.p. bus. and fin., 1984-93; mem. Miss. Ho. of Reps., Jackson, 1993-99; ret., 1999. Mem. Fed. Land Coun., 1997—2003; scoutmaster Boy Scouts Am., 1960—70, chmn. camping and activities Pine Burr area, 1970; bd. dirs., founder Hub Coun., 2000; bd. dirs. Miss. Wild Turkey Fedn., Pine Burr chpt., 2000. 1st lt. pilot USAF, 1953—56. Named Forrest County Tree Farmer of Yr., 1996, Miss. Tree Farmer Yr., 1996; recipient Forestry award Miss. Wildlife Fedn., 1997, Legislator of Yr. Coastal Conservation Assn., 1997. Mem. So. Assn. Collegiate Registrars and Admissions Officers (bd. dirs. 1981, local arrangements chmn. 1981, v.p. admissions and fin. aid 1982-83, pres. 1985-86), Miss. Assn. Collegiate Registrars and Admissions Officers, Miss. Forestry Assn. (exec. bd. dirs. 1992-94, bd. dirs. 1992-94), Soc. Am. Foresters (cert. rev. bd. 2003-05), Am. Legion (life), Miss. Nature Conservancy, Forrest/Lamar Forestry Assn. (pres. 1989-92, 2007—08), Resource Conservation & Devel.(co-chair, 2008-, mem. 2009), Audubon (v.p. Forest County chpt. 2004), Sigma Chi (life), Phi Delta Kappa, Omicron Delta Kappa. Personal E-mail: treefarm43@hotmail.com.

SAULSBURY, FRANK T., pediatric immunologist and rheumatologist; b. Lexington, Nebr., Aug. 27, 1947; MD, U. Nebr. Coll. Medicine, 1972. Diplomate Am. Bd. Pediat. Intern pediat. Johns Hopkins U. Hosp., Balt., 1972—73, resident pediat., 1973—75, fellowship pediat. immunology, 1977—79; med. alumni. prof. pediat. U. Va. Sch. Medicine, 2002—; head divsn. pediat. immunology and rheumatology U. Va. Health Sys. Contbr. articles to profl. jours. Mem.: Am. Pediat. Soc. Office: U Va Sch Medicine Dept Pediat PO Box 800386 Charlottesville VA 22908 Office Phone: 434-924-1906. Office Fax: 434-982-4246. Business E-Mail: fts@virginia.edu.

SAUNDERS, BARRY L., corporate financial executive; BS in acctg., Univ. SC, MBA. CPA. Audit mgr. Ernst & Young; joined Sonoco Products Co., 1989, dir. corp. reporting, dir. fin. European ops. Brussels, staff v.p., corp. contr. Hartsville, SC, 2003—08, v.p, corp. contr., chief acctg. officer, 2008—11, v.p., CFO, 2011—. Office: Sonoco Products Co One N 2nd St Hartsville SC 29550 Office Phone: 843-383-7000. Office Fax: 843-383-7008. Business E-Mail: barry.saunders@sonoco.com.

SAUNDERS, HAROLD HENRY, foundation administrator; b. Phila., Dec. 27, 1930; s. Harold Manuel Saunders and Marian Elizabeth Weihenmayer; m. Barbara Mc Garrigle, May 4, 1963 (dec. Oct. 1973); children: Catherine Elizabeth, Mark Harril; m. Carol Eleanor Jones Cruse, June 2, 1990. AB, Princeton U., 1952; PhD, Yale U., 1956; LittD, New Eng. Coll., 1999; D of Internat. Rels., Dickinson Coll., 2004; D in Pub. Svc., Susquehanna U., 2011; LHD, U. Nebr. With CIA, Washington, 1959—61; sr. staff Nat. Security Coun., Washington, 1961—74; dir. intelligence and rsch., asst. sec. Near East and South Asian affairs Dept. of State, Washington, 1974—81; fellow Am. Enterprise Inst. Brookings Inst., Washington, 1981—91; profl. lectr. Johns Hopkins U., SAIS, George Mason U., 1984—91; dir. internat. affairs Kettering Found., Washington, 1991—; pres. Internat. Inst. Sustained Dialogue, 2002—. Author: The Other Walls: Arab-Israeli Peace Process in Global Perspective, 1985, 91, A Public Peace Process: Sustained Dialogue to Transform Racial and Ethnic Conflicts, 1999, Politics Is About Relationship: Blueprint for the Citizens' Century, 2005, Sustained Dialogue in Conflicts: Transformation and Change, 2011. Trustee Princeton U., 1996—2000; pres. Class of '52, 2002—07; bd. dirs. Hollings Ctr., 2007—; ruling elder Lewinsville Presbyn. Ch., McLean, Va., 1971—; bd. dirs. East-West Inst., NYC, 1981—89, Ptnrs. Dem. Change, San Francisco, 1995—2005, InterNews, Arcata, Calif., 1999—2001. Lt. USAF, 1957—59. Recipient Disting. Fed. Civilian Svc. award Pres. U.S., 1978, Disting. Honor award Dept. of State, 1981, First Disting. Achievement award Germantown Acad., Phila., 2002, Lifetime Achievement award Search for Common Ground, 2004, Annenberg award, Am. Acad. Diplomacy, 2010, Internat. Outstanding Leadership award Assn. Conflict Resolution, 2013. Mem. Internat. Soc. Polit. Psychology (gov. coun. 1991-94), Coun. Fgn. Rels., Princeton Club N.Y., Nassau Club Princeton (NJ), Phi Beta Kappa. Avocation: writing. Home: 2101 Lorraine Ave Mc Lean VA 22101 Office: Kettering Found 444 N Capitol St NW Washington DC 20001

SAUNDERS, MARTHA DUNAGIN, academic administrator; m. Joseph Bailey; 7 children. BA, U. So. Miss., 1969; MA, U. Ga.; PhD in Comm. Theory, Fla. State U. Asst. prof. comm. U. West Fla., dir. Univ. Honors Prog., dean Coll. Arts and Scis., 1999; v.p. Academic Affairs Columbus State U.; chancellor U. Wis., Whitewater, 2005—07; pres. U. So. Miss., Hattiesburg, 2007—. Author: Eastern's Armageddon: Labor Conflict and the Destruction of Eastern Airlines, 1992. Mem.: Pub. Relations Soc. Am. (Silver Anvil award). Avocations: fishing, gardening. Office: U So Miss Office of Pres 118 College Dr Hattiesburg MS 39406-0001

SAUNDERS, RON, state legislator; b. Key West, Fla., Oct. 30, 1954; s. Jack A. Saunders; m. Melodie Saunders; 1 child, Ryan. BS magna cum laude, U. Fla., 1976, JD, 1979. Real estate & investment broker; atty.; mem. Fla. House of Reps., Tallahassee, 1986—94, mem. Dist. 120, 2006—, mem. govt. accountability act coun., joint legis. budget commn., rules and calendar coun., ranking mem. full appropriations coun. on edn. and econ. devel., full appropriations coun. on gen. govt. and health care. Mem. Fla. Tax & Budget Reform Commn., 1991—92. Chmn. Fla. Keys CC Bd. Trustees, 1983—86; pres. Fla. Keys Land and Sea Trust. Mem. Fla. Bar Assn., Monroe County Bar Assn., Mensa, Elks, Key West Rotary (club dir. 1983-84), Key West Jaycees (pres. 1981-82). Democrat. Episcopalian. Office: Overseas Hwy Ste A-90311 Tavernier FL 33070-1947 also: 203 House Office Bldg 402 S Monroe St Tallahassee FL 32399-1300 Office Phone: 305-853-1947, 850-488-9965.

SAVAGE, JAMES FRANCIS, retired editor; b. Boston, July 23, 1939; s. James and Hanora (Enright) S.; m. Sharon Kaye Base, May 29, 1965; 1 son, Sean. AA, Boston U., 1959, BS, 1961. Reporter Quincy (Mass.) Patriot Ledger, 1961-63; reporter Miami (Fla.) Herald, 1963-67, investigative reporter, 1967-78, investigations editor, 1978-84, assoc. editor investigations, 1984—2003. Investigative reporter Boston Herald Traveler, 1967 Served with AUS, 1962. Recipient Nat. Headliners award, 1969, Fla. Press Assn. award, 1972, George Polk Meml. award for investigative reporting, 1973, 80, Pub. Service award Nat. A.P. Mng. Editors, 1974, 80, award Fla. Soc. Newspaper Editors, 1974, 75, Nat. Disting. Service award Sigma Delta Chi, 1979, 87, Pulitzer Prize Staff award for Nat. Reporting, 1987, Outstanding Investigative Reporting award Investigative Reporters and Editors, 1988, Disting. Alumni award Boston U. Coll. Communications, 1990, Pulitzer Prize Staff Pub. Svc. award, 1993; Profl. Journalism fellow Stanford, 1974-75 Home: 1004 Orange Is Fort Lauderdale FL 33315-1651 Office: 1 Herald Plz Miami FL 33132-1609

SAVAGE, WILLIAM WOODROW, JR., historian, consultant, social sciences educator; b. Richmond, Va., Oct. 13, 1943; s. William Woodrow and Margaret Savage; m. Sheila Bobalik, July 30, 1983; 1 child, William Woodrow III. BA in Journalism, U. S.C., 1964, MA in History, 1966; PhD in History, U. Okla., 1972. Instr. Coll. Gen. Studies U. S.C., Columbia, 1966; vis. lectr. history Iowa State U., Ames, 1970; asst. editor U. Okla. Press, Norman, 1972-75; from asst. prof. to assoc. prof. history U. Okla., Norman, 1974—89, prof., 1989—. Tech. adviser Korine-Dunlap Prodns., Nashville, 1982—83; adviser Am. Frontier Project, NYC, 1982—85; bd. cons. editors Popular Culture Librs., Binghamton, NY, 1991—99; mem. editorial advisory bd. Jour. Scholarly Publishing, 2009—. Author: The Cherokee Strip Live Stock Association, 1973, The Cowboy Hero, 1979, Singing Cowboys and All That Jazz, 1983, Comic Books and America, 1945-54, 1990; editor: Indian Life, 1977, Cowboy Life, 1993; co-editor: The Frontier, 1979; editor (newsletter): Comparative Frontier Studies, 1975—86, Norman and Cleve. County Hist. Mus., 1975; co-prodr., host (TV series) Norman Cable TV, 1986—88; columnist: Okla. Gazette, 1993—95, Jour. Scholarly Publ., 2004—; contbr. articles to profl. jours.; editl. bd. Jour. Recipient Spl. Recognition award, Okla. Jazz Hall of Fame, 1993. Mem.: So. Hist. Assn., Okla. Hist. Soc., Phi Alpha Theta, Omicron Delta Kappa, Sigma Delta Chi. Avocations: panelology, mixed media and collage. Office: Univ Okla Dept History 455 W Lindsey Rm 424 Norman OK 73019-2004 Office Phone: 405-325-6001.

SAVARI, SERAP AYSE, engineering educator, researcher; b. Astoria, NY, Nov. 4, 1968; d. Aykut and Sirin Savari. MS, MIT, Boston, 1991, PhD, 1996. Mem. tech. staff Bell Labs., Lucent Techs., Murray Hill, 1996—2003; acad. guest faculty computer sci. and comm. sys. Swiss Fed. Inst. Tech., 2003; assoc. prof. dept. elec. engring. and computer sci. U. Mich., Ann Arbor, 2004—07, Tex. A&M U., College Station, 2008—. Adj. prof. dept. elec. engring. and computer sci. U. Mich., Ann Arbor, 2003. Contbr. articles to profl. jours. Team leader info. processing Internat. Symposium on Info. Theory, 2005; mem program com. Info. Theory Workshop, 2004, 2006—07, mem. program com., 2007, Internat. Symposium in Info. Theory, 2001, 2002, 2004, 2008—10; mem. tech. program com. Data Compression Conf., 2000—; mem. exec. com. Intrernat. Symposium Info. Theory, 2010; bell labs rep. Ctr. Discrete Math. and Theor. Computer Sci., 2001—03. Mem.: SPIE (program com. data compression conf. 2000—, program com. symposium 2001, 2002, assoc. editor Source Coding IEEE Transactions on Info. Theory 2002—05, program com. symposium 2004, team leader program com. info. processing 2005, program com. symposium, recent results session, co chair, exec. com. mem. 2010, intern symposium info theory, program com. symposium 2008—10). Home: 4050 Pendleton Dr Apt 1324 Bryan TX 77802 Office: 308G Wisenbaker Engineering Bldg 3128 TAMU College Station TX 77843-3128 Business E-Mail: savari@ece.tamu.edu.

SAVILLE, PAUL C., construction executive; BBA, Coll. William & Mary, Williamsburg, Va., 1977; MBA, U. Pitts. With automotive ops. Rockwell Internat.; with Ryan Homes, 1981, v.p. bus. planning to CFO; sr. v.p. fin., CFO, treas. NVR Inc., McLean, Va., 1993—2002, exec. v.p., CFO, treas., 2002—05; pres., CEO NVR, Inc., McLean, Va., 2005—. Named to The Va. 100, Va. Bus. mag., 2005. Office: NVR Inc Plaza America Tower 1 11700 Plaza America Dr Ste 500 Reston VA 20190-4792 Office Phone: 703-956-4000. Office Fax: 703-956-4750.

SAVOFF, MARK T., energy executive; BS in Nuclear Engring., U. Fla. Gen. mgr., global Nuclear Fuel bus. General Electric Co.; pres., GE Nuclear Gen. Electric Energy; v.p., corp. officer Gen. Electric Power Sys., pres., 2000—03; v.p., corp. officer GE Nuclear Energy, San Jose, Calif., pres., 2000—03; exec. v.p., ops. Entergy Gulf States Louisiana, LLC, bd. dirs., 2004—05; exec. v.p. Entergy Mississippi, Inc.; bd. dirs. Entergy Miss. Inc., 2004—05; exec. v.p., ops. Entergy New Orleans, Inc., bd. dirs., 2004—05; exec. v.p. Entergy Services, Inc., 2003—; exec. v.p., ops. Entergy Corp., 2004—10, exec. v.p., COO, 2010—. Bd. dirs. Entergy Arkans., 2004—, Entergy La., 2004—, Entergy Tex., 2007—. Bd. dirs. Constrn. Navigator, Electric Power Rsch. Inst., Southeastern Electric Exchange; mem., adv. counsel U. Fla. Coll. of Engring. Office: Entergy Corp 639 Loyola Ave New Orleans LA 70113 Office Phone: 504-576-4000. Office Fax: 504-576-4428. Business E-Mail: msavoff@entergy.com.

SAVRANN, RICHARD ALLEN, lawyer; b. Boston, July 29, 1935; s. Abraham B. and Doris (Curhan) S.; m. Diane Barbara Kleven, Dec. 22, 1957; children: Stephen Keith, Russell Clark. BA, Harvard U., 1956, JD, 1959. Bar: Mass. 1959, U.S. Dist. Ct. Mass. 1963, U.S. Ct. Appeals (1st cir.) 1965, Fla. 1989. Exec. Klev Bro. Mfg., Derry, NH, 1959-63; assoc. Law Office of Jerome Rappaport, Boston, 1963-68; asst. atty. gen. Commonwealth of Mass., Boston, 1968-70; ptnr. Newell, Savrann & Miller, Boston, 1970-75; sr. ptnr. Kunian, Savrann & Miller, Boston, 1976-81, Singer, Stoneman, Kunian & Kurland, P.C., Boston, 1981-88, Singer, Kunian & Kurland, P.C., Boston, 1988-90; sr. ptnr, Curhan, Kunian, Goshko, Berwick and Savrann, P.C., Boston, 1990-92; ptnr. Burns and Levinson, LLP, Boston, 1993—2001, Gargill, Sassoon & Rudolph LLP, Boston, 2001—02, Rudolph Friedmann LLP, Boston, 2002—05, Law Office of Richard A. Savrann, West Palmbeach, 2005—, Boynton Beach, 2005—; spl. magistrates Palm Beach County VAB, 2009—. Active Andover (Mass.) Housing Authority, 1972—90, chmn., 1984—90; pres. Hospice of Greater Lawrence, North Andover, 1984; bd. dirs. Boston Latin Sch. Found., 1987, clk., 1992—98; spl. magistrate Palm Beach County, 2009—; bd. dirs. Comite Internat. de Sci. pour La Santé et l'Environ., Paris, 1993—2000. Mem. Fla. Bar, Mass. Bar Assn., Palm Beach County Bar Assn., Eastpointe Country Club (Palm Beach Gardens, Fla., pres. 2010), Harvard Club (Andover) (pres. 1985-98),

Harvard Club (Palm Beach). Avocations: golf, opera. Home: 13866 Greensview Dr Palm Beach Gardens FL 33418 Home Phone: 561-627-3493; Office Phone: 561-964-6404. Business E-Mail: rsavrann@thednsway.com.

SAWICKI, MARNI L., Mayor, Cape Coral, Florida; children: Brendon, Madisson. B in comm., Ctrl. Mich. U., Mt. Pleasant; MBA, U. Phoenix. With State Farm, Nat. Interstate; mayor City of Cape Coral, 2013—. Office: Office of the Mayor PO Box 150027 Cape Coral FL 33915-0027 Office Phone: 239-574-0436. E-mail: msawicki@capecoral.net.

SAWYER, DOLORES, motel chain executive; b. Shreveport, La., Oct. 16, 1938; d. Orlan B. Greer and Doris Lucile (Sanders) Eckman; m. Raymond Lee Sawyer Jr., June 11, 1960 (dec. Mar. 2007); children: Lisa Kay, Linda Faye. BSN, Northwestern State Coll., 1960; MSN, Tex. Woman's U., 1975. Supr. obstetrics dept. Highland Hosp., Shreveport, La., 1962-64; head nurse (3-11 shift) Scott and White Meml. Hosp., Temple, Tex., 1966-71, dir. of nursing edn., 1975-76; sch. nurse Temple Ind. Sch. Dist., 1971-72; instr. Mary-Hardin Baylor Coll., Belton, Tex., 1972-74; asst. prof., clin. specialist U. Tex. Arlington, 1976-86; v.p. Budget Host Internat., Arlington, Tex., 1986-96, sr. v.p., 1996—, also bd. dirs., chmn. bd., owner. Recipient Amoco Outstanding Tchg. award, 1981. Mem. Sigma Theta Tau. Republican. Methodist. Avocations: reading, scrapbooks, crafts, piano. Office: Budget Host Internat Ste B 2307 Roosevelt Dr Arlington TX 76016-5865 Home Phone: 817-496-4449; Office Phone: 817-861-6088. Personal E-mail: dsawyer@airmail.net. Business E-Mail: dsawyer@budgethost.com.

SAWYER, DOROTHY, healthcare company executive; CEO Havasu Regional Med. Ctr.; regional dir. quality and resource mgmt., chief nursing officer Hosp. Corp. of America, 1988—2000; CEO Maryvale Hosp., Phoenix, 2000—04; pres. Ariz. market IASIS Healthcare Corp., 2008—. Office: IASIS Healthcare Corp Bldg E 117 Seaboard Ln Franklin TN 37067 Office Phone: 615-844-2747. Office Fax: 615-846-3006.

SAWYER, MARY CATHERINE, retired hospital administrator; b. Borger, Tex., Dec. 8, 1931; d. Andrew Rodgers and Mary Elizabeth (Slater) Hill; m. Edmond Eugene Sawyer, Aug. 26, 1963; children: Slater Shane, Anthony Barrett, Maronda Rae. BBA, Tex. Tech U., 1956; cert. in med. records, U. Tex. Med. Br., Galveston, 1957. Registered med. adminstr.; cert. coding specialist. Med. record adminstr. Taylor Hosp., Inc., Lubbock, Tex., 1957-63; pvt. practice cons. Paris, Tex., 1963-79; med. record adminstr., coding specialist St. Joseph's Hosp., Paris, 1979-98; ret., 1998. Mem. DAR (corr. sec. 1989-91, treas. 1991-93, 1st vice regent 1994-96, def. chmn. 1990-96), Gordon Country Club, Phi Gamma Nu. Methodist. Avocation: genealogy. Home: 216 Glover Deport TX 75435-2305

SAWYER, MICHAEL E., library director; b. Martinez, Calif., June 8, 1953; s. William and Shirley (Greenberg) Sawyer. BA in Hist. and Govt., Columbia Coll., Mo., 1974; MLS, U. Pitts., 1976, Cert. of advance study, 1978. Libr. Southern Ohio Correctional Facility, Lucasville, 1977-84; adminstrv. asst. Findlay-Hancock County Pub. Libr., Findlay, Ohio, 1984-85; libr. Chillicothe Correctional Inst., Ohio, 1985-89; dir. Auglaize County Pub. Dist. Libr., Wapakoneta, Ohio, 1989-92, Clinton Pub. Libr., Iowa, 1993-98, Northwestern Regional Libr., Elkin, NC, 1998—2003, Rangeview Libr. Dist., Thornton, Colo., 2003—07; dep. dir. Tulare County Libr., Visalia, Calif., 2007—08; dir. Calcasieu Parish Pub. Libr., Lake Charles, La., 2009—. Author: A Bibliographical Index of Five English Mystics, 1978; co-editor: Classics Jour., 1983—87; contbr. articles to profl. jours. Recipient Bill Butler Meml. award, 1987, US Jaycees Al Marish Meml. award, Correctional Edn. Assn., 1988, Exceptional Svc. award, Assn. Specialized & Coop. Libr. Agy.'s, 1989, Nat. Achievement Citation award, Pub. Libr. Assn., 1994, Future award, ALA Libr., 2002, Merit award, La. Libr. Assn., 2009—, Highsmith Libr. Innovation award, PLA, 2010; named an Outstanding Ohioan, Ohio Jaycees, 1988. Mem.: US JCI Senate (Ohio state pres. 1988—89, historian 1997—), Rotary Club. Office: Calcasieu Parish Pub Libr 301 W Claude St Lake Charles LA 70605 Office Phone: 337-721-7147. Business E-Mail: msawyer@calcasieu.lib.la.us.

SAWYER-MORSE, MARY KAYE, nutritionist, educator; b. Ft. Stockton, Tex. BA in Psychology, S.W. Tex. State U., 1978; MS in Nutrition, Incarnate Word Coll., 1987; PhD, U. Tex., 1997. Lic. dietitian. Nutrition svcs. con. Christian Sr. Svcs., 1985-87, exec. dir., 1987-90; nutrition svcs. cons. Alternative Adult Day Care Ctr., 1989-90; pvt. cons. dietitian, 1990—; cmty. dietitian Health Enhancement Ctr. Humana Hosp. Met., 1990-91; assoc. prof., dietetic program dir. U. Incarnate Word, San Antonio, 1991—2004; dir. Heath Mgmt., UMR, 2004—. Presenter Innovative Nutrition Svc. Model S.W. Tex. Gerontol. Soc. Ann. Meeting, 1988, Diabetic Homebound Svcs. Nat. Conf. Meals-On-Wheels Am., 1989; spkr. in field. Contbr. articles to profl. jours. Recipient Disting. Rsch. award, 1977, 1978, Acad. Excellence award, 1978, Women's Leadership award, YWCA, 1988, Creative Tchg./Rsch. award, 1994; named Tex. Dietetic Educator, 2003; grantee, U.S. Dept. Edn., 1997—2000; Carnation Corp. scholar, 1995. Mem.: Nat. Spkrs. Assn. (devel. dir. 2000—01, Tex. Dietetic Educator of the Yr. 2003), San Antonio Dist. Dietetic Assn., Tex. Dietetic Assn., Am. Dietetic Assn. (sec. 1990—92, mem. nominating com. 1993—94, dietetic educators practice group). Office Phone: 830-997-1552. Personal E-mail: morsemk@msn.com.

SAXON, DON B., state agency administrator; Grad., U. Fla., 1975. Investigative supr. Fla. Dept. Banking and Fin., 1979—81, dir. divsn. investigations, 1981—83, asst. dir. divsn. securities and investor protection, 1983—86, dir. divsn. securities and investor protection, 1986—2003; commr. Fla. Office Fin. Regulation, 2003—08. Recipient Blue Sky award, North Am. Securities Adminstrs. Assn., 1996, 2006. Office Phone: 850-410-9601. Office Fax: 850-410-9663. E-mail: Ofr@fldfs.com.

SAXON, FRANKLIN N., finance executive; b. Charlotte, NC, July 26, 1952; s. James H. and Frances (Shiver) S.; m. Abigail F. Stuckey, June 2, 1979 (div. Feb. 1982). BS in Acctg. with honors, U. N.C., Charlotte, 1977. CPA, N.C. Sr. auditor Coopers and Lybrand, Charlotte, 1979-81, audit supr., 1981-82, audit mgr., 1982-83; v.p., corp. controller Culp, Inc., High Point, N.C., 1983-85, v.p., chief fin. officer, 1985—98, CEO, 2007—. Bd. dirs. Culp, Inc., 2007—. Treas., bd. dirs. Community Health Assn., Charlotte, 1979-81; loaned exec. United Way, High Point, 1985. Scholarship grantee, U. N.C., 1967-77. Mem. Am. Inst. CPA's, N.C. Soc. CPA's, Fin. Execs. Inst. Republican. Presbyterian. Avocations: running, scuba diving, piano. Office: Culp Inc 101 S Main St High Point NC 27260-5239 Business E-Mail: franklin.saxon@culpinc.com.

SAY, BURHAN, retired physician; b. Istanbul, Turkey, Feb. 26, 1923; came to U.S. 1951; s. Ethem Serif and Ayse Say; m. Elizabeth E. Jackson, Nov. 5, 1955; children: Tony, Daniel Demir. MD, U. Istanbul, 1946. Diplomate Am. Bd. Pediatrics, Am. Bd. Med. Genetics. Asst. prof. pediatrics Hacettepe U., Ankara, Turkey, 1960-64, prof. pediatrics, 1964-73; clin. prof. of pediatrics U. of Okla./Tulsa Med. Coll., 1975—; ret. Dir. H.A. Chapman Inst., Tulsa, 1982—; v.p. Children's Med. Ctr., Tulsa, 1988—. Contbr. articles to profl. jours. Pres. Am. Cancer Soc., Tulsa, 1980-90, Great Plains Genetics Soc., Tulsa, 1993. Lt. Turkish Army, 1946-48, Turkey., Fulbright scholar, Boston, 1966—68. Avocation: sports. Home: 6216 E 99th St Tulsa OK 74137-5503 Home Phone: 918-299-5891. Personal E-mail: mbsay@cox.net.

SAYLES, LEONARD ROBERT, management educator, consultant; b. Rochester, NY, Apr. 30, 1926; s. Robert and Rose (Sklof) S.; m. Kathy Ripin; children: Robert, Emily. BA with highest distinction, U. Rochester, 1946; PhD in Econs. and Social Sci., MIT, 1950. Asst. prof. Cornell U., 1950-53, U. Mich., 1953-56; prof. emeritus Grad. Sch. Bus. Adminstrn., Columbia U., 1956-91, prof. bus. adminstrn., 1962—, head div. indsl. relations and orgnl. behavior, 1960-72; adviser to adminstr. NASA, 1966-71. Disting. vis. lectr. McGill U., 1974 Author: (with G. Strauss) The Local Union, 1953, Managerial Behavior, 1964, Human Behavior in Organizations, 1966, (with E. Chapple) Measure of Management, 1961, Behavior of Industrial Work Groups, 1958, Individualism and Big Business, 1963, (with W. Dowling) How Managers Motivate, 1971, (with M. Chandler) Managing Large Systems; Organizations for the Future, 1971, 2d edit., 1993, (with G. Strauss) Personnel, 4th edit, 1980, Managing Human Resources, 2d edit, 1981, Leadership, 1979, (with R. Burgelman) Inside Corporate Innovation, 1985, Managing in Real Organizations, 1989, The Working Leader, 1993, (with K. Ripin) Insider Strategies for Outsourcing Information Systems, 1999, (with C. Smith) The Rise of the Rogue Executive, 2004; mem. editorial bd. Human Orgn., 1957-62 Grant, Nat. Acad. Scis., 1968—70. Fellow Am. Anthropol. Assn.; mem. Phi Beta Kappa. Home Phone: 239-597-7840; Office Phone: 914-693-5158. Personal E-mail: lrsayles@gmail.com.

SAYLOR, MICHAEL J., computer software company executive; b. Lincoln, Nebr., Feb. 4, 1965; BS in Aeronautics & Astronautics, MIT, 1987, BS in Sci., Tech. & Soc. Cons. Federal Group, Inc., 1987—88; venture mgr. E.I. du Pont de Nemours & Co., 1988—89; pres. MicroStrategy, Inc., Vienna, Va., 1989—2000, co-founder, chmn. & CEO, 1989—, pres., 2005—. Named KPMG High Tech Entrepreneur of Yr., 1996, Ernst & Young Software Entrepreneur of Yr., 1997, one of Top 10 Entrepreneurs, Red Herring Mag., 1998; USAF scholar. Avocations: reading, music, studying history and architecture. Office: MicroStrategy Inc 1850 Towers Crescent Plz Vienna VA 22182-6230 Office Phone: 703-848-8600. Office Fax: 703-848-8610. Business E-Mail: msaylor@microstrategy.com.

SCABBIA GUERRINI, MARTINO, apparel executive; Held exec. positions TOD's SpA, Bruno Magli SpA; pres., internat. sportswear & packs VF Corp., Lugano, Switzerland, 2006—09, pres., Sportswear & Contemporary Brands EMEA Coalition, 2009—. Office: VF Corp 105 Corp Ctr Blvd Greensboro NC 27408 Office Phone: 336-424-6000. Office Fax: 336-547-7634. Business E-Mail: martino_scabbia_guerrini@vfc.com.

SCALISE, STEVE (STEPHEN JOSEPH SCALISE), United States Representative from Louisiana, former state legislator; b. New Orleans, Oct. 6, 1965; m. Jennifer Letulle; children: Madison Carol, Harrison Joseph. BS in Computer Programming, La. State U. Software engr., computer programmer, La.; mem. Dist. 82 La. House of Reps., 1996—2007; mem. Dist. 9 La. State Senate, 2008; mem. US Congress from 1st La. Dist., 2008—; chmn. Republican Study Com., 2013—. Bd. mem. Teach For America, New Orleans, American Italian Renaissance Found., Jefferson Sr. Ctr. Recipient Letter of Commendation, US Naval Reserve, Disting. Svc. award, La. Restaurant Assn., Patrick F. Taylor Rep. Leadership award, Bus. Champion award, New Orleans Regional Chamber of Commerce, Outstanding Legislator award, Victims & Citizens Against Crime; named Legislator of Yr., Alliance for Good Govt. Jefferson/New Orleans chap., Citizens Against Lawsuit Abuse, 1999, New Orleans Regional Chamber of Commerce, 2001, Man of Yr., Associated Builders & Contractors, 2001; named a, Ctrl. Metairie Chap. AARP, 1998; named one of The 50 Politicos to Watch, Politico, 2010. Mem.: Young Leadership Coun. New Orleans, La. Young Rep. Republican. Roman Catholic. Office: US House of Representatives 2338 Rayburn House Office Bldg Washington DC 20215 Office Phone: 202-225-3015. Office Fax: 202-226-0386.*

SCANLON, CHARLES FRANCIS, retired military officer, writer, publisher, consultant; b. Nashville, Jan. 31, 1935; s. Francis James Gordon and Dorothy Rose (Compton) S.; m. Barbara Coddington Wall Scanlon, June 18, 2005; children: Teri, Brett, Ashlyn, Kellie. BA in Polit. Sci., U. Fla., 1960; grad., Command and Gen. Staff Coll., Ft. Leavenworth, Kans., 1970, Naval War Coll., Newport, RI, 1977; MA in Am. Studies, U. Hawaii, 1974; postgrad., Pa. State U., 1982, Harvard U., 1984, postgrad., 1992. Commd. 2d lt. U.S. Army, 1960, advanced through grades to maj. gen., 1988; chief collection U.S. Army Europe, Heidelberg, Germany, 1977-78; comdg. officer 66th Mil. Intelligence Brigade, Munich, 1978-80; chief ops. U.S. Army Intelligence and Security Command, Arlington, Va., 1980-82; exec. officer Dept. Army Asst. Chief Staff Intelligence, Washington, 1982-83; dep. commdr. gen. U.S. Army Intelligence and Security Command, Arlington, 1983-85; dir. estimates Def. Intelligence Agy., Washington, 1985-86, dir. attaches, 1986-90; comdg. gen. U.S. Army Intelligence and Security Command, Ft. Belvoir, Va., 1990-93; ret., 1993; pres. Internat. Security, Counterintelligence Cons. Svcs., Fairfax Station, Va., 1993—, Satellite Beach, Fla., 1993—99, Melbourne Beach, Fla., 1999—, Indian Harbour Beach, Fla., 2004—. Decorated Def. D.S.M., Army D.S.M., Nat. Intelligence D.S.M., Legion of Merit with 3 oak leaf clusters, Bronze Star with 2 oak leaf clusters; elected to U.S. Mil. Intelligence Hall of Fame, 1995. Mem. Assn. US Army, Nat. Mil. Intelligence Assn. (pres. 1974-76), 101st Airborne Divsn. Assn., Berlin US Military Vets. Assn., Def. Intelligence Alumni Assn., Sigma Nu, Wuesthoff Health Sys. Found. (bd. mem. 2007-10), Health 1st Found.(bd. mem. 2011-). Presbyterian. Avocations: boating, scuba diving, racquetball, soaring, reading. Home and Office: 208 Lanternback Island Dr Satellite Beach FL 32937 Personal E-mail: chuckscanlon@aol.com.

SCANLON, GEORGE PATRICK, insurance industry executive, accountant; b. Chgo., Sept. 29, 1957; s. George Patrick and Ann Marie (McInerney) S. BBA, U. Notre Dame, 1979; MBA in Fin., U. Miami, 1984. CPA, Ill., Fla. Sr. acct. Price Waterhouse, Chgo., 1979-82, sr. analyst corp. audit dept., 1982-84, mgr. corp. audit dept., 1984-85, sr. mgr. control analysis dept., 1985-87; div. controller, aviation leasing and svcs. div. Aviation Sales Co., Inc., Miami, 1988-90; sr. mgr. acquisition control Ryder Sys., Inc., Miami, Fla., 1982, dir. corp. acctg., 1990-91, group dir. audit svcs., 1991-93, group dir. corp. planning, 1993-95, v.p. corp. planning, 1995-97, sr. v.p. corp. planning, contr., 1997-2000; CFO Seisint, Inc., Boca Raton, Fla., 2000—01, DataCore Software Corp., Ft. Lauderdale, Fla., 2001—04; exec. v.p., CFO, also prin. acctg. officer Levitt Corp., Ft. Lauderdale, Fla., 2004—08; exec. v.p., CFO BFC Fin. Corp., Ft. Lauderdale, Fla., 2007; exec. v.p. fin., CEO Fidelity National Information Services, Inc., Jacksonville, Fla., 2008—10; COO Fidelity National Financial, Inc., Jacksonville, Fla., 2010, CEO, 2010—. Mem. Am. Inst. CPA's, Fla. Inst. CPA's. Clubs: Notre Dame (Miami) (bd. dirs. 1986-95, treas.). Roman Catholic. Avocations: golf, baseball. Office: Fidelity Nat Fin 601 Riverside Ave Jacksonville FL 32204 Business E-Mail: george.scanlon@fnf.com.

SCARBOROUGH, ROBERT HENRY, JR., entrepreneur; b. Hawkinsville, Ga., Mar. 12, 1923; s. Robert Henry and Janet Augusta (Burton) S.; m. Walterene Brant, July 1, 1946; children— Robert Henry, James Burton BS, U.S. Mcht. Marine Acad., 1944; BBA, U. Hawaii, 1969, MBA, 1971; MS, George Washington U., 1971, Armed Forces Staff Coll., 1963, Nat. War Coll., 1971. Commd. lt. (j.g.) USCG, 1949; advanced through grades to vice adm., 1978; chief Office of Ops. USCG, 1974-75, chief of staff, 1975-77, comdr. 9th Coast Guard Dist., 1977-78, vice comdt. Washington, 1978-82, ret., 1982; exec. dir. Navy League U.S., 1982-84; pres. Polaris Potomac Corp., 1985-96. Entrepreneur, 1996—. With USNR, 1942-49 Decorated DSM, Legion of Merit. Mem. Beta Gamma Sigma Office: 5357 37th St N Arlington VA 22207-1312

SCARBOROUGH, WALLACE BERRY, state legislator; b. Charleston, SC, Mar. 25, 1959; s. Robert B. and Elizabeth M. Scarborough; m. Mary Ann Middleton, Nov. 17, 1984; children: Sam, Ross. BS, The Citadel, 1981. Exec. Atlantic Coast Life Ins. Co.; SC State Rep., Dist. 115 SC Ho. of Reps., 2000—, member Agriculture & Natural Resources Committee, chairman, Freshman Caucus, currently. Athletic adv. com. Citadel, 1995—98; chmn. entertainment com. Coastal Carolina Fair, 1998—2000; chmn. Adopt-A-Hwy., Charleston County, 1992—95; chmn. bd. dirs. Trident Acad., 1994—96. Assn. of Citadel, 1st Congressional Dist., 92-95; mem., Citadel Athletic Advisor Committee, 95-98; chairman, Coastal Carolina Fair Entertainment Committee, 98-2000; chairman South Carolina Life, Accident & Health Ins Guaranty Assn., 98-2000; chairman, Adopt-A-Highway, Charleston Co, 92-95. South Carolina Exchange Club; Exchange Club of Charleston (president, 97-98). Republican. Office: State Capitol 306 C Blatt Bldg Columbia SC 29211

SCARMINACH, CHARLES ANTHONY, lawyer; b. Syracuse, NY, Feb. 19, 1944; s. John Louis and Lucy (Egnoto) S.; children: John, Catherine, Karen, Charles, Robert. BA in History, U. Buffalo, 1965; JD, Syracuse U., 1968. Bar: N.Y. 1968, S.C. 1974. Gen. counsel Sea Pines Co., Hilton Head Island, S.C., 1973-78; sole practice Hilton Head Island, 1978-83; ptnr. Novit & Scarminach, P.A., Hilton Head Island, 1983-93, Novit Scarminach & Williams P.A., Hilton Head Island, 1993—2002, Novit, Scarminach & Akins, P.A., Hilton Head Island, 2003—06, Novit & Scarminach PA, Hilton Head Island, 2006—. Bd. dirs. Nations Bank, Hilton Head Island. Chmn. bd. Sea Pines Montessori Sch., Hilton Head Island, 1979-83; bd. trustees Hilton Head Preparatory Sch., 1984-93, chmn. bd. trustees 1986-93; bd. dirs. Hilton Head Island Cmty. Found., 2005-11, Low County Legal Aid, 2003-09. Capt. US Army, 1968—73, major USAR, 1973—82. Mem. ABA, S.C. Bar Assn., N.Y. State Bar Assn., Hilton Head Island C. of C. (bd. dirs. 1996-99), Sea Pines Club. Roman Catholic. Home: 10 Wood Duck Ct Hilton Head Island SC 29928-3010 Office: Novit & Scarminach PA PO Drawer 14 Hilton Head Island SC 29938-0014 Office Phone: 843-785-5850. Business E-Mail: cscarminach@ns-lawfirm.com.

SCARRITT, THOMAS VARNON, newspaper editor; b. Tuscaloosa, Ala., Jan. 28, 1953; s. Charles Wesley and Valerie (Varnon) S.; m. Kathryn Rush Hubbard, Dec. 28, 1973; children: Sara Kathryn, Thomas Varnon Jr. BA in Journalism, U. N.C., 1974; MBA, Samford U., 1995. Reporter The Birmingham (Ala.) News, 1975-79, Washington corr., 1979-83, news editor, 1983-85, editl. page editor, 1986-89, exec. editor, 1989-97, editor, 1997—. Bd. dirs. Workshops Inc. Mem. Am. Soc. Newspaper Editors, Soc. Profl. Journalists, Kiwanis (Birmingham), Phi Beta Kappa. Episcopal. Home: 4240 Clairmont Ave S Birmingham AL 35222-3724 Office: The Birmingham News 2201 4th Ave N Birmingham AL 35203-3840 Home Phone: 205-591-4109; Office Phone: 205-325-2205. E-mail: tscarritt@bhamnews.com.

SCARWID, DIANA ELIZABETH, actress; b. Savannah, Ga. d. Anthony and Elizabeth Scarwid. Grad., Am. Acad. Dramatic Arts, 1975; degree in Theater Arts, Acting, Pace U., 1975. Appeared in films including Pretty Baby, Honeysuckle Rose, Inside Moves, (Oscar award nomination Best Supporting Actress), Mommie Dearest, Rumble Fish, Strange Invaders, Silkwood, Psycho III, Extremeties, Heat, Neon Bible, The Cure, Gold Diggers: The Secret of Bear Mountain, What Lies Beneath, The Angel Doll, A Guy Thing, Party Monster, The Clearing; TV films include Thou Shalt Not Kill, Studs Lonigan, Guyana Tragedy: The Story of Jim Jones, Desperate Lives, A Bunny's Tale, After the Promise, Night of The Hunter, Critical Choices, Bastard Out of Carolina, Angel of Pennsylvania Avenue, Truman (Emmy nomination), If These Walls Could Talk, Ruby Bridges Story, also mini-series From the Earth to the Moon, Before He Wakes; theater prodns. include Key Exchange, Toronto, Can., A Thousand Clowns, Jupiter, Fla., Gethsamanie Springs, Mark Taper Forum, LA, Spoon River Anthology, Ring 'round the Moon, NYC, Nat. Shakespeare Conservancy, NY; (TV films) Down Will Come Baby, Dirty Pictures, Path to War, (series) WonderFalls, Cold Case Lost Law & Order Criminal Mind Heroes, 2009-10 Avocations: reading, bicycling, crabbing, walking.

SCELFO, CHRIS, professional football coach; b. Abbeville, La., Sept. 30, 1963; m. Nancy Caldwell; children: Sarah Beth, Joseph II. BS, Northeast La. U., 1986, MEd, 1988. Asst. coach River Oaks HS, Monroe, La., 1986; grad. asst. Northeast La. U. Indians, 1986-87, U. Okla. Sooners, Norman, 1988—89; offensive line coach Marshall U. Thundering Herd, 1990-95, offensive coord., 1993-95; asst. head coach, offensive line coach U. Ga. Bulldogs, Augusta, 1996-98; head football coach Tulane U. Green Wave, New Orleans, 1998—2006; tight ends coach Atlanta Falcons, 2008—. Co-author: Fourth and New Orleans. Named to Italian Am. Hall of Fame. Office: Atlanta Falcons 4400 Falcon Pky Flowery Branch GA 30542

SCHAAR, SUSAN CLARKE, legislative staff member; d. Garland Lewis and Frances Virginia (Matthews) Clarke; m. William Berkley Schaar, Jr., Nov. 24, 1990. BA, U. Richmond, 1972. Engrossing clk. Senate of Va., Richmond, 1974, legis. rsch. analyst, 1974-77, asst. to the clk., 1977-83, asst. clk., 1983-90, clk., 1990—. Vice chair legis. effectiveness com. Nat. Conf. State Legis., 1996—98, chair, 1998—99, mem. exec. com., 1999—2002, staff vice chmn. standing com., 2002—03, staff vice chair, 2004—05, staff chair, 2005—06; exec. com. Mason's Manual Commn. Mem. model gen. assembly adv. com. YMCA, Richmond, 1990—; bd. trustee U. Richmond, 1990—94, bd. assocs., 1995—2005; pres. Richmond Club Westhampton, 1988—90; bd. dirs. Spider Club Athletic Club, Richmond, 1988—90; govt. counselor Va. Girls State, bd. dirs.; mem. Va. Capitol Found., 2004—. Recipient Disting. Svc. award, U. Richmond, 1994, Legis. Staff Achievement award, NCSL, 2003, Honor award, Richmond Chpt. AIA, Legis. Achievement award, Am. Soc. Legis. Clks. and Secs., 2009, Richmond Bar Liberty award, 2010. Mem.: Coun. Preservation Capitol Sq., Am. Soc. Legis. Clks. and Secs. (mem. exec. com. 1995—99, sec.-treas. 1996, pres.-elect 1997, pres. 1997—98, past pres. 1998—99), Pi Sigma Alpha, Omicron Delta Kappa. Baptist. Office: Senate of Va PO Box 396 Richmond VA 23218-0396 Business E-Mail: sschaar@sov.state.va.us.

SCHABEL, SHAWN S., healthcare industry executive; Degree in Respiratory Therapy, Wichita State U. Joined Lincare Holdings, Inc., 1989, sr. v.p., 1998—2001, COO, 2001—, pres., 2003—. Bd. dirs. Odyssey HealthCare, Inc., 2003—10. Office: Lincare Holdings Inc 19387 US 19 N Clearwater FL 33764 Office Phone: 727-530-7700. Office Fax: 727-532-9692. Business E-Mail: sschabel@lincare.com.

SCHAEFER, BONNIE (E. BONNIE SCHAEFER), retail executive; b. Chgo., Mar. 16, 1963; d. Rowland Schaefer. From sales assoc. to store mgr. Claire's Stores, Inc., 1987—90, v.p., real estate, 1994—2002, bd. dirs., 1998—, co-vice chmn., 1999—2002, co-chmn., co-CEO, 2002—. Bd. dirs. Claire's Nippon. Office: Claires Stores Inc 3 SW 129th Ave Pembroke Pines FL 33027 Office Phone: 954-433-3900. Office Fax: 954-433-3999.

SCHAEFER, GORDON EMORY, food products executive; b. 1932; married. BS, Marquette U., 1956. CPA Wis. With Peat, Marwick, Mitchell & Co., 1955-59; contr., sec. Wells Badger, Badger Carton Co., 1960—64; treas. Pabst Brewing Co., Milw., 1965-72, v.p. adminstrn., 1972-75, v.p. ops., 1975—80, exec. v.p. ops, 1980—85, dir.; pres., dir. Krier Foods Inc., Belgium, Wis., 1981-85, Corrs Beverages, Chgo., 1985-86; dir. bus. devel. Lakeside Packing Co., Manitowoc, Wis., 1989-92; mng. dir. Robertson Assocs., Mfg. Europe Ltd., Cardiff, Wales, 1993-94. Bd. dirs. Fox Fin. Co., Berg Industries, Inc.; fin. and ops. cons. Home: 12600 N Port Washington Rd Apt 3210 Mequon WI 53092-3475 Personal E-mail: gordy5069@yahoo.com.

SCHAEFER, HENRY FREDERICK, III, chemistry professor; b. Grand Rapids, Mich., June 8, 1944; s. Henry Frederick Jr. and Janice Christine (Trost) S.; m. Karen Regine Rasmussen, Sept. 2, 1966; children: Charlotte, Pierre, Theodore, Rebecca, Caleb. BS in Chem. Physics, MIT, 1966; PhD in Chem. Physics, Stanford U., 1969; D (hon.), U. Plovdiv, 1998, U. Sofia, 1999, Beijing Inst. Tech., 1999, Huntington U., 2002, North-Eastern Hill U., Shillong, India, 2008, Babes-Bolyai U., Cluj-Napoca, Romania, 2009. From asst. prof. to prof. chemistry U. Calif., Berkeley, 1969—87; Graham Perdue prof., dir. Ctr. for Computational Quantum Chemistry U. Ga., Athens, 1987—. Apptd. Professeur d'Echange U. Paris, 1977, Gastprofessor Eidgenössische Technische Hochshule, Zürich, 1994, 95, 97, 2000, 02, 04, 06, 08, 10; prof., Ludwig Maximilian U., Munich, 2012, 2013, 14; Wilfred T. Doherty prof., dir. Inst. Theoretical Chemistry, U. Tex., Austin, 1979-80, chemistry prof. emeritus U. Calif., Berkeley, 2004-; lectr. in field. Author: Science and Christianity: Conflict or Coherence? 2010; contbr. articles to profl. jours. including Electronic Structure of Atoms and Molecules: A Survey of Rigorous Quantum Mechanical Results, 1972, Modern Theoretical Chemistry, 1977, Quantum Chemistry, 1983, A New Dimension to Quantum Chemistry, 1994; editor Molecular Physics, 1991-94, editor in chief, 1995-2005. Recipient Pure Chemistry award Am. Chem. Soc., 1979, Leo Hendrik Baekeland award, 1983, Schrödinger Medal, 1990, Centenary medal Royal Soc. Chemistry, London, 1992, Gold medal Comenius U., Bratislava, Slovakia, 2000, Biennial Gold medal U. Sofia, 2009; Sloan fellow, 1972, Guggenheim fellow, 1976-77; named one of 100 Outstanding Young Scientists in Am., Sci. Digest, 1984, named 3d Most Highly cited chemist in world Science Watch, 1992. Fellow AAAS, IUPAC, Am. Phys. Soc., Am. Sci. Affiliation, Am. Acad. Arts and Scis., Royal Soc. Chemistry (London), Am. Chem. Soc. (Peter Debye award, 2014); mem. Internat. Acad. Quantum Molecular Sci., Am. Chem. Soc. (chmn. divsn. phys. chemistry 1992, award in theoretical chemistry 2003, Ira M. Remsen award 2003, Ide P. Trotter prize Tex. A&M U., 2011), World Assn. Theoretical and Computational Chemists (pres. 1996-2005, Joseph O. Hirschfelder prize, 2005, Biennial Grand award, Sofia U. 2008, Alexander von Humboldt award 2012, SURA Disting. Scientist award 2012), Am. Inst. Chemists (Chem. Pioneer award, 2013). Presbyterian. Office: U Ga Ctr Computational Quantum Chemistry Athens GA 30602 Office Phone: 706-542-2067. Business E-Mail: qc@uga.edu.

SCHAEFFER, ANDREW, lawyer; b. Cin., July 31, 1974; BA in Economics, Thomas More Coll., 1996, BA in Hist., 1996, AA in Pre-legal Studies, 1996; JD, U. Ky. Coll. of Law, 1999. Bar: Western Dist. Ky. 1999, Ky. 1999, US Dist. Ct. Eastern Dist. Ky. 2000. Atty. Greenebaum Doll & McDonald PLLC, Cin. Vol. firefighter Burlington Fire Protection Dist., 1990—2000, vice chair, 2002—; trustee Thomas More Coll., 1994—96, mem., Found. Bd. Exec. Com., 1999—; fundraiser United Way Ann. Campaign, 2001; mem., Adv. Com. Conrad and Gunpower Creek Park, 2001—02; fundraiser Muscular Dystrophy Assn., 2002; pres. LEGACY, 2003; co-chair Vision 2015. Named one of 40 Under 40, Cin. Bus. Courier, 2005, Ohio's Rising Stars, Super Lawyers, 2005, 2006. Mem.: Cin. Bar Assn., Northern Ky. Bar Assn., Ky. Bar Assn. (mem., Exec. Com. 2000—, chair, Young Lawyers Sect., mem., Ann. Conv. Planning and CLE Com. 2001—02), ABA (mem., The Young Lawyer Editl. Bd. 2001, vice-chair, Ethics & Professionalism Com. 2001, mem., Del. Credentials Com. 2002—, mem., Resolutions Com. 2002—, chair, Young Lawyers Divsn. Nat. Conf. Team 2004, mem., Leadership Adv. Bd. 2004—, prog. dir., Young Lawyers Divsn. Affiliate Outreach 2005—06). Office: Greenebaum Doll & McDonald PLLC River-Center I 50 E RiverCenter Blvd Ste 1800 Covington KY 41012-2673 Office Phone: 859-655-4200. Office Fax: 859-655-4239.

SCHAEFFER, ERIC D., theater director, performing company executive; b. 1964; BFA, Kutztown U.; continued studies, Crew and Alsager Coll. Visual Arts, Eng. Co-founder, artistic dir. Signature Theatre, Arlington, Va., 1990—; artistic dir. Sondheim Celebration Kennedy Ctr., Washington, 2002, founder Overtures musical theatre inst., 2003. Dir.: (plays) Sweeney Todd, 1991 (Helen Hayes award for Outstanding Musical and Dir., 1992), 2002, Assasins, 1992 (Helen Hayes award for Outstanding Musical and Dir., 1993), Into the Woods, 1994 (Helen Hayes award for Outstanding Musical, 1995), Cabaret, 1995, Passion, 1996 (Helen Hayes award for Outstanding Musical and Dir., 1997), 2002, Sunday in the Park with George, 1997, 2002, Sweet Adeline, 1997, A Little Night Music, 1997, The Rhythm Club, 1998, 2000, Putting It Together, 1998, Witches of Eastwick, 2000, The Gospel According to Fishman, 2002, 110 in the Shade, 2003, Follies, 2003, The Christmas Carol Rag, 2003, Twentieth Century, 2003, Allegro, 2004 (Helen Hayes award for Outstanding Musical and Dir., 2005), One Red Flower, 2004, The Highest Yellow, 2004, Pacific Overtures, 2005; (Broadway plays) Putting It Together, 1999, Glory Days, 2008. Recipient Elizabeth Campbell award for Arts in Arlington, Honored Citizen award, Arlington Sch. Bd., Jonathan Larson Performing Arts Found. award, Profl. Mentor prize, Duke Ellington Sch. Arts; named a Washingtonian of Yr., 2002. Office: Signature Theatre 4200 Campbell Ave Arlington VA 22206 Office Phone: 571-527-1860. Office Fax: 703-845-0236.

SCHAFER, ELIZABETH DIANE, historian, writer; b. Opelika, Ala., Sept. 26, 1965; d. Robert Louis and Carolyn Louise (Henn) S; m. Sean Fitzgerald Allen. BA in History cum laude, Auburn U., 1986, MA in History of Sci., 1988, PhD in History of Tech. magna cum laude, 1993; MA summa cum laude, Hollins Coll., 2003; MFA summa cum laude, Hollins U. Archivist Lee County Hist. Soc. Mus., 1988—. Ind. scholar, 1993—; presenter in field. Author: Exploring Harry Potter, 2000, Lake Martin: Alabama's Crown Jewel, 2002, Auburn: Plainsmen, Tigers and War Eagles, 2003, Auburn Football, 2004; co-author: Women Who Made A Difference in Alabama, 1995, (hist. overview) Alabama Veterinary Medical Assocation Celebrating 100 Years 1907-2007, 2007; cons. editor Ency. of Sci., 1998; freelance editor various tech. docs.; editl. asst. Proceedings of the We. Soc. for French History, 1988-91, Nat. Forum: The Phi Kappa Phi Jour., 1990-91; contbr. History News Svc.; reviewer Children's Lit. database, Magills Literary Annual, 2011, 12; contbr. articles to profl. jours., encys., mags., chpts. to books, Magills Literary Annual, 2011, 2012, 2013. Recipient hon. mention poetry Writer's Digest, 1994 hon. mention children's non-fiction, 1997, children's non-fiction and fiction, 1998, Writer's Digest, Shirley Henn Meml. award Critical scholar, Hollins Coll., 1998. Mem. AAAS, AAUW, Am. Hist. Assn., Orgn. Am. Historians, Soc. History Tech., History Sci. Soc., Women's History Network, N.Y. Acad. Scis., So. Hist. Assn., Soc. Children's Book Writers and Illustrators, Children's Lit. Network, Ala. Poetry Soc., Children's Lit. Assn., Ala. Writer's Forum, Authors Guild, Lancaster Mennonite Hist. Soc., Lee County Hist. Soc. (life mem.), Auburn U. Alumni Assn. (life), Descs. Mex. War Vets., DAR (chpt. historian), Mystery writers of America, Phi Alpha Theta.

SCHAFER, JAMES ARTHUR, physiologist; b. Buffalo, Oct. 10, 1941; s. Joseph James and Gladys Lita (Lighty) S.; m. Margaret Anne Schiefer, Aug. 16, 1964; children: James Arthur Jr., Kirsten Ann. BS, U. Mich., 1963, PhD, 1968. Postdoctoral fellow Gustav-Embden Ctr., Frankfurt, Germany, 1968-69, Duke U., Durham, NC, 1969-70; asst. prof. U. Ala., Birmingham, 1970-72, assoc. prof., 1972-76, prof., 1976—2004, prof. emeritus, 2004—, sr. scientist Nephrology Rsch. and Tng. Ctr. Birmingham, 1980—. Author: (with H. Valtin) Renal Function. Mechanisms Preserving Fluid and Solute Balance in Health, 3d edit., 1994; editor Am. Jour. Physiology: Renal, 1983-89, mem. editl. bd., 2001-07; assoc. editor News in Physiol. Scis., 1997-03; cons. editor Jour. Clin. Investigation, 1998-03; mem. editl bd. Jour. Gen. Physiology, 1979-97, adv. editor, 1998-2007; mem. editl. bd. Kidney Internat., 1990-95; author textbooks on physiology; editor sci. monographs in Membrane Transport in Biology, 1992, Methods in Membrane and Transporter Research, 1994; contbr. articles to profl. jours. Chmn. rsch. com. Nat. Kidney and Urol. Diseases Adv. Bd. U.S. Dept. HHS, 1987-90. Fellow Jane Coffin Childs Meml., 1968-69; recipient Robert F. Pitts. Meml. award Internat. Union Physiol. Scis., Sydney, Australia, 1983, Homer W. Smith award Am. Soc. Nephrology and NY Heart Assn., 1993, Max Planck-Von Humboldt Rsch. award, Govt. of Germany, 1994. Mem. Am. Physiol. Soc. (councilor 1992-95, pres.-elect 1995-96, pres. 1996-97, past pres. 1997-98, Carl W. Gottschalk award 2001, Robert W. Berliner award 2004, Roy G. Daggs award, 2013), Am. Soc. Nephrology (sec.-treas. 1989-92, councilor 1992-95), Am. Soc. Clin. Investigation (hon.), Fedn. Am. Socs. Exptl. Biology (bd. dirs. 1995-99, exec. com. 1996-97, pub. affairs exec. com. 1997-99), Am. Heart Assn. (Established Investigator award, 1971-76), Biophys. Soc., Int. Soc. Nephrol., Soc. Gen. Physiol. Avocations: classical music, mountain hiking, skiing. Office: U Ala Dept Phys & Biophysics 834 MCLM Bldg 1918 University Blvd Birmingham AL 35294-0005 Office Phone: 205-934-7106.

SCHAFER, JOHN STEPHEN, poet; b. NYC, Sept. 5, 1934; s. Stephen James and Siiri (Halmi) S.; m. Gertrud Rosa Fleischmann, June 14, 1958; children: Sylvia F., John Stephen, Karen D., Kristen H. BA, Rutgers U., 1956, MBA, 1963. Advt. research mgr. Union Carbide Corp., NYC, 1959—65; rsch. mgr. Bus. Week, NYC, 1965—66; v.p. Opinion Rsch. Corp., Princeton, NJ, 1966—80; pres. Am. Econ. Found., Cleve., 1981—2002, trustee, 1975—2002; v.p., dir. Ams. for Competitive Enterprise System, Phila., 1970-82. Editor: Linde Electric Welding Progress, 1959-62, ORC Pub. Opinion Index, 1968-72, AEF Straight Talk, 1981-82, Bellcore Exch., 1993-94; works pub. in Famous Poems of the Twentieth Century, 1996, Perceptions in Harmony, 1998, The Communicator, 2000-08, Best Poems and Poets of 2003, 2004, endtimepoet.wordpress.com. Polit. pollster Ed Clark for U.S. Pres., 1980; chmn. N.J. Libertarian party, 1983; nat. dir. U.S. Jaycees, 1965-66, v.p. N.J., 1964-65. Served to 1st lt. U.S. Army, 1957-59. Mem. Jr. Chamber Internat. (hon. life), Philosophean Soc., Scabbard and Blade, Delta Phi Alpha Home: 114 Walton Palm Rd Panama City FL 32413-7311

SCHAFERMEYER, ROBERT WILLIAM, emergency physician, educator, health policy consultant; s. William Jacob and Virginia Rose S.; m. An-ping Yuan, May 12, 1973; children: Christina, David, Matthew, Joseph. Student, St. Louis U., 1966-69; MD, U. Mo., Columbia, 1973. Diplomate Am. Bd. Emergency Medicine, Am. Bd. Pediats., sub-bd. pediat. emergency medicine. With. dept. emergency medicine East Tenn. Children's Hosp., Knoxville, 1979—81; mem. dept. emergency medicine Carolinas Med. Ctr., Charlotte, NC, 1981—; clin. assoc. prof. pediats. U. N.C. Sch. Medicine, Chapel Hill, 1981-85, clin. prof. emergency medicine and pediats., 1994—; assoc. chair dept. emergency medicine Carolinas Med. Ctr., Charlotte, 1982—, chief dept., 2007—13, prof. emeritus dept. emergency medicine. Prof. cons., lectr. and writer, sr. editor Pediat. Emergency Medicine by McGraw Hill, editor Chief PEMSoft by EBSCO, past pres., past bd. mem. Am. Coll. Emergency Physicians, past bd. mem. Soc. Academic Emergency Medicine. Assoc. editor: Pediatric Emergency Medicine Concepts and Clinical Practice, 1992; editor: Pediatric Emergency Medicine: A Comprehensive Study Guide, 1995, 2002, 3rd edit., 2009; contbr. articles and revs. to profl. jours. including Annals Emergency Medicine Jour.; reviewer Pediat. Emergency Medicine, Acad. Emergency Medicine; past mem. editl. bd. Pediat. Emergency Med. Jour., sr. editor fourth edit. Pediatric Emergency Medicine by McGraw Hill. Com. mem. MEMAC Adv., Mecklenberg County, 1991-93; mem. task force Drug Abuse for County Commrs., Mecklenberg, 1989-90. Lt. commdr. USPHS, 1974—76, inactive res., 1976—2012. Recipient: John G Wiegenstein Leadership award, ACEP, George Podgorny Svc. award NC Coll. Emergency Physicians. Fellow Am. Coll. Emergency Physicians (bd. dirs. 1994-2002, pres.-elect 1999-2000, pres. 2000-01, past pres. 2001-02, Weigenstein Outstanding Leadership award 2004)); mem. Am. Acad. Pediats., NC chpt. Am. Coll. Emergency Physicians (councillor 1984-94, bd. dirs. 1983-89, pres. 1986-88, Leadership/Svc. award 1988, George Podgorny Emergency Medicine Svc. award 1996), Soc. Acad. Emergency Medicine (bd. dirs. 2004-07), Mecklenburg County Med. Soc. (bd. dirs. 2009-, pres. elect 2010). Roman Catholic. Avocations: tae kwan do, photography, skiing, gardening. Office: Carolinas Med Ctr 1000 Blythe Blvd Charlotte NC 28203-5812 Office Phone: 704-355-3181.

SCHAFFER, GREGORY PAUL, information technology executive, former federal agency administrator; b. 1963; BA, George Washington U., Washington, 1985; JD, U. Southern Calif. Law Sch., L.A., 1988. Assoc. Skadden, Arps, Slate, Meagher & Flom, 1988—91; assoc. counsel Manatt, Phelps & Phillips LLP, 1991—93, ptnr., 1994—97; assoc. counsel Oldaker, Ryan & Leonard, 1993—94; trial atty. criminal divsn. computer crime & intellectual property sect. US Dept. Justice, Washington, 1997—99; dir. cybercrime prevention & response practice PricewaterhouseCoopers, LLP, 1999—2004; chief info. security officer Alltel Comm., LLC, 2004—06, chief security officer, 2006—07, sr. v.p., chief risk officer, 2007—09; asst. sec. cybersecurity & comm. US Dept. Homeland Security, Washington, 2009—12, 2009—11, acting dep. under sec., nat. protection & programs directorate, 2011; exec. v.p., chief info. security officer Fidelity Nat. Info. Services, Little Rock, 2012—. Office: Fidelity National Information Services 601 Riverside Ave Jacksonville FL 32204 Office Phone: 904-438-6000.*

SCHAFFNER, WILLIAM, medical educator; b. Jersey City, Aug. 12, 1937; BA, Yale U., New Haven, 1957; MD, Cornell U. Med. Coll., NYC, 1962. Diplomate Am. Bd. Internal Medicine, Am. Bd. Preventive Medicine, cert. in infectious diseases. Intern, resident then fellow infectious diseases Vanderbilt U. Med. Ctr., Nashville, 1962—66; epidemic intelligence svc. officer Ctrs. Disease Control, USPHS, 1966—68; faculty Vanderbilt U. Sch. Medicine, 1969—, chief divsn. infectious diseases, 1982—89, now prof. preventive medicine, medicine and infectious diseases and chmn. dept. preventive medicine, Harvic Branscomb disting. prof., 2010. Bd. dirs. Nat. Found. Infectious Diseases, pres., 2010—12; mem. steering com. Nat. Network Immunization Info.; pub. health policy & communicable disease control cons. Tenn. Dept. Health. Mem. editl. bd. Clin. Rsch., 1974—84, Infection, 1985—, Am. Jour. Epidemiology, 1987—97, European Jour. Clin. Microbiology & Infectious Diseases, 1993—2007, sr. assoc. editor Infection Control & Hosp. Epidemiology, 1981—, assoc. editor Jour. Infectious Diseases, 2003—; contbr. articles to profl. jours., chapters to books. Recipient Philip S. Brachman award, Ctrs. Disease Control, 1985, William J. Darby award, Vanderbilt U. Sch. Medicine, 2005, Alumni award, Weill Cornell Med. Coll., 2010, Ronald Davis award, Am. Coll. Preventive Medicine, 2010, Sedwick Meml. medal, APHA, 2010, Duncan Clk. award, Assn. Prevention Tchg. and Rsch., 2011; Ford Found. Scholar, Yale U., 1953—57, Fulbright Scholar, Albert Ludwigs U., Freiburg, Germany, 1957—58. Fellow: Infectious Diseases Soc. America (bd. dirs. 2000—03, Walter Stamm Mentor award 2011); mem.: ACP (master mem., James D. Bruce award 2009), Am. Soc. Microbiology (chair divsn. nosocomial infections 1983—84), Soc. Healthcare Epidemiology America (pres. 1983, Lecturer award 1996). Office: Vanderbilt University Med Ctr Office Ste 2600 Village at Vanderbilt 1500 21st Ave S Nashville TN 37212 Office Phone: 615-322-2037. Business E-Mail: william.schaffner@vanderbilt.edu.

SCHALLY, ANDREW VICTOR, endocrine oncologist, researcher; b. Wilno, Poland, Nov. 30, 1926; arrived in USA, 1957, naturalized, 1962; s. Casimir Peter and Maria (Lacka) Schally; m. Ana Maria Comaru, Aug. 1976 (dec. Sept. 2004). BSc, McGill U., Montreal, Can., 1955, PhD in Biochemistry, 1957; MD (hon.), Tulane Med. Sch., New Orleans, 1978. Rsch. asst. dept. biochemistry Nat. Inst. Med. Research, London, 1949—52; rsch. asst. endocrine unit Allan Meml. Inst. Psychiatry, McGill U., 1952—57; rsch. assoc. dept. physiology Baylor Coll. Medicine/Tex. Med. Ctr., Houston, 1957—60, asst. prof. biochemistry, 1960—62; assoc. prof. Tulane U. Sch. Medicine, 1962—67, prof., 1967—2006; Disting. Leonard Miller prof. pathology Miller Sch. Medicine, U. Miami, 2006—, prof. divsn. hematology/oncology, 2007—. Chief Endocrine, Polypeptide & Cancer Inst., VA Med. Ctr., New Orleans, 1962—2005, VA Med. Ctr., Miami, Fla., 2005—; sr. med. investigator US Dept. Vets Affairs, 1973—99, disting. med. rsch. scientist, 1999—. Author: The Hypothalamus and Pituitary in Health and Disease, 1972; contbr. articles to profl. jours. Recipient Van Meter prize, Am. Thyroid Assn., 1969, Ayerst-Squibb award, Endocrine Soc., 1970, Charles Mickle award, U. Toronto, 1974, Gairdner Found. Internat. award, 1974, Borden award, Assn. Am. Med. Colleges/Borden Co. Found., 1975, Albert Lasker award for basic med. rsch., 1975, Nobel prize for medicine, 1977. Fellow: AAAS; mem.: NAS, Internat. Brain Rsch. Found., Am. Soc. Reproductive Medicine, Am. Chem. Soc., Am. Assn. Cancer Rsch., Royal Acad. Medicine Spain, Acad. Sci. Russia, Nat. Acad. Medicine Venezuela, Nat. Acad. Medicine Brazil, Nat. Acad. Medicine Mex., Internat. Soc. Rsch. Biology & Reproduction, Soc. Exptl. Biology & Medicine, Soc. Biol. Chemists, Am. Physiol. Soc., Endocrine Soc., Mex. Acad. Sci. (corr.), Chilean Endocrine Soc. (hon.), Spanish Soc. Fertility (hon.), Can. Soc. Endocrinology & Metabolism (hon.), Polish Acad. Medicine (hon.), Hungarian Acad. Scis. (hon.), Sigma Xi, numerous other internat. organizations. Achievements include research in TRH, the releasing factor of the thyroid stimulating hormone; hypothalamic luteinizing hormone releasing factor, LH-RH, the brain's master key to the body's control reproductive function; the application of hypothalamic hormones for cancer therapy. Avocations: swimming, soccer. Office: VA Hosp Research 151 1201 NW 16 St Miami FL 33125 Office Phone: 305-575-3477. Office Fax: 305-575-3126. Business E-Mail: andrew.schally@va.gov.

SCHAMBACH, PATRICK, information technology executive; BS in Fin., Fairfield U., 1971; MBA in Info. Sys. Mgmt., George Wash. U., 1977. Asst. dir. Office of Sci. & Tech.; sector pres., Enterprise Acquisition Gateway for Leading Edge Solutions Avaya Government Solutions, Inc.; chierf info. officer US Secret Svc., 1972—96; asst. dir., chief info. officer Bureau of Alcohol, Tobacco, Firearms and Explosives, 1996—2002; founding assoc. under sec., info. tech., chief info. officer, TSA Dept. of Homeland Security, 2002—04; pres., civilian sector Nortel Govt. Solutions, 2004—08; v.p., gen. mgr., N.Am. Pub. Sector, Enforcement, Security and Intelligence Divsn. Computer Sciences Corp., 2008—, v.p., gen. mgr., Homeland Security and Law Enforcement Divsn., 2008—. Bd. dirs. Armed Forces Communication and Electronics Assn. Named one of Top 100 Execs., Fed. Computer Week; recipient Eagle award. Office: Computer Sciences Corp 3170 Fairview Park Dr Falls Church VA 22042 Office Phone: 703-876-1000. Business E-Mail: pschambach@csc.com.

SCHAPIRO, ROBERT ANDREW, dean, law educator; b. NYC, Sept. 6, 1962; s. Donald and Ruth Ellen (Goldman) S.; m. Lillian Rachel Goldstein, Aug. 4, 1990; children: Ruth, Rebecca, Sarah. BA, Yale U., 1984, JD, 1990; MA, Stanford U., Calif., 1986. Bar: Conn. 1990, N.Y. 1992, D.C. 1992, Ga. 1995. Law clk. Pierre N. Leval, NYC, 1990-91, Justice John Paul Stevens, Washington, 1991-92; assoc. Sidley & Austin, Washington, 1992-93; lecturing fellow Duke Law Sch., Durham, N.C., 1993-95; asst. prof. Emory U. Sch. of Law, Atlanta, 1995-98, assoc. prof., 1998—2003, prof., 2003—, assoc. dean faculty, 2006—08, dir. Ctr. on federalism and Intersystemic Governance, 2007—, assoc. faculty dir. Halle Inst. Global Learning, 2008—10, assoc. vice provost academic affairs, 2011, interim dean, 2011—12, dean, Asa Griggs Candler prof. law, 2012—. Mellon fellowship in humanities Stanford U., 1984-86. Office: Emory U Sch of Law 1301 Clifton Rd NE Atlanta GA 30322-1013 Business E-Mail: robert.schapiro@emory.edu.*

SCHAR, DWIGHT C., construction executive; b. 1942; With Ryan Homes, Washington, 1986-77, NVLand, 1977—, NVR Inc., 1980-86, pres., CEO, 1986—2005; chmn. NVR, Inc., 2005—. Bd. dirs. NVCompanies Inc. Named one of Forbes 400: Richest Americans, 2009. Office: Dwight Schar 11700 Plaza America Dr Ste 500 Reston VA 20190-4792

SCHARFF, JOSEPH LAURENT, lawyer; b. New Orleans, Oct. 2, 1935; s. Joseph Roy and Celia Ray S.; m. Mary Susan Greulach, June 29, 1963; children: Catherine Elizabeth, Robert Laurent, Anne Victoria. BS in Journalism, Northwestern U., 1957; JD, Harvard U., 1964. Bar: D.C. 1965, U.S. Supreme Ct. 1970, U.S. Ct. Appeals (D.C. cir.) 1965, U.S. Ct. Appeals (2nd cir.) 1980, U.S. Ct. Appeals (5th cir.) 1973, U.S. Ct. Appeals (10th cir.); U.S. Ct. Claims 1965. From assoc. to ptnr. Pierson, Ball & Dowd, Washington, 1964-89; ptnr. Reed

Smith Shaw & McClay, Washington, 1989-95, counsel, 1996. Mem. ABA (fair trial-free press com. 1973-76, com. reps. media 1985-95, co-chmn. 1989-92), Fed. Comm. Bar Assn., Soc. Profl. Journalists, Radio-TV News Dirs. Assn. (counsel 1965-95, Disting. Svc. award 1987, J. Laurent Scharff Legal Internship established 1996), Media Inst. (First Amendment Adv. Coun. 1993-2003). Home and Office: 12000 Turf Ln Reston VA 20191-2123

SCHAROLD, MARY LOUISE, psychoanalyst, psychiatrist, educator; b. Wichita Falls, Tex., Mar. 3, 1943; d. Walter John and Louise Helen (Hartmann) Baumgartner; m. William Ballew McCollum, Aug. 23, 1964 (div. 1981); m. Harry Karl Scharold, June 19, 1982; children: Margaret Louise, Walter Ballew. BA with highest distinction, U. Kans., 1964; attended, U. Kans. Sch. Medicine, 1964—66; MD, Baylor Coll. Medicine, 1968; attended, Houston-Galveston Psychoanalytic Inst., 1974—76; postgrad., Topeka Inst. Psychoanalysis, 1981. Diplomate Am. Bd. Psychiatry and Neurology, 1975, cert. adult psychoanalysis Am. Psychoanalytic Assn., 1982. Intern Meml. Bapt. Hosp., Houston, 1968-69; resident in psychiatry Baylor Coll. Medicine, Houston, 1969—72, chief resident, 1971-72; psychiatrist Houston, 1972—; psychoanalyst, 1981—. Asst. prof. Baylor Coll. Medicine, Houston, 1973-76, asst. clin. prof., 1981-84, assoc. clin. prof., 1984—2009; dir. Baylor Psychiat. Clinic, Houston, 1973-76; co-dir. Rice U. Psychiat. Svc., Houston, 1981-82; asst. clin. prof. U. Kans. Sch. Medicine, Kansas City, 1977-81; tchg. assoc. Topeka Inst. Psychoanalysis Inst., 1980-81; instr. Houston-Galveston Psychoanalytic Inst., 1984-86, tchg. analyst, 1986-90, tng. and supervising analyst, 1990—2008, emeritus, 2008-10, v.p., 1994-96, pres., 1996-01, bd. dirs., 2001-04; acting pres. bd. trustees Child Devel. Ctr., 2005-06, sec. bd. trustees, 2005-08. Contbr. articles to profl. pubs. Adv. bd. Leavenworth (Kans.) Mental Health Assn., 1977-81 Watkins scholar U. Kans., 1961-64; Grad. Fellowship award, Pi Beta Phi, 1965; recipient Hilltopper, Ten Outstanding Sr. Women, U. Kans., 1963, Greater U. Fund award, 1964, U. Kans., Eugen Kahn award, Outstanding Baylor Psychiatry Resident, 1972, 1st Disting. Svc. award, Houston-Galveston Psychoanalytic Soc., 2004; named Outstanding Woman Med. Student, AMWA, Houston Branch, 1968; named to Best Doctors in America, 1996-. Mem. Am. Psychiat. Assn. (disting. life fellow, mem. com. quality assurance 1986-87, chair Tex. peer rev. 1984-88), Am. Coll. Psychoanalysts, Am. Psychoanalytic Assn. (cert. 1982, peer rev. com. 1985-90, prof. ins. commn. 1986-93, bd. profl. stds. 1994-2001, CME com. 1994-96, exec. coun. 1994-96, cert. com. 1995-98, preparedness and progress com. 1998-2006, chair preparedness and progress com. 2000-06, coordinating com. bd. profl. stds. 2000-06, bylaws com. 2001—09, fin. com. 2003—09, councilor-at-large 2005-09, chair councillors-at-large, 2007—09, hon. membership.com, 2005-09, election oversight com., 2005-09, compliance task force, 2006-07, com. on coun., 2006—2008, annual meeting task force 2008, audit com. 2008—09, mem. taskforce on reform of electron procedure, 2011-12), Am. Group Psychotherapy Assn., Ctr. Advanced Psychoanalytic Studies, Houston Psychiat. Soc. (v.p. 1984-85, pres.-elect 1985-86, pres. 1986-87), Houston-Galveston Psychoanalytic Soc. (sec.-treas. 1984-86, pres.-elect 1986-88, pres. 1988-90, alt. councillor 1994-96), Houston Group Psychotherapy Soc. (adv. bd. 1984-85), Mortar Bd., Phi Beta Kappa, Delta Phi Alpha, Alpha Omega Alpha, Pi Beta Phi Alumni Assn. Republican. Lutheran. Office: 1406 E Main St Ste 200 Fredericksburg TX 78624 Office Phone: 830-992-0315.

SCHAUB, MATT (MATTHEW RUTLEDGE SCHAUB), professional football player; b. West Chester, Pa., June 25, 1981; m. Laurie Schaub. Grad., U. Va., Charlottesville, 2004. Quarterback Atlanta Falcons, 2004—06, Houston Texans, 2007—. Participant Atlanta Falcons Coaches Acad., 2004. Named Player of Yr., Atlantic Coast Conf., 2002, Offensive Player of Yr., 2002, First Team All-Conf., 2002, Pro Bowl MVP, NFL, 2010; named to Am. Football Conf. Pro Bowl Team, 2010, 2012. Achievements include leading the NFL in: passing attempts, completions, yards, 2009. Office: The Houston Texans Two Reliant Pk Houston TX 77054

SCHAUER, FREDERICK FRANKLIN, law educator; b. Newark, Jan. 15, 1946; s. John Adolph and Clara (Balayti) S.; m. Margery Clare Stone, Aug. 25, 1968 (div. June, 1982); m. Virginia Jo Wise, May 25, 1985 (div. Jan., 2009). AB, Dartmouth Coll., 1967, MBA, 1968; JD, Harvard U., 1972; MA, Oxford U., 2007. Bar: Mass. 1972, U.S. Supreme Ct. 1976. Assoc. Fine & Ambrogne, Boston, 1972-74; asst. prof. law W.Va. U., Morgantown, 1974-76, assoc. prof., 1976-78, Coll. William and Mary, Williamsburg, Va., 1978-80, Cutler prof., 1980-83; prof. of law U. Mich., Ann Arbor, 1983-90; Frank Stanton prof. of 1st Amendment Kennedy Sch. of Govt., Harvard U., Cambridge, Mass., 1990—2008, acad. dean, 1997—2002, acting dean, 2001; David and Mary Harrison disting. prof. law U. Va., 2008—. Vis. scholar, mem. faculty law Wolfson Coll. Cambridge (Eng.) U., 1977-78; vis. prof. Law Sch., U. Chgo., 1990, 05; vis. fellow Australian Nat. U., 1993, 98; William Morton Disting. sr. fellow in humanities Dartmouth Coll., 1991; vis. prof. law Harvard Law Sch., 1996, 97, 00, 04, 05, 06, 08; Ewald Disting. vis. prof. law U. Va., 1996, vis. prof. govt. Dartmouth Coll., 1997; disting. vis. prof. law U. Toronto, 2000; Fischel-Neil Disting. vis. prof. law, 2005; George Eastman vis. prof. Oxford U., 2007-08, fellow Balliol Coll., 2007-08. Author: The Law of Obscenity, 1976, Free Speech: A Philosophical Enquiry, 1982 (ABA cert. merit 1983), Supplements to Gunther Constitutional Law, 1983-96, Playing by the Rules: A Philosophical Examination of Rule Based Decision-Making in Law and Life, 1991, The First Amendment: A Reader, 1992, 2d edit., 1995, The Philosophy of Law, 1995, Profiles, Probabilities and Sterotypes, 2003, thinking Like a Lawyer, 2009; editor: Legal Theory, 1995-2000; contbr. articles to profl. jours. Mem. Atty. Gen.'s Commn. on Pornography, 1985-86. Served with Mass. Army N.G., 1970-71. NEH fellow, summer 1980, Guggenheim fellow, 2001-02. Fellow Am. Acad. Arts and Scis., Radcliffe Inst. Adv. Studies; mem. Am. Philos. Assn. (chair com. philosophy and law 2006-2007), Am. Soc. Polit. and Legal Philosophy (v.p. 1996-99), Assn. Am. Law Schs. (chmn. sect. constl. law 1984-86). Office: Univ Va Sch Law 580 Massie Rd Charlottesville VA 22903 Office Phone: 434-924-6777. Business E-Mail: schauer@virginia.edu.

SCHECHTER, ARTHUR LOUIS, lawyer; b. Rosenberg, Tex., Dec. 6, 1939; s. Morris and Helen (Brilling) S.; m. Joyce Proler, Aug. 26, 1965; children: Leslie Schechter Karpas, Jennifer Schechter Rosen. BA, U. Tex., 1962, JD, 1964; postgrad., U. Houston, 1964-65. Bar: Tex. 1964, U.S. Dist. Ct. (ea. and so. dists.) Tex. 1966, U.S. Ct. Appeals (5th cir.), U.S. Supreme Ct. 1976; cert. Tex. Bd. Legal Specialization to Personal Injury Trial Law, 1964-. Pres. Arthur L. Schechter P.C., Houston, 1965—; amb. U.S. to Commonwealth Bahamas; sr. counsel Schechter McElwee Shaffer & Harris LLP, Houston, 2006—. Mediator Arthur Schechter Group, 2006—; spkr. Marine Law Sem., 1983; spkr. in field, chmn. Mayor Com. Internat. Travellers, chmn., Blue Ribbon Com. Term Lemrts. Contbr. articles to profl. jours. Bd. dirs. Theatre Under the Stars, Houston, 1972—78, Congregation Beth Israel, Houston, 1972—84, pres., 1982—84; bd. dirs. Inst. Internat. Edn., 1996—98, S.E.A.R.C.H., 1996—98; pres. Am. Jewish Com., Houston, 1982—84, chmn. fgn. rels. com., chmn. United Jewish Campaign exec. com., chmn., 1993—94; pres. Jewish Fedn. Ctr. Houston, 1994—96; mem. Deans Coun. U. Tex. Law Sch.; chmn. bd. Harris County Met. Transit Authority, 2002—04; chmn. internat. traveler task force Mayor of Houston, 2005; mng. trustee mem. fin. com. Dem. Nat. Com., 1992, fin. chmn. Tex. Clinton/Gore '96; vice chmn. Clinton/Gore Jewish Leadership Coun., 1996; v.p. exec. com. Nat. Jewish Dem. Coun., 1992, chmn., 2004—06; mem. Leadership Ctr. Dem. Senatorial Campaign Com.; trustee mem. Kerry/Edwards and Dem. Nat. Com.; fin. coun. Nat. Dem. Orgn., 1979; chmn. bd. Met. Transit Authority of Harris County, 2002—04; bd. dirs. U. Tex. Med. Sch. Recipient Career and Recovery Resources Barrier Breaker award, United Way Agy., 2003, Search's Outstanding Leadership award, 2003, Israel Bonds Nat. Leadership award, 2004, Lifetime Achievement award, NJDC, 2006, Nat. Jewish Dem. Coun., 2006, Starlight Leadership award, Coun. of Jewish Women, 2006, Houston Treasure award, Social Book, 2007, Leadership award for Lifetime of Svc., Harris Co. Democratic Party, 2008, Interfaith Ministers Forgreater Houston Tapestry award, 2011; named a Tex. Super Lawyer, 2006—12, Local Legend, Jewish Fdn. Greater Houston, 2009, Comm. Leader Am., Am. Biographical Inst., 2007; named one of Houston's Most Fascinating Mems. of the Med. Cmty., 2003, Top 100 Trial Lawyers, Nat. Trial Lawyers Assn., 2012. Home: 1100 Uptown Pk Blvd #273 Houston TX 77056 Home Phone: 713-961-5558; Office Phone: 713-757-7811. Personal E-mail: arthurschechter@gmail.com. Business E-Mail: aschechter@smslegal.com.

SCHECHTER, ROBERT SAMUEL, chemical engineer, educator; b. Houston, Feb. 26, 1929; s. Morris S. and Helen Ruth Schechter; m. Mary Ethel Rosenberg, Feb. 15, 1953; children: Richard Martin, Alan Lawrence (dec.), Geoffrey Louis. BS in Chem. Engring, Tex. A&M U., 1950; PhD in Chem. Engring, U. Minn., 1956. Registered profl. engr., Tex. Asst. prof. chem. engring. U. Tex. at Austin, 1956-60, assoc. prof., 1960-63, prof., 1963—; adminstrv. dir. Ctr. Statis. Mechs. and Thermodynamics, 1968-72, chmn. dept. chem. engring., 1970-73, chmn. petroleum engring., 1975-78, E.J. Cockrell, Jr. prof. chem. and petroleum engring., 1975-81, Dula and Ernie Cockrell prof. engring., 1981-83, Getty prof. engring., 1984-85, Getty Oil Centennial chair in Petroleum Engring., 1985-89, W.A. (Monty) Moncrief Centennial Endowed chair in Petroleum Engring., 1989-97; prof. emeritus U. Tex., 1997. Vis. prof. U. Edinburgh, Scotland, 1965-66; Disting. vis. prof. U. Kans., spring 1968; vis. prof. U. Brussels, 1969; Disting. Lindsay lectr. Tex. A&M U., 1993; cons. in field. Author: Variational Method in Engineering, 1967, (with G.S.G. Beveridge) Optimization: Theory and Practice, 1970, Adventures in Fortran Programming, 1975, (with B.B. Williams and J.L. Gidley) Acidizing Monograph, 1979, (with D.D. Shah) Enhanced Oil Recovery by Surfactants and Polymers, 1979; (with Maurice Bourrel) Microemulsions and Related Systems, 1988, Oil Well Stimulation, 1991; contbr. (with D.D. Shah) numerous articles to profl. jours. Served to 1st lt., Chem. Corps AUS, 1951-53. Decorated Chevalier Order Palmes Academique, 1978; recipient Outstanding Teaching award U. Tex., 1969, Outstanding Paper award, 1973, Gen. Dynamics award for Excellence in Engring. Teaching, Gen. Dynamics Corp., 1987, Sr. Rsch. award Engring. Rsch. Coun. of Am. Soc. Engring. Educators, 1991. Mem. AIME (Industry Edn. award 1998), AIChE (Founders award 1998), Am. Chem. Soc., Soc. Petroleum Engrs. (John Franklin Carll award 1994, Improved Oil Recovery Pioneer 1996), Nat. Acad. Engrs., Sigma Xi, Tau Beta Pi. Achievements include developing methods of measuring surface viscosity and ultra low inter-facial tensions; discovering instability of thermal diffusion. Home: 4700 Ridge Oak Dr Austin TX 78731-4724 Office: U Tex Dept Petroleum & Geosystems Austin TX 78712 Office Phone: 512-471-3245. Business E-Mail: rsschechter@mail.utexas.edu.

SCHECHTERMAN, LAWRENCE, lawyer, chef, freelance travel writer, photographer, teacher of English as a foreign language; b. Elizabeth, NJ, June 23, 1943; s. Josef and Sylvia (Berger) S.; children: Jill Laura, Danielle Sara, Gregory Jared. BA, U. Miami, Fla., 1966; JD, Suffolk U., 1969; LLM, NYU, 1973; AS in Culinary Arts, Art Inst. Ft. Lauderdale, 2001. Cert. tchr. English as a fgn. lang. Tax assoc. Coopers & Lybrand, NYC, 1969-70; assoc. Bendit, Weinstock & Sharbaugh, Newark, 1970-72; pvt. practice East Brunswick, NJ, 1972-81; gen. counsel Equinox Solar, Inc., Miami, 1981-83; mem. Lawrence Schechterman, P.A., Boca Raton, Fla., 1983—94; pres. Ocean Cons. Group divsn. Securities Arbitration Recovery, Inc., Boca Raton, 1993-97; pvt. chef Boca Raton, 2000—; bridgetender C&S Engring., Boca Raton, Fla., 2006—08; assoc. chef Publix Greenwise Market, Boca Raton, 2008—12; tchr. English Extreme Learning Ctr., Arequipa, Peru, 2012, Berlitz Sch. Langs San Luis Potosi Mex., 2013, Academic HS, Boca Raton, Fla., 2013—. Author: In the Mood with Food, A Bachelor's Guide to Wooing Her with Food, 1998, 2000, 01; (poetry) New Dimensions: An Anthology of American Poetry, 1967, Surrounded By Dreams, 1998, Touched by Grace, 1999, Touched by Love, 1999, The Harmony of Silence, 2000, A Trusting Heart, 2000 (Best Poems and Poets award, 2007), Poems of Now and Then: A Collection of Poetry, 2012; contbr. articles to profl. jours. Mem. coun. Twp. of East Brunswick, NJ, 1976—80; pres. B'nai Torah Congregation of Boca Raton Inc., 1987—89, trustee, 1989—91. Mem.: B'nai B'rith Mens Lodge 2935, South Plainfield, NJ (charter pres., co-founder 1973—74). Office: 21218 St Andrews Blvd Unit 160 Boca Raton FL 33433-1716 Business E-Mail: lorenzo1943@hotmail.com.*

SCHECTER, ARNOLD JOEL, public health physician, researcher; b. Chgo., Dec. 1, 1934; s. Benjamin and Leonore Natalie (Lyon) S.; m. Martha-Jean Berenson, Feb. 14, 1964; children: Benjamin, David, Anna. BA in Liberal Arts, U. Chgo., 1954, BS in Physiology-Neurophysiology, 1957; MD, Howard U., 1962; MPH, Columbia U., 1975. Diplomate Am. Coll. Preventive Medicine; med. lic., Ky., N.Y., N.J., N.C. Postdoc. dept. anatomy Harvard Med. Sch., Boston, 1962—64; instr. dept. medicine Mass. Gen. Hosp., Harvard Med. Sch., Boston, 1964-65; intern Beth Israel Hosp., Boston, 1966, US Army Med. Corp., 1967—69; gen. practitioner, sr. aviation med. examiner West Point, Ky., 1969-70; med. dir. inpatient rehab. ctr., drug and alcohol rehab. program Region Eight Mental Health and Mental Retardation Bd., Inc., Louisville, 1971-72; asst. prof. dept. psychiatry, divisional drug and alcohol abuse SUNY Downstate Med. Ctr., Bklyn., 1973-75; clin. assoc. prof. dept. preventive medicine N.J. Med. Sch., Newark, 1975-79; prof. dept. preventive medicine SUNY Upstate Med. Ctr., Binghamton, 1979—98; prof. environ. & occpl. health scis. U. Tex. Sch. Pub. Health, Dallas, 1999—; pres. Zumwalt Inst. for Environ. Health Inc., 1996—; cons. Health Canada, Environment Canada, 2010. Spl. expert Nat. Inst. Environ. Health Scis. NIH, 1997—98; cons. U.S. EPA, Washington, 1985—86, Washington, 1999—2000, WHO, 1986—90; sci. peer reviewer dioxin U.S. EPA, 1995, 2000, 2010—11; peer reviewer A.T.S.D.R. of C.D.C., 1995—2005; dir. clin. rsch. in drug abuse, coord., faculty mem. Career Tchr. Tng. Ctr., SUNY Downstate, 1972—75; assoc. dir. office primary health care edn., office of the dean NJ Med. Sch., 1976—79; advisor Environ. Def. Fund, 1991—92, Nat. Vets. Legal Svcs. Project, 1991—92; co-founder assoc. editor Am. Jour. Drug and Alcohol Abuse, NYC, 1973—78, editl. bd., 1978—86; editl. adv. bd. Substance and Alcohol Actions/Misuse, Elmsford, NY, 1979—85; adj. prof. epidemiology U. N.C. Sch. Pub. Health, 1998—2004; adj. prof. occupl. medicine Duke Med. Ctr., 1998—99; editl. adv. bd. mem. Environ. Health Perspectives, 2008—; mem. USEPA Dioxin Reassessment Panel, 2010—11. Editor: Rehabilitation Aspects of Drug Dependence, 1977, Treatment Aspects of Drug Dependence, 1978, Biomedical Issues in Drug Abuse, 1981, Sociological Issues in Drug Abuse, 1981, Dioxins and Health, 1994, 2d edit., 2003, 3rd edit., 2012; environmental sect.editor Maxcy Rosenau Last Public Health and Preventive Medicine, 14th edit., 1998, 15th edit., 2007; co-editor: Drug Abuse: Modern Trends, Issues and Perspectives, 1978; co-editor: (with H. Alksne, E. Kaufman) Critical Concerns in the Field of Drug Abuse, 1978; contbr. over 200 articles to profl. jours., books. Capt to maj., physician MC US Army, 1967-69. Recipient Pacesetter award Commonwealth Mass., 1990. Fellow: ACP, Am. Coll. Occupl. and Environ. Medicine, Am. Coll. Preventive Medicine; mem.: AAAS, APHA (chair Vietnam caucus), Internat. Soc. Environ. Epidemiology, Internat. Soc. Exposure Scis., Soc. Epidemiology Rsch., Tex. Pub. Health Assn., Soc. Epidemiologic Rsch., Am. Occupl. and Environ. Medicine Assn., Am. Coll. Epidemiology. Achievements include discovery of dioxin and furan levels in US population, US food contaminated with dioxins, dibenzofurans; Polybrominated diphenyl ethers (PBDEs), which are found mainly in meat, fish & diary products; PBDE brominated flame retardant contamination in breast milk of all US mothers tested, and that these levels as well as blood are highest in the world; PCDDs, PCDFs, PCBs can be measured in all total tissues studied; PCB transformer fires can lead to contamination of buildings by dioxins; Agent Orange elevated dioxin body burden exists decades after exposure in some Vietnamese and American Vietnam Veterans; dioxin contamination exists in body tissues of the general population of the US; dioxin hot spots in Vietnam with current contamination of some Vietnamese by contaminated food; development of congener specific tissue dioxin analysis as biomarker for dioxin exposure; developed naltrexone, a narcotic antagonist for rehabilitation of opiate addicts; US food is contaminated with PBDE brominated flame retardants and some contaminated with hexabromocyclododecane, and perfluorinated compounds and Bisphenol A., PFC, Phthalates and BPA. Home: 16606 Loch Maree Ln Dallas TX 75248-1711 Office: U Tex Sch Pub Health 6011 Harry Hines Blvd Dallas TX 75248 Personal E-mail: ajschecter@aol.com. Business E-Mail: arnold.schecter@utsouthwestern.edu.

SCHEDLER, TOM (JOHN THOMAS SCHEDLER), state official, former state legislator; b. New Orleans, Jan. 24, 1950; m. Stephanie Gele; children: Michelle, Rachel, Jessica. BS in Mktg., U. La., Lafayette, 1971. With Sebrite Corp., 1975—77; chmn. Slidell Bd. Zoning & Adjustment, 1984—90; pres. St. Tammany Mcpl. Assn., 1990—96; mem. Dist. 11 La. State Senate, 1996—2008; dir. Slidell Mem. Hosp. Found. & Med. Ctr.; sec. of state State of La., 2010—. Mem.: Greater Slidell Chamber of Commerce, St. Tammany Assn. Retarded Citizens, East Tammany United Way (chmn.), Slidell Boys & Girls Club, Slidell Rotary Club (pres.). Republican. Roman Catholic. Office: Office of Secretary of State PO Box 94125 Baton Rouge LA 70804-9125 Office Phone: 225-342-4479. Office Fax: 225-342-5577. E-mail: admin@sos.louisiana.gov.*

SCHEELER, JAMES ARTHUR, architect; b. Pontiac, Ill., Dec. 20, 1927; s. Aman B. and Jane (Steele) S.; m. Barbara Jean Lloyd, Sept. 2, 1950; children: James Erich, Carl Aman, Orissa Jane Elizabeth; m. Nancy S. Kneece, June 2, 2007. BS with highest honors, U. Ill., 1951, MS, 1952; postgrad., U. Liverpool, 1952-53. Grad. asst. U. Ill., Urbana, 1950-52; draftsman-designer Lundeen & Hilfinger, Bloomington, Ill., 1952-53; designer Skidmore, Owings & Merrill, Chgo., 1955-59; partner Richardson, Severns, Scheeler & Assos., Inc., Champaign, Ill., 1959-65, v.p., treas., 1965-71; vice chmn. bd., dir. Prodn. Systems for Architects and Engrs., Inc., 1973-81. Vis. critic U. Ill., 1959-60. Mem. Plan Commn., Champaign, 1966—71, chmn., 1969-71; mem. Champaign County Regional Planning Commn., 1967-71; bd. dirs. Nat. Center for a Barrier-Free Environment, 1978—81, pres., 1981. Served with USN, 1946-47. Recipient various archtl. awards.; Francis J. Plym fellow, 1953-54; Fulbright fellow, 1953. Fellow AIA (hon.; treas. Ctrl. Ill. chpt. 1967-68, sec. 1968-69, pres. 1970-71, nat. dep. exec. v.p. 1971-76, pres. corp. 1974-78, exec. v.p. 1977-78, program devel. group exec. 1976-85, sr. exec. 1985-88, v.p. design practice group 1989, resident fellow 1990—, Edward D. Kemper award 2000), Internat. Union Archs. Profl. Practice Commn. (sec., co-dir. 1994-2003, internat. union archs. coun. 2005—11), Royal Australian Inst. Architects (hon.), Korean Inst. Archs. (hon.); mem. Ill. Arts Coun. (archtl. adv. bd. 1966-71), Montessori Soc. Champaign-Urbana (dir. 1964-66), Gargoyle, Scarab, Phi Kappa Phi, Lambda Chi Alpha, Lambda Alpha, Cosmos Club, Fedn. Colls. Archs. Republic Mex. (hon.), Japan Inst. Architect (hon.). Episcopalian. Address: 1411 Belcastle Ct Reston VA 20194-1245

SCHEFERMAN, JEFFREY E., defense manufacturing company executive; B in Economics, Ripon Coll., Wis.; MPA, Capitol U., Columbus, Ohio. Dir., internat. devel. bus. HK Sys., Hebron, Ky., 1995—97; mng. dir. Airport Group Internat., Australia, 1997—2000, regional dir., L.Am., 1997—2000; pres., CEO Colliers Sealy Internat., 2000—05; sr. v.p., ops. DynCorp International, Inc., 2005—. Advanced through ranks to through col., USMC. Office: DynCorp International Inc 3190 Fairview Park Dr Ste 700 Falls Church VA 22042 Office Phone: 571-722-0210. Office Fax: 571-722-0252.

SCHEIBLE, DAVID W., paper company executive; BS, MBA, Purdue U. V.p., gen. mgr., Tape Divsn., Automotive Divsn. Avery Denison Corp., 1993—99; pres., Flexible Divsn. Graphic Packaging Internat. Corp., 1999, COO, 1999—2003; exec. v.p., comml. ops. Graphic Packaging Corp., Marietta, Ga., 2003—04, COO, 2004—06; pres., CEO, and dir. Graphic Packaging Holding Corp., Marietta, Ga., 2007—. Office: Graphic Packaging Holding Corp 814 Livingston Ct Marietta GA 30067 Office Phone: 770-644-3000. Office Fax: 770-644-2962. Business E-Mail: david.scheible@graphicpkg.com.

SCHEIN, ROLAND M., critical care medicine; MD, NYU, 1980. Diplomate Am. Bd Internal Medicine, 1983, Am. Bd Internal Medicine-critical care medicine, 2007. Assoc. prof. in critical care medicine Univ. Miami; resident in internal medicine Jackson Meml. Univ. Miami, 1980—83, fellow in critical care medicine, 1983—84, hosp. affiliation includes. Office: University of Miami Jackson Memorial Hospital 1611 NW 12th Ave Miami FL 33136-1094 Office Phone: 305-585-0111.

SCHELL, CATHERINE LOUISE, physician; b. Niskayuna, NY, Jan. 27, 1948; m. Richard J. Rathe, Jan. 7, 1986. BA, Ind. U., 1970, MA, 1974; MLS, Simmons Coll., 1975; MD, Am. U. Caribbean, Montserrat, 1983. Diplomate Am. Bd. Family Practice; cert. CAQ Geriatrics. Libr. Calder Med. Libr., U. Miami, Fla., 1975-78; libr., dir. Mercy Hosp., Miami, 1978-79; libr. Miami-Dade C.C., 1978-80; intern Med. Coll. Ga., Rome, 1983; resident U. Wyo., Cheyenne, 1985-87; staff physician Vets. Hosp., Cheyenne, 1986-88, Dept. of Army, U.S. Dept. Def., Ft. Devens, Mass., 1988-90, Vets. Hosp., Lake City, Fla., 1990-93, staff physician, fellow Gainesville, Fla., 1993-95; fellow in geriatrics U. Fla., 1993-95, fellow in geriatrics internal medicine, 1995, fellow geriatrics internal medicine, 1995; physician Dept. of Navy, 1995-96; pres. Med. Decisions Software, Inc., 1999—; physician Vets. Outpatient Clinic, 2004—, Va. Hosp., 2007—, Bay Pines Va, 2008—12. Tchr. ESL YMCA Internat., Taipei, Taiwan, 1970-71. Title IIB fellow Simmons Coll., 1974-75; Ford Found. grantee, Ind. U., 1969-70. Fellow Am. Acad. Family PRactice; mem. Acad. Health Sci., Med. Libr. Assn.

SCHELL, RICHARD A., federal judge; b. Dallas, 1950; BA, So. Meth. U., 1972, JD, 1975. Bar: Tex. 1975. Asst. dist. atty. Collin County, Tex., 1976; atty. pvt. practice, 1977—81; judge County Ct. Law Collin County, 1982—86, 219th Jud. Dist. Ct. Tex., 1986—88, US Dist Ct. (ea. dist.) Tex., Beaumont, 1988—2003, Sherman, Tex., 2003—08, Plano, Tex., 2008—, chief judge Beaumont, 1994—2001. Instr. rsch. methods and legal writing So. Meth. U., 1975—76; vis. prof. law SMU Dedman Sch. Law, 2010. Mem.: State Bar Tex. Office: US Courthouse Ste 111 7940 Preston Rd Plano TX 75024-2360

SCHELLENBERG, MATTHEW M., councilman; b. Washington, Dec. 2, 1952; s. Bob Schellenberg and Kate Shellenberg; children: Andrew, Perri. BS in Polit. Sci., U. Fla., 1975. Owner Movers Claim Services (MCS), 1991—; councilman Dist. 6 Jacksonville City Coun., 2011—. Bd. mem. Greenscape, 1984—87; mem., chmn. Keep Jacksonville Beautiful. Office: Jacksonville City Council 117 W Duval St Jacksonville FL 32202 Office Phone: 904-630-1388. E-mail: LBoyer@coj.net.

SCHEMBRI, CHRIS, media marketing executive; b. 1971; BA in Comm., U. Windsor, Ont., Can., 1992, MBA, 2005. Regional planner to sr. ptnr., media dir. J. Walter Thompson Co., Detroit, 1997—2004; sr. v.p. media planning & partnerships Discovery Comm. Inc., 2004—08; v.p. media svcs. AT&T Inc., 2008—10; founder, pres. Two Tree Comm. Co., 2010—11; COO Camelot Comm. Ltd., Dallas, 2011—. Office: Camelot Communications 8140 Walnut Hill Ln Ste 700 Dallas TX 75231 Office Phone: 210-821-4105. Office Fax: 210-351-2071.

SCHENCK, ROBERT C., state legislator; b. Somerville, NJ, July 8, 1975; m. Megan Schenck; children: Michael, Isabella. AA, Pasco-Hernando Cmty. Coll., 1995; BS, U. Central Fla., 1998. Tchr. Central High Sch., 1998—; mem. Dist. 44 Fla. House of Reps., 2008—, chair governmental affairs policy com., co-chair joint select com. on collective bargaining, mem. criminal and civil justice policy coun., mem. econ. devel. and cmty. affairs policy coun., energy and utilities policy com., transp. and econ. devel. appropriations com. Dist. 4 rep. Hernando County Commn., 2002. Mem.: Boy Scouts of America (exec. bd. Gulf Ridge coun.), Suncoast YMCA (bd. dirs.). Republican. Methodist. Office: House Office Bldg 402 S Monroe St Rm 214 Tallahassee FL 32399-1300 also: Lincoln Centre 12503 Springhill Dr Spring Hill FL 34609-5069 Office Phone: 850-488-6641, 352-688-5005. Business E-Mail: robert.schenck@myfloridahouse.gov.

SCHENK, JOSEPH BERNARD, museum director; b. Glendale, Ariz., Mar. 28, 1953; m. Jacqueline Van Lierop; children: Brian, Stuart. BA in Mus. Staff Preparation, Huntingdon Coll., 1974; MA in Art Edn., Ball State U., 1979; postgrad., U. Calif., Berkeley, 1986. Exhibits asst. Hunter Mus. of Art, Chattanooga, 1974-75; asst. dir. Alford House/Anderson Fine Arts Ctr., Anderson, Ind., 1976, exec. dir., 1976-79, Okefenokee Heritage Ctr., Waycross, Ga., 1979-83; dir. So. Forest World, Waycross, 1979-83, Chattahoochee Valley Art Mus., LaGrange, Ga., 1983-88, Mobile (Ala.) Mus. of Art, 1988—. V.p. Ala. Mus. Assn., 1994-96, pres., 1996-98; adv. panelist Visual Arts Fellowships, Ala. State Coun. on the Arts, 1994-95, Profl. Touring Panel Ga. Coun. for Arts, 1983-84, PRACSO Panel Ga. Coun. for Arts, 1984-86, Arch. & Environ. Arts Ind. Arts Commn., 1978-79, Mus. Ind. Arts Commn., 1977-79; Ind. rep. Small Mus. Com. Midwest Mus. Conf., 1978-79. Pub. numerous art catalogs; editor newsletter Ga. Assembly of Community Arts Agys., 1987-88. Art juror at numerous pub. and pvt. art shows; bd. dirs. Ga. Alliance for Arts Edn., 1982-84, Assn. Ind. Mus., 1979, Mobile Arts Coun., 1989-90, Ga. Assembly Community Arts Agys., 1986-88; commr. Madison County Hist. Home, Anderson, 1977-79; mem. dedication com., cons. Krannert Fine Arts Ctr., Anderson Coll., 1979; mem. com. forest festival tourism and conventions Waycross/Ware County C. of C., 1979-83; bd. dirs. Southeastern Ga. Travel and Tourism Assn., 1981-83, sec., 1981-82, pres., 1982-83. Grantee Nat. Endowment for Arts, Ala. State Coun. on Arts, Mobile Arts Coun., Ga. Endowment for Humanities, Ga. Coun. Arts, Ala. Arts Found., Inst. Mus. and Libr. Svcs., Ga. Gov.'s Intern Program, others; recipient Spark Plug of Yr. award Waycross Jaycees, 1981; Mus. Mgmt. Inst. scholar, 1986. Mem. Am. Assn. Mus., Southeastern Mus. Conf., Ala. Mus. Assn., Rotary (Paul Harris fellowship 1997), Mobile United (Grad. Leadership Mobile 1998), Mobile Area Mus. Assn. (pres. 1993-95). Home: 4850 Museum Dr Mobile AL 36608-1917 also: 324 Bayshore Dr Corpus Christi TX 78412-2608

SCHENKER, STEVEN, emeritus professor of medicine; b. Poland, Oct. 5, 1929; came to US, 1943, naturalized, 1946, permanent resident; s. Alfred and Ernestyna S.; m. Sally Ann Wood, May 11, 1956; children: Julie C. Schenker Burn, Steven A., David S., Andrew G., Jennifer E. Schenker Campeggi; m. Jo Ann Neumann, Nov. 29, 1985. BA, Cornell U., Ithaca, NY, 1951, MD, 1955. Intern Harvard Service-Boston City Hosp., 1955-56, resident in medicine, 1956-58; asst. prof. medicine U. Cin. Sch. Medicine, 1961-63; asst. prof. U. Tex., Southwestern Sch. Medicine, 1963-67, assoc. prof. medicine, 1967-70; prof. medicine, biochemistry, dir. div. gastroenterology Vanderbilt U. Sch. Medicine, Nashville VA Hosp., 1970-82; prof. medicine and pharmacology U. Tex. Sch. Medicine, San Antonio, 1982—2009, dir. divsn. gastroenterology, 1982—2001, prof. emeritus, 2010—. Chmn. study sect. Nat. Inst. on Alcohol Abuse and Addiction, 1980-83; chmn. study sects. VA, 1985-88. Editor: Hepatology, 1985-90; contbr. numerous articles in field to profl. jours. Recipient Markle award, 1963; Career Devel. award NIH, 1968; Jurzykowski Found. for Research in Medicine award, 1979, Alcoholism Research Soc. award 1987. Mem. Am. Assn. for Study of Liver Diseases (pres. 1980, Disting. Svc. award 1997), Am. Soc. Clin. Investigation, Assn. Am. Physicians, Am. Gastroent. Soc., Am. Soc. Pharm. and Exptl. Therapeutics, Am. Soc. Clin. Nutrition, Internat. Soc. for Study of Liver Diseases, Alpha Omega Alpha. Republican. Home: 26025 Mesa Oak Dr San Antonio TX 78255-3533 Office: U Tex Med Sch San Antonio TX 78284

SCHERGER, STEPHEN R., packaging and container manufacturing company executive; BSBA, Bowling Green State U.; MBA in Fin., U. Cinn. CPA; cert. mgmt. acct. V.p., corp. strategy MeadWestvaco Corp.; fin. analyst Mead Data Ctrl., Inc., Dayton, Ohio, 1986, dir., fin. acctg., Lexis Document Svcs. Springfield, Ill., 1990, dir., bus. mgmt., 1992, dir., corp. planning, 1994; v.p., worldwide, performance, Packaging Sys. Divsn. MeadWestvaco Corp., 1995, v.p., Asia Pacific & L.Am., Packaging Sys. Divsn., 1997, v.p., economics & strategy, Papers Group Dayton, Ohio, 1998, v.p., gen. mgr., The Americas, Packaging Sys. Divsn., 2000, pres., beverage, media & entertainment folding carton ops. Trustee Valentine Richmond History Ctr.; bd. dirs., chmn. United Way of Greater Richmond & Petersburg; bd. dirs. Paperboard Packaging Coun., MeadWestvaco Found., Content Delivery & Storage Assn. Office: MeadWestvaco Corp 501 S 5th St Richmond VA 23219 Office Phone: 804-327-5200. Business E-Mail: Stephen.Scherger@meadwestvaco.com.

SCHERICH, EDWARD BAPTISTE, retired diversified company executive; b. Inland, Nebr., Dec. 3, 1923; s. Clarence H. and Clara E. (Baptiste) S.; m. Hyacinth Rau, Aug. 11, 1945 (dec. 1980); children: Carol, Eileen, John.; m. Antoinette Currera, 1981; 1 stepdau., Sylvia McNamara. BBA, Tulane U., 1948. Acct. Colo. Milling & Elevator Co., Denver, 1948-50; accountant, office mgr. Southdown, Inc., New Orleans, 1950-55, controller, 1955-69; v.p. finance, sec., treas. Southdown Sugars Inc., New Orleans, 1970-73; v.p., sec., treas. Southdown Land Co., New Orleans, 1971-75; sec.-treas. Southdown, Inc., Houston, 1975-78, v.p., sec., 1979-84, treas., 1980-83; ind. fin. cons., 1984—2008; pres. Valmax Inc., 1989—2008. Served in USNR, 1943-45. Mem. Beta Gamma Sigma. Home: 633 Brouilly Dr Kenner LA 70065-1101

SCHERSCHEL, PATRICIA, finance company executive; b. Fishers, Ind. BS in Journalism & Polit. Sci., Ind. U., Bloomington, MBA in Bus. Economics. Assoc. editor US News & World Report, 1977—87; editor, fin. & features Bus. Times, 1987—91; exec. editor Singapore Bus. Mag., 1987—91; v.p., adminstrn. Hudson Inst., 1992—94; v.p., FFELP Strategy SLM Corp.(commonly known as Sallie Mae), 1994; v.p., Loan Consolidation Sallie Mae - SLM Corp., 2005—. Office: SLM Corp 12061 Bluemont Way Reston VA 20190 Office Phone: 703-810-3000. Office Fax: 703-984-5042. Business E-Mail: PScherschel@salliemae.com.

SCHEXNAYDER, CHARLOTTE TILLAR, state legislator; b. Tillar, Ark., Dec. 25, 1923; d. Jewell Stephen and Bertha (Terry) Tillar; m. Melvin John Schexnayder Sr., Aug. 18, 1946; children: M. John Jr., Sarah Holden, Stephen. BA, La. State U., Shreveport, 1944, postgrad., 1947—48. Asst. editor La. Agrl. Extension, Baton Rouge, 1944; editor The McGehee (Ark.) Times, 1945-46, 48-53; editor, co-publisher The Dumas (Ark.) Clarion, 1954-85, pub., 1985-99; mem. Ark. Ho. of Reps., Little Rock, 1985-99, asst. speaker pro tem, 1995—. Pres. Ark. Assn. Women, 1955, Nat. Newspaper Assn., Washington, 1991-92, Ark. Press. Assn., Little Rock, 1982, Nat. Fedn. Press Women, Blue Springs, Mo., 1977-78, Litte Rock chpt. Soc. Profl. Journalists, 1973; mem. pres.'s coun. Winrock Internat., 1990—; chmn. Dumas Area Cmty. Found., 2000-02; pres. Main Street Dumas. Editor: Images of the Past, 1991. 1st woman mem. Ark. Bd. Pardons and Parole, 1975-80; mem. Ark. Legis. Coun., 1985-92; bd. dirs. Women's Found. Ark., sec. 1999—; bd. dirs. Chicot-Desha Port Indsl. Com.; v.p. Desha County Mus., 1989—; dir. Dumas Indsl. Found., 1986—; exec. com. Ark. Ctrl. Radiation Therapy Inst., 1991-92; mem. adv. bd. Ark. Profl. Women Achievement, 1992—; vice chair Ark. Rural Devel. Commn., 1991-96, chair 1996-97; mem. Winrock Internat. Adv. Coun., 1991—; founding incorporator Ark. Waterways Commn., 1996—, bd. dirs.; bd. visitors Manship Sch. Comm., La. State U., 1998—; bd. dirs. Main Street Ark., Hist. Preservation Alliance Ark.; active Ark. Transitional Employment Coun., 1999—, Ark. Transitional Employment Assistance Bd., 2000; sec. Dumas Area Cmty. Fund, 2000—; bd. dirs. Enterprise Corp. for the Delta, 1999-2002, Dumas Main St., v.p.; bd. dirs. Historic Preservation Alliance Ark, 2000—; outstanding bd. mem. Ark. Main St., 2002; outstanding bd. chair Ark. Cmty. Found., 2003. Named Disting. Alumnus Ark. A&M Coll., 1971, Woman of Achievement Nat. Fedn. Press Women, 1970, Outstanding Arkansan C. of C., 1986; recipient Ark. Profl. Women of Distinction award No. Bank, Little Rock, 1990, Emma McKinney award Nation's Top Cmty. Newspaper Woman, 1980, Journalist award Nat. Conf. of Christians and Jews, 1989, Lifetime Achievement award Nat. Fedn. Press Women, 1992, Outstanding Svc. award Ark. Assn. Elem. Prins., Disting. Svc. award Ark. Press Assn., 1993, Disting. Svc. award Internat. Soc. Weekly Newspaper Editors, 1996, Golden Svc. award Ark. Press Assn., 1996, State Leadership award Ark. Waterways Commn., 1996, Horizon award League Women Voters Ark., 1998 Ernie Deane award U. Ark., 2005, Chilcote award Ark. Cmty. Found., 2006; named to La. State U. Alumni Hall of Distinction, 1994, Journalism Hall of Fame La. State U., 1998; named one Top 100 Ark. Women, Ark. Bus., 1995-98; named Outstanding Bd. Mem. of Yr., Main Street Ark., 2002, Outstanding Bd. Mem., Ptnrs. of Ark. Cmty. Found., 2003, Extraordinary Svc. award Ark. Cmty. Found., 2006; honored Outstanding Svc. Women's Found. Ark., 2003, honored, Dumas, Ark. City Coun., 2010. Mem.: Main St. Dumas (pres. 2005), Ark. Delta Coun. (chmn., pres. Dumas Main St., mem. Main St. Ark. adv. bd.), Pi Beta Phi (Crest award 1992). Democrat. Roman Catholic. Home Phone: 870-382-5255. Personal E-mail: cschexnayder@centurytel.net.

SCHEXNAYDER, CLAY, state legislator; Attended, Allen Inst., Atlanta. Owner, operator Car Craft Auto; mem. Dist. 81 La. House of Reps., Baton Rogue, 2012—. Republican. Office: PO Box 267 Sorrento LA 70778 also: La House of Reps 900 N 3rd St Baton Rouge LA 70804 Office Phone: 225-473-6016. Business E-Mail: schexnayderc@legis.la.gov.

SCHIAVO, MARY FACKLER, lawyer; BA cum laude, Harvard U., Cambridge, Mass., 1976; MA, Ohio State U., Columbus, 1977; JD, NYU, 1980. Bar: Mo. 1980, U.S. Ct. Appeals, U.S. Supreme Ct. 1990, D.C. 1993, Md. 1994, SC 2008, Fla., 2009. Asst. U.S. atty., Western Dist. Mo. U.S. Dept. Justice, Kansas City, 1982-85, fed. prosecutor organized crime & racketeering strike force, 1985-86, White House fellow, spl. asst. to U.S. Atty. Gen. Washington, 1987-88; exec. dir. Bush/Quayle '88 Campaign, Mo., 1988; asst. sec., labor-mgmt. stds. U.S. Dept. of Labor, Washington, 1989-90; insp. gen. U.S. Dept. of Transp., Washington, 1990-96; prof., pub. policy & aviation Ohio State U., Columbus, 1997—2002; aviation analyst ABC News, 1996—97; aviation commentator NBC News, 1998—2001, CNN, 2014—; ptnr., transp. liti. Motley Rice, LLC, Mount Pleasant, SC, 2003—. Instr. US Atty. Gen.'s Adv. Inst., Washington, 1986, 88, FBI Acad., Quantico, Va., 1988; guest lectr. NYU Sch. Law, 1986, 88, 91; bd. dirs. Dept. Labor Acad., 1989-90; mem., house of dels. Am. Bar Assn., 1986-1989, assembly del. 1986-1989; mem., bd. govs. Mo. Bar, 1986-1989; chmn. Pro Bono Task Force 1984-1986; bd. dirs. White House Fellows Assn. and Found., 1992-96, 2nd v.p., 1992-93, chair, ann. meeting, 1993, 1st v.p., 1993-94, pres. 1994-95; mem. Pres.'s Coun. on Integrity and Efficiency, 1990-96, Pres.'s Commn. on White House Fellowships, 1994-95; bd. dirs. Worthington Industries 1998-; aviation commmentator CNN, Fox News, NBC, MSNBC, CNBS, ABC, CBS, BBC, CBN, Al Jazerra. Author: Flying Blind, Flying Safe, NY Times Bestseller. Former dir., bd. dirs. Root-Tilden Scholarship Program NYU, 1982-89, Harvard U. Alumni Assn.; former dir., Vis. Nurses Assn. Bd. Dirs. Recipient Thompson award Ohio State U. Alumni, 1988, Aviation Laurel citation Aviation Week and Space Tech. Mag., 1992, Aviation Laurel award Aviation Week and Space Tech. Mag., 1995, Ohio State Outstanding Alumnus award 1997, Truitt award ASPA, 2002, Webster award Internat. Platform Assn., 1997; named one of Top Ten Coll. Women in US, 1975, one of ten Outstanding Young Working Women in America, 1987, Kans. City Career Woman of Yr., 1988, Glamour Mag. Woman of Yr., 1997, Best Lawyers in America, 2010-14, named to NY Times Bestseller List, 1997; Ohio State U. fellow, 1976-77; US-Japan Leadership fellow, 1995; Root-Tilden legal scholar NYU, 1977-79. Mem.: Internat. Soc. Air Safety Investigators, Nat. Air Disaster Alliance and Found., White House Fellows Assn. and Found., Harvard U. and Ohio State U. Alumni Assn. Avocation: pilot. Office: Motley Rice LLC 28 Bridgeside Blvd Mount Pleasant SC 29464-4399 Office Phone: 843-216-9000, 843-216-9138. Office Fax: 843-216-9410. Business E-Mail: mschiavo@motleyrice.com.*

SCHICKEL, JOHN, state legislator; b. Mar. 29, 1954; MPA, Northern Ky. U. Ret. police officer; mem. Dist. 11 Ky. State Senate, 2009—. Republican. Roman Catholic. Office: 702 Capitol Ave Rm 209 Frankfort KY 40601 also: PO Box 991 Union KY 41091 Office Phone: 502-564-8100 Ext. 617, 859-384-7506.

SCHIEBLER, GEROLD LUDWIG, pediatrician, educator; b. Hamburg, Pa., June 20, 1928; s. Alwin Robert and Charlotte Elizabeth (Schmoele) Schiebler; m. Audrey Jean Lincourt, Jan. 8, 1954; children: Mark, Marcella, Kristen, Bettina, Wanda, Michele. BS, Franklin and Marshall Coll., 1950; MD, Harvard U., 1954. Intern pediat. and internal medicine Mass. Gen. Hosp., Boston, 1954—55, resident, 1955—56; resident pediat. U. Minn. Hosp., Mpls., 1956—57, fellow pediatric cardiology, 1957—58, rsch. fellow, 1958—59; rsch. fellow sect. physiology Mayo Clinic and Mayo Found., 1959—60; from asst. prof. pediatric cardiology to prof. emeritus U. Fla., 1960—2001, prof. emeritus, 2001—. Dir. divsn. Children's Med. Svcs. State of Fla., 1973—74, area med. dir., 1974—2000, cons., 2001—. Author (with L.P. Elliott): The X-ray Diagnosis of Congenital Cardiac Disease in Infants, Children and Adults, 1968, 1979; author: (with L.J. Krovetz and I.H. Gessner) Pediatric Cardiology, 1979. Recipient Lifetime Achievement award, Coll. Medicine, 2004; named Children's Med. Svcs. Pediatrician of Decade, Gov. Jeb Bush, 1999. Mem.: AMA (Benjamin Rush award 1993), AAAS, Fedn. State Med. Bds. (Svc. award 2008), Fla. Med. Assn. (past v.p., bd. govs., pres. 1991—92, Cert. Of Merit 2008), Fla. Heart Assn. (past pres.), Fla. Pediat. Soc. (exec. com.), Soc. Pediatric Rsch. (emeritus), Am. Coll. Cardiology, Am. Acad. Pediat. (Abraham Jacobi award 1993), Inst. Medicine NAS, Alpha Omega Alpha, Phi Beta Kappa. Home: 408 Beachside Villas Amelia Island Plantation Amelia Island FL 32034-6551 Home Fax: 904-277-7211. Business E-Mail: gls@health.ufl.edu.

SCHIEFFER, JOHN THOMAS (TOM SCHIEFFER), lawyer, former ambassador; b. Ft. Worth, Oct. 4, 1947; s. John E. and Gladys (Payne) Schieffer; m. Susanne Silber, Sept. 22, 1979; 1 child, Paul Robert. BA in Govt., U. Tex., 1970, MA in Internat. Rels., 1972, JD. Bar: Tex. 1979. Mem. Tex. House of Reps., 1973—79; pvt. law practice, 1979—89; ptnr.-in-charge of ballpark devel. Tex. Rangers Baseball Club, 1990—91, pres., 1991—99, gen. ptnr., 1994—99; pres. J. Thomas Schieffer Mgmt. Co. & Pablo Oper. Co., 1989—2001; US amb. to Australia US Dept. State, Canberra, 2001—05, US amb. to Japan Tokyo, 2005—09; sr. counsel Akin Gump Strauss Hauer & Feld LLP, Washington, 2010—; spl. advisor on behalf of Maj. League Baseball LA Dodgers, 2011—. Mem. advisory bd. US Studies Ctr., U. Sydney; bd. mem. Maureen & Mike Mansfield Found.; bd. councilors US-Japan Council; mem. advisory bd. Japan American Soc. of Dallas/Ft. Worth. Recipient Order of Australia, Govt. of Australia, 2005, Medal for Disting. Pub. Svc., US Dept. Def., 2008. Democrat. Office: Akin Gump Strauss Hauer & Feld LLP 1700 Pacific Ave Ste 4100 Dallas TX 75201 Office Phone: 817-886-5072. Office Fax: 817-887-4288. E-mail: tschieffer@akingump.com.

SCHILLER, JOAN HOFF, oncologist, educator; b. Chgo., Nov. 10, 1954; MD, U. Ill. Coll. Medicine, Chgo., 1980. Diplomate Am. Bd. Internal Medicine, Am. Bd. Internal Medicine, Med. Oncology, cert. Nat. Bd. Med. Examiners. Intern, internal medicine Northwestern Meml. Hosp., Chgo., 1980—81, resident, oncology, 1981—83; fellow, human oncology U. Wis. Clin. Cancer Ctr., Madison, Wis., 1984—86, rsch. assoc.; asst. prof. U. Wis., Madison, Melanie Heald prof., dept. medicine, sect. med. oncology; dep. dir., Harold C. Simmons Comprehensive Cancer Ctr. U. Tex. Southwestern Med. Ctr., Dallas, chair, hematology/oncology, prof., dept. hematology/oncology. Mem. internat. scientific com. 10th World Conf. on Lung Cancer; head, lung cancer disease-orientated working group U. Wis. Hosp. and Cancer Ctr.; spkr. in field. Contbr. articles to profl. jours., chapters to books. Mem. med. com. Joan's Legacy Lung Found.; founder, pres. Women Against Lung Cancer. Mem.: Am. Soc. Clin. Oncology, Eastern Co-operative Oncology Group (chairperson, thoracic oncology com.). Office: U Tex Southwestern Med Ctr at Dallas 5323 Harry Hines Blvd Dallas TX 75390-8852 Office Phone: 214-648-4180. Office Fax: 214-648-1955.

SCHIMEK, JOHN BRADLEY, music educator, musician; b. Houston, Tex., July 21, 1955; m. Pamela J. Schimek; 1 child, Joel. MusB in Edn., U. Wis., 1979; MusM in Double Bass Performance, Rice U., 1981; EdD, La Salle U., 1996; student, U. North Tex. Instr. music Sam Houston State U., 1979—82; dir. orch. Oshkosh Pub. Schs., 1982—86; dir. youth symphony U. Wis., Oshkosh, Wis., 1982—86; instr. music U. North Tex., 1986—92; from asst. prof. music to prof. Okla. City U., 1993—95, prof., 1999—. Adv. bd. Classen H.S. Arts, 1993—, De Vinci Inst., 2003—; lectr. in field. Contbr. articles to profl. jours. and book; musician: Okla. City Philharmonic. Named Outstanding Music Faculty, Okla. City U., 1997. Mem.: AAUP, Coll. Music Soc., Am. Fedn. Musicians, Okla. Music Educators Assn., Music Educators Nat. Conf., Internat. Soc. Bassists, Am. String Tchrs. Assn. Office: Okla City Univ 2501 N Blackwelder Ave Oklahoma City OK 73106

SCHINDLER, ANDREW J., marketing executive; b. Harrisburg, Pa., Aug. 1944; BA, Franklin and Marshall Coll.; MBA, U. Pa. Dir., mfg. Nabisco Foods Co., Parsippany, NJ, 1987—88; with R.J. Reynolds Tobacco Holdings, Inc., 1974—2005; nat. mgr., sales pers. R.J. Reynolds Tobacco Co., Winston-Salem, NC, 1976—78, mgr., orgn. and mgmt. devel. Reynolds Industries parent co., 1978—79, dir., orgn. and mgmt. devel., 1979—82, plant mgr., 1982—87, v.p., pers., 1988—89, sr. v.p., ops., 1989—91, exec. v.p., ops., 1991—94, COO, 1994—95, pres., 1994, CEO, 1995, chmn., 1999; CEO Reynolds America Inc., Winston-Salem, NC, 1999—2004, chmn., 1999—2005, exec. chmn., 2004—05. Mem. adv. bd. Wachovia Bank N.C., N.A. Vice chmn. N.C. Emerging Tech. Alliance; bd. dirs. N.C. Sch. Arts Found., Winston-Salem Bus., Inc.; bd. visitors Wake Forest U. Bapt. Med. Ctr. Capt. U.S. Army, Vietnam. Office: Hanesbrands Inc Bd Directors 1000 E Hanes Mill Rd Winston Salem NC 27105 Office Phone: 336-519-8080. Business E-Mail: andrew.schindler@hanesbrands.com.

SCHLAGETER, ROBERT WILLIAM, museum administrator; b. Streator, Ill., May 10, 1925; s. Herman Pete and Ida (Ladtkow) S.; divorced; children— David Michael, Robert William Diploma, Karl Ruprecht Univ., Heidelberg, Fed. Republic Germany, 1950; BA, U. Ill., Champaign-Urbana, 1950, MFA, 1957. Asst. prof. U. Tenn., Knoxville, 1952-58; dir. Mint Mus. Art, Charlotte, NC, 1958-66; assoc. dir. Downtown Gallery, NYC, 1966, Ackland Art Ctr., U. NC, Chapel Hill, 1967-76; dir. Cummer Gallery Art, Jacksonville, Fla., 1976-92, dir. emeritus, 1992—. Fine arts cons. corp. and pvt. collecting, 1993—. Author: (exhbn. catalogue) Winslow Homer's Florida, George Inness' Florida, Martin Johnson Heade Florida, Robert Henri-George Bellows. Served with U.S. Army, 1943-45, ETO

SCHLAPMAN, KIMBERLY ROADS, singer; b. Cornelia, Ga., Oct. 15, 1969; m. Steven Roads (dec. 2005); m. Stephen Schlapman, Nov. 28, 2006; 1 child, Daisy Pearl. Attended, Samford U., Birmingham, Ala. Co-founder Little Big Town, 1999. Singer: (albums) (with Little Big Town) Little Big Town, 2002, The Road to Here, 2005, A Place to Land, 2007, The Reason Why, 2010, Tornado, 2012, (songs)

Pontoon, 2012 (Single of Yr., Country Music Assn. Awards, 2012, Best Country Duo/Group Performance, Grammy Awards, 2013), Tornado, 2012 (Video of Yr., Acad. Country Music Awards, 2013); host (TV series) Kimberly's Simply Southern, 2012. Named Top New Duo/Vocal Group, Acad. Country Music Awards, 2007, Vocal Group of Yr., Country Music Assn. Awards, 2012, 2013, Acad. Country Music Awards, 2013. Office: c/o Sandbox Entertainment 54 Music Square East Suite 200 Nashville TN 37203*

SCHLEGEL, ERIC M., astrophysicist; BSc in Astronomy and Meteorology, SUNY Albany, 1976; PhD, Ind. U., Bloomington, 1983. Postdoc. rsch. assoc. Ind. U., 1983—86, Harvard Coll. Obs., Cambridge, Mass., 1986—89; rsch. scientist NASA's Goddard Space Flight Ctr. Associated U. Rsch. Astronomy, Greenbelt, Md., 1989—95, Smithsonian Astrophys. Obs., Cambridge, 1995—2005. Author: (book) The Restless Universe: Understanding X-ray Astronomy in the Age of Chandra and Newton. Office: University Tex San Antonio One UTSA Circle San Antonio TX 78249 Business E-Mail: eric.schlegel@utsa.edu.*

SCHLEGEL, HANS, astronaut; b. Uberlingen, Germany, Aug. 3, 1951; m. Heike Schlegel-Walport; 7 children. Diploma in physics, U. Aachen, Germany, 1979. Mem. acad. staff, solid state physicist Rheinisch Westfalische Technische Hochschule, U. Aachen, 1979—86; specialist in non-destructive testing methodology R&D dept. Institut Dr. Förster GmbH & Co. KG, Reutlingen, Germany, 1986—88; basic astronaut tng. German Aerospace Rsch. Ctr., 1988—90, prime payload specialist D-2 mission, 1990—93; payload tng. Cologne, Germany and Johnson Space Ctr., Houston, Tex., 1990—93; cosmonaut candidate. German-Russian Mir-'97 mission, served as crew interface coord. Y.A. Gagarin Tng. Ctr., Moscow, 1995—97, 2nd bd. engr. tng. and cert., 1997—98; astronaut European Astronaut Corps., 1998—; mission tng. specialist NASA, 1998; worked in ISS Branch on mechanisms & structures, on crew equipment and the ISS sys., 1999—2002; worked in the Robotics Branch and as ISS CAPCOM; lead ISS CAPCOM for Increment 10, 2004—05; lead astronaut Johnson Space Ctr., 2005—. Payload specialist STS-55 aboard Space Shuttle Columbia, 1993; crew mem. Atlantis STS-122 mission to deliver the European Space Agency's Columbus Lab. to the ISS, 2008. Contbr. publications and scientific reports in the field of semiconductor physics. Paratrooper, 2nd lt. Fed. Armed Forces. Recipient Fed. Svc. Cross 1st Class, Germany, Medal of Friendship, Russia. Mem.: Am. Field Svc. Germany, German Phys. Soc. Avocations: skiing, scuba diving, flying, reading. Office: NASA Johnson Space Ctr Astronaut Office/CB Houston TX 77058

SCHLEGEL, JOHN FREDERICK, management consultant; b. Ogden, Utah, Dec. 18, 1944; s. Max Joseph and Mary Georgia (Whitaker) S.; m. Priscilla Mary Hecht, Sept. 8, 1967. BS in Pharmacy, U. Pacific, 1967; D of Pharmacy, U. So. Calif., 1972, MS in Edn., 1980; ScD in Pharmacy (hon.), Mass. Coll. Pharmacy, 1984, L.I. U., 1985. Lic. pharmacist, Calif., Nev.; cert. assoc. exec. Chief pharmacist U. So. Calif. Sch. Pharmacy, LA, 1967-73, postdoctoral fellow, 1972—73, dir. pharmacy admissions, 1973-75; dir. office student affairs Am. Assn. Colls. Pharmacy, Alexandria, Va., 1975-77, asst. exec. dir., 1977-81, exec. dir., 1981-84; CEO Am. Pharm. Assn., Washington, 1984-89; exec. v.p., CEO Am. Acad. Facial Plastic and Reconstructive Surgery, Washington, 1989-92; pres. Schlegel & Assocs., 1992—. Cons. in field. Contbr. over 100 articles on pharmacy, health care and assn. mgmt.; presenter in field. Nat. del. White House Conf. on Aging, Washington, 1981.; pres., CEO, founder Alpha Psi Edn., Scholarship & Leadership Found. Disting. alumnus U. So. Calif. Sch. Pharmacy, 1985, U. the Pacific Sch. Pharmacy, 1987. Fellow Am. Soc. Assn. Execs.; mem. Fla. Soc. Assn. Execs., Phi Delta Chi (charter, bd. counsellors), Alpha Psi Ed Found. (pres.). Avocations: tennis, classical music, art, bridge, travel. Office: 3390 Highlands Bridge Rd Sarasota FL 34235-6859 Office Phone: 941-341-0434. Business E-Mail: jschlegel@comcast.net.

SCHLESINGER, HARVEY ERWIN, federal judge; b. NYC, June 4, 1940; BA, The Citadel, 1962; JD, U. Richmond, 1965. Bar: Va. 1965, Fla. 1965, U.S. Supreme Ct. 1968. Corp. counsel Seaboard Coast Line R.R. Co., Jacksonville, Fla., 1968-70; chief asst. US atty. Mid. Dist. Fla., Jacksonville, 1970-75; magistrate judge US Dist. Ct. (mid. dist.) Fla., Jacksonville, 1975-91, US dist. judge, 1991—2006, sr. judge, 2006—. Adj. prof. U. North Fla., 1984-91; mem. Jud. Conf. Adv. Com. Fed. Rules Criminal Procedure, 1986-93; mem. Jud. Conf. Adv. Com. on Adminstrn. of Magistrate Judges Sys., 1996-2003, chmn., 1998-2003; chmn. U.S. Dist. Ct. Forms Working Group, Washington, 1983—, Jud. Conf. Ad hoc Com. on Long Range Planning, 1998-2003; Jud. Conf. Jud. Officers Resources Working Group, 1998-99; 11th Cir. Dist. Judges Assn., 1991—, sec., treas. 1996- 97, v.p. 1997-98, pres.-elect., 1999-2001, pres., 2001-02. Bd. dir. Pine Castle Ctr. for Mentally Retarded, Jacksonville, 1970-87, pres., 1972-74, chmn. bd. dirs., 1973-74; trustee Pine Castle Found., 1972-76, Congregation Ahavath Chesed, Jacksonville, 1970—, v.p., 1975-80, pres., 1980-82; v.p. S.E. Coun. Union Am. Hebrew Congregations, 1984-88; asst. commr. for exploring North Fla. Coun. Boy Scouts Am., 1983-86, exec. com., 1986-98, adv. bd., 1998—; active Boy Scouts Am. Nat. Jewish Com. on Scouting, Irving, Tex., 1986-93, Fla. Sesquicentennial Commn., 1995-96; trustee River Garden Home for Aged, 1982—, sec., 1985-1990; co-chmn. bd. gov. Jacksonville chpt. NCCJ, 1983-1993, presiding co-chmn. 1984-89; nat. bd. trustees, NYC, 1986-93; trustee Jacksonville Cmty. Found., 2000—, vice-chair, 2003-05, chmn. 2006-08. Capt. JAGC, U.S. Army, 1965-68. Recipient Silver Beaver award Boy Scouts Am., 1986; George Washington Medal of Honor, Freedoms Found., Valley Forge, Pa., 1987, Silver Medallion Humanitarian award NCCJ, 1992, Founders award, Fed. Magistrate Judges Assn., 1999, William Green award for profl. excellence U. Richmond Law Sch., 2000, Jurist of Yr. award Am. Bd. Trial Adv., 2001, 08. Mem. ABA (fed. rules of evidence and criminal procedure com. 1979-98, Nat. Conf. Spl. Ct. Judges, 1975-90, conf. newsletter editor, 1988-90, Nat. Conf. Fed. Trial Judges, 1990—2001, chmn. legis. com., 1996-97, Flascher award 1989, Best Trial Judge award), Va. Bar Assn., Fla. Bar Assn., Fed. Judges Assn., Jacksonville Bar Assn.; Fed. Bar Assn. (pres. Jacksonville chpt. 1974, 75, 81-82), Am. Judicature Soc., Chester Bedell Am. Inns of Ct. (pres. 1992-96), Rotary (Paul Harris fellow, pres. S. Jacksonville club), Masons (past master, past venerable master, knights comdr. of Ct. Honour, 33 degree Scottish Rite bodies), Shriners. Office: US Dist Ct Simpson US Courthouse 300 N Hogan St Ste 11-150 Jacksonville FL 32202-4246 Office Phone: 904-549-1990.

SCHLESINGER, SHELDON J., lawyer; b. Bklyn., Aug. 15, 1930; BA, U. Miami, 1952, JD, 1954. Bar: Fla. 1955, DC 1981. Founding ptnr., CEO Sheldon J. Schlesinger, PA, Fort Lauderdale, Fla. Mem. Miami Law Quarterly, 1953—54. Bd. trustees Broward CC, Fla., 1971—87; bd. govs. Nova-Southeastern Law Ctr. With US Army, 1954—56. Named to The Trial Lawyer Hall of Fame, 2011. Mem.: Assn. Trial Lawyers of America, Fla. Trial Lawyers Assn. (mem. bd. dirs. 1976—78), Broward County Trial Lawyers Assn. (pres. 1967—68), DC Bar Assn., Fla. Bar Assn. (former chmn. Standing Com. on Professionalism), Broward County Bar Assn. (mem. trial sect.), Inner Circle of Advocates, Tau Epsilon Rho. Office: 1212 Southeast Third Ave Fort Lauderdale FL 33316 Office Phone: 954-467-8800. Office Fax: 954-523-4803.

SCHLODER, JOHN E., museum director; BS, Duquesne U., 1969; diplôme d'Ancien Elève, L'Ecole du Louvre, Paris, 1973; licence L'Institut d'Art et d'Archéologie, U. Paris-Sorbonne, 1973, doctorat L'Institut d'Art et d'Archéologie, 1988; MPhil, Columbia U., 1980. Chargé de Mission Musée du Louvre, Paris, 1979-82; asst. curator Cleve. Mus. Art Edn Dept., 1982-85, assoc. curator, 1985-86, adminstr. pub. programs, 1986-88, asst. dir. edn. and pub. programs, 1988-92; dir. Birmingham Mus. Art, Ala., 1992-96, Joslyn Mus. Art, Omaha, 1997—2000, Mus. Fine Arts, St. Petersburg, Fla., 2001—. Vis. prof. Colégio Andrews, Rio de Janeiro, Brazil, 1980-81, Vaculdade Candido Mendes, Rio de Janeiro, 1981-82; adj. prof. dept. art history Case Western Res. U., Cleve., 1984-92; lectr. in field. Mus. rep. Northeastern Ohio Inter-Mus. Coun., 1984-92; trustee Cleve. Sch. Arts, 1991-92; active Southeast Mus. Conf., 1992—; mem. Leadership Birmingham, 1994-95; bd. dirs. Op. New Birmingham, 1993—; mem. Birmingham Olympic programming com., mem. outreach com., 1994—. Lurcy Trust fellowship, 1975, Columbia U. Traveling fellowship, 1975, 76, U. Cambridge, Eng. Leverhulme fellowship, 1977, Kellogg Project fellowship Smithsonian Instn., 1987; scholarship J. Paul Getty Trust, 1989; vis. Scholar grantee The Japan Found., 1995; recipient French Govt. award, 1975, award of achievement for best cmty. event Northern Ohio Live Mag., 1991. Mem. Am. Assn. Mus., Assn. Art Mus. Dirs., Internat. Lab. for Visitor Studies, Visitor Studies Assn., Ala. Mus. Assn., Birmingham Area Mus. Assn., Soc. de l'Histoire de l'Art Français, Rotary Club Birmingham. Office: Museum Fine Arts 255 Beach Drive NE Saint Petersburg FL 33701 Business E-Mail: jschloder@fine-arts.org.

SCHLOEGEL, SCOTT P., legislative staff member; b. Berwyn, Ill., Dec. 9, 1967; m. Kirsten L. Bondeson, May 22, 1993; 2 children. BS, No. Mich. U., 1990. Legis. aide to Rep. Bart Stupak Mich. House of Reps., Lansing, 1990, legis. aide to Rep. Ken DeBeausaert, 1991—92; dist. adminstr. to Rep. Bart Stupak, US House of Reps., Washington, 1993—97, chief of staff, 1997—2007, 2007—11; profl. staff mem. US House Com. on Energy and Commerce, Washington, 2007. Avocations: sports, family. Office: Office of Congressman Bart Stupak 2268 Rayburn House Office Bldg Washington DC 20515-0001 Home: 7606 Maritime Ln Springfield VA 22153-1627 Office Phone: 202-225-4735. Office Fax: 202-225-4744. E-mail: scott.schloegel@mail.house.gov.

SCHLUETER, DAVID ARNOLD, law educator; b. Sioux City, Iowa, Apr. 29, 1946; s. Arnold E. and Helen A. (Dettmann) S.; m. Linda L. Boston, Apr. 22, 1972; children: Jennifer, Jonathan. BA, Tex. A&M U., 1969; JD, Baylor U., 1971; LLM, U. Va., 1981. Bar: Tex. 1971, DC 1973, US Ct. Mil. Appeals 1972, US Supreme Ct. 1976. Legal counsel US Supreme Ct., Washington, 1981—83; assoc. dean St. Mary's U., San Antonio, 1984—89, prof. law, 1986—, Hardy prof. trial advocacy, dir. advocacy programs, 2000—; reporter Fed. Adv. Com. on Criminal Rules, 1988—2005. Chmn. JAG adv. coun., 1974-75. Author: Military Criminal Justice: Practice and Procedure, 1982, 8th edit., 2012, Military Crimes and Defenses, 2007, 2nd edit., 2012; (with others) Military Rules of Evidence Manual, 1981, 7th edit., 2011, Texas Rules of Evidence Manual, 1983, 9th edit., 2012, Texas Evidentiary Foundations, 1992, 4th edit., 2011, Military Evidentiary Foundations, 1994, 5th edit., 2013, Military Criminal Procedure Forms, 1997, 3d edit., 2012, Federal Evidence Tactics, 1997, Texas Rules of Evidence Trial Book, 2000, 2nd edit., 2010; editor-in-chief: Emerging Problems Under the Federal Rules of Evidence, 3d edit., 1998; contbr. articles to legal publs. Maj. JAGC, US Army, 1972-81. Fellow Am. Law Inst., Tex. Bar Found. (life), Am. Bar Found. (life); mem. ABA (vice-chmn. criminal justice sect. coun. 1991-94, vice-chmn. com. on criminal justice and mil. 1983-84, chmn. standing com. on mil. law 1991-92, mem. standing com. on armed forces law, chmn. editl. adv. bd., Criminal Justice Mag., 1989-91, 2000-), Tex. Bar Assn. Republican. Lutheran. Office: St Marys U Sch Law 1 Camino Santa Maria St San Antonio TX 78228-8603

SCHLUMBERGER, ROBERT ERNEST, accountant; b. Pitts., Sept. 25, 1951; s. Ernest August Jr. and Barbara Ann (Rodler) S.; m. Mary Cecelia Leahy, Dec. 7, 1974; children: Jennifer Marie Schlumberger Jones, Saralynne Cecelia Schlumberger Miller. BS, Pa. State U., 1974. Mgr. Bradford House Restaurant, Punxsutawney, Pa., 1974-76, Latrobe, Pa., 1976-77, Butler, Pa., 1977-78; owner, acct. Schlumberger Bus. Svcs., Butler, Pa., 1978-88; pres., acct. Schlumberger Acctg. Svcs., Inc., Crystal River, Fla., 1988—. Registered rep. H.D. Vest Investment Securities, Inc., Las Colinas, Tex., 1986—; enrolled agt. IRS, 1983—. Mem. Nat. Soc. Accts., Nat. Assn. Enrolled Agts. Republican. Lutheran. Avocations: flying, fishing, reading, swimming. Home: 720 N Dove Pt Crystal River FL 34429-5339 Office: Schlumberger Acctg Svcs Inc 6220 W Corporate Oaks Dr Crystal River FL 34429-8723 Office Phone: 352-795-3691. E-mail: bob@schlumbergeraccounting.com.

SCHMALZRIED, MARVIN EUGENE, financial consultant; b. Dighton, Kans., Nov. 11, 1924; s. Carl D. and Marie M. (Bahm) S.; m. Jean Landino, Nov. 27, 1946 (dec.); children— Darlene, Candace, Cynthia, Derek, Valerie, Rebecca; m. Judith Reichardt Stuart, Oct. 23, 2004. BBA, Northwestern U., 1949; LL.B., U. Conn., 1955. Bar: Conn. bar 1955; C.P.A., Conn. Acct. Webster, Blanchard & Willard, CPA's (named changed to Price Waterhouse & Co.), Hartford, Conn., 1950-55; contr., asst. treas. J.B. Williams Co., Glastonbury, Conn., 1955-57; treas., sec. Curtis 1000, Inc. (name changed to Am Bus. Products, Inc.), Atlanta, 1957-61; comptroller Wyeth Labs., NYC, 1964-67, v.p., 1967-72, sr. v.p., 1972-84; pres. Venda Vid, Inc., NYC, 1986-90; asst. to pres. Am. Home Products Corp., NYC, 1961—63; sr. v.p. View-Master Ideal Group, Inc., NYC, 1987-90; exec. v.p. Strategics Inc., 1993-95. Recipient Gold medal Conn. Soc. C.P.A.'s, 1953 Mem. AICPA, ABA, Old Greenwich Friday Evening Reading Soc. (pres.) Clubs: Bent Tree Country. Home and Office: 4874 Cherry Laurel Cir Sarasota FL 34241-6442

SCHMANDT, JURGEN A., public affairs educator; b. Mar. 4, 1929; PhD, U. Bonn, Germany, 1956. Prin. adminstr. OECD, Paris, 1960-65; assoc. dir. program sci. and tech. Harvard U., Cambridge, Mass., 1965-71; prof. pub. affairs U. Tex., Austin, 1971—2001; dir. and disting. fellow Houston Advanced Rsch. Ctr., The Woodlands, Tex., 1985—. Author: Acid Rain and Friendly Neighbors, 1988, The Regions and Global Warming, 1992, Scarce Water, 1998, Navigating the Waters of the Paso del Norte, 1999, Sustainable Development, 2000, George Mitchell and The Idea of Sustainability, 2010, The Impact of Global Warmings on Texas, 2011 Home: 300 Bowie Apt 3902 Austin TX 78703-4661 E-mail: jas@harc.edu.

SCHMANDT-BESSERAT, DENISE, archaeologist, educator; b. Ay, France, Aug. 10, 1933; came to U.S., 1965, naturalized, 1970; d. Victor and Jeanne (Crabit) Besserat; m. Jurgen Schmandt, Dec. 27, 1956; children: Alexander, Christopher, Phillip. Ed., Ecole du Louvre, 1965; PhD (hon.), Kenyon Coll., Gambier, Ohio, 2008. Rsch. fellow in Near Eastern Archaeology Peabody Mus. Harvard U., Cambridge, Mass., 1969-71; fellow Radcliffe Inst., Cambridge, 1969-71; asst. prof. Middle Eastern studies U. Tex., Austin, 1972-81, assoc. prof., 1981-88, prof., 1988—2004; acting chief curator U. Tex. Art Mus., 1978—79. Vis. assoc. prof. U. Calif., Berkeley, 1987-88; curator Legacy of the Middle East exhbn. Jeddah (Saudi Arabia) Hist. Preservation Dept. Author: Before Writing, 1992, How Writing Came About, 1996, History of Counting, 1999, When Writing Met Art, 2007, Symbols at Ain Ghazal, edit., 2013; adv. editor Tech. and Culture, 1978-92; editl. adv. bd. Archaeology Odyssey, 2003-06; mem. editl. bd. Written Communication, 1993-95, Visible Lang., 1985—, Explorations in Media Ecology, 2001-13, Ancient Adminstrn., 2001; mem. editl. bd. Near Eastern Archaology, 2005—08, Scripta, 2008-; contbr. articles to profl. jours. Recipient Kayden Nat. U. Press Book award, 1992, Robert W. Hamilton Author award, 1998, 2008, Walter J. Ong award Media Ecology Assn., 2004; named in Am. Scientist, 1999; Wenner-Gren Found. grant, 1970-71, NEA grant, 1974-75, 77-78, ACLS grant, 1984, Deutscher Akademischer Austauschdienst grant, 1986, NEH grant, 1992; NEH fellow, 1979-80, U. Wis. Inst. for Rsch. in Humanities fellow, 1984-85, USIA, Am. Ctr. Oriental Rsch. fellow, 1994-95, 97, 2001, Malone fellow 1997, 99, 2005, Weeks fellow Humanities Rsch. Ctr. Stanford U., 2003—04; ACOR-CAORC fellowship, Amman, Jordan, 2009. Mem. Am. Oriental Soc., Archeol. Inst. Am. (governing bd. 1983-89), Am. Anthropol. Assn., Am. Schs. of Oriental Rsch., Centro Internat. Rsch. Archeologiche Anthropologiche e Storiche (Rome), Com. Philology Polish Acad. Scis, Wroclaw Br. Business E-Mail: dsb@austin.utexas.edu.

SCHMELING, JUDY, corporate financial executive; b. Fla. BS in Acctg., Fla. State U. Various mgmt. positions Deloitte & Touche, 1982—86; mng. dir. Tunstall Consulting Inc., 1986—94; dir., Investor Rels. and operating v.p., fin. HSN Inc., 1994—98, v.p., Strategic Planning and Analysis, 1998—99, sr.v.p., 1999—2002, COO, 2001—02; exec. v.p., CFO HSN, Inc., 2002—. Office: HSN Inc 1 HSN Dr Saint Petersburg FL 33729 Office Phone: 727-872-1000. Business E-Mail: judy.schmeling@hsn.net.

SCHMIDT, PAUL WICKHAM, lawyer; b. Milw., June 25, 1948; s. Edmund Julian and Barbara (Wickham) S.; m. Cathryn Ann Piehl, June 27, 1970; children: Thomas Wickham, William Piehl, Anna Patchin. BA cum laude, Lawrence U., 1970; JD cum laude, U. Wis., 1973. Bar: Wis. 1973, U.S. Dist. Ct. (we. dist.) Wis. 1973, U.S. Supreme Ct. 1982, D.C. 1988. Atty. advisor Bd. Immigration Appeals, Washington, 1973-76; gen. atty. office of gen. counsel Immigration and Naturalization Service, Washington, 1976-78, acting gen. counsel, 1979-81, 86-87, dep. gen. counsel, 1978-87; assoc. Jones, Day, Reavis & Pogue, Washington, 1987-89, ptnr., 1990-92; mng. ptnr. Fragomen, Del Ray & Bernsen, PC, Washington, 1993-95; chmn. Bd. of Immigration Appeals, Falls Church, Va., 1995-2001, mem., 2001—03; judge Arlington (Va.) Immigration Ct., 2003—. Mem. ABA, D.C. Bar Assn., Wis. Bar Assn., Fed. Bar Assn. (immigration sect.). Avocations: gardening, history. Home: 711 S View Ter Alexandria VA 22314-4923 Office: Arlington Immigration Ct 901 N Stuart St Ste 1300 Arlington VA 22203 Business E-Mail: paul.schmidt@usdoj.gov.

SCHMIDT-NIELSEN, BODIL MIMI (MRS. ROGER G. CHAGNON), retired physiologist, educator; b. Copenhagen, Nov. 3, 1918; came to U.S., 1946, naturalized, 1952; d. August and Marie Jorgensen Krogh; m. Knut Schmidt-Nielsen, Sept. 20, 1939 (div. Feb. 1966); children: Astrid, Bent, Bodil; m. Roger G. Chagnon, Oct. 1968 (dec. 2003). DDS, U. Copenhagen, 1941, DOdont, 1946, DPhil, 1955; DS (hon.), Bates Coll., 1983; MD (hon.), U. Aarhus, Denmark, 1997. Mem. faculty Duke U., Durham, NC, 1952-64; prof. biology Case Western Res. U., Cleve., 1964-71, chmn. dept., 1970-71, adj. prof., 1971-74; trustee Mt. Desert Island Biol. Lab., Maine, rsch. scientist Maine, 1971-86, exec. com. Maine, 1978-85, v.p. Maine, 1979-81, pres. Maine, 1981-85; prof. dept. physiology U. Fla., Gainesville, 1985—. Adj. prof. Brown U., Providence, 1971-75, dept. physiol. U. Fla., Gainesville, 1986—; mem. tng. grant com. NIGMS, 1965-71. Author: August and Marie Krogh, Lives in Science, 1995, Danish edit., 1997; editor: Urea and the Kidney, 1970; assoc. editor Am. Jour. Physiology: Regulatory, Integrative and Comparative Physiology, 1978-81. Trustee Coll. of Atlantic, Bar Harbor, Maine, 1972-92. Recipient Career award NIH, 1962-64, John Simon Guggenheim Meml. fellow, 1952-53; Bowditch lectr., 1958, Jacobaeus lectr., 1974. Fellow AAAS (del. coun. 1977-79), NY Acad. Scis., Am. Acad. Arts and Scis.; mem. Am. Physiol. Soc. (coun. 1971-77, pres. 1975-76, Ray G. Daggs award 1989, Orr Reynolds award 1994, August Krogh lectr. 1994, Berliner award 1998), Soc. Exptl. Biology and Medicine (coun. 1967-71). Achievements include research, publications on biochemistry of saliva, water metabolism of desert animals, urea excretion, peristalsis of renal pelvis and concentrating mechanism, comparative kidney physiology, comparative physiology of excretory organs. Office: U Fla Dept Physiology 2015 SW 16th Ave Gainesville FL 32605 also: 2680 SW 53 Ln #1528 Gainesville FL 32608 Business E-Mail: bodil@gator.net.

SCHMITT, KARL MICHAEL, retired political scientist; b. Louisville, July 22, 1922; s. Edward Peter and Mary Ann (Iula) S.; m. Grace Bernadette Leary, June 18, 1949; children: Karl, Edward, Barbara, William, Michael. BA, Cath. U. Am., 1947, MA, 1949; PhD, U. Pa., 1954. Teaching asst. U. Pa., 1948-50; instr. history Niagara U., 1950-54, asst. prof., 1954-55; research analyst U.S. Dept. State, 1955-58; asst. prof. dept. govt. U. Tex., 1958-63, assoc. prof., 1963-66, prof., 1966-91, prof. emeritus, 1991—, chmn., 1975-80. Vis. prof. U. Calif., LA, 1959, Nat. War Coll., 1970-71; vis. sr. fellow U. Manchester, Eng., 1988-89; cons. Dept. of State, 1962-70 Author: Communism in Mexico; A Study in Political Frustration, 1965, Mexico and the United States, 1821-1973: Conflict and Coexistence, 1974, others. Contbr. articles to profl. jours. With US Army, 1943—45. Decorated Purple Heart. Mem. Tex. Cath. Hist. Assn. (pres. 1976-77). Roman Catholic. Home: 11279 Taylor Draper Ln 323 Austin TX 78759

SCHMITT, PATRICIA ANN, health and physical education educator; b. Crystal City, Tex., July 19, 1938; d. Joseph Frances and Clara Constance (Conring) Schmitt. BS, Tex. A&I U., 1960; MA, Tex. Woman's U., 1965, PhD, 1974. Tchr. Driscoll Jr. HS, Corpus Christi Ind. Sch. Dist., Tex., 1960—62, Mary Carroll HS, Corpus Christi, 1962—65; prof. Del Mar Coll., Corpus Christi, 1965—99; ret., 1999. Waterfront dir. Heart o' the Hills Camp, Kerrville, Tex., 1960—63, 1966—71; water safety instr. trainer ARC, Nueces County, 1970—; mem. Fin. Com., 2010—12. Ch. coun.chair, Corpus Christi, 1981—83, 1996—98, 2001—09; chmn. pastor parish rels. com. Wesley United Meth., 2007—10; learning free bd. mem. Wesley United Methodist, 2010—12, chair staff, Parish Rels. Com., 2010—11. Recipient Disting. Svc. award, Tex. Assn. Intercollegiate Athletics for Women, 1981, Honor award, TAHPERD, 1999, District Leader award, Wasley United Meth. Ch., 2012; named Woman of Yr. in Edn., YWCA, 1984. Mem.: Tex. Volleyball Ofcls. Assn. (dist. dir. 1977—83, ofcl.), Tex. Assn. Health, Phys. Edn., Recreation and Dance (life; chmn. coll. adminstrs. sect. 1981). Avocations: walking, gardening, travel, golf. Home: 5005 Maylands Dr Corpus Christi TX 78413-3620

SCHMITZ, SUE, state legislator; m. John Schmitz; children: Davis, Jonathan, Matthew. State rep. Dist. 6, Ala., 1999—; mem. Edn. Com., Elec. Com., Mkt. Com., Madison County Legislature Com., 1999—; state rep. Ala.; co-owner Hardware & Gen. Merchandise Store; sponsor Students Against Drinking & Driving & Close Up Found.;

coach & advisor We The People Program. Mem.: Optimist Club. Democrat. Methodist. Mailing: 4649 Jeff Rd Toney AL 35773 Office: State House Repr 11 S Union St Rm 524-D Montgomery AL 36130 Office Phone: 256-852-7003.

SCHMUDE, RICHARD WILLIS, JR., chemistry professor; b. Washington, June 18, 1958; s. Richard Willis and Winifred Forbes (Delchamps) S. PhD, Tex. A&M U., College Station; MS, BA. Prof. chemistry Gordon State Coll., Barnesville, Ga., 1994—. Contbr. articles to Jour. of the Assn. Lunar and Planetary Observers, Jour. of the Royal Astron. Soc. Can., Tex. Jour. of Sci. Pres. Los Alamos Right to Life, 1990-91. Recipient Walter Haas Observing award, Assn. Lunar and Planetary Observers, 2002, Vol. of Yr. award, Lions Club Lamar County, 2005, Astronomical League award, 2008, Peggy Hans Svc. award, Assn. Lunar & Planetary Observers, 2012. Mem. Am. Astron. Soc. (assoc. mem.), Assn. Lunar and Planetary Observers (acting remote planets recorder 1990, remote planets recorder 1991—), British Astron. Assn. Independent. Roman Catholic. Avocation: hiking. Home: 109 Tyus St Barnesville GA 30204 Office: Gordon Coll 419 College Dr Barnesville GA 30204 Office Fax: 670-359-5850. Business E-Mail: schmude@gordonstate.edu.

SCHMUTZHART, BERTHOLD JOSEF, sculptor, educator; b. Salzburg, Austria, Aug. 17, 1928; came to U.S., 1958, naturalized, 1963; s. Berthold Josef and Anna (Valaschek) S. Student, Acad. for Applied Art, Vienna, Austria, 1956. Cert. fed. tchr., Austria. Prof. Werkschulheim Felbertal, Salzburg, 1951-58; sculptor Washington, 1959-60; tchr. Longfellow Sch., Bethesda, Md., 1960-63; prof., chmn. dept. sculpture Corcoran Sch. Art, Washington, 1963-94, prof. emeritus, 1994—; lectr. Smithsonian Instn., Washington, 1968-84. One-man shows include Fredericksburg Gallery Fine Art, Va., 1967-73, Franz Bader Gallery, Washington, 1978, 81, 83, 86, 88; group shows include Nat. Collection Fine Arts, Washington, 1961-70, High Mus. Art, Atlanta, 1965, Ark. Art Ctr., Little Rock, 1966, Birmingham Mus. Art, Ala., 1967, Hirschhorn Mus. and Sculpture Garden, Washington, 1981, Nat. Gallery Modern Art, New Delhi, 1990; represented in permanent collections Hirschhorn Collection; designer fountain, Gallery of Modern Art, Fredericksburg, 1967; author: The Handmade Furniture Book, 1981; contbr. articles to profl. jours. Fine arts panelist D.C. Commn. for Arts, 1973-79; chmn. bd. Market Five Gallery, Washington, 1978-82; bd. dirs. Franz Bader Gallery, Washington, 1981-86; trustee Arts for the Aging, Inc., Washington, 1990—98; chmn. Franz and Virginia Bader Fund, 2001-06, bd. dirs., 2006-. Recipient 1st prize Washington Religious Arts Council, 1960, for sculpture, Little Rock, 1966, Louisville, 1968, Silver medal Audubon Soc., Washington, 1971 Mem. Guild for Religious Architects, Artists Equity Assn. (pres. D.C. chpt. 1973-75), AAUP, Am. Austrian Soc. (pres. 1968-70, exec. com.), Soaring Soc. Am. Home: 32 Layline Ln Fredericksburg VA 22406-4061 E-mail: gn15bs@earthlink.net.

SCHNABEL, MARTA-ANN, lawyer; b. Butte, Mont., July 15, 1957; m. Kevin O'Bryon; 2 children. BA in History, with honors, Meml. U. Newfoundland, Can., 1978; JD, Loyola U., 1981. Bar: La. 1981, US Dist. Ct. (Ea. Dist. La.), US Dist. Ct. (Mid. Dist. La.), US Dist. Ct. (We. Dist. La.), US Ct. Appeals (5th Cir.). Assoc. Hammett Leake and Hammett, 1981—86, ptnr., 1986; mng. ptnr. Leake & Andersson LLP, 1987—99; shareholder O'Bryon & Schnabel PLC, New Orleans, 2000—. Mem. Alliance for Good Govt., treas., 2000—03; v.p. La. Client Assistance Found., 2003; bd. dirs. New Orleans Legal Aid Bur., 1990—94, sec., 1994—95, v.p., 1997—99; bd. dirs. New Orleans Legal Assistance Corp., 1996—99; mem. bd. trustees St. Martin's Episcopal Sch., 2001—04. Recipient Gillis Long Pub. Svc. award, Loyola Law Sch. Master: New Orleans Bar Assn. Inn of Ct.; fellow: La. Bar Found.; mem.: Def. Rsch. Inst., Assn. Def. Trial Attys., La. Assn. Def. Counsel, La. State Bar Assn. (bd. gov. 1998—2006, ethics adv. svc. com. 2000, editor-in-chief law jour. 2001—03, pres. 2006—07, practice assistance com., improvement com., co-chair access to justice com., com. rules of profl. conduct, Pres. award 1998, 2004), New Orleans Bar Assn. (pres. 1995). Office: O'Bryon & Schnabel PLC Ste 1950 1010 Common St New Orleans LA 70112 Office Phone: 504-799-4200. Office Fax: 504-799-4211.

SCHNAPER, CARA L., diversified financial services company executive; BS, MBA, Cornell U., Ithaca, NY. Head tech. and ops., equities dept. JP Morgan Chase & Co., mng. dir., COO global markets bus.; prin. Market Resolve, LLC; exec. v.p. tech. and ops. TIAA-CREF (Teachers Insurance & Annuity Association-College Retirement Equities Fund), 2008—. Mem. operating com. CHIPCo, ServiceCo; payments risk com. Fed. Res. Bank NY; bd. dirs. Depository Trust & Clearing Corp. Treas. Summit PTA, NJ; mem. Summit Mcpl. Democratic Com., NJ. Office: TIAA-CREF PO Box 1259 Charlotte NC 28201

SCHNATTER, JOHN H., food service executive; b. Jeffersonville, Ind., Aug. 16, 1962; Founder Papa John's International, Inc., Louisville, 1985, pres., 1985—90, 2001—05, exec. chmn., 2005—07, chmn., CEO, 1990—2005, 2009—, interim CEO, 2008—09. Hon. chair Ride to Conquer Cancer, Norton Cancer Inst., Louisville, 2009. Named Nat. Ernst & Young Retail/Consumer Entrepreneur of Yr., 1998; named one of The Outstanding Young Americans for 2000, Nat. Jaycees; named to Jr. Achievement US Bus. Hall of Fame, 2007. Office: Papa Johns International Inc 2002 Papa John's Blvd Louisville KY 40299-2367

SCHNEIDER, EDWIN KAHN, research scientist; b. Philadelphia, Pa., May 6, 1948; s. Abraham and Edna May Schneider; m. Penelope Lee Ganzel, Aug. 5, 1980; children: Andrew Ganzel, Thomas Schmidt. AB, Harvard U., 1970, PhD, 1976. Postdoctoral rsch. assoc. MIT, Cambridge, Mass., 1974—77, prin. rsch. scientist, 1984—84; NATO postdoctoral fellow Reading U., England, 1977—78; rsch. fellow, assoc. Harvard U., Cambridge, Mass., 1978—83; assoc., sr. rsch. scientist U. Md., College Park, Md., 1984—93; sr. rsch. scientist Ctr. for Ocean-Land-Atmosphere Studies, Calverton, Md., 1993—; prof. climate dynamics George Mason U., Fairfax, Va., 2002—; exec. editor Climate Dynamics, 2004—. Author: (book chapter) Climate Change: An Integrated Perspective; contbr. (articles) Encyclopedia of Global Environmental Change; contbr. articles to profl. jours. Grantee, NSF, NOAA, NASA, DOE, EPRI, 1985—; fellow, NSF, 1970—72; Nat. Merit scholar, 1966—70. Fellow: Am. Meteorol. Soc.; mem.: Am. Geophys. Union. Achievements include research in Hadley circulation, El Nino/Southern Oscillation, atmospheric and oceanic dynamics, climate change, climate prediction. Avocations: orchestral violinist, golf. Office: George Mason University 114 Research Hall Mail Stop 2B3 Fairfax VA 22030*

SCHNEIDER, GEORGE T., obstetrician, gynecologist; b. New Orleans; s. George Edmond Schneider and Erna Marie Kraft; 1 child, Lynne Schneider Cantrell. Diploma, U. Heidelberg, Fed. Republic Germany, 1938; BS, Tulane U., 1941, MD, 1944. Intern Touro Infirmary, New Orleans, 1944-45, resident ob-gyn, 1945-47, U.S. Naval Hosp., Creat Lakes, Ill., 1947-48; vice chmn. Ochsner Med. Instns., New Orleans, 1960-86, cons., 1986—. Prof. ob-gyn Sch. Medicine, La. State U., New Orleans, 1965—. Contbr. articles to profl. jours. Bd. dirs. Assn. Internat. Edn., Houston, 1984—, YMCA New Orleans, 1985—, Am. Cancer Soc. La. Lt. USNR, 1945. Recipient Cert. of Merit Cancer Soc. El Salvador, 1980; named hon. counsul Honduras, 1988. Fellow ACS, Am. Coll. Ob-Gyn; mem. Ob-Gyn Soc. New Orleans (past pres.), Internat. Soc. Reproductive Medicine (past pres.), Hospitaliers Order St. Lazarus, Southern Ob-gyn. Seminar (Asheville, NC) (past pres.). Presbyterian. Office Phone: 504-866-1082. Fax: 504-842-4141. E-mail: gtschneidermd@bellsouth.net.

SCHNEIDER, JAYNE BANGS, school librarian; b. Cin., Nov. 9, 1950; d. Neil Kendrick and Edith (Dilworth) Bangs; m. James R. Bronn, June 9, 1973 (div. 1979); m. Arthur Schneider, July 11, 1986; 1 stepdaughter, Heather. BS in Elem. Edn., Ea. Ky. U., 1973; MA in Libr. Sci., Spaulding U., 1978. Tchr. 1st and 2d grades Ruth Moyer Elem. Sch., Fort Thomas (Ky.) Pub. Schs., 1973; libr. Lassiter Middle Sch., Ky., 1973-2000; part-time libr. Jefferson County Pub. Schs., 2003—07; profl. libr. Gheens Acad. Presenter in field. Commr. City of Kingsley. Recipient Outstanding Media Librarian award Jefferson County, 1998; named Superstar Ky. Ednl. TV; Owen Badgett grantee Louisville Community Grant, 1988. Mem. NEA, ALA, AASL, PTSA (life), Nat. Mid. Sch. Assn., Jefferson County Sch. Media Assn. (treas. 1982-83, sec. 1991-92, newsletter editor 1992-93, pres.-elect 1993-94, pres. 1994-95, nomination chairperson 1996-97, bd. dirs. 1997-2000, named Jefferson County's Outstanding Sch. Media Librarian 1998), Ky. Sch. Media Assn. (bd. dirs. 1994-95, 97-98). Presbyterian. Avocations: genealogy, collecting antique glass. Home: 2553 Kings Hwy Louisville KY 40205-2646 Personal E-mail: jaynesch@insightbb.com.

SCHNEIDER, KEVIN D., diversified financial services company executive; BS in Indsl. Labor Rels., Cornell U., Ithaca, NY; MBA, Northwestern U. Kellogg Sch. Mgmt., Evanston, Ill., 1998. Various sales, profit and loss positions Ryder Sys., 1984—92; regional mgr. GATX Corp., 1992—94, v.p. sales, 1994—98; exec. v.p. rail svcs. GE Capital Corp., 1998—2001, quality leader, 2001—02, chief quality officer comml. fin.-Americas, 2003; sr. v.p., chief comml. officer Genworth Mortgage Ins. Corp., 2003—04; pres., CEO US mortgage ins. bus. Genworth Financial, Inc., 2004—, sr. v.p., 2008—. Office: Genworth Financial Inc 6620 W Broad St Richmond VA 23230 Office Phone: 804-281-6000. Office Fax: 804-662-2414. Business E-Mail: Kevin.Schneider@genworth.com.

SCHNEIDER, LAZ LEVKOFF, lawyer; b. Columbia, SC, Mar. 15, 1939; s. Philip L. and Dorothy Harriet (Levkoff) S.; m. Ellen Linda Shiffrin, Dec. 12, 1968; 1 child, David Allen. BA, Yale U., 1961, LLB, 1964; LLM, NYU, 1965. Bar: D.C. 1965, N.Y. 1965, Fla. 1970. Assoc. Fulton, Walter & Duncombe, NYC, 1965-67, Rosenman, Colin Kaye Petschek Freund & Emil, NYC, 1967-69, Kronish, Lieb, Weiner, Shainswit & Hellman, NYC, 1969-70; ptnr. Ruden Barnett McClosky & Schuster, Ft. Lauderdale, Fla., 1970-80; pvt. practice Ft. Lauderdale, 1980-86; ptnr. Sherr, Tiballi, Fayne & Schneider, Ft. Lauderdale, 1986-91, Berger Singerman, Ft. Lauderdale, 1991—2013; ret. Bd. dir. Ocean Biochem. Inc., 1998—2011. Grad. editor Tax Law Rev., 1964-65. Exec. com. Fla. regional bd. Anti Defamation League, 1972—, bd. dirs., Paradise Edn. Found., Inc., 2011-. Mem. Fla. Bar Assn., Broward County Bar Assn. (chmn. sect. corp. bus. and banking law 1978-80), Yale Club (pres. 1977-79). Jewish. Office: 350 E Las Olas Blvd Ste 1000 Fort Lauderdale FL 33301-4215 Home Phone: 954-566-2591; Office Phone: 954-525-9900. Personal E-mail: lazsch@att.net. Business E-Mail: lschneider@bergersingerman.com.

SCHNEIDER, LISA A., lawyer; b. Bklyn., Apr. 24, 1962; BA cum laude, SUNY, Binghamton, 1984; JD, St. John's U. Sch. Law, 1987. Bar: NJ 1987, NY 1988, US Dist. Ct. (so. and ea. dists. NY) 1988, US Dist. Ct. (dist. NJ) 1988, Fla. 1994, cert.: Fla. Bd. (wills, trusts and estates) 2003. Atty. Shea & Gould; positions to shareholder pvt. wealth svcs. dept. Gunster, Yoakley & Stewart, West Palm Beach, Fla., 1994—. Contbr. articles to profl. publs. Mem. profl. adv. com. United Way of Martin County Found. Named one of Best of the Bar, South Fla. Bus. Jour., 2003—04, Fla. Legal Elite, Fla. Trend mag., 2004, Top 100 Attys., Worth mag., 2005, 2007, Top Lawyers, South Fla. Legal Guide, 2006. Mem.: Jewish Women's Found. of Jewish Fedn. of Palm Beach County (founding trustee), Found. of Jewish Fedn. of Palm Beach County (mem. profl. adv. com.), East Coast Estate Planning Coun., Treasure Coast Planned Giving Coun., Martin County Estate Planning Coun., ABA, NY State Bar Assn., NJ State Bar Assn., Martin County Bar Assn. (mem. elder law, probate and guardianship com.). Office: Gunster Yoakley & Stewart Phillips Point 777 S Flagler Dr Ste 500 E West Palm Beach FL 33401 Office Phone: 561-650-0680. Office Fax: 561-655-5677. E-mail: lschneider@gunster.com.

SCHNEIDER, MICHAEL H., SR., federal judge; b. San Antonio, Jan. 6, 1943; AA, Lon Morris Coll., 1963; BS, Stephen F. Austin State U., 1965; JD, U. Houston, 1970; LLM, U. Va., 2001. Asst. dist. atty. Harris County, 1971—75; of counsel Parks & Moss, 1975—76; atty. Dresser Industries, 1976—80; mcpl. judge City of West University Place, 1978—90; v.p., gen. counsel Bawden Drilling Inc., 1980—86; gen. solicitor Union Pacific R.R. Co., 1986—89; of counsel McFall & Sartwelle, 1989—90; presiding judge 157th Civil Dist. Ct. Harris County, 1990—96; chief justice Tex. 1st Ct. Appeals, Houston, 1996—2002; justice Tex. Supreme Ct., 2002—04; judge US Dist. Ct. (ea. dist.) Tex., 2004—. Tchr. Ball HS, Galveston, Tex. Named Trial Judge of the Yr., Tex. Assn. Civil Trial and Appellate Specialists, 1994, 2001. Mem.: ABA, Tex. Bar Found., Houston Bar Found., Houston Bar Assn., State Bar Tex. Methodist.

SCHNEIDER, PETER RAYMOND, retired political scientist; b. Muskogee, Okla., Aug. 8, 1939; s. Leo Frederick and Tillie Oleta (Cannon) S.; m. Anne Larason, Jan. 22, 1964 (div. 1983); children: Christopher, Geoffrey; m. Adrienne Armstrong, Dec. 19, 1986; children: Robbie, Samantha. BS, Okla. State U., 1966, MS, 1968; PhD, Ind. U., 1974. News editor No. Va. Sun, Arlington, 1961-62; news writer AP, Balt., 1962, Balt. News-Am., 1962-65; asst. prof. U. Oreg., Eugene, 1974-76; pres. Inst. of Policy Analysis, Eugene, 1976-83; v.p. Am. Justice Inst., Sacramento, 1983; dir. Ctr. for Assessment of The Juvenile Justice Ctr., Sacramento, 1983; v.p. Nat. Partnership, Washington, 1985; sr. rsch. scientist Pacific Inst. for Rsch. and Evaluation, Bethesda, Md., 1984-92, dir. justice div., 1986-89; pres. Inst. of Policy Analysis, McLean, Va., 1992-95; CEO IPA Internat., Inc., Vienna, 1995—2007. Contbr. numerous articles to profl. jours., chpts. to books. Recipient Julia Lathrop award Am. Criminal Justice Assn., 1985. Mem. Am. Polit. Sci. Assn., Am. Restitution Assn., Pi Sigma Alpha, Sigma Delta Chi, Phi Kappa Phi, Omicron Delta Kappa, Phi Kappa Theta. Avocations: flying, tennis, selling wine, travel. Home: 1345 Woodside Dr Mc Lean VA 22102-1530 Personal E-mail: schneid703@aol.com.

SCHNEIDER, PHILLIP HARRY LEONARD (PHIL SCHNEIDER), healthcare organization executive; b. Saginaw, Mich., Jan. 29, 1947; s. Leonard Franklin and Marjory Avalon (Reed) S.; m. Patricia. BA in Journalism, Ctrl. Mich. U., 1969, BS in Polit. Sci., 1969, MA in Polit. Sci., 1970. Editor-in-chief Midland Daily News, Mich., 1970—75; mgr. fin and pub. rels. Dow Chem. Co., Midland, Mich., 1975-78, mgr. media relations, 1978-82, dir. pub. rels., 1982-86; v.p. corp. comm. Medlantic Healthcare Corp., Washington, 1986—91; v.p. external rels., program devel. Nat. Assn. Chain Drug Stores, Alexandria, Va., 1991—2009; pres. Nat. Assn. Chain Drug Stores Found., 1998—2009; founder, pres. Tier One Assocs., 2009—; strategic initiatives sr. cons. Nat. Cmty. Pharmacists Assn., 2009—. Comm. chmn. Am. Indsl. Health Coun., 1984-86; pub. rels. chmn. Mich. Chem. Coun., Lansing, 1984-86; dir. Am. Found. Pharm. Edn., Pub. Affairs Coun., Washington; chmn. Nat. Coun. on Patient Info. and Edn., Washington; founder, bd. dirs. Sun Safety Alliance. Contbr. articles to profl. jours. Councilman, Midland City Council, 1982-86; bd. dirs. Big Brothers, Jr. Achievement, United Way. Named Outstanding Citizen City of Midland, 1983. Mem.: Assn. Fundraising Profls., Am. Mktg. Assn., Am. Med. Writers Assn., Pub. Rels. Soc. America, Nat. Press Club, Sigma Delta Chi. Roman Catholic. Achievements include playing a key role in establishing and directing the Small Business Coalition on Health Care Reform. Avocations: golf, racquetball, biking, reading.

SCHNEIDER, RICHARD T(HEODORE), optics scientist, researcher, engineer; b. Munich, July 29, 1927; came to U.S., 1961; s. Wilhelm and Martha E. (Hofmann) S.; children: Ursula M. Dyer, Richard W. Diploma in physics, U. Stuttgart, Fed. Republic of Germany, 1958, PhD, 1961. Registered profl. engr. Calif. Sect. chief Allison div. Gen. Motors Corp., Indpls., 1961-65; assoc. prof. U. Fla., Gainesville, 1965-68, prof., 1968—, prof. emeritus, 1988-90; pres. Eye Rsch. Lab., Inc., Alachua, Fla., 1984-90; chief scientist RTS Labs., Inc., Alachua, 1984-92. Cons. Allison div. Gen. Motors Corp., Indpls., 1965-67; IPA assignment Eglin AFB, Ft. Walton Beach, Fla., 1983; liaison scientist USN Office Naval Rsch., London, 1975. Editor: Uranium Plasmas, 1971; patentee in field; contbr. articles to profl. jours. Recipient Medal for Exceptional Sci. Achievement, NASA, 1975, Outstanding Tech. Achievement award, Fla. Engring. Soc., 1978. Mem. Internat. Soc. Optical Engring., Sigma Xi, Tau Beta Pi (Eminent Engr. 1970). Home: 12903 NW 112th Ave Alachua FL 32615-6520 Office Phone: 386-462-2666. Business E-Mail: schneiderlabs@windstream.net.

SCHNEIDER, RYAN M., bank executive; Exec. v.p. US card Capital One Fin. Corp., Va., exec. v.p. auto fin., pres. card, 2007—. Mem.: Capital One Bank Nat. Assn. (dir.). Office: Capital One Financial Corporation 1680 Capital One Dr Mc Lean VA 22102 Office Phone: 703-720-1000.

SCHNEIDER, WILLIAM D., oil and gas company executive; BA in Geology, MA in Geology, Boston U. Geologist Western Gulf Divsn. Tenneco Oil Exploration and Prodn. Co.; founding mem. Newfield Exploration Co., geologist through v.p. internat., tech. coord., 1989—92, mgr. exploration, 1992—97, v.p. onshore Gulf Coast & internat., 2008—. Mem.: Am. Assn. of Geologists. Office: Newfield Exploration Co 363 N Sam Houston Pky E Ste 2020 Houston TX 77060 Office Phone: 281-847-6000. Office Fax: 281-847-6006.

SCHNEIDERBAUER, DIETER, staffing services executive; Attended, Fachhochschule Munchen, Technische Universitat Munchen. Mng. dir. Mercer Mgmt. Consulting; v.p. Booz & Co., ptnr., mng. dir. Munich, Germany; mng. dir. Booz Allen Hamilton Holding Corp. Office: Booz Allen Hamilton Holding Corp 8283 Greensboro Dr Mc Lean VA 22102 Office Phone: 703-902-5000. Office Fax: 703-902-3333. Business E-Mail: schneiderbauer_dieter@bah.com.

SCHNELLE, KARL BENJAMIN, JR., chemical engineering professor, consultant, researcher; b. Canton, Ohio, Dec. 8, 1930; s. Karl Benjamin and Kathryn Emily (Hollingsworth) S.; m. Mary Margaret Dabney, Sept. 8, 1954; children: Karl Dabney, Kathryn Chappell. BS, Carnegie Mellon U., 1952, MS, 1957, PhD, 1959. Registered profl. engr., Tenn. Chem. engr., shift foreman Organics area Pitts. Plate Glass Co., New Martinsville, W.Va., 1952-54; asst. prof. chem. engring. Vanderbilt U., Nashville, 1958—61, assoc. prof., 1961—64; mgr. edn., rsch. Instrument Soc. Am., Pitts., 1964—67; assoc. prof. environ. and air resources engring. Vanderbilt U., 1967—70, prof., 1970—80, chmn. divsn. socio-tech. sys., 1972—75, chmn. environ. and water resources engring., 1975—76, chmn. environ. engring. and policy mgmt. dept., 1976—80, chmn. chem. engring. dept., 1980—88, prof. chem. and environ. engring., 1980—2008, emeritus prof. chem. and environ. engring., 2008—; Alexander Heard disting. svc. prof., 1995-96. V.p. ECCE, Nashville, 1983-88, pres., 1989—95; mem. Air Pollution Control Bd., State Tenn., 1978-82, 82-87; Fulbright prof. U. Liege, Belgium, 1977; invited prof. Universite Catholique de Louvain, Belgium, 1982; vis. prof. chem. engring. Danish Tech. Inst., Lyngby, Denmark, 1988-89. Fellow AIChE (Environmen. Divsn. Svc. award 2009); mem. Air and Waste Mgmt. Assn. (Lyman A. Ripperton Environ. Educator award 2006, Environ. Divsn. award, 2009), Instrument Soc. Am. (mgr. edn. and rsch. 1964-67), Am. Soc. Engring. Edn., Am. Soc. Environ. Engrs., Sigma Xi, Phi Kappa Phi, Tau Beta Pi. Office: Vanderbilt University Dept Chem & Biomolecular Engring PMB 351604 2301 Vanderbilt Pl Nashville TN 37235-1604 Home: 110 Mint Spring Cir Brentwood TN 37027-4996 Office Phone: 615-322-3370. Business E-Mail: karl.b.schnelle@vanderbilt.edu.

SCHNIPPER, DON MARTIN, lawyer; b. Little Rock, Jan. 17, 1939; m. Mary Ann Evans, June 3, 1961; children: Caroline, Elizabeth. AB, U. Ark., 1963, JD, 1964. Bar: Ark. 1964, U.S. Supreme Ct. 1971. Ptnr. Wood, Smith, Schnipper, Clay & Vines, Hot Springs, Ark., 1964—. Spl. assoc. justice Ark. Supreme Ct., 1976-88. V.p. 1st United Meth. Ch., 1976-77, pres. 1977, vice chmn., bd. dirs. 1975-76; chmn. Ouachita Regional Counseling and Mental Health Ctr., 1977, pres., bd. dirs. 1970; bd. dirs. Hot Springs Children's Home. Fellow Am. Bar Found.; mem. ABA, Ark. Bar Assn. (chmn. young lawyers sect. 1969-70, ho. of dels. 1973-76, exec. council 1976-79, chmn. exec. council 1980-81, pres. 1985-86), Garland County Bar Assn. (pres.), Hot Springs C. of C. (bd. dirs. 1966—, pres. 1977, Disting. Svc. award 1970), U. Ark. Alumni Assn. (bd. dirs. 1978-84, nat. pres. 1982-83). Home: 850 Quapaw Ave Hot Springs National Park AR 71901-3926 Office: Wood Smith Schnipper Clay & Vines 123 Market St Hot Springs National Park AR 71901-5398 Office Phone: 501-624-1252. Personal E-mail: donschnipper@aol.com.

SCHNOEBELEN, ANNE MARY, musicologist, educator; b. Tomahawk, Wis., Aug. 4, 1933; d. Herman Sabas and Katherine Alma (Yenor) Schnoebelen; m. John Albert Meixner, May 7, 1980. BA, Rosary Coll., 1958; MusM, U. Ill., 1960, PhD, 1966. From chmn. dept. musicology to prof. emerita Shepherd Sch. Music Rice U., Houston, 1974—2004, interim dean, 1981, 2002—03, prof. emerita Shepherd Sch. Music, 2004—. Author: Padre Martini's Collection of Letters in the Civico Museo Bibliografico Musicale: An Annotated Index, 1979; editor: Cantatas by Maurizio Cazzati in the Italian Cantata in the Seventeenth Century, 1985, Solo Motets from the Seventeenth Century, 10 vols., 1987—89, Seventeenth Century Italian Sacred Music, 10 vols., 1995—99; contbr. articles and reviews to profl. jours. Grantee, NEH, 1969, 1983; fellow, Fulbright, 1964; Travel grant, Am. Coun. Learned Societies, 1984. Fellow: AAUW; mem.: Am. Musicol. Soc. (coun. sec. 1986—88), Soc. 17th-Century Music (hon.). Home: 2001 Holcombe Blvd #702 Houston TX 77030-4214 Business E-Mail: aschnoeb@rice.edu.

SCHNOEBELEN, IAN, chef; b. 1970; Sous chef Commander's Palace, Las Vegas, Lilette, New Orleans; owner, exec. chef Iris, New Orleans, 2006—. Named one of Best New Chefs, Food and Wine Mag., 2007. Office: Iris 320 Decatur St New Orleans LA 70130-1024 Office Phone: 504-299-3944.

SCHOELLKOPF, WOLFGANG, investment company executive; b. Stuttgart, Germany, July 22, 1932; s. Gustav Adolf and Pauline Maria (Weber) S.; m. Margaret F. Weston, Jan. 26, 1964; children—Peter, Michael, Wendy. BA in Econs, U. Calif., 1956; postgrad, U. Munich, W. Ger., 1956-57, Cornell U., 1957-60. Instr. econs. Cornell University, 1960-61; lectr. in econs. Princeton University, 1961-63; sr. v.p. Chase Manhattan Bank (N.A.), 1974-80; exec. v.p., treas. Chase Manhattan Bank, 1979—88; exec. v.p. Shearson Lehman Hutton Inc., 1988—90; CFO First Fidelity Inc., 1990—96; gen. ptnr. PMW Capital Management, LLC, 1996—; ptnr. Ramius Capital Group, 1997—98; CEO US ops. Bank Austria Group, 2000—01; mng. ptnr. Lykos Capital Management, LLC, 2003—. Bd. dirs. SLM Corp. Mem. Am. Econ. Assn., Phi Beta Kappa, Phi Kappa Phi. Office: Lykos Capital Management 909 3rd Ave, 5th Floor New York NY 10022 also: SML Corporation 12061 Bluemont Way Reston VA 20190 Office Phone: 703-810-3000, 646-495-3250. Office Fax: 703-810-5074, 646-495-3249.

SCHOEN, WILLIAM JACK, finance company executive; b. LA, Aug. 2, 1935; s. Jack Conrad and Kathryn Mabel (Stegmayer) S.; m. Sharon Ann Barto, Oct. 1, 1966; children: Kathryn Lynn, Karen Anne, Kristine Lea, William Jack. BS in Fin. magna cum laude, U. So. Calif., 1960, MBA, 1963. Mktg. mgr. Anchor Hocking Glass Co., 1964-68; v.p. sales and mktg. Obear-Nester Glass Co., 1968-71; pres. Pierce Glass Co., Port Allegheny, Pa., 1971-73; pres., chief exec. officer, dir. F.&M. Schaefer Brewing Co., NYC, 1973-81; now chmn., pres. Wilshar Management Co. Inc., Naples, Fla., 1981—; chmn. Health Management Associates, Inc., Naples, 1983—, also bd. dirs. Contbr. to indsl. publns. Founder Marine Corp. Heritage Found.; mem. Bus. Coun. of 100 of Fla.; bd. dir. Internat. Coll. Found.; chmn. Schoen Found.; mem. bd. advisors U. So. Calif. Bus. Sch.; trustee U. So. Calif., 2006-. Served with USMC, 1953-56, Korea. Mem. Hole in the Wall, Naples Yacht Club, Port Royal Club, Teton Springs Club, Phi Kappa Phi. Republican. Lutheran. Office: Health Mgmt Assocs 5811 Pelican Bay Blvd Ste 500 Naples FL 34108-2711 Office Phone: 239-598-3175.

SCHOFIELD, JONATHAN M., aircraft manufacturing company executive; Grad. in Mech. Engring., Carleton U.; MBA, U. Toronto. Cert. profl engr., Can. Assn. Production and Inventory Control. With Altair Avionics Corp.; exec. mgmt. positions Pratt & Whitney divsn. United Technologies Corp.; pres. United Technologies Internat. Corp., 1989—92; chmn., CEO, Airbus N. Am. Holdings Airbus Industries, 1992—2000; chmn. Airbus Americas, Inc., 2000—01. Bd. dirs. Aero Sat, Inc., Douglas Machine, Inc., TurboCombustor Tech., Inc., SS&C Technologies Holdings, Inc., 1997—, Aviall Inc., 2001—, BE Aerospace, Inc., 2001—, Nordam Group, 2007—. Trustee LIFT Trust. Recipient Legion of Honor, French Rep., 2002. Office: BE Aerospace Inc Bd Directors 1400 Corporate Ctr Way Wellington FL 33414 Office Phone: 561-791-5000. Office Fax: 561-791-7900.

SCHOGGEN, PHIL H(OWARD), psychologist, educator; b. Tulsa, Aug. 28, 1923; s. Walter B. and Emma F. (Alexander) S.; m. Maxine F. Spoor, June 28, 1944; children: Leida, Christopher, Ann, Susan. AB in Psychology, Park Coll., 1946; MS, U. Kans., Lawrence, 1951, PhD in Psychology, 1954. Asst. prof. psychology U. Oreg., 1957-62, asso. prof., 1962-66; prof., chmn. dept. psychology George Peabody Coll., 1966-75; prof. York U., Toronto, Ont., Can., 1975-77; prof. human devel. and family studies N.Y. State Coll. Human Ecology, Cornell U., 1977-90, prof. emeritus, 1990—, chmn. dept., 1977-82. Author: (with R. G. Barker) Qualities of Community Life, 1973; Behavior Settings: A Revision and Extension of Roger G. Barker's Ecological Psychology, 1989. Served with USNR, 1944-46, 50-51. Mem. APA. Home: 11 Burton Hills Blvd S-359 Nashville TN 37215 Personal E-mail: schoggph@ourblakeford.com.

SCHOLES, EDISON EARL, military officer; b. McCaysville, Ga., Aug. 16, 1939; s. Alvin L. and Marie (Plemmons) S.; m. Elva E. Bussey, June 4, 1961; children: Juana Kimberly Scholes, Tracy Michele Scholes Heller, Michael Lee. BS in Physics cum laude, No. Ga. Coll., 1961; MS in Ops. Rsch., Naval Postgrad. Sch., 1970; postgrad., Army War Coll., 1980, Harvard Def. Policy Seminar, 1991. Commd. 2d lt. U.S. Army, 1961, advanced through grades to maj. gen., 1991; comdr. A Detachment, 10th Spl. Forces Group U.S. ArmyEurope, 1963-66; comdr. Co. D, 2d Bn.(Abn.), 8th Cav., 1st Cav. Divsn. U.S. Army, Republic of Vietnam, 1967-68, sr. adv. I Corps. Ranger Commd. Vietnam, 1970—71, comdr. 1st Bn., 23d Inf., 2d Inf. Divsn. Republic of Korea, 1976-77, comdr. 2d Tng. Bn., Sch. Brigade, U.S. Army Inf. Sch. Ft. Benning, Ga., 1978-79, comdr. 1st Inf. Tng. Brigade, U.S. Army Infantry Tng. Ctr., 1983-85, dep. commanding gen. chief of staff 3d U.S. Army/U.S. Army Cen. Command Ft. McPherson, Ga., 1986-88, asst. divsn. comdr. 82d Airborne Divsn. Ft. Bragg, NC, 1988-89, chief of staff XVIII Airborne Corps, 1989-90, chief of staff joint task force-south, Op. Just Cause, 1989-90, dep. commanding gen. XVIII Airborne Corps, Operation Desert Shield/Desert Storm Saudi Arabia, Iraq, 1990-91, dep. commanding gen. XVIII Airborne Corps Ft. Bragg, 1991-93; dep. comdr. Allied Land Forces, S.E. Europe NATO, 1993-95; program gen. mgr. Saudi Arabia N.G. Modernization Program, Vinnell Arabia, 1996—2002; pvt. contractor numerous countries, 2002—. Decorated Dept. Def. Disting. Svc. medal, Army Disting. Svc. medal with oak leaf cluster, Silver Star, Legion of Merit with oak leaf cluster, Bronze Star with V device and 4 oak leaf clusters, Purple Heart with oak leaf cluster, 6 Air medals, Army Commendation medal with V device and oak leaf cluster, Armed Forces Expeditionary medal, Combat Infantryman badge, Expert Infantry badge; Cross of Gallantry with Silver and Bronze Stars and Palm (Republic of Vietnam); numerous other US and fgn. awards; inducted into North Ga.'s Coll., State U. Hall of Fame and S. Army Ranger Hall of Fame. Mem. 82d Airborne Divsn. Assn., Spl. Forces Assn., U.S. Army Ranger Assn., Spl. Ops. Assn. Baptist. Avocations: reading, camping, fishing. Office Phone: 850-499-2722. Personal E-mail: eescholes@comcast.net.

SCHOLLANDER, WENDELL LESLIE, JR., lawyer; b. Ocala, Fla., May 17, 1943; 1 child, Wendell Leslie III. BS, U. Pa., 1966, MBA, 1968; postgrad., Stetson U., 1969-70; JD, Duke U., 1972. Bar: NC 1977, Tenn. 1972, Fla. 1987. With Container Corp. Am., Fernandina, Fla., 1968-69; assoc. Miller, Martin, Chattanooga, 1972-75; asst. counsel R.J. Reynolds Industries, Inc., 1975-78, assoc. counsel, 1978-79, sr. assoc. counsel, 1979-82, sr. counsel, 1982-85; gen. counsel RJR Archer, Inc., Winston-Salem, NC, 1979-85; of counsel Finger, Parker & Avram, Winston-Salem, 1985-87; ptnr. Schollander, Winston-Salem, 1987—. Co-author: Forgotten Elegance, 2001, Bankruptcy for Small Business, 2008, Small Business Owners Guide To Bankruptcy, 2002, Bankruptcy Answer Book, 2009. Mem. NC Bar Assn., Forsyth County Bar Assn., Mensa, SAR, Phi Delta Phi, Kappa Sigma. Presbyterian. Office: 2000 W 1st St Ste 308 Winston Salem NC 27104-4225 Office Phone: 336-727-0900.

SCHOLLANDER, WENDELL WES, III, lawyer; b. East Ridge, Tenn., Oct. 15, 1974; BA, U. N.C., Chapel Hill, 1997; JD, Wake Forest Law Sch., Winston-Salem, NC, 2001. Missionary Presbyn. Ch., Guatemala, 1998; pvt. practice Winston-Salem, NC, 2001—; adj. prof. Wake Forest U. Sch. Law, 2009—11. Co-author: Forgotten Elegance, 2001, Small Business Owner's Guide to Bankruptcy, 2002, Bankruptcy for Small Business, 2008, Bankruptcy Answer Book, 2009. Scoutmaster Boy Scouts of Am., Winston-Salem, 2002—04; active Forsyth Soil and Water Commn., 2004—08, vice chmn., 2006—08. Recipient Point of Light award, Pres. George Bush, 1992, Chevron Conservation award, Chevron Award Program, 1992, Take Pride in Am. award, Dept. of Interior, 1991, 1992. Mem.: NC Bar Assn. (bankruptcy sect. 2001—, sect. coun. 2006—09, young lawyers sect.), SAR (awards chair 2002—). Office: Schollander 2000 W 1st St Ste 308 Winston Salem NC 27104

SCHOOLAR, JOSEPH CLAYTON, psychiatrist, pharmacologist, educator; b. Marks, Miss., Feb. 28, 1928; s. Adrian Taylor and Leah (Covington) S.; m. Betty Jane Peck, Nov. 2, 1960; children: Jonathan Covington, Cynthia Jane, Geoffrey Michael, Catherine Elizabeth, Adrian Carson AB, U. Tenn., Knoxville, 1950, MS, 1952; PhD, U. Chgo., 1957, MD, 1960. Diplomate Am. Bd. Psychiatry and Neurology. Chief drug abuse research TRIMS, Houston, 1966-72; assoc. prof. U. Tex. Grad. Sch. Biomed. Scis., Houston, 1968—; prof. psychiatry Baylor Coll. Medicine, Houston, 1975—, prof. pharmacology, 1974—2002, prof. emeritus pharmacology and psychiatry, 2003—, chief div. psychopharmacology, 1973-82; dir. Tex. Research Inst. Mental Scis., Houston, 1972-85. Mem. Nat. Bd. Med. Examiners' Task Force on Drug Abuse and Alcoholism, 1982-; mem. Drug Abuse Adv. Com., FDA, Washington, 1983-85, chmn., 1984; chmn. profl. needs planning task force Nat. Inst. Drug Abuse, Washington, 1977- Editor: Current Issues in Adolescent Psychiatry, 1973, Research and the Psychiatric Patient, 1975, The Kinetics of Psychiatric Drugs, 1979, Serotonin in Biological Psychiatry - Advances in Biochemical Psychopharmacology, 1982. Cons. Parents' League Houston, 1972-74; mem. coordinating com. Citizens Mental Health Service, Houston, 1976; mem. acad. com. for study of violence Houston Police Dept., 1979; bd. dirs. Can-Do-It, Houston, 1982-. Served with U.S. Army, 1945-47, to 1st lt. USAR, 1950-62. Recipient Eugen Kahn award Baylor Coll. Medicine, Houston, 1964, Alumni award for Disting. Svc., U. Chgo., 1995, Psychiat. Excellence award Tex. Soc. Psychiat. Physicians, 1995. Fellow Am. Psychiat. Assn. (disting. life), Am. Coll. Psychiatrists, Am. Coll. Neuropsychopharmacology, Collegium Internationale NeuroPsychopharmacologicum, Am. Soc. Pharmacology and Exptl. Therapeutics. Episcopalian. Home: 1111 Hermann Dr Unit 17E Houston TX 77004-6930 Office: Baylor Coll Medicine PO Box 66575 Houston TX 77266-6575 Home Phone: 713-523-6979; Office Phone: 713-524-9700. E-mail: jschoolar@pol.net.

SCHOOLFIELD, BRENDA THOMPSON, history professor; b. Wichita, Kans., July 5, 1966; d. Richard Dale and Barbara Elaine Thompson; m. William Robnett Schoolfield, Dec. 15, 1989; children: Ellis Richard, Katherine Eunice. PhD, U. SC, Columbia, 2006. Prof., divsn. social sci. Bob Jones U., Greenville, SC, 1988—. Mem., writing panels SC Social Studies Stds., 2011; co-editor SCHA Proceedings, 2013—; pres. Upstate Rep. Women, Greenville, 2003—06. Mem.: SC Geographic Alliance (tchr. cons. 2010—), Soc. Historians Early Am. Republic, Omohundro IEAHC, SC Hist. Assn., Phi Alpha Theata (Beta chpt.), Alpha Delta Kappa (Xi-Phi chpt). Office: Bob Jones Univ 1700 Wade Hampton Blvd Greenville SC 29614 Business E-Mail: bschoolf@bju.edu.*

SCHOONOVER, BRENDA B., ambassador; BA, Morgan State U., Balt.; postgrad., Howard U. Vol. Peace Corps, Philippines, 1961, adminstr. Office Talent Search Washington, assoc. dir. Tanzania, dir. sch. partnership program Washington; affirmative action officer Govt. of Arlington County, Va.; with Fgn. Svc. U.S. Dept. State, Manila, Colombo, Sri Lanka, Tunis, Tunisia, with Bur. Near East and South Asia Washington, 1978-88, chief pers. Bur. European and Can. Affairs, 1988-91, mem. Sr. Seminar, 1996-97; adminstrv. officer, dept. dir. Office Joint Adminstrv. Svcs. Am. Embassy, Brussels, 1992-96; Capstone fellow Nat. Def. U., Washington, 1997; U.S. amb. to Togo Am. Embassy, Lome, 1998-2000; amb.-in-residence Chapel Hill, NC, 2000—01; chargé d'affaires, ad interim min. counselor Am. Embassy, Brussels, 2001—04. Pres. Am. Diplomacy On-line Mag. Ex-officio adv. bd. Global Edn., U. N.C., Chapel Hill. Recipient Order of the Mono award, The Togolese Govt., 2000, Presdl. Meritorious award, U.S., 2003, Sec. of State Career Achievement award, 2004. Mem.: Intra Health Internat. (chair adv. com.). Office: 108 Ironwoods Dr Chapel Hill NC 27516 E-mail: RCSchoon2@aol.com.

SCHORER, STEVEN T., manufacturing executive; BSEE, U. Mass.; MBA course work, Pepperdine U., Malibu, Calif.; grad. exec. mgmt. program, UCLA Anderson Sch. Exec. Mgmt., Am. Grad. Sch. Internat. Mgmt., Phoenix. Positions in engring., program mgmt., internat. bus. devel. and gen. mgmt. Hughes Aircraft Co., Raytheon Co., Lockheed Missiles & Space Co., Allied Aerospace, Inc.; pres., gen. mgr. ocean sys. divsn. L-3 Communications Holdings, Inc.; pres. electronic systems group DRS Technologies, Inc., 2003—08; pres. global platform support solutions DynCorp International, LLC, 2009—. Mem.: Am. Def. Preparedness Assn., US Navy Submarine League, Air Force Assn. Office: DynCorp International LLC Ste 700 3190 Fairview Park Dr Falls Church VA 22042 Office Phone: 571-722-0210. Office Fax: 571-722-0252.

SCHORR, ALVIN LOUIS, social worker, educator; b. NYC, Apr. 13, 1921; s. Louis and Tillie (Godiner) S.; m. Ann Girson, Aug. 21, 1948; children— Jessica Lee, Kenneth L., Wendy Lauren. BSS, CCNY, 1941; MSW, Washington U., St. Louis, 1943; DHL, Adelphi U., 1975. With Family Service No. Va., 1956-58; family life specialist Office Commr. Social Security, 1958-62; vis. prof. London (Eng.) Sch. Econs., 1962-63; acting chief long range research Social Security Adminstrn., 1963-64; dir. research and planning Office Econ. Opportunity, 1965-66; dep. asst. sec. Dept. Health, Edn. and Welfare, 1967-69; prof. social policy, dir. income maintenance project Brandeis U., 1969-70; dean Grad. Sch. Social Work, N.Y.U., 1970-73; gen. dir. Community Service Soc. N.Y., 1973-77; vis. prof. Cath. U. Am., 1977-79; Leonard W. Mayo prof. Case Western Res. U., 1979-92, Leonard W. Mayo prof. emeritus, 1992—. Fulbright sr. rsch. scholar, 1962-63; vist. prof. Hebrew U., Jerusalem, 1986, Fla. Internat. U., 1995, N.Mex. State U., 1996; vis. scholar London Sch. Econs., 1991-92. Author: Filial Responsibility in the Modern American Family, 1961, Slums and Social Insecurity, 1963, Social Services and Social Security in France, 1964, Poor Kids, 1966, Explorations in Social Policy, 1968, Children and Decent People, 1974, Jubilee for Our Times, 1977, Thy Father and Thy Mother, 1980, Common Decency: Domestic Policies After Reagan, 1986, Economic Development in Cleveland: A Dissenting View, 1991; The British Personal Social Services: An Outside View, 1992, Passion and Policy: A Social Worker's Career, 1997, Welfare Reform: Failure and Remedies, 2001. Recipient Disting. Service in Social Welfare award Washington U. Alumni Assn., 1969, Michael Schwerner award, 1972, Lifetime Achievement award Ohio Assn. Social Workers, 1998. Fellow Nat. Acad. Social Ins.; mem. Phi Beta Kappa. Home: 5800 Old Providence Rd No 4306 Charlotte NC 28226

SCHOTTENHEIMER, MARTY (MARTIN EDWARD SCOTTENHEIMER), professional football coach; b. Canonsburg, Pa., Sept. 23, 1943; m. Patricia Schottenheimer; children: Kristen, Brian BA in English, U. Pitts., 1964. Profl. football player Buffalo Bills, 1965-68, Boston Patriots, 1969-70, Pitts. Steelers, 1971, Portland Storm, World League Football, 1974; real estate developer Miami and Denver, 1971-74; linebackers coach NY Giants, 1975-77, defensive coord., 1977; linebackers coach Detroit Lions, 1978-79; defensive coord. Cleve. Browns, 1980-84, head coach, 1985-88, Kans. City Chiefs, 1989-99, Wash. Redskins, 2001, San Diego Chargers, 2002—07; football analyst ESPN, 1999—2000; head coach, gen. mgr. Va. Destroyers, United Football League, Virginia Beach, 2011—. Named Coach of the Year, UPI/AFC, 1995, AP, 2004, Pro Football Weekly, 2004. Office: Virginia Destroyers 2181 Landstown Rd Virginia Beach VA 23456

SCHOULTZ, LARS, political scientist, educator; b. San Gabriel, Calif., Aug. 23, 1942; s. Ture Wilhelm and Bernice (Bowie) S.; m. Jane Volland, Jan. 18, 1969; children: Nils Gibson, Karina Anne. BA, Stanford U., 1964, MA, 1966; PhD, U. N.C., 1973. Prof. Miami U., Oxford, Ohio, 1973—77, U. Fla., Gainesville, 1977—79; William Rand Kenan Jr. prof. polit. sci. U. N.C., Chapel Hill, 1979—. Author: Human Rights and U.S. Policy Toward Latin America, 1981, National Security and U.S. Policy Toward Latin America, 1987, The Populist Challenge, 1983, Beneath the United States, 1998, That Infernal Little Cuban Republic, 2009. Sgt. U.S. Army, 1966-67. MacArthur fellow in internat. peace and security MacArthur Found., 1990-91, Fulbright fellow, Rockefeller Found. fellow, Ford Found. fellow, Social Sci. Rsch. Coun., Woodrow Wilson fellow, 1994-95, Nat. Humanities Ctr. fellow, 1999-00. Mem. Latin Am. Studies Assn. (pres. 1991-92, v.p. 1990-91). Democrat. Home: 250 Glandon Dr Chapel Hill NC 27514-3816 Office: University NC Polit Sci Chapel Hill NC 27599-3255 Office Phone: 919-962-0422. E-mail: schoultz@unc.edu.

SCHOUWEILER, STEVEN HARVEY, insurance company executive; b. St. Paul, Nov. 28, 1946; s. Thomas John and Bette Lou (Hanson) S.; m. Helen Gilbert, Sept. 9, 1967 (div. 1975); m. Jeannette Ann DeLafe, Dec. 22, 1979; children: Christine Marlyn, Christian Paul. BA, U. Minn., 1971. Sr. v.p. John Alden Life Ins. Co., Boise, Idaho, 1973—86; group dir. Coll. Life Ins. Co., Indpls., 1986-87; v.p. Universe Life Ins. Co., Lewiston, Idaho, 1987—88; with Health Brokerage Agy., Lewiston, Idaho, 1989—98; sr. v.p., Health Ins. Ops. American National Insurance Co., 1998—. Author: Alfred Thayer Mahan III, 1979. Served with U.S. Army, 1965-71. Mem. Boise Corvette Club (pres. 1985-86). Republican. Lutheran. Avocations: flying, scuba diving, skiing. Home: 2607 Fra Mauro Ct League City TX 77573-4406 Office: American National Insurance Co 1 Moody Plz Galveston TX 77550-7999 Office Phone: 409-763-4661. Office Fax: 409-766-2912. Personal E-mail: steve.schouweiler@anico.com.

SCHOVER, LESLIE RUTH, psychologist; b. Chgo., Sept. 17, 1952; d. Donald Sanford and Janet June (Moss) Schover; m. Menachem Shoham, Oct. 21, 1990 (div. 2000). BA magna cum laude, Brown U., 1974; MA in Psychology, UCLA, 1975, PhD in Psychology, 1979. Lic. psychologist, Tex. Postdoctoral fellow SUNY, Stony Brook, 1979-81; instr., dept. psychiatry Baylor Coll. Medicine, Houston, 1981; asst. prof. urology (psychology), asst. clin. psychologist M.D. Anderson Hosp. and Tumor Inst., Houston, 1981-86; staff psychologist, dept. urology with joint appointments in the Cancer Ctr. and dept. psychiatry and psychology Cleve. Clinic Found., 1986—99; assoc. prof., behavioral sci. U. Tex. M.D. Anderson Cancer Ctr., 1999—2003, prof., behavioral sci., 2004—. Author: Prime Time: Sexual Health for Men Over 50, 1984, Sexuality and Chronic Illness, 1988; contbr. many articles to profl. jours. Active nat. task force for breast cancer control Am. Cancer Soc., Atlanta, 1988-91. Woodrow Wilson grantee, 1979. Mem. APA, Internat. Acad. Sex Rsch., Am. Soc. Reproductive Med., Phi Beta Kappa. Democrat. Jewish. Office: U Tex MD Anderson Cancer Ctr MDA CPB3 3241 Unit 1330 PO Box 301439 Houston TX 77230-1439 Business E-Mail: lschover@mdanderson.org.

SCHRAGER, MINDY RAE, operations management specialist, life coach; d. Julius Maxwell and Miriam (Max) Schrager; m. Jim Flannery, 1993. BA, Dickinson Coll., 1979; MBA, Babson Coll., 1981. Integrative coaching cert. Ford Inst. JFK U., 2008, cert. NLP Master Practitioner, Aura-Soma Practitioner, Herrmann Brain Dominance Indicator facilitator, Blueprint Coach, spiriitual divorce coach, NLP health practitioner, courage coach. Cons. Nolan Norton & Co., Lexington, Mass., 1981—86; mgr. Logos Corp., Dedham, Mass., 1986—87; resource ctr. supr., customer satisfaction mgr., dir. quality Motorola ISG, Mansfield, Mass., 1987—95; dir. quality, dir. bill payment ops., dir. project mgmt. Fidelity Investments, Boston, 1995—99; sr. program mgr., sr. mgr. collaborative product delivery, dir. program and operational excellence Ascential Software, Westboro, Mass., 1999—2005; mgr., program dir. IBM, Westboro, 2005—07, Rsch. Triangle Pk., 2007—. Author: Stepping Stones to Success. Mem.: NAFE, Internat. Coach Fedn., Assn. Rsch. and Enlightenment. Avocations: coaching, wellness. Home: 307 Capistrane Dr Cary NC 27519 Office: IBM 3039 E Cornwallis Rd PO Box 12195 Research Triangle Park NC 27709-2195 Business E-Mail: mschrager238@msn.com.

SCHRAMM, BERNARD CHARLES, JR., retired advertising agency executive; b. Balt., Jan. 23, 1928; s. Bernard C. and Juliet Marie (Barranger) Schramm; m. Florence Mae Fangman, 1950; children: Stephanie Schramm McDaniel, Carol Schramm Molander, Bernard Charles III, Claudia Schramm Smith. Grad., Balt. Poly. Inst., 1946. Prodn. mgr. Van Sant, Dugdale & Co., Balt., 1946-52; media dir. AWL Advt., Balt., 1952-55; dir. prodn. Henry J. Kaufman Assocs., Washington, 1955-58; exec. v.p. Avalon Hill Co., Balt., 1958-64; v.p. Cargill, Wilson & Acree Advt., Richmond, Va., 1964-68; pres. William Cook Advt. Inc., Jacksonville, Fla., 1968-89, chmn. bd., 1989-97; ret., 1997. Chmn. Otis F. Smith Found., 1991—97. Mem. exec. com., v.p. United Way N.E. Fla., 1982-87, bd. dirs., 1982-93; bd. dirs. N.E. Fla. chpt. ARC, 1976-89, chmn., 1980-81; bd. dirs. F.J.C. Found., 1976-89. Mem.: Am. Assn. Advt. Agys. (chmn. Fla. coun. 1984—85, So. Region Bd. of Govs. 1988—92, chmn. 1989, nat. bd. dirs., agy. mgmt. com. 1989—92), Jacksonville Area C. of C., Rotary Club. Republican. Roman Catholic. Avocations: golf, reading, spectator sports, hunting.

SCHREADLEY, RICHARD LEE, newswriter, retired editor; b. Harrisburg, Pa., Jan. 3, 1931; s. Harry Leroy and Flora Rebecca (McQuilken) S.; m. Doris Arlene Sheaffer, Dec. 18, 1952; 1 child, Rhys Leroy. BA, Dickinson Coll., 1952; MA, Tufts U., 1968, MAL.D., 1969, PhD, 1972. Reporter The News and Courier, Charleston, SC, 1975; asso. editor The Evening Post, Charleston, 1975-76, editorial page editor, 1976-77, editor, 1977-81; exec. editor The Evening Post and The News and Courier, 1981-88; assoc. editor and sr. writer mil. and polit. affairs The News and Courier, 1989. Author: From the Rivers to the Sea, The United States Navy in Vietnam, 1992, Valor and Virtue, The Washington Light Infantry in Peace and in War, 1996. Chmn. Fgn. Affairs Forum of Charleston, 1987-88, mem. steering com., 1989. Served to comdr. USN, 1949-52, 56-73. Mem. Navy League, Ret. Officer Assn., Washington Light Infantry, German

Friendly Soc. Charleston, Army-Navy Club of Washington, Country Club of Charleston. Home: 812 Clearview Dr Charleston SC 29412-4511 Personal E-mail: rlschrea@knology.net.

SCHREIBER, ALAN HICKMAN, lawyer; b. Muncie, Ind., Apr. 4, 1944; s. Ephriam and Clarrisa (Hickman) S.; m. Phyllis Jean Chamberlain, Dec. 22, 1972; children: Jennifer Aline, Brett Justin. Student, DePauw U., 1962-64; BS in Bus., Ind. U., 1966, JD, 1969. Bar: Fla. 1971, U.S. Dist. Ct. (so. dist.) Fla. Asst. State Atty.'s Office, Ft. Lauderdale, Fla., 1971-76; pub. defender 17th Jud. Cir., Ft. Lauderdale, 1976—. Cons. Fla. Bar News on Criminal Law, 1982; lobbyist for indigent funding, Fla., 1980—; apptd. to Supreme Ct. Com. on Racial and Ethic Bias; co-chair Chiles-MacKay task force on criminal justice. Contbr. articles to profl. jours. Mem. Dem. Exec. Com., Ft. Lauderdale, 1980; mem. Plantation Dem. Club, 1983; campaign chmn. Goldstein for Atty. Gen. Fla., 1982. Named Young Dem. of Yr., Broward County Young Dems., 1980; Man of Yr., Jewish War Vets., 1982; recipient B'nai B'rith Pub. Servant award, 1990, Dem. of Yr. award 2000, Harry Galkin Meml. award 2002. Mem. Fla. Bar Assn., Broward County Bar Assn., ABA, Nat. Legal Aid Defenders Assn., Phi Alpha Delta. Business E-Mail: aschveiber2@ausdivv.com, aschreiber2@austin.rr.com.

SCHREIBER, HOWARD E., lawyer; b. Balt., May 18, 1959; BA in Polit. Sci., Dickinson Coll., 1981; JD with honors, Duke U., 1984. Bar: Tex. 1984. Shareholder Jenkens & Gilchrist, P.C., Dallas, 1993—, firm leader real estate practice group. Mem.: ABA, Am. Coll. Mortgage Attorneys, Dallas Bar Assn., Tex. State Bar Assn. Office: Hunton & Williams PC Ste 3200 1445 Ross Ave Dallas TX 75202-2799 Office Phone: 214-855-4370. Office Fax: 214-855-4300. Business E-Mail: hschreiber@jenkens.com.

SCHREIBER, KURT GILBERT, lawyer; b. Milw., Aug. 22, 1946; s. Raymond R. and Mildred L. (Kleist) S.; m. Nelda Beth Van Buren, May 3, 1974; children: Katharine Anne, Matthew Edward. AB in Econs., Cornell U., 1968; JD, U. Mich., 1971; M in Theol. Studies, Vanderbilt U., 2003. Bar: Wis. 1971, Tex. 1979, Tenn. 1997. Internat. atty. Tenneco Internat. Holdings Co., London, 1974-78; atty. Tenneco Inc., Houston, 1978-80; 2d v.p., asst. gen. counsel Am. Gen. Corp., Houston, 1980-83, v.p., gen. counsel, 1983-84, sr. v.p., gen. counsel, 1984-93, sr. v.p., corp. sec., 1993-94; pvt. practice Houston, 1994-96; exec. v.p., gen. counsel Direct Gen. Corp., Nashville, 1996-98, pres., 1998—2001. Bd. dir. Cumberland Trust and Investment Co., Urban Housing Solutions. Fellow Tex. Bar Found.; mem. ABA, Wis. Bar Assn., Tex. Bar Assn., Tenn. Bar Assn. Home: 405 Bushnell St Nashville TN 37206-1820

SCHREIBER, MARK TRAUDT, psychiatrist; b. Denver, Oct. 6, 1947; s. Charles William and Sophie Emily Schreiber; m. Constance Anne Rabe, Nov. 27, 1976; children: Vanessa, Laura, Charles, Anne, John. BS, U. Nebr., Lincoln, 1970; MD, Washington U., St. Louis, Mo., 1975. Diplomate Am. Bd. Psychiatry and Neurology, 1980, Am. Bd. Addictionology, 1986. Resident Barnes Hosp. Washington U., St. Louis, 1975—78; psychiatrist Hearst, Fischer & Schreiber, Virginia Beach, Va., 1978—84, Crossroads Clin., Virginia Beach, 1984—89; CEO Atlantic Psychiatric, Virginia Beach, 1989—. Med. dir. Serenity Lodge, Chesapeake, Va., 1984—91; assoc. med. dir. Va. Beach Psychiat. Ctr., 1991—. Contbr. articles to profl. jours. Dist. coun. bd. mem. & v.p. Boys Scout America, 2008, dist. coun. bd. mem. & pres., 2011—12; elder Bayside Presbyn. Ch., Va. Beach, 1980—, chmn. com., 2008—; chmn. internat. partnership com. Presbytery Ea. Va., Portsmouth, 1982—. Named Am.'s Top Psychiatrists, Consumers' Rsch. Coun. Am. Fellow: Am. Soc. Addiction Medicine (regional chmn. 2000—04), Am. Psychiat. Assn. (Disting. fellow 2005). Avocations: ballroom dancing, skiing, reading, camping, travel. Office: Atlantic Psychiatric 780 Lipshua Pkwy Ste 450 Virginia Beach VA 23452 Office Phone: 757-468-0550.

SCHREIBER, ROBERT, JR., waste management administrator; BSChemE, U. Mo., Columbia. V.p. Lafser and Schreiber Inc.; co-founder Lafser & Schreiber, 1985; pres. Schreiber, Yonley & Associates, 1992—. Dir., Air programs, environ. programs Mo. Dept. of Natural Resources, 1978—85. Office: Perma-Fix Environmental Services Inc Ste 250 8302 Dunwoody Pl Atlanta GA 30350 Office Phone: 770-587-9898. Office Fax: 770-587-9937.

SCHREIBER, SALLY ANN, lawyer; d. Warren Thomas and Joyce (Honey) S.; children: Amanda Honey, Ryan Thorp Luther. BBA, U. N.Mex., 1973; JD, Stanford U., 1976. Bar: Calif. 1976, Tex. 1977. Assoc. Johnson & Swanson, Dallas, 1976-81, ptnr., 1981-89; mem. firm Johnson & Gibbs, P.C., Dallas, 1989-93; of counsel Cox & Smith, Inc., Dallas, 1993-94; shareholder Munsch Hardt Kopf & Harr, P.C., Dallas, 1994—. Spkr. in field. Editor Stanford U. Law Rev., 1975-76; co-author paper Internat. Bar Assn., 1986. Bd. dirs. The Lyric Opera of Dallas, 1982-86; law sch. bd. vis. Stanford (Calif.) U., 1981-84, 2004-06; dir. Tex. Bus. Law Found., 1989—, treas. 1994-96, sec. 1996-98; co-founder Attys. Serving the Cmty. Mem.: Dallas Bar Assn., Calif. Bar Assn., Tex. Bar Assn. (corp. law com. 1981—, vice-chair corp. law com. 1993—97, chair corp. law com. 1997—2001, partnership law com. 1985—, ltd. liability co. com. 1992—, opinion com. 1989—98, codification com. 1997—, bus. law sect. coun. 1996—2007, vice chmn. 2004—05, chair 2005—06). Home: 2737 Purdue Ave Dallas TX 75225-7910 Office: Munsch Hardt Kopf & Harr PC 500 N Akard St Ste 3800 Dallas TX 75201 Office Phone: 214-855-7598. Business E-Mail: sschreiber@munsch.com.

SCHREINER, ROB, pulmonologist; MD, U. Tenn, 1981; grad. Med. Tng. in Internal Medicine, Vanderbilt U., 1985. Fellowship, pulmonary & critical care medicine U. Colo., 1989; pulmonary and critical care medicine physician The SE Permanente Med. Group Inc., 1994; exec. med. dir. The SE Permanente Med. Group, Inc., Ga., 1994—; assoc. med. dir., hospital, splty. and ancillary care, The SE Permanente Med. Group, Inc. Kaiser Permanente, 2005—07, COO, The SE Permanente Med. Group, Inc., 2007—08. Former med. dir., critical care and respiratory care Northside Hosp.; fellow ACP, Am. Coll. Chest Physicians; mem. Our Lady Perpetual Help Home; mem., med. exec. com. Northside Hosp., 1998. Named Educator of the Yr., Specialist of the Year, Adminstr. Physician of the Yr., Physician of the Yr. Avocations: gardening, cooking, exercise. Office: Kaiser Permanente Nine Piedmont Ctr 3495 Piedmont Rd NE Atlanta GA 30305 Office Phone: 404-364-4757. Office Fax: 404-364-4732.

SCHRIEFFER, JOHN ROBERT, retired physics professor; b. Oak Park, Ill., May 31, 1931; s. John Henry and Louise (Anderson) Schrieffer; m. Anne Grete Thomsen, Dec. 30, 1960; children: Anne Bolette, Paul Karsten, Anne Regina. BS, MIT, 1953; MS, U. Ill., 1954, PhD, 1957, ScD, 1974; ScD (hon.), Tech. U., Munich, 1968, U. Geneva, 1968, U. Pa., 1973, U. Cin., 1977, U. Tel Aviv, 1987, U. Ala., 1990. NSF postdoctoral fellow U. Birmingham, England, Niels Bohr Inst., Copenhagen, 1957—58; asst. prof. U. Chgo., 1958—59; asst. prof., then assoc. prof. U. Ill., 1959—62; prof. U. Pa., Phila., 1962—79, Mary Amanda Wood prof. physics, 1964—79; Andrew D. White prof. at large Cornell U., 1969—75; prof. U. Calif., Santa Barbara, 1980—91, Chancellor's prof., 1984—91, dir. Inst. for Theoretical Physics, 1984—89; Univ. prof. Fla. State U., Tallahassee, 1992—2006, chief scientist Nat. High Magnetic Field Lab., 1992—2004, Univ. Eminent Scholar prof., 1995—2006. Pres.'s com. Nat. Medal of Sci., 1996—98. Author: Theory of Superconductivity, 1964. Recipient Comstock prize, NAS, 1968, Nobel prize for Physics, 1972, John Ericsson medal, Am. Soc. Swedish Engrs., 1976, Alumni Achievement award, U. Ill., 1979, Nat. medal of Sci., 1984; fellow Guggenheim, Copenhagen, 1967, Los Alamos Nat. Lab., Exxon faculty, 1979—89. Fellow: Am. Phys. Soc. (v.p. 1994, pres.-elect 1995, pres. 1996, past pres. 1997, Oliver E. Buckley solid state physics prize 1968); mem.: NAS (coun. 1990—), Acad. Sci. USSR, Royal Danish Acad. Scis. and Letters, Am. Acad. Arts and Scis.

SCHROCK, SIMON, wholesale executive; b. Oakland, Md., Dec. 28, 1936; s. Noah and Cora (Burkholder) S.; m. Eva Lena Yoder, June 7, 1959 (dec. Apr. 1962); m. Pauline Yoder, Sept. 29, 1963; children: Janice Yvonne, Eldon Laverne, Ivan Dale. With Eastern States Farm Supply Co., Oakland, Md., 1957-59, Children's Hosp., Washington, 1959-61, Copp Properties, Vienna, Va., 1961-75; pres. Choice Books of No. Va., Fairfax, Va., 1975—. Chmn. Lighthouse Lit., 1976-2001. Author: Get on With Living, 1976, Price of Missing Life, 1981, One-Anothering, 1986, Vow-Keepers Vow-Breakers, A Smoother Journey, 1994, What Shall The Redeemed Wear, 2001, Where Has Integrity Gone, 2001, Don't Throw In the Towel, 2003; contbr. articles to ch. jours. Bishop Faith Christian Fellowship, Catlett, Va., 1981—. Avocations: travel, writing, biking. Office: 10100 Piper Ln Bristow VA 20136 Business E-Mail: schrocks@nva.choicebooks.org.

SCHRODER, JACK SPALDING, JR., lawyer; b. Atlanta, July 10, 1948; s. Jack Spalding Sr. and Van (Spalding) S.; m. Karen Keyworth, Sept. 1, 1973; children: Jack Spalding III, James Edward. BA, Emory U., 1970; JD, U. Ga., 1973. Bar: Ga. 1973, U.S. Dist. Ct. (no. dist.) Ga. 1973, U.S. Ct. Appeals (11th cir.) 1982. Assoc. Alston & Bird, Atlanta, 1973-78, ptnr., 1978—2003, sr. counsel, 2004—07, of counsel, 2007—. Author: Credentialing: Strategies for a Changing Environment/BNA's Health Law and Business Series, 1996; co-editor, contbg. author: Georgia Hospital Law manual, 1979, 84, 92. Bd. dirs. Rsch. Atlanta, 1996-00, pres., 1999, co-chair bd. advisors, 2003-06; participant Leadership Ga., Atlanta, 1986. United Way (chmn. legal divsn.), Atlanta, 1980; bd. dir. Good Samaritan Health and Wellness Ctr., Jasper, Ga., 2006-, vice-chair, 2008. Decorated comdr. S.E. Commandery Mil. and Hospitaller Order of St. Lazarus of Jerusalem. Mem. ABA (vice chmn. medicine and law com. 1989-90), Am. Health Lawyers Assn. (bd. dirs. 1994-99, chmn. med. staff and physician rels. com. 1991-94, vice chair hosps. and health systems law inst. 2001-07), Ga. Acad. Healthcare Attys. (pres. 1981-82), State Bar Ga. (bd. govs. 1987-89), Atlanta Coun. Younger Lawyers (pres. 1977-78), Atlanta Bar Assn. (pres. 1982-83), Atlanta Bar Found. (pres. 1991-95), Mil. and Hospitaller Order St. Lazarus Jerusalem (comdr. S.E. commandery 2003—). Office: Alston & Bird One Atlantic Ctr 1201 W Peachtree St NW Atlanta GA 30309-3424 Office Phone: 404-881-7685.

SCHRODER, JOHN M., state legislator; s. H. Schroder John and Schroder (Mendez) Susie; m. Ellie Daigle; children: Brittany, John. BS in Criminal Justice, Southeastern La. U. Former CID spl. agt. US Army; former ascension parish narcotics detective; businessman; mem. Dist. 77 La. House of Reps., 2008—, mem. adminstrn. of criminal justice com., appropriations com., joint legis. com. on the budget, house com. on homeland security, mem. joint com. on homeland security, spl. com. on mil. and vets. affairs. Republican. Cath. Office: 222 N Vermont Ste K and M Covington LA 70433 also: Capitol Office PO Box 44486 Baton Rouge LA 70804 Office Phone: 985-893-6262, 225-342-6945. Office Fax: 985-893-6261. E-mail: schrodej@legis.state.la.us.

SCHROEDER, CHRISTOPHER HENRY, law educator, former federal agency administrator; b. Springfield, Ohio, 1948; m. Katherine Tiffany Bartlett, Aug. 13, 1975; children: Emily, Ted, Lily. BA, Princeton U., 1968; MDiv, Yale U., 1971; JD, U. Calif., Berkeley, 1974. Bar: Calif. 1974. Assoc. McCutchen, Doyle, Brown & Enersen, San Francisco, 1974—76; dir. energy & environment project Earl Warren Legal Inst., U. Calif. Berkeley, Berkeley, Calif., 1976—77; ptnr. Armour, Schroeder, St. John Wilcox & Goodlin, San Francisco, 1977—79; chief counsel US Senate Judiciary Com., Washington, 1992—93; dep. asst. atty. gen., spl. counsel, Office Legal Counsel US Dept. Justice, Washington, 1993—96, acting asst. atty. gen., 1996—97; assoc. prof. law Duke U. Law Sch., Durham, NC, 1979-85, prof. law, 1985—99, prof. law & pub. policy studies, 1999—, co-chair Ctr. for the Study of the Congress, 1996—, dir. Program in Pub. Law, 2000—, Charles S. Murphy prof. law; asst. atty. gen. Office Legal Policy US Dept. Justice, Washington, 2010—12. Editor-in-chief Calif. Law Review, 1973-74, vis. prof. UCLA, 1985-86, spl. nominations counsel, US Senate Judiciary Com., 1991, 1987-88, impeachment trial counsel for Senator Joe Biden Jr., US Senate, 1998-99, cons. O'Melveny & Myers LLP, 2002-05, of counsel, 2005-09 Author: A New Progressive Agenda for Public Health & the Environment, 2005; co-author (with Curtis A. Bradley): Presidential Power Stories, 2008; co-author: (with Pamela S. Karlan & Goodwin Liu) Keeping Faith with the Constitution, 2009. Office: Duke University School Law 210 Science Dr Box 90360 Durham NC 27708 Office Phone: 919-613-7096. Office Fax: 919-613-7231. E-mail: Schroeder@law.duke.edu.*

SCHROEDER, DAVID J. DEAN, retired psychologist; b. Hutchinson, Kans., Mar. 21, 1942; s. D.J.W. and Louise (Wedel) S.; m. Nevonna Joyce Thomas, May 24, 1964; children: Taryn Dee Schroeder Dye, Anita Joy Fitch. BA, Tabor Coll., 1964; MS, Kans. State Tchrs. Coll., 1967; PhD, U. Okla., 1971. Lic. psychologist, Kans. Rsch. psychologist Civil Aerospace Med. Inst., Oklahoma City, 1970-72, clin. rsch. psychologist, 1980-89, supr., 1989-90, mgr. human factors rsch. lab., 1990-91, mgr. aerospace human factors rsch. divsn., 1991—2008; intern Norfolk (Nebr.) Regional Ctr., 1972-73; clin. psychologist VA Hosp., Murfreesboro, Tenn., 1973-75, Topeka, 1975-80. Co-author: FAA Employee Survey: National Report, 1984, 86, FAA Employee Survey: Regional/Center Reports, 1984, 86, FAA Job Satisfaction Survey National Report, 1988, FAA Job Satisfaction Survey: Regional/Center/Work Group Reports, 1988; mem. adv. editl. bd. Aviation Space and Environ. Medicine, 1993-95, 99-2001, 2006-09. Mem. senate adv. com. Tabor Coll., Hillsboro, Kans., 1987-89; Christian edn. com. chmn. So. Dist. Conf. Mennonite Brethren Ch., Hillsboro, 1989; Sunday Sch. tchr. Western Oaks Christian Ch., Oklahoma City, 1990—; co-chair cmty. investment subcom. United Way Ctrl. Okla., 2006-09, Okla. City Friends Libr. Bd., 2008-09, treas., 2009-11, 13-; vice chair Com. Investment United Way Ctrl. Okla., 2009-11, chair, 2011-14; bd. dirs. United Way Ctrl. Okla., 2011-, mem. United Way Ctrl. Okla. Rsch. and Cmty. Iniatences Adv. com., 2012-, chair United Way Ctrl. Okla. May Turnados Releif Fund Disbursement Com., 2013- Fellow APA, Aerospace Med. Assn. (chmn. sci. program com. 1990-91, mem. coun. 1992-95, v.p. 1996-97, v.p. edn. and rsch. 1999-2002, pres.-elect, 2002-03, pres. 2003-04, program com. chair APA divsn. applied exptl. and engring. psychology 1996-97, sec.-treas. 1998-2001, pres. 2002-03, chair Div 21 fellows com. 2011-12, rep. APA Coun. 2008-10, chmn. aerospace human factors com. 1999-2002, Raymond F. Longacre award for outstanding accomplishments in psychol. and psychiat. aspects of aerospace medicine 1997), Aerospace Human Factors Assn. (pres. 1994-95, sec. 2008-, Henry L. Taylor Founders award 2001); mem. Okla. Psychol. Assn. (bd. dirs. 1988-89, pres.-elect 1991, pres. 1992), Internat. Acad. Aviation and Space Medicine, IAASM Sci. Com. 2007-11, mem. Scholarship com., Nat. Rsch. Coun. Nat. Acads.(mem. Com. Pilot Fatigue 2010-11). Democrat. Achievements include research in assessing the interactive effects of alcohol, age and drugs on dynamic tracking and cognitive performance, personality characteristics and training success of air traffic control students, biofeedback, anxiety and burnout in government employees, human factors of air traffic control operational errors, fatigue and shiftwork. Home: 6109 Walnut Ln Oklahoma City OK 73132 Home Phone: 405-470-1184. Personal E-mail: davids20@cox.net.

SCHROEDER, THOMAS D., federal judge; b. Atlanta, May 26, 1959; Attended, Conservatory of Music, U. Cin., 1977—78; BS, U. Kans., 1981; JD, Notre Dame Law Sch., 1984. Bar: NC 1984. Law clk. for Hon. George E. MacKinnon US Ct. Appeals (DC Cir.), 1984—85; assoc. Womble Carlyle Sandridge & Rice, PLLC, 1985—91, ptnr., 1991—2008, practice group leader, product liability practice group Winston-Salem, NC, 1994—2002, mem. firm mgmt. com., 1996—2007, vice chmn. firm mgmt. com., 2005—07; judge US Dist. Ct (mid. dist.) NC, Winston-Salem, 2008—. Lectr. in field; faculty, trial tng. program Womble Carlyle Sandridge & Rice, PLLC, Winston-Salem, NC. Editor-in-chief Notre Dame Law Review, 1983—84. Mem.: Joseph Br. Inn Ct., 21st Jud. Dist. Bar Assn., Forsyth County Bar Assn., NC Bar Assn., Phi Alpha Delta. Office: US Dist Ct 251 N Main St Winston Salem NC 27101

SCHRUM, JAKE BENNETT, academic administrator; b. Greenville, Tex., Feb. 9, 1946; s. Jake M. and Julia (Bennett) S.; m. Jane Woodman, Dec. 28, 1968; children: Julia Elizabeth, Emily Katharine. BA, Southwestern U., 1968; MDiv, Yale U., 1973; postgrad., Harvard U., 1983. Ordained to ministry Meth. Ch., 1969. Devel. officer Yale U., New Haven, 1973-77; dir. devel. Muhlenberg Coll., Allentown, Pa., 1977-78; v.p. Tex. Wesleyan Coll., Ft. Worth, 1978-82; v.p. univ. rels. Southwestern U., Georgetown, Tex., 1982-85; v.p. Emory U., Atlanta, 1985-91; pres. Tex. Wesleyan U., 1991-2000, Southwestern U., Georgetown, Tex., 2000—. Chmn. CASE, 1995—96, Associated Colls. of the South, 2005—07, Georgetown Project, 2005—06; vice chair higher edn. com. Austin Area Rsch. Orgn.; bd. dirs. Southern U. Conf., Southern Collegiate Athletic Assn., Coun. Pres., Assn. Governing Bds., First Tex. Bank, Edn. and Inst. Insurance Adminstrn., Assn. Tex. Colls. and Univs., Coun. Ind. Colls. Author: Democracy's Last Stand: The Role of the New Urban University, 1999; editor: A Board's Guide to Comprehensive Campaigns, 2000, Justice for All, 2001. Mem. exec. com. Tex. Ind. Coll. Found.; bd. dirs. Georgetown Area Cmty. Found.; chair Georgetown Project. Named Man of Yr., Bnai Brith North Tex., 1995. Mem.: Nat. Assn. Schs. and Colls. of United Meth. Ch., Annapolis Group, Am. Coun. Edn., Philos. Soc. Tex. Avocations: golf, public speaking. Office: Southwestern University Office of President 1001 E University Georgetown TX 78626 Office Phone: 512-863-1454. E-mail: schrum@southwestern.edu.*

SCHRUM, ROGER P., consumer products company executive; Assoc., Fort Scott Cmty. Coll., 1973; BS in Edn. & Journalism, Pitts. State U., 1975; Exec. Devel. Program, Ind. U. Worked, bus. comm. and investor rels. Diamond Shamrock Corp., NorthWestern Corp., Sioux Falls; bus. editor Amarillo Globe-News; dir., media rels. Ashland, Inc., Ashland, 1986—93; gen. mgr., mktg. comm. and pub. SCANA Corp., Columbia, 1993—2001; staff v.p., investor rels. and corp. affairs Sonoco Products Co., 2005—09, v.p., investor rels. and corp. affairs, 2009—. Office: Sonoco Products Co 1 N Second St Hartsville SC 29550 Office Phone: 843-383-7000. Business E-Mail: roger.schrum@sonoco.com.

SCHUBERT, RICHARD FRANCIS, social services administrator, consultant; b. Trenton, NJ, Nov. 2, 1936; s. Yaro and Frances Mary (Hustak) S.; m. Virginia Thomas Austin, Sept. 15, 2000; children: Robyn, David. BA cum laude, Eastern Nazarene Coll., 1958; LLB, Yale U., 1961. Bar: Pa. 1962, U.S. Supreme Ct 1972. Arbitration atty. Bethlehem Steel Corp., Pa., 1961-66, asst. mgr. labor relations, 1966-70; exec. asst. to undersec. labor Washington, 1970; gen. counsel labor, 1971-73; dep. sec. labor, 1973-75; asst. to v.p. indsl. relations Bethlehem Steel Corp., 1973, asst. v.p. public affairs, 1975-77, v.p. public affairs, 1977-79, pres., 1979-80, vice chmn., 1980-82; pres., CEO ARC, 1982-89, Points of Light Found., 1990-95. Bd. dirs. Internat. Ctr. for Religion and Diplomacy, Mgmt. Tng. Corp., Friends Czech Rep., Friends of Zambia. Exec. v.p. EXCN; chmn. emeritus Internat. Youth Found., founding chmn., Nazarene Compassionate Ministries Inc.; co-founder Drucker Found., chmn. Nat. Job Corps Assn. Mem.: Coun. on Fgn. Rels., Northampton County Bar Assn., Pa. Bar Assn., Ea. Nazarene Alumni Assn. (pres. 1969—73), Phi Alpha Delta. Mem. Ch. of Nazarene. Home: 6615 Madison McLean Dr Mc Lean VA 22101-2425 Business E-Mail: rfs@iyfnet.org.

SCHUCKENBROCK, STEVE (STEPHEN FRANCIS SCHUCKENBROCK), computer company executive, former information technology executive; b. 1960; BBA, Elon Coll., 1982. Sales & tech. mgmt. positions IBM Corp., 1983—93; ptnr. Feld Group, 1993—95, COO, 2000—04; chief info. officer Frito-Lay, 1995—98; sr. v.p. info. tech. PepsiCo. Inc., 1998—2000; exec. v.p. global sales & client solutions Electronic Data Systems, Plano, Tex., 2003—06; sr. v.p., pres. global services, chief info. officer Dell, Inc., Round Rock, Tex., 2007—09, pres. large enterprise, 2009—11, pres. Dell Services, 2011—. Office: Dell Inc 1 Dell Way Round Rock TX 78682

SCHUESSLER, MORGAN, human resources specialist; B, NYU; MBA, Emory U. Various positions, sales, mktg., strategy and product mgmt. Am. Express Inc., v.p., global purchasing solutions, 2002—05; sr. v.p., human resources, mktg. and corp. comm. Global Payments, 2005—07, exec. v.p., human resources and corp. comm., 2007—08; exec. v.p., chief adminstrv. officer Global Payments, Inc., 2008—. Dean's adv. bd. Emory U. Goizueta Bus. Sch.; bd. dirs. Ga. C. of C. Mem.: Chastain Park Conservancy (assoc.). Office: Global Payments Inc 10 Glenlake Pkwy NE N Tower Atlanta GA 30328 Office Phone: 770-829-8000. Office Fax: 770-829-8224. Business E-Mail: morgan.schuessler@globalpay.com.

SCHUH, FRANK JOSEPH, oil industry executive, consultant; b. Columbus, Ohio, Feb. 3, 1935; s. Sebastian and Elizabeth (Zorn) S.; m. Alice Virgene Kasler, June 16, 1956; children: Dwain Joseph, Michael James, Barbara Ann. BS in Petroleum Engring., MS in Petroleum Engring., Ohio State U., 1956. Registered profl. engr., Ohio. Drilling and rsch. engr. Atlantic Refining Co., Tex., La., 1956-62; mem. drilling engring. staff, dir. engring. Atlantic Richfield Co., Dallas, 1962-82, mgr. drilling rsch., sr. advisor Plano, Tex., 1982-86; v.p. Enertech Engring. & Tech., Dallas, 1986-87; pres. Drilling Tech., Inc., Plano, 1987—; v.p. Supreme Resources Corp., Dallas, 1988-92. Founder, 1st pres. Drilling Engring. Assn., Dallas, 1983-85; mem. tech. adv. com. Internat. Ocean Drilling Program, 2002—. Author: Drilling Equations, 1975; patentee horizontal drilling, high pressure drilling system, continuous heavy oil production process, 31 other patents. Precinct, region chmn. Rep. Party, Dallas, 1964-74; vol. bldg. com. Mary Immaculate Ch., Dallas, 1965-66; mem. tech. engring. and devel. com. Ocean Drilling Program, Bryan, Tex., 1980-2006. Recipient outstanding achievement in field of engring. award Nat. Engrs. Coun., 1980, Robert Earl McConnell award Am. Inst. Mining Engrs., 1994, Ohio State Univ. Coll. of Engring. Benjamin G. Lamme Meritorious Achievement medel, 1995. Mem. NAE, Soc. Petroleum Engrs. (nat. bd. dirs. 1983-86, Drilling Engring. award 1986, Disting. Mem. award 1989), Am. Petroleum Inst. (chmn. com. 6, 1985-88, svc. citation 1986), Am. Assn. Drilling Engrs., Soc. Ind. Profl. Earth Scientists, Petroleum Engrs. Club (pres. 1974-75), Ohio State U. Alumni Club (pres. 1968-69), Dallas-Ft. Worth Oilman's Club (handicapper 1973-86). Avocations: golf, sailing. Office: Drilling Technology Inc 5808 Wavertree Ln Ste 1000 Plano TX 75093-4513 Office Phone: 972-380-0203. Business E-Mail: schuh1@tx.rr.com.

SCHUKER, STEPHEN ALAN, historian, educator; b. NYC, Feb. 16, 1939; s. Louis A. and Millicent (Milchman) Schuker; m. Elisabeth Glaser, 1998 (dec.); children: Lauren, Daniel. BA summa cum laude, Cornell U., 1959; MA, Harvard U., 1962, PhD, 1969. Asst. head hist. rsch. naval history divsn. Office Chief Naval Ops., 1959—61; instr. history Harvard U., Cambridge, Mass., 1968—69, asst. prof., 1969—74, lectr., 1974—75; vis. assoc. prof. European studies Sch. Advanced Internat. Studies, Johns Hopkins U., Washington, 1977, adj. prof., 1978—83; assoc. prof. history Brandeis U., Waltham, Mass., 1977—82, prof., 1982—91; Commonwealth prof. history U. Va., Charlottesville, 1991—92, William W. Corcoran prof., 1992—. Cons. Nat. Commn. Documents and Records Federal Ofcls., 1976, Rockefeller Found., 1981, Bradley Found., 2008—13. Author: The End of French Predominance in Europe, 1976, American "Reparations" to Germany, 1919-1933: Implications for the Third World Debt Crisis, 1988; editor: Deutschland und Frankreich vom Konflikt zur Aussoehnung, 2000; contbr. articles to profl. jours. Lt. USNR, 1959—61. Recipient George Louis Beer prize, Gilbert Chinard prize; fellowship, NEH, 1972—73, Am. Coun. Learned Socs., 1976—77, DAAD, 1979, 1986, Fulbright fellowship, John D. & Catherine MacArthur Found., 1987—88, Sec. Nav fellow, Naval War Coll., 1992—93, German Marshall Fund, 1998—99, fellow, Historisches Kolleg, Munich, 1996—97. Mem.: Hist. Soc., Soc. Historians Am. Fgn. Relations, Am. Hist. Assn. Office: U Va Corcoran Dept History University Station Charlottesville VA 22908 Office Phone: 434-924-6405. Business E-Mail: sas4u@virginia.edu.

SCHULER, LIZBETH R., healthcare services company executive; Undergraduate in Acctg., U. Louisville, MBA. Various positions, fin. and acctg. Humana, Inc.; dir., fin. Cmty. Health Sys., Inc., 1999—2000, asst. v.p., investor rels., 2000—05; v.p., investor rels. Community Health Systems, Inc., 2005—. Office: Community Health Systems Inc 4000 Meridian Blvd Franklin TN 37067 Office Phone: 615-465-7000. Office Fax: 615-371-1068. Business E-Mail: lizbeth_schuler@chs.net.

SCHULER, THEODORE ANTHONY, retired civil engineer; b. Louisville, July 1, 1934; s. Henry R. and Virginia (Meisner) S.; m. Jane A. Bandy, July 29, 1979; children: Marc, Elizabeth, Eric, Ellen. BCE, U. Louisville, 1957, M Engring., 1973. Registered profl. engr. Tenn. Design constrn. engr. Brighton Engring. Co., Frankfort, Ky., 1960—65; design engr. Hensley-Schmidt Inc., Chattanooga, 1965—68, assoc., 1969—73, sr. assoc., 1973—75, prin., asst. v.p., head Knoxville office, 1975—81; chief planning engr. engring. dept. City Knoxville, 1981—96, ret., 1996. Served to lt. (j.g.) USNR, 1957-60. Fellow: ASCE. Personal E-mail: tschu30447@aol.com.

SCHULMAN, HAROLD, obstetrician, gynecologist; b. Newark, Oct. 26, 1930; m. Rosemarie Vincenti; children: Stanley H., Sandra C., Gina M. BS, U. Fla., 1951; MD, Emory U., 1955. Diplomate Am. Bd. Ob-Gyn., Am. Bd. Maternal and Fetal Medicine; registered diagnostic med. sonographer. Intern Jackson Meml. Hosp., Miami, Fla., 1955-56, resident, 1958-61; instr. dept. ob-gyn. U. Miami (Fla.) Sch. Medicine, 1961; instr., asst. prof. dept. ob-gyn. Temple U. Sch. Medicine, Phila., 1961-65; asst. prof. dept. ob-gyn. Albert Einstein Coll. Medicine, Bronx, 1965-67, assoc. prof., 1968-71, prof., 1971—, acting dept. chmn., 1972—80, chmn., 1973-80; assoc. dir. dept. ob-gyn Bronx Mcpl. Hosp. Ctr., 1967-70, dep. dir., 1970-72; chmn. dept. ob-gyn. Winthrop U. Hosp., Mineola, NY, 1984-93; prof. ob-gyn SUNY, Stony Brook, 1984-93; chmn. dept. ob-gyn. Lawnwood Regional Med. Ctr., Ft. Pierce, Fla., 1995-2000; cons. ob-gyn. Wyckoff Hosp. Med. Ctr., Bklyn., 2002—; clin. prof. Ob-gyn. Rose U., Dominica, 2013—. Author: Techniques of Abortion, 1972, Tipping the Scales, 2005, Women's Secrets, Mens Muscles Unveiled, 2009; contbr. articles to profl. publs. Served to capt. U.S. Army, 1956-58. Am. Cancer Soc. fellow, 1959-60; USPHS trainee, 1965-66 Fellow ACOG (vice chmn. Dist. II 1972-75); mem. Bronx County Obstet. Soc. (pres. 1974), AAAS, Obstet. Soc. (sec. 1978-80, pres. 1982-83), N.Y. Obstetrical Soc., Soc. Maternal Fetal Medicine, Am. Gynecologic and Obstetric Soc., Am. Gynecol. Obstetrics, N.Y. Obstetics Soc. (pres. 1982), Phi Beta Kappa, Alpha Omega Alpha; hon. mem. Miami Ob-Gyn. Soc., South Atlantic Obstetricians and Gynecologists Soc., Buffalo Gynecologic and Obstetric Soc. (E.G. Winkler meml. lectr.), Croatian Ultrasound Soc. (hon.). Democrat. Jewish. Office Phone: 914-747-4168. Personal E-mail: hschulman29@optonline.net.

SCHULMAN, JOSEPH DANIEL, physician, health facility administrator, medical geneticist, educator, reproductive biologist; b. Bklyn., Dec. 20, 1941; s. Max and Miriam (Grossman) S.; m. Dixie A. King; children: Erica N., Julie K. BA, Bklyn. Coll., 1961; MD, Harvard U., 1966. Diplomate Am. Bd. Pediat., Am. Bd. Ob-Gyn., Am. Bd. Med. Genetics. Intern, then resident in pediat. Mass. Gen. Hosp., Boston, 1966-68; clin. assoc. Nat. Inst. Arthritis and Metabolic Diseases, 1968-70; resident in obstetrics and gynecology and fellow in pediatrics N.Y. Hosp.-Cornell Med. Ctr., 1970-73; Gilbert and Nat. Found. fellow Cambridge (Eng.) U., 1973-74; head sect. human biochem. genetics Nat. Inst. Child Health and Human Devel., NIH, Bethesda, Md., 1974-83; dir. med. genetics program NIH, Bethesda, 1979-1983; prof. ob-gyn., pediat., genetics George Washington U., 1983-84; CEO Genetics & IVF Inst., Fairfax, Va., 1984-98, chmn., 1984—2001, 2004—; prof. human genetics, pediat., ob-gyn. Med. Coll., Va. Commonwealth U., 1984—; with dept. ob-gyn. Fairfax Hosp., 1984—. Affiliate prof. ob-gyn. U. Cal., San Diego, 2003—; advisor to numerous govt. and pvt. orgns. Author 4 books; contbr. numerous articles to med. jours.; editorial bd. Molecular Human Reproduction, 1995—2010, numerous other sci. jours. With USPHS, 1968-70, 74-83. Fellow ACOG; mem. Soc. Pediat. Rsch., Soc. Gynecologic Investigation, Am. Soc. Clin. Investigation, Am. Soc. Human Genetics, Am. Fertility Soc., Harvard Club, Cosmos Club, Calif. Club, Phi Beta Kappa, Sigma Xi. Office: 3015 Williams Dr Fairfax VA 22031

SCHULTE, FRANCIS B., archbishop emeritus; b. Phila., Dec. 23, 1926; Grad., St. Charles Borromeo Sem.; MA, Univ. Pa.; postgraduate study, Harvard Univ. Ordained priest Archdiocese of Phila., Pa., 1952, tchr., Cath. schools, 1952—60, asst. supt. schools, 1960—70, supt. schools, 1970—80; pastor St. Margaret parish, Narbeth, Pa., 1980—81; ordained bishop, 1981; aux. bishop, vicar gen. Archdiocese of Phila., 1981—85; bishop Diocese of Wheeling-Charleston, W.Va., 1985—88; archbishop Archdiocese of New Orleans, 1989—2002, archbishop emeritus, 2002—. Past trustee Cath. Univ. Am.; past bd. dir. Cath. Relief Services; past chmn. Com. Bishops & Cath. Coll. & Univ. Presidents. Roman Catholic. Office: c/o 7887 Walmsley Ave New Orleans LA 70125-3431

SCHULTE, JAMES ALLEN, former insurance company executive; b. 1949; Property & casualty group exec. Kemper Corp. Office Phone: 312-661-4600. Office Fax: 312-661-4941. Business E-Mail: jschulte@unitrin.com.

SCHULTE, JEFFREY LEWIS, lawyer; b. NYC, July 24, 1949; s. Irving and Ruth (Stein) S.; m. Elizabeth Ewan Kaiser, Aug. 13, 1977; children: Andrew Riggs, Ian Garretson, Elizabeth Alexandra. BA, Williams Coll., 1971; postgrad., Harvard U., 1971-72; JD, Yale U., 1976. Bar: Pa. 1978, Ga. 1993. Law clk. to hon. John J. Gibbons U.S. Ct. Appeals (3d cir.), Newark, 1976-77; assoc. Schnader, Harrison, Segal & Lewis, Phila., 1977-84, ptnr., 1985-92, founding ptnr. Atlanta, 1992-98, exec. com., 1994-98; ptnr. Morris, Manning & Martin, Atlanta, 1998—. Chair securities law com. Ga. State Bar, 2005—07; mem. exec. com. Business Law Sect., Ga. State Bar, 2005-2007; nat. steering com. lawyers com. to end "Pay-to-Play."; bd. dir. Michael C. Carlos Mus. Emory U.,bd. adv. Cole Sch. Bus. Kennesaw State U. Contbr. articles to profl. jours. Mem.: ABA, State Bar Ga., Weekapaug Tennis Club, Weekapaug Yacht Club R.I., Yale Club of Ga. (bd. dirs. 1996—2002, pres. 2000—01, chmn. of bd. 2001—02), Williams Club Atlanta, Phi Beta Kappa. Office: Morris Manning & Martin Atlanta Financial Center 3343 Peachtree Rd NE Ste 1600 Atlanta GA 30326-1044 Office Phone: 404-233-7000. Business E-Mail: jls@mmmlaw.com.

SCHULTE, MARK J., healthcare service company executive; BA in English, St. Louis U., JD. Lic. Law, New York. Various positions through exec. v.p. The Prime Group, Inc.; pres., CEO Brookdale Senior Living, Inc., 2000—01; chmn. Brookdale Living Cmtys., Inc., 2001—05; CEO Brookdale Senior Living, Inc., 2005—06, co-CEO, 2006—08. Bd. dirs. Brookdale Sr. Living Inc., 2008—. Chmn. Am. Seniors Housing Assn., bd. dirs. Office: Brookdale Senior Living Inc Bd Directors 111 Westwood Pl Ste 200 Brentwood TN 37027 Office Phone: 615-221-2250. Office Fax: 615-221-2289. Business E-Mail: marks@brookdaleliving.com.

SCHULTZ, MARK D., lawyer; b. Detroit, Sept. 5, 1959; s. Roy R. and Nancy (Bowker) S. BA summa cum laude, in econs. and fgn. svc., Alma Coll., 1981; JD magna cum laude, Harvard U., 1984. Bar: Wash. 1984. Assoc. Perkins Coie, Seattle, 1984-90, rep. in Tokyo, 1992-94, ptnr. Seattle, 1990—; spl. assignment Long-Term Credit Bank of Japan, Ltd., Tokyo, 1993-94; mng. ptnr. Sidley, Austin, Brown and Wood, Tokyo; v.p. legal Raytheon Co., Tucson, 2003, former gen. counsel missile systems; former gen. counsel, corp. sec. SRA Internat.; former chief legal and risk officer, corp. sec. MWH Global Inc.; gen. counsel for the Technical Services and Information Technology segment Science Applications Internat. Corp. (SAIC), Inc., 2013—. Contbr. articles to profl. publs. Mem. Wash. State Bar Assn. Republican. Avocation: sumo wrestling. Office: SAIC Inc 1710 SAIC Dr Mc Lean VA 22102 Office Phone: 703-676-4300.*

SCHULTZ, SANDRA L., healthcare educator; PhD in Movement Sci. and Physical Edn., Fla. State U. Volleyball and softball coach Miami Dade Coll., 1977, now prof. biology, health, & wellness, chair North Campus Wellness Day Com., Anastasios and Maria Kyriakides chair. Contbr. articles to profl. jours. Named Fla. Prof. of Yr., Carnegie Found. for Advancement of Tchg. and Coun. for Advancement and Support of Edn., 2009. Office: Miami Dade College Dept Biology, Health and Wellness 300 NE 2nd Ave Miami FL 33132-2204 Office Phone: 305-237-8115. E-mail: sschultz@mdc.edu.

SCHULTZ, STANLEY GEORGE, physiologist, educator, retired dean; b. Bayonne, NJ, Oct. 26, 1931; s. Aaron and Sylvia (Kaplan) S.; m. Harriet Taran, Dec. 25, 1960; children: Jeffrey, Kenneth. AB summa cum laude, Columbia U., NYC, 1952; MD, NYU, 1956. Intern Bellevue Hosp., NYC, 1956-57, resident, 1957-59; research assoc. in biophysics Harvard U., 1959-62, instr. biophysics, 1964-67; assoc. prof. physiology U. Pitts., 1967-70, prof. physiology, 1970-79; prof., chmn. dept. physiology U. Tex. Med. Sch., Houston, 1979-96, prof. dept. internal medicine, 1979—, prof. dept. integrative biol. pharm. physiology, 1997—2010, vice chmn., 1999—2003, Fondren chair in cell signalling, 1999—2009, dean Sch. Medicine, 2003—06, H. Wayne Hightower Dist. prof. biomed. sci., 2005—07, assoc. dean sch. medicine, 2007—10, emeritus prof., 2010—. Cons. USPHS, NIH, 1970—; mem. physiology test com. Nat. Bd. Med. Examiners, 1974-79, chmn., 1976-79 Editor Am. Jour. Physiology, Jour. Applied Physiology, 1971-75, Physiol. Revs., 1979-85, Handbook of Physiology: The Gastrointestinal Tract, 1989-91—; mem. editl. bd. Jour. Gen. Physiology, 1969-88, Ann. Revs. Physiology, 1974-81, Current Topics in Membranes and Transport, 1975-81, Jour. Membrane Biology, 1977—, Biochim. Biophys. Acta, 1987-89; assoc. editor Ann. Revs. Physiology, 1977-81; assoc. editor News in Physiol. Scis., 1989-94, editor, 1994-2003; contbr. articles to profl. jours. Served to capt. M.C. USAF, 1962-64. Recipient Rsch. Career award NIH, 1969-74, Solomon Berson award NYU, 2003; overseas fellow Churchill Coll., Cambridge U., 1975-76, Prince Mahidol award, Thailand, 2007. Mem. Am. Heart Assn. (estab. investigator 1964-68), Am. Physiol. Soc. (councillor 1989-91, pres.-elect 1991-92, pres. 1992-93, past pres. 1993-94, Guyton award 1997, Orr Reynolds award 1999, Daggs award 2003), European Acad. Sci., Fed. Am. Soc. Exptl. Biology (exec. bd. 1992-95), Internat. Cell Rsch. Orgn., Internat. Union Physiol. Scis. (chmn. internat. com. gastrointestinal physiology 1977-80, chmn. U.S. nat. com. 1992-98), Assn. Am. Physicians, Am. Assn. Ob-Gyn. (hon. fellow), Assn. Chmn. Depts. Physiology (pres. 1985-86), Houston Philos. Soc., Phi Beta Kappa, Sigma Xi. Office Phone: 713-500-5012, 713-500-6204. Business E-Mail: stanley.g.schultz@uth.tmc.edu.

SCHULZ, JOHN JOSEPH, communications educator, journalist, book author; b. Great Falls, Mont., Sept. 28, 1940; m. Linda L. Seligman. BA in Journalism, U. Mont., 1962; MPhil, Oxford U., 1979, DPhil, 1981; diploma, Nat. War Coll., Washington, 1985-86. Newswriter, reporter Voice of Am. News, Washington, 1971-72, corr. Hong Kong, 1972-74, bur. chief Tokyo, 1974-77; commentator BBC, London, 1977-79; coverage editor Voice of Am., 1979-82; dep. dir. Voice of Am. News Divsn., 1982—85; South Asia corr. Voice of Am. News, Islamabad, Pakistan, 1987-89; thinktank analyst Oxford Analytica, 1977-79, 84-88; prof. Nat. War Coll., Washington, 1989-91; sr. corr. Voice of Am. News, 1986—87, 1991—92; assoc. dir. publs. The Arms Control Assn., 1992-95; prof. internat. comm. Coll. Comm. Boston U., 1995—97, 2000—03, 2006—09, chair dept. mass. comm., advt., and pub. rels., 1997—2000, dean. Coll. Comm., 2003—06, prof. emeritus, 2009—; editor Arms Control Today, 1992-95. Presenter in field; author, Please Don't Do That: A Guide to Better Writing and Punctuation, 2007 Author Songs From A Distant Cockpit, 2013; editor-in-chief Global Beat Syndicate, 2002-06; contbr. articles to profl. jours.; assoc. editor The Intake Journal of the Super Sabre Society, 2009- Vice chair, bd. dirs. Eastern Shore Rural Health, Inc. With USAF, 1963—71. Decorated 3 DFC, Silver Star, 16 Air medals, 2 Vietnamese Gallantry Crosses; recipient disting. alumni award U. Mont., 1995. Mem.: Eastern Shore Rural Health Inc (bd. v.p.), Intake Mag. (assoc. editor), Super Sabre Soc., American Legion Post 56 (chair, district oratorical contests). Avocations: golf, archery, reading, travel. Business E-Mail: jjschulz@bu.edu.

SCHULZ, MIKE, state legislator; b. Cheyenne, Okla., Mar. 5, 1964; m. Reenie Reid Schulz; children: Benjamin, Abby. BS, Okla. State Univ. Farmer; mem. Dist. 38 Okla. State Senate, 2006—. Mem.: Okla. Farm Bureau (chmn.young farmer and rancher com. 1996, former field rep.), Altus Kiwanis Club. Republican. Methodist. Address: 16830 S County Rd 209 Altus OK 73521-8091 Office: 2300 N Lincoln Blvd Rm 418 Oklahoma City OK 73105 Office Phone: 580-482-0886, 405-521-5612. E-mail: schulz@oksenate.gov.

SCHULZE, ARTHUR EDWARD, biomedical engineer, researcher; b. Richmond, Tex., Nov. 22, 1938; s. Arthur Dorwin and Ida (Bockhorn) S.; m. Sharon Kay Havemann, Sept. 2, 1962; children: Keith E., Mark A. BSEE, U. Tex., 1962, MSEE, 1963; MS Biomed. Sci., U. Tex., Houston, 1968. Registered profl. engr., Tex. Sr. aerosystems engr. Gen. Dynamics, Ft. Worth, 1963-67; rsch. assoc. U. Tex. Grad. Sch. Biomed. Scis., Houston, 1967-68; mgr., biomed. engr. SCI Systems, Inc., Houston, 1968-74; v.p. Telecare, Inc., Houston, 1974-79; gen. mgr. Tex. Sci. Corp., Houston, 1979-81; dir. R & D Narco Bio-Systems, Houston, 1981-84, pres., 1984-86; v.p. Lovelace Sci. Resources, Inc., Houston, 1986-92; pres. Healthcare Tech. Group, 1993—; chmn., founder 20th Century Tech. Mus., 2005—. Contbr. articles to sci. publs. Mem. IEEE, Aerospace Med. Assn., Assn. Advancement Med. Instrumentation, AAAS, Biomed. Technology Club. Avocations: photography, beekeeping. Home: 114 Bluebonnet Ln Wharton TX 77488-3076 Office: Healthcare Tech Group 625 N Fulton St Wharton TX 77488-3941 Office Phone: 979-282-8808. Personal E-mail: schulze@neosoft.com.

SCHULZE, HORST H., hotel company executive; D in Hospitality Mgmt. (hon.), Johnson & Wales U., 1999. Various positions Hilton Hotels; positions from gen. mgr. through corp. v.p. Hyatt Hotels Corp.; charter mem., v.p. ops. Ritz Carlton Hotel Co., 1983—87, exec. v.p., 1987—88, pres., COO, 1988—2001, vice-chmn., 2001—02; founder, pres., CEO West Paces Hotels Group, 2002—, Capella Hotels & Resorts. Bd. dirs. Reliance Trust Co., Travel Inst. Bd. dirs. Cancer Treatment Ctrs. America, InfiLaw Sys., Ga. Family Coun. Recipient Ishikawa medal, 1995; named Corp. Hotelier of World, HOTELS Mag., 1991; named to Internat. Food and Beverage Hall of Fame, 2004. Office: West Paces Hotel Group/Capella Hotels & Resorts 3384 Peachtree Rd Ste 375 Atlanta GA 30326 Office Phone: 404-842-7280. Office Fax: 404-842-7288.

SCHULZE, KEITH E., dermatologist, surgeon; b. Ft. Worth, Nov. 6, 1963; s. Arthur E. and Sharon E. Schulze; m. Betsy S. Nance, Apr. 29, 1989; children: Sarah E., Kristen E. BA in Chemistry summa cum laude, Tex. Luth. U., 1985; MD, U. Tex., 1989. Diplomate Am. Bd. Dermatology, 1993. Physician, ptnr. South Tex. Med. Clinics, P.A., Wharton, 1993—96, sec., treas., 1996—2000; clin. asst. prof. dept. dermatology U. Tex. Med. Sch., Houston, 2000—01; v.p., co-dir. Dermatologic Surgery Ctr., 2001—06; pres. Ft. Bend Skin Cancer Ctr., Sugar Land, Tex., 2006—. Trustee St. Thomas Episcopal Sch., Wharton, Tex., 1999—2001; dir. Wharton C. of C. and Agr., 1996—99. Recipient Eugene D.Jacobson award Highest Achievement Mammalian Physiology, U. Tex. Med. Sch., Houston, 1986, award Highest Achievement Microbiology, 1986. Fellow: Am. Soc. Dermatologic Surgery, Am. Coll. Mohs Micrographic Surgery and Cutaneous Oncology, Am. Acad. Dermatology, Am. Soc. Mohs Surgery; mem.: Houston Dermatologic Soc., Harris County Med. Soc., Tex. Dermatologic Soc., Tex. Med. Assn., Alpha Omega Alpha. Achievements include research in numerous clinical pharmacologic trials. Avocations: fishing, hunting. Office: Ft Bend Skin Cancer Ctr 15400 SW Fwy Ste 150 Sugar Land TX 77478 Office Phone: 281-980-6647.

SCHULZE, RICHARD HANS, environmental engineering executive; b. Buffalo, May 28, 1933; s. Hans Joachim and Lucy (Kawczynska) S.; m. Jacqueline Van Luppen, Nov. 2, 1967 (div. Aug. 1979); children: Richard Hans Jr., Linda Monaco, John; m. Enika Grooters, Aug. 29, 1987. BSME, Princeton U., 1954; MBA, Northwestern U., 1958. Registered profl. engr., Tex. Rsch. analyst U.S. Steel Corp., Pitts., 1958-60; chief engr. G&H Rsch. and Devel., McKeesport, Pa., 1960-62; cons. Mgmt. and Mktg. Inst., NYC, 1962-63, Ill. Inst. Tech. Rsch. Inst. mgmt. consulting divsn., NYC, 1963-64; market analyst Mobil Chem. Co., NYC, 1964-66; market devel. mgr., plastics divsn. Mobil Chem. Co. (now PACTIV), Jacksonville, Ill., 1966-68, dist. sales mgr. Dallas, 1967-71; pres. Ecology Audits, Inc. (Core Labs.), Dallas, 1971-74; pres., CEO, Trinity Cons., Inc., Dallas, 1974-97, chmn. bd. dirs., 1997—, CEO, 2001—. Instr. over 200 short courses on dispersion modeling of air pollutants throughout world; vis. lectr. air quality Princeton U., 1998; adv. bd. Dept. of Environ. Civil Engring, So. Meth. U., 2001—. Contbr. articles to Jour. of Air and Waste Mgmt. Assn., Atmospheric Environ., others; presented papers at sci. symposiums, seminars, confs. Mem. Dallas Symphony Assn., Mus. Art; trustee Dallas Opera, 1993—; elder Preston Hollow Presbyn. Ch., 1996-98; commr. to Grace Presbytery, 1996-98. Lt. (j.g.) USNR, 1954-56. Mem. ASME, Am. Acad. Environ. Engrs. (diplomate, trustee 2001-2003), Am. Chem. Soc., Am. Meteorol. Soc., Air and Waste Mgmt. Assn. (bd. dirs. 1986-89, 90-93, v.p. 1988-89, 1st v.p. 1990-91, pres. 1991-92, past pres. 1992-93, chmn. honors and awards com. 1996-97, vice chmn. planning com. 1999-2000), Soc. Petroleum Engrs. (chmn. environ. health and safety award com. 1994-95), Soc. for Risk Analysis, Verein Deutscher Ingenieure, Assn. Francaise des Ingénieurs et Techniciens Environ., Inst. Profl. Environ. Practice (qualified environ. profl., trustee 1993-95), European Assn. for the Sci. of Air Pollution. Home: 7619 Marquette St Dallas TX 75225-4412 Office: Trinity Cons Inc 12770 Merit Dr Ste 900 Dallas TX 75251 Home Phone: 214-696-5108; Office Phone: 972-419-5606. Business E-Mail: rschulze@trinityconsultants.com.

SCHUMACHER, RICHARD E., JR., tax specialist; BA, Ohio State U.; MA, Capital U. CPA Ohio. With Deloitte & Touche LLP, 1989—99; joined Alliance Data Sys. Corp., 1999; sr. v.p., tax Alliance Data Systems Corp., 2004—. Office: Alliance Data Systems Corp 7500 Dallas Pkwy Ste 700 Plano TX 75024-4006 Office Phone: 972-348-5100. Office Fax: 972-348-5335.

SCHUMAKER-KREIG, DIANE, diversified financial services company executive; BA, Wellesley Coll., Mass.; MBA in Fin., Columbia U., NYC. Positions in corp. fin. Primerica, PepsiCo, Inc.; mgmt. positions in equity capital markets and pvt. equity Dillon, Read & Co., Inc.; mng. dir., co-head US equity rsch. Credit Suisse First Boston, NYC, 1991—2004; mng. dir., head global rsch. Wachovia Securities, 2004—08; global head rsch. and economics Wells Fargo Securities, LLC, 2008—. Named one of 25 Most Powerful Women in Fin., US Banker, 2010, American Banker, 2011. Mem.: Phi Beta Kappa. Office: Wells Fargo Securities LLC 301 S College St Charlotte NC 28202 Office Phone: 704-715-8437. Business E-Mail: diane.schumaker@wellsfargo.com.

SCHUMANN, GREG, publishing executive; BA, Mich. State U., East Lansing. V.p., group pub. Hoyt Pub. Co., Skokie, Ill.; midwest advt. dir., eastern advt. dir., Teen People mag. Time Inc., 1999—2003, pub., Baby Talk mag., 2003—07; v.p., pub. parenting group (includes Parenting, Baby Talk and Conceive magazines) Bonnier Corp., NYC, 2007—11; pub., Southern Living mag. Time Inc., Birmingham, Ala., 2011—. Mem. adv. bd. Nat. Parent Tchr. Assn.; bd. dirs. Juvenile

Products Manufacturers Assn., 2006—08. Mem.: Magazines Publishers America (mem. operating com.). Office: Southern Living 2100 Lakeshore Dr Birmingham AL 35209

SCHUMANN, WILLIAM HENRY, III, corporate financial executive; b. Iowa City, Aug. 28, 1950; s. William Henry Jr. and Eunice Vere (Doak) S. BS, UCLA, 1972; MS, U.Southern Calif., 1973. Program mgmt. analyst Hughes Helicopters, Culver City, Calif., 1973-75; mgr., financial planning Sunkist Growers, Sherman Oaks, Calif., 1975-81; dir., North American ops., Agrl. Products Group FMC Corp., Chgo., 1981, exec. dir., corporate devel., 1990-93, v.p., 1995, sr. v.p., CFO, 1999—2001, FMC Technologies, Inc., 2001—07, exec. v.p., CFO, treas., 2007—11, exec. v.p., 2011—. Bd. dirs. United Agri Products Inc., 2005—, Avnet Inc., 2010—. Republican. Office: FMC Technologies Inc 1803 Gears Rd Houston TX 77067 Office Phone: 281-591-4000. Office Fax: 281-591-4102. Business E-Mail: william.schumann@fmcti.com.

SCHUNK, DALE HANSEN, professor; b. Chgo., Aug. 14, 1946; s. Elmer Charles and Mildred Augusta Schunk; 1 child, Laura Christine. BS, U. Ill., Urbana, 1968; MEd, Boston U., 1974; PhD, Stanford U., Calif., 1979. Asst. prof. edn. U. Houston, 1979—85, assoc. prof. edn., 1985—86, U. NC, Chapel Hill, 1986—91, prof. edn., 1991—93; head dept. ednl. studies Purdue U., W. Lafayette, Ind., 1993—2001; dean sch. edn. U. NC, Greensboro, 2001—11, prof. edn., 2011—. Cons. chpt. 1 reading Spring Br. Ind. Sch. Dist., Tex., 1981—94; mem. bd. trustees NC Tchr. Acad., Durham, 2002—07, 2009—11; mem. task force tchr. retention NC State Bd. Edn., Raleigh, 2004—05. Author: (textbooks) Motivation In Education, 2014, Learning Theories: An Educational Perspective, 2012—; editor: (profl. book) Educational Psychology: A Century of Contributions, 2003; contbr. chapters to books, articles to profl. jours. Sec. parent coun. W. Lafayette Sch. Corp., 1997—99; girls' softball coach W. Lafayette Little League, 1997—2000. Capt. USAF, 1968—74, Sewart AFB, Tenn., Naples, Italy. Recipient Disting. Svc. award, Purdue U. Sch. Edn., 1995, Fulbright Scholar award, New Zealand-US Ednl. Found., 1997, Cmty. Honor Roll, W. Lafayette Sch. Corp., 2000. Fellow: APA (pres. divsn. ednl. psychology 1998—99, Early Career award 1982), Am. Ednl. Rsch. Assn. (program chair 1999—2000). Avocations: tennis, travel. Office: University NC-Greensboro 1300 Spring Garden St Greensboro NC 27402 Home: 1911 Shepherds Way Greensboro NC 27410 Office Fax: 336-334-4120. Business E-Mail: dhschunk@uncg.edu.

SCHUSTER, E. ELAINE, lawyer; b. Oklahoma City, June 8, 1936; d. John Otto and Eula Delone (Campbell) Schuster. AB, Sweet Briar Coll., 1958; MA in Econs. and Fin., U. Okla., 1962, JD, 1968. Bar: Okla. 1968, U.S. Dist. Ct. (we. dist.) Okla. 1969, U.S. Ct. Appeals (10th cir.) 1969, U.S. Dist. Ct. (no. dist.) Okla. 1981, U.S. Dist. Ct. (ea. dist.) Okla. 1991. Prof. econs. Southeastern State U., Durant, Okla., 1961—64; assoc. Whitten & Whitten, Oklahoma City, 1968—71; asst. dist. atty. Oklahoma County, 7th Dist., 1972—78; ptnr. Jones, Schuster & Flaugher, Oklahoma City, 1978—82; prin. E. Elaine Schuster, P.C., Oklahoma City, 1982—. Lectr. in field. Founding bd. dir. Nat. Kidney Found., Okla., 1969—82; active Oklahoma County Bd. Adjustment, 1978—97, chmn., 1984—97; citizen mem. profl. liaison com. City of Oklahoma City, 1980—; bd. edn. Metro Technology Ctrs., Career Tech. Dist. No. 22, Oklahoma City, 1982—, pres., 1984—85, 1991—93, 1998—2000, 2008—10, English Speaking Union, Oklahoma City Br., 1997—2010; scholarship com. Oklahoma City Cmty. Found., 1997—; bd. dir. University Pl. Christian Ch., 1982—86, 1989—92, elder, 1989—92, trustee, 1992; deacon Crown Heights Christian Ch., 2001—04, elder, 2004—07, 2009—, bd. dir., 2001—07, 2009—10; parliamentarian regional bd. Christian Ch. Disciples of Christ, Okla., 2004—; bd. dir. Sweet Briar Coll., 1986—96, trustee emerita, 2005—, disting. alumni, 2012. Recipient Circle of Excellence, Okla. Jour. Record, 2005—; named Outstanding Bus. Woman of Okla., Town Club of Bus. and Profl. women, 1986; named one of Fifty Women Making a Difference, Okla. Jour. Record, 1997, 2001, 2005, fourteen "Ladies in the News, Okla. Hospitality Club, 2006; named to Hon. All State Sch. Bd., Okla. State Sch. Bds. Assn., 1999; grantee GE, U. Va., 1963. Mem.: AAUW (life; br. pres. 1978—80, Okla. divsn. bd. 1981—83, 1985—87, Polished Diamond award S.W. Ctrl. Region 1987), Okla. Career Tech. Adminstrv. Coun., Okla. Assn. Tech. Ctrs. (fiscal officer 2001—05, pres.-elect 2006—09, pres. 2009—10), Okla. Assn. Career Tech. Edn. (fiscal officer 1999—2003, dir. 1999—2005), Sweet Briar Coll. Alumnae Assn. (bd. dir. 1986—90, 1996—2001, Region IX dir. 1996—2001), Okla. County Bar Assn. (ethics com. 1969—71, bench and bar com. 1994—95, long range planning com. 1995—97, bd. dir. 1997—2000, CLE com. 1999—2005, Briefcase pub. com. 2005—11), Okla. Bar Assn. (del. 1996—97, alt. del. 1998—99, del. 2000—01, alt. del. 2002—03, budget com. 2002—03, legal ethics com. 2003—06, professionalism com. 2003—, awards com. mem. 2010—), Oklahoma City-County Hist. Soc. (charter mem.), Kappa Beta Pi Legal Soc., Delta Kappa Gamma (hon.). Avocations: photography, travel, history, genealogy. Office: Heritage Law Ctr 515 NW 13th St Oklahoma City OK 73103-2203 Office Phone: 405-236-8807. Business E-Mail: eeschuster@sbcglobal.net.

SCHUSTER, GARY BENJAMIN, academic administrator, chemistry professor; b. NYC, Aug. 6, 1946; m. Anita C. Schuster, June 16, 1968; children: Eric B., Andrew D. BS in Chemistry, Clarkson Coll. Tech., 1968; PhD in Chemistry, U. Rochester, 1971. Tchg. asst. U. Rochester, 1968-71; NIH postdoctoral fellow Columbia U., NYC, 1973-75; asst. prof. chemistry U. Ill., Champaign, 1975-79, assoc. prof. chemistry, 1979-81, prof. chemistry, 1981—94, head dept. chemistry, 1990-94; prof. chemistry, dean Coll. Sciences Ga. Inst. Tech., Atlanta, 1994—2006, provost, exec. v.p. acad. affairs, 2006—, Vasser Woolley chair of chemistry and biochemistry, interim pres., 2008—09. Symposium chmn. organic chem. physics Pacific Basin Conf., Honolulu, 1984; vice chmn. Gordon Conf. on Organic Photochemistry, 1987, chmn., 1989; vice chmn. Electron Donor Acceptor Interactions Gordon Conf., 1994, chmn., 1996; organizer symposium on photochemistry IUPAC, 1992; mem. vis. com. U. Md., 1991; lectr. in field. Mem. editl. adv. bd. Jour. Organic Chemistry, 1986-91, Advances in Phys. Organic Chemistry, Jour. Am. Chem. Soc., 1991-96; contbr. numerous articles to profl. jours. Fellow Uni-Royal, 1969-71, Alfred P. Sloan Found., 1977-79, Ctr. for Advanced Study, 1979, John Simon Guggenheim Found., 1985-86, Paul Flory fellow IBM, 1990; Dreyfus Tchr. scholar, 1979, A.C. Cope scholar, 1993; recipient Mead Imaging Pres.' award, 1987, Charles Holmes Herty medal, 2006; grantee NIH, 1991-95, NSF, 1991-94, 94-97. Mem. Am. Chem. Soc. (symposium chmn. 1979, 88), Am. Assn. Photochemistry and Photobiology, Inter-Am. Photochem. Soc. (exec. com. 1990), Sigma Xi. Office: Ga Inst Tech Office of Provost 225 N Ave NW Carnegie Bldg Atlanta GA 30332 Office Phone: 404-385-2700. E-mail: schuster@gatech.edu.

SCHUSTERMAN, LYNN, foundation administrator; b. Kansas City, Mo. m. Charles Schusterman (dec. 2000); 3 children. Attended, Univ. Miami. Pres. STAR, B'nai B'right Youth Org.; co-chmn. Internat. Bd. Govs. of Hillel; co-founder & chmn. Charles & Lynn Schusterman Family Found. Former pres & current bd. mem. Jewish Fedn. Tulsa; bd. mem. Parent-Child Ctr, Planned Parenthood, Tulsa Historical Society, Temple Israel Found. Named one of Oklahoma's Most Influential Women, Okla. Family Mag., 2001, 50 Most Influential Jews in North America, The Forward, 2002, Forbes 400: Richest Americans, 2009; named to Oklahoma Women's Hall of Fame, 2003. Office: Two W 2nd St Tulsa OK 74103 Office Phone: 918-591-1090. Office Fax: 918-591-1758.

SCHUTZ, PAMELA S., insurance company executive; BA, Briarcliff Coll.; MS, American Univ. Mgmt. positions GE Capital Comml. Real Estate, 1978—94; pres. GE Capital Realty Group, 1994—97, Harvest Life Ins. Co., 1997—98, Genworth Life & Annuity Insurance Co., 1998—; v.p. General Electric Co., 2000—04; exec. v.p., pres. & CEO retirement income & investments Genworth Financial, Inc., Richmond, Va., 2004—. Bd. mem. Nat. Assn. Variable Annuities, MIB Group Inc. Office: Genworth Financial 6620 W Broad St Richmond VA 23230

SCHUUR, EDWARD ARTHUR GEORGE, ecology professor; BS in Cellular and Molecular Biology, Univ. Mich., 1991; PhD in Ecosystem Ecology, Univ. Calif., Berkeley, 1999. Intern The Land Inst., Salina, Kans., 1992; rsch. assoc. Swedish Agrl. Univ., Uppsala, Sweden, 1993; rsch. asst. Stanford Univ. Tropical Ecosystem Dynamics Field Station, Volcano, Hawaii, 1993—94; grad. tchg. asst. plant population and cmty. ecology Univ. Calif., Berkeley, 1995, postdoctoral researcher Irvine, 1999—2001, NSF postdoctoral fellow in bioformatics, dept. earth system sci., 2000—02; affiliate prof. biology and wildlife dept Univ. Alaska, 2004—; affiliate prof. dept. soil and water sci. Univ. Fla., 2004—, asst. prof. ecosystem ecology, 2002—08, assoc. prof. ecosystem ecology, 2008—. Contbr. of several articles to profl. publications; interviews on global change in high latitude ecosystems for Public Radio, LA Times, Reuters, Science News, Bioscience and many others, manuscript reviewer. Recipient Nat. Ctr. for Ecological Analysis & Synthesis Sabbatical Fellowship, 2008; NASA Earth System Sci. Fellowship, 1997—2000. Office: Dept of Botany Univ Florida 220 Bartram Hall Box 118526 Gainesville FL 32611-8526 Office Phone: 352-392-7913. Office Fax: 352-392-3993. Business E-Mail: tschuur@ufl.edu.

SCHUYLER, MATTHEW W., hotel executive; Degree in bus. adminstrn., Pa. State U.; MBA, U. Mich. Various positions, corp. human resource mgmt. Capital One Financial Corp.; v.p., human resources Cisco Sys., Inc; ptnr., global human resources group. PricewaterhouseCoopers; exec. v.p., COO Hilton Worldwide. Office: Hilton Worldwide 7930 Jones Branch Dr Ste 1100 Mc Lean VA 22102 Office Phone: 703-883-1000.

SCHWARCZ, STEVEN LANCE, lawyer, educator; b. NYC, Nov. 10, 1949; s. Charles and Elinor Schwarcz; m. Susan Beth Kolodny, Aug. 24, 1975; children: Daniel Benjamin, Rebekah Mara. BS summa cum laude in Aero. Engring., NYU, 1971; JD, Columbia U., 1974. Bar: N.Y. 1971, U.S. Dist. Ct. (so. dist.) N.Y. 1975. Assoc. Shearman & Sterling, NYC, 1974-82, ptnr., 1983-89; ptnr., chmn. structured fin. Kaye, Scholer, Fierman, Hays & Handler, 1996—; prof. Duke U. Sch. Law, Durham, NC, 1996—, Stanley A. Star prof., 2004—; spl. counsel Kaye, Scholer, Fierman, Hays & Handler, 1996—2004; faculty dir. Duke Global Capital Markets Ctr.; spl. cons. Kaye Scholer LLP, 2004—07. Adj. prof. law Yeshiva U., Benjamin N. Cardozo Sch. Law, N.Y.C., 1983-92; vis. lectr. Yale Law Sch., 1992-96; lectr. Columbia Law Sch., 1992-96. Contbr. articles to profl. jours. Chmn. Friends of the Eldridge St. Synagogue, N.Y.C., 1979-96, Legis. Drafting Rsch. Fund; founding mem. Internat. Insolvency Inst. George Granger Brown scholar, 1971; NSF grantee in Math., 1969, fellow, Am. Coll. Bnkruptcy. Fellow Am. Coll. Comml. Fin. Lawyers; mem. Am. Law Inst., Assn. of Bar of City of N.Y. (environ. law com. 1975-78, nuc. tech. com. 1979-81, sci. and law com. 1985—, chmn. 1987-90), Am. Law and Econs. Assn., Tau Beta Pi, Sigma Gamma Tau. Jewish. Office: Duke U Sch Law Box 90360 Science Dr & Towerview Rd Durham NC 27708 Office Phone: 919-613-7060. E-mail: schwarcz@law.duke.edu.

SCHWARTZ, CARL EDWARD, artist, printmaker; b. Detroit, Sept. 20, 1935; s. Carl and Verna (Steiner) S.; m. Kay Joyce Hofmann, June 18, 1955 (div.); children: Dawn Ellen, Cari Leigh; m. Celeste Borah, Jan. 1, 2007. BFA, Art Inst. Chgo. Sch.-U. Chgo., 1957. Past tchr. art Chgo. North Shore Art League, Suburban Fine Arts Ctr., Deerpath Art League; faculty Fla. Gulf Coast U. One-man shows include, South Bend (Ind.) Art Center, Feingarten Gallery, Chgo., 1960, Bernard Horwich Center, Chgo., Covenant Club, Chgo., Barat Coll., Chgo. Pub. Library, Alverno Coll., 1020 Art Center, Rosenberg Gallery, Peoria (Ill.) Art Guild, 1977, Ill. State Mus., 1977 Ill. Inst. Tech., 1978, Miller Gallery, Chgo., 1979, Union League Club, Chgo., 1982, Art Inst. Rental and Sale Gallery, Chgo., 1982, Horwich Gallery, Chgo., 1983, Lake Forest (Ill.) Coll., 1983, Campanile-Capponi Contemporary Gallery, Chgo., 1987, Nagata Gallery, Ft. Myers, Fla., 1988, Jan Cicero Gallery, Chgo., 1990, Neopolitan Gallery, Naples, Fla., 1996, 97; group shows include 9th Ann. Michigana Exhbt, Detroit (Cloetingh and Deman award 1959), Hyde Park Art Center, Chgo., 1960 (prize), Spectrum Exhbn. '63, Chgo. (1st prize), New Horizons Exhbt, Chgo., 1960 (Joseph Shapiro award), Nat. Design Center, Chgo., 1965 (New Horizons in Painting 1st prize), 3d Ann. Chgo. Arts Competition, 1962 (1st prize), Union League Club, Chgo., 1967 (2d prize), North Shore Art League, Chgo., 1965 (1st prize), Artists Guild Chgo., 1965 (prize), McCormack Pl., Chgo., 1965 (1st prize), Detroit Art Inst., 1965 (Commonwealth prize), Park Forest (Ill.) Art Exhbn, 1969 (Best of Show), 14th Ann. Virginia Beach (Va.) Show, 1969 (Best of Show), Suburban Fine Arts Center, Highland Park, Ill., 1970 (prize), 15th Ann. Virginia Beach Show, 1970 (prize), 32d Ann. Artists Guild, Chgo., 1970 (2d prize), North Shore Art League, 1970 (prize), 16th Ann. Virginia Beach Show, 1971 (2d prize), Ill. State Fair, 1972 (prize), Artists Guild Chgo., 1972 (1st prize), 17th Ann. Virginia Beach Exhbt, 1972 (1st prize), Artists Guild 50th Fine Art Exhbn., Chgo., 1973 (prize), Dickinson State U., 1973 (prize), North Shore Art League, 1973 (prize), Lakehurst Exhbt, 1974 (prize), Union League Art Exhbt, 1974 (1st prize), 1976 (prize), Artists Guild Fine Arts Exhbn., 1974 (best of Show), Bluegrass Painting Exhbn, Louisville, 1975 (award Washington, Art Inst. Chgo., K. Van Ella, Chgo., Gardner-Colby Gallery, Naples, Fla., Cape Coral Arts Studio, Van Liebig Art Ctr., 2005, Art League of Bonita Springs (Best of Show, Art Focus award 2007), Alliance for the Arts (award), 2007, 50 yr. Retrospective Show Fla. Gulf Coast U. Art Gallery, 2009. Recipient Logan medal, Art Inst. Chgo., 1958. Home: 5825 Briarcliff Rd Fort Myers FL 33912-4204 Office Phone: 239-590-7249. Personal E-mail: carleschwartz@comcast.net.

SCHWARTZ, CHARLES WALTER, lawyer; b. Brenham, Tex., Dec. 27, 1953; s. Walter C. and Annie (Kuehn) S. BS, U. Tex., 1975, MA, 1980, JD, 1977; LLM, Harvard U., Cambridge, Mass., 1980. Bar: Tex. 1977, NY 2007; bd. cert. civil appellate law Tex. Bd. Legal Specialization. Law clk. U.S. Ct. Appeals (5th cir.), Austin, Tex., 1977-79; assoc. Vinson & Elkins LLP, Houston, 1980—86, ptnr., 1986—2003, Skadden, Arps, Slate, Meagher & Flom, 2003—; regent Tex. A & M U. Sys. Bd. mem. Ctr. Am. and Internat. Law. Contbr. articles to law revs. Fellow: Am. Bar Found. (life benefactor fellow), Tex. Bar Found. (sustaining life), Houston Bar Found. (sustaining life), Coll. State Bar Tex.; mem.: ABA, Tex. A&M U. Sys. (regent), Tex. Commn. Lawyer Discipline, Tex. Law Rev. Assn., Am. Law Inst., Bar Assn. of 5th Cir., State Bar Tex. (former chmn. grievance com. 1993—99, bd. dirs. 2000—04, exec. com. 2001—04, chmn. 2002—03, immediate past chmn. 2003—04). Home: 2154 Chilton Rd Houston TX 77019 Office: Skadden Arps Slate Meagher & Flom LLP 1000 Louisiana St Ste 6800 Houston TX 77002 Office Phone: 713-655-5160. Business E-Mail: charles.schwartz@skadden.com.

SCHWARTZ, COLBY, state legislator; b. Okla. City, Apr. 8, 1974; s. Michael and Tally, Michael and Tally; m. Brenda (Black) Schwartz; 1 child, Campbell Faithe. BA in Polit. Sci., Okla. City U., 1995. Worked on several campaigns; worked for Okla. ins. commissioner John Crawford; campaign mgr. for Sen. Mike Johnson; with insurance and investment industry; exec. dir. South OKC Coun. of Neighborhoods; legislature and constituent liaison to Lieutenant Gov. Mary Fallin, 1999—2001; chmn. Canadian County Republican Party, 2000—06; bd. mem. Okla. Republican Party Budget Com.; operates SchINC, LLC; mem. Dist. 43 Okla. House of Representatives, 2007—. Mem.: America Legislature Exch. Coun., Leadership Canadian County, Canadian County Repub. Party, America Legislature Exchange Coun., Leadership Canadian County, Canadian County Repub. Party (chmn. 2000—06, Volunteer of Year 2006). Republican. Address: 12228 SW 7th Cir Yukon OK 73099 Office: 2300 N Lincoln Blvd Rm 329 Oklahoma City OK 73105 Home Phone: 405-354-0555; Office Phone: 405-557-7352. Business E-Mail: colbyschwartz@cox.net, colby.schwartz@okhouse.gov.

SCHWARTZ, ELAINE J., state legislator; b. NYC, Apr. 13, 1943; m. Martin Schwartz; children: Dennis, Deborah, Alison. BA in History, Hofstra U., 1964; JD, NYU, 1968. Bar: NY 1969, Fla. 1982. Atty., advocate Long Term Care Ombudsman Coun., Dist. X; vice chair and commr. Hollywood Housing Authority, Fla.; atty. Fed. Res. Bank NY; asst. city atty. City of Hollywood, Fla.; pvt. practice Law Offices of Elaine J. Schwartz; mem. Dist. 99 Fla. House of Reps., Tallahassee, 2006—, Dem. whip, 2006—08, ranking mem. elder and family svcs. policy com., mem. health and family svcs. policy coun., health care appropriations com., preK-12 policy com. Democrat. Jewish. Office: Old Libr 1st Fl City Hall Cir 2600 Hollywood Blvd Hollywood FL 33020-4807 also: 1402 The Capitol 402 S Monroe St Tallahassee FL 32399-1300 Office Phone: 954-924-3813, 850-488-0465.

SCHWARTZ, GERALD, public relations and fundraising agency executive; b. NYC, June 22, 1927; s. George and Martha F. S.; m. Felice P. Schwartz, June 25, 1950; children: Gary R., Gregg R., Wendy L. Student, N.C. State U., 1944-45; AB, U. Miami, Fla., 1949, BS, 1950; MS in Bus. Journalism & Mass Commn., Fla. Internat. U., Fla., 2009. Staff writer Miami Herald, 1941-44; publicity dir. U.S. Army in Europe, 1946-48; editor Miami Beach Sun, 1950-51; fund raising and pub. rels. counselor Miami, 1952-58; press sec. to Gov. Nebr., 1959—60; exec. v.p. Bar-Ilan U., Ramat Gan, Israel, 1960-61; prin. Gerald Schwartz Agy., Miami, Fla., 1962—. Editor, pub. Jewish Herald Newspaper, 1999-2000; editor, pub. emeritus Jewish Star-Times, 2000-2003. Nat. v.p. Am. Zionist Fedn., 1985—89, 1991—93; pres. Pres.'s coun. Zionist Orgn. Am., 1983—85; nat. chmn. Friends of Pioneer Women/Na'amat, 1984—98; pres. Am. Zionist Fedn. So. Fla., 1970—73, 1986—92; vice chmn. Urban League of Greater Miami, 1983—87, City of Miami Beach Planning Bd., 1953—55; bd. dirs. Greater Miami Symphony, 1982—87, Miami Beach Taxpayers Assn., 1988—89; pres. Civic League Miami Beach, 1985—87; pres. Greater Miami chpt. Assn. Welfare of Soldiers in Israel, 1983—86; chmn. City of Miami Beach Hurricane Def. Com., 1978—86, 1990—97; trustee South Shore Hosp. and Med. Ctr., Miami, 1987—2004, exec. vice-chmn. Miami Beach, 1989—2004; vice chmn. South Shore Med. Ctr. Found., 1989—2004; bd. govs. Barry U., 1985—86; chmn. Econ. Devel. Coun. City of Miami Beach, 1985—91; bd. dirs. Crimestoppers of Dade County, 1991—94; mem. exec. bd. State of Israel Bonds Orgn., 1996—; dep. chmn. Dem. Midwest Conf., 1958—60; bd. dirs. adminstrv. com. Jewish Nat. Fund America, 1995—2010; v.p. Greater Miami region Jewish Nat. Fund of Am., 1996—97; v.p. Jewish Nat. Fund., Fla., 2000—10; bd. dirs. Temple Emanu-El of Greater Miami, Papanicolaou Cancer Rsch. Inst., Miami, 1962—80; bd. dirs. Fla. chpt. Boys Town of Jerusalem, 2006—08; pres. B'nai Zion Chpt. Fla., 2009—12. With US Army, 1944—46. Recipient Jerusalem Peace award State of Israel Bonds, 1978, Jerusalem 3000 award State of Israel, 1996, United Jerusalem medal and Nat. Hon. award State Israel Bonds, 2012. Mem. Pub. Rels. Soc. America (accredited; treas. Southern Fla. chpt. 1962-64, Loyalty award, Miami chpt., 2013, Emeritus award, 2013), Am. Pub. Rels. Assn. (pres. chpt. 1960-61), Am. Assn. Polit. Cons., Nat. Assn. Fund Raising Execs. (pres. chpt. 1977-78), Miami Beach Taxpayers Assn. (bd. dirs. 1994-2000), Miami Internat. Press Club (bd. dirs. 1991-99), Miami Beach C. of C. (v.p. 1978-80, 81-84, 86-87, pres.-elect 1988-90, trustee 1990—), Lead and Ink, Tiger Bay Club (pres. 1986-88), Prime Minister's Club of State of Israel (Greater Miami chmn. 1997—), B'nai B'rith (pres. lodge 1964-66), Theta Omicron Pi, Omicron Delta Kappa, Alpha Delta Sigma (pres. 1965-67), Zeta Beta Tau, Sigma Delta Chi, Soc. Profl. Journalists, Investigative Reporters and Editors, Inc., Jewish War Vets. USA. Office: Gerald Schwartz Agy 21150 Point Pl Unit 406 Aventura FL 33180-4033 Office Phone: 305-792-9711. Personal E-mail: geraldsch62227@aol.com.

SCHWARTZ, JONATHAN E., neonatalogist; MD, U. Miami, 1990. Diplomate Am. Bd. Pediatrics-neonatal-perinatal medicine, 2005. Resident pediat. Jackson Meml. Hosp., 1991—93; fellow neonatal-perinatal medicine Children's Hosp. Med. Ctr., 1993—94; hosp. affiliations include St. Vincent's Med. Ctr., St. Luke's Hosp. Office: St Vincent's Medical Center 1 Shircliff Way Jacksonville FL 32204-2982 Office Phone: 904-308-7300.*

SCHWARTZ, MICHAEL L., plastic surgeon; Attended, Columbia U.; MD, Baylor Coll. of Medicine, Houston, Tex. Diplomate Am. Bd. of Facial Plastic & Reconstructive Surgery, Am. Bd. of Otolaryngology. Internship in gen. surgery Beth Israel Med. Ctr.; resident in otolaryngology, facial plastic surgery Columbia Presbyn. Med. Ctr.; fellow Am. Coll. of Surgeons; hosp. affiliations include Good Samaritan Hosp., St. Mary's Hosp. Office: 1411 North Flager Dr Ste 7600 West Palm Beach FL 33401 Office Phone: 561-829-5212.

SCHWARTZ, RICHARD HARVEY, pediatrician; b. Bklyn., July 6, 1938; s. Hy and Ruth (Marshak) S.; m. Rose Lynne Hass, May 29, 1960; children: Lisa, Keith, Keira. BA, George Washington U., 1960; MD, Georgetown U., 1965. Diplomate Am. Bd. Pediat., Am. Soc. Addiction Medicine. Intern U.S. Army, 1965-66, resident in pediat., 1969-71; pvt. practice, Vienna, Va., 1972—. Contbr. more than 300 articles to med. jours. Maj. U.S. Army, 1965-69. Mem. AMA (Outstanding Contbn. in Adolescent Medicine award 1990), Am. Acad. Pediatrics (rsch. award 1989). Jewish. Avocations: walking, travel. Office: Advanced Pediatrics 100 East St SE Ste 301 Vienna VA 22180 Office Phone: 703-938-5555.

SCHWARTZ, ROBERT PAUL, pediatric endocrinologist; b. Lakeland, Fla., Sept. 29, 1941; s. Sydney and Edythe (Racz) Schwartz; m. Rebecca Chambers, Apr. 29, 1965; children: Sharon, Michael. BS, U. Fla., 1964, MD, 1968. Diplomate Am. Bd. Pediat. Intern, resident Charlotte Meml. Hosp., NC, 1968-70; fellowship pediat. endocrinology Duke U. Med. Ctr., Durham, NC, 1970-71, 73-74; asst. chmn. dept. pediat. Carolinas Med. Ctr., Charlotte, 1974-92; prof., chief pediat. endocrinology Wake Forest U. Sch. Medicine, Winston-Salem,

NC, 1992—. Mem. editl. bd.: Jour. Pediatrics, 1996—2003; contbr. articles to profl. jours. Mem.: Pediat. Academic Soc., Lawson Wilkins Pediat. Endocrine Soc., Am. Diabetes Assn., NC Pediat. Soc. (pres. 1987—89), Am. Bd. Pediat., Am. Acad. Pediat. (chair endocrine sect. 1996—99). Office: Wake Forest U Sch Medicine Med Ctr Blvd Winston Salem NC 27157-0001 Office Phone: 336-716-3199. Office Fax: 336-716-9229. Business E-Mail: rschwrtz@wfubmc.edu.

SCHWARTZ, SANFORD, publishing executive; V.p., gen. mgr. The Atlanta Journal-Constn.; pres., pub. Cox Ariz. Publs., Inc.; with Columbus Citizen Jour., 1974; exec. v.p. Austin-American Statesman, 1996—2001; v.p., bus. devel. Cox Enterprises, Inc., features editor, Tribune Newspapers Mesa, Ariz., 1985, pres., pub., 1995; exec. v.p. Cox Newspapers, 2003; pres. Cox Auto Trader (subs. of Cox Enterprises, Inc.), 2008—, Cox Media Group, Inc. (subs. of Cox Enterprises, Inc.), 2008—. Supervisory bd. dirs. Agora SA. Former chmn. Met. Atlanta Chpt. of the Am. Red Cross; bd. dirs. A.C. Green Youth Found., Los Angeles. Office: Cox Media Group Inc 6205 Peachtree Dunwoody Rd Atlanta GA 30238 Office Phone: 678-645-0000. Business E-Mail: sschwartz@coxenterprises.com.

SCHWARTZ, STEPHEN GREGORY, ophthalmologist; b. Queens, NY, Nov. 28, 1969; s. Charles F. and Patricia Schwartz; m. Melanie Rebak, June 15, 1996; children: Jessica Hope, Reid Alexander, Oliver Mason. BS with honors, Cornell U., Ithaca, NY, 1991; MD, NYU, NYC, 1995; MBA, J.L. Kellogg Sch. Mgmt., Evanston, Ill., 2008. Diplomate Am. Bd. Ophthalmology. Intern Lenox Hill Hosp., NYC, 1995—96; resident NYU Sch. Medicine, NYC, 1996—99; fellow Baylor Coll. Medicine, Houston, 1999—2001; asst. prof. ophthalmology Va. Commonwealth U. Sch. Medicine, Richmond, 2001—04, program dir. ophthalmology, 2002—04; asst. prof. clin. ophthalmology U. Miami (Fla.) Miller Sch. Medicine, 2004—09, assoc. prof. clin. ophthalmology, 2009—; med. dir. Bascom Palmer Eye Inst. Naples, Fla., 2004—. Bd. govs. Prevent Blindness Fla., Tampa, 2006—; bd. dirs. Va. Voice for Print Handicapped, Inc., Richmond, 2002—04. Grantee Investigator award, Prevent Blindness Am., 2005; Nat. Glaucoma Rsch. grantee, Am. Health Assistance Found., 2003. Fellow: Am. Acad. Ophthalmology (Achievement award 2006); mem.: AMA, Retina Soc., Collier County Med. Soc., Fla. Soc. Ophthalmology (bd. dirs. 2006—, pres. 2010—11, Outstanding Young Ophthalmologist Leadership award 2006), Fla. Med. Assn., Assn. Rsch. in Vision and Ophthalmology (members in tng. com. 2003—06), Am. Soc. Retina Specialists. Office: Bascom Palmer Eye Inst 311 9th St N # 100 Naples FL 34102 Office Phone: 239-659-3937. Office Fax: 239-659-3982. Business E-Mail: sschwartz2@med.miami.edu.

SCHWARTZ, STEVE WENDELIN, physician; b. Bethesda, Md., May 16, 1955; s. Wallace John and Gwynne June (Lingenfelter) S. AB in Chemistry summa cum laude, Duke U., 1977, MD, 1981. Diplomate Am. Bd. Family Practice. Rotating intern Med. U. S.C., Charleston, 1981-82, resident in family practice, 1982-84; emergency rm. physician Coastal Emergency Svc., 1985-86; family physician Carolina Health Care, Myrtle Beach, SC, 1984—; CEO Cactus Internat., Inc. Data processing dir. HMI, 1984—; pres. Flu Trends Internat., 2006-10, Unitrends Software Corp., 1989-2003, chief tech officer, 2004-05; rschr. Symbol Theory; programmer langs. Columnist SCO World Mag.; contbr. articles to profl. jours. Del. ann. meeting N.C. Med. Soc., 1980; participant Intramural Soccer, 1977-80; mem. Intramural Track, 1980, Blacknall Meml. Presbyn. Ch., 1977-80; coord. Boy Scouts Phys. Exam. Program, 1983; vol. cmty. health care project for poor East End Cmty. Health Ctr.; tchr. seminars on alcoholism for drug edn. project Holistic Medicine Group, 1980; Bible study coord. Valley of Achor. With USAF. 1973-75. First Place Durham Open Chess Tournament, 1974; recipient Grand Strand Leadership, 1986. Fellow Am. Acad. Family Physicians; mem. AMA (Physicians Recognition award 1986), So. Med. Assn., Horry County Med. Soc., Phi Beta Kappa, Upsilon Pi Epsilon. Achievements include patents for flu nose and throat spray to treat all. Avocations: chess, soccer. Office: Carolina Health Care 4605 Hwy 17 Byp S Myrtle Beach SC 29577-6681 Personal E-mail: steves@sc.rr.com.

SCHWARTZEL, CHARLES BOONE, lawyer; b. Louisville, Jan. 4, 1950; s. Charles Joseph and Rosemary Jane (Redens) S.; m. Rose Marie Carlisi, June 20, 1980; children: Sally Ann, Charles Gerard. BA, Vanderbilt U., 1972; JD, U. Tex., 1975. Bar: Tex. 1975. Atty. Vinson & Elkins L.L.P., Houston, 1975-98, ptnr., 1983-98; pvt. practice Houston, 1998—. Contbr. articles to profl. jours. Councilman City of West University Place, Tex., 1985-89. Fellow Am. Coll. Trust and Estate Counsel; mem. Tex. Bar Assn. Roman Catholic. Office: Attorney at Law 1010 Lamar St Ste 1520 Houston TX 77002-6315 Office Phone: 713-654-1133.

SCHWARZ, BERTHOLD ERIC, psychiatrist; b. Jersey City, Oct. 20, 1924; s. Berthold Theodore Dominick and I. Thyra W. (Ericson) Schwarz; m. Ardis Marilyn Peterson, Jan. 22, 1955; children: Lisa Thyra, Eric Rolf. AB, Dartmouth Coll., 1945; MD, NYU, 1950; MS, Mayo Grad. Sch. Medicine, 1957. Intern Mary Hitchcock Meml. Hosp., Hanover, NH, 1950-51; psychiatrist, researcher pvt. practice, Montclair, NJ, 1955-82; Mayo Found., Rochester, Minn., 1951-55; psychiatrist, researcher pvt. practice, Vero Beach, Fla., 1982—2002. Cons. Essex County Hosp. Ctr., Cedar Grove, N.J., 1965-82, Med. Correctional Assn., Ossining, N.Y., 1960-72; exec. dir. Internat. Psychosomatics Inst., Mountain Lakes, N.J., 1995—. Contbr. articles to med. jours. With USNR, 1943-45. Fellow AAAS, Am. Psychiat. Assn., Am. Soc. Psychical Rsch., Am. Geriatric Soc. Republican. Avocations: ufos, parapsychiatry, swimming, walking. Office: 642 Azalea Ln Vero Beach FL 32963-1832 Home: PO Box 644030 Vero Beach FL 32964-4030 Office Phone: 772-231-5220. Personal E-mail: ardisps@aol.com.

SCHWARZ, CHARLES MICHAEL, family practice physician; MD, Emory U., 1971. Diplomate American Bd. Family Practice, lic. Fla., 1973. Intern family medicine Univ. of Miami Jackson Health System, 1972; resident family medicine Halifax Med. Ctr., 1974; hosp. affiliation includes Venice Regional Med. Ctr. Office: Gulf Coast Medical Group 333 Miami Ave W Ste F-G Venice FL 34285 Office Phone: 941-484-4778.*

SCHWARZ, GLENDA M., oil industry executive; b. 1965; Gen. mgr. downstream fin./performance analysis ConocoPhillips, Houston, gen. auditor, chief ethics officer, 2008—09, v.p., contr. fin., 2009—. Office: ConocoPhillips 600 N Dairy Ashford PO Box 2197 Houston TX 77252 Office Phone: 281-293-1000. Business E-Mail: glenda.m.schwarz@conocophillips.com.

SCHWARZ, MICHAEL L., aircraft manufacturing company executive; BFA in Radio-TV-Film, Tex. Christian U., Fort Worth, Tex., 1971. Various comm. & mktg. positions Pharmacia & Upjohn, Inc.; various positions Northrop Corp., 1976; mgr., internal comm. Northrop Grumman Corp., 1998—2000; dir., corp. comm. Vought Aircraft Industries, Inc., 2000—06, v.p., comm., 2006—. Internat. pres., bd. dirs., chmn. ITVA, vol. leader; adv. bd. pres. Holy Trinity Cath. Sch., Grapevine, Tex. Office: Vought Aircraft Industries Inc 9314 W Jefferson Blvd Dallas TX 75211 Office Phone: 972-946-5298. Business E-Mail: schwami2@voughtaircraft.com.

SCHWARZ, RODERICH EGBERT, surgeon, oncologist; b. Braunschweig, Germany, Aug. 18, 1960; came to U.S., 1987; s. Peter and Ilse Schwarz; m. Margaret A. Schwarz, Feb. 26, 1994; children: Anna Magdalena, Johann Richard, Carla, Liesa, Edward. PhD, Med. Sch. Hannover, Germany, 1985, MD, 1984. Diplomate Am. Bd. Surgery. Resident in gen. surgery U. Pitts., 1989-94; rsch. fellow Pitts. Cancer Ctr., 1987-89; fellow in surg. oncology Meml. Sloan-Kettering Cancer Ctr., NYC, 1994-96; attending surgeon City of Hope Nat. Med. Ctr., Duarte, Calif., 1996—2001; prof., surgical oncology U. Tex. Southwestern Med. Ctr., Dallas, 2007—, pancreatic and gastrointestinal cancer specialist; assoc. prof. surg. oncology UMDN Robert Wood Johnson Med. Sch., NB, NJ, 2001—07. Author chpts. to books; contbr. several articles to profl. jours. Recipient Deutsche Forschungsgemeinschaft Internat. Rsch. Tng. award, 1989. Fellow ACS; mem. Am. Assn. for Cancer Rsch., Am. Soc. Clin. Oncology, Soc. Surg. Oncology(award, 1995), Soc. Surgery of the Alimentary Tract, German Surg. Soc., Soc. U. Surgeons. Avocation: music. Office: U Tex Southwestern Medical Ctr at Dallas 5323 Harry Hines Blvd Dallas TX 75390-8548 also: Simmons Comprehensive Cancer Ctr Seay Bldg 2201 Inwood Rd 3rd Fl Dallas TX 75390 Office Phone: 214-648-5865. Office Fax: 214-648-1118.

SCHWARZSCHILD, JANE L., lawyer; b. Richmond, Va., 1949; BA, Smith Coll., 1971; JD, Univ. Va., 1974. Bar: Va. 1974. Ptnr. Armstrong Bristow Farley & Schwarzschild, PLC, Richmond, Va. Recipient Spl. Achievements and Contributions award, Va. Women Attys. Assn., 1986; named Va. Super Lawyer in Estate Planning & Probate, Richmond Mag., 2006—13; named one of Best Lawyers in Am. Trusts and Estates, 1993—2013; named to Legal Elite in Taxes, Estates, and Trusts, Va. Bus. Mag., 2000—07, 2009, 2011. Mem.: Am. Coll. Trust & Estate Counsel, Richmond Estate Planning Coun., Va. State Bar, Va. Bar Assn. Office: Armstrong Bristow Farley and Schwarzschild PLC 1807 Libbie Ave #200 Richmond VA 23266 Office Phone: 804-282-6170. Office Fax: 804-282-6175. Business E-Mail: jschwarzschild@armstrongbristow.com.

SCHWEINHART, RICHARD ALEXANDER, corporate financial executive; b. Louisville, Sept. 19, 1949; s. John Lawrence and A. Alicia (Kotheimer) S.; m. Margaret Loraine Hobbs, July 17, 1971; children: John Edward, Jennifer Lynn. AB in Acctg., Bellarmine Coll., 1971. CPA, Ky. Staff Coopers & Lybrand (now PricewaterhouseCoopers LLP), 1971-75; asst. contr. Humana, Inc., Louisville, 1975-82, dir. acctg., 1982-83, contr., 1983-85, v.p., contr., 1985-88, v.p. fin., 1988-91, sr. v.p. fin., 1991-93; CFO Galen Health Care, Inc. (spin off of Humana Inc.), Louisville, 1993; sr. v.p., fin. Columbia/HCA Healthcare Corp., Louisville, 1993-95, sr. v.p., new bus. and network devel., 1995; sr. v.p., CFO Kindred Healthcare, Inc., 1998—2002; cons. Ventas, Inc., 2002, sr. v.p., 2002—06, CFO, 2002—, exec. v.p., 2006—. Bd. dirs. Goodwill Industries Ky., 1988-94, treas., 1989-90, vice chmn., 1991-92, chmn., 1992-93; mem. Leadership Louisville, 1987-88. Mem. AICPA, Ky. Soc. CPAs. Democrat. Roman Catholic. Avocations: golf, genealogy. Office: Ventas Inc 353 N Clark St Ste 3300 Chicago IL 60654-4708 Office Phone: 312-660-3800. Office Fax: 312-660-3850. Business E-Mail: rschweinhart@ventasreit.com.

SCHWEITZER, GEORGE KEENE, chemistry professor; b. Poplar Bluff, Mo., Dec. 5, 1924; s. Francis John and Ruth Elizabeth (Keene) S.; m. Verna Lee Pratt, June 4, 1948; children: Ruth Anne, Deborah Keene, Eric George. BA, Central Coll., 1945, ScD in Philosophy, 1964; MS, U. Ill., 1946, PhD in Chemistry, 1948; MA, Columbia U., 1959; PhD in History, NYU, 1964. Asst. Central Coll., 1943-45; fellow U. Ill., 1946-48; asst. prof. chemistry U. Tenn., 1948-52, assoc. prof., 1952-58, prof., 1960-69, Alumni Distinguished prof., 1970—. Cons. to Monsanto Co., Proctor & Gamble, Internat. Tech., Am. Cyanamid Co., AEC, U.S. Army, Massengill, CTI-Siemens; lectr. colls. and univs.; mem. adv. bd. East Tenn. Hist. Soc. Author: Radioactive Tracer Techniques, 1950, The Doctorate, 1966, Genealogical Source Handbook, 1992, Civil War Genealogy, 1993, Tennessee Genealogical Research, 1981, Kentucky Genealogical Research, 1981, Revolutionary War Genealogy, 1982, Virginia Genealogical Research, 1982, War of 1812 Genealogy, 1983, North Carolina Genealogical Research, 1983, South Carolina Genealogical Research, 1984, Pennsylvania Genealogical Research, 1985, Georgia Genealogical Research, 1987, New York Genealogical Research, 1988, Massachusetts Genealogical Research, 1989, Maryland Genealogical Research, 1991, German Genealogical Research, 1992, Ohio Genealogical Research, 1994, Indiana Genealogical Research, 1996, Illinois Genealogical Research, 1997, Missouri Genealogical Research, 1997, Aqueous Chemistry of the Elements, 2010; also 170 articles. Faculty fellow Columbia U., 1958-60. Mem. Am. Chem. Soc., Am. Philos. Assn., History Sci. Soc., Soc. Genealogists, Phi Beta Kappa, Sigma Xi. Home: 407 Ascot Ct Knoxville TN 37923-5807

SCHWENKE, ROGER DEAN, lawyer; b. Washington, Oct. 18, 1944; Son of Clarence Raymond and Virginia Ruth (Gould) S.; m. Carol Lynne Flenniken, Nov. 29, 1980; 1 child: Matthew Robert; stepchildren: Tracy L. Wolf Dickey, M. Montgomery Wolf. BA, Ohio State U., 1966; JD with honors, U. Fla., 1969. Bar: Fla. 1970. Instr. Coll. Law U. Fla., Gainesville, 1969—70; assoc. Carlton Fields, P.A., Tampa, Fla., 1970—74, ptnr., 1975—; adminstr., dept. head Real Estate, Environ. and Land Use Dept., 1978—99. Adj. prof. Coll. Law, Stetson U., St. Petersburg, Fla., 1979-80; mem. faculty U. Miami Coll. of Law Master of Law's in Real Estate Devel. Program, 1994-96. Author chpt. in Environmental Regulation and Litigation in Florida, 1987, chpt. in Florida Real Property Complex Transactions, 1997, 2000, 2005, 2009, 2011, 2013; contbr. articles to profl. jours., chpt. to book. Mem. diocesan coun. Episc. Diocese SW Fla., 1978-86, mem. standing com., 1989-92, chief judge Eccles. Ct., 1996—2011, pres. dissiplinary bd., 2011-; dep. Gen. Convention Episcopal Ch., 1985-2012. Recipient Gertrude Brick Law Rev. prize, U. Fla., 1969. Fellow Am. Coll. Real Estate Lawyers (bd. govs. 1985-88), Am. Coll. Environ. Lawyer, Am. Law Inst.; mem. ABA (liaison to standing com. on environ. law 1980-87, mem. coun. real property sect. 1988-95), Fla. Bar Assn., Order of Coif, Greater Tampa C. of C. (chmn. environ. coun. 1980-81). Democrat. Office: Carlton Fields Jorden Burt PO Box 3239 Tampa FL 33601-3239 Office Phone: 813-229-4152. Business E-Mail: rschwenke@carltonfields.com.

SCIALABBA, LORI L., federal official, lawyer; b. Aug. 1959; BA, U. Md, 1982; JD, Memphis State U., 1985. Trial atty. Immigration and Naturalization Svc. (INS), Chgo., 1985—86, asst. atty. gen. Washington, 1986—89, dep. gen. coun., 1994—98; atty. Office of Immigration Litig., Civil Divsn. US Dept. Justice, Washington, 1989—94, chmn. Bd. Immigration Appeals (BIA), Exec. Office for Immigration Review (EOIR), 1998—99, vice chmn., 1999—2006; assoc. dir. refugee, asylum and internat. ops. US Citizenship and Immigration Svcs. US Dept. Homeland Security (DHS), Washington, 2006—11, sr. adv. for Iraqi refugee affairs, 2007—09; dep. dir. US Citizenship and Immigration Svcs., 2010—13, acting dir., 2013—. Office: US Citizenship and Immigration Services 2675 Prosperity Ave Fairfax VA 22031*

SCOBLE, ROBERT, information technology executive; b. Jan. 18, 1965; m. Maryam Ghaemmaghami; 2 children; 1 child from previous marriage, Patrick. Classes in Journalism, San Jose State U., 1993. Sales support mgr. NEC Mobile Solutions; editor, confs. Fawcette Tech. Publs., Inc., 1997—2001; dir., mktg. UserLand Software, v.p., mktg., 2001—02; tech. evangelist Microsoft Corp., 2003—06; v.p., media devel. PodTech.Network, Inc., Menlo Park, Calif., 2006—08; mng. dir. Mansueto Ventures, 2008—09; video blogger Fast Company, 2008—09, article contbr., 2008; mng. dir. Rackspace Hosting, Inc. (formerly Rackspace Managed Hosting Corp.), 2008—, developer, building43. Co-author: Naked Conversations: How Blogs are Changing the Way Businesses Talk with Customers, 2006; blog writer Scobleizer.com. Named one of Top 25 Web Celebs, Forbes mag., 2006, 2007, 50 Most Important People on the Web, PC World, 2007. Office: Rackspace Hosting Inc 5000 Walzem Rd San Antonio TX 78218 Office Phone: 210-312-4000. Office Fax: 210-447-4300. Business E-Mail: robert.scoble@rackspace.com.

SCOFIELD, CLAY, state legislator; b. Cullman, Ala., May 6, 1980; BS in Agrl., Bus. & Economics, Auburn U., Ala. Owner, farmer Clay Scofield Farms; mem. Dist. 9 Ala. State Senate, 2011—. Mem. Grassy Ch. of Christ. Republican. Office: Alabama State Senate State House Rm 731 11 S Union St Montgomery AL 36130 Office Phone: 334-242-7876. Business E-Mail: clay.scofield@alsenate.gov.

SCOGIN, MACK, architect, educator; BArch, Ga. Inst. Tech., Atlanta, 1966. Registered Ga., Mass., Tex., NY, Conn., cert. NCARB. Sr. design architect Heery & Heery Architects and Engrs., Inc., 1967—81, v.p., coord., 1978—81, pres, COO, dir. design, 1981—84; prin. Scogin Elam and Bray Architects, Inc., Atlanta, 1984—2000, Mack Scogin Merrill Elam Architects, Inc., Atlanta, 2000—. Vis. critic Rice Univ., Houston, 1984, Ga. Inst. Tech., Atlanta, 1987—89, Harvard Univ. Grad. Sch. Design, 1989, chmn., dept. arch., 1990—95, Kajima adj. prof. arch., 1990—; Herbert Baumer disting. vis. prof., sch. of arch. Ohio State Univ., 2003—04. Prin. works include Buckhead Branch Libr., Atlanta (Ga. AIA award of excellence, 1990, Urban Design Commn. award of excellence, 1990, Nat. AIA/ALA award of excellence, 1991, Nat. AIA award of excellence, 1993), Clark Atlanta Univ. Art Galleries (Architectural Record Interiors award, 1996, Atlanta Urban Design Commn. award of excellence, 2000), Lee B. Philmon Branch Libr. (Ga. AIA Design award of excellence, 1999, Nat. AIA/ALA award of excellence, 2003, So. Atlantic Region AIA honor award, 2003). Recipient Arnold W. Brunner Meml. Prize in Archit., Am. Acad. Arts and Letters, 2011. Mem.: NAD (assoc. fellow), Arch. Soc., Atlanta (founding mem., mem. bd. sponsors 1983—88), AIA (nat. com. on design, chmn. steering com. 1987). Office: Mack Scogin Merrill Elam Architects Inc 111 JW Dobbs Ave NE Atlanta GA 30303 Office Phone: 404-525-6869. Office Fax: 404-525-7061.

SCOTT, ANNE BYRD FIROR, history professor; b. Montezuma, Ga., Apr. 24, 1921; d. John William and Mary Valentine (Moss) Firor; m. Andrew Mackay Scott, June 2, 1947; children: Rebecca, David MacKay, Donald MacKay. AB, U. Ga., 1941; MA, Northwestern U., 1944; PhD, Radcliffe Coll., 1958; LHD (hon.), Lindenwood Coll., 1968, Queens Coll., 1985, Northwestern U., 1989, Radcliffe Coll., 1990, U. of the South, 1990, Cornell Coll., 1991; LLD (hon.), Wake Forest U., 2007. Congressional rep., editor LWV of U.S., 1944-53; lectr. history Haverford Coll., 1957-58, U. N.C., Chapel Hill, 1959-60; asst. prof. history Duke U., Durham, N.C., 1961-67, assoc. prof., 1968-70, prof., 1971-80, W.K. Boyd prof., 1980-91, W.K. Boyd prof. emerita, 1992—, chmn. dept., 1981-85; Gastprofessor Universität, Bonn, Germany, 1992-93. Vis. prof. Johns Hopkins U., 1972-73, Stanford U., 1974, Harvard U., 1984, Cornell Coll., 1993, Williams Coll., 1994, U. Miss., 2000; Times-Mirror scholar Huntington Libr., 1995; vice chmn. Nat. Humanities Ctr., 1991-98; mem. adv. com. Schlesinger Libr.; lectr. in field. Author: The Southern Lady, 1970, 1995; author: (with Andrew MacKay Scott) One Half the People, 1974; author: Natural Allies, 1991; editor: Jane Addams, Democracy and Social Ethics, 1964, The American Woman, 1970, Women in American Life, 1970, Women and Men in American Life, 1976, Unheard Voices, 1993, Pauli Murray and Caroline Was, 2006; mem. editl. bd.: Revs. in Am. History, 1976—81, Am. Quar., 1974—78, Jour. So. History, 1978—84; contbr. articles to profl. jours. Chmn. Gov.'s Commn. on Status of Women, 1963-64; mem. Citizens Adv. Council on Status of Women U.S., 1964-68; trustee Carnegie Corp., 1977-85, W.W. Ctr. for Scholars, 1977-84; chmn. bd. dirs. Nat. Cmty. Investment Fund, 1996—2002. AAUW fellow, 1956-57; grantee NEH, 1967-68, 76-77, Nat. Humanities Ctr., 1980-81; grad. medal Radcliffe Coll., 1986, Duke U. medal, 1991, John Caldwell medal N.C. Humanities Coun., 1994; fellow Ctrl. Advanced Study in Behavioral Sci., 1986-87; Fulbright scholar, 1984, 92-93. Fellow Am. Acad. Arts & Sci; mem. Am. Antiquarian Soc., Orgn. Am. Historians (exec. bd. 1973-76, pres. 1983, Disting. Pub. Svc. award 2002), So. Hist. Assn. (exec. bd. 1976-79, pres. 1989), Soc. Am. Historians Assn. (Disting. Scholarly Achievement award, 2008), Phi Beta Kappa. Democrat. Office: Duke U Dept History Durham NC 27708 Personal E-mail: annefiror@gmail.com.

SCOTT, AUSTIN (JAMES AUSTIN SCOTT), United States Representative from Georgia, former state legislator; b. Augusta, Ga., Dec. 10, 1969; s. Jim and Becky Scott; m. Vivian Scott; 1 child, Wells. BBA, U. Ga., Athens, 1993. CLU The American Coll., 1995, CHFC The American Coll., 1995, RHU The American Coll., 2000. Agent Life of South Agency, 1992—93; sr. agent The Prin. Fin. Group, 1993—98; owner, ins. agent & investment salesman The Southern Group, LLC, 1998—; mem. Dist. 165 Ga. State House of Reps., Ga., 1997—2003, mem. Dist. 138, 2003—04, mem. Dist. 153, 2004—10; mem. US Congress from 8th Ga. Dist., Washington, 2011—, US House Agrl. Com., Washington, 2011—, US House Armed Services Com., Washington, 2011—. Mem. American Legis. Exch. Coun., 2004. Mem.: NRA (life), Nat. Assn. Ins. Fin. Advisers. Republican. Baptist. Office: US House of Representatives 516 Cannon House Office Bldg Washington DC 20515 Office Phone: 202-225-6531. Office Fax: 202-225-3013.*

SCOTT, BOB (ROBERT SCOTT), retired chemical engineer, educator; b. Knoxville, Tenn., Dec. 1, 1934; s. Bob and Katherine Scott; m. Julia Scott; children: Robert, Joseph. BS in Chem. Engring., U. Tenn., 1957; MS in Chem. Engring., U. Cin., 1964. Chem. engr. Dupont, Olin, Shell Chem. Co.; staff mem. Oak Ridge Nat. Lab., US Army Signal Corps R&D Lab.; prof. Pellissippi State Tech. Cmty. Coll. Mem. Ch. of the Savior - United Ch. of Christ. Mem.: Audubon Soc., Am. Assn. Retired People, Mensa, Am. Inst. Chem. Engrs., Tenn. Ornithol. Soc., Tech. Soc. Knoxville, Sierra Club. Democrat. Office: 2216 Delta Way Knoxville TN 37919 Office Phone: 865-310-8710. Business E-Mail: scottforcongress@aol.com.

SCOTT, BOBBY (ROBERT CORTEZ SCOTT), United States Representative from Virginia, lawyer; b. Washington, Apr. 30, 1947; s. Charles Waldo and Mae (Hamlin) Scott. BA, Harvard U., Cambridge, Mass., 1969; JD, Boston Coll. Sch. Law, 1973; LLD (hon.), Commonwealth Coll., Hampton, Va., 1988. Lawyer pvt. practice, Newport News, Va., 1973—91; mem. Va. House of Delegates, 1978—83, Va. State Senate, 1983—93, US Congress from 3rd Va. dist., 1993—. Bd. pres. NAACP, Newport News; mem. adv. com. Peninsula Boy Scouts America; chmn. 1st dist. Va. Dem. Party, Va., 1980—85; pres. bd. dirs. Peninsula Legal Aid Ctr., Hampton, Va., 1977—81; bd. dirs. Hampton Roads March of Dimes. Served in USAR, 1970—74, served in Mass. NG, 1974—76. Recipient Brotherhood Citation award, Nat. Conf. Christians & Jews, 1985, Child Advocate award, Va. Acad. Pediat.,

1987, Disting. Svc. award, Va. State Fraternal Order Police, 1987; named an Outstanding Legislator, So. Health Assn., 1989; named one of 100 Most Influential Black Americans, Ebony mag., 2006. Mem.: Peninsula C. of C., Sigma Pi Phi, Alpha Phi Alpha. Democrat. Episcopalian. Office: US House of Representatives 1201 Longworth House Office Bldg Washington DC 20515 also: 2600 Washington Ave Ste 1010 Newport News VA 23607 Office Phone: 202-225-8351.

SCOTT, BRUCE K., retired military officer; b. Ft. Bliss, Tex., Apr. 22, 1950; m. Mary B. Tallman; children: Kate, Andy, Karoline, Kerney, Alec, Adam. BS, U.S. Mil. Acad., 1972; M of Internat. Rels., U. Freiburg, Germany; MPA, Harvard U., 1984. Commd. 2d lt. U.S. Army, 1972, advanced through grades to maj. gen.; dep. dir. strategy, plans and policy Office of the Dep. Chief of Staff for Ops. and Plans, to 1997; chief legis. liaison Office of Sec. of Army, Washington, 1997—2002; v.p. internat. mktg., defense ITT Industries, McLean, Va., 2002—. White House fellow, 1984—85. Decorated Army DSM, legion of Merit with oak leaf cluster, Army Commendation medal, others; Olmsted scholar. Office: ITT Industries, Defense 1650 Tysons Blvd Ste 1700 Mc Lean VA 22102

SCOTT, DAVID ALBERT, United States Representative from Georgia; b. Aynor, SC, June 27, 1945; s. Albert and Mamie (Polite) Scott; m. Alfredia Aaron, Oct. 26, 1969; children: Dayna Dorienda, Marcye Michelle. BA, Fla. A&M U., 1967; MBA, U. Pa., 1969. Pres., owner Dayn-Mark Advt., Atlanta; mem. Ga. House of Reps., Atlanta, 1975-82, Ga. Senate, Atlanta, 1983—2002, chmn. edn. com., 1993, chmn. rules com., 1994—2002; mem. US Congress from 13th Ga. dist., 2003—; mem. Agriculture com., Fin. Svcs. Com. Chmn. Atlanta Fulton Senate Del., 1992—94. Creator, prodr., dir. (film) Langston! (4 Emmy awards, best cultural affairs program award NATAS, spl. recognition Congl. Black Caucus, Bronze Jubilee award), (nat. radio program) Inside Black America (spl. cmty. svc. award Mayor of Chgo., James Weldon Johnson journalism award NAACP, spl. citation City of Highland Park, Mich., spl. broadcasting cmty. svc. award Detroit City Coun., spl. tribute Mich. Ho. of Reps.). Mem. exec. bd. dirs. U. Pa. Wharton Sch. Bus. Recipient Silver Microphone award, 1986, 1992, 1993, 1994, Telly award, 1994; named one of Most Influential Black Americans, Ebony mag., 2006; named to Power 150, 2008. Mem.: NAACP, Black Caucus, Nat. Assn. Black Elected Ofcls., Ga. C. of C. (bd. dirs.), Ga. Bus. Coun., Alpha Phi Alpha. Democrat. Baptist. Avocations: reading, writing, movies, theater. Office: US House of Representatives 225 Cannon House Office Bldg Washington DC 20515 Office Phone: 202-225-2939. Office Fax: 202-225-2939.*

SCOTT, DONALD LAVERN, city manager, librarian, former army officer; b. Hunnewell, Mo., Feb. 8, 1938; s. William Edward and Amanda Beatrice (Dant) S.; m. Betty Jean Forte, Mar. 3, 1962; children: Jeffrey Jerome, Merriell Edward Lavern. BA in Graphic Arts, Lincoln U., 1960; MA in Counseling and Human Devel., Troy State U., 1982. Commd. 2d lt. U.S. Army, 1960, advanced through grades to brig. gen., 1991; bn. comdr. 3d Bn., 47th Inf. Div., Ft. Lewis, Wash., 1978-80; prof. mil. sci. Tuskegee (Ala.) U., 1980-81; dep. insp. gen. U.S. Army Europe, Heidleberg, Fed. Republic Germany, 1982-83; comdr. Hohenfels (Germany) Tng. Ctr., 1983-85; insp. gen. VII U.S. Corps, Stuttgart, Fed. Republic Germany, 1985-86; asst. div. comdr. 1st Cav. Div., Ft. Hood, Tex., 1986-88; chief of staff 2d U.S. Army, Ft. Gillem, Ga., 1988-91; ret. U.S. Army, 1991; chief of staff City of Atlanta, 1991, COO, 1991—; dir., founder AmeriCorps Nat. Civilian Cmty. Corps, 1993—96; mem. Five Star Coun., Vets. History Project, 1996—. Bd. dirs. Atlanta Conv. and Bus. Bur., 1991—; advisor Jimmy Carter's Atlanta Project, 1992; mem. 100 Blackmen, Atlanta, 1992; dep. Libr. of Congress, 1996-; mem. Leg. Br. Coun. Chief Adminstrn. Officers, 1996-. Decorated D.S.M., Legion of Merit, Bronze Star (6), Meritorious Svc. medal. Mem. Assn. U.S. Army, Atlanta C. of C., Kappa Alpha Psi (reporter 1980-82). Avocations: golf, reading, jogging. Office: City of Atlanta Office of Mayor 55 Trinity Ave SW Atlanta GA 30303-3520 E-mail: dscott@loc.gov.

SCOTT, EDWARD T., state legislator; b. Culpeper, Va., Aug. 6, 1965; m. Pauline Scott; 1 child, Danielle. Mem. Madison County Planning Commn., 1992—2000; retail store mgr. Culpeper Farmers' Coop. Inc., 1990—96, field sales rep., 1998—99; mgr., agrl. ops. Culpeper Farmers' Coop Inc., 1998—; dir. govt. affairs Va. Agribusiness Coun., 1996—98; mem. Dist. 30 Va. House of Delegates, Va., 2004—. Trustee St. Luke's Lutheran Sch.; mem. Rappahannock Rapidan Regional Partnership, Va. Tech. Coll. Agr. Leadership Coun. Mem.: Culpeper C. of C. (dir.). Republican. Episcopalian. Office: 206 S Main St Ste 203 Culpeper VA 22701 Office Phone: 540-825-6400. Office Fax: 540-825-6649. Business E-Mail: DelEScott@house.virginia.gov.

SCOTT, HILLARY, singer; b. Nashville, Apr. 1, 1986; d. Linda Davis and Lang Scott; m. Chris Tyrrell, Jan. 7, 2012; 1 child, Eisele Kaye. Founding band mem. Lady Antebellum, 2006—. Singer: (albums) Lady Antebellum, 2008, A Merry Little Christmas, 2010, Need You Now, 2010 (Best Country Album, Record of Yr., Grammy Awards, 2011), Own the Night, 2011 (Best Country Album, Grammy Awards, 2012), On This Winter's Night, 2012, Golden, 2013, (songs) I Run to You, 2009 (Single of Yr., Country Music Assn. Awards, 2009, Best Country Performance by Duo or Group with Vocals, Grammy Awards, 2010), Need You Now, 2009 (Single Record of Yr., Song of Yr., Acad. Country Music Awards, 2010, Group Video of Yr., CMT Music Awards, 2010, Single of Yr., Country Music Assn., 2010, Best Country Performance by Duo or Group with Vocals, Song of Yr., Grammy Awards, 2011, Top Country Song, Billboard Music Awards, 2011), Hello World, 2010 (Group Video of Yr., CMT Music Awards, 2011), We Owned the Night, 2011 (Group Video of Yr., CMT Music Awards, 2012), Downtown, 2013 (Group Video of Yr., CMT Music Awards, 2013). Named Top New Duo or Group, Acad. Country Music, 2008, Top Vocal Group of Yr., 2010, 2011, 2012, New Artist of Yr., Country Music Assn., 2008, Vocal Group of Yr., 2010, 2011, Favorite Country Band, Duo or Group, American Music Awards, 2010, 2011, 2012, 2013, Top Country Artist, Billboard Music Awards, 2012. Office: c/o Capitol Records Nashville 3322 W End Ave #11 Nashville TN 37203*

SCOTT, JAMES M., state legislator; b. Galax, Va., June 11, 1938; s. Fred Sharp and Mary Ruth Bishop Scott; m. Nancy Cromwell, 1976; children: Casey, Mary Alice. BA, U. NC, Chapel Hill, 1960, MA, 1965; MPA, George Mason U., Fairfax, Va., 1982. Exec. dir. Fairfax Cmty. Action Programs, 1966—68, Washington Suburban Inst., 1969—72; mem. bd. supervisors Fairfax County, Va., 1972—86; asst. v.p. Inova Health Sys., cmty. affairs cons.; mem. Dist. 53 Va. House of Delegates, 1992—. Chmn. NACO Cmty. Devel. Steering Com., 1977—83, North Va. Transp. Commn., 1980—81, Met. Washington Water Resources Planning Bd., 1982—85. Co-author: (book) At the Heart of the Problem, 1970. Bd. dirs. Met. Washington Transit Authority, 1982—85. Recipient Human Rights award, Nat. Conf. Christians & Jews, 1980, David & Elizabeth Scull Pub. Svc. award, Metro Washington Coun. Govt., 1983, Disting. Svc. award, NAACP, Fairfax Br., 1983, Pub. Office award, Va. Housing Coalition, 1993, Wayne Anderson Disting. Alumni award, George Mason U., 1997; named Citizen of Yr., Fairfax County, Va., 1991. Mem.: Met. Washington Coun. Governments (bd. dirs. 1993—), United Way (mem. exec. com. 1980—84, 1989—92). Democrat. Methodist. Home: 2827 Maple Ln Fairfax VA 22031-1425 Office Phone: 703-560-8338. Business E-Mail: DelJScott@house.virginia.gov.

SCOTT, JANICE WILKIE, museum director; b. New Haven; d. Valleau Wilkie. Attended, Knox Coll., Galesburg, Ill. Riding instr., NH and Ind.; dir., collections mgr. Sid Richardson Mus., 1982—. Office: Sid Richardson Mus 309 Main St Fort Worth TX 76102 Office Phone: 817-332-6554. Business E-Mail: jan@sidrichardsonmuseum.org.

SCOTT, JOHN LEE, JR., state legislator; b. Richland County, SC, Oct. 21, 1953; s. John L. and Gracie White Scott; m. Joan Crouch Scott, 1975; 1 child, John L. III. BS in Accounting, SC State U., 1975. Owner & broker-in-charge JL Scott Realty County Inc., 1999—; owner, pres. C and S Cons. Group Inc., 1999—; mem. Dist. 77 SC House of Reps., 1999—2009; mem. Dist. 19 SC State Senate, 2009—, mem. Corrections and Penology Com., Gen. Com., Judiciary Com. & Med. Affairs Com. Clk., bd. trustees New Ebenezer Bapt. Ch. Named one of Man of Yr., SC Chpt. Nat. Assn. Real Estate Brokers, 1985—86. Democrat. Baptist. Mailing: 215 Elmont Dr Columbia SC 29203 Office: 612 Gressette Bldg Columbia SC 29201 Home Phone: 803-786-2373; Office Phone: 803-733-5176, 803-212-6048. E-mail: jls@legis.lpitr.state.sc.us.

SCOTT, JOYCE ALAINE, academic administrator; b. Long Beach, Calif., May 21, 1943; d. Emmett Emery Scott and Grace (Evans) Wedum. BA, U. Conn., 1964; MA, U. Va., 1966; PhD, Duke U., 1973. From instr. to assoc. prof. U. Wyo., Laramie, 1971-74, asst. dean, 1974-78, asst. v.p. acad. affairs, 1976-81, assoc. v.p. acad. affairs, 1981-84; provost, v.p. SUNY-Potsdam, 1984-86; exec. v.p. Wichita (Kans.) State U., 1986-90, v.p. on spl. assignment, 1990-91; sr. cons. Am. Assn. State Colls. and Univs., 1991-92, v.p. acad. and internat. programs, 1992-97; dep. commr. Mont. U. Sys., Helena, 1998—2003; provost, v.p. acad. and student affairs Tex. A&M U., Commerce, 2003—06, assoc. prof. dept. ednl. leadership, 2004—. Mem. Commn. on Ednl. Credit and Credentials of Am. Coun. on Edn., Washington, 1982-87; cons. faculty Am. Open U., Lincoln, Nebr., 1981-82. Contbr. articles to profl. jours. Trustee Jones Internat. U. Mem. MLA, Am. Assn. Tchrs. French, Phi Beta Kappa, Phi Kappa Phi, Phi Sigma Iota. Republican. Presbyterian. Office: Dept Educational Leadership PO Box 3011 Commerce TX 75429-3011 Office Phone: 903-886-5503. Business E-Mail: Joyce_Scott@tamu-commerce.edu.

SCOTT, LEE (HAROLD LEE SCOTT JR.), retired retail executive; b. Joplin, Mo., Mar. 14, 1949; s. Harold Lee and Avis Viola (Parsons) S.; m. Linda Gale Aldridge, June 7, 1969; children: Eric Sean, Wyatt Parson. BBA, Pitts. State U., Kans., 1971. Br. mgr. Yellow Freight System, Springdale, Ark., 1972-78; mgr. Queen City Warehouse, Springfield, Mo., 1978-79; dir. transp. Wal-Mart Stores, Inc., Bentonville, Ark., 1979-83, v.p. distbn. to sr. v.p. logistics, 1983—93, exec. v.p. logistics, 1993—95; exec. v.p. merchandise & sales Wal-Mart Stores USA, 1995—98, pres., CEO, 1998—99; vice chmn., COO Wal-Mart Stores, Inc., Bentonville, Ark., 1999—2000, pres., CEO, 2000—09, chmn. exec. com., 2009—11; operating ptnr., mem. investment com. Solamere Capital, Lexington, Mass., 2009—. Bd. dirs. Pvt. Truck Council, 1985—86, Wal-Mart Stores, Inc., 1999—2014, Cooper Industries, 2000—04, The Goldman Sachs Group, Inc., 2010—11. Named an Outstanding Alumni, Pitts. State U., 1995; named one of The 100 Most Influential People in the World, TIME mag., 2004, 2005, The 25 Most Powerful People in Bus., Fortune mag., 2007. Republican. Methodist. Avocations: reading, quail hunting. Office: Wal-Mart Stores Inc 702 SW 8th St Bentonville AR 72716-6299*

SCOTT, MARTIN, state legislator; State rep. Dist. 2, Ga., 2005—. Republican. Mailing: Legis Off Bldg Atlanta GA 30334 Business E-Mail: mscott@legis.state.ga.us.

SCOTT, MELLOUISE JACQUELINE, retired media specialist; b. Sanford, Fla., Mar. 1, 1943; d. Herbert and Mattye (Williams) Cherry; m. Robert Edward Scott, Jr., July 1, 1972; 1 child, Nolan Edward. BA, Talladega Coll., 1965; MLS, Rutgers U., 1974, EdM, 1976, EdS, 1982. Media specialist Seminole County Bd. Edn., Sanford, 1965-72, Edison (N.J.), 1972-98; ret. Edison (N.J.) Bd. Edn., 1999. Mem. ALA, N.J. Ret. Educators Assn., NEA. Baptist. Home: PO Box 1771 Sanford FL 32772-1771

SCOTT, OLOF HENDERSON, JR., priest; b. Phila., May 13, 1942; s. Olof Henderson and Julia Irene (Rutroff) S.; m. Eva Jakowenko, Sept. 13, 1969; children: Lisa Ann, Christopher Olof, Timothy Nicholas. BA in Physics, Franklin and Marshall Coll., 1964; MS in Nuclear Engring., Pa. State U., 1966; postgrad., St. Vladimir's Orthodox Theol. Sem., 1975-76. Ordained deacon Antiochian Orthodox Christian Ch., 1975, priest, 1976, archpriest, 1988. Ops. engr. S3G ops. Knolls Atomic Power Lab., GE Co., Schenectady, N.Y., 1966-68, project engr. S3G ops., 1968-69; lead nuclear engr. Seabrook Nuclear project Pub. Svc. Co. of N.H., Manchester, 1969-70; project engr. VEPCO projects Nuclear Energy Sys. divsn. Westinghouse Elec. Co., Monroeville, Pa., 1970-72, project mgr. VEPCO projects Nuclear Energy Sys. divsn., 1972-74, regional sales mgr. mktg., 1974-75; dean St. George Orthodox Cathedral, Charleston, W.Va., 1976—; dean of clergy Appalachian-Ohio Valley Deanery, 1976—2005, Virginias Deanery, 2005—. Spiritual advisor NAC-SOYO of Archdiocese, 1977-82, vice-chmn. inter-orthodox and inter-faith rels., 1987-2005, chmn., 2005—; exec. bd. W.Va. Coun. Chs., 1977—; bd. govs. Nat. Coun. Chs., 1977-2005, nominating com., 1979-81, exec. com., 1985-96, membership com., 1988-91, unity and rels., 1989-92, ch. world svc., 1997-2005; active West Va. Ecumenical Coalition on Infant Mortality, 1992-96; rep. Christian Chs. Together in the US, 2006—, Steering Comm., 2008- Contbr. articles to profl. jours. Bd. dirs. Religious Coalition for Cmty. Renewal in Charleston, 1987-95, Charleston Ch. Recreation Assn., 1998—, Kanawha Home for Children, 1986-89, pres., 1989; long-range planning com. W.Va. State Rep. Exec. Com., 1985-87; adv. bd. Nat. Ctr. for Human Rels., 1997-98, Charleston Area Religious Leaders Assn., 2004—; del. 8th Assembly of WCC, Harare, Zimbabwe, 1998. Named Hon. West Virginian, 2001; Olof H. Scott Day named in his honor, City of Charleston, W.Va., 2001. Mem. Acad. Parish Clergy (pres. W.Va. chpt. 1983-85), Am. Nuclear Soc., St. Vladimir's Theol. Found., Charleston Ministerial Assn., Order of St. John of Jerusalem-Knights Hospitellers (chaplain 1985—), Order of St. Ignatius of Antioch, Soc. for Preservation and Encouragement Barbershop Quartet Singing in Am. Inc. (v.p. 1984-85), Pa. State Club W.Va. (pres. 1984-88), Alden Kindred of Am., Order DeMolay, Sigma Pi Sigma, Delta Sigma Phi. Avocations: camping, motorcycling, barbershop quartets. Office: St George Orthodox Cathedral PO Box 2044 Charleston WV 25327-2044 Home: 823 Sherwood Rd Charleston WV 25314-1833 Personal E-mail: frolof@suddenlink.net.

SCOTT, OMERIA MCDONALD, state legislator; b. Laurel, Miss., Nov. 21, 1956; m. Charles Scott. Mem. Dist. 80 Miss. House of Reps., 1993—; nursing home administr. Pianist Providence Baptist Ch., Laurel. Democrat. Baptist. Mailing: 615 E 19th St Laurel MS 39440 Home Phone: 601-649-7677; Office Phone: 601-359-3362. Business E-Mail: oscott@house.ms.gov.

SCOTT, RICK (RICHARD LYNN SCOTT), Governor of Florida, investment company executive; b. Bloomington, Ill., Dec. 1, 1952; s. Orba and Esther Scott; m. Annette Holland, 1971; children: Allison, Jordan. BSBA, U. Mo., 1975; JD, Southern Meth. U., 1978. Bar: Tex. Chmn., CEO Columbia/HCA Healthcare Corp., Nashville, 1987-97; pres., CEO Richard L. Scott Investments, LLC, Naples, Fla., 1997—2001; co-founder, chmn. Solantic Corp., Jacksonville, Fla., 2001—11; founder Conservatives For Patients' Rights (CPR), 2009—19; gov. State of Fla., 2011—. Bd. dirs. CyberGuard, 2001—03, Solantic Corp., 2001—11, Secure Computing Corp., 2006—08. Mem. nat. bd. The United Way, 1997—2003. Served in USN, 1971—74. Recipient Second Century award for Excellence in Health Care, Columbia U. Sch. Nursing, 1995, Entrepreneurship award, George Washington U., 2007; named CEO of the Yr., Financial World mag., 1995; named one of The Top 25 Performers, US News & World Report, 1995, America's 25 Most Influential People, TIME mag., 1996. Mem.: Bus. Coun., Bus. Roundtable, Healthcare Leadership Coun. Republican. Christian. Office: Office of Governor PL 05 The Capitol 400 S Monroe St Tallahassee FL 32399-0001 also: Richard L Scott Investments LLC 1400 Gulfshore Blvd N Ste 148 Naples FL 34102 Office Phone: 239-263-9030, 212-398-2020, 850-488-2272. Office Fax: 239-263-9031, 212-398-2033.*

SCOTT, RODERICK HAMPTON (ROD SCOTT), state legislator; s. Percy Scott; m. Carstella Hampton Scott; children: Sara-Valena Morgan Scott, Jordan Elizabeth, Bradlea-roi Shelton Scott. BA in Econs., Yale U., New Haven; MBA, Dartmouth Coll. Amos Tuck Sch. Bus. Adminstrn. Prof. Miles Coll., Birmingham; mem. Dist. 55 Ala. House of Reps., Montgomery, 2006—. Democrat. Office: Miles Coll 5500 Myron Massy Blvd Birmingham AL 35208 also: Ala House of Reps Ala State House 11 S Union St Rm 525-C Montgomery AL 36130 Office Phone: 205-929-1534, 334-242-7752. Business E-Mail: scotthrod@yahoo.com.

SCOTT, SANDRA, state legislator; b. Nov. 14; BS in Bus. Mgmt., Fla. A&M U., Tallahassee; degree in elem. edn., Armstrong Atlantic State U., Savannah, Ga. Educator; mem. Dist. 76 Ga. State of Representatives, 2011—. Mem. Travelers Rest Missionary Ch., Morrow, Ga. Staff sgt. US Army, 1984—89. Democrat. Office: Georgia State of Reps 611 Coverdell Legis Office Bldg Atlanta GA 30334 Office Phone: 404-656-0314.

SCOTT, SENECA, state legislator; b. Tulsa, Okla. m. Anna Scott; children: Harper, Clay. Degree in History/Native Am. Studies, U. Okla. Ops. mgr. Trivestco Energy; precinct chmn. Tulsa Dem. Party; with Service Clearing Co.-Energy Mgmt.; mem. Dist. 72 Okla. House of Representatives, 2008—. Democrat. Office: 2300 N Lincoln Blvd Rm 539 Oklahoma City OK 73105 Home: 3138 E 4th St Tulsa OK 74104-2408 Office Phone: 405-557-7391. Business E-Mail: seneca.scott@okhouse.gov.

SCOTT, T. GORDON, chemistry professor, mathematics professor, writer; b. Laconia, NH, Nov. 27, 1941; s. William Stafford and Jeanne Richardson Scott; m. Elizabeth Mary Winterberg, Mar. 11, 1995. AB, U. Pa., 1963; BA with honours, Cambridge U., England, 1965, MA, 1970; PhD, U. Ill., 1969. Profl. tchg. cert., Pa.; postgrad. tchg. lic., Va. Tchg. asst. U. Ill., Champaign-Urbana, 1965-66; asst. prof. chemistry Oberlin Coll., Ohio, 1969-70; lectr. biochemistry U. Calif., Santa Barbara, 1971; cons. Sci-Math Cons., Uniontown, Pa., 1972-75; supr. secondary studies Westminster Acad., Carmichaels, Pa., 1975-79; asst. prof. chemistry Alderson-Broaddus Coll., Philippi, W.Va., 1981-84; assoc. prof. chemistry Bryan Coll., Dayton, Tenn., 1984-86, Knoxville Coll., Tenn., 1987-89, Union Coll., Barbourville, Ky., 1989-91, Jarvis Christian Coll., Hawkins, Tex., 1992-98; with Chem. Edn. Cons. USA, Hawkins, Tex., 1998-2000; instr. math. Winona Ind. Sch. Dist., Tex., 1998-99; instr. math, chemistry and astronomy Pittsylvania County Schs., Va.; tchr. Dan River HS, Ringgold, Va., 2000—02; adj. prof. chemistry and natural sci.-biochemistry Danville CC, Va., 1999—2004; adj. instr. pharmacology Nat. Coll., Danville, 2001—03; assoc. prof. chemistry Winston-Salem State U., NC, 2004—09; ret., 2009. Rsch. assoc. DuPont Chem. Co., Inc., Phila., 1963, EPA, Phila., 1988, Edgewood-Aberdeen Rsch. US Army, Aberdeen Proving Ground, Md., 1993; vis. prof. La. Coll., Pineville, 1992; adj. sci. instr. Hargrave Mil. Acad., Chatham, Va., 2003; undergrad. rsch. mentor NSF, New Orleans, 2004; cons. with Transition State Assocs., Danville, Va. Author: (with others) Synthetic Procedures in Nucleic Acid Chemistry, 1968, Spectroscopic Model Studies of NAD, 1969; contbr. articles to Jour. Am. Chem., Soc., 1967, 1970, 1972, 2003. Musician with Danville Recorder Consort, Danville Area Choral Arts Soc. Thouron fellow to Cambridge U., 1963-65; Thouron scholar Gonville & Caius Coll., Cambridge U.; grantee NSF, 1996-97, Army Rsch. Orgn., 1993-95, Robert A. Welch Found., 1996-98, NSF, 1997-99. Mem. Am. Chem. Soc., Cambridge U. Chem. Soc., Am. Sci. Affiliation (dir. 1998), Rotary Internat. (chmn. internat. edn. com. 1977-81). Achievements include determined the fluorescent lifetime of coenzyme NADH; research in direct consequence of co-determined this constant six lereditary metabolic diseases were controlled or eliminated at established research stations in the US and Europe; lifetime constant enabled assay times for NADH experiments to be reduced from two to four weeks to about two hours; development of efficient process for formulating. Avocations: baritone vocal solos, exploring ideas, renaissance music (treble and tenor blockflute), astronomy. Home: 3895 Old Vineyard Rd #123 Winston Salem NC 27104 Personal E-mail: ps1388@att.net.

SCOTT, TERRY LEE, communications executive; b. Rockford, Ill., Oct. 21, 1950; s. Wilson C. and Marie G. (Bunger) S.; divorced; children: Andrea, Brady, Tiffany. BS in Acctg. magna cum laude, Bradley U., 1972. CPA Ill., Tex. Audit prin. Arthur Young and Co., Dallas, 1972-82; v.p. fin. and adminstrn., treas. Paging Network Inc., Dallas, 1982-90; sr. v.p. Paging Network, Inc., Dallas, 1990-92, pres., CEO, bd. dirs., 1993-95, Terion Inc., Melbourne, Fla., 1995-97, chmn., CEO, 1997-99, Terry Scott Enterprises, Plano, Tex., 1997—; dir. Chameleon Tech., Inc., Seattle, 2000—03, Metasolv Software, Inc., Dallas, 2003—06; CFO, v.p. Fin. of Chase Med., Inc., 2003—04; pres., CEO, dir. Airimba Wireless, Inc., Plano, Tex., 2004—06. Mem. AICPA, Tex. Soc. CPAs, Phi Kappa Phi, Zeta Pi. Methodist. Home: 5816 Gallant Fox Ln Plano TX 75093-2910 Home Phone: 214-713-7614; Office Phone: 214-718-8927. Personal E-mail: tscott1704@aol.com.

SCOTT, TIM (TIMOTHY EUGENE SCOTT), United States Senator from South Carolina, former United States Representative from South Carolina; b. Charleston, SC, Sept. 19, 1965; s. Ben Scott Sr. and Frances Scott. BS in Polit. Sci., Charleston Southern U., 1988. Owner Tim Scott Allstate, Charleston; ptnr. Pathway Real Estate Group, LLC, Charleston; councilman Charleston County Coun., 1995—2008, chmn., 2007—08; mem. Dist. 117 SC House of Reps., 2008—11; mem. US Congress from 1st SC Dist., Washington, 2011—13, US House Rules Com., Washington, 2011—13; US Senator from SC, 2013—; mem. US Senate Commerce, Sci. & Transp. Com., 2013—, US Senate Energy & Natural Resources Com., 2013—, US Senate Health, Edn., Labor & Pensions Com., 2013—, US Senate Small Bus. & Entrepreneurship Com., 2013—, US Senate Spl. Com. on Aging, 2013—. Co-chmn. financial services com. Allstate Nat. Advisory Bd., 2004—08. Recipient SC Agy. Owner of

Yr. award; named an The 50 Politicos to Watch, Politico, 2010. Republican. Evangelical Christian. Office: US Senate 167 Russell Senate Office Bldg Washington DC 20510 Office Phone: 202-224-6121.*

SCOTT, WILL T., state supreme court justice; b. Ratliff's Creek, Ky., July 20, 1947; s. John H. H. and Betty (Thompson) Scott. Attended, Eastern Ky. U.; BA, Pikeville Coll.; JD, U. Miami, 1974, MS in Taxation, 1975. Bar: Ky., Fla. With trust dept. Pikeville Nat. Bank, 1975—76; atty. priv. practice, 1976—2004; asst. atty. Pike County, 1981—82; judge Pike County Cir. Ct., 1984—88; justice Ky. Supreme Ct., 2005—, dep. chief justice, 2006—10. Served to First Lt. US Army, 1966—69. Decorated Bronze Star, Vietnamese Cross of Gallantry, Combat Infantryman's Badge. Mem.: Ky. Circuit Judges' Assn. (second v.p. 1986). Office: Ky Supreme Ct 700 Capitol Ave Rm 235 Frankfort KY 40601 Office Phone: 502-564-4168.*

SCOTT-RAMIREZ, MICHELLE R., retail executive; BS in bus. adminstrn. mktg. and mgmt., Mid. Tenn. State U., 1981. Dist. sales mgr. Lane Bryant, 1987—2001; regional v.p., retail ops. Cracker Barrel Old Country Store, Inc., 2001—. Recipient Regional v.p. of Yr., 2005—10. Office: Cracker Barrel Old Country Store Inc 305 Hartmann Dr Lebanon TN 37088-0787 Office Phone: 615-444-5533.

SCRIVEN, MARY STENSON, federal judge; b. Atlanta, 1962; d. Marshall and Mary Stenson. BA, Duke U., Durham, NC, 1983; JD, Fla. State U., 1987. Bar: Fla. 1987. Assoc. atty. Carlton Fields, PA, Fla., 1987—95, shareholder Fla., 1995—97; magistrate judge US Dist. Ct. (mid. dist.) Fla., 1997—2008, judge Orlando, 2008—. Assoc. prof. Stetson U. Coll. Law, Gulfport, Fla., 1996—97. Office: US Dist Ct US Courthouse 401 W Central Blvd Rm 5650 Orlando FL 32801 Office Phone: 407-835-3840.

SCROGGS, LARRY KENNETH, lawyer, state legislator; b. Beebe, Ark., Oct. 8, 1941; s. Kenneth Chalmers and Mildred Lorene (McDonald) S.; m. Mary Patricia Rushing, Aug. 25, 1967; children: Larry Kenneth Jr., James Kevin, Michael Kyle. BA, Harding U., 1963; JD, Vanderbilt U., 1971. Bar: Tenn. 1971, U.S. Dist. Ct. (we. dist.) Tenn. 1971, U.S. Ct. Appeals (8th cir.) 1982, U.S. Ct. Appeals (6th cir.) 1989, U.S. Supreme Ct. 1981. Assoc. Law Firm of Leo Bearman, Memphis, 1971-72, Holt, Batchelor, Spicer, Memphis, 1972-76, ptnr., 1976-80, Less & Scroggs, Memphis, 1980-92; pvt. practice, Germantown, Tenn., 1992-96; ptnr. Scroggs & Rogers, Collierville, Tenn., 1997—2003, Burch, Porter & Johnson, Memphis, 2003—06; chief adminstrv. officer, chief counsel Juvenile Ct. Memphis and Shelby County, 2006—. Mcpl. ct. judge City of Germantown, 1980-86; atty. for County Trustee, Shelby County, Memphis, 1990—06. Mem. Tenn. Ho. Reps., Nashville, 1996-2002; Lt. U.S. Navy, 1964-67, Vietnam. Mem. ABA, Tenn. Bar Assn., Memphis Bar Assn. (bd. dirs. 1990-91). Republican. Mem. Ch. of Christ. Avocations: photography, boating, tennis. Office: Juvenile Ct Memphis and Shelby County 616 Adams Ave Memphis TN 38105 Office Phone: 901-405-8518. Business E-Mail: Larry.Scroggs@shelbycountytn.gov.

SCRUGGS, PATRICK A., food service executive; b. 1964; Various positions in the restaurant and retail industries; joined Cracker Barrel Old Country Store, Inc., 1989, v.p. acctg. and tax, chief acctg. officer, 2003—. Office: Cracker Barrel Old Country Store Inc 305 Hartmann Dr Lebanon TN 37088-0787 Office Phone: 615-444-5533. Office Fax: 615-443-9818.

SCULLEY, PATRICK DAVID, retired army officer, director; b. Jamestown, NY, Sept. 12, 1947; s. Claude Francis and Hildegarde Ruth (Anderson) S.; m. Peggy Ann Carroll, Aug. 26, 1967; children: Patricia, Paul, Perry, Peter. BA, Wash. and Jefferson Coll., Pa., 1969; DDS, SUNY, Buffalo, 1973; MA in Health Svcs. Mgmt., Webster U., St. Louis, 1994. Diplomate Fed. Svcs. Bd. Gen. Dentistry, Am. Bd. Oral Medicine, Am. Bd. Gen. Dentistry; cert. Am. Coll. Health Care Execs., Am. Soc. Assn. Execs. Commd. US Army, advanced through grades to maj. gen., 1999; gen. practice resident Kimbrough Army Hosp., Ft. Meade, Md., 1973-74; gen. dentist US Army MEDDAC, White Sands Missile Range, N.Mex., 1974-76; gen. dentistry resident US Army DENTAC, Ft. Knox, Ky., 1977-79, clinic chief Ft. Riley, Kans., 1979-81; comdr. 576th Med. Detachment, Bad Kreuznach, West Germany, 1982-85; staff officer US Army Health Svcs. Command, Ft. Sam Houston, Tex., 1985-86, asst. inspector gen., 1986-88; dental cons. Dept. Army Surgeon Gen.'s Office, Washington, 1988-90; student US Army War Coll., Carlisle Barracks, Pa., 1990-91; comdr. US Army Dental Activity, Ft. Bragg, NC, 1991-92; dir. dental svcs. Health Svcs. Command US Army, 1992-93, comdr. Dental Command, 1993-95, asst. surgeon gen. pers., 1996, commdg. gen. US Army Ctr. Health Promotion and Preventive Medicine, 1996-99, acting dep. surgeon gen., 1998-99, dep. surg. gen./chief Army Dental Corps, chief of staff US Army Med. Command, 1999—2002, ret., 2002; exec. dir. Sigma Xi, 2002—06; dir. sci. and tech. Ctr. for Applied Tech., Tex. A&M U., San Antonio, 2006—. Instr. oral medicine gen. practice residency, Ft. Riley, 1980-81; mem. bd. examiners Fed. Svcs. Bd. Gen. Dentistry, Washington, 1986-90; mem. bd. examiners Am. Bd. of Gen. Dentistry, 1991-95. Asst. high sch. football coach Bad Kreuznach Am. H.S., 1982-83; basketball coach Vienna Youth Inc., Va., 1988-89, Cath. Youth Orgn., San Antonio, 1985-86; softball coach Girls Recreation Softball League, Manhattan, Kans., 1981; mem. adv. coun. Raleigh-Durham USO, 2004-06; mem. steering com. NC Project Lead the Way, 2004-06. Fellow: Internat. Coll. Dentists; mem.: ADA (alt. del. Ho. Dels. 1999—2000), Assn. Mil. Surgeons US (Fed. Healthcare Adminstr. of Yr. 2001), Am. Bd. Gen. Dentistry, Acad. Gen. Dentistry (chmn. self-assessment com. 1988—91, pres. Army chpt. 1988—91, ho. of dels. 1988—91, examination coun. 1988—92, chmn. reference com. on adminstrn. comm. and constrn. bylaws 1990, long range planning coun. 1997—98, chmn. long range planning coun. 1998—99, chmn. strategic advancement com. 1999—2002, Disting. Svc. award 1999), Am. Coll. Health Care Execs., Triangle Area's Rsch. Dirs. Club (vice chmn. 2004—, chmn. 2005), Sigma Xi, Omicron Kappa Upsilon. Independent. Roman Catholic. Avocation: history. Office: Texas Ctr Applied Tech 9350 S Presa St San Antonio TX 78223-4733 Business E-Mail: patrick-sculley@tamu.edu.

SCULLY, MARLAN ORVIL, physics professor; b. Casper, Wyo., Aug. 3, 1939; s. Orvil O. and Thelma G. (Thoms) Scully; m. Judith Bailey, Aug. 16, 1958; children: James, Robert, Steven. AS, Casper Coll., 1959; BS, U. Wyo., 1961; MS, Yale U., 1963, PhD, 1966. Instr. Yale U., New Haven, 1967-69; asst. prof. MIT, Cambridge, 1969-71, assoc. prof., 1971-72; prof. U. Ariz., Tucson, 1972-80; disting. prof. physics U. N.Mex., Albuquerque, 1980—92; Burgess disting. prof. Tex. A&M U., 1996—, prof. physics, 1992—96, prof. elec. engring., 1999—; dir. Ctr. Theoretical Physics, Tex. A&M U., 1995—, Inst. Quantum Studies, Tex. A&M U., 2001—; disting. rsch. chair TEES, 2000—; vis. prof. chemistry Princeton U., 2003—05, prof. mechanical and aerospace engring. and materials sci., 2005—. Dir., co-founder Radtech, 1984; mem. Joint coun. on Quantum Electronics, Internat. Commn. on Optics; mem. program com. VIIth and VIIIth Internat. Conf. on Quantum Electronics (co-chmn. program com.); panel mem. Internat. Conf. on Hot Electrons in Semiconductors, North Tex. State U.; co-dir. VIIth Course of NATO Internat. Sch. Quantum Electronics; mem. program com. for OSA sponsored topical meeting on Picosecons Phenomena, Hilton Head, S.C., 1978; invited lectr. U.S.-Japan Coop. Seminar on Laser Spectroscopy, Hakone, Japan, 1977; mem. NRC panel on electron, atomic and molecular physics; advisor to ARO Nat. Acad. Panel, Los Alamos Physics Div. Author: (with others) Laser Physics, 1974; contbr. articles to profl. jours. Recipient Elliott Cresson medal The Franklin Inst., 1990; John S. Guggenheim fellow, 1970, Alfred P. Sloan fellow, 1972. Fellow AAAS, Am. Acad. Arts and Scis., Optical Soc. Am. (dir. at large 1978-80, publs. com. 1972, Ives medal com. 1976, chmn. Wood prize com. 1978, Adolph E. Lomb medal 1970, Townes award, 1990), Am. Phys. Soc. (Arthur L. Schawlow prize for Laser Sci., 2005); mem. NAS, IEEE (Quantum Electronics award, 2003) Max Planck Soc, Academia Europa. Avocations: cattle ranching, inventing.

SEABAUGH, ALAN T., state legislator, lawyer; m. Laura McClelland; 4 children. BA, La. State U., 1990; JD, La. State U. Law Sch., 1993. Bar: La., US Dist. Ct. (we., mid., ea. districts La.), US Ct. Appeals (5th cir.). Mng. ptnr. Seabaugh & Joffrion LLC, Shreveport, La.; mem. Dist. 5 La. House of Reps., Baton Rouge, 2010—. Mem. ctrl. com. Rep. Party of La.; del., vice chmn. La. delegation Republican Nat. Conv., 2008; mem. Presdl. Electoral Coll., 2008. Former bd. mem. Shreveport Little League; active Broadmoor & Calvary Bapt. Churches, Shreveport; allied atty. Alliance Def. Fund; baseball, softball and T-ball adminstr. Calvary Bapt. Ch.; exec. dir. South Highlands Athletic Assn. Mem.: NRA, La. Bar Assn., Shreveport Bar Assn., Greater Shreveport C. of C., La. Assn. Bus. and Industry, Federalist Soc., Heritage Found. Republican. Office: La State House of Reps 900 N Third St Baton Rouge LA 70804 also: 610 Marshall St Ste 700 Shreveport LA 71101 Office Phone: 318-676-7990. Office Fax: 318-676-7992. Business E-Mail: seabaugha@legis.state.la.us.

SEAL, MARK J., manufacturing executive; BS in Chemistry, U. Cin. With, mgmt. positions Georgia-Pacific Corp.; v.p., Polymer Group Georgia Gulf Corp., 1993—2005, v.p., Chemicals Group, 2005—06, v.p., outdoor bldg. products, 2006—08, v.p. aromatics and additives Atlanta, 2008—. Office: Georgia Gulf Corp 115 Perimeter Ctr Pl Ste 460 Atlanta GA 30346 Office Phone: 770-395-4500. Office Fax: 770-395-4582. Business E-Mail: sealm@ggc.com.

SEALE, ROBERT ARTHUR PETE, lawyer; b. Shreveport, La., July 17, 1942; s. Robert Arthur Sr. and Lucille (Frank) S.; m. Chalon Fontaine; children: Pete A., John Meyers. BBA, La. State U., 1964, JD, 1967. Bar: La. 1967, Tex. 1969. Mem. La. Law Rev., 1965—67; rsch. asst. La. Law Inst. for La. Mineral Code, Baton Rouge, 1967; law clk. U.S. Dist. Ct. (WD-LA), Shreveport, 1967—69; atty./ptnr. Vinson & Elkins, Houston, 1968—97; ptnr. Phelps Dunbar LLP, Houston, 2002—04; of counsel Liskow & Lewis, Houston, 2005—11; ptnr. Vorys, Sater, Seymour and Pease LLP, Houston, 2011—. Trustee and gen. counsel Mus. of Fine Arts, Houston, 1981-89 Pres., trustee The Lyons Found., 1977—; adv. trustee mem. Paul M Hebert Law Ctr.; mem. endowment bd. Child Advocate Inc., Houston; mem. devel. bd. U. Tex. Health Sci. Ctr., Houston, 1995—; trustee Episcopal H.S., Houston, 1985—88. Named one of Best Lawyers in America. Fellow: Houston Bar (life); mem.: ABA, Tex. Bar (sustaining life fellow), Omicron Delta Kappa. Avocations: civic and charitable activities, golf, travel. Office: Vorys Sater Seymour and Pease LLP 700 Louisiana St Ste 4100 Houston TX 77002 Office Phone: 713-588-7006.

SEALS, MARGARET LOUISE CRUMRINE, retired journalist; b. Buckhannon, W.Va., Oct. 27, 1944; d. James Richard and Helen Margaret Crumrine; m. Harry Eugene Seals, Jan. 10, 1975. BS in journalism, W. Va. U., 1966; MS in mass. comm., Va. Commonwealth U., 1983. Reporter, copy editor Democrat & Chronicle, Rochester, NY, 1966-67, Dayton (Ohio) Daily News, 1967-68; copy editor Richmond (Va.) Times-Dispatch, 1968-75, copy desk slot editor, 1975-81, exec. news editor, 1981, asst. mng. editor, 1982-92, dep. mng. editor, 1992-93, mng. editor, 1994—2006. Adj. intr. Va. Commonwealth U. Mass Comm. Sch., 2007—08. Mem. Leadership Metro Richmond, 1986, seminar days co-chair, 2007-08, curriculum com., 2007-08; mem. adv. bd. Sch. Mass. Comm. Va. Commonwealth U., 1988-93, mem. alumni adv. bd. 2004-08; mem. adv. com. Sch. Journalism, W.Va. U., 1999—2011. Named Outstanding Woman in Comms. YWCA Met. Richmond, 1989; recipient Perley Isaac Reed award W.Va. U. Journalism Sch. Alumni Assn., 1996; inducted into Va. Comm. Hall of Fame, 2003. Mem.: Fan Womens Club (Hope in Cities adv. coun. mem.), Va. Press Women Found. (pres. 2008—), Va. Press Women, Ctrl. Va. Chpt. W.Va. U. Alumni Assn. (treas. 2008—09), Richmond Tree Stewards (mem. adv. panel 2009—), Va. Press Assn. (dir. 2001—03, treas. 2003—04, sec. 2004—05, v.p. 2005—06), AP Mng. Editors (editor APME News 1993—94, dir. 1993—95, treas. 1996—97, dir. 1998—2001, Disting. Svc. award 2002, 75th anniversary editor 2008), Va. Press Women (treas. 1986—88, 2nd v.p. 1988—90, pres. 1990—92, Press Woman of Yr. 1986, Communicator of Achievement award 1997), Soc. Profl. Journalists (bd. dirs. Va. profl. chpt. 1998—2003, pres. Va. profl. chpt. 2000—02), Nat. Fedn. Press Women (bd. dirs. 1990—92, Communicator of Achievement award 1997), Phi Kappa Phi. Avocations: hiking, travel, gardening. Personal E-mail: louise.seals@comcast.net.

SEARS, EARL, state legislator; b. Bartlesville, Okla., Sept. 2, 1952; m. Jane Anne Grove; children: Ryan, Hollye. BA, MA, Northeastern State Univ. Former prin. Ctrl. Middle Sch., Bartlesville, Okla.; mem. Bartlesville City Coun.; state rep. Dist. 11 Okla., 2007—. Mem.: Bartlesville Symphony Bd., Bartlesville City Coun., Bartlesville Area Rotary, Bartlesville Sportsman Club. Republican. Address: 1721 Cherokee Pl Bartlesville OK 74003 Office: Oklahoma House of Representatives 2300 N Lincoln Blvd Room 432-D Oklahoma City OK 73105 Office Phone: 405-557-7358. Business E-Mail: earl.sears@okhouse.gov.

SEARS, LEAH WARD, lawyer, retired state supreme court judge; b. June 13, 1955; d. Thomas E. and Onnye J. Sears; married; children: Addison, Brennan. BA, Cornell U., 1976; JD, Emory U., 1980; M in Apellate Jud. Process, U. Va.; LLD (hon.), Morehouse Coll., 1993. Judge City Ct. Atlanta; atty. Alston & Bird, Atlanta; trial judge Superior Ct. Fulton County, Atlanta; justice Ga. Supreme Ct., Atlanta, 1992—2009, chief justice, 2005—09; ptnr. Schiff Hardin LLP, Atlanta, 2009—. Contbr. articles to profl. jours. Bd. dirs. Conf. Chief Justices, southeast chpt. UNICEF, Emory Law Sch. Coun., Woodruff Arts Ctr.; mem. Cornell U. Women's Coun., steering com. Ga. Women's History Month, Children's Def. Fund Black Cmty. Crusade Children; founder Battered Women's Project, Columbus, Ga. Recipient Outstanding Young Alumna award Emory U., Excellence in Pub. Svc. award Ga. Coalition Black Women, 1992, Outstanding Woman of Achievement YWCA Greater Atlanta, One of Under Forty & On the Fast Track, 1993, Ga. Woman of Year Ga. Commn. Women, Margaret Brent Women Lawyer of Achievement ABA, Leadership award Atlanta Bar Assn., Trumpet award for Distinction in Law, Woman Power award Nat. Urban League, Drum Maj. Justice award Southern Christian Leadership Conf., Emory medal, Emory U., 2001, Legal Trailblazers award, Nat. Bar Assn., 2007; named One of The Under Forty & On the Fast Track, 1993, The 100 Most Influential Georgians Ga. Trend mag., 1992, 2004-08; named an Outstanding Woman of Achievement YWCA Greater Atlanta; named Ga. Woman of Year Ga. Commn. Women, Margaret Brent Women Lawyer of Achievement ABA Mem. ABA (chair bd. elections), Nat. Assn. Women Judges, Ga. Bar Assn., Women's Forum Ga., Gate City Bar Assn., Atlanta Bar Assn. (past chair jud. sect.), Ga. Assn. Black Women Attys. (founder, pres.), Fourth Tuesday Group, Jack & Jill Am. (Atlanta chpt.), Links Inc. (Atlanta chpt.), Alpha Kappa Alpha. Office: Schiff Hardin LLP One Atlantic Center Ste 2300 1201 W Peachtree St NW Apt 2300W Atlanta GA 30309 Office Phone: 404-437-7050. Office Fax: 404-437-7100. E-mail: lsears@schiffhardin.com.

SEARS, MARY HELEN, lawyer; b. Syracuse, NY; d. James Louis and Helen Mary (Fitzgerald) Sears. AB, Cornell U., Ithaca, NY, 1950; JD with honors, George Wash. U., Washington, DC, 1960. Bar: Va. 1960, DC 1961, US Supreme Ct. 1963. Chemist Allied Chem. and Dye Corp., Syracuse, 1950-52, Hercules Powder Co., Wilmington, Del., 1952-55; patent examiner US Patent Office, Washington, 1955-60; pvt. practice Washington, 1960—62; assoc. Irons, Birch, Swindler & McKie, Washington, 1962—70; mem. firm Irons & Sears, Washington, 1971—84; chmn. trade regulation practice dept. Memel, Jacobs, Pierno, Gersh & Ellsworth, Washington, 1984-87; ptnr., chmn. intellectual property and unfair competition practice dept. Ginsburg, Feldman & Bress, Washington, 1987-91; ptnr., chmn. intellectual property and telecomm. practice group Reid & Priest, Washington, 1991-94; founder, chmn. M. H. Sears Law Firm, 1994—2007; ret., 2011. Mem. adv. bd. Boardroom Reports, Inc., NYC, 1980-85; mem. Cornell U. Coun., 1981-87, 89-93, life mem., 1995—, mem. adminstrv. bd., 1984-86. Contbr. articles to various publs. Recipient Outstanding Performance award, US Dept. Commerce, 1957, World's Leading Patent Law Experts, Euromoney Publs., PLC, 2001, Belva Lockwood prize, George Wash. U. Law Sch. Assn. for Women, 2007; named one of World's Leading Patent Law Experts, Euromoney Publs., PLC, 1995, 1997, 2003, 2005, 2007. Mem.: ABA (co-chmn. appellate practice com., litigation sect. 1989—92), DC Bar Assn., Va. State Bar Assn., Am. Soc. Internat. Law, Am. Intellectual Property Law Assn., George Wash. U. Law Alumnae Assn. (bd. dirs. 1995—2001), Order of Coif, Phi Alpha Delta. Republican. E-mail: mhsears@mhsears.com, mhsears@verizon.net.

SEARS, ROBERT STEPHEN, finance educator; b. Odessa, Tex., May 27, 1950; s. William Bethel and Leola Vernon (Little) S.; Reva Dana Flournoy, Aug. 17, 1973; children: Matthew Stephen, Elizabeth Rea. AAS, Odessa Jr. Coll., 1970; BA summa cum laude, Tex. Tech. U., 1973, MS, 1976; PhD, U. N.C., 1980. Supr. Bethel Enterprises, Odessa, 1973—74; tchg. asst. Tex. Tech U., Lubbock, 1974—76, dir. Inst. Banking and Fin. Studies, 1988—98; tchg. asst. U. N.C., Chapel Hill, 1976—79; asst. prof. U. Ill., Champaign, 1979—85, assoc. prof., 1985—88; rsch. prof. Bur. Econ. and Bus., Champaign, 1984; tchg. asst. Lubbock Bankers Assn., 1990—2005; chmn. dept. fin. Tex. Tech U., Lubbock, 1997—2001, interim dean Coll. Bus., 2000, sr. exec. assoc. dean, Coll. Bus, 2001—03; Milan Puskar dean Coll. Bus. & Economics W.Va. U., Morgantown, 2005—08, prof. fin., 2005—09; dean Killam dist. prof. fin. Sanchez Sch. Bus. Tex. A & M Internat. U., 2009—. Cons. Cameron Brown Mortgage Co., Raleigh, N.C., 1978-80, Howard Savs. Bank, Livingston, N.J., 1980; asset mgr., trustee, pvt. investors, 1984—. Author: Investment Management, 1993, (chpt), Modern Real Estate, 1980, 84; assoc. editor Rev. of Bus. Studies, 1989-95, Jour. Fin. Rsch., 1990-96, Internat. Chmn. fin. com. Temple Bapt. Ch., Champaign, Ill., 1982, bd. deacons, 1982-88, chmn. deacons, lay leader, 1983; Sunday sch. tchr. Carrboro (NC) Bapt. Ch., 1977-79; bd. deacons Ind. Ave. Bapt. Ch., Lubbock, 1989-96, Sunday sch. tchr., 1991-92, master design com., 1993-96; trustee All Saints Episcopal Sch., 1995-2003, treas., 2000-03; bd. deacons Southcrest Bapt. Ch., Lubbock, 1998-2005, mem. fin. com. Avery United Meth. Ch., Morgantown, 2008-09, mem. strategic planning com., fin. com. chair & sunday sch. tchr., 1st United Meth. Ch., Laredo, 2010, mem. Lavedo Rotary. Rsch. grantee Cameron Brown Mortgage Co., Raleigh, N.C., 1978-80, U. Ill, Champaign, 1980-84, 86-87, Investors in Bus. Edn., Champaign, 1980-81, 84; recipient Excellence in Undergrad. Tchg. award U. Ill. Champaign, 1984-85, Award for Outstanding Coll. Educator Champaign-Urbana, Ill. Jaycees, 1983-84, Coll. of Commerce Alumni Assn. Undergrad. Excellence in Tchg. award U. Ill., 1981-82; Mortar Bd., Omicron Delta Kappa Leadership scholarship and Svc. award Tex. Tech U., 1997-98, Pres.'s Excellence in Tchg. award Tex. Tech U., 1993-94, Acad. Achievement award Tex. Tech U., 1994-95. Mem. Am. Fin. Assn., Southwestern Fin. Assn. (pres. 1989-90, v.p., program chmn. 1988-89, sec., treas. 1986-88, bd. dirs. 1984-86, program com. 1985-86, 89-, Outstanding Educator 2006), Fin. Mgmt. Assn. (program com. 1986, 89-94, 97, 99-2004), So. Fin. Assn. (program com. 1986), We. Fin. Assn. (program com. 1986), Ea. Fin. Assn., Lake Ridge Country Club Republican. Baptist. Avocations: golf, walking, sports. Office: A R Sanchez Jr Sch Bus Tex A & M Internat University 5201 University Blvd Laredo TX 78041 Office Phone: 956-326-2480.

SEATON, DAVID T., engineering company executive; B, U. S.C.; advanced mgmt. program, Wharton Sch. of Bus.; internat. mgmt. program, Thunderbird Univ. Sales & ops. mgmt. positions through v.p. & mng. dir. Fluor Arabia Fluor Corp., Irving, Tex., 1984—2002, sr. v.p. sales, energy & chem., 2002—04; sr. v.p. chem. bus. Fluor Corp., Irving, Tex., 2004—05, sr. v.p. sales, energy & chem., 2005—07; group pres., Energy & Chemicals Fluor Corp., Irving, Tex., 2007—09, sr. group pres. energy & chem., power & govt., 2009, COO, 2009—11, CEO, 2011—. Bd. dirs. The Mosaic Co.; mem. coord. com. oil & gas Nat. Petroleum Coun.; bd. mem. Am. Petroleum Inst., US-Saudi Arabian Bus. Coun. Office: Fluor Corp 6700 Las Colinas Blvd Irving TX 75039 Office Fax: 469-398-7255. Business E-Mail: david.seaton@fluor.com.

SEAVEY, CHRISTOPHER GORDON, psychotherapist, alcohol and drug abuse services professional; b. Syracuse, NY, Dec. 4, 1942; s. Gordon Crowell and Shirley Edith Seavey; m. Eudene Sawyer, Aug. 8, 1965 (div. Mar. 1983); children: Sandra, Sherry, Gordon; m. Nancy Bowen, 1983. BA in Human Svcs., U. Mass., 1986; MA in Rehab. Counseling, U. South Fla., 1991; PhD in Psychotherapy, Internat. U. Grad. Studies, 2001. Sr. counselor Project Turnabout, Hingham, Mass., 1982—86; counselor Coastal Cmty. Counseling, Braintree, Mass., 1986—87, South Shore Coun. on Alcoholism, Quincy, Mass., 1987; chem. dependency counselor II David Lawrence Ctr., Naples, Fla., 1989—90; cons. vocat. rehab. Intracorp, Naples, 1990—96; acting dir. Addiction Recovery Ctr., Ft. Myers, Fla., 1993—98; clin. dir. Assisted Addiction Recovery, Naples, 1995—2004; dir. Christopher Seavey LMHG PA, 2004—. Mem. adv. bd. Naples Rehab. Inc., 1994-97. Chmn. Collier County Depression Coalition, Naples, 1997. Recipient Book award U. Mass., Boston, 1986; U. Calif. San Francisco fellow, 1986; Tobacco Coalition grantee, 1998. Mem. NADAAC, ACA, Internat. Assn. Rehab. Profls., Internat. Coun. on Alcohol and Addictions, Fla. Rehab. Assn. (pres. S.W. Fla. chpt. 1994-95, Svc. award 1999), Fla. Mental Health Counselors, Gulf Coast Mental Health Counselors Assn. (past pres.), Internat. Soc. Study Women's Sexual Health, Am. Assn. Sexuality Educators, Counselors and Therapists, Phi Kappa Phi. Office: 9853 N Tamiami Trail Ste 213 Naples FL 34108 Office Phone: 239-595-7775. Business E-Mail: chriseavey@earthlink.net.

SEAY, FRANK HOWELL, federal judge; b. Shawnee, Okla., Sept. 5, 1938; s. Frank and Wilma Lynn Seay; m. Janet Gayle Seay, June 2, 1962; children: Trudy Alice, Laura Lynn. Student, So. Meth. U.,

1956-57; BA, U. Okla., 1960, LL.B., 1963. Bar: Okla. 1963. Atty., Seminole County, 1963-66; asst. dist. atty., 1967-68; assoc. dist. judge, 1968-74; judge Okla. Dist. Ct. 22, 1974-79; chief judge US Dist. Ct. (ea. dist.) Okla, Okla., 1980—96, judge Okla., 1979—80, 1996—2003, sr. judge, 2003—. Mem. ABA, Okla. Bar Assn., Seminole County Bar Assn. Clubs: Masons, Elks, Lions. Democrat. Office: US Dist Ct PO Box 828 Muskogee OK 74402-0828

SEAY, JOSEPH GARY, healthcare services company executive; Dir., info. sys. Humana, Inc., 1985—87, 1993—96; v.p., managed care sys. EQUICOR, 1987—90; v.p. CIGNA Sys., 1990—93, Cmty. Health Sys., Inc., 1997—2007; chief info. officer Community Health Systems, Inc., 1997—, sr. v.p., 2007—. Mem., CIO adv. coun. HIMSS, Tenn.; bd. dirs. United Way of Williamson County. Office: Community Health Systems Inc 4000 Meridian Blvd Franklin TN 37067 Office Phone: 615-465-7000. Office Fax: 615-371-1068. Business E-Mail: joseph_seay@chs.net.

SEAY, VALENCIA, state legislator; b. Atlanta, Ga., July 6, 1953; m to Walter; children: Vincent & Wendy. Attended, DeKalb Coll., Clayton Coll. & State Univ. Mgmt. positions through asst. v.p. Wachovia Bank, 1979—2001; pres., CEO Seay & Associates; mem. & v.p. Clayton County Bd. Edn., 1993—2000; mem. Dist. 93 Ga. House Reps., 2001—02; mem. Dist. 34 Ga. State Senate, 2003—. Mem. NAACP, Nat. Coun. Negro Women, Nat. Org. Women Legislators; Ga. Assn. Black Elected Officials. Democrat. Baptist. Mailing: PO Box 960008 Riverdale GA 30274 Office Phone: 770-909-9912. Business E-Mail: valencia.seay@senate.ga.gov.

SEBASTIAN, TERESA MOSLEY, lawyer; BS in Sociology, U. Mich., 1978; MBA in Finance, U. North Fla., 1983; JD, Mich. State U., 1993; LLM in Corporate & Finance Law, Wayne State U., 2003. Assoc. Sommers Schwartz PC, 1991—94; sr. corp. counsel CMS Energy, 1994—2001; asst. gen. counsel, asst. corp. sec. DTE Energy Co., 2001—07; sr. v.p., gen. counsel Information Resources, Inc., 2007; v.p., gen. counsel, corp. sec. Veyance Technologies, Inc., 2008—10; sr. v.p., gen. counsel, corp. sec. Darden Restaurants, Inc., 2010—. Office: Darden Restaurants, Inc PO Box 695011 Orlando FL 32869-5011 also: 1000 Darden Center Dr Orlando FL 32837*

SEBERT, KESHA ROSE See KESHA

SECHRIST, CHALMERS FRANKLIN, JR., electrical engineering educator; b. Glen Rock, Pa., Aug. 23, 1930; s. Chalmers F. and Lottie V. (Smith) S.; m. Lillian Beatrice Myers, June 29, 1957; children: Jonathan A., Jennifer N. BE in Elec. Engring., Johns Hopkins U., 1952; MS, Pa. State U., 1954, PhD in Elect. Engring., 1959. Sr. engr. Bendix Corp., summers 1952, 53, 54; instr. elec. engring. Pa. State U., 1954-55; staff engr. HRB-Singer, Inc., State College, Pa., 1959-65; from asst. prof. to prof. elec. engring. U. Ill., Urbana, 1965-96, assoc. head instructional programs dept. elec. and computer engring., 1984-86, asst. dean engring., 1986-96, prof. Emeritus, 1996—; program dir. divsn. undergrad. edn. NSF, Washington, 1992-96; adj. prof. engring. Fla. Gulf Coast U., 1998—2006; mem. adv. bd. Whitaker Coll. Engring., Fla. Gulf Coast U., 2006—. Acting sci. sec. Sci. Com. on Solar-Terrestrial Physics, 1981; chmn. publs. com. Middle Atmosphere Program, 1980-86, editor handbook, 1981-86; mem. adv. com. on tech. edn. Fla. Dept Edn., 2001-2005 Editor: Proc. Aeronomy Confs, 1965, 69, 72; contbr. articles to profl. jours. Grantee NSF. Fellow: IEEE (edn. activities bd. 1990, tech. activities bd. 1991—92, edn. activities bd. 1992—93, chmn. com. on pre-coll. edn. ednl. activities bd. 1997—99, edn. activities bd. 1997—99, awards and recognition com. edn. activities bd. 2000—01, oversight subcom. Virtual Mus. 2000—02, precoll. edn. coord. com. edn. activities bd. 2000—03, pres. edn. soc. 1991—92, Millennium medal 2000); mem.: Am. Soc. Engring. Edn., Am. Geophys. Union, Edn. Soc. of IEEE (v.p. 1989—90, pres. 1991—92, Achievement award 1993). Office Phone: 239-454-0640. Personal E-mail: csechrist@comcast.net.

SECREST, GEORGE MCCALL, JR., (MAC SECREST), lawyer; b. Laredo, Tex., Jan. 5, 1952; BA, U. Houston, 1974; JD with distinction, St. Mary's U. Sch. Law, San Antonio, 1977. Bar: Tex. 1977, US Ct. Appeals (5th cir.) 1981, US Dist. Ct. (so. dist.) Tex. 1982, US Supreme Ct. 1984, US Ct. Appeals (11th cir.) 1989, US Ct. Appeals (6th cir.) 1990, US Dist. Ct. (no. dist.) Tex. 1992, US Dist. Ct. (ea. dist.) Tex. 1994, US Dist. Ct. (we. dist.) Tex. 1997; cert. in criminal law Tex. Bd. Legal Specialization. Briefing atty. Tex. Ct. Criminal Appeals, 1977—78; asst. dist. atty. Harris County, Tex., 1978—81; asst. fed. pub. defender US Attorney's Office (so. dist.) Tex., 1981—83; ptnr. Bennett & Secrest, PLLC, Houston, 1983—. Adj. prof. law South Tex. Coll. Law, 1984, U. Houston, 1990—2003, 2007; mem. Gov.'s Ad Hoc Com. Revise Tex. Code of Criminal Procedure, 1995—96. Contbr. articles to profl. jours. Mem. Tex. Bd. Legal Specialization Exam Commn., 1992—2006. Mem.: Harris County Criminal Lawyers Assn. (treas. 1996—97, Lawyer of Yr. 2007), Nat. Assn. Criminal Def. Lawyers, Tex. Criminal Def. Lawyer's Assn., Houston Bar Assn., State Bar Tex. (Criminal Def. Lawyer of Yr. 1998), Bar Assn. 5th Fed. Cir., John Harlan Soc. Office: Bennett & Secrest PLLC 24th Fl Esperson Bldg 808 Travis St Houston TX 77002 Office Phone: 713-757-0679. Office Fax: 713-650-1602.

SEDAGHAT, HASSAN, mathematician, educator; b. Aug. 19, 1959; m. Seung-Hee Sedaghat. PhD, George Wash. U., 1990. Prof. math. Va. Commonwealth U., Richmond, Va., 1990—. Author: Nonlinear Difference Equations: Theory with Applications to Social Science Models, 2003, Symmetries and Reduction of Order in Difference Equations, 2011—. Recipient Rsch. award, Medtronic Inc., 2005—06. Mem.: AAUP, Internat. Soc. Difference Equations, Math. Assn. America, Am. Math. Soc. Avocations: writing, reading, walking, movies. Office: Virginia Commonwealth University Dept of Math 1015 Floyd Ave PO Box 842014 Richmond VA 23284-2014 Office Phone: 804-828-5806. Business E-Mail: hsedagha@vcu.edu.

SEDGWICK, ALEXANDER, retired historian, educator; b. Boston, June 8, 1930; s. William Ellery and Sarah (Cabot) S.; m. Charlene Mary Maute, June 24, 1961; children— Catherine Maria, Alexander Cameron BA, Harvard U., 1952, PhD in History, 1963. Asst. prof. history Dartmouth Coll., 1962-63; assoc. prof. U. Va., Charlottesville, 1963-66, 1974-79, prof., 1974—, chmn. history dept., 1979-85, dean Coll. Arts and Scis., 1985-90, dean grad. studies Charlottesville, 1990-95, univ. prof., 1995-97, univ. prof. emeritus, 1997—; ret., 1997. Mem. adv. com. in history Sr. Fulbright Awards Council for Internat. Exchange of Scholars. Author: The Ralliment in French Politics 1890-98, 1965, The Third French Republic, 1870-1914, 1968, Jansenism in Seventeenth Century France, Voices in the Wilderness, 1977, The Travails of Conscience. The Arnauld Family and the Ancien Regime, 1998; co-author: Church, State and Society Under the Bourbon Kings of France, 1982, For Want of a Horse, 1985, That Gentle Strength, 1980, Les Discour sur les Révolutions, 1991, History Today, 1991, Chroniques de Port-Royal, 1993, 95. Served with U.S. Army, 1952-54. Fulbright fellow, 1960-62; recipient Am. Coun. Learned Socs. grant-in-aid, 1967-68, Am. Philos. Soc. grant-in-aid, 1971. Mem. AAUP (nat. council 1976-79), Soc. French Hist. Studies (sec. 1979-83, pres. 1983-84), Am. Hist. Assn. Home: 1409 Rugby Rd Charlottesville VA 22903-1240

SEDLACEK, PETR, finance company executive; Dir. gen. Global Payments Europe (subs. of Global Payments, Inc.), chmn., CEO, 2006—. Office: Global Payments Inc 10 Glenlake Pky N Tower Atlanta GA 30328 Office Phone: 770-829-8000. Office Fax: 770-829-8267. Business E-Mail: petr.sedlacek@globalpaymentsinc.com.

SEELY, JAMES MICHAEL, retired military officer, defense consultant, small business owner; b. LA, Oct. 15, 1932; s. Louis K. and Mary Edith (Gleason) S.; m. Gail Margaret Deverman, July 13, 1957; children: Ted Andrew, Nina Marie. BS, UCLA, 1955; MS, George Washington U., 1976. Commd. ensign USN, 1955, advanced through grades to rear adm.; student pilot, 1955-56; attack pilot, 1957-75; comdg. officer Attack Squadron 165, Naval Air Sta. Whidbey Island, Wash., 1972-73; comdr. Carrier Air Wing 9, Naval Air Sta. Lemoore, Calif., 1974-75; comdg. officer U.S. Naval Air Sta., Whidbey Island, 1977-79; dep. dir. DCNO (Air Warfare, OP-50), Pentagon, Washington, 1979-82; dir. Joint Analysis Directorate, Office Joint Chiefs Staff, Washington, 1982-84; comdr. Medium Attack Tactical Electronic Warfare Wing, Pacific Fleet, Naval Air Sta. Whidbey Island, 1984-86; dir. DCNO (Air Warfare, OP-50), Pentagon, 1986-88; dep. comptr. of Navy, Pentagon, 1988-89; ret., 1989; with RRP Def. Cons. Assocs., Arlington, Va., 1989—2002; owner, pres. JMS Cons., 2002—. Vietnam combat duty with Attack Squadrons 93, 152, 165 flying from aircraft carriers USS Enterprise, Hancock, Bon Homme Richard, Shangri-La and Constellation; 447 combat missions. Decorated Defense Superior Service, Legion of Merit (3), D.F.C. (4), Bronze Star, Air Medal (43), Navy Commendation medal with combat v (7). Mem. Naval Inst., Tailhook Assn., Assn. Naval Aviation, Marine Corps Aviation Assn., Red River Valley Fighter Pilots Assn., Navy League, Assn. Old Crows, Golden Eagles, Sigma Pi, Am. legion., Vets Fgn. Wars. Republican. Roman Catholic. Avocations: sports, automobiles. Home: 15552 Legacy Way Haymarket VA 20169-6117 E-mail: jimseely@comcast.net.

SEENITH, SIVASUNDARAM, mathematician, educator; s. Sam Seenith and Tham Kanaga; m. Irene M Siva, May 21, 1973; 1 child, Diantha A Siva. PhD, U. Tex., 1987. Prof. Embry-Riddle Aero. U., Daytona Beach, Fla., 1989—. Organizer, gen. chair various profl. confs. Author: Vector Lyapunov Functions and Stability Analysis of Nonlinear Systems, 1991, College Mathematics for Aviation I, 1992, College Mathematics for Aviation II, 1993, Dynamics Systems on Measure Chain, 1996, Advances in Nonlinear Dynamics, 1997, Nonlinear Problems in Aviation and Aerospace, 2000, Advances in Dynamics and Control, 2004; editor-in-chief Jour. Nonlinear Studies; editor-in-chief: Nonlinear Systems in Aviation, Aerospace and Astronautics Book Series; editor-in-chief Nonlinear Systems in Aviation, Aerospace and Astronautics Series; editor: Proceedings of Nonlinear Problems in Aviation Aerospace, Proceedings of Mathematical Problems in Engineering and Aerospace Sciences, Jour. Aerospace Engineering, Global Jour. Mathematical Analysis, Scientific Journal of Actual Problems of Aviation and Aerospace Systems; author: Advances in Mathematical Problems in Engineering, also Space & Sciences, 2009, Advances in Nonlinear Analysis: Theory Method and Applications, 2009, Advances in Dynamics And Control: Theory Methods And Applications, 2009, World Congress 2010 ICNPAA-.COM, World Congress, 2012, 2014, Mathematical Analysis and Applications in Engineering and Aerospace Sciences, 2012, Work Energies, 2014. Mem.: AAUP, Soc. Indsl. and Applied Math., Internat. Fedn. Nonlinear Analysts (charter), Math. Assn. Am. (charter math. for bus., industry and govt. 1999), Acad. Nonlinear Scis., Am. Math. Soc. Avocations: travel, cricket. Office: Embry-Riddle Aero U 600 S Clyde Morris Blvd Daytona Beach FL 32114 Personal E-mail: seenithi@gmail.com. Business E-Mail: siva@erau.edu.

SEFFRIN, JOHN REESE, health science association administrator, educator; b. Hagerstown, Ind., May 19, 1944; s. Theodore H. and Mary Ellen (Reese) Seffrin; m. Carole Sue Washburn, Apr. 16, 1966; 1 child, Mary. BS in Edn., Ball State U., Muncie, Ind., 1966, DSc (hon.), 1994; MS, U. Ill., Champaign-Urbana, 1967; PhD in Health Edn., Purdue U., West Lafayette, Ind., 1970, D (hon.) in Social Sci., 2003; DSc (hon.), Thomas Jefferson U., Med. Coll. Phila., 2008, Ind. U., Bloomington, 2008. Asst. prof. health edn. Purdue U., 1970—76, assoc. prof., chair health & safety edn., 1976—79; prof., chmn. dept. applied health sci. Ind. U., Bloomington, 1979—92; exec. v.p., chief staff officer Am. Cancer Soc., Atlanta, 1992—95, CEO, 1995—. Trustee Am. Cancer Soc. Found., 1992—; commr.-at-large Nat. Commn. Health Edn. Credentialing, 1995—2000; charter mem., mem. steering com. C-Change (formerly Nat. Dialog on Cancer), 1999; mem. subcom. on cessation HHS, Washington, 2002—03; bd. dirs. Healthcare Inc. Nat. bd. dirs. Am. Lung Assn., 1980—90; treas. Partnership for Prevention of Premature Death, Disease and Disability, 1991—; mem. Pres.'s Commn. on Improving Econ. Opportunity in Cmtys. Dependent on Tobacco Prodn. While Protecting Pub. Health, 2000—01; trustee Ctr. Advancement Health, 2003—05; pres. State Welfare Bd. Ind. Dept. Pub. Welfare, 1979—80, 1982—84; treas. Midwest Nuc. Bd., 1973—75; chmn. cmty. edn. com. Am. Lung Assn., 1981—83, v.p., 1980, pres., 1982; bd. dirs. Nat. Ctr. Tobacco-Free Kids, 1996—; chmn. bd. dirs. Nat. Health Coun., 1998—2000; past pres. Internat. Union against Cancer; bd. dirs. Wabash Ctr. for the Mentally Retarded, 1970—73. Recipient Outstanding Alumnus award, Ball State U., 1982, Surgeon Gen.'s Cert. appreciation, USPHS, 1992, Presdl. citation, Soc. Pub. Health Edn., 2007; named Sagamore of Wabash, State of Ind., 1980, 1988. Fellow: Am. Sch. Health Assn. (mem. governing coun. 1979—81, 1982—89, pres. 1987—88, Howe award 1991); mem.: NAS (Nat. Cancer Policy Bd. 1997—2002), AMA, Am. Acad. Family Physicians (pub. adv. bd. 1999—), Rsch. Am. (bd. dirs. 1996—), Independent Sector (bd. dirs. 1997—2006), Nat. Interagy. Coun. on Smoking and Health (bd. dirs. 1979—), Internat. Union Against Cancer (ex-officio mem. US nat. com. 2000—, pres. 2002—06), Ind. Assn. for Health, Phys. Edn. and Recreation (pres. 1976, Cert. of Appreciation 1977, Honor award 1982), Am. Cancer Soc. (dir. Ind. Divsn. 1977—90, chmn. Ind. Divsn. 1982—85, dir.-at-large to nat. bd. dirs., chmn. nat. pub. edn. com. 1984—87, nat. v.p. 1986—87, chmn. nat. bd. dirs. 1989—91), Ind. Thoracic Soc. (mem. governing coun. 1977—84), Ind. Family Health Coun. (dir. 1979—81, v.p. 1980—81, pres. 1981), Ind. Assn. Health Educators (pres. 1975—76, chair 1997—2000), Assn. for Advancement Health Edn. (bd. dirs. 1989—92), Nat. Assn. State Bds. of Edn. (commn. on sch. cmty. role in improving adolescent health 1989—90), Eta Sigma Gamma, Phi Delta Kappa. Roman Catholic. Office: Am Cancer Soc Inc 250 Williams St NW Atlanta GA 30303 Business E-Mail: john.seffrin@cancer.org.

SEGAL, ROBERT MARTIN, lawyer; b. Atlantic City, Apr. 7, 1935; s. Nathan Albert and Edna (Dutkin) S.; m. Rhoda Sue Luber, June 8, 1958; children: Deborah Ann, William Nathan, Elizabeth Ann Student, Cornell U., 1953-54; BS in Econs., U. Pa., 1957; LLB cum laude, Harvard Law Sch., 1960. Bar: Pa. 1961. Assoc. Wolf, Block, LLP, Phila., 1960—69, ptnr., 1969—2007, sr. counsel, 2007—09, chmn., exec. com., 1978-79, 82-83, 86-87, 89-98. Contbr. articles to profl. jours. and mags. Constable of elections Lower Merion Twp., Pa., 1970-72; bd. dirs. Feinstein Ctr. for Am. Jewish History at Temple U.; bd. govs. Rep. Jewish Coalition; past trustee Hahnemann U., Fedn. Jewish Agys., Phila. Rehab. Plan, Inc., Rosenbach Mus. and Libr., Greater Phila. Urban Affairs Coalition, Jewish Family and Children's Agy., Am. Jewish Com., past pres. Jewish Employment and Vocat. Svc. 2nd lt., Quartermaster Corps US Army, 1958, 1st lt. USAR, 1959—64. Mem. ABA, Pa. Bar Assn., Phila. Bar Assn., Am. Coll. Real Estate Lawyers, Phila. Bar Found. (trustee 1981-87), Am. Law Inst., Harvard Law Sch. Assn. Phila., Chaine des Rotisseurs, Societe Mondiale du Vin, Anglers Club of Absecon Island, La Coquille Club, Harvard Club, Beta Gamma Sigma. Avocation: swimming.

SEGALL, JAMES ARNOLD, lawyer; b. Columbus, Ohio, Aug. 19, 1956; s. Arthur and Greta Helene (Cohen) Segall; m. Kayren Guillory, Dec. 22, 2012; children: Gayle Helene, Aryn Michelle, Craig Lawrence. BA, Coll. of William and Mary, 1978; JD, Washington and Lee U., 1981. Bar: Va. 1981, U.S. Dist. Ct. (ea. dist.) Va. 1981. Assoc. Phelps & King P.C., Newport News, Va., 1981-84, Buxton & Lasris P.C., Yorktown, Va., 1984-85; sole practice Newport News, 1985-89; pres. James A. Segall & Assocs., 1990-91, James A. Segall & Assocs., P.C., 1991-92, Segall & Moody, Newport News, 1992-98; ptnr. Krinick, Segall, Moody & Lewis, Newport News, Va., 1998—2004, Krinick & Segall, 2004—. Lectr. Hampton Roads Regional Acad. Criminal Justice, 1986-89. Bd. dirs. ct.-apptd. Spl. Adv. Program, Newport News, 1986-87; sec. Ruritan, 1985-87; Hampton-Newport News Cmty. Svcs. Bd., 1993-2002, treas., 1995-96, 99-2002, vice-chair, 1996-97, chair 1997-99; participant coop. office edn. program Newport News Pub. Schs., 1987-90; lectr. vol. programs 7th Dist. Ct. Svc. Unit, 1986-89; active City Newport News Cable TV Adv. Commn., 1990-93, Newport News Dem. City Com., 1990-91; bd. dirs. Rodef Sholom Temple, 1992-94, 2006-2010, United Jewish Cmty., Va. Peninsula, Inc., 1990-2010, chmn. spl. activities and fundraising com., 1990-91, chmn. bylaws com., 1992-93, 95-2006, campaign coun., 1995-2010, 2012-, cmty. rels. coun., 1995-98, 2010-, v.p. human svcs., 1998-2000, v.p. fin. and adminstrn., 2002-04, pres. elect, 2004-06, pres. 2006-08, chmn. exec. dir. search com., 2013-14; Sunday sch. tchr. Rodef Sholom Temple, 2001-04; bd. dirs. Newport News Bar Assn., 2011-, sec. 2012-. Mem. Newport News Bar Assn., Va. Trial Lawyers Assn., Va. Assn. Criminal Def. Lawyers, B'nai B'rith (pres. 1989-91). Jewish. Avocations: history, computers, philosophy. Office: Krinick & Segall 11848 Rock Landing Dr Ste 103 Newport News VA 23606-4427 Home: 70 Carriage Hill Dr Poquoson VA 23662 Business E-Mail: jsegall@peninsulalaw.com.

SEGALL, JOSHUA S., lawyer; b. Montgomery, Ala., 1979; BA, Brown U., 2001; JD, U. Ala., 2006. Law clk. for Hon. W. Keith Watkins US Dist Ct. (middle dist.) Ala.; of counsel Memory & Day, Montgomery. Founder Homegrown Ala. Democrat. Office: PO Box 4236 Montgomery AL 36103-4236 Office Phone: 334-265-7999.

SEGARS, KELLY SCOTT, SR., physician, banker; b. Red Bay, Ala., Mar. 11, 1930; s. Dock and Ora (Sims) S.; m. Martha Ann Thompson, oct. 3, 1952; children: kelly Scott, Jr., Mark Thompson, Leigh Ann. BS in Pharmacy, Auburn U., 1952; MD, U. Miss.-Jackson, 1959. Diplomate Am. Bd. Fam. Practice. Intern USPHS Hosp., Norfolk, Va., 1959-60; physician Segars Clinic, Iuka, Miss., 1960—. Founder. pres., chmn. First Am. Nat. Bank, Iuka, 1964—; pres. Segars Communications, Iuka, 1970—, S & G Cablevision, Iuka, 1978—; pres. Tri-State Savs. & Loan, 1963-64; chief med. staff Tishominga County Hosp., Iuka, 1968, 76, 82, dir. coronary care unit, 1970—; chmn. constrn. com. Kelly Segars Field, 1964, Iuka Mcpl. Library, 1971. Exec. coun. Boy Scouts Am., Tupelo, Miss., 1971—. 1st lt. U.S. Army, 1953-55. Decorated Army Commendation medal. Fellow Am. Acad. Family Physicians; mem. AMA, Miss. Med. Assn. (pres.), Flying Physicians assn., Ole Miss Med. Alumni, Rotary (paul Harris Fellowship). Republican. Methodist. Office Phone: 662-423-3656. Personal E-mail: ksegars@fanb.net, hillwinds@hotmail.com.*

SEGNER, EDMUND PETER, III, engineering professor, former natural gas company executive; b. Dallas, Oct. 23, 1953; s. Edmund Peter Jr. and Martha Fairfax (Smith) S.; m. Kathryn Louise Daily, July 10, 1976; children: Peter Michael, Christian James. BSCE, Rice U., 1976; MA in Econs., U. Houston, 1980. CPA, Tex. Acct. Touche Ross & Co., Houston, 1976-78; asst. v.p. planning United Gas Pipe Line Co., Houston, 1978-86; asst. v.p. rsch. Drexel Burnham Lambert, NYC, 1986-88; v.p. pub. and investor rels. Enron Corp., Houston, 1988-90; sr. v.p. pub. and gov. rels., investor Enron Corp, Houston, 1990-92, exec. v.p., chief staff, 1992-98; vice-chmn., chief of staff Enron Oil & Gas Co., 1997-99; pres., chief of staff EOG Resources, Inc., 1999—2007, prin. fin. officer, 2003—07. Prof. civil engring. Rice U., Houston, 1982-84, 97—, bd. dirs. Seahawk Drilling, Inc., 2009-11, Exterran Partners, L.P., 2009-, EOG, 1999-2007, Bill Barrett Corp., 2009-, Laredo Petroleum, 2011-, Midcoast Energy Ptnrs., 2014-. Bd. dirs. Zool. Soc. Houston, 1992-95, Greater Houston Partnership for Ednl. Excellence, 1991-93,; treas. Tex. Nature Conservancy, 1992-99, 2008-, vice-chmn., 1999-2001, chmn., 2001-03; chmn. Cmty. Ptnrs., 1993-95; trustee Houston Mus. Natural Sci., 1999-2004. Mem. River Oaks Country Club. Office: Rice University 6100 Main MS 318 Houston TX 77005-1827 Office Phone: 713-348-2381. Business E-Mail: ed.segner@rice.edu.

SEGUIN, TYLER, professional hockey player; b. Brampton, Ont., Canada, Jan. 31, 1992; s. Paul and Jackie Seguin. Center Plymouth Whalers (Ont. Hockey League), 2008—10, Boston Bruins, 2010—13, Dallas Stars, 2013—. Recipient Red Tilson Trophy, Ont. Hockey League, 2010; co-recipient Eddie Powers Meml. Trophy, 2010; named to NHL All-Star Game, 2012. Achievements include being the second overall draft pick in NHL entry draft, 2010; being a member of Stanley Cup Champion Boston Bruins, 2011. Office: Dallas Stars American Airlines Ctr 2500 Victory Ave Dallas TX 75201*

SEIFERT, KATHI P., printing company executive; b. Appleton, Wis., 1949; m. Steve Seifert; children: Erin, Andrew. BA, Valparaiso U., 1971. Various mktg. positions Procter & Gamble Co., Beatrice Foods, Fort Howard Paper Co.; sr. mng. dir. Brock Capital Group LLC, NYC; chmn. Pinnacle Perspectives LLC, Katapult LLC; product mgr., mktg. dir., Feminine Care Products Kimberly-Clark, Inc., Neenah, Wis., 1978—92, pres., Feminine Care Sector, 1992—94, group pres., N. Am. Consumer Products, 1994—95, group pres., N. Am. Personal Care Products, 1995—98, group pres., Personal Care Products, 1998—99, exec. v.p., group pres., Global Personal Care Products, 1999—2004. Bd. dirs. Eli Lilly and Co., Supervalu, Revlon, Appleton Papers, Lexmark Internat. Inc., 2006—. Bd. dirs. U.S. Fund for UNICEF, Fox Cities Performing Art Ctr., 1999—, chmn. of bd., 2003—; bd. dirs. Theda Health Care Group, Wis. Commn. in Arts Edn. Office: Pinnacle Perspectives 36 Jewelers Park Dr Ste 204 Neenah WI 54956-5904 also: Lexmark International Inc Bd Directors 740 W New Cir Rd Lexington KY 40550 Office Phone: 859-232-2000. E-mail: kpseifert@lexmark.com.

SEIFERT, RACHEL A., lawyer; b. New Brunswick, NJ, 1959; BA, U. Md., 1981, JD, 1985. Bar: Md. 1985. Atty. priv. practice, Dallas, 1985—92; v.p., assoc. gen. counsel Columbia/HCA, 1992—98; sr. v.p. to exec. v.p., sec., gen. counsel Community Health Systems, Inc., Brentwood, Tenn., 1998—. Bd. mem. Women Bus. Leaders of U.S. Health Care Industry Found. Mem.: ABA, Federation of Am. Hospitals, Am. Health Lawyers Assn. Office: Community Health Sys 4000 Meridian Blvd Franklin TN 37067*

SEIFERT, THOMAS J., electronics company executive; b. 1963; m. Gesine Seifert; children: Elena Seifert, Oliver Seifert, Philipp Seifert. Diploma in Bus. Adminstrn., U. Erlangen, Germany; B, MBA, Friedrich Alexander U.; M in Math. & Economics, Wayne State U. Exec. positions Altis Semiconductor; with Siemens AG (Corp. Mgmt. Group), 1990—93; dir., fin. and adminstrn. IBM Corp., Essonnes, France, 1993—96; with White Oak Semiconductor, 1996—2000; COO, CEO, Wireline Comm. Bus. Group Infineon Technologies AG, 2000—04, sr. v.p., gen. mgr., Wireline Bus. Group, 2001—06, group v.p., gen. mgr., Memory Products Group, 2004—06; COO Qimonda AG., 2006—09; interim CFO Qimonda AG, 2008, CFO, 2008—09; sr. v.p., CFO Advanced Micro Devices, Inc., Austin, 2009—, interim CEO, 2011. Bd. dirs. Inotera, Taiwan. Bd. dirs., Va. Commonwealth U. Sch. Engring. Office: Advanced Micro Devices Inc One AMD Pl Sunnyvale CA 94088-3453 also: 7171 Southwest Pkwy Austin TX 78735 Office Phone: 408-749-4000, 512-602-1000. Office Fax: 408-982-6164. Business E-Mail: thomas.seifert@amd.com.

SEIGENTHALER, JOHN MICHAEL, public relations executive, former newscaster; b. Nashville, Dec. 21, 1955; s. John Lawrence and Dolores (Watson) S.; m. Kerry Lynn Brock, Jan. 4, 1992. BA in Pub. Policy, Duke U., 1978. Reporter Nashville Tennesean, 1978-79; advance rep. Kennedy for Pres., Washington, 1979-80; writer WDCN-TV, Nashville, 1980; prodr. WNGE-TV, Nashville, 1980-81; reporter, anchor WSMV-TV, Nashville, 1981-90, KOMO-TV, Seattle, 1990—99; weekend anchor, NBC Nightly News WNBC-TV, NYC, 1999—2007; CEO SPR NY Seigenthaler Pub. Rels., Inc., NYC, 2008—. Reporter, producer documentaries: An Eye for An Eye, 1984 (ABA award), Reflections in Black and White, 1986 (Robert F. Kennedy Journalism award), Breaking Down the Barriers, 1990 (Pres.'s Com. on Employment for Disabled award); reporter, producer pub. affairs programs: Prison Riots, 1985 (Am. assn. TV Program Execs. award). Recipient 2 local Emmy awards, 1986. Mem. NATAS, Soc. Profl. Journalists. Roman Catholic. Avocations: tennis, skiing, water-skiing. Office: Seigenthaler Public Relations Inc 115 29th Ave Nashville TN 37212

SEIGLER, RUTH QUEEN, college nursing administrator, educator, consultant; b. Conway, SC, July 31, 1942; d. Charles Isaac and Berneta Mae (Weaks) Queen; m. Rallie Marshall Seigler, Sept. 1, 1963; children: Rallie Marshall Jr., Scot Monroe. ADN, Lander Coll., 1962; BSN, U. S.C., 1964, M of Nursing, 1980. Pub. health nurse Richland County Health Dept., Columbia, SC, 1964—66; dir. nurses Columbia Area Mental Health Ctr., 1966—69; program nurse specialist Midlands Health Dist., 1969—72; discharge planner Richland Meml. Hosp., 1972—73, clin. dir., 1973—75; exec. dir. S.C. State Bd. Nursing, 1976—83; v.p. nursing dept. Self Meml. Hosp., Greenwood, SC, 1983—86; exec. dir. S.C. Commn. on Aging, Columbia, 1986—95; asst. dean Coll. Nursing U. S.C., Columbia, 1995—96, assoc. clin. prof., 1996—. Cons. intergenerational family studies, 1999—; dir. Cockcroft Leadership Program for Nurse Execs., 2002—. Ctr. for Nursing Leadership, 2004-05, sr. cons., 2005—; bd. dirs. Queen Gas Co., Barnwell, SC; nurse cons. Creative Nursing Mgmt., Mpls., 1984—. Advisor: The Role of Cmty. Mental Health Nurse, 1971. Elder Spring Valley Presbyn. Ch., 2001—04, 2010—; moderator Trinity Presbytery, 2003—. Recipient Disting. Alumni award Lander Coll., 1978, Career Woman Recognition award Columbia YWCA, 1980, William S. Hall award SC Assn. Residential Care Homes, 1988, U. SC Coll. Nursing Disting. Alumni award, 1993, award for excellence SC League for Nursing, 1995, Svc. Recognition award SC AARP, 1995; named one of Ten Women of Achievement, SC March of Dimes, 1987, hon. fellow AVC Leadership, 2002, Excellence in Leadership award, 2004, Ordie P. Taylor Humanitarian award, 2005, Palmetto Gold award Top 100 Nurses in SC, 2006, Spirit of Giving award U. SC Coll Nursing Partnership Bd., 2011. Mem. ANA, APHA, SC Nurses Assn. (sec. 1965-68, bd. dirs. 1986-88, Excellence award 1984, Recognition award 1984), SC Hosp. Assn., SC Gerontol. Soc., SC Nurses Found., SC Healthy People 2000 (vice chair), Partnership for Older South Carolinians (founder, chair bd. dirs.), Columbia Luncheon Club (pres. 1997-98), SC Fedn. Older Ams., Evening Mission Action Group, Bd. Nursing Home Examiners, Pilot Club, Inc. (pres. 1988-89, 97-98), Vols. of Am.-Carolinas (bd. dirs., chair, 1998-00, elder, 1999-01, 2010-), Rotary Internat., Sigma Theta Tau, Beta Sigma Phi (pres. chpt. 1997-98, 2011-12). Presbyterian. Avocations: gardening, travel. Home: 6 Beaver Dam Ct Columbia SC 29223-3100 Office: University SC Coll Nursing Office of Dean Columbia SC 29208-0001

SEILER, CHARLOTTE WOODY, retired education educator; b. Thorntown, Ind., Jan. 20, 1915; d. Clark and Lois Merle (Long) Woody; m. Wallace Urban Seiler, Oct. 10, 1942 (dec. Aug. 2002); children: Patricia Anne Seiler, Janet Alice Seiler Sawyer. AA, Ind. State U., 1933; AB, U. Mich., 1941; MA, Ctrl. Mich. U., 1968. Tchr. elem. schs., Whitestown, Ind., 1933-34, Thorntown, 1934-37, Kokomo, Ind., 1937-40, Ann Arbor, Mich., 1941-44, Willow Run, Mich., 1944-46; instr. English divsn. Delta Coll., University Center, Mich., 1964-69, asst. prof., 1969-77; ret., 1977. Organizer, dir. Delta Coll. Puppeteers, 1972—77. Mem. Friends of Grace A. Dow Meml. Libr., 1974-2000, treas., 1974-75, 77-79, corr. sec., 1975-77; leader Sr. Ctr. Humanities program Midland (Mich.) Sr. Ctr., 1977-94. Fellow AAUW; mem. Mich. Libr. Assn., Harbor Cove Civic Assn., Pi Lambda Theta, Chi Omega. Presbyterian. Home: 9000 Ibis Way # 116 Venice FL 34292-3084

SEILER, JACK P., mayor, Ft. Lauderdale, Florida, prosecutor; b. Fort Collins, Colo., May 27, 1963; m. Susan Rimes; children: Marianna, Jacqueline, Preston, Susanne. BA in Bus. Adminstrn., U. Notre Dame, 1985; JD, U. Miami, 1988. Bar: DC 1988, Fla. Supreme Ct. 1988, US Dist. Ct. (so. Fla. dist.) 1989. Atty. Seiler, Sautter, Zaden, Rimes & Weihe; councilman City of Wilton Manors, Fla., 1993—96, vice mayor, 1996—98, mayor, 1998—2000; mem. Fla. House of Reps. from Dist. 92, Ft. Lauderdale, 2000—06; mayor City of Ft. Lauderdale, 2009—. Com. mem. Policy and Budget, Rules and Calendar, Constitution and Civil Law, Standards of Official Conduct, 2007—08; chmn. Broward Legislative Delegation, 2007—08; gen. counsel Promenade in the Park/Beaux Arts of Ft. Lauderdale Mus. Art, Inc.; guardian ad litem 17th Dist. Cir. Ct. Broward County. Former chmn. City of Wilton Manors Bd. of Adjustments and Appeals, Island City Found. Inc.; former mem. Wilton Manors Visioning Com. and Stakeholders Forum, Ft. Lauderdale High Sch. Pub. Affairs Cluster Adv. Bd., Waiver Review Com. Sch. Bd. of Broward County; mem. Orange Bowl Com., 1994—, Kids in Distress Broward Adv. Coun., Downtown Coun. Steering Com., Marine Industries of South Fla. Manatee Pub. Awareness Team, 2001—02; chmn. Orange Bowl Found.; bd. dirs. Brian Piccolo Chpt. Nat. Football Found. and Coll. Hall Fame Inc., 1988—; bd. dirs. Orange Bowl Com., 1999—; bd. trustees Ft. Lauderdale Mus. Discovery & Sci.; dir. PACE Ctr. for Girls; dir. & adv. Providence Pl. Shelter for Homeless Women and Children, 1998—; lector St. John the Bapt. Cath. Ch. Mem.: Wilton Manors Bus. Assn. (dir.), Broward County Bar Assn. (bench & bar com., chmn. lawyer referral com., profl. responsibility com.), Wilton Manors Elem. PTA, Notre Dame Club Greater Ft. Lauderdale (bd. dirs. 1989—98), Dem. Club (Pompano, Tri-Cities, North Broward, Pine Island & Ft. Lauderdale), St. Thomas More Soc. (bd. dirs.). Democrat. Roman Catholic. Avocations: coaching, golf, fishing. Office: 100 N Andrews Ave Fort Lauderdale FL 33301 Office Phone: 954-828-5000.*

SEITZ, KARL RAYMOND, editor; b. Corpus Christi, Tex., Sept. 26, 1943; s. Kerlin McCullough and Martha Elisabeth (Tillman) S.; m. Patricia Jean Floyd, June 13, 1970; 1 child, Lee Kerlin. BA, Birmingham So. Coll., 1970. Copy editor Birmingham (Ala.) Post-Herald, 1967-70, asst. news editor, 1970-73, chief editorial writer, 1973-78, editor editorial page, 1978—2005. Dir. Birmingham Post-Birmingham Typographical Union Pension Plan, 1983-90, chmn., 1986-90; v.p. Goodfellow Fund, Inc., Birmingham, 1986—2005. Active exec. in residence Birmingham So. Coll., 1987, Leadership Birmingham, 1986—, mem. mem.'s coun., 1998—2001. With USN, 1961—64. Mem. Assn. Opinion Journalists, Acad. Polit. Sci. Home: 1212 30th Street S Birmingham AL 35205-1910 E-mail: kseitz@earthlink.net.

SEITZ, KIMBERLY, audit executive; BSBA in Acctg., U. Ala., Huntsville, 1988; MPA in Acctg., Miss. State U., Starkville, 1996. Cert. internal auditor, info. systems auditor. Tech. asst. Utility Svc. Corp.; experienced mgr. Arthur Andersen LLP; sr. mgr. Protiviti Inc.; dir. internal controls Eagle Global Logistics; v.p. internal audit Helix Energy Solutions Group, Inc. Office: Helix Energy Solutions Group Inc 400 N Sam Houston Pky E Ste 400 Houston TX 77060-3500 Office Phone: 281-618-0400. Office Fax: 281-618-0501. Business E-Mail: kseitz@helixesg.com.

SEITZ, MARK JOSEPH, bishop; b. Milw., Wis., Jan. 10, 1954; Attended, Holy Trinity Sem., Irving, Tex.; BA, Univ. Dallas, 1976, MDiv, 1980, MA, 1982; MA in liturgical studies, St. John's Univ., Collegeville, Minn., 1985. Ordained priest Diocese of Dallas, Tex., 1980; parochial vicar Good Shepherd parish, Garland, Tex., 1980—84; adj. prof. theology Univ. Dallas, 1985—; assoc spiritual dir. & dir. of liturgy Holy Trinity Sem., Irving, Tex., 1986—87, vice rector, dir. liturgy, 1987—93; pastor St. Joseph parish, Waxahachie, Tex., 1993—2002, St. Rita parish, Dallas, 2003—; ordained bishop, 2010; aux. bishop Diocese of Dallas, 2010—. Roman Catholic. Office: Diocese of Dallas 3725 Blackburn St PO Box 190507 Dallas TX 75219 Office Phone: 214-528-2240. Office Fax: 214-528-0287.

SEITZ, PATRICIA ANN, federal judge; b. Washington, Sept. 2, 1946; d. Richard J. and Bettie Seitz; m. Alan Graham Greer, Aug. 14, 1981. BA in History cum laude, Kans. State U., 1968; JD, Georgetown U., 1973. Bar: Fla. 1973, D.C. 1975, U.S. Dist. Ct. (no., mid., so. dists., trial bar) Fla., U.S. Ct. Appeals (5th and 11th cirs.), U.S. Supreme Ct. Reporter Dallas Times Herald, Washington, 1970-73; law clk. to Hon. Charles R. Richey US Dist. Ct., Washington, 1973-74; assoc. Steel, Hector & Davis, Miami, Fla., 1974-79, ptnr., 1980-96; dir. office legal counsel Office of Nat. Drug Control Policy, Exec. Office of Pres., Washington, 1996-97; judge US Dist. Ct. (so. dist.) Fla., Miami, 1998—. Adj. faculty U. Miami Law Sch., Coral Gables, Fla., 1984-88; faculty Nat. Inst. Trial Advocacy, Boulder, Colo., 1982, 83, 95, Chapel Hill, N.C., 1984, 87. Fla. region, 1989; lectr. in field. Contbr. numerous articles to law jours. Mem. Dade Munroe Mental Health Bd., Miami, 1982-84, United Way of Greater Miami comty. devel. com., 1984-87; chmn. family abuse task force United Way of Greater Miami, 1986; chmn. devel. com. Miami City Ballet, 1986-87, bd. dirs., 1986-90. Fellow Am. Bar Found., Am. Bd. Trial Advocacy, Internat. Soc. Barristers; mem. ABA (chmn. various coms. 1979-85, Ho. Dels. 1992-96), Am. Arbitration Assn. (nat. bd. dirs. 1995-97, complex case panel arbitrator), The Fla. Bar (bd. govs. young lawyer divsn. 1981-82, bd. govs. 1986-92, pres. 1993-94, bd. cert. civil trial), Fla. Assn. Women Lawyers, Dade County Bar Assn. (pub. interest law bank). Roman Catholic. Avocations: travel, art. Office: US Dist Ct Ferguson US Courthouse 400 N Miami Ave Rm 11-4 Miami FL 33128 Office Phone: 305-523-5530.

SELBY, JOHN BAYNE, SR., retired radiologist, medical educator; b. Cheyenne, Wyo., Feb. 17, 1924; s. John Edwin Selby and Caroline Lansdale Duckett; m. Jane Claire Dentry, June 11, 1950 (dec. Mar. 3, 2011); children: John Bayne Jr., Henry Gordon, Rebecca Jane. BS, U. Tenn., 1948, MD, 1946; MS in Medicine, U. Minn., 1957. Diplomate Am. Bd. Internal Medicine, Am. Bd. Nuc. Medicine. Asst. in pathology Johns Hopkins U., Balt., 1950—51; intern Evanston (Ill.) Hosp., 1947—48; resident Garfield Hosp., Washington, 1948—50; fellow in pathology Johns Hopkins U., Balt., 1950—51, Mayo Clinic, Rochester, Minn., fellow in medicine, 1954—57, asst. staff mem., 1957; assoc. prof. medicine U. Ky., Lexington, 1958—75; chief nuc. medicine VA Hosp., Lexington, 1966—75, Charleston, SC, 1975—89; prof. radiology Med. U. SC, Charleston, 1995—2000, emeritus prof. radiology, 2001—. Mem. editl. bd. Clin. Nuc. Medicine, Phila., 1985—2005, Jour. SC Med. Assn., Columbia, 2000—06. Author: Self Assessment Nuclear Medicine, 1977, 1981, Mission in Space, 1994. Mem. Med. Discipline Commn., SC, 1985—88; pres. Ky. Diabetes Assn., Lexington, 1968—69; bd. dirs. Sch. Applied Radiol. Sci., Med. U. SC, Charleston, 1984—86. Capt. US Army, 1952—54, Korea, col. USAR, 1956—74. Fellow: ACP; mem.: Soc. Nuc. Medicine, Endocrine Soc., Alpha Omega Alpha. Avocation: astronomy. Home: 2602 Atlantic Ave Sullivans Island SC 29482 Personal E-mail: selbysr2@aol.com.

SELIG, WILLIAM GEORGE, academic administrator; b. Prince Rupert, BC, Can., Sept. 25, 1938; s. George Oliver Selig and Minerva Junuetta (Brand) Goodale; m. Judith Margaret Sprague, June 20, 1964; children: Cheryl, Cynthia. BA, Cen. Washington State Coll., 1961, MA, 1968; CAGS, U. Mass., 1972, EdD, 1973. Tchr. Ketchikan Alaska HS, 1961—62, Sharon (Mass.) High Sch., 1963-64, Hydaburg (Alaska) Grade Sch., 1964-65, W. Puyallup (Wash.) Jr. High Sch., 1966-69; dir. spl. edn. Northampton (Mass.) Schs., 1969-73, 1974-76; asst. prof. Westfield (Mass.) State Coll., 1973; dir. pupil svcs. Longmeadow (Mass.) Pub. Schs., 1976-80; prof. Regent U., Virginia Beach, Va., 1980-83, dean, prof., 1984-89, provost, 1989-2000; Disting. prof. ednl. leadership, 2000—. Bd. dirs. Set Net, Virginia Beach; pres. Motivational Teaching Systems, Inc.; spl. edn. adv. bd. dirs. Virginia Beach Pub. Schs.; bd. trustees Klingberg Family Ctrs., New Britain, Conn., 1991—2000. Author: Training for Triumph, 1984, Loving Our Differences, 1989, Handbook of Individualized Strategies for Classroom Discipline, 1995, Handbook of Individualized Strategies for Building Resilience in At Risk Students, 2005; contbr. chpt. to book. Episcopalian. Avocations: skiing, tennis. Office: Regent University 1000 Regent University Dr Virginia Beach VA 23464-9800 Office Phone: 757-352-4137. Business E-Mail: georsel@regent.edu.

SELIGER, KEL, state legislator; b. Amarillo, Tex. m. Nancy Seliger; children: Jonathan, Matthew. Grad., Dartmouth Coll., Hanover, NH. Lic. comml. pilot, flight instr. Former mem. Amarillo City Commn., Amarillo Civil Svc. Commn.; former mayor City of Amarillo, 1993—2001; mem. Tex. Alcoholic Beverage Commn., 2002; co-owner, v.p. Lake Steel, Inc.; mem. Dist. 31 Tex. State Senate, 2004—. Mem.: NRA, Tex. Farm Bur., Harley-Davidson Owners Group. Republican. Office: 410 S Taylor St Ste 1600 PO Box 9155 Amarillo TX 79101 also: Capitol Extension Room E1.606 State Capitol PO Box 12068 Capitol Station Austin TX 78711 Mailing: PO Box 9155 Amarillo TX 79105 Office: 401 Austin Ste 101 Big Spring TX 79720 also: 6 Desta Dr Ste 3360 Midland TX 79705 also: 4840 E University Ste 205 Odessa TX 79762 Office Phone: 806-374-8994, 432-268-9909, 432-620-0436, 432-550-7476. Office Fax: 512-463-0131.

SELIGSON, MITCHELL A., political science educator; b. Hempstead, NY, Nov. 12, 1945; m. Susan Berk, June 18, 1967; 1 child, Amber Lara. BA cum laude, Bklyn. Coll., 1967; MA, U. Fla., 1968; PhD, U. Pitts., 1974. Vol. U.S. Peace Corps, Costa Rica, 1968-70; asst. prof./assoc. prof. U. Ariz., Tucson, 1974-85; prof. U. Pitts., 1986-93, Daniel H. Wallace prof. polit. sci., 1994—2004, dir. Latin Am. studies, 1986-92, rsch. prof., 1992—2004; Centennial prof. polit. sci. Vanderbilt U., Nashville, 2004—. Dir. L.Am. pub. opinion project; cons. to World Bank, UN Devel. Program, US AID, Inter-Am. Devel. Bank, Guatemala, Honduras, Nicaragua, Costa Rica, Colombia, Dominican Republic, Mex., Ecuador, Jamaica, Panama, El Salvador, Peru, Bolivia, Paraguay, 1980—. Author, editor: Peasants of Costa Rica and the Development of Agrarian Capitalism, 1980, The Gap Between Rich and Poor, 1984, Authoritarians and Democrats, 1987, Elections and Democracy in Central America, 1989, rev. edit. 1995, Development and Underdevelopment, 1993, The Political Economy of Global Inequality, 2003, The Legitimacy Puzzle in Latin America. Fulbright fellow, Costa Rica, 1986, Rockefeller Found. fellow, 1985-86; grantee Social Sci. Rsch. Coun., Ford Found., NSF, Mellon Found., Heinz Endowment. Mem. Am. Polit. Sci. Assn., Latin Am. Studies Assn. (chmn. fin. com. 1991). Office: Vanderbilt U Dept Polit Sci Nashville TN 37235 Office Phone: 615-322-6938. Business E-Mail: m.seligson@vanderbilt.edu.

SELIN, IVAN, entrepreneur; b. NYC, Mar. 11, 1937; s. Saul and Freda (Kuhlman) Selin; m. Nina Kallet, June 8, 1957; children: Douglas, Jessica. BE, Yale U., 1957, ME, 1958, PhD, 1960; DSc, U. Paris, 1962. Rsch. engr. Rand Corp., Santa Monica, Calif., 1960-65; sys. analyst Dept. Def., Washington, 1965-67, dep. asst. sec. def., 1967-69, acting asst. sec. for systems analysis, 1969-70; founder, chmn. bd. Am. Mgmt. Systems, Inc., Arlington, Va., 1970-89; undersec. state Dept. State, Washington, 1989-91; chmn. Nuc. Regulatory Commn., Washington, 1991—95; chmn., CEO Phoenix Internat., Washington, 1995—; chmn. Enumerale Solutions, Inc., 1998—. Lectr. UCLA, 1961-63; chmn. mil. econ. adv. panel to CIA, 1978-89; bd. dirs. BZL Biologics, Inc. Author: Detection Theory, 1964; contbr. articles to profl. jours. Pres. Corp. Against Drug Abuse, 1988-95; bd. dirs., gov. UN Assn. U.S., 1979-89; exec. com. Greater Washington Research Ctr., Fed. City Council; trustee Asia Soc., 1996-98; chmn., bd. dirs. Smithsonian Nat. Mus. of Am. History, 1996—, Yale U. Coun., 2000—. Recipient Disting. Civilian Svc. medal, 1970, Disting. Svc. medal Sec. of State, 1991; Fulbright scholar, 1959-61; Ford Found. grantee, 1952-54. Mem. IEEE (editor Trans. on Info. Theory 1960-65), Coun. Fgn. Rels., Yale Club, Sigma Xi, Tau Beta Pi. Home: 1455 Ocean Dr Apt 1602 Miami Beach FL 33139-4141 Office Phone: 202-337-2337. Business E-Mail: ixs@phnx-intl.com.

SELINGER, JERRY ROBIN, lawyer; b. Peekskill, NY, Nov. 3, 1947; s. Philip R. and Helen D. (Klein) S.; m. Barbara D. Wax, Aug. 2, 1969; children: Elise, Scott. BS in Engring. Sci., SUNY, Buffalo, 1969; MS, Columbia U., 1971; JD, George Washington U., 1975. Bar: Md. 1975, D.C. 1976, U.S. Ct. Appeals (fed. cir.) 1977, U.S. Supreme Ct. 1978, Tex. 1980, U.S. Ct. Appeals (5th cir.) 1981, U.S. Ct. Appeals (3d cir.) 1982. Atty. Arent, Fox, Kintner, Plotkin & Kahn, Washington, 1975-79, Richards, Harris & Medlock, Dallas, 1979-82; mem., dir. Baker, Mills & Glast, Dallas, 1982-90; ptnr. Vinson & Elkins LLP, Dallas, 1990-97; 1997shareholder Jenkens & Gilchrist, Dallas, 1997—2005; ptnr. Morgan Lewis & Bockius LLP, Dallas, 2005—08, Patterson & Sheridan LLP, Dallas, 2008—. Contbr. articles to profl. jours. Bd. trustees Dallas Bar Found., 2001—08. Fellow Dallas Bar (chair 2007); mem. ABA, Tex. Bar Assn. (chair intellectual property law sect. 1996-97, bd. dirs. 1998-01), Dallas Bar Assn. (bd. dirs. 1995-96), Tex. Young Lawyers Assn. (bd. dirs. 1984-86, Pres. award 1986), Am. Intellectual Property Law Assn. (bd. dirs. 2002-05, project award 2008), Dallas Assn. Young Lawyers (sec. 1983, treas. 1984), Order of Coif, Phi Delta Phi. Home: 10414 Woodford Dr Dallas TX 75229-6317 Office: Patterson & Sheridan LLP 1700 Pacific Ste 2650 Dallas TX 75201 Office Phone: 214-272-0957. Business E-Mail: jselinger@pattersonsheridan.com.

SELKIRK, JAMES KIRKWOOD, retired biochemist; b. NYC, Dec. 3, 1938; s. James Kirkwood and Doris (Schuler) S.; m. Carole Ann Bozzone, Sept. 16, 1961; children: James Kirkwood, David Edward. BS in Biochemistry, Coll. Environ. Sci. and Forestry, Syracuse U., NY, 1964; BS in Environ. Sci., Chemistry, Syracuse U., NY, 1964; PhD in Biochemistry, Syracuse U. Upstate Med. Ctr., Syracuse, 1969. Postdoctoral fellow McArdle Lab. Cancer Rsch., U. Wis., Madison, 1969-72; staff fellow Nat. Cancer Inst., NIH, Bethesda, Md., 1972-74, sr. staff fellow, 1974-75; sr. staff scientist unit leader chem. carcinogenesis biology divsn. Oak Ridge (Tenn.) Nat. Lab., 1975-85; chief carcinogenesis and toxicology evaluation br. nat. toxicology program Nat. Inst. Environ. Health Scis., 1985-89, assoc. dir. divsn. toxicology rsch. and testing, 1989-92, chief carcinogen mechanism group Lab. Molecular Carcinogenesis, 1992—97; spl. asst. to sci. dir. for technology devel. Nat. Inst. Evniron. Health Scis., 1997-2000; deputy dir. Nat. Ctr. Toxicogenomics, 2000—09; adj. prof. Oak Ridge Biomed. Grad. Sch., U. Tenn., 1975-85; mem. breast cancer task force NIH, 1979-82; mem. com. on pyrenes and analogs NAS, 1981-83; chmn. Interagy. Testing Commn., 1986-90. Author rsch. articles, chpts. in books; mem. editl. bd. Carcinogenesis Jour., 1984-87, 91-93, Cancer Rsch., 1981-86, Environ. Health Perspectives, 1993-98, contbg. editor, 2003—. Mem. Orange County Planning Bd., 1997—; chmn. Weaver Dairy Precinct, Dem. Party Orange County, 1996-99. With AUS, 1959-61. With chem. corps US Army, 1959—60. Recipient U.S. Interagy. Testing Com. Exemplary Svc. award, 1992. Mem. Am. Cancer Soc. (carcinogenesis study sect. 1975-78, 92-96). Avocations: scuba diving, coin collecting/numismatics, marksmanship. Home: 30119 Settle Dr Chapel Hill NC 27517 Personal E-mail: jselkirk@nc.rr.com.

SELL, CLAY (JEFFREY CLAY SELL), energy company executive, former federal agency administrator; b. 1967; s. George and Judy Sell; m. Alisa M. Sell; children: Jack, Robert, Mary Margaret. BS in Bus. Adminstrn., Tex. Tech. U., 1989; JD, U. Tex. Staff mem. to Rep. Mac Thornberry US House of Representatives, Washington, 1995—97, adminstrv. asst., 1997—99; majority clk. & staff dir. for energy & water sub com. of the Senate Com. on Appropriations US Senate Appropriations Com. Energy & Water Sub Com., Washington, 2000—03; spl. asst. to the Pres. for econ. policy The White House, Washington, 2003—04, spl. asst. to Pres. for legis. affairs, 2004—05; dep. sec. US Dept. Energy, Washington, 2005—08; pres. Hunt Energy Horizons, LLC, Dallas, 2008—; sr. v.p. Hunt Oil Co., Dallas, 2008—. Office: Hunt Energy Horizons LLC 1900 N Akard St Dallas TX 75201 Office Phone: 214-978-8689. Office Fax: 214-978-8671.

SELLERS, BAKARI T., state legislator; b. Sept. 18, 1984; BA, Morehouse Coll., Atlanta, 2005; JD, U. SC Sch. Law, 2008. Congl. intern to congressman Jim Clyburn, 2003; mayoral intern to Shirley Franklin, 2004; mem. Dist. 90 SC House of Reps., 2007—. Bd. trustees Morehouse Coll., 2004—05. Named one of The Politics 40

Under 40, TIME Mag., 2010; named to Power 150, Ebony Mag., 2008. Democrat. Office: 314A Blatt Bldg Columbia SC 29201 Home Phone: 803-793-3637; Office Phone: 803-734-3003. Business E-Mail: SellersB@schouse.org.

SELLERS, PIERS J., astronaut; b. Crowborough, Sussex, Eng., Apr. 11, 1955; married; 2 children. BS in Ecol. Sci., U. Edinburgh, Scotland, 1976; PhD in Biometeorology, Leeds U., Eng., 1981. Astronaut, mission specialist NASA, Johnson Space Ctr., Houston, 1996—. Mem. flight team STS-112 Mission (Atlantis), 2002; crew mem. STS-121 Mission (Discovery), a return-to-flight test mission and assembly flight to the Internat. Space Station, 2006; mission specialist STS-132 Mission (Atlantis)-Last Flight for Atlantis, 2010. Recipient Arthur Fleming award, 1995. Fellow: Am. Meteorology Soc. (Houghton award 1997), Am. Geophys. Union. Achievements include research in how the earth's biosphere and atmosphere interact, computer modeling of climate system, satellite remote sensing studies; field work utilizing aircraft, satellites and ground teams in Kansas, Russia, Africa, Canada and Brazil. Office: Astronaut Office/CB NASA Johnson Space Ctr Houston TX 77058

SELVY, BARBARA, dance instructor; b. Little Rock, Jan. 20, 1938; d. James Oliver and Irene Balmat Banks; m. Franklin Delano Selvy, Apr. 15, 1959; children: Lisa Selvy Yeargin, Valerie Selvy Miros, Lauren Kroll, Franklin Michael, Madison Banks Selvy. Student, U. Ctrl. Ark., Conway, 1955—57. Founder, dir. Carolina Ballet Theater, Greenville, SC, 1973—; pres. Dance Arts Inc. and Incentives, Inc. Mem. adv. bd. dirs. Met. Arts Coun., and S.C. Govs. Sch., St. Marys Cath. Sch. Appeared in numerous TV commls., on Goodson-Toddman game show Play Your Hunch, 1958-59; toured Far East with TV show Hit Parade, 1958; named Miss Ark., 1956, Mrs. S.C., 1981; dir. and staged Mrs. Va., Mrs. N.C., Mrs. S.C. pageants; choreographed Little Theater prodns., Furman U. Opera. Mem. Nat. Rep. Congl. Com., 2003, Pres. Bush Small Bus. Adv. Coun., 2003; Thrift Jhoplon adv. bd. com. mem. St. Francis Cath. Sch. Mem. So. Assn. Dance Masters (ballet adviser, regional dir.), Dance Educators Am., Dance Masters of Am., Profl. Dance Tchrs. Home: 206 Honey Horn Dr Simpsonville SC 29681-5814 Personal E-mail: barbarabselvy@gmail.com.

SELWYN, DONALD, retired engineering administrator, researcher, inventor, educator; b. NYC, Jan. 31, 1936; s. Gerald Selwyn and Ethel (Waxman) Selwyn) Moss; m. Delia Nemec, Mar. 11, 1956 (div. Mar. 1983); children: Laurie, Gerald, Marcia; m. Myra Rowman Markoff, Mar. 17, 1986 BA, Thomas A. Edison Coll. N.J., 1977. Svc. engr. Bendix Aviation, Teterboro, NJ, 1956-59; svc. mgr. Bogue Electric Mfg. Co., Paterson, NJ, 1959; proposal engr. advanced design group Curtiss-Wright Corp., East Paterson, NJ, 1960-64; ind. bioengr., rehab. engring. cons. NYC, 1964-67; pres. bd. trustees, exec. tech. and tng. dir. Nat. Inst. for Rehab. Engring., Hewitt, NJ, 1967—. Cons. N.Y. State Office Vocat. Rehab., 1964—, Pres.'s Com. on Employment of Handicapped, 1966—, bus. and industry and for Am. with Disabilities Act compliance, also numerous state rehab. agys., health depts., vol. groups, agys. for handicapped in fgn. countries; cons., trainer computer applications. Contbr. articles on amateur radio, rehab. of severely and totally disabled to profl., gen. mags. Trustee Nat. Inst. for Rehab. Engring., Rehab. Research Center Trust. Decorated Knight of Malta; recipient Humanitarian award U.S. Ho. of Reps., 1972, Bicentennial Pub. Service award, 1975. Mem. Am. Acad. Consultants, I.E.E.E. (sr.), Soc. Tech. Writers and Pubs. (sr.), Nat. Rehab. Assn., N.Y. Acad. Scis., Mensa. Achievements include being the developer or co-developer field-expander glasses for hemianopsia, tunnel and monocular vision, electronic speech clarifiers, electronically guided wheelchairs, off-road vehicles and cars for quadriplegics, others; patentee indsl., mil. and handicapped rehab. inventions; expert, cons. on handicapped employment, handicapped product safety including design, manufacture, labelling and user instrnl. material, 1990—. Home Phone: 479-885-0840. Personal E-mail: dons@warwick.net. E-mail: nire@warwick.net.

SELZ, NAN, museum director; BA in English, Vassar Coll., Poughkeepsie, NY, 1961; MA in English, U. Ark., Fayetteville, 1967. Cert. fund raising exec. 1990. Exec. dir. ACLU, Ark., 1975—78, Pulaski County Coun. on Aging, Inc., 1978—85, Ark. Sesquicentennial Commn., Inc., 1985—86, Mus. of Discovery, 2004—; dir., devel. Ark. Easter Seal Soc., Inc., 1986—88; pres. Arthritis Found., Ariz., 1988—92, St. Vincent Found., 1992—2004. Mem. women's health adv. bd. St. Vincent Ctr. for Women and Children, 1999—2003; mem. Ark. steering com. Leave a Legacy, 2001—03; bd. dirs. Susan G. Komen Found., 1999—2004. Named an Outstanding Ark. Fund Raising Exec., 1995; named one of Top 100 Women in Ark., 1996—98. Mem.: Nat. Soc. Fund Raising Execs. (pres. Ark. chpt. 1991), Am. Assn. Mus., Aesthetic Club. Office: Mus of Discovery 500 President Clinton Ave Ste 150 Little Rock AR 72201 Office Phone: 501-396-7050 ext. 207. Business E-Mail: nselz@amod.org.

SEMIN, ALEXANDER, professional hockey player; b. Krasnojarsk, Russia, Mar. 3, 1984; Left wing Washington Capitals, 2003—04, 2006—12, HC Lada Togliatti, Russia, 2004—06; right wing Carolina Hurricanes, 2012—. Mem. Team Russia, World Championships, 2005, 2006, 2008, Team Russia, Olympic Games, Vancouver, 2010. Office: Carolina Hurricanes RBC Center 2 1400 Edwards Mill Rd Raleigh NC 27607

SEMRAU, SUE, women's college basketball coach; b. Seattle; Attended, U. Pugent Sound; BS in Comms., U. Calif., San Diego, 1985; MS in Athletic Adminstrn., U. So. Calif., 1988. Pub. rels. dir. Seattle Storm, 1985—86; asst. basketball coach Santa Monica HS, 1986-87; pub. rels. and promotions dir. LA Heat, 1986-87; head women's basketball coach, asst. athletic dir. Occidental Coll., LA, 1987-91; asst. coach No. Ill. U., 1991-93; top asst. coach, recruiting coord. U. Wis., 1993-96; head coach women's basketball Fla. State U., 1997—. Head coach coll. alumni Athletes in Action Spring Australian Tour, 1997; bd. dirs. Women's Basketball Coaches Assn. Office: Fla State Athletic PO Box 2195 Tallahassee FL 32316-2195

SENNEMA, DAVID CARL, arts consultant; b. Grand Rapids, Mich., July 6, 1934; s. Carl Edward and Alice Bertha (Bieri) S.; m. Martha Amanda Dixon, Feb. 22, 1958; children: Daniel Ross, Julia Kathryn, Alice Dixon. BA, Albion Coll., 1956. Mgr. Columbia Music Festival Assn., 1964-67; exec. dir. S.C. Arts Commn., Columbia, 1967-70; assoc. dir. Fed.-State Partnership and Spl. Projects program Nat. Endowment for the Arts, Washington, 1971-73; prof. arts adminstrn., dir. cmty. arts mgmt. program Sangamon State U., Springfield, Ill., 1973-76; dir. SC State Mus., Columbia, 1976-85; bus. mgr. Palmetto Mastersingers, 1988—96; cons. in field, 1997—. Author (short story) Harley Takes a Chance, 2009; co-author: Columbia, S.C. A Postcard History, 1997. Mem. adv. panel Nat. Endowment for the Arts Music, 1968-70; chmn. Springfield Arts Commn., 1975-76, founding music dir. Columbia chpt. SPEBSQSA. Served with US Army, 1957—58. Recipient Verner Lifetime Achievement award, 2006, Short Story Winner, SC Fiction Project, 2009, Disting. Alumni award, Albion Coll., Mich., 2011; named to Order of Palmetto, SC, 1986. Mem. Rotary. Avocations: singing, writing, woodworking, genealogy. Office Phone: 803-782-3581. Personal E-mail: dsennema@att.net.

SENZEL, ALAN JOSEPH, chemist, consultant, music critic; b. LA, May 26, 1945; s. Bernard and Esther Mildred (Shykin) s.; m. Phyllis Sharon Abt, June 22, 1969; children: Richard Steven, Lisa Beth. BS in Chemistry, Calif. State U., Long Beach, 1967; MS, UCLA, 1969, PhD, 1970. Assoc. editor Am. Chem. Soc., Washington, 1970-74; methods editor Assn. Ofcl. Analytical Chemists, Washington, 1974-78; info. dir. Chemistry Industry Inst. Toxicology, Research Triangle Park, NC, 1978-79; pvt. cons. Raleigh, NC, 1978—. Sr. tech. writer Cardinal Health, Morrisville, N.C., 2002-2004; music critic Raleigh News and Observer, 1982-90, Spectator Mag., 1990-94; dep. mgr. Environ. Sys. Group, Environ. Resources Mgmt. Inc., Exton, Pa., 1988; project scientist Agrl. divsn. Residu Chem. dept. CIBA-GEIGY Corp., Greensboro, N.C., 1989-93; analytical contract lab. mgr. Entropy, Inc., 1995-96. Editor: Instrumentation in Analytical Chemistry, 1973, Newburger's Manual of Cosmetic Analysis, 1977 (FDA award 1978), Safety in the Laboratory, 1984 (STC award 1985); assoc. editor: Official Methods of Analysis, 1975; editor Inclusions Quar., 1993-94; publs. mgr. Internat. Union Pure and Applied Chemistry, 1999-2002. Pres. Congregation Sha'arei Israel, 1981-83, Raleigh Chamber Music Guild, 1997-99. Mem. Soc. Tech. Comm. (treas. 1983-85, v.p. 1985-87, achievement award 1985, excellence award 2002), Am. Chem. Soc., Assn. Ofcl. Analytical Chemists, Bridge Club (Raleigh), Capitol Club, Vanderbilt Club, B'nai B'rith. Republican. Jewish. Avocations: music, tennis, basketball, bridge. Home and Office: 7704 Audubon Dr Raleigh NC 27615-3403 Office Phone: 919-559-4814, 919-539-2319. E-mail: asenzel@yahoo.com.

SEPETYS, RUTA ELIZABETH, entertainment company executive, writer; b. Detroit, Nov. 19, 1967; d. George N. and Phyllis Jean (Schefsky) S.; married BS, Hillsdale Coll., Mich.; M. Internat. Mgmt., ICN, Paris. Mgr. Deston Entertainment, Santa Monica, Calif., 1990-94; pres. Sepetys Entertainment Group, Santa Monica, 1994—. Vis. faculty Musician's Inst., Hollywood, Calif., 1994-97; guest spkr. Full Sail Music Sch., Orlando, Fla., 1997. Author: Between Shades of Gray, 2012, Out of the Easy, 2013. Staff mem. Grammys in the Schs., L.A. Mem. Nat. Acad. Rec. Arts and Scis., Rec. Industry Assn. Am., L.A. Music Network. Office: Sepetys Entertainment Group 5543 Edmondson Pike Nashville TN 37211 Address: c/o Sara Ortiz Penguin Group 375 Hudson St New York NY 10014-3657 Office Phone: 615-781-6000.

SEQUEIRA, RAFAEL FRANCIS, cardiologist, educator; b. Nairobi, Kenya, Apr. 10, 1939; came to U.S., 1979; m. Kathleen Patricia Sequeira, Apr. 20, 1975; children: Raphael, Anthony, John. MD, U. Coll. Dublin, 1964. Diplomate Am. Bd. Cardiology. Intern Mater Hosp. Univ. Coll. Dublin (Ireland), 1969-70; resident Stobhill Hosp. Univ. Glasgow (Scotland), 1970-73; fellow in cardiology Univ. Bristol (Eng.) Royal Infirmary, 1974-77; prof. medicine U. Miami, Fla.; prin. investigator divsn. cardiology U. Miami Sch. Medicine. Contbr. articles to profl. jours. Fellow Am. Coll. Cardiology, Royal Coll. Physcians U.K. Office: U Miami Divsn Cardiology PO Box 16960 Miami FL 33101-6960 Home Phone: 305-361-6009; Office Phone: 305-585-5530. Business E-Mail: rsequeir@med.miami.edu.

SERAFIN, DONALD, plastic surgeon, educator; b. NYC, Jan. 18, 1938; s. Stephen Michael and Julia (Sopko) S.; m. Patricia Serafin; children: Allison Elizabeth, Christina Julia, Donald Stephen, Lara Leigh. AB, Duke U., 1960, MD, 1964. Diplomate Am. Bd. Surgery, Am. Bd. Plastic Surgery. Surg. intern Grady Meml. Hosp., Atlanta, 1964-65; resident in surgery Emory U. Hosp., Atlanta, 1965-69; asst. resident in plastic and reconstructive surgery Duke U. Med. Ctr., Durham, NC, 1971-73, chief resident, 1973-74; Christine Kleinert fellow in hand surgery U. Louisville Hosp., 1972-73; practice medicine specializing in plastic surgery, Durham; plastic reconstructional surgery cons. Womack Semy Medicine Ctr., Fort Bragg, NC. Mem. staff N.C. Splty. Hosp., Durham Regional Hosp., Maria Parham Hosp.; asst. prof. plastic, reconstructive and maxillofacial surgery Duke U., 1974-77, assoc. prof., 1977-81, prof., 1981-2000, prof. emeritus, 2000—, chief divsn. plastic reconstructive and maxillofacial and oral surgery, 1985-95, chmn. Plastic Surgery Rsch. Coun., 1983. Assoc. editor Jour. Reconstructive Microsurgery; contbr. articles to profl. jours. Ret. col. USAR, 2004. Decorated Air Force Commendation medal, Army Commendation medal, Army Achievement medal, Army Meritorious Svc. medal. Fellow ACS; mem. AMA, Internat. Soc. Reconstructive Microsurgery, Am. Soc. Plastic Surgeons, Am. Assn. Plastic Surgeons, Am. Soc. Aesthetic Plastic Surgery, Am. Soc. Surgery Hand, Am. Assn. Hand Surgery, Am. Burn Assn., Plastic Surgery Rshc. Coun., N.C. Soc. Plastic, Maxillofacial and Reconstructive Surgeons, Southeastern Soc. Plastic and Reconstructive Surgeons. Office: 511 Ruin Creek Rd Ste 104B Henderson NC 28350 Office Phone: 252-438-8252, 919-220-7711. Personal E-mail: seradonald@aol.com.

SERAFINE, MARY LOUISE, lawyer, educator; b. Rochester, NY, July 2, 1948; BA in Music with honors, Rutgers U., 1970; PhD, U. Fla., 1975; JD, Yale U., 1991. Bar: Calif. 1992, DC 1993, US Tax Ct. 1995, NY 1999, Tex. 2005. Tchg. and rsch. fellow U. Fla., Gainesville, 1970-76; vis. asst. prof. U. Tex., San Antonio, 1976-77, asst. prof. Austin, 1977-79; postdoctoral fellow dept. psychology Yale U., New Haven, 1979-83, lectr., 1981-83; asst. prof. dept. psychology Vassar Coll., Poughkeepsie, N.Y., 1983-88; with O'Melveny & Myers, LA, 1991-96, Chadbourne & Parke, LA, 1996-97, Fried, Frank, Harris, Shriver & Jacobson, LA, 1997-99; pvt. practice, 1999—; nominee Gen. Elec. Tex. Senate Dist. 14, 2010. Author: Music as Cognition: The Development of Thought in Sound, 1988; editl. reviewer Child Devel., Devel. Psychology, Am. Scientist, Jour. Exptl. Child Psychology, Jour. Applied Developmental Psychology, Yale Law Jour.; contbr. articles to profl. jours. Grantee State of Fla., 1974-75, U. Tex.-Austin, 1977, Spencer Found., 1979-85. Republican. Office: PO Box 4342 Austin TX 78765 Office Phone: 512-220-5452. Business E-Mail: mlserafine@earthlink.net.

SEROKA, JAMES HENRY, social studies educator, academic administrator; b. Detroit, Mar. 5, 1950; s. Henry S. and Mary (Wyoral) S.; m. Carolyn Marie White, June 27, 1970; children: Mihail, Maritsa. BA, U. Mich., 1970; MA, Mich. State U., 1972, PhD, 1976. Labor mkt. analyst U.S. Dept. of Labor, Washington, 1970-71; asst. prof. U. N.C., Greensboro, 1976-77, Appalachian State U., Boone, N.C., 1977-79, So. Ill. U., Carbondale, 1979-81, assoc. prof., 1981-87, prof., dir., 1987-88; prof., head div. humanities and social scis. Pa. State U., Erie, 1988-90; prof. U. North Fla., Jacksonville, 1990-98; dir. Ctr. for Pub. Leadership, Jacksonville, 1991-98; vis. prof. internat. security studies U.S. Air War Coll., Maxwell AFB, Ala., 1997-98, 2005—12; prof. Auburn (Ala.) U., 1998—; dir. Ctr. for Govtl. Svcs., Auburn, 1998—2005. Dir. Master of Pub. Affairs Program Soc. Ill. U., 1987-88, Rural and Small Town Adminstrn. Project, 1980-85; asst. dir. Appalachian Regional Bur. Govts., Boone, N.C., 1977-79; manpower planning analyst U.S. Dept. Labor, Washington, 1970-71; exchange prof. Fakultet Politickih Nauka, Univerzitet u Beogradu, Yugoslavia, 1986; vis. prof. Air War Coll., Montgomery, Ala.; sr. researcher Coun. for the Internat. Exchange Scholars Yugoslavia, 1980; mem. state adv. com. Gov.'s Rural Affairs Coun. for State of Ill., 1988; dir. Ctr. Govt. Svcs., Auburn, 1998—. Co-author: Political Organizations in Social Yugoslavia, 1986 (Choice award 1987); editor Rural Public Adminstration, 1986; co-editor: Developed Socialism, 1982, Comparative Political Systems, 1990, Yugoslavia: The Failure of Democratic Transformation, 1992; contbr. numerous articles to profl. jours. Recipient Akademischer Austausch Dienst Lang. scholar Fed. Republic of Germany, 1988 and numerous other grants, traveling fellows. Mem. Am. Polit. Sci. Assn., Internat. Polit. Sci. Assn., Policy Studies Orgn., Acad. Polit. Sci., Hon. Order of Ky. Colonels. Office: Auburn Univ Dept Political Sci 7080 Haley Ctr Auburn AL 36849 Business E-Mail: jseroka@auburn.edu.

SERRANO, DAVE (DAVID SCOTT SERRANO), college baseball coach; b. Torrence, Calif., June 28, 1964; m. Tracy Serrano; children: Kyle, Zachary, Parker. AA, Cerritos Coll., Calif., 1985; BA, Trinity Coll. and Univ., 2003. Asst. baseball coach Cerritos Coll. Falcons, 1988—90, 1992—94, head baseball coach, 1991; asst. baseball coach U. Tenn. Volunteers, 1995—96, head baseball coach, 2012—; pitching coach, recruiting coord. Calif. State U. Fullerton Titans, 1997—2004, head baseball coach, 2007—11, U. Calif. Irvine Anteaters, 2005—07. Named Coach of Yr., South Coast Conf., 1994, Asst. Coach of Yr., Baseball America, 2004, Nat. Coach of Yr., 2007. Office: University of Tennessee Baseball Program Lindsey Nelson Stadium 1511 Pat Summitt Dr Knoxville TN 37996 Office Phone: 865-974-2057. Business E-Mail: dserrano@utk.edu.

SERRA PUCHE, JAIME JOSE, economist; b. Mex. City, Mexico, Jan. 11, 1951; s. Jorge Serra Perayre and Carmen Puche Planes; m. Joanna Wright Abbott. BA in Polit. Sci., Nat Autonomous U. Mex.; MA in Economics, El Colegio de México; PhD in Economics, Yale U., 1979. Undersecretary fin. Mexican Min., 1986—88, sec. trade and industry, 1988—94, sec. fin. and pub. credit, 1994; sr. ptnr. Serra Associates International, 1996—. Former bd. dirs. Grupo Ferroviario Mexicano, Southern Peru Copper Corp.; tchr., economics El Colegio de México, 1979—86; bd. dirs. Grupo Modelo, S.A.B. de C.V., Tenaris S.A., The Mexico Fund, Inc., 1997—, Vitro, S.A.B. de C.V, 1998—, Chiquita Brands Internat., Inc., 2003—; trustee Corp. Yale U.; prin. negotiator N.Am. Free Trade Agreement; guest prof. of several univs. (Barcelona, Bilbao, Madrid and Stanford U.). Author: of several books on econ. theory & evolution of the Mex. econ. Recipient Banamex Nat. award in Econs., Nat. Sci. Rsch. award. Office: Chiquita Brands International Inc 550 S Caldwell St Ste 1010 Charlotte NC 28202-2681 Office Phone: 513-784-8000.

SESSIONS, DAVID, state legislator; m. Lisa Sessions; 3 children. Farmer, co-owner Sessions Farms, Ala.; pres. Grand Bay Water Works, Producers Gin Co. LLC; mem. Dist. 105 Ala. House of Reps., Montgomery, 2011—. Bd. supr. Mobile County Soil and Water Conservation Dist. Mem.: Ala. Pecan Growers Assn. (past pres.). Republican. Office: 13000 Hugh Fort Rd Grand Bay AL 36541 also: Ala House of Reps Rm 625-C 11 S Union St Montgomery AL 36130 Office Phone: 334-242-0947. Personal E-mail: d.r.sessions@att.net.

SESSIONS, JEFF (JEFFERSON BEAUREGARD SESSIONS III), United States Senator from Alabama, former state attorney general; b. Hybart, Ala., Dec. 24, 1946; s. Jefferson Beauregard and Abbie (Powe) S.; m. Mary Montgomery Blackshear, Aug. 9, 1969; children: Mary Abigail, Ruth Blackshear, Samuel Turner BA, Huntingdon Coll., Montgomery, Ala., 1969; JD, U. Ala., 1973. Bar: Ala. 1973. Assoc. Guin, Bouldin & Porch, Russellville, Ala., 1973-75; asst. US atty. (southern dist.) Ala. US Dept. Justice, Mobile, Ala., 1975-77, US atty., 1981-93; assoc. then ptnr. Stockman & Bedsole Attorneys, Mobile, Ala., 1977-81; ptnr. Stockman, Bedsole & Sessions, Mobile, 1993-94; atty. gen. State of Ala., Montgomery, 1995—97; US Senator from Ala., 1997—; ranking mem. US Senate Judiciary Com., 2009—. Mem. U.S. Atty. Gen's. adv. com., 1987-89, vice-chmn. 1989 Presdl. elector State of Ala., 1972; trustee, mem. exec. com. Mobile Bay Area Partnership for Youth, 1981-95; chmn. adminstrv. bd. Ashland Pl. United Meth. Ch., Mobile, 1982; 1st v.p. Mobile Lions Club, 1993-94. Capt. USAR, 1975-85 Recipient U.S. Atty. Gen's. award for significant achievements in the war against drug trafficking, US Dept. Justice, 1992, George (Buck) Gillespie Congl. award, Blinded Americans Veterans Found., 2000, Nat. Leadership award, Civil War Preservation Trust, 2004, Disting. Eagle Scout award, Guardian of Small Bus. award, Minuteman of the Yr. award, Reserve Officers Assn., Svc. to Agrl. award, AL Farmers Fedn., Teddy Roosevelt Environ. award, Watchdog of the Treasury award, Legislative Achievement award, US Chamber of Commerce, 2009 Mem. ABA, Ala. Bar Assn., Mobile Bar Assn. Republican. Methodist. Office: US Senate 326 Russell Senate Office Bldg Washington DC 20510 also: Regions Ctr Ste 802 200 Clinton Ave Huntsville AL 35801 Office Phone: 202-224-4124. Office Fax: 202-224-3149. E-mail: senator@sessions.senate.gov.*

SESSIONS, PETER ANDERSON, United States Representative from Texas; b. Waco, Tex., Mar. 22, 1955; s. William Steele and Alice June (Lewis) Sessions; m. Juanita Diaz, 1984 (div. 2011); children: Bill, Alex. BS in Polit. Sci., Southwestern U., Georgetown, Tex., 1978. Various positions including dist. mgr. mktg. Southwestern Bell Tel. Co., Dallas, 1978—94; v.p. public policy Nat. Ctr. Policy Analysis, Dallas, 1994—95; mem. US Congress from 5th Tex. Dist., 1997—2003, US Congress from 32nd Tex. Dist., 2003—; chmn. US House Rules Com., 2013—, Nat. Republican Congressional Com. (NRCC), 2009—13. Mem. nat. com. Nat. Eagle Scout Assn.; team leader Adopt—A—Shoreline, White Rock Lake, Dallas, 1996—; bd. trustees Southwestern U., 2007—; mem. exec. bd. Cir. Ten Coun. Boy Scouts of America; adv. to pres. Spl. Olympics Tex.; mem. adv. bd. HomeAid Dallas; active United Meth. Ch. Recipient Nat. Disting. Eagle Scout award, 1999, Pub. Svc. award, Assn. Air Med. Services, 2007, Ben Franklin Pub. Policy award, Nat. Assn. Mutual Ins. Companies, 2007, Visionary award, American Acad. Ophthalmology, 2007, Disting. Legis. award, City of Dallas, 2008, Nat. Leadership award, Nat. Down Syndrome Soc., 2008, Guardian of Small Bus. award, Nat. Fedn. Ind. Bus., 2009, Taxpayer Hero award, Citizens Against Govt. Waste, 2009. Mem.: Rotary Club. Republican. Methodist. Avocations: hiking, mountain climbing, running. Office: US House of Representatives 2233 Rayburn House Office Bldg Washington DC 20515 also: Park Ctrl VII 12750 Merit Dr Ste 1434 Dallas TX 75251 Office Phone: 202-225-2231.*

SESSIONS, TRIPP, food service executive; BBA in Mgmt., U. Ga., 1995, MBA, 2006. Dir., info. tech. Zaxby's Franchising, Inc., 2000—08; sr. dir., info. tech. Arby's Restaurant Group, Inc., 2008, Zaxby's Franchising, Inc., 2008; v.p., info. tech. Wendy's/Arby's Group, Inc., 2009—. Office: Wendy's/Arby's Group Inc 1155 Perimeter Ctr W Atlanta GA 30338 Office Phone: 678-514-4100. Business E-Mail: tripp.sessions@wendysarbys.com.

SESSIONS, WILLIAM LAD, philosophy educator, academic administrator; b. Somerville, NJ, Dec. 3, 1943; s. William George and Alice Edna (Billhardt) Sessions; m. Vicki Darlene Thompson, Aug. 28, 1965; children: Allistair Lee, Laura Anne. BA magna cum laude, U. Colo., 1965; MA in Comparative Study of Religion, Union Theol. Sem., NYC, 1967; postgrad., Oxford U., Eng., 1967-68; PhD, Yale U., New Haven, Conn., 1971; postdoctoral studies, Stanford U., Calif., 1976, Harvard U., Cambridge, Mass., 1977-78. Tchg. fellow Yale U., 1969; instr. U. Conn., Waterbury, 1970-71; asst. prof. philosophy Washington and Lee U., 1971-77, assoc. prof., 1977-83, prof., 1983—, Ballengee 250th Anniversary prof., 1999—. Instr. So. Sem., 1972; vis. prof. St. Olaf Coll., 1985—86; assoc. dean Coll. Washington and Lee U., 1992—95, acting dean, 1995—96, 2001—02, head philosophy dept., 1996—2007. Author: The Concept of Faith, 1984, Reading Hume's Dialogues, 2002; contbr. articles to religious and philos. jours. Ruling elder Lexington Presbyn. Ch., Va., 1983—89, 2002—05, tchr. Sunday sch., 1984—. Grantee Glenn grant, Washington and Lee U., 1975—, Babcock Found., 1976, NEH, 1977, 1983, 1986, Mellon Found., 1978—79, Mellon East Asian Studies, 1990. Mem.: Soc. Christian Philosophers (steering com. ea. region 1986—90, 1992—95, 1997—98, exec. com. 1987—90), Soc. for Philosophy of Religion (exec. coun. 1988—94, v.p. 1991, pres. 1992), Va. Philos. Assn., Am. Philos. Assn., Phi Beta Kappa (exec. com. W&L chpt. 1986—95, 1998—2000, v.p. 1989—91, pres. 1991—93). Presbyterian. Office: Washington & Lee U Dept of Philosophy Lexington VA 24450 Business E-Mail: sessionsl@wlu.edu.

SESSOMS, WILLIAM D., JR., mayor, Virginia Beach, Virginia, bank executive; Grad., Va. Commonwealth U. Banker Sovran Bank, Virginia Beach, Va., 1976—84, Wachovia Bank, Virginia Beach, Va., 1984—2004; Virginia Beach pres. TowneBank, 2005—; mem. at-large Virginia Beach City Coun., 1988—92; vice mayor City of Virginia Beach, Va., 1992—2002, mayor, 2009—. Mem. Va. Pub. Sch. Authority, Local Health Benefits Adv. Com., Va., Gov.'s Commn. on Environ. Stewardship, Va. Recipient First Citizen award, Virginia Beach, 2006. Office: City Hall Bldg #1 2401 Courthouse Dr Ste 234 Virginia Beach VA 23456 Office Phone: 757-385-4581, 757-385-4242. Office Fax: 757-427-5626. E-mail: wsessoms@vbgov.com.*

SETHNA, BEHERUZ NARIMAN, academic administrator, educator, management consultant; b. Bombay, July 31, 1948; came to U.S., 1973; s. Nariman Dhanjishaw and Mithu Nariman (Mistry) S.; m. Madhavi Kaji, May 25, 1974; children: Anita B., Shaun B. B in Tech. with honors, Indian Inst. Tech., Bombay, 1971; MBA, Indian Inst. Mgmt., Ahmedabad, 1973; MPhil, Columbia U., 1975, PhD in Bus., 1976; student, Ind. U., 1986, Harvard U., 1991. Cert. computing profl. Inst. for Cert. Computing Profls. Engring. and mgmt. trainee various corps., Bombay, 1968-69, 70-72; case writer, trainee Clarion Advt., Bombay, 1973; project mgr., cons. Lever Bros. Co., NYC, 1974-76; prof., chair mktg. and mgmt. info. systems Clarkson U., Potsdam, NY, 1976-89, dir. grad. programs, 1978-80; mktg., rsch. and strategic planning mgr. Procter & Gamble (India)/Richardson Hindustan (Vicks), Bombay and Westport, Conn., 1980-81; interim exec. v.p. acad. and student affairs; dean Coll. of Bus., chief acad. officer Lamar (Tex.) U., 1989-94, Gulf States Utilities prof. bus., 1991-94; pres. West Ga. Coll., Carrollton, 1994—96, State U. West Ga., 1996—2005, U. West Ga., 2005—; interim sr. vice chancellor Univ. Sys. Ga., 1999—2000, interim exec. vice chancellor, chief acad. officer, 2006—07; pres. Ga. Assn. Colls., Carrollton, 2000—01; commr. Southern Assn. Coll. Schs., 2005—09; pres. Gulf South Conf., 2008—10; vice chair Atlanta Regional Coun. Higher Edn., 2008—09, chair, 2009—; politics & purpose chair Am. Assn. State Coll. U., 2009—10. Mem. adv. coun. SUNY-Canton (N.Y.) Coll., 1975-89; cons. in field. Author: Research Methods in Marketing, 1984; contbr. articles to profl. jours. Scoutmaster Boy Scouts Am., Potsdam, 1987—89, pack com. chair, den leader, 1987—89, mem. dist. bd., 1991—94, mem. exec. bd. Atlanta Area coun., 1997—2003, Pres.'s Scout, Gold Cord, 1966; leader Girl Scouts U.S., Beaumont, 1989—94. Recipient Minority Achiever's award, Role Model award, 1991, Dean's Leadership award, Acad. Bus. Adminstrn., 1993, Nat. Svc. award, 1996, Alumnus award (hon.), 1999, Disting. Alumnus award, Indian Inst. Tech., Bombay, 2000, Carroll County Citizen of Yr., 1999, rated 1st among Carroll County's Movers, Shakers and Newsmakers, 2002, Resolution of Commendation, State Senate, 2003, Instructional Innovation award (hon.), 1984—89, 2004, Cornerstone award, Bd. Regent, 2007, Empowerment award, Ctr. Student Leadership, 2007; named one of 100 Most Influential Georgians, Ga. Trend, 2003, 2006, 2009—10; grantee, US Dept. Energy, 1980, IBM Corp., 1984, AT&T, 1985; Fulbright scholar, U.S. Info. Agy., 1986—87, Paul Harris fellow, Rotary Internat., 1997. Mem. Rotary (polio plus edn. chair). Avocation: scouting. Home: 107 Windsong Ct Carrollton GA 30117-8978 Office: U W Ga Office Pres Carrollton GA 30118-0001 Office Phone: 678-839-6442. Business E-Mail: bsethna@westga.edu.

SETO, LYNN, healthcare company executive; Undergraduate, U. Pa.; med. degree, Jefferson Med. Coll., Phila. Postgraduate tng.residence Albany Med. Ctr., NY; fellow Cleve. Clinic Health Sys., Episcopal Hosp., postgraduate tng.; dir., cardiac robotic surgery Baptist Health, 2009—. Fellow Am. Coll. of Chest Physicians, ACS; with Cleve. Clinic. Office: Baptist Health 9601 Interstate 630 Exit 7 Little Rock AR 72205-7299 Office Phone: 501-202-2000. Office Fax: 501-202-1115. Business E-Mail: lseto@baptistfirst.org.

SETTLE, MARK, information technology executive; BS in Earth & Planetary Sci., MS in Earth & Planetary Sci., MIT; PhD in Geol. Sci., Brown U. Program scientist NASA; various sr. mgmt. positions Atlantic Richfield Co.; dir., sys. integration bus. unit Hughes Aircraft Co.; chief info. officer Corp. Express, Inc., Occidental Petroleum, 1997—99; exec. v.p., sys. & processing through chief info. officer Visa International, 1999—2001; v.p., chief info officer Arrow Electronics, Inc., Melville, NY, 2001; joined BMC Software, Inc., 2008, chief info. officer. Retired USAF. Office: BMC Software Inc 2101 CityWest Blvd Houston TX 77042 Office Phone: 713-918-8800. Business E-Mail: Mark_Settle@bmc.com.

SETZER, MITCHELL S., state legislator; State rep. Dist. 43, NC, 1999—2002; state rep. Dist. 89, 2003—; v.p. Smith, Setzer & Sons, Inc. Mem. Ethics com., Fin. com., Fin. Instns. com., House Select Com. on Small Bus.; vice chmn. Ins. com. Republican. Address: PO Box 416 Catawba NC 28609 Office: North Carolina House of Representatives 16 W Jones St Rm 1206 Raleigh NC 27601-1096 Office Phone: 919-733-4948. E-mail: Mitchell.Setzer@ncleg.net.

SETZLER, ED, state legislator; State rep. Dist. 35, Ga., 2005—. Republican. Mailing: 1555 Boxwood Trace Acworth GA 30102 Office: Legislative Office Bldg Rm 411 Atlanta GA 30334 Home Phone: 770-420-0520; Office Phone: 404-656-0126. Business E-Mail: lesetzler@mactec.com.

SETZLER, NIKKI GILES, state legislator; b. Asheville, NC, Aug. 7, 1945; s. Harry Earl and Verna Leona Parker Setzler; m. Ada Jane Taylor, 1969; children: Tara Nikole, Jamie Leona, Sabra Taylor, Amber Jane. BA, U. SC, 1968, JD, 1971. Atty., 1973—; mem. Dist. 8 SC State Senate, SC, 1977—88, mem. Dist. 26, 1988—, mem. Banking and Ins. Com., Edn. Com., Fin. Com., Interstate Cooperation Com. & Labor, Commerce and Industry Com. Chair Gov.'s Commn. on Tchr. Quality, 1999—, Gov.'s Middle Grades Task Force, 1999—. Recipient Outstanding Leadership & Contbns. award, SC Coun. Elem. Sch. Prins., 1990—91, Supporting Edn. award, Palmetto State Tchrs. Assn., 1991, Outstanding Senator award, SC Sch. Bd. Assn., 1991, Sch. Health Svc. award, Columbia Coll. Bd. Visitors, 1992, Commendation award, SC Counseling Assn., 1994—95, SC Coun. Parents & Tchrs., 1994, Outstanding Svc. award, SC Agr. Edn. Programs, 1994, Richard W. Riley award, SC Consort Gifted Edn., 1995; named Legislator of Yr., Ind. Coll. & Universities SC Inc., 1993, Carl Perkins Humanitarian of Yr., SC, 1995. Mem.: SC Heart Assn., Greater West Columbia-Cayce C. of C. (pres. 1975—76), Lexington Jaycees (dir. 1973), Lexington Country Club (bd. dir. 1974—76), Lions Club (pres. 1977—78, v.p. 1975—77). Democrat. Lutheran. Mailing: 1309 Canary Dr West Columbia SC 29169 Office: 510 Gressette Bldg Columbia SC 29201 Home: 249 Congaree Park Dr West Columbia SC 29169-7647 Home Phone: 803-796-7573; Office Phone: 803-212-6140, 803-796-1285. Business E-Mail: edu@legis.lpitr.state.sc.us.

SEUM, DAN (MALANO), state legislator; b. Jan. 28, 1940; Restaurant owner; state rep. Ky., 1982—88; mem. Dist. 37 Ky. State Senate, 1989—92, mem. Dist. 38, 1995—, majority whip, majority caucus chmn.; mem. Banking & Ins. Com., Econ. Devel. & Tourism Com., Labor & Indsl. Com., Licensing & Occupations Com., Vet. Affairs Com. Recipient Cert. of Merit, Louisville Bd. Alderman, Guardian Small Bus. award, Voice of Democracy award, VFW, Appreciation award, Am. Athletic Assn. Deaf, 1984, Nat. Fed. Ind. Bus. award, 1988, Cert. of Appreciation, Ky. Coalition Against Rape-Sexual Assault, 1988—90; named Dem. of Yr., 1977, Optimist of Yr., 1984. Mem.: Iroquois Amphitheater Assn. (v.p.), Kenwood Optimist (v.p.). Republican. Home: 1107 Holly Ave Fairdale KY 40118 Office: 702 Capitol Ave Annex Rm 242 Frankfort KY 40601 also: 700 Capitol Ave Capitol Rm 319 Frankfort KY 40601 Home Phone: 502-749-2859; Office Phone: 502-564-2450. E-mail: Dan.Seum@lrc.state.ky.us.

SEUNG, THOMAS KAEHAO, philosophy educator; b. Jungju, Republic of Korea, Sept. 20, 1930; m. Kwihwan Hahn, May 29, 1965; children: Hyunjune Sebastian, Kwonjune Justin, Haesue Florence. BA, Yale U., 1958, MA, 1961, PhD, 1965. Instr. Yale U., 1963-65; asst. prof. Fordham U., 1965-66; mem. faculty dept. philosophy U. Tex., Austin, 1966—, prof. in philosophy, 1972—, prof. in govt., 1985—, prof. in law, 1993—, Jesse H. Jones prof. liberal arts, 1987—. Author: The Fragile Leaves of the Sybil, 1962, Kant's Transcendental Logic, 1969, Cultural Thematics, 1976, Structuralism and Hermeneutics, 1982, Semiotics and Thematics, 1982, Intuition and Construction, 1993, Kant's Platonic Revolution, 1994, Plato Rediscovered, 1996, Nietzche's Epic of the Soul, 2005, Goethe, Nietzsche, and Wagner, 2006, Kant, 2007. Served as officer Korean Army, 1950-53. Recipient Wilbur Lucius Cross medal Yale Grad. Sch. Alumni Assn., 1988; Soc. Religion in Higher Edn. fellow, 1969-70; Am. Council Learned Soc. fellow, 1970-71; NEH fellow, 1977-78 Office: U Tex Dept Philosophy Austin TX 78712 Mailing: 3800 Green Trails S Austin TX 78731 Business E-Mail: t.k.seung@austin.utexas.edu.

SEVERINO, MICHELLE A., museum director; BA in Anthropology, George Wash. U., DC, 1992; MA in Art History, George Wash. U., 1995. Asst. dir. Quint Contemporary Art, San Diego, 1994—95; edn. coord. Mus. Contemporary Art, La Jolla, Calif., 1995—96; projects dir. Children's Mus. San Diego, 1996—97; dir. Miller Fine Art Ltd., Alexandria, Va., 1998—99; interim dir. Pensacola Mus. Art, Fla., 1999—2000; cons. U. West Fla., Ctr. Fine Arts & Performing Arts, 2000; mem. faculty Oakloosa-Walton Coll., Niceville, Fla., 2004—; exec. dir. Heritage Mus. Northwest Fla., Valparaiso, Fla., 2006—. Edn. curator Oakloosa-Walton Coll., 2004—05. Writer, editor: Heritage Press, 2006—; contbr. articles to profl. publs. Subcom. mem. Sustainable Emerald Coast Task Force, 2007—; bd. dirs. Mattie Kelly Cultural & Environ. Inst., 2007—. Mem.: Okaloosa County Hist. Mus. Cooperative (founding mem. 2007), Panhandle Hist. Preservation Alliance (founding mem. 2006), Am. Assn. Mus., Mus. Edn. Roundtable, Nat. Trust Hist. Preservation, Fla. Assn. Mus. Office: Heritage Mus Northwest Florida 115 Westview Ave Valparaiso FL 32580 Office Phone: 850-729-5382. Office Fax: 850-678-4547. Business E-Mail: mseverino@co.okaloosa.fl.us.

SEWARD, TROILEN GAINEY, retired psychologist; b. Petersburg, Va., Nov. 26, 1941; d. Troy L. and Mary (Nester) Gainey; m. William E. Seward III, June 29, 1963; children: Susan Blair, William E. IV. BA, Coll. William and Mary, 1963, MEd, EdS, Coll. William and Mary, 1980; MEd, Va. Commonwealth U., 1977. Tchr. elem., Petersburg, 1963—67; tchr. secondary Surry Acad., Va., 1967—76, guidance counselor, 1976—77; headmistress Tidewater Acad., Wakefield, Va., 1977—79; psychologist Peninsula Child Devel. Clinic, Newport News, Va., 1980—82; sch. psychologist Dinwiddie Pub. Sch., Va., 1982—89, dir. pupil pers. svcs., spl. edn., 1990—93, dir. student svcs., 1993—95, supt., 1996—2001; ret., 2001; edn. lobbyist, 2002—. Human rights com. Southside Tng. Ctr., Petersburg, 1986—; cons. in field. Trustee Ritchie Meml. Ch., Claremont, Va., 1971—; mem. Town Coun., Claremont, 1984-90, fin. com., 1984-90, mayor, 2006—10. Mem. Nat. Assn. Sch. Psychologists (del. 1992-94), Va. Assn. Sch. Psychologists (chair cert. and licensure com. 1985-87, legis. chair 1987—1994, pres. 1989-91), Va. Literacy Found. (bd. mem. 2008-), Va. Edn. (adult edn. adv. bd. mem. 2009-, surry county social svcs. bd., 2004-12, chair, 2011-12), Surry County Hist. Soc. (bd. mem. 2006-12), Va. Ret. Sys. (bd. trustees 2013-), Delta Kappa Gamma, Phi Kappa Phi. Episcopalian. Home: PO Box 266 Claremont VA 23899-0266

SEWELL, TERRI ANDREA, United States Representative from Alabama, lawyer; b. Selma, Ala., Jan. 1, 1965; d. Andrew A. and Nancy (Gardner) Sewell. BA, Princeton Univ., 1986; MA with honours, Oxford Univ.; JD, Harvard Univ., 1992. Staff mem. to Rep. Richard Shelby US House of Representatives, Washington; law clk. to Chief Judge U.W. Clemon, US Dist. Ct. (northern dist.) Ala.; staff mem. to Senator Howell Heflin Ala. State Senate; assoc. Davis, Polk & Wardwell, 1994—2004; ptnr. Maynard, Cooper & Gale PC, Birmingham, Ala., 2004—10; mem. US Congress from 7th Ala. Dist., Washington, 2011—, US House Agrl. Com., 2011—, US House Space, Science & Tech. Com., 2011—. Mem. gov. bd. Ala. Coun. on Econ. Edn.; mem. corp. partners coun. Birmingham Art Mus.; bd. mem. Girl Scouts of Cahaba Coun.; bd. treas. & chair fin. com. St. Vincent's Found.; mem. cmty. adv. bd. Birmingham Minority Health & Rsch. Ctr., Univ. Ala. Democrat. Baptist. Office: US House of Representatives 1133 Longworth House Office Bldg Washington DC 20515 Office Phone: 202-225-2665, 202-225-9567.*

SEWRIGHT, CHARLES WILLIAM, JR., mortgage banking advisory services company executive; b. Great Lakes, Ill., Feb. 22, 1946; s. Charles William Sewright Sr. and Selma Joy Kester; m. Bonnie Joyce Knight, July 2, 1967; children: Kimberly Ann, Traci Lynn, Megan Paige. BS in Acctg., Calif. State U., Long Beach, 1969, MBA, 1974. Fin. analyst aeronautic div. Philco-Ford Corp., Newport Beach, Calif., 1969-73; sr. acctg. analyst Calif. Computer Products, Anaheim, 1973-74; product line controller McGaw Labs. div. Am. Hosp. Supply Corp., Irvine, Calif., 1974-75, div. acctg. mgr., 1975-76, fin. planning dir., 1976-80; v.p., controller critical care div. McGaw Park, Ill., 1980-85; v.p., controller EZ Painter Corp., Milw., 1985-86; v.p. dept. mgr. automotive fin. services secondary mkts. Marine Midland Bank, Buffalo, N.Y., 1986-87; pres., chief exec. officer Marine Midland Mortgage Corp., Buffalo, 1987-91, Anchor Mortgage Svcs., Inc., Wayne, NJ, 1991-95; exec. v.p., COO Avondale Fed. Savs. Bank, Chgo., 1997—2000; founder, chmn., CEO Quest Advisors, Inc., Northbrook, Ill., 1995—. Chair credit com. Am. Employees Fed. Credit Union, McGaw Park, Ill., 1980-85; vice chmn. Bd. Am. Employees Fed. Credit Union, 1981-85; mem. Fannie Mae Adv. Bd., 1990-92; speaker in field; mem. bd. trustees Medaille Coll., 1989-92; dir. Avondale Fed. Savs. Bank. Mem. Nat. Assn. Accts., Inst. of Cert. Mgmt. Accts. (cert.), Mortgage Bankers Assn. Am. (legis. com. 1990—), Mortgage Bankers Assn. Am. (bd. govs. 1990-98), Beta Gamma Sigma, Phi Kappa Phi. Avocation: golf. Office: Quest Advisors Inc 75407 Rowan Chapel Hill NC 27517 Business E-Mail: csewright@questadvisors.com.

SEXTON, KELLY J., anatomy and physiology professor; 1 child, Kyle Kennedy. BS, U. Fla., Gainesville, 1981; MS, U. Ark., Fayetteville, 1984; PhD, Auburn U., Ala., 1988. Vis. asst. prof. Tex. Tech U., Lubbock, 1988—91; instr. South Plains Coll., Levelland, Tex., 1991—93; prof. McLennan CC, Waco, Tex., 1993—98, North Lake Coll., Irving, Tex., 1998—. Office: North Lake Coll 5001 N MacArthur Blvd Irving TX 75038 Business E-Mail: ksexton@dcccd.edu.

SEXTON, MELISSA, personal care industry executive; Dir. integrated mktg. planning, adult and feminine care Kimberly-Clark Corp. Former mem. US Olympic Sailing Team. Named a Woman to Watch, Advertising Age, 2011. Office: Kimberly-Clark Corp 351 Phelps Dr Irving TX 75038

SEYMOUR, HARLAN FRANCIS, finance company executive; b. East Saint Louis, Mo., Jan. 25, 1950; s. Harlan Edward and Agnes Wilhelmina (Noakes) S.; m. Ellen Katheleen Schmitt, Aug. 17, 1973; children: Melissa Ann, Harlan Francis Jr. BA in Math., U. Mo., 1973; MBA, Keller Grad. Sch. Mgmt., 1980. Chmn. ACI Worldwide, Inc. (formerly Transaction System Architects, Inc.); corp. v.p. Statis. Tabulating Corp., 1973-80; dist. mgr. Datacorp, 1980-83; exec. v.p. 1st Fin. Mgmt. Corp., 1983-94; pres., CEO 1st Health Svcs. Corp., Richmond, Va., 1989-94; exec. v.p., COO, Trigon Blue Cross/Blue Shield, Richmond, 1994-96; mng. dir. Jefferson Capital Ptnrs. Ltd., Richmond, 1996-97; former bd. dirs. ENVOY Corp. (subs. Quintiles Transnational Corp.), sr. v.p., 1997—99, ind. cons., 1999—2000, exec. v.p., 2000—01; exec. officer HFS LLC, 2001—. Mem. mgmt. info. systems adv. bd. U. Ga., Athens, 1986-89, Va. Commonwealth U., 1991-93; bd. dirs. J. Sargeant Reynoldds C.C., 1991—, Pool Corp., 2003-. V.p. St. Joseph's Home and Sch., Marietta, Ga., 1987-88. Mem. Nat. Assn. Bank Servicers, Bank Mktg. Assn., Richmond Metro C. of C. (former bd. dirs.), Soc. Internat. Bus. Fellows, Assn. for Corp. Growth (bd. dirs. 1996—). Roman Catholic. Avocations: sailing, tennis, jogging. Home: 12106 Country Hills Ct Glen Allen VA 23059-5347 Office: ACI Worldwide Inc 6060 Coventry Dr Elkhorn NE 68022-6482 Office Phone: 402-390-7600. Business E-Mail: harlan.seymour@scppool.com.

SEYMOUR, JAMES B., JR., history professor, department chairman; s. James B. Seymour, Sr. and Joanne Seymour; life ptnr. J. Keith Rawlinson. PhD, Tex. A&M U., College Station, 1997. Chair, social studies St. Stephen's Episcopal Sch., Houston, 2000—03; chair, dept. history and anthropology Cy-Fair Coll., Cypress, Tex., 2003—. Vis. asst. prof. U. Tex., Brownsville, 1998—99, Tex. A&M U., College Station, 1999—2000, Kingsville; divsn. rep. Faculty Senate, 2003—05, sec., 2005—07. Contbr. articles to profl.jours., chapters to books. Hospice vol. Omega Ho., Houston, 2000—07; vestry bd. mem. St. Stephen's Episc. Ch., Houston, 2007—. Grantee Landmarks History Workshop, Nat. Endowment for the Humanities, 2006. Mem.: Am. Fedn. Tchrs., Tex. State Hist. Assn., Western Hist. Assn., East Tex. Hist. Assn., Tex. CC Tchrs. Assn. Office: Cy-Fair Coll 9191 Barker-Cypress Dr Cypress TX 77433

SEYMOUR, MARGARET B., federal judge; b. Washington, 1947; BA, Howard U., 1969; JD, Am. U., 1977. Equal opportunity specialist HEW, 1972—79, EEOC, 1979—80; atty. Office of Civil Rights US Dept. Edn., 1980—88; pvt. practice atty., 1988—90; asst. US atty. US Atty.'s Office (dist. SC), 1990—96, interim US atty., 1993, 1996; magistrate judge US Dist. Ct. SC, 1996—98, judge, 1998—. Office: US Dist Ct Perry Courthouse 901 Richland St Columbia SC 29201 Office Phone: 803-765-5590.

SEYMOUR, STEPHANIE KULP, federal judge; b. Battle Creek, Mich., Oct. 16, 1940; d. Francis Bruce and Frances Cecelia (Bria) Kulp; m. R. Thomas Seymour, June 10, 1972; children: Bart, Bria, Sara, Anna. BA magna cum laude, Smith Coll., 1962; JD, Harvard U., 1965. Bar: Okla. 1965. Practice, Boston, 1965—66, Tulsa, 1966—67, Houston, 1968—69; assoc. Doerner, Stuart, Saunders, Daniel & Anderson, Tulsa, 1971—75, ptnr., 1975—79; judge US Ct. Appeals (10th cir.), Tulsa, Okla., 1979—, chief judge, 1994—2000, sr. judge, 2005—. Mem. US Jud. Conf., 1994—2000, com. defender svcs., 1985—90, chmn., 1987—90, com. to review cir. council conduct and disability, 1996—; joint fed. tribal rels. com. 9th and 10th cirs., 1993—; mem. Okla. State Fed. Tribal Judicial Coun., 1993—94. Task force Tulsa Human Rights Commn., 1972—76; legal adv. panel Tulsa Task Force Battered Women, 1971—77; trustee Tulsa County Law Libr., 1977—78. Recipient Sarah T. Hughes Civil Rights award, Fed. Bar Assn., 2007, medal, Smith Coll., 2010; named to Okla. Women's Hall of Fame, 2008. Mem.: ABA, Am. Inns of Ct. (Council Oak chpt.), Nat. Assn. Women Judges, Fed. Judges Assn., Tulsa County Bar Assn., Okla. Bar Assn. (assoc. bar examiner 1973—79), Phi Beta Kappa. Office: US Courthouse 333 W 4th St Ste 4-562 Tulsa OK 74103-3819

SEYMOUR, THADDEUS, language educator; b. NYC, June 29, 1928; s. Whitney North and Lola Virginia (Vickers) S.; m. Polly Gnagy, Nov. 20, 1948; children: Elizabeth Halsey, Thaddeus, Samuel Whitney, Mary Duffie, Abigail Comfort AB, U. Calif., 1950; MA, U. N.C., 1951, PhD, 1955; D.H.L. (hon.), Wilkes Coll., 1968; LL.D. (hon.), Butler U., 1971, Ind. State U., 1976; LLD (hon.), Wabash Coll., 1984, U. Cen. Fla., 1990, Stetson U., 1990; DHL (hon.), Rollins Coll., 1990. Mem. faculty Dartmouth Coll., 1954-69, prof. English, dean coll., 1959-69; pres. Wabash Coll., Crawfordsville, Ind., 1969-78, Rollins Coll., Winter Park, Fla., 1978-90, prof. English, 1978—. Pres. Ind. Conf. Higher Edn., 1977; v.p. Assoc. Colls. Ind., 1978; vice-chmn. Fla. Ind. Colls. Fund Past mem. Ind. Bicentennial Commn.; trustee Park-Tudor Sch., 1970-78, Bach Festival Soc., Winter Park Pub. Libr., 1998—2004; chmn. Fla. selection com. Rhodes Scholarship Trust, 1983-88; chmn. Habitat for Humanity of Winter Park, 1994—; sec.-treas. Winter Park Health Found., 1998—2005. Mem. Cmty. Found. Ctrl. Fla. (bd. dirs.), Ring 219 (charter), Internat. Brotherhood Magicians, Century Assn., Rotary, Omicron Delta Kappa. Home: 1804 Summerfield Rd Winter Park FL 32792 Office Phone: 407-646-1985. Business E-Mail: tseymour@rollins.edu.

SFORZINI, RICHARD HENRY, aerospace engineer, educator; b. Rochester, NY, July 25, 1924; m. Corinne Lorenz, 1947; children: Richard Jr., Suzanne Simonelli, Deborah Pugh, Michael, Stephen, Andrew, Mark. Degree of Mech. Engr., MIT, 1954; BS, U.S. Mil. Acad., 1947. Instr. ordnance U.S. Mil. Acad., 1954-56, asst. prof., 1956-57; project dir. anti-tank missile sys. R&D Army Rocket and Guided Missile Agy., Redstone Arsenal, Ala., 1958-59; engr. Huntsville divsn. Thiokol Chem. Corp., Ala., 1959-62, mgr. engring. dept. Ala., 1962-64, dir. engring. space booster divsn. Brunswick, Ga., 1964-66; vis. prof. Auburn (Ala.) U., 1966-67, prof., 1967-85, prof. emeritus aerospace engring., 1985—. Home and Office: 912 Cherokee Rd Auburn AL 36830-2723

SGRO, JOSEPH ANTHONY, retired psychologist, educator; b. New Haven, Nov. 22, 1937; s. Fred and Tullia (Francesconi) S.; m. Beverly Ann Huston, Feb. 1, 1964; children: Anthony, Jennifer. BA, Trinity Coll., 1959; MS, Lehigh U., 1961; PhD, Tex. Christian U., 1966. Asst. prof. Old Dominion U., Norfolk, Va., 1965-67, Va. Poly. Inst. & State U., Blacksburg, 1967-71, assoc. prof., 1971-79, prof., 1979-99; prof. emeritus, 1999—; dept. head psychology Va. Poly. Inst. & State U., Blacksburg, 1982-96, mem. exec. bd., sec.-treas., Coun. Grad. Dept. Psychology, 1990-92, chmn., 1992-93; adj. prof. Warren Wilson Coll., 2000, U. NC Asheville, 2004. Vice-chmn. Va. Bd. Psychologists Examiners, Richmond, 1970-75, exec. bd. mem. WNC Communities. Inc., 2009-. Editor: Virginia Tech Symposium on Applied Behavioral Science, 1980. Mem. APA, Southeastern Psychol. Assn. (chmn., Assn. Heads Depts. Psychology 1987-89), Va. Psychol. Assn. (pres. 1974-76), Soc. Indsl. and Orgnl. Psychology, Omicron Delta Kappa, Psi Chi, Sigma Xi. Avocations: golf, cooking, Italian studies. Home: 22 Hilltop Rd Biltmore Forest NC 28803 E-mail: jsgro@charter.net.

SHABANA, YASSER M., plant pathologist professor, research scientist; PhD, Mansoura U., Egypt, 1992. Cert. plant pathologist Mansoura U., Egypt, U. Fla., 1992. Program mgr. weed biocontrol U. Fla., Gainesville, 2006—; demonstrator Mansoura U., 1981—87, rsch. asst., 1987—92, asst. prof., 1992—98, assoc. prof., 1998—2003, prof., head dept. plant pathology, 2003—. Rsch. fellow U. Hohenheim, Stuttgart, Germany, 1999—2001, guest lectr., 2000; vis. scholar U. Fla., Gainesville, 1989—91; vis. prof. Perdue U., West Lafayette, Ind., 2005—06; program mgr. weed biocontrol U. Fla., Gainsville, 2006—; invited spkr. and cons. in field; co inventor US Patents. Contbr. 18 sci. & profl. Socs. Advisor spkr trainer panel mem. IFS, Sweden. Recipient Professorship award, Sauerborn Lab. U. Hohenheim Germany, 2004; grantee, Higher Edn. Enhancement Project Fund, 2004; vis. scholar, U. Fla., Gainsville, 1994—97; Rsch. grant, Third World Acad. Scis., Italy, 1993, Rsch. and Traval grants, Mansoura U., Egypt, 1994, Travel grant, U. Fla., Gainsville, 1998, Equipment grant, Supreme Coun. Egyptian Univs., 1999, Rsch. grant, Danida, Denmark, Cabi Biosci., UK, 2001—02, Equipment grant, Alexander von Humboldt Found., Germany, 2003, Travel grant, U. Hohenheim, Germany, 2000. Mem.: Weed Sci. Soc. America (com. mem. biological control), Internat. Found. Sci. (sci. advisor 1998—, Rsch. grants 1989, 1991, 1994, 2005, Travel grant 1998), Egypt Agrl. Scis. Soc. (assoc.), Egyptian Mycol. Soc. (assoc.), Egyptian Phytopath. Soc. (assoc.), Arab Soc. Plant Protection (assoc.), Internat. Parasitic Plant Soc. (assoc.), Fla. Weed Sci. Soc. (assoc.), Internat. Orgn. Biol. Control (assoc.), Am. Phytopath. Soc. (assoc.), Nat. Profl. Assn. Agriculturists Egypt (assoc.), Egyptian Soc. State Sci. Award Winners (assoc.). Achievements include patents for broad-spectrum bioherbicide for controlling pigweed species; phomopsis species fungus useful as a broad-spectrum bioherbicide to control several species of pigweeds. Office: Univ Fla 1453 Fifield Hall Plant Pathology Dept Gainesville FL 32611 Home Phone: 352-373-4221; Office Phone: 352-392-9055. Personal E-mail: yassershabana2@yahoo.com.

SHABOT, MYRON MICHAEL, hospital system administrator; b. Houston, Aug. 5, 1945; s. Sam and Mona Doris (Stalarow) S.; 1 child, Samuel Laib. Student, Tulane U., 1963-64; BA, U. Tex., Austin, 1966; MD, U. Tex., Dallas, 1970. Intern Parkland Meml. Hosp., Dallas, 1970—71; resident Harbor Gen. Hosp., Torrance, Calif., 1973—78; lectr. surgery UCLA Sch. Medicine, 1977-78, asst. prof., 1978-82, clin. assoc. prof. surgery and anesthesiology, 1983-97, prof. surgery, 1997—; dir. surg. ICU, LA County Harbor Med. Ctr.-UCLA Sch. Medicine, 1980-82; med. dir. Enterprise Info. Svcs. Cedars-Sinai Med. Ctr., LA, dir. surg. ICU, 1982—, vice chief of staff, 2000—01, chief of staff, 2002—03, also bd. dirs. Sec. Cedars-Sinai Med. Ctr. Attending Staff, 1999-2000; bd. dirs. eHealth Initiative and Found., 2006—; adj. prof. U. Tex. Health Scis. Ctr., Houston; supr. sys. chief quality officer Meml. Hermann Healthcare Sys., Houston, 2007, sr. v.p., sys. chief medcial officer, 2007-. Contbr. articles to profl. jours. Served to lt. comdr. USPHS, 1971-73. Fellow ACS (So. Calif. chpt. bd. dirs. 1988—, pres. 1992-93, gov., 1992—), Am. Coll. Critical Care Medicine, Am. Coll. Med. Informatics; mem. Western Surg. Assn., Pacific Coast Surg. Assn., Soc. Critical Care Medicine, Am. Assn. Surgery of Trauma, Soc. Computers in Critical Care and Pulmonary Medicine (bd. dirs. 1988—, treas. 1989—, pres., 1993-94), Soc. Clin. Data Mgmt. Systems (pres. 1985-86), L.A. Surg. Soc. (pres. 1997-98), Phi Eta Sigma. Jewish. Office: 929 Gessner Rd Ste 2700 Houston TX 77024 Home Phone: 713-647-9894. Business E-Mail: michael.shabot@memorialhermann.org.

SHACK, ROBERT BRUCE (BRUCE SHACK), plastic surgeon, department chairman; b. Vernon, Tex., Oct. 7, 1947; s. Nathan Lee and Patsy Lee (Holliday) S.; m. Sharon Summers Frazier, Aug. 16, 1969 (div. 1982); children: Robert David, Nathan Andrew; m. Wanda Kaye, Nov. 11, 1984; children: Jerion Elizabeth, Austin Ryan. BS, Midwestern U., Wichita Falls, Tex., 1969; MD, U. Tex., Galveston, 1973. Diplomate Am. Bd. Surgery, Am. Bd. Plastic Surgery with added qualifications in surgery of the hand. Extern St. Paul's Hosp., Dallas, 1971, St. Bartholomew's Hosp., London, 1971; intern surgery Vanderbilt U. Med. Ctr., Nashville, 1973—74, asst. resident surgery, 1974—77, chief resident surgery, 1977—78, resident plastic surgery, 1978—79, chief resident plastic surgery, 1979—80, asst. prof. plastic surgery, 1982—87, assoc. prof. plastic surgery, 1987—96, interim chmn., assoc. prof. dept. plastic surgery, 1996, chmn. and prof. dept. plastic surgery, 1997—; asst. prof. plastic surgery Johns Hopkins Hosp., Balt., 1980—82, U. Med. Sch. Medicine, Balt., 1981—82. Attending surgeon Children's Hosp. and Ctr. for Reconstructive Surgery, Balt., 1980—82; attending surgeon plastic surgery Md. Inst. for Emergency Medicine, 1980—82, Children's Hosp., Balt., 1980—82, Vanderbilt U. Med. Ctr., Nashville, 1982; attending head and neck surgeon John Hopkins Hosp., Nashville, 1980—82; staff privileges Baptist Hosp., 1982, Centennial Med. Ctr., Nashville, 1982; courtesy privileges in surgery Nashville Gen. Hosp., 1982—93; prof., chmn. dept. plastic surgery Vanderbilt Ctr. for Cosmetic Plastic Surgery; cons. head and neck surgery VA Hosp., 1982—; mem. instrnl. course com. Plastic Surgery Ednl. Found., 1985—86, 1986—87, 1987—88, mem. in svc. exam com., 1985—86, 1987—88, chmn. breast/aesthetic subcom. in-svc. exam. com. plastic surgery, 1988—94, chmn. in-svc. exam com., 1994—97, assoc. vis. prof., 1996; mem. adv. bd. Tenn. chpt. Neurofibromatosis Found., 1990—; sr. guest examiner Am. Bd. Plastic Surgery, 1999—2002, CAQSH exam cons., 1999—2002; mem. carrier adv. com. Tenn. Medicare Part B, 2004—; vis. prof. plastic surgery Scott-White Clinic, Tex. A&M, Temple, 1996; vis. prof. dept. plastic surgery U. Miss., Jackson, 1997; XV Marzoni lectr. and vis. prof. U. Ala., Birmingham, 2000; IX Ann. Coleman lectr. and vis. prof. U. Va., 2001; vis. prof. plastic surgery So. Ill. Sch. Medicine, 2003, Baylor Coll. Medicine, 2003; presenter and lectr. in field. Contbr. chapters to books, articles to profl. jours. Recipient Disting. Alumnus award, Midwestern State U. Divsn. Scis., 1998; named one of Outstanding Young Men in Am., 1969; grantee, LPG, Inc., 1998—99, Aesthetic Surgery Edn. and Rsch. Found., 1998, 1999, Southeastern Soc. for Plastic Surgeons, 2002—03. Fellow: ACS (mem. Tenn. dist. 2 com. on applicants 1990—2000); mem.: AMA, Southern Med. Law (pres. 2009—10), Am. Soc. Plastic and Reconstructive Surgeons (treas. practice rels. commn. 1983—84, mem. fin. com. 1983—84, treas. practice rels. commn. 1984—85, mem. fin. com. 1984—85, 1985—86, socioeconomic com. 1985—86, mem. fin. com. 1986—87, socioeconomic com. 1986—87, 1987—88, v.p. associated mgmt. svcs. 1988—90, chmn. fin. com. 1988—90, mem.-at-large bd. dirs. 1991—93, chmn. profl. liability ins. com. 1991—94, pres. associated mgmt. svcs. 1991—98, chmn. mktg. com. 1995—97, asst. sect. 1997), Tenn. Soc. Plastic and Reconstructive Surgery (pres. 2002—), Tenn. Med. Assn., So. Surg. Assn., So. Med. Assn. (asst. sec. plastic surgery sect. 1984—85, sec. plastic surgery sect. 1986—88, assoc. councilor State of Tenn. 1986—, chmn. elect plastic surgery sect. 1989, chmn. plastic surgery sect. 1990, councilor 2004—, pres. elect 2008—09, pres. 2008—), Southeastern Soc. Plastic and Reconstructive Surgeons (resident and rsch. com. 1984—85, chmn. So. Med. Assn. liaison com. 1986—90, chmn. resident and rsch. com. 1993—95, trustee bd. dirs. 1995—, chmn. spl. edn. com. 1998, 2001—02, pres. 2007, grantee 1998—99), Nashville Surg. Soc. (sec.-treas. 1993—96, pres.-elect 1996, pres. 1996—97), Nashville Acad. Medicine, John Staige Davis Soc. Plastic Surgeons Md., John B. Lynch Soc. (v.p. 1984—85, pres. 1985—), H. William Scott, Jr. Soc. (sec. 1993—97, pres.-elect 1999, pres. 2000—01), Am. Soc. for Aesthetic Plastic Surgery (grantee 1997—98), Am. Soc. for Reconstructive Microsurgery, Am. Soc. Plastic Surgeons (sec. 1998—2001, alt. del. AMA 2000—02, practice commr. 2000—, chmn. by-laws com. 2001—, v.p. 2002), Am. Soc. Maxillofacial Surgeons (mem. fin. com. 1993—98), Am. Cancer Soc., Am. Burn Assn., Am. Assn. Plastic Surgeons, Sigma Xi, Mu Delta, Beta Beta Beta. Republican. Methodist. Avocations: golf, shooting. Office: Vanderbilt U Med Ctr Dept Plastic Surgery 1161 21st Ave S D-4207 MCN Nashville TN 37232-2345 Office Phone: 615-936-0169. Business E-Mail: bruce.shack@vanderbilt.edu.

SHACKELFORD, MARK L., motor and generator manufacturing company executive; Attended, Ark. Tech U., Webster U. Dir., info. svcs., mgr., electronics purchasing, mgr., sys. and ops. Baldor Electric Co., v.p., info. svcs., 2007—. Office: Baldor Electric Co 5711 R S Boreham Jr St Fort Smith AR 72901 Office Phone: 479-646-4711. Office Fax: 479-648-5792. Business E-Mail: mark_shackelford@baldor.com.

SHACKELFORD, RICHARD L., lawyer; BA summa cum laude, JD summa cum laude, U. Ga., Athens. Bar: Ga., US Ct. Appeals (11th cir.), Ga. Mid. & No. Dist. Cts. Ptnr. King & Spalding, Atlanta, mem. healthcare practice and bus. litig. groups. Contbr. of articles to profl. publications. Named The Best Lawyers in America as the Healthcare Lawyer of the Yr. for Atlanta, 2013; named an Outstanding Healthcare Litigator, Nitghtingale's Healthcare News, 2003, 2007; named one of The Best Lawyers in America, The Best of the Best: USA; named to Chambers USA Client Guide, Guide to the Leading US Healthcare Lawyers. Mem.: American Healthcare Lawyers Assn. (vice-chair com. on HMOs and health plans 1998—2000, past chair com. on HMOs and health plans 2000—02, mem. bd. dirs. 2002—12, pres. 2010—11), Ga. Acad. Healthcare Attorneys (past pres. 2001—02), Order of Coif, Phi Beta Kappa. Office: King & Spalding 1180 Peachtree St NE Atlanta GA 30309-3521 Office Phone: 404-572-4995. Office Fax: 404-572-5100. Business E-Mail: rshackelford@kslaw.com.*

SHADDOCK, CARROLL SIDNEY, lawyer; b. Beaumont, Tex., July 7, 1940; s. Carroll Bitting Jr. and Hulda Martha (Gaertner) S.; m. Dorothea Schulze, Nov. 30, 1963; children: Carroll Christian, Peter Eric, Matthew Nolan. BA, Rice U., 1962; JD, Yale U., 1965. Ptnr. Locke Lord LLP, Houston, 1967—2012, Capital Title Tex., Shaddock Co., 2013—. Chmn. Scenic America, Washington, 1985-92; founding chmn. Scenic Tex., 1992—, Trees for Houston, 1982-. Republican. Lutheran. Avocations: music, golf, travel. Home: 2310 Underwood St Houston TX 77030 Office: Capital Title 3040 Post Oak Blvd Ste 150 Houston TX 77056 Business E-Mail: css@shaddocktexas.com.

SHADOIN, ROBERT E., state legislator; BS in Bus. Adminstrn., La. Tech U., Ruston, 1975; JD, La. State U., 1978. Atty., La.; mem. Dist. 12 La. House of Reps., Baton Rogue, 2012—. Republican. Office: 207 W Mississippi Ste 300 Ruston LA 71270 also: La House of Reps 900 N 3rd St Baton Rouge LA 70804 Office Phone: 318-251-5039. Business E-Mail: shadoinr@legis.la.gov.

SHAFER, DAVID J., state legislator; b. De Kalb County, Ga., Apr. 29, 1965; s. James H. and Sarah (McCoy) Shafer; m. Lee Shafer; 1 child, Ellie 1 stepchild, J.W. BA, Univ. Ga. Pres. The Strategies Co., 1997—; mem. Dist. 48 Ga. State Senate, 2003—. Barry Goldwater Mentor Award, Georgia Fedn Col Republican, 92; Republican of Year, Georgia Association Republican Elected Officials, 93. Mem. Lake Lanier Library Bd. Trustees (trustee, 1991-95), Gwinnett Co Library Bd. Trustees (vice chmn., 1991-95), United Cerebral Palsy Greater Atlanta (bd. dir., 1993-95), Partnership Against Domestic Violence (bd. dir., 1996-), Univ. G. Nat. Alumni Assn. (bd. dir., 1997-), Phi Kappa Psi. Republican. Presbyterian. Mailing: PO Box 880 Duluth GA 30096 Office Phone: 770-497-0048. Business E-Mail: david.shafer@senate.ga.gov.

SHAFFER, ANITA MOHRLAND, counselor, educator; b. Racine, Wis., Apr. 5, 1939; d. Milton Arthur and Gudrun Amanda Stoffel. BS magna cum laude, U. Wis., 1961; MEd, U. Wash., 1966; postgrad., Ariz. State U., 1971-76. Cert. in elem. edn., social sci. secondary edn., spl. edn., Tex.; lic. profl. counselor, Tex. Tchr. Racine Unified Dist. 1, 1961-63, Edmonds Sch. Dist. 15, Lynnwood, Wash., 1963-70, Ariz. Dept. Corrections, Phoenix, 1971-77; tchr. spl. edn. Pasadena (Tex.) Ind. Sch. Dist., 1977-78, spl. edn. counselor, 1978-90, elem. counselor, 1990-98; supr. U. Houston, 1998—2008. Ednl. cons., 1998—. Violin, Houston Sinfonietta, 2002—. Mem. Tex. Counseling Assn., Houston Counseling Assn., Mus. Fine Arts Houston (patron), Houston Lic. Profl. Counselors Assn., Pi Lambda Theta, World Affairs Coun. Home: 5905 Woodway Place Ct Houston TX 77057-2005

SHAFFER, BERNARD WILLIAM, mechanical and aerospace engineering educator; b. NYC, Aug. 7, 1924; s. Abraham and Eva (Ellinsky) S.; m. Florence Solow, Feb. 23, 1947 (dec. Oct. 29, 1986); children: Janet Ilene, Roberta Franceen. BME, CCNY, 1944; MSME, Case Inst. Tech. (now Case W. Res. U.), 1947; PhD, Brown U., 1951. Registered profl. engr., N.Y., R.I. Aero. rsch. scientist flight propulsion rsch. lab. NACA (now NASA), Cleve., 1944-47; spl. lectr. applied mechanics Case Inst. Tech. (now Case Western Reserve Univ.), Cleve., 1946-47; rsch. assoc., grad. div. applied math. and engring. instr. Brown U., Providence, 1947-50; asst. prof. mech. engring. NYU, NYC, 1950-53, assoc. prof., 1953-58, prof., project dir. rsch. divsn., 1958-73; prof. dept. mech. and aerospace engring. Poly. Inst. NYU, Bklyn., 1973—93, Farmingdale, prof. emeritus Bklyn., 1993—. Cons. in field; mem. adv. coun. Coll. Aeros., N.Y.C., 1982—; vis. rsch. prof. mech. engring. Fla. Atlantic U., Boca Raton, 1992, Disting. vis. rsch. prof., 1993-95, 97—. Contbr. articles to profl. jours. Bd. dirs. Harbor Hills Civic Assn., Great Neck, N.Y., 1968-71. With USAAF, 1944-47. Recipient various govt. grants; named Order of Engr. Newark Coll. Engring., 1988. Fellow ASME (Richards Meml. award 1968); mem. AIAA (assoc. fellow), Sigma Xi, Tau Beta Pi, Pi Tau Sigma. Avocations: golf, swimming.

SHAFFNER, RANDOLPH PRESTON, retired educator, writer, publisher; b. Winston-Salem, NC, Jan. 17, 1940; s. Emil Nathaniel and Anna Jackson (Preston) S.; m. Margaret Farmer Rhodes; children: Eric Randolph, Edward David, Joseph Andrew, Thomas Matthew, Jackson Rhodes. Student, Davidson Coll., NC, 1958-60; BA in English with honors in writing, U. NC, Chapel Hill, 1962, MA in Comparative Lit., 1969, PhD, 1973. Surveyor's lineman Joyce Mapping Co., Winston-Salem, 1955-58, 62; counselor, scoutmaster Camp Sequoyah, Weaverville, NC, 1959; track repairman Alaska R.R., Anchorage, 1960; case handler Emard Packing Co., Anchorage, 1960, AYR Canneries, Seldovia, Alaska, 1961; tchr. US Peace Corps., Chiengrai, Thailand, 1963-65, St. Christopher's Sch., Richmond, Va., 1969-71; instr. U. NC, 1968-69, 71-73; asst. prof. Fairfield U., Conn., 1973-78, Western Carolina U., 1984, 87, Continuing Edn. program World Masterpieces, Highlands, NC, 1987—89; moderator Highlands lecture series Western Carolina U., 1989-92. Instr. Carolina environ. program U. NC, Chapel Hill, 2003; editor John F. Blair Pub., Winston-Salem, 1966-68; bookseller, owner Cyrano's Bookshop, Highlands, NC, 1978-05; founder, pub. Faraway Pub., 2001; asst. to dean Sch. Libr. Scis. U. NC, Chapel Hill, 1973-74; literary mag. adv., various subcoms. Dept. Eng. Fairfield U., 1973-78. Author: Apprenticeship Novel, 1984, Tree Ordinance for Town of Highlands, 1987, Good Reading Material, Mostly Bound and New: The Hudson Library 1884-1994, 1994, Heart of the Blue Ridge: Highlands, North Carolina, 2001, 2d edit., 2004, Highlands Heritage Trail: A Walking Tour of Many Highlands Historical Buildings and Landmarks, 2003, NC Hwy Hist Marker Thomas G. Harbison, 2003, Highlands Images of America, 2008; (with others) Nineteenth Century Literature Criticism, Vol. 21, 1989; contbr. poetry to NC Poetry Soc. anthology Here's to the Land, 1992; contbr. short stories to mags; contbr. Heritage of Macon Co., NC, Vol. 2, 1999, NC Hwy Hist Marker Andre Michaux, 2013 Lectr. with Alexander, String Quartet, Words & Music, 1989, 92, 94, for Western Carolina U., Highlands lectr. series, 1991-93, 2000; inaugural lectr. Chattooga Watershed Cultural Heritage Series, 2005, Zahner Conservation Lecture Series, 2009; instr. Ctr. for Life Enrichment, 2000, 06-; chmn. ARC Disaster Svcs., Fairfield, 1974-78, Zoning Bd. of Adjustment, Highlands, 1981-83, 85-90; pres., bd. trustees Hudson Libr., Inc., Highlands, 1987-90, 99-2001, chmn. libr. com., 1995-99; trustee Hudson Libr. Bascom-Louise Art Gallery, 1987-90, 95-99, Highlands Land Trust, Inc., 1995-96; bd. dirs. ARC, Fairfield, 1974-78, Highlands Cultural Art Ctr., 1987; fundraising com. Highlands Permanent Endowment Scholarships, 1987-89; Town of Highlands Millennium Com., 1999; historian Highlands Hist. Soc., Inc., 1999—, adv. com., 2001—, archivist, 2005—, webmaster, 2005-; founding mem. Highlands Plateau Greenway, Inc., 2005, v.p., 2007-11, pres., 2013-; chmn. Design Com. NC Small Town Main St. Program, 2010-, exec. com., 2010-, vol., US Forest Svc. Whiteside Mountain, 2010-, mem. Macon County Hist. Preservation Commn. Task Force, 2006, Macon County Heritage Coun., 2006—09; bd. dirs. Friends Mtn. Hist., 2006—09, vice chmn., 2007—09, editor Mtn. Hist. Museums-in-Partnership Newsletter, 2007-09; vice-chmn. bd. missions Greenfield Hill Congl. Ch., Fairfield, Conn., 1977, chmn. scholarship co., 1975-77; chaperon Am. Inst. for Fgn. Study, Grenoble, France, 1970. Recipient God and Country award, 1955, Eagle Scout award, 1957, Outstanding Pres. and Trustee award Hudson Libr. and Bascom-Louise Gallery, 1990, Daniel Boone Coun. Boy Scouts Am. Disting. Citizen award, 2002, Gertrude and Dolly Harbison award, Hudson Libr., 2004; Goethe Inst. scholar German Embassy, Munich, Fed. Rep. Germany, 1965, Univ. Besançon, France, 1965, Named Trail Worker of Yr. Highlands Plateau Greenway, 2009, 10 yrs. Svc. citation Highlands Hist. Soc., 2009. Mem.: NC Writers' Network, Am. Assn. for State and Local History (ann. award for Heart of the Blue Ridge 2005), Highlands Biol. Found. (trustee 1981—2006, fund raising com. 1986, environ. protection com. 1986—88, exec. com. 1986—2004, treas. 1990—2004, adv. com. on Nature Ctr. 1992, hon. trustee 2006—), Highlands Mchts. Assn. (chmn. fin. com., treas. 1984—87, chmn. tree com. and beautification com. 1984—89, greenways com. 2004—), Am. Acad. Poets, NC Poetry Soc., Writers' Workshop, Am. Comparative Lit. Assn., Internat. Comparative Lit. Assn., NC Literary and Historical Assn., Soc. NC Archivists, Highlands-Cashiers Land Trust, Nat. Peace Corps Assn., Highlands Hist. Soc., Highlands C. of C., Clan Morrison Soc., NC Soc. Historians (History Book award 2002, Paul Green Multimedia award 2007, HIstory Book award 2009), Trail Hikers Am., Rotary (Outstanding Vol. award 1989), Lambda Iota Tau (faculty moderator Delta Omicon Ch. 1975—80, founder). Democrat. Moravian. Avocations: reading, travel, hiking, writing. Office: Highlands Hist Soc 524 N 4th St Highlands NC 28741-0670 Home: PO Box 765 189 Cowee Gap Ln Highlands NC 28741-0765 Office Phone: 828-787-1050. Business E-Mail: highlandshistory@nctv.com.

SHAH, NEEL, air transportation executive; b. Balt., Aug. 7, 1969; BA in Economics, Swarthmore Coll.; MBA in Fin. & Strategy, Columbia U. Cons. Beddows & Co., Pa.; cons., mgr., strategy practice Arthur D. Little Inc.; v.p., strategic planning PHP Healthcare Co., Va.; sr. prin., bus. devel. and strategic partnerships UAL Loyalty Svcs., Inc.; analyst, fin. analysis United Airlines Cargo, 1999, v.p., sales and mktg.; joined Delta Air Lines, Inc., 2008, v.p., cargo, 2008—10; SVP, Chief Cargo Officer, 2010—. Mem. Air Transport Assn.; exec. Ga. State Workforce Investment Bd. Office Phone: 404-714-5777. Office Fax: 404-714-5021. Business E-Mail: Neel.Shah@delta.com.

SHAHEEN, JACK GEORGE, communications educator; b. Pitts., Sept. 21, 1935; s. Jack and Nazara (Jacob) S.; m. Bernice Marie Rafeedie, Jan. 22, 1966; children: Michael A., Michele L. BFA, Carnegie Inst. of Tech., 1957; MA, Pa. State U., 1964; PhD, U. Mo., 1969. Entertainment dir. U.S. Spl. Svcs., Berlin, Germany, 1960-63; spl. programs dir. UCLA, 1965-67; asst. instr. mass communications U. Mo., Columbia, 1967-69; prof. mass communications So. Ill. U., Edwardsville, 1969-94. Disting vis. rsch. scholar, NYU,cons. mid. east affairs CBS News, 1994—. Author: The TV Arab, 1984 (Outstanding Book of Yr., Choice Mag. 1984), Reel Bad Arabs: How Hollywood Vilifies A People, 2001, Guilty: Hollywood's Verdict on Arabs After 9/11, 2007, AIS for Arab; editor: Nuclear War Films, 1978; contbr. more than 300 articles, essays to newspapers and mags. Scholar-diplomat Dept. State, 1980; Fulbright scholar, 1975, 82; Oxford Rsch. fellow, 2004. Democrat. Mem. Eastern Orthodox Ch. Avocations: tennis, swimming. Home: One Dahlgren Ln Hilton Head Island SC 29928-3939 Personal E-mail: jgshaheen1@juno.com.

SHAHSHAHANI, AZADEH, legal association administrator; b. Iran; Master's in Modern Middle Eastern and North African Studies, U. Mich., JD, 2004. Muslim/Middle Eastern Cmty. Outreach Coordinator American Civil Liberties Union of NC, 2006—07; interim dir. American Civil Liberties Union of Georgia, 2007—08, dir., Nat. Security/Immigrants' Rights Project, 2008—. Steering com. mem. Georgia Detention Watch; co-founder Human Rights Atlanta, Internat. Tribunal of Conscience of the Global Alternative Forum of Peoples in Movement; chair Refugee Women's Network; co-chair ABA Individual Rights and Responsibilities Sect. Com. on the Rights of Immigrants. Edited several human rights reports:; author of numerous book chapters; author of legal articles on immigration and racial profiling:. Recipient Equal Justice Found. Public Interest Practitioner award, U. Georgia Law Sch., 2009, American Immigration Lawyers Assn. Advocacy award, 2012; UN High Commissioner for Refugees Fellowship, Washington, DC, Rsch. Fellow with a women's rights organization in Iran. Mem.: Nat. Lawyers Guild (pres. 2012—, past co-chair internat. com., past Southern regional v.p.). Office: National Lawyers Guild 132 Nassau St Rm 922 New York NY 10038 also:

American Civil Liberties Union of Georgia 1900 The Exchange Suite 425 Atlanta GA 30339 Office Phone: 212-679-5100, 770-303-9966. Office Fax: 212-679-2811, 770-303-0060. Business E-Mail: president@nlg.org, info@acluga.org.*

SHALALA, DONNA EDNA, academic administrator, former United States Secretary of Health and Human Services; b. Cleve., Feb. 14, 1941; d. James Abraham and Edna (Smith) S. AB, Western Coll., 1962; MSSC, Syracuse U., 1968, PhD, 1970; 44 hon. degrees, 1976—2008. Vol. US Peace Corps, Iran, 1962-64; asst. prof. polit. sci. Bernard M. Baruch CUNY, 1970-72; assoc. prof., chair, program in politics & edn. Tchrs. Coll. Columbia U., 1972-79; asst. sec. for policy devel. & rsch. US Dept. Housing & Urban Devel. (HUD), Washington, 1977-80; prof. polit. sci., pres. Hunter Coll., CUNY, 1980-87; prof. polit. sci. & ednl. policy studies, chancellor U. Wis., Madison, 1987-93; sec. US Dept. Health & Human Services (HHS), Washington, 1993-2001; pres. U. Miami, 2001—, prof. polit. sci., 2001—, secondary faculty Dept. Epidemiology, 2002—. Dir., treas. Mcpl. Assistance Corp. NYC, 1975—77; vis. prof. Yale Law Sch., 1976; co-chair Pres. Commn. on Care for Am. Returning Wounded Warriors, 2007—; bd. dirs. Lennar Corp., 2001—, Gannett Co., Inc, 2001—, MEDNAX, Inc., 2010—. Author: Neighborhood Governance, 1971, The City and the Constitution, 1972, The Property Tax and the Voters, 1973, The Decentralization Approach, 1974. Mem. Trilateral Commn., 1988—92, Knight Commn. on Intercollegiate Sports, 1989—91, Homes for Working Families, 2004—08; bd. govs. American Stock Exch., 1981—87; trustee TIAA, 1985—89, Com. Econ. Devel., 1982—92, Brookings Inst., 1989—92, John F. Kennedy Ctr. for the Performing Arts, Washington, 1993—2001, Henry J. Kaiser Family Found., 2001—11; bd. dirs. Children's Def. Fund, 1980—93, American Ditchley Found., 1981—93, Spencer Found., 1988—92, M&I Bank of Madison, 1991—92, NCAA Found., 1991, Inst. Internat. Econs., 1981—, Gannett Co., Inc., McLean, Va., 2001—, Michael J. Fox Found. for Parkinson's Rsch., 2001—08, United Health Group, Inc., Mpls., 2001—07, Lennar Corp., Miami, 2001—, US Soccer Fedn., 2008—; co-chair (with Ann Veneman) Mother's Day Every Day, 2009—. Recipient Donald C. Stone award, American Soc. for Pub. Adminstrn., 1981, Elizabeth Morrow Cutter award, YWCA of Greater NY, 1982, Disting. Svc. medal, Columbia U. Tchrs. Coll., 1989, Ryan White Youth Svc. award for Outstanding Contributions to the Fight Against Teen HIV/AIDS, 1997, Margaret E. Mahoney award for Outstanding Contributions to Health Policy, NY Acad. Medicine, 1997, League of Women Voters-Disting. Leader award for a Lifetime of Pub. Svc., 2000, U. Calif. San Francisco medal, 2002, American Assn. of Colleges of Nursing John P. McGovern award, 2003, Nat. Conf. for Cmty. & Justice, Silver Medallion award for Svc. to Humanity, 2005, Images in Excellence award, Black Coaches Assn., 2007, Urban Leadership award, U. Pa. Inst. for Urban Rsch., 2008, Statue of Liberty-Ellis Island Found., Ellis Island Family Heritage award in Edn., 2008, Radcliffe medal, Radcliffe Inst. for Advanced Study, Harvard U., 2008, Presdl. Medal of Freedom, The White House, 2008; named Women of the Yr., Glamour mag., 1994; named one of America's 200 Most Influential Women: Legends, Leaders and Trail Blazers, 1998, 100 of America's Most Important Women, 1999, America's Best Leaders, US News & World Report and the Ctr. for Pub. Leadership at Harvard U. Kennedy Sch. Govt., 2005, The 25 Great Pub. Servants, Coun. for Excellence, 2008; Ohio Newspaper Women's scholar, 1958, Western Coll. Trustee scholar, 1958—62, Carnegie fellow, 1966—68, Spencer Fellow, Nat. Acad. Edn., 1972—73, Guggenheim fellow, 1975—76. Fellow American Acad. Polit. & Social Sci., Inst. Medicine (coun. mem.), Nat. Acad. Pub. Adminstrn.; mem. ASPA (Nat. Pub. Svc. award, 1992), American Polit. Sci. Assn.(v.p. 1984-85, Annual Career Achievement award for Disting. Scholarships in Urban Politics, 1992, Hubert Humphrey award, 1994), Nat. Acad. Social Insurance, American Acad. Arts & Sciences, Coun. Fgn. Rels., American Philosophical Soc., Soc. for Women's Health Rsch., Japan Soc.(Leadership Fellow, 1987), Nat. Acad. Edn. Office: U Miami Office Pres 230 Ashe Administration Bldg 1252 Memorial Dr Coral Gables FL 33146 E-mail: dshalala@miami.edu.*

SHALES, THOMAS WILLIAM, former television and film critic, writer, journalist; b. Elgin, Ill., Nov. 3, 1953; s. Clyde LeRoy and Hulda Louise (Reko) Shales. BA, American U., Washington, 1973. Entertainment editor Washington Examiner, 1968-71; writer style sect. Washington Post, 1972—77, chief TV critic, 1977—2006, syndicated columnist, 1979—2010; columnist NewsPro. Author: On the Air!, 1982, Legends: Remembering America's Greatest Stars, 1989; co-author: Live from New York: An Uncensored History of Saturday Night Live, 2002, Those Guys Have All the Fun: Inside the World of ESPN, 2011 (NY Times bestseller). Recipient Disting. Alumnus award, American U., 1978, Pulitzer prize for criticism, 1988, Disting. Writing award, American Soc. Newspaper Editors, 1988.

SHALLCROSS, RICHARD, medical products executive; m. Kim Shallcross; 2 children. BS in Acctg., U. Denver. CPA. Audit mgr. Arthur Andersen & Co.; v.p. fin., CFO Rose Health Care System, Denver; pres., fin. and managed care HCA, Inc., Colo., 1995—96, CFO, Western Group. Mem.: Colo. Soc. CPA's, Health Care Fin. Mgmt. Assn. Office: HCA Inc 1 Park Plz Nashville TN 37203 Office Phone: 615-344-9551. Office Fax: 615-344-2266. Business E-Mail: rshallcross@hcahealthcare.com.

SHAMBAUGH, IRVIN CALVIN, JR., aptitude test firm executive, consultant; b. Harrisburg, Pa., June 7, 1943; s. Irvin Calvin and Viola Mary (Deibler) Shambaugh; m. Amy Willcox Shambaugh, Jan. 3, 1975. BS in Geol. Sci., Pa. State U., 1964; postgrad., MIT, Cambridge, Mass., 1964—65, Tex. Christian U., Ft. Worth, 1974—76, East Tex. State U., 1976—77. Rsch. coord. Johnson O'Connor Rsch. Found., Ft. Worth, 1965—76; pres., chief scientist Aptitude Inventory Measurement Svc., Dallas, 1976—; pres. Aptitude Expertise, Inc., 2009—; test developer Aptitude Inst. Ltd., New Zealand, 2009—. Centennial fellow Coll. Earth and Min. Scis., Pa. State U., 1996. Author: The Test-Taker's Guide to Career Literature, 1982, Test Manual for Selected AIMS Worksamples, 1986, Books About Careers, 1986, Career Facts: Where to Find Them and How to Use Them, 1992, The AIMS Guide to Career Facts, 1997; co-author: AIMS Information About Aptitudes, 1979, The Aptitude Handbook: A Guide to the AIMS Program, 1996, 2004, Career Facts: In Print and on the World Wide Web, 2003, AIMS Guide to Career Information, 2009; co-prodr.: (e-pub.) AIMS Information Disk, 2004—14; editor: You and Your Aptitudes, 1983; developer Activity Preference Questionnaire, 1994, psychometric instrument III Interest Inventory, 1996; contbr. articles to profl. jours.; developer AIMS test battery, 1976—, digital version, 2005—, AIMS Measure of Color Perception, 2005—, AIMS Reasoning Measure, 2006, rev. edit., 2011, 3-D Mental Gymnastics Worksample, 2006, rev. edit., 2011, Spanish Word Assn. Test, 2013. With USMC, 1966—68. Mem.: AAAS, ACA, APA (assoc.), Nat. Assn. Test Dirs., Nat. Assn. Coll. Admissions Counselors, Nat. Coun. Measurement in Edn., Am. Psychol. Soc., Assn. Assessment in Counseling and Edn. Achievements include development of psychometric instruments; SMC online test battery; Shambaugh Hollow structures test. Home: 934 Westbrook Dr Garland TX 75043-5243 Office: Aptitude Inventory Measurement Svc 12160 Abrams Rd Ste 314 Dallas TX 75243-4525

SHAMBUREK, ROLAND HOWARD, physician; b. Adell, Wis., June 7, 1928; s. William and Catherine (Illig) Shamburek; m. Gladys Irene Gibbons, June 21, 1952 (dec. Feb. 5, 2010); children: Steven J., Robert D., Daniel J. Grad., Monroe HS, Wis., 1946; BS, U. Wis., 1950, MD, 1953; MPH, Harvard U., 1961; grad., U.S. Army War Coll., Carlisle Barracks, Pa., 1972. Diplomate Am. Bd. Preventive Medicine. Commd. 1st lt. M.C., U.S. Army, 1953, advanced through grades to col., 1968; intern St. Joseph's Hosp., Marshfield, Wis., 1953-54; grad. U.S. Naval Sch. of Aviation Medicine, Pensacola, Fla., 1957; resident in preventive (aerospace) medicine USAF Sch. Aerospace Medicine, Brooks AFB, 1960-63; service in 216th Field Artillery (Atomic) Battalion, 1954—56, 1966, Office of Army Surgeon Gen., Washington, 1966—70, 1972—75; comdr. 67th EVAC Hosp., Vietnam, 1970-71; comdr. cons. USAR Europe Aviation Medicine, 1963—65; comdr. U.S. Army Med. Pers. Support Agy., 1975-77; ret. U.S. Army, 1977; exec. v.p. Aerospace Med. Assn., 1977-79; clin. practice Pentagon Health Clinic, Washington, 1981-85; med. researcher Office of Army Surgeon Gen., 1985-87; intern Marshfield Hosp., Wis., 1953—54. Med. monitor Canary Island Tracking Sta. for Gemini missions NASA, 1965—66. Contbr. scientific papers in field. Decorated Legion of Merit with oak leaf cluster, Army Commendation medal, Meritorious Svc. medal; recipient Gold Palm Eagle Scout award, Boy Scouts Am., 1945. Mem.: AMA (del. 1978), Internat. Acad. Aviation and Space Medicine, Soc. NASA Flight Surgeons, U.S. Army Flight Surgeons, Soc. Med. Cons. Armed Forces, Aerospace Med. Assn. (v.p. 1968—69), Am. Coll. Preventive Medicine (v.p. 1968—69), Assn. Mil. Surgeons (John Shaw Billings award 1968). Address: 3700 Moss Dr Annandale VA 22003-1915

SHANKLIN, DOUGLAS RADFORD, physician; b. Camden, NJ, Nov. 25, 1930; s. John Ferguson and Muriel (Morgan) S.; m. Virginia McClure, Apr. 7, 1956; children: Elizabeth, Leigh, Lois Virginia, John Carter, Eleanor. Student, Wilson Tchrs. Coll., 1949; AB in Chemistry, Syracuse U., 1952; MD, SUNY, Syracuse, 1955. Intern in pathology Duke U., 1955-56, resident, 1958; resident in pathology SUNY, Syracuse, 1958-60; practice medicine specializing in pathology Gainesville, Fla., 1960-67, 78-83; mem. faculty U. Fla., 1960-67; prof. pathology, ob-gyn. U. Chgo., 1967-78; prof. dept. pathology U. Tenn., Memphis, 1983—2008, prof. obstetrics, 1986—2008, vice chmn. dept. pathology, 1983-90, prof. emeritus, 2008—. Vis. prof. U. Okla., 1967, Duke U., Mich. State U., 1969, Leeds U., Dundee U., Karolinska, 1974, Leeds U., 1978, 85, Emory U., 1980, London U., Edinburgh U., 1981, 85, U. Brit. Coll., 1987; jr. investigator Marine Biol. Lab., Woods Hole, Mass., 1951-54, sr. investigator, 1966—, mem. corp., 1970—, parliamentarian, 1990-94, sr. rschr., 2012-; mem. Marine Resources Adv. Com., 1988-90, mem. election com., 1994-96; chmn. nat. adv. com. W-I-C evaluation U.S. Dept. Agr., 1979-86; lectr. Coll. Law U. Fla., 1963-67, 77-83; cons. Pan Am. Health Orgn., 1973-89; sr. cons. Santa Fe Found., 1976-79, exec. dir., 1979-83; course dir. Ctr. Continuing Edn., U. Chgo., 1980-82. Author: Syllabus for Study of Gynecologic-Obstetric-Pediatric Disease, 1961, Diseases of Woman, Pregnancy, Child, 1964, Maternal Nutrition and Child Health, 1979, 2nd edit., 2000, Tumors of Placenta and Umbilical Cord, 1990; editor Interscience Devel. Disorders, 1971-80; assoc. editor Jour. Reproductive Medicine, 1968-70, 79-85, editor in chief, 1970-75; mem. editl. bd. Exptl. Molecular Pathology, 1999—; contbr. articles to profl. jours. Trustee Coll. Light Opera Co., Falmouth, Mass., 1970—, Hippodrome Theatre, Gainesville, 1975-83, Opera Memphis, 1989-92. With M.C., USNR, 1956-58. Recipient Best Basic Sci. Tchg. award U. Fla., 1967, Excellence in Tchg. award, Grad. Coll. Med. Scis., U. Tenn., 2002, Enid Gilbert-Barness prize, 2010; named freeman citizen of Glasgow, 1981. Fellow: Royal Soc. Medicine (london); mem.: AAAS, Am. Med. Assoc., Coll. Physicians and Surgeons Costa Rica, Internat. Physicians for Prevention Nuc. War, Physicians Social Responsibility, Am. Coll. Ob-gyn., N.Y. Acad. Scis., So. Med. Assn., So. Soc. Pediat. Rsch., Math. Assn. Am., Internat. Acad. Pathologists, Soc. Pediat. Rsch., Am. Coll. Rheumatology (spl. study com. 1995—96), Hosp. Assn., Am. Chem. Soc., Am. Soc. Molecular Marine Biology and Biotech., Am. Soc. Exptl. Pathology, Cosmos Club, Navy League, Pediat. Pathology Club (sec.-treas. 1970—75, pres. 1981—82), Sigma xi, Phi Beta Kappa. Home: PO Box 5758 Gainesville FL 32627-5758 also: PO Box 511 Woods Hole MA 02543-0511 Home Fax: 352-372-5487, 508-457-9635.

SHANNON, HOLDEN E., air transportation executive; Grad., Rice U., Houston, 1985. V.p. corp. real estate and environ. affairs Continental Airlines, Inc., Houston, 1995—2004, sr. v.p. global real estate & security, 2004—. Office: Continental Airlines Inc PO Box 4607 Houston TX 77210 Office Phone: 713-324-5000. Office Fax: 713-324-2637.

SHANNON, MARY LOU, adult health nursing educator; b. Memphis, Apr. 4, 1938; d. Sidney Richmond Shannon and Lucille (Gwaltney) Shannon Cloud. BSN, U. Tenn., 1959; MA, Columbia U., 1963, MEd, 1964, EdD, 1972. Staff nurse City of Memphis Hosps., 1959—60, instr. Sch. Nursing, 1960—62; asst. prof. U. Tenn., Memphis, 1964—70, assoc. prof., 1970—73, prof., 1973—89, acting dean, 1972—73, chair, adult health dept., 1973—77, prof. grad. program, 1977—89; prof., chair adult health dept. Sch. Nursing U. Tex., Galveston, 1989—98, prof. grad. program, 1989—2000, prof. emeritus, 2000—. Bd. dirs. Nat. Pressure Ulcer Adv. Panel, Buffalo, 1987-96; vis. prof. U. Alta., Edmonton, Can., 1982, Union U., Memphis, 2001, Bapt. Coll. Health Scis., 2003, U. Tex., Galveston, 2004; mem. project adv. bd. RAND, Santa Monica, Calif., 1994. Contbr. chpts. to books in field and to periodicals; mem. editl. bd. Advances in Wound Care, 1987-2000. Trustee Nurses Edn. Funds, N.Y.C., 1972-86. Mem. AAAS, ANA, Nat. League Nursing (bd. of rev. 1983-86), Orthopedic Nurses Assn., So. Nursing Rsch. Soc., Am. Assn. for History of Nursing, Sigma Xi, Sigma Theta Tau, Phi Kappa Phi. Avocations: travel, reading.

SHANNON, MICHAEL, finance company executive; BSBA, U. Ctrl. Fla., 1976; MBA in Fin., Ga. State U. Sr. v.p., group contr., North Am. Info. Svcs., sr. v.p., internat. bus. devel., head, mergers & acquisitions Equifax, Inc., gen. mgr., directory bus., v.p., asst. treas., 1992, sr. v.p., corp. devel., 2000—01, mng. dir., UK, 2001—02, group exec., Europe, 2002—06, pres., N.Am. comml. solutions, 2007—. Office: Equifax Inc 1550 Peachtree St NW Atlanta GA 30309 Office Phone: 404-885-8000. Office Fax: 404-885-8682. Business E-Mail: Michael.Shannon@equifax.com.

SHANNON, MICHAEL EDWARD, finance company executive; b. Evanston, Ill., Nov. 21, 1936; s. Edward Francis and Mildred Veronica (Oliver) S.; m. A. Laura McGrath, July 4, 1964; children: Claire Oliver Mary, Kathryn Ann Elizabeth. BA, U. Notre Dame, 1958; MBA, Stanford U., 1960. With Continental Oil Co., Houston, 1960-62, Gulf Oil Corp., 1962-75, asst. treas., 1970-75; treas. Gulf Oil Co. U.S., Houston, 1970-72, Gulf Oil Co.-Ea. Hemisphere, London, 1972-75, Rep. Steel Corp., Cleve., 1975-84, v.p., 1978-82, exec. v.p., 1982-84; pres. ChemLawn Svcs. Corp., Columbus, Ohio, 1989—90; exec. v.p. Ecolab, Inc., St. Paul, 1984, chief fin. and adminstrv. officer, 1984—90, CFO, 1990—92, pres., Residential Svcs. Group, 1990—92, vice chmn., 1992—95, chmn., 1996—99; pres. MEShannon & Assocs., Inc. Bd. dirs. CenterPoint Energy, Inc., Apogee Enterprises, Inc., 2005—07, Clorox Co, NACCO Industries, Inc., 2003—. Bd. dirs. Minn. Orchestral Assn., Mpls., chair. Mem. Fin. Execs. Inst., Nat. Assn. Mfrs. (bd. dirs.), Univ. Club, Rolling Rock Club, Mpls. Club, Minikahada Club, Minn. Club. Roman Catholic. Office: MEShannon & Associates Inc 2001 Kirby Dr Ste 504 Houston TX 77019-6046 Office Phone: 713-874-0700.

SHANNON, STEPHEN C., lawyer, former state legislator; b. Berkeley, Calif., Apr. 5, 1971; m. Abigail Suzanne Hochberg; 1 child, Aidan. BA, Fairfield U., 1993; MA in Pub. Policy, Georgetown U., 1996; JD, U. Va. Sch. Law, 1999. Lic.: Va., DC, US Dist. Ct. (ea. dist.) Va. Atty. Odin, Feldman & Pittleman; mem. Dist. 35 VA. House of Delegates, Va., 2004—10. Co-founder Washington Metropolitan AMBER Alert System, 2001; vice chmn. Fairfax County Consumer Protection Commn., 2002—03. Recipient Lord Fairfax award, 2002, Team Excellence award, Fairfax County Police Dept., 2003; named one of Virginia's Elite, Va. Bus. mag., 2007, 2008. Mem.: Vienna/Tyson Chambers of Commerce, George Mason Inns of Ct. Democrat. Roman Catholic. Office: Odin Feldman & Pittleman PC 1775 Wiehle Ave Ste 400 Reston VA 20190-5159 Office Phone: 703-218-2130. Office Fax: 703-218-2160. E-mail: steve.shannon@ofplaw.com.

SHANNON, T.W., state legislator; m. Devon Shannon; 1 child, Audrey Grace. BA, Cameron Univ.; JD, Okla. City Univ. Staff mem. to US Rep. J.C. Watts & US Rep. Tom Cole; bus. cons.; mem. Dist. 62 Okla. House of Representatives, 2007—. Mem. Chickasaw Nation. Republican. Office: 2300 N Lincoln Blvd Rm 328-A Oklahoma City OK 73105 Mailing: 504 SW 83rd Lawton OK 73505 Office Phone: 405-557-7374. E-mail: tw.shannon@okhouse.gov.

SHAPER, C. PARK, energy executive; BA, BS, Stanford Univ.; MBA, Northwestern Univ. Cons. Boston Consulting Group, Inc., 1995—97; v.p., CFO First Data Corp., 1997—99; pres., bd. dir. Altair Corp., 1999; v.p., CFO Kinder Morgan, Inc., Kinder Morgan Energy Partners LP, Kinder Morgan Management, LLC, Houston, 2000—04, exec. v.p., CFO, 2004—05, pres., 2005—. Bd. dir., treas. Children's Fund, Houston. Office: Kinder Morgan Inc Ste 1000 500 Dallas St Houston TX 77002

SHAPERE, DUDLEY, philosophy educator; b. Harlingen, Tex., May 27, 1928; s. Dudley and Corinne (Pupkin) S.; m. Hannah Hardgrave; children: Hannah Elizabeth, Christine Ann; children by previous marriage: Alfred Dudley, Catherine Lucretia. BA, Harvard U., 1949, MA, 1955, PhD, 1957. Instr. philosophy Ohio State U., 1957-60; asst. prof. U. Chgo., 1960-65, assoc. prof., 1965-67, prof., 1967-72, mem. com. on evolutionary biology, 1969-72, chmn. undergrad. program in history and philosophy of sci., 1966-72, chmn. com. on conceptual founds. sci., 1970-72; prof. U. Ill., Urbana, 1972-75, chmn. program in history and philosophy of sci., 1972-75; prof. U. Md., College Park, 1975-84; Z. Smith Reynolds prof. philosophy and history of sci. Wake Forest U., 1984—2002; ret., 2002. Mem. com. on history and philosophy of sci. U. Md., 1975-84, chmn. program in history and philosophy of sci., 1983-84.; vis. prof. Rockefeller U., 1965-66, Harvard U., 1968; mem. Inst. Advanced Study, Princeton, N.J., 1978-79, 81, 89, Otto Neugebaur fellow, 2001; spl. cons. (program dir.) program in history and philosophy of sci. NSF, 1966-75; Sigma Xi nat. bicentennial lectr., 1974-77. Author: Philosophical Problems of Natural Science, 1965, Galileo: A Philosophical Study, 1974, Reason and the Search for Knowledge, 1984; editorial bd.: Philosophy of Sci., Studies in History and Philosophy of Sci.; rev. bd.: Philosophy Research Archives; contbr. articles to profl. jours. Served with AUS, 1950-52. Recipient Quantrell award for excellence in undergrad. tchg. U. Chgo., 1968; Disting. Scholar-Tchr. award U. Md., 1979-80. Fellow AAAS (sec. sec. 1972); mem. APA, Philosophy of Sci. Assn., History of Sci. Soc., Am. Philos. Assn., Acad. Internat. de Philosophie des Scis. Home: 3125 Turkey Hill Ct Winston Salem NC 27106-4951 E-mail: shapere@wfu.edu.

SHAPIRO, FLORENCE, state legislator; b. NYC, May 2, 1948; d. Martin Nmi and Ann (Spiesman) D.; m. Howard Nmi Shapiro, Dec. 28, 1969; children: Lisa, Todd, Staci. BS in Secondary Edn., U. Tex., 1970. Tchr. Richardson HS, Tex., 1970-72; former owner, advt., pub. rels. exec. Shapiro & Co., Plano, Tex.; former mayor and mem. city coun. City of Plano, Tex.; mem. Dist. 8 Tex. State Senate, 1993—. Bd. dirs. Plano C. of C., Presbyn. and Children's Healthcare Ctr., Plano Econ. Devel. Bd., U. Tex. at Dallas Adv. Coun., The North Tex. Commn., The Dallas Regional Mobility Coalition; mem. nat. bd. dirs. Susan B. Komen Breast Cancer Found.; mem. adv. bd. Children's Edn. Fund Dallas, Dallas County Domestic Violence Task Force, Family Violence Prevention Coun. Injury Prevention Ctr. Greater Dallas. Recipient Plano Vol. of Yr. award, 1983, Plano Citizen of Yr. award, 1985, Athena award Plano C. of C. for Businesswoman of Yr., 1990, Child Advocate award Dallas Children's Advocacy Ctr., 1995, Legislator of Yr. award Tex. Mcpl. League, 1995, 97, Nat. Rep. Legislators Assn., 1997, Tex. Ct. Apptd. Spl. Advs., 1997; Outstanding Legislator of Yr. award Tex. Police Chiefs Assn., 1995, Legislator of Yr. award, 1997, Friend of the Taxpayer award Citizens for a Sound Economy, 1999, Centennial Hero award Plano Ind. Sch. Dist., 1999, Voice of Children award, Ct. Apptd. Spl. Advs. of Collin County, 2001, others; Outstanding Legislator award Tex. Assn. Dist. and County Attys., 1997, Leader of Excellence award Free Market Com., 1997, Senate Statesman award Lonestar Found., 1997, Polit. Courage award John Ben Sheppard Pub. Leadership Forum, 1997; named One of 10 Best Legislators family law session State Bar Tex., 1997, One of 3 State Senators on YCT Honor Roll, 1997, Legis. Star, Tex. Classroom Tchrs. Assn., 1997, Guardian of Free Enterprise, Nat. Fedn. Ind. Bus., 1999, Woman of Yr., Les Femmes du Monde, 2002, Woman of Yr., Women's Transp. Seminar Dallas-Ft. Worth, 2002, others; honored by Texans for Lawsuit Reform, 1997, Assn. Ob-Gyn. and Southwestern Med. Sch., 1997. Mem. Rotary (Paul Harris fellow 1990), Alpha Epsilon Phi (Nat. Outstanding Young Alumnae award). Republican. Jewish. Office: 5000 Legacy Dr Ste 494 Plano TX 75024 also: PO Box 12068 Capitol Station Austin TX 78711 Office Phone: 972-403-3404, 512-463-0108.

SHAPIRO, GARY JOEL, trade association administrator; b. Bethpage, NY, Aug. 28, 1956; s. Jerome and Mildred (Gorby) Shapiro. BA, SUNY, Binghamton, 1977; JD, Georgetown U. Law Ctr., 1980. Bar: DC 1980, Va. 1981, US Dist. Ct. (DC dist.) 1981, US Ct. Appeals (DC cir.) 1981, US Supreme Ct. 1987. Legis. asst. US House of Representatives, Washington, 1977; assoc. Squire Sanders & Dempsey, Washington, 1980-82; v.p. govt. and legal affairs Consumer Electronics Assn. (formerly Electronic Industries Assn./Consumer Electronics Mfrs. Assn.), Arlington, Va., 1982-89, v.p., gen. counsel, sec., 1989-90, group v.p., 1990, now pres., CEO. Bd. dirs. Advanced TV Test Ctr., Alexandria, Northern Va. Tech. Coun., Washington Econ. Club; mem. Commonwealth of Va. Commn. Info. Tech., US Dept. State Adv. Com. Internat. Comm. & Info. Policy; past chmn. Home Recording Rights Coalition. Author: The Comeback: How Innovation Will Restore the American Dream, 2011. Named one of Top Lobbyists in Washington, The Hill, The 100 Most Influential People in Washington, DC, Washington Life mag.; named to Acad. Digital TV Pioneers. Office: Consumer Electronics Association 1919 S Eads St Arlington VA 22202

SHAPIRO, JOSEPH ISAAC, dean, nephrologist; b. Newark, Aug. 24, 1954; s. Leon and Beatrice Mildred Shapiro; m. Mary Ryan, Sept. 23, 1958; children: Anna, Laura. BA, U. Pa., 1976; MD, U. Medicine and Dentistry N.J., 1980. Diplomate Am. Bd. Internal Medicine, Am. Bd. Nephrology. Resident in internal medicine Georgetown U. Hosp., Washington, 1980—83; from fellow in nephrology to assoc. prof. medicine U. Colo., Denver, 1983—97; prof., chief divsn. nephrology U. Toledo Coll. Medicine & Life Sciences, 1997—98; prof., chmn. dept. medicine U. Toledo Coll. Medicine and Life Sciences, 1999—2012, assoc. dean bus. devel., 2006—12; dean Marshall U. Joan C. Edwards Sch. Medicine, Huntington, W.Va., 2012—. Adj. prof. physics Denver U., 1990—97. Contbr. articles to profl. jours., 2001. Fellow: Am. Heart Assn. (vice chmn. kidney & cardiovascular disease coun. 2007—08, Clinician Scientist award 1988, Established Investigator award 1992); mem.: ACP, AAAS, Internat. Soc. Magnetic Resonance in Medicine, Assn. Professors Medicine, Am. Soc. Nephrology, Internat. Soc. Nephrology. Achievements include patents for apparatus and method for analyzing heart sounds. Office: Marshall University Joan C Edwards Sch Medicine Office of the Dean 1600 Medical Center Dr Huntington WV 25701

SHAPIRO, LEE TOBEY, mathematics educator, astronomer; b. Dec. 12, 1943; s. Sydney Harold and Ruth Iva Shapiro; m. Linda Susan Goldman, Aug. 16, 1970; children: Steven Robert, Aaron Edward. BS in Physics, Carnegie Inst. Tech., 1966; MS in Astronomy, Northwestern U., 1968, PhD, 1974. Cert. math. and physics tchr. State Va. Lectr. Adler Planetarium, Chgo., 1967-74; asst. prof. astronomy Mich. State U., East Lansing, 1974-79, assoc. prof., 1979-82; bd. dirs. Abrams Planetarium, 1974-82, Morehead Planetarium U. NC, Chapel Hill, 1982—2002, assoc. prof., 1983—87, adj. prof., 1998—2002; head ednl. and pub. outreach Nat. Radio Astronomy Obs., Charlottesville, 2002—05; tchr. algebra Hermitage HS, Richmond, Va., 2005—; tchr. algebra, physics, geometry Louisa HS, Mineral, Va., 2007—09. Vis. prof. Duke U., Durham, NC, 1987—89, 1993—94, 1996—99, 2005. Fellow Royal Astron. Soc.; mem. Am. Astron. Soc., Am. Assn. Mus., Astron. Soc. of the Pacific, Internat. Planetarium Soc., Gt. Lakes Planetarium Assn. (pres. 1980). Jewish. Home Phone: 434-244-0433.

SHAPIRO, MICHAEL EDWARD, museum director; b. NYC, Nov. 15, 1949; s. Edward Aaron and Sylvia (Fishman) S.; m. Elizabeth Harvey, 1977; 2 children. BA, Hamilton Coll., 1972; MA, Williams Coll., 1976, Harvard U., 1978, PhD, 1980. Asst. prof. dept. art history Duke U., Durham, NC, 1980-84; curator 19th-20th century art St. Louis Art Mus., 1984-92, chief curator, 1987-92; dir. Los Angeles County Mus. Art, 1992-93; dir. mus. programs, chief curator High Mus. Art, Atlanta, 1994-95, dep. dir., chief curator, 1996-99, Nancy and Holcombe T. Green, Jr. dir., 2000—. Author: Bronze Casting and American Sculpture, 1985; contbg. author: Frederic Remington: The Masterworks, 1988, George Caleb Bingham, 1990; mng. curator, editor Rings: Five Passions in World Art, 1996; co-curator Impressionism: Paintings Collected by European Museums, 1998, mng. curator, 1999. Recipient Chevalier, Order Arts & Letters, France, 2005. Office: High Museum Art 1280 Peachtree St NE Atlanta GA 30309*

SHAPIRO, NELSON HIRSH, lawyer; b. Feb. 3, 1928; s. Arthur and Anna (Zenitz) S.; m. Helen Lenora Sykes, June 27, 1948; children: Ronald Evan, Mitchell Wayne, Jeffrey Mark, Julie Beth. BEE, Johns Hopkins U., 1948; JD, George Washington U., 1952. Bar: D.C. 1952, Va. 1981. Patent examiner U.S. Patent Office, 1948-50; patent advisor U.S. Signal Corps, 1950-52; mem. Shapiro & Shapiro, Arlington, Va., 1952-98, Vorys, Sater, Seymour and Pease LLP, Washington, 1998-2001, Miles & Stockbridge, McLean, Va., 2001—. Patentee; contbr. articles to legal publs. and Ency. of Patent Practice and Invention Mgmt., 1964. Mem. ABA, Am. Patent Law Assn., Bar Assn. DC, Order of Coif, Tau Beta Pi. Home: 7001 Old Cabin Ln Rockville MD 20852-4531 Office: 1751 Pinnacle Dr Ste 500 Mc Lean VA 22102-3833 Home Phone: 301-881-0841; Office Phone: 703-610-8687. E-mail: nshapiro@milesstockbridge.com.

SHARAPOVA, MARIA, professional tennis player; b. Nyagan, Russia, Apr. 19, 1987; d. Yuri and Yelena Sharapova. Trained, Bollettieri's Acad., 1996. Prof. tennis player WTA Tour, 2001—; model IMG Modeling Agy., 2003—; winner Wimbledon, 2004, US Open, 2006, Australian Open, 2008, French Open, 2012. Mem. Russian nat. team Summer Olympic Games, London, 2012; founder, gourmet candy brand Sugarpova, 2012—. Recipient Silver medal, women's singles, Summer Olympic Games, 2012; named Newcomer of Yr., WTA, 2003, Most Improved Player of Yr., 2004, Player of Yr., 2004, Female Choice Athlete, Teen Choice Awards, 2006, 2007, Female Athlete of Yr., US Sports Acad., 2006, Whirlpool 6th Sense Player of Yr., 2006; named one of The Most Influential People in the World of Sports, Bus. Week, 2007, The 100 Most Powerful Celebrities, Forbes.com, 2008. Achievements include winning 27 career singles WTA championships; 3 career doubles championships; 4 career ITF Women's Circuit singles titles; winner of 4 Grand Slam singles titles; first Russian woman to win at Wimbledon, 2004; mem. Russian Fed Cup Team, 2008. Avocations: singing, reading, stamp collecting/philately. Office: WTA Tour 100 2nd Ave S Ste 1100 Saint Petersburg FL 33701-4338

SHARER, JOHN DANIEL, lawyer; b. Bklyn., Sept. 19, 1950; s. Albert Robert and Alda Loretta (Tapiro) S.; m. Kathleen Gail Donaldson, Feb. 14, 1981; 1 child, Stephanie Erin. AB summa cum laude, Dartmouth Coll., Hanover, NH, 1972; JD, U. Pa., Phila., 1975. Bar: Pa. 1975, NJ 1975, DC 1976, NY 1989, Va. 1994. Law clk. Superior Ct. Pa., Hon. Edmund B. Spaeth, Jr., Phila., 1975-76; assoc. Sutherland, Asbill & Brennan, Washington, 1976-82, ptnr., 1982-94; counsel Christian & Barton, L.L.P., Richmond, Va., 1994-95, ptnr., 1996-99; sr. counsel Dominion Resources Svcs. Inc., Richmond, 1999—2001, mng. counsel electric delivery, 2001—06, asst. gen. counsel, 2006—. Faculty Va. State Bar Professionalism Course, 2001—04; mem. Third Dist. Disciplinary Comm. Sect. III, 2003—06; grader Va. State Bar Examination, 2003—; mem. Va. State Bar Standing Com. on Professionalism, 2004—, Va. State Bar Coun., 2005—; bd. govs. Va. State Bar Com. on the Edn. Lawyers, 2007—. Bd. dirs. Wakefield Sch., Marshall, Va., 1990-94; pres. Dartmouth Club of Cen. Va., 1997-2003. Named Va. Super Lawyers, 2009. Fellow Va. Law Found. (Va. Super Lawyers 2009); mem. Phi Beta Kappa. Republican. Avocations: classical music, judicial biographies, computers, Norfolk. Home: 12317 Northlake Ct Richmond VA 23233-6635 Office: 120 Tredegar St PO Box 26532 Richmond VA 23261-6532 Office Phone: 804-819-2271. Business E-Mail: john.d.sharer@dom.com.

SHARIPOV, SALIZHAN SHAKIROVICH, cosmonaut; b. Uzgen, Oshsk region, Kirghizia, Aug. 24, 1964; s. Shakirzhan Sharipov; m. Nadezhda Mavlyanovna Sharipova; 2 children. Grad., Air Force Pilot Sch., 1987, Moscow State U. Pilot-instr. teaching 8 cadets; mission specialist STS-89, 1998; cosmonaut-candidate Gagarin Cosmonaut Tng. Ctr., 1990; cosmonaut NASA, 1992—; dir. ops. Russian Space Agy., Johnson Space Ctr., 2005—06. Broke a nearly 30 year tradition of having at least one crewman with previous experience in piloting the capsule. Soyuz Comdr. and Flight Engineer of Expedition-10 headed for the International Space Station with Russian-US crew (with Leroy Chiao and Yuri Shargin) in the Soyuz TMA-5 on October, 2004, landed April, 2005 (with Leroy Chiao and Roberto Vittori). Office: NASA JSC 2101 NASA Rd 1 Houston TX 77058-3691 Office Phone: 281-483-0123.

SHARMA, ANAND, manufacturing executive; Grad. in Adv. Mgmt. Studies, U. Pa.; BS in Mech. Engring., Roorkee U., India; MS in Bus. Adminstrn., Boston U., 1977. V.p., ops. Union Switch & Signal Inc., 1979—87, Am. Std., Inc.; exec. v.p. Productivity Inc.; co-founder, pres., CEO TBM Consulting Group, Durham, NC, 1991—. Spkr. AME Annual Conf.; bd. dirs. Guidon Performance Solutions, 2006—. Author: The Perfect Engine: How to Win in the New Demand Economy by Building to Order With Fewer Resources, 2001; monthly columnist The Manufacturer. Recipient Hero of U.S. Mfg., Fortune, 2001, Donald Burnham Mfg. Mgmt. Award, Soc. Mfg. Engrs., 2002. Office: TBM Consulting Group 4400 Ben Franklin Blvd Durham NC 27704 Office Phone: 919-471-5535. Office Fax: 919-471-5135. Business E-Mail: asharma@tbmcg.com.

SHARP, DAN STEVEN, epidemiologist; s. Darrell Dean Sharp and Stella Louise Morrison-Sharp; m. Carol Lee Thomas, Dec. 26, 1996; m. Caroline Stanley Johnson, June 20, 1970 (div. Apr. 16, 1996); children: Sarah Elizabeth, David Henry. BS in Chemistry, U. Redlands, Calif., 1972; MD, U. Calif., Irvine, 1975; MPH, U. Calif., Berkeley, 1984, PhD in Epidemiology, 1987. Board Certified in Public Health and General Preventive Medicine Am. Bd. of Preventive Medicine, 1990, diplomate Nat. Bd. of Med. Examiners, 1977, Physician's and Surgeon's Certificate Bd. of Med. Quality Assurance, State of Calif., 1977, Certificate of Registration as a Visiting Overseas Doctor Gen. Med. Coun., UK, 1989. Flight surgeon US Army, Natick, Mass., 1977—80; sr. med. epidemiologist Med. Rsch. Coun., Cardiff, Wales, 1988—90; dir., Honolulu heart program Nat. Heart, Lung and Blood Inst., 1992—97; assoc. dir. sci. Health Effects Lab., Nat. Inst. for Occupl. Safety and Health, Morgantown, W.Va., 2000—. Contbr. scientific papers. Capt. US Army, 1977—80, Natick, Massachusetts. Mem.: Soc. for Epidemiologic Rsch. Achievements include research in cardiovascular disease in populations.

SHARP, DOUGLAS ANDREW, secondary school educator; b. Austin, Tex., July 19, 1945; s. Jack Weston and Jean Ernestine (Beeman) S.; m. Marylin Gene Martin, Jan. 20, 1977. BA in Math., Tex. A&M U., 1967, MS in Math., 1970, postgrad., 1969-71; EdD, La Salle U., Mandville, La., 1993. Teaching fellow dept. math. Tex. A&M U., College Station, 1967-71; chmn. math. dept., asst. coach/coach athletics dept. Southfield Sch., Shreveport, La., 1972-73; coach athletics dept. St. John's Sch., Houston, 1975, chmn. math. dept., 1981-93, master teaching chair math., 1987-89; disting. vis. lectr. U. Houston, 1989-90, adj. prof., 1990. Contbr. articles to profl. jours. Recipient Excellence in Teaching award Fin. Dept. U. Houston, 1993, Outstanding Tchr. award Tandy Technol. Scholars, 1993-94. Mem. Am. Math. Soc., Am. Soc. Composer, Authors and Pubs., Am. Statistical Assn., Math. Assn. Am. (Edyth May Stiffe award 1991, 97), Calculus and Elem. Analysis Tchrs. Houston, Nat. Coun. Tchrs. Math., Cum Laude Soc. Office: St John's Sch 2401 Claremont Ln Houston TX 77019-5897

SHARP, GEORGE KENDALL, federal judge; b. Chgo., Dec. 30, 1934; s. Edward S. and Florence S.; m. Mary Bray; children: Florence Kendall, Julia Manger. BA, Yale U., 1957; JD, U. Va., 1963. Bar: Fla. 1963. Atty. Sharp, Johnston & Brown, Vero Beach, Fla., 1963-78; pub. defender 19th Cir. Ct., Vero Beach, 1964-68; sch. bd. atty. Indian River County, Fla., 1968-78; judge 19th Cir. Ct., Vero Beach, 1978-83, US Dist. Ct. (mid. dist.) Fla., Orlando, Fla., 1983—2000, sr. judge, 2000—. Office: US Dist Ct US Courthouse 401 W Central Blvd Rm 6600 Orlando FL 32801

SHARP, KEVIN HUNTER, federal judge, lawyer; b. Memphis, Tenn., Jan. 22, 1963; s. Harmon Thomas and Annette Gray Sharp; m. Holland Ashley Conner, Feb. 9, 2002; 1 child, Sydney Marie. AA, Mesa C.C., 1988; BS summa cum laude, Christian Brothers Coll., 1990; JD, Vanderbilt U. Sch. Law, 1993. Bar: US Dist. Ct. (middle & western dist.) Tenn. 1993, US Ct. Appeals (6th cir.) 1994, Supreme Ct. Tenn. 1993. Assoc. Stokes & Bartholomew, P.A., Nashville, 1993—96, Stokes Bartholomew Evans & Petree, P.A., Nashville, 1997—2000, ptnr., 2000—02; atty. Office of Compliance, US Congress, Washington, 1996—97, dep. gen. counsel, 1997; founding ptnr. Drescher & Sharp, P.C. (formerly Preston & Sharp, P.C.), Nashville, 2003—11; judge US Dist. Ct. (middle dist.) Tenn., Nashville, 2011—. Mem. Cumberland Valley Girl Scout Coun., Nashville, 2002. Mem.: ABA, Nashville Bar Assn., Tenn. Bar Assn., American Legion. Presbyterian. Office: US District Court 801 Broadway Nashville TN 37203 Office Phone: 615-736-5498.

SHARP, WILLIAM, retired advertising executive; b. Chgo., Aug. 1, 1929; s. William and Essie Mae (Kendall) Sharp; m. Doris Ellen Wooten, May 16, 1952; children: William Gregory, Dianne, Michael. Student, Woodrow Wilson Jr. Coll., Chgo., Roosevelt U. Owner, mgr. Card Gifters & Sharp Advt. Agy., Chgo., 1957-65; copywriter Tatham-Laird & Kudner Advt. Agy., 1965-67; copy supr. Leo Burnett Advt. Agy., 1967-68; group creative supr. J. Walter Thompson Advt., 1968-69; dir. communications OEO, Washington, 1969-72; v.p., advt. mgr. Coca-Cola USA, Atlanta, 1972-81; ptnr. Kaiser, Kuhn, Bennett & Sharp Advt. Agy., Atlanta, 1981-83; sr. v.p., gen. mgr. Burrell Advt., Atlanta, 1983—90; founder, pres. Sharp Advt., Inc., Atlanta, 1990; ret. Past chmn. bd. dirs. Am. Advt. Fedn.; adj. mktg. prof. Emory U. Goizueta Bus. Sch., Atlanta. Author: How To Be Black and Get a Job in Advertising Agency Anyway, 1969. Adv. Citizens for Michael Lomax, 1981—89; bd. dirs. Atlanta Coll. Art, Ballethnic Dance Co.; chmn. Atlanta Ednl. Telecomm. Collaborative. Served with US Army, 1952. Recipient NY Art Dir.'s Club award; named Ad Man of Yr., Southern Mag.; named to Advt. Hall of Fame, Am. Advt. Fedn., 2009. Mem.: NAACP (mem. Atlanta branch exec. bd.), Assn. Nat. Advertisers (past. bd. dirs.).

SHARPE, RONALD WESLEY, federal prosecutor; b. Washington, 1965; BS in Mgmt. and Finance, Tulane U., 1987; JD, Stanford U., 1991. Bar: Pa. 1991, DC 1992. Acctg. technician Fed. Nat. Mortgage Assn., Washington, 1987—88; assoc. Jones, Day, Reavis & Pogue, Washington, 1991—95; asst. US atty. DC US Dept. Justice, 1995—2008, first asst. US atty., 2008—09, with Homicide Sect. & Fraud and Pub. Corruption Sect., first asst. US atty. VI, 2008—09, interim US atty., 2009—11, US atty. VI, 2011—. Trial advocacy instr. George Washington U. Law Sch., Office of Overseas Prosecutorial Devel. Assistance and Training (OPDAT). Served in USAF, 1983—84. Mem.: ABA, Stanford Black Alumni Assn. (v.p. 1993—94, bd. dirs. 1999—2005). Office: Federal Building US Courthouse, Room 260 5500 Veterans Dr St Thomas VI 00802-6424 Office Phone: 340-774-5757. Office Fax: 340-776-3474.*

SHARPER, DARREN MALLORY, sportscaster, retired professional football player; b. Richmond, Va., Nov. 3, 1975; s. Harry Sharper. BA in Sociology, Coll. William & Mary, Williamsburg, Va. Defensive back Green Bay Packers, 1997—2004, Minn. Vikings, 2005—08, New Orleans Saints, 2009—10; ret. NFL, 2011; football analyst Sta. WWL-TV, New Orleans, 2012—. TV color commentator NFL Europa, 2004—07. Co-founder Sharper Kids Found. Recipient 1st Team All-Pro, AP, 2009; named Defensive Player of Yr., Yankee Conf., 1996, 1st Team All-Pro, AP, 2000; named to Nat. football Conf. Pro Bowl Team, NFL, 2000, Nat. Football Conf. Pro Bowl Team, 2002, 2005, 2007, 2009, William & Mary Hall of Fame, 2008. Achievements include member of Super Bowl XXXI championship winning Green Bay Packers, 1997; Super Bowl XLIV championship winning New Orleans Saints, 2010; leading the NFL in: interceptions, 2000, 2009; interception return yards, 2002, 2005; interception return touchdowns, 2004, 2005. Office: WWL-TV 1024 N Rampart St New Orleans LA 70116

SHARPSTEIN, RICHARD ALAN, lawyer; b. Boston, Oct. 20, 1950; s. Sidney Joseph and Marilyn (Weitzman) S.; m. Janice Burton, Oct. 20, 1979; children: Jessica Ashley, Katherine Erin, Michael Burton. BA, Tulane U., 1972, JD, 1975. Bar: U.S. Supreme Ct. 1976, Fla. 1976, U.S. Dist. Ct. (no. dist., so. dist., mid. dist.) Fla. 1976, U.S. Ct. Appeals (5th cir.) 1976, U.S. Ct. Appeals (11th cir.) 1980, U.S. Ct. Appeals (3d cir.) 1982, U.S. Ct. Appeals (4th cir.) 1983. Atty. Fla. Bar Assn., Miami, 1976—. Asst. state atty. Dade County, Miami, 1976-79; ptnr., pres. Sharpstein & Sharpstein, P.A., Miami, 1982-2001. Fellow Am. Bd. of Criminal Lawyers; mem. ABA, Acad. Fla. Trial Lawyers, Fla. Criminal Def. Attys. Assn. (v.p. 1985-86, pres. 1986-87, bd. dirs. 1986-92), Am. Inns of Covrt, Omicron Delta Kappa. Home: 1435 W 27th St Miami Beach FL 33140-4208 Office: Akerman Senterfitt One SE 3rd Ave 25th Fl Miami FL 33131 Office Phone: 305-371-2600, 305-374-5600. Business E-Mail: richard.sharpstein@akerman.com. E-mail: ras@jordenusa.com.

SHAUGHNESSY, TIMOTHY THOMAS, state legislator; b. Buechel, Ky., Aug. 22, 1957; s. James W. and Mary Jo Keenan Shaughnessy. Former chmn. Labor & Indsl. Com., Banking & Ins. Com.; intern Gen. Assembly, 1979—80; staff legis. aide for Jim Malone county commr., 1980—83; state senator Dist. 19 Ky., 1989—; mem. Agr. Com., Natural Resources Com., Licensing & Occupations Com., Transp. Com.; mgr. employee rels. Jewish Hosp., 1983—85, mktg. cons. sys., 1985—87, exec. dir. properties, 1987—, asst. pres. health care svc. Recipient Outstanding Young Kentuckian award, 1979; named Class of 89, Ky. Leadership Program. Mem.: C. of C., Holy Cross HS (mem. bd. dir. 1987—). Democrat. Catholic. Mailing: 250 E Liberty Suite 103 Louisville KY 40202 Office: Capitol Annex Rm 229 Frankfort KY 40601 Home Phone: 502-267-5063; Office Phone: 502-584-1920, 502-564-8100 621.

SHAVER, STAN E., state legislator; b. Grafton, W.Va., Sept. 8, 1948; married; 2 children. BS in Phys. Ed. & Social Studies, Alderson-Brouddus Coll., 1970; MS in Secondary Edn., Troy State U., 1975; MA in Edn. Leadership, W.Va., 1999. Coach & instr. Newburg High Sch., 1974—77, Central Preston Jr. High Sch., 1977—91, instr. & prin., 1991—2005; mem. Dist. 46 W.Va. House of Delegates, W.Va., 2000—04, 2006—; prin. Fellowsville Elem. Sch, 2002—03, 2005—06. Democrat. Office: State Capitol Bldg Room 217E Bldg 1 1900 Kanawha Blvd E Charleston WV 25305 also: Rte 1 Box 47B Tunnelton WV 26444 Office Phone: 304-340-3146, 340-892-3866. Business E-Mail: sshaver@mail.wvnet.edu.

SHAW, BRUCE R., gas industry executive; B in Mech. Engring., Tex. A&M Univ.; MBA, Tuck Sch. Bus., Dartmouth Coll. Dir. corp. develop. Holly Corp., Dallas, 1997—2001, v.p. corp. develop., 2001—03, 2004—05, 2007, v.p. mktg. & corp. develop., 2003—04, v.p. crude purchasing & corp. develop., 2005—06, v.p. spl. projects, 2007; pres. Bartos Industries & Standard Supply & Dist. Co. Inc., 2007; sr. v.p., CFO Holly Corp., 2008—11; sr. v.p. strategy & corp. develop. HollyFrontier Corp., Dallas, 2011—. Office: HollyFrontier Corp Ste 1300 2828 N Harwood Dallas TX 75201 Office Phone: 214-871-3555.

SHAW, CAROLE, editor, publisher; b. Bklyn., Jan. 22, 1936; d. Sam and Betty (Neckin) Bergenthal; m. Ray Shaw, Dec. 27, 1957; children: Lori Eve Cohen, Victoria Shaw Locknar. BA, Hunter Coll., 1962. Singer Capitol Records, Hilton Records, Rama Records, Verve Records, 1952-65; TV appearances Ed Sullivan, Steve Allen, Jack Paar, George Gobel Show, 1957; owner The People's Choice, LA, 1975-79; founder, editor-in-chief Big Beautiful Woman mag., Beverly Hills, Calif., 1979—93; on air fashio cons. NBS S Home Show, 1993—95; with Carole Shaw Collectibles The Home Shopping Club, 1993—95; actress Nashville, 2000—; mem. Moonlight & Memories, 2003—. Creator Carole Shaw and BBW label clothing line for large-size women. Author: Come Out, Come Out Wherever You Are, 1982. Avocations: piano, painting, swimming, travel. Office: BBW Mag 6666 Brookmont Ter Ste 412 Nashville TN 37205-4622 Personal E-mail: bibewa@comcast.net.

SHAW, DONALD LESLIE, Spanish language educator; b. Feb. 11, 1930; s. Stephen Leslie and Lily (Hughes) S.; m. Maria Concetta Cristini, June 30, 1958; children: Andrew Leslie, Sylvia Maria Pierina. BA, U. Manchester, Eng., 1952, MA, 1953; PhD, U. Dublin, Ireland, 1960. Asst. lectr. U. Dublin, 1955-57, U. Glasgow, Scotland, 1957-64, U. Edinburgh, Scotland, 1964-69, sr. lectr., 1969-72, reader, prof. spanish, 1972-86; prof. spanish U. Va., Charlottesville, 1986—. Vis. prof. Brown U., Providence, 1967, U. Va., Charlottesville, 1983. Author: Historia de la Literatura Española, Siglo XIX, 1973, La Generación del 98, 1977, Nueva Narrativa Hispanoamericana, 1981, Alejo Carpentier, 1985, Borges' Narrative Strategies, 1992, Antonio Skármeta and the Post-Boom, 1994, The Post-Boom in Spanish American Fiction, 1998, A Companion to Spanish American Fiction, 2001, Spanish American Poetry After 1950, 2007. Served with RAF, 1953-55. Avocation: cycling. E-mail: dls6h@vriginia.edu. Office: U Va 115 Wilson Hall Charlottesville VA 22903-3238 Home: 1830 Jefferson Park Ave #32 Charlottesville VA 22903 Home Phone: 434-296-4528; Office Phone: 434-924-4658. Business E-Mail: dls6h@virginia.edu.

SHAW, HELEN LESTER ANDERSON, nutrition educator, researcher, retired dean; b. Lexington, Ky., Oct. 18, 1936; d. Walter Southall and Elizabeth (Guyn) Anderson; m. Charles Van Shaw, Mar. 14, 1988. BS, U. Ky., Lexington, 1958; MS, U. Wis., Madison, 1965, PhD, 1969. Registered dietitian. Dietitian Roanoke (Va.) Meml. Hosp., 1959-60, Santa Barbara (Calif.) Cottage Hosp., 1960-61; dietitian, unit mgr. U. Calif., Santa Barbara, 1961-63; rsch. asst., NIH fellow U. Wis., Madison, 1963-68; from asst. prof. to prof. U. Mo., Columbia, 1969-88, assoc. dean, prof., 1977-84; prof., chair dept. food and nutrition U. N.C., Greensboro, 1989-94, dean Sch. Human Environ. Scis., 1994-2000; ret., 2000. Cluster leader Food for 21st Century rsch. program U. Mo., 1985-88. Contbr. articles to rsch. publs. Elder First Prebsbyn. Ch., Columbia, Mo., 1974—89, Greensboro, NC, 1992—. Recipient Teaching award Home Econ. Alumni Assn., 1981, Gamma Sigma Delta, 1984, Centennial Legacy medallion U. Ky., 2007; rsch. grantee Nutrition Found., 1971-73, NIH, 1972-75, NSF, 1980-83. Mem. Am. Soc. for Nutrition, Am. Bd. Nutrition, Acad. Nutrition and Dietetics, Sigma Xi, Phi Upsilon Omicron, Kappa Omicron Nu. Democrat. Avocations: singing, volunteering, watercolor painting. Personal E-mail: shaw713helen@aol.com.

SHAW, JAMES GREGORY (GREG), state supreme court justice; b. 1957; s. James Hubert and Ruth (Cooper) Shaw; m. Samantha Shaw, Aug. 1980; children: Gregory, Christopher. BS, Auburn Univ., 1979; JD, Samford Univ., 1982; LLM, Univ. Va., 2004. Bar: Ala. 1982. Atty., private practice, 1982—84; staff atty. Ala. Supreme Ct. Justice Janie Shores, 1984—85, Ala. Supreme Ct. Justice James Gorman Houston, 1985—2000; judge Ala. Ct. Criminal Appeals, 2000—09; chief judge Ala. Ct. of Judiciary, 2007—09; assoc. justice Ala. Supreme Ct., 2009—. Mem. Ala. Chief Justice's Commn. on Professionalism, Ala. State Bar Com. on Archives & History, Jud. Liaison com., Pattern Jury Instructions com., adv. com. criminal procedure. Master: Hugh Maddox Inn of Ct. (hon.); mem.: Kiwanis Club of Montgomery. Methodist. Office: Ala Supreme Ct 300 Dexter Ave Montgomery AL 36104 Office Phone: 334-229-0700.*

SHAW, JASON, state legislator; b. June 29; m. Katy Shaw; 1 child, Anne Harvey Shaw. B in Polit. Sci., U. Ga. Owner Shaw Ins. Svcs., Inc., Lakeland, Ga.; ptnr. Morris & Shaw Ins. Agy., Inc., Nashville, Ga., Ga. Olive Farms, Inc.; mem. Dist. 176 Ga. House of Representatives, 2011—. Republican. Office: 39 Valdosta Rd Lakeland GA 31635 also: Georgia House of Reps 508 Coverdell Legis Office Bldg Atlanta GA 30334 Office Phone: 229-482-3505, 404-656-0213. Business E-Mail: jason.shaw@house.ga.gov.

SHAW, JOHNNY W., state legislator; b. Jan. 5, 1942; married; 6 children. Mem. Dist. 80 Tenn. House of Reps., 2000—; mem. Agr. Com., Children & Family Affairs Com., Fin. Com., Ways & Means Com.; bd chmn. Mayor's 1st Character Program, Brownsville; co-owner Shaw Broadcasting Co. Pastor St. John Missionary Bapt. Ch. Mem.: NAACP, 100 Black Men, Rotary Bolivar, C. of C., Clubs Shaw Singers. Democrat. Baptist. Office: PO Box 191 123 West Market St Bolivar TN 38008 also: 33 Legislative Plz Nashville TN 37243-0180 Office Phone: 615-741-4538, 731-658-8925. Office Fax: 731-658-1682, 615-741-1446. Business E-Mail: rep.johnny.shaw@capitol.tn.gov.

SHAW, JUDY BROWDER, engineer; BS in Chemistry, Harding Coll.; postgrad, Texas Tech U. Process devel. engr. then process engr. mgr. Texas Instruments, 1978—2000, mgr. Silicon Tech. Devel. Process Engring. teams, 2000—07, dir., adv. process modules, 2007—. Co-founder SiTD Women's Network, 2002, Women Tex. Instruments Fund, 2003; mem. SiTD Business Diversity Team, Leadership Tex., 2004; bd. dirs. Real Options for Women, Plano, Tex. Named to Hall of Fame, WITI, 2004.

SHAW, MARK R., lawyer; m. Kristy Shaw; children: Matt, Lindsey. BA in Journalism, U. Tex., 1986; JD, Loyola U. New Orleans Sch. Law, 1990. Atty. Akin, Gump, Strauss Hauer & Feld LLP; with GE Capital Aviation Services, Shannon, Ireland; joined legal dept. Southwest Airlines Co., Dallas, 2000, assoc. gen. counsel corporate & transactions, 2008—13, v.p., gen. counsel, corporate sec., 2013—. Office: Southwest Airlines Co 2702 Love Field Dr Dallas TX 75235 Office Phone: 214-792-4000.*

SHAW, MINOR MICKEL, board member, investment company executive; b. Elberton, Ga; BA, U. NC; DHL (hon.), Wofford Coll., Furman U. Worked C & S Nat. Bank of Ga., C & S Nat Bank of SC; worked (real estate devel.) Manly Investment Group; pres. Micco Corp., Greenville, SC, 1998. Bd. dirs. Piedmont Natural Gas Co., 2004—, BlueCross BlueShield of SC, SC, United States, 2008. Trustee Columbia Nations Funds, The Duke Endowment; bd. dirs. The Palmetto Inst. Named Top 25 Most Influential, The Greenville News, Philanthropist of the Yr., Whitney Young Humanitarian award, Urban League, Greenville C. of C. Chairman award, Order of the Palmetto award, State of SC. Office: Piedmont Natural Gas Co Inc Bd Directors 4720 Piedmont Row Dr Charlotte NC 28210 Office Phone: 704-364-3120. Business E-Mail: minor.shaw@piedmontng.com.

SHAW, NANCY RIVARD, art historian, independent scholar; b. Saginaw, Mich. BA magna cum laude, Oakland U., 1969; MA, Wayne State U., 1973. Asst. curator Am. art Detroit Inst. Arts, 1972-75, curator, 1975-98, curator emerita, specialist in late 19th and early 20th century Am. art, 1998—. Adj. prof. art and art history Wayne State U., Detroit, 1991-98; lectr. in field.; organizer exhibns. Contbg. author: American Art in the Detroit Institute of Arts, Vol. I, 1991, Vol. II, 1997, Vol. III, 2005; contbr. articles to exhbn. catalogues and profl. jours. and chpts. to books. Mem. Wayne State U. Alumni Assn. Avocation: painting. Personal E-mail: nrivardshaw@yahoo.com.

SHAW, RONALD AHREND, physician, educator; b. Toledo, July 20, 1946; s. Harold Michael and Eve Helen (Ganch) S.; m. Carol Ann Rapp, June 13, 1970; children: Robert, Benjamin, Daniel. BS, U. Toledo, 1968; MD, Washington U., 1972. Diplomate Am. Bd. Emergency Medicine. Intern, then resident in surgery St. Luke's Hosp., St. Louis, 1972-73, resident in surgery, 1973; mem. staff Bapt. Med. Ctr.-Montclair, Birmingham, Ala., 1976-81, chief emergency svc., 1979-81; assoc. dir. lifesaver flight ops. Caraway Meth. Med. Ctr., Birmingham, 1981-85; dir. emergency svc. sch. medicine U. Ala., 1985-89; asst. dir. emergency svc. R.I. Hosp., Providence, 1989-95; attending physician emergency dept. Bapt. Med. Ctr., Montgomery, Ala., 1996—; med. dir. emergency dept. Jackson Hosp., 2000—01; sec.-treas., med. staff Bapt. Med. Ctr., 2001—03. Cons. U. Tex., Houston, 1986, Bell Helicopter, Ft. Worth, 1986, Mut. Assurance, Birmingham, 1986-89, NYU, 1988-89, R.I. State Med. Examiners Office, 1991-96, Fla. Dept. Health, EMS Office, 1991—, Joint Underwriters Assocs. of R.I., 1991-96; chmn. adv. bd. emergency svc. Ala. Dept. Pub. Health, 1986-89; med. dir. Emergency Med. Svcs. div. R.I. Dept. Health, 1990-95; med. dir. Health Care Rev., Inc., 1995-96. Bd. dirs. MADD, Ala., 1986, Univ. Emergency Medicine Found., 1995-96; mem. planning com. Youth Baseball, Vestavia Hills, ala., 1986, 87; mem. disaster com. City of Birmingham, 1984-89; mem. 911 Commn., State of R.I., 1991-96. Recipient Disting. Achievement award Birmingham Emergency Med. Svc., 1988. Fellow Am. Coll. Emergency Physicians (bd. dirs. Ala. chpt. 1984-89, steering com. EMS sect. 1991-94, sec.-treas. R.I. chpt. 1995-96); mem. AAAS, ACS (state com. on trauma R.I. chpt. 1990-96), N.Y. Acad. Sci., Med. Assn. Ala. (mem. coun. med. svc. 1985-86). Republican. Avocations: hunting, stamp collecting and computer programming. Office Phone: 334-272-1050. Personal E-mail: kd1hp@msn.com.

SHAW, WILLIAM FREDERICK, statistician; b. Bklyn., Feb. 24, 1920; s. Charles Peter and Josephine Veronica (Seusing) S.; m. Josephine Cannington Kerbey, Jan. 18, 1947; children: William Frederick, Teresa Anne. BBA, U. Miami, 1949; MA, George Washington U., 1953; postgrad. studies in econometrics, math. and computer scis., U.S. Dept. Agr. Grad. Sch., 1964-74; PhD (fellow), Walden U., 1977. Rsch. asst. U. Miami, 1948—49; with Rsch. and Stats. divsn. FHA, Washington, 1950—73, chief statistician Rsch. and Stats. divsn., 1969—; chief statistician, dir. Advanced Statis. Analysis and Computer Applications Staff HUD, 1974—82, chief statistician, dir. housing stats. divsn., 1982—89, chief statistician, dir. info. sys. divsn., 1990—91, chief statistician, dir. Office of Evaluation, 1991—. Pres. Kerbey-Shaw Assos. Served with F.A. AUS, 1943-45. Decorated Bronze Star; recipient Superior Performance award HUD, 1977; named by Info. Resources Adminstrn. Coun. as Fed. Office Sys. Profl. of Yr., 1983. Mem. AAAS, Am. Statis. Assn., Am. Risk and Ins. Assn., Am. Real Estate and Urban Econ. Assn., Am. Econ. Assn., Am. Fin. Assn., N.Y. Acad. Scis., Nat. Assn. Rev. Appraisers and Mortgage Underwriters, Soc. Cost Estimating and Analysis, Res. Officers Assn. U.S., 101st Airborne Divsn. Assn., Air Force Assn., Alpha Kappa Psi. Roman Catholic. Home: 6527 Byrnes Dr Mc Lean VA 22101-5227 Office: HUD 7th and D Sts SW Washington DC 20411-0001

SHEA, BRENT MACK, social sciences educator; b. Oneida, NY, June 3, 1946; s. Mack Evered and Alice May (Meeker) Shea. BA, SUNY, Binghamton, 1968, MA, 1972, PhD, 1977. Vis. instr. Harpur Coll. SUNY, Binghamton, 1975-76, resident dir. Coll.-in-the-Woods, 1976-78, rsch. assoc., 1977-78; from asst. prof. to prof. Sweet Briar Coll., Va., 1978—92, chmn. dept. anthropology and sociology, 1986—90, 1996—99, 2005—06, chmn. dept. sociology, 2007—, prof., 1992—. Vis. fellow Yale U., New Haven, 1984—85, postdoctoral fellow, 1985—86; sci. collaborator Centro studi per l'Evoluzione Umana, Rome, 1990—; vis. scholar Summer Inst. Survey Rsch. U. Mich., 1991; presenter, rschr. in field. Co-editor, contbg. author: Social Psychiatry across Cultures, 1995; editor: conf. procs. Work and Mental Health, 1996; mem. editl. bd. Internat. Scope Rev., 1999—2010; co-editor: Internat. Scope Rev., 2000—01; contbr. articles to profl. jour., chapters to books. Regents scholar, Harpur Coll. SUNY, 1964—68, Faculty Rsch. fellow, Sweet Briar Coll., 1984—85, 1992—93, NIMH Postdoctoral Rsch. fellow, Instn. Social and Policy Studies, Yale U., 1985—86. Mem.: AAUP (chpt. pres. 1996—99, chair state com. on coll. and univ. governance 1998—2001, state exec. com. 1998—2001), Va. Sociol. Assn. (mem. exec. com. 1980—81, pres., co-chmn. conf. program), Ea. Ednl. Rsch. Assn. (dir. rsch. ethics 1979—83, bd. dirs. 1979—85, gen. sec. 1983—85), Ius Primi Viri Internat. Assn., Rome (v.p. bd. 1994—2004, NGO rep. economic and social coun., United Nations Hdqs. 2005—), Internat. Sociol. Assn. (v.p. exec. bd. 1994—98, mental health and illness rsch. com.), Am. Sociol. Assn. (task force on internat. focus of Am. sociology 1999—2003, task force, postdoc in soc. 2013—), Soc. Automotive Historians. Avocations: classical piano, classic cars. Home: PO Box 1 Sweet Briar VA 24595-0001 Office: Sweet Briar Coll Dept Sociology Sweet Briar VA 24595 Office Phone: 434-381-6193.

SHEA, FRANCIS X., energy executive; Mgmt. positions Chase Manhattan Bank, NYC, Hong Kong & Indonesia; pres., COO Trans-Tec Services Inc., 1991—94; dir., sr. adv. Ctr. for Bus. & Advisory Services, Jakarta, Indonesia, 1999—2001; exec. v.p. World Fuel Services Corp., Miami, Fla., 2001—02, exec. v.p., CFO, 2002—05, exec. v.p., chief risk & adminstrv. officer, 2005—, interim CFO, 2006—07. Office: World Fuel Services Corp 9800 NW 41st St Miami FL 33178 Office Phone: 305-428-8000.

SHEA, JOHN J., pharmaceutical executive; BS in chemistry, Bethany Coll. Quality assurance Teledyne Relays, Ortho Diagnostics, Inc., Bio Reagents & Diagnostics, Inc.; dir., corp. quality assurance Hexcel Corp., 1980—87; dir. quality assurance NeoRx Corp., 1987—89; Joined J. Shea Inc., 1989, head, quality assurance mgmt. cons.; quality sys. adviser Quintiles. Bd. dirs. BioDelivery Sciences Internat., Inc. Office: BioDelivery Sciences Internat Inc Ste 210 801 Corporate Center Dr Raleigh NC 27607 Office Phone: 919-582-9050. Office Fax: 919-582-9051. Business E-Mail: john.shea@jfshea.com.

SHEARER, LINDA, museum director; b. LI, NY, Feb. 13, 1946; BA, Sarah Lawrence Coll., Bronxville, NY, 1968. Assoc. curator Solomon R. Guggenheim Mus., NYC, 1969—80; exec. dir. Artists Space, NYC, 1980—85; curator painting and sculpture Mus. Modern Art, NYC, 1985—89; dir. Williams Coll. Mus. Art, Williamstown, Mass., 1989—2004; Alice & Harris Weston dir. Contemporary Arts Ctr., Cin., 2004—06; interim dir. Contemporary Arts Mus Houston, 2007—. Tchr. contemporary art Williams Coll., Sch. Visual Arts, NYC. Bd. trustees Am. Fedn. of Arts; adv. com. Skowhegan Sch. of Painting and Sculpture; chair Phila. Exhibition Initiative, 2003. Mem.: Am. Fedn. of Arts (former trustee), Assn. Art Mus. Dirs. (former trustee). Office: Contemporary Arts Mus Houston 5216 Montrose Blvd Houston TX 77006-6598 Office Phone: 713-284-8250. Office Fax: 713-284-8275.

SHEARER, RICHARD EUGENE, educational consultant; b. Connellsville, Pa., Dec. 30, 1919; s. H.D. and Florence (Prinkey) S.; m. Ruth Mansberger, June 16, 1944 (dec. Mar. 1993); children: Patricia (Mrs. Richard Wilson), Suzanne (Mrs. Terry Jones), Richard J. AB, Eastern Bapt. Coll. and Sem., Phila., 1943, D.D., 1953; B.D., New Brunswick Theol. Sem., 1945; MA, Columbia, 1948, Ed.D., 1959; LL.D., Denison U., 1958; H.H.D., Bishop Coll., 1977. Ordained to ministry Bapt. Ch., 1943; minister Atlantic Highlands, N.J., 1943-45, New Brunswick, N.J., 1945-50; pres. Alderson-Broaddus Coll., Philippi, W.Va., 1951-83; ind. cons., 1983—; cons., interim dir. W.Va. Found. Ind. Colls.; prin. resdl. devel. Bridgeport, W.Va., 1983—; v.p., exec. dir. United Health Found., Clarksburg, W.Va., 1987—; pres. R. Shearer & Assocs., Philippi, W.Va., 1984. Lectr. Mex. Pastor's Conf., summer 1955; past pres. W.Va. Found. Ind. Colls.; mem. Commn. on Instnl. Funding, Am. Bapt. Chs., U.S.A.; coordinator (Central Europe Coll. Program); pres. Am. Bapt. Assn. Sch. and Coll. Adminstrs., 1977; mem. W.Va. Ednl. Found., W.Va. State Scholarship Commn. Author: (book) Miracle on Brownlow Hill. Bd. regents W.Va. Assn. Pvt. Colls.; bd. dirs. W.Va. Found. Independent Colls.; sr. min. Bridgeport (W.Va.) Bapt. Ch., 1988-93; bd. dirs. Eastern Bapt. Theol. Sem., Phila. Named Phi Delta Kappa Profl. Educator of Year, 1964 Mem. Am. Assn. Sch. Adminstrs., W.Va. Assn. Coll. and Univ. Presidents (sec. mem. exec. com. 1963—), Assn. Am. Colls. (commn. coll. and soc.), Kiwanis. Office: 300 Shearerwood Dr Philippi WV 26416 Personal E-mail: rmshearer1@aol.com.

SHEARER, ROBERT K., corporate financial executive; BS in Acctg., Catawba Coll., Salisbury, NC. CPA. Sr. audit mgr. Ernst & Young LLP; pres., outdoor coalition VF Corp., asst. contr. Greensboro, NC, 1986—89, contr., 1989—94, v.p., 1994—98, v.p., fin., 1998—2005, CFO, 1998—, sr. v.p., 2005—. Bd. dirs. Church & Dwight Co. Inc., 2008—. Office: VF Corp 105 Corporate Ctr Blvd Greensboro NC 27408 Office Phone: 336-424-6000.

SHEDD, DENNIS W., federal judge; b. Cordova, SC, Jan. 28, 1953; BA, Wofford Coll., 1975; JD, U. SC, 1978; LLM, Georgetown U., 1980. Bar: SC. Law clerk Harry Dent & Assoc., 1977—78; admin. asst. US Senator Strom Thurmond, 1978—88; chief counsel US Senate Jud. Com., Washington, 1985-86; of counsel Bethea, Jordan & Griffin, Columbia, S.C., 1988-90; pvt. practice, 1989-90; judge US Dist. Ct. SC, Greenville, 1990—2002, US Ct. Appeals (4th cir.), 2002—. Adj. prof. U. SC, 1989-92. Mem. SC Bar Assn., Richland County Bar Assn., Phi Beta Kappa. Office: US Courthouse 1100 Laurel St Columbia SC 29201-2431

SHEEHAN, CHARLES VINCENT, investment banker; b. London, Dec. 19, 1930; came to U.S., 1931; s. Charles Vincent and Mary Margaret (Stokes) S.; m. Susan Ellen Rosar, May 5, 1962. BS, Georgetown U., 1952. Chief fin. officer Gen. Electric Co., Tokyo, Sydney, Australia and Sao Paulo, Brazil, 1962-64, 64-66, 67-71, staff exec. Fairfield, Conn., 1972-83, v.p. corp. exec. office, 1983-87; sr. v.p., chief fin., adminstrn. officer Kidder, Peabody Group, Inc., NYC, 1987-90. Bd. dirs. Fleet Trust Co.; chmn., bd. dirs. Highlands-Cashiers Hosp., Indian River Meml. Hosp. Chmn. Non-partisan Polit. Action Com. for Gen. Electric Co. employees, Fairfield, 1982-83. Served to lt. USN, 1952-54. Mem. Johns Island Club (Vero Beach, Fla.), Quail Valley Golf Club (Vero Beach, Fla.), Wildcat Cliffs Country Club (Highlands, N.C.) (pres. 1998-99). Republican. Roman Catholic. Avocations: golf, boating. Home: 884 Indian Ln Vero Beach FL 32963-1131 Personal E-mail: gecharlie@earthlink.net.

SHEEHAN, JEREMIAH J., former metal company executive; b. NYC, Oct. 21, 1938; m. Mary Rita Sheehan; 3 children. BA in Econs., Hunter Coll.; postgrad., U. Chgo. With Continental Can Co., pres., gen. mgr. beverage packaging; v.p. can divsn. Reynolds Metals Co., Richmond, Va., 1988—90, exec. v.p. consumer and packaging products, 1990—93, exec. v.p. fabricated products, 1993—94, pres., COO, bd. dirs., 1994—96, chmn. bd., CEO, 1996—2000. Bd. dirs. Union Camp Corp., Universal Corp., Richmond, Va., 1998—; fed. resident Bank of Richmond. Mem. Bus. Roundtable, Va. Bus. Coun., Richmond Mgmt. Roundtable; adv. coun. on Rev. Estimates State of Va.; bd. trustees Va. Found. Ind. Colls.; mem. adv. coun. E. Claiborne Robins Sch. Bus., U. Richmond; bd. dirs. Va. Commonwealth U. Sch. Engring. Found., Richmond Met. Coalition Against Drugs; former chmn. bd. Keep Am. Beautiful, Inc.

SHEEN-AARON, JULIA, public health service officer; MPH, Emory U., Atlanta; grad. pub. health cert. program, U. Wash. Sch. Pub. Health and Cmty. Medicine. Dir. chronic disease program VI Dept. Health, St. Thomas, 1993—2004, project mgr., cardiovascular health program, 1993—2004, project coord., behavioral risk factor surveillance systems, 1994—2004, project mgr., breast and cervical cancer program, 1995—98, project mgr., tobacco prevention and control program, 1995—2005, territorial asst. commr., St. Croix dist., 2007—, acting commr., 2009—11. Office: VI Dept Health 48 Sugar Estate St Thomas VI 00802 Office Phone: 340-774-0117. Office Fax: 340-773-6551. Business E-Mail: julia.sheen@usvi-doh.org.

SHEERAN, PAUL W., anesthesiologist, pediatrician, educator; BA in Spanish and Lit. cum laude with honors, Whitman Coll., 1987; MD, U. Wash., 1991. Diplomate Am. Bd. Anesthesiology, Am. Bd. Pediatrics-pediatric critical care medicine, Am. Bd. Pediatrics. Intern Harbor UCLA Med. Ctr., 1992, resident pediat., 1994—97; resident anesthesia UT Southwestern Med. Ctr., 1998—2000; fellow Children's Med. Ctr. of Dallas; fellow, pediatric critical care medicine UT Southwestern Med. Ctr., 1995—97, chief fellow, pediatric critical care medicine, 1997—98, fellow pediatric anesthesia, 2000—01, asst. prof. Office: UT Southwestern Medical Center 5323 Harry Hines Blvd Dallas TX 75390-9003 Office Phone: 214-648-3111.

SHEETS, JEFF W., oil industry executive; b. Bossier City, La., 1958; BS in Chem. Engring., U. Mo., Rolla, 1980; MBA, U. Houston, 1989. Process engr. exploration & prodn. divsn. Conoco Inc., 1980, staff fin. dir., 1990—93, staff fin. dir. exploration & prodn. divsn. Norway, 1993, comml. services mgr. Stavanger, Norway, 1994—97, asst. treas. Houston, 1998—2001, v.p., treas., 2001, ConocoPhillips, Houston, 2002—08, sr. v.p. planning & strategy, 2008—10, sr. v.p. comml. and planning & strategy, 2010, sr. v.p. finance, CFO, 2010—. Bd. dirs. OIL Investment Corp. Ltd. Office: ConocoPhillips PO Box 2197 Houston TX 77252-2197

SHEFFIELD, GREG, media blogger; Co-founder RatherBiased-.com, 2000; editor, NewsBusters.org Media Rsch. Ctr., 2005, now contbr. editor, NewsBusters.org. Work has been featured by CNN, MSNBC, Fox News Channel, New York Times, Washington Post, and New York Mag. Office: Media Rsch Ctr 325 S Patrick St Alexandria VA 22314 E-mail: gsheffield@mediaresearch.org.

SHEFFIELD, MATTHEW, media blogger; Co-founder RatherBiased.com, 2000; media and tech. cons., exec. editor, NewsBusters.org Media Rsch. Ctr., 2005—; pres. Dialog New Media, Washington. Lectr. in field. Work has been featured in NY Times, Washington Post, BBC, Fox News Channel, CNN, MSNBC and the New Yorker, maintains personal blog site matthewsheffield.blogspot.com; exec. prodr.: NewsBusted. Mem. Lds Ch. Office: Media Research Center 1900 Campus Commons Dr Ste 600 Reston VA 20191-1535 Office Phone: 703-683-9733. Office Fax: 703-683-9736. E-mail: msheffield@newsbusters.org.

SHEFFIELD, RALPH, state legislator; b. Waco, Tex., Jan. 11, 1955; m. Debbie Sheffield; children: Ashley, Adrienne, Josh, Ben. Pres., CEO Sheffield, Inc., 1978—; owner Las Casas Restaurant & Catering, Temple, Tex., 1982—; mem. Dist. 55 Tex. House of Representatives, 2008—. Recipient of several awards and honors. Mem.: Tex. Restaurant Assn. (pres. 2002—03, chmn. edn. found.). Republican. Methodist. Office: 3000 S 31st St Ste 505 Temple TX 76502 also: Room E2.314 Capitol Extension PO Box 2910 Austin TX 78768 Office Phone: 254-774-9888, 512-463-0630. Office Fax: 254-771-5775, 512-463-9054.

SHEFFIELD, SCOTT D., oil industry executive; BS in Petroleum Engring., U. Tex. Prodn. and reservoir engr. Amoco Prodn. Co.; petroleum engr. Parker & Parsley Devel. Co., 1979—85, v.p. engring., 1981—85, pres., bd. dirs., 1985—89, chmn., CEO, 1989; pres., bd. dirs. Parker & Parsley Petroleum Co., 1990—97, chmn., CEO, 1990—97; pres., CEO Pioneer Natural Resources, Irving, Tex., 1997—99, chmn., pres., CEO, 1999—2004; chmn., CEO Pioneer Natural Resources Co., Irving, Tex., 2004—. Office: Pioneer Natural Resources 5205 N O'Connor Blvd Irving TX 75039

SHEHEEN, VINCENT A., state legislator; b. Camden, SC, Apr. 29, 1971; s. Fred and Rose Sheheen; m. Amy Renee Uhl, May 13, 1995; children: Austin, Joseph, Anthony. BA, Clemson U., 1993; JD, U. SC, 1996. Law clerk US Dist. Judge, 1996—98; prosecutor City of Camden, SC, 2000; atty. Savage, Royall and Sheheen LLP; mem. Dist. 52 SC House of Reps., 2001—04; mem. Dist. 27 SC State Senate, 2005—, mem. Agr. and Natural Resources Com., Fish, Game and Forestry Com., Gen. Com., Judiciary Com. & Transp. Com. Adj. instr. U. SC Sch. Law, 1998—2001. Democrat. Office: 506 Gressette Bldg Columbia SC 29201 Mailing: PO Drawer 10 Camden SC 29021 Office Phone: 803-432-4391, 803-212-6124. Business E-Mail: VS@scstatehouse.net.

SHEIK, DUNCAN, singer, songwriter; b. Montclair, NJ, Nov. 18, 1969; Degree in semiotics, Brown U., New Providence, RI, 1992. Performed with bands His Boy Elroy, 1993, Liz and Lisa. Singer, musican, co-prodr. (albums) Duncan Sheik, 1996; singer, musician, co-prodr.: albums Humming, 1998, Phantom Moon, 2001, Daylight, 2002, White Limousine, 2006, songs "Wishful Thinking", 1998; TV Appearances: Boston Public, 2003, American Dreams, 2003; composer: (plays) (musical score) The Nightingale, 2006, Nero (Another Golden Rome), 2006, Spring Awakening, 2006 (Drama Desk award outstanding music, 2007, Tony award best original score written for the theatre, 2007, Tony award best orchestrations, 2007, Grammy award for Best Musical Show Album, 2008, Best New Musical award, Laurence Olivier Theatre, 2010). Office: Gold Mountain Entertainment 11 Music Sq E Apt 103 Nashville TN 37203-4353

SHEINER, JONATHAN ROBERT, legislative staff member, lawyer; b. Bklyn., June 24, 1950; s. Bernard and Ethel (Soba) S.; m. Janet Marie Meiburger, Sept. 2, 1972 (div. Dec. 1978); m. Susan White Student, Lehigh U., 1967-68; BA, George Washington U., 1971; JD, NYU, 1974. Bar: N.Y. 1975, D.C. 1977. Atty. Con Edison, NYC, 1974-77, asst. v.p. private affairs, 1979-85; assoc. Lowenstein, Newman, Reis & Axelrod, Washington, 1977-78; atty. Washington Metro. Area Transit Auth., 1978-79; legis. counsel to rep. Charles B. Rangel, 1985—95; dep. asst. sec., congressional and intergovernmental relations US Dept. Housing & Urban Devel., Washington, 1995—98, counselor to asst. sec. for housing, 1997—98; Dem. legis. dir., tax counsel, asst. to chmn Charles B. Rangel US House Ways & Means Com., Washington, 1998—2007, Dem. gen. counsel to rep. Charles Rangel, 2007—. Named a Who's Who in DC, Crain's NY Bus., 2009. Democrat. Office: US House Ways & Means Com 2354 Longworth House Office Bldg Rm 1102 Washington DC 20515 Office Phone: 202-225-4365. Office Fax: 202-225-0818. E-mail: jon.sheiner@mail.house.gov.

SHEINFELD, MYRON M. (MICKEY SHEINFELD), lawyer; b. Mass., Mar. 18, 1930; s. Robert and Sadye (Rosenberg) Sheinfeld; m. Christina Trzcinski, Mar. 30, 1985; children: Scott, Tom. BA, Tulane U., New Orleans, 1951; JD, U. Mich., 1954. Bar: Mich. 1954, Tex. 1956, US Dist. Ct. (we. dist.) Tex. 1980, US Ct. Appeals (5th cir.) 1981, US Ct. Appeals (11th cir.) 1985, US Dist. Ct. (so. dist.) Tex. 1990, US Dist. Ct. (no. dist.) Tex., US Supreme Ct. Rschr. U. Mich. Legis. Rsch. Inst., 1954; asst. US atty. (so. dist.) Tex. US Dept. Justice, 1958-60; law clk. to hon. Ben. C. Connally US Dist. Ct. (so. dist.) Tex., 1960-61; pnr. Strickland, Gordon & Sheinfeld, Houston, 1961-68; co-founder, shareholder Sheinfeld, Maley & Kay, PC, Houston, 1968-96, of counsel, 1996—2001; sr. counsel Akin, Gump, Strauss, Hauer & Feld LLP, Houston, 2001—06, King & Spalding, LLP, Houston, 2007—; mem. Fin. Restructing Group. Adj. prof. U. Tex. Sch. Law, 1975—91; bd. dirs. Nabors Industries Ltd., 1989—; past chmn. Tex. Bankruptcy Adv. Commn.; editl. bd. Practical Lawyer; tchr. U. Tex. Law Sch., U. Houston; mem. Sect. Tax., Corp., Banking & Bus. Law; former chmn. Bus. Law Sect., Bankruptcy Adv. Commn. Tex. Bd. Legal Specialization, Com. Admission and Discipline, US Dist. Ct. Southern Dist. Tex.; former mem. Tex. Bd. Legal Specialization. Co-author: Collier on Bankruptcy Taxation; co-editor: Collier on Bankruptcy; contbr. numerous articles to profl. jours. Svc. with JAG Corps US Army, 1955—58, svc. with USAR, 1965. Named Lawyer of Yr., Houston; named one of Houston's Top Lawyers for the People, H Tex. mag., 2009, Best Lawyers in America, Chambers US. Mem.: ABA, Tex. Bd. Legal Specialization (past chmn.), Nat. Assn. Corp. Directors (bd. dirs., TriCities chpt. 2003—, past pres., TriCities chpt.), State Bar Tex. (past chmn. bus. law sect.), Am. Coll. Bankruptcy, Nat. Bankruptcy Conf., Downtown Club Houston (bd. govs. 1995—), Phi Sigma Alpha, Phi Beta Kappa. Office: King & Spalding LLP 1100 Lousiana St Ste 4000 Houston TX 77002 Office Phone: 713-751-3252. Office Fax: 713-751-3290. Business E-Mail: msheinfeld@kslaw.com.*

SHELBURNE, JOHN DANIEL, pathologist; b. Washington, Aug. 27, 1943; s. Clarence Daniel and Edith (McDanel) S.; m. Katherine Howard Parrish, June 17, 1966; children: Mark, Kerri. BA, U. N.C., 1966; PhD, Duke U., 1971, MD, 1972. Intern, then resident Duke U. Med. Ctr., Durham, NC, 1972-76; asst. prof. Duke U., Durham, 1973-78, assoc. prof., 1978-85, prof. pathology, 1985—; dir. electron microscopy lab. VA Med. Ctr., Durham, 1976-92, chief lab. svc., 1983-99, chief of staff, 1999—. Adv. WHO, Manila, 1990; panel mem. VA Program, Washington, 1987—; participant Nordrhein/Westfalen Exchange, Germany, 1988. Editor: Basic Methods in Biological X-Ray Microprobe, 1983; author, editor: Microprobe Analysis in Medicine, 1989, Biomedical Applications of Microprobe Analysis, 1999. Mem. Appalachian Trail Conf., Harpers Ferry, West, Va., 1970—; bd. dirs. Cen. Carolina Youth Soccer, Durham, 1987-90; founding mem. N.C. Soc. for Electron Microscopy and Microprobe, Research Triangle Park, N.C., 1980—. Recipient Morehead scholarship, 1961-66, AOA Med. Honorary Duke Med. Sch., 1970; named Med. Scientist Tng. Program participant NIH, 1966-72, Shelley Meml. lectr., 1985, Florey Meml. lectr., 1988. Fellow Coll. Am. Pathologists; mem. Am. Assn. Pathologists, Microscopy Soc. Am., Microbeam Analysis Soc. Democrat. Episcopalian. Home: 4302 Malvern Rd Durham NC 27707-5451 Office: Duke U Dept Pathology PO Box 3712 Durham NC 27710-3712

SHELBY, JAMES STANFORD, surgeon, researcher; b. Ringgold, La., June 15, 1934; s. Jesse Audrey and Mable (Martin) S.; m. Susan Rainey, July 15, 1967; children: Bryan Christian, Christopher Linden. BS in Liberal Arts, La. Tech. U., New Orleans, 1956; MD, La. State U., Houston, 1958. Diplomate Am. Bd. Surgery, Am. Bd. Thoracic Surgery. Intern Charity Hosp. La., New Orleans, 1958-59, resident in surgery and thoracic surgery, 1959-65; fellow in cardiovasc. surgery Baylor U. Coll. Medicine, Houston, 1965-66; practice medicine specializing in cardiovasc. surgery Shreveport, La., 1967—2004; ret., 2004. Mem. staff Schumpert Med. Ctr., Highland Hosp., Willis-Knighton Med. Ctr.; assoc. prof. surgery La. State U. Sch. Medicine, Shreveport, 1967—; pres. Shelby Oil and Gas. With M.C., AUS, 1961-62. Recipient Medallion award La. Tech. U., 1982. Mem. AMA, Am. Coll. Cardiology, Soc. Thoracic Surgeons, Am. Heart Assn., Southeastern Surg. Congress, So. Thoracic Surgery Assn. Home: 6003 E Ridge Dr Shreveport LA 71106-2425 Office: 2751 Albert Bicknell Dr Ste 5C Shreveport LA 71103-3970 Office Phone: 318-632-9438.

SHELBY, RICHARD CRAIG, United States Senator from Alabama; b. Birmingham, Ala., May 6, 1934; s. Ozie Houston and Alice L. (Skinner) S.; m. Annette Nevin, June 11, 1960; children: Richard Craig, Claude Nevin. AB, U. Ala., 1957, LLB, 1963. Bar: Ala. 1961, DC 1979. Law clk. Supreme Ct. of Ala., 1961-62; practice law Tuscaloosa, Ala., 1963—78; prosecutor City of Tuscaloosa, 1963—71; spl. asst. atty. gen. State of Ala., 1968—71; magistrate judge US Dist. Ct. (northern dist.) Ala., 1966—70; mem. Dist. 16 Ala. State Senate, 1971—78; mem. US Congress from 7th Ala. Dist., 1979-87; US Senator from Ala., 1987—; chmn. US Senate Select Com. on Intelligence, 1997—2001, US Senate Banking, Housing & Urban Affairs Com., 2003—07. Active Boy Scouts America; pres. Tuscaloosa County Mental Health Assn., 1969-70; bd. govs. Nat. Legis. Conf., 1975-78. Recipient Taxpayer's Friend award, Nat. Taxpayers Union, 1998, Congressional Leadership award, Airports Coun. Internat.-N.Am., 2003. Mem. ABA, Ala. Bar Assn., Tuscaloosa County Bar Assn., DC Bar Assn., American Judiciary Soc., Exch. Club, Tuscaloosa County Mental Heatgh Assn.(former pres.) Republican. Presbyterian. Office: US Senate 304 Hart Senate Office Bldg Washington DC 20510 also: Federal Bldg Ste 240 1118 Greensboro Ave Tuscaloosa AL 35401-2816 Office Phone: 202-224-5744, 205-759-5047. Office Fax: 202-224-3416, 205-759-5067. E-mail: senator@shelby.senate.gov.*

SHELDON, DONNA, state legislator; Mem. Arts & Humanities Com., Banks & Banking Com., Natural Resources & Environment Com.; state rep. Dist. 71 Post 2 Ga., 2003—04; state rep. Dist. 105 Ga., 2004—. Republican. Mailing: 2186 Ewing Chapel Rd Dacula GA 30019 Office: 504 Legis Office Bldg Atlanta GA 30334 Office Phone: 770-963-5472. E-mail: sheldon71@bellsouth.net.

SHELDON, GEORGE FRANK, medical educator; b. Dec. 20, 1934; s. Richard Robert and Helen Irene (Zerzan) S.; m. Ruth Guy, Aug. 28, 1959; children: Anne Anderson, Elizabeth, Julia. BA, U. Kans., Lawrence, 1957, MD, 1961; postgrad., Mayo Clinic Grad. Sch., 1965. Asst. instr. we. civilization U. Kans., 1955—57; intern Kans. U. Med. Ctr.; resident in surgery U. Calif., San Francisco, 1965-69; fellow in surg. biology Harvard Med. Sch. of Peter Bent Brigham Hosp., 1969-71; from asst. to prof. U. Calif., 1971-82; Dr. Zack D. Owens Disting. prof. surgery, dept. chmn. U. NC, Chapel Hill, 1984—2001. Chmn. residency rev. com. accreditation Coun. Grad. Med. Edn.; mem. Coun. Grad. Med. Edn. of Health and Human Svcs., 1986, chmn. 1998; mem. adminstrv. bd. Coun. Acad. Socs., chair, 1998-99; chmn. Merit Rev. Bd. Surgery Va., AAMC, 2000, 01; pres. vis. bd. UN Formed Svcs. U. Health Scis., 2002-03; mem. Coun. on Physician and Nurse Shortage Wharton Sch. Bus. U. Penn. Author: (with J.B. Runnell) Pictorial History of Kansas Medicine, 1961; (with Jill Ridky) Managing in Academics, 1993; editor: (with J.B. Davis) Clinical Surgery, 1995; editor-in-chief: E-Facs.org. With USPHS, 1962-64. Recipient Surgeon's Dist. award for Svc. to Safety, Nat. Safety Coun., 1993, Douglass Stubbs award Nat. Med. Assn., 1991, Disting. Faculty award Med. Alumni Assn. U. N.C., 2001; named Disting. Med. Alumnus, Kans. U., 2000. Fellow Royal Coll. Surgeons of Edinburgh (hon.), Royal Coll. Surgeons Eng., European Surg. Assn., Assn. of Surgeons of Gt. Britain and Ireland, Phila. Acad. Surgeons (Hunterian Orator 2001); mem. ACS (sec. bd. govs., regent 1984-93, pres. 1998, editor-in-chief e.facs.org web portal 2004—, dir. Inst. Health Policy Rsch., Surgeon of Yr. 2001, Fitts Orator, 1987, Scudder Orator Honored Surgeon, editor E facs.org web ponta 2004-), Am. Bd. Surgery (chmn. 1989-90), Nat. Bd. Med. Examiners (test com. 1981-84), Am. Assn. Surgery of Trauma (pres. 1984, Fitts medal), Am. Surg. Assn. (sec. 1989-94, pres. 1994-95), Assn. Am. Med. Colls. (exec. com., chair elect 1999, chair 2000-01, disting. svc. mem.), Soc. Surg. Chmn. (pres.), Coun. Acad. Socs. (chmn. 1998—, com. on gender equity and com. on health workforce), Inst. Medicine (sec. com. on employer based health ins. and tech. assessment edn. bds., Fluid Resuscitation com. on Nation's Physician Workforce 1996, Reviewer Poison Ctrs), Hunter Soc. (172nd Hunterian Orator). Achievements include being recognized as the leading authority on surgical workforce. Office: U NC at Chapel Hill Dept Surgery Campus Bx 7050 4006 Burnett-Womack Bldg Chapel Hill NC 27599-7050 Business E-Mail: gsheldon@med.unc.edu.

SHELL, OWEN GLADSTONE, JR., retired bank executive; b. Greenville, SC, June 19, 1936; s. Owen and Katherine S.; m. Mary Ruth Trammell, Aug. 9, 1980; children: Katherine Sloan, Mary Carroll, Robert Owen, James Walker. BS, U. S.C., 1960; postgrad., Stonier Grad. Sch. Banking, 1971; grad., Advanced Mgmt. Program, Harvard U., 1979. V.p. Citizens & So. Nat. Bank S.C., Columbia, 1968-71, sr. v.p., 1971-74, exec. v.p., 1974-79; pres., dir., chief exec. officer First Am. Nat. Bank, Nashville, 1979-86; vice chmn. bd., dir. First American Corp., 1979-86; chmn., pres., chief exec. officer Sovran Bank/Tenn., Nashville, 1986-91; pres. Nations Bank of Tenn. (formerly Sovran Bank), Nashville, 1992-96; pres. asset mgmt. group NationsBank Corp., St. Louis, 1997-99; pres. Asset Mgmt. Bank of Am., Charlotte, 1997—2002; ret., 2002. Bd. dirs. Nashville br. Fed. Res. Bank, Atlanta, Ctrl. Parking Inc., chmn. bd., Lifepoint Hosp. Inc. Chmn. Leadership Nashville, Tenn. Performing Arts Found., Mid. Tenn. coun. Boy Scouts Am., Vanderbilt U. Owen Grad. Sch. Mgmt.; trustee Met. Nashville Pub. Edn. Found.; chmn. bd. INROADS/Nashville; bd. dirs. Tenn. Bus. Roundtable, Tenn. Tomorrow. Mem.: Assn. Res. City Bankers, Old Warson Country Club (St. Louis), Harvard Club N.Y.C., Belle Meade Country Club (Nashville), Kappa Alpha. Presbyterian. Home: 4412 Chickering Ln Nashville TN 37215-4915

SHELTON, AMY ELIZABETH, health facility administrator; b. Cin., Ohio, Dec. 6, 1973; d. William Marshall and Rebecca Sue Duke; m. Bryan Michael Shelton, Sept. 30, 2000; children: Bennett, Lucas. BBA, Trevecca Nazarene U., Nashville, 1996. Cert. med. practice exec. Budget acctg. analyst Vanderbilt U. Med. Ctr., Nashville, 2002—04, chief bus. adminstr., 2004—. Mem.: NAPW, AIM, Nat. Coun. U. Rsch. Administrators, MGMA. Office: Vanderbilt U Med Ctr 536 Robinson Rsch Bldg Nashville TN 37232-6602 Business E-Mail: amy.shelton@vanderbilt.edu.*

SHELTON, BLAKE TOLISON, musician; b. Ada, Okla., June 18, 1976; s. Richard and Dorothy Shelton; m. Kaynette Williams, Nov. 17, 2003 (div. 2006); m. Miranda Leigh Lambert, May 14, 2011. Musician: (albums) Blake Shelton, 2001, The Dreamer, 2003, Blake Shelton's Barn & Grill, 2004, Pure BS, 2007, Startin Fires, 2008, Hillbilly Bone, 2010, Loaded: The Best of Blake Shelton, 2010, Red River Blue, 2011, Cheers, It's Christmas, 2012, Based on a True Story..., 2013 (Album of Yr., Country Music Assn. Awards, 2013), (songs) (with Trace Adkins) Hillbilly Bone, 2010 (Vocal Event of Yr., Acad. Country Music Awards, 2010, Collaborative Video of Yr., CMT Music Awards, 2010, Vocal Event of Yr., Country Music Assn. Awards, 2010), Who Are You When I'm Not Looking, 2010 (Male Video of Yr., CMT Music Awards, 2011), Sure Be Cool if You Did, 2013 (Male Video of Yr., CMT Music Awards, 2013); writer (songs) Over You, 2011 (Song of Yr., Country Music Assn. Awards, 2012), vocal coach, judge (TV series) The Voice, 2011— (Gene Weed Special Achievement award, Acad. Country Music Awards, 2013). Named Male Vocalist of Yr., Country Music Assn. Awards, 2010, 2011, 2012, 2013, Entertainer of Yr., 2012, Male Vocalist of Yr., Acad. Country Music Awards, 2012, Favorite Country Male Artist, American Music Awards, 2011. Office: PO Box 1511 Ada OK 74821*

SHELTON, HAL TERRY, history professor; b. Brownwood, Tex., July 26, 1935; s. William and Myrtle Shelton; m. Sutthida Chantrasri, July 23, 1976. BE, Tex. A & M U., 1958; MEd, U. Houston, 1972, MA in History, 1985, PhD, 1991. Lt. col. US Army, 1958—79; prof. & assoc. prof., dept. mil. sci. Rice U., Houston, 1969—72; tchg. rsch. fellow, dept. history U. Houston, 1982—89, lectr., dept. history, 1989—91; prof., history San Jacinto Coll., Pasadena, Tex., 1991—, Am. Mil. U., Manassas, Va., 1994—2003. Adj. instr., dept. history North Harris Coll., 1986—88. Author: (books) General Richard Montgomery and the American Revolution, The Use of Site History in Urban Studies, 1988, The Shamrock Hotel Revisited: An Urban History, 1989, (books) From Redcoat to Rebel: General Richard Montgomery and the American Revolution, 1994; assoc. editor: book American History Reader, vol. II, 1992, contbg. editor: book The American Revolution: An Encyclopedia, 1993, Encyclopedia of the American Political Parties and Elections, 1990; contbr. chapters to books & sci. papers. Decorated US Army Meritorious Svs. medal Rice U.; recipient Robert Giesberg award, U. Houston, 1988; David Libr. of Am. Revolution Rsch. grant, 1988. Home: 3414 Summer Bay Dr Sugar Land TX 77478 Office: San Jacinto Coll Ctrl Campus Dept History 8060 Spencer Hwy PO Box 2007 Pasadena TX 77501-2007

SHELTON, HUGH (HENRY HUGH SHELTON), former Chairman of the Joint Chiefs of Staff; b. Tarboro, NC, Jan. 2, 1942; m. Carolyn L. Johnson; children: Jon, Jeff, Mark. BS, N.C. State U.; MS, Auburn U.; grad., Air Command and Staff Coll., Nat. War Coll. Commd. 2d lt. US Army, 1963, advanced through grades to gen., 1996, ret., 2001; with 5th Spl. Forces Group, Vietnam, 173d Airborn Brigade, Vietnam; comdr. 3d Bn., 60th Infantry, 9th Infantry Divsn., Ft. Lewis, asst. chief of staff for ops.; comdr. 1st Brigade, 82d Airborne Divsn., Ft. Bragg, N.C.; chief of staff 10th Mountain Divsn., Ft. Drum, N.Y.; with ops. directorate Joint Staff, Washington, 1987—89; asst. divsn. comdr. for ops. 101st Airborne Divsn., 1989-91; comdr. 82d Airborne Divsn., Ft. Bragg, N.C., XVIIIth Airborne Corps., 1993, US Spl. Ops. Command (USSOCOM), 1996—97; chmn. Joint Chiefs of Staff, US Dept. Def., Washington, 1997—2001; pres., internat. ops. M.I.C. Industries, 2002—06; chmn. Protective Products of America, Inc., 2009—, Red Hat, Inc., Raleigh, NC, 2010—. Bd. dirs. Anheuser-Busch Companies Inc., 2001—08, Anteon Internat. Corp., 2002—06, Red Hat, Inc., 2003—, Protective Products of America, Inc., 2006—, CACI Internat. Inc., 2007—. Co-author (with Ron Levinson & Malcolm McConnell): Without Hesitation: The Odyssey of an American Warrior, 2010. Decorated Def. D.S.M. with three oak clusters, D.S.M. with two oak leaf clusters, Meritorious Svc. medal with two oak leaf clusters, Bronze Star with V device with three oak clusters, Air medal, Army Commendation medal with three oak leaf clusters, Armed Forces Expeditionary medal, Vietnam Svc. medal, Southwest Asia Svc. medal, Vietnam Gallantry cross, Vietnam Campaign medal, Kuwait Liberation medal, Purple Heart, Legion of Merit with one oak leaf cluster, Combat Infantryman badge, Master Parachustist badge, Military Freefall Parachustist badge, Air assault badge, Pathfinder badge, Joint Chiefs of Staff badge, Ranger tab, Spl. Forces tab, Army Svc. ribbon, Army Overseas Svc. ribbon, Presdl. Unit Citation, US Navy Presdl. Unit Citation, Meritorious Unit Commendation, Joint Meritorious Unit award, Vietnam Gallantry Cross Unit Office: Red Hat Inc 1801 Varsity Dr Raleigh NC 27606 Office Fax: 919-754-3701.

SHELTON, JAMES D. (DENNY SHELTON), hospital investment company executive; BA in Polit. Sci. and History, La. State U.; MS in Pub. Adminstrn., U. Mo. Hosp. adminstr. La., Iowa, NC, Ga., Ill., Mo.; exec. dir. Westbank Hosp. Ops. Nat. Med. Enterprises (now Tenet Healthcare Corp.), New Orleans, 1984—86, v.p. ops., 1986—90, sr. v.p. ops., 1990—93, exec. v.p. ctrl. divsn., 1993—94; pres. ctrl. group Columbia/HCA, 1994—98, pres. Pacific group, 1998—99; chmn., CEO Triad Hosps. Inc., 1999—2007; chmn. Legacy Hospital Partners, Inc., 2007—; sr. advisor CCMP Capital Advisors, LLC; interim CEO Omnicare Inc., Covington, Ky., 2010; non-exec. chmn. Omnicare, Inc., Covington, Ky., 2011—. Chmn. Fedn. Am. Hosps., 1999, mem. bd. govs., 1999—2002; bd. dirs. Am. Hosp. Assn., Ventas, Inc., Omnicare, Inc. Office: Legacy Hosp Partners Inc 2800 N Dallas Pky Ste 200 Plano TX 75093

SHELTON, MARK M., state legislator; b. Nov. 8, 1956; m. Mary Ann Shelton; children: Richard, Andrew, Peter, Betsy. BS in Biology, Baylor U., Waco, Tex., 1979; MD, Tex. Agrl. & Mech. U., 1983. Physician Cook's Children's Hosp.; dir. pediatric infectious diseases Cook Children's Med. Ctr.; mem. Dist. 97 Tex. House of Representatives, 2008—. Republican. Office: 1050 Forest Park Blvd Ste 200 Fort Worth TX 76110 also: Room EXT E2.604 Capitol Extension PO Box 2910 Austin TX 78768 Office Phone: 817-927-0061, 412-563-0608.

SHELTON, MIKE, state legislator; b. Tulsa, Okla., Feb. 28, 1973; s. William and Sandra Shelton; m. Clarissa Franklin. BS in agrl. bus. Dir. cmty. relations Okla. County, Langston U.; dist. exec. dir. Boys Scouts of America; claims adjuster State Okla. Ins. Fund.; state rep. Dist. 97 Okla., 2005—. Democrat. Baptist. Office: 2300 N Lincoln Blvd Rm 539 Oklahoma City OK 73105 Mailing: 4125 N Everest Ave Oklahoma City OK 73111 Office Phone: 405-557-7367. E-mail: mikeshelton@okhouse.gov.

SHELTON, ROBERT WARREN, marketing professional; b. Albuquerque, Apr. 26, 1943; s. Eugene and Rusty M. (Jentsch) S.; children: Elise Straus, Samantha; m. Ginger Lee Rapp, Feb. 14, 1984. BBA in Mktg., St. Mary's U., San Antonio, 1969; postgrad., Ga. State U., 1972-73, postgrad. in fin. and internat. bus., 1973. Field mgr. Ford Motor Co., Atlanta, 1969-78; dir. fleet ops. Rollins, Inc., Atlanta, 1978-81; v.p. sales and ops. Lease Plan U.S.A., Atlanta, 1981-85; v.p. mktg. Spencer Services, Inc., Roswell, Ga., 1985-87; v.p. FX-10 Corp., 1987-88; pres. Shiloh Capital Corp., 1989—, USA Calling, Inc. and Canada Calling, Ltd., 1992—95, Innovators.Com, Inc., 2000—. Pres. Victory Svcs., Inc., 1989—. Mem. Lost Forest Civic Assn. (pres. 1980-81). Mem. Nat. Assn. Fleet Adminstrs., Am. Fleet and Leasing Assn., NRA. Republican. Christian. Avocations: golf, racquetball, tennis, shooting. E-mail: rshelton@planetstuff.com.

SHENEFELT, PHILIP DAVID, dermatologist; b. Colfax, Wash., July 31, 1943; s. Roy David and Florence Vanita (Cagle) S.; m. Debrah A. Levenson; children: Elizabeth, Sara, Shaina. BS with honors, U. Wis. Madison, 1966, MD, 1970, MS in Adminstrv. Medicine, 1984. Diplomate Am. Bd. Dermatology, Am. Bd. Med. Hypnosis. Intern U.S. Naval Hosp., Bethesda, Md., 1970-71; gen. practice Oreg. (Wis.) Clinic, 1975; resident in dermatology U. Wis. Hosp., Madison, 1975-78, mem. staff, 1978-87; asst. prof. dermatology U. South Fla., Tampa, 1987—97, assoc. prof., 1997—2011, prof., 2011—. Chief dermatology sect. VA Hosp., Bay Pines, Fla., 1987—89, asst. chief, Tampa, 1988—2002, chief, 2002—07; dermatologist Univ. Health Svc. U. Wis., Madison, 1978—87, VA Hosp., Madison, 1982—85. Served to lt. comdr. USN, 1969-74; capt. USNR (ret.); med. corps officer Submarine and Diving. Kellogg fellow, 1980-82. Mem.: AMA, Fla. Med. Assn., Soc. Clin. Exptl. Hypnosis, Noah Worcester Dermatol. Soc., Fla. West Coast Dermatol. Soc., Fla. Dermatol. Soc., Am. Soc. Clin. Hypnosis, Am. Coll. Physician Execs., Am. Acad. Dermatology. Office: U South Fla Dermatol # 79 12901 Bruce Downs Blvd Tampa FL 33612-4742 Office Phone: 813-974-2188. Business E-Mail: pshenefe@health.usf.edu.

SHENG, QIN, mathematics professor; s. Re and Sh Sheng; m. Helen Huang, Jan. 1, 1962; children: Andy, Danny. BS, U. Nanjing, China, 1982, MS, 1985; PhD, U. Cambridge, England, 1990. Prof. U. Dayton, Ohio, 2001—04, Baylor U., Waco, Tex., 2004—. Editor-in-chief Internat. Jour. Computer Math. Taylor & Francis, 2010—. Rsch. fellow, USAF, 2005—. Mem.: Am. Math Soc., Ctr. Astrophysics, Space Physics and Engring. Rsch. Achievements include research in applied mathematics and computer simulation; splitting computations, parallel computations; computational physics. Avocations: music, paintings, sight-seeing, mountain walks. Office: Dept Math Baylor Univ One Bear Pl Waco TX 76798-7328 Office Phone: 254-710-1241. Office Fax: 254-710-3569. Business E-Mail: qin_sheng@baylor.edu.

SHENKIR, WILLIAM GARY, business educator; b. Three Rivers, Tex., June 27, 1938; s. William and Lydia (Jancik) S.; m. Missy Smith, Jan 1, 1973. BBA, Tex. A & M U., 1960; postgrad. (Rockefeller Bros. Theol. fellow), Drew U. Sem., 1960-61; MBA, U. Tex., 1962, PhD, 1964. Asst. prof. McIntire Sch. Commerce, U. Va., Charlottesville, 1967-69, assoc. prof., 1969-72, prof., 1972—75, dean, 1977-92, Paul Goodloe McIntire prof. Charlottesville, 1977—82; William Stamps Farish prof. McIntire Sch. Commerce U. Va., 1982—2007, William Stamps Farish prof. emeritus, 2007—. Project dir. Fin. Acctg. Stds. Bd., Stamford, Conn., 1973—76; vis. prof. NYU Grad. Sch. Bus., NYC, 1976—77; bd. dirs. ComSonics Corp., Harrisburg, Va., Childrens Youth & Family Svc., Charlottesville, Va., U. Va. Physicians Group, Charlottesville. Editor: Carman Blough: His Professional Career and Accounting Thought, 1978; co-author: The University of

Virginia's McIntire School of Commerce: The First 75 Years, 1921-96, 1996, Open-Book Management: Creating an Ownership Culture, 1998, Making Enterprise Risk Management Pay Off, 2001, Making Enterprise Risk Management Pay Off: How Leading Companies Implement Risk Management, 2002, Enterprise Risk Management: Pulling It All Together, 2002, Enterprise Risk Management, 2007; contbr. articles to profl. jours. Capt. USAF, 1964—67. Mem. AICPA, Am. Acctg. Assn. (former v.p.), Acctg. Edn. Change Commn. (former vice chmn.), Assn. Advance Collegiate Schs. of Bus. (former bd. dirs., pres. 1990-91), Fin. Execs. Inst., Va. Soc. CPAs, Raven Soc., Landfall Club, Farmington Country Club, Phi Delta Kappa, Beta Gamma Sigma, Phi Kappa Phi. Presbyterian. Home: 420 Rookwood Dr Charlottesville VA 22903-4732 Business E-Mail: wgs2Z@virginia.edu.

SHEPARD, DAVID A., state legislator; b. Nashville, Tenn., Oct. 6, 1947; m. Martha Shepard; children: Stacey, Benjamin, Christopher. City councilman, Dickson, 1977—89; vice mayor, 1979—89; clin. pharmacist VA Med. Ctr., 1995—97; mem. Commerce Com., Health & Human Resources Com., Joint Fiscal Rev Com., Bd. Zoning Appeals, Dickson, 1997—; pres., chief exec. officer Cmty. Pharmacy Care Inc., 1981—; mem. Dist. 69 Tenn. House of Reps., 2001—. Mem.: U. Tenn. Bd. Govs., Hickman County C. of C., Dickson County C. of C., High Noon Rotary Club, U. Tenn. Pharmacy Alumni Bd. Democrat. Methodist. Office: 204 McCreary Heights Dickson TN 37055 also: 34 Legislative Plz Nashville TN 37243-0169 Office Phone: 615-741-3513, 615-446-9782. Office Fax: 615-253-0244. Business E-Mail: rep.david.shepard@capitol.tn.gov.

SHEPARD, PHILLIP R., state legislator; Mem. Dist. 15 NC House of Representatives, 2011—. Republican. Office: 111 Vernon Shepard Ln Jacksonville NC 28540 Address: 300 N Salibury St Rm 301H Raleigh NC 27603-5925 Office Phone: 919-733-7928. Business E-Mail: Phil.Shepard@ncleg.net.

SHEPARD, ROBERT C., pharmaceutical executive; BA in Biochemistry & Molecular Biophysics magna cum laudeLaude, Harvard U.; MD, Duke U. Cert. oncology, hematology, internal medicine. Prin. investigator ECOG; various positions, clin. rsch., prin. investigator, Eastern Coop. Oncology Group, 29 oncology clin. trials U. Va.; various positions, clin. rsch. Johns Hopkins University, Tufts U., Harvard University; med. dir., oncology br., CBER The Food and Drug Adminstrn.; med. dir. clin. rsch., devel., oncology AstraZeneca; sr. dir., head, US oncology i3 Oncology; chief medical officer Callisto Pharmaceuticals, Inc., 2006—, Biothera, 2009—. Home: 9124 White Eagle Ct Raleigh NC 27617-7438 Office Phone: 651-675-0300. Office Fax: 651-675-0400. Business E-Mail: rshepard@biothera.com.

SHEPHARD, DANIEL G., construction executive; BS in Acctg., Alfred U. V.p. fin. Magnesia Specialties Martin Marietta Materials, Inc., acctg. dir. Aggregates Divsn., sr. acct., 1989, v.p. asst. treas., 1996—2000, pres. Magnesia Specialties Bus., 1999—2005, treas., 2000—02, v.p. mktg., 2002—04, v.p. bus. devel. and capital planning, 2002—05, regional v.p., gen. mgr. MidAmerica region, 2003—05, sr. v.p., 2004—05, exec. v.p., CEO Magnesia Specialties Bus., 2005—. Office: Martin Marietta Materials Inc 2710 Wycliff Rd Raleigh NC 27607-3033 Office Phone: 919-781-4550. Office Fax: 919-783-4695.

SHEPHERD, BOBBY E., federal judge; b. Arkadelphia, Ark., Nov. 18, 1951; BA, Ouachita Bapt. U., 1973; JD, U. Ark., 1976. Ptnr. Spencer & Spencer, El Dorado, Ark., 1976—81, Spencer, Spencer & Shepherd, 1981—84, Landers & Shepherd, 1987—90; pvt. law practice, 1984—87; circuit-chancery judge Ark. 13th Jud. Dist., 1991-93; magistrate judge US Dist. Ct. (we. dist.) Ark., El Dorado, Ark., 1993—2006; judge US Ct. Appeals (8th cir.), Little Rock, 2006—. Served with US Army Res., 1976-81.

SHEPHERD, JON GLEN, lawyer; b. Des Moines, May 22, 1968; s. Jerry Wayne and Vicki Jean (Clark) S.; m. Stacy Kenna York, May 23, 1992. BA, U. No. Iowa, 1990; JD magna cum laude, U. Mich., 1992. Bar: Tex. 1993, U.S. Ct. Appeals (5th cir.) 1994, U.S. Dist. Ct. (no. dist.) Tex. 1994, U.S. Dist. Ct. (ea. dist.) Tex. 1995. Jud. clk. U.S. Ct. Appeals (5th cir.), San Antonio, 1993-94; assoc. Gibson, Dunn & Crutcher LLP, Dallas, 1994—2003, ptnr., 2003—05; crews Shepherd & McCarty LLP, Dallas, 2006—07, ptnr., 2006—07, Alston & Bird LLP, 2007—. Mem. bd. dirs. Sequoia, Inc., 2005—09, v.p., 2006—07, pres., 2007—09; adj. prof., exec. MBA prog. Tex. Woman's U., 2006—07. Exec editor U. Mich. Law Rev., 1992; sr. editor ABA Antitrust Sec. Antitrust Law Jour., 1997—2006. Mem. Tex. Bar Assn., Dallas Bar Assn., Order of Coif. Avocation: sports. Office Phone: 214-922-3418. Office Fax: 214-922-3899. Business E-Mail: jon.Shepherd@alston.com.

SHEPHERD, MATTHEW, state legislator; b. El Dorado, Ark. m. Alie Shepherd; children: Eli Shepherd, Mary Kate, Libby Shepherd. BS in History & Polit. Sci., Ouachita Baptist U., 1998; JD, U. Ark., 2001. Bar: US Dist. Ct. (so., we., ea. dists.), Ark., US Dist. Ct., La. With, Eighth Circuit US Court of Appeals; mem. Union County Bar Assoc., La. Bar Assoc., Am. Bar Assoc.; atty., ptnr. Thomas, Hickey and Shepherd, LLP; mem. Ark. Bar Assoc.; mem. Dist. 6 Ark. House of Representatives, 2011—. Republican. Office: 423 N Washington Ave El Dorado AR 71730 Office Phone: 870-862-3478. Office Fax: 870-862-7228. Business E-Mail: matthew.shepherd@arkansashouse.org.

SHEPHERD, NICK P., hotel executive, food service executive; b. United Kingdom; B in Catering Sys., Sheffield City Poly. With Whitbread PLC; various positions Grand Met. Plc, Allied Lyons Plc, Kingfisher Plc; chmn., CEO Sagittarius Brands, Inc.; v.p., mng. dir. UK bus. Blockbuster, Inc., joined, 1995, sr. v.p., internat. bus., 1998—2001, chief concept officer, 2001—03, chief mktg. officer, chief merchandising officer, 2003—04, exec. v.p., 2003—07, pres., U.S. stores, 2004—05, pres., N.Am., 2005—07, pres., worldwide stores, 2007, COO, sr. exec. v.p., 2007; pres., CEO Carlson Restaurants, 2009—. Office: Carlson Restaurants Worldwide Inc 4201 Marsh Ln Carrollton TX 75007 Office Phone: 972-662-5400. Office Fax: 972-307-2822. Business E-Mail: nshepherd@carlson.com.

SHEPLEY, MARDELLE MCCUSKEY, architect, educator; b. Bethesda, Md., June 28, 1949; d. E. Scott McCuskey (father) & James R. and Yvonne Hudson S.; m. Laurence Berger, 1974 (div. 1978); m. Michael Curtis Blair, 1981 (div., 2004); children: Colin, Ian, Teal. BA, Columbia U., 1971, MArch, 1974; MA, U. Mich., 1979, DArch, 1981. Registered architect Calif. Urban designer NYC Dept. City Planning, 1972—74; planner Min. Planning & Econ. policy, Panama, Panama, 1975—77; lectr., teaching asst. U. Mich., Ann Arbor, 1977—81; assoc. Tai Assocs. Architects, San Francisco, 1981—85, The Design Partnership, San Francisco, 1985—93; asst. prof. Tex. A&M U., College Station, 1993—97, assoc. prof., 1997—2003, prof., 2003—, coord. PhD program, 1999-2001, assoc. dean for students, 2001—05, interim head dept. architecture, 2005—06. Rsch. com. Ctr. Health Design, Martinez, Calif., 1993—; assoc. dir. Ctr. Health Sys. and Design, 1995—2004, interim dir., 2004—05, dir., 2005—, prin. art and sci., 2006—; dir. design rsch. Shepley Bulfinch Archs., 2006—. Co-author: Healthcare Environments for Children and Their Families, 1998, A Practitioner's Guide to Evidence Based Design, 2008, Design for Critical Care, 2009, author: Health Facility Evaluation for Design Practitioners, 2010, Design for Pediatric and Neontal Critical Care, 2014 Bd. dirs. Assn. for Care of Children's Health, Mt. Royal, NJ, 1998-2000; mem. parent bd. Oakland Montessori Sch., Calif., 1991-93, Skagg Sprague Health Facilities chair, 2012-. Recipient Health Facilities Rsch. award AIA, 1992; Tex. A&M U. scholar, 1998; Tex. A&M U. faculty fellow, 2001-, Skaggs Sprague Endowed Chair, 2012-, William Pena Endowed Prof., 2003-12. Fellow: Am. Coll. Healthcare Architects, Am. Inst. Architects. Office: Tex A&M U Dept Architecture College Station TX 77843-3137 Home: 302 W Dexter Dr College Station TX 77840 Business E-Mail: mshepley@drch.tamu.edu.

SHEPPARD, BLAIR H., finance educator, former dean; m. Martha Putallaz; children: Philip, Christopher. BA, MA, U. Western Ont.; PhD, U. Ill., 1980. Asst. prof. orgn. behavior Fuqua Sch. Bus., Duke U., 1981—86, assoc. prof., 1986—93, prof. mgmt., assoc. dean, dir. exec. edn., 1993—97, sr. assoc. dean academic programs, 1997—2000, dean, 2007—11; CEO Duke Corp. Edn., 2000—07, chmn., 2007—; joined Duke Kunshan U., China, 2011—. Recipient NC NationsBank Outstanding Faculty Award, Outstanding Book Award, Internat. Assn. for Conflict Mgmt.; Can. Coun. Doctoral Fellowship. Office: Duke University Fuqua School of Business 1 Towerview Dr Durham NC 27708 Office Phone: 919-660-4090. Office Fax: 919-684-8742. E-mail: blair.sheppard@duke.edu.

SHEPPE, JOSEPH ANDREW, surgeon; b. Huntington, W.Va., Sept. 24, 1953; m. Kathy Chapman; children: Sheree Nicole, Natalee Marie, Brittany Lee. BS summa cum laude in Chemistry and Zoology, Marshall U., 1975; MD, W.Va. U., 1979. Diplomate Am. Bd. Surgery, Am. Bd. Colon and Rectal Surgery. Intern in gen. surgery Charleston (W.Va.) Area Med. Ctr., 1979-84; fellow in colon and rectal surgery William Beaumont Army Med. Ctr., Royal Oak, Mich., 1984-85; pvt. practice Columbia, SC, 1985—. Physician Bapt. Med. Ctr., Columbia, Providence Hosp., Columbia, Richland Meml. Hosp., Columbia, Lexington Med. Ctr., West Columbia, S.C.; clin. instr. in gen./colorectal surgery U. S.C. Med. Sch. Fellow ACS, Am. Soc. Colon and Rectal Surgery; mem. S.C. Med. Soc., Columbia Med. Soc. Home: 204 Leaning Tree Rd Columbia SC 29223-3009 Office: 1333 Taylor St Ste 4-a Columbia SC 29201-2949 Office Phone: 803-779-5600.

SHEPTOR, JOHN C., sugar company executive; b. 1958; BS, Rensselaer Poly. Inst.; MBA, Tulane U. With Monsanto Co.; COO Partnership for Supple Chaing Mgmt., Inc.; exec. v.p. Merisant Worldwide, Inc., 2001—04; dep. dir., supply chain mgmt. sys. initiative funded under pres., bush's emergency plan, HIV/AIDS Relief Washington, 2005—07; exec. v.p., COO Imperial Sugar Co., Sugarland, 2007, pres., CEO & bd. dirs., 2008—. Office: Imperial Sugar Co 1 Imperial Sq 8016 Hwy 90-A Sugar Land TX 77487 Office Phone: 281-491-9181. Office Fax: 281-490-9530. Business E-Mail: john.sheptor@imperialsugar.com.

SHER, GEORGE ALLEN, philosophy educator; b. NYC, Nov. 10, 1942; s. Daniel and Clara (Landesberg) S.; m. Emily Fox Gordon, July 10, 1972; 1 child, Sarah Constantine. BA, Brandeis U., 1964; PhD, Columbia U., 1972. Instr. philosophy Fairleigh Dickinson U., Teaneck, NJ, 1966—72, asst. prof. philosophy, 1972—74; assoc. prof. philosophy U. Vt., Burlington, 1974-80, prof., 1980-91; Herbert S. Autrey prof. philosophy Rice U., Houston, 1991—, chmn. dept. philosophy, 1993-2000. Mem. Inst. for Advanced Study, Princeton, N.J., 1987-88. Author: Desert, 1987, Beyond Neutrality: Perfectionism and Politics, 1997, Approximate Justice: Studies in Non-Ideal Theory, 1997, In Praise of Blame, 2005, Who Knew? Responsibility Without Awareness, 2009; editor: Moral Philosophy: Selected Readings, 1989, 2d edit., 1996; contbr. articles to profl. jours. Named fellow Nat. Humanities Ctr., Rsch. Triangle Park, N.C., 1980-81. Mem. Am. Philos. Assn. Home: 2425 Dryden Rd Houston TX 77030-1001 Office: Rice U Dept Philosophy MS 14 6100 Main St Houston TX 77251-1892 Office Phone: 713-348-2723. Business E-Mail: gsher@rice.edu.

SHERERTZ, ELIZABETH, dermatologist; MD, U. Va., 1978. Diplomate Am. Bd. Dermatology, 1982. Resident dermatology Duke Univ. Med. Ctr., Durham, NC, 1979—82; clin. prof. dermatology Wake Forest Univ.; hosp. affiliation include Med. Pk. Hosp.; with Winston Salem Dermatology. Office: Winston Salem Dermatology Ste 200 1400 Westgate Center Dr Winston Salem NC 27103 Office Phone: 336-774-8636.

SHERIDAN, DIANE FRANCES, public policy facilitator; b. Wilmington, Del., Mar. 12, 1945; d. Robert Kooch and Eileen Elizabeth (Forrest) Bupp; m. Mark MacDonald Sheridan III, Dec. 7, 1968; 1 child, Elizabeth Anne. BA in English, U. Del., Newark, 1967. Tchr. English Newark Sch. Dist., Del., 1967-68, Lumberton Ind. Sch. Dist., Tex., 1969-71, Crown Point Sch. Dist., Ind., 1972-75; sr. assoc. The Keystone Ctr., Colo., 1986-98; facilitator cmty. adv. panels to chem. plants and refineries Taylor Lake Village, Tex., 1986—. Citizen's adv. coun. La Porte Industry, cmty. adv. panel Alcoa, Alcoa Rockdale Ops., Lyondell and Equistar, cmty. adv. coun. Deer Pk., cmty. adv. panel Luminant, citizen's adv. coun. Pasadena, Bay Area Cmty. Adv. Panel. Oxy Chem Wichita KS Cmty. Involvement Group., 1988-2009, Galena Pk.-Jacinto City Cmty.-Indsl. Partnership, 2010-, chair Keystone Siting Process Local Rev. Com.; pub. adv. panel Chem. Mfrs. Assn. Responsible Care, 1989-97. 1st v.p. LWV, Washington, 1992-94, sec. treas. voters edn. fund, sec. treas. Nat. LWV, 1994-96, bd. dirs. 1996-98; pres. LWV of Tex., 1987-91, chair edn. fund, 1987-91, bd. dirs., 1983-87; pres. LWV of the Bay Area, 1981-83, bd. dirs., 2001—; adv. com. Ctr. for Global Studies of Houston Advanced Rsch. Ctr., The Woodlands, Tex., 1991-97, Ctr. for Conflict Analysis and Mgmt., bd. advisors Environ. Inst.; mem. U. Houston-Clear Lake Devel. Adv. Coun., 1989-95; mem. Bay Area Cmty. Awareness and Emergency Response Local Emergency Planning Com., 1988-92; active Tex. House-Senate Select Com. on Urban Affairs Regional Flooding Task Force, 1979-80, Congressman Mike Andrews Environ. Task Force, 1983-85, Gov.'s Task Force on Hazardous Waste Mgmt., 1984-85; dir. local PTAs, 1981-91; coord. Tex. Roundtable on Hazardous Waste, 1982-87; sec., v.p. Tex. Environ. Coalition, 1983-85; co-chair Tex. Risk Commn. Project, 1986-89; mem. Leadership Tex., Class of 1988; cmty. adv. bd. U. Tex. Med. Br. Ctr. Nat. Inst. Environ. Health Studies, 1998. Mem. LWV (nat. bd. dirs. 1992-98, trustee nat. edn. fund 1992-98), Assn. for Conflict Resolution, Internat. Assn. for Pub. Participation, Mortar Board, East Harris County Mfrs. Assn. (risk mgmt. comm. com. 1994-99, cmty. emergency comm. com., 2003—), Pi Sigma Alpha, Kappa Delta Pi. Office Phone: 281-326-5253. Business E-Mail: dbsheridan@aol.com.

SHERIF, S. A., engineering educator; b. Alexandria, Egypt, June 25, 1952; came to US, 1978; s. Ahmed and Ietedal H. (Monib) S.; m. Azza A. Shamseldin, Feb. 6, 1977 (div.); children: Ahmed S., Mohammad S.; m. Vitrell Lynn McNair, May 30, 2003. BSME (hon.), Alexandria U., 1975, MSME, 1978; PhD in Mech. Engring., Iowa State U., 1985. Tchg. asst. mech. engring. Alexandria U., 1975-78; tchg. assoc. mech. and environtl. engring. U. Calif., Santa Barbara, 1978-79; rsch. asst. mech. engring. Iowa State U., Ames, 1979-84; asst. prof. No. Ill. U., Dekalb, 1984-87, U. Miami, Coral Gables, Fla., 1987—91; assoc. prof. mech. engring. U. Fla., Gainesville, 1991-2001, prof. mech. and aerospace engring., 2001—, mem. doctoral rsch. faculty, 1992—, founding dir. Wayne K. and Lyla L. Masur HVAC Lab., 1995—, asst. dir. Indsl. Assessment Ctr., 2001—, minority mentor, 2004—. ABET coord. for mech. engring., 1997—; coord. for mech. engring. So. Assn. Colls. and Schs., 2001—; affiliate Inst. for Sci. and Health Policy U. Fla., 2001—; cons. Solar Reactor Techs., Inc., Miami, 1988-91, Dade Power Corp., Miami, 1988-91, Ind. Energy Sys., Miami, 1988-91, Carey Dwyer Eckhart Mason Spring Beckham, P.A. Law Offices, Miami, 1988-89, Michael G. Widoff, P.A., Attys. at Law, Ft. Lauderdale, Fla., 1989-93, Law Offices Pomeroy and Betts, Ft. Lauderdale, 1991-92, Ctr. for Indoor Air Rsch., 1994-2000; cons. Fla. Power and Light Co., 1996-98; external examiner U. Roorkee, 1994-95, 98—, Indian Inst. Tech., Delhi, 2002-, Alexandria U., Egypt, 2000-; adj. faculty cons. Kennedy Western U., Thousand Oaks, Calif., 1994-97; resident assoc. Argonne (Ill.) Nat. Lab., Tech. Transfer Ctr., summer 1992; faculty fellow NASA Kennedy Space Ctr., Cape Canaveral, Fla., summer 1993; rsch. assoc. summer faculty rsch. program USAF Office Sci. Rsch., Arnold Engring. Devel. Ctr., Arnold AFB, Tenn., 1994; faculty fellow NASA Marshall Space Flight Ctr., Huntsville, Ala., 1996, 97; ABET coord. for aerospace engring., 2002-; coord. for aerospace engring., So. Assn. Colls. and Schs., 2002-. Co-editor: Industrial and Agricultural Applications of Fluid Mechanics, 1989, The Heuristics of Thermal Anemometry, 1990, Heat and Mass Transfer in Frost and Ice, Packed Beds, and Environmental Discharges, 1990, Industrial Applications of Fluid Mechanics, 1990, rev. edit., 1991, Mixed Convection and Environmental Flows, 1990, Measurement and Modeling of Environmental Flows, 1992, Industrial and Environment Applications of Fluid Mechanics, 1992, rev. edit., 1998, Thermal Anemometry-1993, 1993, Developments in Electrorheological Flows and Measurement Uncertainty-1994, 1994, Heat, Mass and Momentum Transfer in Environmental Flows, 1995, Thermal Anemometry, 1996, Fluid Measurement Uncertainty Applications, 1996, Devices for Flow Measurement and Analysis, 1997, Heat and Mass Transfer in Environmental Flows, 1998, Industrial and Environmental Applications of Fluid Mechanics, 1999, rev. edit., 2001, Measurement and Modeling of Environmental Flows, 2002, Industrial and Environmental Applications of Fluid Mechanics, 2003, Fluid Measurement Uncertainty Applications, 2003; reviewer more than 45 internat. jours., more than 200 conf. procs.; mem. editl. com. SECTAM XXI, 2001-2002; book rev. editor ASME Applied Mech. Revs., 2001—; assoc. tech. editor Solar Energy jour., 2002—; guest editor Solar Energy Jour. Spl. Issue on Hydrogen Prodn., 2003-05; contbr. to 16 book chapters and numerous articles to profl. jours. NASA ambassador, 1996-98, lab. host student sci. tng. program Ctr. for Precollegiate Edn. and Tng., 1997—; mem. environ. awareness adv. com., Dade County Pub. Schs., 1989-91, lab. dir. cmty. lab. rsch. program, 1989-91, also faculty liaison design svcs. dept.; active Com. for Nat. Inst. for Environ., 1992—; mem. senate U. Fla., 1994-95, mem. OUTREACH Spkrs. program, 1996-98. Recipient cert. recognition for rsch. contributions, NASA, 1993, 1996, 1997, E.K. Campbell award of Merit for Outstanding Svc. and Achievement in Tchg., ASHRAE, 1997, Kuwait prize for applied scis., 2002. Fellow ASME (mem. energy resources bd. 2001-03, chmn steering com. internat. energy conversion engring. conf., 2002-03, coord. group fluid measurements, fluids engring. divsn. 1987-03, vice chmn. 1990-92, chmn. 1992-94, fluid measurements and instrumentation tech. com., 2003—, fluids engring. divsn. adv. bd. 1994—, fed. honors and awards com. 1995-01, mem. fluid mechs. tech. com. 1990—, fluid mech. com. 1987-90, K-19 com. on environ. heat transfer 1987—, fluid measurements and instrumentation tech. com., 2003-, chmn. 2003—, mem. K-6 com. on heat transfer in energy systems, 2001—, mem. fluid applications and systems tech. com. 1990—, systems analysis tech. com. advanced energy sys. divsn. 1989—, newsletter editor advanced energy sys. divsn. 1995-98, exec. com., 1999—, mem.-at-large honors awards 1999-00, sec., treas. 2000-01, vice chmn., 2001-02, chmn., 2002-03, sr. mem. and past chmn., 2003-04, fundamentals and theory tech. com. solar energy divsn. 1990-97, chmn. CGFM nominating com. 1992-94, mem. 1994-98, chmn. profl. devel. com. Rock River Valley sect. 1987, tech. activities operating com. Gator sect. 1994-96, MFFCC subcom. 1 on uncertainties in flow measurements 1995-00, certificate of appreciation, 1994, 97. 99, 03), ASHRAE (mem. heat transfer fluid flow com. 1988-92, 93-97, corr. mem. 1992-93, 97—, mem. thermodynamics and psychrometrics com. 1988-92, 96-04, corr. mem. 1992-96, vice chmn. 1990-92, mem. liquid to refrigerant heat exchs. com. 1989-93, 96-97, sec. 1990-92, corr. mem. 1993-96, 97-01, corr. mem. air-to-refrigerant heat transfer com., 2000—, chmn. stds. project com. on measurement of moist air properties 1989-95, corr. mem. refrigeration load calculations com., 1999—, mem. tech. activities com. 2004—, head refrigeration sect., 2004-, E.K. Campbell award of merit for Outstanding Svc. and Achievement in Tchg., 1997, Disting. Svc. award, 2003, certificate of appreciation, 1995), AIAA (assoc., mem. terrestrial energy sys. tech. com. 2001—, certificate of appreciation, 2003); mem. AIChE, Internat. Assn. Hydrogen Energy, Internat. Solar Energy Soc., Am. Soc. for Engring. Edn., Internat. Energy Soc. (mem. sci. coun.), European Assn. Laser Anemometry (ASME/FED rep., mem. steering com.), Internat. Inst. Refrigeration (US nat. com., mem. commn. B1 on thermodynamics and transfer processes), Sigma Xi. Muslim. Achievements include co-inventor two US patents. Avocations: reading, soccer, basketball, history, astronomy. Office: U Fla Dept Mech and Aerospace Engring 232 MAE B 720 Bldg PO Box 116300 Gainesville FL 32611-6300 Home: 3440 NE 41st Pl Ocala FL 34479 Home Phone: 352-629-7410; Office Phone: 352-392-7821. Office Fax: 352-392-1071. Business E-Mail: sasherif@ufl.edu.

SHERLIN, STEPHEN, medical technician; Grad., Ind. U. CFO Athens Cmty. Hosp., Athens, Tenn., Park West Med. Ctr., Knoxville, Tenn., Doctors Hosp.; v.p., CFO Tennessee Divsn., Columbia, 1993—96; sr. v.p., fin. and adminstrn. Team Health Holdings Inc., 1997, exec. v.p., fin. and adminstrn., 1998, exec. v.p., healthcare fin. svcs., 2000; chief compliance officer Team Health Holdings, Inc., 2004—. Office: Team Health Holdings Inc 265 Brookview Ctr Way Ste 400 Knoxville TN 37919 Office Phone: 865-693-1000. Office Fax: 865-539-3073. Business E-Mail: stephen_sherlin@teamhealth.com.

SHERMAN, BEATRICE ETTINGER, hotel executive; b. NYC, May 29, 1919; d. Max and Stella (Schrager) Ettinger; m. Herbert Jacob Howard, Feb. 15, 1942 (dec. 1971); children: Robert David Howard, Carolyn Howard Smith; m. Ernest John Sherman, Dec. 29, 1974 (dec. Oct. 2000). Student, Gulf Park Jr. Coll., Gulfport, Miss., 1934—35, Shimer Jr. Coll., Mt. Carroll, Ill., 1936—38; BA, U. Miami, 1940; postgrad., Harvard U., 1940, Paris-Am. Acad., 1972, Alliance Française, Paris, 1973. Corp. sec., dir. Save Electric Corp., Toledo, 1940—67, Verd-A-Ray Corp., Toledo, 1944—67, Penetray Corp., Toledo, 1962—67; ptnr. Stella Assocs., Newark, 1960—80, BHS Ptnrs., Miami, 1983—; pres. Besman Inc., Miami, 1976—, All Am. Mobile Tel. Co., Coral Gables, 1986—2000; pres., bus. exec. hotelier Besman Hospitality, Gainesville, Fla., 1997—. Vol. worker Jewish Welfare Fedn., Toledo, 1942-69; vol. nurse's aid ARC, 1942-45; nat. spkr. United Jewish Appeal; mem. womens divsn. Greater Miami Jewish Fedn., 1969—, trustee, 1986-95; adv. bd. Miami Bell South; active Miami advertiser adv. bd. Bell South Advt. and Pub. Co.; vol. Nat. Coun. Jewish Women, Toledo, 1946-67, v.p., 1964-67, v.p., Miami, 1970-73; active Toledo chpt. Hadassah, 1943-

67. Recipient Lion of Judah award Greater Miami Jewish Fedn., 1986. Mem. Assn. Telemessaging Svcs. Internat., Pioneers of Miami Beach. Home: 5108 SW 72d Ave Miami FL 33155-5530 Office: PO Box 558446 Miami FL 33255

SHERMAN, DANIEL JAMES, art history professor; b. Ann Arbor, Mich., May 20, 1958; s. Stanley Morton and Claire Richter Sherman; life ptnr. Eduardo deJesus Douglas. AB, MA, Harvard U., 1980, Yale U., 1981, MPhil, 1982, PhD, 1985. Lectr. history, lit., social studies Harvard U., Cambridge, Mass., 1985—88; vis. asst. prof. Cath. U. Am., Washington, 1989; vis. asst. prof. history U. Rochester, NY, 1989—90; asst. prof. French studies and history Rice U., Houston, 1990—94, assoc. prof. French studies and history, 1994—99, prof. French studies and history, 1999—2001; prof. history U. Wis., Milw., 2001—08, dir. Ctr. 21st Century Studies, 2001—08; prof. art history U. NC, Chapel Hill, 2008—. Author: Worthy Monuments: Art Museums and the Politics of Culture in Nineteenth-Century France, 1989, The Constuction of Memory in Interwar France, 1999; editor: Museums and Difference, 2007; co-editor: Museum Culture: Histories, Discourses, Spectacles, 1994, Terror Culture, Politics: Rethinking 9/11, 2006; author: French Primitivism and the Ends of Empire 1945-1975, 2011 (David H. Pinkney prize, 2012, Alf Heggoy Book prize, 2012), The Long 1968: Revisions and New Perspectives, 2013; contbr. articles to profl. jours. Recipient History and Lit. Jr. prize, Harvard Coll., 1978, Laurence Wylie prize, 2000, award, Assn. American Publishers, 2000; grantee, Am. Coun. Learned Socs., 1988; fellow, NEH, 1988, 1990—91, Inst. Advanced Study, 1993—94, John Simon Guggenheim Meml. Found., 2001—02, Inst. d'Etudes Avancées de Paris, 2014; Florence Gould Found. fellowship, Nat. Humanities Ctr., 1999—2000, Paul Mellon fellow, Ctr. Advanced Study Visual Arts, Nat. Gallery Art, 2006—07. Mem.: Soc. French Hist. Studies (mem., editl. bd. 1998—2001, David H. Pinkney prize 2012), Coll. Art Assn., Am. Hist. Assn. (J. Russell Major prize 2000). Jewish. Avocations: travel, photography, cooking. Office: UNC Chapel Hill Dept Art Hanes Art Ctr Campus Box 3405 Chapel Hill NC 27599-3405 Office Fax: 919-962-0722.

SHERMAN, FLOYD F., construction executive; b. Kerhonkson, NY; B, Syracuse U.; MBA, Ga. State U. Chmn., CEO Triangle Pacific, 1992—2001; pres. Builders FirstSource, Inc., Dallas, 2001—06, CEO, bd. dirs., 2006—. Bd. dirs. PGT, Inc., 2005—. Served US Army. Office: Builders FirstSource Inc 2001 Bryan St Ste 1666 Dallas TX 75201 Office Phone: 214-880-3500. Office Fax: 214-880-3599. Business E-Mail: floyd.sherman@bldr.com.

SHERMAN, JEFFREY SCOTT, hospital administrator, lawyer; b. Bklyn., Oct. 26, 1955; s. Martin and Beatrice (Matrick) S.; m. Susan Ellen Ganz, Aug. 13, 1981; children: Elisabeth Faye, Andrew Harris. BA cum laude, SUNY, Albany, 1976; JD magna cum laude, Bklyn. Law Sch., 1980. Bar: NY 1980. Assoc. Proskauer, Rose et al, NYC, 1980-83, Shereff, Friedman, Hoffman & Goodman, NYC, 1983-87, ptnr., 1988—90; v.p., treas. Tenet Healthcare, 1990; joined Wyeth, 1990, v.p., assoc. gen. counsel, 2001—03; v.p., gen. counsel Becton, Dickinson & Co., Franklin Lakes, NJ, 2004—06, sr. v.p., gen. counsel, 2006—; joined LifePoint Hosps., 2009, exec. v.p., CFO. Mem. ABA, Assn. of the Bar of the City of NY (young lawyers com. 1983-86). Office: LifePoint Hospitals Inc 103 Powell Ct Ste 200 Brentwood TN 37027 Office Phone: 614-372-8500. E-mail: jeffrey.sherman@lpnt.net.

SHERMAN, MARY ANGUS, public library administrator; b. Lawton, Okla., Jan. 3, 1937; d. Donald Adelbert and Mabel (Felkner) Angus; m. Donald Neil Sherman, Feb. 8, 1958; children: Elizabeth, Donald Neil II. BS in Home Econs., U. Okla., 1958, MLS, 1969. Br. head Pioneer Libr. System, Purcell, Okla., 1966-76, regional libr. Norman, Okla., 1976-78, asst. dir., 1978—87, dir., 1987—. Bd. dirs. McClain Bank, chair audit com., 1997—. Mem. bd. visitors Coll. Arts and Scis. U. Okla., 1998—2005, mem. internat. programs bd. visitors, 2003—; bd. dirs. U. Okla. Found., 2004—, Women's Resource Ctr., Norman, 1998—2003, pres., 2002. Recipient award of merit, U. Okla. Sch. Libr. and Info. Sci., 2000; named one of Disting. Alumni, Sch. Home Econs. U. Okla., 1980. Mem.: AAUW (pres. Okla. chpt. 1975—77, SW Ctrl. region dir. 1983—85, nat. bd. dirs. 1983—87, v.p. nat. membership 1985—87, Woman of Yr. Purcell chpt. 1982), ALA (councilor 1988—96, internat. rels. round table 1989—, planning and budget assembly 1990—91, internat. rels. com. 1992—96, orientation com. 1998—99, membership com. 1999—2000, chair sister libr. com. 2000—02, exec. bd. 2000—02, internat. rels. com. 2001—05), Okla. Libr. Assn. (pres. 1982—83, interlibr. cooperation com. 1993—95, chair 1994—95, legis. com. 1998—, Disting. Svc. award 1986), Internat. Fedn. Libr. Assns. (standing com. on pub. librs. 1999—), Tech. in Pub. Librs. Com., Pub. Libr. Assn. (divsn. of ALA, pres. pub. policy for pub. librs. sect. 1995—96, chmn. internat. rels. com. 2002—04), Norman Sister City Com., Norman C. of C. (bd. dirs. 1988—96, pres. 1994—95), Norman Soc. Internat. Affairs (v.p. 1998—99, pres. 1999—2001), Norman Assistance League Club (cmty. assoc.), Rotary (program chair 1991—92, bd. dirs. 1993—97, pres. 1995—96, group study exch. leader to Iceland 1996, dist. literacy chair 1998—2000, dist. group study exch. chair 2001—06, dist. gov. nominee 2005—06, dist. gov.-elect 2006—, Paul Harris fellow), Phi Beta Kappa, Beta Phi Mu, Kappa Alpha Theta (pres. Alpha Omicron House Corp. 1984—87, nat. dir. ho. corps. 1987—88), Delta Gamma Mothers (pres. 1978—79). Democrat. Methodist. Office: Pioneer Libr System 225 N Webster Ave Norman OK 73069-7133 Business E-Mail: mary@pls.lib.ok.us.

SHERMAN, RICHARD BEATTY, historian, educator; b. Somerville, Mass., Nov. 16, 1929; s. James Beatty and Hilda Louise (Ford) S.; m. Hanni Fey, June 13, 1952; children: Linda Caroline, Alan Theodore. AB, Harvard U., 1951, PhD, 1959; MA, U. Pa., 1952. Instr. history Pa. State U., State College, 1957-60; asst. prof. Coll. of William and Mary, Williamsburg, Va., 1960-65, assoc. prof., 1965-70, prof., 1970-87, chancellor prof., 1987-92, Pullen prof., 1992-94, prof. emeritus, 1994—. Fulbright prof. Am. history U. Stockholm, 1966-67. Author: The Negro and the City, 1970, The Republican Party and Black America, 1973, The Case of Odell Waller, 1992; co-author: The College of William and Mary: A History, 1993; contbr. articles to profl. jours. Served with U.S. Army, 1952-54. Am. Philos. Soc. grantee, 1964, 66, faculty rsch. grantee Coll. William and Mary, 1962, 63, 65, 80, 87. Mem. ACLU, Phi Beta Kappa. Democrat. Office: Coll William and Mary Dept History Williamsburg VA 23185 Home: Corbridge Course 4201 Williamsburg VA 23188 Personal E-mail: richardsherman@cox.net.

SHERMAN, WILLIAM FARRAR, lawyer, former state legislator; b. Little Rock, Sept. 12, 1937; s. Lincoln Farrar and Nancy (Lowe) S.; m. Carole Lynn Williams, Sept. 2, 1967; children: John, Anna, Lucy. BA in History, U. Ark., 1960; LLB, U. Va., 1964. Bar: Ark. 1964, U.S. Supreme Ct. 1970. Assoc. Smith, Williams, Friday & Bowen, Little Rock, 1964-66; asst. U.S. atty. Ea. Dist. Ark., Little Rock, 1966-69, Ark. Securities Commr., Little Rock, 1969-71; ptnr. Jacoway, Sherman & Pence, Little Rock, 1971—2004; pvt. practice William F. Sherman Law Office, Little Rock, 2005—. Mem. Ark. Ho. of Reps., 1974-84; spl. assoc. justice Supreme Ct., 1991; del. Constnl. Conv. Ark., 1979, mem. First United Methodist Ch., bd. trustees, former mem. Bd. Stewarts. With U.S. Army, 1960-61, now brig. gen. U.S. Army ret. Fellow Ark. Bar Found.; mem. ABA (founding mem. state atty. gen., dept. justice issues com.), Ark. Bar Assn. (sustaining mem.), Pulaski County Bar Assn. Office: 809 North Palm St Little Rock AR 72205 Home Phone: 501-661-1963; Office Phone: 501-372-3148. Personal E-mail: wfsherman@sbcglobal.net.

SHERN, DAVID L., mental health services professional, former dean; b. Pueblo, Colo., Feb. 23, 1951; BA in Psychology, U. Colo., 1973, MA in Social Psychology, 1977, PhD in Social Psychology, 1980; cert. in advanced epidemiologic methods, NIMH Staff Coll., 1980. Asst. dir. research and evaluation sect. Denver Dept. Health and Hosps. Mental Health Programs, 1981-82; research assoc. evaluation services sect. Colo. div. Mental Health, Denver, 1982-84, mgr. sponsored research program, 1984-88; project dir., investigator estimating residential services for chronically mentally ill Colo. divsn. Mental Health, Denver, 1983-87; investigator validation models for estimating mental health need U. Denver, 1983-88; dir. bur. evaluation and svcs. rsch. NY Office of Mental Health, Albany, 1988-95; dean, prof. Louis de la Parte Fla. Mental Health Inst., U. South Fla., Tampa, 1995—2006; pres., CEO Mental Health America, Alexandria, Va., 2006—. Cons. several health facilities, Denver, 1976—88; chmn. Fla. Commn. Mental Health and Substance Abuse, 1999—2000; prin. investigator Treatment Outcome Study, 1988; prin. investigator rsch. grants NIMH Substance Abuse and Mental Health Svcs. Adminstrn., 1988—2000; dir. NIMH Ctr. for Sudy Issues in Pub. Mental Health, 1993—95; mem. Govs. Suicide Prevention Task Force, 2003—06. Contbr. articles to profl. jours. Bd. dirs. Travelers Aid of Denver, 1981-83, Karis Cmty., 1986-88, pres. 1988; founding mem. Albany County Land Conservancy, 1992-95, pres., 1992-95; treas. USF Charter Sch., 1998-2006;active Crisis Ctr. of Tampa Bay, 2004-06. Mem. APA, APHA (chair mental health sect. 1992-93, governing coun. 1995-97), Orgn. for Program Evaluation in Colo. (pres. 1982-83, assoc. editor bull.), Am. Evaluation Assn. Independent. Avocations: hiking, gardening, travel. Office: Mental Health America 2000 N Beauregard St 6th Fl Alexandria VA 22311 Office Phone: 703-838-7500.

SHERN, STEPHANIE MARIE, management consultant; b. Taylor, Pa., Jan. 7, 1948; d. Joseph and Stephanie (Malodovitch) Andrews; m. George Emil Shern, Sept. 25, 1971. AA, Keystone Jr. Coll., 1967; BS, Pa. State U., 1969. CPA, NY. Founder Shern Assocs. LLC; ptnr. Ernst & Young LLP, global and US dir. R&CP markets, various positions, including vice chmn., global dir., retail & consumer products, staff acct. to ptnr., nat. dir. consumer products industry, 1969—2001; sr. v.p. Kurt Salmon Associates, 2001—02. Bd. mem. Gamestop Corp., 2003-, Embarq Corp., 2006-. Contbr. articles to profl. jours. Named Keystonian of Yr., Keystone Jr. Coll., 1984. Mem. AICPA, NY State Soc. CPAs (bd. dirs. 1985-87), Beta Alpha Psi (mem. adv. forum 1984-86). Republican. Ukrainian Orthodox. Home: 11 Green Briar Rd Little Falls NJ 07424-2307 Office: Shern Associates LLC Bd Director 100 CenturyTel Dr Monroe LA 71203 Office Phone: 318-388-9000. Office Fax: 318-388-9562. Personal E-mail: stephanieshern@aol.com. Business E-Mail: shern@centurylink.com.

SHERRER, BEN, state legislator; b. June 18, 1968; m. Margo Sherrer; children: Bennett, Samuel, Delanie. BS, Okla. State Univ.; JD, Okla. City Univ. Auditor Okla. State Auditor And Inspector, 1992—95; baliff Okla. County Dist. Court, 1995—97; town atty. Chouteau; city atty. Pryor; atty. Elliot And Sherrer Law Office, 1997—; mem. Dist. 8 Okla. House of Representatives, 2005—. Mem.: Rotary. Democrat. Mailing: 123 N Hayden Chouteau OK 74337 Office: Oklahoma House of Representatives 2300 N Lincoln Blvd Rm 500 Oklahoma City OK 73105 Office Phone: 405-557-7364. E-mail: bensherrer@okhouse.gov.

SHERRER, JOHN M., III, cultural organization administrator; BA in Eng., Clemson U., SC; MA in Eng., Clemson U.; MA in Applied History, U. SC, Columbia, grad. cert. in mus. mgmt. Hist. interpreter/edn. guide Nat. Trust Hist. Preservation, Drayton Hall Plantation, Charleston, SC, 1994; weekend hist. interpreter Strawberry Banke Mus., Portsmouth, NH, 1995—96; curatorial vol. Old York Hist. Soc., York, Maine, 1994—96, guest curator, 1997, exhibits preparator, 1998; curatorial asst. Hist. Columbia Found., Columbia, SC, 1996—98, coord. vol. & visitor services, 1998—99, acting asst. exec. dir., 1999—2000, dir. collections, 1999—2001, dir. collections & interpretation, 2001—. Instr. Clemson U., Eng. dept., 1991—92; adj. prof. history U. SC, Columbia, 2006. Contbr. articles. Mem. vestry St. John's Episcopal Ch., Shandon, SC, 2004—, jr. warden, vestry, 2006—; mem. Clemson U. Humanities Advancement Bd., 2006—, SC Dept. Archives & History Found., 2007—. Mem.: Anthropology, Mus., Art & Zoo Educators (v.p. 2002), Teaching Am. History Initiative (steering com. 2002), Southeastern Registrar's Assn. (state rep. 2000), S.E. Museums Conf. (scholarship com. 2001, 2004, programs com. 2004), SC Fall Line Consortium, SC Fedn. Museums (profl. devel. com. 1999—2002, chair profl. devel. com. 2001—02, treas. 2002—04, 1st v.p. 2004—06, pres. 2006—), Am. Assn. State & Local History (profl. mentor 2007—, History News editl. vol. 2007—, educators & interpreters com. 2007—). Office: Hist Columbia Found 1601 Richland St Columbia SC 29201 also: SC Fedn Museums PO Box 100107 Columbia SC 29202-3107 Office Phone: 803-252-1770 ext. 28. E-mail: jsherrer@historiccolumbia.org.

SHERRICK, DANIEL NOAH, real estate broker; b. Greenup, Ill., Mar. 28, 1929; s. Conrad Donovan and Helen Lorene (Neeley) S.; m. Dora Ann Moore, Aug. 11, 1957; children: Renata Ann Sherrick McBride, Sherrie Dee Sherrick Sierra BS in Edn., Ea. Ill. U., Charleston, 1956. Owner Midwest Ins. Agy., Greenup, 1956—60; supt. agys. Midwest Life Ins. Co., Lincoln, Nebr., 1960—62; asst. v.p. Gulf Life Ins. Co., Jacksonville, Fla., 1962—71; pres. Bank of Carbondale, Ill., 1971—74, Prescription Learning Corp., Springfield, Ill., 1974—76; exec. v.p. Imperial Industries, Inc., Miami Lakes, Fla., 1976—88, pres., CEO, 1988—90; broker, salesman Coldwell Banker Residential Real Estate, 1990—91, 1993—; pres., bd. dirs. Palmer State Bank, Taylorville, Ill., 1991—93; broker-salesman Coldwell Banker Highlands Properties, 1993—. Pres. Alderman Park Civic Assn., Jacksonville, Ill., 1968, Heritage Hills Home Owners Assn., Carbondale, 1973. With USAF, 1948—52. Mem.: VFW, Greater Sebring C. of C., Am. Legion, Elks, Masons. Presbyterian. Home: 6228 Aquavista Dr Sebring FL 33876 Office: Coldwell Banker Highlands Properties 2521 US Hwy 27 S Sebring FL 33870-2127 Office Phone: 863-382-3157. Personal E-mail: dandora@strato.net.

SHERWOOD, BEVERLY J., state legislator; b. Ossining, NY, May 29, 1947; m. Frank Vincent; 1 child, Alicia S. Mem. Dist. 29 Va. House of Delegates, Va., 1994—; mem. Militia & Pub. Safety Com., Appropriations Com., Rules Com., Agr., Chesapeake and Natural Resources Com. Mem. various Va. commissions and local boards. Mem.: Nat. Conf. State Legislators. Republican. Baptist. Office: 3223 Valley Pike PO Box 2014 Winchester VA 22604 Office Phone: 540-667-8947. Office Fax: 540-667-8960. Business E-Mail: DelBSherwood@house.virginia.gov.

SHESKEY, SUSAN E., venture capitalist and technology executive; b. Oct. 13, 1947; BA, Miami U., Oxford, Ohio, AT&T, Ohio Bell, 1983, Ameritech, 1993. Sr. v.p., chief info. officer Dell, Inc., Round Rock, Tex., 2007; ptnr. Daylight Ptnrs. Venture Capital, 2011; bd. dirs. Stored IQ, Digby, 2011. Spokeperson World Congress Info. Tech., 2006, Diversity Jour. Women Worth Watching, 2006; adv. bd. mem. U. Tex. & Tex. AM U. Named Top 10 Most Powerful Women in Tech., 2007.

SHEUBROOKS, MURIEL W., board member, gas industry executive, retired real estate company executive; Ptnr. Greater Carolinas Real Estate Svcs. Inc., Charlotte, NC; ret.; mng. dir. Piedmont Natural Gas Co. inc. Bd. dirs. Piedmont Natural Gas Co., 1993—. Office: Piedmont Natural Gas Co Inc 4720 Piedmont Row Dr Charlotte NC 28210 Office Phone: 704-364-3120. Home Fax: 704-365-3849. Business E-Mail: muriel.sheubrooks@piedmontng.com.

SHEVARDNADZE, EDUARD AMVROSIYEVICH, former President of Georgia; b. Mamati Lanchkhutsky Raion, Georgia, Jan. 25, 1928; s. Ambrosi Shevardnadze & Sophie Pateishvili S.; m. Nanuli Tsagareishvili, 1950 (dec. Oct. 20, 2004); children: Manana, Paata. Grad., Republican Party Sch. of Cen. Com., Communist Party of Georgia, 1951, Kutaisi Pedagogical Inst., 1959; Degree in Polit. Sci. & Diplomacy (hon.), U. Trieste, 1991, Harvard U. Joined Communist Party Soviet Union, 1948, Komsomol work, 1948-61; 2d sec. Cen. Com. Georgian Komsomol, 1956-57; 1st sec. Cen. Com. Georgian Komsomol, 1957-61; party work, 1961-91; mem. Cen. Com. Georgian Communist Party, 1961-91; 1st sec. Mtskheti Raion Com., 1961-63, Pervomaisky Raion Com., Tbilisi City, Communist Party of Georgia, 1963-64; 1st dep. minister for Protection of Pub. Order, 1961-65; minister (renamed Ministry of Internal Affairs 1968), 1965-72; 1st sec. Tbilisi City Com. of Cen. Com., Communist Party of Georgia, 1972; 1st sec. Cen. Com. Georgian Communist Party, 1972-85; min. fgn. affairs USSR, 1985-90, 91; mem. Cen. Com. of Communist Party Soviet Union, 1976-91; candidate mem. Politburo, 1978-85, dep. to USSR Supreme Soviet, 1978-91; mem. Presdl. Coun., 1990-91; chmn. State Coun. Republic of Georgia, Tbilisi, 1992-93, Pres. of Parliament, head of state, 1992-95, pres., 1995—2003. Author: My Choice, 1991, The Future Belongs to Freedom, 1991, The Great Silk Road, 1999, Thoughts about the Past and the Future, 2006. Decorated Order of Lenin (5), Order of Red Banner of Labour, Hero of Socialist Labour, (2), others.

SHI, DAVID E., gas industry executive, retired academic administrator, historian; s. Joseph and Evelyn Shi; m. Susan Thomson, June 1974; children: Jason, Jessica. BA in polit. sci., magna cum laude, Furman U., 1973; MA in History, U. Va., 1975, PhD in History, 1976; HHD (hon.), Ctr. Coll., 2002. Asst. prof., Frontis W. Johnston prof., chmn. history dept. Davidson Coll., 1976—93; v.p. acad. affairs and dean Furman U., Greenville, 1993—94, pres., 1994—2010; sr. fellow Nat. Humanities Ctr. in Rsch., Triangle Park, NC. Bd. dirs. Nat. Commerce Fin. Corp., Memphis, 2000—, Piedmont Natural Gas Co. Inc., 2003—. Author: Facing Facts: Realism in American Thought and Culture 1850-1920, 1995, In Search of the Simple Life: American Voices, Past and Present, 1986, The Simple Life: Plain Living and High Thinking in American Culture, 1985 (Editors Choice award), Matthew Josephson, Bourgeois Bohemian, 1981; author: (with George Tindall) America: A Narrative History, 4th edit., 1996; contbr. articles to profl. jours. Bd. dirs. Urban League, Greenville. Capt. USAR. Recipient Presdl. Leadership award, James L. Knight Found., 1998, Presdl. award, John Templeton Found., 1999; grantee, NEH, 1980, 1986; fellow, Nat. Humanities Ctr., 1982—83, NEH, 1982—83, 1991—92, Huntington Libr., 1986—87; Andrew Mellon Faculty fellow, 1978, Travel grant, NEH, 1988. Mem.: Greenville C. of C. (bd. dirs.), Commerce Club (bd. dirs.), Omicron Delta Kappa, Phi Beta Kappa. Office: Piedmont Natural Gas Company Inc Bd Directors 4720 Piedmont Row Dr Charlotte NC 28210 Office Phone: 704-364-3120. Office Fax: 704-365-8515. E-mail: david.shi@furman.edu.

SHIELD, GENE, health products executive; Grad., USAF Squadron Officers Sch., Indsl. Coll.; M in Health Care Adminstrn., Med. Coll. Va.; BSBA, The Citadel; MS in Sys. Mgmt., U. Southern Calif. Chief, managed care divsn. Office of Air Force Surgeon Gen.; cons., Surgeon Gen. on managed care, advisor for legis. & CHAMPUS benefits & policy issues; pres., CEO, Humana Mil. Healthcare Svcs. Humana, Inc., Louisville, 1994—2000, sr. v.p., govt. programs, pres. & CEO, Emphesys, 2000—. Office: Humana Inc 500 W Main St Louisville KY 40202 Office Phone: 502-580-1000. Office Fax: 502-580-3677.

SHIELDS, GERALD W., insurance company executive; B in Acctg. & Computer Sci., Baylor U., Waco, Tex., 1980. Chief tech. officer, dir. info. svcs. LifeWay Christian Resources, Nashville; sr. info. tech. positions Electronic Data Sys., 1986—93; v.p. info. tech. enterprises svcs. AFLAC, Inc., Columbus, Ga., 2002—04, dep. chief info. officer, 2004, sr. v.p., chief info. officer, info. tech. Columbus, Ga., 2005—. Mem. inaugural governing body Atlanta Chief Info. Officers Exec. Summit. Bd. trustees Brewton-Parker Coll., Mt. Vernon, Ga.; bd. trustees Cmty. Tech. Adv. Coun. Muscogee County Sch. Dist. Named one of 100 Premier Chief Info. Officers, Computerworld, 2006, 100 Premier Info. Tech. Leaders, 2007. Mem.: Life Mgmt. Inst. Office: AFLAC Inc 1932 Wynnton Rd Columbus GA 31999 Office Phone: 706-323-3431. Office Fax: 706-324-6330. Business E-Mail: gshields@aflac.com.

SHIELDS, JOHN B., chef; b. 1977; m. Karen Shields. Grad., Forest Park Cmty. Coll. Sous chef Charlie Trotter's, Chgo., Alinea, Chgo., 2005; exec. chef Town House, Chilhowie, Va. Named one of America's Best New Chefs, Food & Wine Mag., 2010. Office: Town House 132 E Main St Chilhowie VA 24319 Office Phone: 276-646-8787.

SHIFLET, ANGELA B., mathematics professor; m. George Shiflet. BS in Math., Furman U., Greenville, SC; MS in Math., Clemson U., SC; PhD in Math., Vanderbilt U., Nashville; MS in Computer Sci., U. SC. Rschr. Lawrence Livermore Nat. Lab., 1983—87, 1989—90, Jet Propulsion Lab., 1996—97, Pacific Northwest Lab., 1991—92; Larry H. McCalla prof. in math. and computer sci. Wofford Coll., Spartanburg, SC, chair computer sci. dept. Author: (textbook) Discrete Mathematics for Computer Science, 1986, Elementary Data Structures with Pascal, 1989, Problem Solving in C, Including Breadth and Laboratories, 1995, Data Structures in C++, Including Breadth and Laboratories, 1996, Problem Solving in C++, Including Breadth and Laboratories, 1998; co-author (with G. Shiflet): Introduction to Computational Science: Modeling and Simulation for the Sciences. Recipient Roger Milliken Excellence in the Tchg. of Sci. award, 2007; named SC Prof. of Yr., Carnegie Found. for Advancement of Tchg. and Coun. for Advancement and Support of Edn., 2009. Mem.: Phi Beta Kappa. Office: Wofford Coll 204F Olin Bldg 429 N Church St Spartanburg SC 29303 Office Phone: 864-597-4528. Office Fax: 864-597-4549. Business E-Mail: shifletab@wofford.edu.

SHILLING, ROY BRYANT, JR., academic administrator; s. Roy Bryant and Lila M. (Prestage) S.; m. Margaret Riddle, Oct. 16, 1952; children: Roy Bryant III, Nancy Gale. BA, McMurry U., 1951, HHD, 1982; BD, So. Meth. U., 1957; MS, Ind. U., 1966, PhD, 1967. Presdl. asst. McMurry U., Abilene, Tex., 1959-61; asst. to pres. Tenn. Wesleyan Coll., 1961-64; asst. in devel. Ball State U., 1964-65; rsch. assoc. Ind. U., 1965-67; dir. planning and rsch. Baldwin Wallace Coll., 1967-68; exec. v.p. Southwestern U., 1968-69, pres., 1981-2000, pres. emeritus, 2000—; pres. Hendrix Coll., 1969-81, McMurry Univ., 2002. Mem. Nat. Commn. on United Meth. Higher Edn., 1975-77.

Mem. Ark. Arts and Humanities Coun., 1970-76, chmn., 1974-75; bd. dirs. Ark. Children's Hosp., 1981; mem. bd. higher edn. and ministry United Meth. Ch., 1972-80, mem. univ. senate, 1980-88, v.p. 1983-84, pres., 1984-88; chmn. Gulf dist. Rhodes Scholarship Selection Com., 1992, Ark. chmn., 1973-74, Tex. chmn., 1985-91; mem. Young Pres. Orgn., 1975-81; mem. bd. visitors Air U., 1991-94. With U.S. Army, 1952-54. Recipient Disting. Alumnus award McMurry U., 1980, Perkins Disting. Alumnus award So. Meth. U., 1987, Owen B. Sherrill award for leadership in econ. devel. Georgetown, 1988; named one of Top 100 Most Effective Coll. Pres. in Nation, Bowling Green State U./Exxon Edn. Found., 1986. Mem. North Ctrl. Assn. Colls. and Schs. (vice chmn., chmn. elect 1980-81), Nat. Assn Schs. and Colls. of United Meth. Ch. (v.p. 1975-76, pres. 1976-77), Nat. Coun. Ind. Colls. and Univs. (bd. dirs. 1984-88), So. U. Conf. (exec. com. 1974-78), 79-86, sec.-treas. 1979-86, v.p. 1991-92, pres. 1992-93), Am. Coun. Edn. (bd. dirs. 1989-91; mem. commn. on govt. and pub. rels. 1999-2000, spl. counselor to the pres. 2000-01), Inst. for Humanities (bd. dirs. Salado, Tex. chpt. 1985-91, mem. internat. coun. advs. 1994), NCAA Divsn. III Pres.'s Coun., 1998-2000, Philos Soc. Tex., Rotary, Masons, Alpha Chi, Phi Delta Kappa. Office: 1405 Mesa Ridge Ln Austin TX 78735-1639 E-mail: shilling@southwestern.edu.

SHILLINGBURG, HERBERT THOMPSON, JR., dental educator; b. Mar. 21, 1938; s. Herbert Thompson and Stefi Marie (Schuster) Shillingburg; m. Constance Joanne Murphy, June 11, 1960 (dec. June 28, 2008); children: Lisa Grace, Leslie Susan, Lara Stephanie. Student, U. N.Mex., 1955-58, 65-66; DDS, U. So. Calif., 1962; Dr (hon.), U. Medicine and Pharmacy Targu Mures, Romania, 2006. Gen. practice dentistry, Albuquerque, 1964-67; asst. prof. fixed prosthodontics sect. UCLA Sch. Dentistry, 1967-70, chmn., 1970-72; chmn. dept. fixed prosthodontics U. Okla. Coll. Dentistry, Okla. City, 1972—2003, David Ross Boyd Disting. prof., 1983, prof. emeritus, 2003—. Cons. VA Hosp., Muskogee, Okla., 1975—84, Oklahoma City, 1977—93, U.S. Army Dental Activity, Ft. Knox, Ky., 1980—94. Author: Preparations for Cast Gold Restorations, 1974, Fundamentals of Fixed Prosthodontics, 1976, 2nd edit, 1981, 3d edit., 1997, 4th edit., 2012, Guide to Occlusal Waxing, 1979, 3d edit., 2000, Restoration of the Endodontically Treated Tooth, 1984, Fundamentals of Tooth Preparations for Cast Metal and Porcelain Restorations, 1987; co-editor: Quintessence of Dental Technology, 1984—88; sect. editor: Quintessence Internat., 1988—2001, mem. editl. coun.: Jour. Prosthetic Dentistry, 1996—99. Capt. US Army, 1962—64. Recipient Award for tchg. excellence, UCLA Sch. Dentistry, 1969, 1972, 1973, Okla. Coll. Dentistry, 1976, 1978, 1982, 1987, 1993, 1994, 1997, 1st prize, Am. Med. Writers Assn., 1988, La Mèdaille de la Ville de Paris (èchelon Argent), 1990, Outstanding Profl. Achievement award, O U Coll. Dentristy, 2003, Prof. of Hon., U. Medicine and Pharmacy Targu-Mures, 2004; named Disting. Lectr., O U Assoc., 1989, Herbert T. Shillingburg Endowed Professorship Fixed Prosthodontics, Coll. Dentistry, 2006. Fellow: Am. Coll. Dentists; mem.: ADA, Okla. State Dental Assn., Internat. Assn. Dental Rsch., Am. Coll. Prosthodontists (hon.), Am. Acad. Restorative Dentistry, Am. Acad. Fixed Prosthodontics (George H. Moulton award 1998), Am. Acad. Operative Dentistry, Phi Kappa Phi, Omicron Kappa Upsilon (Stephen H. Leeper award for Tchg. Excellence Supreme Ch. 2000). Independent. Episcopalian. Avocations: travel, photography. Home: 1312 Brixton Rd Edmond OK 73034-3314 Office: U Okla Coll Dentistry PO Box 26901 Oklahoma City OK 73190-0001

SHINDLER, STEVEN M., telecommunications industry executive; m. Mary Kay Shindler; 3 children. BA, U. Mich., 1985; MBA, Cornell U. Various positions through mng. dir., Comm. Fin. Group Toronto Dominion Bank, 1987—96; exec. v.p., CFO NII Holdings, Inc. (formerly Nextel Comm., Inc.), Reston, Va., 1996—2000; CEO NII Holdings, Inc., Reston, Va., 2000—, chmn., 2002—. Recipient Bravo Bus. award as Internat. CEO of the Yr., Latin Trade mag.; named Greater Washington area Entrepreneur of the Yr., Ernst & Young. Office: NII Holdings Inc 1875 Explorer St Ste 1000 Reston VA 20190 Office Phone: 703-390-5100. Office Fax: 703-547-5269. Business E-Mail: steven.shindler@nii.com.

SHINE, KENNETH IRWIN, academic administrator, cardiologist, educator; b. Worcester, Mass., 1935; Grad., Harvard Coll., 1957; MD, Harvard U., 1961. Diplomate Am. Bd. Internal Medicine. Intern Mass. Gen. Hosp., Boston, 1961—62, resident, 1962—63, 1965—66, fellow in cardiology, 1966—67; surgeon USPHS, 1963—65; instr. Harvard Med. Sch., 1968—; asst. prof. medicine UCLA Sch. Medicine, 1971—73, assoc. prof., 1973—77, prof., 1977—92, prof. emeritus, 1993—, dir. CCU, 1971—75, chief div. cardiology, 1975—79, vice chmn. dept. medicine, 1979—81, exec. chmn., 1981—86, dean, 1986—92, provost for med. scis., 1991—92; clin. prof. medicine Georgetown U. Med. Ctr., Washington, 1993; pres. Inst. of Medicine, Washington, 1992—2002; dir. RAND Center for Domestic and International Health Security, 2003; exec. vice chancellor for health affairs U. Tex. Sys., 2003—, interim chancellor, 2008—09. Master: Am. Coll. Physicians; fellow: Am. Coll. Cardiology; mem.: Inst. Medicine, Assn. Am. Med. Colls. (adminstrv. bd. coun. deans 1989—92, exec. bd. 1990—92, chmn. coun. deans 1991—92), Am. Heart Assn. (pres. 1986—87). Office: U Texas Sys O Henry Hall Room 204 601 Colorado St Austin TX 78701 Office Phone: 512-499-4224. E-mail: kshine@utsystem.edu.

SHIPLEY, DAVID ELLIOTT, lawyer, educator; b. Urbana, Ill., Oct. 3, 1950; s. James Ross and Dorothy Jean (Elliott) S.; m. Virginia Florence Coleman, May 24, 1980; 1 child, Shannon C. BA, Oberlin Coll., 1972; JD, U. Chgo., 1975. Bar: R.I. 1975. Assoc. Tillinghast, Collins & Graham, Providence, 1975-77; asst. prof. U. S.C. Sch. Law, Columbia, 1977-81, assoc. prof., 1981-85, prof., 1985-90, assoc. dean, 1989-90; dean U. Miss. Sch. Law, University, 1990-93, U. Ky. Coll. Law, Lexington, 1993-98; prof., dean Sch. Law U. Ga., Athens, 1998—2003, Thomas R. R. Cobb prof., 2003—. Vis. prof. Coll. William and Mary, Williamsburg, Va., 1983-84, Ohio State U. Coll. Law, Columbus, 1986-87. Author: South Carolina Administrative Law, 1983, 2d edit., 1989; co-author Copyright Law, 1992. Pres. Shandon Neighborhood Assn., Columbia, 1988-90, Athens Justice Project, Ga., 2003-05, minority affairs com. law sch. admissions coun., 2001-05, fin. and legal affairs coll., 2005-07, with test R & D, 2007-. Named Prof. of Yr., U. SC Sch. Law, 1990, faculty scholar, 1989-90, O'Byrne award for Student Faculty Rels. U. Ga., 2003-04, 04-05, Hon. Faculty Marshal, 2008, 2009. Mem. ABA, R.I. Bar Assn., S.C. Bar Assn. (assoc.), Ga. Bar Assn. (assoc.). Methodist. Avocations: running, golf, yardwork, gardening, reading. Home: 475 River Bottom Rd Athens GA 30606-6430 Office: U Ga Sch Law 323 Rusk Hall Athens GA 30602-6012 Home Phone: 706-613-0647; Office Phone: 706-542-5184. Business E-Mail: shipley@uga.edu.

SHIPLEY, TONY, state legislator; b. Blountville, Tenn., Aug. 23, 1953; m. Susan Shipley; 5 children. BA, U. Tenn., Knoxville; PGIP, Defense Intelligence Coll., Washington, D.C.; attended, USAF Command & Staff Coll., Maxwell AFB, Ala., USMC Command Staff Coll., Camp Smith, Hawaii. Paramedic Northeast State Cmty. Coll., Blountville; critical care paramedic Roane State Cmty. Coll., Knoxville; mem. Dist. 2 Tenn House of Reps., 2008—, vice chmn. House Public Safety Subcommittee. Ret. USAF. Decorated Bronze Star USAF. Mem.: Masonic Lodge 688, 32nd Degree Mason. Republican. Protestant. Mailing: PO Box 6173 Kingsport TN 37663 Office: 204 War Memorial Bldg Nashville TN 37243 Office Phone: 615-741-2886. Business E-Mail: rep.tony.shipley@capitol.tn.gov.

SHIPP, BRIAN, healthcare company executive; Pres., CEO United Healthcare, Tenn.; CEO, Southeastern Region Amerigroup Corp., 1999—. Mem. Nashville Health Care Coun. Office: Amerigroup Corp 4425 Corporation Ln Virginia Beach VA 23462 Office Phone: 757-490-6900. Office Fax: 757-518-3600. Business E-Mail: bshipp@amerigroupcorp.com.

SHIPP, ROBBIN, prosecutor, former state legislator; b. Feb. 01; 1 child, Alexandria. State rep. Dist. 58, Ga., 2007—09; prosecutor Office of Fulton County Dist. Atty., Atlanta, 2009—. Mem.: Gate City Bar, Georgia Assn. Black Women Atty., Georgia Bar. Democrat. Office: Office Fulton County Dist Atty 136 Pryor St Third Fl Atlanta GA 30303-3477

SHIRER, ROBERT LLOYD, clergyman; b. Ouagadougou, W. Africa, Apr. 14, 1929; s. Wilbert Lloyd and Margaret Peoples S.; m. Juanita Shirer, June 1, 1951 (div. 1971); m. Anne Kleier, Sept. 1, 1973; children: Brenda Margaret, Bruce Robert (dec.). AB magna cum laude, Asbury Coll., 1950; MA, U. Pa., 1951; BD, Princeton Theol. Seminary, 1954; postgrad., NYU, 1955-62. Ordained minister Presbyterian Ch.; CPM Inst. of Real Estate, Maine; real estate broker, Fla. Asst. minister White Plains Presbyn. Ch., NY, 1954—55; minister of edn. Huguenot Meml. Ch., Pelham Manor, NY, 1955—57; pastor First Presbyn. Ch., Peekskill, NY, 1957—62, Maximo Presbyn. Ch., St. Petersburg, Fla., 1962-67; exec. dir. Presbyn. Social Ministries, St. Petersburg, 1967-73; pres. Shirer & Assocs., Inc., Seminole, Fla., 1973—; parish assoc. Good Samaritan Ch., Pinellas Park, Fla., 1996—2003; bd. dirs. Commn. Separation Ch. And State, 2009—. Mem. Suncoast Bd. Realtors, St. Petersburg, 1974—; mem. Inst. Real Estate Mgmt., Chgo., 1975—. Mem. bd. adjustment Indian Rocks Beach, Fla., 1980-81; mem. human rels. adv. com., St. Petersburg, 1965-67; vice-chair Pinellas County Dem. Com., 1996-2002, chmn. grievance com., 2004-06. Named Ky. Col., 1972. Mem. Nat. Assn. Mng. Agts. (bd. dirs. 1974-90), Southeast Assn. of HUD Mng. Agts. (bd. dirs., pres. 1983—), Presbytery of Tampa Bay (pres. trustees 1994-96). Avocation: worldwide travel. Personal E-mail: rlsrascal@tampabay.com.

SHIRK, RICHARD D., retired insurance company executive; b. 1946; married. Grad., Gettysburg Coll. With Equitable Life Assurance, NYC, Houston, 1967-86; pres., southern region Equicor Inc., Nashville, 1987—90, Houston, 1987—90; with Cigna Corp., 1990—92; pres., CEO Blue Cross & Blue Shield of Ga., 1992—2002. Bd. dirs. Amerigroup Corp., 2002—. Bd. trustees Gettysburg Coll. Office: Amerigroup Corp Bd Directors 4425 Corporation Ln Virginia Beach VA 23462 Office Phone: 757-490-6900. Office Fax: 757-222-2330.

SHIRLEY, CRAIG P., public relations executive, writer; b. Syracuse, NY, Sept. 24, 1956; m. Zorine Shirley; children: Taylor, Andrew, Matthew, Mitchell. BA in History & Polit. Sci., Springfield Coll., 1978. Press sec., staff mem. to US Senator Gordon Humphrey, 1978; dir. ind. expenditure campaign Fund for a Conservative Majority, 1980; advertising account exec. NYC, 1981; comm. advisor Rep. Nat. Com., 1982; dir. comm. Nat. Conservative Polit. Action Com., 1984; founder, pres. Craig Shirley & Assocs., 1984—87, 1992—2000; co-founder, CEO Keene, Shirley & Assocs., 1987—92; pres., CEO Shirley & Banister Pub. Affairs (formerly Craig Shirley & Assocs.), 2000—. Bd. dirs. Am. Conservative Union; bd. govs. Reagan Ranch; adv. bd. Patrick Henry Ctr.; lectr. in field. Author: Reagan's Revolution: The Untold Story of the Campaign That Started It All, 2005, Rendezvous with Destiny: Ronald Reagan and the Campaign That Changed America, 2008; editor: Are You a Conservative or a Liberal?, Coaching Youth Lacrosse; contbr. articles to profl. jours. Bd. mem. United Seniors Assn., No. Va. Youth Lacrosse League, Fort Hunt Youth Athletic Assn. Republican. Avocation: sailing. Office: Shirley & Banister Pub Affairs 122 S Patrick St Alexandria VA 22314 Office Phone: 703-739-5920. Office Fax: 730-739-5924. E-mail: info@sbpublicaffairs.com.

SHIRLEY, STACIE, corporate financial executive; Attended, Stephen F. Austin State U. V.p., fin. CompUSA, 1993—2001; v.p., investor rels. Neiman Marcus Group; v.p., fin., treas. Neiman Marcus Group, Inc., 2008—. Office: The Neiman Marcus Group Inc 1618 Main St One Marcus Sq Dallas TX 75201 Office Phone: 214-757-2954. Office Fax: 214-573-5320. Business E-Mail: stacie_shirley@neimanmarcus.com.

SHIRLEY, WILLIAM, state legislator; m. Benita Meadows. Attended, Meridian CC, Miss., Miss. Auctioneer Sch. Restaurant owner The Family Fish Camp, Miss.; mem. Dist. 84 Miss. House of Reps., Jackson, 2012—. Vol. Bellsouth Telephone Pioneers. Republican. Baptist. Office: Miss House of Reps PO Box 1018 Jackson MS 39215 Business E-Mail: wshirley@house.ms.gov.

SHIVER, HARRY, state legislator; Mem. Dist. 64 Ala. House of Reps., Montgomery, 2006—. Mem. Bur. Indian Affairs. Republican. Office: Ala House of Reps Ala State House 11 S Union St Rm 526-D Montgomery AL 36130 Office Phone: 251-937-0240, 334-242-7745. Office Fax: 251-580-1645. Business E-Mail: harryshiver@aol.com.

SHOAF, FORREST (N.B. FORREST SHOAF, NATHAN BEDFORD FORREST SHOAF), lawyer; b. Tenn, 1950; m. Melissa Shoaf; 3 children. BA, West Point Acad., 1972; MA, Vanderbilt U., 1980; JD, Harvard Law Sch., 1987. Ptnr. Bass, Berry & Sims, Nashville; mng. dir. Corp. Fin. Dept. JC Bradford & Co., 1996—2000; mng. dir. Investment Banking Group Morgan Keegan & Co. Inc., 2000—02; head Nashville Corp. Finance Office Morgan Keegan & Co. Inc, 2000—02; mng. dir. Investment Banking Dept. Avondale Partners LLC, Nashville, 2002—05; sr. v.p., gen. counsel, sec. Cracker Barrel Old Country Store, Inc., Lebanon, Tenn., 2005—, interim CFO, 2008—09, 2010—11. Bd. dirs. Logan's Roadhouse, Inc., 2006—. Served to major US Army. Office: CBRL Group Inc PO Box 787 Lebanon TN 37088-0787 Office Phone: 615-443-9869. Office Fax: 615-443-9818.

SHOCHAT, STEPHEN JAY, pediatrician, surgeon; b. Balt., Dec. 17, 1938; s. Albert J. and Rose (Blechman) S.; m. Sheila Floam, July 1960 (div. July 1979); children: Francine Lynne, Alisa Joy; m. Carla Ann Centi, Jan. 26, 1980; children: David Robert, Sarah Elizabeth. Degree, Randolph Mason Coll., 1959; MD, Med. Coll. Va., 1963. Surg. resident Washington U. Med. Ctr., St. Louis, 1963-68; pediatric surg. resident Boston Children's Hosp., 1968-70; thoracic surg. resident Queen Elizabeth Hosp., Birmingham, Eng., 1970, George Washington Hosp., Washington, 1972; chief pediatric surgery Hershey (Pa.) Med. Ctr., 1973-77, Stanford (Calif.) Med. Ctr., 1977-94; sr. surgeon Children's Hosp. Phila., 1994-96; surgeon-in-chief, chmn. dept. surgery St. Jude Children Rsch. Hosp., Memphis, 1996—2009, mem. dept. surgery, 2009—; prof. pediats. and surgery U. Tenn., Memphis, 1996—. Lt. col. USAF, 1970-72. Office: St Jude Children Rsch Hosp Dept Surgery 262 Danny Thomas Pl Memphis TN 38105 Office Phone: 901-595-2911. Business E-Mail: stephen.shochat@stjude.org.

SHOEMAKE, JERRY, state legislator; m. Lynda Shoemake. Attended, Okla. State Univ., Okmulgee. Rancher; mem. Dist. 16 Okla. House of Representatives, 2005—. Democrat. Mailing: 15160 North 310 Rd Morris OK 74445 Office: 2300 N Lincoln Blvd Rm 506 Oklahoma City OK 73105 Office Phone: 405-557-7373. E-mail: jerryshoemake@okhouse.gov.

SHOEMAKER, ROBERT MORIN, retired military officer, commissioner; b. Almont, Mich., Feb. 18, 1924; s. Uriah Beebe and Pomala (Morin) S.; m. Mary A. (Tuke) Rickard, July 17, 1948. BS, U.S. Mil. Acad., 1946; postgrad., U.S. Army Command and Gen. Staff Coll., 1959, Army War Coll., 1967; student, Infantry Sch., Ft. Benning, 1952—53. Commd. 2d lt. U.S. Army, 1946, advanced through grades to gen., 1978, platoon leader, bn. staff officer, co. comdr. 18th Inf., Fed. Republic Germany, 1947-50, co. cmdr. inf., 1950—52, co. comdr., regtl. S2, S3, 23d Inf. Republic of Korea, 1953-54, staff officer inf. br. DA, 1954-56, student, faculty officer U.S. Army Aviation Sch. Ft. Rucker, Ala., 1959-62, project officer Army Concept Team Vietnam, 1962-63, bn. comdr., asst. chief of staff, G-3, 11th Air Assault Div. Ft. Benning, Ga., 1963-65, bn. cmdr., squadron comdr. 1st Cav. Div., Vietnam, 1965-66, chief plans and programs Army Aviation DA, 1967-69, chief of staff, asst. div. comdr. 1st Cav. Vietnam, 1969-70, dep. comdr., chief. of staff III Corps and Ft. Hood, Tex., 1970, dept. comdr. MASSTER Ft. Hood, Tex., 1971-72, comdr. 1st Cav., 1973-75, comdr. III Corps Ft. Hood, 1975-77, dep. comdr. FORSCOM Ft. McPherson, Ga., 1977-78; comdr. U.S. Army Forces Command, 1978-82; ret., 1982; county commr. Bell County, Tex., 1987-94. Decorated D.S.M., Silver Star medal with oak leaf cluster, Legion of Merit, D.F.C., Bronze Star, Air medal with 48 oak leaf clusters, Army Commendation medal with oak leaf cluster, Croix de Guerre (France), Gallantry Cross with palm (Republic of Vietnam), RVN Honor medal 1st class; Robert M. Shoemaker H.S., Killeen, Tex. named in his honor, Aug. 2001; named Disting. Grad., West Point, 2004. Home: 111 Bluff Ln Belton TX 76513-9804 Business E-Mail: bshoe5@embargmail.com.

SHOEMAKER, WILLIAM EDWARD, corporate financial executive; b. Charleston, W.Va., Sept. 17, 1945; s. Robert Edward and Janet Elizabeth (Hoglund) S.; 1 child, Marcus. BBA, U. Notre Dame, 1967. Assoc. buyer Proctor & Gamble, Cin., 1971; gen. mgr. Eastwind Inc., Anchorage, 1972-73; pres., operator Golden Horn Lodge, Inc., Bristol Bay, Alaska, 1973-79; treas. Hawley Resource Group, Inc., Anchorage, 1979-88; treas., chief fin. officer Golden Zone Resources, Inc., Campbell, Calif., 1988-90; ptnr. Resort Mgmt. Corp., Anchorage, 1987-90; pres. Discovery Holdings, Inc., Ft. Lauderdale, Fla., 1991—2005; pres., CEO Foresight Digital Co., 2005—. Bd. dirs. Pacific Art & Design Cons., Inc. Bd. dirs. Anchorage Econ. Devel. Corp., 1988-90, 4 Children's Sake, 1997—; mem. exec. com. Broward Child Welfare Initiative, 2002-06; dir. Lovewell Inst. for Creative Arts, 2004-. Served to lt. USN, 1967—71. Republican. Avocations: boating, skiing, fishing. Office: Foresight Digital Co 1000 Corporate Dr Ste 330 Fort Lauderdale FL 33334 Home: 5121 NE 17th Ter Fort Lauderdale FL 33334-5738 Office Phone: 954-491-0180.

SHOMAKER, SAM (THOMAS SAMUEL SHOMAKER), dean, anesthesiologist, former lawyer; b. Vincennes, Ind. m. Suzanne Yandow; 3 children. Grad. summa cum laude, St. Louis U., 1976; JD, Georgetown U., Washington, 1979; MD, U. Hawai'i John A. Burns Sch. Medicine, 1986. Legis. intern to John. C. Danforth US Senate, legis. asst. to Daniel K. Inouye; intern in surgery U. Hawaii; residency in anestesiology U. Utah, U. Fla.; prof. anestesiology, residency program dir. anestesiology, assoc. dean curriculum & minority affairs, sr. assoc. dean academic affairs U. Utah Coll. Medicine, interim dean, 1998—99; vice dean acad. affairs, COO, v.p. faculty group practice Univ. Clin., Edn. and Rsch. Associates U. Hawaii John A. Burns Sch. Medicine, 2000—06, acting dean, 2005—06; prof. anestesiology U. Tex. Med. Br., 2006—10, dean Austin Programs, 2006—09; Jean and Thomas McMullin dean medicine, v.p. clin. affairs Tex. A&M U. Health Sci. Ctr., 2010—. Lt. USNR. Mem.: Assn. American Med. Colleges. Avocations: Karate, Kung Fu, Ju Jitsu, running, youth soccer coach. Office: Tex A&M Health Sci Ctr Office of Dean 3rd Fl Health Professions Edn Bldg 8447 Hwy 47 Bryan TX 77807 Office Phone: 979-436-0200. Business E-Mail: shomaker@medicine.tamhsc.edu.

SHOOB, MARVIN HERMAN, federal judge; b. Walterboro, SC, Feb. 23, 1923; s. Michael Louis and Lena (Steinberg) S.; m. Janice Paradies, Nov. 14, 1949; children: Michael, Wendy. Student, Ga. Inst. Tech., Va. Mil. Inst., 1942-43, 46; JD, U. Ga., 1948. Bar: Ga. 1948. Ptnr. Brown & Shoob, Atlanta, 1949-55, Phillips, Johnson & Shoob, Atlanta, 1955-56, Shoob, McLain & Merritt, Atlanta, 1956-79; judge US Dist. Ct. (no. dist.) Ga., Atlanta, 1979—91, sr. judge, 1991—. Chmn. Juvenile Ct. Com., 1964-70; mem. Ga. State Bar Grievance Tribunal, 1975-79; chmn. Ga. State Bar Fed. Legislation Com., 1977-79; guest lectr. Continuing Legal Edn., Athens, Ga., 1975-77 Chmn. 5th Dist. Democratic Exec. Com., 1974-76 Mem. Phi Eta Sigma, Phi Kappa Phi Jewish. Office: US Dist Ct 1767 US Courthouse 75 Spring St SW Atlanta GA 30303-3309 Office Phone: 404-215-1470.

SHOOPMAN, PHILLIP W., state legislator; b. Louisville, Ky., Nov. 21, 1968; s. Robert O. and Joyce Shoopman; m. Dawn M. Shoopman; children: Clara M., August W. BSME, Purdue U., 1992, MSE, 1994. Mem. Dist. 18 SC House of Reps., 2007—09; mem. Med. Com., Mil. Com., Pub. & Munic Affairs Com.; mem. Dist. 5 SC State Senate, 2009—, mem. Fish, Game and Forestry Com., Gen. Com., Judiciary Com. & Rules Com. Mem.: Greer C. of C. (vice chmn. 2006). Republican. Office: 504 Gressette Bldg Columbia SC 29201 Home: 2950 N Green Valley Pkwy Apt 814 Henderson NV 89014-0427 Home Phone: 864-895-6446; Office Phone: 803-212-6032. Business E-Mail: ShoopmanP@schouse.org.

SHORT, JOHN W., state legislator; b. Aug. 24, 1964; BA in Bus. Adminstrn. Owner John's Gun & Pawn, Hindman, Ky.; mem. Dist. 92 Ky. House of Reps., Frankfort, 2011—. Democrat. Baptist. Office: PO Box 1133 Hindman KY 41822 also: Kentucky House of Reps Annex Rm 352 702 Capitol Ave Frankfort KY 40601 Office Phone: 606-785-9018, 502-564-8100 ext. 668. Business E-Mail: john.short@lrc.ky.gov.

SHORT, MICHAEL J., automotive executive; Grad., US Naval Acad., Annapolis, Md., 1982; MBA, Columbia U., NYC, 1991. Helicopter pilot, tactics instr. USN, Norfolk, Va.; various fin. positions Univeral Orlando, Joseph E. Seagram & Sons, Inc. and IBM Corp., 1992—2000; exec. v.p., CFO Universal City Devel. Ptnrs., Ltd., 2000—07, AutoNation, Inc., Ft. Lauderdale, Fla., 2007—. Office: AutoNation Inc 110 SE 6th St Fort Lauderdale FL 33301 Office Phone: 954-769-7000.

SHORTAL, TERENCE MICHAEL, retired systems company executive; b. St. Louis, Oct. 13, 1937; s. Harold Leo and Catherine Margaret S.; m. Linda Margaret Elias, May 29, 1965; children: Jennifer, Bradley Alexander. BSEE, U. Mo., 1961; MS, U.S. Naval Postgrad. Sch., 1966; grad. program execs., Carnegie Mellon U., 1979. Commd. ensign USN, 1961, advanced through grades to capt., 1980, asst. officer in charge Engring. Duty Officer Sch. Vallejo, Calif., 1974-77, ship engring. mgr. AEGIS shipbldg. project Naval Ea. Sys. Command Washington, 1977-79, tech. dir. DDGX project, 1979-81, ret., 1981; sr. v.p., dir. Kastle Sys., LLC, 1981—2006. Trustee Cathedral Choral Soc., Washington, 1983-95, 1997-2006, pres., 1986-88, 2000-2002; mem. vestry St. John's Episcopal Ch., McLean, Va., 1982-85; bd. dirs. Langley Sch., McLean, 1984-94, pres. 1986-88. Decorated Meritorious Svc. medal (2), Navy Commendation medal (2); recipient award of merit Cathedral Choral Soc., 1996. Mem. IEEE (life, br. award 1961), Gridiron Club (Washington), Sigma Xi, Phi Kappa Theta, Order St. John., Rotary Club Republican. Episcopalian. Home: 3850 Teesdale Ct Atlanta GA 30350-5054 Personal E-mail: mikeshortal@comcast.net.

SHOSKY, JOHN EDWIN, media consultant, speechwriter; b. Colorado Springs, Colo., Nov. 1, 1955; s. Alexander Matthew and Barbara Marie (Middlekamp) Shosky. BA in Polit. Sci., Colo. Coll., 1979; MA in Philosophy, U. Wyo., 1987; PhD in Philosophy, Am. U., 1992. Dep. dir. media and sports commns. White House Conf. for Drug Free Am., Washington, 1987—88; sr. policy analyst White House Office Pub. Affairs, 1988; cons. to sec. HHS, Washington, 1984—91, cons. to Surgeon Gen., 1991—92; cons. to office of nat. drug control policy Exec. Office of the Pres., Washington, 1992—93, cons. to sec. of edn., 2003—05; pres., sr. writer Roncalli Comm., 1991—; cons. to sec. HUD, 2007—09. Speech writer for govt. ofcls., corp. execs., profl. athletes, congressmen, senators; lectr. in philosophy and internat. studies Am. U., 1987—, asst. prof. philosophy, 1996—97, asst. dir. honors program, 1999—2003; adj. prof. philosophy George Mason U., 1990—94; vis. sr. mem. Linacre Coll., Oxford, England, 1997—; vis. prof. Charles U., Prague, 1998; vis. scholar Ins. of Logic, Acad. Scis., Czech Republic, 1998; vis. fellow Acad. Scis., Czech Republic, 2002—04. Contbr. articles to profl. jours. and publs. Mem.: Mind Assn., Am. Philos. Assn., Austrian Wittgenstein Soc., U. Wyo. Alumni Assn. Republican. Roman Catholic. Home: 1806 Rollins Dr Alexandria VA 22307-1613

SHOUSE, AUGUST EDWARD, lawyer; b. Houston, Aug. 12, 1949; s. Earl Edward Shouse and Mary Ann (Myers) Carrico; m. Deborah Lee Symonds; children: William Bundy, Edwrd Booth, Tucker Clayton. BS, Stanford U., 1971; JD, U. Tex., 1974. Bar: Tex. 1974. From assoc. to ptnr. Vinson & Elkins, Houston, 1974—2004; pvt. practice Houston, 2004—. Bd. dirs. Greater Houston area chpt. ARC. Mem. Order of Coif, Phi Beta Kappa, Tau Beta Pi. Episcopalian. Office: 2001 Kirby Dr Ste 906 Houston TX 77019-6042 Business E-Mail: aes@aeshouse.com.

SHOWALTER, BETSY S., mathematics educator; b. Rockford, Ill., July 25, 1954; d. Donald James and Grace Lutz Curran; children: Thomas, David. BA in Math., U. Okla., Norman, 1976, MA in Math., 1978; PhD in Math. Edn., Okla. State U., Stillwater, 2005. Cert. secondary math. tchr., k-12 library media Okla. Math. tchr. Midwest City HS, Okla., 1978—80, Drumright HS, Okla., 1986—87, Stillwater HS, 1988—91; adj. math. instr. Okla. State U., 1980—86, 1991—93, Southwestern Okla. State U., Weatherford, 1987—88; instr. math. Langston U., Okla., 1993—. Mem.: Math. Assoc. Am., Okla. Coun. Tchrs. Math., Math. Assn. Am., Nat. Coun. Tchrs. Math., Phi Kappa Phi, Kappa Delta Pi. Home: 2402 W 8th Ave Stillwater OK 74074 Office: Langston U Math Dept 202A Jones Hall Langston OK 73050

SHOWS, C. H. (BOBBY), state legislator; b. Laurel, Miss., Aug. 28, 1938; m. Sandra Odom; children: Delfrieda, Sandi, Barnard, Eric, Natalie. Mem. Dist. 89 Miss. House of Reps., 1992—; mem. Adv. Bd. M&M Bank; co-owner Shows Bros. Farm Supply; bd. chmn. Southeastern Miss. Livestock Assn. Mem.: Miss. Arts Fair Handicapped (bd. mem.), Cattleman's Assn., Farm Bur. Democrat. Baptist. Mailing: PO Box 373 Ellisville MS 39437 Home Phone: 601-477-9225; Office Phone: 601-477-3956. E-mail: bshows@house.ms.gov.

SHRADER, RALPH WILLIAM, consulting firm executive; b. Miami, Fla., Sept. 20, 1944; m. Janice Shrader, 1969. BS in Electrical Engring., U. Pa., 1966; MSEE in Math. & Nuc. Physics, U. Ill., PhD in Elec. Engring. Nat. dir. advanced systems planning Western Union; with Booz Allen & Hamilton, McLean, Va., 1974—78, v.p., 1978—94, pres. worldwide tech. divsn. Mc Lean, Va., 1994—99, chmn., CEO, PRES., 1999—. Bd. dirs. ServiceSource Network, 2004—. Bd. dirs. Wolf Trap Found. Nat. Park for Performing Arts, Abilities, Inc.; adv. coun. Character Edn. Partnership; chmn. The Neediest Kids, Inc., Light the Night Walks, Washington, 2004; bd. dirs. Abilities, Inc., ServiceSource, Va. Recipient David Sarnoff award, Armed Forces Communications & Electronics Assn., Cmty. Leadership award, Northern Va. Cmty. Found., 2001; co-recipient Emergence award, Dance Theatre Harlem, 2003. Office: Booz Allen & Hamilton Inc 8283 Greensboro Dr Mc Lean VA 22102 E-mail: shrader_ralph@bah.com.

SHROPSHIRE, WALTER, JR., biophysicist, pastor; b. Washington, Sept. 4, 1932; s. Walter and Mary Virginia (Anderson) S.; m. Audrey Marie McConkey, June 28, 1958; children: Janet Marie, Susan Lynn, Edward Allen. BS in Physics, George Washington U., 1954, MS in Botany, 1956, PhD in Plant Physiology, 1958; MDiv summa cum laude, Wesley Theol. Sem., 1990; postdoctoral fellow biophysics, Calif. Inst. Tech., 1957-59. Ordained to ministry United Meth. Ch., 1977. Physicist Smithsonian Instn., Washington, 1954—63; asst. dir. Smithsonian Environ. Rsch. Ctr., Washington, 1963-86; Gast prof. U. Freiburg, Germany, 1968-69; biophysicist, dir. Omega Lab., Cabin John, Md., 1986—2010. Professorial lectr. botany George Washington U., 1960-85; Gast prof. U. Zurich, Switzerland, 1985-86; part-time adj. prof. Practice Min. and Mission Wesley Theol. Sem., 1990-2008, pres. Wesley Nexus, 2009-. Editor: Phytochrome, 1972, Joys of Research, 1981, Photomorphogenesis, Vol 16A, 16B, 1983, Photobiology, 1984-85, Max Delbrück and New Perception Biology, 1906-1981, 2007; Contbr. 57 articles to profl. jours. Pastor, Foundry United Meth. Ch., Washington, 1991-2003. Recipient Smithsonian Outstanding Performance award, 1967, Smithsonian Research award, 1968, Merit award Soc. John Wesley, 1997, Templeton Sci. and Religion Course prize, 1999, 2002; NSF grantee, 1960-66. Fellow Explorers Club, Am. Solar Energy Soc. Home and Office: Omega Lab Apt 426 300 Westminster Canterbury Dr Winchester VA 22603 Office Phone: 540-665-5748. E-mail: wshrop@erols.com.

SHRUM, KAYSE, dean, educator, pediatrician; AS, Connors State Coll., Warner, Okla., 1992; DO, Okla. State U., 1998. Resident in pediat. Tulsa Regional Med. Ctr., 1998—2001; pvt. practice Muskogee Children's Clinic, Okla., 2001—02; co-course coord. health promotion & disease prevention Okla. State U. Ctr. Health Sciences, 2002—04, asst. residency program dir., 2003—04, asst. prof. dept. pediat., 2002—07, acting chair dept. pediat., 2003, chmn. dept. pediat., 2004—11, St. Francis Health Systems endowed chair pediat., 2004—, assoc. prof. dept. pediat., 2007—09, prof. pediat., 2009—, interim v.p. acad. affairs, 2009—11, provost, dean Coll. Osteopathic Medicine and George Kaiser Family Found. chair in med. excellence and svc., 2011—. Mem. Okla. Med. Res. Corps, 2005—; bd. mem. Tulsa Coalition Children's Health, 2004—; mem. med. exec. com. St. Francis Children's Hosp., 2006—; bd. trustees Okla. State U. Med. Ctr., 2006—08; bd. dirs. Ronald McDonald House Charities, 2006—09. Mem.: Nat. Bd. Osteopathic Med. Examiners, American Osteopathic Bd. Pediat. (bd. trustees 2007—), American Osteopathic Assn. (mem. house dels. 2000, 2009), Okla. Osteopathic Assn. (mem. legis. com. 2002—03, post grad. edn. com. 2003—05, mem. Okla. State genetics bd. 2002—, bd. trustees 2008—, alt. mem. house dels. 2009—, mem. physician grievance com. 2009—10), Phi Theta Kappa, Ark. Alpha Epsilon Delta, Golden Key Honor Soc., Sigma Sigma Phi, Phi Kappa Phi. Office: Okla State University Ctr Health Sciences Office of Provost/Dean 1111 W 17th St Tulsa OK 74107 Office Phone: 918-582-1972. Business E-Mail: kayse.shrum@okstate.edu.

SHUB, HARVEY ALLEN, surgeon; b. Bklyn., Oct. 28, 1942; s. Irving and Sara (Levin) S.; m. Susan Jayne Smith, Dec. 26, 1970; children: Carolyn, Todd. Student, NYU, 1960-61, 64-65; BS in Zoology, Physics, U. Miami, 1964; MD, U. Rome, Italy, 1971. Diplomate Am. Bd. Colon and Rectal Surgery. Intern Beth Israel Med. Ctr., NYC, 1971-72, resident in surgery, 1972-76; fellow in colon and rectal surgery Muhlenberg Hosp., Plainfield, NJ, 1976-77; practice medicine specializing in colon and rectal surgery Orlando, Fla., 1977—; chmn. dept. surgery Fla. Hosp., 1988-89, dept. colon and rectal surgery, 1999—2001. Pres. med. staff Fla. Hosp., 1992-93; asst. cons. prof. dept. surgery Duke U., 1995; mem. staff Winter Park Meml. Hosp., South Seminole Cmty. Hosp., Fla. Hosp. and Med. Ctr., Orlando Regional Healthcare Sys.; clin. asst. prof. dept. family medicine U. South Fla., Tampa, 1982—; med. dir. Brevard Profl. Network, 2002-2004. Consulting editor Jour. Fla. Med. Assn.; contbr. articles to profl. jours. Chmn. pub. edn. com. Am. Cancer Soc. Orange County, 1982—86. Capt. M.C., USAR, 1971-77. Recipient Physician's Recognition awards AMA. Fellow ACS, Am. Soc. Colon and Rectal Surgeons, Internat. Coll. Surgeons, Southeastern Surg. Congress, Internat. Soc. Univ. Colon and Rectal Surgeons; mem. AMA, So. Med. Assn., Fla. Med. Assn. (sect. splty. medicine), Orange County Med. Assn., Piedmont Soc. Colon and Rectal Surgeons (pres. elect 1997, pres. 1998-2000), Orange County Ostomy Assn. (med. adviser), Fla. Soc. Colon and Rectal Surgeons (sec.-treas. 1980-82, pres. 1983-84, sec.-treas. 1986-98, pres. 1998-2000, treas. 2005—), Am. Soc. Gastrointestinal Endoscopy, Am. Soc. Laser Medicine and Surgery, Soc. Am. Gastrointestinal Endoscopic Surgeons. Home: 5252 Vista Club Run Sanford FL 32771-7153 Personal E-mail: tushmd4@aol.com.

SHUFF, RONALD F., lawyer; BA in History, Kenyon Coll., Gambier, Ohio, 1974; MS, MIT Sloan Sch.; JD, Capital U., Columbus, Ohio, 1977. Atty. Columbus & So. Electric Co., 1977-81; sec., gen. counsel Accuray Corp., Columbus, 1981—88; gen. counsel, asst. sec. Duriron Co., 1988—89, gen. counsel, sec., 1989—90; v.p., sec. & gen. counsel Durco Internat. (formerly Duriron Co.), 1990—97; gen. counsel Flowserve Corp., Irving, Tex., 1988—, sec., 1989—, v.p., 1990—2006, sr. v.p., 2006—. Sloan fellow, MIT, 1987-88. Office: Flowserve Corp 5215 N OConnor Blvd Ste 2300 Irving TX 75039 Office Phone: 972-443-6500. Office Fax: 972-443-6800. Business E-Mail: rshuff@flowserve.com.

SHUGAN, STEVEN MARK, business statistics and economics educator; b. Chgo., Apr. 21, 1952; s. David Lester and Charlotte Rose Shugan; m. Irene H. Shugan, Dec. 16, 1973; children: Adam Joshua, Elliot Hillel, Ross Isaac, Henry Andrew. BS in Chemistry, So. Ill. U., 1973, MBA, 1974; PhD in Managerial Econs. and Decision Scis., Northwestern U., 1978. Lectr. Grad Sch. Mgmt., Northwestern U., Evanston, Ill., 1975—76; asst. prof. bus. adminstrn. Grad Sch. Mgmt., U. Rochester, NY, 1977—79; asst. prof. mktg. Grad. Sch. Bus., U. Chgo., 1979—82, assoc. prof., 1982—87, prof., 1987—92; Russ Berrie eminent fellow, mktg. prof. U. Fla., Gainesville, 1991—2010, McKethan-Matherly eminent fellow, 2010—. Chmn., organizer sessions numerous nat. confs., 1979—; cons. various cos., 1976—; chmn. Mktg. Sci. Conf., 1963—96. Editor-in-chief Mktg. Sci., 2002—07; contbr. articles to profl. bus. jours. Recipient numerous awards. Mem.: Am. Statis. Assn., Inst. Mgmt. Scis. (pres. coll. mktg.), Assn. Consumer Rsch., Ops. Rsch. Soc. Am., Am. Mktg. Assn. Office: Univ Fla 209 Bryan Hall Gainesville FL 32611-2014 Business E-Mail: sms@ufl.edu.

SHUGART, JILL, retired school administrator; b. Dallas, July 15, 1940; d. Claude Ernest and Allie Merle (Hamilton) S. BA, Baylor U., 1962; MA, Tex. Woman's U., 1972, PhD, 1980. Middle sch. English tchr. Garland (Tex.) Ind. Sch. Dist., 1962-63, high sch. social studies tchr., 1963-76, high sch. asst. prin., 1976-79, dir. communications, 1979-82, asst. supt., 1982-85, supt., 1985—99, ret., 1999—; exec. dir. Region X Edn. Svc. Ctr., 2004—07. Mem. legis. coun. U. Interscholastic League, Tex., 1989-99; chmn. Dist. III music com., Tex., 1989-99; adj. prof. Tex. Women's U., Denton, 1983; chmn. Region X ESC Adv. Coun., rep. to commr.'s supt.'s com., 1993-95; cons. Richardson and Carrollton-Farmers Br. Sch. Dists., 2000-04; coord. Region 10 ESC Supr.'s Acad., 2000-04, mem. commrs. cabinet regional svcs., 2004-07. Gen. chmn. Boy Scouts Am. Scouting Night, Dallas, 1988-89; chmn. City of Garland Comty. Action Com., 1995-99; sec. Tex. Sch. Alliance, 1995-96, chmn., 1998-99; life mem. Tex. and nat. PTA; pres. Garland br. Am. Heart Assn., 1990-91; co-chmn. sustaining dr. Garland YMCA, 1995-96; mem. Adv. Com. to Gov. and State Legisture, 1998; mem. steering com. Garland Econ. Devel. Partnership, 1994-99, Tex. Fast Growth Sch. Coalition; chair Tex. Sch. Alliance, 1998—. Recipient Lamar award for excellence Masons, Award of Distinction, Tex. Ret. Tchrs. Assn.; named Top 100 Educators to Watch, Executive Educator mag., 1985, Finalist as Outstanding Tex. Sch. Supt., 1990, Woman of Distinction, Soroptomist Club, Disting. Alumnus, Garland H.S., 2005; Paul Harris fellow. Mem. Quality Tex. Bd. Examiners, Garland Edn. Found. (bd. dirs. 1999—), Baylor Med. Ctr. Garland (bd. dirs. 2001—10). Baptist. Avocations: travel, lake activities. Home: 345 Winding Shore Kemp TX 75143 Personal E-mail: jillshugart@aol.com.

SHULA, MIKE (MICHAEL JOHN SHULA), professional football coach, former college football coach; b. Balt., June 3, 1965; s. Donald F. and Mary S. Shula. BA in Labor Rels., U. Ala., 1987. Offensive asst. Tampa Bay Buccaneers, 1988—90, quarterbacks coach, 1990—91, offensive coord., 1996—99; coaches asst. Miami Dolphins, 1991—92, quarterbacks coach, 2001—02; asst. coach Chgo. Bears, 1993—95; head coach U. Ala., 2003—06; quarterbacks coach Jacksonville Jaguars, 2007—10, Carolina Panthers, 2011—. Office: Carolina Panthers 800 S Mint St Charlotte NC 28202

SHULER, ELLIE GIVAN, JR., retired military officer, museum administrator; b. Raleigh, NC, Dec. 6, 1936; s. Ellie Givan and Berta (Williams) S.; m. Annette Fontaine Maury, Mar. 22, 1961; children: Ellie Givan III, Franklin Maury, Gray Hays. BSCE, The Citadel, 1959; MS in Mgmt., Rensselaer Poly. Inst., 1967; grad., Squadron Officer Sch., Maxwell AFB, Ala., 1964; postgrad., Naval War Coll.; grad. command and staff course, Nat. War Coll., 1976; grad. cen. flight instr. course, Castle AFB, Calif. Engr. in tng., S.C. Commd. 2d lt. U.S. Air Force, 1959, advanced through grades to lt. gen., 1988, various positions and locations, 1959-68, F-4C pilot, asst. flight comdr. 558th Tactical Fighter Squadron Cam Ranh Bay AFB, Republic of Vietnam, 1968-69, indsl. engr., then asst. dep. chief Engring. Mgmt. Div., Hdqrs. 2d Air Force Barksdale AFB, La., 1969-71; asst. exec. officer to comdr. in chief U.S. Air Force in Europe, Lindsey Air Sta., West Germany, 1972-73, base civil engr., comdr. 86th Civil Engring. Squadron Ramstein Air Base, Fed. Republic Germany, 1973-75; dir. ops. 3902d Air Base Wing, comdr. 3902d Ops. Squadron Offutt AFB, Nebr., 1976; dir. programs Office Dep. Chief of Staff for Engring. and Services SAC, Offutt AFB, Nebr., 1976-77, exec. to comdr. in chief, 1977-79; vice comdr., then comdr. 19th Bombardment Wing Robins AFB, Ga., 1979-80; comdr. 42d Bombardment Wing Loring AFB, Maine, 1980-81; comdr. 4th Air Div. F.E. Warren AFB, Wyo., 1981-84; comdr. 3rd Air Div. SAC, Andersen AFB, Guam, 1984-86; asst. dep. then dep. chief of staff, ops. SAC Hqrs., Offutt AFB, Nebr., 1986-88; comdr. 8th Air Force SAC, Barksdale AFB, 1988-91; retired, 1991; chmn. bd., CEO 8th Air Force Heritage Mus., 1992—98. Trustee, Longs Peak coun. Boy Scouts Am., 1983-84, chair bd. trustees, 1992-2004; trustee Falcon Found., USAF Acad., 8th Air Force Heritage Mus., 1992—. Lt. gen. USAF. Decorated D.S.M. with oak leaf cluster, Legion of Merit with oak leaf cluster, D.F.C., Air medal with five oak leaf clusters, Air Force Commendation medal with oak leaf cluster; recipient medal of Honor DAR, 2005, Disting. Eagle Scout award Boy Scouts Am., 2006; named Disting. Alumnus, The Citadel, 2007; named to SC Aviation Hall of Fame, 2012. Mem. Soc. Am. Mil. Engrs. (chpt. pres. 1971), Am. Def. Preparedness Assn. (regional bd. dirs. 1981-84), Order of Dadaelians (hon. flight capt. 1981-85), Council on Am.'s Mil. Past, Mil. Order of World Wars, Kiwanis, Tau Beta Pi. Republican. Episcopalian. Avocations: numismatics, hunting, military, history. Home: 5914 Marthas Glen Rd Columbia SC 29209 Home Phone: 803-776-6462. Personal E-mail: egshulerjr@bellsouth.net.

SHULKIN, BARRY, physician; b. Amarillo, Tex., Apr. 2, 1952; s. Stanley and Harriet Shulkin; m. Patricia Ann Mandel, June 17, 1990; children: Zachary David, Jeffrey Daniel. BA, U. Tex., Austin, 1974; MD, U. Tex., Dallas, 1978; MBA, U. Mich., Ann Arbor, 2002. Prof. radiology U. Mich., Ann Arbor, 1999—2004; dir. nuc. medicine St. Jude Children's Rsch. Hosp., Memphis, 2004—. Chair fin. com. Am. Bd. Nuc. Medicine, St. Louis, 2004. Grantee, NIH, 1991—2001. Fellow: ACP. Avocation: running. Office: St Jude Children's Research Hospital 262 Danny Thomas Place Mail Stop 220 Memphis TN 38105

SHULMAN, ALLAN T., architect, architectural firm executive; BArch, Cornell U., Ithaca, NY, 1985; MArch in Suburb & Town Planning, U. Miami, 1992. Assoc. rsch. prof. U. of Miami Sch. of Architecture; founder, prin. Allan T. Shulman Arch., P.A., Miami, 1996—2007; prin. Shulman & Assocs., Miami, 2007—. Rsch. asst. prof. U. Miami Sch. Architecture. Co-author (with Jean-Francois Lejeune): The Making of Miami Beach: The Architecture of Lawrence Murray Dixon 1933-42, 2000; prin. works include Browns Hotel (AIA Fla. Merit award, 2005), Fairwind Hotel (AIA Fla. Honor award, 2006), 354 Washington (AIA Miami Award of Excellence, 2006), Lindemann Residence (Dade Heritage Trust award, 2007), Anglers Resort and Spa (Dade Heritage Trust award, 2007), Chrysler Bldg./Apple Store (Dade Heritage Trust award, 2007, Miami Design Preservation League award, 2007). Office: Shulman & Associate 100 NE 38th St Space 2 Miami FL 33137-3654 Office Phone: 305-438-0609. Office Fax: 305-438-0170. E-mail: allan@shulmanarchitect.com.

SHULMAN, ROBERT JAY, pediatrician, nutritionist, gastroenterologist, educator; b. Newark; s. Irving Jack and Shirley Shulman; children: David Ian, Hannah Rachel. BA, Emory U., 1972; MD, Chgo. Med. Sch., 1976. Diplomate in pediatrics and pediatric gastroenterology Am. Bd. Pediatrics. Asst. prof. pediat. Baylor Coll. Medicine, Houston, 1982-89, assoc. prof., 1989—96, prof., 1996—2008; dir. nutritional support team Tex. Children's Hosp., Houston, 1982—2008. Chmn. sub-bd. in pediatric gastroenterology Am. Bd. Pediatrics, 2003—06; chmn., nutrition com. North Am. Soc. Pediat. Gastroenterology, Hepatology and Nutrition, 2007—08. Author: Young Chef's Nutrition Guide and Cookbook, 1990, Keys to Child Nutrition, 1991; author: (with others) Pediatric Gastroenterology and Nutrition in Clinical Practice, 2001, Principles and Practice of Pediatrics, 2006, Pediatric Nutrition Support, 2007; co-editor: Nutrition in Your Pocket, 2002; mem. editl. bd. Jour. Pediat. Gastroenterology and Nutrition, 1994—96. Fellow: Am. Acad. Pediat.; mem.: Soc. Pediat. Rsch., N.Am. Soc. Pediat. Gastoenterology and Nutrition (exec. coun. 1997—99), Am. Inst. Nutrition, Am. Soc. Patenteral and Enteral Nutrition (chmn. pediatric sect. 1997—99, pres. 1997—99), Am. Gastroent. Assn. Avocation: guitar. Office: Baylor Coll Medicine 1100 Bates Ave Houston TX 77030-2600

SHULMISTER, M(ORRIS) ROSS, lawyer; b. Atlanta, Jan. 6, 1940; s. Morris and Kathryn Sybella (Baker) S.; m. Benita Vee Rosin, Dec. 16, 1974. BEE, U. Fla., 1962, JD, 1973. Bar: Fla. 1973, U.S. Dist. Ct. (so. dist.) Fla. 1974, U.S. Dist. Ct. (mid. dist.) Fla. 1985, U.S. Ct. Appeals (5th and 11th cirs.) 1981. Pvt. practice, Broward County, Fla., 1974—. Spl. master for code enforcement, Pompano Beach, Fla., 1991-92. Mem. Broward County Consumer Protection Bd., 1983-2001, chmn., 1999-2000; chmn. Charter Review Bd., Pompano Beach, Fla., 1994-97; mem. Zoning Bd. Appeals, Pompano Beach, Fla., 2008-; dir. South Pompano Civic Assn., 1989-2000, 2007-, v.p., 1989, pres., 1992-98, 2008-. Lt. col. USAF, 1964-70, ret., USAFR, 1970-93. Mem. Fla. Bar (mem. constrn. law subcom., civil trial cert. 1984-99), Broward County Bar Assn. (bd. dirs. 2003-06). Office: 560 SE 12th St Pompano Beach FL 33060-9409

SHULTIS, ROBERT LYNN, retired finance educator, professional society administrator, consultant, corporate financial executive; b. Kingston, NY, June 30, 1924; s. Albert H. and Dorothy Elizabeth (Jenkins) S.; m. Bernice Elizabeth Johnson, Jan. 20, 1946; 1 son, Robert Lee. BS, Columbia Univ. Sch. Bus., 1949, postgrad., 1949-51. Staff acct. Price Waterhouse, NYC, 1949-52; credit mgr., controller Organon, Inc., West Orange, NJ, 1952-68; v.p., treas., chief fin. officer Arwood Corp., Rockleigh, NJ, 1968-72; v.p., controller Technicon, Tarrytown, NY, 1972-80; exec. dir. Inst. of Mgmt. Accts., Montvale, NJ, 1980-86; faculty, exec. dir. Ctr. for Exec. Devel. Coll. William & Mary, Williamsburg, Va., 1987-91. Instr. Rutgers U., 1964-74, Fairleigh Dickinson U., 1967-68; mem. Fin. Acctg. Standards Adv. Coun., 1981-86; lectr., seminar leader, cons. on controllership, activity-based costing, cost mgmt., cost sys. design Boston U., U. Calif., Berkeley, U. Minn., Michigan State U., So. Meth. U., Baldwin Wallace Coll., George Mason U., James Madison U., U. N.C., Colo. State U., others, 1990—. Editor: Management Accountants' Handbook, and supplements, 1991-94; contbr. articles to profl. jours. Bd. advs. U. Fla. Sch. Accountancy, James Madison U. Sch. Accountancy; fin. and budget com. Kingsmill Cmty. Svcs. Assn.; interpreter Historic Jamestowne Island, 1997-07; Citizens Budget Advisory Com., Williamsburg, James City, With USAF, 1943-45 Decorated Presdl. Unit Citation, ETO Ribbon, eight battle stars. Mem. AAUP, Am. Legion, Fin. Execs. Internat., Inst. Mgmt. Accts., Assn. for Preservation of Va. Antiquities, Kingsmill Club, Beta Alpha Psi (adv. forum). Office Phone: 757-229-6964.

SHUMATE, JABAR, state legislator; b. Tulsa, Okla., Jan. 26, 1976; s. Glenn Shumate and Cleatta Johnson, Joseph Johnson (Stepfather). BA in Public Affairs and Adminstration, Univ. Okla.; MHR in Human Resource Development, Univ. Okla., Tulsa. Mentor Hawthorne Elementary Sch.; former press sec. Univ. Okla.; public relations cons.; mem. Dist. 73 Okla. House of Representatives, 2005—. Democrat. Baptist. Mailing: PO Box 48514 Tulsa OK 74148 Office: 2300 N Lincoln Blvd Rm 510 Oklahoma City OK 73105 Office Phone: 405-557-7406. E-mail: jabarshumate@okhouse.gov.

SHUSTER, FREDERICK, retired internist, gastroenterologist; b. Newark, Sept. 12, 1933; s. Ralph and Anne (Weinstein) S.; m. Jane A. Block, June 11, 1958; children: Alan R., Robert G. BS, Rutgers U., 1955; MD, U. Chgo., 1959. Diplomate Am. Bd. Internal Medicine, Am. Bd. Gastroenterology. Intern U. Mich. Hosp., Ann Arbor, 1959-60, resident internal medicine, 1960-62; resident gastroenterology VA Hosp. U. Miami, Fla., 1962-63; pvt. practice N. Miami Beach, Fla., 1963-97; from clin. instr. to assoc. prof. medicine U. Miami, Fla., 1963—; pvt. practice Aventura, Fla., 1997-98, North Miami Beach; ret., 1998. Chmn. dept. medicine Parkway Regional Med. Ctr., N. Miami Beach, 1967, 70, chief of staff, 1974-75, chief divsn. gastroenterology, 1976-77, chmn. pharmacy and therapeutics com., 1978-98. Chmn. med. advisory com. Crohn's and Colitis Found., S. Fla. chpt., Miami, 1979-81. Major U.S. Army, 1967-69. Recipient Physician's Recognition award in Continung Edn., AMA, Chgo., 1970—. Fellow Am. Coll. Physicians, Am. Coll. Gastroenterology, Alpha Omega Alpha. Jewish. Avocations: bowling, ballroom dancing, stock market research and investing. E-mail: fred991@att.net.

SHUSTERMAN, NATHAN, underwriter, financial consultant; b. Montreal, Que., Can., Aug. 27, 1927; arrived in US, 1950; s. Aaron and Annie (Nulman) S.; m. Norma Thalblum, Jan. 1950; children: Mark D., Claudia S. Student, Sir George Williams Coll., Montreal, 1944-47; grad., N.Y. Inst. Fin. CLU, chartered fin. cons. Retailing mgr. Jefferson Stores, Miami, Fla., 1950-65; gen. agt. Protective Life Ins. Co., Miami, 1965—. Chmn. emeritus field adv. coun., past pres. Protective Club; pres. Am. Fin. Counseling Corp., Miami; instr. estate and tax planning Am. Coll., Bryn Mawr, Pa., 1972—, U. Miami, Coral Gables, Fla., 1972—; registered rep. Pro Equity Services Inc.; cons. in field. Named Man of Yr., Gen. Agts. and Mgrs. Assn., Miami, 1965-67. Mem. North Dade-South Broward Estate Planning Coun., Million Dollar Round Table (life), Top of Table, Assn. Advanced Life Underwriting, Soc. Fin. Svc. Profls. (past pres. Miami chpt.), Nat. Assn. Ins. and Fin. Advisors (Nat. Sales Achievement award, Nat. Quality award), Fla. Assn. Ins. and Fin. Advisors, Miami Assn. Ins. and Fin. Advisors, Internat. Assn. Fin. Planners, Am. Soc. Pension Actuaries (assoc.), Optimists (pres. North Miami Beach, Fla. chpt. 1971), Masons, Shriners, B'nai B'rith (pres. Miami chpt. 1950). Office: Am Fin Counseling Corp 16121 NE 18th Ave Miami FL 33162-4749 Home: 21050 NE 38th Ave Apt 1701 Miami FL 33180-4078 Office Phone: 305-949-0906.

SHUSTERMAN, RICHARD MARC, philosophy educator; b. Phila., Dec. 3, 1949; s. Murray H. and Judith Carol (Weiner) S.; m. Rivka Nahmani, Aug. 16, 1970 (div. Oct. 1987); children: Damon, Aelia, Eden; m. Erica Ando, March 14, 2000; 1 child, Talia. BA magna cum laude, Hebrew U., Jerusalem, 1972, MA magna cum laude, 1974; DPhil, Oxford U., 1979. Lectr. Ben-Gurion U., Beer-Sheva, Israel, 1980-82, sr. lectr., 1983-87; lectr. Bezalel Acad. of Art, Jerusalem, 1980-81, Hebrew U., Jerusalem, 1981-83; assoc. prof. Temple U., Phila., 1985-92, prof., 1992—2004, chair dept. philosophy, 1998—2004; Schmidt eminent scholar chair in humanities Fla. Atlantic U., Boca Raton, 2005—. Vis. fellow St. John's Coll. Oxford U., Eng., 1984-85; vis. prof. Coll. Internat. de Philosophie, Paris, 1990-92, program dir., 1995—; vis. prof. New Sch. Social Rsch., NYC, 1992-2002; vis. prof. Hiroshima U., Japan, 2002-03; dir. d'Etudes associés Ecole des hautes etudes en sciences sociales, Paris, 1990; Fulbright prof., Berlin, 1995-96; vis. prof. U. Paris, 09-10, U. Rome, 2011, U. Lyon, 2011-12. Author: The Object of Literary Criticism, 1984, T.S. Eliot and the Philosophy of Criticism, 1988, Pragmatist Aesthetics, 1992, 2d edit., 2000, L'art à l'état vif, 1992, Kunst Leben, 1994, Sous l'interpretation, 1994, Practicing Philosophy, 1997, Performing Live, 2000, Philosophie als Lebenspraxis, 2001, Vivre la Philosophie, 2001, Surface and Depth, 2002, Conscience du Corps., 2007, Body Conciousness: A Philosophy of Mindfulness and Somaethetics, 2008, Soma-esthétique et architecture, 2010, Thinking through the Body: Essays in Somaesthetics, 2012, Chemins de l'art 2013; editor: Analytic Aesthetics, 1989, Relativism, Interpretation, and the Metaphysics of Culture, 1999, Bourdieu: A Critical Reader, The Range of Pragmatism and the Limits of Philosophy, Aesthetic Experience; mem. editl. bd. Jour. Metaphilosophy, 1993, Yeats-Eliot Rev., 1988, Constellations, 1993, Poetics Today, 1997, Jour. Aesthetics and Art Criticism, 1999, Jour. Speculative Philosophy, 1999, Contemporary Pragmatism, 2010. Recipient Rsch. award Israeli Nat. Lottery Found., 1975; grantee NEH, 1988, Am. Coun. Learned Socs., 1988; fellow NEH, 1990, Fulbright Found., 1995-96, Humboldt Transcoop, 2006-09, French Ordre des Palmes Académique. Fellow: Japan Soc. Promotion Sci., mem. Am. Philos. Assn. (advisor to program com. 1989-92), Am. Soc. for Aesthetics (steering com. 1989-92, trustee 2000-2003), Greater Phila. Philosophy Consortium (assoc. dir. 1991-2004), Soc. Advancement Am. Philosophy, Feldenkrais Guild Democrat. Jewish. Avocations: music, hiking, running, t'ai chi. Office: Fla Atlantic U Coll Arts and Letters 777 Glades Rd Boca Raton FL 33431

SHUTTLEWORTH, THOMAS B., II, lawyer; b. Evanston, Ill., Oct. 27, 1945; BS, Fla. Atlantic U., 1967; JD, Washington & Lee U. Law Sch., Lexington, Va., 1973. Bar: Va. 1973, US Dist. Ct. (ea. dist.) Va. 1973, US Ct. Appeals (4th cir.) 1974, US Supreme Ct. 1976. Shareholder, sr. ptnr. Shuttleworth, Ruloff, Swain, Haddad & Morecock, PC, Virginia Beach, 1987—. Adj. prof. William & Mary Sch. Law, Williamsburg, Va., 1995—98. Named Norfolk Area Best Lawyers Personal Injury Litigator of Yr., 2009; named one of The Legal Elite, Va. Bus. mag., 2003—05, Va.'s Top 50 Superlawyers, Richmond Mag., 2007; named to Best Lawyers in America, 1991—2011. Fellow: Internat. Acad. Trial Lawyers; mem.: AAJ, FBA (pres. Tidewater chpt. 1989), Va. State Bar, Va. Trial Lawyers Assn. (bd. governors 1978—84, 2006—), Million Dollar Advocates Forum. Office: Shuttleworth Ruloff Swain Haddad & Morecock PC 4525 S Blvd Ste 300 Virginia Beach VA 23452 Office Phone: 757-671-6020. Office Fax: 757-671-6004. Business E-Mail: tshuttleworth@srgslaw.com.

SHVEDOVA, YAROSLAVA, professional tennis player; b. Moscow, Nov. 12, 1987; Achievements include winning (singles) Warsaw, 2003, Amiens, 2006; (doubles) Amiens, 2006, Biarritz, 2006, ITF; winning Sony Ericsson Internat., 2007, US Open (with King), 2010, WTA. Office: WTA 100 2nd Ave S Ste 1100 Saint Petersburg FL 33701-4338

SI, QIMIAO, physics professor; b. Zhuji, Zhejiang, China, Jan. 18, 1966; BS in Physics, U. Sci. and Tech. China, Hefei, Anhui, 1986; PhD in Physics, U. Chgo., 1991. Harry C. and Olga K. Wiess prof. physics Rice U., Houston, 1995—. Contbr. articles to sci. jours. Fellow: Am. Phys. Soc., Inst. Physics, Eng., Alfred P. Sloan Found.; mem.: Am. Assn. Adv. Sci. Office: Rice Univ Dept Phys MS61 6100 Main St Houston TX 77005

SIBBALD, JOHN RISTOW, management consultant; b. Lincoln, Nebr., June 20, 1936; s. Garth E.W. and Rachel (Wright) S.; div.; children: Allison, John, Wright. BA, U. Nev., 1958; MA, U. Ill., 1964. Office mgr. Hewitt Assocs., Libertyville, Ill., 1964-66; coll. rels. mgr. Pfizer Inc., NYC, 1966-69; pres., CEO Re-Con Systems, NYC, 1969-70; v.p. Booz, Allen & Hamilton, NYC, 1970-73, Chgo., 1973-75; pres., founder John Sibbald Assocs., Inc., Chgo., 1975. Mem. Nat. Advisory Coun., Nat. Club Assn. Author: The Career Makers, 1990, 92, The New Career Makers, 1995; pub. Club Leaders Forum, Platinum Clubs of America; contbr. articles to profl. jours. Capt. AUS, 1958-64. Mem. St. Louis Club, Anvil Club. Episcopalian. Office: 4246 Sea Grape Dr Apt 1 Lauderdale By The Sea FL 33308 Office Phone: 314-304-8146. Business E-Mail: jsibbald@sibbaldassociates.com.

SIBLEY, JAMES MALCOLM, retired lawyer; b. Atlanta, Aug. 5, 1919; s. John Adams and Nettie Whitaker (Cone) S.; m. Karen Norris, Apr. 6, 1942; children: Karen Mariea, James Malcolm Jr., Jack Norris, Elsa Alexandria Victoria, Quintus Whitaker. AB, Princeton U., 1941; student, Woodrow Wilson Sch. Law, 1942, Harvard Law Sch., 1945—46. Bar: Ga. 1942. Assoc. King & Spalding, Atlanta, 1942-47, ptnr., 1947-91. Bd. dirs. Summit Industries, Inc.; exec. com., mem. pub. affairs com. Coca-Cola Co., 1979-91; chmn. exec. com. John H. Harland Co., 1963-91; chmn. exec. com., mem. compensation com. Trust Co. of Ga., 1975-92; mem. exec. com., mem. compensation com. SunTrust Banks, Inc., 1985-92. Trustee Joseph B. Whitehead Found., Lettie Pate Evans Found., A.G. Rhodes Home, Inc., Robert W. Woodruff Found., Inc. (formerly Trebor Found.); trustee emeritus John H. and Wilhelmina D. Harland Charitable Found., Inc., Berry Coll., The Lovett Sch., Callaway Gardens Found., Emory U. With USAF, 1942—45. Mem. ABA, Ga. Bar Assn., Atlanta Bar Assn., Am. Coll. Probate Counsel, Am. Bar Found., Am. Law Inst., Piedmont Driving Club, Commerce Club. Episcopalian. Home: 3045 Slaton Dr NW Atlanta GA 30305-2006

SICHEWSKI, VERNON ROGER, physician; b. Winnipeg, Man., Can., Dec. 10, 1942; came to U.S., 1980; s. Nicholas and Helen (Sabanski) S. BS, U. Man., 1963; MD, Cairo U., 1979. Diplomate Am. Bd. Emergency Medicine. Resident Charity Hosp. La., New Orleans, 1980-83, Bellevue Hosp., NYC, 1980-83; pvt. practice Broward Gen. Med. Ctr., Ft. Lauderdale, Fla., 1983-86, Trauma Care Assocs., North Miami, Fla., 1986—2003. Flight physician Nat. Jets, Ft. Lauderdale, 1986-1998; mem. Aero Jet Internat. Air Ambulance Profls., 1989-2011; attending physician trauma unit Jackson Meml. Hosp. U. Miami, 1989-97; attending physician Cleve. Clin. Found. Hosp., Ft. Lauderdale, 1999-2006. Flight lt. RCAF, 1963-74. Fellow Am. Coll. Emergency Physicians; mem. AMA, So. Med. Assn. Republican. Roman Catholic. Avocations: stamp collecting/philately, hunting, fishing, antiques. Home: 1108-2841 N Ocean Blvd Fort Lauderdale FL 33308 Personal E-mail: v5561229@comcast.net.

SICIUS, FRANCIS JOSEPH, history professor, writer; b. Phila., Nov. 4, 1949; s. Elizabeth Jane Sicius-Cipollone and Vincent Cipollone (Stepfather); m. Isabel Cristina Valenzuela-Schrader, May 13, 1995; children: Laurie-Anna Regina, Paulina Francisca, Lucia Isabel. BA, Fla. State U., 1971, MA, 1973; PhD, Loyola U., 1979. Prof. history St. Thomas U., Miami Gardens, Fla., 1979—. Author: The Word Made Flesh: The Chicago Catholic Worker and the Rise of Lay Activism in the Catholic Church, 1990, (biography) Peter Maurin Apostle to the World, 2004 (Second Place Biography of Yr. award, 2004), Encyclopedia of American Life 1900-1940, 2008. Fellow, NEH, 1996—97, 2002. Mem.: Am. Cath. Hist. Assn., Am. Hist. Assn. Democrat. Roman Catholic. Office: St Thomas U 16401 NW 37 Ave Miami FL 33179 Office Fax: 305-628-6764. Business E-Mail: fsicius@stu.edu.

SICKLES, MARK D., state legislator; b. Arlington, Va., Feb. 18, 1957; BS in Forest Mgmt., Clemson U., SC, 1981; MS in Indsl. Mgmt., Ga. Inst. Tech., Atlanta, 1984, MS in Tech. and Sci. Policy, 1986. Corp. affairs exec. Weeks Marine Inc. Corp.; chmn. Fairfax County Dem. Com., Va., 1995—98; mem. Dist. 43 Va. House of Delegates, 2004—, minority caucus sec. Recipient Lord Fairfax award, 1999; named Citizen of Week, Springfield Connection. Mem.: United Cmty. Ministries (bd. dir. 1995—2001, pres. 2000), Fairfax County Pub. Library (bd. trustee 1993—2004, chmn. 1998—2000). Democrat. Presbyterian. Office: PO Box 10628 Alexandria VA 22310 Office Phone: 703-922-6440. Office Fax: 703-922-6880. Business E-Mail: DelMSickles@house.virginia.gov.

SIDDALL, PAMELA K., publishing executive; b. Phenix City, Ga., 1968; m. Greg Siddall; 2 children. BA in Acctg., Columbus State U., Ga., 1991. Sr. fin. analyst W.C. Bradley Co., Columbus, 1991—94; contr. lic. product divsn. Russell Corp., 1994—97; CFO Columbus Ledger-Enquirer, 1997—2001, v.p., gen. mgr., 2003—04, pres., pub., 2004—10; v.p., CFO Macon Telegraph, Ga., 2001—03; pub. Birmingham News, Ala., 2010—. Office: The Birmigham News 2200 4th Ave N Birmingham AL 35203

SIDDONS, ANNE RIVERS, writer; b. Atlanta, Jan. 9, 1936; m. Heyward Siddons, 1966; 4 stepchildren. BA, Auburn U., Ala., 1958. Former sr. editor Atlanta mag. Author: (novels) Heartbreak Hotel, 1976, The House Next Door, 1978, Fox's Earth, 1981, Homeplace, 1987, Peachtree Road, 1988, Kings Oak, 1990, Outer Banks, 1991, Colony, 1992, Hill Towns, 1993, Downtown, 1994, Fault Lines, 1995, Up Island, 1997, Low Country, 1998, Nora, Nora, 2000, Islands, 2003, Sweetwater Creek, 2005, Off Season, 2009, Burnt Mountain, 2010, (nonfiction) John Chancellor Makes Me Cry, 1975.

SIDHWA, BAPSI, writer; b. Karachi, Aug. 11, 1938; Grad., Kinnaird Coll. for Women, Lahore. Bd. dirs. Inprint, Houston, 1999—2007, adv. bd.; writer-in-residence Mt. Holyoke Coll., english prof.; spokesperson active women's rights Asian Women's Congress, 1975; tchr. coll.-level english courses St. Thomas Univ., Houston, Rice Univ., The Univ. of Texas; tchr. grad. level Columbia Univ., NY. Author: (novels) Cracking India (LiBeraturepreis award, 1991, listed among the 200 best books in English by The Modern Libr., 1999), The Pakistani Bride, The Crow Eaters (David Higham award), An American Brat, Water (Primo Mondello award, 2007), (plays) Sock 'em With Honey, (anthologies) City of Sin and Splendour: Writings on Lahore, 2006. Recipient Sitara-i-Imtiaz award, Pakistan, 1991, Nat. award for English Lit. by the Pakistan Acad. of Letters, 1991, Patras Bokhari award for Lit., 1992, Lila Wallace-Reader's Digest Writers' award, 1993, Excellence in Lit. award, Zoroastrian Congress, Chicago, 2002, South Asian Excellence awards for Lit., NY, 2008, Houston Cmty. Coll. Asian-Am. Legacy award, 2008; named Zoroastrian Hall of Fame, Houston, 2000; fellow Bunting at Radcliffe/Harvard - Mary Ingraham Inst., 1986—87, Nat. Endowment for the Arts, 1987; vis. scholar Rockefeller Foundn. Study Ctr., Bellagio, Italy, 1991. Mailing: c/o University of St Thomas 3800 Montrose Houston TX 77006-4626

SIEGAL, GENE PHILIP, pathology educator; b. Bronx, NY, Nov. 16, 1948; s. Murray H. and Evelyne (Philips) S.; m. Sandra Helene Meyerowitz, Aug. 3, 1972; children: Gail Deborah, Rebecca Stacey. BA, Adelphi U., Garden City, NY, 1970; MD, U. Louisville, 1974; PhD, U. Minn., 1979; cert. in hosp. mgmt., U. N.C., 1988. Diplomate Nat. Bd. Med. Examiners, Am. Bd. Pathology. Intern, resident, rsch. fellow Mayo Clinic Found., Rochester, Minn., 1974-79; rsch. assoc. Lab. Pathophysiology, Nat. Cancer Inst., NIH, Bethesda, Md., 1979-81; fellow surg. pathology U. Minn., Mpls., 1981-82; asst. prof. pathology U. N.C., Chapel Hill, 1982-88, assoc. prof. pathology, 1988-90; mem. Lineberger Comprehensive Cancer Ctr., Chapel Hill, 1983-90; prof. pathology U. Ala., Birmingham, 1990—2008, prof. cell devel. and integrative biology, prof. surgery, 1991—, sr. scientist, group leader breast, ovary, prostate program, Comprehensive Cancer Ctr., 1993—99, Robert W. Mowry Endowed prof. Pathology, 2008—; exe. vice chair, pathology U. Ala. Health Sys., 2008—. Mem. editl. bd. Yearbook of Pathology, 1983-91, Archives of Pathology and Lab. Medicine, 1990-91, Am. Jour. Clin. Pathology, 1990—, Modern Pathology, 1996—, Advances in Anat. Pathology, 1999-, Am. Jour. Surg. Pathology, 2000-, Annals Diagnostic Pathology, 2003-, Skeletal Radiology, 2003-, Lab. Investigation, 2004-08, Jour. Molecular Medicine, 2005-, CAP Today, 2005-, Human Pathology, 2005-, Am. jour. Translocational Res., 2009-, Open Breast Cancer Jour., 2009-, Musculoskeletal and Spinal Diseases, 2009-, Cancer Growth and Metastasis, 2009-, Clin. Medicine: Pathology, 2009-, Jour. Cytology & Histology, 2010-, The Open Jour. Pathology, 2011-, Frontiers in Pediat. Oncology, 2011-; mem. Children's Cancer Study Group, 1987-90, Pediatric Oncology Group, 1990-2000, Children's Oncology Group, 2001—, mem. Ewing's sarcoma com.; sr. scientist Ctr. for Aging, Cell Adhesion and Matrix Rsch. Ctr., 1995—, Ctr. Metabolic Bone Disease, 1997—, Gene Therapy Ctr., 2000—11; editor-in-chief Lab. Investigation, 2008-. Co-editor: Molecular Antibodies in Diagnostic Immunohistochemistry, 1988, Updates in Diagnostic Pathology, 2003, Frozen Section Library: Bone, 2011, Laboratory Administration for Pathologists, 2011, Atlas of Non-neoplastic Pathology: Non-neoplastic Diseases of Bones & Joints, vol. 9, 2011, Atlas of Bone Pathology, 2013; sr. assoc. editor Am. Jour. Pathology, 2003-08; assoc. editor Archives of Pathology and Lab. Medicine, 1989-90; sect. editor, 2006-. With USPHS, 1979-81. Clin. fellow Am. Cancer Soc., Chapel Hill, 1981-82, jr. faculty fellow, 1983-86, Jefferson-Pilot fellow in acad. medicine, U. N.C., Chapel Hill, 1985-86. Fellow Am. Soc. Clin. Pathologists (bd. dirs. 2005-06, 2011-, chair fellows coun. 2005-06, mem. ann. meeting com. 2004-, membership com. 2005-), Coll. Am. Pathologists (insp. 1990—, mem. surg. pathol. and vice chair pub. coms. 2009-10, chair, pub. com. 2010-13), Royal Soc. Medicine (London); mem. AMA, AAAS, Internat. Skeletal Soc. (exe. com. 2007-10), Am. Soc. for Investigative Pathology (councilor 2002-05, mem. publs. com. 2005-08), U.S. and Can. Acad. Pathology (abstract rev. bd. 1989-91, 2003-05), A.P. Stout Surg. Pathologists (pres. 2005-07, chair exec. com. 2005-09), Metastasis Rsch. Soc., Am. Assn. Cancer Rsch., Assn. Dirs. Anatomic and Surg. Pathology (coun. 2000-05, mem. Castleman award com. 2005-08), Intersoc. Pathology Coun. (sec.-treas. exec. com. 2003-07, chair 2007-09), Sigma Xi (pres. chpt. 1989-90), Alpha Omega Alpha, Phi Beta Delta, Internat. Soc. Bone & Soft Tissue pathology(At-Large officer, 2012-), Mayo Clinic Alumni Assn.(bd. dirs., 2013-) Democrat. Jewish. Office: University Ala at Birmingham Dept Pathology HSB 149 K Birmingham AL 35249 Office Phone: 205-934-6608. Business E-Mail: gsiegal@uab.edu.*

SIEGEL, BETTY LENTZ, president emeritus; b. Cumberland, Ky., Jan. 24, 1931; d. Carl N. and Vera (Hogg) Lentz; m. Joel H. Siegel, June 6; children: David Jonathan, Michael Jeremy. BA, Wake Forest U., 1952; M in Edn., U. NC, 1953; PhD, Fla. State U., 1961; postgrad., Ind. U., 1964-66; doctorate (hon.), Miami U., 1985, Cumberland Coll., 1985, Ea. Ky. U., 1992, Morehead State U., 2002; degree (hon.), Lynchburg Coll., So. Conn. State U. Asst. prof. Lenoir Rhyne Coll., Hickory, N.C., 1956-59; assoc. prof., 1961-64; asst. prof. U. Fla., Gainesville, 1967-70, assoc. prof., 1970-72, prof., 1973-76, dean acad. affairs for continuing edn., 1972-76; dean Sch. Edn. and Psychology Western Carolina U., Cullowhee, N.C., 1976-81; pres. Kennesaw State U., Marietta, Ga., 1981—2006, chair, leaderships, ethics & character; disting. chair Siegel Inst. Leadership, Ethics, and Character. Bd. dirs. Nat. Services Industries; cons. numerous sch. systems. Author: Problem Situations in Teaching, 1971; co-author: Becoming An Invitational Leadership, 2002; contbr. articles to profl. jours. Bd. dirs. United Way Atlanta, Ga. Partnership for Excellence in Edn., Ga. Coun. Econ. Edn., Northside Hosp. Found., Atlanta Ballet; Ga. rep. so. growth policy bd. Commn. on Future of South, 1998. Recipient Disting. Tchr. of Yr. award U. Fla., 1969; Mortar Bd. Woman of Yr. award U. Fla., 1973, Mortar Bd. Educator of Yr., Ga. State U., 1983, CASE award, 1986, Alumna of Yr. award Wake Forest U., 1987, "Grad Made Good" award Fla. State U. Alumni Assn, Omicron Delta Kappa, 1991, Spirit of Life award City of Hope, 1992, Woman of Achievement award Cobb Chamber YWCA, 1992, First Lifetime Achievement award YWCA, N.W. Ga., Oak award outstanding Alumni Ky., 1998, Adminstrv. Leadership award Assn. Gerontology in Higher Edn., 2001, Women in Bus. Lifetime Achievement award, 2001, Peabody award UNC-Chapel Hill Sch. Edn., 2003, Justice Robert Benham award outstanding leadership, svc. and commitment equality of all citizens Black's United for Youth of Cobb County, 2004, Howard Washington Thurman Ecumenical award Morehouse Coll.'s Martin Luther King, Jr. Internat. Chapel, 2005, Leita Thompson Lifetime Achievement award; named 50 Most Influential Women in Ga., One of 100 Most Influential People in State of Ga., Ga. Trend Mag., Outstanding Alumni, Fla. State U. Coll. Edn. Alumni Assn., 1992, Cobb Citizen of Yr., 1996, Ga. Woman of Yr. Ga. Commn. Women, 1997, Divas for Life Bus. to Bus. Mag., 2001, 100 Most Disting. Alumni Cumberland Coll.; named to Jr. Achievement Hall of Fame, 1999, 20 Women Making a Mark on Atlanta Atlanta mag., 20 Yrs., 20 Leaders Ga. Trend mag., Ga. Author of Yr., One Bank GCAPP, 2006, Longest Woman U. Pres., USA, First U. Pres., Ga. Regents U. Mem. Am. Psychol. Assn., Am. Assn. State Colls. and Univs. (bd. dirs., chmn. 1990), Am. Coun. Edn. (bd. dirs., bd. advisors), Am. Inst. Mng. Diversity (bd. dis.), Soc. Internat. Bus. Fellows, Commn. on Women in Higher Edn., Internat. Alliance Invitational Edn. (co-founder, co-dir.), Nat. Ctr. Study of Freshman Yr. Experience, So. Inst. Bus. and Profl. Ethics (mem. gov. bd.), Am. Cancer Soc. (Cobb chpt.), Cobb Exec. Women (founder), Ga. Exec. Women's Network, Internat. Bus. Forum, State Bar Ga., Found. Freedom, Bus./Higher Edn. Forum, mem. exec. com.), Cobb C. of C. (chair 1996), Kiwanis (Atlanta chpt.), Am. Humaries, Inc., Phi Alpha Theta, Pi Kappa Delta, Alpha Psi Omega, Kappa Delta Pi, Pi Lambda Theta, Phi Delta Kappa, Delta Kappa Gamma. Office: Office of the President Emeritus 1000 Chastain Rd MD 91C Kennesaw GA 30144-5591 Office Phone: 678-797-2222. E-mail: b.siegel@kennesaw.edu.

SIEGEL, GEORGE HENRY, management consultant; b. Bklyn., Oct. 8, 1926; s. Samuel S. and Sara Siegel; m. Lenore D. Greenberg, Oct. 28, 1951; children: Arthur B., Ellen S. BEE, CCNY, 1948; MS Indsl. Engring, NYU, 1951. Licensed profl. engr., N.Y. From engr. to gen. mgr. Gen. Electric Corp., Syracuse, Utica and Binghamton, NY, 1951-74; v.p., gen. mgr. flight systems div. Bendix Corp., 1974-77, chief tech. officer, 1977-79, v.p., gen. mgr. diesel engine controls, 1979-82; dir. Engring. Soc. Detroit, 1977—78; v.p., group exec.

Bendix Automation Co., Cleve., 1983-84; v.p. tech. Allied-Signal Internat., Morristown, NJ, 1984-90; founding dir. Nat. Ctr. Mfg. Scis., 1986—87; v.p. Volt Tech. Svcs. Co., NYC, 1991-93; pres. Point North Assocs., Inc., Madison, NJ, 1990—2005. Invited guest lectr. UCLA, 1960-63. Bd. visitors Oakland U., Rochester, Mich., 1977-83. Served with AUS, 1944-46, AF Res., 1946-52. Mem. IEEE (sr., life, sect. chmn. 1965-2007), Soc. Automotive Engrs. Personal E-mail: siegelgh@att.net.

SIEGEL, MATTHEW, retail executive; b. Los Angeles; BS, Northwestern U. With CitySearch, eToys.com, LivePlanet, Warner Brothers Studios; dir., product devel. GameFly.com; dir., product mgmt. Ticketmaster.com; v.p., product mgmt. HSN, Inc., 2003; v.p., E-Retail Strategy HSN.com, 2006—. Office: HSN Inc 1 HSN Dr Saint Petersburg FL 33729 Office Phone: 727-872-1000. Business E-Mail: matthew.siegel@hsn.com.

SIEGEL, PAUL, retired judge; b. Troy, NY, May 7, 1938; s. Benjamin and Mary (Silverman) S.; 1 child, Mark Aron; m. Janique Auvertin, Apr. 30, 1994. BS in Physics magna cum laude, U. Miami, 1958, LLB cum laude, 1962. Bar: Fla. 1963, DC 1964, U.S. Supreme Ct. 1967, U.S. Ct. Appeals (5th cir.) 1967, U.S. Ct. Appeals (11th cir.) 1982; cert. civil trial lawyer Fla. Bar. Mem. gen. counsel's office AEC, Washington, 1962-65; ptnr. Sinclair, Louis, Siegel, Heath, Nussbaum & Zavertnik, P.A., Miami, Fla., 1972-91; judge Dade County (Fla.) Cir. Ct., 1991—2010; mng. mem. Voluntary Trial Resolution LLC, 2011—. Author: Florida Trial Objections, 2004; editor-in-chief, exec. editor: U. Miami Law Rev. Chmn. bd. dirs. Alliance Francaise of Dade County, 1983-87, pres., 1990-92; pres. Pro-Mozart Soc. Greater Miami, 1984-92. Home: 235 E San Marino Dr Miami FL 33139-1151 Office Phone: 786-441-5901. Business E-Mail: privatetrials@me.com.

SIEGEL, SAMUEL, metals company executive; b. Elizabeth, NJ, Oct. 30, 1930; s. Morris and Anna (Fader) S.; m. Raenea Kershenbaum, Mar. 29, 1953; children: Daryl Lynn, Annie Roslyn. BBA, CUNY, 1952. CPA, N.Y. Cost accountant Seaporcel Metals, Inc., Long Island City, NY, 1955-56; asst. to controller Deltown Foods, Inc., Yonkers, NY, 1956-57; sr. accountant Touche Ross, NYC, 1957-61; co-founder, vice chmn., chief fin. officer, treas., sec., dir. Nucor Corp., Charlotte, NC, 1961-99; ret., 2000. Mem. AICPA, Am. Soc. Corp. Secs., Fin. Execs. Inst., Fin. Execes. Intl. Hall Fame. Office: 3421 Windbluff Dr Charlotte NC 28277-9850 Office Phone: 704-542-8000.

SIEGEL, STEVEN L., finance company executive, consultant; b. New Rochelle, NY, Feb. 21, 1962; s. Stuart A. Siegel and Stephanie (Kaplita); m. Elizabeth Ellen Starr, Dec. 12, 1987 (div. Jan. 1993). BS in Fin., Calif. Coast U., MBA in Internat. Fin.; DSc magna cum laude in Internat Fin., So. Calif. U., Santa Ana. Fin. analyst Am. Express, Plantation, Fla., 1982-84; investment banker Kidder Peabody & Co., Ft. Lauderdale, Fla., 1985-87, Shearson Lehman Hutton, Boca Raton, Fla., 1987-89; pres. internat. divsn. Cabe Internat. Cons., Inc., Boca Raton, 1989-92; fin. and adminstv. dir. Ensec, Inc., Boca Raton, 1994-95, Art Collectors Internat., Miami, Fla., 1995-96; CFO, COO Enternet Entertainment Group, Inc., Ft. Lauderdale, 1996—97, S.L. Siegel and Assoc. Consulting Group, 1997—2004, Pan Am., 2004—05, NYAG, 2005—06; mng. dir. Schapiro, Siegel & Co. Capital Ptnrs., 2007—. Mng. dir. Fed. Group Ltd., 2001—02, bd. dir., Bought Deal, Inc.; bd. advisors Howa Telco, 1997—2002; pres., CEO Champion Accessories, 2002—03; mem. Matrix & Green Air Internat. Devel. Negotiated Worlds Hargest REDD Transaction Bolivia, 2009—10; mgr. mem. Green St. Ptnrs. LLC, 2010—. Mem. Lambda Alpha Epsilon. Achievements include designed, negotiated and developed licensing, strategic partnerships, profit sharing, and joint ventures involving paten table technology with international companies including AOL, AT&T, Samsung, Deutsche Telekom, MSN, Sumitomo and Motorola; manufacturing and development of a Vanadium Redox Battery (VRB) technology. Avocations: golf, sailing. Address: 2460 Deercreek CC Blvd Suite 209 Deerfield Beach FL 33442 Office Phone: 917-325-0114. Personal E-mail: drsls@earthlink.net.

SIEVERING, PAUL, retired minister, consultant; b. Zurich, 1941; m. Helena Sievering, 1961 (dec. Sept. 2011); children: Agnes, Damian. AB, Wheaton Coll.; AM, Wheaton Grad. Sch. Theology; MDiv, Grand Rapids Baptist Theological Seminary; ThM, Princeton Theological Seminary. Cert. in clinical pastoral edn. Fitzsimmons Army Med. Ctr. Pastor Bloomfield Hills Baptist Ch., 1970—71, First Baptist Ch., Austin, Minn., 1972—90, Meriks Baptist Ch., 1991—2012, pastoral counselor Metairie, La., 2012—13, pastoral cons., 2013—, head of youth religious education. Contbr. articles to profl. jours.; author: (music books) Songs for Your Flock, 1980, Praise Through Song, 1982; co-author: Praising the Days of Eternity, 2013. Dir. projects Hammond Habitat for Humanity, 2004—; coord. Living Without Borders Outreach, 2012—. Avocations: antiques, reading, yoga, creative writing. Office: Meriks Baptist Church 5000 W Esplanade Ave #205 Metairie LA 70006-2551

SIEVING, CHARLES E., energy executive, lawyer; BA, Denison U.; JD, U. Cin. Ptnr., corp. securities & fin. practice group Hogan & Hartson LLP, 1998; exec. v.p., sec. gen. counsel PAETEC Holding Corp., 2007—08; exec. v.p., gen. counsel FPL Group, Inc., 2008—. Office: NextEra Energy 700 Universe Boulevard North Palm Beach FL 33408 Office Phone: 561-694-4000. Office Fax: 561-694-4999. Business E-Mail: charles_sieving@fpl.com.

SIEWERT, EDGAR ALLEN, retired military non-commissioned officer; b. Slayton, Minn., Nov. 9, 1927; s. Albert William and Matilda Ernestine (Zahn) S.; m. Irene Phyllis Zevenbergen, Apr. 6, 1950; 1 child, Kevin Lee. Grad., Sgt. Maj. Acad., 1974, El Paso CC, Tex., 1978. Lic. real estate agent; cert. pilot, airframe mechanic. Electrician USS Philippine Sea USN, 1945-48; aircraft mechanic Sevedy & Sornsen Aviation, Worthington, Minn., 1948-51; tank platoon sgt. U.S. Army, Ft. Rucker, Ala., 1951-52; aircraft electrician Douglas Aircraft, Tulsa, Okla., 1952-56; self-employed Tulsa, Okla., 1956-61; adminstrn. and supply technician Okla. Nat. Guard, Claremore, 1961-72, ops., tng. and readiness specialist Tulsa, 1972-76, tng. technician Oklahoma City, 1976-87, ret., 1987. State command sgt. maj., 1976-78; comdt. Okla. Nat. Guard Non-Commd. Officers Acad., Oklahoma City, 1978-83; chief ops. sgt. Okla. Mil. Dept., Oklahoma City, 1983-87; sgt. maj. acad. selection bd. Nat. Guard Bur., Edgewood Arsenal, Md., 1979. Scout master Boy Scouts Am., Tulsa, 1962-65; vol. various orgns., 1989—. Mem. Okla. Real Estate Investors Assn., Nat. Guard Assn. (bd. dirs.), Nat. Guard Enlisted Assn. (pres., v.p. 1976-78), Nat. Guard Assn. Okla. (bd. dirs. 1976-77, 83-84), 45th Infantry Div. Assn., USS Philippine Sea Assn., Dale Carnegie Alumni Assn. (pres. 1956-57). Republican. Presbyterian. Avocations: sailing, swimming, marksmanship, travel. Home: 1313 SW 106th Pl Oklahoma City OK 73170-4213 E-mail: esiewert@swbell.net.

SIGAL, ROBERT K., plastic surgeon; Attended magna cum laude, Harvard U., 1977—81; MD, Thomas Jefferson U., 1981—85; post grad., U. Pa., 1987—89. Diplomate Am. Bd. Plastic Surgery. Intern Univ. Calif. LA Med. Ctr., 1985—87, resident gen. surgery, 1989—92; resident plastic surgery Univ. of Pa., 1992—94; hosp. affiliations include Fairfax Hosp., Reston Hosp.; med. dir. Austin-Weston Ctr. for Cosmetic Surgery. Co-author: (publs.) The immunology of silicone in a murine model, 1993, Rejuvenating the Aged Face, 2000, Surgical Treatment of the Aged Mouth, 2003, Lip Recontouring, 2005, and numerous other publications. Recipient Sigma Xi medical student research award, 1984, Clin. Surgery prize, 1985, Basic Sci. award, 1993—94; fellow NIH Cancer and Nutrition Fellowship, 1987—89. Mem.: Nat. Capital Soc. of Plastic Surgeons (former pres.), Va. Soc. of Plastic Surgery, Am. Assn. for the Advancement of Sci., NY Acad. of Sciences, ACS (mem. candidates group), US Rowing Assn., Friends of Harvard Rowing, Univ. Barge Club. Office: Austin-Weston Center for Cosmetic Surgery 1825 Samuel Morse Dr Reston VA 20190 Office Phone: 703-893-6168.

SIGEL, MARSHALL ELLIOT, financial consultant; b. Hartford, Conn., Nov. 25, 1941; s. Paul and Bessie (Somer) Sigel; m. Sybil R. Miller, Nov. 23, 1995. BS in Econs., U. Pa., 1963; JD, U. Miami, 1982, LLM in Taxation, 1983. Exec. v.p. Advo-Sys. divsn. KMS Industries, Inc., Hartford, 1963—69, pres., 1969—72, Ad-Type Corp., Hartford, 1963—69, Ad-Lists, Inc., Hartford, 1963—69; fin. cons. Hartford, 1972—83, Boca Raton, Fla., 1987—; pvt. practice law, 1983—87. Bd. dir. Wharton Sch. Club S. Fla. Mem.: World Pres. Orgn., Saratoga Golf and Polo Club, Boca Grove Club, 100 Club So. Palm Beach County. Home and Office: PO Box 273408 Boca Raton FL 33427-3408

SIGMON, J. LEWIS, JR., medical educator; b. Newton, NC, July 8, 1940; MD, U. N.C., 1966. Intern David Grant USAF Hosp., 1966-67; resident Charlotte (N.C.) Meml. Hosp., 1969-71; chmn. dept. family medicine Carolinas Med. Ctr., Charlotte, 1984-95, clin. coord. Charlotte Ofcl Reg. Primary Care Edn., 1995—2001, sr. ind. cons. in grad. med. edn., family medicine, 2001—, dir. family medicine residency program Monroe, 1997—2001; prof. family medicine U. NC, 1993—2004, prof. emeritus, 2004—. Cons. Residency Assistance Program Family Medicine, Kans. City, Mo., 1989—97; acad. coun. Nat. Inst. for Program Dir. Devel., Kansas City, Mo., 1999—2003; chair Am. Bd. Family Medicine Found., 2000—; residency rev. com. for family medicine ACGME, 1997—2003, specialist site visitor for residency rev. com., 2004—; step 3 test material devel. com. USMLE/NBME, 2005—09, step 3 test devel. com. scriptor, 2009—; mem. Am. Bd. Family Medicine, 1995—2000. Recipient Disting. Svc. award, U. NC Sch. Medicine, 2005. Mem. AMA, N.C. Acad. Family Physicians. Office Phone: 704-578-1416. Personal E-mail: sigmonjr@aol.com.

SIHLER, WILLIAM WOODING, finance educator; b. Seattle, Nov. 17, 1937; s. William and Helen Alice (Wooding) S.; m. Mary Elizabeth Unwin, Aug. 21, 1963; children: Edward Wooding, Jennifer Sihler Zysman. AB summa cum laude in Govt., Harvard U., 1959, MBA with high distinction, 1962, DBA, 1965. Instr., asst. prof. Harvard U. Bus. Sch., 1964-67; asso. prof. Darden Graduate Business School, University Virginia, Charlottesville, 1967-72, prof., 1972-76, A.J. Morris prof., 1976-84, Ronald E. Trzcinski prof., 1984—, assoc. dean acad. affairs, 1972-77; exec. dir. Bankers Assn. Fgn. Trade/Ctr. for Internat. Banking Studies, 1977-91; dir. Tayloe Murphy Ctr. U. Va., 2006—09. Bd. dirs. Curtiss-Wright Corp.; pres. Southeastern Cons. Group, Ltd. Co-author: Financial Management: Text and Cases, 2d edit., 1991, The Troubled Money Business, 1992, Financial Service Organizations: Cases in Strategic Management, 1993, Cases in Applied Corporate Finance, 1994, Building Value with Capital-Structure Strategies, 1998, Financial Turnarounds--Preserving Value, 2001, Smart Financial Management: The Essential Reference for the Successful Small Business, 2004, Realism in Lending, 2011; editor: Classics in Commercial Bank Lending, vol. 1, 1981, vol. 2, 1985; contbr. articles to profl. jours. Vis. com. Sch. Mgmt., Case Western Res. U., 1976-86, bd. overseers, 1980-86. Recipient DeL. K. Jay prize Harvard U., Disting. Prof. award U. Va. Alumni Assn., 1982; C.J. Bonaparte scholar Harvard U.; Sheldon fellow 1959-60. Mem. Fin. Mgmt. Assn., Am. Econ. Assn., Am. Fin. Assn., Eastern Fin. Assn., Univ. Club (N.Y.C.), Harvard Club (N.Y.C.), Greencroft Club (Charlottesville), Phi Beta Kappa, Beta Gamma Sigma. Home: 3215 Heathcote Ln Keswick VA 22947-9160 Office: PO Box 6550 Charlottesville VA 22906-6550 Office Phone: 434-924-7489.

SIKIVIE, PIERRE, physics educator; b. Sint Truiden, Belgium, Oct. 29, 1949; came to U.S. 1970; s. Armand and Claire (Roebroeck) S.; m. Cynthia L. Chennault, July 2, 1980; children: Paul Justin, Michael Chennault. Licencie en Sciences, U. Liege, Belgium, 1970; MS in Physics, Yale U., 1972, PhD in Physics, 1975. Rsch. assoc. dept. physics and astronomy U. Md., College Park, 1975-77; rsch. assoc. SLAC Theory Group, Stanford, Calif., 1977-79; sr. fellow CERN Theory Group, Geneva, Switzerland, 1979-81; asst. prof. physics and math. U. Fla., Gainesville, 1981-83, asst. prof. physics, 1983-84, assoc. prof. physics, 1984-88, prof. physics, 1988—. Lectr. in field. Contbr. numerous articles to profl. jours. Recipient Jesse W. Beams medal, 1996; J.S. Guggenheim Found. fellow, 1997-98, Disting. Prof. Physics, U. Fla., 2012. Fellow Am. Phys. Soc.; mem. AAAS. Home: 3965 NW 30th Pl Gainesville FL 32606-7456 Office: Univ of Fla New Physics Bldg Gainesville FL 32611-8440 Office Phone: 904-392-1923. E-mail: sikivie@phys.ufl.edu.*

SILAS, CECIL JESSE, retired petroleum company executive; b. Miami, Fla., Apr. 15, 1932; s. David Edward and Hilda Videll (Carver) S.; m. Theodosea Hejda, Nov. 27, 1965; children: Karla, Peter, Michael, James. BSChemE, Ga. Inst. Tech., Atlanta, 1953. With Phillips Petroleum Co., Bartlesville, Okla., 1953-94, pres. Europe-Africa, Brussels and London, 1968-74, mng. dir. natural resource group Europe/Africa London, 1974-76, v.p. gas and gas liquids div. natural resources group Bartlesville, 1976-78, sr. v.p. natural resources group, 1978-80, exec. v.p. exploration and prodn., minerals, gas and gas liquids, 1980-82, pres., chief operating officer, 1982-85, chmn., CEO, 1985-94. Bd. dirs. Boys/Girls Clubs Am., Atlanta, parton councillor Atlantic Coun. of the U.S.; bd. dirs. Okla. Found. for Excellence, Ga. Tech. Found.; trustee Frank Phillips Found. Served to 1st lt. Chem. Corps, AUS, 1954-56. Decorated comdr. Order St. Olaf (Norway); inducted into Ga. Inst. Tech. Athletic Hall of Fame, 1959, recipient Former Scholar-Athlete Total Person award, 1988; inducted into Okla. Bus. Hall of Fame, 1989; named CEO of Yr., Internat. TV Assn., 1987. Mem. Am. Petroleum Inst., U.S. C. of C. (past chmn. bd. dirs.), 25 Yr. Club, Phi Delta Theta. Avocations: fishing, golf, hunting. Office: PO Box 2127 Bartlesville OK 74005-2127

SILBIGER, MARTIN L., radiologist, educator, dean; b. Ravenna, Ohio, Mar. 17, 1938; s. Alfred James and Evelyn Norma (Cheswick) Silbiger; m. Ruth Hope Steele, June 4, 1957; children: Martin, Eve, Jonathan, Holly, Wendy. BA, U. Pa., 1958; MD, Western Reserve U., 1962; MBA, U. South Fla., 1989. Diplomate Am. Bd. Radiology, Am. Bd. Nuc. Medicine. Intern Univ. Hosps. Cleve., 1962—63; resident Johns Hopkins Hosp., 1963—66; with NIH, 1966—68; radiologist Tampa (Fla.) Gen. Hosp., 1968—; prof. U. South Fla., Tampa, 1982—; chief of staff Tampa Gen. Hosp., 1978—80; chmn. dept. radiology U. South Fla. Coll. Medicine, 1982—95; dean coll. medicine U. South Fla., 1995—2000, v.p. health scis., 1995—2000. Founder Hillsborough County Med. Assn. Found., Tampa, 1992; treas. Cmty. Found. Tampa, 1993—95; bd. dirs. Moffitt Cancer Ctr., Tampa, 1985—2000, Moffitt Cancer Ctr. Found., 1994—2000. Avocations: reading, rollerblading, golf, tennis. Home: 1827 Bayshore Blvd Tampa FL 33606-3210 Office: 3301 Alumni Dr Tampa FL 33612-9413 also: 1209 Bruce B Downs Blvd PO Box 66 Tampa FL 33601-0066

SILER, EUGENE EDWARD, JR., federal judge; b. Williamsburg, Ky., Oct. 19, 1936; s. Eugene Edward and Lowell (Jones) Siler; m. Christy Dyanne Minnich, Oct. 18, 1969; children: Eugene Edward, Adam Troy. BA cum laude, Vanderbilt U., 1958; LLB, U. Va., 1963; LLM, Georgetown U., 1964, U. Va., 1995. Bar: Ky. 1963, Va. 1963, DC 1963. Pvt. practice, Williamsburg, 1964—65; county atty. Whitley County, Ky., 1965—70; US atty. (ea. dist.) Ky. US Dept. Justice, Lexington, 1970—75; judge (ea. & we. dist.) Ky. US Dist. Ct., 1975—91, chief judge (ea. dist.) Ky., 1984—91; judge US Ct. Appeals (6th Cir.), 1991—2001, sr. judge, 2001—. Trustee Cumberland Coll., Williamsburg, 1965—73, 1980—88; campaign co-chmn. Congressman Tim L. Carter, 1966, 5th Congl. Dist., US Senator J.S. Cooper, 1966; 1st v.p. Ky. Bapt. Convention, 1986—87, 2002—03, pres., 2003—04; bd. dirs. Bapt. Healthcare System Inc., 1990—2004, 2006—. With USN, 1958—60, with USNR, 1960—83. Recipient Freedom's Found. medal, 1968; E. Barrett Prettyman fellow, 1963—64. Mem.: Va. State Bar, DC Bar Assn., Ky. Bar Assn. (Judge of Yr. 1992), Fed. Bar Assn. Republican. Baptist. Home: PO Box 129 Williamsburg KY 40769-0129 Office: US Ct Appeals 310 S Main Street Room 333 London KY 40741

SILLER, BARRY S., gynecologic oncologist, gynecologist, obstetrician; MD, Baylor Coll. of Medicine, Houston, 1988. Diplomate Am. Bd. Ob-Gyn, Am. Bd. Ob-Gyn-gynecologic oncology, lic. Tex. Resident Sch. of Medicine Univ. Ala., Birmingham, 1992, fellow Sch. of Medicine, 1994; hosp. affiliations include Meml. Hermann Katy Hosp., Meml. Hermann NW Hosp., Meml. Hermann Meml. City Med. Ctr., Meth. Hosp., Meth. Sugar Land Hosp., Meml. Hermann-Tex. Med. Ctr. Office: c/o Methodist Hospital Ste 400 Medical Plz 3 915 Gessner Rd Houston TX 77024 Office Phone: 713-242-2575. Office Fax: 713-242-2580.

SILLIMAN, SCOTT LIVINGSTON, federal judge, law educator; b. Newton, Mass., Feb. 14, 1943; s. Scott Alphonso and Dorothy Livingston (Burnett) S.; m. Ernestine Craig, Sept. 11, 1966 (dec. Sept. 1996); children: Craig Livingston, Lisa Silliman Wilson, Kimberly Silliman McMurray. BA in Philosophy, U. N.C., 1965, JD, 1968. Bar: N.C. 1968, US Ct. Mil. Appeals 1969, US Supreme Ct. 1976, US Dist. Ct. (eastern dist.) N.C. 1993. Staff rschr. Inst. Govt., U. N.C., Chapel Hill, 1968; commd. 2d lt. USAF, 1968, advanced through grades to col.; ret., 1993; prof. practice of law, exec. dir. Ctr. Law, Ethics & Nat. Security, Duke U. Sch. Law, Durham, NC, 1993—; judge US Ct. Mil. Commn. Review, 2012—. Contbr. articles to profl. jours. Mem. ABA, Judge Advocate Assn. (bd. dirs. 1977-87). Republican. Avocations: sports, singing. Office: Duke University School of Law PO Box 90360 Durham NC 27708-0360 also: Office of Military Commissions 4800 Mark Center Dr Ste 11F09-02 Alexandria VA 22350 Office Phone: 919-613-7138. Office Fax: 919-613-7231. E-mail: silliman@law.duke.edu.*

SILLS, JOHN, corporate financial executive; Grad., Lehigh U., 1978. Chief adminstrv. officer Unisource Worldwide, Inc., CFO, 2008—. Office: Unisource Worldwide Inc 6600 Governors Lake Pky Norcross GA 30071 Office Phone: 770-447-9000. Office Fax: 770-734-2000. Business E-Mail: john.sills@unisourcelink.com.

SILVAGNI, ANTHONY JOSEPH, dean, osteopath; b. Atlantic City, Apr. 18, 1940; s. Anthony Serafino and Madeline (Valentino) S.; m. Marlene Scherr, Mar. 12, 1961 (div. July 1977); children: Paul, Michelle; m. Dianna Poole, Oct. 1, 1977. BS in Pharmacy, Phila. Coll. of Pharmacy and Sci., 1963, MS in Hosp. Pharmacy, 1966, PharmD, 1970; postgrad., Purdue U., 1963-64; DO, Phila. Coll. Osteo. Medicine, 1982. Resident in hosp. pharmacy Thomas Jefferson U. Hosp., Phila., 1965-66, assoc. dir. pharmacy services, 1969-73; chief pharmacist prescription div. cen. pharm. services Appalachian Regional Hosp., Williamson, W.Va., 1966-67, asst. dir. cen. pharm. services, 1967-68; dir. pharmacy services Presbyn. U. Pa. Hosp., Phila., 1968-69; dir. pharmacy programs Lake Area Health Edn. Ctr., Erie, Pa., 1973-74; assoc. dir. clin. pharmacy services Peter Bent Brigham Hosp., Boston, 1974-76; clin. pharmacist U. Ariz., Tucson, 1976-78; faculty Health Care Edn. Programs Am., Chestnut Hill, Mass., 1980-82; intern Tucson Gen. Hosp., 1982-83; physician Dakota Family Practice, Parkston, S.D., 1983—; dean Nova Southeastern Univ. Coll. of Osteopathic Med., 1998—. Instr. in clin. pharmacy Phila. Coll. Pharmacy and Sci., 1969-73; asst. profl clin. pharmacy U. Ariz., 1977-78; chmn. dept. clin. practice Mass. Coll. Pharmacy, Boston, 1974-76; cons. clin. pharmacy Tucson Gen. Hosp., 1977-78, dir. clin. pharmacy services, 1977-78, vis. cons. staff dept. medicine, 1978; vis. faculty hypertension, Smith, Kline & French, Phila., 1980-82; lectr. to nat., state, county and local health profl. orgns. Contbr. articles to profl. jours. Mem. curriculum com. Mass. Coll. Pharmacy, 1974-76, chmn. PharmD admissions com., 1975-76; mem. bldg. com. U. Ariz. Coll. Pharmacy, 1976-78, grad. thesis com., 1977-78, faculty voting rights com., 1978, chmn. grade grievance com, 1978. Served with U.S. Army, 1961-62. Pa. State U. grantee, VA grantee, Lakes Area Regional Med. Program grantee, Smith, Kline and French grantee; Merck Sharp and Dohme scholar, 1979, Nat. Student Osteo. Med. Assn. scholar, 1980. Fellow Am. Found. for Pharm Edn.; mem. AMA, Am. Acad. Gen. Practitioners, Am. Osteo. Assn. (grantee), Am. Pharm. Assn. (review panel for handbook 1975—, practitioner panel 1973—), Am. Soc. Hosp. Pharmacists (adv. panel on student membership 1975-76), Am. Pharm. Assn. Acad. of Pharmacy Practice (charter), S.D. Med. Assn., Dist. 6 Med. Soc., Kappa Psi, Phi Sigma Gamma, Rho Chi. Avocations: flying, skiing, motorcycling, camping. Office: Nova Southeastern Univ Coll Medicine Rm 1401 Terry Bldg 3200 S University Dr Fort Lauderdale FL 33328

SILVER, BARRY MORRIS, lawyer; b. Mt. Vernon, NY, Nov. 18, 1956; s. Samuel Manuel and Elaine Martha (Shapiro) Silver. BA, Fla. Atlantic U., 1979; JD, Nova U., 1983. Bar: Fla. 1983. Atty. pvt. practice, Boca Raton, 1986—. Tchr. bilingual edn. Palm Beach County Schs., Delray Beach, Fla., 1981—83; faculty Palm Beach Jr. Coll., Boca Raton, 1990—; atty. NOW, South Palm Beach County. Vol. Haitian Refugee Ctr., Miami, 1982; mem. Fla. Ho. Reps., 1997—98; rabbi Congregation L'Dor Va-Dor, Lake Worth, Fla. Mem.: Palm Beach County Bar Assn., Fla. Bar Assn., Sierra Club. Democrat. Jewish. Avocations: languages, tennis, frisbee, chess. Office: 1200 S Rogers Cir Ste 8 Boca Raton FL 33487- Home: 18624 Cape Sable Dr Boca Raton FL 33498-6374 Office Phone: 561-483-6900. Personal E-mail: barryboca@aol.com.

SILVER, DONALD, surgeon, educator; b. NYC, Oct. 19, 1929; s. Herman and Cecilia (Meyer) S.; m. Helen Elizabeth Harnden, Aug. 9, 1958; children: Elizabeth Tyler, Donald Meyer, Stephanie Davies, William Paige. AB, Duke U., 1950, BS in Medicine, MD, 1955. Diplomate Am. Bd. Surgery, Am. Bd. Gen. Vascular Surgery, Am. Bd. Thoracic Surgery. Intern Duke Med. Ctr., 1955-56, asst. resident, 1958-63, resident, 1963-64; mem. faculty Duke Med. Sch., 1964-75, prof. surgery, 1972-75; cons. Watts Hosp., Durham, 1965-75, VA Hosp., Durham, 1970-75, chief surgery, 1968-70; prof. surgery, chmn.

dept. U. Mo. VA Med. Ctr., Columbia, 1975-98, chmn. univ. physicians, 2002—05. Cons. Harry S. Truman Hosp., Columbia, 1975—2000; mem. bd. sci. advisers Cancer Research Center, Columbia, 1975—; mem. surg. study sect. A NIH; dir surg. svcs. U. Mo. Health System, 2001-2003. Contbr. articles to med. jours., chpts. to books; editorial bds.; Jour. Vascular Surgery, Postgrad. Gen. Surgery, Vascular Surgery. Served with USAF, 1956-58. James IV Surg. traveler, 1977 Fellow ACS (gov. 1995-99), Deryl Hart Soc.; mem. AMA, AAAS, Mo. Med. Assn., Boone County Med. Soc., Internat. Cardiovascular Soc., Soc. Univ. Surgeons, Am. Heart Assn. (Mo. affiliate rsch. com.), Soc. Surgery Alimenatry Tract, Assn. Acad. Surgery, So. Thoracic Surg. Assn., Internat. Soc. Surgery, Soc. Vascular Surgery, Am. Assn. Thoracic Surgery, Am. Surg. Assn., Ctrl. Surg. Assn. (pres.-elect 1990-91, pres. 1991-92), Western Surg. Assn., Midwestern Vascular Surg. Soc. (pres. 1984-85), Ctrl. Surg. Assn. Found. (treas. 1992-93, 2d v.p. 1993-94, 1st v.p. 1994-95, pres. 1995-96). Avocations: gardening, hunting, travel. Home: 3 Silver Maple Ct Durham NC 27705-5642 Personal E-mail: retdocsilver3@gmail.com.

SILVER, ELAINE TERRY, lawyer; b. Balt., May 11, 1953; BA with honors, Bucknell U., Lewisburg, Pa., 1974; JD, NYU Sch. Law, 1977. Bar: Conn. 1977, US Dist. Ct. Conn. 1977, US Ct. Appeals (2d cir.) 1978, Fla. 2004; cert. family mediator Fla. Supreme Ct. Assoc. Glazer, Seelig & Glazer, Stamford, Conn., 1977—84; ptnr. Fleisher, Trow & Silver, Stamford, 1984—87; ptnr. divorce, custody & family litig. Silver, Golub & Teitell LLP, Stamford, 1987—2000; founding atty Silver Divorce Ctr., Lake Mary, Fla., 2004—. Vis. lectr. American Constl. & family law Beijing U., 1981—82; adj. family law lectr. U. Bridgeport Sch. Law, Conn., 1989, Barry U. Sch. Law, Orlando, Fla., 2007. Contbr. articles to profl. jours. Vol., contract atty. Guardian Ad Litem Program, Seminole County, 2004—. Recipient Jud. Dept. Svc. Commendation, State of Conn., 1986—87, Cmty. Rels. award, Jewish Fedn. Greater Orlando, 2005; named Agy. Vol. of Yr., United Way Greenwich Conn., 1987. Mem.: ABA, Seminole County Bar Assn., Orange County Bar Assn., Fla. Bar, Ctrl. Fla. Family Law American Inns of Ct., Collaborative Family Law Group Ctrl. Fla. Office: Law Office of Elaine T Silver Esq 1515 International Pkwy St 1019 Lake Mary FL 32746 Office Phone: 407-712-6787. E-mail: ESilver@SilverDivorce.com.

SILVER, LINDA, counseling administrator, educator; b. NYC, Jan. 11, 1954; d. Victor Paul and Mina (Levin) Berk; children: Brooke, Joshua. BA in Spanish and Secondary Edn., Hofstra U., 1976; MS in Guidance and Counseling, Nova U., 1979. Cert. guidance counselor grades K-12, Spanish tchr. grades 7-12. Spanish tchr. Ponus Ridge Middle Sch., Norwalk, Conn., 1976-77, West Hollywood (Fla.) Pvt. Sch., 1977-79; guidance counselor Collins Elem., Dania, Fla., 1979-89; adult edn. tchr. GED-Off Campus, Ft. Lauderdale, Fla., 1989-90; guidance dir. Bethune Elem., Hollywood, 1989-96; family counselor, coord. Family Counseling Ctr., Hollywood, 1990-94; guidance dir. Attucks Middle Sch., 1996—. Ednl. cons. Maimonides Community Sch., Hollywood, 1992—; workshop leader and presenter in field. Active Sister Cities Internat. Youth Summit Task Force. Named Broward County Elem. Counselor of Yr., Broward Counseling Assn., Ft. Lauderdale, 1990, Fla. Elem. Counselor of Yr., Fla. Sch. Counselors Assn., Orlando, 1992. Mem. ACA, Am. Sch. Counselor Assn., Fla. Sch. Counselors Assn., Broward County Counselors Assn., Fla. Counseling Assn., Exec. Bd. Elem. Counselors (co-chairperson 1992-95), Exec. Bd. Maimonides Community Sch. (bd. mem. 1992—), Maimonides Community (chairperson edn. com. 1992-96), Hofstra U. South Fla. Alumni Assn. (pres. 1985), Delta Kappa Gamma, Phi Delta Kappa, Sigma Delta Phi. Office: Attucks Middle Sch 3500 N 22nd Ave Hollywood FL 33020-1298 Home: 3825 SW 50th St Fort Lauderdale FL 33312-8210

SILVERMAN, GARY WILLIAM, investment company executive; b. LA, Nov. 30, 1957; s. Albert and Anna Marie (Robinson) S.; m. Joanne Marie Robinson, Aug. 29, 1976. BS in Psychology Counseling, Miami Christian Coll., Fla., 1987; MBA, U. Dallas, 1992. CFP. Tng. supr. Tex. Utilities, Glen Rose, Tex., 1982-92; registered rep. Waddell & Reed, Ft. Worth, 1990-94; tng. dir. Howmet Refurbishment, Wichita Falls, Tex., 1992-94; owner, fin. planner Personal Money Planning, Wichita Falls, 1993—; with USN, EM1(SS), 1976—82. Owner, cons. Sigma Edn. Sys., 1987—2005; instr. Wayland Bapt. U., 1994-2007, Vernon Coll., 1996-04; fin. course instr. Midwestern State U., 2005; columnist, Your Money, Wichita Falls Times Record News, 2008- Host, commentator TV show Money Cent$ WFTV Time Warner Channel 15, 1995-2012, Falls Informer; editor: Personal Money Planning; editor fin. web site TexasInvest-.com; columnist, Wichita Falls Times Record News. Grad. Leadership Wichita Falls, 1993; loaned exec. Wichita Falls United Way, 1993; instr. ARC, 1983-2003; former chair. North Tex. Workforce Devel. Bd., 2000-10; bd. mem. Mus. North Tex. History; reviewer Jour. Fin. Planning. Mem. Fin. Planning Assn., Sigma Iota Epsilon. Avocation: curling. Office: Personal Money Planning 4245 Kemp Blvd Ste 806 Wichita Falls TX 76308-2822

SILVERMAN, JERRY MARK, political science professor, consultant; b. Chgo., May 17, 1942; s. Maury W. and Rose Silverman; m. Andrea Lee Jones, Aug. 17, 1990; children: Martin Harold, Deanna Michelle Ball, Mauri Sami, Mira Sandrine, Milena Luisa. BA in Polit. Sci., Calif. State Coll., Long Beach, Calif., 1963; PhD in Internat. Rels. Govt., Claremont Grad. Sch. & U. Ctr., Calif., 1967. Sr. planning advisor Devel. Alternatives Inc., Gema Gofa, Ethiopia, chief-of-party Jakarta, Indonesia, 1978—81, Cairo, 1981—82, sr. devel. specialist, 1981—83; instr., polit. sci. Ctrl. Wash. State Coll., Ellensburg, 1965—66; fgn. svc. res. officer US AID, Vietnam, 1967—68, cons. intermittent, 2000—06; asst. prof., polit. sci. McMaster U., Ont., Canada, 1968—72; local govt. advisor Inst. Pub. Adminstrn., Saigon, Vietnam, 1972—73; project specialist social scis. Ford Found. SE Asia Regional Office, Saigon, 1973—75, Bangkok, 1975—77; prin. instl. devel. specialist Africa World Bank, 1983—95, unit mgr., east Asia and pacific Jakarta, Indonesia, 1995—99, cons. intermittent, 2000—03; pvt. practice Lima, Peru, 2002—04, Savannah, Ga., 2004—13; prof. Savannah State U., 2007—09; adj. prof. Armstrong Atlantic State U., Savannah, Ga., 2012—. Vis. fellow Harvard U., 1976, guest spkr., 2000, Duke U., 2002; cons. intermittent Govt. UK & Northern Ireland Dept. Internat. Devel., 2000—03, Asian Devel. Bank, 2000—07. Author: (book) Action-Planning Workshops for Development Management: Guidelines, 1991, Technical Assistance and Aid Agency Staff: Alternative Techniques for Greater Effectiveness; contbr. articles to jours. Vol. mem. United Way of Coastal Empire Assessment Panels; vol. advisor Eastside Concerned Citizens Neighborhood Assn. Savannah, Ga.; bd. mem. Uweza Aid Found. US fgn. svc. officer, dep. province sr. advisor Mil. Assistance Command Vietnam, 1967—68. Named to Alumni Hall of Fame, Claremont Grad. U., 2001. Mem.: Southern Polit. Sci. Assn. Avocation: scuba diving. Personal E-mail: jmsilverman5@comcast.net.

SILVERMAN, MATTHEW, professional sports team executive; b. Dallas, May 20, 1976; s. Ira and Ellen Silverman. B in Economics cum laude, Harvard U., 1998. Assoc., analyst merchant banking divsn. and firmwide strategy group Goldman Sachs Group Inc., 1998—2003; co-founder, CFO Zethus, Inc.; dir. strategic planning Tampa Bay Rays, v.p. planning and devel., pres., 2005—. Bd. mem. Pinellas Edn. Found., Hillsborough Edn. Found., Tampa Bay Partnership. Named one of Forty Under 40, Street & Smith's SportsBus. Jour., 2009. Avocations: running, writing. Office: Tampa Bay Rays One Tropicana Dr Saint Petersburg FL 33705

SILVERMAN, STANLEY WAYNE, chemical company executive; m. Ellen J. Seligsohn, June 7, 1970. BSChemE, Drexel U., 1969, MBA, 1974; AMP, Harvard U., 1989. Process engr. Atlantic Richfield Co. (acquired by BP), Phila., 1969-71, PQ Corp., Phila., 1971-74, mgr. oper. planning Valley Forge, Pa., 1974-76, product mgr., 1976-80, mktg. mgr., 1980-82, nat. sales mgr., 1982-84, pres. Nat. Silicates Ltd. Toronto, 1984-87, pres. Ind. Chem. group Valley Forge, 1987-90, exec. v.p., COO, 1990-99, pres., CEO, bd. dirs., 2000—05; pres. Horizon Venture Group LLC. Bd. dirs. C&D Technologies, Inc., Femco Machine Co., innRoad, Inc., A. Schulman, Inc., 2007—, Met-Pro Corp. Chmn. adv. coun. Drexel U. Coll. Engring, 1991-93, alumni bd. govs., 1998, bd. trustees, 2000—; bd. dirs. Phila. Acad., Inc., 1999—2004. Named among 100 most accomplished grads. Drexel U., 1993; recipient Alumni Achievement award Drexel U., 1995. Mem. Soap and Detergent Assn. (bd. dirs. 2001-05, chmn bd. 2004-05), Am. Chemistry Coun. (bd. dirs. 2001-05), Femco Machine Co. (bd. dirs. 2007-), A. Schulman Inc. (bd. dirs. 2008-). Office: Horizon Venture Group LLC 7580 Britneywoods Cir Arlington TN 38002 Business E-Mail: stanley_silverman@us.aschulman.com.

SILVERS, GERALD THOMAS, retired publishing executive; b. Cin., Aug. 26, 1937; s. Steve Allen and Tina Mae (Roberts) S.; m. Ann Gregory Woodward, July 25, 1964. BA, U. Ky., Lexington, 1960. Asst. rsch. svcs. mgr. Cin. Enquirer, 1963-72, rsch. svcs. dir., 1972-74, rsch. dir., 1974-90, v.p. mktg. svcs., 1990-94, v.p. market devel., 1994—2003; ret., 2003. Active U. Ky. Devel. Coun., Lexington, 1986—; trustee Neediest Kids of All, 1991—; region 5 exec. com. Ohio Sch. to Work, 1997-2000; corps. com. St. Elizabeth Med. Ctr. Found., 1998-2007; bd. overseers Taft Mus. Art, 1999—, treas., bd. govs., 2002—, vice chmn., 2007-2012; 1st lt. U.S. Army, 1960-62. Recipient Thomas H. Copeland award of merit, 1991. Mem. U. Ky. Alumni Assn. Cin. Chpt. (pres. 1985), Newspaper Rsch. Coun. (pres. 1985-86), Internat. Newspaper Market Assn., Am. Mktg. Assn., Am. Art Soc. Cin. (pres. 1999-2001), Cin. MACDowell Soc. Presbyterian. Home: 229 Watch Hill Rd Fort Mitchell KY 41011-1822

SILVERSTEIN, JANET HOPE, pediatrician, educator; b. Bronx, NY, June 21, 1944; d. Jesse and Beatrice (Zuckerman) Fisher; m. Burton Silverstein, Aug. 18, 1978; children: Craig Darryl, Todd Alan. BS, U. Rochester, 1966; MD, U. Pa., 1970. Diplomate Am. Bd. Pediat. Clin. assoc., pediat. Duke U. Med. Ctr., Durham, NC, 1977-78; instr. in pediat., cmty. health U. Fla., Gainesville, 1978-80, asst. prof. pediat., cmty. health, 1980-84, assoc. prof., 1984-90, prof. pediat., 1990—, chief divsn. pediat. endocrinology, 1994—, med. dir., Pediatric Clinic, 1998—2004. Med. dir. Fla. Diabetes Camp, Gainesville, 1988—, Diabetes Project Unit, Gainesville, 1979—2002; gov.'s diabetes adv. coun., Tallahassee, 1984—2000, 2004—; sci. adv. bd. Diabetes Action Rsch. and Edn. Found., Washington, 1990—; program dir. U. Fla. Diabetes Rsch., Edn. and Treatment Ctr., 1991—; com. Am. Bd. Pediat.; mem. editl. bd. Jour. Pediat. & Endocrine Today, 1994—2005. Contbr. articles to profl. jours. Co-creator Diabetes Resdl. Unit for Children Having Trouble Coping with Diabetes; creator Bring a Friend to Camp, After Hours Pediat. Clinic. Named Olympic Torch Bearer, 1996. Mem.: Soc. Pediatric Rsch. (elected), Ambulatory Pediat. Assn., Lawson Wilkins Pediat. Endocrinology Soc. (chair diabetes com. 2000—01, bd. dirs. 2003—07, past chmn. drug, therapeutics com., pres. elect 2010—), Endocrine Soc., Am. Diabetes Assn. (chair coun. on youth 2001—03), Am. Acad. Pediats. (chair exec. com. sect. on endocrinology 2000—04), Am. Pediat. Soc., Nat. Diabetes Edn. Program (chmn. children's work group 2004—). Avocations: jogging, bicycling, art, reading. Home: 1932 NW 24th St Gainesville FL 32605-3848 Office Phone: 352-334-1390.

SILVERSTEIN, LEONARD A., lawyer; b. Mobile, Ala., Apr. 18, 1958; s. Burton Howard and Fannye Mitchell Silverstein; m. Ellen Sue Frauenthal, May 25, 1986; children: Andrew, Laura, Anna. BA magna cum laude, Vanderbilt U., Nashville, 1980; JD, Vanderbilt U., 1983. Bar: Ga. 1983. Assoc./ptnr. Powell Goldstein Frazer & Murphy LLP, Atlanta, 1983—94; ptnr. McKenna Long & Aldridge LLP, Atlanta, 1994—. Mem. Ga. Biomed. Partnership, Atlanta, 2002—; mem., biosciences exec. com. Met. Atlanta C. of C., 2002—. Contbr. articles to profl. jours.; assoc. mng. editor, Vanderbilt Law Rev., 1982—83. Pres. Vanderbilt U. Alumni Club, Atlanta, 1991; co-pres. Bach n' Rollers, Divsn. of The Atlanta Symphony Assocs., 1992—93; bd. mem. and exec. com. mem. Zoo Atlanta, 1996—2001, bd. mem., 2003, Am.-Israel C. of C., S.E. Region, Atlanta, 1995—; bd. mem. and exec. com. mem. Am. Jewish Com., Atlanta, 1999—; bd. of trustees The Atlanta Symphony Assocs., 1992—93. Recipient IPO Rainmaker, IPO Counsel - The Corp. Fin. Inst., 1996. Mem.: Vanderbilt U. Alumni Assn. (bd. dirs. 1992—96), Ga. Bar Assn. (vice chair/chair elect of securities subcom. 2001—02), Atlanta Bar Assn. Achievements include patents pending for Reloadable Rights Plan for Preferred and Common Stock Rights Plans. Avocations: triathlons, golf. Office: McKenna Long & Aldridge LLP 303 Peachtree St Ste 5300 Atlanta GA 30308 Business E-Mail: lsilverstein@mckennalong.com.

SILVERTHORN, ROBERT STERNER, JR., lawyer; b. Okla. City, Dec. 22, 1948; s. Robert Sterner and Marilyn I. Silverthorn; m. Mary Russell Cofer, June 26, 1982; children: Robert Sterner III, Christine Elizabeth. BA, Dickinson Coll., 1969; JD, U. Louisville, 1974; postgrad, Nat. Def. U., 1988, US Army War Coll., 1993. Bar: Ky. 1975, US Dist. Ct. (we. dist.) Ky. 1975, US Tax Ct. 1975, US Dist. Ct. (ea. dist.) Ky. 1980, US Dist. Ct. (so. dist.) Tex. 1981, US Dist. Ct. (no. dist.) Ohio 1983, US Dist. Ct. (so. dist.) Ind. 1993, US Supreme Ct. 1983, US Ct. Appeals (6th cir.) 1995. Pvt. practice, Louisville, 1975; assoc. Pallo White & O'Conner, 1975—76, Hargadon Lenihan & Harbolt, 1976—82; ptnr. White Diamond & Silverthorn, 1982—83; of counsel Nutt & Mayer, 1983—91; mng. ptnr. Morris, Silverthorn & Dutton, 1991—92, Silverhorn Law Offices, 1993—. Commd. 2d lt. US Army, 1970; maj. gen., 2000; comdr. gen. 84th divsn., 1998; comdr. gen. 95th divsn., 2000—04; comdr. ky. col., 2009—11; bd. dirs. Maroco Leasing, Inc., Louisville, Akima Intra-Data, Charlotte, NC, Meth. Retirement Homes Ky. Inc., Lousiville; repeat guest radio talk show Ask the Lawyers Sta. WHAS; mil. commentator WAVE-TV (NBC); cons. Advanced Sys. Tech. Inc., 2009—11; Ky. col.; adv. bd. mem. Salvation Army, Bd. La. With Salvation Army Adv. Bd., 2006—; chair, bd. trustees Christ Ch. United Meth., 2009; dir. Ky. Vietnam Vet. Meml. Found., 2013—; pres. Windhurst Acres Homeowners Assn., St. Matthews, Ky., 1981—85; chmn., pres. Hurstbourne Village Office Condo, Louisville, 2005—; bd. dirs. dePaul Sch., Louisville, 1997—99, Am. Cherokee dist. Boy Scouts Am., 2013—; affiliate dir. Susan G. Komen Louisville, 2008—14, pres., 2009—14, acting exec. dir., 2009—12. Comdr., Butler chpt. Mil. Order World Wars, 2008—11, state chair, dept. def. appontes Kentucky Employer Support Guard and Res., 2008—, ex-com. mem. Ky. Commn. Mil. Affairs, 2010—. Decorated Disting. Svc. medal, Meritorious Svc. medal with 6 oak leaf clusters, Bronze Star with 1 oak leaf cluster, Air medal, Army Commendation medal with 3 oak leaf clusters, Army Achievement medal; recipient Constl. Book award, U. Louisville, 1975; Paul Harris fellow. Mem.: ABA (past vice chair real property sect.), Louisville Area C. of C. (mil. affairs com.), Sr. Army Res. Comdrs. Assn. (pres. 2001—04), Assn. US Army (chmn. Louisville Armed Forces com. 1986—88), Assn. of Century (pres. 1993—95), Res. Officers Assn., Ky. Acad. Trial Attys., Louisville Bar Assn., Ky. Bar Assn. (chmn. civil litigation sect. 2001—02), Kosair Shrine, Scottish Rite, Rotary Club of Jeffersontown, Ky. (pres. 1995—96, dist. 6710 asst. gov. 1997—2000, pres. 2008—09), Jefferson Club, Hurstbourne Country Club, Masons, Sigma Chi, Delta Theta Phi (dean). Methodist. Office: Silverthorn Law Offices Ste 200 2305 Hustbourne Village Dr Louisville KY 40299-1861 Office Phone: 502-495-2300. Personal E-mail: RSilvertho@aol.com. Business E-Mail: silverthornlaw@bellsouth.net.

SIMAAN, MARWAN, electrical engineering educator; m. Rita Simaan. MSEE, U. Pitts., 1970; PhDEE, U. Ill., 1972. Registered profl. engr., Pa. Rsch. engr. Shell Devel. Co., Houston, 1974-76; assoc. prof. elec. engring. U. Pitts., 1976-85, prof., 1985-89, Bell of Pa., Bell Atlantic prof., 1989—2008, chmn. dept. elec. engring., 1991—2008; dean Coll. Engring. & Computer Sci., U. Ctrl. Fla., 2009—; Fla. 21st Century chair, disting. prof. U. Ctrl. Fla. Cons. Gulf Rsch. and Tech., Pitts., 1979-85, ALCOA, Pitts., 1986-89. Editor: Vertical Seismic Profiles, 1984, Two-dimensional Transforms, 1985, Artificial Intelligence in Petroleum Exploration, 1989, Expert Systems in Exploration, 1991, (series) Advances in Geophysical Signal Processing; co-editor jour. Multidimensional Sys. and Signal Processing; mem. editl. bd. profl. jours., including IEEE Procs., IEEE Transactions on Cirs. and Sys., IEEE Transactions on Geosci. and Remote Sensing, Jour. Optimization Theory and Applications, Integrated Computer-aided Engring. Jour., Jour. Cirs., Sys. and Computers; contbr. over 300 articles on signal processing and control to profl. publs. Grantee NSF, NIH, ONR, Def. Advance Rsch. Project Adminstrs., Ben Franklin, Westinghouse, Gulf, ALCOA; recipient Outstanding ECE Alumnus U. Ill., 1995, Coll. Engring., Disting. Svc. award, 2007. Fellow: NAE, AAAS (sec. engring. sect. M 2003—), IEEE (Best Paper award 1985, 1999), Am. Soc. Engring. Edn.; mem.: Am. Assn. Artificial Intelligence, Soc. Exploration Geophysics, Sigma Xi (Best Paper award Alcoa chpt. 1988), Eta Kappa Nu. Achievements include patent in application of signal processing technology in aluminum manufacturing. Office: Univ Ctrl Fla Coll Engring & Computer Sci Orlando FL 32816

SIMBERLOFF, DANIEL, biologist, educator; b. Easton, Pa., Apr. 7, 1942; s. Isaac and Ruth (Koplowitz) Simberloff. AB, Harvard U., 1964, PhD, 1969. Asst. prof. biology Fla. State U., Tallahassee, 1968—73, assoc. prof., 1973—78, prof., 1978—97, Robert O. Lawton Disting. prof., 1986; Nancy Gore Hunger prof. environ. studies dept. ecology and evolutionary biology U. Tenn., 1997—. Vis. prof. U. Mich., 1974, U. Minn., 1980, Hebrew U., Jerusalem, 1984; bd. dirs. Nat. Sci. Bd., 2000—06; mem. species survival commn. Internat. Union Conservation Nature and Natural Resources. Editor: Jour. Biogeography, 1974—, Biodiversity and Conservation; co-editor: Ecological Communities: Conceptual Issues and the Evidence, 1984; co-editor: (with D. Schmitz and T. Brown) Strangers in Paradise: Impact and Management of Nonindigenous Species in Florida, 1997; mem. editl. bd.: Jour. Biogeography, Northeast Gulf. Sci., Environ. and Ecol. Statistics, Raffles Bulletin of Zoology, Ecologia, Oecologia, BioSci., Biol. Invasions; contbr. articles to sci. jours. Recipient Developing Scholar award, Fla. State U., 1977, Rector's medal, U. Helsinki, Finland, 1983, Disting. Statistical Ecologist award, Internat. Assn. Ecology, 1994, Ramon Margalef award for Ecology, Govt. of Catalonia, Spain, 2012. Mem.: NAS, Soc. for Systematic Zoology, Brit. Ecol. Soc., Soc. for Study Evolution, Am. Soc. Naturalists, Ecol. Soc. Am., Nature Conservancy, Soc. Conservation Biology, Brit. Ecol. Soc., American Acad. Arts and Sciences. Jewish. Home: 2145 Indian Hills Dr Knoxville TN 37919-8914 Office: Ecology and Evolutionary Biology 569 Dabney Hall University of Tennessee Knoxville TN 37996-1610 Office Phone: 865-974-0849. Office Fax: 865-974-3067. E-mail: dsimberloff@utk.edu.

SIMEK, JAN F., anthropology professor, former academic administrator; BA, U. Calif., Santa Cruz, 1976; MA, SUNY, Binghamton, 1978, PhD in Anthropology, 1984. Founder Cave Archaeology Rsch. Team U. Tenn., 1996, disting. prof. sci., 2001—, head Anthropology Dept., interim dir. Sch. Art, interim dean Coll. Architecture and Design, 2003—05, chief of staff to chancellor, 2005—08, interim chancellor, 2008—09; interim pres. U. Tenn. Sys., 2009—10. Rsch. assoc., vis. prof. Inst. de Quaternaire, U. Bordeaux, France, 1979—; mem. Commn. 8 on Upper Paleolithic of Europe, Internat. Union of Prehistoric and Protohistoric Scis., 1989; vis. scholar, lectr. Universitat Autonoma de Barcelona, 1991. Contbr. articles to profl. jours. Recipient Certificate of Appreciation for Valuable Svc. to our Nat. Heritage, Tenn. Valley Authority (TVA), 1996. Office: University of Tennessee at Knoxville 250 S Stadium Hall Knoxville TN 37996-0720 Office Phone: 865-974-4408. Business E-Mail: jsimek@utk.edu.

SIMMONS, CHARLES BEDFORD, JR., judge; b. Greenville, SC, Dec. 4, 1956; s. Charles Bedford and Mary Margaret (Mason) S.; children: Charles B. III, Elizabeth S., Mason W. BS magna cum laude, E. Tenn. State U., 1979; JD, U. S.C., 1982. Bar: S.C. 1982, U.S. Dist. Ct. S.C. 1983, U.S. Ct. Appeals (4th cir.) 1986. Law clk. to presiding justice S.C. Cir. Ct., Greenville, 1982-83; with Carter Law Firm, Greenville, 1983-86; ptnr. Wilkins, Nelson, Kittredge & Simmons, Greenville, 1986-89; civil ct. judge Greenville, 1989—; presiding judge 13th Circuit Drug Ct. Mem. bench-bar com. S.C. Supreme Ct., 1992-97; presiding judge 13th cir. Drug Ct; bd. mem. Nat. Assn. Drug Ct. Profls (chmn. bd. 2007-). Mem. adv. com. paralegal program Greenville Tech. Coll., 1989-97, chmn., 1990-91; mem. Friends of 200 Adv. Bd., 1991-99. Named Big Brother of Yr., Big Bros.-Big Sisters, 1988; recipient Svc. to Mankind award Rotary Club, 1989, Outstanding Young Disting. Svc. award Greenville Jaycees, 1990-91. Mem. ATLA, S.C. Bar Assn. (young lawyer liason 1985-89, named Outstanding Young Lawyer of Yr. 1989), Nat. Assn. Drug Ct. Profls. (bd. dirs.), Greenville Bar Assn., S.C. Trial Lawyers Assn., Greenville Young Lawyers (pres. 1988—1990), Gamma Beta Phi, Pi Gamma Mu, Phi Delta Phi. Clubs: Greenville City, Textile (v.p. 1985-87), Revelers (Greenville). Presbyterian. Office: Ste 313 County Courthouse Greenville SC 29601 Office Phone: 864-467-8556. Business E-Mail: csimmons@greenvillecounty.org.

SIMMONS, DAVID, state legislator; b. Nashville, June 13, 1952; m. Alicya V. Simmons; children: Krysia, Alicya. BS, Tenn. Tech. U., 1974; JD, Vanderbilt U., 1977. Atty., ptnr. DeBeaubien, Knight, Simmons, Mantzaris & Neal, LLP, 1980—; former mem. Orange County Rep. Exec. Com., Seminole County Rep. Exec. Com., City Orlando Citizens Rev. Com., US Senator Connie Mack Fed. Jud. Advisor Com., 1989; former chmn. Orlando Landmarks Def Trust; former pres. Orange County Young Reps., Lakeside Alternatives Inc., bd. dir.; vice chmn. Ins. Com.; mem. Procedural & Redistricting Couns. Group A & D, Elder & Long-Term Care & Rules Com., Ethics & Elections Coms., Fla. House of Reps., Fla., 2000—08; mem. Dist. 22 Fla. State Senate, 2011—. Mem.: Orange County Bar Assn., Fla. Bar Assn., Greater Orlando Area C. of C., ABA. Republican. Roman Catholic. Avocations: golf, running, tennis. Office: Ste 304 251 Maitland Ave Altamonte Springs FL 32701 also: Fla State Senate 320 Senate Office Bldg 404 S Monroe St Tallahassee FL 32399-1100 Office Phone: 407-262-7578, 850-487-5050. Business E-Mail: simmons.david.web@flsenate.gov.

SIMMONS, DAVID JEFFREY, real estate executive; b. Greenville, SC, Oct. 12, 1961; s. Wilbur Bernard and Grace (Duncan) S.; m. Georgie Ann Lollis, June 8, 1985. BS in Fin. and Mgmt., U. S.C., 1983. Lic. real estate broker, S.C. V.p. W.B. Simmons and Co., Greenville, 1983—; pres. Simmons Realty and Devel., Greenville, 1983—2002; v.p. Greenville Turf and Tractor, 1987-94, Foothills Turf and Tractor, Easley, SC, 1987-94; pres., CEO Simmons Chevrolet-Geo Inc., Pendleton, SC, 1989-92, Simmons Machinery Co., 2004—. Active March of Dimes, Greenville. Mem. NRA, Nat. Assn. Realtors, S.C. Assn. Realtors, Aircraft Owners and Pilots Assn. Clubs: Poinsett, Commerce (Greenville). Republican. Baptist. Office Fax: 864-269-8730.

SIMMONS, DERRICK T., state senator; b. Greenville, Miss., Dec. 12, 1976; m. CuWanda Flowers. BBA, Jackson State U., Miss., 2000; MBA, Howard U., Washington, 2002, JD, 2005. Bar: Miss. 2006. Trial lawyer Simmons & Simmons PLLC, Greenville, Miss.; senator Dist. 12 Miss. State Senate, Jackson, 2011—. Mem.: ABA, Assn. Trial Lawyers America, Miss. Trial Lawyers Assn., Nat. Bar Assn., Miss. Bar Assn., Magnolia Bar Assn., Greenville Rotary Club, Mason, Kappa Alpha Psi (life). Democrat. Baptist. Office: Miss State Senate Rm 407 PO Box 1018 Jackson MS 39215 Office Phone: 601-359-3221, 662-334-1666. Office Fax: 662-334-1665. Business E-Mail: dsimmons@senate.ms.gov, dtsimmons@simmonspllc.com.

SIMMONS, GLENN REUBEN, management executive; b. Golden, Tex., Jan. 23, 1928; s. Reuben Leon and Fairess (Clark) Simmons; m. Diane Gee Callaway, Dec. 6, 1975; children: Susan, Martha, D'Andra. BS, East Tex. State U., 1950; postgrad., Tex. Christian U. Mgmt. positions LTV Corp., 1949—69; v.p. Contran Corp. & Affiliates, 1969—80; pres. Nat. City Lines & Affiliates, Dallas, 1980—84; res., chief exec. officer Keystone Consol. Industries, Inc., Dallas, 1982—84, dir.; chief exec. officer, dir. Keycon Industries, Inc., 1984—. Dir. LLC Corp. Served with US Army, 1946—47. Mem.: Am. Iron & Steel Inst. Office: Valhi Inc 5430 Lyndon B Johnson Fwy Dallas TX 75240-2601

SIMMONS, HARDWICK, diversified financial services company executive; b. Balt., June 8, 1940; s. Edward Ball and Margaret (Hardwick) S.; m. Sarah Bradlee Dolan, Sept. 9, 1962; children—Elizabeth, Huntington, Benjamin. BA, Harvard U., 1963, MBA, 1966. V.p., Data Processing and Comm. Divsn. Haydens Stone, 1969, mgr., Data Processing and Comm. Divsn., 1970, exec. v.p., retail and sales adminstrn., Data Processing and Comm. Divsn., 1973; sr. exec. v.p., mktg. and sales Shearson/Am. Express, 1977; joined Shearson Lehman Bros. Inc., 1966, regional officer New England, 1972-75, vice chmn., 1975-90, pres., 1983—90; pres., CEO Prudential Securities Inc., 1991—2001; CEO, chmn. The Nasdaq Stock Market Inc., Washington, 2001—03. Former bd. dirs. Chgo. Bd. Options Exch. Inc.; bd. dirs. Stonetex Oil Co., Invivoscribe Technologies, Inc., Raymond James Fin., Inc., 2003—, Lions Gate Entertainment Corp., 2005—, Geneva Acquisition Corp., 2007—09. Trustee Groton Sch. Served, 1960—66, U.S. Marine Corps Res. Mem. Bond Club N.Y.C. Republican. Office: Raymond James Financial Inc 880 Carillon Pky Saint Petersburg FL 33716 Office Phone: 727-567-1000. Office Fax: 727-567-8915. Business E-Mail: hardwick.simmons@raymondjames.com.

SIMMONS, KEITH B., lawyer; b. La Center, Ky., July 14, 1948; m. Kay Simmons; 3 children. BS, U. Ky., 1970; MS, South Dakota State U., 1972; JD, Vanderbilt U., 1976. Bar: Tenn. 1976. Atty. Bass, Berry & Sims PLC, Nashville, 1976—, mng. ptnr., chmn. mgmt. com., 1995—. Bd. dirs. Lex Mundi. Student writing editor: Vanderbilt Law Review, 1975-76. Founding pres. Nashville Pub. Libr. Found., bd. dirs., Rotary Club Nashville, Urban Libraries Coun., Cumberland Region Tomorrow. Lt. USAF, 1970—72. Mem. ABA, Tenn. Bar Assn., Nashville Bar Assn., Nat. Assn. Bond Lawyers. Office: Bass Berry & Sims PLC 150 Third Ave S Ste 2800 Nashville TN 37201 Office Phone: 615-742-6234. Office Fax: 615-742-2734. Business E-Mail: ksimmons@bassberry.com.

SIMMONS, KYLE, lobbyist, former legislative staff member; b. Birmingham, Ala., Apr. 3, 1964; BA, U. Ky., Lexington, 1986, MA, 1988. Account exec. Hill & Knowlton, Inc., Louisville, 1989—95; press sec. to Senator Mitch McConnell US Senate, Washington, 1995, campaign mgr. to Senator Mitch McConnell, 1995—96, chief of staff to Senator Mitch McConnell, 1996—2000, 2002—10; campaign staff mem. Bush-Cheney Presdl. Campaign, 2001; lobbyist Quinn Gillespie Pub. Affairs, Washington, 2002—03; founding mem. The First Group, Washington, 2010—. Named one of The Fabulous 50, Roll Call, 2005, 2009. Republican. Office: The First Group 601 Pennsylvania Ave NW Ste 210 Washington DC 20001 Office Phone: 202-683-6833. E-mail: kyle.simmons@thefirstgroupdc.com.

SIMMONS, MICHAEL ANTHONY, pediatrician; m. Margaret Clare Martindale (div.); children: Kristen Ann, Jeffrey Michael, Jennifer Clare Roe, Jason Davis. AB cum laude, Harvard Coll., 1963, MD, 1967. Diplomate Am. Bd. Pediatrics, Am. Bd. Neonatal-Perinatal Medicine. Intern Harriet Lane Svc., Johns Hopkins Hosp., Balt., 1967—68, asst. resident, 1968—69, sr. asst. resident, 1969; chief resident Dept. Pediatrics, U. Colo. Med. Ctr., Denver, 1971—72, rsch. fellow in perinatal medicine, 1972—74, clin. instr. in pediatrics, 1974—77, assoc. prof. pediatrics, 1977; assoc. prof. pediatrics and obstetrics Johns Hopkins U. Sch. Medicine, Balt., 1977—83; prof., chmn. dept. pediatrics U. Utah Sch. of Medicine, Salt Lake City, 1983—94; dean U. N.C. at Chapel Hill Sch. Medicine, 1994—97, prof. pediatrics, 1994—, interim chief, 1997. Adj. prof. dept. obstetrics and gynecology U. Utah Sch. of Medicine, Salt Lake City, 1984-94; co-dir. newborn svcs. U. Colo. Med. Ctr., Denver, 1974-77, Johns Hopkins Hosp., 1977-83; mem. staff Denver Gen. Hosp., 1976-77, Denver Children's Hosp., 1976-77; vice chmn. clin. affairs dept. pediatrics Johns Hopkins Hosp., 1981-83; chief of pediatrics U. Utah Med. Ctr., Salt Lake, City, 1983-94; med. dir. Primary Children's Med. Ctr., 1983-94; bd. dirs. Triangle Univs. Licensing Consortium, U. N.C. Hosps. Contbr. numerous articles to profl. jours. Fellow Am. Acad. of Pediatrics (excellence in pediatric rsch. com. 1991—, coun. on govt. affairs 1992—); mem. Perinatal Rsch. Soc. (coun. 1982-84, pres.-elect 1985-87, pres. 1989), Western Soc. for Pediatric Rsch. (coun. 1985-86, pres.-elect 1987, pres. 1988), Soc. for Pediatric Rsch., Am. Bd. Pediatrics (sub-bd. of neonatal-perinatal medicine 1983-89, chmn. 1984-88). Office: UNC Health Care 101 Manning Dr Chapel Hill NC 27514 Office Phone: 336-832-6160. Personal E-mail: michael.simmons@mosescone.com.

SIMMONS, RICHARD DE LACEY, mass media executive; b. Cambridge, Mass., Dec. 30, 1934; s. Ernest J. and Winifred (McNamara) S.; m. Mary DeWitt Bleecker, May 20, 1961; children: Christopher DeWitt, Robin Bleecker Turner. Grad., 1951; AB, Harvard Coll., 1955; LLB, Columbia U., 1958. Bar: N.Y. 1959. V.p., gen. counsel Dun & Bradstreet Corp., NYC, 1969-73, exec. v.p., 1976-79, vice chmn., 1979-81; pres. Moody's Investors Svc., NYC, 1973-75, Dun & Bradstreet, Inc., NYC, 1975; pres., chief oper. officer Washington Post Co., Washington, 1981-91; pres. Internat. Herald Tribune, Paris, 1989-96. Bd. dirs. Washington Post Co. Office: 417 S Fairfax St Alexandria VA 22314-3809

SIMMONS, TERRY L., lawyer; b. Santa Anna, Tex. BBA cum laude, Baylor U., Waco, Tex., 1977; JD, Baylor Law Sch., 1978; LLM, So. Meth. U. Dedman Sch. Law, Dallas, 1984. Bar: Tex. 1978, Colo. 1998, NY 2006. With Thompson & Knight, LLP, Dallas. Contbr. articles to profl. jours.; pub., co-editor: Charitable Gift Planning News. Past bd. trustees Bapt. Child & Family Svcs.; bd. trustees Tex. Christian U. Brite Divinity Sch., Adv. Coun. of Dallas Found., Dallas Women's Found. Planned Giving Adv. Com.; founding pres. North Tex. Chpt. Nat. Com. Planned Giving, 1988—97, nat. bd. dirs. Indpls., 1990—92; pres., bd. mem. Charitable Accord, 1994—; bd. dirs. Am. Coun. Gift Annuities. Recipient David M. Donaldson Disting. Svc. award, Planned Giving Grp. New Eng., 1996, Disting. Svc. award, Nat. Com. Planned Giving, 1996; named Planned Giving Profl. of Yr., Planned Giving Today, 1994, Exec. of Yr., The NonProfit Times, 1997; named a Tex. Super Lawyer, Tex. Monthly, 2004—06; named one of Top 100 Attys. in Am., Worth mag., 2005—06. Mem.: ABA. Office: Thompson & Knight LLP One Arts Plaza 1722 Routh St Ste 1500 Dallas TX 75201-2533 Office Phone: 214-969-1419. Office Fax: 214-880-3373. Business E-Mail: Terry.Simmons@tklaw.com.

SIMMONS, WILLIE LEE, state legislator; b. Utica, NY, Mar. 21, 1947; m. Rosie Sibley Simmons; children: Avery, Christopher, Reginald, Sarita. Mem. Dist. 13 Miss. State Senate, 1993—; adminstr. cons. Named Man of Yr., Omega Psi Phi Fraternity, 1993. Mem.: Miss. Assn. Prof. Corrections, Delta State Alumni Assn., Alcorn Alumni Assn., NAACP, Prince Hall Mason, Bolivar County 100 Black Men, America Correctional Assn., Cleve. Area Civic Club. Democrat. Methodist. Mailing: PO Box 297 Cleveland MS 38732 Office Phone: 662-846-7433. Fax: 662-843-0173; Office Fax: 601-359-5957. Business E-Mail: wsimmons@senate.ms.gov.

SIMON, DONALD JOHN, financial planner, theta healer, small business owner; b. Chgo., July 16, 1947; s. Nicholas J. and Alice R. (Olsen) S.; 1 child, Joshua K. BSBA, Oglethorpe U., 1969. CFP, CLU, ChFC. Sales rep. D. W. Shaw, Inc., Berlin, NJ, 1969-74; owner Simon Fin. Co., Vero Beach, Fla., 1975—. Avocations: music, bicycling, boating.

SIMON, HAROLD, radiologist; b. Trenton, NJ, May 13, 1930; s. John and Rae B. Simon; m. Jane L. Ludwig, Feb. 25, 1956; children: Steven Gregg, John Gregory. MD, Duke U., Durham, NC, 1955. Diplomate Am. Bd. Radiology, Am. Bd. Nuc. Medicine. Intern U.S. Naval Hosp., Chelsea, Mass., 1955-56; resident in radiology Mass. Gen. Hosp., Boston, 1958-61, Oak Ridge Inst. Nuc. Medicine, 1959; instr. radiology Med. Sch., Tufts U., Boston, 1961-63, clin. asst. prof., 1965, assoc. clin. prof., 1971-77, clin. prof., 1977-98; pvt. practice Newton Lower Falls, Mass., 1963-95; mem. staff Newton Wellesley Hosp., Mass., assoc. chief radiology, 1977—, radiologist-in-chief, 1987-95; cons. VA Med. Sys., 1997—2009. Dir. Sch. Nuc. Med. Tech.; bd. dirs., mem. CRC com., mem. audit com. Grove Bank, chmn. audit com., 1995—96; bd. dirs., treas. Newell Physicians, Inc., 1986—93; mem. staff Intracoastal Med. Sys., West Palm Beach, Fla., 1997—2001; bd. overseers Newell Health Corp.; cons. VA Hosp., Boston, 1999—2009, Charitas Norwood Hosp., Mass., 1998—2002, Beth Israel Deaconess Hosp., 2007. Contbr. articles to profl. jours. With USNR, 1955—58, med. officer USN, 1956—58 USNR, 1956—58. Fellow: Am. Coll. Radiology; mem.: Palm Beach Civic Assn. (mem. health com. 2009—), CPAC Jewish Fedn., Palm Beach (sub com. chmn. 2007—09, bd. dirs. 2009—, chmn. 2010—13), Mass. Radiology Soc., Mass. Med. Soc. (mem. ins. com. 1992—95), New Eng. Roentgen Ray Soc., Am. Roentgen Ray Soc., Radiol. Soc. N.Am., Banyon Country Club, Belmont Country Club, Pinebrook Country Club (pres. 1982—85), Phi Beta Kappa, Phi Eta Sigma. Home: 252 Atlantic Ave Palm Beach FL 33480-3709

SIMON, H(UEY) PAUL, lawyer; b. Lafayette, La., Oct. 19, 1923; s. Jules and Ida (Rogére) S.; m. Carolyn Perkins, Aug. 6, 1949 (dec. Dec. 1999); 1 child, John Clark. BS, U. Southwestern La., 1943; JD, Tulane U., 1947. CPA La., 1947; bar: La. 1947. Pvt. practice, New Orleans, 1947—; asst. prof. advanced acctg. and taxation U. Southwestern La., 1944-45; staff acct. Haskins & Sells (now Deloitte & Touche), New Orleans, 1945-53, prin., 1953-57; ptnr. Deutsch, Kerrigan & Stiles, 1957-79; sr. founding ptnr. Simon, Peragine, Smith & Redfearn, 1979—. Author: Community Property and Liability for Funeral Expenses of Deceased Spouse, 1946, Income Tax Deductibility of Attorney's Fees in Action in Boundary, 1946, Fair Labor Standards Act and Employee's Waiver of Liquidated Damages, 1946, Louisiana Income Tax Law, 1956, Changes Effected by the Louisiana Trust Code, 1965, Gifts to Minors and the Parent's Obligation of Support, 1968; co-author: Deductions—Business or Hobby, 1975, Role of Attorney in IRS Tax Return Examination, 1978; assoc. editor: The Louisiana CPA, 1956-60; mem. bd. editors Tulane Law Rev., 1945-46, adv. bd. editors, 1992—; estates, gifts and trusts editor The Tax Times, 1986-87. Bd. dirs., mem. fin. com. World Trade Ctr., 1985-86; mem. New Orleans Met. Crime Commn., Coun. for a Better La., New Orleans Met. Area Com., Bur. Govtl. Rsch., Pub. Affairs Rsch. Coun.; co-chmn. NYU Tax Conf., New Orleans, 1976; mem. dean's coun. Tulane U. Law Sch. Named one of Best Lawyers in Am., 1985—. Fellow Am. Coll. Tax Counsel; mem. ABA (com. ct. procedure tax sect. 1958—), AICPA, La. Bar Assn. (com. on legis. and adminstrv. practice 1966-70, bd. cert. tax atty.), New Orleans Bar Assn., Internat. Bar Assn. (com. on securities issues and trading 1970-88), Am. Judicature Soc., Soc. La. CPAs, New Orleans Assn. Notaries, Tulane U. Alumni Assn., New Orleans C. of C. (coun. 1952-66), Tulane Tax Inst. (program com. 1960-96, emeritus 1997-), Internat. House (bd. dirs. 1976-79, 82-85), City Energy Club, New Orleans Country Club, Phi Delta Phi (past pres. New Orleans chpt.). Roman Catholic. Achievements include becoming the 11th attorney-CPA in Louisiana history. Office: 30th Fl Energy Ctr New Orleans LA 70163 Office Phone: 504-258-9177. Personal E-mail: hpsimon@aol.com. Business E-Mail: hpsimon@spsr-law.com.

SIMON, JOSE M., gas distribution company executive; Grad. magna cum laude, Old Dominion U. CPA. Contr. Va. Natural Gas, 1992—96, regional mgr. Newport News, Va., 2002—03, dir., pub. affairs Norfolk, Va., 2003—06, mgr., field svcs.; v.p., contr. Piedmont Natural Gas Co., Inc., 2006—. Office: Piedmont Natural Gas Co 4720 Piedmont Row Dr Charlotte NC 28210 Office Phone: 704-364-3120. Office Fax: 704-365-3849. Business E-Mail: jose.simon@piedmontng.com.

SIMON, LISA, travel association executive; b. Lexington, Ky. BA in Pub. Rels., Eastern Ky. U. Cert. tour profl., in fundraising Ind. U. Various positions Nat. Tour Assn., 1985—98, sr. v.p., 1998—2004, pres., 2006—; exec. dir. Internat. Coach Fedn., 2005—06; sr. v.p. IMG Assns., 2007—. Contbr. articles to profl. jours. Mem.: Tourism Cares US Travel Assn. (bd. mem.), Assn. Mgmt. Companies Inst., Assn. Travel Mktg. Execs., Travel Inst., Am. Soc. Assn. Execs. Office: Nat Tour Assn 546 E Main St Lexington KY 40508 Office Phone: 859-226-4249. Office Fax: 859-226-4404. Business E-Mail: lisa.simon@ntastaff.com.

SIMON, SANDRA RUTH WALDMAN, retired state agency administrator; b. NYC, May 10, 1943; d. Jacob S. and Ann Waldman; m. Sanford R. Simon, Aug. 23, 1964 (div.); m. F. Jerry Lucia, Apr. 30, 1989; children: Hilary G., Taylor M., Pamela Lucia, David Lucia. BA, Barnard Coll., 1965; PhD, Rockefeller U., 1972; MSW, SUNY, Stony Brook, 1985. Postdoctoral rsch. assoc. Brookhaven (N.Y.) Nat. Lab., 1972; rsch. assoc. SUNY, Stony Brook, 1972, Developed and Directed Health Edn. Programs, Islip Town, NY, 1977-81; coord. Suffolk County creative learning program L.I. Regional Adv. Coun. Higher Edn., 1979-80; mng. dir. Pandion Stony Brook Assocs., 1984-87, Tex. Dept. Human Svcs. Evaluation and Planning, Austin, 1987—93; dir. policy analysis and program evaluation Tex. Dept. Human Svcs., 1993—2001, 1993—2001. Lectr., conf. coord. Women's Health Alliance L.I., St. James, N.Y., 1975-77; field instr. U. Tex. Sch. Social Work, 1989, 2000-01. Welfare Reform Evaluation grantee, 1997-2001. Mem. Nat. Coun. Jewish Women, Story Cir. Network Avocations: walking, opera, writing.

SIMON, SCOTT M., state legislator; MArch, Tulane U., 2005. Residential/comml. designer & planner; mem. Dist. 74 La. House of Reps., 2008—, mem. agr., forestry, aquaculture and rural devel. com., commerce com., health and welfare com. Republican. Office: PO Box 1297 Abita Springs LA 70420 also: Capitol Office PO Box 44486 Baton Rouge LA 70804 Office Phone: 985-893-6246, 225-342-6945. Office Fax: 985-893-6247. E-mail: simons@legis.state.la.us.

SIMON, WILLIAM STEVEN (BILL SIMON), retail executive; b. 1959; 2 children. BS in Economics, U. Conn., 1981, MBA, 1988. Various mktg. & devel. positions Cadbury-Schweppes, PepsiCo, Inc., RJR Nabisco, Inc.; v.p. consumer mktg. Diageo PLC, 1998, pres. Southeast region; sec. Fla. Dept. Mgmt. Services, 2003—05; senior v.p. global bus. devel. Brinker Internat., Dallas, 2005—06; exec. v.p. specialty divsn. Wal-Mart Stores Inc., Bentonville, Ark., 2006—07; exec. v.p., COO Wal-mart Stores USA, Bentonville, Ark., 2007—10, pres., CEO, 2010—. Bd. dirs. Miami Project Cure Paralysis, Vol. USA; mem. U. Ark. Sch. Bus. Advisory Bd.; bd. trustees Morehouse Coll.; co-chair Nat. Disaster Relief Fund. Served in USN. Office: Wal-Mart Stores Inc 702 SW Eighth St Bentonville AR 72716 E-mail: bill.simon@walmart.com.

SIMONELLI, LORENZO, diversified technology and services company executive; b. July 27, 1973; BS in Bus. & Economics, Cardiff U., Wales, 1994. With internat. & corporate finance divsn. Mitsubishi Bank, 1991—93; various finance & operational roles General Electric Co., 1994—97, mem. corporate audit staff, 1997—2001, exec. audit mgr. European indsl. bus., 2001—02; financial planning and analysis mgr. GE Consumer & Indsl., Cleve., Louisville, 2002—04, CFO Americas Louisville, 2004—05, gen. mgr. product mgmt., 2005—07, pres., CEO EMEA (Europe, Middle East & Africa) Budapest, Hungary, 2007—08; pres., CEO GE Transp., Erie, Pa., 2008—13, GE Oil & Gas, 2013—. Named one of The 40 Under 40, Fortune mag., 2009, 2010. Office: GE Oil & Gas 4200 Wildwood Pkwy Atlanta GA 30339 Office Phone: 678-844-5407.*

SIMONS, DOYLE R., lumber company executive, lawyer; b. 1964; BBA, Baylor U., 1986; JD, U. Tex., Austin. Assoc. Hutcheson and Grundy, L.L.P.; joined Temple-Inland, Inc., 1992, atty., 1992—94, dir., investor rels., 1994—2003, v.p., adminstrn., 2000—03, chief adminstrv. officer, 2003—05, exec. v.p., 2005—07, chmn., CEO, 2007—. Bd. dirs. Fiserv, Inc., 2007—. Mem., adv. coun. Tex. Meml. Museum, College of Natural Sciences; mem. Governor's Bus. Coun., Tex.; bd. dirs. Am. Forest & Paper Assn. Office: Temple-Inland Inc 3rd Fl 1300 MoPac Expy S Austin TX 78746-6933 Office Phone: 512-434-5800. Office Fax: 512-434-3750. Business E-Mail: doylesimons@templeinland.com.*

SIMONS, ELWYN LAVERNE, physical anthropologist, primatologist, paleontologist, educator; b. Lawrence, Kans., July 14, 1930; s. Verne Franklin and Verna Irene (Cuddeback) S.; m. Friderun Annursel Ankel, Dec. 2, 1972; children: Cornelia Verna Mathilde, Verne Franklin Herbert; 1 child by previous marriage: David Brenton; 1 adopted child Katherine Egan. BS in Biology, Rice U., 1953; MA, Princeton U., 1955, PhD in Paleobiology, 1956; D.Phil., Oxford U., Eng., 1959; MA (hon.), Yale U., 1967; DSc, Oxford U., 1995. Demonstrator, exhibitor Oxford U., 1956-58; lectr. geology Princeton (N.J.) U., 1958-59; asst. prof. zoology U. Pa., Phila., 1959-61; vis. assoc. prof. geology, curator vertebrate paleontology Yale U., New Haven, 1960-61, head divsn. vert. paleontology, 1961-77, prof. paleontology, 1967; prof. geology, curator charge div. vertebrate paleontology Peabody Mus., 1965-77; prof. biol. anthropology, anatomy Duke U., Durham, NC, 1977-82, 1982, prof. zoology, dir. Duke Primate Center, 1977-91, sci. dir., 1991—2001, head, div. fossil primates, 2001—06, dir., div. fossil primates, 2006—. Dir. Paleontol. Expdns., Egypt, 1961—68, Egypt, 1977—2007, India, 1968—69, India, 1996, India, 1998, India, 1999—2000; rsch. expdns. for fossil mammals, Wyo., 1960—96, Wyo., 1998—99, Iran, 1970, Spain, 1971, Madagascar, 1983—2005; Barbour-Schramm Meml. lectr. U. Nebr., 1974; David French lectr. Claremont Coll., 1974; traveling lectr. French Bur. Fgn. Affairs, 1976. Author: Primate Evolution: An Introduction To Man's Place In Nature, 1972; co-editor: Macmillan Series in Physical Anthropology; A Simons Family History in England and America, 1975, Candebec in France and England, 2005, Tarsiers: Past, Present, and Future; contbr. numerous articles to profl. publs. Decorated chevalier Ordre Nat., Madagascar; recipient Annadale Meml. medal, Asiatic Soc. Bengal, 1973, Sr. U.S. Scientist award, Alexander von Humboldt Found., 1975; named hon. citizen, Fayum Province of Egypt, 1981. Mem. AAAS, Am. Philos. Soc., Nat. Acad. Scis., Soc. Vertebrate Paleontology, Inst. Human Paleontology, Am. Assn. Zool. Parks and Aquariums (primate specialist group, advisor prosimian taxon group), Assn. Phys. Anthropology (Charles R. Darwin award 2000), Madagascar Fauna Group (bd. dirs.), Internat. Assn. Human Biologists, Sigma Xi. Democrat. Achievements include research in on early mammals, prosimians and primate and human evolution, with special interest in living prosimians, higher primate and human origin and evolution; discovery of 1st tarsiers and 1st marsupials in Africa; naming of earliest known ape Aegyptopithecus in Oligocene of Africa; discovery of Gigantopithecus in India, 1968; naming of earliest anthropoids Oligopithecus, 1962, Qatrania, 1983, Serapia and Arsinoea, 1992; discovery of and naming of new species of Propithecus: Golden Crowned Sifaka in Madagascar, 1989; conservation of lemurs and rain forest of Madagascar. Office: Duke Lemur Ctr Divsn Fossil Primates 1013 Broad St Durham NC 27705 Office Phone: 919-416-8420 Ext. 27. Office Fax: 919-416-8584. Business E-Mail: esimons@duke.edu.

SIMPSON, ARNOLD, state legislator; b. Apr. 26, 1952; BA, Ky. State U.; JD, U. Ky. Atty.; former mem. Northern Ky. Area Devel. Dist.; mem. St. Elizabeth Med. Ctr., Ky. County Health Dept.; mem. Dist. 65 Ky. House of Reps., 1994—. Mem.: Northern Ky. Arts Coun., Legal Aid Soc., Northern Ky. Cmty. Ctr., Cmty. Chest Northern Ky., Am. Bar Assn., Northern Ky. Bar Assn., Ky. Bar. Assn., Covington Civil Svc. Comn., Ky. County Boys Girls Club. Democrat. Baptist. Address: Shutt Mansion 28 W Fifth St Covington KY 41011 Office: Ky Legislature Rm 357D 702 Capitol Ave Frankfort KY 40601 Office Phone: 859-261-6577, 502-564-8100 ext. 695. Business E-Mail: arnold.simpson@lrc.ky.gov.

SIMPSON, BOB R., energy executive; BS Acctg. with honors, Baylor U., MBA. Tax mgr. Southland Royalty Co., 1976—79, v.p. Fin. & Corp. Devel., 1979—86; co-founder, CEO XTO Energy, Inc.,

Fort Worth, Tex., 1986—96, chmn., CEO, 1996—2008, chmn., 2008—10. Mem. Nat. Petroleum Council; bd. dirs. XTO Energy Inc., 1990—. Office: XTO Energy Inc 810 Houston St Fort Worth TX 76102-6298

SIMPSON, CARTER B., lawyer; b. Pitts., July 19, 1950; s. John W. Simpson; m. Paulette Peters, May 1, 1982; children: Christina B., Carter B. Jr. BSE in Elec. Engring., Princeton U., 1972; JD, U. Mich., 1976. Assoc. Cadwalader, Wickersham & Taft, NYC, 1976—86, counsel, 1986—88; counsel, antitrust and litig. Mobil Corp., Fairfax, Va., 1988—91, sr. counsel, antitrust, 1991—96, sr. counsel, antitrust and trade regulation, 1996—99; downstream antitrust counsel Exxon Mobil Corp., Fairfax, 2000—06; sr. counsel antitrust and trade regulation Downstream Cos., 2006—09; counsel SNR Denton, 2010—13, Dentons, 2013—. Adv. bd. mem.: Antitrust Counselor, Bus. Laws Inc., 1995—2005. Dir. Overlook Condo Assn., Wintergreen, Va., 2005—06. Mem.: ABA Anitrust Sect. (vice chair Clayton Act com. 1995—99, vice chmn. teleseminars com. 2007—10, vice chair programs com. 2009—10, vice chair corporate counseling com. 2010—). Home: 10007 Thompson Ridge Ct Great Falls VA 22066 Office Phone: 202-408-9179. Business E-Mail: carter.simpson@dentons.com.

SIMPSON, CHARLES R., III, federal judge; BA, U. Louisville, 1967, JD, 1970. Bar: Ky. 1970, U.S. Dist. Ct. (we. dist.) Ky. 1971, U.S. Cir. Ct. (6th cir.) 1985. With Rubin, Trautwein & Hays, Louisville, 1971-75, Levin, Yussman & Simpson, Louisville, 1975-77; pvt. practice Louisville, 1977-86; judge US Dist. Ct. (we. dist.) Ky., Louisville, 1986—2001, 2001—, chief judge, 1994—2001. Part-time staff counsel Jefferson County Judge/Exec., 1978-84; adminstr. Jefferson County Alcoholic Beverage Control, 1983-84. Roman Catholic. Office: US Dist Ct 601 W Broadway Rm 247 Louisville KY 40202-2238 E-mail: judgesimpson@kywd.uscourts.gov.

SIMPSON, DANIEL REID, lawyer, mediator; b. Glen Alpine, NC, Feb. 20, 1927; s. James R. and Margaret Ethel (Newton) S.; m. Mary Alice Leonard, Feb. 25, 1930; children: Mary Simpson Beyer, Ethel B. Simpson Todd, James R., II. BS, Wake Forest U., 1949, LLB, 1951. Bar: N.C. 1951, U.S. Dist. Ct. (we. dist.) N.C. 1951, U.S. Ct. Appeals (4th and 5th cirs.) 1980; cert. mediator. Former ptnr. Simpson Aycock PA, Morganton, NC; of counsel Simpson, Kuehnert, Vinay & Jones, P.A., Morganton, Simpson & Simpson Law Firm PLLC. Author: American Angels, 2001. Mem. N.C. Ho. of Reps., 1959-65; mem. N.C. Senate, 1984-96; del. Rep. Nat. Conv., 1968, 76; mem. N.C. Rep. Exec. Com. Served with AUS, 1943-45, PTO, former mem. Courts Commn. Recipient Guardian Small Bus. award Order of Longleaf Pine; named to NRA Legion of Honor; sports complex named in his honor by Town of Glen Alpine, N.C. Mem. N.C. Bar Assn., Burke County Bar Assn., Masons (past master). Baptist. Home: 2358 E Point Rd Nebo NC 28761-9694 also: PO Box 1329 Morganton NC 28680-1329 Office: Simpson & Simpson Law Firm PLLC 401-B South Green St Morganton NC 28655 Office Phone: 828-437-9744. E-mail: jrs@hci.net.

SIMPSON, DAVID JOHN, medical products executive; b. Port Huron, Mich., Aug. 8, 1946; s. John and Gizel (Zotter) S.; m. Carol Ann Leslie, Aug. 31, 1968; children: Matthew, Danielle, Joshua. BBA, Western Mich. U., 1969; attended Advanced Mgmt. Program, Harvard U., 1991. CPA, Mich. Jr. acct., audit mgr. Ernst & Whinney, Kalamazoo, 1969—78; v.p., Fin., treas., sec. & bd. dirs. Clausing Corp., Kalamazoo, 1979—85; treas. Rexnord Inc., Brookfield, Wis., 1985—87, v.p., 1987; v.p., CFO & sec. Stryker Corp., Kalamazoo, 1987—. Bd. dirs. Kinetic Concepts, Inc. Served with USMCR, 1970-76. Mem. Fin. Execs. Inst., Am. Inst. CPAs. Office: Kinetic Concepts Inc Bd Directors 8023 Vantage Dr San Antonio TX 78230-4726 Office Phone: 210-255-6157. E-mail: david.simpson@kci1.com.

SIMPSON, H. RICHARD (DICK SIMPSON), retail merchandiser; b. Oct. 10, 1928; s. Bert M. and Violet K. (Mathias) S.; m. Marion Welty, 1950; children: Carla Sue, Barry Nelson, Richard Drew, Catherine Irene; m. Joan Rose Marshall, March 22, 1970; m. Charlotte S. Fox, Dec. 12, 1999. Student, U. Akron, 1949-50; BS, U. Md., 1955. Mgr. Tex. GMC, Detroit, 1959-62. Pres. Friendly Pontiac, Friendly Toyota, Derrick Chrysler, Simpson Oil Corp., Corp. S., Dick Tiger Homes, Austin, 1962-85, Simpson Hill Country Realty and Builders, 1989-2003, 05, 07. Served to lt. col. USAF, 1953-75; Korea. Decorated D.F.C., Air Medal. Mem. Soc. Automotive Engrs., Res. Officers Assn., Horseshoe Bay Yacht Club, Horseshoe Bay Country Club, Rotary Internat., Masons. Methodist. Office: PO Box 8186 Horseshoe Bay TX 78657-8186 Personal E-mail: dicksimpson_hsb@yahoo.com.

SIMPSON, JACK BENJAMIN, medical technologist, business executive; b. Tompkinsville, Ky., Oct. 30, 1937; s. Benjamin Harrison and Verda Mae (Woods) S.; m. Winona Clara Walden, Mar. 21, 1957; children: Janet Lazann, Richard Benjamin, Randall Walden, Angela Elizabeth. Student, Western Ky. U., 1954-57; grad., Norton Infirmary Sch. Med. Tech., 1958. Asst. chief med. technologist Jackson County Hosp., Seymour, Ind., 1958-61; chief med. technologist, bus. mgr. Mershon Med. Labs., Indpls., 1962-66; founder, dir., officer Am. Monitor Corp., Indpls., 1966-77; founder, pres., dir. Global Data, Inc., Ft. Lauderdale, Fla., 1986—. Mng. ptnr. Astroland Enterprises, Indpls., 1968—2010, 106th St. Assocs., Indpls., 1969-72, Keystones Ltd., Indpls., 1970-82, Delray Rd. Assoc. Ltd., Indpls., 1970-71, Allisonville Assocs. Ltd., Indpls., 1970-82, Grandview Assocs. Ltd., 1977—2010, Rucker Assocs. Ltd., Indpls., 1974—2010; mng. ptnr. Raintree Assocs. Ltd., Indpls., 1978—2010, Westgate Assocs. Ltd., Indpls., 1978—2010; pres., dir. Topps Constrn. Co., Inc., Bradenton, Fla., 1973-91, Acrovest Corp., Asheville, N.C., 1980—; dir. Indpls. Broadcasting, Inc.; founder, bd. dirs. Bank of Bradenton, 1986-92; founder, CFO Biomass Processing Tech., Inc., West Palm Beach, Fla., 1996—2008; also bd. dirs. Mem. Am. Soc. Med. Technologists (cert.), Indpls. Soc. Med. Technologists, Fla. Soc. Med. Technologists, Am. Soc. Clin. Pathologists, Am. Assn. Clin. Chemistry, Royal Soc. Health (London), Internat. Platform Assn., Am. Mus. Natural History, Columbia of Indpls. Club, Harbor Beach Surf Club, Fishing of Am. Club, Marina Bay Club (Ft. Lauderdale), Elks. Republican. Personal E-mail: jack_simpson@msn.com.

SIMPSON, MICHAEL, retired metals service center executive; b. Albany, NY, Dec. 10, 1938; s. John McLaren Simpson and Constance (Hasler) Ames; m. Barbara Ann Bodtke, Jan. 5, 1963; children: Leslie Ann, Elizabeth S. Wessel. BA, U. Mich., 1965, MBA, 1966. Product mgr. Armour & Co., Chgo., 1966-68; with A.M. Castle & Co., Franklin Park, Ill., 1968—, pres. Hy-Alloy Steels Co. divsn., 1974-79, v.p. Midwestern region, 1977-79, chmn. bd., 1979—2004, also bd. dirs.; chmn. emeritus, 2004—. Trustee Rush U. Med. Ctr., Chgo., 1978—, mem. exec. com., 1980—2009, vice chmn., 1991-2009; trustee Oldfields Sch., Glencoe, Md., 1982-87, 95-2003, chmn. bd., 1998-2000; bd. dirs. Lake Forest Hosp. Found. and Lake Forest Hosp., Ill., 1998-2008; chmn. bd. overseers Rush U., Chgo., 1996-2009.

SIMPSON, MICHAEL MARCIAL, science and technology specialist, consultant; b. Honolulu, Sept. 24, 1954; s. Marcial and Beatrice S. AB in Biol. Scis., U. Calif., Berkeley, 1976; MS in Biol. Scis., U. San Francisco, 1977; MS in Energy and Resources, U. Calif., Berkeley, 1979; PhD in Environ. Scis. and Engring., UCLA, 1986. Assoc. researcher NASA, Moffett Field, Calif., 1973; radio program host, producer Sta. KUSF-FM, San Francisco, 1976-78; rsch. asst. Lawrence Berkeley Lab., Berkeley, Calif., 1977-79; rsch. assoc. UCLA/U.S. Dept. Energy, 1979-81; congl. fellow, environ. health U.S. Congress, Washington, 1981-82; specialist in environ. techs., life scis., and terrorism U.S. Congl. Rsch. Svc., Washington, 1982—2006, sci. policy advisor on Homeland Security issues, 2006—; sr. prin. leader, fellow, chair, Coun. Sci. Tech. Engring. Math. CSC Inc., 2006—13; writer Dakota Consultancy, 2013; STEM project mgr. QNA Support of Office Naval Rsch., 2013—. Adv. bd. Banbury Ctr., Cold Spring Harbor, N.Y., 1985—; adj. faculty The Washington Ctr., 1992—. Contbr. articles to profl. jours., chapters to books. Fellow AAAS (Named Congl. Sci. fellow 1981-82), CSC Def. Group; mem. Washington Acad. Sci., Am. Chem. Soc., Am. Nuc. Soc., UCLA in Washington (exec. steering com. 1986-92). Avocations: photography, travel, writing, bicycling. Home: 3464 Mildred Dr Falls Church VA 22042 Business E-Mail: DrMichaelMSimpson22015@yahoo.com.

SIMPSON, MURRAY, electrical engineer, consultant; b. NYC, July 27, 1921; s. George and Sonia Simpson; m. Ethel Gladstein, June 29, 1947; children: David, Mindy, Jonathan. BEE, CCNY, 1942; MEE, Polytech. Inst. of NY, 1952. Engr. ITT, NYC, 1942-44; sr. engr. Raytheon Co., Waltham, Mass., 1946-48; sect. mgr. Fairchild Guided Missles div., Farmingdale, NY, 1948-50; v.p. Maxson Elec. Co., NYC, 1950-62; pres. SEDCO Sys. Inc. subs. Raytheon Co., Melville, NY, 1963-86; cons. M. Simpson Assocs., Ft. Lauderdale, Fla., 1986—. Former chmn. bd. dirs. Radyne Corp. Contbr. articles to profl. jours. Former bd. dirs. United Way, LI. Served to lt. (j.g.) USNR, 1944—46, PTO. Fellow: IEEE (chmn. L.I. sect. 1963—64). Avocations: boating, skiing, golf, tennis.

SIMPSON, ROSS JOSEPH, JR., cardiologist, educator; b. NYC, May 20, 1948; s. Ross Joseph Simpson and Marguarite O'Reilly; m. Christine Barlow, Sept. 13, 1982; children: Christina Elizebeth, Ross Joseph III, Brian Frances, Francesca Alma. BS, Notre Dame U., Ind., 1969; MD, Georgetown U., DC, 1973; MPH, U. NC, Chapel Hill; PhD, Chapel Hill, 1998. Asst. prof. medicne U. NC, 1977—83, assoc. prof. medicine, 1983—91, prof. medicine, 1991—, adj. prof. epidemiology, 1998—, dir. preventive cardiology clinic, 1995—, dir., coronary care unit, 1979—94, med. control officer Carolina air care, 1986—94; prin. clin. coord. Med. Rev. NC, Cary, 1995—. Med. examiner orange county State of NC, Chapel Hill, 1979—86. Contbr. articles to profl. jours. Mem. sorin soc. Notre Dame, Ind., 1985—2009. Grant, NIH, 1980—2003. Fellow: ACP, Am. Coll. Cardiology. Home: 102 Foxridge Rd Chapel Hill NC 27514 Office: University NC 160 Dental Cir CB7075 6033 Burnett-W Chapel Hill NC 27514 Office Phone: 919-966-1743. Business E-Mail: rsimpson@med.unc.edu.*

SIMPSON, STEVEN DREXELL, lawyer; b. Sturgis, Mich., Sept. 20, 1953; s. Rex and Lorraine Simpson; m. Peggy Deibert, Apr. 28, 1979; children: Andrew Drexell, Christine Elizabeth, Marianne Tyner. BA, Hillsdale Coll., Mich., 1975; JD, Wake Forest U., 1978; LLM in Taxation, Georgetown U., 1981. Bar: Fla. 1978, D.C. 1980, N.C. 1984. Assoc. Bradford, Williams et al, Miami, Fla., 1978-80, Webster & Chamberlain, Washington, 1980-82, Fisher, Wayland et al, Washington, 1982-84, Maupin, Taylor & Ellis, P.A., Raleigh, NC, 1984-98; pvt. practice, 1998—2006; counsel Wyrick Robbin Yates & Ponton, LLP, 2007—. Author: Tax-Exempt Organizations: Organizational and Operational Requirements, 2000, Tax-Exempt Organizations: Reporting, Disclosure and Other Procedural Aspects, 2000, Taxable Expenditures, 2000, Tax Compliance for Tax-Exempt Organizations, 2011, Multistate Guides to Regulation and Taxation of Nonprofits, 2011; contbr. articles to profl. jours. Mem. ABA (exempt orgns. com.). Republican. Methodist. Avocations: golf, running. Home: 409 Hillandale Dr Raleigh NC 27609-7036 Office: PO Drawer 17803 4101 Lake Boone Trail Ste 300 Raleigh NC 27619 Home Phone: 919-786-4588; Office Phone: 919-781-4000. Business E-Mail: ssimpson@wyrick.com.

SIMRILL, GARY J., state legislator; b. Rock Hill, SC, May 29, 1966; s. Hugh T. Simrill and Diane Belk; m. Mary Ruth Dobson; children: Mallory Graham, Sarah Kate. BS, Winthrop U., 1991. Pres., CEO Carolina Motorworks; mem. Dist. 46 SC House of Reps., 1993—, asst. majority whip, 1995—; mem. Judiciary Com., Rules Com., Bus. Caucus, Urban Caucus. Recipient Disting. Svc. award, Nat. Fedn. Blind. Mem.: Econ. Forecast Roundtable, Greater Rock Hill United Way (bd. dir. 1995—), Kiwanis Internat., Govt. Action Coun, Lions Club. Republican. Baptist. Address: 1515 Alexander Rd Rock Hill SC 29732 Mailing: 420C Blatt Bldg PO Box 11867 Columbia SC 29201 Office Phone: 803-366-0445, 803-734-3040. Fax: 803-734-2925. Business E-Mail: jgs@scstatehouse.net.

SIMS, BARBARA, state legislator; b. Mar. 18; m. Fred Sims. State rep. Dist. 119, Ga., 2007—. Republican. Office: PO Box 3126 Augusta GA 30904 Office Phone: 706-738-3918, 404-656-0109. E-mail: barbara.sims@house.ga.gov.

SIMS, CHARLES NEIL, state legislator; b. El Paso, Tex., Feb. 19, 1958; s. Charles Neil and Mary Waunelle Vickers Sims; m. Rebbeca Leigh Littleton, 1984; children: Charles Neil III, William Vickers, Caroline Greer. Former state rep. Dist. 167, Ga.; v.p. Sims Funeral Home, Inc., 1985—; ins. & trust agt., 1993—; state rep. Dist. 130 Ga., 2003—04; state rep. Dist. 169 Ga., 2004—; mem. Agr. & Consumer Affairs, 1997—, Ways & Means Com., 1997—, Defense & Vets Affairs Com., 1997—; house rep. Ga. Mem.: Westside Elem Sch. Parent Tchr. Orgn., Soc. Mil. Engrs., Douglas Lions Club (pres. 1997—). Republican. Methodist. Mailing: 9699 W Baker Hwy Ambrose GA 31512 Office: Legis Off Bldg 18 Capitol Sq Rm 607 Atlanta GA 30334 Office Phone: 912-384-1234. Fax: 912-384-1709. Personal E-mail: frawgee1@aol.com. Business E-Mail: c.sims@csims.org, csims@inet.legis.state.ga.us.

SIMS, EDWARD HOWELL, editor, writer; b. Orangeburg, SC, May 29, 1923; s. Hugo Sheridan and Jesse Lucile (Howell) S.; m. Frances Dell Hartt, Jan. 5, 1946; m. Martha Lurene Bass, July 18, 1960; children: Edward H., Robert; m. Bente Thorlund Christensen, Oct. 4, 1969; children: Edward Christian, Frederik. AB, Wofford Coll., 1943; postgrad., Emory U., 1946-47. Mng. editor Orangeburg Times and Democrat, 1946, editor, 1952—; Washington corr., founder Washington bur. for number S.C. dailies, 1947. Dir. Sims Pub. Co., Orangeburg. Columnist: Looking South From Washington, 1948—; Washington Bur. chief: Editor's Copy syndicate, 1950-52; editor-pub., 1952—; radio news analyst: The News of The Week In Washington, 1951—; Author: American Aces, 1958, Greatest Fighter Missions, 1962, The Fighter Pilots, 1967, Fighter Tactics 1914-70, 1972, Aces Over the Oceans, 1987 The German American Tragedy, 2004, The Life & Times of Eduard H. Sims, 2005; contbr. articles to publs. White House corr. covering Pres.''s confs., 1948—; mem. Senate and House press galleries, 1947—; Am. consul Munich, Germany, 1963-65; cons. Exec. Office of White House, 1966-67; consul gen. Zurich, 1992; apptd. mem. Commn. to Preserve Am. Heritage Abroad, 1987. Served to 1st lt. USAF, World War II, fighter pilot Germany. Recipient Young Man of the Year award S.C. Jr. C. of C., 1959 Mem. White House Corrs. Assn., Am. Legion, V.F.W. Clubs: Rotary, Nat. Press; Metropolitan (Washington); R.A.F. (London). Methodist. Home: 3803 Pin Oaks St Sarasota FL 34232-1241 Business E-Mail: mail@editorscopy.com.

SIMS, FREDDIE POWELL, state legislator; m. Norman Sims; 3 children. Ret. middle sch. prin.; mem. Dist. 151 Ga. House Reps., 2005—08; mem. Dist. 12 Ga. State Senate, 2009—. Democrat. Baptist. Mailing: 5377 Goose Hollow Rd Dawson GA 31742 Office Phone: 229-347-0251. Business E-Mail: freddie.sims@senate.ga.gov.

SIMS, MICHAEL B., corporate financial executive; BS in Acctg., Ind. U., Bloomington, Ill., 1977. CPA. Acctg. positions Ernst & Young LLP; audit mgr. Arthur Young & Co., 1980—88; mgr., fin. reporting Staley Continental, Inc., Rolling Meadows, Ill., 1988; joined Chiquita Brands International, Inc., 1988, v.p., investor rels., asst. corp. contr., 1997—99, v.p., fin. and adminstrn., CFO, Europe, 2000—06, v.p., fin. and adminstrn., 2006—07, v.p., corp. devel., 2006—09, treas., 2007—09, sr. v.p., CFO, 2009—. Office: Chiquita Brands International Inc 550 S Caldwell St Ste 1010 Charlotte NC 28202-2681 Office Phone: 513-784-8000. Office Fax: 513-784-8030. Business E-Mail: msims@chiquita.com.

SIMS, ROGER W., lawyer; b. Cleve., Aug. 3, 1950; BA with high honors, U. Fla., 1972, JD, 1974. Bar: Fla. 1975. Mem. Holland & Knight, Orlando, Fla. Mem. Moot Ct. U. Fla.; contbr. to profl mag. and jour. Mem. ABA (mem. standing com. on environ. law 2000-2003), Fla. Bar Assn. (chmn. environ., land use law sect. 1988-89), Fla. Assn. Water Quality Control (pres. 2006-07), Phi Beta Kappa, Phi Kappa Phi, Omicron Delta Kappa, Phi Alpha Delta, Fla. Blue Key. Office: Holland & Knight PO Box 1526 200 S Orange Ave Ste 2600 Orlando FL 32801-3453 Office Phone: 407-425-8500. Business E-Mail: roger.sims@hklaw.com.

SIMS, WILSON, lawyer; b. Nashville, Dec. 24, 1924; s. Cecil and Grace (Wilson) S.; m. Linda Bell, Aug. 12, 1948; children: Linda Rickman, Suzanne, Wilson. BA, U. N.C., 1946; JD, Vanderbilt U., 1948. Bar: Tenn. 1948. Since practiced in, Nashville; ptnr. Bass, Berry & Sims; gen. counsel, dir. of pub. and private rels. Baird Ward Printing Co., Southeastern Capital Corp., Martha White Foods, Synercon Corp., Forrest Life Ins. Co., Charter Co., The Bailey Co., Kenworth of Tenn., Inc. Chmn. Tenn. Commn. for Human Devel., Tenn. Commn. on Continuing Legal Edn.; mem. Tenn. Gen. Assembly, 1959-60; bd. dirs. Nashville YMCA, founder Camp Widjiwagen, United Cerebal Palsy, Kidney Found., Matthew 25, McKendree Village; trustee Meharry Med. Coll.& Webb Sch., Bell Buckle, Tenn.; adv. bd. Jr. League; mem. bd. visitors U. N.C. 1st lt. USMCR, 1942-45, 50-52. Fellow Am. Bar Found. (life), Nashville Bar Found.; mem. ABA, Tenn. Bar Assn. (past spkr. ho. of dels., past pres.), Nashville Bar Assn. (past pres., dir., Pub. Svc. award), Tenn. Bar Found. (past chmn.), Am. Judicature Soc., Am. Acad. Polit. Sci., Vanderbilt U. Law Alumni Assn. (past pres., Disting. Svc. award), Nashville C. of C. (2 terms bd. govs.), Belle Meade Country Club (bd. dirs.), High Hampton Colony Club (bd. dirs., pres., Sr. Golf Champion), Hampton Choral Scramble Soc. (pres.), Hillwood Country Club(bd. dirs.) Methodist. Home: 22 Foxhall Close Nashville TN 37215-1862 Office: Bass Berry & Sims PLC 150 Third Ave S Ste 2800 Nashville TN 37201 Business E-Mail: wsims@bassberry.com.

SIMSON, GARY JOSEPH, dean, law educator; b. Newark, Mar. 18, 1950; s. Marvin and Mildred (Silberg) Simson; m. Rosalind Slivka, Aug. 15, 1971; children: Nathaniel, Jennie Anne. BA summa cum laude, Yale Coll., 1971; JD, Yale U., 1974. Bar: Conn. 1974, NY 1980. Law clk. to Judge J. Joseph Smith US Ct. Appeals (2nd cir.), 1974-75; asst. prof. law U. Tex., 1975—77, prof. law, 1977—80, Cornell U. Law Sch., Ithaca, NY, 1980—2006, prof. law emeritus, 2006, assoc. dean faculty devel., 1997—2000, assoc. dean acad. affairs, 2000—04; dean, Joseph C. Hostetler-Baker & Hostetler prof. law Case Western Reserve U. Sch. Law, 2006—08, Joseph C. Hostetler-Baker & Hostetler prof. law Cleve., 2009—10; dean, Macon chair in law Walter F. George Sch. Law, Mercer U., Macon, Ga., 2010—. Vis. prof. law Cornell U., Ithaca, NY, 1979—80, U. Calif., Berkeley, 1986; chmn. adv. bd. law caseboook series Carolina Acad. Press; bd. trustee Georgia Inst. of Continuing Judicial Edn. Author: Issues and Perspectives in Conflict of Laws: Cases and Materials, 1985, Issues and Perspectives in Conflict of Laws: Cases and Materials, 2nd edition, 1991, Issues and Perspectives in Conflict of Laws: Cases and Materials, 3rd edition, 1997, Issues and Perspectives in Conflict of Laws: Cases and Materials, 4th edition, 2005, Issues and Perspectives in Conflict of Laws: Cases and Materials, 5th edition, 2014; contbr. articles to profl. jours. Mem.: ABA, American Law Inst., ACLU, Phi Kappa Phi, Phi Beta Kappa. Office: Walter F George School Law Mercer University 1021 Georgia Ave Macon GA 31207 Office Phone: 478-301-2602. Business E-Mail: simson_g@law.mercer.edu.*

SINCLAIR, JACK L., retail executive; b. 1960; BA in Economics & Mktg., U. Strathclyde. Trainee Shoppers' Paradise, England, 1982; with Tesco Stores Ltd.; European devel. dir. SB Capital; with McCurrach; various positions Safeway plc, 1990—2004; exec. v.p. grocery divsn. Walmart USA, 2008—10, exec. v.p., food divsn., 2010—. Office: Wal-Mart Stores, Inc 702 SW 8th St Bentonville AR 72716-8611

SINCLAIR, LINDA DRUMWRIGHT, educational consultant; b. Norfolk, Va., Aug. 4, 1942; d. Raymond Edward and Evelyn Elizabeth (Edwards) Drumwright; m. Charles Armstrong Sinclair, Oct. 5, 1962; children: William, Dianne, Sandy. BS, U. S.C., 1974, MA, 1976, postgrad. Cert. tchr. in biology, chemistry, physics. Sci. tchr. Keenan H.S., Columbia, S.C., 1976-77; chemistry/physics tchr. Lexington (S.C.) H.S., 1977-93; talented/gifted tchr. U. S.C., Columbia, 1988; tchr. rsch. program Oak Ridge (Tenn.) Nat. Lab., 1989; rschr. Savannah River Ecology Lab., Aiken, S.C., 1991-92; state sci. edn. cons. S.C. Dept. Edn., Columbia, 1993—; owner Consulting Group: Sci. Edn. Support, LLC. Cons. Prentice Hall Pub., Princeton, N.J., 1992-93. Author: Operation Radon, 1993. Adv. bd. S.C. Forestry Commn., Columbia, 1993—, S.C. Environ. Coalition, Columbia, 1993—, S.C. Sci. Coun., Columbia, 1989—; mem., com. chair Lexington Woman's Club, 1986—; v.p. Lexington Garden Club, 1983—. Named S.C. Sci. Tchr. of the Yr., S.C. Acad. Sci., 1986, Sigma Xi, 1986, S.C. Chemistry Tchr. of the Yr., S.C. Chem. Soc., 1992; recipient Presdl. Award for Excellence in Sci. Teaching, NSF, 1993. Mem. S.C. Sci. Coun. (v.p., pres.), S.C. Chemistry Tchrs. Assn. (bd. dirs. 1987—), S.C. Acad. Sci. (bd. dirs. 1982—), S.C. Jr. Acad. Sci. (bd. dirs. 1980—), S.C. Environ. Edn. Assn. (bd. dirs. 1990—), Nat. Sci. Tchrs. Assn. (bd. dirs. 1992-94), SC Sci. Leadership Assn. (bd. dirs. 1996-), Found. Bd. SC State Mus. Lutheran. Avocations: horseback riding, gardening, swimming, water sports. Home: 107 Hermitage Rd Lexington SC 29072-2221 Office: SC Dept Edn 801-B Rutledge Bldg 1429 Senate St Columbia SC 29201-3730 Business E-Mail: lsinclair@sc.rr.com.

SINCLAIR, ROBERT EWALD, retired physician; b. Columbus, Jan. 19, 1924; s. George Albert and Bertha Florence (Ewald) S.; m. Mary Almira Underwood, Mar. 31, 1945; children: Marcia Ann, Bonnie Sue. BA, Ohio State U., Columbus, 1948, MD, 1952. Lic. physician, Ohio, Colo., Ala., Kans. Intern Mt. Carmel Hosp., Columbus, 1952—53; resident neurology and psychiatry Columbus State Hosp., 1964—66, chief psychiat. resident adolescent unit, 1965—66; pvt. practice medicine Columbus, 1953—57, Granville, Ohio, 1957—64; dir. student health svc., prof. health edn., team physician Denison U., 1957—64; dir. student health svc., team physician U. Cin., 1966—70; dir. Lafene Student Health Ctr. and U. Hosp.; team physician Kans. State U., Manhattan, 1970—80; dir. Russell Student Health Ctr. and Hosp.; prof. medicine U. Ala., University, 1980—88, ret., 1988. Physician Westinghouse Electric Corp., Columbus, 1953-57; asst. zone chief Civilian Def., Columbus, 1954-57; mem. Licking County Bd. Health, Ohio, 1958-59. Bd. dirs. social health com. Cin. and Hamilton County, Ohio, 1967-70, drug abuse and edn. com., 1968-70. With USNR, 1943-46. Named Hall of Fame, West High Alumni Assn., Columbus, Ohio., 2004. Mem. AMA, Ohio Med. Soc., Kans. Med. Soc., Ala. Med. Soc., Columbus Acad. Medicine, Licking County Med. Soc., Riley County Med. Soc. (Kans.), Tuscaloosa County Med. Soc., Nat. Athletic Trainers Assn., Ohio Coll. Health Assn. (editor Newsletter 1968-70, pres. 1970-71), Central Coll. Health Assn. (pres. 1972-73), So. Coll. Health Assn. (pres. 1986), St. Andrews Soc., So. Medicine Assn., Delta Tau Delta (faculty advisor), Nu Sigma Nu, Nu Sigma Nu Ohio State Alumni Assn. (pres. 1953-54), Kiwanis, Rotary. Home: 1 Rollingwood Tuscaloosa AL 35406-2261 Personal E-mail: unsink2@comcast.net.

SING, WILLIAM BENDER, lawyer; b. Houston, Oct. 16, 1947; s. William Bender, Sr. and Alice Irene Sing; m. Doris Anne Sing, Sept. 1, 1967; children: Erin Elaine, Emily Elizabeth. BS cum laude, U. Houston, 1968, JD magna cum laude, 1971; MLA, U. St. Thomas, 1995. Bar: Tex. 1971. Assoc. Fulbright & Jaworski, LLP, Houston, 1973-80, ptnr., 1980—. Past pres., bd. dirs. St. Andrew's Presbyn. Sch., Houston; past pres. Houston CC Place civic Assn.; elder, trustee St. Andrew's Presbyn. Ch., Houston. 1st lt. US Army, 1971—77. Mem.: ABA, Houston Bar Assn., Tex. Bar Assn., U. Houston Alumni Orgn. (life), Order of Barons Law Honor Soc., Omicron Delta Epsilon, Phi Kappa Phi, Phi Delta Phi (life). Avocations: history, literature. Office: Fulbright and Jaworski LLP 1301 Mckinney St Houston TX 77010-3095 Office Phone: 713-651-3709.

SINGER, DAVID VINCENT, food products executive; b. Northumberland, Pa., June 18, 1955; s. Harold William and Dolores Elizabeth (Galonian) S.; m. Barbara Brown, Feb. 19, 1983; children: Brian, Andrew. BS, Pa. State U., 1977, MBA, 1979. Mgmt. trainee Mellon Bank, Pitts., 1979—81, corp. fin. lending officer, 1981—86; v.p., treas. Coca-Cola Bottling Co. Consol., Charlotte, NC, 1986—87, v.p., CFO, 1986—2001; exec. v.p., CFO Coca-Cola Bottling Co. Consol, 2001—05; bd. dirs. Lance, Inc., 2003—, pres., CEO, 2005—. Bd. dirs. Flowers Foods, Inc., 2010—. Avocation: golf. Home: 3401 Royden Pl Charlotte NC 28226-1111 Office: Lance Inc 13024 Ballantyne Corporate Pl Ste 900 Charlotte NC 28277 Office Phone: 704-554-1421. Office Fax: 704-554-5562. E-mail: dsinger@lance.com.

SINGH, K. PAUL, telecommunications industry executive; MSEE, SUNY, Stony Brook; MBA, Harvard U. Founder Cygnus Satellite Corp.; v.p., Strategic Planning M/A-Com Corp.; found., chmn., CEO Overseas Telecom., Inc., 1984—91; v.p., global product mktg. M.C.I., 1991—94; founder, chmn., pres., CEO Primus Telecom. Group, 1994—. Office: Primus Telecommunications Group 7901 Jones Branch Dr Ste 900 Mc Lean VA 22102 Office Phone: 703-902-2800. Office Fax: 703-902-2814. Business E-Mail: psingh@primustel.com.

SINGH, MANJIT MANMOHAN, corporate financial executive; BS in Math. & Computer Sci., SUNY, Binghamton; MS in Computer Sci., Indiana U., Bloomington. Selection mgr. Procter & Gamble, Co.; chief info. officer Wakul, Inc; dir., strategic bus. alliances Broadwing, 2001—02; dir., Asia Pacific Bus. Sys., regional chief info. officer The Gillette Co. (acquired by Procter & Gamble Co.), Singapore, 2002—06; v.p., corp. & comml. info. tech. Chiquita Brands International, Inc., 2006, v.p., chief info. officer, 2006—. Office: Chiquita Brands International Inc 550 S Caldwell St Ste 1010 Charlotte NC 28202-2681 Office Phone: 513-784-8000. Office Fax: 513-784-8030. Business E-Mail: msingh@chiquita.com.

SINGH, NARENDRA, cardiologist, researcher, medical educator; b. Saraiya, Uttar Pradesh, India, June 10, 1963; Can., US; s. Rudra Prasad and Manorma Singh; m. Mitra Kumari Kandhal, June 26, 1993; children: Shailin Raj, Ishaan Vivek, Vrushali Kumari. BS in Biochemistry, Dalhousie U., Halifax, Can., 1983, MD, 1987. Diplomate Am. Bd. Internal Medicine, Am. Bd. Cardiovascular Disease, Cert. Bd. Nuclear Cardiology, NASPE Testamur. Rotating intern St. Michael's Hosp., U. Toronto, 1987—88, resident in internal medicine, 1988—91, cardiology fellow, 1991—93; cardiologist Centenary Cardiology Assocs., Toronto, Ont., Canada, 1994—2002, Northside Cardiology P.C., Atlanta, 2002—10, Atlanta Heart Specialists LLC, 2010—; dir. clin. rsch. Atlanta, 2002—; dir. Scarborough Cardiology Rsch., Toronto, 1996—2002; cardiology sect. chair Northside Hosp., Atlanta, 2003—06. Lectr. U. Toronto, 1994—2002; med. dir. Pacemaker/ICD Programme, 1995—2002, Cardiac Cath Lab., 1999—2001; co-founder Greater Toronto Area Cmty. Cardiologists, 1995—2001; clin. asst. prof. Emory U. Sch. Medicine, Atlanta, 2002—11, Ga. Regents U.; mem. nat. adv. bd. Pfizer, Canada; nat. spkrs. bur. Pfizer, GSK, Novartis, Sanofi Aventis, Boehringer Ingelheim; heart failure adv. bd. Saint Joseph's Hosp.; vice chair Saint Joseph's Rsch. Inst., 2009—10; CME chairperson GA Am. Coll. Cardiology, 2006—10; sr. clin. scientist Can. Cardiovascular Rsch. Network, 2011—. Contbr. articles to profl. jours. Bd. dirs. Hosp. Found., Toronto, 1998—2002. Recipient award plaque in recognition for contbns., Greater Toronto Area Cmty. Cardiologists, Leadership award, Northside Hosp., 2006, Disting. Svc. award, Ga. chpt.-ACC, 2010; scholar, Dalhousie U., 1981, 1983, 1985; Rsch. fellow, U. Toronto, 1993. Fellow: Am. Coll. Cardiology (councillor, Atlanta region, Ga. chpt. 2008—, mem. nat. needs assessment working group), Royal Coll. Physicians and Surgeons Can. (cert. in cardiology/internal medicine), Am. Heart Assn. (bd. dirs. Atlanta 2008—09); mem.: Am. Soc. Nuc. Cardiology, Med. Assn. Ga., Can. Med. Assn., Med. Staff Soc. (bd. govs., mem. med. adv. com. 1995—97, pres. Centenary site, mem. strategic planning com. 1996), Can. Cardiovasc. Soc. (coun. mem. 1999—2002, nat. sec. 2000—02, coun., mem. exec. com., chairperson membership com. 2000—02). Avocations: travel, golf, theater. Office: Atlanta Heart Specialists LLC 1505 Northside Blvd Ste 2500 Cumming GA 30041 Home: 6350 Haddington Ln Johns Creek GA 30024 Office Phone: 678-679-6800. Office Fax: 678-679-6804. Business E-Mail: info@heartdrsingh.com.

SINGH, RAJENDRA, electrical engineering educator, researcher; b. Saharanpur, India, July 13, 1946; arrived in US, 1979; s. Kartar Singh and Savitri Devi; m. Reeta Sinha, Aug. 15, 1976; children: Rupalika, Rupangini. BS in Physics, Agra U., India, 1965; MS in Electronics, Meerut U., India, 1968; MS in Super Conductivity, Dalhousi U., Can., 1974; PhD in Solar Cells, McMaster U., Can., 1979. Lectr. Meerut U., 1968—73; vis. asst. prof. U. Waterloo, Ont., Canada, 1979, Colo. State U., Ft. Collins, 1979—80; sr. rsch. scientist Energy Conservation Devices, Troy, Mich., 1980—82; assoc. prof. elec. engring. and computer sci. U. Okla., Norman, 1982—86, prof. elec. engring. and computer sci., 1986—; cons. Howard U., Washington, 1978—79, Arco Solar, Inc., Chatsworth, 1983—86; high speed semiconductors and superconducting electronics, solar cells, nuclear detectors, superconductivity computers. Contbr. articles to profl. jours. Vol. Can. Red Cross, Hamilton, 1977—79. Recipient Faculty Excellence award, U. Okla., 1983—84, award Outstanding Instrn. and Svc., 1984, Young Faculty Devel. award, 1984, 1985, Engring. Excellence award, 1987, 1988. Mem.: IEEE (Disting. Lectr. award 1983, Disting. Technologist 1987). Hindu. Home: 112 Santee Trail Clemson SC 29631-2833

SINGH, VIJAY, professional golfer; b. Lautoka, Fiji, Feb. 22, 1963; m. Andrea Seth Singh; 1 child, Qass Seth. Profl. golfer, 1993—. Mem. internat. team The President's Cup, 1994, 1996, 1998, 2000, 2003, 2005, 2007, 2009; player World Cup, 2002. Hon. chairperson Nat. Golf Day, 1999. Recipient Samman award, Pravasi Bharatiya Divas, 2005, Byron Nelson award, PGA of America, 2004, Vardon Trophy, 2004; named Rookie of Yr., PGA Tour, 1993, Player of Yr., PGA European Tour, 2004, PGA of America, 2004, PGA Tour, 2004; named to World Golf Hall of Fame, 2006. Achievements include having 34 career PGA Tour victories and 14 European and Asian Tour victories; winning PGA Tour Major Championships: PGA Championship, 1998, 2004, Masters Tournament, 2002; winning World Golf Championships: Buick Classic, 1993, 1995, Phoenix Open, 1995, 2000, Meml. Tournament, 1997, Buick Open, 1997, 2004, 2005, Spirit Internat., 1998, Honda Classic, 1999; Shell Houston Open, 2000, 2004, 2005, The Tour Championship, 2000, EDS Byron Nelson Championship, 2003, John Deere Classic, 2003, FUNAI Classic, 2003, AT&T Pebble Beach Nat. Pro-Am, 2004; HP Classic, 2004, Deutsche Bank Championship, 2004, 2008, Bell Canadian Open, 2004, 84 Lumber Classic, 2004, Chrysler Championship, 2004, Sony Open, 2005, Wachovia Championship, 2005; Barclays Classic, 2006, Mercedes Championships, 2007, Arnold Palmer Invitational, 2007, Bridgestone Invitational, 2008, The Barclays, 2008; ranked number 1 golfer in the world by the Official World Golf Ranking, 2004-05; holds record for: most wins on PGA Tour after the age of 40, most wins by an international player. Avocations: snooker, cricket, rugby, soccer. Office: PGA Tour 112 TPC Blvd Ponte Vedra Beach FL 32802

SINGLETARY, ALVIN D., lawyer; b. Sept. 27, 1942; s. Alvin E. and Alice (Pastoret) Singletary; m. Judy Louise Singletary, Dec. 3, 1983; children: Kimberly Dawn, Shane David, Kelly Diane. BA, La. State U., 1964; JD, Loyola U., New Orleans, 1969. Bar: La. 1969, U.S. Dist. Ct. (ea. dist.) La. 1972, U.S. Ct. Appeals (5th cir.) 1972, U.S. Ct. Appeals (11 cir.) 1981, U.S. Ct. Internat. Trade 1981, U.S. Ct. Customs and Patent Appeals 1982, U.S. Supreme Ct. 1978. Instr. Delgado Coll., New Orleans, 1976—77; sole practice Slidell, La., 1970—. Spl. asst. dist. atty 22d Judicial Dist. Ct., Parish of St. Tammany, La.; sec., treas. St. Tammany Pub. Trust Fin. Authority, 1978—2002. Chmn. sustaining membership enrollment Cypress dist. Boy Scouts Am., 1989—; treas. Slidell Centennial commn.; councilman-at-large City of Slidell, 1978—2002, interim mayor, 1985; mem. Dem. State Ctrl. Com., 1978—82; mem. Rep. State Ctrl. Com. Dist. 76, La., 1996—2000; del. La.Constl. Conv., 1972—73; chmn. Together We Build Program First Baptist Ch. of Slidell, La.; bd. dir. St. Tammany Coun. on Aging. Mem.: Lions, Delta Theta Phi. Baptist. Office: 1659 Sgt Alfred Dr PO Box 1158 Slidell LA 70458-1158 Office Phone: 985-643-9800. Personal E-mail: asingl1@bellsouth.net.*

SINGLETON, BOBBY, state legislator; b. Greensboro, Ala. BS, Ala. State U., Montgomery; JD, Miles Law Sch. Mem. Dist. 72 Ala. House of Reps., Montgomery, 2003—05; mem. Dist. 24 Ala. State Senate, Montgomery, 2005—; owner Black Belt Technologies, LLC. Field dir. Campaign 2000 & Beyond; dist. 7 chmn. Hale County, Ala.; mem. Greenleaf Missionary Bapt. Ch., Greensboro; chmn. WARAC Econ. Devel. Com.; mem. Ala. Emergency Comm. Dist. Long-Range Study Commn. Mem. Ala. NewSouth Coalition, Ala. Dem. Conf. Democrat. Office: Ala State Senate Ala State House 11 S Union St Rm 732-B Montgomery AL 36130 Office Phone: 334-242-7935. Office Fax: 334-242-7191. Business E-Mail: bsingle164@yahoo.com.

SINGLETON, DAVID MICHAEL, chemist, researcher, retired; b. Upton, Poole, Dorset, Nov. 3, 1939; came to US, 1965; s. Hubert Frederick and Marjorie Clare S.; m. Elizabeth Ann Sloan, Sept. 14, 1962; children: David Arthur, Katherine Ann. BSc, U. London, 1960; PhD, McMaster U., Hamilton, Ont., Can., 1965. Postdoctoral fellow Case Inst. Tech., Cleve., 1965-67; rsch. chemist Shell Devel. Co., Emeryville, Calif., 1967-72, Houston, 1972-74, sr. rsch. chemist, 1974-75, 76-92; exch. scientist Shell Rsch. BV, Amsterdam, The Netherlands, 1975-76; sr. rsch. chemist Shell Chem. Co., Houston, 1992-99, ret., 1999. Adj. prof. U. Houston, 1985-91; mem. adv. bd. Tex. State Tech. Coll., Waco, 1994—2009; chmn. organometallic chemistry Gordon Conf., Newport, R.I., 1987; lectr. McMaster U., Queen's U., RWTH Aachen, Tulane U., U. Houston. Contbr. articles to profl. jours., chpt. to book. Fellow Royal Soc. Chemistry, Am. Chem. Soc. (chair Greater Houston sect. 1998, councilor 2003—; SW Regional Indsl. Innovation award, 2003, ACS Fellow, 2012), S.W. Catalysis Soc. (sec. 1978, chair 1982), Archaeol. Inst. Am., Coun. on Brit. Archaeology, N.Y. Acad. Scis. (mem. adv. bd. Catalysis Conf. 1978), Curling Club Houston (treas. 1995-2007), ACS. Achievements include 24 US patents and 2 British patents. Avocations: history, archaeology, music, art, sports. Personal E-mail: dsingleton5@yahoo.com.

SINGLEY, JOHN EDWARD, JR., retired environmental scientist, consultant; b. Wildwood, NJ, July 31, 1924; s. John Edward Singley and Dorothy Mae (Pfrommer) S.; children: Gladys, Ann, Margaret, Patricia; m. June Walden Calohan, Apr. 28, 2001 (dec.); stepchildren: Daniel(dec.), Christopher Calohan. BS, Ga. Inst. Tech, 1950; MS, Ga. Inst. Tech., 1952; PhD, U. Fla., 1966. Chemist Redstone Arsenal, Huntsville, Ala., 1950-51; dir. tech. svs. Tenn. Corp., College Park, Ga., 1951-64; lectr. chemistry Ga. State U., Atlanta, 1954-64, assoc. prof., 1964-67; prof. environ. engring. sci. U. Fla., Gainesville, 1967-90, prof. emeritus, 1990—; dir. TREEO Ctr., Gainesville, 1978-86; v.p. James M. Montgomery, Cons. Engrs., Inc., Gainesville, 1984-93, Montgomery Watson Cons. Engrs. Inc., Gainesville, 1993-96; sr. v.p. Environ. Scis. Engring. Inc., Gainesville, 1977-84; prin. Water and Air Rsch., Gainesville, 1970-77; v.p. Metcalf & Eddy, Gainesville, 1996-99; ret., 1999. Cons. Carollo Engrs., Sarasota, Fla., Jones, Edmunds Assocs., Gainesville. Patentee in field of polymers. Mem. Fulton County Rep. Exec. Com., 1962-64; mem. founding bd. Water for People, 1990-92. With USN, 1943-45. Recipient Donald R. Boyd award Met. Water Agys., 1992. Fellow Am. Inst. Chemists, Inst. Water and Environ. Mgmt.; mem. Am. Water Works Assn. (hon., life, bd. dirs. 1984-87, exec. com. 1986-87, 89-93, v.p. 1989-90, pres.-elect 1990-91, pres. 1991-92, Fuller award 1974, rsch. award 1983, Abel Wolman Excellence award 1995, Disting. Pub. Svc. award 1995, Water Industry Hall of Fame 2000), Fla. Water and Pollution Control Operators Assn. (Flanigan award 1979), Nat. Lime Assn. (Recognition award), Internat. Water Supply Assn., Nat. Assn. Corrosion Engrs., Internat. Ozone Assn. (bd. dirs. 1985-93). Clubs: Gainesville, Civitan (pres. 1972, lt. gov. Fla. dist. 1973-76), Elks Lodge. Presbyterian. Home: 8015 NW 28th Pl Apt A118 Gainesville FL 32606-6274 Office Phone: 352-372-7797. Personal E-mail: h2odoceds@aol.com.

SINISGALLI, PETER F., information technology executive; b. 1956; B in Economics, Cornell U., MBA. Pres., CEO NewRoads, Inc.; CFO Nielsen Media Rsch. divsn. Dun and Bradstreet; exec. v.p., CFO Dun & Bradstreet Corp; sr. v.p., group fin. Dun & Bradstreet Corp.; v.p., CFO Dun & Bradstreet Software, 1994—96; v.p. Check Free Holdings Inc., Norcross, Ga., 1996—99, pres., COO, 1999; COO Manhattan Associates, Inc., 2004, pres., CEO & bd. dirs., 2004—. Office: Manhattan Associates Inc 2300 Windy Ridge Pkwy Ste 1000 Atlanta GA 30339 Office Phone: 770-955-7070. Office Fax: 770-955-0302. Business E-Mail: psinisgalli@manh.com.

SINK, ALEX (ADELAIDE ALEXANDER SINK), former state treasurer, retired bank executive; b. Mt. Airy, NC, June 4, 1948; d. Kester and Adelaide (Bunker) Sink; m. Bill McBride, 1987 (dec. Dec. 22, 2012); children: Bert, Lexi. BS in Mathematics, Wake Forest U. Joined NationsBank, Charlotte, 1974; pres. NationsBank Fla., Tampa, 1993—97; pres. Fla. ops. Bank of America, Fla., 1993—2000; CFO State of Fla., Tallahassee, 2007—10; sr. adv. Hyde Park Capital, Tampa, 2011—. Democratic nominee for Gov. State of Fla., 2010; bd. dirs. C1 Bank, 2013—, Health Ins. Innovations, Inc., 2013—. Founder, chair Fla. Next Found. Recipient Jewish Nat. Fund Tree of Life award, Champion of Bus. award, Associated Industries of Fla., Disting. Alumnus award, Wake Forest U.; named Volunteer of the Yr., Fla. Chamber of Commerce; named to The Tampa Bay Bus. Hall of Fame. Democrat. Presbyterian.*

SINNAMON, WALTER BRUCE, college administrator, biology educator, biologist, educator; b. Phila., Dec. 27, 1947; m. Carol Sinnamon; 1 child, Michel. BS in Zoology, Houghton Coll., 1969; postgrad., SUNY, Geneseo, 1975-77; PhD in Zoology, Clemson U., 1985. Cert. tchr. biology, chemistry, phys. sci., gen. sci., NY, radiation safety officer. Sci. instr. Houghton Acad., NY, 1969-77, bus. mgr., 1973-77; grad. teaching asst. dept. zoology Clemson U., SC, 1977-82; asst. prof. So. Wesleyan U., 1982-85, assoc. prof., 1985-90, prof. biology, 1990—, spl. asst. to the pres., 1993—2003, dean Coll. Arts Sci., 2005—, dept. chair, 2003—. Grant writer US Dept. Edn., Washington, 1990, Cannon Found., Kannapolis, N.C., 1991, JanIrve Found., Asheville, N.C., 1991, NSF, Washington, 1991, Consortium for Advancement of Pvt. Higher Edn; mem. advisory com., Tri County Tech. Coll., 2002-; coun. mem., Coll. Arts & Scis.; mem. instl. biosafety com., Clemson U. Contbr. articles to profl. jours. Recipient Gov.'s Distinguished Prof. award, So. Wesleyan U., 2007, Prof. of the Yr., 2008, Excellence in Tchg. award, SI Ind. Coll., U., 2008. Mem. Am. Assn. Advancement of Sci., History of Sci. Soc., Nat. Assn. Advisors for Health Profls., Affiliation Christian Biologists, Human Anatomy and Physiology Soc., Am. Sci. Affiliation, Soc. Integrative Comparitive Biology, S.C. Acad. Sci., Gideons Internat., Wycliff Assocs., Sigma Xi. Home: 423 Pin Du Lac Dr Central SC 29630-9435 Office: So Wesleyan U PO Box 1817 Central SC 29630-0407 Office Phone: 864-644-5265. Business E-Mail: wsinnamon@swu.edu.

SINNETTE, KEVIN, state legislator; b. Mar. 2, 1962; BS, Eastern Ky. U., 1984; JD, Salmon P. Chase Coll. Law, 1988. Asst. atty. City of Ashland, Ky., 1990—2008; mem. Dist. 100 Ky. House of Reps., 2009—. Democrat. Baptist. Office: Ky Legislature Annex Rm 316C 702 Capitol Ave Frankfort KY 40601 Mailing: PO Box 1358 Ashland KY 41105 Office Phone: 502-564-8100 ext. 703.

SINNOTT, JOHN THOMAS, internist, educator; b. Reading, Pa., May 16, 1948; s. John Thomas and Josephine (Mallon) S.; m. Barbara Ballentine, May 30, 1970. BA, Columbus Coll., Ga., 1971; MA, U. South Fla., 1973; MD, U. South Ala., 1978. Diplomate Am. Bd. Internal Medicine, Am. Bd. Infectious Diseases. Resident in internal medicine U. South Fla. Coll. Medicine, Tampa, 1978-81, infectious disease resident, 1981-83, asst. prof., 1983-87, assoc. prof., 1987-92, prof. and dir. infectious diseases, 1991—, James Cullison prof. medicine, 2000—, assoc. dean internat. affairs, 2005—; dir. epidemiology Tampa Gen. Healthcare, 1985—, mem. med. exec. bd., 1992—, vice chief staff, 1992-94, chief staff, 1994-96. Dir. S.W. Fla. Tissue Bank, 1987—, dir. epidemiology Shriners Hosp. for Children, 1987; co-founder CHART India, 1998-; mem. adv. bd. Lifelink Fla., 1988-; trustee Tampa Gen. Hosp. Found., 2000-, Hillsborough C.C. Found., 2003-; mem. bd. dirs. FoodTech, 2002- chmn. 2005- Editor jour. Infections in Medicine, 1994—. Recipient hon. alumnus award U. South Fla. Coll. Medicine, 1998, Outstanding Clin. Prof. award, 1986-92; Humanism in Medicine award NBI Healthcare Found., 1998, award For AIDS Care Today, 1998; John T. Sinnott Outstanding Clin Prof. award named in his honor U. So. Fla. Coll. Medicine, 1992. Fellow ACP, Infectious Disease Soc. Am. (fin. com. 1998—); mem. Soc. Hosp. Epidemiology (fin. com. 1998—), Alpha Omega Alpha. Avocations: fishing, flying. Home: 9666 Oak St NE Saint Petersburg FL 33702-2610 Office: Tampa Gen Hosp Dept Infectious Disease Tampa FL 33601-1289

SINOR, HOWARD EARL, JR., lawyer; b. New Orleans, Sept. 6, 1949; s. Howard E. and Beverly M. (Bourgeois) S.; m. Katy K. Sinor; children: Sally, Vera Sue, Sarah, Sadie. BA with honors, U. New Orleans, 1971; JD cum laude, Harvard U., 1975. Bar: La. 1975, U.S. Supreme Ct. 1983, U.S. Ct. Appeals (5th and 11th cir.), U.S. Dist. Ct. (Ea., Middle, We.) Dist. La. Ptnr. Jones, Walker, Waechter, Poitevent, Carrere & Denegre, 1975-98, Gordon Arata, New Orleans, 1999—. Contbg. author: La. Appellate Practice Handbook, 1990, 97; editor: CLE Manual of Recent Developments, 1985; contbr. articles to profl. jours. Recipient Pres.'s award, La. State Bar Assn., 1987. Fellow La. Bar Found.; mem. ABA, FBA, La. State Bar Assn. (chmn. antitrust sect. 1987-89). Avocations: golf, hiking.

SIPIORA, LEONARD PAUL, retired museum director, art appraiser; b. Lawrence, Mass., Sept. 1, 1934; s. Walter and Agnes S.; m. Sandra Joyce Coon, 1962; children— Alexandra, Erika. AB cum laude, U. Mich., 1955, MA, 1956. Dir. museums, City of El Paso, Tex., 1967-90; ret. Co-founder, pres. El Paso Arts Coun., 1969-71; sec.-treas. El Paso Coun. Internat. Visitors, 1968-71; trustee El Paso Mus. Art; bd. dirs. Tex. Com. Humanities, Assn. Southwestern Humanities Coun.; adv. bd. S.W. Arts Found.; expert Antiques Roadshow-U.S.A. Bd. dirs. Cmty. Concert Assn. El Paso, El Paso Symphony Orch., El Paso Hist. Soc. Mem. Assn. Mus. Dirs., Mountain Plains Mus. Assn. (pres. 1978-79), Tex. Assn. Museums (pres. 1977-79), Appraisers Assn. Am., Knights of Malta (decorated Grand Cross), Prior of Tex., Kappa Pi. Republican. Lutheran. Home: 1012 Blanchard Ave El Paso TX 79902-2727

SIPLIN, GARY ANTHONY, state legislator; b. Orlando, Fla., Oct. 21, 1954; m. Victoria Pierre; children: Gary Jr., Angelika, Joshua, Jacobe. BA, Johnson C. Smith U., 1975; M in Pub. and Internat. Affairs, U. Pitts., 1976; JD, Duquesne U., 1981. Law clk. to presiding justice US Dist. Ct., Miami, Fla., 1981-82; asst. county atty. County Atty.'s Office, Miami; mem. Fla. House of Reps., Tallahassee, 2000—02; mem. Dist. 19 Fla. State Senate, Tallahassee, 2002—, chair joint legis. com. on Everglades oversight, vice chair cmty. affairs com., edn. preK-12 appropriations com., govtl. oversight and accountability com., mem. policy and steering com. on energy, environment and land use, policy and steering com. on social responsibility, criminal justice com., mem. policy and steering com. on ways and means, reapportionment com., rules com., transp. com. Judge Dade County Bar Moot Ct., Miami, 1983-84. Author: Prosecutorial Misuse of Peremptory Challenges on Black Veniremen: The Reasons, Impacts and Remedies, 1981. Asst. co-dir. Ctr. for Internat. Policy, Washington, 1976; staff writer Dade County Bar Bull., 1985; bd. dirs.

Informed Families, 1985; chairperson Inner City Task Force, 1985. Named one of Outstanding Young Men in Am., 1984. Mem. ABA, Dade County Bar Assn. (bd. dirs. young lawyers sect.), Nat. Bar Assn., Dade County Nat. Bar Assn. (chairperson jud. reception com. 1984, bd. dirs., bd. govs. 1985), Omega Psi Phi. Democrat. Office: 1436 N Pine Hills Rd Orlando FL 32808 also: 205 Senate Office Bldg 404 S Monroe St Tallahassee FL 32399-1100 Office Phone: 407-297-2071, 850-487-5190. Business E-Mail: siplin.gary.web@flsenate.gov.

SIPLING, PHILIP J., mining executive; Grad., Juniata Coll., Pa.; MS in Geological Sci., PhD in Geological Sci., Brown U. V.p., mktg. Martin Marietta Materials, Inc., 1985—87, v.p., aggregates ops., 1987—93, exec. v.p., aggregates bus., 1993—, v.p., Magnesia Specialties unit, sr. v.p., 1993—97, chmn., Magnesia Specialties Bus., 1997—2005, exec. v.p., 2001—. Bd. dirs. Indsl. Microwave Sys. Inc., Nat. Asphalt Pavement Assn. Bd. dirs. Ind. Coll. Fund NC. Office: Martin Marietta Materials Inc 2710 Wycliff Rd Raleigh NC 27607 Office Phone: 919-781-4550. Office Fax: 919-783-4695.

SIRCHIO, JOHN KRISTIN, food products executive; B in Polit. Sci., Duke U., Durham, NC; MBA, Southern Meth. U., Dallas, Tex. Various mktg. & leadership positions, European ops. Procter & Gamble Co.; global head, profl. products Syngenta AG, Basel, Switzerland; chief mktg. officer Brown-Forman Corp., 2009—. Office: Brown Forman Corp 850 Dixie Hwy Louisville KY 40210 Office Phone: 502-585-1100. Office Fax: 502-774-7876. Business E-Mail: john_sirchio@b-f.com.

SIRICA, ALPHONSE EUGENE, pathology educator; b. Waterbury, Conn., Jan. 16, 1944; s. Alphonse Eugene and Elena Virginia (Mascolo) S.; m. Annette Marie Murray, June 9, 1984; children: Gabrielle Theresa, Nicholas Steven. MS, Fordham U., 1968; PhD in Biomed. Sci., U. Conn., 1977. Asst. prof. U. Wis., Madison, 1979-84; assoc. prof. Med. Coll. Va., Va. Commonwealth U., Richmond, 1984-90, prof. of pathology, 1990—, divsn. chair exptl. pathology, 1992-99, divsn. chair cellular and molecular pathogenesis, 1999—. Vis. prof. Pa. State U. Coll. Medicine, 2000, Mayo Clinic, 2011; regular mem. sci. adv. com. on carcinogenesis and nutrition Am. Cancer Soc., Atlanta, 1989—92; metabolic pathology study sect. NIH, Bethesda, 1991—95, ad hoc mem. study sect., 1997—2006, 2008, 2010—12, 2012; mem. bd. dir. CanLiv, Hepatobiliary Cancer Found., 2008—11; presenter Dr. & Mrs. Michael A Gerbar Meml. Lectr. Tulane U. Health Scis. Ctr., 2012. Editor, author: The Pathobiology of Neoplasia, 1989, The Role of Cell Types in Hepatocarcinogenesis, 1992, Cellular and Molecular Pathogenesis, 1996; co-editor, author: Biliary and Pancreatic Ductal Epithelia: Pathobiology and Pathophysiology, 1997; mem. editl. bd. Pathobiology, 1990-99, Hepatology, 1991-94, Exptl. and Molecular Pathology, 1999—, World Jour. Gastroenterology, 2006-09, Annals Clin. & Lab. Sci., 2010-; rev. bd. In Vitro Cellular and Devel. Biology-Animal, 1987—; contbr. articles to profl. jours. including Am. Jour. Pathology, Cancer Rsch., Hepatology, and other. Organizer, chair FASEB Summer Rsch. Conf. on Growth Factor Receptor Tyrosine Kinases in Mitogenesis, Morphogenesis, and Tumorigenesis, 1999, 2001. Recipient Rsch. Recognition award, Va. Commonwealth U. Sch. Medicine, 2002, 2007. Fellow: Am. Gastroent. Assn.; mem.: AAAS, Am. Soc. Clin. Pathology, Soc. Toxicology, Han. Popper Hepatopathology Soc., Soc. Exptl. Biology and Medicine, NY Acad. Scis., Am. Assn. Study Liver Diseases (chair conf. pathobiology of biliary epithelia and cholangiocarcinoma), Am. Soc. Investigative Pathology (chair program com. 1994—96), Assn. Clin. Scientists, Soc. for In Vitro Biology, Am. Assn. Cancer Rsch. (chmn. Va. state legis. com. 1992—95, mem. 2014, mem. prog. com. 2014, ann. meeting program com. 2013—14), Am. Soc. Cell Biology. Achievements include development of collagen gel-nylon mesh system for culturing hepatocytes; first establishment and characterization of hyperplastic bile ductular epithelial cells in culture; research in hepato- and biliary carcinogenesis, pathobiology of hepatocyte and biliary epithelial cells and molecular pathogenesis and experimental therapeutics of biliary cancer. Office Phone: 804-828-9549. Business E-Mail: asirica@mcvh-vcu.edu.

SIRILLA, GEORGE M., lawyer; b. Perryopolis, Pa., May 1, 1929; s. Michael and Helen Sirilla; m. Floranne Zalewski Sirilla, Nov. 23, 1968; children: Michael George, Joseph David. BSME, Rensselaer Poly. Inst., Troy, NY, 1952; LLB, Georgetown Law Sch., Washington, JD, 1956. Bar: Va. 1956, DC 1956. Assoc. Cushman, Darby & Cushman, Washington, 1955—59, ptnr., 1960, 1968—96, Pillsbury, Madison & Sutro, 1996—, Pillsbury Winthrop, McLean, Va., 2001—05, Pillsbury Winthrop Shaw Pittman, 2005—. Adj. prof. George Washington Law Sch., Washington, 1982—83; mem. mng. bd. Cushman, Darby & Cushman, 1988—89, Pillsbury, Madison & Sutro, 1999—2000. Contbr. articles to law revs. Sgt. US Army, 1946—47, Korea. Named Master, Giles S. Rich Inn of Ct., 1992—2001. Fellow: Am. Coll. Trial Lawyers. Office: Pillsbury Winthrop Shaw 1650 Tysons Blvd Mc Lean VA 22102 Office Phone: 703-770-7784.

SISITSKY, TODD B., investment company executive; Undergraduate summa cum laude, Dartmouth Coll.; MBA, Stanford Grad. Sch. Bus. With Oak Hill Capital Partners, Forstmann Little & Co., 2001—03; assoc. TPG Capital, LP, 2003—07, ptnr., 2007—. Bd. dirs. Axcan Pharma, Inc., Fenwal, Inc., IASIS Healthcare Corp., Biomet, Inc, 2007—, Surg. Care Affiliates, 2007—. Office: TPG Capital LP 301 Commerce St Ste 3300 Fort Worth TX 76102 Office Phone: 817-871-4000. Office Fax: 817-871-4010.

SISLEY, NINA MAE, physician, public health service officer; b. Jacksonville, Fla., Aug. 19, 1924; d. Leonard Percy and Verna (Martin) S.; m. George W. Fischer, May 16, 1962 (dec. 1990). BA, Tex. State Coll. for Women, 1944; MD, U. Tex., Galveston, 1950; MPH, U. Mich., 1963. Intern City of Detroit Receiving Hosp., 1950-51; resident in gen. practice St. Mary's Infirmary, Galveston, Tex., 1951-52; sch. physician Galveston Ind. Sch. Dist., 1953-56; dir. med. svcs. San Antonio Health Dept., 1960-63, acting dir., 1963-64; resident in pub. health Tex. Dept. Pub. Health, San Antonio, 1963-65; dir. cmty. health svcs. Corpus Christi-Nueces County Dept. Health, Tex., 1964-67; dir. Tb control region 5 Tex. Dept. Health, Corpus Christi, 1967-73; chief chronic illness control City of Houston Health Dept., 1973-78; dir. pub. health region 11 Tex. Dept. Health, Rosenberg, 1978-87; dir. Corpus Christi-Nueces County Dept. Pub. Health, 1987—2002. Lectr. Incarnate Word Coll., San Antonio, 1963-64; adj. prof. U. Tex. Sch. Pub. Health, Houston, 1980—2002; adj. prof. Tex. A&M U., Corpus Christi, 1997—2002; pvt. practice Galveston, Stockdale, Hereford and Borger, Tex., 1952-59; mem. adv. bd. Cmty. Adv. Coun.; clin. instr. U. Tex. Health Sci. Ctr., San Antonio, 1997-2002 Mem. Nueces County Child Fatality REv. Com.; mem. adv. com. Nueces County Hosp. Dist.; mem. adv. bd. Alzheimers Assn.; mem. health adv. bd. Corpus Christi Ind. Sch. Dist.; bd. dirs. Coastal Bend chpt. ARC, Corpus Christi, 1990—94, 2003—07, pres., 1990—91; bd. dirs. United Way-Coastal Bend, Coastal Bend Coalition on AIDS, 1988—94, Charlie's Place Alcohol and Drug Rehab. Ctr. Fellow Am. Coll. Preventive Medicine; mem. Tex. Med. Assn., Nueces County Med. Soc. (pres. 1997-98), Tex. Assn. Pub. Health Physicians, Tex. Pub. Health Assn. (pres. 1991-92), Local Emergency Planning Assn., Long Term Health Assn., Asthma Coalition. Episcopalian. Avocations: fishing, crossword puzzles, raising african violets. Home: 6410 Meadowvista Dr Apt 510 Corpus Christi TX 78414-2655 E-mail: nsisley@sbcglobal.org.

SISNEY, SHERLEEN SUE, secondary school educator; b. Stillwater, Okla., Oct. 19, 1946; m. Lee Sisney, June 11, 1969; 1 child, Shara Lee. BS in Secondary Edn., Okla. State U., 1968; MEd, U. Louisville, 1975. Tchr. Merrill Jr. HS, Denver, 1968—69, Monterey HS, Calif., 1969—71, Ballard HS, Louisville, 1971—92; exec. dir. Ky. Gov.'s Scholard Program; dir. Career Acad., Louisville; mem. pub.'s adv. coun. Quantum Comm., Inc.; dir. New Founds. in Edn., 1984—. Mem. adv. coun. tchr. and edn. disn. Met. Life Found.; mem. Gov's Coun. on Edn. Reform, Joint Coun. Econ. Edn.; mem. task force social studies Ky. Dept. Edn. Mem. Okla. State U. Centennial Adv. Commn., Jr. League Louisville. Recipient Chris Mattingly Outstanding Leadership in Ky. award, U. Louisville, 1999; named Nat. Tchr. of Yr., 1984. Mem.: Ky. Edn. Assn. (Outstanding Tchr. 1979—80), Phi Delta Kappa. Home: 8002 Montero Ct Prospect KY 40059-9424 Office: Gov Scholars Program Ste 210 1024 Capital Ctr Dr Frankfort KY 40601

SISSOM, LEIGHTON ESTEN, engineering educator, dean, consultant; b. Manchester, Tenn., Aug. 26, 1934; s. Willie Esten and Bertha Sarah (Davis) S.; m. Evelyn Janelle Lee, June 13, 1953; children: Terry Lee, Denny Leighton. BS, Middle Tenn. State Coll., 1956; BS in Mech. Engring., Tenn. Technol. U., 1962; MS in Mech. Engring., Ga. Inst. Tech., 1964, PhD, 1965. Diplomate Nat. Acad. Forensic Engrs.; registered profl. engr., Tenn. Draftsman Westinghouse Electric Corp., Tullahoma, 1953-57; mech. designer ARO, Inc., Tullahoma, 1957-58; instr. mech. engring. Tenn. Technol. U., Cookeville, 1958-62, chmn. dept. mech. engring., 1965-79, dean engring., 1979-88, dean of engring. emeritus, 1988—; prin. cons. Sissom & Assocs., Cookeville, Tenn., 1962—. Bd. dirs. Accreditation Bd. Engring. and Tech., N.Y.C., 1978-86, treas., 1982-86. Author: (with Donald R. Pitts) Elements of Transport Phenomena, 1972, Heat Transfer, 1977, 1,000 Solved Problems in Heat Transfer, 1991; contbr. An Attorney's Guide to Engineering, 1986; contbr. articles to various publs. Fellow ASME (sr. v.p. 1982-86, gov. 1986-88, Golden medallion), Am. Soc. Engring. Edn. (bd. dirs. 1984-87, pres. 1991-92), Accreditation Bd. Engring. and Tech.; mem. NSPE, Soc. Automotive Engrs., Nat. Engring. Deans Coun. (chmn. 1984-87), Order of the Engr. (chmn. bd. govs. 1994-96), Tau Beta Pi (v.p. 1986-89, councillor 1986-89). Home and Office: 1151 Shipley Church Rd Cookeville TN 38501-7730 Office Phone: 931-526-9123. Business E-Mail: sissom@frontiernet.net.

SIVERD, ROBERT JOSEPH, lawyer; b. July 27, 1948; s. Clifford David and Elizabeth Ann (Klink) S.; m. Bonita Marie Shulock, Jan. 8, 1972; children: Robert J. Jr., Veronica Leigh. AB in French, Georgetown U., 1970, JD, 1973; postgrad., The Sorbonne, Paris, 1969. Bar: N.Y. 1974, US Dist. Ct. (southern & eastern districts) N.Y. 1974, US Ct. Appeals (2d cir.) 1974, US Supreme Ct. 1980, US Dist. Ct. (eastern dist.) Pa. 1984, US Ct. Appeals (3d cir.) 1984, US Ct. Appeals (6th cir.) 1985, Ohio 1991, Ky. 1992. Assoc. Donovan Leisure Newton & Irvine, NYC, 1973-83; staff v.p., litigation counsel American Financial Group, Inc., Greenwich, Conn., 1983-85, v.p. litigation counsel, 1986-87, v.p. assoc. gen. counsel Cin., 1987-92; sr. v.p., gen. counsel, sec. General Cable Corp., Newport, Ky., 1992-94, exec. v.p., gen. counsel, sec., 1994—. Mem. Ky. Bar Assn. Republican. Office: General Cable Corp 4 Tesseneer Dr Newport KY 41076-9167 Office Phone: 859-572-8000. Business E-Mail: rsiverd@generalcable.com.

SIZEMORE, CAROLYN T., controller; BBA in Acctg., U. Richmond. CPA. Acct. Ernst and Young LLP; various positions, mgr.,Corp. Acctg., dir., Budgets and Performance Analysis, and sr. dir., Fin. and Strategic Measures CSX Corp., acct., 1989, asst. v.p., Fin. Planning, 1999—2001, asst. v.p., asst. contr., 2001—02, v.p., contr., 2002—, CSX Transportation, Inc., 2002—. Office: CSX Corp 15th Fl 500 Water St Jacksonville FL 32202 Office Phone: 904-359-3200. Office Fax: 904-633-3450. Business E-Mail: carolyn_sizemore@csx.com.

SIZEMORE, MICHAEL MAYNARD, architectural firm executive; b. Detroit, July 20, 1943; s. Arthur Logan and Evelyn (Willer) S.; m. Christine Wick, June 1, 1968; children: Christine Corsaut, James Gawne. BArch, Ga. Inst. Tech., 1966; MArch in Urban Design, Carnegie-Mellon U., 1968. Registered arch. Owner Sizemore & Assocs., Atlanta, 1974-76; v.p. CRS, Sizemore/CRS, Houston and Atlanta, 1976-78; sr. prin. Sizemore Floyd (now Sizemore Group), Atlanta, 1973—. Mem. bd. advisors dist. coun. Urban Land Inst.; trustee The Ga. Conservancy. Author: Energy Planning in Buildings, 1979; prin. works include redesign of hqrs. AIA, Washington, Emory U. Clinic, Hale Ctr. Theatre, Salt Lake City, Atlanta C. of C., master plan of Centennial Olympics, Atlanta, 1996, master plan, feasibility Centennial Olympic Park, hqrs. Atlanta Com. Olympic Games, Smyrna Town Ctr. Design and Devel. (Nat. award Urban Land Inst. 1997). Fellow AIA; mem. Atlanta C. of C. (bd. advisors). Office: 1700 Commerce Dr NW Atlanta GA 30318-3123 Home Phone: 404-355-0839; Office Phone: 404-605-0690.

SIZEMORE, WILLIAM HOWARD, JR., journalist; b. South Boston, Va., Dec. 18, 1948; s. W. Howard and Genevieve T. (Walton) S.; m. Mary K. Lamont, Jan. 29, 1972; children: Justin, Jennifer, Julie. BA in Philosophy, Coll. William and Mary, 1971. Editor The Clarksville (Va.) Times, 1972-75; reporter The Roanoke (Va.) Times, 1975-76, The Times-Herald, Newport News, Va., 1976-81; editor, pub. The York Town Crier, Yorktown, Va., 1981-88; copy editor The Ledger-Star, Norfolk, Va., 1982-89, news editor, 1989-95; writer, editor The Virginian-Pilot, Norfolk, Va., 1995—. Recipient various Journalism awards Va. Press Assn., 1972-2012. Avocations: tennis, music, bicycling, camping. Home: 4704 Yarrow Ct Williamsburg VA 23188-2427 Office: Virginian-Pilot 150 W Brambleton Ave Norfolk VA 23510-2075 Office Phone: 757-446-2276. Business E-Mail: bill.sizemore@pilotonline.com.

SKAFF, DOUG, JR., state legislator; b. South Charleston, W.Va., Nov. 10, 1976; BS in Mktg., W.Va. U., 2000, MA in Indsl. Labor rels. & Human Resources, 2001. Sales mgr. Owens Corning, 2002—05, human resource Specialist, 2005—06; dist. mgr. Norandex, Saint Gobain, 2006—; mem. Dist. 30 W.Va. House of Delegates, 2008—, mem. Banking and Ins. Com. & Govt. Orgn. Com. Democrat. Office: State Capitol Complex Rm 230E, Bldg 1 Charleston WV 25305 Mailing: 2809 Ranch Rd Charleston WV 25303 Home Phone: 304-744-2957; Office Phone: 304-340-3362, 304-549-2171. E-mail: dskaff@mail.wvnet.edu.

SKAGGS, KAREN GAYLE, elementary school educator; b. Campbellsville, Ky., Sept. 29, 1956; d. E. Edward and Mary Virginia (Kearney) Davis; m. Stephen Douglas Skaggs, July 30, 1976. BA in English, French and Journalism, Campbellsville Coll., 1977, elem. edn. endorsement 1-8, 1989; MA in Secondary Edn. and Psychology, Western Ky. U., 1980, reading specialist degree, 1986, rank 1 in edn., 1990. Cert. secondary tchr., Ky. Tchr. English, French, journalism Taylor County Bd. Edn., Campbellsville, 1978-81, adult edn. tchr., 1981-89; elem. tchr. Campbellsville Bd. Edn., 1989—2012. Bdlg. coord. Extended Sch. Svcs., 1998—2010 Co-owner operator Steve & Karen Skaggs Photography. Mem. Campbellsville Site Based Coun., 1993-98, 99-2002. Recipient Outstanding Tchr. award State Dept. of Edn. Mem. Internat. Reading Assn., Taylor County Lit. Coun. (pres.), Taylor County Bus. and Profl. Women's Club (chmn. young careerist com. 1987-88, Outstanding Young Career Woman award 1987, Tchr. of Yr. award 1993, Excellence in Tchg. award 1994). Democrat. Baptist. Avocations: reading, country music, decorating, internet. Home: 901 S Columbia Ave Campbellsville KY 42718-2410 Office Phone: 270-465-4561. Personal E-mail: sskaggs01@windstream.net. Business E-Mail: karen.skaggs@cville.kyschools.com.

SKAGGS, RICKY, musician; b. Cordell, Ky., July 18, 1954; s. Hobert and Dorothy Skaggs; m. Sharon White, 1981; 4 children. Mandolin player Ralph Stanley's Clinch Mountain Boys, 1969; with Country Gentlemen, J.D. Crowe & New South, Emmylou Harris' Hot Band, 1977, The Whites; founder Boone Creek; joined Grand Ole Opry, 1982. Musician: (albums) Waitin' for the Sun to Shine, 1981, Highways and Heartaches, Don't Cheat in Our Hometown, Country Boy, 1984, Favorite Country Songs, Live in London, Love's Gonna Get Ya!, Comin' Home To Stay, 1988, Kentucky Thunder, 1989, My Father's Son, 1991, Super Hits, 1993, Solid Ground, 1998, Ricky Skaggs Portrait, 1992, Life Is a Journey, 1997, Bluegrass Rules, 1998 (Grammy award for Best Bluegrass Album, 1999), Ancient Tones, 1999 (Grammy award for Best Bluegrass Album), Soldier of the Cross, 2000 (Grammy award for Best Bluegrass Gospel Album), Big Mon-The Songs of Bill Monroe, 2000, The Essential Ricky Skaggs, 2003, Brand New Strings, 2004, Instrumentals, 2006 (Grammy award for Best Bluegrass Album, 2007), Ricky Skaggs & Bruce Hornsby, 2007, Salt of the Earth, 2007 (Grammy award for Best Bluegrass Gospel Album, 2008), Honoring the Fathers of Bluegrass: Tribute to 1946 & 1947, 2008 (Grammy award for Best Bluegrass Album, 2009), The High Notes, 2008, Solo: Songs My Dad Loved, 2009, Mosaic, 2010, Country Hits: Bluegrass Style, 2011, Love's Gonna Get Ya! / Comin' Home to Stay, 2011, A Skaggs Family Christmas, Vol. 2, 2011, (songs) Wheel Hoss, 1984 (Grammy award for Best Country Instrumental Performance), Raisin' the Dickens, 1986 (Grammy award for Best Country Instrumental Performance), Restless, 1991 (Grammy award for Best Country Collaboration with Vocals), Same Old Train, 1998 (Grammy award for Best Country Collaboration with Vocals), A Simple Life, 2003 (Grammy award for Best Country Group Vocal Performance). Recipient Horizon award for Best Newcomer, Country Music Assn., 1982, Male Vocalist of Yr. award, 1982, Best Instrumental Group award, 1983, 1984, best instrumental group award, 1985, 6 Country Music Assn. awards including Entertainer of Yr. award, 1985, Vocal Event of Yr. award, 1991, 6 Acad. of Country Music awards, MusicDove award, Gospel Music Assn., Edison award, 1987, 50th Anniversary award, USO, 1989, various awards Music City News, Cash Box, Radio and Records, Musician of Yr. award, Christian Country Music Assn., 1994, Instrumental Group of Yr. award (with Kentucky Thunder, Internat. Bluegrass Music Awards, 1998—2006; named Playboy Reader's Poll Best Country Instrumental Performance, 1989, Eng.'s Country Music Round Up Most Popualr Internat. Male, 1986—87, Christian Country Artist of Yr., Gospel Voice Mag., 1993. Address: Skaggs Family Records 329 Rockland Rd Hendersonville TN 37075-3423

SKAGGS, WAYNE GERARD, retired diversified financial services company executive; b. Bonneterre, Mo., Dec. 12, 1929; s. Jasper Pinkney and Lattie May (Duren) S.; m. Hana Kaneko, June 1, 1952; children: Robert Kenneth, Melody Jane, Joy Elizabeth. Student, Mo. Inst. Acctg. and Law, 1947-48, U. Mo., Columbia, 1954-55. With Advantage Capital Corp. (formerly Am. Capital Corp.), Houston, 1955-96, ret., 1996; pres., COO Mktg. Group of Cos., Houston, 1976-80, corp. v.p., cons., 1972-90. Served with USAF, 1950-54, Korea. Mem. Nat. Assn. Securities Dealers (nat. vice-chmn. 1977, dist. chmn. 1972), Nat. Bus. Conduct (gov., chmn. 1976), Investment Co. Inst., Am. Legion (life), VFW (life), Optimists (life, pres. 1966). Home: PO Box 726 Wimberley TX 78676-0726 Personal E-mail: hanawayn@vownet.net.

SKAINS, THOMAS E., gas industry executive; BBA, Sam Houston State Univ.; JD, Univ. Houston. Sr. atty. Trans-Continental Gas Pipeline Corp., 1981—86, v.p., 1986—89, sr. v.p. transp. & customer svc., 1989—95; sr. v.p. mktg. & supply svc. Piedmont Natural Gas, Charlotte, NC, 1995—2002, pres., COO, 2002—03; chmn., pres., CEO Piedmont Natural Gas Co., Inc., 2003—. Bd. dir., mem. exec. com. Am. Gas Assn.; chmn. So. Gas Assn.; regional bd. adv. Wachovia Bank. Bd. dir., mem. exec. com. Charlotte C. of C.; bd. mem. United Way Ctrl. Carolinas; chmn. bd. trustees Providence Day Sch. Mem.: State Bar Tex. Office: Piedmont Natural Gas 4720 Piedmont Row Dr Charlotte NC 28210 Mailing: Piedmont Natural Gas PO Box 33068 Charlotte NC 28233

SKALKA, MICHAEL B., insurance company executive, lawyer; b. 1951; BA, Long Island U. C.W. Post Coll.; JD, Kent Coll. of Law, Chicago, 1977. Bar: Ill. 1977. Chmn. Stewart Title Ltd.; pres. Stewart Title Insurance Co., NY, 1988—93, chmn., CEO NY, 1993—; pres. Stewart Title Guaranty Co., exec. v.p., gen. counsel, 1993—2005, exec. v.p. internat., 2005—; chmn., CEO Stewart International, 2005—. Mem.: ABA, NY State Land Title Assn. (past pres.), Am. Land Title Assn. (mem. underwriting counsel Com., mem. indian lands com.). Office: Stewart Internat 1980 Post Oak Blvd Ste G Houston TX 77056-3819 Office Phone: 713-625-4100. Office Fax: 713-625-4129.

SKAMBIS, CHRISTOPHER CHARLES, JR., lawyer; b. Painesville, Ohio, Jan. 21, 1953; s. Christopher Charles and Anne (Haritos) S.; m. Susan Elaine Adrianson, Dec. 18, 1976 (div. Mar. 1997); m. Kathleen Louise Maloney, Feb. 1999; children: Adrianne Elaine, Christopher Roy. Student, U. Pa., 1970-72; BA, U. Conn., 1972-74; JD, Ohio State U. Coll. Law, Columbus, 1975-78. Bar: Fla. 1978, US Dist. Ct. (mid. dist.), 1979, US Dist. Ct. (no. and so. dists.) 1997, US Ct. Appeals (5th and 11th cir.) 1981, US Supreme Ct. 1989. Assoc. VandenBerg, Gay & Burke, Orlando, Fla., 1978-81, ptnr., 1982, VandenBerg, Gay, Burke, Wilson & Arkin, Orlando, Fla., 1982-85, Foley & Lardner, Orlando, Fla., 1985—95, Moran & Shams PA, Orlando, Fla., 1996-99, The Skambis Law Firm, Orlando, 2000—. Mem. Orange County Bar Assn., Orlando, Fla., 1978, Fla. Bar 9D Grievance Commn., Orlando, Fla., 1989; arbitrator Fla. Bar 9th Cir. Fee Arbitration Commn., Orlando, 1987; co-chair Federal and State Trial Practice Co., Orlando, 1992-93, radio operator WB8TID. Mem. ABA. Avocation: amateur radio. Office: The Skambis Law Firm 720 Rugby St Ste120 Orlando FL 32804 Office Phone: 407-649-0090. Office Fax: 407-649-0191. Business E-Mail: cskambis@skambislaw.com.

SKEEN, DAVID RAY, systems engineer, consultant, engineering executive, educator; b. Bucklin, Kans., July 12, 1942; s. Claude E. and Velma A. (Birney) S.; m. Carol J. Stimpert, Aug. 23, 1964; children: Jeffrey Kent, Timothy Sean, Kimberly Dawn. BA in Math., Emporia State U., Kans., 1964; MS, Am. U., DC, 1972; grad., Fed. Exec. Inst., 1983, Naval War Coll., 1984; DSc in Engring. Mgmt., George Washington U., DC, 1998. Cert. office automation profl. Computer sys. analyst to comdr.-in-chief U.S. Naval Forces-Europe, London, 1967-70; computer sys. analyst Naval Command Sys. Support Activity, Washington, 1970-73; dir. data processing Office Naval Rsch.,

U.S. Navy Dept., Arlington, Va., 1973-78; dir. mgmt. info. sys. Naval Civilian Pers. Command, Washington, 1978-80; dep. dir. manpower, pers. tng. automated sys. Dept. Naval Mil. Pers. Command, Washington, 1980-85; dir. manpower, pers. tng. info. resource mgmt. Chief Naval Ops., Washington, 1985-91; assoc. dir. Office of IRM, USDA, Washington, 1992-96; dir. modernization of adminstrn. processes program, 1996-98; dep. dir. office of ops. USDA, Washington, 1998; sr. engrng. mgr., cons. Lockheed Martin, Washington, 1998—2004; sys. engr., cons. GCI, 2004—07; cons. Enterprise Bus. Solutions, 2008—. Lectr. Inst. Sci. and Pub. Affairs, 1973-76; cons. Electronic Data Processing Career Devel. Programs, 1975—; detailed to Pres.'s Reorgn. Project for Automated Data Processing, 1978, spl. Navy IRM studies, SECNAV, 1991, USDA/Office of Mgmt. and Budget IRM, 1993, spl. USDA Field Structure Studies, 1997; adj. prof. Sch. Engring. and Applied Sci. George Washington U., 1985—, Dept. Pub. Adminstrn. George Mason U., 2005—; mem. Pres.'s Fed. Automated Data Processing Users Group, Washington, 1978-80 Contbr. articles to profl. jours. Capt. USNR, 1960-91. Recipient Outstanding Performance award Interagy. Com. Data Processing, 1976, Adminstrv. Staff Performance award, 1998, Sec.'s cert. Appreciation, 1998. Mem. Internat. Coun. on Sys. Engring., Sr. Exec. Assn., Assn. Fed. IRM, Naval Res. Assn., Pres. Fed. Automated Data Processing Users Group. Avocations: travel, photography, reading. Personal E-mail: docskeen@embarqmail.com.

SKEES, WILLIAM LEONARD, JR., lawyer; b. Indpls., Jan. 26, 1947; s. William Leonard and Marian Catherine (Fagan) S.; m. Cindy Lee Keeton; children: Kristina Suzanne Carlsen, Elizabeth Ann Garrison, Catherine Fagan, William Leonard III (dec.), Samuel Jackson. BA, Ball State U., 1969; JD magna cum laude, Ind. U., 1971. Bar: Ind. 1971, Ky. 1981. Law clk. U.S. Dist. Ct. (no. dist.), Fort Wayne, Ind., 1971-72; mem. Frost Brown Todd, LLC, Louisville, 1981—. Contbr. articles to jours. in field. Mem. bd. visitors Ind. U. Sch. Law, 1975-91; bd. dirs., past pres. Louisville Housing Partnership, 1978—; bd. dirs. Stage One, Louisville Children's Theatre, pres., 1990-91; bd. dirs. Ky. chpt. Nat. SIDS Found.; grad. Leadership Ky., 1996. Mem. ABA, Ky. Bar Assn., Ind. Bar Assn., Louisville Bar Assn., Nat. Assn. Bond Lawyers. Office: Frost Brown Todd LLC 400 W Market St Fl 32D Louisville KY 40202-3346 Office Phone: 502-568-0301. Business E-Mail: bskees@FBTLaw.com.

SKELLAND, ANTHONY HAROLD PETER, chemical engineering professor; b. Birmingham, Eng., Feb. 21, 1928; came to U.S., 1959; s. Harold and Hilda Skelland. BSChemE, U. Birmingham, 1948, PhD in Chem. Engring., 1952. Mgr. Procter and Gamble, Eng., 1954-56, R&D engr., 1956-59; asst. prof. Ill. Inst. Tech., Chgo., 1959-62; assoc. prof. U. Notre Dame, South Bend, Ind., 1962-66, prof., 1966-69; Ashland prof. U. Ky., Lexington, 1969-79; prof. Ga. Inst. Tech., Atlanta, 1979—. Cons. Monsanto, Babcock and Wilcox, Union Carbide, E.I. duPont de Nemours, FMC Corp., Westinghouse and others. Author: Non-Newtonian Flow and Heat Transfer, 1967, Diffusional Mass Transfer, 1974; contbr. over 90 articles to profl. jours. Fellow AIChE, Inst. Petroleum; mem. Royal Soc. Chemistry (Eng.), Inst. Chem. Engrs. (Eng.). Avocations: tennis, theater, dining out.

SKELLY, MICHAEL, energy executive; b. Oct. 19, 1961; m. Anne Skelly; 3 children. Degree, U. Notre Dame, Harvard Bus. Sch. Owner Horizon Wind Energy, Houston. Mem. Peace Corps. Mem. Mayor White's green bldg. adv. com. Mem.: Am. Wind Energy Assn. (bd. mem.). Democrat. Cath. Office: Horizon Wind Energy 808 Travis Ste 700 Houston TX 77002

SKELTON, B. R., state legislator; b. Westminster, SC, Jan. 21; s. Hattie Tallulah Vaughan Skelton; m. Vickie Lynn Roach Skelton, Oct. 27, 1990; children: Ginger, Dana, Will, John. Emeritus econs. prof. Clemson U.; mem. Clemson City Coun., 1971—74, Pickens County Planning Commn., 1980, Accommodations Tax Subcom., 1984—88, Pickens County Econ. Devel. Alliance, 1996; chmn. Pickens County Transp. C Fund Com., 1995—; mem. Dist. 3 SC House of Reps., 2003—. Republican. Office: 418C Blatt Bldg Columbia SC 29201 E-mail: SkeltonBR@scstatehouse.net.

SKELTON, WILLIAM DOUGLAS, physician; MD, Emory U., 1963. Sr. v.p. rsch. and health affairs Mercer U., Macon, Ga., 1985—2004; dist health dir. Coastal Health Dist., Savannah, Ga., 2004—. Office: Coastal Health Dist 24 Oglethorpe Professional Blvd Savannah GA 31416 Home Phone: 912-598-0762; Office Phone: 912-356-2233, 912-644-5210. Business E-Mail: wdskelton@dhr.state.ga.com.

SKEMP, SHEILA L., history professor; b. Oak Park, Ill., Aug. 21, 1945; d. Kenneth W. and Lucy W. Skemp; m. Murphy A. Richardson, July 7, 1998. PhD, U. Iowa, Iowa City, 1974; BA in History, U. Mont., Missoula, 1967. Vis. asst. prof. U. Iowa, 1979—80; prof. history U. Miss., University, 1980—. Dir. Sarah Isom Ctr. Women, University, Miss., 1998—2000. Mem.: Omohundro Inst. Early Am. History Culture (assoc.; adv. coun. 2003—06). Democrat. Office: Univ Miss History Dept Bishop 310 University MS 38677 Personal E-mail: sskemp@olemiss.edu.

SKENE-STIMAC, PHYLLIS, corporate financial executive; Attended, Regis U. V.p. AML compliance, global programs-internat. Western Union, dep. chief compliance officer; sr. dir. comm. Blockbuster; sr. v.p., chief compliance officer MoneyGram Internat. Office: MoneyGram International 2828 N Harwood Fl 15 Dallas TX 75201 Office Phone: 800-666-3947.

SKINNER, JAMES E., retail executive; b. 1952; m. Alice Skinner; children: Allison, Claire, Suzanne. BS in Acctg., Tex. Tech U., 1974. CPA. Ptnr. Ernst & Young LLP, 1987—91; chief acctg. officer CompUSA, 1991—94, exec. v.p., treas., CFO, 1994—2000; sr. v.p., CFO CapRock Comm. Corp., 2000—01; sr. v.p. The Neiman Marcus Group, Inc., 2001—07, CFO, 2001—, exec. v.p., 2008—, COO, 2010—. Bd. dirs. Fossil Inc., 2007—. Office: The Neiman Marcus Group Inc 1618 Main St Dallas TX 75201 Office Phone: 214-743-7600. Business E-Mail: james_skinner@neimanmarcus.com.

SKINNER, JAMES LISTER, III, retired language educator; b. Emory, Ga., Sept. 24, 1938; s. James Lister and Josephine Norvell (Fry) S.; m. Ramona Ann York Skinner, Apr. 2, 1961; 1 child, James Lister Skinner IV. AB in English, N. Ga. Coll., Dahlonega, 1960; MA in English, U. Ark., Fayetteville, 1962, PhD in English, 1965. Comdr. Headquarters and Headquarters Battery 28th Artillery Group, Selfridge AFB, Mich., 1964-65; assoc. prof. English Presbyn. Coll., Clinton, SC, 1965-70, prof. English, 1970-92, Charles A. Dana prof. English, 1992—2003, chmn. The Russell Program, 1986-98, co-chmn. English dept., 1996-99, sr. faculty coun., 1995-98, chair sr. faculty coun., 1997-98, chair English dept., 1999-2001, Charles A. Dana prof. English emeritus, 2003—. NDEA fellow U. Ark., Fayetteville, 1960-63; NEH summer fellow Yale U., New Haven, Conn., 1976; hon. vis. fellow Leicester (Eng.) U., 1983; sec. Presbyterian Coll. Faculty, Clinton, S.C., 1995-98; opening spkr. 43rd Anniversary, Rep. Coll.'s Lit. Mag., Figs and Thisthas, 1967, 50th Anniversary Celebration, Boys Farm, 2010. Author: Boys Farm: A History, 2002; editor: The Autobiography of Henry Merrell: Industrial Missionary to the South, 1991, The Refugees: Roswell, 2004; co-editor: The Death of a Confederate, 1996. 1st lt. U.S. Army, 1963-65. Recipient Commendation medal U.S. Army, 1965; named Presbyterian Prof. of Yr. Presbyterian Coll., Clinton, S.C., 1991, State Prof. of Yr. Coun. for Advancement and Support of Edn., 1991, Gov's. Prof. of Yr., Gov. of S.C., Columbia, 1991, DAR History Award medal, 1998, Alumni Hall of Fame award No. Ga. Coll. and State U., 2004. Mem. Phi Beta Kappa, Omicron Delta Kappa, Alpha Psi Omega, Phi Alpha Theta, Sigma Tau Delta. Democrat. Presbyterian. E-mail: jskinner@presby.edu.

SKINNER, JEFF, professional hockey player; b. Markham, Ont., Canada, May 16, 1992; s. Andrew and Elizabeth Skinner. Center Carolina Hurricanes, 2010—. Recipient Calder Meml. Trophy, 2011; named Rookie of Yr., Sporting News, 2011, The Hockey News, 2011; named to NHL All-Star Game, 2011. Achievements include being the youngest All-Star selection ever in the four major North American sports, 2011. Office: Carolina Hurricanes Hockey Club RBC Center 1400 Edwards Mill Rd Raleigh NC 27607

SKINNER, MICHAEL DAVID, lawyer, lobbyist, consultant; b. Shreveport, LA, Jan. 5, 1950; s. Roger Gilman and Jerry Ann (Sneed) S.; m. Janet Louise Horaist, Jan. 7, 1978. JD, La. State U., 1976. Bar: La. 1977, U.S. Dist. Ct. (we. dist.) La. 1978, U.S. Ct. Appeals (5th and 11th cirs.) 1978, U.S. Dist. Ct. (mid. dist.) La. 1982, U.S. Supreme Ct. 1982, U.S. Dist. Ct. (so. dist.) Tex. 1983. Pvt. practice, Lafayette, La., 1976-84; asst. dist. atty. Lafayette Parish, 1983—84; ptnr. Guilliot, Skinner & Everett, 1984-86; asst. parish atty. Lafayette Parish, 1988—93; ptnr. Goode, Skinner & Hawkland, 1986-93; U.S. atty. West Dist. La., 1993-2000; atty. Onebane Law Firm, Lafayette, La., 2001—07, Skinner Law Firm, 2007—. Chmn. La. Democratic Party, 2003—05. Mem. La. State Bar Assn. (mem. ho. of dels.). Democrat. Office: 600 Jefferson St Ste 810 Lafayette LA 70501 Office Phone: 337-354-3030. Business E-Mail: mike@law.glacoxmail.com.

SKLAR, WILLIAM PAUL, lawyer, educator; b. NYC, Sept. 10, 1958; s. Morris and Helen (Meyers) S.; m. Lori Ann Hodges, Jan. 5, 1985. BBA magna cum laude, U. Miami, 1977, JD, 1980. Bar: Fla. 1980, N.Y. 1986, U.S. Dist. Ct. (so. dist.) Fla. 1981, U.S. Tax Ct. 1980, U.S. Ct. Appeals (5th cir.) 1980, U.S. Ct. Appeals (11th cir.) 1981. Assoc. Wood, Cobb, Murphy & Craig, West Palm Beach, Fla., 1980-85, ptnr., 1985-88, Foley & Lardner, West Palm Beach, 1989—2006, ptnr.-in-charge, 1995—2002; counsel Edwards Angell Palmer and Dodge, 2006—. Adj. prof. law Sch. Law, U. Miami, Coral Gables, Fla., 1980—; dir. Inst. on Condo. and Cluster Devels., Inst. on Real Property Law, 1986—. Co-author: Cases and Materials in Condominium and Cluster Developments, 1980; author, co-editor; Florida Real Estate Transactions, 1983; contbr. articles to profl. jours. Atty. adv. bd. Morse Geriatric Ctr., West Palm Beach, 1984-88. Mem. ABA (chmn. subcom. on condominium and coop. housing sect. gen. practice 1983-88), Fla. Bar (com. condominium and planned devels. 1980—, bd. cert. real estate lawyer 1994, exec. coun. mem. real property, probate and trust law sect. 1997—), Palm Beach County Bar Assn., Coll. Cmty. Assn. Lawyers, Am. Coll. Real Estate Lawyers, Phi Delta Phi, Pi Sigma Alpha. Republican. Avocations: travel, tennis. Home: 7238 Montrico Dr Boca Raton FL 33433-6930 Office: Edwards Angell Palmer and Dodge Ste 400 One N Clematis St West Palm Beach FL 33401 Office Phone: 561-820-0270.

SKLENAR, HERBERT ANTHONY, industrial products manufacturing company executive; b. Omaha, June 7, 1931; s. Michael Joseph and Alice Madeline (Spicka) S.; m. Eleanor Lydia Vincenz, Sept. 15, 1956; children: Susan A., Patricia I BSBA summa cum laude, U. Omaha, 1952; MBA, Harvard U., 1954; LLD (hon.), Birmingham-So. Coll., 1996. CPA W.Va. V.p., comptr. Parkersburg-Aetna Corp., W.Va., 1956—63; v.p., dir. Marmac Corp, Parkersburg, 1963-66; mgr. fin. control Boise-Cascade Corp., Idaho, 1966-67; exec. v.p. fin. and adminstrn., sec. Cudahy Co., Phoenix, 1967-72; v.p. fin. Vulcan Materials Co., 1972, exec. v.p. fin. and adminstrn., 1974, chmn. emeritus Birmingham, Ala., 1972-97, chmn. bd. dirs. emeritus, 1997—. Author (with others): The Automatic Factory: A Critical Examination, 1955. Recipient Alumni Achievement award U. Nebr.-Omaha, 1977, cert. merit W.Va. Soc. CPAs, Elizah Watts Sells award AICPA, 1965, Brotherhood award NCCJ, 1993; inductee Ala. Acad. Honor, 1997; Named to Birmingham Bus. Hall of Fame, 2013 Mem.: Rotary Club Birmingham (past-pres.), Birmingham Country Club, Phi Eta Sigma, Phi Kappa Phi, Omicron Delta Kappa, Delta Sigma Pi. Republican. Presbyterian.

SKOOG, GERALD DUANE, science educator; b. Sioux City, Iowa, Feb. 27, 1936; s. Paul and Mary Ann Skoog; m. Elizabeth Ann Lee, Dec. 28, 1962; children: Jeffrey, John, Sarah. BS in Sci. Edn., Curriculum & Instr., U. Nebr., Lincoln, 1958; MA, U. Northern Iowa, 1969. Tchr. various schs., Nebr., Ill., 1958-69; instr. U. Nebr., Lincoln, summer 1969; asst. prof. curriculum and instrn. Tex. Tech U., Lubbock, 1969-72, assoc. prof., coordinator program, 1972-74, assoc. prof., chmn. secondary edn., 1976-80, prof., chmn. secondary edn., 1980-90, prof., chmn. curriculum and instrn., 1990-97, Helen DeVitt Jones prof., 1997-2001, pres. faculty senate, 1986-87, dean Coll. Edn., 2002—03, Paul Whitfield Horn prof., 2000—04, prof. emeritus, 2005; dir. Ctr. Integration Sci. and Edn. Rsch., 2004—. Vis. prof. We. Ill. U., summer 1972; lectr. in field; participant, facilitator numerous workshops; cons. Contbr. numerous articles to profl. jours., also reviewer articles and papers; co-author secondary sch. science textbooks. Bd. dirs. Gloria Dei Luth. Ch., Lubbock, 1971-74, 92-93, 2013-; bd. dirs. Luth. Coun. Cmty. Action, 1970-71, 2013-14, Good Neighbor Ministry, 1982-84; leader Boy Scouts Am., 1978-79; foster parent Luth. Social Svcs. Tex.; bd. dirs. Triangle Coalition for Sci. and Tech., 1986-95. Recipient Pres.'s Faculty Achievement award Tex. Tech. U., 1986, Disting. Leadership award, 1996, Award of Excellence, U. Nebr., Lincoln Tchrs. Coll. Alumni Assn., 2003; named Notable Alumnus, U. Nebr., Lincoln, Tchrs. Coll., 1998; named to Tex. Sci. Hall of Fame, 2000. Fellow AAAS, AERA (inaugral fellow 2009); mem. Friend Darwin, NCSE, NSTA (life, bd. dirs. 1977-79, pres. 1985-86, various coms., Disting. Svc. to Sci. Edn. award 1994, Robert H. Carleton award 2004), Nat. Assn. Rsch., Sci. Tchrs. Assn. Tex. (hon., past pres., Skoog Cup award), Nat. Assn. Biology Tchrs., Tex. Assn. Biology Tchr.(hon. mem.). Lutheran. Office: Tex Tech U Coll Edn Lubbock TX 79409 Home: 4709 116th St Lubbock TX 79424 Office Phone: 806-834-2543.

SKRÖDER, CHRISTIAN E., consumer products company executive; Sr. v.p., worldwide market devel. Tupperware Brands Corp., 2001—09, group pres., Asia Pacific, 2009—. Office: Tupperware Brands Corp 14901 S Orange Blossom Trail Orlando FL 32837 Office Phone: 407-826-5050.

SKUNDA, ROBERT T., life science organization administrator; b. Flint, Mich., Sept. 22, 1946; BArch, U. Mich., 1969, MA in Urban Planning, 1970. Prin., mng. dir. Dewberry & Davis, Fairfax, Va., 1979—93; sec. of commerce & trade Commonwealth of Va., 1993—97; pres., CEO Virginia Biotechnology Research Park, Richmond, 1997—. Bd. dirs. LandAmerica Fin. Group, Inc., 2001—, Greater Richmond Tech. Coun. Office: Virginia BioTechnology Research Park 800 E Leigh St Richmond VA 23219 Office Phone: 804-828-5390. Office Fax: 804-828-8566. Business E-Mail: rts@vabiotech.com.

SKUTA, GREGORY LOUIS, ophthalmologist, educator; b. Benton, Ill., June 22, 1956; s. Richard Louis and Jacquelyn Gail (Weaver) S.; m. Anne Marie (Phelan), May 26, 1984; children: Jonathan Richard, Catherine Anne, Matthew Gregory. BS, U. Ill., 1977, MD, 1981. Intern St. Joseph Mercy Hosp., Ann Arbor, Mich., 1981—82; ophthalmology resident U. Wis., Madison, 1982—85; glaucoma fellow Bascom Palmer Eye Inst., Miami, Fla., 1985—87; asst. prof. ophthalmology U. Mich., Ann Arbor, 1987—92; clin. assoc. prof., dean McGee Eye Inst. U. Okla. Coll. Medicine, Oklahoma City, 1992—98, James P. Luton clin. prof., dep. dean, 1998—2009; pres., CEO Dean McGee Eye Inst., 2009—; Edward L. Gaylord prof., chair, dept. ophthalmology U. Okla. Coll. Medicine, Okla. City, 2009—. Dir. Am. Bd. Ophthalmology 2001-08; bd. govs. World Glaucoma Assn., 2004-07. Contbr. articles to profl. jours., chapters to books. Recipient Okla. Super Drs., 2013—; named one of Best Doctors in Am., 1994—, America's Top Ophthalmologists, 2002—, America's Top Drs., 2013—. Fellow Am. Acad. Ophthalmology (sec. ophthalmic knowledge 2001-06, sr. sec. clin. edn. 2007—12, pres. 13 bd. trustees, 2007-, Life Achievement Hon. award 2013); mem. AMA, Assn. Rsch. Vision and Ophthalmology, Pan Am. Assn. Ophthalmology, Am. Glaucoma Soc. (v.p. 2003-04, pres. 2005-06), Okla. State Med. Soc., Okla. Acad. Ophthalmology, Am. Eye Study Club (pres. 2001-02), Glaucoma Rsch. Soc., Phi Beta Kappa, Phi Kappa Phi, Alpha Omega Alpha. Methodist. Avocations: music, theater, tennis, travel, history. Home: 1516 Sweetbriar Ct Edmond OK 73034-6555 Office: Dean McGee Eye Inst 608 Stanton L Young Blvd Oklahoma City OK 73104 Office Phone: 405-271-6363. Business E-Mail: greg-skuta@dmei.org.

SKVORETZ, JOHN VINCENT, sociologist, educator; b. Allentown, Pa., Sept. 8, 1947; s. John Vincent and Ruth Elizabeth (Heffelfinger) Skvoretz; m. Sharon Louise Anthony Skvoretz, Aug. 31, 1968 (div. Oct. 1998); children: Jonathan, Christopher, Matthew; m. Gretchen Elizabeth Koehler, May 15, 1999. BA in Sociology, Lehigh U., 1969, BA in Math., 1969; PhD in Sociology, U. Pitts., 1976. Prof. sociology U. SC, Columbia, 1976—2005; chmn. dept. sociology U. South Fla., 1984—94, dean, Coll. Liberal Arts, 2003—05, prof. sociology, 2005—, dean, Coll. Arts & Sci. Assoc. editor Jour. Math. Sociology, 1993—. Contbr. articles to profl. jours. Fellowship, NSF, 1969—72. Mem.: Internat. Network Soc. Network Analysis, Southern Sociol. Soc., Am. Sociol. Assn., Phi Beta Kappa. Democrat. Office: USF Dept Sociology 4202 E Fowler Ave CPR 107 Tampa FL 33620-5550 Office Phone: 813-974-7288.

SKVORTSOV, ALEKSANDR ALEKSANDROVICH, cosmonaut; b. Russia, May 6, 1966; m. Skvortsova Elena Georgievna; 1 child, Anna. Grad., Stavropol Air Force Pilot and Navigator Sch., 1987, Mil. Red Banner ZhukovAir Def. Acad., 1997. Aircraft pilot Russian Air Force, sr. pilot, chief aircraft formation, col.; test cosmonaut NASA, Russia. Decorated 70 years of Soviet Armed Forces medal, Russian Armed Forces Meritorious Svc. Medal of the 1st, 2nd and 3rd degree, Commendation Medal of 3rd degree, Mil. Superior Svc. medal of 2nd degree. Office: National Aeronautics and Space Administration Lyndon B Johnson Space Ctr Houston TX 77058

SKYLER, JAY S., medical educator, consultant; b. Phila., Feb. 14, 1947; m. Mercedes Armas Bach, Aug. 9, 2003; children: Jennifer Anne, Alexandra Regina Bach, Marcus Richard Bach. BS, Pa. State U., 1967; MD, Jefferson Med. Coll., 1969. Diplomate in internal medicine, also endocrinology, diabetes and metabolism Am. Bd. Internal Medicine. Intern, resident in internal medicine, fellow in endocrinology and metabolism Duke U., Durham, NC, 1969—73, assoc. then asst. prof., 1972—76; assoc. prof. then prof., medicine, pediatrics and psychology, divsn. endocrinology, diabetes and metabolism, dept. medicine U. Miami, Fla., 1976—. Pres. Am. Diabetes Assn., Alexandria, Va., 1991—92; v.p. Internat. Diabetes Fedn., Brussels, 1994—2000; bd. dirs. Amylin Pharms., San Diego, Dex-Com, Inc, San Diego. Founding editor-in-chief (med. jour.) Diabetes Care, 1978—82, scientific editor Internat. Diabetes Monitor, 1989—2010, sr. editor Diabetes Technology & Therapeutics, 2006—. With USPHS, 1973—75. Master: ACP (mem. bd. regents 1996—99, chmn., coun. of subspecialty societies); mem.: Internat. Diabetes Fedn. (past v.p.), So. Soc. for Clin. Investigation, Internat. Diabetes Immunotherapy Group, Am. Diabetes Assn. (past pres.). Independent. Achievements include research in multiple developments for treatment of diabetes. Office: Univ of Miami Diabetes Research Institut Ste 3054 1450 NW 10th Ave Miami FL 33136 Office Fax: 305-243-4484. Business E-Mail: jskyler@miami.edu.

SLADE, ROY, artist, college president, museum director; came to U.S., 1967, naturalized, 1975; s. David Trevor and Millicent (Stone) S. N.D.D., Cardiff Coll. Art, 1954; A.T.D., U. Wales, 1954; D of Arts, Art Inst. So. Calif., 1994. Tchr. art and crafts Heolgam High Sch., Wales, 1956-60; lectr. art Clarendon Coll., Nottingham, Eng., 1960-64; sr. lectr. fine art Leeds Coll. Art, Eng., 1964-67; prof. painting Corcoran Sch. Art, Washington, 1967-68, assoc. dean, 1969-70, dean, 1970-77; dir. Corcoran Gallery of Art, Washington, 1972-77; pres., dir. Cranbrook Acad. Art, Bloomfield Hills, Mich., 1977-94, now dir. emeritus, lectr. art show juror, exhibition judge; judge Old Fla. Celebration Arts, Cedar Key, Fla., 2011. Sr. lectr. Leeds Coll. Art, England, 1968—69; vis. Boston Mus. Fine Arts, 1970; dir. emeritus Cranbrook Art Mus., 2000—. Exhibited one-man shows Howard Roberts Gallery, Cardiff, Wales, 1958, New Art Ctr., London, 1960, U. Birmingham, 1964, 69, Herbert Art Gallery and Mus., Coventry, 1964, Va. State Art League, 1967, Mus. of Arts and Crafts, Columbus, Ga., 1968, Jefferson Place Gallery, Washington, 1968, 70, 72, 73, Park Sq. Gallery, Leeds, 1969, St. Mary's Coll., Md., 1971, Guelph U., Ont., Can., 1971, Hood Coll., 1974, Pyramid Gallery, Washington, 1976, Robert Kidd Gallery, 1981, 92, Herman Miller, Inc., Mich., 1985; group shows in U.K., Washington, Can.; represented in permanent collections Arts Council Gt. Brit., Contemporary Art Soc., Nuffield Found., Ministry of Works, Eng., Brit. Embassy, Washington, Brit. Overseas Airways Corp., U. Birmingham, Wakefield City Art Gallery, Clarendon Coll., Cadbury Bros., Ltd., Eng., Lord Ogmore, Local Edn. Authorities, judge, All Fla. Show, Boca Raton Mus. Art, Fla., 2009, juror, Nat. Invitational Katherine Butler Gallery, Sarasota, Fla.; contbr. articles to profl. jours. Mem. D.C. Commn. on Arts.; bd. dirs. Artists for Environment Found., Nat. Assn. Schs. Art; chmn. Nat. Council Art Adminstrs., 1981; lectr., jury in art exhbn. Fla., Hawaii, Mich., Honolulu Acad. Arts, Flint Mus. Art, The Ringling Mus. Art, 1995-2011; judge Art Festival Beth-Ei, St. Petersburg, Fla., 2008; juror Nat. Invitational, Katherine Butler Gallery, Sarasota, Fla., 2009; judge, Ann. Art Festival Boca Raton Mus. Art, 2008, judge, All Fla. Show 2009, advisor Trustees Search Com., 2011; judge Old Fla. Celebration Arts, Cedar Key, 2011. Served with Brit. Army, 1954-56. With Brit. Army, 1954—56, Malayan Campaign GSM. Decorated knight 1st class Order of White Rose (Finland), Royal Order of Polar Star (Sweden); recipient award Welsh Soc., Phila., 1974, Gov.'s Arts Orgn. award, 1988; Fulbright scholar, 1967-68. Mem. Nat. Soc. Lit. and Arts, AIA (hon. Detroit chpt.), Assn. Art Mus. Dirs. (hon.). Anglican. Home: 31 Island Way Apt 801 Clearwater FL 33767-2206 Personal E-mail: royslade@royslade.com.

SLANSKY, JERRY WILLIAM, investment company executive; b. Chgo., Mar. 8, 1947; s. Elmer Edward and Florence Anna (Kosobud) S.; m. Marlene Jean Cannella, Jan. 29, 1950; children: Brett Matthew, Blake Adam. BA, Elmhurst Coll., 1969; MA, No. Ill. U., 1971. Mktg. rep. Bantam Book Co., Chgo., 1972-73, Charles Levy Circulating Co., Chgo., 1973-76; account exec. Merrill Lynch, Chgo., 1976-77, Oppenheimer & Co., Inc., Chgo., 1977—, asst. v.p., 1978, v.p., 1979, sr. v.p., 1981, mng. dir., 1986, ptnr., 1986—. Bd. dirs. Lake Geneva (Wis.) Beach Assn., 1987-02, Glen Ellyn Youth Ctr., Glenbard West H.S., pres., 1998-99, Booster Club; bd. dirs. Buttonwood Cove, Longboat Key, Fla., 2006-08; mem. bus. affairs com. Presbytery of Chgo., 1999-04. Mem. Nat. Assn. Securities Dealers (arbitrator 1988—), N.Y. Stock Exch., Chgo. Bd. Options, Am. Arbitration. Assn, Omaha C. of C. Presbyterian. Avocations: swimming, water-skiing, golf, skiing, kayaking. Office: Oppenheimer & Co Ste 4000 500 W Madison St Chicago IL 60661 Office Phone: 312-360-5553. Personal E-mail: jerry.slansky@opco.com.

SLATE, JOE HUTSON, psychologist, educator; b. Hartselle, Ala., Sept. 21, 1930; s. Murphy Edmund and Marie (Hutson) S.; m. Rachel Holladay, July 1, 1950; children: Marc Allan, John David, James Daryl. BS, Athens Coll., 1960; MA, U. Ala., 1965, PhD, 1970. Mem. Faculty Athens State U., 1965—92; prof., psychology, chair, Behavioral Scis. Divsn., 1974—92; dir., Instnl. Effectiveness, 1988—92; pvt. practice, 1970—; author, 1988—. Author: Psychic Phenomena, 1988, Self-Empowerment, 1991, Psychic Empowerment, 1995, Psychic Empowerment for Health and Fitness, 1996, Astral Projection, 1998, Aura Energy for Health Healing, and Balance, 1999, Rejevenation: Strategies for Living Younger, Longer and Better, 2001, Psychic Vampires, 2002, Beyond Reincarnation, 2005, Connecting to the Power Nature, 2009, Self-empowerment for Everyone, 2009, Self-empowerment Through Self Hypnosis, 2010, Self Empowerment and Your Subconscious Mind, 2010, Doors to Past Lives and Future Lives, 2011, Llewellyn Complete Book of Psychic Empowerment, 2011, Astral Projection for Psychic Emposwermentp, Clairvoyance and Psychic Empowerment, 2013. Named hon. prof. U. Montevallo, 1973, prof. emeritus Athens State U., 1992. Mem. APA, Am. Soc. Clin. Hypnosis, Inst. Parapsychol. Rsch. (founder), Coun. for Nat. Register Health Svc. Providers in Psychology, NEA, Ala. Edn. Assn., Delta Tau Delta, Phi Delta Kappa, Kappa Delta Pi. Home: 210 Main St West Hartselle AL 35640-4442 Office: 110 Sparkman St S Hartselle AL 35640 Office Phone: 256-773-0116. Personal E-mail: jhslate@aol.com.

SLATER, GARY, automotive executive; BS in Bus., U. San Francisco. With Anderson Racking, Calif., Cal-Rak, Calif.; v.p., sales Unarco Material Handling, Inc. (subs. of The Renco Group, Inc.), 1999—2005, pres., 2005—. Pres. RMI (Rack Manufacturer's Inst.); active Material Handling Supply Association, Calif.; bd. dirs. Material Handling Equipment Distbrs.Assn. (MHEDA). Office: Unarco Material Handling Inc 701 16th Ave E Springfield TN 37172-3305 Office Phone: 615-384-3531. Office Fax: 615-382-2782. Business E-Mail: gslater@unarcorack.com.

SLATER, THOMAS GLASCOCK, JR., lawyer; b. Washington, Mar. 15, 1944; s. Thomas G. and Hylton R. Slater; m. Scott Newell Brent, Aug. 31, 1996; children: Thomas Glascock, Tacie Holden Norris, Andrew Fletcher. BA, Va. Mil. Inst., 1966; LLB, U. Va., 1969. Bar: Va. 1969, US Dist. Ct. (ea. dist.) Va. 1970, US Ct. Appeals (4th cir.) 1975, DC 1980, US Ct. Appeals (5th cir.), US Ct. Appeals DC 1980, US Supreme Ct. 1981. Assoc. Hunton & Williams LLP, Richmond, Va., 1969-76, ptnr., 1976—. Group head litig., intellectual property competition and labor group Hunton & Williams LLP; bd. dirs. Tredegar Industries. Pres. VMI Found., 1995—97; with VMI Bd. Visitors, 2003—, pres., 2008—; bd. trustees Va. Hist. Soc.; bd. dirs. Central Va. Legal Aid Soc. Fellow: Va. Law Found., Am. Coll. Trial Lawyers, Am. Bar Found.; mem.: Richmond Bar Assn. (pres. 1989—90), DC Bar Assn., Va. State Bar Coun. (exec. com.), 4th Cir. Jud. Conf., Va. Mil. Inst. Alumni Assn. (past pres.). Office: Hunton & Williams LLP Riverfront Plz East Tower 951 E Byrd St Richmond VA 23219-4074 Office Phone: 804-788-8475. Business E-Mail: tslater@hunton.com.

SLATTERY, EDWARD JAMES, bishop; b. Chgo., Aug. 11, 1940; Student, St. Mary of the Lake Sem., Mundelein, Ill., Loyola U., Chgo. Ordained priest Archdiocese of Chgo., Ill., 1966; v.p. Cath. Ch. Ext. Soc., 1971-76, pres., 1976-94; ordained bishop, 1994; bishop Diocese of Tulsa, 1994—. Roman Catholic. Office Phone: 918-294-1904. Office Fax: 918-252-1168.

SLAUGH, LYNN H., retired chemist; BS, Bringham Young U., 1952; PhD, U. Wash., 1956. With Shell Devel. Co., Houston, 1956—98; ret., 1998. Contbr. articles to profl. jours. Recipient Indsl. Chemistry award Am. Chem. Soc., 1995. Achievements include 162 patents; development of two indsl. processes.

SLAUGHTER, ALEXANDER HOKE, lawyer; b. Charlottesville, Va., Nov. 24, 1937; s. Edward Ratliff and Mary (Hoke) S.; m. Virginia Borah, 1964 (div.); 1 child, David A.; m. Mary Peeples, 1971. BA, Yale U., 1960; LLB, U. Va., 1963. Counsel McGuire, Woods, Richmond, Va. Episcopalian. Home: 3016 Rugby Rd Richmond VA 23221-3936 Office: McGuire Woods One James Ctr 901 E Cary St Richmond VA 23219-4030 Home Phone: 804-353-1405; Office Phone: 804-775-4346. E-mail: aslaughter@mcguirewoods.com.

SLAUGHTER, EDWARD RATLIFF, JR., lawyer; b. Raleigh, NC, Sept. 15, 1931; s. Edward Ratliff and Mary McBee (Hoke) S.; m. Anne Limbosch, July 25, 1957; children: Anne-Marie, Hoke, Bryan. AB, Princeton U., 1953; postgrad. (Rotary Found. fellow), U. Brussels, 1955-56; LLB, U. Va., 1959. Bar: Va. 1959, D.C. 1981. Assoc. firm McGuire, Woods & Battle (now McGuire Woods) and predecessors, Charlottesville, Va., 1959-64; ptnr. McGuire, Woods & Battle and predecessors, 1964-79, head dept. litig., 1964-79, spl. asst. for litig. to atty. gen. U.S., 1979-81; ptnr. firm Whitman & Ransom, Washington, 1981-84; prin. Slaughter & Redinger, P.C., Charlottesville, 1984-95, Slaughter, Izakowitz, Clarke & Nunley, P.C., 1995-96, Woods, Rogers & Hazlegrove, P.L.C., 1996—2002, of counsel, 2002—03, Michie, Hamlett, Lowry, Rasmussen, & Tweel, PLLC, 2003—. Vis. lectr. trial advocacy U. Va., 1970-77, Va. procedure, 1986-91; disting. lectr. U. Tunis, 1996; mem. standing com. on commrs. of accounts Jud. Coun. of Va., 1993—, chmn., 1995-2001. Chmn. Albemarle County (Va.) Dem. Com., 1969-73; pres. Charlottesville-Albemarle United Way, 1972; commr. accounts Albemarle County, 1986—; trustee Lime Kiln Arts, Inc., 1992-98. Served with USNR, 1953-55. Recipient William J. Brennan award U. Va. Trial Advocacy Inst., 1996. Fellow Am. Bar Found., Am. Coll. Trial Lawyers; mem. D.C. Bar, Charlottesville-Albemarle Bar Assn. (pres. 1976-77), Va. Bar Assn. (pres. 1978), Va. State Bar (bd. govs. internat. practice sect. 1992-2000, bd. govs. sr. lawyers conf. 2004—08), Thomas Jefferson Inn Ct. (pres. 1995-96), Farmington Country Club. Home: 200 Tuckahoe Farm Ln Charlottesville VA 22901-5531 Office: Michie Hamlett Lowry Rasmussen & Tweel PLLC 500 Court Sq Ste 300 PO Box 298 Charlottesville VA 22902-0298 Home Phone: 434-975-3079; Office Phone: 434-295-8310. Business E-Mail: eslaughter@mhlrt.com.

SLAUGHTER, RALPH, academic administrator; BS in Acctg. and Fin., MPA, PhD in Pub. Policy. CPA. V.p. Southern U. System. Chmn. bd. dirs. LA Cap. Fed. Credit Union. Mem. Mount Zion First Bapt. Ch. Named to Power 150, Ebony mag., 2008. Mem.: Treasury Mgmt. Assn., Soc. La. Cert. Pub. Accountants, Am. Inst. Cert. Pub. Accountants, Am. Soc. Pub. Administrators (pres. La. chpt.), Prince Hall Masons La. (grand master, CEO, imperial potentate Prince Hall Shriners, grand chancellor United Supreme Coun., Southern Juristriction). Office: Southern U System PO Box 10878 Baton Rouge LA 70813

SLAYTON, GUS, foundation administrator; b. Pocahontas, Ark., Jan. 20, 1937; s. Alvin M. and Eula Inis (Milam) S.; m. Ruth Virginia Furr, May 27, 1961 (dec. Nov. 1989). BA, U. Md., College Park, 1973. Enslited U.S. Army, 1957, commd. 2nd lt., 1963, advanced through grades to lt. col., 1978; various operational and research and devel. assignments, including The Pentagon, 1974-78; ret., 1980; exec. dir. Assn. of Old Crows, Alexandria, Va., 1980-92, AOC Ednl. Found., 1992—. Decorated Legion of Merit (2), Bronze Star (2) Republican. Avocation: real estate investment. Home: 152 Mill Cove Ln Ponte Vedra Beach FL 32082-4135 Personal E-mail: slaytonag@comcast.net. E-mail: slaytonag@earthlink.net.

SLEDD, ROBERT C., real estate company executive; b. 1952; Pres., CEO Taylor & Sledd Industries, 1984—87; pres. Performance Food Group Co., 1987—95, CEO, 1987—2001, 2004—06, chmn., 1995—2008; sr. econ. adv. to Gov. State of Virginia, Richmond, 2010; mng. ptnr. Pinnacle Ventures, LLC, Sledd Properties, LLC. Bd. dirs. Taylor & Sledd Industries, 1974—87, Performance Food Group, 1987—2008, SCP Pool Corp., 1996—, Union Bankshares Corp., 2003—, Owens & Minor, Inc., 2007—, Universal Corp., 2009—. Vice chmn. Homeward, 2000—; bd. dirs. Better Housing Coalition, 2000—, Va. Found. for Performing Arts; trustee Va. Found. of Independent Colleges; chmn. bus. adv. bd. Hilliard House. Republican. Office: Sledd Properties LLC 9860 W Broad St Glen Allen VA 23060 Office Phone: 804-527-1643. Business E-Mail: rsledd@pinnacleven.com.

SLEDGE, CHARLES M., oil industry executive; BS in Accounting, La. State U.; grad., Advanced Mgmt. Program, Harvard Bus. Sch. CPA. With Price Waterhouse LLP, 1989—96; v.p., controller Stage Stores Inc., 1996—99, sr. v.p. fin., treas., 1999—2001; corp. controller Cameron International Corp., Houston, 2001—08, v.p., CFO, 2008, sr. v.p., CFO, 2008—. Office: Cameron Internat Corp 1333 W Loop S, Ste 1700 Houston TX 77027

SLICE, KIMBO (KEVIN FERGUSON), boxer; b. Nassau, Bahamas, Feb. 8, 1974; s. Rosemary Clarke; 6 children. Attended, Bethune-Cookman Coll., Daytona Beach, Fla., U. Miami, Coral Gables, Fla. Bodyguard RK Netmedia, Miami; underground street fighter Miami; mixed martial arts fighter EliteXC, Ultimate Fighting Championship, 2007—10; profl. boxer, 2011—. Winner by submission vs. Bo Cantrell EliteXC: Renegade, 2007; winner by knockout vs. Tank Abbott EliteXC: Street Certified, 2008; winner by tech. knockout vs. James Thompson EliteXC: Primetime, 2008; loser by tech. knockout vs. Seth Petruzelli EliteXC: Heat, 2008; winner by decision vs. Houston Alexander The Ultimate Fighter 10 Finale, 2009; loser by tech. knockout vs. Matt Mitrione Ultimate Fighting Championship 113, 2010. Office: Team Kimbo 1031 N Miami Beach Blvd Miami FL 33162

SLINKARD, MARY, state legislator; Mem. Dist. 100 Ark. House of Reps., 2009—. Republican. Baptist. Office: State Capitol Rm 350 Little Rock AR 72201 also: 10422 Virden Ln Gravette AR 72736 Office Phone: 501-682-6211, 501-682-7771, 479-787-6120. E-mail: slinkardm@arkleg.state.ar.us.

SLIVA, CHRIS, food products executive; 2 children. BSBA in Mktg. & Psychology, Wash. U., St. Louis. Various positions Procter & Gamble Co., Fort James Corp.; v.p., retail sales, v.p., US sales Eastman Kodak Corp., v.p., gen. mgr., Americas Output; with White Wave Foods Co.; sr. v.p., sales and chief customer officer Dean Foods Co., 2006, COO, Morningstar Divsn., 2008—10, pres., Morningstar Divsn., 2010—. Office: Dean Foods Co 2515 McKinney AveSte 1200 Dallas TX 75201 Office Phone: 214-303-3400. Office Fax: 214-303-3499. Business E-Mail: chris_sliva@deanfoods.com.

SLIVE, MICHAEL LAWRENCE, sports association executive, lawyer; b. Utica, NY, July 26, 1940; m. Elizabeth Slive; 1 child, Anna. BA, Dartmouth Coll., 1962; JD, U. Va. Sch. Law, 1965; LLM, Georgetown U. Law Ctr., 1966. Asst. dir. athletics Dartmouth Coll., 1966—69; ptnr. Stebbins & Bradley, Hanover, NH, 1969—77, Coffield Ungaretti & Harris, Chgo., 1986—91; jud. master, clerk Grafton County Superior Ct., NH, 1977—79; asst. exec. dir. Pacific-10 Conf., 1979—81; dir. athletics Cornell U., 1981—83; pvt. practice, 1983—86; commr. Great Midwest Conf., 1991—95, Conf. USA, 1995—2002, Southeastern Conf., 2002—. Judge Hanover Dist. Ct., 1972—77; sr. ptnr., founder Slive-Glazier Sports Group, 1990—91; coord. Bowl Championship Series, 2007—. Named one of Most Influential People in the World of Sports, Bus. Week, 2008; E. Barrett Prettyman fellowship in trial advocacy. Mem.: Nat. Assn. Collegiate Dirs. of Athletics (mem. exec. com.), Collegiate Commrs. Assn. (pres. 2001—03), Sports Lawyers Assn. (bd. dirs. 1997—2001). Office: Southeastern Conf 2201 Richard Arrington Blvd N Birmingham AL 35203 Office Phone: 205-458-3000. Office Fax: 205-458-3031.

SLOAN, O. TEMPLE, JR., (ORRIS TEMPLE SLOAN JR.), automotive executive; b. Sanford, NC, Feb. 21, 1939; s. Orris Temple and Thelma (Hamilton) S.; m. Carol Carson (dec.); children: C. Carson Henline, O. Temple Sloan III, Mark H. Sloan; m. Carolyn Myers. BA in Bus. Adminstrn., Duke U., 1961; LLD (hon.), Northwood U., Midland, Mich., 2007. Co-founder, chmn. Highwoods Properties, Inc., Raleigh; founder, chmn. Gen. Parts Internat., Inc., Raleigh, NC, 1961—2008, chmn., 2008—; founder, chmn. Trailcreek Investments. Bd. dirs. Golden Corral, Bank of America Corp., 1996-2008, Lowe's Companies Inc., 2004-11; chair Raleigh YMCA Ann. Campaign, 2011-. Former trustee Boys & Girls Homes N.C., Lake Waccamaw, 1973; campaign chmn. Wake County United Way, 2001; mem. Centennial Authority, 1995—2005, trustee, former chmn. fin. com.; elder Presbyn. Ch.; exec. bd., Occoneechee coun., v.p., supply Boy Scouts Am., capital campaign chmn. Occoneechee coun., 2004—05, past v.p.Occoneechee coun., past treas. Occoneechee coun.; bd. visitors Peace Coll., Raleigh, 1985—87, trustee, 1987—97, vice chmn. bd. trustees. Recipient Silver Beaver, Silver Antelope, Silver Buffalo, Eagle Scout award, Nat. Bd., Officer Boy Scouts America, Disting. Eagle Scout award Boy Scouts Am., Disting. Svc. citation Automotive Hall of Fame, 1997, Lifetime Achievement award Ernst & Young Entrepreneur of Yr., 2008,; named Northwood U. Outstanding Bus. Leader, 1999; named to NC Bus. Hall of Fame, 2010. Mem. Automotive Warehouse Distbrs. Assn. Inc. (dir. 1969—, chmn. 1976-77, Scholarship award 1977, Automotive Man of Yr. award 1989), The Fifty Group (past pres.), Carolina Country Club (Raleigh), Desert Mountain Club, Abaco Club. Avocations: fishing, hunting, ranching. Office: Trail Creek Investments 4800 Falls Neuse Rd Ste 315 Raleigh NC 27609 Office Phone: 919-573-3000, 919-573-3105. Office Fax: 919-573-3551. Business E-Mail: sloan@generalparts.com, orsloan@trailcreekinv.com, orsloan@gpi.com.

SLOAN, ROBERT BRYAN, JR., academic administrator; b. Coleman, Tex., 1949; m. Sue Collier; children: Charissa, Bryan, Eraina, Michael, Alathea, Sophia, Paul. BA cum laude, Baylor U., 1970; MDiv magna cum laude, Princeton Theol. Sem., 1973; doktor der theologie insigni cum laude, U. Basel, 1978. Faculty Hardin-Simmons U., Abilene, Southwestern Bapt. Theol. Sem., Fort Worth, 1980—83; faculty, religion Baylor U., Waco, Tex., 1983, George W. Truett chair in Evangelism, 1990—95, dean Truett Sem., 1993—95, pres., CEO, 1995—2005, chancellor, 2005—06; pres. Houston Baptist U., 2006—. Mem. Cooper Found. Bd., Compass Bank Adv. Bd.; pastor, interim pastor over 20 chs., Tex., Okla., N.J., Germany; mem., treas. Big 12 Exec. Com.; bd. dirs. Salado Inst. for the Humanities. Inducted Little League Hall of Excellence. Mem. Studiorum Novi Testamenti Societas, Soc. of Bib. Lit., Inst. for Bib. Rsch. Office: Houston Baptist U 7502 Fondren Rd Houston TX 77074-3298 Office Phone: 281-649-3450.

SLOAN, ROBERT D., law educator, director; b. Ill., Oct. 27, 1947; m. Dauphine de Montlaur Sloan; children: Alexandra, Caroline, Edward. BA, U. Mich., 1969; JD, Harvard U., 1972. Asst. gen. counsel and then gen. counsel to the Minority U.S. Senate Permanent Subcommittee on Investigations, 1973—77; legal adviser, worked on nuclear non-proliferation and politico-military matters U.S. State Dept.'s Office of Legal Adviser, 1977—82; gen. counsel Multinational Force and Observers, Rome, 1982—84; v.p., head dir. Sovereign Credit Mgmt. Divsn. First Nat. Bank Chgo., 1984—87; ptnr. Pepper, Hamilton and Sheetz Law Firm, Washington, 1987—92, Sloan, Lehner & Ruiz; mng. ptnr. Brussels office McKenna. Long, Aldridge LLP, 1993—98; v.p., gen. counsel GE Indsl. Sys., Plainville, Conn., 1998—2003; exec. v.p., gen. counsel, sec. Entergy Corp., New Orleans, 2003—12; dir. La. State U. John P. Laborde Energy Law Ctr., 2012—; prof. profl. practice La. State U. Paul M. Herbert Law Ctr., 2012—; counsel, Energy Advisory Practice Group McDermott Will & Emery, Washington. Adj. prof. law Georgetown Law Ctr., Washington; adv. bd. mem. Energy Policy Inst., U. Chgo. (EPIC), sr. fellow. Bd. dir. Ctr. for Internat. Bus. Edn., U. Mich., New Orleans Ballet Theatre. Office: Paul M Herbert Law Ctr 1 East Campus Dr Office 430 Louisiana State University Baton Rouge LA 70803-1000 Address: McDermott Will & Emery The McDermott Building 500 North Capitol St NW Washington DC 20001 Office Phone: 225-578-6411, 202-756-8109. Office Fax: 202-756-8000. Business E-Mail: robert.sloan@law.lsu.edu, rsloan@mwe.com.*

SLOANE, STANTON D., security systems company executive; B in Profl. Studies, Barry U.; M in Human Resources Mgmt., Pepperdine U.; D in Mgmt., Case Western Res. U. Joined GE Aerospace, 1984, various positions in engring., program mgmt. and bus. devel.; various bus. devel. positions in Greece, England and Australia Lockheed Martin Corp., v.p. radar, sensor sys., ocean radar and sensor sys. Syracuse, NY, dep. exec. v.p. IS and S, v.p. comm. sys., mgmt. and data sys. Global Telecom., sr. v.p. network sys. devel. Global Telecom., 1998—2000, exec. v.p. mgmt. and data sys., 2000—03, pres. mgmt. and data sys., 2003—04, exec. v.p. integrated sys. and solutions, 2004—07; COO SRA Internat., Inc., 2007; pres., CEO SRA International, Inc., 2007—11; dir., pres., CEO Decision Sciences Internat. Corp., 2011—. Bd. dirs. Profl. Services Coun. Aero. maintenance officer USN, 1976—81. Office: Decision Sciences 14900 Conference Center Dr Ste 125 Chantilly VA 20151

SLOCUM, DONALD WARREN, chemist, educator, researcher; m. Laurel Hopper, 1990 (dec. May 1997); children from previous marriage: Warren, Matthew. BS in Chemistry, U. Rochester, NY, 1956, BA in English, 1956; PhD in Chemistry, NYU, 1963. Postdoctoral rsch. assoc. Duke U., Durham, NC, 1963—64; asst. prof. chemistry Carnegie Inst. Tech., Pitts., 1964—65; from asst. to assoc. prof. chemistry So. Ill. U., Carbondale, 1965—72, prof., 1972—81, adj. prof., 1981—84; program dir. chem. dynamics sect., chemistry divsn. NSF, Washington, 1984—85; program leader divsn. ednl. programs, sr. scientist chem. tech. divsn. Argonne Nat. Lab., Ill., 1985—90; head dept. chemistry We. Ky. U., Bowling Green, 1990—95, prof. chemistry, 1995—2005, rsch. prof. chemistry emeritus, 2005—. Sr. scientist Gulf R&D Co., Pitts., 1980-82; vis. prof. U. Ill., 1970, U. Bristol, Eng., 1973, U. Cin., 1976; vis. fellow U. Bristol, 1972; vis. lectr. Carnegie-Mellon U., 1983-84, U. Pitts., 1983-84; organizer symposia on organometallic chemistry and catalysis; bd. dir. Ctrl. States Univs., Inc., 1986-88, Arts at Argonne, 1988-90; mem. nat. organizing com. XV Internat. Conf. on Organometallic Chemistry Wayne State U., Detroit, 1990; mem. internat. adv. bd. XV Internat. Conf. on Organometallic Chemistry, Warsaw, 1992; mem. NSF/EPSCoR subcom., Ky., 1993-94; mem. coun. on undergrad. rsch. Instnl. Liaison Rep. to We. Ky. U., 1995-2005; cons. in field. Co-editor: Advances in Chemistry Series of Am. Chem. Soc., Vol. 230, 1992, Methane and Alkane Activation (Plenum), 1995; mem. editl. bd. Synthesis and Reactivity in Inorganic, Metal-Organic and Nano-Metal Chemistry, 1971—, Natural Product Rsch., 2006—; regional editor Letters in Organic Chemistry, 2004-05, mem. editl. bd., 2005—; contbr. over 85 articles to profl. jours., chpts. to books Recipient Rsch./Creativity award Ogden Coll. of Sci., Tech. and Health, We. Ky. U., 1996, Sci. award honoring Brian Andreen, Cottrell Coll. Sci., 1999. Mem. Am. Chem. Soc. (sec. gen. elect catalysis and surface sci. secretariat 1992, sec. gen. 1993, organic divsn. rep. to catalysis and surface sci. secretariat, 1993-98, co-chmn. symposium, San Diego, 1994), Chem. Soc. Gt. Britain, Catalysis Soc., Bowling Green Chamber Singers, Sigma Xi. Avocations: music, literature, sports. Office: Western Ky U Dept Chemistry Bowling Green KY 42101 Office Phone: 270-745-5239. Business E-Mail: donald.slocum@wku.edu.

SLONE, JORDAN E., real estate company executive; Chmn., CEO Harbor Group Internat., Norfolk, Va. Bd. dirs. Hampton Roads Bankshares Inc., 2006—. Office: Harbor Group International LLC Ste 2300 999 Waterside Dr Norfolk VA 23510 Office Phone: 757-640-0800. Office Fax: 757-640-0817. Business E-Mail: jordanslone@gwfh.com.

SLOSBERG, IRVING, state legislator; b. Chgo., Ill., Aug. 26, 1947; children: Dori (dec.), Wendy, Emily. BSBA, Roosevelt U., Chgo., 1970. Pres. Slosberg Report Israel; mem. Fla. State House of Representatives, 2001—06, mem. Dist. 90, 2011—. Democrat. Jewish. Office: 9045 LaFontana Blvd Ste 117 Boca Raton FL 33433-5641 also: Fla House of Reps 1402 The Capitol 402 S Monroe St Tallahassee FL 32399-1300 Office Phone: 561-470-6644, 850-488-1302.

SLOVIN, BRUCE, printing company executive; b. NYC, 1935; BA, Cornell U., 1957; JD, Harvard U. Law Sch., 1960. Pres., bd. dirs. MacAndrews & Forbes Holdings, Inc.; pres., COO, bd. dirs. Revlon Group, Inc.; pvt. practice NYC, 1960—64; with Kane Miller Corp., 1964—74, Hanson Industries, Inc., 1974—80; Joined MacAndrews & Forbes Group, Inc., 1980. Dir. Oak Hill Sportswear Corp., Gulf Resources & Chem. Corp., Moore Med. Corp., Four Star Internat. Inc.

Office: Revlon Group 555 SW 12th Ave Pompano Beach FL 33069-3500 also: Revlon Group Inc 35 E 62nd St New York NY 10021-8032 Office: M & F Worldwide Corp 35 E 62nd St New York NY 10021 Office Phone: 212-572-8600. Office Fax: 212-572-8650.

SLUTSKY, BERNICE, agricultural products executive; PhD in Biology, U. Iowa. Rsch. asst. Plant Genetic Sys., Gent, Belgium; rsch. assoc., plant rsch. labs. Mich. State U.; with biotechnology staff EPA, sci. policy advisor, fgn. agrl. svc.; asst. v.p., internat. & regulatory affairs Pharm. Rsch. & Mfrs. Am.; sr. advisor to sec. USDA, 2004—06; spl. asst. to sec., biotechnology, 2004—06; v.p., sci. & internat. affairs American Seed Trade Association, Inc., 2006—. Office: American Seed Trade Association Inc 1701 Duke St Ste 275 Alexandria VA 22314-3492 Office Phone: 703-837-8140. Office Fax: 703-837-8165. Business E-Mail: bslutsky@amseed.org.

SMAGORINSKY, PETER, education educator; b. Princeton, NJ, Oct. 24, 1952; s. Joseph and Margaret (Knoepfel) Smagorinsky; m. Anne O'Gorman, July 10, 1982 (dec. Aug. 1982); m. Jane E. Farrell, Oct. 12, 1985; children: Alysha, David. BA, Kenyon Coll., 1974; MA in Tchg., U. Chgo., 1977, PhD, 1989. English tchr. Westmont (Ill.) H.S., 1977-78, Barrington (Ill.) H.S., 1978-85, Oak Park (Ill.) and River Forest H.S., 1985-90; asst. prof. U. Okla., Norman, 1990-95, assoc. prof., 1995-98, U. Ga., Athens, 1998-2001, prof., 2001—. Author: Standards in Practice, 1996, Tchg. English by Design, Handbook on Adolescent Rsch., 2008, The Discourse of Character Edn., 2005, Rsch. on Composition, Reflective Tchg., Reflective Learning, 2005; co-author: How English Teachers Get Taught, 1995, The Language of Interpretation, 1995; co-editor: Rsch. Tchg. English, 1996—2003, Reading Rsch. Quar. Rev. Ednl. Rsch., Am. Jour. Edn., Written Comm., Reading and Writing Quar. Recipient Steve Cahir award for Rsch. in Writing, Am. Ednl. Rsch. Assn., 1991, Raymond B. Cattell award for Disting. Programmatic Rsch., 1999, ATE Disting. award for rsch. in tchr. edn., 2008, Edward B. Fry Book award, 2009, Russell H. Rsch. award, 2009, Disting. Rsch. Mentor award, UGA Coll., 2011, Sage Citation Excellence award, 2011, Disting. Rsch. Prof., U. Ga., 2011—, Sylvia Scribner award, AERA. Mem.: Am. Ednl. Rsch. Assn., Nat. Coun. Tchrs. English (chair standing com. rsch. 1995—96, co-chair assembly rsch. 1996, trustee rsch. found. 1997—2003, chair 2000—03, pres. nat. conf. rsch. lang. and literacy 2001, English Jour. Writing award 1989, Edwin M. Hopkins award 2000, Janet Emig award 2003). Home: 121 Inverness Rd Athens GA 30606 Office: U Ga 315 Aderhold Hall Athens GA 30602 Office Phone: 706-542-4507. Business E-Mail: smago@uga.edu.

SMALL, CLARENCE MERILTON, JR., lawyer; b. Birmingham, Ala., July 24, 1934; s. Clarence Merilton and Elva (Roberts) S.; m. Gretchen Reeves, Sept. 23, 1935; children: William Stephen, Elizabeth Ann, Laura Carol. BS, Auburn U., 1956; LLB, U. Ala., 1961. Founding ptnr. Christian & Small, Birmingham, 1961—. Served to 1st lt., arty. AUS, to capt. JAGC. Fellow Am. Bar Found., Internat. Acad. Trial Lawyers, Am. Coll. Trial Lawyers, Ala. Law Found.; mem. ABA (ho. of dels. 1984-86), Ala. Bar Assn. (pres. 1992-93), Birmingham Bar Assn. (pres. 1979), Ala. Def. Lawyers Assn., Internat. Assn. Def. Counsel. Office: 1800 Financial Ctr Birmingham AL 35203-4611 Home Phone: 205-871-5994; Office Phone: 205-795-6588. Business E-Mail: cmsmall@csattorneys.com.

SMALL, PARKER ADAMS, JR., pediatrician, educator; b. Cin., July 5, 1932; s. Parker Adams and Grace (McMichael) S.; m. Natalie Settimelli, Aug. 26, 1956; children: Parker Adams, Peter McMichael, Carla Edmea. Student, Tufts U., 1950-53; MD, U. Cin., 1957; BS extraordinem, 1986. Med. intern Pa. Hosp., Phila., 1957-58; rsch. assoc. Nat. Heart Inst. NIH, Washington, 1958-60; rsch. fellow St. Mary's Hosp., London, 1960-61; sr. surgeon NIMH, Washington, 1961-66; prof. immunology and med. microbiology U. Fla., 1966-95, chmn. dept., 1966-75, prof. pediat., 1979—2003, prof. emeritus, 2003—, prof. pathology, 1995—2003, prof. emeritus, 2003—, adj. clin. prof. large animal sci., 1999—2003; pres. PigVax Inc., 2000—01. Dir. Ctr. for Coop. Learning for Health Sci. Edn., U. Fla., 1988-2003; vis. prof. U. Lausanne, Switzerland, 1972, U. Lagos, Nigeria, 1982, Al Hada Hosp., Saudi Arabia, 1983; vis. scholar Assn. Am. Med. Colls., Washington, 1973; assoc. life scis. panel Nat. Acad. Scis., 1981-88, co-chmn., 1982-83; bd. dirs. Biol. Sci. Curriculum Study, 1984-90, exec. bd., 1987-90; mem. edn. adv. com. Nat. Fund Med. Edn., 1984-87; mem. study com. Nat. Bd. Med. Examiners, 1983-85, mem. nat. vaccine adv. com., 1987-91, chmn. subcom. on new vaccines, 1987-91; v.p. smallgroupconsultants.com, 2003-; mem. Truro Shellfish Advisory Com.; cons. in field. Creator patient oriented problem solving system/POPS, for tchg. immunology and coop. learning to med. students and Team Packs for tchg. K-12 & coll. students health edn. and coop. learning; co-dir. Fla. Ptnrs. in Prevention of Substance Abuse, 1997-2003; editor: The Secretory Immunologic System, 1971; mem. editl. bd. Infection and Immunity, 1974-76, Jour. Med. Edn., 1978-80; cons. editor Microbios, Cytobios; patentee in field; contbr. more than 150 articles to profl. jours. Sec., treas. Oakmont, Md., 1964-65, mayor, 1965-66; chmn. Citizens for Pub. Schs. Gainesville, Fla., 1969-70; mem. Teen Pregnancy Prevention Action Com., 1998-2000, Truro Shellfish Adv. Com., 2004-. With USPHS, 1958-60, 61-66. Named Tchr. of Yr. U. Fla. Coll. Medicine, 1978-79, Disting. Lectr. AMA, 1986; recipient Presdl. medallion U. Fla., 1987, Nat. Basic Sci. Disting. Tchg. award Alpha Omega Alpha, 1993, Jacob Ehrenzeller award, 1995, Pres.'s Faculty Humanitarian award U. Fla., 1996, Pep award U. Fla., 1998, Lifetime Achievement award U. Fla. Coll. Medicine, 2003; NIH spl. fellow, 1960-61, rsch. grantee, 1966-91, U. Fla. Tchr./Scholar and commencement spkr., 1987; invited lectr. Assn. Am. Med. Colls., 1992. Mem. AAAS, Am. Assn. Immunologists (edn. com. 1983-86), Physicians for Social Responsibility, Fla. Med. Assn., Phi Beta Kappa, Sigma Xi, Alpha Omega Alpha, Theta Delta Chi. Office: U Fla Coll Med PO Box 100275 Gainesville FL 32610-0275 Personal E-mail: smallgroup2@aol.com. Business E-Mail: small@pathology.ufl.edu.

SMALL, WILLIAM EDWIN, JR., association and recreation executive; b. Jackson, Mich., Jan. 18, 1937; s. William Edwin and Lena Louisa (Hunt) S.; m. Ruth Ann Toombs, Mar. 28, 1959; children: Suzanne Marie, William Edwin III, Bryan Anthony. AS, Jackson C.C., 1959; BS in Geology, Mich. State U., 1961, MA in Journalism, 1964. Reporter Sci. Svc., Washington, 1961-62; writer sci. U. Chgo., 1963-64; sci. info. officer Pa. State U., State College, 1964-66; corr. McGraw-Hill, Washington, 1966-69; staff com. pub. works U.S. Senate, 1969—71; founding editor Biomed. News, 1969-71; dir. pub. info. Nat. Bur. Standards, Washington, 1972-76; editor Am. Pharmacy Jour., 1979-82; dir. media and info. svcs. AMA, Washington, 1982-86; exec. dir. Nat. Found. Infectious Diseases, Washington, 1986-91, Assn. Biotech. Cos., 1991-93; CEO, Bioconfs. Internat., Bethesda, Md., 1993-95; exec. dir. Va. Biotech. Assn., 1996—2000, Va. Campground Assn., 2001—03; CEO, WESmall & Assocs., Assn. Execs., Louisa, Va., 1976—. Owner recreation resort Small Country Campground, Louisa, 1976—; developer Weswood Estates properties, Louisa, 2004-. Author: Third Pollution, 1971. With Security Agy., AUS, 1955-59. Recipient Superior Accomplishment award U.S. Dept. Commerce, 1974. Fellow AAAS; life mem. Nat. Assn. Sci. Writers. Office: PO Box 343 Louisa VA 23093-0343 Office Phone: 540-967-2431. Personal E-mail: wesmall@hotmail.com.

SMART, RITA H., state legislator; b. Jessamine County, Ky., Nov. 13, 1948; m. Richard Smart. BS, Ea. Ky. U., Richmond; MS, U. Ky., Lexington. Owner Bennett House Bed and Breakfast; mem. Dist. 81 Ky. House of Reps., Frankfort, 2011—. Democrat. Office: Kentucky House of Reps Annex Rm 352 702 Capitol Ave Frankfort KY 40601 Office Phone: 502-564-8100 ext. 607. Business E-Mail: rita.smart@lrc.ky.gov.

SMART, SHAKA, men's college basketball coach; b. Madison, Wis., Apr. 8, 1977; s. Monica King; m. Maya Payne, May 20, 2006; 1 child, Zora Sanae. BA in History, magna cum laude, Kenyon Coll., Gambier, Ohio, 1999; M in Social Sci., Calif. U., Pa., 2001. Asst. basketball coach Calif. U. Vulcans, 1999—2001; dir. basketball ops. U. Dayton Flyers, 2001—03; asst. basketball coach U. Akron Zips, 2003—06, Clemson U. Tigers, 2006—08, U. Fla. Gators, 2008—09; head basketball coach Va. Commonwealth U. Rams, 2009—. Achievements include head coach of the College Basketball Invitational tournament winning Virginia Commonwealth University Rams, 2010. Office: Va Commonwealth Mens Basketball Siegel Ctr 1200 W Broad St Richmond VA 23284-3013 Office Phone: 804-828-1278. Business E-Mail: vcuhoops@vcu.edu.

SMARTT, BILL, air courier company executive; CFO DHL Airways Inc., Redwood City, Calif.; exec. v.p., CFO, chief administrv. officer DHL Worldwide Express, Redwood City, Calif. Office: DHL 1200 S Pine Island Rd Ste 170 Plantation FL 33324-4469

SMEETON, THOMAS ROONEY, government affairs consultant; b. Evanston, Ill., Sept. 26, 1934; s. Cecil Brooks, Jr. and Florence Mary (Rooney).; m. Susan Diane Tollefson, Feb. 23, 1963; children: Sean, Timothy, Shannon, Brendan, Colin. BS in History, Marquette U., 1958; postgrad., U. Notre Dame, 1958-59; grad., Armed Forces Staff Coll., 1972. Intelligence officer U.S. CIA, Langley, Va., 1962-73; vp., gen. mgr. Nowicki Fla. Devel. Corp., Ft. Lauderdale, 1973-75; cons. spl. projects com. on fgn. affairs US House of Representatives, Washington, 1975-86, minority counsel permanent select com. on intelligence, 1986-92, minority staff dir. Iran/Contra com., 1987-88, exec. dir. Rep. policy com., 1993-94; adminstr., chief investigator House Judiciary Com., Washington, 1995-96; govtl. affairs cons., 1996—2013. Contbg. author: (with Hyde) For Every Idle Silence, 1985. Bd. dirs. Sylvan Beach Found. With U.S. Army, 1959-62. Recipient Agy. Seal medallion CIA, 1993. Mem. Assn. Former Intelligence Officers, Ctrl. Intelligence Retirees Assn., Am. Legion, Amelia Island Club, Capitol Hill Club, The Notre Dame Club of North Fla., KC. Republican. Roman Catholic. Avocation: golf. Home and Office: 3401 Sea Marsh Rd Amelia Island FL 32034-5059

SMELSER, RONALD E., dean, mechanical engineer, educator; b. Celina, Ohio, Nov. 17, 1947; s. Raymond H. and Gertrude Celina Smelser; m. Barbara Ann Schmalz, Sept. 2, 1972; children: Elizabeth Ann Fox, Peter Christopher. BSME, U. Cin., 1971; SMME, MIT, Cambridge, Mass., 1972; PhD, Carnegie Mellon U., Pitts., 1978. Cert. profl. engr., Ohio, Idaho, NC. Asst. prof. U. Pitts., 1978—81; rsch. scientist US Steel Rsch. Lab., Monroeville, Pa., 1981—83; sci. assoc. Alcoa Tech. Ctr., Alcoa Ctr., Pa., 1983—93; prin. tech. staff Concurrent Techs. Corp., Johnstown, Pa., 1993—94; prof. U. Idaho, Moscow, 1994—2003; prof., assoc. dean U. NC Charlotte, 2003—. Vis. rsch. scientist Colo. State U., Ft. Collins, 1990. Co-author (with G. T. Mase & G. E. Mase): Introduction to Continuum Mechanics; contbr. articles to profl. publs. Ordained elder, deacon Presbyn. Ch., Pitts., 1986. Fellow: ASME. Office: University NC Charlotte 310 Duke Centennial Hall 9201 University City Blvd Charlotte NC 28223-0001 Office Phone: 704-687-8244. Office Fax: 704-687-8267. Business E-Mail: rsmelser@uncc.edu.*

SMERAGLINOLO, ANTHONY, aerospace and defense manufacturing company executive; B in Bus. Mgmt., Fairfield U., 1970; MBA in Fin., Fla. Inst. Tech., 1982. Various fin., operational leadership positions, Govt. Comm. Divsn. Harris Corp., 1980—99; sr. v.p., bus. ops. DRS Technologies, 1999—2001; v.p., programs Harris Tech. Svcs., 2001—06; sr. v.p., gen. mgr., nat. solutions bus. area, Intelligence Solutions Divsn. L-3 Comm., 2006—07, pres., Intelligence Solutions Divsn., 2007—08; pres., global stabilization, devel. solutions segment DynCorp International, Inc., 2009—. Office: DynCorp International Inc Ste 700 3190 Fairview Park Dr Falls Church VA 22042 Office Phone: 571-722-0210. Office Fax: 571-722-0252.

SMETANKA, SALLY S., small business owner; b. Athens, NY, Aug. 26, 1944; AS, Valencia C.C., Orlando, Fla., 1981; BA, Rollins Coll., Winter Park, Fla., 1991. With labor rels. Walt Disney World, Orlando, Fla., 1978—81, asst. to pres.; owner Carriage House Antiques, Winter Park, Fla., 1983—. Home and Office: Carriage House Antiques 937 Aragon Ave Winter Park FL 32789 Home Phone: 321-217-1687. Personal E-mail: sallysmetanka@yahoo.com.

SMIDDY, JOSEPH CHARLES, retired academic administrator; b. Jellico, Tenn., June 20, 1920; s. Joseph F. and Sara Nan (Tye) Smiddy; m. Reba Graham, Sept. 6, 1985; children: Joseph F., Elizabeth Lee. BA, Lincoln Meml. U., 1948, LHD (hon.), 1970; MA, Peabody Coll., 1952; LLD, U. Richmond, 1975; LHD (hon.), Coll. William and Mary, 1986; DAm (hon.), Cumberland Coll., 1993. Tchr. Jonesville HS, 1948—51, prin., 1951—52; sec.-treas. Powell Valley Oil Co., Big Stone Gap, Va., 1952—53; prof. biology Clinch Valley Coll., U. Va., Wise, 1956—57, dean, 1957—68, dir., 1968—85, chancellor, 1968—85, chancellor emeritus, 1985—. Mem. Charter Day Award Emory and Henry Coll., 1980; mem. Commonwealth Day Award James Madison U., 1985. Musician, singer. Trustee Lincoln Meml. U. With US Army, 1942—45, PTO. Recipient Laurel Leaves award, Appalachian Consortium, 1995, Kanto Ednl. award, Wise County, 1995. Mem.: Bapt. Gen. Assn. Va. (pres. 1974—), Kiwanis, Shriners, Masons. Home: Ridgefield Acres Wise VA 24293 Office: PO Box 3160 Wise VA 24293-3160

SMITH, A. ROBERT, editor, author; b. York, Pa., Feb. 13, 1925; s. Arthur R. and Inez (Dunnick) S.; m. Yvonne Franklin, 1945 (div. 1965); 1 child, Dana C.; m. Elizabeth McDowell Morgan, 1967 (div. 1988); children: Philip S. Morgan IV, Edward A. M. Morgan, Elizabeth A. Morgan; m. Jane Dreifus, 1993 (dec. 1999). BS, Juniata Coll., 1950; postgrad., George Washington U., 1950. Reporter Huntingdon (Pa.) Daily News, 1947, Evening Star, Washington, 1950; Washington corr. Eugene (Oreg.) Register-Guard, 1951-78, Portland Oregonian, 1952-72, King Broadcasting, 1976-78; assoc. editor Virginian-Pilot, Norfolk, 1978-83; editor Venture Inward, Assn. Rsch. and Enlightenment mag., Virginia Beach, Va., 1984—2003. Author: The Tiger in the Senate, 1962, Hugh Lynn Cayce: About My Father's Business, 1988, The Lost Memoirs of Edgar Cayce, 1997, Misdiagnosed: Was My Wife a Casualty of America's Medical Cold War?, 2001, No Soul Left Behind, 2005, God Gave Me A Mulligan: A Journalist's Life In War and Peace, 2012, Ben Franklin's Secret Love, 2013; co-author: (with Eric Sevareid and Fred J. Maroon) Washington: Magnificent Capital, 1965; (with James V. Giles) An American Rape, 1975 With USNR, 1943-46, PTO. E-mail: abob@cox.net.

SMITH, A.J. (ALBERT J. SMITH), professional sports team executive; b. Feb. 28, 1949; m. Susan Smith; children: Andrea, Kyle. BS in Health & Phys. Edn., Ky. Wesleyan Coll., Owensboro, 1971. Tchr. health & phys. edn. Providence Jr. HS Sys., 1971—85; asst. coach Cranston West HS, RI, 1971—76, U. RI, 1978; wide receiver Attleboro Kings, Eastern Football League, Mass., 1972—74; head coach RI Kings, Eastern Football League, 1976; vol. part-time scout NY Giants, 1977; part-time scout New Eng. Patriots, 1978—80, Houston Oilers, 1981; scouting position Chgo. Blitz., US Football League (USFL), 1982—83, Pitts. Maulers, US Football League (USFL), 1984; dir. pro pers. San Diego Chargers, 1985—86; area scout Buffalo Bills, 1987—89, asst. dir. coll. scouting, 1989—93, dir. pro pers., 1993—2000; asst. gen. mgr., dir. pro pers. San Diego Chargers, 2001—03, exec. v.p., gen. mgr., 2003—12; sr. exec. Washington Redskins, 2013—. Named NFL Exec. of Yr., Pro Football Weekly, 2004, Profl. Football Writers of Am., 2004, FoxSports.com, 2004, CBSSportsline.com, 2004; named to The American Football Assn. Minor/Semi-Pro Football Hall of Fame, 1990. Office: Washington Redskins 21300 Redskin Park Dr Ashburn VA 20147*

SMITH, ALEXANDER W., retail executive; BSc, U. East Anglia, UK. Chmn. Winners Merchant Internat. LP; mdse. dir. Owen Owen plc, Singapore, 1987—90, mng. dir., 1990—93, Lane Crawford Ltd., 1994—95; pres. UK ops., mng. dir. T.J. Maxx, 1995—2001; exec. v.p. and group exec. internat. The TJX Companies Inc., 2001—04, sr. exec. v.p. and group pres. internat., 2004—07; pres., CEO Pier 1 Imports, Inc., 2007—. Bd. dirs. Papa John's Internat. Inc., 2007—, Pier 1 Imports, Inc., 2007—. Office: Pier 1 Imports Inc 100 Pier 1 Pl Fort Worth TX 76102 Office Phone: 817-252-8000. Office Fax: 817-252-8174. Business E-Mail: asmith@pier1.com.

SMITH, ALISON LEIGH, lawyer; b. Brownsville, Tex., Sept. 24, 1952; d. Arthur Lee and June (Allen) Smith; m. Dean A. Burkhardt, Apr. 24, 1981. B in Journalism summa cum laude, U. Tex., 1974, JD cum laude, 1977. Bar: Tex. 1977, US Dist. Ct. (so. dist.) Tex. 1978, US Ct. Appeals (5th cir.) 1981, US Dist. Ct. (no. dist.) Tex. 1987, US Ct. Appeals (DC cir.) 1989. Assoc. Vinson & Elkins LLP, Houston, 1977-84, ptnr., 1984—89, 1991—2004; dep. asst. atty. gen. antitrust divsn. U.S. Dept. Justice, Washington, 1989-91; ptnr. Dewey Ballantine LLP, Houston, 2004—05, Haynes and Boone, LLP, Houston, 2005—10, Mc Dermott Will & Emery LLP, Houston, 2010—. Adj. prof. law U. Tex., Austin, 1992-93. Alternate del. Rep. Nat. Conv., New Orleans, 1988; mem. ethics com. City of Houston, 1988-89; chair Mayor's Animal Protection Task Force, 2005. Mem. ABA (antitrust law sect., chair transp. industry com., 1992-95, co-chmn. pvt. antitrust litig. com. 2001-04, long range planning task force, 2002, vice chmn. Sherman Act sect. one com. 2004-05, econ. evidence task force 2005-06, editl. bd. State Antitrust Practice and Statutes, 2006-09, Internat. Cartel Task Force, 2010-, liason dispute resolution sect., 2009-10), Am. Law Inst., Tex. Bar Found., Houston Bar Assn. Home: 2125 Bolsover St Houston TX 77005-1617 Office: Mc Dermott Will & Emery LLP 1000 La St Ste 3600 Houston TX 77002-5005 Home Phone: 713-520-1979; Office Phone: 713-653-1753. Business E-Mail: alsmith@mwe.com.

SMITH, ALLIE MAITLAND, retired engineering educator; b. Lumberton, NC, June 9, 1934; s. Allie McCoy and Emma Hattie (Wright) S.; m. Sarah Louise Whitlock, June 16, 1957; children: Sara Leianne, Hollis Duval, Meredith Lorren. BME with honors, N.C. State U., Raleigh, 1956, MS, 1961, PhD, 1966. Assoc. engr. Martin Co., Balt., 1956-57; devel. engr. Western Electric Co., 1957-60; mem. tech. staff Bell Tel. Labs., Burlington, NC, 1960-62; instr., then asst. prof. extension N.C. State U., 1958-62; rsch. project engr. Rsch. Triangle Inst., Durham, NC, 1962-66; rsch. supr. Sverdrup/ARO, Inc., Arnold Air Force Sta., Tenn., 1966-79; adj. prof. U. Tenn., Tullahoma, 1967-79; prof. mech. engring. U. Miss., University, 1979—2008, dean Sch. Engring., 1979—2000, emeritus prof., 2008—, emeritus dean, 2000—. Bd. dirs., scholarship bd. Miss. Mineral Resources Inst.; exec. chmn. 14th conf. Southeastern Conf. on Theoretical and Applied Mechanics, exec. com. 13th-16th confs., ops. com. and policy com., 1990-99, session chair, 1994; organizing com., internat. sci. adv. bd., plenary session presiding officer Internat. Conf. on Hydrosci. and Engring., 1993, 95; organizing com., plenary session chair Conf. on Mgmt. of Landscapes Disturbed by Channel Incision, 1997; keynote lecture and plenary sessions chair, 3rd Internat. Conf. on Hydrosci. and Engring., Berlin, 1998 Author: Fundamentals of Silicon Integrated Device Technology, Vol. I: Oxidation, Diffusion and Epitaxy, 1967, also articles, revs.; editor: Radiative Transfer and Thermal Control, 1976, Thermophysics of Spacecraft and Outer Planet Entry Probes, 1977, Fundamentals and Applications of Radiation Heat Transfer, 1987, Developments in Theoretical and Applied Mechanics, Vol. XIV, 1988, Radiation Heat Transfer: Fundamentals and Applications, 1990, Fundamentals of Radiation Heat Transfer, 1991, Radiative Heat Transfer: Theory and Applications, 1993, Solution Methods for Radiative Heat Transfer in Participating Media, 1996, Radiative Heat Transfer, 1997. Fellow AIAA (chmn. thermophysics tech. com. 1975-77, ASME (aerospace heat transfer com. 1975-2007; chmn. radiative heat transfer I and II sessions, Pitts. 2000, chmn. radiation heat transfer II session, St. Louis, 2002, chmn. terrestrial energy sys. tech. com. 1979-81, chmn. confs. 1975, 79, assoc. editor jour. 1975-77, 1986-2007, nat. publ. com. 1979-83, Nat. Thermophysics award 1978, Hermann Oberth award 1984-85, Space Shuttle Flag Challenger plaque 1984, supernumerary dir. Ala.-Miss. sect. 1994-2000); mem. AAUP, NSPE (pres. N.E. Miss. chpt. 1990-91), Am. Soc. Engring. Edn. (host Nat. Engring. Deans' Inst. 1991), NY Acad. Scis., Sigma Xi, Phi Kappa Phi, Tau Beta Pi, Pi Tau Sigma, Upsilon Pi Epsilon, Sigma Pi (scholar 1955), Order of the Engr., Notable. Achievements include discovery of anomalous refraction maxima phenomenon. Mailing: PO Box 4601 Chapel Hill NC 27515-4601 Office Phone: 919-542-0164. Personal E-mail: enas0609@gmail.com.

SMITH, ANDREA B., bank executive; BS in Economics, So. Meth. U. Joined Bank of America Corp., Charlotte, NC, 1988, team leader consumer and comml. bank, consumer products and asset mgmt. group staffing teams, 1994, sr. personnel exec. risk mgmt., 2002, sr. human resources exec. global banking and markets, global tech. and ops. and chief adminstrv. officer group, global human resources exec., 2010—. Former mem. bd. dirs. Youth Homes, Inc., Charlotte. Office: Bank of America Corp 100 N Tryon St, 18th Fl Charlotte NC 28255

SMITH, ANDREW (THOMAS ANDREW SMITH), lawyer; b. Calif., 1960; m. Janette Smith; children: Shelby, Caroline, Mack. BA, Vanderbilt U., 1982; JD, Southern Methodist U. Dedman Sch. Law, 1985. Chmn. healthcare group and mem., corp. & securities group Bass, Berry & Sims PLC, Nashville, 1985—2006; exec. v.p., gen. counsel, sec. Brookdale Senior Living, Inc., Chgo., 2006—. Avocations: golf, cooking. Office: Brookdale Senior Living Inc 111 Westwood Pl Ste 200 Brentwood TN 37027 Office Phone: 615-221-2250. E-mail: andysmith@brookdaleliving.com.

SMITH, B. SCOTT, automotive executive; Grad., Rollins Coll., 1991. Gen. mgr. Town & Country Ford, Charlotte, NC, 1992—97; pres., COO Sonic Automotive, Inc., Charlotte, NC, 1997—2002, vice chmn., chief strategic officer, 2002—07, pres., chief strategy officer, 2007—. Office: Sonic Automotive Inc 5401 Independence Blvd Charlotte NC 28212

SMITH, BAKER ARMSTRONG, management executive, lawyer; b. Oct. 3, 1947; s. William Armstrong and Priscilla (Baker) S.; m. Deborah Elizabeth Ellis, Nov. 13, 1982; children: Ellis Armstrong, Elizabeth Anne(Lewis), Everett Baker, Emery Manning. BS, U.S. Naval Acad., 1969; MBA, Northeastern U., 1975; JD cum laude, Suffolk U., 1977; LLM in Labor, Georgetown U., 1981. Bar: Ga. 1977, D.C. 1978, U.S. Supreme Ct. 1980; cert. turnaround profl., 1994; fellow Family Firm Inst. Commd. ensign USN, 1969, advanced through grades to lt., 1974; exec. dir., founder Ctr. on Nat. Labor Policy, Inc., North Springfield, Va., 1977-81; asst. to sec., dir. labor rels. U.S. Dept. HUD, Washington, 1981-83; exec. v.p. U.S. Bus. and Indsl. Coun., Nashville, 1983-84; pres. Am. Quality Builders, Inc., Nashville, 1984-86; v.p. Hopeman Bros., Inc., Waynesboro, Va., 1986-88, Morris, Anderson, Atlanta, 1988—2008, BDO Consulting, LLC, Atlanta, 2008—. Sec., founder US Constnl. Rights Legal Def. Fund, Inc., Atlanta, 1983—; trustee Leadership Inst., Arlington, Va., 1978-2013, v.p., 1998-2013, Turnaround Mgmt. Assn., Chgo., 1998-99, 2009; pres. Assn. Cert. Turnaround Profls., Chgo., 1997-98; mem. Coun. for Nat. Policy, Washington, 1981—, Civil Rights Reviewing Authority US Dept. Edn., Washington, 1984-88; transition team leader Office of the Pres.-Elect of US, NLRB, Occupl. Safety and Health Rev. Commn., Fed. Mediation and Conciliation Svc., Nat. Mediation Bd., Fed. Labor Rels. Authority, Washington, 1980-81; instr. law, faculty sec. Northern Va. Law Sch., Alexandria, Va., 1980-83; instr. law DC Law Sch., Washington, 1978-80. Contbg. author: Mandate for Leadership, 1981; contbr. articles to profl. jours. Bd. dirs. Atlanta Opera, 2006—13. Recipient Outstanding Contbn. to the Turnaround Profession award, 1999. Fellow Family Firm Inst.; mem. ABA (Nat. Law Day chmn. 1976-77, Silver Key award 1977), St. George's House, Windsor Castle (assoc.), Phila. Soc., U.S. Supreme Ct. Hist. Soc., Federalist Soc., Beta Gamma Sigma, Phi Delta Phi (pres. 1989-91), Capitol Hill Club (Washington), Piedmont Club (Winston-Salem). Republican. Anglican. Home: 3360 E Terrell Branch Ct Marietta GA 30067-5164 Business E-Mail: bsmith@bdocca.com.

SMITH, BARBARA, bank executive; b. Bryan County, Ga. m. Gary Smith. Teller The Heritage Bank, Hinesville, Ga., 1972, sr. v.p. Vol. fundraiser United Way, Am. Cancer Soc., Am. Heart Assn., Am. Diabetes Assn. Named one of 25 Most Powerful Women in Banking, US Banker, 2006. Mem.: Independent Cmty. Bankers Am. Avocation: quilting. Mailing: The Heritage Bank PO Box 1009 Hinesville GA 31310 Office Phone: 912-408-6102. Office Fax: 912-369-9397. E-mail: bsmith@the-heritage-bank.com.

SMITH, BARBARA R., metal products executive; BS in Acctg., Purdue U. CPA State of Tennessee. CFO Gerdau Ameristeel Corp., 2007, Alcoa Fujikura Ltd., dir. internal audit; sr. v.p. and CFO FARO Technologies Inc.; CFO Comml. Metals Co., 2011—, sr. v.p., 2011—. Office: Commercial Metals Company PO Box 1046 Dallas TX 75221-1046 Office Fax: 214-689-5869.

SMITH, BRADLEY E., anesthesiologist; b. Cedar Vale, Kans. MD, U. Okla., 1957. Diplomate Am. Bd. Anesthesiologists. Resident U.S. Naval Hosp., NYC, 1957-60; fellow Columbia Presbyn. Hosp., NYC, 1960—61; faculty Yale U., 1962-63, U. Miami, 1963-69; chmn., prof. dept. anesthesiology Vanderbilt U., Nashville, 1969-93, prof., 1993—, prof. emeritus, 2004—, prof. clin. anesthesiology, 2005—08; trustee Wood Libr. Mus. Anesthesiology, 2008—. Mem.: AMA, ACOG (assoc.), Anesthesia History Assn. US (pres. 2012—), Am. Soc. Anesthesiologists. Office: Vandy Med Ctr Rm 209 Oxford House Nashville TN 37232-4245 Office Phone: 615-936-0718.

SMITH, BRANDON, state legislator; b. June 14, 1967; V.p. Hazard Food Mart, Inc.; owner Daniel Boone Investments; retail operation dir. Perry Oil Co.; commr. Hazard, 1993—98; state rep. Dist. 84 Ky., 2001—; state senator Dist. 30 Ky., 2008—; mem. Econ. Devel. & Tourism Com., Local Govt. Mem.: Boy Scouts America (dist. commr., den leader pack 1990), Shriner, Lions Club (former pres.), Mason. Republican. Presbyterian. Office: Capitol Annex Rm 429B Frankfort KY 40601 Home: PO Box 846 Hazard KY 41702-0846 Home Phone: 606-436-4526; Office Phone: 502-564-8100 697. Fax: 606-436-2398.

SMITH, C. THOMAS, JR., medical products executive; b. Little Rock, Apr. 10, 1938; s. Carl Thomas and Mary Elizabeth (Singleton) S.; m. Martha Nell Fincher, June 24, 1961; children: Laura, Adam. BA, Baylor U., 1960; MBA, U. Chgo., 1962; DSc (hon.), U. Bridgeport, 1986; DHL (hon.), Quinnipiac Coll., 1988. Asst. to chmn., Psychology Dept. Baylor U., Waco, Tex., 1959—60; adminstrv. extern Ark. Bapt. Med. Ctr., Little Rock, 1958, acting personnel dir., 1960; adminstrv. extern Bapt. Meml. Hosp., Memphis, 1959, adminstrv. resident, 1961—62, adminstrv. asst., 1962—63, adminstrv. assoc., 1963—67; assoc. dir. U. Minn. Hosp., Mpls., 1967—71; coord., Health Sciences Planning University of Minnesota, Mpls., 1969—71; assoc. exec. dir. Henry Ford. Hosp., Detroit, 1971—74, v.p., exec. dir., 1974—77, trustee, 1974—77; pres. Yale-New Haven Hosp., 1977—91, trustee, 1978—91; pres., bd. dirs. Yale-New Haven Health Svcs. Corp., 1983—91; pres., CEO VHA Inc., Irving, Tex., 1991—2003. Lectr. health care adminstrn. U. Minn., 1969-71; lectr. dept. epidemiology and pub. health Sch. Medicine, Yale U., 1977-91; lectr. Sch. Orgn. and Mgmt., Yale U., 1979-91; preceptor grad. programs in hosp. and health care adminstrn. Yale U., 1977-91; speaker in field; trustee Nat. Com. Quality Health Care, 1978-98, Hosp. Rsch and Ednl. Trust, 1987-94; bd. dirs. Hosp. Rsch. and Devel., Inc., 1983-89; bd. dirs., exec. com. Vol. Hosps. Am., Inc., 1983—; U.S. del. King Edward's Hosp. Fund for London, 1983-88; mem. coun. on health care tech. Inst. Medicine, NAS, 1986-88; bd. dirs. Vol. Hosps. Am. of Southern New Eng., 1985-91, Vol. Hosps. Am. Enterprises, 1988-91; bd. dirs. Kinetic Concepts Inc., Genetech, Inc., 1986-99, New Haven Savs. Bank, 1978-91. Mem. editorial bds. Jour. Med. Edn., 1974-78, Health Care Mgmt. Rev., 1982-88, Health Services Research, 1984-88 Bd. dirs. United Way Greater New Haven, 1984-89, campaign chmn., 1986; bd. dirs. Sci. Pk. Devel. Corp., New Haven, 1983-91; trustee U. Bridgeport, 1987-89. Mem. Am. Hosp. Assn. (trustee 1987-92, chmn. 1991), Assn. Am. Med. Colls. (adminstrv. bd. council teaching hosps. 1982-86, chmn. 1986), Am. Coll. Healthcare Execs., Conn. Hosp. Assn. (trustee 1982-86). Presbyterian. Home: 17703 Cedar Creek Canyon Dr Dallas TX 75252-4969 Office: Kinetic Concepts Inc Bd Directors 8023 Vantage Dr San Antonio TX 78230-4726 Office Phone: 210-255-6157. E-mail: c.smith@kci1.com.

SMITH, CATHERINE H., investment company executive; b. 1953; 2 children. BA, Hampshire Coll.; M in Pub. and Pvt. Mgmt., Yale Sch. Orgn. and Mgmt. Sr. positions in investment and healthcare, 1983—98; CFO Aetna Fin. Services; pres., healthcare, edn., govt. distbn. ING US Worksite Fin. Services, COO, broker dealer ops., customer svc., USFS retail and worksite bus. groups; pres. US retail fin. services ING Group, CEO US ins. bus., CEO US retirement services, 2009—. Bd. mem. Outward Bound USA, Conn. Fund for Environment; adv. Conn. Trust for Pub. Land. Named one of 25 Women to Watch, US Banker, 2006, 2008, 25 Most Powerful Women in Fin., 2009, 2010. Avocations: hiking, skiing. Office: ING North Am Ins Corp 5780 Powers Ferry Rd NW Atlanta GA 30327-4390

SMITH, CATHERINE R., corporate financial executive; BS in Bus. Economics, U. Calif., Santa Barbara; MBA, U. So. Calif. Various fin. positions including v.p., CFO intelligence & info. systems bus. Raytheon Co., 1986—2003; exec. v.p., CFO Bell Systems Textron, Inc., 2003—05; exec. v.p., CFO Kennametal, Inc., 2005—06, Centex Corp., Dallas, 2006—09, GameStop Corp., Grapevine, Tex., 2009—10; CFO Wal-Mart International, 2010—. Bd. dirs. Dick's Sporting Goods, Inc., 2009—. Office: Wal-Mart 702 SW 8th St Bentonville AR 72716-8611

SMITH, CECE, venture capitalist; b. Washington, Nov. 16, 1944; d. Linn Charles and Grace Inez (Walker) S.; m. John Ford Lacy, Apr. 22, 1978. BBA, U. Mich., 1966; M in Liberal Arts, So. Meth. U., 1974. CPA, Tex. Staff acct. Arthur Young & Co. (CPAs), Boston, 1966-68; staff acct., then asst. to contr. Wyly Corp., Dallas, 1969-72; contr., treas. subs. Univ. Computing Co., Dallas, 1972-74; contr. Steak and Ale Restaurants Am., Inc., Dallas, 1974-76, v.p. fin., 1976-80, exec. v.p., 1980-81, Pearle Health Services, Inc., 1981-84, pres. Primacare divsn., 1984-86; gen. ptnr. Phillips-Smith-Machens Venture Ptnrs., 1986—2007; pres. Le Sportsac Dallas, Inc., 1981-87. Bd. dirs. Brinker Internat. Inc., Pier 1 Imports, Inc.; chmn. Fed. Res. Bank Dallas, 1994—96; past v.p., dir. IWF-Dallas; past mem. pres. adv. group U. Mich.; mem. exec. bd. Dallas Symphony Assn. Past co-chmn. pres.'s rsch. coun. U. Tex. S.W. Med. Ctr. Dallas; past vis. com. U. Mich. Bus. Sch.; past exec. bd. So. Meth. U. Cox Sch. Bus.; past v.p., bd. dirs. Jr. Achievement Dallas; past pres. Charter 100; past treas. Dallas Assembly. Home: 3710 Shenandoah St Dallas TX 75205-2121 Office: Cece Smith 3710 Shenandoah St Dallas TX 75205-2121 Office Phone: 972-387-0725.

SMITH, CHARLES EDWIN, computer science educator; b. Columbia, Mo., Apr. 15, 1950; s. William Walter and Nelletha Pearl (Lavendar) S.; m. Mary L. Davis, July 27, 1991. AA, Edison C.C., Ft. Myers, Fla., 1971; BS, Troy State U., 1979; MA, Webster U., St. Louis, 1989. Adj. instr. Manatee C.C., Venice, Fla., 1989-90, Edison State Coll., Punta Gorda, Fla., 1989—92, prof. computer sci., 1992—, Charles O'Neill endowed chair astronomy, 1997—2001. Cons. Charles E. Smith Consulting, North Port, Fla., 1989-91. Served to maj. USAF, 1975-79, USAFR, 1979-96. Mem. Fla. Assn. C.C.s, Mil. Officers Assn. Am., Air Force Assn., Am. Legion, USGA, Elks. Avocations: reading, fishing, boating, astronomy, golf. Office: Edison State Coll 26300 Airport Rd Punta Gorda FL 33950-5748

SMITH, CHARLES ISAAC, geology educator; b. Hearne, Tex., Feb. 9, 1931; s. Walter Lee and Nellie Lucille (Clearwater) S.; m. Anita Lou Howell, Aug. 22, 1961; children: Lanita Maylene, James Emmett, Timothy Stephen, Sheila Nell. BS, Baylor U., 1952; MA, La. State U., 1955; PhD, U. Mich., 1966. Geologist Shell Devel. Co., Houston, 1955-60, 62-65; prof. geology U. Mich., Ann Arbor, 1965-77, chmn. dept., 1970-77; prof. geology U. Tex., Arlington, 1977-93, prof. emeritus, 1994—, chmn. dept., 1977-89, cons. geologist, 1993—. Contbr. articles to profl. jours. Home: 3814 Tridens Trl San Angelo TX 76904-7223 Office: Univ Tex Dept Geology Arlington TX 76019-0001

SMITH, CHARLES LYNWOOD, JR., federal judge; b. Talladega, Ala., Feb. 25, 1943; s. Charles Lynwood and Ann Lou (Riley) Smith; m. Missy Ming; children: Ashley Lauren, Carlton Riley. Student, Ga. Inst. Tech., 1961—63; BA, U. Ala., 1966, JD, 1971; MA, Rutgers U., 1967. Bar: Ala. 1971, Ala. (US Dist. Ct. (no. dist.)) 1971, Tex. 1974, (US Ct. Appeals (5th cir.)) 1973. Cons. Fla., Miss. and Ala. State Legislatures, 1968—70; law clk. to Hon. Frank H. McFadden US Dist. Ct. (no. dist. Ala.), Birmingham, 1971—72; mem. Bell, Richardson, Cleary, McLain & Tucker, Huntsville, Ala., 1972—75, Hornsby, Blankenship, Smith & Robinson, 1975—81; judge Madison County Dist. Ct., Huntsville, Ala., 1981, 23d Jud. Cir. Ct. Ala., 1981—95, US Dist. Ct. (no. dist. Ala.), 1995—. Instr., lectr. polit. sci. Rutgers U., 1968—69, U. Ala., Huntsville, 1972—75; mem. Madison County Dem. Exec. Com., 1974—81; pres. Madison County Young Dems., 1977—78. Author: Strengthening the Florida Legislature, 1970; contbr. articles to profl. jours. Dist. chmn. Chickasaw Dist., Tenn. Valley Coun., Boy Scouts Am., 1981—82. Recipient Henderson M. Somerville Law prize, U. Ala. Law Sch., 1971; named Outstanding Grad., Phi Delta Phi, U. Ala., 1971. Mem.: ABA, Pi Sigma Alpha, Omicron Delta Kappa, Ala. Trial Lawyers Assn., Fed. Bar Assn., Ala. Assn. Cir. Judges, Ala. State Bar, Rotary (Huntsville). Methodist. Office: US Dist Ct No Dist Ala Hugo Black Courthouse 1729 5th Ave N Birmingham AL 35203

SMITH, CHARLOTTE REED, retired music educator; b. Eubank, Ky., Sept. 15, 1921; d. Joseph Lumpkin and Cornelia Elizabeth (Spenser) Reed; m. Walter Lindsay Smith, Aug. 24, 1949; children: Walter Lindsay IV, Elizabeth Reed. MusB, Tift Coll., 1941; MA in Mus. Theory, Eastman Sch. Music, 1946; postgrad., Juilliard Sch., 1949. Asst. prof., theory Okla. Bapt. U., 1944—45, Washburn U., 1946—48; prof., music Furman U., Greenville, SC, 1948—92; chmn., dept. music, 1987—92. Editor: Seven Penitential Psalms with Two Laudate Psalms, 1983; author: Manual of Sixteenth-Century Contrapuntal Style, 1989. Mem.: AAUP (sec. & treas., Furman chpt. 1984—85), Soc. Music Theory, Am. Musicological Soc., Internat. Musicological Soc., Nat. Fedn. Music Club, Pi Kappa Lambda. Republican. Baptist.

SMITH, CHRISTOPHER L., state legislator; b. Ft. Lauderdale, Fla., Mar. 15, 1970; m. Desorae Giles-Smith; children: Christopher, Christian. BS in Polit. Sci., Johnson C. Smith U., 1992; JD, Fla. State U., 1995. Atty. Johnson, Anselmo, Murdoch, Burke & George; mem. Fla. House of Reps., 1998—2006, majority leader, 2004—06; mem. Dist. 29 Fla. State Senate, 2008—, vice chair banking and ins. com., higher edn. com., reapportionment com., mem. policy and steering com. on commerce and industry, comm., energy and pub. utilities com., rules com., transp. & econ. devel. appropriations com., mem. joint com. on pub. counsel oversight. Mem. Ft. Lauderdale City Commn. Planning & Zoning Bd., 1995. Mem. Broward Workforce Devel. Bd., Ft. Lauderdale Downtown Coun.; adv. bd. Fla. Martin Luther King, Jr. Inst. for Nonviolence; bd. dirs. Ft. Lauderdale Cmty. Devel. Corp., Friends of Children, Youth, & Families Inc., Mus. Discovery & Sci. Recipient Nat. Champion, Moot Ct., 1995, Legis. Champion of Justice award, Fla. Assn. Criminal Defense Lawyers; named Citizen of Yr., Omega Psi Phi Frat., 1999; named one of 30 Leaders Under 30, Ebony Mag. Mem.: NAACP (youth adv.), Johnson C. Smith U. Gold Coast Alumni Chpt., Alpha Phi Alpha (Zeta Alpha Lambda chpt.). Democrat. Baptist. Office: Senate Office Bldg 404 S Monroe St Rm 220 Tallahassee FL 32399-1100 also: 1101 NE 40th Ct Ste 1 Oakland Park FL 33334 Home: 1101 NE 40th Ct Ste 1 Oakland Park FL 33334-3093 Office Phone: 850-487-5112, 561-650-6801, 954-267-2114. Office Fax: 561-650-6819, 954-267-2116. Business E-Mail: smith.chris.web@flsenate.gov.

SMITH, CLARK C., energy executive; BBA, MBA, U. Tex., Austin. Various positions Enron Corp.; pres., CEO Coastal Gas Mktg. Co., Engage Energy, Inc., 1997—2000; exec. v.p. El Paso Corp., 2000—03; pres. El Paso Mcht. Energy Group, 2000—03; mng. dir. Engage Investments, L.P., 2004—07; pres., COO Buckeye Partners, LP, Houston, 2009—12, pres., CEO, 2012—. Bd. dirs. Pipestream Inc. Office: Buckeye Partners LP One Greenway Plz Ste 600 Houston TX 77046*

SMITH, CRAIG R., health products executive; m. Cynthia Smith; 2 children. BA, Univ. So. Calif. With Owens & Minor, Inc., Glen Allen, Va., 1989—; divsn. v.p., group v.p., sr. v.p. distbn. and info. sys. Owens & Minor, Glen Allen, Va., 1989—95, exec. v.p., COO, 1995—99, pres., COO, 1999—2005; pres., CEO Owens & Minor, Inc., Glen Allen, Va., 2005—. Bd. mem. Inst. for Diversity in Health Mgmt., Health Ind. Dist. Assn.; mem. bd. vis. St. Gertrude High Sch., Richmond; mem. bus. council Va. Mus. Fine Arts; bd. dir. Greater Richmond YMCA. Office: Owens & Minor Inc 9120 Lockwood Blvd Mechanicsville VA 23116

SMITH, CULLEN, lawyer; b. Waco, Tex., May 31, 1925; s. Curtis Cullen and Elizabeth (Brient) S.; m. Laura Risher Dossett, Mar. 6, 1948 (dec.); children: Sallie Smith Wright, Alethea Risher Smith Gilbert, Elizabeth Brient Smith; m. Ann Brown Parsons, Jan. 3, 2009. Student, Emory U., 1943-44, Duke U., 1944; BBA, Baylor U., 1948, JD, 1950. Bar: Tex. 1950. Ptnr. firm Smith, McIlheran & Smith, Weslaco, Tex., 1950-53, Naman, Howell, Smith & Lee PLLC, Waco, 1953—. Lectr. law Baylor U. Sch. Law, 1964-72 Contbr. articles to legal publs. Mem. standing com. Episcopal Diocese of Tex., 1960-63, 74-75; trustee Episcopal Theol. Sem. of S.W., 1962-67, M.J. Hanna Found., 2013-; mem. Waco City Coun., 1983-86; chmn. bd. Vanguard Sch., 1975; bd. dirs. G.H. Pape Found., 1993-94; bd. dirs., vice chmn. Tex. Ctr. for Legal Ethics and Professionalism, 1994-99; mem. adv. coun. Baylor U. Coll. Arts and Scis., 1998-2003. 1st lt. USMCR, 1943—46, inactive, 1946—58. Named one of 5 Outstanding Young Texans Tex. Jr. C. of C., 1957, Baylor Lawyer of Yr., 1980; recipient Disting. Alumnus award Waco Ind. Sch. Dist. Edn. Found., 2002; named Outstanding Mentor of Tex., Tex. Young Lawyers Assn., 2007. Fellow Am. Bar Found., Tex. Bar Found. (chmn. bd. 1973-74, 50 Yr. Lawyer award 2000), fellow Coll. of Law Practice Mgmt.; mem. ABA (chmn. standing com. econs. law practice 1965-69, chmn. spl. com. on law book pub. practices 1970-72, chmn. gen. practice sect. 1973-74, mem. house of dels. 1974-81), Am. Law Firm Assn. (chmn. 1989-90), Waco-McLennan County Bar Assn. (pres. 1956-57), Mont. Bar Assn. (hon.), State Bar Tex. (pres. jr. bar 1957-58, chmn. profl. econs. com. 1959-61, chmn. spl. com. on revision Tex. Canons Ethics 1969-71, dir. 1971-74, pres. 1978-79), Philos. Soc. Tex., Baylor U. Law Alumni Assn. (pres. 1962-63), Order of Coif, Delta Sigma Phi, Phi Delta Phi, Am. Inns Ct. (master), Ridgewood Country Club (pres. 1965), Hedonia Club (pres. 1957), Rotary. Avocation: photography. Home: Oak Grove Farm 447 Meandering Way China Spring TX 76633-2905 Office: Naman Howell Smith & Lee LLP Tex Ctr PO Box 1470 Waco TX 76703-1470 Office Phone: 254-755-4100.

SMITH, DAVE, human resources specialist; b. Ind. m. Beckie Smith; 2 children. Attended, Grace Coll. & Sem., 1969; BA in Behavioral Sciences, Ind. U.; MA in Indsl. Rels., St. Francis Coll., 1980. Cert. profl. Compensation, WorldatWork. Pers. mgr. US Steel Corp., 1974—87; dir., compensation & benefits AON Corp. (AON Brokerage Group), 1990—92; dir., human resources, comml. govt. and indsl. sys. sector Motorola, Inc., 1993—2000; v.p., global rewards and recognition Delta Air Lines, Inc., 2000—05; joined AGL Resources, Inc., 2005, v.p., human resources. Mgr., compensation Am. Hosp. Assn., 1987-90; human resources adv. coun. Willow Creek Cmty. Ch., 1998-04; bd. dirs. Consumer Credit Counseling Svcs.; teaching faculty, vice chmn. WorldatWork; vol. Northpoint Cmty. Ch., 2000-. Office: AGL Resources Inc Ten Peachtree Pl NE Atlanta GA 30309 Office Phone: 404-584-4000. Office Fax: 404-584-3945. Business E-Mail: dsmith@aglresources.com.

SMITH, DAVID EDWARD, small business owner, aerospace engineer, aerospace scientist; b. Battle Creek, Mich., Sept. 16, 1939; s. Hebdin Leslie and Dureatha Rosella (Stephens) S.; m. Margaret Eugenia Clark, June 13, 1964; 1 child, Wendy Leigh. Student, Kellogg C.C., 1957—58; BSME, Mich State U., 1962; MS in Real Estate Investing (hon.), Meta U., Salt Lake City, 1992. Engr., scientist Douglas Aircraft Co., Santa Monica, Calif., 1962-63, McDonnell Douglas Astronautics Co., Cape Kennedy, Fla., 1963-78; broker salesman Cape Kennedy Realty, Inc., Cape Canaveral, Fla., 1978-87; pres., founder Cash Flow Seminars, Merritt Island, Fla., 1979—, Cash Flow Systems, Inc., Merritt Island, Fla., 1983—; prof. fin. Meta U., Salt Lake City, 1992-94. Lectr. fin. convs. and orgns. including Fed. GSA, Pub. Bldg. Svc., Am. League of Savs., Fin. Instns. Mktg. Assn., Acad. Real Estate, Am. Congress Real Estate; prof. fin. Meta U., Salt Lake City, 1992-94; distbr. Hewlett Packard Corp., 1985-88; dir. comml. investment divsn. CKBOR, Merritt Island, 1978-79; adv. bd., lectr. Fin. Freedom Report, Nat. Inst. Fin. Planning, both Salt Lake City, 1985-92; instr. Fla. Real Estate Commn., La. Real Estate Commn., Fla. Bd. Accountancy, Am. Inst. Real Estate Appraisers. Author: Turbo-Diesel, The Time Value of Money, Creative Financing Techniques; contbr. articles to profl. jours. and mags. Mem.: Internat. Platform Assn., Fla. Real Estate Exchangors, Motorcycle Iron Butt Assn. (master traveler), Gold Wing Rd. Riders Assn. Republican. Avocations: flying, transcontinental bicycling, motorcycling. Office: Cash Flow Seminars PO Box 540634 Merritt Island FL 32954-0634

SMITH, DAVID ENGLISH, pathologist, educator; b. San Francisco, June 9, 1920; s. David English and Myrtle (Goodin) S.; m. Margaret Elizabeth Bronson, June 9, 1948; children: Ann English Smith Elbert, David Bronson, Mary Margaret. AB, Central Coll. Mo., 1941; MD cum laude, Washington U., St. Louis, 1944. Intern, resident pathology Barnes Hosp., St. Louis, 1944-46; instr. pathology Washington U. Med. Sch., 1948-51, asst. prof., 1951-54, asst. head dept., 1953-54, assoc. prof., 1954-55; prof. pathology U. Va. Sch. Medicine, 1955-73, chmn. dept., 1958-73; dir. div. U. Va. Sch. Medicine (Cancer Studies), 1972-73; prof. pathology Northwestern U. Sch. Medicine, 1974-75, U. Pa. Sch. Medicine, 1976-80, Tulane U. Sch. Medicine, 1980-85, assoc. dean, 1980-85; prof. pathology U. Tex. Med. Br., 1986—. Assoc. dir. Am. Bd. Med. Spltys., 1974-75; v.p., sec., dir. undergrad. evaluation Nat. Bd. Med. Examiners, 1975-80; trustee Am. Bd. Pathology, 1966-73, v.p., 1973; mem. Nat. Bd. Med. Examiners, chmn. pathology test com., 1966-72; chmn. test com. Ednl. Commn. for Fgn. Med. Grads., 1979-91; eligibility & due process com. Nat. Commn. Cert. Physician Assts., 1990-2001. Editor: Survey of Pathology in Medicine and Surgery, 1966-70; contbr. articles to profl. publs. Pres. Va. div. Am. Cancer Soc., 1967-69. Served from 1st lt. to capt. M.C. AUS, 1946-48. Recipient Preclin. Tchr. award, U. Tex. Med. Br., 1999; named Disting. Alumnus, Wash. U. Med. Sch., 2004; Paul Brindley Disting. scholar, U. Tex. Med. Br., 1997. Mem. Va. Soc. Pathology (pres. 1960), Am. Assn. Pathologists, Internat. Acad. Pathology (council 1956-59, pres. 1964-65), Am. Soc. Clin. Pathologists (co-dir. self assessment program 1970-75, Path Educator award 2000), AMA, Am. Assn. Neuropathologists, AAAS, Sigma Xi, Alpha Omega Alpha, Phi Beta Pi, Alpha Epsilon Delta. Home: 9701 Sorrento Court Austin TX 78759-5611 E-mail: descolpkga@aol.com.

SMITH, DAVID JOHN, JR., plastic surgeon; b. Indpls., Feb. 20, 1947; s. David John and Carolyn (Culp) S.; m. Nancy Loonsten, June 7, 1975; children: Matthew, Peter, Hadley. BA, Wesleyan U., 1969; MD, Ind. U., 1973. Diplomate Am. Bd. Plastic Surgery. Resident

Emory U.-Grady Hosp., Atlanta, 1973-78; resident Ind. U. Med. Ctr., Indpls., 1978-80; Christine Kleinert fellow in hand surgery, 1979; asst. prof. surgery Ind. U. Sch. Medicine, 1980-84; assoc. prof. of surgery Wayne State U. Sch. Medicine, 1984-87; assoc. prof. plastic surgery, surgery sect. head U. Mich. Med. Ctr., Ann Arbor, 1987-92, prof. surgery sect. head, 1992—2001; prof. surgery Coll. Medicine U. South Fla., 2004—, Juan Bolivar chair in surg. oncology, dir. divsn. plastic and reconstructive surgery, 2004—; interim chair, dept. surgery USF. Mem. Residency Rev. Com. for Plastic Surgery, 1992-2000, vice chmn., 1994, chmn. 1996-99; vis. prof. Ctr. Cutaneous Rsch. Queen Mary U., London, Eng., 2004—, Anglia Polytech. U., Cambrige, Eng., 2004—. Mem. editl. bd. Jour. of Surg. Rsch., 1989-95, Annals of Plastic Surgery, 1992-2002, assoc. editor, 1994-2002, Yearbook of Hand Surgery, 1989—; guest reviewer Surgery, 1988—, Plastic and Reconstructive Surgery, 1988—; contbr. articles to profl. jours. Recipient numerous grants. Fellow ACS (com. mem.), Am. Assn. Plastic Surgeons, Am. Surg. Assn., Am. Bd. Plastic Surgeons (vice chmn. 1997-98, chair-elect 1998-99, chmn. oral exam 1995-97, chmn. 1999-2000), Ctrl. Surg. Assn., Am. Soc. for Surgery of the Hand, Am. Soc. Plastic Surgeons, Plastic Surgery Ednl. Found. (bd. dirs. 1988-99, treas. 1994, v.p., pres.-elec., pres., chair nominating com. 1997-98), Plastic Surgery Rsch. Coun., Am. Burn Assn. (chmn. com. on organization and delivery of burn care 1995-98), Am. Burn Life Support Nat. Faculty, Am. Assn. for Hand Surgeons (pres. 1994), Assn. Acad. Chmn. Plastic Surgery (pres.-elect 1997, pres. 1998-99, chmn. nominating com. 1999-2000). Home: 3107 Prospect Rd Tampa FL 33629 Office: Divsn Plastic Surgery 4 Columbia Dr Ste 650 Tampa FL 33606 Home Phone: 813-250-9160. Business E-Mail: dsmith3@health.usf.edu.

SMITH, DAVID LEE, retired media executive; b. Shelby, Ohio, Apr. 4, 1939; s. Ferris Francis and Rita Ann (Metzger) Smith; m. Betty Stewart Walker, Sept. 10, 1960; children: Stacie Lynn, Stefanie Linn, David Lee II(dec.). Student, Pontifical Coll. Josephinum, Worthington, Ohio, 1953-56, Ohio State U., Mansfield, 1961. Sports writer Mansfield News-Jour., 1960-61; sports editor Ashland Times-Gazette, Ohio, 1961-63, Miami News, Fla., 1963-67, Ft. Lauderdale News, Fla., 1967-70, Boston Globe, 1970-78, Washington Star, 1978-81; dep. mng. editor, exec. sports editor Dallas Morning News, 1981—2005, sports dir. AH Belo pub. and new media divsns., 1998—2003, v.p., 2003—05; ret., 2005. Condr. seminars. Mem. adv. bd. Dallas Stars Found., Dallas Alliance for the Mentally Ill, SMU Athletics, Jesuit Sch. Found.; bd. chmn. Bethesda Home Boys, Savannah, Ga.; bd. dirs. Field Scovell Scholarship Found., Doak Walker Nat. Running Back Award, GTE-SMU Athletic Forum. With USMC, 1957—60. Mem.: Golf Writers Assn., Football Writers Assn., Baseball Writers Assn. (Red Smith award for major contbns. to sports journalism 1990), AP Sports Editors Assn. (1st pres. 1974—75), SMU Athletic Forum (bd. dirs.), Salesmanship Club Dallas, Bent Tree Country Club. Roman Catholic. Home: 19 Deleqal Rd Savannah GA 31411 Personal E-mail: studie.dave@gmail.com.

SMITH, DAVID THORNTON, lawyer, educator; b. Pawtucket, RI, Dec. 11, 1935; s. Herbert Jeffers and Harriet Amelia (Thornton) S.; m. Sandra June Gustavson, Dec. 20, 1958; children: David T., Douglas A., Daniel H. BA, Yale U., 1957; JD cum laude, Boston U., 1960. Bar: Mass. 1961, U.S. Supreme Ct. 1964. Instr. law Ind. U., Bloomington, 1960-62; asst. prof. law Duquesne U., Pitts., 1962-63, Case Western Res. U., Cleve., 1963-65, assoc. prof., 1965-68; assoc. prof. law U. Fla., Gainesville, 1968-69, prof., 1969—2003, prof. emeritus, 2003—. Vis. prof. law U. Ga., 2004, Wake Forest U., 2006, Stetson U., 2007. Author: (with M. Sussman and J. Cates) The Family and Inheritance, 1970, Florida Probate Code Manual, 1975. Mem. Am. Bar Assn., Mass. Bar Assn., Am. Law Inst., Am. Judicature Soc., AAUP (past pres. U. Fla. chpt.), Fla. Blue Key, Selden Soc., Omicron Delta Kappa, Phi Alpha Delta. Lutheran. Office: University Fla College Law Gainesville FL 32611

SMITH, DEAN EDWARDS, retired men's college basketball coach; b. Emporia, Kans., Feb. 28, 1931; s. Alfred Dillon and Vesta Marie (Edwards) S.; m. Ann Cleavinger, 1954 (div. 1973); children: Sharon, Sandy, Scott; m. Linnea Weblemoe, May 21, 1976; children: Kristen, Kelly. BS in Math. & Phys. Edn., U. Kans., 1953. Asst. basketball coach USAF Acad., 1955-58; asst. basketball coach U. N.C., 1958-61, head basketball coach, 1961-97. Mem. U.S. and Canadian Basketball Rules Com., 1967-73; U.S. basketball coach Olympics, Montreal, Que., Can., 1976; lectr. basketball clinics, Germany, Italy. With USAF, 1954-58. Recipient Joe Lapchick Character award, 2008, Presdl Medal of Freedom The White House, 2013; named Coach of Yr., Atlantic Coast Conf., 1967, 68, 71, 76, 77, 79, Nat. Basketball Coach of Yr., 1977, Nat. Coach of Yr., US Basketball Writers, 1979, named one of The Top 5 Coaches of the 20th Century, ABC-TV and ESPN; named to The Naismith Basketball Hall of Fame, 1982, Nat. Collegiate Basketball Hall of Fame, 2006. Mem. Nat. Assn. Basketball Coaches (Nat. Basketball Coach of Yr. 1976, dir. 1972—, pres. 1981-82), Fellowship Christian Athletes (dir. 1965-70) Democrat. Baptist. Office: U NC Basketball Office PO Box 2126 Chapel Hill NC 27515-2126*

SMITH, DONNIE, food products executive; b. 1959; BS in Animal Sci., U. Tenn., Knoxville, 1980. Various live poultry prodn. jobs Tyson Foods, Inc., 1980—87, joined commodities purchasing group, Hdqs. office Springdale, Ark., 1987, various positions including v.p. purchasing, 1995, exec. v.p. and gen. mgr. supply chain & mgmt., 1999—2001, sr. v.p. supply chain & mgmt., 2001—05, sr. v.p., chief info. officer, 2005—06, sr. v.p. info. systems, purchasing & distbn., 2006—07, group v.p. logistics & ops. services, 2007—08, group v.p. consumer products, 2008—09, group v.p. poultry & prepared foods, 2009, pres., CEO, 2009—. Office: Tyson Foods Inc PO Box 2020 Springdale AR 72764 Business E-Mail: Donnie.Smith@tyson.com.*

SMITH, E. ASHLEY, lawyer, insurance company executive; LLM, U. Houston; JD, U. Tex., Austin. Gen. counsel, v.p. Southwestern Group Fin.; pres., CEO Inst. for Rehab. and Rsch. (TIRR); vice chancellor govtl. rels. and policy U. Tex. Sys.; exec. v.p., chief legal officer Stewart Info. Svcs. Corp., 2006—. Mem. Tex. Ho. of Reps., Harris County. Office: Stewart Info Svcs Corp 1980 Post Oak Blvd Houston TX 77056

SMITH, EARNEST, state legislator, nuclear energy industry executive; m. Patricia Childs; 1 child, Marki. BBA in Mktg., Augusta State U. Hull Sch. Bus., Ga.; attended, SC State U., Orangeburg. Cert. project mgr. Exec. liaison stakeholder strategist Savannah River Nuc. Solutions, Savannah River Site, Aiken, SC; state rep. Dist. 122 Ga. House of Reps., Atlanta, 2009—. Former hostage negotiator Wackenhut Nuc. Security, Aiken. Singer: Wisdom (The Distinguished Men of Gospel); host: (radio talk show) Community Matters. Mem. Second Bapt. Ch.; bd. dirs. Christ Cmty. Health Services, Augusta; former pres. Olde Town Neighborhood Assn., Augusta. Air traffic contr., air traffic control liaison coord. USAF. Mem.: Am. Assn. Aviation Executives, Omega Psi Phi, Upsilon Gamma Gamma Grad. Chpt. Democrat. Office: 253 Greene St Augusta GA 30901-1616 also: Ga Gen Assembly 511 Coverdell Legis Office Bldg Atlanta GA 30334 Office Phone: 404-656-6372. Personal E-mail: ma1027@aol.com.

SMITH, EDWARD KENDRICK, lawyer; b. Atlanta, Dec. 9, 1956; s. Alexander Wyly and Elizabeth (Haverty) Smith; m. Caryl Greenberg Smith, Oct. 16, 1983; children: Gina Leigh, Jacob Ryan. BA, U. NC, Chapel Hill, 1974—78; JD, U. Ga., Athens, 1978—81. Bar: Ga. 1981, US Ct. Appeals (4th and 11th cirs.), US Dist. Ct. (no., mid. & so. dists.), US Supreme Ct. Ptnr. Smith Gambrell & Russell, LLP, Atlanta, 1981—2005, Jones Day, Atlanta, 2005—. Instr. Lorman Bus. Inst, 1989—, Inst. Continuing Legal Edn., Nat. Bus. Inst., Inc., Tax Exec. Inst., Faculty for Advanced Tax Sch., Leadership Atlanta, 1997. Chmn. Rsch. Atlanta, 1993—97; program chair Leadership Ga., Atlanta, 1997—98; chmn. Servants Relief for Incurable Cancer, Atlanta, 2000—; mem. exec. com. Atlanta Downtown Partnership, 1990—92; pres. The Bridge, Atlanta, 1991—99; trustee SW Hosp. & Med. Ctr., Atlanta, 1991—2002; bd. dirs. Ctrl. Atlanta Progress, Atlanta, 1994—, Zoo Atlanta, Atlanta, 2004—; mem. bd. visitors U. Ga. Law Sch., Athens, 2004—07; co-chmn. Fernbank Soc., 2005—06; pres. Tate Mt. Assocs., 2005—06; trustee John & Mary Franklin Found., 2002—. Recipient Ga. Legal Elite, Ga. Trend Mag., 2003, 2004, 2005, 2006, Ga. Super Lawyer, Atlanta Mag., 2003—, Ga. Legal Leader, James Mag., 2005, 2006, Top Ga. Lawyer, 2007, Leaders in the Field, Chambers USA, 2008—09, Best Lawyers America, 2009. Mem.: ABA, Inst. Profls. Taxation, Ctrl. Atlanta Progress, Piedmont Driving Club. Avocations: squash, hiking, piano, bicycling. Office: Jones Day 1420 Peachtree St Ste 800 Atlanta GA 30309 Office Fax: 404-581-8330. Business E-Mail: eksmith@jonesday.com.

SMITH, ELAINE DIANA, foreign service officer; b. Glencoe, Ill., Sept. 15, 1924; d. John Raymond and Elsie (Gelbard) S. BA, Grinnell Coll., 1946; MA, Johns Hopkins U., 1947; PhD, Am. U., 1959. Commd. fgn. svc. officer U.S. Dept. State, 1947; assigned to Brussels, 1947-50, Tehran, Iran, 1951-53, Wellington, New Zealand, 1954-56, Dept. State, Washington, 1956-60, Ankara, Turkey, 1960-69, Istanbul, Turkey, 1969-72, Dept. Commerce Exch., 1972-73; dep. examiner Fgn. Svc. Bd. Examiners, 1974-75; Turkish desk officer Dept. State, Washington, 1975-78. Consul gen., Izmir, Turkey, 1978—. Author: Origins of the Kemalist Movement, 1919-1923, 1959. Recipient Alumni award Grinnell Coll., 1957. Mem. U.S. Fgn. Svc. Assn., Phi Beta Kappa. Office: Lynn House 4400 braddock Rd Alexandria VA 22304-1010

SMITH, ELIZABETH A. (LIZ SMITH), restaurant chain company executive, former cosmetics company executive; BA, U. Va., Charlottesville, 1985; MBA, Stanford U. Grad. Sch. Bus., Calif. Pvt. placement fin. analyst Paine Webber, Inc., 1986; gen. mgr., category bus. mgr. Callard & Bowser-Suchard, Inc.; asst. brand mgr. Kraft Foods, Inc., 1990, exec. v.p. Kraft Foods North America (KFNA), gen. mgr. beverages, 2000—02, pres. US beverages & grocery, 2004; exec. v.p., brand pres. Avon Products, Inc., 2005, exec. v.p., pres. North America, 2005—07, pres. Avon Products, Inc., 2007—09; CEO OSI Restaurant Partners, LLC, 2009—. Bd. dirs. Carter's Inc., 2004—08, Staples, Inc., 2008—, Cosmetic, Toiletry & Fragrance Assn., Personal Care Products Coun. Bd. dirs. Big Brothers Big Sisters. Named a Top Marketer, Advt. Age, 1996; named one of The 50 Most Powerful Women in Bus., Fortune mag., 2007, 2008, 2009, The 25 Leaders Reshaping NY, Crain's NY mag., 2008, The World's 100 Most Powerful Women, Forbes mag., 2009. Mem.: Phi Beta Kappa. Office: OSI Restaurant Partners LLC 2202 N West Shore Blvd 5th Fl Tampa FL 33607 Office Phone: 813-282-1225.

SMITH, ELLEN LOUISE, retired language educator; b. Tulsa, Feb. 25, 1935; d. Joe D. and Laura Betty (McBrien) Hurt; m. Robert Lester Smith. BA, Ctrl. State Coll., Edmond, Okla., 1955; MA, U. Okla., Norman, 1958; PhD, U. Oreg., Eugene, 1964. Acting dir. publs. Ctrl. State Coll., Edmond, Okla., 1956-57; tchg. asst. U. Okla., Norman, 1957-59; instr. English U. Oreg., Eugene, 1959-64; asst. prof. English U. Calif. Santa Barbara, 1964-66; instr. English U. Granada, Spain, 1967-70; Fulbright lectr. English U. Valladolid, Spain, 1973-74; dep. dir. Spanish Fulbright Commn., Madrid, 1974-75; prof. English Stetson U., DeLand, Fla., 1977—2003. Contbr. articles to profl. jours. Mem. Nat. League Am. Pen Women, Delta Kappa Gamma. Democrat.

SMITH, ELMER, telecommunications industry executive; Grad., Tulane U. Various positions Berry Co. (now BellSouth Corp.), pres., CEO, pres., advt. and pub. Atlanta, 2001—. Mem.: Assn. Directory Mktg. (bd. dirs.), Yellow Pages Integrated Media Assn. (chmn. 2003—04). Office: BellSouth Corp 675 W Peach St Ste 4200 Atlanta GA 30309 Office Phone: 404-249-2000. Office Fax: 404-249-3839.

SMITH, FERR, state legislator; b. Leake County, Sept. 10, 1941; m. Shirley McFarland; children: Cassandra Holt, Latasha, Ferri, Rochelle. Former Leake county supr.; mem. Dist. 27 Miss. House of Reps., 1993—; bd. dir. Ctrl. Miss. Legal Svc.; atty. Mem.: Miss. Valley State U. Found. (chmn.), Leake County Devel. (pres.), Inter-Alumni Coun. Democrat. Baptist. Mailing: 2480 Hwy 16 W Carthage MS 39051 Office Phone: 601-859-6500. Business E-Mail: fsmith@house.ms.gov.

SMITH, FREDERICK WALLACE, delivery service executive; b. Marks, Miss., Aug. 11, 1944; s. Frederick C. Smith & Sally (Wallace) S.; m. Linda Black Grisham, 1969 (div. 1977), 2 children; m. Diane Avis; 8 children BS in Econs., Yale U., 1966. Cert. comml. pilot. Owner Ark Aviation, 1969-71; founder FedEx Corp., Memphis, 1971, pres., 1971—75, CEO, 1977—98, chmn. bd., 1975—98, chmn. bd., pres., CEO, 1998—. Bd. dirs. FedEx Corp. (formerly FedEx Express Corp), 1971—. Served with USMC, 1966-70, co-chmn. WWII Meml. Campaign. Decorated Silver Star, Bronze Star, Purple Heart; recipient Peter F. Drucker Strategic Leadership award, 1997, Eagle of Aviation award, Embry-Riddle Aero. award, 2001, Champion of Workplace Learning and Performance award, Amer. Soc. Tng. and Devel., 2002, Bower award for Bus. Leadership, Franklin Inst., 2008; named CEO of Yr., Chief Executive Mag., 2004, Person of Yr., French-Am. C. of C., 2006; named one of Forbes 400: Richest Americans, 2006—. Office: FedEx Corp 942 S Shady Grove Rd Memphis TN 38120-4117*

SMITH, G. RICHARD, psychiatry educator; BS in Chem.-Biology, Rhodes Coll., Memphis, Tenn., 1973; MD, U. Ark. Coll. Medicine, Little Rock, 1977. Intern, resident psychiatry U. Hosp., Little Rock, 1977—80; fellow, instr., psychiatry and med., med./psych liaison group U. Rochester, NY, 1980—81; asst. prof., psychiatry and medicine U. Ark. Med. Sch., Little Rock, 1981—85, dir., residency tng., dept. psychiatry and behavioral sciences, 1982—86, assoc. prof., medicine, 1985—97, assoc. prof., psych, dept. psychiatry and behavioral sciences, 1985—2001, vice-chmn., dept. psychiatry and behavioral sciences, 1985—2001, prof., psychiatry, dept. psychiatry and behavioral sciences, 1991—2001, prof. medicine, 1997—, Marie Wilson Howells prof. & chair, dept. psychiatry and behavioral sciences, 2001—, dir., Ctrs. for Mental Healthcare Rsch., dept. psychiatry and behavioral sciences, 1989—2001, prof., dept. health policy and mgmt., Coll. Pub. Health, 2001—; vis. scholar LBJ Sch. Pub. Affairs, U. Tex., Austin, 1997—98; CEO Psychiatric Assessment Systems, 2004—. Mem. NIMH Initial Review Group Services Rsch., 1989—93, chair, 1991—93; mem. NIMH Nat. Mental Health Adv. Coun., 1995—98, coordinating mem., 1996—98. Contbr. several articles to profl. jours. Office: U Ark Coll Pub Health 4301 WMarkham # 820 Little Rock AR 72205

SMITH, GARRY R., state legislator; b. Aiken, Ga., Mar. 4, 1957; m. Brenda Smith; children: Michael Grady, Dana, Michelle. BA, U. SC, 1979, MPA, 1983. Mng. ptnr. Nin Tai Enterprises; v.p. Burkhold Smith Planning & Mgmt.; mem. Dist. 27 SC House of Reps., 2003—, second vice chair Judiciary Com., mem. Ops. and Mgmt. Com., Ways and Means Com. Republican. Office: 534 Blatt Bldg Columbia SC 29211 Mailing: 210 Foxhound Rd Simpsonville SC 29680 Home Phone: 864-963-0337; Office Phone: 803-734-3045. E-mail: SmithG@schouse.org.

SMITH, GARY L., state legislator; b. Mena, Ark., Oct. 19, 1951; m. Rebecca Smith; children: Kelly, Teresa, Aaron. BBA, Southern Ark. U., 1972; MBA, Henderson State U., 1978. Staff adminstr. Ark. Law Enforcement Training Acad., 1978—82; acctg. supr. Ark. Devel. Dist. Svcs., 1982—83; sr. electrician & buyer Gen. Dynamics Camden, 1983—93; mgr. & owner Garry's Plumbing & Elec. Inc., 1993—; adj. prof. Econ. Southern Ark. U. Tech. Inst., Camden, 1994—; mem. Dist. 7 Ark. House of Reps., 2008—. Bd. dirs. Harmony Grove Sch. Bd., 1983—91; instr. Ark. Hunter Edn. Vol., 1987—; bd. dirs. Ouachita County Fire Dist. 1, 2004—; mem. Ouachita County Farm Bureau, 2008—. Mem.: Ouachita County Cattleman's Assn. (treas. 1996—), Camden Lodge Number 1 F & AM (master mason 1972—), Scottish Rite Free Masonry SJ USA (32 degrees 1982—). Democrat. Office: State Capitol Rm 350 Little Rock AR 72201 also: 600 Ouachita 31 Camden AR 71701 Office Phone: 501-682-6211, 501-682-7771, 870-574-1792.

SMITH, GARY L., JR., state legislator; Assoc. Tareza & Gelderman LLC; atty. Sole Piad; mgr. Magnolia Holdings Inc.; mem. Dist. 56 La. House of Reps., 2000—12; mem. Dist. 19 La. State Senate, 2012—. Mem.: Lions Club. Democrat. Baptist. Office: PO Box 189 Norco LA 70079 also: La State Senate 900 N 3rd St Baton Rouge LA 70804 Office Phone: 985-764-9122. Business E-Mail: smithgl@legis.la.us.

SMITH, GEORGE MURRELL, JR., lawyer, state legislator; b. Florence, SC, May 15, 1968; s. G. Murrell and Jody Hill Smith; m. Mary Smith. BA, Wofford Coll., 1990; JD, U. SC, 1993. Asst. pub. defender, 1995—98; pvt. practice; mem. Dist. 67 SC House of Reps., 2001—. Mem.: ABA, Sumter County Defender Assn. (sec. 1998—2000), S.C. Bar Assn., Sumter County Bar Assn. (exec. com.), Rotary. Republican. Methodist. Office: State Capitol 420B Blatt Bldg Columbia SC 29211 Address: PO Box 580 Sumter SC 29151

SMITH, GODFREY TAYLOR (BUCK SMITH), college president; b. Newton, Miss., Nov. 12, 1935; s. Taylor and Edna (Blanton) S.; m. Joni Eaton, Sept. 1, 1956; children: Paul Brian, Sherry Lynn. BA, Coll. of Wooster, 1956; MPA with distinction, Cornell U., 1960; LLD (hon.), Bethany Coll., 1979. Assoc. dir. devel. Cornell U., Ithaca, NY, 1960-62; dir. devel. Coll. Wooster, Ohio, 1962-66, v.p., 1966-77; pres. Chapman U., Orange, Calif., 1977-88, pres. emeritus, 1988—; exec. dir. Talaris Rsch. Inst., Seattle, 2001—03; pres. Bethany Coll., Bethany, W.Va., 2004—08, Davis & Elkins Coll., W.Va., 2008—13, pres. emeritus, 2013—. Lectr. in field. Contbr. numerous articles to profl. publs. Bd. dirs. Wayne County (Ohio) Indsl. Devel. Corp., 1966-72, World Affairs Coun. Orange Coun., Calif., 1978-89, Orange County chpt. NCCJ, 1979-86, Orange County coun. Boy Scouts Am., 1980-85, Coun. Ind. Colls., 1985-87; bd. dirs. div. higher edn. Christian Ch. (Disciples of Christ), 1977-88, chmn., 1984-86; bd. dirs., mem. exec. com. Ind. Colls. So. Calif., 1979-88, pres., 1981-82; mem. exec. com. Assn. Ind. Calif. Colls. and Univs., 1980-88, treas., 1982-87. Recipient William A. Galpin prize The Coll. Wooster, 1956, Steuben Apple award for tchg. excellence Coun. for Advancement and Support Edn., 1984, Disting. Alumnus award Coll. of Wooster, 1991, Faith and Reason award Christian Ch. (Disciples of Christ), 1993, Laureate award for Lifetime Achievement Inst. for Charitable Giving, 1997; named Person of Yr., Boy Scouts America Allohack Coun., Highland Dist., 2012, Educator of Yr., Randolph County C. of C., 2013; Smith Hall dedicated at Chapman U., 1988; Alfred P. Sloan fellow Cornell U., 1960. Office: Davis & Elkins Coll 100 Campus Dr Elkins WV 26241 Home: 6430 Pineridge Dr Medford OR 97504-7200 Personal E-mail: buck1956@gmail.com. Business E-Mail: buck@dewv.edu.

SMITH, GREGORY DALE, lawyer, judge; b. Knoxville, Feb. 1, 1963; s. James C. and Essie Pearl (Norman) S.; m. Cynthia Luckett, Oct. 15, 1988; children: Leora, Philip. BS, Middle Tenn. State U., 1985; JD, Cumberland Law Sch., 1988. Bar: Tenn., U.S. Supreme Ct., U.S. Ct. Appeals (fed. crct.), U.S. Ct. Mil. Appeals, U.S. Dist. Ct. (mid., ea. and we. dists.) Tenn., Army Ct. of Mil. Rev., U.S. Ct. Vet. Appeals. Mcpl. magistrate City of Birmingham, Ala., 1987-88; assoc. Marks, Marks & Shell, Clarksville, Tenn., 1988-89; juvenile referee Montgomery County Juvenile Ct., Clarksville, Tenn., 1992-95; assoc. Richardson & Richardson, Clarksville, Tenn., 1989-93; pvt. practice Clarksville, 1993—; mcpl. judge Pegram, Tenn., 2004—06. Adj. prof. Austin Peay State U., Clarksville, 1989-93; lectr. in field; hearing officer Tenn. Bd. Profl., 1993-2001; mcpl. judge, Pleasant View, Tenn., 1997-, Pegram Tenn., 2001- Author: The TACDL Guide to Defending Juvenile Cases in Tennessee, 1993, Tennessee Municipal Judges Benchbook, 2013; co-author: Juvenile Courts in Tennessee, 1998; editor: Tennessee Judicial Ethics Opinions Handbook, 2012; presenter Tenn. Jud. Acad., 2013; contbr. articles to profl. jours. Bd. dirs. Treehouse Daycare Ctr., 1991-95, sec., 1992, v.p., 1993, pres. 1994; Leadership Clarksville; participant UN conf. juvenile drug prevention, 1994. Named Internat. Man of the Yr. Internat. Biog. Ctr., Cambridge, Eng., 1992, Outstanding Young Alumnus, Middle Tenn. State U., 1999. Mem. ABA (juvenile justice com. nat. chmn. 1990-92, nat. vice chmn. litigation 1992-93), Tenn. Assn. Criminal Def. Lawyers (chmn. juvenile justice com. 1991-95, chmn. ethics com. 1995-97), Montgomery County Young Lawyers (pres. 1991-92), Tenn. Bar Assn. (assoc. gen. counsel 1995-2001, Pro Bono Atty. of Yr. 2001), Tenn. Young Lawyers Conf. (bd. dirs. 1992-94), Tenn. Mcpl. Judges Assn. (pres. 2002-04), Tenn. Ct. of the Judiciary, 2005-09. Office: 331 Franklin St Ste 1 Clarksville TN 37040-3448 Office Phone: 931-647-1299. Personal E-mail: gregorydsmith@prodigy.net.

SMITH, GREGORY EDWARD, finance company executive; Grad. in Economics with honors, Brown U., 1978; doctoral, U. Chgo., 1981. Investment banker, v.p., fin. svcs., tech. Thomson McKinnon, 1985; pres., founder Indepth Data Inc. (acquired by Dow Jones & Co.), 1985—97; sr. v.p., content Dow Jones Markets (acquired by Bridge Information Sys. Inc.), 1997; pres., CEO, founder Cicada Corp. (acquired by Chi-X Global Inc.), 1998; vice chmn. Chi-X Global, Inc., 2009—. Bd. dirs. China Holdings Acquisition Corp. Office: Chi-X Global Inc 525 Ctrl Park Dr Ste 500 Oklahoma City OK 73105 Office Phone: 405-609-3800. Office Fax: 405-524-3734. Business E-Mail: gregory.smith@chi-x.com.

SMITH, GRIFFIN, newspaper editor; b. Fayetteville, Ark., June 29, 1941; s. Griffin and Mildred Smith; m. Mary Elizabeth Routh, Sept. 1, 1979. BA in History, Rice U., Houston, 1963; MA in Polit. Sci., Columbia U., NYC, 1965; JD, U. Tex. Sch. Law, 1969. Bar: Tex. 1969, US Dist. Ct. (ea., we., no. and so. dists.) Tex. 1969, Ark. 1981,

US Dist. Ct. (ea. and we. dists.) Ark. 1981. Spl. asst. to rep. J. William Fulbright US Senate, Washington, 1968-69; atty. estate & gift tax divsn. IRS, Houston, 1970; chief counsel constl. amendments com. Tex. Senate, 1971, chief counsel drug law reform com., 1971-73; sr. editor Tex. Monthly mag., 1973—77; Presdl. speech writer The White House, 1977-78; ptnr. Smith & Nixon (formerly Smith, Smith, Nixon & Duke), Little Rock, 1981—92; exec. editor Ark. Democrat-Gazette, Little Rock, 1992—. Media fellow Hoover Instn., Stanford U., Calif., 2006. Author: (book) A Consumer Viewpoint on Taxation, 1971, Marijuana in Texas, 1972, The Best of Texas Monthly, 1978, Texas Monthly's Political Reader, 1978, 1980, Journey into China, 1982, Forgotten Texas: A Wilderness Portfolio, 1983, The Great State of Texas, 1985. Recipient Disting. Alumni award, Rice U., 1999; Woodrow Wilson fellow, 1964. Mem.: Tex. Inst. Letters (award for best work of journalism in Tex. 1974, 1976), State Bar Tex. Episcopalian-Reformed. Office: Ark Democrat-Gazette 121 E Capitol Ave Little Rock AR 72201-3819 also: Ark Democrat-Gazette PO Box 2221 Little Rock AR 72203

SMITH, GROVER CLEVELAND, JR., language educator; b. Atlanta, Sept. 6, 1923; s. Grover C. and Lillian Julia (McDaniel) S.; m. Phyllis Jean Snyder, June 19, 1948 (div. 1965); children: Alice Elizabeth, Charles Grover; m. Dulcie Barbara Soper, Dec. 29, 1965; children: Stephen Kenneth, Julia Margaret. BA with honors, Columbia U., 1944, MA, 1945, PhD, 1950. Instr. English Rutgers U., 1946-48, Yale U., 1948-52, Duke U., 1952-55, asst. prof., 1955-61, assoc. prof., 1961-66, prof., 1966-93, prof. emeritus, 1993—. Mem. summer faculty CUNY, 1946, 47, 48, Columbia U., 1963, 64, NYU, 1963, Wake Forest U., 1966, vis. lectr., 1963, 64; instr. coll. entrance exam bd. Summer Inst. Commn. on English, 1962. Author: The Poems of T.S. Eliot 1909-1928: A Study in Symbols and Sources, 1950, T.S. Eliot's Poetry and Plays: A Study in Sources and Meaning, 1956 (Poetry Chapbook award) rev. edit., 1974, Archibald MacLeish, 1971, Ford Madox Ford, 1972, The Waste Land, 1983, T.S. Eliot and the Use of Memory, 1996; editor: Josiah Royce's Seminar, 1913-1914: As Recorded in the Notebooks of Harry T. Costello, 1963, Letters of Aldous Huxley, 1969. Mem. Christian Gauss Award com., 1973-75; mem. com. of sponsors Sir Julian Huxley Tribute, NY Soc. for Ethical Culture, 1975. With U.S. Army, 1943. Alexander M. Proudfit fellow Columbia U., 1945-46; Guggenheim fellow, 1958; Am. Philos. Soc. grantee, 1965; Am. Learned Socs. grantee, 1965; NEH grantee, 1979, fellow, 1980. Mem. T.S. Eliot Soc. (hon., 2000-, Eliot Meml. Lectr. 1986, bd. dirs. 1986-94, 96-99, v.p. 1986-88, editor News and Notes, 1987-88, 90-91, pres. 1989-91, supr. elections 1992-94, sec. 1996-99), Am. Lit. Assn. (rep. to coun.of Am. Author Socs. 1990-91), Nat. Assn. Scholars. Home: 2 Silver Maple Ct Durham NC 27705-5642

SMITH, HAROLD HASKEN, university administrator; b. Cin., Mar. 16, 1942; s. Harold C. and Ruth V. (Hasken) S.; m. Karen A. Willis, Dec. 20, 1969; children: Amy Elizabeth, Andrew David, Anne Cameron. AB, Centre Coll., 1964; MBA, Am. U., 1968; LLD (hon.), Cumberland Coll., 2003; LHD (hon.), Pikeville Coll., 2010. Admissions counselor Centre Coll., Danville, Ky., 1964-66, assoc. dir. admissions, 1968-70, dir. admissions, 1970-73, dean admissions, 1973-80, v.p., den students, 1980-83, lectr. econs. mgmt., 1973-80; v.p. devel. Muskingum Coll., New Concord, Ohio, 1983-97; pres. Pikeville Coll. and Coll. Osteo. Med., Ky., 1997—2009, pres. emeritus, 2009—; pres. Gov.'s Scholars Found., 2009. Cons. in edn. Dir. Boyle-Mercer County YMCA, Ky., 1979-83, Ky. Athletic Hall of Fame, 2009-, Presby. Homes/Svcs. Ky., 2009-, Nativity Acad., 2011-; mem. bd. trustees Southeast Ohio Regional Med. Ctr., 1987-97; bd. dirs. Southeast Ohio Symphony Orch., 1983-97, Renew Environment of New Concord, 1983-97, Leadership Ky., 2002—. Recipient Disting. Chmn. award Rotary Found., 1981-82; named Bus. Person of Yr. Pike County C. of C., 2001, Disting. Alumnus Centre Coll., 2006; named to Pikeville Coll. Athletic Hall of Fame, Pikeville Coll., 2009. Mem. Ctr. Coll. Athletic Hall of Fame, 1994, Assn. Ind. Ky. Colls. and Univs. (exec. com. 2004—), Nat. Assn. Student Personnel Adminstrs., Am. Coll. Personnel Assn., Nat. Assn. Intercollegiate Athletics (coun. pres. 2004—), Cambridge C. of C. (bd. dirs. 1984-97), Nat. Assn. Coll. Admissions Counselors, So. Assn. Colls. and Schs. (commr. coll. commn. 2005—), Rotary (pres. 1979-80, dist. gov.'s rep. 1981-82), Zanesville Country Club, Green Meadow Country Club, Cardinal Club Office: Pres's Office Govs Scholars Found Frankfort KY 40601 Home Phone: 502-896-6740. Business E-Mail: halsmith64@gmail.com.

SMITH, HARRI ANNE, state legislator; b. Slocomb, Ala., Jan. 20, 1962; m. Charlie Smith. BBA, Troy State U., Ala. Councilwoman City of Slocomb, mayor; mem. Dist. 29 Ala. State Senate, 1998—; exec. v.p. Slocomb Nat. Bank, Friend Bank. Mem. First Bapt. Ch. Recipient Wal-Mart Hometown Hero award; named Slocomb Woman of Yr., 1998, Role Model of Yr., Girls, Inc., 1998. Mem. NRA, Assn. US Army, Southern Ala. Regional Coun. on Aging Bd., State Ala. Agribusiness Coun., Dothan Area C. of C., Cmty. & Ala. Bankers Assns., Nat. Fedn. Ind. Bus., Geneva County United Way Bd., Houston County Young Rep., Houston County Rep. Women's Assn. Republican. Baptist. Office: PO Box 640 Slocomb AL 36375 also: Ala State Senate Ala State House 11 S Union St Rm 735 Montgomery AL 36130 Office Phone: 334-886-2367, 334-242-7879. Business E-Mail: harriannesmith@graceba.net.

SMITH, HILARY CRANWELL BOWEN, investment banker; b. Balt., Nov. 1, 1937; s. Henry Bowen and Clayton (Cranwell) S.; m. Janet Simmons, June 9, 1962; children: Kent C.B., Kendall S., Hillary E. BA, Colgate U., 1960; MBA, U. Va., 1967. V.p. Merc. Safe Deposit & Trust, 1967—69, Goldman, Sachs & Co., NYC, 1969-74, E. F. Hutton & Co., NYC, 1974-77; sr. v.p. Blyth Eastman Dillon, NYC, 1977—79; mng. dir. Salomon Bros., NYC, 1979—90, UBS, NYC, 1990—2004; sr. advisor Greenhill & Co., NYC, 2004—08, Houlihan Lokey, 2009—10, cons. TAP advisors, 2012—; CFO, bd. mem. United Stem Cell Techs., 2011—. Trustee Wheaton Coll., 1997-2003, Chesapeake Maritime Mus., 1998-2004, Greenwich Acad., 1988-94, Mystic Seaport, 2005, Nat. Maritime Hist. Soc., 2004-12, treas., 2006-10, overseer, 2013, Riverside Theater, 2007-12; bd. dirs. Forest 2 Market, 2000-. Lt. USN, 1960-63. Office Phone: 917-602-3891.

SMITH, HOWARD WELLINGTON, education educator, retired dean; b. Granby, Mo., Jan. 19, 1929; s. Howard W. and Margaret L. (Sanderson) S.; m. Margaret E. Bell, Mar. 1, 1953; 1 child, Christopher Alan. BS, S.W. Mo. State U., 1954; MEd, U. Mo., 1955, EdD, 1959. Tchr. Newton County (Mo.) Pub. Schs., 1948-51; instr. U. Mo., Columbia, 1955-59; asst. prof. So. Meth. U., Dallas, 1959-61; from asst. to full prof. U. North Tex., Denton, 1961-97, dean emeritus. Assoc. dean Coll. Edn. U. North Tex., 1972-76, assoc. v.p. acad. affairs, 1976-79, v.p. acad. affairs, 1979-82, interim dean, 1994-97; interim chancellor U. North Tex. Coll. Osteo. Medicine, Denton and Ft. Worth, 1981; sr. cons. Am. Assn. State Colls. and Univs., Washington, 1982; cons. Srinakharinwirot U., Thailand, 1986, Tex. Internat. Edn. Consortium, Austin, 1992, sr. author Operation Manual Al Akhawayn U., 1993; vis. prof. Shanxi Ednl. Coll. Taiyuan, China, 1993, Action Team Coll. Edn. U. North Tex. Capital Campaign. Contbr. articles to ednl. jours. Prin. investigator Micro Tchg. Lab., 1967—69; chair Ret. Instrs., Pers. and Spouses U. North Tex., 2001; accreditation cons. Art Inst. Dallas, 2001—10; chair Denton County Hist. Soc., 1999—2004; exec. coun. U. North Tex. Friends of Libr., 2005—09; trustee Art Inst. Dallas, 2005—10; adv. bd. Coll. Edn. U. North Tex., 1997—2005, adv. bd. Bill J. Priest Ctr. for C.C. Edn., 1999—2002, Coll. of Edn. devel. bd., 1999—2002, devel. bd. Coll. Edn., 2006—; pres. bd. dirs. Tex. Lakes Trail, 2002—04; bd. dirs. HOPE, Inc., 2007—09. With USAF, 1951—53. Democrat. Presbyterian. Avocations: travel, reading. Office: U North Tex Coll Edn PO Box 311337 Denton TX 76203-1337

SMITH, JAMES EMERSON, JR., state legislator; b. Columbia, SC, Sept. 9, 1967; s. James Emerson and Nina Geddes Smith; m. Mary Kirkland Thomas, 1991; children: James Emerson II, Thomas Bridges. BA, U. SC, 1990, JD, 1995. Atty. Nelson, Mullins, Riley Scarborough LLP, 1995—96; pvt. practice, 1996—2000; shareholder Smith Ellis and Stuckey, PA, 2000—; mem. Dist. 72 SC House of Reps., SC, 1997—, chair Ethics Com. Mem. Success by 6 United Way. 1st lt. USAR, 1996—. Recipient Outstanding Young Alumni award, U. SC, 1997. Mem.: Am. Bar Assn., Ga. Bar Assn., Sierra Club, Columbia Rotary Club. Democrat. Episcopal. Address: PO Box 50333 Columbia SC 29250 Mailing: 335C Blatt Bldg PO Box 11867 Columbia SC 29201 Home Phone: 803-256-3582; Office Phone: 803-933-9800, 803-734-2997. Fax: 803-312-0087. Personal E-mail: JESmithII@msn.com.

SMITH, JAMES ROLAND, state legislator; b. Aiken, SC, Feb. 26, 1933; s. Mae Bel Smith Craig; m. Peggy C. Cato; children: Garry R., Todd D., Caroline M. DD, Universal Bible Inst. Pastor, 1960—98; with US Post Office, 1966—86; mem. Dist. 84 SC House of Reps., 1989—. Mem.: Midland Valley C. of C., Beech Island Hist. Soc. (hon.), Beech Island Agriculture Clubs, Midland Valley Lion's Club. Republican. Mailing: 183 Edgar St Warrenville SC 29851 Office: 519B Blatt Bldg Columbia SC 29201 Home Phone: 803-593-2359; Office Phone: 803-734-3114, 803-593-8987. E-mail: JS@schouse.org.

SMITH, JEFFERY W., architect; m. Nancy Smith. Grad., La. State U., Baton Rouge. Pres. Obst Assocs., 1985, Smith Architectural Group, Inc., Palm Beach, Fla., founder, prin., 1989—. Prin. works include La Follia, 1993, Villa Venezia, La Reverie, Serenity (Elizabeth L. and John H. Schuler award, Preservation Found. Palm Beach, 2007). Chmn. Palm Beach Archtl. Commn., Landmark Preservation Commn. Mem.: AIA. Office: Smith Architectural Group Inc 206 Phipps Plz Palm Beach FL 33480 Office Phone: 561-832-0202. Office Fax: 561-832-3443.

SMITH, JEFFREY A., lawyer; b. Trenton, Tenn., Sept. 27, 1963; s. Nathan L. and Mary Jane (Ledsinger) S. BS in Acctg., U. Tenn. at Martin, 1985; JD, MBA, Memphis State U., 1991. Cost acct. Goodyear Tire & Rubber, Union City, Tenn., 1986-88; atty. Bill Barron, Atty., Trenton, Tenn., 1991-93, Kizer, Bonds, Crocker & Hughes, Milan, Tenn., 1993-95, Jeffrey A. Smith, Trenton, Tenn., 1995—. City atty. City of Dyer, Tenn., 1993-95, City of Kenton, Tenn., 1996—; bd. dirs. United Way of West Tenn., Jackson, 1997—. Elected mem.-alderman Bd. of Mayor & Aldermen, Rutherford, Tenn., 1993-00; elected mem.-commr. Gibson County Bd. County Commrs., 1994-02. Office: Jeffrey A Smith Atty PO Box 126 Trenton TN 38382 Home: 16 Mcwherter Ln Rutherford TN 38369-9605

SMITH, JEFFREY C., state legislator; b. Loundes County, Dec. 6, 1949; m. Laura Terrell; children: Todd, Corky, Day, Caitlyn. Prosecutor Lowndes County, 1980—89; mem. Dist. 39 Miss. House of Reps., 1992—; mem. Joint Study Commn. Statutory Salaries; deacon First Bapt. Ch., Columbus; atty. Mem.: Lowndes County Bar Assn., C. of C., Coll. Arts Coun., Swim Columbus (pres.), Steens Civic Club (bd. pres.). Democrat. Baptist. Mailing: PO Box 681 Columbus MS 39703 Office Phone: 601-359-1541, 601-328-2711. Fax: 601-328-0745. Business E-Mail: jsmith@house.ms.gov.

SMITH, JEFFREY CHIPPS, art educator; MA, Columbia U., 1975, MPhil, 1977, PhD, 1979. Kay Fortson chair in European art U. Tex., Austin, 1979—; pres. Interdisciplinary Internat. Acad. Group, 2008—. Co-editor Jour. Historians Wetherlandish Art, 2009—. Author: Nuremberg, A Renaissance City, 1500-1618, 1983, German Sculpture of the Later Renaissance, c. 1520-1580: Art in an Age of Uncertainty, 1994, Sensuous Worship: Jesuits and the Art of Early Catholic Reformation in Germany, 2002, The Northern Renaissance, 2004, The Art of the Goldsmith in Late Fifteenth Century Germany: The Virgin and Her Bishop, 2006; editor: New Perspectives on the Art of Renaissance Nuremberg: Five Essays, 1985; editor: (introduction to) E. Panofsky, The Life and Art of Albrecht Durer, 1943—2005; co-editor: The Essential Dürer, 2009; reviewer in field, —; contbr. articles to profl. jours. Alexander von Humboldt-Stiftung fellow, Bonn, Germany, ACLS grantee, NEH grantee, Getty Found. grantee, Guggenheim Found. grantee, Kimbell Art Found. grantee, Zentralinstitut Kunstgeschicht fellow. Mem.: Sixteenth Century Soc. and Conf. (bd. dir. 2004—07), Renaissance Soc. Am. (bd. dirs. 2000—, editor Renaissance Quarterly 2003—06), Coll. Art Assn. (bd. dir. 1996—2000). Office: U Tex Dept Art and Art History Austin TX 78712 Home Phone: 512-451-0097; Office Phone: 512-232-2609. Business E-Mail: chipps@mail.utexas.edu.

SMITH, JEFFREY MICHAEL, lawyer; b. Mpls., July 9, 1947; s. Philip and Gertrude E. (Miller) S.; 1 son, Brandon Michael. Student, U. Malaya, Kuala Lumpur, 1967—68; BA summa cum laude, U. Minn., Mpls., 1970, JD magna cum laude, 1973. Bar: Ga. 1973. Assoc. Powell, Goldstein, Frazier & Murphy, 1973-76; ptnr. Rogers & Hardin, 1976-79, Bondurant, Stephenson & Smith, 1979-85, Arnall, Golden & Gregory, 1985-92, Katz, Smith & Cohen, 1992-98; prin. shareholder Greenberg Traurig LLP, 1998—; hon. prof. Ctrl. U. Fin. and Economics, Beijing, 2009—. Vis. lectr. Duke U., 1976-77, 79-80, 89-93; adj. prof. Emory U., 1976-79, 81-82; lectr. Vanderbilt U., 1977-82. Editor, reviewer Accountant's Legal Liability, 1981; co-author: Preventing Legal Malpractice, 1999, Legal Malpractice, 2013, Legal Opinions in Business Transactions, 2012. Bd. dirs. Atlanta Cmty. Food Bank, 2007-10; bd. trustees UNICEF, USA, 2007-09; Bd. visitors Law Sch. U. Minn., 1976-82. Mem. ABA (vice-chmn. com. profl. liability 1980-82, mem. standing com. lawyers's profl. liability 1981-85, chmn. 1985-87, standing com. lawyer competency 1993-95), State Bar Ga. (chmn. profl. liability and ins. com. 1978-89, trustee Inst. Cont. Legal Edn. in Ga. 1979-80), Order of the Coif, Phi Beta Kappa. Home: 145 15th St NE Unit 811 Atlanta GA 30309-3559 Office Phone: 678-553-2333. Business E-Mail: smithj@gtlaw.com.

SMITH, JERRY EDWIN, federal judge; b. Del Rio, Tex., Nov. 7, 1946; s. Lemuel Edwin and Ruth Irene (Henderson) Smith; m. Mary Jane Blackburn, June 4, 1977; children: Clark, Ruth Ann, J.J. BA, Yale U., 1969, JD, 1972. Bar: Tex. 1972. Law clk. to judge US Dist. Ct. (no. dist.) Tex., Lubbock, 1972—73; assoc. then ptnr. Fulbright & Jaworski, Houston, 1973—84; dir. Harris County housing auth., Tex., 1978—80; special asst. office of atty. gen., Tex., 1981—82; Chmn. Houston Civ. Svc. Comm., 1982—84; city atty. City of Houston, 1984—87; judge US Ct. Appeals (5th cir.), Houston, 1988—. Chmn. Harris County Rep. Party, Houston, 1977—78; committeeman State Rep. Exec. Com., Tex., 1976—88. Mem.: Houston Bar Assn., State Bar Tex. Methodist. Office: US Ct Appeals Bob Casey US Courthouse 515 Rusk St Rm 12621 Houston TX 77002-2698

SMITH, JESSE E., facial plastic surgeon; b. Fort Worth, Tex. BA in Biology minor in Chemistry, magna cum laude, Baylor U., Waco, Tex., 1990—94; MD, U. Tex. Southwestern Med. Ctr., Dallas, Tex., 1994—98. Lic. physician Calif. State Bd. Med. Examiners, Tex. State Bd. Med. Examiners, diplomate Am. Bd. Head & Neck Surgery, Am. Bd. Facial Plastic Surgery. Intern in gen. surgery Univ. Tex. Southwestern Med. Ctr., Dallas, 1998—99, resident in otolaryngology head & neck surgery, 2000—04, asst. clin. prof. otolaryngology dept.; fellow in facial plastic & reconstructive surgery Univ. Calif. Los Angeles Med. Ctr., Calif., 2004—05, Santa Barbara, 2004—05; joined Tex. Health Network, Fort Worth, 2005. Plastic surgeon CRISP Found. Recipient Disting. Chemist award, Baylor Univ., 1990, Academic Scholar Athlete, 1990—94, Outstanding Sr. in Biology, 1993—94, Outstanding Sr. Man, 1994, Golden Key, Nat. Honor Soc., Resident Tchg. award, Univ. Tex. Southwestern Med. Ctr., 2006, Outstanding Dr. award, Fortworth Tex. Mag., 2009. Avocations: bicycling, running, travel. Office: Jesse E Smith M D FACS 923 PA Ave Fort Worth TX 76104 Office Phone: 817-920-0484. Office Fax: 817-920-0068.

SMITH, JIMMIE T., state legislator; b. Ridgewood, NJ, Oct. 12, 1965; children: Ashton, Gabriella. Ret. US Army; security officer; mem. Dist. 43 Fla. House of Reps., Tallahassee, 2011—. Mem.: VFW, Sertoma of Inverness, Citrus County Veterans Coalition, Disabled American Veterans. Republican. Office: 591 E Gulf to Lake Hwy Lecanto FL 34461-9392 also: Fla House of Reps 1003 The Capitol 402 S Monroe St Tallahassee FL 32399-1300 Office Phone: 352-560-6020, 850-488-0805.

SMITH, JOANNE, marketing executive; Mgr. aviation mktg. & cargo sales DHL, v.p. mktg. planning; v.p. mktg. customers Song Airlines, 2003—05, pres., 2005—06; v.p. mktg. Delta Air Lines Inc., 2006—07, sr. v.p. flight services & global product devel., 2007—. Named a Woman to Watch, Advt. Age, 2007; named one of 50 Women to Watch, The Wall St. Jour., 2008. Office: Delta Air Lines Inc PO Box 20706 Atlanta GA 30320-6001 Office Phone: 404-715-2600.

SMITH, JOHN R., state legislator; b. Dec. 29, 1945; m. Pamela Arnondin. Pvt. practice; mem. La. State Dem. Ctrl. Com., 1980—83, La. House of Reps., 1988—2008; mem. Dist. 30 La. State Senate, 2008—, vice chair senate and govtl. affairs com., mem. agr., forestry, aquaculture and rural devel. com., fin. com., natural resources com. Mem.: C. of C., Lion Club, Mason. Democrat. Methodist. Office: 611-B S Fifth St Leesville LA 71446 also: Capitol Office La State Senate PO Box 94183 Baton Rouge LA 70804 Office Phone: 318-238-2709, 225-342-2040. Business E-Mail: smithj@legis.state.la.us.

SMITH, JOSEPH A., JR., urologic surgeon; b. Memphis, July 13, 1949; s. Joseph A. Smith and Virginia E. (Redd) Mulroy; m. Barbara Bradford, June 14, 1974; children: Carolyn, Bradford J., Christiane. BS, U. Tenn., Knoxville, 1971; MD, U. Tenn., Memphis, 1974. Diplomate Am. Bd. Urology. Intern Parkland Meml. Hosp./U. Tex. Southwestern Med. Sch., Dallas, 1974—75, resident surgery, 1975—76; resident urology U. Utah, Salt Lake City, 1976—79; urologic oncology fellow Meml. Sloan-Kettering Cancer Ctr., NYC, 1979—80; asst. prof. surgery U. Utah Health Scis. Ctr., 1980—83, assos. prof. surgery, 1983—88, prof. surgery, 1988—91; William L. Bray prof. surgery & chmn. dept. urol. surgery Vanderbilt U. Med. Ctr., Nashville, 1991—, vice-chmn. sect. surg. scis., 1992—93, interim chmn. sect. surg. scis., 1993—95, assoc. dir. sect. surg. scis., 2004—06. Oral examiner Am. Bd. Urology, 1993—, trustee, 1998—2005, pres., 2004—05; chmn Am. Found. Urologic Disease, 1995—2003. Assoc. editor Investigative Urology, 1989—92, Endourology, 1990—, Jour. Urology, 2006—, Jour. Robotic Surgery, 2006—, mem. editl. bd. Lasers in Surgery and Medicine, 1995—, Prostate Cancer and Prostatic Diseases, 1995—, Primary Care Update, 1996—, Jour. Evolution in Clin. Practice, 1997—, Current Urology Reports, 2000—; contbr. articles to profl. jours., chapters to books. Recipient Outstanding Alumnus award, U. Tenn. Coll. Medicine, 2003; named one of Best Doctors in America, Castle Connelly Med. Ltd., 1988—2007, Am. Health Mag., 1996, Woodward White, Inc., Best 400 Doctors in America, Good Housekeeping, Best Med. Specialists in N.Am., Town & Country mag., Top 10 Am. Surgeons, US News & World Report. Fellow: ACS; mem.: AMA (vice-chmn. 1996, chmn. 1998—2000), Vanderbilt Urology Soc., Nashville Surg. Soc., Soc. Univ. Urologists (mem. exec. com. 2001—04), Tenn. Urologic Assn. (pres. 1999—2001), Nashville Acad. Medicine, Clin. Soc. Genitourology Surgeons, Am. Cancer Soc., Soc. Basic Urologic Rsch., Am. Assn. Clin. Urologists, Internat. Soc. Laser Surgery, Utah Urologic Soc. (pres. 1981—83), Am. Soc. Lasers in Medicine & Surgery, James Ewing Soc. Surg. Oncology, Soc. Urologic Oncology (sec. 1995—98, pres. 2001—03), Am. Assn. Genitourology Surgeons, Am. Soc. Clin. Oncology, Am. Urol. Assn. (pres. Southeastern sect. 2004—05, Disting. Contbn. award 2004), Alpha Omega Alpha. Office: Vanderbilt U A 1302 Med Ctr N Nashville TN 37232-0001 Office Phone: 615-343-0234.

SMITH, JULIOUS PERRY, JR., lawyer; b. Richmond, Va., Jan. 10, 1943; s. Julious Perry and Mary Inez (Whitlow) S.; m. Sherrill Marie Poehler, July 28, 1967; children: Julious P. III, S. Hayes, Sarah Graham. BS, Hampden-Sydney Coll., Va., 1965; LLB, U. Va., 1968. Bar: Va. 1968, U.S. Dist. Ct. (ea. dist.) Va. 1969. Assoc. Williams Mullen, Richmond, 1968-73, shareholder, 1973—, chmn., CEO, 1984—2010, chmn., 2010—11, chmn. emeritus, 2011—. Bd. dirs. LandAm. Fin. Group, Inc., 2000—08, Hilb Rogal and Hobbs Co., 2000—08, U. Va. Alumni Assn., 2013—; spkr. Joel A. Rose Conf. on Law Firm Mgmt., 1995, 1998, 2000, 2004, 2009; bd. mem. Mut. Assurance Soc. Va., 1986—, chmn., 2008—12; mem. State Coun. Higher Edn. Va., 2010—; chair econ. develop. authority City of Richmond, 2013—. Author: Herding or Leading, Mng. Ptnr. Mag., 2010; contbg. editor: Managing Partner Mag., 2010—. Chmn. profl. divsn. United Way, 1990—92, campaign chmn., 1994—95, de Tocqueville Chair, 2000; Va. state chair U.S. Olympic Com., 1996—2000; trustee Hampden-Sydney Coll., 1996—2005, vice chmn., 2004—06; bd. dirs. Theater Va., pres., 2001—02; chair Multiple Sclerosis Dinner, 2002, CCA-Fin.-Am. Cancer Soc. Golf Championship, 2004; mem. sch. bd. St. Bridget's Cath. Ch., Richmond, 1981—88, chmn. capital fund raising campaign, 1991. Recipient Micheli award Richmond Touchdown Club, 1981, Patrick Henry award Hampden-Sydney Coll., 2003, Outstanding Alumnus award, 2010, Keating medal, 2014; named Living Legacy City Richmond Pub.Schs., 2014; named to Salvation Army Boys and Girls Club Hall of Fame, 1997 Fellow: Va. Law Found., Am. Coll. Trust and Estate Coun.; mem.: ABA, Va. Found. Independent Coll. (former trustee), Chambers Internat. Lawyers, Va. Super 50 Lawyers, Best Lawyers in Am., Va. Legal Elite, Richmond Mgmt. Round Table, Soc. Internat. Bus. Fellows (Va. chair 1996—97), Richmond Bar Assn. (chmn. young lawyers sect. 1973—74, bd. dirs. 1985—87, 1989—92, pres. 1995—96, Hill-Tucker Pub. Svc. award 2005), Va. Bar Assn., Kinloch Golf Club, Farmington Country Club, Forum Club, Country Club Va., Commonwealth Club (bd. govs. 1997—2000, v.p. 2005—07, pres. 2007—09). Roman Catholic. Avocations: reading, sports, travel. Office: Williams Mullen Williams Mullen Ctr 200 S 10th St Richmond VA 23219 Office Phone: 804-420-6408. Office Fax: 804-420-6507. Business E-Mail: jsmith@williamsmullen.com.

SMITH, KENNETH MICHAEL (MIKE), state legislator; b. June 1, 1948; m. Linda Clardy. Tchr., 1972—74; state senator Dist. 31 La., 1996—. Mem.: Masons. Democrat. Baptist. Address: 406 W Main Winnfield LA 71483 Mailing: PO Box 1381 Winnfield LA 71483 Home Phone: 318-628-6887; Office Phone: 318-628-3075. Fax: 318-628-9032.

SMITH, KEVIN ANDREW, state legislator, non-profit corporation executive; b. Helena, Ark., Mar. 12, 1962; s. LeVaughn Andrew and Joann Marjorie (Dawson) S.; m. Virginia Carroll Fagan, Feb. 22, 1989; children: Andrew Whittington, Nathaniel DuVal. BA in Internat. Affairs, George Washington U., 1984. News editor Phillips County Progress, Helena, Ark., 1984-85; staff asst. Senator David Pryor, Washington, 1985, Senator Dale Bumpers, Washington, 1985-87; press sec. Senator Small Bus. Com., Washington, 1987-89; dir. govt. affairs Lower Miss. Delta Devel. Commn., Memphis, 1989-90; exec. dir. Ark. Delta Coun., Stuttgart, 1990—; senator Ark. State Senate, Little Rock, 1993—. Dir. Catfish Farmers of Ark., Stuttgart, 1990—. Recipient Excellence in Mil. Hist. award Assn. of U.S. Hist., Washington, 1982. Mem. Lions Club Internat., Ducks Unltd. Internat. (bd. mem. 1991). Episcopalian. Avocations: golf, fishing, writing. Office: 135 Waverly Wood Dr Helena AR 72342-1638

SMITH, KIP, state legislator; b. Apr. 28; m. Caroline Smith. Comml. real estate broker; rep. Dist. 129 Ga. House of Reps., Atlanta, 2009—. Republican. Office: PO Box 551 Columbus GA 31902 also: Ga Gen Assembly 508 Coverdell Legis Office Bldg Atlanta GA 30334 Office Phone: 404-656-0213.

SMITH, LAMAR SEELIGSON, United States Representative from Texas; b. San Antonio, Nov. 19, 1947; s. Campbell and Eloise Keith (Seeligson) Smith; m. Elizabeth Lynn Schaefer, Mar. 20, 1992; children from previous marriage: Nell Seligson, Tobin Wells. BA, Yale U., New Haven, 1969; JD, Southern Methodist U. Sch. Law, Dallas, 1975. Mgmt. intern Small Bus. Adminstrn., Washington, 1969-70; bus. writer Christian Sci. Monitor, Boston, 1970-72; assoc. Maebius & Duncan, Inc., San Antonio, 1975-76; chmn. Bexar County Republican Party, San Antonio, 1978—82; mem. Dist. 57 Tex. House of Reps., 1981-82; Bexar County commr., 1982—85; mem. US Congress from 21st Tex. Dist., 1987—; chmn. US House Standards of Official Conduct Com., 1999—2001, US House Judiciary Com., 2011—13, US House Sci., Space & Technology Com., 2013—. Ptnr. Lamar Seeligson Ranch, Premont, Tex., 1975—. Republican. Christian Scientist. Office: US House of Representatives 2409 Rayburn House Office Bldg Washington DC 20515 also: 1100 NE Loop 410 Ste 640 San Antonio TX 78209 Office Phone: 202-225-4236.*

SMITH, LANTY LLOYD, bank executive, lawyer; b. Sherrodsville, Ohio, Dec. 11, 1942; s. Lloyd H. and Ellen Ruth (Newell) S.; m. Margaret Hays Chandler, June 11, 1966; children: Abigail Lamoreaux Presson, Margaret Ellen Smith-Rhee, Amanda Prescott Lacoff. BS in Math. with honors, Wittenberg U., Springfield, Ohio, 1964; LLB with honors, Duke U., 1967. Bar: Ohio 1967. Assoc. Jones, Day, Cockley & Reavis, Cleve., 1967-73; ptnr. Jones, Day, Reavis & Pogue, Cleve., 1974-77; exec. v.p., sr. gen. counsel Burlington Industries, Inc., Greensboro, NC, 1977-86, pres., 1986-88; chmn. Precision Fabrics Group Inc., Greensboro, NC, 1988—, Wachovia Corp., Charlotte, NC, 2008, interim CEO, 2008. Pres., CEO MediWave Star Tech. Inc., 1999—; chmn., CEO Tippet Capital, 2007—, Scion Neurostim, 2007—. Mem. bd. visitors Duke U. Sch. Law; vice chmn. exec. com. Duke U. Mgmt. Co. Mem.: NC Inst. Medicine. Home: 3150 Cone Manor Ln Raleigh NC 27613-6606

SMITH, LOVIE, professional football coach; b. Gladewater, Tex., May 8, 1958; m. MaryAnne Smith; children: Mikal, Matthew, Miles. BA, U. Tulsa, 1979. Defensive coord. Big Sandy HS Football Team, 1980; asst. coach defensive backs/wide receivers Cascia Hall Prep, Tulsa, 1981; linebackers coach U. Tulsa, 1983—86, U. Wis., 1987, Ariz. State U., 1988—91, U. Ky, 1992; defensive backs coach U. Tenn., 1993—94, Ohio State U., 1995; linebacker coach Tampa Bay Buccaneers, 1996—2001; defensive coord. St. Louis Rams, 2001—03; head coach Chgo. Bears, 2004—12, Tampa Bay Buccaneers, 2014—. Named NFL Coach of Yr., AP, 2005; named to The Tex. Sports Hall of Fame, 2012. Christian. Achievements include being one (of two) African-American head coaches to lead a NFL team to the Super Bowl, 2007. Office: Tampa Bay Buccaneers One Buccaneers Pl Tampa FL 33607*

SMITH, LUCINDA B., human resources specialist; BA in History, Scripps Coll., Claremont. Various mgmt. positions domestic & internat. human resource Ga.-Pacific Corp., Cendian Corp., Lend Lease Corp.; global dir., human resources AJC Internat. Inc.; v.p., global talent mgmt. & rewards AGCO Corp., dir., orgnl. devel. & compensation, 2006, sr. v.p., human resources, 2009—. Advisor, global expertise panel Soc. for Human Resource Mgmt. Office: AGCO Corp 4205 River Green Pky Duluth GA 30096 Office Phone: 770-813-9200. Office Fax: 770-813-6118. Business E-Mail: lucinda.smith@agcocorp.com.

SMITH, LYNN, state legislator; b. Orlando, FL, Aug. 30, 1945; m. Charles Smith; children: Martha Lynn, Jackie. BS in Secondary Edn., Georgia U. Chmn. Newnan-Coweta C. of C., Ga., Newnan Carnegie Libr., Ga., Coweta Econ. Develop. Partnership, Ga., Shenandoah Ga. Youth Sci. and Tech. Ctr., Ga., Natural Resources and Environ. Com., Ga.; exec. bd. mem. Women's Legis. Network of the Nat. Conf. of the State Legis., Ga., 2004; mem. Dist. 70 Ga. House of Reps., 1997—. Republican. Catholic. Avocation: gardening. Office: 228 State Capitol Atlanta GA 30334 also: Eight Evergreen Dr Newnan GA 30263 Office Phone: 404-656-7149. E-mail: lynn.smith@house.ga.gov.

SMITH, MARGARET DONALDSON, state legislator; b. Weston, W.Va., Aug. 10, 1952; d O.E. and Geraldine (Robinson) C.; m. Michael Clay Smith Apr. 5, 1982; 1 child, Melissa Jean Arbogast Riley. BA cum laude, W.Va. Wesleyan U., 1976; MA, W.Va. U., 1979, EdD, 1982, JD, 1986. Bar: W.Va. 1986, Miss. 1986. Tchr. Lewis County Pub. Schs., Weston, 1976-79, prin., 1980-81; asst. to state treas. State of W.Va., Charleston, 1982-84; law clk. W.Va. Supreme Ct. Appeals, Charleston, 1985; lawyer W.Va. Edn. Assn., Charleston, 1986; prof. law U. So. Miss., Hattiesburg, dir. Edn. Law Inst.; mem. Dist. 38 W.Va. House of Delegates, Charleston, 2008—, mem. Edn. Com., Roads and Transp. Com. & Vet. Affairs and Homeland Security Com. Cons. Hattiesburg Drug Prevention Program, 1987-88; mem. publs. com. Nat. Orgn. on Legal Problems in Edn., Topeka, 1987-88; atty. Petal Bd. Edn., Miss. Editor: Teaching the Law to High School Students in Mississippi, 1989, Mississippi High Students & the Law, 1989; contbr. articles to legal jours., chpts. to books. Candidate Va. Ho. of Dels., 1978; mem. Lewis County Dem. Exec. Com., 1978-86, W.Va. State Dem. Exec. Com., 1985-86; v.p. LWV, 1986-88. U.S. Dept Edn. grantee, 1986-91. Mem. Assn. Trial Lawyers Am. Democrat. Episcopalian. Avocation: sailing. Mailing: 518 Center Ave Weston WV 26452-2121 Office: State Capitol Complex Rm 228E Bldg 1 Charleston WV 25303 Office Phone: 304-340-3123. E-mail: mdsmith@mail.wvnet.edu.

SMITH, MARK EUGENE, nuclear engineering service company executive; b. Wareham, Mass., Apr. 1, 1951; s. Mark Alvin and Evelyn Marie (Somers) S.; m. Brigid Ann Murray, Oct. 17, 1979; children: Hugh Talmidge, Patrick Morgan. AS, New England Inst. Tech., 1981. Owner Marks Motor Co., Wareham, 1965-69; chief designer HF Scientific Instrument, Ft. Myers, Fla., 1981-83; chief designer HVE Keltron Corp., Waltham, Mass., 1984-85; CEO Home Svcs., Ft. Myers, 1985-90, Gen. Capitol, Mocksville, N.C., 1990—. Cons. Underwood & Assocs., Cape Coral, Fla., 1981-89, Shaban Mfg. Co., Ft. Myers, 1982-83; chief designer Keltron Corp., Waltham, 1984-85; sr. designer Proctor & Schwartz, Lexington, NC, 1990-99; lead discipline designer Mixed Oxide Fabrication Facility (MOX-MFFF), Shaw, Ariva Mox Svcs., Aiken, SC, 2003—. Co-author: The Art of Custom Painting, 1978. With USMC, 1969-72. Named Advanced Designer, Metalflake Design Group, Springfield, Mass., 1977. Mem. Soc. Mech. Engrs., Soc. Automotive Engrs., Am. Inst. Design and Drafting (nat. drafting award 1981), Am. Nuc. Soc. Republican. Avocations: antiquarian, numismatics. Home: PO Box 906 Jackson SC 29831-0906 Office Phone: 803-819-8600. Personal E-mail: markussmithium@email.com. Business E-Mail: mesmith@moxproject.com.

SMITH, MICHAEL R., dean, academic administrator; BA, U. Mich., 1975; JD, U. NC, Chapel Hill, 1978. Faculty mem. Inst. Govt. U. NC, Chapel Hill, 1978, dir. Inst. Govt., 1992—2001, dean Sch. Govt., 2001—, vice chancellor pub. svc. and engagement, 2006—. Recipient C. Knox Massey Disting. Svc. Award, 1999. Office: U NC School of Government Knapp Sanders Bldg Campus Box 3330 Chapel Hill NC 27599-3330 Office Phone: 919-966-4107. Office Fax: 919-962-0654. E-mail: msmith@sog.unc.edu.*

SMITH, MIKE, professional football coach; b. Chgo., June 13, 1959; m. Julie Smith; 1 child, Logan. Student, East Tenn. U., 1977—81. Linebacker Winnipeg Blue Bombers, 1982; part-time asst. coach San Diego State U. Aztecs, 1982, linebackers coach, 1983—85; def. line coach, recruiting coord. Morehead State U. Eagles, 1986; def. line coach Tenn. Tech U. Golden Eagles, 1987, spl. teams coord., 1988—95, def. coord., linebackers coach, 1996—98; def. asst., def. line coach Balt. Ravens, 1999—2001, linebackers coach, 2002; def. coord. Jacksonville Jaguars, 2003—07; head coach Atlanta Falcons, 2008—. Named NFL Coach of Yr., AP, 2008. Achievements include being a member of Super Bowl XXXV winning Baltimore Ravens, 2001. Office: Atlanta Falcons 4400 Falcon Pky Flowery Branch GA 30542 Office Phone: 770-965-3115.

SMITH, MORTON HOWISON, religious organization administrator, educator; b. Roanoke, Va., Dec. 11, 1923; s. James Brookes and Margaret Morton (Howison) S.; m. Lois Virginia Knopf, July 7, 1925; children: Samuel Warfield, Susanne Rochet Margaret. BA, U. Mich., 1947; BD, Columbia Theol. Sem., 1953; ThM, ThD, Free U., Amsterdam, The Netherlands, 1962. Ordained to ministry Presbyn. Ch., 1954. Pastor Springfield-Roller Presbyn. Chs., Carroll County, Md., 1954; prof. bible Belhaven Coll., Jackson, Miss., 1954-63; guest lectr. Westminster Theol. Sem., Phila., 1963-64; prof. Reformed Theol. Sem., Jackson, 1964-79; stated clk. gen. assembly Presbyn. Ch. in Am., Decatur, Ga., 1973-88; prof. systematic theology Greenville Presbyn. Theol. Sem., 1987—, dean faculty, 1987-98. Moderator gen. assembly Presbyn. Ch. Am., 2000-01; advisor to bd. dirs. Greenville (S.C.) Presbyn. Theol. Sem., 1986-98, bd. dirs.; mem. bd. dirs. Presbyn. Jour., Asheville, N.C., 1965-87; lectr. on theology Republic of So. Africa, June-July, 1988, Riga, Latvia, 1992, Budapest, Hungary, 1994, Prague, Czech Republic, 1994, 95, Trinidad and Tobago, 1995, Zlin, Czech Republic, 1998, 99, on missions, Republic of Korea, June-July, 1989, Munkton, Can., 1998, 99, Recife, Brazil, 1998, 2002, Reformed Sem., St. Petersburg, Russia, New Zealand, 2003. Author: Studies in Southern Presbyterian Theology, 1962, 2d edit. 1987, How Is the Gold Become Dim, 1973, republished 1998, (pamphlet) Reformed Evangelism, 1970, Testimony, 1986, Commentary on the Book of Church Order of the Presbyterian Church in America, 1990, Harmony of the Westminster Confession and Catechisms, 1990, Systematic Theology, 1994; contbr. articles to profl. jours. Trustee Covenant Coll., Lookout Mountain, Tenn., 1982-90. 1st lt. USAAF, 1942-45. Fulbright fellow U.S. Govt., 1958. Mem. N.Am. Presbyn. and Reformed Coun. of Chs. (sec. 1977-92). Presbyterian. Avocations: flying, travel, genealogy. Office: Greenville Presbyn Theol Sem PO Box 690 Taylors SC 29687-0014 Office Phone: 864-322-2717. Personal E-mail: wcflcsc@mtnisp.com.

SMITH, MYRON JOHN, JR., librarian, author; b. Toledo, May 3, 1944; s. Myron John and Marion Oliva (Herbert) S.; 1 son, Myron John III. Student, Coll. Steubenville, 1962; AB, Ashland Coll., 1966; MLS, Western Mich. U., 1967; MA, Shippensburg U., 1969; postgrad., U. Wis., Purdue U.; LittD, Cardinal Newman Coll., 1982. Rsch. librarian G.W. Blunt White Libr., Mystic Seaport, Conn., 1967-68; asst. librarian Western Md. Coll., Westminster, 1969-72; libr. dir. Huntington (Ind.) Pub. Libr., 1972-76; prof. history and libr. sci., dir. libr. Benedum Libr. Salem-Teikyo U.; dir., then assoc. dir. aviation program Salem (W.Va.) Coll., 1976-90; prof. history and libr. sci., libr. dir. Tusculum Coll., Greeneville, Tenn., 1990—. Mem. Am. Com. on History 2d World War, Assn. for Bibliography of History Author: American Naval Bibliography Series, 1972-74, Huntington Centennial Handbook, 1973, The Sophisticated Lady: The Battleship Indiana in World War II, 1973, World War II at Sea: A Bibliography of Sources in English, 1976, (with Robert Webber) Sea Fiction Guide, 1976, The Cloak and Dagger Bibliography, 1976, World War I in the Air, 1977, Air War Chronology 1939-45, 1977, Air War Bibliography Series, 1977—, The Mountain State Battleship: USS West Virginia, 1979, Air War Southeast Asia, 1979, The Soviet Navy, 1941-1978, 1979, The Secret Wars Series, 1980-81, The Soviet Air and Strategic Rocket Forces, 1941-1980, 1981, The Soviet Army, 1941-1980, 1981, Equestrian Studies: The Salem College Guide, 1981, The Cloak and Dagger Fiction Guide: An Annotated Guide to Spy Thrillers, 1981, (with Terry White) 3d edit., 1994, The Mountaineer Battlewagon: USS West Virginia, 1982, The Keystone Battlewagon: USS Pennsylvania, 1983, The Golden State Battlewagon: USS California, 1983, Watergate: A Bibliography, 1983 World War II: Mediterranean and European Theaters, 1984, The United States Navy and Coast Guard, 1946-1983: A Bibliography of English Language Works and 16mm Films, 1984, U.S. Television Network News: A Guide to Sources in English, 1984, Battleships and Battlecruisers, 1884-1984: A Bibliography and Chronology, 1985, Baseball: A Comprehensive Bibliography, 1986, 99th Infantry Division Bibliography, 1986, The Airline Bibliography: The Salem College Guide to Sources on Commercial Aviation, Vol. I, The United States, 1986, Vol. II, Airliners and Foreign Carriers, 1987, Passenger Airliners of the United States, 1926-86: A Pictorial Guide, 1987, rev. edit. through 1991, 1991, 3d rev. edit. through 1995, 4th revised edit., 2002, Brooklyn/Los Angeles Dodgers: A Bibliography, 1987, American Warplane Bibliography, 1989, Volunteer Battlewagon: The U.S.S. Tennessee (BB-43), 1989; editor: Sports Teams and Players Bibliography Series, 1987, Battle and Leaders Bibliography Series, 1988, 100 Years of Opportunity: A Pictorial History of Salem College, 1888-1988, 1988, Pro Football Bio-Bibliography, 1920-1988, 1989, Pearl Harbor, December 7, 1941: An Annotated Bibliography, 1991, Battles of the Coral Sea and Midway, 1942: A Bibliography, 1991, World War II at Sea, 1974-1989: A Bibliography, 1990, Professional Football: The Official Pro Football Hall of Fame Bibliography, 1993, Baseball: A Comprehensive Bibliography-1st Supplement: 1985-1991, 93, The College Football Bibliography, 1994, Glimpses of Tusculum College: A Pictorial History, 1794-1994, 1994, Baseball: A Comprehensive Bibliography-2d Supplement: 1992-1997, 1998, The Airline Encyclopedia, 1909-2000, 2002, The Baseball Bibliography, 2d edit., 2006, Le Roy Fitch: The Civil War Career of a Union River Gunboat Commander, 2007, The Timberlands in the Civil War: The Lexington, Tyler and Conestog on the Western waters, 2008, Tinclads in the Civil War: Union Light-Draught Gunboat Operations on Western Waters 1862-1865, 2009, The Uss Carondelet: A Civil War Ironclad on Western Waters, 2010, CSS Arkansas: A Confederate Ironclad on Western Writers, 2011, The Fight for the Yazoo, August 1862-July 1864: Swamps, Forts and Fleets on Vicksburg's Northern Flank, 2012; contbr. articles to various jours. Recipient Nelson Ross award Profl. Football Rsch. Assn., 1993; 1st Am. recipient Richard Franck Gold medal Bibliothek für Zeitgeschichte, Stuttgart, Fed. Rep. Germany, 1981. Mem. ALA, U.S. Naval Inst., U.S. Mil. Inst., U.S. Air Force Found., Assn. Bibliog. of History (pres. 1981-82), Alliance of Librs. in Northeast Tenn. (pres. 1997—), Beta Phi Mu, Phi Alpha Theta. Clubs: Optimist. Office: Tusculum Coll PO Box 5005 60 Shiloh Rd Greeneville TN 37743-0001 Home Phone: 423-639-7364; Office Phone: 423-636-7320.

SMITH, O. BRUTON, automotive company executive; Founder Charlotte Motor Speedway, 1959, CEO & dir., 1975—; chmn., CEO Sonic Automotive, Inc., Charlotte, NC, 1997—, Speedway Motor Sports, Inc., Charlotte, 1994—; owner operator Town and Country Ford and various other pvt. bus., Charlotte, NC. Founder Speedway Children's Charities, 1984. Recipient Award of Excellence, NASCAR, 1997; named to, Greater Charlotte Sports Hall of Fame, 2005. Office: Sonic Automotive Inc 4401 Colwick Rd Charlotte NC 28211-2311

SMITH, PATRICIA H., library association director; B, Austin Coll., Sherman, Tex.; MLS, U. Tex., Austin. Exec. dir. Tex. Libr. Assn. Mem.: Austin Conv. and Visitors Bur. (bd. dirs. 2007—), Tex. Soc. Assn. (execs. ex bd. vice chmn. 2002—06, 2007—09), Com on Legislation (chmn. 2000—01), Coun. for 6 Terms (budget chmn. 2001—05), Tex. Libr. Assn. (Libr. of Yr. 1989, Disting. Svc. award 1994), ALA (mem. exec. bd. 1995—99, 2005—08). Office: Tex Libr Assn 3355 Bee Cave Rd Ste 401 Austin TX 78746-6763 Office Phone: 512-328-1518. Office Fax: 512-328-8852. Business E-Mail: pats@txla.org.

SMITH, PATRICIA HAYNES, state legislator; b. Baton Rouge, La. m. Freddie Smith Jr.; 6 children. BE, Kent State U.; attended, Yougstown U., Louisiana State U. Former employee Exon/Mobil Pub. Affairs; former tchr. East Baton Rouge Parish Sch.; mem. East Baton Rouge Parish Sch. Bd., v.p. Baton Rouge; mem. Dist. 67 La. House of Reps., 2008—, mem. appropriations com., edn. com., labor and indsl. rels. com., joint legis. com. on the budget. Democrat. Office: Capitol Office PO Box 44486 Baton Rouge LA 70804 also: 251 Florida St Ste 300 Baton Rouge LA 70801 Office Phone: 225-342-7106, 225-342-6945. Office Fax: 225-342-7117. E-mail: smithp@legis.state.la.us.

SMITH, PAUL VERGON, JR., retired gas industry executive; b. Lima, Ohio, Apr. 25, 1921; s. Paul Vergon and Aleta Rose (Bowers) S.; m. Alta Fern Chipps, Mar. 2, 1945; children: Douglas, Marsha, Jeffrey, Alison AB, Miami U., Oxford, Ohio, 1942; MS, U. Ill., 1943, PhD, 1945. With Exxon Rsch. & Engring. Co., 1946—66; with Exxon Rsch. & Engring Co., 1972—86, mgr. pub. affairs, 1972—86, mgr. ednl. and profl. soc. rels. Florham Park, NJ, 1981—86; asst. dir. chem. rsch. Esso Petroleum Co., Abingdon, England, 1966—67; dir. chem. rsch. Esso Rsch. S.A., Brussels, 1967—71; mem. adv. bd. Cache, Inc., Austin, Tex., 1979—86; pres. APS Assocs., Westfield, NJ, 1986—90. Bd. dirs., treas. Jets, Inc., Alexandria, Va.; dir. CENTCOM, Ltd.; mem. exec. bd. N.J. Bus./Industry/Sci. Edn. Consortium Patentee in field; contbr. numerous articles to profl. jours., chpts. to books Bd. dirs. United Way Union County, N.J., 1980-86; chmn. rsch. adv. coun. Miami U., 1980-84 Recipient Pres.'s award Am. Assn. Petroleum Geologists, 1955; Spl. award N.J. Sci. Tchrs. Assn., 1985 Mem. AAAS, Am. Chem. Soc. (dir. 1978-86, chmn. bd. 1984-86; Belden award 1984), Am. Soc. Engring. Edn. (dir. 1980-86, v.p. 1980-86), Country Club Naples, Phi Beta Kappa, Sigma Xi, Omicron Delta Kappa, Phi Eta Sigma, Alpha Chi Sigma, Pi Mu Epsilon, Sigma Pi Sigma, Phi Lambda Upsilon Republican. Methodist. Home Phone: 239-262-4901.

SMITH, PETE A., lawyer; b. St. Marys, Ohio, Mar. 29, 1969; BA, U. Cin., 1991; JD, U. Notre Dame, 1994. Bar: Ohio 1994, Ky. 1995. Ptnr. Strauss & Troy, Cin. Pro-bono legal adv. Covington Cmty. Ctr.; mem., Bd. Dirs. Southland Hall Assn. Named one of Ohio's Rising Stars, Super Lawyers, 2006. Mem.: ABA, Ky. Bar Assn., Ohio State Bar Assn., Cin. Bar Assn., Omicron Delta Kappa, Pi Kappa Alpha, Phi Beta Kappa. Office: Strauss & Troy 50 E River Center Blvd Covington KY 41011 Office Phone: 513-621-8900. Office Fax: 513-629-9444.

SMITH, PETER K., cardiothoracic surgeon; b. Cleve., Ohio, Aug. 20, 1951; MD, Duke U. Sch. Medicine, 1977. Cert. Am. Bd. Thoracic Surgery, Am. Bd. Surgery. Intern Duke U. Med. Ctr., Durham, NC, resident, cardiovascular rsch., 1987, divsn. chief; asst. prof., surgery Duke U., Durham, NC, 1987, prof. surgery, thoracic and cardiovascular surgery. Contbr. several articles to profl. jours. Tchg. Scholar, Am. Heart Assn. Clinician Scientist Awardee, Duke U. Med. Ctr., NC, 1980—83. Office: Duke U Med Ctr Box 3442 Durham NC 27710 Office Phone: 910-684-2890. Office Fax: 919-681-7905.

SMITH, PHILIP B., gas industry executive; BS in Mech. Engring., Okla. State U.; MBA, U. Tulsa. Exec. v.p., gen. counsel Sonat Inc., 1999; exec. v.p. El Paso Corp., 1999—2002; CEO, chmn. Prize Energy Corp., Grapevine, Tex., 1999—2002; mng. dir., ptnr. Galway Group, L.P., 2002; various positions Eagle Rock Energy G&P, LLC, 2002—06. Bd. dirs. El Paso Pipeline GP Co., LLC, MESA, Inc., 1996—99, Pioneer Natural Resources Co., 1996—99, HS Resources, Inc., 1996—99, Eagle Rock Energy G&P, LLC, 2006—. Office: Eagle Rock Energy Partners L P PO Box 2968 Houston TX 77252-2968 Office Phone: 281-408-1200. Office Fax: 281-408-1399. Business E-Mail: philip.smith@eaglerockenergy.com.

SMITH, PHILIP DANIEL, academic administrator, education educator; b. Dayton, Ohio, Dec. 25, 1933; s. Hubert Edgar and Edith (Parker) S.; m. Marilyn Brown, Nov. 25, 1953; children: Carolyn Smith Graybeal, Norman Daniel, Stanley Nathan. BS cum laude, Bob Jones U., 1955; MEd, Miami U., Oxford, Ohio, 1956; EdD, Pa. State U., 1964. Dean coll. arts and sci. Bob Jones U., Greenville, SC, 1961-65, registrar, 1965-81, prof. edn., 1956—2005, provost, 1981—2005, provost emeritus, 2005—; project coord. Bob Jones Acad. Internat., Zhejiang, China, 2013. Mem. edn. adv. bd. One Touch Systems, Inc., 1995-96; ednl. analyst Bible Colls., Gospel Fellowship Missions Assn., 2007—; academic advisor West Africa Bapt. Coll., 2011-. Cons. for BJ Help Network, BJ Linc, and BJU Press books Beginnings for Christian Schools, English Skills for Christian Schools, Handwriting for Christian Schools. Pres. Bob Jones U. Alumni Assn., Greenville, 1970-71; mem. coll. parallel adv. com. Tri-County Tech. Coll., Pendleton, S.C., 1973-86. Mem. Assn. Ednl.

Communications and Tech. (life mem.; membership coord. profl. assns. 1969-72, vice chair nat. membership com. 1972-73, chair nat. membership com. 1973-75, council del. S.C. chpt. 1972-73, audiovisual instrn. editorial adv. com. 1974-75, del. to Lake Okoboji ednl. media leadership conf. 1972, 74), Assn. Ednl. Communications and Tech. of S.C. (bd. dirs. 1970-75, pres. 1972-73, award for outstanding contbns. and service 1971), Am. Assn. Collegiate Registrars and Admissions Officers, Phi Delta Kappa. Republican. Baptist. Office: Bob Jones U Office Provost Greenville SC 29614-0001 Office Phone: 864-242-5100. Business E-Mail: psmith@bju.edu.

SMITH, PHILIP WILLIAM, surgeon, educator; married. BA in Physics, U. Va., Charlottesville, 1999, MD, 2003. Diplomate Am. Bd. Surgery, 2010. Asst. prof., surgery U. Va. Dept. Surgery, Charlottesville, 2010—. Office: University Va Dept Surgery Box 800709 Charlottesville VA 22908*

SMITH, PHILLIPS GUY, banker; b. Orange, NJ, Sept. 15, 1946; s. Phillips Upham and Helen Ottilie (Voderberg) S.; m. Ann Dixon Schickhaus, Dec. 29, 1973; children: Guy Dixon, William Schickhaus, Louisa Upham. B in Engring., Stevens Inst. Tech., Hoboken, NJ; MBA, U. Pa., 1975. Comml. banking rep. The Bank of N.Y., NYC, 1976-78, asst. treas., 1978-79, asst. v.p., 1979-80, v.p., 1980-85, sr. v.p., 1985-93; mng. dir. Internat. Strategy Svcs., Inc., NYC, 1993-2000, Ctr. Capital Advisors LLP, Greenwich, 2008—10; prin. Sippican Group LLC, Greenwich, Conn., 2000—08, Novahill Partners LLC, 2010—. Vestryman Ch. of The Heavenly Rest, N.Y.C., 1983-88, treas., 1985-87; trustee Tabor Acad., Marion, Mass., 1987—, treas., 1991—. Lt. USN, 1970-74, Vietnam. Mem. Racquet and Tennis Club, Down Town Assn., Rockaway Hunting Club, Nantucket Yacht Club. Episcopalian. Office: Novahill Partners LLC 1765 Duke St Alexandria VA 22314 Business E-Mail: psmith@novahillpartners.com.

SMITH, PRESTON, retired minister, small business owner; s. Arthur W. and Syble M. Smith; children: Cynthia Ann Smith Jones, Carey R. BS, Little Rock U., 1959; BA in Religion, Campbell Coll., 1973; MDiv in Pastoral Care, S.E. Sem., 1978; postgrad., East Carolina U., 1994; D of Ministry, Grad. Theol. Found., 1997. Cert. chaplain, ordained to ministry Free Will Bapt. Ch., 1968. Pastor Welcome Home Ch., Beaufort, N.C., 1968-71, Rains Crossroads, Princeton, N.C., 1972-76, Piney Grove, Kenly, N.C., 1976-78; res. chaplain U. N.C. Hosp., Chapel Hill, 1978-80, fellow in pastoral care, 1980-81; dir. of pastoral care Nash Gen. Hosp., Rocky Mount, NC, 1981—2003; owner Walker Enterprises and Silver Dollar Press, Inc., Hot Springs Village, Ark., 2003—. Cons. for ch. conflict Presbyn. Chs., Rocky Mount, N.C., 1984-87, N.C. Chaplains Assn., 1986-2003; bioethics bd. Nash Health Care Sys., 1994-2003; bd. dirs. Down East Christian Ins., 1996; mem. sci. textbook selection com. Ark. Coun. Tchrs. Math., Little Rock, Ark., 1983. Author, pub.: Free E-Book About Free E-Books, 2004, How to Adjust and Repair Your Sewing Machine, 2005. Bd. dirs. Kiwanis, Rocky Mount, 1988-90; mem. United Way, Rocky Mount. Mem. N.C. Chaplains Assn. (pres. v.p., sec. exec. com. 1986-94, Outstanding Leadership award 1994), Coll. of Chaplains (state rep. 1991-96, chair mem. svc. coun., bd. dirs. 1996), Order of De Molay (master councillor). Democrat. Avocations: woodworking, candle making. Office: PO Box 8394 Hot Springs Village AR 71910

SMITH, R. GORDON, lawyer; b. Roanoke, Va., May 28, 1938; BA with highest honors, U. Va., 1960; LLB magna cum laude, Harvard U., 1964. Bar: Va. 1964. Law clk. to judge U.S. Ct. Appeals (5th cir.), 1964-65; ptnr. McGuire, Woods, Battle & Boothe, Richmond, Va., 1969—. Exec., legislation editor Harvard Law Rev., 1963-64; bd. dirs. Scott & Stringfellow Fin., Inc., Trigon Healthcare, Inc., Va. C. of C., mem. coun., Virginia Inst. Marine Sci. Fellow Am. Bar Found.; mem. Va. Bar Assn. (pres. 1987-88), Am. Law Inst., Phi Beta Kappa, Omicron Delta Kappa. Office: McGuire Woods 901 E Cary St Richmond VA 23219-4057 Office Phone: 804-775-4347.

SMITH, RALPH HARRISON, II, lawyer, consultant; b. Albuquerque, Nov. 2, 1951; s. Robert Tatum and Harriet Smith; m. Helen Elizabeth Oakley, July 13, 1974; children: Harrison, William, Robert BA, Washington and Lee U., 1973; MA, Oxford U., 1976; JD, Yale U., 1979. Bar: D.C. 1979, Ala. 1982. Assoc. Covington & Burling, Washington, 1979—82, Cabaniss, Johnston, Gardner, Dumas & O'Neal, Birmingham, Ala., 1982—84; ptnr. Johnston, Barton, Proctor & Powell LLP, Birmingham, 1984—2004; gen. counsel U. Ala. Sys., 2004—12; pres., CEO Ralph Smith Group, 2013—; spl. counsel Jones Walker, 2013—. Disting. lectr. law U. Ala. Law Sch., 2005—2013; co-founder Global Innovation Alliance, 2012; pres.'s adv. coun. Birmingham So. Coll., 1987-88; leadership coun. U. Ala., Birmingham, 1988-91, Med. Clinics Bd., Birmingham, 1997; dir. Comm. on Fgn. Rels., Birmingham, 1996-2002; selection com. Rhodes Scholarship, 1982-87, 98—; Ala. sec. Rhodes Scholarship Trust, 2003-04, dist. sec., 2005—; dir. Assn. Am. Rhodes Scholars, 2006—, exec. com. 2008-, admin. Am. Trust for Oxford U., 2008-; mem. Am. Bar. Assn. Ctr. for Racial & Ethnic Diversity, 2008-10. Trustee Highland's Day Sch., Birmingham, 1985-89; pres. bd. St. Martin's in the Pines Nursing Home, Birmingham, 1990; dir. Ala. Sch. Fine Arts Found., Birmingham, 1993-98, Farrah Law Soc., U. Ala. Law Sch. Found., 2008-; mem. Leadership Birmingham, 1988, membership coun., 1998-2001; chancellor Episcopal Diocese of Ala., 2000-200, Rhodes scholar, 1973. Mem. Birmingham Bar Assn., Tuscaloosa Bar Assn., D.C. Bar Assn., Birmingham C. of C. (trustee 1993-2004), Am. Assn. Rhodes Scholars (dir. 2006—), Rotary Club Birmingham (dir., v.p. 1989-91, 90-91, 2001-02, 10-12, Paul Harris fellow 2001), Order of St. John; fellow Ala. Bar Found. Episcopalian. Home: 3519 Country Club Rd Birmingham AL 35213-2826 Office: 1819 5th Ave N Ste 1100 Birmingham AL 35203 Business E-Mail: ralph@ralphsmithgroup.com.

SMITH, RALPH K., state legislator; b. Roanoke, Va., July 19, 1942; 4 children. Attended, Nashville Auto Diesel Coll. Pres. Ralph Smith, Inc., 1966—; mayor City of Roanoke, 2000—04; mem. Dist. 22 Va. State Senate, 2008—12, mem. Dist. 19, 2012—, mem. Rules Com., Transp. Com., Edn. and Health Com., Local Govt. Com. & Privileges and Elections Com. Served in USCG, 1964—70. Republican. Office: Senate of Virginia PO Box 396 Richmond VA 23218 also: PO Box 91 Roanoke VA 24002 Office Phone: 540-206-3597, 804-698-7522. Office Fax: 804-698-7651. E-mail: district19@senate.virginia.gov.

SMITH, RALPH LEE, writer, musician; b. Phila., Nov. 6, 1927; s. Hugh Harold and Barbara (Schatkin) S.; m. Betty H. Smith, Sept. 1954 (div. Jan. 1963); children: David Bruce, Robert Hugh; m. Mary Louise Hollowell, 1971 (div. 1977); m. Shizuko Maruyama, 1977; 1 child, Lisa Koyuki. BA, Swarthmore Coll., Pa., 1951; MEd, U. Va., Charlottesville, 1987. Folk musician on Appalachian dulcimer; recs. include Dulcimer: Old Time and Traditional Music, 1973, Tunes of the Blue Ridge and Great Smoky Mountains, 1983, Across the Blue Ridge, 2005; author: The Story of the Dulcimer, 1986, Appalachian Dulcimer Traditions, 1997, Songs and Tunes of the Wilderness Road, 1999, Folk Songs of Old Kentucky, 2003, Greenwich Village: The Happy Folksinging Days, 2008, Folk Songs of Old Virginia, 2009, Song Treasures of the Cumberland Mountains, 2011, Smoky Mountain Memories, 2013. Recipient writing awards Columbia U. Grad. Sch. Journalism, U. Mo. Grad. Sch. Journalism, AMA, Western Carolina U. Home: 1662 Chimney House Rd Reston VA 20190-4302 E-mail: ralphleesmith@comcast.net.

SMITH, REBECCA BEACH, federal judge; b. 1949; BA, Coll. William and Mary, 1971; postgrad., U. Va., 1971-73; JD, Coll. William and Mary, 1979. Assoc. Wilcox & Savage, 1980-85; U.S. magistrate Ea. Dist. Va., 1985-89; dist. judge U.S. Dist. Ct. (ea. dist.) Va., Norfolk, 1989—. Exec. editor Law Review, 1978-79. Active Chrysler Mus. Norfolk, Jean Outland Chrysler Libr. Assocs., Va. Opera Assn., Friends of the Zoo, Friends of Norfolk Pub. Libr., Ch. of the Good Shepherd. John Marshall Soc. fellow; recipient Acad. Achievement and Leadership award St. George Tucker Soc.; named one of Outstanding Women of Am., 1979. Mem. ABA, Va. State Bar Assn., Fed. Bar Assn. Supreme Ct. Hist. Soc., Fourth Cir. Judicial Conf., The Harbor Club, Order of Coif., Phi Beta Kappa. Office: US Dist Ct US Courthouse 600 Granby St Ste 358 Norfolk VA 23510-1915

SMITH, RICHARD F., financial services company executive; BS, Purdue Univ., 1983. Sales rep. Owens Corning, Inc., Kans. City, Kans., 1981—83; various mgmt. positions General Electric Co., 1983—2005; sales rep. GE Plastics Bus. Group, Itasca, Ill., mktg. mgr., gen. mgr.; pres., CEO GE Capital Modular Space, Malvern, Pa., GE Capital Fleet Services, Eden Prairie, Minn., GE Global Property & Casualty Reinsurance, Overland Park, Kans.; COO GE Ins. Solutions, Overland Park, Kans.; pres., CEO Equifax, Inc., Atlanta, 2005, chmn., CEO, 2006—. Office: Equifax Inc 1550 Peachtree St NW Atlanta GA 30309 Mailing: Equifax Inc PO Box 4081 Atlanta GA 30302

SMITH, RICHARD H., state legislator; b. Wrightsville, Ga., Mar. 9, 1945; State rep. Dist. 131, Ga., 2005—. Republican. Baptist. Mailing: Legis Off Bldg Atlanta GA 30334 E-mail: richard@smithforgeorgia.com.

SMITH, RICHARD J., energy executive; BS in Acctg., Ind. U. and Purdue U.; MBA, U. Indpls. V.p. fin. Energy Svcs. bus. unit Cinergy Corp., Cin., 1996—99, v.p. energy svcs., 1999, pres. Cinergy Resources, Inc., 1999; sr. v.p. transition mgmt. Entergy Corp., 1999—2000, pres. Retail, 2000, group pres. Utility Ops., pres., COO, 2007—10, pres. wholesale commodity bus., 2010—. Office: Engery Corp 1340 Echelon Pkwy Ste 100 Jackson MS 39213-8210 Office Phone: 504-576-4000.

SMITH, RICK, professional sports team executive; b. Petersburg, Va., Sept. 3, 1969; m. Tiffany Smith; children: Robert LaMar, Avery Jordan. BA, Purdue U., Ind., 1992. Asst. strength and conditioning coord. Purdue U. Boilermakers, 1992—93, tight ends coach, 1993—94, secondary coach, 1994—96; asst. defensive backs coach Denver Broncos, 1996—99, head, pro pers. ops., 1999—2005, asst. gen. mgr., 2006; gen. mgr. Houston Texans, 2006—. Mem. NFL Gen. Mgrs. Adv. Com., NFL Competition Com., 2008—. Recipient Tank Younger award, Fritz Pollard Alliance, 2008. Mem.: Fellowship Christian Athletes. Office: Houston Texans Two Reliant Park Houston TX 77054 Office Phone: 832-667-2000.

SMITH, ROBERT LEONARD, pastor, religious studies educator, retired theology studies educator; b. San Antonio, Dec. 23, 1924; s. Leonard and Alice Jewel (Horton) S.; m. Ethelyn Hughes, Feb. 8, 1945; children: Robert Leonard, Judy Claire Smith George. BS, Centenary Coll., Shreveport, La., 1947; BDiv, Southwestern Seminary, 1953, MDiv, 1987; DD (hon.), Ouachita U., 1961; DDiv, Howard Payee U., 2012. Ordained to ministry, Bapt. Ch., 1953. Pastor First Bapt. Ch., Crossett, Ark., 1953-55, Pine Bluff, Ark., 1955-65, Houston, 1965-69, Pompano Beach, Fla., 1969-84; disting. prof. preaching and ch. adminstrn., dean Howard Payne U., Brownwood, Tex., 1984-94, dean emeritus, sch. ch. studies, 2007, adj. prof. old & new testament, 2009—11. Mem. Bapt. Sunday Sch. Bd., Nashville, 1957-65; presented Sermons in Art in 38 states. Author: Successful Chalk-Talk, 1972; author, prodr. (TV series) The Art of Living, 1960-67; contbr. articles to religious jours.; oil and watercolor artist; one man shows include Stetson U., Deland, Fla., 1984, Lighthouse Point Nat. Bank, Fla., 1975, First Nat. Bank, Pompano Beach, Fla., 1976, Citizens Nat. Bank, Brownwood, Tex., 1991, Howard Payne U., Brownwood, 1994; exhibited at Jefferson County Fair, Pine Bluff, Ark., 1964, First Meth. Ch., Pompano Beach, 1974. Mem. Ark. Exec. Bd., Little Rock, 1954-62, Tex. Exec. Bd., Dallas, 1966-80, Fla. Exec. Bd., Jacksonville, 1966-80; trustee Pine Bluff (Ark.) Mental Health Ctr., 1959, Henderson Mental Health Clinic, Ft. Lauderdale, Fla., 1971-75, Stetson U., DeLand, Fla., 1978-82. Named Artist of the Yr., 2007. Mem. Rotary Internat. Avocations: oil and watercolor painting, flying, golf. Home: 3 Quail Creek Rd Brownwood TX 76801-6309

SMITH, ROBERT VICTOR, academic administrator, educator; b. Glendale, NY, Feb. 16, 1942; s. Robert Arthur and Marie Marlene (Florence) S. BS in Pharm. Sci., St. John's U., Jamaica, NY, 1963; MS in Pharm. Chemistry, U. Mich., 1964, PhD in Pharm. Chemistry, 1968. Asst. prof., then assoc. prof. U. Iowa, Iowa City, 1968-74; assoc. prof., asst. dir. U. Tex., Austin, 1974-77, area coordinator basic pharmaceutics, 1975-76, assoc. dir. Drug Dynamics Inst., 1977-78, dir. Drug Dynamics Inst., Coll. Pharmacy, 1979-85, James E. Bauerle Centennial prof. Coll. Pharmacy, 1983-85; prof., dean Coll. Pharmacy, Wash. State U., Pullman, 1985-86, vice provost for rsch., dean Grad. Sch., 1987-97; vice provost for rsch. and grad. edn., dean Grad. Sch., U. Conn., Storrs, 1997-2000; provost, vice chancellor acad. affairs U. Ark., Fayetteville, 2000—08, provost, vice chancellor emeritus and prof., chemistry, 2008—09; provost, sr. v.p. Tex. Team U. Lubbock, 2009—. Cons. E.R. Squibb, New Brunswick, N.J., 1979-82, Upjohn Co., Kalamazoo, 1982-85, Ministry Higher Edn., Saudi Arabia, 2010; external examiner U. Malaysia, Penang, 1981-82; mem. sci. adv. bd. Biodecision Labs., Pitts., 1985-86; Wash. Exposition Sci. Tech. Found., 1989-90; mem. noms. com. Coun. Grad. Schs., Washington, 1990-91, 96-97; accreditation evaluator Northwest Assn. Schs. and Colls., Seattle, 1991-97; mem. exec. com. grad. deans African-Am. Inst., N.Y., 1992-2000; bd. dirs. Coun. Grad. Schs., 1998, Grad. Record Exam, 1999-2003; exec. sec. U. Ark. 2010 Commn., 2000-08; chair Southeastern Conf. Provosts Group, 2003-04. Author: Textbook of Biopharmaceutic Analysis, 1981, Graduate Research: A Guide for Students in the Sciences, 1998, Development and Management of University Research Groups, 1986, The Elements of Great Speechmaking: Adding Drama and Intrigue, 2004, Pedestals, Parapets and Pits: The Joys, Challenges and Failures of Professional Life, 2005, Where You Stand is Where You Sit: An Academic Administrator's Handbook, 2006. Bd. dirs. Wash. Tech. Ctr., 1990-92; exec. sec. 2010 Commn. Grantee NIH, 1974-83; fellow Acad. Pharm. Scis., 1981, Am. Assn. Pharm. Scientists, 1987; recipient Disting. Alumnus award Coll. Pharmacy U. Mich., 1990, Outstanding Svc. award Wash. State U., Grad. and Profl. Student Assn., 1993, 95. Mem. Am. Assn. Colls. Pharmacy (chmn. research and grad. affairs com. 1983-84), U.S. Pharmacopeia (revision com. 1985-90), Acad. Pharm. Scis. (chmn., vice chmn. 1983-85, 90, Presdl. citation 1985), Wash. Rsch. Found. (bd. dirs. 1989-97). Unitarian Universalist. Office: CHEM 119 Fayetteville AR 72701 Home: 10501 Utica Ave Lubbock TX 79424-7305 Office Phone: 806-742-2184. Business E-Mail: bobsmith@ttu.edu.

SMITH, ROBIN, former political organization administrator; b. Ga., 1963; m. Scott Smith; children: Callie, Caleb. Grad., U. Tenn., 1985. Critical care/transplant nurse U. Ala. Med. Ctr., Birmingham; chmn. Hamilton County Rep. Party, 1998—2002, Tenn. Rep. Party, 2007—09; commr. Tenn. Human Rights. Del. Rep. Nat. Conv., 2004; candidate for US Congress Tenn., 2010; mem. Hixson Ctrl. Baptist. Republican. Home: PO Box 23805 Chattanooga TN 37422-3805

SMITH, ROD (RODNEY WARREN SMITH), lawyer, former political organization administrator; b. Southwest City, Mo., Nov. 15, 1949; m. Deidra Painter; children: Alison, Jesse, Dylan. BA, U. Tulsa, 1971; JD, U. Fla. Coll. Law, 1975. Bar: Fla. Atty. Fla. Public Employees Relations Commn.; pvt. practice Alachua County, Fla.; state atty. Eighth Judicial Cir. State of Fla., 1993—2000; mem. Dist. 14 Fla. State Senate, 2001—06; ptnr. Avera & Smith LLP, Gainesville, 2000—; chmn. Fla. Democratic Party, 2011—13. Adj. prof. Levin Coll. Law, U. Fla. Recipient Disting. Svc. award, Fla. Coun. Crime & Delinquency, Fla. Profl. Firefighters, Harry S. Truman "Buck Stops Here" award, Champion of Justice award, North Ctrl. Fla. Police Benevolent Assn.; named Person of Yr., Gainesville Sun, 1994. Democrat. Office: Avera & Smith LLP 2814 SW 13th St Gainesville FL 32608

SMITH, RODNEY WIKE, retired engineering executive; b. Havre de Grace, Md., July 29, 1944; s. Marshall Thomas and Ellen Nora (Wike) S.; m. Mary Katherine Trent, Dec. 20, 1967; children: Scott Walker, Craig Duncan. BS, Va. Poly. Inst. and State U., 1972. Registered profl. engr., Va., N.C. Project engr. Hercules Inc., Radford, Va., 1967-72; planning engr. Va. state Water Control Bd., Richmond, 1972; project mgr. Cen. Shenandoah Planning Dist. Commn., Staunton, 1972-76; v.p., br. office mgr. Patton, Harris, Rust & Assocs., Bridgewater, Va., 1976-82, prin. in charge office Buchanan, W.Va., 1980-82; sr. v.p. Copper & Smith, PC, Harrisonburg, Va., 1982-88; pres. R.W. Smith & Assocs. PC, Verona, Va., 1988-95, Va. Sports Tech., Verona, Va., 1995—, Intellectual Properties Inc., Hampton, Va., 1996—; sr. project mgr. Olver, Inc., Blacksburg, Va., 1998—2003; pres., owner Value Built LLC, 2000—05; ret., 2005. Contbr. articles to profl. jours.; 4 patents in field. Apptd. to Va. Resources Authority Citizens Adv. Commn., 1987-91. Named Exec. of Yr. Profl. Secs. Internat.; Copper and Smith listed among fastest growing pvt. cos. by Inc. mag., 1987. Mem. Nat. Soc. Profl. Engrs., Water Polllution Control Fedn. Republican. Lutheran. Home: 3238 Northfork Rd Elliston VA 24087-3632

SMITH, ROGER WINSTON, retired political theory educator; b. Birmingham, Ala., July 9, 1936; s. Buford Houston and Sarah Louise (Trucks) S.; m. Martha Christin Daniels, Jan. 16, 1960; children: Louisa, David AB magna cum laude, Harvard U., 1958, postgrad. in law, 1958—59; MA in Polit. Sci., U. Calif., Berkeley, 1963, PhD in Polit. Sci., 1971. Teaching assoc. U. Calif.-Berkeley, 1965-66; asst. prof. govt. Coll. William and Mary, Williamsburg, Va., 1967-72, assoc. prof., 1972-80, prof, 1980-2001, prof. emeritus, 2001—. Sr. lectr. politics Glasgow U., 1977-78; lectr. NEH, 1988; cons. Nelson-Hall Pubs., Chgo.; mem. coun. Inst. Internat. Conf. on the Holocaust and Genocide, Jerusalem; chair acad. adv. bd., dir. genocide and human rights univ. program Zoryan Inst., Toronto; v.p. Inst. Study of Genocide, NY. Co-author, editor: Guilt: Man and Society, 1971; co-author: Genocide and the Modern Age, 1987, Genocide, vol. 2, 1991, Bearing Witness to the Holocaust, 1939-89, 1987, The Coming Age of Scarcity, 1998, Pioneers of Genocide Studies, 2002, When Will Genocide Ever End?, 2002, On the Edge of Scarcity, 2002, Race and Ethnic Relations, 15th ann. edit., 2005, Encyclopedia of Genocide and Crimes Against Humanity, 2004, Geniciur Matters, 2013; editor: Genocide, 1999; contbg. editor Internet on the Holocaust and Genocide; contbr. articles to profl. jours. Served to 1st lt. U.S. Army, 1960-62, Japan Fellow NSF, 1966, College of William and Mary, 1977; recipient: award, 2008, Rep. Armania award, 2008. Mem. Internat. Assn. Genocide Scholars (co-founder, v.p., past pres.), Human Rights Watch, PETA. Democrat. Avocations: gardening, walking, opera. Home: 102 Lake Dr Williamsburg VA 23185-3113 Office: Coll William and Mary Dept Govt Williamsburg VA 23187

SMITH, ROLAND C., movie theatre company executive, former food service company executive; b. 1954; BS in Engring., US Mil. Acad., West Point, NY, 1978. Various mgmt. positions KFC Internat., Schering-Plough Corp., Pepsi Cola Internat., Procter & Gamble Co.; pres., CEO Arby's, Inc., 1997—99, AMF Bowling Worldwide, Inc., 1999—2003, American Golf Corp. & Nat. Golf Properties, 2003—05, Arby's Restaurant Group, Inc., 2006—08, Wendy's/Arby's Group, Inc., 2007—11, Wendy's Co., 2011; non-exec. chmn. Carmike Cinemas, Inc., 2009—; interim pres. Arby's Restaurant Group, Inc., 2010—11. Bd. dirs. Dave Thomas Found., Carmike Cinemas, Inc., 2002—, Wendy's/Arby's Group, Inc., 2007—11. Platoon leader transp. and aviation corps, dep. dir. Army progs., aide-de-camp, maintenance officer, pilot US Army. Office: Carmike Cinemas Inc PO Box 391 Columbus GA 31904

SMITH, ROLAND CARROLL, SR., construction executive; m. Jacqueline M. Smith. Pres., CEO Hearndon Constrn. Corp., Chesapeake, Va. Bd. dirs. Hampton Roads Bankshares Inc., 2006—. Office: Hearndon Construction Corp 2010 Old Greenbrier Rd Chesapeake VA 23320 Office Phone: 757-523-2569. Business E-Mail: rolandsmith@gwfh.com.

SMITH, SHARMAN BRIDGES, state librarian; BS, Miss. U. for Women, Columbus, 1972; MLS, George Peabody Coll., Nashville, 1975. Head libr. Clinton (Miss.) Pub. Libr., 1972-74; asst. dir. Lincoln-Lawrence-Franklin Regional Libr., Brookhaven, Miss., 1975-77, dir., 1977-78; info. svcs. mgr. Miss. Libr. Commn., Jackson, 1978-87, asst. dir. libr. ops., 1987-89, dir. libr. svcs. div., 1989-92; state libr. State Libr. Iowa, Des Moines, 1992—2001; exec. dir. Miss. Libr. Commn., Jackson, Miss., 2001—. Recipient Friend of Edn. award, Iowa Computer Using Educators, 1995, Mem. of Yr. award, Iowa Libr. Assn., 1996, Peggy May award, MS Libr. Assn., 2010. Office: Miss Libr Commn 3881 Eastwood Dr Jackson MS 39211 Office Phone: 601-432-4039. Business E-Mail: sharman@mlc.lib.ms.us.

SMITH, SHERWOOD HUBBARD, JR., retired electric utilities executive; b. Jacksonville, Fla., Sept. 1, 1934; s. Sherwood Hubbard and Catherine Gertrude (Milliken) S.; m. Eva Hackney Hargrave, July 20, 1957; children: Marlin Hamilton Dohlman, Cameron Hargrave Callaway, Eva Hackney Davis. AB, U. N.C., 1956, JD, 1960; D civil laws, St. Augustine's Coll., 1988; LDD, Campbell U., 1990; HHD, Francis Marion Coll., 1990. Bar: N.C. 1960. Assoc. Lassiter, Moore & Van Allen, Charlotte, 1960-62; ptnr. Joyner & Howison, Raleigh, 1962-65; assoc. gen. counsel Carolina Power & Light Co., Raleigh, 1965-70, sr. v.p., gen. counsel, 1971-74, exec. v.p., 1974-76, pres., 1976-92, CEO, 1979-96, chmn. bd., 1980-99, chmn. emeritus, 1999—; with Progress Energy Co., 2005—. Former dir. NorTel Network, Northwestern Mut. Life Ins. Co., Wachovia Corp., Durham Corp., Springs, Ind. Trustee Z Smith Reynolds Found., 1978-96, Nat. Humanities Ctr., 1990-93; bd. dirs. NC Citizens Bus. and Industry, chmn., 1985-86; bd. dirs. Rsch. Triangle Found. NC, NC Inst. Medicine; mem. bd. govs. Ctr. Creative Leadership; mem., chmn. Triangle Univs. Ctr. Advanced Studies, 1986—; dir. Franklin St.

Ptnrs.; former chmn. bd. trustees, chmn. Rex Hosp.; gov. Boys and Girls Clubs Am. Recipient Nat. Humanitarian award Am. Lung Assn., 1993, Outstanding Leadership award in Mgmt. scis. Am. Soc. Mech. Engrs., 1983, A.E. Finley Disting. Svc. award Greater Raleigh C. of C., 1985, Disting. Citizenship award N.C. Citizens Bus. and Industry, 1997; named to N.C. Bus. Hall of Fame, 1999. Mem.: Greater Raleigh C. of C. (pres. 1979), Phi Beta Kappa. Home: 408 Drummond Dr Raleigh NC 27609-7006 Office: Progress Energy Co PO Box 1551 Raleigh NC 27602-1551

SMITH, SIDNEY CRAWLE, JR., cardiologist, educator; b. Wilmington, Del., 1941; MD, Yale U., 1967. Diplomate Nat. Bd. Med. Examiners, 1969, Am. Bd. Internal Medicine, 1972, Cardiovascular Disease, 1973. Intern Peter Bent Brigham Hosp., Boston, 1967—68, resident cardiology, 1968—69, fellowship, 1969—71, Harvard Med. Sch., Boston, 1969—71; dir. cardiovascular labs. U. Colo. Health Sci. Ctr., 1973—77; dir. San Diego Cardiac Ctr. at Sharp Healthcare, 1977—94; chief cardiology U. NC, Chapel Hill, 1994—2001, dir. Ctr. Cardiovascular Sci. and Medicine, 1996—. Asst. prof. U. Colo., Denver, 1973—77; asst. clin. prof. medicine U. San Diego, 1977—85, assoc. clin. prof., 1985—90, clin. prof., 1990—94; prof. U. NC Sch. Medicine, 1994—. Contbr. articles to med. jours. Recipient Eugene Drake Award, 2003, Award Spl. Recognition, Nat. Heart, Lung, and Blood Inst., NIH, 2003. Mem.: Am. Coll. Cardiology, Am. Heart Assn. (chief sci. officer 2001—03, nat. pres. 1995—96, Physician of Yr. Award 1993, Disting. Nat. Leadership Award 1996, Gold Heart Award 2000), Inter Am. Soc. Cardiology (v.p.), World Heart Fedn. (exec. com. mem.), World Heart Forum (chmn.). Office: U NC / Divsn Cardiology CB #7075 160 Dental Circle Chapel Hill NC 27599-7075 Office Phone: 919-966-0732. Office Fax: 919-966-1743. E-mail: scs@med.unc.edu.

SMITH, STANLEY BERTRAM, clinical and anatomic pathologist, allergist, immunologist; b. Phila., 1929; MD, Washington U., St. Louis, 1956. Diplomate Am. Bd. Clin. Pathology, Am. Bd. Allergy and Immunology, Am. Bd. Anatomic Pathology. Intern Barnes Hosp., St. Louis, 1956—57; resident in pathology Jackson Meml. Hosp., 1957—62; fellow in immunology Sch. Medicine Yale U., New Haven, 1963—65; pathologist Miami (Fla.) Children's Hosp., 1966—. Mem. AAAS, AMA, Internat. Acad. Pathology, Am. Soc. Clin. Pathology, Coll. Am. Pathologists, Am. Soc. Hematology. Office: Miami Children's Hosp 3100 SW 62nd Ave Miami FL 33155-3009 E-mail: Stanley.Smith@mch.com.

SMITH, STEPHEN JAMES, federal marshal; BS, Armstrong Atlantic State U., Savannah, Ga., 1975, MSc, 1987; Grad., FBI Nat. Acad., 1990. Various positions, rose to the rank of Capt. Savannah Police Dept., comdr. Chatham-Savannah Counter Narcotics Team, 1996—2002, chief of police Thunderbolt, Ga., 2002—05, Meml. Health U. Med. Ctr., 2005—07; US Marshal (so. dist.) Ga. US Marshals Svc., US Dept. Justice, Savannah, Ga., 2010—. Served with US Army, 1967—69, Vietnam. Decorated Bronze Star (2), Purple Heart; grantee Fulbright Scholarship, 1995. Office: Dist Ct Ga Hdqs 125 Bull St Savannah GA 31401

SMITH, STEVEN DELANO, sportscaster, retired professional basketball player; b. Highland Park, Mich., Mar. 31, 1969; Student, Mich. State U. Guard Miami Heat, 1991-94, Atlanta Hawks, 1994-99, broadcast analyst, 2005—08; guard Portland Trailblazers, 1999—2001, San Antonio Spurs, 2001—03, New Orleans Hornets, 2003—04, Miami Heat, 2004—05; ret., 2005; studio analyst NBA TV, 2008—. Named Sporting News All-Am. First Team, 1990, 91, NBA All-Rookie Team, 1992, Dream Team II, 1994; recipient J. Walter Kennedy Citizenship award, 1996, NBA Sportsmanship award, 2002; Olympic Gold Metalist, 2000. Office: NBA TV 1065 Williams St NW Atlanta GA 30309

SMITH, STEVEN ESCAR, library director; b. Nuremberg, Germany; married; 2 children. BA in English Lit., U. SC, 1987, MA in English Lit., 1990, ML in Librarianship, 1990; PhD in English Lit., Tex. A&M U., 2001. Reference grad. asst. U. SC Thomas Cooper Libr., 1988—90; humanities reference librarian Tex. A&M U. Libraries, 1990—91, bibliographic instrn. librarian, 1991—92, spl. collections librarian, 1992—2001, assoc. dean for advancement, dir. Cushing Meml. Libr. and Archives, 2001—07, assoc. dean collections and svcs., 2007—10, interim exec. assoc. dean, 2010—11; prof., dean libraries U. Tenn., Knoxville, 2011—. Bd. dirs. Tex. Digital Libr., 2010—. Mem. editl. bd.: Libraries and the Cultural Record, 2004—; contbr. articles to profl. jours., chapters to books. Served with SC Army Nat. Guard, 1982—90. Recipient Disting. Librarianship award, Tex. A&M Assn. Former Students, 1997. Mem.: ALA, Assn. Coll. and Rsch. Libraries, Tex. Libr. Assn., Soc. American Archivists, Bibliographic Soc. America, Tex. Philosophical Soc., Grolier Club. Office: University of Tennessee Libraries 1015 Volunteer Blvd Knoxville TN 37996-1000 Office Phone: 865-974-6600. Business E-Mail: stevensmith@utk.edu.

SMITH, STEVEN LEE, judge; b. San Antonio, Apr. 19, 1952; s. Bill Lee and Maxine Rose (Williams) S.; m. Rebecca Ann Brimmer, Aug. 5, 1978 (dec. Apr. 2005); children: William Christopher, Laura Charlotte. B in Music Edn. magna cum laude, Abilene Christian U., 1974; JD, U. Tex., 1977. Bar: Tex. 1977. U.S. Dist. Ct. (so. dist.) Tex. 1979, U.S. Dist. Ct. (we. dist.) Tex. 1980; cert. civil trial lawyer, Tex. Bd. Legal Specialization. Assoc. Dillon & Giesenschlag, Bryan, Tex., 1977-80, ptnr., 1980-84, Dillon, Lewis, Elmore & Smith, Bryan, 1985-88, Hoelscher, Lipsey, Elmore and Smith, College Station, Tex., 1988-94; asst. mcpl. judge City of College Station, 1988-91, presiding mcpl. judge, 1992-95; judge Brazos County Ct. at Law # 1, Bryan, 1995-98, 361st Dist. Ct., Bryan, 1999—; past chair Jud. Sect. State Bar Tex. Past chair Nat. Conf. Spl. Ct. Judges. Chmn. Brazos Valley chpt. March of Dimes, 1983-84; Leadership Brazos Devel. Program, Bryan/Coll. Sta. C. of C., 1984-85; pres. Meml. Student Ctr. Opera and Performing Arts Soc., College Station, 1985-86; trustee Abilene Christian U., 2001—. Recipient Charles Plum Disting. Svc. award Tex. A&M U., 1986; Sustaining Life fellow Tex. Bar Found. Mem. U. Tex. Law Sch. Alumni Assn. (dist. dir. 1986-89), U. Tex. Ex-Students Assn. Exec. Coun. (club rep. 1987-88); fellow Am. Bar Found. Avocations: golf, flying. Home: 3840 Cedar Ridge Dr College Station TX 77845-6275 Office: 361st Dist Ct 300 E 26th St Ste 305 Bryan TX 77803-5361 Office Phone: 979-361-4380. E-mail: ssmith@co.brazos.tx.us.

SMITH, SUE FRANCES MUECK (MUECK SMITH), retired newspaper editor; b. Lockhart, Tex., July 4, 1940; d. Monroe John Baylor and Myrtle (Krause) Mueck; m. Michael Vogtel Smith, Apr. 20, 1963 (div. July 1977); 1 child, Jordan Meredith; m. Kirkland Gideon Smith, Apr. 17, 1999. B of Journalism, U. Tex., 1962. Feature writer, photographer Corpus Christi Caller-Times, 1962—64; soc. reporter, feature writer, editor Chgo. Tribune, 1964-76; features editor Dallas Times Herald, 1976-82; sales assoc. Bumpas Assocs., Dallas, 1982-83; asst. mng. editor for features Denver Post, 1983-84, assoc. editor, 1984-91; asst. mng. editor in charge of Sunday paper Dallas Morning News, 1991-94, asst. mng. editor Lifestyles, 1994-96, dep. mng. editor Lifestyles, 1996—2001, dep. mng. editor recruiting/devel., 2001—06. Coun. pres., 1993; juror Pulitzer Prize, 2002, 03. Mem. Am. Assn. Sunday and Feature Editors (pres. 1993), Soc. Features Journalism Found. (bd. mem.), Newspaper Features Coun. (pres. 2002), Tex. AP Mng. Editors (pres. 1999-00, Jack Douglas award disting. svc. 2005), Delta Gamma Sorority, Mayborn Lit. Nonfiction Conf. (adv. bd. mem.), Beta Sigma Phi. Home: PO Box 1542 Lockhart TX 78644-1423 Business E-Mail: kgsmith41@msn.com.

SMITH, SUSAN, bank executive; b. 1961; married; 2 children. Exec. Boatmen's Ark. Bank (now Regions Bank); sr. exec. v.p., COO Met. Nat. Bank. Chmn. Ark. Commitment Scholarship Program. Named one of 25 Most Powerful Women in Banking, Fortune Mag., 2004, 25 Women to Watch, US Banking, 2007. Office: Metropolitan National Bank 425 W Capitol Little Rock AR 72201 Office Phone: 501-377-7600. Office Fax: 501-377-7608.

SMITH, THOMAS F., immunologist; b. July 14, 1949; s. Oney Percy and Evelyn Fugate Smith; m. Jane S. Snoddy, May 24, 1975; children: Thomas Bryan, Amanda Catherine, Christopher Evan. BA, U. Va., Charlottesville, 1971, MD, 1974. Diplomate Am. Bd. Pediat., Sub-Bd. Pediatric Pulmonology, 1975, Nat. Bd. Med. Examiners, 1975, Am. Bd. Pediat., 1979, Am. Bd. Allergy & Immunology, 1979, Am. Bd. Med. Lab. Immunology, 1983, Amer Bd. Allergy & Immunology, Diagnostic Lab. Immunology, 1990. Intern and resident in pediat. Vanderbilt U. Hosp., Nashville, 1974—77; fellow in pediatric allergy & clin. immunology Nat. Jewish Hosp. & Rsch. Ctr., Denver, 1977—80; instr. pediat. U. Colo. Sch. Medicine, Denver, 1979; assoc. prof. pediat., asst. prof. medicine, asst. prof. microbiology & immunology Emory U. Sch. Medicine, Atlanta, 1980—93, dir. allergy & immunology tng. program, 1986—93; prof. pediat. Wash. U. Sch. Medicine, St. Louis, 1993—98; chief allergy sect. Austin Diagnostic Clinic, Tex., 1998—. Ctrl. region bd. mem. Am. Lung Assn. Tex. Mem. editl. bd. Jour. Allergy and Immunology, 1997—2002; contbr. 67 articles to profl. jours. With Boy Scouts Am., 1967—2007. Recipient Hal M. Davidson Meml. award, Southeastern Allergy Assn., 1982, Cross & Flame award, United Meth. Ch., 1986, Scoutmaster's Merit award, Boy Scouts Am., 1988, Dist. Merit award, 1989; named Tex. Super Dr., Key Profl. Media, Inc., 2005—08; named one of Best Doctors in Am., Best Doctors, Inc., 1992—2008; grantee Rsch. grants, NIH, 1983—89, 1991—98. Mem.: Am. Acad. Pediat., Joint Coun. Allergy, Asthma and Immunology, Am. Coll. Allerg, Asthma and Immunology, Am. Acad. Allergy, Asthma and Immunology, Tex. Allergy and Immunology Soc., Tex. Med. Assn., Sigma Xi, Alpha Phi Omega, Phi Beta Kappa. Episcopalian. Avocations: photography, art, camping, hiking, reading.

SMITH, TODD, state legislator; b. Arlington, Tex., Mar. 23, 1963; m. Nancy Smith; children: Spencer, Sawyer. BA in Polit. Sci., magna cum laude, So. Meth. U., Dallas, 1985; JD with honors, U. Tex. Sch. Law, 1988. Assoc., ptnr. Locke, Purnell, Rain, & Harrell; mem. Euless City Coun., Tex., 1991—96; mem. Dist. 92 Tex. House of Representatives, 1996—. Recipient of several awards and honors. Mem.: Hurst-Euless-Bedford C. of C., Hurst-Euless Bedford Rotary, Mid-Cities Optimist Club. Republican. Baptist. Office: 1608 Airport Freeway Ste 100 Bedford TX 76022 also: Room CAP 4S.06 Capital PO Box 2910 Austin TX 78768 Office Phone: 817-283-3131, 512-463-0522.

SMITH, TOMMY, state legislator; b. Dec. 15, 1950; Del. Dem. Nat. Conv., 1968; Ga. state rep. Dist. 152, 1978—92; Ga. state rep. Dist. 169, 1993—2002; chmn. Legislature & Congl. Reapportionment Com.; mem. appropriations & health & ecol. com.; house rep. Ga.; Ga. State Rep. Dist. 129, 2003—04; Ga. State Rep. Dist. 168, 2004—. Democrat. Meth. Mailing: 197 Campground Church Rd Nicholls GA 31554 Office: 135 State Capitol Atlanta GA 30334 Office Phone: 404-656-5105.

SMITH, TONY, state legislator; b. Jackson, Miss., Dec. 14, 1962; m. Angie Taylor; children: Lauren, Alexis, Addison. BS, U. So. Miss., Hattiesburg. Owner Stonewalls BBQ & Catering, Miss.; mem. Dist. 47 Miss. State Senate, Jackson, 2012—. Mem.: Miss. Restaurant Assn., Nat. BBQ Assn., Picayune C. of C. Republican. Office: Miss State Senate PO Box 1018 Jackson MS 39215 Business E-Mail: tsmith@senate.ms.gov.

SMITH, TRACEY, real estate broker; b. Ft. Worth, June 23, 1948; married; 4 stepchildren. BA in Economics, U. Tex. Austin, 1970; MA in Journalism, Ohio State U., 1974. Journalist KDFW-TV, 1978—80; comml. real estate broker, 1984—. Precinct chmn. Dem. Party. Democrat. Office: 1100 Miller Ave Fort Worth TX 76105

SMITH, TUBBY (ORLANDO SMITH), men's college basketball coach; b. Scotland, Md., June 30, 1951; s. Guffrie & Parthenia Smith; m. Donna Smith; children: Orlando, Shannon, Saul, Brian. BS in Health & Phys. Edn., High Point Coll., 1973; HD (hon.), U. Ky., Lexington, 2008. Head coach Great Mills HS, Md., 1973-77, Hoke County HS, Raeford, NC, 1977-79; asst. coach Va. Commonwealth U. Rams, 1979-86, U. SC Gamecocks, 1986-89, U. Ky. Wildcats, Lexington, 1989-91, head coach, 1997—2007, U. Tulsa Golden Hurricane, 1991-95, U. Ga. Bulldogs, Athens, 1995-97, U. Minn. Golden Gophers, Mpls., 2007—13, Tex. Tech U. Red Raiders, 2013—. Asst. basketball coach US Men's Nat. Basketball Team, 1999; head coach US Olympic Basketball Team, Sydney, 2000; bd. dirs. Nat. Assn. Basketball Coaches. Founder The Tubby Smith Found., 1987—. Recipient Henry Iba award, 2003; named Jim Phelan Coach of Yr., 2005, Naismith Coll. Coach of Yr., 2003. Coached the U. Ky. to five Southeastern Conf. Titles, 1998-2001, 2003-2004 & 1 NCAA Men's Divsn. I Basketball Championship, 1998. Office: Texas Tech University Basketball Program TTU Box 42220 1701 Indiana Ave Lubbock TX 79409 Office Phone: 806-742-7700.

SMITH, VANCE CARLTON, state agency administrator, former state legislator; b. Columbus, Ga., Feb. 27, 1952; s. Vance Carlton and Reba Simmons Smith; m. Michele Holler, 1973; children: Vance Carlton III, Suzanne Grayce, John Andrew. Chmn. Harris Co. Rep. Com., 1985—87; bd. commr. Harris Co., Ga., 1987—90, chmn. Ga., 1989—90; state rep. Dist. 102 Ga., 1993—2002; mem. Human Relations & Aging Com., Retirement & Transp. Com.; house rep. Ga.; state rep. Dist. 110 Ga., 2003—04; state rep. Dist. 129 Ga., 2004—09; v.p. Vance Smith Constrn. Co., 1975—; bd. mem. First Union Bank, 1987—, W. Ga. Tech. Sch., 1991—; mem. Harris Co. Rep. Com.; commr. Ga. Dept. Transp., 2009—. Mem.: Assn. Co. Commr. Ga. (transp. bd. mem.), Harris Co. Cmty. Leadership Prog. (charter mem.), LaGrange Acad. (bd. mem. 1991—92), Harris Co. Pub. Lib. (bd. mem. 1987—), Flint River Acad. (bd. mem. 1985—87), Pine Mountain & Harris Co. C. of C. Republican. Baptist. Office: Ga Dept Transp One Georgia Ctr 600 W Peachtree NW Atlanta GA 30308 Office Phone: 404-631-1990. Office Fax: 404-631-1844.

SMITH, VME EDOM (VERNA MAE EDOM SMITH), social sciences educator, freelance photographer, writer; b. Marshfield, Wis., June 19, 1929; d. Clifton Cedric and Vilia Clarissa (Patefield) Edom; children: Teri Smith Freas, Anthony Thomas, Lynn Smith Simpson. AB in Sociology, U. Mo., 1951; MA in Sociology, George Washington, 1965; PhD in Human Devel., U. Md., 1981. Tchr. Alcohol Safety Action Program Fairfax County, Va., 1973-75; instr. sociology No. Va. C.C., Manassas, 1975-77, asst. prof., 1977-81, assoc. prof., 1981-84, prof., 1984-94, prof. emerita, 1995, coord. coop. edn., 1983-89, Chancellor's Commonwealth prof., 1991-93; adj. faculty Tidewater C.C., 1996—2002; freelance writer, editor and photographer, 1965—; dir. Truth With a Camera (photography workshops), 1994—2007; hon. dir., 2008—. Asst. prodr. history of photography program Sta. WETA-TV, Washington, 1965; rsch. and prodn. asst., photographer, publs. editor No. Va. Ednl. TV, Sta. WNVT, 1970—71; cons. migrant divsn. Md. Dept. Edn., Balt., 1977; rschr. photographer Roundabout presch. high sch. series Am. Values Sta. WNVT, 1970—71; documentary photographer Portsmouth (Va.) Redevel. and Housing Authority, 1998—2000; dir. Edom Found. Photojournalism Edn., 1994—2013. Author, photographer Middleburg and Nearby, 1988; co-author: Small Town America, 1993; contbr. photographs and articles to various publs.; author: Photojournalism, Child Growth and Development; exhibitions include Nat. Press Photographers Assn., Gordon Parks Internat. Competition, others. Mem. ednl. adv. com. Head Start, Warrenton, Va. Recipient Emmy, Ohio State Children's Programming award; Fulbright-Hays Rsch. grantee, 1993, Va. Found. Humanities and Pub. Policy grantee, 1997—99. Mem.: Va. Assn. Coop. Edn. (com. mem.). Democrat.

SMITH, WALTER JOHN, lawyer; b. Omaha, Apr. 19, 1948; s. Walter H. and Margaret A. (Ortman) S.; m. Mary Lou Dreves, June 20, 1970; children: Benjamin, Michael, Jeffrey. JD, Creighton U., 1972; LLM, Harvard U., 1975. Bar: Nebr. 1972, Tex. 1975. Law clk. to Judge E.A. Tamm US Ct. Appeals (DC cir.), 1972-73; assoc. Monen, Seidler, McGill, Festerson & Koley, Omaha, 1973-74; ptnr. Baker Botts LLP, Houston, 1975—2003, mng. ptnr., 2003—. Editor in chief Creighton Law Rev. Dir. Ctrl. Houston Inc., Fund for Tchrs., Greater Houston Partnership; trustee Riverview Sch., Ea. Sandwich, Mass.; dir. devel. bd. U. Tex. Health Sci. Ctr., Houston; bd. visitors The Univ. Cancer Found. Named a Tex. Super Lawyer, 2003—10; named one of The Best Lawyers in America, 1991—2010. Fellow: Tex. Bar Found., Houston Bar Found. (life); mem.: Houston Bar Assn., Coronado Club. Office: Baker & Botts LLP One Shell Plz 910 Louisiana St Houston TX 77002-4995 Office Phone: 713-229-1614. Office Fax: 713-229-7714. Business E-Mail: wsmith@bakerbotts.com.

SMITH, WALTER SCOTT, JR., federal judge; b. Marlin, Tex., Oct. 26, 1940; s. Walter S. and Mary Elizabeth Smith; children— Debra Elizabeth, Susan Kay BA, Baylor U., 1964, JD, 1966. Bar: Tex. Assoc. Dunnam & Dunnam, Waco, Tex., 1966-69; ptnr. Wallace & Smith, Waco, 1969-78, Haley & Fulbright, Waco, 1978-80; judge Tex. Dist. Ct., 1980-83; U.S. magistrate US Dist. Ct. (We. Dist.) Tex., 1983-84, judge Waco, 1984—2003, 2010—, chief judge, 2003—10. Named Outstanding Young Lawyer of Yr., Waco-McLennan County Bar Assn., 1976. Office: US District Courthouse 800 Franklin Ave Waco TX 76701

SMITH, WAYNE, state legislator; b. Aug. 17; m. Barenda Smith; 2 children. Lic. profl. engr.; registered pub. land surveyor. Pres. Wayne Smith & Associates, Inc. Consulting Engineers; mem. Dist. 128 Tex. House of Representatives, 2002—. Construction chmn. of bd. dirs. Harris County-Houston Sports Authority; dir. Gulf Coast Waste Disposal Authority and Coastal Water Authority. Served with US Army, Vietnam. Republican. Office: Room E2.708 Capitol Extension PO Box 2910 Austin TX 78768 also: 909 Decker Dr Ste 104 Baytown TX 77520-4441 Office Phone: 832-556-2002, 512-463-0733.

SMITH, WAYNE THOMAS, healthcare company executive; b. Jan. 29, 1946; BS, Auburn Univ, 1968, MS, 1969; M in Hosp. Adminstrn., Trinity U.; postgrad., King's Fund Coll. Hosp. Adminstrn. With Trinity Univ, 1971-73, Humana Inc, Louisville, 1973-96, v.p. ctrl. hosp. region, 1978-80, sr. v.p., 1980-85, exec. v.p., 1985-86, pres., COO group health divsn., 1986-96, also bd. dirs.; exec. v.p. Humana Health Care Ops., Louisville, 1991-96; ret. Humana, Inc., 1996; pres. CEO Community Health Systems, Brentwood, Tenn., 1996—, chmn. bd., 2001—. Exec. v.p. health plan ops., bd. dirs. Humana Health Plan, Inc., Louisville; pres. Humana Health Ins. Nev., Inc., Humana Health Plan Fla., Inc., Humana Health Plan Ohio, Inc., Humana Health Chgo. Ins. Co., Humana Kansas City, Inc.; pres., COO Humana Health Plan Tex., Prime Health Mgmt. Svcs.; pres., bd. dirs. HMPK, Inc.; bd. dirs. Praxair, Inc.; chmn. bd. Fedn. Am.'s Hosps. Bd. dirs. Gov.'s Scholars Program, Ky., Actors Theatre of Louisville, Ky. Ctr. for the Arts, The Louisville Orchestra; bd. overseers U. Louisville; mem. exec. com. Greater Louisville Fund for the Arts; past chair bd. dirs. Louisville Collegiate Sch. With U.S. Army, 1969-73, capt., 1973. Mem. Group Health Assn. Am. (bd. dirs.), Health Ins. Assn. Am. (bd. dirs.). Office: Community Health Sys 4000 Meridian Blvd Franklin TN 37067

SMITHART-OGLESBY, DEBRA LYNN, restaurant chain executive; b. Apr. 24, 1959; BA in Acctg., U. Tex.; MBA, So. Methodist U. Asst. contr. Brinker Internat., Inc., Dallas, 1985—86, contr., 1986—88, v.p., contr., 1988—91, v.p. fin., 1991, exec. v.p., CFO, 1991—97; pres. corp. services, CFO First Am. Autootive Inc., 1997—99; pres. Dekor, Inc., 1999—2000, O/S Partners, 2000—06; chmn. Denny's Corp., Spartanburg, SC, 2006—. Bd. dirs. Brinker Internat., Inc., 1991—97, Denny's Corp., 2003—, Noodles & Co. Office: Dennys Corp 203 E Main St Spartanburg SC 29319

SMITH BECKER, NANCY WOOLVERTON, public relations executive, art appraiser; b. San Antonio, July 31, 1947; d. Tillman Louis and Enid Maxine (Woolverton) Brown; m. William F. Pry II, Mar. 7, 1998 (div. July 31, 2003); m. Lawrence Becker, June 2, 2007; 1 child from previous marriage, Christina Elizabeth Woolverton Jones. Student, Ecole Nouvelle de la Suisse, Romande, Lausanne, Switzerland, 1962, Vanderbilt U., 1964; BA, So. Meth. U., 1968, postgrad., 1969-70. Cert. S.E. Paralegal Inst., Ancien Regime Christie's (London), antiques and residential contents. Tchr. spl. edn. Hot Springs Sch. Dist. (Ark.), 1970-72; reporter, soc. editor Dallas Morning News, 1974-82; soc./celebrity columnist Dallas Times Herald, 1982-91; owner, pub. High Society, Society Fax; bus. editor DFW Cmty. Newspapers divsn. Lionheart Newspapers Inc., Plano, Tex., 1999—2003; co-founder Decorative Arts Soc. Dallas, For Worth; pub. Decorative Arts Mag.; owner Personal Property Appraisal Svc., 2005—; realtor Keller Williams. Realtor, Ebby Halliday Realtors; stringer Washington Post, 1978; owner Nancy Smith Pub. Rels. Contbg. editor Ultra mag., Houston, 1981-82, Tex. Woman mag., Dallas, 1979-80, Profl. Woman mag., Dallas, 1979-80; mem. bd. advisors Ultra Mag., 1985—; columnist North Dallas People; appeared on TV series Jocelyn's Weekend, Sta. KDFI-TV, 1985, Author: Napoleon III, Empress Eugenie and Her Secret Duke of Sestoi Imperial Wedding of Old Paris: Napoleon III, Empress Eugenie and her Secret Duke of Sesto, Imperial Triangle of Napoleon III Empress Eugenie and the Intriguing Duke of Sesto: Love, Power and Rewage in Old Paris and Medrid, 2011, Napoleon III Empress Eugenie and The Duke of Sesto, Moments of Extraordinary Violence and Intensity, Dallas International with J.R. Ewing: History of Dallasites on the Original Years of Dallas, Southfork and the 1980's Gold Rush, 2013. Bd. dirs. TACA arts support orgn., Dallas, 1980—, asst. chmn. custom auction, 1978-83; judge Miss Tex. USA Contest, 1984; bd. dirs. Am. Parkinson Disease Assn. (Dallas chpt.), mem. adv. bd. Cattle Baron's Ball Com., Dallas Symphony Debutante presentations; mem. bd. dirs. Dallas Opera Women's Bd., Northwood Inst. Women's Bd., Dallas Symphony Leauge; mem. Friends of Winston Churchill Meml. and libr., Dallas Theatre Ctr. Women's Guild, Childrens' Med. Ctr. Aux.; mem. women's com. Dallas Theatre Ctr.; hon. mem. Crystal Charity Ball Com.; mem. Cmty. Coun. Greater Dallas Cmty. Awareness Goals Com. Impact '88, 1985—; com. mem. Dallas Arboretum, Preservation Dallas; co-chmn. Multiple Sclerosis San Simeon Gala, 1988; celebrity co-chmn. Greer Garson Gala of Hope 1990-91; gala chmn. Greer Garson Gala of Hope for Am. Parkinson's Disease Assn., 1991-93; chmn. gala benefit Northwood U., 1994; co-chmn. star-studded stomp Mar. Dimes, 1994; mem. Femmes du Monde spl. activities com., 1999 luncheon com., com. Dallas Coun. World Affairs; bd. dirs. Dallas Ballet's Lone Star Adagio; pub. rels. vol. Habitat for Humanity, 2005. Mem.: DAR (2nd v.p., Highland Pk. chpt. 2011—), Dallas Internat. Soc. (v.p.), Internat. Soc. Appraisers (accredited; antiques and residential contents cert.), Nat. Press Club, Soc. Profl. Journalists (v.p. coms. 1978—79), Winterthur, Flagler Mus., City of Plano Sister Cities Com., Dallas Opera Guild, Daus. of Republic of Tex. (registrar 1972), Dallas So. Meml. Assn., Dallas County Heritage Soc. (bd. dirs.), Dallas Mus. Art League, Lancaster Hist. Soc., French Heritage Soc., Decorative Arts Soc. Dallas/Ft. Worth (CEO, appraiser, co-founder), Mes Amis (1st v.p. 2007), Preservation Soc. Newport County, Dallas Glass Club (bd. dirs. Internat. Soc., recording sec.), Dallas Knife and Fork Club, Thalia Club, Rondo/Carrousel Club, The 500 Club (Dallas), Argyle Club (sec. 1983—84, 1st v.p. 2005—, pres. 2008), Pub. Affairs Luncheon Club, Trippers Club (pres. 2010—11, v.p.), Tower Club, Pk. Cities Rotary (gala chmn. 2007). Home: 5727 Covehaven Dr Dallas TX 75252-4934 Home Phone: 972-381-0418; Office Phone: 214-625-1162. Personal E-mail: nancywoolvertonsmith@tx.rr.com, decorativeartssociety@gmail.com.

SMITHEE, JOHN TRUE, state legislator, lawyer; b. Amarillo, Tex., Sept. 7, 1951; s. John J. and Mildred B. (True) S.; m. Becky Collins, Aug. 18, 1979; children: Jennifer, Rebecca, John True. BBA, West Tex. State U., Canyon, 1973; JD, Tex. Tech U., 1976. Bar: Tex. 1976, U.S. Supreme Ct., 1983. Atty. Templeton, Smithee, Hayes, Heinrich & Russell, Amarillo, Tex., 1976—; mem. Dist. 86 Tex. House of Representatives, Austin, 1985—. Mem. State Bar Tex., Amarillo Bar Assn. Republican. Office: Templeton Smithee Hayes Fields Young & Heinrich PO Box 15010 Amarillo TX 79105-5010 also: Room CAP 1W.10 Capitol PO Box 2910 Austin TX 78768 Address: 320 S Polk 1st Fl Amarillo TX 79101 Office Phone: 806-376-4641, 512-463-0702, 806-372-3327.

SMITHERAM, MARGARET ETHERIDGE, health facility administrator, director; d. Philip Fitzgerald and Mary Catharine (Dwyer) E.; m. Roy Charles McCracken, May 5, 1975; m. William Bertram Smitheram, Aug. 17, 1985. BA, Emory U., 1960; M in Health Adminstrn., Washington U., St. Louis, 1973. Registered record administr., 1960-71; spl. asst. to dir. VA Med. Ctr., Roseburg, Oreg., 1973-74; hosp. adminstrn, specialist VA Central Office, Washington, 1974-75; asst. dir. trainee VA Med. Ctr., Phila., 1976, assoc. dir. Hampton, Va., 1976--80, Buffalo, 1980-81; presdl. exchange exec. Kimberly Clark Corp., Neenah, Wis., 1981-82, Roswell, Ga., 1981-82; dir. VA Med. Ctr., Grand Island, Nebr., 1982-94; interim dir. Grand Island-Hall County Health Dept., 1996-97; instr. Cerritos Coll., 1969-70. Bd. dirs. Project 2M Coordinating Coun., Inc., Grand Island, 1985-87, Hall County Leadership Unlimited, Inc., 1990. Bd. dirs. Grand Island Area United Way, 1987-90, pres., 1989; bd. dirs. Grand Island Concert Assn, 1987-92, Ctrl. Nebr. Goodwill Industries, Inc., 1987-93, pres. 1991-92; hon. adm. Gt. Navy State of Nebr., 1987. Named Woman of Yr., Beta Sigma Phi Woman's Profl. Sorority, 1988, Bus. and Profl. Women's Club, Grand Island, Nebr. chpt., 1990, Grand Island, NE Independent Newspaper, 1991, The Independent Newspaper. Fellow Am. Coll. Healthcare Execs. (life); mem. rev. bd. State of Nebr. Foster Care, Am. Hosp. Assn., Fed. Exec. Assn. (pres. Grand Island chpt. 1987), Nebr. Hosp. Assn., Grand Island C. of C. (bd. dirs. 1988-92, legis. affairs com 1984-85, priorities com. 1984-85, govtl. affairs com. 1984-88, nominating com. 1991-92, 94-95, audit com. 1992-93, pres. club 1993-94), Rotary Internat. Club #1485 (v.p. 1998-2000, pres. 2000-2001, District 5630 Group Study Exchange Team Leader to South Korea District 3710, 1999, Paul Harris fellow). Home: 221 Trail of the Flowers Georgetown TX 78633

SMITHERMAN, RODGER MELL, state legislator; b. Montgomery, Ala., Mar. 2, 1953; m. Carole Catlin; children: Rodger II, Tonya Renee, Mary Elaine, Crystal Nicole. BBA, U. Montevallo; JD, Miles Law Sch. Atty.; law prof. Miles Coll. Law Sch.; mem. Dist. 18 Ala. State Senate, Montgomery, 1994—, pres. pro tempore, 2009—. Elder Presbyn. Ch. Mem. Birmingham C. of C., Ala. Trial Lawyers Assn., Birmingham Bar Assn. Democrat. Presbyterian. Office: 2029 Second Ave N Birmingham AL 35203 also: Ala State Senate Ala State House 11 S Union St Rm 722 Montgomery AL 36130 Office Phone: 205-322-0012, 334-242-7870. Business E-Mail: rodger.smitherman@alsenate.gov.

SMITHIES, OLIVER, geneticist, educator; b. Halifax, Eng., June 23, 1925; naturalized; m. Nobuyo Maeda. MA, PhD in Biochemistry, Balliol Coll., Oxford U., Eng., 1951; DSc (hon.), U. Chgo., 1991, Duke U., Durham, NC, 2004, U. São Paulo, 2008. Postdoc. fellow in phys. chemistry U. Wis., Madison, 1951—53, asst. prof. genetics, 1960—61, assoc. prof., 1961—63, prof., 1963—71, Leon J. Cole prof. genetics & med. genetics, 1971—80, Hilldale prof. genetics & med. genetics, 1980—88; Excellence prof. pathology and lab. medicine U. NC Sch. Medicine, Chapel Hill, 1988—. Rsch. asst., assoc. Connaught Med. Rsch. Lab., Toronto, Canada, 1953—60; mem. nat. adv. med. scis. coun. NIH, 1985—90. Contbr. articles to profl. jours. Recipient William Allen Meml. award, Am. Soc. Human Genetics, 1964, Karl Landsteiner Meml. award, Am. Assn. Blood Banks, 1984, Gairdner Found. Internat. award, 1990, 1993, NC award for sci., 1993, Alfred P. Sloan award, GM Found. Cancer Rsch. Found., 1994, CIBA award, Am. Heart Assn., 1996, Bristol-Meyers Squibb award for disting. achievement in cardiovasc./metabolic disease rsch., 1997, Internat. Okamoto award, Japan Vascular Disease Rsch. Found., 2000, Albert Lasker award for basic med. rsch., 2001, Oliver Max Gardner award, U. NC, 2002, Massry prize, 2002, Wolf prize in medicine, Israel, 2003, Nobel prize in physiology/medicine, 2007. Fellow: AAAS; mem.: NAS, Royal Soc. London (fgn.), Inst. Medicine, Genetics Soc. America (v.p. 1974, pres. 1975), Am. Acad. Arts & Scis. Office: U NC Dept Pathology & Lab Medicine CB #7525 Brinkhous Bullitt Bldg Chapel Hill NC 27599-0001 Office Phone: 919-966-6913. E-mail: oliver.smithies@pathology.unc.edu.

SMOAK, JOHN RICHARD, JR., (RICHARD SMOAK), federal judge; b. Columbus, Ga., 1943; BA, US Mil. Acad., West Point, NY, 1965; JD, U. Fla., Gainesville, 1972. Pvt. practice atty., Fla., 1973—2005; judge US Dist. Ct. (no. dist.) Fla., Panama City, 2005—. Mem. US Army, 1965—70. Office: US Dist Ct US Courthouse 30 W Government St Panama City FL 32401 Office Phone: 850-785-9761.

SMOAK, LEWIS TYSON, lawyer; b. Orangeburg, SC, Feb. 11, 1944; s. William B. and Louise (Dempsey) Smoak; m. Elizabeth Adams Babb, July 16, 1966; children: Katherine, Blair, Tyson. BA, Furman U., 1966; JD, U. SC, 1969. Bar: SC 1969, DC 1982. Founder Ogletree, Deakins, Nash, Smoak and Stewart, Greenville, SC, 1969—. Recipient Ellis Island Honor medal, 2006, Ellis Island Medal of Honor, 2006; named Supper Lawyers, Chambers USA; named one of Best Lawyers in America, 2006—07. Fellow: Coll. Labor and Employment Lawyers; mem.: ABA, Greenville Country Club, Poinsett Club, DC Bar Assn., SC Bar Assn., Greenville County Bar Assn., Doonbeg Golf Club (Ireland), Wade Hampton Golf Club (Cashiers, NC). Office: 300 N Main St Greenville SC 29601 Office Phone: 864-271-1300.

SMOAK, RANDOLPH DUNCAN, JR., surgeon; b. Bamberg, SC, May 5, 1933; MD, Med. Coll. S.C., 1959. Diplomate Am. Bd. Surgery. Intern Grady Meml. Hosp., Atlanta, 1959-60; resident surgery Med. U. S.C.-Teaching Hosps., 1962-65, resident, tchg. fellow, 1965-66; fellow surgery MD Anderson Cancer Ctr., Houston, 1966-67; surg. staff Orangeburg (S.C.) Calhoun Regional Hosp., 1967-87, emeritus staff, 1987; clin. prof. surgery Med. U. SC, Charleston, 1987—2006, emeritus clin. prof. surgery, 2006; clin. prof. surgery U.S.C. Sch. Medicine, Columbia, 86—. Fellow ACS; mem. AMA (pres. 2000-01), So. Med. Assn., Soc. Head and Neck Surgeons, So. Soc. Clin. Surgeons, Soc. Clin. Oncology. Office: 112 Cloister Cove Orangeburg SC 29115 Personal E-mail: randysmoak@earthlink.net. Business E-Mail: smoak@ama-assn.org.

SMOCK, RAYMOND WILLIAM, historian; b. Jeffersonville, Ind., Feb. 8, 1941; s. Richard and Lottie (Paciorek) S.; m. Phyllis Lee Chadwick, Feb. 12, 1961 BA, Roosevelt U., Chgo., 1966; PhD, U. Md., College Park, 1974. Rsch. asst. Md. Constl. Conv., Annapolis, 1967-68; lectr. in history U. Md., College Park, 1968-72; co-editor The Booker T. Washington Papers, 14 vols., 1972-83; pres. Instructional Resources Corp., Lanham, Md., 1976-83, Rsch. Materials Corp., College Park, 1982-83, dir., 1982-85; historian, dir. Office for Bicentennial, U.S. Ho. of Reps., Washington, 1983-89, Office of Historian, U.S. Ho. of Reps., Washington, 1989-95. Mem. editl. advisors Md. Historian, College Park, 1971—95; exec. dir. Robert C. Byrd Ctr. for Legis. Studies, Shepherd U., Shepherdstown, W.Va., 2002—. Author: A Talent for Detail: The Photographs of Miss Frances Benjamin Johnston 1889-1910, 1974, Booker T. Washington: Black Leadership in the Age of Jim Crow, 2009; co-editor: A Guide to Manuscripts in the Presidential Libraries, 1985, Masters of the House, 1998; editor: Booker T. Washington in Perspective: The Essays of Louis R. Harlan, 1988, Congress Investigates: A Critical History with Documents, 2011; author, editor: Landmark Documents on the U.S. Congress, 1998. Ford Found. fellow, 1970; recipient Philip M. Hamer award Soc. Am. Archivists, 1979 Mem. Nat. Coun. Pub. History, Assn. for Documentary Editing (pres. 1983-84), Orgn. Am. Historians, So. Hist. Assn., Soc. History in Fed. Govt. (v.p./pres.-elect 2000—), Assn. Ctrs. for Study of Congress (pres. 2005-08), W.Va. Humanities Coun. (bd. mem. 2006—), Nat. Hist. Publs. and Records Commn., Contemporary American Theatre Festival (bd. mem. 2010-). Avocations: photography, astronomy. Office Phone: 304-876-5665. Personal E-mail: raysmock@aol.com. Business E-Mail: rsmock@shepherd.edu.

SMOLEN, ROBERT LEE (BOB SMOLEN), retired military officer; b. 1952; married; 3 children. BA in Comm., Allegheny Coll., Meadville, Pa., 1974; student in Operational Readiness Tng., Vandenberg AFB, Calif., 1974; student, Air Command and Staff Coll., Maxwell AFB, Ala., 1984—85, Air War Coll., 1991—92; M in Pub. Adminstrn., U. Okla., 1976; M in Internat. Rels., Auburn U., 1985. Advanced through grades to maj. gen. USAF, 2003; Minuteman missile sys. crew mem., instr. and evaluator 91st Stategic Missile Wing, Minot AFB, ND, 1974—77; airborne missile ops. officer 4th Airborne Command Control Squadron, Ellsworth AFB, SD, 1977—79; aide to comdr. North Am. Aerospace Def. Command, Colorado Springs, 1979—80; congl. liaison officer to spl. asst. to dir. of legislative liaison Dept. Air Force, Washington, 1980—83; chief inter-agy. ops. plans branch, def. sys. mobilization planning activity US Dept. Def., 1983—84; internat. polit.-mil, affairs officer spl. actions branch Air Force Internat. Affairs, 1985—88; asst. chief of staff Air Tng. Command, Randolph AFB, Tex., 1988, exec. officer to comdr., 1988—89; dep. comdr. 12th Air Base Group, Randolph AFB, 1989—91; comdr. 750th Support Squadron, Onizuka AFB, Calif., 1992—93, 51st Support Group, Osan Air Base, Republic of Korea, 1993—95; chief inquiry divsn. Sec. of Air Force Office of Legis. Liaison, Washington, 1995, chief Senate Liaison Office, 1995—96; comdr. 72nd Air Base Wing, Tinker AFB, Okla., 1996—98; dep. dir. nuc. and counterproliferation Office of Dep. Chief of Staff of Air and Space Ops. Hdqs. USAF, Washington, 1998—99, dir. nuc. and counterproliferation, 2002—04; dir. manpower & personnel The Joint Staff, US Dept. Def., 2000—02; dir. strategic policy & arms control Nat. Security Coun., 2004—06; comdr. Air Force Dist. Washington, Bolling AFB, 2006—07; dep. adminstr. for def. programs Nat. Nuc. Security Adminstrn. US Dept. Energy, 2007—09. Decorated Disting. Svc. medal USAF, Def. Superior Svc. medal with oak leaf cluster, Legion of Merit, Def. Meritorious Svc. medal, Meritorious Svc. medal with three oak leaf clusters, Joint Svc. Commendation medal, Air Fore Commendation medal with oak leaf cluster, Joint Svc. Achievement medal, Air Force Achievement medal, Combat Readiness medal, Nat. Def. Svc. medal with two bronze stars, Global War on Terrorism Svc. medal, Korea Def. Svc. medal; Nat. and Internat. Security Program fellow, John F. Kennedy Sch. Govt., Harvard U., 2000.

SMOLENSKI, LISABETH ANN, physician; b. Pitts., Oct. 1, 1950; d. Anthony Edward and Betty Jean (Gross) S.; m. William Ward Daniels, May 24, 1980; 1 child, Kathryn Elizabeth. BA, Carlow Coll., Pitts., 1972; MD, Hahnemann U., Phila., 1982. Diplomate Am. Bd. Family Practice. Resident in family practice West Jersey Health Sys., Voorhees, N.J., 1982-85; pvt. practice, Somerville, Tenn., 1985-90, Memphis, 1990—2003; with Spectrum Pain Clinics, Franklin-Nashville, Tenn., 2003—04, Cumberland Back Pain Clinic PC, Cookeville, Tenn., 2005—, Clarksville, Tenn., 2005—. Sec. exec. com. med. staff Meth. Hosp. Somerville, 1988-90. Fellow: Am. Acad. Family Physicians. Republican. Avocation: reading. Office: Cumberland Back Pain Clinic PC 271 Med Park Dr Clarksville TN 37043-6310 also: Cumberland Back Pain Clinic PC 120 Walnut Commons Ln Ste D Cookeville TN 38501-6037 Office Phone: 931-520-8104, 931-647-5747. Business E-Mail: lsmolenski@painmgmtcenters.com.

SMOLLA, RODNEY ALAN, academic administrator, law educator; b. Pueblo, Colo., Mar. 13, 1953; s. Richard Paul and Harriet (Waskowiak) S. BA, Yale U., 1975; JD, Duke U., 1978. Bar: Ill. 1979, US Supreme Ct. 1987. Law clk. to presiding judge U.S. Ct. Appeals, Jackson, Miss., 1978-79; assoc. Mayer, Brown & Pratt, Chgo., 1979-80; asst. prof. De Paul U. Sch. Law, Chgo., 1980-81, U. Ill. Coll. Law, 1981-83; prof. U. Ark. Sch. Law, 1983-87; vis. prof. U. Denver Coll. Law, 1987-88; Arthur B. Hanson prof. constl. law Coll. of William and Mary, Williamsburg, Va., 1988-98, dir. Inst. Bill of Rights Law, 1988-96; George E. Allen prof. U. Richmond Sch. Law, Va., 1998—2007, dean, 2003—07; dean, Roy. L. Steinheimer prof. law Wash. and Lee U. Sch. Law, Lexington, Va., 2007—10; pres. Furman U., 2010—. Author: Suing the Press: Libel, The Media & Power, 1986 (cert. of merit ABA 1987), Law of Defamation, 1986, Jerry Falwell V. Larry Flynt: The First Amendment on Trial, 1988; (with Banks and Braveman) Constitutional Law: Structure and Rights in Our Federal System, 1991, 3rd edit., 1996, Free Speech in an Open Society, 1992 (William O. Douglas Prize 1993), Smolla and Nimmer on Freedom of Speech, 1994, 3rd edit., 1996, Federal Civil Rights Acts, 1994; editor: A Year in the Life of the Supreme Court, 1995 (ABA Silver Gavel award), Deliberate Intent: A Lawyer Tells the True Story of Murder by the Book, 1999. Fellow, cons. Annenberg Washington Program in Comm., 1987-96; project dir. Annenberg Libel Reform Task Force, 1988-89; reporter Bill of Rights Adv. Com. to the Commn. on the Bicentennial of US Constitution, 1989. Recipient Recipient Disting. Prof. of Yr. award, U. Ark., 1986, Outstanding Faculty award, Va. State Coun. Higher Edn., 2002. Mem. ABA, AAUP (mem. litigation com.), Ill. Bar Assn. Office: Furman University Office of President 3300 Poinsett Highway Greenville SC 29613 Office Phone: 864-294-2000.*

SMULIAN, ANDREW M., lawyer; BA, Yale U., New Haven, 1968; JD, U. Pa. Law Sch., Phila., 1974. Bar: NJ, NY, Fla. Ptnr. Akerman Senterfitt LLP, Miami, Fla., 1995—, former chmn. real estate practice, chmn., CEO of firm, 2008—. Advisor Bricknell Ave. Literary Soc.; mem. Zell-Lurie Real Estate Ctr. at Wharton. Named one of South Florida's Top Lawyers, Miami Metro Mag., Legal Elite, Fla. Trend, 2005—06, Best Lawyers in America, Fla. Real Estate Law, 2006—11, Leading Lawyers in America, Fla. Real Estate, Chambers USA, 2008—10. Mem.: Urban Land Inst. Office: Akerman Senterfitt LLP One SE Third Ave 25th Fl Miami FL 33133 Office Phone: 305-982-5613. Office Fax: 305-374-5095. Business E-Mail: andrew.smulian@akerman.com.

SMYRE, CALVIN, state legislator; b. Ga., May 17, 1948; div.; 1 child. BS in Bus. Adminstrn., Fort Valley State U. Exec. v.p. corp. affairs Synovus Fin. Corp.; mem. Dist. 92 Georgia House of Reps., Atlanta, 1974—92, asst. adminstrn. floor leader Dist. 92, 1983, mem. Dist. 132, 1993—; mem. Dem. Nat. Com., 1984, adminstrn. floor leader. Chmn. univ. sys. Ga. com.; mem. appropriations com., rules com.; chmn. rules com., Ga. Dem. Party, 2001—; mem. appropriations com., ethics com., higher edn. com., spl. rules com. Nat. sec. Nat. Black Caucus State Legislators; bd. trustees Med. Coll. Ga. Found., Morehouse Sch. Med., Jack D. Hughston Found.; chmn. bd. trustees Fort Valley State U. Found.; former nat. pres. Fort Valley State U. Nat. Alumni Assn.; bd. advisors Atlanta U. Sch. Social Work. With U.S. Army. Served in US Army, 1970. Named to Power 150, Ebony mag., 2008. Democrat. Methodist. Office: Dist 132 PO Box 120 Columbus GA 31902-0120 also: 409-G Coverdell Legislative Office Atlanta GA 30334 Office Phone: 706-563-1794. Business E-Mail: calvinsmyre@synovus.com.

SMYTH, RICH, publishing executive; b. Bronx, NY; married; 2 children. BA in Comm., Boston Coll. Dist. sales mgr. Carnation Co. (now Nestle USA), Dallas, 1985—88; advt. rep., account mgr. Southern Living mag. Southern Progress Corp. (subs. Time Inc.), NYC, 1988—92, NY mgr., 1992—96, nat. advt. dir., 1996—2000, v.p., advt. dir., 2000, v.p., pub., 2000—11; pres. Seek Publishing, Birmingham, Ala., 2011—. Office: Seek Publishing 3500 Blue Lake Dr Ste 330 Vestavia AL 35243-1910

SMYTHE, CHEVES MCCORD, internist, geriatrician, educator, dean; b. May 25, 1924; Student, Yale Coll., 1942—43; MD cum laude, Harvard, 1947. Diplomate Am. Bd. Internal Medicine, Am. Bd. Geriatrics. Intern, asst. resident Harvard Med. Svc., Boston City Hosp., 1947—49, chief resident, 1954—55; resident chest svc. Bellevue, 1949—50; rsch. fellow Presbyn. Hosp., NYC, 1950—52; assoc. medicine Med. Coll. S.C. Sch. Medicine, 1956—58, asst. prof. medicine, 1958—60, assoc. prof. medicine, 1960—66, dean, 1963—65; attending physician Wesley Meml., Cook County North Side VA Hosps., Chgo., 1967—70; with Aga Khan U. Hosp., Karachi, Pakistan, 1990—91; dean faculty health scis., prof. medicine Aga Khan U., Karachi, Pakistan, 1982—85, prof., chmn. dept. medicine, 1990—91; chief Med. Svcs. at LBJ Hosp., Houston, 1991—95; prof. divsn. gen. medicine dept. internal medicine U. Tex. Med. Sch., Houston, 1970—, dean, 1970—75, dean pro tem, 1995—96. Assoc. med. dir. Hermann Hosp., 1996—. Bd. dirs. Assn. Am. Assoc. Med. Colls., Office: U Tex Med Sch 6431 Fannin St 1-108 Houston TX 77030-1501

SNAPP, ELIZABETH, librarian, educator; b. Lubbock, Tex., Mar. 31, 1937; d. William James and Louise (Lanham) Mitchell; m. Henry Franklin Snapp, June 1, 1956 (div. Dec. 2001). BA magna cum laude, North Tex. State U., Denton, 1968, MLS, 1969, MA, 1977. Asst. to archivist Archive of New Orleans Jazz Tulane U., 1960-63; catalog libr. Tex. Woman's U., Denton, 1969-71, head acquisitions dept., 1971-74, coord. readers svcs., 1974-77, asst. to dean Grad. Sch., 1977-79, instr. libr. sci., 1977-88, acting Univ. libr., 1979-82, dir. librs., 1982—2002, dir. librs. emeritus, 2002—, univ. historian, 1995—2002; adj. prof. dept. history and govt. Tex. Woman's U., Denton, 2002—; rsch. assoc. Tex. Woman's U. Libr., Denton, 2002—. Chair-elect Tex. Coun. State U. Librs., 1988—90, chmn., 1990—92; adv. com. on libr. formula Coord. Bd. Tex. Coll. and Univ. Sys., 1981—92; Libr. Sys. Act adv. bd. Tex. State Libr. and Archives Commn., 1999—2002; del. OCLC Nat. Users Coun., 1985—87, by-laws com., 1985—86, com. on less-than-full-svcs. networks, 1986—87; trustee AMIGOS Libr. Svcs., 1994—2000, sec. bd. trustees, 1996—97, vice-chmn. bd. trustees, 1997—99, chair bd. trustees, 1999—2000; project dir. NEH consultancy grant on devel. core curriculum for women's studies, 1981—82; chmn. Blue Ribbon com. 1986 Gov.'s Commn. for Women to select 150 outstanding women in Tex. History; project dir. math./sci. anthology project Tex. Found. Women's Resources; co-sponsor Irish Lecture Series, Denton, 1968, 1970, 1973, 1978. Asst. editor Tex. Academe, 1973—76; co-editor: Read All About Her! Texas Women's History: A Working Bibliography, 1995; contbg. author Women in Special Collections, 1984, Special Collections, 1986, book reviewer Libr. Resources and Tech. Svcs., 1973—2002; contbr. articles to profl. jours. Trustee, treas. Adult Day Care of North Tex., 2002—04, v.p., 2004; sec. Denton County Dem. Caucus, 1970. Recipient Ann. Pioneer award, Tex. Woman's U., 1986, Women's Studies Vision award, 1998. Mem.: AAUW (legis. br. chmn. 1973—74, br. v.p. 1975—76, br. pres. 1979—80, state historian 1986—88, treas. 1998—99), ALA (stds. com. 1983—85), AAUP, Tex. Assn. Coll. Tchrs. (pres. Tex. Woman's U. chpt. 1976—77), So. Conf. Brit. Studies, Women's Collecting Group (chmn. ad hoc com. 1984—86), Tex. Hist. Commn. (judge for Farenbach History prize 1990—93), Tex. Libr. Assn. (program com. 1978, Dist. VII chmn. 1985—86, archives and oral history com. 1990—92, co-chair conf. program com. 1994, Tall Texan selection com. 1995—96, treas. exec. bd. 1996—99, Centennial com. 2000—02), AAUW Ednl. Found. (rsch. and awards panel 1990—94), Alliance Higher Edn. (chair coun. libr. dirs. 1993—95), Rotary Internat. (sec. local chpt. 1999—2002), Soroptomist Internat. (pres. Denton chpt. 1986—88), Women's Shakespeare Club (pres. 1967—69), Pi Delta Phi, Alpha Lambda Sigma (pres. 1970—71), Alpha Chi, Beta Phi Mu (pres. chpt. 1976 1978, sec. nat. adv. assembly 1978—79, pres. 1979—80, nat. dir. 1981—83). Methodist. Office: TWU Sta PO Box 424093 Denton TX 76204-4093 Personal E-mail: esnapp@verizon.net.

SNAPP, HARRY FRANKLIN, historian, educator; b. Bryan, Tex., Oct. 15, 1930; s. H.F. and Ethel (Manning) Snapp; m. Elizabeth Mitchell, June 1, 1956 (div. Dec. 20, 2001). BA, Baylor U., 1952, MA, 1953; PhD, Tulane U., 1963. Instr. U. Coll. Tulane U., 1960—62; asst. prof. history Wofford Coll., 1963—64, U. North Tex. (formerly North Tex. State U.), Denton, 1964—69, assoc. prof., 1969—94; dir. Tex. Rsch. Ctr. Biog. Study of Women, Denton, 1995—; pres., dir.

Read All About Her Tex. Women's Biographic Ctr., Inc., 1995—2012. Editor: Brit. Studies Mercury, 1970—84, Tex. Acad., 1973—76; co-editor: Read All About Her! Texas Women's History: A Working Bibliography, 1995, enlarged edit., 1997; author (with others): West Texas Historical Assn. Year Book, 1994, 1996; contbr. articles to profl. jours. Mem. Bridwell Assocs. of So. Meth. U., Friends of Southwestern Art, Am. Com. Irish Studies; mem. adv. com. on acad. freedom and tenure policy, coord. bd. Tex. Coll. and Univ. System. Recipient North Tex. State U. Faculty Rsch. award, 1966, 1967. Mem.: AAUP (pres. North Tex. chpt. 1968—69, pres. Southwestern regional conf. 1971—72, pres. Tex. conf. 1974—76, nat. coun. 1976—86), Butler Soc. (Ireland), Northamptonshire Record Soc., Libr. History Round Table, Libr. Rsch. Round Table, Hist. Assn. (London), Tex. State Hist. Assn., Panhandle-Plains Hist. Soc., West Tex. Hist. Assn. (bd. dirs. 1997—), Am. Hist. Assn., So. Conf. Brit. Studies (sec.-treas. 1969—84), Tulane U. Alumni Assn., Lambda Chi Alpha, Alpha Chi. Democrat. Methodist.

SNAREY, JOHN ROBERT, psychologist, educator; BS, Geneva Coll., Beaver Falls, Pa., 1969; MA, Wheaton Coll., Ill., 1973; EdD, Harvard U., Cambridge, Mass., 1982. Postdoctoral rsch. fellow dept. psychiatry Harvard U., Cambridge, Mass., 1982-84; assoc. rsch. psychologist Wellesley Coll., 1984-85; assoc. prof. human devel. and edn. Northwestern U., Evanston, Ill., 1985-87; prof., human devel. and ethics Sch. Theology and dept. psychology Emory U., Atlanta, 1987—2013, Franklin Parker prof., human devel. and ethics Sch. Theology and dept. psychology, 2014—. Mem. senate Emory U., 2001—05, pres., 2003—04, dir. moral cognition and devel. lab., 2005—. Author: How Fathers Care for the Next Generation, 1993; contbr. articles to profl. jours.; editor: Conflict and Continuity: A History of Ideas on Social Equality and Human Development, 1981, Remembrance of Lawrence Kohlberg, 1988, William James: The Varieties of Religious Experience and Moral Formation, 2003, Race-ing Moral Formation: African Am. Perspectives on Care and Justice, 2004; mem. editl. bd. Harvard Ednl. Rev., 1979—81, Jour. Psychology and Theology, 1986—90, Jour. Moral Edn., 1998—2011, Am. Ednl. Rsch. Jour., 2001—04, Fathering: A Journal of Theory, Research, and Practice, 2002—, William James Studies, 2005—. Recipient Exemplary Dissertation award, Nat. Coun. Social Studies, 1982, Kuhmereker Dissertation award, Assn. Moral Edn., 1983, Outstanding Human Devel. Rsch. award, Am. Ednl. Rsch. Assn., 1988, James D. Moran Book award, Assn. Family and Consumer Sci., 1994, Marie C. Keel, Excellence in Mentoring award, 2003, Albert Levy Sci. Rsch. award, 2007. Fellow: APA, Am. Ednl. Rsch. Assn. (divsn. E exec. bd. 1990—2000, moral devel. and edn. spl. interest group co-chair 1994—96, sec. divsn. E 1997—99, Moral Devel. and Edn. Book award 2006); mem.: William James Soc., Assn. Moral Edn. (exec. bd. 1986—2007, program chair 1997, treas. 2001—04, pres. 2004—07). Office: Emory University Rita Anne Rollins Bldg 1531 Dickey Dr Ste 354 Atlanta GA 30322-0001 Office Phone: 404-727-4185. Business E-Mail: jsnarey@emory.edu.

SNEAD, DAVID L., history professor; s. Marilyn M. Snead; m. Lori H. Hughes, May 11, 1991; children: Reagan Lindsey, Delaney Nicole, Darel Connor. PhD in History, U. Va., Charlottesville, 1997. Asst. prof. Tex. Tech U., Lubbock, 1999—2004; assoc. prof. Liberty U., Lynchburg, Va., 2004—08, chair dept. history, 2007—, prof., 2008—. Author: The Gaither Committee, Eisenhower, and the Cold War; editor: In Hostile Skies: An American B-24 Pilot in World War II, An American Soldier in World War I. Mem.: Western Front Assn., Soc. Mil. History, Soc. Historians Am. Fgn. Rels. Republican. Baptist. Home: 1385 Brandon Ct Forest VA 24551 Office: Liberty Univ Dept History Lynchburg VA 24502 Business E-Mail: dlsnead@liberty.edu.

SNEAD, GEORGE MURRELL, JR., military officer, research scientist, consultant; b. San Diego, Nov. 6, 1922; s. George Murrell and Helen (Olsen) S.; m. Kathleen Hill Dawson, Apr. 26, 1947; children: George Murrell III, James M., William M., John P., Edward W. BS, Va. Mil. Inst., 1943; MS, U. Ill., 1948; PhD, U. Va., 1953. Commd. 2d lt. U.S. Army, 1943, advanced through grades to brig. gen., 1969; with Central Germany campaign 805th Signal Co., Europe, 1945-46; Aleutian sector comdr. Alaska Communication System, 1948-50; sta. at Electronic Warfare Center Ft. Monmouth, N.J. and Ft. Huachuca, Ariz., 1953-56; student U.S. Army Command and Gen. Staff Coll., 1956-57; signal adviser MAAG Vietnam, 1957-58; signal officer Dept. Army, 1958-60; acting dir. research ballistic missile def. Advanced Research Projects Agy., 1960; with U.S. Army Satellite Communications Agy. Ft. Monmouth, 1960-63; student Nat. War Coll., 1963-64; div. signal officer 24th Inf. Div., 1964-65; comdg. officer 7th Signal Group, 1965; dir. Communication /ADP Lab. Ft. Monmouth, 1966-68; exec. asst. chief of staff Communications Electronics, Dept. Army, 1968; dir. army research Dept. Army Washington, 1968-71; comdr. Army Rsch. Offices-Europe, Asia and Durham, 1968—71; mem. Def. Rsch. Coordinating Com., 1968—71; chmn. Army Ops. Rsch. Symposia, 1969—71, Nat. Jr. Sci. and Humanities Symposia, 1969—71; dep. comdr. Army Strategic Communications Command, 1971-73; prin. scientist Gen. Research Corp. McLean, Va., 1973-82; pres. Nat. Sci. Ctr. Found., Burke, Va., 1982-84. Chmn. bd. Am. Fed. Savs. & Loan Assn., Lynchburg, Va., 1985-86; sci./bus. cons., 1986—. Active Boy Scouts Am., 1958-68; bd. dirs. Ctrl. Youth Summer Activities, Ft. Monmouth, 1960-63, Arthritis Found., Washington, 1981-84, Lynchburg Symphony, 1990-95; pres. Acad. Music Theatre, Lynchburg, 1985-95; trustee, vice chmn. bd. dirs. Westminster-Canterbury, Lynchburg, 1991-99; trustee Sci. Mus. Va., 1995-2001; elder Presbyn. Ch., 1986—. Decorated D.S.M., Legion of Merit with two oak leaf clusters, Six Campaign medals, Army Commendation medal with 4 oak leaf clusters, Galantry Cross, Republic Vietnam Civil Actions medal. Mem. Assn. U.S. Army, Armed Forces Communications and Electronics Assn. (sec. Washington chpt. 1968-69), Sigma Xi, Kappa Alpha. Office: PO Box 3306 Lynchburg VA 24503-0306

SNEAD, THOMAS G., JR., healthcare executive; b. Halifax County, Va. BS in Acctg. with honors, Va. Commonwealth U., 1976. CPA Va. Soc., Am. Inst. Staff pub. acctg., fin. exec. KPMG LLP, Richmond; with KPMG, 1976; mgr., fin. Trigon Healthcare, Inc., 1985, CFO, sr. v.p., 1990, pres., COO, 1997—2000, CEO, chmn., 2000—02; CEO Anthem Southeast Inc. (subs. of WellPoint Inc.), 1999—2002, chmn., 2000—02; pres. Anthem Health Plans of Va., Inc., 2001—, WellPoint Inc., 2002—04; CEO, pres., southeast region, fin. compliance dir., acctg. and budget dir. and group bus. fin. officer Wellpoint Inc., 2004—06; chmn. LandAmerica Fin. Group Inc., 2009; treas. Va. Commonwealth U. Health System Authority. Bd. dirs. Va. Commonwealth U. Health System Authority., America's Health Ins. Plans., Anthem Southeast, Inc., 1999—, LandAmerica Fin. Group Inc., 2001. Mem. Va. Commonwealth U. Bus.Coun.; bd. dirs. Am. Assn. of Health Plans, Johns Hopkins Medicine, Maymont Found., Richmond Renaissance, SunTrust Regional Bd., Blue Cross Blue Shield Assn. Health Policy, Forum Club, St. Catherine's Sch. Office: Anthem Health Plans of Virginia Inc 2015 Staples Mill Rd Richmond VA 23230 Office Phone: 804-354-7000. Office Fax: 804-354-2578. Business E-Mail: thomas@vhcf.org.

SNEDEKER, BRANDT, professional golfer; b. Nashville, Dec. 8, 1980; m. Mandy Snedeker; 1 child. Grad. in Comm., Vanderbilt U., Nashville, 2004. Mem. Nationwide Tour, 2004—06, PGA Tour, 2007—. Mem. US team Ryder Cup, 2012. Named Male Golfer of Yr., Southeastern Conf., 2003, Rookie of Yr., PGA Tour, 2007, FedEx Cup Champion, 2012. Achievements include winning Nationwide Tour events including: Scholarship America Showdown at Somerby, 2006, Permian Basin Charity Golf Classic, 2006; winning PGA Tour events including: Wyndham Championship, 2007; The Heritage, 2010; Farmers Insurance Open, Tour Championship, 2012. Office: c/o PGA Tour 112 PGA TOUR Blvd Ponte Vedra Beach FL 32082

SNEED, RONALD ERNEST, retired project engineer, educator; b. Oxford, NC, Nov. 23, 1936; s. Henry Ernest and Jewel Leigh (Hughes) S.; m. Shelba Jean Walters, June 8, 1958; children: Kathy Geneva Grosvenor, Jennie Leigh Berrier. BS in Agrl. Engring., N.C. State U., 1959, PhD in Biol. and Agrl. Engring., 1971. Registered profl. engr., NC; cert. irrigation designer, contractor, landscape irrigation auditor, and irrigation specialist. Sales trainee John Deere Co., 1959-60; ext. specialist NC State U., 1960-62, ext. instr., 1962-69, 70, ext. asst. prof., 1971-75, ext. assoc. prof., 1971-80, prof., 1980-92, prof. emeritus, 1993—; project engr. Agri-Waste Tech., Inc., 1993-2000, Irrigation Consulting, Inc., 1995—; project engr. divsn. soil and water NC Dept. Environment and Natural Resources, 1997-99, project engr. divsn. water quality, 2003—05, Carolina Turkeys, 2004—06, NC Dept. Adminstrn., 2004—05. Maj. gen. U.S. Army, 1960-95, ret. Recipient Outstanding Paper award So. region Am. Soc. Hort. Sci., 1986, 91; Ronald E. Sneed Irrigation Soc., Inc. scholarship established in his honor, 1991, Dr. Ronald Sneed Excellence award, Carolinas Irrigation Assn. Fellow Am. Soc. Agrl.& Bio Engrs. (ednl. aids competition Blue Ribbon 1963-64, 68, 78-79, 85, 89, 91-92, Gunlogson Countryside Engring. award 1992, Outstanding Paper award 1984, Heermann Sprinkler Irrigation award 2009.), The Irrigation Assn. (life tech. mem., Man of Yr. 1981), NC Irrigation Soc., Inc. (Oustanding Contbn. to Irrigation award 1973, former tech. advisor), Soil and Water Conservation Soc., Carolinas Irrigation Assn. (hon.), NC Irrigation Contractors Licensing Bd. (chairperson 2008-), Res. Officers Assn. (life), Civitan (Civitan of Yr. 1998). Democrat. Baptist. Office: 3405 Malibu Dr Raleigh NC 27607-6505 Office Phone: 919-782-7867. Business E-Mail: rsneed2@bellsouth.net.

SNEED, THOMAS K., oil industry executive; b. Dayton, Ohio; B in Computer and Info. Sci., Ohio State U. Computer applications programmer Marathon Oil Corp., Findlay, Ohio, 1981—84, data base mgmt., 1984—92, supr., corp. sys. and programming, 1992—97, mgr. info. tech. svcs., 1997—98; mgr. computer svcs. Speedway SuperAmerica, LLC, Enon, 1998—2000, v.p. info. tech. svcs., 2000—02; mgr. info. tech. svcs. Marathon Ashland Petroleum, LLC, Findlay, 2002—03; chief info. officer Marathon Oil Corp., Houston, 2003—. Office: Marathon Oil Corp Headquarters 5555 San Felipe Rd Houston TX 77056-2723

SNIDER, JAMES RHODES, radiologist; b. Pawnee, Okla., May 16, 1931; s. John Henry and Gladys Opal (Rhodes) S.; m. Lynadell Vivion, Dec. 27, 1954; children: Jon, Jan. BS, U. Okla., 1953, MD, 1956. Intern Edward Meyer Meml. Hosp., Buffalo, 1956—57; resident radiology U. Okla. Med. Ctr., 1959—62; radiologist Holt-Krock Clinic and Sparks Regional Med. Ctr., Ft. Smith, Ark., 1962—66; dir. Fairfield Comty. Land Co., Little Rock, 1968—87, Fairfield Comtys., Inc., 1968—87. Assoc. editor: Computerized Tomography, 1976—88. Mem. Ark. Bd. Pub. Welfare, 1969—71; bd. visitors U. Okla.; bd. dirs. U. Okla. Assn., 1967—70, U. Okla. Alumni Devel. Fund, 1970—74. Lt. comdr. USNR, 1957—62. Mem.: AMA, Am. Roentgen Ray Soc., Radiol. Soc. N.Am., Am. Coll. Radiology, Phi Beta Kappa, Alpha Epsilon Delta, Beta Theta Pi. Home: 5814 Cliff Dr Fort Smith AR 72903-3845 Office: 1500 Dodson Ave Fort Smith AR 72901-5128

SNIDER, ROBERT LARRY, management consultant; b. Muskogee, Okla., Aug. 10, 1932; s. George Robert and Kathryn (Smiser) S.; m. Gerlene Rose Tipton, Nov. 26, 1953; children: Melody Kathryn Porter, Rebecca Lee. BS in Indsl. Engring., U. Houston, 1955, postgrad., 1956, Pomona Coll., 1960. Cert. mgmt. cons. Instr. U. Houston Coll. Engring., 1955—58; sr. indsl. engr. Sheffield Steel Corp., Houston, 1958—59, Kaiser Steel Co., Fontana, Calif., 1959-60; cons. Arthur Young & Co., LA, 1960-61; mgmt. analyst Iranian Oil Exploration & Producing Co., Masjidi-Suliman, Iran, 1961—65; v.p., Dallas office mgr. operating methods divsn. Booz, Allen & Hamilton, Inc., 1966—68, v.p. internat. prodn. and inventory control divsn., 1968—69; prin., gen. cons. practice Peat Marwick Mitchell, CPAs, Houston, 1969-71; exec. v.p. mfg. Sterling Electronics Corp., Houston, 1971-72, COO, pres., 1972-77; sr. electronics CEO, pres. Rapoca Energy Corp., Cin., 1977-79; mng. ptnr., cons. Coopers & Lybrand, Southwest, Houston, 1979-81; mng. dir. S.W. region Korn Ferry Internat., Houston, 1981—83; ptnr.-in-charge Houston Mgmt. Cons. Practice, 1983—91; ptnr. cons. Southwest Enterprise Coopers & Lybrand, Houston, 1991-92, ptnr. S.W. Mfg. Cons. Process Improvement Group, 1992-93, internat. cons. ptnr., 1993-95; mng. ptnr. RLS Profl. Svcs. LLC, 1995—. Chmn., dir L&G Snacks, 1997—2000. Trustee Gene Cragg Caring Forever Found., 1997—99; sr. trustee R. Larry and Gerri R. Snider Native Am. scholarship trust Cullen Coll. Engring., U. Houston, 2004—; sr. trustee Melody Snider, Womens Indsl. Engring. scholarship trust U. Houston, Cullen Coll. Engring., 2006—; mem. Cullen Coll. Leadership bd. U. Houston, 1995—; past chmn. bd. mem. found. bd. and adminstrv. bd. Chapelwood Meth.Ch.; former mem. adminstrv. bd. Memorial Dr. Meth. Ch., Houston, 1997—99; sr. trustee United Meth. Found. Remainder Trust, 2002—; mem. stewardship com. 1st United Meth. Ch., Conroe, Tex., 2005—, mem. prayer & healing team, 2009—, mem. Conroe Pastor Parish Comittee and Usher, 2010—; deacon, steward 1st Christian Ch., Conroe, Tex., 2003—05; mem. pastor Danish Com., 2010—; past bd. dirs., exec. com. Houston Jr. Achievement; ret. exec. com. Houston Grand Opera, bd. dirs.; sr. trustee Tipton-Snider Minister Edn. Fund., 1999—; mem. Bridge Builder Soc. Cullen Coll. Engring. U. Houston, 2006—, mem. dean's advisory com. Cullen Coll Engring., 2005—. With C.E. AUS, 1956. Recipient Outstandng Mil. Engr. award Soc. Mil Engrs., 1955; named Disting. Alumni, Cullen Coll. Engring., U. Houston, 1991, Disting. Alumni Lifetime Achievement award, 2013, named Disting. Indsl. Engring. Alumni, U. Houston Cullen Coll. Engring., 2005. Mem.: Cherokee Hist. Soc., First United Meth. Ch. Conroe, U. Houston Alumni Assn. (life; exec. com. 1985—94, pres. and chmn. bd. 1990—93, mem. Cir. of Excellence 2003—, bd. dir.), Phi Kappa Phi, Phi Theta Kappa. Republican. Methodist. Avocations: travel, fishing. Home and Office: 9387 Escondido Dr Willis TX 77318-6621 Personal E-mail: rlarry32@yahoo.com. Business E-Mail: rlarry32@hotmail.com.

SNIDER, STEPHEN A., oil industry company executive; Gen. mgr., Air Compressor Ops. Tidewater Compression, 1975, worked, Western US Ops., 1981—83, sr. v.p., Compression, 1991; pres. Exterran GP, LLC, 2006; COO Exterran Partners LP, 2008; pres., CEO Exterran Holdings, Inc., 1998, pres., 2007—08, COO, 2008; pres. Universal Compression Holdings GP, LLC, 2006; chmn. Universal Compression Holdings Inc., 2006; COO Universal Compression Holdings GP, LLC, 2008, chmn., CEO, 2006—; chmn. Exterran Inc. (formerly Universal Compression Inc.), 2006—09; CEO Exterran Holdings Inc. (formerly Universal Compression Holdings Inc.), 2007—09; chmn. Seahawk Drilling, Inc., Houston, 2009—. Former bd. dirs. T-3 Energy Svcs. Inc., 2003; bd. dirs. Exterran Holdings Inc., 1998—, Energen Corp., 2000—; chmn. UCO GP LLC, 2006—. Bd. dirs. Meml. Hermann Hosp. Sys. Mailing: Seahawk Drilling Inc Ste 2700 5 Greenway Plz Houston TX 77046 Office Phone: 281-836-7000. Business E-Mail: Stephen.Snider@exterran.com.

SNIVELY, STEPHEN WAYNE, lawyer; b. Danville, Ill., Apr. 27, 1949; s. Roberts Eyster and Margaret Louise Snively; m. Heather Lea Patten, Mar. 19, 1988; children: Toby, Ben, Madeline, Taylor. BA, U. Ill., 1971, JD, 1975. Bar: Ill. 1975, US Supreme Ct., Fla. 1980. Assoc. Kavanagh, Scully, Sudow, White & Frederick, Peoria, Ill., 1975-80, Maguire, Voorhis & Wells, P.A., Orlando, Fla., 1980—; merged with Holland & Knight LLP, Orlando, 1998—. Seminar speaker, 1987, hon. consul Namibia, Fla., 2007-, founder, pres. scholarships Namibia, Inc. Contbr. articles to profl. jours. Bd. dirs. Found. for Orange County Pub. Schs., Orlando, 1987-96, officer, 1987-96, pres., 1993-94, chmn., 1994-96; bd. dirs. Found. for Hospice of Ctrl. Fla., Inc., 1995-96; treas., bd. dirs. HCF Found., Inc., 1996—, pres., 1998—. Mem. ABA (retail leasing com.), Fla. Bar (liaison to land surveyor com. 1982—), Orange County Bar Assn., Internat. Coun. Shopping Ctrs., Fla. C. of C. (Leadership Fla. 1991-92), Fla. Zool. Soc. (sec., bd. dirs. 1991-96), Tiger Bay Club, Phi Beta Kappa, Northland-A Ch. Distributed. Republican. Avocations: running, writing, photography. Office: Holland & Knight LLP 200 S Orange Ave Ste 2600 Orlando FL 32801-3453 Office Phone: 407-244-1112. E-mail: stephen.snively@hklaw.com.

SNOW, JOHN J., state legislator; b. Asheville, NC, Oct. 24, 1945; s. John J. Snow and Dorothy Nix Snow Mason; m. Sheila Gossett Snow. Atty., 1971—72; ct. judge, 30th jud. Dist., 1976—86; chief dist. ct. judge, 1986—2004; state senator Dist. 50 NC, 2005—10. Democrat. Methodist. Office Phone: 919-733-5875. Business E-Mail: John.Snow@ncleg.net.

SNOWDEN, GREG (ELTON GREGORY SNOWDEN), state legislator; b. Meridian, Miss., May 30, 1954; s. Elton Monroe and Almeta (Civington) Snowden; m. Renee Campbell, Dec. 20, 1975; children: Emily Gay, Katharine Covington. BA in Hist., magna cum laude, U. Ala., 1976; JD, Vanderbilt U., Nashville, 1979. Bar: Fla. 1979, US Ct. Appeals (5th cir.) 1979, Miss. 1981, US CT. Appeals (11th cir.) 1981. Assoc. Holland & Knight, Bartow, Fla., 1979—80, Lakeland, Fla., 1980—81, Bourdeaux & Jones, Meridian, Fla., 1981—84, ptnr., 1984—99; mem. Dist. 83 Miss. House of Reps., 2000—. Del. Rep. Nat. Conv., 1988. Mem.: ABA, U. Ala. Nat. Alumni Assn. (nat. v.p. 1990—92), Vanderbilt U. Alumni Assn., Fla. Bar, Miss. Bar, U. Ala. Million Dollar Band Assn. (pres. 1995—97), Downtown Meridian Optimist Club, Greater Meridian Jaycees (pres. 1985), Phi Beta Kappa. Republican. Baptist. Mailing: PO Box 3807 Meridian MS 39303-3857 Office Phone: 601-693-5700. Business E-Mail: gsnowden@house.ms.gov, greg@gregsnowden.com.

SNOWDEN, LAWRENCE FONTAINE, retired air transportation executive, retired military officer; b. Charlottesville, Va., Apr. 14, 1921; s. Lawrence Fontaine Snoddy and Beatrice M. (Huffman) S.; m. Martha Roselyn Ham, Nov. 17, 1942; children: John Stephen, Brian Fontaine. Student, Stetson U., 1938-39; BS, U. Va., 1942; MA, Northwestern U., 1950; postgrad., Harvard U., 1968; grad., Indsl. Coll. Armed Forces, 1967. Commd. 2d lt. USMC, 1942, advanced through grades to lt. gen., 1975; comdr. 7th Marine Regt., Vietnam, 1966; ops. officer III Marine Amphibious Force, Vietnam, 1967; asst. dir. personnel Hdqrs. Marine Corps, Washington, 1968-69, dir. systems support group, 1969-70; dir. Marine Corps Devel. Ctr., Quantico, Va., 1970-72; chief of staff U.S. Forces, Japan, 1972-75; U.S. chmn. UN Bd., Japan, 1973-75; chief of staff Hdqrs. U.S. Marine Corps, 1977-79; ret., 1979; v.p. Far East Internat. Service Co. Hughes Aircraft Co., 1979-86, group v.p. Internat. Ground Systems Group Fullerton, Calif., 1986-88; pres. Snowden Internat. Assocs., Tallahassee, Fla., 1988—. Recipient Silver Beaver award Boy Scouts Am., Disting. Eagle Scout award; decorated Disting. Svc. medals (2), Legion of Merit (5), Army Commendation medal, Navy Commendation medal, Purple Heart (2), Cross of Gallantry (3) Vietnam, Second Order of Sacred Treasure Japan) Mem. Marine Corps League, Am. C. of C. in Japan, Marine Corps Assn., Econ. Club Fla., Sigma Nu. Home and Office: 4425 Meandering Way Tallahassee FL 32309

SNYDER, CHARLES AUBREY, lawyer; b. Bastrop, La., June 19, 1941; s. David and Shirley Blossom (Haas) S.; m. Sharon Rae Veta, Aug. 29, 1963; children: David Veta, Shelby Haas, Claire Frances. BBA, Tulane U., 1963; JD, La. State U., 1966. Bar: La. 1966. Assoc. firm. Milling Benson Woodward, LLP and predecessors, New Orleans, 1966-69, ptnr., 1969—. Bd. dirs. Terre aux Boeufs Land Corp., Kemper and Leila Williams Found., v.p., 2004-07, pres., 2007—. Bd. dirs. New Orleans Speech and Hearing Ctr., pres., 1978-80; bd. dirs. City Pk. Commn., 1991-98, pres., 1995, dir. emeritus, 1999—; bd. dirs. New Orleans Mus. Art, 1996-2002, 04—, v.p., 1998-99, 2007—m sec., 1999-2000. Fellow Am. Bar Found., La. Bar Found.; mem. ABA, La. Bar Assn. (chmn. sect. on corp. and bus. law 1982-83), New Orleans Bar Assn., Am. Law Inst., La. Law Inst. (coun. 2000—), Plimsoll Club, Bienville Club, Beta Gamma Sigma. Home: 74724 River Rd Covington LA 70435-2222 Office Phone: 504-569-7230. E-mail: csnyder@millinglaw.com.

SNYDER, DANIEL, professional sports team owner; b. Nov. 23, 1964; m. Tanya Snyder. Founder, chmn., CEO Snyder Comm., Inc. (sold to Havas), 1985—2000; chmn. bd., owner Washington Redskins, 1999—; non-exec. chmn. Six Flags Inc., 2005—; founder, investor Red Zone LLC, 2005—. Bd. dirs. McLeod USA, Ventiv Health; mem., broadcast com. and ventures com. NFL. Bd. dirs. Ctr. for Missing and Exploited Children, Parents in Charge; exec. leadership cabinet Martin Luther King, Jr. Nat. Meml. Found. Project; bd. dirs. Wash. Children's Nat. Med. Ctr.; founder Wash. Redskins Leadership Coun. Named one of The Most Influential People in the World of Sports, Bus. Week, 2007, The Most Powerful People in D.C., GQ mag., 2007, Forbes 400: Richest Americans, 2009. Mem.: Wash. Bd. Trade, Bus. Executives for Nat. Security. Office: c/o Washington Redskins 21300 Redskin Park Rd Ashburn VA 20147

SNYDER, DONALD EDWARD, SR., finance company executive; b. Rochester, NY, Nov. 10, 1928; s. Benjamin Orman and Arlien Henrietta (Wing) S.; m. Dorothy Edna Stanke, Oct. 16, 1954; children— Donald Edward, Anne Arlien Snyder Marone, Barbara Lynn Snyder Mitchell, Richard John Snyder. AB, Cornell U., 1950, JD, 1952; postgrad., Ind. U., 1962. Bar: N.Y. 1953. Pvt. practice law, 1953-56; with Eastman Savs. and Loan Assn., 1956-68, pres., 1970-75, chmn. bd., 1979-88; asst. to treas. Eastman Kodak Co., Rochester, 1968-70, gen. credit mgr., 1975-77, with Comptroller's div., 1977-78, asst. treas., 1978-79, treas., 1979-88; chmn. Eastman Kodak Credit Corp., 1985-88; chief exec. officer, chmn. bd., pres. Corp. Officers and Dirs. Assurance Ltd., Hamilton, Bermuda, 1990-93. Bd. dirs. Greater Rochester chpt. Epilepsy Found. Am., 1979-85, Allendale Mut. Ins. Co., 1983-92; bd. dirs. Luth. Ch.-Mo. Synod, 1983-95; vice chmn. bd., chmn. fin. com., mem., chmn. audit com., 1989-95; bd. dirs., mem. exec. com. ACE Ltd., 1985-90, EXEL Ltd., 1985-90, CODA Ltd., 1986-93; mem. investment rev. com. United Way of Greater Rochester, 1979-2000; trustee Seneca Zool. Soc., 1983-90. With USNR, 1946-48. Mem. N.Y. State Bar Assn., Monroe County Bar Assn., Rochester C. of C. (trustee 1980-86), Cornell Club (Rochester),

Phi Kappa Tau (nat. fin. advisor, mem. nat. coun. 1988-95, treas., mem. exec. com. Phi Kappa Tau Found. 1991-2002), Nat. Assn. Corporate Treas.(founding dir., first chmn. 1982). Home and Office: 14 Hidden Springs Dr Pittsford NY 14534-2897 also: 2700 N A1A Ste 705 Fort Pierce FL 34949

SNYDER, HERB, state legislator; b. Winchester, Va., Sept. 7, 1953; m. Stephanie Shaffer; children: Jason, Rod, Terra, Mariah, Herb II, Joseph. BS, Shepherd Coll., 1977. Owner, dir. Hydrochem Labs.; mem. Dist. 16 W.Va. State Senate, Charleston, 1996—2004, 2009—, vice chair Govt. Orgn. Com. & Interstate Cooperation Com., mem. Agr. Com., Econ. Devel. Com., Health and Human Resources Com., Judiciary Com. & Labor Com. Chmn. Jefferson County Solid Waste Authority, 1991-96; mem. Jefferson County Commn., 1991-96. Democrat. Methodist. Office: State Capitol Complex Rm 217W, Bldg 1 1900 Kanawha Blvd E Charleston WV 25305-0009 Mailing: PO Box 400 Shenandoah Junction WV 25442 Office Phone: 304-357-7957. E-mail: herb.snyder@wvsenate.gov.

SNYDER, JAMES C., JR., lawyer, consumer products company executive; BA, Wake Forest Univ.; JD, George Washington Univ. Bar: Ga., DC, Pa. Ptnr. litigation practice King & Spalding, Atlanta, 1989—2001; corp. counsel Home Depot, Atlanta, 2001—04, v.p. litigation, 2004—06, v.p., assoc. gen. counsel legal & risk mgmt., 2006—09, acting gen. counsel, 2007; sr. v.p., gen. counsel, sec. Family Dollar Stores, Inc., Matthews, NC, 2009—. Bd. dir. Spl. Olympics, Atlanta. Mem.: ABA, State Bar Ga. Mailing: Family Dollar Stores Inc PO Box 1017 Charlotte NC 28201-1017*

SNYDER, JOHN JOSEPH, bishop emeritus; b. NYC, Oct. 25, 1925; s. John Joseph and Katherine Marie (Walsh) Snyder. Ordained priest Diocese of Bklyn., NY, 1951, sec. to bishops, 1957-72; assoc. pastor St. Mel's Parish, Flushing, NY, 1951-57; ordained bishop, 1973; aux. bishop Diocese of Bklyn., 1973—79; bishop Diocese of St. Augustine, Fla., 1979—2000, bishop emeritus, 2000—. Roman Catholic. Office: 5 Casa San Pedro 1714 State Rd 13 Ste 6 Jacksonville FL 32259 Office Phone: 904-262-3200. Office Fax: 904-262-0698.

SNYDER, JOHN L., music educator; b. Spokane, Wash., Jan. 1, 1950; s. John L. and Katherine Snyder. MusB, Mich. State U., East Lansing, 1972, MusM, 1974; PhD, Ind. U., Bloomington, 1982. Vis. instr. music Okla. State U., Stillwater, 1974—75; vis. asst. prof. music U. Wis., Milw., 1982—83; asst. prof. music Nicholls State U., Thibodaux, La., 1983—85, U. Houston, 1987—93, assoc. prof. music, 1993—2010, prof., music, 2010—. Author: Theinred of Dover's De legitimis ordinibus pentachordorum et tetrachordorum: A Critical Text and Translation, with an Introduction, Annotation, and Indices, 2006; editor: Samuel Coleridge-Taylor, Symphonic Variations on an African Air, 2007, Samuel Coleridge-Taylor, Symphony in A minor, Opus 8, with the Earlier Finales and Idyll, Opus 44, 2013; contbr. chapters to books, articles to profl. jours. Fellow: Mannes Inst. Advanced Studies in Music Theory; mem.: Plainsong and Mediaeval Music Soc., Tex. Soc. Music Theory (pres. 1994—97), Internat. Musicological Soc., Am. Musicological Soc., Soc. Music Theory, Pi Kappa Lambda (sec. zeta tau chpt. 1989—94), Phi Mu Alpha Sinfonia. Avocations: birdwatching, hiking, photography, canoeing, camping. Office: Univ Houston 120 Moores Sch Music Bldg Houston TX 77204-4017 Business E-Mail: jlsnyder@uh.edu.*

SNYDER, ROBERT ALAN, paper company executive; b. North Tonawanda, NY, June 14, 1948; s. Milton U. and Monica M. (McKernan) Snyder; m. Carmel Mary Brady, June 13, 1970; children: Jacqueline Maureen, Robert Milton. BS, SUNY, Syracuse, 1970. Various positions Kruger, Inc.; gen. mgr. KTG USA (subs. Kruger, Inc.); various positions Alliance Forest Products US Corp.; process supr. Kimberly-Clark, Niagara Falls, NY, 1970—72; various positions, including product devel. engr. Great Northern Paper Co., Millinocket, Maine, 1972—75; gen. supt. Midtec/Nitec, Niagara Falls, 1975—77; coating supt., gen. supt. Mead Paper Corp., Chillicothe, Ohio, 1977—83; gen. supt., coated north mill Boise Cascade Co., Rumford, Maine, 1983—85; prodn. mgr. Bear Island Paper Co., Doswell, Va., 1985; bd. dirs. Orchids Paper Products Co., pres., CEO, 2007—. Contbr.: articles to profl. jours. Bd. dirs. March of Dimes, Chillicothe, 1980—82. Recipient Dept. Safety award, Mead Paper Corp., 1981—82, Gold Star award, 1981. Mem.: Paper Industry Mgmt. Assn., TAPPI (additives com. 1985—). Roman Catholic. Avocations: skiing, golf. Home: 105 Riverside Dr Ashland VA 23005-3110 Office: Orchids Paper Products Co 4826 Hunt St Pryor OK 74361 Office Phone: 918-825-0616. Business E-Mail: rasnyder@orchidspaper.com.

SNYDER, ROBERT LYMAN, materials scientist, educator; b. Plattsburgh, NY, June 5, 1941; s. George Michael and Dorothy (Lyman) M.; m. Sheila Nolan, Sept. 1, 1963; children: Robert N., Kristina Gardner. BA, Marist Coll., 1963; PhD, Fordham U., 1968. Postdoctoral fellow NIH U. Pitts., 1968; NRC fellow NASA Elec. Rsch. Ctr., Cambridge, Mass., 1969; asst. prof. ceramic sci. Alfred (N.Y.) U., 1970-77, assoc. prof., 1977-83, prof., 1983-96, dir. Inst. Ceramic Superconductivity, 1987-96; prof., chmn. dept. materials sci. and engring. Ohio State U., Columbus, 1996—2002; prof., chmn. Sch. Materials Scis. and Engring. Ga. Inst. Tech., Atlanta, 2003—. Vis. prof. Lawrence Livermore (Calif.) Lab., 1977, 78, U.S. Nat. Bur. Stds., Gaithersburg, Md., 1980, 81, Siemens AG Ctrl. Rsch. Labs., Munich, 1983, 91; invited prof. U. Rennes, France, 1995. Author: Introduction to X-Ray Powder Diffractometry, 1996; author, editor 8 books; contbr. chpts. to books and over 300 articles to profl. jours. Deputy mayor Village of Alfred, 1973-77; pres. Alfred Vol. Fire Co., 1979-88. Recipient Chancellor's award SUNY, 1980, numerous research grants; named Faculty Exch. scholar SUNY, 1978-96. Fellow Am. Ceramic Soc. (Outstanding Educator award 1999), Am. Soc. Metals (disting.), Internat. Ctr. Diffraction Data (Hanawalt award, 2004); mem. TMS (Leadership award 2002, Educator award 2008), NAS (U.S. nat. com. on crystallography 1991-95, Codata 2001—06), Nat. Inst. Ceramic Engrs., Am. Crystallography Assn. (chmn. applied crystallography div. 1988-92), Materials Rsch. Soc., Ceramic Ednl. Coun., Internat. Ctr. Diffraction Data (bd. dirs. 1986-92, elected chmn. bd. dirs. 1996-2000), Internat. X-ray Analysis Soc. (pres. 2000-2001), Edward Orton Jr. Ceramic Found. (bd. dirs. 1996—), Alfred and Allegany County Fire Assn., Sigma Xi, Phi Kappa Phi. Democrat. Achievements include numerous patents for practical superconductors. Office: Ga Inst Tech Sch Materials Sci and Engring 771 Ferst Dr Atlanta GA 30332-0245 Home: 195 14th St NE Ste 1 Atlanta GA 30309-2682 Office Phone: 404-894-2888. Business E-Mail: robert.snyder@mse.gatech.edu.

SNYDER, SHARON VETA, management consultant, educator; d. G. John and Margaret Veta; m. Charles A. Snyder, Aug. 29, 1963 (dec. Oct. 2010); children: David Veta, Shelby Snyder Hammer, Claire Frances. BA, La. State U., Baton Rouge, 1965; MBA, U. New Orleans, 1981. Adj. faculty, coll. bus. adminstrn. U. New Orleans, 1985—; dir. to v.p. Veta Land and Investment, Inc., Wyo.; asst. vice chancellor, tech. transfer La. State U. Med. Ctr. (now La. State Health Scis. Ctr.), 1989—92; pres., founder SVS Inc. Mgmt. Consultants, Covington, La., 1992—2003. Contbr. articles to profl. jours. Com. mem. La. Philharm. Symphony, New Orleans, 2007. Mem.: New Orleans Mus. Art, Statewide Adv. Coun., Northshore Out-Reach (co chair 2008—11), Rotary Club New Orleans (program chmn. 2004—05), Beta Gamma Sigma, Phi Kappa Phi. Office: U New Orleans COBA 2000 Lakaeshore Dr New Orleans LA 70148

SNYDER, WILLIAM BURTON, insurance company executive; b. Clarksburg, W.Va., July 9, 1929; s. William Burton and Mary Catherine (Cornwell) Snyder; m. Georgie Gaye, Oct. 27, 1951 (dec.); children: William Burton, Melissa Ann; m. Sally Marie Snyder, May 17, 2003. BBA in Acctg. cum laude, Tex. Tech U., 1955. With Travelers Ins. Co., 1955-77, v.p., 1970-77; with Govt. Employees Ins. Co., Washington, 1977-93; chmn., pres., CEO GEICO Corp., 1985-93. Dir. Nat. Capital Area coun. Boy Scouts Am. Capt. USAF, 1950—53. Decorated Air medal. Republican. Baptist.

SNYDER, WILLIAM D., state legislator; b. NYC, Sept. 6, 1952; children: David, John, Laura. AA in Criminal Justice, Miami-Dade CC, Fla., 1976; grad., U. Va. FBI Acad., 1999; attended, Fla. Gulf Coast U., Ft. Meyers. Dir. law enforcement Martin County Sheriff's Office; mem. Dist. 82 Fla. House of Reps., Tallahassee, 2006—, chair criminal and civil justice policy coun., mem. criminal and civil justice appropriations com., fin. and tax coun., policy coun. Bd. dirs. Am. Red Cross, Martin County; adv. bd. Big Brothers Big Sisters, Martin County; maj. Civil Air Patrol. Republican. Protestant. Office: 2400 S Federal Hwy Ste 250 Stuart FL 34994-4590 also: 410 House Office Bldg 402 S Monroe St Tallahassee FL 32399-1300 Office Phone: 772-221-4904, 850-488-8832.

SOBEL, ELEANOR, state legislator; b. Brooklyn, NY, Feb. 11, 1946; m. Stuart Sobel; children: Emily, Rachel. BA in Hist., Brooklyn Coll., 1967; MA, CUNY, 1968, Columbia U., 1975; grad. Cert. Leadership, JFK Sch. Govt. Harvard U., 2003; grad., Foreign Policy Inst. State Legislators, 2006. Pres. Emrelle Skin Care Ltd.; mem. Fla. House of Reps., 1998—2006, dem. rules & calendar coun. lead, 2004—06; mem. Dist. 31 Fla. State Senate, 2008—, vice chair environ. preservation and conservation com., health regulation com., mem. policy and steering com. on energy, environment and land use, policy and steering com. on ways and means, commerce com., rules com., mem. govtl. oversight and accountability com., health and human svcs. appropriations com., select com. on Fla.'s economy, joint legis. sunset com. Commr. City of Hollywood, Fla., 1992—98; mem. Dist. 1 Broward County Sch. Bd., 2006—08. Guardian ad litem Broward County Courts, 1983—87; founding mem. Hollywood C. of C. Travel & Tourism Com., 1991—2006; coord. Hurricane Andrew Emergency Relief, 1992; chmn. Broward County Met. Planning Org., 1995—97; city rep. Hollywood Econ. Growth Corp., 1997—98; bd. dirs. Hollywood Art & Culture Ctr., 1998—; bd. mem. Tri-County Regional Transp. Org., 1998; hon. chmn. Crohn's & Colitis Found. America, 2004. Mem.: South Broward Med. Assn. Aux. (chmn. scholarship com. 1987—90), Nat. League of Cities (alt. del. 1993—98), Broward League of Cities (alt. del. 1993—98), Nat. Coun. Jewish Women (pres. Hollywood section 1988—90, pres. state pub. affairs 1990—92), Oaks Condominium Assn. (pres.), Hollywood Police Athletic League (bd. dirs. 1992—2006), Hills Dem. Club (pres. 1996—99). Democrat. Jewish. Office: Senate Office Bldg 404 S Monroe St Rm 224 Tallahassee FL 32399-1100 also: The Old Libr 2600 Hollywood Blvd Hollywood FL 33020 Office Phone: 850-487-5097, 954-924-3693. Office Fax: 954-924-3695. Business E-Mail: sobel.eleanor.web@flsenate.gov.

SOBEL, STUART A., dermatologist; b. Bklyn. BA in Biology, CUNY: Bklyn. Coll.; MD, Tufts U., 1972. Diplomate Am. Bd. Dermatology, 2009. Med. internship Montefiore Hosp.; resident dermatology Mt. Sinai Hosp., NYC, 1973—76, chief resident, 1975—76, faculty mem.; with Sobel & Sofman; hosp. affiliation include Meml. Regional Hosp. Named one of America's Best Doctors, Castle and Connelly's, 2001—. Mem.: Broward County Med. Assn., Fla. Med. Assn., Am. Med. Assn., Am. Contact Dermatitis Soc., Broward Dermatologic Assn., Fla. Soc. of Dermatology, Am. Acad. of Dermatology. Office: Sobel and Sofman Ste 101 4340 Sheridan St Hollywood FL 33021-3511 Office Phone: 954-983-5533.

SOBIESKI, JAROSLAW, aerospace engineer; b. Wilno, Poland, Mar. 11, 1934; came to U.S., 1966; naturalized, 1971. s. Stanislaw and Sabina Sobieszczanski; m. Wanda Dlugosz, Dec. 31, 1958; children: Margaret Ann, Ian Patrick. BS aeros., Tech. U. Warsaw, 1955, MS aeros., 1957, DEng, 1964. Cons. Polish Aircraft Industries, Warsaw, 1957-64; asst. and adj. prof. Tech. U. Warsaw, Warsaw, 1955-64; rsch. assoc. Tech. U. Norway, Trondheim, 1964-66; assoc. prof. St. Louis U., 1966-71; aerospace engr. NASA Langley Rsch. Ctr., Hampton, Va., 1971-89, head rsch. office, 1979-93, chief scientist, 1993—96, multidisciplinary rsch. coord., 1994—2001, mgr. Computational AeroScis. team, 1996—2001, sr. rsch. scientist, 2001—06, disting. rsch. assoc., 2006—. Mem. faculty George Washington U., 1971-2003, U. Va., 1992-99, Va. Poly. Inst., 2004—, mem. PhD coms. MIT, 2009-, Tech. U. Delft, Netherlands, 2010-; pres. and cons. engr. Tech. Analysis Optimization, Inc. Hampton, Va., 1982-02, lectr. presentations USA UK Australia, China, Japan, Brasil. Germany, Norway, Denmark, France, Portugal, Belgium, Israel & Holland. Co-editor: Structural Optimization jour., 1989-2005; contbr. articles to profl. jours. Recipient Engring. Achievement medal NASA, 1988, Exceptional Svc. medal, 2004, Wright Bros. medal, SAE, 2000, Fellow AIAA (founding chmn., Nat. Multidisciplinary Design Optimization award 1996); mem. International Soc. for Structural and Multidisciplinary Optimization (founding mem. exec. bd. 1992—2003). Achievements include research in and problem solving for aeronautics, space flight, and high performance computing; multidisciplinary design optimization. Home: 518 Elizabeth Lake Dr Hampton VA 23669-1724 Office: NASA Langley Rsch Ctr MS 188E Hampton VA 23681-0001 Personal E-mail: ysobieskiy@gmail.com. E-mail: jaroslaw.sobieski-1@nasa.gov.

SOBOL, STEVEN E., otolaryngologist; MD, McGill U., Can., 1997. Cert. Pediat. Otolaryngology, 2003. Intern McGill U., Canada, 2001, resident, 2002; fellow Children's Hosp. Phila., Pa., 2004; asst. prof., dir. pediat. otolaryngology Emory U. Hosp., 2004—. Contbr. several articles to profl. jours. Recipient James H. Birkett Meml. Scholarship (excellence in the field of otolaryngology, 1997, Glaxo Traveling Scholarship, best scientific paper presented at a nat. meeting, 2000, First prize resident rsch. competition, Assn. Otorhinolaryngology and Maxillofacial Surgery Quebec, 2001, William P. Potsic Basic Sci. Rsch. prize, Am. Soc. Pediat. Otolaryngology. Mem.: Royal Coll. Physicians and Surgeons of Canada, Am. Coll. Physician Executives, Soc. for Ear, Nose and Throat Advances in Children, Am. Acad. Otolaryngology-Head and Neck Surgery, AMA, Am. Acad. Pediat. Office: Emory Childrens Center 2015 Uppergate Dr Atlanta GA 30322 Address: Emory Childrens Center 2040 Ridgewood Drive NE Atlanta GA 30322 Office Phone: 404-727-1368.

SODERBERG, NANCY, foundation administrator, former ambassador; b. San Turce, PR, Mar. 13, 1958; d. Lars Olof and Nancy (MacGilvrey) S. BA in French and Econs., Vanderbilt U., 1980; MS in Fgn. Svc., Georgetown U., 1984. Del. selection asst. Mondale-Ferraro Com., Washington; dep. issues dir. fgn. policy Dukakis for Pres. Com., Boston, 1988; fgn. policy advisor to Senator Edward M. Kennedy US Senate, Washington, 1985-88, 89-92; fgn. policy dir. Clinton/ Gore Campaign, Little Rock, 1992; dep. asst. dir. transition nat. security Bill Clinton Presdl. Transition Team, Little Rock, 1992-93; dep. asst. to Pres. for nat. security affairs NSC, Washington, 1993—97; amb. (alt. rep.) to UN US Dept. State, NYC, 1997—2001; v.p., dir. Internat Crisis Group, NYC, 2001—05; dist. vis. scholar U. North Fla., Jacksonville, 2006—; pres., CEO Soderberg Global Solutions, Jacksonville, Fla., 2007—; pres. Connect US Fund, Washington, 2009—13. TV and radio commentator; mem. advisory bd., Nat. Com. on Am. Fgn. Policy, Tannenbaum Ctr.; adj. prof., Columbia U. Sch. Internat. & Pub. Affairs, 2003. Author: The Superpower Myth: The Use and Misuse of American Might, 2005; co-author (with Brian Katulis): The Prosperity Agenda: What the World Wants from America and What We Need in Return, 2008. Bd. mem. Concern Worldwide; pres. Sister City Program, NYC, 2002—06. Mem.: Coun. Fgn. Rels. Office: Soderberg Solutions 1031 1st St S Apt 1005 Jacksonville Beach FL 32250-6557*

SODERLING, ROBIN, professional tennis player; b. Tibro, Sweden, Aug. 14, 1984; s. Bo and Britt-Inge Soderling. Profl. tennis player ATP, 2001—. Achievements include winning 5 career singles titles, 1 career doubles title, ATP; winning (singles) Lyon, 2004, 2008, Milan, 2005, Båstad, 2009, Rotterdam, 2010, (doubles) Båstad, 2008. Office: c/o ATP Tour Inc 201 Atp Tour Blvd Ponte Vedra Beach FL 32082-3211

SODERQUIST, DONALD G., entertainment company executive; b. Chgo., 1935; BA, Wheaton Coll., 1955. Pres. Ben Franklin Stores div. City Products Co., 1963-80; sr. v.p. Wal-Mart Stores Inc., Rogers, Ark., 1980, exec. v.p., ops. adminstrn., 1981-88, vice-chmn., COO & sr. vice chmn., 1988. Bd. dirs. First Nat. Bank, Rogers, Internat. Mass. Retail Assn., Cinemark Holdings, Inc. Home: 91 Woodridge Ln Rogers AR 72756-9264 also: Cinemark Holdings Inc Bd Directors 3900 Dallas Pky Ste 500 Plano TX 75093 Office Phone: 972-665-1000. Office Fax: 972-665-1004. Business E-Mail: dsoderquist@cinemark.com.

SODOLSKI, JOHN, retired professional society administrator; b. Menasha, Wis., Apr. 11, 1931; s. L.V. and L.W. (Pinkowski) S.; m. C.J. Eppard BS, U. Wis., 1953. Vice pres. Electronic Industries Assn., Washington, 1961-83; pres. U.S. Telephone Assn., Washington, 1983-93; ret., 1993. Served to 1st lt. USMC, 1955 Home: PO Box 1014 Middleburg VA 20118-1014

SOETEBER, ELLEN, journalist, editor; b. East St. Louis, Ill., June 14, 1950; d. Lyle Potter and Norma Elizabeth (Osborn) S.; m. Richard M. Martins, Mar. 16, 1974. BJ, Northwestern U., 1972. Edn. writer, copy editor Chgo. Today, 1972-74; reporter Chgo. Tribune, 1974-76, asst. met. editor, 1976-84, assoc. met. editor, 1984-86, media editor, 1986, met. editor, 1987-89, assoc. mng. editor for met. news, 1989-91, dep. editor editorial page, 1991-94; mng. editor South Fla. Sun-Sentinel, Ft. Lauderdale, 1994-2001; editor St. Louis Post-Dispatch, 2001—05. Vis. faculty Poynter Inst. Media and diversity Studies, 2006-; presenter in field; Gaylord vis. prof. journalism ethics, Ariz. State U., 2008. Recipient Pulitzer prize; named to Hall of Achievement, Medill Sch. Journalism, 2003; Journalism fellow, U. Mich., Ann Arbor, 1986—87. Office Phone: 954-533-9248. Personal E-mail: ellsoeteber@aol.com.

SOFFA, MARY LOU, computer science and engineering educator; BS in Math. magna cum laude, U. Pitts., PhD in Computer Sci., 1977; MS in Math., Ohio State U. Asst. prof. dept. computer sci. U. Pitts., 1977—83, assoc. prof., 1983—90, prof., 1990—2004, dean grad. studies, Coll. Arts & Scis., 1991—96; Owen R. Cheatham prof. & chair dept. computer sci. U. Va., Charlottesville, 2004—. Vis. assoc. prof., dept. elec. engring. and computer sci. U. Calif., Berkeley, 1987. Mem. editl. bd. Computer Languages, 1987, Internat. Jour. Parallel Programming, 1995—2003, South African Jour. Computing, 1996—, Jour. Empirical Software Engring., 2003—, Transactions on Software Engring. Methodology, 2003—; contbr. articles to numerous profl. jours. Recipient Presdl. award for excellence in sci., math. & engring., The White House, 1999; named a Girl Scout Woman of Distinction, 2003. Fellow: Assn. Computing Machinery; mem.: Computer Rsch. Assn. (bd. dirs. 1996—2006, vice-chair 1997—2001, Nico Habermann award 2006). Office: U Va Dept Computer Sci 151 Engineers Way PO Box 400740 Charlottesville VA 22904-4740 Office Phone: 434-982-2277. Office Fax: 434-982-2214. Business E-Mail: soffa@cs.virginia.edu. E-mail: soffa@virginia.edu.

SOFTNESS, JOHN, public relations executive, speechwriter; b. Bklyn., Nov. 7, 1930; s. Burt H. and Ida (Kaiser) S.; m. Leona R. Softness (dec.); m. Carol Brady Blades; children: Barney, David, Daniel. BA, U. Miami, 1955. Reporter Miami Herald, 1953; reporter Sta. WTVJ, Miami, Fla., 1954; pub. relations dir. aviation dept. Shell Oil Co., NYC, 1958-60; pres., chief exec. officer The Softness Group, Inc., NYC, 1960-91, chmn., 1992-98; spl. asst. to dean Sch. Bus. U. Miami, 1998-2000; speechwriter Mayor Alex Penelas, Miami-Dade, Fla., 2000—04, writer prodr. musical reviews, 2009—11. Spl. counselor to Bklyn. Borough pres., 1966-76; adj. prof. comm. arts St. John's U., 1981-98; adj. prof. speechwriting U. Miami, 2006; counselor comms. com. N.Y. Heart Assn.; mem. comm. coun. U. Miami. Author: (autobiography) Boy Outta Brooklyn. Dir. Alliance for Ethical Govt., Miami. Served to capt. USAF, 1955-59. Mem. Pub. Rels. Soc. Am., Pride and Alarm (chmn.), Counselors' Acad. Home and Office: 2 Grove Isle Dr Apt 210 Coconut Grove FL 33133-4102 Personal E-mail: jsoftness@gmail.com.

SOJOURNER, MELANIE, state legislator; b. Centreville, Miss., Jan. 5, 1968; Attended, Copiah-Lincoln CC, Wesson, Miss., La. State U. Cattle prodr.; small bus. owner; mem. Dist. 37 Miss. State Senate, Jackson, 2012—. Active Natchez Regional Med. Ctr. Found. Mem.: Miss. Farm Bur. Fedn., Miss. Cattlemen's Assn., Coun. State Govt., Kiwanis, Official Miss. Women's Club. Republican. Baptist. Office: Miss State Senate PO Box 1018 Jackson MS 39215 Business E-Mail: msojourner@senate.ms.gov.

SOKOL, JOEL S., engineering educator; BA inn Math and Computer Sci., Rutgers U., 1994, BS in Applied Sciences in Engring., 1994; PhD in Ops. Rsch., MIT, 1999. Applied rsch. intern Bellcore (Bell Comm. Rsch.), 1996—97; tchg. asst., Sloan Sch. Mgmt. MIT, 1996—99, rsch. asst., Ops. Rsch. Ctr., 1994—99; asst. prof. Sch. Indsl. and Systems Engring. Ga. Inst. Tech., 1999—. Affiliated faculty mem., Ctr. for the Study of Systems Biology Ga. Inst. Tech., affiliated faculty mem., Algorithms, Combinatories, and Optimization, affiliated faculty mem., Logistics Inst.; cons. Conrad Group, 2000—01, SP Newsprint, 2001, Hartsfield Internat. Airport, 2001, NatureWorks, LLC, 2005. Contbr. chapters to books, several articles to peer-reviewed journals; several TV, Radio, Internet and print media appearances, assoc. editor INFORMS Transactions on Education, INFORMS Journal on Computing spl. issue on OR models in music, vice-chair for programs INFORMS OR in Sports Subdivision, 2004—, referee for several journals. NSF Grad. Rsch. Fellowship, 1994—97. Mem.: Math. Programming Soc., Inst. for Ops. Rsch. and Mgmt. Sci. (INFORMS) (mem. Optimization, Logistics and OR in Sports Subdivision, INFORM-ED, Jr. Faculty Insterest Group), Golden Key, Tau Beta Pi. Office: Georgia Inst Technology Sch of Indsl and Systems Engring Groseclose Building Room 418 Atlanta GA 30332 Office Phone: 404-894-6484. Business E-Mail: jsokol@isye.gatech.edu.

SOKOLOFF, DANIEL O., dermatologist; married; 2 children. Grad. with honors, Tulane U.; MD, George Wash. U., 1977. Diplomate Am. Bd. Dermatology, 1982. Resident dermatology Baylor Med. Ctr., Houston, 1979—82; staff Good Samaritan Hosp., St. Mary's Hosp., Palm Beach Gardens Hosp. Named one of South Fla. Top Doc, Castle Connolly, 2000—11. Mem.: Palm Beach Dermatology Soc., Fla. Soc. of Dermatology, Am. Acad. of Dermatology. Office: Palm Beach Dermatology Ste 2 4475 Medical Center Way West Palm Beach FL 33407 Office Phone: 561-863-1000.

SOLARI, LARRY THOMAS, private equity firm executive; b. Stockton, Calif., July 30, 1942; s. John Fredrich and Elizabeth (Rubino) Solari; m. Patricia Harlan, Feb. 5, 1966 (div. 1978); m. Deirdre Duff, Apr. 9, 1980; children: Chris, Ryan, Erin, Brad. BS in Indsl. Mgmt., San Jose State U., Calif., 1965, MBA, 1966. Mfg. trainee Owens Corning Fiberglas, Santa Clara, Calif., 1966—67, salesman San Francisco, 1967—69, product mgr. Toledo, 1970—73, mktg. mgr., 1974—78, gen. mgr., v.p., 1979—84, oper. v.p., 1985—88, pres. constrn. products group, 1986—94; pres. bldg. materials group Domtar, Inc., 1994—96; chmn., CEO Sequentia, Inc., 1996—97, BSI Holdings, Inc., Carmel, Calif., 1998—2001; ptnr. Kenner & Co., Inc., 2002—. Bd. dirs. Beazer Homes USA, Inc., 1994—, Flooring America, Inc., 1999—, Atrium Companies, Inc., 2003—, vice chmn., 2005—10, chmn., 2010—. Served with US Army, 1966—72. Republican. Roman Catholic. Office: Kenner & Company Inc 437 Madison Ave New York NY 10022 Mailing: Beazer Homes USA Inc Bd Directors 1000 Abernathy Rd Ste 1200 Atlanta GA 30328 Office Phone: 770-829-3700. Office Fax: 770-481-2808. Business E-Mail: lsolari@beazer.com.

SOLCHER, STEPHEN B., computer company executive; B in Adminstrn., Tex. A&M U. Audit mgr. Arthur Andersen & Co.; corp. treas. BMC Software, Inc., Houston, 1992—2000, asst. treas., 1991—92, v.p. fin., 2000—05, treas., 2000, interim CFO, 2005, sr. v.p., CFO Houston, 2005—. Office: BMC Software Inc 2101 City West Blvd Houston TX 77042-2827 Office Phone: 713-918-8800. Office Fax: 713-918-8000. Business E-Mail: stephen_solcher@bmc.com.

SOLIS, JORGE ANTONIO, federal judge; b. 1951; BA, McMurray Coll., 1973; JD, U. Tex., 1976. Clk. Indsl. Accident Bd., 1975-76; asst. criminal dist. atty. U.S. Attys. Office, 1976-81; with Moore & Holloway, 1981-82; criminal dist. atty. U.S. Attys. Office, 1983-87, spl. prosecutor narcotics task force, 1988; judge 350th Dist. Ct., 1989-91, US Dist. Ct. (no. dist.) Tex., 1991—. Bd. dirs. HRC Drug Abuse Treatment Ctr., Abilene, Tex., 1979—, pres. bd. dirs., 1982-83, Meals on Wheels, 1984—, Abilene (Tex.) Girls Home, 1985—; active Gov. Task Force on Drug Abuse, 1987—. Mem. State Bar Tex., Abilene Bar Assn. (past bd. dirs.), Abilene Young Lawyers Assn. (sec.-treas. 1977-78), Tex. Dist. and County Attys. Assn. Office: US Dist Ct 1100 Commerce St Ste 16g36 Dallas TX 75242-1495

SOLLS, MARK A., lawyer; b. 1956; married; 3 children. BA in Fin., U. Ill., 1977; JD, Southern Ill. U., 1980. Bar: Ill. 1980, Tex. 1982, cert.: mediator. V.p., gen. counsel, sec. Pronet, Inc., 1993—97, Dal-Tile Internat., Inc., 1998—2002; exec. v.p., general counsel, sec. Wyndham Internat., Inc., 2002—06, Concentra, Inc., 2006—. Office: Concentra Inc 5080 Spectrum Dr Ste 1200 W Addison TX 75001 Office Phone: 972-364-8000. Office Fax: 972-387-0019. Business E-Mail: mark.solls@concentra.com.

SOLOMON, BARRY J., human services administrator, consultant; b. Boston, May 16, 1934; s. Samuel and Ethel (Fleishman) Solomon; m. C. Priscilla Fugate, June 29, 1958; children: R. Stephen, Jon, Julie Ellen. BS in Biology and Chemistry, Tufts U., Medford, Mass., 1955; MBA in Health Care Adminstrn., Xavier U., Cin., 1960; MPH in Health Care Adminstrn., U. NC, 1989. Chief med. record adminstr. USPHS Hosp., Lexington, Ky., 1956-59; asst. dir. Union Meml. Hosp., Balt., 1960-61; asst. adminstr. James Lawrence Kernan Hosp., Balt., 1961-67; asst. to dean, lectr. health edn. and med. care sects. Yale U. Sch. Medicine, New Haven, 1967-70; dir. health svcs., clin. asst. prof. pharmacy adminstrn. U. RI, Kingston, 1970-76; assoc. dir. for adminstrn. USPHS Hosp., Norfolk, Va., 1976-81; dir., COO, sr. fellow in social medicine Montefiore Hosp., Bronx, NY, 1981-84; assoc. v.p. for med. affairs, mem. exec. coun. of Med. Sch. U. South Fla., Tampa, 1984-89; assoc. prof., acting chmn. dept. comprehensive medicine U. So. Fla., Tampa, 1984-89, assoc. prof. Coll. Pub. Health, 1984-89; cons. in health adminstrn., Columbia, Md., 1989-93; v.p. for acad. affairs North Broward Hosp. Dist., Ft. Lauderdale, Fla., 1993-96; chmn. bd. dirs. Sr. Benefit Ctrs. Am., Inc., 1998-2000; cmty. rep., mem. safety com. North Broward Med. Ctr., 2007—. 1st v.p. bd. trustees, CEO Count and Countess de Hoernle Alzheimer's Pavillion, 2000—06, cons. to bd. dirs., 2006—; pres. Villa D'Este Condominium, Inc., 1999—2001; exec. com., nominating com. Vis. Nurse Assn. Tampa Bay, 1987—90; planning com. bd. trustees Hillsborough County Hosp. Authority, 1986—88; profl. affairs com. bd. trustees H. Lee Moffitt Cancer Ctr. and Rsch. Inst., 1986—88; affiliation com. S.W. Fla. Blood Bank, 1988—89; instr. hosp. adminstrn. Xavier U., 1960; course asst., instr. Am. Med. Record Assn., 1962—72; instr. Howard U. Coll. Continuing Edn., Washington, 1993; cons. St. Elizabeth Hosp., Covington, Ky., 1959, City Hosp. Ctr. Elmhurst, 1965, Hall-Brooke Hosp., Westport, Conn., 1968—69, Conn. Mental Health Ctr., New Haven, 1969—70, South County Hosp., Wakefield, RI, 1970—76, Centurion Hosp., Tampa, 1989, Primary Care Svcs., Tampa, 1991, Holland & Knight, Tampa, 1991, NCC Internat., Colchester, England, 1991, F. W. Assocs., Tampa, 1989—92, Decking Design, Norfolk, 1986—93, SMinc., Columbia, 1993, Internat. Flooring & Protective Coatings, Inc., Norfolk, 1993—; sr. cons. Meisel Assocs., Inc., NYC, 1983—; bd. dirs. Care Source, Inc., 2007—; patient safety strategic team North Broward Med. Ctr., 2007—. Contbr. articles to profl. jours. Mem. Nat. Com. Religion and Health, 1982—84; mem., vice chmn. Chariho Sch. Bd., Richmond, RI, 1974—76; mem. Broward Econ. Devel. Coun., Inc.; trustee Montefiore-Mosholu Cmty. Ctr., 1981—84. Lt. USPHS, 1956—59, capt. USPHS, 1976—81. Recipient citation, Suncoast chp. Am. Heart Assn., 1988. Fellow: Am. Coll. Healthcare Execs.; mem.: APHA. Avocation: tennis. Home: 2863 Via Venezia Deerfield Beach FL 33442-8633 Personal E-mail: prisandbj@bellsouth.net.

SOLOMON, CARL L., lawyer; BS, Fla. State U.; JD, U. SC, 1994. Bar: SC 1995, US Dist. Ct., SC 1996. Ptnr. Solomon Law Group, LLC, Columbia, SC. Pro bono prosecutor SC Atty. Gen.'s Office Criminal Domestic Violence Program. Bd. mem. SC Commn. on Higher Edn., Mid-Carolina Commn. Recipient Compleat Lawyer Award, U. SC Sch. Law, 2005. Mem.: ABA, SC Bar Assn. (pres. 2010—11), Nat. Bar Assn., Columbia Lawyers Assn. (former pres.), American Assn. for Justice, SC Assn. for Justice, Richland County Bar Assn. Office: Solomon Law Group, LLC 1519 Richland St Columbia SC 29202-1866 Office Phone: 803-779-8080. Office Fax: 803-256-1816.

SOLOMON, IRA, dean, business educator; b. Nov. 2, 1952; m. Susan Sharpe; 3 children. BBA in Acctg., U. Tex., Austin, 1973, MPA in Acctg., 1974, PhD in Acctg., 1979. CPA Tex., 1974. Mem. audit staff Peat, Marwick, Mitchell & Co., Houston, 1974—76; tchg. asst. dept. acctg. U. Tex., Austin, 1976—78; asst. prof. dept. acctg. U Ariz., Tucson, 1978—83; assoc. prof. accountancy U. Ill., Urbana-Champaign, 1983—87, KPMG Peat Marwik disting. prof. accountancy, 1987—2001, co-dir. office acctg. rsch., 1991—95, assoc. head dept. accountancy, 1998—2001, R.C. Evans endowed chair in bus., 2001—11, head dept. accountancy, 2002—11; dean, Debra and Rick Rees prof. bus. Tulane U. A.B. Freeman Sch. Bus., New Orleans, 2011—. Audit rsch. fellow KPMG Peat Marwick Exec. Office, Montvale, NJ, 1990, 1991; vis. disting. scholar & lectr. Macquarie U., Sydney, 2011. Contbr. chapters to books, articles to profl. jours. Mem.: AICPA (mem. governing coun. 2008—11, Outstanding Achievement in Acctg. Education award 2009), Tex. Soc. CPAs, Ill. CPA Soc. (Spl. Merit award 2009), American Acctg. Assn. (v.p. 2009—11, Outstanding Auditing Educator award 1997). Office: Tulane University AB Freeman School Business Goldring/Woldenberg Hall Rm 440F 7 McAlister Dr New Orleans LA 70118 Office Phone: 504-865-5407. Business E-Mail: isolomon@tulane.edu.

SOLOMON, KERRY D., ophthalmologist, surgeon, consultant; s. Alan M. and Sheila M. Solomon; m. Cynthia Loiacano Solomon, June 12, 1992; children: Brandon, Coleman. BA in Psychology, U. Vt., 1983, MD, 1987. Diplomate Am. Bd. Ophthalmology, 1993, lic. ophthalmologist SC, 1993. Felow in ophthalmic pathology U. Utah, Salt Lake City, 1987—88; intern Yale U. Hosp. St. Raphael, New Haven, 1988—89; resident in ophthalmology U. Ky., Lexington, 1989—92; fellow in cornea, external disease, anterior segment surgery Wilmer Inst. Johns Hopkins Hosp., Balt., 1992—93; staff Med. U. SC, 1993—, from asst. prof. to assoc. prof. ophthalmology, 1993—2002, prof. ophthalmology, 2002—. Dir. Magill Laser Ctr., SC, 1994—, ophthalmology ambulatory care com. liaison, 1994—99; chmn. hosp. laser com. Med. U. SC, 1999—, dir. cornea/refractive surgery svc., SC, 2000—; co-med. dir. SC Lions Eye Bank, 1996—2001, Magill Rsch. Ctr., SC, 2000—; lectr., presenter in field. Editor: Refractive Surgery Quar.; mem. editl. bd.: Ocular Surgery News, Phaco and Foldables, Ocular Therapeutics, Ophthalmic Practice, Cataract and Refractive Surgery Today; contbr. articles to profl. jours. Ednl. com. Internat. Soc. Refractive Surgery. Recipient Pierre Guatier Jenkins award, Med. U. SC, 2006—07; grantee, Allergan, 1994—95, 1998—2001, Chiron Vision, 1994—97, Akorn, Inc., 1997—99, Alcon Labs., 1997—, Pharmacia and Upjohn, 1997—98, Pharmacia, 1999—2000, JAEB Ctr. for Health Rsch., 1999—2004, Otsuka Md. Rsch. Inst., 2004—05, Advanced Med. Optics, 2004—; fellow, Heed Ophthalmic Found., Wilmer Eye Inst., Johns Hopkins Hosp., 1992; Rsch. grant, Nat. Soc. to Prevent Blindness, Wilmer Eye Inst., Johns Hopkins Hosp., 1992. Fellow: Am. Acad. Ophthalmology (Honor award 1998, Sr. Achievement award 2005); mem.: Charleston County Med. Soc., Charleston Ophthalmol. Soc., SC Soc. Ophthalmology, SC Med. Assn., Wilmer Resident Assn., Refractive Surgery Interest Group, Johns Hopkins Univ. Sch. Medicine Alumnae, Internat. Soc. Refractive Keratoplasty, Heed Ophthalmic Found., Eye Bank Assn. Am., Assn. for Rsch. in Vision and Ophthalmology, Am. Soc. Cataract and Refractive Surgery (program com., practice mgmt. com., FDA com., Best Paper award 1995, Grand prize 1997, Video award 1998, Best Paper award 2000, Lee T. Nordan Achievement award 2006). Avocations: golf, travel. Office: Storm Eye Inst 167 Ashley Ave Charleston SC 29403-5836

SOLOMON, ROB, retail executive; b. NY; BS in Mgmt., Pepperdine U. Various sr. positions Continental Guest Svcs., NY, Electronic Processing Source Inc.; v.p., call center ops. Ticketmaster Corp., exec. v.p., contact centers and retail locations, 2000; sr. v.p., customer care HSN, Inc., 2003—09, exec. v.p., ops., 2009—. Office: HSN Inc 1 HSN Dr Saint Petersburg FL 33729 Office Phone: 727-872-1000. Office Fax: 727-872-6615. Business E-Mail: rob.solomon@hsn.net.

SOLOMONS, BURT R., state legislator; b. Oct. 31, 1950; m. Jamie Solomons; 1 child, Haley. BA in Govt., Tex. Tech U.; MPA, So. Meth. U.; JD, U. Tulsa. Atty. Denton County, Tex., 1978—, pvt. practice atty. North Carrollton, Tex., 1986—; asst. atty. City of Denton, acting city atty.; gen. counsel Lawyers for Title Denton and Lewisville; presiding mcpl. judge City of Carrollton, Tex., 1987—93; alt. mcpl. judge Lewisville and Flower Mound, Tex.; legal counsel Greater Lewisville Assn. Realtors, 1990—; of counsel Bell, Nunnally & Martin, LLP, Dallas; mem. Dist. 65 Tex. House of Representatives, 1994—. Recipient of several awards and honors. Republican. Office: 1029 Rosemeade Pky Ste 108 Carrollton TX 75007 also: Room 1W.11 Capitol PO Box 2910 Austin TX 78768 Office Phone: 972-394-3904, 512-463-0478. Office Fax: 972-394-5638.

SOLOSKI, JOHN, journalism and communications educator; AB cum laude, Boston Coll., 1974; MA in Journalism, U. Iowa, 1976, PhD, 1978. Copy editor, reporter Iowa City Press Citizen, 1977-78; instr. Univ. Iowa, 1977-78, asst. prof. sch. journalism and mass communication, 1978-84, assoc. prof. sch. journalism and mass communication, 1984-85, assoc. prof., head of grad. studies, 1985-92, prof., head of grad. studies, 1992-94, prof., acting dir., 1994-95, prof. sch. of journalism and mass communication, 1995-96, prof., dir. sch. of journalism and mass communication, 1996—, prof. law, 1996—2001; dean Grady Coll. Journalism and Mass Comm. U. Ga., 2001—04, prof. Grady Coll. Journalism and Mass Comm., 2004—. Con. Ottumwa Courier, 1976-77, Iowa City Press-Citizen, 1976-77; speaker in field; vis. prof. Univ. Tech., Sydney, Australia, 1995. Co-author: Reforming Libel Law, 1992, Libel and the Press: Myth and Reality, 1987, Taking Stock: Journalism nad the Publicly Traded Newspaper Company, 2001; contbr. numerous articles to profl. jours.; editor: Journalism and Communication Monographs, 1994—. Recipient Soc. of Profl. Journalists Disting. Svc. award, 1988; numerous rsch. grants. Mem.: Assn. Schs. Journalism and Mass Comm. (pres. 2003—04). Office: Henry W Grady College of Journalism and Mass Communication The University of Georgia Athens GA 30602-3018 Office Phone: 706-542-1704. Business E-Mail: jsoloski@uga.edu.

SOLOWAY, MARK STEPHEN, urologist, urologic oncologist; b. Balt., Jan. 24, 1943; s. Louis and Ada (Yoffee) S.; m. Cynthia T. Teper, May 30, 1966; children: Scott, Deanna. Student, Northwestern U.; MD, Case Western Reserve U., 1968. Diplomate Am. Bd. Urology; lic. MD, Tenn., Fla. Clin. assoc. surgery br. Nat. Cancer Inst., 1970-72; resident in urology Univ. Hosps., Cleve., 1972-75; asst. prof. urology U. Tenn., Memphis, 1975-78, assoc. prof. urology, 1978-91; prof., chair dept. urology U. Miami (Fla.) Sch. Medicine, 1991—. Mem. med. staff Cedars Med. Ctr., Miami, 1991—, mem. operating room com., 1991—, acad. affairs com., 1991—; mem. med. staff Jackson Meml. Hosp., Miami, 1991—, VA Hosp., Miami, 1991—; vis. prof. various univs. in U.S. and internat.; presenter and spkr. over 350 confs. and lectures in field. Editor Current Urology Reports; mem. editl. bd. Urology, Organo Ufficiale Suicmi (Italy); mem. internat. adv. bd. Progres en Urologie; reviewer Jour. Urology, Investigative Urology, 1978—, Cancer, Jour. Am. Med. Assn.; contbr. over 500 articles to profl. jours., over 35 chpts. to books in field. Lt. comdr. USPHS, 1970-72. Grantee NIH, 1975-87; Clin. fellow Am. Cancer Soc., 1973-74, Jr. Facility Clin. fellow, 1976-79; recipient 1st prize Cleve. Urol. Soc. Essay Contest, 1974. Mem. ACS, Am. Urol. Assn. (Southeastern sect., Gold Cystoscope award 1984, North Ctrl. Sect. Traveling fellow 1972-73), Am. Soc. Clin. Oncology, Am. Assn. Cancer Rsch., Soc. Surg. Oncology, Urol. Rsch. Soc., Soc. Urol. Oncology, Greater Miami Urol. Soc., Dutch Urol. Soc. (hon.), Buffalo Urol. Soc. (hon.), Phi Beta Kappa. Home: 9601 Collins Ave Apt 1410 Miami FL 33154-2213 Office: PO Box 16960 Miami FL 33101-6960 Office Phone: 305-243-8090.

SOLTERO-HARRINGTON, LUIS RUBÉN, retired surgeon, educator; b. San Juan, Sept. 4, 1925; s. Augusto Rafael Soltero and Anna Lila Harrington; m. Alice Joyce Carpenter, Apr. 24, 1958; children: Luis Ruben, Kathleen Ann, Susan Joyce, Robert Richard, Sharon Theresa. BS in Agr., U. P.R., Rio Piedras, 1945; BM, MD, Northwestern U., Chgo., 1949. Diplomate Am. Bd. Surgery, Nat. Be. Med. Examiners, P.R. Rd. Med. Examiners. Intern Michael Reese Hosp., Chgo., 1949-50; resident in gen. surgery Aguadilla (P.R.) Dist. Hosp., 1950-51; resident in gen. surgery, instr. Baylor U. Coll. Medicine and Affiliated Hosps., Houston, 1954-59; resident in gen. surgery Jefferson Davis, VA and M.D. Anderson Hosps., Houston, 1954-57; resident in pediatric, thoracic and cardiovasc. surgery St. Luke's-Tex. Children's Hosp., Houston, 1957-59; asst. prof. surgery U. P.R. Sch. Medicine, 1960-64, assoc. clin. prof., 1972-73, assoc. clin prof., 1973—, in charge devel. heart surgery program, 1960-64, dir. surgery residency tng. program, 1961-64; pvt. practice San Juan, 1959—2003; ret., 2003; prof. San June Bautisa Sch. Medicine, 2006—. Prof. surgery U. del Caribe Sch. Medicine, Cayey, P.R., 1981—, San Juan Bautista Sch. Med., 2006-; cons. in cardiovasc. and thoracic surgery Med. Examing Bd. P.R., San Juan, 1989; chief thoracic and cardiovasc. surgery Tchrs. Hosp., San Juan, from 1959; dir. surgery residency tng. program Univ. Hosp., Rio Piedras, from 1961-64; cons. in thoracic and cardiovasc. surgery San Juan City Hosp., 1962—, cons. in surgery, 1964—; cons. in surgery Presbyn. Hosp., 1972—, Mimiya's Hosp., 1987—; cons. in thoracic and cardiovasc. surgery Indsl. Hosp., San Juan, 1975—, Hosp. Met., 1982—, Clinic Fernández García, 1983—; chief surgery Ruiz Arnau Hosp., Bayamon, P.R., 1978—; asst. dir. ICU, Hosp. del Maestro, 1987—; bd. dirs. Rsch. Found. Cardiovasc. Surgery Tex., 1984—, Am. Cancer Soc., 1974; mem. Nat. Adv. Cun. Mended Hearts, Inc., 1969. Author: (textbook) The Management of the Acutely Ill Patient, 2002; contbr. articles to med. jours.; patentee partial occlusion vascular clamp to be used in small blood vessels; inventor respirator for infants based on electronic equipment. Capt., M.C., USAF, 1953-54. Recipient award for outstanding work in cardiovasc. surgery Lions Club, Hato Rey, 1961. Fellow Am. Acad. Pediat., Am. Coll. Legal Medicine (assoc.); mem. AMA (physician recognition award 1986); mem. Denton A. Cooley Cardiovasc. Surg. Soc., Michael E. De Bakey Internat. Cardiovasc. Soc., Pan Am. Med. Assn. (coun. pediatric surgery), P.R. Soc. Cardiology, Am. Heart Assn., P.R. Hear Assn., Phi Chi. Avocations: travel, horticulture, bridge.

SOLTMAN, RONALD P., lawyer, surgical hospital company executive; JD cum laude, U. Mich., 1971. Asst. gen. counsel Hosp. Affiliates Internat., 1978—81; v.p. & asst. gen. counsel Hosp. Corp. Am., 1981—94; sr. v.p., gen. counsel & sec OrNda HealthCorp, 1994—97; bd dirs. Vanguard Health Sys., Inc., 1997—2004, exec. v.p., gen. counsel & sec., 1997—. Office: Vangard Health Systems Inc Ste 100 20 Burton Hills Blvd Nashville TN 37215 Office Phone: 615-665-6000. Office Fax: 615-665-6099. Business E-Mail: rsoltman@vanguardhealth.com.

SOLYMOSY, EDMOND SIGMOND ALBERT, marketing professional, manager, retired military officer; b. Budapest, Pest, Hungary, Sept. 3, 1937; came to U.S., 1949; s. Sigmond Ladislas and Gabrielle (Lindelof) S.; m. Mary Ellen Via, Sept. 9, 1961; children: Edmond S.A. Jr., Stephan G., Philip A. BSME, Tex. A&M U., 1960, BBA, 1961, MBA, 1970; postgrad., Mich. U., 1985, Harvard U., 1991. Commd. 2d lt. U.S. Army, 1961, advanced through grades to gen., 1985; student Nat. Def. U., Washington, 1980-81; comdr. 1st Air Def. Arty. Brigade, Ft. Bliss, Tex., 1981-83; chief of staff U.S. Army Air Def. Ctr., Ft. Bliss, 1983; dir. Human Resources Directorate, Hdqrs. Dept. Army, Washington, 1983-85; dep. comdr. U.S. Army Community and Family Support Ctr., Alexandria, Va., 1985-86; chief of staff U.S. Army I Corps, Ft. Lewis, Wash., 1986-88; chief exec. U.S. Office of Def. Coop., Athens, Greece, 1988-91; ret., 1991; pres. Global Project Mgmt., Houston, 1991—, Am. Southwest Properties Inc., 1993-95, Prime Daniel Asset Mgmt. Corp., 1997-2001; sr. ptnr. Solymosy Investment Assocs., 2000—; owner Bar-O-S Ranch. Advisor Sec. of Army Panel, Washington, 1983-86, Hellenic-Am. C. of C., Athens, 1988-91; bd. dirs. Am. Ikarus Inc., Maxoil Inc., So. Nat. Bank Tex., SNB Bankshares, Tex. A&M U. Rsch. Found., Fin. Literacy Found.; hon. consul Republic of Hungary; chmn. Houston Com. on Fgn. Rels. Author: Continental Economic Alliances, 1981. Sponsor Spl. Olympics, Ft. Lewis, 1986; advisor Mil. Mus., Ft. Lewis, 1986-88; regional v.p. Mediterranean coun. Boy Scouts Am., Athens, 1988-91; mem. devel. com. Tex. A&M U., College Station, 1991, advisor Ctr. for Internat. Bus.; mem. bd. advisors Mosher Inst. for Internat. Policy Studies; mem. Mil. Com., Houston, mem. bd. dirs., MINT Natul Bank, Kingwood, Tex. Decorated D.S.M., Def. D.S.M., Combat Infantryman's Badge, Airborne Parachutist's Badge, Army Ranger, Legion of Merit (3); recipient U.S. and Vietnamese awards for heroism, Greek Disting. Svc. award, 1991. Mem.: VFW, Assn. U.S. Army (Svc. to Soldiers award 1985), Am. Quarter Horse Assn., Armed Forces YMCA (chmn. com. 1982, nat. vol. of yr. award 1983), Am. Palomino Horse Breeders Assn., Internat. Propeller Club (Greece advisor 1989), Kiwanis Club Houston, Hungarian Knights Hospitaller of Order of St. John. Republican. Lutheran. Avocations: sports, jogging, sailing, fishing, hunting, western horsemanship. Personal E-mail: essglobal@aol.com.

SOMERHALDER, JOHN W., II, energy executive; m. Rebecca Somerhalder; 4 children. BSCE, Univ. Ariz. Sr. v.p. El Paso Corp., Houston, 1992—96, pres. El Paso Energy Resources Co., 1996, exec. v.p. pipeline group, pres. pipeline group, 1999—2005, exec. v.p., 1999—2005; pres., CEO AGL Resources, Inc., Atlanta, 2006—07, chmn., pres., CEO, 2007—. Bd. dir., past chmn. Interstate Natural Gas Assn. Am.; bd. dir. Interstate Nat. Gas Assn. Am.; bd. mem. & first vice chmn. Am. Gas Assn. Bd. mem. Metro Atlanta C. of C., Ga. C. of C. Office: AGL Resources Inc 10 Peachtree Pl Atlanta GA 30309 Mailing: AGL Resources Inc PO Box 4569 Atlanta GA 30302-4569

SOMMERFELD, JUDE THOMAS, chemical engineer, educator; b. Cin., Ohio, Feb. 4, 1936; s. Henry Anthony and Hilda Catherine (Diffley) S.; m. Rosemary Sniatkowski, May 17, 1958 (div. 1983); children: Loretta, Margaret, Maria, Joanna; m. Elizabeth Ryder, Apr. 18, 1992. B in Chem. Engring., U. Detroit, 1958; MS in Engring., U. Mich., 1960, PhD, 1963. Registered profl. engr., Ga. Sys. engr. Monsanto Co., St. Louis, 1963-66; dir. process engring. BASF-Wyandotte Corp., Mich., 1966-70; assoc. prof. Ga. Inst. Tech., Atlanta, 1970-75, prof., 1975—2002, cons., 2002—. Contbr. numerous articles to profl. jours. Fellow AIChE. Roman Catholic. Avocations: tennis, guitar, classical music, whitewater rafting. Business E-Mail: jude.sommerfeld@che.gatech.edu.

SOMMERFELDT, JOHN ROBERT, historian, educator; b. Detroit, Feb. 4, 1933; s. Melvin John and Virginia Zita (Gruenheck) S.; m. Patricia Natalie Levinske, Aug. 25, 1956; children: Ann, James, John, Elizabeth. AB, U. Mich., 1954, AM, 1956, PhD, 1960. Instr. history Stanford U., 1958-59; from instr. to prof. Western Mich. U., 1959-78; prof. history U. Dallas, 1978—2010, emeritus prof., 2010—, chmn.

dept. history, 1984-87, univ. pres., 1978-80. Dir. Medieval Inst., Western Mich. U., 1961-76; exec. dir. Inst. Cistercian Studies, 1973-78; dir. Center Contemplative Studies, 1976-78; pres. Cistercian Publs., 1973-79, chmn. bd., 1976-79. Author: The Spiritual Teachings of Bernard of Clairvaux, 1991, Bernard of Clairvaux On the Life of the Mind, 2004, Bernard of Clairvaux On the Spirituality of Relationship, 2004, Aelred of Rievaulx: Pursuing Perfect Happiness, 2005, Aelred of Rievaulx On Love and Order in the World and in the Chuch, 2006, Christianity in Culture, 2009; editor: Studies in Medieval Culture, 12 vols., 1964-78, Studies in Medieval Cistercian History, II, 1977, Cistercian Ideals and Reality, 1978, Simplicity and Ordinariness, 1980, The Chimaera of His Age: Studies in Bernard of Clairvaux, 1980, Abba: Guides to Wholeness and Holiness, East and West, 1981, Erudition at God's Service, 1987, Bernardus Magister, 1992, Studiosorum Speculum, 1993, Studies in the Theology of St. Thomas Aquinas, 1995. Fulbright scholar, 1954-55; Univ. fellow U. Mich., 1956-57. Mem. Medieval Acad. Am., Am. Catholic Hist. Assn., Am. Soc. Ch. History, Phi Beta Kappa, Phi Eta Sigma, Phi Kappa Phi. Republican. Roman Catholic. Office: 2809 Warren Cir Irving TX 75062 also: University Dallas Dept History 1845 E Northgate Dr Irving TX 75062-4736 Home: 3412 Bellah Ct Irving TX 75062 Home Phone: 972-258-5812; Office Phone: 972-255-0608. Business E-Mail: jrsommer@udallas.edu.

SOMMESE, JAMES, wholesale distribution executive; BA, SUNY, Stony Brook, 1993. Sales & product mgr. Arrow Electronics/Gates-Arrow Distbg. Inc., 1994—98, dir. asset mgmt., 2001—03; product mgr. ScanSource, Inc., 1998—2001, dir. reverse logistics, 2003—, dir. sys. integration, 2005—. Office: ScanSource Inc 6 Logue Ct Greenville SC 29615 Office Phone: 864-288-2432. Office Fax: 864-288-1165.

SONBERG, STEVEN, lawyer; b. NYC, May 10, 1947; BS in Acctg., NYU Leonard N. Stern Sch. Bus., 1969; JD, U. Miami Sch. Law, 1972; LLM in Taxation, NYU Sch. Law, 1973. Bar: Fla. 1972, US Tax Ct. 1979. Ptnr. Holland & Knight LLP, Miami, Fla., 1992—, co-chair corp. governance nat. practice group, chmn. bus. law sect., 2003—08, mng. ptnr., 2008—. Spkr. in field. Contbr. articles to profl. jours. Bd. trustee U. Miami; bd. dir. Diabetes Rsch. Inst. Found., Inc., 1980—, pres., 1984—86, chmn. bd. dirs., 1990—96. Named a Top Lawyer, South Fla. Legal Guide, 2006—11; named one of The Best Lawyers in America-Corp. Governance & Compliance Law, Corp. Law and Securities Law, 2006—11, America's Leading Bus. Lawyers-Corp. Mergers and Acquisitions, Chambers USA, 2008—10; named to Fla. Super Lawyers, 2006—10, Super Lawyers-Corp. Counsel Edit., 2006—10. Mem.: Am. Bar Found., Fla. Bar (mem. bus. law sect., internat. law sect., tax sect.), ABA (mem. bus. law, internat. and tax sects.), Dade County Bar Assn., Broward County Bar Assn. Office: Holland & Knight LLP 701 Brickell Ave Ste 3000 Miami FL 33131 Address: Holland & Knight LLP One East Broward Blvd Ste 1300 Fort Lauderdale FL 33301 Office Phone: 305-789-7794, 954-468-7816. Business E-Mail: steven.sonberg@hklaw.com.

SONDOCK, RUBY KLESS, retired judge; b. Apr. 26, 1926; d. Herman Lewis and Celia (Juran) Kless; m. Melvin Adolph Sondock, Apr. 22, 1944; children: Marcia Cohen, Sandra Marcus. AA, Cottey Coll., Nevada, Mo., 1944; BS, U. Houston, 1959, LLB, 1961. Bar: Tex. 1961, U.S. Supreme Ct. 1977. Pvt. practice, Houston, 1961-73, 89—; judge Harris County Ct. Domestic Rels. (312th Dist.), 1973-77, 234th Jud. Dist. Ct., Houston, 1977-82, 83-89; justice Tex. Supreme Ct., Austin, 1982; of counsel Weil Gotshal and Manges, 1989-93, Houston Ctr., 1993—. Mem. ABA, Tex. Bar Assn., Houston Bar Assn., Houston Assn. Women Lawyers, Order of Barons, Phi Theta Phi, Kappa Beta Pi, Phi Kappa Phi, Alpha Epsilon Pi. Address: 1111 Caroline St #2608 Houston TX 77010 Office Phone: 713-655-1111.

SONFIELD, ROBERT LEON, JR., lawyer; b. Houston, Oct. 28, 1931; s. Robert Leon and Dorothy Harriett (Huber) S.; 1 dau., Sheree. BA, U. Houston, 1956, LLB, JD, 1959; PhD (hon.), U. Eastern Fla., 1962; LLD (hon.), London Inst. Applied Rsch., 1973; cert. fed. taxation, NYU, 1973; cert. securities regulation, Harvard U., 1983. Bar: Tex. 1959, U.S. Supreme Ct. 1959, U.S. Dist. Ct. Tex. 1960, U.S. Tax Ct. 1960, U.S. Ct. Appeals 1960, U.S. Ct. Claims 1974. Mng. dir. Sonfield & Sonfield, Houston, 1959—. Mem. nat. adv. coun. Nat. Fedn. Ind. Bus. Author: Corporate Financing by Sale of Securities to the Public, 1969, Mergers and Acquisitions, 1970, Student Rights, 1971, The Limited Partnership as a Vehicle for Real Estate Investment, 1971, Integration of Partnership Offerings, 1974, The Grantor Trust Rules After The Tax Reform Act of 1986, Incentive Equity Program, Corporate Name Protection Along With Name Registration, A Guide to SEC Corporate Filing, Organizational Professionals' Residual Litigation and Investment Strategy, Comparing California, Delaware and Nevada: Corporate Laws in Light of California Corporations Code Section 2115 and Offering of Unregistered Securities Only to Accredited Investors, Disclosure Policies, Practices and Procedures For Public Companies, Regulation of Franchises, How to Become a Publicly Held Company Via the Registered Ditribution of a Percentage of Your Company's Stock to Shareholders, numerous others. Recipient St. John Garwood award, 1957, Frio-Finnegan Outstanding Alumnus award, 1970-71, citation for outstanding contbn. to legal profession, 1971. Mem. Am. Tax Lawyers Assn. (pres.), Lawyers Soc. Houson, Am. Judicature Soc., ABA, Tex. Bar Assn. (dist. com. on admission to state bar, chmn. clients security fund com.), Houston Bar Assn. (com. chmn. coun., tax sect.), Tex. Equal Access to Justice Found., Houston Bar Found., Real Estate Securities and Syndication Inst., Huguenot Soc. of London, Order Stars and Bars, SAR, Sons Confederate Vets., Mil. Order World Wars, Mil. and Hospitaller Order St. Lazarus of Jerusalem, Knightly Assn. St. George the Martyr, Smithsonian Assocs., Houston Heritage Soc., Houston Mus. Fine Arts, Newcomen Soc. N.Am., Phi Delta Phi, Delta Sigma Phi, Met. Club (N.Y.C.), Argyle Club (San Antonio), Houston Club, Houstonian Club. Office: Sonfield & Sonfield 2500 Wilcrest Dr Ste 300 Houston TX 77042-2754 Office Phone: 713-877-8333. Personal E-mail: robert@sonfield.com.

SONGER, MARK ANTHONY, energy executive; b. Warren, Pa., Nov. 8, 1959; s. Robert Sylvester and Mary Jane (Kuzminski) S.; m. Cynthia Lynn Campbell, July 27, 1981; children: Ashley Renee, Amber Nichol, Rachel Brianne, Dylan Michael. BS, Ark. State U., 1981; MBA, U. Wyo., 1990. Engr. trainee B.J. Hughes, Dickinson, ND, 1981-82, dist. tech. sales, 1982-84, sr. dist. engr., 1984-85, region sales engr. Casper, Wyo., 1985-88; dist. mgr. BJ Svcs. Co., Casper, Wyo., 1988-92, region mgr., West Coast-Alaska ops., 1992—96, regional mgr., ops., Northeastern US, 1996—2008; pres., pumpco divsn. Complete Production Services, Inc., 2008—10, pres., appalachian divsn., 2010—. Mem. API, SPE, U.Wyo. Alumni Assn. Republican. Roman Catholic. Avocations: family, basketball, tennis, music, art. Home: 3715 Misty Cv Little Elm TX 75068-3117 Office: Complete Production Services Inc 1001 Louisiana St Houston TX 77002-5089 Office Phone: 281-372-2300. Office Fax: 281-372-2301. Business E-Mail: msonger@completeproduction.com.

SONI, PAUL J., corporate financial executive; Acctg. positions Price Waterhouse LLP; contr., internat. divsn. Savannah Foods & Industries, Inc.; corp. contr., US, L. Am. Oxford Industries, Inc.; v.p., contr. Roper Industries, Inc., 2002—, chief acctg. officer. Office: Roper Industries Inc Ste 200 6901 Professional Pky E Sarasota FL 34240 Office Phone: 941-556-2601. Office Fax: 941-556-2670.

SONNENFELD, GERALD, microbiology and immunology educator; b. NYC, Oct. 14, 1949; s. Otto Arthur and Ann (Perelman) S.; m. Elizabeth; 3 children, Jennifer, Jessica, Susan. BS, CCNY, 1970; PhD, U. Pitts., 1975. Postdoctoral fellow Stanford (Calif.) U. Sch. Medicine, 1976-78; assoc. guest worker Ames Rsch. Ctr. NASA, Moffett Field, Calif., 1976-78; asst. prof. microbiology and immunology U. Louisville, 1978-83, from assoc. prof. to prof. microbiology and immunology, 1983-93; dir. rsch. immunology Carolinas Med. Ctr., Charlotte, NC, 1994—98. Prof., chair dept. microbiology and immunology, assoc. dean basic scis. & grad. studies Morehouse Sch. Med., Atlanta, 1999-2004; v.p. rsch. Binghamton U., SUNY, 2004-10, Clemson U., 2010-. Assoc. editor Jour. Interferon Cytokine Rsch., 1981—; contbr. over 150 articles to profl. jours. Grantee NASA, 1978—2008, Environ. Protection Agy., 1980-82, U.S. Army, 1983-87, NIH, 1984-87. Mem. Internat. Soc. for Interferon Rsch., Am. Assn. Immunologists (Lifetime Svc. award, 2010), Am. Soc. Microbiology, Am. Soc. Gravitational and Space Biology (governing bd. 1992-95, pres.-elect 1996-97, pres. 1997-1998), Sigma Xi. Avocation: railroading. Office: Clemson University 300 Brackett Hall Clemson SC 29634-5701

SONNENFELD, JEFFREY ALAN, construction executive; b. Phila., Apr. 1, 1954; s. Burton David and Rochelle (Galant) S. AB, Harvard Coll., 1976; MBA, Harvard U., 1978, D in Bus. Adminstrn., 1980. Mcht., Retail Clothing The Heir & Gentry Shop, Hatboro, Pa., 1968—72; pres. Harvard Radio Broadcasting, Cambridge, Mass., 1974—76; mgmt. intern Scott Paper, IBM, Phila., Armonk, 1976—78; adv., tutor Harvard Coll., Cambridge, 1976—80; rsch. asst. Harvard University, Cambridge, 1977—80, asst. prof., 1980—84; assoc. prof. Harvard Business School, Cambridge, 1984—89; prof. Emory U., Atlanta, 1989, dir., Ctr. Leadership & Career Studies, 1989—97; sr. assoc. dean, Exec. Programs Sch. Mgmt. Yale U., New Haven, 2001, Lester Crown prof., Mgmt. Practice, 2001. Bd. dirs. Eastgate Pub., NYC, Kloster Cruises Ltd., Miami, Levity HR, Inc., TheStreet.com., Lennar Corp., Miami, 2005-, founder, pres. Yale Chief Exec. Leadership Inst., 1989-. Author: Corporate Views of the Public Interest: Perceptions of the Forest Products Industry, 1981, Managing Career Systems: Channeling the Flow of Executive Careers, 1984, The Hero's Farewell: What Happens When CEOs Retire, 1988 (best seller 1989), Concepts of Leadership, The International Library of Management, 1995; co-author: (with R. Gandossy) Leadership and Governance from the Inside Out, 2004, (with Andrew Ward) Firing Back: How Great Leaders Rebound After Career Disasters, 2007; mem. bd. editors Acad. Mgmt. Jour., Acad. Mgmt. Exec., Orgnl. Dynamics, Jour. Occupational Behavior; contbr. articles to profl. jours., chpts. to books. Adv., dir. Am. Assn. Ret. Persons, Washington, 1992; mem. Anti-Defamation League, Washington, 1992, Am. Jewish Com., NYC, 1992; trustee Sacred Heart U. Recipient AT&T-Hawthorne award for Social Sci., 1980, Standout New Mgmt. Book award Bus. Week, 1988. Mem. Acad. Mgmt. (dir., trustee, Outstanding Rsch. in Social Issues award 1981, 84, Award for Best Article, 2005), Kiwanis, Havard Alumni Assn., Harvard Bus. Sch. Club. Democrat. Office: Lennar Corp Bd Directors 700 NW 107th Ave Miami FL 33172 Office Phone: 305-559-4000. Office Fax: 305-228-8383. E-mail: jsonnenfeld@lennar.com.

SONTANY, JANIS BAIRD, state legislator; b. Aug. 9, 1946; 2 children. Former pres. Nashville Women's Polit. Caucus; mem. Children & Family Affairs Com., Human Resources Com., Transp. Com.; bd. mem. Outlook Nashville, Nashville Thermal Transfer Corp.; customer svc. rep. DuPont Corp.; mem. Nashville Met. Coun., 1995—; mem. Dist. 53 Tenn. House of Reps., 2003—. Mem.: Divsn. County Dem. Women. Democrat. Office: 188 Chilton St Nashville TN 37211 also: 32 Legislative Plz Nashville TN 37243-0153 Office Phone: 615-741-6861. Office Fax: 615-253-0325. Business E-Mail: rep.janis.sontany@capitol.tn.gov.

SOOD, ANIL K., oncologist, researcher; MD, U. N.C., 1991. Diplomate Am. Bd. Obstetrics and Gynecology 1999. Intern in ob-gyn. U. Fla., Gainesville, Fla., 1991—93, resident in ob-gyn., 1993—95; fellow in gynecol. oncology U. Iowa, Iowa City, 1995—98; asst. prof. U. of Iowa, 1998—2002; assoc. prof. gynecologic oncology and cancer biology M.D. Anderson Cancer Ctr., U. Tex., Houston, 2002—06, dir. ovarian cancer rsch., 2005—, prof. gynelogic oncology and cancer biology, 2006—. Editl. adv. bd. Cancer, 2003—; editl. bd. Current Cancer Therapy Reviews, 2003—, Cancer Biology and Therapy, 2005—, Obstetrics and Gynecology, 2006—. Recipient Reproductive Scientist Devel. award, NIH, 1999—2001, Rsch. award, Gynecologic Cancer Found., 2001, Am. Cancer Soc./U. Iowa, 1998, phase 2 RSDP award, Gynecologic Cancer Found., 2001, James F. Nolan award, Western Assn. Gynecologic Oncologists, 2002, 2004, Charles A. Hunter Jr. prize, Am. Gynecological and Obstetrical Soc., 2003, Faculty Scholar award, M.D. Anderson Cancer Ctr., 2006—09. Mem.: ACOG, Am. Soc. Clin. Investigation, Am. Soc. Clin. Oncology, Soc. of Gynecologic Oncologists, Am. Assn. for Cancer Rsch. Office: UTMD Anderson Cancer Ctr Dept Gyn Oncology 1515 Holcombe Blvd 440 Houston TX 77030

SOOUDI, MATTHEW M., retired surgeon; b. Iran, Oct. 24, 1934; came to U.S., 1962; s. Yahya and Iran (Nicknejad) S.; m. Joyce J. Sooudi, Oct. 2, 1965; 2 children. MD, U. Iran, 1962. Diplomate Am. Bd. Surgery, Am. Bd. Colon and Rectal Surgery, Internat. Bd. Proctology. Intern. Bon Secours Hosp., Grosse Pointe, Mich., 1962-63; resident Grace Hosp., Detroit, 1963-67, Ferguson Clinic, Grand Rapids, Mich., 1967-68; pvt. practice St. Elizabeth Hosp., Tex., Beaumont (Tex.) Med. Hosp., Bapt. Hosp., Tex.; ret., 1996. Fellow ACS, Am. Soc. Colon and Rectal Surgeons, Internat. Assn. Proctologists; mem. AMA, Am. Assn. Phys. Surgeons, So. Med. Assn., Tex. Med. Assn., Tex. Soc. Colon and Rectal Surgeons. Address: 980 Thomas Rd Beaumont TX 77706-4621

SORFLEET, DIANA B., human resources executive, former electric power industry executive; b. 1964; BA in Comm., Loyola U. Chgo.; M in Mgmt. & Human Resources Devel., Nat. Louis U.; MBA, Northwestern U. Human resources rep. Carson Pirie Scott; v.p., human resources, mgr., employee rels. Exelon Nuc., mgr., human resources Byron; OD, mng. dir., human resources, employee comm., recruiting, labor postions Exelon Generation Co., LLC (subs. Exelon Corp.), mgr., human resources Zion, v.p., human resources; dir., leadership devel. Exelon Corp., v.p., strategic human resources planning, devel., v.p., diversity, devel.; v.p., chief human resources officer CSX Corp., Jacksonville, Fla., 2011—. Office: CSX Corp 500 Water St 15th Fl Jacksonville FL 32202 Office Phone: 904-359-3200.

SORGE, KAREN LEE, printing company executive, consultant; b. Warwick, NY, May 27, 1958; d. Wesley Thomas and Margaret Anne (Storms) Kervatt; m. David W. Farquhar, July 16, 1982 (div. Feb. 1990); 1 child: Lauren Nicole; m. Thomas E. Sorge, May 16, 1997; children: Natalie MaKalen Sorge, Ryan Thomas. AS, Roger Williams Coll., 1978, BS cum laude, 1980. Office mgr. Price-Rite Printing Co., Dover, NJ, 1975—76; cons. SBA, Bristol, RI, 1978—80; account exec. P.M. Press Inc., Dallas, 1980—90, sales trainer, 1984—85; v.p. KDF Bus. Forms Inc., Dallas, 1984—90; account exec. Jarvis Press, Dallas, 1990—2008, Ussery Printing, Dallas; pres. Print Trends, Dallas, 1990—. Printer Tex. Aux. Charity Auction Orgn., Dallas, 1985, Cystic Fibrosis, Dallas, 1989—93, Life Enhancement Assn. Programs Found., 1992—, Dallas Soc. Visual Comm., 1992, AIDS Resources Com., Dallas chpt. Cerebral Palsy, 1994, Lloyd-Paxton AIDS Benefit, 1994, Feast for the Eyes Gala-Benefit to Prevent Blindness, 2001, Genesis Women's Shelter, 2002, others. Recipient award, Clampitt Paper Co., Dallas, 1982, P.M. Press Inc., 1983—89, Mead Paper Co., 1985—96, Feast for the Eyes Gala, 2001, Gold award, Adrian Advt., 2004, Silver award, 2005, 2006. Mem. Printing Industry in Am. (recipient Judges Favorite award 1992, Best of Show Hon. Mention award 1994, gold award Best of Tex. 1996), Internat. Assn. Bus. Communicators, Nat. Bus. Forms Assn. Republican. Baptist. Avocation: piano. Home: 2600 Raintree Dr Southlake TX 76092-5536 Office Phone: 817-424-5252. Business E-Mail: printtrends@mac.com.

SORIA, JOAKIM AGUSTIN, professional baseball player; b. Monclova, Mexico, May 18, 1984; Relief pitcher Kansas City Royals, 2007—12, Tex. Rangers, 2013—. Mem. Mex. nat. team World Baseball Classic, 2009. Recipient Spl. Achievement award, Kans. City Sports Commn. and Found., 2009; named to Am. League All-Star Team, Maj. League Baseball, 2008, 2010. Office: Texas Rangers 1000 Ballpark Way Arlington TX 76011

SORKIN, ROBERT DANIEL, psychologist, industrial engineer, educator; b. NYC, May 24, 1937; s. Harry and Cynthia (Erdreich) S.; m. Nancy Jayne Sloan, July 3, 1960; children: David, Susan. BEE, Carnegie Inst. Tech., 1958; PhD, U. Mich., 1965. Engr. human factors Martin Co., Balt., 1958—60; assoc. rsch. engr. Cooley Labs. U. Mich., Ann Arbor, 1960—65; asst. prof. psychology Purdue U., West Lafayette, Ind., 1965—68, assoc. prof., 1968—73, prof. dept. psychol. scis., 1973—88; prof., chair dept. psychology U. Fla., Gainesville, 1988—95, prof. dept. psychology, indsl. and sys. engring. dept., 1995—2008, emeritus prof., dept. psychology, indsl. and system engring., 2008—. Asst. dean sch. humanities, social scis. and edn. Purdue U., 1973-75; dir. psychobiology program NSF, Washington, 1975-76; chair Coun. Grad. Depts. Psychology, Blacksburg, Va., 1994-95; mem. com. on hearing and bioacoustics NRC, Washington, 1987-90; mgr. cognition program Air Force Office Scientific Rsch., Va., 2002-2005; sr. scientist Human Effectiveness Directorate, Air Force Rsch. Lab., Wright-Patterson AFB, Ohio, 2005-07. Author: (software) Laboratory Projects in Experimental Psychology, 1998; co-author: Human Factors: Understanding People-System Relationships, 1983; contbr. articles to profl. jours.Jour. Acoustical Soc. Am., Perception and Psychophysics, Jour. Exptl. Psychology, Human Factors, Psychol. Rev., Psych. Sci. With US Army, 1960. Fellow Acoustical Soc. Am., APA, Am. Psychol. Soc.; mem. Human Factors Soc., European Assn. Decision Making, Soc. for Judgment and Decision Making Home: 159 Marine St Apt 205 Saint Augustine FL 32084

SOROKULOVA, IRYNA, microbiologist, educator; b. Kiev, Ukraine, June 3, 1949; d. Boris Kalmanovsky and Varvara Khomenko; m. Valeriy Sorokulov, Aug. 10, 1973; 1 child, Volodymyr Sorokulov. Degree summa cum laude, Kiev U., 1971; PhD, Inst. Microbiology and Virology, Kiev, 1983, DSc, 1999. Cert. WHO, 1998. Asst. prof. Inst. Microbiology and Virology, 1974—91, assoc. prof., 1991—2000, prof., 2000—02; vis. prof. Auburn U., Ala., 2002—07, rsch. prof., 2007—12, prof., 2012—. Head dept. Com. Biol. Products, Kiev, 1996—2002. Author: (book) Guide for Isolation and Identification of Bacteria of the Bacillus Genus from Human and Animals, Probiotic Subalin — New Approach to Treatment of Bacterial and Viral Infections; contbr. articles to numerous profl. jours. Recipient State prize, Ukraine Sci. and Tech., Govt. of Ukraine, 1995, Cert. of Recognition, Ministry of Health Ukraine, 2001, Mechnikov's prize, NAS Ukraine, 2002; grantee, Ukrainian Ministry of Sci. and Tech., 1997—98, NIH, 2003—05. Russian Orthodox. Achievements include patents for biosporin for prophylaxis and treatment of human enteric diseases; method of correction of vaginal microflora; method of eubiotic Biosporin production; probiotic preparation with complex activity; bacillus licheniformis strain with antiviral and antibacterial activity; souche bacillus subtilis CU1, son utilization comme agent immunomodulateur du systeme immunitaire et vaccin vivant recombinant contre Helicobacter pylori la contenant; method for enhancing the efficacy of antitumor vaccine; phage ligand sensor devices and uses theirof; strain of bacillus subtilis exhibiting the antiviral and antibacterial activity. Avocation: travel. Office: Auburn Univ 109 Greene Hall Auburn AL 36849 Business E-Mail: sorokib@auburn.edu.*

SORRELL, ROZLYN, singer, actress, theater director, educator; b. Bklyn. d. Nathaniel Otis and Cupid Viola (Logan) S. BA in Theatre, CUNY, 1976, MS in Edn., 1985. Cert. tchr. Calif., NY. Tchr. LA Unified Sch. Dist., 1997, Sylvan Learning Ctr., LA, 1998, Westmark Sch., Encino, Calif., 2000, Achievement Sch., Raleigh, NC, 2002, Easter Seals UCP, NC, 2006. Bus. cons., LA, 1989—; voice tchr., LA, 1992—; mem. Albert McNeil Jubilee Singers, LA, 1994—2000. Actress various TV programs, commls., stage prodn. and films, 1986—; soloist Temple of Music and Art, Tucson, 1990, El San Juan (PR) Hotel, 1985, Hour of Power, Glory of Christmas, Glory of Easter, Garden Grove, Calif., 1994—, Miyazaki Civic Culture Hall, Japan, 1996, Anaheim Pond, Calif., 1997, Honolulu Symphony, 1998, Hollywood Bowl, Calif., 1998, Gospel Recording Artist, 2000, Harris Teeter Harvest Festival, Raleigh Conv. Ctr., 2004, Carolina Theatre, Durham, NC, 2005, Spiritual Awakening, WRAL-TV, NC, 2004, Pops in the Park, Regency Theatre, Cary, NC, 2004, 05, 06, Summerfest, Koka Booth Amphitheater, Cary, NY,2008, African Am. Cultural Ctr., Raleigh, NC, 2004, Greensboro Coliseum, 2005, Progress Energy Ctr. Performing Arts, Meymandi Concert Hall, Raleigh, NC, 2006, 07, 08, 09, 11, Mint Raleigh NC 2008, NC Fairgrounds, 2006, Hayes Barton Baptist, Raleigh, NC, 2007, 09, Garner Hist. Auditorium, NC, 2007, 2008; guest artist, soloist NC Symphony, 2006, 08, 13-City Tour, 2010, 2011, 1st Annual Gospel Christians Spectacular NC Symphony, 2007, Blues in the Night Summerfest Koka Booth Amphitheatre, 2008; soloist Durham Symphy, 2010, 11, Music dir., Parchman Hour World Premiere PlayMakers Repertory Co. Inc., Chapel Hill, 2011, NC Theatre Cabaret Night, 2008, CMP Gospel Showcase, Dallas Conv. Ctr., 2007; featured soloist Artsplosure Moore Square Park, Raleigh, 2007, Paramount Theatre, Goldsboro, NC, 2009, 12, The Parchman Hour, 2011, The Parchman Hour Winston Salem State U., 2012, Whiteville, NC, 2012, numerous others; music dir., Parchman Hour Playmakers Repertory Co., solo concert Where The Spirit Leads, Sampson Ctr. Stage, Clinton, NC, 2008; dir. Storms of Life, 2005, Country Club NC (Pinehurst), 09, 11, Pinehurst Resort & Hotel, 2012, Kinston Arts Ctr, Kinston, NC, 2012, pub. spkr., Communicate With Conf. Clarity & Conviction and Concert, soloist, 32nd Annual MLK Prayer Breakfast Sheraton Imperial Hotel & Convention Ctr., Durham, 2012, 14, Clover Sch. Dist. Auditorium Clover (SC), Hampton St. Auditorium Waterboro (SC), 2009, 11, Black Nativity, Justice Theater Project, Raleigh, NC, 2012, Ctr. Performing and Visual Arts, Newnan, Ga., 2013, Ruined, Burning Coal Theatre, Raleigh, 2013, Black Pearl Sings! Temple Theatre, Sanford, NC, 2014, Music & Musicians NC, Carolina Theatre, Durham, Durham Symp. Orch., 2014, Explorations in the Arts, Craven CC, 2013, The

First Lady, St. Augustina's U., Seby Jones Auditorium, Raleigh, 2014. Mem. AFTRA, SAG, Actors Equity Assn, Theater Pk. Raleigh, NC, Performing Arts Exchange Juried Showed Roper Performing Art Ctr. Norfolk, Va. Avocations: dance, walking, theater, exercise. Office Phone: 919-329-8070. Personal E-mail: rozlyn@rozlynsorrell.com. Business E-Mail: info@vocalprecision.com.

SORRENTINO, CHARLES ALAN, manufacturing executive; b. Beloit, Wis., Oct. 9, 1944; s. Charles Andrew and Virginia Mary (Morgan) S.; m. Mary Kay Potts, Nov. 25, 1972; children: Michael, Robert. BS in Mech. Engring., Southern Ill. U., 1970; MBA, U. Chgo., 1978. Subs. pres., divsn. v.p. & region v.p. PepsiCo, Inc.; engr. Sundstrand Corp., Rockford, Ill., 1970—72, sales engr., 1972—74, sales mgr. Dowagiac, Mich., 1974—78, dir., Mktg. Bristol, Va., 1978—79; v.p. Bristol Corp., Bristol, 1979—83; group gen. mgr. Reed Industries, Atlanta, 1983—84; sr. mgmt. designate Pizza Hut, Atlanta, 1984—86, region v.p., 1986—88, pres., divsn. v.p. Boca Raton, Fla., 1988; pres. Pameco Corp., 1994—98; pres., CEO & bd. dirs. Houston Wire & Cable, 1998—. Avocations: golf, reading, outdoor sports. Home: 2920 Cason St Houston TX 77005-3916 Office: Houston Wire & Cable Co 10201 N Loop E Houston TX 77029 Office Phone: 713-609-2100. Office Fax: 713-609-2101. E-mail: csorrentino@houwire.com.

SORRENTINO, TONY, wholesale distribution executive; Attended, Clemson U., SC. Account mgr. Henderson Advt.; dir. merchandising POS & barcoding sales unit ScanSource, Inc.; v.p. merchandising ScanSource Security, 2004—08, v.p. sales ScanSource Security, 2008—. Office: ScanSource Inc 6 Logue Ct Greenville SC 29615 Office Phone: 864-288-2432. Office Fax: 864-288-1165.

SOSTILIO, ROBERT FRANCIS, office equipment marketing consultant; b. Boston, Nov. 17, 1942; s. Natale J. and Louise Sostilio; m. Gail Marie McGuinness, Apr. 17, 1966. Student, U. Maine, 1960—61, Broward Jr. Coll., Ft. Lauderdale, 1967—70, Miami-Dade Jr. Coll., 1979. Product assurance engr. Saxon Copystatics, Miami, Fla., 1970-77; internat. svc. mgr. Saxon Export Corp., Miami, 1977-80; nat. svc. mgr. Cybernet Internat., Warren, N.J., 1980-81; mgr. nat. copier svc. Monroe Systems for Bus., Morris Plains, N.J., 1981-82; nat. OEM mgr. Panasonic Indsl. Co., Secaucus, N.J., 1982-86; assoc. dir. copier rsch. Dataquest, San Jose, Calif., 1987-90; mgr. product program Ricoh Corp., West Caldwell, N.J., 1986-87, dir. copier mktg., 1990-94, dir. strategic planning, 1994-96; group svc. dir. converging digital peripherals Cap Ventures, 1996—2000; pres., CEO Sostilio and Assocs. Internat. Inc., Ocala, Fla., 2002—. Editor-in-chief Knights Colombus Newsletter Coun. 9649, 2006—09. Editor: (newsletter) Multifunctionality, 1987, Color Copiers, 1989; editor: (pub.) SAI Digest, 2002—. Block capt. Meadow Ridge Civic Assn., Basking Ridge, NJ, 1985—87; sgt.-at-arms UNICO Nat., San Jose, 1990. With USN, 1964—67. Roman Catholic. Avocations: woodworking, home remodeling, dog breeding, travel, cooking. Office: Sostilio & Assocs Internat PO Box 830190 Ocala FL 34483 Office Phone: 352-624-2625.

SOSTMAN, DIRK, physician, clinical researcher, medical educator; b. NYC, Nov. 20, 1948; s. Henry and Theodora (Slokker) S.; m. Maria Preka, Sept. 1, 2003; 1 child Erik Alexandros. MD, Yale University, New Haven, 1977. Diplomate Am. Bd. Radiology, Nat. Bd. Med. Examiners. Intern and resident Yale-New Haven Hosp., 1977—82; prof., chair Weill Med. Coll. Cornell U., NYC, 1995—2005, exec. vice dean, 2003—; exec. v.p. The Meth. Hosp., Houston, 2005—; CEO Meth. Physician Orgn., 2006—. Mem. lung scan interpretation panel and nuclear medicine working group Prospective Investigation of Pulmonary Embolism Diagnosis Study, Nat. Heart, Lung and Blood Inst., 1984-88; cons. Fluoromed Pharms, 1988, Am. Cancer Soc., 1992; mem. Duke Comprehensive Cancer Ctr., 1993—; program dir. Duke Winter Imaging Course, 1993-94; vis. prof. U. Pisa, 1993, U. Milan, 1993; dir. Imaging Rsch. Lab. Yale U. Sch. Medicine, 1981-84, dir. MR Imaging, 1983-87; mem. numerous adv. panels. Assoc. editor: Yearbook of Nuclear Medicine, 1984-92; mem. editorial bd.: Investigative Radiology, 1984—, Magnetic Resonance Imaging, 1985—, Jour. Thoracic Imaging, 1985—; manuscript referee; contbr. chpts. to books and numerous articles to profl. jours. Recipient Fales prize Rutgers U., 1972, Dolgan Meml. award Yale U., 1972; Yale U. summer fellowship, 1975, Lamport Biomed. Rsch. award, 1976; Winchester Chest fellow in radiology; grantee in field. Fellow Am. Coll. Chest Physicians, Am. Coll. Radiology; mMem. Fleischner Soc. (George Simon Meml. award 1982, exec. com. 1987-90, mem. Simon award com. 1991—), Soc. MRI (edn. com. 1984-86), Assn. Univ. Radiologists (Pres. 2001, Stauffer award 1988, Stauffer award com. 1983), Radiol. Soc. N.Am., Soc. Thoracic Radiology (founding mem.), Sigma Xi, Phi Beta Kappa, others. leadership in major clinical trials of venous thromboembolism diagnosis. Office: Dunn 200 6565 Fannin St Houston TX 77030 Office Phone: 713-441-2192. Business E-Mail: dsostman@tmhs.org.

SOTO, ARMANDO, plastic surgeon; MD, Johns Hopkins Sch. of Medicine. Diplomate Am. Bd. of Plastic Surgeon. Tng. gen. and plastic surgery The Barnes-Jewish Hosp. of Wash. Univ.; tng. advanced techniques for breast enhancement and reconstruction The Harry and Jeanette Weinberg Ctr. for Women's Health and Medicine, Baltimore; fellow Am. Coll. of Surgeons. Named one of Top 40 under 40, Baltimore Bus. Jour. Mem.: Am. Soc. for Aesthetic Plastic Surgery, Am. Soc. of Plastic Surgeons. Office: Aesthetic Enhancement Suite 100 7009 Dr Phillips Blvd Orlando FL 32819 Office Phone: 407-218-4550.

SOTO, DARREN, state legislator; b. Ringwood, NJ, Feb. 25, 1978; BA in Econ., Rutgers U., 2000; JD, George Washington U. Law Sch., 2004. Fin. analyst Prudential Insurance, 1998—2001; summer assoc. L.A. Gonzalez Law Offices, 2002—04; pres. D. Soto Law Offices, 2005—; mem. Dist. 49 Fla. House of Reps., 2007—, ranking mem. civil justice and courts policy com., mem. criminal and civil justice appropriations com., energy and utilities policy com. Mem. Hispanic C. of C. Met. Orlando, 2006—, City of Orlando Civil Svc. Bd., 2006—. Mem.: Orange County Democrats (treas. 2007), Orange County Young Democrats (v.p. comm. 2007). Democrat. Office: 402 S Monroe St Rm 1402 Tallahassee FL 32399-1300 also: 5425 S Semoran Blvd Ste 1-B Orlando FL 32822-1751 also: Kissimmee City Hall 101 N Church St 3rd Fl Kissimmee FL 34741-5054 Office Phone: 850-488-9240, 407-249-4743, 407-846-5187. Business E-Mail: darren.soto@myfloridahouse.gov.

SOTO, GEOVANY, professional baseball player; b. San Juan, Jan. 20, 1983; Catcher Chgo. Cubs, 2005—12, Tex. Rangers, 2012—. Mem. Puerto Rican nat. team World Baseball Classic, 2009. Named Rookie of Yr., The Sporting News, 2008, Nat. League Outstanding Rookie, Maj. League Baseball Players Assn., 2008, Nat. League Rookie of Yr., Maj. League Baseball, 2008; named to Nat. League All-Star Team, 2008. Achievements include being the first rookie catcher in Major League Baseball history to start in the All-Star Game, 2008; catching Carlos Zambrano's no-hitter against the Houston Astros, September 14, 2008. Office: Texas Rangers 1000 Ballpark Way Arlington TX 76011

SOTOMORA-VON AHN, RICARDO FEDERICO, pediatrician, educator; b. Guatemala City, Guatemala, Oct. 22, 1947; s. Ricardo and Evelyn (von Ahn) S.; m. Eileen Marie Holcomb, May 9, 1990; m. Victoria Monzon, Nov. 26, 1971; children: Marisol, Clarisa, Ricardo III, Charlotte Marie. MD, San Carlos U., 1972; MS in Physiology, U. Minn., 1978. Diplomate Am. Bd. Pediats., Am. Bd. Pediat. Cardiology, Am. Bd. Neonatology-Perinatal Medicine. Rotating intern Gen. Hosp., Guatemala, 1971-72; pediat. intern U. Ark., 1972-73, resident, 1973-75; fellow in pediat. cardiology U. Minn., 1975-78; rsch. assoc. in cardiovasc. pathology United Hosps., St. Paul, 1976; fellow in neonatal-perinatal medicine St. Paul's Children's Hosp., 1977-78, U. Ark., 1981-82; instr. pediats. U. Minn., 1978-79; pediat. cardiologist, unit cardiovasc. surg. Roosevelt Hosp., Guatemala City, 1979-81; asst. prof. pediats. cardiology and neonatology U. Ark., Little Rock, 1981-83; pvt. practice Little Rock, 1983—. Fellow: Am. Coll. Angiology, Am. Coll. Chest Physicians, Am. Coll. Cardiology, Am. Acad. Pediat.; mem.: AAAS, ABA, Soc. Critical Care Medicine, So. Soc. Pediat. Rsch., Ctrl. Ark. Pediat. Soc., Guatemala Coll. Physicians and Surgeons, Soc. Pediat. Echocardiology, Am. Heart Assn., NY Acad. Scis., Ark. Med. Soc., Soc. Genealogists London, Guatemala Acad. Genealogy, Heraldry and Hist. Studies (corr.), The Country Club of Little Rock. Home: 3 River Ridge Ct Little Rock AR 72227-1523 Office: The Pediatric Clinic 3401 Spring Mill Dr Ste #245 North Little Rock AR 72117 E-mail: rfsotomora@aol.com.

SOTTILE, F. MICHAEL, state legislator; b. Rock Hill, SC, June 7, 1948; s. Frank J. and Tommie Lee Sottile; m. Loraine Johnson, Sept. 17, 1977; 1 child, Amy L. Attended, Bapt. Coll., Charleston. Pres. Ind. Ins. Agts. Charleston, 1986; bd. of dirs. Ind. Aents SC, Charleston, 1986—89; councilman City of Isle of Palms, 1990—2001, mayor, 2001—08; bd. mem. Mcpl. Assn. SC, 2004—07; mem. Dist. 112 SC House of Reps., SC, 2008—. Republican. Bapt. Home and Office: Dist/Home Office 132 Sparrow Dr Isle Of Palms SC 29451 Office: Capitol Office 306D Blatt Bldg Columbia SC 29201 Home Phone: 843-886-8759; Office Phone: 843-884-3159, 803-212-6880. E-mail: mikescottile@schouse.org.

SOTUNDE, TUNDE, medical insurance company executive, pediatrician; MBA, U. Memphis; MD, U. Ibadan, Nigeria. Med. dir. Cigna Healthcare; residency in pediatrics Howard U.; chief pediatrics Syracuse Cmty. Health Ctr., NY; v.p., chief med. officer, Southeast Region United Healthcare, 2001—07; chief med. officer The Little Clinic, Nashville, 2007—08; CEO, Cmty. Care of Ga. Amerigroup Corp., 2008—. Office: Amerigroup Corp Ste 100 4425 Corporation Ln Virginia Beach VA 23462 Office Phone: 757-490-6900. Office Fax: 757-518-3600. Business E-Mail: tsotunde@amerigrp.com.

SOUCEK, DANIEL F., state legislator; m. Kim Soucek; children: Lucy Soucek, Isaac Soucek, Janie Ann Soucek. BA, US Mil. Academy, 1991. Tchr. Alliance Bible Fellowship Sunday Sch.; Co. Comdr., Internat. Mil. Student office US Army, 1991—99; dir. Young Life Area for Watauga, 1999—2004, Ashe, 1999—2004; cross-country track coach Watauga High Sch., 2001—03; candidate, Dist. 93 NC House of Representatives, 2008; mem. Dist. 45 NC State Senate, 2010—. Republican. Office: 313 Williams Ridge Rd Boone NC 28607 Address: NC Senate 300 N Salisbury St Room 310 Raleigh NC 27603-5925 Office Phone: 919-733-5742, 828-773-6197. Business E-Mail: Dan.Soucek@ncleg.net.

SOUERWINE, DAVID A., healthcare company executive; BS in Math. & Economics, Dickinson Coll., Carlisle, Pa.; MBA, U. Rochester, NY. Pres. proprietary Rx & OTC pharm. Bausch & Lomb, Inc., Rochester, NY; corp. v.p. Spectrascan Imaging Svcs., Inc., Windsor, Conn.; divsn. pres. Horizon Med. Products; pres. Neostar Med. Technologies; pres. Automation divsn. McKesson Corp., Cranberry Township, Pa., 2002—, pres. Provider Technologies divsn. Atlanta, 2010—. Office: McKesson Provider Technologies 5995 Windward Pky Alpharetta GA 30005 also: McKesson Automation Inc 500 Cranberry Woods Dr Cranberry Township PA 16066 E-mail: dave.souerwine@mckesson.com.

SOULES, CARLTON, councilman; b. San Antonio, Tex. m. Laura Soules; children: Joe, Jennifer. Grad., Southern Methodist U. Councilman Dist. 10 San Antonio City Coun., 2011—. Mem. San Antonio Local Devel. Co., San Antonio Housing Authority, Austin Highway Revitalization Project, San Antonio Parks and Recreation Bd. Mem. San Antonio Food Bank Bd. Office: City Hall PO Box 839966 San Antonio TX 78283 also: 1635 NE Loop 410, Suite 604 San Antonio TX 78209 Office Phone: 210-207-7276, 210-207-0999. Office Fax: 210-207-8777, 210-207-0994.

SOUTHARD, EDWARD L., state legislator; b. Cornelia, Ga., Oct. 1, 1946; s. Don L. and Helen B.; m. Patricia Pressley, June 9, 1967; children: Edward L. Jr., Jason B. Mem. Berkeley County Planning and Zoning Com., Trident Workforce Bd.; charter mem. Berkeley County Landowners' Assn.; mem. Berkeley County Adv. Bd. for Roper Hosp.; business owner; mem. Dist. 100 SC House of Representatives, 2011—. Mem. SC Nat. Guard, 1966—71. Republican. Home: 1511 Dennis Blvd Moncks Corner SC 29461 Office: 530D Blatt Office Bldg Columbia SC 29201 Home Phone: 843-899-6162; Office Phone: 803-212-6930, 843-761-4366.

SOUTHERLAND, S. DUANE, manufacturing executive; b. Durham, NC, Apr. 24, 1949; s. Sydney Duane and Beatrice Marie (Carver) S.; m. Linda F. Lewis, Jan. 5, 1974, 1 child, S. Duane III. BSE, Duke U., 1971, MS in Engring., 1973, MBA, 1974. Ops. analyst Cooper Group Div. Cooper Industries, Apex, NC, 1974-78, planning analyst Houston, 1978-81, dir. fin. Cooper Electronics Div. Nashua, NH, 1981-83, gen. mgr. Conn. ops. Kirsch Div. Beacon Falls, Conn., 1983-87, pres. Kirsch Div. Sturgis, Mich., 1987-94; pres., CEO Conso Products Co., Union, SC, 1995-98; pres., CEO, dir. Equality Specialties, Inc., NYC, 1999—2001; pres., CEO Conso Products, Union, SC, 2002—, Taos, LLC, Spartanburg, 2005—. Republican. Baptist.

SOUTHERLAND, STEVE, state legislator; b. Mar. 8, 1955; 1 child, Mattea. Mem. Dist. 1 Tenn. State Senate, 2003—; sec. Transp. Com.; mem. Environ. Com., Govt. Operation, Joint Fiscal Rev. Com. Mem.: Rotary Club, Morristown Area C. of C., NRA. Republican. Baptist. Office: 322 West Hillcrest Dr Morristown TN 37813 also: 10 Legislative Plz Nashville TN 37243-0201 Office Phone: 615-741-3851. Office Fax: 615-253-0330. Business E-Mail: sen.steve.southerland@capitol.tn.gov.

SOUTHERLAND, STEVE (WILLIAM SOUTHERLAND II), United States Representative from Florida; b. Nashville, Tenn., Oct. 10, 1965; m. Susan Southerland; children: Samantha, Stephanie, Allison, Abby. AA in Mortuary Sci., Jefferson State CC, Birmingham, Ala.; BS in Bus. Mgmt., Troy State U., Ala. Lic. ins. agent; funeral dir. Co-owner, pres. Southerland Family Funeral Homes; founding ptnr. Genesis Granite and Stone, LLC, K&B Land and Timber Co., LLC; mem. US Congress from 2nd Fla. Dist., Washington, 2011—, US House Agrl. Com., 2011—, US House Transp. & Infrastructure Com., Washington, 2011—. Former mem. Early Edn. and Care Adv. Bd., Coun. on Aging Adv. Bd., Bay Def. Alliance, Covenant Hospice Found Bd., Bay Edn. Found., Fla. State Devel. Bd. Panama City Campus, Bay County Econ. Devel. Allliance; fundraiser American Heart Assn., American Cancer Soc., Jr. Svc. League; apptd. mem. Fla. Bd. Funeral Directors; charter mem. former trustee Northstar Ch.; former chmn. Early Childhood Learning Coalition NW Fla., Bay County C. of C., former chmn. mil. affairs com.; former mem. and chmn. Salvation Army Adv. Bd. Mem.: NRA, Nat. Funeral Directors Assn., Fla. Funeral Directors Assn., Leaders Network, Bay Patriots. Republican. Baptist. Office: US House of Representatives 1229 Longworth House Office Bldg Washington DC 20515 Office Phone: 202-225-5235.*

SOUTHERN, ROBERT ALLEN, lawyer; b. Independence, Mo., July 17, 1930; s. James Allen and Josephine (Ragland) S.; m. Cynthia Agnes Drews, May 17, 1952; children: David D., William A., James M., Kathryn S. O'Brien. BS in Polit. Sci., Northwestern U., 1952, LL.B., 1954. Bar: Ill. 1955. Assoc. Mayer, Brown & Platt (now Mayer Brown LLP), Chgo., 1954-64, ptnr., 1965-96, mng. ptnr., 1978-91, LA, 1991-96; CEO So. Assocs., Grayslake, Ill., 1997—2004, Chapel Hill, NC, 2004—09. Editor in chief Northwestern U. Law Rev., 1953-54. Trustee, v.p., gen. counsel LaRabida Children's Hosp. and Rsch. Ctr., Chgo., 1974-89; trustee Kenilworth (Ill.) Union Ch., 1980-88; pres. Joseph Sears Sch. Bd., 1977-79; trustee Rush U. Med. Ctr., 1983-91, life trustee, 1991—; bd. dirs. Boys and Girls Clubs Chgo., 1986-91; governing mem. Orchestral Assn. Chgo., 1988-93. With U.S. Army, 1955-57. Mem. Carolina Club (Chapel Hill, NC), Lawyers Club Chgo., Order of Coif. Home: 3000 Galloway Ridge Apt K 304 Pittsboro NC 27312-5519 Personal E-mail: rsouthern@nc.rr.com.

SOUTHERN, TERRY KEITH, engineering executive; b. Shelbyville, Tenn., USA, Aug. 29, 1954; s. Harry Jerome Southern and Mary Millinea Jones; m. Tinya Leigh Rose Butler, Dec. 1981 (div. Sept. 12, 1988); children: Jeremy Ryan, James Aaron, Amanda Renee. BS in Aviation Mgmt., Southern Ill., 1989; BS in Fire Sci., Norcross, Ga., 2007; degree in Fire Sci., Ala. Fire Coll., Tuscaloosa. Cert. fire ins., fire fighter II, fire instr. I/II, fire officer I. Master sgt. US Marine Corps., Wash., DC, 1971—92; fire commander Fire Dept. Lexington, Ala., 1995—2000; fire engr. insp. Killen Fire Dept., Killen, Ala., 2000—07; fire officer Boeing Aircraft, Ala., 2002—05; fire engr. insp. Wackenttut IRAQ, 2005—. Pres. Enferno Marina Del Rey, Calif., 2007—. Decorated Navy Cotmnendation medal, Marine Corps Expeditionary medal, Presidential Svc. Badge, Nat. Defense medal, Overseas Deployment Ribbon; recipient award, Am. Assn. Airport Executives, 1980, Fire Dept. Safety Assn., 2007, Congressional Fire Svcs. Inst., 2008, Marine Corps Good Conduct medal. Mem.: Congressional Fire Svc. Inst., Fire Dept. Safety Officers Assn., Am. Assn. Airport Executives, Pine Ridge Hunt Club. Avocations: hunting, fishing, woodworking. Office: Wackenhut Svcs WSI Fire Emergency Svcs Mosul Fire Dept St 2 Mosul AL 09334 Home Phone: 818-451-8414. Personal E-mail: tksouth4@yahoo.com.

SOUTHWICK, FREDERICK SEACREST, epidemiologist, internist, medical educator, medical researcher; s. Jessie Ann and Wayne Orin Southwick; m. Kathleen Bzoch Southwick, Nov. 26, 2000; children: Peter Frederick, Ashley Ann, Robyn Rowe, Karli Rowe. BA, Yale U., New Haven, 1968; MD, Columbia Coll. Physicians and Surgeons, NYC, 1973; BS (hon.), U. Pa., Phila., 1990. Diplomate in internal medicine Am. Bd., 1973, in infectious diseases Am. Bd. Internal Medicine, 2000; cert. in advanced leadership initiative Harvard Bus. Sch., 2011. Asst. prof. medicine Harvard Med. Sch., Cambridge, Mass., 1982—85, U. Pa. Sch. Medicine, 1985—90, assoc. prof. medicine, 1990—91, chief infectious disease, 1991—2011, prof. medicine, 1991—; mgr. patient care quality projects U. Fla. Coll. Medicine, Gainesville, Fla., 2011—. Author: (med. textbook) Infectious Diseases in 30 Days, Infectious Diseases Quick Glance, Infectious Diseases: A Clinical Short Course, 2013; contbr. over 100 articles to profl. jours.; author: (med. textbook) Critically Ill: A 5-point Plan to Cure Healthcare Delivery, 2012; editor: Clinical Decision Support:Infectious Diseases. Fundraising campaign rep. Yale U.; campaign mgr. Congressman Allard Lowenstein, Baldwin, NY, 1970. Recipient Clin. Rsch. prize, U. Fla. Coll. Medicine, 1998, Ann. Maxwell Finland spkr., Infectious Diseases America, 1999; Med. Sch. Leadership fellowship, Edward J. Noble Found., 1968—73, Rsch. grants, Nat. Inst. Health, 1981—. Fellow: ACP; mem.: Am. Clin. and Climatologic Assn., Am. Assn. Physicians, Am. Soc. Clin. Investigation. Liberal. Congregationalist. Achievements include patents for use of the proteomic signature of peripheral white blood cells to detect anthrax infection. Avocations: rowing, bicycling, writing, travel, canoeing. Office: Univ Fla Box 100277 Gainesville FL 32610 Office Phone: 352-273-9511. Personal E-mail: fsouthwick@gmail.com.

SOUTHWICK, LESLIE HARBURD, federal judge, lawyer; b. Edinburg, Tex., Feb. 10, 1950; s. Lloyd M. and Ruth (Tarpley) S.; m. Sharon E. Polasek, Aug. 18, 1973; children: Philip, Catherine. BA cum laude, Rice U., 1972; JD, U. Tex., 1975. Bar: Tex. 1975, Miss. 1977. Law clk. to Hon. John F. Onion Jr. Tex. Ct. Criminal Appeals, Austin, 1975-76; law clk. to Hon. Charles Clark US Ct. Appeals (5th cir.), Jackson, Miss., 1976-77, judge, 2007—; assoc. Brunini, Grantham, Grower & Hewes, Jackson, 1977-83, ptnr., 1983-89; dep. asst. atty. gen. civil divsn. US Dept. Justice, Washington, 1989—93; judge Miss. Ct. Appeals (Dist. 4), 1995—2006. Adj. prof. Miss. Coll. Sch. Law, Jackson, 1985-89, 98-; mem. Miss. Constn. Study Commn., 1985-86. Author: Presidential Also-Rans and Running Mates, 1984, 2nd edit, 1998 (ALA Best Reference Book award 1985). Pres. Hinds County Mental Health Assn., Jackson, 1981-82, Jackson Servant Leadership Corp.; Miss. campaign mgr. George Bush for Pres., 1980, 88; alternate del. Rep. Nat. Conv., 1984, del., 1988; mem. State Rep. Exec. Com., 1988. Served in USAR, 1992—97 Miss. Army Nat. Guard, 1997—, dep. staff judge advocate US Army, 2004—05, staff judge advocate, 2006. Named Vol. of Yr., Hinds County Mental Health Assn., 1981, 85; recipient Miss. Bar Jud. Excellence award, 2004. Mem. ABA, Miss. Bar Assn. Lodges. Roman Catholic. Office: US Ct Appeals 245 E Capital St Jackson MS 39201

SOUTHWORTH, LOUIS SWEETLAND, II, lawyer; b. Huntington, W.Va., Sept. 4, 1943; s. Louis Sweetland and Mary (Davis) S.; m. Sharon Johnson, June 13, 1964; children: Laura Elizabeth, Brian Scott. AB, Marshall U., 1965; JD, W.Va. U., 1968; LLM, NYU, 1970. Mem., tax atty. Jackson & Kelly, Charleston, W.Va., 1968—, mem. exec. com., 1999—, chmn. exec. com., 2001—. Trustee U. Charleston, Greater Kanawha Valley Found., Charleston, CAMC Found., Charleston, Highland Hosp. Found.; bd. mem. Clay Found. Named Corp. Lawyer of Yr., W.Va. Best Lawyers, 2009; named one of Best Lawyers in America, 1993—2011. Fellow Am. Coll. Tax Counsel, W.Va. Bar Found.; mem. ABA, W.Va. Bar Assn., Kanawha County Bar Assn., W.Va. Tax Inst., Order of Coif, Edgewood Country Club, Rotary. Democrat. Methodist. Avocations: golf, tennis, skiing, squash. Office: Jackson & Kelly PLLC 500 Lee St E Ste 1600 PO Box 553 Charleston WV 25322 Office Phone: 304-340-1231. Office Fax: 304-340-1093. Business E-Mail: lsouthworth@jacksonkelly.com.

SOWARDS, JOHN A., lawyer; m. Elizabeth Sowards; 2 children. BA magna cum laude, U. Tenn., 1975; JD cum laude, U. SC, 1982. Bar: SC. Atty. Nexsen Pruet, Columbia, 1980—, chmn. of bd., 2010—. Former troop leader Boy Scouts America; former youth sports coach; active Saluda Shoals Found.; commr. Irmo Chapin Recreation Commn., 2004—. 2d lt. US Army, reservist USAR.

Recipient Outstanding HS Mentor award, Lexington-Richland Sch. Dist. Five, 2003, Outstanding Bd. Mem. award, Columbia Urban League, 2004. Office: Nexsen Pruet 1230 Main St Ste 700 Columbia SC 29201 Office Phone: 803-771-8900. Office Fax: 803-727-1426. Business E-Mail: jsowards@nexsenpruet.com.

SOWELL, JOSEPH A., III, hospital administrator, lawyer; b. Sept. 20, 1956; m. Joanne Sowell; children: Jacob Sowell, Joseph Sowell. B, U. Ala., 1978, JD, 1981; LLM, U. Fla., 1982. Co-mgr., corp., comml. transactions practice Waller Lansden Dortch & Davis, ptnr., 1987—96, 1999—2009; COO Arcon Healthcare; with Arcon Healthcare (Devel.), 1996—99; sr. v.p., chief devel. officer HCA, Inc., 2009—. Active Room In the Inn-Campus for Human Devel., St. Luke's Cmty. House. Mem.: ABA, Nashville Bar Assn. (health law comm.), Tenn. Bar Assn. Office: HCA Inc 1 Park Plz Nashville TN 37203 Office Phone: 615-344-9551. Office Fax: 615-344-2266. Business E-Mail: joseph.sowell@hcahealthcare.com.

SPACKMAN, THOMAS JAMES, radiologist; b. Oak Park, Ill., Apr. 24, 1937; s. Thomas Frederick and Louise Mary (Kaiser) Spackman; m. Donna S. Stewart, June 25, 1960; children: Kirsten, Thomas James, Victoria. BA, DePauw U., 1959; MD, Western Res. U., 1964; diploma in bus. studies, London Sch. Econs., 1987. Intern, then resident in internal medicine Yale-New Haven Med. Ctr., 1964-66, resident in diagnostic radiology, 1966-68, fellow clin. rsch. tng. unit, 1968-69; instr., then asst. prof. radiology Yale U. Med. Sch., New Haven, 1969-74; assoc. prof. U. Pa. Med. Sch., 1974-78; prof. radiology U. Conn. Med. Sch., Farmington, 1978—, head dept., 1978-90; dir. radiology St. Francis Hosp. and Med. Ctr., Hartford, Conn., 1992-93; pres. Elscint, Inc., Hackensack, NJ, 1993-97; sr. v.p. Elscint, Ltd., Haifa, Israel, 1993-97; pres. Spackman Assocs., Vero Beach, Fla., 1997—; chmn. Xicon Technologies LLC, Vero Beach, 1997-98; v.p. physician affairs Quorum Health Resources, 2000—02, Cambio Health Solutions LLC, 2002—05; chmn. Navix Diagnostix, Inc., 2002—; mng. dir. FTI Cabmrio Health Solutions, 2005—07. Mem. Conn. Med. Exam. Bd., 1980—86; bd. dirs. Elscint, Inc. Mem. editl. adv. bd. Diagnostic Imaging, 1989—92; contbr. articles to profl. jours., chapters to books. Fellow: Am. Coll. Radiology; mem.: Indian River Hosp. Dist. (Fla.) (trustee 2009—, chmn. 2010—12), Environ. Learning Ctr. (trustee 2007—), Soc. Pediatric Radiology, Assn. U. Radiolgoists. Office Phone: 772-388-4631. Business E-Mail: tspackman@bellsouth.net.

SPAHN, GARY JOSEPH, lawyer; b. NYC, July 23, 1949; s. Harry G. and Mary (Hopkins) S.; m. Lois Luttinger, Aug. 9, 1975; children: Gary J. Jr., Lori J. BA, L.I. U., 1971, MA, 1976; JD, U. Richmond, 1975. Bar: Va. 1975, U.S. Ct. Appeals (4th cir.) 1975, U.S. Supreme Ct. 1980. Law clk. to Hon. Judge Dortch U.S. Dist. Ct. (ea. dist.) Va., Richmond, 1975—77; from assoc. to ptnr. Troutman Sanders LLP (formerly Mays & Valentine), Richmond, 1977—; now ptnr. Troutman Sanders LLP, Richmond, past chmn. products liability and ins. sect. Lectr. in field, 1980—; mem. jud. conf. U.S. Ct. Appeals (4th cir.). Co-author: Virginia Law of Products Liability, 2000 Pres. Southhampton Citizens Assn., Richmond, 1982-85; bd. dirs. Southhampton Recreation Assn., Richmond. 1983, Chesterfield County Crime Solvers. With USAF, 1967-73. Named to Best Lawyers Am. Products Liability, 2007. Mem. ABA (litig. and tort and ins. sects.), Internat. Assn. Def. Counsel (co-chair litig. sect. Products Liability com.), Def. Rsch. Inst., Va. Assn. Def. Attys., Va. Mfrs. Assn., Products Liability Adv. Counsel, Va. Power Boat Assn. (commodore). Avocations: boating, basketball, racquetball, guitar. Office: Troutman Sanders LLP PO Box 1122 1001 Haxall Point Richmond VA 23218-1132 Office Phone: 804-697-1400. Business E-Mail: gary.spahn@troutmansanders.com.

SPAHN, JAMES FRANCIS, marketing professional; b. Dubuque, Iowa, Oct. 4, 1957; s. Ervin Henry and Denise Marie (Shuhert) S.; m. Beverly Joan Burns, Oct. 22, 1983. Grad., Brown Inst. Tech., 1977. Lic. real estate commn.; cert. mktg. dir. Mktg. dir., cert. shopping ctr. mgr. The Cafaro Co., Dubuque, 1979-80; mktg. dir. The Herring Marathon Group, Dallas, 1980-83, Dusco Property Mgmt., Inc., Lancaster, Pa., 1983-87, Jim Wilson and Assocs., Montgomery, Ala., 1987—2004; dir. mktg. Bayer Properties Inc., Birmingham, Ala., 2004—07; v.p. mktg. Colonial Properties Trust, Birmingham, 2007—13; dir. mktg. TRG Mgmt. Co. LLC, Weston, Fla., 2013—. Co-author: Operating Shopping Centers, 1984. Mem. Cen. Bus. Dist. Revitalization Task Force, Savannah, Ga., 1984-86, Transit Task Force, Savannah, 1985-86; bd. dirs. Conv. and Vis. Bur., Savannah, 1986-87. Recipient Addy awards Dubuque Advt. Club, 1980. Mem. Internat. Coun. Shopping Ctrs. (Maxi award 1982, Maxi finalist 1987, 89, 90, 94, 2002, 03), Savannah Advt. Club (bd. dirs. 1984-87), Birmingham Advt. Club (Addy awards 1983-87, 89). Roman Catholic. Avocations: camping, bicycling. Home: 601 NW 82nd Ave 301 Plantation FL 33324

SPALDING, ANDREW FREEMAN, lawyer; b. Toledo, June 24, 1951; s. Dean and Shirley Louise (Maitland) S.; m. Adele Taylor, May 17, 1980; children: Amy Louise, Adam Freeman, Audrey Wade, Abigail Maitland. BA, U. Calif., Berkeley, 1973; JD, So. Meth. U., 1977. Bar: Tex. 1977, NY 2006, US Dist. Ct. (so., ea. and we. dists.) Tex. 1978, US Ct. Appeals (5th cir.) 1978; bd. cert. civil trial law, personal injury trial law. Assoc. Bracewell & Giuliani, LLP, Houston, 1977-84, ptnr., 1985—. Notes and comments editor So. Meth. U. Law Jour., Dallas, 1976-77. Fellow Tex Bar Found., Houston Bar Found.; mem. State Bar Tex., Houston Bar Assn., Tex. Assn. Def. Counsel, Def. Rsch. Inst., Am. Bd. Trial Advocates (assoc.), Knights Momus, Krewe Maximilian, Pan Tex. Assembly, Allegro, Houston Country Club. Office: Bracewell & Giuliani LLP 2300 S Tower Pennzoil Pla 711 Louisiana St Ste 2300 Houston TX 77002-2770 Office Phone: 713-221-1220. Business E-Mail: Andrew.Spalding@bgllp.com.

SPALDING, WILLIAM R. (BILL SPALDING), lawyer, former pharmaceutical executive; Grad., Dartmouth Coll., 1981; JD, Washington & Lee U., 1984. Law clk. to Hon. Ellsworth A. Van Graafeiland US Ct. Appeals (2nd Cir.); sr. ptnr. King & Spalding, LLP, Atlanta, 2001—05, ptnr., 2010—; exec. v.p. strategic initiatives Caremark Rx, LLC (formerly Caremark Rx, Inc.), 2005—07; exec. v.p. strategy & managed care CVS Caremark Corp., 2007—10; co-founder, prin. The Crawford Spalding Group, 2008—; chmn. MedVantx, Inc. Bd. dirs. PharMEDium Healthcare Corp., 2010—, SecureWorks, Inc. Office: King & Spalding LLP 1180 Peachtree St Atlanta GA 30309 Office Phone: 404-572-4600. Office Fax: 404-572-5100. E-mail: kingspalding@kslaw.com.

SPANGLER, CLEMMIE DIXON, JR., construction company executive; b. Charlotte, NC, Apr. 5, 1932; s. Clemmie Dixon and Veva C. (Yelton) S.; m. Meredith Jane Riggs, June 25, 1960; children: Anna Wildy, Abigail Riggs. BS, U. N.C., 1954; MBA, Harvard U., 1956; LHD (hon.), Queens Coll., 1985; LLD (hon.), Davidson Coll., 1986, Furman U., 1993; LLD U. N. Carolina (hon.), 2003. Pres. C.D. Spangler Constrn. Co., Charlotte, 1958-86, Golden Eagle Industries, Inc., 1968-86; chmn. bd. Bank of N.C., Raleigh, 1973-82; dir. NCNB Corp., 1983-86; chmn. N.C. Bd. Edn., 1982-86; pres. U. N.C., Chapel Hill, 1986-97; CEO, chmn. C.D. Spangler Constrn. Co., Charlotte, 1997—. Bd. dirs. BellSouth Corp., Atlanta; chmn. bd. dirs. Nat. Gypsum Co., Charlotte. Past deacon Myers Park Bapt. Ch., vice-chmn. Charlotte-Mecklenburg Bd. Edn., Charlotte, 1972-76; past trustee Charlotte Symphony Orch., Crozer Theol. Sem.; past chmn. Charlotte adv. bd. Salvation Army; past bd. dirs. YMCA, Equitable Life Assurance Soc., Jefferson-Pilot Corp.; pres. bd. trustees Mint Mus. Art; bd. dirs. Union Theol. Sem., 1985-90, Assocs. Harvard Bus. Sch.; pres. bd. overseers Harvard Coll., 2003. With U.S. Army, 1956-58. Recipient Liberty Bell award Mecklenburg County Bar Assn., 1985, Alumni Achievement award Harvard Bus. Sch., 1988; named one of Forbes 400: Richest Americans, 2006-. Mem. Assn. Am. Univs., Bus. Higher Edn. Forum, Harvard Club (N.Y.C.), Univ. Club (N.Y.C.), Quail Hollow Country Club (Charlotte). Office: CD Spangler Constrn Co Office of Chmn Box 36007 Charlotte NC 28236-6007

SPANN, CYRIL O., JR., gynecologic oncologist, educator; MD, Meharry Med. Coll., Nashville, 1981. Diplomate Am. Bd. Ob-Gyn, 1987, Am. Bd. Ob-Gyn-gynecologic oncology, 1992. Intern Emory Univ. Affiliated Hosps., Atlanta, 1982, resident, 1985; fellow Univ. NC Affiliated Hosps., Durham, 1989; prof. gynecology and obstetrics dept. Emory Clinic; joined Emory Univ. Hosp. Midtown, 1989; hosp. affiliation includes Grady Meml. Hosp. Co-author: Effect of sleep deprivation on medical resident and student function: A prospective study, 2003, Predictors of cervical dysplasia after the loop electrosurgical excision procedure in an inner-city population, 2004. Mem. Gynecologic Cancer Found. Named one of the Top Doctors, Atlanta Mag., 2009. Mem.: ACS, ACOG, Am. Assn. of Gynecologic Laparoscopists, Southern Med. Assn., Nat. Med. Assn., Ga. Obstet. and Gynecol. Soc., Dekalb Med. Soc., Atlanta Obstet. and Gynecol. Soc., Am. Assn. of Gynecologic Endoscopists. Office: Emory University Hospital Midtown Medical Office Tower 9th Fl 550 Peachtree St NE Atlanta GA 30309 Office Phone: 404-778-3401.

SPANN, GEORGE WILLIAM, management consultant; b. Cuthbert, Ga., July 21, 1946; s. Glinn Linwood and Mary Grace (Hiller) S.; m. Laura Jeanne Nason, June 10, 1967; children: Tanya Lynne, Stephen William. BS in Physics with honors, Ga. Inst. Tech., 1968, MS, 1970, MS in Indsl. Mgmt., 1973. Engr. Martin Marietta Corp., Orlando, Fla., 1968-70; rsch. scientist Engring. Exptl. Sta., Ga. Inst. Tech., 1970-75; v.p., dir. Metrics, Inc., mgmt. and engring. cons., Atlanta, 1973-78, pres., dir., 1978—; v.p., dir. Exec. Data Sys., Inc., 1981—. Mem. Ga. Energy Policy Coun., Ga. Metrication Coun., NASA applications survey group for Landsat follow-on; mem. com. on practical applications of remote sensing from space Space Applications Bd. NRC; market rsch. cons. NOAA, NASA, pvt. cos. Contbr. articles to profl. jours. Regents scholar, 1964. Mem. Am. Soc. Photogrammetry, Urban and Regional Info. Sys. Assn., Atlanta Jaycees, Tau Beta Pi, Phi Kappa Phi, Sigma Pi Sigma. Home: 3475 Clubland Dr Marietta GA 30068-2509 Office: Bldg 27 #100 1640 Powers Ferry Rd SE Marietta GA 30067-5491

SPANO, ROBERT, conductor, music director; b. Conneaut, Ohio, May 7, 1961; Grad., Oberlin Conservatory Music, Ohio; student, Curtis Inst. Music, Phila.; D (hon.), Bowling Green State U., 2004. Dir. orchestral activities Bowling Green State U., Ohio, 1985—89; faculty Oberlin Conservatory Music, 1989—; asst. condr. Boston Symphony Orch., 1990—93; music dir. Bklyn. Philharm. Orch., 1996—2004, artistic adv., prin. guest condr., 2004—07; music dir. Atlanta Symphony Orch., 2001—. Head conducting fellowship program Tanglewood Music Ctr., Mass., 1998—2002, dir. Festival Contemporary Music, 2003—04; guest condr. Chgo. Symphony Orch., Boston Symphony Orch., Houston Symphony Orch., San Francisco Symphony Orch., Cleve. Orch., LA Philharm., Nat. Symphony Orch., Phila. Orch., Royal Opera Covent Gardens, Welsh Nat. Opera, Orch. Filharmonica della Scala, City of Birmingham Symphony. Musician (piano): (chamber concerts) Atlanta Symphony, Brooklyn Philharm, Boston Symphony, Oberlin Conservatory; recordings include Rimsky-Korsakov: Scheherazade and Vaughan Williams: A Sea Symphony, Del Tredici: Paul Revere's Ride and Theofanidis: The Here and Now, Berlioz Requiem, Atlanta Symphony Orch. (Grammy award for Best Choral Performance, 2005), Golijov's Ainadamar: Fountain of Tears (Grammy award for Best Opera Performance, 2007), featured on (TV series) City Arts, PBS, Breakfast with the Arts, A&E, Late Show with David Letterman, CBS, Sunday Morning, (TV special) Sound Choices - Inside the ASO with Monica Kaufman, WSB-TV. Recipient Conductors award, Seaver Inst./NEA, 1994, Ditson Conductor's award, Columbia U., 2008. Office: Atlanta Symphony Hall 1280 Peachtree St NE Atlanta GA 30309-3552 Mailing: c/o Jason Bagdade Opus 3 Artists 470 Park Ave 9th Fl N New York NY 10016

SPARKMAN, BRANDON BUSTER, educator, consultant, writer; b. Hartselle, Ala., Aug. 2, 1929; s. George Olan and Mary Louise (Jones) S.; m. Wanda Phillips, Sept. 13, 1952(dec.); children— Ricky Brandon, Rita Sharon, Robert Lee; m. Anne Jayler. BS, U. North Ala., 1952; MA, U. Ala., 1958, EdS, 1961; EdD, Auburn U., Ala., 1970. Tchr., asst. prin. Phllips High Sch., Bear Creek, Ala., 1954-57; prin. Tuscumbia, Ala., 1957-65; asst. supt., 1965-69; ednl. cons. Auburn Center, 1969-70; mem. faculty dept. sch. adminstrn. Auburn U., 1970; asst. supt. for staff personnel devel. Jackson (Miss.) Pub. Schs., 1970-71, supt., 1971-73; sch. supt. Richland County Sch. Dist. 1, Columbia, SC, 1973-75; asst. supt. instruction Hartselle (Ala.) City Schs., 1975-80; supt. Guntersville (Ala.) City Schs., 1980-88; CEO The Right Combination Pub. & Ednl. Svcs. Corp., Guntersville, Ala., 1984-93. Adj. prof. U. Ala., Birmingham, 1998-2000; writer, cons. in field. Sr. author: Blueprint for a Brighter Child, 1973, STEPS (System for Teacher Evaluation of Pre-reading Skills), 1974; co-author: Preparing Your Preschooler for Reading, 1977, Competency Tests for Basic Reading Skills, 1978, Soaring High with Science, 1985, Soaring High with Social Studies, 1985; author: How Well Does Your Child Read, 1979, Writing Composition Made Easy, 1991, Blueprint for Expository Writing, 1993, Reading Skills Competency Tests, 1999, Called to Jackson, Mississippi, The Last Bastion of Segregation, 2011; editor: The In-Between Years, 1979; creator: CORE (Program Management Through Computer Systems), 1975; editor, contbg. author: The Advantaged, A Preschool Program for the Disadvantaged, 1969; contbr. articles to profl. jours. Bd. dirs. Morgan County chpt. ARC, United Givers Fund, Colbert-Lauderdale Child Study Center, Sheffield-Tuscumbia Credit Union; bd. govs. Jackson Symphony Orch.; adv. bd. Jackson Mental Health Center. Served with AUS, 1952-54. Recipient Human Relations award Jackson. Mem. Am., Ala assns. sch. adminstrs. (past pres.), Ala. Council Sch. Adminstrn. and Supervision (past pres.), Assn. Supervision and Curriculum Devel., Ala. Assn. Supervision and Curriculum Devel. (past pres.), Florence State U. Alumni Assn. (past pres.) Methodist (ch. sch. tchr., supt., chmn. ofcl. bd., chmn. commn. edn.). Home and Office: 285 Lake View Dr Muscle Shoals AL 35661

SPARKMAN, STEVEN LEONARD, lawyer; b. Sarasota, Fla., May 30, 1947; s. Simeon Clarence and Ursula (Wahlstrom) S.; m. Terry Jeanne Gibbs, Aug. 23, 1969; children: Joanna Jeanne, Kevin Leonard. BA, Fla. State U., 1969, JD, 1972. Bar: Fla. 1972. Legal rsch. asst. Office Gen. Counsel, Fla. Dept. Revenue, Tallahassee, 1971; legis. intern com. on cmty. affairs Fla. Ho. of Reps., Tallahassee, 1971-72; jud. rsch. aide Fla. 2d Dist. Ct. Appeals, Lakeland, 1972-73; asst. county atty. Hillsborough County, Tampa, Fla., 1973-75; assoc. Carlton, Fields, Ward, Emmanuel, Smith & Cutler, P.A., Tampa, 1975-80, sr. atty., 1980-2001; pvt. practice Plant City, Fla., 2001—. Mem. bd. visitors Fla. State U. Coll. Law, 1994—2000. Trustee Fla. Bapt. Children's Homes, Inc., 2004—09; deacon 1st Bapt. Ch., Plant City, 1980—; sec., bd. dirs. Bapt. Towers Plant City, Inc., 1981—84; bd. dirs. Tampa Kiwanis Found., 1997—2000. 1st lt. USAFR, 1973. Fellow: Am. Bar Found.; mem.: ABA, Plant City Bar Assn. (sec. treas 2003—05, treas. 2005—08, v.p. 2008—09), Fla. Bar Assn. (exec. coun. local govt. law sect. 1978—79), Kiwanis (life; bd. dirs. 2003—06, George F. Hixsen fellow 2008). Democrat. Office: 102 W Reynolds St Ste 201 Plant City FL 33563 Office Phone: 813-759-1444. Business E-Mail: sls@sparklaw.com.

SPARKS, JOHN, state legislator; m. Elizabeth Sparks; 2 children. BA, Harvard Univ., 1991; JD, Univ. Okla., 1994. Intern for Senator David Boren; legislative aide to Okla. Congressman Bill Brewster; with Crowe & Dunlevy, Foliart, Huff, Ottaway & Bottom; founding ptnr. Odom, Sparks & Jones; former pres. Cleveland County Workforce Investment Bd.; founder Corner Post Mgmt. & Consulting LLC; bd. dirs. Health For Friends, Thunderbird Clubhouse; mem. Dist. 16 Okla. State Senate, 2006—. Mem.: Cleveland County Cattlemen's Assn., Okla. Cattlemen's Assn., Okla. Farm Bur, Norman C. of C., Norman Sooner Rotary Club, United Way Norman, Cleveland County Bar Assn. (pres.). Democrat. Methodist. Address: PO Box 368 Norman OK 73070-0368 Office: 2300 N Lincoln Blvd Rm 533 Oklahoma City OK 73105 Office Phone: 405-364-2006, 405-521-5553. Business E-Mail: sparks@oksenate.gov.

SPARKS, SAM, federal judge; b. 1939; BA, U. Tex., 1961, LLB, 1963. Aide Rep. Homer Thornberry, 1963; law clk. to Hon. Homer Thornberry U.S. Dist. Ct. (we. dist.) Tex., 1963-65; assoc. to ptnr., shareholder Hardie, Grambling, Sims & Galatzan (and successor firms), El Paso, Tex., 1965-91; judge US Dist. Ct. (we. dist.) Tex., 1991—. Fellow Am. Coll. Trial Lawyers, Tex. Bar Found. (life); mem. Am. Bd. Trial Advocates (advocate), State Bar Tex Office: US Dist Ct Judge 200 W 8th St Ste 100 Austin TX 78701-2333 Office Phone: 512-916-5230.

SPARKS, SAM, construction executive, lawyer; BS in Urban Life & Criminal Justice, Ga. State U., 1975; JD in Law, Woodrow Wilson Coll., 1978. Regional pres., Lennar Land And Homebuilding Lennar Corp., 2006—. Office: Lennar Corp 700 NW 107th Ave Miami FL 33172 Office Phone: 305-559-4000. Office Fax: 305-226-4158. Business E-Mail: sam.sparks@lennar.com.

SPATZ, KENNETH CHRIS(TOPHER), JR., statistics educator; b. Tyler, Tex., Mar. 25, 1940; s. Kenneth Christopher and Mary E. (Harton) S.; m. Thea Siria, May 31, 1961; children: Mark C., Kenneth S., Ann Spatz Nichols. BA, Hendrix Coll., 1962; PhD, Tulane U., 1966. Asst. prof. U. of South, Sewanee, Tenn., 1966-69; assoc. prof. U. Ark., Monticello, 1971-73, Hendrix Coll., Conway, Ark., 1973—85, prof., 1985—2003. Author: Basic Statistics: Tales of Distributions, 1976, 10th edit., 2011; co-author: Research Methods in Psychology: Ideas, Techniques and Reports, 2008. Fellow U. Calif., Berkeley, 1969-71. Office: Hendrix Coll Dept Psychology Conway AR 72032 Home: 615 Davis St Conway AR 72034 Business E-Mail: Spatz@hendrix.edu.

SPAULDING, KARLA RAE, lawyer; b. Breckenridge, Mich., 1954; d. Donald Hugh and Shirley Ann (Federspiel) S. BA magna cum laude, Western Mich. U., 1975; JD, Northwestern U., 1980. Bar: Ohio 1980, Fla. 1987. Vis. prof. Grand Valley State Colls., Allendale, Mich., 1975-76; asst. U.S. atty. U.S. Atty. Office, Tampa, Fla., 1983—92, Grand Rapids, Mich., 1988-89, Houston, 1992—93, chief maj. drug trafficking sect. Mid. Dist. Fla. Tampa, 1989-90, chief appellate div. Mid. Dist. Fla., 1990-92; chief fraud and econ. crime sect. So. Dist. Tex. U.S. Atty. Office, Houston, 1992-93; pvt. practice, 1980—83, 1994—97; U.S. magistrate judge, U.S. Dist. Ct. (mid. dist.) Fla., Orlando, 1997—. Bd. editor's, dep. editor-in-chief Fed. Bar Jour., 1992-95; exec. editor Jour. Criminal Law and Criminology; contbr. articles to profl. publs. Recipient Dir.'s award IRS, 1988. Mem. FBA, Orange County Bar Assn., Hillsborough County Bar Assn. Office: US Courthouse 401 W Ctrl Blvd Ste 5-500 Orlando FL 32801-0550*

SPEAR, TIMOTHY L., state legislator; Ret. clerk Superior Court; state rep. Dist. 2 NC, 2007—. Democrat. Office: North Carolina House of Representatives 300 N Salisbury St Room 402 Raleigh NC 27603-5925 Office Phone: 919-715-3029. Business E-Mail: Tim.Spear@ncleg.net.

SPEARING, ANTHONY COLIN, English literature educator; b. London, Jan. 31, 1936; came to U.S., 1987; s. Frederick and Gertrude (Calnin) S. MA, Cambridge U., Eng., 1960; PhD (hon.), Lund U., Sweden, 2011. W.M. Tapp rsch. fellow Gonville-Caius Coll. Cambridge U., 1959-60, asst. lectr. in English, 1960-64, official fellow Queens' Coll., 1960-87, life fellow, 1987—, dir. studies in English, 1967-85, lectr. in English, 1964-85, reader in medieval English lit., 1985-87; vis. prof. English U. Va., Charlottesville, 1979-80, 84, prof. English, 1987-89, Kenan prof. English, 1989—. William Matthews lectr. Birkbeck Coll., London, 1983—84; invited lectr. numerous colls. and univs. Eng., Europe, Can., U.S.; Lansdowne vis. fellow U. Victoria, 1993; Benjamin Meaker vis. prof. U. Bristol, 2003; Conway lectr. U. Notre Dame, 2007. Author: Criticism and Medieval Poetry, 1964, rev. edit., 1972; (with Maurice Hussey and James Winny) An Introduction to Chaucer, 1965; The Gawain-Poet: A Critical Study, 1970, 2010, Chaucer: Troilus and Criseyde, 1976, Medieval Dream-Poetry, 1976, 2012, Medieval to Renaissance in English Poetry, 1985, 2009, Readings in Medieval Poetry, 1987, 2010, The Medieval Poet as Voyeur, 1993, 2009, Textual Subjectivity, 2005, Medieval Autographies, 2012; editor: The Pardoner's Prologue and Tale (Chaucer), 1965, rev. edit., 1994, The Knight's Tale (Chaucer), 1966, rev. edit., 1995, The Franklin's Prologue and Tale (Chaucer), 1966, rev. edit., 1994; co-editor: (with Elizabeth Spearing) Shakespeare: The Tempest, 1971, Poetry of the Age of Chaucer, 1974, The Reeve's Prologue and Tale (Chaucer), 1979, Julian of Norwich: Revelations of Divine Love, 1998; translator: The Cloud of Unknowing and Other Works, 2001; contbr. numerous articles to profl. jours. Mem. Medieval Acad. Am., Internat. Assn. U. Profs. English, New Chaucer Soc. (trustee 1986-90). Office: Univ Va Dept English 219 Bryan Hall PO Box 400121 Charlottesville VA 22904-4121 Business E-Mail: acs4j@virginia.edu.

SPEARMAN, KENNETH ALBERT, federal agency administrator; b. 1944; m. Maria Spearman; children: Michelle, Rochelle, Kenneth. BS in Acctg., Ind. U.; MBA, Governers State U., University Park, Ill. Formerly with Arthur Andersen & Co.; co-founder acctg. firm. Chgo.; contr. Citrus Ctrl., Inc., Orlando, Fla., 1980—91; dir. internal audit Fla.'s Natural Growers, Inc., 1991—2008, ret., 2008; bd. mem. Farm Credit Adminstrn., 2009—; chmn. Farm Credit System Ins. Corp., 2009—. Bd. dirs. AgFirst Farm Credit Bank, Columbia, SC, 2006—09. Mem.: Nat. Soc. Accountants for Cooperatives, Inst. Internal Auditors. Office: Farm Credit Adminstrn 1501 Farm Credit Dr Mc Lean VA 22102*

SPEARMAN, MAXIE ANN, financial analyst, administrator; b. Piedmont, SC, Sept. 14, 1942; d. J. Mac and Margaret Cecille S. BS, U. SC, 1965; postgrad., Ga. State U., 1985, U. Ga. Acct. Shell Oil Co., Atlanta, 1965-66; internal auditor Sears, Roebuck & Co., Atlanta,

1966-67; acct. Econ. Opportunity Atlanta, Atlanta, 1967-68, City of Atlanta, 1968-78, fin. analyst, 1978-89, sr. fin. analyst planner, 1989—. Investment cons., Atlanta, Conyers, Ga., 1980—. Mem. Rep. Presdl. Task Force, 1985—, U.S. Senatorial Club, Rep. Nat. Com., 1988—, Ga. Rep. Party, 1990—, Atlanta Safety Com., 1985—, Mayor's Spl. Events Task Force, 1990; charter founder Ronald Reagan Rep. Ctr., 1988; del.-at-large Rep. Platform Planning Com., 1992, 94. Recipient safety award Atlanta City Govt., 1990, Presdl. Commn. Exec. Com. of Republican Party award, 1992; Order of Merit award Nat. Rep. Senatorial Com., 1996. Mem. AAUW, NAFE, Am. Mgmt. Assn., Ga. Assn. Med. Victims, Inc. (sec., treas. 1985—), Nat. Trust for Historic Preservation. Methodist. Avocations: writing, tennis, decorating, investing. Home: 1280 Vineyard Dr SE Conyers GA 30013-2466

SPEARMAN, ROBERT WORTHINGTON, lawyer; b. Durham, NC, Jan. 24, 1943; s. Walter and Mary Elizabeth (Dale) S.; m. Patricia Hinds, June 2, 1973; children: Madolyn Marschall, Dorothy Marschall. BA in Polit. Sci., U. N.C., 1965; MA in Philosophy/Econs., Oxford U., 1967; LLB, Yale U., 1970. Bar: NC 1971, DC 1979, U.S. Dist. Ct. (ea., mid. and we. dists. NC), U.S. Ct. Appeals (4th and 5th cirs.), U.S. Supreme Ct. Law clk. to Justice Hugo L. Black U.S. Supreme Ct., Washington, 1971; assoc. Adams, McCullough & Beard, Raleigh, 1971-75, ptnr., 1975—90; ptnr. litig., antitrust & bus. torts practice group leader Parker Poe Adams & Bernstein LLP, Raleigh, 1990—. Adj. prof. Law Sch., U. N.C., Chapel Hill, 1982-83. Vice chmn. corrections planning com. N.C. Crime Control Commn., 1979-81; chmn. Wake County Democratic Com., 1979-81, N.C. Elections Bd., 1981-85. Vice chmn. corrections planning com. N.C. Crime Control Commn., 1979-81; chmn. Wake County Dem. Com., 1979-81, N.C. Elections Bd., 1981-85. Morehead Found. scholar, 1961, Rhodes scholar, 1965; Razor Walker award, 2002, Defender Justice award NC Justice Ctr., 2004; named one of Woodward White's Best Lawyers in Am., 2000-08, Legal Elite, NC, 2003-08. Fellow Am. Coll. Trial Lawyers (mem. NC State Com. 2003-05); mem. ABA, N.C. Bar Assn. (chmn. comml. litigation com. 1982-83), Phi Beta Kappa. Presbyterian. Office: Parker Poe Adams & Bernstein LLP Ste 1400 150 Fayetteville St PO Box 389 Raleigh NC 27602-0389 Office Phone: 919-828-0564. Office Fax: 919-835-4560. Business E-Mail: bobspearman@parkerpoe.com.

SPEARS, ALEXANDER WHITE, III, tobacco company executive; b. Grindstone, Pa., Sept. 29, 1932; s. Alexander White and Eva Marie (Elliott) S.; m. Shirley Pierce; 1 child, Craig Stewart. BS, Allegheny Coll., Meadville, Pa., 1953; PhD, SUNY, 1960. Research asso., then research fellow SUNY, Buffalo, 1956-58; instr. Millard Fillmore Coll., Buffalo, 1958-59; with Lorillard Corp., Greensboro, N.C., 1959-2000, v.p. R & D, 1971-74, sr. v.p. ops. and rsch., 1975-79, exec. v.p. ops. and rsch., 1979-91, vice chmn., COO, 1991-95, chmn., CEO, 1995-99; chmn. Lorillard Tobacco Co., Greensboro, 1999-2000, also bd. dirs. Asst. prof. Guilford Coll., 1961-65, mem. bd. assocs., 1990, 91, trustee, 1995—. Patentee in field; past editor: Tobacco Sci. Jour. Chmn. Coun. on Edn., 1974, mem. exec. com., 1987; chmn. model sch. task force Greensboro Bd. Edn. and Greensboro C. of C., 1975; mem. N.C. Humanities Coun., 1978-81, Piedmont Triad Airport Authority, 1993-99, treas., 1995-97, vice chmn., 1997-99; bd. dirs. United Way of Greensboro, 1980-85, 97—, chmn., 2000, chmn. campaign cabinet, 1999; bd. dirs. N.C. Bus. Com. on Edn., 1983-84, Greensboro Devel. Corp., 1985—, pres., 1992-94, exec. commn., 1987—; chmn. Greensboro Area United Negro Coll. Fund, 1982, N.C. AT&T St. U., Focus on Excellence campaign, 1984-86, Greensboro Pub. Sch. Fund, 1987; capital campaign chmn. Greensboro Area Girl Scouts U.S., 1987; bd. dirs. N.C. A&T U. Found., 1985-93, trustee, 1990—, sec., 1995-97, vice chmn., 1997-99, chmn., 2000—; bd. dirs. Greensboro NCCJ, 1990-92, chmn. ann. dinner, 1991, N.C. Citizens for Bus. and Industry, 1984-88, YMCA, 1989-96, chmn., 1993-95; chmn. Hayes-Taylor Capital Campaign, 1990; bd. dirs. Ctr. Indoor Air Rsch., 1988-99, chmn., 1991-95, Coun. for Tobacco Rsch., 1990-99; mem. U.S. Tech. Study Group Cigarette Safety Act of 1984, U.S. Study CPSC Tech. Adv. Group Cigarette Safety Act. of 1990; adv. bd. U. N.C., Greensboro, 1988-94; chmn. fundraiser campaign Greensboro Hist. Mus., 1988-89, trustee, 1989—; mem. Forward Guilford II Exec. Com., 1998—; chmn. bd. visitors Greensboro Coll., 1990-94; mem. Greensboro Cmty. Initiative, 1996—; mem. adv. coun. N.C. Ctr. for Nonprofits, 1999—. Recipient Disting. Achievement award in tobacco sci. Philip Morris, 1970, Nat. Brotherhood award NCCJ, 1999, Citation award N.C. Piedmont Triad region, 1999; named to Jr. Achievement Bus. Leaders Hall of Fame, 1994, and YMCA Hall of Fame, 1994, hon. life mem. YMCA, 1996—. Mem. AAAS, Am. Chem. Soc., Soc. Applied Spectroscopy, Am. Mgmt. Assn., N.Y. Acad. Scis., Am. Judicature Soc. (hon.), Internat. Coop. Ctr. Sci. Rsch. Relative to Tobacco (sci. com. 1972), Greensboro C. of C. (bd. dirs. 1974-75, 86-87, 96-99, chmn. 1997, Nathaniel Greene award 1975, hon. chmn. 1994 Kmart Greater Greensboro Open). Presbyterian. Office: Lorillard Tobacco Co 714 Green Valley Rd Greensboro NC 27408-7018 also: PO Box 10529 Greensboro NC 27404-0529

SPEARS, JAE, state legislator; b. Latonia, Ky. d. James and Sylvia (Fox) Marshall; m. Lawrence E. Spears; children: Katherine Spears Cooper, Marsha Spears-Duncan, Lawrence M., James W. Student, U. Ky. Reporter Cin. Post, Cin. Enquirer newspapers; rschr. Stas. WLW-WSAI, Cin.; tchr. Jiya Gakuen Sch., Japan; lectr. U.S. Mil. installations East Anglia, England; del. State of W.Va., Charleston, 1974-80; mem. W.Va. Senate, Charleston, 1980-1993. Mem. vis. com. W.Va. Extension and Continuing Edn., Morgantown, 1993-2000; advising bd. mem., W.Va. U. Sch. Medicine, 1992—; with state sen., 1980-93; apptd. to Jud. Hearing Bd., 1993-2000. Chmn. adv bd. Sta. WNPB, 1992-94; congl. liaison Am. Pub. TV Stas. and Sta. WNPB-TV, 1992-97; mem. coun. W.Va. Autism Task Force, Huntington, 1981-90; mem. W.Va. exec. bd. Literacy Vols. Am., 1986-90, 94—, pres., 1990-92; mem. Gov.'s State Literacy Coun., 1991-97; bd. dirs. Found. Ind. Colls. W.Va., 1986—; mem. regional adv. com. W.Va. Gov.'s Task Force for Children, Youth and Family, 1989; mem. USS W.Va. Commn., 1989; mem. exec. com. W.Va. Employer Support Group for Guard and Res., 1989, mem. steering com., 1990-92. Decorated Purple Heart (hon.); recipient Susan B. Anthony award NOW, 1982, edn. award Profl. Educators Assn. W.Va., 1986, ann. award W.Va. Assn. Ret. Sch. Employees, 1985, Meritorious Svc. award W.Va. State Vets. Commn., 1984, Vets. Employment and Tng. Svc. award U.S. Dept. Labor, 1984, award W.Va. Vets. Coun., 1984; named Admiral in N.C. Navy, Gov. of N.C., 1982, hon. Brigadier Gen. W.Va. N.G., 1984, One of 11 Women Pioneers of W.Va. Legislature, W.Va. U. Inst. for Pub. Affairs, 1997, Disting. West Virginian, Gov. W.Va., 2005, Comm. award W.Va. Womens Comm., 2006. Mem. DAR, VFW (aux.), Bus. and Profl. Women (Woman of Yr. award 1978), Nat. League Am. Pen Women (Pen Woman of Yr. 1984), Nat. Order Women Legislators, Am. Legion (aux.), Delta Kappa Gamma, Alpha Xi Delta. Democrat. Home and Office: PO Box 98 Shinnston WV 26431 Office Phone: 304-558-0070.

SPEARS, RONALD E., telecommunications industry executive; Grad., US Mil. Acad., West Point, NY; M in Pub. Svc., We. Ky. U. Mgr. AT&T Long Lines, 1978; pres. Midwest divsn. MCI WorldCom, Inc., 1984—90; corp. v.p. Citizens Utilities Co., 1995—98; pres., COO e.spire Comm. Inc., 1998—99; pres., CEO CMGI Solutions, 1999—2000, Vaultus, Inc., 2000—02; v.p. signature client grp. AT&T Inc. (merger of SBC Communications & AT&T Corp.), 2002—06, exec. v.p. bus. sales, 2006—07, grp. v.p. global bus. svcs., 2007—08, pres., CEO bus. solutions, 2008—10, sr. exec. v.p. exec. ops., 2010—. Bd. dirs. MCF Corp., San Francisco, 2000—08, RateXchange, Inc., 2000—, USA Broadband, Inc., 2002—. Officer US Army, 1970—78. Office: AT&T Hdqs 208 S Akard St Dallas TX 75202 Office Phone: 210-821-4105. Business E-Mail: respears@att.com.

SPEARS, SALLY, lawyer; b. San Antonio, Aug. 29, 1938; d. Adrian Anthony and Elizabeth (Wylie) S.; m. Tor Hultgreen, July 15, 1961 (div. Jan. 1983); children: Dagny Elizabeth, Sara Kirsten, Kara Spears. BA, U. Tex., 1960, LLB, 1965. Bar: Tex. 1961, Ill. 1971. Practice law, Stamford, Conn., 1966-67, Chgo., 1970-71, Northbrook, Ill., 1972-73, Toronto, Ont., Canada, 1973-81; assoc. firm Cummings & Lockwood, Stamford, 1966-67, Kirkland & Ellis, Chgo., 1970-71; sr. atty. Allstate Ins. Co., Northbrook, Ill., 1971-73; gen. counsel, sec. Reed Paper Ltd., Reed Ltd., Toronto, 1973-78, Denison Mines Ltd., Toronto, 1978-81; pvt. practice law San Antonio, 1981—. Apptd. by Sec. of Def. to serve on Def. Adv. Com., Women in the Svcs., 1997—99. Author: Call Sign Revlon: The Life and Death of Navy Fighter Pilot Kara Hultgreen, 1998. Mem. Tex. Bar Assn., San Antonio Bar Assn., Bankruptcy Bar Assn., San Antonio Country Club, The Club at Sonterra. Democrat. Home: 433 Evans Ave San Antonio TX 78209-3725 Office: Ste 106 8151 Broadway San Antonio TX 78209-1938 Home Phone: 210-822-4682; Office Phone: 210-826-7020. Personal E-mail: sespears@swbell.net.

SPECHT, ALICE WILSON, university libraries dean; b. Caracas, Venezuela, Apr. 3, 1948; (parents Am. citizens); d. Ned and Helen (Lockwood) Wilson; m. Joe W. Specht, Dec. 30, 1972; 1 child, Mary Helen. BA, U. Pacific, 1969; MLS, Emory U., 1970; MBA, Hardin-Simmons U., 1983. Libr. social scis. North Tex. State U., Denton, 1971-73; reference libr. Lubbock (Tex.) City and County Libr., 1974-75; system coord. Big Country Libr. System, Abilene, 1975-79; assoc. dir. Hardin-Simmons U., 1981-88, dir. univ. librs., 1988—, dean univ. librs., 2002—. Apptd. Mayor's Task Force Libr. Svcs., 1995-96; mem. adv. bd. Libr. Sys. Act, 2001-07; mem. vision task force TLA, 2007-. Author bibliog. instrn. aids, 1981-90; editor; The College Man, For Pilots Eyes Only. Mem. mayor's task force Abilene Pub. Libr., 1995—96; bd. trustees Grace Mus., 2009—; mem. Libr. Sys. Act. Bd., Tex., 2000—07. Recipient Boss of Yr., Am. Bus. Women's Assn., 1994. Mem.: ALA, Texshare Adv. Bd., Abilene Libr. Consortium (chair adminstrv. coun. 1990, coord. nat. conf. 1991, 1993, libr. sys. act adv. bd. 2001—, coord. nat. conf. 2002, chair adminstrv. coun. 2006), Tex. Libr. Assn. (chair com. 1978—84, sec.-treas. coll. and univ. librs. divsn. 1993—94, legis. com. 1994—, exec. bd. 2009—12), Texshare Ednl. Working Group (chair 1999). Home: 918 Grand Ave Abilene TX 79605-3233 Office: Hardin-Simmons U PO Box 16195 2341 Hickory St Abilene TX 79698-6195 Business E-Mail: aspecht@hsutx.edu.

SPECTOR, DANIEL EARL, historian, educator; b. Pensacola, Fla., Dec. 19, 1942; s. Rabbi Joseph and Dorothy Margaret (Givens) S.; m. Esta Gelda Rappaport, Aug. 9, 1964; children: Warren Leigh, Susan Artemis (dec.). BA, George Washington U., 1963; postgrad., U. Fla., 1963-64; MA, U. Tex., 1972, PhD, 1975. Adj. instr. Jacksonville (Ala.) State U., 1975-77; chief skill qualification test br. U.S. Army Mil. Police Sch., Ft. McClellan, Ala., 1975-80; supr. edn. specialist U.S. Army Chem. Sch., Ft. McClellan, 1980-82; chief U.S. Army Chem. Sch. Standardization & Analysis Div., Ft. McClellan, 1982-84; dep. dir. U.S. Army Chem. Sch. Directorate of Tng. & Doctrine, Ft. McClellan, 1984-88; adj. prof. U. Ala., Birmingham, 1986—2001; chem. corps historian U.S. Army Chem. Sch., Ft. McClellan, 1988-94; adj. prof. Troy State U., Ft. Benning, Ga., 2003—05. Accreditation coord. U.S. Army Chem. Sch., Ft. McClellan, 1984-90; accreditation team chief So. Assn. Colls. and Schs., Atlanta, 1985-90; U.S. Army rep. EURO-NATO nuc., biol. and chem. workgroups, 1984-90. Author: Chemical School Annual Historial Reviews, 1988—92; contbr. numerous revs., articles and ency. entries to several profl. jours. and encyclopedias pubs. Mem. Jacksonville Kiwanis, 1981-92. Road scholar Ala. Humanities Found., 2002-10; NDEA fellow U. Fla., 1963-64, NDFL fellow U. Tex. 1972-73. Mem. Middle Eastern Studies Assn., Middle East Inst., Am. Hist. Assn., Soc. Mil. History, Ala. Assn. Historians, MENSA, Temple Beth-El, Scottish Rite, Hiram Lodge 52, Ala. Master Gardener, Calhoun County Sheriff's Garden (advisor), Legion of Honor, Chapel of Four Chaplains, Jacksonville Garden Club (treas.), Phi Alpha Theta. Democrat. Jewish. Avocations: gardening, fishing, reading. Home: 1317 7th Ave NE Jacksonville AL 36265-1174 Personal E-mail: drspector@cableone.net.

SPECTOR, MICHAEL JOSEPH, agribusiness executive; b. NYC, Feb. 13, 1947; s. Martin Wilson and Dorothy (Miller) S.; m. Margaret Dickson, Sept. 14, 1977. BS in Chemistry, Washington and Lee U., 1968. Rsch. chemist Am. Viscose, Phila., 1968-69; pres. MJS Entertainment Corp., Miami, Fla., 1970-84; also MJS Internat., Inc.; ptnr. Old Town Key West Devel. Ltd., Fla., 1977—2002. Pres. MJS Entertainment of Can., Inc., Toronto, Margo Farms, MJS Prodns., Inc., NYC; chmn., CEO Margo Caribe, Inc., Dorado, PR, 1981—, bd. dir.; pres. Costa Del Norte Devel., Inc., Dorado, 1998—; bd. dir. Goodwill Industries So. Fla., v.p. fin., 1980; bd. dir. Plz. Bank of Miami; hon. Consul Belgium in P.R., U.S. V.I., Turks & Caicos Islands, West Indies, 2000—13; dir. Consular Corp. of P.R., 2002, vice-dean, 2003—04, dean, PR, 2004. Internat. judge The Floralies Exhbn., Gent, Belgium, 1995, 2000, 05; knight Sociedad Heraldica Espanola, 2003—. With AUS, 1969-70. Robert E. Lee rsch. grantee Washington and Lee U., 1967-68; named Agri-bus. Exec. of Yr., Govt. of P.R., 1999; knighted Order of King Leopold II, King of Belgium, 2005. Mem. Nat. Assn. Record Merchandisers (dir. Nova divsn., chmn. one-stop distbn. com. 1982-83), Country Music Assn., Dorado Beach Golf and Tennis Club, Ocean Reef Club, Key Largo, Univ. Club, Sawgrass County Club Achievements include patent for synthetic stretching process. Business E-Mail: mspector@margocaribe.com.*

SPECTOR, ROSE, former state supreme court justice; BA, Columbia U.; JD, St. Mary's Sch. Law, 1965. Judge County Ct. at Law 5, 1975-80, 131st Dist. Ct., 1981-92; justice Tex. Supreme Ct., 1993-98; atty. Bickerstaff, Heath, Delgado, Acosta, LLP, Austin, Tex., 1998—. Office Phone: 512-404-7867.

SPECTOR, WARREN E., console and personal computer game developer; b. Oct. 2, 1955; BS in Speech, Northwestern U.; MA in Radio-TV-Film, U. Tex., Austin. Exec. prodr. Electronic Arts; assoc. editor to editor-in-chief Steve Jackson Games; mgr., Game Divsn, editor & developer TSR, Inc., game editor, game writer, 1987—89; exec. prodr. ORIGIN Sys, Inc., assoc. prodr., 1989—97; exec. prodr., gen. mgr. LookingGlass Technologies, 1997; studio dir., ptnr. ION Storm, 1997—2004; v.p. Disney; v.p., creative dir. Disney Interactive Studios; founder, pres. Junction Point Studios, Inc., Austin, Tex., 2004—. Bd. dir. ION Storm, 1999—2004; spkr. in field. Credited with the following games Space Rogue, ORIGIN Systems, Inc., 1989, Wing Commander: The Secret Missions, 1990, Wing Commander, 1990, Ultima VI: The False Project, 1990, Bad Blood, 1990, Wing Commander: The Secret Missions 2-Crusade, 1991, Wing Commander II: Vengeance of the Kilrathi, 1991, Ultima: Worlds of Adventure 2: Martian Dreams, 1991, Ultima Underworld: The Stygian Abyss, 1992, Ultima Underworld II: Labyrinth of Worlds, 1992, Wing Commander: Privateer-Righteous Fire, 1993, Ultima VII, Part Two: Serpent Isle, 1993, CyberMage:Darklight Awakening, 1995, Crusader: No Remorse, 1995, Ultima VII, Part Two: The Silver Seed, Electronic Arts, Inc., 1993, Wings of Glory, 1994, Cel Damage, 2002, System Shock, Electronic Arts, Inc. and ORIGIN Systems, Inc., 1994, Dragonsphere, MicroProse Software, Inc., 1994, Thief: The Dark Project, Eidos Inc., 1998, Whiplash, 2003, Deus Ex:Invisible War, 2003, Backyard Wrestling:Don't Try This at Home, 2003, Thief: Deadly Shadows, 2004, Deus Ex, Eidos Interactive, Inc., 2000, Deus Ex (Game of Year Edition), 2001, Frequency, SCEA, 2001. Mem.: Internat. Game Developers Assn. (bd. dir.). Avocations: guitar, reading, board games, basketball. Business E-Mail: wspector@junctionpoint.com.

SPEECE, RICHARD EUGENE, civil engineer, educator; b. Marion, Ohio, Aug. 23, 1933; s. Irvin Ward S. and Desta May (Speece); m. Jean Margaret Edscorn, Nov. 15, 1969; children: Eric Jordan, Lincoln Dana. BCE, Fenn. Coll., 1956; M of Engring., Yale U., 1958; PhD, MIT, 1961. Assoc. prof. civil engring. U. Ill., Urbana, 1961-65; prof. N.Mex. State U., 1965-70, U. Tex., Austin, 1970-74; Betz chair prof. environ. engring. Drexel U., Phila., 1974-88; Centennial prof. Vanderbilt U., Nashville, 1988—. Vis. scholar Cambridge (Eng.) U., 1994; cons. to govt., industry. Contbr. articles to profl. jours.; patentee in field. Recipient hon. mention for best paper Trans. Am. Fisheries Soc., 1973, Founders award Assn. Environ. Engrs. Profs., 2005., Assoc. Environ. Engr. Profs. Founders award 2005. Mem. ASCE (J. James Cross medal 1983), Assn. Environ. Engring. and Sci. Profs. (disting. lectr. 1978, trustee 1981-83, Disting. Faculty award 1970, Engring. Sci. award 1982, Founders award 2005, 06), Am. Soc. Microbiologists, Water Environ. Fedn. (Harrison Prescott Eddy medal 1966), U.S. ANC (Founders award 1991), Internat. Assn. on Water Pollution Rsch. and Control. Office: Vanderbilt Univ Dept Civil Engring Nashville TN 37235 Office Phone: 615-343-6328, 317-371-1977. Business E-Mail: dick.speece@vanderbilt.edu.

SPEER, JACK ATKESON, publisher; b. Wichita, Kans., July 3, 1941; s. Jack Shelley and Shannon C. Speer; m. Judith Ann Fuller, Aug. 5,1967; children: Martin Fuller, Elizabeth Speer Goodwin. BSBA, Kans. State U., Emporia, 1966; ML, Kansas. State U., 1967; postgrad., U. Mo., 1967, U. So. Calif., 1969; IBM Pres.'s Class, Harvard U., 1980. Mem. advt., editorial, mech. staffs Wichita Eagle-Beacon, 1954-64; photographer, editl. asst. Emporia (Kans.) Gazette, 1964—65; supr. libr. data processing Kans. State U., Emporia, 1965-67, mgr. data processing ctr. Manhattan, 1967-69; mgr. systems and programming John Wiley Inc.-Becker & Hayes Inc., Bethesda, Md., 1969-72; dir. libr. info. systems Informatics Inc. Info. Systems Group, Rockville, Md., 1972-77; v.p. ops. Arcata Real Estate Data Inc., Miami, Fla., 1977-79; mgr. electronic info. systems Arcata Publs. Group, Norwalk, Conn., 1979-83; v.p. mktg./sales, data imaging group The William Byrd Press, Richmond, Va., 1983-84; sr. v.p. ops. NewsBank Inc., New Canaan, Conn., 1984-85; pres., pub. Buckmaster Pub., Mineral, Va., 1986—. Mem. faculty Cath. U. Am. Libr. Sch., Kans. State U. Libr. Sch.; customer adv. coun. U.S. Postal Svc., 1996—. Author: Amateur Radio Call Directory Ham Call, 1982—, Buckmaster's Ann. Stockholder Reports, 1986—, Front-Page-News (CD-ROM and Internet), 1989, HamCall (CD-ROM and Internet), 1988—; compiler Libraries and Automation: A Bibliography, 1967, The Living Bible Concordance, 1972. Trustee Jefferson-Madison Regional Libr., 1990-91; commr. Louisa County Planning Commn. 1992-; pres. Louisa County Libr. Found. 2003-; bd. mem. J. Sargeant Reynolds CC, 2009-2013. Mem. ALA, NRA, Am. Radio Relay League, Nat. Info. Standards Orgn. (CD-ROM com), D.C. Libr. Assn. (pres.), Rotary, Sigma Tau Gamma. Office: Buckmaster Pub 6196 Jefferson Hwy Mineral VA 23117-3425 E-mail: speerj@buck.com.

SPEER, KEVIN PAUL, surgeon; b. Evansville, Ind., June 8, 1959; m. Marcy Carlson Speer, Mar. 24, 1984; children: Casey, Kira. MD, Johns Hopkins U., 1985. Lic. physician N.C., 1992. Assoc. prof. orthopedics Duke U. Med. Ctr., Durham, NC, 1992—2000; pvt. practice Southeastern Orthopedics, Raleigh, NC, 2000—. Fellow, Am. Orthop. Assn., 1992. Fellow: AAOS. Office: Southeastern Orthopedics 3404 Wake Forest Rd Ste 201 Raleigh NC 27609 Business E-Mail: kspeer@nc.rr.com.

SPEESE, MARK E., rental company executive; Student, Western Mich. U. Regional mgr. Thorn Americas, 1979—86; from v.p. N.J. Ops. to chmn., CEO Rent A Center, Plano, Tex., 1986—2001; chmn., CEO Rent-A-Center, Inc., 2001—. Bd. dirs. Rent A Ctr. Office: Rent A Center 5501 Headquarters Dr Plano TX 75024-5837

SPELLACY, WILLIAM NELSON, obstetrician, gynecologist, educator; b. St. Paul, May 10, 1934; s. Jack F. and Elmyra L. (Nelson) Spellacy; m. Lynn Larsen; children: Kathleen Ann, Kimberly Joan, William Nelson. BA, U. Minn., 1955, BS, 1956, MD, 1959. Diplomate subsplty. cert. in maternal and fetal medicine Am. Bd. Ob-Gyn. Intern Hennepin County Gen. Hosp., Mpls., 1959—60; resident U. Minn., Mpls., 1960—63; practice medicine specializing in ob-gyn. Mpls., 1963—67, Miami, Fla., 1967—73, Gainesville, Fla., 1973—79, Chgo., 1979—88; prof., dept. head U. Ill. Coll. Medicine, Chgo., 1979—88; dept. chmn. U. So. Fla. Coll. Medicine, Tampa, 1988—2002, prof., 1988—. Prof. dept. ob-gyn. U. Miami, 1967—73; prof., chmn. dept. U. Fla., 1973—79. Contbr. articles to med. jours. Mem.: ACOG, AMA, Inst. Medicine, Ill. Med. Soc., Soc. Perinatal Obstetricians, Ctrl. Assn. Obstetrics and Gynecology, South Atlantic Soc. Obstetrics and Gynecology, Perinatal Rsch. Soc., Am. Diabetes Assn., Assn. Profs. Gynecology and Obstetrics, Am. Fertility Soc., Endocrine Soc., Am. Assn. Obstetricians and Gynecologists, Soc. Gynecol. Investigation, Am. Gynecol. and Obstet. Soc., Am. Gynecol. Soc., Rotary. Episcopalian. Office: Univ South Fla Coll Medicine Dept OBGYN 2A Tampa General Cir Tampa FL 33606-3589 Home: 516 Mirabay Blvd Apollo Beach FL 33572 Office Phone: 813-259-8542.

SPENCE, JAMES ROBERT, JR., television executive, educator, mediator; b. Bronxville, NY, Dec. 20, 1936; s. James Robert and Mary Jeffery (Grant) Spence; m. Betsy Jo Viener, June 16, 1992. BA, Dartmouth Coll., 1958. Prodn. asst. ABC Sports, Inc. (known as Sports Programs, Inc. through 1966), NYC, 1960-63; asst. to exec. prodr. ABC's Wide World of Sports, 1963-66, coordinating prodr., 1966-70; v.p. program planning ABC Sports, Inc., 1970-78, sr. v.p., 1978-86; pres. Sports Television Internat., Inc., NYC, 1986—2006, exec. prodr., 1986—2006. Adj. assoc. prof. broadcasting NYU Sch. Continuing and Profl. Studies, NYC, 1999—2003; vis. scholar Coll. William and Mary, Williamsburg, Va., 2004—; instr. Christopher Wren Assn., Williamsburg, Va., 2008—; cert. mediator Gen. Dist. Ct., Va., 2008—. Author: Up Close & Personal - The Inside Story of Network Television Sports, 1988. With US Army, 1958—60. Mem.: Golden Horseshoe Golf Club (Williamsburg, Va.), Two Rivers Country Club (Williamsburg, Va.), Westchester Country Club (Rye, NY).

SPENCE, PAUL HERBERT, librarian; b. Geraldine, Ala., Dec. 25, 1923; s. John Clardy and Leila (Carrell) S.; m. Ruth Schmidt, May 9, 1954 (dec. Aug. 2003); children: John Carrell, Peter Schmidt, Robert McCollough AB, Emory U., 1948, MA, 1956; PhD, U. Ill., 1969. Asst. reference librarian Emory U., Atlanta, 1950-53; periodical reference librarian Air U., Maxwell AFB, 1953-56; dir. library Air Force Inst. of Tech., Wright-Patterson AFB, Ohio, 1957-58; asst. dir. social studies U. Notre Dame, South Bend, Ind., 1959-60, U. Nebr., Lincoln, 1960-63; history and polit. sci. librarian U. Ill., Urbana, 1963-66; assoc. dir. libraries U. Ga., Athens, 1966-70; dir. libraries U. Ala., Birmingham, 1970-84, collection devel. librarian, 1985-89, prof. emeritus, 1989—, libr. cons., 1990—. Bd. dirs. Southeastern Library Network, Atlanta, 1973-75. Served with U.S. Army, 1943-46, ETO Mem. ALA (council mem. 1976-78), Ala. Library Assn. (treas. 1975-76), Southeastern Library Assn. (pres. 1980-82) Democrat. Presbyterian. Home: 614 Warwick Rd Birmingham AL 35209-4426 Office: U Ala at Birmingham 172 Sterne Libr Birmingham AL 35294-0001 Personal E-mail: paulhspence@aol.com. Business E-Mail: pspence@beowulf.mhsl.uab.edu.

SPENCE, ROY MILAM, JR., advertising executive; b. Brownwood, Tex., Oct. 10, 1948; m. Mary Spence; children: Courtney, Ashley, Shay. BA in Govt., U. Tex., 1971. Co-founder GSD&M's Idea City (formerly GSD&M Advt.), Austin, Tex., 1971, pres., 1971—2007, chmn., CEO, 2007—. Mem. devel. bd. U. Tex., Austin, mem. adv. coun. McComb Sch. Bus. Featured in Fortune, The Wall St. Jour., The New York Times, USA Today. Mem. Wal-Mart Lit. Coun. Recipient Disting. Alumnus award, U. Tex., 2004. Office: GSD&M's Idea City 828 W 6th St Austin TX 78703-5420

SPENCER, ALBERT FRANKLIN, physical education educator; b. Pitts., Pa., Dec. 31, 1943; s. Albert Clair and Ann Mary (Kielbas) Spencer; m. Sue Spencer; stepchildren: Flannery Heath, Russell Yopp. BS in Edn., Slippery Rock State Coll., Pa., 1966; MS in LS, Clarion State U., Pa., 1981; PhD in LS, Fla. State U., Tallahassee, 1985, PhD in Phys. Edn., 1991. Departmental dir. Kmart, 1972—74; phys. edn. tchr., libr., coach St. John's Indian Sch., Komatke, Ariz., 1976-77, Duncan HS, Ariz., 1977-79; tchr. math. and sci. Army and Navy Acad., Carlsbad, Calif., 1979-80; phys. edn. tchr., libr., coach Baboquivari HS, Sells, Ariz., 1980-81; asst. men's intercoll. basketball coach Fla. State U., Tallahassee, 1981-83; asst. prof. phys. edn., dir. audiovisual svcs. St. Leo Coll., Fla., 1983-86; asst. prof. Atlanta U. and Emory U., Atlanta, 1986-87; assoc. prof. phys. edn./athletics, libr. dir., coach Ga. Mil. Coll., Milledgeville, 1987-90; asst. prof. edn. U. Nev., Las Vegas, 1991-94, 2000; asst. prof. phys. edn., dept. human performance/health scis. Rice U., Houston, 1994—98; prof. phys. edn. & sport mgmt. Limestone Coll., 2000—; invited spkr. Oxford Round Table, 2012, 2014. Dir. athletics YMCA, Kittanning, Pa., 1969; cons. ednl. tech. Atlanta Pub. Schs., 1986-87; profl. basketball scout Bertka Agy. and LA Lakers, 1985-91; chair ethics com. Am. Alliance for Health, Phys. Edn., Recreation and Dance, 2005-08. Contbg. author: Twentieth-Century Young Adult Writers, 1994; contbr. articles and revs. to profl. jours. Fundraiser KC, Sacred Heart, Gaffney, SC, patriotic degree and recruitment dir., 1991-; vol. coach for youth league St. Anthony Elem. Sch., San Antonio, Fla.; asst. scoutmaster Boy Scouts America, New Kensington, 1968-70; fundraiser St. Jude's Children's Hosp., 1968-70; mem. Southeastern Cherokee Fedn.; vol. elem. sch. reader Reading is Fundamental, 1991-; event. coord. Spl. Olympics, Limestone Coll., Cherokee County, SC, 2000-08; candidate US Congress, 2004, 08. Mem. AAHPERD, ALA, Am. Libr. and Info. Sci. Educators, Fla. Assn. for Health, Phys. Edn., Recreation and Dance, U.S. Phys. Edn. Assn., Beta Phi Mu, Omicron Delta Kappa. Republican. Roman Catholic. Avocations: writing, golf, basketball, hiking. Office: Limestone Coll WGPE Building Gaffney SC 29340-3615 Home Phone: 864-489-4300; Office Phone: 864-488-4563. Business E-Mail: aspencer@limestone.edu.

SPENCER, EDGAR WINSTON, geology educator; b. Monticello, Ark., May 27, 1931; s. Terrel Ford Spencer and Allie Belle (Shelton) S.; m. Elizabeth Penn Humphries, Nov. 26, 1958; children: Elizabeth Shawn, Kristen Shannon. Student, Vanderbilt U., Nashville, 1949—50; BS, Wash. and Lee U., Lexington, Va., 1953; PhD, Columbia U., NYC, 1957. Lectr. Hunter Coll., 1954-57; mem. faculty Washington and Lee U., 1957—2001, prof. geology, head dept., 1962-95, Ruth Parmly prof. Pres. emeritus Rockbridge Area Conservation Coun., 1978-79, co-pres. 1992-98, bd. dirs., 1999-; NSF sci. faculty fellow, New Zealand and Australia; dir. grant for humanities and pub. policy on land use planning Va. Found., 1975; dir. grant Petroleum Rsch. Fund, 1981-82; leader field trip Ctrl. Appalachian Mts. Internat. Geol. Congress, 1989. Author: Basic Concepts of Physical Geology, 1962, Basic Concepts of Historical Geology, 1962, Geology: A Survey of Earth Science, 1965, Introduction to the Structure of the Earth, 1969, 3d edit., 1988, The Dynamics of the Earth, 1972, Physical Geology, 1983, Geologic Maps, 1993, 2nd edit., 2000, Geologic Maps of the Buena Vista and Glasgow Quadrangle, Virginia, 2000, Earth Science-Understanding Environmental Systems, 2003; co-author: Geologic Map and Report on the Geology of Rockbridge County, Virginia, 2007, Geologic Map of THe Natural Bridge Quadrangle, 2010. Vice pres. Rockbridge Area Conservation Coun.; dir. pub. forum Va. Found., 1975; with Va. Found for the Humanities and Pub. Policy. Recipient Va. Outstanding Faculty award Va. Coun. of Higher Edn., 1990, Anna Jonas 2013 award Virginia Geological Field Conf., Disting. Alumnus award, Washington and Lee U. Fellow Geol. Soc. Am., Am. Geophys. Union, Yellowstone-Bighorn Rsch. Assn., Phi Beta Kappa (hon.), Omicron Delta Kappa (hon.), Sigma Xi. Avocations: music, hiking, photography. Home: PO Box 1055 Lexington VA 24450-1055 Office Phone: 540-458-8866. Business E-Mail: spencere@wlu.edu.

SPENCER, GEORGE HENRY, lawyer; b. Vienna; s. Frank Henry and Lillian (Godin) S.; m. Joan Betty Spencer, Sept. 16, 1956 (dec.); children: Lucy, Margaret, Robert, Nancy; m. Mollie Cole Sabol, Oct. 31, 1987; stepchildren: Jeanne, Marta. BE, Yale U., 1948; JD, Cornell U., 1952. Bar: D.C., N.Y. Examiner U.S. Patent Office, 1952-54; sole practice NYC, Washington, 1954-62; ptnr. Spencer & Frank, Washington, 1962-98, Venable, LLP, Attys. at Law, Washington, 1998—2003. Master of bench Giles S. Rich Am. Inn of Ct.; lectr. World Trade Inst. Served to capt. JAGC, U.S. Army, 1956-62. Mem. ABA, Am. Patent Law Assn., Lawyer-Pilots Bar Assn., Internat. Trade Commn. (mem. panel of mediators), World Intellectual Property Orgn. (panel of arbitrators and mediators), Cosmos Club (Washington). Avocations: aviation, music, German and French language studies, poetry. Home: 1102 Flor Ln Mc Lean VA 22102-1737 Office: Antonelli Terry Stout & Kraus LLP 1300 N 17th St Ste 1800 Arlington VA 22209 Office Phone: 703-312-6697. Business E-Mail: gspencer@antonelli.com.

SPENCER, JAMES R., federal judge; b. 1949; BA magna cum laude (hon.), Clark Coll., 1971; JD, Harvard U., 1974, MDiv, 1985. Staff atty. Atlanta Legal Aid Soc., 1974-75; asst. US atty. Washington, 1978, US Dist. Ct. (Ea. Dist.) Va., 1983, judge, 1986—, chief judge, 2004—. Adj. prof. law U Va., 1987—. Capt. JAGC US Army, 1975—78, Res. JAGC US Army, 1981—86. Mem.: Old Dominion Bar Assn., Wash. Bar Assn., Richmond Bar Assn., Va. State Bar, State Bar Ga., Nat. Bar Assn., ABA, Sigma Pi Phi, Omega Psi Phi. Office: US Courthouse 401 Courthouse Sq Alexandria VA 22314 Office Phone: 804-916-2250. Office Fax: 276-957-8203.

SPENCER, JAN B., health products executive; b. Rostrup, Germany, 1955; m. Miriam Spencer; 3 children. B in Textile Tech. & Mgmt. Sciences, U. Manchester Inst. Sci. & Tech. Comml. sales rep. Kimberly-Clark Corp., Manchester, England, 1979, product mgr., bus. analyst, bus. mgr., 1980—88, various positions including dir., washroom bus., VSE to UCTAD project mgr. and Scott merger integration mgr., 1988—96, v.p., rsch., devel. & engring., Away From Home, 1996—98, v.p., wiper bus., 1998—2000, v.p., European Ops., Engring., Supply Chain in Profl. sector, 2000—02, pres., Kimberly-Clark Profl., Europe, 2002—03, pres., Kimberly-Clark Profl., N.Am., 2003—04, pres., Kimberly-Clark Profl., North Atlantic, 2004—06, pres., Global Kimberly-Clark Profl., 2006—10, sr. v.p. continuous improvement, global sourcing & sustainability, 2010—. Office: Kimberly Clark Corp 351 Phelps Dr Irving TX 75038 Office Phone: 972-281-1200. Office Fax: 972-281-1490. Business E-Mail: jspencer@kcc.com.

SPENCER, JASON, state legislator; b. Offutt AFB, Nebr., Nov. 14; m. Melaney Spencer; children: Madeline, Vera. Attended, Abraham Baldwin Agrl. Coll., Tifton, Ga.; B in Sports Medicine, U. Ga., 1995; B, South U., Savannah, Ga., 2001; M, U. Nebr., 2005. Emergency dept. physicians asst.; mem. Dist. 180 Ga. House of Representatives, 2011—. Mem.: NRA (life). Republican. Avocation: tennis. Office: 28 Yachtsman Ct Woodbine GA 31569-4083 also: Georgia House of Reps 411 Coverdell Legis Office Bldg Atlanta GA 30334 Office Phone: 912-576-5810, 404-656-0126. Business E-Mail: jason.spencer@house.ga.gov.

SPENCER, JILL WILEMON, bank executive; b. 1952; BA in History, U. Tex., Austin, 1973; JD, So. Meth. U., 1977. With Fed. Home Loan Bank of San Francisco, 1979—97, sr. v.p., gen. counsel; pvt. practice, 1998—2002; exec. v.p., gen. counsel, corp. sec. Fed. Home Loan Bank of Atlanta, 2002—04, exec. v.p., COO, 2004—08, corp. sec., 2007—, exec. v.p., gen. counsel, chief strategy officer, 2008—, interim pres., CEO, 2010—. Office: Federal Home Loan Bank of Atlanta PO Box 105565 Atlanta GA 30348-5565 Office Phone: 404-888-8000.

SPENCER, RICHARD THOMAS, III, health products executive; b. Oak Park, Ill., Mar. 18, 1936; s. Richard Thomas Spencer Jr. and Lois Anne (Pollock) Spencer; m. Andrea B. Schlickeiser, June 26, 1962; 1 child, Richard Thomas IV. BA, U. Mich., 1959; postgrad., U. Pa., 1976, Stanford U., 1984, Clemson U., 1985. Mktg. group Mobil Oil Co., Detroit, 1962; internat. trade specialist U.S. Dept. Commerce, Detroit, 1963—64; account exec. J. Walter Thompson Co., Detroit, 1965—66; sales mgr. Sarns Inc., Ann Arbor, Mich., 1967—69; v.p. mktg. Cordis Dow Corp., Miami, Fla., 1970—81; pres. mktg. divsn. Cordis Corp., Miami, 1982—87; pres., CEO Uni-Med Internat. Corp., Miami, 1988—2000; exec. v.p., COO, bd. dirs. World Med. Mfg. Corp., Sunrise, Fla., 1995—2000. Bd. dirs. Viacor Corp., Wilmington, Mass., Bioheart, Inc., Weston, Fla., Oxira Med., Inc., Boca Raton, Fla.; cons. in field. Contbr. articles to profl. jours. With CIC US Army, 1959—61. Republican. Avocations: skiing, golf, running, stereo equipment, geopolits. Home and Office: 3641 N 47th Ave Hollywood FL 33021-2211 Home: 811 E Hill Rd North Troy VT 05859 Office Phone: 954-558-3689. Personal E-mail: richardtspencer@yahoo.com.

SPENCER, ROGER FELIX, psychiatrist, educator; b. Apr. 19, 1934; came to U.S., 1941; s. Eugene S. Spitzer and Santa Spencer; m. Barbara Ann Houser, Aug. 18, 1958; children: Geoffrey, Jennifer, Rebecca. BS, Yale Coll., 1956; MD, Harvard Med. Sch., 1959. Diplomate Am. Bd. Psychiatry. Intern N.C. Meml. Hosp., Chapel Hill, 1959-60, resident in psychiatry, 1960-63; instr. U. N.C. Sch. Medicine, Chapel Hill, 1963-66, asst. prof., 1966-69, assoc. prof., 1969-76, prof., 1976—. Dir. of liaison and cons., U. N.C., 1967-77, dir. out patient psychiatry, 1977-95. Contbr. articles to profl. jours.;, author short stories. Recipient Career Tchr. award NIMH, 1965-67. Fellow Am. Psychiat. Assn. (life), Am. Psychoanalytic Assn.; mem. N.C. Psychoanalytic Soc. (past pres.), N.C. Psychiat. Assn. (past pres.). Office: UNC Hosps Dept Psychiatry CB 7160 Chapel Hill NC 27599-7160 Home Phone: 919-929-6192; Office Phone: 919-966-5772. Office Fax: 919-843-6102. Business E-Mail: roger_spencer@med.unc.edu.

SPENCER, VIVIAN L., gallery director; BA in Art Edn., U. West Fla., Pensacola; MFA, Md. Inst. Coll. Art, Balt. Profl. tchg. cert. Fla. Chair, instr., art dept. Washington HS, 1984—2001; edn. curator Pensacola Mus. Art, 2001—03; exec. dir. Belmont Arts and Cultural Ctr., 2003—05; gallery dir. Pensacola Jr. Coll., 2005—. Adj. prof. Pensacola Jr. Coll., 1997—, U. West Fla., 2003—05; vis. artist, Hagiwara, Japan, 1998, Hagiwara, 2000. Contbr. articles to profl. jours. Vol. Big Brothers and Big Sisters, Belmont Arts and Cultural Ctr., Arts Coun. Northwest Fla. Recipient Centerstage award, Arts Coun. Northwest Fla., 1999, Edna Rivers Humanitarian award, Washington HS, 2000. Mem.: Fla. Arts in Edn., Fla. Art Edn. Assn., Nat. Art Edn. Assn., Alpha Delta Kappa. Office: Anna Lamar Switzer Ctr for Visual Arts Pensacola Jr Coll 1000 College Blvd Pensacola FL 32504 Office Phone: 850-484-2048. Office Fax: 850-484-2564. Business E-Mail: vspencer@pjc.edu.

SPENDLOVE, G. SCOTT, energy executive; B in Acctg., Brigham Young U.; MBA, Calif. State U., Fresno. Various positions, investor rels., acctg., fin., forecasting & planning Unocal Corp., Ultramar Diamond Shamrock Corp. (acquired by Valero), v.p., investor rels., corp. devel.; v.p., fin. Tesoro Corp., 2002—03, v.p., fin., treas., 2003—06, v.p., contr., 2006, v.p., strategy, long-term planning, 2006—07, v.p., asset enhancement, planning, 2007—08, sr. v.p., risk mgmt., 2008—10, sr. v.p., CFO, treas., 2010—11, sr. v.p., CFO, 2011—. Office: Tesoro Corp 19100 Ridgewood Pky San Antonio TX 78259-1828 Office Phone: 210-626-6000. Office Fax: 210-579-4574. Business E-Mail: sspendlove@tsocorp.com.

SPERBER, MATTHEW ARNOLD, direct marketing company executive; b. NYC, Dec. 17, 1938; s. Raymond and Sylvia (Pollock) S.; m. Jane L. Trautman; children: Sean S., Dawn E. BS in Architecture, CUNY, 1961. Mgr. advt. IBM, White Plains, N.Y., 1967-78; mgr. advt. and promotion Exxon Office Systems, Lionsville, Pa., 1979-81; dir. advt. and promotion Wang, Lowell, Mass., 1981-83; dir. mkgt. communication Datapoint, San Antonio, 1983-85; pres. Bus. to Bus. div. Harte Hanks Direct Mktg., San Antonio, 1985-88; pres. Internat. Direct Mktg., San Antonio, 1988—. Mgr. IBM Copier, 1970, QYX Electronic Typewriter, 1980; dir. Wang Personal Computer, 1982, Datapoint 32 Mini Computer, 1985. With U.S. Army, 1961-63. Mem. Am. Mktg. Assn. (exec.), Direct Mktg. Assn. (Best Indsl. Direct Mktg. award 1978). Republican. Avocations: tennis, basketball, aerobics, music, travel. Office: Internat Direct Mktg 8045 Antoine Dr Ste 109 Houston TX 77088-4301 Home: 142 Turnberry Way San Antonio TX 78230 Office Phone: 713-850-4808.

SPERLING, SHELDON JAY, former federal prosecutor; b. 1949; m. Marvetta Sperling; 2 children. BA, Northeastern State Coll., 1971; JD, U. Tulsa, 1979. Pvt. practice, Tulsa, 1979—82; asst. dist. atty. Okla. Dist. Atty.'s Office, 1983—85; asst. US atty. (ea. dist.) Okla. US Dept. Justice, Muskogee, Okla., 1985—89, 1st asst. US atty., criminal chief, 1989—2000, US atty. (ea. dist.) Okla., 2000—10. Mem. Tulsa County Bar Assn., 1979—82, ABA, 1979—86, Okla. Dist. Atty.'s Assn., 1983—85, Nat. Dist. Atty.'s Assn., 1984, Nat. Assn. Asst. US Attorneys, 1994—2001, exec. dir., regional dir., del. Recipient Special Commendations, FBI Dir. William S. Sessions, 1993, FBI Dir. Louis J. Freech, 1998, FBI Dir. Robert S. Mueller III, 2002, US Dept. Justice Dir. award, 1994. Mem.: Bar of Northern Dist. Okla., Bar of Eastern Dist. Okla., Phi Rho Pi, Rho Theta Sigma, Delta Theta Phi.

SPERRY, LEN THOMAS, psychiatrist and preventive medicine educator; b. Milw., Dec. 1, 1943; s. Leonard V. and Wanda R. (Sadowski) S.; m. Patricia L. Garcia, June 11, 1977; children: Tracy, Christen, L. Timothy, Steven, Jonathan. BA, St. Mary's U. Minn., Winona, Minn., 1966; PhD, Northwestern U., 1970; MD, CETEC U., 1981; MA, Loyola U., 1984; D in Ministry, Barry U., 2001. Diplomate Am. Bd. Profl. Psychology, Am. Bd. Psychiatry and Neurology, Am. Bd. Preventive Medicine. Asst. prof. Marquette U., Milw., 1971-74; assoc. prof. U. Wis., Milw., 1974-75, Alliant Internat. U., San Diego, 1976-78; resident in psychiatry and preventive medicine Med. Coll. Wis., Milw., 1982-85; fellow in behavioral medicine U. Wis. Med. Sch., Milw., 1984-85; assoc. prof. psychiatry, preventive medicine Med. Coll. Wis., Milw., 1986-92, prof., 1992-2000, prof. cmty. and family medicine, 1998-2000, vice chair dept. psychiatry, 1997-2000, clin. prof. psychiatry, 2000—; prof. health adminstrn., prof. psychology Barry U., Miami Shores, Fla., 2000—02, dir. doctoral program in counseling, 2003; prof. Fla. Atlantic U., 2003—; dir, clin. tng., 2012—. Author: Learning Performance and Individual Differences, 1972, Contract Counseling, 1974, You Can Make It Happen: Self-Actualization and Organization, 1977, Together Experience, 1978, Aderian Counseling and Psychotherapy, 1987, Psychiatric Case Formulations, 1992, Psychopathology and Psychotherapy, 1993, 2d edit., 1996, Psychiatric Consultation in the Workplace, 1993, Handbook of Diagnosis and Treatment of DSM-IV Personality Disorders, 1995, Psychopharmacology and Psychotherapy, 1995, Treatment Outcomes in Psychotherapy and Psychiatric Interventions, 1996, Aging in the 21st Century, 1996, Family Therapy: Ensuring Treatment Efficacy, 1997, The Disordered Couple, 1997, The Intimate Couple, 1998, Brief Therapy Strategies with Individuals and Couples, 2000, Ministry and Community, 2000, Integrative and Biopsychosocial Therapies, 2000, Spirituality in Clinical Practice, 2001, Transforming Self and Community, 2002, Effective Leader, 2002, Becoming an Effective Therapist, 2003, Becoming an Effective Health Care Manager, 2003, Sex, Priestly Ministry and the Church, 2003, Executive Coaching, 2004, Spiritually-Oriented Psychotherapy, 2005, Couple and Family Assessment, 2005, Health Promotion and Health Counseling, Couples Therapy (2d edit.), 2005, Family Therapy Techniques, 2005, Cognitive Behavior Therapy of DSM-TR Pesonality Disorders, 2006, Psychological Treatment of Chronic Illness, 2006, The Ethical and Professional Practice of Counseling and Psychotherapy, 2007, Dictionary of Ethical and Legal Terms and Issues, 2007, Treatment Chronic Med. Conditions, 2008, Highly Effective Therapy Developing Essential Clinical Conptency, 2010, Recovery of Intimacy, 2011, Core Competency in Counseling and Psychotherapy, 2010, Spirituality in Clinical Practice, 2nd edit., 2011-, Mobbing: Causes, Consequences, and Solutions, 2012, Family Assessment, 2012, Case Conceptualization, 2012, Inner Life of Priests, 2012, Behavioral Health, 2013, How Master Therapists Work, 2013, Overcoming Mobbing, 2013, Cognative Behavior Therapy of DSM-5 Personality Disorders, 2013; contbr. articles to profl. jours. Bd. dirs. Am. Coun. on Sci. and Health, Nat. Acad. for Certified Family Therapists, St. Camillus Health Ctr., 1996-2000, Cath. Health Svcs., 2001—; cons. dir. Staff Devel. Am. Appraisal Assn., Milw., 1972-76. Northwestern U. fellow, 1969, Med. Coll. Wis. grantee, 1981, Named U. Scholar of Yr., 2012-13 Fellow APA (Harry Levinson award 1998), Am. Psychiat. Assn. (chair com. on psychiatry in workplace 1998—, fellow, 1987-2001, disting. fellow, 2001-11, disting. life fellow 2011-), Am. Coll. Preventive Medicine, Am. Coll. Psychiatrists, Am. Bd. Profl. Psychology, Am. Bd. Psychiatry and Neurology, Acad. Orgnl. and Occupational Psychiatry (v.p. 1993-96, Alan McLean lifetime achievement award 2000), Group for Advancement of Psychiatry, Coalition for Family Diagnosis, North Am. Soc. Adleran Psychology(achievement award, 2013) Avocations: reading, racquet sports, music. Office: Fla Atlantic U 777 Glades Rd Boca Raton FL 33431 Business E-Mail: lsperry@fau.edu.

SPICER, MARK J., oil and gas company executive; BS in Geological and Petroleum Engring., N.Mex. Inst. Mining and Tech. With Amerada Hess Corp.; mgr. info. tech. Newfield Exploration Co., 2005, v.p. info. tech., 2005—. Mem.: Soc. Petroleum Engrs. Office: Newfield Exploration Co 363 N Sam Houston Pky E Ste 2020 Houston TX 77060 Office Phone: 281-847-6000. Office Fax: 281-405-4242.

SPIEGEL, ALDONA J., plastic surgeon; d. Stanislaw Richard and Elizabeth Helena Jedrysiak; m. Spiegel Noah Damon, Sept. 22, 2001; 2 children. MD, U. Ottawa, Can., 1994. Diplomate in plastic surgery Am. Bd. Plastic Surgery, 2002. Dir. Meth. Hosp., Ctr. Breast Restoration, Houston, 2005—; asst. prof. Weill Med. Coll., Cornell U., NYC, 2006—. Contbr. articles to profl. jours. Mem.: AMA, Plastic Surgery Rsch. Coun., World Soc. Reconstructive Microsurgery, Am. Soc. Reconstructive Microsurgery, Am. Soc. Plastic Surgery. Achievements include patents for medical device. Office: Methodist Hosp 6560 Fannin Ste 800 Houston TX 77030 Office Fax: 713-790-2085. Business E-Mail: aspiegel@tmhs.org.

SPIEGEL, LAWRENCE HOWARD, advertising executive; b. NYC, Oct. 9, 1942; s. Melvin Arthur and Rose (Black) S.; m. Christy Mansfield; children from previous marriage: Robert, David. BA, NYU, 1963. Print buyer William Esty Co., NYC, 1964-65, broadcast buyer, 1965-66; media planner Batten, Barton, Durstine & Osborn, Inc., NYC, 1966-67, media supr., 1967-68, assoc. media dir., 1969-72, v.p., 1972-74; media group head Jack Tinker & Ptnrs., NYC, 1968-69; v.p. Tracy-Locke, Dallas, 1974-80, sr. v.p., 1980-84, exec. v.p., 1984-89; prin. The Richards Group, Dallas, 1989—. Pres. Tex. Coun. Advt., 1991-97, Leading Agy. Network, 1997—; dir. Dream Fund, 1999—; charter mem. broadband video adv. bd. AOL. Guest editor Mktg. and Media Decision mag., June 1982. Mem. Dallas Cable Bd., 1983-86; chmn. mktg. com. U. Tex., Dallas, 1984-89; pres. Cable Access Dallas, Inc., 1985-86; trustee Dallas Symphony Assn., 1978—; bd. dirs. Equest Inc., 1991-92, DREAM Fund, 1999—. Staff sergeant US Army. Recipient Excellence award, Am. Women in Radio and TV, 2006. Mem. Assn. Broadcasting Execs. Tex. (pres. 1975-76), Am. Women in Radio and TV, Inc. (bd. dirs. 1992-93), Dallas Ad League. Republican. Avocations: skiing, sailing. Office: The Richards Group 1307 W Main St Suite B-109 Gun Barrel City TX 75156 Office Phone: 214-891-5843. Personal E-mail: larry_spiegel@embarqmail.com.

SPILLANE, TIMOTHY J., medical insurance company executive; m. Anne Spillane; 3 children. BS, U. Va., 1989; MBA in Fin., UCLA, 1991. Anlayst Dean Witter Reynolds, 1989—91; dir. Pricewaterhouse-Coopers Securities, 1993—2000; founder, mng. dir. Envest Capital Advisors, 2000—02; joined Amerigroup Corp., 2002, v.p. corp. devel., 2005, sr. v.p., corp. devel. Bd. dirs. Cavalier Golf and Yacht Club. Office: Amerigroup Corp 4425 Corporation Ln Virginia Beach VA 23462 Office Phone: 757-490-6900. Office Fax: 757-222-2330. Business E-Mail: tspillane@amerigroupcorp.com.

SPINELLA, JUDY LYNN, health care operations consultant; b. Ft. Worth, Apr. 8, 1948; d. Gettis Breon and Velrea Inez (Webb) Prothro; m. Peter E. Veruki; children: Scott Slater, Jennifer Spinella Kochan. BS in Nursing, U. Tex., Austin/Galveston, 1971; MS in Nursing, Tex.

Woman's U., Dallas, 1973; MBA, Vanderbilt U., Nashville, 1993. RN, Tex. Asst. prof. U. Tex., Arlington, 1976-81; dir. emergency svcs. San Francisco Gen. Hosp., 1981-84, assoc. adminstr. for clin. svcs. and chief nursing officer, 1984—88; exec. dir. for nursing svcs. and chief nursing officer Vanderbilt U. Med. Ctr., Nashville, 1988—93, dir. patient care svcs. and chief nursing officer, 1993—94; dir., COO Vanderbilt U. Hosp., Nashville, 1994-96; sr. assoc. cons. APM/CSC Healthcare, Inc., NYC, 1996—98; interim chief nursing officer Caritas Med. Ctr., Louisville, 2000—01; v.p. ops. The Meth. Hosp., 2001—04; pres., CEO Gunnison Valley Hosp., Colo., 2004—05; chief nursing officer U. N. Mex. Hosp., 2005—08; prin. cons. Houston Healthcare Ops., LLC, 2009—11, 2012—; v.p. B.E. Smith, Lenexa, Kans., 2011—12. Asst. clin. prof. UCSF, San Francisco; asst. dean and clin. prof. Vanderbilt U. Sch. Nursing, Nashville. Active Emergency Nurses Assn., 1976—82; founding chairperson Bd. Cert. Emergency Nursing. Fellow Am. Acad. HealthCare Execs., Regent N.Mex., Am. Coll. Healthcare Execs., St. Martin's Episcopal Ch., Houston, Wharton fellow Johnson & Johnson, 1987. Mem. Am. Orgn. Nurse Execs.; fellow Am. Coll. Healthcare Execs., Emergency Nurses Assn. (bd. dirs., treas. 1979-86), Sigma Theta Tau. Avocations: hiking, travel, ballet. Business E-Mail: jlspinella@aol.com.

SPIRES, L. KIT, state legislator; b. Columbia, Feb. 21, 1954; s. Lucoe and Cornelia Spires; children: Kevin, Kristin. BS, U. SC Coll. Pharmacy, 1976. Mem. Pelton Town Coun., 1999—2003, mayor pro tempore, Town of Pelion, 1999—2003; mem. Dist. 96 SC House of Reps., 2007—. Mem. bd. trustees Lexington Med. Ctr., 1987—97. Republican. Address: PO Box 396 Pelion SC 29123 Office: 326D Blatt Building Columbia SC 29201 Home: 833 Forts Pond Trail Pelion SC 29123 Home Phone: 803-894-4440; Office Phone: 803-894-4010, 803-734-3010. Business E-Mail: SpiresK@schouse.org.

SPITZER, CARY REDFORD, avionics consultant, electrical engineer; b. New Hope, Va., July 31, 1937; s. Clyde Burke and Marion Jeanette (Redford) S.; m. Carrie Laura Ruth Logan, June 18, 1960; 1 child, Stiegel Logan (dec.). BSEE, Va. Poly. Inst. & State U., 1959; MS in Engring. Mgmt., George Washington U., 1970. Rsch. engr., engring. mgr. Langley Rsch Ctr., NASA, Hampton, Va., 1962-94; founder, pres. AvioniCon, Inc., 1993—. Lectr. UCLA, 1989—, George Washington U., 1994. Author: Viking Orbiter Views of Mars, 1981, Digital Avionics Systems, 1987, 2d edit., 1993, Avionics Handbook, 2000, Digital Avionics Handbook, 2007; contbr. articles to sci. publs. 1st lt. USAF, 1959-62. Recipient Volare award Airline Avionics Inst., 1988; named Va. Peninsula Engr. of Yr., 1993; recipient Digital Avionics award Am. Inst. of Aeronautics and Astronautics, 1994; nominated Collier Trophy, 1991. Fellow: IEEE (Centennial medal 1984, Millennium medal 2000), AIAA (assoc.); mem.: Aerospace and Electronic Systems Soc. of IEEE (pres. 1973—74, editor-in-chief Trans. 1996—99, chmn. IEEE-USA aerospace policy com. 1997—2000), Exch. Club (pres. Williamsburg 1985). Methodist. Avocations: kite flying, car mechanics. Home and Office: 3409 Foxridge Rd Williamsburg VA 23188-2499 Home Phone: 757-229-8296; Office Phone: 757-221-8031.

SPITZLI, DONALD HAWKES, JR., lawyer; b. Newark, Mar. 19, 1934; s. Donald Hawkes and Beatrice (Banister) S.; children: Donald Hawkes III, Peter Gilbert, Seth Armstrong. AB, Dartmouth Coll., 1956; LLB, U. Va., 1963. Bar: Va. 1963. Assoc. Willcox, Savage, Lawrence, Dickson & Spindle, Norfolk, Va., 1964-67, 68-70, ptnr., 1971-77; atty. Eastman Kodak Co., Rochester, N.Y., 1967-68; pres. Marine Hydraulics Internat., Inc., Chesapeake, Va., 1978-80; sole practice Virginia Beach, Va., 1980—. Owner Chieftain Motor Inn, Hanover, N.H., 1980-87. Comdr. USNR, 1956-70. Episcopalian. Office: 4445 Corporation Ln Ste 200 Virginia Beach VA 23462-3262 Office Phone: 757-213-6914. Personal E-mail: airbuzzard24@aol.com.

SPITZNAGEL, JOHN KEITH, retired microbiologist, immunologist, physician; b. Peoria, Ill., Apr. 11, 1923; s. Elmer Florian and Anna S. (Kolb) S.; m. Anne Moulton Sirch, Feb. 2, 1947; children: John, Jean, Margaret, Elizabeth, Paul. BA, Columbia U., 1943, MD, 1946. Diplomate Nat. Bd. Med. Examiners, Am. Bd. Internal Medicine. Intern Johns Hopkins Hosp., Balt., 1946-47; resident in internal medicine Barnes Hosp., St. Louis, 1949-51; vis. investigator Rockefeller Inst., NYC, 1952-53, Nat. Inst. Med. Research, London, 1967-68; mem. faculty U. N.C., Chapel Hill, 1957-79, prof. microbiology and infectious diseases, prof. medicine, 1957-79; cons. N.C. Meml. Hosp., Chapel Hill, 1974-79; ad hoc adviser NIH, 1971—; prof. microbiology and immunology, chmn. dept. Emory U., Atlanta, 1979-93, prof. emeritus microbiology and immunology, 1993—, assoc. dean rsch., 1997-98; co-founder, attending physician Good Samaritan Health and Wellness Ctr., Jasper, Ga., 2002—12, chmn. exec. bd., CEO, 2004—06. Mem. study sect. bacteriology and mycology NIH, 1975-79, 85-89, chmn., 1977-79. Editor: Infection and Immunity, 1970-80, Jour. Immunology, 1973-80, Jour. Reticuloendothelial Soc, 1973-80. Served with M.C. AUS, 1947-57. Recipient Research Career Devel. award USPHS, 1957-67, Disting. Service award Sch. Medicine U. N.C., Chapel Hill, 1987; USPHS postdoctoral fellow, 1968; USPHS and AEC grantee; lectureship named in his honor, Spitznagel Lectureship on Host Antimicrobial Def., Emory U., 1998. Fellow ACP, Infectious Disease Soc.; mem. AAAS (life), Am. Soc. Microbiology (div. group councilor 1977-79), Am. Assn. Immunologists, Reticuloendothelial Soc. (pres. 1982), Infectious Disease Soc., So. Soc. Clin. Rsch., Assn. Am. Med. Sch. Microbiology and Immunology Chmn. (pres. 1990-91), Sigma Xi, Kiwanis KP. Achievements include research on cell biology of human neutrophil polymorphonuclear leukocytes, and oxygen ind. mechanisms of antimicrobial phagocytoses; first to demonstrate cationic antimicrobial proteins of polymorphonuclear leukocytes granules; co-discoverer of a cationic protein of polymorph granules with antimicrobial action and a powerful attractant for mononuclear phagocytes.

SPOELSTRA, ERIK, professional basketball coach; b. Evanston, Ill., Nov. 1, 1970; s. Jon and Lisa Spoelstra. Degree in comm., U. Portland, 1992. Player, coach Tus Herten, Germany; video coord. Miami Heat, 1995—97, asst. coach, video coord., 1997—99, asst. coach, advance scout, 1999—2001, asst. coach, dir. scouting, 2001—08, head coach, 2008—. Head, individual player devel. program Miami Heat, summer league coach, 2005—07. Achievements include head coach of NBA Finals championship winning Miami Heat, 2012, 2013. Office: Miami Heat 601 Biscayne Blvd Miami FL 33132*

SPOONER, EDWARD M., federal marshal; b. 1950; Intern Fla. Highway Patrol, 1973; officer Tallahassee Police Dept., Fla.; dir. pub. safety Quincy Police Dept., Fla., 1979—91; chief dep. Gadsden County Sheriff's Office, Fla.; training acad. dir. Fla. Dept. Law Enforcement, Fla., asst. spl. agent in charge Fla., 2010—11; interim sheriff Okaloosa County Sheriff's Office, Fla., 2009, sheriff Fla., 2009—10; US marshal (northern dist.) Fla. US Marshals Svc., US Dept. Justice, 2011—. Interim dir. Pat Thomas Law Enforcement Acad., 1999; former mem. Fla. Parole Commn., Parole Commn. Qualifications and Selection Com., Criminal Justice Standards and Training Commn. Mem.: Fla. Peace Officers Assn., Big Bend Law Enforcement Officers Assn., Fla. Sheriff's Assn. Office: US Marshals Service US Courthouse 111 N Adams St, Room 277 Tallahassee FL 32301 Office Phone: 850-942-8400.

SPORN, PAUL ANDREW, obstetrician, gynecologist; MD, NY Med. Coll., 1981. Lic. Fla., 1985, diplomate American Bd. Ob-Gyn, 1987. Resident ob-gyn. Nassau Univ. Med. Ctr., 1981—85; hosp. affiliations include Univ. Cmty. Hosp., St. Joseph's Women's Hosp., St. Joseph's Hosp. Fellow: American Congress of Obstetricians and Gynecologists. Office: St Joseph's Hospital 3001 W Martin Luther King Blvd Tampa FL 33607-6387 Office Phone: 813-870-4000.*

SPRANSY, JOSEPH WILLIAM, corporate lawyer; b. Durham, NC, July 17, 1946; s. George Brower and Marion Elizabeth (Dibble) S.; m. Lillian Drew Darden, Aug. 8, 1970; children: Katherine Leigh, Joseph William II. AB in Math., King Coll., Bristol, Tenn., 1968; JD, U. N.C., 1973. Bar: Ala. 1973, US Dist. Ct. (no. dist.) Ala. 1973, US Ct. Appeals (5th cir.) 1976, US Supreme Ct. 1980, US Ct. Appeals (11th cir.) 1981. Math. tchr. Castlewood HS, Va., 1968—70; program dir. Camp Monroe, Laurel Hill, NC, 1968-70; assoc. Bradley, Arant, Rose & White, Birmingham, Ala., 1973-79; corp. counsel US Pipe and Foundry Co., 1979—2003, v.p., 1999—2003; pvt. practice, 2003—. Vice moderator Birmingham Presbytery, Presbyn. Ch. USA, 1986, moderator, 1987, trustee, Sheppards Hapsley Presbyn. Ch., 2012-; elder Mountain Brook Presbyn. Ch., 1982-84, 1986-88, 91-94, 98-2000, trustee 2008-11, pres. trustee, 2011-; asst. scoutmaster, Boy Scouts Am., 1994-2006, troop 320 com. chair, 1994-97. Mem. ABA, Ala. State Bar Assn. (chair labor and employment sect. 1992-93, chair bus. law sect. 1999-2000), Birmingham Bar Assn. (chair mem. com. 1997-2003, 2010, bd. mem. small firm sect. 2008-09), Assn. Corp. Counsel in Am. (bd. dirs. Ala. chpt. 1985-91, 1998-2003, sec.-treas. 2002), U. NC Alumni Assn. (pres. Ala. chpt. 1983-84, 95), Phi Alpha Delta. Clubs: Birmingham Sailing(comdr. 1992), Birmingham Tip Off Club (bd. dirs. 1992-96), Ruffner Mountain Nature Ctr. (bd. dirs. 2004—10, treas. 2005-06, sec. 2007—09, exec. com.). Avocations: woodworking, sailing. Home: 4000 Hunters Ln Birmingham AL 35243-5820 Office: Law Office Joseph W Spransy 2320 Arlington Ave S Birmingham AL 35205 Office Phone: 205-930-9800. Business E-Mail: jwspransy@spransylaw.com.

SPRAY, PAUL ELLSWORTH, retired surgeon; b. Wilkinsburg, Pa., Apr. 9, 1921; s. Lester E. and Phoebe Gertrude (Hull) S.; m. Mary Louise Conover, Nov. 28, 1943 (dec. Jun 12, 2008); children: David C., Thomas L., Mary Lynn (Mrs. Thomas Branham). BS, U. Pitts., 1942; MD, George Washington U., Washington, DC, 1944; MS, U. Minn., 1950. Diplomate Am. Bd. Orthop. Surgery. Intern U.S. Marine Hosp., SI, 1944-45; resident Mayo Found., Rochester, Minn., 1945-46, 48-50; practice medicine specializing in orthop. surgery Oak Ridge, Tenn., 1950-98; ret., 1998; vol. physician Knoxville Interfaith Clinic, 1998—2008. Mem. active staff Oak Ridge Hosp., 1950-98, hon. staff, 98-; courtesy staff Harriman Hosp., Tenn., ret., 1998; vol. vis. cons. CARE Medico, Jordan, 1959, Nigeria, 1962, 65, Algeria, 1963, Afghanistan, 1970, Bangladesh, 1975, 77, 79, Peru, 1980, U. Ghana, 1982; AMA vol. physician, Vietnam, 1967, 72; vis. assoc. prof. U. Nairobi, 1973; mem. tchg. team Internat. Coll. Surgeons to Peru, 1979, 84; vis. prof. orthop. surgery U. Khartoum, 1976; hon. prof. San Luis Gonzaga U., Ica, Peru, 1979; AmDoc vol. cons. U. Biafra Tchg. Hosp., 1969; vis. prof. Mayo Clinic, 1988; sec. orthops. overseas divsn. CARE Medico, 1971-76, sec. Medico adv. bd., 1974-76, vice chmn., 1976, chmn., 1977-79, v.p. CARE, Inc., 1977-79, pub. mem. CARE bd. dirs., 1980-90, mem. bd. overseers, 1991-99; chmn. Orthops. Overseas, Inc., 1982-86, treas., 1986-88, emeritus mem., 1994; mem. U.S. organizing com. 1st Internat. Acad. Symposium on Orthops., Tianjin, China, 1983; mem. CUPP Internat. Adv. Coun., 1986-99; invited guest spkr. Japan Orthop. Assn., 1994; mem. curriculum com. Oak Ridge Inst. Continual Learning, 1999-2007; bd. dirs. MMC Oak Ridge Found., chmn., 2003-04, emeritus, 2007. Mem. editl. bd. Contemporary Orthopedics, 1984-96. Pres. Anderson County Health Coun., 1976—77, v.p., 1975, hon. bd. dirs.; pres. health commn. Coun. So. Mountains, 1958—65, sec., bd. dirs., 1965—66; Tenn. pres. UN Assn., 1966—67; vice-chmn. bd. Camelot Care Ctr., Tenn., 1979—82, chmn. Tenn., 1982—86; hon. mem. World Orthopedic Concern, 1990; with del. to Vietnam People to People, citizen amb. to Vietnam, 1993; del. to Oak Ridge's Sister City, Obninsk, Russia Obninsk, Russia, 1993; trustee Vietnam Am. Scholarship Fund, 1992—95; Rotary vol. orthopaedic surgeon Kikuyu Hosp. Rehab. Ctr. of East Africa Presbyn. Ch., 1998; vol. Habitat for Humanity, 2004; bd. dirs. Hope of East Tenn., 2002—06, Clinch River Home Health Assn., 2005—08. Capt. MC, 1946—48. Recipient Svc. to Mankind award, Serotoma, 1967, Humanitarian award, Lions Club, 1968, Freedom Citation, Sertoma, 1978, award, Amb. Goodwill Lions Club, 1979, Medico Disting. Svc. award, 1990, 1st Ann. Vocat. Svc. award, Oak Ridge Rotary, 1979, Tech. Comm. award, East Tenn. chpt. Soc. for Tech. Comm., 1983, Individual Achievement award, Meth. Med. Ctr. of Oak Ridge, 1991, Humanitarian award, Orthopaedics Overseas, 1992, Biographic Exhibit recognition, Mus. Appalachia Hall of Fame, Norris, Tenn., Humanitarian award, Mayo Clinic Alumni Soc., 2013; named to Anderson County Hall of Fame for Philanthropy, 2007; fellow Melvin Jones fellow, Lions Club, 1993. Fellow Am. Coll. Surgeons, Internat. Coll. Surgeons (Tenn. regent 1976-80, bd. councilors 1980-84, hon. chmn. bd. trustees 1981-83, trustee 1983-84, v.p. US sect. 1982-83, mem. surg. teams com. 1983-90, Humanitarian award 1992); mem. AMA (Humanitarian Svc. award 1967, 72), Société International Chirugie Orthopèdique et de Traumuatologie, So. Orthop. Assn., Western Pacific Orthop. Assn., Am. Fracture Assn., Am. Acad. Orthop. Surgeons (mem. com. on injuries 1980-86), Tenn. Med. Assn. (com. on emergency med. svcs. 1978-97), Peru Acad. Surgery (corr.), Peruvian Soc. Orthop. Surgery and Traumatology (corr.), Clin. Orthop. Soc., Mid-Am. Orthop. Soc., Rotary Club (Oak Ridge chpt., chmn. cmty. and world svc. com. 2000-04, Paul Harris fellow). Home: 507 Delaware Ave Oak Ridge TN 37830-3902 Personal E-mail: spray507@aol.com.

SPRAYBERRY, ROSLYN RAYE, retired secondary school educator; b. Newnan, Ga., June 29, 1942; d. Henry Ray and Grace (Bernhard) S. BA, Valdosta State Coll., 1964; MA in Teaching, Ga. State U., 1976, EdS in Spanish, 1988; EdD, Nova U., 1993. Cert. tchr., Ga. Tchr. history Griffin (Ga.) High Sch., 1964-65; tchr. 6th grade Beaverbrook Elem Sch., Griffin, 1965-66; tchr. Spanish, chair fgn. lang. dept. Forest Park (Ga.) High Sch., 1969-77, Riverdale (Ga.) High Sch., 1977-99; ret., 1999. Correlator Harcourt, Brace, Jovanovich, 1989; adv. bd. So. Conf. Lang. Teaching, 1992-99; lectr. and speaker in field. Contbr. articles to The Ednl. Resource Info. Ctr. Clearinghouse on Langs. and Linguistics, Ctr. for Applied Linguistics, Washington; designed courses for the Gifted, Ga. Dept. of Edn. Cnvener Acad. Alliances-Atlanta II, Clayton County, Ga., 1982-99; advisor, workshop leader Ga. Fgn. Lang. Camp, Atlanta, 1983; dir. Clayton County Fgn. Lang. Festival, 1990-91. Recipient STAR Tchr. award Ga. C. of C., 1982; Fulbright-Hays scholar, 1978; NEH grantee, 1977, 84. Mem. NEA, Am. Coun. Tchrs. Fgn. Langs., Am. Assn. Tchrs. Spanish and Portuguese, Ga. Assn. Educators, Fgn. Lang. Assn. Ga. (treas. 1977-85, assoc. editor jour. 1981-86, Tchr. of Yr. award 1976), Clayton County Edn. Assn., So. Conf. Lang. Teaching. Methodist. Avocations: travel, music. Home: 104 Hickory Trail Stockbridge GA 30281-7361

SPRECHER, JEFFREY C., stock exchange executive; b. 1955; m. Kelly Loeffler, 2004. BSChemE, U. Wis., Madison, 1978; MBA, Pepperdine U., Malibu, Calif. Pres. Western Power Group., Inc., 1983—97; owner Continental Power Exch., 1997—2000; founder IntercontinentalExchange, Inc., Atlanta, 2000—, chmn., CEO, 2002—. Dir. NY Bd. Trade, 2007—, ICE Futures US, Inc.; serves on US Commodity Futures Trading Commission Global Market Adv. Com.; mem. Energy Security Leadership Coun. Named a Top Entrepreneur, Ernst & Young, 2002; named one of five finalists, CEO of the Year, MarketWatch, 2006. Mem.: Energy Security Leadership Coun. Office: Intercontinental Exchange Inc 2100 Riveredge Pky Ste 500 Atlanta GA 30328*

SPRIGGS, JAMES, sales executive; Co-founder, COO Apex Home Healthcare Svcs. (acquired by Almost Family, Inc.); v.p., Sales and Devel. Almost Family, Inc., v.p., mktg., NE Fla. region, 2008, v.p., sales and mktg., 2010—. Office: Almost Family Inc 9510 Ormsby Sta Rd Ste 300 Louisville KY 40223 Office Phone: 502-891-1000. Office Fax: 502-891-8067. Business E-Mail: jamesspriggs@almostfamily.com.

SPRINGER, DAVID WILLIAM, social sciences educator; b. NYC, Sept. 1, 1968; s. Paul David and Elizabeth Springer; 1 child, Aidan David. BA, Fla. State U., 1990, MSW, 1992, PhD, 1997. LCSW Tex., ACSW. Clin. social worker Univ. Behavioral Ctr., Orlando, Fla., 1992—94; rsch. assoc. Fla. State U., Tallahassee, 1994—97; asst. prof. U. Tex., Austin, 1997—2000, assoc. prof., 2000—02, assoc. dean, 2002—11, disting. tchg. prof., 2005—. Author: Substance Abuse Treatment for Criminal Offenders, 2003, Handbook of Forensic Mental Health with Victims and Offenders, 2007, Juvenile Justice and Delinquency, 2011. Bd. dirs. Austin Child Guidance Ctr., 1998—2003, Great Wall China Adoption, 2007—, Hogg Found. Mental Health, 2006—. Recipient Outstanding Grad. Tchg. award, U. Tex. at Austin, 2003; named to Acad. Disting. Tchrs., 2005, Who'w Who in Social Scis. Higher Edn., 2004. Mem.: NASW, Tex. Assn. Social Work Deans and Dirs. (pres. 2005—07), Coun. Social Work Edn., Soc. Social Work and Rsch. Democrat. Avocations: guitar, camping, hiking, surfing, running. Office: U Tex at Austin Sch Social Work Austin TX 78712 Office Fax: 512-471-9600. Business E-Mail: dwspringer@austin.utexas.edu.

SPRINGER, KARL, school system administrator; b. Hollywood, Calif., Sept. 27, 1948; m. Catherine Springer, 1972; children: Andrea, Nathan. BA in Edn., Calif. State U., Chico, 1970; EdM, Northeastern State U., Tahlequah, Okla., 1980; attended, US Army War Coll., Carlisle Barracks, Pa., 1997. Tchg. cert. Calif. State U. Chico, 1971. Track & cross-country coach Butte Coll., Oroville, Calif., 1970—71; supr. Container Corp. of America, Santa Clara, Calif., 1974—77; tchr. Muskogee Pub. Schs., 1977—84; spl. edn. tchr. Norman Pub. Schs., Okla., 1984—89, asst. dir. spl. svcs. Okla., 1989—95; asst. supt. Chickasha Pub. Schs., Okla., 1995—2000; supt. Mustang Pub. Schs., Yukon, Okla., 2000—08, Oklahoma City Pub. Schs., 2008—. Bd. dirs. Mustang C. of C., 2001—. Lt. USMC, 1971—74, capt. res. USMC, 1974—77, served up to col. (ret.) USAR, 1977—2002. Named Dist. 14 Coop. Coun. for Okla. Sch. Adminstrn. Ctrl. Adminstr. of Yr., 2006. Mem.: Okla. Assn. Sch. Administrators. Office: Oklahoma City Public Schools 900 N Klein Oklahoma City OK 73106 Office Phone: 405-587-0000.*

SPRINGER, MARLENE, retired academic administrator; b. Murfreesboro, Tenn., Nov. 16, 1937; d. Foster V. and Josephine Jones; children: Ann Springer, Rebecca Springer. BA in English and Bus. Adminstrn., Centre Coll., 1959; MA in Am. Lit., Ind. U., 1963, PhD in English Lit., 1969. Chair English dept. U. Mo., Kansas City, 1980-81, acting assoc. dean grad. sch., 1982; Am. Coun. of Edn. Adminstrn. fellow U. Kans., Lawrence, 1982-83; dean grad. sch. U. Mo., Kansas City, 1983-84, assoc. vice chancellor acad. affairs & grad. studies, 1985-89; vice chancellor acad. affairs East Carolina U., Greenville, NC, 1989-94; pres. Coll. Staten Island, CUNY, 1994—2007. Author: Edith Wharton and Kate Chopin: A Reference Guide, 1976; What Manner of Woman: Essays, 1977, Thomas Hardy's Use of Allusion, 1983, Plains Woman: The Diary of Martha Farnsworth, 1986 (Choice award 1986), Ethan Frome: A Nightmare of Need, 1993. Huntington Libr. fellow, 1988. Mem.: Coun. Grad. Schs. (chair 1986—88), Assn. Tchr. Educators (chair 1992), Acad. Leadership Acad. (exec. com. 1992—94), Am. Assn. State Colls. and Univs., Am. Coun. on Edn. (profl. devel. com. 1991—, invited participant Nat. Forum 1984, bd. dirs. 2001—). Business E-Mail: springer@mail.csi.cuny.edu.

SPRINGER, NEIL ALLEN, consulting services executive; b. Fort Wayne, Ind, May 2, 1938; s. Roy V. and Lucille H. (Gerke) S.; m. Janet M. Grotrian, Sept. 3, 1960; children: Sheri Lynn, Kelly Jean, Mark Allen. BS, U. Ind, 1960; MBA, U. Dayton, 1966. CPA, Ill. Staff asst. acctg. Internat. Harvester Co. (now Navistar Internat. Corp.), Bridgeport, Conn., 1966-68, asst. comptroller Fort Wayne, Ind., 1968-70, staff asst. Chgo., 1970-75, asst. corp. compt., 1975-77, v.p. fin., 1977-79, v.p. gen. mgr. trucks, 1979-81, pres. truck group, 1981-84, pres., chief operating officer, 1984-87; chmn., pres., chief exec. officer Navistar Internat. Transp. Corp., Chgo., 1987-90; pres., chief oper. officer Navistar Internat. Corp./Navistar Internat. Transp. Corp., Chgo., 1990; pres., cen. region Alexander Proudfoot, Deerfield, Ill., 1991; mng. ptnr. Springer & Assocs., LLC, mng. dir., 2005—. Bd. dirs. Century Cos. Am.; Waverly, Iowa; TNT Freightsways, Rosemont, Ill.; CUNA Mut. Group; CUNA Mut. Ins. Soc.; USF Corp.; Walter Energy, Inc.; IDEX Corp., Northbrook, Ill., 1990-; Mueller Water Products, Inc., 2006-. Active bus. dean's adv. coun. Ind. U., 1988—. Mem. Ill. Soc. CPAs. Office: Mueller Water Products Inc Bd Directors 1200 Abernathy Rd NE Ste 1200 Atlanta GA 30328 Office Phone: 770-206-4200. Office Fax: 770-206-4235. Business E-Mail: nspringer@muellerwaterproducts.com.

SPRINGER, WAYNE GILBERT, computer company executive; b. El Paso, Tex., Oct. 6, 1951; s. Wayne Gill and Constance A. (Courtney) S.; m. Dianne Louise Slaydon, Jan. 3, 1981; children: Courtney Lee, Carol Jeanne, Kent Slaydon. BS in Engring., U.S. Mil. Acad., 1973; MBA, So. Meth. U., Dallas, 1979, MSCE, 1980. Registered profl. engr. Commd. 2d lt. U.S. Army, C.E., 1973, advanced through grades to capt., 1977, resigned, 1978; grad. sch. instr. So. Meth. U., 1978-80; engr. Fluor Corp., Irvine, Calif. and Houston, 1980-82; coord. project devel. United Energy Resources, Houston, 1982-83; founder Computer Leasing Exch. Corp., Houston, 1983—. Founder Computer Helpline, Houston, 1984—, Network Systems Tech. Corp., 1993—; pres., founder Laser Express Corp., 1991; pres. Atiwa Computing, Inc., 1995—; ptnr. Springer Cons., Houston and Whittier, Calif., 1980-86. Author: Your Road Map to E-Commerce Success, 2000; contbr. articles to profl. jours.; inventor mech. devices. Mem. Houston Conv. and Visitors Coun., 1983—; mem. technology com. United Way. Mem. MIT Enterprise Forum, West Point Alumni Assn., Houston C. of C., Computer and Audio Visual Execs. Assn. (founder 1989), Nat. Speakers Assn. (pres.), Rotary Club, Mensa, Plaza Oaks Club. Avocations: skiing, tennis. Office: Atiwa Computing Inc STE 125 6950 Portwest Dr Ste 100 Houston TX 77024-8020

SPRINKLE, ROBERT LEE, JR., podiatrist; b. Winston-Salem, NC, July 13, 1932; s. Robert Lee and Elton Elizabeth Sprinkle; children: Robert III, Karen, Ralph, Richard, Roy, Randy, Drouin; m. Nancy House Dixon. Student, Salem Coll., 1952; BS, Ohio Coll. Podiatry, 1956; DPM, Pa. Coll. Podiatry, 1970. Diplomate Am. Bd. Disability Analysts, Am. Coun. Cert. Podiatric Phys. and Surgeons, Sr. Acad. Ambulatory Podiatric Surgeons. Pvt. practice, Winston-Salem, 1957—. Chmn. N.C. Bd. Podiatry Examiners, 1968-74; clin. assoc. prof. Dr. William M. School Coll. Podiatric Medicine; researcher reconstructive surgery human foot and ankle; bd. dirs. Cmty. Gen. Hosp. Found., Thomasville, N.C.; bd. dirs. Am. Coun. Cert. Podiatric Phys. and Surgeons. Chmn. Mayor's Com. on Hiring the Handicapped, 1963-64; commr. Old Hickory Coun., Boy Scouts Am., 1970-71, v.p., 1973-74, Silver Beaver award, 1969, mem. adv. bd. Old North State Coun.; pres. St. Leo's Parochial Sch. PTA, 1969-70; dir. Halfway House, 1965-66; chmn. Bishop McGuiness PTA, 1976. Recipient St. George medal Charlotte Diocese, Roman Cath. Ch., 1971, Order of the Long Leaf Pine, State of NC, 2006; Schering grantee, 1972-74. Mem. APHA, Am. Podiatric Med. Assn. (life mem.), N.C. Podiatry Assn. (past pres., Podiatrist of Yr. 1976), Piedmont Podiatry Assn., Acad. Ambulatory Podiatric Surgeons (life mem.), Internat. Analgesia Soc., Forsyth Country Club, Colonial Country Club, Twin City Club, KC (4th degree), SAR (life; NC state registrar, past pres. Bethabara chpt., N.C. state pres. 2002—, mem. George Washington Found.), SCV, NRA (life), Rotary (Paul Harris fellow, dist. gov. 1976-77), St. Andrew's Soc., Sons of the Revolution (life; state chpt. sec. pres. NCSSR). Republican. Roman Catholic. Home: 10 Mock St Thomasville NC 27360-4622 Office: Abc Family Foot Ankle 10 Mock St Thomasville NC 27360-4622 Office Phone: 336-848-2240. Business E-Mail: foot1@northstate.net.

SPRINTHALL, NORMAN ARTHUR, psychology educator; b. Attleboro, Mass., Aug. 19, 1931; s. William Archie and Edith Jarvis (Clark) S.; m. Barbara Weller (div. 1974); children: Douglas, Jayne, Carolyn; m. Lois Mae Thies. AB magna cum laude, Brown U., 1954, MA, 1959; EdD, Harvard U., 1963. Dir. fin. aid Brown U., 1955-60; asst. prof., then asso. prof. psychology, program chmn. counseling Harvard U., 1963-72; mem. faculty U. Minn., Mpls., 1972-82, prof. ednl. psychology, 1973-82, program chmn. counseling, 1972-74; prof. psychology, head counselor edn. program N.C. State U., Raleigh, 1982-87, prof., counselor, 1987-95, prof. emeritus, 1995—. Co-dir. Ethical Reasoning Project in Pub. Adminstrn., U.S. and Poland, 1993-95, Russia, 1998-99. Co-author: Educational Psychology: Readings, 1969, Guidance for Human Growth, 1971, Educational Psychology: A Developmental Approach, 7th edit., 1998, Value Development as the Aim of Education, 2d edit., 1981, Adolescent Psychology: A Developmental View, 1984, 2d rev. edit., 1988, 3d edit., 1995, International Eds. Portugal Psicologia Educational, 1993, Psicologia do adolescente, 2003, Spain Psicologia De La Education, 1996; co-author: Stewart-Sprinthall Management Survey (SSMS) Ethics and Public Administration, others; mem. editl. bd. profl. jours. Bd. dirs. Josephson Inst. Advancement of Ethics, 1986-90, mem. bd. advisors Character Counts Coalition, 1994—2004. Co-recipient with Dr. Lois M. Thies, Kuhmerker Career Rsch. award, Assn. Moral Edn., 2005. Fellow APA (Disting. Sr. Contbr. award); mem. Phi Beta Kappa. E-mail: nlsprint@aol.com.

SPROTT, JAMES D., lawyer; b. Auburn, Ind., Mar. 13, 1949; BA, Hendrix Coll., 1970; JD, So. Methodist U., 1973. Bar: Ark. 1973, US Ct. Appeals (8th Cir.), US Dist. Ct. (We. Dist. Ark.), US Dist. Ct. (Ea. Dist. Ark.). Ptnr. Sprott & Golden, Harrison, Ark., 2005—. Mem.: Ark. Bar Found. Inc. (pres. 1998—99), Ark. Trial Lawyers Assn., Ark. Bar Assn. (chmn. bd. gov. 2002—03, pres.-elect 2005—06, pres. 2006—07), ABA, Boone County Bar Assn. Office: Sprott & Golden 502 N Walnut PO Box 1800 Harrison AR 72601 Office Phone: 870-741-3633. Office Fax: 870-741-5479.

SPROUSE, VIC, state legislator; b. Altoona, Pa., Apr. 29, 1968; s. Lawrence and Mary Sprouse; m. Rachel Sprouse; 1 child, Marie Anne. Former chmn. Kanawha County Young Rep.; former mem. South Charleston Bd. Zoning Appeals; former state del. Dist. 30 W.Va.; state senator Dist. 97, 1997—; minority leader; mem. Fin. Com., Health & Human Resources Com., Pensions Com., Rules Com., Small Bus. Com., Banking & Ins. Com.; chem. engr. Republican. Catholic. Mailing: WVa Senate 1900 Kanawha Blvd E Bldg 1 Rm 245M Charleston WV 25305 Home: PO Box 8635 Charleston WV 25303-0635

SPRUELL, ALYCE MANLEY, lawyer; BA, Vanderbilt U., 1980; JD, U. Ala., 1983. Bar: Ala. 1983, US Dist. Ct. (northern dist.) Ala. 1984, US Dist. Ct. (southern dist.) Ala. 1984, US Dist. Ct. (middle dist.) Ala. 1994, US Ct. Appeals (11th cir.) 1985, US Supreme Ct. 1986. Assoc. Phelps, Jenkins, Gibson & Fowler, 1983—88; asst. dean, dir. law devel. U. Ala. Sch. Law, 1988—94, adj. prof. trial advocacy, 1991—2002; pvt. practice Ala., 1995—2001; mng. mem. Spruell & Powell, LLC, 2002—; co-owner Main Ave. Title Co., 2002—. Mem.: ABA, Tuscaloosa County Bar Assn. (past pres.), Supreme Ct. Commn. on Alternative Dispute Resolution (charter mem., sec.), Ala. Acad. of Atty. Mediators (charter mem.), Ala. Def. Lawyers Assn. (mem. bd. dirs. 2001—), Ala. State Bar Assn. (pres. 2010—11), American Arbitration Assn. (mem. Comml. Panel 1998—). Office: Spruell & Powell LLC PO Box 1010 Tuscaloosa AL 35403 Office Phone: 205-345-8755. Office Fax: 205-345-8793. E-mail: alyce@tuscaloosalaw.net.

SPRUILL, LIONELL, state legislator; b. South Norfolk, Va., Dec. 28, 1946; m. Charlene Joyner; children: Lionell Jr., Tony, Clayton, Nadia. Former mem. Chesapeake City Coun.; former house del. off technician Bell Atlantic Telephone Co.; state del, Dist. 77 Va., 1994—; mem. Edn. Com., Counties Com., Cities & Towns Com., Health Com., Welfare & Inst. Com., Labor Com., Commerce Com., Claims Com. Mem.: founder First Black Security, Chesapeake Forward, Knights Pythagoras (former state dir.), Prince Hall Grand Lodge Va. (former grand master), NAACP. Democrat. Methodist. Mailing: PO Box 5403 Chesapeake VA 23324-0403 Home Phone: 757-543-1988; Office Phone: 757-523-2373. E-mail: Del_Spruill@house.state.va.us.

SPRUILL, MARCUS C., retired mathematics professor; b. Oakland, Calif., Nov. 14, 1944; s. Marcus C. Spruill and Eunice Rayburn; m. Elizabeth Irvin, Aug. 23, 1969; children: Robert C., David W. BS, Old Dominion Coll., 1966; MS, Purdue U., Lafayette, 1969, PhD, 1973. Prof. math. Ga. Inst. Tech. Sch. Math., Atlanta, 1973—2005. Stats. program adminstr. Ga. Inst. Tech., 1982—2002. Contbr. articles to profl. jours. Mem.: Inst. Math. Stats. Office: Georgia Inst Tech Sch Math 686 Cherry St Atlanta GA 30332-0160 Business E-Mail: spruill@math.gatech.edu.

SPURRIER, STEVE (STEVEN ORR SPURRIER), college football coach; b. Miami Beach, Fla., Apr. 20, 1945; s. John Graham and Marjorie Spurrier; m. Jerrie Spurrier. Grad., U. Fla. Quarterback San Francisco 49'ers, 1967-75, Tampa Bay Buccaneers, 1976; quarterbacks coach U. Fla. Gators, 1978, Ga. Tech. Yellow Jackets, 1979; asst. coach Duke U. Blue Devils, 1980—82; head coach Tampa Bay Bandits, US Football League, 1983—85, Duke U. Blue Devils, 1987—89, U. Fla. Gators, Gainesville, 1990—2001, Wash. Redskins, 2002—03, U. South Carolina Gamecocks, Columbia, 2005—. Recipient Heisman trophy, 1966; named Atlantic Coast Conf. Coach of Yr., 1988, 1989, Southeastern Conf. Coach of Yr., 1990, 1991, 1994, 1995, 1996, 2005; named to Hall of Fame, U. Fla., Athletic Hall of Fame, Gator Football Ring of Honor, 2006. Mem.: Alpha Tau Omega. Achievements include being the only coach in Southeastern Conference history and one of only three coaches in major college history to lead a team to 12 consecutive seasons of nine or more wins (1990-2001); being the only coach in Southeastern Conference history to win eight conference games in a season for four straight years (1993-96); being the only coach in Southeastern Conference history and one of only two coaches in major college history to lead a team to six straight seasons of 10 or more wins (1993-1998). Office: Rex Enright Athletic Center 1300 Rosewood Drive Columbia SC 29208

SQUIBB, SAMUEL DEXTER, chemistry professor; b. Limestone, Tenn., June 20, 1931; s. Benjamin Bowman and Lou Pearl S.; m. JoAnn Kyker, Dec. 15, 1951; children: Sandra Lavanne, Kevin Dexter. BS, E. Tenn. State U., 1952; PhD, U. Fla., 1956. Assoc. prof., dir. chemistry Western Carolina U., Cullowhee, NC, 1956-60; asst. prof., dir. chemistry Eckerd Coll., St. Petersburg, Fla., 1960-63, asso. prof., 1963-64; prof. chemistry U. N.C., Asheville, 1964-94, prof. emeritus, 1994—, chmn. dept., 1964-94. Vis. prof. U. NC, Chapel Hill, 1976-81, 83-87, 92-95, Clemson U., SC, 1982; cons. So. Assn. Colls. and Schs., State of W.Va. Author: Experimental Organic Chemistry, 1972, Understanding Chemistry One, 1979, rev. 1990, Two, 1981, rev. 1991, Three, 1981, rev. 1992, Four, 1981, rev. 1992, Five, 1981, rev. 1989, Six, 1984, Chemistry One, 1976, rev. 1987, Two, 1980, rev. 1990, Experimental Chemistry One, 1976, rev. 1988, Two, 1981, rev. 1991; contbr. articles to profl. jours. Mem. Grose United Meth. Ch. Disting. Tchr. award U. N.C.-Asheville, 1983; S.D. Squibb Disting. Chemistry Lectureship U. N.C., Asheville, established 1997; named to We. Carolina Fedn. Square and Round Dancing Hall of Fame, 2001; recipient Pres.'s Svc. award, Folk, Round and Square Dancing Fedn. N.C., 2001. Fellow Am. Inst. Chemists (life, nat. publs. bd. 1988-92); mem. Am. Chem. Soc. (Charles H. Stone award Carolina Piedmont sect. 1979, Disting. Chemist award Western Carolinas sect. 1993, chmn. Tampa Bay subsect. 1963, Western Carolina sect. 1981, editor Periodic News Western Carolina sect. 1980-2007), NC Inst. Chemists (pres. 1977-79, sec. 1975-77, 85-91, Disting. Chemist award 1986), Land of Sky Sq. Dance Club, Silver Spurs Advanced Sq. Dance Club, Jerry's Kids Advanced Sq. Dance Club, Skylarks Round Dance Club, Phi Beta Kappa.

SQUIRES, ARTHUR MORTON, chemical engineer, educator; b. Neodesha, Kans., Mar. 21, 1916; s. Charles Loren and Vera Amber (Moore) S. AB with distinction in Chemistry, U. Mo., 1938; PhD, Cornell U., 1947. Design engr. M.W. Kellogg Co., NYC, 1942-46; asst. dir. process devel. Hydrocarbon Research, Inc., NYC, 1946-51, dir. process devel., 1951-59; cons. chem. process industries NYC, 1959-67; prof. chem. enging. CUNY, 1967-74, disting. prof., 1974-76, chmn. dept. chem. enging., 1970-73; Vilbrandt prof. chem. enging. Va. Poly. Inst. and State U., Blacksburg, 1976-82, disting. prof., 1978-86, disting. prof. emeritus, 1986—. Author: The Tender Ship, 1986, From Toumai to G. Stein and O. Wilde, 2011; editor: (with D.A. Berkowitz) Power Generation and Environmental Change, 1971; contbr. articles to profl. jours.; patentee in field Mem. N.Y. Pro Musica, 1953-60 Fellow Am. Acad. Arts and Scis., AAAS; mem. ASME, NAE, AIChE (inst. lectr.), Am. Chem. Soc. (Henry H. Storch award 1973), Internat. Soc. for Human Ethology, Human Behavior and Evolution Soc., Sigma Xi, Tau Beta Pi Avocation: performing medieval and renaissance music. Home: 2710 Quincy Ct Blacksburg VA 24060-4124 Office: Va Poly Inst and State U Dept Chem Engring Blacksburg VA 24061 Home Phone: 540-951-8369. Business E-Mail: verasqu@vt.edu.

SQUIRES, BURT, retail executive; b. Indpls., 1949; V.p. Dillard's, Inc., 1984—, corp. v.p. stores Ark. divsn., 1998. Office: Dillard s Inc 1600 Cantrell Rd Little Rock AR 72201 Office Phone: 501-376-5200. Office Fax: 501-399-7831. E-mail: burt.squires@dillards.com.

SQUIRES, JAMES A., rail transportation executive; Atty. Norfolk Southern Corp., Va., 1992, sr. gen. counsel, 2002—03, v.p. law, 2003—04, sr. v.p. law, 2004—06, sr. v.p. fin. planning, 2006—07, exec. v.p. fin., 2007—, CFO, 2007—. Office: Norfolk So Corp Three Commercial Pl Norfolk VA 23510-2191 Office Phone: 757-629-2680.

STAAB, THOMAS ROBERT, consumer product company financial executive; b. Beaver Falls, Pa., Apr. 23, 1942; s. Henry Louis and Margaret Constance (Clarke) S.; m. Angela Maria Simon, Aug. 6, 1965; children: Thomas II, Jennifer, Thea. BBA, U. Pitts., 1964, MBA, 1965. CPA, Pa. Sr. audit mgr. Price Waterhouse & Co., Pitts., 1970-77; practice fellow Fin. Acctg. Standards Bd., Stamford, Conn., 1978-80; dir. corp. acctg. and taxes Fieldcrest Cannon Inc., Eden, NC, 1981-84, asst. contr., 1985, contr., 1986-91, v.p. fin., 1992-93, CFO, 1994-97; bd. dirs., sr. v.p., CFO Lorillard, Inc., Greensboro, NC, 1998—2008, sr. v.p. chief acctg. officer, 2009—. Served to lt. USN, 1966-70. Mem. AICPA, Pa. Inst. CPAs. Independent. Roman Catholic. Home: 3726 NC # 65 Reidsville NC 27320 Office: Lorillard Inc PO Box 10529 714 Green Valley Rd Greensboro NC 27404-0529

STAAL, ERIC, professional hockey player; b. Thunder Bay, Ont., Canada, Oct. 29, 1984; s. Henry and Linda Staal; m. Tanya Vanden-Broeke, Aug. 3, 2007; 1 child, Parker Lucas. Center Carolina Hurricanes, 2003—, capt., 2010—. Mem. Team Canada, Olympic Games, Vancouver, 2010. Recipient NHL All-Star Game, 2009; named MVP, NHL All-Star Game, 2008; named to NHL YoungStars Game, 2004, NHL All-Star Game, 2007, 2008, 2011, Second All-Star Team, NHL, 2006. Achievements include being a member of Stanley Cup Champion Carolina Hurricanes, 2006; being a member of gold medal winning Canadian Hockey Team, Vancouver Olympics, 2010. Office: Carolina Hurricanes RBC Ctr 2 1400 Edwards Mill Rd Raleigh NC 27607

STAAL, JORDAN, professional hockey player; b. Thunder Bay, Ont., Canada, Sept. 10, 1988; s. Henry and Linda Staal; m. Heather Staal, June 22, 2012. Center Pitts. Penguins, 2006—12, Carolina Hurricanes, 2012—. Recipient Player's Player award, 2010; named to NHL YoungStars Game, 2007, All-Rookie Team, NHL, 2007. Achievements include being the youngest player in NHL history to score two shorthanded goals in one game and the youngest player to score on a penalty shot, 2006; being the youngest player in NHL history to score a hat trick, 2007; being a member of Stanley Cup Champion Pittsburgh Penguins, 2009. Office: Carolina Hurricanes RBC Ctr 2 1400 Edwards Mill Rd Raleigh NC 27607

STAATS, THOMAS ELWYN, neuropsychologist; s. Percy Anderson and Julia (Bourmorck) S.; m. Debra R. (dec. Aug. 28, 2011); children: Lauren Malu, Kara Kristyn, Stacy Rhnea, Ronald Derek. BA cum laude, Emory U., 1970; MA, U. Ala., 1972, PhD, 1974; postgrad., U. Tex., Tyler, 1992. Diplomate Am. Bd. Prof. Disability Cons.; lic. psychologist. Dir., chief psychologist Caddo Parish Diagnostic Ctr., Shreveport, La., 1974-81; exec. dir. Doctors Psychol. Ctr., Shreveport, 1979-91, Comprehensive Assessments, 1991—2013. Cons. to Charter Forest Hosp., 1989-2000, Shreveport Impairment and Disability Evaluation Ctr., 1993—2010; clin. assoc. prof. psychology La. State U., Shreveport, 1977-1990; clin. assoc. prof. psychiatry La. State U. Sch. Medicine, Shreveport, 1980-92, 2003—; neuropsychol. cons. to dept. psychiatry, 1992-2002; mem. faculty Am. Acad. Disability Evaluating Physicians, 1986—2001, Health South Impairment Evaluation Lectr. Series, 1998—2000. Author: Manual for the Stress Vector Analysis Test Series, 1983, The Doctors Guide to Instant Stress Relief, 1987, Stress Management and Relaxation Training System Handbook; contbr. articles to profl. jours. and popular mags. Mem. Gov.'s Com. of 1000, La., 1979. Recipient AADEP award, 1991; Grad. Rsch. Coun. fellow, 1974. Fellow Am. Inst. Stress; mem. APA, Nat. Acad. Neuropsychology, Nat. Register of Health Svc. Providers, Am. Acad. Neuropsychology. Episcopalian. Avocations: scuba diving, gun collecting, camping, boating, paintball competition. Office: 4300 Youree Dr Ste 200 Shreveport LA 71105 Home: 6005 Kateland Cir Bossier City LA 71111-6986 Office Phone: 318-861-0194. Personal E-mail: drtomstaats@bellsouth.net.

STABLER, LEWIS VASTINE, JR., retired lawyer; b. Greenville, Ala., Nov. 5, 1936; s. Lewis Vastine and Dorothy Daisy Stabler; m. Monteray Scott, Sept. 5, 1958; children: Dorothy Monteray Scott, Andrew Vastine, Monteray Scott Smith, Margaret Langston. BA, Vanderbilt U., 1958; JD with distinction, U. Mich., 1961. Bar: Ala. 1961. Assoc. Cabaniss & Johnston, Birmingham, Ala., 1961-67; assoc. prof. law U. Ala., 1967-70; ptnr. Cabaniss, Johnston, Gardner, Dumas & O'Neal (and predecessor firms), Birmingham, 1970-91, Walston, Stabler, Wells, Anderson and Bains, Birmingham, 1991-97; pvt. practice, Birmingham, 1997—. Mem. com. of 100 Candler Sch. Theology, Emory U. Bd. editors: Mich. Law Rev, 1960-61. Fellow Am. Bar Found. (life); mem. Am. Law Inst. (life), Ala. Law Inst. (mem. coun., dir. 1968-70), ABA, Ala. Bar Assn., FINRA (arbitrator), Birmingham Bar Assn., Am. Assn. R.R. Trial Counsel, Order of Coif. Meth. (cert. lay speaker). Clubs: Country of Birmingham, Rotary. Home: 531 Old English Ln Birmingham AL 35223-1080 Personal E-mail: vstabler@gmail.com.

STACEY, WESTON MONROE, JR., nuclear engineer, physicist, educator; b. Birmingham, Ala., July 23, 1937; s. Weston Monroe and Dorothy (Toole) S.; m. Penelope Smith; children: Helen Lee, Weston Monroe III, Lucia Katherine. BS in Physics, Ga. Inst. Tech., 1959, MS in Nuc. Sci., 1963; PhD in Nuc. Enging., MIT, 1966. Nuc. engr. Knolls Atomic Power Lab., Schenectady, NY, 1962-64, 66-69; assoc. dir. applied physics divsn. and dir. fusion program Argonne Nat. Lab., Chgo., 1969-77; Callaway Regents prof. Ga. Inst. Tech., Atlanta, 1977—; vice chair IAEA INTOR Workshop leading to ITER Project, 1978—88. Author: Modal Approximation in Reactor Physics, 1967, Space-Time Nuclear Reactor Kinetics, 1969, Variational Methods in Nuclear Reactor Physics, 1972, Fusion Plasma Analysis, 1981, Fusion, 1984, 2nd edit., 2010, Nuclear Reactor Physics, 2001, 2d edit., 2007, Fusion Plasma Physics, 2005, 2nd edit., 2012, Quest for a Fusion Energy Reactor, 2010, From Midway Church to Nuclear Fusion, 2011; contbr. 300 articles to profl. jours. Recipient Cert. Appreciation Dept. Energy, 1981, 88, Disting. Assoc. award Dept. Energy, 1990, Rsch. award Sigma Xi, 1998; Disting. Career award Fusion Power Assn., 2009. Fellow: AAAS, Am. Nuc. Soc. (bd. dirs. 1974—77, Outstanding Achievement award 1981, 1996, Seaborg medal 2001, Wigner award 2003), Am. Phys. Soc.; mem.: Am. Soc. Engring. Edn. Office: Ga Inst Tech Nuclear Engring Dept 0745 Atlanta GA 30332-0745 Business E-Mail: weston.stacey@nre.gatech.edu.

STACK, STEVEN JOSEPH, emergency physician; b. Cleve. m. Tracie Stack; 1 child. Grad. magna cum laude, Coll. Holy Cross, Worcester, Mass.; MD, Ohio State U., Columbus, 1998. Diplomate American Bd. Emergency Medicine. Intern, resident Ohio State U. Hosp., 1998—2001; emergency physician, med. dir. emergency dept. Baptist Meml. Hosp., Memphis, 2001—06; emergency medicine physician St. Joseph Hosp. East, Lexington, Ky., 2006—, chair, med. dir. Dept. Emergency Medicine, 2006—10. Mem.: AMA (bd. trustees 2006—, sec. 2010—11, chair-elect 2011—), Ohio State Med. Assn., Emergency Medicine Residents' Assn. Office: St Joseph Hosp East Dept Emergency Medicine 150 N Eagle Creek Dr Lexington KY 40509 Office Phone: 859-967-5176. Office Fax: 859-967-5784.

STACKHOUSE, DAVID WILLIAM, JR., retired furniture systems installation contractor; b. Aug. 29, 1926; s. David William and Dorothy Frances (Snider) Stackhouse; m. Shirley Pat Smith, Dec. 23, 1950; 1 child, Stefan Brent. BS, Lawrence Coll., Appleton, Wis., 1950. Indsl. designer Globe Am. Co., Kokomo, Ind., 1951—53; product designer, chief engr. Midwest Foundry and Workwall divsn. L.A. Darling Co., Bronson, Mich., 1954—66; contract mgr. Brass Office Products, Indpls., 1966—73; mfrs. rep. Nashville, Ind., 1973—78; mktg. exec. Brass Office Products, Indpls, 1978—80; office furniture systems installation contractor, 1980—92. Creator This Great House, The Story of this Home, 1995; founder Half-High Hill Prodns., Inc., 1996. With USNR, 1944—46. Mem.: VFW, Am. Legion, Masons, Lions, Shiners, Beta Theta Pi. Achievements include patents for interior structural systems. Home: 410 Pocono Ct Arden NC 28704-8475 E-mail: davenshirleypat@bellsouth.net.

STACY, DENNIS WILLIAM, architect; b. Council Bluffs, Iowa, Sept. 22, 1945; s. William L. and Mildred Glee (Carlsen) S.; m. Judy Annette Long, Dec. 28, 1968; 1 child: Stephanie. BArch, Iowa State U., 1969; postgrad., U. Nebr., 1972. Registered arch., Iowa, Tex., Colo., Mo., Nat. Coun. Architectural Registration Bds. Cert. Designer Troy & Stalder Archs., Omaha, 1967, Archs. Assocs., Des Moines, 1968-69, Logsdon & Voelter Archs., Temple, Tex., 1970; project arch. Roger Schutte & Assocs., Omaha, 1972-73; arch., assoc. Robert H. Burgin & Assocs., Council Bluffs, 1973-75, Neil Astle & Assocs., Omaha, 1975-78; owner, prin. Dennis W. Stacy, AIA, Arch., Glenwood, Iowa, 1978-81; pres. Stacy Archs., Inc., Dallas, 1981—2001, Stacy Archtl. Studio, PLLC, 2002—. Mem. organizing com. symposium Tex. A&M U., 1991—2010. Archtl. works include: Davies Amphitheater, 1980, Addison Nat. Bank Bldg., 1985, Villa Roma, 1988, C.U. Performing Arts Ctr., 1989, Mercedes-Benz Distbn. Ctr., 1987, Dallas Chpt. AIA Offices, 1990, Janadria Festival Arena, 1994, Physicians Consultants Clinic, 1994, Horizon Pain Mgmt. Ctr., 1995, Rheumatology Assoc. Clinic, 1996, Addison Nat. Br. Bank, 1996, Cummins So. Plains Distbn., Fabrication and Corp. Offices Ctr., 1998, Arthur Murray Dance Studios, 2001,03, 06, Tatum Residence, 2001, Big Glee Office Plz., 2006, Heart First Med. Office, 2008, Zashin Rheumatology Office, 2009, Frater med. office, 2009, Nolan Residence, 2013; co-author Guide to Dallas Architecture, 1999, Transformations-The Architects, Buildings and Events That Shaped Dallas Architecture, 2008. Mem. City of Dallas Urban Design Adv. Com., 1992-96, chmn., 1995-96; dir. Greater Dallas Planning Coun., 1997-05; chmn. Glenwood Zoning Bd. Adjustment, 1979-81; chmn. Mills County Plant Iowa Program, 1979-81; mem. S.W. Iowa Citizen's Adv. Com., Iowa State Dept. Transp., 1977-81; regional screening chmn. Am. Field Svc. Internat./Intercultural Programs, 1974-79, Iowa-Nebr. rep., 1978-80. With U.S. Army, 1969-71. Decorated Nat. Def. Svc. medal, Vietnam Svc. medal, Vietnam Campaign medal, Army Commendation medal, Good Conduct medal, Disting. Alumnus Design Achievement award Iowa State U., 1999. Fellow AIA (chmn. nat. conv. 2000, Tex. Regional rep. coll. fellows2011-, Iowa Design Honor award 1981, Dallas AIA commendation awards 1990, 92, 95-98, 2007, 2009 (2), Citation of Honor award 1991-92, 96, 2001, 08, Dallas Design awards 1991, (2), 96,97, Tex. Design

Honor award 1992, Dallas AIA Firm award 1992, Nat. Presdl. Citation 2000, Dallas commr. design 1991, chmn. Dallas design awards 1992, pres. Dallas AIA 1996; Dallas Pres. medal 2011), Tex. Soc. Archs. (environ. resource com. 1994-95, chmn., Tex. arch. pub. com., 1992-98, chmn. 1997, 98, convention chmn., 2011, Flowers Media award 2009), Nat. Coun. Archtl. Registration Bds., Iowa State U. Adv. Coun. (1997-2000, 05-07, chmn. 1999-2000). Home and Office: 4148 Cobblers Ln Dallas TX 75287-6725 Office Phone: 972-250-1909. Business E-Mail: dstacyarch@aol.com.

STACY, JOHN WILL, state legislator; b. Mar. 29, 1953; BS, Morehead State U.; JD, Salmon P. Chase Coll. Law. Bus. owner; mem. Dist. 71 Ky. House of Reps., Ky., 1993—, majority whip. Democrat. Mailing: PO Box 135 West Liberty KY 41472 Office: 702 Capitol Ave Annex Rm 315 Frankfort KY 40601 Office Phone: 502-564-7756, 800-372-7181.

STACY, MARK ALLEN, neurologist; b. Cape Girardeau, Mo., May 4, 1959; s. Billy Wayn and Jane Cooper S.; m. Tina Estrada, June 26, 1982; children: Bryan, Andrea. BS, S.E. Mo. State, 1981; MD, U. Mo., 1986. Diplomate Am. Bd. Neurology. and Psychiatry. Intern in internal medicine St. Mary's Hosp., St. Louis, 1986-87; resident in neurology Hahnemann U., Phila., 1987-90, chief resident, 1989-90, clin. instr., 1989-90; asst. prof. neurology U. Mo., 1991-96, dir. Parkinson's Disease Clinic and Movement Disorders Ctr., 1992-96; neurologist Barrow Neurol. Inst., St. Joseph's Hosp., 1996, dir. Muhammad Ali Parkinson Rsch. Ctr., 1997; assoc. prof. neurology, dir. movement disorders prog. Duke U., Durham, NC, dir. Neurology Clin. Rsch. Ctr. Cons. neurology Harry S. Truman Meml. Vet. Hosp., 1991-96; adv. bd. DuPont Pharma, 1996—, Athena Pharm., 1997—, SmithKline Beecham, 1999, Elan Pharm., 1999; assoc. med. dir. Nat. Parkinson Found., 1997—; mem. Dystonia Study Group, 1996—, Parkinson Study Group, 1997—, WeMove, LME, adv. com., 1998—. Author: (chpt.) Current Pediatric Therapy, Vol. 16, 1999; co-author: (chpt.) Current Therapy in Neurologic Disease-3, 1990, Pathology of the Aging Nervous System, 1991, Neurobehavioral Aspects of Parkinson's Disease, 1992, Movement and Allied Disorders in Childhood, 1995, Adult Neurology, 1997, Textbook of Clinical Neurology, 1998; ed.: The Handbook of Dystonia; mem. editl. bd. Neurology Network Commentary, 1996—, Movement Disorders, 1997—; editl. bd. Southern Medical Jour. ad hoc reviewer, 1999—; contbr. articles to profl. jours. Mem. counseling staff Mo. Boys State, 1979—, dean of counselors, 1993—, bd. dirs., 1993—; mem. adv. bd. Physician's Home Health & Hospice Network, 1993-95, WE Move, 1998—; advisor Greater Mo. Tourette Syndrome Chpt., 1991-96, Am. Parkinson's Disease Assn., Columbia, Mo., 1992-96, bd. dirs. Fight Night Found., 1999—, Dystonia Med. Rsch. Found., 1993-96, Multiple Sclerosis Inst., 1993-96, Benign Essential Blepharospasm Found., 1997—; bd. deacons First Bapt. Ch., Columbia, 1995-96; mem. Internation Congress of Parkinsons Disease. 1999. Recipient Outstanding Young Alumni award S.E. Mo. State U., 1995, Caregivers award Nat. Parkinson Found.; Movement Disorders fellow Baylor Coll. Medicine, 1990-91; grantee DuPont Pharma, 1992, 93, Childrens Miracle Network Telethon, 1993, Sandoz Pharm., 1993, Berlex Pharm., 1994, Allergan, Inc., 1995-96, MDS Harris and Scherer DDS, 1997, Eli Lilly Pharm., 1997-98, Amgen, Inc., 1997, 98, Smith Kline Beecham, 1998—, NIH, 1998—, Pentech Pharm., Inc., 1999, Teva Pharm. USA, 1999, Roberts Pharm., 1999, others. Mem. Am. Acad. Neurology (movement disorders sect. 1995—, liaison com. 1995—), Movement Disorders Soc., Ariz. State Med. Assn., Maricopa County Med. Soc. Office: DUMC 3333 Durham NC 27710 Office Phone: 919-668-7600, 919-668-2493. Office Fax: 919-681-4935.

STADTER, PHILIP AUSTIN, classicist, educator; b. Cleve., Nov. 29, 1936; s. John M. and Mary Louise (Jones) S.; m. Lucia Angela Ciapponi, July 6, 1963; children: Paul, Maria, Mark. BA, Princeton U., 1958; MA, Harvard U., 1959, PhD, 1963. Instr. U. N.C., Chapel Hill, 1962-64, asst. prof., 1964-67, assoc. prof., 1967-71, prof., 1971—, chmn. dept. classics, 1976-86, prof. comparative lit., 1991—2003, Falk prof. humanities, 1991—2003, prof. emeritus, 2003—. Author: Plutarch's Historical Methods, 1965, The Public Library of Renaissance Florence, 1972, Arrian of Nicomedia, 1980, A Commentary on Plutarch's Pericles, 1989; editor: The Speeches of Thucydides, 1973, Plutarch and the Historical Tradition, 1992, Sage and Emperor, 2003. Fulbright fellow Rome, 1960-61; Guggenheim fellow Florence, Italy, 1967-68; NEH fellow, 1974-75; fellow Am. Council Learned Socs., Oxford, Eng., 1982-83 Fellow Nat. Humanities Ctr.; mem. Am. Philol. Assn. (dir. 1977-80), Am. Assn. Ancient Historians. Democrat. Roman Catholic. Office: University NC Dept Classics Chapel Hill NC 27599-3145 Home: 3000 Galloway Ridge Apt K206 Pittsboro NC 27312

STAELIN, RICHARD, business administration educator; b. Larchmont, NY, Aug. 3, 1939; s. Richard Carl and Dorothy (Potts) S.; m. Julie Ann Fischer, Aug. 24, 1963; children: Adam, Kate. BSME, U. Mich., 1961, BS in Math., 1962, MBA, 1963, PhD, 1969. Market planner IBM, Harrison, NY, 1963-66; prof. Carnegie-Mellon U., Pitts., 1969-82; Edward and Rose Donnell prof. Duke U., Durham, NC, 1982—, assoc. dean faculty affairs, 1982-91, assoc. dean exec. edn., 2000—02, dep. dean, 2002—04; exec. dir. Teradata CRM Ctr., 2004—; mng. dir. GEMBA, 1995-97; exec. dir. Mktg. Sci. Inst., Cambridge, Mass., 1991-93. Vis. prof. Australian Grad. Sch., Kensington, 1980—81. Author: Consumer Protection Legislation and the U.S. Food Industry, 1980; mem. editl. bd. Jour. Mktg. Rsch., 1974-82, Jour. Consumer Rsch., 1976-87; area editor Mktg. Sci., 1983-88; editor-in-chief Mktg. Sci., 1995-97. Mem. Pitts. Exec. Bd.; treas. Pitts. Arts and Crafts Ctr., 1976-79; bd. dirs. Dispute Settlement Ctr., Chapel Hill, NC, Bio Electronics, Frederick, Md., 2005—; bd. vis. drama dept. Duke U., 1990-96. Recipient Best Mktg. Paper award Inst. Mgmt. Sci., 1985, NCNB Faculty award 1990, AMA/Irwin Disting. Mktg. Educators award, 1996, O'Dell award JMR, 1998, Manyard award, 2006; HEW grantee, 1972-74, NSF grantee, 1973-79. Mem.: INFORMS Soc. Marketing Sci. (pres. elect 2006—07), INFORMS (pres. 2008—), Assn. Consumer Rsch., Am. Mktg. Assn. (Converse award 2000). Office: Fuqua Sch of Bus Science Dr Rm 339 Durham NC 27706-2597 Home Phone: 919-382-9977; Office Phone: 919-660-7824. E-mail: rick@staelin.com.

STAFFORD, CYNTHIA A., state legislator; b. Miami, Fla., July 11, 1967; BA in Comm. Arts, St. Thomas U., Miami, 1993, JD, 1999. Aide to Carrie P. Meek US House of Representatives, Washington; atty.; mem. Dist. 109 Fla. House of Representatives, 2011—. Democrat. Baptist. Avocation: reading. Office: 3550 Biscayne Blvd Miami FL 33137-3854 also: Fla House of Reps 1401 The Capitol 402 S Monroe St Tallahassee FL 32399-1300 Office Phone: 305-571-2100, 850-488-0625.

STAFFORD, WILLIAM HENRY, JR., federal judge; b. Masury, Ohio, May 11, 1931; s. William Henry and Frieda Gertrude (Nau) S.; m. Nancy Marie Helman, July 11, 1959; children: William Henry III, Donald Helman, David Harrold. BS, Temple U., 1953, LLB, 1956. Bar: Fla. 1961, U.S. Ct. Appeals (5th cir.) 1969, U.S. Supreme Ct. 1970. Assoc. Robinson & Roark, Pensacola, 1961-64; individual practice law Pensacola, 1964-67; state atty., 1967-69; US atty., 1969-75; judge U.S. Dist. Ct. (no. dist.) Fla., Tallahassee, 1975—81, 1993—96, chief judge, 1981-93, sr. judge, 1996—, Fgn. Intelligence Surveillance Ct., 1996—2003. Instr. Pensacola Jr. Coll., 1964, 68; mem. judicial council U.S. Ct. Appeals (11th cir.), 1986-89; apptd. com. on intercircuit assignments, 1987-92, subcom. on fed. jurisdiction, 1983-87; adj. prof. Fla. State U. Coll. Law, 1992-97. Lt. (j.g.) USN, 1957-60. Mem. Fla. Bar (mem. numerous coms., bench/bar commn. 1991-92, bench/bar implementation commn. 1993), Dist. Judges Assn. 11th Cir. (pres. 1984-85), State Fed. Judicial Council Fla., William H. Stafford Am. Inn Ct., Tallahassee Bar Assn., Tallahassee Inn (founding pres. 1989-91), Mason (33d degree), Sigma Phi Epsilon, Phi Delta Phi. Republican. Episcopalian. Office: US Dist Ct US Courthouse 111 N Adams St Tallahassee FL 32301-7730 Office Phone: 850-521-3611.

STAFFORD, WILLIE RANSOME, III, federal marshal; b. 1953; BA in American History & Psychology, U. NC, Greensboro, 1975, MPA, 1988. Various positions including asst. chief of police Western Ops. Bur., Greensboro Police Dept., 1975—2004, background investigator, 2004—10; US marshal (mid. dist.) NC US Marshals Svc., US Dept. Justice, Greensboro, 2010—. Office: US Courthouse 324 W Market St Rm 234 Greensboro NC 27401 Office Phone: 336-332-8700.

STAGG, THOMAS E., JR., federal judge; b. Shreveport, La., Jan. 19, 1923; s. Thomas Eaton and Beulah (Meyer) S.; m. Margaret Mary O'Brien, Aug. 21, 1946; children: Julie, Margaret Mary. BA, La. State U., 1943, LLB, 1949. Bar: La. 1949. With firm Hargrove, Guyton, Van Hook & Hargrove, Shreveport, 1949-53; pvt. practice law Shreveport, 1953-58; sr. ptnr. firm Stagg, Cady & Beard, Shreveport, 1958-74; judge US Dist. Ct. (we. dist.) La., Shreveport, 1974—84, 1991—92, chief judge, 1984—91, sr. judge, 1992—. Mem. Shreveport Airport Authority, 1967-73, chmn., 1970-73; chmn. Gov.'s Tidelands Adv. Council, 1969-70; del. La. Constl. Conv., 1973-74; chmn. rules com., com. on exec. dept.; mem. Gov.'s Adv. Com on Offshore Revenues, 1972-74 Active Republician party, 1950-74, del. convs., 1956, 60, 64, 68, 72; mem. Nat. Com. for La., 1964-72, mem. exec. com., 1964-68; Pres. Shreveport Jr. C. of C., 1955-56; v.p. La. Jr. C. of C., 1956-57. Served to capt., inf. AUS, 1943-46, ETO. Decorated Bronze Star, Purple Heart with oak leaf cluster, Combat Inf. badge. Mem. Am., La., Shreveport bar assns. Office: US Dist Ct 300 Fannin St Ste 4100 Shreveport LA 71101-3123 Office Phone: 318-676-3260. Business E-Mail: tom_stagg@lawd.uscourts.gov.

STAGGERS, HARLEY ORRIN, JR., (BUCKEY STAGGERS), lawyer, former United States Representative from West Virginia; b. Washington, Feb. 22, 1951; s. Harley Orrin Sr. and Mary (Casey) S.; m. Leslie Sergy, 1986; c. Elizabeth Clare and Harley Orrin III. BA, Harvard U., 1974; JD, W.Va. U., 1977. Asst. atty. gen. State of W.Va, Charleston, 1980; mem. W.Va. State Senate, 1980-82, US Congress from 2nd W.Va. Dist., 1982—92; atty. Staggers & Staggers, Keyser, W.Va. Democrat. Roman Catholic. Office: Staggers & Staggers PO Box 876 Keyser WV 26726 Office Phone: 304-788-5749.*

STAHL, DALE O., economics professor, department chairman; PhD, U. Calif., Berkeley, 1981. Malcolm Forsman centennial prof. dept. economics U. Tex., Austin, 1996—, chmn. dept. economics, 2007—. Author: (book) The Economics of Electronic Commerce; contbr. articles to profl. jours. Mem.: Am. Economics Assn. Office: Univ Texas Dept Economics Austin TX 78712

STAKEL, JOHN, corporate financial executive; BS in bus. adminstrn., U. Fla. Worked NationsBank Corp., Alamo-Rent-A-Car, Inc., Bruno's, Inc.; v.p., treas. John H. Harland Co., 2000—03; COO DataScan Technologies, 2003—07; sr. v.p., treas. Rock-Tenn Co., 2008—. Office: Rock-Tenn Co 504 Thrasher St Norcross GA 30071 Office Phone: 770-448-2193. Office Fax: 678-291-7666. Business E-Mail: jstakel@rocktenn.com.

STALCUP, JOE ALAN, retired lawyer, dean; b. Hooker, Okla., Feb. 13, 1931; s. Herbert I. and Ruby (Gantt) S.; m. Nancy Jo Vaughn, Sept. 3, 1950; children: Melinda, Sondra Jo, Cheri Ann. BBA cum laude, So. Methodist U., 1951, JD magna cum laude, 1959, M.Th. magna cum laude, 1978. Bar: Tex. 1959. Tchr. Dallas Ind. Sch. Dist., 1951-57; assoc. atty. firm Locke, Purnell, Boren, Laney & Neely, Dallas, 1959-66; assoc. atty., partner firm Geary, Brice & Lewis, Dallas, 1966-67; founder, sr. partner firm Stalcup, Johnson, Meyers & Miller (and predecessor firm), Dallas, 1968-75; dean Sch. Theology for the Laity, 1978—80, 1992—96, 2003—06. Pres. Dallas County Young Democrats, 1952-54; Bd. dirs., mem. exec. com. N. Tex. Christian Communications Commn., 1972-78; bd. dirs., v.p. Greater Dallas Council Chs., 1972-75; bd. dirs., chmn. Christian Ch. Found., 1976-84, 86-91, Christian Bd. Publ., 1991-98. Mem. ABA, Tex. Bar Assn., Dallas Bar Assn., Am. Judicature Soc., Phi Alpha Delta. Mem. Disciples of Christ (minister). Home and Office: 7528 Benedict Dr Dallas TX 75214-1903

STALEY, DAWN MICHELLE, women's college basketball coach, retired professional basketball player; b. Phila., May 4, 1970; d. Estelle. Grad., U. Va., 1992. Profl. basketball player Brazil, France, Italy, Spain, Richmond Rage, ABL, 1996—98, Charlotte Sting, 1999—2005, Houston Comets, 2005—06; ret., 2006; head women's basketball coach Temple U. Owls, 2000—08, U. SC Gamecocks, 2008—. Mem. US Women's Sr. Nat. Basketball Team, 1989—2004, asst. coach, 2008. Founder Dawn Staley Found. Recipient Spectrum Award, ARC, 1998, Entrepreneurial Spirit Award, WNBA, 1999, Sportsmanship Award, 1999, Woman One award, 2005; named USA Basketball Female Athlete of Yr., 1994, 2004, MVP, Goodwill Games, 1994, Phila. Big Five Coach of Yr., 2002, Atlantic 10 Coach of Yr., 2004, 2005; named to First Team All-ABL, 1997, WNBA All-Star Team, 2001, 2002, 2003, Women's Basketball Hall of Fame, 2011, Naismith Meml. Basketball Hall of Fame, 2013. Achievements include being a member of US Women's Basketball Olympic gold medal team, Atlanta, 1996, Sydney, 2000, Athens, 2004; having her number retired at U. Va; being the first women in professional basketball history to record 1,000 career assists; serving as Olympic Flag bearer, Athens Olympic Games, 2004. Office: U SC c/o Dept Athletics Roost Bldg B 1322 Heyward St Columbia SC 29208 Office Phone: 803-777-5204. Office Fax: 803-777-2967.

STALEY, JOHN R., JR., health products executive; MD, U. Tenn. Other ACLS; Other ATLS. Intership, internal medicine U. Tenn Med. Ctr., 1981; pres. Team Health Atlantic. Mem.: AMA (assoc.). Office: Team Health Holdings 265 Brookview Ctr Way Ste 400 Knoxville TN 37919 Office Phone: 865-693-1000. Office Fax: 865-539-3073. Business E-Mail: john_staley@teamhealth.com.

STALEY, THOMAS FABIAN, literature and language professor, museum director; b. Pitts., Aug. 13, 1935; s. Fabian Richard and Mary (McNulty) S.; m. Carolyn O'Brien, Sept. 3; children: Thomas Fabian, Caroline Ann, Mary Elizabeth, Timothy X. AB, BS, Regis Coll., 1957; MA, U. Tulsa, 1958; PhD, U. Pitts., 1962; D.H.L., Regis Coll. Asst. prof. English Rollins Coll., 1961-62; mem. faculty U. Tulsa, 1962-88, prof. English, 1969-88, dean Grad. Sch., 1969, dean Coll. Arts and Scis., 1981-83, provost, v.p. acad. affairs, 1983-88, McFarlin prof. modern lit., 1988; prof. English, dir. Ransom Humanities Rsch. Ctr. U. Tex., Austin, 1988—, Chancellor's Centennial prof. of the Book, 1989—92, Harry Huntt Ransom chair liberal arts, 1992—. Fulbright prof., Italy, 1966-67; Fulbright lectr., 1971; Danforth assoc., 1962-67; chmn. Internat. James Joyce Symposium; dir. Grad. Inst. Modern Letters, 1970-81. Author: James Joyce Today, 1966, James Joyce's Portrait of the Artist, 1968, Italo Svevo: Essays on His Work, 1969, (with H.J. Mooney) The Shapeless God: Essays on the Modern Novel, 1968, (with B. Benstock) Approaches to Ulysses: Ten Essays, 1970, Approaches to Joyce's Portrait: Ten Essays, Jean Rhys: A Critical Study; editor: Il Punto Su Joyce, 1973, Dorothy Richardson, Ulysses: Fifty Years, 1974, Twentieth-Century Women Novelists, 1982, British Novelists, 1890-1929, Traditionalists, Dictionary of Lit. Biography, Vols. 34, 36, 70, 77, An Annotated Critical Bibliography of James Joyce, 1989, Joyce Studies: An Annual edit., 1990-2003, Studies in Modern Literature Series, 1990—, Reflections on James Joyce: Stuart Gilbert's Paris Journal, 1993, Writing the Lives of Writers, 1998, James Joyce Quar., 1963-89; adv. editor Twentieth-Century Lit., 1966—, Jean Rhys Rev., 1986—; bd. dirs. Eighteenth-Century Short Title Catalogue/North America, 1990; mem. editl. bd. Tulsa Studies in Women's Literature, Jour. Modern Lit., 1989—, Mailer Rev., 2007—; contbr. articles to profl. jours. bd. dirs. Tulsa Arts Coun., 1969-76, NCCJ, 1979—, Christopher Isherwood Found.; pres. James Joyce Found., 1968-72; chmn. bd. Undercroft Montessori Sch., 1968-70, Marquette Sch., 1969-70; bd. dirs. Cascia Hall Prep. Sch.; chmn. disting. authors com. Tulsa Libr. Trust, 1984; mem. bd. commrs. Tulsa City-County Libr., chmn., 1980-82; mem. adv. coun. Tex. Inst. for Humanities; trustee Regis U., 1992—; bd. dirs. Libr. of Am., 1994—, Harlick Trust, 1994—; mem. symposium com. Lyndon Baines Johnson Presdl. Libr., 1993—; mem. AFI Dallas Internat. Film Festival Bd., 2006—. Recipient Am. Council Learned Socs. award, 1969, 80 Mem. MLA, Internat. Assn. Univ. Profs. English, Anglo-Irish Studies Assn., Am. Com. for Irish Studies, Assn. Internat. de Bibliophilie, James Joyce Soc., Hopkins Soc., Tex. Philos. Soc. (bd. dirs. 1991—), Internat. James Joyce Found. (hon. trustee), LBJ Centennial Hist. Soc., US Tennis Assn., Tulsa Tennis Club, Westwood Country Club, The Athenaeum Club (London), Grolier Club (N.Y.), Edgecomb Tennis Club (Kennebunk, Maine), Tarry House, Phi Beta Kappa. Business E-Mail: TFS@mail.utexas.edu.

STALL, WILLIAM M., weed scientist, educator; b. Apr. 14, 1944; BS, Ohio State U., 1967; MS, U. Fla., 1969, PhD, 1973. Ext. agt. Dade County Cooperative Ext. Svc., 1974-80; assoc. prof. U. Fla., Gainesville, 1980-85, prof., 1985—2009; prof. emeritus, 2009—. Author chpts. to books; contbr. articles to profl. jours. Mem. Am. Soc. Hort. Scis. (chmn. weed sci. and IPM working group 1986, Extension Edn. Aids award, 1994, 2000), Weed Sci. Soc. Am. (mem. minor use com. 1991-94, Outstanding Ext. award 1995), Fla. State Hort. Soc. (dir.-at-large 1977, v.p. vegetable sect. 1983), Fla. Weed Sci. Soc. (dir. 1985-89, pres. 1994-95, Outstanding Weed Scientist award, 2000), Fla. Fruit and Vegetable Assoc. (Outstanding Rsch. award, 2001). Office: U Fla Hort Scis Dept Inst Food and Agrl Scis PO Box 110690 Gainesville FL 32611-0690

STALLARD, HUBERT R., retired telephone company executive; b. Norton, Va., Jan. 31, 1937; s. Nathaniel Winfield and Evelyn (Stewart) S.; m. Alice Cheatwood, Aug. 1, 1959; children: Craig Winston, Brian Kendrick, Mark Brian. BS, Hampden-Sydney Coll., 1959. Successively staff asst. engr., foreman svc., plant supr., foreman supr., dist. plant supr., dist. plant mgr. Chesapeake and Potomac Telephone Co. of Va., Richmond, Roanoke, Newport News, Norfolk, 1960-68; staff supr. Chesapeake and Potomac Telephone Cos., Washington, 1968-69; from staff supr. to div. plant mgr. Chesapeake and Potomac Telephone Co. of Va., Northern and Culpeper, 1969-73; gen. plant mgr. Chesapeake and Potomac Telephone Co. of Washington, 1973-77; from gen. engring. mgr. to gen. mgr. network engring. and provisioning, Richmond Chesapeake and Potomac Telephone Co. of Va., Richmond, 1977-80, asst. v.p. revenue requirements, 1980-82, asst. v.p. external affairs, 1982-85, v.p., 1985-88, pres., 1988-90, pres., chief exec. officer, 1990; pres., CEO Bell Atlantic Va., Richmond, 1990—2000; ret. Bd. dirs. Universal Corp., Richmond, Va., 1991—. Exec. adv. bd. Jr. Achievement of Richmond, 1981; adv. bd. U. Richmond, 1982; bd. dirs. Richmond Renaissance, 1985, Va. Literacy Found., 1989; mem. Va. Bus. Coun., Richmond, 1985, corp. bd. YMCA of Greater Richmond, 1986, capital funds bd. United Way Greater Richmond, 1988—; trustee Va. Found. for Ind. Colls., 1986, Hampden-Sydney (Va.) Coll., 1987. Lt. comdr. Va. C.G., 1960—. Named Chief Exec. Officer of Yr. Minority Devel. Coun., 1989, Bus. Man of Yr. Va. Literacy Found., 1989. Mem. Va. Mfrs. Assn., Va. Telephone Assn. (bd. dirs. 1984-85). Presbyterian. Office: Bell Atlantic Va 600 E Main St Ste 1000 Richmond VA 23219-2442

STALLINGS, GENE (EUGENE CLIFTON STALLINGS JR.), retired college football coach; b. Paris, Tex., Mar. 2, 1935; s. Eugene C. and Neil (Moye) S.; m. Ruth Ann Jack, Dec. 1, 1956; children: Anna Lee, Laura Nell, John Mark, Jacklyn Ruth, Martha Kate BS, Tex. A&M U., 1958. Asst. football coach U. Ala. Crimson Tide, 1958-64; head football coach, dir. athletics Tex. A&M U. Aggies, 1964-72; asst. coach Dallas Cowboys, 1972-85; head football coach St. Louis Cardinals, 1986-89, U. Ala. Crimson Tide, 1990—96. Dir. Bank of A&M, College Station, Tex., Rolling Internat., Inc., Dallas; sports cons. Spalding. Co-author (with Sally Cook): Another Season: A Coach's Story of Raising an Exceptional Son, 1997. Mem. Sam Houston Coun. Boy Scouts Am.; trustee Abilene Christian U., Tex.; bd. regents Tex. A&M U., 2005- Recipient Munger award, Maxwell Football Club, 1992, Eddie Robinson award, Football Writers Assn. America, 1992, Walter Camp Coach of Yr. award, Walter Camp Football Found., 1992, Paul "Bear" Bryant Coach of Yr. award, Nat. Sportscasters & Sportswriters Assn., 1992; named Dallas Father of Yr., 1983, Coach of Yr., Am. Football Coaches Assn., 1992, Southeastern Conf., 1992, 1994; named to Tex. A&M U. Hall of Fame, 1982, Hall of Fame, Ala., Cotton Bowl, Gatton Bowls, Tex., Am. Football Found. Mem. Nat. Assn. Collegiate Dirs. Athletics, Am. Football Coaches Assn., Fellowship Christian Athletes Mem. Ch. of Christ Achievements include head coach of NCAA football national championship winning University of Alabama Crimson Tide, 1992. Office: Tex A&M University Bd Regents 200 Technology Way College Station TX 77845

STALLINGS, KEVIN, men's college basketball coach; m. Lisa Stallings; children: Jacob, Alexa, Jordyn. B in Bus. Mgmt., Purdue U., West Lafayette, Ind., 1982, M, 1985. Asst. coach Purdue U. Boilermakers, 1983—88, U. Kans. Jayhawks, 1989—94; head basketball coach Ill. State U. Redbirds, 1994—99, Vanderbilt U. Commodores, 1999—. Named Coach of Yr., Southeastern Conf., 2007, 2010, Dist. XXI Coach of Yr., Nat. Assn. Basketball Coaches, 2010. Office: Vanderbilt U Athletics McGugin Ctr 2601 Jess Neely Dr Nashville TN 37212 Office Phone: 615-343-8482.

STALLINGS, RONALD DENIS, lawyer; b. Evansville, Ind., Feb. 22, 1943; s. Denis and Gertrude (Tong) S.; m. Vicki Lee Chandler, Aug. 21, 1965; children: Courtnay, Claire, Ryan. B in Indsl. Engring., Ga. Inst. Tech., 1965; LLB, U. Va., 1968. Bar: Ga. 1968. Assoc. Powell, Goldstein, Frazer & Murphy LLP, Atlanta, 1968—75, ptnr., 1976—2000, co-counsel, 2001—05; exec. v.p., gen. counsel, corp. sec. Reliance Fin. Corp. and Reliance Trust Co., Atlanta, 2001—. Co-author: Georgia Corporate Forms, 1988. Mem. ABA, Ga. Bar Assn., Atlanta Bar Assn., Nat. Assn. Bond Lawyers, Am. Soc. Corp. Secs., Phoenix Soc. Atlanta (trustee 1987-93). Roman Catholic.

Home: 4601 Polo Ln NW Atlanta GA 30339-5345 Office: Reliance Trust Co 500 Northpark Ste 400 1100 Abernathy Rd NE Atlanta GA 30328-5646 Business E-Mail: rstallings@relico.com.

STAM, PAUL B., state legislator; b. Princeton, NJ, Sept. 5, 1950; m. Dorothy Stam; 2 children. Attended, US Armed Forces Inst., UNC, Greensboro, East Carolina U.; BS, Mich. State U., 1972; JD, UNC Law Sch., Chapel Hill, 1975. Clk. Justice James G. Exum Jr. NC Supreme Ct., 1975—76; atty. Stam, Fordham & Denchi, 1976—2006, Town of Apex, 1992—95; mem. Dist. 62 NC House of Reps., 1989—90, mem. Dist. 37, 2003—, minority leader, 2006—. Adj. prof. family law Campbell U., 1978. Auth, Legal Articles, The Equal Access Act, Campbell Law Observer, Search and Seizure at Sea, Sea Grant, Judging the American Constitution, NC Policy Coun Press, 1989, The End of the State Abortion Fund, Campbell Law Review, 1999. Cpl. USMC, 1968—70. Wake Co & NC Bar Asns; Christian Legal Soc of NC; Wake Co Right to Life; Southern Baptist Theological Sem (trustee, 1988-98). Republican. Baptist. Office: 16 W Jones St Rm 2301 Raleigh NC 27601-1096 Office Phone: 919-733-2962. Business E-Mail: Paul.Stam@ncleg.net.

STAMATOPLOS, ANTHONY, librarian, educator; s. John and Joanne Stamatoplos; m. Kari Ann Kudlas. BA, Eastern Wash. U., Cheney, 1980; MA, Wash. State U., Pullman, 1985; MLS, Ind. U., Bloomington, 1989. Vis. asst. libr. Ind. U., Bloomington, 1989—90; assoc. reference libr. Irwin Libr., Butler U., Indpls., 1990—92, head reference libr., 1992—94, acting assoc. dir. pub. svcs., 1993—94; asst. libr. Ind. U., Purdue U. Indpls., 1994—2000, assoc. libr., 2000—13; rsch. dir. Ctr. Rsch. and Learning Ind. U. Purdue U., Indpls., 2004—09; assoc. libr. Scholarly Support Svcs. Spl. Projects U. South Fla., St. Petersburg, 2013—. Book reviewer Behavioral & Social Scis. Libr., 1991, Collection Mgmt., 1993—96, Reference and User Svcs. Quar., 1998—; asst. prof. Ind. U. Sch. Libr. & Info. Sci., Indpls., 2000—13; lectr. in field; sr. faculty mem. U. Coll., Ind. U.-Purdue U. Indpls., 2010—13. Co-author: (books) The Chinese Economy: A Bibliography of Works in English, 1995, International and Area Studies Resources: A Selected Guide, 1998; actor: ComedySportz Indianapolis, 1996—2013; contbr. articles to profl. jours., chapters to books. Mem., documentary screening com. Heartland Film Festival, Indpls., 2011—12, mem., hospitality com., 2011—12. Recipient Tchg. Excellence Recognition award, Ind. U., Purdue U., 1997—2000, Libr. Instrn. Roundtable's Top 20 Instrn., 1999, Ind. U. Trustees Tchg. award, 2002, 2009; grantee, NSF, 2006—10. Mem.: ALA, Fla. Libr. Assn., Soc. Cultural Anthropology, Am. Anthropological Assn., Coun. on Undergrad. Rsch., Ind. Libr. Fedn. (chair, awards & honors com. 2007—10, sec., reference divsn. 2007—10), Assn. Coll. & Rsch. Librs. (mem., instrn. sect., rsch & scholarship com. 2011—13, mem., instrn. and info. literacy com. 2012—, mem., anthropology and sociology sect.), Beta Phi Mu (Chi Chpt. pres. 2008—11). Avocation: theater. Office: Nelson Poynter Memorial Libr University South Fla 140 USFSP Harborwalk Avenue S Saint Petersburg FL 33701

STAMELMAN, RICHARD HOWARD, French and humanities educator; b. Newark, Mar. 7, 1942; s. Louis Robert and Golda (Senzer) S.; children: Emily, Gibson, Jeremy White. BA, Hamilton Coll.; PhD, Duke U. Asst. prof. French and humanities Wesleyan U., Middletown, Conn., 1967-74, assoc. prof., 1974-79, prof., 1979-93, William R. Kenan Jr. prof. humanities, 1983-92, dean humanities, 1986-89, dir. Ctr. for the Humanities, 1976-82, dir. humanities devel., 1982-85; dir. Weston Ctr. for Fgn. Langs., Lits. and Cultures Williams Coll., Williamstown, Mass., 1992-97, prof. Romance langs., comp. lit., 1992—2007; chmn. dept. French and Italian U. Colo., Boulder, 1991-92; vis. prof. comp. lit. Dartmouth Coll., 2008—12; exec. dir. Kenneth & Harle Montgomery Endowment Dartmouth Coll., 2008—. Organizer study group Ecrire le Livre: Autour d'Edmond Jabès, Cerisy-la-Salle, France, 1987; co-dir. Edouard Morot-Sir Summer Inst. for French Cultural Studies, Hanover, NH, 1994; academic cons. Making Scents: The Art and Passion of Fragrance, Longwood Gardens, Pa., 2007-10. Author: The Drama of Self in Guillaume Apollinaire's Alcools, 1976, Claude Garache: Prints, 1965-85, 1985, Lost Beyond Telling: Representations of Death and Absence in Modern French Poetry, 1990, Perfume: Joy, Obsession, Scandal, Sin A Cultural History of Frangrance from 1750 to the Present, 2006; editor: Contemporary French Poetry, Studies in 20th Century Literature, 1989, Ecrire le Livre: Autour d'Edmond Jabès, 1989, Italian transl., 1991, French Poetry since the War, L'Esprit Créateur, 1992; editor, prin. translator: The Lure and the Truth of Painting, Selected Essays by Yves Bonnefoy, 1995; translator: The Grapes of Zeuxis and Other Fables by Yves Bonnefoy, 1987, Once More the Grapes of Zeuxis by Yves Bonnefoy, 1989, The Last Grapes of Zeuxis by Yves Bonnefoy, 1993, Transmorphoses by Yves Bonnefoy, 1998; mem. editl. bd. French Forum; contbr. articles to profl. jours. Recipient Chevalier dans l'ordre des Palmes Académiques award French Govt., 1993; NEH fellow, 1973, John Simon Guggenheim Meml. Found. fellow, 1999; Am. Council Learned Socs. grantee, 1983 Mem. MLA (regional del. 1987-90, mem. program com. 1996-99), Societe Francaise des Parfumeurs. Home: 21 Sussex Ct Williamsburg VA 23188-1555 Business E-Mail: rstamelman@wm.edu.

STAMKOS, STEVEN, professional hockey player; b. Markham, Ont., Canada, Feb. 7, 1990; Center Tampa Bay Lightning, 2008—, capt., 2014—. Mem. Team Canada, World Jr. Championships, Czech Republic, 2008. Co-recipient Maurice Richard Trophy, 2010; named to NHL YoungStars Game, 2009, NHL All-Star Game, 2011, 2012, Second All-Star Team, NHL, 2011. Achievements include being the first overall draft pick in NHL entry draft, 2008; being a member of Gold Medal Team Canada, World Junior Championships, 2008. Office: Tampa Bay Lightning Hockey Club St Pete Times Forum 401 Channelside Dr Tampa FL 33602*

STAMP, FREDERICK PFARR, JR., federal judge; b. Wheeling, W.Va., July 24, 1934; s. Frederick Pfarr Sr. and Louise (Aul) Stamp; m. Joan A. Corson, Sept. 20, 1975; children: Frederick Andrew, Joan Elizabeth. BA, Washington & Lee U., Lexington, Va., 1956; LLB, U. Richmond T.C. Williams Sch. Law, 1959, LLD (hon.), 2006. Bar: Va. 1959, W.Va. 1959, Va. Supreme Ct. Appeals 1959, US Dist. Ct. (no. dist.) W.Va. 1960, US Ct. Appeals (4th cir.) 1962, W.Va. Supreme Ct. Appeals 1966, US Supreme Ct. 1973, US Tax Ct. 1973, US Dist. Ct. (so. dist.) W.Va. 1975, Pa. 1986, US Dist. Ct. (we. dist.) Pa. Assoc., then ptnr. Schrader, Stamp, Byrd, Byrum & Companion, Wheeling, 1960-90; judge US Dist. Ct. (no. dist.) W.Va., Wheeling, 1990—2006, chief judge, 1994—2001, sr. judge, 2006—. Mem. W.Va. Commn. Uniform State Laws, Nat. Conf. Commissioners Uniform State Laws. Mem. W.Va. Bd. Regents, Charleston, 1970—77; bd. trustees Linsly Sch., Wheeling, U. Richmond; mem. W.Va. House of Delegates, 1966—70. Pvt. US Army, 1959—60, 1st lt. USAR, 1960—67. Fellow: American Coll. Trial Lawyers, American Bar Found.; mem.: W.Va. Bar Assn. (pres. 1981—82). Office: US Courthouse 1125 Chapline St PO Box 791 Wheeling WV 26003 Office Phone: 304-233-1120.

STAMPS, JEFFREY M., pharmaceutical executive; BS in Pharmacy magna cum laude, U. Cin. Joined Omnicare Inc., 1990, regional v.p., sr. regional v.p., pharmacy ops. group, 1990, sr. regional v.p., pharmacy ops. group, Eastern Region, 2001—05, corp. v.p., sr. v.p., pharmacy ops. group, Ctrl. divsn., 2005—07, corp. v.p., sr. v.p., field ops., pharmacy ops. group, 2007—09; sr. v.p., pharmacy ops. Omnicare, Inc., 2009—; currently serving as pres. D & R Pharm. Svcs. Inc. Office: Omnicare Inc 100 E RiverCenter Blvd 1600 RiverCenter II Covington KY 41011 Office Phone: 859-392-3300. Office Fax: 859-392-3333. Business E-Mail: Jeffrey.Stamps@omnicare.com.

STAMPS, LEIGHTON ELDERKIN, psychology educator; b. Pitts., Mar. 10, 1947; s. Ranzie Washington and Florence Elderkin (Cromlish) Stamps; children: Jason, Lauren, Christopher, Justin. BA in Eonomics, Westminster Coll., 1969; MA in Psychology, W.VA. U., 1972, PhD, 1974. Lic. psychologist La. Asst. prof. to prof., psychology U. New Orleans, 1974—, dept. chmn., 1982—84, 2003—07; pvt. practice La., 1978—; prof. Belmont Abbey Coll., 2007—. Contbr. articles to profl. jours. Mem.: APA, La. Psychol. Assn. (chmn., sci. affairs com. 1984). Office: Belmont Abbey Coll Dept Psychology Belmont NC 28012 Home: 2004 Gladelynn Ct Belmont NC 28012 Office Phone: 704-461-6821. Business E-Mail: lstamps@uno.edu.

STANCELL, ARNOLD FRANCIS, chemical engineering educator, retired oil industry executive; b. NYC, Nov. 16, 1936; s. Francis and Maria (Lucas) S.; m. Constance Newton, Apr. 21, 1973; 1 child, Christine. BChemE magna cum laude, CCNY, 1958; ScD, MIT, Cambridge, 1962. Lic. profl. engr., NY, Conn. Rsch. scientist, rsch. mgr. Mobil Oil Corp., Edison, NJ, 1962—72, chem. planning assoc., mgr. NYC, 1973—75, v.p. chem. divsn. Macedon, NY, 1976—79, mgr. corp. planning NYC, 1980—81, regional exec. mktg. and refining London, 1982—84, planning v.p. mktg. and refining NYC, 1985—86, v.p. U.S. exploration and prodn. Fairfax, Va., 1987—88, v.p. internat. exploration and producing, 1989—93; prof. and endowed chair prof. chem. engring. Ga. Inst. Tech., Atlanta, 1994—2004. Vis. prof. MIT, Cambridge, 1970, 1998, adv. bd., 1976-2006; adv. bd. CCNY, 1990-2004, Carnegie Mellon U., 1999-2003, cons., 2005-; cons. US Sec. of Interior on BP Oil Spill; apptd. mem. Nat. Sci. Bd., Pres. Obama, 2011-. Contbg. author: Polymer Science and Materials, 1971; contbr. articles to Jour. Applied Polymer Sci., AIChE Symposia Series, Jour. Macromolecular Sci. Recipient Profl. Achievement award, Nat. Orgn. Black Chemists and Chem. Engrs., 1975, Career Achievement award CCNY, 1993, Townsend Harris medal, 2009. Fellow AIChE (Chem. Engring. Practice award 1997, One of One Hundred Chem. Engrs. of Modern Era, 1940-); mem. Nat. Acad. Engring. (councillor 2009-), Nat. Rsch. Coun. (governing bd. mem. 2011-), Tau Beta Pi. Achievements include research in new chemical processes and management and growth of large domestic and international businesses in chemicals, oil and natural gas; patents for petrochemical and polymer processes and plasma processes at surfaces. Business E-Mail: arnold.stancell@chbe.gatech.edu.

STANCZAK, STEPHEN PHILLIP, environmental services administrator, lawyer; b. Waukegan, Ill., June 19, 1957; BS magna cum laude, W.Va. U., 1979; JD magna cum laude, U. Ill., 1982. Bar: Ill. 1982, U.S. Dist. Ct. (no. dist.) Ill. 1984. Counsel Amoco Corp., 1982-86; assoc. legal counsel Evang. Health Sys., 1986-87; corp. counsel Waste Mgmt. Inc., 1987-90; v.p., sec., assoc. gen. counsel Wheelabrator Techs., Inc., 1990-95; v.p. legal affairs, co. sec. Waste Mgmt. Internat. Plc, 1995-98; exec. v.p., gen. counsel, sec. U.S. Filter Corp., Palm Desert, Calif., 1999—. Mem. ABA, Internat. Bar Assn., U.K. Inst. Co. Secs., Am. Corp. Counsel Assn., Am. Soc. Corp. Secs., Ill. State Bar Assn. Office: US Filter Corp 14950 Heathrow Forrest Pkwy Ste 200 Houston TX 77032-3846

STANISLAWSKI, GARY M., state legislator; m. Dayna Stanislawski, 1982; 1 child, Shawn; 1 child, Kristie. BS in Bus. Admin., Oregon State U.; MA, Oral Roberts U. Pres. Regent Financial Services, Inc.; mem. Dist. 35 Okla. State Senate, 2008—. Pilot USAF, 1984—92. Mem.: Financial Planning Assn. Republican. Office: 2300 N Lincoln Blvd Rm 427A Oklahoma City OK 73105 Address: 6119 E 91st St Ste 300 Tulsa OK 74137 Office Phone: 405-521-5624, 918-493-4190. Business E-Mail: stanislawski@oksenate.gov.

STANKEY, JOHN T., telecommunications industry executive; b. Calif. m. Shari Stankey; 3 children. B in Fin., Loyola Marymount U., LA, 1985; MBA, UCLA, 1991. Exec. dir. advanced comm. network, local wholesale ops. Pacific Bell, 1985—98; v.p. industry markets SBC Comm. Inc., 1998—2000, pres. industry markets, 2000—02, pres., CEO SBC Southwestern Bell, 2002—03, sr. exec. v.p., chief tech. officer, 2003—06, AT&T Inc., 2006—07, grp. pres. ops. support, 2007, grp. pres. telecomm. ops., 2007—. Named one of Premier 100 IT Leaders, Computerworld, 2006, Top 25 Chief Tech. Officers, InfoWorld mag., 2006. Office: AT&T Inc 175 E Houston St San Antonio TX 78205

STANKEY, JOHN T., telecommunications industry executive; BA in Fin., Loyola Marymount U., 1985; MBA, UCLA, 1991. V.p. industry markets SBC Telecommunications, 1998; joined Pacific Bell, 1985, exec. dir. advanced comm. network; pres. industry markets SBC Southwest, 2000, pres., CEO, 2001; pres. bus. comm. svcs. SBC Southwestern Bell, 2001; sr. exec. v.p., chief info. officer SBC Comm., Inc.; sr. exec. v.p., chief tech. officer AT&T Inc. (merger of SBC Communications & AT&T Corp.), 2004, group pres. ops. support, group pres. telcom ops., 2007—08, pres., CEO AT&T Ops., Inc., 2008—10, pres., CEO bus. solutions, 2010—. Office: AT&T Inc 208 S Akard St Dallas TX 75202

STANLEY, MARGARET KING, performing arts administrator, educator, designer; b. San Antonio, Dec. 11, 1929; d. Creston Alexander and Margaret (Haymore) King; children: Torrey Margaret, Jean Cullen. Student, Mary Baldwin Coll., 1948-50; BA, U. Tex., Austin, 1952; MA, U. Incarnate Word, 1959. Cert. elem. tchr. Tex. Elem. tchr. San Antonio Ind. Sch. Dist., 1953-54, 55-56, Arlington County Schs., Va., 1954-55, Ft. Sam Houston Schs., San Antonio, 1956—58; art and art history tchr. St. Pius X Sch., San Antonio, 1959-60; originator, founding chairwoman Student Music Fair, San Antonio, 1963; English tchr. Trinity U., 1963-65; designer-mfr., owner CrisStan Clothes, Inc., San Antonio, 1967-73; founder, exec. dir. San Antonio Performing Arts Assn., 1976-92; founding chmn. Joffrey Workshop, San Antonio, 1979; radio host On Stage with Margaret Stanley Sta. KTRU-FM, San Antonio, 1983-98. Founder MKS Designs, 2002. Orginator with the Joffrey Ballet Jamboree, 1984. Mem. Met. Opera Nat. Coun., 1969—80, 2009—; founder Arts Coun. San Antonio, 1962, v.p., 1975, Originator Symphony Belles Program, 1972; pres. San Antonio Symphony League, 1971—74; v.p., founder San Antonio Opera Guild, 1974—, pres., 2002—05; bd. govs. Artists Alliance San Antonio, 1982; founding exec. dir. San Antonio Performing Arts Assn., 1968—90; founder San Antonio Early Music Festival, 1990—92; artistic advisor, dir. presentation, dir. devel. San Antonio Symphony, 1992—94; founding organizer Musica San Antonio, 1997—98; v.p. Instnl. Devel. Carver Cultural Ctr., 1998—2000; adv. bd. Hertzberg Circus Collection, San Antonio Dance Umbrella, Houston Early Music, Morgan-Scott Ballet, Hot Springs Mus. Festival; pres. Univ. Roundtable, 1995—97. Recipient Outstanding Tchr. award, Arlington County Sch. Dist., 1954, Emily Smith award for outstanding alumni, Mary Baldwin Coll., 1973, Today's Woman award, San Antonio Light Newspaper, 1980, Woman of the Yr. in Arts award, San Antonio Express News, 1983, Erasmus medal, Dutch Consulate, 1992, Mary Baldwin Sesquicentennial medallion, 1992, Opera Guild Founder's award, 2000, Vol. Achievement award, Opera Vols. Internat., 2005, Music Support award, Cactus Pear Festival, 2006, Hon. award, San Antonio Symphony League, 2010, Arts San Antonis award, 2014; named to Women's Hall of Fame, San Antonio, 1984, Disting. Alumnae, St. Mary's Hall, 1990; Tchg. fellow, Trinity U., San Antonio, 1964—66. Mem.: Founder Opera Guild Edn. Program, Opera Guild (v.p. edn. 2006—11), S.W. Performing Arts Presenters (chmn. 1988—92), Battle Flowers Assn., Jr. League San Antonio (Vol. Extraodinaire 2001), Women in Comm. (Headliner award 1982), Assn. Performing Arts Presenters (award for commn.of Jamboree 1984), Internat. Soc. for Performing Arts (hon.; regional rep. 1982—85, bd. dirs. 1991—97). Avocations: travel, reading, cooking, music, dance. Office Phone: 210-601-4855. Business E-Mail: mkingstanley@att.net.

STANLEY, SCOTT, JR., editor; b. Kansas City, July 11, 1938; s. Winfield Scott and Irene Mae (Flint) S.; m. Janice Johns, Aug. 30, 1959 (dec. July 1992); children: Leslie, Scott, Margaret; m. Cynthia Ward, Dec. 30, 1995; 1 child, Elizabeth. BA, Earlham Coll., 1960. Mng. editor Am. Opinion mag., Boston, 1961-85; editor Rev. of The News mag., Boston, 1965-85; editor-in-chief Conservative Digest, Washington, 1985-88, Am. Press Internat., Washington, 1987—; pres. USA Tech., 1991-92, 2006—; mng. editor Nutrition and Healing, 1994-2000; dep. editor Insight on the News, Washington, 1995—2005. Founding mem. nat. bd. dirs. Young Ams. for Freedom, 1960-62; public speaker and univ. lectr., 1962— Keynote speaker Am. Party Nat. Conv., 1976; pres. Ams. Legal Def. Fund, 1977—; bd. govs. Council for Nat. Policy, 1981—; nat. sec. bd. dirs. Free Congress Polit. Action Com., 1985-88, bd. trustees, nat. sec. Conservative Caucus Found., 2006—; pres. Scott Stanley Real Estate Trust, 1988— Recipient award of merit Young Ams. for Freedom, Freedom award Nat. Congress for Freedom. Mem.: Nat. Press Club. Episcopalian. Personal E-mail: scottstanley711@yahoo.com.

STANLEY, TIM, information technology executive; BS in Engring., U. Washington; degree in Internat. Bus. & Tech. Mgmt., Thunderbird U., Ariz. State U. CEO Innova Tech; mgr., Bus. Devel., Product Mgmt., Mktg. Intel Corp.; various positions, Internat. Rsch. & Devel., Med. and Consumer Products, Internat. Ops. Kimberly-Clark Corp.; v.p. info. sys. Nat. Airlines, chief info. officer, v.p., Info. Tech.; assic. ptnr. Optima/KPMG; ptnr. USWeb (now marchFIRST), USWeb / CKS; v.p., info. tech. devel. Harrah's Entertainment, Inc., Las Vegas, 2001—03, chief info. officer, sr. v.p., Innovation, Gaming, Tech., 2003; chmn., dir., Advisor & Investor Newco in Stealth / Startup mode; mem., Investor. Advisor Tech Coast Angels; pres. Tekexecs; prof., lectr., Paul Merage Sch. Bus. University of California, Irvine. Bd. dirs. Multimedia Games. With USAF. Named one of the Top 25 Unsung Heroes of the Internet, Interactive Week Mag., Top 25 Chief Tech. Officers, InfoWorld mag., 2006. Office: Multimedia Games Bldg B 4th Fl 206 Wild Basin Rd Austin TX 78746 Office Phone: 512-334-7500. Office Fax: 512-334-7695. Business E-Mail: tim.stanley@uci.edu.

STANLEY, WILLIAM MARTIN, JR., state legislator, lawyer; b. Milton, Fla., July 21, 1967; s. William Martin Sr. and Diane (Davies) S.; m. Lorraine Haire, Dec. 17, 1994. BA, Hampden-Sydney Coll., 1989; JD, D.C. Sch. law, 1994. Bar: Va. 1994, U.S. Dist. Ct. (we. and ea. dists.) Va. 1995, U.S. Ct. Appeals (4th cir.),1994. Assoc. atty. Davis & Assocs., Fairfax, Va., 1994-96, Cohen, Gettings, Dunham & Davis, Arlington, Va., 1996-98; ptnr. Davis & Stanley, LLC, Fairfax, Bird & Stanley, LLC, Moneta, Va., Stanley & Stanley, Moneta; mem. Dist. 19 Va. State Senate, Richmond, 2011—12, mem. Dist. 20, 2012—. Bd. dirs. The Paralegal Inst., Fairfax, 1991—, prof., 1991—; bd. dirs. Cambridge Sta. Assn., Farifax, 1996—. Mem. Fairfax City Rep. Com., 1996—. Mem. ATLA, Va. Trial Lawyers Assn., Fed. Bar Assn., Va. State Bar Assn. Methodist. Avocations: golf, fishing. Office: Senate of Virginia PO Box 396 Richmond VA 23218 also: Bird & Stanley LLC 13508 Booker T Washington Hwy Moneta VA 24121-5766 Office Phone: 804-698-7520, 540-721-6028. Office Fax: 540-721-6405. Business E-Mail: district20@senate.virginia.gov.

STANLEY-TURNER, LANETT LORRAINE, state legislator; b. Atlanta, Nov. 5, 1962; d. Archie and Ethel Francis (Dixon) S. BS, U. Tenn., 1985; postgrad., Carver Bible Coll., Atlanta, 1991—. State rep. Dist. 33, Ga., 1987—92; state rep. Dist. 50, 1993—2002; state rep. Dist. 43, 2003—04; state rep. Dist. 53, 2004—; vice chmn. Interstate Coop. Com.; sec. Rules Com.; mem. Ethics Com., Legislature & Congl. Reapportionment Com., Spl. Rules Com., Ways & Means Com.; journalist; cons. Mem. Nat. and Ga. Legis. Black Caucus, 1987. Bd. dirs. West End Med. Ctrs., Inc., 1988—, Southside Youth Athletic Acad. Assn., 1991—. Fellow: Nat. Orgn. State Legislators, Fulton County Young Dem., Christian Athletes; mem.: Assn. Black Communicators. Democrat. Baptist. Avocations: public speaking, swimming, bible study, travel, modeling. Mailing: 712 Gary Rd NW Atlanta GA 30318-6216 Office: 415 State Capitol Atlanta GA 30334 Office Phone: 404-794-8357, 404-656-5024. Business E-Mail: lstanley@legis.state.ga.us.

STANOS, PETER, healthcare company executive; Assoc. adminstr. & dir. Quality & Resource, Materials, Pharmacy & Risk Mgmt. HCA, 1997—2000, Triad Hosps. Inc., 1997—2000; chief quality officer Province Healthcare Corp., 2000—02, Havasu Regional Med. Ctr., regional dir., Quality & Resource Mgmt., 2000—03; dir., clin. ops. IASIS Healthcare, LLC, v.p., Ethics & Bus. Practices, 2003—; chief med. officer Physician Group Ariz., 2010—. Greek Orthodox. Office: Iasis Healthcare LLC Bldg E 117 Seaboard Ln Franklin TN 37067 Office Phone: 615-844-2747. Office Fax: 615-467-1270. Business E-Mail: pstanos@iasishealthcare.com.

STANTON, DONALD SHELDON, retired academic administrator; b. Balt., June 8, 1932; s. Kenneth Gladstone and Dorothy Erma (Hetrick) S.; m. Barbara Mae Hoot, June 25, 1955; children: Dale Richard, Debra Carol, Diane Karen. AB, Western Md. Coll., 1953; Litt.D., Oglethorpe U., 1999; LLD, Western Md. Coll., 1981; MDiv magna cum laude, Wesley Theol. Sem., 1956; MA, Am. U., 1960; Ed.D., U. Va., 1965; L.H.D., Columbia Coll., 1979; Litt.D., Albion Coll., 1983. Ordained to ministry United Methodist Ch., 1956; pastor Balt. and Va. confs. United Meth. Ch., 1953-59; dir. Richmond (Va.) Area Wesley Found., 1959-63; chaplain, dean of students Greensboro Coll., 1963-65; chaplain Wofford Coll., 1965-69; dir. office coll. services United Meth. Div. Higher Edn., Nashville, 1969-75; v.p. for devel. Wesleyan Coll., 1975-78; pres. Adrian Coll., 1978-88, Oglethorpe U., Atlanta, 1988-99, pres. emeritus, 1999—; interim pres. Haywood Cmty. Coll., 2005—06. Adminstr., prof. European internat. ednl. programs, summers 1960, 69-71, 73; chmn. pres.'s assn. Mich. Intercollegiate Athletic Assn., 1986-87. Contbr. articles, revs. to profl. publs. in U.S., Japan, Argentina, chpts. to books; editor: Faculty Forum, 1972-74; bass-baritone soloist. Bd. dirs. Toledo Symphony, 1980-83, Lewanee County Jr. Achievement, 1980-83, Found. Ind. Higher Edn., 1996-99, Nat. Conf. for Cmty. and Justice, Atlanta Region, Atlanta Area coun. Boy Scouts Am.; chair bd. trustees U. Ctr. Ga., 1994-96; chair So. Collegiate Athletic Conf., 1994-95. Adminstrn. bldg. at Adrian Coll. named in honor of Stanton and his wife, 1988. Mem. Am. Assn. Univ. Adminstrs. (bd. dirs. 1990-93), Ga. Assn. Colls. (pres. 1992), Soc. Wesley (Disting. Alumni Recognition award 1988), Ga. Found. for Ind. Colls. (vice chair 1992), Nat. Assn. Ind. Colls. and Univs. (past mem. pub. rels. com.), Assn. Pvt. Colls.

and Univs. Ga. (treas. 1996-97), Lake Junalusha Assembly (bd. dir. 2008-), Rotary, Omicron Delta Kappa, Order of Omega, Tau Kappa Epsilon, Psi Chi, Phi Eta Sigma. Home: 312 Tillman Rd Lake Junaluska NC 28745-9779 Personal E-mail: stantons2@earthlink.net.

STANTON, EDWARD LESLEY, III, federal prosecutor; b. Memphis, Tenn., 1972; BA, U. Memphis, 1994, JD, 1997. Bar: Tenn. 1997, US Dist. Ct. (we. dist.) Tenn., US Dist. Ct. (so. dist.) Tex., US Dist. Ct. (ea. dist.) Mo. 2003, US Dist. Ct. (no. dist.) Tex., US Ct. Appeals (5th cir.), US Ct. Appeals (2nd cir.). Law clk. Office Legal Counsel U. Memphis, 1995—97; law clk. to Hon. James E. Swearengen Cir. Ct. of Shelby County, Memphis, 1996—97; assoc. atty. Law Offices of Charles E. Carpenter, PC, 1997—2000; asst. city atty. Law Divsn. City of Memphis, 2000—01; assoc. atty. Armstrong Allen PLLC, 2001—02; sr. counsel Litig. Dept. Fed. Express Corp., 2002—10; US atty. (western dist.) Tenn. US Dept. Justice, 2010—. Contbr. articles to law jours. Vol. AmeriCorps, 1994; bd. mem. Memphis-Shelby County Ctr. City Commn., 2005—, bd. sec., 2008—09; bd. mem. Memphis Ctr. City Devel. Corp., 2008—09. Fellow: Memphis and Shelby County Bar Found.; mem.: NAACP, ABA, Am. Inn of Cts., Fed. Bar Assn., Tenn. Bar Assn., Memphis Bar Assn., Nat. Bar Assn. - Ben F. Jones Chap. Office: US Attorneys Office 167 N Main St, Ste 800 Memphis TN 38103 Office Phone: 901-544-4231. Office Fax: 901-544-4230.*

STANTON, JOHN JEFFREY, editor, director, journalist, non profit administrator educator; b. Wichita Falls, Tex., July 19, 1956; s. John Joseph Jr. and Joan (Marley) S.; m. Scylla Maria Silva, Jan. 6, 1981; 1 child, Damien Kristian. BS in Pub. Adminstrn. and Bus. Adminstrn., Nichols Coll., 1978; M in Pub. Adminstrn., U. Detroit, 1980. Rsch. asst. Am. Enterprise Inst., Washington, 1977; rep. aide R.I. Ho. of Reps., Providence, 1977-78; mng. editor Am. Politics, Washington, 1982, assoc. editor, 1983, corp. advisor, 1984, sr. editor, 1985-87; editor, govt. programs mgr. ENTEK, Alexandria, Va., 1988-90; govt. programs dir., cons. Tech. Group, Springfield, Va., 1991; analyst, writer Nat. Security Issues, Arlington, Va., 1991—; program dir. Comm. Group, McLean, Va., 1991—93; Washington corr., mem. editl. bd. Tech. Transfer Jour., 1994-98; editor Tech. Transfer Newsletter; asst. to pres., info. transfer specialist Am. Def. Preparedness Assn., Arlington, 1994-97; contbg. writer Nat. Def. Mag., 1996—2004; adminstrn. dir. Nat. Def. Indsl. Assn., Arlington, 1997—2004; Washington corr. Australian Def. Mag., 1998-99; editor Voice of the Indsl. Base NDIA, 1998—2000; tchr., adminstr. St. Stephens & Agnes, 2005—; rsch. assoc. Rsch. Inst. for European and Am. Studies, 2006—; mem. Triangle Inst. for Security Studies, 2007—, Internat. Inst. Strategic Studies. Creator, co-host (radio) Power Breakfast, Sta. WNTR, Washington, 1987, Am. Politics Radio, 1987; commentator WAMU-NPR, WBAL, KPFA, Am. Talk Live, NYC, Radio 101, Croatia, Radio Adelaide, KCMO, Kansas City, WNTR, WAMU, WBAC, Balt.; polit.-mil. analyst CBS News, CNN, ABC, 2001—, Russia TV Today. Author: A Power But Not Super, 2004, Talking Politics with God and the Devil in Washington, DC, 2007, The Inside Story of the US Army's Human Terrain System, 2009, The Raptor's Eye, JIEDDO, MISO, General P and The Prophet Smith, 2012, Cyber Noodles, Orphan Nukes and the Failure of the US National Security State, 2013; co-author: America's Nightmare, 2003; contbr. articles to profl. jours., popular mags. Polit. campaign cons. to Glenn Tenney, 1992—; commr. Arlington Little League Baseball, 1993, coach 1997—; mentor Arlington County Ct. Sys., 1997; varsity football coach Wakefield H.S., Arlington, Va., 1998-2002, St. Stephen's Agnes, 2003—. Recipient Doers Honoree The Washington Times, 1988. Mem.: IG, INSA, NDIA (life). Avocation: coaching youth sports programs. Office: St Stephens St Agnes 1000 St Stphenn Rd Alexandria VA 22304 Office Phone: 703-212-2774. Personal E-mail: cioran123@yahoo.com. Business E-Mail: jstanton@sssas.org.

STANTON, MICHAEL J., lobbyist; BA in English, Wheeling Jesuit Coll., W.Va.; MSA in Fin. Mgmt., George Wash. U., Washington. Fed. & state issues rep. Motor Vehicle Manufacturers Assn.; dir. fed. govt. affairs American Automobile Manufacturers Assn.; v.p. govt. and internat. affairs Alliance Automobile Manufactures Assn.; pres., CEO Assn. Internat. Automobile Manufacturers. Active mem. of several auto-industry related boards; expert on issues affecting the auto industry. Officer USN, Vietnam. Named a Govt. Affairs All-Star, Automotive News, 2008; named one of Washington's Top Lobbyists, The Hill, 2010. Office: Assn Internat Automobile Manufacturers 2111 Wilson Blvd Ste 1150 Arlington VA 22201 Office Phone: 703-525-7788. Office Fax: 703-525-8817.

STANTON, ROBERT PAGE, orthopedic surgeon; b. Aurora, Colo., 1948; s. Donald Raymond and Elizabeth Mary Stanton; m. Betty Ruth Williams, June 0, 1970; children: Christopher Graeme, Steven Donald, Scott Phillip, Amanda Page. BS, U. Fla., Gainesville, 1970, MD, 1976. Diplomate Am. Bd. Orthpedic Surgery, 1981. Surgeon in chief Nemours Childrens Clinic, Pensacola, Fla., 2003—. Contbr. articles to various med. jours. Col. Nat. Guard US Army, 2001—07, Del. Fellow: ACS, Am. Acad. Orthop. Surgeons; mem.: Pediatric Orthop. Soc. N.Am. Office: Nemours Childrens Clinic 5153 N 9th Ave Pensacola FL 32504

STAPLES, DONALD EDWARD, radio, film and television educator; b. NYC, Apr. 15, 1934; s. Edward Daniel and Ethlyne Babcock Staples; m. Diane Staunton, June 2, 1956 (div. July 1980); children: Douglas Arthur, Daniel Charles; m. Kristen Petersen, Nov. 26, 1982; stepchildren: Julia Lynn Smith, Susan Smith Milner. BS in Speech, Northwestern U., 1955; MA in Cinema, U. So. Calif., 1959; PhD, Northwestern U., 1967. Instr. So. Ill. U., Carbondale, 1959-63; lectr. Northwestern U., Evanston, Ill., 1963-65; asst. prof. Ohio State U., Columbus, 1965-68, assoc. prof., 1968-69; prof. NYU, NYC, 1969-79, Vassar Coll., Poughkeepsie, N.Y., 1972-74, U. North Tex., Denton, 1979—2004, prof. emeritus, 2004—. Author, editor: American Cinema, 3d edit., 1991; co-author: Film Encounter, 1973; contbr. articles, film revs. to profl. jours. Mem. Greater Denton Arts Coun., 1980—, Denton Cmty. Theatre, 1980—; bd. dirs. Nat. Mus. Comms., Irving, Tex., 1983-93; juror film festivals, 1969—; mem. adv. bd. Arts and Humanities Citation Index, Phila., 1979—. Lt. (j.g.) USN, 1955-57. Univ. scholar U. So. Calif., 1957-59, Northwestern U., 1963-65; Danforth Found. assoc., 1968-85. Mem. SAG, Soc. for Cinema Studies (pres. 1974-75), Univ. Film and Video Assn. (pres. 1975-77, life mem.), Internat. Congress of Schs. of Film and TV (v.p. 1982-86), Univ. Film and Video Found. (trustee emeritus), Dallas Corinthian Yacht Club (bd. dirs. 1995-98). Methodist. Avocations: sailing, golf. Home: 2901 Montecito Dr Denton TX 76205-8513 Office: U North Tex Dept Radio/TV/Film Denton TX 76203 Personal E-mail: dkstaples2@verizon.net.

STAPLES, GARY VICTOR, state legislator; b. Laurel, Miss., Jan. 16, 1940; m. Betty Norton. Former mem. bd. edn. Jones Co.; mem. Dist. 88 Miss. House of Reps., 1988—92, 2004—; technician S Cent Bell. Mem.: Nat. Rifle Assn., Cmty. Concert Assn., America Legion, Vol. Fire Dept., Jr Livestock Assn., Farm Bur., Miss & Jones Co. Cattlemen's Assn. Republican. Baptist. Mailing: 366 Forest Rd Laurel MS 39443 Home Phone: 601-649-4972; Office Phone: 601-359-2434. E-mail: gstaples@house.ms.gov.

STAPLETON, HARVEY JAMES, physics professor; b. Kalamazoo, Dec. 22, 1934; s. Herbert James and Viola Delia (Early) S.; m. Joan Eilleen Sylvander, June 22, 1957; children: Patricia Lynne, Susan Joan, Jeffrey Denis. BS, U. Mich., 1957; PhD, U. Calif., Berkeley, 1961. Faculty physics U. Ill., Urbana, 1961—, prof., 1969-95, prof. emeritus, 1995—, assoc. dean Grad. Coll., 1980-95, assoc. vice chancellor for rsch., 1987-95; interim dean Grad. Coll., 1992; interim vice chancellor for rsch. U. Ill., 1992. Alfred P. Sloan fellow, 1962-64 Contbr. articles to profl. jours. Fellow Am. Phys. Soc.; mem. Phi Beta Kappa, Sigma Xi, Phi Sigma Kappa, Phi Kappa Phi, Phi Eta Sigma. Roman Catholic. Home: 3806 Gulf Of Mexico Dr Unit 310 Longboat Key FL 34228-2733 Personal E-mail: hjstapleton@comcast.net.

STARCHER, LARRY VICTOR, retired state supreme court justice; b. Rocksdale, W.Va., Sept. 25, 1942; m. Rebecca Wiles; children: Mollianne, Victor, Amy. AB cum laude, W.Va. U., 1964, JD, 1967. Bar: W.Va. 1967. Judge and chief judge W.Va. Ct. (17th jud. cir.), 1977—96; justice W.Va. Supreme Ct. Appeals, 1997—2008, chief justice, 1999, 2003. Pvt. practice, Morgantown, 1976—; dir. North Ctrl. W.Va. Legal Aid Soc., 1969-76; former instr. law, pub. adminstrn., and history W.Va. U.; contract adminstr. W.Va. U., 1966-67, asst. to v.p., 1967-69. Editor W.Va. Law Rev.; contbr. articles to profl. jours. Mem. City Coun. Morgantown, 1971-72; mem. W.Va. Martin Luther King, Jr. Holiday Commn. Fellow Harvard U., summer 1978. Mem. ATLA, Am. Correctional Assn., W.Va. Jud. Assn., W.Va. State Bar, Monongalia County Bar Assn., Kanawha County Bar Assn., Conf. Chief Justices, Beta Theta Pi, Phi Delta Phi, Phi Alpha Theta, Pi Sigma Alpha. Avocations: carpentry, gardening.

STARGEL, KELLI, state legislator; b. Tampa, Fla., Mar. 23, 1966; m. John Stargel; 5 children. Grad., Tallahassee Cmty. Coll., 1991. Mem. Dist. 64 Fla. House of Reps., 2008—, vice chair preK-12 appropriations com., mem. edn. policy coun., preK-12 policy com., pub. safety and domestic security policy com. Mem. Achievement Acad. Adv. Bd., Commn. Marriage & Family Support Initiatives. Mem.: USF Adv. Bd., The Well of Central Fla., Rep. Women's Club Lakeland. Republican. Baptist. Office: 405 House Office Bldg 402 S Monroe St Tallahassee FL 32399-1300 also: 2000 E Edgewood Ste 109 Lakeland FL 33803-3639 Mailing: PO Box 2839 Lakeland FL 33806-2839 Office Phone: 850-488-2270, 863-614-9156. Business E-Mail: kelli.stargel@myfloridahouse.gov.

STARKE, HAROLD EUGENE, JR., lawyer; b. Richmond, Va., Aug. 1, 1944; BA, Randolph-Macon Coll., Ashland, Va., 1967; JD, U. Richmond, 1971; LLM in Taxation, NYU, 1973. Bar: Va. 1971, DC 1981. Ret. ptnr. Troutman Sanders LLP, Richmond, 1977—2011. Adj. prof. law Wash. and Lee Law Sch. Editor U. Richmond Law Rev., 1970-71. Bd. trustees Randolph-Macon Coll., 1983-85, 95-97, 99—11. Fellow Am. Coll. Tax Counsel, Am. Bar Found., Va. State Bar (chmn. taxation sect. 1985-86), DC Bar, Richmond Estate Planning Coun., McNeill Honor Soc., Phi Delta Phi. Office: Troutman Sanders LLP Troutman Sanders Bldg 1001 Haxall Point PO Box 1122 Richmond VA 23218-1122 Office Phone: 804-697-1287.

STARKEY, BOB (ROBERT G. STARKEY), women's college basketball coach; b. Sept. 7, 1959; m. Sherie Hayslett. Asst. coach Winfield HS, W.Va. Coll., 1984—87, Poca HS, W.Va.; asst. coach women's basketball Marshall U., Huntington, W.Va., 1988—89; asst. coach men's basketball La. State U., 1990—96, adminstrv. asst. men's and women's basketball, 1996—97, asst. coach women's basketball, 1998—2007, acting head coach women's basketball, 2007, assoc. head coach, 2007—11; asst. coach U. Ctrl. Fla., 2011—. Office: University Ctrl Fla Womens Basketball 4000 Central Florida Blvd Orlando FL 32816-3555 Office Phone: 407-823-5807. Business E-Mail: bstarkey@athletics.ucf.edu.

STARKEY, ELIZABETH LARUFFA, accountant; b. Franklin, Ky., May 23, 1947; d. Albert A. LaRuffa and Alma L. (Duer) LaRuffa (dec.); m. Jerry L. Starkey, June 14, 1969; children: James, Jonathan. AA, Miami-Dade Jr. Coll., 1967; BS in Math., Fla. State U., 1969; MS in Acctg., U. Houston, 1984. CPA; cert. math. tchr. Tchr. Dade County, Miami, Fla., 1969-75; mgr. Ernst & Young, Houston, 1984-90, Starkey & Co., Houston, 1990—2008; E.C. Starkey CPA, 2009—. Bd. dirs. St. Thomas HS Found., 1994—2000, Miami-Dade CC Found., 1997—99, Am. Cancer Soc., Houston, 1985—87, 1990—2000, mem. legacy and planned giving com.; mem. Houston Estate and Fin. Forum. Mem.: AICPA, Tex. Soc. CPAs (Houston chpt.), U. Houston Alumni Orgn. (treas. 2000—03, bd. dirs. 2000—06, planned giving adv. bd. 2007—), Omicron Delta Kappa, Beta Alpha Psi, Beta Gamma Sigma. Roman Catholic. Home: 4410 Merwin St Houston TX 77027-6714 Office: Elizabeth Starkey CPA PO Box 22548 Houston TX 77227-2548 Office Phone: 713-877-8488. Personal E-mail: elizabethstarkey@hotmail.com.

STARKEY, JERRY L., real estate developer; BBA, North Tex. State U., Denton; JD, Tex. Tech. U., Lubbock. Bar: Tex. Pres., sec. Fla. Design Cmtys., 1994—2005, Ashton Care Sys. Inc., 1996—98; COO Watermark Communities LP (WCI), Bonita Springs, Fla., 1998—2005, pres., CEO, 2005—. Bd. trustees Fla. Gulf Coast Univ., 2001—. Office: Watermark Communities LP (WCI) 24301 Walden Ctr Dr Bonita Springs FL 34134 Office Phone: 239-947-2600. Business E-Mail: jerry.starkey@wci.wcicommunities.com.

STARKS, CHARLES WILEY, minister; b. Bastian, Va., June 27, 1954; s. Clarence Eugene and Mattiline Mae (Compton) S.; m. Angela D. Marshall; 1 child, Olivia Grace Starks. BA, Emory and Henry Coll., 1976; MDiv, Emory Univ., 1979, D of Ministry, 1988. Lic. to ministry, 1972; ordained to ministry United Meth. Ch. as deacon, 1977, as elder, 1981. Pers. recruiter and trainer A Christian Ministry in the Nat. Parks, NYC, 1979—80; min. Meadowview United Meth. Ch., Meadowview, Va., 1980—84, Pleasant View United Meth. Ch., Abingdon, Va., 1984—93, First United Meth. Ch., Newport, Tenn., 1993—97, Asbury United Meth. Ch., Greeneville, Tenn., 1997—2002; supt. Wytheville dist. United Meth. Ch., Va., 2002—09, dean Holston Conf. Cabinet, 2006—07; sr. pastor First United Methodist Ch., Morristown, Tenn., 2009—. Adj. prof. of philosophy/religion Va. Highlands Cmty. Coll., Abingdon, 1986-93; coord. Abingdon Dist. Youth, 1980-84; New Life Missioner, 1983—; apptd. counseling elder Holston Conf., supervising pastor, 1985—; mem. Abingdon Dist. Com. on Superintendency, 1985-93, Holston Conf. Bd. of Ordained Ministry exec. com., 1985-92, chmn. psychol. testing and assessment com., 1987-92, com. on the Episcopacy, 1990-97, task force on conf. strategy and structure for ministry and mission, 1990-92; mem. alumni exec. com. Candler Sch. Theology; dean Holston Conf. Cabinet, 2006-07. Vol. Big Bro., Washington County Big Bro./Big Sister Orgn., 1985-88; chmn. Washington County Office on Youth Svcs. Citizens Bd., 1988-90; mem. Washington County Commonwealth Alliance for Drug Rehab. and Edn., 1989-90, Washington County Multi-Discipline Bd., 1989-90, Washington County Fed. Emergency Mgmt. Authority Bd., 1987-93; mem. bio-med. ethics com. Johnston Meml. Hosp., 1991-93; bd. dirs. Holston Home for Children, 1993-97; bd. trustees Hiwassee Coll., 1997-2003; mem. Helping Overcome Poverty's Existence, 2004-09, vice chair, bd. dirs.; chaplain Morristown-Hamblen County C. of C., 2010-11; mem. Leadership Morristown, 2010; mem. bd. dirs. Ministerial Area Temporary Shelter, 2011-, Tri Vista Villas Homeowners' Assoc., 2009-, pres. bd. dirs., 2011-; mem. Morristown-Hamblen County C. of C. Bd Tourism, 2011-. Named to Outstanding Young Men in Am., 1985, Chaplain of Day US Senate, Washington, 1989, 2009. Mem. United Meth. Assn. of Ch. Bus. Adminstrs., Kiwanis (religious affairs com. 1988), Mason, others. Home: 2295 Regency Cir Morristown TN 37814-2796 Office: First United Methodist Ch 101 E First N St Morristown TN 37814 Office Phone: 423-581-2180.

STARKWEATHER, FREDERICK THOMAS, retired data processing executive; b. Sioux City, Iowa, Feb. 24, 1933; s. Fred Ervin and Gertrude Faye (Madden) S.; m. Margot Glassen, Nov. 19, 1959; children: Thomas Frederick, Jerry Russell, Michael Glassen. BA in Math. and Physics, U. Nebr., Omaha, 1955. Mathematician Flight Determination Lab., White Sands Missile Range, N.Mex., 1955-56; supervisory mathematician Analysis & Computation, White Sands Missile Range, 1956-81; chief data scis. divsn. Nat. Range Ops., White Sands Missile Range, 1981—93; co-owner B and T Managed Care, LLC, 2001—; owner The Spotlight Restaurant, 2002—12; part owner KCKM-Am. Radio; co-owner KTXO FM Radio, Vis. Angels of the Permian Basin, 2010—12. Nat. coun. rep. Am. Def. Preparedness Assn., Washington, 1980-93; pres. White Sands Pioneer Group, White Sands Missile Range, 1983-86; bd. dirs. Assn. U.S. Army, Washington. Author hist. and geneal. books; contbr. book revs. and articles to newspapers and mags. Chmn. El Paso City Planning Commn., Tex., 1980-84; bd. dirs. El Paso County Hist. Soc., 1983-87; active El Paso County Hist. Commn., 1983-2000. With USAR, 1955-63. Recipient Profl. Secs. Internat. Exec. of Yr. award, 1987, Conquistador award City of El Paso, 1980; named Disting. Alumnus U. Nebr., Omaha, 1985; named to Hon. Order of St. Barbara U.S. Field Arty. Assn., 1988; cited for svcs. to mankind El Paso chpt. Sertoma, 1985. Mem. Fed. Mgrs. Assn. (bd. dirs.), Freedom Found. at Valley Forge (pres. El Paso chpt., George Washington Hon. medal 1982), El Paso C. of C. (assoc. dir. 1984-92, bd. dirs.), Toastmasters (dist. gov. 1970-71), Masons, Tau Kappa Epsilon (Hall of Fame 1986). Avocations: coin collecting/numismatics, genealogy, reading. Home Phone: 915-449-5082.

STARLING, LARRY EUGENE, consultant; s. Thomas Edward and Montoria (Dickson) S.; m. Deborah Denise Askins, Sept. 8, 1984; children: Ryan Thomas, Sean Michael. BS, Tenn. State U., 1979. Tax auditor III State Tenn., Nashville, 1979-83; tax analyst No. Telecom Inc., Nashville, 1983-90; state tax specialist Burlington Industries, Inc., Greensboro, NC, 1990—2007, Psychiatric Solutions Inc., 2007—10, Universal Health Svc., 2010—11; contractor, 2012—. Avocations: tennis, bass. Personal E-mail: istarlin@att.net.

STARNES, CLARKE R., III, bank executive; b. Greenville, NC, July 29, 1959; BSBA, U. NC, Chapel Hill; attended, U. Del. Joined BB&T Corp. (Branch Banking and Trust Co.), 1982, with, loan officer devel. program, credit analyst dept., regional loan adminstr., corp. accts., direct retail lending risk mgr., various positions including bus. svcs. mgr., regional sr. credit officer, mgr., Specialized Lending Group, 2000—08, chief credit officer, 2008—09, sr. exec. v.p., chief risk officer, 2008—. Dir., Consumer Credit Counseling Svcs. Forsyth County, NC; mem. New Hope Presbyterian Ch., Clemmons, NC; mem., Regulatory Rels. Coun. Risk Mgmt. Assn.; bd. dirs. Consumer Bankers Assn. Office: BB&T Corp 200 W Second St Winston Salem NC 27101 Office Phone: 336-733-2000. Office Fax: 336-721-3499. Business E-Mail: cstarnes.iii@bbrandt.com.

STARNES, EARL MAXWELL, retired urban and regional planner, architect, educator; b. Winter Haven, Fla., Sept. 14, 1926; s. Thomas Lowe and Kathryn Maxwell (Gates) Starnes; m. Dorothy Jean Prather, Aug. 21, 1949; children: Tom, Will, Janet, Patricia. Student, Fla. So. Coll., 1946—48; BArch cum laude, U. Fla., 1951; MS in Urban and Regional Planning, Fla. State U., 1973, PhD, 1977. Registered arch., Fla. Assoc. Courtney Stewart, Ft. Lauderdale, Fla., 1951-52, William Bigoney, Ft. Lauderdale, 1952-53, William T. Vaughn, Ft. Lauderdale, 1953, Alfred B. Parker, Miami, Fla., 1953-55, Rufus Nims, Miami, 1955-57; ptnr. Starnes & Rentscher, Miami, 1957-63, Starnes, Rentscher & Assocs., Miami, 1963-71; dir. divsn. mass transp. Fla. Dept. Transp., Tallahassee, 1971-72; dir. divsn. state planning Fla. Dept. Adminstrn., 1972-75; engaged in rsch. and cons. svc. Tallahassee, 1975; prof., chmn. urban and regional planning Coll. Architecture U. Fla., Gainesville, 1976-88, prof. urban and regional plan coord., doctoral studies, 1989-93, prof. emeritus, 1993—. Instr. architecture U. Miami, 1953; adj. asst. prof. dept. urban and regional planning Coll. Social Scis., Fla. State U., 1971—74; mem. adv. panel B8-15 Nat. Coop. Hwy. Rsch. Program, Transp. Rsch. Bd., NRC-Nat. Acad. Scis., 1974—; mem. adv. bd. Pub. Tech., Inc., 1974—; mem. N. Ctrl. Fla. Regional Planning Com., 1980—85, Fla. Substate Dist. Com., 1985—87; co-chmn. Joint Liaison Com. Divsn. Responsibility Urban Svcs., Dade County, Fla., 1965—71; chmn. joint policy com. U. Miami-Dade County Jackson Med. Ctr., 1966—71; chmn. Cape Fla. State Pk. Adv. Coun., 1966—69, Dade County Landscape Ordinance Study Com., 1967—70, S. Fla. Everglades Area Planning Coun., 1969—71; vis. lectr. Calif. Poly. State U., San Luis Obispo, 1988—89; cons. Urban Planning Fla. and Caribbean. Prin. works include 1st Unitarian Ch., Miami; co-author: Growth Management, 1992, Rural Sustainability in America, 1996; co-author: (with Richard Rubino) History of Planning in Florida, 2008; contbr. articles to profl. jours., chapters to books. Active Nat. Task Force Natural Resources and Land Use Info. and Tech., 1973—74, Cape Fla. Acquisition Com., 1966, South Dade Mental Health Soc., 1967—68, Dade County Downtown Govtl. Ctr. Com., 1967—71, Miami Downtown Devel. Authority, 1970, Gov.'s Task Force Resource Mgmt., 1971—72, Fla. Gov.'s Commn. Property Rights, 1993—94, Fla. Greenway's Commn., 1991—93, Fla. Greenway Coordinating Coun., 1998—99; bd. dirs., chmn. retirement and compensation com. State Assn. County Commrs., 1968—71; mem. Alachua County Budget Study Com., 1978, Fla. Land Use Adv. Com. Phosphate Lands, 1978—80, Suwanee River Water Mgmt. Bd., 1982—87, 1991—98, chmn., 1987—88, Fla. Inst. Phosphate Rsch., 1984—87; bd. dirs. 1000 Friends Fla., 1986—2003; mem. gov.'s adv. commn. coastal mgmt., 1997; county commr. Dist. 7 Dade County, 1964—71; vice mayor, 1964, 1968. With USCG, 1944—46. Fellow: AIA (urban design com. 1976—80), Assn. Collegiate Schs. Planning (bd. dirs. 1986—88), Nat. Inst. Bldg. Scis. (steering com. for rsch. 1979—80), Am. Inst. Cert. Planners, Gargoyle Soc.; mem.: Phi Kappa Phi. Democrat. Unitarian Universalist. Office: PO Box 234 Cedar Key FL 32625-0234 Personal E-mail: earldorothy@bellsouth.net.

STARNES, EDGAR VANCE, state legislator; b. Hickory, NC, Sept. 3, 1956; s. Ray Coolidge and Sara Capshaw Starnes; m. Marilyn Starnes. Farmer, Granite Falls, NC, 1978—; chmn. Caldwell County Young Rep., 1979—80, Young Rep. State Archives, 1980; mem. Caldwell County Rep. Exec. Com., 1979—87, Agr. Stabilization & Conservation Svc. Com., 1981—84; state rep. Dist. 46 NC, 1987—89; state rep. Dist. 91, 1997—2002; state rep. Dist. 87, 2002—; investment broker. Mem.: Blue Key, Coble Dairy Young Co-operators (bd. dir. 1985—), Caldwell County Farm Bur. Republican. Southern Baptist. Office: North Carolina House of Representatives 300 N Salisbury St Rm 419A Raleigh NC 27603-5925 Office Phone: 919-733-5931. Business E-Mail: Edgar.Starnes@ncleg.net.

STARNES, WILLIAM HERBERT, JR., chemist, educator; b. Knoxville, Tenn., Dec. 2, 1934; s. William Herbert and Edna Margaret (Osborne) Starnes; m. Maria Sofia Molina, Mar. 4, 1986. Attended, Union Coll., Ky., 1950—52; BS with honors, Va. Poly. Inst., Blacksburg, 1955; PhD, Ga. Inst. Tech., Atlanta, 1960; DSc (hon.), Union Coll., Ky., 2013. Rsch. chemist Esso Rsch. & Engring. Co., Baytown, Tex., 1960—62, sr. rsch. chemist, 1962—64, polymer additives sect. head, 1964—65, rsch. specialist, 1965—67, rsch. assoc., 1967—71; instr. and rsch. assoc. dept. chemistry U. Tex., Austin, 1971—73; mem. tech. staff AT&T Bell Labs., Murray Hill, NJ, 1973—85; prof. chemistry Poly. U., Bklyn., 1985—89, head dept. chemistry and life scis., 1985—88, assoc. dir. polymer durability ctr., 1987—89; Floyd Dewey Gottwald Sr. prof. chemistry Coll. William and Mary, Williamsburg, Va., 1989—2006, Floyd Dewey Gottwald Sr. prof. chemistry emeritus, 2006—, prof. applied sci., 1990—2006. Invited lectr. nineteen fgn. countries and US; ofcl. guest USSR Acad. Scis., 1990, Russian Acad. Scis., 1992; disting. vis. prof. Beijing Inst. Tech., 1996; vis. scientist Tex. Acad. Scis., 1964—67; mem. bd. doctoral thesis examiners Indian Inst. Tech., New Delhi, 1988, McGill U., Montreal, 1989, MacQuarie U., Sydney, 1991, McMaster U., Hamilton, Canada, 1994; panelist, reviewer NSF Acad. Rsch. Facilities Modernization Program, 1990; channel program mentor U. Cairo, 1994—95; mem. opinion leader panel Wall St. Jour., 1995—; charter mem. dept. chemistry adv. coun. Va. Poly. Inst. and State U., 1998—; sci. advisor European Multinational Environ. Rsch. Project on PVC in Soil and Landfills, 1995—99; cons. numerous indsl. cos., govtl. and pvt. agys.; course dir. continuing edn. Editor-in-chief: Jour. Vinyl and Additive Tech., 1998—, mem. adv. bd., bd. reviewers: Jour. Vinyl Tech., 1981—83, mem. editl. bd.: Jour. Chem. and Biochem. Kinetics, 1992—, Polymer Degradation and Stability, 1997—, Internat. Jour. Coatings Sci., 2001—, The Chemist, 2003—, guest editor: Procedia Chemistry, 2012; contbr. chapters to books, articles to profl. jours. Recipient Profl. Progress award, Soc. Profl. Chemists and Engrs., 1968, Disting. Tech. Staff award, AT&T Bell Labs., 1982, Polymer Sci. Pioneer award, Polymer News, 1988, Honor Scroll award, N.J. Inst. Chemists, 1989, Excellence in Innovation award, Hampton Rds. Tech. Coun., 2004, Outstanding Alumnus, Ga. Inst. Tech. Sch. Chemistry and Biochemistry, 2012; named honoree Plastics History and Artifacts Program, Plastics Pioneers Assn., 2001, Disting. Alumni Scholar, Union Coll., 2009, Hon. Order of Ky. Cols., 2009; named to Southwest Va. Walk of Fame, 2008, Hall of Distinction, Va. Tech. Coll. Sci., 2013; grantee, NSF, 1989—, Nat. Bur. Stds. Ctr. Fire Rsch., Internat. Copper Rsch. Assn., Va. Ctr. Innovative Tech., GenCorp Found., several indsl. cos.; fellow, NSF, 1958—60. Fellow: AAAS (Project 2061 1985—86, chmn. chemistry subpanel 1985—86, mem. panel on phys. scis. and engring. 1985—86), Soc. Plastics Engrs. (nat. pubis. com. 1998—2001, 2006—, Best Thesis Advisor Nat. award vinyl plastics divsn. 1996, 1998, ANTEC Best Student Paper Advisor Nat. award vinyl plastics divsn. 2007, ANTEC Best Paper Nat. award vinyl plastics divsn. 2009, Tech. Contbns. Vinyl Nat. award 2009, ANTEC Best Tech. Paper Nat. award Vinyl Plastics Divsn. 2011, Elliott Weinberg Vinyl Commn. Nat. award 2011, hon. grantee), NY Acad. Scis., Am. Inst. Chemists (life); mem.: Legacy Soc. Union Coll., Soc. Chem. Industry, Va. Acad. Sci., Am. Chem. Soc. (bd. dirs. southeastern Tex. sect. 1970, spkrs. bur. divsn. polymer chemistry 1976—, mem.-at-large exec. com. Va. sect. 1995), N.Am. Thermal Analysis Soc., Ut Prosim Soc. Va. Tech, Phi Lambda Upsilon (pres. Va. Poly. Inst. chpt. 1954—55), Sigma Xi (M. A. Ferst award Ga. Inst. Tech. chpt. 1960), Phi Kappa Phi (life). Achievements include patents in field; invention of ester thiol stabilization technology for poly(vinyl chloride); research in degradation, stabilization, flammability, microstructures and polymerization mechanisms of synthetic polymers, especially poly(vinyl chloride); mechanistic organic chemistry and free radical chemistry; carbon-13 nuclear magnetic resonance and organic synthesis; subspecialities include organic chemistry, polymer chemistry. Office: Coll William and Mary Dept Chemistry PO Box 8795 Williamsburg VA 23187-8795 Business E-Mail: whstar@wm.edu.

STARNES, WILLIAM STANCIL, insurance company executive, lawyer; b. Tuscaloosa, Ala., Sept. 3, 1948; s. Stancil R. and Mary Margaret (Lee) Starnes; m. Joan White, Aug. 4, 1979; 1 child, Amanda. BS, U. Ala., 1969; JD summa cum laude, Samford U., 1972. Bar: Ala. 1972, US Dist. Ct. (no. and so. dists.) Ala. 1972, US Ct. Appeals (11th cir.) 1982. Adv. Am. Bd. of Trial Advocacy; assoc. Cabaniss, Johnston, Birmingham, Ala., 1972—74; sr., founder & mng. ptnr. Starnes & Atchinson, Birmingham, 1975; with Med. Assurance, 1979; pres., corp. planning adminstrn. Brasfield & Gorrie, LLC, 2006; chmn., CEO ProAssurance Corp., 2007—. Mem. adv. com. Supreme Ct. Ala. Ala. Rules of Civil Procedure. Fellow Am. Coll. of Trial Lawyers; life mem. Ala. Bar Found. Mem.: ABA, Birmingham Bar Assn., Ala. Bar Assn., Ala. Def. Lawyers Assn., Def. Rsch. Inst., Am. Bd. Trial Advocacy, Fedn. Ins. Counsel, Internat. Assn. Ins. Counsel, Country Club (Birmingham), Kiwanis. Episcopalian. Office: ProAssurance Corp 100 Brookwood Pl Ste 500 Birmingham AL 35209 Office Phone: 205-877-4400. Office Fax: 205-802-4710. Business E-Mail: william.starnes@ProAssurance.com.

STARR, KENNETH WINSTON, academic administrator, law educator, lawyer; b. Vernon, Tex., July 21, 1946; s. W. D. and Vannie Maude (Trimble) Starr; m. Alice Jean Mendell, Aug. 23, 1970; children: Randall Postley, Carolyn Marie, Cynthia Anne. BA, George Washington U., 1968; MA, Brown U., 1969; JD, Duke U., 1973; LLD (hon.), Hampden Sydney Coll., 1992, Shenandoah U., 1993, John Marshall Coll. Law, 1993, Pepperdine U., 1996. Bar: Calif. 1973, D.C. 1979, Va. 1979. Law clk. to Judge David Dyer U.S. Ct. Appeals (5th cir.), Miami, Fla., 1973—74; assoc. Gibson, Dunn & Crutcher, Los Angeles, 1974—75, assoc. ptnr. Washington, 1977—81; law clk. to Chief Justice Warren E. Burger US Supreme Ct., Washington, 1975—77; counselor to atty gen. US Dept. Justice, Washington, 1981—83; judge US Ct. Appeals (DC cir.), Washington, 1983—89; solicitor gen. US Dept. Justice, Washington, 1989—93; ptnr. Kirkland & Ellis LLP, Washington, 1993—2005, of counsel LA, 2005—10; ind. counsel for Whitewater, 1994—99; Duane and Kelly Roberts Dean and Dean, prof. law Pepperdine U. Sch. of Law, Malibu, Calif., 2004—10; pres. Baylor U., Waco, Tex., 2010—. Author: First Among Equals: The Supreme Court in American Life, 2002; contbr. articles to legal jours. Legal advisor CAB transition team office of pres.-elect, 1980—81, SEC transition team, 1980—81; bd. adv. Duke Law Jour. Recipient Disting. Alumni awards, George Washington U., Duke U., Atty. General's award for Disting. Svc., US Dept. Justice, 1993, American Values award, US Indsl. Coun. Ednl. Found., 1993; named one of The 75 Best Lawyers In Washington, Washingtonian survey mag., 2002. Fellow: Am. Bar Found. (jud. fellows com., jud. conf. com. on bicentennial of U.S. constn.); mem.: ABA, Am. Inns of Court, Va. Bar Assn., D.C. Bar Assn., Calif. Bar Assn., Supreme Ct. Hist. Soc., Inst. Jud. Adminstrn. (pres.), Am. Judicature Soc., Am. Law Inst., Phi Delta Phi (Hughes chpt. Man of Yr. 1973), Order of Coif. Republican. Office: Baylor University Office of President One Bear Place #97096 Waco TX 76798-7096 Office Phone: 254-710-3555.*

STARR, MARTIN KENNETH, management educator; b. NYC, May 21, 1927; s. Harry and Melanie (Krauss) S.; m. Polly Exner, Apr. 3, 1955; children: Christopher Herschel, Loren Michael. BS, MIT, 1948; MS, Columbia U., 1951, PhD, 1953. Ptnr., dir. M.K. Starr Assocs., 1956-61; prof. mgmt. sci. Columbia U., NYC, 1961-96, dir. Ctr. for the Study of Ops., 1980-95, dir. Ctr. for Enterprise Mgmt., 1995-96, vice dean Grad. Sch. Bus., 1974-75; Disting. prof. ops. mgmt. Crummer Grad. Sch. Bus. Rollins Coll., Winter Park, Fla., 1996—2003, prof. emeritus, 2003—, dir. Ctr. for Enterprise Mgmt., 1996—2001; prof. emeritus Columbia U., 1996—. Lectr. in field; cons. in field. Author: (with David W. Miller) The Structure of Human Decisions, 1967, (with David W. Miller) Inventory Control-Theory and Practice, 1972, Product Design and Decision Theory, 1963, (with David W. Miller) Executive Decisions and Operations Research, 2d edit., 1969, Systems Management of Operations, 1971, Management: A Modern Approach, 1971, Production Management: Systems and Synthesis, 2d edit., 1972, (with Irving Stein) The Practice of Management Science, 1976, Operations Management, 1978, (with David G. Dannebring) Management Science: An Introduction, 1981, (with Earl K. Bowen) Statistics for Business and Economics, 1982, (with Marion Sobol) Statistics for Business and Economics: An Action Learning Approach, 1983, Managing Production and Operations, 1989, Global Corporate Alliances and the Competitive Edge, 1991, (with Marion Sobol) Introduction to Statistics for Executives, 1993, Operations Management: A Systems Approach, 1996, CD-text rev., 2000, Production and Operations Management, 2004, 2nd edit., 2008, Foundations of Production and Operations Management, 2007, Executive Readings in Management Science, 1965, (with Milan Zeleny) Multiple Criteria Decision Making, 1977; editor: Global Competitiveness: Getting the U.S. Back on Track, 1988; editor-in-chief Mgmt. Sci., 1967-82; mem. editl. bd. Behavioral Sci., 1970-2002, Internat. Jour. Flexible Mfg. Sys., 1989-2010; mem. editl. adv. bd. Jour. Ops. Mgmt., 1983-2009; editl. adviser Operational Rsch. Quar., 1970-85, (with Sushil K. Gupta)Production and Operations Management Systems, February; cons. editor: Columbia Jour. World Business: Focus: Decision Making, fall, 1977, Quantitative Methods in Mgmt.; contbr. articles to profl. jours. and publs. Recipient Kimball award, 1983, Sushil K. Gupta POMS Disting. Svc. award, 2013. Fellow AAAS, Inst. for Ops. Rsch. and the Mgmt. Scis., Inst. Mgmt. Scis. (pres. 1974-75), Prodn. and Ops. Mgmt. Soc. (pres.-elect 1994—, pres. 1995, past pres., bd. dirs. 1996—, chair Coun. of Pres. 1999-, bd. mem., Coll. Behaviour Ops. Mgmt. 2009-, Coll. Humanitarian Ops. and Crisis Mgmt., 2010-), Prodn. and Ops. Mgmt. Soc. (Disting. Svc. award 2013); mem. Beta Gamma Sigma. Achievements include having an annual award for practitioner excellence in operations named in his honor by the Production and Operations Management Society. Home: 100 S Interlachen Ave #304 Winter Park FL 32789-4450 Office: Rollins Coll 120 Crummer Grad Sch Bus Winter Park FL 32789 Office Phone: 407-212-1118. Office Fax: 407-644-2394. Business E-Mail: starr@columbia.edu.

STARR, WADE, state legislator; b. Nov. 08; m. Linda Starr. State rep. Dist. 78, Ga., 2007—. Mem.: Clayton County Branch NAACP (founding mem.). Democrat. Office: Capitol Suite 611 Coverdell Legislative Office Atlanta GA 30334 also: 1348 Government Circle Jonesboro GA 30236 Office Phone: 404-656-0314, 770-477-3748. Fax: 770-473-3907. E-mail: wade.starr@co.clayton.ga.us.

STARRETT, MELVIN KEITH, federal judge; b. McComb, Miss., July 15, 1951; s. Melvin and Mary (Roberts) S.; m. Barbara O'Neal, Dec. 18, 1971; children: Josh, Whit, Leah Claire. BS, Miss. State U., 1972; JD, U. Miss., 1974. Bar: Miss. 1974, U.S. Dist. Ct. (no. and so. dists.) Miss. 1974. Ptnr. Statham, Watkins & Starrett, Magnolia, Miss., 1975-79; pvt. practice Magnolia, 1980-89, McComb, 1989-92; cir. judge 14th Cir. Dist. Miss., McComb, 1992—2004; judge US Dist. Ct. (So. dist.) Miss., Hattiesburg, 2004—. Baptist. Avocations: backpacking, jogging, canoeing. Office: US Dist Ct 701 Main St Ste 228 Hattiesburg MS 39401 Office Phone: 601-583-4422. Business E-Mail: keith_starrett@mssd.uscourts.gov.

STASNEY, C. RICHARD, otolaryngologist, director; s. Homer R. and Eska Gage Stasney; m. Susan Pitzer Pitzer, June 8, 1968; children: Kathryn Stasney Childers, Elizabeth Stasney Moriarty, W. Spencer. BA, Yale U., New Haven, 1965; MD, Baylor Coll. Medicine, Houston, 1969. Diplomate Am. Bd. Otolaryngology, 1974. Dir. Tex. Voice Ctr., Houston, 1977—; chmn. Ctr. Performing Arts Medicine, Houston, 2001—. Contbr. articles to profl. jours. Bd. mem. Tex. State Bd. Med. Examiners, Austin, 1987—93, Mus. Health & Med. Sci., Houston, 2001—06. Lt. comdr. USN, Oakland. Recipient Physician of yr., Houston Acad. Communicative Disorders, 1998, Disting. Surgeon of Yr., Assn. Oper. Rm. Nurses, 2006; named one of America's Top Physicians, Consumer's Rsch. Coun. Am., 2001—09. Achievements include research in medical problems of performing artists. Office: Tex Voice Ctr 6550 Fannin Ste 2025 Houston TX 77030 Office Fax: 713-796-2349.*

STATON, CECIL, state legislator; b. Greenville, SC; m. Catherine Staton; children: Trey, William. BA, Furman Univ.; PhD, Oxford Univ. Pub., broadcaster; mem. Dist. 18 Ga. State Senate, 2005—. Republican. Baptist. Mailing: PO Box 26427 Macon GA 31221 Office Phone: 478-757-0983. Office Fax: 478-757-1305. Business E-Mail: cecil.staton@senate.ga.gov.

STAUB, W. ARTHUR, health care products executive; b. Detroit, Dec. 25, 1923; s. Edward Elmer and Emma Josephine (Fleury) S.; m. Alla Elizabeth Edwards, June 26, 1948; children: James Randall, Sally Ann, David Scott. BS, Dartmouth Coll., 1944; MD, Temple U., 1947. Intern Muhlenberg Hosp., Plainfield, NJ, 1947-48; resident in pediatrics Abington (Pa.) Meml. Hosp., 1950-51; practice medicine specializing in pediatrics Westfield (N.J.) Med. Group, 1948-63; assoc. med. dir. Ciba Pharm. Co., Summit, NJ, 1963-66; med. dir., v.p. life sci. div. Becton-Dickinson and Co., Rutherford, NJ, 1966-70; v.p. med. affairs C. R. Bard Co., Murray Hill, NJ, 1970-88, also bd. dirs. Bd. dirs. Crestmont Fed. Savs. and Loan Assn., Edison, N.J., Colonial Trust Nat. Bank, North Palm Beach, Fla.; cons. Children's Specialized Hosp., Westfield, 1948-88, Overlook Hosp., Summit, 1948-88. Contbr. articles to profl. jours. Deacon Presbyn. Ch., Westfield, 1959—. Ensign USNR, 1944—50, to capt. USAF, 1950—53. Fellow Am. Coll. Physician Execs.; mem. AAAS, Assn. Advancement Med. Instrumentation, Health Industry Mfrs. Assn. (chmn. med. and sci. steering com.). Clubs: Echo Lake Country (Westfield) (bd. trustees 1984-88); Lost Tree (North Palm Beach, Fla., bd. govs. 1989-94, sec. 1989-94); Skytop (Pa.). Republican. Presbyterian. Avocations: golf, physical fitness, reading, sailing, travel. Home: 3330 Devonshire Way Palm Beach Gardens FL 33418 E-mail: DoctorWAS@aol.com.

STAVRINAKIS, LEONIDES EMMANUEL (LEON STAVRINAKIS), state legislator; b. Charleston, Jan. 5, 1966; s. Emmanuel and Merofia Stavrinakis; m. Anne Heinsohn; children: Clare Anne, Emmanuel. BA, Coll. Charleston, SC, 1988; JD, U. SC Sch. Law, 1992. Asst. solicitor, 9th cir., 1993—96; councilman Charleston County Coun., 1999—2006, chmn., 2005—06; mem. Dist. 119 SC House of Reps., 2007—. Democrat. Home: 375 Meadow Breeze Ln Charleston SC 29414 Office: 420D Blatt Building Columbia SC 29201 Home Phone: 843-573-0491; Office Phone: 843-724-1060, 803-734-3039. Business E-Mail: StavL@schouse.org.

STEA, DAVID, environmental psychologist urban planner, educator; b. Bklyn., Dec. 12, 1936; s. Armand and Henriette (Lipsky) S.; children: Kalisa, Kevin, Damon. BS, Carnegie Inst. Tech., 1957; MS, U. N.Mex., 1960; PhD, Stanford U., 1964. Human factors engr. Sandia Corp., Albuquerque, 1957-60; engring. psychologist Lockheed Missiles & Space Corp., Sunnyvale, Calif., 1961; postdoctoral fellow Brown U., Providence, R.I., 1964-66, Escuela Nacional de Arquitectura, Mexico, 1966-67; asst. prof. geography and psychology Clark U., Worcester, Mass., 1967-69, assoc. prof., 1969-71; assoc. prof. architecture, urban design and planning UCLA, 1971-74, prof., 1974-82; disting. prof. architecture U. Wis., Milw., 1982-88, sr. scientist Urban Rsch. Ctr., 1982-86; adj. prof. planning U. N.Mex., 1986—; dir. Internat. Ctr. for Culture and Environment, Santa Fe, 1985-89; Enrique O. Aragon Disting. Prof. Univ. Nacional Autonoma de Mexico, 1989; sr. prof. rsch. Univ. Autonoma Metropolitana, 1989-90; dir. Centro Internacional Para La Cultura y El Ambiente, Mex., 1989—; prof. U.S. Internat. U. and Universidad de las Americas, Mexico, 1991—. Vis. disting. prof. Gadjah Mada U., Yogyakarta, Indonesia, 1986; vis. scholar Latin Am. Inst., U. N.Mex., 1987-89; co-founder Miniversity, 1970; cons. Fed. U. Tech., Yola, Nigeria, 1982-84, Inst. Am. Indian Arts, 1983-88; vis. lectr. U. Waikato, New Zealand, 1978, 94, Mid-East Tech. U., Turkey, 1981, U. Melbourne, Australia, 1982, U. Autonoma de Baja Calif., Mex., 1983, U. Auckland, 1990; vis. prof. Technion-Israel Inst. Tech., 1992, Ramapo Coll. N.J., 1992-93, Mt. Holyoke Coll., 1994. Author: Environmental Mapping; co-author: Placemaking; co-editor: Maps in Minds, Image and Environment, The Fourth World; mem. editorial bd. Environ. and Behavior, 1969-80, Human Ecology, 1971-76, Jour. Environ. Psychology and Non-Verbal Behavior, 1976-80, Geog. Rsch. Forum, 1982—, profl. geographer, 1998-2008; mem. editorial bd. Ethnoscapes series Avebury Press, U.K., 1987—, Ency. of Contemporary Peoples, 1993. Cons. community planning Sawtelle Community, L.A., 1972-75, Navajo Nation and Pima/Maricopa Salt River Community, 1974—, Ngati Awa, Tainui Maori, 1978, 90, 94, Confederated Tribes of the Umatilla, 1980, San Ysidro del Norte, N.Mex., 1985—, Costilla, N.Mex., 1987, Tierra Amarilla, N.Mex., 1988, Colonia Miguel Hidalgo, Mex., 1989-90, AIA Regional/Urban Design Assistance Team, 1976-94. Grantee NSF, 1994-2002, 2004-09, Social Sci. Research Council, 1966-67, Shell Found., 1969, U.S. Dept. Edn., 1968-71, 85-88. Mem. AIA (assoc.), Assn. Am. Geographers, Sociedad Interamericana de Psicologia, Internat. Assn. Impact Assessment, Com. of Latin-Americanist Geographers, Assn. Borderlands Scholars, Environ. Design Rsch. Assn., Internat. Soc. for Environ. Ethics. Office: 5802 Bob Bullock Loop, CL #84-147 Laredo TX 78041 Home: Calle Del Angel *1 Los Frailes Sammjyuel De Alleude Gto Mex. City Mexico

STEARNS, FRANK WARREN, lawyer; b. Washington, July 20, 1949; s. Robert Maynard and Ermyntrude (Vaiden) S.; m. Judith Anne Ketcheson, Sept. 7, 1974; children: Frank W. Jr., Brian S., Joe G. BA, Washington & Lee, 1971; JD with honors, George Washington U., 1974. Bar: Washington DC 1975, Va. 1980, Supreme Ct. Va., U.S. Dist. Ct. (DC 1975, ea. dist. Va.), U.S. Ct. Appeals (DC cir. 1975, 4th cir. 1985), U.S. Supreme Ct. Law clk. Superior Ct. D.C., Washington, 1974-75; asst. corp. counsel Office of the Corp. Counsel, Washington, 1975-79; asst. county atty. County Atty's Office, Fairfax County, Va., 1979-80; mng. ptnr. Wilkes Artis P.C., Fairfax, Va., 1984-2001; ptnr., Real Estate, State & Local Govt., Communications practices Venable LLP, Vienna, Va., 2001—. Bd. dirs. No. Va. Bldg. Industry Assn., 1987-94; trustee Greater Washington Bd. Trade-P.A.C., 1987-2003; chmn. tech. adv. com. NVBIA, Loudoun, Va., 1986-90, mem. Econ. Devel. Commn. Arlington County, Va. Coun. Excellence in Govt., Washington, 1989—98; Commr. Arlington County Econ. Devel. Commn., Arlington, Va., 1987—91. Mem. ABA, Va. State Bar Assn., Va. Trial Lawyers Assn., DC Bar Assn., Fairfax County Bar Assn., Barristers, Counsellors, Fairfax C. of C. (PAC trustee 2003—). Avocations: tennis, golf. Office: Venable LLP Ste 300 8010 Towers Crescent Dr Vienna VA 22182 Office Phone: 703-760-1956. Office Fax: 703-821-8949. Business E-Mail: fwstearns@venable.com.

STEARNS, STEWART WARREN, charitable association executive; b. Denver, Apr. 8, 1947; s. Vinton H. and Marjorie L. (Tedro) S.; m. Marjorie L. Fuller, Jan. 25, 1969; children: Theresa Lyn, Gregory Robert. BS, Ea. N.Mex. U., 1970; MA, No. Ill. U., 1973; postgrad., SUNY, Albany, 1974—. Mng. editor Studies in Linguistics, DeKalb, Ill., 1972-73; instr. No. Ill. U., DeKalb, 1972-73; cons. AID, Guatemala, 1973-74; instr. Skidmore Coll., Saratoga Springs, N.Y., 1975; OAS fellow Guatemala, 1976-77; asst. dir. Chaves County Cmty. Action Program, Roswell, N.Mex., 1977-78; exec. dir. United Way Chaves County, Roswell, 1978-83, Levi Strauss Found., Dallas, 1983-85, Cmty. Trust Met. Tarrant County, Ft. Worth, 1985-88; pres., CEO Cmty. Found., Sarasota County, 1988—2010. NDEA fellow, Dallas, 1970-71. Personal E-mail: stearnsconsulting@verizon.net.

STEBBINS, PAUL H., energy executive; b. 1965; 3 children. BA Govt., Georgetown Univ., 1979. Bunker broker Gary Bunkering Services, Inc.; with Trans-Tec Services, 1985; joined World Fuel Services, Inc. (subs. World Fuel Services Corp.), 1995, sr. v.p., 1995—97, exec. v.p., 1997—2000, pres., COO, 2000—02, chmn., CEO, 2002—12, chmn., 2012—. Planning coord. Internat. Energy Corp. Office: World Fuel Services Ste 400 9800 NW 41st St Miami FL 33178

STEDMAN, W. DAVID, textile manufacturing company executive; m. Sarah Elizabeth White; children: Sarah Elizabeth, Nancy Jane, Anne Louise. AB in Economics, Duke U., 1942; IA, Harvard U., 1943; MA in Astronomy, Georgetown U., 1962. Exec. v.p. Stedman Mfg. Co., Asheboro, NC, 1954—60; pres. Stedman Hosiery Mills, Inc., Asheboro, 1955—66, Caraway Investment Corp., Asheboro, 1956—58, Anson Mfg. Co., Wadesboro, NC, 1967—69, Stedman Corp., Asheboro, 1960—, chmn. bd., 1978—. Instr. astronomy U. NC-Greensboro, 1960—61, vis. counselor physics dept., 1960—62; chmn. Internat. Knitting Congress, 1983; bd. dirs. U.S. Apparel Coun., 1981—83; trustee Enterprise Am., 1981—83. Contbr. articles to profl. publs. Mem. budget amendment com. Nat. Taxpayers Union (Fed. Budget Constl. Amendment), 1980—; bd. dirs. Asheboro Meml. Found., 1958—64, v.p., 1959—60; bd. dirs. Asheboro (Randolph) Devel. Corp., 1958—59, mem. exec. com., 1960—61; chmn. Randolph County dist. Boy Scouts Am., 1949, bd. dirs. Gen. Greene Coun., 1949; mem. Asheboro Bd. Edn., 1959—67; mem. state evaluation com. on tchr. edn., mem. stds. com. of adv. coun. on tchr. edn. N.C. Bd. Edn., 1963—71; trustee Inst. for Homiletical Studies Meth. Ch., 1965—79; mem. citizens adv. com. City of Asheboro, 1967—68; mem. gov.'s adv. com. for Piedmont Crescent State of N.C., 1967—68; mem. exec. com. Randolph Hosp., Asheboro, 1969—80; trustee, mem. exec. com. Pfeiffer Coll., Misenheimer, NC, 1969—83, chmn. bd. trustees, 1974—79; bd. visitors St. Andrews Presbyn. Coll., Laurinburg, NC, 1969—79; trustee Meth. Coll., Fayetteville, NC, 1970—75; mem. adv. coun. Sch. Bus. Adminstrn. U. N.C., Charlotte, 1970—74; bd. dirs., mem. exec. com., treas. Zool. Soc., 1970—77, sec., 1976; trustee N.C. Com. on Econ. Edn.; bd. dirs. Ctr. for Study Human Values, 1973—79, v.p., 1974; mem. exec. com. N.C. Zool. Pk. Coun., 1974—79; mem. Divs. Sch. fellow Duke U., 1975, mem. hosp. adv. bd., 1980—; bd. dirs. N.C. Symphony Assn., 1979, 1982, mem. exec. com., 1982; mem. N.C. Coun. on Econs. Edn., 1980—; bd. dirs. United Fund, Asheboro, 1958—60, Randolph County Ctr. for Exceptional Children, 1961—62, Maryfield Nursing Home, High Point, 1969—79, Bus. Found. N.C., 1979—, N.C. Mus. Art, 1981, N.C. Zool. Authority, 1973—74; mem. Tomorrow's Am. Found. Bd., 1979—; lay leader 1st United Meth. Ch., Asheboro,

1958—62, mem. adminstrv. bd., 1950—, chmn., 1974, trustee, 1969—72, High Point-Randolph dist. Western N.C. Conf. Meth. Ch., 1960—72, mem. adv. coun. on pub. rels. and Meth. info., 1962—65, trustee Meth. Found., 1968—69, mem. coll. coordinating coun., 1974—79, mem. exec. com. coll. coordinating coun., 1975—79, mem. United Meth. home com. Triad area, 1975—76, del. to annual conf., 1975, 1986, del. to Southea. Jurisdictional Conf., 1976, del. to gen. conf., 1976; treas. Meth. Ch., 1971—79, trustee bd. homes and hosps., 1968—77, trustee bd. health and welfare ministries, 1968—71, mem. TV, radio and film commn., 1967—69. Recipient Silver Beaver award, Boy Scouts Am., 1951, Disting. Svc. award, US Jr. C. of C., 1957, spl. appreciation award, Pfeiffer Coll. Alumni Assn., 1974, achievement award, Knitting Industry Mag., Nat. Knitwear Mfrs. Assn., 1978; named hon. alumnus, Pfeiffer Coll., 1975, Honor Scouter, 1981, Appalachian State U.'s Free Enterprise Hall of Fame award, 1981. Fellow: AAAS; mem.: NAM (indsl. problems com. 1963—66, bd. dirs. 1981), Bus. Leader Group (rotating chmn. 1981), Nat. Knitwear Mfrs. Assn. (bd. dirs. 1975, vice chmn. 1981, exec. com. 1981—82, bd. dirs. 1981—83, chmn. 1982), NC Acad. Scis., Am. Astron. Soc., Order Silver Spoon, NC Citizens for Bus. and Industry (exec. com. 1969—, 1st vice chmn. 1981, chmn. 1982), US C. of C. (pub. affairs com. 1981), Newcomen Soc., Duke U. Alumni Assn. (pres. local chpt. 1970), Asheboro C. of C. (bd. dirs. 1958—66, chmn. total devel. com. 1967—69, bd. dirs. 1970—72, 1977—80, pres.-elect 1978, exec. com. 1978—80, pres. 1979), Rotary (bd. dirs. 1958), Phi Beta Kappa. Office: Sara Lee Corporation 100 Industrial Park Ave Asheboro NC 27205-7324

STEED, JOHN DAVID, retail executive; B in Mktg., Western Carolina U. Joined Lowe's Companies, Inc., 1973, v.p., merchandising fashion plumbing & elec., 1998—99, v.p., merchandising western divsn., 1999—2001, sr. v.p., gen. merchandising mgr., bldg. products, 2001—. Office: Lowe's Companies Inc 1000 Lowe's Blvd Mooresville NC 28117 Office Phone: 704-758-1000. Office Fax: 336-658-4766. Business E-Mail: john.steed@lowes.com.

STEEL, NATE, state legislator; m. Shay Steel. BA in Psychology, U. Ark., JD. Bd. advisors CASA for Children; bd. dirs. U. Ark. Found., Howard Meml. Hosp. Found; dep. prosecutor Ariz.; v.p. Cossatot Cmty. Coll.; ptnr. Steel and Steel, 2007—; mem. Dist. 21 Ark. House of Representatives, 2011—. Democrat. Office: 102 N Main St Nashville AR 71852 Office Phone: 870-845-1870. Office Fax: 870-845-3355. Business E-Mail: nate.steel@arkansashouse.org.

STEELE, (MARGARET) ANITA MARTIN, law librarian, educator; b. Haines City, Fla., Dec. 30, 1927; d. Emmett Edward and Esther Majulia (Phifer) Martin; m. Thomas Dinsmore Steele, June 10, 1947 (div. 1969); children: Linda Frances, Roger Dinsmore, Thomas Garrick, Carolyn Ann; m. James E. Beaver, Mar. 1980 (dec. Feb. 1996). BA, Radcliffe Coll., 1948; JD, U. Va., 1971; M in Law Librarianship, U. Wash., 1972. Asst. prof. law U. Puget Sound, Tacoma, 1972—74, assoc. prof. law, 1974—79, prof. law, 1979—98, dir. law libr., 1972—98; prof. law, dir. law libr. Seattle U., Tacoma, 1994—98, prof. law emerita, 1998—. Author: (book) Martin and Carmichael Descendants in Ga., 1811-1994, 1994; contbr. articles to profl. jours.; mem. editorial adv. bds.: various law book pubs. Treas. Congl. Campaign Orgn., Tacoma, 1978, 1980. Mem.: DAR, Nat. Assn. Parliamentarians, Colonial Dames XVII Century. Republican. Home: 3582 Roanoke Rd Daleville VA 24083-3209

STEELE, CHARLES, JR., retired civil rights association executive, former state legislator; b. Tuscaloosa, Ala., Aug. 3, 1946; m. Cathelean Annette; children: LeKeisha, Charla. Student, Miss. Valley State, Oakland U.; BA, Am. Internat. U.; LHD (hon.), Stillman Coll.; Ph.D (hon.), Am. Internat. U. Co-owner Van Hoose and Steele Funeral Home; mem. Tuscaloosa City Coun., Ala. State Senate from Dist. 24, Montgomery, 1995—2004; pres., CEO So. Christian Leadership Conf. (SCLC), Atlanta, 2004—09, cons., 2009—. Mem. Local Legis. No. 1 Com., Fiscal Responsibility and Accountability Com., Fin. and Taxation Gen. Fund Com., Fin. and Taxation Edn. Com., Agr. and Forestry Com., Health and Human Resources Com., Oil and Gas subcom. Commerce, Transp., and Utilities Com., Indsl. Devel. and Recruitment Com., Small Bus. and Rural Devel. Com., Constitution, Campaign Fin., Ethics, and Elections Com., Postsecondary and Higher Edn. subcom. Edn. Com., Law Enforcement and Victims Rights subcom., Violence in Schs. subcom. Judiciary Com.; chairperson Rural Devel. subcom. Small Bus. and Rural Devel. Com., Mental Health subcom. Health and Human Resources Com. Named one of Most Influential Black Americans, Ebony mag., 2006. Mem. Nat. Assn. Funeral Dirs. and Morticians, Ala. Funeral Dirs. and Morticians Assn. Democrat. Baptist. Avocations: walking, reading.

STEELE, FITZ, state legislator; b. June 19, 1965; married; 3 children. Mem. Dist. 84 Ky. House of Reps., 2009—. Democrat. Baptist. Office: 702 Capitol Ave Rm 316B Frankfort KY 40601 also: 176 Woodland Ave Hazard KY 41701 Office Phone: 502-564-8100 Ext.697, 606-439-0556. Office Fax: 606-439-0556.

STEELE, HOWARD LOUCKS, economic development consultant, author; b. Pitts., Jan. 27, 1929; s. Howard Bennington and Ruby Alberta (Loucks) S.; m. Sally E. Funk, June 6, 1952 (div. 1977); children: John F., David A., Patricia A.; m. Jane R. Cornelius, July 30, 1977 (div. 1996); 1 child, Jennifer L.; m. Elaine Haddock, Aug. 23, 1997. BS, Washington and Lee U., 1950; MS, Pa. State U., 1952; PhD, U. Ky., 1962. Sales mgr. Greenville (Pa.) Dairy Co., 1952-56; owner H.L. Steele Bulk Milk Hauling, Greenville, 1955-60; asst. prof. Clemson (S.C.) U., 1956-57, assoc. prof., 1957-64, Ohio State U., Columbus, 1964-71; with Fgn. Agrl. Svc./Internat. Coop. and Devel. U.S., Dept. Agr., Washington, 1971-97; ret.; econ. devel. cons., 1997—. Project mgr. AID, Guatemala, 1976-77, Bolivia, 1977-80, Honduras, 1980-82, Sri Lanka, 1982-84, Bur. L.Am. and Caribbean USAID, Washington, 1984-88, office of the dir. tech. assistance divsn., 1988-90, with office of dep. adminstr., 1990-97; USDA liaison officer Inter-Am. Inst. Coop. in Agr., 1993-97; instr. U. Md., College Park, 1974-76; vis. prof. U. Sao Paulo, Piracicaba, Brazil, 1964-66; ptnr. Kingwood Acres Farm, Rockwood, Pa., 1966-98. Author: Commercializacao Agricola, 1971, A 200 Year History of Some Descendents of the Pioneer James Steel of Castleblaney, Ireland and Mt. Pleasant, Pennsylvania, 1994, Your Tax Dollars at Work (I'd Rather Have Gone Business Class!), 1998, Food Soldier, 2002, Bushels and Bales: A Food Soldier in the Cold War, 2008, More Food Soldier Encounters, 2010; contbr. articles to profl. jours. Recipient Nat. Forensic Union award; named One of Outstanding Young Men U.S., U.S. Jaycees, 1965; cert. of merit Dept. Agr., 1975, 92. Mem.: SAR, Masons, Internat. Assn. Agrl. Economists, Agrl. & Applied Economics Assn., Shriners, Sigma Nu, Gamma Sigma Delta. Home: 5204 Holden St Fairfax VA 22032-3418 Office Phone: 703-978-4066. Personal E-mail: ehsteele@verizon.net.

STEELE, JOHN E., federal judge; b. Detroit, 1949; BA, U. Detroit, 1971, JD, 1973. Asst. pros. atty., Wayne County, 1974-77, Ingham County, 1977-80; asst. US atty. US Dist. Ct. (we. dist.) Mich., 1980-81, US Dist. Ct. (mid. dist.) Fla., Jacksonville, 1981-88, magistrate judge, 1991—2000, judge Fort Myers, 2000—; assoc. Mahoney, Adams & Criser, 1988-91. Mem. FBA, State Bar Fla., State Bar Mich. Office: US Dist Ct 2110 First St Ste 6-109 Fort Myers FL 33901 Office Phone: 239-461-2140. Office Fax: 239-461-2149.

STEELE, KENNETH FRANKLIN, JR., hydrologist; b. Statesville, NC, Jan. 16, 1944; s. Kenneth Franklin and Ruth Virginia (Wilhelm) Steele; m. Sheila Kay Stumpf, Sept. 3, 1966 (dec.); children: Krista Robin, Celisa Anne; m. Beth Vaughan-Wrobel, Sept. 24, 2005. BS in Chemistry, U. N.C., 1966, PhD in Geology, 1971. Registered profl. geologist, Ark., registered hydrogeologist Am. Inst. Hydrology. From instr. to prof. geology U. Ark., Fayetteville, 1970—83, dir. Ark. Water Resources Ctr., 1988—2001, prof. emeritus, 2007. Mem. State Bd. Registration for Profl. Geologists, 1992-96, 2000-2004, chmn., 1996, 2002-03, vice chmn., 2001-02; cons. in field. Contbr. numerous articles to profl. jour., chpts. to books; editor: Animal Waste and the Land-Water Interface. Mem. Internat. Order St. Luke the Physician. Summer faculty fellow Oak Ridge Associated Univ., 1981, 83, 85. Mem. Nat. Ground-Water Assn., Internat. Assn. Hydrologists, Am. Inst Hydrology, Assn. Applied Geochemists, Soc. Environ. Geology & Health, Geol. Soc. Am. (regional bd. dir. 1980-82, 84-86), Am. Water Resources Assn. (bd. dirs. 1991-94), Ark. Ground Water Assn. (bd. dir. 1988-90, 93-95, v.p. 1991, pres. 1992), Nat. Assn. Water Inst. Dirs. (counselor 1990-93), Nat. Inst. Water Resources (bd. dir. 1998-2001). Achievements include research on the importance of rainstorms on ground and surface water chemistry in karstic terrain, nitrate and pesticide contamination of ground water, and evolution of ground water chemistry with emphasis on iron and arsenic. Office: U Ark Dept Geoscis 113 Ozark Hall U Ark Fayetteville AR 72701-4040 Home: PO Box 1065 Fayetteville AR 72702 Office Phone: 479-575-7937. Business E-Mail: ksteele@uark.edu.

STEELE, KRIS, state legislator; b. Ardmore, Okla., Mar. 11, 1973; m. Kellie Kursar; children: Mackenzie, Madison. BA in Religion, Okla. Baptist Univ., 1996; MEd in Sch. Counseling, Ea. Ctrl. Univ., 2006. Assoc. minister Wesley United Methodist Church, Shawnee, Okla.; mem. Dist.26 Okla. House of Representatives, 2001—. Assoc. min. Wesley United Meth. Ch., Shawnee, Okla. Mem.: Rotary Club. Republican. Methodist. Office: Oklahoma House of Representatives 2300 N Lincoln Blvd Rm 411 Oklahoma City OK 73105 Mailing: 1211 Cambridge Dr Shawnee OK 74804 Office Phone: 405-878-0514, 405-557-7345. E-mail: krissteele@okhouse.gov.

STEELE, RODNEY REDFEARN, judge; b. Selma, Ala., May 22, 1930; s. C. Parker and Miriam Lera (Redfearn) S.; m. Frances Marion Blair, Aug. 1, 1964; children: Marion Scott, Claudia Redfearn, Parker Blair. AB, U. Ala., 1950, MA, 1951; LLB, U. Mich., 1954. Bar: Ala. 1954, U.S. Dist. Ct. (mid. dist.) Ala. 1959, U.S. Ct. Appeals (5th cir., now 11th cir.) 1981. Law clk. Ala. Ct. Appeals, 1956-57; assoc. Knabe & Nachman, Montgomery, Ala., 1957-61; asst. U.S. atty. Dept. Justice, Montgomery, 1961-66; staff atty. So. Bell T&T Co., Atlanta, 1966-67; judge U.S. Bankruptcy Ct., Mid. dist. Ala., Montgomery, 1967—, chief judge, 1985-99; ret., 1999—. Served with U.S. Army, 1954-56, Korea. Mem. ABA, Ala. State Bar, Montgomery County Bar Assn. Democrat. Episcopalian. Home: 1227 Magnolia Curv Montgomery AL 36106-2136

STEELE, TRACY, state legislator; b. Mar. 8, 1953; Degree in Polit. Sci., Rice U., Houston. Former exec. dir. Ark. Martin Luther King Jr. Commn., Little Rock; mem. Dist. 59 Ark. House of Reps., 1999—2002, mem. Dist. 39, 2011—; mem. Dist. 34 Ark. State Senate, 2003—11, majority leader, 2007—09, asst. pres. pro tempore, 2009—11; founder, CEO STAND Found., Inc., North Little Rock, 2006—. Recipient Legislator of Yr. award, Nat. Directors Chronic Diseases/American Heart Assn., 2003, Pub. Health Through Pub. Policy award, U. Ark. Med. Scis. Fay W. Boozman Coll. Pub. Health, 2009, Pub. Health Heroes award, Ark. Dept. Health, 2009, Cmty. Champion award, MADD, 2009, Disting. Legislator award, Ark. Mcpl. League, 2009, Legis. Champion award, Cmty. Health Centers, 2009. Democrat. Baptist. Mailing: Dist Address PO Box 9267 North Little Rock AR 72119 Office: STAND Foundation Inc 601 Main St North Little Rock AR 72114 Office Phone: 501-374-8788. Office Fax: 501-374-8780. Business E-Mail: repsteele@yahoo.com.

STEELE, WILLIAM H., federal judge; b. Tuscumbia, Ala., 1951; BA, U. Southern Miss., 1972; JD, U. Ala., 1980. Law clk., bailiff Tuscaloosa County Dist. Ct., 1981; asst., chief asst. dist. atty. Mobile County Dist. Atty.'s Office, Mobile, Ala., 1981-87; asst. US atty. US Atty.'s Office (So. Dist. Ala.), 1987—89; pvt. practice Mobile, 1988-90; magistrate judge US Dist. Ct. (so. dist.) Alab., Mobile, 1990—2003; judge US Dist. Ct. (so. dist.) Ala., 2003—10, chief judge, 2010—. With USMC, 1972-78, USNG, 1978-90. Mem. Nat. Assn. Magistrate Judges, Ala. Bar Assn., Mobile Bar Assn. Office: US Dist Ct So Dist Ala 113 Saint Joseph St Mobile AL 36602-3606 Fax: 334-694-4668.

STEEN, DONALD E., healthcare company executive; Undergraduate, U. Mo., Columbia; M, St. Louis U. CPA. Founder Med. Care Internat., Inc., 1982; pres., CEO Med. Care America, Inc., 1982—94; pres. Western Group, 1994—95, HCA Inc. (formerly HCA Healthcare Corp.), 1995—97, Internat. Group of Columbia, 1995—97; founder United Surg. Ptnrs. Internat., Inc., 1998, CEO, 1998—2004, chmn.; sr. oper. ptnr. Welsh, Carson, Anderson & Stowe; chmn., CEO AmeriPath, Inc., 2004—. Bd. dirs. Horizon Health Corp., 1995—, United Dental Care Inc., 1996—, Kinetic Concepts, Inc., 1998—. Office: AmeriPath Inc 7111 Fairway Dr Ste 400 Palm Beach Gardens FL 33418 Office Phone: 561-712-6200. Office Fax: 561-845-0129. Business E-Mail: dsteen@ameripath.com.

STEEN, FRED F., II, state legislator; Cost analyst., cons.; state rep. Dist. 76 NC, 2005—. Mem. Agrl. com., Alcoholic Beverage Control com., Appropriations com., Commerce, Small Bus. and Entrepreneurship com., Local Govt. I, Transp. com.; vice chmn. Appropriations Subcom. on Gen. Govt., Wildlife Resources com. Republican. Office: North Carolina House of Representatives 300 N Salisbury St Rm 305 Raleigh NC 27603-5925 Office Phone: 919-733-5881. E-mail: Fred.Steen@ncleg.net.

STEEN, JOHN THOMAS, JR., state official, lawyer; b. San Antonio, Dec. 27, 1949; s. John Thomas and Nell (Donnell) S.; m. Ida Louise Clement, May 12, 1979; children: John T. III, Ida Louise Larkin, James Higbie Clement. AB cum laude, Princeton U., NJ, 1971; JD, U. Tex., 1974; Honor grad., US Army Mil. Police Sch., 1974. Bar: Tex. 1974, US Dist. Ct. (western dist.) Tex. 1976, US Ct. Appeals (5th cir.) 1989. Assoc. Matthews & Branscomb, San Antonio, 1977—82; ptnr. Soules, Cliffe & Reed, San Antonio, 1982—83; sr. v.p., gen. counsel, dir. Commerce Savings Assn., San Antonio, 1983—88; pvt. law practice San Antonio, 1988—2012; sec. of state State of Tex., Austin, 2012—14; mem. Tex. Higher Edn. Coordinating Bd., Austin, 2014—. Trustee San Antonio Acad., 1976-81, 87-93, chmn. bd., 1989-91, advisory coun., 1991—; v.p. Bexar County Easter Seal Soc., San Antonio, 1976-77; trustee, vice-chmn. San Antonio C.C. Dist., 1977-82; bd. dirs. Tex. Easter Seal Soc., Dallas, 1977-80, San Antonio Rsch. and Planning Coun., 1978-81, Cmty. Guidance Ctr., 1983-84, Accord Med. Found., 1987-92; vice-chmn. Leadership San Antonio, 1978-79; dir. Fiesta San Antonio Commn., 1982-83, 93-96, 98-2001, 2003—09, v.p., 2004-06, pres. 2007-08; commr. Bexar County, San Antonio, 1982, Tex. Commn. on Economy & Efficiency in State Govt., 1985-89; adv. bd. Freeman Coliseum, 1985-91, chmn. bd. 1990-91; pres. San Antonio Performing Arts Assn., 1984-85; trustee World Affairs Coun. San Antonio, 1982—2009, chmn. bd., 1984-86, disting. leaders coun., 2009-; trustee United Way, San Antonio, 1985-92, Tex. Cavaliers Charitable Found., 1994-97, 2003-05, Austin Coll., 1996-2001; trustee, Tex. State History Mus. Found., 2009-; mem. Tex. Comptrs. Bus. Adv. Coun., 2011-; bd. dirs. Houston Livestock Show and Rodeo; adv. bd. U. Tex., San Antonio, 1987—, vice chmn., 2008-; exec. com. chancellor's coun. U. Tex. Sys., 2005—; active Pan-Tex. Assembly, 1985-2002; chmn. Tex. Alcoholic Beverage Commn., 2003-08, commr., 1998-2008; commr. Tex. Dept. Public Safety, 2008-12, coord., Tex. Border Commerce, 2012-; exec. com. Rep. Eagles, 2000-01; dir. and exec. com. mem., Assoc. Reps. Tex., 2009-12, hon. dir. San Antonio Livestock Exposition, Inc.; bd. dirs. Fiesta Commn. Charitable Corp., 2004-09, chmn., pres., 2007-08. lt. USAR, hon. Tex. ranger capt., 2012. Named Chevalier Confrérie de Chevaliers du Tastevin, Sous-Commanderie de So. Tex., 1994—; Philanthropy award, Tex. Assn. Against Sexual Assault, 2007. Fellow San Antonio Bar Found., Tex. Bar Found. (life); mem. Tex. Bar Assn., San Antonio Acad. Alumni Assn. (pres. 1976-77, Disting. Alumnus award 2009), Ivy Club (Princeton, NJ), San Antonio German Club (pres. 1982-83), Order of Alamo, Order of Cascaron, Tex. Cavaliers (bd. dirs. 1989-92, 94-97, comdr. 1994-95, King Antonio LXXIV 1996-97, Kings coun. 1997—, vice chmn. 2003-04, chmn. 2004-05), San Antonio Country Club (bd. govs. 1990-93, v.p. 1992-93), Argyle Club, Conopus Club (bd. dirs. 1989-90), Princeton Club San Antonio and South Tex. (pres. 1980-81), Maclean Soc. at Princeton U., Sons of Republic of Tex. (life), Phi Delta Phi. Republican. Presbyterian. Office: Texas Higher Education Coordinating Board PO Box 12788 Austin TX 78711 Office Phone: 512-427-6101. Office Fax: 512-427-6127.*

STEENBERGEN, EWOUT, insurance company executive; M in Actuarial Sci., U. Amsterdam, Netherlands; MBA, U. Rochester, NY. Head corp. strategy, gen. mgr. Retail Czech Rep.; CEO RVS; cons. Ten Pas (known as Mercer); head corp. strategy, gen. mgr. Slovakia; dir., employee benefits, nationale-nederlanden ING Life Ins. Co., Netherlands; regional gen. mgr. ING Group, Hong Kong; CFO, chief risk officer ING Asia Pacific; CFO, exec. v.p. ING Life Ins. and Annuity Co.; CFO, ING Ins. US ING Group, 2010—. Bd. dirs. ING Life Ins. and Annuity Co. Office: ING North America Insurance Corp 5780 Powers Ferry Rd NW Atlanta GA 30327 Office Phone: 770-980-5100. Office Fax: 770-980-3301. Business E-Mail: ewout.steenbergen@ing.com.

STEENLAND, DOUGLAS M., food products executive; b. 1951; married; 2 children. BA in History, Calvin Coll., Grand Rapids, Mich., 1973; JD, George Washington U., 1976. Sr. ptnr. Verner, Liipfert, Bernhard, McPherson & Hand, Washington, 1978—91; v.p., dep. gen. counsel Northwest Airlines Corp., Eagan, Minn., 1991—94, sr. v.p., gen. counsel, 1994—98, exec. v.p., gen. counsel & alliances, 1998—99, exec. v.p., chief corp. officer, 1999—2001, pres., 2001—08, CEO, 2004—08; chmn. Internat. Lease Fin. Corp., 2009—, Performance Food Group, Richmond, Va., 2010—. Bd. dirs. MAIR Holdings, Inc., 2004—05, Am. Internat. Group, Inc. (AIG), 2009—, Chrysler Group LLC, 2009—, Digital River, Inc., 2009—. Bd. dirs. Guthrie Theater, Mpls., Minn. Symphony Orch.; mem. Super Bowl XL-Detroit 2006 Host Com.; chmn. Air Transport Assn., 2006—08. Office: Performance Food Group 12500 W Creek Pky Richmond VA 23238 Office Phone: 804-484-7700. Office Fax: 804-484-7701. Business E-Mail: dsteenland@pfgc.com.

STEENSLAND, RONALD PAUL, library consultant; b. Dothan, Ala., Dec. 16, 1946; s. Maurice John and Claire Folkes S.; m. Nancy Hollister, Dec. 20, 1970; 1 child, Ronald Paul. BA, Fla. State U., 1969, MS, 1970; postgrad., Miami U., Ohio, 1972, U. Md., 1980, US Army War Coll., 1995. Dir. Davidson County Pub. Libr., Lexington, N.C., 1970-73, Hidalgo County Libr. System, McAllen, Tex., 1973-76, Los Alamos County Libr., 1976-77, Lexington Pub. Libr., 1977—2003, Bay County Libr. Friends of Libr., 2003—; exec. v.p. Libr. Max Consultants, 2012—. Chmn. John Cotton Dana Library Public Relations Awards, 1977 Treas. Hildago County chpt. ARC, 1975. Served as co. comdr., bn. comdr., brigade comdr., asst. divsn. comdr., col., US Army, USAR, 1969-2005. Recipient Service award United Way. Mem. ALA, Res. Officers Assn. (sec.-treas. chpt. 100), Assn. U.S. Army (sec. Bluegrass chpt.), U.S. Chess Fedn., Southeastern Library Assn., Ky. Library Assn., Lexington C. of C., Alpha Tau Omega. Clubs: Lafayette, Pres.'s, Lexington Chess, Rotary. Baptist. Office: Lexington Pub Libr 140 E Main St Lexington KY 40507-1318 Personal E-mail: ron2085@yahoo.com.

STEEPLES, DOUGLAS WAYNE, retired university dean, professor consultant; b. Great Bend, Kans, Mar. 30, 1935; s. Marion Wayne and Dorothy Augusta (King) S.; children from previous marriage: Donald Bruce, John Douglas, Sheila Margaret; m. Christine McInnes Webster, Dec. 8, 1990. BA summa cum laude, U. Redlands, 1957; MA, U. NC, 1958, PhD, 1961; cert., Inst. Ednl. Mgmt., Harvard U., 1981. Asst. prof. history Calif. State U., North Ridge, 1961—64; prof. history Earlham Coll., Richmond, Ind., 1963-80; acad. v.p. Wartburg Coll., Waverly, Iowa, 1979-80; exec. v.p. Westminster Coll., Salt Lake City, 1980-83; provost Ohio U., Delaware, Ohio, 1983-85, acting pres., winter 1984; dean Coll. Liberal and Fine Arts, U. So. Colo., Pueblo, Colo., 1985-89; v.p. for acad. affairs Aurora U., Ill., 1989—93, v.p. acad. planning, 1993—94; dean, prof. history Coll. Liberal Arts, Mercer U., Macon, Ga., 1994-2000, ret., 2000; proctor, participant clin. practice program Mercer U. Med. Sch., Macon, 2005—08. Cons. higher edn. mgmt.; cons., reader advanced placement program Ednl. Testing Svc., Princeton, NJ, 1976-93; cons., evaluator North Ctrl. Assn. Sch. and Coll., Chgo., 1985-1994; mem. Accreditation Rev. Commn., 1992-94; bd. dirs. Western Ind. Coll. Fund, Salt Lake City, 1980-83; bd. dirs. Am. Conf. Acad. Deans, 1995-2000, sec.-treas., 1998-99; trustee Econ. and Bus. Hist. Soc., 1995-2000, pres., 1998-99; bd. dirs. Associated New Am. Colls., 1994-00, bd. mem., Pueblo Symphony Orch., 1987-89. Editor, contbg. author: Institutional Revival: Case Histories, 1986, Successful Strategic Planning: Case Studies, 1989, Mng. Change in Higher Ed., 1990; author: Treasure from the Painted Hills: Calico Calif., 1882-1907, 1999, Advocate for American Enterprise: William Buck Dana and the Commercial and Fin. Chronicle, 1865-1910, 2001; (with David O. Whitten) Democracy in Desperation: The Depression in the 1890s, 1998 (Choice Mag. Acad. Book of Yr. award), David James Steeples: Kansas Pioneer Family Patriarch, 2012; editor John Randolph Spears, Illustrated Sketches of Death Valley, 2000; assoc. editor Bus. Libr. Rev., 1996-2001; occasional columnist for Macon Telegraph; contbr. over 50 articles to profl. jours.; contbr. over 100 book revs. Adv. bd. Pueblo Symphony Orch., 1987—89; allocations com. United Way, Richmond, 1976—79, Pueblo, 1988—89, Aurora, 1990—94; vol. in svc., spl. cons. to pres. Ho-Chunk Wis./ Winnebago Nation, 2001; mem. Mayor's Commn. Restoration Ft. Hawkins, Macon, Ga., 1997—2003; pipe maj. Mercer U. Pipes and Drums, 2002—06, pipe sgt., 2006—09; scout master, chmn. Troop Commn. Eagle Scout, dist. committeeman, neighborhood commr., wood badge, unit commr., 2008—; vice chair East Ctrl. Dist., 1976—79, lectr., adult edn. tchr.; pres. Luth. Inter-parish Coun., Richmond, 1975—78; eucharistic min. St. Francis Episcopal Ch., Macon; bd. dir. Soc. for Use and Preservation of Resources, Richmond, 1976—79. Scholar U. Redlands, Calif., 1953-57; Danforth fellow, 1957-61; Woodrow Wilson fellow, 1957-58; Found. for Econ. Edn. Fellow in Bus., 1963; Am. Philos. Soc. grantee, 1966 Mem. Am. Hist. Assn., Orgn. Am. Hist., So. Hist. Assn., Soc. for Values in Higher Edn., Sierra Club, Rotary (bd. dirs. 1983-84), Palaver Club, Phi Beta Kappa (senator united chpt. 1973-79, sec.-treas. mid-Ga. alumni assoc. 1996-2000, pres. east ctrl. dist. 2003-04), Omicron Delta Kappa, Phi Kappa Phi, Alpha Mu Gamma. Republican. Avocations: mountain climbing, walking, bagpipes, travel, writing. Office: 656 River North Blvd Macon GA 31211-6340 Office Phone: 478-750-1051. E-mail: douglassteeples@att.net.

STEFANYSHYN-PIPER, HEIDEMARIE M., astronaut; b. St. Paul, Feb. 7, 1963; d. Michael and Adelheid Stefanyshyn; m. Glenn A. Piper; 1 child. BS in Mech. Engring., MIT, 1984, MS in Mech. Engring., 1985. Tng. as Navy basic diving officer and salvage officer Naval Diving and Salvage Tng. Ctr., Panama City, Fla.; several tours of duty as an engring. duty officer in area of ship repair and maintenance; underwater ship husbandry ops. officer for the supr. of salvage and diving Naval Sea Systems Command; astronaut, mission specialist NASA Johnson Space Ctr., 1996—. Crew mem., will perform spacewalks Space Shuttle Atlantis (STS-115), 2006; crew mem. STS-126 Endeavour Mission, 2008. Recipient Meritorious Svc. medal, Navy Commendation medal, Navy Achievement medal. Mem.: Am. Soc. Mech. Engineers. Achievements include being the first woman to be assigned as lead spacewalker for a shuttle flight on STS-126 mission in 2008. Avocations: scuba diving, swimming, running, rollerblading, ice skating. Office: Astronaut Office CB NASA Lyndon B Johnson Space Ctr Houston TX 77058

STEGER, CHARLES WILLIAM, academic administrator; b. Richmond, Va., June 16, 1947; s. Charles William and Virginia Belle (Garrett) S.; m. Janet Grey Baird, Sept. 13, 1969; children: Christopher B., David C. BArch, Va. Poly. Inst. & State U., 1970, MArch, 1971, PhD, 1978. Registered architect, Va. Project planner, architect Wiley & Wilson Inc., Lynchburg, Va., 1971-72, mgr. urban planning dept., 1973-74; dir. Environ. Design Consortium Inc., Blacksburg, Va., 1974-85; inst. grad. urban design program Coll. Architecture and Urban Studies, Va. Poly. Inst. and State U., Blacksburg, 1974-76, chmn. grad. urban design program, 1976-81; dean Coll. Architecture and Urban Studies, Va. Poly. Inst. and State U., Blacksburg, 1981-93; acting v.p. for pub. svc. Va. Poly. Inst. and State U., Blacksburg, 1990-93, v.p. for devel. and univ. rels., 1993-99; pres. Va. Tech. U., 2000—. Bd. dirs. Va. Found. Architecture, Richmond, Innovative Tech. Authority; mem. Gov.'s Secure Va. Tech. Initiative, 2001-02; mem. Gov.'s Va. Preparedness and Security Panel, 2001-02; bd. mem. Va. Advanced Shipbuilding and Carrier Integration Ctr., 2001-. Contbr. articles to jours. in field. Bd. dirs. Hollins Coll., Roanoke, Va., 1987-96, Boswil Found., Switzerland, 1986—, Ctr. in the Square, Roanoke, 1993-99; v.p. Va. Tech. Found., Inc., 1993-99; adv. coun. Va. Ctr. on Rural Devel., 1992—; commr. Govs. Commn. on Population Growth and Devel., Richmond, 1989-94; pres. Endowment Found. for We. Va. Found. for Arts and Scis. Fellow AIA (bd. dirs. ACSA Health Facilities Rsch. Program, Washington 1989—, ACSA Coun. on Arch. Rsch., 1987—); mem. Am. Planning Assn., Am. Inst. Cert. Planners, Commonwealth Club (Richmond, Va.), Shenandoah Club (Roanoke, Va.). Avocations: cattle farming, golf, canoeing. Office: Virginia Tech Office of President 210 Burruss Hall Blacksburg VA 24061 Office Phone: 540-231-6231. E-mail: president@vt.edu.*

STEHLING, ROBERT, chef; m. Nunally Kersh. Attended, U. NC. Dishwasher Crook's Corner, Chapel Hill, NC, chef, 1987, Magnolia Grill, Durham, NC, Arizona 206 & Cafe, NYC, Sarabeth's, NYC, Monkey Bar and Home, NYC; owner, exec. chef Hominy Grill, Charleston, SC, 1996—. Named Best Chef: Southeast, James Beard Found., 2008. Office: Hominy Grill 207 Rutledge Ave Charleston SC 29403 Office Phone: 843-937-0930.

STEIB, JAMES TERRY, bishop; b. Vacherie, La., May 17, 1940; Ordained priest Soc. of Divine Word, 1967; ordained bishop, 1984; aux. bishop Archdiocese of St. Louis, Mo., 1984—93; bishop Diocese of Memphis, Tenn., 1993—. Roman Catholic. Office: Diocese of Memphis 5825 Shelby Oaks Dr PO Box 341669 Memphis TN 38184-1669 Office Phone: 901-373-1200. Office Fax: 901-373-1269.

STEIDLEY, JUAN DWAYNE, lawyer, judge; b. Claremore, Okla., Mar. 8, 1959; s. J.D. and Gwendolyn Ann (Barnes) S.; m. Teresa Ann Brim, July 31, 1987; 1 child, Terrence. BA, Okla. State U., 1981; JD, Tulsa U., 1984. Bar: Okla. 1985. Judge, 1999—. Mem. Ho. of Rep. Okla. Ho. of Reps., Oklahoma City, 1986-98; past chmn. Sequoyah Dist. Boy Scouts Am. Methodist. Home: 2710 Highwood Ct Claremore OK 74017-4872 Office: Rogers County Court House 219 S Miss Divs II Claremore OK 74017

STEIN, BARRY EDWARD, medical educator; BA, CUNY, Queens, 1966, MA, 1969; PhD, CUNY, 1971. Prof. dept. physiology Med. Coll. Va.-Va. Commonwealth U., Richmond, 1982-94, affil. prof., 1994—; prof., chair dept. neurobiology and anatomy Wake Forest U Sch. Medicine, Winston-Salem, NC, 1994—. Bd. trustees The Gwendolyn Hardy Williams and Oliver Williams Found., Inc., 1992—; lectr. in field. Co-author: The Merging of the Senses, 1993; contbr. chpts. to books including The Cognitive Neurosciences, 1995, 99, Electrophysiology of Vision, 1991, The Development of Intersensory Perception: Comparative Perspectives, 1994, others; co-editor: The Handbook of Multisensory Processes, 2004; mem. editl. bd. Jour. Cognitive Neuroscience, The Behavioral and Brain Sciences; contbr. numerous articles to profl. pubs. including Jour. Neurophysiology, Jour. Neurosci., Sci., Jour. Comparative Neurology, others. Home: 1825 Georgia Ave Winston Salem NC 27104-3101 Office: Wake Forest Sch Medicine Med Ctr Blvd Winston Salem NC 27157-0001 Business E-Mail: bestein@wfubmc.edu.

STEIN, JOSH, state legislator; b. Washington, Sept. 13, 1966; m. Anna Stein; 3 children. BA in Hist., Dartmouth Coll.; MA in Pub. Policy & Law, Harvard U., 1995. Tchr. Danhiko High Sch., Zimbabwe, 1988—90; real estate project mgr. Self-Help Credit Union, 1995—97; legal counsel Senator John Edwards, 1999—2000; sr. dep. atty. gen. Atty. Gen. Roy Cooper, 2001—; mem. Dist. 16 NC State Senate, 2009—. Democrat. Jewish. Office: NC Senate 16 W Jones St Room 1113 Raleigh NC 27601-2808 Office Phone: 919-715-6400. Business E-Mail: Josh.Stein@ncleg.net.

STEIN, KATHY W., state legislator; b. Jan. 31, 1955; m. Alan Marcus; children: Wade Hampton Hancock, Scooter, Hadley Darin. State rep. Dist. 75, Ky., 1995—; state senator. Dist. 13 Ky., 2009—; mem. Edn. Com., Health & Welfare & Judiciary Com.; atty.; bd. dir. Fayette County Domestic Violence Prevention Bd.; bd. trustees Ohavay Zion Synagogue; mem. adv. com. Appalachian Sch. Law. Mem.: Am. United Separation Ch. & State. Democrat. Jewish. Mailing: 364 Transylvania Park Lexington KY 40508 Office: Capitol Annex Rm 429I Frankfort KY 40601 Home Phone: 859-252-1500; Office Phone: 859-225-4269, 502-564-8100 ext. 675. E-mail: kathy.stein@lrc.ky.gov.

STEIN, MARK RODGER, allergist; b. Phila., Apr. 24, 1943; s. Eli and Norma Stein; m. Phyllis Feinstein, Dec. 27, 1964; children: Amy Lynn, Philip Warren. BA, LaSalle Coll., Phila., 1964; MD, Jefferson Med. Coll., Phila., 1968. Diplomate Nat. Bd. Med. Examiners, Am. Bd. Internal Medicine, Am. Bd. Allergy and Immunology. Intern Abington Meml. Hosp., Pa., 1968-69; resident internal medicine Letterman Army Med. Ctr., San Francisco, 1972-75; fellow allergy and clin. immunology Fitzsimons Army Med. Ctr., Denver, 1975-77; pvt. practice West Palm Beach, Fla., 1979—. Asst. prof. depts. medicine and pediatrics Uniformed Svcs. U. Health Scis. Sch. Medicine, Bethesda, Md., 1978—79; clin. asst. prof. dept. internal medicine U. South Fla. Coll. Medicine, Tampa, 1979—83, Tampa, 1997—2000; clin. care cons. Clin. Ctr., NIH, Bethesda, 1978—79; mem. active staff Good Samaritan Hosp., West Palm Beach, Fla., chief svc. dept. allergy, 1990—98, chief svc. allergy, 2001—; chief dept. allergy St. Mary's Hosp., West Palm Beach, 1985—98; mem. active staff Palm Beach Gardens Med Ctr.; chief allergy svc. Intracostal Health Sys., 2000—01. Editor Gastroesophageal Reflux Disease and Airway Disease, 1999; contbr. articles to profl. jours. Trustee Am. Lung Assn., West Palm Beach, 1984-93, 95-2007. Fellow ACP, Am. Acad. Allergy, Asthma and Immunology, Am. Coll. Allergy, Asthma and Immunology (chmn. geriat. com. 1988-90), Am. Assn. Cert. Allergists, Am. Coll. Chest Physicians; mem. Am. Thoracic Soc., Mil. Allergists, Fla. Med. Assn., Palm Beach County Med. Assn., Asthma and Allergy Found. Am., Fla. Allergy and Immunology Soc. (pres. 1987-88), Southeastern Allergy Assn. Jewish. Avocations: tennis, golf. Office: 840 Us Highway 1 North Palm Beach FL 33408-3830 Home Phone: 561-622-2728; Office Phone: 561-626-2006. Personal E-mail: latallergy@aol.com.

STEIN, SAM LEE, lawyer; b. Cherokee, Okla., Nov. 19, 1958; s. Leroy Clark and Rosevelyn Edith (Peterson) Stein; m. Kelly Lee Pelter, Dec. 27, 1980; children: Patrick Leroy, Kelsy Lee. BS in Agr., Okla. State U., 1981; JD with honors, U. Okla., 1987, Gerry Spence's Trial lawyers Coll., 2006. Bar: Okla. 1987, U.S. Dist. Ct. (we. dist.) Okla. 1987, U.S. Dist. Ct. (no. dist.) Tex. 1987, Tex. 1988, U.S. Dist. Ct. (we. dist.) Tex. 1989, U.S. Ct. Appeals (5th cir.) 1993, U.S. Ct. Appeals (10th cir.) 2007, cert.: Nat. Bd. Trial Advocacy, Civil Trial Adv., Tex. Bd. Legal Specialization (civil trial and consumer and comml. lawl) 1994, bar: Tex. 2011, US Dist. Ct. (so. dist.) Tex. Assoc. Morris, Moore, Dalrymple, et. al., Amarillo, Tex., 1987—89, Templeton & Garner, PC, Amarillo, 1989—90; shareholder Garner, Stone & Lovell, Amarillo, 1990—94; mng. shareholder Garner, Lovell & Stein, PC, Amarillo, 1994—97; prin. Garner & Stein, LLP, Cherokee, Okla., 1997—2001, Garner, Stein & Dean, LLP, Cherokee, 2001—04, Whittenburg, Whittenburg, Garner & Stein, P.C., Cherokee, 2004—07. Asst. scoutmaster Troop 335 Boy Scouts Am., Cherokee, 1997—, bd. dirs. Cimarron Coun. Enid, Okla., 1999—. Recipient Profl. Responsibility award, U. Okla., 1987. Mem.: OAAJ, AAJ, ABA, Okla. Bar Assn., State Bar Tex. Office: Law Office Sam L Stein PLLC 305 S Grand Cherokee OK 73728 Home Phone: 580-596-2830; Office Phone: 580-596-3000. E-mail: sstein@steinlaw-ok.com.*

STEINBAUM, BERNICE, art dealer; b. Flushing, NY, Jan. 3, 1941; d. Julius Dov and Sarah (Lasker) Aptowitz; m. Harold Steinbaum; children: Jeremy, Sarah, Carrie. BA, Queens Coll., 1961; MA, Hofstra U., 1965; PhD in Art Edn., Columbia U., 1977. Tchr. Iowa Pub. Sch. System; assoc. prof. Drake U., Iowa; prof. Hofstra U., NYC; gallery dir. Bernice Steinbaum Gallery, NYC. Curator numerous exhbns. and traveling mus. shows; speaker in field; juror numerous art shows. Host: Art Time with Mrs. Steinbaum, Iowa; contbr. articles to profl. pubis., mags., and newspapers; author: The Rocker, 1992. Recipient Lifetime Achievement award, Women's Caucus for Art's, 2012; Named Woman of Yr. NOW, 1988. Office: Bernice Steinbaum Gallery 2101 Tigertail Ave Miami FL 33133-3243 Office Phone: 305-573-2700. Personal E-mail: bernicefla@bellsouth.net.

STEINBERG, LAWRENCE EDWARD, lawyer; b. Dallas, Nov. 25, 1935; s. Oscar J. and Pearl L. (Soloman) S.; children: Adam Joseph, Ilana Sara, Oliver David. BBA, U. Tex., 1958; JD, So. Meth. U., 1960. Bar: Tex. 1960. Since practiced in Dallas; ptnr. firm Steinberg Soloman & Meer, 1971-88, Johnson & Steinberg, Dallas, 1988-93; chmn., CEO Eagle Equity, Inc., Dallas, 1991—; of counsel Jenkins & Gilchrist, Dallas, 1993—98; mem. US Commn. Preservation of America's Heritage Abroad, 2007—11. Active program Dallas Ind. Sch. Dist., 1974-76; regional bd. chmn. Anti-Defamation League of B'nai Brith, 1974-77, nat. exec. com., 1977—, nat. law com., 1974-87; trustee Edna Gladney Home, 1975-92; v.p., trustee Shelton Sch., 1987-90; trustee Temple Emanu-El, 1992-94, 2008-12, Dallas Jewish Cmty. Found., 1990-2001, 2005—12; pres. U. Tex. Hillel Found., 2001-2003, mem. exec. com., 2001—09; bd. dirs. Jewish Fedn. Greater Dallas, 1984-87, 91-94, Dallas Coun. on World Affairs, 1998-2007, Stephen Wise, Acad., 1998-2002, Dallas Holocaust Ctr., 1998—10, Jewish Inst. Nat. Securities Affairs, 1999—, Dallas Furniture Bank, 2003—12; v.p. Am. Jewish Commn., 2003-06; regional bd. chmn. Am. Israel Pub. Affairs Com., 1997-2001, nat. exec. com., 1998-2008; mem. Dallas Com. Fgn. Rels. 2d lt. U.S. Army, 1959-60. Mem. Honors Golf Club, Masons, Shriners, Zeta Beta Tau, Phi Delta Phi, Beta Gamma Sigma, Pi Tau Pi (nat. pres. 1964-66). Home: 10131 Hollow Way Rd Dallas TX 75229-6634 Office: 5420 LBJ Fwy Ste 570 Dallas TX 75240

STEINBERG, LEV, mathematics professor; b. Kishinev, Moldova, Oct. 30, 1950; life ptnr. Vera Nisla. PhD, Acad. Scis., Russia, 1988. Prof. U. PR, Mayaguez, 1988—. Office: University PR Dept Mathematical Sciences Mayaguez PR 00681-9000 Personal E-mail: levste@gmail.com.*

STEINBERG, MARTY, lawyer; b. Balt., May 13, 1945; BS cum laude in Pharmacy, U. Pitts., 1968; JD cum laude, Ohio State U., 1971. Bar: Ohio 1971, Fla. 1974; U.S. Supreme Ct. 1981; Registered Pharmacist Ohio 1968. Atty. US Dept. Justice, Washington, Miami, 1972-78, atty. in charge NY regional offices Washington, 1978-79; chief counsel, permanent subcommittee on investigations US Senate, Washington, 1979-82; ptnr. Holland & Knight, Miami, Fla.; mng. ptnr., litig., intellectual property, antitrust Hunton & Williams LLP, Miami, 1999—. Inst. Canisius Coll. Buffalo, N.Y. 1978-79, SUNY Buffalo 1978-79, Am. U. Washington D.C. 1980-81. Contbr. articles to profl. jours. Bd. dirs. Miami Citizens Against Crime. Recipient Am. Jurisprudence award. Mem. ABA, Fla. Bar Assn., Ohio State Bar Assn., Am. Law Inst. (chmn. civic justice adv. com.), Fellow, Am. Coll. Trial Lawyers, Am. Bar Found., Am. Pharm. Assn., Am. Assn. Corporate Counsel. Office: Hunton & Williams LLP 1111 Brickell Ave Ste 2500 Miami FL 33131 Office Phone: 305-810-2500. Office Fax: 305-810-2460. Business E-Mail: msteinberg@hunton.com.

STEINER, DAVID P., waste management executive; BS in Acctg., La. State U., Baton Rouge, 1982; JD with honors, UCLA, 1986. Assoc. Gibson, Dunn & Crutcher, San Jose; ptnr. Phelps Dunbar, New Orleans; v.p., dep. gen. counsel Waste Management, Inc., Houston, 2000—01, sr. v.p., gen. counsel, corp. sec., 2001—03, exec. v.p., CFO, 2003—04, CEO, 2004—10, pres., CEO, 2010—. Mem.: ABA, Calif. Bar Assn., La. Bar Assn. Office: Waste Mgmt Inc 1001 Fannin St Ste 4000 Houston TX 77002 Office Phone: 713-512-6200.

STEINER, SARAH, school librarian; MA in Libr. & Info. Sci., U. South Fla., Tampa, 2004; MA in English Literary Studies, Ga. State U., Atlanta, 2011. Reference & instrn. librarian Johnson & Wales U., 2004—05; learning commons librarian Ga. State U., Atlanta, 2005—09, social work and virtual services librarian, 2009—. Co-founder Carterette Webinar Series. Assoc. editor: Ga. Libr. Quar.; co-editor: The Desk and Beyond: Next Generation Reference Services, 2008. Named a LYRASIS NextGen Librarian, 2009; named to Movers & Shakers, Libr. Jour., 2011. Mem.: ALA, Libr. Soc. of World, Assn. Coll. & Rsch. Libraries, Ga. Libr. Assn. (Bob Richardson award 2010), American Folklore Assn. Office: Georgia State University Library North 2d Fl 100 Decatur St SE Atlanta GA 30303-3202 Office Phone: 404-413-2808. Business E-Mail: ssteiner@gsu.edu.

STEINHART, RONALD G., board member, retired bank executive; b. Beaumont, Tex., June 15, 1940; s. Werner and Marga (Steinhart); m. Phyllis Yonet; children: David Alan, Kenneth Jason, Barry Joel. BBA in Acctg., U. Tex., MBA in Fin. CPA. Pres. Dallas Bank & Trust, 1965-69, Main St. Nat. Bank, Dallas, 1969-77; chmn. Town North Nat. Bank, Dallas, 1972-75, Dallas Fort Worth Airport Bank, 1972-75; pres. Valley View Bank, Dallas, 1977-80; chmn. Equitable Bank, Dallas, 1979-80; vice chmn. InterFirst Corp., Dallas, pres., COO, 1980-86; vice chmn. First RepublicBank Corp., Dallas, 1986-88; founder Team Bank, 1988; chmn., CEO Team Bancshares, Inc. (merged with Bank One, Tex., N.A. in 1992), 1988—92; pres., COO Bank One, Tex., N.A., Dallas, 1992—94; chmn., CEO Bank One, Tex. N. A., 1995—96; chmn., CEO, Commercial Banking Group Bank One Corp., 1996—2000. Prin. rep. Assn. Bank Holding Cos.; former prin. RepublicBank Assn.; bd. dirs. NCH Corp., 2000-, Penske Automotive Group, Inc., 2001-, Susser Holdings Corp., 2009-, Carreker Corp. 2001-05, Penson Worldwide, Inc., 2006-08, Tex. Industries Inc., 2007-, Animal Health Internat., Inc., 2007-, Chase Paymentech Solutions, LLC(formerly known as Paymentech, Inc.), Pension Worldwide, Inc. 2006-08; trustee MFS, Sun Life Series Trust; bd. mgrs. Compass Variable Accounts, Prentiss Properties Trust; mem. adv. bds. JP Morgan Chase Dallas, SunTx Capital Partners, Red McCombs Sch. Bus., bd. dirs. Mem. Edwin L. Cox Sch. Bus. assoc. bd. So. Meth. U.; mem. exec. bd., chmn. 1983 and 1984 Scout show Circle Ten council Boy Scouts Am.; sec./treas. Dallas Citizens Council; dir. Jewish Welfare Fedn. Found., Dallas Zoolog. Soc., State Fair of Tex., United Way of Dallas, Dallas Mus. Art, Dallas Ctr. for Performing Arts, US Holocaust Meml. Mus.; chmn. bd. trustees Tchr. Retirement Sys. of Tex., housing authority City of Dallas; mem. Cotton Bowl Council. Served with USAF, 1958-68, with res. Recipient 2009 J. Erik Jonsson Ethics award, So. Methodist U. Cary M. Maguire Ctr. for Ethics and Pub. Responsibility. Mem. Tex. Bankers Assn., Tex. Assn. Bank Holders Cos., Dallas Clearing House Assn. (dir.), Tex. Soc. C.P.A.s., Assn. Res. City Bankers, Young Pres. Orgn. Office: Susser Holdings Corp 4525 Ayers St Corpus Christi TX 78415-1401 Office Phone: 361-884-2463. Office Fax: 361-884-2494. Business E-Mail: rsteinhart@txi.com.

STEINHAUS, JOHN EDWARD, retired anesthesiologist, educator; b. Omaha, Feb. 23, 1917; s. Emil F. and Pearl (Haynie) S.; m. Mila Jean Pinkerton, Feb. 21, 1943; children: Kathryn, Carolyn, Barbara, William, Elizabeth. BA, U. Neb., Lincoln, 1940, MA, 1941; MD, U. Wis., Madison, 1945, PhD, 1950. Diplomate Am. Bd. Anesthesiologists. Pvt. practice specializing in anesthesiology, Madison, Wis., 1951-58, Atlanta, 1958—; faculty U. Wis., 1951-58; mem. faculty Emory U., Atlanta, 1958—, prof. anesthesiology, 1959-87, prof. emeritus, 1987—, chmn. dept., 1959-85; chief anesthesiology service Grady Meml. Hosp., 1959-77, Emory U. Hosp., 1958-85; ret., 1987. Author: Medical Care Divided; contbr. articles to profl. jours. Past pres. Anesthesia Found. Mem. Am. Soc. Anesthesiologists (past pres., Disting. Service award 1982), So. Soc. Anesthesiologists (past pres.), AMA, AAAS, Assn. U. Anesthetists (past pres.), Anesthesiology History Assn. (past pres.), Soc. Pharm. Exptl. Therapeutics, Phi Beta Kappa, Sigma Xi, Alpha Omega Alpha. Home: 15605 Freemanville Rd Alpharetta GA 30004-2798 Office Phone: 404-741-5325.

STEINHAUSER, BRENDAN MICHAEL, political campaign administrator; b. 1981; BA, U. Tex., 2004; MA in American Fgn. Policy, Inst. of World Politics, 2011. Dir. fed. & state campaigns FreedomWorks, 2005—12; dir. comm. Right on Crime Initiative Tex. Public Policy Found., 2012—; mgr. Senator John Cornyn's Re-Election Campaign, 2013—. Author: The Conservative Revolution: How to Win the Battle for College Campuses, 2004. Co-founder ISI Alumni Network, Washington; guest lectr. LI Youth Leadership Sch. Recipient Free Republic Collegiate Eagle award; named one of The Politics 40 Under 40, TIME Mag., 2010, The 35 Under 35 Who Changed DC, MSNBC Beltway Power List, 2010. Mem.: Golden Key Internat. Honour Soc. Conservative.*

STEINHORN, IRWIN HARRY, lawyer, corporate financial executive, educator; b. Dallas, Aug. 13, 1940; s. Raymond and Libby L. (Miller) Steinhorn; m. Deborah Kelley Steinhorn, Apr. 7, 2002; 1 child, Leslie Robin. BBA, U. Tex., 1961, LLB, 1964. Bar: Tex. 1964, U.S. Dist. Ct. (no. dist.) Tex. 1965, Okla. 1970, U.S. Dist. Ct. (we. dist.) Okla. 1972. Assoc. Oster & Kaufman, Dallas, 1964-67; ptnr. Parness, McQuire & Lewis, Dallas, 1967-70; sr. v.p., gen. counsel LSB Industries, Inc., Oklahoma City, 1970-87; v.p., gen. counsel USPCI, Inc., Oklahoma City, 1987-88; ptnr. Hastie & Steinhorn, Oklahoma City, 1988-95; sr. ptnr., dir. Conner & Winters, Okla. City, 1995—. Adj. prof. law Oklahoma City U. Sch. Law, 1979—; lectr. in field. Mem. adv. com. Okla. Securities Commn., 1986—; mem. exec. adv. bd. Oklahoma City U. Sch. Law, 2000—; bd. dirs. Okla. Venture Forum, 2000—. Served to capt. USAR, 1964-70. Recipient Law award, 2009. Mem.: ABA, Jewish Fedn. Okla. City, Com. to Revise Okla. Bus. Corp. Act, Okla. Bar Assn. (bus. assn. sect., sec., treas. 1986—87, chmn. 1988—89), Tex. Bar Assn., Rotary, Phi Alpha Delta. Republican. Jewish. Home: 224 NW 18th St Oklahoma City OK 73103 Office: Conner & Winters One Leadership Sq 211 N Robinson Ave Ste 1700 Oklahoma City OK 73102-7136 Home Phone: 405-524-5621; Office Phone: 405-272-5711. Business E-Mail: isteinhorn@cwlaw.com.

STEINKAMPF, MICHAEL P., physician; m. Stephanie Steinkampf. MA in Chemistry, Princeton U., NJ, 1977; MD, LSU Sch. Medicine, New Orleans, La., 1981. Cert. in reproductive endocrinology, infertility Am. Bd. Ob-Gyn., 1989. Prof. ob-gyn. U. Ala., Birmingham, 1987—2004; dir. Ala. Fertility Specialists, Birmingham, 2004—. Named one of Best Dr. in Am., 1994—. Office: Alabama Fertility Specialists 2700 Hwy 280 S Ste 370E Birmingham AL 35223

STEINMETZ, DEBORAH SUSAN, interior designer; b. New Orleans, Nov. 29, 1951; d. Donald Frederick and Estelle Margaret (Ulmer) Tossell; m. Robert Steinmetz, Dec. 29, 1973. BFA, La. State U., 1973. Interior designer David Grinnell Architect, 1973—75; pvt. practice Columbus, Ga., 1975—77; designer Dameron-Pierson, New Orleans, 1977—79; v.p. interior design Interior Environments, Inc., New Orleans, 1979—83; pres., owner Steinmetz & Assocs., 1983—. Interior design curriculum com. Dominican Coll., New Orleans, 1981—82; interior design adv. com. Delgado CC, New Orleans, 1982—; chmn. membership Preservatin Resource Ctr., 1988. Dir. profl. devel. Nat. Coun. Interior Design Qualification, 1994—95;

Visual arts com. Contemporary Art Ctr., 1980—81. Mem.: La. State Interior Design Alumni (sec. 1987), Interior Designers of La. (treas. 1987), La. State Bd. Interior Design Examiners, Internat. Interior Design Assn., Am. Soc. Interior Designers (bd. dirs. 1993—94, bd. dirs. La. chpt. 1982—, newsletter editor 1982, chain membership/admissions 1984, treas. 1985—87, sec. 1988, chmn. New Orleans chpt. 1980—81, Presdl. citation), La. Landmarks Soc., Nat. Trust Hist. Preservation. Roman Catholic. Office: 225 Baronne St Ste 207 New Orleans LA 70112-1704

STEINMETZ, JON DAVID, health facility administrator, psychologist; b. NYC, June 4, 1940; s. Lewis I. and Rose (Josefsberg) S.; m. Jane Audrey Hilton, Dec. 24, 1964; children: Jonna Lynn, Jay Daniel. BA, NYU, 1962; MA, Bradley U., 1963. Lic. psychologist, Ill. Intern in psychology Galesburg (Ill.) State Rsch. Hosp., 1963-64; staff psychologist Manteno (Ill.) State Hosp., 1964-68, program dir., 1968-70, asst. dir., 1970-72; dep. dir. Manteno Mental Health Ctr., 1972-80, Tinley Park (Ill.) Mental Health Ctr., 1980-88; dir. Chgo. Read Mental Health Ctr., 1988-91; ret., 1991. Clin. dir. Jane Addams Hull House Assn., 1992-98. Trustee Village of Park Forest, Cook, Will Counties, Ill.; officer, bd. dirs. various civic orgns., Park Forest; dir. SOS Children's Village Ill., Lockport, 2004—05. Home: 38 Springside Ct Hendersonville NC 28791-6406

STEINORTH-POWEL, CHRISTINA ENNI, psychotherapist, author; m. Russell A. Powel, Oct. 28, 2014. BA, Calif. State U., Northridge, 1990; MA in Marriage and Family Therapy, Phillips Grad. Inst., 1995. Cert. in profl. counselling Internat. Assn. Behavioral Medicine, Counseling & Psychotherapy. Pvt. practice, Santa Barbara, Calif., 2000—13, Dallas, 2014—. Media relationship expert Wall St. USA Today Playboy, Womans Day Mag., NBC News, Fox News Frequent & Popular Radio Personality. Author: (book) Cue Cards For Life, Cue Cards for Men. Mem.: Tex. Assn. Marriage and Family Therapists, Calif. Assn. Marriage & Family Therapists (Santa Barbara chpt. & Ventura County chpt. clin. mem.), Am. Assn. Marriage & Family Therapists (clin. mem.). Avocations: writing, reading, art, painting. Office: 1512 Flintwood Dr Richardson TX 75081 Office Phone: 805-320-6624. Office Fax: 972-850-9222. Business E-Mail: SteinorthC@aol.com.*

STELLAR, ARTHUR WAYNE, school system administrator; b. Columbus, Ohio, Apr. 12, 1947; s. Fredrick and Bonnie Jean (Clark) S. BS, Ohio U., 1969, MA, 1970, PhD, 1973. Tchr. Athens City Schs., Ohio, 1969-71; curriculum coord., tchr. Belpre City Schs., Ohio, 1971-72; prin. elem. schs., head tchr. learning disabilities South-Western City Schs., Grove City, Ohio, 1972-76; dir. elem. edn. Beverly Pub. Schs., Mass., 1976-78; coord. spl. projects and system-wide planning Montgomery County Pub. Schs., Rockville, Md., 1978-80; asst. supt. Shaker Heights, Ohio, 1980-83; supt. schs. Mercer County Pub. Schs., Princeton, W.Va., 1983-85, Oklahoma City Pub. Schs., 1985-92, Cobb County, Ga., 1992-93, Kingston Sch. Dist., NY, 1996—2001; dep. supt. Boston Pub. Schs., 1993-95, acting supt., 1995-96; pres., CEO High/Scope Ednl. Rsch. Found., Ypsilanti, Mich., 2001—03; v.p., chief edn. officer Renaissance Learning, Madison, Wis., 2003—04; sr. assoc. Proact Search, Inc., Milw., 2004—09; rep. Docufide, Inc., LA, 2004—05, also adv. bd. dirs., 2004—05; supt. Taunton Pub. Schs., Mass., 2005—09, Burke Co. Pub. Schs., NC, 2009—. Mem. ednl. adv. bd. Tchrs. Support Network, 2004-08; adj. prof. Lesley Coll., Cambridge, Mass., 1976-78; adj. faculty Harvard U., 1992-93; assoc. Sch. Match, Ohio, 2004—09. Author: Educational Planning for Educational Success; Effective Schools Research: Practice and Promise; editor: Effective Instructional Management; cons. editor, book rev. editor Jour. Ednl. Pub. Rels.; mem. editl. bd. Jour. Curriculum & Supervision, Reading Today's Youth; contbr. articles to profl. jours. Mem. Urban Ctr. Ednl. Adv. Bd., US Dept. Edn. Urban Supt. Network, Coun. Great City Schs. Bd., Urban Edn. Clearing House Adv. com., U. Okla. Adminstrn. cert. program com., Cmty. Literacy Coun. Bd.; chmn. bd. dirs. Langston U.; bd. dirs. Oklahoma County chpt. ARC, Jr. Achievement Greater Oklahoma City Bd., Okla. State Fair Bd., Horace Mann League, 1993—, v.p. 2000-01, pres.-elect, 2001-02, pres. 2002-03, past pres. 2003-04, mem. found. com., 2003-05; v.p. Last Frontier Coun. Bd., v.p. NY State PTA, 1996-2000, Kingston chpt. Rip Van Winkle Coun.; v.p. Boy Scouts Am., 1996-2001, membership chmn., 1996-97; exec. bd. Nat. Dropout Prevention Ctr. Network, 1998-2008, chmn., 2003-07; curriculum com. NY State Coun. Sch. Supts., 1996-2001; bd. dirs. Friends Historic Kingston, 1996-2001, Friends Senate House, Kingston, 1996-2001, Project Contemporary Competitiveness Inc., 2005-09. Recipient Silver Beaver award, Boy Scouts Am., 1990, Amb. award, Horace Mann League, 1995—2009, Crystal Star Leadership award, NDPC/N, 2007, Disting. Svc. award, Pub. Edn. Mass., Tech. award, JFY Networks, 2008; named a Friend, Horace Mann League, 2006; named to Linden McKinley H.S. Acad. Hall of Fame, 2003; fellow, Charles Kettering Found. IDEA, 1976, 1978, 1980, NEH, Danforth Found., 1987—88. Mem. ASCD (life, exec. coun., pres. 1994-95, rev. coun. 1997-2002), Mich. ASCD, Mass. ASCD, Ohio ASCD, Okla. ASCD (Publ. award 1989), NY ASCD, Wis. ASCD, Internat. Soc. Ednl. Planning, Internat. Reading Assn. (govt. rels. com. 2003-04), Nat. Soc. Study Edn., Nat. Planning Assn., Nat. Assn. Gifted Children (life), Nat. Assn. Edn. Young Children (life), Nat. Coun. Tchrs. English (life), Music Educators Nat. Conf. (life), Nat. Orgn. Legal Problems Edn., Nat. Policy Bd. Ednl. Adminstrn., Am. Assn. Sch. Adminstrs. (life, Leadership for Learning award 1991, Dr. Effie Jones Humanitarian award 2007), Coll. Bd. Advanced Placement Spl. Recognition award 1991, Nat. Assn. Elem. Sch. Prins. (life), Am. Edn. Fin. Assn., Nat. Assn. Edn. Young Children (life), Nat. Sch. Pub. Rels. Assn. (Honor award 1991), Am. Mus. Natural Hist. (assoc.), Mass. Assn. for Sch. Supts., Mass. Assn. for Edn. of Young Children, Harvard U. Roundtable of Supts., Mass. Urban Supts., Nat. Sch. Pub. Rels. Assn., Taunton Area C. of C., World Coun. Curriculum and Instrn. (life, bd. dirs. N.Am. chpt. 1996-2000, pres. 2000-02), Coun. Basic Edn., Ohio Assn. Elem. Sch. Adminstrs., Buckeye Assn. Sch. Adminstrs., Ohio U. Coll. Edn. (disting. alumnus award 1991), Okla. Assn. Sch. Adminstrs., Mass. Assn. Sch. Adminstrs., Okla. Coalition Pub. Edn., Okla. Commn. Ednl. Leadership, Urban Area Supts. (Okla. br.), Ohio U. Alumni Assn. (nat. dir. 1975-78, pres. Ctrl. Ohio chpt. 1975-76, pres. Mass. chpt. 1976-78, life mem. trustees acad.), World Future Soc. (life) Greater Oklahoma City C. of C. (bd. dirs.), Okla. Heritage Assn., Heritage Hills Assn. (bd. dirs.), Victorian Soc. (New England chpt.), Nat. Eagle Scout Assn. (life), Aerospace Found. (hon. bd. dirs.), PLATO, Learning, Inc. (bd. dirs. 2000-03), Tchrs. Support Network (adv. bd. dirs. 2004-08), Am. Bus. Card Club, Coca Cola Collectors Club, Internat. Club, Mgmt. Consortium (bd. advisors),Fulbright Alumni Assn. (life), Tau Kappa Epsilon Alumni Assn. (regional officer Mass. 1976-78, named Alumni Nat. Hall of Fame 1986, Nat. Alumnus of Yr. 1993, Excellence in Edn. award 1993), Kappa Delta Pi (life; advisor Ctrl. Okla. chpt., nat. publs. com.), Phi Delta Kappa (life; mem. Fulbright tchr. and adminstr. exch. program to Mexico, 2009, mem. Fulbright tchr. and adminstr. exch. program to Brzil, 2009). Methodist. Office Phone: 508-922-6389. Personal E-mail: artstellar@yahoo.com. Business E-Mail: astellar@tauntonschools.org.

STELLING, KESSEL D., JR., bank executive; b. 1956; m. Carol Stelling; 2 children. BBA in Banking & Fin., U. Ga., Athens, 1978; grad., La. State U. Grad. Sch. Banking of South, 1988. With First Railroad and Banking Co.; sr. v.p. First Nat. Bank of Cobb County; chmn., CEO Riverside Bancshares, Inc. and Riverside Bank; pres., COO Bank of North Georgia, 2006—08; regional CEO, Atlanta market Synovus Financial Corp., Atlanta, 2008—10, pres., COO, 2010, pres., CEO, 2010—, chmn., 2011—. Bd. dirs. Wellstar Health Systems, Synovus Financial Corp., 2010—. Past chmn. Regional Bus. Coalition; past pres. YMCA Cobb County; mem. Devel. Authority Bd. Cobb County; bd. mem. Cumberland Cmty. Improvement Dist., Univ. Sys. Ga. Bd. Regeants Sixth Congl. Dist., Metro Atlanta C. of C., Cobb C. of C., Cobb Cmty. Found., The Georgian Club; mem. dean's adv. coun. U. Ga. Terry Sch. Bus.; trustee Kennesaw State U.; campaign chmn. United Way Cobb County, 2002. Recipient Disting. Alumni award, U. Ga. Terry Coll. Bus.; named Cobb County Citizen of Yr., Marietta Daily Jour., 2003; named one of The 100 Most Influential Georgians, Ga. Trend mag., 2009, 2010. Office: Synovus Financial Corp Ste 500 1111 Bay Ave Columbus GA 31901 Office Phone: 706-649-5220. Office Fax: 706-641-6555.

STEPHEN, CRAIG A., JR., food products executive; BSBA, U. Cin., 1980. CPA 1985. Sr. mgr. Ernst & Young LLP, Cin.; v.p., CFO, middle east/Australia region Chiquita Brands International, Inc., corp. planner, 1990, v.p., fin., planning, 1997, pres., COO, fresh group far and middle east/Australia region, 1997—. Office: Chiquita Brands International Inc 550 S Caldwell St Ste 1010 Charlotte NC 28202-2681 Office Phone: 513-784-8000. Office Fax: 513-784-8030. Business E-Mail: cstephen@chiquita.com.

STEPHENS, BOBBY GENE, college administrator, consultant; b. Glendale, SC, Mar. 8, 1935; s. Dewey and Bertha Cordelia (Mott) S.; m. Sandra Elizabeth White, June 27, 1957; children: Elaine, Ward, Todd, Adam. BS, Wofford Coll., Spartanburg, SC, 1957; MS, Clemson U., SC, 1961, PhD, 1964; LHD, MacMurray Coll., Jacksonville, Ill., 1987. Textile chemist Reeves Bros., Fairforest, SC, 1957-58; grad. asst. Clemson U., 1960-63; instr. chemistry Wofford Coll., Spartanburg, SC, 1963-64, asst. prof., 1964-67, assoc. prof., 1967-72, prof., v.p. acad. affairs, 1972-80; pres. MacMurray Coll., Jacksonville, Ill., 1980-86; v.p. research and enrollment Wofford Coll., Spartanburg, SC, 1986-91, v.p. sci. and tech., 1991—, prof. chemistry emeritus, 2000—. Project dir. Howard Hughes Med. Inst., 1992—; pres. BGS Cons.; cons. in field Contbr. articles to sci. jours.; inventor extractions with propylene carbonate, 1975; producer: TV series The Psychology of Interpersonal Behavior, 1974. Co-chmn. Daniel Morgan Restoration Com., 1986-88; vice chmn. Spartanburg County Pollution Control Authority, 1970-74; bd. dirs. SC Lung Assn., Spartanburg, 1970-75; sect. maj. United Way, 1975-77; chair SC State Libr. Bd., 2004—. 1st lt. US Army, 1958-60. Recipient Jefferson award SC Acad. Sci., 1969; recipient 1st prize graphics div. 2d Edit. Art Contest, 1971, 2d and 3d prizes Lawson's Fork Creek Photography Contest, 1978, Alumni Disting. Svc. award Wofford Coll., 2001; USPHS grantee; NSF grantee Mem. Am. Chem. Soc. (chair Western Carolinas sect. 2003), Nat. Assn. Gifted Children, Assn. Ednl. Communications and Tech., Phi Beta Kappa. Methodist. Home: 460 S Fairview Ave Spartanburg SC 29302 Office: Wofford College 429 N Church St Spartanburg SC 29303-3663 Office Phone: 864-573-8844. Personal E-mail: bgsphd@bellsouth.net. Business E-Mail: stephensbg@wofford.edu.

STEPHENS, EDWARD MICKEY, state legislator; b. Savannah, GA, Apr. 14; m. Gloria Stephens; children: Edward Jr., Karlis. Attended Savannah State Coll.; MS in Edn., Cambridge Coll. Mem. Dist. 124 Ga. House of Reps., 2002—04, mem. Dist 161, 2004—. Democrat. Catholic. Office: 409-D Coverdell Legislative Office Bldg Atlanta GA 30334 also: PO Box 5485 Savannah GA 31414 Office Phone: 404-656-0117. E-mail: mickey.stephens@house.ga.gov, mickey.stephens@gmail.com.

STEPHENS, JERRY WAYNE, librarian, director; b. Birmingham, Ala., Sept. 10, 1949; s. William Larkin and Odell (Kerr) S.; m. Lisa Brown, June 2, 1972; children: Jeramy Wayne, Elizabeth Ashley, John Larkin BS in Acctg., U. Ala.-Birmingham, 1974, MBA, 1976; M.L.S., U. Ala., 1977, PhD in Adminstrn. Higher Edn., 1982. Svc. mgr. Hammond Organ Studios, Birmingham, 1973-74; acct. Mervyn Sterne Libr., U. Ala., Birmingham, 1974-75, asst. to dir., 1975-76, asst. dir., 1976-85, libr., dir., 1985—; interim fiscal officer Univ. Coll. U. Ala., Birmingham, 1982, interim asst. v.p. for acad. affairs, 1989-91. Vice chmn. Network Acad. Librs., 1985-86, 95-96, chmn., 1986-88, 96, 2000-01; cons. Birmingham Pub. Libr., 1977—; cons. Southeastern Libr. Assn., Atlanta, 1979-80; bd. dirs. Southeastern Libr. Network, treas., 1992-93, chmn., 1993-94; mem. user's coun. Online Computer Libr. Ctr., 1997—, pres.-elect, 2000-01, pres., 2001-2002, bd. trustees, 2002—. Contbr. articles to profl. publs. Sponsored exec. United Way, Birmingham, 1978, sr. exec., 1982; foster parent Dept. Pensions and Securities, Birmingham, 1982-83; elder Homewood Cumberland Presbyn. Ch., Birmingham, 1982-84, 88-90. With USN, 1972-73 Named one of Outstanding Young Men Am., U.S. Jaycees, 1978, 79 Mem. ALA, SE Libr. Assn., Ala. Libr. Assn. (treas. 1977-78), Am. Mgmt. Assn. Avocations: camping, softball. Office: U Ala-Birmingham Mervyn H Sterne Libr 1530 3d Ave South Birmingham AL 35294-0014 Office Phone: 205-934-6360. Business E-Mail: jwstephens@uab.edu.

STEPHENS, JOHN J., telecommunications industry executive; m. Michele Stephens; 6 children. BSBA in acctg., Rockhurst Coll.; JD, St. Louis Univ. Tax acct. Peat Marwick & Mitchell, Kans. City; sr. tax. mgr. Ernst & Young, St. Louis; dir. Fed. taxes SBC Comm. (now AT&T Inc.), Dallas, 1992—95; mng. dir. taxes AT&T Inc., Dallas, 1995—2000, v.p. taxes, 2000—01, sr. v.p., contr., 2001—11, sr. exec. v.p., CFO, 2011—. Bd. dir. Telmex, America Movil. Mem. adv. bd. Mays Bus. Sch., Tex. A&M Univ. Office: AT&T Inc 208 S Akard St Dallas TX 75202 Office Phone: 210-821-4105.

STEPHENS, LAURENCE DAVID, JR., linguist, investor, oil industry executive; b. Dallas, July 26, 1947; s. Laurence D. Sr. and Amy Belle (Schickram) S.; m. Susan Leigh Foutz, Apr. 16, 1988; 1 child, Laurence David III. MA, Stanford U., 1972, PhD, 1976. Cert. minerals mgr. Nat. Assn. Royalty Owners, 2003. Vis. fellow Yale U., New Haven, summer 1979; rsch. fellow U. SC, Columbia, 1980; asst. prof. U. NC, Chapel Hill, 1982-88, assoc. prof., 1989—; pres. Colgate Mgmt. Co., Inc., Dallas, 1997—; gen. ptnr. Moorman, Schickram & Stephens, Ltd., Dallas, 1997—; mem.-mgr. Stephens Resources, LLC, 2004—. Co-author: Two Studies in Latin Phonology, 1977, Language and Metre, 1984, The Prosody of Greek Speech, 1994, Discontinuous Syntax, 1999, Latin Word-Order: Structured Meaning and Information, 2006, Semantics for Latin, 2013; editor ann. vol. L'Année Philologique, 1987-92; contbr. numerous articles to profl. jours. Mem. University Park Cmty. League, Park Cities Hist. Soc., Nat. Trust for Hist. Preservation, Washington, 1989—, The Dallas Symphony Assn. Ann. Fund, Metro. Opera Guild, N.Y.C., 1992—, Wythe County VA Hist. Soc., 1998—. Grantee L'Année Philologique, NEH, 1987-89, 89-91, 91-93. Mem. Am. Philol. Assn., Greek and Latin Linguistic Assn. (chmn. 1987-92), N.Y. Acad. Scis., Indogermanische Gesellschaft, Internat. Soc. Bibliographie Classique, Arabian Horse Assn., Nat. Assn. Royalty Owners, Sigma Xi. Achievements include discovery of language universal regularities concerning labiovelar phonemes, laws of palatalization, the law of catathesis in Greek (pitch lowering), and grammatical, semantic, pragmatic (information structure) regularities of discontinuous constituency and nonconfigurational syntactic structures in Greek and Latin; co-developer of Justeson-Stephens probability distribution for cognates between unrelated languages, Justeson-Stephens probability distribution of the numbers of vowels, consonants, and total phonological inventory size in the languages of the world; research on the law of the quantitative form of diachronic polysemy growth, semantic universals of aspect and modality, universals of writing systems and their evolution. Home: 2785 Turnpike Rd Lexington VA 24450 also: 3319 Greenbrier Dr Dallas TX 75225 Office: 30 Crossing Ln Ste 204 Lexington VA 24450 Office Phone: 540-463-3146. Personal E-mail: lsteph8694@aol.com.

STEPHENS, RON, state legislator; Former state rep. Dist. 150, Ga.; house rep. Ga.; state rep. Dist. 123 Ga., 2003—04; mem. Appropriations Com., Industry Rels., Transp. Com.; state rep. Dist. 164, 2004—. Republican. Address: 103 Anford Dr Garden City GA 31418 Mailing: 507 Legis Off Bldg Atlanta GA 30334 Office Phone: 912-966-5665. Fax: 912-964-9699. E-mail: quickrxdrg@aol.com.

STEPHENS, SCOTT, art educator; BFA in Printmaking, Wash. U., St. Louis; studied grad. work, Sch. of Art Inst. Chgo.; MFA, U. Ala. Prof. fine art Montevallo U., 1983—. Exhibitions include Montgomery Mus. Fine Art, U. Montevallo, residencies, Centrum vor Grafiek Frans Masereel in Kasterlee, Belgium, Tamarind Summer Workshop in Traditional Lithography. Named U.S. Prof. Yr. State Ala., Carnegie Found. Advancement of Teaching, 2006; fellow So. Arts Fedn., NEA, Ala. State Coun. Arts. Office: Dept Arts U Montevallo Montevallo AL 35115

STEPHENS, SLOANE, professional tennis player; b. Plantation, Fla., Mar. 20, 1993; d. John Stephens and Sybil Smith. Profl. tennis player WTA Tour, 2008—. Achievements include winning singles and doubles (with Mallory Burdette), Grade 1 USTA Internat. Spring Championships, 2009; winning doubles (with Tímea Babos), Jr. Wimbledon Championships, 2010, Jr. French Open Championships, 2010, Jr. US Open Championships; winning Camparini Gioielli Cup, 2011; being the youngest player in the year-end Top 20 rankings (World No. 17), 2013. Office: WTA Tour 100 2nd Ave S Ste 1100 Saint Petersburg FL 33701-4338*

STEPHENS, WARREN A., bank executive; BA, Washington & Lee U., 1979; MBA, Wake Forest U., 1981. V.p., corp. fin. dept. Stephens, Inc., 1981—86, chmn., CEO, pres., 1986—. Bd. dirs. Dillards Inc., 2002—. Named one of Forbes 400: Richest Americans, 2009. Office: Stephens Inc 111 Center St Little Rock AR 72201-4402 Office Phone: 501-377-2000. Office Fax: 501-377-2470. Business E-Mail: wstephens@stephens.com.

STEPHENS, WILLIAM A. (DEAN STEPHENS), computer consultant; b. NC, Mar. 30, 1945; BBA, Ga. State U., Atlanta. Sales mgr.; product mgr., advanced Internet technologies KLA Tencor; dir. mgmt. info. systems Allied Signal Corp., 1981—89; dir. systems devel. EMI Music, Inc., 1989—91; v.p. mgmt. info. systems Print Tech., Inc.; co-founder, CEO The Seminars Group; CFO First Commerce Mortgage; mng. ptnr. William Stephens & Associates, 1992—2001; founder, computer cons. ASL Computing, 2003—. Republican. Achievements include patents for word processing and Internet to bank network bridge technologies. Office: ASL Labs PO Box 325 Colerain NC 27924 Office Phone: 252-325-3125.

STEPHENSON, KENT R., lawyer; b. 1949; BA in Finance, Mich. State U., 1971; JD, U. Tenn., 1975. Sr. v.p., gen. counsel Zapata Corp.; v.p., gen. counsel, sec. Pioneer Americas, 1993—95, Pioneer Companies, Inc., 1995—2006; sr. v.p., dep. gen. counsel Dynegy, Inc., Houston, 2007—11, exec. v.p. adminstrn., gen. counsel, 2011—. Office: Dynegy Inc Ste 5800 601 Travis St Ste 1400 Houston TX 77002-3253 Office Phone: 713-507-6400. Office Fax: 713-507-6808. Business E-Mail: kent.r.stephenson@dynegy.com.

STEPHENSON, MASON WILLIAMS, lawyer; b. Atlanta, May 29, 1946; s. Donald Grier and Katherine Mason (Williams) S.; m. Linda Frances Partee, June 13, 1970; children: Andrew Mason, Walter Martin. AB cum laude, Davidson Coll., 1968; JD, U. Chgo., 1971. Bar: Ga. 1971, U.S. Dist. Ct. (no. dist.) Ga. 1985. Assoc. Alston, Miller & Gaines, Atlanta, 1971-76, ptnr., 1976-77, Trotter, Bondurant, Griffin, Miller & Hishon, Atlanta, 1977-82, Bondurant, Miller, Hishon & Stephenson, Atlanta, 1982-85, King & Spalding, LLP, Atlanta, 1985—, mng. ptnr. Atlanta office, 2001—. Fin. com. Atlanta Olympic Organizing Com., 1988—90. Mem. ABA (sect. bus. law, real property, probate and trust sect.), Am. Coll. Real Estate Lawyers, State Bar Ga. (exec. com., real property law sect. 1989-97, chair intangible rec. tax com. 1994-97), Atlanta Bar Assn. (chair real estate sect. 1981-82), Causeway Club, Capital City Club, Phi Beta Kappa, Phi Delta Phi. Avocations: boating, skiing, jogging. Office: King & Spalding LLP 1180 Peachtree St Atlanta GA 30309 Office Phone: 404-572-4600. Office Fax: 404-572-5100. Business E-Mail: mstephenson@kslaw.com.

STEPHENSON, MIMOSA SUMMERS, literature and language professor; b. Huntsburg, Ohio, Nov. 18, 1939; d. Philip Sidney Summers and Edna Elizabeth White; m. William Alva Stephenson, Apr. 2, 1988; m. Ronald Gene Schraer, May 29, 1968 (div. Dec. 9, 1983); children: Mimosa Schraer Flores, Amanda Schraer Lopez, Adam David Schraer. PhD, Tex. Technol. Coll., Lubbock, 1965. Lectr. Hong Kong Bapt. Coll., 1965—67; assoc. prof. William Jewell Coll., Liberty, Mo., 1967—73; prof. English U. Tex. Brownsville, 1973—. Fulbright lectr. Xiamen U., China, 2000—01. Contbr. articles to profl. jours. Missionary journeyman So. Bapt. Conv., Hong Kong, 1965—67. Recipient Chancellor's Outstanding Tchg. award, U. Tex. Sys., 1992, NISOD award, 2004; Nat. Def. fellowship, 1961—64. Mem.: Am. Studies Assn. Tex., Am. Humor Studies Assn., Assn. Lit. Scholars and Critics, Nathaniel Hawthorne Soc., SW Conf. Christianity and Lit. (pres. 2004—05). Baptist. Office: Univ Texas Brownsville One W University Blvd Brownsville TX 78520 Office Fax: 956-882-7064. Personal E-mail: willsteph@aol.com. Business E-Mail: mimosa.stephenson@utb.edu.

STEPHENSON, PAM, state legislator; Former state rep. Dist. 60, Ga.; mem. Banks & Banking Com., Pub. Utilities Com.; sec. Govt. Affairs Com.; state rep. Dist. 92 Ga., 2004—. Mem.: Fulton-DeKalb Hosp. Authority (trustee), State Med. Edn. Bd. (vice chmn.), Nat. Coalition 100 Black Women (pres. Decatur-DeKalb chpt.). Democrat. Mailing: 411 Legis Office Bldg Atlanta GA 30334 Office: 3262 Herrenhut Rd Lithonia GA 30038 Office Phone: 404-656-0254, 770-436-0699. E-mail: pstephenson@legis.state.ga.us.

STEPHENSON, RANDALL L., telecommunications industry executive; b. Oklahoma City, Apr. 22, 1960; m. Lenise H. Stephenson. BS in Acctg., Ctrl. State U., Edmond, Okla., 1982; MS in Acctg., U. Okla., Norman. With Southwestern Bell Tel. Co., Oklahoma City, 1982, area mgr. corp. taxes, 1986—91, dist. mgr. fin. analysis, 1991—92; dir. fin. SBC Internat. SBC Comm., Inc., Mexico City,

1992—96, contr. San Antonio, 1996—97, v.p., contr., 1997, sr. exec. v.p., CFO, 2001—04; chmn. Cingular Wireless, LLC, 2003—04; COO SBC Comm., Inc., 2004—05, AT&T Inc. (merger of SBC Communications & AT&T Corp.), San Antonio, 2005—07, chmn., pres., CEO, 2007—. Bd. dirs. Cingular Wireless LLC, 2001—06, AT&T Inc., 2005—, Emerson Electric, 2006—; mem. audit com. H.E. Butt Grocery Co. Mem. nat. exec. bd. Boy Scouts Am.; mem. exec. com., audit com. United Way San Antonio; bd. mem. San Antonio Met. Missions Bd. Named one of 50 Who Matter Now, Business 2.0, 2007. Mem.: Okla. Soc. CPAs. Office: AT&T Inc 175 E Houston St PO Box 2933 San Antonio TX 78299-2933*

STEPHENSON, THOMAS A., publishing executive; b. SD; BS in Economics, Northern State U., Aberdeen, SD; MBA, U. Minn. With Knight Ridder Newspapers, 1975—97; sr. v.p. ops. & adminstrn. San Antonio Express-News, 1997—2005, pres., pub., 2005—12; pub. The Houston Chronicle, 2012—. Bd. dirs. United Way, San Antonio, Econ. Devel. Found, San Antonio, The Chamber, San Antonio. Mem.: Tex. Daily Newspaper Assn. (legis. affairs com.). Office: The Houston Chronicle 801 Texas Ave PO Box 4260 Houston TX 77210-4260

STEPONAITIS, VINCAS PETRAS, archaeologist, anthropologist, educator; b. Boston, Aug. 10, 1953; s. Vincas and Elena (Povydis) S.; m. Laurie Cameron, Dec. 31, 1976; children: Elena Anne, Lillian Kazimiera. AB in Anthropology magna cum laude, Harvard U., 1974; MA in Anthropology, U. Mich., 1975, PhD in Anthropology, 1980. From lectr. to assoc. prof. dept. anthropology SUNY, Binghamton, 1979-87; assoc. prof. U. N.C., Chapel Hill, 1988-94, prof., 1995—, dir. Rsch. Labs. Archaeology, 1988—, chair, Curriculum in Archaeology, 2009—. Guest worker Nat. Bur. Stds., 1979; adj. lectr. dept. anthropology SUNY, Binghamton, 1979; lectr. and presenter in field. Author: Ceramics, Chronology, and Community Patterns, An Archaeological Study at Moundville, 1983, Archaeology of the Moundville Chiefdom, 1998, (CD-Rom) Excavating Occaneechi Town, 1998; editor Southeastern Archaeology, 1984-87; regional editor Investigations in Am. Archaeology, 1987-91; mem. editl. bd. Prehistory Press, 1990-97, Southern Cultures, 1992—, Am. Archaeology, 1996-2000; contbr. articles to profl. jours. Smithsonian Instn. fellow, 1978-79; grantee NSF, 1978-80, 83, 89-92, 94, 2000, 05, IMLS, 2003, Wenner-Gren Found., 1981, 86-88, Nat. Geographic Soc., 1987-88, Z. Smith Reynolds Found., 1992-94, Alcoa Found. 2005. Fellow Am. Anthrop. Assn.; mem. Soc. Am. Archaeology (Presdl. Recognition award 1993-94, exec. com. 1983-84, treas. 1992-94, pres. 1997-99), Archaeological Conservancy (bd. dirs. 2000-11, chmn. 2003-07), NAGPRA (rev. com. 2004-09), Ctr. Maya Rsch. (bd. dirs. 2002-), Southeastern Archaeol. Conf. (editor 1984-87, pres. 1990-92), N.C. Archaeol. Soc. (exec. sec. 1988-91, sec. 1991-96), N.C. Archaeol. Coun. (exec. com. 1988-92), Archaeol. Soc. S.C., Ala. Archaeol. Soc., Miss. Archaeol. Soc., La. Archaeol. Soc. Office: U NC Rsch Labs Archaeology Alumni Bldg Cb 3120 Chapel Hill NC 27599-3120

STEPP, JOHN R., management executive; b. Bluefield, W.Va., Sept. 24, 1941; s. Freeman and Nancy P. Stepp; m. Tali R. Stepp; children: Leslie Catherine, Anne Allison, Nancy Meredith. BS in Indsl. Mgmt., Ga. Inst. Tech., 1963; MBA, Emory U., 1965; PhD in Bus. Adminstrn., U. Ga., 1971. Mem. faculty Coll. Indsl. Mgmt., Ga. Inst. Tech., 1966—75; commr. Fed. Mediation and Conciliation Svc., Atlanta, 1975—78, nat. rep., tech. assistance coord. Washington, 1978—80; dir. Office Labor-Mgmt. Rels. Svcs. Dept. Labor, Washington, 1980—84, assoc. dep. under sec. for Labor-Mgmt. Rels. and Coop. Programs, 1984—88, dep. under sec., 1988—90; pres. Bill Usery & Assocs., Inc., Washington, 1990—92, Restructuring Assocs., Inc., 1992—. Contbr. numerous articles to profl. jours. With USCG, 1963—64. Office: Restructuring Assocs Inc 1150 17th St NW Washington DC 20036-4603

STEPTOE, ROBERT MASON, JR., lawyer; b. Martinsburg, W.Va., July 7, 1943; s. Robert Mason and Sarah Virginia (Duff) S.; m. Mary Patricia Thompson, Feb. 20, 1966; children: Robert Mason III, Katherine Van Lear, Elizabeth Wetherell, Anne Pendleton. BA in English, U. Va., 1965; JD, W. Va. U., 1970. Bar: W.Va. 1970, Va. 1970, DC 1971, US Dist. Ct. (no. and so. dists.) W.Va. 1970, US Ct. Appeals (3d and 4th cirs.), US Supreme Ct. 1983. Assoc. Cole, Zylstra & Raywid, Washington, 1970-71, Steptoe & Johnson, Clarksburg, W.Va., 1971-74, ptnr., 1975—, past CEO, chmn. of firm, 2009—. Mem. 4th Cir. Jud. Conf.; adj. prof. appellate advocacy W.Va. U. Sch. Law. Mem. W.Va. Ethics Com.; chmn. vis. com. W.Va. U. Coll. Law, Morgantown, 1985—86; pres., campaign chmn. United Way Harrison County, W.Va.; bd. mem. United Hosp. Ctr., Inc., West Liberty U.; chmn. bd. trustees The Nature Conservancy, W.Va. Lt. USNR, 1965—67. Mem. ABA, W.Va. State Bar (pres. 1987-88), W.Va. Bar Found. (past pres.), Va. Bar Assn., DC Bar Assn., W.Va. C. of C. (past chmn.), Harrison County C. of C. (pres. 1985-86). Democrat. Episcopalian. Office: Steptoe & Johnson PLLC 400 White Oaks Blvd Bridgeport WV 26330 Office Phone: 304-933-8142. Office Fax: 304-933-8183. Business E-Mail: bob.steptoe@steptoe-johnson.com.

STERIN, STEVEN M., chemicals executive; m. Ellen Sterin; 2 children. BBA, Univ. Tex., Austin, 1995, M in acctg., 1995. CPA Tex., NC. Tax acct. Price Waterhouse; fin. mgmt. positions through v.p. fin. Reichold Inc., 1997—2003; dir. fin., contr. chem. bus. Celanese Corp., Dallas, 2003—05, v.p., corp. contr., 2005—07, sr. v.p., CFO, 2007—. Office: Celanese Corp 1601 W LBJ Freeway Dallas TX 75234

STERLING, ANNE D., not-for-profit developer; b. Evanston, Ill., Aug. 24, 1938; d. Theodore Craig and Barbara (Cox) Diller; m. Keir B. Sterling, Apr. 3, 1961; children: Duncan D., Warner S., Theodore C. BA in History, NYU, 1964. Editl. staff Columbia U. FORUM Quar. Jour., NYC, 1969; asst. editor Columbia U. Sch. Bus. Hermes Mag., NYC, 1970; assoc., rights and permissions Random House Pub., NYC, 1974, assoc., inst. human resources, 1975; writing asst. Robert B. Parker, Syndicated Columnist, 1975; notes editor Vassar Coll. Quar. Mag., Poughkeepsie, NY, 1977—80; cmty. editor Rhinebeck Gazette-Advertiser, NY, 1979—80; writing instr., BOCES program gifted children Poughkeepsie Pub. Schs., 1982—83. Lectr. Open U. Richmond, 2012—. Chair selection com. Am. Field Svc. Fgn. Exch. Student Program, 1979—80; outreach parent Johns Hopkins U. Ctr. Talented Youth, 1986—88; pres. Bel Air Mid. Sch. PTA, Md., 1986—88; mem. Harford County Bd. Edn., Md., 1988—94, v.p., 1992—93; parent representative Phillips Acad., Andover, Mass., 1993—2007; pres. Harford County Bd. Edn., Md., 1993—94; exec. com. Friends of Boatwright Libr., U. Richmond, 1997—2000, 2004—08, 2012—; chair Va. Women's Network, 1998—2000, lobbyist, 2000—02; mem. adv. bd. County of Henrico Pub. Libr., Va., 1998—2011; pres. Coll. Hills Civic Assn., Richmond, 1998—99, Coll. Hills Women's Club, Richmond, 1999; del. UN NGO Conf., NYC, 1999, 2001, 2003, 2007; dir. Internat. Assn. Torch Clubs, 2000—04, pres.-elect, 2004—06, pres., 2006—08; editor ALTA Voice, Am. Libr. Assn. Trustees and Advocates Divsn., 2003—05, pres.-elect, 2005—06, pres., 2006—07; del. UN conf. on the status of women; League Women Voters, US, 2004, nominating com., 2006—08; project team facilitator Leadership Met. Richmond, 2004, mem. programs com., 2007—08; trustee Torch Found., 2011—; commr. Henrico County Pks. and Recreation Adv. Commn., 2012—. Recipient Gold award, Internat. Assn. Torch Clubs, 2010. Mem.: NOW, ACLU, AAUW (Va., v.p. pub. policy 2002—04, chair Centennial state convention 2009), ALA, Va. Libr. Assn., World Affairs Coun. Greater Richmond, UN Assn., League Women Voters, Va. (legis. coord. 2005—, adminstr. Va. Gen. Assembly women's round table 2006—, 2nd. v.p. state bd. 2007—11, sec., Richmond Met. Area 2008—11, 1st v.p. 2011, pres. 2011), Va. Redistricting Coalition, Women's Club Richmond, Vassar Club Richmond. Episcopalian. Home: 7104 Wheeler Rd Richmond VA 23229 Office Fax: 804-285-9133. Personal E-mail: nimbleleap@aol.com.

STERLING, KEIR BROOKS, historian, educator; b. NYC, Jan. 30, 1934; s. Henry Somers and Louise Noel (de Wetter) S.; m. Anne Cox Diller, Apr. 3, 1961; children: Duncan Diller, Warner Strong, Theodore Craig. BS, Columbia U., 1961, MA, 1963, profl. diploma, 1965, PhD, 1973. Asst. to dean Sch. Gen. Studies Columbia U., NYC, 1959-65; rsch. grantee England, 1965-66; adj. instr. history Pace U., NYC and Pleasantville, NY, 1966-71, from asst. adj. prof. to assoc. adj. prof., 1971-77, adj. prof., 1977-83; ordnance br. historian U.S. Army Ordnance Ctr. and Sch., Aberdeen Proving Ground, Md., 1983-94, Ft. Lee, Va., 1994-98; historian U.S. Army Combined Arms Support Command, Ft. Lee, 1998—2008; ind. historian, author, 2008—; open U. lectr. Richmond, Va., 2012—. Lectr. gen. counseling Bklyn. Coll., CUNY, 1967-68; asst. acad. dean, adj. asst. prof. history, coord. Am. studies program, dir. summer session Marymount Coll., Tarrytown, N.Y., 1968-71; asst. dean Rockland C.C., SUNY, Suffern, 1971-73; vis. prof. Mercy Coll., Westchester C.C., King's Coll., Nyack Coll., U. Wis., 1971, 75, 78-80, 83, Harford (Md.) C.C., 1987-94; instr. Army Logistics Mgmt. Coll., Ft. Lee, 1995—2008; co-project dir. Am. Ornithologists Union Centennial Hist., Project, 1976-89; cons. Arno Press, Inc., 1973-78, Grad. Sch. State Colls. of N.J., 1974-75, NSF, 1983—, Am. Trust for Brit. Libr., 1986-89; active Columbia U. Seminar on History and Philosophy of Sci., 1976-83; archivist, historian mem. steering com. sect. mammalogy Internat. Union Biol. Scis., 1985-2007; chair historian/archivist com. Internat. Fedn. Mammalogy, 2007-; judge Ann. Nat. History Day Competition U. Md., 1993-; chair Adams-Pendleton Book Prize Com., Soc. History Fed. Govt., 02-, grant reviewer Tchg. Am. History Program U.S. Dept. Edn., 2003-05. Author: Last of the Naturalists: The Career of C. Hart Merriam, 1974, 77; editor: Notes on the Animals of North America (B.S. Barton), 1974; assoc. editor: Am. Nat. Biog., 1989-98; editor, contbr.: Natural Sciences in America, 1974, 68 vols., 1974, Biologists and Their World, 1978, 77 vols.; gen. editor, contbr.: The International History of Mammalogy, 1987—; sr. editor, contbr. (with R. Harmond, G. Cevasco, and L. Hammond) Biographical Dictionary of American and Canadian Naturalists and Environmentalists, 1997; contbg. author: Ground Warfare: An International Encyclopedia, 2002, Dictionary of Am. History, 3d edit., 2003, Encyclopedia of World Environmental History, 2003, Science in Uniform, Uniforms in Science, 2007, Military Comm. Ancient Times to the 21st Century, 2007; editor, contbr. to numerous works in history, Am. natural scis., and Am. mil. history. Boy scout leader, Seattle, Ft. Devens, Mass., NYC, Tarrytown, NY, 1953—77; pres. Rhinebeck, NY Hist. Soc., 1982—83; co-v.p. Coll. Hills Civic Assn., Richmond, Va., 2006—07. With US Army, 1954—56. Grantee Theodore Roosevelt Meml. Fund, Am. Mus. Natural History, 1967, Nat. Geog. Soc., 1977, NSF/Am. Soc. Mammalogists, 1978, Pace U., 1980, 81, NSF, 1981-82, IREX, 1982; recipient Editor's Quill Award, Internat. Assn. of Torch Clubs, 2003. Mem.: Soc. History Fed. Govt., History of Sci. Soc., Orgn. Am. Historians, Am. Hist. Assn., Assn. Bibliography of History (mem. coun. 1994—98), Am. Soc. Environ. History (sec., mem. governing bd., editor newsletter), Am. Ornithologists Union (co-chmn. centennial hist. com., mem. archives com., grantee 1976, 1977), Am. Soc. Mammalogists (mem. archives com., mem. 75th ann. com.), Phi Delta Kappa, Sigma Tau Delta, Phi Alpha Theta. Democrat. Episcopalian. Avocations: reading, travel. Home and Office: 7104 Wheeler Rd Richmond VA 23229-6939 Business E-Mail: kbs1934@cs.com.

STERN, DAVID MARK, dean, medical educator; b. Great Neck, NY; s. Robert and Florence Stern; m. Kathleen Shirley Stern; children: Eric David, Alan Robert. BS, Yale U., 1973; MD, Harvard U., 1978. Mem. faculty Coll. Physicians and Surgeons, Columbia U., NYC, 1983—2002, named Gerald & Janet Carrus Prof. of Surg. Sci., 1998, dir. Ctr. Vascular and Lung Pathobiology, dir. Juvenile Diabetes Rsch. Ctr.; dean sch. medicine, sr. v.p. clin. activities Med. Coll. Ga., Augusta, 2002—05, prof. medicine, physiology and grad. studies, 2002—05; Christian R. Holmes prof. medicine U. Cin. Coll. Medicine, 2005—10, dean, 2005—10, v.p. health affairs, 2008—10; exec. dean, prof. physiology U. Tenn. Coll. Medicine, Memphis, 2011—; vice chancellor clin. affairs U. Tenn. Health Sci. Ctr., Memphis, 2011—. Mem.: Am. Assn. Physicians, Am. Soc. Clin. Investigation. Office: University Tenn Health Sci Ctr 910 Madison Ave #1048 Memphis TN 38163 Office Phone: 901-448-5529. Business E-Mail: dstern@uthsc.edu.

STERNAD, KEN, delivery service executive; b. Norwalk, Conn. m. Judy Sternad; 3 children. B in Journalism & Polit. Sci., Ohio Wesleyan U.; grad. work in Corp. & Polit. Comm., Fairfield U. V.p., pub. rels. United Parcel Svc. of America, Inc., comm. supr., 1977—82, pub. rels. mgr., 1982—85, dir., media rels., 1985—90, with, pub. rels. dept., 1990; pres. The UPS Found., 2009—. Bd. trustee Arthur Page Soc.; scoutmaster Boy Scouts of America; chmn., alumni rep. Ohio Wesleyan U. Office: United Parcel Service of America Inc 55 Glenlake Pky NE Atlanta GA 30328 Office Phone: 404-828-6000. Business E-Mail: KSternad@ups.com.

STERNBERG, PAUL, ophthalmologist, researcher; b. Chgo., Apr. 30, 1953; s. Doris Feitler and Paul Sternberg; m. Gloria May, Oct. 17, 1987; children: Matthew Gregory, Zachary Ian. BA, Harvard Coll., Cambridge, Mass, 1971—75; MD, U. Chgo., 1975—79. Diplomate Nat. Bd. Med. Examiners, 1980, cert. Am. Bd. Ophthalmology, 1985. Thomas Aaberg prof. ophthalmology Emory U. Sch. Medicine, Atlanta, 1985—2002; G.W. Hale prof., chmn. dept. ophthalmology Vanderbilt U. Sch. Medicine, Nashville, 2003—. Bd. sci. counselors Nat. Eye Inst., Bethesda, Md., 2003—06, bd. trustees, Assn. Rsch. in Vision and Ophthalmology, Rockville, Md., 2005—. Bd. trustees Cheekwood Bot. Garden & Mus. of Art, Nashville, 2003—06. Mem.: Am. Acad. Ophthalmology (life; sec. of comm. 2000—05, bd. trustees 2005—). Office: Vanderbilt Eye Inst 1215 21st Ave S Nashville TN 37232-8808 Business E-Mail: paul.sternberg@vanderbilt.edu.

STERNBERG, ROBERT JEFFREY, president professor psychology education; b. Newark, Dec. 8, 1949; s. Joseph Sternberg and Lillian Myriam (Politzer) Weingast; m. Karin Sternberg; children: Seth, Sara, Samuel, Brittany, Melody. BA summa cum laude, Yale U., 1972; PhD in Psychology, Stanford U., 1975; D honoris causa (hon.), Complutense U., Madrid, 1994, U. Cyprus, 2000, U. Paris, 2000, U. Leuven, Belgium, 2001, Constantine the Philosopher U., Nitra, Slovakia, 2004; DSc, U. Durham, Eng., 2006, St. Petersburg U., Russia, 2006, U. Tilburg, Netherlands, 2007, Ricardo Palma U., 2008, Eureka Coll., 2008, U. Conn., 2009, LaSalle U., Philippines, 2011, U. Huelva, Spain, 2012. Mem. faculty dept. psychology Yale U., New Haven, 1975—2005, asst. prof., 1975—80, assoc. prof., 1980—83, prof. psychology, 1983-86, dir. grad. studies, 1983—88, IBM prof. psychology and edn., 1986—2005, acting chmn. dept. psychology, 1992, dir. Yale Ctr. Psychology of Abilities, Competencies and Expertise, 2000—05, prof. Sch. Mgmt., 2003—10; dean Sch. Arts and Scis. Tufts U., Medford, Mass., 2005—10, prof. psychology & edn., 2005—10; hon. prof. U. Heidelberg, 2007—; sr. scholar Ctr. for Pub. Leadership, Kennedy Sch. Govt., Harvard U., 2006—10; provost & sr. v.p. Okla. State U., 2010—13; prof. psychology, 2010—13; chair, leadership ethics Kaiser Family Found.; pres. U. Wyo., 2013; prof. human devel. Cornell U., 2014—. Disting. assoc. Psychometrics Ctr., Cambridge, England, 2007—; chair ethical leadership George Kaiser Family Found. Editor-in-chief Ency. of Human Intelligence, Psychol. Bull., 1991-96, Contemporary Psychology, 1999-2004; cons. editor Learning and Individual Differences, 1992—, Intelligence, 1977—, Devel. Rev., 1987-91, Jour. Personality and Social Psychology, 1989-91, Psychol. Rev., 1989-91; assoc. ed. Ann. Rev. of Psychology, 2008-; author: Intelligence, Information Processing and Analogical Reasoning, 1977, Beyond IQ, 1985, The Triarchic Mind, 1988, Metaphors of Mind, 1990, In Search of the Human Mind, 1995, 98, (with T. Lubart) Defying the Crowd, 1995, Successful Intelligence, 1997, Pathways to Psychology, 1997, Thinking Styles, 1997, Intelligence, Heredity and Environment, 1997, Love is a Story, 1998, Cupid's Arrow, 1998, Handbook of Intelligence, 2000, Psychology 101-1/2, 2002, Wisdom, Intelligence, and Creativity Synthesized, 2003; co-author (with Karin Sternberg): The Nature of Hate, 2008, College Admissions for the 21st Century, 2010. Recipient award for Excellence Mensa Edn. and Rsch. Found., 1989, Disting. Lifetime Contbn. to Psychology Conn. Psychology Assn., 1999, Disting. Scientist and Scholar award Positive Psychology Network, 2002, Anton Jurovsky award, Slovak Psychol. Soc., 2004, Interam. Psychologist award Interam. Psychol. Soc., 2005, E. Paul Torrance award, 2006, Sir Francis Galton award Internat. Assn. Empirical Aesthetics, 2008; Guggenheim Found. fellow, 1985-86. Fellow AAAS, APA (bd. dirs. 2002-04, pres. 2003, past pres. divsns. 1, 10, 15, 24, trustee ins. trust 2004, McCandless Young Scientist award divsn. devel. psychology 1982, Disting. Sci. award for early career contbn. 1981, pres. 2003, Farnsworth award, Arthur W. Staats award, E.L. Thorndike award 2003, Arnheim award, 2005, Disting. Lifetime Contribution to Pub. U. Psychology award, 2008), Nat. Acad. Edn., East Psychol. Assn. (bd. dirs.2007-2009, pres. 2007—2008), Am. Psychol. Found. (trustee 2005—07), Internat. Assn. Cognitive Edn. and Psychology (pres. 2009-11), Fedn. Behavioral & Brain Scis.(pres. 2012-), Assn. of Am. Coll. & Univ. (bd. dir. 2007-2013, treas, 2011-2013), Am. Acad. Arts and Scis., Am. Psychol. Soc., Soc. Exptl. Psychologists; mem. Am. Ednl. Rsch. Assn. (Rsch. Rev. award 1986, Outstanding Book award 1987, Sylvia Scribner award 1996, James McKeen Cattell award 1999), Soc. Multivariate Exptl. Psychology (Cattell award 1982), Nat. Assn. Gifted Children (Disting. Scholar award 1985, E. Paul Torrance award 2006), Phi Beta Kappa, Kappa Delta Pi (Laureate chpt. 2003). Achievements include theory of successful intelligence; balance theory of wisdom; theory of mental self government; investment theory of creativity; triangular theory of love; duplex theory of hate; wics theory of leadership. Avocations: exercise, travel, reading, cello. Home: 1120 t Ivinson St Laramie WY 82070 Office: Cornell University Human Devel B44 MVR Ithaca NY 14853 Personal E-mail: robert.sternberg@gmail.com.

STERNBERG, STUART L., professional sports team executive, retired finance company executive; b. Bklyn. s. Sam and Beverly Sternberg; married; 4 children. Degree in fin., St. John's U., Queens, NY. Equities trader Am. Stock Exch.; ptnr. Spear, Leeds & Kellogg, Goldman Sachs Group, Inc.; prin. owner Tampa Bay Rays, 2004—. Former mem. various coms. and adv. bds. in the fin. securities industry. Mem. nat. bd. advisors H. Lee Moffitt Cancer Ctr. & Rsch. Inst., 2006—. Office: Tampa Bay Rays One Tropicana Dr Saint Petersburg FL 33705

STERNBLITZ, DAVID H., retail executive; BA in Fin., U. Tex. Coll. Bus. Adminstrn., Arlington, 1991, MBA, 1993. Various adminstrv. positions Bank of America Corp., 1989—94; sr. budget analyst City of Dallas, 1994—95, cash mgr., 1995—98; treasury mgr. Zale Corp., 1998—2001, dir. investor rels., 2001—02, sr. dir. investor & pub. rels., 2002—04, v.p., treas., 2004—. Office: Zale Corp 901 W Walnut Hill LnMS 5B-12 Irving TX 75038-1003 Office Phone: 972-580-5047. Office Fax: 972-580-5266. Business E-Mail: dsternbl@zalecorp.com.

STEUBE, GREG, state legislator; b. Bradenton, Fla., May 19, 1978; 1 child, Ethan Gregory. BS in Animal Sci., U. Fla., 2000, JD, 2003. Intern US House of Representatives, 2000; atty.; mem. Dist. 67 Fla. House of Representatives, 2011—. Served with US Army, 2004—08, Iraq. Republican. Methodist. Office: Ste 5830 5830 Lakewood Ranch Blvd S Sarasota FL 34240-8479 also: Fla House of Representatives 1102 The Capitol 402 South Monroe St Tallahassee FL 32399-1300 Office Phone: 941-907-2810, 850-488-6341.

STEVENS, CURTIS, construction materials company executive; BA in Economics, U. Calif., L.A., MBA in Finance. With Deloitte Haskins & Sells, 1976—83, Planar Systems, Inc., 1983—91, exec. v.p., treas., asst. sec., 1991—97; v.p., treas. CFO Louisiana-Pacific Corp., Portland, Oreg., 1997—2002, exec. v.p. adminstrn., CFO, 2002—11, interim exec. v.p., COO Nashville, 2011—. Bd. dirs. Welch Allyn Protocol Inc., 1998—, Longview Fibre Paper & Packaging, Inc., 2006—, Quanex Building Products Corp., 2010—. Office: Louisiana-Pacific Corp 414 Union St Ste 2000 Nashville TN 37219 Office Phone: 615-986-5600. Office Fax: 615-986-5666.

STEVENS, DAVID D., board member; Pres., COO Southern Health Sys., Inc., 1983—96; chmn., CEO Accredo Health (subs. of Medco Health Solutions, Inc.), 1996—2005; bd. dirs. Medco Health Solutions, Inc., 2006—. Mem. bd. dir. Thomas & Betts Corp., 2004—, Wright Medical Group, Inc., 2004—. Office: Thomas & Betts Corp Bd directors 8155 T&B Blvd Memphis TN 38125 Office Phone: 901-252-8000. Office Fax: 901-252-1354. Business E-Mail: david.stevens@tnb.com.

STEVENS, EARL PATRICK, minister; b. Vicksburg, Miss., Nov. 21, 1925; s. Elton Alva and Mary Elizabeth (Keathley) S.; m. Vonda Jean Tuttle, Aug. 7, 1949; children: Teresa Darlene, Deborah Lalene, Earl P. II, David Paul. BA, Abilene Christian U., 1949; BRE, Coll. of the Bible, 1966; MA, MRE, Nat. Christian U., 1968, ThM, PhD, ThD, Nat. Christian U., 1969; DD (hon.), Ohio Christian Coll., 1968. Ordained to ministry Ch. of Christ, 1943; cert. neuropsychiat. technician. Minister Ch. of Christ, Olden, Tex., 1946-49, Barrackville, W.Va., 1949-62, Parkersburg, W.Va., 1962-66, St. Mary's, W.Va., 1966-77, Shinnston, W.Va., 1977-90, Fairmont, W.Va., 1990-96, Mt. Nebo, W.Va., 1990-96, Pleasant Valley, W.Va., 1996—. Instr. Ohio Valley Coll., Parkersburg, 1964-66; prof. Nat. Christian U., Ft. Worth, 1968-78. Author: The Glory of Christ, 1963, Doctrinal Study of I Timothy, 1987, 100 Years Preaching, 1995, Doctrines of Scripture Preservation, 1997, 26 other books. Served with USN, 1944-46. Named to Eagle Scout, Boy Scouts Am., 1942; recipient Golden Record award Word Records, 1968, Colin Anderson award Colin Anderson Ctr., 1968. Mem. So. Assn. Marriage Counselors, Am. Numismatic Assn. Democrat. Avocations: writing, stamps, hunting and fishing, golf, bowling. Home and Office: 204 Russell St Fairmont WV 26554-1860

STEVENS, ELISABETH GOSS (MRS. ROBERT SCHLEUSSNER JR.), writer, graphic artist; b. Rome, NY, Aug. 11, 1929; d. George May and Elisabeth (Stryker) Stevens; m. Robert Schleussner,

Jr., Mar. 12, 1966 (dec. 1977); 1 child, Laura Schleussner Stevens Forné. BA, Wellesley Coll., 1951; MA with high honors, Columbia U., 1956. Editl. assoc. Art News Mag., 1964-65; art critic and reporter Washington Post, Washington, 1965-66; freelance art critic and reporter Balt., 1966—; contbg. art critic Wall Street Jour., NYC, 1969-72; art critic Trenton (NJ) Times, 1974-77; art and architecture critic The Balt. Sun, 1978-86; critic-at-large srqradio.com, 2004—; art correspondent Sarasota Herald Tribune, 2005—07; contbg. writer The Senses mag., 2007. Author: Elisabeth Stevens' Guide to Baltimore's Inner Harbor, 1981, Fire and Water: Six Short Stories, 1982, Children of Dust: Portraits and Preludes, 1985, Horse and Cart: Stories from the Country, 1990, The Night Lover: Art & Poetry, 1995, In Foreign Parts, 1997, Household Words, 1999, 2d edit., 2000, Eranos, 2000, Cherry Pie & Other Stories, 2001, Long Trail Winding: New & Collected Upstate Stories, 2008, 10 Large Etchings, 2008, Ragbag, 2010, Sirens' Songs, 2010, Impossible Interludes: Three Short Plays, 2012, Ride a Bright and Shining Pony, 2013, numerous poems; contbr. articles short stories to jours., newspapapers and popular mags.; one-woman shows include Coll. Notre Dame of Md., 1997, Galerie Francoise, Lutherville, Md., 2000, Kirkland Libr., Clinton, NY, 2007, Sarasota Art Ctr., Sarasota, Fla., 2008, Utica Pub. Libr., Utica, NY, 2008, Stakenborg Fine Art, Sarasota, Fla., 2011, Bright Hill Literary Ctr., Treadwell, NY, 2012, exhibited in group shows at Corcoran Gallery of Art, Washington, Towson State U., Balt., Atelier A/E, NYC, Stephen Gang Gallery, Govt. Ho., Annapolis, U. Minn., Morris, Cooperstown Art Assn., NY, Armory Art Ctr., West Palm Beach, Fla., Venice Art Ctr., Fla., Ft. Meyers Alliance for the Art, Katharine Butler Gallery, Sarasota, Fla., 2004, Combined Talents: Fla. Internat., Tallahassee, 2005, Mus. Fine Arts, Tallahassee, 2005, Silvermine Guild Arts Ctr., Wilton, Conn., 2006, N.Mex. Printmakers, Santa Fe, 2006—07, Kirkland Libr., Clinton, NY, 2007, Old Print Shop, NYC, Binghamton U. Art Mus., 2008—09, Rome, NY Art Ctr, 2010; contributing arts writer: Sarasotas, Arts and Culture Mag., 2006—07; author: Sirens Songs, 2011, The Secret Painting Elizabeth Stevens; Stakenborg Fine Art, Sarasota, Fla., 2011, 2013, FukinSei Art Lab., Sarasota, 2013. Recipient A.D. Emmart award for journalism, 1980, Critical Writing citation Balt.-Washington Newspaper Guild, 1980, fiction awards Md. Poetry Rev., 1992, 93, 94, 2d prize Lite Circle, 1994, 1st prize in fiction Lite Circle, 1995, 96, Balt. Writers Alliance Play Writing Contest award, 1994; art critics' fellow NEA, 1973-74, fellow MacDowell Colony, 1981, Va. Ctr. for Creative Arts, 1982-85, 88-90, 92, 93, 95, 97, 2000, 07, Ragdale Found., 1984, 89, Yaddo, 1991, Villa Montalvo, 1995; Work-in-Progress grantee for poetry Md. Art Coun., 1986, Creative Devel. grantee for short fiction collection Balt. Mayor's Com. on Art and Culture, 1986. Mem. Coll. Art Assn., Authors Guild, Soc. Am. Graphic Artists, NY Soc. Etchers, Women Contemporary Artists Sarasota. Home: Bards Castle 5353 Creekside Trail Sarasota FL 34243 Personal E-mail: gosspress@comcast.net.

STEVENS, GLADSTONE TAYLOR, JR., retired industrial engineer, retired educator; b. Brockton, Mass., Dec. 16, 1930; s. Gladstone Taylor and Blanche Ruth S.; m. Jane A. Crouch, July 20, 1953; children— Robert, Bartlett. BSM.E., U. Okla., 1956; MSM.E., Case Inst. Tech., 1962; PhD in Indsl. Engring, Okla. State U., 1966. Registered profl. engr., Tex., Okla. Project engr. E.I. duPont, Orange, Tex., 1956-59; research engr. Thompson-Ramo-Wooldridge, Cleve., 1960-62; asst. prof. mech. and indsl. engring. Lamar U., Beaumont, Tex., 1962-64; asst. prof. to asso. prof. indsl. engring. Okla. State U., Stillwater, 1966-75; prof., chmn. dept. indsl. engring. U. Tex., Arlington, 1975-98; ret., 1998. Author: (with J.E. Shamblin) Operations Research: A Fundamental Approach, 1974, Economic and Financial Analysis of Capital Investments, 1993; Engineering Economy, 1983. Served with AUS, 1948-52. Recipient E.L. Grant award, 1974, AMOCO Teaching award, 1979, Wellington award, 1992. Fellow Am. Inst. Indsl. Engrs.; mem. Sigma Xi, Alpha Pi Mu (nat. pres.), Tau Beta Pi, Sigma Tau, Omicron Delta Kappa. Home: 2501 Spanish Trl Apt 212 Arlington TX 76016-1410

STEVENS, JAMES C., chemist; BA, Coll. Wooster, Ohio, 1975; PhD in Organic Chemistry, Ohio State U., 1979. Tchg. asst. Ohio State U., 1975—79; rsch. fellow performance polymers and chems. R & D Dow Chem. Co. Contbr. articles to profl. jours. Recipient Inventor of Yr. award, Mich. Saginaw Valley Patent Lawyers Assn., 1992, Carothers award, Am. Chem. Soc., Del. sect., 2004, Indsl. Chemistry award, Am. Chem. Soc., 2006, Perkin medal, Soc. Chem. Industry, 2006; co-recipient US Nat. Inventor of Yr. award, 1994; named one of 50 R & D Stars, Industry Week Mag., 1994; fellow, U. Calif. Berkeley, 2007—08. Mem.: NAE. Achievements include patents in field. Mailing: Dow Chem Co 2301 N Brazosport Blvd Freeport TX 77541

STEVENS, JEFF A., oil industry executive; m. Sharon Stevens. V.p. supply & mktg. Phoenix Fuel, 1993—97; sr. v.p. supply & mktg. Giant Industries, 1997—2000; exec. v.p. Western Refining Co., El Paso, Tex., 2000—08, exec. v.p., COO, 2008—09, pres., COO, 2009—10; pres., CEO Western Refining, Inc., El Paso, Tex., 2010—. Office: Western Refining Co 6500 Trowbridge Dr El Paso TX 79905

STEVENS, JOHN PAUL, retired United States Supreme Court Justice; b. Chgo., Apr. 20, 1920; s. Ernest James and Elizabeth (Street) Stevens; m. Elizabeth Jane Sheeren, June 7, 1942 (div. 1979); children: John Joseph(dec.), Kathryn Stevens Jedlicka, Elizabeth Jane Stevens Sesemann, Susan Roberta Stevens Mullen; m. Maryan Mulholland Simon, Dec. 1979. AB, U. Chgo., 1941; JD magna cum laude, Northwestern U., 1947. Bar: Ill. 1949. Practiced in, Chgo.; law clk. to Justice Wiley B. Rutledge US Supreme Ct., Washington, 1947—48; assoc. Poppenhusen, Johnston, Thompson & Raymond, 1949—52; assoc. counsel, Subcommittee to Study Monopoly Power US House Judiciary Com., Washington, 1951—52; ptnr. Rothschild, Stevens, Barry & Myers, 1952—70; judge US Ct. Appeals (7th Cir.), Chgo., 1970—75; assoc. justice US Supreme Ct., Washington, 1975—2010. Lectr. anti-trust law Northwestern U. Sch. Law, 1953—54, U. Chgo. Law Sch., 1955—58; mem. Atty. Gen.'s Nat. Com. to Study Anti-Trust Laws, 1953—55; chief counsel to commn. investgating the judgment of People v. Isaacs Ill. Supreme Ct., 1969; appellate judge seminar NYU Sch. Law, 1972. Contbr. articles to profl. jours.; author: Five Chiefs: A Supreme Court Memoir, 2011, Six Amendments: How and Why We Should Change the Constitution, 2014. With USNR, 1942—45. Decorated Bronze Star; recipient Presdl Medal of Freedom, The White House, 2012. Fellow: American Acad. Arts & Sciemces; mem.: American Law Inst., Fed. Bar Assn., Ill. Bar Assn., American Bar Assn., Chgo. Bar Assn. (2d v.p. 1970), Order of Coif, Phi Delta Phi, Psi Upsilon, Phi Beta Kappa. Protestant.*

STEVENS, RICHARD GORDON, political scientist, educator; b. Chgo., Dec. 29, 1925; s. Philip Jacob and Almyra (DeVillery) Solomon; m. Norma Jean Duncan, Oct. 14, 1949; children: Dennis Gordon, Laura Louise, Patricia Jean. AM in Polit. Sci., U. Chgo., 1956, PhD in Polit. Sci., 1963. Asst. prof. Coll. William and Mary, Williamsburg, Va., 1959-62; tutor honors divsn. U. Santa Clara, Calif., 1963-66; asst. prof. U. Wash., Seattle, 1966-69; assoc. prof. U. Waterloo, Ont., Can., 1969-73; prof., chmn. Rockford Coll., Ill., 1973-75; prof. Georgetown U., Washington, 1981-85; prof., assoc. dean Def. Intelligence Coll., Washington, 1984-92; prof. Nat. Def. U., Washington, 1992-94; lectr. Inst. World Politics, Washington, 1994-2000; adj. prof. Am. U., Washington, 1994—, Gettysburg Coll., 2003—09. Cons. Pub. Adminstrn. Svc., McLean, Va., 1975—, Office Sec. Def., Washington, 1977. Author: The American Constitution and Its Provenance, 1997, Frankfurter and Due Process, 1987, Sober as a Judge, 1999, Reason and History in Judicial Judgment, 2008, Political Philosophy: an Introduction, 2010; co-author: American Political Thought, 1973, 83; co-editor: American Political Thought, 1970, 2nd edit., 1983, 3rd edit., 2010, Sober as a Judge, 1999; contbr. articles to profl. jours. Comdr. USNR, 1943—85. Carnegie fellow in law and govt. Harvard Law Sch., Cambridge, Mass., 1962-63, Fulbright fellowship, Faculty Law, Hong Kong U., 1986-87; Salvatori fellow Free Congress Found., Washington, 1994-95. Mem. Am. Polit. Sci. Assn., Nat. Assn. Scholars, Assn. of USN, Assn. Former Crewmembers USS Intrepid, Harvard Law Sch. Assn., Mil. Officer's Assn. America, Marines Meml. Club. Home: 8350 Greensboro Dr # 307 Mc Lean VA 22102

STEVENS, RICHARD YATES, attorney, former state senator; b. Raleigh, NC, Dec. 12, 1948; s. Floyd L. and Luna (Yates) Stevens; m. Jere Ann Gilmore, Sept. 13, 1980; children: Charles Andrew, Katherine Elizabeth Billington. BA in Polit. Sci., U. N.C., 1970, JD, 1974, MPA, 1978. Bar: N.C. 1974. Asst. dean men U. NC, Chapel Hill, 1970-71, asst. residence dir., 1971-75, asst. Office Student Affairs, 1973-75, adj. instr., 2008; pvt. practice Chapel Hill, NC, 1974-76; adminstrv. asst. City of Durham, NC, 1975-76, budget officer, 1976-78, dir. adminstrn., 1978-79, dir. fin. and program devel., 1979-80; from asst. county mgr. to county mgr. Wake County, NC, 1980—2000; mem. Dist. 17 NC State Senate, 2003—12. Coord. NC State Govt. Intern Program, Inst. Govt., 1971; adj. prof. polit. sci. NC State U., 1980, 1992, 1994; sr. budget advisor NC Gov.'s Transition Team, 2000—01. Bd. visitors U. N.C., Chapel Hill, 1991—95, trustee, 1995—2003, chmn., 1997—99; chmn. bd. dirs. U. N.C. Endowment Fund, 1997—99; chmn. U. N.C. Found., 1997—99. Recipient William R. Davie award, U. NC, 2010. Mem.: ASPA (Nat. Pub. Svc. award 2000), NC Mus. Natural Scis. Soc. (bd. dirs. 1987—88, treas. 1988—89, pres.-elect 1989—90, pres. 1990—91), NC City-County Mgmt. Assn. (bd. dirs. 1991—92, 2d v.p. 1997—98, 1st v.p. 1999—99, pres. 1999—2000), NC Bar, Nat. Assn. County Adminstrs. (bd. dirs. 1989—92), Internat. City-County Mgmt. Assn. (life), Yates Mill Assn. (bd. dirs. 2001—07), Cary Acad. (bd. dirs. 2001—13), U. NC Gen. Alumni Assn. (dir. 1978—80, 1983—88, treas. 1988—98, chmn.-elect 1999—2000, chmn. 2000—01, Disting. Svc. medal 1994), U. NC Pub. Adminstrn. Alumni Assn. (pres. 1977—79, dir. 1982—84, Disting. Pub. Svc. award 1998), Carolina Club (vice chmn. 1993—94, chmn. 1994—98, 2002—12). Office: Wells Fargo Capital Ctr PO Box 2611 150 Fayetteville St Ste 2300 Raleigh NC 27602-2611 Office Phone: 919-851-0228.

STEVENS, SARAH, state legislator; Atty. pvt. practice; mem. Dist. 90 NC House of Reps., 2009—. Mem. Appropriations com., Appropriations Subcom. on Justice and Pub. Safety, House Select Com. on Civil Custody Guardians, Judiciary I com., Juvenile Justice com., Sci. and Tech. com., Ways and Means/Broadband Connectivity com. Republican. Office: North Carolina House of Representatives 300 N Salisbury St Rm 509 Raleigh NC 27603-5925 Home: 2161 Margaret Dr Mount Airy NC 27030 Home Phone: 336-789-0639; Office Phone: 919-715-1883. Business E-Mail: Sarah.Stevens@ncleg.net.

STEVENS, SCOTT R., investment company executive; BA with highest honors, U. NC; MBA, Stanford U. Analyst Comm. and Media Fin. Group First Union Securities, 1997—99; joined Wachovia Capital Ptnrs. (now Pamlico Capital), 1999, v.p., prin., 2007—10, ptnr. Bd. dirs. Southern Bay Oil and Gas LLC, MACTEC Inc., TMW Sys. Inc., HostMySite Inc., Express Energy Svcs Oper. LP, Lightower, USA Compression Ptnrs. LP; bd. mgrs. Southern Bay Energy LLC, 2005—10; bd. dirs. GeoResources Inc., 2007—10. Office: Pamlico Capital 150 North College St Ste 2400 Charlotte NC 28202 Office Phone: 704-414-7198. Office Fax: 704-374-6711. Business E-Mail: scott.stevens@pamlicocapital.com. E-mail: scott.stevens@wachovia.com.

STEVENS, TRISH, public relations executive, advertising executive; Owner, pres., CEO Ascot Media, Inc. Blogger trishstevens.com. Office: Ascot Media Inc PO Box 133032 The Woodlands TX 77393 Office Phone: 281-333-3507. Office Fax: 832-813-5154. Business E-Mail: tstevens@ascotmedia.com.

STEVENSON, BEN, performing company executive; b. Portsmouth, Eng., Apr. 4, 1936; arrived in U.S., 1968; s. Benjamin John and Florence May; m. Joan Toastivine. Grad., Arts Ednl. Sch., London, 1955. Co-dir. Nat. Ballet, Washington, 1971—74; artistic dir. Chgo. Ballet, 1974—75, Houston Ballet, 1973—2003, Tex. Ballet Theater, 2003—. Mem. dance panel Tex. Commn. Arts, 1977; guest tchr. Am. Ballet Theatre, Joffrey Ballet, Royal Ballet; hon. faculty Beijing Dance Acad.; hon. facutly Shenyang Conservatory of Music. Dancer Theatre Arts Ballet, London, 1952-54, Sadler's Wells Theatre Ballet, 1955-56, Royal Ballet, 1956-60, London Festival Ballet, 1960-62; appearances in Wedding in Paris, 1954-55, Music Man, London, 1962-63, Half a Sixpence, also, Boys in Syracuse, London, 1964; prin. dancer, ballet master, London Festival Ballet, 1964-68; prin. ballets choreographed include Three Faces of Eve, 1965, Cast Out, 1966, Sleeping Beauty (full length), 1967, 71, 76, 78, Fervor, 1968, Three Preludes, 1968, Forbidden, 1969, Cinderella (full length), 1969, 71, 73, 74, 76, Bartok Concerto, 1970, Nutcracker (full length), 1972, 76, Symphonetta, 1972, Courant, 1973, Swan Lake (full length), 1977, L, 1978, Britten Pas de Deux, 1979, Four Last Songs, 1979, Space City, 1980, Peer Gynt (full length), 1981, Zheng Ban Qiao, 1982, The Prince of Pagodas, 1986 Recipient 1st Prize, London Choreographic competitions, 1965—67, Internat. Ballet Competition, Bulgaria, 1972, Gold medal for choreography, Internat. Ballet Competition, 1982, Dance mag. award, 2000; named to Order of Brit. Empire, 1999. Mem.: Royal Acad. Dancing (assoc. Adeline Genee Gold medal 1955). Office: Tex Ballet Theatre 1600 Green Oaks Rd Fort Worth TX 76116-1504 Office Phone: 817-763-0207. E-mail: bstevenson@texasbalettheater.org.

STEVENSON, BRYAN ALLEN, legal institute administrator, law educator; b. Milton, Del., Nov. 14, 1959; s. Howard Carlton and Alice Gertrude (Golden) S. BA, Eastern Coll., St. Davids, Pa., 1981; MPP, John F. Kennedy Sch. Govt., Harvard U., Cambridge, Mass., 1985; JD, Harvard Law Sch., 1985. Bar: Ga. 1985, Ala. 1987. Staff atty. So. Prisoners Def. Com., Atlanta, 1985-89; exec. dir. Ala. Capital Representation Resource Ctr., Montgomery, 1989-95; dir. Equal Justice Initiative of Ala., Montgomery, 1995—, exec. dir.; asst. prof. clin. law NY U. Sch. Law, 1998, assoc. prof. clin. law, 2002, prof. of clin. law, 2003—. Vis. prof. law NYU Sch. Law, 1997, U. Mich. Law Sch., 1995. Recipient Nat. Human Rights award Reebok Human Rights Found., 1989, ACLU Medal of Liberty, 1991, ABA Wisdom Award for Pub. Svc., 1991, Gleitsman Found. Citizen Activist award, 200, Olof Palme prize, 2000, Gruber Prize for Justice, Gruber Found., 2009, Nat. Pub. Svc. award Stanfor U. Law Sch., 2010, William Robert Ming Advocacy award NAACP, 2010, Visionaries award Ford Found., 2011; named a MacArthur Fellow, The John D. & Catherine T. MacArthur Found., 1995 Avocations: music, piano and keyboards. Office: Equal Justice Initiative of Alabama 122 Commerce St Montgomery AL 36104-2538 also: NYU Sch Law 245 Sullivan St 628 New York NY 10012 Office Phone: 212-998-6456, 334-269-1803. Office Fax: 212-995-4031, 334-269-1806. Business E-Mail: bstevenson@eji.org.

STEVENSON, JOSIAH, IV, management consultant; b. Jamaica, NY, Oct. 4, 1935; s. Josiah and Ruth Lillian (Leech) S.; m. Jane Margaret Kupfer, Sept. 1, 1957; children: Josiah V., Todd Sander. AB, Dartmouth Coll., 1957; MBA, Amos Tuck Sch. Bus., 1958. Instr. U. Md.-Far East, 1959—61; account supr. Benton & Bowles, Inc., NYC, 1961—66; group product mgr., gen. mgr. Japan Chesebrough-Pond's Inc., Greenwich, Conn., 1967—77; dir. devel. Dartmouth Coll., 1977—84, Boston Symphony Orch., 1984—95; v.p. Curtis Inst. Music, Phila., 1995—2003; mng. ptnr. Dover Stevenson & Assocs., 1987—; bd. trustees NC Symphony Found., 2010—. V.p. Opera North, trustee, Sphinx Found., Inst. Preservation Med. Tradition, bd. dirs. Weymouth Ctr. for the Arts & Humanities, 2013- With USAF, 1958—61. Mem. US C. of C., Assn. Fund Raising Profls. (Mass. chpt. bd. dirs., v.p. 1993-95, Greater Phila. chpt. bd. dirs., v.p. fin. 1996-2003), Dartmouth Club, Tokyo Lawn Tennis Club, Yale-Dartmouth Club (NYC), Badminton and Tennis Club (Boston), Pinehurst Country Club. Episcopalian. Home: 6 Squires Ln Pinehurst NC 28374-6866 Home Phone: 910-420-2596. Personal E-mail: jstevensoniv@nc.rr.com.

STEVENSON, PAUL MICHAEL, physics professor, researcher; b. Denham, Eng., Oct. 10, 1954; came to U.S., 1983; s. Jeremy and Jean Helen (Jennings) S. BA, Cambridge U., Eng., 1976; PhD, Imperial Coll., London, 1979. Rsch. assoc. U. Wis., Madison, 1979-81, 1983-84; fellow European Orgn. for Nuclear Rsch., Geneva, 1981-83; sr. rsch. assoc. Rice U., Houston, 1984-86, asst. prof. physics, 1986-89, assoc. prof., 1989-93; prof. physics, 1993—. Contbr. articles to profl. jours. Avocation: music. Office: Rice U Dept Physics 6000 Main St Houston TX 77005-1826 Business E-Mail: stevenson@rice.edu.

STEVERSON, JODY, state legislator; m. Lauren Bailey. Attended, NE Miss. CC, Booneville, Miss. State U. Dir. voice and data Ripley Video Cable Co.; mem. Dist. 4 Miss. House of Reps., Jackson, 2012—. Mem. career path experience adv. com. Tippah County Career and Tech. Ctr., Miss. Mem.: Tippah County Devel. Assn., Ripley Main St. Assn., Tippah County Miss. State U. Alumni Assn. Democrat. Presbyterian. Office: Miss House of Reps PO Box 1018 Jackson MS 39215 Business E-Mail: jsteverson@house.ms.gov.

STEVES, GALE C., marketing professional, writer, editor-in-chief, publishing executive; d. William Harry and Ruth (May) Steves; m. David B. Stocker, Mar. 31, 1972 (div. Apr. 1978); m. Philip L. Perrone, Aug. 14, 1983. BS, Cornell U., 1964; MA, NYU, 1966. Editl. asst. Ladies Home Jour., NYC, 1966-69; seafood consumer specialist U.S. Dept. Commerce, NYC, 1969-73; editor food Homelife mag., NYC, 1973-74; editor food and equipment Co-Ed mag., NYC, 1974-76, Am. Home mag., NYC, 1976-78; editor kitchen design and equipment Woman's Day mag., NYC, 1979-83; editor-in-chief Woman's Day Spls., NYC, 1983-91; v.p., editor-in-chief Home Mag. Group, NYC, 1991—2001; pres. Open House Prodns., NYC, 2001—03, 2005—; v.p., editl. dir., pub. AMI Mini Mags. Group, NYC, 2003—05. Bd. dirs. Les Dames d'Escoffier, Coun. Sr. Ctrs. and Svcs. N.Y.C., Catskill Ctr. Cons. and Econ. Devel. Author: Game Cookery, 1974, The International Cook, 1980, Creative Microwave Cooking, 1981; author: (with Lee M. Elman) Country Weekend Cooking, Home Magazine's Best Little Houses, 1998; mem. editl. bd. Sr. Summary, N.Y.C., 1982—88; author: Right String Your Home, 2011. Co-chmn. Alder Lake Restoration Soc.; bd. mem. Human Soc. Greater Savanah, 1998—2011; chmn. alumni adv. bd. Coll. Human Ecology, Cornell U., 1993—97, mem. univ. coun., 1996—2000, mem. pres.'s coun. Cornell Women; mem. adv. bd. Cornell Plantations, 1998—2005; bd. mem. Catskill Ctr. Conservation and Econ. Devel. Mem.: Garden Writers Assn. Am., Am. Soc. Mag. Editors, Internat. Furnishings and Design Assn., Acad. Women Achievers YWCA N.Y.C. Home: 304 E Gaston St Savannah GA 31401-5614

STEWART, BUTCH (GORDON B. STEWART), hotel executive; b. Kingston, Jamaica, July 6, 1941; m. Erica Stewart (div.); children: Brian, Bobby, Jonathan(dec.); m. Penelope Jane Stewart; children: Jamie, Adam, Sabrina, Kelly, Gordon. Sales mgr. Curacoa Trading Co.; founder Appliance Traders, Ltd., Kingston, Jamaica, 1968; founder, chmn. Sandals Resorts Internat., 1981—; former co-owner Air Jamaica. Recipient Lifetime Achievement Award, Caribbean World Mag.; named Travel Man of the Millennium, World Travel Awards, 2000; named a Trendsetters of Yr., Modern Bride, 2006. Mem.: Jamaica Hotel and Tourist Assn. (pres. 1984—88). Office: Sandals Resorts Internat 4950 SW 72nd Ave Miami FL 33155

STEWART, CARL E., federal judge; b. Shreveport, La., Jan. 2, 1950; s. Corine and Richard Stewart; m. Jo Ann Southall; 3 children. BA magna cum laude, Dillard U., 1971; JD, Loyola U., New Orleans, 1974. Atty. Piper & Brown, Shreveport, La., 1977—78; staff atty. La. Atty. General's Office, Shreveport, 1978—79; asst. US atty. (western dist.) La. US Dept. Justice, Shreveport, 1979—83; prin. Stewart & Dixon, Shreveport, 1983—85; spl. asst. dist. atty., asst. prosecutor City of Shreveport, 1983—85; judge La. Dist. Ct., 1985—91, La. Ct. Appeals (2d cir.), 1991—94, US Ct. Appeals (5th cir.), 1994—, chief judge, 2012—. Bd. trustees Cmty. Found. Shreveport-Bossier, Shreveport, La., 1994—2004, American Inns. Ct. Found.; chmn. nat. search com. Boy Scouts America. Capt. JAGC other, 1974—77, Ft. Sam Houston, Tex. Recipient American Silver Buffalo award, Boy Scouts America, 2002, A.P. Tureaud Achievement award, Loyola U. Sch. Law Black Law Students Assn., 2008, Times Leadership award, Shreveport Times & Alliance for Edn., 2008. Mem.: La. State Bar Assn. (bench/bar liaison com.), La. Conf. Ct. Appeal Judges, Black Lawyers Assn. Shreveport-Bossier, American Inns of Ct. (Harry Booth/Henry Politz chpt. Shreveport), Nat. Bar Assn., Omega Psi Rhi (Rho Omega chpt.). Office: US Court Appeals 300 Fannin St Ste 2299 Shreveport LA 71101-3124 Home Phone: 318-636-4829; Office Phone: 318-676-3765.*

STEWART, CHARLES E., chemicals executive; b. Kewanee, Ill., 1935; married. BS, Marquette U., 1957. Exec. v.p. Occidental Chem. Corp.; various indsl. chem. sales positions Diamond Shamrock Corp., Dallas, 1958—63, asst. product mgr., electro-chem. div., 1963—65, new products mgr., 1965—66, product and mktg. mgr., electro-chem. div., 1967—73, v.p., gen. mgr., soda products div., 1973—75, v.p., gen. mgr., process chem. div., 1975—78, corp. v.p., planning and devel., 1978—80, exec. v.p., pres., 1980. Bd. dirs. Albemarle Corp., 1997—. Office: Albemarle Corp Bd Directors 451 Florida St Baton Rouge LA 70801 Office Phone: 225-388-7402. Office Fax: 255-388-8924. Business E-Mail: charles.stewart@albemarle.com.

STEWART, DAVID MARSHALL, librarian; b. Nashville, Aug. 1, 1916; s. David and Mary (Marshall) Stewart; m. Gladys Carroll, June 9, 1947; 1 child, James Marshall. BA, Bethel Coll., 1938; BSLS, George Peabody Coll., 1939. Circulation asst. Vanderbilt U. Library, 1938-39; county librarian Ark. Library Commn., 1939-40; Tenn. supr. WPA library service projects, 1940-42; librarian Memphis State U., 1942-46; spl. asst. to chief card div. Library of Congress, Washington,

1947; librarian CIA, Washington, 1948-60; chief librarian Nashville Pub. Library, 1960-85; Instr. Peabody Library Sch., 1966-80. Bd. dirs. Coun. Cmty. Agys., Nashville, Friends Chamber Music, Nashville, Traverlers Aid, Nashville; v.p. bd. Mid.-E. Tenn. Arthritis Found. Served to lt. comdr. USNR, 1942—46. Mem.: ALA, Pub. Libr. Assn. Am. (chmn. stds. com. 1964—65, pres. 1966—67), Southeastern Libr. Assn., Tenn. Libr. Assn. (chmn. legis. com. 1961—65, v.p. 1965, pres. 1966, Honor award 1983), Alumni Assn. Bethel Coll. (dir., Disting. Alumni award 1992), Coffe House Club (Nashville), Kiwanis. Democrat. Mem. United Meth. Ch. Home: 6342 Torrington Rd Nashville TN 37205-3157

STEWART, ERIC, state legislator; b. Dec. 6, 1972; married; 2 children. Attended, Austin Peay State U. Former commr. Franklin Co., former mem. Dem. Party Exec. Com., mem. C of C.; owner ins. agency; mem. Dist. 14 Tenn. State Senate, 2008—, sec. Environ., Conservation & Tourism Com. Former Rotarian Fayetteville/ Lincoln Co. Mem.: Masons. Democrat. Baptist. Mailing: 300 Bobby Holt Ln Belvidere TN 37306 Office: 310A War Memorial Bldg Nashville TN 37243 Office Phone: 931-967-1462, 615-741-6694. Business E-Mail: sen.eric.stewart@capitol.tn.gov.

STEWART, JIM, III, state legislator; b. Oct. 21, 1958; m. Maryanne Bingham; 1 child, James S. IV. Farmer; mem. Dist. 86 Ky. House of Reps., 1997—. Republican. Baptist. Office: Capitol Annex Rm 429G 702 Capitol Ave Frankfort KY 40601 Office Phone: 502-564-8100 ext. 690. E-mail: jim.stewart@lrc.ky.gov.

STEWART, JOAN HINDE, academic administrator; b. NYC, Aug. 11, 1944; d. Wade and Dorothy (Ronning) H.; m. Philip Robert Stewart, Jan. 31, 1970; children: Anna Faye, Justin. Student, Université Laval Summer Sch, Quebec, 1963, Middlebury Coll. Summer Sch., 1964-65; BA summa cum laude, St. Joseph's Coll., 1965; student, Salzburg Summer Sch., Austria, 1966; MPhil, Yale U., 1969, PhD, 1970. Tchg. assoc. French Yale U., New Haven, 1967—69, acting instr. French, 1969—70; instr. French Wellseley Coll., 1970—71, asst. prof. French, 1971—72, NC State U., Raleigh, 1973—77, assoc. prof. French, 1977—81, prof. French, 1981—99, asst. head dept. fgn. langs. and lits., 1978—82, asst. dean rsch. and grad. programs, 1983—85, acting head dept. fgn. langs. and lits., 1984—85, head dept. fgn. langs. and lit., 1985—97; prof., dean liberal arts U. SC, 1999—2003; prof. French, pres. Hamilton Coll., Clinton, NY, 2003—. Author: The Novels of Mme Riccoboni, 1976, Colette, 1983, 1996, Gynographs: French Novels by Women of the Late Eighteenth Century, 1993; editor: Mme Riccoboni's Lettres de Mistriss Fanni Butlerd, 1979; co-editor: Isabelle de Charrière's Lettres de Mistriss Henley, 1993, Marie Riccoboni's Histoire d'Ernestine, 1998. Chmn. N.C. Humanities Coun., 1988-89. Fellow Camargo Found., Cassis, France, 1979, Nat. Humanities Ctr., 1982-83, (sr.) ctr. for humanities Wesleyan U., 1990; NEH summer seminar fellowship, Princeton U., 1980; NEH fellowship Coll. Tchrs. and Ind. Scholars, 1990-91, 1994-95; fellow Ctr. d'Etude du XVIII Siecle, U. Paul Valery, Montpellier, France, 1995, Liguria Study Ctr. for the Arts and Scis., Bogliasco, Italy, 1997, Beinecke Rare Book and Manuscript Libr., Yale U., 1997; stipend younger humanists NEH, 1973; travel grantee ACLS, 1983; travel to collections grantee NEH, 1984; vis. scholar European Humanities Rsch. Ctr., Oxford U., 1995. Mem. AAUP, MLA, Am. Assn. Tchrs. French. Office: Hamilton College Office of President 198 College Hill Rd Clinton NY 13323 Office Phone: 315-859-4104. E-mail: jstewart@hamilton.edu.*

STEWART, JOHN MURRAY, retired bank executive; b. Summit, NJ, Apr. 2, 1943; s. Robert John Stewart and Mary Catherine Grabhorn; m. Sandra Meyers Frazier, 1966 (div. 1997); children: Jennifer Bricar Crone, Catherine Dorothy Lochead; m. Rebecca Marie Mellen, July 10, 1998. BA, U. Va., Charlottesville, 1965; MBA, NYU, 1983. Trust officer, v.p. Bankers Trust Co., NYC, 1965-82, Morgan Guaranty Trust Co., NYC, 1982-83; mgr., pres., dir. Morgan Trust Co. Fla., Palm Beach, 1983-89; pres., dir. Bankers Trust Co. Fla., 1989-93; founder, pres. pvt. capital group SunTrust Bank, Orlando, Fla., 1993-96; pres., dir. Harris Trust/Bank of Montreal, West Palm Beach, 1996—2001; contbg. writer Cannon Fin. Inst., 2004—06; sr. trust advisor Wachovia Bank, 2006—13. Campaign chmn. Palm Beach Cmty. Chest, 1985, 1986; exec. com. Tampa Bay and Palm Beach County Local Initiatives Support Corp.; mem. planned giving coun. U. Va., 1997—, pres. alumni club, 1990—98; vestryman Bethesda By the Sea Ch., Palm Beach, 1986—89, 1992—94, treas., 1986—87, Cathedral Ch. of St. Luke, Orlando, 1996, St. Philips Ch., Pinellas Pk., 2014—; bd. dirs. Orlando Opera Co., 1994—96, Palm Beach Opera Co., 1996—2001. Mem. Fla. Bankers Assn. (chmn. trust bus. devel. com. 1989, planning commn., chmn. trust legis. com. 1990, named to Hall of Fame, 2014), NY State Bankers Assn. (mem. trust bus. devel. com. 1978-82), NY Yacht Club (NYC), St. Petersburg Yacht Club, Monmouth Boat Club (Red Bank, NJ), SAR (pres. Palm Beach chpt. 1997-98, St. Petersburg chpt. 2009-13, chair Knight Essay Comm. Fla.). Home: 1121 32nd Ave N Saint Petersburg FL 33704

STEWART, JOHN RICHARD, manufacturing company executive; b. North Wilksboro, NC, Nov. 2, 1947; s. George and Jean (Walker) Stewart; m. Elizabeth Dickerson. BS, U. NC, 1973. Staff acct. Coopers & Lybrand, Charlotte, NC, 1973—77; with Aeronca, Inc., Pineville, NC, 1977—, treas., 1980—. Lectr. in field. With USNR, 1969—71. Mem.: AICPA, Nat. Assn. Accts., N.C. Assn. CPAs, Soc. of 49ers, Alpha Kappa Psi. Republican. Episcopalian. Home: 8034 Bush Ln Denver NC 28037-8866

STEWART, JON DOUGLAS, lawyer; b. Chicopee, Ga., Sept. 8, 1938; s. Marvin Jones and Lillian Monteen (Cozens) S.; m. Helen Helms, Feb. 22, 1964; children: Jon Douglas Jr., William Andrew. BA, Emory U., 1960, LLB, 1962. Bar: Ga. 1962, U.S. Dist. Ct. (no. dist.) Ga. 1962, U.S. Ct. Appeals (5th cir.) 1962, U.S. Dist. Ct. (mid. dist.) Ga. 1964, U.S. Supreme Ct. 1968, U.S. Dist. Ct. (so. dist.) Ga. 1976, U.S. Ct. Appeals (11th cir.) 1982. Assoc. Green, Buckley, De Rieux & Jones, Atlanta, 1962-68; ptnr. Stewart Melvin & Frost, Gainesville, Ga., 1968—. Chair Gainesville Cmty. Concert, 1973; chair adminstrv. bd. Gainesville 1st United Meth. Ch., 1979-81, tchr. Serendipity Sunday Sch.; chmn. Emory Univ. Law Alumni Assn. Fellow Am. Bar Found. (life), Ga. Bar Found. (mem., chair bd. trustees 1983-93), Ga. Lawyers Found. (life); mem. ABA (Ga. state del. ho. of dels. 1985-2005, bd. gov. 2002-2005), State Bar of Ga. (pres.-elect, pres., treas., bd. govs., Disting. Svc. award 1992). Avocations: acting, singing. Office: Stewart Melvin & Frost Suite 600 Hunt Tower 200 Main St NW Gainesville GA 30501-3649 Office Phone: 770-536-0101. Business E-Mail: dstewart@smf-law.com.

STEWART, JONATHAN T., construction executive; b. Ohio; Grad., Ohio U. With Internat. Harvester; joined Martin Marietta Corp., 1982, dir. personnel, 1984, v.p. human resources Materials Group, 1992; v.p. human resources Martin Marietta Materials, Inc., 1993—2001, sr. v.p. human resources, 2001—. Bd. dirs. Clarence E. Lighter Youth Found.; bd. trustees Raleigh Bus. & Tech. Ctr. Office: Martin Marietta Materials Inc 2710 Wycliff Rd Raleigh NC 27607 Office Phone: 919-781-4550. Office Fax: 919-783-4695.

STEWART, J.W., energy executive, lawyer; b. Mar. 2, 1944; BSEE, Univ. Tex., Arlington, 1966; JD, Univ. Houston, 1973. V.p. legal, sec. Hughes Tool Co.; chmn., pres., CEO BJ Services (merged with Baker Hughes), Houston, 1990—2010. Bd. dir. Baker Hughes Inc., 2010—. Mailing: Baker Hughes Inc Bd Directors PO Box 4740 Houston TX 77210-4740

STEWART, KENNETH L., lawyer; b. Nashville, Ark., Feb. 26, 1954; BSBA in Acctg., U. Ark., 1976; JD, Vanderbilt U., 1979. Bar: Tex. 1979. Ptnr.-in-charge Dallas office, mem. corp. banking and bus. practice Fulbright & Jaworski, LLP, Dallas, 1979—. Editor: Vanderbilt Law Rev. Chmn. Dallas Bus. Hall of Fame, 2001, Jr. Achievement Dallas Inc., 2002—03. Mem. ABA, Dallas Bar Assn., State Bar Tex., Dallas Citizens Coun., Greater Dallas C. of C. (dir. 2005-06), Order of Coif. Office: Fulbright & Jaworski LLP 2200 Ross Ave Ste 2800 Dallas TX 75201-2784 Office Phone: 214-855-8060. Office Fax: 214-855-8200. Business E-Mail: kstewart@fulbright.com.

STEWART, KENT KALLAM, analytical biochemistry educator; b. Omaha, Sept. 5, 1934; s. George Franklin and Grace S.; m. Margaret Reiber, June 10, 1956; children: Elizabeth, Cynthia, Richard, Robert. Student, U. Chgo., 1951-53; AB, U. Calif., Berkeley, 1956; PhD, Fla. State U., 1965. Guest investigator Rockefeller U., NYC, 1965-67, research assoc., 1967-68, asst. prof., 1968-69; research chemist U.S. Dept. Agr., Beltsville, Md., 1970-75, lab. chief Nutrient Composition Lab., 1975-82; prof., head dept. food sci. and tech. Va. Poly. Inst. and State U., Blacksburg, 1982-85, prof. biochemistry, anaerobic microbiology, food sci./tech., 1985—96, prof. emeritus of biochemistry; adj. prof. dept. chemistry and biochemistry U. Tex., Austin, 1996—2004. Editor Jour. Food Composition and Analysis, 1987-97, also 3 books; contbr. articles to profl. jours., co-author book; patentee in field. Capt. USMCR, 1956—59. Fellow AAAS, Inst. Food Technologist. Home: 3900 Glengarry Dr Austin TX 78731-3812 Office Phone: 512-458-1072. Personal E-mail: stewart.kent@gmail.com.

STEWART, MIKE, state legislator; b. Jan. 30, 1965; m. Ruth Stewart; children: Will, Joseph, Eve. BA in History, U. Pa., 1987; JD, U. Tenn. Coll. Law, 1994. Atty. Waller Lansden Dortch & Davis; ret. Tenn. Valley Authority; mem. Dist. 52 Tenn. House of Reps., 2008—. Served US Army, 1988—91, vet., Operation Desert Storm. Recipient Distinguished Leader Award, US Eighth Army. Democrat. Methodist. Mailing: 412 North 16th St Nashville TN 37206 Office: 22 Legislative Plaza Nashville TN 37243 Office Phone: 615-741-2184. Business E-Mail: rep.mike.stewart@capitol.tn.gov.

STEWART, PATRICIA CARRY, foundation administrator; b. Bklyn., May 19, 1928; d. William J. and Eleanor (Murphy) Carry; m. Charles Thorp Stewart, May 30, 1976. Student, U. Paris, 1948—49; BA, Cornell U., 1950. Fgn. corr. Irving Trust Co., NYC, 1950-51; with Janeway Rsch. Co., NYC, 1951-60, sec., treas., 1955-60; with Buckner & Co. and successor firms, NYC, 1961-73, ptnr., 1962-70, v.p., treas., 1970-71, pres., treas., 1971-73, Knight, Carry, Bliss & Co., Inc., NYC, 1971-73, G. Tsai & Co., Inc., 1973, 1992; v.p. Edna McConnell Clark Found. Inc., 1974-92; bd. dirs. Trans World Airlines, 1973—95, F. W. Woolworth Co., 1973—75, Continental Corp., 1974—95, Borden Inc., 1974—96, Bankers Trust Co., 1977—99, Morton Norwich, 1978—81, CVS Corp., 1986—98. Dir. Cmty. Found. Palm Beach and Martin Counties, 1993-2001, chair, 1998, 2000; allied mem. N.Y. Stock Exch., 1962-73; past mem. nominating com. Am. Stock Exch., N.Y. Stock Exch., N.Y.C. Fin. Svcs. Corp.; dir. emeritus, past chmn. Investor Responsibility Rsch. Ctr. Trustee, vice chair Cornell U., 1967-95, mem. bd. life overseers Cornell Med. Coll.; mem. vis. com. Grad. Sch Bus., Harvard U., 1974-80; bd. dirs. NOW Legal Def. and Edn. Fund, 1984-92, Women in Founds./Corp. Philanthropy, 1980-86; v.p. fin. com. Women's Forum, 1982-90; vice chmn. CUNY, 1976-80. Mem. Country Club of Fla. (bd. dirs.), Univ. Club (N.Y.C), Gullane Golf Club (Scotland), North Berwick Golf Club (Scotland), Dunbar Golf Club (Scotland), St. Andrews Club (Delray Beach, Fla.), Phi Beta Phi. Home and Office: 2613 N Ocean Blvd Delray Beach FL 33483-7367

STEWART, RANDY, state legislator, high school teacher; b. Nashville, Ark., Oct. 28, 1951; m. Marla Stewart; children: Sara, Jason, Lee. BS, Henderson State Univ., 1973, MSE, 2002. Cattle farmer; adminstr. & fed. tech. Ark. Nat. Guard, 1991—95; tchr. Kirby High Sch., 1996—; mem. Dist. 23 Ark. House of Reps., 2007—. Advanced to Lt. Col. US Army, USAR, Ark. Nat. Guard, 1974—2002. Democrat. Church Of Christ. Address: PO Box 23 Kirby AR 71950 Office Phone: 870-398-4630. Business E-Mail: stewartr@arkleg.state.ar.us.

STEWART, ROBERT S., construction executive; B, MBA, U. Wash. With Weyerhaeuser Co., 1977—2000; sr. v.p. strategic planning and mktg. Centex Corp., Dallas, 2000—05, sr. v.p. strategy and corp. devel., 2005—09; exec. v.p. strategy, corp. develop., comm. Eagle Materials Inc., Dallas, 2009—. Bd. dirs. Tex. Bus. and Edn. Coalition. Office: Eagle Materials Inc 3811 Turtle Creek Blvd Dallas TX 75219 Office Phone: 214-432-2000.

STEWART, TONY (ANTHONY WAYNE STEWART), professional race car driver; b. Columbus, Ind., May 20, 1971; s. Nelson Stewart and Pam Boas. Race car driver NASCAR Joe Gibbs Racing, 1999—2008, Stewart-Haas Racing, 2009—; owner World of Outlaws, Eldora Speedway, Rossburg, Ohio, 2004—; co-owner Paducah Internat. Raceway, Ky., Macon Speedway, Ill. 1st pl. Exide NASCAR Select Batteries 400 Richmond Internat. Raceway, 1999, 1st pl. Pontiac Excitement 400, 2001, 2002; 1st pl. Checker Auto Parts/Dura Lube 500 Phoenix Internat. Raceway, 1999; 1st pl. Pennzoil 400 Homestead-Miami Speedway, 1999, 2000, 1st pl. Ford 400, 2011; 1st pl. MBNA Platinum 400 Dover Internat. Speedway, 2000, 1st pl. MBNA.com 400, 2000; 1st pl. Kmart 400 Mich. Internat. Speedway, 2000; 1st pl. thatlook.com 300 NH Internat. Speedway, 2000, 1st pl. New Eng. 300, 2005, 1st pl. Sylvania 300, 2011; 1st pl. NAPA Autocare 500 Martinsville Speedway, 2000, 1st pl. DirecTV 500, 2006, 1st pl. Tums Fast Relief 500, 2011; 1st pl. Dodge/Save Mart 350 Infineon Raceway, 2001, 2005; 1st pl. Sharpie 500 Bristol Motor Speedway, 2001; 1st pl. MBNA Am. 500 Atlanta Motor Speedway, 2002, 1st pl. Bass Pro Shops 500, 2006, 1st pl. Emory Healthcare 500, 2010; 1st pl. Sirius at the Glen Watkins Glen Internat. Raceway, 2002, 2004, 2005, 1st pl. Centurion Boats at the Glen, 2007, 2009; 1st pl. Pocono 500 Pocono Raceway, 2003, 2009; 1st pl. UAW-GM Quality 500 Lowe's Motor Speedway, 2003, 1st pl. NASCAR Sprint All-Star Race, 2009; 1st pl. Tropicana 400 Chicagoland Speedway, 2004, 1st pl. USG Sheetrock 400, 2007, 1st pl. Chicagoland 400, 2011; 1st pl. Pepsi 400 Daytona Internat. Speedway, 2005, 2006, 1st pl. Coke Zero 400, 2009, 2012; 1st pl. Allstate 400 at The Brickyard Indpls. Motor Speedway, 2005, 2007; 1st pl. Banquet 400 Kans. Speedway, 2006, 1st pl. Kans. 400, 2009; 1st pl. Dickies 500 Tex. Motor Speedway, 2006, 1st pl. AAA Tex. 500, 2011; 1st pl. Amp Energy 500 Talladega Superspeedway, 2008; 1st pl. Pepsi Max 400 Auto Club Speedway, Fontana, Calif., 2010, 1st pl. Auto Club 400, 2012; 1st pl. Kobalt Tools 400 Las Vegas Motor Speedway, 2012. Founder Tony Stewart Found., 2003. Recipient ESPY award for best driver, 2006; named NASCAR Driver of Yr., The Sporting News, 2002, 2005, NASCAR Winston Cup Champion, 2002, NASCAR Nextel Cup Champion, 2005, 2011, NASCAR Nationwide Series Champion, 2009; named one of The Most Influential People in the World of Sports, Bus. Week, 2007. Mailing: Tony Stewart Found 5644 W 74th St Indianapolis IN 46278 Office: Stewart-Haas Racing 6001 Haas Way Kannapolis NC 28081 Office Phone: 704-652-4227.

STICE, JAMES EDWARD, chemical engineer, educator; b. Fayetteville, Ark., Sept. 19, 1928; s. F. Fenner and Charlotte (Anderson) S.; m. Patricia Ann Stroner, Sept. 22, 1951 (dec.); children: Susan Emily, James Clayton; m. Betty B. Gowdy, Aug. 3, 1996. BS, U. Ark., 1949; MS, Ill. Inst. Tech., 1952, PhD, 1963. Registered profl. engr., Ark. Process engr. Visking Corp., North Little Rock, Ark., 1951-53; chem. engr. Thurston Chem. Co. div. W.R. Grace & Co., Joplin, Mo., 1953-54; asst. prof. chem. engring. U. Ark., 1954-57, from assoc. prof. to prof., 1962-68; instr. chem. engring. Ill. Inst. Tech., Chgo., 1957-62; dir. Bur. Engring. Teaching, assoc. prof. chem. engring. U. Tex., Austin, 1968-73, prof. engring. edn. in chem. engring., 1973-85, T. Brockett Hudson prof. chem. engring., 1985-90, Bob R. Dorsey prof. engring., 1990-96, dir. Ctr. for Teaching Effectiveness, 1973-89; dir. Effective Teaching Inst. U. Tex. System, summer 1970; prof. emeritus, 1996—. Vis. prof. U. Iberoamericana, Mexico City, summer 1977; disting. vis. prof., H.T. Person chair engring. U. Wyo., Laramie, 1996; summer cons. E.I. duPont de Nemours & Co., Inc., Savannah River Plant, Aiken, S.C., 1955, Humble Oil & Refining Co., Baytown, Tex., 1956, Universal Oil Products Co., Des Plaines, Ill., 1957, 58, Phillips Petroleum Co., Bartlesville, Okla., 1963, Ethyl Corp., Baton Rouge, 1965, U. Wis., Eau Claire, 1970-97; vis. scholar in NSF and Am. Soc. for Engring. Edn. programs to improve engring./sci. tchg. at various univs. Author: (with B.S. Swanson) Electronic Analog Computer Primer, 1965, Computadoras Analogicas Electronicas, 1971, Expansion of Keller Plan Instruction in Engineering and Selected Other Disciplines, 1975, Developing Critical Thinking and Problem-Solving Abilities, 1987. Recipient Jour. award, Instrument Soc. Am., 1966, Outstanding Engring. Advisor award, U. Tex., 1993, Gen. Dynamics award for excellence in engring. tchg., 1980, Disting. Alumni award, U. Ark. Coll. Engring., 2006, Profl. Achievement award, Ill. Inst. Tech., 2006, Charles W. Pierce Disting. Alumni award, Dept. Chem. and Biol. Engring., IIT, 2011; named Outstanding Chem. Engring. prof., U. Tex., 1977, 1979, 1988, 1991, 1993, 1996, Disting. Alumnus, U. Ark., 1995; tchg. fellow, Friar Soc., 1993—94. Fellow Am. Soc. Engring. Edn. (life; elected dir. 1983-85, chmn. chem. engring. div. 1988-89, bd. dirs. 1990-92, v.p. 1991-92, Western Electric Fund award for excellence in engring. tchg. 1981, Chester F. Carlson award for innovation in engring. tchg. 1984, Donald Marlowe award for leadership in engring. edn. 1999, Lifetime Achievement award in chem. engring. 2002, Benjamin Garver Lamme award, 2010); mem. AIChE, Ark. Acad. Chem. Engrs., bd. dirs., 2005-07, U. Tex. Ret. Faculty-Staff Assn. (pres. 2000-01), Scabbard and Blade, Scholia (pres. 1989-90), Fayetteville Pub. Schs. Sys. (Hall of Honor, 2011), Sigma Xi, Delta Sigma, Sigma Chi, Phi Eta Sigma, Pi Mu Epsilon, Alpha Chi Sigma, Tau Beta Pi, Omicron Delta Kappa, Phi Lambda Upsilon, Phi Kappa Phi. Home: 4205 North Hills Dr Austin TX 78731-2827 Home Phone: 512-794-8046.

STICKLER, DANIEL LEE, health care management consultant; b. Fairmont, W.Va., Jan. 4, 1938; s. Elmer Daniel and Ruby Lee (Ball) S.; m. Donna Lou Johnson, Apr. 16, 1960; children— Dwight Lorne, Dwayne Lee, Douglas Lynn BS in Civil Engring., W.Va. U., 1960; M.P.H. in Health Adminstrn., U. Pitts., 1970. Registered profl. engr., Tex. Asst. dir. Presbyn.-Univ. Hosp., Pitts., 1970-71, assoc. dir., 1971-72, adminstr., chief operating officer, 1972-76, exec. dir., chief exec. officer, 1976-83, pres., chief exec. officer, 1983-86; pres., CEO, The Cedars Med. Ctr., Miami, Fla., 1986-91; pres. DLS Assocs., Inc., Miami, 1991-95; sr. v.p. The Hunter Group, 1996—. Adj. assoc. prof. Grad. Sch. Pub. Health, U. Pitts., 1976-86. Fellow Am. Coll. Hosp. Adminstrn.; mem. Palmaire Country Club (bd. gov. mem.). Methodist. Avocations: golf, gardening. Home and Office: 5803 Fairwoods Cir Sarasota FL 34243-3821 Business E-Mail: dstickle@tampabay.rr.com.

STIEBING, WILLIAM HENRY, JR., retired history professor; b. New Orleans, Dec. 21, 1940; s. William Henry and Eunice Sophie Stiebing; m. Ann Erma Thompson, Sept. 11, 1965; 1 child, Kimberly Ann Heston. BA, U. New Orleans, 1962; PhD, U. Pa., 1970. Instr. history U. New Orleans, 1967—70, asst. prof. history, 1970—73, assoc. prof. history, 1973—85, prof. history, 1985—2001, Seraphia D. Leyda tchg. prof. history, 2001—05. Staff mem. excavations Archaeological Expdn., U. Pa. Mus., Tell Es-Sa'idiyeh, Jordan, 1965; coord. European history U. New Orleans, 1974—83; pottery supr. excavations Archaeological Expdn., U. Pa. Mus., Sarafand, Lebanon, 1974. Author: (scholarly book) Ancient Astronauts, Cosmic Collisions and Other Popular Theories About Man's Past, 1984, Out of the Desert?: Archaeology and the Exodus/Conquest Narratives, 1989 (Named one of Choice Mag.'s Outstanding Acad. Books, 1990), Uncovering the Past: A History of Archaeology, 1993, Ancient Near Eastern History and Culture, 2003, 2008. Bd. dirs., v.p., pres., treas. Salem United Ch. of Christ, New Orleans, 1970—2005. Recipient Disting. Faculty award, La. State U. Alumni Fedn., 1985, Career award for Excellence in Rsch., U. New Orleans Alumni Assn., 2003; NDEA fellow, U. Pa., 1962—65. Mem.: Soc. Bibl. Lit., Archaeol. Inst. Am. (sec. New Orleans chpt. 1983—88), Am. Hist. Assn. Mem. Protestant Episcopal Ch. Avocation: travel. Home Fax: 501-767-3636.

STIFF, ROBERT MARTIN, newspaper editor; b. Detroit, Aug. 25, 1931; s. Martin L. and Gladys (Mathews) S.; m. Cindy Rose, Aug. 30, 1980; children: David Alan, Amy Anne, Kirsten Marie. BA in Radio and Journalism, Ohio State U., 1953. All-Am. sports editor Ohio State U., Daily Lantern, 1952—53; reporter, bur. chief, city editor Painesville Telegraph, Ohio, 1953-61; deskman, asst. city editor, sports editor, city editor, day editor, state editor, asst. mng. editor St. Petersburg Times, Fla., 1961-67; editor St. Petersburg Evening Ind., 1967-84; dir. St. Petersburg Times Pub. Co., 1969-84; exec. editor, v.p. Tallahassee Democrat, 1985-91; pres. Bob Stiff & Assocs., Tallahassee, 1991-95; exec. editor JMT Assocs., 1991—92, 1994—95; mng. editor About Fla., 1991-94; editor Lexington (NC) Dispatch, 1995—2006. Mem. Pulitzer Prize Jury, 1982-83; dir. devel. and pub. rels. Fla. Taxwatch Inc., 1992-94; bd. dirs. NC AP News Coun., 1995-2001, v.p., 1997-99, pres., 1999-2000; pres. Empty Stocking Fund, 1995-2006; news cons. ultant Asheville Citizen-Times, 1985, Capital Outlook, 2010. Bd. dirs. Cancer Svcs. Davidson County, 1996—2004, NC Open Govt. Coalition, 2004—06, U. NC, Chapel Hill, Sch. Journalism Found., 2004—06; pres. Capital Press Assn., 1998—2001; bd. dirs. NC Daily Newspaper Assn., 1995—2006, v.p., 1998—99, pres., 1999—2000. Mem.: Fla. Supreme Ct. Cnstl. Revision Commn., Nat. Coun. Editl. Writers, NC Press Assn. (bd. dirs. 1999—2000, 2002—05), AP Mng. Editors Assn., Fla. Bar Found. (bd. dirs. 1990—92), Fla. Soc. Newspaper Editors (pres. 1975—76, dir. 1971—84, 1990—93), Am. Soc. Newspaper Editors Found. (bd. dirs., treas. 1986—90), Am. Soc. Newspaper Editors (dir. 1981—87), AP Assn. Fla. (pres. 1970—71), Fla. Econ. Club, Lexington Kiwanis (bd. dirs. 1996—2000, 2003—06), Sigma Delta Chi (pres. West Coast chpt. 1970—71). Personal E-mail: bobstifffla@aol.com.

STIKA, RICHARD F., bishop; b. St. Louis, Mo., July 4, 1957; BS, Univ. St. Louis; MA, Cardinal Glennan Coll.; MDiv, Kenrick Sem. Ordained priest Archdiocese of St. Louis, Mo., 1985; parochial vicar Mary Queen of Peace parish, Webster Groves, Mo., 1986—91, St.

Paul parish, Fenton, Mo., 1991—92; spiritual dir., assoc. dir. vocations CYO Archdiocese of St. Louis, 1991—94; parochial vicar Cathedral parish, St. Louis, 1992—94; chancellor Archdiocese of St. Louis, 1994—2004, sec. to archbishop & master of ceremonies, 1994—97, vicar gen. & vicar for religious, 1997—2004, coord. of the Papal visit, 1998—99, vicar for priests, 2002—05, vicar for child & youth protection, 2004—09; pastor Church of the Annunziata parish, Ladue, Mo., 2004—09; ordained bishop, 2009; bishop Diocese of Knoxville, Tenn., 2009—. Roman Catholic. Mailing: Diocese of Knoxville PO Box 11127 Knoxville TN 37939-1127 Office: Diocese of Knoxville The Chancery 805 Northshore Dr SW Knoxville TN 37939 Office Phone: 865-584-3307. Office Fax: 865-584-7538.

STILL, CHARLES HENRY, SR., lawyer; b. Lubbock, Tex., Sept. 22, 1942; s. Charles Alphonso and Henri Sue S.; m. Frances Eugenia Odell, Apr. 29, 1967; children: Charles Henry Jr., Kathryn Elizabeth. BBA in Acctg., Tex. Tech. U., 1965; JD with honors, U. Tex., 1968. Bar: Tex. 1968. Assoc. Fulbright & Jaworski, Houston, 1968-75, ptnr., 1975—2008, head corp. dept., 1984-99, mem. exec. com., 1992-99. Speaker numerous confs. and meetings; bd. dirs. Oyo Geospace Corp. Comment editor Tex. Law Rev., 1967-68. Bd. dirs. St. Luke's Episcopal Hosp., Houston, 1991—, Catalyst Found., Houston, 1992—; mem. vestry Christ Ch. Cathedral, Houston, 1981-84, sr. warden, 1983, chancellor, 1986-2002. Fellow Am. Bar Found., Tex. Bar Found., Houston Bar Found.; mem. ABA (bus. law sect. 1968—, corp. laws com. 1983-89, fed. regulation of securities com. 1976—, com. on legal opinions 1989—, law firms com. 1990—, chmn. 1998-2000, ethics 2000 task force 1999-2002, multiple disciplinary practice task force 1998—, profl. conduct com. 2002—), Am. Law Inst., State Bar Tex. (chmn. bus. law sect. 1984-85, mem. coun. 1982-86, chmn. securities law com. 1981-83, Forest Club, Petroleum Club, Order of Coif, Phi Delta Phi, Phi Kappa Phi, Gamma Phi Beta, Beta Alpha Psi, Phi Delta Theta, Phi Eta Sigma. Avocations: hunting, reading. Office: Fulbright & Jaworski 1301 Mckinney St Ste 5100 Houston TX 77010-3095 Home: 16 Pine Briar Cir Houston TX 77056-1113

STILL, JAY P., oil industry executive; BS in Mech. Engring., Texas A&M U.; MBA, Loyola U. With Mobil; dir. engring. devel. Parker & Parsley, 1995; v.p. ops. Pioneer Natural Resources Co., Argentina, 1997—2001, v.p. Gulf of Mexico, 2001—04, v.p. Western Divsn., 2004—05, exec. v.p. Western Divsn., 2005, exec. v.p. domestic ops., 2007—. Office: Pioneer Natural Resources Co Ste 200 5205 N O Connor Blvd Irving TX 75039 Office Phone: 972-444-9001. Office Fax: 972-969-3576.

STILLMAN, CORY, professional hockey player; b. Peterborough, Ont., Can., Dec. 20, 1973; m. Mara Stillman; children: Riley, Madison, Chase. Left wing Calgary Flames, 1995—2001, St. Louis Blues, 2001—03, Tampa Bay Lightning, 2003—04, Carolina Hurricanes, 2005—08, Ottawa Senators, 2008, Fla. Panthers, 2008—. Achievements include being a member of Stanley Cup Champion Tampa Bay Lightning, 2004, Carolina Hurricanes, 2006. Office: Fla Panthers One Panther Parkway Sunrise FL 33323

STILLMAN, GREGORY N., lawyer; b. Portsmouth, Va., Apr. 29, 1948; BA in English, U. Richmond, 1969; JD, Washington & Lee U., 1974. Bar: Va. 1974. Mng. ptnr. Norfolk office, litig, intellectual property, antitrust Hunton & Williams LLP, Norfolk, Va., mem. exec. com. Contbr. The Va. Lawyer, 1980-86. Burls scholar. Fellow Am. Coll. Trial Lawyers (Va. State chmn., 1998-2000); mem. Va. Bar Assn., Fed. Bar Assn., Richmond Bar Assn., Va. Assn. Def. Attys., Norfolk-Portsmouth Bar Assn., Phi Delta Phi. Office: Hunton & Williams PO Box 3889 Crestar Bank Bldg 500 E Main St Ste 1000 Norfolk VA 23510-2204 Office Phone: 757-640-5314. Business E-Mail: gstillman@hunton.com.

STILLWAGON, GARY BOULDIN, radiation oncologist; b. Memphis, Dec. 30, 1951; s. Jack Wright and Ida Jean (Bouldin) S. BS in Physics, Ga. Inst. Tech., 1974, MS in Nuclear Engring., 1975, PhD, 1978; MD, U. Tenn., 1983. Diplomate Nat. Bd. Med. Examiners, Am. Bd. Radiology in Radiation Oncology; cert. FLEX, 1983. Med. physicist Meth. Hosp., Memphis, 1974; rsch. asst. Ga. Inst. Tech., Atlanta, 1975-78; radiation safety officer, physicist VA Med. Ctr., Memphis, 1978-80, cons. radiation safety, 1980-83; fellow in radiation oncology Johns Hopkins U. and Hosp., Balt., 1983-87; asst. prof. oncology and radiology Johns Hopkins U. Sch. Medicine, Balt., 1987—; pres. house staff John Hopkins Hosp., 1986—87. Vis. rschr. radiobiology lab. U. Utah, 1978; com. mem., site visitor, radiation therapy oncology group, coop. group Nat. Cancer Inst., 1989—; cons. in field. Contbr. articles to profl. jours. CEO & founder charity Struggling Kids Inc., Boy Scouts Am., Bapt. Ch. Dept. of Energy fellow, 1976-78, Clin. fellow Am. Cancer Soc., 1986-87. Fellow Am. Coll. Radiology; mem. Health Physics Soc., Am. Assn. Physicists in Medicine, Am. Soc. Therapeutic Radiology and Oncology, Am. Soc. Clin. Oncology, Sigma Xi. Republican. Home: 655 River Chase Rdg NW Atlanta GA 30328-3568 Office: 320 Parkway NE Atlanta GA 30312

STILLWELL, WALTER BROOKS, III, lawyer; b. July 30, 1946; s. Walter Brooks Jr. and Selpha T. (Everson) S.; m. Carolyn E. Laws, Dec. 20, 1992; children: Walter, Haviland. BA cum laude, Wake Forest U., 1968; JD, U. Ga., 1971. Bar: Ga. 1971, U.S. Dist. Ct. (so. dist.) Ga. 1971, U.S. Ct. Appeals (D.C. cir.) 1976, U.S. Ct. Appeals (11th cir.) 1981, U.S. Dist. Ct. (no. dist. 1996) Ga., U.S. Supreme Ct., 1977. Assoc. Hunter, Maclean, Exley & Dunn, P.C., Savannah, Ga., 1971-74, ptnr., 1974—. Dir. Savannah (Ga.) Econ. Devel. Authority, 2008- Alderman City of Savannah, 1974-92, mayor-pro-tem, 1990-92; chmn. Chatham County Bd. Elections, 1999-2002. Mem. State Bar of Ga. (real property sect., exec. com. 1986-93, chmn. 1992), Am. Coll. Real Estate Lawyers, Savannah Bar Assn. (pres. 1999-2000). Office: Hunter Maclean Exley & Dunn PC 200 E Saint Julian St Savannah GA 31401-2700

STILWELL, JOHN P., mining company executive; BS in Pub. Adminstrn., U. Southern Calif., MBA. CPA, Idaho. Exec. v.p., CFO Hecla Mining Co., internal auditor Couer d'Alene, Idaho, 1985; exec. v.p., CFO Drummond Co., Inc., 2000—. Office: Drummond Co Inc 1000 Urban Ctr Dr Ste 300 Birmingham AL 35242 Office Phone: 205-945-6300. Office Fax: 205-945-6440. Business E-Mail: jack.stilwell@drummondco.com.

STILWELL, WILLIAM EARLE, III, psychology educator, retired military officer; b. Cin., July 28, 1936; s. William Earle Jr. and Frances (Hunt) S.; m. Doris Ann Nowak; children: Jane Belen Stilwell Angel, William Earle IV. AB, Dartmouth Coll., Hanover, NH, 1958; MS, San Jose State U., Calif., 1966; PhD, Stanford U., Calif., 1969. Lic. counseling psychologist, Ky., 2006; cert. profl. qualification in psychology Assn. State of Provincial Psychology Bds. Transp. engr. Hiller Aircraft, 1958—59; with, active duty Patrol Squadron 9, Alameda, 1960—63; active res., 1965—83; exec. officer Units DC Area; ret., 1983; rsch. assoc. Am. Inst. Rsch., Palo Alto, Calif., 1967-69; prof. psychology U. Ky., Lexington, 1969—2006; prof. emeritus, 2006; cons. accreditation and internet U. Ky., Coll. Edn., 2006—. V.p. Ednl. Skills Devel., Lexington, 1969-85. Author: Psychology for Teachers and Students, 1981; mem. editl. bd. Counsel Edn. and Supervision, 1980-87; contbr. numerous (25) articles to profl. jour., chpts. to books. Assigned to patron nine, USNR, 1960—63; webmaster Coll. Edn., 1995—. Recipient Nat. Def. and Armed Forces Res. with cluster, Tchr. Who Makes a Difference award, UK Coll. Edn., 1998, 2002, Svc. award, Coun. Univ. Depts. Clin. Psychology, 1998, Study Web Academic Excellence award, 1999, 2000, Web Homework Spot award, 2000, Svc. award, Coun. Dirs. of Sch. Psychology Programs, 2004, Coun. Counseling Psychology Tng. program, 2001; Henry Stites Barker fellow, U. Ky. Mem. APA (life; Svc. award 2010), Soc. Counseling Psychology, (Svc. award 2010), Coun. Counseling Psychology Tng. Programs (Svc. award 2001), Am. Ednl. Rsch. Assn. (v.p. 1980-82), Ky. Psychol. Assn., Ky. Sch. Counseling Assn. (v.p. 1979-80, 81-82), Ohio Soc. of the Colonial Wars, Hon. Order Ky. Cols., Res. Officers Assn. US (life), Stanford Alumni Assn. (life). Achievements include Kentucky Department of Education inaugural Stilwell award for personal dedication and outstanding service in educational technology to the teachers and children of the Commonwealth 2008. Avocation: fishing in ontario. Home: 1919 Williamsburg Rd Lexington KY 40504-3013 Address: Treetenders PO Box 4382 Midway KY 40347 Home Phone: 859-278-7086; Office Phone: 859-257-5997. Business E-Mail: westil3@uky.edu.

STIMPERT, MICHAEL ALAN, retired agricultural products company executive; b. Madisonville, La., Aug. 21, 1944; s. Warren Eugene and Louisa (Beale) S.; m. Kim Kathleen Agee, Apr. 17, 1970 (div. 1985); 1 child, Kelly Kathleen; m. Helen Marie Evans, June 27, 1987; children: Katherine Helen, Michael Adam. Student, Washburn U., 1962-64, U. Copenhagen, 1964; BA, Western Res. U., 1967; MBA, Harvard U., 1974. Asst. to group v.p. Gold Kist Inc., Atlanta, 1974, mgr. internat. div., 1975-80, dir. spl. markets and staff services, 1980-81, group v.p., 1982-86; v.p. ops. and govt. affairs Golden Peanut Co., Atlanta, 1986-89, exec. v.p., 1989-95; sr. v.p. Gold Kist Inc., Atlanta, 1996—2007. Chmn. bd. dirs. Sunpower, Inc., Athens, Ohio, 2000-2008, Fundatropicos, Turrialba, Costa Rica, pres. Treas. Tropics Found., Atlanta. Lt. (j.g.) USN, 1967-72, Vietnam. Mem. Harvard Bus. Sch. Club Atlanta, Cherokee Town and Country Club. (bd. dirs.), Buckhead Rotary Club. Democrat. Roman Catholic.

STIMPSON, SANDY, Mayor, Mobile, Alabama, lumber company executive; m. Jean Stimpson, 1975; 4 children. BCE, U. Ala., Tuscaloosa, 1975. Positions up to exec. v.p. Scotch Gulf Lumber (formerly Gulf Lumber Co.); mayor City of Mobile, 2013—. Mem. President's Cabinet U. Ala.; mem. Ashland Pl. United Meth. Ch.; bd. mem. UMS-Wright Prep. Sch., 1982—; chair bd. dirs. Prichard Prep. Sch., 2008—; bd. mem. Ala. Alliance of Bus. and Industry, Boys and Girls Club, Mobile Area C. of C. Office: Office of the Mayor PO Box 1827 Mobile AL 36633-1827 Office Phone: 251-208-7395. Office Fax: 251-208-7548. E-mail: mayorstimpson@cityofmobile.org.

STINE, KATIE KRATZ, state legislator; b. Dec. 6, 1956; BS, U. Cin.; JD, No. Ky. U.; attended, Salmon P. Chase Coll. Law. Atty., homemaker; former state rep. Dist. 68 Ky.; state rep. Dist. 24 Ky., 1995—98; state senate mem. Dist. 24 Ky., 1999—; pres. pro tempore, 2005—. Mem. Campbell County Rep. Com.; bd. mem. Fort Thomas Weekday Religious Edn. Program; former vice chmn. Fort Thomas Bd. Adjustments. Mem.: Ky. Bar Assn., Northern Ky. Right Life, Jr. League Cin., Parent Tchrs. Assn., Homemakers, Fort Thomas Garden Club, Episcopal Ch. Women. Republican. Episcopalian. Mailing: 21 Fairway Dr Newport KY 41071-3023 Office: 702 Capitol Ave Annex Rm 236 Frankfort KY 40601 also: 700 Capitol Ave Capitol Rm 328 Frankfort KY 40601 Home Phone: 859-781-5311; Office Phone: 502-564-3120.

STINSON, ALAN LYNN, insurance company executive; b. 1945; BA, U. Tex., 1968. CPA. Ptnr. Deloitte & Touche LLP, 1980—94; exec. v.p., CFO Alamo Title Holding Co., 1994—98; exec. v.p. fin. ops. Fidelity National Financial, Inc., Jacksonville, Fla., 1998—99, exec. v.p., CFO, 1999—2006, exec. v.p., CFO, COO, 2006, exec. v.p., COO, 2006—07, CEO, 2007—10, exec. v.p., 2010—. Mem.: Am. Inst. CPAs. Office: Fidelity Nat Fin Inc 601 Riverside Ave Jacksonville FL 32204-2950

STINSON, STACY L., food service executive; V.p. ops. initiatives Cracker Barrel Old Country Store, Inc., dir. Personal Achievement Responsibility tng. program. Office: Cracker Barrel Old Country Store Inc 305 Hartmann Dr Lebanon TN 37088-0787 Office Phone: 615-444-5533. Office Fax: 615-443-9476.

STIPANCICH, JOHN K., lawyer; Undergraduate in Acctg., U. Toledo; JD, Ohio State U. Exec. v.p., gen. counsel Evenflo Co., Inc. (formerly Kohlberg Kravis Roberts & Co.); assoc. Squire, Sanders & Dempsey, LLP; atty., tools, hardware & comml. products group Newell Rubbermaid, Inc., 2004; sr. v.p., gen. counsel & corp. sec. Newell Rubbermaid Inc., 2010—. Office: Newell Rubbermaid Inc 3 Glenlake Pky Atlanta GA 30328 Office Phone: 770-418-7000. Office Fax: 770-677-8662. Business E-Mail: john.stipancich@newellco.com.

STIPANOVICH, CHUCK, metal products executive; V.p. plates and shapes Canton Metals USA Holdings Corp., Ohio. Office: Metals USA Holdings Corp Plates and Shapes Canton 6991 Freedom Ave NW Canton OH 44720 Office Phone: 330-966-3401.

STIPANOVICH, JOHN MCKAGER (MAC STIPANOVICH), lobbyist, lawyer; b. Ocala, Fla., Nov. 26, 1948; BA with honors, U. Fla., 1972; JD with high honors, U. Fla. Levin Coll. Law, 1974. Bar: Fla. 1975. Dir. numerous mayoral/gov. campaigns Fla. rep. Bob Martinez, Tallahassee, Tampa, 1979—90; chief of staff to Gov. Bob Martinez Tallahassee, 1987—91; sr. adv. Jeb Bush for Gov. Campaign, Tallahassee, 1993—94; practicing atty., shareholder Fowler White Boggs PA, Tallahassee. Named one of Fla. Super Lawyer, 2006—08, The Best Lawyers in America, 2007—09. Mem.: ABA, Fla. Bar Assn. Republican. Office: Fowler White Boggs PA 101 N Monroe St Ste 1090 Tallahassee FL 32301 Office Phone: 850-681-0411. Office Fax: 850-681-6036. Business E-Mail: mckager@fowlerwhite.com.

STIRITZ, MARETTE MCCAULEY, English language educator, consultant; b. Center Point, Ark., Dec. 9, 1931; d. Edrie Delos and Lucyle Virginia (Dautrieve) McCauley; m. Charles Wayne Jackson, July 1, 1950 (dec. June 1986); children: Charles, Retta, Shelia; m. John David Stiritz, Dec. 3, 1992. BSE, Ark. State U., 1962; MA, U. Ark., 1965, PhA, 1986. Tchr. elem. Plum Bayou (Ark.) Pub. Schs., 1950—52; tchr. Laura Connor H.S., Augusta, Ark., 1955-59, Swifton (Ark.) Elem. Sch., 1959-60, Swifton H.S., 1962-63; prof. English So. Ark. U., Magnolia, 1965-78, U. Cen. Ark., Conway, 1978—96; cons., 1996—. Cons. high schs., Conway, Morrilton, Vilonia, 1983—, Ark. Dept. Edn., Little Rock, 1982, 84; lectr. U. Chile, Santiago, 1989, Moscow Pedagogical U., 1991, 92, Academica Inst. Chileno-Norteamericano, Santiago, 1994; speaker 8th Bi-ann. Conf. Profs. Fgn. Langs., Chile, 1992, 9th Conf., Chile, 1994. Author: A Grammar for All Seasons, 1996, Using Language Effectively, 1996; editor: What the American Children Like to Read, 1995, Study Guide Russian Schs., 2000; contbr. articles to profl. jours.; book reviewer Ark. Elem. Coun., 1980—. Del. Faulkner County Dems., Conway, 1984; exec. sec., founder Columbia Tchrs. Eng., Magnolia, 1974-78. Mem. Ark. Coun. Tchrs. English (pres. 1979-80, bd. dirs. 1989-93), Ark. Philol. Assn., Nat. Coun. Tchrs. English, Ark. Coll. Tchrs. English (pres. 1992-93), Conway Rotary Internat. Breakfast Club (charter), Conway Shakespeare Club (v.p. 2005-06, pres. 2006-2008, parliamentarian 2008-10, program chmn., 2010-11), Alpha Chi (region II v.p. 1992-93). Democrat. Methodist. Office Phone: 501-269-0919. Personal E-mail: JorMStiritz@conwaycorp.net.

STIVERS, ROBERT, state legislator; b. Dec. 24, 1961; m. Nancy O. Stivers; children: Joshua Pierce, Caroline Marie, Margaret Eleanor. Asst. commonwealth atty., 1989—93; state senator Dist. 25 Ky., 1997—; mem. Edn. Com., Appropriations & Revenue Com., Banking & Ins. Com., Ky. State Senate; atty.; bd. trustees Sue Bennett Jr. Coll. Mem.: Sue Bennett Jr. Coll. Alumni., Masons. Republican. Presbyterian. Mailing: 207 Main St Manchester KY 40962 Office: Capitol Annex Rm 225 Frankfort KY 40601 Home Phone: 606-598-8575; Office Phone: 606-598-2322. Fax: 606-598-2357. E-mail: robert.stivers@lrc.state.ky.us.

STOBER, WILLIAM JOHN, II, economics professor; b. Boston, Mar. 24, 1933; s. Ralph William and Marjorie Cairncross (Duthie) S.; m. Jeannine Lynn Defries, Sept. 10, 1955. B.Sc., Washington and Lee U., 1955; MA, Duke U., 1957, PhD, 1965. Instr., then asst. prof. econs. N.C. State U., Raleigh, 1959-65; asst. prof., then asso. prof. La. State U., 1965-69, acting head dept. econs., 1968-69; mem. faculty U. Ky., 1969—, prof. econs., 1974-97, chmn. dept., 1979-86, 90-95, dir. grad. studies, 1979-86, prof. emeritus, 1997—. Mem. Beta Gamma Sigma. Democrat. Home: 3051 Rio Dosa Dr Apt 332 Lexington KY 40509-1543

STOBO, JOHN DAVID, academic administrator, physician; b. Somerville, Mass., Sept. 1, 1941; BA, Dartmouth Coll., 1963; MD, SUNY, Buffalo, 1968. Intern Osler Med. Services, Johns Hopkins, Balt., 1968-69, asst. med. resident, 1969-70, chief med. resident, 1972-73; research assoc. NIH, Bethesda, 1970-72; asst. prof. Mayo Clinic and Research Found., Rochester, Minn., 1973-76; assoc. prof. Moffitt Hosp., San Francisco, 1976-82, prof., head section rheumatology, clin. immunology, 1982-85; William Osler prof. medicine, chmn. dept. medicine John Hopkins Hosp. and Univ., Balt., 1985-94, vice dean clin. sci., assoc. v.p. medicine, 1994—97; v.p. Johns Hopkins Health System, Balt., 1994—97; chmn., CEO Johns Hopkins Healthcare LLC, Balt.; pres. U. Tex. Med. Br., Galveston, 1997—. Mem. transp. and immunobiology adv. com. NIAID, 1976—81; vice chmn. rsch. com. Arthritis Found., 1982—84, chmn. rsch. com., 1984—86, sr. investigator, 1974—77; mem. bd. sci. counselors Nat. Cancer Inst., 1982—; mem. sci. adv. bd. exec. com. Lupus Rsch. Inst.; mem. rsch. adv. bd. DuPont Co., 1987—94. Mem. editl. bd.: Jour. Immunology, 1981—86, Jour. Lab. and Clin. Investigation, 1977—82, Arthritis and Rheumatism, 1980—85, Jour. Reticuloendothelial Soc., 1982—84, Jour. Clin. Investigation, 1981—86, Jour. Clin. Immunology, 1982—87, Jour. Molecular and Cellular Immunology, 1984—86, Rheumatology Internat., 1984—86, Jour. Immunology, 1875—1987; contbr. numerous articles to profl. jours. Recipient Merck award, 1967, Maimonides Med. Soc. award, 1968. Fellow: ACP, Am. Clin. and Climatol. Assn.; mem.: AAAS, Assn. Profs. Medicine (sec.-treas. 1991—92, pres. 1994—95), Am. Soc. Clin. Investigation, Am. Fedn. Clin. Rsch., Assn. Am. Physicians, Am. Assn. Immunologists, Am. Rheumatism Assn. (sec., treas., 1st v.p. 1985—89), Am. Coll. Rheumatology (pres. 1989—90), Inst. Medicine, Md. Soc. Internal Medicine, Interurban Clin. Club, Balt. City Med. Soc., Alpha Omega Alpha. Office: U Texas Med Br Pres Office 301 University Blvd Galveston TX 77555-5302

STOCK, ELANE B., consumer products company executive; b. 1964; BA in Polit. Sci. with honors, U. Ill., 1986; MBA, U. Pa. Whaton Sch. Bus., 1992. Ptnr., mng. dir. McKinsey & Co., Dublin, 2005—07; regional mgr. Georgia Pacific's (Koch Industries), 2007—08; sr. v.p., chief strategy officer Kimberly-Clark Corp., 2010—12; pres. Kimberly-Clark Professional, 2012—. Fellow Internat. Economics, Victoria Univ. Wellington, New Zealand. Mem.: American Cancer Soc. (nat. v.p. strategy 2008—10). Office: Kimberly-Clark Corp 351 Phelps Dr Irving TX 75038

STOCKARD, JAMES ALFRED, lawyer; b. Lake Dallas, Tex., Aug. 4, 1935; s. Clifford Raymond and Thelma Gladys (Gotcher) S.; m. Mary Sue Hogan, Aug. 17, 1956; children— Bruce Anthony, James Alfred, Paul Andrew. BA with honors, N. Tex. State U., Denton, 1956; LLB magna cum laude, So. Methodist U., 1959. Bar: Tex. 1959. Pvt. practice, Dallas, 1959-62; with Employers Casualty Co., Dallas, 1962-65; v.p. Southland Life Ins. Co., Dallas, 1965-77, sr. v.p., gen. counsel, dir., 1977-87; exec. v.p., gen. counsel, sec. Southland Fin. Corp., Dallas, 1978-87; dir. Tex. Life, Accident, Health and Hosp. Svc. Ins. Guaranty Assn., 1978-84, chmn. bd., 1980-84; ptnr. Butler & Binion, Dallas, 1987-2000; pvt. practice Dallas, 2000—; counsel Employers Gen. Ins. Group, Inc., 1994—2006. Bd. dirs. Ins. Systems Am., Atlanta; pres., bd. dirs. Dallas County Mcpl. Utility Dist. 1, Irving, Tex.; gen. counsel, bd. dirs. Lone Star Life Ins. Co., 1988-99. Contbr. legal jours. Mem. exec. com., precinct chmn. Dallas County Dem. Com., 1971. Mem.: ABA, Tex. Bar Assn., Dallas Bar Assn., Assn. Life Ins. Counsel. Methodist. Home: 3607 Asbury St Dallas TX 75205-1848 Personal E-mail: alstockas@sbcglobal.net.

STOCKBAUER, ROGER LEWIS, retired physicist, researcher; b. Victoria, Tex., Feb. 3, 1944; s. Fred Ferdinand and Elizabeth (Nitschman) S.; m. Catherine Pauline Jones, June 10, 1972; children: Robbin Renee, Kathryn Elizabeth, Marc Daniel. BA, Rice U., 1966; MS, U. Chgo., 1968, PhD, 1973. Rsch. assoc. U. Chgo., 1972-73; rsch. physicist Nat. Inst. Stds. and Tech., Gaithersburg, Md., 1973-89; prof. physics La. State U., Baton Rouge, 1989—2005; ret., 2004. Editor: High Tc Superconducting Thin Films, 1990; contbr. articles to profl. jours. Recipient Silver medal US Dept. Commerce, 1983; NRC fellow, 1973-75. Fellow Am. Phys. Soc., Am. Vacuum Soc.; mem. AAAS, AAUP, Materials Rsch. Soc., Sigma Xi. Personal E-mail: rlstockbauer@mac.com.

STOCKBURGER, JEAN DAWSON, retired lawyer; b. Scottsboro, Ala., Feb. 4, 1936; d. Joseph Mathis Scott and Mary Frances (Alley) Dawson; m. John Calvin Stockburger, Mar. 23, 1963; children: John Scott, Mary Staci, Christopher Sean. Student, Gulf Park Coll., 1954-55; BA, Auburn U., 1958; M in Social Work, Tulane U., 1962; JD, U. Ark., Little Rock, 1979. Bar: Ark. 1979, U.S. Dist. Ct. (ea. dist.) Ark. 1980. Assoc. Mitchell, Williams, Selig, Gates & Woodyard and predecessor, Little Rock, 1979-85, ptnr., 1985-94, of counsel, 1994—2010. Bd. dirs., sec. Cen. Ark. Estate Coun., Little Rock, 1984—85, 2d v.p., 1985—86, pres., 1987—88. Assoc. editor: U. Ark. Law Rev., 1978—79. Bd. dirs. Little Rock Cmty. Mental Health Ctr., 1994—, v.p., 1996—99, pres., 1999—2001; bd. dirs. Sr. Citizens Activities Today, Little Rock, 1983—88, treas., 1986—88; bd. dirs. Vol. Orgn. for Ctrl. Ark. Legal Svcs., 1986—91, sec., 1987—88, chmn., 1989—91, H.I.R.E. Inc., 1994—2001. Mem. ABA, Ark. Bar Assn. (chmn. probate and trust law sect. 1986-88), Pulaski County Bar Assn. (bd. dirs. 1994-97), Ark. Bar Found., Am. Coll. Trust and Estate Counsel. Democrat. Methodist. Personal E-mail: jeands@aol.com.

STOCKDALE, BRYAN K., tobacco manufacturing company executive; b. Painesville, Ohio; m. Debra Stockdale; children: Jason Derek, Rachel Nicole. Grad. in Strategic Mktg. Mgmt. Program, Darden Bus. Sch.; BBA in Mktg., High Point U., NC. Dir., retail & wholesale trade mktg. R.J. Reynolds Tobacco Co. (subs. Reynolds Am. Inc.), Winston-Salem, various mgmt. positions, field sales, sr. mktg. mgr., Camel, Winston & Salem cigarette brands, area sales rep., 1979, nat. sales planning mgr., 1988—90, mktg. mgr., 1990—94, dir., wholesale strategies & program devel., 1994—96, v.p., trade mktg., v.p., sales strategy & ops., 1996—2005, sr. v.p., consumer & trade mktg. ops., 2006—09; pres., CEO Am. Snuff Co. LLC; chmn. Lane Ltd. Subs. Reynolds Am. Inc., 2009—10. Avocation: basketball. Office: American Snuff Company LLC 813 Ridge Lake Blvd Memphis TN 38101-0127 Office Phone: 901-761-2050. Office Fax: 901-767-1302. Business E-Mail: bryan.stockdale@americansnuff.com.

STOCKHOLDER, JESSICA, sculptor; b. Seattle, 1959; BFA, Univ. Victoria, 1982; MFA, Yale Univ., New Haven, Conn., 1985. Instr., dept. Sculpture NYU, 1992, Bard Coll., 1993; prof., dir. grad. studies in sculpture Yale U., 1999—. One-woman shows include, Renaissance Soc., U. Chgo., 1991, Weatherspoon Gallery, U. NC, 1994, Jay Gorney Modern Art, NYC, 1995, 1997, Dia Ctr. Arts, NYC, 1995, Galerie Nathalie Obadia, Paris, 1995, 1998, 2001, 2004, White Cube, London, 1998, Gorney Bravin + Lee, NYC, 2001, 2003, Rice U. Art Gallery, Houston, 2004, P.S.1 Contemporary Art Ctr., NYC, 2006, 1301 PE, LA, 2007, one-woman shows include retrospective Kissing the Wall, U. Houston, Weatherspoon Art Gallery, and Blaffer Art Gallery, 2004—06, exhibited in group shows at Making a Clean Edge, P.S.1 Contemporary Art Ctr., 1989, Contingent Realms, Whitney Mus. Am. Art at Equitable Ctr., 1990, Whitney Biennial, Whitney Mus. Am. Art, NYC, 1991, 2004, Heart, Mind, Body, Soul: Am. Art in the 1990s, 1997, As Long As It Lasts, Witte de With, Rotterdam, 1992, Simply Made in America, Aldrich Mus. Contemporary Art, Conn., 1993, Biennial Exhbn. Contemporary Am. Painting, Corcoran Gallery Art, Washington, 1996, What I Did On My Summer Vacation, White Columns, NYC, 1996, Colorflex, Apex Art, NYC, 1997, Pop/Abstraction, Pa. Acad. Fine Arts, Phila., 1998, Now and Later, Yale U. Art Gallery, 1998, Objective Color, 2001, SiteLines, Addison Gallery Am. Art, Andover, Mass., 2002, Under Pressure, Cooper Union Sch. Art, NYC, 2003, Ann. Invitational Exhbn. Contemporary Am. Art, Nat. Acad. Mus., NYC, 2004, Conn. Contemporary, Wadsworth Atheneum, Hartford, 2007. Recipient Lucelia Artist award, Smithsonian Am. Art Mus., 2007; grantee NEA award for Sculpture, 1988, NY Found. Arts grant in Painting, 1989; fellow Guggenheim Found., 1996. Office: c/o Blaffer Gallery 120 Fine Arts Building Univ Houston Houston TX 77204

STOCKMAN, JAMES ANTHONY, III, medical association administrator, pediatrician; b. Phila., 1943; MD, Jefferson Med. Coll., 1969. Diplomate Am. Bd. Pediat. Intern Childrens Hosp., Phila., 1969—70, resident, 1970—71, chief resident in pediat., instr. dept. pediat., 1971—72, vis. fellow divsn. oncology, 1972; fellow in pediatric hematology/oncology SUNY, Syracuse, 1972—74, asst. prof. pediat., 1974—77, assoc. prof., vice-chmn. pediat., 1977—81, prof. pediat., 1981—84; prof., chair dept. pediat. Northwestern Med. Sch., Chgo., 1984—92; chair medicine, physician-in-chief and Women's Bd. Centennial chair in pediat. Children's Meml. Hosp., Chgo., 1984—92; chief pediat., assoc. dean hosp. academic affairs McGaw Med. Ctr., Chgo., 1984—92; pres., CEO American Bd. Pediat., 1992—; clin. prof. pediat. Duke U. Sch. Medicine, Durham, NC, U. NC, Chapel Hill. Author: Clinical Facts and Curios; editor: Year Book of Pediatrics, The Child's Doctor; editor-in-chief: Current Problems in Pediatrics, Focus and Opinion: Pediatrics; contbr. articles to profl. jours., chapters to books. Office: Office of the Pres Am Bd Pediatrics 111 Silver Cedar Ct Chapel Hill NC 27514-1512 Office Phone: 919-929-0461.

STOCKMAN, JAMES D., retail executive; V.p. ladies' apparel merchandising Dillard's, Inc., 2006, gen. mdse. mgr. product devel. Office: Dillards Inc 1600 Cantrell Rd Little Rock AR 72201 Office Phone: 501-376-5200. Office Fax: 501-399-7831. E-mail: jim.stockman@dillards.com.

STOCKMAN, STEVE (STEPHEN ERNEST STOCKMAN), United States Representative from Texas; b. Bloomfield Hills, Mich., Nov. 14, 1956; m. Patti F. Ferguson, Dec. 10, 1988. Attended, San Jacinto Coll., 1985—86; BS in Acctg., U. Houston-Clear Lake, 1990. Acct. computer sales & lab researcher divsn. IBM Corp.; acct., tech. McKee Environ. Health, Inc., 1991-93; mem. US Congress from 9th Tex. Dist., 1995—97; v.p. exec. development Leadership Inst., 2005—07; mem. US Congress from 36th Tex. Dist., Washington, 2013—, US House Fgn. Affairs Com., US House Sci., Space & Technology Com., 2013—. Recipient Taxpayer's Best Friend award, Citizens for Tax Reform, Taxpayer's Hero award, Citizens Again Govt. Waste. Republican. Southern Baptist. Office: US House of Representatives 326 Cannon House Office Bldg Washington DC 20515 also: 907 E Houston St Cleveland TX 77327 Office Phone: 202-225-1555, 409-883-8028. Office Fax: 202-226-0396.*

STOCKS, WILLIAM L., federal judge; Bar: N.C. Bankruptcy judge for mid. dist. N.C. U.S. Bankruptcy Ct., Greensboro, 1993—. Office: US Bankruptcy Ct 101 S Edgeworth St Greensboro NC 27401-2219 Office Phone: 336-358-4080.

STOCKTON, DAVID A., lawyer; BA, Emory U., 1978; JD with honors, U. NC, Chapel Hill, 1982. Bar: Ga. 1982. Ptnr. Corp. Group Kilpatrick Stockton LLP, Atlanta. Editor (review): UNC Ch. Law. Mem.: ABA (mem. Fed. Regulation of Securities sub-com.), Atlanta Bar Assn., State Bar of Ga. (chmn. Bus. Law Sect.), Order of the Coif. Office: Kilpatrick Stockton LLP Ste 2800 1100 Peachtree St Atlanta GA 30309 Office Phone: 404-815-6500. Office Fax: 404-541-3402. E-mail: DStockton@KilpatrickStockton.com.

STOCKTON, DICK, sportscaster; b. Phila., Nov. 22, 1942; s. Joseph William and Beatrice Stokvis; m. Lesley Visser. BS, Syracuse U., 1964. Newscaster Sta. KYW-AM, Phila., 1965-67; sportscaster Sta. KYW-TV, Phila., 1966-67; dir. sports Sta. KDKA-TV, Pitts., 1967-71, Sta. WBZ-TV, Boston, 1971-73; NFL post game commentator CBS Sports, 1967-73, host, CBS Sports Spectacular, 1978-80, play-by-play announcer, NCAA basketball, 1978—94, Maj. League Baseball broadcaster, 1990—92; play-by-play announcer Boston Celtics, 1972-75, NY Knicks, 1975-76; TV broadcaster Boston Red Sox, 1975-78; commentator 1975 World Series; host NHL series, 1978; play-by-play announcer NBA Game of Week, 1981—90; TV broadcaster Oakland Athletics, 1993—95; play-by-play announcer, NFL FOX Sports, 1994—, play-by-play announcer, NHL, 1996, play-by-play announcer, MLB, 2003—; play-by-play announcer, NBA Turner Sports, 1995—, play-by-play announcer, MLB, 2007—. Recipient Harold Waldron Meml. award Syracuse Club of Buffalo, 1981, Curt Gowdy Electronic Media award Basketball Hall of Fame, 2001; named one of Top 50 Sportscasters Am. Sportscasters Assn., 2009. Mem. Sigma Delta Chi. Office: Turner Sports One CNN Ctr 13 S Tower Atlanta GA 30303

STODOLA, MARK ALLEN, mayor, Little Rock, Arkansas, former prosecutor; b. Mpls., May 18, 1949; s. Robert Allen and Elizabeth (Abeler); m. Jo Ellen Stodola; children: Allison, Robert, John Mark. BA in Journalism and Polit. Sci., U. Iowa, 1971; JD, U. Ark., 1974. Bar: Ark. 1974, US Dist. Ct. (we. and ea. dists.) Ark. 1975, US Ct. Appeals (8th cir.). Assoc. Givens & Buzbee, Little Rock, 1974-75; dep. pub. defender Pulaski County, Little Rock, 1975-76; pub. defender City of North Little Rock, Ark., 1976-85; ptnr. Stodola & Smith, North Little Rock, 1976-85; city atty. City of Little Rock, Ark., 1985—90, prosecuting atty., 1990—96, mayor, 2007—. Instr. criminal justice U. Ark., Little Rock, 1976—85; lectr. in Argentina & Russia Nat. Dist. Atty. Assn. Mem. exec. com. Dem. State Com., Little Rock, 1976—, Dem. Nat. Com., Washington, 1981—83; nat. pres. Young Dems. Am., Washington, 1981—83; vol. Big Brothers & Big Sisters; bd. mem. Ark. Repertory Theatre; pres. Quapaw Quarter Assn., Hist. Preservation Alliance of Ark.; mem. Heights Neighborhood Assn. 2nd lt. USAFR, 1969—74. Mem.: Internat. Mcpl. Lawyers Assn. (former chmn.), Ark. City Atty. Assn. (former pres.), Ark. Pros. Atty. Assn. (former pres.), Nat. Dist. Attys. Assn. (former v.p.), Am. Trial Lawyers Assn., Nat. Inst. Mcpl. Law Officers, Pulaski Bar Assn. (Lawyer's award 1981), Ark. Bar Assn., ABA, Rotary. Avocations: rugby, hist. preservation. Office: City Hall 500 W Makham Rm 203 Little Rock AR 72201 Home Phone: 501-666-6630; Office Phone: 501-371-4510, 501-371-4791. Office Fax: 501-371-4498. Business E-Mail: mayor@littlerock.org, mstodola@castlaw.com.*

STOFFEL, PAUL T., investment company executive; m. Gayle Stoffel. MBA, Harvard Bus. Sch. Various positions to bd. dirs. Centex Corp.; chmn. Triple S Capital Corp., 1985—, Paul Stoffel Investments, 1985—; dir. HollyFontier Corp., 2011—. Bd. dirs. Holly Corpn., Dallas, 2001—. Co-founder Gayle and Paul Stoffel Found.; bd. mem. Dallas Symphony Orch., Southwestern Med. Found., Zale Lipshy Hosp., St. Paul U. Hosp.; bd. dirs. Dallas Symphony Assn., Dallas Symphony Found. Named one of Top 200 Collectors, ARTnews mag., 2005—12. Mailing: 5949 Sherry Ln Ste 1465 Dallas TX 75225

STOKELY, JOHN E., information technology executive; CFO Richfood Holdings, Inc. (merged with Supervalu, Inc.), Richmond, Va., 1990-93, v.p., fin. & adminstrn., 1993-95, chmn., pres. & CEO, 1997—99; pres. JES, Inc., 1999—. Bd. dirs. Performance Food Group Co., Nash Finch Co., ACI Worldwide, Inc. (formerly Transaction Sys. Architects, Inc.), Pool Corp., 2000—. Mailing: JES Inc PO Box 71745 Richmond VA 23255 Office Phone: 804-335-1470. Business E-Mail: john.stokely@scppool.com.

STOKES, JAMES SEWELL, environmental services administrator, not-for-profit developer; b. Englewood, NJ, Jan. 24, 1944; s. James Sewell III and Doris Mackey (Smith) S.; m. Esther Moger, Aug. 19, 1967; children: Jessica Neale, Elizabeth Sewell BA, Davidson Coll., NC, 1966; LLB, Yale U., 1969. Bar: Ga. 1969. Asst. to gen. counsel Office Gen. Counsel of the Army, Washington, 1969-72; assoc. Alston, Miller & Gaines, Atlanta, 1972-77; ptnr. Alston & Bird (previously Alston, Miller & Gaines), Atlanta, 1977—2005, chmn. environ. group, 1987—96, chmn. bus. devel. com., 1996—2005; mem. ptnr.'s com. Alston & Bird, Atlanta, 1995-98; chmn. mgmt. com., Atlanta, 1998; pres. Ga. Conservancy, Atlanta, 2005—. Mem. Gov.'s Environ. Adv. Coun., 1991-2004, chmn., 1997-99; chmn. Gov.'s Conf. on Pollution Prevention and the Environment, 1997; spkr. in field Contbr. articles to profl. jours. Mem. Metro Atlanta Chamber Clean Water Initiative, 2000, Ga. Future Forestry Commn., 2005, Atlanta Regional Commn. Environ. & Land Use Com., 2005—; exec. com. Livable Cmtys. Coalition, 2005—; chmn. Metro Atlanta Chamber Water Com., 2002; mem. Trust for Public Land Ga. Bd., 1986-91; co-chmn. Spotlight on Ga. Artists V, 1986; mem. City of Atlanta Zoning Rev. Bd., 1978-85, chmn., 1984-85; bd. dirs. Brookwood Hills Civic Assn., 1975-77, pres., 1977; bd. dirs. Nexus Contemporary Arts Ctr., Atlanta, 1987-92, vice chmn. capital campaign, 1989, chmn. nominating com., 1988, chmn. fundraising com., 1987-88; bd. dirs. Butler St. YMCA N.W. br., 1973-75, Dynamo Swim Club, 1988-91, Arts Festival Atlanta, 1994-98; trustee Inst. Continuing Legal Edn., Athens, 1980-81, Trinity Sch., Atlanta, 1998, 1997-2003, Charles Loridans Found., 1994-2005; mem. session Trinity Presbyn. Ch., 1986-89, 1997-2000, clk. of session, 1988-89, chmn. cmty. concerns com., 1987-88, chmn. pers. com., 1989-90, 1999-2005, chmn. assoc. pastor search com., 1991-92, 2004-05; bd. dirs. Park Pride, 1992, Ga. C. of C., 1998-2005, Hambidge Ctr., 2000-2003, chmn. environ. com., 1987-92, environ. legal counsel, 1981-87; mem. spl. program Leadership Atlanta, 1979-80, Leadership Ga., 1985, Inst. Ga. Environ. Leadership, 2004. Capt. U.S. Army, 1969-72 Decorated D.S.M.; recipient Spl. award Atlanta chpt. AIA, 1988, Mayor Andrew Young, 1985; named one of 96 Most Influential Atlantans, Atlanta Bus. Chronicle, 2005, One of 100 Most Influential Georgians, Ga. Trend Mag., 2006. Mem. ABA (natural resources sect.), State Bar Ga. (chmn. environ. law sect. 1979-82), Atlanta Bar Assn., City of Atlanta Hist. Preservation (policy steering com. 1989), Atlanta C. of C. (water resources task force 1982-87, solid waste task force 1989, air quality task force 1993-97, environ. affairs com. 1998—2005), Ga. Indsl. Developers Assn. (hazardous waste com. 1983-84), Phi Beta Kappa, Omicron Delta Kappa. Avocations: swimming, bird watching, community activities, travel. Office: Ga Conservancy Ste 200 817 W Peachtree St Atlanta GA 30308 Office Phone: 404-876-2900 ext. 200. Office Fax: 404-872-9229. Business E-Mail: jim.stokes@alston.com.

STOKES, MACK BOYD (MARION), bishop; b. Wonsan, Korea, Dec. 21, 1911; arrived in U.S., 1929; s. Marion Boyd and Florence Pauline (Davis) Stokes; m. Ada Rose Yow, June 19, 1942; children: Marion Boyd III, Arch Yow, Elsie Pauline. Student, Seoul Fgn. High Sch., Korea; AB, Asbury Coll., 1932; BD, Duke, 1935; postgrad., Boston U. Sch. Theol., 1935-37, Harvard, 1936-37; PhD, Boston U., 1940; LLD, Lambuth U., Jackson, Tenn., 1963; DD, Millsaps Coll., 1974. Resident fellow systematic theology Boston U., 1936-38, Bowne fellow in philosophy, 1938-39; ordained to ministry Meth. Ch., deacon, 1938, elder, 1940; vis. prof. philosophy and religion Ill. Wesleyan U., 1940-41; prof. Christian doctrine Candler Sch. Theology, Emory U., 1941-56, asso. dean, Parker prof. systematic theology, 1956-72, chmn. exec. com. div. of religion of grad. sch., 1956-72; acting dean Candler Sch. Theology, Emory U. (Candler Sch.), 1968-69; bishop-in-residence Peachtree Rd. United Meth. Ch. Atlanta, 1988—. Faculty mem. Inst. Theol. Studies Oxford U., 1958; del. Meth. Ecumenical Conf., 1947, 1952, 1961, 1971, Holston, Gen. confs., S.E. Jurisdictional Conf., 1956, 1960, 1964, 1968, 1972; chmn. com. ministry Gen. Conf. Meth. Ch., 1960; nat. com. Nature Unity We Seek, 1956—; mem. gen. com. ecumenical affairs theol. study com. United Meth. Ch., 1968—72, com. on Cath.-Meth. rels., 1969—, bishop, 1972—. Author: (book) Major Methodist Beliefs, 1956, Major Methodist Beliefs, rev. 15th edit., 1990, The Evangelism of Jesus, 1960, The Epic of Revelation, 1961, Our Methodist Heritage, 1963, Crencas Fundamentals Dos Methodistas, 1964, Study Guide on the Teachings of Jesus, 1970, The Bible and Modern Doubt, 1970, Major United Methodist Beliefs, 1971, Major United Methodist Beliefs, Korean transl., 1977, Major United Methodist Beliefs, rev. with added study guide, 1998, The Holy Spirit and Christian Experience, 1975, The Holy Spirit and Christian Experience, Korean transl., 1985, Twelve Dialogues on John's Gospel, 1975, Jesus, The Master-Evangel, 1978, Can God See the Inside of an Apple?, 1979, Questions Asked by United Methodists, Philippine transl., 1980, The Bible in the Wesleyan Heritage, 1981, Respuestas A Preguntas Que Hacen Los Metodistas Unidos, 1983, The Holy Spirit in the Wesleyan Heritage, 1985, The Holy Spirit in the Wesleyan Heritage, Spanish transl., 1992, The Holy Spirit in the Wesleyan Heritage, Korean transl., 1992, Scriptural Holiness of the United Methodist Christian, 1988, Talking with God: A Guide of Prayer, 1989, Theology for Preaching, 1994, Questions and Answers about Life and Faith, 2000, Person-to-Parson, 2007. Trustee Emory U., Millsaps Coll., Rust Coll., Wood Jr. Coll. Methodist. Home: Unit EPH2C 13597 Perdido Key Dr Pensacola FL 32507-2659

STOKES, PAUL MASON, lawyer; b. Miami Beach, Fla., July 16, 1946; s. Walter Johnson and Juanita (Hemperley) S.; m. Carol Crocker, Sept. 12, 1970; children: Macon Lanford, Walter Ashley, Mary Juanita. BA, Duke U., 1968; JD, U. Chgo., 1971. Bar: Fla. 1971. Law clerk to hon. Milton Pollack U.S. Dist. Ct. (so. dist.) N.Y., NYC, 1971—72; assoc. Smathers and Thompson, Miami, Fla., 1972—77, ptnr., 1977—88, Kelley Drye & Warren L.L.P., Miami, 1988—99, Stokes McMillan Antúnez P.A., Miami, 1999—. Adj. prof. law U. Miami, Coral Gables, Fla., 1987-94, 2005-10; pub. defender City of Miami Springs, Fla., 1974, City of Hialeah, Fla., 1974-75. Mem. Code Enforcement Bd. Miami Springs, 1990-92; regent Trinity Internat. U., Deerfield, Ill., 1989-98; mem. Permanent Jud. Commn., Presbytery of Tropical Fla., 1997-00; bd. dirs. Greater Miami Youth for Christ; com. on ministry, Presbytery of Tropical Fla., 2007-. Fellow Am. Coll. Trust and Estate Coun.; mem. Dade County Bar Assn. (probate and guardianship ct. com. 1988—, bd. dirs. 1989-92, 94-2000, 2004—05), Fla. Bar (cert. wills, trusts and estates), Phi Beta Kappa, Order of Coif. Democrat. Presbyterian. Office: Stokes McMillan Antúnez P A One SE 3d Ave Ste 1750 Miami FL 33131 Home Phone: 305-887-0643; Office Phone: 305-379-4008. Business E-Mail: pstokes@smpalaw.com.

STOKOE, KENNETH H., II, civil engineer, educator; BSCE, U. Mich., 1966, MSCE, 1967, PhD, 1972. Instr. Univ. Mich., 1971; asst. prof. Univ. Mass., 1972—73, Univ. Tex., Austin, 1973—78, assoc. prof., 1978—83, prof. civil engring., 1983—85, Brunswick Abernathy Regents prof., 1985—97, Cockrell Family Regents Chair, 1997—99, Jennie C. and Milton T. Graves chair in engring., 2000—. Contbr. articles to prof. jours. Mem.: Nat. Acad. Engring., Am. Soc. Civil Engineers, Am. Soc. Nondestructive Testing, Am. Soc. Testing & Materials, Earthquake Engring. Rsch. Inst., Internat. Soc. Soil Mech. & Geotechnical Engring., Seismological Soc. Am., Soc. Exploration Geophysicists, Transp. Rsch. Bd., Soc. Profl. Engineers. Office: U Tex at Austin Dept Archl and Environ Engring 1 Univeristy Sta C1792 Austin TX 78712-0280

STOLEN, ROGERS HALL, optics scientist; b. Madison, Wis., Sept. 18, 1937; BA, St. Olaf Coll., 1959; PhD in Physics, U. Calif., Berkeley, 1965. Fellow U. Toronto, 1964-66; mem. tech. staff solid state optics AT&T Bell Labs., Holmdel, 1966—68; with Va. Inst. Tech., Blacksburg, 1998—2005; foreign mem. Russian Acad. Sci., 2009; with Clemson U., SC, 2005—. Recipient of R.W. Wood Prize, 1990, Optical Soc. Am. Mem. Am. Phys. Soc., Optical Soc. Am. (R. W. Wood prize 1990). Achievements include research in nonlinear properties of optical fibers, polarization preserving optical fibers, light scattering in glass. Office: Clemson University COMSET 91 Technology Dr Anderson SC 29625 Home: 1042 Issac Franklin Dr Gallatin TN 37066 Office Phone: 615-504-6540. Business E-Mail: rstolen@clemson.edu.

STOLLE, CHRISTOPHER P., state legislator, physician; b. Norfolk, Va., Apr. 1, 1958; m. Lisa Stolle; children: Patricia, Christopher, Graham, Andrew, Kevin. BS, US Naval Acad., Annapolis, Md., 1981; MD, Uniformed Services U. of Health Sciences, Md., 1988; MBA, Coll. William and Mary, Williamsburg, Va., 2004. Cert. Am. Coll. Physician Execs. Internship and residency in ob-gyn Naval Med. Ctr., Portsmouth, Va., chmn. ob-gyn dept.; dept. head ob-gyn Naval Hosp., Jacksonville, Fla.; small bus. owner Va., 2005—; v.p. med. affairs Riverside Regional Med. Ctr.; house del. Dist. 83 Va. House of Dels., Richmond, 2010—. Nuc. engr., physician USN, 1981—2005. Fellow: Am. Coll. Obstetrics and Gynecology; mem.: Med. Soc. Va. Republican. Roman Catholic. Office: Va House of Dels Gen Assembly Bldg Rm 422 PO Box 406 Richmond VA 23218 also: 1037 Ducking Point Trail Virginia Beach VA 23455 Office Phone: 804-698-1083, 757-651-5035. Office Fax: 804-698-6783. Business E-Mail: delcstolle@house.virginia.gov.

STOLLE, KENNETH W., protective services official, former state legislator; b. Washington, Oct. 7, 1954; m. Deborah L. Stolle. Atty.; chmn. Va. Beach Rep. Party, 1990—92; state senator Dist. 8 Va., 1992—2009; mem. Agr., Conservation & Natural Resources, Commerce & Labor, Courts of Justice & Fin. Com.; sheriff City of Va. Beach, 2009—. Recipient Silver Star for Bravery & Medal of Merit, Va. Beach Police Dept., Silver Star for Bravery, America Law Enforcement Officers Assn.; named Senator of Yr., Fraternal Order of Police. Mem.: Fraternal Order of Police, Va. Trial Lawyers Assn., K of C. Republican. Roman Catholic. Office: Va Beach Sheriff's Office Mcpl Ctr Bldg 7 Virginia Beach VA 23456 Office Phone: 757-385-4073. Office Fax: 757-385-5037. Business E-Mail: planteigne@vbso.net.

STOLLE, RUSSELL ROBERT, chemicals executive; b. Houston; BA, Valparaiso U., Ind., 1984; JD with honors, U. Tex., 1987. Bar: Tex. 1987, US Patent and Trademark Office 1988. Intern Tex. Supreme Ct., Austin, Tex., 1987; assoc. Baker & Botts, LLP, Houston, 1987-89; patent atty. Texaco Inc., Austin, 1990-94; chief patent and licensing counsel Huntsman Corp., Austin, 1994—2000, v.p., chief tech. counsel, 2000—02, v.p., dep. gen. counsel, 2002—06, sr. v.p., dep. gen. counsel, 2006—. Mem. Am. Intellectual Property Law Assn., Licensing Execs. Soc., Austin Intellectual Property Law Assn. Office: Huntsman Corp 10003 Woodloch Forest Dr The Woodlands TX 77380 Office Phone: 281-719-6000.

STOLTZFUS, DAN P., critical care medicine, educator; MD, U. Tex. Health Sci. Ctr., Houston, 1983. Cert. anesthesiology 1987, critical care medicine 2005. Resident in anesthesiology Walter Reed Hosp., Washington, 1983—87, fellow in critical care anesthesiology, 1987—88; asst. clin. prof. anesthesiology Univ. Fla.; hosp. affiliations include Orlando Regional Med. Ctr., Orlando South Seminole Hosp. Office: Orlando South Seminole Hospital 555 W State Rd 434 Maitland FL 32750-4999

STOLZBERG, MARK ELLIOTT, psychologist; b. NYC, Apr. 30, 1944; s. Seymour and Ruth (Petesky) S.; m. Marilyn Goldberg, Mar. 18, 1972; children: Susan Beth Swinkin, David Jonathan, Daniel Jason. BA, Hofstra U., Hempstead, NY, 1966, PhD; MA in Exptl. Psychology, C.W. Post Coll., Greenvale, NY, 1970; postgrad. in clin. psychology, SUNY, Albany, 1973. Diplomate in clin. psychology Am. Bd. Profl. Psychology. Intern in clin. psychology Maimonides Hosp., Bklyn., 1972-73; pres. Stolzberg Rsch., LLC, Stony Brook, NY, 1976—. Adj. lectr. Bklyn. Coll., 1973; faculty Coll. Optometry, SUNY, 1985-86; cons. psychologist in numerous clinical and business settings, 1994—, pilot US Coast Guard Air Aux. Contbr. articles to numerous profl. jours. Co-pres. North Shore SEPTA, 1999-2001;

founder, past pres. Ind. Practitioners Geropsychology. Grad. fellow SUNY, Albany, 1970-72, N.Y. State War Svc. scholar; recipient Disting. Achievement award for Rsch., NY State Optometric Assn. Mem. NY State Psychol. Assn. (pres., adult devel. & aging divsn. 2004), Nat. Aeronautics Assn. Achievements include two US transcontinental speed records for piston-engine aircraft. Home and Office: 6759 Shamrock Trail Boynton Beach FL 33437

STONE, BILL, state legislator; b. Memphis, Dec. 29, 1965; m. Debbie Samples. Attended, NE CC, U. Miss. Real estate broker/appraiser; mem. Dist. 2 Miss. State Senate, 2008—. Democrat. Baptist. Home: PO Box 63 Ashland MS 38603 Office: PO Box 1018 Jackson MS 39215 Home Phone: 662-224-3949; Office Phone: 662-224-3300, 601-359-4090. E-mail: bstone@senate.ms.gov.

STONE, EDMUND CRISPEN, III, banker; b. Charleston, W.Va., Nov. 29, 1942; s. Edmund C. and Sallie Ragland (Thornhill) S.; m. Annette Margarethe Isaksen, Nov. 26, 1965 (div.); 1 child, Kristine Margarethe; m. Barbara J. Sarff, June 15, 2000. BS, U.S. Mil. Acad., 1964; MBA, U. Va., 1972. V.p. Wachovia Bank, Winston-Salem, N.C., 1972-81; exec. v.p. First Am. Corp., Nashville, from 1981; vice chmn. First Am. Nat. Bank Nashville, 1988; exec. v.p. Regions Fin. Corp. (formerly First Ala. Bancshares, Inc.), Birmingham, 1988—2005; chief credit officer First Nat. of Nebr. Inc.; ret. Contbg. author: The International Banking Handbook, 1983. Mem. export policy task force U.S. C. of C., 1980-81. With inf. U.S. Army, 1964-70, Vietnam, Iran. Decorated Bronze Star (Valor) with oak leaf cluster, Vietnamese Cross of Gallantry, others; hon. mem. Imperial Iranian Spl. Forces, 1968. Mem. Assn. of Grads. U.S. Mil. Acad. (trustee 1992-93, 98-2001, 2001—08). Republican. Avocations: golf, sailing, hunting, fishing. E-mail: crisstone@bellsouth.net.

STONE, JACQUELYN ELOIS, lawyer; b. Williamsburg, Va., Jan. 7, 1958; d. William Thomas and Sara Elizabeth (Cumber) Stone. BA in Am. Govt., U.Va., 1980; JD, Harvard U., 1985. Bar: Va. 1985. Legis. asst. US House of Representatives, Washington, 1980-82; assoc. McGuire, Woods, Battle & Boothe, LLP (now McGuireWoods LLP), Richmond, Va., 1985—94, ptnr., 1994—, mem. bd. partners, firmwide hiring ptnr. & recruiting com. chair, mem. diversity com. Bd. mem. Arts Coun. of Richmond, past pres.; bd. mem. Jr. Achievement of Ctrl. Richmond, Richmond Eye & Ear Hosp., Venture Richmond, asst. sec.; exec. com. mem. Va. Performing Arts Found.; mem. local adv. com. Local Initiatives Support Corp.; bd. mem. Va. Commn. for the Arts. Recipient Outstanding Woman Award, YWCA, 2000, Women of Achievement award, Met. Richmond Women's Bar Assn., 2005, Themis award, DuPont Women's Lawyer Network, 2005. Mem.: ABA (mem. bus. law sect. 1985—), Am. Immigration Lawyers Assn., Old Dominion Bar Assn. (mem. exec. com. 1990—92), Va. Bar Assn. (exec. com. young lawyers sect. 1988—90, chmn. membership com. 1988—90), Va. State Bar. Baptist. Avocation: travel. Office: McGuireWoods LLP One James Ctr 901 E Cary St Richmond VA 23219-4030 Office Phone: 804-775-1046. Office Fax: 804-698-2183. Business E-Mail: jstone@mcguirewoods.com.

STONE, JESSE, state legislator; b. Augusta, Ga., Mar. 21; m. Amanda Stone; 3 children. B, MBA, JD, U. Ga. Co-founder, atty. Merill & Stone Law Firm; mayor City of Waynesboro, Ga., 2003; mem. Dist. 23 Ga. State Senate, 2011—. Republican. Office: 642 Liberty St Waynesboro GA 30830 also: Ga State Senate 320B Coverdell Legis Office Bldg Atlanta GA 30334 Office Phone: 478-237-7029, 404-463-1314. Business E-Mail: jesse.stone@senate.ga.gov.

STONE, MARVIN JULES, hematologist, oncologist, educator; b. Columbus, Ohio, Aug. 3, 1937; s. Roy J. and Lillian (Bedwinek) S.; m. Jill Feinstein, June 29, 1958; children: Nancy Lillian, Robert Howard. Student, Ohio State U., 1955-58; SM in Pathology, U. Chgo., 1962, MD with honors, 1963. Diplomate Am. Bd. Internal Medicine, (Hematology, Med. Oncology). Intern ward med. svc. Barnes Hosp., St. Louis, 1963-64, asst. resident, 1964-65; clin. assoc. arthritis and rheumatism br. Nat. Inst. Arthritis and Metabolic Diseases, NIH, Bethesda, Md., 1965-68; resident in medicine, ACP scholar Parkland Meml. Hosp., Dallas, 1968-69; fellow in hematology-oncology, dept. internal medicine U. Tex. Southwestern Med. Sch., Dallas, 1969-70, instr. dept. internal medicine, 1970-71, asst. prof., 1971-73, assoc. prof., 1974-76, clin. prof., 1976—, chmn. bioethics com., 1979-81; mem. faculty & steering com. Immunology Grad. Program, Grad. Sch. Biomed. Scis., U. Tex. Health Sci. Ctr., Dallas, 1975, adj. mem., 1976—2008; dir. oncology med. edn., quality & safety, assoc. dir. Cancer Ctr., 2008—. Dir. Charles A. Sammons Cancer Ctr., chief oncology, dir. immunology, co-dir. divsn. hematology-oncology, attending physician Baylor U. Med. Ctr., Dallas, 1976—; v.p. med. staff Parkland Meml. Hosp., Dallas, 1982, dir. Oncology Med. Edn. Quality and Safety, 2008-, assoc. dir., Baylor Charles A. Sammon Cancer Ctr. Contbr. chpts. to books, articles to profl. jours. Chmn. com. patient-aid Greater Dallas/Ft. Worth chpt. Leukemia Soc. Am., 1971-76, chmn. med. adv. com., 1978-80, bd. dirs., 1971-80; mem. v.p. Dallas unit Am. Cancer Soc., 1977-78, pres., 1978—; mem. adv. bd. Baylor U. Med. Ctr. Found., Marvin J. Stone Libr., Baylor Inst. Immunology Rsch., 1999. With USPHS, 1965-68. Recipient Wings of Eagles award, Baylor Health Care Sys., 2001, Disting. Svc. award, U. Chgo., 2002, Lifetime Achievement award, Internat. Soc. Study of Waldenstrom's Macroglobulinemia, 2004. Master ACP (gov. No. Tex. 1993-97, laureate Tex. chpt. 2000); fellow Royal Soc. Medicine (London); mem. AMA, Am. Assn. Immunologists, Am. Soc. Hematology, Internat. Soc. Hematology, Coun. Thrombosis, Am. Heart Assn. (established investigator 1970-75), Am. Soc. Clin. Oncology (edn. com. 2002-05, career devel. com. 2002-05), Am. Osler Soc. (bd. govs. 1997-2000, 2005—, v.p. 2001-03, pres. 2003-04), Am. Assn. for Cancer Rsch., So. Soc. Clin. Investigation, Tex. Med. Assn., Dallas County Med. Soc., Clin. Immunology Soc., Phi Beta Kappa, Sigma Xi, Alpha Omega Alpha. Office: Baylor U Med Ctr Charles A Sammons Cancer Ctr 3500 Gaston Ave Dallas TX 75246-2096 Business E-Mail: marvins@baylorhealth.edu.

STONE, MICHAEL C., state legislator; m. Jennifer Stone; children: Gabrielle Stone, Connor Stone. AAS in Bus. & Acctg., Ctrl. Carolina Cmty. Coll. Owner O'Connell's Grocery Store; bd. dirs. Four Oaks Bank; co-owner TBS enterprise; mem. Ctrl. Carolina Jaycees; chaplain Sanford Elks Lodge, 2002; exec dir. Sanford Chamber, 2003—07; vice chmn. Public Policy Com., 2004; candidate Dist. 44 NC House of Representatives, 2002, mem. Dist. 51, 2011—. Republican. Avocation: Lee Parks and Rec. Address: PO Box 3729 Sanford NC 27331 also: 1123 Winterlocker Dr Sanford NC 27330 Office: North Carolina House of Representatives 16 W Jones St Room 1008 Raleigh NC 27601-1096 Office Phone: 919-775-8202, 919-715-3026, 919-777-8419. Business E-Mail: Michael.Stone@ncleg.net.

STONE, ROBERT G., JR., water transportation executive; BA, Harvard U., 1947. Lead investor Industrial Capital Group lead investor, Intersouth Partners, Morgan Holland Venture Partners, Mayfield Fund; chmn. & pres. States Marine Lines; chmn. Kirby Corp., 1983—95, bd. dirs., 1995—. Bd. dirs. Chubb Corp., Core Industries Inc., Corning Inc., NovaCare Inc., Pittston Co., Russell Reynolds Assoc., Tandem Computers Inc., Tejas Gas Corp.; mem. bd. adv. Arcadia Partners. Fellow Harvard Corp., 1975—95, sr. fellow, 1995—2002. With US Army, 1943—45. Fellow: Am. Acad. Arts & Sci.; mem.: N.Y. Yacht Club (commodore), Augusta Nat. Golf Club. Achievements include world record in 2000 meter heavyweight crew, captain, 1947. Office: Kirby Corp 55 Waugh Dr Ste 1000 Houston TX 77007 Office Phone: 713-435-1000. Office Fax: 713-435-1464.

STONE, ROGER JASON, JR., political consultant; b. Norwalk, Conn., Aug. 22, 1952; s. Roger J. and Gloria Rose (Corbo) Stone; m. Ann E. Wesche, 1974 (div. 1991). Attended, George Washington U. Scheduler Com. to Re-Elect the President, 1971—72; dir. Presdl. Inauguration Com., 1972—73; spl. asst. Senator Bob Dole, 1974—75; nat. youth dir. Citizens for Reagan, 1976; co-founder Nat. Conservative Polit. Action Com., 1978; Eastern region campaign dir. Reagan/Bush, 1980, 1984; strategic cons. Mayor Ed Koch, NYC, 1981, Gov. Thomas Kean, NJ, 1981, NJ, 1985, Rep. Matt Rinaldo, NJ, 1982, NJ, 1984, NJ, 1986, Rep. Jim Courter, NJ, 1982, NJ, 1986, Rep. Jack Kemp, NY, 1986, Rep. Charles Douglas, NJ, 1988; sr. polit. cons. Jack Kemp for President, 1987—88, Bush/Quayle Calif. Campaign, 1988; polit. cons. Black Manafor & Stone, 1980; co-founder Republicans for Choice, 1989; pres. Arlen Specter presdl. campaign, 1996; founder Citizens United Not Timid, 2008; press and PR mgr. Rothstein Rosenfeldt Adler Attorneys at Law, Ft. Lauderdale, NYC. Author: (blogs) The Stone Zone. Chmn. DC Fedn. Coll. Republicans, 1971—72; exec. com. Nat. Fedn. Young Republicans, 1974—75, chmn.; mem. Alexandria Republican City Com., Va., 1976—78. Named Man of Yr., Va. Young Republican Fedn., 1977; named one of 25 Most Influential Republicans, Newsmax Mag., 2008. Republican. Roman Catholic. Office: Rothstein Rosenfeldt Adler Ste 1650 101 NE 3rd Ave Ste 1800 Fort Lauderdale FL 33301-1252

STONE, WILSON, state legislator; b. Scottsville, Ky., Nov. 16, 1952; m. Lanna Stone; 1 child, Catherine. BS, Western Ky. U., 1974, MS, 1978. Farmer, 1983—; trainer Ky. Sch. Bd. Assn., 2002—; mem. Dist. 22 Ky. House of Reps., 2009—. Democrat. Office: 702 Capitol Ave Rm 329A Frankfort KY 40601 also: 1481 Jefferson School Rd Scottsville KY 42164 Office Phone: 502-564-8100 Ext. 672, 270-622-5054.

STONECIPHER, HARRY CURTIS, former aerospace transportation executive; b. Robbins, Tenn., May 16, 1936; s. Harry Sheldon and Jennie Mae Stonecipher; m. Joan Stonecipher; 2 children. BS, Tenn. Poly. Inst., 1960; DSc (hon.), Washington U., 2002. With GE, 1960—61, 1962—79, Martin Aircraft Co., 1961-62; v.p., gen. mgr., comml. & mil. transp. ops. GE, 1979—84, v.p., gen. mgr., aircraft engine ops. Evendale, Ohio, 1984—87; exec. v.p. Sundstrand Corp., 1987, pres., COO, 1987-88, pres., CEO, 1988-94, chmn., 1991-94, also past bd. dirs.; pres., CEO McDonnell-Douglas Corp., St. Louis, 1994-97; pres., COO The Boeing Co., 1997—2001, vice chmn., 2001—02, pres., CEO, 2003—05. Bd. dirs. PACCAR, Inc., The Boeing Co., 1997-2005. Bd. trustees Mus. Contemporary Art; bd. dirs. Lyric Opera Chgo.; bd. mem. US-China Bus. Coun., US-Saudi Arabia Bus. Coun., exec. com. mem. Recipient John R. Allison award, 1996, Rear Adm. John J. Bergen Leadership medal Navy League, 1996, Wings Club Disting. Achievement award, 2001, John W. Dixon award, U.S. Army Assn., 2002. Fellow Royal Aero. Soc., 1998.

STONER, DOUG, state legislator; m Della; children: Gray & Honor. BS, Kennesaw State Univ. No. Am. distbr. Exeloo; mem. Dist. 34 Ga. House Reps., 2003—04; mem. Dist. 6 Ga. State Senate, 2005—. Cobb Transit Advisor Bd (chairman); Smyrna Downtown Develop Authority; Georgia Regional Transportation Authority (tracking comt for Northwest Connectivity Study); King Springs PTA (president, formerly), advisor board; Kennesaw State Univ Sch of Arts (chairman alumni comt); Smyrna Bus Association. Democrat. Methodist. Mailing: PO Box 1781 Smyrna GA 30081 Office Phone: 770-436-0699. Business E-Mail: doug.stoner@senate.ga.gov.

STONESTREET, JANA, nursing administrator; b. Apr. 4, 1953; BS, Kent State U., 1976; MS, U. Tex., 1979. Dir. nursing St. David's Cmty. Hosp., Austin, 1985-86; asst. dir. nursing St. Luke's Episcopal Hosp., Houston, 1986-89, v.p. nurisng, 1989-91; exec. dir., chief nursing Officer U. Tex. Med. Br., Galveston, 1991—. Office: Univ Tex Med Br Hosps 301 University Blvd # 18 Galveston TX 77555-5302

STONEY, LEVAR M., state official; b. Long Island, NY, 1981; married. BA in Political Sci., James Madison U., 2004; Completed, Va. Commonwealth U. Minority Political Leadership Inst., 2006. Staff mem. to Senator R. Creigh Deeds Va. State Senate; political party dir. Democratic Party of Va., 2006—08, exec. dir., 2008; dep. campaign mgr. Terry McAuliffe Gubernatorial Campaign, 2013; dep. dir. Terry McAuliffe Gubernatorial Transition Team; sec. commonwealth State of Va., Richmond, 2014—. Democrat. Office: Secretary of Commonwealth PO Box 2454 Richmond VA 23218 Office Phone: 804-786-2441. Office Fax: 804-371-0017. E-mail: socmail@governor.virginia.gov.*

STOOKSBURY, WILLIAM CLAUDE, minister; b. Knoxville, Tenn., June 6, 1947; s. William Claude and Vera Faye (Hudman) S.; m. Mary Jayne Moyer, Mar. 21, 1970; 1 child, William David. BS, U. Tenn., Chattanooga, 1980; MDiv, Vanderbilt U., 1987; PhD (hon.), Pennington U., 2001. Ordained to ministry Bapt. Ch., 1978; ordinations transfered to Unithed Meth. Ch., 1988. Min. of visitation 1st Bapt. Ch., Chattanooga, 1975-78; pastor Beacon Bapt. Ch., Rossville, Ga., 1978-80; asst. min. Ea. Pkwy. Bapt. Ch., Louisville, 1980-81; pastor 1st Bapt. Ch., Fisherville, Ky., 1981-84, Baker's Grove Bapt. Ch., Mt. Juliet, Tenn., 1984-86, Fairgarden United Meth. Ch., Sevierville, Tenn., 1988-92, Lonsdale United Meth. Ch., Knoxville, 1992—2000, St. Luke's United Meth. Ch., Knoxville, 2000—05; sr. pastor 2nd United Meth. Ch., Knoxville, 2005—09; bd. missions Holston Conf. United Meth. Ch. Design team urban ministry Holston Conf., Meth. Ch., Knoxville, 1992. Mem. search com. dean of human svcs. U. Tenn., Chattanooga, 1980; co-chair area II, Campbellsville Coll. Fund-raising, Ky., 1983; mem. steering com. Tenn. Alliance Strong Cmtys., Nashville, 1989—; charter mem. Ams. for Change, Washignton, 1993—; mem. nat. steering com. Clinton/Gore '96 Campaign. Named one of Outstanding Young Men of Am., Outstanding Young Assn., 1982, Dyer scholarship Vanderbilt Div., 1986. Mem. Am. Acad. Religion, Long Run Bapt. Assn. (chair asn. message com. 1984, com. to study ordination 1982, exec. bd. dirs. 1981-84), People for the Am. Way, The Interfaith Alliance, Internat. Platform Assn. Democrat. Avocation: reading. Home: 885 General George Patton Rd Nashville TN 37221-2574

STOOPS, BOB, college football coach; b. Youngstown, Ohio, Sept. 9, 1960; s. Ron and Evelyn Stoops. BS, Univ. Iowa, 1983. Grad. asst. coach U. Iowa Hawkeyes, 1983—84, vol. coach, 1985—87; asst. coach Kent State U. Golden Flashes, 1988; defensive backs coach Kans. State U. Wildcats, 1989—90, co-defensive coord., 1991—95; def. coord., asst. head coach U. Fla. Gators, 1996—98; head football coach U. Okla. Sooners, 1998—. Recipient Paul "Bear" Bryant award, Nat. Sportscasters & Sportswriters Assn., 2000, George Munger award, Maxwell Football Club, 2000, Eddie Robinson award, Football Writers Assn. America, 2000; named Coach of Yr., AP, 2000, Woody Hayes Nat. Coach of Yr., 2000, 2003, Nat. Coach Yr., Am. Heart Assn., 2000, Football News, 2000, Walter Camp awards, 2000, 2003, Big 12 Coach Yr., 2000, 2003, Dallas Morning News, 2004, 2006, Region IV Coach of Yr., AFCA, 2003, Bobby Dodd Nat. Coach of Yr., 2003. Achievements include coaching the University of Oklahoma Sooners to the BCS National Championship, 2000. Office: Univ Okla Football 180 W Brooks St Norman OK 73019

STOOPS, JAMES KING, biochemistry researcher; b. Charleston, W.Va., Sept. 15, 1937; s. William Nelson and Mary Alice (Duncan) S.; m. Pamela Ann Moore, Aug. 18, 1962; children: Timothy, Mary. BS, Duke U., 1960; PhD, Northwestern U., 1966. Adj. prof. Baylor Coll. of Medicine, Houston, 1990—2007; prof. U. Tex. Health Sci. Ctr. Med. Sch., Houston, 1990—. Contbr. articles to profl. jours. Grantee NIH, 1990, 91, 94. Mem. AAAS, Am. Chem. Soc., Am. Soc. for Biochemistry and Molecular Biology. Presbyterian. Achievements include contbn. to understanding of structure-function relationships of the enzymes involved in lipid metabolism; determination of three-dimensional structures of human alpha-2-macroglobulins, pyruvate dehydrogenase, Cam kinases and the fatty acid synthase which indicate how these macromolecules function, propose novel therapy for pulmonary TB. Home: 10310 Cliffwood Dr Houston TX 77035-3610 Office: U Tex Health Sci Ctr 6431 Fannin St Houston TX 77030-1501 Office Phone: 713-500-5345. Business E-Mail: james.k.stoops@uth.tmc.edu.

STOOPS, MARK, college football coach; b. Youngstown, Ohio, July 9, 1967; s. Ron and Evelyn Stoops; m. Chantel Stoops; children: Will, Zack. B, U. Iowa, Iowa City, 1989. Grad. asst. U. Iowa Hawkeyes, 1990—91; athletic dir., asst. football coach Nordonia Hills HS Knights, Ohio, 1992—95; defensive backs coach U. South Fla. Bulls, 1996, U. Wyo. Cowboys, 1997—99; co-defensive coord., safeties coach U. Houston Cougars, 2000; defensive backs coach U. Miami Hurricanes, Fla., 2001—03; defensive coord., defensive backs coach U. Ariz. Wildcats, 2004—09; defensive coord. Fla. State U. Seminoles, 2010—12; head football coach U. Ky. Wildcats, 2013—. Office: University of Kentucky Football Program Joe Craft Center 338 Lexington Ave Lexington KY 40506-0604 Office Phone: 859-257-3611.*

STOOPS, MIKE (MICHAEL J. STOOPS), college football coach; b. Youngstown, Ohio, Dec. 31, 1961; s. Ron and Evelyn Stoops; m. Nicole Stoops; children: Payton, Colton. Grad., U. Iowa, Iowa City, 1986. Defensive back Chgo. Bears, Pitts. Gladiators, Arena Football League; grad. asst. coach U. Iowa Hawkeyes, 1986—87, vol. coach, 1988—91; defensive ends coach Kansas State U. Wildcats, 1992—95, co-defensive coord., 1996—97, asst. head coach, 1998; assoc. head coach U. Okla. Sooners, 1999—2003, assoc. head coach, defensive coord., defensive backs coach, 2012—; head coach U. Ariz. Wildcats, 2004—11. Named First Team All-American, UPI, 1984, First Team All-Conf., Big 10 Conf., 1983, 1984; finalist Asst. Coach of Yr., American Football Coaches Assn., 2001. Office: University of Oklahoma Football Program McClendon Ctr Intercollegiate Athletics 180 W Brooks Norman OK 73019*

STORDAHL, ANN M., retail executive; BS, NYU, 1975. Nurse's aide; sr. v.p., gen. mgr. Magnin-Bullocks Wilshire, LA, 1989; v.p., divisional mdse. mgr. Neiman Marcus Stores, 1992—95, sr. v.p., divisional mdse. mgr., 1995—2004, gen. mdse. mgr.,women's apparel, 1995—, exec. v.p., Women's Apparel, 2004—. Office: Neiman Marcus Inc One Marcus Sq 1618 Main St Dallas TX 75201 Office Phone: 214-743-7600. Business E-Mail: ann_stordahl@neimanmarcus.com.

STOREY, DEBBIE, telecommunications industry executive; BA in Psychology, U. Ga., 1980, MBA, 2004—06. V.p. and gen. mgr. Steven Graphics, 1983—97, Bellsouth, 1996—98; v.p. pub. Bellsouth Advt. and Pub. Corp., 1998—2001, v.p. ops., 2000—05; v.p. broadband transormation BellSouth Corp., 2005—06, v.p. merger integration, 2006—07; v.p. consumer sales AT&T, 2007—09, sr. v.p. centers support, 2009—11, sr. v.p. talent devel., 2011—, chief diversity officer, 2011—. Office: AT&T Corporate Office 208 S Akard St Dallas TX 75202 Office Phone: 2108214105.

STORK, TRAVIS LANE, emergency physician; b. Fort Collins, Colo., Mar. 9, 1972; Grad. magna cum laude, Duke U.; MD with honors, U. Va. Resident Vanderbilt U., Nashville; physician Emergency Dept. Vanderbilt Med. Ctr., Nashville; host The Doctors, 2008—. Co-author: Don't Be That Girl: A Guide to Finding the Confident, Rational Girl Within, 2008, The Lean Belly Prescription: The fast and foolproof diet and weight-loss plan from America's top urgent-care doctor, 2010; author: The Doctor Is In: A 7 Step Prescription for Optimal Wellness, 2011, The Doctor's Diet: Dr. Travis Stork's STAT Program to Help You Lose Weight & Restore Your Health, 2014. Avocations: hiking, kayaking. Office: Dept Emergency Medicine 1313 21st Ave S 703 Oxford House Nashville TN 37232-4700*

STORM, WILLIAM JOHN, restaurant chain executive; b. Chgo., Feb. 13, 1925; s. Josef and Rose (Steirer) Somogyi; m. Barbara L. Larson, June 13, 1953; children: Michael, David, Cynthia, Caroline, Julie, Matthew, Sara. BSME, U. Ill., 1947; MBA, U. Chgo., 1953. Registered profl. engr., La. Engr. Western Electric Co., Chgo., 1950—53, US Army CE, Chgo., 1953—54; cons. engrng. New Orleans, 1954—68; ptnr. Alexander Grant & Co., New Orleans, 1968—78; sr. v.p. Church's Fried Chicken, San Antonio, 1978—83; pres. & CEO Tokyo Bowl Restaurants, Inc., Denver, 1983—. Mem. faculty Tulane U., Loyola U., 1955—65. Contbr. articles to profl. jours. Mem.: NSPE. Republican. Presbyterian. Office: 355 Spencer Ln # San Antonio TX 78201-2019 Home: 6105 McKinstry Rd Moscow TN 38057-6103

STORMONT, RICHARD MANSFIELD, hotel executive; b. Chgo., Apr. 4, 1936; s. Daniel Lytle and E. Mildred (Milligan) S.; m. Virginia Louellen Walters, Nov. 21, 1959; children: Stacy Lee Freeman, Richard Mansfield, John Frederick. BS, Cornell U., 1958. Cert. hosp. adminstrn.; cert. hosps. industry profl. Food cost analyst, sales rep. Edgewater Beach Hotel, Chgo., 1957-58; asst. sales mgr. Marriott Hotels, Inc., Washington, 1962-64, dir. sales Atlanta, 1964-68, resident mgr., 1969-71; gen. mgr. Marriott Hotel, Dallas, 1971-73, Phila., 1973-74, Atlanta, 1974-79; pres. Hardin Mgmt. Co., 1979-80; v.p. Marriott Franchise div. Marriott Corp., Washington, 1980-83, v.p. ops. Courtyard by Marriott, 1981-83; pres. The Stormont Cos. Inc., 1984—2014; chmn. Stormont Trice Corp., 1993-2000, Stormont Noble Devel. LLC, 2004—06; pres. The Stormont Cos., LLC, 2004—14. Pres. Atlanta Conv. and Visitors Burs., 1975-76, vice chmn. bd., 1976-77, chmn., 1998-99, chmn. bd. exec. com., 1998-2000; trustee Young Harris Coll.; bd. dirs. Better Bus. Bur.; exec. com. Ctrl. Atlanta Progress, 1979-80; exec. coun. Boy Scouts Am.; bd. dirs., chmn. tourism divsn. Ga. Dept. Industry, Trade and Tourism, 1999-2001; chmn. bd. trustees Lenbrook Square Found., Inc., 2007—; chmn. bd. dirs. Atlanta St. Patricks Day Found., 2005-06. Paul Harris fellow Rotary Internat., 2006-07; recipient Disting. Salesman of Yr. award Marriott, 1967, Obi T. Brewer award for Decade of Outstanding Svc., 1979, Atlanta Hospitality Hall of Fame award, 2006. Mem. Sales and Mktg. Execs. (exec. v.p. 1969-70, pres. Atlanta 1970-71), Am. Hotel-Motel Assn. (exec. com., bd. dirs. 1993-95, Most Valuable Vol. Ga. 1999), Ga. Hospitality and Travel Assn. (founder 1975, bd. dir., pres. 1989-90, chmn. bd. 1991-92, Hotelier of Yr. award 1977, Hall of

Fame 2001), Ga. Bus. and Industry Assn. (bd. dirs.), Atlanta Hotel Assn. (pres. 1976), So. Innkeepers Assn., Atlanta C. of C. (v.p. 1978-79), Gwinnett C. of C. (bd. dirs.), Cornell Soc. Hotelmen (pres. Ga. chpt. 1976, regional v.p. 1989-91), Cornell U. Hotel Soc. (SE Hotelier of Yr.), Rotary Club Atlanta (Atlanta, bd. dirs. 1999-2007, pres. 2007-08, chmn. bd. 2008-09). Home: 3747 Peachtree Rd NE Apt 723 Atlanta GA 30319-1330 E-mail: dstormont@bellsouth.net.

STORMS, RONDA, state legislator; b. Des Moines, Iowa, Sept. 05; m. David Storms; 2 children. BA, U. South Fla., 1988; JD, Stetson U. Coll. Law, 1995. Tchr.; atty.; businesswoman; mem. Dist. 10 Fla. State Senate, Tallahassee, 2006—, chair children, families and elder affairs com., co-chair joint legis. sunset com., mem. banking and ins. com., cmty. affairs com., edn. preK-12 com., fin. and tax com., reapportionment com., rules com. Republican. Baptist. Office: 413 Senate Office Bldg 404 S Monroe St Tallahassee FL 32399-1100 also: Lithia Oaks Bus Ctr 421 Lithia Pinecrest Rd Brandon FL 33511-6138 Office Phone: 813-651-2189, 850-487-5072. Business E-Mail: storms.ronda.web@flsenate.gov.

STORY, LESLIE (ERIC STORY), oil industry executive; b. Wichita Falls, Tex., Nov. 4, 1956; m. Cheri Story; 2 children. Positions in oilfield svc. including mgr. global support services Smith Internat., Inc., Houston, 1983—. Alt. del. Rep. Nat. Convention, 2004; dep. voting registrar Tex. Congl. Dist. 29, precinct chair, precinct convention chair; del. Rep. Dist. Convention, State Rep. Convention; min. Assemblies of God. Mem.: NRA, US Border Watch, Tex. Rifle Assn., Gun Owners America, Christian Motorcyclists Assn., Patriot Guard Riders. Republican. Mailing: PO Box 62488 Houston TX 77205 Office: Smith Internat Inc PO Box 60068 Houston TX 77205

STORY, RICHARD WAYNE, federal judge; b. Augusta, Ga., May 3, 1953; s. Lawrence Farr and Erline (Helmly) S.; m. Nancy Gail Duffey, Aug. 14, 1976; children: Laura Catherine, Elizabeth Ruth, William Richard. BA, LaGrange Coll., 1975; JD, U. Ga., Athens, 1978. Bar: Ga. 1978, US Dist. Ct. (no. and so. dists.) Ga. 1978, US Ct. Appeals (11th cir.) 1984. Ptnr. Hulsey, Oliver and Mahar, Gainesville, Ga., 1978-86; part-time spl. asst. atty. gen. State of Ga., 1980—84; part-time judge Juvenile Ct. Hall County, Ga., 1985-86; chief judge Northeastern Jud. Cir. Superior Ct. Ga., Gainesville, 1986—97; judge US Dist. Ct. (no. dist.) Ga., Atlanta, 1998—. Pres. Gainesville-Hall County Girls Club, 1987. Mem. Gainesville Northeastern Bar Assn., Coun. Superior Ct. Judges, Gainesville-Hall County C. of C. (assoc. dir. 1980, Silver Shovel award 1984), Jaycees (pres. Gainesville chpt. 1982-83, Young Man of Yr. award 1985). Methodist. Home: 3710 Timberwalk Dr Gainesville GA 30506-3667 Office: US Dist Ct 2121 US Courthouse 75 Spring St SW Atlanta GA 30303-3309 Office Phone: 404-215-1350.

STOSCH, WALTER ALLEN, state legislator; b. Fredericksburg, Va., Aug. 18, 1936; m. Eleanor Herbert. Prin. Stosch, Dacey & George P.C.; ret. ptnr. Deloitte & Touche; Va. State Del., Dist. 73, 1983—92; former mem. Edn. Com., Fin. Com., Claims Com.; senator Dist. 12 Va. State Senate, 1992—, former chmn. transp. com., majority leader, 1998—; mem. Commerce & Labor Com., Fin. Com., Rules Com.; chmn. Gen. Laws Com. Contbr. articles to profl. jours. Recipient Nat. Achievement award, AICPA; named Outstanding CPA in Va., 1980. Mem.: Richmond Area Heart Assn. (former chmn.), Va. Soc. of CPAs (former pres., former bd. mem. Richmond chpt.), America Inst. CPAs, America Legion, Dominion Club (founding bd.mem.). Republican. Bapt. Address: 12101 Country Hills Way Glen Allen VA 23060 Mailing: Dist Off Innsbrook Centre 4551 Cox Rd Ste 110 Glen Allen VA 23060-6740 Home Phone: 804-360-0300; Office Phone: 804-527-7780. Office Fax: 804-527-7740. Business E-Mail: district12@sov.state.va.us.

STOSUR, SAMANTHA, professional tennis player; b. Brisbane, Australia, Mar. 30, 1984; d. Tony and Dianne. Profl. tennis player WTA, 1999—. Recipient ITF World Women's Doubles Champions award (with Lisa Raymond), 2006; named Doubles Team of Yr. (with Lisa Raymond), Stars for Stars, 2006, WTA 2005 Player Awards, WTA 2006 Player Awards. Achievements include winning 3 career singles titles, 23 career doubles titles, WTA; winning 4 career singles titles, 11 career doubles titles, ITF; member Australian Fed Cup Team, 2003-05, Australian Olympic Team, 2004; winning Grand Slam singles event: US Open, 2011. Office: WTA Hdqs One Progress Plz Ste 1500 Saint Petersburg FL 33701

STOTT, GRADY BERNELL, lawyer; b. Bailey, NC, Sept. 19, 1921; s. William Willard and Zettie Harriett (Bissette) S.; m. Mays Beal, May 9, 1952; children: Sue J., Caroline Beal. AB, Duke U., 1947, JD, 1952. Bar: N.C. 1952. Dist. atty. 27th Jud. Dist., Gastonia, NC, 1957-62; partner firm Stott, Hollowell, Palmer & Windham, Gastonia, 1960—. Served with USMC, 1943-48. Fellow Am. Bar Found., Am. Coll. Trial Lawyers; mem. N.C. State Bar (pres. 1978-79), Am. Bar Assn. (del. 1980), N.C. Bar Assn., Assn. Ins. Attys. Clubs: Masons. Democrat. Methodist. Office: 401 E Franklin Blvd Gastonia NC 28054-7152 Office Phone: 704-864-3425. Personal E-mail: gbs@shpw.com.

STOTTLEMYER, DAVID LEE, federal official; b. Waynesboro, Pa., June 1, 1935; s. Omar Samuel and Miriam (Noll) S.; m. Jane Ann Hembree, Aug. 26, 1961; children: Todd Andrew, Kristen Elizabeth, Kathryn Ann. AB, Miami U., Oxford, Ohio, 1959; M. Pub. and Internat. Affairs (NDEA fellow), U. Pitts., 1964, also postgrad. Program and budget analyst Exec. Office of Pres., Office of Mgmt. and Budget, Washington, 1964-69; sr. mgmt. officer UN, NYC, 1969-70; adviser internat. orgn. affairs US Mission to UN, NYC, 1971-72, counsellor internat. orgn. affairs, 1973-75, counsellor UN resources mgmt., 1976-77; also mem. U.S. del. 26th-31st gen. assemblies, mem. UN Com. on Contbns., 1971; mem. UN Adv. Com. on Adminstrv. and Budgetary Questions, 1973-77; dir. policy mgmt. staff Bur. Internat. Orgn. Affairs, US Dept. State, Washington, 1977-80, exec. asst. to asst. sec. of state for internat. orgn. affairs, 1980; mem. staff Office of Vice-Pres., Washington, 1981-83; dir. adminstrv. mgmt. service UN, NYC, 1984-85; exec. asst., dir. Office of Under-Sec.-Gen. for Adminstrn. and Mgmt., UN, NYC, 1986-87; pvt. practice as cons., 1987-90; dir. industry rels. NASA, Washington, 1990-91, dir. office nat. svc., 1992-93; retired, 1993; cons. pvt. practice, 1993—. Served with AUS, 1953-56. Recipient Superior Honor award State Dept., 1975 Mem. Am. Fgn. Svc. Assn. Home and Office: 12363 Grantley Ct Lake Ridge VA 22192 Office Phone: 703-967-0216. Personal E-mail: davestot@comcast.net.

STOUDAMIRE, DAMON LAMON, men's college basketball coach, retired professional basketball player; b. Portland, Oreg., Sept. 3, 1973; s. Willie Stoudamire and Liz Washington. Student, U. Ariz. Drafted Toronto Raptors, 1995, point guard, 1995—98, Portland Trail Blazers, 1998—2005, Memphis Grizzlies, 2005—08, asst. coach, 2009—11; point guard San Antonio Spurs, 2008; asst. coach U. Memphis Tigers, 2011—. Co-recipient Pac-10 Player of Yr., NCAA, 1995; named Schick NBA Rookie of Yr., 1996, Rookie All-Star Game MVP, 1996. Office: University of Memphis Basketball Program c/o Athletic Dept 570 Normal AOB Rm 230 Memphis TN 38152

STOUSE, MARK, information technology executive; BA in Journalism & Polit. Sci., Baylor U., Waco, Tex., 1987, MA in Internat. Rels., 1989. Spl. projects writer, stringer Newsweek, 1986—88; account exec. Edelman Pub. Rels. Worldwide, 1989—90; sr. account exec. Hill & Knowlton, 1990—91; account mgr. Goswick Advt., 1991—92; v.p., gen. mgr. Delstar Corp., 1992—2000; sr. v.p. Neale-May & Ptnrs., 2000—01; sr. dir., worldwide external comm., enterprise storage & solutions Compaq Computer Corp., 2001—02; sr. dir. worldwide competitive intelligence & comm. Hewlett Packard Co., 2002—03, sr. dir. worldwide external comm., personal sys. goup, 2003—04, sr. dir. worldwide external comm., pub. sector health and edn., 2004—05; global comm. dir. BMC Software, Inc., Houston, 2006—. Office: BMC Software Inc 2101 CityWest Blvd Houston TX 77042 Office Phone: 713-918-2714. Office Fax: 713-918-8000. Business E-Mail: mark_stouse@bmc.com.

STOUT, JOHN T., milling company executive; b. Paoli, Ind., Jan. 29, 1923; s. Raymond and Sarah (Oakes) S.; m. Elizabeth Moore, Feb. 4, 1945; children: John T., Elmer, Sarah Catherine. BA, Earlham Coll., 1943; MBA, Harvard U., 1947. Treas. Dixie Portland Flour Mills, Memphis, 1950-65, pres., 1965-79, chmn., bd. dirs., 1979—, exec. v.p., 1984—90; pres. Manildra Milling Corp., 1991—98, Manildra Energy Corp., 1991—98; CEO Plaza Belmont Mgmt. Group LLC, 1998. Bd. dirs. The Andersons, Inc., 2009—. Served to lt. (j.g.) U.S. Navy, 1943-46. Office: Dixie Portland Flour Mills PO Box 17236 Memphis TN 38187-0236 also: The Andersons Inc Bd Directors 480 W Dussel Dr Maumee OH 43537 Office Phone: 419-893-5050. Office Fax: 419-891-6670. Business E-Mail: john_stout@andersonsinc.com.

STOVALL, JERRY COLEMAN, insurance company executive; b. Houston, July 31, 1936; s. Clifford Coleman and Maxine (Lands) S.; m. Elsie Hostetter, June 20, 1959; 1 child, Brent Allen. BBA, U. Houston, 1968. Adminstr. home office Am. Gen. Life, Houston, 1955-63, agt., agy. mgr., 1963-66, agy. mgr., regional dir. agys., regional v.p., 1969-74; sr. brokerage cons. Conn. Gen. Life, Houston, 1966-69; sr. v.p., dir. mktg. Capitol Life Ins. Co., Denver, 1974-78; v.p., dir. mktg. Integon Life Ins. Corp., Winston-Salem, N.C., 1978-81; pres. Life of Mid-Am. Ins. Co., Topeka, 1981-85, Victory Life Ins. Co., Topeka, 1981-85, chmn., pres., chief exec. officer, 1981-87; pres., retired chief exec officer Integon Life Ins. Co., Winston-Salem, N.C., 1987-91; pres. Lamar Life Ins. Co., 1992-95, ret., 1995; pres., CEO Am. Pub. Holding Inc., 1996-2000, ret., 2000. Bd. dirs., vice-chmn., Ga. Internat. Life; vice-chmn. Mktg. One Inc., bd. dirs. Boy Scout Miss., 1987-91, Bank Topeka, Kans., 1981-87, Firstcitizens Bank, NC, 1987-91, adv. bd., Internat. Assn. Fin. Planners, 1975-78. Bd. dirs. Jr. Achievement Miss., Inc.; bd. trustees Miss. Bapt. Found. With U.S. Army, 1955-57. Mem. Nat. Assn. Life Cos., Nat. Assn. Life Underwriters, Am. Soc. CLUs (Gold Key soc.), Am. Coun. Life Ins., Exec. Round Table (chmn. 1995), The Country Club of Jackson. Home: 1406 Mossycup Ln Livingston TX 77351-3074

STOVER, JILL S., school librarian, writer; BA in History, Ohio State U., 2001; MS in Libr. Sci., U. NC, 2004; student in Mktg., Va. Commonwealth U., Richmond, 2005—. Undergraduate svcs. libr. James Branch Cabell Libr. Va. Commonwealth U. Contbr. articles to profl. publs. Mem.: ALA, Reference and User Svcs. Assn., Assn. Coll. and Rsch. Librs., Phi Beta Kappa. Office: Va Commonwealth U Librs 901 Park Ave PO Box 842033 Richmond VA 23284-2033 Office Phone: 804-828-8964. E-mail: jsstover@vcu.edu.

STOVERN, BRETT A., gas industry executive; B in Acctg., Calif. State Polytechnic U., 1987. CPA. Sr. auditor Arthur Andersen, 1987—91; v.p., contr., treas., mergers & acquisitions Pratt Industries, 1991—99; sr. bus. cons. AGL Resources, Inc., 2000—02, asst. treas., 2002—04, mng. dir., fin., 2004—05, v.p., treas., 2005—. Bd. dirs. AGL Resources Pvt. Found. Office: AGL Resources Inc 10 Peachtree Pl NE Atlanta GA 30309 Office Phone: 404-584-4000. Office Fax: 404-584-3714. Business E-Mail: Bstovern@aglresources.com.

STOWE, HAROLD CROSBY, investment company executive; b. Charlotte, NC, June 22, 1946; s. George Washington and Kathryn (Crosby) S.; m. Claudia Carr Blair, Aug. 4, 1974; children: Harold Crosby, Claudia Blair, Patrick Board. BS in Commerce, Washington and Lee U., Lexington, Va., 1968; MBA, Harvard U., 1970. Joined Nat. Bank of NC, Charlotte, 1970, v.p., corp. banking mgr., 1976-77; fin. analyst Springs Mills, Inc., Fort Mill, SC, 1977-78, treas., 1978-80; mng. ptnr. Springfield Assos., Charlotte, 1980; exec. v.p., dir. Springs Co., Lancaster, SC, 1986; pres., CEO Canal Holdings, LLC, Conway, SC, 2001—06; mng. mem. Stowe-Monier Management, LLC, 2007—. Dir. Charter Properties, Inc., Kitty Hawk Capital Co., Leland Computer Services, Inc., S.E. Huffman Inc., Springs Leasing Corp., Springs Mortgage Corp., Kanawha Ins. Co., Cen. Re Corp. Bd. dirs. Elliott White Springs Meml. Hosp., S.C. Downtown Devel. Assn.; chmn. The Catawba Sch., Rock Hill, S.C. Mem. Greater Fort Mill C. of C. Presbyterian. Home: 8246 Forest Lake Dr Conway SC 29526-9000 Office: Ruddick Corp 301 S Tryon St Ste 1800 Charlotte NC 28202 Office Phone: 704-372-5404. Office Fax: 704-372-6409. Business E-Mail: hstowe@ruddickcorp.com.

STOWE, ROBERT LEE, III, textile company executive; b. Charlotte, NC, July 3, 1954; s. Robert Lee Jr. and Ruth Link (Harding) S.; m. Christine Ruth Edwards, Jan. 15, 1983; children: Christine Ruth, Lillian Rhyne. BA, Davidson Coll., NC, 1976. Dir., mgmt. trainee R.L. Stowe Mills, Inc., Belmont, N.C., 1976-77, v.p., 1977-79, exec. v.p., 1979-84, chmn. bd., 1984—. Sec., treas. Lakeview Farms, Inc.; pres. Robrt Lee Stowe Jr. Found., Belmont, 1978—; bd. mgrs. Wachovia Bank of N.C., Gaston County; mem.-mgr. McAdams & Stowe, LLC; bd. dirs. John Locke Found. Trustee Belmont Abbey Coll., 1987-90, Mint Mus. Art, Charlotte, 1989-92, Crossnore (N.C.) Sch., 1987-98, Sci. Museums, Charlotte, 1989-91, Gaston Day Sch., 1994-97, Gaston County C. of C., 1992-95, Mis. of New South; trustee Daniel Jonathan Stowe Conservancy, 1990, pres., 1996-2000, vice-chmn., 2000; deacon, elder local Presbyn. Ch.; bd. dirs. Downtown Belmont, Inc., Gaston County Edn. Found., Gaston County YMCA, John Locke Found., 2005—; trustee Presbyn. Hosp. Found., Charlotte, N.C. Named one of Outstanding Young Men Am., 1979. Mem. Am. Textile Mfrs. Inst. (bd. dirs. 1989-92), Newcomen Soc. U.S., N.C. Textile Found. (bd. dirs. 1986—), Met. Club N.Y., Charlotte Country Club, Gaston Country Club. Republican. Avocations: golf, boating, church activities. Office: RL Stowe Mills Inc 100 N Main St Belmont NC 28012-3104 Home: 135 N Main St Belmont NC 28012-3122 Home Phone: 704-825-1235; Office Phone: 704-825-5314. Business E-Mail: rlstowe3@rlstowe.com.

STOWERS, CARLTON EUGENE, writer; b. Brownwood, Tex., Apr. 14, 1942; s. Ira Milton and Fay Eloise (Stephenson) S.; m. Patricia Ann Folks, Mar. 2, 1981; children: Anson, Ashley. Student, U. Tex., Austin, 1961-63. Sportswriter Abilene (Tex.) Reporter News, 1963-64; sports editor Roswell (N.Mex.) Daily Record, 1964-65; sportswriter Lubbock (Tex.) Avalanche Jour., 1965-67; sports editor Amarillo (Tex.) Globe News, 1967-72; reporter, columnist Dallas Morning News, 1972-81; freelance writer Cedar Hill, Tex., 1981—. Editor Dallas Cowboys Weekly, 1985-89. Author: The Randy Matson Story, 1971, Spirit, 1973; author: (with Trent Jones) Where the Rainbows Wait, 1978; author: (with Wilbur Evans) Champions, 1978; author: The Overcomers, 1978; author: (with Roy Rogers and Dale Evans) Happy Trails, 1979; author: pub. softcover as Terlingua Teacher, 1982, 2005, The Unsinkable Titanic Thompson, 1982, softcover, 1988, Journey to Triumph, 1988, Partners in Blue: The 100-Year History of the Dallas Police Department, 1983; author: (with Billy Olson) Reaching Higher, 1984; author: The Dallas Cowboys: The First 25 Years, 1984, The Cowboy Chronicles, 1984; author: (ghosted for Pam Lontos) Don't Tell Me It's Impossible Until I've Already Done It, 1988; author: Careless Whispers, 1986 (Edgar Allan Poe award Mystery Writers Am.), The Cotton Bowl: The First 50 Years, 1986; author: (with William C. Dear) Please...Don't Kill Me: The True Story of the Milo Murder, 1989; author: (with Larry Wansley) The FBI Undercover: The True Story of Special Agent 'Mandrake', 1989; author: Innocence Lost, 1990, A Hero Named George, 1991, Hard Lessons, 1994, Open Secrets, 1994, Sins of the Son, 1995; author: (with Marcus Allen) Marcus, 1997; author: To the Last Breath, 1998 (Edgar Allan Poe award Mystery Writers Am.); author: (with Rev. Carroll Pickett) Within These Walls, 2002 (Violet Crown award, 2002, PEN S.W. Book award finalist, 2005); author: Scream at the Sky, 2003, Death in a Texas Desert, 2003, Where Dreams Die Hard, 2005, Oh, Brother How They Played the Game, 2007, Staubach: Portrait of the Brightest Star, 2010. Recipient numerous journalism awards. Mem.: Big County Athletic Hall of Fame, Tex. Lit. Hall of Fame, Tex. Inst. Letters. Home: 1015 Randy Rd Cedar Hill TX 75104-3035 Office Phone: 972-291-4831. E-mail: cstowers1@att.net.

STOWERS, JOSH, state legislator; b. Spartanburg, SC, Jan. 1, 1979; s. Barry, Brenda; m. Jennifer Stowers; 1 child, Reilly. BS, Concord Coll.; MA, Marshall U. Mem. Dist. 19 W.Va. House of Delegates, 2008—. Democrat. Protestant. Office: Rm 218E, Bldg 1 Charleston WV 25305 Office Phone: 304-340-3384. E-mail: jstowers@mail.wvnet.edu.

STRADA, SAMUEL J., dean, pharmacologist, educator; Attended, Rockhurst Coll., Kansas City, 1959—60; BSc in Pharmacy with distinction, U. Mo., Kansas City, 1964, MSc in Pharmacology, 1966; PhD in Pharmacology, Vanderbilt U., Nashville, 1970. Post-grad. tng. lab. pre-clinical pharmacology St. Elizabeth's Hosp., Nat. Institutes Mental Health, Washington, 1970—72; grad. faculty mem. U. Tex. Grad. Sch. Biomed. Sciences, 1972—83; asst. prof. pharmacology U. Tex. Med. Sch., Houston, 1972—75, assoc. prof. pharmacology, 1975—81, prof. pharmacology, 1981—83, acting chmn. dept. pharmacology, 1982; sabbatical dept. biochemistry U. Dundee Med. Sciences Inst., Scotland, 1979—80; prof. pharmacology U. South Ala. Coll. Medicine, Mobile, 1983—, chmn. designate dept. pharmacology, 1983, chmn. dept. pharmacology, 1983—94, acting dir. grad. program in basic med. sciences, 1990—92, acting head dept. psychiatry, 1992, sr. assoc. dean, 1993—2005, acting dean, 2005—07, dean, 2007—. Cons. in biology rsch., pharmacology divsn. Ciba-Geigy Corp., Summit, NJ, 1984—86. Mem. editl. bd.: Jour. cyclic Nucleotide and Protein Phosphorylation Rsch., 1974—85, Second Messengers and Phosphoproteins, 1985—94, Substance and Alcohol Actions/Misuse, 1980—84, Patient Oriented Problem-Solving System in Pharmacology, 1993—98, CNS Drug Reviews, 1994—; contbr. articles to profl. jours., chapters to books. Mem.: AAAS, Ala. Acad. Sci., American Soc. Pharmacology and Expt. Therapeutics, Assn. Med. Sch. Pharmacology, Assn. Univ. Tech. Managers, Basic Sci. Edn. Forum, Found. Advanced Edn. in the Sciences, Internat. Assn. Med. Sci. Educators, NY Acad. Sci., Soc. Neurosciences, Tissue Culture Assn., Southeastern Pharmacology Soc. (life), Sigma Xi. Office: University South Ala Sch Medicine 2015 Med Sciences Bldg 5851 USA Dr N Mobile AL 36688 Office Phone: 251-460-6041. Office Fax: 251-460-6073. Business E-Mail: sstrada@jaguar1.usouthal.edu.

STRAFER, G. RICHARD, lawyer; b. Evanston, Ill., Jan. 19, 1951; BA, U. Wis.-Madison, 1976; JD, Northeastern U., 1980; LLM, Georgetown U., 1983. Bar: DC, U.S. Dist. Ct., DC, U.S. Ct. Appeals, DC Cir. 1980, Fla. 1984. Appellate law fellow Appellate Litig. Clin. Prog. Georgetown U. Law Ctr., 1981—83; pvt. practice G. Richard Strafer, PA. Contbr. articles to law jours. Mem.: ABA, Fla. Assn. Criminal Defense Lawyers, Nat. Assn. Criminal Defense Lawyers. Office: 201 S Biscayne Blvd Ste 1380 Miami FL 33131 Office Phone: 305-374-9091. Office Fax: 305-377-9937.

STRAIT, GEORGE, musician; b. Poteet, Tex., May 18, 1952; m. Norma Voss, Feb. 23, 1972; children: George Bubba Jr., Jennifer (dec.). Degree in Agr., SW Tex. State U., San Marcos, PhD (hon.), 2006. Musician: (albums) Strait Country, 1981, Strait from the Heart, 1982, Right or Wrong, 1983, Does Fort Worth Ever Cross Your Mind, 1984, Something Special, 1985, Strait Country, 1985 (Country Music Assn. award for Album of Yr. 1985), #7, 1986, Ocean Front Property, 1987, If You Aint Lovin' (You Aint Livin'), 1988, Beyond the Blue Neon, 1989, Livin' It Up, 1990, Ten Strait Hits, 1991, Chill of An Early Fall, 1991, Pure Country, 1992, Holding My Own, 1992, Easy Come, Easy Go, 1993, Greatest Hits Volume I, II, Lead On, 1994, Strait Out of the Box, 1995, Blue Clear Sky, 1996 (Country Music Assn. award for Album of Yr. 1996), Carrying Your Love With Me, 1997 (Country Music Assn. award for Album of Yr. 1997), One Step at a Time, 1998 (Country Music Assn. award for Album of Yr. 1998), Always Never the Same, 1999, Merry Christmas Wherever You Are, 1999, Latest Greatest Strait Greatest Hits, 2000, George Strait, 2000, The Road Less Traveled, 2001, 20th Century Masters, 2002, Honkytonkville, 2003, 50 Number Ones, 2004, Somewhere Down in Texas, 2005, It Just Comes Natural, 2006 (Country Music Assn. award for Album of Yr. 2006), Live at Texas Stadium, 2007, George Strait 22 More Hits, 2007, Troubadour, 2008 (Country Music Assn. award for Album of Yr. 2008, Grammy Award for Best Country Album 2009), Classic Christmas, 2008, Twang, 2009, Here for a Good Time, 2011, Love Is Everything, 2013; (songs) Good News Bad News (Duet with Lee Ann Womack), 2005 (Country Music Assn. award for Musical Event of Yr. 2005), Give It Away, 2006 (Country Music Assn. awards for Single Record of Yr., Song of Yr. 2007), I Saw God Today, 2008 (Country Music. Assn. award for Single of Yr. 2008); actor: (films) The Soldier, 1982, Pure Country, 1992, Grand Champion, 2002. Served with US Army until 1975. Named Top Male Vocalist, Acad. Country Music Awards, 1984, 1985, 1988, Entertainer of Yr., 1990, 2014, Artist of Decade, 2011, Male Vocalist of Yr., Country Music Assn. Awards, 1985, 1986, 1996, 1997, Entertainer of Yr., 1989, 1990, 2013, Top Country Vocalist, Am. Music Awards, 1991, Tex Ritter Award for Pure Country, 1993, Voice of Yr. award, ASCAP, 1995, SRO Touring Artist of Yr., 1990, #1 in top 25 country singers of the past 25 years, Billboard, 2010; named to Country Music Hall of Fame, 2006; recipient Legend of Live award, Billboard Touring awards, 2013. Office: George Strait Productions Inc PO Box 792063 San Antonio TX 78279*

STRAMA, MARK, state legislator; b. Sept. 10, 1967; m. Crystal Strama; children: Victoria Rose, Caroline. Grad., Brown U., Providence, 1990. Chief staff to Senator Rodney Ellis Tex. State Senate; program dir. Rock the Vote; mem. Dist. 50 Tex. House of Representatives, 2004—. Adv. bd. mem. Clean Energy Incubator, Environmental Sciences Inst., U. Tex.; bd. mem. Challah for Hunger; founding bd.

mem. Hope Street Group. Recipient of several awards and honors. Democrat. Office: Room E2.822 Capitol Extension PO Box 2910 Austin TX 78768 Office Phone: 512-463-0821. Office Fax: 512-463-0821.

STRANCH, JANE BRANSTETTER, federal judge; b. Nashville, Sept. 17, 1953; m. James G. Stranch III; 4 children. BA summa cum laude, Vanderbilt U., Nashville, 1975; JD Order of the Coif, Vanderbilt U. Law Sch., 1978. Bar: Tenn. 1978, Tenn. Supreme Ct. 1978, US Dist. Ct. (mid. dist.) Tenn. 1979, US Tax Ct. 1980, US Ct. Appeals (6th cir.) 1982, US Dist. Ct. (ea. dist.) Tenn. 1991, US Supreme Ct. 1996, US Dist. Ct. (dist. Colo.) 2002, US Dist. Ct. (ea. dist.) Mich. 2005, US Dist. Ct. (we. dist.) Tenn. 2008, US Ct. Appeals (9th cir.) 2008. Law clk. Branstetter, Stranch & Jennings, PLLC, Nashville, 1975—78, assoc., 1978—94, ptnr., 1994—2010; judge US Ct. Appeals (6th cir.), 2010—. Lectr. labor law Belmont U., Nashville, 1981—83. Fellow: Tenn. Bar Found., Nashville Bar Found.; mem.: ABA, Lawyers' Assn. Women, Tenn. Bar. Assn., Nashville Bar Assn., Phi Alpha Delta, Phi Beta Kappa. Office: US Court of Appeals 701 Broadway Nashville TN 37203

STRANDJORD, MARY JEANNINE, telecommunications industry executive; b. Kansas City, Mo., Dec. 21, 1945; d. Vincent Stanley and Clara Lucille (Aylward) Kerwin; m. David Christian Strandjord, June 24, 1978; 1 child, Katie Marie. BSBA, Kans. U., 1968; postgrad., U. Mo., Kansas City, 1976. CPA, Mo. Mem., audit staff Enrst & Whinney, Kansas City, 1968—71; with Kansas City Power & Light, 1971—81, dir., asst. controller, 1979—81; dir., asst. controler Macy's Midwest, 1981—82, v.p. acctg., budget and expense, 1982—85; v.p. fin. & ops. AmeriSource, Inc., Westwood, Kans., 1986—90; sr. v.p., treas. Sprint Corp., 1990—98, sr. v.p., fin. global markets group, 1998—2003, sr. v.p. financial services, 2003, sr. v.p., chief integration officer, 2003—05; v.p., treas. & bd. dirs. Ctrl. Tel. Co. Bd. dirs. Charming Shoppes, Inc., 2006—10, DST Sys., Inc., 1996—, Euronet Worldwide, Inc., 2001—. Treas. St. Health Ctr. Found., Kansas City, 1986—; mem. exec. com., acct. adv. coun. Kans. U., Lawrence, 1989—, Named Woman of Yr., YMCA, 1987. Mem. AICPA, Fin. Exec. Inst., Blue Hills Country Club. Roman Catholic. Avocations: reading, walking, interior design, skiing. Office: Central Telephone Co 100 Centurylink Dr Monroe LA 71203-2041 Office Phone: 913-323-4637. Business E-Mail: mary.strandjord@dstsystems.com.

STRANG, STEPHEN EDWARD, communications executive, editor; b. Springfield, Mo., Jan. 31, 1951; s. A. Edward and Amy Alice (Farley) S.; m. Joy Darlene Ferrell, Aug. 19, 1972; children: Cameron Edward, Chandler Stephen. BS in Journalism, U. Fla., Gainesville, 1973; LittD (hon.), Lee U., Tex., 1995. Reporter Orlando Sentinel Star, Fla., 1973-76; editor Charisma mag. Calvary Assembly, Winter Pk., Fla., 1976-81; founder, CEO Charisma Media (formerly Strang Comm. Co.), Lake Mary, Fla., 1979—, pres., 1981—. Founding editor, pub. Charisma mag., 1975, Ministries Today mag., 1983, Christian Retailing mag., 1986, Creation House Books 1986, CharismaLife Pubs., 1990, CharismaLife Learning Resources, 1990, New Man mag., 1994, (in Spanish) Vida Cristiana, 1996, others; author: Old Man, New Man, 2000. Mem. steering com. N.Am. Renewal Svcs. Com., 1985—; trustee Internat. Charismatic Bible Ministries, 1986—; pres. Christian Life Missions, 1991—; bd. dirs. World Relief, 2001—. Recipient First Pl. award Nat. Writing Championship, William Randolph Hearst Found., 1973, Alumnus of Distinction award U. Fla. Coll. Journalism and Comm., 1994, Industry of Yr. award for Seminole County, Fla., Econ. Devel. Commn. Mid-Fla., 1994; named one of 25 Most Influential Evangelicals in America, TIME mag., 2005. Mem. Internat. Pentecostal Press Assn., Christian Booksellers Assn., Fla. Mag. Assn. (pres. 1979-80), Evang. Christian Pubs. Assn., Evang. Press Assn. Republican. Mem. Assemblies of God. Avocations: racquetball, golf. Office: Charisma Media 600 Rinehart Rd Lake Mary FL 32746-4898 E-mail: info@strang.com.

STRANGE, H. ANTHONY, healthcare company executive; B, U. SC. Various mgmt. positions Glass Rock Home Healthcare; various mgmt. positions including regional mgr., v.p., devel. The Healthfield Group, Inc. (acquired by Gentiva Health Svcs., Inc.), 1990—2001, pres., COO, 2001—06; exec. v.p., pres., home health divsn. Gentiva Health Services, Inc., 2006—07, COO, 2007—08, pres., 2007—, CEO, bd. dirs., 2009—. Office: Gentiva Health Services Inc 3350 Riverwood Pkwy Ste 1400 Atlanta GA 30339 Office Phone: 770-951-6450. Business E-Mail: tony.strange@gentiva.com.

STRANGE, LUTHER JOHNSON, III, state attorney general; b. Birmingham, Ala., Mar. 1, 1953; m. Melissa Strange; 2 children. BA, Tulane U., New Orleans, 1975; JD, Tulane U. Law Sch., New Orleans, 1979. Ptnr. Bradley Arant Boult Cummings LLP; founder, atty. Strange LLC, Birmingham; atty. gen. State of Ala., 2011—. Eagle scout Boy Scouts America; mem. adv. bd. US Merchant Marine Acad., Kings Point, NY. Named one of The Best Lawyers in Ala., Birmingham Mag., The Best of the Bar, Birmingham Bus. Jour. Mem.: Rotary. Republican. Episcopalian. Office: State of Alabama Attorney Generals Office PO Box 300152 501 Washington Ave Montgomery AL 36130-0152 Office Phone: 334-242-7300.*

STRANGE, ROY, agricultural cooperative executive; Pres. Dairymen, Inc., Louisville, dir. Office: Dairymen Inc 10140 Linn Station Rd Louisville KY 40223-3813

STRANGE, TODD, mayor, Montgomery, Alabama; m. Linda Davis; children: Jennifer Strange Crumpton, Elizabeth Strange Burt. BA in Polit. Sci., U. Montevallo. With South Central Bell Co.; pres., CEO Blount Devel. Corp.; sr. v.p. adminstrn. Blount Internat., Ltds.; pres., CEO, co-owner Blount Strange Automotive Group; dir. Ala. Devel. Office; chmn. Montgomery County Commn.; mayor City of Montgomery, Ala., 2009—. Pres., campaign chmn. Montgomery United Way; pres. Ala. Inst. for the Deaf and Blind Found.; mem. bd. dirs., vice chmn. Montgomery Bus. Com. for Arts; mem. bd. trustees U. Montevallo; chmn. bd. dirs. Montgomery C. of C.; bd. chmn. Montgomery Riverfront Devel. Com. Recipient Outstanding Cmty. Leader award, AUM, Quality Dealer award, Ala., Time Mag.; named Bus. and Profl. Women Boss of Yr., River Region Citizen of Yr., March of Dimes. Mem.: Capital City Club (chmn.). Office: City Hall Rm 206 103 North Perry St Montgomery AL 36104 Office Phone: 334-241-2000. Office Fax: 334-241-2600. Business E-Mail: mayor@montgomeryal.gov.*

STRANGES, ANTHONY NICHOLAS, science history educator; b. Niagara Falls, NY, Sept. 28, 1936; s. Victor Anthony and Maria Theresa (Serianni) S.; m. Sonya Michelene Rudy, Aug. 24, 1963; children: Krista Stranges Fazzino, Kara Stranges Holmgreen. BS in Chemistry, Niagara U., 1958, MS in Chemistry, 1964; PhD in History of Sci., U. Wis., 1977. Secondary tchr. Notre Dame Coll. Sch., Welland, Ont., Can., 1959-63, Lewiston-Porter H.S., Youngstown, N.Y., 1963-69; prof. Tex. A&M U., College Station, 1977—. Author: Electrons and Valence, 1982, Technological Transformation of Gilded Age America, 2014; contbr. articles to profl. jours. Recipient Faculty Disting. award for Tchg. Assn. of Former Students, Tex. A&M U., 1987. Mem. Am. Hist. Assn., Can. Sci. and Tech. History Assn., Soc. for the History of Tech., Hist. of Sci. Soc. Democrat. Roman Catholic. Avocations: music, stamp collecting/philately. Home: 1205 Barak Ln Bryan TX 77802-3202 Office: Tex A&M U Dept History College Station TX 77843-4236 Office Phone: 979-845-7151. Business E-Mail: a-stranges@tamu.edu.

STRASNICK, BARRY, otolaryngologist, health facility administrator, educator; b. Malden, Mass., Nov. 16, 1958; m. Victoria S. Strasnick; children: Evan, Ryan. BA in Biology summa cum laude, Boston U., 1980; MD, Baylor U., 1985. Diplomate Am. Bd. Otolaryngology. Intern Baylor Coll. Medicine, Houston, 1985—86, resident, 1986—87, UCLA Sch. Medicine, 1987—90; clin. prof. Vanderbilt U., 1991—92; from asst. prof. to assoc. prof. Ea. Va. Med. Sch., Norfolk, 1993—99, prof., 2000—, chmn., 1999—; dir. Hearing & Balance Ctr. DePaul Med. Ctr., Norfolk, 1993—; dir. pediatric otology divsn. Children's Hosp. King's Daus., Norfolk, 1993—. Co-author: (book) English Textbook of Otolaryngology, 1994, Ololaryngology, 1997, Pediatric Otolaryngology - H/N Surgery, 1998, The Ear: A Textbook of Otology, 2000. Chmn. Va. State Adv. Commn. Universal Newborn Hearing Screening, Richmond, 1998—; bd. dirs. Ear Ctr., Norfolk, 2000—. Fellow, Head/neck Surgery Found., 1997—. Fellow: Am. Acad. Otolaryngology; mem.: Norfolk Acad. Medicine, Tidewater Otolaryngology & Ophthalmology Soc., Va. Soc. Otolaryngologists (bd. dirs. 1997—), Va. Med. Soc. (Dr. Clarence A. Holland award 2001), Soc. Univ. Otolaryngologist. Office: Ea Va Med Sch 600 Gresnam Dr 1100 Norfolk VA 23507 Office Phone: 757-388-6200. Business E-Mail: strasnb@evms.edu.

STRASSMANN, JOAN ELIZABETH, evolutionary biologist; b. Washington, May 6, 1953; d. Wolfgang Paul and Elizabeth Marsh (Fanck) S.; m. David Charles Queller, Jan. 2, 1988; children: Anna Strassmann Mueller, Daniel Strassmann Mueller, Philip Strassmann Queller. BS with distinction and honors in Zoology, U. Mich., 1974; PhD, U. Tex., Austin, 1979. NSF postdoctoral fellow U. Tex., Austin, 1979—80; asst. prof., biology dept. Rice U., Houston, 1980-85, assoc. prof., 1985-93, prof., 1993—, chair, ecology and evolutionary biology dept., 2003—, Harry C. & Olga K. Wiess prof. ecology and evolutionary biology, 2005—. Field experience U. Mich. Biol. Station, 1972—73, Costa Rica, 1974, Tex., 1976—, Venezuela, 1988—2001, Brazil, 1996—2000, Italy, 1997—, So. Appalachians, 2000—; spkr. in field. Contbr. articles to Science, Nature; editl. bd. mem. Animal Behavior, 1995-97, Insectes Sociaux, 2000-2006, American Naturalist, 2000-03, Ecology Letters, 2004-07, BMC Evolutionary Biology, 2005-, Journal Evolutionary Biology, 2005-, Ecology, Ethology, and Evolution 2006- John Simon Guggenheim Meml. Fellow, 2004. Fellow: AAAS, Animal Behavior Soc., Am. Acad. Arts & Scis.; mem.: Cambridge Entomological Soc., Houston Philos. Soc., Nat. Assn. Biology Teachers, Nat. Ctr. for Sci. Edn., Internat. Soc. Hymenopterists, Internat. Union for the Study Social Insects (pres., N.Am. sect. 2001), Am. Soc. Microbiologists, Internat. Soc. for Behavioral Ecology, Soc. for the Study Evolution (councilor 2002—04), Am. Soc. Naturalists, Associazione Italiana per lo Studio degli Artopodi Sociali e Presociali (hon.), Phi Kappa Phi, Sigma XI. Achievements include research in society of temperate and tropical wasps. Office: Rice U Dept Ecology and Evolutionary Biology MS 170 133E Anderson Biology Lab 6100 Main St Houston TX 77005-1892 Office Phone: 713-348-4922. Office Fax: 713-348-5232. Business E-Mail: strassm@rice.edu.

STRATHE, MARLENE I., academic administrator; BS, Iowa State U., MS in Counseling Psychology, PhD in Ednl. Rsch. and Measurement; EdS in Ednl. Psychology, U. No. Iowa, 1973. Faculty mem., assoc. dean Coll. Edn., asst. v.p. academic affairs U. No. Iowa; provost U. ND, 1993—98; provost, v.p. academic affairs U. No. Colo., 1998—2003; provost, sr. v.p. Okla. State U., Stillwater, 2003—, interim sys. CEO, pres., 2007—08. Exec. com. mem. Higher Learning Commn. Bd. Trustees. Contbr. articles to profl. jours. Recipient Fulbright Award, 1995, Virgil Lagomarcino Award for Excellence in Edn., Iowa State U. Office: Okla State U 101 Whitehurst Stillwater OK 74078 Office Phone: 405-744-5627. E-mail: marlene.strathe@okstate.edu.

STRATTON, ROBERT, retired electronics executive; b. Vienna, Aug. 14, 1928; came to U.S., 1959, naturalized, 1966; s. Kenneth Kurt and Eugenie (Schwatzer) S.; m. Elfriede Karlberger, Jan. 11, 1980; children: David Alexander, Valerie Pam. B.Sc. in Physics, Manchester U., 1949, PhD in Theoretical Physics, 1952. Rsch. physicist Met. Vickers Elec. Co., Manchester, Eng., 1952-59; with Tex. Instruments, Inc., Dallas, 1959-94, dir. physics rsch. lab., 1963-71, assoc. dir. cen. rsch. labs., 1971-72, dir. semiconductor R & D, 1972-75, dir. cen. rsch. labs., 1975-77, asst. v.p., dir. cen. rsch. labs., 1977-82, v.p. corp. staff, dir. cen. rsch. labs., 1982-94; dir. Indsl. Outreach Elec. Materials Sci. Tech. Ctr., dir. Engring. and Tech. Inst., U. Tex., Austin, 1994-96. Contbr. articles to profl. jours. Bd. dirs. Indsl. Rsch. Inst., 1985-88, Coun. on Superconductivity for Am. Competitiveness, 1987-90; adv. bd. dirs. Tex. Ctr. for Superconductivity, 1989-2000. Fellow IEEE, Inst. Physics (U.K.), Am. Phys. Soc.; mem. NAE. Personal E-mail: rstratton@tx.rr.com.

STRAUB, CHESTER JOHN, JR., state agency administrator, former federal agency administrator; b. Charlottesville, Va., Oct. 4, 1960; s. Chester John and Patricia (Morrissey) S.; m. Erin Mary Norton, Apr. 21, 1990. BA in History, Tufts U., 1982. Asst. to exec. dir. Friends of Mario M. Cuomo, Inc., NYC, 1986; dep. exec. dir. N.Y. State Dem. Com., NYC, 1987-89, exec. dir., 1989-90; corp. sec. Battery Park City Authority, NYC, 1990-93; dep. asst. sec. Econ. Devel. Adminstrn. US Dept. Commerce, Washington, 1999—2001, acting asst. sec., 1999—2000; pres. Ulster County Devel. Corp. (UCDC), 2001—06; exec. dir. Technological Rsch. & Devel. Authority (TRDA), Miami, 2007—. Dir. campaign ops. Clinton/Gore Coordinated Campaign, N.Y., 1992. Democrat. Roman Catholic. Office: Technological Rsch & Devel Authority (TRDA) 1050 W Nasa Blvd Melbourne FL 32901 Office Phone: 321-872-1050. Office Fax: 321-872-1051. E-mail: cstraub@trda.org.

STRAUB, PETER THORNTON, lawyer; b. St. Louis, Mar. 27, 1939; s. Ralph H. and Mary Louise (Thornton) S.; m. Wendy B. Cubbage, Dec. 29, 1964; children: Karl Thornton, Philip Hamilton, Ellen Elizabeth. AB, Washington and Lee U., 1961, LLB, 1964. Bar: Mo. 1964, Va. 1964, US Dist. Ct. (ea. dist.) Mo. 1967, US Circuit Ct. Appeals (8th cir.) 1969, US Supreme Ct. 1970. US Circuit Ct. Appeals (DC cir.) 1971, Ct. Mil. Appeals 1970, US Tax Ct. 1971, US Bankruptcy Ct. 1991. Assoc. Evans & Dixon, St. Louis, 1966-68; asst. pub. defender St. Louis County, St. Louis, 1968-69; asst. US Atty. St. Louis, 1969-71; trial atty. internal security div. Dept. Justice, Washington, 1971-72, atty.-adviser office of dep. atty. gen., 1972-73, dir. office criminal justice, spl. asst. to atty. gen., 1974; minority counsel com. on judiciary US House of Representatives, Washington, 1973-74; gen. counsel SSS, Washington, 1974-76; pvt. practice Law Offices of Peter T. Straub, Alexandria, Va., 1976—2010; of counsel Life & Estate Planning Law Ctr. PLLC, 2010—11; ret., 2011. Pres., gov. bd. Alexandria Cmty. Mental Health Ctr., 1982—95; mem. No. Va. Estate Planning Coun., 1981—2011; pres.'s coun. Trinity Coll., Washington, 1980—87; adv. bd. Am. Heart Assn., Alexandria, 1991—92, Salvation Army, Alexandria, 1991—, v.p., 1994—96, chmn., 1997—99, Alexandria Cmty. Shelter Adv. Bd., 1995—97; Va. escheat atty. City of Alexandria, 1994—2002; dist. chmn. Boy Scouts Am., 1998—2001, risk mgmt. com. Nat. Capital Area coun., 2006—11; adv. bd. Hospice No. Va., 2000—09; mem. Econ. Opportunity Commn. City of Alexandria, 2006—10; bd. dirs. Friends of the Washington and Old Dominion Trail, 2002—, Parc East Condominium, 1990—2009, sec., 1992—2006; bd. dirs. Sigma Nu Ednl. Found., Inc., 2000—08; charter mem. bd. dirs. Alexandria Country Day Sch., 1983—90; charter mem., bd. dirs. Charter JAG Am. Legion Greenspring Post 123, 2010—, comdr., 2012—; charter mem. bd. dirs. Greenspring Vill. Residents Adv. Coun., 2011—. With US Army, 1964—66, capt. USAR, 1966—72. Recipient certificate of award Dept. Justice, 1970, certificate of appreciation Law Enforcement Assistance Adminstrn. Dept. Justice, 1974, Silver Beaver award Boy Scouts Am., Washington, 1987, Collins award Alexandria Coun. Persons with Disabilities, 1993, Cmty. Svc. award Am. Indian Alliance, 1995. Mem.: FBA, ABA, Nat. Acad. Elder Law Attys., Va. Trial Lawyers Assn., Alexandria Bar Assn., Mo. Bar Assn., Bar Assn. Met. St. Louis, Va. State Bar Assn., Optimists (bd. dirs., pres. Alexandria chpt. 1984, lt. gov. Nat. Capitol Va. Dist. 1987—89, treas. 1999—2001), Nat. Eagle Scout Assn., Sigma Nu. Republican. Congregationalist. Avocations: scouting, reading, bicycling. Office: 1225 Martha Custis Dr # 103 Alexandria VA 22302-2040 Home: 7416 Spring Village Dr Apt T17 Springfield VA 22150 Office Phone: 703-820-3600. Office Fax: 703-820-8602. Business E-Mail: pstraub@lifeandestateplanninglaw.com. E-mail: psfranb@aeitv.net.

STRAUCH, KATINA PARTHEMOS, college librarian, publishing executive; m. Bruce Strauch; children: Raymond, Ileana. MLS, U. NC-Chapel Hill. Head libr., collection dept. Coll. Charleston Librs., SC; founder, dir. Charleston Conf., 1980—; founder, editor Against the Grain, 1989—. Chair bd. Charleston Report, 1996—, Charleston Advisor, 1999—; bd. dirs. Inst. Mus. & Libr. Svc., 2004—. Author: Legal and Ethical Issues in Acquisitions, 1990. Recipient Disting. Alumnus award, U. NC-Chapel Hill Sch. Libr. and Info. Sci., 1992, SC Outstanding Libr. award, 1996. Mem.: ALA, Reference and User Svcs. Assn. (Louis Shores-Greenwood Pub. Group award 2007), Assn. Libr. Collections and Tech. Svcs. (Leadership in Libr. Acquisitions award 1997). Office: Coll Charleston Librs 66 George St Charleston SC 29424 also: Charleston Info Group LLC MSC 98 The Citadel Charleston SC 29409 Office Phone: 843-953-8020, 843-953-8020. Office Fax: 843-953-8019. Personal E-mail: kstrauch@comcast.net, katina.strauch@gmail.com. Business E-Mail: strauchk@cofc.edu.

STRAUGHAN, WILLIAM THOMAS, structural engineering consultant, educator; b. Shreveport, La., Aug. 2, 1936; s. William Eugene and Sara Chloetilde (Harrell) S.; m. Rubie Ann Barnes, Aug. 20, 1957; children: Donna Ann, Sara Arlene, Eugene Thomas. BS, MIT, 1959; MS, U. Tex., 1986; PhD, Tex. Tech. U., 1990. Registered profl. engr., Fla., Ill., Iowa., La., Tex., Wash.; cert structrl. engr. Project engr. Gen. Dynamics Corp., Chgo., 1959—60; chief project, design engr. Gen. Foods Corp., Kankakee, Ill., 1960—64; mgr. plant engring. Std. Brands Inc., Clinton, Iowa, 1964—66; regional mgr. Air Products & Chems., Inc., Creighton, Pa., 1966—68; gen. mgr. Skyline Corp., Harrisburg, NC, 1968—70; cons. Charlotte, NC, 1970—72; dir. engring. and Fla. ops. Zimmer Homes Corp., Pompano Beach, 1972—73; v.p. engring. and mfg. Nobility Homes, Inc., Ocala, Fla., 1973—78, Moduline Internat., Inc., Lacey, Wash., 1978—85; rsch. engr. U. Tex., Austin, 1985—86; lectr., rschr. Tex. Tech. U., Lubbock, 1987—90; assoc. prof. U. New Orleans, 1990—92; asst. prof. dept. civil engring. La. Tech. U., Ruston, 1992—98. Tchr. 30 different courses, 1987—; adj. prof. Coll. Engring., La. Tech. U., 2001-05, vis. prof., 2005-10; cons. in field, Dubach, La., 1992—; condr. workshops in field; apptd. spokesman Mfrd. Housing Industry before U.S. Congress. Contbr. articles to numerous profl. jours. Vol. engring. svcs. Lubbock Fire Safety House, 1990; judge sci. fair Ben Franklin H.S., New Orleans, 1990. Recipient T.L. James Svc. award La. Tech. U., 1994; grantee Urban Waste Mgmt. and Rsch. Ctr., New Orleans, 1991, Shell Devel. Co., 1993, La. Edn. Quality Support Fund, Insituform Techs., Inc., Trenchless Tech. Ctr., PABCO, Inc., InLiner USA, Inc., 1995, others; numerous grants in field. Mem. ASME (life), ASCE (Student chpt. Tchr. of Yr. award 1995, 98, 2009), Nat. Coun. Structural Engrs. Assns., Structural Engrs. Assn. La., Phi Kappa Phi, Sigma Xi, Chi Epsilon. Avocations: flying, skiing, motorcycling, camping, reading, photography. Personal E-mail: drtomstraughan@msn.com.

STRAUGHTER, RUFUS E (PETE), state legislator; b. May 4, 1937; m. Mattie Banks Straughter; children: Rona, Robert Grantham, Eldevon. Mem. Dist. 51 Miss. House of Reps., 1996—; educator. Mem.: NAACP, Nat. Coun. Tchrs. Math, Nat. Edn. Assn., Elks Lodge. Democrat. Protestant. Address: 107 Van Buren St Belzoni MS 39038 Home Phone: 601-247-2728; Office Phone: 601-359-3396. E-mail: rstraughter@house.ms.gov.

STRAUS, JOE, III, state legislator; b. Sept. 1, 1959; m. Julie Brink; children: Sara, Robyn. BA in Polit. Sci., Vanderbilt U. Former mem. mgmt. com. Bexar County Rep. Party; former precinct chmn. Terrell Hills, Tex.; former campaign mgr. to Rep. Lamar Smith US House of Representatives, 1986; former asst. to commr. customs US Dept. Commerce, dep. dir. bus. liason, 1989—91; prin. Watson, Mazur, Bennett & Straus, LLC; mem. Dist. 121 Tex. House of Representatives, 2005—, spkr. of house, 2009—. Recipient of several awards and honors. Republican. Office: 7373 Broadway Ste 202-A San Antonio TX 78209 also: Room CAP 2W.13 Capitol PO Box 2910 Austin TX 78768 Office Phone: 912-463-0686, 512-463-1000, 210-828-4411.

STRAUS, ROBERT, behavioral sciences educator; b. New Haven, Jan. 9, 1923; s. Samuel Hirsh and Alma (Fleischner) Straus; m. Ruth Elisabeth Dawson, Sept. 8, 1945; children: Robert James, Carol Martin, Margaret Dawson, John William. BA, Yale U., 1943, MA, 1945, PhD, 1947. Asst. prof. Yale U., 1948—51, rsch. assoc. applied physiology, 1951—53; acting dir. Conn. Child Study and Treatment Home, New Haven, 1952—53; assoc. prof. preventive medicine SUNY Upstate Med. Ctr., 1953—56; prof. med. sociology U. Ky., Lexington, 1956—59, prof. dept. behavioral sci. Coll. Medicine, also chmn. dept., 1959—87; dir. for sci. devel. Med. Rsch. Inst. San Francisco, 1991—93. Vis. fellow Yale U., 1968—69; vis. prof. U. Calif., Berkeley, 1978, 1986; sec. Com. Med. Sociology, 1955—57; chmn. Coop. Com. Study Alcoholism, 1961—63, Nat. Adv. Com. on Alcoholism, 1966—69; mem. Nat. Adv. Coun. on Alcohol Abuse and Alcoholism, 1984—87; trustee Med. Rsch. Inst. San Francisco, 1988—93; mem. Calif. Pacific Med. Ctr. Rsch. Coun., 1993. Author: Medical Care for Seamen, 1950; author: (with S.D. Bacon) Drinking in College, 1953; author: Alcohol and Society, 1973, Escape From Custody, 1974, A Medical School is Born, 1996; co-editor: Medicine and Society, 1963; mem. editl. bd.: Jour. Studies on Alcohol, 1950—2000. Pres. Bluegrass R.R. Mus., 1980. Mem.: Inst. Medicine NAS, Acad. Behavioral Medicine Rsch., Am. Pub. Health Assn. (lifetime achievement award sect. on alcohol, tobacco and other drugs 1993), Assn. Behavioral Scis. and Med. Edn. (pres. 1974), Am. Sociol. Assn. (chmn. med. sociology sect. 1967—68, Leo G. Reeder award Disting. Contbn. to Med. Sociology 1998), Sigma Xi, Phi Beta Kappa. Home: 690 Mason Headley Rd Apt 312 Lexington KY 40504-2386

STRAUSER, ROBERT WAYNE, lawyer; b. Little Rock, Aug. 28, 1943; s. Christopher Columbus and Opal (Orr) S.; m. Atha Maxine Tubbs, June 26, 1971 (div. 1991); children: Robert Benjamin, Ann

Kathleen; m. Terri D. Seales, Oct. 17, 1998. BA, Davidson Coll., NC, 1965; postgrad., Vanderbilt U., Nashville, 1965-66; JD, U. Tex., Austin, 1968. Bar: Tex. 1968, U.S. Ct. Mil. Appeals 1971. Staff atty. Tex. Legis. Coun., Austin, 1969-71; counsel Jud. Com., Tex. Ho. of Reps., Austin, 1971-73; chief counsel Jud. Com., Tex. Constl. Conv., Austin, 1974; exec. v.p. and legis. counsel Tex. Assn. Taxpayers, Austin, 1974-85; assoc. Baker Botts, LLP, Austin, 1985-87, ptnr., 1988—2008; pvt. practice, 2009—. Assoc. editor Tex. Internat. Law Jour., 1968. Mem. Tex. Ho. Speakers Econ. Devel. Com., Austin, 1986-87; mem.-at-large McDonald Obs. Bd. Visitors, 1988-; bd. dirs. Tex. Assn. Bus. and C. of C., 2000-2002; bd. dirs. Austin Symphony Orch. Soc., 1985—, v.p., 1993-94, nominating com., 1998-2002. Capt. USNR, ret. Named Rising Star of Tex., Tex. Bus. Mag., 1983. Fellow Tex. Bar Found. (life); mem. State Bar of Tex., Headliners Club (Austin). Office: 1005 Congress Ave Ste 1040 Austin TX 78701 Personal E-mail: robert.strauser@gmail.com.

STRAUSS, ALBRECHT BENNO, retired English professor, editor; b. Berlin, May 17, 1921; came to U.S., 1940; s. Bruno and Bertha (Badt) S.; m. Nancy Grace Barron, July 30, 1978; 1 child, Rebecca Ilse; stepchildren: Carolyn, Kathryn BA, Oberlin Coll., 1942; MA, Tulane U., 1948; PhD, Harvard U., 1956. Instr. English Brandeis U., 1951-52; teaching fellow gen. edn. Harvard U., 1952-55; instr. English Yale U., 1955-59; asst. prof. English U. Okla., Norman, 1959-60, U. N.C., Chapel Hill, 1960-64, assoc. prof., 1964-70, prof., 1970-91, prof. emeritus, 1991—; lectr. Duke Inst. for Learning in Retirement, 1993—2005. Editor Studies in Philology, 1974-80; sec. editorial com. Yale Edit. of Works of Samuel Johnson, 1975-2008; mem. editorial com. Ga. Edit. Works of Tobias Smollett, 1973-95; contbr. articles to lit. publs. Served with U.S. Army, 1942-46 Recipient Tanner Teaching award U. N.C., 1966; Fulbright fellow, Germany, 1983-84 Mem. MLA, South Atlantic MLA, Am. Soc. Eighteenth-Century Studies (pres. Southeastern group 1980-81), Johnsonians. Republican. Jewish. Home: 396 Lakeshore Ln Chapel Hill NC 27514-1728 Personal E-mail: strausshaus@mindspring.com.

STRAUSS, JEROME FRANK, III, dean, medical researcher, educator; b. Chgo., May 2, 1947; s. Jerome Frank (Jr.) and Josephine (Newberger) Strauss; m. Catherine Blumlein, June 20, 1970; children: Jordan L., Elizabeth J. BA, Brown U., 1969; MD, U. Pa., 1974, PhD, 1975. Asst. prof. U. Pa. Sch. Medicine, Phila., 1976—83, assoc. prof., 1983—85, prof., 1985—, assoc. chair, 1987—, assoc. dean, 1990—98; Luigi Mastroianni jr. prof. and founding dir. Ctr. Rsch. on Women's Health and Reproduction, Phila., 1990—94; prof. Inst. Medicine NAS, 1994—; dean, exec. v.p. med. affairs, prof. ob-gyn. Va. Commonwealth U. Sch. Medicine, Richmond, 2005—. Biochem. endocrinology study sect. NIH, 1983—87, Nat. Adv. Child Health and Human Devel. Coun., 2002—06; chmn. population rsch. com. NICHHD, 1989—92; chair Reproductive Scientist of the Ams. Network, 1995—; dir. Ctr. Excellence in Women's Health, 1996—2002; co-chair Indo-U.S. Joint Working Grp. on Reproductive Sci. and Contraceptive Tech., 1999—; bd. dirs. Burroughs Wellcome Fund, 2003—; trustee Berlex Found., 2005—; Cheung Kong lectr., prof. Heilongjiang U. Chinese Medicine, 2006—08; clin. rsch. adv. com. NIEHS, 2009—. Editor: Lipoprotein and Cholesterol Metabolism in Sterodogenic Tissues, 1985, Current Topics in Membrane Research, 1987, Uterine and Embryonic Factors in Early Pregnancy, 1991, New Achievements in Research of Ovarian Function, 1995, Cell Death in Reproductive Physiology, 1997, Molecular Biology in Reproductive Medicine, 1999, Ovarian Function Research: Present and Future, 1999, Reproductive Medicine Molecular, Cellular and Genetic Fundamentals, 2002, New Frontiers in Contraceptive Research, 2004, Yen and Jaffe's Reproductive Endocrinology, 2004, Preterm Birth, 2007, Steroids jour., 1993—; assoc. editor Ency. of Reproduction, 1998—, assoc. editor, mem. editl. bd. Jour. Lipid Rsch., 1982—90, corr. editor Jour. Steroid Biochem. and Molecular Biology, 1990—99, mem. editl. bd. Endocrinology, 1986—90, 1997—2000, Biology of Reprodn., 1986—90, 1999—2003, Jour. of Women's Health, 1991—, Jour. Soc. Gynecologic Investigation, 1993—, Placenta, 1995—98, Trends in Endocrinology and Metabolism, 1999—2008, Reference en Gynecologie Obstetrique, 1999—, Seminars in Reproductive Endocrinology, 2000—, Jour. Endocrinology, 2000—06, Human Reproduction Update, 2001—05, Science, 2004—, assoc. editor Molecular Human Reproduction, 2007—. Recipient Transatlantic medal, Brit. Endocrine Soc., 1998, Disting. Grad. award, U. Pa., 2005, NAS Inst. Medicine, 2005, Rectoral medal, U. Chile, 2009. Fellow: Internat. Acad. Human Reproduction; mem.: Perinatal Rsch. Soc., Am. Soc. for Reproductive Medicine, Soc. for Study of Reproduction (bd. dirs. 1989—91, Rsch. award 1992), Endocrine Soc., Soc. Gynecologic Investigation (pres. 2003, Pres.'s Achievement award 1990, Disting. Scientist award 2006). Home: 2808 Monument Ave Unit 3 Richmond VA 23221 Office: Va Commonwealth U Dean's Office Sch Medicine 1101 E Marshall St Rm 1-070 Richmond VA 23298 Business E-Mail: jfstrauss@vcu.edu.

STRAUSS, JEROME MANFRED, lawyer, trust company executive, professional private fiduciary, author; s. Emanuel and Loraine Strauss; children: Martha Lynn, Jared Lee, David Aaron. BA with honors, Ind. U., 1956; JD, NYU, 1959; cert in Advanced Estate Planning, Harvard Sch. Law, Cambridge, 1964. Bar: Ind. 1959, Fla. 1996, U.S. Dist. Ct. (so. dist.) Ind. 1959, U.S. Tax Ct. 1965, U.S. Ct. Appeals (7th cir.) 1969. Lawyer Ice Miller Donadio & Ryan, Indpls., 1959—93, ptnr., 1969-93; sr. v.p. and regional trust mgr. Merrill Lynch Trust Co., 1993-95; with Mershon, Sawyer, Johnston, Dunwody & Cole, Miami, Palm Beach, Naples, 1995-96; established Wollman, Strauss & Assocs., P.A., 1997; of counsel Grant Fridkin, Pearson, Athan & Crown PA, NAples, 2011; founder Midwest Tax and Estate Planning Inst., Indpls., 1976—; pvt. Fiduciary JMSLEGAL, LLC, 1996—. Pres. Indpls. U. Student Govt., Bloomington, 1955—56; chmn. Big Ten U. Student Govt., 1955—56. Co-author: Marital Deduction Trusts, 1963, Real Estate in an Estate, 1963, Durable Powers of Attorney, 1993; contbr. articles to profl. jours. Bd. dirs. Orton Soc., Indpls., 1970-72, Indpls. 1970-72, Indpls. Hebrew Congregation, 1979-85, Planned Giving Group of Ind., Indpls., 1988-95, Ind. Continuing Legal Edn. Forum, 1989-94; devel. com. Collier County, Fla. Cmty. Found., 1995-2002; mem. Planned Giving Com. of Lee County, Fla., 1995-2002, Fla. Planned Giving Coun., 1995—; estate planning coun. Naples, Fla., 1996—. Recipient Golden Career award, Ind. State Bar, 2010; Fulbright scholarship, 1956. Fellow, Am. Coll Trust and Estate Counsel (charitable com., estate and gift tax com. 1996-2001); mem. Internat. Acad. Estate and Trust Law (academician 1987—), Ind. State Bar Assn. (sec. 1979-80, chmn. probate, trust and real property sect. 1970-71) Jewish. Home and Office: 1056 Diamond Lake Cir Bay 385 Naples FL 34114-9211 Office Fax: 239-732-9006. Business E-Mail: jerry@jeromemstrauss.com.

STRAUSS, JON CALVERT, academic administrator; b. Chgo., Jan. 17, 1940; s. Charles E. and Alice C. (Woods) S.; m. Joan Helen Bailey, Sept. 19, 1959 (div. 1985); children: Susan, Stephanie; m. Jean Anne Sacconaghi, June 14, 1985; children: Kristoffer, Jonathon. BSEE, U. Wis., 1959; MS in Physics, U. Pitts., 1962; PhD in E.E., Carnegie Inst. Tech., 1965; LLD (hon.), U. Mass., 1996. Assoc. prof. computer sci., elec. engring. Carnegie Mellon U., Pitts., 1966-70; dir. computer ctr., prof. computer sci. Tech. U. Norway, Trondheim, Norway, 1970; vis. assoc. prof. elec. engring. U. Mich., Ann Arbor, 1971; assoc. prof. computer sci. Washington U., St. Louis, 1971-74, dir. computing facilities, 1971-73; dir. computing activities U. Pa., Phila., 1974-76, faculty master Stouffer Coll. House, 1978-80, prof. computer, info. scis., prof. decision sci. Wharton Sch., 1974-81, exec. dir. Univ. Budget, 1975-78, v.p. for budget, fin., 1978-81; prof. elec. engring. U. So. Calif., Los Angeles, 1981-85, sr. v.p. adminstrn., 1981-85; pres. Worcester Poly. Inst., Mass., 1985-94, pres. emeritus; v.p., chief fin. officer Howard Hughes Med. Inst., Chevy Chase, Md., 1994-97; pres. Harvey Mudd Coll., Claremont, Calif., 1997—2006, pres. emeritus, 2006—; interim dean Edward E. Whitacre Jr. Coll. Engring., Tex. Tech U., Lubbock, 2009—. Cons. Electronics Assocs., Inc., 1965, IBM Corp., 1960—64, Westinghouse Elec. Corp., 1959—60; bd. dirs. Transamerica Income Fund, Variable Ins. Fund, United Educators Ins.; mem. Nat. Sci. Bd., NSF, chair Subcommittee on Polar Issues. Contbr. articles on computer systems and university mgmt. to profl. jours.; co-holder patent. Bd. dirs. Presbyn.-U. Pa. Med. Ctr., Phila., 1980-81, U. So. Calif. Kenneth Norris Jr. Cancer Hosp., L.A., 1981-85, Med. Ctr. of Ctrl. Mass., 1986-94, Worcester Acad., 1986-91, Mass. Biotech. Rsch. Inst., 1985-94. Mem. New. Eng. Assn. Schs. and Colls., Inc., Commn. on Instns. of Higher Edn., Nat. Collegiate Athletic Assn. (pres.'s commn. 1990-94). Avocations: hiking, running, swimming. Office: Whitacre College of Engineering Texas Tech University Box 43103 Lubbock TX 79409-3103 Office Phone: 806-742-3451. Office Fax: 909-321-8360. Business E-Mail: jon_strauss@hmc.edu. E-mail: jon.strauss@ttu.edu.

STRAWSER, JERRY R., dean; BBA in Acctg., Tex. A&M U., 1983, MS in Acctg., 1984, PhD in Acctg., 1985. CPA Tex., 1985. Asst. prof. La. State U., 1985—90, Arthur Andersen & Co. rsch. fellow, 1989—90; assoc. prof. Conn. Bauer Coll. Bus., U. Houston, 1990—97, assoc. dean academic and rsch. programs, 1995—99, prof. and Arthur Anderson & Co. alumni prof. acctg. and taxation, 1997—2001, interim dean, 1999—2001; dean Mays Bus. Sch., Tex. A&M U., 2001—, Devel. Coun. chair bus., 2001—, Leland/Weinke chair acctg., 2001, now KPMG chair acctg. Mem. editl. bd. Issues in Acctg. Edn., 1998—. Co-author: (books) Auditing Theory and Practice, 1985—2001, Managerial Accounting, 1990—2000, Auditing & Assurance Services, 2004. Recipient Outstanding Tchg. award, Alpha Kappa Psi, 1985, George W. Fair award for tchg. excellence, 1986, Melcher award for rsch. excellence, 1992, 1995, Master Tchg. award, NationsBank, 1994, Disting. Faculty award, Exec. MBA Alumni Assn., 2000; Arthur Andersen rsch. fellowship, 1989, Melcher tchg. fellow, 1991, Melcher svc. fellow, 1993. Mem.: Am. Assn. Acctg., Assn. to Advance Collegiate Schools of Bus. Office: Tex A&M U Mays Bus Sch 4113 TAMU 3003 Wehner College Station TX 77843-4113 Office Phone: 979-845-4711. Office Fax: 979-845-6639. Business E-Mail: jstrawser@tamu.edu.

STRECKER, DAVID EUGENE, lawyer; b. Carthage, Mo., Nov. 29, 1950; s. Eugene Albert and Erma Freida (Wood) S.; m. Katherine Ann Pugh; children: Charles David, Carrie Christina. BA, Westminster Coll., 1972; JD, Cornell U., 1975, M in Indsl. Labor Rels., 1976. Bar: NY 1976, Okla. 1981, US Dist. Ct. (no. dist.) NY 1976, US Dist. Ct. (ea. dist.) Okla. 1984, US Dist. Ct. (we. dist.) Okla. 2000, US Dist. Ct. (we. and ea. dists.) Ark. 2000, US Ct. Appeals (no. dist.) Okla. 1981, US Ct. Appeals (10th cir.) 1982, US Ct. Appeals (6th cir.) 1990, US Supreme Ct. 1991, US Dist. Ct. (ea. dist.) Tex. 2006. Assoc. Conner & Winters, Tulsa, 1980-85, ptnr., 1985-91, Shipley, Inhofe & Strecker, Tulsa, 1991-95, Strecker & Assocs. P.C., Tulsa, 1995—; adj. prof. Negotiation U. Tulsa, 2009—10; mediator Resolution Ctr. Mediation & Arbitation, 2011—. Instr. paralegal program Tulsa Jr. Coll., 1985—, mem. adv. com., 1986-91; mem. Cornell Secondary Schs. Com., Tulsa, 1985—; instr. labor rels. Okla. State U., 1995—; instr. St. Gregory's U., 2010-, instr. bus. law, Rogers State U.; master Am. Inns of Ct. Author: Labor Law: A Basic Guide to the National Labor Relations Act, 2011. Bd. dirs., v.p. Tulsa Sr. Svcs., 1988-91; mem. pers. com. Philbrook Art Mus. Capt. JAGC, U.S. Army, 1976-80. Mem. ABA, Okla. Bar Assn. (chmn. labor sect. 1990-91), Tulsa County Bar Assn. (continuing legal edn. com. 1981—), Soc. for Human Resource Mgmt., Tulsa Area Human Resources Assn. (gen. counsel 1989-2000, v.p. 1994-98, bd. dirs. family and children's svcs. 2000—04), Kappa Alpha. Democrat. Episcopalian. Avocations: walking, sailing, fishing. Home: 5112 E 107th St Tulsa OK 74137-7238 Office: Midcontinent Tower 401 S Boston Ste 2150 Tulsa OK 74103-4009 Home Phone: 918-298-4652; Office Phone: 918-582-1716. E-mail: destreck@juno.com, david.strecker@streckerlaborlaw.com.*

STREDLER, JEFFREY L., lawyer; BA, JD, U. Va. Ptnr. Williams Mullen; sr. v.p., sr. litigation counsel Amerigroup Corp., 2008—. Office: Amerigroup Corp 4425 Corporation Lane Virginia Beach VA 23462 Office Phone: 757-490-6900. Office Fax: 757-518-3600. Business E-Mail: jstredler@amerigroupcorp.com.

STREEB, GORDON LEE, diplomat, economist; b. Windsor, Colo., Dec. 24, 1935; s. Gerhard O. and Amelia (Martin) S.; m. Alice Junette Thomas, Aug. 11, 1962; children: Kurt, Kent, Kerry-Lynn. BSBA, BSChemE, U. Colo., 1959; PhD in Econs., U. Minn., 1978. Fgn. service officer U.S. Dept. State, Berlin, 1963-65; vice consul Am. Consulate, Guadalajara, Mex., 1965-67; instr. econs. U. Minn., 1968; examiner Bd. Examiners, 1972-73; internat. economist for trade policy Bur. Econ. and Bus. Affairs, Washington, 1973-77; econ. counselor U.S. mission European Office of the UN and other internat. orgns., Geneva, 1977-80; exec. asst. to undersec. of state on econ. affairs Washington, 1980-81; dep. asst. sec. state for econ. and social affairs Bur. Internat. Orgn. Affairs, Washington, 1981-84; dep. chief mission Am. Embassy, New Delhi, 1984-88; sr. inspector Dept. State, Washington, 1988-90; amb. to Zambia Am. Embassy, Lusaka, 1990-93; diplomat-in-residence The Carter Ctr., Atlanta, 1994-95, assoc. exec. dir. peace program, 1995—2004; vis. prof. Emory U., Atlanta, 2004—. Mem. Coun. on Fgn. Rels.; mem. adv. bd. Engrs. Without Borders-USA. Home: 2680 Churchwell Ln Tucker GA 30084-2402 Business E-Mail: gstreeb@emory.edu.

STREET, DARON G., gynecologic oncologist; MD, U. Okla., Tulsa. Diplomate Am. Bd. Ob-Gyn, Am. Bd. Ob-Gyn-gynecologic oncology. Resident Coll. Medicine Univ. Okla., Tulsa, physician; fellow gynecologic oncology Loyola Univ. Med. Ctr., Chgo.; gynecologic oncologist St. Francis Hosp., Hillcrest Med. Ctr.; physician Cancer Care Assocs.; pvt. practice Women's Clinic. Named one of the Top Doctors, Okla. Mag., 2011. Office: Saint Francis Hospital 6161 S Yale Ave Tulsa OK 74136 Office Phone: 918-494-2200.

STREET, GORDON P., JR., iron foundry executive; b. 1938; married. AB, U. N.C., 1960. Adminstrv. officer N.Am. Royalties Inc., Chattanooga, 1960—66, v.p. oil & gas divsn., 1966—68, exec. v.p., 1968—73, pres., dir., 1973—, chmn., 1982—. Treas., dir. Nat. Park Found.; bd. dirs. First Tenn. Nat. Corp., Cin., Provident Life & Accident Ins. Co.; adv. dir. First Tenn. Bank Chattanooga; mem. adv. bd. Ctr. Strategic & Internat. Studies; mem. Norfolk Southern Adv. Bd. Trustee Baylor Sch., Tenn. Camp Diabetic Children, Chattanooga Neighborhood Inc.; bd. visitors U. NC Chapel Hill; bd. dirs. Gordon St. Found. Office: N Am Royalties Inc 200 E 8th St Chattanooga TN 37402-2201

STREET, WILLIAM MAY, retired beverage company executive; b. Louisville, 1938; Grad., Princeton U., 1960; MBA, Harvard U., 1963. Pres., COO Brown-Forman Beverage Co. Divsn., Louisville, 1986-94; pres., CEO Brown-Forman Beverages Worldwide Divsn., 1994—2003; sr. v.p. Brown-Forman Corp., Louisville, 1977, pres., 2000—03. Vice chmn. Brown-Forman Corp., 1987—2000, bd.dirs., 1971—, Papa John's Internat., 2003—. Chmn. Ky. Horse Racing Authority. Office: Brown-Forman Corp 850 Dixie Hwy Louisville KY 40210 Home Phone: 502-897-7320; Office Phone: 502-585-1100. Office Fax: 502-774-6633.

STREETER, RICHARD BARRY, academic official; b. Albany, NY, Aug. 6, 1940; s. Lyle Tyler and Marion Downey Streeter; m. Janet Grace Marsteller, July 31, 1971; children: Jonathan Lyle, Stephanie Lyn. BA, U. Fla., 1962, MEd, 1963; EdD, U. Miami, Coral Gables, Fla., 1972. Assoc. dir. fin. aid U. Miami, 1970—73; dir. fin. aid Portland State U., Oreg., 1973—76, asst. dean grad. studies, dir. sponsored rsch., 1976—80; dir. office rsch. Lehigh U., Bethlehem, Pa., 1980—90; asst. v.p. rsch., dir. U. South Fla., Tampa, 1990—96; dir. USDOE/USF Tech. Deployment Ctr., 1994—; exec. dir. econ. devel. USF, 1996—. Bd. dirs., chair fin. and audit com. Oak Ridge Associated Us. Bus. mgr. Quality Life Maintenance Orgn., 1976—80; mem. Easton area Sch. Bd., 1984—90; bd. trustees Northampton County Area C.C., 1986—90; del. Pa. Fed. of C.C. Trustees. Mem.: AAAS, Archontes, Coun. Rsch. and Tech. (rsch. policy com., commercialization task force), Soc. Rsch. Adminstrs., Nat. Coun. U. Rsch. Adminstrs., Phi Delta Kappa, Omega. Republican. Presbyterian. Office: U South Fla 4202 E Fowler Ave Tampa FL 33620-8000 Home: PO Box 979 Inglis FL 34449-0979

STREETMAN, BEN GARLAND, engineering professor, former dean; b. Cooper, Tex., June 24, 1939; s. Richard E. and Bennie (Morrow) Streetman; m. Lenora Ann Music, Sept. 9, 1961; children: Paul, Scott. BS, U. Tex., 1961, MS, 1963, PhD, 1966. Fellow Oak Ridge Nat. Lab., 1964-66; asst. prof. elec. engring. U. Ill., 1966-70, assoc. prof., 1970-74, prof., 1974-82; rsch. prof. Coordinated Sci. Lab., 1970-82; prof. elec. engring. U. Tex., Austin, 1982—, dir. Microelectronics Rsch. Ctr., 1984—96, Dula D. Cockrell Centennial chair engring., 1989—2010, dean Cockrell Sch. Engring., 1996—2008. Bd. dirs. Nat. Instruments., 1997—2009. Author: Solid State Electronic Devices 6th edit., 2005. Recipient Frederick Emmons Terman award, Am. Soc. Engring. Edn., 1981, AT&T Found. award, 1987, Aldert van der Ziel award, 2005; named Disting. Alumnus, U. Tex. at Austin, 1998. Fellow: IEEE, Electrochem. Soc., Tau Beta Pi; mem.: NAE, Sigma Xi, Am. Acad. Arts and Scis., Eta Kappa Nu. Office: Universit of Texas at Austin Electrical & Computer Engineering 2501 Speedway Austin TX 78712-0240 Office Phone: 512-471-1640. E-mail: bstreet@mail.utexas.edu.

STREKOWSKI, LUCJAN, chemistry professor; came to U.S., 1981; s. Antoni and Janina S.; m. Alewtina Smirnova, Oct. 14, 1967; children: Rafal, Anna. BS in Polymer Chemistry with distinction, Mendeleev Inst. Chemistry, Moscow, 1967; PhD in Organic Chemistry, Polish Acad. Scis., 1972; DSc in Chemistry, Adam Mickiewicz U., Poznan, Poland, 1976. Instr. organic chemistry Adam Mickiewicz U., Poznan, 1971-72, asst. prof. dept. chemistry, 1972-78, assoc. prof. dept. chemistry, 1978-81; rsch. assoc. dept. chemistry U. Fla., Gainesville, 1981-84; asst. prof. dept. chemistry Ga. State U., Atlanta, 1984-89, assoc. prof. dept. chemistry, 1989-96, prof. dept. chem., 1996—2011, prof. emeritus, dept. chemistry, 2011—. Vis. prof. U. Fla., Gainesville, 1979-80, 81, Australian Nat. U., 1980, U. Kans., Lawrence, 1972-73. Editor: Pyridine-Metal Complexes, Vol. 14, Part 6, 1985, Synthetic and Biophysical Studies of DNA Binding Compounds, 2008, Hetrocyclic Polymethine Dyes, 2008; editor-in-chief Heterocyclic Comms., 2010-; mem. editl. bd. Arkivoc; contbr. more than 350 articles to profl. jours. Recipient award, Polish Ministry Sci., 1977, Polish Chem. Soc., 1973, Polish Acad. Scis., 1972, Ga. State U., 1993; grantee Am. Chem. Soc.-Petroleum Rsch. Fund, 1985—2006, Solvay Pharms., 1992—93, Nat. Diagnostics, 1991—93, NIAID/NIMH, 1988—89, Rohm and Hass Co., 1988, Am. Cancer Soc., 1987—89, Rsch. Corp., 1985—94, Milheim Found. Cancer Rsch., 1985—86, DuPont Co., 1996—2000, Small Bus. Innovation Rsch. Program, 2000—02, FBI, 2002—07, Coley Pharms., 2003—04, Ga. Rsch. Alliance, 2004—05, Harvard U. Med. Sch., 2007—. Achievements include patents in field. Avocation: classical music. Office: Ga State Univ Dept Chemistry Atlanta GA 30302 Office Phone: 404-413-5509. Business E-Mail: lucjan@gsu.edu.

STRENG, WILLIAM PAUL, lawyer, educator; b. Sterling, Ill., Oct. 17, 1937; s. William D. and Helen Marie (Conklen) S.; children: Sarah, John. BA, Wartburg Coll., 1959; JD, Northwestern U., 1962. Bar: Iowa 1962, Ill. 1962, Ohio 1964, Tex. 1975. Law clk. to U.S. circuit judge Lester L. Cecil, Cin., 1963-64; assoc. firm Taft, Stettinius & Hollister, Cin., 1964-70; atty.-advisor Office Sec. Tax Policy, Office Tax Legis. Counsel, Dept. Treasury, Washington, 1970-71; dep. gen. counsel Export-Import Bank U.S., Washington, 1971-73; prof. law Sch. Law, So. Methodist U., Dallas, 1973-80; vis. prof. Coll. Law Ohio State U., Columbus, 1977; ptnr. firm Bracewell & Patterson, Houston, 1980-85; Vinson & Elkins prof. of law U. Houston Law Ctr, 1985—. Vis. prof. Rice U., NYU Law Sch., 1990, U. Tex. Sch. Law, 2002, Yokohama (Japan) Nat. U., 2005; disting. vis. prof. U. Hong Kong Law Faculty, 1992; Fulbright prof. U. Stockholm Law Faculty, 1993; vis. fellow law faculty Victoria U., Wellington, New Zealand, 1996; vis. law lectr. U. Leiden, Netherlands, 1997, 1998, 2000, 2007, 2009; cons. Bracewell & Patterson (now Bracewell & Giuliani), 1985—2011; lectr. various confs. Am. Law Inst., World Trade Inst., Practicing Law Inst., Internat. Fiscal Assn., ABA, Tex. State Bar. Author: International Business Transactions-Tax and Legal Handbook, 1978, Estate Planning, 1991, 2006, 2013, International Business Planning: Law and Taxation, 3 vols., 2011, Tax Planning for Retirement, 2001, revised edit., 2012, Doing Business in China, 1990, 1996, Federal Income Taxation of Corporations and Shareholders--Forms, 1995—2013, Choice of Entity, 1994, 1999, 2007, U.S. International Estate Planning, 1996, revised, 2006. Served with USMC, 1962. Lutheran. Home: 1903 Dunstan Rd Houston TX 77005-1619 Office: U Houston Law Ctr Houston TX 77204-6060 Office Phone: 713-743-2148. Business E-Mail: wstreng@uh.edu.

STRENGLIS, WILLIAM A., business services company executive; Grad., U. Minn., 1976. Various exec. positions Schwan's Bakery, Inc. (formerly Mrs. Smith's Bakeries), divsn. v.p., 1999, exec. v.p., 1999—2002, pres., COO, 2002—04; pres. DI Foodservice Companies, 2004—05, Unified Brands, Inc. (subs. of Dover Corp.), 2005—. Office: Unified Brands Inc 1055 Mendell Davis Dr Jackson MS 39272 Office Phone: 601-372-3903. Business E-Mail: bills@dovercorp.com.

STRICK, JEREMY ADAM, art museum director; b. 1955; BA in Hist. of Art,with highest honors, U. Calif., Santa Cruz, 1977; student, Harvard U. Asst. curator 20th Century art Nat. Gallery Art, Washington, 1986-89, assoc. curator 20th Century art, 1989-93, acting dept. dept. 20th Century art, 1992-93, curator Nat. Sculpture Garden project, 1989-93; curator modern art St. Louis Art Mus., 1993-96; Frances and Thomas Dittmer curator 20th Century painting and sculpture Art Inst. Chgo., 1996-99; dir. Mus. Contemporary Art (MOCA), L.A., 1999—2008, Nasher Sculpture Ct., Dallas, 2009—. Curator NY Interpreted: Joseph Stella and Alfred Stieglitz, Nat.

Gallery Art, 1987, Milton Avery, 1990, Mark Rothko: The Spirit Myth, 1990-95, asst. curator A Century of Modern Sculpture: The Patsy and Raymond Nasher Collection, 1987, co-curator Twentieth-Century Art: Selections for the Tenth Anniversary of the East Building, 1987; curator Brice Marden: A Painting, Drawings, Prints, St. Louis Art Mus., 1993, Currents 58: Susan Crile—The Fires of War, 1994, Louise Bourgeois: The Personages 1946-1954, 1995, Currents 60: Jerald Ieans, 1994, Masterworks from Stuttgar: The Romantic Age in German Art, 1995, Currents 66: Michael Byron, 1996, Currents 67: Leonardo Drew, 1996; curator The Sublime Is Now: The Early Work of Barnett Newman, Walker Art Ctr., Mpls., Pace Gallery, N.Y.C., 1994; curator In the Light of Italy: Corot and Early Open-Air Painting, Nat. Gallery Art, Bklyn. Mus., St. Louis Art Mus., 1996; lectr., symposia participant and organizer, 1980—; juror Showhegan awards, 1995. Contbg. author: Works by Antoine-Louis Barye in the Collection of the Fogg Art Museum, Vol. IV, 1982; contbr. articles to exhbn. catalogs, newspapers, mags., ency. Instnl. fellow Samuel H. Kress Found., Paris, 1983-85, fellow Mrs. Giles Whiting Found., 1985-86. Office: Nasher Sculpture Ctr 2001 Flora St Dallas TX 75201 Office Phone: 214-242-5103. E-mail: jstrick@nashsculpturecenter.org.

STRICKER, STEVE, professional golfer; b. Edgerton, Wis., Feb. 23, 1967; m. Nicki Stricker; 1 child, Bobbi Maria. Grad., U. Ill., 1990. Profl. golfer, 1990—. Mem. US team Alfred Dunhill Cup, 1996, Presidents Cup, 1996, 2007, 2009, 2011, Ryder Cup, 2008, 2010, 2012. Named PGA TOUR Comeback Player of Yr., 2006, 2007. Achievements include winning international events: Victoria Open, Canada, 1990; Canadian PGA Championship, 1993; winning PGA Tour events: Kemper Open, 1996; Motorola Western Open, 1996; Accenture Match Play Championship, 2001; The Barclays, 2007; Crowne Plaza Invitational at Colonial, 2009; John Deere Classic, 2009, 2010, 2011; Deutsche Bank Championship, 2009; Memorial Tournament, 2011; Hyundai Tournament of Champions, 2012; being a member of the Ryder Cup winning US team, 2008. Office: PGA Tour 112 PGA Tour Blvd Ponte Vedra Beach FL 32082

STRICKLAND, FRANK B., lawyer; b. Washington, July 12, 1936; BA, Vanderbilt U., 1958; LLB, Emory U., 1966. Bar: Ga. 1966, US Dist. Ct., no. mid. & so. dists. Ga., US Ct. Appeals, 11th circuit, US Supreme Ct. Ptnr. Wilson Strickland & Benson, Atlanta, 1971—2000, Holland & Knight, Atlanta, 2000—01, Strickland Brockington Lewis, Atlanta, 2001—. Mem. State Ethics Commn., Ga., 1987—90, pres. Ga., 1989—90; mem. Jud. Nominating Commn., Ga., 2003—; trustee Atlanta Metro Grp.; mem. Fulton County Bd. Registration & Elections; trustee Inst. Continuing Edn., Ga.; gen. counsel Rep Party, Ga., 1993—95; chmn. bd. Legal Svcs. Corp., 2003—10; dir. Atlanta Legal Aid Soc. & Fed. Def. prog., 1984—88. Comdr. (ret.) USCGR. Mem.: Rep. Nat. Lawyers Assn. (bd. gov., chmn. Ga. chptr. 2002—), Federalist Soc. (chmn. Atlanta lawyers chptr. 1996—), Nat. Assn. Coll. & Univ. Attys., Lawyers Club Atlanta, State Bar Ga. (bd. gov. 1985—), Atlanta Bar Assn. (pres. 1985—86), ABA (ho. del. 1985—87), Atlanta Vanderbilt Alumni Assn. (past pres.). Republican. Office: Strickland Brockington Lewis LLP Midtown Proscenium 1170 Peachtree St NE Ste 2200 Atlanta GA 30309-7200 Office Phone: 678-347-2211. E-mail: fbs@sbllaw.net.

STRICKLAND, ROBERT LOUIS, retired retail executive; b. Florence, SC, Mar. 3, 1931; s. Franz M. and Hazel (Eaddy) S.; m. Elizabeth Ann Miller, Feb. 2, 1952; children: Cynthia Anne, Robert Edson. AB, U. N.C., 1952; MBA with distinction, Harvard U., 1957. Bd. dirs. Lowe's Cos., Inc., North Wilkesboro, NC, 1961—2000, sr. v.p., 1970—76, exec. v.p., 1976—78, chmn. bd., 1979—98, chmn. exec. com., 1988—98, mem. office of pres., 1970—78, chmn. emeritus, 1999; founder Sterling Advt., Ltd., 1966. V.p., mem. adminstrv. com. Lowe's Profit-Sharing Trust, 1961-87, chmn. ops. com., 1972-78; mgmt. com. Lowe's ESOP Plan, 1978-97; prior bd. dirs. Lowe's Cos., Wilkesboro, NC, T.Rowe Price Assocs., Balt., 1991-2001, Hannaford Bros. Co., Portland, Maine, Krispy Kreme Corp., Winston-Salem, NC, Wholesale Club, Indpls., Summit Comms., Atlanta; vice chair, bd. dirs. Revelstoke Co., Calgary, Can.; panelist investor rels. field, 1972-99; spkr., panelist employee stock ownership, 1978-2000; spkr. on investor rels., London, Edinburgh, Glasgow, Paris, Zurich, Frankfurt, Milan, Vienna, Singapore, Tokyo. Author: Lowe's Cybernetwork, 1969, Lowe's Living Legend, 1970, Ten Years of Growth, 1971, The Growth Continues, 1972, 73, 74, Lowe's Scoreboard, 1978; contbr. articles to profl. jours. Mem. NC Ho. of Reps., 1962-64, Rep. Senatorial Inner Circle, 1980-95; exec. com. NC Rep. Com., 1963-73; trustee U. NC, Chapel Hill, 1987-95, chmn. bd., 1991-93; dir., dep. chmn. Fed. Res. Bank of Richmond, 1996-98; com. on bus. laws and the economy NC, 1994-97; dir. US Coun. Better Bus. Burs., 1981-85; bd. dirs., v.p. Nat. Home Improvement Coun., 1972-76; bd. dirs. NC Sch. Arts Found., 1975-79, NC Bd. Natural and Econ. Resources, 1975-76; bd. dirs., govt. affairs com. Home Ctr. Inst., co-chmn. Home Ctr. to Israel Del., 1984; trustee, sec. bd. Wilkes CC, 1964-73; chmn., pres. bd. dirs. Do-It-Yourself Rsch. Inst., 1981-89; pres. Hardware Home Improvement Coun. City of Hope Nat. Med. Ctr., LA, 1987-89; co-founder Home Safety Coun., 1993. With USN, 1952—55, lt. res. USN, 1955—62. Named Wilkes County NC Young Man of Yr., Wilkes Jr. C. of C., 1962; recipient Bronze Oscar of Industry award Fin. World, 1969-74, 76-79, Silver Oscar of Industry award, 1970, 72-74, 76-79, Gold Oscar of Industry award as best of all industry, 1972, 87, Excellence award in corp. reporting Fin. Analysts Fedn., 1970, 72, 74, 81-82, cert. of Distinction Brand Names Found., 1970, Retailer of Yr. award, 1971, 73, Disting. Mcht. award, 1972, Spirit of Life award City of Hope, 1983, Free Enterprise Legend award Students Free Enterprise, 1994; named to Home Ctr. Hall of Fame, 1985, Golden Hammer Hall of Fame, 2007. Mem. Nat. Assn. Over-Counter Cos. (bd. advisers 1973-77), Newcomen Soc., Employee Stock Ownership Assn. (pres. 1983-85, chmn. 1985-87), James Madison Club, Federalist Soc., Forsyth Country Club, Piedmont City Club, Ponte Vedra Inn and Club (Fla.), Harvard Club (NY), Scabbard and Blade, Phi Beta Kappa, Pi Kappa Alpha. Home: 226 N Stratford Rd Winston Salem NC 27104-3132 also: 721 5th Ave Apt GH New York NY 10022 Office: 2000 W 1st St Winston Salem NC 27104-4225 Home: 67 Ponte Vedra Blvd Ponte Vedra Beach FL 32082

STRICKLAND, ROD (RODNEY STRICKLAND), men's college basketball coach, retired professional basketball player; b. Bronx, NY, July 11, 1966; m. Cheryl Strickland; 4 children. B, De Paul U., Chgo., 1988. Guard NY Knicks, 1988—90, San Antonio Spurs, 1990—92, Portland Trailblazers, 1992—96, 2001, Washington Bullets, 1996—97, Washington Wizards, 1997—2001, Miami Heat, 2001—02, Minn. Timberwolves, 2002—03, Orlando Magic, 2003—04, Toronto Raptors, 2004, Houston Rockets, 2004—05; ret. NBA, 2005; dir. student athlete devel., mgr. U. Memphis Tigers, 2006—08, dir. basketball ops., 2008—09; asst. coach U. Ky. Wildcats, 2009—. Named to NYC Basketball Hall of Fame, 2008. Achievements include leading the NBA in: assists per game (10.5), 1997-98. Avocation: bowling. Office: University of Ky Basketball Joe Craft Ctr 338 Lexington Ave Lexington KY 40506-0604 Office Phone: 859-257-1916.

STRICKLAND, SAMUEL RAY, corporate financial executive; b. Norfolk, Va., Sept. 15, 1950; s. Algrin Perry and Ruth Jordan (Furlough) S.; m. Paula Katherine Parkinson, Jan. 7, 1984; children: Katherine Elizabeth, Sarah Clayton. AB in Bus. Adminstrn., Coll. William and Mary, 1972. CPA. Acct. Price Waterhouse Inc., Washington, 1972-78; fin. project mgr. Arabian Bus. and Mgmt. Services, Dhahran, Saudi Arabia, 1978-79; v.p., contr. BDM Internat. Inc., McLean, Va.; joined Booz Allen Hamilton, McLean, 1996, exec. v.p., CFO, chief adminstrv. officer, dir., 2004—. Bd. trustees George Mason U. Found., Inova Health Services; chmn. bd. trustees Capital Hospice. Mem. Am. Inst. CPAs, Fin. Execs. Inst. Office: Booz Allen Hamilton 8283 Greensboro Dr Mc Lean VA 22101

STRICKLAND, WILLIAM JESSE, lawyer; b. Newport News, Va., Mar. 21, 1942; BSBA, U. Richmond, 1964, JD, 1969. Bar: Va. 1969, US Dist. Ct. Ea. Dist. Va., US Dist. Ct. We. Dist. Va., US Ct. Appeals 4th Cir., US Ct. Claims, US Tax Ct., Bar Brussels, Solicitors Regulation Authority of England & Wales. Mem McGuire Woods LLP, Richmond, Va., 1969—, mng. ptnr., 1996—2007. Bd. dirs. Cableform Inc., Zion Crossroads, Va., Eimeldingen Corp., Indpls, Greater Richmond. Mem. exec. com. Va. Found. for Rsch. & Econ. Edn., Inc., bd. dirs. U. Richmond Law Sch. Found.; mem. coun. Va. Inst. Marine Sci.; founder Marine Corps Heritage Found.; bd. dirs. World Affairs Coun. Greater Richmond; chmn. Am. Club Brussels. Capt. USMC, 1964—67. Mem. ABA (com. on tax exempt fin.), Va. Bar Assn., Richmond Bar Assn., Nat. Assn. Bond Lawyers, Va. Govt. Fin. Officers Assn., Va. Local Govt. Attorneys Assn., Va. Bond Club. Office: McGuire Woods LLP One James Ctr 901 E Cary St Richmond VA 23219-4030 Office Phone: 804-775-4350. Office Fax: 804-698-2185. Business E-Mail: wstrickland@mcguirewoods.com.

STRICKLER, HOWARD MARTIN, physician, director; b. New Haven, Oct. 26, 1950; s. Thomas David and Mildred Laing (Martin) S.; m. Susan Hunter, May 2, 1982; children: Hunter Gregory, Howard Martin Jr. BA, Berea Coll., 1975; MD, Univ. Louisville, 1979. Cert. Am. Assn. Med. Rev. Officers, 1993, diplomate Am. Bd. Addiction Medicine. Resident Anniston (Ala.) Family Practice Residency, 1979-82; pvt. practice Monteagle, Tenn., 1982-85; fellow in addictive diseases Willingway Hosp., Statesboro, Ga., 1985-86; faculty devel. fellow Univ. N.C., Chapel Hill, 1985-86; pvt. practice Birmingham, Ala., 1986-90; pres. Employers Drug Program Mgmt., Inc., Birmingham, 1990—; med. dir. Am. Health Svcs., Inc., 1993—2007. Med. dir. Bradford Facilities, Birmingham, 1987-90, New Life Clinic, Bessemer, Ala., Physicians Smoke Free Clinic, Birmingham, 1988-90, Am. Health Svcs., Inc., 1993-2008; chmn. dept. family practice and emergency medicine Bessemer Carraway Med. Ctr., 1993-95. Mem. tennis anti-doping appeals com. ATP Tour, Inc., 1997; bd. dirs. Ala. Vets. Meml. Found. With U.S. Army, 1969-72, Vietnam. Decorated Bronze Star, Vietnam Campaign medal, Vietnam Svc. medal 3 Stars; Named Small Bus. Person of Yr., Birmingham Regional C. of C., 2007. Fellow Am. Acad. Family Physicians; mem. Am. Soc. Addiction Medicine (cert.), Am. Assn. Med. Rev. Officers (cert.), Med. Assn. State of Ala., Phi Kappa Phi. Methodist. Avocations: flying, tennis, golf. Home: 868 Tulip Poplar Dr Birmingham AL 35244-1633 Office: Howard M Strickler Md 505 20th St N Ste 1200 Birmingham AL 35203-4610 Home Phone: 205-985-9928; Office Phone: 205-326-3100. Business E-Mail: drs@edpm.com.

STRINGER, JOHNNY WILLIAM, state legislator; b. Bay Springs, Miss., Feb. 1, 1950; m. Joan B. Weir; children: John, John Robert. Mem. Dist. 87 Miss. House of Reps., 1980—; farmer. Mem.: SAR, Jasper County Econ. Devel. Assn., Farm Bur., Charolais Cattle Assn. Democrat. Baptist. Mailing: HCR64 PO Box 39 Montrose MS 39338 Office: Dist Off 167 CR 2349 Montrose MS 39338 Home Phone: 610-739-3663; Office Phone: 601-359-3340. Business E-Mail: jstringer@house.ms.gov.

STRINGER, TOMMY, state legislator; b. Greer, SC, July 1, 1966; s. L.W. "Duck" and Joyce Price Springer; m. Carrie Cureton, Nov. 16, 1993; children: Rupert Winford Max(dec.), Thomas Hugh Montgomery. BS, Bob Jones U., 1989. Deacon First Presbyn. Church, 2005—07; mem. Academic Affairs Com., 2006—07, Fin. Com., 2007—08; trustee Coastal Carolina U., 2006—08, bd. sec., 2007—08; chmn. Audit Com., 2007—08; pension cons./businessman; mem. Dist. 18 SC House of Reps., 2008—. Republican. Presbyn. Office: Dist/Home Office 4040 Hwy 414 Landrum SC 29356 also: Capitol Office 312A Blatt Building Columbia SC 29201 Address: PO Box 2078 Greer SC 29652 Office Phone: 864-877-9511, 864-895-9896, 803-212-6881. E-mail: tommystringer@schouse.org.

STRODE, JOSEPH ARLIN, lawyer; b. DeWitt, Ark., Mar. 5, 1946; s. Thomas Joseph and Nora (Richardson) S.; m. Carolyn Taylor, Feb. 9, 1969; children: Tanya Briana, William Joseph. BSEE with honors, U. Ark., 1969; JD, So. Meth. U., 1972. Bar: Ark. 1972. Design engr. Tex. Instruments Inc., Dallas, 1969-70; patent agent Tex. Instruments, Dallas, 1970—72; assoc. Bridges, Young, Matthews, Drake, Pine Bluff, Ark., 1972-74, ptnr., 1975—. Chmn. Pine Bluff Airport Commn., 1993; bd. dirs. United Way Jefferson County, Pine Bluff, 1975-77, campaign chmn., 1983, pres., 1986, exec. com., 1983-87; bd. dirs. Leadership Pine Bluff, 1983-85. Mem. Ark. Bar Assn., Jefferson County Bar Assn. (pres. 1995), Pine Bluff C. of C. (dir. 1981, 84, 94, 97), Ark. Wildlife Fed. (dir. 1979-81), Jefferson County Wildlife Assn. (dir. 1973-80, pres. 1974-76), Kiwanis (lt. gov. Mo.-Ark. divsn. 1983-84, chmn. lt. govs. 1983-84), Order of Coif, Tau Beta Pi, Eta Kappa Nu. Home: 7600 Jay Lynn Ln Pine Bluff AR 71603-9387 Office: 315 E 8th Ave Pine Bluff AR 71601-5005 Office Phone: 870-534-5532. Business E-Mail: joestrode@bridgesplc.com.*

STROM, J. PRESTON, JR., lawyer; b. May 21, 1959; s. Grace and J.P. Sr. S.; m. Donna Savoca, Oct. 5, 1985; children: Margaret, Caroline. BA, U. S.C., 1981, JD, 1984; Program for sr.exec., Harvard U., Cambridge, 1995. Bar: S.C. 1984, U.S. Dist. Ct. S.C., 1986, U.S. Ct. Appeals (4th cir.) 1986. Law clerk to Hon. Frank Eppes 13th cir. Judge, 1984—85; asst. solicitor 5th Jud. Cir., S.C., 1985-86; ptnr. Leventis, Strom & Wicker, 1986-88, Strom Law Firm, 1988-90, Bolt, Popowski, McCulloch & Strom, 1990-93; acting U.S. atty. Office U.S. Atty., S.C., 1993, U.S. atty. S.C., 1993-96; atty. Strom Law Firm, LLC, Columbia, S.C., 1996—; ptnr. Strom & Young, L.L.P., Columbia, SC. Chmn. Law Enforcement Coord. Com.; juvenile justice and child support enforcement subcom. U.S. Dept. Justice; active Atty. Gen. Adv. Com. Contbg. articals to profl. jour. Chmn. Juvenile Justice and Child Support Enforcement Subcom. (U S Dept. of Justice), 1993, SC Law Enforcement Coordinating Com., 1993. Recipient James Pickett Fellowship in Criminal Justice, 1993—95; named Who's Who in American Law, 1994. Mem. S.C. Bar, S.C. Trial Lawyers Assn., Richland County Bar Assn. (chmn. criminal law sect.), Criminal def. Lawyers Assn., 4th Cir. Judicial Conf. Nat. Assn., former U S attys. Nat. Crime Victim Bar Assn., SC Trial Lawyers Assn.legis. streering Com., 1993-1994, atty. gen. adv. com. U S Dept. of Justice, 1993-1994, pres. Kappa Sigma Fraternity, 1981. Office: Strom Law Firm, LLC Ste A 2110 Beltline Blvd Columbia SC 29204 Office Phone: 888-490-2847. Office Fax: 803-252-4801.

STROM, LELAND A. (LEE STROM), federal agency administrator; b. 1956; m. Twyla Strom; 3 children. A, Kishwaukee Coll., Malta, Ill.; attended, Northern Ill. U. Bd. mem. 1st Farm Credit Svcs., chmn.; mem. adv. coun. on agr., labor, and small bus. Fed. Reserve Bank, Chgo., 2000—06; mem. country mutual fund trust bd. Ill. Farm Bur.; bd. mem. Farm Credit Adminstrn., 2006—, chmn., CEO, 2008—12; bd. dirs. Farm Credit System Ins. Corp. (FCIS), 2006, chmn., 2006—07. Mem. Restructuring Task Force of the Sixth Farm Credit Dist.; bd. mem. Northern F.S., Inc., AgriBank, FCB, Farm Credit Coun. Mem. State Young Farmer Com., 1981—85. Office: Farm Credit Administn 1501 Farm Credit Dr Mc Lean VA 22102-5090*

STROMQUIST, GARY D., corporate financial executive; m. Jeri I. Stromquist. B in Acctg., U. Ky.; MBA, Xavier U. Held various acctg., fin. and mgmt. positions IBM Corp.; prin. acctg. officer Lexmark Internat. Inc., dir., corp. planning, CFO, 1997—98, v.p., fin., consumer printer divsn., 1998—99, v.p., OEM and alliances, consumer printer divsn., 1999—2001, v.p., corp. contr., 2001—09; v.p., corp. fin., v.p., fin., printing solutions and svcs. divsn. Lexmark International, Inc., 2009—. Office: Lexmark International Inc 740 W New Cir Rd Lexington KY 40550 Office Phone: 859-232-2000. Office Fax: 859-232-2403. Business E-Mail: gstromquist@lexmark.com.

STRONACH, NEIL, air transportation executive; BS in Aerospace Engring., Tex. A&M U. Various structural engring., supply chain mgmt., prodn. control, prodn. & engring. positions Am. Airlines, Inc., 1988—98; dir. engring programs Delta Air Lines, Inc., 1998—99, dir. reliability engring., 1999—2000, dir. aircraft base maintenance, 2000—04, v.p. ops. planning, control & reliability divsn., 2004—08, sr. v.p. ops. control, 2008—. Office: Delta Air Lines Inc PO Box 20706 Atlanta GA 30320-6001 Office Phone: 404-715-2600. Office Fax: 404-715-5042. E-mail: neil.stronach@delta.com.

STRONG, CHARLIE (CHARLES R. STRONG), college football coach; b. Batesville, Ark., Aug. 2, 1960; m. Victoria Lovallo; children: Hailee, Hope. BEd, U. Ctrl. Ark., Conway, 1982; M in Phys. Edn., Henderson State U., Arkadelphia, Ark., 1983; M & Ednl. Specialists Degree in Curriculum & Instrn., U. Fla., Gainesville, 1985. Grad. asst. U. Fla. Gators, Gainesville, 1983—84, outside linebackers coach, 1988—89, asst. head football coach, defensive tackles coach, 1994, defensive coord., 2003—09, defensive ends coach, 2003—04, interim head football coach, 2004, asst. head football coach, 2005—07, linebackers coach, 2005—09, assoc. head football coach, 2008—09; grad. asst. Tex. A&M U. Aggies, College Station, 1985; wide receivers coach Southern Ill. U. Salukis, Carbondale, 1986—87, U. Miss. Rebels, University, 1990; intern New Orleans Saints, 1993, Detroit Lions, 1994; defensive line coach U. Notre Dame Fighting Irish, South Bend, Ind., 1995—98; defensive coord. U. SC Gamecocks, Columbia, 1999—2002; head coach U. Louisville Cardinals, 2010—13, U. Tex. Longhorns, Austin, 2014—. Named Big East Conf. Coach of Yr., 2010, 2012, Region I Coach of Yr., American Football Coaches Assn., 2012. Achievements include assistant coach for NCAA football Bowl Championship Series National Championship winning University of Florida Gators, 2007, 2009. Office: University Texas Longhorns PO Box 7399 Austin TX 78713*

STRONG-TIDMAN, VIRGINIA ADELE, marketing professional; b. July 26, 1947; d. Alan Ballentine and Virginia Leona (Harris) Strong; m. John Fletcher Tidman, Sept. 23, 1978 (dec. Aug. 10, 2009). BS, Albright Coll., Reading, Pa., 1969; postgrad., U. Pitts., 1970-73, U. Louisville, 1975-76. Exec. trainee Pomeroy's divsn. Allied Stores, Reading, 1969-70; mktg. rsch. analyst Heinz U.S.A., Pitts., 1970-74; new products mktg. mgr. Ky. Fried Chicken, Louisville, 1974-76; dir. Pitts. office M/A/R/C, 1976-79; assoc. rsch. dir. Henderson Advt., Inc., Greenville, SC, 1979-81; sr. v.p., dir. rsch. Bozell, Jacobs, Kenyon & Eckhardt, Inc., Dallas, 1981-86, sr. v.p., dir. rsch. and strategic planning Atlanta, 1986-88; sr. v.p., dir. mktg. svcs. Bozell, Inc., Atlanta, 1988-91; sr. v.p., mng. ptnr. Henderson Adv., Inc., 1991-95; prin. Ender-Ptnr., Inc., 1995-96; v.p. mktg. Booth Rsch. Svcs., Inc., 1996-98; COO Moore & Symons, Inc., 1998—2009; ret., 2009. Cons. mktg. rsch. Greenville Zool. Soc., 1981; adj. prof. So. Meth. U., 1984-85. Mem. Oconee Hospice Foothills (bd. mem. 2012-, advocates quality devel. bd. mem., 2009-, Effie award N.Y. chpt. 1982). Republican. Episcopalian. Home: 146 Northshores Dr Seneca SC 29672

STROTHMAN, JAMES EDWARD, editor-in-chief; b. Pitts., Mar. 27, 1939; s. Edward Charles and Harriet Hope (Jones) S.; m. Eleanor Shawfield Jacobs, Sept. 9, 1961 (dec. Nov. 8, 2005); children—Joseph, Jill, Stuart. BA in Journalism, Pa. State U., University Park, 1961. Asst. city editor, city hall reporter Williamsport Grit, Pa., 1961-64; with Miami Herald, Fla., 1964-67; aerospace writer AP, Cape Kennedy, Fla., 1967-69; reporter Los Angeles bur. Electronic News, 1969-71, sr. editor computer news sect., 1971-73, mng. editor, 1973; sr. info. rep. corp. hdqrs., then program adminstr. data processing divsn. hdqrs. IBM Corp., 1973-77, mgr. ea. area comm. data processing divsn., 1977-79, field comm. mgr. data processing divsn., 1979-81, mgr. comm. rsch. divsn., 1981; free-lance writer and cons. Strothman Assocs., 1981-82; editor-in-chief MIS Week, NYC, 1982-88; free-lance writer, cons., 1988-89; editor-in-chief Computer Pictures, Chappaqua, NY, 1989-94; news editor InTech Mag. and ISA On Line Instrument Soc. Am. (ISA), Research Triangle Park, NC, 1994-2000. Online editor, eCommerce Bus. Mag., 2000-01; assoc. editor InTech Mag., 2001-02; freelance writer, mktg. comm. cons., 2003—. Presbyterian.

STROUD, JOHN FRED, JR., judge; b. Hope, Ark., Oct. 3, 1931; s. John Fred and Clarine (Steel) S.; m. Marietta Kimball, June 1, 1958; children: John Fred III, Ann Kimball, Tracy Steel. Student, Hendrix Coll., Conway, Ark., 1949-51; BA, U. Ark., 1959, LLB, 1960. Bar: Ark. 1959, Tex. 1988, US Supreme Ct. 1963, cert.: Ark. (mediator). Ptnr. Stroud & McClerkin, 1959-62; city atty. City of Texarkana, Ark., 1961; legis. asst. to US Senator John L. McClellan, 1962-63; ptnr. Smith, Stroud, McClerkin, Dunn & Nutter, 1963-79, 81-95; assoc. justice Ark. Supreme Ct., Little Rock, 1980; judge Ark. Ct. Appeals, Little Rock, 1996—2001, chief judge, 2001—04. Chmn. Texarkana Airport Authority, 1966-67, Texarkana United Way Campaign, 1988; pres. Caddo area coun. Boy Scouts Am., 1971-73; former trustee Ark. Nature Conservancy; former bd. dirs. Ark. Cmty. Found.; mem. adv. bd. Donald W. Reyonds Inst. On Aging, bd. United Meth. found. of Ark.; former pres. Red River Valley Assn.; former commr. Red River Compact Commn.; past vice chmn. Ark. Water Code Study Commn.; chmn. bd., chmn. coun. ministries Meth. Ch. Lt. col. USAF, 1951-56, Res. ret. Recipient award of exceptional accomplishment Ark. State C. of C., 1972, 86, Silver Beaver and Disting. Eagle awards Boy Scouts Am., Joint Presdl. award of excellence Ark. Bar Assn. and Ark. Bar Found., 2007; named Outstanding Young Man of Texarkana, 1966, One of Five Outstanding Young Men of Ark., 1967, Outstanding Alumnus of U. Ark. Law Sch., 1980. Fellow Am. Bar Found. (chmn. Ark. chpt.); mem. ABA, Ark. Bar Assn. (chmn. exec. coun. 1979-80, pres. 1987-88, C.E. Ransick award of excellence 1990-91, Presdl. award of excellence and Charles L. Carpenter Meml. award 1997-98, Golden Gavel award 2006), Four States Area Estate Planning Coun. (past chmn.), State Bar Tex., Miller County Bar Assn. (past pres.), Texarkana Bar Assn. (pres. 1982-83), Ark. Bar Found. (chmn. 1974-75, chmn. trust com. 2003-06), Am. Coll. Trust and Estate Counsel (chmn. Ark. chpt. 1986-91), S.W. Ark. Bar Assn., N.E. Tex. Bar Assn., Assn. Atty.-Mediators, Texarkana C. of C. (pres. 1969, C.E. Palmer award 1979), U. Ark. Law Alumni Soc. (bd. dirs.), Texarkana

Country Club (pres. 1990-92), Rotary (pres. Texarkana 1965-66) Avocations: tennis, golf, hunting, fishing. Office: 405 Walnut Texarkana AR 71854 Office Phone: 870-772-0718. Personal E-mail: jstroudadr@yahoo.com.

STROUD, ROBERT EDWARD, lawyer; b. Chester, SC, July 24, 1934; s. Coy Franklin and Leila (Caldwell) S.; m. Katherine C. Stroud, Apr. 8, 1961; children: Robert Gordon, Margaret Lathan. AB, Washington and Lee U., 1956, LLB, 1958. Bar: Va. 1959, U.S. Ct. Appeals (4th cir.) 1967, U.S. Tax Ct. 1959. Assoc. McGuire Woods, LLP, Charlottesville, Va., 1959-64; ptnr. McGuire Woods, LLP, Charlottesville, Va., 1964—2002, exec. com., 1978-89. Lectr. math. Washington and Lee U., Lexington, Va., 1957-59; lectr. bus. tax Grad. Bus. Sch., U. Va., Charlottesville, 1969-87, lectr. corp. taxation Law Sch., U. Va., Charlottesville, Va. 1985-91; lectr. to legal edn. insts., lectr. in corp. law Washington and Lee Law Sch., Lexington Va., 1984. Co-author: Buying, Selling and Merging Businesses, 1975; editor-in-chief Washington and Lee Law Rev., 1959; editor: Advising Small Business Clients, Vol. 1, 1978, 4th edit., 1994, Vol. 2, 1980, 3d edit., 1990; contbr. articles to profl. jours. Pres. Charlottesville Housing Found., 1968-73; mem. mgmt. coun. Montreat Conf. Ct., NC, 1974-77; trustee Presbyn. Found., 1972-73, Union Theol. Sem., Va., 1983-91; bd. dirs. Presbyn. Outlook Found., 1968-02, pres., 1985-88; mem. governing coun. Presbyn. Synod of the Virginias, 1973-78, moderator of coun., 1977-78, moderator of Synod, 1977-78; trustee, v.p. Va. Tax Found., 1984-95; adv. bd. Westminster Orgn. Concert Series, 1989-93; bd. dirs. Shannon Found. for Excellence in Pub. Edn., Charlottesville, 1996—; adv. bd. Ashlawn-Highland Summer Festival, 1989-03, pres., 1994-00; bd. dirs. Ash Lawn Opera Festival Found., 2003-05, gov. coun. Presbyn. Presbytery of the James, 1993-96, moderator of coun., 1995-96; moderator of presbytery, 1997; dir. Nat. Soc. Arts and Letters, Va. and NC chpt., 2005-08, treas., 2006-08. Capt. inf. US Army, 1958, with res. 1958-70. Recipient Outstanding Law Alumnus award, Lee Law Sch., 2008. Fellow Am. Bar Found., Va. Law Found.; mem. ABA, Am. Judicature Soc., Va. State Bar, Va. Bar Assn., Washington and Lee Law Sch. Assn. (Lexington, Va.) (governing coun. 1974-80, pres. 1979-80), Order of the Coif (hon.), Phi Delta Sigma, Omicron Delta Kappa, Phi Delta Phi. Democrat. Home: 345 Terrell Ct Charlottesville VA 22901-2171 Office: McGuire Woods LLP PO Box 1288 Charlottesville VA 22902-1288 E-mail: rstroud@mcguirewoodseueritus.com.

STROUSTRUP, BJARNE, computer science and engineering professor; b. Aarhus, Denmark, 1950; m. Marian Stroustrup; children: Annemarie, Nicholas. Grad., U. Aarhus, 1975; PhD in Computer Sci., Cambridge U., 1979. Joined Computer Sci. Rsch. Ctr., Bell Telephone Labs., Murray Hill, NJ, 1979; mem. AT&T Bell Labs. Rsch., head Large-Scale Programming Rsch. Dept., mem. Info. and Sys. Software Rsch. Lab., AT&T Bell Labs. fellow, 1993—96, AT&T fellow, 1996—; prof. computer sci., chmn. coll. engring., mem. Parasol group in the computer sci. dept. Tex. A&M U., College Station, Tex., 2002—, disting. prof., 2010—. Author: The C++ Programming Language, 1985, 1991, 1997, 2000; contbr. articles to profl. jours. Recipient ACM Grace Murray Hopper award, 1993; named one of Am.'s twelve top young scientists, Fortune Mag., 1990. Fellow: IEEE (Computer Entrepreneur Award 2004), Assn. Computing Machinery, Computer Hall of Fame; mem.: NAE, Tex. Acad. of Medicine, Engring. and Sci., Sigma Xi (William Procter Prize for Scientific Achievement 2005). Achievements include designer and original implementer of C++ programming language. Avocations: hiking, running, music, travel. Office: Tex A&M U Dept Computer Sci TAMU 3112 College Station TX 77843-3112 also: AT&T Rsch 180 Park Ave Florham Park NJ 07932-0971 E-mail: bs@cs.tamu.edu.

STRUBBE, THOMAS R., insurance industry executive; b. Ft. Wayne, Ind., Mar. 30, 1940; s. Rudolph C. and Maverne E. (Wagoner) S.; children: Tracy Lynn, Patrick Thomas, Christina Lee. BS, Ind. U., 1962; JD, Tulane U., 1965. Bar: Ind. 1965, Ill. 1969. Atty. Lincoln Nat. Life Ins. Co., Ft. Wayne, Ind., 1965-66, asst. counsel, 1967-68; with Washington Nat. Corp., Evanston, Ill., 1968-90, counsel, 1968-73, gen. counsel, 1973-79, corp. sec., 1970-84, v.p., 1975-79, sr. v.p., 1979-83, exec. v.p., 1983-84, pres., 1984-90, also bd. dirs., mem. exec. com.; pres., CEO Osborn Labs. Inc., Olathe, Kans., 1990-98, Guarantee Res. Life Ins. Co., Chgo., 1998-99, also bd. dirs., ret., 2000. V.p., bd. dirs., exec. com. Chgo. chpt. Epilepsy Found. Am., 1975—79; trustee Glencoe Union Ch., Ill., 1984—87; Stephen leader Trinity Luth. Ch., Kans., 2003—08; bd. dirs. Assn. Retarded Citizens Ill., 1985—89, Northlight Theater, 1984—89. Lt. USNR, 1965—71. Lincoln Found. grantee, 1964. Mem. ABA, Assn. Life Ins. Counsel, Nat. Investor Rels. Inst., Am. Soc. Corp. Secs., Home Office Life Underwriters Assn., Ind. Bar Assn., Ill. Bar Assn., Skokie Country Club (Ill.), Shadow Glen Golf Club (Kans.), Hallbrook Country Club (Kans.), Hideaway Beach Club (Fla.), Rotary, VFW, Lambda Chi Alpha, Delta Sigma Pi. Home (Summer): 9210 Oak Valley Dr De Soto KS 66018-7994 Home (Winter): 6000 Royal Marco Way Unit 350 Marco Island FL 34145 Personal E-mail: tomstrubbe@yahoo.com.

STRUELENS, MICHEL MAURICE JOSEPH GEORGES, political science professor, consultant; b. Brussels, Mar. 10, 1928; m. Godelieve De Wilde, Aug. 2, 1949; children: Alain, Patricia, Brigitte, Bernard, Jean Paul (dec.). BA, Coll. St. Pierre, Brussels, 1944; MA, Antwerp U., Belgium, 1949; PhD, Am. U., Washington, 1968. Insp. econ. affairs Congo Govt., Leopoldville, 1950-54, chief insp. econ. affairs, 1954-55, dep. commr. transp., 1955-57; dir. Info. and Public Relations Office for Congo, Brussels, 1957-58, Congo Tourism Pavillion, Internat. World's Fair, Brussels, 1958-59; dir. gen. Belgian Congo and Ruanda Urundi Tourist Office, Congo, 1959; chmn. African Commn. Internat. Union Ofcl. Travel Orgns., Geneva, 1959-60; ofcl. Katanga rep. in U.S., NYC, 1960-63; dir. gen. Internat. Inst. for African Affairs in Can., 1963-64; spl. asst. to prime minister Democratic Republic Congo, fgn. affairs minister, adviser to Congo UN del., adviser Congo embassy Washington, NYC, 1964-66; dir. Eurafrica, Consultants on Fgn. Affairs, Washington, 1966—; prof. polit. sci., French, internat. bus. Am. U., 1968-93; prof. emeritus, 1993; dir. Ctr. Rsch and Documentation on European Community Am. U., 1971—, chmn. faculty rels. com., 1986-87, chmn. grad. studies com., SIS, 1989-90; dir. E.C. Inst. in Europe, 1978-93, U. Antwerp Exchange Program, 1979-83. Dir. EPSCI/ESSEC (France) Exchange Program, 1980-84, chmn. internat. bus. dept., 1980-84; dir. exchange program Bus. Sch. of Poly., U. Madrid, 1981-84; investment adviser, 1977—; adminstr. French Parish,, 1974-75, Ctr. Studies on Internat. Relations, 1987-96, Econs. and Bus., La Rochelle, France, 1987-96; exec. v.p. Eglise St. Louis Corp., French-Speaking Union, Washington, 1974-75; mgr. by agreement with European Communities, European Documentation Ctr. (CERDEC), accessing by satellite EC Data Banks, 1985— and providing through WCL Libr. of Am. U., On Line Pub. Access Cataloging, 1991—. Author: (with Inforcongo) Congo Belge et Ruanda-Urundi, 1958; monograph Le Canada à l'Heure de l'Afrique, 1964; The United Nations in the Congo - or ONUC and International Politics, 1976. Recipient Internat. Union Ofcl. Travel Orgns. Poster award Brussels, 1958, Etoile de Service en Argent King of Belgium, 1956; chevalier de l'Ordre Royal du Lion, 1957; Faculty award for outstanding contbn. to acad. program devel. Coll. Bus. Adminstrn., Am. U., 1979; Faculty award for outstanding teaching, 1980, 82, 84; Faculty award for outstanding service to Am. U., 1981 Mem. Golden Key, Phi Sigma Alpha. Clubs: Cosmos (Washington) (Emeritus nominee); Bukavu Royal Sports (founder 1950, pres. 1951-54, hon. pres. 1957) (Congo). Lodges: Rotary. Home: 1374 Woodside Dr Mc Lean VA 22102-1536 Office: Am U 4400 Mass Ave NW Washington DC 20016-8071

STRUNK, ORLO CHRISTOPHER, JR., psychology professor; b. Pen Argyl, Pa., Apr. 14, 1925; s. Orlo Christopher and Katherine Elizabeth (Glasser) S.; m. Mary Louise Reynolds, July 3, 1947; children: Laura Louise, John Christopher. Certificate, Churchman Bus. Coll., Easton, Pa., 1948; AB, W. Va. Wesleyan Coll., Buckhannon, 1953; S.T.B., Boston U., 1955, PhD, 1957. Exec. sec. Inst. Pastoral Care, Mass. Gen. Hosp., 1955-57; grad. asst. Boston U., 1955-57, instr. psychology of religion, 1956; instr. Boston U. (Sch. Theology), 1957-58, 62; assoc. prof. psychology W. Va. Wesleyan Coll., 1957-60, dean, prof. psychology, 1959-69; prof. psychology of religion Boston U., 1969-86; also faculty counselor, supr. Albert V. Danielsen Inst. Part-time faculty Webster U., 1994—; pastoral psychotherapist The Coastal Samaritan Ctr., Myrtle Beach, S.C., 1986—2003; assoc. dir., staff psychologist Ecumenical Counseling Svc., Inc., Melrose, Mass.; rsch. cons. Religion in Edn. Found., Calif. Author: Readings in the Psychology of Religion, 1959, Religion: A Psychological Interpretaton, 1962, Mature Religion: A Psychological Study, 1965, The Choice Called Atheism, 1969, The Psychology of Religion, 1971, Dynamic Interpersonalism for Ministry, 1973, The Secret Self, 1976, Privacy: Experience, Understanding, Expression, 1983, three-Two Count, 2005, An Ever-Fixed Mark, 2007, Satan's Angels, 2009, The Geriatric Murders, 2010, The Forerun Winter, 2010, The Intelligentia Connection, 2011; mng. editor: Jour. Pastoral Care and Counseling, 1979-2007, mng. editor emeritus, 2009. Served with USAAF, 1943-46. Decorated Air medal with five oak leaf clusters. Fellow Am. Psychol. Assn.; mem. W.Va. Assn. Acad. Deans (pres.) Methodist (elder). Home: 1068 Harbor Dr SW Calabash NC 28467-2300 Office Phone: 910-579-5084. Personal E-mail: glass@atmc.net.

STRUSZ, DANIEL A., insurance company executive; BS in Acctg., Winona State U., Minn., 1981. Various mgmt. positions Allianz Life Ins. Co., Nat. Benefits Resources, Inc., Fortis Benefits Ins. Co.; underwriting supr. Paul Burke & Assocs.; Northwest region underwriting mgr. HCC Benefits Corp., Mpls., 2001—03, v.p. Midwest region Plymouth, Minn., 2003—08; exec. v.p. HCC Life Insurance Co., 2008—. Office: HCC Life Insurance Co Corp Hdqs 225 Townpark Dr NW Ste 350 Kennesaw GA 30144-3710 Office Phone: 770-973-9851. Office Fax: 770-973-9854. Business E-Mail: dstrusz@hcclife.com.

STRYKER, SHELDON, sociologist, educator; b. St. Paul, May 26, 1924; s. Max and Rose (Moskevitz) S.; m. Alyce Shirley Agranoff, Sept. 7, 1947 (dec. Aug. 4, 2009); children: Robin Sue, Jeffrey, David, Michael, Mark. BA summa cum laude, U. Minn., 1948, MA, 1950, PhD, 1955. Mem. faculty Ind. U., 1951—, prof. sociology, 1964—, disting. prof. sociology, 1985—2002, disting. prof. emeritus, 2002—; dir. Inst. Social Rsch., 1965—70, 1989—94, chmn. dept. sociology, 1969—75; co-dir. Ctr. Social Rsch., 1989—94. Cons. in field; mem. social scis. research rev. com. NIMH, 1974-79, chmn., 1976-79, mem. research scientist devel. award com., 1981-85 Editor: Rose Monograph Series of Am. Sociol. Assn., 1971-73, Am. Sociol. Rev., 1982-85, Sociometry, 1967-69; assoc. editor: Social Problems, 1957-59; author books, monographs, articles, chpts. in books. Served with AUS, 1943-46. Fellow Social Sci. Research Council, 1959-60, Ctr. Advanced Behavioral Scis., 1986-87; Fulbright research scholar Italy, 1966-67. Mem. Am. Sociol. Assn. (nat. coun. 1965-67, 80-81, chmn. social psychology sect. 1978-79, chmn. publs. com. 1991-93, Cooley-Mead award 1986, WE DeBois award 2009), Soc. Study Symbolic Interaction (George Herbert Mead award 2000), Ohio Valley Sociol. Soc. (coun. 1965-67), North Ctrl. Sociol. Assn. (pres. 1978-79), Sociol. Rsch. Assn. (coun. 1978-84, pres. 1983-84), Phi Beta Kappa, Internat. Soc. Self and Identity (Lifetime Career award, 2006). Office: Sheldon Stryker Dept Sociology Ind University Bloomington IN 47405 Home (Winter): 3319 Highlands Bridge Rd Sarasota FL 34235

STRYKER, STEVEN CHARLES, lawyer; b. Omaha, Oct. 26, 1944; s. James M. and Jean G. (Grannis) S.; m. Gina; children: Ryan, Kevin, Gerrit, Courtney. BS, U. Iowa, 1967, JD with distinction, 1969; postgrad. studies, Northwestern U. Grad. Sch. Bus, 1969-70, DePaul U., 1971. Bar: Iowa 1969, Tex. 1986; CPA Ill., Iowa. Sr. tax acct. Arthur Young & Co., Chgo., 1969-72; fed. tax mgr. Massey Ferguson, Des Moines, 1972-74; fed., state tax mgr. FMC Corp., Chgo., 1974-78; gen. tax atty. Shell Oil Co., Houston, 1978-81, asst. gen. tax counsel, 1981-83, gen. mgr., 1983-86, v.p., gen. tax counsel, 1986—2000; pvt. practice Houston, 2000—. Mem. ABA, Tex. Bar Assn., Tax Execs. Inst. Home and Office: 2117 Del Monte Houston TX 77019

STUART, CHARLES EDWARD, electrical engineer, oceanographer; b. Durham, NC, Feb. 9, 1942; s. Charles Edward and Wilma Kelly Stuart; m. Margaret Ann Robinson, Jan. 9, 1982; children: Marjorie Kelly, Heather Alison BSEE, Duke U., 1963; degree in Bus. and Mktg., Alexander Hamilton Inst., NY, 1969. Engr. Westinghouse Electric Corp., Balt., 1963—65; sr. engr. Booz Allen Hamilton, Bethesda, Md., 1966—68; rsch. dir. B-K Dynamics Inc., Huntsville, Ala., 1969—78; oceanographer Office of Naval Rsch., Arlington, Va., 1979—84; dir. Maritime Sys. Tech. Office Advanced Rsch. Projects Agy., Arlington, 1985—98; with Def. Programs US Dept. Energy, Washington, 1998—99; pres. Competitive Enterprise Solutions, LLC, Arlington, Va., 2000—04, Slidell, Va., 2005—. Contbr. articles to profl. jours. Recipient Am. Def. Preparedness Assn. Bushnell award career contbns. undersea warfare, 1996 Mem. (life) IEEE (sr., ad. com. 1991-93), Assn. Unmanned Vehicle Systems (trustee 1989-93), Nat. Def. Indsl. Assn., Yatch Club (Washington), Capital Yatch Club Methodist. Achievements include rsch. in antisubmarine warfare, cybersecurity and unmanned undersea vehicle technology. Office: Competitive Enterprise Solutions LLC 55 Inlet Dr Slidell LA 70458 Office Phone: 985-290-9261. Business E-Mail: cstuart@cesllc.com.

STUART, DABNEY, poet, language educator; b. Richmond, Va., Nov. 4, 1937; s. Walker Dabney Jr. and Martha (vonSchilling) S.; m. Sandra Westcott, Jan. 20, 1983; children: Martha, Nathan vonSchilling, Darren Wynne. AB, Davidson Coll., 1960; AM, Harvard U., 1962. Instr. Coll. William and Mary, Williamsburg, Va., 1961-65; prof. English Washington and Lee U., Lexington, Va., 1965—2002, S. Blount Mason Jr. prof. English, 1991—2002. Vis. prof. Middlebury (Vt.) Coll., 1968-69, Ohio U., Athens, 1975, U. Va., Charlottesville, 1981-83. Author: The Diving Bell, 1966, A Particular Place, 1969, The Other Hand, 1974, Friends of Yours, Friends of Mine, 1974, Round and Round, 1976, Nabokov: The Dimensions of Parody, 1978, Rockbridge Poems, 1981, Common Ground, 1982, Don't Look Back, 1987, Narcissus Dreaming, 1990, Sweet Lucy Wine, 1992, Light Years: New and Selected Poems, 1994, Second Sight: Poems for Paintings by Carroll Cloar, 1996, Long Gone, 1996, The Way to Cobbs Creek, 1997, Settlers, 1999, Strains of the Old Man, 1999, No Visible Means of Support, 2001, The Man Who Loves Cezanne, 2003, Family Preserve, 2005, Tables, 2009, Open the Gates, 2010, Greenbrier Forest, 2012, Time's Body: New & Selected Poems, 1994-2014. Recipient Dylan Thomas prize Poetry Soc. Am., 1965, Gov.'s award State of Va., 1979; NEA lit. fellow, 1975, 82, Guggenheim fellow, 1987-88, Individual Artist fellow Va. Commn. for Arts, 1995, resident fellow Rockefeller Study and Conf. Ctr., Bellagio, Italy, 2000, Libr. Va. Poetry award, 2006. Avocations: food, travel, painting. Home: 160 Kendal Dr 1019 Lexington VA 24450-1904

STUART, LYN (JACQUELYN STUART), state supreme court justice; b. Atmore, Ala., Sept. 23, 1955; m. George Stuart; children: Tucker, Shepard, Kelly. BA in Sociology and Edn., Auburn U., 1977; JD, U. Ala., 1980. Asst. atty. gen. State of Ala.; exec. asst. to commr. and spl. asst. atty. gen. Ala. Dept. Corrections; asst. dist. atty. Baldwin County; dist. judge, 1989—97; judge Ala. Cir. Ct., 1997—2001; assoc. justice Ala. Supreme Ct., 2001—. Faculty advisor Nat. Judicial Coll., Reno; former pres. Ala. Council of Juvenile & Family Ct. Judges; pres. Blue Ridge Inst. for Juvenile & Family Ct. Judges, 2002. Former pres. Heritage Junior Women's Club, Bay Minette Kiwanis Club, Jubilee Woman's Club; bd. mem. Ala. Federation of Women's Clubs. Republican. Office: Ala Supreme Ct 300 Dexter Ave Rm 3-215 Montgomery AL 36104-3741 Office Phone: 334-229-0626. Business E-Mail: lstuart@appellate.state.al.us.*

STUART, MICHAEL B., lawyer, former political organization administrator; b. Philippi, W. Va. m. Katrina Pileggi; children: Isabella Grace, Audrey Frances. BA, BSBA, Univ. W. Va.; JD, Boston Univ., 2000. Bar: W. Va. Acct. Coopers & Lybrand, Pitts., 1995; atty. K&L Gates, Boston, 2000—03, Spilman Thomas & Battle, Charleston, W.Va., 2003—05; mem. Steptoe & Johnson, Charleston, W.Va., 2005—; founder, publ. WVInc. mag, 2005. Bd. dir. Liberty Hydrologic Systems Inc.; vice-chmn. W. Va. Republican Party, chmn., 2010—12. Past mem. adv. bd. W. Va. Small Bus. Develop. Ctr.; mem. econ. develop. & energy com. W. Va State C. of C.; founder, pres., bd. dir. W. Va. Conservative Found. Republican. Office: Steptoe & Johnson PLLC Chase Tower 8th Fl 707 Virginia St E Charleston WV 25301 Office Phone: 304-353-8107. Business E-Mail: mike.stuart@steptoe-johnson.com.

STUART, RICHARD H., state legislator; b. Fredericksburg, Va., Jan. 6, 1964; m. Lisa Stuart; 3 children. BA, Va. Wesleyan Coll.; JD, U. Richmond, 1991. Atty. Westmoreland County Sch. Bd., 2006—; mem. Dist. 28 Va. State Senate, 2008—. Trustee Westmoreland County Vol. Fire Dept., 1999—; mem. bd. of dirs. George Washington Nat. Memorial Found.; bd. chmn. Woodland Acad., 2002—. Republican. Office: PO Box 1146 Montross VA 22520 Home: Senate of Virginia PO Box 396 Richmond VA 23218 Office Phone: 804-493-8892, 804-698-7528. Office Fax: 804-493-8897, 804-698-7651. E-mail: district28@senate.virginia.gov.

STUART, ROBERT, container manufacturing executive; b. Oak Park, Ill., Aug. 3, 1921; s. Robert S. and Marie (Vavra) Solinsky; m. Lillian C. Kondelik, Dec. 5, 1962 (dec. May 1978); m. Lila Winterhoff Peters, May 21, 1982, (dec., Dec. 07). BS, U. Ill., Chgo., 1943, LLD, 1982. Sec.-treas., gen. mgr. Warren Metal Decorating Co., 1947-49; asst. to gen. mgr. Cans, Inc., 1950-52; asst. to v.p., then v.p. Nat. Can Corp., Chgo., 1953-59, exec. v.p., 1959-63, pres., 1963-69, chief exec., 1966-69, chmn. bd., CEO, 1969-73, chmn. bd., 1973-83, chmn. fin. com., 1983, mem. corp. devel. com., until 1986, chmn. emeritus, 1986—. Past pres., bd. dirs. Corp. Responsibility Group of Greater Chgo. Past pres., bd. dirs. Chgo. Crime Commn.; past dir. Nat. Crime Prevention Coun.; founding chmn. Nat. Minority Supplier Devel. Coun., 1972-73, Lloyd Morey Scholarship Fund: Freedoms Found. at Valley Forge, past trustee; past mem. adv. bd. Salvation Army, Broader Urban Involvement and Leadership Devel.; chmn. emeritus World Federalist Assn.; past bd. dirs., past moderator Millard Congl. Ch.; past pres. Ctrl. Ch. Chgo.; chmn. emeritus Assn. to Unite the Democracies. Capt. AUS, 1943-46. Mem.: Seventh-day Adventists Ch. (Cape Coral, Fla.), Cape Coral Gold Coast Rotary Club, Rotary (past pres. Chgo. club, past dist. gov.), Yacht Club, Chgo. Club, Little Ship Club (London), Masons (32d degree, Red Cross of Constantine), Alpha Kappa Lambda (past nat. pres.). Home and Office: 233 SW 43d Ter Cape Coral FL 33914

STUART, ROBERT KENNETH, internist, hematologist, oncologist, educator; b. Baton Rouge, July 6, 1948; s. Walter Bynum and Rita Bess (Kleinpeter) S.; m. Gail Elaine Wiscarz, June 12, 1971 (div. Dec. 1988); children: R. Morgan, Elaine C.; m. F. Charlene Gates, Nov. 2, 1991. BS, Georgetown U., 1970; MD, Johns Hopkins U., Balt., 1974. Diplomate Am. Bd. Internal Medicine. Resident in medicine Johns Hopkins Hosp., Balt., 1974-76, oncology fellow Oncology Ctr., 1976-78; rsch. fellow Sloan-Kettering Inst., NYC, 1978-79; asst. prof. Johns Hopkins U., Balt., 1979-84, assoc. prof., 1984-85; prof. medicine Med. U. S.C., Charleston, 1985—; assoc. dir. Hollings Cancer Ctr., Charleston, 1993-97; chmn. dept. oncology King Faisal Specialist Hosp and Rsch. Ctr., Riyadh, Saudi Arabia, 1997-2001; prof. medicine Med.U. S.C., Charleston, 2001—. Bd. dirs. Aplastic Anemia Found., Balt., 1982-93, med. adv. bd., 1993-98; mem. nat. team Tour of Hope, 2004. Recipient Champions Advocacy award, Am. Soc. Hematology, 2004, Partners in Progress award, Leukemia and Lymphoma Soc., 2004, Physician Healthcare Hero award, Charleston Regional Bus. Jour., 2007, Disting. Faculty Svc. award, Med. U. SC, 2012; named one of Best Dr. Am., 2007—. Democrat. Roman Catholic. Office: Medical Univ of South Carolina 171 Ashley Ave Charleston SC 29425-0100 Office Phone: 843-792-9300. E-mail: stuartrk@musc.edu.

STUART, WALTER BYNUM, III, retired banker; b. Baton Rouge, Oct. 5, 1922; s. Walter Bynum and Rosa (Gauthreaux) S.; m. Rita Kleinpeter, May 20, 1944; children: Walter Bynum IV, Robert, Douglas, Ronald, Scott. BS, La. State U., 1943. Adminstrv. mgr. Kaiser Aluminum & Chem. Corp., 1946-63; v.p. First Nat. Bank Commerce, New Orleans, 1963-65, sr. v.p., 1965, exec. v.p., 1965-73; vice chmn. bd., dir. 1st Nat. Bank Commerce, New Orleans, 1973-78; exec. v.p. 1st Commerce Corp., New Orleans, 1972-73, pres., 1973-75, vice-chmn. bd., 1975-78, dir., 1973-78; pres. Am. Bank & Trust Co., Lafayette, La., 1978-86, cons., ret., 1986. Assoc. dir., mem. faculty Sch. Banking La. State U., 1973-75, dir., 1975-78; mem. Faculty Assemblies for Bank Dirs. Campaign group chmn. industry com., mem. United Fund for Greater New Orleans Area, 1974; mem. research com. Pub. Affairs Research Council La., 1973-76, v.p., trustee, 1973-76; bd. dirs. Bur. Govtl. Research, 1973-77, Council Better La., 1975—; pres. New Orleans Indsl. Devel. Bd., 1973-75. Served to lt. (j.g.) USNR, 1943-46. Mem. C. of C. of Greater New Orleans Area (v.p. 1973-75, bd. dirs.), Am. Bankers Assn., La. Bankers Assn. (pres. 1977), Am. Mgmt. Assn., Kappa Alpha, Delta Sigma Pi, Beta Gamma Sigma. Democrat. Roman Catholic. Home: 10100 Hillview Dr Apt 2109 Pensacola FL 32514-5481

STUBBLEFIELD, GARY, state legislator; m. Kathi Stubblefield. Mem. Br. Bapt. Ch., County Line Sch. Bd., Dairy Farmer, Franklin County Quorum Ct., Milk Adv. Com.; mem. Dist. 67 Ark. House of Representatives, 2011—. Republican. Office: 2542 Skeets Rd Branch AR 72928 Office Phone: 479-635-4314. Business E-Mail: gary.stubblefield@arkansashouse.org.

STUBBS, CHARLES J., internet company executive; B, Cornell U.; MBA, Vanderbilt U. Pres. BellSouth IntelliVentures Co.; exec. v.p. InfoSpace Inc.; with Intelligent Media Ventures LLC, 1996; pres.,

CEO YellowPages.com LLC, 2004—08; pres., CEO, bd. dirs. PRIMEDIA, Inc., 2008—. Office: PRIMEDIA Inc 3585 Engineering Dr Ste 100 Norcross GA 30092 Office Phone: 678-421-3000. Business E-Mail: CStubbs@primedia.com.

STUBBS, DACE BROWN, beverage manufacturing company executive; b. Louisville; m. William King Stubbs. Bd. dirs. Brown-Forman Corp., 1999—. Non-voting mem. bd. trustees St. Francis Sch., Goshen, Ky., 2010—11; bd. dirs. Indian River IMPACT 100; bd. mem. Treasure Coast Wine Festival, Vero Beach Cmty. Found.; mem. adv. bd. McKee Bot. Garden. Office: Brown-Forman Corp 850 Dixie Hwy Louisville KY 40210 Office Phone: 502-585-1100. Office Fax: 502-774-6633. Business E-Mail: dace_brownstubbs@b-f.com.

STUBBS, GERALD, biochemist, educator; b. Hobart, Australia, May 9, 1947; came to the US, 1976; m. Rebecca Lynn Harris; children: Andrew, Tamsin, Anneliese, Rachel. BSc, Australian Nat. U., 1968; DPhil, U. Oxford, 1972. Sci. asst. Max Planck Inst., Heidelberg, Germany, 1973-76; rsch. assoc. Brandeis U., Waltham, Mass., 1976-83; asst. prof. Vanderbilt U., Nashville, 1983-87, assoc. prof., 1987-90, prof., 1990—. Contbr. articles to profl. jour. Achievements include determination of molecular structure of tobacco mosaic virus. Office Phone: 615-322-2018. Business E-Mail: gerald.stubbs@vanderbilt.edu.

STUBBS, KENDON LEE, retired librarian; b. Washington, Apr. 6, 1938; s. Donald and Rosalee S.; m. Patricia Townsend, June 3, 1961; children: Christopher, Peter, Timothy. BA, St. John's Coll., Annapolis, Md., 1960; MA, U. Va., 1964; MS, Columbia U., 1965. Sr. asst. in manuscripts U. Va. Libr., Charlottesville, 1965, reference libr., 1966-76, acting acquisitions libr., 1967-68, assoc. univ. libr., 1976-87, assoc. univ. libr. for pub. svcs., 1987-92, acting univ. libr., 1993, assoc. univ. libr., 1994-98, dep. univ. libr., 1998—2003, ret., 2003. Cons. US Dept. Edn., Washington, 1982—84. Author: Quantitative Criteria for Academic Research Libraries, 1984; editor: Cumulated Assn. Research Libraries Statistics, 1981, Rsch. Libr. Statistics, 1990, ARL Statistics, 1992-95, Japanese Text Initiative on World Wide Web, 1995-2003; contbr. articles on library stats., rsch. to profl. publs., Internet. Recipient Thomas Jefferson award, U. Va., 1998, Bronze medal, Am. Rhododendron Soc., Mid. Atlantic chpt., 2002, Libr. Assessment Career Achievement award, Assn. Rsch. Librs., 2010, Shoden Cert., Chikushikai Koto Sch., Fukuoka, Japan, 2012. Mem. Assn. of Rsch. Librs. (mem. stats. com., vis. program officer 1995-97), Bibliog. Soc. U. Va. (pres. 1975-78, v.p. 1978-99).

STUBBS, WILLIAM W., interior designer; b. Gonzales, Tex. Attended, Internat. Inst. Design, Washington, DC. Owner, pres., designer William W. Stubbs & Assocs., Houston, 1987—. Author: I Hate Red, You're Fired! The Colorful Life of an Interior Designer, 2004; host (TV series) A Moment of Luxury, 2008—. Recipient Houston Chronicle & Am. Soc. Interior Design award, Prizm award, Great Houston Builders Assn., Golden Nugget - Best in the West award, Champion of Literacy award; named one of 100 World's Top Designers and Architects, Archtl. Digest. Mem.: Internat. Interior Design Assn. (Outstanding Design award). Office: WIlliam W Stubbs & Assocs 1502 Augusta Dr Ste 150 Houston TX 77057-7402 Office Phone: 713-780-7772. Office Fax: 713-977-1151. Business E-Mail: Bill.Stubbs@wwstubbs.com.

STUBER, CHARLES WILLIAM, retired genetics educator, researcher, director; b. St. Michael, Nebr., Sept. 19, 1931; s. Harvey John and Minnie Augusta (Wilks) S.; m. Marilyn Martha Cook, May 28, 1953; 1 child, Charles William Jr. BS, U. Nebr., 1952, MS, 1961; PhD, N.C. State U., 1965. Vet., agrl. instr. Broken Bow HS, 1956-59; rsch. asst. U. Nebr., Lincoln, 1959-61; rsch. geneticist Agrl. Rsch. Svc., USDA, Raleigh, NC, 1962-75, supervisory rsrch. geneticist, rsch. leader, 1975-98, collaborator, 1998—; prof. genetics & crop sci. NC State U., Raleigh, 1975-98, prof. emeritus, 1998—, dir. Ctr. Plant Breeding and Applied Plant Genomics, 2006—. Assoc. editor Crop Sci. Jour., 1979-82, tech. editor, 1984-86, editor, 1987-89; contbr. over 200 articles to profl. jour., chpt. to books. Chmn. coun. on ministries and numerous offices Highland United Meth Ch., Raleigh. Lt. USN, 1952-56. Named Outstanding Sci. of Yr., USDA-ARS, 1989; recipient Genetics and Plant Breeding award Nat. Coun. Comml. Plant Breeders, 1995, Award of Merit, U. Nebr. Alumni Assn., 1997, Outstanding Alumnus award Coll. Agr. & Life Scis., NC State U., 2010, Disting. Alumnus award, 2012, Lifetime Achievement award Nat. Assn. Plant Breeders, 2012; inductee USDA-Agrl. Rsch. Svc. Sci. Hall of Fame, 1999; Vol. 45 of MAYDICA dedicated to Charles W. Stuber, 2000. Fellow: Crop Sci. Soc. Am. (editor-in-chief 1987—91, pres. 1992—93, Crop Sci. Rsch. award 1995, DeKalb Genetics Crop Sci. Disting. Career award 1999), Fellow Am. Soc. Agronomy (pres. 2002); mem.: Am. Genetic Assn. (sec. 1984—86), Genetics Soc. Am., Phi Kappa Phi, Sigma Xi. Avocations: windsurfing, water-skiing. Home: 1800 Manuel St Raleigh NC 27612-5510 Office: NC State University NC Agril Res Svc 4124 A Williams Hall Raleigh NC 27695-7620 Office Phone: 919-515-5834. Office Fax: 919-515-7959. Personal E-mail: cstuber2@aol.com.

STUDER, WILLIAM ALLEN, security consultant, retired military officer; b. Chgo., July 27, 1939; s. William Gotlieb and Annette Elizabeth (Bruzek) S.; m. Donna Barnes Bray, Dec. 26, 1961; children: Scott, Shannon. BS in Indsl. Mgmt., Ga. Tech., 1962; MS in Guidance and Counseling, Troy State U., 1975, MS in Mgmt., 1978; graduate, Air War Coll., Maxwell AFB, Ala., 1981, Air Command and Staff Coll., 1975. Commd. 2d lt. USAF, 1961, advanced through grades to maj. gen., 1989; legis. liaison U.S. Senate, Washington, 1981-83; dir. fighter ops./tng. USAF Hdqrs. Europe, Ramstein AB, Fed. Republic Germany, 1983-84; vice comdr. 10th Tactical Reconnaissance Wing RAF USAF, Alconbury, Eng., 1984-85, comdr. 10th Tactical Reconnaissance Wing RAF, 1985-86, cmdr. 81st Tactical Fighter Wing RAF Bentwaters, Eng., 1986-87, comdr. 316th Air Div/Kaiserslautern Ramstein AB, Fed. Republic Germany, 1987-88, vice comdr. 12th Air Force/U.S. So. Command Bergstrom AFB, Tex., 1988-90, comdr. 13th Air Force Clark AFB, The Philippines, 1990-91; dir. ops. CENTCOM/J-3, MacDill AFB, Fla., 1992-94; ret. USAF, 1994; dir. pub. safety dept. Hillsborough County, Tampa, Fla., 1994—2005, emergency preparedness cons., 2005—; pres. Studer & Assoc., Tampa. Decorated D.S.M., Legion of Merit with oak leaf cluster, DFC with three oak leaf clusters, Bronze Star, Air medal with 35 oak leaf clusters; Legion of Honor, Bronze Cross medal (The Philippines). Mem. Daedalians, Quiet Birdmen, Rotary. Avocations: golf, reading, hiking. Office: Studer & Assoc Tampa FL 33611 Home: 3301 Bayshore Blvd Unit 604 Tampa FL 33629-8842 Office Phone: 813-758-5106. Personal E-mail: williedonnastuder@gmail.com.

STUEWER, SHERRI K., oil industry executive; BS in Engring., Cornell U., 1973, MS in Engring., 1975. Mgr. Baytown refinery ExxonMobil Corp., gen. mgr. Exxon Co. USA supply dept., strategic planning mgr., v.p. safety, health, and environ., v.p. environ. policy & planning. Pres., bd. mem. Houston Regional Monitoring Corp.; mem. bd. trustees Engring. Coll. Coun. Cornell U.; chmn. industry adv. bd. Internat. Energy Agy.; bd. mem. Galveston Bay Found. Bd. mem. Baytown C. of C., YMCA Met. Dallas. Office: Exxon Mobil Corp Hdqs 5959 Las Colinas Blvd Irving TX 75039-2298

STUFFLEBEME, SHARON S., retail executive; married; 3 children. B, U. Dallas, 1983; MBA, U. Texas, 1986. Various positions Andersen Consulting, Hitachi Consulting, Michaels Stores; ptnr. with Arthur Andersen Bus. Cons.; sr. v.p., chief info. officer 7-Eleven, Inc., 2004—09, RadioShack Corp., 2009—. Nat. bd. mem. Network Exec. Women, 2008—10; adv. bd. mem. Arthritis Found., North Tex., SMU Cox Sch. Bus., ITOM, TCU Neeley Sch. Bus. CIO. Mem.: Network Exec. Women, Bd. Connection. Office: RadioShack Corp 300 RadioShack Cir Fort Worth TX 76102 Office Phone: 817-415-3700. Business E-Mail: sharon.stufflebeme@radioshack.com.

STUKENBERG, MICHAEL WESLEY, lawyer; b. Freeport, Ill., Feb. 22, 1951; s. Wesley W. and Nancy Jack (Baker) S.; m. Amanda Reed Eggert, July 21, 1973; children: Sarah Reed, William Robinson. BA, Princeton U., 1973; JD, Vanderbilt U., 1976. Bar: Tex. 1977, U.S. Tax Ct. 1977, U.S. Dist. Ct. (so. dist.) Tex. 1982. Assoc. firm Branscomb P.C., Corpus Christi, Tex., 1976-81, shareholder, 1981—. Gov. Art Mus. South Tex., Copus Christi, 1990-96; dir., pres. Corpus Christi Estate Planning Coun., 1989-98; trustee, chair bd. trustees YMCA Corpus Christi, 1997-. Fellow Am. Coll. Trust and Estate Counsel; mem. ABA, Tex. Bar Assn. (tax sect.), Tex. Acad. of Probate and Trust Lawyers, Coll. of State Bar of Tex., Corpus Christi Yacht Club. Episcopalian. Home: 3502 Aransas St Corpus Christi TX 78411-1302 Office Phone: 361-888-9261. E-mail: mstukenberg@branscombpc.com.

STULTS, WALTER BLACK, management consultant, trade association administrator; b. Hightstown, NJ, Oct. 25, 1921; s. C. Stanley and Nettie M. (Black) S.; m. Ann D. Haynes, June 28, 1947 (dec. 2002); children: Andrew Haynes, Thomas Stanley; m. Jean Morris Curtin, 2003. BA, Williams Coll., 1943; MA (Woodrow Wilson fellow), Princeton U., 1949. Teaching asst. Princeton (N.J.) U., 1946-49; legis. asst. to U.S. Senator Robert Hendrickson, Washington, 1949-50; staff dir. U.S. Senate Small Bus. Com., Washington, 1950-61; pres. Nat. Assn. Small Bus. Investment Cos., Washington, 1961-86; prin. W.B. Stults, Cons., Chapel Hill, NC, 1979-99. Dir. Pardee & Curtin Lumber Co., Pardee Resources Co., Phila.; chmn. Coun. Small and Ind. Bus. Assns., 1976-81. Pres. Carol Woods Residents Assn.; dir. Carol Woods Retirement Comty., 1995-97, 2001-06. With USAAF, 1943-46. Mem. Am. Soc. Assn. Execs., The Exchequer Club, Masons. Congregationalist.

STUMP, JOHN SUTTON, retired lawyer; b. Clarksburg, W.Va., Aug. 7, 1929; s. John Sutton and Helen (Mannix) S.; m. Elaine Claire Scammahorn, Sept. 14, 1968; children— John Sutton IV, James Felix. Student, Washington and Lee U., 1946-47, LL.B., 1957; BS in Commerce, U. N.C., 1951. Bar: W.Va. 1957, Va. 1957, D.C. 1983. Assoc. Jackson, Kelly, Holt & O'Farrell, Charleston, W.Va., 1957-58, Boothe, Dudley, Koontz & Boothe, Alexandria, Va., 1958-61, Boothe, Dudley, Koontz & Blankingship, Fairfax and Alexandria, Va., 1962-63; ptnr. Boothe, Dudley, Koontz, Blankingship & Stump, Fairfax and Alexandria, 1963-71, Boothe, Prichard & Dudley, 1971-87, McGuire, Woods, Battle & Boothe LLP, 1987-99. Served to lt. comdr. USNR, 1951-54, 61-62. Fellow Am. Coll. Trial Lawyers; mem. Am. Law Inst. Office: 1750 Tysons Blvd Mc Lean VA 22102-4208 Home: 21145 Cardinal Pond Ter Apt 130 Ashburn VA 20147 Office Phone: 703-712-5457. Business E-Mail: jstump@mcguirewoodsemeritus.com.

STUMPF, WALTER ERICH, cell biology and pharmacology professor, researcher; b. Oelsnitz, Sachsen, Germany, Jan. 10, 1927; arrived in U.S., 1963; m. Ursula Emily Schwinge, May 20, 1961; children: Andrea, Martin, Carolin, Silva. MD summa cum laude, Humboldt U., Berlin, 1952; PhD in Pharmacology, U. Chgo., 1967; D of Human Biology (hon.), U. Ulm, Germany, 1987. Resident in neurology and psychiatry Humboldt U., Berlin, 1954-57, U. Marburg, Germany, 1957-61, resident in radiobiology, 1961-62; rsch. assoc. U. Chgo., 1963-67, asst. prof., 1967-70; assoc. prof. U. N.C., Chapel Hill, 1970-73, prof., 1973-95, mem. labs. for reproductive biology and neurobiology program, mem. Cancer Rsch. Ctr., Carolina Population Ctr., mem. curriculum in toxicology. Vis. psychiatrist Maudsley Hosp., London, 1959; vis. prof. Max-Planck Inst. for Cell Biology, Wilhelmshaven, Germany, 1975, U. Ulm, 1981, U. Sao Paulo, Brazil, 2000-02; rsch. advisor Chugai Pharm. Co., Ltd., Tokyo, 1992-95; lectr. U. São Paulo, 1997, 2000, Ain Shams U., Cairo, 1998; cons. Harris Mfg. Co., North Billerica, Mass., Rsch. Triangle Inst., Chemistry and Life Scis. Divsn., Rsch. Triangle Park, N.C., Merck Sharp and Dome, Westpoint, Pa., Glaxo Wellcome, Rsch. Triangle Park; exec. com. NRC, Inst. of Lab. Animal Resources, NAS, 1979-81, coun. Inst. of Lab. Animal Res., 1978-81, com. Soc. for Exptl. Biology and Medicine, 1987-92, founder Internat. Inst. Drug Distbn. Cytopharmacology and Cytoxicology, Chapel Hill, 1995—. Editor: Autoradiography of Diffusible Substances, 1969, Anatomical Neuroendocrinology, 1975, Autoradiography and Correlative Imaging, 1995; author: Drug Localization in Tissues and Cells, 2003; mem. editl. bd. Neuroendocrinology Letters, 1979-87, Exptl. Aging Rsch., 1975-85, Jour. Histochemistry and Cytochemistry, 1982-90, Cell and Tissue Rsch., 1982-88, Molecular and Cellular Neurosci., 1989-94, Biomed. Rsch., 1991-94, Histochemistry, 1992-96; contbr. articles to profl. jours. Recipient Humboldt Found. award, 1989. Mem. AAAS, Am. Assn. Anatomists, N.Y. Acad. Scis., Soc. for Exptl. Biology and Medicine, Soc. for Neurosci., Endocrine Soc., Internat. Brain Rsch. Orgn., Am. Soc. Zoologists, Histochem. Soc. (coun. 1977-81), Histochem. Gesellschaft (Feulgen lectureship 1982), Internat. Soc. Study Xenobiotics (charter), Internat. Inst. Drug Distbn. Cytopharmacology and Cytotoxicology (founder). Home: U NC Sch Medicine 2612 Damascus Church Rd Chapel Hill NC 27516-8043 Office: Internat Inst Drug Distribution Cytopharmacology & Cytotoxicology Chapel Hill NC 27516 Office Phone: 919-942-8646. Business E-Mail: stumpfwe@email.unc.edu.

STURDIVANT, JAMES M., lawyer; b. Tulsa, Sept. 14, 1937; s. Ben S. and Elizabeth (Carlock) S.; m. Carol A. Baker, 1961 (div. Feb. 1975); children: Anne Carol, Catherine Abby; m. Barbara Dunn, Feb. 4, 1978; children: David Andrew, John Michael. BBA, U. Okla., 1959, JD, 1964. Bar: Okla. 1964, U.S. Tax Ct. 1964, U.S. Ct. Claims 1964, U.S. Dist. Ct., no. we. & so. dist. Okla. 1964, U.S. Ct. Appeals, 10th circuit 1971, U.S. Supreme Ct. 1975. Lawyer Gable & Gotwals, Inc., Tulsa, 1964—. Trustee River Parks Authority, Tulsa County, Okla., 1989-97; Okla. Jud. Nomin. Commn. 1981-87, chmn. 1985-87; Ctr. Am. & Internat. Law, trustee 1997-, rsch fellow 2000-; bd. dir. Tulsa Area United Way 2003- (exec. comm. 2003-, Alexis de Tocqueville Soc. chmn. 2004); bd. visitors Univ. Okla. Coll. Arts & Sci. 1997-, Coll. Law 2002-. Officer infantry USMC, 1959—61. Mem. ABA (house del. 1992-04, bd. govs. 2004-07); Am. Coll. Trial Lawyers (fellow, state chmn. 2000-02), Okla. Bar Assn. (v.p., bd. gov. 1976, chmn. profl. responsibility commn. 1978, chmn. adminstrn. justice comm.1994-97, mem. tort reform task force, 2004), Okla. Bar Found. (trustee 1988—); Tulsa County Bar Assn.(Dist. Svc. award, 1992, Outstanding Young Lawyer, 1968). Life Fellow, Am. Bar Found; Okla. Bar Found; Am. Inns of Ct. (founding master, Hudson-Hall-Wheaton chptr.). Republican. Methodist. Office: Gable & Gotwals 1100 ONEOK Plz 100 W 5th St Tulsa OK 74103-4217 Home Phone: 918-747-1234; Office Phone: 918-595-4800. Business E-Mail: jsturdivant@gablelaw.com.

STURGIS, KATHY ANN, judge; b. NYC, Aug. 28, 1952; d. Irv DeKoff and Belle DeKoff Shouse; m. Radford Russell Sturgis, May 30, 1976. BA, Mt. Holyoke Coll., 1977; JD cum laude, Stetson U., 1986. Bar: Fla. 1986. Family services aide Dept. Health and Rehab. Services, Ft. Myers, Fla., 1974-77; legis. aide Fla. Ho. of Reps., Ft. Myers and Tallahassee, 1977-79; exec. dir. Voluntary Action Ctr., Lee County, Fla., 1979-80; owner Dance Fitness Unltd., Cape Coral, Fla., 1980-83; law clk. to circuit judges Fla. 20th Jud. Cir., Ft. Myers, 1985; assoc. Peper, Martin, Jensen, Maichel & Hetlage, Ft. Myers, 1986—92; gen. master mediator Division of Adminstrv. Hearing, Fort Myers, 1996—2006; judge compensation claims Ft. Myers Dist., 2006—. Admissions rep. Mt. Holyoke Coll., SW Fla., 1982—86; secretariat mem. Gulf Coast Cursillo, Lee County, 1983; campaign coordinator Com. to Retain Judge Sturgis, Lee County, 1982; bd. dirs. Edison Women's Ctr., Lee County, 1978, Imaginarium Group Inc., 1990-95, sch. bd. chmn. SW Fla. Christian Acad., mem. SW Fla. Cmty. Found. Women's Legacy Fund, 2007-, co chair, 2009-. Charles A. Dana scholar Stetson U., 1985-86. Mem. Lee County Bar Assn. (pres. 1992), Fla. Bar Assn. (law related edn. com. 1987—92), Women Legacy Fund (co-chair, 2009-10, chair, 10-11), Clubs: Rotary, Calusa Inns of Ct., P.E.O. Presbyterian. Avocations: ballroom dancing, watching football, hockey, reading. Office Phone: 239-938-1159. Office Fax: 239-938-1169. Business E-Mail: kathy.sturgis@doah.state.fl.us.

STURLEY, MICHAEL F., law educator; b. Syracuse, NY, Feb. 14, 1955; s. Richard Avern and Helen Elizabeth (Fisher) S.; m. Michele Y. Deitch, July 2, 1989; children: Jennifer Diane, Elizabeth Claire. BA, Yale U., 1977, JD, 1981; BA in Jurisprudence, Oxford U., 1980, MA, 1985. Bar: NY 1984, US Dist. Ct. (so. and ea. dists.) NY 1984, US Supreme Ct. 1987, US Ct. Appeals (11th cir.) 2001, US Ct. Appeals (2nd cir.) 2004. Law clk. to Judge Amalya L. Kearse US Ct. Appeals for 2nd Cir., NYC, 1981-82; law clk. to Justice Lewis F. Powell, Jr. US Supreme Ct., Washington, 1982-83; assoc. Sullivan & Cromwell, NYC, 1983-84; asst. prof. law U. Tex. Law Sch., Austin, 1984-88, prof., 1988—. Vis. prof. Queen Mary and Westfield Coll., U. London, 1990, advisor Restatement (3rd) of Property (servitudes), 1989-2000; sr. adv., US Del. to Working Group III, United Nations Commn. Internat. Trade Law, 2002-09. Author: (with Tomotaka Fujita and Gertjan van der Ziel) The Rotterdam Rules: The UN Convention on Contracts for the International Carriage of Goods Wholly or Partly by Sea, 2010; (with David W. Robertson and Steven F. Friedell) Admiralty and Maritime Law in the United States, 2001, 2nd edit., 2008; compiler, editor: The Legislative History of the Carriage of Goods by Sea Act and the Travaux Préparatoires of The Hague Rules, 3 vols., 1990; mem. editl. bd. Jour. Maritime Law and Commerce, 1989—, book rev. editor, 1993—; contbg. author: Benedict on Admiralty, 1990—; contbr. articles to legal jours. Mem. Am. Law Inst., Maritime Law Assn. (proctor), Comité Maritime Internat. (titulary). Office: University Tex Sch Law 727 E Dean Keeton St Austin TX 78705-3224 Office Phone: 512-232-1350.

STURTEVANT, RUTHANN PATTERSON, anatomist, educator; b. Rockford, Ill., Feb. 7, 1927; d. Joseph Hyelmun and Virginia (Wharton) Patterson; m. Frank Milton Sturtevant Jr., Mar. 18, 1950 (dec.); children: Jill Sturtevant Rovani, Jan Sturtevant Cassidy; m. Richard Kiegler, Aug. 8, 2010. BS, Northwestern U., Evanston, Ill., 1949; MS, Northwestern U., 1950; PhD, U. Ark., Little Rock, 1972. Instr. life scis. Ind. State U., Evansville, Ind., 1965—72, asst. prof., 1972—74; asst. prof. anatomy Ind. U. Sch. Medicine, Evansville, 1972—74, U. Evansville, 1972—74; lectr. anatomy Northwestern U., Chgo., 1974—75; asst. prof. anatomy and surgery Loyola U., Maywood, 1975—81; assoc. prof. Loyola U. Sch. Medicine, Maywood, 1981—88, prof., 1988—90, prof. emerita, 1990—. Contbr. articles to profl. jours.; mem. editl. bd. Chronobiology Internat., 1988-90; reviewer numerous profl. jours. Active Mayor's Task Force on High Tech. Devel., Chgo., 1983-85; exec. bd. Anatomical Gifts Assn. Ill., Chgo., instr. Mote Marine Labs; vol. many cmty. svcs.; docent Mote Rsch. Aquarium, 1992-. Grantee Pott's Found., NIH, others, 1978—. Mem. Am. Assn. Anatomists, So. Soc. Anatomists (councillor 1978-80), Internat. Soc. Chronobiologists, Am. Soc. Pharmacology and Exptl. Therapeutics, Soc. for Exptl. Biology and Medicine, Am. Assn. Clin. Anatomists, League of Underwater Photographers, Sarasota Scuba Club, Sigma Xi. Avocations: photography, scuba diving, flying, community volunteering. Address: 5760 Midnight Pass Rd Unit 610-D Sarasota FL 34242 Personal E-mail: patty5760@verizon.net.

STUZIN, JAMES M., plastic surgeon; b. Miami, Fla., June 1, 1952; BA, U. Fla., Gainesville, 1974, MD, 1978. Cert. in gen. surgery 1985, in plastic surgery 1989. Intern, gen. surgery U. Wash. Hosps., Seattle, 1978—79, resident, gen. surgery, 1979—83; fellow, plastic surgery NYU Hosps., NYC, 1984—86; craniofacial fellow U. Miami Hosps., Fla., 1986, UCLA Sch. Medicine, 1987, asst. clin. prof., plastic surgery, 1987; clin. instr., dept. plastic surgery U. Miami Sch. Medicine, Fla., 1989—95, clin. asst. prof., plastic surgery, 1995—. Chmn. Am. Bd. Plastic Surgery, 2008—. Mem. editl. bd. Annals of Plastic Surgery, 1993—; co-editor: Jour. of Plastic and Reconstructive Surgery; co-author: Facial Skin Resurfacing, 1998. Mem.: Am. Soc. for Aesthetic Plastic Surgery (pres. 2006), Alpha Omega Alpha, Phi Beta Kappa. Office: 3225 Aviation Ave Ste 100 Coconut Grove FL 33133 Office Phone: 305-854-8828.

STYSLINGER, LEE JOSEPH, JR., manufacturing executive; b. Birmingham, Ala., June 28, 1933; s. Lee Joseph and Margaret Mary (McFarl) S.; m. Catherine Patricia Smith, Apr. 30, 1960; children: Lee Joseph III, Jon Cecil, Mark Joseph. Student, U. Ala., 1952. Pres., chief exec. officer Altec, Inc., Birmingham, 1956-89, chief exec. officer, chmn. bd., 1989-92, chmn., 1992—2011, mem. bd. dirs., 2011—. Bd. dirs. Altec Inc., Jemison Investment Co., Birmingham, Ala., chmn., 1992-2011. Mem. Country Club Birmingham, Mountain Brook Club, Shoal Creek Club, Willow Point Golf and Country Club, Jupiter Island Club (Hobe Sound, Fla.), Seminole Golf Club (Juno Beach, Fla.), Lyford Cay Country Club (Bahamas), Rotary, NY Yacht Club (N.Y.C.). Roman Catholic. Home: 3260 E Briarcliff Rd Birmingham AL 35223-1305 Office: 210 Inverness Center Dr Birmingham AL 35242-4834

SU, LISHAN, medical educator; married. PhD, Harvard U. Prof. U. NC, Chapel Hill, 1996—. Office: University NC 22-048 LCCC UNC-CH Chapel Hill NC 27599-7295 Business E-Mail: lsu@med.unc.edu.*

SU, SAMUEL (JING-SHYH S. SU), restaurant chain company executive; Grad., Nat. Taiwan U.; MS in Chem. Engring., Pa. State U.; MBA, U. Pa. With Procter & Gamble, Germany, Taiwan; internat. dir. mktg. North Pacific Region, KFC Yum! Brands, Inc. (formerly TRICON Global Restaurants, Inc.), 1989, v.p. North Asia, KFC and Pizza Hut, 1993—97, vice chmn. bd., 2008—; pres. Yum! Restaurants China, Shanghai, 1997—2010, chmn., CEO, 2010—. Non-exec. dir. Little Sheep Group Ltd., 2009—. Office: Yum! Brands, Inc 1441 Gardiner Lane Louisville KY 40213 also: Little Sheep Group Ltd Kun District No 9 Wulan Rd Bautou China Office Phone: 502-874-8300. Office Fax: 502-454-2410.

SUBOLESKI, STANLEY C., mining executive; b. 1941; BS, Pa. State U., 1963, PhD in Mining Engring., 1978; MS, Va. Tech. U., 1968. Pres. United Coal Co.; mining engr. North American Coal Corp., 1963—65; gen. supt. Underground Mines, Ctrl. Div. Consolidation Coal Co., 1969—74; v.p. mining divsn. Continental Ill. Nat. Bank, 1977—81; v.p. mining devel, treas. A.T. Massey Coal Co., 1981—88, v.p., ops. strategy, 1993—97; cons. mining engr., 2000—01; exec. v.p., interim COO Massey Energy Co., 2001—03; commr. Fed. Mine Safety and Health Review Commn., Washington, 2003—06. Instr. Pa. State U., 1974—77, Centennial prof. mining engring., chmn. Mining Engring. Sect., 1988—93; instr. Va. Tech. U., 1965—69; prof., head Dept. Mining Engring. Va. poly. Inst. & State U., 1998—2001; bd. dirs. Massey Energy Co., 2008—. Mem.: NAE, Soc. Mining, Metallurgy and Exploration (mem. exec. com. Coal and Energy Div.). Office: Massey Energy Co 4 N 4th St Richmond VA 23219 Office Phone: 804-788-1800. Office Fax: 804-788-1870. Business E-Mail: stanley.suboleski@masseyenergyco.com.

SUCATO, DANIEL J., orthopaedic surgeon; s. Justin and Ilde Sucato; m. Lisa Sucato; children: Daniel, Emma, Matthew. BA magna cum laude, Canisius Coll., Buffalo, 1987; MD, U. Buffalo, 1991, MS in Biophysics, 1997. Orthopaedic resident U. Buffalo, 1991—97, basic sci. rsch. fellow, 1992—93; pediatric orthopaedic surgery fellow Tex. Scottish Rite Hosp., Dallas, 1997—98, prof. orthop. surgery, U. Tex. at Southwestern Med. Ctr., Dallas, 1998—. Active staff mem. Children's Med. Ctr. Dallas. Contbr. articles to profl. jours., including Jour. Bone and Joint Surgery; cons. reviewer Spine, Jour. of Spinal Cord Medicine, Jour. of Bone and Joint Surgery, Jour. Pediat. Orthop., mem. editl. bd. Spine Universe. Active smem. Recipient Dr. William Beaumont award, AMA, 2005; Hip Preserving fellowship, Bern, Switzerland, 1998, SRS Internat. Traveling Fellow, 2003. Mem.: N.Am. Spine Soc., Tex. Med. Assn., Pediatric Orthopaedic Soc. N.Am., Am. Acad. Orthopaedic Surgeons, Scoliosis Rsch. Soc. Office: Texas Scottish Rite Hosp 2222 Welborn St Dallas TX 75219 Office Fax: 214-559-7570. Business E-Mail: dan.sucato@tsrh.org.

SUDHIVORASETH, NIPHON, pediatrician, immunologist, allergist; b. Bangkok, 1940; MD, Chulalongkorn Hosp. U., Bangkok, 1966. Diplomate Am. Bd. Pediatrics, Am. Bd. Allergy and Immunology. Intern Ch. Home Hosp., Balt., 1967-68; resident in pediatrics St. Lukes Hosp., NYC, 1968-69, Beth Israel Hosp., NYC, 1969-70; fellow in allergy Metro Hosp., N.Y. Med. Coll., NYC, 1970-72; staff Marshall Meml. Hosp., Tex., 1978—; pvt. practice. Mem. AMA, Am. Acad. Allergy, Asthma, and Immunology, Am. Acad. Pediats., Am. Coll. Allergy and Immunology. Office: PO Box 2087 705 S Grove St Marshall TX 75670-5220 Personal E-mail: drniphonsudhi@yahoo.com.

SUGG, JEANNE D., library director; m. John Sugg; 1 child, James; 1 child, Jeff. BA, Trevecca Nazarene U., Nashville; MLS, Vanderbilt U. Peabody Coll. Libr. coord. Arabian-Am. Oil Co., Saudi Arabia, 1981—89; dir. pub. svcs. Tenn. State Libr. & Archives, Nashville, 1989, dir., 1991, asst state libr., archivist for admin., 1992—2005, state libr. & archivist, 2005—. Mem.: ALA, Tenn. Historical Soc., Tenn. Libr. Assn., Chief Officers State Libr. Agencies. Office: Tenn State Libr & Archives 403 7th Ave N Nashville TN 37243 Office Phone: 615-741-7996. Office Fax: 615-532-9293. Business E-Mail: jeanne.sugg@state.tn.us.

SUGHRUE, MICHAEL EDWARD, neurosurgeon; b. Provo, Utah, Oct. 23, 1978; s. Edward Lawrence and Marilyn Sughrue; m. Kanokkorn Phooprasartporn, Feb. 14, 2014. MD, Columbia U., NYC, 2005. Neurosurgeon U. Calif., San Francisco, 2011, U. Okla., 2012—. Office: 1000 N Lincoln Blvd Ste 400 Oklahoma City OK 73151 Business E-Mail: mes261@columbia.edu.*

SULLEBARGER, JOHN THOMPSON, internist, cardiologist, educator; b. Plainfield, NJ, May 2, 1957; s. Franklyn Jackson and Joanne Abbott (Aspinall) S.; m. Lorrie Jeanne Miller, June 14, 1980; children: Jeffrey Franklyn, Melissa Jeanne. Student, U. Mainz, 1977; AB, Dartmouth Coll., 1979; MD, Johns Hopkins U., 1983. Intern U. Rochester, NY, 1983-84, resident in medicine, 1984-86, fellow in cardiology, 1986-89, from sr. instr. to asst. prof., 1989-92; asst. prof. U. South Fla., Tampa, 1992-96, assoc. prof., 1997-99; dir. CCU Tampa Gen. Hosp., 1997—; clin. assoc. prof. U. South Fla., Tampa, 2004—. Dir. Cardiac Catheterization Lab. James Haley VA Hosp., Tampa, 1992—99; dir. interventional cardiology U. South Fla., 1994—99; attending physician Strong Meml. Hosp., Rochester, 1989—92; pres. Fla. Cardiovascular Inst., 2004—; chief cardiology Tampa Gen. Hosp., 2008—. Author: (with others) book chapters; contrb. articles to profl. jours. Chmn. Bd. Christian Svc., 1st Bapt. Ch., Rochester, 1991-92. Fellow ACP, 1992, Am. Coll. of Cardiology, 1991, Counc. on Clin. Cardiology of Am. Heart Assn., 1991, N.Y. Cardiological Soc., 1992. Fellow ACP, Soc. Cardiac Angiography and Interventions, Am. Coll. Cardiology, N.Y. Cardiol. Soc.; mem. Am. Heart Assn. (fellow coun. on clin. cardiology), Tampa Internat. Heart Found. (founder 2004-). Avocation: music. Office: 509 S Armenia Ste 200 Tampa FL 33609 Home: 3476 Marlinspihe Dr Tampa FL 33607 Office Phone: 813-353-1515.

SULLENBARGER, DANIEL JAMES, oil industry executive, lawyer; b. Greenville, Ohio, Apr. 25, 1951; s. James Lee and Doris Evelyn (Roark) S.; m. Lauren Jean Drehs, Aug. 10, 1974; children: Jennifer Ann, Erin Michelle, Kylie Marie. BA, Bowling Green State U., 1973; JD, Ohio No. U., 1976. Bar: Ohio 1976, U.S. Dist. Ct. (no. dist.) Ohio 1977, U.S. Ct. Appeals (7th cir.) 1978, U.S. Ct. Appeals (5th cir.) 1985, Tex. 1985. Atty. pipeline div. Marathon Oil Corp., Findlay, Ohio, 1976-78, atty. mktg. div., 1978-80, legal adviser prodn. div. London, 1980-84, atty. prodn. div. Houston, 1984-86, sr. counsel refining, mktg., supply, transp. and adminstrn., 1986-88, sr. counsel offshore and Gulf Coast prodn., 1988-90, sr. counsel adminstrn. and spl. projects, 1990-91, gen. atty. refining, mktg. supply and transp. Findlay, Ohio, 1991—94, group counsel-Worldwide Exploration & Production Houston, 1994—98, v.p. Human Resources and Environment, 1998—2000, v.p. Health, Environment, Safety, 2000—05, v.p. corp. responsibility, 2005—08, v.p. corp. compliance & ethics, 2008—. Mem. gen. com. Am. Petroleum Inst.; chmn. exec. com. Internat. Petroleum Ind. Environ. Conservation Assn. Bd. dirs. Hancock County Mental Health Assn., Findlay, 1976-80; chmn. City of Findlay Bd. of Zoning Appeals, 1978-80; mem. exec. com. Houston Clean City Commn. Recipient awards for Excellence Lawyer's Coop. Pub. Co., 1975,76. Mem. ABA, Ohio State Bar Assn., Tex. State Bar Assn., Houston Bar Assn. Avocation: recreational and competitive running. Office: Marathon Oil Corp 5555 San Felipe Rd Houston TX 77056

SULLIVAN, DANIEL EDMOND, fundraising executive; b. Alexandria, La., Jan. 22, 1946; s. Edmond James and Ruth (Morris) S.; m. Camille Lafleur Broussand, June 13, 1970; children: Daniel Edmond Jr., Parish Coughlin. Student, La. State U., 1964-67; BS, Northwestern State U., Natchitoches, La., 1968. Field underwriter N.Y. Life Ins. Co., New Orleans, 1968-70; asst. dir. Tulane U. Alumni Fund, New Orleans, 1970-71; assoc. dir. La. Civil Svc. League, New Orleans, 1971-73, exec. v.p., 1973—, also bd. govs., 1973—; bd. of gov. La. Orgn. for Jud. Excellence, 1992—2008, v.p., 1995—2008. Mem. com. La. Joint Legis. Com., 1982-2008, La. Atty. Disciplinary Bd., 2009-; mem. pub. adminstrn. tng. adv. com. U. New Orleans, 1983-90; trustee LA Jud. Excellence Found., 2002-. Bd. dirs. Young Audiences New Orleans, 1974-78. Named Hon. Alumnus Tulane U., 1977. Mem. Nat. Soc. Fund Raising Execs. (cert.), Am. Arbitration Assn. (panel of arbitrators), Royal Soc. St. George, Northwestern State U. Alumni Assn. (bd. dirs. 1974-84), New Orleans Lawn Tennis Club (bd. govs. 1978-80), La. Polit. Hall of Fame Found. (bd. dirs. 2011-), Stratford Club, Pickwick Club. Republican. Roman Catholic. Home: 919 Short St New Orleans LA 70118-2730 Office: La Civil Svc League 810 Union St Ste 305 New Orleans LA 70112-1426

SULLIVAN, DANIEL S., former state legislator, lawyer; b. Tulsa, Okla., Mar. 12, 1963; s. Frank and Karen Sullivan; m. Melanie Pouncey. BS cum laude, Northeastern State Univ., 1985; JD, Univ. Tulsa, 1988. Bar: Okla. 1988, US Dist. Ct. No. Ea. We. Okla., US Ct. Appeals 10th Cir. Of counsel Pierce Couch Hendrickson Baysinger & Green, Tulsa, Okla.; mem. Dist. 71 Okla. House of Representatives, 2005—11. Mem.: ABA, Okla. Bar Assn., Okla. Assn. Def. Counsel, Internat. Assn. Def. Counsel, Def. Rsch. Inst., Christian Legal Soc. Republican. Mailing: 1338 E 43rd Ct Tulsa OK 74105 Office Phone: 405-557-7361. E-mail: danielsullivan@okhouse.gov.

SULLIVAN, DOUGLAS BURNS, retail executive; b. Summit, NJ, Jan. 23, 1951; s. Miles Vincent and Evelyn Catherine (Burns) S.; m. Rebeccah Beck, Dec. 8, 1955; children: Anna Burns, Lauren Beck, Rebeccah Anne. BA, Wake Forest U., 1973, JD, 1976. Bar: N.C. 1977. V.p. real estate Family Dollar Stores, Inc., Charlotte, NC, 1977—88; joined Michael Stores, 1988, exec. v.p. devel., pres. COO. Office: Michaels Stores 8000 Bent Branch Dr Irving TX 75063

SULLIVAN, HARRY TRUMAN, retired research scientist; b. Camden, Ala., Mar. 21, 1952; s. Ernest Curley and Luticia Ann (Aaron) B.; m. Sandra Carol Jackson, Nov. 13, 1976; 1 child, Asha Nicole. AA, So. Tech. Inst., Marietta, Ga., 1976; BS in Computer Sci., Ga. State U., 1989. Instrumentation technician Ga. Power Co., Baxley, 1976-78; electronic technician Micromeritics Instrument Corp., Atlanta, 1978-80, GEC Avionics, Inc., Atlanta, 1980-82; electronic technician II Ga. Inst. of Tech., Atlanta, 1982—2010. Mem. IEEE, Assn. for Computing Machinery. Avocation: tang soo do. Personal E-mail: harrysul@bellsouth.net.

SULLIVAN, JAMES E., corporate financial executive; BA in Economics, MA in Economics, SUNY, Binghamton. CPA. Sr. audit mgr. PricewaterhouseCoopers, LLP; sr. dir., fin. reporting Brinker Internat., Inc., 2001—06; asst. contr. Affiliated Computer Services, Inc. (ACS) (acquired by Xerox Corp.), 2006—07; v.p., fin. reporting and compliance Zale Corp., 2007—09, v.p., chief acctg. officer, contr., 2009—. Office: Zale Corp 901 W Walnut Hill Ln Irving TX 75038 Office Phone: 972-580-4000. Office Fax: 972-580-5547.

SULLIVAN, JERRY STEPHEN, electronics executive; b. Havre, Mont., July 17, 1945; s. Patrick Joseph and Evangeline (O'Neil) S.; m. Sharon Lee Horton, June 17, 1967; children: Garrett, Mindy, Darren. BS, U. Colo., 1967, MS, 1969, PhD, 1970; advanced mgmt. program, Harvard U. Bus. Sch., 1986. Tech. mgr. N.V. Philips Co., Eindhoven, Netherlands, 1971-75; group dir. N.Am. Philips Corp., Briarcliff Manor, NY, 1975-80; dir. Tektronix, Beaverton, Oreg., 1981-83, div. gen. mgr., 1983-85, corp. dir., 1985-88; v.p. Microelectronics & Computer Tech. Corp., Austin, Tex., 1988-92; pres., CEO, Design Techs. Inc., Austin, 1992—. Chmn. bd. MBA Techs., Inc., Phoenix; bd. dirs. Sherpa Corp., San Jose, Calif., Ontos, Inc. Boston, MBA Tech. Inc., Phoenix; mem. adv. bd. Ctr. Integrated Sys., Stanford U., Palo Alto, Calif., 1982—. Mem. adv. com. Coll. Engring., U. Tex., Austin, 1989—, bd. dirs. Edn. Found., 1990—. Mem. IEEE, Am. Phys. Soc., Assn. Computing Machinery, Am. Mgmt. Assn., Nat. Assn. Corp. Dirs. Avocations: scuba diving, golf, chess, sailing. Office: Design Techs Inc 107 Ranch Rd 620 S Austin TX 78734-3942

SULLIVAN, KEVIN A., lawyer; BBA magna cum laude, North Tex. State U., Denton, 1979; JD cum laude, U. Tex. Sch. Law, 1982. Bar: Tex. 1982. Shareholder Winstead PC, Dallas, chmn. real estate structured fin. practice, chmn., CEO of firm. Named one of The Best Lawyers in America, Real Estate and Structured Fin. Law, 2004—11, The Best Lawyers in Dallas, D Mag.; named to Tex. Super Lawyers, Tex. Monthly, 2010. Mem.: ABA, State Bar Tex., Dallas Bar Assn., Comml. Mortgage Securities Assn., Leadership Dallas, Dallas C. of C. (life). Office: Winstead PC 5400 Renaissance Tower 2728 N Harwood St Ste 500 Dallas TX 75201-1743 Office Phone: 214-745-5292. Office Fax: 214-745-5390. Business E-Mail: ksullivan@winstead.com.

SULLIVAN, LEONARD, realtor, state representative; b. Dale, Okla., Dec. 12, 1934; s. Leonard F. and Willie Lee (Stone) Sullivan; m. Marilyn S. West; children: Diana L. Wood, Lee Ann Crull. BA, Okla. State U. Mgr. Kroger Super Markets, Okla. City; sales mgr. Kimberly Clark, Neenah, Wis.; v.p. sales and mktg. Carousel Fashions; realtor Leonard E. Sullivan Co., Okla. City, 1975—; rep. Ho. Reps., State of Okla., 1987—. Mem. banking and fin., higher edn., retirement laws, transp. coms. Okla. Ho. Reps., Okla. City, 1987—. Capt. US Army. Republican. Office: 2300 N Lincoln Blvd Rm 540 Oklahoma City OK 73105 Home and Office: 4117 NW 122d St Oklahoma City OK 73120 E-mail: sullivanle@lsb.state.ok.us.

SULLIVAN, LOUIS WADE, medical educator, former United States Secretary of Health & Human Services; b. Atlanta, Nov. 3, 1933; s. Walter Wade and Lubirda Elizabeth (Priester) S.; m. Eve Williamson, Sept. 30, 1955; children: Paul, Shanta, Halsted. BS magna cum laude, Morehouse Coll., Atlanta, 1954; MD cum laude, Boston U., 1958. Diplomate: Am. Bd. Internal Medicine. Intern N.Y. Hosp.-Cornell Med. Ctr., NYC, 1958-59, resident in internal medicine, 1959-60; fellow in pathology Mass. Gen. Hosp., Boston, 1960-61; rsch. fellow Thorndike Meml. Lab. Harvard Med. Sch., Boston, 1961-63; instr. medicine Harvard Med. Sch., 1963-64; asst. prof. medicine N.J. Coll. Medicine, 1964-66; co-dir. hematology Boston U. Med. Ctr., 1966; assoc. prof. medicine Boston U., 1968—73; dir. hematology Boston City Hosp., 1973-75; prof. medicine & physiology Boston U., 1973—75; dean Sch. Medicine, Morehouse Coll., Atlanta, 1975—83; pres. Morehouse Sch. Medicine, Morehouse Coll., Atlanta, 1981—89, 1993—2002, pres. emeritus, 2002—; sec. US Dept. Health & Human Services, Washington, 1989-93. Non-exec. dir. GM, 1993-2002; bd. dirs. 3M Co., Henry Schein Inc., Bristol-Myers Squibb Co., CIGNA Corp., Equifax Inc., Georgia-Pacific Corp., United Therapeutics Corp., Emergent Biosolutions, BioSante Pharm.; mem. sickle cell anemia adv. com. NIH, 1974-75; ad hoc panel on blood diseases Nat. Heart, Lung Blood Disease Bur., 1973, Nat. Adv. Rsch. Coun., 1977; mem. med. adv. bd. Nat. Leukemia Assn., 1968-70, chmn., 1970, Pres. Commn. on HIV and AIDS, 2001-06, Pres. Commn. on Hist. Black Colleges and Universities, 2002-09, Nat. Health Mus., Atlanta, Sullivan Alliance to Transform America's Health Professionals, Washington; mem. Sec. of Edn.'s Commn. on Future of Edn., 2005. John Hay Whitney Found. Opportunity fellow, 1960-61; recipient Honor medal Am. Cancer Soc., 1991. Mem. Assn. Am. Physicians, Am. Soc. Hematology, Am. Soc. Clin. Investigation, Clin. and Climatological Soc., Inst. Medicine, Phi Beta Kappa, Alpha Omega Alpha. Episcopalian. Achievements include research in suppression of hematopoiesis by ethanol, pernicious anemia in childhood, folates in human nutrition. Office: Morehouse Sch Medicine Office of the Pres Emeritus 133 Peachtree St Ste 4040 Atlanta GA 30303 Office Phone: 404-752-1933.

SULLIVAN, MICHAEL EVAN, investment company executive; b. Phila., Dec. 30, 1940; s. Albert and Ruth (Liebert) S. BS, N.Mex. State U., 1966, MA, 1967; BS, U. Tex., 1969; MBA, U. Houston, 1974; MS, U. So. Calif., 1976, MPA, 1977; BS in Acctg., U. La Verne, Calif., 1981; PhD in Adminstrn., U. So. Calif., 1983. Sr. adminstrv. and tech. analyst Houston Lighting & Power Co., 1969—74; electronics engr. US Govt., Point Mugu, Calif., 1974—77; mem. tech. staff Hughes Aircraft Co., El Segundo, Calif., 1977—78; staff program adminstr. Ventura divsn. Northrop Corp., Newbury Park, Calif., 1978—79; divsn. head engring. Navastrogru, Point Mugu, 1978—82; br. head, divsn. head spl. programs head operational sys. Pacific Missile Test Ctr., Calif., 1983—90, head tech. devel. office, head capability devel., 1993—98; regional coord. far west, exec. com., exec. bd. Fed. Lab. Consortium, 1999—. CNO, dir. rsch., devel. and acquisiiton The Pentagon, Washington, 1987-88, dir. rsch. devel. test and evaluation and tech., 1990-93; pres., chmn. bd. Diversified Mgmt. Sys., Inc., Camarillo, Calif., 1978—. Author: The Management of Research, Development, Test and Evaluation Organizations; Organization Behavior Characteristics of Supervisors-Public versus Private Sectors; Self-Actualization in RDT & E Organizations: Self-Actualization in a Health Care Agency; others. V.p., bd. dirs. Ventura County Master Chorale and Opera Assn.; bd. dirs. So. Calif. Assn. of Pub. Adminstrn. (also mem. fin. com., programs com., student aid com., exec. bd., exec. com. fed. lab. consortium). Served with U.S. Army, 1958-62. Ednl. Rsch. Info. Clearing House fellow, 1965-67, Ednl. Rsch. Tng. Program fellow N.Mex. State U., 1967. Mem. IEEE, Am. Math. Soc., Math. Assn. Am., Am. Statis. Assn., IEEE Engring. Mgmt. Soc., Am. Soc. Pub. Adminstrn., So. Calif. Assn. Pub. Adminstrn. (bd. dirs., various coms.), Assn. Fedn. Tech. Transfer Execs., Fed. Mgrs. Assn., Am. Assn. Individual Investors, Mcpl. Mgmt. Assts. So. Calif., Acad. Polit. Sci., Internat. Soc. for the Sys. Scis., Assn. MBA Execs., Tech. Transfer Soc., Internat. Fedn. for Sys. Rsch., Phi Kappa Phi, Pi Gama Mu. Home and Office: Dr Mike Sullivan PO Box 1532 Sarasota FL 34230-1532

SULLIVAN, MICHAEL L., publishing executive; Sr. exec. positions News Group, Murdoch Magazines, TV Guide, Globe Mktg. Services; exec. v.p. Hearst Distbn. Group; pres., CEO Comag Mktg. Group, 2000—10; CEO Source Interlink Companies Inc., Bonita Springs, Fla., 2010—. Bd. dir. Source Interlink Companies Inc., 2010—, Internat. Periodical Distributors Assn.; mem. GMDC Mdse. Adv. Bd.; mem. retail adv. coun. Mag. Publishers of America. Office: Source Interlink 27500 Riverview Ctr Blvd Bonita Springs FL 34134

SULLIVAN, MIKE, councilman, small business owner; m. Kim Sullivan; 1 child. Lic. real estate broker. Owner, pres. Mar-Max Supply, Inc., Channelview, Tex.; mgr. First World Realty, Houston; councilman, Dist. E Houston City Coun., 2008—. Bd. trustees Humble Ind. Sch. Dist., 2004—; ex-officio dir. Bay Area Houston Econ. Partnership. Active Good Shepherd Episcopal Ch., Kingwood, Tex.; bd. dirs. Hosp. Corp. America, Kingwood Med. Ctr. Office: City Hall Annex 900 Bagby 1st Fl Houston TX 77002 Office Phone: 832-393-3008. Office Fax: 832-393-3279. Business E-Mail: districte@cityofhouston.net.

SULLIVAN, PATRICIA, corporate financial executive; Dir. pub. rels. Pizza Hut; sr. v.p. mktg. and media rels. Tex. Capital Bank; sr. dir. comm. Blockbuster Inc.; sr. v.p. comm. MoneyGram, 2011—. Office: MoneyGram International 2828 N Harwood Fl 15 Dallas TX 75201 Office Phone: 800-666-3947.

SULLIVAN, PRESTON E., state legislator; b. Tupelo, Miss., June 8, 1947; m. Linda Buchanan Sullivan. Mem. Dist. 22 Miss. House of Reps., 2004—, vice chair appropriations com., mem. agr. com., banking and fin. svcs. com., county affairs com., oil, gas and other minerals com., pub. property com., transp. com. Mem.: NRA, Farm Bur., Miss. Cattleman's Assn., Mason. Democrat. Baptist. Address: 1601 CR 410 Okolona MS 38860 Office Phone: 601-359-3340. E-mail: psullivan@house.ms.gov.

SULLIVAN, TERESA ANN, academic administrator, law and sociology educator; d. Gordon Hager and Mary Elizabeth S.; m. H. Douglas Laycock, June 14, 1971; children: Joseph Peter, John Patrick. BA, Mich. State U., 1970; MA, U. Chgo., 1972, PhD, 1975. Asst. prof. sociology U. Tex., Austin, 1975-76, assoc. prof. sociology, 1981-87, dir. women's studies, 1985-87, prof. sociology, 1987—, prof. law, 1988—, assoc. dean grad. sch., 1989-90, 1992-95, chair dept. sociology, 1990-92, vice provost, 1994-95, v.p., grad. dean, 1995—2002; asst. prof. sociology U. Chgo., 1977-81; exec. vice-chancellor acad. affairs U. Tex. Sys., 2002—06; provost, exec. v.p. academic affairs U. Mich., Ann Arbor, 2006—10; pres. U. Va., 2010—. Pres. Southwestern Sociol. Assn., 1988-89; mem. faculty adv. bd. Hogg Found. Mental Health, 1989-92; mem. sociology panel NSF, 1983-85. Author: Marginal Workers Marginal Jobs, 1978; co-author: As We Forgive Our Debtors, 1989 (Silver Gavel 1990), Social Organization of Work, 1990, 5th edit., 2011; co-author: The Fragile Middle Class, 2000; contbr. articles and chpts. to profl. jours. Bd. dirs. Calvert Found., Chgo., 1978, CARA, Inc., Washington, 1985; mem. U.S. Census Bur. Adv. Com., 1989-95, chmn., 1991-92; mem. sociology panel NSF, 1983-85; trustee St. Michael's Acad., 1996-2001. Leadership Tex. 1994. Fellow AAAS (liaison to Population Assn. Am. 1989-91, chair sect. K 1996), Sociol. Rsch. Assn., Am. Sociol. Assn. (sec. 1995—, editor Rose Monograph Series 1988-92), Philos. Soc. Tex., Soc. Study of Social Problems (chair fin. com. 1986-87), Population Assn. Am. (bd. dirs. 1989-91, chair fin. com. 1990-91), Assn. Grad. Schs. (pres. 2001-2002). Roman Catholic. Avocation: reading. Home and Office: University of Virginia Office of President 1910 Carr's Hill Rd Charlottesville VA 22903 Office Phone: 434-924-3337. Personal E-mail: president.sullivan@virginia.edu.*

SULLIVAN, TIMOTHY E., bank executive; B, U. Ill.; MBA, U. Calif., Berkeley. Various tech. and ops. mgmt. positions including chief info. officer First Interstate Bank, Ariz.; chief info. officer Kaiser Found. Health Plan; exec. v.p., group tech. exec. Wells Fargo, San Francisco; corp. exec. v.p., chief info. officer SunTrust Banks, Inc., Atlanta, 2003—. Office: SunTrust Banks Inc PO Box 4418 Atlanta GA 30302-4418 Office Phone: 404-588-7711. Office Fax: 505-827-6173.

SULLIVAN, TIMOTHY JACKSON, museum administrator, retired academic administrator, educator; b. Ravenna, Ohio, Apr. 15, 1944; s. Ernest Tulio and Margaret Elizabeth (Caris) Sullivan; m. Anne Doubet Klare, Jan. 21, 1973. AB, Coll. William and Mary, Williamsburg, Va., 1966; JD, Harvard U., Cambridge, Mass., 1969; LLD (hon.), U. Aberdeen, Scotland, 1993, Old Dominion U., Norfolk, Va., 2005, Centre Coll., Danville, Ky., 2007. Asst. prof. law Coll. William and Mary, Williamsburg, Va., 1972—75, assoc. prof., 1975—78, prof., 1978—85, Bryan prof. law, dean, 1985—92, pres., 1992—2005, pres. emeritus, 2005—; exec. asst. for policy to Gov. Charles S. Robb State of Va., Richmond, Va., 1982—85; atty. Freeman, Drapers' Co., London, 1992; pres., CEO The Mariners Mus., Newport News, Va.,

2006—. Vis. prof. law U. Va., Charlottesville, 1981; exec. dir. Gov.'s Commn. on Va.'s Future, Richmond, 1982—84; vice-chmn. Gov.'s Commn. on Fed. Spending, Richmond, 1986; mem. Gov.'s Fellows Selection Com., 1985—90, Gov.'s Commn. on Sexual Assault and Substance Abuse on the Coll. Campus (chmn. enforcement subcom.), 1991—92; counsel Commn. on Future of Va.'s Jud. Sys., 1987—89; chair VA Rhodes Scholarship Commn., 1998—2003; mem. Livery Drapers Co., 2003; chair appeals panel Internat. Commn. Holocaust Era Ins. Claims, 2002—06. Mem. Va. State Bd. Edn., Richmond, 1987—92; chair Gov.'s Task Force on Intercollegiate Athletics, 1992—93; pres. The Mariner's Mus., Newport News, Va., 2006—. Decorated Bronze Star; named Outstanding Virginian, Va. 4-H Found., 1999. Fellow: Va. Bar Fedn., Am. Bar Fedn.; mem.: ABA, Va. Bar Assn., Va. State Bar, Am. Arbitration Assn. (bd. dirs. 2000—03), Cosmos Club, Univ. Club (Washington), Bull and Bear Club, Omicron Delta Kappa, Phi Beta Kappa. Democrat. Avocations: wine, swimming, reading, golf. Office: Coll William and Mary Office of Pres Emeritus PO Box 8795 Williamsburg VA 23187-8795 also: The Mariners Museum 100 Museum Dr Newport News VA 23606 Home Phone: 757-220-0423. Business E-Mail: tjsull@wm.edu, tsullivan@marinersmuseum.org.

SULLIVAN, TIMOTHY JOHN, allergist, immunologist, educator; MD, U. Miami, 1966. Diplomate Am. Bd. Allergy and Immunology, 1979. Intern Univ. of Miami Jackson Health System, 1967; resident internal medicine Barnes Hosp., 1971—73, fellow allergy & immunology, 1971—73; assoc. clin. prof. pediat. Med. Coll. of Ga.; hosp. affiliations include Atlanta Med. Ctr., Children's Healthcare of Atlanta, DeKalb Med. Ctr., Northside Hosp., Wellstar Kennestone Hosp., St. Joseph's Hosp. Office: Northside Hospital NE 1000 Johnson Ferry Rd Atlanta GA 30342-1611 Office Phone: 404-851-8000.

SULT, JOHN R., corporate financial executive; BS in Commerce, U. Lexington, Va. CPA. Sr. v.p., CFO and contr. ANR Pipeline Co.; v.p., contr. Halliburton Energy Svcs., 2004—05; CFO, contr. El Paso's Pipeline Group, sr. v.p., CFO and contr., 2005—09; bd. dirs. El Paso Pipeline GP Co., LLC, contr., 2007—09, sr. v.p., CFO, 2007—, El Paso Pipeline Partners, LP, 2007—, bd. dirs., 2009—; sr. v.p., contr. El paso Corp., 2005—09, prin. acctg. officer, 2007—10; CFO El Paso Corp., 2009—, exec. v.p., 2010—; sr. v.p., CFO Southern Natural Gas Co., 2009—. Mem.: AICPA, Texas Soc. CPAs, Fin. Execs. Internat. (mem. com. on corp. reporting). Office: El Paso Corp El Paso Bldg 1001 Louisiana St Houston TX 77002 Office Phone: 713-420-2600. Office Fax: 713-420-4417. Business E-Mail: John.Sult@elpaso.com.

SUMLIN, KEVIN, college football coach; b. Indpls., Aug. 3, 1964; m. Charlene Sumlin; children: Courtney, Shelby, Jackson, Joey. B in Criminology and Criminal Justice, Purdue U., West Lafayette, 1988. Grad. asst. coach Wash. State U. Cougars, 1989—90; wide receivers coach U. Wyo. Cowboys, 1991—92, U. Minn. Golden Gophers, 1993—96, quarterbacks coach, 1997; wide receivers coach Purdue U. Boilermakers, 1998—2000; asst. head coach, wide receivers coach Tex. A&M U. Aggies, 2001, asst. head coach, offensive coord., wide receivers coach, 2002; spl. teams coord., tight ends coach U. Okla. Sooners, 2003—05, co-offensive coord., wide receivers coach, 2006—07; head football coach U. Houston Cougars, 2008—11, Tex. A&M U. Aggies, 2011—. Named Conf. USA Coach of Yr., 2011, Southeastern Conf. Coach of Yr., 2012, Region II Coach of Yr., American Football Coaches Assn., 2012; finalist Paul "Bear" Bryant Nat. Coach of Yr. award, 2009. Office: Tex A&M Football Program c/o Athletic Dept PO Box 90017 College Station TX 77842-3017

SUMMERS, GERALD HOWARD (JERRY), lawyer; b. Chattanooga, May 28, 1941; s. Homer Howard and Millie (Dean) Summers. BA in Bus. Adminstrn. with honors, Auburn U., U. of South, 1963; LLB, U. Tenn., 1966. Bar: Tenn. 1966, US Ct. Appeals (6th cir.) 1970, US Supreme Ct. 1972. Asst. dist. atty., Chattanooga, 1966—69; sole practice; ptnr. Summers & Wyatt; mem. Tenn. Law Revision Commn., 1976, Tenn. Supreme Ct. Com. Jud. Planning, 1976, Commn. on Advt., 1978; judge Soddy-Daisy, Tenn., 1976—83. Mem. bd. advisors paralegal program Cleve. State CC, 1975—76; mem. faculty polit. sci. U. Tenn., 0982; mem. Law Enforcment Commn. Hamilton County; bd. dirs. Project First Offender; memb. br. adv. bd. United Bank Chattanooga; mem. Speedy Trial Planning Commn. for Eastern Dist. Tenn., 1977—78, Commn. on Criminal Rules, Tenn. Supreme Ct., 1982—83; lectr. in field. Author: Law Office Management Manual, 1974. Named Young Man of Yr., Chattanooga Jaycees, 1973, 1976—77, Outstanding Young Man Am., US Jaycees, 1974. Fellow: Am. Bd. Criminal Lawyers, Internat. Soc. Barristers, Am. Bd. Trial Advocates (founding mem., pres. Tenn. chpt. 1986—87), Tenn. Bar Found.; mem.: NACDL (gov. 1975—76), ABA, Ctrl. High Alumni Assn. (pres. 1971—73), Chattanooga Trial Lawyers Assn. (pres. 1972—73), Chattanooga Bar Assn. (mem. bd. govs. 1978, sec. 1981, pres.-elect 1982, pres. 1983—84), Tenn. Assn. Criminal Def. Lawyers (pres. 1975—76), Tenn. Trial Lawyers Assn. (v.p. 1972—73, pres. 1977—78), Assn. Trial Lawyers Am. (chmn. young lawyers sect. 1975, bd. govs. 1985—87), Tenn. Bar Assn. (chmn. criminal justice sect. 1976), Civitan (Chattanooga), Phi Gamma Delta (v.p. chpt. 1962—63). Office: Summers & Wyatt PC The James Bldg 735 Broad St, Ste 800 Chattanooga TN 37402-2913 Office Phone: 423-266-2385. Office Fax: 423-266-5211. E-mail: jsummers@summersandwyatt.com.

SUMMERS, LORRAINE DEY SCHAEFFER, retired librarian; b. Phila., Dec. 14, 1946; d. Joseph William and Hilda Lorraine (Ritchey) Dey; m. F. William Summers, Jan. 28, 1984. BA, Fla. State U., 1968, MS, 1969. Ext. dir. Santa Fe Regional Libr., Gainesville, 1969-71; pub. libr. cons. State Libr. of Fla., Tallahassee, 1971-78, asst. state libr., 1978-84; dir. adminstrv. svcs. Nat. Assn. for Campus Activities, Columbia, SC, 1984-85; asst. state libr. State Libr. of Fla., Tallahassee, 1985—2001, ret., 2001—. Bd. dirs., sec. Southeastern Libr. Network, Inc.; cons. in field. Contbr. articles to profl. jours. Del. Pres.'s Com. on Mental Retardation Regional Forum, Atlanta, 1975; del. Fla. Gov.'s Conf. on Libr. and Info. Svcs., 1978, 90, treas. Zonta Cares, 2012-14. Mem. ALA (orgn. com. 1979-83, coun. 1982-84, 93-97, resolutions com. 1983-85, mem. legislation com. 1993-95, nominating com. 1996, awards com. 1998-99, Spectrum awards jury 1999-2000), Assn. Specialized and Coop. Libr. Agys. (dir. 1976-82, chmn. planning and orgn. com. 1976-80, chmn. nominating com. 1980-81, chmn. by laws com. 1985-86, exec. bd. state libr. agy. sect. 1983-86, pres. 1987-88, chmn. stds. rev. com. 1990-92), Southeastern Libr. Assn. (exec. bd. 1976-80, v.p., pres.-elect 1994-96, pres. 1996-98, past pres. 1998-2000, nominating com. 2000-02), Fla. Libr. Assn. (sec. 1978-79, dir. 1976-80, nominating com. 1995-96), Zonta (dir. 1992-95, sec. 1999-2001, mem. svc. com. 2007-), United Nat. Comm.(chmn. 2009-10), Status Women Com. (chair 2011-12), Zonta Cares, Inc.(treas 2012-14). Democrat. Methodist. Personal E-mail: lorrainesummers@comcast.net.

SUMMERS, TIM, state legislator; m. Peggy Summers. Dir. Decision Point; mem. Dist. 99 Ark. House of Reps., 2009—. Fin. chmn. Bentonville City Coun.; mem. Benton County Quorum Ct. Pres. Bentonville-Bella Vista C. of C.; cert. lay speaker Living Waters Meth. Ch. Mem.: Thomas Jefferson Parent-Tchr. Assn. (pres.), Farm Bur., Bentonville Kiwanis. Republican. Meth. Office: State Capitol Rm 350 Little Rock AR 72201 also: 1805 Kimberly Pl Bentonville AR 72712 Office Phone: 501-682-6211, 501-682-7771, 479-273-0773. Business E-Mail: summerst@arkleg.state.ar.us.

SUMMITT, PAT (PATRICIA SUE SUMMIT), retired women's college basketball coach; b. Henrietta, Tenn., June 14, 1952; d. Richard and Hazel Head; m. R.B. Summitt (div.); 1 child, Ross Tyler. BS in Phys. Edn., U. Tenn., Martin, 1974; MS in Phys. Edn., U. Tenn., Knoxville, 1975. Head coach U. Tenn. Lady Volunteers, Knoxville, 1974—2012, head coach emeritus, 2012—. Head coach 1st US Jr. Nat. team, 1977 (2 gold medals in internat. play), US Nat. team William R. Jones Cup Games, 1979, World Championships, 1979, Pan American Games, 1979 (2 gold medals, 1 silver medal); asst. coach US Women's Olympic Basketball team, 1980-84, head coach, 1984 (gold medal); assoc. athletics dir., U. Tenn.; past v.p. USA BASKETBALL; past Olympic rep. adv. com. to USA BASKETBALL; bd. trustees Basketball Hall of Fame; bd. dirs. Women's Basketball Hall of Fame. Author: Reach For The Summit, 1998, Raise the Roof, 1998, Sum It Up: A Thousand and Ninety-Eight Victories, a Couple of Irrelevant Losses, and a Life in Perspective, 2013. Active Big Bros./Big Sisters; active spokesperson United Way, Race for the Cure, Juvenile Diabetes; hon. chair Tenn. Easter Seal Soc., 1985, 87, 88, 89; Tenn. chair Am. Heart Assn., 1994. Recipient Silver medal, US World U. Games, 1973, Gold medal, Pan American Games, 1975, Silver medal, Olympic Games, 1976, Wooden award, 1997, ARETE Award for Courage in Sports, 1999, Dick Enberg award, Coll. Sports Info. Directors America, 2007, John R. Wooden Award's Legends of Coaching award, 2008, ESPY award, Best Coach-Mgr., ESPN, 2008, Joe Lapchick Character award, 2008, Presdl. Medal of Freedom, The White House, 2012; named Women's Basketball Coaches Assn./Converse Coach of Yr., 1983—95, NCAA Coach of Yr., 1983, 1987, 1989, 1994, 1995, 1998, 2004, SEC Coach of Yr., 1993, 1995, 1998, 2001, 2003, 2004, 2007, 2011, Naismith Coach of Century, 2000, Sportswoman of Yr., Sports Illus., 2011, Women of Yr., Women in Sports and Events, 1999; named one of America's Best Leaders, US News & World Report, 2007; named to Women's Sports Found. Hall of Fame, 1990, The Nat. Assn. Sport & Physical Edn. Hall of Fame, 1996, The Women's Basketball Hall of Fame, 1999, The Naismith Meml. Basketball Hall of Fame, 2000. Mem. Chi Omega. Achievements include leading the Lady Vols to the NCAA Championship, 1987, 89, 91, 96, 97, 98, 2007, 2008; led the Lady Vols to the Southeastern Conf. Championship, 1980, 85, 90, 93, 94, 95, 98, 99, 2000, 01, 02, 03, 04, 07, 10, 11; became the all-time winningest coach in NCAA basketball history, March 21, 2005; first Division 1 coach to record 1,000 career victories, Feb. 5, 2009. Avocations: cooking, golf, running, water-skiing, boating. Office: University Tennessee 207 Thompson-Boling Ctr and Arena 1600 Phillip Fulmer Way Knoxville TN 37996-4610 Office Phone: 865-974-0600.

SUN, YUEFENG, research scientist, educator; b. Liangshan, Shandong, China, Apr. 5, 1962; s. Xueqian Sun and Shuyuan She; m. Lilai Yan; 1 child, Yusha Yan Sun. BS, Petroleum U. China, Donying, Shandong, 1981; MS, Columbia U., NYC, 1988, PhD, 1994. Geophysicist China Nat. Petroleum Corp., Urumqi, Xinjiang, 1982—87; grad. tchg. fellow Columbia U., NYC, 1988—94; postdoctoral fellow Lamont Doherty Earth Obs., Columbia U., Palisades, 1995—97, Doherty rsch. scientist, 1998—2005; assoc. prof. The Petroleum Inst., Abu Dhabi, 2005—06, Tex. A&M U., College Station, 2007—. Mem.: Am. Assn. Petroleum Geologists, Soc. Exploration Geophysicists (assoc.), Am. Geophys. Union (assoc.). Achievements include invention of work on relating permeability to wave velocity implemented and referred to as the Sun model by Shell Oil Co., which improves world hydrocarbon reserves and production; research in theory invention; patents for method of estimation of gas hydrates; systems and methods of detecting living organisms in rocks. Office: TAMU 3115 College Station TX 77843 Home: 721 Aster Dr College Station TX 77845 Personal E-mail: yfsun3@yahoo.com. Business E-Mail: sun@geo.tamu.edu.

SUNAHARA, YUKIO, electronics executive; b. Japan, 1938; BA, Keio U., 1961. Joined Tokyo Broadcasting System Inc., 1961, bd. dirs., 1993—96, pres., 1996—2002, chmn., 2002; owner Yokohama BayStars, 2002—03; tax officer Tokyo Electron America, Inc. Mem.: Internat. TV Acad. Arts & Sciences (bd. dirs.). Office: Tokyo Electron America Inc 2400 Grove Blvd Austin TX 78741-6500 Office Phone: 512-424-1000. Office Fax: 512-424-1001.

SUND, RICK (RICHARD W. SUND), professional sports team executive; b. Elgin, Ill., 1951; s. Bob Sund; m. Lea E. Sund; children: Hali, Patrick. Student, Northwestern U.; M in Athletic Adminstrn., Ohio U., 1974. With Milw. Bucks, 1974—78; player pers. dir. to v.p. ops. Dallas Mavericks, 1979—93; player pers. cons. Seattle SuperSonics, 1994—95, gen. mgr., 2001—07, cons., 2007—08; v.p. player pers. to exec. v.p. basketball ops. Detroit Pistons, 1995—2001; exec. v.p., gen. mgr. Atlanta Hawks, 2008—12, sr. advisor, basketball ops., 2012—. Named to Ill. HS Basketball Coaches' Hall of Fame. Avocation: golf. Office: Atlanta Hawks Centennial Tower 101 Marietta St NW Ste 1900 Atlanta GA 30303*

SUNDBERG, RICHARD JAY, chemistry professor; b. Sioux Rapids, Iowa, Jan. 6, 1938; BS, U. Iowa, 1959; PhD, U. Minn., 1962. Faculty dept. chemistry U. Va., Charlottesville, 1964-74, prof., 1974—. Author (with F. A. Carey) Advanced Organic Chemistry, 5th edit., 2007. Served to 1st lt. U.S. Army, 1962-64 Mem. Am. Chem. Soc. Lutheran. Office: U Va Dept Chemistry Box 400319 Charlottesville VA 22904-4319 Office Phone: 434-924-3233. Personal E-mail: rjs1d@virginia.edu.

SUNDEL, MARTIN, management consultant, psychologist, educator; b. Bronx, NY, Sept. 22, 1940; s. Louis and Pauline (Brotman) S.; m. Sandra Stone, Aug. 22, 1971; children: Adam Daniel, Jenny Rebecca, Ariel Pauline. BA cum laude, St. Mary's U., 1961; MSW., Our Lady of the Lake Univ., 1963; MA, PhD, U. Mich., 1968. Social group work supr. Valley Cities Jewish Cmty. Ctr., Van Nuys, Calif., 1963-65; asst. prof. U. Mich. Sch. Social Work, Ann Arbor, 1968-71; dir. rsch. and evaluation River Region Mental Health-Mental Retardation Bd., Louisville, 1972-77; assoc. clin. prof. dept. psychiatry and behavioral sci., adj. prof. Kent. Sch. Social Work, U. Louisville, 1974—77; sr. research assoc. The Urban Inst., Washington, 1977-80; pvt. practice psychology Dallas, 1980-95; Dulak Disting. prof. U. Tex., Arlington, 1980-89, prof., 1980-95, Fla. Internat. U., Miami, Fla., 1995-2000; faculty assoc. S.E. Fla. Ctr. on Aging, 1996-2000; pres. Sundel Cons. Group, 2000—. Mental health cons. UN High Commn. for Refugees in Cyprus, 1993-95; profl. adv. coun. Dallas Geriatric Rsch. Inst., 1980-89; long-range planning com. Dallas Jewish Coalition for the Homeless, 1986-95; coordinating com. Arlington Human Svcs. Project, 1981-90, Mayor's Forum on Human Svc. Needs Assessment, Ft. Worth, 1983-86; vis. prof. U. So. Calif. Sch. Social Work, spring 1985, mem., Gen. Sys. Theory rsch. Group, Neuropsychatric Inst., UCLA, 1985; sr. consortium rsch. fellow, Dept. Def., 1996-99. Author: (with Sandra Stone Sundel) Behavior Change in the Human Services, 1975, 5th edit., 2005; Be Assertive, 1980; co-author: Women at Midlife, 2002; co-editor: Assessing Health and Human Service Needs, 1983, Individual Change Through Small Groups, 2d edit., 1985, Midlife Myths, 1989; mem. editl. bds. and cons. to profl. jours. Named Nat. Table Tennis Champion, U1600 Round Robin Age Group of 40 Yrs. and Older, 2005; fellow, Harvard U. Lab. Cmty. Psychiatry, Boston, 1971—72. Fellow Prescribing Psychologists Register (diplomate), Internat. Coun. Prescribing Psychology (diplomate in psychopharmacology); mem. Behavior Therapy and Rsch. Soc. (charter clin. fellow). Home: 3804 Barbados Ave Hollywood FL 33026-4659 Personal E-mail: sundelm@bellsouth.net.

SUNDERLAND, RICHARD H., electrical engineer, freelance/self-employed lawyer; b. Jan. 17, 1933; BSEE, Tenn. Tehhnol. U., Cookeville, 1955; MSEE, U. Tenn., 1965; JD, U. San Francisco, 1990; LLM in Tax Law, NYU, 1994. Lic. atty. Tenn., DC, cert. pub. acct. Tenn., registered profl. engr. Tenn. Platoon leader US Marine Corps., Va., 1955—57; elec. engr. Tenn. Valley Auth., Chattanooga, 1957—75; chief procurement Tenn. Valley Auth, 1975—86; assoc. prof. bus., dir. Small Bus. Ctr., Valley City State U., 1991—92; prof. taxation Marist Coll., Poughkeepsie, NY, 1994—95. Dir. TVA'Retirement Sys. Knoxville, 1976; adj. prof. elec. engring. U. Tenn., 1965—73. Commr. USMC, 1955, served in US and Caribbean Area, 1955—57. Recipient Student Bar Assn. award, USF Law Sch., 1990; named one of Young Engr. of Yr., Tenn. Soc. Profl. Engrs., 1968. Mem.: ABA, IEEE (life; sr. mem., v.p. 1960—), Tenn. Bar Assn., Chattanooga Bar Assn., Tenn. Soc. Prof. Engrs. (chmn. ann. meeting 1962—86). Avocations: golf, guitar. Home: 8908 Brow Lake Rd Soddy Daisy TN 37379-4506

SUNDSTROM, HAROLD WALTER, public relations executive; b. Chgo., Jan. 26, 1929; s. Elmer A. and Rosalind Lillian (Busse) S.; m. Mary Olin, Oct. 1, 1955; children: Geoffrey Lee, Lori Lynn, Deborah. AA, Wright Jr. Coll., 1949; BA, Mich. State U., 1952, MA, 1954. Fgn. svc. info. officer USIA, Tokyo, Jakarta, Seoul, 1955-61; sr. pub. rels. assoc. Eli Lilly and Co., Indpls., 1962-66; v.p., dir. pub. rels. Eisenhower People to People Program, Kansas City, Mo., and Copenhagen, 1966-68; govt. and pub. affairs rep. North Ctrl. States Automobile Mfrs. Assn., Kansas City, 1968-69; speechwriter, pub. rels. cons. Commdr.-in-Chief U.S. Pacific Forces, Aiea, 1969-75; pres. No. Ariz. Comm., Inc., Flagstaff, 1975-79; asst. sec., dir. pub. affairs U.S. Internat. Trade Commn., Washington, 1977-87; v.p. pub. affairs and publs. Export-Import Bank U.S., Washington, 1987-89; pres. Halamar, Inc., Manassas, Va. and Easley, SC, 1983—, Silver Springs, Fla., 1983-98; assoc. dir. Mich. Citizenship Clearing House, MSU, East Lansing, Mich., 1954—55. Mem. Pres.'s Consumer Affairs Couns., 1977-89; freelance writer and poet. Author: The American West, 1956, Indonesia: Its People and Politics, 1957, Why Vietnam, 1961, Garuda, Introducing Indonesia, 1962, Faces of Asia: Korea, 1965, The Northern Arizona Scene, 1976, American Collie Champions, Vol. I, 1979, Vol. II, 1980, Vol. III, 1987, Collies - A Complete Pet Owners Manual, 1994, 2d edit., 2005; editor, pub. Hawaiian Dog Rev., The Alaska Cir., The Arizona Cir., Internat. Lhasa Apso Rev., Sandwich Isles Dog Gazette, 1972-76, Collie Cues, 1983-86, Travel Writer, Honolulu Sun Press, 1972-76. Active Civil War Preservation Trust, Colonial Williamsburg, Hist. Mount Vernon, Va. With U.S. Army, 1947-48, 52-53. Recipient People to People Disting. Svc. award, 1967, George Washington Honor medal Freedom Found., 1968, Silver Beaver award Boy Scouts Am., 1975. Fellow Japan Soc. N.Y., Pub. Rels. Soc. Am. (past pres. Hawaii chpt., Silver Anvil award 1973); mem. Dog Writers Assn. Am. (pres. 1984-92, Disting. Svc. award 1993), Dog Writers Ednl. Trust (vice chmn., chmn. 1999-2005), Collie Club Am. (pres. 1984-86), Collie Club Am. Found. (life, pres. 1990-92), Am. Kennel Club (del. 1987—; 25 Yr. AKL medal, 2012), Pi Sigma Alpha, Phi Kappa Sigma. Republican. Avocations: travel, photography. Home and Office: 1 Wadsworth Ct Greer SC 29651

SUPERNEAU, DUANE WILLIAM, geneticist, physician; b. Ogden, Utah, Dec. 31, 1950; s. Richard Edwin and Mary Ellen Superneau; children: Adam, Ashley, Allison. BA, Carroll Coll., 1973; MD, U. Wash., 1977. Diplomate Am. Bd. Pediat., Am. Bd. Med. Genetics. Asst. prof. dept. med. genetics U. So. Ala., Mobile, 1982-87, assoc. prof. dept. med. genetics, 1987-91; chief sect. med. genetics Ochsner Clinic, New Orleans, 1991—2005; dir. Genetic Svcs. La., Baton Rouge, 2005—10, Our Lady of the lake Genetics Svcs., Baton Rouge, 2010—. Clin. asst. prof. La. State U., New Orleans, 1992—. Bd. dirs. The ARC Greater New Orleans, 1991—, pres. 1994-96; bd. dirs. ARC of La., 1994—, pres., 1999-2001; bd. dirs. Jefferson Parish Human Svcs. Authority, Jefferson Parish, La., 1992-99. Roman Catholic. Office: Olol Genetics Svcs 8415 Goodwood Blvd Ste 202 Baton Rouge LA 70806-7851 Home: 981 Tifton De Baton Rouge LA 70815 Office Phone: 225-231-5381. Business E-Mail: duane.superneau@womans.org.

SUPINA, JOHN, aerospace and defense manufacturing company executive; B in Aviation Maintenance Mgmt. Various exec. positions, including v.p., contract adminstrn., govt. svcs. divsn., sr. v.p., state ops. dept. & gen. mgr. DIFZ, Dubai, United Arab Emirates; joined Dynalectron, 1980; sr. v.p., bus. adminstrn. DynCorp International, Inc., 2007—. Served USN. Office: DynCorp International Inc 3190 Fairview Park Dr Ste 700 Falls Church VA 22042 Office Phone: 571-722-0210. Office Fax: 571-722-0252.

SURAWICZ, BORYS, physician, educator; b. Moscow, Feb. 11, 1917; came to U.S., 1951, naturalized, 1956; s. Josef and Mathilda (Soloweczyk) S.; m. Frida G. Van Klaveren, July 19, 1946; children: Christina M., Nina M., Tanya S., Serge J. MD, Stefan Batory U., Wilno, Poland, 1939. Mem. staffs hosps., Germany, Norway, 1945-49; staff De Goesbriand Meml. Hosp., Burlington, Vt., 1951-53, Phila. Gen. Hosp., 1953-55; instr. cardiology U. Pa., Phila., 1954-55; instr. U. Vt., Burlington, 1955-57, asst. prof. clin. and expt. medicine, 1957-62; chief div. cardiology U. Ky. Coll. Medicine, Lexington, 1962-81, assoc. prof. medicine, 1962-66, prof., 1966-81; prof. medicine Ind. U. Sch. Medicine, Indpls., 1981—. Cons. VA Hosp., Indpls. Editor: (with E.D. Pellegrino) Sudden Cardiac Death, 1964, (with C. Fisch) Digitalis, 1969; (with E. Prystowsky, C.P. Reddy) Tachycardias, 1985, Electrophysiologic Basis of ECG and Cardiac Arrhythmics, 1995, Chou's Electrocardiography in Clinical Practice, 2001, 2008, Doctors in Fiction Lessons from Literature, 2009; mem. editl. bds. profl. jours. Recipient award, U. Ky. Rsch. Found., 1971, Cummings Humanitarian award, 1975, NASPE Disting. Scientist award, 1992, Merit award, Hungarian Cardiac Soc., 1995, award, Cardiac Electrophysiology Soc., 2006. Mem. AMA, ACP, Am. Heart Assn., Assn. Univ. Cardiologists (pres. 1978), Am. Coll. Cardiology (master; pres. 1979), Am. Physiol. Soc., Sigma Xi. Personal E-mail: bsurawic@yahoo.com.

SURAYEV, MAXIM, cosmonaut, pilot; b. Chelyabinsk, May 24, 1972; m. Suraeva Anna Alexandrovna; children: Arina, Ksenia. Grad. with honors as pilot engr., Kachin Air Force Pilot Sch., 1994; grad. with honors as pilot-engr.-researcher, Zhukovski Air Force Acad., 1997; JD, Russian Acad. Civil Svc., 2007. Maj. Russian Air Force; completed basic space tng., 1997—99; qualified as a test-cosmonaut Yuri Gagarin Cosmonaut Tng. Ctr., 1999—. Back-up crew mem. Internat. Space Station Expedition 17, 2006—08, Internat. Space Station Expedition 19, 2008—09; flight engr., cosmonaut Internat. Space Station Expedition 21 and 22 and TMA-16 mission, 2009. Avocations: sports, reading. Office: NASA Johnson Space Ctr 2101 NASA Parkway Houston TX 77058

SURBER, DAVID FRANCIS, media consultant, syndicated television producer, journalist; b. Covington, Ky. s. Elbert and Dorothy Kathryn (Mills) Surber. BA in Physics, Thomas More Coll., Covington, Ky., 1960; LLD (hon.), London Inst. Applied Rsch., 1973. Owner P.R. Co., pub. affairs counseling, Covington, 1960—. Judge Brit. Airways Tourism Tomorrow awards, London, 2000—. Spl. corr.: Am. newspapers to Vatican II, 1965; prodr.: (TV series) Make Peace with Nature, Sta. WKRC-TV, 1973—, Strip Mining: Two Views, 1972, Energy: Where Will It Come From, How Much Will It Cost, 1975, Atomic Power for Ohio, 1976, A Conversation with the Vice President, 1976, The Bad Water, 1977, The Trans-Alaska Pipeline: A Closeup Report, 1977, Acid Rain: A World View, 1986—89, Energy Independence in the U.K., 1992, Unhappy Prospects: Acid Rain & Global Climate Change, 1995, The Kyoto Summit: Was It Global and Will It Work, 1997—98. Apptd. by Sec. of Energy to Nat. Coal Coun., 1992, 1994, 1996, 1998, 2000, 2002, 2004, 2006, 2008, 2010, 2012, chmn. comm. com., 1999—; mem. Bd. Zoning Appeals, Covington, 1964—84, chmn., 1971—84, Covington Environ. Commn., 1971—72, Commn. Strip Mining, 1967—68; pub. interest adv. com. Ohio River Valley Water Sanitation Commn., 1976—82; water quality adv. com. Ohio-Ky.-Ind. Regional Coun. Govts., 1975—82; environ. adv. coun. City of Cin., 1981—84; rehab. com. Cmty. Chest Greater Cin., 1972—78, mem. agy. admissions com., 1972—78, mem. priorities com., 1972—78; pres. bd. dirs. Cathedral Found., 1968—70; trustee Montessori Learning Ctr., 1973—75, Bklyn. Spanish Youth Choir; founding mem. Mayor's Task Force on the Environment, Cin., 1972—73; mem. Ky. Nature Preserves Commn., 1976—79; Dem. candidate for U.S. Ho. Reps., 1972. Recipient Cmty. Svc. award, Thomas More Coll., 1975. Mem.: ACLU, AFTRA, Nat. Inst. Urban Wildlife (bd. dirs. 1987—96), Tri-State Air Com. (chmn. 1973—74), Mousquetaires d'Armagnac, Izaak Walton League (pres. Ky. 1973—98, bd. dirs. Ky., nat. bd. dirs.). Office: PO Box 15555 Latonia KY 41015-0555 Office Phone: 859-491-5000. Business E-Mail: surber@surber.com.*

SURBER, JOSEPH A., III, gas industry executive; m. Yancey Surber; 3 children. B, U. Ga. With Bank South, IBM Corp.; sr. ptnr. Intellinet Corp.; mng. dir. AGL Resources, Inc., v.p., chief info. officer, 2008—. Chmn., tech. divsn. Metro Atlanta United Way, 2009-. Mailing: AGL Resources Inc P O Box 4569 Atlanta GA 30302-4569 Office: AGL Resources Inc 10 Peachtree Pl NE Atlanta GA 30309 Office Phone: 404-584-4000. Office Fax: 404-584-3714. Business E-Mail: jsurber@aglresources.com.

SURGNIER, DAVID HERAL, gas company executive; b. Feb. 8, 1949; s. Florida Belle (Hair) S.; m. Mar. 20, 1973 (div. Nov. 1988); children: Jonathan, Angela, Nicholas. BS in Math., U. Okla., 1971, BS in Petroleum Engring., 1972; MS in Petroleum Engring., U. Tex., 1982. Registered profl. engr., Tex., Okla. Petroleum engr. Can. and mid-continent region Atlantic Richfield, Plano, Tex., 1972-75, mgr. spl. projects Houston, 1975-82; ops. mgr. Westwind Prodn., Oklahoma City, 1982-85; completion specialist Tex. Iron Workers, Oklahoma City, 1985-86; pres. David H. Surgnier, Inc., Oklahoma City, 1986-88; tech. sales rep. mid-continent area CTC (Completion Tool Co.) Internat., Oklahoma City, 1988-90, Rocky Mountain regional mgr. Denver, 1990-92; CEO Delta Gas Corp., Ada, Okla., 1992—; environ. cons. Environ. Resource Mgmt., Biotreatment, Inc., Aarow Environ., Inc., Argonne Nat. Lab., University of Chicago. Cons. Naval Oil Shale Res. 3, U.S. Dept. Energy, 1993.; bd. dirs.Sun River Energy, Inc., 2002-. Inventor and patentee in field. Trustee, pub. rels. chmn. Okla. chpt. Nat. Multiple Sclerosis Soc.; voting mem. Choctaw Indian Tribe. Mem. NSPE, Soc. Profl. Well Log Analysts, Geol. Soc. Am., Oklahoma City Geol. Soc. Office: Delta Gas Corp 6950 County Rd Ada OK 74820-2152 Office Phone: 405-332-3110.

SURLES, CAROL D., academic administrator; b. Pensacola, Fla., Oct. 7, 1946; d. Elza Allen and Versy Lee Smith; divorced; children: Lisa Surles, Philip Surles. BA, Fisk U., 1968; MA, Chapman Coll., 1971; PhD, U. Mich., 1978. Personnel rep. U. Mich., Ann Arbor, 1973-78, vice-chancellor-adminstrn. Flint, 1987-89; exec. asst. to pres., assoc. v.p. for human resources U. Ctrl. Fla., Orlando, 1978-87; v.p. acad. affairs Jackson State U., Miss., 1989-92; v.p. adminstrn. and bus. Calif. State U., Hayward, 1992-94; pres. Tex. Woman's U., Denton, 1994-99, Ea. Ill. U., Charleston, 1999—2001. Trustee Pub. Broadcasting Ch. 24, Orlando, 1985-87; bd. dirs. First State Bank, Denton, Tex., Tex.-N.Mex. Power Co., TNP-Enterprise. Recipient Outstanding Scholar's award Delta Tau Kappa, 1983. Mem. AAUW, Am. Assn. Colls. and Univs., Golden Key Honor Soc., Mortar Bd. Soc., Dallas Citizens' Coun., Dallas Women's Found., Coun. of Pres. (Austin, Tex.), Phi Kappa Phi, Alpha Kappa Alpha. Episcopal. Avocation: piano. Home: 1120 W La Rua St Pensacola FL 32501-3761

SURLES, RICHARD HURLBUT, JR., retired law librarian; b. Norfolk, Va., Mar. 28, 1943; s. Richard H. and Elda Florine (Belvin) S.; m. Judith Louise Coffin, May 29, 1964; children— Stephanie Anne, Richard H. BA, Tex. A&M U., 1963; JD, U.Houston, 1967; M.L.L., U.Wash., 1969. Bar: Colo. 1971. Asst. to law librarian U. Houston, 1966-68; asst. to law librarian King county Law Library, Seattle, 1968-69; dir. of law library, prof. law U. Denver, 1969-71, U. Tenn., Knoxville, 1971-76, U. Oreg., Eugene, 1976-81, U. Ill., Champaign, 1981—98; ret., 1998. Author: Legal Periodical Management Data, 1977 Mem. Am. Assn. Law Libraries Republican. Personal E-mail: Beretta@KTC.com.

SUROVELL, SCOTT A., state legislator, lawyer; m. Erinn Marie Madden; children: Eva, Leia, Mara, Colin. BA, James Madison U., Harrisonburg, Va., 1993; JD, U. Va. Sch. Law, 1996. Intern office records and registration Office of Clk. of US House of Reps., Washington, 1990; constituent svc. intern to Rep. Jim Moran US House of Representatives, 1991, legis. asst. to Rep. Ron Wyden Washington; co-founding ptnr., owner Surovell Markle Issacs and Levy PLC, Fairfax, Va.; mem. Dist. 44 Va. House of Dels., Richmond, Va., 2010—. Mem. Mt. Vernon Dem. Com., 2001—, co-chmn., 2004—05, dist. chmn., 2006—08; chmn. Fairfax County Dem. Com., 2008—09; mem. cmty. adv. coun. Fairfax County Pub. Schools, mem. leadership coun.; sec. Fifth Dist. Atty. Discipline Com. Named a Rising Star, Va. Superlawyer mag.; Governors' fellow, 1993. Mem.: Va. Trial Lawyers Assn. Family Law Sect., Fairfax Bar Assn., Lee-Mt. Vernon C. of C., Tauxemont Cmty. Assn. Democrat. Office: Va House of Dels Gen Assembly Bldg PO Box 406 Richmond VA 23218 also: PO Box 289 Mount Vernon VA 22121 Office Phone: 804-698-1044, 571-249-4484. Office Fax: 804-698-6744. Business E-Mail: delssurovell@virginia.house.gov.

SUROWIEC, ANDREW JULIUS, biophysicist, researcher; b. Lwów, Poland, Apr. 13, 1940; arrived in US, 1986; s. Jan Jakub and Maria (Knobloch) S.; m. Irene Regina Baranowski, Apr. 27, 1977; 1 child, Caroline Maria. Engr., Tech. U., Gliwice, Poland, 1962, MS, 1964; PhD, Silesian U., Katowice, Poland, 1972. Cert. elec. engring. Asst. prof. Silesien Sch. Medicine, Katowice, 1964-82; postdoctoral fellow Ctr. d'Etude L'Energie Nucleaire, Mol, Belgium, 1973-74; disting. vis. scientist U. Ottawa, Ont., Canada, 1983-87; asst. prof. Bowman U. Sch. Medicine, Winston-Salem, NC, 1987-88, U. So. Calif., LA, 1988-93; sr. physicist Centennial Med. Ctr., Nashville, 1993—2005. Peer reviewer: Cancer, Internat. Jour. Am. Cancer Soc., 1993; contbr. articles to Physics in Medicine and Biology, Bioelectromagnetics, IEEE Transactions Biomed., Internat. Jour. Hyperthermia, Biopolymers, Jour. Chem. Soc. Faraday Transactions. Grantee Nat. Sci. and Engring. Rsch. Coun., 1985. Fellow Radiation Rsch. Soc.; mem. Internat. Clin. Hyperthermia Soc., N.Y. Acad. Scis. Achievements include patent for recording system for rotating viscometer; finding of simulated materials for electromagnetic studies and cancer treatment; findings of dielectric spectroscopy of normal and cancer tissues; finding of dielectric and hydrodynamic properties of DNA. Personal E-mail: andsur@aol.com.

SURWIT, RICHARD SAMUEL, psychology professor; b. Bklyn., Oct. 7, 1946; s. David and Ethel S.; m. Sandra E. Cummings, May 23, 1982; children: Daniel Alan, Sarah Jeanne. AB, Earlham Coll., 1968; PhD, McGill U., Montreal, Que., Can., 1972; postgrad., Harvard U., Boston. Cert. clin. psychology Am. Bd. Profl. Psychology. Postdoctoral fellow Harvard Med. Sch., 1972-74, instr., 1974-76, asst. prof., 1976-77; assoc. prof. psychiatry Duke U. Med. Ctr., Durham, NC, 1977-83, prof., 1980, 1983—2012, vice chmn., 1993—2012; chief divsn. med. psychology Duke U., 1997—2012, prof. psychology, 1991—; chmn. bd. dir. ZyCare Inc. (formerly Healthware Corp.), Chapel Hill, 1983—2009; CEO Sengenix Inc., 2012. Author: Fear: Learning to Cope, 1978, Behavioral Approaches to Cardiovascular Diseases, 1982, The Mind-Body Diabetes Revolution, 2004. Recipient rsch. devel. award NIMH, 1980, rsch. scientist award NIMH, 1993, Sr. Career Award, Divsn. 38, Am. Psychological Assn., 2010 Fellow APA, Soc. Behavioral Medicine (pres. 1994, Disting. Scientist award 2012), Acad. Behavioral Medicine Rsch. Achievements include co-discovery in 1997, of UCP2, a novel gene related and diabetes and immunity; co-developer of the Diacare diabetes disease management system, Coag-Care anticoagulation management system; patents in field. Home: 3804 Sweeten Creek Rd Chapel Hill NC 27514-9706 Office: Duke U Med Ctr PO Box 3842 Durham NC 27702-3842 Office Phone: 919-684-4317.

SUSANIN, TIMOTHY SCOTT, lawyer, health products executive; b. 1963; m. Barbara Susanin. BA in History with honors, Franklin & Marshall Coll., 1985; JD, Villanova U., 1988. Asst. US atty. (ea. dist.) Pa. US Dept. Justice, asst. US atty. DC; ptnr. Gibbons PC, 2001—08; v.p., chief counsel, dispute mgmt. WellCare Health Plans Inc., 2008; sr. v.p., gen. counsel, sec. WellCare Health Plans, Inc., 2009—. Assoc. ind. counsel US Senate Whitewater Investigation, 1998—2000. Worked US Navy Judge Adv. General's Corps, 1988—92. Office: WellCare Health Plans Inc 8735 Henderson Rd Tampa FL 33634 Office Phone: 813-290-6200. Office Fax: 813-262-2802. Business E-Mail: timothy.susanin@wellcare.com.

SUSMAN, MORTON LEE, lawyer; b. Aug. 6, 1934; m. Nina Meyers, May 1, 1958; 1 child, Mark Lee. BBA, So. Meth. U., 1956, JD, 1958. Bar: Tex. 1958, U.S. Dist. Ct. (so. dist.) Tex. 1961, U.S. Ct. Appeals (5th cir.) 1961, U.S. Supreme Ct. 1961, U.S. Ct. Appeals (11th cir.) 1981, DC 1988, U.S. Ct. Appeals (DC cir.) 1988, N.Y. 1990, Colo. 1996. Asst. U.S. atty., Houston, 1961-64; 1st asst. U.S. atty., 1965-66; U.S. atty., 1966-69; ptnr. Weil, Gotshal & Manges and predecessor firm Susman & Kessler, Houston, 1969-97; ret., 1998. Lt. USNR, 1958—61. Fellow: Am. Coll. Trial Lawyers, Tex. Bar Found.; mem.: FBA (dir., Younger Fed. Lawyer award 1968), ABA, Tex. Bar Assn. Democrat.

SUSMAN, STEPHEN DAILY, lawyer; b. Houston, Jan. 20, 1941; m. Ellen Spencer, 1999; children: Stacy Kuhn, Harry. BA magna cum laude, Yale U., 1962; JD with highest honors, U. Tex., 1965. Bar: Tex. 1965, US Supreme Ct. 1970, DC 1999, NY 2000, Colo. 2002. Law clk. to Hon. John R. Brown US Ct. Appeals (5th cir.), New Orleans, 1965-66; law clk. to Justice Hugo L. Black US Supreme Ct., Washington, 1966-67; ptnr. Fulbright & Jaworski LLP, Houston, 1966-75; spl. counsel to atty. gen. Mandell & Wright, P.C., Houston, 1975-80; founding ptnr. Susman Godfrey LLP, Houston, 1980—. Vis. prof. law U. Tex., Austin, 1975; chmn. adv. com. on discovery Tex. Supreme Ct. Contbr. articles to profl. jours. Mem. Nat. Coun. of Human Rights First; mem. bd. visitors Anderson U. Cancer Found.; mem. devel. bd. U. Tex. Health Sci. Ctr.; mem. Yale Art Gallery, Yale Devel. Found. Recipient ADL Jurisprudence award, 1995, Disting. Counselor award, State Bar Tex., 2005; named one of The Nation's Top Litigators, The Nat. Law Jour., 1989, 2006 Mem. ABA (antitrust sect., mem. coun. litig. sect., chmn. task force on fast track litig.), Houston Bar Assn., Dallas Bar Assn., DC Bar Assn., NY Bar Assn., Colo. Bar, State Bar Tex., Am. Law Inst., Assn. Trial Lawyers Am., Am. Bar Trial Advs., Houston Bar Assn., Southwestern Legal Found. Rsch. Fellows, Yale Club (Houston, NYC), Houston Trial Lawyers Assn. (dir.), Tex. Assn. Civil Trial and Appellate Specialists (former pres., dir.), Order of the Coif, Friars, Phi Delta Phi. Avocations: skiing, bicycling. Office: Susman Godfrey LLP Ste 5100 1000 Louisiana St Houston TX 77002-5096 Office Phone: 713-653-7801. Office Fax: 713-654-6670. Business E-Mail: ssusman@susmangodfrey.com.

SUSSER, SAM L., oil industry and consumer products company executive; married; 3 children. BBA in Fin., U. Tex., Austin. Vice chmn., dir. Corpus Christi Regional Econ. Devel. Corp.; with, Corp. Fin. Divsn., mergers and acquisitions group Salomon Brothers, Inc., NYC and Dallas, 1985—87; founder Susser Holdings Corp. (formerly Southguard Corp.), 1988, gen. mgr., v.p., ops., 1988—92, pres., CEO and dir., 2005—. Mem. adv. coun. Tex. A&M U. Coll. Bus., Corpus Christi; trustee Driscoll Found.; dir. Tex. State Aquarium, USS Lexington Mus. Office: Susser Holdings 4525 Ayers St Corpus Christi TX 78415-1401 also: Susser Holdings Corp 4525 Ayers St Corpus Christi TX 78415-1401 Home Phone: 361-884-2463. Office Fax: 361-884-2494. Business E-Mail: ssusser@susser.com.

SUSSMAN, HARVEY MARTIN, educator; b. NYC, Dec. 7, 1943; s. Morris and Rose Sussman; m. Sandra Rae Klayman, June 22, 1969; children: Zachary Michael, Hannah Elizabeth. PhD, U. Wis., Madison, 1970. Endowed prof. U. Tex., Austin, 1970—. Rsch. grant, NIH. Fellow: Acoustical Soc. Am. Home: 21 North Peak Rd Austin TX 78746 Office: Univ Texas Austin TX 78712 Office Fax: 512-471-4340. Business E-Mail: sussman@mail.utexas.edu.

SUSTANA, MARK, lawyer, construction company executive; b. Berea, Ohio, July 18, 1961; m. Susan Sustana; children: David, Kathleen. BA, U. NC, 1983; JD, U. NC Sch. Law, 1986. Bar: NY 1987, US Dist. Ct. (so. dist) NY 1991. Atty. Dunnington, Bartholow & Miller, 1986—92; with Russ Berrie & Co. Inc., 1992—94, J.M. Huber Corp., 1994—98; chief legal officer, corp. sec. GenTek, Inc., 1998—2005; sec., gen. counsel Lennar Corp., Miami, Fla., 2005—. Mem.: NY State Bar Assn. Office: Lennar Corp 700 NW 107th Ave Ste 400 Miami FL 33172 Office Phone: 305-559-4000. Office Fax: 305-228-8383. E-mail: mark.sustana@lennar.com.

SUTHERLAND, ALAN ROY, business educator; b. NYC, Jan. 15, 1944; s. Arthur Abbott and Margaret Louise S. BFA, Pratt Inst., Bklyn., 1964; MPA, NYU, 1969, PhD, 1984. Personnel dir. Manhattan Psychiat. Ctr., NYC, 1966-72; dep. dir. Rockland Children's Psychiat. Ctr., Orangeburg, NY, 1972-74, L.I. Devel. Ctr., Melville, NY, 1974-78, dir., 1978-80; program dir. Vols. Am., NYC, 1983-86; sr. staff officer Nat. Acad. Scis., Washington, 1986-88; dep. dir. U.S. Interagy. Coun. on Homeless, Washington, 1988-89; exec. dir. Travelers Aid Internat., Washington, 1989-91, AIDS Ctr. of Queens County, Rego Park, NY, 1992-96; chair dept. mgmt. studies Southeastern U., Washington, 1998-99. Prof. U. Md., College Park, 1998—, program dir. U. Md. U. Coll., Adelphi, Md., 1998-. Editor: Homlessness, Health and Human Service Needs. Recipient citation N.Y.C. Coun., 1986, Stanley J. Drazak Excellence in Tchg. award U. Md., 2004. Mem. ASPA, World Futurist Soc. Lutheran. Avocation: weightlifting. Office: Univ of Maryland 3501 University Blvd E Adelphi MD 20783-7998

SUTPHEN, JAMES L., pediatrician; b. Aug. 9, 1946; MD, Columbia U., NYC, 1972. Cert. in pediat., in pediatric gastroenterology 2005. Residency in pediat. Johns Hopkins U., Balt.; fellowship in clin. nutrition, pediatric gastroenterology Harvard Med. Sch. Boston Children's Hosp.; prof., dept. pediat. U. Va. Health Sys., Charlottesville, head, divsn. pediatric gastroenterology, nutrition. Contbr. articles to profl. jours. Named to Best Doctors in America, Best Doctors, Inc. Office: Univ Va Health Sys Divsn Pediat Gastroenterology Nutrition PO Box 800386 Charlottesville VA 22908-0386 Office Phone: 434-924-2457. Office Fax: 434-924-8798. Business E-Mail: jls5z@virginia.edu.

SUTTHOFF, JOHN, delivery service executive; Sr. v.p., COO UPS Logistics Group (subs. of United Parcel Svc., Inc.), 1998—2002; v.p., global mktg. & new product devel. UPS Supply Chain Solutions (subs. of United Parcel Svc., Inc.), 2002—. Office: UPS Supply Chain Solutions 12380 Morris Rd Alpharetta GA 30005 Office Phone: 913-693-6151. Office Fax: 913-469-8824. Business E-Mail: jsutthoff@ups.com.

SUTTON, BEVERLY JEWELL, psychiatrist; b. Rockford, Mich., May 27, 1932; d. Beryl Dewey and Cora Belle (Potes) Jewell; m. Harry Eldon Sutton, July 7, 1962; children: Susan, Caroline. MD, U. Mich., 1957. Diplomate Am. Bd. Pediat., Am. Bd. Psychiatry and Neurology. Rotating intern St. Joseph Mercy Hosp., Ann Arbor, Mich., 1958; resident in child psychiatry Hawthorne Ctr., Northville, Mich., 1958-62; resident in pediat. U. Hosp./U. Mich. Med. Ctr., Ann Arbor, 1959-61; resident in psychiatry Austin (Tex.) State Hosp., 1962-64, dir. children's svc., 1964-89, dir. psychiat. residency program, 1989—, dir. tng. and rsch., 1993-98. Cons. in field. Contbr. articles to profl. jours. Active numerous civic orgns. Recipient Outstanding Achievement award, YWCA, 1989, Jackson Day award, Tex. Soc. Child and Adolescent Psychiatry, 1989, Showcase award, Tex. Dept. Mental Health/Mental Retardation, 1990. Fellow Am. Acad. Child and Adolescent Psychiatry (life), Am. Psychiat. Assn. (Disting. fellow), Am. Pediatric Assn.; mem. Group for Advancement Psychiatry, Tex. Soc. Child and Adolescent Psychiatry (pres. 1979-80, Jackson Day award), Tex. Soc. Psychiat. Physicians (Disting. Svc. award 1990), AMA, Tex. Med. Soc., Am. Genetics Soc. Office: Seton Shoal Creek Hosp 3501 Mills Ave Austin TX 78731 Business E-Mail: bsutton@seton.org.

SUTTON, DOUGLAS HOYT, nursing educator; b. McHenry, Ill., Oct. 27, 1962; s. Hoyt Douglas and Barbara Sutton. Cert. in emergency med. tech., Polk C.C., Winter Haven, Fla., 1985; ADN, SUNY, Albany, 1990, BS in Psychology, 1993; MSN, U. Fla., 1995; MPA, Troy State U., 1998; EdD, Fla. Internat. U., 2004, master's cert., 2003. RN Calif., cert. adult health nurse practitioner, adult clin. nurse specialist. Paramedic Polk County Emergency Med. Svcs., Bartow, Fla., 1984—88; edn. cons. Moore Pubs., 1990—94; mgr. orthopedics and skilled care programs Columbia Healthcare, Inc., Gainesville, Fla., 1995—97; dir. med. surg. nursing U. Cmty. Hosp., Tampa, Fla., 1997—98; dir. patient svcs. Bethesda Meml. Hosp., Fla., 1998—2000; asst. prof. nursing Broward C.C., Ft. Lauderdale, Fla., 2000—02, Barry U., Miami, Fla., 2002—05; posdoctoral fellow Wash. State U., Spokane, 2003; assoc. prof. nursing Fla. Atlantic U., Boca Raton, Fla., 2005—06, DON programs Broward campus, 2006—07. Mem.: Nat. Assn. Bariatric Nurses, Am. Acad. Nurse Practitioners (cert. adult health nurse practioner 2004—), Nat. League of Nursery (cert. nurse educator), Sigma Theta Tau. Home: 1747 NE 45 St Fort Lauderdale FL 33334 Office Phone: 561-297-2872. Business E-Mail: dsutton@fau.edu.

SUTTON, HARRY ELDON, geneticist, educator; b. Cameron, Tex., Mar. 5, 1927; s. Grant Edwin and Myrtle Dovie (Fowler) S.; m. Beverly Earlene Jewell, July 7, 1962; children: Susan Elaine, Caroline Virginia. BS in Chemistry, U. Tex., Austin, 1948, MA, 1949; PhD in Biochemistry, U. Tex., 1953. Biologist U. Mich., 1952-56, instr., 1956-57, asst. prof. human genetics, 1957-60; assoc. prof. zoology U. Tex., Austin, 1960-64, prof., 1964-99, chmn. dept. zoology, 1970-73, asso. dean Grad. Sch., 1967-70, 73-75, v.p. for research, 1975-79, Ashbel Smith prof. emeritus molecular genetics and microbiology, 2000—. Mem. adv. council Nat. Inst. Environ. Health Scis., 1968-72, council sci. advs., 1972-76; mem. various coms. Nat. Acad. Scis.-NRC; cons. in field; bd. dirs. Associated Univs. for Research in Astronomy, 1975-79, Argonne Univs. Assn., 1975-79, Univ. Corp. for Atmospheric Research, 1975-79, Associated Western Univs., 1978-79 Author: Genes, Enzymes, and Inherited Disease, 1961, An Introduction to Human Genetics, 1988, Genetics: A Human Concern, 1985; editor: First Macy Conference on Genetics, 1960, Mutagenic Effects of Environmental Contaminants, 1972, Am. Jour. Human Genetics, 1964-69. Trustee S.W. Tex. Corp. Public Broadcasting, 1977-80, sec., 1979-80; bd. dirs. Ballet Austin, 1978-84, 98-2004; mem. Austin Arts Commn., 1991-95. Served with U.S. Army, 1945-46. Mem. AAAS, Am. Soc. Human Genetics (dir. 1961-69, pres. 1979), Genetics Soc. Am., Am. Soc. Biochem. and Molecular Biology, Am. Chem. Soc., Tex. Genetics Soc. (pres. 1979), Am. Genetic Assn., Headliners Club (Austin), Town and Gown Club. Achievements include research and publications in human genetics. Home: 1103 Gaston Ave Austin TX 78703-2507 Office: Univ Tex Sect Molecular Genetics & Microbiology Austin TX 78712 Business E-Mail: eldon.sutton@mail.utexas.edu.

SUTTON, JAY, gas industry executive; B in Mech. Engring., Clemson U. Registered profl. engr., Ga. V.p., gen. mgr., Coastal Region Florida City Gas, Atlanta Gas Light (subs. of AGL Resources Inc.); various engring. leadership positions AGL Resources, Inc., dir., strategic alliances, 2006, v.p., engring. svcs. and supply chain, 2009—. Bd. dirs. Fla. Natural Gas Assn. Office: AGL Resources Inc 10 Peachtree Pl NE Atlanta GA 30309 Office Phone: 404-584-4000. Office Fax: 404-584-3714. Business E-Mail: jsutton@aglresources.com.

SUTTON, JEFFREY PAUL, physician, scientist, administrator; b. NYC, July 6, 1958; MD, U. Toronto, Ontario, Can., 1982, MSc in Med. Sci., 1985, PhD in Physics, 1988. Resident Harvard Med. Sch., Boston, 1988-91; vis. scientist brain & cognitive scis. MIT, Cambridge, 1988-95; facaulty Harvard Med. Sch., Boston, 1991—2002; founder. dir. neural sys. grp. Mass. Gen. Hosp., 1995—2002; pres., inst. dir. Nat. Space Biomed. Rsch. Inst., Houston, 2001—. Recipient Career Rsch. Scientist award, NIH, Presidents Citation, Soc. NASA Flight Surgeons. Office: National Space Biomedical Research Institute One Baylor Plaza NA 425 Houston TX 77030 Office Phone: 743-798-7412. Office Fax: 743-798-7413.

SUTTON, JOHN SCHUHMANN, JR., retired purchasing consultant; b. Louisville, July 12, 1931; s. John Schuhmann and Ruth Evelyn (Roby) S.; m. Doris Jean Hornung, Dec. 12, 1953; children: Deborah Ann, Francis Eugene, Thomas Gerard. BA in Zoology, U. Louisville, 1953, MA in Math., 1965. Cert. purchasing mgr. Quality control technician Brown-Forman Corp., Louisville, 1956-64, mgr. quality control, 1964-80, asst. dir. purchasing, 1980—83, dir. purchasing, 1983-85, asst. v.p. purchasing, 1985-88, v.p. purchasing, 1988-91; cons. in field, 1991-95; ret., 1995. Cons. in field. Author poems. With U.S. Army, 1953-55. Mem. Am. Soc. Quality Control, Nat. Assn. Purchasing Mgrs., Purchasing Mgrs. Assn. Louisville, Jefferson Club. Democrat. Roman Catholic. Avocations: sports, fishing, poetry, writing. Home: 1106 Grazing Meadows Ln Louisville KY 40245 E-mail: suttonjss@aol.com.

SUTTON, JOHNNY KEANE, lobbyist, former prosecutor; b. June 1960; B in Internat. Bus., U. Tex., 1983, JD, 1987. Criminal trial prosecutor Harris County Dist. Atty. Office; asst. dist. atty. Harris County Dist. Atty.'s Office, 1987—95; criminal justice policy dir. to Gov. State of Tex., 1995—2000; assoc. dep. atty. gen. US Dept. Justice, Washington, 2001; policy coord. Bush-Cheney Transition Team, US Dept. Justice; US atty. (we. dist.) Tex. US Dept. Justice, 2001—09; ptnr. The Ashcroft Group, LLC, Washington, 2009—. Avocation: baseball (played for the Longhorns, starting lef-fielder on 1983 Nat. Championship team).

SUTTON, LYNN SORENSEN, librarian; b. Detroit, July 31, 1953; d. Leonard Arthur Edward and Dorothy Ann (Steele) Sorensen. AB, U. Mich., 1975, MLS, 1976. Dir. Med. Libr. South Chgo. Cmty. Hosp., 1976-77; corp. dirs. libraries Detroit-Macomb Hosp. Corp., Detroit, 1977-86; dir. librs. Harper Hosp., Detroit, 1987-88; dir. Sci. and Engring. Libr. Wayne State U., Detroit, 1989-95, dir. undergrad. libr., 1996—2004; dean Z. Smith Reynolds Libr. Wake Forest U., Winston-Salem, NC, 2004—. Cons. Catherine McAuley Health Sys., Ann Arbor, Mich., 1993. Contbr. articles to profl. jours. Mem. ALA, Assn. Coll. and Rsch. Librs. (budget and fin. com. 1995—), Mich. Health Scis. Librs. Assn. (pres. 1987-88), Met. Detroit Med. Libr. Group (pres. 1983-84), Phi Beta Kappa, Beta Phi Mu. Office: Z Smith Reynolds Libr Wake Forest U PO Box 7777 Winston Salem NC 27109 Office Phone: 336-758-5090. Business E-Mail: suttonls@wfu.edu.

SUTTON, MARK S., paper company executive; Engr. International Paper Co., Pineville, La., 1984, gen. mgr. pressure sensitive products, sales and mktg. mgr., indsl. papers and mgr., Thilmany Mill, v.p., gen. mgr. corrugated packaging ops., European, 2002—05, v.p. strategic planning, 2005—07, v.p. supply chain, 2007—08, sr. v.p. supply chain, 2008—09, sr. v.p. printing and comm. papers, Americas, 2010—11, sr. v.p. indsl. packaging, 2011—; former sr. v.p. supply chain Shorewood Packaging Corp. Office: International Paper Co 6400 Poplar Ave Memphis TN 38197 Office Phone: 901-419-9000. Office Fax: 901-214-9682.

SUTTON, NEAL S., lawyer, energy executive; b. Grand Forks, ND, Sept. 9, 1945; BA, U. Houston, 1969, JD, 1972. Bar: Tex. 1972, US Ct. Appeals (5th cir.) 1972. Atty. pvt. practice; gen. counsel, sec. Cameron Iron Works (acquired by Cooper Industries Inc.), 1977—89; assoc. gen. counsel Cooper Industries, Inc., 1989—91; v.p. Smith International, Inc., 1991—92, sec., gen. counsel, 1991—2006, v.p., adminstrn., 1992—94, sr. v.p., adminstrn., 1994—2006, sr. v.p., law, 2006—. Adj. assoc. prof. adminstrv. sci. Rice U. Jones Grad. Sch. Adminstrn., 1989—93; gulf coast dist. dir. Petroleum Equipment Suppliers Assn. Bd. dirs. Harris County Edn. Found., 1997—. Mem.: Am. Corp. Counsel Assn. (dir. Houston chpt. 1984—87, pres. Houston chpt. 1985—86, mem. nat. bd. dirs. 1988—96), State Bar Tex., Houston Bar Assn. (dir. corp. counsel sect. 1991—93), ABA. Office: Smith International Inc 16740 E Hardy Rd Houston TX 77032 Office Phone: 281-443-3370. Office Fax: 281-233-5199. Business E-Mail: nsutton@smith-intl.com.

SUZUKI, HIDETARO, violinist; b. Tokyo, June 1, 1937; arrived in U.S., 1956; s. Hidezo and Humi (Sakai) S.; m. Zeyda Ruga, May 16, 1962; children: Kenneth Hideo, Nantel Hiroshi, Elina Humi. Diploma, Toho Sch. Music, Tokyo, 1956, Curtis Inst. Music, 1963. Prof. violin Conservatory Province Que., Canada, 1963-79, Laval U., Quebec, Canada, 1971-77, Butler U., Indpls., 1979—. Concertmaster Que. Symphony Orch., 1963-78, Indpls. Symphony Orch., 1978-2005; performed as concert violinist Can., U.S., Ea. and Western Europe, Cuba, Japan, S.E. Asia, India, USSR 1951-; guest condr. orchs. in numerous concerts, broadcasts, 1968—; mem. jury Mont. Internat. Competition, 1979, Internat. Violin Competition, 1979, jury for Internat. Violin Competition of Indpls., 1982, 86, 90, 94; artistic dir. Suzuki and Friends chamber music series, 1980-, founder Pro Musica Washington, 2007-; rec. artist (CDs, violin and piano) Dialogue, Dialogue II, Pas de deux.

SUZUKI, HOWARD KAZURO, retired anatomist, educator; b. Ketchikan, Alaska, Apr. 3, 1927; s. Goerge K. and Tsuya S.; m. Tetsuko Fujita, Sept. 12, 1952; children: Georganne, Joan, James, Stanley. BS, Marquette U., 1949, MS, 1951; PhD, Tulane U., 1955. Instr. anatomy Yale U. Sch. Medicine, 1955-58; asst. prof. anatomy U. Ark. Med. Center, Little Rock, 1958-62, asso. prof., 1962-67, prof., 1967-70; prof. anatomy, asso. dean health related professions U. Fla., Gainesville, 1970-71; prof. anatomy U. Fla. (Coll. Medicine), 1970-71; dean U. Fla. (Coll. Health Related Professions), 1971-79; prof. anatomy U. Fla. (Coll. Medicine and Health Related Professions), 1979-90, ret., 1990. Cons. NIH, VA, NASA; vis. research prof. U. Utah Sch. Medicine, 1962 Contbr. articles to profl. jours. Bd. dirs. Civitan Regional Blood Bank, 1977—; regional v.p. Fla. Retarded Citizens Assn., 1974-76; mem. Fla. Adv. Council on Vocat. Edn., 1978-86, chmn., 1981; active United Way. Fellow AAAS; mem. Soc. Exptl. Biol. Medicine, Am Assn. Anatomists, Am. Soc. Allied Health Professions, Am. Soc. Marine Artists, Sigma Xi. Episcopalian. Home: 4331 NW 20th Pl Gainesville FL 32605-3436 E-mail: hksuzuki@aol.com.

SWAID, SWAID N., neurosurgeon, educator; BS in Biology summa cum laude, U. Ala., 1973, MD cum laude, 1976. Diplomate American Bd. Neurol. Surgery, 1983, lic. Calif., 1978. Intern in gen. surgery Univ. Calif. San Diego, 1976—77; chief. neurosurgical resident Univ. Ala. Med. Ctr., resident in neurol. surgery, 1977—81; hosp. affiliation includes: Brookwood Med. Ctr., Baptist Med. Ctr., St. Vincent's Hosp.; assoc. prof. neurol. surgery Univ. Ala. Fellow: American Coll. of Surgeons; mem.: AMA, Jefferson County Med. Soc., Southern Med. Assn., Ala. Neurosurgical Assn. Office: Swaid N Swaid MD FACS Ste 372 513 Brookwood Blvd Birmingham AL 35209 Office Phone: 205-949-1800, 888-884-9528. Office Fax: 205-870-7735.*

SWALLOW, EDWARD M., aerospace and defense manufacturing company executive; BEE, Syracuse U.; B in Physics & Astronomy, SUNY (State U. NY), Oneonta; M in Sys. Mgmt., U. S.C.; grad., Squadron Officer's Sch., Air Command and Staff Coll. With Logicon, Space Applications Corp.; v.p., bus. devel. Steven Myers and Assocs. Govt. Svcs. Group; dir., strategic devel. Northrop Grumman Corp., TASC; with info. systems sector; v.p. Strategic Capture and Campaigns, 2010, Bus. Devel. and Civil Cyber Lead Civil Systems Divsn. Bd. mem., pres. Nat. Defense Indsl. Assn., Washington Chpt., 2004; bd. mem., chmn. NDIA Space Divsn., 2003—05; founder and chmn. NDIA Science Tech. Engring. & Math. Workforce Divsn.; bd. mem. and asst. treas. Soc. Manufacturing Engineeris Edn. Found.; bd. mem. Nat. Guard Youth Found. Office: Northrop Grumman Corp 7575 Colshire Dr Mc Lean VA 22102 Office Phone: 703-556-2239. Business E-Mail: edward.swallow@ngc.com.

SWAN, GEORGE STEVEN, law educator; b. St. Louis; s. Raymond Albert and Lorene Catherine (Kennedy) Swan. BA, Ohio State U., 1970; JD, U. Notre Dame, 1974; LLM, U. Toronto, 1976, SJD, 1983. Bar: Ohio 1974, U.S. Dist. Ct. (so. dist.) Ohio 1975, U.S. Supreme Ct. 1987, U.S. Ct. Appeals (6th and 11th cirs.) 1993, U.S. Ct. Appeals (10th cir.) 1994, DC 1997, Ga. 1997, Fla. 1997, U.S. Dist. Ct. (no. dist.) Ga. 1997, Minn. 1998, La. 1999, Mass. 1999, Nebr. 1998, US Ct Appeals, 7th cir. 1998; CLU, ChFC, CFP, CPFFE, CRCMP. Asst. atty. gen. State of Ohio, Columbus, 1974-75; jud. clk. Supreme Ct. Ohio, Columbus, 1976-78; asst. prof. Del. Law Sch., Wilmington, 1980-83, assoc. prof., 1983-84; prof. law St. Thomas U. Law Sch., Miami, Fla., 1984-88; jud. clk. U.S. Ct. Appeals (7th cir.), Chgo., 1988-89; assoc. prof. N.C. Agrl. & Tech. State U., Greensboro, 1989—. Vis. prof. John Marshall Law Sch., Atlanta, 1996—97, 2000—01. Contbr. articles to profl. jours. Mem.: Global Assn Risk Profs., Global Assn. Risk Profs., Internat. Assn. Risk & Compliance Profs., Am. Assn. Univ. Profs., Am. Assn. Family & Consumer Sci., Acad. Mgmt., Minn. Bar Assn., Am. Polit. Sci. Assn., Fin. Planning Assn., Soc. Fin. Svc. Profls., La. State Bar Assn., Nebr. State Bar Assn., Mass. Bar Assn., Fla. Bar, State Bar Ga., DC Bar, Ohio State Bar Assn., Phi Kappa Phi. Office: Merrick Hall 1601 E Market St Greensboro NC 27411 Business E-Mail: swan@ncat.edu.

SWAN, IVE ARLINGTON, territorial supreme court justice; b. St. Thomas, VI; m. Gertrude Niles Drue. BA, Morgan State U., Balt., 1967; JD, Howard U. Sch. Law, 1970; course completion, U. Nev. Nat. Jud. Coll., Reno, Am. Acad. Jud. Edn. Bar: US Supreme Ct., US Ct. Appeals (DC), US Ct. Appeals (3rd cir.), US Dist. Ct. (DC), VI. Legal intern VI Dept. Justice, dep. asst. atty. gen., asst. atty. gen., criminal and family law divsns. civil and adminstrv. law divsns., atty. gen., 1978—81; pvt. practice atty., 1981—87; judge Territorial Ct. the VI, 1987—2006, Superior Ct. VI, 2006; assoc. justice Supreme Ct. VI, 2006—. Mem.: Soc. Atty. Generals Emeritus, Am. Judges Assn., Nat. Bar Assn., VI Bar Assn., Washington, DC Bar Assn. Office: Supreme Ct the VI PO Box 590 St Thomas VI 00804*

SWAN, MICHAEL K., lawyer; b. Kilgore, Tex. BBA, Tex. A&M, 1964; LLB, Univ. Tex., 1967. Bar: Tex. 1967, US Supreme Ct. 1971, US Dist. Ct. (so., no., we., ea. districts) Tex., US Ct. of Appeals Fed. Cir., US Dist. Ct. Colo., US Ct. of Appeals (5th and 9th Dist.), cert.: Civil Trial Law, Tex. Bd. Legal Specialization. Assoc. Reynolds White Allen & Cook, 1971—75, mng. ptnr., 1981—88; ptnr., gen. litig. Andrews Kurth, 1988—92, ptnr. in charge, 2000—07; head ptnr. litig. practice Akin Gump Strauss Hauer & Feld LLP, Houston, 1992—. Spkr. in field. Bd. dirs. YMCA. Mem. JAGC US Army, 1967—71. Fellow: Houston Bar Found., Tex. Bar Found.; mem.: ABA, Am. Bd. Trial Advocates, State Bar of Tex. (dir. 1982—85), Houston Bar Assn., Phi Alpha Delta. Office: Akin Gump Strauss Hauer & Feld LLP 44th fl 1111 Louisiana St Houston TX 77002-5200 Office Phone: 713-220-5862. Office Fax: 713-236-0822. Business E-Mail: mswan@akingump.com.

SWAN, PATRICIA BRINTNALL, academic administrator, researcher; b. Hickory, NC, Oct. 21, 1937; d. Philip Earle and Mary Lucille (Farmer) Brintnall; m. James Byron Swan, Apr. 23, 1962; children: Kathryn Ann, Deborah Lee. BS, U. N.C., 1959; MS, U. Wis., 1961, PhD, 1964. Rsch. assoc. U. Wis., Madison, 1963—64, U. Minn., St. Paul, 1964—65, asst. prof., 1965—68, assoc. prof., 1968—73, prof., 1973—89; assoc. dean U. Minn. Grad. Sch., Mpls., 1987—89; prof. Iowa State U., Ames, 1989—2001, prof. emeritus, 2002—, vice provost, dean, 1989—91, 1992—99, interim provost, 1991—92. Program coord. SEA-USDA, Washington, 1979-80; bd. dirs. Fedn. of Am. Socs. for Exptl. Biology, Bethesda, Md., 1988-91; mem. Bd. Agr., NRC, Washington, 1992-94; mem. Grad. Rsch. Examination Bd., 1996-2002. Contbr. over 80 tech. articles to profl. jours.; author Managing Intellectual Property. Pres. U. Minn. Faculty Polit. Action Com., Mpls., 1984-87; bd. dirs. Ames Econ. Devel. Commn., 1991-99. Recipient Disting. Alumni award U. Wis., 1994. Fellow Am. Soc. Nutrition Sci., Am. Inst. Nutrition (sec. 1981-84, historical and biographical editor Jour. Nutrition); mem. Nat. Agrl. Biotech. Coun. (chair 1996-97), Rsch. Coun. of Iowa (pres. 1994-96). Home: 1301 Crest Ridge Ct Nashville TN 37221-4336 E-mail: pswan@iastate.edu.

SWANBERG, CHRISTOPHER GERARD, environmental engineer; b. NYC, Jan. 31, 1958; s. Clifford Duane and Margaret Mary (Spillane) S.; m. Sherrie Joy Shuler, Mar. 3, 1979; children: Daniel Christopher, Sarah Elizabeth. BS in Environ. Engring., Western Ky. U., 1981; MBA, U. Tulsa, 1991. V.p. Sage Environ. Consulting; environ. engr. Atlantic Richfield (ARCO), Louisville, 1981-82, environ. project engr. Russellville, Ky., 1982-84, coord. environ. affairs Independence, Kans., 1984-86, sr. environ. engr. Anaheim, Calif., 1986-88, mgr. environ. engring. LA, 1988-90; mgr., Regulatory and Legis. Affairs Lyondell-Citgo Refining; v.p. Heritage Environ. Svc., Inc., Tulsa, 1990-91; sr. v.p. Separation and Recovery Systems, Inc., Irvine, Calif., 1991; v.p., Environ.l, Health and Safety Coffeyville Resources, LLC, 2005; v.p., Environ., Health and Safety CVR Energy, Inc.; mng. gen. ptnr. CVR Ptnrs., LP. Contbr. articles to profl. publs. Asst. commr. Am. Youth Soccer Orgn., Laguna Niguel, Calif., 1992; bd. dirs. Independence Day Care, 1985; advisor Jr. Achievement, Louisville, 1984. Achievements include development of thermal disorption technology to meet EPA land disposal restrictions for petroleum refining wastes, EPA accepted physical and chemical standards for solidification and stabilzation of organic wastes, first water based coatings for aluminum foil packaging industry to reduce air pollution; designer aluminum industry's zero process discharge rolling mill complex. Office: CVR Energy Inc 2277 Plz Dr Ste 500 Sugar Land TX 77479 Office Phone: 281-207-3200. Business E-Mail: cgswanberg@cvrenergy.com.

SWANN, RICHARD ROCKWELL, lawyer, banker; b. Orlando, Fla., May 7, 1940; s. Pervie P. and Maesther (Mears) Swann; m. Doris Orr (dec. Oct. 1983); children: Dorothy Orr, Christian Mears, Campbell Thornal, Doris Reed. AB, Duke U., 1961, JD, 1963. Bar: Fla. 1963. Mem. Swann & Haddock, Orlando, 1963—90, Swann & Hadley, 1990—2011, Swann Hadley Stump Dietrich & Spears, P.A., 2011—. Mem. Jr. Achievement Bd., Orlando, 1964—68; jr. achievement bd. Downtown Orlando Coun., 1969—71; appointee of Gov. Askew Orange County Budget Commn., Orlando, 1971, Orange County Expy. Authority, Orlando, 1973—75; dir. Overseas Pvt. Investment Corp., Washington, 1977—82; bd. govs. Overseas Investment Ress, 1978—82; dir., appointed by Gov. Graham Fla. High Speed Rail Commn., Orlando, 1984—88; bd. visitors Terry Sanford Sch. Inst. Pub. Policy, Duke U., 1989—92; gen. counsel, dir. Am. Heritage Homes USA, Inc., 1995—2000, Jefferson Nat. Title Ins. Co., 1997—2003; dir. Property Gen., Inc., Orlando, 2003—, Comml. Vehicle Ins. Co. SC, 2004—, Surrey Homes, LLC, Orlando, 2008—, Fla. Next Found., 2011—; former chmn. bd. 1st Fidelity Savs. & Loan, Orlando, Am. Pioneer Savs. Bank, Orlando, Am. Pioneer, Inc., Orlando. Mem.: ABA, Fla. Bar Assn., Orange County Bar Assn. Democrat. Office: 1031 W Morse Blvd Ste 350 Winter Park FL 32789 Office Phone: 407-647-2777. Business E-Mail: rswann@swannhadley.com.

SWANSON, AL, oil industry executive; Internal audit & acctg. positions Apache Corp., 1986—92; acctg. mgr. Snyder Oil Corp., 1992—97, contr. SOCO Offshore, 1997—98, dir. corp. fin., 1998—99; treas. Santa Fe Snyder Corp., 1999—2000, Plains All American Pipeline, LP, Houston, 2001—04, v.p., treas, 2004—05, v.p. fin., treas., 2005—07, sr. v.p. fin., treas., 2007—08, sr. v.p., CFO, 2008—11, exec. v.p., CFO, 2011—; sr. v.p., CFO PAA Nat. Gas Storage LP, 2010—. Office: Plains All Am Pipeline LP 333 Clay St Ste 1600 Houston TX 77002 Office Phone: 713-646-4100. Business E-Mail: apswanson@paalp.com.

SWANSON, DONALD FREDERICK, retired food company executive; b. Mpls., Aug. 6, 1927; s. Clayton A. and Irma (Baiocchi) S.; m. Virginia Clare Hannah, Dec. 17, 1948; children— Donald Frederick, Cynthia Hannah, Janet Clare Webster. BA, U. Minn., 1948. With Gen. Mills, Inc., 1949-85, div. v.p., dir. marketing flour, dessert and baking mixes, 1964-65, v.p., gen. mgr. grocery products div., 1965-68, v.p., corporate adminstrn. officer consumer foods group, fashion div., transp. and purchasing depts., advt. and marketing services, 1969, exec. v.p. craft, game and toy group, fashion group, direct marketing group, travel group, dir., 1968-76, sr. exec. v.p. consumer non-foods, 1976-85, chief financial officer, 1977-79, sr. exec. v.p. restaurants and consumer non-foods, 1980-81, vice chmn. restaurants and consumer non-foods, 1981-85. Ret. chmn. bd. Soo Line Corp. Served with AUS, 1946-47. Mem. Mpls. Club, Wayzata Country Club, Royal Poinciana Golf Club, Phi Kappa Psi. Home: 2171 Gulf Shore Blvd N Apt 504 Naples FL 34102-4685

SWANSON, DOUGLAS E., retired oil industry executive; BA, Cornell Coll. CPA. Chmn. Boots & Coots Internat. Well Control Inc.; pres. Cliffs Drilling Co., exec. v.p., 1978—92, chmn., CEO, 1992—99. Bd. dir. Flint Energy Svcs. Ltd.; pres., CEO Oil States Internat., Inc., 2000—07; bd. dirs. Oil States Internat., Inc, 2000—. Office: Boots & Coots International Well Control Inc 5th Fl 7908 N Sam Houston Pky W Houston TX 77064 Office Phone: 281-931-8884. Business E-Mail: douglas.swanson@oilstatesintl.com.

SWANSON, JACQUELINE V., academic administrator, women's health nurse practitioner, educator; b. Houston, Feb. 12, 1944; d. Ivan Jack and Edith Wilson; m. James Swanson, Aug. 21, 1965; children: Jim, Charlotte, Robert, Guy, Danny. BS, Tex. Woman's U., 1967, MS, 1974; PhD, U. North Tex., Denton, 1989. Cert. clin. nurse specialist, in maternal-newborn health, women's health nurse practitioner Planned Parenthood of Rocky Mountains, sexual assault nurse examiner. Various clin. nursing positions, Tex., Kans., Montana, Okla., Tex., 1967-73; supr. obstet. and nursery Harris County Hosp. Dist., Houston, 1970-73; instr. Prairie View (Tex.) A&M U., 1973-75; asst. prof. Tex. Woman's U., Denton, 1975-85; labor and delivery nurse Tarrant County Hosp. Dist., Ft. Worth, 1987-89; assoc. prof., chmn. dept. nursing Ft. Hays State U., Hays, Kans., 1989-94; dir. BS nursing program Lamar U., Beaumont, Tex., 1994-95; prof., dean Coll. Nursing, Mont. State U. No., Havre, 1995—98, prof. nursing, 1998-2000; assoc. prof. nursing Tarleton State U., 2000—03, women's health nurse practioner Student Health Clinic, 2003—04; clin. instr. Tex. Christian U., 2005; dean Sch. Nursing Bacone Coll., 2005—07, Hometown Hosp., 2007—08, North Tex. VA Healthcare, 2008—. Contbr. articles to profl. jours.; presenter U.S. and internat. Mem. Denton Area War on Drugs. Mem. AAUP, ANA, Nat. Assn. Nurse Practioners Women's Health, Assn. Women's Health, Obstetric and Neonatal Nurses, Kans. State Nurses Assn., Tex. Nurses Assn., Tex. Nurse Practioner's Assn., Mont. Nurses Assn., Internat. Coun. on Women's Health Issues, Internat. Soc. for Univ. Nurses, Sigma Theta Tau. Home: 315E 9th Bonham TX 75418

SWANSON, JEFFREY, sociologist, researcher, educator; b. St. Paul, Mar. 24, 1957; s. Wallace Leroy and Charlotte Dillon Swanson; m. Pamela Ruth Mydske, Aug. 23, 1983; children: Angela Nicole, Alexandra Jane, Matthew Thomas. BA, Westmont Coll., Santa Barbara, Calif., 1979; PhD, Yale U., New Haven, 1985. Asst. prof. psychiatry and behavioral scis. U. Tex. Med. Br., Galveston, 1985—91; postdoctoral fellow U NC, Chapel Hill, NC, 1991—93, Duke U. Med. Ctr., NC, 1991—93; prof. psychiatry and behavioral scis. Duke U. Sch. Medicine, Durham, 1993—; mem. John D. and Catherine T. MacArthur Found. Rsch. Network on Mandated Cmty. Treatment, 2002—. Author: Echoes of the Call: Identity and Ideology among American Missionaries in Ecuador, 1995; contbr. over 130 articles to profl. and acad. jours. Grantee Ind. Rsch. Scientist Career Award, NIMH, 2004—. Progressive. Achievements include seminal research studies on links between violent behavior and severe mental illnesses, effectiveness of involuntary outpatient mental health treatment, and psychiatric advance directives. Office: Duke Univ Sch Medicine Dumc 3071 Durham NC 27701

SWANSON, LARRY, manufacturing executive; CFO Beaulieu Group, Dalton, Ga., 1997-99. Office: Beaulieu Group PO Box 1248 Dalton GA 30722-1248

SWANSON, PEGGY EUBANKS, retired finance educator; b. Ivanhoe, Tex., Dec. 29, 1936; d. Leslie Samuel and Mary Lee (Reid) Eubanks; m. B. Marc Sommers, Nov. 10, 1993. BBA, U. North Tex., 1957, M. Bus. Edn., 1965; MA in Econs., So. Meth. U., 1967, PhD in Econs., 1978. Instr. El Centro Coll., Dallas, 1967-69, 71-78, bus. div. chmn., 1969-71; asst. prof. econs. U. Tex., Arlington, 1978-79, asst. prof. fin., 1979-84, assoc. prof., 1984-86, chmn. dept. fin. and real estate, 1986-88, prof. fin., 1987—, interim dean Coll. Bus. Adminstrn., 1999—2000, John and Judy Goolsby disting. prof., 2004—11, prof. emeritus, 2012—. Expert witness various law firms, primarily Tex. and Calif., 1978—; cons. Internat. Edn. Program, 1992-99; curriculum cons. U. Monterrey, Mexico, 1995, New Saudi Arabia U., 1999. Contbr. articles to acad. profl. jours. Vol. Am. Cancer Soc., Dallas, Arlington, 1981—, Meals on Wheels, Arlington, 1989—; mem. adv. bd. Ryan/Reilly Ctr. for Urban Land Utilization, Arlington, 1986-88. Mem. Fin. Exec. Inst. (chmn. acad. rels. 1987-88), Internat. Bus. Steering Com. (chmn. 1989-91), Am. Fin. Assn., Am. Econ. Assn., Fin. Mgmt. Assn. (hon. faculty mem. Nat. Honor Soc. 1985-86, program com. 1998-99), Southwestern Fin. Assn. (program com. 1987-88, 96), Midwest Fin. Assn. (program com. 1997-98, 98-99), Acad. of Internat. Bus. (program com. 1992-95), Acad. Disting. Tchrs., Phi Beta Delta (membership com. 1987-89). Republican. Episcopalian. Avocations: tennis, gardening. Home: 4921 Bridgewater Dr Arlington TX 76017-2729 Office: U Tex at Arlington PO Box 19449 Arlington TX 76019-0001 Office Phone: 817-272-3841. Business E-Mail: swanson@uta.edu.

SWANSON, RALPH WILLIAM, aerospace executive, consultant, engineer; b. Mpls. m. Virginia May Peoples (dec.); children: John W., Timothy R.; m. Patricia Anne Smith. BS in Aero. Engring., U. Minn., 1947; MS in Nuclear Engring., N.C. State U., 1954; PhD in Engring., Kennedy-Western U., 1989. Design engr. Los Alamos (N.Mex.) Sci. Lab., 1948-52; asst. prof. physics Air Force Inst. Tech., Wright

Patterson AFB, Ohio, 1954-56; chief radiation div. armed forces spl. weapons project Pentagon, Washington, 1957-61; dep. chief staff plans and programs Air Force Eastern Test Range, Patrick AFB, Fla., 1961-64; dep. for programs and requirements Air Force Nat. Range Div., Patrick AFB, Fla., 1962—65; mgr. advanced programs IBM Corp., Kennedy Space Center, Fla., 1965-75; chief engr. Planning Rsch. Corp., Kennedy Space Center, 1975-79, dep. project mgr., gen. mgr., 1979-87; project mgr. Bamsi, Inc., Kennedy Space Center, 1987-93. Freelance cons., Cocoa Beach, Fla., 1987—; pres. R&A Cons. Corp., Cocoa Beach. Bd. dirs. Brevard Achievement Ctr., Rockledge, Fla., 1970—. Col. USAF, 1941-65, ETO and Korea, ret. Named one of Seven AFO Officers, Los Alamos Rsch. Lab. Mem. Air Force Assn., Assn. AFIT Grads., Masons, Shriners, Sigma Xi, Sigma Pi Sigma. Republican. Avocations: scuba diving, under water photography, jogging. Office Phone: 321-783-8780. Personal E-mail: rswanson1@cfl.rr.com.

SWANSON, ROY JOEL, lawyer; b. Houston, Feb. 21, 1945; s. Roy J. and Daisy Lee (Peper) S.; m. Lynn Northway, Apr. 5, 1986; children: Emily Rebecca, Nell Cameron. BSChemE, U. Tex., 1967; MBA, JD, Harvard U., 1972. Bar: Tex. 1972. Assoc. Baker & Botts, Houston, 1972-80, ptnr., exec. com., sr. v.p., 1980; pvt. practice Houston. Office: 3000 One Shell Plz Houston TX 77002 Office Phone: 713-229-1330. Business E-Mail: joel.swanson@bakerbotts.com.

SWANSON, SHIRLEY JUNE, retired emergency room nurse; b. Dade City, Fla., Feb. 26, 1942; d. Allen John and Ollie Mae (Jackson) S.; m. J.A. Whatley, 1960 (div. 1962); m. Jerald Ward Steen, June 7, 1963. AA, Hillsborough C.C., 1974; BA, U. South Fla., 1975; AS, Gupton-Jones Coll., 1992, No. Maine Tech. Coll., 1996. RN, cert. in elem. and adult edn. scis. Underwriter Home Ins. Co., NYC, 1979—82; with L.L. Bean, Freeport, Maine, 1988—90. Owner/breeder hosannachows; spkr. in field. Author, editor Coffee Break, 1963-64. Ofcl. spinner Fla. State Fair, Tampa, 1984-85; spinner East Animal Farm/Westshore Mall, Tampa, 1984-85 Billerica, Mass. O.E.S. scholar, 1975, Am. Bd. Funeral Svc. Edn. scholar, 1992, Caribou Adult Edn. Sys. scholar, 1995. Mem. DAR, Phi Theta Kappa, Pi Sigma Eta. Avocations: spinning, weaving, quilting.

SWANSON, STEVEN R., astronaut; b. Syracuse, NY, Dec. 3, 1960; s. Stanley and June Swanson; m. Mary Drake Young; 3 children. BS in Engring. Physics, U. Colo., 1983; MAS in Computer Sys., Fla. Atlantic U., 1986; PhD in Computer Sci., Tex. A&M U., 1998. Software engr. GTE, Phoenix; sys. engr. aircraft ops. divsn. NASA, Johnson Space Ctr., Houston, 1987—89, flight simulation engr. for shuttle tng. aircraft, 1989—98, astronaut, mission specialist candidate, 1998—. Crew mem., spacewalker STS-117 Atlantis Mission, 2007; mission specialist STS-119 Discovery Mission, 2009. Recipient NASA Exceptional Achievement medal, Johnson Space Ctr. Cert. Accomodation, Flight Simulation Engring. award. Mem.: Phi Kappa Phi. Avocations: mountain biking, basketball, skiing, weightlifting, running, woodworking. Office: Astronaut Office/CB NASA Johnson Space Ctr Houston TX 77058

SWARTLING, DAVID R., food service executive; Regional v.p. restaurant ops. Cracker Barrel Old Country Store, Inc. Office: Cracker Barrel Old Country Store Inc 305 Hartmann Dr Lebanon TN 37087 Office Phone: 615-444-5533. Office Fax: 615-443-9476.

SWARTZ, JON DAVID, psychologist, educator; b. Houston, Dec. 28, 1934; s. Orville Elmo and Nina June (Baker) S.; m. Carol Joseph Hampton, Oct. 20, 1966; children: Eric Jason McFarland, Sally Katherine Baker, Edward Joseph Bryson. BA, U. Tex., Austin, 1956, MA, 1961, PhD, 1969, postgrad., 1973-74. Rsch. and tng. asst. dept. psychology U. Tex., 1956-62, asst. prof. dept. ednl. psychology, 1969-72; assoc. prof. psychology, chmn. U. Tex.-Permian Basin, 1974-78, chmn. anthropology and sociology, 1975-78, field dir., 1962-65; asst. dir. Austin Longitudinal Rsch. project, 1965-69, co-dir., 1969-74; research scientist Hogg Found. for Mental Health, 1972-74; prof. edn. and psychology Southwestern U., Georgetown, Tex., 1978-90, vis. prof. psychology, 1991, dir. testing and guidance, 1978-81, holder Brown vis. chair, 1978-82, assoc. dean for librs. and learning resources, 1981-90; coord., adminstrv. head Killeen office Cen. Counties Ctr. for MHMR Svcs., Temple, Tex., 1990-91; chief psychol. svcs. Temple, Tex., 1991-99; pvt. practice Tex., 2000—. Lectr. Nat. U., Mexico, 1962, U. Ctrl. Tex., 1994, Temple Coll., 1994. Author: (with W.H. Holtzman) Inkblot Perception and Personality, 1961, (with C.C. Cleland) Mental Retardation: Approaches to Institutional Change, 1969, Administrative Issues in Institutions for the Mentally Retarded, 1972, Exceptionalities Through the Lifespan: An Introduction, 1982, Multihandicapped Mentally Retarded, 1973, (with W.H. Holtzman, R. Diaz-Guerrero) Personality Development in Two Cultures, 1975; editor: (with C.C. Cleland, L.W. Talkington) Profoundly Mentally Retarded, 1976, (with R.K. Eyman, C.C. Cleland) Research with the Profoundly Retarded, 1978, Holtzman Inkblot Technique: An Annotated Bibliography (supplement), 1988, (with R.C. Reinehr, W.H. Holtzman) Holtzman Inkblot Technique: An Annotated Bibliography 1956-1982, 1983, (with R.C. Reinehr) Handbook of Old-Time Radio, 1993, Holtzman Inkblot Technique: Research Guide and Bibliography, 1999, Southwestern University Bibliographic Series, 1986-1990, Historical Dictionary of Old-Time Radio, 2008, A To Z of Old Time Radio, 2010, Pseudonyms of Science Fiction, Fantasy and Horror Authors, 2010, Buck Rogers Big Little Books and Other Collectibles, 2013; The Hugo Awards for Best Novel, 2013; contbr.: Handbook of Texas, 1996; editl. assoc. Current Anthropology, 1971-77; assoc. editor: Am. Corrective Therapy Jour., 1971-81, Exceptional Children, 1982-84; mem. editl. bd. Tex. Psychologist, 1979-83, Phi Kappa Phi Jour./Nat. Forum, 1976-80; editl. cons. Mental Retardation, 1972-77; rev. editor Jour. Biol. Psychology, 1972-80, Revista Interamericana de Psicologia, 1983-89; reviewer Sci. Books, Films, 1978-; cons. editor Jour. Personality Assessment, 1981-90; spl. features editor: Scientifiction: The First Fandom Report, 2002-; rev. editor The National Fantasy Fan, 2003-10; frequent contbr. Paperback Parade, 2004-;contbr. Big Little Times, 2008-, contbg. editor Fan Dominion, 2008-; Fancyclopedia 3, 2013-; editor, The Ultraverse, 2006-; contbr. more than 500 articles to profl. jours. and 400 popular culture publs. Mem. Mayor's Drug Abuse Panel, Odessa, Tex., 1975-78; chmn. adv. bd. Human Potentials Ctr., Permian Basin Cmty. Ctrs. for Mental Health and Mental Retardation, Odessa and Midland, Tex., 1975-78; bd. govs. Mood-Heritage Mus., 1984-90. US Office Edn. fellow, 1964-66, U. Tex. fellow, 1973-74; recipient Franklin Gilliam prize Humanities Rsch. Ctr. U. Tex., 1965, Spencer Rsch. award Nat. Acad. Edn., 1972, Faculty Fellowship award Southwestern U., 1981. Fellow: AAAS, Am. Psychol. Soc., Soc. Personality Assessment (life); mem.: Western Rsch. Conf. Mental Retardation, Am. Acad. Mental Retardation, Southwestern Psychol. Assn., Bell County Psychol. Assn., Sigma Xi, Psi Chi, Mu Alpha Nu, Delta Tau Kappa, Phi Kappa Phi, Phi Delta Kappa, Nat. Fantasy Fan Fedn.: Club Historian (mem. directorate, 2007-10, 2012-2014, pres. 2010-12; Franson award 2005, 07, Kaymar award, 2010), First Fandom, Carboniferous Amateur Press Alliance (CAPA). Avocation: chess. Personal E-mail: jon_swartz@hotmail.com.

SWARTZLANDER, EARL EUGENE, JR., engineering educator, former electronics company executive; b. San Antonio, Feb. 1, 1945; s. Earl Eugene and Jane (Nicholas) S.; m. Joan Vickery, June 9, 1968. BSEE, Purdue U., 1967; MSEE, U. Colo., 1969; PhD, U. So. Calif., 1972. Registered profl. engr., Calif., Colo., Tex. Devel. engr. Ball Bros. Rsch. Corp., Boulder, Colo., 1967-69; Hughes fellow, mem. tech. staff Hughes Aircraft Co., Culver City, Calif., 1969-73; mem. rsch. staff Tech. Svc. Co., Santa Monica, Calif., 1973-74; chief engr. Geophys. Systems Corp., Pasadena, Calif., 1974-75, staff engr. to sr. staff engr., 1975-79, project mgr., 1979-84, lab. mgr., 1985-87; dir. ind. R&D TRW Inc., Redondo Beach, Calif., 1987-90; Schlumberger Centennial prof. engring. dept. elec. and computer engring. U. Tex., Austin, 1990—2006, prof., 2006—. Gen. chmn. Internat. Conf. Wafer Scale Integration, 1989, Internat. Conf. Application Specific Array Processors, 1990, 94, 2011, 11th Internat. Symposium on Computer Arithmetic, 1992, 31st Ann. Asilomar Conf. on Signals, Sys., and Computers, 1997, others; chmn. 3d Internat. Conf. Parallel and Distributed Sys., Taiwan, 1993, 12th Internat. Conf. on Application-Specific Sys., Architectures and Processors, 2000, 23rd Internat. Conf. on Application-Specific Sys., Architectures and Processors, 2011; mem. tech. adv. bd. ECIT, Queen's U., Belfast, 2005— Author: VLSI Signal Processing Systems, 1986, Design of Semiconductor QCA Systems, 2013; editor: Computer Design Development, 1976, Systolic Signal Processing Systems, 1987, Wafer Scale Integration, 1989, Computer Arithmetic Vol. 1 and 2, 1990, Application Specific Processors, 1996; editor-in-chief Jour. of VLSI Signal Processing, 1989-95, IEEE Transactions on Computers, 1991-94, IEEE Transactions on Signal Processing, 1995; editor: IEEE Transactions on Computers, 1982-86, IEEE Transactions on Parallel and Distributed Systems, 1989-90; hardware area editor ACM Computing Revs., 1985—; assoc. editor: IEEE Jour. Solid-State Circuits, 1984-88; contbr. more than 394 articles to profl. jours. and tech. conf. procs., chpts. to books. Bd. dirs. Casiano Estates Homeowners Assn., Bel Air, Calif., 1976-80, pres., 1978-80; bd. dirs. Benedict Hills Estates Homeowners Assn., Beverly Hills, Calif., 1984-2006, pres., 1990-95. Recipient Disting. Engring. Alumnus award Purdue U., 1989, U. Colo., 1997, Outstanding Elec. Engr. award Purdue U., 1992, knight Imperial Russian Order St. John of Jerusalem (Knights of Malta), 1993. Fellow: IEEE (hist. com. 1996—2004, fellows com. 2000—03, 3d Millennium medal 2000)); mem.: Assn. for Computing Machinery, IEEE Solid-State Cirs. Coun. (bd. govs. 1986—91, sec. 1992—93, treas. 1994—97), IEEE Signal Proc. Soc. (bd. govs. 1992—94), IEEE Computer Soc. (bd. govs. 1987—91, Golden Core award 1996), Omicron Delta Kappa, Sigma Tau, Eta Kappa Nu. Achievements include patents in field. Office: U Tex Austin Dept Elec Computer Engring Austin TX 78712 Home: 8105 Hickory Creek Dr Austin TX 78735 Office Phone: 310-702-5756. Business E-Mail: e.swartzlander@ieee.com.

SWAYZE, CHARLES J., JR., lawyer; b. Greenwood, Miss., May 14, 1944; m. Jo Claire Swayze; 4 children. BBA, Univ. Miss., 1966, JD, 1969; LLM, George Washington Univ., 1973. Bar: Miss. 1969, US Ct. Mil. Appeals 1969, US Supreme Ct. 1973. Prosecuting atty. City of Greenwood, Miss., 1974—75, Leflore County, 1976—2000; mem. Whittington, Brock & Swayze PA, Greenwood, Miss. Pres. Southern Conf. of Bar Pres., Nat. Caucus State Bar Assn.; mem. ABOTA. Past pres., fellow Rotary Club. Capt. JAGC US Army, 1969—73. Decorated Army Commendation award. Fellow: Miss. Bar Found., Am. Bar Found.; mem.: ABA (house of del.), Miss. Bar Assn. (pres. 2004), Phi Delta Phi. Avocation: golf. Office: Whittington Brock & Swayze PA 308 Fulton St PO Box 941 Greenwood MS 38930*

SWEENEY, JACK, publishing executive; b. Jersey City; m. Ellie Sweeney; children: Jake, Jessica. BA in English, King's Coll., Wilkes-Barre, Pa. Various advt. positions Washington Post, 1968—74; advt. dir. Trenton Times, NJ, 1974—78, Boston Herald, 1978—80, Houston Chronicle, 1980—83, dir. sales & mktg., 1983—86, v.p. sales & mktg., 1986—91, v.p., gen. mgr., 1991—98, assoc. pub., 1998—2000, pres., 1998—2012, pub., 2000—12, chmn., 2012—. Exec. com., bd. trustees United Way Tex. Gulf Coast, campaign chmn., 2002—03; exec. com., bd. dirs. Greater Houston Partnership; hon. mem. bd. dirs. Greater Houston Conv. & Visitors Bur.; chmn. Be A Super Host Com. Super Bowl 2004, Houston. Mem.: Tex. Daily Newspaper Assn. (Tex. Newspaper Leader of Yr./Pat Taggart Meml. award 2000), Newspaper Assn. America. Office: Houston Chronicle 801 Texas Ave Houston TX 77002

SWEENEY, WILLIAM ROBERT, JR., information technology executive; b. Portland, Maine, Feb. 1, 1951; s. William Robert and Mary (Farrell) S.; m. Susan Read, Apr. 23, 1983; children: Caitlin Elizabeth, Sarah Lister. BA, Am. U., 1973. Rsch. dir., then exec. dir. Dem. Congl. Campaign Com., Washington, 1974-81; dep. chmn. Dem. Nat. Com., Washington, 1981-85; pres. Washington Resources & Strategy, 1985; joined Electronic Data Sys. (EDS), Plano, Tex., 1991, v.p. global govt. affairs, 1999—. Mgr. 1982 Dem. Party Conf.; mem. nat. adv. bd., Ctr. Nat. Policy, Am. Coun. Young Polit. Leaders. Mem. Am. Assn. Polit. Cons., US Coun. Internat. Bus., Info. Tech. Assn. America, European-Am. Bus. Coun. Democrat. Roman Catholic. Office: EDS 5400 Legacy Dr Plano TX 75024

SWEET, JAMES BROOKS, oral and maxillofacial surgeon; b. Darlington, Pa., Mar. 28, 1934; s. Lufay Anderson and Margaret Jean (Brooks) S.; m. N. Gayle Laird, Oct. 11, 1958; children: James Brooks II, Laird Anderson, Bradley Stephen. BA, Lafayette Coll., 1956; DDS, U. Pitts., 1964, DMD, 1974; MS in Dentistry, NYU, 1975. Aviation flight officer USNR, 1957; advanced through grades to dir. USPHS; rotating intern USPHS Hosp., Staten Island, N.Y., 1964-65, resident oral and maxillofacial surgery, 1970-73; chief dept. dentistry Fed. Correctional Inst. Hosp., Ashland, Ky., 1965-67, Terminal Island, Calif., 1967-70; chief oral and maxillofacial surgery Clin. Ctr. NIH, Bethesda, Md., 1973-80; chief dept. dentistry and oral and maxillofacial surgery USPHS Hosp., Nassau Bay, Tex., 1980-81; ret. USPHS, 1981; assoc. prof. dept. oral and maxillofacial surgery Health Sci. Ctr. U. Tex., Houston, 1981-84, prof., 1984—95, prof. emeritus, 2002—. Asst. clin. prof. med. br. U. Tex., Galveston, 1980-2002, prof. emeritus, 2002--; assoc. attending physicianBen Taub Gen. Hosp., Houston, 1984-95; cons. oral and maxillofacial surgery self study guides, Stoma Press, Seattle, 1983-; cons. VA Hosp., Houston, 1986-. Contbr. articles to profl. jours.; editorial reviewer: Annals of Internal Medicine, 1977-. Coach basketball Olney (Md.) Boys Club, 1975-80; mem. aim rev. Tex. area USCG, 1981-82. Lt. USNR, 1957-64. Fellow Am. Assn. Oral and Maxillofacial Surgeons; mem. Tex. Soc. Oral and Maxillofacial Surgeons, Houston Soc. Oral and Maxillofacial Surgeons, Am. Assn. Dental Schs., USPHS Profl. Assn., NIH Sailing Club, Omicron Kappa Upslion (pres. Mu Mu chpt. 1993-94). Presbyterian. Avocations: sailing, swimming, real estate, travel. Home: 2013 Sweet St Navarre FL 32566-3042 Office: University Tex Health Sci Ctr 7500 Cambridge St Houston TX 77054 Business E-Mail: jamesbsweet@mediacombb.net.

SWEET, PHILLIP, singer; b. Cherokee Village, Ark., Mar. 18, 1974; m. Rebecca Arthur, Mar. 30, 2007; 1 child, Penelopi Jane. Attended, Ark. State U., Jonesboro. Co-founder Little Big Town, 1999. Singer: (albums) (with Little Big Town) Little Big Town, 2002, The Road to Here, 2005, A Place to Land, 2007, The Reason Why, 2010, Tornado, 2012, (songs) Pontoon, 2012 (Single of Yr., Country Music Assn. Awards, 2012, Best Country Duo/Group Performance, Grammy Awards, 2013), Tornado, 2012 (Video of Yr., Acad. Country Music Awards, 2013). Named Top New Duo/Vocal Group, Acad. Country Music Awards, 2007, Vocal Group of Yr., Country Music Assn. Awards, 2012, 2013, Acad. Country Music Awards, 2013. Office: c/o Sandbox Entertainment 54 Music Square East Suite 200 Nashville TN 37203*

SWENSON, ERIC D., SR., information technology executive; BA, U. Calif., LA. Legis. asst. to US Congressmen, Washington; exec. v.p., Southern Calif. regional Property Insight LLC, Lender's Svc. Inc., Nat. Relocation, Chgo. Title Ins. Co. (acquired by Fidelity Nat. Fin., Inc.); mng. dir. Fin. Svc. Solutions, Inc.; exec. v.p., Southern Calif. regional Fidelity Nat. Default Solutions, Fidelity Nat. Lender Solutions; joined Fidelity National Financial, Inc., 2000; pres., COO Fidelity Nat. Info. Solutions, Inc. (subs. Fidelity Nat. Fin., Inc.), 2001—02, exec. v.p., 2002—03; exec. v.p. through regional mgr. Fidelity National Financial, Inc., 2004—06; pres., Lender Outsourcing divsn. Fidelity National Information Services, Inc., 2004—06, exec. v.p., Mortgage Info. Svcs. divsn., 2006—08; exec. v.p., co-COO Lender Processing Svcs., Inc. Office: Lender Processing Services Inc 601 Riverside Ave Jacksonville FL 32204 Office Phone: 904-854-5100. Office Fax: 904-854-4124. Business E-Mail: eric.swenson@lpsvcs.com.

SWENSSON, EARL SIMCOX, architect; b. Nashville, July 28, 1930; s. Earl Ebenezer and Viola Lazelle (Simcox) Swensson; m. Suzanne Dickenson, June 6, 1953; children: Krista, Lin, Kurt. BS in Bldg. Design, Va. Poly. Inst. and State U., 1952, MSArch, 1953, U. Ill., 1955. Founder, prin. Earl Swensson Assocs., Inc., Nashville, 1961—. Adj. prof. Va. Poly. Inst. and State U., Blacksburg, 1971—72, Auburn U., 1976—83; lectr. in field; apptd. chairholder Jennings and Rebecca Jones Chair of Excellence in Urban and Regional Planning, Mid. Tenn. State U., 1999—2008. Contbr. articles to profl. jours.; author (with Richard L. Miller): (books) New Directions in Hospital and Healthcare Facility Design, 1995; author: Hospital and Healthcare Facility Design 2d edit., 2002, A Passion for Design, Human-Centered Architecture and Synergenial Practice, 2008, The Sketches of Earl S. Swensson, FAIA, 2010. Mem. arch. program adv. coun. Auburn U., 1990—94; bd. dirs. Metro Arts Commn., 1979—86; Middle Tenn. Health Systems (pres. 1972) AIA, 1984—; bd. advisors U. Tenn. Sch. Arch., 1982, chmn., 1985—88. Recipient Jefferson award, Am. Inst. Pub. Svc. (Nashville chpt.), 1985, Hall Fame, Nashville Alliance Pub. Edn., 2008; named Outstanding Nashvillian of Yr., Downtown Kiwanis Club, 1992, One of Top 100 Alumni of Greatest Distinction Throughout 128-yr. History, Va. Poly. Inst. and State U., 2001. Presbyterian. Achievements include patents for systamodule for pharmacies. Office: Earl Swensson Assocs 2100 W End Ave Ste 1200 Nashville TN 37203-5239 Office Phone: 615-329-9445.

SWETMAN, CHEVIS, bank executive; m. Marcia Swetman; children: Tanner Swetman. BS in Fin., U. Southern Miss., MBA. Chmn. The Peoples Bank; pres., CEO Peoples Bank, 1971—, Peoples Financial Corp., 1971—, chmn., 1994—. Bd. dirs. Peoples Fin. Corp., 1984. Chmn. Pine Burr Area Coun. Boy Scouts, Memorial Hosp. Gulfport Found., MS GC C. of C. With US Army, 1969-71. Named Outstanding Civic Leader, 2003. Office: Peoples Financial Corp 152 Lameuse St Biloxi MS 39530 Office Phone: 228-435-5511. Office Fax: 228-435-8418. Business E-Mail: cswetman@thepeoples.com.

SWETMAN, GLENN ROBERT, literature and language professor, poet; b. May 20, 1936; s. Glenn Lyle and June (Read) S.; m. Margarita Ortiz, Feb. 8, 1964 (div. 1979); children: Margarita June, Glenn Lyle Maximilian, Glenda Louise. BS, U. So. Miss., 1957, MA, 1959; PhD, Tulane U., 1966. Instr. U. So. Miss., 1957-58, asst. prof., 1964-66; instr. Ark. State U., 1958-59, McNeese U., 1959-61; instr. English Univ. Coll. Tulane U., 1961-64, spl. asst. dept. elec. engring., 1961-64; assoc. prof. La. Inst. Tech., 1966-67; prof., head dept. langs. Nicholls State Coll., Thibodaux, La., 1967-69, head dept. English, 1969-71, prof., 1971-91; prof. emeritus William Carey U., Gulfport, Miss., 1991—. Writer in residence, prof. English William Carey U., Gulfport, 1991—; ptnr. Breeland Pl., Biloxi, 1960—; stringer, corr. Shreveport Times, La., 1966—; ptnr. Ormuba, Inc., 1975—; cons. tech. writing Union Carbide Corp., Am. Fedn. Tchrs. State v.p. Nat. Com. to Resist Attacks on Tenure, 1974—. Book reviewer Jackson State Times, Miss., 1961; contbr. poetry to various publs. including Poet, Prairie Schooner, Trace, Ball State U. Forum, Film Quar., Poetry Australia, numerous others worldwide; author: (books of poems) Tunel de Amor, 1973, Deka #1, 1973, Deka #2, 1979, Shards, 1979, Concerning Carpenters, 1980, Son of Igor, 1982, Poems of the Fantastic, 1990, Oh What Tangled Web, 2007, Deka 3, 2008, Biloxi:A Bankers Day Book, 2nd edit., 2010, History of the People's Bank of Biloxi, 2010; contbr. numerous articles to encys.; cons. editor (poetry) Paon Press, 1974—, Scott-Foresman, 1975; mem. editl. bd. Scholar and Educator, 1980—. Subdivsn. coord. Rep. Party, Hattiesburg, Miss., 1964. With AUS, 1957. Recipient Poetry awards KQUE Haiku contest, 1964, Coll. Arts contest, LA, 1966, Black Ship Festival, Yoqosuka, Japan, 1967, Green World Brief Forms award Green World Poetry Editors, 1965. Mem. MLA, S. Cen. MLA, So. Literary Festival Assn. (v.p. 1975-76, 82-83, pres. 1984-85), Coll. Writers Soc. La. (pres. 1971-72, exec. dir. 1983—), IEEE, Am. Assn. Engring. Edn., La. Poetry Soc. (pres. 1971-74, 86—), Internat. Boswellian Inst., Nat. Fedn. State Poetry Socs. (2d v.p., nat. membership chmn. 1972-74, pres. 1976-77), Nat. Soc. Scholars and Educators (bd. dirs. 1982—, sec. exec. bd. 1986—, sec. bd. dirs. 1968—, sec. soc. 1989—, exec. edn. 2001-), Am. Fedn. Tchrs. (chpt. pres. 1973-78), Nat. Fedn. State Poetry Socs. (1st v.p. 1975-76, exec. bd. 1972—), Phi Eta Sigma, Omicron Delta Kappa. Home: PO Box 146 Biloxi MS 39533-0146 Office: William Carey University Traditions Campus Gulfport MS 39507-1508

SWIENTON, GREGORY T., transportation company executive; BBA in Mktg., Loyola U., Chgo., 1971; MBS in Bus. Admin., U. Chgo. Various sales and mktg. positions Ill. Bell and AT&T, Chgo., Mpls., 1971-82; former v.p., gen. mgr. DHL Airways, Inc., Chgo. and Houston; mng. dir. We. & Ea. Europe DHL Worldwide Express, Brussels, 1988—90, exec. dir. Europe and Africa, 1991—94; exec. v.p. Intermodal Bus.Unit Burlington No. Railroad, 1994—95; sr. v.p. Industrial Bus. Unit Burlington Northern Santa Fe Corp., 1995—99; pres., COO Ryder System, Inc., Miami, 1999—2000, chmn., CEO, 2000—. Mem. bd. dir. St. Thomas Univ. Bd. Trustees. Office: Ryder System Inc PO Box 20816 Miami FL 33102-0816

SWIFT, DAVID L., manufacturing executive; b. Wilbraham, Mass. married. BA in Math. & Physics, Amherst Coll., Mass., 1980; M in Electronics Engring., Dartmouth Coll., Hanover, NH; MBA, Harvard U., 1999. Chmn., pres., Greater Asia Region Eastman Kodak Co., pres., Kodak Profl. Group; exec. v.p., N.Am. Region Whirlpool Corp., Benton Harbor, Mich., 2001—05, pres., Whirlpool N.Am., bd. dirs., 2006—07; pres., CEO & bd. dirs. Goodman Global, Inc., 2008—. Office: Goodman Global Inc 5151 San Felipe Blvd Ste 500 Houston TX 77056 Office Phone: 713-861-2500. Office Fax: 713-861-3207. Business E-Mail: david.swift@goodmanmfg.com.

SWIFT, JOHN D., manufacturing executive; CFO Mohawk Industries Inc., Calhoun, Ga. Office: Mohawk Industries Inc 160 S Industrial Blvd Calhoun GA 30701-3030

SWIFT, ROBERT J., lawyer; b. Wilmington, Del., Jan. 17, 1948; BA, U. Del., 1972; JD, South Tex. Coll. Law, 1977. Bar: Tex. 1977. Assoc. Fulbright & Jaworski L.L.P., Houston, ptnr., 1985—, and co-head health law-litig. and adminstrn. dept. Mem. ABA, Am. Soc. Healthcare Risk Mgmt., State Bar Tex. (mem. health litigation/med. malpractice com.), Tex. Assn. Def. Counsel, Houston Bar Assn., Greater Houston Soc. Healthcare Risk Mgmt. Office: Fulbright & Jaworski LLP 1301 McKinney St Ste 5100 Houston TX 77010-3031 Office Phone: 713-651-5151. Office Fax: 713-651-5246. Business E-Mail: rswift@fulbright.com.

SWIFT, TAYLOR, singer, songwriter; b. Wyomissing, Pa., Dec. 13, 1989; d. Scott Kingsley and Andrea Gardner (Finlay) Swift. Spokesmodel CoverGirl, Diet Coke, Keds, American Greetings, Sony Electronics; launched fragrance Wonderstruck. Singer: (albums) Taylor Swift, 2006, Songs of the Season, 2007, Fearless, 2008 (Album of Yr., Acad. Country Music Awards, 2009, Favorite Country Album, American Music Awards, 2009, Album of Yr., Country Music Assn. Awards, 2009, Choice Country Album, Teen Choice Awards, 2009, Top Country Album of Yr., Billboard Music Awards, 2009, Album of Yr., Best Country Album, Grammy Awards, 2010), Speak Now, 2010 (Top Country Album, Billboard Music Awards, 2011, Favorite Country Album, American Music Awards, 2011), Speak Now: World Tour Live, 2011, Red, 2012 (Top Country Album, Billboard Music Awards, 2013, Favorite Country Album, American Music Awards, 2013), (songs) Tim McGraw, 2006 (Breakthrough Video of Yr., CMT Music Awards, 2007), Teardrops On My Guitar, 2006 (Country Song of Yr., BMI Awards, 2008), Our Song, 2006 (Video of Yr., Female Video of Yr., CMT Music Awards, 2008), Love Story, 2008 (Music Video of Yr., Country Music Assn. Awards, 2009, Country Song of Yr., BMI Awards, 2009, Video of Yr., Female Video of Yr., CMT Music Awards, 2009), White Horse, 2008 (Best Female Country Vocal Performance, Best Country Song, Grammy Awards, 2010), Fifteen, 2009 (Choice Country Song, Teen Choice Awards, 2010), You Belong with Me, 2009 (Best Female Video, MTV Video Music Awards, 2009, Country Song of Yr., BMI Awards, 2010, Favorite Song, Nickelodeon Kids' Choice Awards, 2010), Mine, 2010 (Video of Yr., CMT Music Awards, 2011), Mean, 2010 (Best Country Solo Performance, Best Country Song, Grammy Awards, 2012), Sparks Fly, 2010 (Choice Country Song, Teen Choice Awards, 2012), Eyes Open, 2012 (Choice Single by a Female Artist, Teen Choice Awards, 2012), We Are Never Getting Back Together, 2012 (Top Country Song, Billboard Music Awards, 2013), (with The Civil Wars) Safe & Sound, 2012 (Best Song Written for Visual Media, Grammy Awards, 2013), (featured vocals on Tim McGraw's track) Highway Don't Care, 2013 (Musical Event of Yr., Music Video of Yr., Country Music Assn. Awards, 2013, Video of Yr., Acad. Country Music Awards, 2014); actress: (films) Hannah Montana: The Movie, 2009, Valentine's Day, 2010 (Choice Breakout Female, Teen Choice Awards, 2010), (voice) Dr. Suess' The Lorax, 2012 (Choice Movie Voice, Teen Choice Awards, 2012); guest appearance (TV series) CSI: Crime Scene Investigation, 2009. Recipient Horizon award, Country Music Assn. Awards, 2007, Internat. Artist Achievement award, 2009, Pinnacle award, 2013, Internat. Artist Achievement award, 2013, Crystal Milestone award, Acad. Country Music Awards, 2009, Jim Reeves Internat. award, 2011, Hal David Starlight award, Songwriters Hall of Fame, 2010, Best Female Video for the song I Knew You Were Trouble, MTV Video Music Awards, 2013; named Top New Female Vocalist, Acad. Country Music Awards, 2008, Entertainer of Yr., 2011, 2012, Favorite Country Female Artist, American Music Awards, 2008, 2009, 2010, 2011, 2012, 2013, Artist of Yr., 2009, 2011, 2013, Favorite Adult Contemporary Artist, 2009, Favorite Pop/Rock Female Artist, 2009, Entertainer of Yr., Country Music Assn. Awards, 2009, Female Vocalist of Yr., Country Music Assn., 2009, Entertainer of Yr., AP, 2009, Entertainment Weekly, 2010, Country Music Assn. Awards, 2011, Artist of Yr., Billboard Music Awards, 2009, 2013, Top Country Artist, 2011, 2013, Top Female Artist, 2013, Top Billboard 200 Artist, 2013, Choice Female Artist, Teen Choice Awards, 2009, 2012, Choice Female Country Artist, 2010, Favorite Female Artist, People's Choice Awards, 2010, Favorite Country Artist, 2011, 2012, 2013, 2014, Favorite Female Singer, Nickelodeon Kids' Choice Awards, 2010, Favorite Internat. Solo Artist of Yr., Ind. Music Awards, 2011, Woman of Yr., Billboard mag., 2011; named one of The 100 Most Beautiful People, People mag., 2008—10, The 25 Most Intriguing People, 2009, The 100 Agents of Change, Rolling Stone mag., 2009, The 100 Most Influential People in the World, TIME mag., 2010, The 100 Most Powerful Women in Entertainment, Hollywood Reporter, 2013. Achievements include recognition as the youngest artist to ever be nominated for and win the Country Music Association Entertainer of the Year award in 2009; the eighth and youngest female artist to win the Academy of Country Music Entertainer of the Year award in 2011. Office: c/o Troy Tomlinson Sony/ATV Tree Publishing 8 Music Sq W Nashville TN 37203*

SWIGER, ANDREW P., oil industry executive; m. Sherry Swiger. BSc in Petroleum Engring., Colo. Sch. Mines, Golden, 1978. Ops. engr. to various staff and managerial upstream assignments Mobile Oil, 1978—96, gen. mgr. mfg. Singapore, 1996—99, pres., gen. mgr., Mobil Oil Can., 1999—2001; corp. prodn. advisor ExxonMobil Corp., Irving, Tex., v.p. Africa London, 2001—03, chmn., prodn. dir., ExxonMobil Internat. Ltd., lead country mgr., UK and Ireland, 2003—04, exec. v.p., ExxonMobil Prodn. Co., pres., ExxonMobil Gas & Power Mktg. Co., sr. v.p., 2009—. Chmn. Esso Exploration and Prodn., Mobil North Sea. Bd. dirs. US-Kazakhstan Bus. Assn.; mem. Greater Houston Partnership Bus. Issues Adv. Com. Mem.: Internat. Assn. Oil and Gas Prodrs. (vice chmn. bd. dirs.). Office: ExxonMobil Corp 5959 Las Colinas Blvd Irving TX 75039-2298

SWIGER, ELIZABETH DAVIS, chemist, educator; b. Morgantown, W.Va., June 27, 1926; d. Hannibal Albert and Tyreeca Elizabeth (Stemple) Davis; m. William Eugene Swiger, June 2, 1948 (dec.); children: Susan Elizabeth Swiger Knotts-Case, Wayne William; m. James E. Coleman, Dec. 11, 2004. BS in Chemistry, W.Va. U., 1948, MS in Chemistry, 1952, PhD in Chemistry, 1964. Instr. math. Fairmont State Coll., 1948-49, instr. math. and phys. sci., 1956-57, instr. chemistry, 1957-60, from asst. prof. to assoc. prof., 1960—66, prof., 1966-92, chmn., divsn. sci., math, and health careers, 1991-92; NSF fellow rsch. W.Va. U., Morgantown, 1963-64, prof. emerita, 1992. Advisor Am. Chem. Soc. student affiliates, 1965-88. Author: Morton Family History, 1984-2004, Davis-Winters Family History, 1994—, Civil War Letters and Diary of Joshua Winters, 1991, 2d edit., 1996; contbr. articles to profl. jour. Chmn. Blacks Chapel Meml. Found., 1993—; rep. adv. coun. to Bd. Regents Fairmont State Coll., Charleston, W.Va., 1977—78, rep. instl. bd. advisors, 1990—92. NSF grantee, 1963; named Outstanding Prof. W.Va. Legislature, Charleston, 1990. Mem.: Am. Chem. Soc. (advisor student affiliates 1965—88, sec. chmn. North W.Va. 1975—83), W.Va. Acad. Sci. (life; pres. 1978—79, exec. com. edn. chmn. 1990—93), Nature Conservancy (bd. dir. W.Va. chpt. 1970—86, chmn. 1980—82), Prickett's Fort Meml. Found. (life; bd. dir. 1988—2000, chmn. elect 1990—92, chmn. 1992—96, bd. dir 2002—), Marion County Hist. Soc. (life; sec. 2013—), Fairmont Lions Club, Morning Gardeners Garden Club (pres. 1999—2003, 2013—). Republican. Methodist. Avocations: local history, genealogy, gardening, quilting. Home (Winter): 242 Laird Dr Freeport FL 32439 Home: 1599 Hillcrest Rd Fairmont WV 26554-4807

SWIGGER, KEITH, library and information scientist, educator; b. Hutchinson, Kans., Feb. 3, 1943; s. Paul Clarke and Loneta (Miller) S.; children: Jessica, Nathaniel; m. Cindy Johnson Potter, Nov. 29, 1997. BA, U. Chgo., 1965, MA, 1975, Ind. U., 1967; PhD, U. Iowa, 1973. Sketchwriter Marquis Who's Who, Chgo., 1963-67; teaching asst. Ind. U., Bloomington, 1967, U. Iowa, Iowa City, 1968-73, lectr., 1973-74, libr., 1976-77; asst. prof. East Tex. State U., Commerce, 1977-81; asst. prof. libr. scis. Tex. Woman's U., Denton, 1981-85, assoc. prof., 1985-89, prof., 1989—, interim dean Sch. Libr. Sci., 1991-92, dean Sch. Libr. and Info. Studies, 1992-2000, dir. Sch. Libr. and Info. Studies, 2001—02, dir. Ctr. for Consulting and Planning, 1997—2010, dean Coll. Profl. Edn., 2000—03, dir. Gear Up fed. grant program, 2002—03. Mem. adv. com. continuum libr. edn. We. Coun. State Librs., 2003—07; cons. in field. Co-editor Jour. of Youth Svcs., 1997-2000, author The MLS Project: An Assessment after 60 Years, 2010; contbr. numerous articles to profl. jours. Bd. dirs. ACLU, Denton, 1990-92, Emily Fowler Pub. Libr., Denton, 1995-97, vice chair, 1997; mem. Tex. Edn. Tech. Coord. Coun., 2000-03; delegate Tex. Dem. Party state convention, 2004. Rsch. grantee OCLC, Inc., 1990-91, Career Tng. grantee U.S. Office Edn., 1990-98; postdoctoral fellow Coun. on Libr. Resources U. Chgo., 1974-75; recipient Svc. award Nat. Storytelling Assn., 1998. Mem. ALA, Lib. Leadership & Mgmt Assn., Nature Conservancy, Nat. Audubon Soc. Democrat. Office: Tex Womans U Sch Libr Info Studies PO Box 425438 Denton TX 76204-5438 Personal E-mail: kswigger@alumni.uchicago.edu.

SWIMMER, ROSS OWEN, former federal official; b. Oklahoma City, Oct. 26, 1943; s. Robert Otis and Virginia Marie (Pounder) S.; m. Margaret Ann McConnell, June 30, 1965; children: Joseph Ross, Michael David. BA, U. Okla., 1965, JD, 1967. Bar: Okla. 1967. Ptnr. Hanson, Peterson, Thompkins, Oklahoma City, 1967-72; counsel Cherokee Nation, Tahlequah, Okla., 1972-74, prin. chief, 1975-85; exec. v.p. 1st Nat. Bank, Tahlequah, 1974, pres., 1974-84; asst. sec. for Indian affairs US Dept. Interior, Washington, 1985-89, spl. trustee for American Indians, 2003—09; of counsel Hall, Estill, Hardwick, Gable, Golden & Nelson, Tulsa, 1989—92; founder Swimmer Group LLC, 2009—; ptnr. NAFA Capital Markets, 2009—. Bd. dirs. First National Bank & Trust Co., 2009—. Mem. ABA, Okla. Bar Assn., Cherokee Nat. Hist. Soc. (pres. 1979-80), Okla. Hist. Soc. Republican. Personal E-mail: rswimmer@sbcglobal.net.

SWINKER, MARIAN LEA, public health service officer, state official; b. Phila., Jan. 10, 1951; d. Robert J. and Margaret P. Swinker; m. Allen C. Schlobohm, Dec. 11, 1981. BS, U. Pitts., 1971, MPH, 1972; MD, Pa. State U., 1978. Diplomate American Bd. Preventive Medicine, American Bd. Family Medicine. Chem. technologist Pa. Dept. Environ. Rsch., Pitts., 1973-74; intern W.Va. U. Hosp., Morgantown, 1978-79, resident, 1981-83; physician Nat. Health Svc. Corps, Burton, W.Va., 1979-81; prof. medicine W.Va. U., Morgantown, 1983-94, East Carolina U., Greenville, NC, 1994—2011; commr. W.Va. Dept. Pub. Health, Charleston, 2011—. Hysterectomy panelist RAND, Santa Monica, Calif., 1993-95; bd. dirs. Eastern region N.C. Dept. Labor Safety Sch., Greenville, 1995-97. Contbr. chpt. to book. Mem. American Coll. Occup. & Environ. Medicine (occup. infection com. 1998—), American Acad. Family Physicians, N.C. Med. Soc. (occup. and environ. med. com. 1996—), N.C. Spine Soc., N.C. Occupl. Medicine Assn., Pitt County Med. Soc. Avocations: horseback riding, golf, gardening. Office: West Virginia Department Public Health Room 702 350 Capitol St Charleston WV 25301 Office Phone: 304-558-2971. Office Fax: 304-558-1035.*

SWINNEY, DABO, college football coach; b. Ala., Nov. 20, 1969; m. Kathleen Bassett, 1994; children: Will, Drew, Clay. B in Commerce & Bus. Adminstrn., U. Ala., 1993, MBA, 1995. Grad. asst. coach U. Ala. Crimson Tide, 1993—95, wide receivers, tight ends coach, 1996—97, tight ends coach, 1997—98, wide receivers coach, 1998—2001; pvt. bus. Ala., 2001—03; wide receivers coach Clemson U. Tigers, 2003—08, interim head coach, 2008, head coach, 2008—. Office: Clemson Univ Athletic Dept PO Box 31 Clemson SC 29633

SWISHER, STEPHEN R., corporate financial executive; BBA, Fla. Atlantic U.; MBA, U. Miami. CPA. Mgr., divsn. acctg. Burger King Corp.; audit mgr. Deloitte & Touche LLP; dir., fin. BE Aerospace, Inc., 1994—96, contr., 1996—, v.p., fin., 1999—. Mem. AICPA, Fla. Inst. of CPAs. Office: BE Aerospace Inc 1400 Corp Ctr Way Wellington FL 33414 Office Phone: 561-791-5000. Office Fax: 561-791-7900.

SWOAP, DAVID BRUCE, government and state agency administrator, consultant, art director; b. Kalamazoo, Aug. 12, 1937; s. Orlo Frederick and Aileen Esther (Hempy) S. BA in Govt. with honors, Denison U., 1959; MA in Govt., Claremont Grad. Sch., 1961; DSc (hon.), U. Osteo. Medicine and Health Scis., Des Moines, 1981. Asst. sec. Calif. State Pers. Bd., Sacramento, 1972-73; chief dep. dir., acting dir. Calif. State Dept. Social Welfare, 1973, dir., 1973-74, Calif. State Dept. Benefit Payments, 1974-75; sr. rsch. asso. Rep. Study Com., U.S. Ho. of Reps., Washington, 1975-76; profl. staff mem. U.S. Senate Com. on Fin., 1976-79; legis. dir. U.S. Senator William L. Armstrong, 1979-81; dep. sec. HHS, 1981-83; sec. health and welfare State of Calif., Sacramento, 1983-85; ptnr. Franchetti & Swoap, San Francisco, 1985-90; owner Mana Olana Farms, Hakalau, Hawaii, 1989—97; vice chmn. Sacramento Advs., 1991-98; owner The David Bruce Gallery, Carlsbad, Calif., 1995-97. Chmn. bd. Hope Unltd. for Children, Los Alamitos, Calif., 1991—96, bd. mem., 2007—, mem. adv. bd., 1996—2007, chmn. adv. bd., 1996—2003. Elder Presbyn. Ch.; bd. dirs. Friends of SOS Children's Villages, 1989-91; bd. regents John F. Kennedy U., 1990-93; mem. Healthy Families Dorchester adv. bd., 2002-05, Md. State Bd. of Physicians, 2003-05. Rotary Club Found. fellow, 1961-62 Mem. Wycliffe Assocs., Phi Beta Kappa, Delta Upsilon. Republican.

SWOFFORD, DONALD ANTHONY, architect; b. Houston, Apr. 14, 1947; s. Harry and Henrian (Engbrock) Swofford; 1 child, James McShea. BArch, Tex. A&M U., 1969; MArch, U. Va., 1976. Registered arch., Va., Tex., DC, Nat. Coun. Archtl. Registration Bd.; lic. instrument pilot. Arch., urban designer City of Dallas, 1970-72, Office Milton L. Grigg, FAIA, Archs., 1972-78; prin., owner DASA, PLC, Charlottesville, Va., 1978—. Author: Dallas Historical Landmark Program, 1972; prin. works include Flovanna County Courthouse, Joseph Jarvis residence, 1978, Shrinemont Conf. Ctr., Episcopal Diocese Va., Orkney Springs, 1981, United Coal/Martha Washington Inn, Bristol, Va., 1985, Montpelier, home of James Madison, 1986, restoration Farley, Culpeper, Va., 1987 (Nat. Trust Hist. Preservation Gt. Homes Am., 1985), restoration St. Francis Assisi Cath. Ch., Stanton, Va., 1988, restoration and additions Goochland County (Va.) Courthouse, 1989, George M. McMath residence, Locustville, Va., 1991, restoration of Highlands, home of James Monroe, Charlottesville, 1991, restoration of Clover Hill Tavern, Appomattox, Va., 1994, hist. rehab. of Danville (Va.) Rail Passenger Sta., restoration of Gen. George C. Marshall Home, Leesburg, Va., 1994, Danville City Courthouse, 1995, Danville Cts. and Jails Bldg., 1999, Congl. Cemetery, Washington, 1999, Nottoway County Courthouse, 1999, Ct. Sq. F&M Bank, Winchester, Va. (Nat. Honor award Nat. Trust Hist. Preservation), McGlothlin Family Mus., 2001, Tom McGlothlin residence, 2003, FT Pickett Officer's Club, 2003, James and Cella Rutt residence, 2004. Cub master Pack 119, Stonewall Jackson Coun. Boy Scouts Am., 1994—98. Recipient Design award, Tex.-AIA, 1969—70, Loudoun County award for Jarvis Residence, 1985. Fellow: AIA; mem.: Assn. Preservation Tech., Soc. Archtl. Historians, Nat. Trust Hist. Preservation, Albemarle County Hist. Soc. Office: Don Swofford And Asso 1860 Bentivar Dr Charlottesville VA 22911-8229 Office Phone: 434-979-7407. Personal E-mail: dons@dasaonline.com.

SWOFFORD, JOHN, sports association executive; b. North Wilkesboro, NC, Dec. 6, 1948; m. Nora Swofford; children: Amie, Chad, Autumn. B in Psychology and Indsl. Rels., U. NC, Chapel Hill, 1971; M in Athletic Adminstrn., Ohio U., 1973. Athletic ticket mgr., asst. to the dir. athletic facilities and fin. U. Va., 1973—76; asst. athletic dir., bus. mgr. U. NC, Chapel Hill, 1976—79, asst. athletic dir., exec. v.p. of Ednl. Found., 1979—80, dir. athletics, 1980—97; commr. Atlantic Coast Conf., 1997—. Pres. Nat. Assn. Collegiate Dir. Athletics, 1993—94; mem. exec. com. NCAA, mem. TV com., chmn. comm. com., chmn. spl. events/post season bowl com., chmn. divsn. I championship com., mem. spl. com. to study a divsn. 1-A football championship; coord. Bowl Championship Series, 2000—01. Named to NC Sports Hall of Fame, 2009; Morehead scholar, U. NC. Office: Atlantic Coast Conf PO Drawer ACC Greensboro NC 27417-6724 Office Phone: 336-854-8787.

SWOPE, DALE M., lawyer; b. Tampa, Fla., Apr. 6, 1954; s. Samuel Morris and Betty (Rentz) Swope. BS with honors, U. South Fla., 1975; JD, U. Fla. Fredric G. Levin Coll. Law, 1978. Bar: Fla. 1978, US Dist. Ct. (no., so. and mid. dists.) Fla., cert. civil trial specialist. Assoc. Law Office Ron Sales, P.A., West Palm Beach, Fla., 1978-79; founder, ptnr. Swope, Rodante P.A., Tampa, 1979—. Contbr. articles to profl. jours. Bd. trustees Fla. Lawyer's Action Group, 1999—. Recipient Champion for Children award, 2005; named one of Legal Elite in Ins. Law, Fla. Trend Mag., 2008. Mem.: ABA, AAJ, Tampa Bay Trial Lawyers Assn. (founding mem., pres. 2000—02), Fla. Justice Assn. (bd. dirs. 1998—2004, Silver Eagle award 1997, 1999, Crystal Eagle award 2005), American Bd. Trial Advocates, Southern Trial Lawyers Assn. (bd. dirs. 1998—), American Law Inst., Hillsborough County Bar Assn. (founder & chmn. Solo Practioner's Com. 1991—92, Outstanding Young Lawyer award 1988), Fla. Bar Assn. Office: Swope Rodante PA 1234 5th Ave E Tampa FL 33605 E-mail: swope@swopelaw.com.

SYED, IBRAHIM BIJLI, medical educator, physicist, founder evidence based religion; b. Bellary, India, Mar. 16, 1939; came to US, 1969, naturalized, 1975; s. Syed Ahmed Bijli and Mumtaz Begum (Maniyar) S.; m. Sajida Shariff, Nov. 29, 1964; children: Mubin, Zafrin. BS with honors, Veerasaiva Coll., Bellary U., Mysore, 1960; MS with honors and distinction, Bangalore U., Mysore, 1962; diploma, U. Bombay, 1964; DSc, Johns Hopkins U., Balt., 1972; PhD (hon.), Malta, 1985; DSc (hon.), VSK U., Bellary, India, 2013. Cert. hazard control officer, 1980, internat. health care safety profl., 1980; diplomate Am. Bd. Radiology, Am. Bd. Health Physics. Lectr. physics Veerasaiva Coll., Bellary U., Mysore, 1962-63; med. physicist, radiation safety officer Victoria Hosp., India, 1964-67, Bowring and Lady Curz on Hosp. & Postgrad. Med. Rsch. Inst., Bangalore, India, 1964-67; cons. med. physicist, radiation safety officer Ministry of Health, Govt. of Karnataka, India, 1964-67, Bangalore Nursing Home, India, 1964-67; med. physicist, radiation safety officer Baystate Med. Ctr., Springfield, Mass., 1973-79; assoc. prof. Springfield Tech. C.C.; also adj. prof. radiology Holyoke C.C., Mass., 1973-79; asst. clin. prof. nuclear medicine U. Conn. Sch. Medicine, Farmington, 1975-79; cons. med. physicist Mercy Hosp., Springfield, 1973-79, Wing Meml. Hosp., Palmer, Mass., 1973-79; med. physicist, radiation safety officer VAMC, Louisville, 1979—, exec. officer radiation safety com., 1979—; prof. medicine U. Louisville Sch. Medicine, 1979—, dir. nuclear med. scis., 1980—; mem. Instl. Review Bd. Veterans Admin. Medical Ctr., Louisville, 2000—. Guest lectr. religious studies program U. Louisville, 1979—; vis. prof. Bangalore U., 1987—88, Gulbarga U., India, 1987—88; vis. scientist Bhabha Atomic Rsch. Ctr., Bombay; invited spkr. Veerasaiva Coll., Bellary, India, 1996, Vijayanagar Coll., Hospet, 1996, Vajayanagar Inst. Med. Scis., Bellary, 1996, Deccan Coll. Med. Scis., Hyderabad, India, Bhabha Atomic Rsch. Ctr., Bombay, 1997, 15th Ann. Islamic Conf. New Eng., Islamic Coun. New Eng., 1999, Coun. for a Parliament of the World's Religions, Cape Town, South Africa, 1999, Garden City Coll. Bangalore, 2000, Veerasaiva Coll., Bellary, 2000, Islamic Rsch. Found., Mumbai, India, 2001, Islamic Assn. of Essex, England, 2001, Assn. Muslim Social Scientists, Detroit, 2001, Darus Salam, Bangalore, India, 2005; invited faculty Assn. Muslim Social Scientists, Dallas, 2005; invited spkr. Islamic Orgn. Med. Scis., Cairo, 2002; PhD thesis examiner Allahabad U., 1996—; course dir. licensing for nuclear cardiologists U. Louisville, 1980—, mem. admissions com. nuclear medicine program, 1980—; guest relief examiner Am. Bd. Radiology, 1991, 2005; examiner in radiol physics, 1995, 1997, 1998, 2000; examiner in radiol. physics, 2003, 2005, 2006; mem. panel of examiners Am. Bd. Health Physics; PhD thesis examiner U. Delhi, Internat. Inst. for Advanced Study, Clayton, Mo., 1985—, Allahabad (India) U., 1996—2005; faculty mem. Med. Physicists of India Ann. Meeting, 1987; IAEA tchr. expert in nuclear medicine on mission to People's Republic of Bangladesh, 1986; to Guatemala, 1994; founder, pres. Islamic Rsch. Found. Internat., Louisville, 1988—; convener Internat. Conf. on Islamic Renaissance: Action Plan for the 21st Century, Chgo., 1995; cons. Coun. Sci. and Indsl. Rsch., Govt. India, 0809—, Am. Coun. Sci. and Health, 1980—; cons. gastroenterology and urology divsn. FDA, HHS, 1988—, cons. radiopharm. divsn., 1989—; cons. Govt. India in nuclear medicine, diagnostic radiol. physics, therapeutic radiol. physics and radiation safety, 1992; cons. radiol. and med. nuc. physics Govt. India, Un Devel. Program, 1992; convenor Internat. Conf. on Islamic Renaissance, Chgo., 1995; guest spkr. Muslim Cmty. Ctr., Chgo., 1988; invited spkr. objective studies and Islamic voice, Bangalore, 1996, Parliament of World Religions, Chgo., 1993, Cape Town, South Africa, 1999, Cooper Mosque, Mississauga, Ont., Canada, 2002; invited faculty Assn. of Muslim Social Scientists, Dallas, 2005; invited spkr. Internat. Conf. on Alternative Medicine, Cairo, 2002, Darus Salam, Bangalore, India, 2005, Internat. Conf. on Alternative Med., Cairo, 2002, Bellari Inst. Tech. and Mgmt., Berrary, India, 2013, Vijayanagara Sri Krishnadevaraya U., Berrary, 2013, Vijayanagar Inst. Med. Scis., Berrary, 2013, Integral U., Lucknow, India, 2013, Sri Ram Mohan Lohia Inst. Med. Scis., Lucknow, 2013, Garden City Coll., Bangalore, India, 2013, Raichur Dist. Tchrs. Confs., India, 2013, Islamic Voice Ter. Gardens, Bangalore, 2013. Author: Radiation Safety for Allied Health Professionals, Radiation Safety Manual, 1979, Intellectual Achievements of Muslims, 2002, Qur'anic Inspirations, 2007; contbg. editor Jour. of Islamic Food and Nutrition Coun. of Am., 1986—, health and sci. column Muslim Jour., 1989—; freelance writer Minaret Biweekly, NYC, 1975—, Islamic Voice, India, 1988—, Al-Balaagh, Lenasia, South Africa, 1989—, AL'FURQAN Internat., Norcross, Ga., 1990, Message Internat., Jamaica, NY, 1990, Minaret Monthly Mag., LA, 1995—, The Message, London, 1998—, The Minaret, Botswana, 1998—; editor: Science and Technology for the Developing World, 1988; mem. editl. bd. Jour. Islamic Med. Assn., 1981—, columnist, sci. editor The Indian Muslim Observer; regular contbr. Pres.'s Page; manuscript reviewer for sci. and med. jours., 1973; assoc. editor AAlim, 1998—; contbr. more than 100 articles to sci. jours.; pub. internat. more than 400 articles on various topics of Islam in jours. and mags. Moderator fgn. policy workshop U.S. Dept. State, Louisville, 2000; spkr. Dayton Islamic Ctr., Dayton, 2000, Muslim Student Assn. U. Cin., 2000, Muslim Cmty. Ctr., Chgo., 2001; invited spkr. Muslim Assn. of Cleve. East, 2002, Biotech. Conf., Kuala Lumpur, Malaysia, 2007; adv. bd. Partnership to Prevent Child Abuse, Louisville, 2007—; bd. dir. Nur Islamic Sch., Louisville, 2003, Am. Muslim Assn. Louisville, 2003—; commr. Human Rels. Commn. Metro Louisville Ky. Govt., 2010; bd. dirs. Islamic Ctr. of Louisville, 1992—; founder, mgr., trustee Bijli Found. Charitable Trust, Bellary, India, 2005—. Recipient Disting. Cmty. Svc. award India Cmty. Found., 1982, Hind Rattan Jewel of India Title award North Soc. New Delhi, 1984, Disting. Svc. award, Am. Bd. radiology, 2008, Mus. Jour. Muslim Civilization Advancement award, 2010; WHO fellow, Govt. India scholar Bhabha Atomic Rsch. Ctr., Bombay, 1963-64; USPHS fellow Johns Hopkins U., 1969-72. Fellow Inst. Physics (UK), Am. Inst. Chemists, Royal Soc. Health, Am. Coll. Radiology, Internat. Acad. Med. Physics; mem. Am. Assn. Physicists in Medicine, Am. Coll. Nuclear Medicine, Health Physics Soc., Am. Acad. Health Physics, Soc. Nuclear Medicine (faculty mem. ann. meeting 1987, convenor internat. conf. 1995), Nat. Assn. Ams. of Asian Indian Descent (chmn. state pub. rels. com. 1982—), Islamic Med. Assn. N.Am. (life, faculty 1994, 96, 98), Internat. Inst. Islamic Medicine (faculty Orlando, Fla. 1996, 97, Birmingham, UK 1998), Islamic Soc. N.Am. (faculty Chgo. 1998), Islamic Soc. Balt. (founding mem.), Islamic Cultural Ctr.(sec. 1999-), Louisville, Islamic Assn. Maritime Provinces Can., Halifax, N.S. (asst. sec. 1967-69), Health Physics Soc. (chmn. med. health physics com. 1989—, affirmative action com. 1984—), Am. Assn. Physicists in Medicine (biol. effects com.), Assn. Muslim Scientists and Engrs. N.Am. (program chmn. ann. conf. 1987, treas. 1987-88, sec. 1988—), AAUP, Soc. Nuc. Medicine India (life, faculty mem. ann. meeting 1987, invited spkr. and faculty ann. meeting 1996), Assn. Med. Physicists India (life, invited spkr. and faculty ann. meeting Madras 1996), Med. and Biol. Physics (divsn. Can.) Assn. Physicists, Hosp. Physicists Assn., NY Acad. Scis., Islamic Assn. Maritime Provinces of Can., Ky. Med. Assn., Jefferson County Med. Soc. (assoc.), Am. Muslim Assn. Louisville (bd. dirs. 2003—), Assn. Muslim Social Scientists, Sigma Xi Islamic. Home: 7102 W Shefford Ln Louisville KY 40242-4642 Office: 3rd Fl ACB Bldg 710 S Jackson St Louisville KY 40202 Office Phone: 502-423-1988.

SYKES, ANTHONY, state legislator; BA, JD, Okla. Univ. Bar: Okla. 2000. Atty.; mem. Dist. 24 Okla. State Senate, 2006—. Republican. Address: 1807 SW 24 St Moore OK 73170 Office: 2300 N Lincoln Blvd Rm 426 Oklahoma City OK 73105 Office Phone: 405-521-5569. E-mail: sykes@oksenate.gov.

SYKES, GWENDOLYN, academic administrator, former federal agency administrator; b. West Point, NY, 1965; BS in Acctg., Cath. U., 1987; MPA, American U., 2001. Cert. govt. fin. mgr. With Def. Contract Audit Agy.; legis. correspondent to Senator Ted Stevens US Senate, 1982—87; sr. program analyst, Office Under Sec. US Dept. Def.; dep. CFO NASA, 2002—03, CFO, 2003—07, Yale U., New Haven, 2007—09; v.p. bus. & fin. Morehouse Coll., Atlanta, 2009—. Bd. mem. Assn. Govt. Accountants, 1989—2009. Recipient Exceptional Achievement medal, NASA, 2003; named one of The 50 Most Powerful Women in Bus., Black Enterprise mag. Office: Morehouse Coll 830 Westview Dr SW Atlanta GA 30314

SYKES, RICHARD NESBIT, retired history professor, department chairman; b. Charlotte, NC, Jan. 11, 1942; s. Richard Nesbitt and Sarah Elizabeth (Hovis) Sykes. AB in History and English summa cum laude, So. Wesleyan U., 1964; MA in Social Sci. and Reading Spec., Appalachian State U., 1965; PhD in History, Greenwich U., 2001. Cert. educator NC, SC. Instr. history and polit. sci. Gordon State Coll., Barnesville, Ga., 1965—67; asst. prof. history and reading Gardner-Webb U., Boiling Springs, NC, 1967—69; instr. history and reading Ctrl. Piedmont C.C., Charlotte, 1969—70; coord. secondary reading Chester County Schs., 1971—73; reading specialist Williamsburg County Schs., 1973—74; reading diagnostician Chesterfield County Schs., 1974—79; tchr., reading specialist Lancaster County Schs., SC, 1979—90; prof. history Aiken Tech. Coll., SC, 1990—2005, dept. chair, 2001—05, ret., 2006. Recipient medal, Nat. Inst. Staff and Orgnl. Devel., 2000, Gov.'s Disting. Prof. award, S.C. Commn. on Higher Edn., 2000; named Faculty Mem. of Yr., Aiken Tech. Coll., 1999. Mem.: SC State Employees Assn., SC Tech. Edn. Assn. (Educator of Yr. Aiken Tech. Coll. 1991—92), Nat. Geog. Soc., Smithsonian Instn. Avocations: reading, walking, fishing. Home: 838 Osbon Dr Aiken SC 29801-4154

SYKES, ROBIN ALEXIS, plastic surgeon; b. McKeesport, Pa., May 17, 1954; d. Robert T. and Joyce P. Sykes; m. Thomas Richard Rowe, Aug. 12, 1989; children: Galen, Alexis. BA in Biology, Wells Coll., 1976; MD, Johns Hopkins U., 1980; postgrad., U. Miami, 1983, U. Kans., 1985. Diplomate Am. Bd. Med. Specialties. Pvt. practice, Jupiter, Fla., 1985—. Reporter Healthvision TV Sta. WPBF, 2001—02; spkr. in field. Recipient Top Docs award, Jupiter Mag., 2013—14. Mem.: Palm Beach County Plastic Surgeons, Am. Soc. for Laser and Medicine and Surgery, Am. Med. Womens Assn., Fla. Soc. Plastic Surgeons, Am. Soc. Plastic Surgeons, Fla. Med. Assn. Avocations: music, reading, travel, theater, movies. Office: Jupiter Plastic Surgery Ctr 2055 Military Tr Ste 305 Jupiter FL 33458 Office Phone: 561-746-9400. Personal E-mail: drrasplastic@aol.com, rartists@aol.com.

SYLVER, DONNA, accountant; BS in Acctg., Wesleyan Coll., NC, 1989; MBA, U. NC, Chapel Hill. With dept. budgeting Pioneer Savs. Bank, budget mgr., v.p., contr. & CFO; fin. mgr. Consol. Diesel Co.; asst. contr. Safety Kleen Environ. Svcs.; with three banking firms, 1998—2004; sr. v.p., CFO Mut. Cmty. Savs. Bank, Durham, NC, 2004; sr. mng. mem. Sylver CPA, PLLC. Named one of 25 Most Powerful Women in Banking, USBanker Mag., 2005. Mem.: United Way African Am. Leadership Initiative. Office: Sylver CPA PLLC 9 Pinestraw Way Durham NC 27713-9176 Office Phone: 919-688-1308. Business E-Mail: dsylver@sylvercpa.com.

SYMONS, JOSEPH KEITH, bishop emeritus; b. Champion, Mich., Oct. 14, 1932; Student, St. Thomas Sem., Bloomfield, Conn., St. Mary Sem., Balt. Ordained priest Diocese of St. Augustine, Fla., 1958; ordained bishop, 1981; aux. bishop Diocese of St. Petersburg, Fla., 1981—83; bishop Diocese of Pensacola-Tallahassee, Fla., 1983-90, Diocese of Palm Beach, Fla., 1990—98, bishop emeritus, 1998—. Roman Catholic. Office: PO Box 109650 Palm Beach Gardens FL 33410-9650

SYNEK, MIROSLAV, physicist, chemist, world affairs consultant; b. Prague, Czech Republic, Sept. 18, 1930; came to U.S., 1958, naturalized, 1963; s. Frantisek and Anna (Kokrment) S.; children: Mary Rose, Thomas Robert. Cert., Indsl. Chemistry Tech. Sch., Prague, 1946-50; cert. in liberal arts, Prague, 1951; MS in Physics with distinction, Charles U., Prague, 1956; PhD in Physics, U. Chgo., 1963. Analytical chemist Indsl. Medicine Inst., Prague, 1950-51; rsch. physicist Acad. Scis., Prague, 1956-58; from asst. to assoc. prof. De Paul U., Chgo., 1962-67; prof. Tex. Christian U., Ft. Worth, 1967-71; lectr., rschr. U. Tex., Austin, 1971-75; tenured faculty U. Tex., San Antonio, 1975-95. Sci. advisor Tex. Edn. Agy., Austin, 1971-73, U. Tex., 1971-73; advisor Student Physics Soc., active numerous univ. coms. Contbr. numerous articles to sci. jours., abstracts to presentations. Campaigner United Way, San Antonio, 1975-95; judge Alamo Sci. Fairs and Tex. Acad. of Sci. Fairs, annually; grand award judge Internat. Sci. and Engring. Fairs, 1998, 99. Rsch. grantee Robert A. Welch Found., 1968-71, 76-83, 93-95. Fellow AAAS, Am. Phys. Soc. (life), Tex. Acad. Sci., Am. Inst. Chemists; mem. NEA, Tex. State Tchrs. Assn., AAUP, DAV Comdrs. Club, Am. Assn. Physics Tchrs., Am. Acad. Polit. Sci., Am. Mus. Natural History, Libr. Congress, Smithsonian Instn., Nat. Trust Hist. Preservation, N.Y. Acad. Scis., Am. Chem. Soc. (San Antonio edn. com. chmn.), Czechoslovak Nat. Coun. Am. (dist. sec. Chgo. 1961-63, chmn. 1967), Czechoslovak Soc. Arts and Scis. Am., Internat. Soc. Poets (disting. mem.), Sheriffs' Assn. Tex. (assoc.), San Antonio Astron. Assn., World Affairs Coun. San Antonio (diplomat mem.), Bexar County Czech Heritage Soc. of Tex., Sigma Xi (life), Sigma Pi Sigma (sustaining). Roman Catholic. Achievements include research in atomic structure calculations of laser-active lanthanides, analytical relativistic self-consistent field theory, approximate estimate of the extra-terrestrial intelligence probability, nuclear age requiring free elections, democracy is a historical urgency in the age of inter-continental nuclear missiles, main dangers of our times, suggested priorities for human society. Home and Office: Independent Consultant 602 Babcock Rd San Antonio TX 78201 Personal E-mail: m.synek@juno.com.

SYPOLT, GARY L., energy executive; m. Janet Sypolt; 2 children. B in Elec. Engring., W. Va. U. Joined CNG Transmission Corp., 1975; pres., transmission Va. Electric & Power Co., 2003—06, pres., COO, transmission, 2006—07; sr. v.p., transmission Dominion Transmission, Inc. (formerly CNG Transmission Corp.), 1999, pres., transmission, 2003—09, CEO; pres. Dominion Transmission, Inc., 2009—; CEO Dominion Energy, Inc., 2009—. Vice chmn. INGAA Found.; bd. dirs. Southern Gas Assn. Office: Dominion Resources Inc 120 Tredegar St Richmond VA 23219 Office Phone: 804-819-2000. Office Fax: 804-819-2233. Business E-Mail: gary_sypolt@dom.com.

SYRING, JAMES D., federal agency administrator, military officer; BS in Marine Engring., US Naval Acad., 1985; MS in Mech. Engring., Naval Postgrad. Sch., 1992. Engring. duty officer USN, auxiliaries, elec., and electronics material officer USS Downes (FF 1070), ship supt. USS Port Royal (CG 73), Aegis test officer for new constrn. DDG 51 class ships, combat sys., test, and trials officer DDG 51 Aegis Shipbuilding Program Office, combat sys. baseline mgr. Aegis Tech. Divsn., dir. surface combatants Office of Asst. Sec. Navy for rsch., devel., and acquisition, tech. dir. DDG 1000 Shipbuilding Program, DDG 1000 maj. program mgr., program exec. officer Integrated Warfare Sys.; dir. Missile Def. Agy., Fort Belvoir, Va., 2012—. Ensign to vice adm. USN. Decorated Disting. Svc. Medal, Legion of Merit, Meritorious Svc. Medal, Navy Commendation Medal, Navy Achievement Medal. Office: Missile Defense Agency Blddg 245 5700 18th St Fort Belvoir VA 22060-5573

SZALKOWSKI, CHARLES C., lawyer; b. Amarillo, Tex., Apr. 14, 1948; s. Chester Casimer and Virginia Lee Szalkowski; m. Jane Howe, Dec. 28, 1971; children: Jennifer Lee, Stephen Claude. BA, BS in Acctg., Rice U., 1971; MBA, JD, Harvard U., 1975. Bar: Tex. 1975. Assoc. Baker Botts L.L.P., Houston, 1975-82, ptnr., 1983—, gen. coun., 2006—. Speaker in field. Chmn. ann. fund campaign Rice U., Houston, 1991-93, chmn. Fund Coun., 1995-96, bd. trustees, 2010-; chmn. adminstrv. bd. St. Luke's United Meth. Ch., Houston, 1994, chmn. bd. trustees, 1997, 2003, 10; chmn. DePelchin Children's Ctr., Houston, 2002-04; bd. dirs. Meth. Children's Home, Waco, 1998-2001, 03-. Mem.: ABA (fed. regulation of securities com.), BioHouston (chmn. assoc. adv. bd. 2007—), Tex. Bus. Law Found. (chmn. 1998—2000, bd. dirs.), Harvard Law Sch. Assn. Tex. (pres. 1983—84), Houston Bar Assn. (corp. counsel sect. 1989—90, chmn.), State Bar Tex. (chmn. bus. law sect. 1991—92), Am. Law Inst., Assn. Rice U. Alumni (bd. dirs. 1999—2002, pres. 2007—08, bd. dirs. 2010—), Harvard Bus. Sch. Club (Houston) (bd. dirs. 2000—04, 2006—09). Office: Baker Botts LLP 1 Shell Plz 910 Louisiana St Ste 3000 Houston TX 77002-4991 Office Phone: 713-229-1480.

SZEFTEL, IVAN, corporate financial executive; grad., B, U. Cape Town. CPA Pa.; chartered acct., South Africa. Exec. v.p., CFO Charming Shoppes, Inc, 1981—96; COO Forman Mills, Inc., 1996—98; joined Alliance Data Sys., Inc., 1998, exec. v.p., pres. retail credit svcs. Mem. bd. dirs. Forman Mills, Inc., 1996—98. Office: Alliance Data Systems Inc 7500 Dallas Pkwy Ste 700 Plano TX 75024-4006 Office Phone: 972-348-5100.

SZOSTAK, (M.) ANNE, consulting firm executive, former bank executive; b. London, June 23, 1950; BA in sociology, Colby Coll., Waterville, Maine, 1972; student, Husson Coll., 1992. Pres. Fleet Nat. Bank, Providence, 1980—82; sr. v.p. Fleet Nat. Bank, 1982—85, exec. v.p., 1985—88, corp. v.p., head human resources, 1988—91; pres., COO Fleet Bank Maine, 1991—94; sr. v.p., human resources FleetBoston Fin. Corp., 1994—98, exec. v.p., dir. human resources & diversity, 1998—2004; chmn., CEO Fleet Bank RI, RI, 2001—03; pres., CEO Szostak Partners LLC, 2004. Bd. dirs. Tupperware Corp., 2000-, Belo Corp., 2004-, Spherion Corp., 2005-, Choicepoint, Inc., 2005-, Cadbury Schweppes plc, 2008-. Chmn. Boys & Girls Clubs of Am., 2003—; bd. mem. United Way Women's Leadership Com. Recipient Disting. Alumni Award, Colby Coll., Leadership Award, New England Coun., 1993, Athena Award, YWCA Outstanding Women's Gala, 2002; named to Human Resources Honor Roll, Human Resources Exec. Mag., 2001. Office: 17 Virginia Ave Providence RI 02906 also: Dr Pepper Snapple Group Inc 5301 Legacy Dr Plano TX 75024 Office Phone: 972-673-7000. Office Fax: 972-673-7980. Business E-Mail: aszostak@bgca.org.

SZULIK, MATTHEW J., information technology executive; With Sapiens Internat., MapInfo Corp.; pres. Relativity Technologies, 1997—98; COO Red Hat, Inc., Raleigh, NC, 1998—99, pres., CEO, 1999—2007, chmn., 2002—. Chmn., sci. and tech. bd. State NC Econ. Devel. Bd. Recipient 20/20 Vision award, CIO mag. Mem.: NC Electronics and Information Technologies Assn. (past chmn. and exec. dir.). Office: Red Hat Inc 1801 Varsity Dr Raleigh NC 27606-2072 Office Phone: 919-754-3700. Office Fax: 919-754-3701. Business E-Mail: MSzulik@redhat.com.

SZYGENDA, STEPHEN A., electrical and computer engineering educator, researcher; b. McKeesport, Pa., Oct. 5, 1938; s. Stephen A. Sr. and Elizabeth B. (Zolczer) S.; m. Marie A. Deli, Apr. 2, 1960; children: Stepahnie Burden, Diana Easton, Mark. BS, Fairleigh Dickinson U., 1965; MS, Northwestern U., 1967, PhD, 1968. Registered profl. engr., Tex. Engr. Comprehensive Design, NJ, 1959-62; mem. tech. staff Bell Tel. Labs., NJ, Ill., 1962-68; assoc. prof. elec. engring. and computer engring. U. Mo., Rolla, 1968-70; prof. elec. engring. and computer engring. So. Meth. U., Dallas, 1970-73, U. Tex., Austin, 1973-86, dir. Ctr. for Tech. Tng., 1986-89, Clint Murchison Sr. Chair of Free Enterprise prof., 1986-96, chmn. elec. and computer engring. dept., 1993-96; dean Sch. Engring. U. Ala., Birmingham, 1996-2000, So. Meth. U., Dallas, 2000—04, Cecil H. Green chair, 2004—. Pres. CCSS, Austin, 1972-81, Comsat Gen. Internat. Sys., Austin, 1981-83, SBI, Inc., Austin, 1985—; pres., CEO Rubicon Group, Austin, 1983-85; active Tex. Gov. Coun. for Sci. and Tech., 1984-87. Contbr. articles to profl. jours. Dir. Laguna Gloria Mus., Austin, 1981-83; pres. bd. Austin Ballet, 1983. With USN, 1956-59. Fellow IEEE (bd. dirs. 1973-75 Svc. awards 1977, 79, 83, 87, 96), IC2, Soc. for Design and Process Sci.; mem. Assn. Computing Machinery (Svc. award 1975, 79, 87, 88, Disting. lectr. 1991-95). Roman Catholic. Achievements include pioneering in CAD, simulation, fault tolerant computing, telecommunications, entrepreneurship, and software engineering. Home: 5227 Beckington Ln Dallas TX 75287 Office: Southern Methodist Univ Sch of Engring Dallas TX 75275 Office Phone: 214-768-3959. Personal E-mail: szygenda@msn.com.

TABATZNIK, BERNARD, retired cardiologist; b. Mir, Poland, Jan. 8, 1927; arrived in US, 1959, naturalized, 1966; s. Max and Fay (Ginsberg) T.; m. Marjorie Turner, Jan. 8, 1956; children: Darron Mark, Keith Donald, Ilana Wendy; m. Charline Edwards Harmon, Aug. 7, 1992. BSc, U. Witwatersrand, South Africa, 1945, MB, BChir, U. Witwatersrand, South Africa, 1949. Intern Baragwanath Hosp., Johannesburg, 1950-51, Hillingdon Hosp., Ashford Hosp., also rsch. unit Can. Red Cross Meml. Hosp., Taplow, England, 1951-54; med. registrar Ashford Hosp., 1954-56, Johannesburg Gen. Hosp., 1956-58; physician Baragwanath Hosp., 1958-59; fellow in medicine Sch. Medicine Johns Hopkins U., Balt., 1959-60, fellow in cardiology, 1960-61, asst. prof. medicine, 1966-97, ret., 1997; head cardiopulmonary divsn. Sinai Hosp., Balt., 1961-72, assoc. chief medicine, 1964-72; chief cardiology dept. North Charles Gen. Hosp., Balt., 1972; also dir. med. edn., dir. Postgrad. Inst., coord. ambulatory svcs.; med. dir. Nurse Practitioner-Physician Asst. Program Ch. Hosp., Balt., 1987-90. Contbr. articles to profl. jours. Recipient Save-A-Heart Humanitarian award, 1977, Maimonides award, 1983, Shaarei Zion Humanitarian award, 1987. Fellow Royal Coll. Physicians (London); mem. South African Cardiac Soc., Am. Heart Assn., Md. Heart Assn. (chmn. health careers 1964-66), Am. Coll. Cardiology. Home: 63 Oakridge Dr Monterey VA 24465-2350 Personal E-mail: btabatznik@aol.com.

TABB, WALLER CROCKETT, retired allergist, immunologist; b. Richmond, Va., 1935; MD, U. Va., 1959. Diplomate Am. Bd. Internal Medicine, Am. Bd. Allergy and Immunology. Intern U. Va. Hosp., Charlottesville, 1959-60, resident in internal medicine, 1964-66, fellow in allergy/immunology and pulmonary medicine, 1966-67; mem. staff Lakeland (Fla.) Regional Med. Ctr., 1967—; pvt. practice Watson Clinic, Lakeland, ret., 1997. Fellow ACP, Am. Acad. Allergy and Immunology, Am. Coll. Chest Physicians; mem. Alpha Omega Alpha. Address: PO Box 178 Ware Neck VA 23178-0178 Home: 6102 WAre Neck Rd Ware Neck VA 23178 Personal E-mail: aroca2@earthlink.net.

TABER, DAVID O., urological surgeon; b. Panama City, Panama, June 30, 1938; s. Alden Pugh and Virginia (Kresler) Taber; m. Rebecca M.; children: Sharon Taber Silverman, Jeffrey, Andrew, Richard; m. Rebecca M. Taber, Dec. 20, 1987. BA, Syracuse U., 1959; MD, George Washington U., 1963. Diplomate Am. Bd. Urology. Urologic surgeon, El Paso, Tex., 1973—2009; pvt. practice County Med. Soc., 2008—09; pres. El Paso County Med. Soc., 2008—; intern. Walter Reed Gen. Hosp., 1968—69, urological resident, 1965—69; chief urology 130th Gen. Hosp., Nurnberg, 1969—73. Chief med. staff Columbia West Hosp., El Paso, 1975-76, chief of urology, 1998-99; chief of surgery Sierra Med. Ctr., El Paso, 1977-78, chief of urology, 1995-97; prof. urology Tex. Tech Sch. Medicine, El Paso, 1998—. Mem. state com. on prostate cancer Am. Cancer Soc., Austin, 1998-99, bd. dirs. El Paso unit, 1999; mem. Tex. Rangers Found., Waco, 1998-2005; judge Santa Fe Indian Market; med. exec. com. El Paso County; founder Am. Mus. Served to lt. U.S. Army, 1963-72. Lt. col. US Army. Named one of Best Doctors in Tex., 2010. Fellow ACS; mem. AMA, Urol. Soc. Internat., Urostomy Assn. (adv.), Tex. Urol. Soc., Am. Urol. Assn., Tex. Med. Assn. (del. 2009), Am. Fertility Soc., Am. Lithotripsy Soc., El Paso Med. Soc. (exec. com. 2004- sec. 2006-, pres. elect, 2007, pres., 2008-, named in Best Doctors in Am., Best Doctors in Tex.), Mason (32 degree), Elmaida Shrine, Rotary, Alpha Epsilon Delta, Pi Sigma. Episcopalian. Avocations: photography, diving instructor. Office: 2201 N Stanton St El Paso TX 79902 Personal E-mail: dotabermd@yahoo.com.

TABOR, CURTIS HAROLD, JR., retired librarian, minister; b. Atlanta, July 3, 1936; s. Curtis Harold and Gerturde Olive (Casey) Tabor; m. Dorothy May Corbin, June 30, 1957 (dec. June 1996); m. Paulene C Pennington, July 12, 1997; children: Timothy M, John M. AA, Fla. Coll., Temple Ter., 1957; BA, Harding Coll., Ark., 1960; MA, Butler U., Indpls., 1969; MDiv, Bapt. Missionary Assn. Theol. Sem., Jacksonville, Tex., 1974; MLS, Tex. Woman's U., Denton, Tex., 1977. Min. Ch. of Christ, Bowling Green, Ky., 1960-61, Hamilton, Ont., Canada, 1961-64, Indpls., 1964-67, Nacogdoches, Tex., 1967-75, Dallas, 1976-77, Columbus, Miss., 1977-79, Tampa, Fla., 1993-97, Maryville, Tenn., 1997—; reference libr. Blount County Pub. Libr., 1998—2006; ret., 2006. Tchr. Great Lakes Christian Coll., Beamville, Ont, Canada, 1961—64; Bible chair dir Stephen F Austin State U., Nacogdoches, Tex., 1967—75; participant archeological excavations, Tell Gezer, Israel, 1969, Tell Lachish, Israel, 1980; profl. libr. sci. Fla. Coll., Temple Terrace, 1979—85, libr. dir., 1985—97; prin., owner Tabor Properties, Inc., 2005—08. Author (with others): (book) Resurrection, 1973, Biblical Authority, 1974, The Lord of Glory, 1980, Making A Difference: Florida College, the First Fifty Years, 1996. Cub master Boy Scouts Am, Nacogdoches, Tex., 1970—75; pres Nacogdoches Baseball Asn, 1974—75; vol driving instr 55 Alive AARP, 1998—2001. Recipient Scouters Key, Cub Scouts Ams, 1975. Mem.: SAR, Tampa Bay Libr. Consortium (treas 1986—89), Beta Phi Mu, Eta Beta Rho. Republican. Mem. Ch. Of Christ. Home: 2359 Six Mile Rd Maryville TN 37803-2739 Personal E-mail: haltabor@yahoo.com.

TACHMES, LEONARD, plastic surgeon; BS, Duke U.; MD, Jefferson Med. Coll. Diplomate Am. Bd. of Plastic Surgery, 1997, recertification 2008. Fellow Meml. Sloan Kettering Cancer Ctr., Manhattan; resident plastic and reconstructive surgery Univ. Chgo. Hosps.; resident gen. surgery Brookdale Hosp. Med. Ctr., Bklyn.; internship surgery Mary Imogene Bassett Hosp., Cooperstone, NY; hosp. affiliations include Jackson North Med. Ctr., Fla. Med. Ctr., North Shore Hosp. Med. Ctr. Mem.: Am. Soc. of Plastic Surgeons. Office: Miami Beach Plastic Surgery Center and MedSpa Suite 204 1674 Meridian Ave Miami Beach FL 33139 Office Phone: 305-531-9800. Office Fax: 305-531-9801.

TADDEO, ANNETTE, language services professional; b. Barrancabermeja, Columbia, Apr. 7, 1967; m. Eric Goldstein; 3 children. BA, U. North Ala., 1992; grad. exec. edn. prog., Dartmouth Tuck Sch. Bus., Hanover, NH. Founder, CEO comprehensive lang. svcs. co. LanguageSpeak, Miami, 1993—. Mem. exec. bd. Women Impacting Pub. Policy. Recipient Entrepreneurial Diversity award, Women Impacting Pub. Policy, Latina Excellence award, Hispanic Mag.; named Businesswoman of Yr., South Fla. Bus. Jour., Women in Internat. Trade; named one of Top 50 Latina Entrepreneurs in US, Hispanic Mag. Mem.: Miami-Dade County Women's C. of C., Dade-County C. of C. Democrat. Office: LanguageSpeak Hdqs 5975 Sunset Dr Ste 803 Miami FL 33143 Office Phone: 305-668-9797. Office Fax: 305-668-0435.

TAFT, THOMAS FLEMING, state senator, retail executive, real estate developer; b. Greenville, NC, Dec. 29, 1945; s. Edmund Hoover and Helen Irene (Fleming) Taft; m. Kathy Arnold Taft, Jan. 30, 1982; children: Jessica, Paige, Thomas, Jonathan. AB, Duke U., 1968; JD, UNC, 1972. Bar: NC; cert. London Coll., 1971. Legal counsel to lt. gov. Office of Lt. Gov., Raleigh, 1972—74; state senator NC, 1985—90; ptnr. Taft, Taft & Haigler, Greenville, NC, 1974—; pres. Eastern Lumber & Supply Co., Winterville, NC, dir., Hardware Suppliers Am., Inc., Winterville, Mercer Glass Co., Inc., Greenville; chmn. bd. dirs. NC Ports Authority, 1978—85; mem. 9th Dist. NC Senate, 1985—. With USAR, 1968—74. Recipient Disting. Svc. award, Greenville Jaycees, 1980, Legis. award, Am. Acad. Pediat., 1986, N.C. Pediat. Soc., 1987; named one of Outstanding Men America, 1977. Mem.: ABA, Am. Trial Lawyers Assn., NC Acad. Trial Lawyers, Pitt County Bar Assn., NC Bar Assn., Kiwanis, Jaycees. Democrat. Methodist. Avocation: boating. Office: Taft Taft & Haigler 2217 Stantonsburg Rd Greenville NC 27834-2841

TAFT, TIMOTHY NED, orthopedist, surgeon, sports medicine physician; s. Samuel Milton and Helen Taft; m. Judith Ann Huffman, Sept. 13, 1971; children: Todd Daniel, Rebecca Lynn Fecher. AB, Princeton U., NJ, 1964; MD, U. Mo., Columbia, Mo., 1969. Diplomate Am. Bd. Orthopaedic Surgery, 1978, lic. physician N.C., 1978. Intern, resident in orthopedics U. N.C., NC, 1969—74, prof., 1974—, dir. sports medicine, 1991—. Mem.: Spl. Olympics N.C. (chmn., bd. dirs.). Office: University of North Carolina 3154 Bioinformatics CB 7055 Chapel Hill NC 27599 Office Phone: 919-966-6730; Home Fax: 919-967-6750. Business E-Mail: ttaft@med.unc.edu.

TAGLE, HILDA GLORIA, federal judge; b. Corpus Christi, Tex., Dec. 18, 1946; d. Manuel Cisneros and Dolores (Cipriano) T.; 1 child, Santiago. AA, Del Mar Coll., Corpus Christi, 1968; BA, East Tex. State U., 1969; MLS, North Tex. State U., 1971; JD, U. Tex., 1977. Bar: Tex. 1977, U.S. Dist. Ct. (so. dist.) Tex. 1989, U.S. Supreme Ct. 1985. Asst. city atty. City of Corpus Christi, 1977-78; asst. county atty. Nueces County, 1978-79; asst. dist. atty. Nueces County Dist. Atty., 1979-81; pvt. practice law Corpus Christi, 1981-85; judge Nueces County Ct. at Law No. 3, Corpus Christi, 1985—94, 148th Dist. Ct., Tex., 1995—98, US Dist. Ct. (we. dist.) Tex., Brownsville, 1998—. Mem. State Commn. on Jud. Conduct, Austin, Tex., 1989—; mem. Gov's. Commn. for Women; mem. jud. edn. exec. com. Supreme Ct. Tex., Austin, 1987-89. Recipient Good Gals award Tex. Women's Polit. Caucus, 1990. Mem. Corpus Christi Bar Assn. (chmn. lawyers for literacy com. 1989-90, Women Lawyers of Coastal Bend, State Bar Tex. (co-chmn. ann. meeting planning com. 1991), Alpha Lambda Sigma. Mem. Christian Ch. (Disciples Of Christ). Office: US Dist Ct US Courthouse 600 E Harrison St Brownsville TX 78520 Office Phone: 956-548-2510.

TAGLIARENI, JOSEPH M., corporate financial executive; Attended, James Madison U. CFO, v.p., fin., adminstrn., Mid-Atlantic Region United Healthcare; v.p., corp. officer, fin. Coventry Healthcare; sr. v.p., med. fin. ops. Amerigroup Corp., 2009—. Office: Amerigroup Corp 4425 Corporation Ln Virginia Beach VA 23462 Office Phone: 757-490-6900. Office Fax: 757-222-2330. Business E-Mail: jtagliareni@amerigrp.com.

TALBERT, CHARLES HAROLD, theologian, educator; b. Jackson, Miss., Mar. 19, 1934; s. Carl E. and Audrey (Hale) T.; m. Betty O'Neal Weaver, June 30, 1961; children: Caroline O'Neil, Charles Richard. BA, Samford U., 1956, LittD (hon.), 1990; BD, So. Bapt. Theol. Sem., Louisville, 1959; PhD, Vanderbilt U., 1963. Asst. prof. Wake Forest U., Winston-Salem, NC, 1963-68, assoc. prof., 1968-74, prof., 1974-89, Wake Forest prof., 1989-96; disting. prof. religion Baylor U., Waco, Tex., 1996—2011. Author: Reading Luke, 1982, Reading Corinthians, 1987, Learning Through Suffering, 1991, Reading John, 1992, The Apocalypse, 1994, Reading Acts, 1997, Romans, 2002, Reading Luke-Acts in its Mediterranean Milieu, 2003, Reading the Sermon on the Mount, 2004, Literary Patterns, Theological Themes and the Genre of Luke-Acts, 2005, Paideia: Ephesians and Colossians, 2007, Paideia: Matthew, 2010, The Development of Christology during the First Hundred Years, 2011, Getting Saved the While Story of Salvation in the New Testament, 2011. Postdoctoral fellow U. N.C., 1968-69, Soc. for Values in Higher Edn., 1971-72. Mem. Soc. Bibl. Lit. (editor SBL Dissertation Series, N.T. 1984-86, 87-89, editorial bd. jour. 1984-89), Cath. Bibl. Assn. (assoc. editor Cath. Bibl. Quar. 1991-98, pres. 1999-00), Nat. Assn. Bapt. Profs. Religion (pres. 1985), Studiorum Novi Testamenti Societas. Independent. Baptist. Home: 9602 Old Farm Rd Waco TX 76712-6402 Office: Baylor Univ Dept Religion PO Box 97284 Waco TX 76798-7284 Office Phone: 254-710-8622. Business E-Mail: charles_talbert@baylor.edu.

TALBERT, WINSTON M., oil and gas industry executive; BBA, So. Meth. U., Dallas; MBA, Emory U., Atlanta. Various mgmt. positions in corp. devel. & fin. Halliburton Energy Svcs. (formerly Kellogg, Brown & Root), Dallas, Destec Energy, Inc., Houston; mgr. internat. fin. Pennzoil Co.; asst. treas. PennzEnergy Co., Ocean Energy, Inc., 1999—2001, v.p., treas., 2001—03; v.p. fin. & investor rels. Plains Exploration & Prodn. Co., 2003—04, v.p. fin., treas., 2004—06; exec. v.p., CFO Plains Exploration and Production Co., 2006—. Office: Plains Exploration & Production Co Ste 3100 700 Milam Houston TX 77002 Office Phone: 713-579-6000. Office Fax: 713-579-6611.

TALBOT, KIRK, state legislator; m. Julie Talbot. BBA, U. Miss. Businessman; mem. Dist. 78 La. House of Reps., 2008—, mem. commerce com., ins. com., labor and indsl. rels. com. Republican. Cath. Office: 9523 Jefferson Hwy Ste B River Ridge LA 70123 also: Capitol Office PO Box 44486 Baton Rouge LA 70804 Office Phone: 504-736-7299, 225-342-6945. Office Fax: 504-736-7113. E-mail: talbotk@legis.state.la.us.

TALBOT, LEE MERRIAM, ecologist, educator, administrator; b. New Bedford, Mass., Aug. 2, 1930; s. Murrell Williams and Zenaida (Merriam) T.; m. Martha Walcott Hayne, May 16, 1959; children: Lawrence Hayne, Russell Merriam. BA, U. Calif., Berkeley, 1953, MA, PhD, U. Calif., Berkeley, 1963. Biologist Arctic Research Lab., Point Barrow, Alaska, 1951; staff ecologist Internat. Union for Conservation, Brussels, 1954-56; ecologist, dir. East African ecol. research project Nat. Acad. Scis., Govts. of Kenya and Tanzania, 1959-63; wildlife advisor UN Spl. Fund, Africa, 1963-64; dir. S.E. Asia project Internat. Union for Conservation, 1964-65; resident ecologist, field rep. for internat. affairs Smithsonian Instn., Washington, 1966-70; sr. scientist, dir. internat. activities Pres.'s Council on Environ. Quality, Washington, 1970-78; sr. sci. advisor Internat. Council Sci. Unions, Paris, 1978-83; dir. conservation, spl. sci. advisor World Wildlife Fund Internat., Switzerland, 1978-80; dir. gen. Internat. Union for Conservation of Nature and Natural Resources, Gland, Switzerland, 1980-83; research fellow Environ. and Policy Inst., East West Ctr., 1983-87; vis. fellow World Resources Inst., Washington, 1984-89; sr. environ. advisor World Bank, 1984—; pres. Lee Talbot Assocs. Internat., 1991—; sr. prof. environ. scis., internat. affairs and pub. policy George Mason U., Va., 1994—, affiliate prof. geography, 2007—. Cons. UNESCO, World Bank, Asian Devel. Bank, Nat. Geog. Soc., Inter-Am. Devel. Bank, The Nature Conservancy, U.S. Govt., U. Calif., UN Spl. Fund, WHO, UN Environment Program, UN Univ., UN Devel. Programme, African and Asian Govts.; conservation coord. Internat. Biol. Program, 1965-70; bd. dirs. Defenders of Wildlife, Inst. Pks.; mem. corp. NY Bot. Gardens; mem. sci. adv. inst. parks coun. Nat. Pks. Conservation Assn., Bailey Wildlife Compensation Trust; founding trustee Inst. Ecosys. Studies, NY, 2006; mem. pres.'s coun. Population Reference Bur., 2007—. Author 17 books and monographs; contbr. more than 295 articles to profl. jours. Active Boy Scouts Am., Geneva, 1980-82, Washington, 1987-95. With USMC, 1953-54. Decorated officer Order of Lion (Senegal); recipient Regents Lectureship award U. Calif., Santa Barbara, 1986, Pierre Chaleur prize French Acad. Scis., 1993, Festschrift Career Accomplishments award George Mason U., 2003, World Commn. Protected Areas East Asia award, 2005; named Disting. Alumnus, 1953 Officer Candidate Sch., USMC, 2003; Centenary Symposium named in his honor Bombay Natural History Soc., 2003, Explorers Club Flag award, 2003-05,07, 11; Excellence in Achievment award U. Calif., 2008, Explorers medal Explorers Club, 2009, Roll of Honor award, Species Survival Commn. IUCN, 2010, named Driver of Yr., Sportscar Vintage Racing Assn., 2010, US Sec. State Sec. Interior award, For Devel. & Implementing The World Heritage Convention, 2012, Benton Box Nat. award, Clemson U., 2013. Fellow Royal Geog. Soc., Royal Soc. Arts, AAAS, N.Y. Zool. Soc.; mem. Am. Inst. Biol. Scis. (Disting. Scientist award 1979), Acad. Medicine, World Conservation Union (hon.), Am. Assn. for Club of Rome, Am. Soc. Mammalogists, Ecol. Soc., Wildlife Soc. (Outstanding Publ. award 1963), Soc. for Conservation Biology, Internat. Soc. for Ecol. Econs., Boone and Crockett Club (N.Y.C.), Explorers Club (N.Y.C., medal, 2009), Cosmos Club (Washington), Sigma Xi, Phi Kappa Sigma. Achievements include incorporation of ecological principles in international development; development of new principles for management of wild living resources; biodiversity conservation; definition of ecosystem dynamics of tropical savannahs including role of fire, feeding habits and migrations of wild herbivores; development and negotiation of national legislation and international agreements for environmental protection. Home: 6656 Chilton Ct Mc Lean VA 22101-4422

TALBOTT, CLOYCE A., oil industry executive, retired energy executive; BS in Petroleum Engring., Tex. Tech U., Lubbock. Cofounder, bd. dirs. Patterson-UTI Energy, Inc., Snyder, Tex., 1978; v.p. Patterson-UTI Energy, Inc. (formerly Patterson Drilling Co. and then Patterson Energy before merging with UTI Energy), 1978—83, chmn., 1983—2001, CEO, 1983—2007, pres., 2006—07; cons. Patterson-UTI Energy, Inc. Bd. dirs. Patterson-UTI Energy, Inc., 2007—. Office: Patterson-UTI Energy Inc 450 Gears Rd Ste 500 Houston TX 77067 Office Phone: 281-765-7100. Office Fax: 281-765-7113. Business E-Mail: talbottc@patenergy.com.

TALBOTT, FRANK, III, retired lawyer; b. Danville, Va., Mar. 26, 1929; s. Frank and Margaret (Jordan) Talbott; m. Mary Beverley Chewning, July 11, 1952; children: Beverley, Frank IV. BA, U. Va., 1951, LLB, 1953. Bar: Va. 1952. With firm Meade, Talbott & Tate, Danville, 1956—59; ptnr. firm Talbott, Wheatley & Talbott, Danville, 1959—66; with Dan River Inc., 1966-76, v.p., gen. counsel, 1968-76; ptnr. firm Clement, Wheatley, Winston, Talbott & Majors, Danville, 1977-78; individual practice law Danville, 1979-92; gen. counsel Va. Mfrs. Assn. Inc., 1983-92; of counsel Woods, Rogers PLC, Danville, Va., 1992—2010. Chmn. adv. bd. NationsBank, Danville, 1984-94. Vice-chmn. Danville Sch. Bd., 1964-70; trustee Va. Student Aid Found., 1963-68; bd. dirs. United Fund Danville, 1959-63, Meml. Hosp., Danville, 1977-90. Served with AUS, 1953-56. Decorated Commendation medal. Fellow Am. Bar Found. (life); mem. Va. Bar Assn. (v.p. 1965-66, exec. com. 1967-70), Danville Bar Assn. (pres. 1965-66), Am. Judicature Soc., Newcomen Soc., U. Va. Alumni Assn. (bd. mgrs.), Danville Golf Club, Farmington Country Club, Country Club Va., Delta Psi, Phi Alpha Delta. Methodist. Home: 1500 Westbrook Ct Apt 4146 Richmond VA 23227

TALBOTT, JOSEPH B., state legislator; b. Webster Springs, W.Va., Jan. 23, 1933; s. William R. and Opal Jarvis, William R. and Opal (Jarvis) Talbott; m. Sue Legg Talbott; children: Kelli, Sherri Wong. BS, MA, W.Va. Wesleyan. Mem. Dist. 36 W.Va. House of Delegates, 1992—96, 2002—, chmn. Constl. Revision, 2001—03. Mem. W.Va. Pvt. Industry Coun., W.Va. State Job Training Coun. Served with USMC, 1955—59. Mem.: NRA, Marine Corps League, Retired Teachers Assn., Vets. of Fgn. Wars, Lions, Webster Sportsman's Club, Am. Legion. Democrat. Methodist. Office: State Capitol Complex Rm 205E Bldg 1 Charleston WV 25305 also: 148 Webster Ave Webster Springs WV 26288 Office Phone: 304-340-3116, 304-847-2503. Business E-Mail: jtalbott@mail.wvnet.edu.

TALLANT, STEVEN HALL, academic administrator, social worker; b. Winston-Salem, NC, Dec. 29, 1948; s. Daniel Hoge and Wanda Jean (Nance) T.; m. Karen Marie Snider, June 29, 1974; children: Matthew Hoge, Sean Edward. AA, Paris Jr. Coll., 1969; BA, U. Fla., 1975; MSW, U. Utah, 1977; PhD in Social Welfare, U. Wis., 1985. Lic. social worker. Unit social worker Sacred Heart Home, Pueblo, Colo., 1977-78; chief social work svcs. USAF Hosp., Ellsworth AFB, S.D., 1978-82, dir. alcoholism rehab. ctr. Scott AFB, Ill., 1985-87; dir. family support ctr. 1605 Air Base Group, Lajes Field, Portugal, 1987-89, 3380 Air Base Group, Keesler AFB, Miss., 1989; chief Air Force Family Rsch. The Pentagon, Washington, 1991—94; prof. social work U. Wis., Eau Clair, 1994—2000, assoc. vice chancellor, dir. grad. programs, 2000—04, assoc. vice chancellor academic affairs, 2004, interim provost, vice chancellor academic affairs, 2004, 2005—07, provost, vice chancellor academic affairs, 2007—08; pres. Tex. A&M U., Kingsville, 2008—. Contbr. articles to profl. jours. Lt. col. USAF, 1978-94. Named to Alpha Kappa Delta, 1975, Phi Kappa Phi, 1975, Phi Kappa Phi, 1977; recipient Charles I. Schottland award U. Utah, 1977. Mem. NASW. Democrat. Avocations: camping, hiking, golf, fishing. Office: Tex A&M U - Kingsville Office of Pres 700 University Blvd Kingsville TX 78363

TALLEDO, OSCAR EDUARDO, medical educator; b. Sullana, Piura, Peru, Aug. 1, 1929; s. Jorge Antonio and Flora Natividad (Cordova) T.; m. Jeanette McCarley, June 8, 1959; children: Roy Anthony, Paul Frederick, Linda Jeanette. BS, San Marcos U., 1948, MD, 1955. Diplomate Am. Bd. Ob-Gyn., Am. Bd. Laser Surgery. Intern Crawford W. Long Hosp., Atlanta, 1956-57, resident, 1957-58, Med. Coll. Ga., Augusta, 1958-60, fellow in gynecology, 1960-61, chief gynecologic oncology, 1961—, prof. ob-gyn, 1970—, instr., 1961-63, asst. prof., 1963-68, assoc. prof., 1968-71, prof., 1971—, acting chmn., 1981-82. Nat. Heart Inst. grantee, 1965 Fellow Am. Coll. Ob-Gyn, ACS, Gynecologic Oncology Soc.; mem. Soc. Gynecologic Investigation, AMA, Am. Fertility Soc., Richmond County Med. Soc., Ga. Ob-Gyn Soc., So. Med. Assn., S. Atlantic Assn. Ob-Gyn, Gyn-Urology Soc., Ga. Med. Assn. Clubs: Augusta Country. Lodges: Rotary (chmn. world community service com., Augusta 1983). Presbyterian. Home: 817 Aumond Pl W Augusta GA 30909-3106 Personal E-mail: cordoba@comcast.net. Business E-Mail: ctalledo@mail.mcg.edu.

TALLEY, CHARLES RICHMOND, retired bank executive; b. Richmond, Va., Dec. 23, 1925; s. Charles Edward and Marie (Thorckmorton) Talley; m. Anne Marie Smith, June 4, 1948 (dec. Feb. 16, 2007); children: Laurie Anne, Charles Richmond Jr. BA in Econs, U. Richmond, 1949; postgrad., Rutgers U., 1959-61, Northwestern U., 1954-55; grad. exec. program, U. Va., 1974. Asst. cashier 1st & Mchts. Nat. Bank, Richmond, 1955-57, asst. v.p., 1957-63, v.p., 1963-69, sr. v.p., 1969-73, exec. v.p., 1973-84; corp. exec. officer Sovran Bank N.A., 1984-86, ret., 1986. Bd. dirs. Security Atlantic Life Ins. Co.; v.p., bd. dirs. Security Atlantic Ins. Agency; bd. dirs. Sovran Properties Inc.; vice-chmn., bd. dirs. Va Edn. Loan Authority, 1983—87, chmn., 1988—91; v.p., mem exec. com. Richmond Eye and Ear Hosp., pres., 1988—91. Pres Richmond Jr Cof C, 1960—61; treas Richmond chpt Nat Found, 1956—; pres Baptist Extension Bd Va, 1973—75; bd dirs Commonwealth Eye and Ear, 1986—89, Richmond Symphony Orchestra, Richmond Better Bus Bur. With USNR, 1944—46. Mem.: Richmond Clearing House Asn (pres 1977), Richmond Metropolitan CofC (bd dirs 1979—89), The Tartan Golf Course (Irvington, Va), Bull and Bear Club, Willow Oaks Country Club Richmond (pres 1971), Rotary (bd dirs Richmond 1981—83). Home: 4301 Stratford Rd Richmond VA 23225-1060 also: Bldg 2 Unit 2 The Green At Tides Lodge Irvington VA 22480

TALLEY, JOSEPH EUGENE, psychologist; b. Springfield, Mass., May 27, 1949; s. Joseph Addison and Miriam Louise (Ayers) T.; m. Vibeke Absalon, Jan. 3, 1981; children: Kirsten, David, Jonathan. BA, U. Richmond, 1971; MA, Radford Coll., 1973; PhD, U. Va., 1978. Diplomate in counseling psychology Am. Bd. Profl. Psychology, 1986, in clin. psychology, 2002; lic. psychologist, NC; cert. health svc. provider, NC. Faculty Duke U. Med. Ctr., Durham, NC, 1977—, prof. med. psychology, dept. psychiatry, 2005—, with counseling and psychol. svcs., 1977—, asst. dir., 2006—, assoc. dir., adminstrn., 2013—; gen. practice psychotherapy Durham, 1980—. Author: Study Skills, 1981, Performance Prediciton of Law Enforcement Personnel, 1990, The Predictors of Successful Very Brief Psychotherapy, 1992, Seeking Something Sacred: Managing Our Frustrations, Losses and Fears, 2001, Practicing Notes and Tools For Brief and Very Brief Integrative Psychodynamic Psychotherapy, 2013; author, editor: Counseling and Psychotherapy Services, 1985, Counseling and Psychotherapy with College Students: A Guide to Treatment, 1986, Multicultural Needs Assessment with College and University Populations, 1995; contbr. articles to profl. jours. Bd. deacons Hillsborough Presbyn. Ch., NC, 1983-85, chmn., 1985, bd. elders, 1987-94, 2002-07, v.p. bd. trustees, 1992-94; bd. dirs. Orange County Mental Health Assn., Chapel Hill, NC, 1982-83, mem. legis. com., 1983, APA site visitor for accreditation. Recipient Disting. Contbn. award, ABPP, 2002; named Disting. Practitioner, Nat. Acads. Practice, 2009. Fellow APA (awards com. divsn. 17, 2002-05, chair awards com. 2006-07, chair Leona Tyler lifetime achievement award com., 2007-08, mem. external interface bd. 2009-), Am. Acad. Clin. Psychology, Am. Acad. Counseling Psychology, Am. Acad. Counseling Psychology (pres. 1995-97, pres. emeritus 2007, Disting. Svc. award 2002); mem. Am. Bd. Profl. Psychology (sec., treas. coun. of pres.'s psychology splty. acads. 1997-98, chmn., CEO 2000-03, spl. liaison to related groups 2003—, past chmn., CEO 2003-05, exec. bd. and spl. liaison to congress and related profl. groups, 2005—, Disting. Contbns. award 2002, chair and CEO emeritus, 2008-), NC Psychol. Assn., Nat. Soc. Clin. Hypnosis (cert. and approved cons., supr. and practitioner, ethics com. 1995-97), Phi Kappa Phi, Omicron Delta Kappa, Psi Chi, Phi Kappa Sigma. Democrat. Presbyterian. Home: 134 E Tryon St Hillsborough NC 27278-2550 Office Phone: 919-660-1000. Business E-Mail: jtalley@duke.edu.

TALLEY, NICHOLAS JOSEPH, medical educator, research scientist, physician; b. Perth, Australia, Jan. 9, 1956; arrived in U.S., 1986; s. Nicholas Alexander and Irene Mary Talley; m. Catherine Elizabeth Davies, Dec. 30, 2004; children: Nicholas Stephen, Matthew Jonathon, Nicole Sarah, Luke James. MB, BS, U. NSW, 1979; PhD, U. Sydney, 1987; MD, U. NSW, 1993, M in Med. Sci., 2003. Resident med. officer/registrar Prince of Wales Hosp., Sydney, 1979—83; rsch. fellow, prof. registrar Royal North Shore Hosp., Sydney, 1983—87; rsch. fellow Mayo Clinic, Rochester, Minn., 1987—88, asst. prof. medicine, 1988—91, assoc. prof., 1991—93; head divsn. medicine, prof. medicine Nepean Hosp., Sydney, 1993—2001; area dir. medicine Westworth Area Health Svc., Nepean Hosp., Sydney, 2001—02; prof. medicine, cons. Mayo Clinic Coll. Medicine, Rochester, 2003—10, prof. epidemiology, 2007—10; chair dept. internal medicine Mayo Clinic, Jacksonville, 2007—10, adj. prof. medicine, 2010—; pro vice chancellor, prof., faculty health and medicine U. Newcastle, Australia, 2010—, acting dep. vice chancellor rsch., 2013—14. Adj. prof. Karolinska Inst., Stockholm, 2010—. Author: Examination Medicine, 1985, 6th edit., 2010, Clinical Examination, 1988, 7th edit., 2013, Internal Medicine, 1990, 2d edit., 2000, Clinical Gastroenterology, 1996, 3rd edit., 2010, Multiple Choice Questions in Clinical Examination, 1996, Pocket Clinical Examination, 1998, 3d edit., 2009, Conquering Irritable Bowel Syndrome, 2006, 2nd edit., 2012, GI Epidemiology, 2007, 2nd edit., 2014, Handbook of Gastroenterology, 2007, 2nd edit., 2013, Practical Gastroenterology and Hepatology, Vol. 1, 2 and 3, 2010; asst. editor Am. Jour. Gastroenterology, 1992-97; co-editor-in-chief, Am. Jour. Gastroenterology, 2004-09; mem. editl. bd. Gastroenterology, 1993-98, Jour. Clin. Gstroenterology, 1994-2008, Alimentary Pharmacology and Therapeutics, 1995-03, editor-in-chief, 2009-, Jour. Gastroenterology and Hepatology, 1994-98, editor, 1998-03; contbr. articles and revs. to profl. jours., chpts. to books. Pres. Miranda br. Young Liberals, Sydney, 1976, pres.-elect Royal Australasian Coll. Physicians, 2012-; wing comdr. Royal Australia Air Force, 2000. Postgrad. rsch. scholar Nat. Health and Med. Rsch. Coun., Australia, 1984-85. Fellow ACP, Royal Australasian Coll. Physicians, Am. Coll. Gastroent., Australian Faculty Pub. Health Medicine (founding mem.), Royal Coll. Physicians (London and Edinburgh); fellow Am. Gastroent. Assn., Gastroent. Soc. Australia, Brit. Soc. Gastroenterology, Functional Brain Gut Rsch. Group (pres.), Royal Australasian Coll. Physicians (pres. elect., 2012-). Avocations: tennis, writing, travel, jogging, martial arts. Office: Mayo Clinic 4500 San Pablo Rd Jacksonville FL 32224 Personal E-mail: talley5173@msn.com. Business E-Mail: talley.nicholas@mayo.edu, nicholas.talley@newcastle.edu.au.

TALLON, DALE, professional sports team executive, former professional hockey player; b. Rouyn-Noranda, Can., Oct. 19, 1950; m. Meg Tallon; children: Lauren, Kristen. Defenseman Vancouver Canucks, 1970—73, Chgo. Blackhawks, 1973—78, Pitts. Penguins, 1978—80; color analyst Chgo. Blackhawks, 1981—97, dir. player personnel, 1998—2002, color analyst, 2002—03, asst. gen. mgr., 2003—05, gen. mgr., 2005—09, sr. advisor hockey ops., 2009—10; gen. mgr. Fla. Panthers, 2010—. Named to NHL All-Star Team, 1971, 1972. Office: Florida Panthers One Panther Parkway Sunrise FL 33323

TALLON, EDWARD R., SR., state legislator; b. Baltimore, Md., Oct. 30, 1944; s. Perseghin and M. Ray Tallon; m. Linda Roberts, June 20, 1971; children: Emily Tallon, E. Ray Tallon Jr. AA, Spartanburg Methodist Coll., 1970; BA, Limestone Coll., 1971. CERT. fraud examiner. Mem. Am. Legion; chmn. Freshman Caucus; mem. House Judiciary Com., Internat. Assn. of Chiefs of Police, Morningside Baptist Ch., Nat. Rifle Assn., SC Law Enforcement Divsn. (SLED); pres. The Tallon Group, Inc.; mem. SC Law Enforcement Officers Assn., 1982—, pres., 1988—89, Nat. Food Svc. Security Coun. Bd., 1996—97, mem., 1996—2006; spokesperson Nat. Food Svc. Security Coun., 2006—08; mem. Dist. 33 SC House of Representatives,

2011—. With USAF, 1963-67. Named Optimist Law Enforcement Officer of the Yr., 1972, Lion of the Yr., 1981. Republican. Office: South Carolina House of Representatives District 33 402A Blatt Bldg Columbia SC 29201 Address: 140 Bagwell Farm Rd Spartanburg SC 29302 Home Phone: 864-596-1478; Office Phone: 803-212-6893, 864-380-8777.

TALTON, WILLIE L., state legislator; m. Annie Mae Talton; 2 children. AA in Edn., Middle Ga. Coll., 1974; BA in Criminal Justice, Fort Valley State U. Chief dep. sheriff City of Warner Robbins, Ga.; interim police chief Centerville Police Dept.; mem. Dist. 145 Ga. House of Reps., 2005—, mem. Banks and Banking Com., Edn. Com., Legis. and Congl. Reappointment Com. & Ways and Means Com. Bd. dirs. Flint Electric Corp. Republican. Mailing: 1126 S David Dr Warner Robins GA 31088 Office: 601-E Coverdell Legislative Office Bldg Atlanta GA 30334 Office Phone: 404-656-0254. E-mail: willie.talton@house.ga.gov.

TAMAYO, JAMES ANTHONY, bishop; b. Brownsville, Tex., Oct. 23, 1949; BA magna cum laude, U. St. Thomas, Houston, MA; grad., St. Mary's Sem., Houston. Ordained priest Diocese of Corpus Christi, Tex., 1976; assoc. pastor St. Patrick Parish, 1976—81, adminstr., 1981; asst. pastor Corpus Christi Cathedral, 1981—82; assoc. pastor St. Pius X Parish, 1982—85; pastor St. Andrew by the Sea Parish, 1986—90, Blessed Sacrament Parish, Laredo, Tex., 1990—93; vicar, adminstr. Western vicariate Diocese of Corpus Christi, Tex., 1993; ordained bishop, 1993; aux. bishop Archdiocese of Galveston-Houston, Tex., 1993—2000; bishop Diocese of Laredo, Tex., 2000—. Staff mem. Cath. Charities, 1975—81; v.p., bd. dirs. Cath. Legal Immigration Network. State chaplain Cath. Daughters Am.; state coun. chaplain Knights of Columbus, Tex.; nat. episcopal advisor Cursillo Movement, Tex.; regional exec. bd. mem., mem. Hispanic com. on scouting Boy Scouts Am.; mem. Leadership Houston; bd. dirs. United Way of Tex. Gulf Coast, Houston; mem. fin. com. Inst. Hispanic Culture, Houston. Chaplain with the rank of major USAFR. Mem.: US Conf. Cath. Bishops (subcom. on Youth of the Secretariat 1996—99, Internat. Policy com. 1996—99, com. on Hispanic Affairs 1999—, subcom. on Hispanic Liturgy 1999—, com. on Pastoral Practices 1999—), US Cath. Conf., Nat. Conf. Cath. Bishops (Nat. Adv. coun. 1996—99, Adminstrv. bd. 1996—99), US Res. Officers Assn. (life), USAF Assn. (life). Roman Catholic. Address: Diocese of Laredo 1901 Corpus Christi St PO Box 2247 Laredo TX 78043-2247 Office Phone: 957-727-2140. Office Fax: 956-727-2777.

TAN, WILLIAM W., electronics executive; 1 child, Mimi. Chmn., pres., CEO Zunicom, Inc., 1997—; chmn. AlphaNet, 1999—, Universal Power Group, Inc., 1999—. Office: Universal Power Group Inc 488 S Royal Ln Coppell TX 75019-3820 Office Phone: 469-892-1122. Office Fax: 469-892-1123. Business E-Mail: twilliam@alphanet.org.

TANCER, EDWARD F., lawyer, utilities executive; b. 1961; BA in Polit. Sci., U. Fla., Gainesville, JD. Bar: Fla. 1985. Atty. FPL Energy, Juno Beach, Fla., 1988, v.p., gen. counsel, 2001—05; asst. sec. FPL Group, Inc., Juno Beach, Fla., 1997—, assoc. gen. counsel, 2003—05, v.p., gen. counsel, 2005—08; asst. sec. Florida Power & Light Co., 1997—, sr. v.p., gen. counsel, 2005—08, vice chmn., sr. v.p. state govt. affairs, 2008—10; ptnr., corp. law practice Gunster Law, West Palm Beach, Fla., 2011—. Mem.: Fla. Bar Assn. Office: Gunster Law Ste 500 E 777 S Flager Dr West Palm Beach FL 33401-6194 Office Phone: 561-650-0687. Office Fax: 561-655-5677. Business E-Mail: etancer@gunster.com.

TANDON, RAJIV, psychiatrist, educator; b. Kanpur, India, Aug. 3, 1956; arrived in US, 1984, naturalized, 1988; s. Bhagwan Sarup and Usha (Mehrotra) T.; m. Chanchal Nammi Vohra; children: Neeraj, Anisha, Gitanjali. Student, St. Xavier's Coll., Bombay, India, 1974; BS, All India Inst., New Delhi, 1980; MD, Nat. Inst. of MH, India, 1983. Sr. resident Mental Health and Neuro-Scis., India, 1983-84; resident U. Mich. Hosps., Ann Arbor, 1984-87, attending psychiatrist, 1987-2000. Dir. schizophrenia program, dir. hosp. svcs. divsn. U. Mich., Ann Arbor, 1987—2000, assoc. prof., 1993—99, prof., 1999—2004; cons. Lenawee County Cmty. Mental Health, Adrian, Mich., 1985—99. Author: Biochemical Parameters of Mixed Affective States; Negative Schizophrenic Symptoms: Pathophysiology and Clinical Implications; contbr. over 250 articles to profl. jours. Recipient Young Scientist's award Biennial Winter workshop on Schizophrenia, 1990, 92, Travel award Am. Coll. Neuropsychopharmacology/Mead, 1990, Rsch. Excellence award Am. Assn. Psychiatrists from India, 1993, Sci. award, Best Drs. in Am. award, 1994-98, Gerald Klerman award for outstanding rsch. by a Nat. Alliance for Rsch. in Schizophrenia and Depression young investigator, 1995, FuturPsych award CINP, 1997. Mem. Am. Psychiat. Assn. (Wisniewski Young Psychiatrist Rschr. award 1993), World Fedn. Mental Health, Soc. for Neurosci., N.Y. Acad. Scis., Soc. Biol. Psychiatry, Mich. Psychiat. Soc. Independent. Hindu. Office: University Fla 140 SW 128th St 301 Jonesville FL 32669 Home: 140 SW 128th St Apt 301 Newberry FL 32669-3396 Office Phone: 352-294-0400, 352-376-1611 ext. 7611. Business E-Mail: tandon@ufl.edu.

TANENBAUM, ALLAN JAY, lawyer; b. Savannah, Ga., Aug. 9, 1946; s. Nathan and Gertrude Sadie (Palefsky) Tanenbaum; m. Elaine Kruger Tanenbaum, Aug. 8, 1971; children: Louis, Sharon, Stephen, Eric. BS in Economics, U. Pa., 1967; JD, U. Va., 1971. Bar: Ga. 1972. Ptnr. Frankel, Hardwick, Tanenbaum, Fink, PC, Atlanta, 1972—96, Cohen Pollock Merlin Axelrod & Tanenbaum, 1996—2001; gen. counsel AFC Enterprises Inc., 2001—; mng. dir. Lawyer Reference Svc. Atlanta, 1977—87. Trustee Congregation B'nai Torah; sec., exec. com., bd. dirs. Jewish Family & Career Svcs. Inc. With USAR, 1968—74. Fellow: Am. Bar Found.; mem.: ABA (house dels., chair gen. practice sect., spkr. young lawyers divsn., lawyer referral & info. svc., chair pub. edn. divsn., chair com. scope correlation work, chair fellows young lawyers divsn, chair coun. fund justice & edn. 2003—, nominating com. 2003—, Ga. state del. to house dels.), Atlanta Coun. Younger Lawyers (past pres.), Atlanta Bar Assn. (past sec., del.), Lawyers Club Atlanta. Office: Afc Enterprise Inc 400 Perimeter Center Ter NE Ste 1000 Atlanta GA 30346-1234 Office Phone: 770-353-3321. Business E-Mail: atanenbaum@afce.com.

TANG, IRVING CHE-HONG, mathematician, educator; b. Macau, China, Dec. 29, 1931; came to U.S., 1948; s. Man-yan and Susie Wei-chun (Chung) T. BS, U. Calif., Berkeley, 1952; MS, U. Ill., 1953; DS, Washington U., St. Louis, 1965. Chartered engr., Brit. Engring. Coun. Design engr. Friden Calculators, San Leandro, Calif., 1955-56; staff engr. IBM Corp., San Jose, Calif., 1956-66; postdoctoral fellow U. Oslo, 1966-68; head math. dept. NSW Inst. Tech., Sydney, 1969-76, Hong Kong Poly., 1977-89; prof. math. Phillips U., Enid, Okla., 1989-91, Oklahoma City C.C., Rose State Coll., 1991-94, Okla. State U., Oklahoma City, 1994—97, 1999—2009, Ednl. Testing Svc., Princeton, N.J., 1997-99, Kaplan U., 2009—10. Contbr. articles to profl. jours. Mem. Hong Kong Math. Soc. (pres. 1977-81), Sigma Xi, Tau Beta Pi, Eta Kappa Nu. Home: 1116 SW 100 Terrace Oklahoma City OK 73139 Home Phone: 405-692-2771. Personal E-mail: tangic31@gmail.com.

TANKERSLEY, JAN B., state legislator; b. Jan. 12; m. Hughie Tankersley; 2 children. Attended, Ga. So. U., Statesboro. Hospice care profl. Willingway Hosp.; councilwoman Brooklet City Coun., Ga.; commr. Bulloch County Bd. Commissioners; mem. Dist. 158 Ga. House of Representatives, 2011—, Republican. Office: PO Box 187 Brooklet GA 30415 also: Georgia House of Reps 601 Coverdell Legis Office Bldg Atlanta GA 30334 Office Phone: 912-842-5512, 404-656-0254. Business E-Mail: jan.tankersley@house.ga.gov.

TANKERSLEY, MICHAEL WAYNE, bank executive; b. Dallas, Apr. 5, 1956; s. Ewell L. and Sylvia (Sikes) T.; m. Lisa Dunlevy, May 20, 1978; children: Jennifer Lauren, Amy Elizabeth, Rowland Lake, James Reagan. BA, Rice U., 1977, M in Acctg., 1978; JD with high honors, U. Tex., 1980. Bar: Tex. 1981; CPA, Tex. Assoc. Hughes & Luce LLP, Dallas, 1980-86, ptnr., 1986—99, Bracewell & Patterson LLP, 1999—2005, Bracewell & Giuliani LLP, 2005—07; insp. gen. Export-Import Bank US, Washington, 2007—09; exec. v.p., gen. counsel CSG Investments, Inc., Plano, 2009—; interim CFO Charter Bank, Albuquerque, 2010—. Adj. prof. law U. Tex., 1987— Contbg. author: Texas Corporation Law and Practice, 1984; editor, contbr. articles Bull. of Corp. Banking and Bus. Law, 1985-87. Chmn. Tex. Bus. Law Found., 2000—02. Mem. Tex. Bar Assn. (chmn. communications and newsletter com. 1985-86, coun. 1987—, bus. law sect.), Dallas Bar Assn., Dallas Assn. Young Lawyers (bd. dirs. 1986-87), Tex. Bus. Law Found. (bd. dirs. 1988—, chmn. legis. com.), Leadership Dallas, Order of Coif, Chancellors. Office: CSG Investments Inc 6000 Legacy Dr Plano TX 75024 Office Phone: 469-467-5563.

TANNENWALD, PETER, lawyer; b. Washington, Apr. 8, 1943; s. Judge Theodore and Selma (Peterfreund) T.; m. Carol B. Baum, May 25, 1969; 1 child, Jonathan Mark. AB, Brown U., 1964; LLB, Harvard U., 1967. Bar: U.S. Dist. Ct. D.C. 1968, U.S. Ct. Appeals (D.C. cir.) 1968, U.S. Supreme Ct. 1972, Va., 2008. Assoc. Arent, Fox, Kintner, Plotkin & Kahn, Washington, 1967-74, ptnr., 1975-94; v.p. Irwin, Campbell & Tannenwald, P.C., Washington, 1995—2007; mem. Fletcher, Heald & Hildreth, 2008—. Columnist The LPTV Report, 1988-92. Mem. cmty. coun. Sta. WAMU-FM, Washington, 1986-93, 94-97, 2003—; dir. Brown Broadcasting Svc., Inc., Providence, 1970-2014; chmn. maj. law firms divsn. Nat. Capital Area affiliate United Way, 1977-79. With USCG, 1967—73. Mem. Harvard Law Sch. Assn. D.C. (pres. 1979-80), Harvard Law Sch. Assn. (sec. 1982-84). Avocations: electronics, photography. Office: Fletcher Heald & Hildreth PLC 1300 N 17th St 11th Fl Arlington VA 22209-3801 Office Phone: 703-812-0400. Business E-Mail: tannenwald@fhhlaw.com.

TANNER, RAY (DONALD RAY TANNER JR.), college baseball coach; b. Smithfield, NC, Mar. 25, 1958; m. Karen Donald; children: Bridgette Grace, Margaret Pearl, Joseph Luke. BS in Recreation Resources Adminstrn., NC State U., Raleigh, 1980, MPA, 1983. Asst. to the athletics dir., asst. athletics dir. in charge of games ops., asst. coach NC State U. Wolfpack, 1980—87, head baseball coach, 1988—96, U. SC Gamecocks, 1997—. Asst. coach USA Nat. Baseball Team, 1993, 1995, 1996, 2000, head baseball coach, 2003; asst. coach US nat. team Summer Olympic Games, Atlanta, 1996, Sydney, 2000. Named Coach of Yr., Atlantic Coast Conf., 1990, Southeastern Conf., 1998, 2000, 2011, Atlantic Region Coach of Yr., Am. Baseball Coaches Assn., 1993, South Region Coach of Yr., 2002, Nat. Coach of Yr., 2000, Collegiate Baseball, 2010, US Nat. Coach of Yr., 2003. Achievements include head coach of NCAA College World Series national championship winning University of South Carolina Gamecocks, 2010, 2011. Office: University SC Baseball Rex Enright Athletics Ctr 1300 Rosewood Dr Columbia SC 29208 Office Phone: 803-777-7830.

TANNER, W(ALTER) RHETT, lawyer; b. Athens, Ga., May 16, 1938; s. Johnnie Bryson and Walterette (Arwood) T.; m. Carolyn Laverne Watson, Nov. 11, 1967; 1 child, Walter Rhett (dec. 1989). AB cum laude, U. Ga., 1960, JD cum laude, 1962. Bar: Ga. 1961. With Hansell & Post, Atlanta, 1964—89, Jones, Day, Atlanta, 1989—99. Panelist Am. Arbitration Assn., 1995—. Bd. dirs. Atlanta Symphony Orch., 1975—95, mem. exec. com., 1977—86, v.p., 1978, chmn. maj. gifts campaign, 1980, bd. counsellors, 1996—; mem. Leadership Atlanta, 1980, Leadership Ga., 1982; mem. bd. visitors Grady Meml. Hosp., 1983—92; trustee Ga. Legal History Found., 1986—, pres., 1996—2008; hon. chmn. Atlanta Decorators Show House, 2002; mem. Rotary Club, 2003—08; hon. chmn. Meal To Remember, 2005; bd. dirs., vice chmn. Sr. Citizens Svc. Met. Atlanta, Inc., 2000—, chmn., Highlands-Cashiers Chamber Music Festival, 2006—08, Sr. Citizens Found., 2000—11. Lt. comdr. USNR, ret. Mem. Atlanta Bar Assn. (bd. dirs. 1982-87, exec. com. 1983-87), State Bar Ga. (vice chmn. bar and media com. 1979-82), Atlanta Bar Found. (trustee 1985-91), U. Ga. Alumni (pres. chpt. 1973-74, chmn. Atlanta/Met. coun. 1975, mem. state bd. mgrs., v.p. 1976-78), Gridiron, Capital City Club, Phi Beta Kappa, Omicron Delta Kappa, Phi Kappa Phi, Phi Delta Phi, Delta Tau Delta.

TANSKY, BURTON M., retail executive; b. 1938; married. BA, U. Pitts., 1960. With Kaufmann's, 1961-67; asst. store mgr. Filenes, 1967—71, store mgr., 1971; mdse. mgr. Rikes, Dayton, Ohio, 1971-74; v.p. Forbes and Wallace, Springfield, Ohio, 1974, I. Magnin, 1974—77; sr. v.p. Saks & Co., 1977—80, exec. v.p., 1980, pres., 1980—94, chmn., CEO, 1990—94, Neiman Marcus Stores (subs. of The Neiman Marcus Group, Inc.), Dallas, 1998; exec. v.p. Neiman Marcus Group, Inc., 1998, COO, 1998—2001, pres., CEO, 2001—10, interim CEO, Bergdorf Goodman, 2004, chmn., 2010—. Bd. dirs. Internat. Flavors & Fragrances Inc., 2003. Named a Chevalier de la Legion d'Honneur, Govt. France, 2002. Office: The Neiman Marcus Group Inc 1618 Main St Dallas TX 75201-4720 Office Phone: 214-741-6911. Office Fax: 214-573-5789. Business E-Mail: Burton_Tansky@neimanmarcus.com.

TANT, ALLISON (ALLISON TANT RICHARD), political organization administrator; b. Jacksonville, Fla. m. Barry Richard. Grad., Fla. State U. Lobbyist Steel, Hector & Davis, Holland & Knight; intern for Senator Bob Graham US Senate; investing founder Project New Fla.; chair Leon County Dem. Exec. Com., Fla. Dem. Party, 2013—. Found. bd. dirs. Tallahassee Cmty. Coll.; mem. state found. bd. Children's Home Soc. Fla. Democrat. Office: Florida Democratic Party 214 South Bronough St Tallahassee FL 32301

TANZBERGER, ERIC D., corporate financial executive; BBA, U. Notre Dame. CPA. Acct. Coopers & Lybrand L.L.P.; asst. corp. contr. Kirby Marine Transp. Corp., 1996; mgr., budgets & fin. analysis Svc. Corp. Internat., 1996—2000, asst. corp. contr., 2000—02, corp. contr., 2002—06; sr. v.p., CFO Service Corp. International, 2006—, treas., 2007—. Office: Service Corporation International 1929 Allen Pky Houston TX 77019 Office Phone: 713-522-5141. Office Fax: 713-525-5586.

TAPLEY, BYRON DEAN, aerospace engineer, educator; b. Charleston, Miss., Jan. 16, 1933; s. Ebbie Byron and Myrtle (Myers) T.; m. Sophia Philen, Aug. 28, 1959; children: Mark Byron, Craig Philen. BS in Mech. Engring., U. Tex., Austin, 1956, MS in Engring. Mechanics, 1958, PhD in Engring. Mechanics, 1960. Registered profl. engr., Tex. Engr. Structural Mechanics Rsch. Lab. U. Tex., Austin, 1954-58, instr. mech. engring., 1958, prof. aerospace engring. and engring. mechanics, 1960—, chmn. dept. aerospace engring. and engring. mechanics, 1966-77, Woolrich prof. engring., 1974-80, dir. Ctr. Space Rcsh., 1983—, Clare Cockrell Williams Centennial chair aerospace engring., 1984—; dir. Tex. Space Grant Consortium, 1990—2001. Mem. adv. com. on guidance control and nav. NASA, 1966-67, com. on space rsch., panel 1, 1974-76, chmn. region IV, engring. coun. on profl. devel., 1974-76; chmn. geodesy com. NRC, 1981-84, mem. aeros. and space engring. bd., 1984-86, mem. space sci. bd., chmn. com. on earth studies, 1988-91; mem. Mission PI, Grace Mission, 1997-, NASA Adv. Coun. Com., 2006-09; vice chair NAC Sci. Com., 2009-13; chair NAC Earth Sys. Subcom., 2009-13, AGU Whitten Medal Selection Com., 2009-10; panel mem. NRC, NASA Tech. Roadmap Investigation. Author: Statistical Orbit Determination, Elsevier; editor: Celestial Mech. Jour., 1976-79; assoc. editor: Jour. Guidance and Control, 1978-79; assoc. editor: Geophys. Revs, 1979-81. Recipient Exceptional Sci. Achievement medal, NASA, 1983, Pub. Svc. medal, 1995, Exceptional Pub. Svc. medal, 2009. Fellow: AAAS, AIAA (chmn. com. astrodynamics 1976—78, Mechanics and Control of Flight award 1989), Am. Geophys. Union (pres. geodesy sect. 1984—86, Charles A. Whitten medal 2001); mem.: Internat. Astron. Union, Soc. Engring. Sci., Am. Astronautical Soc. (pres. divsn. dynamic astronomy 1988—89, Dirk Brouwer award 1995), Am. Acad. Mechanics, IEEE, ASME, NAE, Tau Beta Pi, Phi Kappa Phi, Sigma Gamma Tau, Pi Tau Sigma, Sigma Xi. Avocations: sailing, cross country biking, backpacking. Office: University Tex Ctr Space Research 3925 W Braker Ln Ste 200 Austin TX 78759 Business E-Mail: tapley@csr.utexas.edu.*

TAPLIN, WINN LOWELL, historian, retired federal agency administrator; b. Saint Albans, Vt., Oct. 3, 1925; s. Winn Lowell and Elinor (Cunningham) T.; m. Ellajean Allard, July 16, 1949; children: Leslie Taplin Baumann, Mark Allard. BSCE, U. Mich., 1946, AB, 1948, AM, 1950, PhD, 1956. Oper. officer CIA, Washington, Saigon, Bucharest, Geneva, Bangkok, 1955-81; cons. Stowe, Vt., 1981-94, Sarasota, Fla., 1994—; tchr. Am. & intelligence history U. South Fla.-Sarasota Campus, 2007—09. Author: Secret New England: Spies of the American Revolution, 1991, We Vermonters, 1992. Mem. U.S. del. to UN Commn. on Human Rights, 1969; pres. Vt. Hist. Soc., 1989-93, trustee, 1983-96; mem. Sarasota Geneal. Soc., v.p., 1999-2001, pres., 2001—03; pres. Mansfield View Water Corp., Stowe, 1989-92. 1st lt. USMC, 1943-46, 50-52, Korea. Decorated Bronze Star, Intelligence Medal of Merit, Korean War Purple Heart, 1951. Mem. DAV, Central Intelligence Retirees Assn., Assn. Former Intelligence Officers, First Day Cover Soc., Am. Philatelic Assn., Soc. Mayflower Descendants (Sarasota Tilley chpt., dir. 2005-11), Am. Legion, U. Mich. Club Sarasota (dir. 1994-04, pres. 2009-11), Sigma Chi. Avocations: historical research, genealogy, classical music, stamp collecting/philately. Home: 4468 Calle Serena Sarasota FL 34238-5641 Home Phone: 941-924-7719. Personal E-mail: winn.ej@verizon.net.

TARBUTTON, LLOYD T., hotel executive, consultant; DCS in Mktg., Pacific Western U. Grad. Realtors Inst.; cert. franchise exec., La. State U., cert. hotel adminstr. Divsn. sales mgr. Reuben H. Donnelley Corp. (advt. agy.), Norfolk, Va., 1953-58; chmn. bd., dir. Tarbutton Assocs., Inc., Norfolk, 1962—; founder, dir., pres., chmn. bd. Econo Lodges of Am., Norfolk, 1967-83; chmn. bd. emeritus Econo Lodges of Am. (formerly Econ-Travel Motor Hotel Corp.), Norfolk, 1983—. Co-founder, chief judge Franchising Hall of Fame, Washington, 1979-82; co-founder, chmn. Coun. Franchise Suppliers, Washington, 1986-88. Author: Franchising--The How To Book, 1986. Trustee Edn. Found. Old Dominion U., 1979-86, chmn. bd. trustees Ctr. Econ. Edn., Old Dominion U., 1983-84. Recipient Hon. Tchr. award Maury High Sch., Norfolk, 1959. Mem. Internat. Franchise Assn. (hon. life, chmn. bd. dirs., chmn. 1st Asian Symposium on Franchising, Tokyo 1978, 1st European Symposium on Franchising, Amsterdam 1978, 1st So. Pacific Symposium on Franchising, Jakarta 1991), 1st Ea. Europe Franchise Symposiums (Varna, Bulgaria, 2000, inducted into Franchise Hall of Fame 2000), Internat. Coun. Hotel/Motel Mgmt., Realtor's Inst. Norfolk (chmn. 1965), Internat. Sales Execs. Club (Distinguished Sales award 1957), Internat. Platform Assn., Airplane Owners and Pilots Assn., Cavalier Golf and Yacht Club, Town Point Club, Naples Grande Resort Hotel & Tennis Club, The Club at Pelican Bay. Presbyterian. Office Phone: 239-877-3000.

TARLETON, JESSE S., retired business educator; b. Upper Darby, Pa., Nov. 1, 1928; s. Leslie Sauren and Jessie Dorothy (Sommers) T.; m. Lavonne Catherine Olson, June 25, 1955; children: Lesley Omary., David T. BS in Chem. Engring., Pa. State U., 1952; PhD in Chem. Engring., Cornell U., 1958; MBA, Coll. William and Mary, 1970; postgrad., Am. Grad. Sch. Internat. Mgmt., (Thunderbird), 1974. Cert. planning commr., Va.; cert. US Track and Field ofcl. Tchg. asst. Sch. Chem. Engring. Cornell U., Ithaca, NY, 1952-53, 55-57; rsch. engr. E.I. duPont de Nemours, Wilmington, Del., 1957-59; various positions in prodn. and engring. to sr. engr. Dow Badische Co. formerly Dow Chem. Co., Williamsburg, Va., 1959-70; from asst. prof. to prof. bus. adminstrn. Coll. William and Mary, Williamsburg, Va., 1970—97, prof. emeritus, 1997—. Spkr. in field. Sports editor, Camp newspaper, 1946-48; contbr. chpts. to books, articles to profl. jours. Rep. Richmond Rd. transp. study group City of Williamsburg, 1992-94, regional issues com., 1991-95, mem. beautification adv. com., 1987-91, mem. planning commn., 1987-95, vice chmn., 1994-95, mem. econ. devel. authority, 1996-2007, chmn. 2003-05; mem. investment bd. Greater Peninsula Workforce, 2004—08. With US Army, 1946—48. Standard Oil of Ind. fellow, 1953-55. Mem. AIChE, Acad. of Mgmt., Acad. Internat. Bus., Decision Scis. Inst., Am. Prodn. and Inventory Control Soc., James River Assn., Nat. Ry. Hist. Soc., Nat. Assn. Railroad Passengers, Kiwanis Club of Williamsburg (sec. 1965-74, dir., com. chmn.), Colonial Road Runners, Phi Kappa Phi, Tau Beta Pi, Sigma Tau, Phi Lambda Upsilon, Alpha Chi Sigma. Avocations: travel, railroading, reading, walking. Home: 500 Elmington Ave Apt 306 Nashville TN 37205-2520 Personal E-mail: thetarletons@gmail.com.

TARPGAARD, PETER THORVALD, naval architect; b. Knoxville, Tenn., Sept. 25, 1937; s. Peter Thorvald and Edith Margurite (Mees) T.; m. Judith Ann Burgess; 1 child, Andrew Christian. BS, U.S. Naval Acad., 1959; MSME, MIT, 1968, naval engr., 1968, PhD, 1970. Spl. project asst. Office Chief of Naval Devel., Washington, 1970—73; profl. staff U.S. Arms Control & Disarmament Agy., Washington, 1973—76; design supr. Portsmouth Naval Shipyard, Portsmouth, NH, 1976—79; prin. analyst Congressional Budget Office, Washington, 1979—85; mgr. submarine programs Draper Lab., Cambridge, Mass., 1985—92; prof. U.S. Naval War Coll., Newport, RI, 1992—97; mgr. Noesis Inc., Arlington, Va., 1997—. Cons. Congressional Office of Tech. Assessment, Washington, 1991-92. Contbr. articles to profl. jours. With U.S. Navy, 1959-79. Mem. Soc. Naval Architects & Marine Engrs., Assn. for Public Policy Analysis & Mgmts., U.S. Naval Inst. Episcopalian. Home: 5 Longmeadow Ave Middletown RI 02842-5225 Office: Noesis Inc 4100 N Fairfax Dr Ste 800 Arlington VA 22203-1663 Business E-Mail: ptarpgaard@alum.mit.edu.

TARR, KENNETH J., retired investment company executive; b. 1945; BA, U. Pa., 1967; MBA, Columbia U., 1971. With Chem. Bank, NYC, 1971-72; asst. v.p. Standard and Poors/Inter Capital, NYC, 1972-74; founder, mgr. S&P/Market Insights, NYC, 1974-75; v.p. Kuhn Loeb and Co., NYC, 1975-77; asst. v.p. Bessemer Trust Co., NYC, 1977-80, v.p., 1980-82, sr. v.p., 1982-91, dir. rsch., 1984; pres., dir. Suisse Asset Mgmt., Inc., NYC, 1991-93; mng. prin. Weiss, Peck & Greer, LLC, NYC, 1994-97; exec. v.p., regional head pvt. banking Am.'s Deutsche Bank AG, NYC, 1997-99; ret., 2000. Mem.: NY Yacht Club.

TARRANCE, VERNON LANCE, JR., research and development company executive; b. Harlingen, Tex., Dec. 4, 1940; s. Vernon Lance Sr. and Mary Gilmore (Rea) T.; m. Eugenia Aline McCuistion, July 2, 1966 (dec.), Debora, July 14, 2007; children: Vernon Lance III, Haloway McCuistion (dec.), Kyle Rea. BA, Washington & Lee U., 1962; postgrad., U. Mich., 1971; MA with distinction, American U., 1973; postgrad., Harvard U., 1973-74. Dir. rsch. Tex. Republican Com., Austin, 1964-67, Republican Nat. Com., Washington, 1969-70; spl. asst. to dir. US Census Bur., Washington, 1970-73; v.p. Decision Making Info. Inc., Santa Ana, Calif., 1974-77; pres., founder Tarrance, Hill, Newport & Ryan, Houston, 1977-92; pres., mng. dir. Gallup China Ltd., Beijing, 1993-95; vis. prof. polit. sci. Tex. A&M U., College Station, 1995-96; scholar in residence Washington & Lee U., Va., 1996; mng. dir. Burson-Marsteller, Washington, 1997-99. Bd. dirs. Gallup Orgn., 1987-92; cons. Gallup Internat. Rsch. Ctr., Lincoln, Nebr.; co-chmn. adv. adjustment panel U.S. Census, 1990. Co-author: The Ticket Splitter, 1972, Checked and Balanced, 1998, How Republicans Can Win in a Changing America, 2014; editor: Texas Precinct Votes '66, '68, '70. Sr. strategist, sr. advisor Senator John McCain for Pres. 2008. Fellow John F. Kennedy Inst. Politics Harvard U., 1973-74; named one of The 150 People Who Influence Fed. Govt. Nat. Jour. Mag., 1986; named to Hall of Fame, Am. Assn. Polit. Consultants, 2013. Mem.: Raleigh Tavern Philos. Soc. (founder), Am. Polit. Sci. Assn., Kappa Sigma. Avocations: mountain trekking, golf, aviculture, travel.

TARTT, BLAKE, lawyer; b. Houston, Mar. 16, 1929; s. Herbert Blake and Bernice (Schwalm) T.; m. Barbara Jean Moore, Jan. 30, 1960; children: Blake III, Courtnay Elias. BBA, So. Meth. U., Dallas, 1949, JD cum laude, 1959. Bar: Tex. 1959. Assoc. Fulbright & Jaworski, Houston, 1959-70, ptnr., 1970-2000, Beirne, Maynard & Parsons, LLP, Houston, 2000—. Mem. Tex. Commn. on Jud. Conduct, 1996-2001; bd. dirs. Nat. Judicial Coll. Bd. dirs. Mus. Fine Arts, Houston; mem. bd. visitors Nat. Jud. Coll. Served to 1st lt. USAF, 1951-55, Korea. Decorated Air medal. Fellow Am. Bar Found. (chmn. fellows 1987, life), Tex. Bar Found. (chmn. bd. 1974-75, chmn. fellows 1978-79, life), Am. Coll. Trial Lawyers; mem. ABA (ho. of dels. 1976-99, state del. 1990-99, standing com. fed. jud. 1996-99, chair 1997, bd. govs. 2001-04), Am. Bd. Trial Advocates (advocate), Houston Bar Found. (life., chmn., bd. dirs. 1992), Fed. Bar Assn., Internat. Assn. Def. Counsel, Am. Judicature Soc. (bd. dirs. 1984-88), So. Conf. Bar Pres. (pres. 1984), State Bar Tex. (dir. 1972-75, exec. com. 1975-76, pres. elect 1982-83, pres. 1983-84), Houston Bar Assn., Am. Law Inst., Tex. Jud. Commn., Citizens Commn. on the Tex. Judiciary, Tex. Commn. Jud. Conduct, Houston Philos. Soc., Coronado Club, Forest Club, Argyle Club (San Antonio), Reform Club (London), Delta Theta Phi, Alpha Tau Omega. Episcopalian. Office: Beirne Maynard & Parsons 1300 Post Oak Blvd Houston TX 77056-3028 Office Phone: 713-960-7331. Business E-Mail: btartt@bmpllp.com.

TARVER, EDWARD J., federal prosecutor, former state legislator; b. Augustz, Ga., July 22, 1959; m. Beverly Tarver; children: Edward Jr., Beverly Elizabeth. BA, Augusta Coll., 1981; JD, Univ. Ga., 1991. Bar: Ga. 1991, Ga. Ct. Appeals, Ga. Supreme Ct., US Dist. Ct. So. Mid. & No. Dist. Ga., US Ct. Appeals 11th Cir. Law clk. Judge Dudley Bowen, US Dist. Ct., So. Dist. Ga., 1991—92; assoc. Hull, Towill, Norman, Barrett & Salley PC, Augusta, Ga., 1992—99, ptnr., 1999—2009; mem. Dist. 22 Ga. State Senate, 2005—09; US atty. (southern dist.) Ga. US Dept. Justice, 2009—. Served to capt. field artillery US Army, 1982—89. Alvin W Vogtle Volunteer of the Year, 1995; 2002 Leadership Augusta Community Service Award. Mem. ABA, Nat. Bar Assn., State Bar Ga., Augusta Bar Assn., Augusta Metro C. of C., Leadership Georgia Found., Leadership Augusta Bd., Acad. Richmond County Boosters Club, St. John's Towers Adv. Bd.; past pres. Augusta Tech. Coll. Bd. of Directors, East Georgia Easter Seals Soc. Office: US Attorneys Office 100 Bull St 2nd Fl Savannah GA 31401 Office Phone: 912-652-4422. Office Fax: 912-652-4388.*

TARVER, GREGORY WILLIAMS, SR., state legislator; b. Mar. 30, 1946; m. Velma Jean Kirksey-Tarver. Attended, Centenary Coll. La., Shreveport, Grambling State U., La. Pres. J.S. Williams Funeral Home and Ins. Cos.; mem. Dist. 39 La. State Senate, Baton Rouge, 1984—2004, 2012—. Former mem. Caddo Parish Police Jury; councilman Shreveport City Coun., 1978—84. Served with US Armed Forces, Germany, Vietnam. Democrat. Office: 1024 Pierre Ave Shreveport LA 71103 also: La State Senate 900 N 3rd St Baton Rouge LA 70804 Office Phone: 318-227-1499. Business E-Mail: tarverg@legis.la.gov.

TASH, PAUL CLIFFORD, publishing executive; b. South Bend, Ind., July 17, 1954; s. Robert and Barbara (Eller) Tash; m. Karyn Krayer, Aug. 19, 1983; children: Kaley Marie, Kendyl Barbara. BA summa cum laude, Ind. U., 1976; LLB magna cum laude, Edinburgh U., Scotland, 1978. Reporter St. Petersburg Times, Fla., 1978-83, city editor, 1983-86, metro editor, 1986-89, Washington bur. chief, 1991-92, exec. editor, 1992-2000, dep. chmn., 1997—2004, editor, pres., 2000—04, editor, 2004—10; editor, pub. Fla. Trend Mag., 1990-91; chmn., CEO Times Pub. Co., 2004—. Chmn. Poynter Inst. Media Studies, St. Petersburg. Chmn. Fla. First Amendment Found.; mem. adv. bd. Ind. U. Sch. Journalism; bd. dirs. Newspaper Assn. America, Com. Protect Journalists. Recipient Kappa Tau Alpha Hall of Fame award, U. So. Fla. Sch. Mass Comm., 2009; Marshall scholar, 1976—78. Mem.: Fla. First Amendment Found., Tampa Bay Area Com. on Fgn. Rels., Am. Soc. Newspaper Editors, Fla. C. of C. Office: Tampa Bay Times 490 1st Ave S Saint Petersburg FL 33701-4204 Mailing: PO Box 1121 Saint Petersburg FL 33731-1121 Office Phone: 727-893-8887. Office Fax: 727-892-2328. E-mail: ptash@tampabay.com.

TASMAN, ALLAN, psychiatry educator; b. Louisville, Feb. 8, 1947; s. Goodman and Zelda Tasman; m. Cathy Faye Goldstein, May 24, 1970. BA in Chemistry, Franklin and Marshall Coll., 1969; MD, U. Ky., 1973. Diplomate Am. Bd. Psychiatry and Neurology. Resident in psychiatry U. Ky. Med. Sch., Lexington, 1973—74, U. Cin. Med. Ctr., 1974—76; asst. prof. psychiatry U. Conn. Med. Sch., Farmington, 1976—82, assoc. prof. psychiatry and tenure, 1982—88, prof. psychiatry, 1988—91; prof. psychiatry and behavioral scis., tenure and chmn. U. Louisville Sch. Medicine, 1991—; dir. Cognitive Neurosci. Lab., 1991—. Editor: Annual Review of Psychiatry, 1989-92, Clinical Challenges in Psychiatry, 1993, Less Time to Do More, 1993; sr. editor: Textbook of Psychiatry, 1997, 2d edit., 2003, 3rd edit., 2008, assoc. editor Am. Jour. Psychotherapy, 2002-; founding dep. editor Jour. Psychotherapy Practice and Rsch., 1992-2001; founding editor Asia Pacific Psychiatry, 2009-; contbr. articles of profl. jours. Recipient Alpha Omega Alpha Faculty award, 2002, Nat. Alliance Mental Illness Exemplary Psychiatrist award, 2002, Pres.'s Disting. Faculty award for svc. to the profession, U. Louisville, 2003, St. Clair award, Ky. Psychiat. Assn., 2007, Disting. Alumnus award, U. Ky. Coll. Medicine, 2008, Frankilin and Marshall Coll., 2012, Pres. Disting. Faculty award, U. Louisville, 2013. Fellow RCP, Am. Psychiat. Assn. (disting. fellow, v.p. 1996-98, pres.-elect 1998-99, pres. 1999-2000, Nancy Roeske award for excellence in med. student edn. 1991, Irma Bland award for excellence in resident tchg. 2005), Royal Coll. Psychiatrists, Am. Assn. Dirs. Psychiat. Residency Tng. (pres. 1993-94), Assn. Acad. Psychiatry (pres. 1993-94, Educator of Yr. award 2000), Am. Assn. Chmn. Depts. Psychiatry (pres. 1996-97, 97-98), World Psychiat. Assn. (hon.; bd. dirs. 2002-11, sec. for edn. 2005-11), Pacific Rim Coll. Psychiatrists (pres. 2006—08, pres. Ky. med. reciprocal risk retention group, 2004-, pres. U. Louisville med. sch. fund, 2009-, treas. U. Healthcare, 2011-).

TATA, ROBERT, state legislator; b. Detroit, Jan. 27, 1930; m. Martha Jeraldine Morris; children: Robert M., Anthony J., Kendall. State del. Dist. 85, Va., 1984—; mem. Edn. Com., Appropriations Com., Corps. Com., Ins. & Banking Com., Labor & Commerce Com., Mil. & Police Com.; Counselor HS; coach. Republican. Roman Catholic. Mailing: 4536 Gleneagle Dr Virginia Beach VA 23462 Home Phone: 757-499-2490; Office Phone: 757-340-3510. E-mail: Del_Tata@house.state.va.us.

TATE, HAROLD SIMMONS, JR., lawyer; b. Taylors, SC, Sept. 19, 1930; s. Harold Simmons and Cleone (Clayton) T.; m. Elizabeth Anne Coker, Dec. 22, 1952; children— Mary Elizabeth Anne, Martha Coker, Virginia Clayton. Degree in internat. law and rels. cum laude, Harvard U., 1951, postgrad., 1954, JD, 1956; MA, U. SC, 2005; PhD, U. SC., 2008. Bar: S.C. 1956. Ptnr. Haynsworth Sinkler Boyd, PA, Columbia, SC, 1962—. Chmn. adv. com. US Dist. Ct. (SC), 1984-2006; lectr. Am. Law Inst.-ABA seminars; adv. com. on rules and procedures US Ct. Appeals (4th cir.), 1990-95. Co-author: South Carolina Appellate Practice, 1985; bd. editors Federal Litigation Guide Reporter, 1985—; co-draftsman S.C. Rules of Evidence, 1995; contbr. articles and book revs. to profl. jours. Chmn. Richland County Mental Health Ctr., 1965-66; co-chmn. Columbia Hearing and Speech Ctr., 1962-64; mem. admission and scholarship com. Harvard U., 1961—; chmn. subcom. on legislation, legislation and fin. study commn. Gov.'s Adv. Group on Mental Health Planning, 1963-65; chmn. Columbia Bd. Supervisors of Registration, 1961-70; pres. Columbia Philharm. Orch., 1966-67, Town Theatre, 1967-70; bd. trustee Richland County Pub. Libr., 1973-78, Hist. Columbia Found., 1971-75, Caroliniana Soc., 1978—, Bostick Charitable Trust, 1968—, Archaeol. Rsch. Trust, 2000-2003; bd. mgrs. SC Hist. Soc., 1993-99, 2002-2008; commr. SC Commn. of Archives and History, 1995—; bd. dirs. Charleston Libr. Soc., 2009-; former mem. Harvard Club, NYC, Assn. Bar City NY, Harvard Law Sch. Assn. SC, sec. treas., 1968-70, pres., 1988; former mem. Palmetto Club, sec. 1963-70, pres. 1973-76. Capt. US Army, 1951—53. Recipient DuRant award Disting Pub. Svc., 2001. Fellow: Am. Coll. Trial Lawyers; mem.: ABA, Am. Law Inst., Am. Judicature Soc., SC Bar Assn., Richland County Bar Assn., Columbia Drama Club (pres. 1963-64), Forum Club, Harvard Club SC, Carolina Yacht Club. Episcopalian. Office: Haynsworth Sinkler Boyd PA Fl 22 1201 Main St Ste 2200 Columbia SC 29201-3232 Home: 41 King St Charleston SC 29401 Office Phone: 803-779-3080. Business E-Mail: state@hsblawfirm.com.

TATE, HORACENA, state legislator; b. Griffen, Ga., May 8, 1956; BS, Univ. Ga., 1977; MA, Atlanta Univ., 1988; EdD, Clark-Atlanta Univ., 1992. With Ga. Dept. Labor, United Airlines, Apollo Travel Services; pres. Tate, Marsh & Associates; mem. Dist. 38 Ga. State Senate, 1999—. Rosalie Wright Community Coun (v.p.); United Methodist Women. Democrat. Methodist. Mailing: 201 Joseph E Lowery Blvd NW Atlanta GA 30314 Office Phone: 404-577-5609. Business E-Mail: horacena.tate@senate.ga.gov.

TATE, JOHN TORRENCE, retired mathematics professor, researcher; b. Mpls., Mar. 13, 1925; married; 3 children. BA, Harvard U., 1946; PhD, Princeton U., 1950. With Harvard U., 1954—90; Sid W. Richardson chair math. U. Tex., Austin, 1990—2009. Recipient Cole prize in number theory, Am. Math. Soc., 1956, Leroy P. Steele prize for Lifetime Achievement, Am. Math. Soc., 1995; co-recipient Wolf prize in math. Wolf Found., Israel, 2003, Abel prize, Norwegian Acad. Sciences and Letters, 2010. Mem. NAS, Academie des Scis. (Paris), hon. mem. London Mathematical Society. Office: Univ Texas at Austin Dept Math 1 University Station C1200 Austin TX 78712-0257 Office Phone: 512-471-7127, 512-471-7711. Office Fax: 512-471-9038. E-mail: tate@math.utexas.edu.

TATE, REGINALD, state legislator; State senator Dist. 33, Tenn., 2007—; vice-chmn. Edn. Com.; mem. Commerce Com., Labor Com., Agr. Com. Democrat. Office: 320 War Memorial Bldg Nashville TN 37243-0033 Office Phone: 615-741-2509. Office Fax: 615-253-0167. Business E-Mail: sen.reginald.tate@capitol.tn.gov.

TATE, SAMUEL LESTER, III, lawyer; b. Cedartown, Ga., Sept. 13, 1961; s. Samuel L. Jr. and Ruth Opal (Edwards) T.; children: Samuel Lester Tate IV, Grace Anderson Tate. BS, Ga. Inst. Tech., 1982; JD, U. S.C., 1987. Bar: Ga. 1987, U.S. Dist. Ct. (no. dist.) Ga. 1988, U.S. Dist. Ct. (mid. dist.) Ga. 1995. Staff mem. to Senator Sam Nunn US Senate, Washington, 1983—84; press sec. to Rep. George Darden US House of Representatives, Washington, 1984—85; assoc. Savell & Williams, Atlanta, 1988-90, Goodman, McGuffey, Aust & Lindsey, Atlanta, 1990-91; pvt. practice Akin & Tate, PC, Cartersville, Ga., 1991—. Bd. govs. State Bar Ga., 1996—, bd. dirs. gen. practice and trial sect. Bd. dirs. Advocates for Bartow's Children, Cartersville, past treas.; active Boston County Dem. Com. Mem.: ABA, State Bar Ga. (bd. govs. 1996—, exec. com. 2005—, treas. 2007—09, pres.-elect 2009—10, pres. 2010—11), American Assn. Justice, Cartersville-Bartow County Bar Assn., Ga. Trial Lawyers Assn., Altanta Bar Assn., Bartow County Bar Assn. Baptist. Avocations: reading, running. Home: PO Box 2139 Cartersville GA 30120-1686 Office: Akin & Tate PLC 11 Public Square PO Box 878 Cartersville GA 30120 Office Phone: 770-382-0780. Office Fax: 770-386-1452.

TATE, TOM, healthcare company executive; V.p. aviation Cmty. Health Sys., Inc. Office: Community Health Systems Inc 4000 Meridian Blvd Franklin TN 37067 Office Phone: 615-465-7000. Office Fax: 615-371-1068. Business E-Mail: tom_tate@chs.net.

TATUM, BEVERLY DANIEL, academic administrator, writer, psychology and education educator; b. Tallahassee, Sept. 27, 1954; d. Robert Alphonse and Catherine Faith (Maxwell) Daniel; m. Travis James Tatum, July 28, 1979; children: Travis Jonathan Daniel, David Alexander Daniel. BA, Wesleyan U., 1975; MA in Psychology, U. Mich., 1976, PhD, 1984; MA in Religious Studies, Hartford Seminary. Lic. clin. psychologist. Asst. prof. Dept. Psychology Westfield State Coll., Mass., 1983—86, assoc. prof. Mass., 1986—89; assoc. prof. Dept. Psychology and Edn. Mt. Holyoke Coll., South Hadley, Mass., 1989—96, prof., 1996—, dept. chair, 1997—98, dean, v.p. student affairs, 1998—2002, acting pres., 2002; pres. Spelman Coll., Atlanta, 2002—. Lectr. dept. black studies U. Calif., Santa Barbara, 1980-83, counseling psychologist, 1979-83; vis. scholar Stone Ctr., Wellesley Coll., 1991-92; chair, bd. dirs. Equity Inst., Emeryville, Calif., 1987-89; bd. dirs. Ga. Power, 2008- Author: Assimilation Blues: Black Families in a White Community, 1987, Why Are All the Black Kids Sitting Together in the Cafeteria?: And Other Conversations About Race, 1997, Can We Talk About Race?: And Other Conversations in an Era of School Resegregation, 2007; contbr. articles to profl. jours. Recipient Brock Internat. Prize in Edn., 2005; named one of The 100 Most Influential Georgians, Ga. Trend mag., 2008; fellow APA Minority Program, 1976—79, U. Calif., 1980—81, Ford Found., 1991. Mem. APA, Am. Psychol. Soc., Ea. Psychol. Assn., Mass. Psychol. Assn., Assn. Women in Psychology, Assn. Black Psychologists, Atlanta Rotary Club, Metro Atlanta C. of C. Office: Spelman College Office of Pres 350 Spelman Lane SW Atlanta GA 30314-4399 Office Phone: 404-270-5001.*

TAUB, EDWARD, psychology researcher; b. Bklyn., Oct. 22, 1931; s. Samuel Hart and Ida Pearl (Kimmel) T.; m. Mildred Allen Taub, Aug. 13, 1959. BA, Bklyn. Coll., 1953; MA, Columbia U., 1959; PhD, NYU, 1969. Rsch. asst. Columbia U., NYC, 1956; rsch. asst. dept. exptl. neurology Jewish Chronic Disease Hosp., NYC, 1957-60, rsch. assoc., 1960-68; dir. Behavioral Biology Ctr., Inst. for Behavioral Rsch., 1968-83; assoc. dir. Inst. for Behavioral Rsch., 1978-83; univ. prof. psychology U. Ala., Birmingham, 1986—2000, 2000—; standing guest prof. U. Konstanz, Germany, 1995—2002; guest prof. U. Jena, Germany, 1996—2002. Asst. prof. dept. psychiatry Johns Hopkins U., Balt., 1972-82; vis. prof. grad. program dept. psychology CUNY, 1984-85; vis. prof. U. Tuebingen, U. Muenster, Humboldt U., Germany, 1993—2001. Contbr. articles to profl. jours. Recipient Pioneering Rsch. Contbn. award, 1989, Disting. Scientist of 1998 award, Assn. of Applied Psychophysiology and Biofeedback, Ireland prize for scholarly distinction, U. Ala., Birmingham, 1997, Humboldt Rsch. award, 2000; fellow Guggenheim Found., 1983—84. Fellow AAAS (pres. psychol. sect. 2009), APA (exec. com. divsn. 6, Disting. Sci. award for the applications of psychology 2004), Soc. for Behavioral Medicine, Am. Psychol. Soc. (charter, William James Fellow award 1997); mem. Soc. for Neurosci. (named one of 10 leading translational rsch. projects in neurosci. in the 20th Century 2003), Biofeedback Soc. Am. (pres. 1978-79, Outstanding Rsch. Contbn. award 1988), Am. Physiol. Soc. (exec. com. neurosci. sect. 1988-91). Achievements include invention of technique of thermal biofeedback; Constraint-Induced Movement therapy for rehabilitation for stroke, traumatic brain injury, spinal cord injury, cerebral palsy and other motor disorders due to neurological injury. Office: U Ala at Birmingham 712 CPM 1530 3d Ave S Birmingham AL 35294-0018 Office Phone: 205-934-2471. Business E-Mail: etaub@uab.edu.

TAULBEE, THOMAS LESTER, psychotherapist, educator; b. Normal, Ill., June 12, 1947; s. Marion L. and Marjorie S. T. BS, Ill. State U., 1970; MS, Tex. A&M U., 1971, EdD, 1973. Cert. marriage and family therapist; cert. sports counselor; ordained min. Psychotherapist Human Resource Devel. Ctr., Dallas, 1974-76; prof. psychology Richland Coll., Dallas, 1976—, prof. history, 1994—. North Tex. regl. dir. Nat. Inst. Sports, 2000-2003, nat. coord. of divsn. chmn., 2002-03; bd. advisors Revival Fires Ministries, Branson West, Mo., 1997-99, bd. dirs. Sports Sys. Internat., 2001-2003, mem. sports chaplaincy adv. com. U.S. Coun. for Sports Chaplaincy, 2002-2003, exec. dir., exec. v.p., chief orgnl. officer, 2003; pres., founder Internat. Escorted Tour Svc., 2004—; internat. tour guide, with nat. and internat. cos., 1980—. Co-author: Psychology from a Personal Perspective, 1992, rev. edit., 1997; editor, co -author: Personal Applications of Psychology, 1997. Dir. Superior Student Roundtable, Parker, Tex., 1993, 1996—; bd. dirs. U.S. Coun. for Sports Chaplaincy, 2003—. Recipient Nat. Inst. for Staff and Orgnl. Devel. excellence award U. Tex., 2004; Ctr. for Behavioral Studies U. North Tex., Denton, 1973-74; named Basketball All-Am., Ill. State U., 1969; named to Ill. State U. Athletic Hall of Fame. Mem. Tex. Jr. Coll. Teachers Assn., Nat. Assn. Scholars, Assn. Behavior Analysis. Avocations: world travel, scuba diving, cooking. Office: Richland Coll 12800 Abrams Rd Dallas TX 75243-2173 E-mail: ttaulbee@verizon.net.

TAYLOE, DAVID T., JR., pediatrician; b. Phila., Mar. 24, 1949; MD, U. NC Sch. Medicine, 1974. Intern pediat. St. Christopher's Hosp. Children, Phila., 1974—75, resident pediat., 1975—76; resident NC Meml. Hosp., Chapel Hill, 1976—77; pvt. practice pediatrician Goldsboro, NC, 1977—. Contbr. articles to profl. jours. Fellow: Am. Acad. Pediat. (NC chpt. pres. 1993—95, nat. pres. 2008—09). Address: Goldsboro Pediat 2706 Medical Office Pl Goldsboro NC 27530 Office: AAP Nat Hdqs 141 Northwest Point Blvd Alden IL 60001

TAYLOR, ANTHONY BASIL, bishop; b. Ft. Worth, Apr. 24, 1954; s. Basil and Rachel (Roth) Taylor. Attended, Univ. Okla.; BA, St. Meinrad Sem., Ind.; attended, No. Am. Coll., Rome, 1976—80; D in Biblical Theol., Fordham Univ., 1989. Ordained priest Archdiocese of Oklahoma City, 1980; assoc. pastor Sacred Heart parish, Okla. City, 1980—82, Queen of All Saints Mission, Sayre, Okla., 1982—86, Holy Rosary parish, Bronx, NY, 1986—88; vicar for ministries Archdiocese of Oklahoma City, 1988—2008; founding pastor St. Monica parish, Edmond, Okla., 1993—2003; pastor Sacred Heart parish, Okla. City, 2003—08; ordained bishop, 2008; bishop Diocese of Little Rock, Ark., 2008—. Roman Catholic. Office: Diocese of Little Rock PO Box 7565 2500 N Tyler St Little Rock AR 72217 Office Phone: 501-664-0340. Office Fax: 501-664-9075.

TAYLOR, ASHLEY L., JR., lawyer, former federal commissioner; b. Washington, 1968; BA in Economics, Va. Mil. Inst., Lexington, 1990; JD, Washington & Lee Sch. Law, Lexington, 1993. Bar: Va., US Ct. Appeals (4th cir.) 1999, US Dist. Ct. (ea. Va. dist.) 1999, US Supreme Ct. Law clk. to hon. David A. Faber US Dist. Ct., 1993—95; assoc. Kaufman & Canoles, Norfolk, Va., 1995—98; dep. atty. gen. State of Va., 1998—2001; assoc. Troutman Sanders LLP, Richmond, Va., 2001—02, ptnr., 2003—, mem. exec. com., 2004—; commr. US Commn. on Civil Rights, 2004—10. Former dir. Va. Mil. Inst. Athletic Assn. Contbr. articles to profl. jours. Mem. Commn. on Va. Courts in the 21st Century. Named a Va. Super Lawyer, 2006—09; named one of Top 40 Under 40, Style Weekly, 2007, 50 Most Influential Minority Lawyers in America, Nat. Law Jour., 2008. Mem.: ABA (chmn. state atty. gen. subcom., former mem. exec. coun., young lawyers divsn., State and Local Govt. Sect. Up and Comer of Yr. 1999), Va. Bar Assn. (former mem. exec. com., young lawyers divsn., mem. com. on fed. judgeships, ea. dist.). Republican. Office: Troutman Sanders LLP 1001 Haxall Point PO Box 1122 Richmond VA 23218-1122 Office Phone: 804-697-1286. Office Fax: 804-698-6018. Business E-Mail: ashley.taylor@troutmansanders.com.

TAYLOR, BILL, state legislator; m. Donna Taylor; children: Kasey Taylor Craven, Ryan Taylor. Cons. George H.W. Bush White House; v.p., assoc. broker and realtor Meybohm Realtors, Aiken; mem. Aiken Rotary Club, Aiken County Shrine Club, Millbrook Bapt. Ch.; vice chmn. Aiken County Chpt. of the Am. Red Cross; mem. Dist. 86 SC House of Representatives, 2011—. Republican. Office: South Carolina House of Representatives District 86 PO Box 2646 Aiken SC 29802 Address: 416D Blatt Bldg Columbia SC 29201 Office Phone: 803-270-2012. E-mail: Bill@TaylorSCHouse.com.

TAYLOR, BRYAN, state legislator, lawyer; m. Jessica Taylor; 1 child, Samuel. BA, U. Ala., 1998; JD, U. Tex., 2001. Prosecutor JAG; policy dir. and legal counsel to Bob Riley Office of Gov., Ala., 2006—10; mem. Dist. 30 Ala. State Senate, 2011—. Founder Tex. Law Republicans; mem. Prattville United Meth. Ch. Capt. US Army, Iraq, maj. Ala. Army Nat. Guard. Republican. Methodist. Office: 150 S Perry St PO Box 2069 Montgomery AL 36102-2069 also: Ala State Senate State House Rm 733 11 S Union St Montgomery AL 36130 Office Phone: 334-242-7883. Business E-Mail: bryan.taylor@alsenate.gov.

TAYLOR, CINDY B., oil industry executive; BBA in Acctg., Tex. A&M U., 1984. CPA. Acctg. mgmt. positions Ernst & Young LLP, 1984—92; v.p., contr. Cliffs Drilling Co., 1992—99; CFO L.E. Simmons & Associates, 1999—2000; sr. v.p., CFO Oil States International, Inc., Houston, 2000—06, pres., COO, 2006—07, pres., CEO, 2007—. Bd. dirs. Boots & Coots Internat. Well Control Inc., Global Industries Ltd., 2006—09, Boots & Coots, Inc., 2006—07, Oil States International, Inc., 2007—, Tidewater Inc., 2008—, AT&T Inc., 2013—. Office: Oil States Internat 333 Clay St Houston TX 77002*

TAYLOR, DANIEL J., film company executive; Sr. tax mgr. Arthur Andersen & Co.; exec. Tracinda Corp.; with Metro-Goldwyn-Mayer Inc (MGM), LA, 1985—91, exec. v.p.-corp. fin., 1997, pres., 2005—06, sr. exec. v.p., CFO, 1997—2005; chmn. Delta Petroleum Corp., 2009—. Bd. dirs. MGM Mirage, 2007—. Office: Delta Petroleum Corp 1301 McKinney St Ste 2025 Houston TX 77010-3089 Office Phone: 303-293-9133. Office Fax: 303-298-8251. Business E-Mail: danieltaylor@mirage.com.

TAYLOR, DARLENE K., state legislator; b. Jan. 29; m. John Taylor; 2 children. Benefit coord. Flowers Industries, Inc., 1980—82; claims mgr. Sunnyland Foods/Employer Svc., 1982—87; pres., CEO Adminstrv. Claims Svcs./North Am. Adminstrs., 1987—2000; v.p., client svcs. Employee Benefit Svcs., Inc., 2000—01; pres., owner Taylor Benefit Resources, Inc., 2001—; mem. Dist. 173 Ga. House of Representatives, 2011—. Republican. Office: 100 Town Ct Thomasville GA 31792 also: Georgia House of Reps 501 Coverdell Legis Office Bldg Atlanta GA 30334 Office Phone: 229-226-9943, 404-656-0177. Business E-Mail: darlene.taylor@house.ga.gov.

TAYLOR, DAVID H., corporate financial executive; BA in Bus. Adminstrn. & Acctg., Furman U. Sr. mng. dir. FTI Palladium Ptnrs.; exec. v.p., CFO Guilford Mills, Inc., 2002—05; treas. Eddie Bauer LLC; interim CFO Eddie Bauer Holdings, Inc., 2006—07; exec. v.p., fin. and planning, CFO, bd. dirs. Lorillard, Inc., 2008—. Office: Lorillard Inc 714 Green Valley Rd Greensboro NC 27408-7018 Office Phone: 336-335-7000. Office Fax: 336-335-7550. Business E-Mail: dtaylor@lortobco.com.

TAYLOR, DWAYNE L., state legislator; b. Daytona Beach, Fla., Nov. 13, 1967; children: Dwayne Jr., D'Ambra. AS, Daytona State Coll.; BS, U. Central Fla. Commr. City of Daytona Beach, 2003—08; mem. Dist. 27 Fla. House of Reps, 2008—, ranking mem. health care svcs. policy com., mem. gen. govt. policy coun., ins., bus. and fin. affairs policy com., joint legis. auditing com., roads, bridges and ports policy com. Trustee Daytona Beach Police & Fire Pension Bd.; vice chmn. Volusia/Flagler MPO, 2007—08; chmn. East Volusia Regional Water Authority Oversight Com., 2008. Mem.: Fla. Black Caucus Local Elected Officials (first v.p. 2006—08), Volusia League of Cities, Nat. League of Cities, Fla. League of Cities, Leadership Fla. (Class X). Democrat. Office: Capitol Office 402 S Monroe St Rm 1401 Tallahassee FL 32399-1300 also: 732 Orange Ave Daytona Beach FL 32114-4773 Office Phone: 850-488-0580, 386-239-6202. Business E-Mail: dwayne.taylor@myfloridahouse.gov.

TAYLOR, FRANCIS MICHAEL, auditor, municipal official; b. Munich, 1960; came to the U.S., 1961; BS, Va. Tech., 1982. CPA Va., cert. internal auditor. Pub. acct. Brown, Edwards, Co., Roanoke, Va., 1982-84; controller ARC Roanoke, Inc., Roanoke, 1984-87; audit supr. City of Roanoke, 1987-94; city auditor City of Stockton (Calif.), 1994—. Nat. coord. com. Key Nat. Indicators Initiative; GAO adv. coun. Govt. Auditing Standard. Mem. AICPA, Assn. Local Govt. Auditors (past chair peer review com., past pres.), Calif. Soc. CPAs, Inst. Internal Auditors, Bay Area Local Govt. Auditors, Brookside Country Club (mem. fin. com.).

TAYLOR, GEORGE B., JR., lawyer, electric power industry executive; BEE, Ga. Inst. Tech., 1975, MSEE, 1976; MBA, Ga. State U., 1984, JD, 1994. Bar: Ga. 1995. Planning engr. Oglethorpe Power Corp., Tucker, Ga., 1976—79, sec. mgr., Power Supply, 1979—84, dept. mgr., Power Contracts, 1984—86, sr. negotiator, 1986—92, mgr., Regulatory Compliance, 1992—96, legal advisor to CEO, 1996—2003, v.p., 2003—05, sr. v.p., strategic initiatives, 2005—. Office: Oglethorpe Power Corp PO Box 1349 2100 E Exchange Pl Tucker GA 30085-1349 Office Phone: 770-270-7600. E-mail: george.taylor@opc.com.

TAYLOR, GEORGE KIMBROUGH, JR., lawyer; b. Atlanta, Aug. 28, 1939; s. George Kimbrough and Helen Whiteside (Shepard) T.; m. Carol Ann McKinney, July 1, 1961 (div. 1976); children: George Kimbrough III, Thomas Haynes; m. Triska Ashley Drake, Oct. 2, 1981. BA, Emory U., 1961; LLB, U. Va., 1964. Bar: Ga. 1964, U.S. Dist. Ct. (no. dist.) Ga. 1964, U.S. Ct. Appeals (11th cir.) 1964. Assoc. Kilpatrick & Cody, Atlanta, 1964-70, ptnr., 1970-96, Kilpatrick Stockton LLP (formerly Kilpatrick & Cody), 1997—2010; sr. counsel Kilpatrick Townsend & Stockton LLP (formerly Kilpatrick Stockton). Bd. dirs. Ont. Reins. Co. Ltd., Atlanta; chmn., bd. dirs. MFI Am., Inc., Atlanta, 2003—06. Chmn. bd. dirs. Spl. Audiences, Inc., Atlanta, 1985-87; bd. dirs. Atlanta Symphony Orch., 1986—; trustee Woodruff Arts Ctr., Atlanta, 1997—; bd. dirs. Atlanta Opera, 1995—, Ga. Humanities Coun., Atlanta, 1986-93, Ga. Conservancy, 1979-85; bd. dirs. Ga. Trust for Hist. Preservation, 2002—, vice chair, 2004-2008; chair 2008-11; bd. dirs. Ga. Coun. Internat. Visitors, Atlanta, 1987-94, pres., 1993; bd. dirs. Brit.-Am. Bus. Group, 1989-95, pres., 1994; bd. visitors Emory U., Atlanta, 1993-96, Brit.-Am. Bus. Coun., 1997—, chmn. 1997-98; mem. alumni coun. U. Va. Law Sch., 1995-98; active Leadership Atlanta. Woodrow Wilson fellow, 1961. Mem. ABA, Internat. Bar Assn., Atlanta Bar Assn., Order of Coif, Soc. Internat. Bus. Fellows, Capital City Club, Phi Beta Kappa, Omicron Delta Kappa. Democrat. Avocations: sailing, skiing. Office: Kilpatrick Townsend & Stockton LLP 1100 Peachtree St NE Ste 2800 Atlanta GA 30309-4530 Office Phone: 404-815-6500. Business E-Mail: ktaylor@kilpatricktownsend.com.

TAYLOR, HAROLD ALLEN, JR., industrial minerals consultant; b. San Jose, Calif., June 27, 1936; s. Harold Allen and Marie Anna (Briody) T.; m. Theresa Josephine Kustritz, Aug. 29, 1963; children: Harold Allen III, Ruth F., Jonathan L.E. BA, Brown U., 1958; MA, U. Minn., 1968. Project leader Office Mineral Supply, U.S. Bur. Mines, Mpls., 1968-70, commodity specialist divsn. ferrous metals Washington, 1970-74; commodity analyst U.S. internat. Trade Commn., Washington, 1974-80; sr. commodity specialist br. indsl. minerals U.S. Bur. Mines, Washington, 1980-95; pres. Basics Mines, Summit Point, W.Va., 1995—. Pub., editor Dimension Stone Advocate News, Graphite Advocate News, Bismuth Advocate News, Indium Advocate News, 2000-, Compendium of World Dimension Stone Data, 2009; contbr. articles to profl. jours. & to stone-related wikis on Wikipedia. Pres. Arlington (Va.) Interfaith Coun., 1994, 95. Mem. AIME (sec 1983-84, 1st vice chmn. 1984-85, chmn. 1985-86, exec. adv. bd. mineral econs. subsect. 1981-83, 87-91), ASTM (chmn. subcom. nomenclature of com. on dimension stone 1987-2004, sec. of com. 1990-95), Soc. Govt. Economists (chmn. materials policy panels, 1979-84), Capitol Metals Forum (steering com. 1979-85), Toastmasters (pres. 1978, 81, 87, 91, asst. area gov. 1978-79, area gov. 1979-80, dep. divsn. lt. gov. 1989-90), Sigma Gamma Epsilon Address: PO Box 185 Summit Point WV 25446-0185 Office Phone: 304-725-6619. E-mail: bmhtayl@earthlink.net.

TAYLOR, IVY R., councilwoman; BA, Yale U., 1992; M in City and Regional Planning, U. NC, Chapel Hill, 1998. With Housing and Cmty. Devel. Dept., San Antonio, Neighborhood Action Dept., San Antonio; v.p. Merced Housing Tex.; councilwoman, Dist. 2 San Antonio City Coun., 2009—. Mem. San Antonio Planning Commn.; commr. San Antonio Urban Renewal Agency; lectr. pub. adminstrn. program U. Tex., San Antonio, 2009—. Adv. bd. mem. Ctr. for Women in Ch. and Soc., Our Lady of the Lake; bd. mem. Martinez St. Women's Ctr., Haven for Hope. Named a Rising Star, San Antonio Bus. Jour., 2004. Office: 4458 E Houston St San Antonio TX 78220 also: City Hall PO Box 839966 San Antonio TX 78283 Office Phone: 210-207-0950. E-mail: district2@sanantonio.gov.

TAYLOR, JACKIE A., educational association administrator; 1 child. PhD candidate, U. Tenn. Coll. Edn., Health & Human Sciences. Tchr. Families First welfare reform program, Nashville; rsch. assoc. U. Tenn. Ctr. Literacy Studies, Knoxville, 2001—. Chmn. Assn. Adult Literacy Profl. Developers. Recipient Literacy Leadership award, Nat. Coalition Literacy, 2006. Office: Ctr Literacy Studies Ste 312 600 Henley St Knoxville TN 37996 Office Fax: 865-974-3857. E-mail: jataylor@utk.edu.

TAYLOR, JERRY, state legislator; b. Rison, Ark., Oct. 9, 1937; m to Linda; children: Pam & Kelly. Ret. land surveyor & real estate broker; alderman City of Pine Bluff, Ark., 1980—92, mayor, 1992—2000; mem. Dist. 10 Ark. House of Reps., 2001—04; mem. Dist 23 Ark. State Senate, 2005—. Democrat. Baptist. Home: 4591 Shoal Creek Dr Benton AR 72019-8266 Office Phone: 870-879-3233. Office Fax: 870-535-7970. Business E-Mail: taylorj@ark.leg.state.ar.us.

TAYLOR, JIMMY LYNN, retired family practice physician, administrator; b. Franklin County, NC, May 11, 1936; s. Herman Benjamin and Ruby Lynn (Perry) T.; m. Dorothy Keenum, Sept. 4, 1960; children: Gregory Scott, Sonya Lynn Taylor Loper. AA, Mars Hill Coll., 1956; BS, Wake Forest U., 1958; MD, Wake Forest U. Sch. Medicine, 1962. Postdoctoral fellow Greenville (S.C.) Gen. Hosp., 1962-63; staff physician USPHS Indian Hosp., Pine Ridge, SD, 1963-65, chief of obstetrics, 1964-65; family physician, co-founder Monroe (N.C.) Family Med. Ctr., 1965, family physician, ptnr., 1965-95; student physician Wingate (N.C.) U., 1987-94; med. dir. Brian Ctr. Nursing Facility, Monroe, 1992-95. H.S. team physician, 1965—75. Lt. comdr. USPHS, 1963-65. Recipient Head Start Child Care Achievement award N.C. Head Start Assn., 1990. Fellow Am. Acad. Family Physicians; mem. Am. Bd. Family Practice (diplomate), N.C. Acad. Family Physicians, N.C. Med. Soc., Union County Med. Soc. (pres. 1976-77). Republican. Baptist. Avocations: golf, fishing, gardening, bridge, collecting autographed first edition books. Home: 1657 Pageland Hwy Monroe NC 28112-8737 Office: Monroe Family Med Ctr 5231 John Tyler Hwy Williamsburg VA 23185-2553 Personal E-mail: jtaylor28112@yahoo.com, jtaylor6@carolina.rr.com.

TAYLOR, LARRY, state legislator; b. June 25; m. Kerri Taylor; children: Trudy, Carly, Jake. BBA, Baylor U., 1982. Owner Truman Taylor Ins. Agency, Friendswood; mem. Dist. 24 Tex. House of Representatives, Tex., 2002—. Republican. Office: 174 Calder Rd Ste 116 League City TX 77573 also: Room E2.322 Capital Extension PO Box 2910 Austin TX 78768 Office Phone: 281-338-0924, 512-463-0729. Office Fax: 281-554-9240, 512-474-2398.

TAYLOR, LAWRENCE A., science educator; BS in Chemistry, Ind. U., MS in Geography; PhD in Geology and Material Scis., Lehigh U. Postdoc. fellow Carnegie Inst. Wash., 1968—70; fullbright fellow & humboldt stiftung Max-Plant-Inst. Kemphysik, Heidelburg, 1970—71; asst. prof. dept. geosci. Purdue U. W Lafayette, 1971—73; assoc. prof. dept. geol. sci. U. Tenn., Knoxville, 1973—77, prof. dept. geol. sci., 1977—, dir. planetary geosci., 1993—. Office: Dept Geol Sci Planetary Geosci Inst Univ Tenn 402 GS Bldg Knoxville TN 37996 Office Phone: 865-974-6013. Office Fax: 865-974-6022. E-mail: lataylor@utk.edu.

TAYLOR, LYNDON CLINT, lawyer, energy executive; b. Lawton, Okla., June 9, 1958; s. Clinton Harold and Doris Lee (Nance) T. BS of Indsl. Engring., Okla. State U., 1981; JD, U. Okla., 1984. Bar: Okla. 1984, U.S. Dist. Ct. (we. dist.) Okla. 1985, D.C. 1986. Assoc. Watson & McKenzie, Okla. City, 1984-86; assoc. through mng. ptnr. energy practice Skadden, Arps, Slate, Meagher & Flom LLP, Houston, 1986—2005; dep. gen. counsel Devon Energy Corp., Okla. City, 2005—07, exec. v.p., gen. counsel, 2007—. Republican. Avocation: golf. Office: Devon Energy Corp 333 W Sheridan Ave Oklahoma City OK 73102-5010*

TAYLOR, NICOLE RENÉE (NIKI TAYLOR), model, shop owner; b. Miami, Fla., Mar. 5, 1975; d. Ken and Barbara Taylor; m. Matt Martinez (div. 1996); children: Jake Martinez, Hunter Martinez; m. Burney Lamar, Dec. 27, 2006; children: Ciel Taylor Lamar, Rex Harrison Lamar. With Tri Star Sports and Entertainment Group, Brentwood, 2006—; owner Abbie and Jesse's, Cool Springs, Tenn., 2006—, Franklin, Tenn., 2006—. Contracts with L'Oreal, 1990-92, Cover Girl Makeup, Liz Claiborne, Gap, Pantene; appeared in Seventeen (cover girl) 1989, Vogue, Elle, Mademoiselle, Harper's Bazaar; modeled for Yves Saint Laurent, Karl Lagerfeld; modeled swimsuit Sports Illus., 1997, cover Sports Illus. Calendar, 1998; co-host, Make Me a Supermodel, 2008. Founder Begin Found. for Advancement of Women in Business. Named to 50 Most Beautiful People, People mag., 1991. Achievements include appearing on over 320 magazine covers worldwide; youngest model to appear on the cover of Vogue; holds the world record for being the youngest model to receive a six figure deal. Office: TriStar Entertainment Group Suite 200 1222 16th Ave S FL 3 Nashville TN 37212-2926 Office Phone: 615-309-0969. Business E-Mail: tristar@tristarse.com.

TAYLOR, PEYTON TROY, JR., oncologist, educator; b. Tuscaloosa, Ala., July 21, 1941; s. Peyton Troy, Sr. and Frances (Sutter) Taylor; m. Helena Ström, Sept. 23, 1967; children: Annika, Karin, Sarah. BS, U. Ala., 1963, MS, 1968; MD, Med. Coll. Ala., 1968. Intern U. Va. Hosp., Charlottesville, 1968-69, resident, 1969-70, 72-75; asst. prof. ob-gyn. U. Va., Charlottesville, 1976-79, assoc. prof., dir. divsn. ob-gyn. Health Scis. Ctr., 1981-87, Richard N. and Louise R. Crockett prof., 1987—2011, Richard N. and Louise R. Crockett prof. emeritus, 2012—, med. dir. Cancer Ctr. Charlottesville, 1996—2008, dep. med. dir. Cancer Ctr., 2008—11, emeritus, 2012—; clin. assoc. surgery Nat. Cancer Inst., Bethesda, Md., 1970-72; cons. prof. ob-gyn. Duke U., Moshi, Tanzania, 2012—. Assoc. prof. U. Ala., Birmingham, 1979—81. Contbr. articles to profl. jours. With USPHS, 1970—72. Recipient Disting. Alumnus, U. Ala. Med. Alumni Assn., 2000. Fellow: ACS, Am. Coll. Obstetricians and Gynecologists; mem.: So. Surg. Assn., Internat. Gynecol. Cancer Soc., Am. Assn. Cancer Rsch., Am. Soc. Clin. Oncology, Soc. Surg. Oncology, Soc. Gynecol. Oncologists, Assn. Acad. Surgeons. Episcopalian. Avocations: sports, travel. Office Phone: 434-924-9933. Personal E-mail: pttivy@aol.com. Business E-Mail: peyton.taylor@virginia.edu. E-mail: peyton.taylor@dm.duke.edu.

TAYLOR, PHILIP RAYMOND, lawyer; b. Dublin, Ga., Nov. 1, 1933; s. Evan Augustus and Eula Bush Taylor; children: Emily Taylor Fendig, Lester Taylor Odachowski. AB, Mercer U., Macon, Ga., 1955, JD, 1957. Bar: Ga. Ptnr. Harris, Watkins, Taylor & Davis, Macon, Ga., 1958—80, Fendig, McLemore, Taylor, Whitworth & Durham, Brunswick, Ga., 1980—2001; sr. ptnr. Taylor, Odachowski, Schmidt & Crossland, St. Simons, Ga., 2001—. Bd. visitors Mercer U. Law Sch., Macon, Ga., 1998—2004, chmn. bd. visitors, 2002—04. Mem. editl. bd Mercer Law Rev., 1956—57. Mem. Ga. State Ho. of Reps., Atlanta, 1961—62; chmn. Macon-Bibb County Dem. Exec. Com., Macon, Ga., 1964—68, Macon-Bibb County Bd. of Elections, Macon, Ga., 1969—80. Capt. USAR, 1962—78. Fellow: Am. Coll. Trial Lawyers, Am. Bd. Trial Lawyers; mem.: ABA, Am. Acad. Healthcare Attys., Def. Rsch. Inst., Ga. Acad. Healthcare Attys., Brunswick-Glynn County Bar Assn., Ga. Def. Lawyers Assn. (bd. dirs. 1967), Delta Theta Phi. Avocations: travel, fishing, hunting. Office: Taylor Odachowski Schmidt & Crossland 300 Oak St Saint Simons Island GA 31522 Office Phone: 912-634-0955. Business E-Mail: ptaylor@toslaw.com.

TAYLOR, PRISCILLA ANN, county official; b. Dec. 31, 1949; children: Vita, Sean. BS, Barry U., Miami Shores, Fla., 1997; MBA, Palm Beach Atlantic U., Fla., 1999. Owner, ins. agency; mem. Dist. 84 Fla. House of Reps., Tallahassee, 2004—10, Dem. whip, 2004—06; commr. Dist. 7 Palm Beach County. Chairwoman Port of Palm Beach Commn.; commr. Port of Palm Beach. Southeast dist. gov. Nat. Assn. Negro Bus. and Profl. Women; bd. mem. Columbia Hosp., Criminal Justice Commn., Epilepsy Found., Workforce, Urban League. Democrat. Episcopalian. Office: Palm Beach County 301 N Olive Ave Ste 1201 West Palm Beach FL 33401 Office Phone: 561-355-2207. E-mail: ptaylor@pbcgov.org.

TAYLOR, RASHAD, state legislator; b. Mar. 21; Pub. rels. cons.; mem. Dist. 55 Ga. House of Reps., 2009—. Democrat. Office: 509 Coverdell Legislative Office Bldg Atlanta GA 30334 Home: PO Box 11078 Atlanta GA 30310-0078 Office Phone: 404-656-0220. Business E-Mail: rashadjtaylor@gmail.com.

TAYLOR, RAYMOND MASON, lawyer, educator, former government official; b. Washington, NC, Jan. 1, 1933; s. Thaddeus Raymond and Mary Ada (Mason) T.; m. Rachel High; 1 dau., Elizabeth Lee Taylor Garber (Mrs. Kenneth Richard Garber). AB, U. NC-Chapel Hill, 1955, JD, 1960. Cert. law librarian Am. Assn. Law Libraries, 1968. Bar: NC 1960, US Dist. Ct. (ea. dist.) NC 1960, US Supreme Ct. 1970, US Ct. Appeals (4th, 5th, 6th, 7th, 8th and 9th cirs.) 1977, US Ct. Internat. Trade 1978, US Ct. Appeals (11th cir.) 1981, US Ct. Appeals (DC cir.) 1983, US Ct. Mil. Appeals 1983. Staff reporter Washington Daily News, NC, 1952, 54; adminstrv. asst. CD, Winston-Salem and Forsyth County, NC, 1955; adminstrv. intern City of Winston-Salem, 1958; rsch. asst. Assoc. Justice NC Supreme Ct., Raleigh, 1960-61; assoc. Gardner, Connor & Lee, Wilson, NC, 1961-64; adj. instr. bus. law Atlantic Christian Coll. (now Barton Coll.), Wilson, 1962-63, adj. prof., 1963-64; marshal, librarian NC Supreme Ct., 1964-77; sole practice Raleigh, NC, 1977—81, 1983—84, 1988—. Asst. US atty., chief of appellate sect. Eastern Dist. NC, 1981-82; supt. documents of US, asst. pub. printer of US, assoc. gen. counsel US GPO, Washington, 1982-83; ptnr. Hall, Hill, O'Donnell, Taylor, Manning & Shearon, 1985-87; vis. lectr. econs. and bus. law NC State U., Raleigh, 1967-85; project dir. Fed. Jud. Ctr. Study of Fed. Ct. Libraries, 1976-77; dir. NC Law Research Facilities Study, 1970; chmn. State and Ct. Law Libraries of the US and Can., 1973-74; mem. Info. Industry Coun. to Pub. Printer of US, 1981-83. Author: Federal Court Libraries, 1981. Mem., sec. southeastern area coun. Am. Jr. Red Cross, 1949-50, internat. study visitor, Europe, 1950; chmn. Parents' Day Campbell U., 1979, chmn. Parents Fund, 1981-82; mem. Wake County Libr. Commn., 1979-81. Served with CIC, US Army, 1955-57. Recipient NC Soc. County and Local Historians award, 1955, Tar Heel of Week award, 1971, Excellence award Soc. Tech. Communication, 1976. Mem. ABA, NC Bar Assn. (chmn. legis. com. elder law sect. 2002-03), Nat. Acad. Elder Law Attys. (state coord. 1991-95), SCV, Order Golden Fleece (pres. 1958-59), West Raleigh Rotary (pres. 1992-93, Paul Harris fellow 1992, Holoman Disting. Svc. award 1997), Pi Sigma Alpha, Phi Delta Phi, Omicron Delta Kappa, NC Supreme Ct. Hist. Soc. (trustee 1999-), Golden Tar Heel Soc. Carolina Law. Home: 3073 Granville Dr Raleigh NC 27609-6917

TAYLOR, RHONDA M., lawyer; B in Polit. Sci., Birmingham-Southern Coll., 1989; JD, U. Va., 1992. With Stokes & Bartholomew, Nashville, Ford & Harrison, Memphis; atty., labor law and employment litigation dept. Ogletree, Deakins, Nash, Smoak & Stewart, 1997—2000; employment atty. Dollar General Corp., 2000—01, sr. employment atty., 2001—04, dep. gen. counsel, 2004—10, v.p., asst. gen. counsel, 2010—13, sr. v.p., gen. counsel, 2013—. Mem.: Tenn. Bar Assn. Office: Dollar General Corporation 100 Mission Ridge Goodlettsville TN 37072 Office Phone: 615-855-5151.*

TAYLOR, ROBERT BROWN, physician, educator, writer; s. Olaf C. Taylor and Elizabeth (Place) Brown; m. Anita Dopico; children: Diana Taylor Root, Sharon Taylor Oliverio. Student in science, Bucknell U., Lewisburg, Pa, 1954-57; MD, Temple U., Phila., Pa., 1961. Diplomate Am. Bd. Family Medicine. Gen. practice medicine, New Paltz, NY, 1964-78; faculty physician Sch. Medicine Wake Forest U., Winston-Salem, NC, 1978-84; prof. dept. family medicine Oreg. Health Scis. U. Sch. Medicine, Portland, 1984—, chmn., 1984-98, prof. emeritus family medicine, 1998—. Mem. comprehensive part II com. Nat. Bd. Med. Examiners, Phila., 1986-91. Author: Common Problems in Office Practice, 1972, A Primer of Clinical Symptoms, 1973, The Practical Art of Medicine, 1974; editor: Family Medicine: Principles and Practice, 1978, 6th edit., 2003, Health Promotion: Principles and Clinical Applications, 1982, Difficult Diagnosis, 1985, Difficult Medical Management, 1991, Difficult Diagnosis II, 1992, Fundamentals of Family Medicine, 1996, 3rd edit, 2003, Manual of Family Practice, 1997, 2d edit., 2002, Taylor's Review of Family Medicine, 1998, Manual of Ten-Minute Diagnosis, 2000, The Clinician's Guide to Medical Writing, 2004, Taylor's Diagnostic and Therapeutic Challenges, 2005, Taylor's Cardiovascular Diseases, 2006, Academic Medicine: A Guide for Clinicians, 2006, Taylor's Musculoskeletal Problems and Injuries, 2006, White Coat Tales: Medicine's Heroes, Heritage and Misadventures, 2008, Medical Wisdom and Doctoring: The Art of 21st Century Practice, 2010, Essential Medical Facts Every Clinician Should Know, 2011, Diagnostic Principles and Applications, 2013; contbg. editor Physicians Mgmt. Mag., 1972-99; editl. bd. Family Practice Research Jour., 1980-90, Female Patient, 1984-2006, American Family Physician, 1990-98, Jour. Family Practice, 1990-93, Med. Tribune, 1993-99.

Served as surgeon USPHS, 1961-64. Recipient Outstanding Sci. Paper award, American Acad. Family Physicians, 1982, Certificate of Excellence, Soc. Teachers Family Med., 1989, J. David Bristow MD award, Oreg. Health Scis. U., 1993, John G. Walsh Lifetime Achievement award, 2003, F. Marian Bishop Leadership award, Soc. Tchrs. Family Medicine Found., 2007, Disting Faculty award, Oreg. Health Scis. U., 2010. Fellow Am. Acad. Family Physicians (sci. program com., Thomas W. Johnson award 1998, bd. curators found. archives, John G. Walsh Lifetime Achievement award 2003, Outstanding Sci. Paper award 1982); mem. Soc. Tchrs. Family Medicine (bd. dirs., Cert. Excellence 1989), Assn. Am. Med. Colls., World Orgn. Family Doctors (chmn. sci. program com.), Phi Beta Kappa (award 1957), Alpha Omega Alpha (award 1961). Avocations: medical writing, editing. Office: 3100 Shore Dr Ste 941 Virginia Beach VA 23451-7318 Business E-Mail: taylorr@ohsu.edu.

TAYLOR, ROBERT LEWIS, management consultant; b. Pitts., Dec. 10, 1939; s. Robert William and Elinor (Miller) T.; m. Linda Taylor Shapiro, Oct. 28, 1988; 1 step child, Kara; children by previous marriage: Rob, Mike. AB in Am. Studies, cum laude, Allegheny Coll., 1961; MBA, Ohio State U., 1966; D in Bus. Adminstrn., Mgmt., Ind. U., 1972. Asst. prof., dir. rsch. USAF Acad., Colorado Springs, Colo., 1971-77, assoc. prof., dir. instrn. dept. econ., geography, mgmt., 1977-79, prof. mgmt., head dept. econs., geography, mgmt., 1980-81; assoc. dean Coll. Letters and Sci., head div. Bus. and Econs., Carl N. Jacobs Prof. of Bus. U. Wis., Stevens Point, 1981-84; dean Coll. Bus. Pub. Adminstrn. U. Louisville, 1984—2003, dean emeritus and prof. of mgmt., 2003—12; sr. cons. Oliver Group La., Ky., 2012—. Chmn. bd. dirs. Ky. Wood Floors, Louisville, 1988-98; bd chair AACSB: Internat., Tampa, Fla., 1999-2000; bd. advisors Rawlings Co., Louisville; bd. dirs. Stock Yards Bancorp, 2003-10; cons., advisor Kellogg Nat. Fellowship Program, Kellogg Found., Battle Creek, Mich., 1985-89; bd. dirs. Innovative Productivity Inc., La. Ky., 2007-12. Co-editor: Contemporary Issues in Leadership, 1984, 6th edit., 2006, 7th edit. 2012, Leadership Challenges for Today's Manager, 1988, Military Leadership: In Pursuit of Excellence, 6th edit., 2009; contbr. articles to profl. jours Chmn. Mayor's Strategic Planning Group, Louisville, 1986—; mem. Gov.'s Econ. Devel. Com., Frankfort, Ky., 1987-89, exec. com. Bus. Advs., 1988-92, task force on econ. devel. Ky. Legis. Rsch. Coun., 1991, Leadership Louisville, 1986, Leadership Ky., 1987; bd. dirs. Metro United Way, 1999—, Ctr. Nonprofit Excellence, 2005—12, Louisville Public Media, 2006—; bd. trustees Jewish Hosp. Healthcare Svcs., Louisville, 2000—07; active St. Michael Orthodox Ch., mem., Parish Coun., 2010-12. Lt. col. USAF, 1961—81. Mem. Acad. Mgmt. (proceedings editor 1976-77, newsletter editor 1983-86), Louisville C. of C. (bd. dirs., exec. com 1990-94), Sigma Xi, Beta Gamma Sigma, Pi Gamma Mu. Democrat. Avocations: travel, stamp collecting/philately, exercise, reading. Home: 1516 Sylvan Way Louisville KY 40205-2408 Personal E-mail: rltayl01@gmail.com. Business E-Mail: btaylor@olivergroup.com.

TAYLOR, ROWAN H., food products executive; Counsel Alston & Jones, Jackson, Miss., First Am. Title Ins. Co., Santa Ana, Calif.; adv. dir. Trustmark Corp.; pres. Miss. Valley Title Ins. Co., 1975—89, chmn., CEO, 1989—92; adv. dir. Trustmark Nat. Bank, Jackson, Miss., 1995. Bd. dirs. Sanderson Farms, Inc., 1989—. Office: Sanderson Farms Inc 127 Flynt Rd Laurel MS 39440 Office Phone: 601-649-4030. Office Fax: 601-426-1461. Business E-Mail: rtaylor@sandersonfarms.com.

TAYLOR, STEVEN W., state supreme court justice; b. Henryetta, Okla., June 7, 1949; m. Mary Taylor; 1 child. BA in Polit. sci., Okla. State U., 1971; JD, U. Okla. Coll. Law, 1974. Atty. Gotcher, Gotcher & Taylor, Okla., 1978—84; councilman McAlester City, 1980—82, mayor, 1982—84; judge Okla. Dist. Ct., 1984—94; dist. judge, chief judge 18th Jud. Dist., 1994—2004; presiding judge E. Ctrl. Jud. Adminstrv. dist., 1997—2003; justice Okla. Supreme Ct., Oklahoma City, 2004—, vice chief justice, 2009—10, chief justice, 2011—12. Pres. Okla. Jud. Conf., 1990. Mem. bd. dirs. Okla. Heritage Assn., Okla. Med. Rsch. Found. Served atty. & judge USMC, 1970—78. Named to Hall of Fame, Okla., 2009. Mem.: Pittsburg County Bar Assn., Okla. Bar Assn. (Jud. Excellence award 2003, Outstanding Okla. Judge of Yr. 2003). Office: Oklahoma Supreme Ct Okla Judicial Ctr 2100 N Lincoln Blvd Ste 4 Oklahoma City OK 73105-4907 Office Phone: 405-521-3844. Business E-Mail: steven.taylor@oscn.net.*

TAYLOR, SUSAN L., former magazine editor, philanthropist; b. NYC, Jan. 23, 1946; d. Lawrence and Violet (Weekes) Taylor; m. William Bowles (div.); 1 child, Shana Nequai; m. Khephra Burns, 1989. BA in Sociology, Fordham U., 1991; doctorate (hon.), Spelman Coll., Bennett Coll., U. Del., Fisk U., Lincoln U., Dillard U. Founder, rschr., developer, pres. Nequai Cosmetics, 1970—72; freelance writer, beauty editor Essence Mag., NYC, 1970—71, fashion, beauty editor, 1971—80, editor-in-chief, 1980—2000, editl. dir., 2000—08; founder, dir. Nat. Cares Mentoring Movement (formerly Essence Cares Initiative), 2006—. Exec. prodr. and host to exec. coord., v.p. TV prog. Essence Essence Comm. Inc. Author: In the Spirit: The Inspirational Writings of Susan L. Taylor, 1993, Lessons in Living, 1995; co-author (with husband Khephra Burns): Confirmation: The Spiritual Wisdom That Has Shaped Our Lives, 1997; contbr. articles to mags.; exec. prodr.: Essence Awards and Essence Music Festival; spkr. in field. Mem. rsch. com. in black edn. Assn. Ednl. Rsch.; co-chair Danny Glover for Shared Interest (to raise money to build housing in rural areas of S. Africa); bd. dir. Joint Ctr. for Polit. and Econ. Studies, Washington; mem. adv. bd. Black Adminstr. in Child Welfare; mem. La. Recovery Authority. Recipient Henry Johnson Fisher award, 1998, President's award, NAACP Image award, 2006; named to Power 150, Ebony mag., 2008. Mem.: Women in Comm. (Matrix award), Am. Soc. Mag. Editors (inducted into Hall of Fame 2002), Nat. Assn. Black Journalists. Office: Nat Cares Mentoring Movement PO Box 56129 Atlanta GA 30343-0129 Office Phone: 404-584-2744. Office Fax: 404-525-6222.

TAYLOR, TOM, marketing executive; Assoc. Outside Garden Dept. Home Depot, Inc., Miami, dept. head, asst. store mgr. to mgr., dist. mgr., regional v.p., S.W. Divsn., 1996, merchandising v.p., N.W. Divsn., 1999, divsn. pres., N.W., 1999, sr. v.p., PRO Bus., 2001—02, pres., Ea. Divsn., 2002—05, exec. v.p., Home Depot stores, 2002—05, exec. v.p. merchandising and mktg. Atlanta, 2005—06, cons., 2006—. Named one of Top 20 Southerners to Watch, The Fin. Times, 2003. Office: Home Depot Inc 2455 Paces Ferry Rd NW Atlanta GA 30339-4024 Office Phone: 770-433-8211. Office Fax: 770-384-2356.

TAYLOR, TOM, state legislator; b. Boca Raton, Fla., Feb. 20; m. Wendi Taylor; 1 child, Keith. B in Internat. Rels. & Economics, Ga. State U., MBA in Internat. Bus. Sr. mgmt. positions DynCorp Internat., Rockwell Internat. Tactical Sys., AT&T; city councilman City of Dunwoody, 2008—10; mem. Dist. 79 Ga. House of Representatives, 2011—. Served with USN. Republican. Office: 4926 Four Oaks Ct Dunwoody GA 30360 also: Georgia House of Reps 401 Coverdell Legis Office Bldg Atlanta GA 30334 Office Phone: 404-656-0152. Business E-Mail: tom.taylor@house.ga.gov.

TAYLOR, TOMMY, state legislator; Mem. Dist. 28 Miss. House of Reps., Jackson, 2012—. Served with US Armed Forces, Vietnam. Republican. Office: Miss House of Reps PO Box 1018 Jackson MS 39215 Business E-Mail: ttaylor@house.ms.gov.

TAYLOR, WENDY HALL, auditor; b. Cohasset, Mass., Oct. 1, 1959; d. Robert Sterling and Barbara Ruth (Sparks) Hall; m. James Allen Taylor, Nov. 28, 1986. Student, Salem Coll., 1977-79; BS in Acctg., U. N.C., Greensboro, 1987. CPA, N.C. Staff auditor Deloitte & Touche, Greensboro, N.C., 1987-90, sr. auditor Winston Salem, N.C., 1990-93, audit mgr., 1993—2000, ptnr. enterprise risk services Charlotte, NC, 2000—10; v.p. internal audit Goodrich Corp., Charlotte, NC, 2010—. Mem. Leadership America N.C. Devel. Com., 2001. Mem. AICPA, Nominahons Com. (Blue Diamond award 2001). Democrat. Episcopalian. Avocation: golf. Office: Goodrich Corp Four Coliseum Centre 2730 W Tyvola Rd Charlotte NC 28217 Office Phone: 704-423-7000. Office Fax: 704-423-7002.

TEAFF, GRANT, sports association administrator; m. Donell Teaff; children: Tammy Bookbinder, Layne Pittman, Tracy. Attended, San Angelo Jr. Coll., Tex., 1951—53; BS in Phys. Edn., McMurry U., Abilene, Tex., 1956, MS in Adminstrv. Edn., 1957, HHD, 1975. Asst. football coach Lubbock HS, Tex., 1956; asst. football coach, head track coach McMurry U., 1957—59, head football coach, head track coach, 1960—65; asst. football coach, recruiting coord. Tex. Tech. U. Red Raiders, 1966—68; head football coach Angelo State U. Rams, Tex., 1969—71, Baylor U. Bears, 1972—92; athletic dir. Baylor U., 1992—93; exec. dir. Am. Football Coaches Assn., 1994—. Various com. appointments NCAA, 1982—; chmn. ethics com. Am. Football Coaches Assn., 1982—92, bd. trustees, 1987—92; mem. exec. com. NCAA Football; mem. bd. dirs. Football USA, Nat. Football Found., 1995—, SBC Cotton Bowl Classic, 1997—, Am. Sports Medicine Inst., 1997—, Football Fedn. USA, 1999—. Author: I Believe, Winning, Seasons of Glory, Coaching in the Classroom, Grant Teaff with the Master Coaches. Active Multiple Sclerosis Soc., Muscular Dystrophy Soc., Red Cross, Friends for Life, Camp Success; deacon, Sunday sch. tchr. First Bapt. Ch., Waco; mem. Downtown Waco Devel Bd. Recipient Achievement award, Football Writers Assn. America, 1993, Morris Frank Touchdowner of Yr. award, 1993, Gen. Robert R. Neyland Meml. award, 1993, Disting. Svc. award, Tex. HS Coaches Assn., Amos Alonzo Stagg award, Am. Football Coaches Assn., 2006; named Nat. Coach of Yr., 1974, Football Writers Assn. America, 1974, Six-time Coach of Yr., Southwest Conf., Alumnus Honoris Causa, Baylor Univ.; named one of Most Powerful Administrators in Coll. Athletics, The Sporting News, 2002, Most Influential People in Coll. Sports, Street & Smith's Sports Bus. Jour., 2004; named to Baylor Univ. Athletics Hall of Fame, 1993, Blue-Gray All-Star Football Classic Hall of Fame, 1993, Tex. Sports Hall of Fame, Southwest Conf. Hall of Honor, Coll. Football Hall of Fame, 2001. Mem.: Fellowship Christian Athletes. Office: Am Football Coaches Assn 100 Legends Ln Waco TX 76706 Office Phone: 254-754-9900. Office Fax: 254-754-7373.

TEAGUE, A. JAMES, energy executive; Mem., sr. mgmt. teams Shell Oil Co., MAPCO Inc.; pres., mktg. and trading MAPCO, Inc., 1997—98; pres. Tejas Natural Gas Liquids, LLC, 1998—99; exec. v.p. Enterprise Products GP, LLC, 1999—2010, chief comml. officer, 2008—10; exec. v.p., COO Enterprise Products Holdings LLC, 2010—. Bd. dirs. EPE Holdings, LLC (subs. Dan Duncan LLC), 2009—. Office: Enterprise Products Holdings LLC 10th Fl 1100 Louisiana St Houston TX 77002 Office Phone: 713-381-6500. Business E-Mail: ajteague@enterprisegp.com.

TEAGUE, LARRY, state legislator; b. Nashville, Ark. m. Debbie Teague; children: Larry Jr., Shelley. Attended, U. Ark., Texarkana Cmty. Coll. Asst. mgr. Skaggs Alpha Beta; owner & mgr. Teague & Teague Insurance Family, 1985—; alderman Nashville City Coun., Ark.; mem. Ark. House of Reps., 1996—2002; asst. to pres. pro tem. Senator Jim Hill, 2003; mem. Ark. State Senate from Dist. 20, 2008—. Mem. Hope-Hempstead County C. of C., Mena/Polk County C. of C., Murfreesboro C. of C. Bus.; mem. & former pres. Nashville C. of C.; bd. mem. Mine Creek Soil & Water Conservation Dist., Southwest Ark. Counseling; Sunday sch. tchr. & lay speaker First United Meth. Ch. Mem.: NRA (life), Mental Health Ctr. Ark. Cattlemen's Assn., Ark. Ind. Insurance Agents Assn. (bd. mem.), Delta Waterfowl, Ducks (life), Hempstead, Polk & Sevier County Dem. Women (assoc.), Rotary Internat. (former pres.). Democrat. Methodist. Office: State Capitol Rm 320 Little Rock AR 72201 also: PO Box 903 Nashville AR 71852 Office Phone: 501-682-2920, 501-682-6107, 870-845-5303. Business E-Mail: teaguel@arkleg.state.ar.us.

TEASLEY, SAM, state legislator; b. Cobb County, Ga., Apr. 29; m. Michelle Teasley; 3 children. Real estate broker Atlanta Communities Real Estate Brokerage; mem. Dist. 38 Ga. House of Representatives, 2009—. Republican. Office: PO Box 670051 Marietta GA 30066 also: Georgia House of Reps 501 Coverdell Legis Office Bldg Atlanta GA 30334 Office Phone: 404-656-0177. Business E-Mail: sam.teasley@house.ga.gov.

TEBBETTS, JOHN BERYL, plastic surgeon; b. Ruston, La., Nov. 9, 1946; BS, Tulane Univ., 1968; MD, Univ. Tex. Med. Branch, Galveston, 1972. Cert. Am. Bd. Gen. Surgery, 1978, Am. Bd. Plastic Surgery, 1980, lic. Tex., 1972, Wyo., 1987. Intern LDS Hosp., Salt Lake City, 1972—73; resident in surgery Univ. Utah Affiliated Hospitals, 1973—77; resident in plastic surgery Southwestern Med. Sch., Dallas, 1977—79; asst. clin. prof. in plastic surgery Southwestern Univ.; attending staff plastic surgery Mary Shiels Hosp., Baylor Univ. Med. Ctr., Longview Regional Hosp.; plastic surgeon Board Certified Surgery-Dallas. Contbr. articles to profl. jours.; co-author (with Terrye B. Tebbetts): The Best Breast. Recipient Ralph Millard award, Canadian Soc. for Aesthetic Plastic Surgery, 1994. Mem.: AMA, Am. Assn. Plastic Surgeons, Am. Coll. Surgeons, Am. Coll. Emergency Physicians, Am. Soc. Plastic & Reconstructive Surgery, Am. Cleft Palate Assn., Am. Soc. Aesthetic Plastic Surgery (Walter Scott Brown award 1984, 1990, Simon Fredericks award 1990), Tex. Soc. Plastic Surgeons, Tex. Med. Assn., Dallas Soc. Plastic Surgeons, Dallas County Med. Soc. Office: Board Certified Surgery-Dallas Ste W-300 2801 Lemmon Ave Dallas TX 75204 Office Phone: 972-220-2712, 888-888-8769. Office Fax: 214-969-0933.

TEDDER, THOMAS FLETCHER, immunology educator, researcher; b. Chateauroux, France, May 14, 1956; came to U.S. 1959; s. Raymond Percy and Barbara (Hagemann) T. AA, Okaloosa-Walton C.C., Niceville, Fla., 1976; BS with honors, U. Fla., 1978, MS, 1980; PhD, U. Ala., Birmingham, 1984. Rsch. fellow in pathology Harvard Med. Sch., Boston, 1984-85, instr. pathology, 1986-88, asst. prof. pathology, 1988-93; assoc. prof. pathology Harvard U. Med. Sch., Boston, 1993; prof. immunology Duke U. Med. Ctr., Durham, NC, 1993—, chmn. dept. immunology, 1993—. Alter Geller prof. rsch. in immunology Duke U. Med. Ctr., 1997—, founder, Collective Therapeutics, Inc.; co-founder Angelica Therapeutics, Inc.; cons. in field. Assoc. editor Jour. Immunology, 1989-93, sect. editor, 1993-98, dep. editor, 2004-08; contbr. numerous articles to med. jours., including Jour. Immunology, Nature, Cell, Lancet, Immunity. Recipient LeRoy Collins Disting. Alumnus award Fla. Assn. C.C.'s; named 25th Anniversary Disting. Alumnus, Okaloosa-Walton C.C., 1989; Damon Runyon-Walter Winchell rsch. fellow, 1985-87; scholar Leukemia Soc. Am., 1991-96, Stohlman scholar, 1995-96. Mem. Am. Soc. for Microbiology (Pres. fellow 1982), Am. Assn. Immunologists, Sigma Xi, Phi Kappa Phi. Achievements include identification and determination of structure and function of many human B lymphocyte cell-surface molecules. Office: Duke U Med Ctr Dept Immunology PO Box 3010 Durham NC 27710-0001 Office Phone: 919-684-3681. E-mail: thomas.tedder@duke.edu.

TEDFORD, JEFF (JEFFREY R. TEDFORD), professional football coach, former college football coach; b. Lynwood, Calif., Nov. 2, 1961; BS in Physical Edn., Fresno State U., 1983. Profl. football player Hamilton, Calgary, Saskatchewan, and Winnipeg, Can. Football League, 1983—87; vol. asst. coach Calif. State U. Fresno Bulldogs, 1987—88, quarterbacks coach, 1992—97; asst. coach Calgary Stampede, Can. Football League, 1989—91; offensive coord. U. Oreg. Ducks, 1998—2001, Tampa Bay Buccaneers, 2014—; head football coach U. Calif. Golden Bears, 2002—12. Named Pac-10 Coach of the Yr., 2002. Achievements include winning the Insight Bowl (2003), Las Vegas Bowl (2005); creating a team that earned the school's highest national ranking (No. 4) since 1952 and registered its best regular-season record (10-1) in 54 years. Office: Tampa Bay Buccaneers One Buccaneers Pl Tampa FL 33607*

TEEPEN, THOMAS HENRY, editor, journalist; b. Nashville, Jan. 19, 1935; s. Albert George and Elizabeth Blanche (Winfree) T.; m. Nancy Irene Roux, Feb. 2, 1957 (div. 1974); children— Kristina Lynn, Jeremy Roux; m. Sandra Jean Richards, May 14, 1975; 1 stepchild, Jennifer Koerlin BS in Journalism, Ohio U., Athens, 1957. Reporter Urbana (Ohio) Daily Citizen, 1957-58; asst. editor Kettering-Oakwood Times, Dayton, Ohio, 1958-59; from reporter to editorial writer Dayton Daily News, 1959-68, editorial page editor, 1968—82, Atlanta Constitution, 1982-92; nat. corr. Cox Newspapers, Atlanta, 1992-2000, columnist, 2000—09. Contbg. columnist Liberal Opinion Week; contbr. The Bluegrass Reader. Former pres. Joel Chandler Harris Assn., Atlanta; mem. Atlanta Opera, 1985—2009, Joint Internat. Observer Group, Ethiopian Elections, 1992; mem. internat. adv. com. The African-Am. Inst., N.Y.C., 1985-97; former bd. trustees Freedom to Read Found., Chgo; former Mayor's Cmty. Cultural Steering Com., Atlanta. Profl. journalism fellowship Stanford Univ. Calif., 1967, Writing award Ga. Press Assn., 1989, Ace award Women Comm., Ga., 1991, Best Editl. award United Press Internat., Ga.,1987, Human Rights award State Com. Life and History of Black Georgians, 1987, Civil Libertarian award Am. Civil Liberties Union Ga.,1989, Veterans Day award Friends of Andersonville and All Ex-POWs, 1990, award Anti-Defamation League, Commitment to Dem. Ideals, Atlanta, 2000 Mem.: Portofino Club (Atlanta). Home and Office: 900 Charles Allen Dr NE Atlanta GA 30308-1722 Home Phone: 404-874-1421; Office Phone: 404-874-1421. Personal E-mail: tteepen@earthlink.net.

TEER, DIANE, food packaging company executive; b. 1960; B, U. Western Ontario, 1982; MBA, McMaster U., 1984. Brand mgr. The Procter & Gamble Co., 1985—89; v.p. mktg. The Nabob Coffee Co., 1989—94; dir. coffee divsn. Kraft Foods Inc., Canada, 1994—96; v.p. gen. mgr. beverage divsn. The Campbell Soup Co., v.p. North American soup innovation, pres. new growth divsn. & mktg. services; pres. culinary products ConAgra Foods, Inc., Omaha, 2006—08, pres. consumer frozen foods, 2008—10; pres. World Kitchen, LLC, Rosemont, Ill., 2010—11; pres. food packaging bus. MeadWestvaco Corp., Richmond, Va., 2011—. Bd. dirs. American Frozen Food Inst., 2006—. Office: MeadWestvaco Corp 501 S 5th St Richmond VA 23219

TEHLE, DAVID M., retail executive; b. 1956; BA in Econs., U. Wis., 1978; MBA in Fin. and Acctg., U. Mich., 1980. Fin. acctg. Texas Instruments, Inc., 1980—86; fin. mgmt. Ryder Sytem, Inc., 1987—93; v.p., CFO Hat Brands, Inc., 1993—96; v.p. fin. divsn. The Stanley Works, 1996—97; exec. v.p., CFO Haggar Corp., 1997—2004, Dollar General Corp., 2004—. Bd. dirs. Jack in the Box, Inc., 2004—. Mem.: Am. Apparel & Footwear Assn. Office: Dollar Gen Corp 100 Mission Ridge Dr Goodlettsville TN 37072 Office Phone: 615-855-4000. Office Fax: 615-855-5180.

TEITELBAUM, PHILIP, psychologist; b. Bklyn., Oct. 9, 1928; s. Bernard and Betty (Schechter) T.; m. Osnat Boné; children: Benjamin, Daniel, David, Jonathan, Gideon. BS, CCNY, 1950; MA, Johns Hopkins U., 1952, PhD, 1954. Instr., asst. prof. physiol. psychology Harvard U., 1954-59; assoc. prof. psychology U. Pa., Phila., 1959-63, prof., 1963-73; prof. psychology U. Ill.-Urbana-Champaign, 1973-85, emeritus prof., 1985—, Disting. prof. Ctr. Advanced Studies, 1980-85; grad. research prof. U. Fla., Gainesville, 1984—. Author: Fundamental Principles of Physiological Psychology, 1967; editor: (with E. Satinoff) Motivation: Handbook Behavioral Neurobiology, 1983, (with Osnat Teitelbaum) Does Your Baby Have Autism, 2008; contbr. chpts. to books; contbr. articles to profl. jours. Fellow Ctr. for Advanced Study in Behavorial Scis., Stanford U., 1975-76, Fulbright fellow Tel Aviv U., 1978-79, Guggenheim fellow, 1984-85, Carnegie Found. fellow Inst. Neurol. Scis., U. Pa. Med. Sch., 1958-59. Fellow APA (pres. div. physiol. psychology, disting. sci. contbn. award 1978), Am. Psychol. Soc. (William James fellow); mem. NAS, AAAS, Am. Physiol. Soc., Soc. for Neurosci., Soc. Exptl. Psychology. Home: 2239 NW 17th Ave Gainesville FL 32605-3909 Personal E-mail: teitelb@hotmail.com.

TEIXEIRA, ARTHUR ALVES, food engineer, educator, consultant; b. Fall River, Mass., Jan. 30, 1944; s. Arthur Araujo and Emelia (Alves) T.; m. Jean E. Lamb, Dec. 26, 1966 (dec. Dec. 1983); children: A. Allan, Scott C.; m. Marjorie St. John, June 28, 1986; 1 stepchild, Craig St. John. PhD, U. Mass., 1971. Registered profl. engr., Fla., Mass. Rsch. engr. Ross Labs., Columbus, Ohio, 1971-73, R&D group leader, 1973-77; sr. cons. Arthur D. Little, Inc., Cambridge, Mass., 1977-82; assoc. prof. U. Fla., Gainesville, 1982-89, prof., 1989—. Sci. advisor Escola Superior de Biotecnologia, Porto, Portugal, 1991-96, FMC Corp., Santa Clara, Calif., 1989-92; internat. cons., Albania, Australia, Belgium, Brazil, Bulgaria, Chile, Cuba, Eng., France, Germany, Hungary, Indonesia, Ireland, Israel, Kenya, Netherlands, Poland, Portugal, Peru, Romania, South Africa, Spain, China; reviewer USDA, Washington, 1991—. Author: Computerized Food Processing Operations, 1989, Food Physics, 2007; contbr. 14 chpts. to books, 70 articles to profl. jours. Judge Internat. Sci. Fair, Orlando, Fla., 1991. Recipient Fulbright scholar award, Portugal, 1990—91, Golden Retort award of Merit, IFTPS, 1994, Sr. Faculty award, U. Fla. chpt. Gamma Sigma Delta, 1996, Tchr. of Yr. award, U. Fla. Coll. Engring., 1996, Fulbright scholar award, Peru, 2000, Disting. Food Engr. award, IAFIS/FPEI/ASAE, 2001, Marvin Tung Achievement award, 2005, Disting. Alumni award, Durfee H.S., 2007; named Internat. Educator of Yr., U. Fla., 2009; internat. fellow, U. Fla. chpt. Gamma Sigma Delta. Fellow Am. Soc. Agrl. Engrs. (dir. 1988-90, Paper awards 1988-89, 2001, assoc. editor Transactions of ASAE 1985—), Inst. Food Technologists; mem. AIChE, Am. Soc. Agr. and Biol. Engrs., Inst. Food Technologists (mem. editl. bd. 1980-83, 2003—), Am. Soc. Engring. Edn., Inst. Thermal Process Specialists, Coun. on Agrl. Sci. and Tech., R & D Assocs., Gamma Sigma Delta (chpt. pres. U. Fla. 1999-2000), Sigma Xi, Alpha

Epsilon, Tau Beta Pi. Roman Catholic. Achievements include design of on-line process control system to assure safety of sterilized canned foods; tech. and economic feasiblity for radiation sterilization of disposable feeding devices; research in computer optimization and control of food sterilization processes, mathematical modelling of bacterial spore population dynamics in processed foods, and anaerobic composting for solid waste management on long-term NASA space missions. Office: U Fla Rogers Hall Gainesville FL 32611-0570 Home Phone: 352-335-3608; Office Phone: 352-392-1864. E-mail: atex@ufl.edu.

TEJA, AMYN SADRUDIN, chemical engineering educator, consultant; came to U.S., 1980, naturalized. s. Sadrudin N. and Amina T.; m. Carole Rosina Thurlow, July 3, 1971; children: Kerima, Adam. BSc in Engring., Imperial Coll., London, 1968, PhD, 1972. Rsch. fellow in chem. engring. Loughborough U. Tech., England, 1971-74, chem. engring. lectr., 1974-80; assoc. prof. chem. engring. Ga. Inst. Tech., Atlanta, 1980-83, prof., 1984-90, dir. Fluid Properties Rsch. Inst., 1985—2006, regents prof. Sch. Chem. Engring., 1990—2012, regent prof. emeritus, 2013—, regents prof. Woodruff Sch. Mech. Engring., 1991—2001, co-dir. Specialty Separations Ctr., 1992—, assoc. chair grad. studies, 1994—2011; prof. Grassman Found., 2011—12. Vis. assoc. prof. chem. engring. U. Del., Newark, 1978—79, Ohio State U., 1980; presenter in field, reviewer various jours.; cons. Various Cos. Editor: Chemical Engineering and the Environment, 1981; mem. editl. bd. Reports on the Progress of Applied Chemistry, 1972-76, Critical Reports on Applied Chemistry, 1976-80, Jour. Chem. and Engring. Data, 1991-96, Chem. Engring. Rsch. Compendium, 1990—, Jour. Supercritical Fluids, 1990-2000; assoc. editor The Chem. Engring. Jour., 1973-2003; contbr. more than 275 articles to profl. jour. Recipient Hinchley medal Instn. Chem. Engrs., 1968, IBM Rsch. scholarship, 1968-71, Gas Coun. Rsch. scholarship, 1968-71, Brit. Coun. Younger Rsch. Workers award, 1977, Outstanding Tchr. award Omega Chi Epsilon, 1990, award Excellence in Industrial Gases Tech., Am. Inst. Chem. Engrs. Inst., 2002. Fellow AIChE (pub. com. 1992—, jour. rev., Inst. Award 2002, Excellence in Indsl. Gases Award 2002); Sigma Xi (v.p. Ga. Tech. chpt. 1991-92. pres. 1992-93, Supr. Outstanding MS Thesis in Engring. 1984, 90, Supr. Outstanding PhD Thesis 1993, 96, Sustained Rsch. award 1987). Avocations: tennis, theater, science fiction. Home: 6282 Indian Field Norcross GA 30092-1372 Office: Ga Inst Tech Sch Chem Engring Atlanta GA 30332-0100 Home Phone: 770-300-9891; Office Phone: 404-894-3098. Business E-Mail: amyn.teja@chbe.gatech.edu.

TEMERLIN, LIENER, advertising executive; b. Ardmore, Okla., Mar. 27, 1928; s. Pincus and Julie (Kahn) T.; m. Karla Samuelsohn, July 23, 1950; children: Dana Temerlin, Lisa Temerlin Gottesman. BFA, U. Okla., 1950. Assoc. editor Sponsor Mag., NYC, 1950-51; from copywriter to COO Glenn Advt. Inc., Dallas, 1952—74; pres. Glenn, Bozell & Jacobs, Inc., 1974-79; chmn. bd. dirs. Bozell & Jacobs Inc., 1979-86, Bozell, Jacobs, Kenyon & Eckhardt, Dallas, 1986-89; chmn. Bozell, 1989-92, Temerlin McClain, Irving, Tex., 1992—2001; pres. Temerlin Cons., 2001—. Bd. dirs. East/West Inst. Chmn. Winston Churchill Found. award dinner, 1986; chmn. Dallas Symphony Assn., 1986-88, pres., 1984-86, bd. govs., 1982-84, pres. coun., 1989—; mem. Blair House Restoration Com., 1987-88; vice-chmn. Am. Film Inst., 1992-93, bd. dirs., 1992-2000, hon. trustee, 2000; bd. dirs. United Way of Met. Dallas Exec. Com., 1986-89, Dallas Bus. Com. for Arts, 1989, Dallas Citizen's Coun., 1984-86, 92; trustee Southwestern Med. Found., 1988—, mem. adv. com., 2003—; trustee com. univ. devel. So. Meth. U., mem. exec. bd., 1990-91, bd. dirs. Tate lectr. series, 2002—; trustee and chmn. of devel. com. Dallas Mus. Art, 1993-96; steering com. Susan G. Komen Found., 1989-91, art acquisition com. Meyerson Symphony Ctr., 1989-92, exec. coun. Daytop/Dallas, 1989—; chmn. grand opening fortnight Morton H. Meyerson Symphony Ctr., 1989; active Madison Coun. Libr. Congress, Washington, 1991-2002; hon. chair rsch. dinner Am. Lung Assn. Tex., 1996; corp. chmn. Sr. Citizens Greater Dallas for Spirit of Generations Award to Stanley Marcus, 1997; fundraising campaign chmn. Lieberman Rsch. Bldg., Baylor Med. Ctr., 1997; hon. chmn. ann. dinner Make A Wish Found., 1998; exec. bd. Meadows Sch. Arts, So. Meth. U., 2001; co-chair ann. fundraising event Vogel Alcove Child Care Ctr. for the Homeless, 2001; adv. cons. Dallas Ctr. Performing Arts, 2003-; chmn., founder & festival dir., Am. Film Inst. Dallas Internat. Film Festival, 2006-08. Lt. field arty. US Army, Korea. Decorated Bronze Star; recipient Bill D. Kerss award Dallas Advt. League, 1983, Brotherhood award NCCJ, 1984, Susan G. Komen Found. for Breast Cancer Rsch. Cmty. award, 1989, Neiman Marcus (formerly James K. Wilson) Silver Cup award, 1990, Linz award 1990, Silver Medal award Dallas Advt. League, 1991, Vol. Fundraiser of Yr. award Nat. Soc. Fundraising Execs., 1991, Inst. Human Rels. award Am. Jewish Commn., Dallas, 2003; named Dallas Father of Yr., 1991, Best Man in Advt. award McCall's Mag., 1992; named Temerlin Advt. Inst. for Edn. and Rsch. in his honor So. Meth. U. Sch. Advt., 2001; inducted into Am. Advt. Hall Fame, 2004. Mem.: Am. Film Inst. (hon. trustee), Dallas CC Dist. (bd. dir. 1982), Dallas Citizens Coun. (bd. dir. 1984—86, 1992—95), Dallas C. of C. (bd. dir. 1982), Dallas Ambassadors Forum (adv. coun. 1993), Am. Heart Fund (chmn. Cmty. Relation Com. and Keystone Gifts Com. 1977, Dallas chpt. bd. dir.). Business E-Mail: connie.beebe@temerlinconsulting.com.

TEMPLE, DONALD, retired allergist, dermatologist; b. Chgo., May 21, 1933; s. Samuel Leonard and Matilda Eve (Riff) T.; m. Sarah Rachel Katz, Sept. 29, 1957; children: Michael A., Matthew D., Madeline B. AB in Biology cum laude, Harvard U., 1954; MD, U. Chgo., 1958. Diplomate Am. Bd. Allergy and Immunology, Am. Bd. Dermatology, Nat. Bd. Med. Examiners; lic. Intern Michael Reese Hosp., Chgo., 1958-59; resident in dermatology U. Chgo. Hosps., 1959-62; clin. asst., dept. dermatology Boston U., 1963-64; clin. instr., dermatology dept. Stanford U. Sch. Medicine, 1965; preceptee in allergy Offices of Leon Unger, M.D., and Donald Unger, M.D., Chgo., 1965-69; pvt. practice Des Plaines, Ill., 1969-76; with allergy dept. Glen Ellyn (Ill.) Clinic, 1972-97; ret., 1997. Dermatology and allergy staff Louis A. Weiss Hosp., Chgo., 1965-73, allergy sect. Loyola U. Med. Ctr., Maywood, Ill., 1977-80, exec. and contract medicine coms. Glen Ellyn; clin. asst. prof. dermatology Abraham Lincoln Sch. Medicine, U. Ill., 1972-75; clin. asst. prof. medicine sect. allergy and dermatology, Loyola U., 1977-85; mem. staff Cen. DuPage Hosp., Winfield, Ill., 1973-97, Glen Oaks Med. Ctr., Glendale Heights, Ill., Glendale Heights Cmty. Hosp., 1980-92. Contbr. articles to profl. jours. Bd. dirs. Am. Lung Assn., DuPage, McHenry counties, 1980-91; chmn. Contract Medicine, HMO Com., Glen Ellyn Clinic, 1985, mem. exec. com., 1988-92. Fellow Am. Coll. Chest Physicians, Am. Assn. Cert. Allergists, Am. Coll. Allergists, Am. Acad. Allergy, Ill. Soc. Allergy and Clin. Immunology, Chgo. Dermatol. Soc.; mem. AMA, Ill. State Med. Soc., DuPage County Med. Soc., Chgo. Med. Soc., Fla. Med. Assn. Collier County Med. Soc. Jewish. Avocations: sailing, investing. Home: 6585 Nicholas Blvd Ph 3 Naples FL 34108-7210 E-mail: don.temple@post.harvard.edu.

TEMPLE, LARRY EUGENE, lawyer; b. Plainview, Tex., Dec. 26, 1935; s. Herman Edward and Grace Eileen (Ivey) T.; m. Laura Louann Atkins, Feb. 23, 1963; children: Laura Allison, John Lawrence. BBA, U. Tex., 1957, LLB with honors, 1959; LLD (hon.), Lamar U., 1985. Bar: Tex., U.S. Dist. Ct. (we. dist.) Tex., U.S. Ct. Appeals (5th cir.), U.S. Supreme Ct. Law clk. to justice Tom Clark U.S. Supreme Ct., Washington, 1959-60; assoc. Powell, Rauhut, McGinnis, Reavley & Lochridge, Austin, Tex., 1960-63; legal adminstrn. asst., exec. asst. (chief of staff) Tex. Gov. John B. Connally, Austin, 1963-67; spl. counsel to pres. Lyndon Baines Johnson, Washington, 1967-69; pvt. practice Austin, 1969—. Bd. dirs. Temple-Inland, Inc., Guaranty Bank, 1991-2008. Mem. U. Tex. Cancer Found., Houston, 1978-84, U. Tex. Devel. Bd., Austin, 1980-85, 90—, chmn., 1993-95; pres. U. Tex. Ex-Students Assn., 1997-98; mem. Tex. Higher Edn. Coordinating Bd., Austin, 1983-89, chmn., 1983-87; chmn. Select Com. for Higher Edn., Austin, 1985-87; bd. dirs. Lyndon B. Johnson Found., 1986—, vice chmn., 1989-2000, pres., 2000-10, chmn., 2010-; trustee U. Tex. Law Sch. Found., 1989-2007. Recipient Faculty award U. Tex. Law Sch., 1987, Humanitarian award Austin region NCCJ, 1988, Santa Rita award U. Tex. System, 1989, Disting. Alumnus award U. Tex., Austin, 1990, Mirabeau B. Lamar medal Assn. Tex. Colls. and Univs., 1990, Pro Bene Meritis award U. Tex., 1991 Outstanding Alumnus award U. Tex. Law Sch., 1999, Presdl. Citation award U. Tex., 2001, Leon Green award Tex. Law Rev., 2003; named a Tex. Super Lawyer, 2003-; Named one of Best Lawyers in Am., 1994—, Outstanding 50yr. Lawyer award, Tex Bar Found. 2011 Mem.: ABA, Tex. Bar Assn. (chmn. legis. com. 1980, 1983—86), Tex. Jr. Bar Assn. (chmn. bd. dirs. 1967), Austin Bar Assn. (Disting. Lawyer award 2004). Democrat. Episcopalian. Home: 2606 Escondido Cv Austin TX 78703-1610 Office: 400 W 15th St Ste 705 Austin TX 78701-1647 Home Phone: 512-453-7936; Office Phone: 512-477-4467. Business E-Mail: larry@larrytemple.com.

TEMPLET, RICKY JAMES, county official, former state legislator; b. New Orleans, La., Feb. 4, 1963; m. Christine Templet; 1 child, Ryan. Owner/operator R&C Templet Enterprises; councilman City of Gretna, 2001—; mem. Dist 85 La. House of Reps., 2008—12, mem. adminstrn. of criminal justice com., ways and means com., joint legis. com. on capital outlay; mem. Dist. 1 Jefferson Parish Coun., 2012—. Republican. Cath. Office: Jefferson Parish Council General Government Building 200 Derbigny St, 6th Floor Gretna LA 70053-5850 Office Phone: 504-361-6013, 225-342-6945. Office Fax: 504-361-6687. E-mail: templetr@legis.state.la.us.

TEMPLETON, CATHERINE B., state agency administrator; JD, U. SC. Human resources mgr. Milliken & Co.; former asst. to the dir. SC Dept. Labor, Licensing and Regulation, dir., 2011—12; atty. Ogletree Deakins; dir. SC Dept. Health & Environ. Control, 2012—. Nat. coord. iCivics. Mem., Sunday sch. tchr. St. Michael's Episc. Ch., Charleston, SC; bd. mem. Boy Scouts America, SC Trial Attorneys Assn., Carolina Arts Assn. Gibbes Mus. Art Women's Coun. Recipient Compleat Lawyer award, U. SC Sch. Law Alumni Assn. Office: SC Dept Health & Environmental Control 2600 Bull St Columbia SC 29201

TEMPLETON, MARK B., information technology executive; BA in Product Design, NC State U., 1975; MBA, U. Va., 1978. V.p., mktg. Keyfile Corp., 1991—93; exec. v.p. Softblox, Inc., 1993—94; group dir., corp. mktg. UB Networks, Inc., 1994—95; v.p., mktg. Citrix Sys., Inc., 1995—98, pres., 1998—2001; pres., CEO Citrix Systems., Inc., 2001—. Former bd. dirs. Active Word Sys., Inc.; bd. dirs. Citrix Sys., Inc., 1998—, Equifax, Inc., 2008—. Recipient Excalibur award, Businessperson of the Yr., AeA Abacus award. Office: Citrix Systems Inc 851 W Cypress Creek Rd Fort Lauderdale FL 33309 Office Phone: 954-267-3000. Office Fax: 954-267-9319. Business E-Mail: Mark.Templeton@citrix.com.*

TEMPLETON, RICHARD K., electronics executive; BSEE, Union Coll., NY, 1980. Various positions Texas Instruments, Inc., Dallas, 1980—91, v.p. semiconductor group, 1991—94, mgr. worldwide application specific products, 1993—96, sr. v.p. semiconductor group, 1994—96, exec. v.p., pres. semiconductor group, 1996—2004, COO, 2000—04, pres., CEO, 2004—08, chmn., pres., CEO, 2008—. Bd. dirs. Tex. Instruments, Inc., 2003—, Semiconductor Industry Assn. Mem. Bus. Roundtable, Dallas Chief Exec. Roundtable. Office: Tex Instruments Inc PO Box 660199 Dallas TX 75266-0199 Office Phone: 972-995-2011. Office Fax: 972-995-4360.

TENEN, S. MARK, endocrinologist, educator; b. New Haven, 1959; Grad., U. Toronto, 1977—79, MD, 1979—83. Cert. Med. Coun. of Canada, 1983, Nat. Bd. of Med. Examiners, 1984, Royal Coll. of Physicians and Surgeons of Canada, 1987, diplomate American Bd. Internal Medicine, 1986, American Bd. Internal Medicine-endocrinology, diabetes and metabolism, 1989. Tchg. asst., computer sciences Univ. of Toronto, Canada, 1978—79; intern medicine St. Michael's Hosp.-Univ. of Toronto, Canada, 1983—84, chief med. resident; med. resident Toronto Gen. and St. Michael's Hosps.-Univ. of Toronto, Canada, 1984—86; clin. endocrinology fellow Univ. of Toronto, Canada, 1987—88; med. staff fellow endocrinology NIH, Bethesda, Md., 1988—89; attending physician Georgetown Univ. Med. Ctr., Washington, 1989—92; physician Endocrine Assocs., McLean, Va., 1989—; supporting instr. Internat. Diabetes Ctr. of Va., Falls Church, 1989—; clin. instr. Georgetown Univ., Washinton, 1989—94, clin. asst. prof., divsn. endocrinology, 1994—; staff The Arlington Hosp., Va., 1989—98, Reston Hosp. Ctr., Va., 1989—2005, INOVA Fairfax Hosp., Falls Church, Va., 1989—, courtesy staff, 1994—. Contbr. articles to profl. publs. Recipient Pearce Meml. award, 1980, Haist award, 1980, Saddington medal, 1981, Bruce medal, 1983, Cody Silver medal, 1983, Physician's Recognition award, AMA, 1989, 1992, 1995, 1998, 2001, 2004, 2007. Fellow: American Coll. of Endocrinology; mem.: ACP, Polycystic Ovary Syndrome Assn., Med. Soc. of Va., Endocrine Soc., American Diabetes Assn., American Assn. of Clin. Endocrinology. Office: Endocrine Associates Ste No 320 7921 Jones Branch Dr Mc Lean VA 22102 Office Phone: 703-448-6010. Office Fax: 703-506-6726.*

TENENBAUM, INEZ MOORE, lawyer, former federal agency administrator, former school system administrator; b. Hawkinsville, GA, Mar. 8, 1951; m. Samuel J. Tenenbaum. BS in Edn., U. Ga., Athens, 1972, MSE in Edn., 1974; JD, U. S.C. Law Sch., Columbia, 1986. Tchr. Elementary Sch.; dir. rsch. S.C. House of Reps., 1977-83; atty. Sinkler & Boye, P.A., Columbia, SC, 1986-92; supt. S.C. Dept. Edn., Columbia, SC, 1999—2007; chmn. US Consumer Product Safety Commn. (CPSC), Bethesda, Md., 2009—13; ptnr. Nelson, Mullins, Riley & Scarborough, LLP, Washington, 2013—. Mem. Southern Regional Edn. Bd., 1999—2008, SC Ednl. Television Commn., 1999—2007; bd. dirs. SC Chamber of Commerce, 2005—06, SC Governor's Sch. Arts & Humanities Found., 2007—09; mem. nat. advisory bd. Milken Family Found. Nat. Inst. for Excellence in Tng., 2007—09. Founder S.C. Ctr. Family Policy. Named one of The 100 Most Powerful Women in DC, Washingtonian mag., 2009. Democrat. Methodist. Office: Nelson Mullins Riley & Scarborough LLP Meridian 17th Fl 1320 Main St Columbia SC 29201 Office Phone: 803-255-9243. E-mail: inez.tenenbaum@nelsonmullins.com.*

TENNANT, NATALIE E., state official; b. Fairmont, W.Va., Dec. 25, 1967; m. Erik Wells, June 20, 1998; 1 child, Delaney. BA in Journalism, W.Va. U., 1991, MA in Corporate & Organizational Comm., 2002. TV anchor, reporter WBOY-TV, Clarksburg, W.Va., WCHS-TV, Charleston, W.Va.; co-owner Wells Media Group LLC, Charleston; sec. of state State of W.Va., 2009—. Mem.: American Heart Assn. (bd. mem. Great Rivers Affiliate). Democrat. Office: Office of the Secretary of State Building 1 Suite 157 K 1900 Kanawha Blvd E Charleston WV 25305-0770 Office Phone: 304-558-6000. Office Fax: 304-558-0900. Business E-Mail: wvsos@wvsos.com.*

TENNIES, ROBERT HUNTER, headmaster; b. Bogotá, Colombia, Aug. 19, 1952; s. Leo C. and Ruth (Winston) T.; m. Ruth Ellen Fischer, June 14, 1975; children: Debbie, Julie. BS, Wheaton Coll., Ill., 1973; MA, U. South Fla., 1975; EdS, Fla. Atlantic U., 1978, EdD, 1982. Sci. tchr. Cypress Lake Middle Sch., Ft. Myers, Fla., 1973-77, Boca Raton (Fla.) Christian Sch., 1977-78, asst. adminstr., 1978-84, headmaster, 1984—, min. of children, 1984-90; interim. min. of edn., 1991-93. Spkr. Internat. Conf. Religious Edn., Petrozavodsk, Russia; mem. Nat. Rev. Panel Blue Ribbon Schs., 1999. Recipient Excellence in Edn. award Nat. Assn. Elem. Prins., 1990, 97, Presentation award, Internat. Children Educators Conf., Hong Kong, China, 2008. Mem. Assn. of Christian Schs. Internat. (chair Fla. accreditation commn., 2007), Nat. Assn. Elem. Sch. Prins. Avocation: camping. Home: 2415 NW 30th Rd Boca Raton FL 33431-6214 Office: Boca Raton Christian Sch 315 NW 4th St Boca Raton FL 33432-3739 Office Phone: 561-391-2727. Business E-Mail: bocachristian@bocachristian.org.

TENNYSON, FIONNUALA, food products executive; Dir., corp. and govt. affairs, European union region Kraft Foods, Inc.; v.p., pub. affairs and comm., European group Coca-Cola Enterprises, Inc. Office: Coca-Cola Enterprises Inc 2500 Windy Ridge Pky Atlanta GA 30339 Office Phone: 770-989-3000. Office Fax: 770-989-3788. Business E-Mail: ftennyson@cokecce.com.

TERILLI, SAMUEL A., JR., newspaper publishing executive; Gen. Coun. Miami Herald, Fla.; of cousel Ford Harrison LLP, Fla., 2000—. Office: Ford Harrison LLP 25 SE 2nd St Ste 516 Miami FL 33131-2102

TERRACCIANO, ANTHONY PATRICK, board member, consumer products company executive, finance company executive; b. Bayonne, NJ, Oct. 27, 1938; s. Patrick and Grace Teracciano; m. Rity Cuddy, Apr. 20, 1963; children: Laura, Karen, Kenneth. BS in Economics, St. Peters Coll., 1960; MA in Philosophy, Fordham U., 1962. Exec. v.p. internat. Chase Manhattan Bank, NYC, 1974—76, exec. v.p., CFO, 1983—84, vice chmn., global banking, 1985—87; pres., COO Mellon Bank Corp., 1987—90; chmn., pres. and CEO First Fidelity Bancorp, Newark, 1990—96; pres., banking ops. First Union Nat. Bank, Summit, NJ, 1996—97; vice chmn. Am. Water Works Co. Inc., 1998—2003; chmn. Dime Bancorp, Inc., NYC, 1999—2002, Riggs Nat. Corp., Washington, 2004—05, Sallie Mae - SLM Corp., Reston, Va., 2008—. Bd. dirs. Polypore Internat. Inc., TradeCard, Inc., 1999—, Bell Atlantic Corp., 2000—02, Avaya, Inc., 2002—, Ikon Office Solutions, Inc., 2003—, Fortent Inc., 2003—, Knoll, Inc., 2004—, CIT Group Inc., 2010—. Bd. dirs. N.Y. Philharm., Metro Newark C. of C.; mem. exec. coun. Better Bus. Bur., Newark; trustee Renaissance Newark, Inc., U. Medicine & Dentistry NJ, 2006-, Monmouth Med. Ctr.; mem. Coun. Fgn. Rels. 1st lt. U.S. Army, 1962-64., NJ State Investment Coun. Mem. N.J. Bankers Assn. (exec. com.). Avocations: music, reading. Office: SLM Corp 12061 Bluemont Way Reston VA 20190 Office Phone: 703-810-3000. Office Fax: 703-984-5042. Business E-Mail: anthony.terracciano@salliemae.com.

TERRACINA, ROY DAVID, entrepreneur; b. Chgo., Aug. 24, 1946; s. Angelo R. and Josephine T.; divorced; children: Joseph, Vincent, Angela, Peter, Paul. BS in Fin., Marquette U., 1968, MBA, 1972. Officer First Wis. Nat. Bank, Milw., 1968-71; account exec. Robert W. Baird Co., Milw., 1971-74; v.p. mktg. Midwest Retail Group, Milw., 1974-76; mgmt. cons. Anderson-Roethle, Milw., 1976-77; v.p., treas. Farm House Foods Corp., Milw., 1977-84; pres. Sterling Foods, Inc., San Antonio, 1984-93, pvt. investor, 1994—. Instr. personal fin. Marquette U.; instr. fin. Trinity U.; bd. dir. US Global Investors, JP Morgan Chase, San Antonio. Roman Catholic. Office: 7900 Callaghan Rd San Antonio TX 78229-2327

TERRELL, G. IRVIN, lawyer; b. Houston, Sept. 28, 1946; s. George I. and Adella (Weichert) T.; m. Karen Steenberg, Jan. 8, 1984; 1 child, Katharine. BA, U. Tex., 1968, JD, 1972. Bar: Tex., US Supreme Ct., US Ct. Appeals (3d and 5th cirs.), US Dist. Ct. (so., no. and ea. dists.) Tex., US Dist. Ct. (we. dist.) Pa, US Dist. Ct. (so. dist.) NY. Assoc. Baker & Botts LLP, Houston, 1972-79, ptnr., 1980—. Mem. ABA, Houston Bar Assn., Internat. Soc. Barristers. Office Phone: 713-229-1231. Business E-Mail: irv.terrell@bakerbotts.com.

TERRELL, KARENANN, retail executive; b. 1961; Attended, Kettering U.; BSEE, Gen. Motors Inst., 1986; MSEE, Purdue U., 1988. Dir., eConnect platform, Chrysler Group DaimlerChrysler Corp., Auburn Hills, Mich., dir., managed svcs. & internat. process sys., dir., e-business, v.p., chief info. officer, Chrysler Group & Mercedes Benz N.Am., 2005—06; v.p., chief info. officer Baxter International, Inc., 2006—10; exec. v.p., asst. chief info. officer Wal-Mart Stores, Inc., Bentonville, Ark., 2010—12, exec. v.p., chief info. officer, 2012—. Mem. adv. bd. Women in Tech. Internat. Recipient Women's Corp. Tech. award, Women in Tech. Internat., 2005, Office Depot Bus. Woman of the Yr.; named one of The 100 Influential Women in Automotive Bus., Automotive News. Office: Wal-Mart Stores 702 SW Eighth St Bentonville AR 72716-8611 Office Phone: 847-948-2000. Office Fax: 847-948-3948. Business E-Mail: karenann_terrell@baxter.com.

TERRILL, RANDY, state legislator, law educator; b. Alva, Okla., Sept. 29, 1969; m. Angela Fitzgerald; children: Elizabeth, Randal. BA summa cum laude, Univ. Ctrl. Okla.; JD, Univ. Okla. Prof. govt. history & law Hillsdale Coll., Moore; former press intern to Gov. Henry Bellmon; former legis. asst. to former House Republican Leader Larry Ferguson; former dir. legis. research & special projects to Gov. Frank Keating; self-employed business and legal cons.; mem. Dist. 53 Okla. House of Representatives, 2005—. Mem.: Order of the Coif. Republican. Baptist. Office: 2300 N Lincoln Bldg Rm 407 Oklahoma City OK 73105 Home: 504 SW 30th Cir Moore OK 73160-6072 Office Phone: 405-557-7346. E-mail: randyterrill@okhouse.gov.

TERRY, ANNE CURTIS, lawyer, writer; d. Charles and Florine Curtis; m. Edward H. Terry; children: Edward, Ellyn. BA, Fla. State U., Tallahassee, 1970; MA, U. Tex., Austin, 1972; JD, U. Fla., Gainesville, 1978. Bar: Fla. 1979. Tchg. asst./lectr. dept. geography U. Tex., Austin, 1972—74; appellate law clk. 1st Dist. Ct. of Appeals, Tallahassee, 1978—79; asst. atty. gen. Office of Fla. Atty. Gen., Tallahassee, 1980—86; staff counsel Fla. Legislature, Tallahassee, 1986—89; solo practitioner/firm owner Law Office of Anne Curtis Terry, Tallahassee, 1993—2009. Co-author: The Spirit in the South, 2006, author (contbr.) legal opinions to ann. report of atty. gen. Fla. NDEA Title VI fellow, Inst. Latin Am. Studies, U. Tex., 1971-1972. Mem.: Phi Alpha Delta, Phi Kappa Phi. Democrat. Methodist. Achievements include represented Southern Christian Leadership Conference in First Amendment litigation; represented numerous plaintiffs in employment discrimination cases, based on disability, harrassment race and gender; represented plaintiff-relators in state and federal qui tam litigation ongoing; research in model ordinance for regulation of noise pollution, high & low frequency vibrations. Avocations: travel, genealogy, photography, poetry, cooking.

TERRY, DAVID L., JR., health insurance company executive; BS in Stats., Colo. State U., Fort Collins, 1973; MS in Actuarial Sci., U. Nebr., Lincoln, 1975. Sr. cons. Reden & Anders, Ltd., 2000—03; various positions including chief actuary NewQuest, LLC, 2003—05; sr. v.p., chief actuary HealthSpring, Inc., 2005—. Office: HealthSpring Inc 9009 Carothers Pky Ste 501 Franklin TN 37067 Office Phone: 615-291-7000. Office Fax: 615-401-4566.

TERRY, JASON EUGENE, professional basketball player; b. Seattle, Sept. 15, 1977; s. Curtis Terry and Andrea Cheatham; m. Johnyika Terry; 4 children. BA in Gen. Studies, U. Ariz., Tucson, 1999. Guard Atlanta Hawks, 1999—2004, Dallas Mavericks, 2004—12, Boston Celtics, 2012—13, Bklyn. Nets, 2013—. Mem. US nat. team Goodwill Games, Brisbane, Australia, 2001. Founder Jason Terry Found. Recipient Cmty. Asst. award, NBA, 2002, Image Leader Award In Sports, Building Leaders for Tomorrow, 2007; named NCAA 1st Team All Am., AP, 1999, Nat. Player of Yr., Sports Illus., Basketball Times, 1999, Player of Yr., Pac-10 Conf., 1999, Sixth Man of Yr., NBA, 2009. Achievements include member of the NCAA Men's Basketball Championship winning University of Arizona Wildcats, 1997; member of the NBA Finals Championship winning Dallas Mavericks, 2011. Office: Brooklyn Nets 15 MetroTech Ctr 11th Fl Brooklyn NY 11201 also: The Jason Terry Found PO Box 3095 Loganville GA 30052*

TERRY, WAYNE GILBERT, retired healthcare educator, hospital administrator; b. Plymouth, Mass., Oct. 2, 1932; s. Lawrence Arthur and Betty Frances (Boutemain) Terry; m. Barbara Aileen Bromwell, Sept. 20, 1980; children: Karleton Wayne, Dale Duane, Kendrick Shane, Kristen Alayne, Tammye Van Clief, Wade Bromwell Delk. AA in Gen. Adminstrn., Allan Hancock Coll., Santa Maria Calif., 1960; BBA in Bus. Mgmt., U. Hawaii, Honolulu, 1966; MHA, Med. Coll. Va., Va. Commonwealth U., Richmond, 1973; PhD in Health Svcs. Mgmt., LaSalle U., 1999; PhD, Manderville, La., 1999. Commd. 2d lt. USAF Med. Svc. Corps, 1967, advanced through grades to maj., 1976; asst. adminstr. for registrar activities USAF Hosp., Orlando AFB, Fla., 1966-67; assoc. adminstr. aeromed. evacuation activities USAF, Hickam AFB, Hawaii, 1967-71; adminstrv. resident USAF Regional Hosp., Langley AFB, Va., 1972-73; CEO USAF Hosp., Columbus AFB, Miss., 1973-75; nat. health edn. and tng. program advisor Office of Surgeon Gen., Dept. of Air Force, Washington, 1975-78; dir. health professions pers. planning and policy divsn. Office of Asst. Sec. Def. for Health Affairs, The Pentagon, Washington, 1978-80; dep. project mgr./adminstrv. dir. King Faisal U. Teaching Hosp., Al-Khobar, Saudi Arabia, 1980-82; dep. project mgr., hosp. dir. North Yemen Healthcare Project, As-Salem Hosp., Sadah, Yemen Arab Republic, 1982-83; hosp. dir., CEO western area Armed Forces Hosps., Khamis Mushayt, Saudi Arabia, 1983-84; chief adminstr./commissioning team chief Orbit Summit Health, Ltd., Riyadh, Saudi Arabia, 1984-85; hosp. dir., adminstrv. dir. Truk State Dept. Health Svcs., Moen, Federated States of Micronesia, 1985-87; assoc. adminstr. support svcs. King Fahad Hosp., Saudi Arabian N.G., Riyadh, 1987-90; project mgr., CEO N.W. Armed Forces Hosps. Program, Tabuk, Saudi Arabia, 1990-98, cons. in health svcs. mgmt., 1998-99; cons., mediator in health svcs. mgmt. Crozet, Va., 1999-2000; exec. dir., CEO Southside Area Health Edn. Ctr. Longwood U., Farmville, Va., 2000—14; ret. Apptd. mil. cons. healthcare planning to the Air Force Surgeon Gen., 1979; apptd. preceptor program in healthcare adminstrn. U. Mich. for adminstrv. residents at N.W. Armed Forces Hosps. Programs, Tabuk, Saudi Arabia, 1993; mem. supervisory bd. Royal Coll. Surgeons in Ireland, Dublin, 1990-98; cert. sr. grant specialist, reviewer, cons.; lectr., cons. in field. Contbr. articles to profl. jours. Warden to Am. Cmty. N.W. Region of Yemen Arab Republic to Am. Embassy in Sanaa, 1982-83, warden to Am. Cmty. N.W. Region of Saudi Arabia to Am. Embassy in Riyadh, 1990-99; mem. Internat. Sch. Sys. Coord. Com., Tabuk, 1990-99; bd. dirs. Taif Sch. Dist. Sys., Saudi Arabia, 1981-82; chmn., exec. com., bd. dirs. Ctrl. Va. Health Planning Agy., Richmond, Va., 2001-08; bd. dirs. Va. Tobacco Settlement Found., Regional Adv. Bd., Richmond, Va., 2001—09, Southside Area Health Edn. Ctr., Longwood U., Farmville, 2001—13; leadership and planning group Nat. Area Health Edn. Ctr. Assn., Balt., 2003-04, Va. Dept. Health Commr's. Healthcare Workforce Devel. Authority, 2008-12, chmn., program adv. group. Va. Statewide AHEC Program, 2008-12, adv. bd. mem., Region 8 Govs. Health Scis. Acad. Soothside CC Ksysuille, Va., 2013-. Decorated Def. Meritorious Svc. medal, Air Force Meritorious Svc. medal with 3 Oak Leaf Clusters, Air medal with 3 Oak Leaf Clusters, Air Force Commendation medal with 3 oak leaf clusters, Republic of Vietnam Gallantry Cross with palm, Republic of Vietnam Svc. medal with 11 svc. stars, Korean Def. Svc. medal, Sec. of Def. Svc. medal/badge, Air Staff Svc. Badge Dept. Air Force, Air Force Chief Med. Svc. Corps badge; recipient Citation of Appreciation Nat. Coun. Social Welfare, Seoul, Republic of Korea, 1963, Citation of Appreciation award Suchan Province Gov., Choong Nam, Republic of Korea, 1963, award of merit Pacific Air Forces Command, Hickam AFB, Hawaii, 1965, Outstanding Jr. Officer in 22nd Air Force, USAF, 1970, Outstanding Rsch. award Med. Coll. Va., 1973, Personality of the South award, 1975, Men of Achievement award, Cambridge, Eng., 1982, Citation of Appreciation Gov. Truk State, Federated States of Micronesia, 1987, Citation of Merit Internat. Red Cross Commn., Bern, Switzerland, 1991, N.W. Armed Forces Hosps., Ministry Def. and Aviation, Tabuk, 1991, Citation of Appreciation Presidency of Gen. Staff Hdqs., Ministry of Def. and Aviation, Tabuk, 1992-93, 95-99, Disting. Alumni award Allan Hancock Coll., Santa Maria, 2000, Citation of Appreciation Longwood U., Va., 2006, 2010, 2014, Commitment to Excellence award, Air Force Surgeon Gen., Wash., Outstanding Svc. Med. Svc. Corps. Officer award, ACHE Congress Chgo., Washington, 2011, Dedicated Svc. Air Force Med. Svc. Corps. Assn., 2005-11, Scottsdale, Ariz., 2011. Fellow Am. Coll. Healthcare Execs. (life), Ctrl. Va. Assn. Healthcare Execs. Group (2007-), Royal Soc. Health; mem. Am. Hosp. Assn., Am. Mgmt. Assn. (life), Air Force Med. Svc. Corps. Assn. (life, membership and awards com. 2003-2005, bd. dirs., 2005-2011, newsletter editor 2005-, decorated plaque 2011), Assn. Mil. Surgeons of U.S., Air Force Assn; life mem., Vets. of Foreign Wars (life), The American Legion (2007-), Military Officer's Assn. of Am., Piedmont Region (2001-). Republican. Baptist. Avocations: tennis, coin collecting/numismatics, hiking. E-mail: terrywg@longqwood.edu.

TERWILLIGER, J. RONALD, real estate company executive; Grad., US Naval Acad.; MBA (hon.), Harvard U. Pres., COO Sea Pines Plantation Co., Hilton Head Plantation Co.; chmn., CEO & prin. Trammell Crow Residential, 1986—; prin. Tcr Gateway Inc.; nat. mng. ptnr. Fla. Rs Inc.; CEO Tauer Constrn. I Ltd.; bd. dirs. Tcr Collinwood Ltd. Partnership, Tcr Magnolia Ptnrs. Ltd. Partnership, Tcr Maxey Ptnrs. Ltd. Partnership, Tcr Jefferson Three Ptnrs. Ltd. Partnership, Tcr Affordable Housing Ltd. Partnership; CEO, v.p. Tcr Sca Constrn. Inc. Chmn. emeritus Wharton Real Estate Ctr.; mem. Fannie Mae Adv. Coun.; owner Atlanta WNBA team, 2007—. Mem. internat. bd. dirs. Habitat for Humanity; vice chmn. Atlanta Neighborhood Devel. Partnership; dir. Naval Acad. Found. Baker scholar, Harvard Grad. Sch. Bus. Mem.: Real Estate Roundtable, Urban Land Inst. (immediate past chmn.). Office: Trammell Crow Residential Co Two Buckhead Plz 800 Mount Vernon Hwy NE Ste 475 Atlanta GA 30328-4261 Office Phone: 770-801-1600. Office Fax: 770-801-1256.

TERZIAN, GRACE PAINE, communications executive; b. Boston, Oct. 19, 1952; d. Thomas Fite and Grace Hillman (Benedict) Paine; m. Philip Henry Terzian, Oct. 20, 1979; children: William Thomas Hillman, Grace Benedict Paine. BA in Art History, Williams Coll., Williamstown, Mass., 1974. Art dir. The New Republic, Washington, 1976-78; asst. editor The Chronicle of Higher Edn., Washington, 1978-79; rsch. editor Archtl. Digest, LA, 1982-85; pub. The Women's Quar., Arlington, Va., 1994—2004; exec. dir. Allergy and Asthma Network Mothers of Asthmatics, 2004—06; v.p. comm. Hudson Inst., Washington, 2006—. Editor Ex Femina, 1996—2004; sr. v.p. Ind. Women's Forum, 1998-2004. Mem. Soc. Colonial Dames in Am., Phi Beta Kappa. Episcopalian. Home: 10505 Adel Rd Oakton VA 22124-1605 Office: The Hudson Inst 1015 15th St NW 6th Fl Washington DC 20005 Home Phone: 703-938-7321; Office Phone: 202-974-2400. Personal E-mail: gterzian@cox.net. Business E-Mail: gracet@hudson.org.

TERZIAN, PHILIP HENRY, journalist; b. Kensington, Md., July 5, 1950; s. L. A. and Louise (Anderson) Terzian; m. Grace Barrett Paine, Oct. 20, 1979; children: William Thomas Hillman, Grace Benedict Paine. BA in English, Villanova U., 1973; DTS, Episcopal Theol. Sem., Va., 1995; postgrad., Oxford U., Eng., 1976. Desk editor Reuters, Washington, 1973, U.S. News & World Report, Washington, 1973-74; asst. editor The New Republic, Washington, 1974-78; mem. policy planning staff Dept. State, Washington, 1978-79; asst. editor Anniston (Ala.) Star, 1979-80; assoc. editor Lexington (Ky.) Herald, 1980-82; asst. editor of editl. pages L.A. Times, 1982-86; editor of editl. pages Providence Jour., 1986-92, assoc. editor, syndicated columnist, 1992—2005; lit. editor The Weekly Standard, Washington, 2005—. Panelist Washington Wk. in Rev., C-SPAN, Fox News, Nat. Pub. Radio, Voice Am. Contbr. articles to newspapers and jours.; author: Architects of Power: Roosevelt, Eisenhower, and the American Century, 2010. Pres. Providence Com. Fgn. Rels., 1989—92. Recipient Edn. Writers award, Edn. Writers Am., 1981, Svc. to Preservation award, Ida Lee Willis Found., 1982, juror, Pulitzer Prize, 1994—95; named finalist Disting. Commentary, 1991; Travelling fellow, Am. Journalism Found. Mem.: Pvt. Librs. Assn., The Lit. Soc. Washington DC, Va. Hist. Soc., Am. Coun. on Germany, Va. Soc. Ornithology, Assn. Literary Scholars and Critics, Order Hosp. St. John of Jerusalem, St. Andrew's Soc. Washington, Soc. King Charles the Martyr, Wolver Beagles (hon. whip), Sons of Union Vets. of Civil War, Nat. Press Club, Univ. Club, Nat. Beagle Club. Republican. Episcopalian. Home: 10505 Adel Rd Oakton VA 22124-1605 Office: The Weekly Standard 1150 17th St NW Washington DC 20036 Office Phone: 202-293-4900. E-mail: pterzian@weeklystandard.com.

TERZOTIS, JUDI, advertising executive; Attended, U. of Tennessee, 1980—84. Gen. mgr. Mid. Ten. Cmty. Newspaper, 1998—2004; pub. The Daily News journal Gannett Co., 2004—07, advt. dir., 2007—, pres. and pub. The Fort Collins Coloradoan; advt. dir. The Clarion-Ledger, 2007—09. Mem.: Am. Heart Assn. Go Red for Women (chair). Office: Gannett Company 7950 Jones Branch Dr Mc Lean VA 22107-0150 Office Phone: 703-854-6000.

TESELLE, EUGENE ARTHUR, JR., religion educator; b. Ames, Iowa, Aug. 8, 1931; s. Eugene Arthur and Hildegarde (Flynn) TeS.; m. Sallie McFague, Sept. 12, 1959 (div. Oct. 1976); children: Elizabeth, John; m. Penelope Saunders, Mar. 4, 1978; children: William, James, Thomas. BA, U. Colo., Boulder, 1952; BD, Princeton Theol. Sem., NJ, 1955; MA, Yale U., New Haven, Conn., 1960, PhD, 1963. Commr. to gen. assembly Presbyn. Ch. in U.S.A., 1993. Issues analyst Witherspoon Soc., 1987-93, 99-2005, pres., 1996-99; chmn. global missions com. Presbytery Mid. Tenn., 1989-93, mem. nominating com., 2002-05. Author: Augustine, the Theologian, 1970, Augustine's Strategy as an Apologist, 1974, Christ in Context, 1975, Thomas Aquinas: Faith and Reason, 1988, Living in Two Cities: Augustinian Trajectories in Political Thought, 1998, Augustine (Abingdon Pillars of Theology), 2006. Incorporator Belmont-Hillsboro Neighbors, Nashville, 1971, Consumer Coalition for Health, Nashville, 1980, Nashville Local, Dem. Socialists Am., 1983, Cen. Am. Solidarity Assn., Nashville, 1986. Presbyn. Grad. fellow, 1958, Rockefeller doctoral fellow, 1960, Kent fellow, 1961; recipient Thomas Jefferson award Vanderbilt U., 1996. Mem. Am. Acad. Religion, Am. Soc. Ch. History, Soc. for Values in Higher Edn., Workgroup on Constructive Christian Theology, Witherspoon Soc. (pres. 1995—99), Phi Beta Kappa. Home: 1925 19th Ave S Nashville TN 37212-3805 Home Phone: 615-297-2629. Personal E-mail: teselle@bellsouth.net.

TESLIK, SARAH ANNA BALL, oil industry executive; b. Oberlin, Ohio, July 31, 1953; d. George Hudson and Nancy Ann (Cronon) Ball; m. Kennan Teslik, Aug. 21, 1976; children: Lee, William. BA, Whitman Coll., 1974; BA, MA, Oxford U., Eng., 1976; JD, Georgetown U., 1983. Bar: D.C. 1983. Assoc. Stroock and Stroock and Lavan, Washington, 1983-85, Wilkie, Farr and Gallagher, Washington, 1985-88; head Washington Office Hiscock and Barclay, 1988-91; exec. dir. Coun. Instl. Dirs., Washington, 1988—2004; pvt. practice law Washington, 1992—; CEO, cert. fin. planner bd. Stds. Inc., 2004—06; sr. v.p. policy and governance Apache Corp., 2006—. Office: Coun Instl Investors 1730 Rhode Island Ave NW Washington DC 20036-3101 also: Apache Corp 2000 Post Oak Blvd Ste 100 Houston TX 77056-4400 Office Phone: 713-296-6000. Office Fax: 713-296-6496. Business E-Mail: sarah.teslik@apachecorp.com.

TETER, CLAY, retail executive; V.p., Real Estate Family Dollar Stores, Inc., 1991—2004, Tractor Supply Co., 2004—. Office: Tractor Supply Co 200 Powell Pl Brentwood TN 37027 Office Phone: 615-440-4000. Business E-Mail: cteter@tractorsupply.com.

TETHER, ANTHONY JOHN, aerospace executive; b. Middletown, NY, Nov. 28, 1941; s. John Arthur and Antoinette Rose (Gesualdo) T.; m. Nancy Engle Pierson, Dec. 27, 1963 (div. July 1971); 1 child, Jennifer; m. Carol Suzanne Dunbar, Mar. 3, 1973; 1 child, Michael. AAS, Orange County C.C., Middletown, NY, 1961; B, Rensselaer Poly Inst., 1964; MSEE, Stanford U., Calif., 1965, PhD, 1969. V.p., gen. mgr. Sys. Control Inc., Palo Alto, Calif., 1968-78; dir. nat. intelligence Office Sec. of Def., Washington, 1978-82; dir. strategic tech. DARPA, Washington, 1982-86; corp. v.p. Ford Aerospace, Newport Beach, Calif., 1986-90, LORAL, Newport Beach, 1990-92; corp. v.p., gen. mgr. Sci. Application Internat., Inc., San Diego, 1992-94; CEO Dynamics Tech. Inc., Torrance, Calif., 1994-96; CEO, pres. Sequoia Group, Newport Beach, Calif., 1996-2001, pres., 2009—; dir. def. advanced rsch. project agy. Office of Sec. of Def., Washington, 2001—09; disting. fellow Coun. Competitiveness, Washington, 2009—. Bd. dirs. Condyne Tech., Inc., Orlando, Fla., 1990—92, chmn., 1990—92; dir. Orincon, La Jolla, Calif., 1996—99, Evans & Sutherland, Salt Lake City, 2001; bd. dirs. Qteros, 2009—10, Aurora, 2009—, Tessera, 2010—13; mem. def. sci. bd. Army Sci. Bd. Task Forces, 1998—2002; cons. Army Sci. Bd., Def. Sci. Bd. Contbr. articles to profl. jours.; mem. editl. adv. bd. Sigma Space, MAXID. Recipient Nat. Intelligence medal DCI, 1986, Civilian Meritorious medal U.S. Sec. Def., 1986, Outstanding Pub. Svc. medal, Sect. Def., 2009. Mem. IEEE (sr., life), Cosmos Club, DACOR, Sigma Xi, Eta Kappa Nu, Tau Beta Pi. Avocations: amateur radio, skiing, golf. Personal E-mail: ttether@aol.com.

TEW, E. JAMES, JR., management services company executive; b. Dallas, July 7, 1933; s. Elmer James and Bessie Fay (Bennett) T.; children: Teresa Annette, Linda Diane, Brian James. Student, Arlington State Jr. Coll., 1955—57; BBA in Indsl. Mgmt., So. Meth. U., 1969; MS in Quality Systems, U. Dallas, 1972, MBA in Mgmt., 1975; EdD in Adult Edn., Nova Southeastern U., 1986. Registered profl. engr., Calif. Mgr. quality assurance ops. Tex. Instruments Inc., Dallas, 1957-98; chmn. corp. metric implementation com. Texins Credit Union, co-chmn. credit com. Adj. faculty Richland Coll. Mountain View Coll., LeTourneau U., 1998-; precinct chmn., election judge, del. several county and state convs.; bus. computer info. systems adv. bd. U. North Tex., bd. dirs. ctr. for quality and productivity U. North Tex.; bd. examiners Malcolm Baldridge Nat. Quality award, U.S. Dept. Commerce, Nat. Inst. Standard and Tech., 1988, 89, 90, 91, 95, 96; chmn. panel judges, fellow Tex. Quality Award, 1993-2001; cons. nat. quality award Govt. Singapore, 1994; spkr. in field; bd. examiners Presdl. Quality Award, 1994-96, judge 1997-2000; quality examiner U.S. Army, 1996—; sr. quality examiner USAF, 1995-98; postdoc. edn. and arbitration edn. Nova Southeastern U., 1987, 89, in mediation, 1998, 99; vol. mediator for dispute mediation svc., 1998—. Spkr. in field. Contbr. articles to profl jours. Decorated Army Commendation medal with oak leaf cluster, Meritorious Svc. medal, Legion of Merit. Fellow Am. Soc. Quality Control (cert. quality auditor, cert. quality mgr., cert. as quality and reliability engr., chmn. Dallas-Ft. Worth sect. 1974-75). Fellow U.S. Metric Assn. (cert., chmn. cert. bd. 1986-87); mem. U.S. Res. Officers Assn., Dallas C. of C. (chmn. world mfg. com. 1974-77, chmn. spl. tasl force career edn. adv. bd. 1973-74), Property Owners Assn. Lakeview (pres. 2009-13), Dal-Tech. Alumni Assn. (pres. 2010-12), Mensa (mem. air force blue ribbon commn. on assesments and evaluations 1996-98), Sigma Iota Epsilon, Phi Delta Kappa. Baptist. Clubs: Texins Rod and Gun (pres. 1969-70), Texins Flying, Masons (32 degree).

TEWELL, JOSEPH ROBERT, JR., retired electrical engineer; b. Albany, NY, May 19, 1934; s. Joseph Robert and Florence Edna Tewell; m. Barbara Ann Johnson, Nov. 20, 1960; children— Patricia Ann, Donna Lynn, Joseph Robert, III. B.E.E., Rensselaer Poly. Inst., 1955, M.E.E., 1958. Rsch. engr. N.Am. Aviation, Inc., Downey, Calif., 1955; assoc. rsch. engr. Lockheed Aircraft Corp., Burbank, Calif., 1956; instr. Rensselaer Poly. Inst., 1957-64; sr. rsch. scientist Martin Marietta Corp., Denver, 1964-79, mgr. advanced programs Michoud, La., 1979-87, mgr. shuttle-C project, 1988-90, mgr. computer-aided productivity, 1991-93, mgr. sys. engring., 1994-96; ret., 1996. Cons. in field. Contbr. articles to profl. jours. Founding sponsor Challenger Ctr. Served with Army Security Agy., 1957. Recipient NASA Manned Awareness citation, 1970, NASA Skylab Achievement award, 1974, NASA New Tech. award, 1976, Tech. Achievement award Martin Marietta Corp., 1977, Sustained Performance award Martin Marietta Corp., 1981, NASA cert. of recognition, 1977, Author of Yr. award, 1986, also 38 publ. awards, 1965— Fellow Explorers Club; mem. AIAA, Smithsonian Assocs., Air and Space Mus., Unmanned Vehicle Sys., Nat. Audubon Soc., Sigma Xi, Eta Kappa Nu, Tau Beta Pi, Theta Chi. Achievements include invention of dual action single drive actuator; spacecraft docking and retrieval mechanism. Home and Office: 619 Legendre Dr Slidell LA 70460-3427

THACKER, STEPHANIE DAWN, federal judge; b. Huntington, W.Va., Aug. 22, 1965; BA, Marshall U., 1987; JD, W.Va. U. Coll. Law, 1990. Assoc. Kirkpatrick & Lockhart, Pitts., 1990—92, King, Betts & Allen, Charleston, W.Va., 1992—94; asst. atty. gen. environmental divsn. State of W.Va., Charleston, W.Va., 1992; asst. US atty. (southern dist.) W. Va. US Dept. Justice, Charleston, W.Va., 1994—99, trial atty. child exploitation & obscenity section Washington, 1999—2002, dep. chief of litigation, 2002—04, prin. dep. chief of litigation, 2004—06; ptnr. Guthrie & Thomas, Charleston, W.Va., 2006—12; judge US Ct. Appeals (4th Cir.), 2012—. Office: US Court Appeals 300 Virginia St E Rm 7404 Charleston WV 25301*

THACKER, STEPHEN BRADY, medical association administrator, epidemiologist; b. Independence, Mo., Dec. 30, 1947; m. 1976; 2 children. AB, Princeton U., 1969; MD, Mt. Sinai Sch. Medicine, 1973; MSc, London Sch. Hygiene and Tropical Medicine, 1984. Chief consolidated surveillance and commn. activity epidemiol. program office Ctrs. Disease Control and Prevention, Atlanta, 1978-83, dir. surveillance and epidemiol. studies, 1983-86, asst. dir. sci. Ctr. Environ. Health and Injury Control, 1986-89, dir. Epidemiol. Program Office, 1989—2004, acting dir. Nat. Ctr. Environ. Health, 1993-95, acting dep. dir., 1998, acting dir. Nat. Ctr. Injury Prevention and Control, 1999-2000, dir. Office Workforce and Career Devel., 2004—10, acting dir. Nat. Ctr. Pub. Health Informatics, 2009, dep. dir., 2010—, dir. Office Surveillance Epidemiology & Lab. Services, 2010—. Mem. steering com. Assn. Behavioral Sci. Med. Edn., 1971-74; assoc. Dept. Cmty. Medicine, Med. Ctr. Duke U., Durham, N.C., 1975-76; lectr. Cmty. Ctr. Mt. Sinai Sch. Medicine, N.Y.C., 1978—, Sch. Medicine Emory U., Atlanta, 1985-86; cons. epidemiology Arab Republic Egypt, 1979-91; clin. asst. prof. cmty. health Sch. Medicine Emory U., 1986-91; adj. prof. Emory U. Sch. Pub. Health, 1992—. Editor: Epidemiologic Revs., 1990-2003. Clin. scholar Robert Wood Johnson Found., 1974-75; recipient Mosby Book award for excellence, 1973, Pub. Health Svc. Outstanding Svc. medal, 1987, Pub. Health Svc. Meritorious Svc. medal, 1988, 2002, Saul Horowitz Jr. Meml. award, 1990, Supervisory award for contbr. advantage of women, 1991, Pub. Health Svc. Commendation medal, 1991, Pub. Health Svc. Disting. Svc. medal, 1993, 2006, Pub. Health Svc. Surgeon Gen.'s Exemplary Svc. medal, 1993, Pub. Health Svc. Disting. Svc. medal, 1997, Medal of Excellence William C. Watson, Jr., 1996, Ray E. Brown award Assn. Mil. Surgeons of U.S., 2003, Lifetime Sci. Achievement award CDC, 2009. Achievements include rsch. public health surveillance, infectious disease, environ. health, injury prevention, alcohol abuse, health care delivery, meta-analysis, technology assessment. Office: Ctrs for Disease Control and Prevention MS E94 1600 Clifton Rd NE Atlanta GA 30333 Business E-Mail: sbt1@cdc.gov.

THACKSTON, EDWARD LEE, civil engineering educator; b. Nashville, Apr. 29, 1937; s. Guy Carleton and Sydney Virginia (Adams) T.; m. Betty Tucker, Mar. 19, 1961; children: Carol Elizabeth Thackston Nixon, Leah Virginia Thackston Hawkins. BE summa cum laude, Vanderbilt U., 1961; MS, U. Ill., 1963; PhD, Vanderbilt U., 1966. Registered profl. engr., Tenn. City engr. City of Lebanon, Tenn., 1959; design engr. City of Nashville, 1961-62; instr. Vanderbilt U., Nashville, 1965-66, asst. prof., 1966-69, assoc. prof., 1969-75, prof. engring., 1975-2000, chmn. dept. civil and environ. engring., 1980-99. Asst. to gov. for environ. affairs, State of Tenn., 1972-74; cons. in field. Author book, tech. reports; contbr. to profl. publs. Bd. dirs. Tenn. Environ. Coun., Nashville, 1971-76; bd. dirs. Tenn. Conservation League, Nashville, 1974-2003, v.p., 1977, pres., 1978-80; trustee Cumberland Mus., Nashville, 1986-92; trustee Cumberland U., Lebanon, 1996—, mem. exec. com., 1996-2002, 04—, sec.-treas., 2000-02, 04-07, chmn. 07—. Recipient Tenn. Lifetime Environ./Conservation Stewardship award State Tenn. 1996, Engr. of Yr. Mid. Tenn. Tenn. Soc. Prof. Engring., 2001, Landmark Paper award Assn. Environ.

Engring. and Sci. Profs., 2001; named Tenn. Conservationist of Yr., 1974, Distinguished Alumnus Vanderbilt Univ. Sch. Engring., 2007. Fellow ASCE; mem. Am. Water Works Assn. (life), Water Environ. Fedn. (life), Assn. Environ. Engring. Profs. (emeritus, Landmark Paper award 2001), Tenn. Hist. Soc., Hillwood Country Club, Tau Beta Pi, Chi Epsilon. Republican. Episcopalian. Avocations: genealogy, history, photography, weightlifting. Business E-Mail: elt@vuse.vanderbilt.edu.

THADANI, UDHO, physician, cardiologist; b. Hyderabad, India, Apr. 1, 1941; came to U.S., 1980; s. Vensimal Mulchand and Gopi Thadani; m. Dorothy Ann Thadani, 1974; 1 child, Emma Sarala. MBBS, All India Inst. Med. Scis., New Delhi, 1964. Lic. physician, Okla., Ont., Can., Eng., India; cert. internal medicine, U.K., Can.; cert. cardiology, Can.; diplomate in internal medicine and cardiovasc. diseases Am. Bd. Internal Medicine. Intern All India Inst. Med. Scis., New Delhi, 1964-65, house physician, surgeon, 1965-66; house physician in medicine Joyce Green Hosp., Dartford, Kent, England, 1966-67; sr. house physician in medicine Kingston Gen. Hosp., Hull, England, 1967-69, registrar, rsch. fellow in medicine and cardiology, 1969-71, U. Leeds (Eng.), The Gen. Infirmary at Leeds, 1971-75; sr. rsch. fellow, clin. asst. medicine Queen's U., Kingston Gen. Hosp., Ont., Canada, 1975-78; asst. prof. medicine Queen's U., Kingston, 1978-80; staff physician Kingston Gen. Hosp., 1978-80; assoc. prof. medicine U. Okla. Health Scis. Ctr., Oklahoma City, 1980-83; prof. medicine Okla. U. Health Scis. Ctr., Oklahoma City, 1983—2001, prof. emeritus medicine, 2001, mem. cardiology fellowship com., 1980-82; dir. clin. cardiology Okla. U. Health Scis. Ctr. and VA Med. Ctr., Oklahoma City, 1980-87, cons. cardiologist, 1980—, vice chief cardiovasc. sect., 1981-99, dir. clin. rsch., 1987-99. Vice-chmn. rsch. and devel. com. VA Med. Ctr., Oklahoma City, 1989-92, chmn. physiology-pharmacology categorical rev. com., 1989-94, chmn. rsch. and devel. com., VA Med. Ctr. Oklahoma City, 1992-94, 2003-05; sr. rsch. fellow Ont. Heart Found., 1978-80, rsch. fellow, 1976-78; rsch. fellow dept. medicine Queen's U., Kingston, Ont., 1975-76; rsch. fellow U. Leeds, Pub. Health and Ciba Found., dept. medicine and cardiovasc. sect. Leeds Gen. Infirmary, 1971-75. Editor: Medical Therapy of Ischemic Heart Disease, 1992, Nitrates Updated, 1996; mem. editl. bd. panel Cardiology Drug Facts and Comparison, 1989; contbg. rev. panel Drug Facts and Comparisons, 1989-2012; mem. editl. bd. Internat. Jour. Cardiology, 1987-93, Cardiovascular Drugs and Therapy, 1987-2004, Heart Diseases, 1999-2004, Am. Jour. Pharmacology, 2000-04, Am. Jour. Cardiovasc. Drugs, 2003—, Cardiology, 2005—; reviewer Circulation, Jour. Am. Coll. Cardiology, Am. Jour. Cardiology, Brit. Heart Jour., Internat. Jour. Cardiology, Can. Jour. Cardiology, European Heart Jour., Annals of Internal Medicine, New Eng. Jour. Medicine, Archives of Internal Medicine, Cardiovasc. Drugs and Therapy, Drugs, European Jour. Pharmacology, Clin. Pharmacology and Therapeutics; contbr. over 200 articles to profl. jours., chpts. to books. Recipient Provost Rsch. award, OUHSC, 1995, James F. Hammarsten award for physicians of excellence award, VA Med. Ctr., Okla., 2003, Melvin L. Marcus Meml. Physicians Excellence award, Internat. Acad. Cardiology, 2008. Fellow: Coun. Clin. Cardiology Am. Heart Assn. (coun. rep. Okla. 1989—2000), Am. Coll. Cardiology (mem. cardiovasc. drug com. 1990—94), Royal Soc. Medicine London; mem.: Can. Cardiovasc. Soc., Royal Coll. Phycisians U.K., Phi Kappa Phi (mem. FDA cardiovasc. and renal drugs adv. com. 1995—99). Avocations: gardening, tennis, travel. Office: Okla U Health Sci Ctr Cardiology Sect 920 SL Young WP 3120 Oklahoma City OK 73104 Office Phone: 405-271-4742. Business E-Mail: udho-thadani@ouhsc.edu.

THALLER, SETH RAY, plastic surgeon; b. NYC, June 22, 1949; m. Patricia Thaller; children: Cody, Lexi. BA, Lafayette Coll., 1971; MD, U. Louisville, 1975; DMD, Boston Sch. Dentistry, 1978; resident gen. surgery, St. Vincent's Hosp., 1978-80. Intern in internal medicine SUNY, Buffalo, 1975-76; resident in gen. surgery St. Vincent's Hosp., NYC, 1978-80; resident otalaryngology/head and neck surgery Mass. Eye and Ear Infirmary, 1980-83; resident in plastic surgery Albert Einstein Coll. Medicine Affiliated Hosps., 1983—85; craniofacial fellowship UCLA Sch. Medicine, 1986; clin. instr. NYU Sch. Dentistry, NYC, 1984-86; adj. asst. prof. plastic surgery U. Calif., LA, 1986, asst. prof. plastic surgery, 1987-93, acting chief divsn. plastic surgery, 1989, assoc. prof. plastic surgery Davis, 1993-95; prof. and chief divsn. plastic surgery U. Miami/Jackson Meml. Hosp. Mem.: ACS, Am. Assn Plastic Surgeons, Assn. Academic Chmn. Plastic Surgeons, Am. Soc. Maxillofacial Surgeons, Am Soc. Plastic & Reconstructive Surgeons, Am. Cleft Palate Craniofacial Assn., Am. Society for Aesthetic Plastic Surgery, AMA. Home: 11010 Paradela St Coral Gables FL 33156-4244 Office: Univ Miami Jackson Meml Hospital PO Box 16960 Miami FL 33101-6960 Office Phone: 305-585-5285.

THAMES, RICK, newspaper editor; b. Laurinburg, NC; m. Debbie Thames; children: Nathan, Hunter, Lucy. AB in English, Pfeiffer U., Misenheimer, NC; MS in Comm., U. Tenn., Knoxville. Reporter Fayetteville Observer, NC, 1978—80; reporter, local news editor Miami News, Fla., 1980—88; various positions including govt. editor, city editor, assist. mng. editor & pub. editor Charlotte Observer, NC, 1988—96, v.p., editor, 2004—; editor Wichita Eagle, Kans., 1997—2004. Chmn. adv. bd. Elliot Sch. Comm., Wichita State U. Fellow News Leadership 2009, Knight Digital Media Ctr. Mem.: NC Press Assn. (pres.), American Soc. Newspaper Editors (mem. Freedom of Info. Com.), Kans. Press Assn. (bd. dirs.). Office: The Charlotte Observer PO Box 32188 600 S Tryon St Charlotte NC 28202 Office Phone: 704-358-5000. E-mail: rthames@charlotteobserver.com.

THAPAR, AMUL ROGER, federal judge; b. Detroit, 1969; BS, Boston Coll., 1991; JD, U. Calif. Berkeley, 1994. Law clk. to Hon. S. Arthur Spiegel US Dist. Ct. (so. dist.) Ohio, 1994—96; law clk. to Hon. Nathaniel R. Jones US Ct. Appeals (6th Cir.), 1996—97; assoc. Williams & Connolly LLP, Washington, 1997—99, Squire, Sanders & Dempsey, Cin., 2001—02; asst. US atty. DC US Dept. Justice, Washington, 1999—2000; gen. counsel Equalfooting.com, 2000—01; asst. US atty. (so. dist.) Ohio US Dept. Justice, Cin., 2002—06, US atty. (ea. dist.) Ky. Lexington, 2006—07; judge US Dist. Ct. (ea. dist.) Ky., London, 2008—. Founder Street Law Inc., Cin., 1995; adj. prof. law U. Cin. Coll. Law, 1996—97, 2002—06; trial advocacy instr. George U. Law Ctr., 1999—2000. Office: US Dist Ct Ste 444 310 S Main St London KY 40741

THARPE, FRAZIER EUGENE, journalist; b. Panama City, Fla., Jan. 10, 1941; s. Henry Clayton and Margaret Jane (Jenkins) T.; m. Barbara Ann Hembree, Oct. 30, 1971. BA in Polit. Sci. and History, Vanderbilt U., Nashville, 1963. Reporter Miami (Fla.) News, 1963; reporter U.P.I., Atlanta and Columbia, SC, 1964; pub. relations exec. Atlanta, 1965-69; fin. editor Atlanta Constn., 1969-73. Editl. assoc., columnist, 1974-83, columnist Helpline, ConsumerWatch, 1983-98; editor Homefinder, 1999-2002.

THAXTON, MARY LYNWOOD, librarian, researcher; b. Detroit, Dec. 27, 1944; d. Osceola Alvin Jr. and Mary Phlegar (Penn) T. BA, Emory and Henry Coll., 1966; MLn, Emory U., 1967; AS, Ga. State U., 1978, MA, 1983, PhD, 1989. Reference libr. Coll. of William and Mary, Williamsburg, Va., 1967-71; reference libr., asst. prof. Ga. State U., Atlanta, 1971-77, social sci. bibliographer, assoc. prof., 1977-89; pvt. practice psychotherapy, gerontol cons., Tucker, Ga., 1989-91; gerontol. cons., psychotherapist in pvt. practice Marietta, Ga., 1991-95; Atlanta, 1996-99; behavioral sci. liaison, assoc. prof. Ga. State U., Atlanta, 1999—. Editor bibliography: Metropolitan Atlanta Rapid Transit Authority, 1982, Community Mental Health Services to the Elderly, 1984 (Libr. award 1984); contbr. articles to profl. jours. Office: Ga State U Pullen Libr University Plz Atlanta GA 30303 Home Phone: 404-463-9946. E-mail: lthaxton@gsu.edu.

THAYER, ANNE J., state legislator; b. Greenville, SC, Apr. 13; d. Bobby G. and Vivian I. Williams; m. Mark W. Thayer, 1990; children: Brenn Thayer, Johnston Thayer, Jordan Thayer. BA, Marycrest Coll., 1990. Owner Thayer Properties, LLC; mem. Anderson County Foster Care Review Bd., 2003—, State Foster Care Review Bd., 2005—08; mem. Dist. 9 SC House of Representatives, 2011—. Republican. Office: South Carolina House of Representatives District 9 436D Blatt Bldg Columbia SC 29201 Address: 225 Ansonborough Plantation Belton SC 29627 Office Phone: 803-212-6889.

THAYER, CHARLES JAMES, investment banker; b. Abilene, Kans., Feb. 28, 1944; s. Bruce V. and Neoma (Obermeyer) T.; 1 child, Travis J. Grad., U. Kans., 1967. Exec. v.p., CFO Citizens Fidelity Bank, Louisville, 1977—87; exec. v.p. fin. PNC Bank Corp., Pitts., 1987—89; chmn., mng. dir. Chartwell Capital Ltd., Ft. Lauderdale, Fla., 1989—; interim chmn., CEO Sunbeam-Oster, Providence, 1993. Adv. dir. Louisville Cmty. Devel. Bank, 1997—2013, Keefe Mgrs. Inc., NYC, 1990-2002; chmn. Am. Assn. Bank Dirs., 2007-2013; chmn. emeritus Am. Assn. Bank Dirs., 2013-; bd. dirs. BB&T Bank, Fla., 2004-06, Republic Bank, St. Petersburg, Fla., 1999-04; bd. dirs. CogenAmerica, 1996-1999, MainSource Fin., 2011-; trustee Cystic Fibrosis, 1980-. Trustee Cystic Fibrosis Found., Washington, 1980—; chmn. Cystic Fibrosis Svcs., Washington, 1994-04. Mem. Nat. Assn. Corp. Dirs. (Fla. bd. dirs. 2005). Avocation: sailing. Office: Chartwell Capital Ltd 702 SW Falcon St Palm City FL 34990 Business E-Mail: cjt@chartwellcapital.com.

THAYER, DAMON, state legislator; b. Sept. 16, 1967; State senator Dist. 17, Ky., 2003—; mem. Agr. & Nat Resources Com., Transportation Com., Licensing Com., Occupations Com., Adminstrn. Regulations Com.; chmn. State & Local Govt. Com.; mem. Ky. State Senate; v.p. Breeder's Cup Event Mgmt. Mem.: NRA, League Ky. Property Owners, Ky. Col., Scott County C. of C., Ky. Right to Life, Nat. Thoroughbred Racing Assn. Republican. Roman Catholic. Address: 102 Grayson Way Georgetown KY 40324 Office: 214 Capitol Annex Frankfort KY 40601 Office Phone: 502-564-8100 644. Fax: 502-504-5508. Business E-Mail: damon.thayer@lrc.ky.gov.

THELIN, JOHN ROBERT, historian, educator, researcher, sportsman; b. West Newton, Mass., Oct. 15, 1947; s. George Willard and Rozalija Katherine (Komarec) T.; m. Anna Sharon Blackburn, June 24, 1978. AB cum laude, Brown U., 1969; MA, U. Calif., Berkeley, 1972, PhD, 1973. Rsch. asst. Brown U., Providence, 1968-69; rschr., lectr. U. Calif., Berkeley, 1972-74; asst. prof. U. Ky., Lexington, 1974-77; asst. dean Pomona Coll., Claremont, Calif., 1977-79; from asst. dir. to rsch. dir. Assn. Ind. Calif. Colls. and Univs., Santa Ana, 1979-81; chancellor prof. Coll. William and Mary, Williamsburg, Va., 1981-93, pres. faculty assembly, 1990-91; prof. higher edn. and philanthropy Ind. U., Bloomington, 1993-96; prof. ednl. policy and history U. Ky., Lexington, 1996—, disting. univ. rsch. prof., 2001—; adj. faculty Martin Sch. Pub. Policy, 2010—. Vis. prof. grad. sch. Claremont U., 1978—81; vis. scholar U. Calif., Berkeley, 1995; curator Marquandia Soc., 1971—2006; essay rev. editor Rev. of Higher Edn., 1979—91; rsch. cons. NSF, Washington, 1991; mem. faculty senate U. Ky., 1997—; guest faculty Coll. Bus. Mgmt. Inst., 1998—2006; chair social sci. com. Grad. Coun., U.K., 1998—2001; cons. Booz, Allen & Hamilton, 2004—05; rsch. cons. Am. Enterprise Inst., 2005—06; keynote spkr. U. Ga., 2010; spkr. NASPA Nat. Conf., 2007; invited spkr. Princeton U. Woodrow Wilson Sch. Symposium, 2009; ann. McBee lectr., Higher Edn. U. Ga., 2012; invited spkr., higher edn. Manhattan Inst., 2012; keynote spkr. Strategic Planning Initiative, U. Ky., Provost, 2014. Author: Higher Education and Its Useful Past, 1982, The Cultivation of Ivy, 1976, Higher Education and Public Policy, 1991, Games Colleges Play, 1994, A History of American Higher Education, 2004, Revised Edit., 2011, The Rising Costs of Higher Education, 2013, Brown University Wrestling: A Centennial History, 1912 to 2012; author: (with others) The Old College Try, 1989, One Hundred Classic Books About Higher Education, 2001; assoc. editor (jour.) Higher Edn.: Theory and Rsch., 1983—91, guest columnist Lexington Herald-Leader, 2001; contbr. chpts. to books and articles to profl. publs.; author: Essential Documents in the History of American higher Education, 2014. Pres., bd. dirs. United Way, Williamsburg, 1987-89; pres. Friends of Williamsburg Libr., 1989. Grantee Spencer Found., 1989-91, 99-2001, Ky. Humanities Coun., 2003-05, Rsch. grant Aspen Inst., 2008-09; Regents fellow U. Calif., 1972; recipient Outstanding Faculty Rsch. award Coll. of Edn., U. Ky., 2000, Great Tchrs. award U. Ky., 2004, Provost's Tchg. award U. Ky., 2006, Exch. acad. award Nat. Edn. Assn., 2007, Democracy Higher Edn. prize, State Local History Rsch. award Ky. Hist. Soc., 2006; named Berkeley Campus Cross Country Champion, U. Calif., 1973, 1974, Va. State Masters Ten Mile Running Champion, 1992, Nat. TAC Sr. 8k Second, 1993, Ky. Blue Grass Games Sr. 5k Champion, 2004; Outstanding Scholar Athlete Alumnus for Ivy League, 2006, Coun. Advancement & Support Edn. Nat. Rsch. award, 2013, Stukgiv award, 2014 Mem. Assn. Study of Higher Edn. (bd. dirs. 1988-90, keynote spkr. 1994, pres. 1999-2000, Outstanding Rsch. award, 2011), Am. Ednl. Rsch. Assn. (Exemplary Rsch. Higher Edn. award 2007), Nat. Coll. Athletic Assn. (chpt. mem., rsch. adv. bd. 2008-10), History of Edn. Soc. (editl. bd. 1988-91), Order of Ky. Cols., Lexington Club, Phi Beta Kappa (elected mem., Alpha of RI, 1969, Faculty award for advancement of scholarship Alpha of Va. 1986), Omicron Delta Kappa (Nat. Roark Meritorious Svc. award, 2008), Brown U. Wrestling Alumni Assn., Am. Enterprise Inst. Working Group Higher Edn. Avocations: long-distance running, history of Los Angeles and California, sports history. Home: 1745 Richmond Rd Lexington KY 40502 Office: U Ky Edn Policy Studies Lexington KY 40506-1 Home Phone: 859-269-0125; Office Phone: 859-257-4996. Business E-Mail: jthelin@uky.edu.

THEODORE, JOSE, professional hockey player; b. Laval, Que., Canada, Sept. 13, 1976; m. Stephanie Cloutier; 1 child, Romy. Goaltender Montreal Canadiens, 1995—2006, Colo. Avalanche, 2006—08, Washington Capitals, 2008—10, Minn. Wild, 2010—11, Fla. Panthers, 2011—. Mem. Team Can., World Cup of Hockey, 2004. Recipient Vezina Trophy, 2002, Hart Meml. Trophy, 2002, Bill Masterton Meml. Trophy, 2010; named Fredericton's Player of Yr., Am. Hockey League; named to NHL All-Star Game, 2002, 2004. Achievements include being a member of World Cup Champion Team Canada, 2004. Office: Florida Panthers BankAtlantic Center One Panther Parkway Sunrise FL 33323

THEON, JOHN SPERIDON, meteorologist, researcher; b. Washington, Dec. 12, 1934; s. Lewis and Merope Theon; m. Joanne Edens, July 31, 1965; children: Christopher James, Catherine. BS in Aero. Engring, U. Md., 1957; BS in Meteorology, Pa. State U., 1959, MS, 1962; PhD in Engring. Sci. and Mechanics, U. Tenn., 1985. Aero. engr. Douglas Aircraft Co., Santa Monica, Calif., 1957-58; engr. U.S. Naval Ordnance Lab., White Oak, Md., 1962; rsch. meterologist, 1962-74; head meterology br. NASA Goddard Space Flight Center, Greenbelt, Md., 1974-77; asst. chief lab. Atmospheric Scis., 1977-78, Nimbus project scientist, 1972—78; program scientist Global Weather Rsch. Program NASA Hdqrs., Washington, 1978—82, chief atmospheric dynamics and radiation program, program scientist Spacelab 3 mission, 1982—90; program scientist Tropical Rainfall Measuring Mission, 1984—95; chief climate processes rsch. program NASA Hdqrs., 1990—94, exec. sec. interagency task force on observations and data mgmt., 1994—95, cons., 1995—2012. Cons. Orbital Scis. Corp., 1995—96, Inst. Global Environ. Strategies, 1995—2005, Cal Tech Jet Propulsion Lab., 1997—99, George Washington U., Washington, 2005—12, NASA, 2005—09. Contbr. articles to profl. jours. With USAF, 1958—60. Recipient Goddard Exceptional Performance award, 1978, Exceptional Performance award, NASA, 1986, Radio Wave award, Ministry of Posts & Telecom. Japan, 1995; named Disting. Alumnus, U. Tenn., 1989. Fellow: Am. Meterol. Soc. Presbyterian.

THERNSTROM, ABIGAIL, federal commissioner; b. NYC, Sept. 14, 1936; d. Ferdinand and Helen Mann; m. Stephan Thernstrom, Jan. 3, 1959; children: Melanie, Samuel. BA, Barnard Coll., NYC, 1958; MA, Harvard U., Cambridge, Mass., 1961, PhD, 1975. Lectr. Harvard U., Cambridge, Mass., 1975-78; project dir. The Twentieth Century Fund, NYC, 1981-86; stringer The Economist, London, 1988-92; sr. fellow The Manhattan Inst., NYC, 1993—2009; commr. US Commn. on Civil Rights, 2001—, vice chair, 2004—; adj. scholar Am. Enterprise Inst., Washington, 2007—. Vis. lectr. Harvard U., 1988—89, Boston Coll., 1990; adj. prof. Boston U. Sch. Edn., 1991—93; mem. domestic strategy group Aspen Inst., Colo., 1992—97; mem. edn. policy com. Hudson Inst., Indpls., 1994—97; mem. Mass. State Bd. Edn., 1995—2006, Citizen's Initiative Race & Ethnicity, 1998—2002; mem. bd. advisors US Election Assistance Commn., 2006—. Author: Whose Votes Count?: Affirmative Action and Minority Voting Rights, 1987 (Anisfield Wolf Book award, 1987, ABA Cert. of Merit, 1988, Best Policy Book of Yr., Polit. Studies Orgn., 1987, Benchmark Book award, Ctr. Jud. Studies, 1987), School Choice in Massachusetts, 1991, Voting Rights--and Wrongs: THe Elusive Quest for Racially Fair Elections, 2009; co-author (with Stephan Thernstrom): America in Black and White: One Nation Indivisible, 1997 (NY Times Notable Book, 1997), No Excuses: Closing the Racial Gap in Learning, 2003 (one of Best Books of 2003-LA Times, A. Sch. Bd. Jour., Fordham Found prize, 2007); editor: A Democracy Reader, 1992; co-editor: Beyond the Color Line: New Perspectives on Race and Ethnicity in America, 2002; contbr. articles to profl. jours. Co-recipient Peter Shaw Meml. award, Nat. Assn. Scholars, 2004, Outstanding Achievement award, Bradley Found., 2007. Republican. Office: 5920 Woodley Rd Mc Lean VA 22101-3343 Address: US Commission on Civil Rights 1331 Pennsylvania Ave NW Ste 1150 Washington DC 20425 Office Phone: 703-237-1599.*

THEUNISSEN, GERALD (JOSEPH THEUNISSEN), state legislator; b. Aug. 19, 1933; m. Pat Reaud Theunissen. Mem. La. Advisor Com. Pesticides, 1985—91; state rep. Dist. 37 La., 1992—96; state senator Dist. 25, 1996—; owner Aviation Co.; mgr. Jennings Airport. Recipient Outstanding Cmty. Svc. award, Jennings Rotary Club, 1985. Mem.: VFW, Jennings Indsl. Devel. Bd., Welsh & Lake Arthur C. of C., Ret. Officers Assn., Jefferson Davis Rice Growers Assn., Jefferson Davis Farm Bur., America Legislature Exch. Coun., Greater Jennings C. of C. (pres.), Nat. & La. Agr. Aviation Assns. Democrat. Roman Catholic. Address: 436 Second St Jennings LA 70546 Mailing: PO Box 287 Jennings LA 70546 Home Phone: 318-824-1153; Office Phone: 318-824-0376. Fax: 318-824-4780.

THIBAUT, MAJOR, state legislator; Degree, La. State U., 1999. Ins. & fin. svcs.; mem. Dist. 18 La. House of Reps., 2008—, mem. commerce com., edn. com. Democrat. Office: State Capitol PO Box 44486 Baton Rouge LA 70804 Mailing: 2004 False River Dr New Roads LA 70760 Office Phone: 225-342-6945, 225-638-3811. Office Fax: 225-638-2952. Business E-Mail: thibautm@legis.state.la.us.

THIELE, DWAIN LOUIS, medical educator, department vice chairman; b. Kingsville, Tex., Dec. 22, 1952; s. Louis and Olivia Thiele; m. Elizabeth Crosser, Oct. 30, 1954; children: Alan, Kyle. BA, Rice U., 1974; MD, Baylor Coll. Medicine, 1977. Diplomate Am. Bd. Internal Medicine, 1980, in gastroenterology Am. Bd. Internal Medicine, 1983. Internship, residency Duke U. Med. Ctr., 1977—80; fellow gastroenterology, hepatology U. Tex. Southwestern Med. Ctr., Dallas, 1980—83, from asst. prof. internal medicine to prof., 1983—95, prof. internal medicine, 1995—, chief hepatology, 1998—2005, interim chief digestive, liver diseases, 2002—05, vice chair internal medicine, 2005—. Mem.: Assn. Am. Physicians, Am. Soc. Clin. Investigation. Office: University of Texas Southwestern Med Ctr 5323 Harry Hines Blvd Dallas TX 75390 Office Fax: 214-648-5607. E-mail: dwain.thiele@utsouthwestern.edu.

THIERRY, LEDRICKA JOHNSON, state legislator; m. Travis Thierry. JD, Southern U. Law Sch., 2003. Atty.; mem. Dist. 40 La. House of Reps., 2010—, mem. Acadiana del., Dem. caucus, La. Legis. Women's caucus. Democrat. Office: 8202 Hwy 182 Opelousas LA 70570 Office Phone: 337-948-0369. Office Fax: 337-948-0384. E-mail: thierryl@legis.state.la.us.

THIESSEN, MARC A., journalist, former federal official; b. Jan. 1967; m. Pamela Thiessen; 4 children. AB in Polit. Sci., Vassar Coll., 1989; studied at, US Naval War Coll. Rsch. assoc. Black, Manafort, Stone & Kelley, 1989—91, dep. dir. comm., 1991—93; press. sec. Huffington for Senate, 1994; asst. to pres. Empower America, 1993—94; press spokesman, sr. policy advisor US Senate Fgn. Rels. Com., 1995—2001; chief speechwriter to sec. US Dept. Def., 2001—04; spl. asst. to Pres., sr. speechwriter The White House, 2004—05, spl. asst. to Pres., dep. dir. speechwriting, 2005—06, dep. asst. to Pres., dep. dir. speechwriting, 2006—08, asst. to Pres for speechwriting, chief speechwriter, 2008—09. Mem. Coun. on Fgn. Rels. Contbr. articles to Wall St. Jour., Washington Post, LA Times, Weekly Standard, Nat. Review, NY Post, NY Times, Fin. Times, Fgn. Affairs, Nat. Interest, USA Today; author: Courting Disaster: How the CIA Kept America Safe and How Barack Obama Is Inviting the Next Attack, 2010. Republican.

THIGPEN, ALTON HILL, transportation executive; b. Kinston, NC, Feb. 3, 1927; s. Kirby Alton and Alice (Hill) T.; m. Rebecca Ann Braswell, May 16, 1953; children: David Alton, Jennifer Ann, Steven Roy. BS in Indsl. Engring., N.C. State U., 1950. With Assoc. Transport, Inc., Burlington, NC, 1950-71, engr., 1950-57, asst. terminal mgr. Phila., 1957-58, terminal mgr. Knoxville, Tenn., 1959, regional mgr. Valley region, 1960-62, South region, 1962-68, v.p.,dir. So. divsn., 1968-71; v.p. R.S. Braswell Co. Inc., Kannapolis, NC, 1971-80, pres., 1980—, Hartford Motor Inn Inc., North Myrtle Beach, SC, 1982—, A.T. Developers, Inc., North Myrtle Beach, 1983-97. Pres. Cherokee 2 Inc., Shelby, N.C., 1986-95, bd. dirs.; bd. dirs. Wachovia Bank, Earl Ownsby Studios Inc., Shelby. Bd. regents Berkshire Christian Coll., Lenox, Mass., 1975—; mem. adv. bd. Salvation Army, chmn. adv. bd., 1997-99. Served with USNR,

1945-46. Mem. Motor Carriers Va. (pres. 1967-68), N.C. Motor Carriers Assn. (dir. 1968-), Masons (32d degree), Lions, Sigma Chi, Tau Beta Pi. Mem. Advent Christian Ch. Office: PO Box 1197 Kannapolis NC 28082-1197 Home: 6131 Pagemont Rd Kannapolis NC 28081-8790 Office Phone: 704-933-2269.

THIGPEN, JAMES TATE, oncologist, educator; b. Columbia, Miss., June 8, 1944; m. Louisa Berdie Kessler, June 14, 1969; children: Monroe Tate, James Howard, Samuel Calvin, Richard Allen, David Albert. BS, U. Miss., 1964, MD, 1969. Cert. Am. Bd. Internal Medicine, Oncology Subspecialty Bd. Am. Bd. Internal Medicine, Hematology Subspecialty Bd. Am. Bd. Internal Medicine. Intern Strong Meml. Hosp., U. Rochester, NYC, 1969-70; resident U. Miss. Sch. Medicine, 1970-71, prof., dir. divsn. med. oncology dept. internal medicine, 1973—. Nat. med. del. from Miss. Am. Cancer Soc., 1983-85, nat. pub. issues com., 1983-85; cancer clin. investigations rev. com. Nat. Cancer Inst., 1990-95, chmn., 1993-95. Nat. bd. govs. ARC, 1981-87; group chmn. NRG Oncology, 2013-. Fellow divsn. hematology/oncology dept. medicine, 1971-73. Fellow ACP; mem. AMA, Miss. Med. Assn., Ctrl. Med. Soc., Jackson Acad. Medicine, Miss. Acad. Scis., SW Oncology Group, Gynecologic Oncology Group (group vice chmn. sci. 1988—), Am. Fedn. Clin. Rsch., Am. Assn. Cancer Edn., Am. Soc. Clin. Oncology, Am. Assn. cancer Rsch., Am. Soc. Hematology, Soc. Gynecologic Oncologists, Soc. Assn. Oncology (pres. 1988-90), Am. Radium Soc., Optimists (internat. v.p. 1983-84, internat. pres. 1990-91). Republican. Baptist. Home: 3601 Kings Hwy Jackson MS 39216-3322 Office: Univ Physicians 2500 N State St Jackson MS 39216-4500 Office Phone: 601-984-5590. Personal E-mail: jtthigpen@att.net.

THIGPEN, RICHARD ELTON, JR., retired lawyer; b. Washington, Dec. 29, 1930; s. Richard Elton and Dorothy (Dotger) Thigpen; m. Nancy H. Shand, Dec. 15, 1951; children: Susan T. Carlson, Richard M. AB, Duke U., 1951; JD, U. N.C., 1956. Bar: NC 1956, U.S. Ct. Appeals (4th cir.) 1960, U.S. Ct. Appeals (5th cir.) 1960, U.S. Ct. Appeals (10th cir.) 1974, U.S. Tax Ct. 1958, U.S. Ct. Claims 1978, U.S. Supreme Ct. 2003. Lawyer FTC, Washington, 1956-58, Thigpen & Hines, Charlotte, NC, 1958-84, Moore & Van Allen, Charlotte, 1984-88, Poyner & Spruill, Charlotte, 1988-93; gen. counsel Richardson Sports, 1994-98; ret. Bd. dirs. OrthoCarolina Rsch. Inst., 2001—08, dirs. emeritus, 2008—; bd. dirs. Charlotte-Mecklenburg YMCA, 1964—88, Heineman Med. Rsch. Ctr., Charlotte, 1970—, chmn., 2010—; bd. dirs. Charlotte C. of C., 1982—85. Lt. USNR, 1951—53. Fellow: Am. Coll. Tax Counsel (regent 1989—95, vice chmn. 1992, chmn. 1993—94); mem.: ABA, Sports Lawyers Assn. (bd. dirs. 1995—2007, pres. 2003—05, dir. emeritus 2007—), N.C. Bar Assn. (chmn. tax sect. 1976—80, pres. 1988—89), N.C. State Bar. Avocations: golf, travel. Home: 8919 Park Rd DC 30 Charlotte NC 28210 Personal E-mail: thigpenhouse@carolina.rr.com.

THILL, HOWARD J., energy executive; b. Bartlesville, Okla. B in Acctg. & Mktg., Okla. State U., MBA. CPA. Various mgmt. positions in natural gas ops., fed. & internat. tax, chem. acctg., internat fin., bus devel. Phillips Petroleum Co., 1982—2002; mgr., investor rels. Marathon Oil Corp., 2002—03, dir., investor rels., 2003—07, v.p., investor rels. and pub. affairs, 2008—. Mem. Okla. State U. Alumni Assn., past chapter pres.; mem. Nat. Investor Rels. Inst.; bd. dirs. Jr. Achievement, Houston, Tex. Office: Marathon Oil Corp 5555 San Felipe Rd Houston TX 77056-2723 Office Phone: 713-629-6600. Office Fax: 713-296-2952. Business E-Mail: hjthill@marathonoil.com.

THIRSK, ROBERT BRENT, astronaut; b. New Westminster, BC, Can., Aug. 17, 1953; m. Brenda Biasutti; 3 children. BSc in Mech. Engring., U. Calgary, 1976; MSc in Mech. Engring., MIT, 1978; MD, McGill U., 1982; MBA, MIT, 1998; LLD (hon.), U. Calgary, 2009; DSc (hon.), U. NB, 2010. Resident Queen Elizabeth Hosp., Montreal, Canada, 1982—83; astronaut Can. Astronaut Program, 1984—; sabbatical yr. Victoria, B.C., Canada, 1994—95; chief astronaut Can. Space Agy., 1993—94; astronaut NASA, Houston, 1998—. Dir. Can. Found. Internat. Space U., 1992—; crew comdr. CAPSULS mission, 1994; astronaut Space Shuttle mission STS-78, 1996; crew comdr. NEEMO 7 undersea mission, 2004; backup astronaut STS-41G space shuttle mission, 1984, Soyuz 10 S taxi mission, 2005; astronaut Soyuz Mission TMA-15 & ISS Expeditions 20 & 21, 2009. Recipient Disting. Alumni award, U. Calgary, 1985, Space Flight medal, NASA, 2009, Disting. Pub. Svc. medal, 2009. Mem.: Coll. Physicians and Surgeons B.C., Coll. Physicians & Surgeons Ontario, Aerospace Med. Assn., Can. Aeronautics & Space Inst., Can. Coll. Family Physicians, Assn. Profl. Engrs. Ontario (Gold Medal award 1997). Avocations: hockey, squash, playing the piano. Office: Astronaut Office CB NASA Johnson Space Center Houston TX 77058

THOMAN, ROY EDWARD, political scientist, educator; b. Evansville, Ind., Mar. 11, 1938; s. Joseph Henry and Nell Yates Thoman; m. Judith Ann Schiff, May 20, 1967 (div. Apr. 18, 1985); 1 child, Mark; m. Jan Brister, May 21, 2005. BA magna cum laude, U. Evansville, 1960; MA, Ind. U., 1964; PhD, U. Ky., 1967. Asst. prof. West Tex. A&M U., Canyon, 1968—70, assoc. prof., 1970—76, prof., 1976—. Contbr. articles to profl. jours.; consulting editor World Affairs, 1979—82. Recipient scholarship medal, Pi Gamma Mu, 2000, endowed scholarship in his name, Phi Eta Sigma, 2000; grantee, Tex. Ednl. Assn., 1972—75. Mem.: KC, Am. Polit. Sci. Assn. Republican. Roman Catholic. Office: West Tex A&M U WT Box 725 Canyon TX 79016 Home: 3816 Doris Dr Amarillo TX 79109-5505 Office Phone: 806-352-6140. Business E-Mail: rthoman@mail.wtamu.edu.

THOMAS, ANDREA B., retail executive; B, U. Utah; MBA, Brigham Young U., Provo, Utah. Dir., new product mktg. Pizza Hut, Inc.; v.p. retail mktg. and promotions Fritos/Tostitos brands, then v.p. innovation Frito-Lay, Inc.; v.p. global innovation Hershey Co., 2006; sr. v.p. pvt. brands Wal-Mart Stores, Inc., 2007—10, sr. v.p. sustainability, 2010—. Named one of 25 Masters of Innovation, Business-Week. Office: Wal-Mart Stores Inc 702 SW 8th St Bentonville AR 72716 Office Phone: 479-273-4000. Office Fax: 479-277-1830.

THOMAS, BEVERLY D., healthcare company executive; BA in Journalism, U. Ga., 1967, M in Pub. and Nonprofit Adminstrn., 1976, MPA, 1991. Reporter Atlanta Jour.-Constn., Columbus Enquirer, Ga.; staff Atlanta Housing Authority; dir. pub. rels., then v.p. comm. & pub. rels. Grady Health Sys., Atlanta, 1982—93; v.p. comm. & pub. affairs Kaiser Permanente, 1994—. Bd. dirs. AID Atlanta, Atlanta Women's Found. Office: Kaiser Permanente Nine Piedmont Ctr 3495 Piedmont Rd NE Atlanta GA 30305 Office Phone: 404-364-7000. Office Fax: 404-364-4998. Business E-Mail: beverly.thomas@kp.org.

THOMAS, BEVERLY IRENE, special education educator, counseling administrator, educational diagnostician; b. Del Rio, Tex., Nov. 12, 1939; d. Clyde and Eve Whistler; m. James Thomas, Jan. 28, 1972; children: Kenneth (dec.), Wade, Robert, Darcy, Betty Kay, James III, Debra, Brenda, Michael. BM summa cum laude, Sul Ross State U., 1972, MEd in Music, 1976, MEd in Counseling, 1992, MEd in Mid. Mgmt., 1996. Cert. music, 1972, elem. edn., 1974, music edn., 1976, learning disabilities, 1976, spl. edn. generic, 1976, ednl. diagnosis, 1976, ednl. counseling, 1996, spl. edn. counseling and mid. mgmt., 1995, anger resolution therapist, 1995; cert. correctional justice addictions profl.; lic. chem. dependency counselor, 2006. Tchr. Pecos-Barstow-Toyah Ind. Sch. Dist., 1974—92, 1992—2000; edn. diagnostician West Tex. State Sch., Tex. Youth Commn.; tchr. spl. edn. and enhanced 5th grade Pecos-Barstow-Toyah Ind. Sch. Dist., 2000—01; youth counselor Tex. Workforce Ctr., Pecos, 2000; substance abuse counselor Reeves County Detention Ctr., 2001—09, tchr., 2012—; LCDC Clover House Inc, 2004—12. Gifted-talented coordinator 5th grade, Pecos-Barstow-Toyah Ind. Sch. Dist., 1999-2000. Mem. ASCD, NEA, MENSA, Assn. for Children with Learning Disabilities (local sec. 1974), Tex. State Tchrs. Assn. (treas. 1991-94), Tex. Ednl. Diagnosticians Assn., Tex. Profl. Ednl. Diagnosticians, Reeves County Assn. of Children with Learning Disabilities, Nat. Coun. Tchrs. of Maths., Nat. Coun. Tchrs. English, Learning Disabilities Assn., Nat. Coun. for Geog. Edn., Learning Disabilities Assoc., Tex., Coun. for Exceptional Children, Tex. Counseling Assn., Am. Correctional Assn., Alpha Chi, Kappa Delta Pi, Chi Sigma Iota.

THOMAS, BRAD, gallery director, curator; B in Creative Arts, U. NC, Charlotte, 1992; grad., Penland Sch. Crafts, NC, 1998. Exhbn. coord. Light Factory, Charlotte, 1998—99; gallery dir., curator Van Every/Smith Galleries, Davidson Coll., NC, 1999—. Pub. art commr. Arts and Sci. Coun. Mecklenburg County, Charlotte, 2006—. Office: Van Every/Smith Galleries Davidson Coll PO Box 1720 Davidson NC 28036 Office Phone: 704-894-2519. Business E-Mail: brthomas@davidson.edu.

THOMAS, BRIAN W., state legislator; b. Paterson, NJ, Jan. 15, 1961; BA in History and Philosophy, Wofford Coll., 1983; MA, Wake Forest U., 1991; PhD in Anthropology, SUNY, Binghamton, 1995. Archaeologist Nat. Park Svc., 1991—92, The Hermitage, 1994—96, SW Mo. State U., 1997—99; ops. mgr. TRC Garrow Assocs., Inc., 1999—; mgr. Cultural Resources Co.; mem. Dist. 100 Ga. House of Reps., 2005—, mem. Def. and Vets. Affairs Com., Edn. Com., Natural Resources and Environ. Com. & Subcommittee on Academic Support. Bd. mem. Am. Cultural Resources Assn., 2004—, Ga. Coun. Profl. Archaeologists. Capt. mil. intelligence divsn. US Army, 1983—87, major USAR, 2000. Democrat. Office: 612-B Coverdell Legislative Office Bldg Atlanta GA 30334 Home: 101 Coley Cove Rd Lamoine ME 04605-7906 Office Phone: 404-656-0325. E-mail: brian.thomas@house.ga.gov.

THOMAS, CHERYLL C., epidemiologist, federal agency administrator; BS in Biochemistry, UCLA, 1995; MPH, Emory U., Atlanta, 1999. Staff rsch. assoc. UCLA Med. Ctr., 1995—97; epidemiologist American Cancer Soc., 1999—2004; epidemiologist, divsn. cancer prevention & control US Centers Disease Control & Prevention, Atlanta, 2004—. Contbr. articles to profl. jours. Office: Centers Disease Control & Prevention 1600 Clifton Rd Atlanta GA 30333 Business E-Mail: zzg3@cdc.gov.

THOMAS, COLIN GORDON, JR., surgeon, medical educator; b. Iowa City, July 25, 1918; s. Colin Goudenz and Eloise Kinzer (Brainerd) T.; m. Shirley Forbes, Sept. 14, 1946 (dec.); children: Karen, Barbara, James G., John F. BS, U. Chgo., 1940, MD, 1943. Diplomate Am. Bd. Surgery. Intern U. Iowa Hosp., 1943-44, resident surgery, 1944-45, 47-50; assoc. in surgery U. Iowa Med. Sch., 1950-51, asst. prof., 1951-52; mem. faculty U. N.C. Med. Sch., Chapel Hill, 1952—, prof. surgery, 1961—, Byah Thomason Doxey-Sanford Doxey prof. surgery, 1982—, chmn. dept., 1966-84, chief div. gen. surg., 1984-89, part-time prof., 1991—. Contbr. surg. texts, numerous articles to med. jours. Served to capt., M.C. AUS, 1945-47. Recipient Prof. award U. N.C. Sch. Medicine, 1964, Disting. Svc. award U. Chgo., 1982, Med. Alumni Disting. faculty award U. N.C., 1984; Berryhill lectr. U. N.C., 1989; recipient Fleming Fuller award U. N.C. Hosps., 1994, Disting. Alumnus award, Shattuck, St. Marys Sch., Minnesota, 2011, Order of Long Leaf Pime, NC, 2012. Mem. AMA, ACS (Disting. Leadership award N.C. chpt. 1990), AAUP, Am. Thyroid Assn., Am. Assn. Cancer Research, Am. Assn. Endocrine Surgeons (pres. 1989-90), Soc. Univ. Surgeons, So. Surg. Assn. (v.p. 1989-90), N.Y. Acad. Scis., Halsted Soc., Am. Surg. Assn., Womack Surg. Soc. (pres. 1981-83), Soc. Internationale de Chirurgie, Soc. Surgery Alimentary Tract, N.C. Surg. Assn., Internat. Assn. Endocrine Surgeons, Kiwanis (pres. Tarheel Golden Kiwanis 2004), Alpha Omega Alpha. Episcopalian (warden 1961-62). Home: 621 Cedars Club Cir Chapel Hill NC 27517 Office: Univ NC Chapel Hill 4005 Burnett-Womack CB 7228 Chapel Hill NC 27599-7228 Business E-Mail: cqt@med.unc.edu.

THOMAS, DAVID L., state legislator; b. Westminster, SC, Sept. 10, 1949; s. Harry Lee and Mary Brown Thomas; m. Fran Thressia Bauman, 1984. BA, U. NC, Charlotte, 1971; MDiv, Southwestern Baptist Theol. Seminary, 1975; MA, Tex. Christian U., 1979; JD, U. SC, 1995. Atty.; mem. Greenville City Coun., SC, 1979—83, mayor pro tem SC, 1983—84; mem. Dist. 8 SC State Senate, 1985—, chair Banking and Ins. Com., mem. Corrections and Penology Com., Fin. Com. & Med. Affairs Com. Republican. Baptist. Address: 23 Wade Hampton Blvd Greenville SC 29609 Office: 410 Gressette Bldg Columbia SC 29201 Office Phone: 803-212-6240, 864-271-6371. Fax: 803-212-6299. Business E-Mail: sbi@scsenate.org.

THOMAS, DAVID LAMARR, surgeon, educator; b. Phila., Oct. 13, 1945; MD, U. Miami Sch. Medicine, 1970; JD, Stetson U. Coll. Law, 1995. Dep. sec., dir. health svcs., Fla., 1994—2003; prof., chair dept. surgery, divsn. correctional medicine Nova Southeastern U., 2003—, prof. pub. health. Mem. fla. ho. reps. Fla. Legislature, 1984—94; bd. govs. exec. com. Am. Correctional Assn., 2005. Recipient Better Life award, Fla. Health Care Assn., 1985, Disting. Svc. award, Am. Correctional Health Care Assn., 2002, Spl. Achievement award, Fla. Soc. Ophthalmology, award, Fla. Juvenile Justice Blueprint Commn., Outstanding Legislative Efforts award, Am. Lung Assn. Fellow: Am. Coll. Ophthalmology. Avocation: boating. Office: 3200 S University Dr Ste 1443 Fort Lauderdale FL 33328 Office Fax: 954-262-3271. Business E-Mail: davithom@nova.edu.*

THOMAS, ELLIOTT GRIFFIN, bishop emeritus; b. Pitts., July 15, 1926; Ordained priest Diocese of St. Thomas, USVI, 1986; ordained bishop, 1993; bishop Diocese of St. Thomas, USVI, 1993-99, bishop emeritus, 1999—. Roman Catholic. Office: PO Box 301825 Charlotte Amalie VI 00803-1825 Office Phone: 340-776-3166. Office Fax: 340-774-5816. E-mail: chancery@islands.vi.

THOMAS, ELWYN, state legislator; b. Feb. 18, 1943; m. Linda Thomas; 1 child, Teresa Ratliff. Attended, Lincoln Grad. Ctr., Ala. Bankers' Seminars. Real estate evaluator, east ctrl. divsn. Colonial Bank; mem. Dist. 34 Ala. House of Reps., 1998—. Mem. Blount County C. of C., St. Clair County Bd. Realtors, First Bapt. Ch., Oneonta, Ala. Mem.: Ala. Realtors' Assn., Gideons. Republican. Baptist. Office: Ala House of Reps Ala State House 11 S Union St Rm 541-B Montgomery AL 36130 Home: 2007 Home Park Trl Apt 111 Prattville AL 36066-7785 Office Phone: 205-237-4672, 334-242-7762.

THOMAS, FAYE EVELYN J., elementary and secondary school educator; b. Summerfield, La., Aug. 3, 1933; d. Reginald Felton and Atlee (Hunter) Johnson; m. Archie Taylor Thomas, Sept. 8, 1960; 1 child, Dwayne Andre. BA, So. U., 1954; student, Tuskegee Inst., 1958, student, 1969, U. Detroit, 1961, student, 1962, student, 1963, Ctrl. Mich. U., 1965; MS, U. Ctrl. Ark., 1971, Cleve. State U., 1979. Tchr. Cullen (La.) Elem. Sch., 1957; tchr. English and social studies Charles Brown H.S., Springhill, La., 1957—70; tchr. English, Upward Bound Program, Grambling State U., 1968; tchr. English, Springhill H.S., 1970; elem. intermediate tchr. Riveredge Elem. Sch., Berea, Ohio, 1971—93; tchr. 7th grade English, Ford Mid. Sch., 1993—94; interventionist Brown Upper Elem. Sch., Springhill, La., 2009—; instr. GED, Springhill. Tchr. asst. elem. coun. curriculum and instrn. Berea Sch. Dist., 1984—85. Author: When the Time Is Right, Move On, 2002, A Journey to the Mountain Top, 2003. Program dir. teen pregnancy prevention program First Bapt. Ch., Cullen, La., 2003—04. Grantee, EDPA, 1970—71, Internat. Paper Found., 1958, 1960, NDEA, 1965; scholar Martha Holden Jennings scholar, 1984—85. Mem.: ASCD, NEA, N.E. Ohio Tchrs. Assn., Berea Edn. Assn., Ohio Edn. Assn., Ohio Motorists Assn., Charles Brown Soc. Orgn. (trustee 1984—), Black Caucus NEA, People United to Save Humanity, Toastmasters, Order Eastern Star. Democrat. Baptist. Office: 311 Henrietta White Blvd Springhill LA 71075-8407

THOMAS, FRANK M., JR., corporate financial executive; BSBA, U. SC. Co-chmn. Aiken Downtown Devel. Assn.; sr. v.p., comml. lending, sr. v.p., Aiken area exec. Security Federal Corp., bus. devel. officer, 1994, exec. v.p.; treas. U. of SC. Bd. dirs. Security Fed. Corp., Aiken Downtown Devel. Assn. Bd. dirs., treas. Greater Aiken C. of C.; bd. dirs, U. of SC Aiken Partnership Bd.; bd. dirs., Free Medical Clinic Aiken County; working Aiken Cmty. Office: Security Federal Corp 238 Richland Ave W Aiken SC 29801 Office Phone: 803-641-3000. Office Fax: 803-641-3046.

THOMAS, GINNI (VIRGINIA LAMP THOMAS), public policy analyst; b. Feb. 23, 1957; d. Donald and Marjorie Lamp; m. Clarence Thomas, May 30, 1987. BA in Polit. Sci. and Bus. Comm., Creighton U., 1979, JD, 1983. Legis. aide then legis. dir. to Rep. Hal Daub US House of Representatives, Washington, 1981; atty., labor rels. specialist US C. of C., 1985—89, mgr. employee rels., 1989; joined Legis. Affairs Office US Dept. Labor, 1991; policy analyst for Rep. Dick Armey US House of Representatives; White House liaison Heritage Found., now cons.; assoc. v.p. Washington campus Hillsdale Coll., 2008—09; founder, pres., CEO Liberty Ctrl., Inc., 2009—. Alumni adv. bd. Creighton U. Sch. Law. Republican. Episcopalian. Office: Liberty Central, Inc Suite 302 5765-F Burke Center Parkway Burke VA 22015

THOMAS, HERMAN L., school system administrator; Asst. supt. Arkadelphia Sch. Dist., Ark., 1992—. Recipient Blue Ribbon Sch. Award, 1990-91. Office: Arkadelphia Sch Dist 235 N 11th St Arkadelphia AR 71923-4903

THOMAS, HUW FRANCIS, dean, dental educator; BDS, U. London, Guy's Hosp., 1975; MS in Dental Rsch., U. Rochester, 1978; PhD in Biomedical Sci., U. Conn., 1986. Cert. pediatric dentistry Eastman Dental Ctr., U. Rochester, 1978. Postdoctoral fellow. NIH, 1980—84; asst. prof. pediatric dentistry U. Tex. Health Sci. Ctr., San Antonio, 1978—80; assoc. prof. pediatric dentistry dept. U. Conn. Health Ctr., Conn., 1980—92; prof., chmn. dept. pediatric dentistry U. Tex. Health Sci. Ctr., San Antonio, 1992—2003, prof. dept. pediat. & cellular and structural biology; prof., dean Sch. Dentistry, U. Ala., Birmingham, 2004—. Sci. cons. ADA Commn. on Dental Accreditation. Reviewer: American Journal of Anatomy, Archives of Oral Biology, Journal of Dental Education. Recipient New Investigator Research award, NIH, 1985. Fellow: Internat. Coll. Dentists, Am. Coll. Dentists, Am. Acad. Pediat. Dentistry; mem.: AAAS (mem. at large sec. on dentistry and oral health sci.), Am. Assn. Dental Rsch. (mem. nominating com.), Am. Acad. Pediat. (mem. exec. com. pediat. dentistry sect.), Omicron Kappa Upsilon. Office: U Ala Birmingham Sch Dentistry SDB 406 1530 3rd Ave S Birmingham AL 35294-0007 Office Phone: 205-934-4720. Office Fax: 205-975-6544. Business E-Mail: hft@uab.edu.

THOMAS, JOYCE CAROL, author, educator; b. Ponca City, Okla., May 25, 1938; children: Monica, Gregory, Michael, Roy. BA, San Jose State Coll., Calif., 1966; MS, Stanford U., 1967. Asst. prof. San Jose State Coll., 1969—72, reading prog. dir., 1979—82, prof., 1982—83; tchr. Contra Costa Coll., Calif., 1973—75; prof. St. Mary's Coll., Moraga, Calif., 1975—77; prof. English U. Tenn, 1989—. Vis. prof. English Purdue U., West Lafayette, Ind., 1984. Author: Bittersweet, 1973, Crystal Breezes, 1974, Blessing, 1975, Black Child, 1981, Inside the Rainbow, 1982, Marked by Fire, 1982 (Before Columbus Book award, 1982, Best Book for Young Adults, ALA, 1982, Nat. Book award, 1983), Bright Shadow, 1983, Water Girl, 1986, The Golden Pasture, 1986, Journey, 1988, A Gathering of Flowers: Stories About Being Young in America, 1990, When the Nightingale Sings, 1992, Brown Honey in Broomwheat Tea: Poems, 1993, Gingerbread Days: Poems, 1995, Cherish Me, 1998, I Have Heard of a Land, 1998 (Notable Book award, ALA, 1999, Tchr.'s Book award, Internat. Reading Assn., 1999), You Are My Perfect Baby, 1999, Hush Songs: African-American Lullabies, 2000, The Bowlegged Rooster: And Other Tales That Signify, 2000, House of Light, 2001, A Mother's Heart, A Daughter's Love, 2001, The Gospel Cinderella, 2001, The Blacker the Berry: Poems, 2001, Crowning Glory: Poems, 2002, (plays) A Song in the Sky, 1976, Look! What a Wonder!, 1976, Magnolia, 1977, Ambrosia, 1978, When the Nightingale Sings, 1991. Recipient Arrell Gibson Lifetime Achievement award, Okla. Ctr. For the Book, 2001; named Okla. Poet Laureate, 1996—2000. Office: Tenn Authors Project UT Librs Knoxville TN 37996 Personal E-mail: JCTauthor@aol.com.

THOMAS, LARRY S., transportation executive; m. Lynn Thomas; 2 children. BSEE, U. Evansville, Evansville, Ind. Info. tech. positions IBM Corp., Whirlpool Corp., Kimbal Internat.; dir., Info. Svc. Landstar System Inc., 1994, v.p., Rsch. & Engring., 2000—01; v.p., chief info. officer Landstar System, Inc., 2001—. Named one of Premier 100 IT Leaders, Computerworld, 2006. Office: Landstar System Inc 13410 Sutton Park Dr S Jacksonville FL 32224 Office Phone: 904-398-9400. Office Fax: 904-390-1437. Business E-Mail: lthomas@landstar.com.

THOMAS, LAURA W., corporate financial executive; BA in French & Bus., Radford U.; MBA, George Wash. U. V.p., fin. Concert Comm., acting CFO; dir., fin. MCI Comm.; v.p., fin. XO Holdings, Inc. (formerly XO Communications), 2000—09, sr. v.p., CFO, 2009—. Office: XO Holdings Inc 13865 Sunrise Valley Dr Herndon VA 20171 Office Phone: 703-547-2000. Office Fax: 703-547-2881. Business E-Mail: laura.thomas@xo.com.

THOMAS, LEE MULLER, investment company executive, former government official; b. Ridgeway, SC, June 13, 1944; s. Robert Walton and Laura (Muller) Thomas; m. Dixie Gay Smily, June 20, 1981; children: Jordan, Braden; children: Lee, Elliott. BA, U. South, 1967; MEd, U. SC, 1971. Ind. cons. Criminal Justice Planning, 1977-79; exec. dir., criminal justice program Office Gov., Columbia, SC, 1972-77, dir., pub. safety programs, 1979-81; assoc. dir., state and local programs and support FEMA, Washington, 1981-82, dep. dir., 1982-83; asst. adminstr. EPA, Washington, 1983-85, adminstr., 1985-89; chmn., CEO Law Companies Environ. Group Inc., 1989—93;

joined Ga. Pacific Corp., 1993, sr. v.p., paper, 1995—96, exec. v.p., paper & chemicals, 1997—2000, exec. v.p., consumer products, 2000—02, pres., bldg. products & distribution, 2002, pres., 2002—03, pres., COO, 2003—05; pres., CEO Rayonier, Inc., Jacksonville, Fla., 2007—. Bd. dirs. Resolve Inc., Fed. Res. Bank, Atlanta, Airgas Inc., 1998—, Regal Entertainment Inc., 2006—. Bd. dir. World Resources Inst., Washington, Nat. Merit Scholarship Corp., Ga. Environ. Facilities Authority. Mem.: SC Law Enforcement Officers Assn., SC Corrections Assn., Nat. Criminal Justice Assn. (chmn. 1979—81), Sigma Nu. Office: Rayonier Inc 1301 Riverplace Blvd Ste 2300 Jacksonville FL 32207-9062 Office Phone: 904-357-9100. Office Fax: 904-357-9101. Business E-Mail: lee.thomas@rayonier.com.

THOMAS, LINDSEY KAY, JR., research ecology biologist, educator, consultant; b. Salt Lake City, Apr. 16, 1931; s. Lindsey Kay and Naomi Lurie (Biesinger) T.; m. Nancy Ruth Van Dyke, Aug. 24, 1956; children: Elizabeth Nan Thomas Reid, David Lindsey, Wayne Hal, Dorothy Ann Thomas Brown. BS, Utah State Agrl. Cultural Coll., Logan, 1953; MS, Brigham Young U., Provo, Utah, 1958; PhD, Duke U., Durham, NC, 1974. Park naturalist Nat. Capital Pks., Nat. Pk. Svc., Washington, 1957—62, pk. naturalist (rschr.) Region 6, 1962—63, rsch. pk. naturalist Nat. Capital Region, 1963—66; rsch. biologist S.E. Temperate Forest Pk. Areas, Washington, 1966, Durham, NC, 1966—67, Great Falls, Md., 1967—71, Nat. Capital Pks., Great Falls, 1971—74, Nat. Capital Region, Triangle, Va., 1974—93, Washington, 1985—93; rsch. biologist, Patuxent Environ. Sci. Ctr. Nat. Biol. Survey, 1993—94, Nat. Biol. Svc., Washington, Triangle, 1995—96; resource mgmt. specialist Balt.-Washington Pkwy., Greenbelt, Md., 1996, Nat. Capital Parks-East, 1996—98; rsch. ecologist emeritus and cons. Nat. Capital Region, Nat. Park Svc., 1998—. Bd. dirs. Prince William County Svc. Authority, Va., 1996-2004; adj. prof. George Mason U., Fairfax, Va., 1988—, George Washington U., Washington, 1992-98; instr. US Dept. Agr. Grad. Sch., 1964-66; aquatic ecol. cons. Fairfax County Fedn. Citizens Assns., Va., 1970-71; guest lectr. Washington Tech. Inst. (now U. DC), 1976. Contbr. articles to profl. jours. Wildlife mgmt. cons. Girl Scouts Am., Loudoun County, Va., 1958; preservation and mgmt. cons. McAteean Magnolia Bogs, Save Araby, Mattawoman and Mason Springs in Charles County, Md., 2002-06, Nat. Resources Divsn., Arlington County, Va., 2004—; asst. scoutmaster, scoutmaster, merit badges counselor Boy Scouts Am., 1958—, Scouters Tng. award, 1961. Recipient Incentive awards Nat. Park Svc., 1962, Superior Performance award, 1989; rsch. grantee Washington Biologists' Field Club, 1977, 82. Mem.: AAAS, The Book of Mormon Archaeological Digest, Md. Native Plant Soc., Nat. Trust for Historic Preservation, Washington Biologists' Field Club, Southern Appalachian Botanical Soc., The Nature Conservancy, George Wright Soc., Ecol. Soc. Am., Bot. Soc. Washington, Sigma Xi. Mem. Lds Ch. Home and Office: 13854 Delaney Rd Woodbridge VA 22193-4654

THOMAS, LIZANNE, lawyer; BA cum laude, Furman U., 1979; JD, Washington & Lee U., 1982. Bar: Ga. 1982. Ptnr. mergers and acquisitions practice Jones Day, Atlanta, firmwide adminstrv. ptnr., 2003—07, ptnr.-in-charge Atlanta office, 2008—. Lectr. corp. fin. U. Calif., Berkeley and Davis; pres. Law Alumni Assn. Washington and Lee U., 2001—02; bd. dirs. Krispy Kreme Doughnuts, 2004—. Recurring panelist Directors' Inst. of the Conf. Bd. Bd. mem. NYSE s Corp.; bd. trustees Furman U.; exec. bd. dirs. Atlanta C. of C. Mem.: State Bar of Ga. Office: Jones Day 1420 Peachtree St NE Ste 800 Atlanta GA 30309-3053 Office Phone: 404-581-8411. Office Fax: 404-581-8330. Business E-Mail: lthomas@jonesday.com.

THOMAS, REGINA, state legislator; b. Savannah, Ga., Dec. 05; m. Ervine J. Thomas. Former state rep. Dist. 148, Ga.; former mem. Banking Com., Children & Youth & Jour. Com.; house rep. Ga.; tax assoc. H & R Block; mem. Commerce Pathway Tchg., Savannah State U.; vol. Ralph Mark Gilbert Civil Rights Mus., Chatham-Savannah Citizen Advocacy Office; state senator Dist. 2 Ga., 2003—08; mem. Def. Com., Sci. & Tech. Com., Vets. & Consumer Affairs Com., Appropriations Com., Edn. Com., Reapportionment Com. Democrat. Mailing: 313-A Legis Office Bldg Atlanta GA 30334 Office: 1406 E 35th St Savannah GA 31404 E-mail: rthomas@legis.state.ga.us.

THOMAS, ROBERT EGGLESTON, retired manufacturing executive; b. Cuyahoga Falls, Ohio, July 28, 1914; s. Talbott E. and Jane S. (Eggleston) T.; 1 child, Barbara Ann. BS in Econs, U. Pa., 1936. Asst. to gen. mgr., sec., mgr. r.r. investments Keystone Custodian Funds, Boston, 1936-53; v.p. Pennroad Corp., NYC, 1953-59; chmn. exec. com., dir. M.-K.- T. R.R., 1956-65; mem. exec. com. MAPCO Inc., 1960-84, dir., chief exec. officer, 1960-80, pres., 1960-76, chmn. bd., 1973-84. Adv. bd. BancOkla. Corp. Mem.: Newcomen Soc., Nat. Mining Assn. (hon. dir.), Am. Petroleum Inst. (hon. dir.), Desert Horizons Country Club (Indian Wells, Calif.), San Diego Yacht Club, Summit Club (Tulsa), So. Hills Country Club (Tulsa), Chgo. Club. Episcopalian. Office: Williams Cos PO Box 4679 Tulsa OK 74159-0679 Home Phone: 918-499-1695; Office Phone: 918-573-8100. E-mail: Robert.Thomas@williams.com.

THOMAS, ROBERT PAIGE, lawyer; b. Columbus, Ohio, July 31, 1941; s. Charles Marion and Elsie (Cavanaugh) Thomas; children: Paige Cason, Park Cavanaugh. BA, Vanderbilt U., 1963, MA, 1965, JD, 1970. Bar: Tenn. 1970, US Dist. Ct. (mid. dist.) Tenn. 1970, US Ct. Appeals (6th cir.) 1977. Assoc. Bradley Arant Boult Cummings LLP, Nashville, 1970—74, ptnr., 1974—, mng. ptnr., 1977—84, Bradley Arant Boult Cummings, 2009—; chmn. Tenn. Dem. Party. Mem. Bill Clinton's Nat. Fin. Com.; fin. chmn. Sen. Jim Sasser. Mem.: ABA, Nashville Bar Assn., Tenn. Bar Assn., Belle Meade Country, Yale NYC. Office: PO Box 340025 Nashville TN 37203 Home Phone: 615-383-1907; Office Phone: 615-252-2314. Business E-Mail: bthomas@babc.com.

THOMAS, ROBIN, mathematics professor; Prof. math. Ga. Inst. Tech., Atlanta. Office: Ga Inst Tech Math Dept 225 North Ave NW Atlanta GA 30332-0002

THOMAS, SARA RICHARDSON, state legislator; b. Indianola, Miss., Apr. 21, 1941; m. Arthur Lee Thomas. Mem. Dist. 31 Miss. House of Reps., 1999—. Mem.: Crepe Myrtle Garden Club, Regulette Civic & Social, Miss. Valley State U. Alumni Assn., Miss. Ret. Tchrs., Miss. & Nat. Assn. Educators. Democrat. Baptist. Mailing: 512 BB King Rd Indianola MS 38751 Office Phone: 601-359-9465, 662-887-2628. E-mail: sthomas@house.ms.gov.

THOMAS, TIM, professional hockey player; b. Flint, Mich., Apr. 15, 1974; m. Melissa Thomas; children: Kiley, Kelsey, Keegan. Grad., U. Vt., 1997. Goaltender Boston Bruins, 2002—03, 2005—13, Providence Bruins (Am. Hockey League), 2003—04, Fla. Panthers, 2013—14, Dallas Stars, 2014—. Mem. Team USA, Olympic Games, Vancouver, 2010. Recipient Vezina Trophy, 2009, 2011, Conn Smythe Trophy, NHL, 2011; co-recipient William M. Jennings Trophy, 2009; named NHL Goalie of Yr., Sporting News, 2009; named to East Second All-Am. Team, NCAA, 1995, East First All-Am. Team, 1996, NHL All-Star Game, 2008, 2009, 2011, 2012, All-NHL Team, Sporting News, 2009, First All-Star Team, NHL, 2009, 2011. Achievements include being a member of silver medal winning US Hockey Team, Vancouver Olympics, 2010; being a member of Stanley Cup Champion Boston Bruins, 2011. Office: Dallas Stars American Airlines Center 2500 Victory Ave Dallas TX 75201*

THOMAS, WAYNE LEE, lawyer; b. Sept. 22, 1945; s. W. M. and June F. Thomas; m. Patricia H. Thomas, Mar. 16, 1968; children: Brigitte Elisabeth Williams, Kate Adelaide Culpepper. BA, U. Fla., 1967, JD cum laude, 1971. Bar: Fla. 1971, U.S. Supreme Ct. 1975, U.S. Ct. Appeals (5th cir.) 1975, U.S. Ct. Appeals (11th cir.) 1981, U.S. Ct. Claims 1976, U.S. Dist. Ct. (mid. dist.) Fla. 1973, U.S. Dist. Ct. (so. dist. trial bar) Fla. 1975; cert. mediator and arbitrator. Law clk. U.S. Dist. Ct. (mid. dist.) Fla., 1971—73; assoc. Trenam, Simmons, Kemker, Scharf, Barkin, Frye & O'Neill, PA, Tampa, 1973—77, ptnr., 1978—81; founder, pres. McKay & Thomas, PA, Tampa, 1981—89; ptnr. Carlton, Fields, Ward, Emmanuel, Smith & Cutler, PA, 1989—95; pvt. practice Tampa, 1995—2008; ptnr. Akerman Senterfitt, 2008—. Bd. mem. State of Fla. 13th Jud. Cir. Indigent Svcs. Com., 2006—07. Mem. ABA, Fla. Bar (chmn. sect. gen. practice 1981-83, ethics com., vice chmn. unauthorized practice law com. 1994-98, 2000-04, chmn. 2004-06, vice chmn. fed. practice com. 1995-96, chmn. 1996-97, bd. bar examiners 1986-91, chmn. 1990-91, chmn. unauthorized practice law com. 13A 1998-2001), Nat. Conf. Bar Examiners (multistate profl. responsibility exam. policy com. 1994-2004), Hillsborough County Bar Assn. (chmn. grievance com. 1985-86), J.C. Cheatwood Am. Inn of Ct. (pres. 2007-08), Order of Coif, Fla. Blue Key, Phi Kappa Phi, Omicron Delta Kappa. Democrat. Office: Akerman Senterfitt 401 E Jackson St Ste 1700 Tampa FL 33602 Business E-Mail: wayne.thomas@akerman.com.

THOMAS, ZACH MICHAEL (ZACHARY MICHAEL THOMAS), retired professional football player; b. Pampa, Tex., Sept. 1, 1973; m. Maritza Thomas. BS in Exercise Sci., Tex. Tech. U., 1996. Linebacker Miami Dolphins, 1996—2008, Dallas Coyboys, 2008, Kansas City Chiefs, 2009; ret. NFL, 2010; owner Zach's Club 54, Amarillo, Tex., Zach's Club, Lubbock, Tex. Named Am. Football Conf. Defensive Rookie of Yr., 1996, 1st Team All-Pro, AP, 1998, 1999, 2002, 2003, 2006; named to Am. Football Conf. Pro-Bowl Team, NFL, 1999—2003, 2005, 2006, Tex. Tech. U. Red Raiders Hall of Fame, 2006. Avocations: weightlifting, basketball. Office: Zachs Club 54 6022 SW 48th Amarillo TX 79109

THOMASHOW, STEVEN ROY, military and intelligence officer, global business leader, counsel, law enforcer; b. Bronx, NY, Jan. 27, 1957; s. Isaac Tom and Dorothy (Cuillino Bodsky) T. Accredited, U.S. Mil. Acad. Cert. US blackbelt, Israel combat expert. Commd. United States of the World, adm., with spl. ops., 1988—; served with Israeli War USN, served with Gulf War. Recipient Pres. Nat. Medal of Patriotism; named to Am. Police Hall of Fame, 1996. Fellow Nat. Law Enforcement Acad. (hon.); mem. Am. Fedn. Police. Avocations: Karate (black belt), torah studies, boxing, reading. Home and Office: US of the World/Recon One 4644 Myrtle Ln West Palm Beach FL 33417-5316 Home Fax: 561-640-4359.

THOMPSON, BENNIE G., United States Representative from Mississippi; b. Bolton, Miss., Jan. 28, 1948; m. London Johnson; 1 child, BendaLonne. BA in Polit. Sci., Tougaloo Coll., Miss., 1968; MS in Ednl. Adminstrn., Jackson State U., Miss., 1972; grad., U. So. Miss. Alderman, Bolton, Miss., 1969—73; mayor, 1973—79; supr. Hinds County, Miss., 1980-93; mem. US Congress from 2nd Miss. Dist., 1993—; chmn. US House Homeland Security Com., 2007—11. Presdl. appointee Nat. Coun. Health Planning and Devel. Bd. trustees Tougaloo Coll.; bd. dirs. So. Regional Coun., Housing Assistance Coun. Named one of 100 Most Influential Black Americans, Ebony mag., 2006; named to Power 150, 2008. Mem.: Miss. Assn. Black Suprs. (founding mem.), Miss. Assn. Black Mayors (founding mem.). Democrat. Methodist. Office: US House of Representatives 2466 Rayburn House Office Bldg Washington DC 20515 also: 107 W Madison St Bolton MS 39041 Office Phone: 202-225-5876. Office Fax: 202-225-5898. E-mail: thompsonms2nd@mail.house.gov.*

THOMPSON, BRUCE R., bank executive; BA, Allegheny Coll., Meadville, Pa.; MBA, U. Va. Darden Sch. Bus. Formerly with Kidder, Peabody & Co.; mng. dir. high yield orgn. group Banc of America Securities, 1996, head US leveraged fin. debt capital markets, 2006; mng. dir., head global capital markets Bank of America Merrill Lynch; chief risk officer Bank of America Corp., Charlotte, NC, 2010—11, CFO, 2011—. Bd. mem. United Way Central Carolinas. Office: Bank of America Corp 100 N Tryon St Charlotte NC 28255 Business E-Mail: bruce.thompson@bankofamerica.com.

THOMPSON, CURT B., state legislator, lawyer; b. Decatur, Ga., Dec. 15, 1968; m. Sascha Thompson. BA, Am. Univ., Washington, 1990; JD, Ga. State Univ., 1992. Bar: Ga. 1993. Staff atty. Internat. Assn. Firefighters, Internat. Brotherhood Police Officers, Svc. Employees Internat. Union; mem. Dist. 69 Ga. House Reps., 2003—04; mem. Dist. 5 Ga. State Senate, 2005—. Friends Sch of Atlanta (board director, 1995-); Georgia Abortion Rights Action League (board director, 1995); Gunnett Habitat for Humanity (board director, 1994-95); Gunnett Co Democratic Party. Democrat. Lutheran. Mailing: 6320 Glenbrook Dr Tucker GA 30084-8707 Office Phone: 404-575-2223. Business E-Mail: curt.thompson@senate.ga.gov.

THOMPSON, DAVID RUSSELL, engineering educator, dean; b. Cleve., Apr. 4, 1944; s. Dwight L. and Ella Caroline (Wolff) T.; m. Janet Ann Schall, Aug. 27, 1966; children: Devin Mathew, Colleen Michelle, Darin Michael. BS in Agrl. Engring., Purdue U., 1966, MS in Agrl. Engring., 1967; PhD in Agrl. Engring., Mich. State U., 1970. Asst. prof. agrl. engring., food sci. and nutrition depts. U. Minn., St. Paul, 1970-75, assoc. prof., 1975-81, prof., 1981-85; prof. agrl. engring., head dept. Okla. State U., Stillwater, 1985-91, assoc. dean Coll. Engring., Architecture and Tech., 1991—. Engr. ops. dept. Green Giant Co., La Sueur, Minn., 1978-79; reviewer Colo. State U., Coop. State Rsch. Svc., USDA, Ft. Collins, 1989, foods, feeds and prodn. cluster U. Mo., Columbia, 1989, 93, dept. agrl. engring. Pa. State U., University Park, 1990, Tex. A&M U., College Station, 1992, Utah State U., Logan, 1993, USAF, Tyndall, Fla. and San Angelo, Tex., 1994-95, 97, Wash. State U., Pullman, 1995, U. Ga., Athens, 1996, S.D. State U., 1997, U. Fla., 1998, U. Del., 1998, U. Neb., 1999, U. Wis., 2000, U. Idaho, 2001, Rutgers U., 2003, Lake Superior State U., Sault St. Marie, 2003, Auburn U., 2004, U. Tenn., 2005, Western New Eng. Coll., 2005, So. Ill. U., Carbondale, 2006, St. Petersburg Coll., 2006, U. of the Pacific, 2006, U. New Orleans, 2007, Tex. Tech. U., 2007, Eastern Ky. U., 2008, Sultan Qaboos U., 2008, U. Louisville, 2009, U. San Martín Porres, 2009, others; reviewer USDA, 1983; vis. scholar Va. Poly. Inst. and State U., Blaksburg. Author: The Influence of Materials Properties on the Freezing of Sweet Corn, 1984, Mathematical Model for Predicting Lysine and Methionine Losses During Thermal Processing of Fortified Foods; contbr. over 50 articles to profl. jours. including Jour. Food Sci. Fellow Am. Soc. Agrl. Engrs. (divsn. chmn. 1976-77, bd. dirs. 1981-84, 87-89, v.p. 1994-98, stds. coun. chmn. 1997-98, Farm and Indsl. Equip. Inst., Young Rschr. award 1983, Pres.'s citation 1989, 98); mem. ASHRAE, NSPE (chair Okla. mid-north sect. 1994-95), Okla. Soc. Profl. Engrs. (v.p. 2000-01), Inst. Food Technologists (program com. 1982-85, state officer 1987-89), Am. Soc. Engring. Edn. (chair Midwest sect. 1994-95), Engring. Accreditation Commn. ABET Inc., Sigma Xi, Phi Kappa Phi, Tau Beta Pi, Alpha Epsilon, Phi Eta Sigma, Gamma Sigma Delta. Office: Okla State U Coll Engring Arch & Tech 201 Adv Tech Rsch Ctr Stillwater OK 74078-5010 Home Phone: 405-377-5263; Office Phone: 405-744-5140. Business E-Mail: dthomps@okstate.edu.

THOMPSON, DAVID WALKER, manufacturing executive; b. Phila., Mar. 21, 1954; s. Robert H. and Nancy S. (Walker) T.; m. Catherine K. Ahulii, April 16, 1983. B in Aeronautics & Astronautics, MIT, 1976; M in Aeronautics, Calif. Inst. Tech., 1977; MBA, Harvard U., 1981. Project engr. Jet Propulsion Lab., Pasadena, Calif., 1976; with, space shuttle projects, Langley Rsch. Ctr. & Johnson Space Ctr. NASA, aerospace engr., advanced rocket engines, Marshall Space Flight Ctr., 1977, project mgr. Huntsville, Ala., 1977-79; spl. asst. to pres., Missile Sys. Group Hughes Aircraft Co., Los Angeles, 1981-82; pres. Orbital Sciences Corp., Dulles, Va., 1982—99, co-founder, chief exec. officer & chmn., 1982—. Cons. Rockwell Internat., Thousand Oaks, Calif., 1980-81, Rand Corp., Santa Monica, Calif., 1982. Mem. US Nat. Acad. of Engring. Recipient Nat. award Space Found., Houston, 1981, Nat. Medal Tech. U.S Dept. Commerce Tech. Adminstrn., 1991, Nat. Air & Space Mus. Trophy Smithsonian Instn., 1990, George M. Low Space Transportation award, Am. Inst. Aeronautics and Astronautics, 1994, World Tech. award for Space, Economist Mag.; fellow Hertz Found., 1976, NSF fellow, 1976, Rockwell Internat. fellow, Harvard U. fellow, 1979; named Va. Industrialist Yr., 1991, Satellite Exec. of Yr. Via Satellite Mag., Satellite Mag., 1990, High-Tech. Entrepreneur Yr. Fellow AIAA (assoc., Young Engr./Scientist Yr. award 1984, George M. Low Space Trans. award 1994), Am. Astronautical Soc., Royal Aeronautical Soc.; mem. Nat. Space Club, Internat. Acad. Astronautics, NAE. Office: Orbital Sciences Corp 21839 Atlantic Blvd Dulles VA 20166 Office Phone: 703-406-5000. Business E-Mail: thompson.david@orbital.com.

THOMPSON, EDWARD IVINS BRADBRIDGE (BRAD EDWARD), biological chemistry and genetics educator, endocrinologist; b. Burlington, Iowa, Dec. 20, 1933; s. Edward Bills and Lois Elizabeth (Bradbridge) T.; m. Lynn Taylor Parsons; children: Elizabeth Lynn, Edward Ernest Bradbridge. BA with distinction, Rice U., 1955; postgrad., Cambridge U., 1957-58; MD, Harvard U., 1960. Intern The Presbyn. Hosp., NYC, 1960-61, asst. resident internal medicine, 1961-62; rsch. assoc. Nat. Inst. Mental Health, NIH, Bethesda, Md., 1962-64; rsch. scientist Nat. Inst. Arthritis and Metabolic Diseases, NIH, Bethesda, Md., 1964-68, Lab of Biochemistry, Nat. Cancer Inst., NIH, Bethesda, Md., 1968-73, sect. chief, 1973-84; prof., chmn. dept. human biol. chemistry and genetics U. Tex. Med. Br., Galveston, 1984—2003, I.H. Kempner prof., 1984—2005, prof. internal medicine, 1984—, interim dir., Sealy Ctr. for Molecular Sci., 1996—2003, prof., dept. biochem. & molecular biology, 2003—09, J.P. Saunders prof., 2006, prof. emeritus, 2009—; sr. res. prof. Ctr. Nuc. Receptors & Cell Signaling, Dept. Biol. & Biochem, U. Houston, 2009—; vis. prof. dept. biol. Jhon Hopkins U., 2013—. UNESCO vis. expert Inst. Genetics, Hungarian Acad. Sci., Szeged, Hungary, 1976; attending physician Nat. Naval Med. Ctr., Bethesda, 1978-80; chmn. hormones and cancer task force NIH, Bethesda, 1978-80; co-chmn. Gordon Rsch. Conf., 1980; mem. adv. com. on Biochem. and Chem. Carcinogenesis, Am. Cancer Soc., 1982-86; mem. revision com. Endocrinology adv. panel U.S. Pharmacopoeial Conv., Inc., 1980-85; mem. coun. for clin. investigation and rsch. awds., Am. Cancer Soc., 1989-93; bd. sci. overseers Pennington Nutrition Rsch. Ctr. La. State U., 1991-98; Fulbright prof., Marburg, Germany. 1992-93; mem. edn. bd. Am. Med. and Grad. Depts. Biochemistry, 1999-2003; co-organizer FASEB Summer Conf., 2006, mem. Bd. Scitific Overseers, Mt. Desert Is. Biological Lab. 2010-; vis. prof. dept. biol. Johns Hopkins U., 2013-. Co-editor Gene Expression and Carcinogenesis in Cultured Liver, 1975, Steroid Receptors and the Management of Cancer, 1979, DNA: Protein Interactions and Gene Regulation; other vols. in field; assoc. editor Cancer Rsch. jour., 1976-86; corr. editor Jour. Steroid Biochemistry, 1977-85; founding editor-in-chief Molecular Endocrinology Jour., 1985-92; editor-in-chief Endocrine Reviews, 2001-05; mem. editl. bd. Steroids, 1995, Endocrinology, 2011-, Molecular Endocrinology, 1998; sect. editor: Handbook of Cell Signalling, 2004, 05; contbr. over 270 sci. articles to profl. jours. Mem. troop com. Girl Scouts U.S., Rockville, Md., 1970-76; mem. PTA, Rockville, 1967-77, Wilderness Soc., Washington, 1964-75; initiator sci. edn. liaison program Galveston Pub. Schs., 1991; mem. pres.'s cabinet U. Tex. Med. Br., mem. ext. res. bd. Mt. Desert Inst. Biol. Lab., 2010-. Served as med. dir. USPHS, 1962-84. Grantee NIH, Walls Rsch., Nat. Inst. Diabetes and Digestive and Kidney Diseases, Nat. Cancer Inst.; Am. Cancer Soc. scholar, 1992-93; Fulbright scholar; named Disting. alumnus Rice U., 2001; honored Signalling Life and Death Symposium, 2004; recipient J.G. Sinclair award Sigma Xi, 1997, Educator award Endocrine Soc., 2004; finalist 2d Pl. age group triathlon Sr. Olympics, 2013, fellow Am. Assn. Advi Sci., 2005. Mem.: Galveston Cmty. Chorus, Am. Coll. Med Genetics (affiliate), Endocrine Soc., Am. Soc. Biol. Chemists, Am. Assn. Cancer Rsch., Bar Harbor Yacht Club, Phi Kappa Phi, Alpha Omega Alpha, Phi Beta Kappa, Sigma Xi. Achievements include patent on anti-tumor activity of a modified fragment of glucocorticoid receptor. Office: University Tex Med Br Dept Biochem & Molecular Biology Galveston TX 77555-0857 also: University Houston 3007 Sci & Engineering Rsch Ctr Houston TX 77204 Business E-Mail: bthompso@utmb.edu.

THOMPSON, FRANCES MCBROOM, mathematics professor, writer; BS in Edn., Abilene Christian U., Tex., 1963; MA, U. Tex., Austin, 1967; EdD, U. Ga., Athens, 1973. Math. cons., tchr., 1963—84; math. prof. Tex. Woman's U., Denton, 1984—. Author: (tchr. resource books) Hands on Math for Grades 4-8, 1994, Hands on Algebra for Grades 7-12, 1998, Math Proficiency Lessons and Activities, Fourth Grade, 2003, Math Essentials, Middle School Level, 2005, Math Essentials, High School Level, 2005, Math Essentials, Elementary School Level, 2007. Bible class coord.; tchr., 1982—95. Recipient Mary Mason Lyon Jr. Faculty award, Tex. Woman's U., 1992, Alumni Citation for achievement, Abilene Christian U., 1998, Grover C. Morlan Outstanding Educator award, 2005, Distinction in Svc. award, Tex. Woman's U., 2006. Mem.: Rsch. Coun. for Math. Learning, Tex. Coun. Tchrs. Math., Tex. Assn. Suprs. Math., Math. Assn. Am., Nat. Coun. Tchrs. Math. Office: Tex Woman's U PO Box 425886 Denton TX 76204-5886 Business E-Mail: fthompson@twu.edu.

THOMPSON, FRANCIS C., state legislator; b. Delhi, La., Oct. 29, 1941; s. Clyde Coleman and Frances Nolan Thompson; m. Marilyn Bryant, 1962; children: Francis Todd, Brant, Mary Melissa. Mem., southern edn. bd.; asst. prof. Northeast La. U.; tchr., 1963—65; v.p. Delcraft Mfg. Corp., 1965—72; mem. Parish Sch. Bd., 1968—75; mem., com. law enforcement, 1973—74; mem., dept. edn. La., 1974—75; asst. prof., 1974—75; mem. Dist. 19 La. House of Reps., 1975—2007; mem. Am. Legislature Coun., 2000—; mem. Dist 34 La. State Senate, 2008—, chair agr., forestry, aquaculture and rural devel. com., interim mem. fin. com., mem. labor and indsl. rels. com., select com. on homeland security, joint legis. com. on the budget. Mem.: Edn. Com. of States, Richland Parish Farm Bur., Delhi Presbyn. Ch., Retarded Children's Assn., Mason, La. Mental Health Drug Adv. Coun., Lions Club. Democrat. Presbyterian. Address: 456 Robinhood

Ln Delhi LA 71232 Mailing: PO Box 68 Delhi LA 71232 Home Phone: 318-878-5612; Office Phone: 318-878-9408. Fax: 318-878-5650. Business E-Mail: larep019@legis.state.lg.us. thompsof@legis.state.la.us.

THOMPSON, GERALDINE F. (GERI THOMPSON), state legislator; b. New Orleans, Nov. 18, 1948; m. Emerson R. Thompson; children: Laurise A. Thomas, Emerson R. III, Elizabeth R. AA, Miami-Dade CC, Fla., 1968; BEd, U. Miami, Fla., 1970; MS, Fla. State U., Tallahassee, 1973. Ret. coll. adminstr.; museum founder; mem. Dist. 39 Fla. House of Reps., Tallahassee, 2006—, Dem. leader pro tempore, 2008—10, ranking mem. econ. devel. and cmty. affairs policy coun., mem. econ. devel. policy com., state univs. and pvt. colls. appropriations com. Commr. Fla. Commn. on Human Rels.; mem. Orange County Ednl. Facilities Authority. Founder New Day Enterprises Inc.; bd. mem. Ctrl. Fla. YMCA, Holocaust Meml. and Edn. Ctr., Orlando Performing Arts Ctr. Mem.: NAACP, Assn. to Preserve African Am. Soc., History and Tradition, Inc. (founding pres.). Democrat. Baptist. Office: 511 W South St Ste 204 Orlando FL 32805-2761 also: 316 The Capitol 402 S Monroe St Tallahassee FL 32399-1300 Office Phone: 407-245-1511, 850-488-0760. Business E-Mail: geraldine.thompson@myfloridahouse.gov.

THOMPSON, HUGH P., state supreme court chief justice; b. Montezuma, Ga., July 7, 1943; married; 2 children. JD, Mercer U., 1969. Bar: Ga. 1970. Pvt. practice, Milledgeville, Ga., 1970—71; judge Recorder's Ct. of Milledgeville, 1971—79, Baldwin County Ct., 1973—78, Superior Ct. of Ga., 1979—94; chief judge Ocmulgee Jud. Cir., 1987—94; justice Ga. Supreme Ct., Atlanta, 1994—, presiding justice, 2012—13, chief justice, 2013—. Instr. bus. law Ga. Coll., 1971—72; pres. Coun. Superior Ct. Judges, 1993—94. Communicant St. Stephen's Episcopal Ch. Recipient Disting. Svc. award, Baldwin County Jaycees, 1972, Outstanding Alumnus award, Mercer U. Law Sch., 1994, Disting. Svc. award, Ga. Coll. and State U., 2002; named Outstanding Young Man of Baldwin County, 1972. Mem.: ABA, Bleckley Inn of Ct., Ga. Bar Found., State Bar Ga., Charles Longstreet Weltner Family Law Inn of Ct., Old War Horse Lawyers Club, Lawyers Club Atlanta. Avocations: hunting, gardening, golf, fishing. Office: Supreme Ct Ga State Judicial Bldg 244 Washington St SW Rm 572 Atlanta GA 30334-9007*

THOMPSON, IAN MURCHIE, JR., urologist, oncologist; b. Montgomery, Ala., May 18, 1954; m. BS, US Mil. Acad., West Point, NY, 1976; MD, Tulane U. Sch. Medicine, New Orleans, 1980. Diplomate Am. Bd. Urology. Intern surgery Brooke Army Med. Ctr., San Antonio, 1980—81, resident urology, 1982—85; clin. fellow urologic oncology Meml. Sloan-Kettering Cancer Ctr., NYC, 1985—88; clin. assoc. prof. Uniformed Svcs. U. Health Scis., Bethesda, Md., 1992—; prof. and chair dept. urology, Henry B. & Edna Smith Dielmann meml. chair urologic sci. U. Tex. Health Sci. Ctr., San Antonio, 1998—, also Glenda & Gary Woods disting. chair in genitourinary oncology, Cancer Therapy & Rsch. Ctr. Chmn. divsn. urology & dept. surgery Brooke Army Med. Ctr., 1992—98; chmn. GU task force Am. Joint Commn. on Cancer, Chgo., 1999—. Contbr. articles to profl. jours., chapters to books. Col. US Army, 1976—2000. Mem.: Soc. Urologic Oncology (pres. 2004, Huggins medal 2008), Am. Urol. Assn. (chmn. prostate cancer panel 1994—, Disting. Contbn. award 1997). Office: Univ Tex Health Science Ctr 7703 Floyd Curl Dr San Antonio TX 78229 Office Phone: 210-567-5643. Business E-Mail: thompsoni@uthscsa.edu.

THOMPSON, JAMES NICHOLAS, academic administrator, former medical association administrator; b. Cin., Oct. 20, 1944; m. Carol Washburn; children: Carrie, David, Victoria, Deborah. BA, DePauw U., 1966; MD, Ohio State U., 1971. Lic. otolaryngologist NC, diplomate Am. Bd. Otolaryngology. Intern Mercy Hosp., Pitts., 1971—72, resident in gen. surgery, 1972—73, resident in otolaryngology, 1973—76; fellow in otolaryngology U. Calif., Irvine, 1976—77; asst. prof. surg. scis., otolaryngology Bowman Gray Sch Medicine, Winston-Salem, NC, 1979—81, assoc. prof. surg. scis., otolaryngology, 1981—88, dep. assoc. dean, 1986—87, assoc. dean, 1987—94, prof. surg. scis., otolaryngology, 1988—2002, assoc. sports medicine, 1989—2002, assoc. pediat., 1991—2002, dean, 1994—97; v.p., dean Wake Forest U. Sch. Medicine, 1994—2001, spl. adv. to exec. v.p. for health affairs, 2001—02, dean emeritus, 2002—, prof. emeritus, 2002—; pres., CEO Fedn. of State Med. Bds. of U.S., Inc., Dallas, 2002—08; interim pres. Med. Coll. of Ga., 2009—10. Libr. and learning resources com. Wake Forest U. Sch. Medicine, 1981—82, clin. skills workshops and rev., 1982, 1984, admissions and pre-med. rels. com., 1984—86, clin. faculty adv. coun., 1985—2001, chair dept. clinics computer adv. com., 1985—87, faculty exec. coun., 1986—2002, vice chair, 1993—94, chair, 1994—2001, clin. svcs. coord. com., 1988—89, chair clin. scis. bldg. com., 1988; profl. ins. com. Risk and Ins. Mgmt. Adv. Coun., 1989—2001, affirmative action com., 1990—2001, compliance com., 1999—2001; acad. coun. Wake Forest U., 1987, adminstrv. coun., 1987, affirmative action com., 1990, long range planning standing com., 1993, intra-univ. ops. com., 2001, exec. coun., 1994, univ. ofcl. for animal care, 1997, audit and compliance com., 1999; clin. prof. otolaryngology U. Tex. S.W. Med. Ctr., Dallas, 2002—09; composite com. U.S. Med. Licensing Exam., 2002—, budget com., 2002—08. Contbr. chapters to books, articles to profl. jours. Chair med. adv. com. Wake Forest U. Sch. Medicine/VA Med. Ctr., Salisbury, NC, 1995—2001; med. audit/utilization rev. com. NC Bapt. Hosp., 1982—84, capital equipment com., 1984—92, chiefs of profl. svcs. com., 1984—2001; bd. trustees The Med. Found., 1984—2001, Wake Forest Sch. Medicine, 1984—2001, NC Bapt. Hosp., 1984—2001, Arts Coun. Winston-Salem and Forsyth County, 1992; bd. visitors Wake Forest U. Bapt. Med. Ctr., 1997—2001; internat. med. edn. cons. to China China Med. Bd. N.Y., Inc., 2000; bd. govs. Bermuda Run Country Club, 1982—84; indsl. devel. and econ. authority City of Winston-Salem, 1998—99; mem. planning com. Crosby Golf Classic, Bermuda Run, NC, 1987; bd. advisors Here's Life Winston-Salem, 1985—87; corp. recruitment chair Juvenile Diabetes Found. Winston-Salem, 2000; mem. Leadship Winston-Salem, 1987—88, health and human svc. day com., 1988—89, co-chair health and human svc. day com., 1991—92; dinner of champions com. Nat. Multiple Sclerosis Soc., Ctrl. NC chpt., 1999; campaign coord. surgery dept., otolaryngology sect. United Way Forsyth County, 1983—84, mem. med. ctr. com., 1987, health care campaign divsn. chair, 1989, vice chmn. divsn. III, 1992, mem. campaign cabinet, 1997—99, cmty. chair Forsyth County Cmty. Campaign, 2001—02, bd. dirs. Forsyth County, 2001—02; bd. dirs. Forsyth County Day Sch., 1987—90, Greater Winston-Salem C. of C., 1995—97. With USAR, 1972—78. Recipient Alumni Achievement award, Ohio State U. Coll. Med., 2006, Depauw U., 2006, Disting. Svc. award, Nat. Bd. Med. Examiners, 2009, Spl. Recognition award, Assoc. Am. Med. Colls., 2009. Mem.: Tex. Med. Assn., Dallas County Med. Soc., Am. Acad. Med. Ethics, Am. Coll. Physician Execs., Am. Acad. Med. Dirs., Am. Laryngological, Rhinological and Otological Soc., Am. Acad. Otolaryngology, Head and Neck Surgery, So. Med. Assn., Christian Soc. Otolaryngology, Head and Neck Surgeons, Christian Med. and Dental Assns., Bapt. Med./Dental Fellowship. Office: Medical College of Georgia 1120 15th St Augusta GA 30912 also: 18523 Carnegie Overlook Blvd Davidson NC 28036

THOMPSON, JANE JOHNSON, retail executive; b. Charleston, W.Va., July 13, 1951; d. Robert Paul and Phyllis Jane (Judson) Johnson; m. T. Stephen Thompson, Aug. 28, 1976; children: Robert Baker, Catherine Brooke. BBA, U. Cin., 1973; MBA, Harvard Coll., 1978. Brand mgr. Procter & Gamble Co., Cin., 1973-77; prin., ptnr. McKinsey & Co., Inc., Chgo., 1978-88; v.p. Sears Specialty Merchandising div. Sears Roebuck & Co., Chgo., 1988-89; v.p. planning Sears Roebuck & Co., Chgo., 1989-90, v.p. corp. and mdse. group planning, mem. corp. mgmt. com., 1990-93; exec. v.p. credit, gen. mgr., mem. exec. com. Sears Merchandise Group, 1993-96, pres. home svcs., mem. exec. com.; pres. fin. and consumer services Wal-Mart Stores, Inc. Bd. dirs. ConAgra, Inc. Bd. dirs. Lincoln Park Zoo Soc. Aux., 1988—; bd. dirs., exec. com., head strategic planning com. Boys and Girls Club of Chgo., 1992—. Named one of 25 Most Powerful Women in Fin., US Banker, 2010; Baker scholar, Harvard U., 1978. Mem. Chgo. Network, Econ. Club Chgo., Nat. Retail Fedn. (credit. coun., bd. dirs.), Internat. Credit Assn. (bd. dirs.). Office: Walmart 702 SW 8th St Bentonville AR 72716-8611

THOMPSON, JANET ANN, history professor; b. Balboa, Panama Canal Zone; BA, U. Cin., 1974, MA, 1976; MSLS in Archival Adminstrn., Case Western Res. U., 1984; PhD, U. Cin., 1987. History prof. Tallahasssee C.C., 1990—. Founder, dir. Friends of Gypsy, Inc., Tallahassee, 2003—07. Independent. Office: Tallahassee CC 444 Appleyard Dr Tallahassee FL 32304 Business E-Mail: thompsja@tcc.fl.edu.

THOMPSON, JEFF R., state legislator; BS in Bus. Adminstrn., NE La. State U., 1988; JD, Tulane U., New Orleans, 1995. Atty.; mem. Dist. 8 La. House of Reps., Baton Rogue, 2012—. Republican. Office: 1527 Doctors Dr Bossier City LA 71111 also: La House of Reps 900 N 3rd St Baton Rouge LA 70804 Office Phone: 318-741-2850. Business E-Mail: thompsonj@legis.la.gov.

THOMPSON, JEROME WALTER, otolaryngologist; b. Blytheville, Ark., Jan. 8, 1950; MD, UCLA, 1976, MBA, 1994. Prof., chmn. ear, nose and throat dept. U. Tenn. Health Sci. Ctr., Memphis; pediat. ear, nose and throat surgeon LeBonhowe Children's Med. Ctr., Memphis; clin. lectr. U. Southern Calif., Sch. Medicine, LA, 1981—86, asst. clin. prof., 1986—94, assoc. clin. prof., 1994; assoc. prof. pediat. U. Tenn., Memphis, Sch. Medicine, 1994—; assoc. prof. Otolaryngology - head and neck surgery U. Tenn., 1994—2001; head UT div. Pediat. Otolaryngology, LeBonheur Children's Hosp., U. Tenn., 1994—; assoc. dean Grad. Med. Edn., U. Tenn., 1999—2002; interim chair Dept. Otolaryngology, U. Tenn., 2000—01; program dir. otolaryngology, head and neck surgury U. Tenn., 2006—, program dir. otolaryngology, head and neck surgery, 2001—03, prof. otolaryngology, head and neck surgery, 2001—, chair, otolaryngology, head and surgery, 2001—; faculty mem. Dept. Allergy & Immunology, U. Tenn., 2001—. Chmn. Meth. U. Hosps., Memphis, 2004—; adj. assoc. prof. U. Memphis, Dept. Hearing and Speech Pathology, 1998—; adj. clin. faculty mem. St. Jude Children's Rsch. Hosp., 2001—; cons. appointment Telemedicine Hosp. U. Tenn., 2008. Clin. faculty mem., vol. Vanderbilt U. Sch. Nursing, Nashville, 2004—. Fellow: Am. Acad. Pediat.; mem.: Am. Soc. Pediat. Otolaryngologist (past pres.), Am. Acad. Otolaryngology (mem. audit com. 2006—). Office: 910 Madison #430 Memphis TN 38163 Office Phone: 901-448-5885.

THOMPSON, JERRY E., gas industry executive, former oil industry executive; BS, Colo. Sch. Mines. V.p., refining CITGO Petroleum Corp., 1987—98, sr. v.p., 1998—2003, COO, 2003—06; pres., CEO and gen. ptnr. TEPPCO Partners, LLP, 2006—. V.p., past chmn. Nat. Petrochemical & Refiners Assn.; bd. dirs. Tex. Eastern Products Pipeline Co., LLC, Susser Holdings Corp., 2006—. Office: TEPPCO Partners 1100 Louisiana St 1600 Houston TX 77002 Office Phone: 713-381-3636. Business E-Mail: jthompson@susser.com.

THOMPSON, JILL LYNETTE LONG, federal agency administrator, former United States Representative from Indiana; b. Warsaw, Ind., July 15, 1952; m. Don Thompson, 1995. BBA, Valparaiso U., 1974; MBA, Ind. U., 1978, PhD, 1984. Asst. instr., lectr. Ind. U., Bloomington, 1977—80; asst. prof. Valparaiso U., 1981—88; mgmt. cons. Campbell & Pryor, 1985-86; mem. US Congress from 4th Ind. Dist., 1989-95; under sec. for rural devel. USDA, Washington, 1995—2001; CEO Nat. Ctr. for Food & Agrl. Policy, Washington, 2003—08; bd. mem. Farm Credit Adminstrn., McLean, Va., 2010—, chair, CEO, 2012—; bd. dirs. Farm Credit Sys. Ins. Corp. (FCSIC), 2010—. Adj. prof. Indiana U.-Purdue U. Ft. Wayne, 1987-89; Manchester Coll., 2002-03 asst. prof. Valparaiso U. Councilwoman City of Valparaiso, Ind., 1984-86; chair Congrl. Rural Congress. Fellow: Inst. of Politics. Democrat. Methodist. Office: Farm Credit Administration 1501 Farm Credit Dr Mc Lean VA 22102-5090*

THOMPSON, JOHN ALBERT, JR., dermatologist; b. Austin, Tex., June 5, 1942; s. J. Albert Sr. and Elizabeth (Brady) T. BA, Georgetown U., 1963; MD, Bowman Gray Sch. Medicine, 1967; Dermatology Fellowship, U. N.C., 1971-73. Diplomate Am. Bd. Dermatology. Resident in internal medicine N.C. Baptist Hosp., Winston-Salem, NC, 1967-69; resident in dermatology N.C. Meml. Hosp., Chapel Hill, NC, 1971-73; pvt. practice Charlotte, NC, 1974—; clin. prof. dermatology Dept. Dermatology, U. N.C. Sch. Medicine, Chapel Hill, 1974—. Author profl. papers. Lt. comdr. USNR, 1969-71, Vietnam. Mem. Am. Acad. Dermatology (chmn. subcom. for sch. health edn. 1976-79, task force--nat. health ins.), Carolinas-Va. Dermatology Assn. (adv. bd. council rep. 1976-79), Charlotte Dermatology Assn., Mecklenburg County Med. Soc., N.C. Med. Soc., North Am. Clin. Dermatology Soc. Southern Med. Assn., Southeastern Consortium for Continuing Dermatol. Edn. (steering com. 1983—2003), South Cen. Dermatol. Congress (organizing com. 1982-86), Am. Soc. Dermatol. Surgery, Am. Dermatol. Soc. Allergy and Immunology, Am. Soc. Laser Medicine and Surgery, Inc. Democrat. Episcopalian. Home: 2633 Richardson Dr Apt 8A Charlotte NC 28211-3346 Office: Dermatol Laser Ctr Dermatologic Laser Ctr 2310 Randolph Rd Charlotte NC 28207-1526 Office Phone: 704-376-9849.

THOMPSON, KATHY C., bank executive; 2 children. From. sr. v.p. to exec. v.p. Stock Yards Bancorp Inc., Louisville, 1992—96, exec. v.p.; sr. v.p., dir. trust co., dir. sales, services and mktg. Stock Yards Bancorp Inc. Active Home of the Innocents. Named No. 3 Fast Tracker in the Industry, US Bankers mag., 2003; named one of 25 Women to Watch, 2007. Office: Stock Yards Bancorp Inc 1040 East Main St Louisville KY 40206

THOMPSON, KEIFER, musician; b. Miami, Okla. m. Shawna Thompson. Solo musician; co-founder band Thompson Square, 2010—; with Stoney Creek Records, 2010—. Musician: (albums) Thompson Square, 2011, Just Feels Good, 2013, (songs) Are You Gonna Kiss Me or Not, 2010 (Best Single by a Duo or Group, Best Single by a Breakthrough Artist, Best Music Video by a New Artist, Am. Country Awards, 2011), I Got You, 2011 (Duo Video of Yr., CMT Music Awards, 2012). Named Vocal Duo of Yr., Acad. Country Music Awards, 2012, 2013, Country Music Assn. Awards, 2012, New Vocal Duo or Group of Yr., Acad. Country Music Awards, 2013. Office: c/o William Morris Agency 1600 Division St Suite 300 Nashville TN 37203-2755

THOMPSON, KIRK, transportation executive; CPA, Ark. With J.B. Hunt Transport Services, Inc., Lowell, Ark., 1973-78, v.p. fin., 1979-84, exec. v.p., CFO, 1984-85, pres., COO, 1986-87, pres., CEO, 1987—2010, chmn., 2011—. Office: JB Hunt Transport Svcs Inc 615 JB Hunt Corporate Dr Lowell AR 72745

THOMPSON, LARRY DEAN, lawyer; b. Hannibal, Mo., Nov. 15, 1945; s. Ezra W. and Ruth L. (Robinson) T.; m. Brenda Anne Taggart, June 26, 1970; children: Larry Dean, Gary E. BA cum laude, Culver-Stockton Coll., Canton, Mo., 1967; MA, Mich. State U., 1969; JD, U. Mich., 1974. Bar: Mo. 1974, Ga. 1978. Indsl. rels. rep. Ford Motor Co., Birmingham, Mich., 1969-71; atty. Monsanto Co., St. Louis, 1974-77; assoc. King & Spalding LLP, Atlanta, 1977-82, ptnr., 1986—2001; US atty. (northern dist.) Ga. US Dept. Justice, Atlanta, 1982-86; dep. atty. gen. US Dept Justice, Washington, 2001—03; head Corporate Fraud Task Force US Dept. Justice, Washington, 2002; sr. fellow Brookings Instn., Washington, 2003—04; sr. v.p., govt. affairs, gen. counsel, corporate sec. PepsiCo, Inc., Purchase, NY, 2004—11, exec. v.p. govt. affairs, gen. counsel, corporate sec., 2012—; Sibley prof. in corporate & bus. law U. Ga. Law Sch., Athens, Ga., 2011—. Ind. counsel US Dept. Housing & Urban Devel. (HUD), 1995-98; vis. prof., U. Ga Sch. Law, 2004 Editor: Jury Instructions in Criminal Antitrust Cases 1976-80, 1982. Chmn. Atlanta Urban League; mem. Ga. Bd. Edn., 1997; bd. dirs. Ga. Republican Found., pres., Nat. Security Coordination Coun., 2002., chmn., bipartisan Jud. Review Commn. on Fgn. Asset Control, 2000, atty., Southern Organized Crime Drug Enforcement Task Force, atty. gen., Econ. Crime Coun. Recipient Outstanding Achievement award FBA, 1992., Edmund Jennings Randolph award, Litigator award, Fed. Bar Assn., A. T. Walden award, Gate City Bar Assn. Mem. ABA, Nat. Bar Assn. Republican. Presbyterian. Office: PepsiCo Inc 700 Anderson Hill Rd Purchase NY 10577 Office Phone: 914-253-2000. Office Fax: 914-253-2070. Business E-Mail: larry.thompson@pepsi.com.*

THOMPSON, MACK EUGENE, historian, educator; b. Burley, Idaho, Feb. 24, 1921; s. Eugene and Nora (McFate) T.; m. Helen Goldhamer, Oct. 30, 1945. AB, Queen's Coll., CUNY, 1948; MA, Brown U., 1951, PhD, 1955. Instr. history Brown U., 1954-55; asst. prof. Calif. Inst. Tech., 1955-56, U. Calif. at Riverside, 1956-62, asso. prof., 1962-66, prof., 1966-77; emeritus prof., 1977—; chmn. div. humanities U. Calif. at Riverside, 1961-63, asso. univ. dean acad. planning, 1965-66, dean, div. undergrad. studies, 1971-74; exec dir. Am. Hist. Assn., Washington, 1974-81. Chmn. editorial bd. Experiment and Innovation: New Directions in Edn., U. Calif., 1966-68 Author: The Ward-Hopkins Controversy and the American Revolution in Rhode Island: An Interpretation, 1959, Moses Brown, Reluctant Reformer, 1962, Causes and Circumstances of the Du Pont Family's Emigration, 1969. Bd. dirs. Harry S. Truman Libr. Inst., 1974-81. With AUS, 1942-45. Home: 1378 River Oaks Ct Oldsmar FL 34677-4828 Home Phone: 727-787-6983. E-mail: pwobrien@aol.com.

THOMPSON, MICK, state banking agency administrator; b. Oct. 11, 1976; BA, Southeastern Okla. State U., Durant; MEd, Northeastern State U., Tahlequah, Okla.; grad. in Banking, U. Colo., Boulder. Exec. v.p. Ctrl. Nat. Bank, Poteau, Okla., 1977—90; dir. legis. and govtl. rels. Okla. Gov.'s Office; commr. Okla. State Banking Dept., Oklahoma City, 1992—. Mem. Okla. House Reps., Poteau, 1976—84, chmn. banking and fin. com., mem. appropriations and budget com., majority floor leader, 1983—84; pres. Okla. Cmty. Bankers Assn., 1988—90; bd. dirs. UICI, North Richland Hills, Tex., 2004—. Mem. adv. coun. Southeastern Okla. State U. Bus. Sch., Durant; adv. to bd. trustees U. Colo. Grad. Sch. Banking, Boulder. Mem.: Conf. State Bank Suprs. (chmn. 2003, chmn. emeritus). Republican. Office: Oklahoma State Banking Department 2900 N Lincoln Blvd Oklahoma City OK 73105 Office Phone: 405-521-2782. Office Fax: 405-522-2993. E-mail: rmt1@onenet.net.

THOMPSON, MYRON HERBERT, federal judge; b. Tuskegee Institute, Ala., 1947; BA, Yale U., 1969, JD, 1972. Asst. atty. gen. State of Ala., 1972-74; sole practice Montgomery, Ala., 1974—80; ptnr. Thompson & Faulk, Montgomery, 1979-80; judge US Dist. Ct. (mid. dist.) Ala., Montgomery, 1980—81, 1998—, chief judge, 1991—98. Mem. ABA, Ala. Bar Assn., Nat. Bar Assn., Ala. Lawyers Assn. Office: US Dist Ct 203 US Courthouse PO Box 235 Montgomery AL 36101-0235

THOMPSON, NEAL PHILIP, food science and nutrition educator, dean; b. Bklyn., July 18, 1936; s. Thomas I. and Ellenor (Backie) T.; m. Beverly Ethel Godshall, Oct. 4, 1958; children: Erick, Victor, Clifford, Karen, Stuart. BS, Wheaton Coll., 1957; MA, Miami U., 1962; PhD, Princeton U., 1965. Asst. prof. U. Fla., Gainesville, 1965-70, assoc. prof., 1970-76, prof., 1976—, asst. dean, 1980-86, assoc. dean, 1986-93. Capt. USNR, ret. Office: U Fla Inst Food & Agrl Scis Food & Environ Toxicology Gainesville FL 32611-0720 Home: 1224 Chestnut Dale Rd Newland NC 28657-9254

THOMPSON, PAUL MICHAEL, lawyer; b. Dubuque, Iowa, Aug. 30, 1935; s. Frank W. and Genevieve (Cassutt) T.; m. Mary Jacqueline McManus, Jan. 30, 1960; children: Anne, Tricia, Paul, Tim, Jim. BA magna cum laude, Loras Coll., 1957; LLB, Georgetown U., 1959. Bar: Iowa 1959, DC 1959, Va. 1966. Atty. appellate ct. br. NLRB, Washington, 1962-66; assoc. Hunton & Williams, Richmond, Va., 1966-71, ptnr., 1971—. Adj. prof. The T.C. Williams Sch. Law U. Richmond; adj. prof. law sch. Coll. William and Mary Sch. Law. Served with JAGC, USAF, 1960-62. Mem. ABA, Va. State Bar, Va. Bar Assn., Commonwealth Club. Roman Catholic. Office: The TC Williams School Law University of Richmond Richmond VA 23173 Office Phone: 804-289-8856. Personal E-mail: thompmerrypoint@comcast.net. Business E-Mail: pthomps3@richmond.edu.

THOMPSON, PETER J., manufacturing executive; Pres. U.S. opers. Schweitzer-Mauduit Internat., Inc., Alpharetta, Ga., 1995—. Office: Schweitzer-Mauduit Internat Inc 100 N Point Ctr E Ste 600 Alpharetta GA 30022-8263

THOMPSON, PHILIP C., lawyer, investment advisor, private equity fund manager, educator, journalist; b. Balt., Oct. 21, 1945; s. Earl Clinton and Virginia Thompson; m. Julia Ann Young, June 10, 1948; children: Kathryn Adair, Julia Hamilton, Philip Clinton Jr. BA, Washington and Lee U., 1967, BS, 1968, JD, 1971. Bar: Ga. 1973. Law clk. to Hon. Walter E. Hoffman US Dist. Ct. (ea. dist.) Va., 1971—72, 9th Cir., 1972; ptnr. Jones, Day, Reavis & Pogue, Atlanta, 1973—86, Dow, Lohnes & Albertson, Atlanta, 1986—94, Arnall, Golden, Gregory LLP, Atlanta, 1994—2014, Duane Morris LLP, Atlanta, 2004—09, Nelson Mullins, Atlanta, 2010—; lectr. in fileds. Vis. lectr. Emory U. Goizueta Bus. Sch., Atlanta, 2003—04; adj. prof. Ga. State Robinson Coll. Bus., Atlanta, 2007—11; bd. trustee Robinson Coll. Bus., 2010—12. Capt. res. US Army, 1972—73. Mem.: Capital City Club. Reformed Anglican. Avocations: youth programs, prison ministry. Office: 201 17th St Ste 1700 Atlanta GA 30363

THOMPSON, RALPH GORDON, retired federal judge; b. Okla. City, Dec. 15, 1934; m. Barbara Irene Hencke, Sept. 5, 1964; children: Lisa, Elaine, Maria. BBA, U. Okla., 1956, JD, 1961. Bar: Okla. 1961.

Spl. agt. Office of Spl. Investigations, USAF, 1957—60; ptnr. Thompson, Thompson, Harbour & Selph (and predecessors), Oklahoma City, 1961-75; judge U.S. Dist. Ct. for Western Dist. Okla., Oklahoma City, 1975—2008; chief judge U.S. Dist. Ct. (we. dist.) Okla., 1986-93. Mem. Okla. Ho. of Reps., 1966-70, asst. minority floor leader, 1969-70; spl. justice Supreme Ct. Okla., 1970-71; tchr. Harvard Law Sch. Trial Advocacy Workshop, 1981-2008; apptd. by chief justice of U.S. to U.S. Fgn. Intelligence Surveillance Ct., 1990-97; elected to jud. conf. of the U.S., 1997; apptd. to Edward J. Devitt Disting. Svc. Justice award selection com., 1997-99; apptd. by chief justice of U.S. to exec. com. of Jud. Conf. of the U.S., 1998-2000; coord. Long Range Planning for Fed. Judiciary, 1999-2000. Co-author: Mr. Integrity, Bryle Harlow, Counsellor to Presidents, Bob Burke and Ralph G. Thompson, 2000. Rep. nominee for lt. gov., Okla., 1970; chmn. bd. ARC, Oklahoma City, 1970-72; chmn., pres. Okla. Young Lawyers Conf., 1965; mem. bd. visitors U. Okla., 1975-78, U. Okla. Honors Coll., 2007—. Lt. USAF, 1957-60, col. Res., ret. Decorated Legion of Merit; named Oklahoma City's Outstanding Young Man, Oklahoma City Jaycees, 1967, Outstanding Young Oklahoman, Okla. State Jr. C. of C., 1968, Outstanding Fed. Trial Judge, Okla. Trial Lawyers Assn., 1980; recipient Regents Alumni award U. Okla., 1990, Disting. Svc. award, 1993, Jour. Record Pub. Co. award for Disting. Svc., 2001, Humanitarian award Oklahoma City Pub. Schs. Found., 2003; inducted Okla. Hall of Fame, 1995, Fellow Am. Bar Found.; mem. ABA, Fed. Bar Assn., Okla. Bar Assn. (chmn. sect. internat. law and gen. practice 1974-75), Oklahoma County Bar Assn. (Jud. Svc. award 1988), Jud. Conf. U.S. (com. on ct. adminstrn. 1981-89, com. on fed.-state jurisdiction 1988-91), U.S. Dist. Judges Assn. 10th Cir. (pres. 1992-94), Rotary (hon.), Order of Coif, Am. Inns of Ct. (pres. XXIII 1995-96), Phi Beta Kappa (pres. chpt. 1985-86, Phi Beta Kappa of Yr. 1991), Beta Theta Pi, Phi Alpha Delta, Nat. Conf. of Commrs. on Uniform State Laws, Judge Fed. Arbitration Inc.; mem. bd. of visitors, U. Oklahama Honours Coll., U. Oklahama Coll. of Law. Episcopalian.

THOMPSON, RICHARD L., retired manufacturing executive; B in Engring., Stanford U. With Caterpillar, Inc., 1983—2004, v.p. Customer Services, Solar Turbines Inc., pres. Solar Turbines Inc., v.p. engring. divsn., 1990-95, group pres., 1995—2004; ret., 2004. Bd. dir. Gardner Denver, Inc., Lennox Internat., 1993—, vice chmn., 2005—06, chmn., 2006—12, lead dir., 2012—. Office: Lennox Internat 2140 Lake Park Blvd Richardson TX 75080

THOMPSON, ROBERT, III, state legislator, lawyer; b. Paragould, Ark., June 19, 1971; BA summa cum laude, Hendrix Coll., 1993; post-grad. Rotary Found. Internat. Scholarship, Univ. St. Andrews, Scotland, 1993—94; JD with high honors, Univ. Ark., 1997. Bar: Ark. 1997. Law clk. Judge Richard Arnold, US Ct. Appeals 8th Cir., 1997—98; mem., civil & comml. litigation Branch, Thompson, Philhours & Warmath, Paragould, Ark.; mem. Dist. 78 Ark. House of Reps., 2005—06; mem. Dist. 11 Ark. State Senate, 2007—. Editor (in chief): Ark. Law Rev., 1996—97. Mem.: ABA, Ark. Bar Assn., Green-Clay County Bar Assn. Democrat. Methodist. Mailing: 414 W Court St Paragould AR 72450 Office Phone: 870-239-9581. Office Fax: 870-239-4859. Business E-Mail: thompsonr@arkleg.state.ar.us.

THOMPSON, RONALD L., finance company executive, former manufacturing company executive; BBA, U. Mich.; MS, PhD, Mich. State U. Chmn., CEO Evaluation Techs., Inc.; chmn. bd. dirs., pres. GR Group Inc., 1980—93; chmn., CEO Midwest Stamping & Mfg. Co. (subs. of GR Group Inc.), Bowling Green, Ohio, 1993—2005. Bd. trustee, Teachers Ins. & Annuity Found. Coll. Retirement Equities Fund (TIAA-CREF), 1995-, chmn., 2008-; bd. dirs., Chrysler Group LLC, 2009- Recipient Nat. Minority Entrepreneur of Yr. award U.S. Dept. Commerce, 1989, Disting. Svc. to Edn. award Harris-Stowe State Coll., 1991, disting. Cmty. Svc. award So. Ill. U., Edwardsville, 1990. Office: TIAA-CREF PO Box 1259 Charlotte NC 28201*

THOMPSON, SANDRA GUERRA, lawyer, educator; BA, Yale U., 1985, JD, 1988. Asst. dist. atty. NY County Dist. Atty.'s Office, 1988—90; prof. U. Houston Law Ctr., 1990—, dir. Mexican Legal Studies Program, 2000; dir. Criminal Justice Inst., Univ. Houston. Co-author: The Law of Asset Forfeiture; contbr. articles to prof. jour. Mem.: Assn. Am. Law Sch. (chair, Criminal Justice sect. 2001), Hispanic Bar Assn. (mem. bd. dir.), Houston Bar Assn., Am. Law Inst. (mem. bd. adv. Model Penal Code: Sentencing project). Office: Criminal Justice Institute 100 Law Ctr 4800 Calhoun Rd Houston TX 77204 Office Phone: 713-743-2134. E-mail: sgthompson@Central.uh.edu.

THOMPSON, SCOTT L., automotive executive; BBA, Stephen F. Austin State U. CPA. Exec. v.p., oper. and fin. KSA Ind., Inc., 1991—96; sr. v.p., CFO, treas. Group1 Automotive, Houston, 1996—2002, exec. v.p., CFO, treas., 2002—05; sr. exec. v.p., CFO Dollar Thrifty Automotive Group, Tulsa, Okla., 2008; pres., CEO Dollar Thrifty Automotive Group, Inc., Tulsa, Okla., 2008—. Bd. dir. Dollar Thrifty Automotive Group, Conn's Inc.; non-exec. chmn. Houston Wire & Cable Co.; bd. dir. UAP Holding Co., 2007—08. Mailing: Dollar Thrifty Automotive Group PO Box 35985 Tulsa OK 74135-0985

THOMPSON, SENFRONIA, state legislator; b. Booth, Tex., Jan. 1, 1939; d. Lindsey and Thelma Waterhouse Paige; 2 children. BS in Biology, MEd, LLM in Internat. Law. Former pub. sch. tchr.; atty. Houston; mem. Dist. 141 Tex. House of Representatives, 1973—. Recipient of several awards and honors; named one of Longest Serving Female House Mem. in Tex. Mem.: NAACP, YWCA, N. Harris County C. of C., Nat. Bar Assn., United Negro Coll. Fund, Women's Polit. Caucus, Nat. Orgn. Women, Black Women Lawyers Assn., Nat. Coun. Negro Women, Cath. Daughters America. Democrat. Roman Catholic. Office: 10527 Homestead Rd Houston TX 77016 also: Room 3S.6 Capitol PO Box 2910 Austin TX 78768 Office Phone: 713-633-3390, 512-463-0720.

THOMPSON, SHAWNA, singer; b. Chatom, Ala. m. Keifer Thompson. Solo musician; co-founder band Thompson Square, 2010—; with Stoney Creek Records, 2010—. Singer: (albums) Thompson Square, 2011, Just Feels Good, 2013, (songs) Are You Gonna Kiss Me or Not, 2010 (Best Single by a Duo or Group, Best Single by a Breakthrough Artist, Best Music Video by a New Artist, Am. Country Awards, 2011), I Got You, 2011 (Duo Video of Yr., CMT Music Awards, 2012). Named Vocal Duo of Yr., Acad. Country Music Awards, 2012, 2013, Country Music Assn. Awards, 2012, New Vocal Duo or Group of Yr., Acad. Country Music Awards, 2013. Office: c/o William Morris Agency 1600 Division St Suite 300 Nashville TN 37203-2755

THOMPSON, STEVE, state legislator; b. Atlanta, Ga., Dec. 22, 1950; m. Karen Lynch; 1 child, Amy Hill. AS, Kennesaw Univ., 1984. Positions through v.p. Ga. State Bank, 1977—86; owner Affiliates Group A Bus. Services Co., 1986—; mem. Ga. House Reps., 1980—90; mem. Dist. 33 Ga. State Senate, 1991—. Served USN, 1969—71. Leadership Georgia, 84; Five Outstanding Young Men of Georgia, 84; Georgia Coun Children's Friend Children Award, 86 & 87; Legislator of Year, Georgia Coun Child Abuse, 86; Cobb Democratic of Year, 88. S Cobb Optimist Club; Marietta Kiwanis; S Cobb Jaycees (president, formerly); life member Georgia Parent Teachers Association; life member Cobb Co Chamber of Commerce; Masons; life member Georgia Jaycees; Cobb Co Develop Authority. Democrat. Baptist. Office: 1170 Longwood Drive Marietta GA 30008 Office Phone: 770-427-2600. Business E-Mail: steve.thompson@senate.ga.gov.

THOMPSON, TOMMY, state legislator; b. Cabot, Ark. m. Diane Thompson; 6 children. Attended, U. Ark. With Agri Co-op Supply, Morrilton, Agr. Cons., Morrilton; rep. Ark. State House of Representatives, 2010—; mem. Dist. 60 Ark. House of Representatives, 2011—. Democrat. Baptist. Office: 15 Ashley Dr Morrilton AR 72110 Office Phone: 501-208-2007. Business E-Mail: tt4rep@att.net.

THOMPSON, TOMMY N., state legislator; b. Owensboro, Ky., 1948; m. Judi Thompson Thompson; children: Nick, Wes, Hunter. Mgr. Thompson Homes, Inc., 1975—80, pres., 1980—; mem. Dist. 14 Ky. House of Reps., 2003—. Recipient Mayor's award, 1994; named Outstanding Young Man of Owensboro, 1977, Outstanding Young Men of America, 1981, State Ky. Housing Hall of Fame, 2000, Nat. Housing Hall of Fame, 2000. Mem.: Home Builders Assn. Ky. (pres. 1983), Nat. Assn. Home Builders (pres. 1994), Nat. Pk. Found. (bd. dir.), US Small Bus. Assn. (bd. dir.), Fed. Nat. Mortgage Assn. (advisor mem.). Democrat. Mailing: PO Box 458 Owensboro KY 42303 Office: Capitol Annex Rm 429D Frankfort KY 40601 Office Phone: 270-926-1740 ext. 16, 502-564-8100 ext. 664. Office Fax: 270-685-3242. Business E-Mail: tommy@thompsonhomesinc.com.

THOMPSON, WARREN M., food franchise executive; BS, Hampden-Sydney Coll.; MBA, U. Va. V.p. Host Internat. divsn. Marriott Corp.; pres., CEO Thompson Hospitality, Reston, Va. Office: Thompson Hospitality Corp 1741 Business Center Dr Ste B Reston VA 20190-5352

THOMPSON, ZACHARY, city health department administrator; AS, El Centro Coll.; BS in Social Work, U. Tex., Arlington; MS, Amberton U., Garland, Tex. With W. Dallas Cmty. Ctr.; dep. dir. Dallas Co. Dept. Health and Human Svcs., Dallas, 1997—2004, dir., 2004—. Office: Dallas Co Dept Health and Human Svcs 2377 N Stemmons Fwy Dallas TX 75207-2710

THOMSEN, TODD, state legislator; Mem. Dist. 25 Okla. House of Representatives, 2007—. Republican. Address: 1021 E 6th St Ada OK 74820 Office: Oklahoma House of Representatives 2300 N Lincoln Blvd Rm 408 Oklahoma City OK 73105 Office Phone: 405-557-7336. E-mail: todd.thomsen@okhouse.gov.

THOMSON, BASIL HENRY, JR., lawyer; b. Amarillo, Tex., Jan. 17, 1945; m. Margaret Shepard, May 4, 1985; children: Christopher, Matthew, Robert. BBA, Baylor U., 1968, JD, 1973. Bar: Tex. 1974, U.S. Ct. Mil. Appeals 1974, U.S. Supreme Ct. 1977, U.S. Dist. Ct. (we. dist.) Tex. 1988, U.S. Ct. Appeals (fed. cir.) 1990. Oil title analyst Hunt Oil Co., Dallas, 1971-73; atty., advisor Regulations and Adminstrv. Law divsn. Office of Chief Counsel USCG, Washington, 1973-77; dir. estate planning devel. dept. Baylor U., Waco, Tex., 1977-80, gen. counsel, 1980—2002; ret., 2002; assoc. gen. counsel So. Meth. U., Dallas, 2002—. Adj. prof. law Baylor U.; lobbyist legis. Ind. Higher Edn., 71st Session of Tex. Legislature; mem. legis. com. Gov.'s Task Force on Drug Abuse; dir. govtl. rels. Baylor U.; spkr. at meetings of coll. and univ. adminstrs., chair, legal svcs. review panel, Nat. Assn. Independent Colls. & U.; assisted in drafting legis. for Texan's War on Drugs Tex. Legislature; mem. legal adv. com. United Educators Ins. Risk Retention Group, 1994-96, asst. area dir. US naval Acad. Active Longhorn Coun. Boy Scouts of Am.; vice chair planning and zoning commn. City of Woodway, 2004—10, mem. bd. adjustment, 1998—2004; bd. dirs. Heart of Tex. Coun. on Alcohol and Drug Abuse, 1987—91. Recipient Pres.'s award Ind. Colls. and Univs. of Tex., 1994, Dist. award of merit Boy Scouts Am. Fellow Coll. State Bar Tex.; mem. FBA, Nat. Assn. Coll. and Univ. Attys. (fin., nominations and elections coms. 1994-95, bd. dirs. 1988-91, 2000—, pres. 2004-05), Nat. Assn. Ind. Colls. and Univs. (chair, legal svcs. rev. panel), Tex. Bar Assn., Waco McLennan County Bar Assn., Owners Assn. of Sugar Creek, Inc. (bd. dirs. 1991-95). Baptist. Avocations: backpacking, running, environmental concerns, historical reinactment. Home: 100 Sugar Creek Pl Waco TX 76712-3410 Office: So Meth U PO Box 750132 Dallas TX 75275-0137 Home Phone: 254-772-7706; Office Phone: 214-768-3233. Business E-Mail: bthomson@smu.edu.*

THOMSON, ROGER F., restaurant chain executive, lawyer; b. Detroit, Apr. 4, 1949; m. Carol M. Barger. BA, Miami U., Oxford, Ohio, 1971; JD, Southern Meth. U., Dallas, 1974. Bar: Tex. 1974, US Dist. Ct. (no. dist.) Tex., US Ct. Appeals (5th cir.). Legal counsel S&A Restaurant Corp., 1978—80, corp. counsel, 1980—82, v.p., 1982—84, gen. counsel, 1982—88, sec., 1983—88, sr. v.p., 1984—85, exec. v.p., 1985—88; sr. v.p., gen. counsel Burger King Corp., Miami, Fla., 1988—93; sr. v.p., gen. counsel, sec. Brinker International Inc., Dallas, 1993—94, exec. v.p., gen. counsel, sec., 1994—, chief adminstrv. officer, 1996—. Bd. dirs. Brinker Internat. Inc., 1993—95. Mem.: State Bar Tex. Office: Brinker International Inc 6820 LBJ Freeway Dallas TX 75240 Office Phone: 972-980-9917. Office Fax: 972-770-9593. Business E-Mail: roger.thomson@brinker.com.

THORN, TERENCE HASTINGS, energy executive, consultant, writer; b. Takoma, Md., July 6, 1946; s. John Hastings and Norine R. (Freytag) T.; m. Judith Carol Bailey, Aug. 15, 1970; children: Kristin Lynn, Matthew Hastings. BA, U. Md., 1969, MA, 1973. Dir. congl. rels. Am. Gas Assn., Arlington, Va., 1975-79; dir. govt. rels. J. Walter Thompson Co., Washington, 1979-81; v.p. govt. rels. Houston Natural Gas Co., Washington, 1981-85; exec. v.p., chmn. bd. Mojave Pipeline Co., Houston, 1986-89; pres., CEO Transwestern Pipeline Co., Houston, 1993—; sr. v.p., exec. mgmt. com. bd. Enron Corp., Houston, 1993-98, exec. v.p. internat. govt. rels. and environ. affairs, 1998—2001, mng. dir. Middle East, 2001; cons. Houston Tex. Energy, Environment, Tech.; pres. JKM Cons., Houston, 2001—. Cons. in field. Contbr. articles to profl. jours. Bd. dirs. Houston Pops, 1989-90, Pin Oak Charities, Houston, 1991-93, Greater Houston chpt. YMCA, 1994; city alderman, 1992-93; mem. Hermann Soc., 1993—, Energy Industry Sector Adv. Com. U.S. Dept. Commerce; prin. liason Pres.'s Coun. Sustainable Devel.; chmn. internat. com. Bus. Coun. of Sustainable Devel.; mem. adv. com. Commn. for Environ. Cooperation; trustee Tomas Rivera Policy Inst.; chmn. Internat. Gas Ctr. Mem. Pacific Coast Gas Assn. (chmn. 1994-95), Internat. Gas Union (chmn. com. 9), U.S. C. of C. (mem. internat. policy com.), Coun. of the Ams. (adv. com.), Wildlife Conservation Soc. (trustee), Nature Conservancy (trustee, bd. Greater Houston area for smog prevention, industry profl. for clean air). Avocation: international energy development writing.

THORNBERRY, MAC (WILLIAM MCCLELLAN THORNBERRY), United States Representative from Texas; b. Clarendon, Tex., July 15, 1958; m. Sally Thornberry; 2 children. BA in History, summa cum laude, Tex. Tech U., Lubbock, 1980; JD, U. Tex. Law Sch., 1983. Legis. coun. Staff of US Rep. Tom Loeffler, 1983-85; chief of staff to US Rep. Larry Combest, 1985-88; dep. asst. sec. legis. affairs US Dept. 0State, 1988-89; def. atty. Peterson, Farris, Doores & Jones, Amarillo, Tex., 1989-94; mem. US Congress from 13th Tex. dist., 1995—. Mem.: Southwestern Cattle Raisers Assn., Tex. Cattle Raisers Assn. Republican. Presbyterian. Office: US House of Representatives 2329 Rayburn House Office Bldg Washington DC 20515 also: 905 S Fillmore St Ste 520 Amarillo TX 79101 Office Phone: 202-225-3706.*

THORNBURG, FREDERICK FLETCHER, lawyer executive, educator; s. James F. and Margaret R. (Major) T.; children: James Brian, Charles Kevin, Christian Sean, Christopher Herndon; m. Patricia J. Malloy, Dec. 4, 1981. AB, DePauw U., 1963; postgrad., U. Notre Dame, 1965; JD magna cum laude, Ind. U., 1968. Bar: Ind. 1968, U.S. Tax Ct. 1970, U.S. Ct. Appeals (7th cir.) 1970, U.S. Supreme Ct. 1971. Tchr., coach U.S. Peace Corps, Colombia, 1963-65; law clk. to chief judge U.S. Ct. Appeals (7th cir.), 1968-69; assoc. Thornburg, McGill, Deahl, Harman, Carey & Murray Barnes & Thornburg, South Bend, 1969—75; ptnr. Thornburg, McGill, Deahl, Harman, Carey & Murray, South Bend, 1975—81; v.p. systems and svcs. group The Wackenhut Corp., Coral Gables, Fla., 1981-82, sr. v.p. adminstrn., 1982—86, exec. v.p., 1986-88, bd. dirs. exec. com.; pres. Wackenhut Internat. Corp. and Wackenhut Svcs., Inc.; v.p., legal counsel St. Thomas U., 1988-90, adj. prof. law, 1989-90; pres., CEO PropServ, Inc., 1991-94; CEO Practice Resources Corp., 1996-97; CEO, of counsel Stephens, Lynn, Klien & McNicholas, P.A., 1998-2000; dean CAU Bus. Sch., 2006—07; ceo FFS Inc., 2010—. Cons. MSC, Am. Tel. Corp., GMMG Inc.; mem. bd. advisors Publix Supermarkets, Inc., 1994—95; legal and mgmt. cons., mem. bd. advisors St. Thomas U., 1990—95, 2001—06; bd. dirs., mem. exec. com., trustee RFBD, Inc.; bd. dirs. YEI, Inc., 2000—09, Carlos Albizu U. Found., 2002—09; trustee U. Cmty. Hosp. Found., 1991—94; adj. prof. bus. St. Mary's Coll., 1975—78; vis. prof. CTA, 1985—95; vice chmn., pvt. sec. adv. coun. Fla. Sec. of State, 1985—90; chair ethics com. Miami-Dade County Pub. Schs., 2002—05; legal and mgmt. cons., mem., chair bd. advisors WLRN-PBS Radio and TV, 2003—; adj. prof. bus. St. Thomas U., 1999—2000, Carlos Albizu U., 2004—09, St. Thomas U. Law Sch., 1989—90; chair Audit Budget Com. Miami-Dade County Pub. Schs., 2008—. Assoc. editor in chief Ind. Law Jour., 1967-68; contbr. articles to legal and bus. jours. Former dir. Civic Ctr. Found.; past pres. Jaycees, 1974; mem. MDCPS Superintendents Bus. Adv. Coun., 2009—; past chair, cmty. adv. bd. WLRN Pub. Radio and PBS TV; past mem. U. Hosp. Found. Bd., Tampa, Fla.; trustee RFD&D, Inc.; former bd. dirs. Michiana YMCA; past mem. exec. comm. bd. dirs. PBS Channel 34; former bd. dirs. Symphony Orch. Assn., 1974—80, Michiana Bd. Boy Scouts of USA; bd. dirs., mem. exec. com. Doral and West Airport C. of C.; former trustee Greater Miami-Dade C. of C.; past mem. bd. dirs., sec. New World Sch. Arts Found., 2006—11; past chair M-DCPS Ethics Com.; exec. bd. NWSA, 2008—; mem., former chair Miami Dade Sch. Sys. Audit & Budget. Com.; former vice chair FL State Security Adv. Coun.; past mem. Coral Gables Com. 21; former bd. mem. Carlos Albizu U. Found.; former mem. St. Thomas U. Adv. Bd., Ind. U. Sch. Law Alumni Bd., Class Agent; past pres. Doral Park Country Club; past mem. Ind. Soc. Chgo.; bd. dirs. Miami-Dade County PTA-PTSA; past bd. mem. Merry Lee Found.; former peace corps vol. Finalist for United Way Dorothy Shula Cmty. Vol. of Yr. award, 2010; recipient award Keys to City of South Bend, IN for civic and charitable Endeavors, Outstanding Legal Article of Yr. Ind. Bar Assn's Res Gestae, Honoree award Civic Ctr. Found., Disting. Alumni award Phi Gamma Delta Fraternity, DePauw U., American Jurisprudence awards Criminal Law and Future Interests; Adminstr. of Yr. award St. Thomas U. Mem. ABA, Ind. Bar Assn., Doral Park Golf and Country Club (bd. dirs., pres. 2004-06), Order of Coif, Phi Delta Phi, Alpha Delta Sigma, Lambda Phi Gamma Delta (Disting. Alumni award) Office: 10005 NW 52nd Ter Miami FL 33178-2608 Home Phone: 305-591-1898; Office Phone: 305-591-1898. Office Fax: 305-591-6560.

THORNELL, JACK RANDOLPH, photographer; b. Vicksburg, Miss., Aug. 29, 1939; s. Benjamin O. and Myrtice (Jones) T.; divorced; children— Candice, Jay Randolph. Student pub. schs. Photographer Jackson (Miss.) Daily News, 1960-64; with A.P., 1964—, assigned Dominican Republic, 1965, Selma, Ala., 1965, Democratic Nat. Conv., 1968. Served with AUS, 1958-60. Recipient Pulitzer prize for news photography of shooting of James Meredith, 1967; Headliners Photography award, 1967 Office: 3800 Howard Ave New Orleans LA 70125-1429

THORNER, MICHAEL OLIVER, medical educator; b. Beaconsfield, Eng., Jan. 14, 1945; came to U.S., 1977; s. Hans and Ilse T.; m. Prudence Maria Ross, July 7, 1966; children— Benjamin Bruno, Anna Rosa MB, BChir, U. London, 1970. Intern, resident Middlesex Hosp., St. Bartholomew's Hosp., London; lectr. chem. pathology St. Bartholomews Hosp., London, 1974, research fellow, 1974-75, lectr. medicine, 1975-77; assoc. prof. medicine U. Va., Charlottesville, 1977-82, prof. medicine, 1982-90, head div. endocrinology and metabolism, 1986-98, dir. Clin. Research Ctr., 1984-97, assoc. dir. CRC, 1981-84, Kenneth R. Crispell prof. in internal medicine, 1990-98, chmn. dept. internal medicine, 1998—2006, Henry B. Mulholland prof. internal medicine, 1998—2006, David C. Harrison prof. internal medicine, 2006—. Contbr. articles to profl. jours. Recipient Albion O. Bernstein award, 1984, Virginia Scientist of Yr. award, 1985, Gen. Clin. Rsch. Ctrs. program award, 1995, The Pituitary Soc. Annual award for contbns. to understanding pituitary disease, 1995, Theodore E. Woodward Award 1996. Master Am. Coll. Physicians; fellow ACP (John Phillips Meml. award 1999), AAAS, Royal Coll. Physicians, Soc. Endocrinology (Dale medal 2009), Endocrine Soc. (Edwin B. Astwood award 1992, Konrad Koch award 2013), Assn. Am. Physicians, Am. Soc. Clin. Investigations; fellow: Am. Acad. Arts & Scis. Office: U Va Health Sys Dept Internal Medicine Endocrinology PO Box 801411 Charlottesville VA 22908 Home: 906 Fendall Terr Charlottesville VA 22903 Fax: 434-982-0147. E-mail: mot@virginia.edu.

THORNHILL, ARTHUR H., JR., retired publishing executive; b. Boston, Jan. 1, 1924; s. Arthur Horace and Mary Josephine (Peterson) T.; m. Dorothy M. Matheis, Oct. 28, 1944(dec. Feb.4, 2013); children: Sandra Susanne Thornhill Brushart, Arthur Horace. AB magna cum laude, Princeton U., 1948. With Little, Brown & Co., Inc., Boston, 1948-88, v.p., 1955-58, gen. mgr., 1960-87, chief exec. officer, pres., 1962-87, chmn. bd., 1970-87; chmn., pres., dir. Little, Brown & Co. (Can.), Ltd., 1955-84; v.p. Time, Inc., 1968-87; vice chmn. Time-Life Books, Inc., 1976-86. Mem. adv. council history dept. Princeton U., 1964-85; trustee, treas. Princeton U. Press, 1972-85; chmn. N.Y. Graphic Soc., 1974-79. Trustee Bennington Coll., 1969-76; fellow emeritus Ctr. for Creative Photography U. Ariz.; bd. dirs. Am. Book Pubs. Council, 1964-67. Served to 1st lt. USAAF, World War II. Decorated Air medal; recipient Princeton U. Press medal, 1985, Disting. Alumni award Dwight-Englewood Sch., 1998. Mem. Assn. Am. Pubs. (bd. dirs. 1978-81), Edgartown Yacht Club, Edgartown Reading Room (pres. 1990-92), Union Club (N.Y.C.), Century Club (N.Y.C.), Publs. Lunch Club (N.Y.C.)(pres. 1969-70), St. Botolph (Boston). Home: Apt 5303 250 Pantops Mountain Rd Charlottesville VA 22911-8703

THORNSBERRY, CLYDE, microbiologist; b. Pippa Passes, Ky., June 20, 1930; s. Columbus B. and Ollie Mae (Sparkman) T.; m. Glenda L. Martin, May 13, 1952; children: Teresa, David, Robert. BS, U. Ky., Lexington, 1958, PhD, 1966. Chief Antimicrobial Investigations Br. Ctrs. for Disease Control, Atlanta, 1966-89; dir. Inst. for

Microbiol. Rsch., Franklin, Tenn., 1989-93, Focus BioInova, Inc., Franklin, 1993—; dirt. Eurofins Medinet, Inc., Franklin. Lectr. in field; chmn., vice-chmn. Intersci. Conf. Anti-Agts., Washington, 1989-94; adv. bd. several pharm. cos., 1980—. Contbr. articles to profl. jours. Recipient awards USPHS, Washington, 1982, 87. Fellow Infectious Disease Soc. of Am.; mem. Am. Soc. Microbiology (BD award for Rsch. in Clin. Microbiology 2003), Am. Acad. Microbiology, NY Acad. Scis., WHO Coms. on Antibiotics, Nat. Com. Clin. Lab. Stds. Democrat. Achievements include patent-use of antimicrobial agts. to sterilize tissue for implanting; study of antimicrobials, antimicrobial resistance, and in vitro testing of antimicrobial activity; lab. was designated a WHO lab. for antimicrobial agts. Home: 5228 Forsyth Rd #202 Macon GA 31210 Personal E-mail: clyde.thornsberry@gmail.com.

THORNTON, J. RONALD, technology consultant; b. Fayetteville, Tenn., Aug. 19, 1939; s. James Alanda and Thelma White (McGee) T.; m. Mary Beth Packard, June 14, 1964 (div. Apr. 1975); 1 child, Nancy Carole; m. Martha Klemann, Jan. 23, 1976 (div. Apr. 1982); 1 child, Trey; m. Bernice McKinney, Feb. 14, 1986; 1 child, Paul Leon. BS in Physics and Math., Berry Coll., 1961; MA in Physics, Wake Forest Coll., 1964; postgrad., U. Ala., 1965-66, Rollins Coll., 1970. Rsch. physicist Brown Engring. Co., Huntsville, Ala., 1963-66; sr. staff engr. Martin Marietta Corp., Orlando, Fla., 1966-75; dep. dir. NASA, Washington, 1976-77; exec. asst. Congressman Louis Frey, Jr., Orlando, 1978; pres. Tens Tec, Inc., Orlando, 1978-79; dir. So. Tech. Applications Ctr. U. Fla., Gainesville, Fla., 1979—2002. Bd. dirs., treas. North Fla. Tech. Innovation Ctr., 1994—2004; mem. light wave tech. com. Fla. High Tech. and Indsl. Coun., Tallahassee, 1986—93, NASA Tech. Transfer Exec. Com., Washington, 1987—, Javits Fellowship Bd., Washington, 1986—91, Gov.'s New Porduct Award Com., Tallahassee, 1988—94, Fla. K-12 Math., Sci. and Computer Sci. Edn. Quality Improvement Adv. Coun., 1989—94, Fla. Sci. Edn. Improvement Adv.Com., 1991—92; bd. dirs. North Fla. Enterprise Corp., 2001—04. Pres. Orange County Young Rep. Club, Orlando, 1970-71; treas. Fla. Fedn. Young Reps., Orlando, 1971-72; chmn. Fla. Fedn. Young Reps., Orlando, 1972-74; pres. Gainesville Area Innovation Network, 1988-89; mem. Berry Coll. Alumni Coun., 2006—. Named Engr. Exhibiting Tech. Excellence and Accomplishment ctrl. Fla. chpt. Fla. Engring. Soc., 1975, Achievement award NASA, 1977; named to Berry Coll. Hall of Fame, 2005. Mem. IEEE, Soc. Mfg. Engrs., Tech. Transfer Soc. (pres. 1999, bd. dirs. 1996—2001, Thomas Jefferson award 1999), Nat. Assn. Mgmt. and Tech. Assistance Ctrs. (bd. dirs. 1988, pres. 1992), Covenant Pres. Ch. (Gainesville, Fla.)(elder). Republican. Avocations: music, travel, reading, golf. Home and Office: 17829 NW 20th Ave Newberry FL 32669-2143 Office Phone: 352-472-6026. Personal E-mail: ronthornton@cox.net.

THORNTON, JAMES F., plastic surgeon, former military officer; b. Orange, NC, Jan. 4, 1961; m. Katherine Thornton; 5 children. BA, Austin Coll., 1982; MD, Univ. Tex. Southwestern Med. Ctr., 1989. Cert. Am. Bd. Plastic Surgery, 2000. Intern Univ. Tex. Southwestern Med. Ctr., 1989—90, resident in surgery, 1993—97; fellow in plastic surgery Emory Univ., 1997—99; assoc. prof. Univ. Tex. Southwestern Med. Ctr., Dallas, 2000—; staff mem. Parkland Meml. Hosp., Zale Lipshy Univ. Hosp., Children's Med. Ctr., St. Paul Med. Ctr. Comdr., flight surgeon Air Training Wing USN, & USNR. Decorated Navy & Marine Corps Commendation Medal, Nat. Defense Medal Dept. of the Navy; recipient Armed Forces Reserve Medal with M device, 2003; named a Top Doctor - Plastic Surgery, Redbook Mag., 2001. Fellow: Am. Coll. Surgeons; mem.: AMA, Tex. Med. Assn., Dallas County Med. Soc., Am. Soc. Plastic Surgeons, AO No. Am. Maxillofacial Faculty, Am. Soc. Maxillofacial Surgeons, Jurkiewicz Soc., Parkland Surgical Soc. Office Phone: 214-645-3113. Office Fax: 214-645-3140. Business E-Mail: james.thornton@utsouthwestern.edu.

THORNTON, JOSEPH SCOTT, research and development company executive, materials scientist; b. Sewickley, Pa., Feb. 6, 1936; s. Joseph Scott and Evelyn (Miller) T.; divorced; children: Joseph Scott III, Chris P. BSME, U. Tex., 1957, PhD, 1969; MSMetE, Carnegie Mellon U., 1962. Engr. Walworth Valve Co., Boston, 1958; metall. engr. Westinghouse Astronuclear Lab., Large, Pa., 1962-64; instr., teaching assoc. U. Tex., Austin, 1964-67; group leader Tracor Inc., Austin, 1967-69, dept. dir., 1973-75; dept. mgr. Horizons Rsch., Inc., Cleve., 1969-73; founder, bd. mem. Tex. Rsch. Internat., Inc. (formerly Tex. Rsch. Inst., Inc.), Austin, 1975—. Contbr. numerous tech. papers to profl. publs.; editor: WANL Materials Manual, 2 vols., 1964; patentee in field. Founder, bd. mem. Cmtys. Recovery 501 (c) Social Profit Corp., Austin, 2004—. Recipient IGS award, 2002; fellow Alcoa, Austin, 1964, RC Baker Found., 1967;Dr. Stewart Nemir Friend of Recovery Recognition Award, 2010; Pres.'s Call to Service Award, Lifetime 2010. Mem.: ASTM, Internat. Geosynthetics Soc. (award 2002), Adhesion Soc., Am. Soc. Metals Internat. (exec. com. 1965—66). Office: Tex Rsch Internat Inc 9063 Bee Caves Rd Austin TX 78733-6201 Office Phone: 512-615-4440. Business E-Mail: jst@cforr.org. E-mail: jst@tri-intl.com.

THORNTON, SPENCER P., ophthalmologist, educator; b. West Palm Beach, Fla., Sept. 16, 1929; s. Ray Spencer and Mae (Phillips) T.; m. Annie Glenn Cooper, Oct. 6, 1956; children: Steven Pitts, David Spencer, Ray Cooper, Beth Ellen. BS, Wake Forest Coll., 1951, MD, 1954. Diplomate: Am. Bd. Ophthalmology. Intern Ga. Bapt. Hosp., Atlanta, 1954-55; resident gen. surgery U. Ala. Med. Center, 1955-56; resident ophthalmology Vanderbilt U. Sch. Medicine, 1960-63; practice medicine specializing in ophthalmic surgery Nashville, 1960—; med. dir. Thornton Eye Ctr., 1995-99; clin. prof. ophthalmology U. Tenn., Memphis, 2002. Disting. vis. prof. dept. ophthalmology U. Tenn., Memphis 2001, Ridley medal lectr., 2001; mem. staff Bapt. Hosp., chief ophthalmology svc., 1982-87; guest prof., vis. lectr. U. Toronto, 1990-92, U. Paris, 1989, Rothchilds Inst., Paris, 1992, 94, U. Pretoria, 1991, 93, others; instr. Moscow Inst. Eye Microsurgery, 1981; instr. ophthalmic surgery Am. Acad. Ophthalmology Ann. Courses; lectr. lens implant symposiums Eng., Spain, Australia, Switzerland, Can., Sweden, Greece, Germany, France, Republic of South Africa, Japan; Berzelius lectr. U. Lund, Sweden, 1992; P.J. Hay Gold medal lectr. North of Eng. Ophthal. Soc., Scarborough, 1992; pres. Biosyntrx Inc., 2002—. King Features syndicated newspaper columnist, 1959-60, feature writer, NBC radio and TV, 1958-60; author, co-author textbooks on cataract and refractive surgery; mem. editl. bd. Jour. Refractive and Corneal Surgery, Jour. Cataract and Refractive Surgery, Video Jour. Ophthalmology, Ocular Surgery News (Ophthalmologist of Yr. 1996), Ophthalmic Practice (Can.), Eye Care Tech. Mag. (Lifetime Achievement award 1996); contbr. articles to profl. jours.; inventor instruments and devices for refractive and lens implant surgery. Named one of 100 Best Ophthalmologists in Am., Ophthalmology Times mag., 1996; recipient Honor award Can. Implant Assn., 1993, Outstanding Achievement award Bowman Gray Sch. Medicine, 1995, Ridley medal U. Tenn., Memphis, Tenn., 2001, Epstein medal lectr. Durban S. Africa, 2005. Fellow: ACS (life), Am. Coll. Nutritional Medicine (pres. 2000—), Am. Acad. Ophthalmology (honor award 1995); mem.: Am. Soc. Cataract and Refractive Surgery (pres. 1997—99), Can. Implant Soc. (life), South African Intraocular Implant Soc. (life), Am. Med. Soc. Vienna (life), Delta Kappa Alpha, Phi Rho Sigma. Baptist. Home: 5031 Hillsboro Pike Apt 314 Nashville TN 37215-1535 Business E-Mail: sthornton@biosyntrx.com.

THORP, BENJAMIN A., III, retired paper company executive; b. Albany, NY, May 31, 1938; s. Benjamin A. Jr. and Anna C. (Head) T.; m. Barbara Sue Tellock, Aug. 1, 1964 (div. Mar. 1986); 1 child, Benjamin A. IV; m. Laurie Diane Murdock, Oct. 25, 1987. Student in elec. engring., Rensselaer Poly. Inst., 1956-61, postgrad. in mgmt., 1967-68; BS in Physics, U. Md., 1964; postgrad. in engring., U. Bridgeport, 1966; postgrad. in mktg., U. Tenn., 1970. Product devel. mgr. Huyck Formex div. Huyck, Greenville, Tenn., 1969-71, mktg. mgr., 1971-73, v.p., gen. mgr., 1973-75, Huytech Systems div., Wake Forest, NC, 1975-78; v.p., dir. research Huyck Corp., Rensselaer, NY, 1978-80; pres. Benjamin A. Thorp Inc., Albany, 1980-82, POYRY-BEK Inc., Raleigh, NC, 1982-84; v.p. engring. BE&K Inc., Birmingham, Ala., 1984-85, James River Corp., Richmond, Va., 1985—95; v.p. mfg. tech. Chesapeake Corp., Richmond, Va., 1996-97; dir. pulp and paper engring. Ga. Pacific, Atlanta, 1998—2004, ret., 2004; pres. Flambeau River Biorefinery, 2006—07, renewable energy cons., 2004—. Mem. exec. com. Pulp and Paper Found. Bd., Ga. Inst. Tech., 1991-95, pres., 1993-95; mem. indsl. adv. bd. Forest Web.com, 2000—03, Peregrine Energy, Greenville, SC, 2002-08; chmn. bd. Besicorp.-Empire Newsprint LLC, 2004-07; bd. dirs. K.P. Products, chmn. bd. dirs., Bioenergy Deployment Constorium Co-author: Pulp and Paper Energy Best Practice Guidebook, 2d edit., 2006; tech. editor Paper Machine Operations, Vol. 7, 3d edit., 1991; contbr. more than 200 articles to profl. jours.; patentee in field. Bd. dirs. Richmond Math. and Sci. Ctr., 1987-93, Sic. Mus. of Va. Found., 1989-98; chmn. papermaking project adv. com. Inst. Paper Sci. and Tech., 1990-94. Fellow TAPPI (chmn. papermakers com. 1984-86, vice chmn. paper and bd. divsn. 1988-90, chmn. 1990-92, bd. dir., Leadership award 1994); mem. Paper Industry Mgmt. Assn. (pres. 1996-97, chmn. bd. trustees 1999—2003, Glen T. Rinnegar award 1999), PIMA-CPBIS Mgmt. Excellence award 2003, Exptl. Aircraft Assn., Meadowbrook Estates Civic Assn. (bd. dirs. 1996-98, pres. 2003-04, 2010), Meadowbrook Country Club (bd. dirs. 2005-08). Presbyterian. Personal E-mail: bathorp@comcast.net.

THORP, JAMES SHELBY, electrical engineering educator; b. Kansas City, Mo., Feb. 7, 1937; s. Joseph Chester and Ruth Vefe (McNamara) T.; m. Barbara Anne Curit, June 27, 1959 (div. July 1976); children: Jeffrey Barton, Elizabeth Anne; m. Christine Annette Moore, Aug. 10, 1980 (div. 1995); children: Gregory, William. BEE, Cornell U., 1959, MS, 1961, PhD, 1962. Asst. prof. Cornell U., Ithaca, NY, 1962-66, with, 1962—2004, assoc. prof., 1966-75, prof., 1975—94, assoc. dir. Sch. Elec. Engring., 1991-94, dir. Sch. Elec. Engring., 1994, Charles N. Mellowes prof. engring., 1994—2001; faculty intern Am. Electric Power Svc. Corp., NYC, 1976-77; fellow Churchill Coll., U. Cambridge, 1988; Hugh P. and Ethey C. Kelley prof. elec. and computer engring. Va. Polytechnic and State U., Blackburg, Va., 2004—, dept. head, Bradley Dept. Elec. and Computer Engring., 2004—. Cons. Am. Electric Power Svc. Corp., 1977-83, Dowty Control Techs., Boonton, N.J., 1988—. Author: Computer Relaying for Power Systems, 1988; assoc. editor IEEE Transactions on Circuits and Sys., 1985-87; editor IEEE Transactions on Power Delivery 1998-2001, mem. editl. bd.; contbr. chpts. to books, articles to profl. jours. Co-recipient Benjamin Franklin medal in Elec. Engring., Franklin Inst., 2008. Fellow IEEE (Power Engring. Soc. Outstanding Power Engring. award, Career Svc. award, mem. power sys. relaying com.), NAE, Eta Kappa Nu, Tau Beta Pi and Sigma Xi Achievements include patents in field. Avocation: golf. Office: Va Tech 302 Whittemore Hall (0111) Blacksburg VA 24061 Office Phone: 540-231-6646, 540-231-3363. Business E-Mail: jsthorp@vt.edu.

THORP, JOHN MERCER, JR., physician; b. Rocky Mountain, NC, Aug. 31, 1957; BA in Zoology, U. NC, Chapel Hill, 1979; MD, East Carolina Univ., 1983. Intern Univ. NC Sch. Medicine, Chapel Hill, 1983, resident ob-gyn., 1983-87, fellow maternal-fetal medicine, 1987-89, clin. asst. prof., divsn. maternal-fetal medicine, dept. ob-gyn., 1989—90, asst. prof., divsn. maternal-fetal medicine, dept. ob-gyn., 1990—95, assoc. chair, dept. ob-gyn., 1995—99, assoc. prof., divsn. maternal-fetal medicine, dept. ob-gyn., 1995—2000, co-dir., Inst. Generalist Physician, 1999—2000, sr. rsch. fellow, Cecil G. Sheps Ctr. for Health, Svcs. Rsch., 1999—, co-dir., NC program for women's health rsch., Cecil G. Sheps Ctr. for Health Svcs. Rsch., 1999—2004, prof., dept. ob-gyn., 2000—, Hugh McAllister Disting. prof. ob-gyn, dept. ob-gyn., 2001—, interim and dep. dir., Ctr. for Women's Health Rsch., Cecil G. Ships Ctr. for Health Svc. Rsch., Dept. Epidemiology, Sch. Pub. Health, Dept. Ob-gyn, 2004—. Med. dir., HORIZONS Perinatal Substance Abuse Program U. NC, Chapel Hill, 1993—; adj. prof., dept. epidemiology, sch. pub. health and tropical medicine Tulane U., 2003—; adj. prof., dept. epidemiology, sch. pub. health U. NC, Chapel Hill, 1999—2004, Chapel Hill, 2004—, fellow, Carolina Population Ctr., 2003—, dir., biomedical core, Carolina Population Ctr., 2004—. Contbr. several articles to profl. jours. Recipient NC Divsn. Mental Health Develop. Disabilities and Substance Abuse Recogntion award for Outstanding Svc. to Women and Children, 1999, Perinatal Health Model of Excellence NC Dept. Health and Human Svcs. in Conjunction with the March of Dimes, 1999; named Mcallister Disting. Prof. Ob-gyn., 2002. Fellow: Am. Gynecological and Obstetrical Soc.; mem.: Soc. for Maternal-Fetal Medicine, Assn. Professors Gynecology and Obstetrics, Soc. Gynecologic Investigation, South Atlantic Assn. Ob-gyn., Am. Fertility Soc., Am. Coll. Ob-gyn. Office: Dept Ob-Gyn 4012 Old Clinic Bldg CB #7570 Chapel Hill NC 27599-7570 Office Phone: 919-843-7850. Office Fax: 919-843-6938. Business E-Mail: thorp@med.unc.edu.

THORSTEINSSON, GUDNI, physiatrist; b. Vestmannaeyjar, Iceland, Aug. 5, 1941; came to U.S., 1971; s. Thorsteinn and A. G. Einarsson; m. Elin Klein, Apr. 10, 1965; children: Arnar Karl, Asdis Thora. BS, Reykjavik (Iceland) Coll., 1961; candidatus med. et chirurg., U. Iceland, Reykjavik, 1968; MS, U. Minn., 1976. Diplomate Am. Bd. Phys. Medicine and Rehab. Dist physician Icelandic Govt., Djupivogur, 1970-71; resident dept. phys. medicine and rehab. Mayo Found., Rochester, Minn., 1972-75, mem. consulting staff, 1975-80; chair dept. Nat. Hosp., Reykjavik, 1980-81; dir. rehab. Mayo Clinic/St. Mary's Hosp., Rochester, 1981-85; dir. out-patient rehab. Mayo Clinic, Rochester, 1985-88, chair dept., 1987-91, chair dept. phys. medicine and rehab. Jacksonville, Fla., 1991-99. Physiatrist cons. Mayo Clinic, Rochester, 81-91, Jacksonville, 1991—. Author: (with others) Efficacy of Transcountaneous Electrical Stimulation, 1977, Placebo Effect of Transcountaneous Electrical Stimulation, 1978, Electrical Stimulation for Anagesia, 1983, Management of Post Polio Syndrome, 1997. Mem. Am. Acad. Phys. Medicine and Rehab. Office: Mayo Clinic Jacksonville 4500 San Pablo Rd S Jacksonville FL 32224-1865

THORUP, SHAWNA SAAVEDRA, librarian; b. Torrance, Calif., Mar. 29, 1969; d. Larry Dean and Sylvia Louise (Saavedra) Westphal; m. John Lindstrom Thorup, Dec. 1, 1995; child, Sean. AA in English, El Camino Coll., Torrance, 1989; BA in English, U. Calif., Berkeley, 1991; MLS, UCLA, 1993. Children's libr. L.A. Pub. Libr., Venice, Calif., 1993-96; sr. libr. Torrance Pub. Libr., 1996—2005; asst. dir. Fayetteville Pub. Libr., Ark., 2005—09, exec. dir., 2009—. Christian Fiction columnist Libr. Jour., 2002—03. Named one of the Movers & Shakers, Libr. Jour., 2007. Mem. ALA, AAUW, Libr. Adminstrn. and Mgmt. Assn., Pub. Libr. Assn., Southestern Libr. Assn., Assn. for Libr. Trustees, Advs., Friends & Founds. Office: Fayetteville Public Library 401 W Mountain St Fayetteville AR 72701 Office Phone: 479-856-7000. Office Fax: 479-571-0222. Business E-Mail: sthorup@faylib.org.

THRASH, THOMAS WOODROW, JR., federal judge; b. Birmingham, Ala., May 8, 1951; s. Thomas Woodrow and Catherine (Pope) Thrash; m. Margaret Lines Thrash, June 20, 1981; children: Andrew Stiles, Margaret van Buren. BA, U. Va., 1973; JD with cum laude, Harvard U., 1976. Bar: Ga. 1976. Assoc. McClain, Mellen, Bowling & Hickman, Atlanta, 1976—77; asst. dist. atty. Atlanta Jud. Dist., 1977—81; assoc. Finch, McCranie, Brown & Thrash, Atlanta, 1981—85, ptnr., 1985—97; judge US Dist. Ct. (no. dist.) Ga., Atlanta, 1997—. Adj. prof. litigation Ga. State U., 1986—; instr. Atlanta Law Sch., 1977, Atlanta Coll. Trial Advocacy, 1984—85. Contbr. articles to profl. jours. Active High Mus. Art, Atlanta, 1982—, Atlanta Hist. Soc., 1977—; bd. dirs. Current Historians, 1983—87, Ga. Conservancy, 1982—; alt. del., 1988, Dem. Nat. Conv. Mem.: Atlanta Bar Assn., Ga. Bar Assn., Lawyers Club Atlanta. Democrat. Episc. Home: 2850 Vinings Way NW Atlanta GA 30339-5312 Office: US Dist Ct 2188 US Courthouse 75 Spring St SW Atlanta GA 30303-3309 Office Phone: 404-215-1550.

THRASHER, FAY C., clinical psychologist; b. Wynne, Ark., Dec. 17, 1935; d. Andrew J. and Joy M. (Charles) Thrasher; children: Jeffrey K. Mitchell, Sidney J. Guidroz Jr. MEd, McNeese State U., 1963; MA, La. State U., 1967, PhD, 1970. Lic. psychologist. Chief psychologist Cmty. Mental Health, Lake Charles, La., 1970-73; clin. psychologist VA Hosp., Salisbury, NC, 1973-76; chief psychologist VA Opt Clinic, San Antonio, 1976-77, Alvin C. York VA Med. Ctr., Murfreesboro, Tenn., 1977-87; clin. psychologist VA Med. Ctr., Alexandria, Va., 1990-95, chief psychologist, 1995—. Bd. dirs. Oasis Ministry, Pineville, La. Chmn. Combined Fed. Campaign, Murfreesboro, 1985—86. Mem.: APA, La. Psychol. Assn., Nat. Register. Avocations: bridge, antiques, art, music. Home: 303 Rain Tree Pl Pineville LA 71360-5472 Office Phone: 318-473-0010 2626.

THRASHER, JOHN, state legislator, former political organization administrator; b. Columbia, SC, Dec. 18, 1943; m. Jean Moore; children: Jennifer, Jon, Julie. BS, Fla. State U., 1965; JD with honors, Fla. State U. Coll. Law, 1972. Bar: Fla. Mem. Fla. House of Reps., 1992—2001, co-chmn. rules, resolutions & ethics com., 1996-97, spkr. of the house, 1999—2000; of counsel Smith, Hulsey & Busey, Jacksonville, Fla., 1996—2008; ptnr. Southern Strategy Group, Tallahassee, 2001—08; gen. counsel. Jacksonville Chamber of Commerce, 2009; mem. Dist. 8 Fla. State Senate, 2009—; chmn. Republican Party of Fla., 2010—11. Mem. Clay County Sch. Bd., 1986—90, vice chmn., 1988, chmn., 1989—90; v.p. govtl. affairs Clay County Chamber of Commerce, 1989—92; bd. dirs. Clay Police Athletic League, Clay YMCA. Served in US Army, 1966—70, Germany, Vietnam. Decorated Army Commendation Medal, Bronze Star with oak leaf cluster; recipient Raymond B. Stewart Gavel of Authority award, Fla. Assn. Sch. Administrators, 1994. Republican. Presbyterian. Avocations: golf, basketball, reading. Office: 212 Senate Office Bldg 404 S Monroe St Tallahassee FL 32399-1100 also: 113 Nature Walk Pkwy Unit 106 Saint Augustine FL 32092-3066 Office Phone: 904-727-3600, 850-487-5030. Office Fax: 904-727-3603, 850-487-5368. E-mail: thrasher.john.web@flsenate.gov.

THREEFOOT, SAM ABRAHAM, physician, educator; b. Meridian, Miss., Apr. 10, 1921; s. Sam Abraham and Ruth Frances (Lilienthal) Threefoot; m. Virginia Rush, Feb. 6, 1954; children: Barbara Jane Stockton Mattingly, Ginny Ruth Threefoot Lindberg, Tracyann Threefoot Esenstad, Shelley Ann Cowan. BS, Tulane U., New Orleans, 1943, MD, 1945. Diplomate: Am. Bd. Internal Medicine. Intern Michael Reese Hosp., Chgo., 1945-47; asst. vis. physician Charity Hosp. New Orleans, 1947-50, vis. physician, 1950-57, sr. vis. physician, 1957-69, cons., 1969-70, 76-91; clin. asst. dept. medicine Touro Infirmary, New Orleans, 1953-56, jr. asst., 1956-60, sr. asst., 1960-63, dir. med. edn., 1953-63, dir. research, 1953-70, sr. dept. medicine, 1963-70; fellow dept. medicine Tulane U., 1947-49, instr., 1948-53, asst. prof., 1953-59, asso. prof., 1959-63, prof., 1963-70, 76-91, prof. emeritus, 1991—, asst. dean, 1979-91, adj. prof. emeritus Sch. Pub. Health & Tropical Medicine, 1993—; chief of staff VA Hosp. (Forest Hills div.), Augusta, Ga., 1970-76; asso. chief staff VA Hosp., New Orleans, 1976-79, chief of staff, 1979-91, cons., 1991—97; asst. dean Med. Coll. Ga., 1970-76, prof. medicine, 1970-76. Cons. physician Lallie Kemp Charity Hosp., Independence, La., 1951-53 Editor: Lymphology, 1967-70, sr. mem. editl. bd.; Contbr. articles profl. jours. With US Army, 1943—45. La. Heart Assn. grantee, 1953-55; John A. Hartford Found. grantee, 1956-74; Am. Heart Assn. grantee, 1959-61; USPHS grantee, 1953-66 Fellow ACP, Am. Coll. Cardiology, NY Acad. Sci.; mem. Am. Heart Assn. (v.p. 1970, fellow council on circulation), Central Soc. Clin. Research, So. Soc. Clin. Investigation (pres. 1967), AAAS, Internat. Soc. Lymphology, Soc. Exptl. Biology and Medicine, Soc. Nuclear Medicine, Microcirculatory Conf., Inc., Am. Fedn. Clin. Research, La. Heart Assn. (pres. 1967), Nat. Assn. VA Chiefs of Staff (pres. 1987-88), Phi Beta Kappa, Sigma Xi. Jewish. Avocation: writing. Home: 1750 St Charles Ave Unit 616 New Orleans LA 70130 Office Phone: 504-524-3668. Personal E-mail: threefoot@bellsouth.net.

THRO, WILLIAM EUGENE, general counsel; b. Elizabethtown, Ky., Nov. 8, 1963; s. Ernest Guernsey and Joan (Young) T.; children: Sandra Lucinda Grace Edwards-Thro, William Thomas Daniel Edwards-Thro, Noah Christopher James Edwards-Thro.; m. Julie Urback, Sept. 04, 2004. BA, Hanover Coll., Ind., 1986; MA, U. Melbourne, Australia, 1988; JD, U. Va., Charlottesville, 1990. Bar: Ky. 1990, Colo. 1991, Va. 1998, US Dist. Ct. (we. dist.) Ky. 1990, US Dist. Ct. Colo. 1991, US Ct. Appeals (6th and 10th cirs.) 1991, US Ct. Appeals (3d cir.) 1993, US Supreme Ct. 1993, US Ct. Appeals (4th cir.) 1997, US Dist. Ct. (ea. dist.) Va. 1998, US Dist. Ct. (we. dist.) Va. 1998, US Ct. Appeals (DC cir.) 1999, US Bankruptcy Ct. (ea. and we. dists.) Va. 1999, US Dist. Ct. (ea. dist.) Ky. 2003, US Dist. Ct. (no. dist.) Ill. 2003, US Ct. Appeals (7th cir.), 2005, US Ct. Appeals (8th cir.), 2006. Jud. clk. Judge Ronald E. Meredith, US Dist. Ct. (we. dist.) Ky., Louisville, 1990-91; asst. atty. gen. State of Colo., Denver, 1991-97, Commonwealth Va., Richmond, 1997—99, U. Counsel Christopher Newport U., Newport News, 2000—04, 2008—12; asst. prof. Govt. Christopher Newport U., 2008—11, assoc. prof. constl. studies, 2011—12; solicitor gen. Commonwealth Va., 2004—08, dep. solicitor gen., 2002—04; gen. counsel U. Ky., 2012—, Pub. U. Author: Why You Cannot Sue State U: A Guide to Sovereign Immunity, 2001, 2d edit., 2007; co-author: Race Conscious Admissions and Financial Aid After the University of Michigan Decisions, 2004; co-editor: The NACUA Handbook for Lawyers New to Higher Education, 2003, 2d edit., 2007, 3rd edit 2009, Free Speech in Higher Education, 2008; mem. editl. bd. Coll. and Univ. Law, 2000—, vice chair, 2004-05, chair, 2005-08; mem. editl. bd. Encyclopedia of Edn. Law, 2005-08, Internat. Jour. Edn. Reform, 2008-; adv. bd. mem. Ency. Higher Edn. Law, 2008-10; mem. author's com. West's Edn. Law Reporter, 1992-2007, mem. editl adv. com., 2007-; contbr. articles to profl. jours. Gen. counsel adv. bd. NCAA, 2001—04, 2010; mem. Com. Ministry, Presbytery Eastern Va., 2011—12, LaCrosse Presbyn. Ch.; elder Presbyn. Ch. USA, 2007—13, moderator permanent jud. commn., presbytery Eastern Va., 2010—12. Recipient Best

Brief award, Nat. Assn. Attys. Gen., 2003—04, 2009—10, Hardin County Sch. Disting. Alumni award, 2004; fellow, Nat. Assn. Coll. U. Attorneys, 2007, Nat. Edn. Fin. Conf., 2012; scholar U.S. Senate Youth scholar, Hearst Found., 1982, Harry S Truman scholar, Truman Scholarship Found., 1984, Rotary Internat. Ambassadorial scholar, Melbourne, 1987. Mem.: Va. Bar Assn. (bd. govs. edn. lawyers sect. 2010—13, chair appellate practise sect. 2011—12), South Africa Edn. Law Assn., Edn. Law Assn. (bd. dirs. 2008—, pres. 2012—13), Nat. Assn. Coll. and U. Attys., Ky. Bar Assn., Am. Red Cross (chair, York Poquoson Chapt. 2011—12), Federalist Soc., Nat. Eagle Scout Assn., Hon. Order of Ky. Cols. Republican. Presbyterian. Home: 4209 Clearwater Way Lexington KY 40515 Office: University Ky 301 Main Blog Lexington KY 40506 Personal E-mail: william.thro@gmail.com.

THUESEN, GERALD JORGEN, industrial engineer, educator; b. Oklahoma City, July 20, 1938; s. Holger G. and Helen S. T.; m. Harriett M. Thuesen; children: Karen T. Hannah, Dyan T. Jacobus. BS, Stanford U., 1960, MS, 1961, PhD, 1968. Engr. Pacific Tel. Co., San Francisco, 1961-62, Atlantic Richfield Co., Dallas, 1962-63; asst. prof. indsl. engring. U. Tex., Arlington, 1963, 67-68; assoc. prof. indsl. and sys. engring. Ga. Inst. Tech., Atlanta, 1968-76, prof., 1976-96, prof. emeritus, 1996—. Author: Engineering Economy, 4th edit., 1971, 9th edit., 2001, Economic Decision Analysis, 1974, 3rd edit., 1998; assoc. editor: The Engring. Economist, 1974-80, editor, 1981-91. NASA/Am. Soc. Engring. Edn. summer faculty fellow, 1970. Fellow Inst. Indsl. Engrs. (dept. editor Trans. 1976-80, v.p. publs. 1979-80, divsn. dir. 1978-80, Wellington award 1989, Publs. award 1990, bd. trustees 1979-81), Am. Soc. Engring. Edn. (bd. dirs. 1977-79, Eugene L. Grant award 1977, 91); mem. Sigma Xi. Office: Ga Inst Tech Sch Indsl & Sys Engring Atlanta GA 30332-0205 Business E-Mail: gthuesen@isye.gatech.edu.

THURMAN, KAREN L., lobbyist, former United States Representative from Florida; b. Rapid City, SD, Jan. 12, 1951; d. Lee Searle and Donna (Altfillisch) Loveland; m. John Patrick Thurman, 1973; children: McLin Searl, Liberty Lee. AA, Santa Fe CC, Gainesville, Fla.; BA, U. Fla., Gainesville, 1973. Mem. Dunnellon City Coun., Fla., 1975—83, mayor City of Dunnellon, 1979-81; mem. Fla. State Senate, 1983—93, US Congress from 5th Fla. dist., 1993—2002, mem. ways & means com., agrl. com., 1996—2002; lobbyist eAppeals, Miami, 2004—, Freedom Healthcare, Hollywood, Fla., 2004—; chairwoman Fla. Democratic Party, Tallahassee, 2005—10. Del. Dem. Nat. Conv., 1980. Mem.: Dunnellon C. of C. (bd. dirs., Svc. Above Self award 1980), Fla. Horseman's Children's Soc. (charter mem.). Democrat. Episcopalian. Office Phone: 850-222-3411. Office Fax: 850-222-0916.

THURMOND, GEORGE MURAT, judge; b. Del Rio, Tex., Oct. 22, 1930; s. Roger H. and Day (Hamilton) T.; m. Elsiejean Davis, June 27, 1959; children: Carolyn Day, Georganna, Sarah Gail. BA, U. of the South, 1952; JD, U. Tex., 1955. Bar: Tex. 1955. Ptnr. Montague & Thurmond, Del Rio, 1955-69; judge Tex. Dist. Ct. (63rd dist.), Del Rio, 1970-2000, sr. judge, 2001—. Presiding judge 6th Adminstrv. Region, Del Rio, 1983-87; chmn. jud. sect. State Bar Tex., 1988-89. Staff: U. Tex. Law Review, 1955. Rep. Tex. Ho. of Reps., 1955-58. Mem.: ABA, Fifth US Ct. Appeals, Tex. Bar Assn. Republican. Anglican. Avocations: exercise, traditional jazz, model railroading. Office Phone: 830-775-3710. Business E-Mail: gthurmand@stx.rr.com.

THURSTON, BONNIE BOWMAN, religious studies educator, minister, poet; b. Bluefield, W.Va., Oct. 5, 1952; d. Ernest Venoy and Eleanor Sabina (King) Bowman; m. Burton Bradford Thurston, May 29, 1980 (dec. Nov. 1990). BA summa cum laude, Bethany Coll., 1974; MA, U. Va., 1975, PhD, 1979; postgrad., Harvard Div. Sch., 1983, Eberhard Karls U., Germany, 1983—84, Ecole Biblique, Jerusalem, 1993. Ordained to ministry Disciples of Christ Ch., 1984. Instr., asst. dean U. Va., Charlottesville, 1979—80; adj. prof. Wheeling Coll. (now Wheeling Jesuit U.), W.Va., 1980—81, assoc. prof., chair dept. theology, 1985—95; asst. prof. Bethany Coll., W.Va., 1981—83; assoc. prof. N.T. Pitts. Theol. Sem., 1995—99, William F. Orr prof., 1999—2002. Vis. scholar Harvard U. Div. Sch., Cambridge, Mass., 1983; tutor Inst. Study of Christian Origins, Tubingen, Germany, 1983—85. Author: (books) The Widows, 1989, Wait Here and Watch, 1989, Spiritual Life in the Early Church, 1993, Women in the NT, 1998, To Everything a Season, 1999, Preaching Mark, 2002, Philippians and Philemon, 2005, Religious Vows, the Sermon on the Mount, And Christian Living, 2006, The Spiritual Landscape of Mark, 2008, For God Alone: A Primer on Prayer, 2009, (books of poetry) The Heart's Land, 2001, Hints and Glimpses, 2004; contbr. articles to profl. jours., poetry to jours. Mem.: Soc. for the Study of Christian Spirituality, Disciples Hist. Soc., Soc. for Buddhist-Christian Studies, Internat. Thomas Merton Soc., Soc. Bibl. Lit., Cath. Bibl. Assn. Avocations: gardening, music, cooking. Office: PO Box 2258 Wheeling WV 26003

THURSTON, PERRY E., JR., state legislator; b. Pompano, Fla., Jan. 30, 1961; m. Dawn Board; children: Alison, Perry E. III. BA in Fin., Morehouse Coll., Atlanta, 1982; JD, U. Miami, Fla., 1987. Atty.; mem. Dist. 93 Fla. House of Reps., Tallahassee, 2006—, ranking mem. fin. and tax coun., mem. criminal and civil justice appropriations com., criminal and civil justice policy coun., policy coun., rules and calendar coun., mem. select policy coun. on strategic and econ. planning. Democrat. Baptist. Office: 410 House Office Bldg 402 S Monroe St Tallahassee FL 32399-1300 also: 331 NW 27th Ave Fort Lauderdale FL 33311-8632 Office Phone: 954-762-3746, 850-488-1084.

THUSTON, WILLIAM LEE, lawyer; BA, U. Va.; JD, Samford U., Birmingham, Ala.; LLM, NYU, NYC. Bar: Ala., Tenn. Law clk. to Hon. Richard L. Jones Ala. Supreme Ct.; ptnr. Burr & Forman LLP, Birmingham, mng. ptnr. of firm. Former mem. nat. bd. dirs. Girls Inc., former pres. bd. dirs. of ctrl. Ala.; bd. dirs. Ala. Automotive Manufacturers Assn., Ala. Wildlife Fedn., Met. Devel. Bd., U. Ala. at Birmingham Comprehensive Cancer Care Ctr. Named one of The Best Lawyers in America, Gen. Corp. Law and Econ. Devel., Leading Lawyers for Bus., Chambers USA; named to Ala. Super Lawyers. Fellow: American Bar Found., Ala. Law Found.; mem.: ABA (mem. taxation and bus. law sections), Ala. State Bar, Birmingham Bar Assn. (sec., treas. 1994, pres. 2005), Tenn. Bar Assn. Office: Burr & Forman LLP 420 N 20th St Ste 3400 Birmingham AL 35203 Office Phone: 205-458-5143. Office Fax: 205-244-5712. Business E-Mail: lthuston@burr.com.

THYER, CHRISTOPHER R., federal prosecutor, former state legislator; b. 1969; BA, Ark. State U., 1991; JD, U. Ark.Sch. Law, 1995. Solo law practice, 1995—97; ptnr. Mooney Law Firm, 1997—2005, Halsey & Thyer, PLC, 2005—07, Stanley & Thyer, P.A., 2007—11; mem. Dist. 74 Ark. House of Reps., Little Rock, 2003—09; vice chmn. Ark. State Agencies & Govt. Affairs Com., Little Rock, 2003—04; US atty. (eastern dist.) Ark. US Dept. Justice, Little Rock, 2010—. Mem.: Ark. Trial Lawyers Assn., American Trial Lawyers Assn., Ark. Bar Assn., Craighead County Bar Assn. Democrat. Baptist. Office: US Attorney's Office PO Box 1229 Little Rock AR 72203 Office Phone: 501-340-2600. Office Fax: 501-340-2728.*

T.I., See **HARRIS, CLIFFORD JR.**

TIAN, LI, investment company executive, educator; arrived in U.S., 1996; m. Min Shi, Apr. 20, 2001. B in Engring., Tsinghua U., Beijing, 1993; M in Engring., Beijing U. Aeronautics & Astronautics, 1996; MS in Info. Sys., George Mason U., 1999; MBA, U. Chgo. Grad. Sch. Bus., 2008. Cert. sys. engr., database adminstr., solution developer Microsoft; project mgmt. profl. Project Mgmt. Inst. Gen. mgr. multimedia tech. Beijing Feitian Inst. New Tech., 1993—96; software engr. GTSI Corp., Chantilly, Va., 1998; project cons. MCI Comm. Corp., Pentagon City, Va., 1998; supr. systems/infrastructure Airlines Reporting Corp., Arlington, Va., 1998—2006; faculty U. Phoenix, 2002—; founder, CEO Dcom Solutions, Llc, Fairfax, Va., 2001—. Industry advisor and virtual mentor Mgmt. Leadership Tomorrow, NYC, 2005—; dir. Internat. Rsch. Assn., Cambridge, Mass., 2005—; treas. Fairfax Ctr. Recreation Assn., Inc., 2005—; team leader beta program Microsoft, 2001—; v.p. project mgmt. Inst. Diversity SIG, Newtown Sq., Pa., 2005—. Vol. Ctr. Internat. Disaster Info., Arlington, 2003—; pres. Washington organizing com. U.S.-China People Friendship Assn., Fairfax, 2005—. Recipient Software Excellence award, 1996. Mem.: IEEE (sr.), Project Mgmt. Inst., Assn. Computing Machinery (Spl. Interest Group MIS), PA SQL Server, IEEE Control Sys. Soc. (sr.), IEEE Info. Theory Soc. (sr.), IEEE Engring. Mgmt. Soc. (sr.), IEEE Edn. Soc. (sr.), IEEE Computer Soc. (sr.), IEEE Comm. Soc. (sr.). Achievements include development of GTSI.COM, GTSIEXPRESS.COM and MCI ISC Online; C/C++ class libraries for modeling and operation of dimensions and tolerances; computer aided road design system; multimedia general information management software system. Home: 7007 Kilworth Ln Springfield VA 22151-4008 Personal E-mail: ltian01@gmail.com.

TIBBS, SUE, state legislator; b. Tulsa, Okla., Oct. 6, 1934; d. Clyde and Frances (VanSlyke) Sloan; m. Milton Homer Tibbs; children: Debra West, Kelli Dodd. Attended, Tulsa Jr. Coll. Mem. Dist. 23 Okla. House of Representatives, 2001—. Named Woman of Yr. Republican. Mailing: Oklahoma House of Representatives 2300 N Lincln Blvd Rm 303-A Oklahoma City OK 73105 also: 10902 E 28th St Tulsa OK 74129-7603 Office Phone: 405-557-7379, 918-663-3915. Business E-Mail: suetibbs@okhouse.gov.

TICE, DOUGLAS OSCAR, JR., retired federal judge; b. Lexington, NC, May 2, 1933; s. Douglas Oscar Sr. and Lila Clayton (Wright) T.; m. Janet N. Capps, Feb. 28, 1959 (div. Sept. 1976); children: Douglas Oscar III, Janet E.; m. Martha Murdoch Edwards, June 8, 1996. BS, U. N.C., 1955, JD, 1957. Bar: N.C. 1957, U.S. Ct. Appeals (4th cir.) 1964, Va. 1970, U.S. Dist. ct. (ea. dist.) Va. 1976, U.S. Bankruptcy Ct. (ea. dist.) Va. 1976. Exec. sec. N.C. Jud. Coun., Raleigh, 1958-59; assoc. Baucom & Adams, Raleigh, 1959-61; trial atty. Office Dist. Coun., IRS, Richmond, Va., 1961-70; corp. atty. Carlton Industries, Inc., Richmond, 1970-75; ptnr. Hubard, Tice, Marchant & Samuels, P.C., Richmond, 1975-87; judge U.S. Bankruptcy Ct. (ea. dist.), Richmond, Norfolk, Alexandria, Va., 1987-99, chief judge, 1999—2012. Author: author: Collier On Bankrupty, 2010-; co-author: Monument & Boulevard, Richmond's Grand Avenues, 1996; contbr. articles to profl. jours. Vice pres. Richmond Pub. Forum, 1976-80, com. chmn. Richmond Forum, Inc., 1986-2001; past pres. Richmond Civil War Roundtable, mem., 1965—; bd. dirs. Epilepsy Assn. Va., Inc., 1976-87. Capt. USAR, 1957-66. Fellow Am. Coll. Bankruptcy; mem. ABA, Va. Bar Assn., City of Richmond Bar Assn., Am. Bankruptcy Inst., Nat. Conf. Bankruptcy Judges (bd. govs. 2005—08), So. Hist. Assn., Va. Hist. Soc., Old Dominion Sertoma (pres. Richmond chpt. 1967), Comml. Law League Am., Supreme Ct. Hist. Soc., Am. Inn of Ct., Hist. Soc. of U.S. Dist. Ct. for Eastern Va. (asst. sec., bd. dir. mem. 2006—). Home: 5 Foxmere Dr Richmond VA 23238 Home Phone: 804-740-1265. Personal E-mail: thetices2@comcast.net.

TICE, RAPHAEL DEAN, military officer; b. Topeka, Dec. 4, 1927; s. Arthur Taylor and Mamie (McDonald) T.; m. Eunice Miriam Suddarth, Dec. 23, 1946; children: Karen Ann Tice Claterbos, William Dean. BS in Mil. Sci., U. Md., 1963; MSBA, George Washington U., 1970. Served as enlisted man U.S. Army, 1946-47; commd. 2d lt., 1947; advanced through grades to lt. gen., 1981; platoon leader and co. comdr. 1st Inf. div., W.Ger., 1949-52; co. comdr., regimental adj. 8th Inf. divsn., 1955-56; tng. advisor Vietnam, 1956-57; mem. staff Office of Dep. Chief of Staff for Pers., Dept. Army, 1960-63; chief pers. mgmt. divsn. Office of Under Sec. of Army, 1963-64; plans Officer So. Command, Panama, 1965-67; dep. comdr. 3rd Brig., 4th Inf. Divsn., 1967; comdr. 2nd Bn., 12th Inf. of 25th Inf. divsn., Vietnam, 1968; exec. for pers. procurement Office of Sec. Def. for Manpower and Res. Affairs, 1968-69; comdr. 1st Brig., 1st Inf. divsn., 1970, chief of staff, 1971; dep. dir. mil. pers. mgmt. Dept. Army, 1972-73; comdg. gen. Berlin Brigade, 1974-76; dep. chief of staff personnel U.S. Army Europe, 1976-77; comdg. gen. 3rd. Inf. divsn., 1977-79; dep. asst. sec. def. for mil. pers. and force mgmt. Dept. Def., 1979-85; exec. dir. Nat. Recreation and Pk. Assn., 1986—2001; ret., 2001. Spl. adviser Pres.'s Coun. on Phys. Fitness and Sports; bd. dirs. Sports Pub. LLC, Class 6 Kayak, Inc. Decorated Silver Star, Legion of Merit with 2 oak leaf clusters, Air medal with V and 7 oak leaf clusters, Bronze Star with V, Vietnam Cross of Gallantry with Palm, Purple Heart., Def. Disting. Service medal, Army Disting. Service medal Mem. Assn. U.S. Army, Am. Chess Found. (hon. pres.) Home: 18077 Clendenning Cir Round Hill VA 20141-2580 Home Phone: 540-338-7194. Personal E-mail: ticepunky@aol.com.

TIDEMAN, T. NICOLAUS, economics educator; b. Chgo., Aug. 11, 1943; s. Robert and Jane Catherine (Schmidt) T.; m. Lisa Nicole Woodside, Jan. 29, 1965 (div. Jan. 1971); m. M.J. Estill Putney, Jan. 19, 1971. BA, Reed Coll., 1965; PhD, U. Chgo., 1969. Asst. prof. Harvard U., Cambridge, Mass., 1969—73; sr. staff economist Pres.'s Coun. Econ. Advisors, Washington, 1970-71; postdoctoral fellow Ctr. for Study of Pub. Choice, Blacksburg, Va., 1973-75; assoc. prof. Va. Tech., Blacksburg, 1975-85, prof. econs., 1985—; pres. Schalkenbach Found., NYC, 1996—2002. Cons. Bur. of the Budget, Washington, 1969, U.S. Treasury, Washington, 1973-75, various law firms, Boston, also Roanoke, Va., 1972-96. Contbr. articles to profl. jours. Recipient Disting. Rsch. in Edn. award Va. Edn. Assn., 1976. Mem. Am. Econ. Assn. (nominating com., 1992), Mt. Tabor Ruritan Club (pres. 1995).

TIDEY, R. SCOTT, sales executive, marketing executive; BS in Bus. Mgmt., Va. Poly. Inst. & State U., 1983. Sales planning mgr. Wyeth Consumer Healthcare, 1987—93, Hamilton Beach Brands, Inc. (subs. NACCO Industries, Inc.), 1993—94, mgr., channel devel., 1994—96, dir., spl. markets, 1996—2001, v.p., nat. account sales, 2001—07, v.p., internat., 2005—07, v.p., consumer sales, 2007—08, v.p., sales, N.Am., 2008—09, v.p., mktg., N.Am., 2009; sr. v.p., sales and mktg., N.Am. Hamilton Beach Brands, Inc., 2009—. Office: Hamilton Beach Brands Inc 4421 Waterfront Dr Glen Allen VA 23060 Office Phone: 804-273-9777. Office Fax: 804-527-7142.

TIDWELL, GEORGE ERNEST, federal judge; b. Atlanta, Aug. 1, 1931; s. George Brown and Mary (Wooddall) T.; m. Carolyn White, July 1, 1961; children: Thomas George, Linda Carol, David Loran. LLB, Emory U., 1954. Bar: Ga. 1954. With John J. Westmoreland Sr. and Jr., Atlanta, 1954-58, Slaton, Brookins, Robertson & Tidwell, Atlanta, 1958-66; exec. asst. atty. gen. Atlanta, 1966-68; judge Civil Ct., Fulton County, Ga., 1968-71, Superior Ct., Atlanta Jud. Circuit, 1971-79, US Dist. Ct. (no. dist.) Ga., Atlanta, 1979—96, chief judge, 1996—99, sr. judge, 1999—. Mem. ABA, State Bar Ga., Am. Judicature Soc., Atlanta Bar Assn. Office: US Dist Ct 1967 US Courthouse 75 Spring St SW Ste 1967 Atlanta GA 30303-3331

TIDWELL, JOHN CHARLES, state legislator; b. Murg Co, Tenn., Aug. 15, 1941; s. James Wesson and Margaret Jewel Atkins Tidwell; m. Charlotte Faye Tyler Tidwell, 1964; children: John Charles, Nicole Tyler. Mem. Transp. Com.; chmn. Tenn. State House; area mgr. & civil engr. Ei Dupont, New Johnsonville, 1966—; city councilman New Johnsonville, Tenn., 1970—78; regional planning commr., 1974—90; county commr. Humphreys County, Tenn., 1978—94; mem. River Port Authority, Waverly, Tenn., 1980—86, Humphreys County Solid Waste Bd., 1992—; state rep. Dist. 74 Tenn., 1996—; sect. mem. Conservancy Com.; mem. Pub. Safety & Rural Rds. Subcom.; chmn. House Pks. & Tourism Com. Democrat. Methodist. Office: 158 Harbor Cir New Johnsonville TN 37134 also: 22 Legislative Plz Nashville TN 37243-0174 Office Phone: 931-535-2619, 615-741-7098. Office Fax: 615-741-4324. Business E-Mail: rep.john.tidwell@capitol.tn.gov.

TIEFEL, WILLIAM REGINALD, hotel company executive; b. Rochester, NY, Mar. 30, 1934; s. William Reginald and Mary Hazel (Cross) T.; m. Vada Morell, Dec. 30, 1985 (dec. Apr. 1999); m. Norma Gewirz Kline, Nov. 25, 2000. Student, Williams Coll., 1952-54; BA with honors, Mich. State U., 1956; postgrad., Harvard Bus. Sch.; DBA in Hospitality Mgmt. (hon.), Johnson and Wales U. Gen. mgr. Marriott Hotels, 1964—71, regional v.p. Washington, 1971-80; exec. v.p. Marriott Hotels and Resorts, Washington, 1980-88; pres. Marriott Hotels, Resorts and Suites, 1988-92, Marriott Lodging Group, 1992-98; vice chmn. Marriott International, 1998—2002; chmn. Ritz-Carlton Hotel Co, 1998—2002; chmn. emeritus Ritz-Carlton Hotel Co, 2002—; dir. Bulgari Hotels and Resorts, 2001—07. Bd. dir. CarMax Inc., 2002—, chmn., 2007—. Bd. visitors Valley Forge Mil. Acad. and Jr. Coll., 1976-79, chmn., 1979, trustee, 1982-92; chmn. Campaign Valley Forge, 1985-88, chmn. com. on trustees, 1989-91, hon. life trustee; trustee Johnson and Wales U., 2001-09, Norton Mus. Art, 2004-08, adv. coun. Wilmer Eye Inst., Johns Hopkins U.; trustee Town Palm Beach United Way, 2005-11. With US Army, 1956. Mem. Am. Hotel and Lodging Assn. (dir. Ednl. Inst., Arthur Landstreet award 1997), Soc. of the Four Arts (Palm Beach), Club Colette (Palm Beach), Cosmos Club (Washington), Tavern Club (NYC). Independent. Roman Catholic. Home: 159 Via Del Lago Palm Beach FL 33480-4916

TIEN, JAMES M., dean, engineering educator, consultant; b. NYC, Mar. 27, 1945; s. Yu-Shih Tien and Tien-Lun Li; m. Ellen S. Weston, Aug. 27, 1981; children: Lee, Rex. BEE, Rensselaer Poly. Inst., 1966; SM in Systems Engring. and Ops. Rsch., MIT, 1967, PhD in Systems Engring. and Ops. Rsch., 1972. Mem. tech. staff Bell Labs., Holmdel, NJ, 1966-69; rsch. project dir. Rand Corp., NYC, 1970-73; area dir. Urban Sys. Rsch. & Engring., Cambridge, Mass., 1973-75; prin., v.p. Structured Decisions Corp., Cambridge, 1975—; prof. Dept. Elec., Computer, and Sys. Engring. Rensselaer Poly. Inst., Troy, NY, 1977—2007, Yamada Corp. prof., acting chair, 1986—87, founding chair Dept. Decision Scis. and Engring. Sys., 1988, acting dean engring., 1992—94, 1998—99; dean Coll. Engring. U. Miami, 2007—, disting. prof. Recipient IBM Faculty award, 2005. Fellow AAAS, INFORMS, IEEE (bd. dirs. 2000-04, v.p. in charge of publication services and products bd. 2001-02, mem. ednl. activities bd. 2003-04, Joseph G. Wohl Oustanding Career award 1998, Major Ednl. Innovation award 2000, Norbert Weiner award, 2004, Richard M. Emberson award, 2010), NAE. Office: U Miami Coll Engring PO Box 248294 Coral Gables FL 33124

TIERNEY, CINDY B., construction executive; b. Atlanta, Ga. BS, Ga. Southern U. Sr. v.p., global strategic adv. svcs. Comdisco; dir., bus. sys. & planning Office Depot, Inc.; chief info. officer National Service Industries; sr. v.p., chief info. officer Beazer Homes USA, Inc. Office: Beazer Homes USA Inc 1000 Abernathy Rd NE Ste 260 Atlanta GA 30328-5648 Office Phone: 770-829-3700. Office Fax: 770-481-2808.

TILFORD, JOSEPH P., scenic and lighting designer, educator; b. Cin., Jan. 27, 1949; s. Kenneth William and Jeanne Mae (Redditt) T.; w. Deborah Wentworth; children: Molly Tilford, Michael Tilford. BGS, U. Cin., 1975, MA, 1976. Assoc. prof. Northwestern U., Evanston, Ill., 1990—2003; dean U. NC, Sch. Arts, 2003—. Freelance theatrical designer sets & lighting over 300 designs for profl. theatres including Cin. Playhouse in the Park, Goodman Theatre, Mo. Repertory Theatre, Chgo. Shakespeare, Cleve. Playhouse, Asolo Theatre, Off-Broadway. Bd. mem. US Inst. Theatre Tech. Mem. United Scenic Artists. Avocations: outdoors, baseball. Office: UNC School of the Arts 1533 South Main St Winston Salem NC 27127 Office Phone: 336-770-3214. Business E-Mail: tilford@uncsa.edu.*

TILLAR, THOMAS CATO, JR., academic administrator, consultant; b. Radford, Va., Sept. 9, 1947; s. Thomas Cato Sr. and Ruth (Wiemer) T. BS in Biology, Va. Poly. Inst., 1970, MA in Edn., 1973, EdD, 1978. Cert. fund raising executive. Program director Va. Poly. Inst., Blacksburg, 1970-73, coord. student programs, 1973-74, grad. teaching asst., 1974-75, dir. alumni svcs., 1975-78, dir. corp. foundn. prog., 1978-80, dir. ann. giving, 1980-90, dir. alumni rels., 1990-95, v.p. alumni rels., 1996—. Cons. Colo. State U., Fort Collins, 1982, Va. Mil. Inst., Lexington, 1983, Datatel Minicomputer Co., Alexandria Va., 1985-86. Editor: (book) A Pictorial History of Virginia Tech, 1984. Bd. dirs. Montgomery Regional Hosp., 1998—2003, Blacksburg Shelter Home; pres. Smithfield Preston Found., 2000—, Blacksburg Health and Fitness. Mem. Nat. Soc. Fund Raising Execs., Nat. Edn. Alumni Trust (pres.), Coun. Advancement and Support of Edn., Alumni Assn. Execs. (mem. coun.), Rotary (pres. 1990-91), Ctr. in the Square (bd. dirs. 2004—), Pi Kappa Alpha (pres., trustee edn. found., Memphis 1986—). Presbyterian (elder). Avocations: running, golf, travel. Home: 3010 Stradford Ln Blacksburg VA 24060-8176 Office Phone: 540-231-6285. Business E-Mail: ttillar@vt.edu.

TILLERSON, REX W., oil company executive; b. Wichita Falls, Tex., Mar. 23, 1952; s. Robert Tillerson; m. Renda St. Clair; 4 children. BS in Civil Engring., U. Tex., Austin, 1975. Joined Exxon Co., U.S.A., 1975, various positions, prodn. dept., 1975—87, bus. devel. mgr., natural gas dept., 1987—89, gen. mgr., ctrl. prodn. divsn., 1989—92; prodn. adv. Exxon Corp., Dallas, 1992; coord., affiliate gas sales Exxon Co. Internat., Florham Park, NJ, 1992—95; pres. Exxon Yemen Inc., Esso Exploration and Prodn. Khorat Inc., 1995—98; v.p. Exxon Ventures Inc., 1998—99; pres. Exxon Neftegas Ltd., 1998—99; exec. v.p. ExxonMobil Development Co., 1999—2001; sr. v.p. ExxonMobil Corp., 2001—04, pres., 2004—06, chmn., CEO, 2006—. Mem. adv. bd. Engring. Found., U. Tex. at Austin; bd. dirs. Exxon Mobil Corp., 2004—. Dir. United Negro Coll. Fund; bd. trustee Ctr. Strategic and Internat. Studies; mem. nat. exec. bd. Boy Scouts Am.; mem. exec. bd. Circle Ten Coun.; mem. engring. found. adv. coun. U. Tex. Austin. Named a Disting. Engring. Grad., U. Tex., 2006; named one of The 25 Most Powerful People in Bus., Fortune Mag., 2007, Bus. People of Yr., 2010, The Global Elite, Newsweek mag., 2008, The World's Most Powerful People, Forbes mag., 2009—13.

Mem.: U.S.-Russia Bus. Coun. (dir.), Soc. Petroleum Engineers, American Petroleum Inst., Ford's Theatre Soc. (vice-chmn.). Office: ExxonMobil Corp 5959 Las Colinas Blvd Irving TX 75039-2298*

TILLEY, NORWOOD CARLTON, JR., federal judge; b. Rock Hill, SC, 1943; s. Norwood Carlton and Rebecca (Westbrook) Tilley. BA, Wake Forest U., 1966, JD, 1969. Bar: NC 1969, admitted to practice: US Dist. Ct. (Mid. Dist.) NC 1971. Law clk. to Hon. Eugene A Gordon US Dist. Ct. (middle dist.) NC, Greensboro, NC, 1969-71; ptnr. Osteen, Adams, Tilley & Walker, Greensboro, NC, 1977-88; asst. US atty. (middle dist.) NC US Dept. Justice, Greensboro, NC, 1971-73, US atty., 1974-77; judge US Dist. Ct. (mid. dist.) NC, Greensboro, NC, 1988—99, 2006—08, chief judge, 1999—2006, sr. judge, 2008—. Instr. Wake Forest U. Sch. Law, 1980. Office: US District Court 324 West Market St Greensboro NC 27401 Office Phone: 336-332-6000.

TILLINGHAST, NANCY, library director; b. Buckhannon, W.Va., Mar. 2, 1946; children: Beth Norman, Mark. BS, W.Va. Univ., 1969; MLIS, Univ. SC, 1991. Asst. libr. Roane County Libr., Spencer, W.Va., 1982—90; children's & pub. services libr. Thomas County Pub. Libr. Sys., Thomasville, Ga., 1991—94, asst. dir., 1994—96, dir., 1996—. Chmn. Libr. Council SW Ga. Tech. Coll., mem. Literacy Council; chmn. Certified Literate Cmty. Prog. Thomas County. Chmn. United Way Thomas County; mem. Family Connections, Hands on Thomas County. Recipient Libr. award, NY Times, 2006, Cmty. Svc. award, Zion Christian Bible Inst.; named Woman of the Yr., Thomasville-Thomas County C. of C., 2007. Mem.: ALA, Pub. Libr. Assn., Ga. Libr. Assn., Rotary. Avocations: gardening, cross stitch, reading. Office: Thomas County Pub Libr Sys 201 N Madison St Thomasville GA 31792 Office Phone: 229-225-5252. Office Fax: 229-225-5258. Business E-Mail: nancy@tcpls.org.

TILLIS, THOM, state legislator; m. Susan Tillis; children: Lindsay, Ryan. Former ptnr. Pricewaterhousecoopers; head IBM Corp., 2002—; state rep. Dist. 98 NC; bd. commr. Cornelius, 2003—05; pres. Parent Tchr. Student Assn., Hopewell High Sch., 2005—06; bd. mem. United Way Cent Carolinas; chmn. bd, dirs. Lake Norman/Mooresville United Way; founder Hopewell High Sch. Project Hope. Recipient Duke Power Citizenship & Svc. award. Republican. Office: North Carolina House of Representatives 16 W Jones St Rm 2304 Raleigh NC 27601-1096 Address: PO box 32186 Charlotte NC 28232 Office Phone: 919-733-5828, 919-733-3451. E-mail: Thom.Tillis@ncleg.net.

TILLMAN, AUDREY BOONE, insurance company executive, lawyer; married; 3 children. BA in Polit. Sci., U. NC, Chapel Hill; JD, U. Ga. Law clk. to Judge Richard C. Erwin US Dist. Ct. NC; assoc. Smith, Helms, Mulliss and Moore, Greensboro, NC, 1990—93; assoc. prof. NC Ctrl. U. Sch. Law; mem. legal dept. AFLAC, Inc., Columbus, Ga., 1996—97, second v.p., 1997—2000, v.p., sr. assoc. counsel legal divsn., 2000—01, sr. v.p., dir. human resources, 2001—05, sr. v.p. to exec. v.p. corp. services, 2005—. Dir.-at-large Soc. Human Resource Mgmt. Mem. Workforce Devel. Task Force State of Ga. Recipient Corp. Governance award, Celebrating Excellence in Leadership Orgn., Office Depot Visionary award, 2007; named one of Top 100 Blacks in Corp. Am., Black Profls. mag. Mem.: Bar DC, NC State Bar, State Bar Ga. Office: AFLAC Inc 1932 Wynnton Rd Columbus GA 31999 Office Phone: 706-323-3431.

TILLMAN, JERRY W., state legislator; Ret. sch. adminstr.; state senator Dist. 29 NC, 2003—; rep. whip. Mem. Agrl., Environ., and Natural Resources com., Appropriations on Edn./Higher Edn. com., Appropriations/Budget com., Edn./Higher Edn. com., Fin. com., Judiciary I com., Transp. com. Republican. Office: NC Senate 300 N Salisbury St Rm 627 Raleigh NC 27603-5925 Office Phone: 919-733-5870. E-mail: Jerry.Tillman@ncleg.net.

TILLMAN, LEE MARK, oil industry executive; b. 1961; BS in Chemical Engring., Tex. A&M U., 1983; PhD in Chemical Engring., Auburn U., 1989. Rsch. engineer Exxon Production Rsch. Co., Houston, 1989—93; engring. specialist Exxon Corp., Houston, 1993, Esso project cons. Aberdeen, Scotland, 1993—95; ops. supt. Exxon New Orleans Production Organization, 1998—2001; ops. mgr. Mobil Equatorial Guinea, Malabo, 2001—03; offshore divsn. mgr. Exxon-Mobil Upstream Rsch. Co., Houston, 2005—07, acting v.p., 2006—07; production mgr. North Sea Production Organization (NSP), mng. dir Esso Norge AS Exxon Corp., Stavanger, Norway, 2007—10; v.p. engring. Exxon Mobil Development Co, 2010—13; pres., CEO Marathon Oil Corp., Houston, 2013—. Bd. dirs. Marathon Oil Corp., 2013—. Mem.: Soc. Petroleum Engineers. Office: Marathon Oil Corp 5555 San Felipe Rd Houston TX 77056*

TILLMAN, MARY NORMAN, urban affairs consultant; b. Atlanta, Jan. 31, 1926; d. Mary Nellie Shehee; m. James A. Tillman Jr., Apr. 11, 1952; children: James A., Gina G. BA, Morris Brown Coll., 1947; postgrad., U. Minn., 1964, Old Dominion U., 1975—. Asst. bus. mgr. Morris Brown Coll., Atlanta, 1947-53; race rels. and urban affairs cons. Tillman Assocs. Cons. Social Engrs., Atlanta and Syracuse, NY, 1963—, sr. ptnr., treas., from 1965, now pres. Bd. dirs. The Tillman Inst. of Human Rels., Inc.; clin. prof. United Theol. Sem., New Brighton, Minn.; adj. prof. Gordon-Conwell Theol. Sem., South Hamilton, Mass. Author: What is Your Racism Quotient?, 1964, A Common Sense Approach to Racism and Other Exclusivities, 1998, (with James A. Tillman, Jr.) Why America Needs Racism and Poverty, 1972, Black Intellectuals, White Liberals and Race Relations: An Analytic Overview, 1973; What is your Exclusivity Quotient, 1978, A Common Sense Approach to Racism and Other Exclusivities, 2001; contbr. articles to profl. jours. Adv. coun. to urban ministries dept. So. Bapt. Conv., Cmty. Rels. Commn., Atlanta; bd. dirs. Christian Coun. Met. Atlanta, Tillman Inst. Human Rels. Mem. Tidewater Assn. Pub. Adminstrs. (dir.), Am. Acad. Cons., Nat. Black Writers Consortium (v.p.), Joint Ctr. for Polit. Studies. Home: 12061 Fm 466 Seguin TX 78155-8242 Office Phone: 404-665-7757.

TILLMAN, MASSIE MONROE, mediator, arbitrator, art gallery owner, retired judge; b. Corpus Christi, Tex., Aug. 15, 1937; s. Clarence and Artie Lee (Stewart) T.; m. Karen Wright, July 2, 1993; children: Jeff, Holly. BBA, Baylor U., 1959, LLB, 1961. Bar: Tex. 1961, US Dist. Ct. (no. dist.) Tex. 1961, US Ct. Appeals (5th cir.) 1969, US Supreme Ct. 1969, formerly bd. cert. personal injury trial law: Tex., Ind.; hearing examiner Tex. Edn. Agy. Pvt. practice, Ft. Worth, 1961—87; chief US bankruptcy judge Ft. Worth divsn. No. Dist. Tex., 1987—2001; mediator, arbitrator, 2001—. Author: Tillman's Trial Guide, 1970,-1990, comments editor, case notes editor; editl. bd. Baylor Law Rev., 1960-61. Recipient AV Rating award, Martindale Hubble, 1967—. Fellow Tex. Bar Found., Am. Bd. Trial Advocates (founding mem.); mem. Ft. Worth/Tarrant County Bar (bd. dirs. 1969-70, v.p. 1970-71, mentor program), Trial Attys. Am., Arbitration Assocs., Coll. State Bar Tex. (alternative dispute resolution sect. sch. law sect.), Tarrant County Trial Lawyers Assn. (founding mem.). Baptist. Avocation: quail hunting. Address: 6805 Vista Ridge Dr East Fort Worth TX 76132 Office Phone: 817-683-1422. Personal E-mail: tillmanmediator@yahoo.com.

TIMMCKE, ALAN EDWARD, colon and rectal surgeon; b. Madison, Wis., July 7, 1949; s. Wesley Eugene Timmcke; m. Teresa Ann Watkins, Dec. 31, 1977; children: Gretchen Kristine, Alan Edward Jr. BS, Dickinson Coll., 1971; MD with honors, Temple U., 1975. Diplomate Am. Bd. Surgery, Am. Bd. Colon and Rectal Surgery; lic. physician, Pa., La., Fla. Intern in surgery Nat. Naval Med. Ctr., Bethesda, Md., 1975-76, resident in gen. surgery, 1976-79; rsch. fellow in colon and rectal surgery Jewish Hosp./Washington U. Med. Ctr., St. Louis, 1985-86, clin. fellow in colon and rectal surgery, 1986-87; asst. in surgery Washington U. Sch. Medicine, St. Louis, 1985-87; staff colon and rectal surgeon Ochsner Clinic, New Orleans, 1987—. Staff surgeon Nat. Naval Med. Ctr., Bethesda, 1979, Naval Regional Med. Ctr., Newport, R.I., 1979-82, dept. colon and rectal surgery Lahey Clinic Med. Ctr., Burlington, Mass., 1984-85; staff surgeon Rumford (Maine) Community Hosp., 1982-84, med. staff v.p., 1983-84; instr. surgery Uniformed Svcs. U. of Health Scis., Bethesda, 1978-79; lectr. in field. Assoc. editor Diseases of the Colon and Rectum, 2002—08; contbr. articles and abstracts to profl. jours. Lt. comdr. M.C., USN, 1975-82. Recipient Harry E. Bacon Found. award for best original paper, 1987; NIH Summer Rsch. fellow, 1972. Fellow ACS, Am. Soc. Colon and Rectal Surgeons; mem. New Orleans Surg. Soc., Surg. Assn. of La., Internat. Soc. Univ. Colon and Rectal Surgeons, Soc. of Am. Gastrointestinal Endoscopic Surgeons, Alpha Omega Alpha. Office: Ochsner Clinic Dept Colon/Rectal Surgery 1514 Jefferson Hwy New Orleans LA 70121-2483 Office Phone: 504-842-4060. Personal E-mail: atimmcke@aol.com.

TIMMERMAN, JOSÉ R., consumer products company executive; Sr. v.p. worldwide ops. Tupperware Brands Corp., 1997—2009, sr. v.p. supply chain worldwide, 2009—10, exec. v.p. supply chain worldwide, 2010—. Office: c/o Tupperware Brands Corp 14901 S Orange Blossom Trail Orlando FL 32837 Office Phone: 407-826-5050. Office Fax: 407-826-8874.

TIMMERMAN, WILLIAM B., retired utilities executive, accountant; b. Columbia, SC, Nov. 12, 1946; s. William Bledsoe and Helen (Speissegger) T.; m. Janet Russell, Sept. 15, 1971; children: William III, Catherine Lucille. BA in Pub. Acctg., Duke U., 1968; postgrad., Harvard U., 1990. CPA, N.C. Auditor Arthur Andersen & Co., Charlotte, NC, 1968-78; sr. v.p. Carolina Energies, Inc., Columbia, 1978-82; v.p. S.C. Electric & Gas Co., Columbia, 1982-83, v.p., group exec., 1983-84; chief fin. officer, sr. v.p. SCANA Corp., Columbia, 1984—94, exec. v.p., CFO, contr., 1994—95, pres., 1995—97, COO, 1996—97, chmn., pres., CEO, 1997—2011. Exec. adv. com. Edison Electric Inst.; acctg. and fin. exec. com. Southeastern Electric Exchange; bd. dir. SCANA Corp., Liberty Corp., Preholding Inc., Palmetto Bus. Forum; past dir. Powertel Inc., SouthernNet/Telecom USA, Wachovia Bank SC, Palmetto Seed Corp.; chmn. bd. Standard Fed. Savs. Bank, Columbia; past chmn. SC Rsch. Authority. Trustee United Way of Midlands, Columbia, 1985—; vice chmn. fin. ARC, Columbia, 1986—; adv. bd. Sch. Bus. U. SC, 1985—, Duke Neighbordhood Partnership; bd. dir. Duke U., the Fuqua Sch.; past dir. Benedict Coll., SC State Ports Authority. Served with USN, 1968-72.

TIMMONS, SEAN ABBOTT, lawyer; b. Washington, Aug. 4, 1967; s. James Donald and Anita Abbott Timmons; m. Sheri Lynn Outlaw, June 8, 1996; children: Elizabeth Kelly Ross, Sean Abbott. BA, Williams Coll., 1989; JD, Duke U. Sch. Law, 1994. Bar: NC 1998, US Dist. Ct. (ea. dist.) NC 1998, US Ct. Appeals (4th cir.) 2001. Atty. Smith, Anderson, Blount, Dorsett, Mitchell & Jernigan, LLP, Raleigh, 1998—2006, ptnr., 2006—. Contbr. articles to profl. jours. Mem.: NC Bar Assn., Am. Health Lawyers Assn. Avocation: trombone. Home: 2902 Everett Ave Raleigh NC 27607 Office: Smith Anderson Blount Dorsett Mitchell & Jernigan LLP 150 Fayetteville St Cte 2300 PO Box 2611 Raleigh NC 27602-2611 Office Phone: 919-821-1220. Office Fax: 919-821-6800. Business E-Mail: stimmons@smithlaw.com.

TIMONEY, PETER JOSEPH, veterinarian, educator, virologist, consultant; b. Dublin, June 5, 1941; came to U.S., 1983; s. John Francis and Evelyn Norah (Whittle) T.; m. Katherine Mary Murphy, Sept. 11, 1971; children: Peter, Caroline, Sarah, David. MVB, Nat. U., Dublin, 1964; MS, U. Ill., 1966; PhD, U. Dublin, 1974. Rsch. assoc. U. Ill., Urbana, 1964-66; rsch. officer Vet. Rsch. Lab., Abbotstown, Ireland, 1966-72; sr. rsch. officer head equine diseases sect. Veterinary Rsch. Lab., Abbotstown, Ireland, 1972-79; assoc. prof. diagnostic lab., dept. microbiology Cornell U., Ithaca, NY, 1979-81; sci. dir. Irish Equine Ctr., Johnstown, Ireland, 1981-83; assoc. prof. virology vet. sci. dept. U. Ky., Lexington, 1983-87, prof. virology, assoc. chair for rsch., 1987-89, Frederick Van Lennep chair, 1988—, acting chair, 1989-90, chair, 1990-99, 2002—08, U. Ky. Gluck Equine Rsch. Hall of Fame Inductee, 2009; OIE designated expert Equine Viral Arteritis, 1991—, Equine Rhinopneumonitis, 2010—. Cons. Daryl Labs., Inc., Santa Clara, Calif., 1981-86, Ft. Dodge (Iowa) Animal Health Lab., 1986-92, 94—2009. Fellow Royal Coll. Vet. Surgeons, World Equine Vet. Assn. (pres. 1995-99); mem. Am. Assn. Equine Practitioners, Am. Soc. Microbiology, Am. Soc. Virology, U.S. Animal Health Assn., Am. Assn. Vet. Lab. Diag., Am. Vet. Med. Assn., Royal Coll. Vet. Surg. Avocations: reading, gardening. Office: Gluck Equine Rsch Ctr 128E Gluck Ctr Lexington KY 40506-0099 Office Phone: 859-218-1094. Business E-Mail: ptimoney@uky.edu.

TIMPERLAKE, EDWARD THOMAS, writer; b. Perth Amboy, NJ, Nov. 22, 1946; s. James Elwood Timperlake Jr. and Joan Dorothy (Conkling) Maurer; m. Barbette Runckel, Aug. 10, 1969 (div. 1993); children: Tara, Kimberly; m. Cathryn Porcelli Gekas, Apr. 8, 2000. BS, U.S. Naval Acad., 1969; MBA, Cornell U., 1977. Commd. 2d lt. USMC, 1969, advanced through grades to lt. col., ret., 1993; asst. venture mgr. Exxon Enterprise, NYC, 1977-78; sect. mgr. T.A.S.C., Arlington, Va., 1978-81; dep. dir. Nat. Dir. Vietnam Vets. Leadership Program, Action Agy., Washington, 1981-83; dir. mobilization plans and requirements Office of Sec. Def., Washington, 1984; campaign staff George Bush for Pres., 1988; asst. sec. Dept. Vets. Affairs, Washington, 1989-93; pres. T-9 Group, 1993-95; profl. staff rules com. US House of Representatives, Washington, 1996—99; dir. tech. assessment internat. tech. security Office of the Sec. of Def., The Pentagon, Washington, 2003—09; rsch. fellow USMC War Fighting Lab., 2012—. Author: Year of the Rat, 1998, Red Dragon Rising, 1999, Showdown, 2006; prin., writer, editor SLD Forum Com; contbr. articles to profl. jours. Mem.: Disabled Am. Vets. (life), Naval Acad. Alumni Assn., Cornell Club (DC), Army-Navy Club. Home: 1027 22d St Arlington VA 22202

TINDELL, HARRY J., state legislator; b. Oct. 30, 1960; Mem. Knox Co. Bd. Edn., 1986—91; state rep. Dist 13 Tenn., 1991—; businessmen. Democrat. Baptist. Mailing: PO Box 27325 Knoxville TN 37927-7325 Office: 33 Legislative Plz Nashville TN 37243-0113 Office Phone: 865-524-7200, 615-741-2031. Business E-Mail: rep.harry.tindell@capitol.tn.gov.

TINDELL, SEAN J., state legislator; b. Gulfport, Miss., Oct. 5, 1973; m. Claire Tindell; children: Sam, John Thomas, Meredith. Attended, U. So. Miss., Hattiesburg. Atty.; mem. Dist. 49 Miss. State Senate, Jackson, 2012—. Active Harrison County Rep. Party, Miss. Mem.: Miss. Assn. Realtors, Gulfport Bus. Club, Rite Masons, Kappa Sigma. Republican. Baptist. Office: Miss State Seante PO Box 1018 Jackson MS 39215 Business E-Mail: stindell@senate.ms.gov.

TINGLEY, F. WARREN, retired internist; b. Charlotte, NC, Nov. 22, 1933; s. Floyd Warren Sr. and Janie (Suggs) T.; m. Sandra Carpenter, Aug. 20, 1955 (div. Dec. 1984); children: Sheryl Tingley Hagen, David Alan; m. Johnette Hill, Apr. 5, 1985. BA in English, Emory U., 1955, MD, 1959. Diplomate Am. Bd. Internal Medicine (bd. govs. 1986-92). Intern USAF Hosp., Lackland AFB, Tex., 1959-60; resident in internal medicine Parkland Meml. Hosp., Dallas, 1963-65, fellow in cardiology, 1965-66; pvt. practice specializing in internal medicine Arlington, Tex., 1966-88; med. dir. southwestern region Met. Life Ins. Co., Irving, Tex., 1988-90; regional practice leader William M. Mercer Inc., 1990-91; v.p., sr. med. dir. Provident Life and Accident Co., Chattanooga, 1991-92; v.p., nat. med. dir. Travelers Ins. Cos., Hartford, Conn., 1992-94; sr. v.p., chief med. officer Kemper Nat. Svcs., Plantation, Fla., 1995-2000; med. dir. Mednet Connect, 2005—07, Fairpay Solutions, 2007—09. Apptd. Tex. Commn. on Health Care Reimbursement Alternatives, 1987; bd. dirs. Riverside Nat. Bank, Grand Prairie, Tex. Contbr. articles to profl. jours. Pres. Arlington YMCA, 1971; chmn. budget com. Family Services, Ft. Worth, 1973; participant Health Policy Agenda for Am. People, Chgo., 1984-87; trustee Tex. Med. Liability Trust, Austin, 1987-88. Capt. USAF, 1958-63. Fellow ACP (pres. Tex. chpt. 1981); mem. AMA (chmn. sect. coun. internal medicine, 1979-88), Am. Soc. Internal Medicine (pres. 1986-87), Tex. Med. Assn. (treas. 1978-85, alt. del. to AMA 1985-91, commendation 1985), Tarrant County Med. Soc. (pres. Arlington br. 1974, del. to Tex. Med. Assn., Community Svc. award 1983). Presbyterian. Avocations: photography, sailing, gardening. Home: 1912 Channing Park Dr Arlington TX 76013

TINKER, THOMAS EATON, retired headmaster; b. Providence, May 24, 1941; s. George Milan and Ruth (Eaton) T.; m. Roslyn May Silverman, Dec. 21, 1968. BA, Columbia U., 1963; MA, Brown U., 1968. English instr. Tabor Acad., Marion, Mass., 1964-66; history instr. Wheeler Sch., Providence, 1967-77; headmaster Broadmeadow Sch., Middletown, Del., 1977-82, St. Paul's Sch., Garden City, N.Y., 1982-89, The Barnard Sch., NYC, 1989-93; assoc. head sch. Trevor Day Sch., NYC, 1993—2003, head sch., 2003—05, ret., 2005. Evaluator Mid. State Assn. Colls. and Schs., Phila., 1978—. Trustee Barnard Sch. Found., 1993—; bd. dirs. Univ. Club L.I., 1984-86. With USAR, 1963-69. Mem. Nat. Assn. Ind. Schs., N.Y. State Assn. Ind. Schs., L.I. Episcopal Sch. Assn. (v.p./treas. 1984-89), Del. Assn. Ind. Schs. (sec. 1978-82). Episcopalian. Avocation: sailing. Home: 3911 Lucina Ct Fort Myers FL 33908

TINSLEY, BARBARA V., lawyer; BA magna cum laude, Emory U., 1971, JD with distinction, 1975. Asst. US atty. US Dept. Justice; with Ga.-Pacific, 1987—92, chief counsel, distbn. divsn., 1992—98; corp. compliance officer Home Depot, 1998—2000; asst. gen. counsel Mitsubishi Electric and Electronics USA, Inc., 2000—02; assoc. gen. counsel Cendian Corp., 2002—04; gen. counsel, sec. BlueLinx Holdings, Inc., Atlanta, 2004—, sr. v.p. Office: BlueLinx Corp 4300 Wildwood Pky Atlanta GA 30339 Office Phone: 770-953-7000. Office Fax: 770-221-8160. Business E-Mail: Barbara.Tinsley@BlueLinxCo.com.

TINSLEY, RICHARD L., personal care industry executive; CPA; Other Certified Law. Sr. mgr. Yum! Brands, Inc.; v.p., compliance and bus. devel. Almost Family, Inc.; chief devel. officer ResCare, Inc., 2007—. Office: Res Care Inc 9901 Linn Station Rd Louisville KY 40223-3808 Office Phone: 502-394-2100. Office Fax: 502-394-2206. Business E-Mail: rtinsley@rescare.com.

TINTEROW, GARY H., museum director; b. 1954; BA, Brandeis U., 1976; MFA, Harvard U., 1983; MBA, Columbia U. Bus. Sch., 2008. Chmn. dept. contemp. art Metropolitan Mus. Art, 1983—2011; dir. Mus. Fine Arts Houston, Tex., 2011—. Organized (exhibitions) Degas, 1988, Origins of Impression, 1994, Manet/Velázquez: The French Taste for Spanish Painting, 2003, Francis Bacon: A Centenary Retrospective, 2009, Picasso in the Metropolitan Mus. Art, 2010; contbr. over 60 major exhib. catalogues. Recipient Chevalier French Legion Hon., 2000, Officer of the French Order of Arts and Letters, 2003. Mem.: Historic Preservation Commn. Marbletown NY (chmn.), Thomas Moran Trust, Assn. Art Mus. Curators (founding pres.). Office: Museum Fine Arts Houston 1001 Bissonnet Houston TX 77005*

TIPLER, FRANK JENNINGS, III, physicist; b. Andalusia, Ala., Feb. 1, 1947; s. Frank Jennings Jr. and Anne (Kearley) T.; m. Jolanta Rokicka; children: Allison Anne, Caroline Nicole. S.B., MIT, 1969; PhD, U. Md., 1976. Rsch. mathematician U. Calif., Berkeley, 1976-79; sr. rsch. fellow Oxford (Eng.) U., 1979; rsch. assoc. U. Tex., Austin, 1979-81; assoc. prof. physics and math. Tulane U., New Orleans, 1981-87, prof., 1987—. Vis. sr. scientist Max-Planck Inst. Astrophysics, Munich, 1987; vis. fellow U. Sussex, Brighton, Eng., 1987; vis. prof. Inst. Astrophysics, Liege, Belgium, 1988, U. Bern, Switzerland, 1988, U. Vienna, Austria, 1992. Author: l'Homme et le Cosmos, 1984, The Anthropic Cosmological Principle, 1986, The Physics of Immortality, 1994, The Physics of Christianity, 2007; editor: Essays in General Relativity, 1980; contbr. articles to profl. jour. Rsch. grantee NSF, 1984, 86. Libertarian. Office: Tulane Univ Physics Dept St Charles ave New Orleans LA 70118 Office Phone: 504-862-3449. Business E-Mail: tipler@tulane.edu.

TIPPINS, LINDSEY, state legislator; b. June 26, 1949; m. Ann Scott; children: Rebekah, Nathan. BBA, Ga. State U., 1971; JD, Woodrow Wilson Coll. of Law, 1978. Founder, owner Tippins Contracting Co., 1969—; mem. Dist. 37 Ga. State Senate. Mem.: Ga. Utility Contractor Assn. (bd. dirs., pres.). Republican. Office: 139 Midway Rd Marietta GA 30064 also: Ga State Senate 302B Coverdell Legis Office Bldg Atlanta GA 30334 Office Phone: 770-424-2700, 404-657-0406. Business E-Mail: lindsey.tippins@senate.ga.gov.

TIRYAKIAN, EDWARD ASHOD, sociologist, educator; b. Bronxville, NY, Aug. 6, 1929; s. Ashod Haroutioun and Keghinee (Agathon) T.; m. Josefina Cintron, Sept. 5, 1953; children: Edmund Carlos, Edwyn Ashod. BA summa cum laude, Princeton U., 1952; MA, Harvard U., 1954, PhD, 1956; PhD (hon.), U. Rene Descartes, Paris, 1987. Instr. Princeton U., 1956—57, asst. prof., 1957—62; lectr. Harvard U., 1962—65; assoc. prof. Duke U., Durham, NC, 1965—67, prof., 1967—2004, chmn. dept. sociology and anthropology, 1969—72, dir. internat. studies, 1988—91, prof. emeritus, 2004—. Vis. lectr. U. Philippines, 1954-55, Bryn Mawr Coll., 1957-59; vis. scientist program Am. Sociol. Assn., 1967-70; vis. prof. Laval U., Quebec City, Que., Can., 1978, Inst. Polit. Studies, Paris, 1992, Free U., Berlin, 1996; summer seminar dir. NEH, 1978, 80, 93, 89, 91, 96; lectr. Kyoto Am. Studies Summer Seminar, 1985, project leader Fulbright New Cent. Scholars Program, 2002-03. Author: Sociologism and Existentialism, 1962, For Durkheim: Essays in Historical and Cultural Sociology, 2009; Editor: Sociological Theory, Values and Sociocultural Change: Essays in Honor of P.A. Sorokin, 1963, new edit., 2013, The Phenomenon of Sociology, 1971, On the Margin of the Visible: Sociology, the Esoteric, and the Occult, 1974, The Global Crisis: Sociological Analyses and Responses, 1984; co-editor: Theoretical Sociology: Perspectives and Developments, 1970; New Nationalisms of the Developed West, 1985; Rethinking Civilizational Analysis, 2004. Fellow Ctr. for Advanced Study in Behavioral Scis., 1997-98; recipient Fulbright rsch. award, 1955; Ford faculty rsch. fellow, 1971-72, fellow Ctr. for Advanced Study in Behavioral Scis., 1997-98, Disting. New Century scholar Fulbright Scholar Program, 2002-03. Mem. Am. Sociol. Assn., African Studies Assn., Am. Soc. for Study Religion (co uncil 1975-78, pres. 1981-84), Assn. Internationale des Sociologues de Langue Française (v.p. 1985-88, pres. 1988-92), Soc. for Phenomenology and Existential Philosophy, Phi Beta Kappa. Clubs: Princeton. Home: 16 Pascal Way Durham NC 27705-4924 Office Phone: 919-660-5632. Business E-Mail: durkhm@soc.duke.edu.

TISCH, JAMES SOLOMON, diversified holding company executive, energy executive; b. Atlantic City, Jan. 2, 1953; s. Laurence A. and Wilma (Stein) T.; m. Merryl Hiat; children: Jessica, Benjamin, Samuel. BA, Cornell U., Ithaca, NY, 1975; MBA, U. Pa. Wharton Grad. Sch., 1976. Joined Loews Corp., 1977, exec. v.p., 1987-94, COO, 1994—99, pres., CEO, 1999—; chmn. Diamond Offshore Drilling, Inc., 1995—, CEO, 1998—2008; chmn. Educational Broadcasting Corp., 2006—. Bd. dirs. Loews Corp., 1986-, CNA Financial Corp., 1999-, Fed. Reserve Bank NY, 2010-, General Electric Co. 2010-. Bd. dirs. Fedn. Employment & Guidance Svc., NYC, 1985; trustee Edn. Broadcasting Corp. 2003-, chmn. 2006; trustee NY Pub. Libr., Mt. Sinai Med. Ctr./NYU Med. Ctr., NYC, 1988—; mem. bd. overseers, U. Pa. Wharton Sch. Bus.; mem. exec. com. Partnership for NYC. Mem.: Coun. Fgn. Rels., Phi Beta Kappa. Office: Diamond Offshore Drilling Inc 15415 Katy Freeway Houston TX 77094 Office Phone: 281-492-5300. Office Fax: 281-492-5378. Business E-Mail: jtisch@dodi.com.

TISHER, CHARLES CRAIG, nephrologist, educator, former dean; MD, Wash. U., St. Louis, 1961. Resident Barnes Hosp., St. Louis, U. Wash. affiliated Hosps., Seattle; fellow in nephrology U. Wash., Seattle; positions at Walter Reed Hosp. and Walter Reed Army Inst. Rsch., Washington; joined faculty Duke U. Sch. Medicine, 1969; prof. medicine and pathology U. Fla. Coll. Medicine, Gainesville, Fla., 1980—, chief divsn. nephrology, hypertension and transplantation, 1980—87, named Ctrl. Fla. Kidney Ctr. Eminent Scholar Chair in Nephrology, 1989, prof. anatomy and cell biology, sr. assoc. dean, 1998—2002, Folke H. Peterson Disting. Professorship, 1999—, dean, 2002—07, assoc. v.p. program devel., 2007—; dir. Ctr. Clin. Trials Rsch U. Fla. Founding asst. editor Kidney Internat. jour.; chmn. med. adv. board Bioavailability Systems Inc., Cocoa Beach, Fla. Recipient Faculty Rsch. Prize in Clin. Scis., U. Fla., 1985. Mem.: Internat. Soc. Nephrology, Am. Soc. Nephrology (pres. 1990—91, jour. editor 1996—2001, John P. Peters Award 2001). Office: U Fla Divsn Nephrology Box J224 JHMHC Gainesville FL 32610 also: U Fla PO Box 100215 Gainesville FL 32610-0215 Office Phone: 352-273-7508. Business E-Mail: tisher@ufl.edu.

TISHLER, JOHN C., lawyer; BA cum laude, Vanderbilt U., Nashville, 1980; JD with honors, U. Tenn., 1988. Bar: Tenn., Calif., US Dist. Ct. (we., mid., ea. dists.) Tenn., US Dist. Ct. (ctrl. dist.) Calif., US Ct. Appeals (6th cir.), US Supreme Ct. Assoc. sports info. dir. U. Miss., 1980—82; law clk. to Hon. Julia Smith Gibbons US Dist. Ct. (We. Dist.) Tenn., 1988—89; sports news coord. Tex. A&M U., 1980—84; ptnr. Waller, Lansden, Dortch & Davis, Nashville, bd. dirs., 2004—, chmn. of the firm, 2007—. Mem. adv. com. US Ct. Appeals (6th Cir.). Bd. dirs., legal counsel Goodwill Industries Mid. Tenn., Inc.; bd. dirs. St. Mary Villa. Named Best of Bar, Nashville Bus. Jour.; named one of The Best Lawyers in America. Mem.: ABA, Tenn. Bar Assn., Nashville Bar Assn., American Bankruptcy Law Inst., Turnaround Mgmt. Assn. (pres. Tenn. chpt. 2003—). Office: Waller Lansden Dortch & Davis LLP Nashville City Ctr 551 Union St Ste 2700 Nashville TN 37219 Office Phone: 615-850-8756. Business E-Mail: john.tishler@wallerlaw.com.

TISSUE, MIKE, medical educator, respiratory therapist; b. Garfield, Wash., Aug. 24, 1941; s. Altha Lester and Fern Adeline (Willard) T.; m. Marjorie Lena Atkinson, Feb. 24, 1961 (div. June 1991); children: Sue Tipton, Pam Kromholtz, Paul, Donna Leach; m. Mary Emma Napier, Aug. 24, 1998. AAS (4 degrees) with honors, Spokane CC, Wash., 1985; BS in Respiratory Therapy cum laude, Loma Linda U., Calif., 1987; MS in Respiratory Care, Ga. State U., 1999. Registered cardiovasc. invasive specialist; registered cardiac sonographer; registered respiratory therapist-neonatal pediat. specialist; registered pulmonary function technologist, respiratory care practitioner; diplomate sr. disability analyst. Respiratory intern, NICU therapist Loma Linda (Calif.) U. Med. Ctr., 1985-87; educator, therapist Riyadh (Saudi Arabia) Armed Forces Hosp., 1987-91; head dept. respiratory care Security Forces Hosp., Riyadh, 1991-93; asst. prof., dir. clin. edn. respiratory therapy program Morehead (Ky.) State U., 1993-94; program dir. assoc. degree respiratory therapy Chattahoochee Tech. Coll., Marietta, Ga., 1994—98; clin. instr. Ga. State U., Atlanta, 1999-2001; dir. respiratory therapy program Nat. Inst. Tech., Atlanta, 2001—08. Pres., founder Riyadh Cardiorespiratory Soc., 1988-93; rschr. Loma Linda U., 1987, Riyadh Armed Forces Hosp., 1988; instr. and affil.various heart assns. at various times cons. ARC, Tacoma, 1984, instr. standard and advanced first aid, and CPR, Inland Empire chpt., Spokane, 1975-94; instr. first aid San Bernardino/Redlands Svc. Ctr., Loma Linda, 1985-87, Am. Cmty. Svcs. U.S. Embassy, Riyadh, 1987-93, U.S. Mil. Operation Desert Storm, Riyadh, 1991-93; instr. Freedom From Smoking Clinic Program Am. Lung Assn., Calif., 1985-87, Saudi Arabia, 1987-93, Smyrna, Ga., 1994-96; mem. several coms. Chattahoochee Tech. Coll., 1994-98. Contbr. articles to profl. jours. Bd. dirs. Am. Heart Assn., Spokane, 1976-83, chair fin. com., 1981-83; chair programming and spkrs. bur. Am. Lung Assn., Smyrna, Ga., 1994-98, chmn. bd. dirs., 1995-96; sec. Cobb County Cmty. Coun., Marietta, 1995-96, spkr., 1995, v.p., 1996, pres. 1997; vol. Ga. Internat. Cultural Exch., 1995; registry exam. sr. proctor Cardiovasc. Credentialing Internat./Nat. Bd. Cardiovasc. Technologists, Riyadh, 1987-90; commr. Boy Scouts Am., Spokane, 1973-82. Named Citizen of Day, KGA Radio, Spokane, 1983. Mem. AAUP (legis. com. Atlanta 1995-96), Am. Assn. Respiratory Care (therapist-driven protocol rev. com. 1994, ad hoc com. on patient-driven protocol rev. com. 1996, ad hoc com. for sects. rev. 1995-96, job analysis, neonatal pedit. specialist 2002), Applied Measurement Profls., Alliance of Cardiovasc. Profls., Ga. Soc. Respiratory Care (chmn. cardiopulmonary com. 1994-95, edn. com., smoking and health com.), Phi Delta Kappa (pub. rels. com. 1995-96). Avocations: photography, travel. Home: 1881 Arnold Dr SW Austell GA 30106-2907 Personal E-mail: miketissue@hotmail.com.

TITUS, BRUCE EARL, lawyer; b. NYC, June 5, 1942; BA, Coll. William and Mary, 1964, JD, 1971. Bar: Va. 1971, D.C. 1972, Md. 1984. Asst. dir. torts br., civil divsn. U.S. Dept. Justice, 1971-82; mem. Jones, Waldo, Holbrook and McDonough, Washington; ptnr. Venable, Baetjer and Howard, LLP, McLean, Va., 1986—97; prin. Rees, Broome PC, Vienna, Va., 1997—. Exec. editor William & Mary Law Review, 1970-71. Mem. ABA, Va. State Bar, D.C. Bar, Fairfax Bar Assn. (pres. 1999-2000), Md. State Bar, Phi Delta Phi, Omicron Delta Kappa. Office: Rees Broome PC 1900 Gallows Rd Ste 700 Tysons Corner VA 22182 Office Phone: 703-790-1911.

TITZMAN, DONNA M., energy executive; BBA in Acctg., U. Tex. CPA. Acct. natural gas liquids Valero Energy Corp., San Antonio, 1986—89, various positions with fin. dept., 1989, v.p., treas., 1999—. Office: Valero Energy Corpn PO Box 696000 San Antonio TX 78269-6000

TJOFLAT, GERALD BARD, federal judge; b. Pitts., Dec. 6, 1929; s. Gerald Benjamin and Sarita (Romero-Hermoso) Tjoflat; m. Sarah Marie Pfohl, July 27, 1957 (dec.); children: Gerald Bard, Marie Elizabeth; m. Marcia Penman Parker, Feb. 21, 1998. Student, U. Va., 1947—50, U. Cin., 1950—52; LLB, Duke U., 1957; DCL (hon.), Jacksonville U., 1978; LLD (hon.), William Mitchell Coll., 1993. Bar: Fla. 1957. Pvt. practice, Jacksonville, Fla., 1957—68; judge 4th Jud. Cir. Ct., Fla., 1968—70, US Dist. Ct. Mid. Dist., Jacksonville, 1970—75, US Ct. Appeals (5th cir.), Jacksonville, 1975—81, US Ct. Appeals (11th cir.), Jacksonville, 1981—, chief judge, 1989—96. Mem. Adv. Corrections Coun. U.S., 1975—87, Jud. Conf. U.S., 1989—96, mem. com. adminstrn. probation sys., 1972—87, chmn., 1978—87; mem. Fed. Jud. Ct. Com. on Sentencing, Probation and Pretrial Svcs., 1988—90; U.S. del. 6th and 7th UN Congress for Prevention of Crime and Treatment of Offenders. Hon. life mem., bd. visitors Duke U. Law Sch., 2000; pres. North Fla. coun. Boy Scouts Am., 1976—85, 2000—01, chmn., 1985—90; trustee Jacksonville Marine Inst., 1976—90, Episc. H.S., Jacksonville, 1975—90; mem. vestry St. Johns Cathedral, Jacksonville, 1969—71, 1973—75, 1977—79, 1981—83, 1985—87, 1993, 1995—96, sr. warden, 1975, 1983, 1987, 1991, 1992. With US Army, 1953—55. Recipient Merit award, Duke U., 1990, Fordham-Stein prize, 1996. Mem.: ABA, Am. Judicature Soc., Am. Law Inst., Fla. Bar Assn. Episcopalian. Office: US Courthouse 300 N Hogan St Ste 14-200 Jacksonville FL 32202-4257 Office Phone: 904-301-6570.

TOAL, GERARD, political science professor; b. Clones, Monaghan, Ireland, Sept. 11, 1962; s. Toal; m. Sabine Durier, Sept. 13, 2006; 1 child, Sirin. PhD, Syracuse U., NY, 1989. Dir., govt. internat. affairs Sch. Pub. and Internat. Affairs, Alexandria, Va., 2000—. Author: (Book) Critical Geopolitics. Office: Virginia Tech 1021 Prince St Alexandria VA 22314 Business E-Mail: toalg@vt.edu.

TOAL, JEAN HOEFER, state supreme court chief justice; b. Columbia, SC, Aug. 11, 1943; d. Herbert W. and Lilla (Farrell) Hoefer; m. William Thomas Toal; children: Jean Toal Eisen, Lilla Toal Mandsager. BA in Philosophy, Agnes Scott Coll., 1965; JD, U. S.C., 1968; LHD (hon.), Coll. Charleston, 1990; LLD (hon.), Columbia Coll., 1992, The Citadel, 1999, Francis Marion U., 1999, U. S.C., 2000, Charleston Sch. Law, 2007, Columbia Coll., 2008. Bar: S.C. Assoc. Haynsworth, Perry, Bryant, Marion & Johnstone, 1968—70; ptnr. Belser, Baker, Barwick, Ravenel, Toal & Bender, Columbia, 1970—88; assoc. justice SC Supreme Ct., Columbia, 1988—2000, chief justice, 2000—. Mem. S.C. Human Affairs Commn., 1972-74; mem. S.C. Ho. of Reps., 1975-88, chmn. house rules com., constitutional laws subcom. house judiciary com.; mem. parish coun. and lector St. Joseph's Cath. Ch.; chair S.C. Juvenile Justice Task Force, 1992-94; chair S.C. Rhodes Scholar Selection Com., 1994; bd. dirs. Nat. Ctr. State Cts., 2005-09, chair, 2007-2008; pres. Conf. Chief Justices, 2007-08. Mng. editor S.C. Law Rev., 1967—68. Bd. visitors Clemson U., 1978; trustee Columbia Mus. Art, 1980-85; bd. trustees Agnes Scott Coll., 1996—2008. Recipient Disting. Svc. award, S.C. Mcpl. Assn., 1980, U. Notre Dame award, 1991, Algernon Sydney Sullivan award, U. S.C., 1991, Agnes Scott Coll. Outstanding Alumna award, 1991, John W. Williams award, Richland County Bar Assn., 1995, Jean Galloway Bissell award, S.C. Women Lawyers Assn., 1995, Margaret Brent Women Lawyers of Achievement award, 2004; named Outstanding Legislator of Yr., Greenville News, 1976, Woman of Yr., U. S.C. Mortar Bd., 1989; named one of Top 25 Doers, Dreamers & Drivers, Govt. Tech. Mag., 2002. Mem. ABA, S.C. Women Lawyers Assn., S.C. Bar Assn., John Belton O'Neall Inn of Ct., Phi Beta Kappa, Mortar Bd., Order of the Coif Office: Supreme Ct SC PO Box 11330 Columbia SC 29211-2456 Business E-Mail: jtoal@sccourts.org.*

TOBEN, BRADLEY J.B., dean, law educator; m. Beth Toben; children: John, Sarah Beth. BA in Polit. Sci. with honors, U. Mo., St. Louis; JD with honors, Baylor U., 1977; LLM, Harvard U., 1981. Bar: Tex., Mo. Tchr. Ind. U. Sch. Law, Indpls.; of counsel Dawson & Sodd (Dallas and Corsicana); with faculty Baylor Law Sch., 1983—, dean, 1991—, Gov. Bill and Vara Faye Daniel prof. law, 1991, M.C. & Mattie Caston chair of law. Gov. apptd. tax commr. Nat. Conf. of Commrs. on Uniform State Laws. Recipient Disting. Alumni Polit. Sci. Award, U. Mo.-St. Louis; named a Outstanding Young Alumnus, Baylor U., Disting. Alumnus, U. Mo.-St. Louis. Fellow: Tex. Bar Found., American Bar. Found.; mem.: American Law Inst., State Bar of Tex. Office: Baylor U 1114 S University Parks Drive One Bear Place #97288 Waco TX 76798 Office Phone: 254-710-1911. Business E-Mail: Brad_Toben@baylor.edu.*

TOBIA, JOHN, state legislator; b. Honolulu, Hawaii, Jan. 6, 1978; 1 child, Taylor. AA Brevard Cmty. Coll., 1996; BA, MA, U. Fla. Mem. Dist. 31 Fla. House of Reps., 2008—, mem. criminal and civil justice appropriations com., fin. and tax coun., health care svcs. policy com., joint legis. auditing com., mem. state univs. and pvt. colls. policy com. Republican. Office: House Office Bldg 402 S Monroe St Rm 209 Tallahassee FL 32399-1300 also: 1901 S Harbor City Blvd Ste 508 Melbourne FL 32901-4770 Office Phone: 850-488-2528, 321-984-4848. Business E-Mail: john.tobia@myfloridahouse.gov.

TODD, CURRY, state legislator; b. Juno, Tenn., Dec. 31, 1947; married; 1 child. Legis. liaison-lobbyist Memphis Police Dept., Memphis Police Assn., 1976—88, Tenn. Fraternal Order Police, 1982—87; state rep. Dist. 95 Tenn., 1999—; mem. Legislature Study Coms. Corrections & Criminal Justice Tenn. Gen. Assembly, 1981—84, Memphis & Shelby County Job Conf., 1982—83, Shelby County Rep. Party Steering Com.; adv. bd. Tenn. Correction Vol. Mem.: Memphis Zoological Soc., M-Club U. Memphis, Collierville Rotary Club, Fisherville Civic Club, Collierville Rep. Club. Republican. Baptist. Office: 891 Lancelot Cir Collierville TN 38017 also: 209 War Memorial Bldg Nashville TN 37243-0195 Office Phone: 615-741-1866, 901-853-1348. Office Fax: 615-532-8221. Business E-Mail: rep.curry.todd@capitol.tn.gov.

TODD, JAMES DALE, federal judge; b. Scotts Hill, Tenn., May 20, 1943; s. James P. and Jeanette Grace (Duck) T.; m. Jeanie M. Todd, June 26, 1965; 2 children. BS, Lambuth Coll., 1965; M Combined Scis., U. Miss., 1968; JD, Memphis State U., 1972. Bar: Tenn. 1972, US Dist. Ct. (we. dist.) Tenn. 1972, US Ct. Appeals (6th cir.) 1973, US Supreme Ct. 1975. Tchr. sci., chmn. sci. dept. Lyman High Sch., Longwood, Fla., 1965-68, Memphis U. Sch., 1968-72; ptnr. Waldrop, Farmer, Todd & Breen, P.A., 1972-83; cir. judge div. II 26th Jud. Dist., Jackson, Tenn., 1983-85; judge US Dist. Ct. (we. dist.) Tenn., Jackson, 1985—, chief judge, 2001—07, sr. judge, 2008—. Recipient Law & Liberty award, Jackson Madison County Bar Assn., 1988, Lifetime Achievement award Lambuth U., 2001; named Alumnus of Yr. Lambuth Coll. Alumni Assn., 1985 Fellow Tenn. Bar Found.; mem. Fed. Judges Assn. (bd. dirs. 1998-2002), Fed. Bar Assn., Jackson Madison County Bar Assn. (pres. 1978-79), Dist. Judges Assn. of 6th Cir. (pres. 2000-2001). Methodist. Office: US Dist Ct Rm 448 111 S Highland Ave Jackson TN 38301-6107

TODD, LEE TROVER, JR., retired academic administrator, electrical engineer; b. Earlington, Ky., May 6, 1946; s. Lee T. Todd; m. Patricia Brantley; children: Troy, Kathryn. BSEE, U. Ky., 1968; MS, MIT, 1970, PhD in Elec. Engring., 1973. IBM postdoctoral fellow MIT, 1973-74; asst. prof. engring. U. Ky., Lexington, 1974-78, assoc. prof., 1978-87, pres., 2001—11; chmn., chief exec. officer DataBeam Corp., Lexington, 1983—2000; v.p. Hughes Display Products, Lexington, 1993—93; sr. v.p. pres. Lotus Devel. Corp., 2000—01. Chmn. Ky. Sci. & Tech. Coun., Lexington, 1987—; mem. Ky. Epscor Com., 1985—, Ky. Acad. Sci., 1988; chair Southeastern Conf. Com. on Academic Initiatives; mem. Cou. of Edn. Commn. Contbr. articles to profl. jours. Chmn., deacon Calvary Bapt. Ch., Lexington, 1989; bd. dirs. Ky. Econ. Devel. Corp., Frankfort, Georgetown Coll., Ky. Named Entrepreneur of Yr., INC mag., 1989; recipient Outstanding Alumnus award U. Ky. Coll. Engring., 1989, Small Bus. of Yr. award Lexington C. of C., U.S. Gt. Tchr. award, 1983; Hertz Found. fellow, 1968-73. Mem. NSF, Ky. Soc. Profl. Engrs. (Award of Achievement 1990), U. Ky. Alumni Assn., Leadership Ky., Louisville Adv. Tech. Coun. Baptist. Achievements include patents in field. Office Phone: 859-257-1701. Office Fax: 859-257-1760. E-mail: ltodd@email.uky.edu.

TODD, PATRICIA, state legislator; life ptnr. Jennifer Clarke. MPA, U. Ala., Birmingham. Mem. Dist. 54 Ala. House of Reps., Montgomery, 2006—. Sec. Crestwood Neighborhood Assn.; del. Dem. Nat. Convention; former sec. Episc. Ch. Women at Grace Episc. Woodlawn; bd. mem. Equality Ala., Episc. Pl., Greater Birmingham Ministries, Sidewalk Film Festival. Named one of Top 40 Under 40, Birmingham Bus. Jour., 1992. Mem.: NAACP, League Women Voters. Democrat. Office: Ala House of Reps Ala State House 11 S Union St Rm 541-C Montgomery AL 36130 Office Phone: 205-324-9822, 334-242-7718. Business E-Mail: reptodd@gmail.com.

TODHUNTER, JOHN ANTHONY, toxicologist, consultant; b. Cali, Valle, Colombia, Oct. 9, 1949; s. John Arthur and Teresa Maria (Torres) T.; divorced, 1986; children: Jennifer, Julia; m. Holli Wilson, Apr. 19, 1986; 1 child, Jacqueline Rose. BSc, UCLA, 1971; MSc, Calif. State U., 1973; PhD, U. Calif., Santa Barbara, 1976. Diplomate Am. Bd. Toxicology, Am. Bd. Forensic Examiners. Instr. Calif. State U., LA, 1972-73; rsch. asst. U. Calif., Santa Barbara, 1973-76; fellow Roche Inst. Molecular Biology, Nutley, NJ, 1976-78; asst. prof. Cath. U. Am., Washington, 1978-81, chmn. Biochemistry Program, 1980-81; asst. adminstr. U.S. EPA, Washington, 1981-83; cons. Sci. Regulatory Svcs. Internat., Washington, 1983-91; pres. SRS Internat. Corp., 1991—2010, SRS Internat. Health Care Group, 1995—2010; CEO Assura Pharms., 2006—11; chief sci. officer, sr. v.p. R & D SinoFresh HealthCare, Inc., 2010—. Expert advisor European regional office WHO, Stockholm, 1984; mem. Hazardous Waste Siting Bd., Annapolis, Md., 1980-81. Contbr. articles to profl. jours. Bd. dirs. Reagan Alumni Assn., Washington, 1985—; vol. Am. Cancer Soc., Washington, 1988-93; mem. Presdl. Transition Team, Washington, 1980. U. Calif. Bd. Regents fellow, 1975, B.R. Baker Meml. fellow dept. chemistry U. Calif., Santa Barbara, 1976. Fellow Am. Inst. Chemists (dir. at large 1989-92, vice chmn. bd. 1992); mem. Soc. of Toxicology, Am. Chem. Soc., Soc. for Risk Analysis, N.Y. Acad. Sci. Business E-Mail: todhunter@svsinternational.com.

TODOROFF, CHRISTOPHER M., lawyer, insurance company executive; BA, Rutgers Univ., 1984; JD, Cornell Univ., 1987. Bar: 1988. Law practice in NY & Fla., 1988—95; legal positions through v.p. & sr. corp. counsel Aetna, Inc., 1995—2008; sr. v.p., gen. counsel Humana, Inc., Louisville, 2008—. Editor: Cornell Law Rev. Office: Humana 500 W Main St Louisville KY 40202*

TOFTELAND, CURT L., producer, director; b. Martin, ND, Apr. 30, 1952; s. Donald Morris and Jona Georgine (Goodman) T.; m. Marcia Tarbis, May 30, 1981; 1 child, Joshua Tarbis. BFA in Music, U. N.D., 1974; MFA, U. Minn., 1978. Actor Asolo Touring Theater, Sarasota, Fla., 1978-79; assoc. artistic dir. Stage One, Louisville, 1979-85; pres. Joshua Prodns., Louisville, 1985-89; producing dir. Ky. Shakespeare Festival, Louisville, 1989—. Adj. faculty U. Louisville, 1987—, Ind. U. S.E., 1993—, Bellarmine Coll., 1994—, Jefferson C.C., 1998—; cons. Ky. Arts Coun., Frankfort, 1985—, Ky. Humanities Coun., Lexington, 1988, Very Spl. Arts Ky., Frankfort, 1987—, Jefferson C.C., 1998—. Playwright six plays. Al Smith fellow, 1988. Mem. Ky. Allinace for Arts in Edn., Ky. Citizens for the Arts, Actors' Equity Assn. Office: Ky Shakespeare Festival 323 W Broadway Ste 400 Louisville KY 40202-2180 Office Phone: 502-637-4933.

TOLCHIN, SUSAN JANE, political science professor, writer; b. NYC, Jan. 14, 1941; d. Jacob Nathan and Dorothy Ann (Markowitz) Goldsmith; m. Martin Tolchin, Dec. 23, 1965; 1 child, Karen Rebecca. BA, Bryn Mawr Coll., 1961; MA, U. Chgo., 1962; PhD, NYU, 1968. Lectr. in polit. sci. CCNY, NYC, 1963-65, Bklyn. Coll., 1965-71; adj. asst. prof. polit. sci. Seton Hall U., South Orange, NJ, 1971-73; assoc. prof. polit. sci., dir. Inst. for Women and Politics, Mt. Vernon Coll., Washington, 1975-78; prof. pub. adminstrn. George Washington U., Washington, 1978-98; prof. sch. pub. policy George Mason U., Fairfax, Va., 1998—. Disting. lectr. Indsl. Coll. Armed Forces, 1994. Author: The Angry American: How Voter Rage is Changing the Nation, 1996, 2d edit., 1998; author: (with Martin Tolchin) To the Victor: Political Patronage from the Clubhouse to the White House, 1971, Clout--Womanpower and Politics, 1974, Dismantling America--The Rush to Deregulate, 1983, Buying Into America--How Foreign Money Is Changing the Face of Our Nation, 1988, Selling Our Security--The Erosion of America's Assets, 1992, Glass Houses--Congressional Ethics and the Politics of Venom, 2001, A World Ignited: How Apostles of Ethnic, Religions and Racial Hatred Torch the Globe, 2006, Pinstripe Patronage: Political Favoritism from the Clubhouse to the White House and Beyond, 2010. Bd. dirs. Cystic Fibrosis Found., 1982-98; county committeewoman Dem. Party, Montclair, N.J., 1969-73. Recipient Founder's Day award NYU, 1968, Trachtenberg award for rsch. George Washington U., 1998; named Tchr. of Yr., Mt. Vernon Coll., 1978; Dilthey fellow George Washington U., 1983, Aspen Inst. fellow, 1979. Fellow Nat. Acad. Pub. Adminstrn.; mem. Am. Polit. Sci. Assn. (pres. Women's Caucus for Polit. Sci. 1977-78), Am. Soc. Pub. Adminstrn. (chair sect. natural resources and environ. adminstrn. 1982-83, Marshall Dimock award 1997). Democrat. Office: Sch Pub Policy George Mason U 3401 Fairfax Dr Arlington VA 22201

TOLLEFSON, TERRENCE ALFRED, retired educator and consultant; b. Pontiac, Mich., May 1, 1938; s. Alfred and Iva Denice Tollefson; m. Bonnie Lou Bradley, 1961 (dec. 1990); children: Katherine Marie, Michelle Suzanne Miller, Bradley Alfred. BA in Edn. and Soc. Studies, U. Mich., Ann Arbor, 1961; PhD, U. Mich., 1975; MBA in Mktg., Mich. State U., East Lansing, 1963. Assoc. prof. dept. adult and CC edn. NC State U., Raleigh, 1986—93; prof., interim chair dept. ednl. leadership and policy analysis East Tenn. State U., Johnson City, 1993—2007, prof. emeritus, 2007—08, faculty senate pres., 2003—04. Home: 4100 Prescott Dr Johnson City TN 37601

TOLLESON, THORBORN ROSS, JR., state legislator; b. Perry, Ga., Apr. 26, 1956; son of Thornborn Ross Tolleson Sr. & Mary Shannon; married to Sally Funk; children: Trip, Ansley & Kelly (twins). Attended, Univ. Ga. Past v.p. Tolleson Supply Co.; founder, past bd. dir. Crossroads Bank, Perry, Ga.; founding ptnr. Shepley-Tolleson Fin. Group; fin. adv. UBS Paine Webber, Macon, Ga.; mem. Dist. 18 Ga. State Senate, 2003—. Mem. Perry C. of C. (past bd. dir.). Republican. Methodist. Office: PO Box 1356 Perry GA 31069 Office Phone: 478-988-1206. Business E-Mail: ross.tolleson@senate.ga.gov.

TOLLEY, AUBREY GRANVILLE, psychiatrist, health facility administrator; b. Lynchburg, Va., Nov. 15, 1924; married. Student, Duke U., 1942—43, U. Va., 1946—48, MD, 1952. Diplomate Am. Bd. Psychiatry and Neurology. Intern St. Elizabeths Hosp., Washington, 1952-53; asst. resident psychiatry U. Va. Hosp., Charlottesville, 1953-54; resident psychiatry VA Hosp., Roanoke, Va., 1955-56; instr. U. NC Sch. Medicine, 1956—61, asst. prof., 1961—66, clin. asst. prof. psychiatry, 1966—72, clin. assoc. prof., 1972—76, clin. prof., 1976—2010, adj. prof. psychiatry, 2010—; dir. psychotherapy Dorothea Dix Hosp., Raleigh, NC, 1962-67, dir. hosp., 1973-88. Dir. resident tng. John Umstead Hosp., Butner, N.C., 1966-67; dir. profl. tng. and edn. N.C. Dept. Mental Health, Raleigh, 1967-72, asst. dir., 1972-73; prin. investigator USPHS grant, 1957-59; cons. VA Hosp., Fayetteville, N.C., 1957-78; sr. cons., supervising faculty, cmty. psychiatry sect. dept. psychiatry U. N.C. Sch. Medicine, 1971-88; exec. sec. Multiversity Group, 1968-73 Trustee Found. Hope, Raleigh, 1984—. Served with USNR, 1943-46. Recipient The Order of the Long Leaf Pine, State of N.C., 1982. Fellow Am. Psychiat. Assn. (disting. life; assembly rep. N.C. Dist. br. 1969-82, 86-2000, mem. joint commn. on pub. affairs 1984-87, mem. constl. membership com. 1990-96, mem. commn. on subspecialization 1990-94, Warren Williams award 1987), Am. Coll. Psychiatrists (life); mem. AMA, N.C. Med. Soc. (life), Durham-Orange County Med. Soc., N.C. Psychiat. Assn. (pres. 1984-85, Lifetime Disting. Svc. award 1999), N.C. Hosp. Assn. (life), George C. Ham Soc. (Disting. Alumni award 1992). Home and Office: 110 Laurel Hill Rd Chapel Hill NC 27514-4323

TOLLEY, EDWARD DONALD, lawyer; b. San Antonio, Jan. 31, 1950; s. Lyle Oren and Mary Theresa Tolley; m. Beth Dekle Tolley; 1 child, Edward Spencer. BBA, U. Ga., 1971, MBA, 1974, JD, 1975. Bar: Ga. 1975, U.S. Dist. Ct. (5th cir.) 1976, U.S. Supreme Ct. 1978, U.S. Ct. Appeals (11th cir.) 1981. Ptnr. Cook, Noell, Tolley and Bates, Athens, Ga., 1975—. Lectr. various colls., univs., civic and profl. groups. Mem. Family Counseling Assn. of Athens, Inc., mem. Gov.'s Commn. on Criminal Sanctions and Correctional Facilities, 1988-90; past bd. dirs. Am. Cancer Soc.; pres. Clarke County Bd. Edn., 1992-93. Recipient award for cmty. svc. Chief Justice Ga. Supreme Ct., 2000, Lifetime Achievement award, State Bar Ga., 2008. Fellow Ga. Bar Found., Am. Bd. Criminal Lawyers (bd. dirs. 1987, pres. 1996); mem. Fed. Bar Assn. (sec. 1983, treas. 1985, pres. Macon chpt. 1997-98), State Bar Ga. (chmn. law office and econ. com., bd. govs. 1985—, formal adv. opinion bd., Professionalism award 2002), Ga. Trial Lawyers (v.p.), Ga. Assn. Criminal Def. Lawyers (pres. 1985, Indigent Def. award 1983, 88), Athens Bar Assn. (past pres.), Am. Judicature Soc., Order of Barristers (Cmty. Svc. award Chief Justice Ga. Supreme Ct., 2000). Office: Cook Noell et al 304 E Washington St Athens GA 30601-2751 Home Phone: 706-546-9972; Office Phone: 706-549-6111.

TOLLEY, JERRY RUSSELL, academic administrator; b. Goldsboro, NC, Nov. 6, 1942; s. Elva Russell Tolley and Clara (Smith) Tolley-Bunch; m. Joan Morrison, June 8, 1965; children: Jerry R. Jr., Justin Clay. BS, East Carolina U., 1965, MEd, 1966; EdD, U. NC, Greensboro, 1982; exec. mgmt. courses, Duke U. Tchr., coach Fayetteville Sr. HS, NC, 1966; asst. football coach, head track and tennis coach Elon Coll., NC, 1967-77, head football coach, 1977-81, dir. athletic sholarship fund, 1982, dir. corp. and ann. resources, 1983, coordinator Pride II Capital Campaign, 1984, assoc. dir. devel., 1985, officer corp. and major gifts, maj. gifts officer, 1999, dir. ann. giving, 2003; dir Elon Soc., NC, 2008; asst. v.p. tng., nat. dir. tng. & pub. affairs Lab. Corp. of Am., Burlington, NC, 1986—. Author: Intercollegiate History of Athletics and Elon College, 1982, American Football Coaches Guidebook to Championship Football Drills, 1985, 101 Winning Football Drills -From the Legends of the Game, 2003, The Complete Book of Defensive Football Drills, 2005, The Complete Book of Offensive Football Drills, 2005, The Complete Book of Speed and Agility Drils, 2007; co-author: 101 Winning Plays, 1977, Leadership Education: A Source Book, 1989; contbr. articles. Treas. Town of Elon Coll., 1984-87, mayor protem, 1988, mayor, 1990-98, 2006, mayor emeritus, 1998-2006, chmn. recreation commn.; mayor Town of Elon, 2006; convenor City County Govt. Assn., 1987-98, 2006-, Alamance County, NC, 1986—; mem. exec. bd. dir. Cherokee Coun. Boy Scouts Am., 1986, Thomas E. Powell Jr. Biology Found.; pres. Alamance Found.; exec. bd. NC Health & Fitness Found.; bd. visitors Elon Coll.; mem. exec. com. Alamance County Ptnrs. in Edn.; bd. govs. 2 Those Who Care; dir. Alamance Edn. Alliance; bd. dir. Cmty. Found. Greensboro; chmn. Citizens for Schs.; mktg. advisory com. Village of Brookwood; bd. advisors Randolf Bank. Named one of Outstanding Young Men Am., 1980, Internat. Men of Achievement, 1990, Cmty. Leaders Am., 1990, Mayors Hall of Fame, 1995; recipient HHP Centenential Leadership medellian, Dwight D. Eisenhower award Nat. Football Hall of Fame, 1980, 81, Nat. Collegiate Football Championship award Eastman Kodak, Meritorious Svc. award Tom Sawyer-Huck Finn Tennis Classic, 1986, Order of the Long Leaf Pine, 1997, Laurel Wreath award State of NC, 2002, Old North State award, 2007; named Nat. Football Coach of Yr., Nat. Assn. Intercollegiate Athletics, 1980, Elon Coll. Sports Hall of Fame, East Carolina U. Athletic Hall of Fame, 1991, East Carolina U. Ednl. Hall of Fame, 2008, East Carolina U. Centenial Leadership medalian, 2008 Mem.: All-Am. Football Found. (Lifetime Achievement award 2003, Hall of Fame 2009), Coun. Advancement of Edn., Am. Football Coaches Assn. (life), Omicron Delta Kappa, Phi Delta Kappa, Sigma Delta Psi. Avocations: writing, racquet sports, jogging. Home: 1322 Westbrook Ave Elon NC 27244-9358 Office: Elon Univ 2600 Campus Box # 2600 Elon NC 27244-2010 Office Phone: 336-278-7447. Business E-Mail: tolleyj@elon.edu.

TOLLISON, GRADY FRANKLIN (GRAY), state legislator; b. Memphis, Sept. 8, 1964; m. Farish Percy Tollison. Mem. Dist. 9 Miss. State Senate, 1996—. Democrat. Episcopalian. Office: PO Box 1216 Oxford MS 38655-1216 Home Phone: 662-234-8395; Office Phone: 662-234-7070, 601-359-3425. Fax: 662-234-7095; Office Fax: 601-359-2879. Business E-Mail: gtollison@senate.ms.gov.

TOLLISON, NINA STUBBLEFIELD, lawyer; BM, U. Miss.; JD, Miss. Coll. Sch. Law. Bar: Miss. 1982, US Dist. Ct. (northern dist.) Miss., US Dist. Ct. (southern dist.) Miss., US Ct. Appeals (5th cir.). Pvt. practice, Oxford, Miss. Mem.: The Miss. Bar (pres. 2010—11). Office: Tollison Law Firm, PA PO Box 1216 100 Courthouse Square Oxford MS 38655 Office Phone: 662-234-7070. E-mail: ninatollison@bellsouth.net.

TOLSON, JOE PAT, state legislator; m. Janice Tolson. Ret. educator; state rep. Dist. 71 NC, 1997—2002; state rep. Dist. 23 NC, 2003—. Mem. Agrl. com., Edn. com., Edn. Subcom. on Cmty. Colleges, Ethics com., Pensions and Retirement com.; vice chmn. Sci. and Tech. com., Energy and Energy Efficiency com.; chmn. Appropriations com. Democrat. Address: PO Box 1038 Pinetops NC 27864 Office: North Carolina House of Representatives 300 N Salisbury St Rm 608 Raleigh NC 27603-5925 Office Phone: 919-715-3024. E-mail: Joe.Tolson@ncleg.net.

TOMASI, CARLO, computer science professor; Degree in Elec. Engring., with honors, U. Padova, Italy, 1981, D, 1987; MS in Elec. and Computer Engring., U. Mass., Amherst, 1984; PhD, Carnegie Mellon U., Pitts., 1991. Asst. prof. Cornell U., Ithaca, NY, 1991—93, Stanford U., Calif., 1994—2001; assoc. prof. Duke U., Durham, NC, 2001—04, prof., 2004—, chair dept. computer sci., 2010—. Software architect Canesta, Inc., 2001—04. Contbr. articles to profl. jours. Office: Duke U Dept Computer Sci Levine Sci Rsch Bldg D315A Box 90129 Durham NC 27708 Office Phone: 919-660-6505. Office Fax: 919-660-6502. E-mail: tomasi@cs.duke.edu.

TOMBLIN, EARL RAY, Governor of West Virginia, former state legislator; b. Logan County, W.Va., Mar. 15, 1952; s. Earl and Freda M. (Jarrell) Tomblin; m. Joanne Jaeger, Sept. 8, 1979; 1 child, Brent Jaeger. BS, W.Va. U.; MBA, Marshall U., Huntington, W.Va.; D (hon.), Southern W.Va. Cmty. & Tech. Coll. Mem. Dist. 16 W.Va. House of Delegates, Charleston, 1974-80; mem. Dist. 7 W.Va. State Senate, 1980—, pres., 1995—2011; lt. gov. State of W.Va., 2000—11, acting gov., 2010—11, gov., 2012—. Chmn. Southern Legis. Conf., 1999; vice chmn. Nat. Coun. State Governments, 2004—05, chmn., 2005; mem. exec. com. Nat. Conf. State Legislatures; mem. nat. bd. dirs. Senate Presidents' Forum. Mem. Logan County Devel. Authority; past pres. bd. dirs. Appalachia Ednl. Lab., Inc. Mem.: Kappa Alpha. Democrat. Presbyterian. Office: Office of the Governor State Capitol 1900 Kanawha St East Charleston WV 25305 Office Phone: 304-558-2000.*

TOMÉ, CAROL BUCHENROTH, consumer products company executive; b. Jackson, Wyo., Jan. 8, 1957; m. Ramon E. Tomé. BS in Comm., U. Wyo., 1979; MBA in Finance, U. Denver, 1981. Comml. lender United Bank Denver (now Wells Fargo); dir. banking Johns-Manville Corp.; v.p., treas. Riverwood Internat. Corp., 1992—95, The Home Depot, Inc., Atlanta, 1995—2000, sr. v.p. finance, 2000—01, exec. v.p., CFO, 2001—07, exec. v.p. corporate services, CFO, 2007—. Bd. dirs. United Parcel Svc., Inc. (UPS), 2003—, Fed. Res. Bank Atlanta, 2008—, United Home Systems, Inc., 2012—. Bd. dirs. Girls Inc.; trustee Ga. Substance Abuse Adv. Coun., Home Fund; chair Metropolitan Atlanta Chamber of Commerce, 2012—. Recipient Lettie Pate Whitehead Evans award, BDN Network, 2009, Disting. Alumni award, U. Wyo., 2011; named CFO of the Yr. award, CFO Roundtable, 2009; named a Laureate, Metropolitan Atlanta Chamber of Commerce, 2013; named one of The Next 20 Female CEOs, Pink Mag. & Forté Found., 2006, The 100 Most Powerful Women, Forbes mag., 2008, The 50 Most Powerful Women in Bus., Fortune mag., 2001—02, 2012—13, The Best CFO's in Corporate America, The Wall St. Journal, 2012; named to The Jr. Achievement of Ga. Bus. Hall of Fame, 2013. Office: The Home Depot Inc 2455 Paces Ferry Rd Atlanta GA 30339-4029*

TOMKO, EDWIN JOSEPH, lawyer; b. McKeesport, Pa., Oct. 23, 1943; s. John Edwin and Madeline Kusic Tomko; m. Katherine Ramm Tomko, July 11, 1970; children: Alexandra, Stuart. BA, Washington and Jefferson Coll., Washington, Pa., 1965; JD, Vanderbilt U., Nashville, 1968. Bar: Pa. 1968, D.C. 1980, Tex. 1984, U.S. Dist. Ct. (we. dist.) Pa. 1968, U.S. Dist. Ct. (D.C. dist.) 1980, U.S. Dist. Ct. (no., ea. and we. dist.) Tex. 1988, U.S. Ct. Appeals (5th cir.) 2006. Asst. dist. atty. trial divsn. Allegheny County, Pitts., 1969—73; trial atty. Spl. Counsel to the Chief Fraud sect., Criminal divsn. Dept. Justice, Washington, 1973—82; asst. regional adminstr. SEC, Houston, 1982—86, chief Office Criminal Ref., asst. chief litigation counsel Divsn. of Enforcement Washington, 1986—87; dep. chief fraud sect., criminal divsn. Dept. Justice, Washington, 1987—88; ptnr. Doke & Riley, LLP, Dallas, 1988—92, Baker Botts LLP, Dallas, 1993—2001, Akin, Gump, Strauss, Hauer & Feld, Dallas, 2001—03, McManemin & Smith, Dallas, 2003—05, Curran Tomko LLP, Dallas, 2006—13, Dykema Gossett PLLC, Dallas, 2013—. Mem. Bank Fraud Working Group, Washington, 1987—88, Securities Fraud Working Group, Washington, 1987—88. Mem.: ABA, Dallas Bar Assn., Tex. Bar Assn. Republican. Episcopalian. Office: Dykema Gossett PLLC 1717 Main St Ste 4000 Dallas TX 75201 Office Fax: 888-462-6401. Business E-Mail: etomko@dykama.com.

TOMLINSON, ABEL, columnist; b. Kingston, Ark., Oct. 5, 1980; m. Amanda Tomlinson; 1 child, Anna. BS in Horticulture Sci., U. Ark., Fayetteville, 2005. Rsch. asst. greenhouse horticulture U. Ark., 2002—05, rsch. asst. plant pathology, 2005—07; polit. columnist The Traveler, 2007—08. Vol. Global Warming Task Force. Green Party. Office: 915 W Lawson St Fayetteville AR 72703 Office Phone: 479-799-1492. E-mail: atomlin@abelforcongress.com.

TOMLINSON, CAROL ANN, education educator, writer; d. James M. and Louise Askins Windham. BA, U. SC, Columbia, 1965; MEd, U. Va., Charlottesville, 1973, EdD, 1991. Tchr. Lee County Pub. Schs., Sanford, NC, 1967—68; dir. Clarendon Child Devel. Ctr., Arlington, Va., 1968—70; tchr. and adminstr. Fauquier County Pub. Schs., Warrenton, Va., 1970—90; Parish prof. & chair of ednl. leadership, foundations, and policy U. Va., Charlottesville, 1990—. Author: (books) How to Differentiate Instruction in Mixed Ability Classrooms, The Differentiated Classroom: Responding to the Needs of All Learners, Fulfilling the Promise of the Differentiated Classroom: Strategies and Tools for Responsive Teaching. Recipient Outstanding Tchr. award, Warrenton Jr. HS, 1973, Outstanding Prof., Curry Sch. Edn., U. Va., 1994, All U. Tchg. award, U. Va., 2008; named Tchr. of Yr., Va. Dept. Edn., 1974. Mem.: Nat. Assn. Gifted Children (pres.), Nat. State Tchrs. of Yr. Avocations: literature, writing, travel.

TOMLINSON, PHILIP W., diversified financial services company executive; Grad., La. State U. Sch. Banking. Various mgmt. positions General Electric Co., Columbus Bank & Trust Co., Ga., 1974—82; exec. v.p. Total System Services, Inc., 1982—92, pres., 1992—2003, CEO, 2003—, chmn., 2006—. Bd. dirs. Total System Services Inc., 1982—, Synovus Fin. Corp., 2008—. Mem. adv. bd. Ga. Inst. Tech., Columbus State Cunningham Ctr. Leadership Devel.; bd. trustees Columbus State U.; bd. dirs. Am. Cancer Soc., United Way, Muscogee Ednl. Excellence Found. Mem.: Greater Columbus C. of C. (chmn. 2006). Office: Total System Services Inc 1 TSYS Way Columbus GA 31902-2567 Office Phone: 706-649-2310. Office Fax: 706-649-2267.

TOMLINSON, TERESA, mayor, Columbus, Georgia; m. Wade H. Tomlinson. Grad., Sweet Briar Coll., Va., 1987, Emory U. Sch. Law, Ga., 1991. Atty. Pope, McGlamry, Kilpatrick and Morrison, LLC, 1990—2006; exec. dir. Midtown, Inc.; owner Tomlinson Properties LLC, The Butler's Pantry, Inc.; mayor City of Columbus, Ga., 2011—. Mem. Met. Planning Org. Citizen Adv. Com., Columbus. Bd. dirs. Columbus Regional Med. Ctr. Found.; bd. trustees RiverCenter; ex officio mem. Greater Columbus C. of C. Bd. Office: Office of the Mayor 6th Fl Government Center Tower Columbus GA 31901 Office Phone: 706-653-4712. Office Fax: 706-653-4970.*

TOMLINSON, WILLIAM HOLMES, management educator, retired military officer; b. Thornton, Ark., Apr. 12, 1922; s. Hugh Oscar and Lucy Gray (Holmes) T.; m. Dorothy Payne, June 10, 1947 (dec.); children: Jane Axtell, Lucy Gray, William Payne; m. Florence Mood Smith, May 1, 1969 (div.); m. Suzanne Scollard Gill, Mar. 16, 1977. Student, Centenary Coll., Shreveport, LA, 1938—39; BS, US Mil. Acad., West Point, NY, 1943; grad., Field Arty. Sch., 1951, Air Command Staff Coll., 1958; MBA, U. Ala., 1960; MS in Internat. Affairs, George Wash. U., Washington, DC, 1966; grad., US Army War Coll., 1966, Indsl. Coll. Armed Forces, 1968; PhD in Bus. Adminstrn., Am. U., Washington, DC, 1974; grad. Advanced Mgmt. Program, Harvard Bus. Sch., Cambridge, Mass., 1968-69; BAS, U. North Fla., Jacksonville, 1988. Commd. 2d lt. US Arty, 1943; advanced through grades to Col., Field Arty. US Army, 1966; combat svc. in Leyte and Cebu Philippines 246 Field Arty. Bn. Americal Divsn., 1945; aide de camp to comdg. gen. Robert Eichelberger 8th US Army, Japan, 1945-48; comdr. Btry A, 319th FA Bn and Btry A, 39th FA Bn, 3d Divsn., Ft. Benning, Ga., 1948—50; exec. officer 34 FA Bn, ops. officer 9th Divsn. Arty. Germany and Ft. Carson, Colo., 1954-57; with ODCSPER, 1960—61, Office of Undersec. Army, The Pentagon, Washington, 1961-64; comdr. 2d Bn. 8th Arty. and 7th Divsn. Arty. UN Comd. South Korea, 1964-65; faculty Indsl. Coll. Armed Forces, Ft. McNair, Washington, 1966-72, U. North Fla., Jacksonville, 1972—2002, prof. mgmt., prof. emeritus, 2002—. Vis. prof. U. Glasgow, Scotland, 1987; vis. lectr. Moscow Linguistics U., Plekhanov Econ. Acad., Moscow State U. Ulyanovsk, Ulyanovsk, Russia, 1993; mem. Nat. Def. Exec. Res., Fed. Emergency Mgmt. Agy., 1976—. Author: Assessment of the National Defense Executive Reserve, 1974; co-author: International Business, Theory and Practice, 1991, Business Policy and Strategy, 2000; contbr. articles to profl. jours. Mem. exec. bd. Jacksonville Campus Ministry, 1991—, pres., 2002-04. Decorated Bronze Star, Legion of Merit, Philippine Liberation medal, Japanese Occupation, Asiatic Pacific with Invasion Arrow; recipient Freedom Found. award, 1967-71, Lifetime Sr. Profl. in Human Resources, Outstanding Faculty Tchg. & Svc. Awards Fellow Soc. Antiquaries Scotland; mem. SAR, Sons Confederate Vets., Soc. Human Resource Mgmt., Acad. Mgmt., Indsl. Rels. Rsch. Assn., Acad. Internat. Bus., European Internat. Bus. Assn., Internat. Trade and Fin. Assn., Exec. Svc. Corp. Bd., Co. Mil. Historians, Nat. Eagle Scout Assn., N.E. Fla. Employee Svcs. Mgmt. Assn. (charter pres. 1987-89), Stewart Soc. Edinburgh (regional commr. FL, GA), West Point Soc. North Fla. (pres. 1976-77), Mil. Order Stars and Bars (comdr. 1980-90), Army Navy Club, Fla. Yacht Club, Masons, Shriners, Rotary, Beta Gamma Sigma (pres. 1988-89), Kappa Alpha. Presbyterian (elder, trustee). Office: 1890 Shadowlawn St Jacksonville FL 32205-9430 Office Phone: 904-388-1148. Personal E-mail: 1tommytomlinson@comcast.net.

TOMNITZ, DONALD J., construction executive; V.p. RepublicBank Dallas, N.A., Crow Devel. Co.; v.p. various divsns. D.R. Horton, Inc., Fort Worth, Tex., 1983—94, v.p. western region, 1994, pres. homebuilding divsn., 1996—98, exec. v.p., 1998, vice chmn., CEO, 1998—2000, vice chmn., pres., CEO, 2000—. Capt. US Army. Office: DR Horton Inc DR Horton Tower 301 Commerce St Ste 500 Fort Worth TX 76102

TOMPKINS, ALAN W., lawyer; b. Ky., 1961; m. Julie R. Tompkins. B in Economics, U. Southern Ind., 1983; MBA, Southern Meth. U., 1983; M in Acctg., U. Tex., Dallas, 1990; JD, Southern Meth. U., 1993. CPA 1988. Atty. Malouf Lynch Jackson Kessler & Collins, Weil, Gotshal & Manges, Secore & Waller; gen. counsel Attenza, Inc., Nukote Internat.; asst., bankruptcy reorganization efforts RepublicBank Corp., 1988; assoc. gen. counsel Richmont Corp., 1997—2001; atty. Hance, Scarborough, Wright, Ginsberg & Brusilow, 2002—03; v.p., gen. counsel Unity Hunt, Inc., 2003—, Hunt Capital Group (subs. of Unity Hunt, Inc.), 2003—, Hunt Sports Group (subs. of Unity Hunt, Inc.), 2003—. Adj. prof. bus. law Edwin L. Cox Sch. Bus. Southern Meth. U., 1991—97, lectr. acctg., 1991—97. Bd. dirs. Pegasus Theatre, 1995—2005, USA Film Festival, 1999—2006, For The Love of the Lake Found., 1999—2003, AFI-Dallas Internat. Film Festival, 2006—; mem City of Dallas Judicial Nominating Commn., 1997—2005. Office: Unity Hunt Inc 1601 Elm St Ste 4000 Dallas TX 75201-7202 Office Phone: 214-720-1600. Business E-Mail: atompkins@unityhunt.com.

TOMPKINS, ANNE MAGEE, federal prosecutor; b. Waynesboro, Va., 1962; BA in Polit. Sci., U. NC, Charlotte, 1984; MPA, U. NC, Chapel Hill, 1988, JD, 1992. Bar: NC 1992, US Ct. Appeals (4th cir.) 2001, US Dist. Ct. (middle dist.) NC 2006, US Dist. Ct. (eastern dist.) NC 2006. Adminstr. Dept. Parks and Recreation, Charlotte, NC, 1986—87; budget analyst Office of Budget and Evaluation, 1987—89, rschr., 1990; summer law clk. Horack, Talley, Pharr & Lowndes, Charlotte, 1991; asst. dist. atty. Mecklenburg County Dist. Atty.'s Office, Charlotte, 1992—97, 1997—2000; atty. Fialko & Tompkins, PLLC, Charlotte, 1997; asst. US atty. (western dist.) NC US Dept. Justice, Charlotte, 2000—05, US atty., 2010—; ptnr. Litig. and Trial Practice Group Alston & Bird, LLP, Charlotte, 2005—10. Adj. prof. criminal procedure Charlotte Sch. Law, 2007, adj. prof. white collar crime, 2008; bd. advisors NC Conf. for Women, 2008—10. Contbr. articles to law jours. Mem.: ABA, Nat. Assn. Criminal Def. Lawyers, Nat. Assn. Women Lawyers, NC Bar Found., Mecklenburg County Bar Assn., NC Bar Assn., Mecklenburg County Bar Found. Office: US Attorneys Office 227 W Trade St, Ste 1650 Charlotte NC 28202 Office Phone: 704-344-6222.*

TOMS, DAVID, professional golfer; b. Monroe, La., Jan. 4, 1967; m. Sonya Toms; 2 children. Student, La. State U., Baton Rouge. Profl. golfer, 1989—; mem. PGA Tour, 1992—. Mem. US team World Cup, 2002, Ryder Cup, 2002, 2004, 2006, Presidents Cup, 2003, 2005, 2007, 2011. Founder David Toms Found., 2003. Co-recipient Charlie Bartlett Award, Golf Writers Assn. America, 2006. Achievements include winning PGA Tour events: Quad City Classic, 1997, Sprint Internat., 1999, Buick Challenge, 1999, Michelob Championship, 2000, 01, Compaq Classic of New Orleans, 2001, PGA Championship, 2001; Wachovia Championship, 2003 FedEx Classic, 2003, 04, World Golf Championships-Accenture Match Play Championship, 2005, Sony Open in Hawaii, 2006, Crowne Plaza Invitationa, 2011. Office: c/o PGA Tour 100 Avenue of the Champions Palm Beach Gardens FL 33410 also: David Toms Found 1545 E 70th St Ste 201 Shreveport LA 71105

TOMS, PAUL B., JR., consumer products company executive; Joined Hooker Furniture Corp., 1983, v.p., sales, 1987—93, sr. v.p., sales & mktg., 1993—94, exec. v.p., mktg., 1994—99, pres., COO, 1999—2000, chmn., CEO, 2000—, pres., 2006—. Bd. dirs. Hooker Furniture Corp., 1993—, Yahoo! Inc. Bd. dirs. NC Home Furnishings Export Coun., Hooker Ednl. Found., Internat. Woodworking Fair, The Harvest Found., pres., 2010. Recipient Pub. Pvt. Partnership award, Va. Commonwealth U. L. Douglas Wilder Sch. Govt. and Pub. Affairs, 2009. Mem.: Am. Furniture Mfgs. Assn. (bd. dirs.). Office: Hooker Furniture Corp 440 E Commonwealth Blvd Martinsville VA 24112 Office Phone: 276-632-0459. Office Fax: 276-632-0026. Business E-Mail: ptoms@hookerfurniture.com.

TONG, FRANK, science educator; s. You-Tan and Shu-Chin Tong; m. Adriane Seiffert, June 17, 2000; 1 child, Katharine Adriane. PhD, Harvard, Cambridge, Mass., 1999. Asst. prof. Princeton U., NJ, 2000—04, Vanderbilt U., Nashville, 2004—07, assoc. prof., 2007—. Recipient Young Investigator award, Cognitive Neurosci. Soc., 2006, Vision Scis. Soc., 2009; co-recipient Troland Rsch. award, NAS, 2010; Cognitive Neuroscience grant, McDonnell Found. & Pew Charitable Trusts, 1999—2002, grant, NIH, 2002—06, 2007—, NSF, 2007—. Achievements include research in brain imaging studies of human visual perception, neural decoding and visual mind reading, neural correlates of visual consciousness. Office: Vanderbilt Univ 301 Wilson Hall Nashville TN 37240 Business E-Mail: frank.tong@vanderbilt.edu.

TONIETTE, SALLYE JEAN, physician; b. Sulphur, La., 1929; d. Eugene Augusta and Sallye (Tanner) T. Student, John McNeese Jr. Coll., 1946-47; BS, La. State U., 1949, tchrs. cert., 1950, MD, 1955. Intern Crawford W. Long Meml. Hosp., Emory U., Atlanta, 1955-56, resident in ob-gyn., jr., sr., chief residencies, 1956-59; practice in ob-gyn. Sulphur, La., 1959—. Mem. med. staff West Calcasieu Cameron Hosp., 1959—. Dir. Calcasieu Parish Cancer Soc., 1963-67. Named Woman of Distinction, Calcasieu Parish Police Jurors, also Bus. and Profl. Women's Club of West Calcasieu, 1969, named to Hall of Fame Sulphur HS, 2013; Queen of Krewe of Cosmos, 1963, Mardi Gras. Fellow Am. Coll. Ob-Gyn.; mem. La. Med. Assn., Calcasieu Parish Med. Soc., La. Wildlife Fedn., Am. Quarter Horse Assn., Assn. Am. Physicians and Surgeons, Bayou Oaks Country Club (v.p., bd. dirs. 1974—), Krewe de Bon Coer, Krewe of Cosmos, Alpha Chi Omega, Beta Tau Mu, Iota Sigma Pi, Phi Theta Kappa, Beta Sigma Phi. Republican. Methodist. Home: 4917 La Paix Dr Sulphur LA 70665 Office: 521 Cypress St Sulphur LA 70663-5049

TONKIN, INA LYNN DYER, physician, cardiovascular radiologist, educator; b. Louisville, Apr. 26, 1944; d. Robert S. and Nancy E. (Camp) Dyer; m. Allen K. Tonkin, June 29, 1968; children: Allison Elizabeth-Ann, Kieth Allen. BA, DePauw U., 1966; MD, U. Louisville, 1970. Diplomate Am. Bd. Radiology, 1974; Am. Bd. Vascular Interventional Radiology, 1994; Am. Bd. Pediatric Radiology, 1996. Pediatric intern U. Fla., Gainesville, 1970-71, resident in radiology, 1971-73, fellow in cardiovasc. radiology, 1974-75; asst. prof. U. Ariz. Health Sci. Ctr., Tucson, 1975-77, U. Ala.-Birmingham, 1977-79; assoc. prof. radiology U. Tenn., Memphis, 1979-84, prof., 1984—, prof. pediat., 1985—. Exec. com. LeBonheur Children's Med. Ctr., Memphis, 1981-85, chief med. staff, 1987; disting. scientist Armed Forces Inst. Radiologic Pathology, Washington, 1992-93; prof. radiology & pediat. U. Tenn. Hlth. Sci. Ctr., Memphis; lectr. nat. and internat. Editor: (book) Pediatric Cardiovascular Imaging, 1992; contbr. chpts. to books, rsch. articles to profl. jours. Recipient Disting. Alumnus award U. Louisville Med. Sch., 1999. Fellow Soc. Interventional Radiology, Am. Coll. Radiology, Cardiovasc. Coun. Am. Heart Assn.; mem. Soc. Pediat. Radiology (treas.), Jour. Rev. Club Memphis (sec. 1984, pres. 1985), Soc. Interventional Radiology, N.Am. Soc. Cardiac Imaging (pres. 1991). Methodist. Home: 3415 Chambers Chapel Rd Lakeland TN 38002-9573 Office: LeBonheur Children's Med Ctr 50 N Dunlap St Memphis TN 38103-4909 also: Univ Tenn Health Sci Ctr Prof Radiology and Pediat 50 N Dunlap St Memphis TN 38103-4909 Personal E-mail: drstonkin@mindspring.com.

TONNING, KEN, broadcast executive; With news adminstrn. ABC's Network, New York, 1966; account exec., Atlanta WXIA-TV (acquried Gannett Co., Inc.), 1974; v.p., station mgr. & gen. mgr. KUSA-TV, gen. sales mgr. Denver, 1985, pres., 1987; pres., gen mgr. WJXX-TV (subs. Gannett Co., Inc.), Jacksonville, 1989—, WTLV (subs. Gannett Co., Inc.), Jacksonville, 1989—; pres., gen. mgr. WTSP-TV (subs. Gannett Co., Inc.), St. Petersburg, FL, 2008—, Tampa, FL, 2008—. Office: Gannett Co Inc 7950 Jones Br Dr Mc Lean VA 22107-0150 Office Phone: 703-854-6000. Office Fax: 703-854-2053. Business E-Mail: ktonning@10connects.com.

TONNISON, JOHN, information technology executive; b. England; Various exec. mgmt. positions in U.S., Germany, England Log 2000; various exec. mgmt. positions Mancos Computers, Ameriquest, Frontline Distbn., TSN; v.p., worldwide e-business Tech Data Corp., 2001—06, sr. v.p., info. tech., The Americas, 2006—10, exec. v.p., chief info. officer, 2010—. Office: Tech Data Corp 5350 Tech Data Dr Clearwater FL 33760-3122 Office Phone: 727-539-7429. Office Fax: 727-538-7803. Business E-Mail: john.tonnison@techdata.com.

TOOLE, MCLAIN R., state legislator; b. Columbia, SC, Mar. 8, 1946; s. Leon and Juanita W. Toole; m. Linda R. Roland, Oct. 24, 1969; children: Karlayne, Chris. AS, Midlands Tech. Coll., 1966. Mem. Lexington Sch. Bd., Dist. 2, SC, 1996—2000, Lexington County Coun., Dist. 5, 2001—02; mem. Dist. 88 SC House of Reps., 2003—, second vice chair Labor, Commerce and Industry Com., mem. Ops. and Mgmt. Com., Subcommittee on Bus. and Commerce & Subcommittee on Pub. Utility. Mem. dist 2 Lexington Sch. Bd., 1996—2000; mem. Lexington County Coun. Dist. 5, 2001—; deacon Trinity Bapt. Ch., dir. Mem.: SC Small Bus. C. of C., SC Cattle Assn., SC Sportsmen's Coalition, Mothers Against Drunk Driving, SC Sheriff Assn., SC Citizens for Life. Republican. Office: 323D Blatt Bldg Columbia SC 29211 Mailing: 180 Dogwood Cir West Columbia SC 29170 E-mail: TooleM@schouse.org.

TOOTHE, KAREN LEE, elementary and secondary school educator; b. Seattle, Dec. 13, 1957; d. Russell Minor and Donna Jean (Drolet) McGraw; m. Edward Frank Toothe, Aug. 6, 1983; 1 child, Kendall Erin. BA in Psychology with high honors, U. Fla., 1977, MEd in Emotional Handicaps and Learning Disabilities, 1979. Cert. behavior analysis Fla. Dept. Profl. Regulation, behavior analyst Nat. Behavior Analyst Bd., crisis prevention intervention trainer, 2011, local assistive tech. specialist, 1995-2010. Alternative edn. self-contained tchr. grades 2 and 3 Gainesville Acad., Micanopy, Fla., 1979; emotional handicaps self-contained tchr. Ctr. Sch. Alternative Sch., Gainesville, Fla., 1979-80; learning disabilities resource tchr. grades 2 and 3 Galaxy Elem. Sch., Boynton Beach, Fla., 1980-81, learning disabilities self-contained tchr. grades 1-3, 1981, varying exceptionalities self-contained tchr. grades 3-5, 1981-83, chpt. one remedial reading tchr. grades 3 and 4, 1982-83; sec. and visual display unit operator Manpower, London, 1983-84; dir. sci./geography/social studies program Fairley House Sch., London, 1984-86, specific learning difficulties self-contained tchr. ages 8-12, dir. computing program, 1984-89; specific learning difficulties resource tchr. ages 8-16 Dyslexia Inst., Sutton Coldfield, Eng., 1990; behavior specialist, head Exceptional Student Edn. dept. Gateway High Sch., Kissimmee, Fla., 1990, behavior specialist, head ESE dept., 1991, resource compliance specialist, head ESE dept., 1991-93, tchr. summer youth tng. and enrichment program, 1993, Osceola High Sch., Kissimmee, 1992; resource compliance specialist, program specialist for mentally handicapped, physically impaired, occupational and phys. therapy programs St. Cloud (Fla.) Mid. Sch., 1993-96, local augmentative/assistive tech. specialist, 1995—; resource compliance specialist, program specialist physically impaired occupl./phys. therapy programs, local augmentative/assistive tech. specialist Hickory Tree Elem. Sch., 1996-97, program specialist assistive tech., occpl., and phys. therapy, physically impaired programs, 1997-99, program specialist assistive tech., 1999—2010, program specialist behaviour support, 2010—11, ind. program specialist, 2011—. Sch. rep. CREATE, Alachua County, Fla., 1979-80, Palm Beach County South Area Tchr. Edn. Ctr. Coun., 1980-83, chmn., 1982-83; mem. writing team Title IV-C Ednl. Improvement Grant, Palm Beach County, Fla., 1981; mem. math. curriculum writing team Palm Beach County (Fla.) Schs., 1983; mem., co-dir. Fairley House Rsch. Com., 1984-90; co-founder, dir. Rsch. Database, London, 1984-89; co-chmn. computer and behavior/social aspects writing teams Dyslexia Inst. Math., Staines, Eng., 1990; lectr., course tutor Brit. Dyslexia Assn., Crewe, Eng., 1990; mem. Vocat.-Exceptional Com., 1991-93; mem. Osceola Reading Coun., 1991-98; mem. sch. adv. com. Gateway High Sch., 1991-93, St. Cloud Mid. Sch., 1993-96; mem. sch. adv. com. Hickory Tree Elem. Sch., 1999-2000, Ctr. for Ind. Living Assitance for Tech. Divsn.; presenter in field. Mem. bd. assistive tech. divsn. Ctr. for Ind. Living. Recipient Disney's Teacherific Spl. Judges award, 1997, Outstanding Svcs. to Coun. for Exceptional Children award, 2002, 2003, Outstanding Related Svcs. Tchr. of Yr., 2003, Outstanding Support Svcs. award, 2003; named Mid. Sch. Profl. of Yr. Osceola chpt. Coun. Exceptional Children, 1995, 96, Profl. Recognized Spl. Educator, 1997. Mem. CEC (exec. com. 1997-, pres. 2007-08, 10-12, Pres.'s award, 2007, Mini-Grant winner); C.A.N. rep. 1997-99, pres.-elect 1999-2000, 06, pres. 2000-01, 07, named local chpt. Mid. Sch. Profl. of Yr. 1995, 96, Outstanding Svcs. to CEC award 2002, 03, Outstanding Related Svcs. Tchr. of Yr. 2003, Outstanding Support Svcs. award 2003, 25 Yrs. Svc. award 2006, Hall of Fame 2005-06), Fla. Soc. for Augmentative and Alt. Comm., Phi Beta Kappa. Avocations: travel, reading, exercise, scuba diving, crafts. Home: 2175 James Dr Saint Cloud FL 34771-8830 Office: Osceola Dist Schs ESE Adminstrv Annex 805 Bill Beck Blvd Kissimmee FL 34744-4492 Office Phone: 407-518-8147. Business E-Mail: toothek@osceola.k12.fl.us.

TOPAZI, ANTHONY J., utilities executive; b. 1950; BSEE, Auburn U., Ala. Coop. edn. student Ala. Power Southern Co., 1969, various positions including Western divsn. v.p. and Birmingham divsn. v.p. Ala. Power, sr. v.p. Southern Power, exec. v.p. Southern Co. Generation and Energy Mktg., pres., CEO Miss. Power, 2004—10, exec. v.p., COO, 2010—. Bd. dirs. Hancock Bank. Mem. steering com., co-chair econ. devel. work group Blueprint Miss.; chmn. Momentum Miss.; vice chmn. Miss. Partnership for Econ. Devel.; mem. Miss. Gulf Coast Econ. Devel. Coun., Miss. Gulf Coast C. of C., DeToqueville Soc. of United Way of Am.; bd. trustees Nature Conservancy Miss.; bd. dirs. Miss. Econ. Coun., Gulf Coast Cmty. Found., Miss. World Trade Ctr. Office: Miss Power Co 2992 W Beach Blvd Gulfport MS 39501 Office Phone: 866-251-1943.

TOPHAM, SALLY JANE, performing arts educator; b. NYC, June 2, 1933; d. William Holroyd and Marion Phyllis (Thomas) Topham; m. Joseph Vincent Ferrara, Dec. 27, 1958 (div. 1977); children: Gregory Paul Ferrara, Mark Edward Ferrara. Student Ballet Theatre Sch., Royal Acad. Dance, London, diploma in tchg.; trained in Europe. Registered tchr.; cert. advanced tchg. Royal Acad. Dance, tchg. RAD, ATC, RTC. Freelance profl. dancer ballet, opera ballet, summer stock, 1956—60; founder, dir. Monmouth Sch. Ballet, N.J., 1963-83; dir. Shore Ballet Theatre Sch., 1986-95; freelance tchr., choreographer Metro Lyric Opera. Tchr., dir. Mount Allison U. Summer Sch., New Brunswick, Canada, 1973—77; dir. Westfield Sch. Ballet, NJ, 1976—77; artistic dir. Shore Ballet Co., 1986—95, 1977—2001; prof. ballet Monmouth Coll., West Long Branch, NJ, 1981—83; founder Ctrl. Jersey Acad. Ballet, Red Bank, NJ, 1983—85; dir. Acad. Shore Ballet, 1995—2000; cons. formulation dance curriculum for N.J. pub. schs. State Bd. Edn., 1997; freelance tchr. Colts Neck Dance Acad., 2000—03; tchr. Middletown Dance Acad., 2003—, Spring Lake Sch. Dance, 2003—07; faculty Internat. Ballet Acad. Cary, NC, 2011. Choreographer (ballets) Nutcracker, 1985, Homage to Bournonville, 1977, Shubert Songs, 1980, Coppelia, 1981, 1990, 1996, Cinderella, 1988; staged numerous ballets and opera ballets including Firebird, Les Sylphides, Carnival. Bd. dirs. Monmouth Arts Found., Red Bank, 1972—85; founder Shore Ballet Co., Red Bank, 1976—2000; founder, bd. dirs. Monmouth Civic Ballet, Red Bank, 1972—75; mem., bd. dirs. English-Speaking Union, Raleigh, NJ, 2000—07, treas. NJ; mem. bd. English-Speaking Union Rsch. Triangle Br., NC, 2007—. Mem.: English Speaking Union, Royal Acad. Dance (assoc.). Avocations: theater, music, books, travel, gardening, opera, films, ballet. Personal E-mail: sjtballet06@yahoo.com.

TOPLIN, ROBERT BRENT, history professor, television producer; b. Phila., Sept. 26, 1940; s. Maurice Cunningham and Janet Rachel (Belsinger) T.; m. Karin Bendel, Dec. 26, 1996; children: Cassandra, Jennifer. BS, Pa. State U., 1962; MA, Rutgers U., 1965, PhD, 1968. Asst. prof. Denison U., Granville, Ohio, 1968-74, assoc. prof., 1976-78; assoc. prof. and program dir. U. Houston-Clear Lake City, 1974-76; assoc. prof. U. N.C. at Wilmington, 1978-80, prof. history, 1980; spkr. Orgn. Am. Hist. Disting. Lectureship Program, 2004—. Vis. prof. U. N.C.-Chapel Hill, 1983; media advisor NEH; lectr. in field. Project dir.: A House Divided (TV series) U.S.A.; A Television history, Pres.'s in Crisis, The Am. Frontier; author: The Abolition of Slavery in Brazil, 1972, Unchallenged Violence: An American Ordeal, 1975, Freedom and Prejudice: The Legacy of Slavery in the United States and Brazil, 1982, History By Hollywood: The use and Abuse of the American Past, 1996; author: Reel History: In Defense of Hollywood, 2002, Michael Moore's Fahrenheit 9/11: How One Film Divided a Nation, 2006, Radical Conservatism: The Right's Political Religion, 2006; editor: Slavery and Race Relations in Latin America, 1974; editor anthology: American History Through Film, 1983, Ken Burns's The Civil War: Historians Respond, 1996, Oliver Stone's USA: Film, History and Controversy, 2000, Masters at The Movies, 2006; contbg. editor: Jour. Am. History, 1986—2007, Perspectives, Am. Hist. Assoc., 1995 - 2000, 2007-; contbr. articles to profl. jours.; book reviewer various jours.; project dir.: (PBS TV) Denmark Vesey's Rebellion 1982, Solomon Northup's Odyssey, 1984; Charlotte Forten's Mission, 1985; (films) The War to End All Wars, 1985, Lincoln and the War Within, 1992; broadcast appearances on PBS TV, CBS TV, The History Channel, Turner Classic Movie Channel, C-SPAN. Pres. Williston Jr. H.S. PTA; v.p. New Hanover County PTA, New Hanover County Bd. Edn. Grantee or fellow Ford Found., 1967, NEH, 1970, 77-80, 82-89, 90-91, Am. Philos. Soc., 1970m 81, Denison U. Rsch. Found., 1972, Annenberg/Corp. for Pub. Broadcasting, 1983-84; grantee Ill. Humanities Coun., 1991; fellow Am. Coun. Learned Soc., 1991. Mem. Am. Hist. Assn. (tchg. com. 1990-93), Orgn. Am. Historians (mem. com. on radio, TV, film media 1978-80, Erik Barnouw prize 1985, 87-89), Conf. on Latin Am. History (com. on tchg. materials 1978), Erik Barnouw prize com. 1987-88. Democrat. Jewish. Home Phone: 434-989-3564. Business E-Mail: toplinrb@uncw.edu.

TORBETT, JOHN A., state legislator; Vol. East Gaston High Sch.; coach Stanley Dept. of Parks & Recreation; chmn. Gaston County Rep. Party; assoc. mem. Gaston County Rep. Womens Club, Gaston County Young Republicans; pres. Kiser Elem. Sch. PTO; supporting mem. Smithsonian Air & Space Mus., Wash., DC; pres. Stanley Athletic Assn.; mem. Tech. Assn. of Pulp & Paper Inst. (TAPPI), Stanley Recreational Adv. Bd., Gaston County Rep. Mens Club, Gaston County Drug & Crime Task Force, Gaston County Water & Sewer Adv. Bd., Assn. of Ind. Corrugated Converters, Internat. Assn. of Die makers & Die Cutters (IADD), Rep. Nat. Com., NCGOP Ctrl. Com., NCGOP Exec. Com., NC Rep. Party; chmn. Dist. 9 US Congl.; mem. Dist. 9 US Congl. Com.; pres. Stanley Middle Sch. PTO; v.p., bus. devel. Def. Technologies, Inc.; chmn. NC Rep. Party Resolutions Com., 2001, mem., 2002; commrs. Gaston County Bd. of Commrs., 2002, 2006; v.p., ops. Def. Technologies, Inc., NC, 2003; mem. Dist. 108 NC House of Representatives, 2011—. Recipient Gaston County Rep. of the Yr., 2002 Republican. Office: 210 Blueridge Dr Stanley NC 28164 Address: North Carolina House of Representatives 300 N Salisbury St Room 537 Raleigh NC 27603-5925 Office Phone: 704-866-3196, 919-733-5868, 704-263-9282. Office Fax: 704-866-3147. Business E-Mail: jtorbett@co.gaston.nc.us, John.Torbett@ncleg.net.

TORCIVIA, S. JAMES, food service executive; Attended, Rutgers U., New Brunswick, NJ, 1964—68. Dir. real estate and devel. The Wills Group, 1992—94; dir. real estate, v.p. devel. Cracker Barrel Old Country Store, Inc., 1994—. Office: Cracker Barrel Old Country Store Inc 305 Hartmann Dr Lebanon TN 37088-0787 Office Phone: 615-444-5533. Office Fax: 615-443-9476.

TORGERSEN, PAUL ERNEST, academic administrator, educator; b. NYC, Oct. 13, 1931; s. Einar and Frances (Hansen) T.; m. Dorothea Hildegarde Zuschlag, Sept. 11, 1954; children: Karen Elizabeth, Janis Elaine, James Einar. BS, Lehigh U., 1953, DEng, 1994; MS, Ohio State U., 1956, PhD, 1959. Grad. tchg. asst. Ohio State U., Columbus, 1957, instr., 1957-59; asst. to assoc. prof. Okla. State U., Stillwater, 1959-66; prof., dept. head, dean Coll. Engring. Va. Tech, Blacksburg, 1967-93, pres., 1993-2000, John W. Hancock chair of engring. Dir. Roanoke (Va.) Electric Steel, 1986-2001, Luna Innovations, 2000—, EDD, 1996—. Author 5 books. Mem. Gov. Mark Warner's Commn. on Bd. of Visitor Appts., Richmond, Va., 2002--; So.State Energy Bd., Richmond, 1986-90. 1st lt. USAF, 1953-55. Fellow Am. Soc. Engring. Edn. (Lamme medal 1994), Inst. Indsl. Engring (Frank and Lillian Gibreth award 2001); mem. Nat. Acad. Engring. (coun. 1999--). Avocation: tennis. Office: Va Tech 201 Durham Hall Blacksburg VA 24061-0118 Business E-Mail: tennis@vt.edu.

TORGERSEN, TORWALD HAROLD, architect, consultant; b. Chgo., Sept. 2, 1929; s. Peder and Hansine Malene (Hansen) T.; m. Dorothy Darlene Peterson, June 22, 1963. BS in Archtl. Engring. with honors, U. Ill., 1951. Gargoyle Archtl. hon., Sigma Tau Engring. hon., Lic. architect Ill., D.C., real estate broker, Ill., interior designer, Ill., pvt. pilot, scuba diver; registered architect Nat. Coun. Archtl. Registration Bds. Ptnr. Coyle & Torgersen Architects-Engrs., Washington, Chgo. and Joliet, Ill., 1955—56; project coord. Skidmore, Owings & Merrill, Chgo., 1956—60; corp. architect, dir. architecture, constrn. and interiors Container Corp. Am., Chgo., 1960—86; prin. in charge of orgn. and adminstrn. Jack Train Assocs. Inc., Chgo., 1987—88; cons. Torwald H. Torgersen, AIA, FASID, Chgo., 1988—. Guest lectr. U. Wis. Capt. USNR, 1951-82, US Naval War Coll., 1967 Recipient Top Ten Design award Factory mag., 1964 Fellow Am. Soc. Interior Designers; mem. AIA, Naval Res. Assn., Rear Admiral, United Air Million Miler, Chgo. Marathon, Ill. Naval Militia, Rear Admiral, Ill., Am. Arbitration Assn., Am. Soc. Mil. Engrs., Paper Industry Mgmt. Assn. (hon.), Sports Car Club Am., Nat. Eagle Scout Assn., 20 Fathoms Club, Chgo. Marathon. Home and Office: 4625 Whisper Way Pensacola FL 32504

TORIAN, LUKE E., state legislator, minister; b. Roxboro, NC, May 30, 1958; m. Clarice Jones; 1 child, Constance A. BA, Winston-Salem State U., NC, 1980; MDiv, Va. Union U., Richmond, 1984; PhD, Howard U. Sch. Divinity, Washington, 1987. Pastor First Mount Zion Bapt. Ch., Dumfries, Va.; mem. Dist. 52 Va. House of Delegates, Richmond, 2010—. Founder Virginians Organized Interfaith Cmty. Engagement. Recipient James Floyd Jenkins Pillar of Faith award, Howard Univ., 2002. Mem.: Eastern Prince William Ministerial Assn. (co-pres.), Omega Psi Phi (Third Dist. Citizen of Yr. award 2000, Psi Nu Citizen of Yr. award 2001). Democrat. Office: Va House of Dels Gen Assembly Bldg Rm 716 PO Box 406 Richmond VA 23218 also: 15653 Neath Dr Woodbridge VA 22193 Office Phone: 804-698-1052, 703-785-2224. Office Fax: 804-698-6752. Business E-Mail: deltorian@house.virginia.gov.

TOROK, KEN, delivery service executive; Grad., NC State U. Delivery driver United Parcel Service, Inc. (UPS), 1975, transp. mgr. UPS Europe, 1994—97, mng. dir. Utah ops., 1998, mng. dir. South Fla. ops., pres. Asia Pacific Region Singapore, 2003—08, pres. global freight forwarding ops., 2009—11. Office: UPS, Inc 55 Glenlake Parkway, NE Atlanta GA 30328

TORRAS, JOSEPH HILL, pulp and paper company executive; b. Americus, Ga., Nov. 14, 1924; s. Fernando Joseph and Nell Wilson (Hill) T.; m. Mary Ravenel Robertson, Sept. 20, 1952; children: Mary Martin, Fernanda Maria, Joseph Hill. S.B., Yale U., 1948; MBA, Harvard U., 1950; D in Bus. Adminstrn., Piedmont Coll., 1997. Asst. to fin. v.p. Seatrian Lines, Inc., 1950—51; with St. Regis Paper Co., 1951—60, sales mgr. printing papers div., 1956—60; exec. v.p. Brown Co., Boston, 1960—64; pres., chmn. bd. Premoid Corp., West Springfield, Mass., 1964—87; pres. Precon, Inc., Ludlow, 1967—87, Astro Tissue Co., Battleboro, Vt., 1968—72; chmn. bd. Whitman Products, Ltd., West Warwick, RI, 1976—89; pres., CEO, Preco Corp., Amherst, Mass., 1976—98; chmn., CEO Lincoln Pulp & Paper Co., Lincoln, Maine, 1968—2004, Eastern Fine Paper, Inc., Brewer, Maine, 1989—2004. CEO, Shelburne Corp., 1999—; adv. dir. Liberty Mut. Ins. Mem. Mass. Gov.'s Bus. Adv. Coun., 1985—89; devel. bd. Yale U.; bd. govs. Mass. Gen. Hosp., 1985—96; bd. dirs. Mass. Taxpayers Assn., 1976—86; trustee Hist. Deerfield, 1990—2004, Piedmont Coll., Ga., 1991—99; dir. Inst. of World Politics, 1990—. Lt. (j.g.) aviator USNR, 1943—46. Mem. Tissue Paper Mfrs. Assn. (dir. 1963-64), Am. Pulp and Paper Mill Supts. Assn., Salesman's Assn. Paper Industry, NAM (dir. 1981-85), Colony Club, Carolina Yacht Club, Yale Club (NYC). Home: 12 Tradd St Charleston SC 29401 Home Phone: 843-722-4978.

TORRES, DAVID, retired Spanish language educator; b. Laredo, Tex., Oct. 30, 1934; PhD, U. Ill., 1969. Cert. tchr., Tex. Prof. Spanish Angelo State U., San Angelo, Tex., 1979—96. Author: Los Prólogos de Leopoldo Alas, 1984, Studies on Clarín, 1987; contbr. articles to profl. publs. Grantee Nat. Endowment Humanities, 1977, Angelo State U., 1981, 84; Southland Corp. scholar, 1986. Mem. Am. Assn. Tchrs. Spanish and Portuguese, Tex. Assn. Coll. Tchrs., Sigma Delta Pi.

TORRES, JOHN D., lawyer, manufacturing executive; B, U. Notre Dame; JD, U. Chgo. Sr. counsel Motorola, 1996, v.p., gen. counsel, 2001; sr. v.p., gen. counsel & sec. Freescale Semiconductor Inc., Austin, Tex.; exec. v.p., chief legal officer & sec. Lennox International, Inc., 2008—. Bd. dirs. Greater Austin C. of C. Office: Lennox International Inc 2140 Lake Park Blvd Richardson TX 75080 Office Phone: 972-497-5000. Office Fax: 972-497-5292. E-mail: john.torres@lennoxintl.com.

TORRES, RAYMOND, professor; PhD, U. Calif., Berkeley, 1996. Prof. U. SC, Columbia, 1997—. Office: Univ South Carolina 701 Sumter St EWS617 Columbia SC 29208

TORTORELLA, JOHN, former professional hockey coach; b. Boston, June 24, 1958; s. William and Rita Tortorella; m. Christine Tortorella; children: Brittany, Dominick. Degree, U. Maine, 1981. Coach Va. Lancers (Atlantic Coast Hockey League), 1986—88; asst. coach Buffalo Sabres, 1989—95; head coach Rochester Am. (Am. Hockey League), 1995—97; asst. coach Phoenix Coyotes, 1997—99, NY Rangers, 1999—2001, head coach, 2009—13, Tampa Bay Lightning, 2001—08, Vancouver Canucks, 2013—14; analyst TSN, 2008—09. Head coach Team USA, IIHF World Hockey Championship, 2008; asst. coach Team USA, Olympic Games, Vancouver, 2010. Recipient Jack Adams Award, NHL, 2004; named Coach of Yr., Atlantic Coast Hockey League, 1986—87, NHL Coach of Yr., Sporting News, 2004. Achievements include being the coach of Stanley Cup Champion, Tampa Bay Lightning, 2004.*

TOSCA, CARLOS, professional baseball coach; m. Geraldine Tosca; children: Jessica, Lauren, Matthew. B in Phys. Edn., U. South Fla., Tampa. Tchr. McLane Mid. Sch., Brandon, Fla.; pitching coach King HS Lions, Tampa; coach Oneonta Yankees, NY-Penn League, 1978—79; mgr. Bradenton Yankees, Gulf Coast League, 1980—82, Greensboro Hornets, So. Atlantic League, 1983—84, Sarasota Yankees, Gulf Coast League, 1985, Royals, Gulf Coast League, 1988—90, Baseball City Royals, Fla. State League, 1991, Marlins, Gulf Coast League, 1992, Kane County Cougars, Midwest League, 1993, Portland Sea Dogs, Ea. League, 1994—96, Charlotte Knights, Internat. League, 1997; bench coach Ariz. Diamondbacks, 1998—2000, third base coach, 2005—06; mgr. Richmond Braves, Internat. League, 2001; third base coach Toronto Blue Jays, 2002, mgr., 2002—04; bench coach Fla. Marlins, 2007—10, Atlanta Braves, 2011—. Named Carl Barger Player Devel. Person of Yr., 1995, Minor League Mgr. of Yr., Baseball America, 1996. Office: Atlanta Braves 755 Hank Aaron Dr Atlanta GA 30315

TOSCANO, DAVID J., state legislator; b. Syracuse, NY, June 28, 1950; m. Nancy M. Tramontin; 1 child, Matthew T. BA, Colgate U., Hamilton, NY, 1968; PhD, Boston Coll., 1972; JD, U. Va. Sch. Law, 1986. Pvt. practice atty.; councilman Charlottesville City Coun., Va., 1990—2002; mayor City of Charlottesville, 1994—96; mem. Dist. 57 Va. House of Delegates, Va., 2006—; mem. Cts. Justice Com., 2006—, Sci. and Tech. Com., 2006—, Transp. Com. Mem.: Charlottesville Regional C. of C., Thomas Jefferson United Way, Charlottesville & Albemarle NAACP. Democrat. Roman Catholic. Office: 211 E High St Charlottesville VA 22902 Office Phone: 434-220-1660. Business E-Mail: DelDToscano@house.virginia.gov.

TOSCHES, PETER L., janitorial service company executive; BA in Comm., Fordham U. Coord., employee comm. Blue Cross & Blue Shield of Conn.; mgr., employee comm. GE Co., v.p., corp. comm., consumer fin., 1997—2005; v.p., corp. comm. Cendant Timeshare Resort Group, 2005; dir., internal comm., N.Am. Mars Inc., Hackettstown, NJ, 2005—07; v.p., corp. comm. Servicemaster Co., Servicemaster Global Holdings, 2007—. Recipient Creative Gold award, MarCom. Office: The ServiceMaster Co 860 Ridge Lake Blvd Memphis TN 38120 Office Phone: 901-597-1400. Office Fax: 630-663-2001. Business E-Mail: peter.tosches@servicemaster.com.

TOSKES, PHILLIP PAUL, gastroenterologist, educator, researcher; b. Balt., Jan. 4, 1940; s. John F. and Mary R. (Vonelli) T.; m. Patricia A. Sponsel, June 3, 1961; children: Tammy Lynn Price, Tracey Lynn, Steven D. BA, Johns Hopkins U., 1961; MD, U. Md., 1965. Diplomate Am. Bd. Internal Medicine (bd. dirs.), Am. Bd. Gastroenterology. Intern, resident U. Md. Hosp., Balt., 1965-68; fellow in gastroenterology Hosp. U. Pa., Phila., 1968-70; asst. prof. medicine U. Fla., Gainesville, 1973-75, assoc. prof. medicine, 1975-78, prof. medicine, 1978—, dir. divsn. gastro, hepatology, 1978-97, prof., chmn. dept. medicine, 1997—2002. Chief gastro sect. Gainesville VA Med. Ctr., 1973-92; chmn. Nat. Digestive Disease Adv. Bd., Washington, 1992-94. Author chpts. to books. Maj. U.S. Army, 1970-73. Recipient Disting. Achievement award Can. Gastroenterol. Assn., 1982. Fellow ACP (Meade Johnson scholar 1966-68); mem. Am. Soc. Clin. Investigation, Am. Fedn. Clin. Rsch., Am. Gastroenterol. Assn. (pres. 1997-98). Avocations: travel, swimming, boating. Office: U Fla Box 100214 1600 SW Archer Rd Gainesville FL 32610-3001 Home: 202 NW 114th Way Gainesville FL 32607-1122 Office Phone: 352-392-2877. Business E-Mail: toskepp@medicine.ufl.edu.

TOTENBERG, AMY MIL, federal judge; b. NYC, Dec. 29, 1950; d. Roman and Melanie (Shroder) T.; m. Ralph Green, Sept. 27, 1980; children: Sonya, Naomi, Emily, Clara. BA, Harvard U., 1974; JD, Harvard Law Sch., 1977. Bar: Ga. 1977, U.S. Dist. Ct. (no. and mid. dists.) Ga. 1977, U.S. Ct. Appeals (5th cir.) 1977, U.S. Ct. Appeals (11th cir.) 1982, U.S. Supreme Ct. 1988. Ptnr. Law Project, Atlanta, 1977—82; sole practice Atlanta, 1982—94, 1998—2011; pro hac vice judge Atlanta Mcpl. Ct., 1988—93; gen. counsel Atlanta Pub. Sch. System, Atlanta, 1994—98, arbitrator, mediator, 1999—2010; spl. master US Dist. Ct., Md., 2000—10, monitor, 2006—11, judge, 2011—. Adj. prof. law Emory U. Sch. Law, 2004-07 Mem. Ga. Bar Assn. (vice chmn. individual rights sect. 1985-85, sec. individual rights sect. 1985-86). Office: US District Court 2388 Richard B Russell Federal Building 75 Spring St SW Atlanta GA 30303

TOTTEN, HERMAN LAVON, dean, library and information science educator; BA, Wiley Coll.; MLS, U. Okla., PhD in Edni. Media/Libr. Sci. Chief libr. Wiley Coll., academic dean Marshall, Tex.; assoc. dean Coll. Libr. and Info. Sci., U. Ky.; prof., dean U. Oreg.; faculty mem. Sch. Libr. and Info. Scis., U. North Tex., Denton, 1977—, Regents prof., 1991—, assoc. dean, dean, 2005—; faculty exec. asst. to pres. U. North Tex., Denton. Commr. US Nat. Commn. on Librs. and Info. Sci., 2004—. Co-editor: Administrative Effects of Education for Librarianship, 1975; co-author: Culturally Diverse Library Collections for Children, 1995, Model Policies for Small and Medium Public Libraries, 1998, rev. edit., 2008. Mem.: ALA (life; past pres., Melvil Dewey Award 2001), Libr. Quarterly Editl. Bd., Am. Records Mgmt. Assn., Tex. Libr. Assn., Phi Kappa Phi. Office: University North Texas College Information 1155 Union Cir #311068 Denton TX 76203-1068

TOTTEN, PATRICIA A., lawyer; b. Cleve. BA in Philosophy, Eckerd Coll.; MEd, Kent St. U., Ohio; JD, So. Tex. Coll. Law, 1983. Bar: Tex. Former v.p. mktg. Verizon Wireless; former gen. coun. Houston Data Svc. Co.; dep. gen. counsel Enterprise Products Partners L.P, 2002—06; v.p., gen. coun., corp. sec. TEPPCO Partners, L.P., 2006—. Office: TEPPCO 1100 Louisiana St Houston TX 77002

TOTTENHAM, TERRY OLIVER, lawyer; b. Dallas, June 5, 1944; s. Edwin Pier and Ruth Elizabeth (Paris) T.; m. Carolyn Sue Lewis, July 7, 1967; children: Leslie Jo, Dana Elizabeth, Jessica Leigh. Student, Blinn Jr. Coll., 1962-67; BS in Pharmacy with high honors, U. Tex.-Austin, 1967, JD with honors, 1970; LL.M., George Washington U., 1973. Bar: Tex. 1970, U.S. Ct. Mil. Appeals 1971. Assoc. Fulbright, Crooker & Jaworski, Houston, 1970; ptnr. Fulbright & Jaworski LLP, Austin, Tex., 1978, head Pharm. and Med. Device Litig. Group, of cousnel. Mem. faculty South Tex. Coll. Law, U. Houston; vis. prof. med. jurisprudence Baylor U.; vis. prof. health law Tex. Women's U.; adj. prof. law U. Tex. Sch. Law; speaker profl. groups Author: Texas Medical Jurisprudence; editor: Patients Rights Handbook, 1980. Served to capt. USMC, 1971-75. Recipient Gene Cavin award, 1992; named Outstanding Young Lawyer Houston, 1981, Outstanding Young Lawyer Tex., 1981. Fellow: Tex. Bar Found. (life; trustee 1986—); mem.: ABA, Tex Young Lawyers Assn. (chmn. 1979—80), Houston Young Lawyers Assn. (dir. 1975—77), State Bar Tex. (chmn. Health Law Sect. & Litig. Sect., bd. dirs. 1985—86, pres. 2010—11), American Acad. Hosp. Attys. (bd. dirs. 1989—), Nat. Health Lawyers Assn., American Soc. Pharmacy Law, American Soc. Law and Medicine, Tex. Assn. Def. Counsel, Tex. Ex-Students Assn. (life). Democrat. Episcopalian. Office: Fulbright & Jaworski LLP 600 Congress Ave Ste 2400 Austin TX 78701-3271 Office Phone: 512-536-4555. Office Fax: 512-536-4598. Business E-Mail: ttottenham@fulbright.com.

TOUBY, KATHLEEN ANITA, lawyer; b. Miami Beach, Feb. 20, 1943; d. Harry and Kathleen Rebecca (Hamper) T.; m. Joseph Thomas Woodward; children: Mark Andrew, Judson David Touby. BS in Nursing, U. Fla., 1965, MRC in Rehab. Counseling, 1967; JD with honors, Nova U., 1977. Bar: Fla. 1978, D.C. 1978. Counselor Jewish Vocat. Svc., Chgo., 1967-68; rehab. counselor Fla. Dept. Vocat. Rehab., Miami, 1968-70; spl. asst., asst. U.S. atty. U.S. Dept. Justice, Miami, 1978-80; assoc. Pyszka & Kessler, P.A., Miami, 1980-83; ptnr. Touby & Smith, P.A., Miami, 1983-89, Touby, Smith, DeMahy & Drake, P.A., Miami, 1989-94, Touby & Woodward, P.A., Miami, 1994—; of counsel Law Offices Maria L. Rubio P.A. Chmn. adv. exec. bd. Paralegal Edn. program Barry U., 1986-87; lectr. Food and Drug Law Inst., 1987-89, 91; lectr. environ. law Exec. Enterprises, 1987-88; lectr. trial techniques, Hispanic Nat. Bar Assn., St. Thomas Law Sch.; adj. prof. product liability Can. Govt., U.S. Trade and Mktg. Dept., 1989-95, of counsel law offices Marial L. Rubio P.A., 2011- Coauthor: The Environmental Litigation Deskbook, 1989; contbr. chpts. to books, articles to profl. jours. Mem. ABA, Am. Inns of Ct. (pres. 1998-99, pres.-elect St. Thomas Law Sch. chpt. 1997-98, pres. 1998-99), Dade County Bar Assn. (legal aid, pub. svcs. com. 1988), Fed. Bar Assn. (bd. dirs. 1989—2010, v.p. 1991-92, pres.-elect So. Fla. chpt. 1992-93, pres. 1993-94), Cuban-Am. Bar Assn., Phi Delta Phi (province pres. 1982-85, bd. dirs. 1985-87). Roman Catholic. Home: 8721 SW102 St Miami FL 33176 Office: Touby & Woodward PA One Datran Ctr 9100 S Dadeland Blvd Ste 1510 Miami FL 33156 Office Phone: 305-670-1164.

TOULMIN, PRIESTLEY, retired geologist; b. Birmingham, Ala., June 5, 1930; s. Priestley and Catharine Augusta (Carey) T.; m. Martha Jane Slason, Aug. 30, 1952 (dec. Jan., 2008); children: Catharine Bosier (Mrs. Robert G. Gibson), Priestley Chewning (dec. Dec. 2011). AB, Harvard U., 1951, PhD, 1959; MS, U. Colo., 1953. With U.S. Geol. Survey, Washington, 1953-56, 57-89, staff geologist for exptl. geology, 1966, chief br. exptl. geochemistry, 1966-71, geologist geologic div., 1971-89, Reston, Va., 1974-89, ret., 1989; also leader inorganic chemistry team NASA (Viking Project). Adj. prof. Columbia U., 1966; rsch. asso. in geochemistry Calif. Inst. Tech., 1976-77; vis. lectr. Am. Geol. Inst.; dir. petrogenesis and mineral resources program NSF, 1985; bd. dirs., treas. 28th Internat. Geol. Congress, 1985-86 Mng. sci. editor Geochemistry Internat., 1965-68; assoc. editor Am. Mineralogist, 1974-76; contbr. articles to profl. jours. Mem. adv. com. spl. edn., Alexandria, Va., 1977-80. Recipient Exceptional Service medal NASA, 1977; Meritorious Service award U.S. Dept. Interior, 1978 Fellow Geol. Soc. Am., Mineral Soc. Am. (bd. assoc. editors 1974-76), Soc. Econ. Geologists, Explorers Club(bd. dirs. Wash. DC Group); mem. AAAS, Geol. Soc. Washington (2d v.p. 1977, councillor 1973-74, 90-91, 1st v.p. 1981, pres. 1982), Am. Geophys. Union, Soc. Mayflower Descs., Jamestowne Soc. (bd. dirs. 2012-), S.R., SAR, Soc. Colonial Wars (DC), Aztec Club of 1847, St. Andrews Soc. (Washington), Cosmos Club (pres. 1993-94, found. trustee 1994—, chmn. 1996-2001), Sigma Xi, Sigma Gamma Epsilon. Home: 418 Summers Dr Alexandria VA 22301-2449 Office: PO Box 183 Alexandria VA 22313-0183

TOUPS, JOHN M., information technology executive; BS in Civil Engring., U. Calif., Berkeley, 1949. Registered civil engr., Calif., Md. Interim chmn. & CEO Nat. Bank of Washington; interim chmn., CEO Washington Bancorp; various mgmt. positions Planning Rsch. Corp., McLean, Va., 1970—78, pres. & CEO, 1978—87, chmn., 1982—87, GTSI Corp., 2007—. Former bd. dirs. Dinte Resources, Inc., Halifax Corp., Va., CACI Internat. Inc; bd. dirs. Dewberry & Davis, NVR, Inc., 1993—, Willdan Group, Inc., 2007—; bd. trustees Inova Health System, 2009—. Fellow Am. Soc. of Civil Engrs. Office: GTSI Corp 2553 Dulles View Dr Ste 100 Herndon VA 20171 Office Phone: 703-502-2000. Office Fax: 703-463-5101. Business E-Mail: john.toups@gtsi.com.

TOUR, JAMES M., chemistry educator, researcher; b. NYC, Aug. 18, 1959; s. Eli and Hedi T.; m. Shireen Grace Massey, May 29, 1982; children: Ambreen, Sabrina, Josiah, Benaiah. BS in Chemistry, Syracuse U., Syracuse, NY, 1981; PhD in Synthetic Organic and Organometallic Chemistry, Purdue U., West Layafette, Ind., 1986. Undergraduate student, dept. chemistry Syracuse U., 1977—81; grad. student, dept. chemistry Purdue U., 1981—86; postdoctoral fellow in organometallic chemistry U. Wis., 1986—87; NIH postdoctoral fellow in synthetic organic chemistry Stanford U., 1987—88; asst. prof. dept. chemistry and biochemistry U. SC, Columbia, 1988—92, assoc. prof. dept. chemistry and biochemistry, 1992—94, prof. dept. chemistry and biochemistry, 1994—96, Guy F. Lipscomb prof. chemistry, 1996—99; Disting. faculty assoc. Hanzen Coll. Rice U., Houston, 1999—2000; T.T. and W.F. Chao prof. of chemistry Smalley Inst. for Nanoscale Sci. and Technology, Rice U., 1999—, prof. mech. engring. and materials sci., 1999—, prof. computer sci., 1999—; co-founder, v.p. Molecular Electronics Corp., Houston, 1999—; also bd. dirs.; co-founder NanoComposites, Inc., 2004—, RJAC-10, LLC, 2007; founder, principal NanoJtech Consultants, LLC, 2007. One week vis. lectr. polymer divsn. IBM, Almaden Rsch. Ctr., 1988; vis. scholar dept. chemistry Harvard U., 1994; mem. CAREER program adv. com. NSF, 1995, mem. adv. com. Materials Rsch. Ctr., 1996—97; Weissberger-Williams lectr. Eastman Kodak Corp., Rochester, NY, 1995; mem. adv. bd. Gov.'s Math. and Sci., SC, 1996—98; Abbott Disting. lectr. Colo. State U., 1997; mem. tech, adv. bd. Calif. Molecular Electronics Corp., 1998—99; mem. Nat. Def. Sci. Study Group, 1997—99, MD Anderson Cancer Rsch. Ctr. Competitive Grant Renewal Bd., 2007—, Def. Sci. Bd. Chem/Nano Study Sect., 2007, Dept. Commerce Emerging Technology and Rsch. Adv. Com., 2008—; adj. prof., dept. chemistry and Ctr. for Nanoscale Sci. and Technology Rice U., Houston, 1999; dir. Carbon Nanotechnology Lab., 2005—07; bd. dirs. Ariel Ministries, 2006—; cons. in field. Author: Molecular Electronics: Commercial Insights, Chemistry, Devices, Architecture, and Programming; mem. adv. bd. Chemical Reviews, 1999—2002; contbr. of several articles to publications. Mem. Def. Sci. Study Group, 2003; bible study tchr. Broad River Maximum Security Prison, Columbia, SC, 1989—99. Recipient George Wiley award in Organic Chemistry, 1979, award, Am. Inst. Chemists, 1981, Office of Naval Rsch. Young Investigator award in polymer chemistry, Office of Naval Rsch., 1989-1992, NSF Presdl. Young Investigator award in polymer chemistry, 1991-1996, Exxon Ednl. Found. rsch. and tng. award, 1994, Russell Rsch. award in Sci., Math. and Engring., U. SC, 1997, Honda Innovation award for Nanocars, 2005, Alan Berman Rsch. Publication award, Dept. Navy, 2006, Small Times Mag. Innovator of the Yr. award, 2006, Nanotech Briefs Nano 50 Innovator award, 2006, George R. Brown award for Superior Tchg., 2007, NASA Space Act award for develop. of carbon nanotube reinforced elastomers, 2008, Feynman prize in Experimental Nanotechnology, 2008, Disting. Alumni award, Purdue U., 2009, Houston Technology Ctr. Nanotechnology award, 2009; named one of Top 10 Chemists in the World over the past decade, Thomson Reuters Citations per Publication Index Survey, 2009; Celanese Corp. grad. fellowship in chemistry, Purdue U., 1981-1982, IBM Corp. full grad. fellowship in polymer chemistry, 1985-1986. Fellow: AAAS; mem.: Materials Rsch. Soc. (assoc.), Am. Chem. Soc. (assoc.; assoc. dir. polymer divsn. materials rsch. secretariat 1991—95, mem. editl. adv. bd. chem. revs. 1999—2003, Arthur C. Cope Scholar award 2007, Southern Chemist of the Yr. award 2005). Achievements include patents in field; patents pending in field. Avocations: Bible study, target shooting. Office: Rice U Smalley Inst for Nanoscale Science & Technology 6100 Main St MS 222 Houston TX 77005 Office Phone: 713-348-6246. Office Fax: 713-348-6250. Business E-Mail: tour@rice.edu.

TOVELL, WILLIAM, wholesale distribution executive; Pres. Conn. Distbrs., Inc.; v.p., mktg. Sunbelt Beverage Corp.; vice chmn. Ben Arnold Beverage Co., L.P. (subs. of The Charmer Sunbelt Group), pres., 2000—09, chmn., 2009—. Office: Ben Arnold Beverage Co LP 101 Beverage Blvd Ridgeway SC 29130 Office Phone: 803-337-3500. Office Fax: 803-337-5310. Business E-Mail: wtovell@c-sg.com.

TOVEY, JOSEPH, investment banker; b. Tel Aviv, Nov. 5, 1938; came to U.S., 1940, naturalized, 1947; s. Samuel and Rachel (Weiman) T.; m. Anita Beverly Losice, Feb. 20, 1961; children: David, Debra, Nissan Chaim, Seth Reuven, Shaina Nava. BS in Acctg & Economics summa cum laude with honors, Bklyn. Coll., 1959; MBA in Taxation, NYU, 1961, PhD in Investment, Corp. Fin., Taxation, Accg. & Economics, 1969. CPA. Staff acct. Machtiger Green & Co., NYC, 1959—60, Loeb & Troper, NYC, 1960—61; tax rschr. Lybrand, Ross Bros. & Montgomery, 1961—63; planning assoc. Mobil Oil Corp., NYC, 1963—67; asst. v.p. A.G. Becker & Co., N.Y.C., 1967—70; assoc. Roth, Gerard & Co., N.Y.C., 1970—73; v.p. Faulkner, Dawkins & Sullivan, Inc., NYC, 1973—76, Shields Model Roland, Inc., NYC, 1976—77; mng. ptnr., CEO Tovey & Co., NYC, 1977—; contract CEO, CFO Glen Rose Petroleum Corp., 2009—10. Pres. Joint Trading Ltd., 1977-83, Tovey & Co., Inc., 1978-96, Midwood Petroleum Corp., 1980-91, Joint Trading (Del.) Ltd., 1984-96; chmn. Midwood Asset Mgmt. Co., Inc., 1985-96; CEO Terra Link Comm. Corp., 1997-2001; mem. exec. bd. Agudath Israel Am., 1963-67; CEO Hearthside Comm. Ltd. LLC, 1998-2001; adj. asst. prof. fin. Sy Syms Sch. Bus., 2002—09. Author: (with H.C. Smith) Federal Tax Treatment of Bad Debts and Worthless Securities, 1964; assoc. editor Tax Letter, 1961-66; contbr. articles to profl. jours. Mem. NYU Alumni Assn., Bklyn. Coll. Alumni in Fin. Office: 40 Wall St New York NY 10268-1524

TOWER, ALTON G., JR., pharmacist; b. Buffalo, Jan. 16, 1927; m. Nan R. Spinner, Aug. 15, 1953; children: Adrienne, Michele, Renee. BS in Pharmacy, U. Buffalo, 1953. Registered pharmacist. Pharmacist Woldmans Drug Store, Buffalo, 1946-53; med. svc. rep. Strasenburgh Lab., Rochester, N.Y., 1953-66; pharmacist, mgr. Eckerd Drugs, Clearwater, Fla., 1966—, 2nd v.p. abilities guild, 2012—. Bd. dirs. Am. Cancer Soc. Pinellas County, Fla., 1976—, pres., 1988-89, Life Saver award, 1988, life mem., 1995—, dir. cmty. affairs Pinellas Pharmacist Soc.; charter mem. Smoke Free Class of 2000, Pinellas County, 1988—. Recipient Vol. of Yr. award Am. Cancer Soc. Pinellas County, 1987, 97, Willis G. Gregory award U. Buffalo Sch. Pharmacy, 2004, IPA Corrons Motivation & Inspiration award, 2010. Mem. Am. Cancer Soc. (life, Lifesaver award Pinellas County chpt. 1988, named Vol. of Yr. 1997), Am. Pharm. Assn., Fla. Pharmacy Assn. (bd. dirs. 1981-85, speaker ho. of dels. 1986, chmn. bd. trustees, R.Q. Richards award 1989, Bowl of Hygeia award 1990, Sid Simkowitz Involvement award 1991, named Pharmacist of Yr. 1992), Pasco Hernando Pharmacists Assn. (James Beal award 1992), Pinellas County Pharmacy Soc. (life; dir. 1968-73, 78-81, 89-91, pres. 1973, 88, Pharmacist of Yr. 1973), Fla. Pharmacy Found. (pres. 1999, Jean Lamberti Mentorship award 2003), Phi Lambda Sigma. Avocations: gardening, hiking, travel.

TOWNES, TIM M., science educator, researcher; b. 1951; BS, U. Tenn., 1973, MS in Zoology, 1975, PhD in Microbiology, 1980. With U. Cin., U. Ala., Birmingham, 1984—, chmn., prof. biochemistry and molecular genetics. Contbr. articles to profl. jours. Office: Kaul Human Genetics Bldg Rm 537 720 South 20th St Birmingham AL 35294-0024 Office Phone: 205-934-5294. Office Fax: 205-934-2889. Business E-Mail: ttownes@uab.edu, ttownes@bmg.bhs.uab.edu.

TOWNS, JOE, state legislator; State rep. Dist. 84, Tenn., 1995—. Mem.: Men Progess, Kax Fraternity. Democrat. Christian. Office: 36 Legislative Plz Nashville TN 37243-0184 also: 4528 Saint Honore Memphis TN 38116 Office Phone: 901-332-7009, 615-741-2189. Office Fax: 615-253-0201. Business E-Mail: rep.joe.towns@capitol.tn.gov.

TOWNSEND, DAVID W., physicist, radiology professor; b. Jan. 13, 1945; BS in Physics, U. Bristol, Eng., 1966; PhD in Exptl. High Energy Physics, Westfield Coll., U. London, 1971. Docent in med. imaging U. Geneva, 1987. Rsch. assoc. Westfield Coll., 1969—70; sci. programmer, data handling divsn. European Orgn. Nuc. Rsch. (CERN), Geneva, 1970—78; vis. sci. cons., med. imaging processing group SUNY, Buffalo, 1978—79; physicist, computer analyst divsn. nuc. medicine Univ. Hosp. Geneva, 1979—93; assoc. prof. dept. radiology U. Pitts. Sch. Medicine, 1993—99, prof., 2000—03; prof. depts. medicine & radiology, dir. molecular imaging and translational rsch. program U. Tenn. Sch. Medicine, Knoxville, 2003—09, prof. dept. anesthesiology, 2006—09, adj. prof., 2009—; prof. radiology Yong Loo Lin Sch. Medicine, Nat. U. Singapore, 2009—, dir. Clin. Imaging Rsch. Ctr., 2010—. Hon. vis. scientist PET (positron emission tomography) group Hammersmith Hosp., London, 1987—2000; sr. scientist PET facility U. Pitts. Med. Ctr., 1993—2003, acting co-dir. PET facility, 1996—2001; head SPECT/PET devel. Singapore Bioimaging Consortium, 2009—. Assoc. editor Transactions in Med. Imaging, Jour. Nuc. Medicine, mem. editl. bd. Current Med. Imaging Reviews, mem. internat. editl. bd. Annals Nuc. Medicine, Japan; contbr. articles to profl. jours. Named one of 100 Names You Need to Know, Health Imaging & IT, 2004. Fellow: IEEE (Medal for Innovations in Healthcare Tech. 2010); mem.: Acad. Molecular Imaging (bd. dirs., treas. 2004, Disting. Clin. Scientist of Yr. 2004), Soc. Nuc. Medicine, Swiss Soc. Radiology & Nuc. Medicine. Achievements include with electrical engineer Ronald Nutt, implementing design, commercial development and clinical implementation of hybrid PET/CT scanners, named TIME Magazine's Invention of the Year in 2000; patents in field. Mailing: Univ Tenn Sch Medicine 1924 Alcoa Hwy Box 93 Knoxville TN 37920 Office Phone: 865-305-6181. E-mail: DTownsend@mc.utmck.edu.

TOWNSEND, JOHN L., III, private investor; b. Lumberton, NC, Aug. 9, 1955; s. John L. Jr. and Beverley C. Townsend; m. Marree Shore, June 23, 1977; children: Merritt Moore, Louise Rice. AB in English Lit. and American History, U. NC, Chapel Hill, 1977; MBA, Kenan-Flagler Bus. Sch., U. NC, 1982. Mgr. Townsend Farms,

Lumberton, 1977—80; v.p. Donaldson Lufkin Jenrette, 1982—87; various positions Goldman Sachs & Co., 1987—2002, gen. ptnr., 1992—99, mng. dir., 1999—2002; sr. advisor Stone Point Capital, LLC; mng. ptnr., COO Tiger Management, LLC, 2010—. Bd. dirs. Belk, Inc., 2005—, Internat. Paper Co., 2006—, Castle Point Capital Mgmt., LLC., 2006—; mem. exec. com. U. NC Investment Fund. Bd. trustees US Ski & Snowboard Team Found., Grand Teton Nat. Park Found., U. NC; chmn. bd. dirs. Episcopal HS. Republican. Episcopalian. Avocations: running, golf, mountain climbing. Mailing: Tiger Management LLC 101 Park Ave New York NY 10178 also: Stone Point Capital LLC 20 Horseneck Ln Greenwich CT 06830 also: Belk Inc 2801 W Tyvola Rd Charlotte NC 28217-4500 Office Phone: 704-357-1000. Office Fax: 704-357-1876. Business E-Mail: john_townsend@belk.com.

TOWNSEND, MILES AVERILL, aerospace and mechanical engineering educator; b. Buffalo, Apr. 16, 1935; s. Francis Devere and Sylvia (Wolpa) T.; children: Kathleen Townsend Hastings, Melissa, Stephen, Joel, Philip. BA, Stanford U., 1955; BS MechE, U. Mich., 1958; advanced cert., U. Ill., 1963, MS in Theoretical and Applied Mechanics, 1967; PhD, U. Wis., 1971. Registered profl. engr., Ill., Wis., Tenn., Ont. Project engr. Sundstrand, Rockford, Ill., 1959-63, Twin Disc Inc., Rockford, 1963-65, 67-68; sr. engr. Westinghouse Electric Corp., Sunnyvale, Calif., 1965-67; instr., fellow U. Wis., Madison, 1968-71; assoc. prof. U. Toronto, Ont., Canada, 1971-74; prof. mech. engring. Vanderbilt U., Nashville, 1974-81; Wilson prof. mech. and aerospace engring. U. Va., Charlottesville, 1981—, chmn. dept., 1981-91. Ptnr., v.p. Endev Ltd., Can. and U.S., 1972—; cons. in field. Contbr. numerous articles on dynamics, design dynamical systems, controls and optimization to profl. jours.; 7 patents in field. Recipient numerous research grants and contracts. Fellow ASME, AAAS; mem. N.Y. Acad. Scis., Sigma Xi, Phi Kappa Phi, Pi Tau Sigma. Avocations: running, reading, music. Home: 212 Alderman Rd Charlottesville VA 22903-1704 Office: U Va Dept Mech and Aerospace Engring Thornton Hall Charlottesville VA 22903-2442 Business E-Mail: mat@virginia.edu.

TOWNSEND, WILLIAM JACKSON, lawyer; b. Grayson, Ky., June 4, 1932; s. Robert Glenn and Lois Juanita (Jackson) Townsend. BS, Wake Forest U., Winston-Salem, NC, 1954; student, U. Ky., Lexington, 1957, U. Louisville, 1958; JD, U. NC, Chapel Hill, 1960. Bar: NC 1965. Claims adjuster State Farm Ins. Co., 1963; pvt. practice, Fayetteville, NC, 1965—; pub. adminstr. Robeson County, NC, 1966; dir., treas. Colonial Foods, Inc., St. Paul, NC, 1959—; tax atty. City of Lumberton, 1966-67. Served as 1st lt. U.S. Army, 1954-56. Mem.: Cumberland County Bar Assn., NC State Bar, NC Bar Assn., Scabbard and Blade (pres.), Kiwanis (treas. Fayetteville 1973—82), Delta Theta Phi. Presbyterian. Office: PO Box 584 Fayetteville NC 28302 Office Phone: 910-483-4462.

TRABER, PETER GEORGE, medical educator, former academic administrator; b. Johnstown, NY, Apr. 6, 1955; m. K. Bobbi Traber; 2 children. Grad., U. Mich., 1977; MD, Wayne State U. Med. Sch., 1981; completed Mgmt. Devel Program for Physician Exec., Wharton Sch. U. Pa. Resident in internal medicine Northwestern U. Med. Sch., Chgo., fellow in gastroenterology, U. Mich. Sch. Medicine, faculty mem. Ann Arbor, 1987—92; chief gastroenterology U. Pa. Sch. Medicine, 1992—97, T. Grier Miller prof. medicine, 1993—97, Frank Wistar Thomas prof. and chair dept. medicine, 1997—2000, interim dean Phila., 2000; interim CEO U. Pa. Health Sys., Phila., 2000; sr. v.p. clinical devel. & med. affairs & chief med. officer GlaxoSmith-Kline, 2000—03; pres., CEO, prof. medicine Baylor Coll. Medicine, Houston, 2003—08, exec. dean, 2008—, pres. emeritus, 2008—. Bd. dirs. Tanox Inc., 2004—. Bd. trustees Baylor Coll. Medicine; bd. dirs. Houston Branch Fed. Res. Bank Dallas. Recipient Disting. Alumni award, Wayne State U. Sch. Medicine. Mem.: Assn. Am. Physicians, Am. Soc. Clinical Rsch., Am. Gastroenterologic Assn. Office: Baylor Coll Medicine BCM100 One Baylor Plz Houston TX 77030 Office Phone: 713-798-6363. Office Fax: 713-798-6353. E-mail: pgtraber@bcm.tmc.edu.

TRACY, JIM, state legislator; b. 1956; m. Trena Tracy; children: Chad, Craig, Connor. State senator Dist 16, Tenn., 2004—; vice chmn. Transp. Com., 2004—; sec. Edn. Com., 2004—; mem. Govt. Ops. Com., 2004—; state senate Tenn.; asst. floor leader Senate Repub. Caucas. Mem.: NCAA Basketball (official), Bedford Co. C. of C., Rutherford Co. C. of C., Bedford Co. Sch. Bd., NFIB Leadership Coun. Republican. Church Of Christ. Office: 106 Finch Ln Shelbyville TN 37160-2157 also: 2 Legislative Plz Nashville TN 37243-2016 Office Phone: 615-741-1066. Office Fax: 615-741-2255. Business E-Mail: sen.jim.tracy@capitol.tn.gov.

TRACY, MIKE, director; BA in Economics, Brown U.; MBA, U. Pa. Co-founder Fieldstone Mktg.; exec., consumer brand portfolio mgmt., mktg. Disney, Home Depot, Inc., PepsiCo, Inc., Lenox, Inc. Pres. Montgomery Acad. Found., 2009—; bd. trustee Montgomery Acad., 2009—. Office: Montgomery Academy 3240 Vaughn Rd Montgomery AL 36106 Office Phone: 334-272-8210. Office Fax: 334-277-3240.

TRAFICANTI, JOSEPH J., lawyer, food products executive; b. Cheyenne, Wyo., Feb. 11, 1951; s. Joseph John and Lodema LaVerne (Atwell) T.; m. Kathi McKee, June 7, 1974; 1 child, Nathan. BS, USAF Acad., 1974; JD, Creighton U., 1981. Bar: Nebr. 1981, US Dist. Ct. (dist. Nebr.) 1981, Colo. 1984. Fed. prosecutor, law prof., spl. counsel, staff of the sec. USAF, advanced through grades to maj.; chief legal counsel USAF Comiso Air Sta., Sicily, Italy; trial lawyer civil litig. USAF, commd. 2nd lt., 1974, pilot, 1974—78, prosecuter, 1981—82, def. atty., 1982—83; assoc. prof. law USAF Acad., Colo., 1983; mil. asst. and spl. counsel to USAF gen. counsel Pentagon; trial lawyer McGuire Woods, LLP, Richmond, Va., 1993—96; assoc. gen. counsel Owens & Minor, Inc., Richmond, Va., 1996—2007; sr. v.p., gen. counsel, chief compliance officer, corp. sec. Performance Food Group, 2004—09; sr. v.p., gen. counsel, chief compliance officer & corp. sec. United Natural Foods, Inc., 2009—. Briefer, rschr. mil. investment and estate planning USAF Acad., 1984. Assoc. editor Creighton U. Law Rev., 1979-81. Mem. ABA. Republican. Avocations: golf, hiking. Office: United Natural Foods Inc 313 Iron Horse Way Providence RI 02908 Office Phone: 401-528-8634. Business E-Mail: jtraficanti@unfi.com.

TRAINOR, CINDI, school librarian; BA in English, U. Ky., Lexington, 1992, MLIS, 1994; BFA, Ea. Ky. U., Richmond. Reference/technical services librarian Rend Lake Coll., Ina, Ill., 1994—95; desktop support/electronic resources librarian U. Ky. Libraries, Lexington, 1995—98, team leader, electronic resources/support, 1998—2001; dir. libr. & info. tech. Libraries of Claremont Colleges, Calif., 2001—07; coord. rsch. & instrnl. services divsn. Eastern Ky. U., 2007—08, coord. libr. tech. & data services divsn., 2008—. Spkr. in field. Mem. editl. bd.: Jour. Electronic Resources Librarianship, 2007—, Practical Academic Librarianship, 2009—; contbr. articles to profl. jours. Libr. vol. Lexington Montessori Sch., Ky., 2009—. Named to Movers & Shakers, Libr. Jour., 2011. Mem.: ALA, Libr. Info. Tech. Assn. (bd. mem. at-large 2010—), Ky. Libr. Assn. Office: Eastern Kentucky University 103 Libraries Complex 521 Lancaster Ave Richmond KY 40475 Office Phone: 659-622-2033. Business E-Mail: cindi.trainor@eku.edu.

TRAMMELL, BRADLEY ELLIS, lawyer; b. Opelika, Ala., Jan. 11, 1961; s. Herman Bruce and Laura Elizabeth Trammell; m. Katherine Farrell McClintock, Apr. 11, 1992; children: William McClintock, Henry Ellis. BA cum laude, U. of South, Sewanee, Tenn., 1983; JD, U. Ala., Tuscaloosa, 1989. Bar: Tenn. 1989, Ala. 1991. Acct. exec. Travelers Ins. Co., Plantation, Fla., 1983—86; shareholder Baker, Donelson, Bearman, Caldwell & Berkowitz, Memphis, 1989—, chair Memphis office recruiting com., 2002—06. Campaign chmn. Travelers South Fla. offices United Way, 1984; chmn. ann. ptnrs. campaign Downtown YMCA, Memphis, 1993; jr. warden St. John's Episcopal Ch., Memphis, 2002, vestry mem., 2001—03. Recipient Best Lawyers award, Am. Comml. Litig., 2010. Mem.: ABA, Memphis Bar Assn. Young Lawyers (bd. dirs. 1991—93), Memphis Bar Assn., Ala. Bar Assn., Tenn. Bar Assn., Omicron Delta Kappa. Office: Baker Donelson Bearman Caldwell & Berkowitz 165 Madison Ave Ste 2000 Memphis TN 38103 Office Phone: 901-577-2121. Office Fax: 901-557-0781. Business E-Mail: btrammell@bakerdonelson.com.

TRAN, DAT T., lawyer, gas industry executive; 3 children. B in Acctg., U. Conn., 1990, MBA, 1993, JD, 1994. Various mgmt. positions Duke Energy, Kinder Morgan Inc.; asst. gen. counsel, CMS Energy's Energy Mktg. Unit CMS Mktg. Svcs. and Trading; joined AGL Resources, Inc., 2003, assoc. gen. counsel, unregulated businesses, 2007, Pivotal Energy Development (divsn. of AGL Resources), Sequent Energy Mgmt. Office: AGL Resources Inc Ten Peachtree Pl NE Atlanta GA 30309 Office Phone: 404-584-4000. Office Fax: 404-584-3714. Business E-Mail: dat.tran@aglresources.com.

TRAN, LONG TRIEU, industrial engineer; b. Saigon, Vietnam, Oct. 10, 1956; arrived in US, 1973; s. Nguyen Dinh and Thiet Thi (Nguyen) Tran; m. Khanh Thi-Hong Phan, Aug. 3, 1988. BSME with honors, U. Kans., 1976; MSME, MIT, 1980; MBA with honors, U. Louisville, 1993. Cert. quality engr., mfg. engr., project mgmt. profl. Tchg. asst. U. Kans., 1975-76, U. Calif., Berkeley, 1977; rsch. asst. Lawrence Berkeley Labs., 1977, MIT, 1977-80; libr. staff Harvard U. Med. Sch. Libr., 1977-78; mem. staff New England Deaconess Hosp., Boston, 1978-80; prodn. programming engr. GE, Cleve., 1980-81, advanced mfg. engr. Louisville, 1981-82, quality sys. engr., 1982-84, quality control engr., 1984-86, sr. quality info. equipment engr., 1986-89, sr. quality indsl. engr., 1990-94, sr. supplier tech. assistance engr., 1995-96, sr. advanced supplier quality engr., 1996-98, program mgr. purchased material quality, 1999, combo blackbelt leader supplier quality, 1999-2000, Six Sigma program mgr., 2000—02, sr. purchased material quality engr., 2003—. Exec. advisor Jr. Achievement, Inc., Louisville, 1983—84; monitor/reader Rec. for Blind, 1994—; fundraiser Dream Factory Inc., 1994—. Vol. NCCJ, 1994—, Clothe-A-Child, 1993—, Dare-To-Care, 1994—, Ronald McDonald House, 1994—. Mem.: ASME, AAAS, Heritage Found., Am. Assn. Individual Investors, Ctr. for Positive Thinking, Cato Inst., Ctr. Positive Thinking, Indsl. Computing Soc. (founding), N.Y. Acad. Scis., Am. Mgmt. Assn., Robotics Internat. (charter), Robot Inst. Am., Am. Prodn. and Inventory Control Soc., Computer and Automated Sys. Assn. (charter), Am. Soc. Quality Control, Instrument Soc. Am. (sr.), Soc. Mfg. Engrs. (sr.), U.S. Libr. Congress Assocs. (founding), Nat. Pks. Conservation Assn. (founding), Assn. Compassion (life), Internat. Platform Assn., PGA Tour Ptnrs. Club, Handyman Club Am. (life), Sigma Xi, Beta Gamma Sigma, Phi Kappa Phi, Tau Beta Pi, Pi Tau Sigma. Republican. Achievements include research in grinding processes and material surface analysis, mfg. project mgmt., supplier quality mgmt. Home: 3642 Windward Way Louisville KY 40220-1818 Office: Gen Electric Co Appliance Park AP1-162A Louisville KY 40225-0001 Office Phone: 502-452-7082. Business E-Mail: long.tran@ge.com.

TRAN, THOMAS L., health products executive; B in Acctg., Seton Hall U., South Orange, NJ; MBA in Fin., NYU, NYC. V.p. fin., contr. CIGNA Healthcare; CFO Blue Cross and Blue Shield Mass.; sr. v.p., CFO ConnectiCare, Inc.; sr. v.p., CFO Uniprise UnitedHealth Group, Inc.; pres., COO, CFO Careguide, Inc.; sr. v.p., CFO WellCare, 2008—. Office: WellCare Group 8725 Henderson Rd Renaissance One Tampa FL 33634 Office Phone: 813-290-6200.

TRANQUILL, CHRIS, information technology executive; BS, US Naval Acad. With CyberRep, Inc., Capital One; call ctr. dir., v.p., info. tech., v.p., ops., divsn. v.p. and region v.p. Affiliated Computer Services, Inc. (ACS) (acquired by Xerox Corp.), mng. dir., comm. and consumer goods, sr. v.p., group pres., Bus. Process Solutions, 2009—. Office: Affiliated Computer Services Inc 2828 N Haskell Dallas TX 75204 Office Phone: 214-841-6111. Business E-Mail: chris.tranquill@acs-inc.com.

TRANSOU, LYNDA LOU, advertising art administrator; b. Atlanta, Dec. 11, 1949; d. Lewis Cole Transou and Ann Lynette (Taylor) Putnam; m. Lue Gregg Loso, Oct. 25, 1991. BFA cum laude, U. Tex., 1971. Art dir. The Pitluk Group, San Antonio, 1971, Campbell, McQuien & Lawson, Dallas, 1973-74, Bozell & Jacobs, Dallas, 1974-75; art dir., ptnr. The Assocs., Dallas, 1975-77; art dir. Belo Broadcasting, Dallas, 1977-80; creative dir., v.p. Allday & Assocs., Dallas, 1980-85; owner Lynda Transou Advt. & Design, 1986—; cons., creative dir. Woodbine Devel. Corp., Dallas, 2001—. Recipient Merit award, N.Y. Art Dirs. Show, 1980, Gold award, Dallas Ad League, 1980, Silver award, 1980, 1981, 1982, 2 Merit awards, Houston Art Dirs. Club, 1978, Dallas Ad League, 1986, Merit award, Broadcast Designers Assn., 1980, Merit awards, Dallas Ad League, 1978, 1987, Silver award, Houston Art Dirs. Show, 1982, Gold award, Tex. Pub. Rels. Assn., 1985, N.Y. One Show, 1982, Creativity awrd, Art Direction mag., 1986, Print award, Regional Design Annual, 1988, 2 Gold Adrian awards, 1997, Katy award, Dallas Press Club, 2001. Dallas Soc. Visual Comm. (Bronze award 1980, Merit award 1978-86), Delta Gamma (historian 1969-70).

TRAUGER, ALETA ARTHUR, federal judge; b. Denver, 1945; BA in English magna cum laude, Cornell Coll., Iowa, 1968; MAT, Vanderbilt U., 1972, JD, 1976. Tchr., Tenn., Eng., 1970-73; assoc., law clk. Barrett, Brandt & Barrett, P.C., Nashville, 1974-77; asst. U.S. atty., first asst., chief of criminal divsn. Mid. Dist. Tenn., 1977-82, No. Dist. Ill., 1979-80; assoc. Hollins, Wagster & Yarbrough, P.C., Nashville, 1983-84; legal counsel Coll. of Charleston, SC, 1984-85; counsel, ptnr. Wyatt, Tarrant, Combs, Gilbert & Milom, Nashville, 1985-91; judge Tenn. Ct. of the Judiciary, 1987-93; chief of staff Mayor's Office, Nashville, 1991-92; bankruptcy judge U.S. Bankruptcy Ct. (mid. dist.) Tenn., Nashville, 1993-98; judge US Dist. Ct. (mid. dist.) Tenn., Nashville, 1998—. Mem. hearing panel bd. profl. responsibility Tenn. Supreme Ct., 1983-84, mem. adv. com. on rules of civil and appellate procedure, 1989-96; lectr. Vanderbilt U. Sch. Law, 1986-88, mem. Law Sch. alumni bd., 1989-92; master of bench Harry Phillips Am. Inn of Ct., 1990-94; mem. Internat. Women's Forum, 1993—, v.p. Tenn. chpt., 1996-97; trustee Cornell Coll., 1998-2007. Bd. dirs. Nashville Inst. for Arts, 1992-99, Miriam's Promise (adoption agy.), 1995-98, Renewal House, 1996-98; mem. Vanderbilt Law Sch. Nat. Coun., 2004-10. Fellow: Nashville Bar Found., Tenn. Bar Found. (life), Am. Bar Found. (life); mem.: FBA (v.p. 1983—84, 1985—86), ABA, Dist. Judges Assn. 6th Cir. (pres. 2008—09), Nat. Conf. Bankruptcy Judges (chmn. ethics com. 1994—98), Fed. Judges Assn., Nat. Assn. Women Judges (liaison to ABA commn. on the status of women in the profession 2000—01), Tenn. Lawyers Assn. for Women (v.p. 1988—89, pres. 1989—90, bd. dirs. 1990—91), Lawyers Assn. for Women (pres. 1982—83, bd. dirs. 1983—84, 1986—88), Nashville Bar Assn. (bd. dirs. 1984, 1989—91). Office: 825 US Courthouse 801 Broadway Nashville TN 37203-3816 Office Phone: 615-736-7143.

TRAVIS, ANTONIO D. (TONY TRAVIS), career military officer; b. 1968; m. Andrea Lawrence; children: Brittany, Amanda, Emily. Svc. with USMC, 1985—93, USAF, 1993—, rose through ranks to chief master sgt., sr. combat controller, chief enlisted mgr. Air Force Spl. Ops. Training Ctr. Hurlburt Field, Fla. Named one of The 100 Most Influential People in the World, TIME mag., 2010. Achievements include as one of the first US military members on the ground at the international airport in Port au Prince, Haiti 30 hours after the 2009 earthquake, led a team of special tactics Airmen for 12 days, 24 hours a day, running the airport without computers or electricity; led the largest single-runway operation in history, using hand-held radios to control thousands of aircraft and a card table set up next to the airport's runway as the air traffic control tower; coordinating with Miami FAA officials via text messaging on his Blackberry, his ingenuity paid massive dividends as priority aircraft transited the small airport, delivering lifesaving water, food and medical supplies. Office: Air Force Special Operations Training Center 220 Cody Ave Hurlburt Field FL 32544 Office Phone: 850-884-5515.

TRAVIS, JAY A., III, lawyer; b. McComb, Miss., June 8, 1940; s. J.A. and Katharine (Brennan) T., Jr.; m. Judith Thompson, Sept. 8, 1965; children: Kathy, John E., William. BBA, U. Miss., 1962, JD, 1965. Bar: Miss. 1965, US Dist. Ct. (so. dist.) Miss. 1967, US Ct. Appeals (5th cir.) 1970. Assoc. Thompson, Alexander & Crews, Jackson, Miss., 1967-69; ptnr. Butler, Snow, O'Mara, Stevens & Cannada, Jackson, 1969—. Chmn. Miss. Law Inst., 1974; pres. Estate Planning Coun. Miss., 1975-76. Mem. vestry, cathedral warden St. Andrew's Episc. Ch., 1983-87. Capt. JAGC, USAR, 1965-73; bd. dirs U. of Miss. Found., 1999-2007. Fellow Am. Coll. Trust and Estate Counsel (bd. regents, 1994-00, state chmn. 1987-92) Am. Coll. Trust and Estate Counsel Found. (bd. dirs. 2006—10), Am. Bar Found.; mem. ABA (fellow young lawyers sect.), Miss. State Bar (pres. young lawyers sect. 1975-76), Miss. Bar Assn. (chmn. estates and trusts sect. 1987-88), Hinds County Bar Assn. (pres. 1988-89), River Hills Club, Phi Delta Phi. Office: PO Box 6010 Ridgeland MS 39158-6010 Office Phone: 601-948-5711. Business E-Mail: jay.travis@butlersnow.com.

TRAVIS, ROBERT M., lawyer; b. Lyons, Ga., Dec. 12, 1945; BA, Univ. NC, Chapel Hill, 1968; JD, Univ. Ga., 1972. Bar: Ga. 1972. Ptnr., Litig. Dept. Powell Goldstein LLP, Atlanta. Editor (assoc.): Ga. Law Rev. Vice chmn. bd., chmn. devel. com. YMCA, Ga.; mem. Episcopal Diocese Atlanta Registrar, 1988—90. Mem.: ABA, State Bar Ga., Def. Rsch. Inst., Ga. Def. Lawyers Assoc. (former chair litig. dept.), Ga. Def. Lawyers Assn. (pres., past pres.), Atlanta Bar Assn., Lawyers Club Atlanta, Bleckley Inns of Ct. (Master), U. NC Alumni Assn. (life), YMCA (vice chmn. bd. Ga. chpt., chmn. devel. com.), Phi Delta Phi. Office: Bryan Cave LLP 1 Atlantic Ctr 14th Fl 1201 W Peachtree St NW Atlanta GA 30309-3488 Home Phone: 404-315-0089; Office Phone: 404-572-6646. Office Fax: 404-572-6999. Business E-Mail: robert.travis@bryancave.com.

TRAVIS, TONI-MICHELLE C., political scientist, educator; d. Mark E. and Ada Deans Chapman; m. Theodore W. Travis. BA, Bard Coll., Annandale-on-Hudson, NY, 1969; MA, U. Chgo., 1973, PhD, 1983. Asst. prof., govt. George Mason U., Fairfax, Va., 1984—90, asst. dean, Coll. Arts & Scis., 1993—95, host, prodr., Capital Region Roundtable, 1998—2002, assoc. prof., govt., 1990—2004; vis. prof. Simmons Coll., Boston, 1998—2000. Pres. Women's Caucus, Washington, 1994—95. Co-author: The Meaning of Difference, 1996; author: 4th edit., 2005, Virginia Almanac of Politics, 2006; editor: (book series) Race and Politics, 1995—2002; co-editor: Virginia Almanac of Politics, 2005. Active Higher Edn. Group, Washington, 1997—2003; bd. dirs. Make Women Count, Richmond, Va., 1998—2000; bd. govs. Bard Coll. Alumni Assn., 2004—. Fellow, Rothermere Am. Inst., Oxford U., 2007—; John Bard scholar, Bard Coll., 1968, Ford Found fellow, U. Chgo., 1969—73, Fenwick fellow, George Mason U., 2006—07. Mem.: Com. on Internat. Polit. Sci., Nat. Capital Area Polit. Sci. Assn. (pres. 1994—95), Am. Polit. Sci. Assn. (coun. mem. 1994—96, mem. com. on internat. polit. sci. 2003—), Fairfax Com. of 100. Avocation: walking. Office: Dept Pub and Internat Affairs George Mason Univ MS 3F4 4400 University Dr Fairfax VA 22030 Business E-Mail: ttravis@gmu.edu.

TRAXLER, WILLIAM BYRD, JR., federal judge; b. Greenville, SC, May 1, 1948; s. William Byrd and Bettie (Wooten) Traxler; m. Patricia Alford, Aug. 21, 1972; children: William Byrd III, James McCall. BA, Davidson Coll., 1970; JD, U. SC, 1973. Assoc. William Byrd Traxler, Greenville, 1973—75; asst. solicitor 13th Jud. Ct., Greenville, 1975—78, dep. solicitor, 1978—81, solicitor, 1981—85, resident cir. judge, 1985—92; US Dist. judge Dist. of SC, Greenville, 1992—98; judge US Ct. Appeals (4th cir.), Greenville, 1998—, chief judge, 2009—. Recipient Outstanding Svc. award, Solicitors Assn., SC, 1987, Leadership award, Probation, Parole & Pardon Svcs., SC, 1990. Office: US Ct Appeals 300 E Washington St Ste 222 Greenville SC 29601-2431

TRAYNHAM, JAMES GIBSON, chemist, educator; b. Broxton, Ga., Aug. 5, 1925; s. James G. and Eddie Louise (Greer) T.; m. Margaret A. Egert, 1948; children: David F., Peter C.; m. Gresdna A. Doty, 1980. Student, South Ga. Coll., 1942-43; BS, U. N.C., 1946; PhD, Northwestern U., 1950. Instr. Northwestern U., 1949-50; asst. prof. Denison U., 1950-53; mem. faculty La. State U., Baton Rouge, 1953—, prof. chemistry, 1963-88, prof. emeritus, 1988—, chmn. dept. chemistry, 1968-73, vice chancellor for advanced studies and rsch., dean Grad. Sch., 1973-81. Postdoctoral research fellow Ohio State U., 1951-53; oral history cons. Chem. Heritage Found., 1997-2002. Author: Organic Nomenclature: A Programmed Introduction, 1966, 6th edit., 2009; editor: Essays on the History of Organic Chemistry, 1987; contbr. articles to profl. jours. Bd. dirs. Council Grad. Schs. in U.S., 1981. Recipient Petroleum Research Fund-Am. Chem. Soc. Type D award Eidg. Technische Hochschule, Zurich, Switzerland, 1959-60; Charles E. Coates award Baton Rouge sects. Am. Chem. Soc. and Am. Inst. Chem. Engrs., 1965; NATO sr. fellow in sci. Universität des Saarlandes, Saarbrücken, Fed. Republic Germany, 1972; named to Hall of Distinction, La. State U. Coll. Basic Scis., 2007. Fellow Am. Chem. Soc. (past councilor, past chmn. Baton Rouge sect., chmn. divsn. history of chemistry 1988); mem. La. Acad. Sci., Internat. Union Pure and Applied Chemistry (former titular mem. commn. on nomenclature of organic chemistry, sec. 1994-99), Phi Beta Kappa, Sigma Xi, Phi Lambda Upsilon, Phi Kappa Phi (past pres. La. State U. chpt.). Home: 122 Highland Trace Dr Baton Rouge LA 70810-5061

TREADAWAY, BENJAMIN (ALLEN TREADAWAY), state legislator; b. Sept. 25, 1961; m. Susan Treadaway; children: Kelsey, Erin, Tyler, Ally, Cody. Recipient Peace Officers Stds. and Tng. Commn., Birmingham Police Acad. Police lt. City of Birmingham; mem. Dist. 51 Ala. House of Reps., Montgomery, 2006—. Past dir. Toys for Tots; dir. Birmingham Retirement & Relief Sys.; mem. Enon Bapt. Ch.

Named Officer of Yr. City of Birmingham, 1992, Most Outstanding Mem. of Yr. Ala. State Fraternal Order Police, 2004-05. Mem. Birmingham Fraternal Order Police (past pres.). Republican. Baptist. Office: PO Box 126 Morris AL 35116 also: Ala House of Reps Ala State House 11 S Union St Rm 536-D Montgomery AL 36130 Office Phone: 205-254-1720, 334-242-7685. Business E-Mail: bsketa@aol.com.

TREADWAY, CHARLES L., electronics executive; BSEE, U. La.; MSEE, Clemson U.; MBA, Harvard U. Engr. Square D; pres., Groupo Tesa Mexico Yale Security Inc., Guadalajara, N.Mex.; pres., automotive Prettl Internat.; pres., CEO custom sensors & tech. Schneider Electric; sr. v.p., group pres., elec. Thomas & Betts Corp., 2009—11, pres., COO, 2011—12, CEO, 2012—. Office: Thomas & Betts Corp 8155 T&B Blvd Memphis TN 38125 Office Phone: 901-252-8000. Office Fax: 901-680-5112. Business E-Mail: charles.treadway@tnb.com.

TREADWELL, MARC THOMAS, federal judge; b. Ft. Campbell, Ky., 1955; BA, Valdosta State U., Ga., 1978; JD, Mercer U., Macon, Ga., 1981. Assoc. Kilpatrick & Cody, Atlanta, 1981—85, Chambless, Hidgon & Carson LLP, Macon, 1985—87, ptnr., 1987—2000, Adams, Jordan & Treadwell PC, Macon, 2000—10; judge US Dist. Ct. (mid. dist.) Ga., 2010—. Adj. prof. Mercer U. Walter F. George Sch. Law, 1998—2010. Fellow: Internat. Acad. Trial Lawyers; mem.: William Augustus Bootle Inn of Ct. (pres.). Mailing: William A Bootle Fed Bldg & US Courthouse PO Box 128 475 Mulberry St Macon GA 31202 also: CB King US Courthouse 201 W Broad Ave Albany GA 31701

TREAT, GREG, state legislator; m. Marissa Treat; children: Mason, Cooper, Olivia. BA in Polit. Sci. and History, U. Okla. Legis. dir. to Lt. Gov. Mary Fallin; legis. advisor to Representative Fred Morgan; regional dir. to Senator Tom Corburn's re-election campaign; field representative and state govt. liaison to Tom Corburn; mem. Dist. 47 Okla. State Senate, 2011—. Cortez A.M. Ewing Fellowship, 1999. Republican. Avocations: hunting, fishing, reading. Mailing: 2300 N Lincoln Blvd Rm 530 Oklahoma City OK 73105 Office Phone: 405-521-5632. Business E-Mail: treat@oksenate.gov.

TREBILCOCK, JAMES R., beverages industry executive; m. Janet Trebilcock; children: Scott, Zachary. BA in Mktg., MBA in Mktg., Mich. State U. Mktg. positions, Big G cereal divsn. Gen. Mills Inc.; various regional sales and mktg. positions Coca-Cola Bottling Co. Consol.; dir., promotions, v.p., mktg., sr. v.p., mktg. svcs. Dr. Pepper Snapple Group Inc. (formerly Cadbury Schweppes Americas Beverages), Cherry 7 UP brand mgr., 1987, sr. v.p., consumer mktg., 2003—08, exec. v.p., mktg., 2008—. Office: Dr Pepper Snapple Group Inc 5301 Legacy Dr Plano TX 75024 Office Phone: 972-673-7000. Office Fax: 972-673-7980. Business E-Mail: james.trebilcock@drpeppersnapplegroup.com.

TREBILCOCK, JOHN, state legislator; b. Tulsa, Okla., Aug. 17, 1973; son of Jon Trebilcock & Sondra Phillips T; BA, Okla. State Univ., 1996; JD, Univ. Tulsa, 2001. Former high sch. history tchr.; atty. of counsel Sprouse, Shrader, Smith PC; mem. Dist. 98 Okla. House of Representatives, 2003—. Broken Arrow Schools, New Teacher of Year, 1997; Tulsa Univ, Order of Curule Chair. Oklahoma State Univ Alumni Association; Jaycees; Broken Arrow Chamber of Commerce; Tulsa Co Republican Men's Club. Republican. Mailing: 2300 N Lincoln Blvd Rm 404 Oklahoma City OK 73105 Address: 1721 S 1st Pl Oklahoma City OK 73105 Home: 7425 E Jackson St Broken Arrow OK 74014-7310 Office Phone: 406-557-7362, 918-258-8184. E-mail: johntrebilcock@okhouse.gov.

TREFIL, JAMES STANLEY, physicist researcher author; b. Chgo., Sept. 10, 1938; s. Stanley James and Sylvia (Mestek) T.; m. Elinor Pletka; children: James Karel, STefan; m. Jeanne L. Waples, Oct. 17, 1972; children: Dominique, Flora, Tomas; m. Wanda T. O'Brien, 2005. BS, U. Ill., 1960; BA, MA, Oxford U., Eng., 1962; MS, Stanford U., 1964, PhD, 1966. Rsch. assoc. Stanford (Calif.) Linear Accelerator Ctr., 1966; Air Force Office Sci. Rsch. postdoctoral fellow CERN, Geneva, 1966-67; asst. prof. physics U. Ill., Urbana, 1968-70; assoc. prof. physics U. Va., Charlottesville, 1970-75, prof. physics, 1975-87, Univ. prof. physics, 1987; C.J. Robinson prof. physics George Mason U., Fairfax, Va., 1987—. Sci. adv. bd. Nat. Pub. Radio; sci. cons. Smithsonian Mag.; tech. cons. Am. Heritage Dictionary; cons. Adler Planetarium. Author: Dictionary of Cultural Literacy, 2002, 3rd edit., 1993, Reading the Mind of God, 1989, Science Matters, 1991, 2nd edit., 2009, Facts of Life: Science and the Abortion Controversy, 1992, A Scientist in the City, 1994, The Sciences: An Integrated Approach, 1995, 6th edit., 2009, Edge of the Unknown, 1996, Are We Unique, 1997, Human Nature, 2004, Why Science, 2008, Science in World History, 2011; contbg. editor: USA Weekend Principle Science; illustrator Atlas, 2013. Chmn. Beta Kappa Sci. Book Award Com. NSF fellow Stanford U., 1966; recipient Sci. Journalism award AAAS-Westinghouse, 1983; John Simon Guggenheim fellow, 1987-88; Marshall scholar Oxford U., 1962; recipient Gemant award Am. Inst. Physics, 2007, Sci. Journalism award, 2008. Fellow Am. Phys. Soc., World Econ. Forum, Am. Assn. For Advancement Sci. Office: George Mason U 207 E Bldg Fairfax VA 22030 Office Phone: 703-993-2183.

TREFRY, JOHN H., III, chemical oceanographer, educator; b. Boston, Sept. 2, 1947; s. John H. Trefry, Jr. and Phyllis Nelson Trefry; m. Susan E. Page, July 20, 1969; 1 child, Caroline Page Kempf; 1 child, John H. IV. BA, Syracuse U., 1969; MS in Chem. Oceanography, Tex. A&M U., 1973, PhD in Chem. Oceanography, 1977. Asst. prof. Fla. Inst. Tech., Melbourne, Fla., 1978—82, assoc. prof., 1982—87, prof., 1987—. Vis. scientist MIT, Cambridge, Mass., 1987—88. Editor (assoc.): Marine Chemistry. Grant, NSF, 1990—94, NOAA, 1977—85, 1995—2000, US Dept Interior, 1997—. Mem.: Coastal Soc., Outer Continental Shelf Scientific Com., U.S. Dept. of Interior, Minerals Mgmt. Svc., Fla. Acad. Sci. (pres. 2005—07, medalist 2002), Am. Chem. Soc., Am. Geophys. Union. Achievements include first to co-discover deep-sea hydrothermal vents in the Atlantic Ocean; show positive impact of banning lead in gasoline to the Mississippi River and Gulf of Mexico; extensive global research in environmental studies of offshore oil exploration and production. Office: Florida Inst Tech 150 W Univ Blvd Melbourne FL 32901 Office Fax: 321-674-7212. Business E-Mail: jtrefry@fit.edu.

TRELEASE, ALLEN WILLIAM, historian, educator; b. Boulder, Colo., Jan. 31, 1928; s. William, Jr. and Helen (Waldo) T.; children: William C. (dec. 1990), Mary E., John A. AB, U. Ill., 1950, MA, 1951; PhD, Harvard U., 1955. Mem. faculty Wells Coll., Aurora, NY, 1955-67, prof. history, 1965-67, chmn. dept. history and govt., 1963-67; prof. history U. NC, Greensboro, 1967-94, head dept., 1984-92, prof. emeritus, 1994—. Author: Indian Affairs in Colonial New York: The Seventeenth Century, 1960, White Terror: The Ku Klux Klan Conspiracy and Southern Reconstruction, 1971, Reconstruction: The Great Experiment, 1971, The North Carolina Railroad, 1849-1871, and the Modernization of North Carolina, 1991, Changing Assignments: A Pictorial History of the U. of N.C. at Greensboro, 1991, Making North Carolina Literate: The University of North Carolina at Greensboro, from Normal School to Metropolitan University, 2004. Mem. Am., So. Hist. assns., Orgn. Am. Historians, Hist. Soc. NC (pres. 1986-87), AAUP, Phi Beta Kappa, Phi Kappa Phi, Phi Eta Sigma, Phi Kappa Psi. Personal E-mail: atrelease@triad.rr.com.

TREMAINE, THOMAS R., finance company executive; b. Fla. Attended, U. South Fla., St. Petersburg Jr. Coll. Staff acct. Jacob & Mills, PA, St. Petersburg, Fla.; contr., treas., sr. v.p. Raymond James & Associates, Inc., tax cons., 1983, exec. v.p., ops & administration, 2009—. Mem., ops. com. Security Industry Assn., mem.; mem. BayCare Health System; bd. dirs. St. Anthony's Health Care; bd. dirs., treas. Children's Dream Fund. Office: Raymond James & Associates Inc 880 Carillon Pkwy Saint Petersburg FL 33716-1102 Office Phone: 727-567-1000. Office Fax: 727-567-8915. Business E-Mail: thom.tremaine@raymondjames.com.

TREMBLEY, DAVE, professional baseball coach; m. Patti Trembley; 1 child, Kevin. BPE, EdM, SUNY, Brockport; grad. student in Sports Psychology, Pa. State U. Tchr., baseball coach Daniel Murphy HS, LA, 1977—79; head baseball coach Antelope Valley Coll., Calif., 1980—84; LA area scout, minor league instr. Chgo. Cubs Orgn.; coach Wytheville, Appalachian League, Va.; minor league mgr. Kinston Eagles, Carolina League, 1986, Navajoa, Mex. Pacific League, 1986—87, Harrisburg Senators, Ea. League, 1987—89; third base coach Magallanes, Venezuelan Winter League, 1987—89; dir. day-to-day ops., minor league complex and spring tng. facility Pitts. Pirates, Bradenton, Fla., 1990; minor league mgr. Charleston Rainbows, South Atlantic League, 1991—92, Wichita Wranglers, Tex. League, 1993, Daytona Cubs, Fla. State League, 1995—96, Orlando Rays, So. League, 1997, West Tenn. Diamond Jaxx, So. League, 1998—99, Iowa Cubs, Pacific Coast League, 2000, Daytona Cubs, Fla. State League, 2001—02, Bowie Baysox, Ea. League, 2003—04, Ottawa Lynx, Internat. League, 2005—06; bullpen coach, bench coach, field coord. Balt. Orioles, 2007, mgr., 2007—10; field dir. Atlanta Braves, 2010—12; bench coach Houston Astros, 2013—. Named Ea. League Mgr. of Yr., 1987, Fla. State League Mgr. of Yr., 1995, So. League Mgr. of Yr., 1999; named one of Minor League Baseball's Top Five Mgrs. of the Previous 20 Yrs., Baseball Am., 2001. Office: Houston Astros 501 Crawford St Houston TX 77002

TREML, VLADIMIR GUY, economist, educator; b. Kharkov, USSR, Mar. 27, 1929; came to U.S., 1950, naturalized, 1953; s. Guy Alexey and Lydia Vladimir (Timofeev) T.; m. Emma Miro, July 12, 1952; children— Irene Treml Cagney, Tatiana, Alexey. BA in Econs, Bklyn. Coll., 1955; MA in Econs, Columbia U., 1956; PhD in Econs, U. N.C., 1963. Dept. supr. Bache & Co., NYC, 1953-58; research asso. Inst. for Social Scis., U. N.C., Chapel Hill, 1958-61; asso. prof. econs. Franklin and Marshall Coll., 1961-66; research asso. Inst. Study USSR, Munich, Germany, 1966-67; prof. econs. Duke U., 1967—; dir. Ctr. for Slavic Studies U.S. Dept. Edn. of Duke U., 1991—. Cons. in field; expert Dept. Commerce, The World Bank, other fed. agys., 1971—; vis. Ford research prof. U. Calif., Berkeley, 1984-85; vis. research prof. U. Hokkaido, Sapporo, Japan, 1985. Author: (with others) Structure of the Soviet Economy, 1972, Input-Output Analysis and the Soviet Economy, 1975, Western Sovietology in the Soviet Union, 1999; contbr. reports to publs. of Joint Econ. Com., U.S. Congress; contbr. articles to profl. publs.; editor: Soviet Economic Statistics, 1972; editor, contbg. author: Studies in Soviet Input-Output Analysis, 1977, Alcohol in the USSR, 1982; contbg. editor: Soviet Economy Jour. Trustee Nat. Council for Soviet and East European Research, Inc., Washington, 1978-84. Served with USMC, 1951-53. Grantee Ford Found., 1972-81, Dept. Def.-Advanced Rsch. Project Agy., 1975-76, Dept. State, 1976-77, Dept. Def., 1985-90, Georgetown U., 1984-86, Olin Found., 1989, Internat. Rsch. and Exch. Bd., 1993-96, Nat. Coun. for Eurasian Rsch., 1996-98; Fulbright fellow Moscow U., 1992. Mem. So. Econ. Assn., Am. Econ. Assn., Assn. Comparative Econ. Studies (exec. com. 1972-74), Am. Assn. Advancement Slavic Studies, So. Conf. on Slavic Studies (pres. 1977-78), Phi Beta Kappa. Democrat. Eastern Orthodox. Home: 3719 Albritton Dr Durham NC 27705-7381 Office Phone: 919-684-1800, 919-660-1800. Business E-Mail: treml@econ.duke.edu.

TRENGA, ANTHONY JOHN, federal judge; b. Wilmerding, Pa., 1949; m. Rita Marie FlorCruz; children: Elizabeth, Anthony. AB, Princeton U., NJ, 1971; JD, U. Va. Sch. Law, 1974. Bar: Va. 1974. Law clerk to Hon. Ted Dalton US Dist. Ct. (we. dist.) Va., 1974—75; assoc. Sachs, Greenebaum & Tayler, Washington, 1975—82, ptnr., 1982—87, Hazel & Thomas, P.C., Fairfax, Va., 1987—98; chmn. litigation dept. Miller & Chevalier Chartered, 1998—2008; judge US Dist. Ct. (ea. dist.) Va., Alexandria, 2008—. Mem.: Am. Coll. Trial Lawyers. Office: US Dist Ct 401 Courthouse Sq Alexandria VA 22314 Office Phone: 703-229-2113.

TRENNEPOHL, GARY LEE, finance educator, academic administrator; b. Detroit, Dec. 6, 1946; s. Leo Donald and Wilma Mae (Tiensvold) T.; m. Sandra K. Yeager, June 9, 1968; children: Paige E., Adrienne A. BS, U. Tulsa, 1968; MBA, Utah State U., 1971; PhD, Tex. Tech. U., 1976. Asst. prof. aero. studies Tex. Tech. U., Lubbock, 1972-74; asst./assoc. prof. fin. Ariz. State U., Tempe, 1977—82; prof. U. Mo., Columbia, 1982-86, dir. Sch. Bus., 1984-86; prof., head dept. fin. Tex. A&M U., College Station, 1986-91, assoc. dean Coll. Bus., 1991-93, Peters prof. fin., 1992-95, exec. assoc. dean, 1994-95; dean Coll. Bus. Okla. State U., Stillwater, 1995-99; pres. Okla. State U. at Tulsa, 1999—2009, fin. prof., 2011—, ONEOK chair, fin., 2012. Mem. faculty options inst. Chgo. Bd. Options Exch., 1987—; chair Blue Cross/Blue Shield Okla.; adv. bd. Tulsa Air and Space Mus. Author: An Introduction to Financial Management, 1984, Investment Management, 1993; assoc. editor Jour. Fin. Rsch., 1983-96; contr. chpts. Encyclopedia of Investments, Options: Essential Concepts; contbr. articles to profl. jours. Trustee chair Okla. Tchrs. Retirement Sys., 2009—. Capt. USAF, 1968—74. Decorated Commendation medal with oak leaf cluster, Vietnam Svc. medal. Mem. Fin. Mgmt. Assn. (v.p. program 1993, pres. 1993-94). Lutheran. Office: Okla State U Tulsa 700 N Greenwood Ave Tulsa OK 74106-0702 Home Phone: 918-523-8563. Business E-Mail: gary.trennepohl@okstate.edu.

TRENT, B. KEITH, lawyer, energy executive; b. Little Rock, Oct. 16, 1959; m. Lucy Trent; 2 children. BSEE with honors, So. Methodist U., 1981; JD with high honors, U. Tex., 1987. Bar: Tex. 1987, US Ct. Appeals (5th cir.), US Supreme Ct., NC. Reservoir/prodn. engr. Arco Oil & Gas, Houston, 1982; atty. Jackson Walker, Dallas; ptnr. Snell Brannian & Trent, Dallas, 1991—2002; gen. counsel litig. Duke Energy, Charlotte, NC, 2002—05, group v.p., gen. counsel, sec., 2005, group exec., chief devel. officer, 2006, group exec., chief strategy and policy officer Charlotte, NC, 2006—07, group exec., chief strategy, policy and regulatory officer, 2007—09, group exec., pres. comml. bus., 2009—. Mem. exec. com. Internat. Inst. Conflict Prevention & Resolution; bd. dirs. NAM. Editor (assoc.): Tex. Law Rev. Bd. visitors Wake Forest U. Babcock Grad. Sch. Mgmt.; mem. Youth Edn. Coun. United Way of Ctrl. Carolinas. Mem.: Mecklenburg County Bar, NC State Bar, ABA, Assn. Corp. Counsel, Tex. State Bar, Dallas Bar Assn., Houston Bar Assn., Dallas Inn of Ct., Order of the Coif, Tau Beta Pi. Office: Duke Energy 526 S Church St Charlotte NC 28202-1904 Office Phone: 704-594-6200.

TRENT, ROBERT HAROLD, retired business educator; b. Norfolk, Va., Aug. 3, 1933; s. Floyd Murton and Myrtle Eugenia (White) T.; m. Joanne Bell, Aug. 17, 1951; 1 child, John Thomas BS, U. Richmond, 1963; PhD, U. N.C., 1968. Asst. prof. U. N.C., Chapel Hill, 1968-69; assoc. prof. commerce McIntire Sch. Commerce U. Va., Charlottesville, 1970-74, prof. commerce, 1975-84, Ralph A. Beeton prof. free enterprise, 1985-91; C. & P. Telephone Co. prof. commerce U. Va., Charlottesville, 1991-98, prof. commerce emeritus, 1998—. Co-author: Marketing Decision Making, 1976, 4th edit., 1988; editor: Developments in Management Information Systems, 1974 Mem.: Omicron Delta Kappa, Beta Gamma Sigma. Home Phone: 434-293-3761.

TREPP, GREGORY H., consumer products company executive; BS, U. Richmond; MBA, U. Conn. Interim pres., CEO The Kitchen Collection, Inc. (subs. NACCO Industries, Inc.), CEO, bd. dirs., 2009—10; dir., mktg. Hamilton Beach Brands, Inc. (subs. NACCO Industries, Inc.), 1998—99, v.p., product mgmt., 1999—2002, v.p., mktg., 2004—08, v.p., global mktg., 2008—10; pres., CEO, bd. dirs. Hamilton Beach Brands, Inc., 2010—. Office: Hamilton Beach Brands Inc 4421 Waterfront Dr Glen Allen VA 23060 Office Phone: 804-273-9777. Office Fax: 804-527-7142. Business E-Mail: greg.trepp@hamiltonbeach.com.

TRETHEWEY, NATASHA, poet, literature educator; b. Gulfport, Miss., 1966; d. Eric Trethewey and Gwendolyn Ann Turnbough; m. Brett Gadsden. BA in English, U. Ga., Athens; MA in English and Creative Writing, Hollins U., Roanoke, Va.; MFA in Poetry, U. Mass., Amherst. Asst. prof. English Auburn U., Ala., 1997—2001; assoc. prof. English, creative writing Emory U., Atlanta, Phyllis Wheatley disting. chair in poetry, Charles Howard Candler prof. English and creative writing; poet laureate of Miss., 2012—; US poet laureate cons. in poetry Libr. of Congress, Washington, 2012—. Vis. Lehman Brady joint chair prof. documentary and American studies Duke U. and U. NC-Chapel Hill, 2005—06; James Weldon Johnson fellow in African American studies Yale U. Beinecke Libr., New Haven, 2009—10; Louis D. Rubin writer-in-residence Hollis U., 2012. Author: Domestic Work, 2000 (Cave Canem Poetry prize, 1999, Miss. Inst. of Arts and Letters Book prize, 2001, Lillian Smith award for peotry, 2001), Bellocq's Ophelia, 2002, Native Guard, 2006 (Pulitzer Prize for Poetry, 2007), Beyond Katrina: A Meditation on the Mississippi Gulf Coast, 2010, Thrall, 2012; contbr. poetry to publs. including Agni, Am. Poetry Review, Callaloo, Gettysburg Review, Kenyon Review, New Engl. Review. Recipient Disting. Young Alumna award, U. Mass., Julia Peterkin award, Converse Coll., Grolier Poetry prize, Grolier Bookstore, Cambridge, Mass., Margaret Walker award for poetry, Poets and Writers mag. and QBR: The Black Book Rev., Jessica Nobel-Maxwell Meml. award for poetry, Am. Poetry Rev., Miss. Gov. Excellence in Arts award, 2008; named Ga. Woman of Yr., 2009; named to Fellowship of So. Writers, 2009, Ga. Writers Hall of Fame, 2011; fellow, John Simon Guggenheim Meml. Found., 2003, Nat. Endowment for the Arts, Ala. State Coun. on the Arts, Money for Women/Barbara Deming Meml. Fund; Bunting fellow, Radcliffe Inst. for Advanced Study, Harvard U., 2000—01. Office: Emory Univ Creative Writing Program 537 Kilgo Cir Atlanta GA 30322 Office Phone: 404-727-4683. Office Fax: 404-727-4672. E-mail: creativewriting@emory.edu.

TREVOR, ALEXANDER BRUEN, information technology consultant; b. NYC, Apr. 12, 1945; s. John B. Jr. and Evelyn (Bruen) T.; m. Ellen Ruth Armstrong, Sept. 21, 1974; children: Anne Wood Roebel, Alexander Jay Bruen. BS, Yale U., 1967; MS, U. Ariz., 1971. Rsch. asst. U. Ariz., Tucson, 1971; systems analyst CompuServe Inc., Columbus, Ohio, 1971-73, dir. systems, 1973-74, v.p., 1974-81, exec. v.p., chief tech. officer, 1981-96, also bd. dirs., 1985-96; pres. Nuvocom, Inc., Columbus, 1996—. Bd. dirs. State Auto Fin. Corp., Columbus. Author (software program) CB Simulator, 1980. Trustee Aviation Safety Inst., Worthington, Ohio. 1st lt. Signal Corps, U.S. Army, 1968-70, Vietnam. Decorated Bronze Star. Mem. IEEE (sr.), SAR (Fla.), Union Club (N.Y.). Republican. Episcopalian. Home: 1987 My Tern Ct Sanibel FL 33957

TREXLER, EDGAR RAY, minister, editor; b. Salisbury, NC, Sept. 17, 1937; s. Edgar Ray and Eula Belle (Farmer) T.; m. Emily Louise Kees, Aug. 21, 1960; children: David Ray, Mark Raymond, Karen Emily. AB, Lenoir-Rhyne U., 1959, LittD, 1978; MDiv, Luth. Theol. So. Sem., 1962; MA, Syracuse U., 1964; student, Boston U., 1960, Luth. World Fedn. Study Project, Geneva, 1977, Luth. World Fedn. Study Project, 1981; LittD (hon.), Midland Coll., 1990; DD, Wittenberg U., 1994. Ordained to ministry United Luth. Ch. Am., 1962; pastor St. John's Luth. Ch., Lyons, NY, 1962-65; features editor Luth. Mag., Phila., 1965-72, assoc. editor, 1972-78, editor, 1978-87, Chgo., 1988-99. Sec. Commn. Ch. Papers, Luth. Ch. Am., 1971-72, mem. staff team comm., 1972-78; chmn. Interch. Features, 1971-76; chmn. postal affairs com. Assoc. Ch. Press, 1983-90, Work Group on New Ch. Periodical, 1985-86; Evangelical Luth. Ch. Am. Cabinet of Execs., 1988-99. Author: Ways to Wake Up Your Church, 1969, Creative Congregations, 1972, The New Face of Missions, 1973, Mission in a New World, 1977, LWF/6, 1978, Anatomy of a Merger, 1991, High Expectations: Understanding the ELCA's Early Years, 1988-2002, 2003; mem. edit. adv. bd. The New World, Roman Cath. Archdiocese of Chgo., 1994-96. Pres. Lyons Coun. Chs., 1964; trustee Lenoir Rhyne U., 1975-84, 97-2006, Luth. Theol. So. Sem., 2003—09; vol. Interfaith Assistance Ministries, 2000-07; bd. dirs., 2007-13, Grace Lutheran Ch. Coun., 2011-13, pres., 2013. Recipient Disting. Alumnus award Lenoir-Rhyne U., 1991, Disting. Svc. award Newberry Coll., 1992, Bachman award for disting. leadership Luth. Theol. So. Sem., 1993, Mauney Leadership Awd., Luth. Theol. So. Seminary (alumni awd.), 1999, award of merit for editls. Assoc. Ch. Press, 1991, 98, award of merit for articles in mission mags. Assoc. Ch. Press, 1974, hon. life mem., Assoc. Ch. Press, 1999. Mem. Nat. Luth. Editors Assn. (pres. 1975-77). Home: 2504 Carriage Falls Ct Hendersonville NC 28791-1816 E-mail: etrexler@bellsouth.net.

TRIBBLE, DAVID, JR., state legislator; b. Decatur, Ga., Mar. 10, 1955; s. David and Dot Tribble; m. Leta Meole, Jan. 1, 1977; children: Perrin Tribble, Chandler Tribble, Blakely Tribble, David M. Tribble. BA, Presbyn. Coll., 1977; MPA, Clemson U., 2010. Mem. Med., Mil., Pub. & Mcpl. Affairs Com.; mayor Clinton, 1981—86; bd. dirs. Mcpl. Assn., 1982—85, Laurens County Healthcare System, 1988—92; chmn. Printing Industry of the Carolinas, 1991; candidate Dist. 15 SC House of Representatives, 2002; mem. Laurens County Coun., 2004—10; mem. Dist. 15 SC House of Representatives, 2011—. Recipient Outstanding Young Alumni, Presbyn. Coll., 1991. Office: South Carolina House of Representatives District 15 434A Blatt Bldg Columbia SC 29201 Address: PO Box 1456 Clinton SC 29325 Office Phone: 803-212-6890. E-mail: dtribble@charter.net.

TRICHE-MILAZZO, JANE MARGARET, federal judge; b. Napoleonville, La., Mar. 2, 1957; d. Risley and Clara Caballero Triche; m. Kurt J. Perque (div.); children: Richard G., Anne Louise, Jerome F., K. Joseph Jr.; m. John W. Milazzo, Jr., Sept. 25, 1999; stepchildren: John W. III, Jennifer S. BA magna cum laude, Nicholls State U., 1977; JD, La. State U., 1992. Bar: La. Paralegal Law Office Risley Triche, LLC, Napoleonville, 1986—89, law clk., 1989—92, assoc., 1992—98, ptnr., 1998—2008; judge 23rd Judicial Dist. Ct. La.,

Donaldsonville, 2008—11, US Dist. Ct. (eastern dist.) La., 2011—. Mem., del. Democratic State Ctrl. Com., 2000—04, 2004—. Mem.: ABA, La. Dist. Ct. Judges Assn., Nat. Assn. Women Judges, Baton Rouge Bar Assn., 23rd Judicial Dist. Bar Assn., Fifth Cir. Ct. Appeals Bar Assn., La. Trial Lawyers Assn., Assumption Parish Bar Assn. (former pres.), JDC Bar Assn., La. State Bar Assn. (chair Legis. Com. 2007). Democrat. Roman Catholic. Avocations: reading, cooking. Office: US District Court 500 Poydras St Rm C406 New Orleans LA 70130

TRIGIANI, LUCIA ANNA, lawyer; b. Easton, Pa. BA, St. Mary's Coll., 1980; JD, U. Richmond, 1983. Bar: Va. 1983, DC 1988. Prin. MercerTrigiani, Alexandria, Va. Mem. Va. Real Estate Bd., 1992—96, vice chair, 1995—96. Contbr. articles to law jours. Mem.: DC Bar Assn., Alexandria Bar Assn., Va. State Bar, Va. Bar Assn. (chair Real Estate Coun. 2001—04, bd. dirs. 2006—, chair bd. govs. 2009, pres.-elect 2010, pres. 2011, mem. Adminstrv. Law Coun.). Office: MercerTrigiani 112 S Alfred St Alexandria VA 22314 Office Phone: 703-837-5008. Office Fax: 703-837-5018. E-mail: pia.trigiani@mercertrigiani.com.

TRIMBLE, JAMES TRAVIS, JR., federal judge; b. Bunkie, La., Sept. 13, 1932; s. James T. Sr. and Mabel (McNabb) T.; m. Murel Elise Biles, Aug. 18, 1956; children: Elise Rumsey, Mary Olive Beacham, Martha McNabb Elliott, Sarah Trimble Moritz. Student, U. La., Lafayette, 1950-52; BA in Law, La. State U., 1955, LLB, 1956. Bar: La. 1956. With Gist, Murchison & Gist (now Gist, Methvin, Hughes & Munsterman), 1959-78, Trimble, Percy, Smith, Wilson, Foote, Walker & Honeycutt, 1979-86; magistrate US Dist. Ct. (we. dist.) La., 1986—91, judge, 1991—2002, sr. judge, 2002—. Lt. USAF, 1956-59. Mem. Southwest La. Bar Assn., La. Bar Assn., La. Bar Found. Office: US Dist Ct 611 Broad St Ste 237 Lake Charles LA 70601-4380 Office Phone: 337-437-3884.

TRIMBLE, PRESTON ALBERT, retired judge; b. Salina, Okla., Aug. 27, 1930; s. James Albert and Winnie Louella (Walker) T.; m. Patricia Ann Beadle; children: Todd, Beth, Amy. BA, U. Okla., 1956, LL.B., 1960. Bar: Okla. 1960. Practice law, 1960; asst. county atty. Cleveland County, Okla., 1960-62; county atty., 1962-67; dist. atty., 1967-79; dist. judge, 1979-91. Spl. instr. S.W. Center Law Enforcement Edn.; cons. prosecution mgmt. Mem. Jud. Council Okla.; chmn. Okla. Corrections Workshop; mem. planning com. Nat. Inst. Crime and Delinquency; mem. com. on multi-agy. problems in criminal justice Appellate Judges Conf. Bd. dirs. Okla. U. Crisis Ctr., 1970—, ARC, Lake Murray Conservation Assn.; pres. Okla. Amateur FTA; trustee Nat. Assn. Pretrial Svc. Agys. Resource Ctr., Sarkeys Found., 1994—. With USNR, 1948-52; col. USAFR. Mem. Okla., Cleveland County bar assns., Nat. Dist. Attys. Assn. (past pres.), Okla. Dist. Attys. Assn. (past pres.), Nat. Coll. Dist. Attys. (bd. regents), Am. Legion, Lions, Amateur Field Trial Clubs Am. (trustee 2002—, v.p. 2005—, pres. 2011) Democrat. Roman Catholic. Home: 1886 Trailview Dr Norman OK 73072-6655 Office: 231 S Peters Ave Norman OK 73069-6035 Office Phone: 405-321-8272. Personal E-mail: trimble@coxinet.net.

TRIMBLE, VANCE HENRY, retired newspaper editor; b. Harrison, Ark., July 6, 1913; s. Guy L. and Josephine (Crump) T.; m. Elzene Miller, Jan. 9, 1932; 1 dau., Carol Ann. Student pub. schs., Wewoka, Okla. Cub reporter Okemah (Okla.) Daily Leader, 1928; worked various newspapers in Okmulgee, Muskogee, Tulsa and, Okla.; successively reporter, rewrite man, city editor Houston Press, 1939-50, mng. editor, 1950-55; news editor Scripps-Howard Newspaper Alliance, Washington, 1955-63; editor Ky. Post and Times-Star, Covington, 1963-79. Author: The Uncertain Miracle, 1974, Sam M. Walton, 1990, (biography) E.W. Scripps, 1992, Frederick Smith of Federal Express, 1993, An Empire Undone: Rise and Fall of Chris Whittle, 1995, Alice & J.F.B.-The Hundred Year Saga of Two Seminole Chiefs, 2006, Choctaw Kisses Bullets & Blood, 2007; co-author: Happy Chandler Autobiography, 1989; editor: Scripps-Howard Handbook, 1981. Trustee Scripps-Howard Found., 1974-79. Recipient Pulitzer prize for nat. reporting, 1960, Raymond Clapper award, 1960, Sigma Delta Chi award for disting. Washington correspondence, 1960, Frank Luther Mott award for journalism book rsch. U. Mo., 1993; named to Okla. Journalism Hall of Fame, 1974. Mem. Am. Soc. Newspaper Editors, Nat. Press Club (Washington), Press Club (Houston), Wewoka Country Club. Baptist. Home: 25 Oakhurst Rd Wewoka OK 74884-3714 Personal E-mail: vhtrimble@aol.com.

TRINGALE, ANTHONY ROSARIO, insurance executive; b. Syracuse, NY, Apr. 20, 1942; s. Anthony and Assunta Maria Cerio Tringale; children: Anthony William, Michael Paul, Mark David, Amber Marie. BSFS, Georgetown U., 1967. CLU. Office mgr. trainee NY Life Ins. Co. No. Va., 1965-66, office mgr. Fairfax, Va., 1966, field underwriter, 1966-68; mgmt. asst. home office NY Life Ins. Co., NYC, 1973, gen mgr. Pitts., 1973-76; gen. mgr. Acacia Mut. Life Ins. Co., Annandale, Va., 1976-83, fin. and ins. planner, mgmt. and mktg. cons., 1983-86; from field rep. to mktg. com. Acacia Mut. Life, Annandale, Va., 1983-86; prin. Benefits-By-Design, Fairfax, Va., 1986—; pres. Acacia Prodn. Clubs, 1984, 86. Mem. steering com. Entrepreneurship Forum, Washington, 1980-; founding bd. mem. Commonwealth Va. DECA Found., 2003-; nat. adv. bd. Entrepreneurship Inst., Columbus, Ohio, 1985—; mem. supts. bus. and industry adv. coun. Fairfax County Pub. Schs., 1989-2004, mem. mktg edn. adv. bd., 1980-2004, chmn. 1983-84, 90-91; lectr. in field. Contbr. articles in field of personal and bus. fin. strategies to Md. Bus. Observer, Washington Bus. Jour., NALU's Life Assoc. News; radio host Basically Bus. Sta. WGMS-FM, Washington, 1988-91. Trustee SME-1 Accreditation Inst. U. Memphis, 1990—99, Syracuse U., 1995—99; past liaison rep. Am. Soc. CLUs, Bryn Mawr, Pa., 1988—98; arbitrator Fairfax County Dept. Consumer Affairs; pres., bd. dir., exec. com. The Jeane Dixon Children to Children Found., 1980—; chmn. VIP panel DC, 1988—92, Vt., 1988—92; pres. VIP panel, DC, 1992—94, Va., 1992—94, Birch Pond Homeowners Assn., 1998—2000; bd. dir., exec. com., pres. United Cerebral Palsy of D.C. and No. Va., 1985—2006; pres., adv. bd. Fairfax County Corps of Salvation Army, 1996—2004, Front Royal Corps, 2004—, elected bd. mem., life mem. emeritus, 2011; pres. United Cerebral Palsy of D.C. and No. Va., 2002; dir. at large Nat. Christopher Columbus Quincentary Jubilee Adv. Bd., 1995—; active Nat. Italian-Am. Found. Coun. of 1000, 1989—; mem. Italian Am. Leaders Com. Venture Clinic; bd. mem. emeritus, 2011; founding vice chmn. Fairfax Orgn. Christians/Jews United in Svc.; lector, extraordinary minister Basilica Nat. Shrine Immaculate Conception, 1980—2003; bd. dirs., v.p. exec. com., chmn. grants com. No. Va. Cmty. Found., 1979—2004; bd. dir. Summer Opera Theater Co., 1996—98, Nat. Cath. Cmty. Found., 1996—97; adv. bd., grants com. No. Va. Cmty Found., 2004—12; adv. bd. Salvation Army, Fairfax, Va., 1995—2004; adv. bd., life mem. Front Royal Waren County Corps., 2004—; bd. dirs. edn. and conf. ctr. 4-H, Front Royal, Va., 2007—. Recipient 2000 Crystal award No. Va. Cmty. Found., Cmty. Svc. award NAACP, 2013, Citizen of Yr., 2013. Mem. No. Va. Soc. CLUs (past pres.), Am. Soc. CLUs, No. Va. Assn. Life Underwriters (treas. 1972, nat. com. 1997-99, Pres.' Cup 1991-92), Assn. Advanced Life Underwriting, Sales and Mktg. Execs. Met. Washington (pres. 1979-80, 95-97, treas. 1989-92, bd. dirs. 1990-2000, sr. v.p. profl. devel. 1993-95, Man of Yr. 2000), Nat. Assn. Life Underwriters (Nat. Mgmt. award Gen. Agts. and Mgrs. Conf. 1976-83, exec. com. 1984-85, life qualifying), No. Va. Estate Planning Coun. (exec. com. 1985-92, pres. 1990-91), Internat. Platform Assn. (trustee, bd. govs. 1990-2002), No. Va. Gen. Agts. and Mgrs. Assn. (pres. 1980-81, dir. 1982-83), Greater Washington Area Health Underwriters, Fairfax County C. of C. (dir. small bus. 1989-90, dir. membership 1990-91, exec. com. dir. at large 1991-92, Small Bus. Adv. of Yr. award 1990), Million Dollar Round Table (life), John Carroll Soc. Ins. Club Washington (pres. 1997-98) Office Phone: 540-622-2244. Personal E-mail: tonyt33@embarqmail.com.

TRIPATHI, RAM KISHORE, physicist, researcher; b. Rae Bareli, India, Jan. 1, 1942; arrived in U.S., 1966; s. Shiva Kumar and Devi Mani Tripathi; m. Pushpa Shukla Tripathi, May 26, 1966; 1 child, Sanjay. BS, U. Lucknow, 1961, MS, 1963; PhD, U. Kans., 1970. Asst. prof. U. Ky., Lexington, 1970—71, prof., 1986—87; scientist Kern Forschungsanlage, Juelich, Germany, 1971—73; sr. faculty fellow U. Sussex, Brighton, England, 1973—76; fellow Tata Inst. Fundamental Rsch., Bombay, 1975—78; prof. Dept. Energy/Inst. Physics, Bhubaneswar, India, 1978—85, U. Tuebingen, Germany, 1980—82, U. Liege, Belgium, 1985—86; sr. radiation physicist NASA Langley Rsch. Ctr., Hampton, Va., 1987—. Contbr. numerous articles to profl. jours. Pres. internat. cultural activities U. Kans., Lawrence, 1966-68. Fulbright fellow USIA, Washington, 1966-70, Sr. NRC fellow NAS, Washington, 1999; grantee NASA, Dept. of Def., Dept. of Energy, NSF. Fellow AIAA (assoc.), Am. Phys. Soc. (life), AAAS, Am. Nuc. Soc. (life), Inst. Physics. Avocations: jogging, travel, anthropology. Home: 13 Natalie Dr Hampton VA 23666-5565 Office: NASA Langley Rsch Ctr Ms 188 E Hampton VA 23681-0001 Personal E-mail: rk_tripathi@hotmail.com.

TRIPATHI, RAMESH CHANDRA, ophthalmologist, researcher, educator; b. Jamira, India, July 1, 1936; came to U.S., 1977, naturalized, 1983; s. Arjun and G. Tripathi; m. Brenda Jennifer Lane, May 20, 1969; children: Anita, Paul. ISc, Lucknow Christian Coll., 1954; MD, Agra U. Med. Coll., 1959; M of Surgery in Ophthalmology, Lucknow U., 1963; PhD, U. London, 1970. Ophthalmic resident in surgery and demonstrator Lucknow U. Med. Coll., Kanpur, 1959—63; asst. surgeon, med. officer in charge casualty dept. Rly Hosp., Delhi, 1963; fellow Univ. Eye Clinic, Ghent, Belgium, 1964; ophthalmic registrar Southwest Middlesex Hosp., 1965-68; Hayward fellow, registrar, chief clin. asst. Inst. Opthalmology and Moorfields Eye Hosp., London, 1968-72; lectr. U. London Inst. Opthalmology, 1968-70; sr. lectr. U. London, 1970-77; cons. ophthalmologist and pathologist Moorfields Eye Hosp., London, 1972-77; prof. ophthalmology U. Chgo., 1977-93, The Coll. prof., 1979-93, sec. dept. ophthalmology, 1977-87, cons. pediatric tumor bd., 1978-80; attending ophthalmologist, attending ocular pathologist, mem. med. staff U. Chgo. Med. Ctr., 1977-93, dir. Eye Pathology Labs., 1977-93; prof. ophthalmology U. S.C., Columbia, 1993—2006, chmn., 1993—98, endowed chair ophthalmology Columbia, 2000—; dir. ophthalmology edn. Richland Mem. Hosp., SC, 1993—98; prof. The Graduate Sch., 1996—2006; adj. prof. pathology and microbiology, 2002—06; emeritus disting. prof., 2006—. Cons., attending ophthalmologist Oak Forest (Ill.) Hosp., 1986-93, dir. ophthalmology resident program, 1986-89, chmn. instnl. rev. bd., 1988; quality assurance com. U. Chgo. Hosp., 1979-93, med. curriculum com. U. Chgo., 1990-93; cons. Nat. Eye Inst. NIH, 1981—, Fight for Sight Rev. Bd., 1990-91; vis. prof. Yeshiva U., NYC, 1973, U. Wurzberg, Germany, 1974, U. Toronto, 1979, Jefferson U., Phila., 1979, Columbia U., NYC, 1981, U. Oxford, Eng., 1984, 86, 89, Nat. Autonomous U. Mex., Mexico City, 1981, Hotel Dieux de Paris, 1975, U. Tex. Med. Br., Galveston, 1990, Kresge Eye Inst. Wayne State U., Detroit, 1991, NY Eye and Ear Infirmary, NYC, 1991, Boston U. Dept. Ophthalmology, New Eng. Eye Ctr., Tufts U., Boston, 1991, Mayo Clinic Dept. Ophthalmology, Rochester, Minn., 1992, others; preceptor MS and PhD degree candidates in ophthalmology and visual sci., U. Chgo., 1977-93, U. SC, 1993—; mem. coun. Ill. Asian-Am. Adv. Com. to Gov. State of Ill., 1989-93; rep. to AMA & Chgo. Med. Soc. from Oak Forest Hosp./Cook County Hosp. Med. Staff, 1987-93, alt. del. Ill. State Med. Soc., 1991-93; del. Bd. Govs. Southeastern Chgo. Med. Soc. from U. Chgo. Hosp. & Clinics, 1991-93; faculty basic and clin. sci. course Am. Acad. Opthalmology, 1991-2003; attending ophthalmologist WBJ Dorn VA Hosp., 1993—2006; vis. prof. Harvard Med. Sch. Eye and Ear Infirmary, Boston, Mass., 1997-. Author: Wolff's Anatomy of the Eye and Orbit, 1997; exec. editor Exptl. Eye Rsch., 1973—2000, sect. editor, 1987—99, mem. editl. bd. Ophthalmic Literature, 1974—76, sect. editor, mem. editl. bd. Cornea, 1981—86, assoc. editor Afro-Asian Jour. Ophthalmology, 1981—93, Drug Devel. Rsch., 1988—92, Lens and Eye Toxicology Rsch., 1989—93, Sci. Rsch. Jour., 1990—; contbr. over 600 articles to profl. jours., over 60 chpts. to books and monographs. Chmn. Med. Coun. Assn. Indians in Am., Chgo., 1983-93, v.p., 1986-88; bd. dirs. Indo-Am. Ophthal. Soc. World Eye Found.; mem. Chgo. Found. for Med. Care, 1977-93; pres. Vision Rsch. Found., 1987—; mem. exec. bd. Assn. Scientists of Indian Origin in Am. Recipient Ophthalmology prize Royal Soc. Medicine London, 1971, Royal Eye London prize Ophthal. Soc. London, 1976, Resolutions Commendation, Ill. State Gen. Assembly, 1987, 88, Outstanding US Citizen award, 1984, Internat. prize Alcon Rsch. Inst., 1987; Med. Rsch. Coun. London grantee, 1972-75, Nat. Eye Inst. USPHS grantee, 1977—; named Litchfield endowed lectr. U. Oxford (Eng.), 1986, Ida Mann Gold medal U. Oxford, 1989, Disting. Physician of Am., 1990. Fellow: ACS (diplomate), Am. Acad. Ophthalmology (sect. 2 fundamentals and principles of ophthalmology 1991—2001, chair and past chair, basic and clin. sci. com., Honor award 1984, sr. honor award 1997), Internat. Coll. Surgeons (diplomate, vice regent U.S. 1984—), Royal Coll. Ophthalmologists London (diplomate), Royal Coll. Pathologists (diplomate), Nat. Acad. Scis. of India (life), Royal Soc. Medicine London (coun. 1973—76); mem.: AAUP, AMA, Ill. Med. Soc. (alternate del.), Internat. Soc. Ocular Toxicology (sec., treas. 1993—97, bd. dirs. 1993—, pres. 1998—2000, founder Hockwin-Green Meml. Endowment Fund 2002), Chgo. Ophthal. Soc., S.C. Ophthal. Soc., Glaucoma Soc., Electron Microscopical Soc. Am., Am. Assn. Ophthalmic Pathologists, Am. Assn. Pathologists, Internat. Acad. Pathologists, Contact Lens Assn. Ophthalmologist, Oxford Ophthal. Soc., Ophthal. Soc. U.S., Assn. for Rsch. Vision and Ophthalmology, Pan-Am. Assn. Ophthalmology, Royal Microscopical Soc., Assn. Eye Rsch. Europe (guest of honor 1974), Indian Med. Assn. U.S.A. (bd. dirs. 1984—85, Disting. Physician award 1987), Chgo. Med. Soc. (v.p. 1993, bd. dirs. Southea. br., pres. 1993), Assn. Indians in Am. (v.p. 1988—90, honor award 1986), Fedn. Am. Soc. Exptl. Biology, Physiol. Soc. London, Royal Coll. Physicians and Surgeons (diplomate, conjoin bd.). Achievements include research in pathophysiology, diagnosis and medical and surgical treatment of various ocular disorders including corneal diseases, glaucoma, cataract, vitreoretinopathy; optic nerve; orbital diseases & ocular toxicology; pioneer in the field of aqueous humor and cerebrospinal fluid dynamics, growth factors, contact lens spoilage and fibrinolytic therapy of the eye. Avocations: photography, swimming. Office: Univ South Carolina Sch Medicine Dept Opthalmology 4 Medical Pk Ste 300 Columbia SC 29203 Office Fax: 803-749-4554. Business E-Mail: ramesh.tripathi@uscmed.sc.edu.

TRIPLETT, E. EUGENE, editor; b. La Jolla, Calif., Mar. 12, 1949; s. Erbin Eugene Triplett and Marjorie Ann (Aldrich) Heath; m. Vannie Carol Crow, July 19, 1968; 1 child, Aaron Eugene. BA in Journalism, Ctrl. State U., 1975. Reporter, columnist The Okla. Jour., Oklahoma City, 1976-80; entertainment editor The Daily Oklahoman, Oklahoma City, 1981-85, asst. city editor, 1985-89, city editor, 1989-99, sr. feature writer, columnist, 1999—. Bd. dirs. Crime Stoppers Oklahoma City; mem. comm. com. Okla. Heart Assn., 1989-92. With U.S. Army, 1969-71, Vietnam. Recipient 1st pl. Feature Writing award Soc. Profl. Journalists, 1987, 97-98, Great Plains Journalism Competition, 2009, 1st Pl., 1999-2000, inducted Okla. Music Hall of Fame, 2011. Mem. AP/Okla. News Exec. (pres.-elect 1994-95, pres. 1995-96, 2nd pl. Feature Writing award 1988, 1st pl. Feature Writing award, 2002, 1st pl. Rev. Writing award 2003, 1st Pl. Entertainment Feature, Gt. Plains Journalism Competition, 2009). Democrat. Avocations: collecting recorded music, feature films, vintage tv shows. Home: 8116 NW 118th St Oklahoma City OK 73162-1113 Office: The Daily Oklahoman 9000 Broadway Ext Oklahoma City OK 73114-3799 Office Phone: 405-475-4105. E-mail: etriplett@oklahoman.com, geneoat@cox.net.

TRIPODI, JOSEPH V., beverage company executive; b. Aug. 7, 1955; BA, Harvard U., 1977; MS, London Sch. Econs., 1981. Various mgmt. positions IBM Corp., 1977—81, Mobil Oil Corp., 1981—88; exec. v.p. global mktg. MasterCard International, 1989—98; chief mktg. officer Seagram Spirits & Wine Group, 1999—2002, Bank of New York, 2002—03; sr. v.p., chief mktg. officer Allstate Ins. Co., Northbrook, Ill., 2003—07; sr. v.p., chief mktg. & comml. officer Coca-Cola Co., Atlanta, 2007—09, exec. v.p., chief mktg. & comml. officer, 2009—. Bd. mem. Ad Council; past. chmn. Assn. Nat. Advertisers. Trustee Field Mus., Chgo. Named a Power Player, Advt. Age, 2008, 2009. Office: The Coca Cola Co 1 Coca Cola Pl Atlanta GA 30313

TRIPODO, ANTHONY, corporate financial executive; BA summa cum laude, St. Thomas U., Miami. Various positions, CFO, Baker Performance Chemicals and the Baker Oil Tools divsns. Baker Hughes; exec. v.p., CFO Tesco Corp.; dir., Petroleum Geo-Svcs. Vetco Internat. Ltd.; pres., North and South Am. Group Veritas DGC, Inc., exec. v.p., CFO, treas., 1997—2001, exec. v.p., 2002—03; mng. dir. Arch Creek Advisors LLC, 2003—06; exec. v.p., CFO Helix Energy Solutions Group, Inc., 2008—. Bd. dirs. Helix Energy Solutions Group, Inc., 2003—. Office: Helix Energy Solutions Group Inc Ste 400 400 N Sam Houston Pky E Houston TX 77060 Office Phone: 281-618-0400. Office Fax: 281-618-0501.

TRITT, TRAVIS, musician; b. Marietta, Ga., Feb. 9, 1963; s. James and Gwen Tritt; m. Karen Ryon, Sept. 1983 (div. 1984); m. Jodi Barnett (div.); m. Theresa Nelson, Apr. 12, 1997; children: Tristan James, Tarian Nathaniel, Tyler Reese. Recording artist Warner Bros., 1990-99, Sony Music, Nashville, 1999—. Singer: (albums) Country Club, 1990 (platinum), It's All About to Change, 1991 (platinum), T-R-O-U-B-L-E, 1992 (platinum), A Travis Tritt Christmas: Loving Time of the Year, 1992 (with Marty Stuart, Hank Williams Jr., Waylon Jennings) Ten Feet Tall and Bulletproof, 1994, Restless Kind, 1996, No More Looking over My Shoulder, 1998, Down the Road I Go, 2000, Strong Enough, 2002, My Honky Tonk History, 2004, The Storm, 2007; #1 singles The Whiskey Ain't Workin' (Grammy award with Marty Stuart 1993), Here's a Quarter (Call Someone Who Cares), Anymore, Can I Trust You with my Heart; actor: (films) The Cowboy Way, 1993, Sgt. Bilko, 1996; (TV films) Rio Diablo, 1993, Following Her Heart, 1994, A Holiday for Love, 1996, The Long Kill, 1999; (TV appearances) Teh Jeff Foxworthy Show, 1995, Touched by an Angel, 1999, Yes, Dear, 2004, Battleground Earth, 2008; author: (with Michael Bane) 10 Foot Tall and Bullet Proof, 1994. Named Billboard's Top New Male Country Artist, 1990; recipient Horizon award Country Music Assn., 1991, (with Marty Stuart) Vocal Event of Yr. award Country Music Assn., 1992, (with George Jones) 1993, (with Marty Stewart) 1996, Grammy award, Best Country Collaboration with Vocals, 1999; inductee Grand Ole Opry, 1992. Republican. Office: c/o Agency for the Performing Arts 3017 Poston Ave Nashville TN 37203

TROOST, BRADLEY TODD, neurologist, educator; b. July 5, 1937; s. Henry Bradley and Elizabeth (Todd) Troost; m. Elizabeth Gail Godet Troost, Apr. 17, 1976; children: Elizabeth Claire, Laurie Anne. BS in Biophysics with honors, Yale U., 1959; MD, Harvard U., 1963. Diplomate Am. Bd. Psychiatry & Neurology. Intern Colo. Gen. Hosp., Denver, 1963—64; resident in neurology U. Colo., Denver, 1966—69. Asst. prof. U. Miami, Fla., 1970—76; assoc. prof. U. Pitts., 1976—80; prof. Case Western Res. U., Cleve., 1980—83; prof., chmn. dept. neurology Wake Forest U. Sch. Medicine, Winston-Salem, NC, 1983—; chief dept. neurology VA Med. Ctrs., Pitts., Cleve. Contbr. articles to profl. publs. Bd. dirs. Greater Miami Epilepsy Found., 1973—76. Served to capt. USAR, 1964—66. NIH fellow, U. Calif.-San Francisco, 1969—70. Fellow: Am. Acad. Neurology; mem.: Barany Soc., Am. Assn. Univ. Profs. Neurology, Am. Neurol. Assn. Republican. Episcopalian.

TROPEZ-SIMS, SUSANNE, pediatrician, educator; b. New Orleans, Apr. 13, 1949; d. Maxwell Sterling and Ethel (Ross) Tropez; m. James Carnell White, Apr. 10, 1971 (div. 1992); children: Lisa, Janifer, James Carnell; m. Michael Milroy Sims, Feb. 18, 1995. BS, Bennett Coll., 1971; MD, U. N.C., 1975, MPH, 1982. Diplomate Am. Bd. Pediatrics. Resident pediat. N.C. Meml. Hosp., Chapel Hill, 1975—76, 1977—79; pediatrician Darnell Army Hosp., Ft. Hood, Tex., 1976—77; acting dir. pediat. day clinic Wake County Med. Ctr., Raleigh, NC, 1979—82; dir. pediat. day clinic, asst. prof. U. N.C., Chapel Hill, 1982—88; assoc. prof. pediat. La. State U. Med. Ctr., New Orleans, 1988—97; dir. divsn. pediat. emergency rm. La. State U., New Orleans, 1988—89, chief divsn. ambulatory care, 1989—97; chmn. and prof. dept. pediat. Meharry Med. Coll., Nashville, 1997—2005; chair Meharry Med. Svc. Found., Nashville, 2000—02; chair curriculum com. Meharry Med. Coll., Nashville, 2003—, assoc. dean acad. support, 2005—06, assoc. dean clin. affiliation, 2006—, Joy McCann prof., 2006—10, pediatric clearkship dir., 2005—. Clin. dir. maternal and child health units New Orleans Health Dept., 1992-97, chief divsn. cmty. pediat. and adolescent medicine, 1992-97; pediatrician Shelly Child Devel. Ctr., Raleigh, 1981-88, child med. examiner program, 1979-88; chair sch. health com. local chpt. AAP, 1993-96; mem. Nat. Com. Sch. Health, 1992-99; chair health info. network bd. Nat. Edn. Assn., 2000-02, 2011-; vice chair pediat. sect., Nat. Med. Assn., 2009-11, chair pediat. sect., 2011-13, Dom Com., 2011-, chair, Health Network Bd. NEA, 2011-12, chair, Pediat. Sect. NMA, 2009-11, chair, 2011-12. Contbr. articles to profl. jour. Chair adminstrv. bd. Cornerstone U.M.C., 1993-96, chair edn. com., 1991-92; mem. United Meth. Women, Walnut Terr. Child Devel. Ctr., Raleigh, 1981-83, chmn., 1982-83; chmn. pastor parish com. Longview Ch., Raleigh, 1982-84, 87-88, chmn. membership care com.; chair bd. trustees Clark Meml. United Meth. Ch., 2001-06, chair bldg. com., 2005-10; with L.D.M. Com., 2011-. Fellow preventive medicine, 1979-82, Faculty Devel. fellow U. NC Sch. Medicine, 1985-87; named America's Top Pedistrician Consumer Rsch. America, 2009, Pre Alumnae Clinical Faculty of Yr. Tchg. award, 2011-12. Fellow Am. Acad. Pediatrics (mem. sch. health com.); mem. N.C. Pediatric Soc. (com. child abuse and neglect, adolescent pregnancy), La. Pediatric Soc., Ambulatory Pediatric Assn., Adolescent Pregnancy Coalition United Way, Bennett Coll. Alumnae Assn., A. P. Gold Humanism Hon. Soc., 2013 Democrat. Office Phone: 615-327-6925, 615-327-5915, 615-327-6332. Business E-Mail: stsims@mmc.edu.

TROTTER, IDE PEEBLES, financial planner, investment manager; b. Colombia, Mo., Oct. 27, 1932; s. Ide Peebles and Lena Ann (Breeze) T.; m. Luella Ruth Haupt, June 9, 1956; children: Ruth Elizabeth, Arrenia Ann, Catherine Suzanne. BS, Tex. A&M U., 1954; MA, Princeton U., 1957, PhD, 1960. Registerd investment advisor Tex. Various tech. positions Exxon Research & Engring. Co., 1958-65, sect. head Baytown, Tex., 1965-67; advisor refining hdqrs. and corp. planning Exxon Co. USA, Houston, 1967-70, tech. supt. Billings, Mont., 1970-72, process supt., 1972-74; sr. advisor logistics Exxon Corp., NYC, 1974-78; gen. mgr. logistics Esso Sekiyu, Tokyo, 1978-81; mgr. feedstock & energy Exxon Chem. Internat., Brussels, 1981-86; dean Coll. Mgmt. & Free Enterprise Dallas Bapt. U., 1986-89, prof. fin., 1989-90; pres. Trotter Capital Mgmt. Inc., Duncanville, Tex., 1990—. Chmn. Met. Bapt. Ministries, NYC, 1976—78, bd. dirs., 1976—78, Visionwalk Internat. Ministries, 1997—, chmn., bd. dirs., 2000; bd. regents Midwest Bapt. Theol. Sem., 2005—; bd. dirs. Dallas Life Found., 1996—2002, vice-chmn., 2001, chmn., 2002; bd. dirs. Probe Ministries, 2004. 1st lt. US Army, 1960. NSF fellow, 1954; recipient Profl. Progress award Soc. Profl. Chemists & Engrs., 1964. Mem. Am. Inst. Chem. Engrs., Am. Chem. Soc., Am. Fin. Assn. (registered investment adviser). Republican. Baptist. Achievements include patents in field. Avocations: skiing, hiking, fishing, camping. Home and Office: 1215 Rock Springs Rd Duncanville TX 75137-2839

TROTTER, TEDDY N., state representative, consumer products company executive; b. Pickens, SC, May 30, 1957; s. Olie and Sally (Hayes) Trotter; m. Lisa D. Durham, Nov. 5, 1983; children: Lynzie, Tyler, Lexis. Grad., Pickens H.S., 1975. Owner/operator Teddy's Gas & Fuel, Trotter Mobile Home Pk., Trotter Strawberry Farm; state rep. dist. 4 S.C. Legis., 1993—, mem. ways and means com. SC. Republican. Office: State Capitol 418C Blatt Bldg Columbia SC 29211 Home: 232 Florence St Pickens SC 29671 E-mail: TNT@scstatehouse.net.

TROTTER, WILLIAM T., mathematics professor; MA, U. Ala., 1967; BS with first class honors, The Citadel, 1965; PhD, U. Ala., 1969. Asst. prof. The Citadel, 1969—72, U. SC, 1973—75, assoc. prof., 1975—80, prof., 1980—86, Carolina rsch. prof., 1986—87; prof. Ariz. State U., 1987—92, Regent's prof., 1992—2002; prof. Ga. Inst. Tech., 2002—, chair, Sch. Math., 2002—09. Vis. lectr. Stillman Coll., 1969; vis. asst. prof. Dartmouth Coll., 1972—73; asst. dean, Coll. Sci. and Math. U. SC, 1976—79, chair, dept. math., computer sci. and stats., 1979—80, chair, dept. math. and stats., 1980—85; chair, dept. math. Ariz. State U., 1987—91, 1995—97, vice provost acad. affairs, 2000—02; vis. scholar MIT, 1981; dir. combinatorics and optimization rsch. group Bell Comm. Rsch., 1991—94. Contbr. articles to profl. jours. Office: Chair Sch Math Ga Inst Tech Atlanta GA 30332

TROUBH, RAYMOND STANLEY, financial consultant; b. Portland, Maine, May 3, 1926; s. Maurice J. and Sadye (Brickman) T.; m. Jean Loeb, May 28, 1971; children: Amy, John. AB, Bowdoin Coll., Brunswick, Maine, 1949; LLB, Yale U., 1952. Lawyer Sullivan & Cromwell, NYC, 1954-58; investment banker Lazard Frères & Co., LLC, NYC, 1958-73; fin. cons. Troubh & Co., NYC, 1974—. Bd. dirs. Applied Power Inc., Becton, Dickinson & Co., Manville Inc., Time Warner Inc., Diamond Offshore Drilling, Inc., Gen. Am. Investors Co., Gentiva Health Services, Inc., Wendy's Arby's Group, Inc., 1994-. Mem. Bd. Overseers Bowdoin Coll. Mem. Legal Aid Soc. Office: Wendy's/Arby's Group Inc Bd Directors 1155 Perimeter Ctr W Atlanta GA 30338 Office Phone: 678-514-4500. Business E-Mail: raymond.troubh@wendysarbys.com.

TROUT, MAURICE ELMORE, diplomat; b. Clifton Hill, Mo., Sept. 17, 1917; s. David McCamel and Charlotte Temple (Woods) T.; m. Margie Marie Mueller, Aug. 24, 1943; children: Richard Willis, Babette Yvonne. BA, Hillsdale Coll., 1939; MA in Pub. Adminstrn, St. Louis U., 1948, PhD in Polit. Sci, 1950. Joined U.S. Fgn. Service, 1950; assigned Paris, 1950-52, Vienna, 1952-55, London, 1955-59, Vientiane, Laos, 1959-61; with Office Exec. Dir. Bur. Far Eastern Affairs, Dept. State, Washington, 1961-65; Am. consulate gen. Munich, 1965-69; 1st sec., consul Am. embassy, Bangkok, 1969—72; dep. office dir. Bur. Politico-Mil. Affairs, Dept. State, Washington, 1972-75; Dept. State advisor Armed Forces Staff Coll., Norfolk, Va., 1975-77. Bd. dirs. Internat. Sch., Bangkok, 1970-72. Served with USCG, 1939-45; capt. USAFR, 1951-55. Recipient Achievement award, Hillsdale Coll., 1962. Mem. Am. Fgn. Service Assn., Diplomatic and Consular Officers Ret., Delta Tau Delta, Delta Theta Phi, Pi Gamma Mu. Home: 6203 Hardy Dr Mc Lean VA 22101-3114

TROUT, MONROE EUGENE, health facility administrator; b. Harrisburg, Pa., Apr. 5, 1931; s. David Michael and Florence Margaret (Kashner) T.; m. Sandra Louise Lemke, June 11, 1960; children: Monroe Eugene, Timothy William. AB, U. Pa., 1953, MD, 1957; LLB, Dickinson Sch. of Law, 1964, JD, 1969; LLD (hon.), Dickinson Sch. Law, 1996, Bloomfield Coll., 1994, Cumberland Coll., 2003. Intern Great Lakes (Ill.) Naval Hosp., 1957-58; resident in internal medicine Portsmouth (Va.) Naval Hosp., 1959-61; chief med. dept. Harrisburg State Hosp., 1961-64; dir. drug regulatory affairs Pfizer, Inc., NYC, 1964-68; v.p., med. dir. Winthrop Labs., NYC, 1968-70; med. dir. Sterling Drug, Inc., NYC, 1970-74, v.p., dir. med. affairs, 1974-78, sr. v.p., dir. med. affairs, bd. dirs., mem. exec. com., 1978-86; pres., CEO Am. Healthcare Sys., Inc., 1986-95, chmn., 1987-95; also bd. dirs. Am. Healthcare Systems, Inc.; chmn. emeritus Am. Healthcare Sys., Inc., 1995—; interim CEO Cytran Inc., 1996. Chmn. bd. dirs. Cytyc Inc., 1998—2002, Ineed MD, Inc., Am. Excess Ins. Ltd., 1990—95; adj. assoc. prof. Bklyn. Coll. Pharmacy; spl. lectr. legal medicine, trustee Dickinson Sch. Law, 1970—93; trustee Ariz. State U. Sch. Health Adminstrn., 1988—91; mem. rsch. bd. Sterling Winthrop, 1977—86; mem. Joint Commn. Prescription Drug Use, 1976—80; sec. Commn. on Med. Malpractice, HEW, 1971—73; co-chmn. San Diego County Health Commn., 1992—94; chairs in pharmacology and surgery U. Calif., San Diego, Vision Rsch., U. WI; prof. history Westminster Coll. Author, Winter Galley, 2008; mem. editl. bd. Hosp. Formulary Mgmt., 1969-79, Forensic Sci., 1971—, Jour. Legal Medicine, 1973-79, Reg. Tox. and Pharmac, 1981-87, Med. Malpractice Prevention, 1985—; editl. reviewer Annals of Internal Medicine; contbr. articles to profl. jours. Exec. com. White House Mini Conf. on Aging, 1980; mem. Nat. Health Adv. Bd. AAA; chmn. bd. Am. Coll. Legal Medicine Found., 1983—87; mem. N.Y. State Commn. Substance Abuse, 1978—80, Town Coun., New Canaan, 1978—86, vice chmn., 1985—86; trustee Cleve. Clinic, 1971—87, Albany Med. Coll., 1977—86, St. Vincent DePaul Ctr. for the Homeless, 1987—90, U. Calif.-San Diego Thornton Hosp. and Med. Ctr., 1990—97, San Diego Mus. Art, 1996—98, Bapt. Health Sys. Found., Knoxville, 1999—2007; trustee, vice chmn. Morehouse Med. Sch., 1980—89; assoc. trustee U. Pa.; bd. visitors U. Pa. Sch. Nursing, 1988—92; pres. bd. trustees U. Calif. San Diego Found., 1994—97; vice chmn. Med. Commn. for Food and Shelter, Inc.; chmn. Internat. B'nai B'rith Dinner, 1989, 1994; Rep. dist. leader New Canaan, 1966—68; bd. dirs. New Canaan Interchurch Svc. Com., 1965—69, Athletes Kidney Found., Cir. in the Sq. Theatre Inc., 1984—86, Knoxville Symphony Soc., 2001—04, Knoxville Opera Co., 2001—04, East Tenn. Hist. Soc., 2003—04. Recipient Alumni award of merit U. Pa., 1953, Disting. Alumni award Dickinson Sch. Law, 1989, Nat. Healthcare award Internat. B'nai B'rith, 1991, Entrepreneur of Yr. award San Diego, 1994, Horatio Alger award, 1995, Salvation Army Tradition of Caring award, 1996, Civis Universitatus award U. Calif. San Diego, 1997, Gold Medal award, Am. Coll. Legal Medicine, 1999, Bapt. Health Sys. Visionary award, 2002, Knoxville Philanthropist of Yr., 2004, Cumberland Coll. Caring Servant award, 2005, Leadership award U. Cumberlands, 2014; Monroe E. Trout Day named in his honor, Knox County, Tenn., Mar. 13, 2007; Churchill fellow, 2013. Master: Bridge (life); fellow: Am. Coll. Legal Medicine (v.p., pres., bd. govs.); mem. AMA (Physician's Recognition awards 1969, 72, 76, 82, 85, 88, 92), Med. Execs. (pres. 1975-76), Delta Tau Delta (Alumni Achievement award 1996, Named to 100 Most Influential Delts of Twentieth Century 2000), Founding Sponsor Rossini Festival (Knoxville). Lutheran. Achievements include Appleton Art Center, Wisconsin renamed Trout Museum of Art in honor of Sandra Lemke Trout and Monroe Eugene Trout. Office: 2110 Cove View Way Knoxville TN 37919

TROUTMAN, HOLMES RUSSELL, lawyer; b. Beckley, W.Va., July 27, 1933; s. Holmes Fielding and Florence Lillo (Wallett) T.; m. Patricia Lee Bullion, Nov. 12, 1954; children: Holmes Russell, Richard Byron, Teresa Lee. AB, Marshall U., 1955; postgrad., Stetson Law Sch., 1955-56; JD, U. Miami, 1958. Bar: Fla. 1958. Assoc., ptnr. firm Akerman, Turnbull, Senterfitt & Eidson, Orlando, Fla., 1958-62; ptnr. firm Fishback, Davis, Dominick & Troutman, Orlando, 1962-69, Troutman, Williams, Irvin, Green, Helms, and Polich, Winter Park, Fla., 1969—. Spl. city prosecutor, City of Winter Park, 1965, city atty., 1968-72, acting county solicitor, 1967-69; spl. counsel Fla. Turnpike Authority, 1968-70, Fla. Pub. Svc. Commn., 1978-79; mem. Fla. Supreme Ct. Nominating Commn., 1978-82, chmn., 1981-82; chmn. bd. trustees Fla. Supreme Ct. Historical Soc., 2000—. Author: Undiscovered Poems; contbr. articles to profl. jours. Host, prodr. Discussion programs Sta. WFTV, 1968-85. Pres. Friends of Orlando Pub. Libr., 1971-73, Fla. Supreme Ct. Hist. Soc., 1997-99; mem. Orange County Charter Study Commn., 1973-74; chmn. Winter Park Charter Study Commn., 1982-83; chmn. bd. advisors Rollins Coll. Hamilton Holt Sch., 1996-98, chmn. emeritus Hamilton Holt Sch. Bd. Rollins Coll.; pres. Fla. Supreme Ct. Hist. Soc., 1997-99; commencement spkr. Rollins Coll., 1999. Recipient Orlando Jr. C. of C. Good Govt. award, 1969, Marshall U. Alumnus Civic Contbrn. award, 1979, Winter Park C. of C. Good Govt. award, 1985, Outstanding Past Pres. Fla. Counsel Bar Assn., 1984, Lifetime Achievement award Fla. Supreme Ct. Hist. Soc., 2009. Mem. ABA (mem. ho. of dels. 1978-80), Am. Acad. Trial Lawyers, Fla. Acad. Trial Lawyers, Fla. Bar (mem. bd. govs. 1972-78, pres. 1977-78), Orange County Bar Assn. (mem. exec. coun. 1966-68, pres. 1968-69, driving force and co-founder Legal Aid Soc. 1969), Orlando Tiger Bay Club (pres. 1988-89). Home: 1600 Barcelona Way Winter Park FL 32789-5615 Office: Troutman Williams Irvin Green & Helms PA 311 W Fairbanks Ave Winter Park FL 32789-5094 Home Phone: 407-620-5009; Office Phone: 407-647-2277. Business E-Mail: rtroutman@troutmanwilliams.com.

TROUTT, KENNY, communications executive; b. Mt. Vernon, Ill., Jan. 8, 1948; s. Nadine Adams; m. Lisa Troutt; 3 children. BS, Southern Ill. U. Founder Excel Comm., 1988, CEO, chmn., vice chmn.; co-owner WinStar Farms, Ky.; dir. Mt. Vernon Investments, Inc. Vice chmn. Teleglobe, bd. dirs.; trustee Thoroughbred Owners & Breeders Assn.; bd. dirs. Breeders' Cup. Coach boys' basketball. Named one of Forbes 400: Richest Americans, 2006—. Christian. Mailing: WinStar Farms 3001 Pisgah Pike Versailles KY 40383 Office Phone: 859-873-1717. Office Fax: 859-873-1612.

TROUTT, WILLIAM EARL (BILL TROUTT), academic administrator; b. Bolivar, Tenn., June 13, 1949; s. Jack and Earline (Shearin) Troutt; m. Carole Pearson, Nov. 26, 1970; children: Carole Anne, Jack. BA, Union U., Jackson, Tenn., 1971; MA, U. Louisville, 1972; PhD, Vanderbilt U., 1978. Admissions counselor Union U., 1973—75; asst. dir. Tenn. Higher Edn. Commn., Nashville, 1975—78; sr. assoc. McManis Assocs. Inc., Washington, 1978—80; exec. v.p. Belmont Coll., Nashville, 1981—82, pres., 1982—99, Rhodes Coll., Memphis, 1999—. Chmn. Am. Coun. on Edn. Chmn. Jacob Javits Fellowship Bd., Nat. Assn. Ind. Colls. & Univs., Nat. Commn. Cost Higher Edn. Named one of Nation's Most Effective Coll. Pres., Exxon Found. Study, 1986. Mem.: So. Assn. Colls. and Schs. (commnr. commn. colls. 1986—), Tenn. Ind. Colls. Fund (sec.-treas. 1986—), Tenn. Coun. Pvt. Colls. (chmn.), Nashville Area C. of C. (bd. dirs. 1985—), Rotary. Office: Rhodes College Office of President 2000 N Parkway Memphis TN 38112-1690*

TROWBRIDGE, JOHN PARKS, physician; b. Dinuba, Calif., Mar. 24, 1947; s. John Parks and Claire Dovie (Noroian) Trowbridge; children: Sharla Tyann, Lyndi Kendyll. AB in Biol. Scis., Stanford U., 1970; MD, Case Western Res. U., 1976; postgrad., Fla. Inst. Tech., 1983-85. Diplomate in Preventive Medicine, Am. Bd. Clin. Metal Toxicology (examiner for bd. 1987—, protocol coun. 1996-98), Am. Bd. Biologic Reconstructive Therapy (examiner for bd. 1994-97), Am. Bd. Anti-Aging Medicine, 1998, Nat. Bd. Med. Examiners. Intern in gen. surgery Mt. Zion Hosp. & Med. Ctr., San Francisco, 1976-77; resident in urol. surgery U. Tex. Health Sci. Ctr., Houston, 1977-78; pvt. med. practice, health recovery unit, pain relief unit, life long health unit Life Celebrating Health, Humble, Tex., 1978—. Chief corp. med. cons. Tex. Internat. Airlines, Houston, 1981-83; immunology rsch. asst. Stanford U. Med. Ctr., Stanford, Calif., 1967-70; night lab. supr. Kaiser Found. Hosp., Redwood City, Calif., 1971-72; advisor to bd. dirs. Am. Inst. Med. Preventics, Laguna Hills, Calif., 1988-90; sr. aviation med. examiner FAA, 1983-96; invited guest lectr. Taipei Med. U., Taiwan, 2005, invited guest lectr., XXV Congresso Internat. Pratica Ortomolecular E Radicals Livers Sao Paolo, 2011, invited guest lectr. multiple profl. groups, Ehlers Damlos Nat. Edn., 2009; lectr., cons. in field. Co-author: The Yeast Syndrome, 1986, Chelation Therapy, 1985, 2d edit., 1990, Yeast Related Illnesses, 1987, Do What You Want to Do, 1996, The Rumble in Humble: Heart Surgery and All That Jazz, 1997, Living Well Past 50: Rejuvenate Your Heart and Arteries, 1998;prodr. narrator: Dozen CDs DVDs Alternative Integrative Medicine Topics, 2004-, contbr. Challenging Orthodoxy: America's Top Medical Preventives Speak Out, 1991, pain pain go away, 2008, The Osteopathic Medicine Advantage: How Medical Miracles Are Made Faber, 2011; weekly radio show host (KBME-AM): Feeling Better...Naturally, with Dr. John Trowbridge, Houston, 2003-2004; contbr. articles to profl. jours. Adv. bd. Tex. Chamber Orchestra, Houston, 1979-80; med. dir. Humble unit Am. Cancer Soc., 1980-81; med. cons. personal fitness program Lake Houston YMCA, 1981-83. Nat. Merit scholar, 1965-69, Calif. State scholar, 1967-69; recipient Resolution of Commendation house of dels., 1974 Am. Podiatry Assn., Spl. Profl. Svc. Citation bd. trustees, 1976, Am. Podiatry Students Assn. Fellow: Am. Coll. Advancement in Medicine (v.p. 1987—89, pres.-elect 1989—91), Am. Soc. for Laser Medicine and Surgery; mem.: AMA, Aposthe Ecclesiaste, Sacred Med. Ch. Hope, TMA, Neuro Cranial Reconstruction Rsch. Inst. (pres. 2002—03, rsch. inst. pres. 2003—11), Metabolic Syndrome Assn. (pres. 2008—), Knight Chevalier Sacred Med. (prof. mem. 2010—, Order of Knights Hope 2008), Pastoral Med. Assn., Internat. Acad. Biol. Dentistry and Medicine (bd. dir. 2007—, pres. 2009—11), Advanced Med. Edn. and Svcs. Physician Assn., Am. Bd. Clin. Metal Toxicology (bd. dirs. 2006—, sec. bd. dirs. 2007—, sec. 2007—), Neuro Cranial Restructuring Drs. Assn., Am. Soc. Life Ext. Physicians (founding), Am. Assn. Nutritional Cons., Am. Acad. Thermology, Nat. Health Fedn. (chmn. bd. govs. 1989), Am. Soc. Gen. Laser Surgery, Am. Acad. Environ. Medicine, Legal and Edn. Found. Am. Preventive Med. Assn. (bd. dirs. 1996—99, charter), Am. Preventive Medicine Assn. (bd. dirs. 1992—99, charter), Am. Coll. Preventive Medicine, Internat. Coll. Integrative Medicine (editor newsletter 2000—01, bd. dirs. 2000—, sec. 2002—08), N.Am. Cervicogenic Headache Soc., Royal Soc. Medicine (sect. orthop.), Soc. for Orthomolecular Medicine, Great Lakes Coll. Clin. Medicine (bd. dirs. 1991—95, med. rsch. instnl. rev. bd., v.p. 1993—94, pres. 1994—95, program chair Advanced Tng. Seminar in Heavy Metal Toxicology 1996—98, bd. dirs. 1999—2000), Huxley Inst. for Biosocial Rsch., Inst. Health Freedom (founding bd. dirs. 1997—2001), Arthritis Trust Am. (med. adv. bd. 1995—), Internat. Acad. Bariatric Medicine, NY Acad. Scis., Aerospace Med. Assn., Houston Acad. Medicine, Harris County Med. Soc., Tex. Med. Assn., Am. Acad. Anti-Aging Medicine, Assn. Am. Physicians and Surgeons. Avocations: private piloting, computer applications. Office: Life Celebrating Health Assn 9816 Memorial Blvd Ste 205 Humble TX 77338-4206 Home Phone: 281-540-2255; Office Phone: 281-540-2329. Personal E-mail: jptlch@earthlink.net. Business E-Mail: info@healthchoicesnow.com.

TROY, ANTHONY FRANCIS, lawyer; b. Hartford, Conn., Apr. 16, 1941; children: Anthony John, Francis Gerard II, Silvio Connor A. BA in Govt., St. Michael's Coll., Vt., 1963; LLB, U. Richmond, Richmond, Va., 1966. Bar: Va. 1966, D.C. 1972, U.S. Dist. Ct. (ea. dist.) Va. 1966, U.S. Dist. Ct. (we. dist.) Va. 1967, U.S. Ct. Appeals (4th cir.) 1967, U.S. Supreme Ct. 1969. Asst. atty. gen. Commonwealth of Va., Richmond, 1966-72, atty. gen., 1977-78; assoc. Colson & Shapiro, Washington, 1972-74; ptnr., govtl. law, spl. investigations Troutman, Sanders LLP, Richmond, 1978—, and mem., exec. com. Conard Mattox Disting. adj. prof. chair law U. Richmond Law Sch. Contbr. articles to profl. jours. Trustee Sci. Mus. Va. Fellow Am. Law Found., Va. Law Found. Office: Troutman Sanders LLP 1001 Haxall Point Richmond VA 23219 Home Phone: 804-513-7200; Office Phone: 804-697-1318. Office Fax: 804-698-5162. Business E-Mail: tony.troy@troutmansanders.com.

TRUDELL, JULIE LOFTUS, medical insurance company executive; V.p., investor rels. Amerigroup Corp., sr. v.p., investor rels. Office: Amerigroup Corp National Support Ctr 1330 Amerigroup Way Virginia Beach VA 23464 Office Phone: 757-490-6900. Business E-Mail: jtrudell@amerigroupcorp.com.

TRUDNAK, STEPHEN JOSEPH, landscape architect; b. Nanticoke, Pa., Feb. 25, 1947; s. Stephen Adam and Marcella (Levulis) T.; m. Arden Batchelder Weill, Sept. 6, 1980. BS in Landscape Arch., Pa. State U., 1970. Jr. landscape arch. Kling Partnership, Phila., 1970-72; mem. landscape arch. firm Keith French Assocs., Washington, 1972-73; head dept. landscape arch. Linganore Ctr. Design, Frederick, Md., 1973-74, Toups and Loiederman, Rockville, Md., 1974-76; project landscape arch. Kaiser Transit Group, So. Calif. Rapid Transit Dist., Dade County Transit Improvement Program, Metro Rail Transit Cons.; v.p. Harry Weese & Assocs., Ltd., Miami, Fla., 1976-84; v.p. landscape arch. Canin Assocs., Orlando, Fla., 1984-87; dir. planning and design Bonita Bay Properties, Inc., Bonita Springs, Fla., 1987-91; prin. Stephen J. Trudnak, P.A. Landscape Arch. and Land Planning, 1991—2006; sr. landscape arch. Johnson Engring., Inc., Ft. Myers, Fla., 2006—. Bd. dirs., v.p. Koreshan State Hist. Site, 1989—94; mem. "not for profit" com. Bonita Springs Cmty. Redevel. Agy., 1994—97; v.p. Bonita Springs Mainstreet Program, 1996, 2000, pres., 1997—98; bd. dirs. Bonita Springs YMCA, 1999—2005, mem. exec. com., 2000—03, chair facilities design task force, 2000—04; del. for Congressman Porter Goss Congl. Small Bus. Summit, 1998, 2000; del. representing Fla. state rep. Carol Green Fla. Small Bus. Summit, 1999. Recipient Alumni Achievement award, Pa. State U., Dept. Landscape Architecture, 2003. Fellow Am. Soc. Landscape Archs. (pres. Fla. chpt. 1983, chpt. adv. bd. 1984-85, elections task force 1986, publs. task force 1987, trustee 1987-89, membership task force, chmn. 1989-90, nat. v.p. chpt. and mem. svcs. 1992-94, non-dues revenue task force 1994-95, ASLA On-Line com. 1997-2005, chair 1999, specifications task force 1998-99, Fla. chpt. ann. vice chair 2009), Nat. Xeriscape Coun. (Fla. steering com.), Nat. Speleol. Soc. SCARAB; mem. Bonita Springs C. of C. (chair beautification com. 1991-92, 94-95, chair awards task force 2000, bd. dirs. 1995-2000, v.p. edn. divsn. 1996-98, vice chmn. cmty. devel. divsn. 1998-99, chmn. tech. com. 2003-04, Affiliate of Yr. 1997, Citizen of Yr. 1999, Charter Class Leadership Bonita Grad. 2000). Office: 2122 Johnson St Fort Myers FL 33901 Office Phone: 239-334-0046. E-mail: strudnak@johnsoneng.com.

TRUE, ROY JOE, lawyer; b. Shreveport, La., Feb. 20, 1938; s. Collins B. and Lula Mae (Cady) T.; m. Patsy Jean Hudsmith, Aug. 29, 1959; children: Andrea Alane, Alyssa Anne, Ashley Alisbeth. Student, Centenary Coll., 1957; BS, Tex. Christian U., 1961; LLB, So. Meth. U., 1963, postgrad., 1968—69. Bar: Tex. 1963. Pvt. practice, Dallas, 1963—; pres. Invesco Internat. Corp., 1969-70, True & Shackelford and predecessors, 1975—2002; of counsel Shackelford, Melton & McKinley, 2002—. Bus. adviser, counselor Mickey Mantle, 1969-95; former dir. The Mickey Mantle Found., 1995-98. Mem. editl. bd. Southwestern Law Jour., 1962-63. With AUS, 1956. Mem. ABA, Dallas Bar Assn., Tex. Assn. Bank Counsel, Phi Alpha Delta. Home: 5837 St Marks Circle Dallas TX 75230 Office: 3333 Lee Pkwy 10th Fl Dallas TX 75219 Home Phone: 214-369-0606; Office Phone: 214-780-1400. Business E-Mail: rtrue@shacklaw.net.

TRUE, SUSAN JANE, federal agency administrator; d. Arthur James Krauss and Marie Anna Krauss nee Rehrig; m. Paul Douglas True, Sept. 10, 1977; 1 child, Vanessa Marie Shoop. MEd, Kutztown State Coll., Pa., 1973. Edn. dir. Planned Parenthood of Broome and Chenango Counties, Binghamton, NY, 1975—85; program mgr. NY State Dept. Health, Albany, 1985—96, dir. bur. chronic disease svcs., 1996—2000; chief program svcs. br., divsn. cancer prevention and control CDC, Atlanta, 2000—06; chief program svcs. br., divsn. state and local readiness CDC, Coord. Office Terrorism Preparedness and Emergency Response, Atlanta, 2006—. Contbr. articles to profl. jours. Recipient Svc. award, Nat. Cancer Inst., 2004. Methodist. Avocations: reading, travel. Office: Ctr Disease Control and Prevention 1600 Clifton Rd Atlanta GA 30333 Business E-Mail: smt7@cdc.gov.

TRUEMPER, JOHN JAMES, JR., retired architect; b. Helena, Ark., June 18, 1924; s. John James and Mary Ann (Jacob) T.; m. Julia Clare Wood, Nov. 21, 1956; children: Zachary Wood, John James III, Ann Truemper Rogers. BS in Arch., U. Ill., 1950; DHL (hon.), Lyon Coll., 1995. With archtl. firm Cromwell, Truemper, Levy, Thompson, Woodsmall Inc. (and predecessors), Little Rock, 1950-94, v.p., 1972-74, pres., 1974-81, chmn. bd., 1980-89; ret., 1994. Mem. Ark. Bd. Architects, 1974-82, pres., 1980 Prin. works include Ark. system for edn. and tng. mentally retarded, 1956-78, Winrock Farm, Morrilton, Ark., 1953-58, Ark. State Parks, 1955-75, Ark. Power & Light Co., 1961-89, Lyon Coll., Batesville, 1983-94; author: A Century of Service, 1885-1985, 1985. Pres. Ark. Arts Ctr., 1979, chmn. bd., 1980; mem. Little Rock Bldg. Code Bd. Appeals, 1961-86, chmn., 1971-86; mem. Ark. Hist. Preservtion Rev. Bd., 1987-99; bd. dirs. Little Rock Met. YMCA, 1975-84; pres.Ctrl. YMCA; mem. Friends of Libr. Bd., U. Ark., Little Rock, 1989-99, pres. 1995-97; bd. dirs. Greater Little

Rock C. of C., 1986-88. With USAAF, 1943-46. Recipient Winthrop Rockefeller Meml. award Ark. Arts Center, 1980 Fellow: AIA (pres. Ark. chpt. 1968); mem.: Sigma Chi. Roman Catholic. Home: 6502 Cantrell Rd Little Rock AR 72207-4219

TRUESS, JAMES W., corporate financial executive; BBA, U. Wash.; M in Fin., Seattle U. CFA. CFO, treas. Group Health Coop., 1997—2006; exec. v.p., CFO Amerigroup Corp., 2006—. Office: Amerigroup Corp National Support Ctr 1330 Amerigroup Way Virginia Beach VA 23464 Office Phone: 757-490-6900. Business E-Mail: jim.truess@amerigrp.com.

TRUITT, VICKI, state legislator; m. Jim Truitt; 2 children. Healthcare cons., Tex.; mem. Dist. 98 Tex. House of Representatives, 1999—. Recipient of several awards and honors; Rotary Paul Harris fellow. Republican. Office: Room CAP GW.18 Capitol PO Box 2910 Austin TX 78768 also: PO Box 2910 Austin TX 78768-2910 Office Phone: 817-488-4098, 512-463-0690. Office Fax: 817-488-4099.

TRUJILLO, CARLOS, state legislator; b. LI, NY, Feb. 25, 1983; m. Carmen Mir; 1 child, Carlos Manuel. BS in Internat. Bus., Spring Hill Coll.; JD, Fla. State U. Asst. state atty. 11th Jud. Circuit of Fla.; mem. Dist. 116 Fla. House of Representatives, 2011—. Republican. Office: 13550 SW 88th St Miami FL 33186-1541 also: Fla House of Reps 1301 The Capitol 402 S Monroe St Tallahassee FL 32399-1300 Office Phone: 305-596-3030, 850-488-5047.

TRUJILLO, DAVID, investment company executive; BA, Yale U.; MBA, Stanford U. Investment banker Merrill Lynch & Co., Inc.; assoc. GTCR Golder Rauner, LLC., 1998—2000, v.p., 2002—06; joined TPG Capital (formerly Texas Pacific Group), 2006, prin. Bd. dirs. Triad Fin. Corp., HSM Electronic Protection Svcs., Inc., Sorenson Comm., Inc., Fenwal Transfusion Therapies, Inc., Univision Comm. Inc., 2009—. Office: TPG Capital LP Ste 3300 301 Commerce St Fort Worth TX 76102 Office Phone: 817-871-4000. Office Fax: 817-871-4001.

TRUNNELL, THOMAS NEWTON, dermatologist; b. Waterloo, Iowa, May 7, 1942; s. Thomas Lyle and Vivian (Dahl) T.; m. Patricia Rautiala, Aug. 2, 1974; children: Suzanne, Thomas, Sarah. AB cum laude, Princeton U., 1964; MD, U. Iowa, 1968. Diplomate Am. Bd. Dermatology, 1973. Intern U. So. Calif., LA, 1969; resident NYU, 1969—72; pvt. practice dermatology Tampa, Fla., 1974—; asst. clin. prof. U. S. Fla., Tampa, 1975—. Contbr. articles to profl. jours. Maj. USAF, 1972—74. Mem.: AMA, Fla. Dermatology Soc., Fla. Soc. Dermatological Surgeons (pres. 1993), Fla. Med. Assn., Am. Acad. Dermatology. Republican. United Methodist. Avocations: fishing, hunting. Office Phone: 813-977-1024.

TRUSTY, DAVID L., energy and services company executive; b. Portland, Oreg., 1958; BS in Economics, U. Tenn, Knoxville, 1979; MBA, Vanderbilt U., Nashville, 1981. Mgmt. intern Nashville Gas Co., 1980—83, mktg. svcs. mgr., 1983—84, dir. residential mktg., 1984—87, asst. v.p. mktg., 1987—89, v.p. mktg. Nashville divsn., 1989—97; v.p. mktg. Piedmont Natural Gas Co., Inc., Charlotte, NC, 1997—2004, v.p. corp. comm., 2004—. Office: Piedmont Natural Gas Co Inc 4720 Piedmont Row Dr Charlotte NC 28210 Office Phone: 704-731-4391. Office Fax: 704-365-3849. Business E-Mail: david.trusty@piedmontng.com.

TRUSTY, SHARON, former state legislator; b. Oregonia, Ohio, Aug. 27, 1945; m to Fritz; children: Katherine, Jonna & Jessica. Attended, Ark. Tech. Univ. Businesswoman Trusty & Assoc. Inc.; legis. liaison for Ark. Gov. Huckabee, 1999; mem. Dist. 4 Ark. State Senate, 2000—09. Bd. mem. Simmons First Bank; commr. Ark. Dept. Econ. Develop.; bd. mem. Ark. Dept. Work Force Edn. Bd. mem. Ark. Next Step Edn. Found., Ark. River Valley Arts Ctr., Child Develop. Inc.; bd. chmn. St. Mary's Regional Med. Ctr.; co-chair Ark. State Rep. Party, 1984—86. Republican. Baptist. Home: 8 Pine Forest Dr Russellville AR 72801-4514

TRYBULSKI, JOANN, adult nurse practitioner, educator; d. Anthony Pagliaro and Fannie DeCicco; m. Edmund Trybulski, Nov. 16, 1974; 1 child, Sarah. AAS in Nursing, Excelsior Coll., Albany, NY, 1978; BS in Biology, Fordham U., Bronx, NY, 1972; MS in Nursing, Simmons Coll., Boston, 1982; PhD, Boston Coll., Boston, 2001. Cert. adult nurse practitioner, Am. Nurse's Credentialing Ctr., 1982. Nurse practitioner Cmty. Health Plan, Peabody, Mass., 1984—95, asst. chief nursing, 1993—95; clin. asst. prof. MGH Inst. Health Professions, Boston, 1995—2002; asst. prof. U. Miami, Coral Gables, Fla., 2002—, assoc. dean master's programs, 2007—. Editor: Primary Care: A Collaborative Practice (Book of Yr. Clin. Practice, 1999, 2008). Acad. mem. Nat. Academies Practice, 2007. Mem.: Sigma Theta Tau (Pearl Rosendahl award Nursing Edn. Alpha Omega chpt. 2002). Roman Catholic. Achievements include research in women's long term responses to elective pregnancy termination - a phenomenological study; hispanic women's contraceptive choices, their origins and influences. Avocations: travel, cooking, exercise, golf.

TRYTHALL, HARRY GILBERT, music educator, composer; b. Knoxville, Tenn., Oct. 28, 1930; s. Harry Gilbert and Clara Hannah (Akre) T.; m. Jean Marie Slater, Dec. 28, 1951 (div. 1976); children: Linda Marie, Karen Elizabeth; m. Carol King, Sept. 19, 1985. BA, U. Tenn., 1951; MusM, Northwestern U., 1952; DMA, Cornell U., 1960. Asst. prof. music Knox Coll., Galesburg, Ill., 1960-64; prof. music theory and composition George Peabody Coll. Tchrs., Nashville, 1964-75; dean Creative Arts Ctr., 1975-81; prof. music W.Va. U., Morgantown, 1975-96; ret., 1997. Vis. prof. U. Federal do Espiritu Santo, Vitoria, Brazil, 1999-2000; adj. prof. Brookhaven Coll., Dallas, 2002-. Author: Principles and Practice of Electronic Music, 1974, Eighteenth Century Counterpoint, 1993, Sixteenth Century Counterpoint, 1994; past mem. editorial bd. Music Educators Jour.; composer orchestral music, chamber and electronic music. With USAF, 1953-57. Personal E-mail: htrythal@yahoo.com.

TSCHINKEL, VICTORIA JEAN, energy executive; b. Mt. Vernon, NY, Oct. 30, 1947; d. William Aaron and Edith (Meyerson) Nierenberg; m. Walter Rheinhardt Tschinkel, June 15, 1968; 1 child, Erika Lotte Elizabeth. AB in Zoology, U. Calif., Berkeley, 1968. Biologist, libr. Tall Timbers Rsch. Sta., Tallahassee, 1970—74; field insp., trustees Internal Improvement Trust Fund, 1974—76; environ. specialist Dept. Environ. Regulations, 1976, asst. to sec., 1976—77, asst. sec., 1977—81, sec., 1981—87; mem., energy rsch. adv. bd. Dept. Energy, 1979—86; mem. adv. panel on energy, city bldgs. Office Tech. Assessement, 1980—81; chmn. Solar Energy Inst., 1985—88; sr. environ. cons. Landers and Parsons, 1987—2002. Bd. govs. Argonne Nat. Lab., 1986—; bd. dirs. Phillips Petroleum, 1993—, ConocoPhillips, 2002—. Bd. dirs. NAS Site Selection Com. for Superconducting Supercollider; mem. energy rsch. adv. bd. Dept. Energy, 1979—86; mem., Adminstrv. Toxic substances Adv. Coun. EPA, 1982—84; mem. Capital Womens Network, Tallahassee, 1983—84, NRC, Washington, Space Applications Bd, 1983—85, Electric Power Rsch. Inst. Adv. Coun., 1986—92; bd. dirs. Fla. Defenders Environment, 1987—90; mem. adv. com. Nuclear Facility Safety, 1988—91; mem. Gas Rsch. Adv. Coun., Chgo., 1983—; bd. dirs. Environ. and Energy Inst., Washington, 1984—, Environ. & Energy Study Inst., 1986—, 1000 Friends of Fla., 1988—; trustee German Marshall Fund, 1989—. Named North Fla. Pub. Aminstr. of Yr., Am. Soc. Pub. Adminstrs., 1984. Fellow: Nat. Acad. Pub. Adminstrn.; mem.: Women Execs. State Govt. Office: ConocoPhillips Bd Directors 600 N Dairy Ashford Houston TX 77079 Office Phone: 281-293-1000. Personal E-mail: victoria.tschinkel@conocophillips.com.

TSEGAYE, THEODROS SOLOMON, biomedical researcher, medical doctor, educator; MD in Human Medicine, Jimma U. Sch. Medicine, 2006; PhD in Molecular Medicine, Hannover Biomed. Rsch. Sch., Germany, 2011. Intern doctor, human medicine Jimma U. Hosp., 2005—06; lectr., epidemiology and biostatistics Jimma U., 2006—07; rsch. scientist Hannover Med. Sch., 2007—11; postdoc. rsch. scientist CDC, 2011—. Recipient Young Investigator award, 16th Conf. on Retroviruses and Opportunistic Infections; Rsch. fellowship, Am. Soc. Microbiology. Mem.: Internat. Soc. Infectious Diseases, Ethiopian Med. Students Assn. Achievements include research in HIV-1 attachment and interaction with platelets. Avocations: travel, movies. Office: CDC 1600 Clifton Rd NE Bldg 17 Level 3 MS A25 Atlanta GA 30333 Personal E-mail: tedysol@yahoo.co.uk.*

TSENG, YANI, professional golfer; b. Taiwan, Jan. 23, 1989; Profl. golfer LPGA, 2007—. Named LPGA Tour Rookie of Yr., 2008, LPGA Player of Yr., 2010, Female Player of Yr., Golf Writers Assn. America, 2010; named one of The 100 Most Influential People in the World, TIME mag., 2012. Achievements include winning LPGA major tournaments: LPGA Championship, 2008, 2011; Kraft Nabisco Championship, 2010; Women's British Open, 2010, 2011; winning LPGA events: LPGA Corning Classic, 2009, P&G NW Arkansas Championship, 2010, Honda LPGA Thailand, LPGA State Farm Classic, 2011; becoming the first player from Taiwan to win a LPGA major championship, 2008; becoming the the youngest player to win five career LPGA major championships, 2008-11. Avocations: pool, movies. Office: LPGA 100 International Golf Dr Daytona Beach FL 32124

TSHUDY, DOUG, mining executive; Dir., bus. devel., Massey Metallurgical Coal Massey Energy Co. Office: Massey Energy Co 4 N 4th St Richmond VA 23219 Office Phone: 804-788-1800. Office Fax: 804-788-1870. Business E-Mail: doug.tshudy@masseyenergyco.com.

TSONGA, JO-WILFRIED, professional tennis player; b. Le Mans, France, Apr. 17, 1985; s. Didier and Evelyne Tsonga. Profl. tennis player ATP, 2004—. Mem. French nat. team Summer Olympic Games, London, 2012. Recipient Silver medal, men's doubles, Summer Olympic Games, 2012. Achievements include winner 8 career singles titles, 4 career doubles titles, ATP. Office: c/o ATP Tour 201 ATP Tour Blvd Ponte Vedra Beach FL 32082

TU, LAWRENCE P., lawyer, broadcast executive; b. NYC, Aug. 23, 1954; AB summa cum laude, Harvard Univ., 1976, JD magna cum laude, 1981; BA, Magdalen Coll., Oxford Univ., 1978. Bar: DC 1983, US Supreme Ct. 1988, Hong Kong 1996. Law clk. Judge Walter R. Mansfield, US Ct. Appeals, 2d cir., 1981—82, Justice Thurgood Marshall, US Supreme Ct., 1982—83; gen. counsel, Asia Pacific Goldman Sachs; spl. asst. to legal adviser U.S. Dept. State, 1985—86; assoc. O'Melveny & Myers LLP, 1986—89, ptnr., 1990—2001, mng. ptnr. Hong Kong office, 1995—2000; exec. v.p., gen. counsel NBC Universal, 2001—04; sr. v.p., gen. counsel Dell, Inc., 2004—14; sr. exec. v.p., chief legal officer CBS Corp., Los Angeles, Calif., 2014—. Editor (notes): Harvard Law Rev., 1979—81. Rhodes Scholar. Mem.: ABA, Minority Corp. Counsel Assn. Bd., DC Bar. Office: CBS Corporation 7800 Beverly Blvd Los Angeles CA 90036*

TUBB, JAMES CLARENCE, lawyer; b. Corsicana, Tex. s. Cullen Louis and Sarah Elmore (Chapman) T.; m. Suzanne Alice Smith, Nov. 25, 1954; children: James Richard, Sara Elizabeth, Daniel Chapman. BA, So. Meth. U., 1951, JD, 1954. Bar: Tex. 1954, U.S. Dist. Ct. (no. dist.) Tex. 1955, U.S. Ct. Appeals (5th cir.) 1959, U.S. Supreme Ct. 1978; cert. comml. real estate specialist, 1983; lic. Tex. real estate broker; cert. mediator Dallas Bar Assn. With legal dept. Schlumberger Well Surveying Corp., Houston, 1954-55; claims atty. Franklin Am. Ins. Co., Dallas, 1957-58; ptnr. Vial, Hamilton, Koch, Tubb & Knox and predecessor firm Akin, Vial, Hamilton, Koch & Tubb, Dallas, 1958-84; dir., ptnr. Winstead, McGuire, Sechrest & Minick, Dallas, 1984-90; pvt. practice Dallas, 1990—. Guest lectr. on real estate broker liability Real Estate Ctr., Tex. A&M U., 1987. Mem. bd. deacons Highland Park Presbyn. Ch., Dallas, 1972—78, ruling elder, 1978—84, 1988—91; mem. permanent jud. commn. Grace Presbytery, 1984—90; bd. dirs. Christian Concern Found., 1965—71, Dallas County affiliate Am. Diabetes Assn., 1991—95. With Tex. Air N.G., 1949—51, 1st lt. JAGC, SAC USAF, 1955—57, 1st lt. USAF, ret. Recipient Outstanding Student award Student Bar Assn., 1954. Fellow Tex. Bar Found.; mem. ABA (chmn. comml. law com. gen. practice sect. 1982-84, real estate probate and trust law sect.), Tex. Bar Assn., Am. Arbitration Assn. (sec. comml. arbitration panelist), Dallas Country Club, Dallas County Rep. Men's Club (sec. 1978-79). Home and Office: 3407 Haynie Ave Dallas TX 75205-1842 Office Phone: 214-232-8964.

TUBESING, RICHARD LEE, library director; b. Kansas City, Mo., Nov. 25, 1937; s. Clarence and Letha (Thacker) T. BA, Yale U., 1959; MA, U. Chgo., 1969; MSL, Western Mich. U., 1972. Asst. to dir. U. Louisville, 1972-73; reference libr. Ga. Tech. Libr., Atlanta, 1973-76; head bus. and sci. Atlanta Pub. Libr., 1976-79; libr. dir. Lewis U., Romeoville, Ill., 1979-81; collection devel. coord. U. Toledo Libr., 1981-86; libr. dir. Coll. of the Southwest, Hobbs, N.Mex., 1986-89; libr. dir., dir. libr. sci. program Glenville (W.Va.) State Coll., 1989-99; ret., 1999. Part-time libr. Gilmer Pub. Libr., Glenville, W.Va. Author: Architectural Preservation, 1978, Architectural Preservation and Urban Renovation, 1982. Program coord. Lea County Archaeol. Soc., Hobbs, 1987-89. Lt. j.g. USNR, 1960-63. Mem. W.Va. Libr. Assn., Lea County Libr. Assn. (v.p. 1987-88, pres. 1988-89). Home: 351 E Valley Dr Glenville WV 26351-9416

TUCHMAN, ALAN, publishing executive; V.p. Alliance Entertainment Corp., 1991—96, pres., COO, 2000—05, sr. v.p. strategic planning, 1996—97, pres. AEC One Stop Group, Inc., 1997—2000, pres., COO, 2000—05; exec. v.p., pres. Alliance divsn. Source Interlink Cos., 2005—06, interim co-CEO, 2006—08; pres. distbn. Source Interlink Companies, Inc., 2008—. Office: Source Interlink Cos 27500 Riverview Center Blvd Bonita Springs FL 34134 Office Phone: 239-949-4450.

TUCK, GRAYSON EDWIN, retired real estate agent, gas industry executive; b. Richmond, Va., May 11, 1927; s. Bernard Okly and Erma (Wiltshire) T.; m. Rosalie Scroggs, June 6, 1947; children—Janice Lorrain, Kenneth Edwin, Carol Lynn. BS, U. Richmond, 1950. Payroll clk., cost clk. Gen. Baking Co., Richmond, 1948-51; jr. accountant Commonwealth Natural Gas Corp., Richmond, 1951-55, sr. accountant, 1956-57, accounting supr., 1957-58, asst. treas., 1959-62, asst. sec., asst. treas., 1963-64, treas., asst. sec., 1965-77; treas. Commonwealth Natural Resources, Inc., 1977-81, CNG Transmission Co. subs., 1977-79; sec.-treas. Air Pollution Control Products, Inc., Richmond, 1970-73; asst. treas., asst. sec. Commonwealth Gas Distbn. Corp., Richmond, 1969-79; mgr. taxes and cash mgmt. Commonwealth Gas Pipeline Corp., subs. Columbia Gas System Inc., 1981-86; investor, realtor Bill Eudailey & Co., 1986—2010; realtor Keller Williams Realty, 2010—11. Active Boy Scouts Am., 1965—69; bd. dirs. Henrico Area Mental Health Retardation Svcs., 1983—85; active Elpis Christian Ch., 2001—; deacon Presbyn. Ch., 1958—86, elder, 1986—2001, treas., 1968—70. With USNR, 1945—46. Mem.: Nat. Assn. Accts. (assoc. dir. 1963—64). Home: 2923 Oakland Ave Richmond VA 23228-5827 Personal E-mail: realtortuck1@comcast.net.

TUCKER, ANNE WILKES, curator, historian, photographer, critic; b. Baton Rouge, Oct. 18, 1945; BA in Art History, Randolph-Macon Women's Coll., Lynchburg, Va., 1967; AAS in Photographic Illustration, Rochester Inst. Tech., 1968; MFA in Photographic History, SUNY, Buffalo, 1972. Rsch. asst. Internat. Mus. Photography at the George Eastman House, Rochester, NY, 1968—70; rsch. assoc. Gernsheim Collection U. Tex., Austin, 1969, 1970; curatorial intern dept. photography Mus. Modern Art, NYC, 1970—71; photography cons. Creative Artists Pub. Svc. Program, NYC, 1971—72; vis. lectr. New Sch. for Social Rsch., NY, 1973; dir. photography lecture series Cooper Unionn Forum, NYC, 1972—75; lectr. Cooper Union for Advancement of Arts and Sci., NY, 1972—75; vis. lectr. Phila. Coll. Art, 1973—75; affiliate artist U. Houston, 1976—80; curator photography Mus. Fine Arts, Houston, 1976—; Gus and Lyndall Wortham cur., photographic historian and critic, lectr., 1984—. Trustee Visual Studies Workshop, 1980—, Houston Ctr. Photography, 1991—96, Houston Foto Fest, 1988—, art adv. bd., 1987—, bd. dirs., 1990—; trustee Randolph Coll., 2008—, FotoFest, 1990—; visual arts panel The Houston Festival, 1981—83; adv. bd. Randolph-Macon Woman's Coll. Art Gallery, 1982—84; bd. trustees Am. Leadership Forum, 1992—94, co-chair selection com., 1993—94; dir. numerous exhbns. and workshops; lectr. in field; mem. numerous juries and panels. Author: (books and catalogues) Walker Evans: Photographs, 1971, The Woman's Eye, 1973; author: (with Lee Witkin) Rare Books and Photographs, Catalogue 1, The Witkin Gallery, 1973; author: (with William C. Agee) The Target Collection of American Photography, 1977; author: Target II: 5 American Photographers, 1981, Target III: In Sequence, 1982; author: (with Philip Brookman) Robert Frank: New York to Nova Scotia, 1986; author: A Photographic Portrait, Vol. 1: Historic Texas; Vol. II: Contemporary Texas, 1986; author: (with Maggie Olvey) The Sonia and Kaye Marvins Portrait Collection, 1986; author: Photo Notes & Filmfront, 1977; author: (with other curators) The Museum of Fine Arts, Houston: A Guide to the Collection, 1981; author: Unknown Territory: Photography by Ray K. Metzker, 1957-83, 1984, Fifth Annual International Fine Art Photography Exposition, 1984; author: (with Andy Grundberg) American Prospects: The Photographs of Joel Sternfeld, 1987, 2d edit., 1994; author: (with Willie Morris) American Classroom: The Photographs of Catherine Wagner, 1988; author: Five Jerome Artists, 1988; author: (with Pamela Allara) Crosscurrents/Crosscountry, 1988; author: The Art of Photography 1839-1989, 1989, A Permanent Legacy: 150 Masterpieces From the Museum of Fine Arts, Houston, 1989; author: (with other authors) Money Matters: A Critical Look at Bank Architecture, 1990; author: The Blue Man: Photographs by Keith Carter, 1990; author: (with Pete Daniel) Carry Me Home: Photographs by Debbie Fleming Caffery, 1990; author: George Krauze, 1991, Ansel Adams: American Icons, 1992, Tradition and the Unpredictable: The Allan Chasanoff Photographic Collection, 1994, Quest for the Moon and other stories: Three Decades of Astronauts in Space, 1994, Toshio Shibata: Landscape, 1996 (Photo-Eye Best Contemporary Monograph award, 1996), Crimes and Splendors: The Desert Cantos of Richard Misrach, 1996 (Golden Light award, 1996), Charles Schorre, 1997, Myths, Dreams and Realities: Contemporary Argentine Photographs, 1997, Irving Penn, 1999, Mario Carvo Neto, 1999, Amy Blakemore, 1999, Irving Penn Dancer: Photographs of Alexandra Bellar, 2001, Heart and Soul: The Photographs of Ray Carrington III 1993-2002, 2002, Joe Mills: Inner City, 2003, History of Japanese Photography 1853-2000, 2003 (Golden Light award), First Down Houston, Birth of An NFL Franchise, 2003, La Oscura Piel De La Luz; La Obra Fotografica De Mario Cravo Neto, 2003, David Carol: 40 Miles of Bad Road, 2004, Alec Soth: Sleeping by the Mississippi, 2004, Documenting Poetry Contemporary Latin American Photography, 2005, Icons of Photography, 2005, On Assignment, 2005, Mark Cohen: Grim Street, 2005, David Maisel: Terminal Mirage, 2005, (exhbns. and catalogues) A Fotographia Na Arte Contemporanea, 1995;: The Sonia and Kaye Marvins Portrait Collection, 1995, Keith Carter: Reinventing the World, 1995, Illuminations: Women writing on Photography from the 1850's to the present, 1996, Brassai: The Eye of Paris, 1999, Louis Faurer, 2001 (Mus. Pub. Design Competition First prize, 2002), This Was the Photo League: Compassion and the Camera from the Depression to the Cold War, 2001 (Photo-Eye runner-up Best Visual Anthology, 2001), History of Japanese Photography, 2003 (named to Top 12 Photo Books of 2003, Spl. Commendations from Kraszna-Krausz Photography Book Awards, 2005); co-prodr. (video) Fire in the East: The Portrait of Robert Frank, 1986; editor: (books and catalogues) The Anthony G. Cronin Memorial Collection, 1979, (manual) Suzanne Bloom and Ed Hill, 1980, (exhbns. and catalogues) Reframings, New American Feminist Photographies, 1995, The Photo League, 1987, Czech Modernism 1900-1945, 1990, Paul Strand: Essays on His Life and Work, 1990, George Krause, 1992; co-editor: Building a Photographic Library, 2001; singer (photographer): Caught in Act: Lou Stoumen Vintage Photographs, 1995, Crimes and Splendors: The Desert Cantos of Richard Misrach, 1996, Brassai: The Eye of Paris (1999); History of Japanese Phtoography 1853-2000, The Great Wall of China: Photographs by Chen Changfen, 2006, Chaotic Harmony: Contemporary Korean Photography, 2009, Robert Mapplethorpe: eros and order, 2010, Images of Armed Conflict and its Aftermath, 2012; contbr. articles to numerous profl. jours. and mags., essays to books; subject of numerous interviews and articles. Recipient Third Ann. Publ. award, Internat. Ctr. Photography, 1987, Bronze Apple award, Am. Film and Video Festival, 1987, John Simon Guggenheim Meml. Alumna Achievement award, Randolph-Macon Woman's Coll., 1993, Alumnae Achievement award, 1993, Lifetime Achievement award, Griffin Mus., 2006, Kraszna-Krausz Foundation Book award, Images of Armed Conflict and its Aftermath, 2013, Aperture Found. - Paris Photo Special Jury Mentio, 2014; named Best Curator, TIME Mag., 2001; named to The 100 Most Important People in Photography, American Photo Mag., 2005; grantee Nat. Endowment Arts grantee, 1976, 1986, 1989; fellowship for mus. profls., Nat. Endowment Arts, 1990, John Simon Guggenheim Meml. Found. fellowship award, 1983—84, Rsch. Support grant, The Getty Ctr. for the History of Art and the Humanities Resource Collections, 1995. Mem.: Houston Ctr. for Photography (adv. bd 1980—90, bd. trustees 1990—93, sec. 1990—93, adv. bd. 1994—95, exhbn. com. pres. 1999—), Art Table, Inc., Coll. Art Assn., Soc. Photographic Edn. (nat. bd. dirs. 1976—80, sec. nat. bd. 1977—79). Office: Mus Fine Arts Houston PO Box 6826 Houston TX 77265 Office Phone: 713-639-7347. Business E-Mail: atucker@mfah.org.

TUCKER, DAVID E., energy executive; BS in Fin., Bentley Coll., Waltham, 1984. Gen. mgr., Power Svc. General Electric Energy, gen. mgr., Bus. Devel., 2001—04; v.p., GE Capital Audit Staff, v.p., CFO, GECS Equipment Mgmt. Svc., sr. v.p., CFO, Vendor Fin. Svcs., GE Comml. Fin., exec. audit mgr. GE Co.; COO, VetcoGray Inc. General

Electric Co., 2007—. Office: VetcoGray Inc Ste 300 3010 Briarpark Ave Houston TX 77042 Office Phone: 713-683-2400. Office Fax: 713-683-2421. Business E-Mail: david.tucker@ge.com.

TUCKER, DON EUGENE, retired lawyer; b. Rockbridge, Ohio, Feb. 3, 1928; s. Beryl Hollis and Ruth (Primmer) T.; m. Elizabeth Jane Parke, Aug. 2, 1950; children: Janet Elizabeth, Kerry Jane, Richard Parke. BA, Aurora Coll., 1951; LL.B., Yale, 1956; LHD, Aurora U., 2011. Bar: Ohio 1956. Since practiced in, Youngstown, Ohio; asso. Manchester, Bennett, Powers & Ullman, 1956-62, ptnr., 1962-73, of counsel, 1973-87; gen. counsel Comml. Intertech Corp., Youngstown, 1973-75, v.p., gen. counsel, 1975-83, also dir., sr. v.p., gen. counsel, 1983-87, sr. v.p., 1987-93; ret., 1993. Solicitor Village of Poland, Ohio, 1961-63; former chmn. bd., pres., trustee United Cerebral Palsy Assn., Youngstown and Mahoning County; trustee Mahoning County Tb and Health Assn.; former trustee, pres. Indsl. Info. Inst.; former pres., trustee Ea. Ohio Lung Assn.; trustee, former chmn. Cmty. Corp.; trustee, former pres. Butler Inst. Am. Art. With USMCR, 1946-48, 51-53. Mem. Ohio Bar Assn., Mahoning County Bar Assn. (pres. 1972, trustee 1970-73), Youngstown Area C. of C. (chmn. bd. dirs. 1979). Methodist. Home: 3000 Galloway Rdg Apt E-208 Pittsboro NC 27312-8689

TUCKER, HERBERT, English professor; BA, Amherst Coll., 1971; PhD, Yale U., 1977. Fellow Tchg. and Tech. Initiative, Va., 2008—09; John C. Coleman prof. english dept. Univ. of Va. With shannon ctr. for advanced studies Univ. of Va., 1986—88, 1997; Margaret Bundy Scott vis. prof. Williams Coll., 2006. Series editor (jour.) Victorian Lit. and Culture, Va., 1989, assoc. editor New Lit. History, 1996; editor: (book) Critical Essays on Alfred Lord Tennyson, 1993, Under Criticism, 1998, A Companion to Victorian Literature and Culture, 1999, Victorian Literature, 2001; author: Browning's Beginnings: The Art of Disclosure, 1980, Tennyson and the Doom of Romanticism, 1988, Britain's Heroic Muse, 2008, (articles) Epic, Ever a Fighter: Browning's Struggle with Conflict, 2010, Elizabeth Barrett and Robert Browning, 2010, and numerous others. Danforth Fellow, 1973—77, Whiting Fellow, 1976—77, MLA-ACLS Fellow, 1982—83. Office: University Va Department of English 219 Bryan Hall Charlottesville VA 22904-4121 Office Fax: 434-924-1478.

TUCKER, HOWARD MCKELDIN, investment banker, consultant; b. Washington, Apr. 1, 1930; s. Howard Newell and Bessie Draper (McKeldin) T.; m. Julia Spencer Merrell, Feb. 1, 1952 (div. 1975); children: Deborah, Mark, Alexander, Howard David; m. Megan Evans, Aug. 17, 1979. BA, U. Va., 1954; postgrad., NYU, 1956; MBA, Stern Sch. CFA., 1965. With J.P. Morgan & Co., 1954—61, Mackall & Coe, Washington, 1961—69, Legg Mason & Co., Washington, 1969—79, Govt. Rsch. Corp./Nat. Jour., 1979—82, Potomac Asset Mgmt., 1982—91; ptnr., mng. dir. Capital Insights Group, Washington, 1991—2001; with Skillsmith, LLC, 2002—05. Mem. task force balance-of-payments U.S.Treasury Dept., 1967-72; cons. County Natwest (Washinton Analysis Corp.), 1985-90; bd. dirs. Monarch Enterprises, Inc., Uniflight, Inc., Sci. Mgmt. Assocs., Inc., Jeffrey Bigelow Assocs. USA Nica Wind Power. Author: Literature in Medicine, In Memoriam, Michael Halberstam, M.D., 1984; book reviewer Washington Post; contbr. articles to profl. jours. Dir. Washington Area Coun. Chs., 1962-65; vestryman Christ Episcopal Ch., Georgetown, 1962-65; mem. chpt. Washington Nat. Cathedral, 1966-72; del. Va. Republican Conv., 1968; trustee Nat. Cathedral Sch. for Girls, 1972-78; chmn. Missionary Devel. Fund Episcopal Diocese D.C., 1974; co-dir. Andover-Exeter Washington Intern Program, 1976-86; co-organizer U.S.-German Parliamentary Exchange, 1980-82; observer OECD, 1980-82; spl. overseas visitor Australian Govt., 1982; patron West Europe program Woodrow Wilson Ctr., 1985-86; bd. dirs. Am. Hort. Soc., 1998-2008. With USNR, 1950—56. Mem.: CFA, DumPlings Club, Fin. Analysts Fedn., Washington Soc. Investment Analysts, Nat. Economists Club, Cogswell Soc., Hist. Alexandria Found., Alexandria Seaport Found., Old Dominion Boat Club, Naval and Mil. Club London, Nat. Press Club, Saints and Sinners Club, Georgetown Visitation Tennis Club, Beta Theta Pi. Home: 4 Potomac Ct Alexandria VA 22314-3821 Personal E-mail: hmcktucker@yahoo.com.

TUCKER, J. WALTER, JR., manufacturing executive; Vice chmn. Keystone Consolidated Industries, Inc., Dallas, chmn., 1987—. Office: 3 Lincoln Ctr 5430 LBJ Fwy Ste 1740 Dallas TX 75240-2697 Fax: 972-458-8108.

TUCKER, JOHN MARK, librarian, educator; s. Paul Marlin and Edith Tucker; m. Barbara Ann Wilson, Mar. 22, 1968. BA, David Lipscomb Coll., 1967; MLS, George Peabody Coll. Tchrs., 1968, specialist in edn., 1972; PhD, U. Ill., 1983. Head libr. Freed-Hardeman Coll., Henderson, Tenn., 1968-71; reference libr. Wabash Coll., Crawfordsville, Ind., 1973-79, Purdue U., West Lafayette, Ind., 1979-82, asst. prof. libr. sci., 1979-85, assoc. prof. libr. sci., 1985-89, sr. reference libr. Humanities, Social Sci. and Edn. Libr., 1982-90, prof. libr. sci., 1989—2003, libr. Humanities, Social Sci. and Edn. Libr., 1990—2003, prof. emeritus library sci., 2003—; dean libr., info. resources Abilene Christian U., 2003—. Mem. grantee com. instl. coop. NEH, 1991—94. Co-editor: Reference Services and Library Education, 1983, User Instruction in Academic Libraries, 1986, American Library History, 1989, Reading for Moral Progress, 1997; editor: Untold Stories: Civil Rights, Libraries and Black Librarianship, 1998; mem. editl. bd. Dictionary of American Library Biography, 2002; mem. editl. bd.: Libr. Issues; contbr. articles to profl. jours.; co-editor: Libraries & Culture: Historical Essays Honoring the Legacy of Donald G. Davis, Jr., 2006; mem. editl. bd. Libraries & the Cultural Record. Thomas S. Wilmeth grantee, 1988, Frederick B. Artz Rsch. grantee, Oberlin Coll. Archives, 1991, Rsch. fellow, Coun. Libr. Resources, 1990. Mem.: SCV, ALA (chair libr. history round table 1993—94), Disciples of Christ Hist. Soc., Assn. Coll. and Rsch. Librs., Beta Phi Mu, Phi Kappa Phi. Democrat. Mem. Ch. Of Christ. Home: 1687 Bent Tree Dr Abilene TX 79602 Office: Brown Libr Abilene Christian U Box 29208 Abilene TX 79699-9208 Office Phone: 325-674-2387. Business E-Mail: mark.tucker@acu.edu.

TUCKER, LAUREY DAN, lawyer; s. Floyd A. and Harriet Kathleen (Graves) T.; m. Katherine Washburn, June 21, 1958; children: Laurie Tucker Diaz, Dana Tucker Kleine. BSChemE, U. Okla., Norman, 1959, LLB, 1962. Bar: Okla. 1962, Tex. 1972. Patent atty. Phillps Petroleum Co., Bartlesville, Okla., 1964—67, Monsanto Co., St. Louis, 1967—70, patent mgr. Texas City, Tex., 1970—74; ptnr. Hubbard, Tucker & Harris, Dallas, 1974—94, Harris, Tucker & Hardin, Dallas, 1994—97, Locke Purnell Rain Harrell, Dallas, 1997—98, Locke Liddell & Sapp LLP, Dallas, 1999—2006. Past pres. Dallas-Ft. Worth Patent Assn. Capt. USAR, 1959—69, 1st lt. US Army, 1962—64. Mem.: State Bar Tex. (past officer Intellectual Property Law Section), Okla. Bar Assn. Republican. Episcopalian. Avocations: fishing, hunting, travel. Personal E-mail: tucker_dan@sbcglobal.net.

TUCKER, LAURIE A., marketing executive; b. 1957; m. John Tucker; 2 children. BBA, U. Memphis, 1978, MBA, 1983. Fin. analyst FedEx Corp., 1978—83, mgr. pricing, 1983—89, mng. dir. customer automation & invoicing, 1989, sr. v.p. logistics, electronic commerce & catalog divsn., 1996, sr. v.p. corp. mktg., 2000—. Bd. dirs. Iron Mountain, Inc., Boston, 2007—. FedEx co-chair March of Dimes; mem. United Way Alexis de Tocqueville Soc., 1998—; bd. visitors U. Memphis. Recipient inaugural Diversity Champion award, FedEx Services, Woman of Achievement award, The Women's Project, 2008, Disting. Alumni award, U. Memphis, 2001; named Outstanding Alumna, Fogelman Coll. Bus. and Econ.; named one of Who's Who in B2B Advt., BtoB Mag., 2008, 2009, The 25 Best Marketers, 2009. Office: FedEx Corp 942 S Shady Grove Rd Memphis TN 38120

TUCKER, N(IMROD) H(OLT), III, physician; b. Columbus, Ga., Nov. 22, 1947; s. Nimrod Holt Jr. and Sarah Elizabeth (King) T.; m. Kathryn Gail Waddle, June 6, 1976; children: Jennifer Leigh, Nimrod Holt IV. BS, Auburn U., Ala., 1969; MD, U. Ala., 1973. Diplomate Am. bd. Internal Medicine. Intern and resident ednl. program Jacksonville Hosp. U. Fla., 1973-76; pvt. practice Jacksonville, Fla., 1976—; mem. med. staff St. Vincent's Hosp., Jacksonville, 1976—. Bd. dirs. Profl. Found. for Health Care, Tampa, Fla. Bd. dirs. Fla. C.C. Found., Jacksonville, 1986—, St. Vincent's Hosp. Heart and Lung Inst., 1989—, Fla.-Ga. Blood Alliance, 1999—; chair bd. dirs., 2008. Fellow ACP (bd. dirs. Fla. chpt. 1988—); mem. Fla. Soc. Internal Medicine (bd. dirs. 1988-, v.p. 1998), AMA, Fla. Med. Assn. (del. 1987, 89), Duval County Med. Soc. (pres. 1999), Jacksonville C. of C. (bd. dirs. 1999), Timuquana Country Club, Fla. Yacht Club, River Club. Methodist. Avocations: racquetball, tennis, golf, poker, bridge. Office: 2149 St Johns Ave Jacksonville FL 32204-4418 Office Phone: 904-384-2525.

TUCKER, RICHARD A., airport terminal executive; Exec. dir. Huntsville (Ala.) Internat. Airport, Huntsville, AL, 1995—. Office: Huntsville Internat Airport 1000 Glenn Hearn Blvd Box 20008 Huntsville AL 35824

TUCKER, RUSSELL B., insurance company executive; V.p. Am. Income Life Ins. Co., Inc.; cons. Torchmark Corp., v.p. Birmingham, Ala., 1997—2001, exec. v.p., chief investment officer, 2001. Office: Torchmark Corp PO Box 8080 3700 S Stonebridge Dr Mc Kinney TX 75070-8080 Office Phone: 972-569-4000.

TUCKER, THOMAS JAMES, retired investment company executive; b. Atlanta, Sept. 5, 1929; s. Thomas Tudor and Carol (Govan) T.; m. Margaret Guerard. BA, U. of the South, 1952. With CIT Corp, NYC, 1957—72; pres., CEO AmSouth Fin. Corp., Birmingham, Ala., 1972—82, chmn. bd., 1982, dir., 1972—93; exec. v.p. AmSouth Bank N.A., Birmingham, 1982—93, chief credit officer, 1992—93; prin. Tucker Investments, Birmingham, 1994—2003; ret., 2003. Exec. v.p. AmSouth Bancorp, Birmingham, 1982-93; bd. dirs. Alabanc Properties Corp., Birmingham, chmn., 1991-93; bd. dirs. Birmingham Broadway Series Inc., treas., 1996-97, pres., 1997-99, chmn., 1999-2001; co-founder Garland-Govan Scholarship Fund, Sewanee-U. of the South. Photographer gen. interest mags., 1970—; contbr. articles on credit and leasing to trade jours. Bd. dirs. Birmingham Cmty. Devel. Corp.; chmn. bd., 1990-93. 1st lt. USAF, 1952-56. Mem.: Birmingham Art Mus. Assn., Birmingham Bot. Soc., Friends of Emmt O'Neal Libr., Cahaba River Soc. (adv. bd. 1991-92, bd. dirs. 1993-98, v.p. orgnl. devel. 1995-98), Manigault Soc., Order of Purple/Sewanee-U. of the South, Never Failing Succession of Benefactors/Sewanee-U. of the South, Carolynne Scott Writers Group (2d pl. 2006, 3rd pl. 2007, Hackney Short Fiction awards), The Club, Silhouettes Club. Episcopalian. Avocations: photography, writing. Home: 415 Club Pl Birmingham AL 35223 Office: 6 Office Park Cir Ste 208 Birmingham AL 35223-2541

TUCKER, TOMMY, SR., state legislator; Attended, NC State U. Factory representative Internat. Comfort Products, 1987—2000; owner Parks Heating and Cooling, 2000—; councilman, mayor pro tem City of Weddington, 1994—96; commissioner Union County, 1996—2000; state senator Dist. 35 NC, 2010—. With USN. Republican. Mailing: 1206 Rosehill Dr Waxhaw NC 28173 Office: NC Senate 300 N Salisbury St Room 311 Raleigh NC 27603-5925 Office Phone: 919-733-7659, 704-654-8410. Business E-Mail: Tommy.Tucker@ncleg.net.

TUCKER, WILLIAM EDWARD, academic administrator, minister; b. Charlotte, NC, June 22, 1932; s. Cecil Edward and Ethel Elizabeth (Godley) T.; m. Ruby Jean Jones, Apr. 8, 1955; children: Janet Sue, William Edward, Gordon Vance. BA, Barton Coll., Wilson, NC, 1953, LLD (hon.), 1978; BD, Tex. Christian U., Ft. Worth, 1956; MA, Yale U., New Haven, Conn., 1958, PhD, 1960; LHD (hon.), Chapman U., Orange, Calif., 1981, Ky. Wesleyan Coll., Owensboro, 1989; DH (hon.), Bethany Coll., W.Va., 1982; DD (hon.), Austin Coll., Sherman, Tex., 1985. Ordained to ministry Disciples of Christ Ch., 1956; prof. Barton Coll., 1959-66, chmn. dept. religion and philosophy, 1961-66; mem. faculty Brite Div. Sch., Tex. Christian U., 1966-76, prof. ch. history, 1969-76, dean, 1971-76, chancellor, 1979-98, chancellor emeritus, 1998—. Pres. Bethany (W.Va.) Coll., 1976-79; dir. RadioShack Corp., 1985-2003, Brown and Lupton Found.; mem. gen. bd. Christian Ch. (Disciples of Christ), 1971-74, 75-87, adminstrv. com., 1975-81, chmn. theol. edn. commn., 1972-73, mem. exec. com., chmn. bd. higher edn., 1975-77; dir. Christian Ch. Found., 1980-83; moderator Christian Ch. (Disciples of Christ), 1983-85 Author: J.H. Garrison and Disciples of Christ, 1964, (with others) Journey in Faith: A History of the Christian Church (Disciples of Christ), 1975; also articles. Bd. dirs. Van Cliburn Found., 1981—; bd. trustees Amon Carter Mus. Mem. Exch. Club, Phi Beta Kappa. Home: 2337 Colonial Pky Fort Worth TX 76109-1030 Office: 777 Taylor St Ste P2-J Fort Worth TX 76102 Office Phone: 817-347-3220. Business E-Mail: w.tucker@tcu.edu.

TUFFY, JANET, human resources specialist; BA in Psychology, 1975. Dir., human resources Alfa Romeo, 1986—90; v.p., human resources Castrol N.Am., 1992—2000; v.p., exec. talent American Express Co., 2001—06; exec. v.p., human resources King Pharmaceuticals, Inc. Office: King Pharmaceuticals Inc 501 5th St Bristol TN 37620 Office Phone: 423-989-8000. Office Fax: 423-274-8677. Business E-Mail: janet.tuffy@kingpharm.com.

TUGGLE, CLYDE CEBRON, beverage company executive; b. Atlanta, Apr. 9, 1962; s. Arthur Coleman and Nelle (Martin) Tuggle. Student, Ludwig-Maxillian U., Munich; grad. exec. program, U. VA. Darden Sch. Bus.; BA in German Studies and Econs., Hamilton Coll., Clinton, NY, 1984; MDiv, Yale U., 1988. Market analyst Scott, Fitton & Co., New Haven, 1987-88; editor, corp. issues comm. dept. Coca-Cola Co., Atlanta, 1989—92, mng. editor, 1992, exec. asst. to chmn., CEO, 1992—98, dir. ops. devel., dep. to div. pres., region mgr. Vienna, 1998—2000, exec. asst. for chmn. and CEO to v.p. Atlanta, 2000—03, dir., worldwide comm., 2001—02, sr. v.p., worldwide pub. affairs/comm., 2002—05, pres. Russia, Ukraine, Belarus bus. unit Moscow, 2005—. Bd. dirs. Sledco, Inc., Ga. Rsch. Alliance; mem. exec. com. Coca-Cola Co., 2003—. Bd. dirs. Yale U. Divinity Sch., So. Ctr. Internat. Studies, Atlanta Symphony Orch., East Lake Cmty. Found., High Mus. Arts; trustee Agnes Scott Coll.; bd. vis. Emory U. Mem.: Metro Atlanta C. of C. (bd. dirs.), US Austrian C. of C., Coun. Fgn. Rels. Episcopalian. Office: Co Hdqs 1 Coca Cola Plz Atlanta GA 30313-1734 Office Phone: 404-676-2121.

TUGGLE, DAVID W., pediatric surgeon; b. Tex. BS with highest honors, Abilene Christian U., Tex., 1975; MD, U. Tex. Southwestern Med. Sch., 1979. Diplomate Am. Bd. Surgery, cert. Spl. Competence in Pediat. Surgery and Added Qualification in Surgical Critical Care, lic. Tex., 1979, Okla., 1985. Resident, gen. surgery Parkland Meml. Hosp., Dallas, 1979—82, 1983—84, chief resident, gen. surgery, 1984—85; surgical rsch. fellow U. Tex. Health Sci. Ctr., Dallas, 1982—83; chief resident, pediat. surgery Okla. Children's Meml. Hosp., 1985—87; coord., surgical critical care Children's Hosp. Okla., 1987—; clin. asst. prof., dept. pediat. U. Okla., 1987—, asst. prof. surgery, dept. surgery, sect. pediat. surgery, 1987—92, assoc. prof. surgery, dept. surgery, sect. pediat. surgery, 1992—99, chief, sect. pediat. surgery, dept. surgery, 1995—, prof. surgery, dept. surgery, sect. pediat. surgery, 1999—, Paula Milburn Miller, Children's Med. Rsch. Inst., chair pediat. surgery, 2001—, vice-chmn., dept. surgery, 2002—. Trauma med. dir. Okla. U. Med. Ctr., Level 1 Trauma Ctr., 1999—2001; dir., Extracorporeal Membrane Oxygenation Ctr. Children's Hosp. Okla., 1992—97. Peer-reviewer Archives of Surgery, Journal Pediatric Surgery; contbr. several articles to profl. jours. Recipient Weigelt-Wallace award for exemplary med. care for performing an on-site amputation to free a victim from the debris of the Olka. City bombing, 1995. Fellow: Am. Acad. Pediat. (Spl. Achievement award 1996), Am. Coll. Critical Care Medicine, ACS (com. on trauma 1997—2003, liaison to Am. Acad. Pediat. com. on pediat. emergency 2002—, Okla. Dist. #1 com. on applicants 1994—99, verification review com. 1995—2003); mem.: Okla. Chpt. ACS (vice-pres. 1995—96, pres.-elect 1996—97, pres. 1997—98, Spl. Achievement award 1996), Am. Assn. Surgery of Trauma, AMA, Am. Pediat. Surgical Assn. (critical care com. 1992—93, publications com. 1995—98, trauma com. 1998, chmn. 2004—05), Am. Soc. for Parental and Enteral Nutrition, Am. Trauma Soc., Assn. for Academic Surgery, Ctrl. Okla. Pediat. Soc., Okla. City Surgical Soc., Okla. County Med. Assn., Okla. Organ Sharing Network, Okla. State Med. Assn., Okla. Surgical Assn., Parkland Surgical Soc., Soc. for Critical Care Medicine (sec./treas., surgical sect. 1987—90, chmn. surgical sect. 1991—92), Southwestern Surgical Congress, So. Surgical Assn., Alpha Omega Alpha. Achievements include being part of surgical team who separated what is believed to be the first known American Indian conjoined twins in 2008. Office: U Okla Dept Surgery PO Box 26901 CHO 2B 2403 Oklahoma City OK 73126 Office Phone: 405-271-5922. Office Fax: 405-271-3278. Business E-Mail: David-Tuggle@ouhsc.edu.

TUGGLE, MARK M., state legislator; married; 1 child. MS in Mgmt., Faulkner U., Montgomery, Ala. Profl. forester; mem. Dist. 81 Ala. House of Representatives, 2011—. Mem.: Alexander City Lions Club, Dadeville Kiwanis Club. Republican. Avocations: hunting, reading. Office: 110 Calhoun St Ste 108 Alexander City AL 35010 also: Ala House of Reps Rm 524-C 11 S Union St Montgomery AL 36130 Office Phone: 334-242-7219. Personal E-mail: tughd81@gmail.com.

TUKE, ROBERT DUDLEY, lawyer, educator; b. Rochester, NY, Dec. 5, 1947; s. Theodore Robert and Doris Jean (Smith) T.; m. Susan Devereux Cummins, June 21, 1969; children: Andrew, Sarah. BA with distinction, U. Va., 1969; JD, Vanderbilt U., 1976. Bar: Tenn. 1976, U.S. Dist. Ct. (mid. dist.) Tenn. 1976, U.S. Ct. Appeals (6th cir.) 1976, U.S. Ct. Appeals (4th cir.) 1978, U.S. Ct. Appeals (fed. cir.) 1993, U.S. Supreme Ct. 1986, U.S. Ct. Internat. Trade 1993. Assoc. Farris, Warfield & Kanaday, Nashville, 1976—79, ptnr., 1980—94, Tuke Yopp & Sweeney, Nashville, 1994—99, Trauger, Ney & Tuke, Nashville, 2000—05, Trauger & Tuke, Nashville, 2006—; candidate US Senate, 2008. Adj. prof. law Vanderbilt U. Law Sch., Nashville. Author: (with others) Tennessee Practice, 1992—; editor-in-chief Vanderbilt Law Rev.; contbr. articles to profl. jours. Mem. Tenn. Adoption Law Study Commn., 1993-96, Metro CATV Com.; chmn. Tenn. Dem. Party, 2005-07. Capt. USMC, 1969-73. Decorated Cross of Gallantry; Patrick Wilson Merit scholar. Mem. ABA, Am. Health Law Assn., Nat. Assn. Bond Lawyers, Am. Acad. Adoption Attys. (past pres.), Tenn. Bar Assn., Nashville Bar Assn., Order of Coif. Democrat. Episcopalian. Avocations: rowing, running, bicycling, hiking, travel. Office: 222 4th Ave N Nashville TN 37219-2115 Home Phone: 615-385-2786; Office Phone: 615-256-8585. Business E-Mail: rtuke@tntlaw.net.

TULLIS, BILL, sound recording engineer, music company executive; b. Valdosta, Ga., Feb. 3, 1953; BA, Valdosta State Coll., 1974, Ga. State U., 1976. Audio and music dir. Turner Broadcasting System, Inc., Atlanta, 1975—2001; CEO Creative Svcs. Co., Atlanta, 2001—, mgr., CEO, 2001—. Recipient Emmy award, 1980, 81, 84, 88, Clio award, 1987, 88, Aurora award (2). 2000, 01, 06, Chgo. Internat. TV award, 2003, Axis award, 2003. Mem. IEEE, NARAS, Audio Engring. Soc., Nat. Assn. Broadcasters. Avocations: architecture, music collecting and appreciation. Office: Creative Svcs Co Sounds Atlanta Recording/Mastering PO Box 49266 Atlanta GA 30359 Office Phone: 404-329-9438. Personal E-mail: btullis497@aol.com, soundsatlanta@aol.com.

TUMAY, MEHMET TANER, geotechnical engineering educator, researcher, consultant; b. Feb. 2, 1937; arrived in US, 1959; s. Bedrettin and Muhterem (Uybadin) T.; m. Karen Nuttycombe, June 15, 1962; children: Peri, Suna. BSCE, Robert Coll. Sch. Engring., Istanbul, Turkey, 1959; MSCE, U. Va., 1961; postgrad., UCLA, 1963—64; PhD, Tech. U. Istanbul, 1971. Lic. civil engr., La., Ga., SC, Turkish Chamber of Civil Engring. Instr. civil engring. U. Va., Charlottesville, 1961-62; asst. prof. civil engring. U. Louisville, 1962-63; tchg. fellow UCLA, 1963-64; asst. prof. civil engring. Robert Coll. Sch. Engring., Istanbul, 1966-71; assoc. prof. dept. civil engring. Bogazici U., Istanbul, 1971-75; Fugro-Cesco postdoctoral rsch. fellow U. Fla., Gainesville, 1975-76; Ga. Gulf disting. prof. La. State U., Baton Rouge, 1976—2005, prof. emeritus, 2005—. Adv. prof. U. Vicosa, Minas Gerais, Brazil, 1991—, Tongji U., Shanghai, 1991—; adj. prof. Bogazici U., Istanbul, Turkey, 2005-; dir. geomechanics program NSF, Washington, 1990-94; dir. rsch. La. Transp. Rsch. Ctr., Baton Rouge, 1994-97; assoc. dean rsch. and grad. studies Coll. Engring., La. State U., 1997-2004; maitre de conferences Ecole Nationale des Ponts et Chaussees, Paris, 1980-94; geotech. cons. Sauti, Spa, Cons. Engrs., Italy, 1969-72, SOFRETU-RATP, Paris, 1972-73, D.E.A., Cons. Engrs., Istanbul, 1974-75, BOTEK, Ltd., Istanbul, 1975—, Senler-Campbell Assocs., Louisville, 1979-90, Fugro Gulf-Geogulf, Houston, 1980-83, Fugro Onshore Geotechnics, Fugro Cons., Inc., Baton Rouge, 2010-; cons. in field. Contbr. articles to profl. jours. AID scholar, 1975-76, French Ministry External Rels. scholar, 1982. Fellow: ASCE; mem.: ASTM (diplomate), Acad. Geo-Profls., Transp. Rsch. Bd. of the Nat. Acads, (emeritus), Internat. Soc. Soil Mechanics and Found. Engring., Turkish Chamber Civil Engrs., Turkish Soil Mechanics Group (charter mem.), La. Engring. Soc., Am. Soc. Engring. Edn., Tau Beta Pi, Chi Epsilon, Sigma Xi. Home: 2217 Dove Hollow Dr Baton Rouge LA 70809-1275 Office: La State U Coll Engring Baton Rouge LA 70803-0001 Home Phone: 225-927-7719; Office Phone: 225-578-9165. Business E-Mail: mtumay@eng.lsu.edu.

TUMLINSON, JAMES H., III, agriculturist; BS in Chemistry, Va. Mil. Inst., Lexington, 1960; MS in Organic Chemistry, Miss. State U., 1966, PhD in Organic Chemistry, 1969. Chemist Boll Weevil Rsch.

Lab. USDA-Agrl. Rsch. Svc., State Coll., Miss., 1964-69, rsch. chemist, Insect Attractants, Behavior, and Basic Biology Rsch. Lab. Gainesville, Fla., 1970-72, rsch. leader Ctr. Med., Agrl., and Vet. Entomology, 1972—2003; postdoctoral NY State Coll. Forestry, Syracuse, 1969—70; adj. asst. prof. U. Fla. Inst. Food Agr., Gainesville, 1970—75, adj. assoc. prof., doctoral faculty, 1975—82, adj. prof., doctoral faculty, 1982—; Ralph O. Mumma prof. entomology Pa. State U., U. Pk., 2003—. FAO cons. Nuclear Rsch. Ctr., Demokritos, Greece, 1974; mem. Boll Wevil Pheromone Devel. Group, 1975; rsch. leader Insect Chemistry Rsch. Group, 1983. Recipient Superior Svc. award, USDA, 1975, 1983, Sec. Agrl. award, 1995, award Outstanding Rsch. and Leadership, Agrl. Rsch. Svc., 1979, Disting. Scientist of Yr., 1984, Hall of Fame, 1998, Burdick and Jackson Internat. award, Am. Chem. Soc., 1986, Disting. Lectr. in Life Scis., Boyce Thompson Inst. Plant Rsch., 1998, Kenneth A. Spencer award, 2002, listed in top 1% of environment/ecology citations, ISI Essential Sci. Indicators, 2002, Presdl. Rank award as Meritorious Sr. Profl., USDA, Agrl. Rsch. Svc., 2003, Jean-Marie Delwart Found. prize, 2003; co-recipient Ann. Rsch. award, Fla. Entomol. Soc., 1991, Wolf Found. prize in Agr., Israel, 2008; Agrl. Rsch. Svc. fellowship, Ctr. Insect Sci., U. Ariz., 1989. Fellow Entomol. Soc. Am. (J.E. Bussart Meml. award 1990, Recognition award 2000); mem. NAS, Internat. Soc. Chem. Ecology (v.p. 1997, pres. 1998). Office: Usda Ars 1600 SW 23rd Dr Gainesville FL 32608-1067

TUMMINELLO, PETER I., gas industry executive; b. La. married; 2 children. BS in Petroleum Engring., La. Tech. U.; MBA, U. Southwestern La. With energy mktg. and storage and transp. asset mgmt. TPC Corp.; v.p., energy supply Green Mountain Energy Co.; v.p., asset mgmt. and origination Sequent Energy Management, LP, 2003; v.p., corp. devel. AGL Resources, Inc., 2005—; exec. v.p., bus. devel. and support Sequent Energy Management, LP, 2007—. Office: AGL Resources Inc Ten Peachtree Pl NE Atlanta GA 30309 Office Phone: 404-584-4000. Office Fax: 404-584-3714. Business E-Mail: Ptumminello@aglresources.com.

TUNE, LARRY E., geriatric psychiatrist, educator; MD, U. Va., 1975. Diplomate Am. Bd. Psychiatry and Neurology, 1991, Am. Bd. Psychiatry and Neurology-geriatric psychiatry, 2004. Resident psychiatry Johns Hopkins Hosp., 1976—79, resident neurology, 1981—83; fellow in psychopharmacology Johns Hopkins Univ., 1979—81; hosp. affiliation includes: Emory Univ. Hosp.; prof. psychiatry Emory Univ. Office: Emory University Hospital 1364 Clifton Rd NE Atlanta GA 30322-1102 Office Phone: 404-712-2000.

TURANCHIK, MICHAEL, research and development director; Dir. R&D Editek, Inc. (now named Medtox Diagnostics), Burlington, N.C. Office: Medtox Diagnostics 1238 Anthony Rd Burlington NC 27215-8936

TURBIDY, JOHN BERRY, investor, management consultant; b. Rome, Ga., Oct. 18, 1928; s. Joseph Leo and Louyse (Berry) T.; m. Joan Marsales, Dec. 19, 1958 (dec.); children: John Berry, Trevor Martin; m. Jaquelin Lamond Schulter, June 8, 1996 Grad., Darlington Sch., 1945; BA, Duke U., 1950; postgrad., NYU, 1952, Emory U., 1954-56. Various positions Lockheed Aircraft, Marietta, Ga., 1951-56; gen. mgmt. cons. McKinsey & Co., NYC and London, 1956—62; v.p. adminstrn. ITT Europe, Inc., Brussels, 1963, v.p., group exec. European consumer products, 1963—65, v.p., group exec. for No. Europe, 1965-67; corp. v.p. adminstrn. Celanese Corp., NYC, 1967-68; pres., mng. dir. SIACE, SP.A. subs., Milan, 1968-69; chmn. bd., pres. Vecta Group, Kalamazoo, 1970-74; sr. v.p. corp. devel. IU Internat. Corp., Phila., 1974-78, exec. v.p., 1978-83; pres., chief exec. officer Pitcairn Fin. Mgmt. Group, Jenkintown, Pa., 1984-90; chmn. Office John Turbidy, 1990-95; mng. dir. Friedman, Turbidy & Co., Inc., NYC, 1995—2000. Bd. dirs. Statute of Liberty Ellis Island Found., 1982-2004, chmn. 2003-08. Served with USNR, 1952 Mem. Sea Island Club. Address: 113 Biltmore Saint Simons Island GA 31522 Personal E-mail: jbturb@hotmail.com.

TURCOT, MARGUERITE HOGAN, medical researcher; b. White Plains, NY, May 19, 1934; d. Joseph William (dec.) and Marguerite Alice (dec.) Barrett) Hogan; children: Michael J., Susan A. Turcot, William R. Student, Syracuse U., 1951-54; BSN, U. Bridgeport, 1968. RN, Conn., N.C. Nurse Park City Hosp., Bridgeport, Conn., 1968-69, Meml. Mission Hosp., Asheville, N.C., 1969-70; instr. St. Joseph's Hosp., Asheville, 1970-71, oper. rm. nurse, 1973-77, charge nurse urology-cystoscopy, 1977-85; tchr. Asheville-Buncombe Tech. Coll., Asheville, 1971-72, Buncombe County Child Devel., Asheville, 1972-73; rschr. VA Med. Ctr., Asheville, 1988—; owner Reed House Bed & Breakfast, Asheville, 1985—2001. Bd. dirs. RiverLink, Quality Foreward. Charter mem. French Broad River Planning Com., Asheville, 1987—, Biltmore Village Hist. Mus.; mem. Asheville Bicentennial Commn., 1990-93; exec. dir. Preservation Soc. Asheville and Buncombe County. Recipient Griffin award, 1994, Friend of the River award, Land of Sky Regional Coun., 1995, Sondley award, Hist. Resources Commn. Asheville and Buncombe County, 1996, Vol. of Yr. award, RiverLink, 2001, Critical Link award, 2003; grantee U. Bridgeport, 1967—68; scholar Syracuse U. Faculty, 1951—54. Mem. Am. Urology Assn. (presenter VA urology workshop Asheville chpt. 1981, nat. meeting allied), Am. Bd. Urologic Allied Health Profls., Nat. Trust for Hist. Preservation, Preservation Found. N.C., Blue Ridge Pkwy. Assn., Preservation Soc. Asheville and Buncombe County (bd. dirs., past pres.), Asheville Newcomers Club (founder, 1st pres.), Earthwatch, Friends of Blue Ridge Pkwy. Inc. Republican. Roman Catholic. Avocations: preservation, history, architecture, sewing, hiking. Office: Preservation Soc Asheville & Buncombe County PO Box 2806 Asheville NC 28802

TURINSKY, PAUL JOSEF, nuclear engineer, educator; b. Hoboken, NJ, Oct. 20, 1944; s. Paul J. and Wilma A. (Budig) T.; m. Karen Ann DeLuca, Aug. 29, 1966; children: Grant Dean, Beth Noelle. BS, U. R.I., 1966; MSE, U. Mich., 1967, PhD, 1970; MBA, U. Pitts., 1979. Asst. prof. Rensselaer Poly. Inst., Troy, NY, 1971-73; engr., mgr. nuc. design Westinghouse Elec. Corp., Pitts., 1973—78, mgr. core devel., 1978-80; head dept. nuc. engring. NC State U., Raleigh, 1980—88, 1999—2006, prof., 1980—, dir. Electric Power Rsch. Ctr., 1989—2008; pres. Nuclear Fuel Mgmt. Assocs., 1994—2007; chief scientist Consortium Advanced Simulation of Light Water Resources, 2010—. Bd. dir. Quantum Rsch. Svcs.; cons. Electric Power Rsch. Inst., Palo Alto, Calif., 1980-98, Sci. Applications Internat. Corp., 1990-92, US Dept. Energy, 1993; tech. specialist Internat. Atomic Energy Agy., Vienna, Austria, 1982—; mem. nuc. safety rev. bd. Duke Power Co., Charlotte, NC, 1986-2001; cons. Can. Nuc. Safety Commn., 2000-, Western Svcs. Corp., 2006-; mem. nuc. sci. advisory bd. Commissariat l'Energie Atomique, France, 2006-. Author: (with others) CRC Handbook of Nuclear Reactor Calculations, 1986; contbr. more than 100 articles to tech. jours. Recipient Outstanding Tchr. award, NC State U., 1985, RJR award, 2007, Supercomputer award, IBM, 1991, Alcoa Disting. Rschr. award, 1993, E.O. Lawrence award in nuc. tech., U.S. Dept. Energy, 2002, Merit award, Alumni Soc. U. Mich., 2003. Fellow: Am. Nuc. Soc. (chmn. reactor physics divsn. 1987—88, chmn. math. and computer divsn. 1995—96, bd. dirs. 1990—93, Mark Mills award 1971, Eugene E. Wigner Reactor Physics award 2003, Arthur Holly Compton award 2004, Presdl. Citation award 2009); mem.: AAAS (math. com.), Soc. Indsl. and Applied Math., Edison Electric Inst. (Power Engring. Educator award 1992), Am. Soc. Engring. Educators (chmn. nuc. engring. divsn. 1984—85, Glenn Murphy award 1990). Office: NC State U Dept Nuclear Engring PO Box 7909 Raleigh NC 27695-7909 Business E-Mail: turinsky@ncsu.edu.

TURK, JAMES CLINTON, federal judge; b. Roanoke, Va., May 3, 1923; s. James Alexander and Geneva (Richardson) T.; m. Barbara Duncan, Aug. 21, 1954; children: Ramona Leah, James Clinton, Robert Malcolm Duncan, Mary Elizabeth, David Michael. AB, Roanoke Coll., 1949; L.L.B., Washington and Lee U., 1952. Bar: Va. 1952. Assoc. Dalton & Poff, Radford, Va., 1952-53; ptnr. Dalton, Poff & Turk, Radford, 1953-72; state senator from Va., 1959-72; judge US Dist. Ct. (we. dist.) Va., Roanoke, 1972-73, 1993—2002, chief judge Roanoke, 1973—93, sr. judge, 2002—. Dir. 1st & Mchts. Nat. Bank of Radford Mem. Va. Senate, from 1959, minority leader.; Trustee Radford Community Hosp., 1959—. Served with AUS, 1943-46. Mem.: Order of Coif, Omicron Delta Kappa, Phi Beta Kappa. Baptist (deacon). Home: 1002 Walker Dr Radford VA 24141-3018 Office: US Dist Ct 246 Franklin Rd SW # 220 Roanoke VA 24011-2214 Home Phone: 540-639-2055; Office Phone: 540-857-5122. Office Fax: 540-857-5123. Business E-Mail: jamest@vawd.uscourts.gov.

TURK, JAMES CLINTON, JR., lawyer; b. Radford, Va., Oct. 27, 1956; s. James Clinton and Barbara (Duncan) T.; m. Allison Blanding, Oct. 16, 1993; children: Lindsey Leigh, Katherine Alexandra, Alana Rae. BA in Econs., Roanoke Coll., 1979; JD, Samford U., 1984. Bar: Va. 1984, US Dist. Ct. (ea. and we. dists.) Va. 1984, US Bankruptcy Ct. 1985, US Ct. Appeals (4th cir.) 1985, US Supreme Ct. 1988; cert. specialist in civil and criminal trial advocacy Nat. Bd. Trial Advocacy; cert. players agt. Nat. Basketball Players Assn.; cert. players agt./contract advisor NFL. Ptnr. Harrison & Turk, Radford, 1985—. Adj. prof. criminal justice dept. Radford U.; bd. dirs. New River brs. SunTrust Bank, Va. Tech. Found., Intrexon Transcriptional Therapeutics Corp.,2006-07, Synchrony, Inc, 2008-. Sec. Radford Rep. Com., 1984—; fundraising chmn. Am. Heart Assn., Radford, 1986—; bd. dir. New River Valley Workshop, Inc., v.p., 1990-92, pres., 1992-93; bd. dirs. new River CC Ednl. Found.; apptd. chmn. and dir. Va. Student Assistance Authorities by Gov. George Allen, 1994—; escheator City of Radford and Pulaski County; rep. western dist. CJA Panel Atty., Va.; mem. 4th Cir. Jud. Conf., 2000-01; bd. dirs. Va. Tech. Athletic Found. Recipient Bill Geimer Capital Defender award, Va. Capital Case Clearinghouse, 2000—01; named a Va. Super Lawyer, 2006—07, 2007. Mem. ATLA (sustaining, fellow Coll. of Advocacy), Ted Dalton Am. Inn Courts (barrister), ABA, Am. Bd. Trial Adv., Am. Coll. Barristers, Am. Triple Lawyers Assn., Va. Bar Assn. (civil litig. sect. coun. 1991—, criminal litig. sect. coun. 1994—), Nat. Assn. Criminal Def. Lawyers (life; death penalty com. and indigent def. com.), Va. Trial Lawyers Assn., Inn of Cts., Jaycees, Am. Inn of Ct., Rotary. Republican. Roman Catholic. Avocations: weightlifting, golf, travel, flying, scuba diving. Home: 460 Quailwood Dr Blacksburg VA 24060-6724 Office: Harrison And Turk Pc 1007 E Main St Radford VA 24141-1745 Office Phone: 540-639-9056. Personal E-mail: jimturk@aol.com.

TURK, THOMAS LIEBIG, arts consultant; b. Indpls., July 4, 1936; s. Laurel Herbert and Esther Lucille (Liebig) T.; m. Judith Ann Prochnow, July 26, 1969; children: Martisha Emily, Benjamin Edward. AB, DePauw U., 1958; MA, Mich. State U., 1960; cert., Harvard U., 1973. Promotion and publicity dir. Sta. WMSB-TV Mich. State U., East Lansing, 1961, asst. editor news bur., 1962-63, fine arts assoc. producer Sta. WKAR-TV, 1963-68, fine arts producer Sta. WKAR-TV, 1969-81; acting dir. publicity DePauw U., Greencastle, Ind., 1961-62; exec. dir. Cultural Activities Ctr., Temple, Tex., 1981-91, Met. Nashville Arts Commn., 1993—2003, Tennesseans for the Arts, 2003—06; mng. dir. Texarkana (Tex.) Regional Arts & Humanities Coun., 1991-93. Pres. Met. Lansing (Mich.) Fine Arts Coun., 1975-77, Mich. Assn. Comm. Arts Agys., East Lansing, 1979-81; Gov. apptd. mem. Mich. Coun. for Arts, 1979-81; chmn. Mich. Arts Forum, 1980-81; pres. U.S. Urban Arts Fedn., 1999-00; mem. State Arts Action Network Coun., 2005-06. Producer, co-producer: 400 programs for local, nat. and internat. distbn. on pub. TV, 1963-81. Bd. dir. Alias Chamber Music Ensemble, 2006—11, Univ. Club Nashville, 2006—10. With USAF, 1960. Mem.: Tennesseans for Arts (bd. dirs. 2000—03), Nat. Assembly Local Arts Agys. (bd. dirs. 1979—85), Rotary, Sigma Chi. Episcopalian. Home and Office: 643 Harpeth Trace Dr Nashville TN 37221-3147 Personal E-mail: turktj@comcast.net.

TURKOGLU, HEDO (HIDAYET), professional basketball player; b. Istanbul, Turkey, Mar. 19, 1979; Basketball player Turkish Profl. League Efes Pilsen, Istanbul, 1996—2000; guard-forward Sacramento Kings, 2000—04, Orlando Magic, Fla., 2004—09, 2010—, Toronto Raptors, 2009—10, Phoenix Suns, 2010. Mem. Turkish nat. team FIBA European Championships, France, 1999, Turkey, 2001, Sweden, 2003, Serbia and Montenegro, 2005, Spain, 2007, Poland, 2009, Lithuania, 2011, FIBA World Championships, United States, 2002, Turkey, 2010. Recipient Silver medal, FIBA European Championship, 2001, FIBA World Championship, 2010; named NBA Most Improved Player, 2008. Avocations: reading, music, movies, video games. Office: Orlando Magic 400 W Church St # 250 Orlando FL 32801-2515

TURLEY, STEWART, retired retail company executive; b. Mt. Sterling, Ky., July 20, 1934; s. R. Joe and Mavis S. Turley; children from previous marriage: Carol Cohen, Karen Shockley; m. Linda A. Mulholland; stepchildren: Kathleen Smiley, Kristine Johnson. Student, Rollins Coll., 1952-53, U. Ky., 1953-55. Plant mgr. Crown Cork & Seal Co., Orlando (Fla.), Phila., 1955-66; mgr. non-drug ops., dir. corporate employee rels. and spl. svcs. Eckerd Corp. (formerly Jack Eckerd Corp.), Clearwater, Fla., 1966-68; v.p. Eckerd Corp., Clearwater, Fla., 1968-71, sr. v.p., 1971-74, dir., 1971-97, pres., chief exec. officer, 1974-96, chmn. bd., 1975-97. Past bd. dirs. WCI Cmtys., Inc., Sprint Corp., Marine Max, Inc., Springs Industries, Inc., Barnett Banks, Inc. Past chmn. U.S. Ski Team Found.; bd. dirs. Vilar Ctr. Found., Vail Valley Found.; bd. visitors Duke U.; bd. dirs. Steadman-Hawkins Sports Medicine Found. Mem. Nat. Assn. Chain Drug Stores (chmn. bd. 1978-79, 88-89), Fla. Coun. 100 (past chmn.), Carlouel Yacht Club, Belleair Country Club, Eagle Springs Golf Club, Kappa Alpha. Office: 1465 S Fort Harrison Ave Ste 201 Clearwater FL 33756-2505

TURNAGE, FRED DOUGLAS, retired lawyer; b. Ayden, NC, Sept. 24, 1920; s. Fred C. and Lou (Johnson) T.; m. Margaret Futrell, Aug. 21, 1943 (div. Nov. 1980); children: Betty Lou Griffith, Douglas C.; m. Elizabeth Louisa Turnage, Jan. 23, 1981. Grad. Naval Sch. on Far Eastern Civil Affairs, Princeton U., 1945; LLB, Wake Forest U., 1948, LLD, 1970. Bar: N.C. 1948, U.S. Supreme Ct. 1953, U.S. Dist. Ct. D.C. 1965, U.S. Ct. Appeals (D.C. cir.) 1967, U.S. Ct. Appeals (4th and 7th cirs.) 1979. Trial atty. antitrust div. U.S. Dept. Justice, Kansas City, Mo., 1948-51, sr. trial atty. antitrust div. Washington, 1951-65, spl. asst. to atty. gen., 1965; sr. ptnr. Cleary, Gottlieb, Steen & Hamilton, Washington, 1968—, counsel, 1990—2004, ret., 2004. Lectr. continuing legal edn. courses, 1973-77. Contbr. articles to profl. jours. Bd. Visitors Wake Forest U. Sch. Law, Winston-Salem, N.C., 1980—. Served to 1st lt. AUS, 1942-46. Recipient Disting. Service in Law citation Wake Forest U., 1979. Mem. ABA (antitrust and litigation sects.), Fed. Bar Assn., Adv. Bd. Antitrust Bulletin, Wake Forest U. Alumni Assn. (pres. 1977), Nat. Lawyers Clubs. Methodist. Avocations: fishing, golf, writing, law.

TURNBULL, MARJORIE REITZ, educational consultant, state legislator; b. Madison, Wis., July 4, 1940; d. J. Wayne anf Frances H. (Millikan) R.; m. Augustus Bacon Turnbull, Nov. 26, 1965 (dec. Nov. 1991). Student, Agnes Scott Coll., 1958-60; BA, U. Fla., 1962; MA, U. Ga., 1968. Legis. analyst Fla. Ho. of Reps., Tallahassee, 1973-85, staff dir. com. on health and rehab. svcs., 1975-78, exec. asst. to speaker, 1978-80; asst. dir. Devel. Svc. Program Office, Tallahassee, 1980-82; dep. asst. sec. Health Planning State Fla., 1982-84; ind. cons. legis. mgmt. and planning, Tallahassee, 1984-95; ednl. cons., person assoc. Tallahassee C.C. Found.; state rep. legis. mgmt. and planning, Tallahassee, 1994-2000; found. dir. and v.p, Instl. Advancement, Tallahassee CC, 1995—2007. County commr. Leon County, Tallahassee, 1988-94; bd. dirs. Fla. Assn. Counties, Tallahassee, 1993-94, pres. 1994, Tallahassee Symphony Orch., 1992-98, chair State Juvenile Justice Found., 2007-08; mem. Found. Fla. CC; trustee Esward Waters Coll. Named Woman of Yr., AAUW, Tallahassee, 1991, County Champion in the Legislature, Fla. Assn. Counties, 1995, Legislator of Yr., Fla. Assn. Sch. Supts., 1999; recipient Girl Scout Woman of Distinction award, 1999, Disting. Svc. award Fla. Student Assn., 2000, Disting. Citizens award Boy Scout Coun., 2000, Meritorious Achievement award Fla. A&M U., 2000, Legis. Advocacy award Fla. Coalition Against Domestic Violence, 2000, Freedom from Violence Leadership awrd, 2000, Model of Achievement award Tallahassee C.C., 2001. Mem. Rotary (program com. 1992—), Zonta Internat., Fla. Blue Key. Democrat. Presbyterian. Avocations: scuba diving, travel, cultural activities. Office: Tallahassee C C 444 Appleyard Dr Tallahassee FL 32304 Home: 3935 Meandering Ln Tallahassee FL 32308-5953 E-mail: turnbulm@tcc.fl.edu.

TURNER, DAVID J., JR., corporate financial executive; B in acctg., Univ. Ala., Tuscaloosa; attended, Tulane Univ. CPA. Acctg. positions from staff auditor to audit ptnr. Arthur Andersen; audit ptnr. KPMG LLC, 2002—06; head internal audit divsn. Regions Financial Corp., Birmingham, Ala., 2006—10, sr. exec. v.p., CFO, 2010—. Bd. dir. Jr. Achievement Greater Birmingham. Mem.: Am. Inst. CPAs, Ala. Soc. CPAs. Office: Regions Fin Corp 1900 5th Ave N Birmingham AL 35203 Office Phone: 205-944-1300.

TURNER, DOUGLAS LAIRD, writer, editor, columnist; b. Buffalo, Jan. 5, 1932; s. Henry Albert and Effie Donna (McIndoo) T.; m. Mary Joan Hassett, July 7, 1962; children: Christopher Henry, Mary Julia, Albert William. BA, Brown U., 1954; postgrad., Stanford U., 1968. Reporter Buffalo (N.Y.) Courier-Express, 1957-60, state capital corr., 1960-64, fin. editor, 1964, city editor, 1964-70, exec. editor, 1971-80, Washington bur. chief, 1981-82; Washington corr. Buffalo (N.Y.) Evening News, 1982, Washington columnist, 1983, Washington bur. chief, 1989—2006, sr. corr., 2007. Founder, dir. Friends of Williamsburg Rowing Inc., 1993—. Mem. U.S. Olympic Rowing Team, 1956. With U.S. Army Counter Intelligence Corps, 1956-57. Nation champion four-oared shell with cox, 1956; winner Hanlan Trophy, Royal Can. Henley Regatta, 1956 Mem. Nat. Press Club (former gov. 1988), Potomac Boat Club, Gridiron Club (Wash.). Roman Catholic. Home: 7923 Saint George Ct Springfield VA 22153-2741

TURNER, ELIZABETH ADAMS NOBLE (BETTY TURNER), real estate company executive, author, architect; b. Yonkers, NY, May 18, 1931; d. James Kendrick and Orrel (Baldwin) Noble; m. Architect Jack Rice Turner, July 11, 1953; children: Jay Kendrick, Randall Ray. BA, Vassar Coll., 1953; MA, Tex. A&I U., 1964. Ednl. cons., Tex. sales mgr. Noble & Noble Pub. Co., NYC, 1956-67; psychometrist Corpus Christi Guidance Ctr., 1967-70; psychologist Corpus Christi State Sch., 1970-72, dir. programs, asst. supt., 1972, dir. devel. and vol. svc., 1972-76, dir. rsch. and tng., 1977-79; psychologist Tex. Mental Health and Mental Retardation, 1970-79; dir., alumni affairs Corpus Christi State U., 1976—78; pres. Turner Co., 1975-82; mayor pro tem Corpus Christi, 1981-85; mayor, 1987-91; CEO, pres. Corpus Christi C. of C., 1991; pres., broker, owner Betty Turner Real Estate, 1999—. V.p. bus. and govt. rels. ctrl. and south Tex. divsns. Columbia Healthcare Corp., 1994—99; G. Clifford Noble paternal grandfather co-founder Namesake, Barnes and Noble, NYC. Author: The Noble Legacy. Bd. dirs. Nat. AARP, 2002—04; coord. vols. Summer Head Start Program, Corpus Christi, 1967; chmn. spl. gifts com. United Way, Corpus Christi, 1970; founder Com. 100, Goals for Corpus Christi, Bay Area Sports Assn., Coastal Bend Mayor's Alliance, Mayor's Commn. on Disabled, Mayor's Task Force on Homeless; pres. Mayor's Interagy. Coun.; bd. dirs. USO, Coastal Bend Coun. Govts., Corpus Christi Mus., Harbor Playhouse, Cmtys. in Schs., YWCA, Y-Teen Sponsor, Del Mar Coll. Found., 1998—2005, Tex. A&M at Corpus Christi Pres. Coun., Hispanic C. of C., TAMACC Corp. Ptnrs. Bd., Salvation Army, Jr. League, Coun. Deaf Silent Found., 2001—, Am. Heart Assn., 1999—2000, Bethune Day Care Nursery, 1999—2004, Jr. League Cmty. Adv. Coun., 1999—2000, 21st Century Charter Sch. Bd., 2001—02, Boys and Girls Club Corpus Christi, bd. mem., 2002—05; bd. dirs. Food Bank, bd. pres., 2004—05, Adm. Tex. Navy; mem. Gov.'s Commn. Women, 1984—85, Leadership Tex. Class I, Corpus Christi, Class II; fund-raising chair Port Aransas Leadership Cmty. Performing Arts Theater; libr. bd. Port Aransas Charter Rev. Commn.; bd. mem. Port Aransas C. of C., 2009; mem. Corpus Christi City Coun., 1979—91; elder Cmty. Presbyn. Ch., 2004—07; bd. dirs. Southside Cmty. Hosp., 1987—93; mem. strategic planning com. Meml. Hosp., 1992, Tex. Capital Network Bd., 1992—95, Humana Hosp., Physician Relocation and Condo Sales; bd. dirs. Rehab. Hosp., St. David's/Austin and Medth. Healthcare Sys., San Antonio, 1997—99; adv. coun. Sch. Nursing U. Tex., 1998—99; bd. dirs. Gulfway Bank and Pacific Southwest Bank, 1997—2000. Recipient Love award, YWCA, 1970, Y's Women Careers award, 1988, Recognition award, Rotary, 1991, Comdr.'s award for pub. svc., U.S. Army, Scroll Honor award, Navy League, Tex. Hwy Dept., Road Hand award, Tex. Hwy. Commn., Women of Distinction award, Pres. award, Corpus Christi Food Bank, 2008, DAR Cmty. Svc. award, 2009; named Newsmaker of Yr., 1987. Mem.: NAACP (life), Tex. Assn. Realtors, Tex. Bookman's Assn., Tex. Mcpl. League (bd. dirs.), Psychol. Assn. (pres., founder), Tex. Psychol. Assn. (pres., mem. exec. bd.), Jr. League Corpus Christi, Jr. Cotillion Club, Corpus Christi Town Club, Kappa Kappa Gamma, Delta Kappa Gamma (hon.). Home: 403 Blue Heron Dr Port Aransas TX 78373 Office Phone: 361-877-1111. Personal E-mail: bettyturner@centurytel.net.

TURNER, HARRY SPENCER, preventive medicine physician, educator; b. Dayton, Ohio, July 25, 1938; s. Eli and Daphne (Cunagin) T.; m. Jan (Fairley) T.; children: Michael, Mary, Daniel. BA, Manchester Coll., North Manchester, Ind., 1960; MD summa cum laude, Ohio State U., 1963, MS in Preventive Medicine, 1968. Diplomate Am. Bd. Preventive Medicine. Resident in preventive (aerospace) medicine Ohio State U., Columbus, 1966-69, chief resident, 1968-69, clin. asst. prof. dept. preventive medicine, 1969-80, dir. Univ. Health Svc., 1970-80; pvt. practice Dayton, 1980-90; dir. Univ. Health Svc., head team physician U. Ky., Lexington, 1991—2003, prof. preventive medicine and environ. health, 1991—2003, prof. emeritus, 2003, dir. emeritus, 2003; med. dir.

Starting Point Behavioral Health, 2003—. Editor: (textbook) History and Practice of College Health, 2002; contbr. articles and papers to profl. jours. and meetings. Bd. dirs. Blue Shield, 1981-86; mem. Cin. Internat. Chorale, 1989-94; mem. Lexington Singers, 1992—2003, Island Chamber Singers, 2005-11. Capt. U.S. Army, 1964-66. Recipient Army Commendation medal. Fellow Am. Coll. Preventive Medicine, Am. Coll. Health Assn. (pres. 1980, Ruth Boynton award 1982, Edw. Hitchcock award 1996, Lifetime Achievement award 2003), Alpha Omega Alpha Avocation: music. Personal E-mail: hsturner904@comcast.net.

TURNER, HUGH JOSEPH, JR., lawyer; b. Paterson, NJ, Oct. 5, 1945; s. Hugh Joseph and Louise (Sullivan) T.; m. Charlene Chiappetta, Feb. 11, 1983. BS, Boston U., 1967; JD, U. Miami, Coral Gables, Fla., 1975. Bar: Fla. 1975, U.S. Dist. Ct. (so., no. and mid. dists.) Fla. 1975, U.S. Ct. Appeals (11th cir.) 1981, U.S. Supreme Ct. 1984. Tchr. Browne & Nichols, Cambridge, Mass., 1968-72; ptnr. Smathers & Thompson, Miami, Fla., 1981-87, Kelley Drye & Warren, Miami, 1987-93, English, McCaughan & O'Bryan, Ft. Lauderdale, 1993—2001, Redgrave & Turner LLP, Boca Raton, Fla., 2001—03, Akerman Senterfitt, Ft. Lauderdale, 2003—. Chmn. Fla. Bar internat. law sect., 1988-89. Contbg. author book on internat. dispute resolution Fla. Bar, 1989; contbr. articles to profl. jours. Bd. dirs. Japan Soc. South Fla., Miami, 1989-97; mem. Sea Ranch Lakes Village Coun., 1997-2000; mayor Sea Ranch Lakes, 2000-02. Mem.: ABA, Def. Rsch. Inst. Avocation: running. Office: Akerman Senterfitt Ste 1600 350 E Las Olas Blvd Fort Lauderdale FL 33301-2229 Home Phone: 954-942-8073; Office Phone: 954-463-2700. Business E-Mail: hugh.turner@akerman.com.

TURNER, JANINE, political commentator, radio personality, actress; b. Lincoln, Nebr., Dec. 6, 1963; d. Turner & Janice Gaunt.; 1 child, Juliette Attended, Pepperdine U. Founder, co-chair Constituting America, Colleyville, Tex., 2010—; host, The Janine Turner Show 570 KLIF-AM, Dallas, 2011—; guest commentator FOX News. Mem. President's Coun. on Svc. & Civic Participation, 2006—08. Actress: (TV appearances) Dallas (3 episodes), 1980-81, Mr. Merlin, 1981, The Love Boat, 1982, The Paper Chase, 1983, The Happy Days, 1983, Boone, 1983, The Master, 1984, Santa Barbara, 1984, The New Mike Hammer, 1984, The A-Team, 1985, Knight Rider, 1985, Quantum Leap, 1989, Law & Order: Special Victims Unit, 2008, Friday Night Lights (8 episodes), 2008-09; (TV series) Behind the Screen, 1981-82, General Hospital, 1982-83, Another World, 1986-87, Northern Exposure, 1990-95, Strong Medicine, 2000-02; (films) Young Doctors in Love, 1982, Knights of the City, 1985, Tai-Pan, 1986, Monkey Shines: An Experiment in Fear, 1988, Steel Magnolias, 1988, The Ambulance, 1990, Cliffhanger, 1993, Leave It to Beaver, 1997, The Curse of the Inferno, 1997, Dr. T and the Women, 2000, Birdie and Bogey, 2004, No Regrets, 2004, Night of the White Pants, 2006, Maggie's Passage, 2009, Black Widow, 2010; (TV movies) Stolen Women, Captured Hearts, 1997, Circle of Deceit, 1998, Beauty, 1998, Fatal Error, 1999, A Secret Affair, 1999, Walker, Texas Ranger: Trial By Fire, 2005, Primal Doubt, 2007; actor, dir.: (short films) Trip in a Summer Dress, 2004; author: Holding Her Head High: Inspiration from 12 Single Mothers Who Championed Their Children and Changed History, 2008 Recipient Women at Work award, Nat. Commn. on Working Women. Republican. Office: Constituting America.org PO Box 1988 Colleyville TX 76034

TURNER, JERRY R., state legislator; b. Tupelo, Miss., Nov. 16, 1941; m. Mary Ellen Blaylock Turner. Mem. Dist. 18 Miss. House of Reps., 2004—, mem. agr. com., banking and fin. svcs. com., conservation and water resources com., municipalities com., pub. property com., ways and means com. Mem.: Cmty. Devel. Found., Miss. Cattlemans Assn. Republican. Church Of Christ. Address: 1290 Carrollville Ave Baldwyn MS 38824 Office Phone: 662-365-8484. E-mail: jturner@house.ms.gov.

TURNER, JOHN T., finance company executive; m. Amandah Turner; 3 children. Attended, St. Luke United Meth. Church; grad., Vanderbilt U. Bd. dirs. W.C. Bradley Co., Columbus Bank and Trust, Total System Svcs., Inc., 2003—. Trustee Trees Columbus, Midtown Project, United Way, Uptown Columbus, Ga. Conservancy, Ctr. for Servant Leadership, Chattahoochee Valley Land Trust, Voyage Discovery, South Columbus Task Force, Chattahoochee Riverkeeper; trustee, chmn. Brookstone Sch. Office: Total System Services Inc One TSYS Way Columbus GA 31901 Office Phone: 706-649-2310. Office Fax: 706-644-8065. Business E-Mail: jturner@tsys.com.

TURNER, JOHNNY RAY, state legislator; b. Dec. 19, 1949; BA, MA, Morehead State U. Mem. Dist. 29, Ky., 2001—; mem. Appropriations & Revenue Com., Edn. Com., Local Gov. & State Gov. Coms., Ky. State Senate; minority caucus chmn., 2003—. Democrat. Baptist. Office: 702 Capitol Ave Annex Rm 254 Frankfort KY 40601 also: 700 Capitol Ave Capitol Rm 330 Frankfort KY 40601 Home: 849 Crestwood Dr Prestonsburg KY 41653-8039 Home Phone: 606-377-6962; Office Phone: 502-564-6136.

TURNER, KATHLEEN J., communications educator, consultant; d. Josiah Shelden Turner and Anne A. Alexander; m. Raymond Sprague. BA in Comm. and English, U. Kans., 1974; MA in Comm., Purdue U., 1976, PhD in Comm., 1978. Asst. prof. comm. Denison U., Granville, Ohio, 1978—79, U. Notre Dame, Ind., 1979—85; assoc. prof. comm. U. Tulsa, Okla., 1985—86, Tulane U., New Orleans, 1986—2000; prof. comm. Queens U. Charlotte, NC, 2000—04, Knight-Crane prof. comm., 2001—04; prof. comm. studies Davidson Coll., 2004—. Media/pub. rels. cons. La. Vocal Arts Chorale, New Orleans, 1993—99; Wayne Thompson vis. prof. Professor, Western Ill. U., 2001; Annabel Hagood vis. prof. U. Ala., 2003; vis. prof. Communication and Gender, Randolph-Macon Coll., 2005, Group Presentations, Randolph-Macon Coll., 2006, Savannah Coll. Art and Design, 2008, Lyndon Johnson, Tex. State U., 2008; residence scholar Nat. Comm. Assn. Inst. Faculty Devel., 2008, 2010, leader, 2010; spkr. in field. Author: Lyndon Johnson's Dual War: Vietnam and the Press, 1985; editor: Doing Rhetorical History: Concepts and Cases, 1998, Insinuating the Product into the Message: An Historical Context for Product Placement, 2006, Reporting the Darkness: The Role of the Press in the Vietnam War, 1998, The Only Thing I've Learned: The Central Tenet of a Liberal Arts Education, 2004, Descendence, Ascendence, Transcendence: Critiquing Popular Film, 2006, The Glory of Rhetorical Analysis: Communication as a Process of Social Influence, 2013; co-author (with Raymond Sprague): (books) Musical and Visual Invention in Miami Vice in Vande Berg and Wenner, Television Criticism, 1990, Diary of a Generation: The Rhetoric of Sixties Protest Music in Savage and Nimmo, Politics in Familiar Contexts, 1990; contbr. chapters to books, articles to profl. jours. Recipient Svc. to Pub. award, Nat. Communication Assn., 1990, Ecroyd award, 2007, Preston award, 2010, Turner Advocacy award, 2011, Hobgood Svc. award, 2012, Osborn Tchr.-Scholar award, Southern States Communication Assn., 2011; fellowship, Purdue U., 1974—76. Mem.: Nat. Assn. Comm. Ctrs., Pub. Rels. Soc. Am., Popular Culture Assn., Southern States Comm. Assn. (Osborn Tchr. award 2011), Ctrl. States Comm. Assn. (life Fedn. prize 1985), Nat. Comm. Assn. (life; elect. 1st v.p. 2013, Ecroyd Outstanding Teaching Higher Edn. award 2007, Turner award 2011), Phi Beta Kappa. Office: Davidson Coll Comm Studies Box 7066 Davidson NC 28035-7066 Business E-Mail: katurner@davidson.edu.*

TURNER, LESLIE MARIE, lawyer; b. Neptune, NJ, Oct. 2, 1957; BS, NYU, 1980; JD, Georgetown U. Law Ctr., 1985; LLM, American U. Law clk. Cole, Raywid & Braverman, Washington, 1984-85; jud. clk. to Hon. William C. Pryor US Ct. Appeals (DC cir.), Washington, 1985-86; assoc. Akin, Gump, Strauss, Hauer & Feld, LLP, Washington, 1986-93, ptnr., 1996—2006; asst. sec. for territorial & internat. affairs US Dept. Interior, Washington, 1993—95, counselor to sec., 1995—96; gen. counsel Coca-Cola North America, Atlanta, 2006—12; sr. v.p., gen. counsel, sec. The Hershey Co., Hershey, Pa., 2012—. Bd. dirs. Close Up Found., Georgia Appleseed, The Student Conservation Assn. Mem.: ABA, DC Bar Assn., NY State Bar Assn., The Washington Lawyer's Com. on Civil Rights & Urban Affairs (trustee, Wiley A. Branton award 2008). Office: The Hershey Company 100 Crystal A Dr Hershey PA 17033

TURNER, LISA PHILLIPS, human resources executive; b. Waltham, Mass., Apr. 10, 1951; d. James Sinclair and Virginia Turner. BA in Edn. and Philosophy magna cum laude, Washington Coll., Chestertown, Md., 1974; AS in Electronics Tech., AA in Engring., Palm Beach Jr. Coll., 1982; MBA, Nova U., 1986, DSc, 1989; PhD, Kennedy Western U., 1990. Cert. sr. profl. in human resources; cert. quality engr., designated airworthiness rep. Fed. Aviation Adminstrn., 2007; lic. USCG capt.; lic. pvt. pilot FAA, IFAA lic. airframe and powerplant mechanic, 2004; cert. Black Belt, 2006. Founder, pres. Turner's Bicycle Svc., Inc., Delray Beach, Fla., 1975-80; electronics engr., quality engr. Audio Engring. and Video Arts, Boca Raton, Fla., 1980-81; tech. writing instr. Palm Beach Jr. Coll., Lake Worth, Fla., 1981-82; adminstr. tng. and devel. Mitel Inc., Boca Raton, 1982-88; mgr. comm. and employee rels. Modular Computer Systems, Inc., Ft. Lauderdale, Fla., 1988-89; U.S. mktg. project mgr. Mitel, Inc., Boca Raton, 1990-91; v.p. human resources Connectronics, Inc., Ft. Lauderdale, 1991-93; sr. mgr. human resources Sensormatic Electronics Corp., Boca Raton, 1993-98, dir. human resources, 1998—2001; chief tng. officer and dir. human resources Tyco Fire and Security Svcs., Inc., Boca Raton, 2001—05, Six Sigma black belt, 2005—06; pres. Turner Bus. Svcs., Inc., Hayesville, NC, 2007—08; owner, insp. Your Inspection Expert, Inc., 2008; mfg. engr. Moog Inc., Murphy, NC, 2009—. Contbg. author Kitplanes Mag. With USCG Aux. Recipient Human Resources Profl. Excellence award, Soc. Human Resource Mgmt., 1999. Mem. Soc. for Human Resource Mgmt., Internat. Assn. Quality Cirs., Am. Soc. Quality Control, Fla. Employment Mgmt. Assn., Am. Acad. Mgmt., Employment Assn. Fla., Am. Capts. Assn., Citizens Police Acad., Aircraft Owners and Pilot's Assn., Exptl. Aircraft Assn., Fla. Aero. Club, Soc. Mfg. Engrs. Achievements include being the first female to construct, complete and fly a pulsar XP aircraft. Office: Moog Inc Components Group Murphy Operations 1995 NC Hwy 141 Murphy NC 28906-6864 Office Phone: 828-837-5115 ext. 216. Business E-Mail: lturner2@moog.com.

TURNER, MARTA JONES, food products executive; Various comm. positions Flowers Foods, Inc. (formerly Flowers Industries, Inc.), 1978, v.p., pub. affairs Thomasville, Ga., 1998, v.p., comm. & investor rels., 2002—04, sr. v.p., corp. rels., 2004—08, exec. v.p., corp. rels., 2008—. Office: Flowers Foods Inc 1919 Flowers Cir Thomasville GA 31757 Office Phone: 229-226-9110. Business E-Mail: mturner@flowersfoods.com.

TURNER, MICHAEL, professional football player; b. Waukegan, Ill., Feb. 13, 1982; BA, No. Ill. U., DeKalb. Running back San Diego Chargers, 2004—08, Atlanta Falcons, 2008—. Named 1st Team All-Pro, AP, 2008; named to All-Joe Team, USA Today, 2006, Nat. Football Conf. Pro Bowl Team, NFL, 2008, 2010. Achievements include leading the NFL in: rushing attempts, 2008, 2010. Office: Atlanta Falcons 4400 Falcon Pky Flowery Branch GA 30542

TURNER, MICHAEL DAN, academic administrator; b. Pasadena, Tex., Sept. 14, 1966; s. Daniel Lee and Freda Gayle (Cullie) Turner; m. Lisa Dawn Bowers, July 19, 1997; children: Madison, Megan. AAS, Okla. State U., Okmulgee, 1988; BS, Northeastern State U., 1991, MS, 1998. Univ. rep. Northeastern State U., Tahlequah, Okla., 1995—97, spl. asst. to pres., 1999—2003; dir. admissions and prospective student recruitment 199 Okla. State U., Okmulgee, Okla., 1997—99; v.p. student affairs Rogers State U., Claremore, Okla., 2003—07; pres. Southeastern Okla. State U., Durant, 2008—. Bd. trustees Claremore Pub. Schs. Found; exec. com. mem. Okla. Coun. on Student Affairs. Vol. Okla. Spl. Olympics, 1988—95; event chmn. Am. Cancer Soc., 1997—98; chmn. bd. dirs. Claremore C. of C. Capt. USMC, 1991—97. Named to Outstanding Young Men of Am., 1989. Mem.: Okmulgee Rotary Club, Okmulgee C. of C. (cmty. image and pub. rels. coms. 1997—98), Northeastern State U. Alumni Assn., Okla. State U.-Okmulgee Alumni Assn., Pi Kappa Alpha (chpt. advisor 1995—97). Methodist. Avocations: golf, water-skiing, softball, classic car restoration. Office: Southeastern Okla State U Office of Pres 1405 N 4th Durant OK 74701 Home: 1401 N 6th Ave Durant OK 74701-2724 Office Phone: 580-745-2000.

TURNER, MICHAEL L., state legislator; b. Feb. 6, 1955; married; 3 children. Mem. House Consumer & Employee Affairs Com., House Consumer Affairs Subcom.; state rep. Dist. 51 Tenn., 2001—. Mem.: Tenn. Fire Fighters Emergency Relief Fund (bd. dir., treas.), Tenn. Fire Commn. (bd. dir.), Tenn Profl. Fire Fighters (pres.), Tenn. AFL-CIO, Nashville Fire Fights Assn. (v.p.), Donelson C. of C., Madison C. of C., Old Hickory C. of C., Old Hickory Village Assn., Mason. Democrat. Methodist. Office: 1408 Hadley Ave Old Hickory TN 37138 also: 18 Legislative Plz Nashville TN 37243-0151 Office Phone: 615-847-0002, 615-741-3229. Office Fax: 615-741-4322. Business E-Mail: rep.mike.turner@capitol.tn.gov.

TURNER, PHILIP MICHAEL, academic administrator, writer; b. West Acton, Mass., Nov. 26, 1948; s. William Albert and Evelyn Olena (Peterson) T.; m. Lis Jane VanderBeke, Aug. 16, 1969; children: Gabrielle, Adrienne. BS in Edn., Boston State Coll., 1970; MS, U. Wis. at La Crosse, 1972; MSLS, EdD, East Tex. State U., 1977. Tchr. math. Edgewood Jr. High Sch., Merritt Island, Fla., 1969-71; ptnr. Video Guide Prodn. Co., Denver, 1973; libr. media specialist Edison Jr. High Sch., Green Bay, Wis., 1973-76; prof. libr. sci. U. Ala., Tuscaloosa, 1977-88; dean Sch. Libr. and Info. Studies U. North Tex., Denton, 1996—2004; asst. vice chancellor acad. affairs U. Ala. System, 1991-96; assoc. v.p. for acad. affairs for distance edn. U. North Tex., Denton, 1996—2004, vice provost learning enhancement, 2004—. Chair distance edn. adv. com. Tex. Higher Edn. Coordinating Bd., 2004—. Author: Handbook for In-School Media Personnel, 1980, Helping Teachers Teach, 1985, 3d edit., 2003. Vol. Meals on Wheels, Tuscaloosa, 1987-96. Recipient Outstanding Commitment To Teaching award U. Ala. Alumni Assn., 1979, Outstanding Svc. award Ala. Libr. and Media Prodrs., 1987, publ. award Div. Sch. Libr. Media Specialist, 1987, award for mng. info. tech., 1994, Ala. Libr. Assn. Disting. Svc. award, 1996; named Libr. of Yr., Beta Phi Mu, 1991. Mem. ALA (mem. accreditation com. 2000—04), Assn. Sch. Librs. (chair rsch. com. 1987-90, bd. dirs. 1990-94). Unitarian Universalist. Office: Coll Info 1155 Onion Cir 311068 Denton TX 76203-5017 Home: 1802 Teesley Ln Denton TX 76203 Home Phone: 940-484-8214, 910-533-4310; Office Phone: 940-565-4462. Business E-Mail: pturner@unt.edu.

TURNER, R. GERALD (ROBERT GERALD TURNER), academic administrator; b. Atlanta, Tex., Nov. 25, 1945; s. Robert B. and Oreta Lois (Porter) T.; m. Gail Oliver, Dec. 21, 1968; children: Angela Jan, Jessica Diane AA, Lubbock Christian Coll., 1966, LLD (hon.), 1985, Pepperdine U., 1989; BS, Abilene Christian U., 1968; MA, U. Tex., 1970, PhD, 1975. Tchr. Weatherford High Sch., Tex., 1968-69; tchr. Lanier High Sch., Austin, Tex., 1969-70; instr. psychology San Antonio Coll., 1970-72; instr. Prairie View A & M U., Tex., 1973-75; asst. prof. psychology Pepperdine U., Malibu, Calif., 1975-78, assoc. prof. psychology, 1978-79, dir. testing, 1975-76, chmn. social sci. div., 1976-78, assoc. v.p. univ. affairs, 1979; assoc. prof. psychology U. Okla., Norman, 1979-84, exec. asst. to pres., 1979-81, acting provost, 1982, v.p. exec. affairs, 1981-84; chancellor U. Miss., University, 1984-95; pres. So. Meth. U., Dallas, 1995—. Pres. Southeastern Conf., 1985-87; trustee Pepperdine U., 1994-95; mem. Pres.'s Commn., NCAA, 1989-92, chmn., 1991-92; mem. Knight Commn. on Intercollegiate Athletics, 1991—; chmn. pres. coun. Miss. Assn. Colls., 1985-86; mem. def. adv. com. Svc. Acad. Athletic Programs, 1992—; bd. dirs. J.C. Penney Co.,Inc., 1995- Author: (with L. Willerman) Readings About Individual and Group Differences, 1979. Contbr. articles to profl. jours. Recipient Outstanding Alumni award Abilene Christian U., 1989; named to New Boston HS Athletic Hall of Fame, 1993. Mem. Young Pres. Orgn., Sigma Xi, Beta Alpha Psi, Phi Theta Kappa, Alpha Chi, Phi Kappa Phi. Mem. Ch. of Christ. Avocations: reading, tennis, golf, travel. Office: Southern Methodist Universtiy Office of President 6425 Boaz Lane Dallas TX 75275-0001 Office Phone: 214-768-3300.*

TURNER, ROBERT FOSTER, law educator, writer, former government official; b. Atlanta, Feb. 14, 1944; s. Edwin Witcher and Martha Frances T. AB, Ind. U., Bloomington, 1968; postgrad., Stanford U., 1972-73; JD, U. Va., 1981, SJD, 1996. Bar: Va. 1982, U.S. Supreme Ct. 1986. Rsch. assoc., pub. affairs fellow Hoover Instn. on War, Revolution and Peace, Stanford U., 1971-74; spl. asst., legis. asst., nat. security advisor U.S. Sen. Robert P. Griffin, 1974-79; co-founder, assoc. dir. Ctr. for Nat. Security Law U. Va., Charlottesville, 1981, 87—; sr. fellow, 1985-86; spl. asst. undersec. for policy Dept. Def., 1981-82; counsel Pres.'s Intelligence Oversight Bd., White House, 1982-84; prin. dep. asst. sec. for legis. and intergovtl. affairs Dept. State, 1984, acting. asst. sec., 1984—85; pres. U.S. Inst. Peace, Washington, 1986-87; lectr. in law and in govt. and fgn. affairs U. Va., Charlottesville, 1988-93, assoc. prof., 1993-97, prof., 1997—; Charles H. Stockton prof. internat. law Naval War Coll., 1994-95. Disting. lectr. U.S. Mil. Acad., West Point, 1995. Author: Myths of the Vietnam War: The Pentagon Papers Reconsidered, 1972, Vietnamese Communism: Its Origins and Development, 1975, The War Powers Resolution: Its Implementation in Theory and Practice, 1983, Nicaragua v. United States: A Look at the Facts, 1987, Repealing the War Powers Resolution: Restoring the Rule of Law in U.S. Foreign Policy, 1991, The ABM Treaty and the Senate: Issues of International and Constitutional Law, 1999; editor: The Jefferson-Hemings Controversy, 2011, (with John Norton Moore) The Legal Structure of Defense Organization, 1986, International Law and the Brezhnev Doctrine, 1987, Readings on International Law, 1995, The Real Lessons of the Vietnam War, 2002, National Security Law, 1990, 2nd edit., 2005, Legal Issues in the Struggle Against Terror, 2010, (with John Norton Moore and Guy B. Roberts) National Security Law Documents, 1995, 2nd edit., 2006, (with John Norton Moore and Ross A. Fisher) To Oppose Any Foe: The Legacy of US Intervention in Vietnam, 2006. Pres. Endowment of U.S. Inst. Peace, 1986-87; trustee Intercollegiate Studies Inst., 1986-92; bd. dirs. Thomas Jefferson Inst. for Pub. Policy, 1997—; chmn. scholars commn. on Jefferson-Hemings matter Thomas Jefferson Heritage Soc., 2000-01. Capt. US Army, 1968—71, Vietnam. Grantee Hoover Press, 1972, Earhart Found., 1980, 1989-90, 2013-14, Inst. Ednl. Affairs, 1980, Carthage Found., 1980. Mem. ABA (chmn. com. on exec.-congl. rels., sec. internat. law and practice 1983-86, adv. com. on law and nat. security 1984-86, standing com. on law and nat. security 1986-92, chmn. 1989-92, editor ABA Nat. Security Law Report 1992-99), Federalist Soc. (chmn. subcom. on nat. security law 1998—), Com. on the Present Danger, 2005-, Bd. Rsch. Cons., Inst. Fgn. Policy Analysis, Mensa, Am. Soc. Internat. Law, Nat. Eagle Scout Assn., Coun. on Fgn. Rels., Acad. of Polit. Sci., Am. Polit. Sci. Assn., Am. Hist. Assn., Soc. Mil. History, Soc. Historians Early Am. Republic. Office: Univ Va Sch of Law Ctr for Nat Security Law 580 Massie Rd Charlottesville VA 22904-7362 Home Phone: 434-978-7838; Office Phone: 434-924-4083. Business E-Mail: bobturner@virginia.edu.

TURNER, ROBERT G., JR., publishing executive; b. Columbus, Ga. m. Dottie Turner; children: Stephanie Turner, Robert Turner. Degree in Bus., U. South Fla. Advt. sales rep. Columbus Ledger-Enquirer, Ohio, 1973; retail advt. mgr. The Bradenton Herald (subs. of The McClatchy Co.), Fla., 1979, advt. dir. Fla., 1983—88, gen. mgr. Fla., 1988—96, v.p., ops. Fla., 1996—2008, pres., pub. Fla., 2008—. Recipient President's Disting. Citizen award, U. South Fla., 2005. Mem.: Manatee C. of C.(chmn., Econ. Devel. Coun. 2008-; (former bd. dirs., Econ. Devel. Coun. 2000; (former chmn. 1994; (bd. dirs. 1990-95). Office: The Bradenton Herald 1111 3rd Ave W Ste 100 Bradenton FL 34205-7834 Office Phone: 941-748-0411. Business E-Mail: rturner@bradenton.com.

TURNER, RON, college football coach; b. Martinez, Calif., Dec. 5, 1953; m. Wendy Turner; children: Morgan, Cameron, Callan, Madison. BA, U. Pacific, 1977. Grad. asst. coach U. Pacific Tigers, 1977; wide receivers coach U. Ariz. Wildcats, 1978—79, running backs coach, 1980; coach Northwestern U. Wildcats, 1981-82; receivers coach U. Pitts. Panthers, 1983-84; quarterbacks coach U. Southern Calif. Trojans, 1985, quarterbacks coach, offensive coord., 1986, wide receivers coach, 1987; quarterback coach Tex. A&M U. Aggies, 1988-89; offensive coord., quarterbacks coach Stanford U. Cardinals, 1989-92; head coach San Jose State U. Spartans, 1992-93; offensive coord., quarterbacks coach Chgo. Bears, 1993-96, 2005—10; head coach U. Ill. Fighting Illini, 1996—2004; wide receivers coach Indpls. Colts, 2010, quarterbacks coach, 2011, Tampa Bay Buccaneers, 2012; head coach Fla. Internat. U. Golden Panthers, 2013—. Named Big Ten Coach of Yr., 2001; named to The Diablo County Cmty. Coll. Hall of Fame, 2009. Office: Florida International University 11200 SW 8th St Miami FL 33199 Office Phone: 305-348-4155.

TURNER, STEPHEN PARK, philosopher, sociologist, educator; b. Chgo., Mar. 1, 1951; s. Lawrence Lynn and Natalie (Stephens) Turner; m. Kimberly Anne Wills, Apr. 21, 1990; children: Evan Wills, Douglas Carrera. AB, U. Mo., Columbia, 1971, AM in Sociology, 1971, AM in Philosophy, 1972, PhD in Sociology, 1975. Asst. prof. U. South Fla., 1975—80, assoc. prof., 1980—84, prof., dept. sociology, 1984—87, grad. rsch. prof., dept. of sociology, 1987—89; vis. prof. Boston U., 1987; grad. rsch. prof. dept. philosophy U. South Fla., Tampa, Fla., 1989—; dir. Ctr. Social and Polit. Thought, 1994—. Simon hon. prof. U. Manchester, 1996—97; vis. prof. Va. Poly. Inst. and State U., Blacksburg, 1982, U. Notre Dame, 1985. Author: (books) Sociological Explanation as Translation, 1980, The Search for a Methodology of Social Science: Durkheim, Weber, and the 19th Century Problem of Cause, Probability, and Action, 1986, The Social Theory of Practices: Tradition, Tacit Knowledge, and Presuppositions, 1994, Brains/Practices/Relativism: Social Theory after Cognitive Science, 2002, Liberal Democracy 3.0: Civil Society in an Age of Experts, 2003, Explaining the Normative, 2010, Understanding the Tacit, 2014, Politics of Expertise, 2014, American Sociology: From Pre-Disciplinary to Post-normal, 2014; co-author (with F. Weed): (books) Conflict in Organizations, 1983; co-author: (with R. Factor) Max Weber and the Dispute Over Reason and Value: A Study in Philosophy, Ethics, and Politics, 1984; co-author: (with Jonathan Turner) The Impossible Science: An Institutional Analysis of American Sociology, 1990; co-author: (with Regis A. Factor) Max Weber: The Lawyer as Social Thinker, 1994; editor: The Cambridge Companion to Weber; editor: (with Dirk Käsler) Sociology Responds to Fascism, 1992; editor: Emile Durkheim: Sociologist and Moralist, 1993, Causality, 2010; co-editor (with M. Wardell): Sociological Theory in Transition, 1986; co-editor: (with Alan Sica) The Disobedient Generation: Social Theorists in the Sixties, 2005; co-editor: (with Mark Risjord) Philosophy of Anthropology and Sociology, 2007; co-editor: (with William Outhwaite) The SAGE Handbook of Social Sci. Methodology, 2007; co-editor: (with Gerard Delanty) Routledge International Handbook of Social and Political Theory, 2011; co-editor: (with Seven Eliaeson, Patricia Mindus) Axel Hagersfrom and Modern Social Thought, 2014; collaborating editor: jour. Social Studies of Science, 1986—; contbr. articles to profl. jours., NEH fellow, 1991-1992, Swedish Collegium for Advanced Study in Social Scis. fellow, 1992, 1998. Mem.: Soc. Social Studies Sci., Am. Sociol. Assn., Am. Philos. Assn., St. Petersburg Yacht Club. Office: U South Fla Dept Philosophy Tampa FL 33620 Office Phone: 813-974-5549.

TURNER, SYLVESTER, state legislator; b. Sept. 27, 1954; 1 child, Ashley Paige. Attended, U. Houston, Harvard U. Law Sch. Former del. chmn. Harris County Legislature, Tex.; founder, atty. Law Office of Barnes & Turner, 1983—; mem. Dist. 139 Tex. House of Representatives, 1988—. Adj. prof. Thurgood Marshall Sch. Law; lectr. U. Houston Law Sch., South Tex. Coll. Law. Recipient Rising Star award, Harris County Dem.; named Legislator of Yr., Houston Police Patrolman's Union, Tex. Monthly, 1995, Rookie of Yr., One of Five Outstanding Houstonian, Houston Jaycees. Mem.: Acres Homes Citizens C. of C., Coalition Sch. Improvement, Am. Cancer Soc. (bd. mem.), United Negro Coll. Fund. Democrat. Baptist. Office: 6915 Antoine St Ste E Houston TX 77091 also: Room CAP 1W.06 Capitol PO Box 2910 Austin TX 78768 Office Phone: 713-683-6363, 512-463-0554.

TURNER, TED (ROBERT EDWARD TURNER III), retired broadcast company executive, philanthropist; b. Cin., Nov. 19, 1938; s. Robert Edward and Florence (Rooney) Turner; m. Judy Nye, 1960 (div. 1964); children: Laura Lee, Robert Edward IV; m. Jane Shirley Smith, June 1965 (div. 1988); children: Beau, Rhett, Jennie; m. Jane Fonda, Dec. 21, 1991 (div. May 22, 2001). Attended, Brown U., 1957—60; DSc in Commerce (hon.), Drexel U., 1982; LLD (hon.), Samford U., 1982, Atlanta U., 1984; D Entrepreneurial Sci. (hon.), Cen. New Eng. Coll. Tech., 1983; D in Pub. Adminstrn. (hon.), Mass. Maritime Acad., 1984; D in Bus. Adminstrn. (hon.), U. Charleston, 1985; BA in Philosophy (hon.), Brown U., 1989, LHD (hon.), 1993; D (hon.), Trinity Coll., 2001. Account exec. Turner Advt. Co., Atlanta, 1961—63, pres., COO, 1963—70; pres., chmn. bd. Turner Broadcasting Sys., Inc. (TBS), Atlanta, 1970—96; chmn. Turner Found. Inc., 1990—; vice chmn. Time Warner Inc. (merger Turner Broadcasting Sys.), 1996—2000; vice chmn., sr. advisor AOL Time Warner (merger of Time Warner Inc. and AOL, Inc.), 2001—03; chmn. Turner Enterprises, Inc., 2003—; owner Atlanta Braves, 1976—. Bd. dirs. Time Warner, 1996—2001, Time Warner Inc. (formerly AOL/Time Warner), 2001—06. Co-author (with Bill Burke): (autobiography) Call Me Ted, 2008; prodr.: (films for prodn. companies) Ted Turner Pictures, Ted Turner Documentaries. Co-founder, co-chair Nuclear Threat Initiative, Washington, 2001—; bd. dirs. Martin Luther King Ctr., Atlanta; donations to a number of non-profit foundations, including Turner Found., Inc., Endangered Species Fund, UN Found. and the Nuclear Threat Initiative. Recipient Outstanding Entrepreneur of Yr. award, Sales Mktg. & Mgmt. Mag., 1979, Pvt. Enterprise Exemplar medal, Freedoms Found. Valley Forge, 1980, Communicator of Yr. award, Pub. Rels. Soc. America, 1981, NY Broadcasters, 1981, Nat. News Media award, VFW, 1981, Disting. Svc. in Telecomm. award, Ohio U. Coll. Comm., 1982, Carr Van Anda award, Ohio Sch. Journalism, 1982, Spl. award, Edinburgh Internat. TV Festival, Scotland, 1982, Bd. Govs. award, Atlanta chpt. NATAS, 1982, Media Awareness award, United Vietnam Vets. Orgn., 1983, Dinner of Champions award, Ga. chpt. Multiple Sclerosis Soc., 1983, Praca Spl. Merit award, NY Puerto Rican Assn. Cmty. Affairs, 1983, World Telecomm. Pioneer award, NY State Broadcasters Assn., 1984, Golden Plate award, Am. Acad. Achievement, 1984, Outstanding Supporter Boy Scouting award, Nat. Boy Scout Coun., 1984, Lifetime Achievement award, NY Internat. Film & TV Festival, 1984, Corp. Star of Yr. award, Nat. Leukemia Soc., 1985, Disting. Achievement award, U. Ga., 1985, Tree of Life award, Jewish Nat. Fund, 1985, Bus. Exec. of Yr. award, Ga. Security Dealers Assn., 1985, Life Achievement award, Popular Culture Assn., 1986, George Washington Disting. Patriot award, SAR, 1986, Mo. Honor medal, U. Mo. Sch. Journalism, 1987, Golden Ace award, Nat. Cable TV Acad., 1987, Sol Taishoff award, Nat. Press Found., 1988, Citizen Diplomat award, Ctr. Soviet-Am. Dialogue, 1988, Chmn.'s award, Cable Advt. Bur., 1988, Directorate award, NATAS, 1989, Paul White award, Radio & TV News Dirs. Assn., 1989, Bus. Marketer of Yr. award, Am. Mktg. Assn., 1989, Disting. Svc. award, Simon Wiesenthal Ctr., 1990, Glasnost award, Vols. America/Soviet Life mag., 1990, Carnegie Medal of Philanthropy, 2001, Bower award for Bus. Leadership, Franklin Inst., 2006, Silver Satellite award, Am. Women in Radio and TV; named Man of Yr., TIME mag., 1991, Cable & Broadcasting's Man of Century, 1999, Yachtsman of Yr. 4 times; named one of 50 Most Generous Philanthropists, Fortune mag., 2005, Forbes 400: Richest Americans, 2006—, The World's Most Influential People, TIME mag., 2009; named to Promotion & Mktg. Assn. Hall of Fame, 1980, Nat. Assn. Sport & Phys. Edn. Hall of Fame, 1986, Advt. Hall of Fame, 2004, Jr. Achievement US Bus. Hall of Fame, 2007; won America's Cup in his yacht 'Courageous', 1977. Mem.: NAACP (life; bd. dirs. Atlanta chpt.), Nat. Cable TV Assn. (Pres.'s award 1979, 1989, Regional Employer of Yr. award 1976), Cousteau Soc., Nat. Audubon Soc., Bay Area Cable Club (hon.). Achievements include launching TBS Superstation concept, CNN, built a portfolio of unrivaled cable TV news and entertainment; opened first Teds Montana Grill. Avocations: sailing, fishing. Office: Turner Enterprises Inc 133 Luckie St NW Atlanta GA 30303 Personal E-mail: info@tedturner.com.

TURNER, TODD, lawyer, former political organization administrator; m. Becca Arnold; children: Harper, Cannon. BA magna cum laude, Ouachita Bapt. U., Arkadelphia, Ark., 1988; JD, U. Ark., Little Rock, 1992. Bar: Ark., US Dist. Ct. (ea., we. and fed. dist.) Ark., US Ct; Appeals (8th cir.), US Supreme Ct. Law clk. to hon. Robin Mays Ark. Supreme Ct., 1992; ptnr. Arnold, Batson, Turner & Turner, P.A., Arkadelphia; chmn. Ark. Dem. Party, 2009—11. Dep. prosecuting atty. Ninth East Jud. Dist., Ark., 1993—2002, 2007—. Contbr. articles to profl. jours. Bd. dirs. Clark County United Way, 1995—97, Ark. Better Bus. Bur., 2006—, Arkadelphia C. of C.; chmn. Clark County Dem. Com., 2007—. Officer Ark. Army Nat. Guard, Army Res., 1989—99. Mem.: Nat. Assn. Consumer Advocates, Clark County Bar Assn. (pres. 1994—96), Ark. Bar Assn. (mem. House of Delegates 1998—2006, pres. Southwest chpt. 2003, bd. govs. 2006—), Ark. Trial Lawyers Assn. (Consumer Advocate award 2000). Democrat. Office: Arnold Batson Turner & Turner 501 Crittenden St PO Box 480 Arkadelphia AR 71923 Office Phone: 501-374-2361. Office Fax: 501-376-8409. Business E-Mail: Todd@ArnoldBatsonTurner.com.

TURNER, TOMMY, state legislator; b. Aug. 8, 1952; m. Donna Turner; children: Christopher, Nicole. Factory worker & farmer; mem. Dist. 85 Ky. House of Reps., 1997—. Republican. Baptist. Mailing: 175 Clifty Grove Church Rd Somerset KY 42501-5532 Office: Capitol Annex Rm 413F 702 Capitol Ave Frankfort KY 40601 Office Phone: 502-564-8100 ext. 716. Business E-Mail: tommy.turner@lrc.ky.gov.

TURNER, V(ERAS) DEAN, retired dean; b. Tompkinsville, Ky., Oct. 19, 1925; s. Hubert B. and Hazel Pearl (Craig) T.; m. Maxine H. Henson, June 30, 1946; children: Sharon Kay, Ruth Diane. BS, Northwestern U., 1946; MA, U. Ill., 1949; PhD, U. Okla., 1968. Instr. dept. math. Moark Bapt. Coll., West Plains, Mo., 1949-51; instr. chair of math. dept. Champaign (Ill.) Jr. H.S., 1953-56; spl. instr. math. U. Okla., Norman, 1965-66; prof. Mankato (Minn.) State U., 1956-73, chairperson, dept. math., 1973-77, dean, 1977-89, dean emeritus, Coll. of Natural Scis., Math, Home Econs., 1989—2014. Chairperson external affairs subcom. on internat. math. edn. Upper Midwest Danforth Found., 1974-77; cons. Haldingford (Minn.) Sch., Assn. of Math. Tchrs. in Mex., Toluca; faculty senate, fiscal affairs com. Mankato State U., Sch. Arts and Scis. exec. com., curriculum com., dean selection com., chmn. task force on consolidation; mem. Study Group to Peoples Republic of China, 1980; mem. Minn. Coun. of Engring. Deans; mem. State U. Systems task force on admissions requirements. Co-author: Introduction to Mathematics, 1972, Principles of Mathematics, 1972. Comdr. USN, 1944, WWII, Korean War. Mem. Nat. Coun. of Tchrs. of Math., Math. Assn. of Am., Minn. Coun. of Tchrs. of Math., Sch. Sci. and Math. Assn., Phi Delta Kappa (pres. Mankato State U. chpt. 1984-85), Sigma Xi. Republican. Baptist. Home: 1034 Siena Oaks West Palm Beach Gardens FL 33410 Personal E-mail: vturner@aol.com.

TURNER, WILLIAM BRAD, JR., retired consumer products company executive; s. Bill Turner. Pres. W.C. Bradley Co., 1987—2008, ret., 2008, mem. adv. bd. Bd. dirs., emeritus dir. Total Sys. Services, Inc., Synovus Fin. Corp., ret. chmn. exec. com. Office: W C Bradley Co 1017 Front Ave Columbus GA 31902 Office Phone: 706-571-6080. Office Fax: 706-571-6081.

TURTZ, STEVEN, bank executive; BS, SUNY, Brockport. Registered rep., SunTrust Investment Svcs. Inc. Sr. v.p., western regional mgr. Wells Fargo Ins.; v.p., sales Highland Capital Brokerage; pres., v.p. & nat. sales dir. Comerica Bank Ins. Svcs.; pres., SunTrust ins. svcs. SunTrust Banks, Inc., 2009—. Mem. Inst. Bus. and Estate Planners. Office: SunTrust Banks Inc 303 Peachtree St NE Atlanta GA 30308 Office Phone: 404-588-7711. Office Fax: 404-332-3875. Business E-Mail: steven.turtz@suntrust.com.

TUSZYNSKI, DANIEL J., JR., sales, management and marketing consultant; b. Erie, Pa., Aug. 22, 1947; s. Daniel and Dorothy (Tylman) T. Grad., Iroquois Trade Sch., 1968; AA, L.A. City Coll., 1971; BS, Calif. State U., 1975; MBA, Gannon U., 1979; postgrad., The Cons. Inst., 1989. Cert. profl cons. Indsl. engr. Gen. Electric Co., Erie, Pa., 1965-75; sales mgr. Burroughs Corp., Culver City, Calif., 1975-76; regional sales mgr. Gen. Electric Co., Erie, 1976-81; dir. sales, mktg. Peerless Mfg. Co., Inc, Dallas, 1981-85; v.p. sales, mktg. Consumat Systems, Inc., Richmond, Va., 1985-88; v.p. mktg. Sutton Holding Co., Richmond, 1988-89; pres., chief exec. officer Tech. Mktg. Inc., Richmond, 1989—; v.p. sales and mktg. Hobart Tafa Technologies, Inc., Concord, N.H., 1990-91; pres. Music Treasures Co., Richmond, 1991—. Author: (manual) Peerless Air Inlet Systems, 1984. 1st lt. USNG, 1968-75. Mem. Am. Mktg. Assn., Am. Cons. League, Porsche Club Am. Roman Catholic. Avocations: sailing, carpentry, skiing, flying. Home: 11227 Linderwood Dr Mechanicsville VA 23116-3137 Office: Music Treasures Co PO Box 9138 Richmond VA 23227-0138 Office Phone: 804-730-8800 ext. 10. Business E-Mail: musict@musictreasures.com.

TUTOR, TYRA H., consulting company executive; CPA. Dir. Office of Chmn. MPS (Modis Professional Services) Group, Inc. (acquired by Adecco), 1997—2000, v.p. Office of Chmn., 2000—01, v.p. fin. and corp. devel., 2001—03, sr. v.p. fin. and corp. devel., 2003—05, sr. v.p. corp. devel., 2005—. Office: MPS Group Inc Ste 2500 1 Independent Dr Jacksonville FL 32202 Office Phone: 904-360-2000. Office Fax: 904-360-2350. Business E-Mail: tyra.tutor@mpsgroup.com.

TUTTLE, JEREMY BALLOU, neuroscientist; s. John Bauman and Charlotte Marion (Root) T.; m. Sara Jane Stasko, Mar. 26, 1971. AB, U. Rochester, 1969; PhD, Johns Hopkins U., 1977. Postdoctoral fellow U. Conn., Storrs, 1976-79, vis. asst. prof., 1980, asst. prof. in residence, 1981-84; asst. prof. physiology U. Va., Charlottesville, 1984-87, asst. prof. neuroscience, 1987-90, rsch. asst. prof., 1990-93, assoc. prof. urology neuroscience, 1993-98, prof., 1998—. Contbr. articles to Devel. Biology, Science, Jour. Neuroscience, others; mem. editl. bd. Investigative Urology, Jour. Urology, Jour. Hypertension. Chmn. mem. Common Area Planning Commn., 1984-87; pres. bd. Earlysville Forest Homeowner's Assn., 1986-89, Earlysville, Va.; chmn. urology spl. emphasis panel NIH, 1996-2001; chmn. spl. emphasis panel on female pelvic floor disorders Nat. Inst. Child Health and Human Devel., 1999; mem. promotion and tenure com. U. Va., 2004—10. U. Rochester Hon. scholar, 1965-69, Regent's scholar for Medicine, 1969, NIH predoctoral fellow, 1971-75, Nat. Rsch. Svc. fellow, 1976-79, Nat. Spinal Cord Injury Found. rsch. fellow, 1979-80; recipient Rsch. Career Devel. award Nat. Inst. Neurol. Disease/NIH, Muscular Dystrophy Assn. Rsch. award, 1990—; Am. Heart Assn. grantee, 1987-89, 90—, fellowship, Fogarty Internat. Ctr. for Rsch. NIH, Japan, 1997. Mem.: AAAS, Am. Soc. Cell Biology, Biophys. Soc., Soc. Neuroscience, Sigma Xi. Achievements include research on NGF dynamics in hypertrophic disease, carbon dioxide transport and chemosensitivity, molecular mechanisms of quantal synaptic transmission, nerve growth factor synthesis by vascular smooth muscle, trophic regulation of motor neurons, neurodegenerative diseases. Office: U Va Med Sch PO Box 801392 Charlottesville VA 22908-1392 Office Phone: 434-924-5634. Business E-Mail: tuttle@virginia.edu.

TWAIN, SHANIA (EILLEEN REGINA EDWARDS), singer, musician; b. Windsor, Ontario, Can., Aug. 28, 1965; d. Sharon and Jerry Twain (Stepfather), Clarence Edwards; m. Robert John Lange, Dec. 28, 1993 (div. 2008); 1 child, Eja; m. Frederic Thiebaud, Jan. 1, 2011. Singer: (albums) Shania Twain, 1993, The Woman in Me, 1995 (Album of Yr., Can. Country Music Assn. Awards, 1995, Album of Yr., Acad. Country Music Awards, 1996, Country Album of Yr., Billboard Music Awards, 1996, Best Country Album, Grammy Awards, 1996, Top Selling Album Spl. Achievement award, Can. Country Music Assn. Awards, 1997), Come on Over, 1997 (Album of Yr., Can. Country Music Assn. Awards, 1998, Best Selling Country Record of Yr., Nat. Assn. Record Merchandisers, 1999), Up!, 2002 (Album of Yr., Can. Country Music Assn. Awards, 2003), Greatest Hits, 2004, (songs) You're Still the One, 1998 (Best Selling Country Single, Billboard Music Awards, 1998, Single of Yr., Can. Country Music Assn. Awards, 1998, VH1 Viewer's Choice award, 1998, Best Country Song, Best Female Country Vocal Performance, Grammy Awards, 1999), From This Moment On, 1998 (Vocal/Instrumental Collaboration of Yr., Can. Country Music Assn. Awards, 1999), That Don't Impress Me Much, 1998, Man! I Feel Like a Woman!, 1999 (Best Female Country Vocal Performance, Grammy Awards, 2000), Come on Over, 1999 (Best Country Song, Grammy Awards, 2000); author: (autobiography) From This Moment On, 2011; featured in (reality documentary series) Why Not? With Shania Twain, OWN Network, 2011. Recipient Outstanding Musical Achievement award, First Americans in the Arts, 1996, Juno Internat. Achievement award, Can. Acad. Recording Arts & Scis., 1997, Songwriter/Artist of Yr. award, Nashville Songwriters Assn. Internat., 1998, Double-Diamond award, Acad. Country Music Awards, 1999, Internat. Artist Achievement award, Country Music Assn. Awards, 1999, Star on Canada's Walk of Fame, 2003, Songwriter award, Can. Radio Music Awards, 2004, Star on the Hollywood Walk of Fame, 2011; named Female Video Artist of Yr., ABC Radio Networks Country Music Awards, 1995, Best Female Artist, Country Music Radio Awards, 1995, Female Vocalist of Yr., Can. Country Music Assn. Awards, 1995, 1996, 1998, 1999, 2003, Fan's Choice Entertainer of Yr., 1996, 1998, 1999, World's Best Selling Female Country Artist, World Music Awards, 1996, Entertainer of Yr., Juno Awards, Can. Acad. Recording Arts & Scis., 1996, Country Female Vocalist of Yr., 1996, 1997, 1998, Best Country Female Vocalist, 1999, Best Country Female Artist, 2000, Best Songwriter, 2000, Artist of Yr., 2003, Top New Female Vocalist, Acad. Country Music Awards, 1996, Entertainer of Yr., 2000, Favorite New Country Artist, American Music Awards, 1996, Favorite Female Country Artist, 1997, 1999, 2000, Favorite Female Pop/Rock Artist, 2000, Female Country Artist of Yr., Billboard Music Awards, 1996, Female Artist of Yr., 1998, Country Artist of Yr., 2003, Female Artist of Yr., Country Music TV (CMT) Awards, 1996, 1998, 1999, Entertainer of Yr., Country Music Assn. Awards, 1999, Favorite Female Musical Performer, People's Choice Awards, 2000, Favorite Country Female Singer, 2005; named one of 40 Greatest Women in Country Music, Country Music TV, 2002; named to Canadian Music Hall of Fame, 2011. Office: Mercury Records 66 Music Sq W Nashville TN 37203-4315 Address: Shore Fire Media c/o Georgette Pascale 32 Court St Fl 16 Brooklyn NY 11201-4404 Office: c/o Q Prime 131 S 11th St Nashville TN 37206

TWEARDY, DAVID JOHN, physician, scientist, educator; b. Monessen, Pa., Feb. 12, 1952; s. John Tweardy Sr. and Helen Kotch Tweardy; m. Ruth Falik, Jan. 21, 1982; children: Samuel David, Benjamin John, Daniel James. AB in Chemistry, Princeton U., 1974; MD, Harvard U., 1978. Diplomate Am. Bd. Internal Medicine, 1983, Am. Bd. Infectious Diseases, 1984. Asst. prof. medicine U. Pitts. Sch. Medicine, 1987—93, assoc. prof. medicine, 1993—99; prof. medicine Baylor Coll. Medicine, Houston, 1999—, chief sect. infectious diseases, 1999—. Grantee, NIH, 1997—2005, 2002—, 2004—. Mem.: Am. Clin. and Climatalogical Assn., Assn. Am. Physicians. Home: 3769 Nottingham St Houston TX 77005 Office Phone: 713-798-8918. E-mail: dtweardy@bcm.edu.

TWISDALE, HAROLD WINFRED, dentist; b. Roanoke Rapids, NC, Apr. 28, 1933; s. James Robert and Elma (Smith) T.; m. Barbara Ann Edmonds, Aug. 2, 1958 (div. Apr. 1974); children: Harold Winfred, Leigh Ann.; m. Frances Jean Winstead, July 1983. BS in Dentistry, U. N.C., 1955, D.D.S., 1958. Individual practice dentistry, Charlotte, NC, 1961—; head, dept. dental prosthetics Meml. Hosp., 1964-66; lectr. dental subjects.; pres., gen. mgr. WCTU-TV, Charlotte Telecasters, Inc., 1967-69, WATU-TV, Augusta, Ga., Augusta Telecasters, Inc., 1968-69, Television Presentations, Inc., Charlotte, 1967-69; partner Twisdale and Steel Assos., Charlotte, 1965-70; propr. Twisdale Enterprises, Charlotte, 1965-70. Pres. Memphis Telecasters, Inc., 1966-76, Va. Telecasters, Inc., Richmond, 1966—, Durham-Raleigh Telecasters, Inc., Durham, N.C., 1966-70, Gentil Elite, Inc., 1979— Transp. chmn. Miss N.C. Pageant, 1965; v.p. N.C. Jaycees, 1963-64; Trustee Boys Home, Lake Waccomaw, N.C., 1966-67. Served to capt. USAF, 1958-60. Recipient various awards Charlotte Jaycees, 1962-66. Fellow Acad. Dentistry Internat.; mem. ADA, N.C. Dental Found., N.C. Dental Soc., Charlotte Dental Soc. (chmn. various coms. 1961—), Am. Analgesia Soc., Internat. Analgesic Soc. (dir. 1980-85), N.C. Dental Soc. Anesthesiology (v.p. 1983-84), Charlotte Analgesia Study Club (co-founder 1970), N.C. 2d Dist. Dental Soc., Metrolina Dental Soc. (founder 1994, pres. 1994-95), U. N.C. Dental Alumni Assn., Southeastern Analgesia Soc. (founder 1972, pres. 1972-74), Lambda Chi Alpha, Delta Sigma Delta. Republican. Methodist. Office: 3104 Weddington Rd Ste 200 Matthews NC 28105 Home Phone: 704-841-3605; Office Phone: 704-849-2595. Personal E-mail: twisdds@aol.com.

TWITTY, H. R., hospital administrator; b. Columbia, SC, May 9, 1941; s. Archie Hazel Twitty and Sara (Murphy) Avritt; m. Marlene Faye Wingate, June 9, 1961; children: William Thomas, Michael David. BA, Tenn. Temple Coll., 1964. Cert. profl. for hosp. material mgmt. Mgr. store room Erlanger Hosp., Chattanooga, 1961-69; purchasing agt. Meml. Hosp., Chattanooga, 1969-71, dir. facility svcs., 1999—2001, dir. material, 1972-99, bd. dirs. credit union, 1986-92, 2008, CSR coord. Chattanooga, 2002—, exec. to United Way, 2001; mem. Manicharse Hosp. Meml. Hikson Hosp. Bd. dirs. Credit USA. United Way Loaned Exec., 2001; deacon Duncan Park Bapt. Ch., Chattanooga, 1986—88, 1991—92, 1995—96, 1997—2000, 2003—06, chmn. bd. deacons, 1983, 1988, mem. leadership com., 1995—96, chmn. bd. deacons, 1998—2000, supt. Sunday sch., 1975—2007, 2007—08, 2010—. Mem. Am. Hosp. Assn. Purchasing Mgrs. (cert. sr.), Internat. Hosp. Soc. Material Mgrs. (Disting. Profl.), Tenn. Hosp. Soc. Material Mgrs. (bd. dirs. region III 1979-82, pres. 1983-84, 89-92, Mgr. of Yr. award 1991, bd. dirs. 1994-2005), Chattanooga Area Purchasing Soc. (pres. 1985-87), Optimist. Home: 369 Prater Rd Rossville GA 30741-4692 Office: Meml North Park Hosp 2051 Hamill Rd Hixson TN 37343- Business E-Mail: hrtwitty@memorial.org.

TYGRETT, HOWARD VOLNEY, JR., judge, lawyer; b. Lake Charles, La., Jan. 12, 1940; s. Howard Volney and Hazel (Wheeler) T.; m. Linda Lee; children: Carroll Diane, Howard V. III. BA, Williams Coll., 1961; LLB, So. Methodist U., 1964. Bar: Tex. 1964. Gen. atty. SEC, 1964-65; law clk. to chief judge U.S. Dist. Ct. No. Dist. Tex., 1965-67; ptnr. Tygrett & Walker and predecessors, Dallas, 1968-98; state dist. judge, 86th dist. Kaufman County, Tex., 2003—. Bd. dirs. Routh St. Ctr., 1976-83, Theatre Three, 1974-75, Shakespeare Festival, 1978-81, Suicide and Crisis Ctr., 1983-88, Kaufman County Civic Theatre, 2005—, Terrell Christian Acad., 2006-08; bd. dirs. Dallas Ctr. for Developmentally Disabled, pres., 2006-08; chmn. Terrell Hist. Preservation Commn., 2000-03. Mem. Tex. Bar Assn., Civitan (lt. gov. Tex. dist. 1976-77, gov. 1979-80), Terrell Heritage Soc. (v.p.

1999—2008), Delta Phi, Delta Theta Phi. Episcopalian. Home: 505 Pacific Ave Terrell TX 75160-2073 Office: Kaufman County Courthouse 100 W Mulberry Kaufman TX 75142

TYLER, BRETT MERRICK, geneticist, researcher; b. Vancouver, BC, Canada, Aug. 29, 1955; s. Neil Merrick and Melva May Tyler; m. Catherine Jeanette Tyler; children: Eric David Lajeunesse, Christopher Merrick. PhD, U. Melbourne, Australia, 1981. Rsch. fellow Australian Nat. U., Canberra, Act, 1984—88; prof. U. of Calif., Davis, 1988—2002, Va. Poly. Inst. State U., Blacksburg, 2002—. Author 76 sci. jours. articles, (ednl. software for children) Germ Wars, Guerra de Germenes. Recipient Biol. Scis. Directorate Disting. Lectr., US NSF, 2006; fellow Lectureship, Fulbright Found., 2004; fellow, Willie Commelin Scholten Found. (The Netherlands), 1999-2000, 8 Sci. Rsch. Grants, US NSF, 2001-2011, 15 Sci. Rsch. Grants, US Dept. Agr., 1989-2010, 3 Sci. Rsch. Grants, US NIH, 1988-1995. Master: Internat. Phytophthora Genome Initiative (chair 1997—2001), Internat. Fungal Genetics Policy Com. (chair 1993—97), Internat. Oomycete Molecular Genetics Rsch. Collaboration Network (coord. 2001—); mem.: Internat. Soc. for Molecular Plant-Microbe Interactions, Am. Phytopathological Soc., Internat. Fungal Genetics Policy Com. (mem. 1991—97). Achievements include discovery of genome sequences of phytophthora pathogens. Avocations: travel, skiing, ballroom dancing, kayaking.

TYLER, DAVID EARL, veterinary medical educator; b. Carlisle, Iowa, July 12, 1928; s. Guy Earl and Beatrice Virginia (Slack) T.; m. Alice LaVon Smith, Sept. 6, 1952; children: John William, Anne Elizabeth. BS, Iowa State U., 1953, D.V.M., 1957, PhD, 1963; MS, Purdue U., 1960. Instr. dept. vet. sci. Purdue U., 1957-60; asst. prof. dept. pathology Coll. Vet. Medicine, Iowa State U., 1960-63, asso. prof., 1963-66; prof., head dept. pathology and parasitology Coll. Vet. Medicine, U. Ga., 1966-71, head dept. pathology, 1971-79, prof., 1971-91, prof. emeritus, 1991—; ret., 1991. Co-founder internat. vet. pathology slide bank, 1984, co-dir., 1984-98; apptd. discussant Charles L. Davis Found. for Advancement Vet. Pathology, 1977-91. Cub Scout master, 1967-69, scout com. chmn., 1970-72; elder Disciples of Christ Ch., 1968—, chmn. ch. bd., 1973-74, 92-94; mem. citizens com. to County Bd. Edn., 1968-70; bd. dirs. Christian Coll., Ga., 1974-77. With AUS, 1946-48. Recipient Borden award Gail Borden Co., 1956, Norden Disting. Teaching award Norden Labs., 1964, 69, 81, 85, 91, Prof. of Yr. award Coll. Vet. Medicine, Iowa State U., 1965, Outstanding Prof. award Coll. Vet. Medicine, U. Ga., 1970, 76, 80-81, 83, 86, 87-88, 90, Joshia Meigs Teaching award, 1985, Stange award Coll. Vet. Med., Iowa State U., 1987, Phi Zeta Teaching award, 1985, N.Am. Outstanding Tchr. award, 1991, Omicron Delta Kappa Outstanding Prof. award U. Ga., 1981, Harold W. Casey award C.L. Davis Found., 1995. Mem. AVMA, Farm House, Am. Coll. Vet. Pathologists (mem. council 1975-77, exam. com. 1982-85), Am. Assn. Vet. Med. Colls. (chmn. com. teaching-learning materials 1975-77), Nat. Program for Instructional Devel. in Vet. Pathology (adv. com. 1976-77), Aghon, Sigma Xi, Phi Eta Sigma, Alpha Zeta, Gamma Sigma Delta, Phi Kappa Phi, Phi Zeta (chpt. sec.-treas. 1982-84), Omega Tau Sigma. Home: 406 Garnet Ct Fort Mill SC 29708-7892 Personal E-mail: dtyler4689@compotium.net.

TYLER, LINDA, state legislator; m. Hugh Tyler; children: Doug, Melissa. Personnel mgmt. Carrier Air Conditioning, United Broadcasting Corps., United Technologies; sr. organizational devel. leader Acxiom Corp., 1988—; mem. Dist. 45 Ark. House of Reps., 2009—. Former bd. mem. Conway Regional Health Sys.; bd. mem. Conway Regional Health Found., Faulkner County Libr., U. Central Ark. Found.; adv. com. chmn. U. Ark. Med. Sci. Kidney Inst. Capital Campaign. Mem.: Faulkner County United Way, Nat. Kidney Found. Ark. (pres.), Nat. Kidney Found., Am. Heart Assn. Democrat. Methodist. Office: State Capitol Rm 350 Little Rock AR 72201 also: 40 Richland Hills Dr Conway AR 72034 Office Phone: 501-682-6211, 501-682-7771, 501-329-8644. Business E-Mail: tylerl@arkleg.state.ar.us.

TYLER, RONNIE CURTIS, art historian, former museum director; b. Temple, Tex., Dec. 29, 1941; s. Jasper J. and Melba Curtis (James) T.; m. Paula Eyrich, Aug. 24, 1974. BSE, Abilene Christian Coll., TEx., 1964; MA, Tex. Christian U., 1966, PhD (Univ. fellow), 1968; DHL, Austin Coll., 1986. Instr. history Austin Coll., Sherman, Tex., 1967-68, asst. prof., 1968-69; curator history Amon Carter Mus., Ft. Worth, 1969, dir. publications, asst. dir. history and publications, asst. dir. collections and programs, 1984—86, dir., 2006—11; prof. history U. Tex., Austin, 1986—2006. Adj. prof. history Tex. Christian U., 1971-72; dir. Tex. State Hist. Assn., 1986-2005; cons. visual materials Western. Am. art. Author: Santiago Vidaurri and the Confederacy, 1973, The Big Bend: The Last Texas Frontier, 1975, The Image of America in Caricature and Cartoon, 1975, The Cowboy, 1975, The Mexican War: A Lithographic Record, 1974, The Rodeo Photographs of John Addison Stryker, 1978, Visions of America: Pioneer Artists in a New Land, 1983, Views of Texas: The Watercolors of Sarah Ann Hardinge, 1852-56, 1988, Nature's Classics: John James Audubon's Birds and Animals, 1992, Audubon's Great National Work: The Royal Octavo Edition of the Birds of America, 1993, Prints of the West, 1994, Alfred Jacob Miller: Artist as Explorer, 1999; (with Paula Eyrich Tyler) Texas Museums: A Guidebook, 1983; editor: (with Lawrence R. Murphy) The Slave Narratives of Texas, 1974, Posada's Mexico, 1979, Alfred Jacob Miller: Artist on the Oregon Trail, 1982, Wanderings in the Southwest in 1855 (J.D.B. Stillman), 1990, Prints and Printmakers of Texas, 1997. Pres. Tarrant County (Tex.) Hist. Soc., 1975-77. Good Neighbor Commn. scholar Instituto Tecnologico Monterrey, Mex., 1967; Am. Philos. Soc. grantee, 1970-71; recipient H. Bailey Carroll award, 1974; Coral H. Tullis award, 1976, Alonso de León medal Sociedad Nuevoleonsa História Geografía y Estadistica, 2002. Mem. Am. Antiquarian Soc., Tex. Inst. Letters (Friends of Dallas Pub. Libr. award), Philos. Soc. Tex. (sec. 1990), Phi Beta Kappa. Home Phone: 817-377-1297; Office Phone: 817-989-5095. Business E-Mail: ron.tyler@cartermuseum.org.

TYLER, ROSLYN C., state legislator; b. Greensville Co, Va., June 18, 1961; m. Rufus Edmond Tyler Jr.; children: Rufus Jr., Ronecia, Rosche, Rameka. Supr. Sussex County Bd., 1985—96; state del. Dist. 75 Va., 2006—; mem. Edn. Com., 2006—, Gen. Laws Com., 2006—, Militia Police and Pub. Safety Co., 2006—. Mem. Chapel Hill Bapt. Ch. Mem.: Head Start Health Adv. Bd., Sussex County Bd. Social Svcs., Am. Physical Therapy Assn. Democrat. Baptist. Office: 25359 Blue Star Hwy Jarratt VA 23867 Home Phone: 434-246-4246; Office Phone: 434-336-1710. E-mail: DelRTyler@house.state.va.us.

TYMINSKI, DAN, musician; b. Rutland, Vt., 1967; Former mem. Green Mountain Bluegrass; mem. Lonesome River Band, 1988, Alison Krauss and Union Sta., 1992—93, 1994—; musician, recording engr., prodr. Doobie Shea Records, Boones Mill, Va. Singer, musician (songs) When You Say Nothing at All, Man of Constant Sorrow, 2001 (Country Music Awards Single of Yr., 2001), Carry Me Across the Mountain, 2001 (Assn. for Ind. Music award, 2001), (albums) Looking for Yourself, Carrying the Tradition, 1991 (Internat. Bluegrass Music Assn. Album of Yr., 1991), Old Country Town, 1994, O Brother Where Art Thou?, 2001 (Country Music Awards Album of Yr., 2001); prodr.: (albums) Bowman' Cold Virginia Night, The Man I'm Tryin' To Be, Stanley Gospel Tradition (Internat. Bluegrass Music Awards Gospel Recorded Performance of Yr., 1998), many others; contbg. vocalist Dolly Parton, Clint Black, Randy Travis, others. Recipient awards (4), Internat. Bluegrass Music Assn., 2001, Mainstream Song of Yr., Christian Country Music Awards, 2001; co-recipient Grammy awards (4), Country Music Assn. award, Nashville Music Awards (2), Entertainer of Yr., Internat. Bluegrass Music Assn. Office: Doobie Shea Music 2008 Sadie Ln Goodlettsville TN 37072-4249 Business E-Mail: publicity@doobieshea.com.

TYNES, ROBERT DICK, artist, educator; b. Chgo., Jan. 7, 1953; s. Marion F. and Faye Tynes Dick; m. Bette L. Bates, June 13, 1981; children: Alison Hayley, Robin Elizabeth. BA with hons. in Art, Rhodes Coll., Memphis, Tenn., 1975; MFA in Painting, East Carolina U., Greenville, NC, 1981. Lectr. art East Carolina U., 1981—82, Humboldt State U., Arcata, Calif., 1982—84; vis. asst. prof. art U. Hawaii Manoa, Honolulu, 1986—87; artist-in-residence U. NC, Asheville, 1987—91, from asst. prof. to prof. art, 1991—2004, prof. art, 2004—. Dir. S. Tucker Cooke Gallery U. NC, 1993—2013. Over 25 solo exhbns., over 150 group shows, one-man shows include Fay Gold Gallery, Atlanta, Ga., 2001, Lee Hansley Gallery, Raleigh, NC, 2004, Gallery at Carillon, Charlotte, NC, 2005, Blue Spiral, Asheville, NC, 2006, Represented in permanent collections Charlotte Pub. Arts Commn., IBM Corp., Field Engring. Ctr., Atlanta, Ga. Chair Black Mountain Coll. Mus. and Art Ctr., Asheville, NC, 1993—95; dir. Asheville Area Arts Coun., 1994—2002, sec., 2000—02; dir. Black Mountain Ctr. Arts, NC, 2003—04, sec., 2004. Recipient We. NC Regional Juried Exhbn. 1st prize, Asheville Art Mus., 1993; fellow, Roswell Mus. and Art Ctr., Roswell, N.Mex., 1985, 1991, Ucross Found. Residency Program, Wyo., 1986. Democrat. Unitarian Universalist. Achievements include development of original style of painting juxtaposing abstract brush marks with hyperrealistic trompe l'oeil illusionism; original style of cutout paintings. Avocation: hiking. Office: Dept of Art Univ of NC Asheville One University Heights Asheville NC 28804 Business E-Mail: rtynes@unca.edu.

TYRRELL, GERALD GETTYS, banker; b. Canton, China, Dec. 27, 1938; came to U.S., 1940. s. Gerald Fraser and Virginia Lee (Gettys) T.; m. Jane Haldeman, June 1961 (div. Aug. 1975); children: Gerald F., Jane N., Robert M.; m. Elizabeth Ann Drautman, Mar. 31, 1978. BA, Yale U., 1960; MA, Rutgers U., 1971. Cert. real estate financier. With 1st Nat. Bank of Louisville, 1961—89, sr. v.p., 1975—81, exec. v.p., 1981—89; pres., chmn. Churchill Mortgage Corp., 1975—77; chief fin. cons. City of Louisville Office of Downtown Devel., 1989—2000; exec. v.p. Univ. Group, Consultants for Bus., Prospect, 2000—06, assoc., 2006—08. Vice chmn. bd. dirs. Porcelain Metals Corp., 2001—06; assoc. Venture Resource Bus. Brokers, 2006—; adv. bd. Skyway LLC, 2007—08, chief fin. officer, 2008—09, mem., bd. dirs., sec., 2009—11; chief fin. officer Near Directions Housing Corp., 2012—. Author: A Positive Approach to Financing Black Business, 1972 Trustee, treas. Patton Mus., Ft. Knox, Ky., 1970—96; mem. exec. bd. Boy Scouts Am., 1983—; bd. dirs. The Louisville Orch., 1984—90, Crane Ho., The Asia Inst., 1988—, pres., 1995—97; bd. dirs., chmn. fin. com. Glassworks Found., Inc., 2001—03; bd. dirs. Thomas Merton Found., 2003—05. Served to capt. US Army, 1960—68. Recipient Disting. Service Ribbon Ky. Nat. Guard, 1966 Mem. Robert Morris Assocs., Nat. Soc. Real Estate Fin. (bd. govs), Soc. Colonial Wars Commonwealth Ky. (treas. 1970-89, sec. 1996-99, gov. 2000-05), Gen. Soc. Colonial Wars (treas. gen. 2004-07, lt. gov. gen. 2007—10, vice gov. gen. 2010-13, gov. gen., 2013-), Louisville Country Club. Democrat. Avocations: fine wines, tennis. Personal E-mail: geraldgtyrrell@gmail.com.

TYSON, CYNTHIA HALDENBY, academic administrator; b. Scunthorpe, Lincolnshire, Eng., July 2, 1937; came to U.S., 1959; d. Frederick and Florence Edna (Stacey) Haldenby; children: Marcus James, Alexandra Elizabeth. BA, U. Leeds, Eng., 1958, MA, 1959, PhD, 1971; DHL (hon.), Mary Baldwin Coll., 2003, Queens U., Charlotte, 2006. Lectr. Brit. Council, Leeds, 1959; faculty U. Tenn., Knoxville, 1959-60, Seton Hall U., South Orange, NJ, 1963-69; faculty, v.p. Queens Coll., Charlotte, NC, 1969-85; pres. Mary Baldwin Coll., Staunton, Va., 1985—2003, pres. emerita, 2003—; pres. Robert Haywood Morrison Found., 2002—. Pres. adv. cir. Queens U., Charlotte, NC, 2005—09, trustee, 2009—; WDAV radio adv. bd. Davidson (NC) Coll., 2005—. Contbr. articles to profl. jours. Mem. Va. Internat. Trade Commn., Richmond, 1987; trustee Am. Frontier Culture Mus., Va.; mem. Va. Lottery Bd., 1987-94; chair selection com. State of Va. Rhodes Scholarship Competition, 1993-97; bd. dirs. Cmty. Found. Staunton, Augusta County and Waynesboro, 1993-98; mem. adv. bd. WDAV Radio of Davidson Coll., 2005—; mem. pres.'s adv. cir. Queens U. of Charlotte, NC, 2005—. Fulbright scholar, 1959; Ford Found. grantee Harvard U., 1981; Shell Oil scholar Harvard U., 1982. Mem.: Assn. Presbyn. Colls. and Univs. (bd. dirs. 1998), So. Assn. Colls. and Schs. (vice chair 1998, pres.-elect 2001, pres. 2002), Assn. Va. Colls. and Univs. (pres. 1997—98), So. Assn. Colls. for Women (pres. 1980—81), Mary Baldwin Coll. (hon.), Phi Beta Kappa. Republican. Office: Robert Haywood Morrison Found 1409 East Blvd # 3C Charlotte NC 28203-5817

TYSON, JOHN H., food products executive; b. Springdale, Ark., Sept. 5, 1953; s. Don and Jean Tyson; m. Kimberly McCoy; children: John Randal, Olivia Laine. BBA, So. Meth. U., 1975. Complex mgr. N.C. area Tyson Foods, Inc., Springdale, Ark., v.p. mktg. corp. accounts, purchasing mgr., retail sales mgr. N.E. states, pres. beef and pork divsn., pres., chmn., 1998-00, pres., chmn., CEO, 2000—01, chmn., CEO, 2001—06, chmn., 2006—. Polit. liaison to Washington and Little Rock Tyson Foods, Inc. Bd. dirs. Area United Way; supporter Farm Aid; vol. activities for well-being and edn. of Ark. children. Named Man of Yr., Ark. Poultry Industry, 1994. Mem.: Ark. Poultry Fedn. (past pres.), Am. Meat Inst., Nat. Assn. Mfrs. Avocations: deep sea fishing, music, golf. Office: Tyson Foods Inc 2200 W Don Tyson Pkwy Springdale AR 72762-6901*

TYURIN, MIKHAIL, cosmonaut; b. Kolomna, Russia, Mar. 2, 1960; m. Tatiana Anatoleyvna; 1 child, Alexandra. Grad. with a degree in engring. and specialization in creating math. models related to mechanical flight, Moscow Aviation Inst., 1984. Engr. Energia Corp.; began cosmonaut tng., 1993; started tng. as flight engr. for Expedition-3 crew, 1998. Served as back-up crew mem. for the first Internat. Space Station (ISS) mission STS-105 Discovery, 2001; Soyuz-13 (TMA-9) comdr., flight engr. on the Expedition-14 mission to the Internat. Space Station, 2006; performed spacewalk to repair antenna on Russian cargo ship, 2007. first person to strike a lightweight golf ball from outside international space station in a promotional stunt for golf club manufacturer E21 Golf on November 22, 2006.

UBERALL, HERBERT MICHAEL STEFAN, physicist, professor emeritus; b. Neunkirchen, Austria, Oct. 14, 1931; arrived in U.S., 1953, naturalized, 1963; s. Michael and Stefanie U.; m. Reyna Tosta, 1981; children by previous marriage: Bernadette Chauvallon, Bertrand. PhD, U. Vienna, Austria, 1953, Cornell U., 1956; PhD (honoris causa), U. Le Havre, France, 1987. Staff mem. Signal Corps Labs., Ft. Monmouth, NJ, 1953-54; research asst. Cornell U., 1954-56; research fellow Nuclear Physics Research Lab., U. Liverpool, Eng., 1956-57; Ford Found. fellow CERN, Geneva, 1957-58; research physicist Carnegie Inst. Tech., Pitts., 1958-60; asst. prof. U. Mich., Ann Arbor, 1960-64; assoc. prof. Cath. U. Am., Washington, 1964-65, prof. physics, 1965-94, prof. emeritus, 1994—2008. Vis. prof. U. Paris VII Jussieu, 1984-85, U. Le Havre, 1990, 92, 94, 96, U. Bordeaux, 1993, 95, U. Aix-Marseille II and Lab. Mech. Acoustics, 1995, Ecole Centrale de Lille, 1997, Tech. U. Denmark, 1998; cons. Naval Rsch. Lab., Washington, 1966-92. Author: Electron Scattering from Complex Nuclei, 1971; co-author: Giant Resonance Phenomena, 1980, Nuclear Pion Photoproduction, 1991; editor: Acoustic Resonance Scattering, 1992; co-editor: Long Distance Neutrino Detection, 1979, Classical and Quantum Dynamics, 1991, Coherent Radiation Sources, 1985, Coherent Radiation Processes in Strong Fields, 1991, Radar Target Imaging, 1994; contbr. 300 articles to profl. jours. Recipient Fgn. medal French Soc. Acoustics, 1996. Fellow (life) IEEE, (life) Am. Phys. Soc., Acoustical Soc. Am., Washington Acad. Scis. (Achievement award 1984); mem. AAUP, Am. Acad. Mech., Electromagnetics Acad., Internat. Union Radio Sci. Personal E-mail: uberallh@msn.com.

UCHIN, ROBERT ALLEN, dean, endodontist; b. Phila., Apr. 19, 1933; s. Harry and Doris (Goodman) U.; m. Marlene Florence Neiman; children: Andrew, Richard, Carol. Student, Franklin and Marshall Coll., 1951-53; DDS, Temple U., 1957. Diplomate Am. Bd. Endodontics. Fellow research teaching. dept. endodontics Temple U., Phila., 1959-60, instr. Sch. of Dentistry, 1960-69; co-chmn. endodontic sect. Dade County (Fla.) Dental Research Clinic, 1961-75; founding v.p., chmn. Endodontic sect. Broward County (Fla.) Dental Research Clinic, 1974-79; clin. assoc. Sch. of Dentistry U. Fla., Gainsville, 1970; practice dentistry specializing in endodontics Ft. Lauderdale, Fla., 1960—2000; assoc. dean, dir. extramural programs Coll. Dental Medicine, Nova Southeastern U., Ft. Lauderdale, Fla., 1996—2000, dean, 2000—. Chmn. Endodontic sect. Atlantic Coast Research Clinic, 1971-75; vis. lectr. Emory U., 1965, U.N.C., 1970, 72, U. Wash., 1972, U. Pitts., 1974, U. Pa., 1973-89; cons. VA Hosp., Miami, 1968-86, Cen. Office, 1972-84, dir. endodontic residency, 1972-79; bd. dirs., founding chmn. Gold Coast Savs. and Loan Assn. of Fla., 1984-90, Commonwealth Savs. and Loan of Fla., Ft. Lauderdale, 1979-84; adv. dir. Landmark First Nat. Bank, Ft. Lauderdale, 1974-81; vice chmn. Fla. Dental Assn. Services, Inc. Assoc. editor Jour. Endodontics and Traumatology, 1981-89; contbr. numerous articles to profl. jours. Pres., Temple Emanu-El Reform Congregation, Ft. Lauderdale, 1967-69; trustee, Vanguard Sch., Haverford, Pa., 1971-77; bd. dirs., Vanguard Sch., Ft. Lauderdale, 1970-73, Performing Arts Found., Broward County, Fla., 1986-90. Served to capt. USAF, 1957-59. Fellow: Am. Assn. Endodontists (pres. 1976), Internat. Coll. of Dentists, Am. Coll. of Dentists; mem.: Broward County Dental Assn. (pres. 1982), Fla. Dental Assn. (past pres.), Am. Dental Assn. Holding Co. (past pres.), Fla. Assoc. of Endodontics, So. Endodontic Study Group, Am. Dental Assn., Rotary (pres. Ft. Lauderdale 1969—70). Republican. Jewish. Avocations: fly fishing, stamp collecting/philately, orchids. Office: Coll Dental Medicine Nova Southeastern U 3200 S Univ Dr Fort Lauderdale FL 33328 Office Phone: 954-262-7312. Office Fax: 954-262-1782. Business E-Mail: ruchin@nova.edu.

UDAGAWA, TAKESHI, physicist, researcher; b. Tokyo, May 3, 1932; arrived in U.S., 1970; s. Saheiji Udagawa and Teruko (Yamazaki) Urayama; m. Yukiko Amano, Mar. 20, 1960 (dec. Oct. 1989); children: Yoichi, Taturo; m. Mami Eto, Apr. 15, 1991. BS, Tokyo Inst. Sci., 1957; MS, Tokyo U. of Edn., 1959, PhD, 1962. Instr. Tokyo Inst. Tech., 1962-64; rsch. assoc. Fla. State U., Tallahassee, 1964-66; rsch. fellow Niels Bohn Inst., Copenhagen, 1966-68; assoc. prof. Kyoto (Japan) U., 1968-70; prof. dept. physics U. Tex., Austin, 1970—. Rsch. fellow Kernforschungsanlage, Juelich, Germany, 1981—95. Contbr. articles to profl. jours. Decorated Order of Sacred Treasure, Gold Rays with Neck Ribbon Govt. of Japan; recipient Fgn. Mins. commendation in Commemoration of 150th Anniversary Japan/U.S. Relationship, 2004; Rsch. grantee, Dept. Energy, Washington, 1970—96. Mem.: Japanese Phys. Soc., Am. Phys. Soc. Achievements include contributions to various aspects of nuclear reaction theories. Home: 4018 Amy Cir Austin TX 78759-8146 Office: U Tex Dept Physics Austin TX 78712 Home Phone: 512-795-8191; Office Phone: 512-471-1984. Business E-Mail: udagawa@physics.utexas.edu.

UDELL TURSHEN, ROCHELLE MARCIA, marketing executive; b. NYC, Nov. 29, 1944; d. Julius David and Beatrice Kafka; m. James Edward Udell, Oct. 12, 1969 (div. 1976); m. Doug Edward Turshen, Mar. 9, 1980; children: Ben, Julia. BA, Bklyn. Coll., 1966; MA, Pratt Inst., 1967. Tchr. Sheepshead Bay High Sch., Bklyn., 1967-70; asst. art dir. N.Y. Mag., NYC, 1970-71; art dir. MS. Mag., 1970-71, Vogue, 1971-77; creative dir. Calvin Klein Advt., 1975-84; art dir. House & Garden, Self, GQ, 1982-84; agy. pres. Della Femina Travisano & Ptnrs., 1984-88; assoc. editorial dir. Conde Nast Publications, Inc., 1988-95, editor-in-chief, 1995-99; sr. v.p. brand devel. The Limited., 1999—2002; exec. v.p. creative devel. & design, chief creative officer Revlon, Inc., 2002—06; chief talent officer Arnell Group, 2006—09; sr. v.p., creative dir. Chico's FAS, Inc., 2009—. Lectr. Fashion Group, Women in Communications, Advt. Women in NY and Radcliffe Pub Course. Author: How to Eat an Artichoke. Bd. dirs. Bklyn. Coll., Am. Mus. of the Moving Image. Recipient Matrix Award, Women in Comms., Herb Lubalin Award of Excellence; named to Art Dir.'s Club Hall of Fame. Mem. Am. Soc. Mag. Editors, Women in Need, Japan Soc., Fashion Group. Democrat. Jewish. Avocations: reading, running, tennis. Office: Chico's FAS Inc 11215 Metro Parkway Fort Myers FL 33912

UDOFF, ERIC JOEL, diagnostic radiologist; AB, Washington U., 1969; MD, U. Rochester, 1973. Intern, resident in diagnostic radiology U. Chgo., 1973-77; instr. in cardiovasc. radiology Johns Hopkins U., Balt., 1977-79; radiologist Sinai Hosp., Balt., 1979-86, Mt. Sinai Med. Ctr., Milw., 1986-88, Sinai Hosp., Balt., 1988-90; asst. prof. radiology Johns Hopkins U. Hosp., 1990-91; radiologist North Fulton Regional Hosp., Roswell, Ga., 1991-97; instr. thoracoabdominal imaging U. Va., 1997-98, Radiologist, Diagnostic Imaging Specialists, Atlanta, 1998—. Mem. AMA, Am. Roentgen Ray Soc., Am. Coll. Radiology, Radiol. Soc. N.Am., Ga. Radiol. Soc., Phi Beta Kappa. Avocations: reading, tennis. Office: 6000 Lake Forrest Dr Ste 475 Atlanta GA 30328 Office Phone: 404-459-8440. Personal E-mail: ejurad@yahoo.com.

UDOGU, E. IKE, social sciences educator, researcher; s. Onya Olisa and Cicelia Udogu; m. Ahante A. Diamond; 1 child, Eric. PhD, So. Ill. U., Carbondale, 1980. Prof. Francis Marion U., Florence, SC, 1985—2003; prof. and faculty fellow Appalachian State U., Boone, NC, 2003—. Mem. editl. bd. Collegiate Press, San Diego, 1990-92, cons., 1992—; reviewer Jour. of Third World Studies, Columbus, Ga., 1990—, Can. Rev. of Studies in Nationalism, Charlottetown, Can., 1994—. Guest editor Jour. Asian & African Studies, 1996; dir., Rsch. & Publ. African Studies and Rsch. Forum, 1996-2007; Author: Liberating Namibia, 2012; contbr. chapters to books, articles to profl. jours. Polit. analyst, guest speaker Black History Month, CBS-TV-13, Florence, 1988, PBS-Ch. 27, Sumter, S.C., 1991, ABC-TV-15, Florence, S.C., 1992, Kingstree (S.C.) High Sch., 1991; pres. Coalition of Black Networking, Florence, 1990-91. Nat. Endowment Humanities fellow U. Wis., 1983; recipient cert. Outstanding Young Men of Am.,

1982, 84, cert. appreciation Senate of the State of S.C., Columbia, 1990, cert. merit Collegiate Press, San Diego, 1991, Minority Recruiter Positive Image award, 1992; named to Athletic Hall of Fame, Appalachian State U., Boone, N.C., 1986., Outstanding Scholars of 21st Century, Internat. Biographical Ctr., Cambridge, Eng., 2000, Tops African Ctr. Scholars Decade award, 2012. Mem. Internat. Studies Assn., Internat. Soc. Study European Ideas, African Studies Assn. (pres.), Assn. 3rd World Studies, S.C. Polit. Sci. Assn. (bd. mem. 1983-85), S.C. Consortium for Internat. Studies. Avocations: writing fiction, soccer, tennis, jogging. Office: Appalachian State Univ Anne Belk Hall Boone NC 28608-2107 Office Fax: 828-262-2947. Business E-Mail: udoguei@appstate.edu.*

UDOLF, BRUCE LEE, lawyer; s. Roy Joseph and Marcelle Udolf; m. Sheryl Singer Udolf, Oct. 24, 1992; 1 child, Hayley. BA, Hofstra U., 1973; JD, Emory U. Sch. Law, 1979. Bar: Ga. 1979, US Dist. Ct. (no. dist.) Ga. 1979, US Ct. Appeals (11th cir.) 1982, Fla. 1991, US Dist. Ct. (so. dist.) Fla. 1998, US Dist. Ct. (mid. dist.) Fla. 1999, US Supreme Ct. 1983. Atty. Mishan, Sloto, Greenberg, Hellinger & Udolf, P.A., Miami, Fla., 1998—2000, Eckert, Seamans, Cherin and Mellott, LLC, Ft. Lauderdale, 2000—01, Ruden McClosky, P.A., 2001—06, Berger Singerman, Ft. Lauderdale, 2006—10, Bruce L. Udolf, P.A., 2010—; law clerk to Hon. Arthur W. Fudger Tallapoosa Jud. Cir. Ga., 1979—80; asst. dist. atty. Northeastern Jud. Cir. Ga., 1980—83, dist. atty., 1983—87; asst. US atty. US Atty.'s Office, So. Dist. Fla., 1987—98, appellate divsn., 1987; major crimes sect. US Dept. Justice, 1987—88, narcotics sect., 1988, pub. corruption sect., 1988—97, chief pub. corruption sect., 1992—97, assoc. ind. counsel Office Ind. Counsel Washington, 1997—98. Lectr. Law Edn. Inst., 2002, US Dept. Treasury, Office Tech. Assistance, US Dept. Justice, Office Profl. Devel. and Tng. Corruption and Organized Crime Symposium, St. Petersburg, Russia, Fla. Internat. U., Ctr. Adminstrn. Justice Pub. Corruption Seminars in La Paz, Bolivia; Caracas, Venezuela; Tegucigalpa, Honduras, Atty. Gen.'s Advocacy Inst., Washington, Nat. Inst. Trial Advocacy, Trial Techs. Program, Emory U. Sch. Law, Atlanta, Fla. Bar CLE, Professionalism and Ethics Symposium, U. Miami Sch. Law, "Mortgage Fraud Now on the Rise" Nat. Law Jour., 2007; mem. Fla. Bar Atty. Client Privilege Task Force; mem. adv. com. on rules on procedures US Dist. Ct., So. Dist. Fla. Recipient commendation, Bur. Alcohol, Tobacco and Firearms, 1989, Dirs., FBI, 1991, 1994, Drug Enforcement Adminstrn., Office Profl. Responsibility, 1994, US Customs Svc., Office Internal Affairs, 1997, Outstanding Achievement award, US Dept. Justice, 1990, 1991, 1994. Mem.: Fla. Legal Elite, AV Preeminent, Martindale Hubbell (Best Lawyers in America, Super Lawyers), Fla. Bar (criminal law sect. edn., ethics subcom.), Fla. Bar Criminal Procedure Rules com. (chair subcom. I, fast track subcom., chair joint appellate, civil, criminal rules subcom.), Palm Beach County Bar Assn., Broward County Bar Assn., Dade County Bar Assn. (chair meetings com., vice chair fed. practice com.), ABA (mem. criminal justice sect., white collar crime com.), Fla. Assn. Criminal Def. Lawyers, Nat. Assn. Criminal Def. Attys., Eugene Spellman Am. Inns of Ct., Fed. Bar Assn. (past pres., v.p., dir. Broward County chpt., asst.), US Atty.'s Assn. (past pres.). Office: Broward Financial Ctr 500 E Broward Blvd Ste 1400 Fort Lauderdale FL 33394 Business E-Mail: budolf@udolflaw.com.

UEHARA, KOJI, professional baseball player; b. Neyagawa, Japan, Apr. 3, 1975; Grad., Osaka Taiiku U. Pitcher Yomiuri Giants, 1998—2008, Balt. Orioles, 2009—11, Tex. Rangers, 2011—. Mem. Japanese nat. team Summer Olympic Games, Athens, Greece, 2004, World Baseball Classic, San Diego, 2006. Recipient Eiji Sawamura award, Nippon Profl. Baseball, 1998, 2002, Bronze medal, baseball, Summer Olympic Games, 2004, Gold medal, World Baseball Classic, 2006, Ctrl. League Gold Glove, Nippon Profl. Baseball, 1998, 2003; named Ctrl. League Rookie of Yr., 1998, Japan Series MVP, 2002; named to Ctrl. League All-Star Team, 1999—2005, 2007. Achievements include member of Nippon Professional Baseball's Japan Series championship winning Yomiuri Giants, 1999, 2002. Office: Tex Rangers 1000 Ballpark Way Arlington TX 76011 Office Phone: 03-3295-7711.

UFFELMAN, MALCOLM RUCJ, electronics executive; b. Clarksville, Tenn., Oct. 22, 1935; s. Malcolm C. and Margaret Lillian (Davidson) U.; m. Sarah White Barksdale, June 11, 1957; children: Malcolm Rucj Jr., Katharina White, Davidson Barksdale, Jefferson Churchill. BS, Vanderbilt U., 1957; MS, George Washington U., 1963. Engr. Melpar, Inc., Falls Church, Va., 1957-60; v.p. Scope, Inc., Reston, Va., 1960-73; sr. cons. MRI, Inc., McLean, Va., 1973-78; v.p. Racal Communications Inc., Rockville, Md., 1978-80; sr. cons. MRJ, Inc., Fairfax, Va., 1980-82; v.p., gen. mgr., Ctr. Advanced Planning and Analysis E-Systems Inc., Fairfax, 1982-96; US del. NATO Indsl. Adv. Group, 1993—97; v.p. Constellation Comm., Inc., Fairfax, 1996-99; patent agt., 1999—2000; exec. v.p. Contact Corp., 2000—08, bd. dir., 2009—; trustee Camco Fund, 2002—10. Contbr. numerous articles to profl. jours.; holder 7 patents in field. Scoutmaster Troop 183 Boy Scouts Am., Oakton, Va., 1973-79; Capt. USAR, 1957-69. Fellow IEEE; mem. Cosmos Club (Washington), Internat. Brotherhood Magicians. Episcopalian. Avocations: sailing, reading, travel, magic, fly fishing. Personal E-mail: rucj@ieee.org.

UFFINDELL, COLIN M., consumer products company executive; V.p., trade mktg. R.J. Reynolds Tobacco Co., 2006—07; v.p., trade & consumer mktg. Santa Fe Natural Tobacco Co. (subs. Reynolds Am. Inc.). Office: Reynolds American Inc 401 N Main St Winston Salem NC 27101-2990 Office Phone: 336-741-2000. Office Fax: 336-741-4238.

UHLMANN, FREDERICK GODFREY, securities trader; b. Chgo., Dec. 31, 1929; s. Richard F. and Rosamond G. (Goldman) U.; m. Virginia Lee Strauss, July 24, 1951; children: Richard, Thomas, Virginia, Karen, Elizabeth. BA, Washington and Lee U., 1951. Ptnr. Uhlmann Grain Co., Chgo., 1951-61; v.p. Uhlmann & Co., Inc., Chgo., 1961-65; sr. v.p. H. Hentz & Co., Chgo., 1965-73, Drexel Burnham Lambert Inc., Chgo., 1973-84; exec. v.p., dir. bus. futures Dean Witter Reynolds Inc., Chgo., 1984-85; sr. v.p., mgr. commodity dept. Bear, Stearns & Co., Inc., Chgo., 1985-88; exec. v.p. Rodman & Renshaw, Inc., 1988-95; sr. v.p. LIT-Divsn. of First Options Inc., Chgo., 1995-98; chmn. Chgo Bd. Trade, Ill., 1973-74; dir., officer H. P. Ill. Hosp., 1985—95; sr. v.p., exec. dir. MAN Financial, 1998—. Ptnr. Uhlmann Price Securities LLC. Bd. dir. Dist. 113 H.S. Found., 1990—, Mt. Sanai Hosp. Inst., Chgo., 1999—2008. Mem. Nat. Futures Assoc. (dir. 1981-2000, vice chair 1998-2000), Futures Industry Assn. (bd. dir., chmn. 1975-76), Futures Industry Inst. (bd. dir.). Home: 783 Whiteoaks Ln Highland Park IL 60035-3656 Office: 119-1 Nautical Way Jupiter FL 33477 Home Phone: 847-432-5122; Office Phone: 847-828-8147.

UHRIG, ROBERT EUGENE, nuclear engineer, educator; b. Raymond, Ill., Aug. 6, 1928; s. John Mathew and Anna LaDonna (Fireman) U.; m. Paula Margaret Schnepf, Nov. 27, 1954; children: Robert John, Joseph Charles, Mary Catherine, Charles William, Jean Marie, Thomas Paul, Fredrick James. BS with honors, U. Ill., 1948; MS, Iowa State U., Ames, 1950, PhD, 1954; grad. Advanced Mgmt. Program, Harvard U., Cambridge, Mass., 1976. Registered profl. engr., Iowa, Fla. Instr. engring. mechanics Iowa State U., 1948-51; assoc. engr., rsch. asst. Inst. Atomic Rsch. (at univ.), 1951-54, assoc. prof. engring. mechanics and nuc. engring., also group leader, 1956-60; prof. nuc. engring., chmn. dept. U. Fla., Gainesville, 1960-68, on leave, 1967-68, dean Coll. Engring., 1968-73, dean emeritus, 1989—; dep. asst. dir. rsch. Dept. Def., Washington, 1967-68; dir. nuc. affairs Fla. Power & Light Co., Miami, 1973-74, v.p. for nuc. affairs, 1974-75, v.p. nuc. and gen. engring., 1976-78, v.p. advanced systems and tech., 1978-86; disting. prof. engring. U. Tenn., Knoxville, 1986—2002, disting. prof. engring. emeritus, 2003—; disting. scientist Oak Ridge Nat. Lab., 1986—2002, disting. scientist emeritus, 2003—. Instr. engring. mechanics US Mil. Acad., 1954-56; rep. Dept. Def. to com. on acad. sci. and engring. Fed. Coun. Sci. and Tech., 1967; chmn. engring. adv. com. NSF, 1972-73; bd. dirs. Engring. Coun. Profl. Devel., 1968-72; mem. commn. edn. for engring. profession Nat. Assn. State Univs. and Land Grant Colls., 1969-72; apptd. mem. adv. com. on reactor safeguards US Nuc. Regulatory Commn., 1997-2001. Author: Random Noise Techniques in Nuclear Reactor Systems, 1970, trans. into Russian, 1974; co-author: (with Lefteri H. Tsoukalas) Fuzzy and Neural Approaches in Engineering, 1997—. Served to 1st lt. USAF. Recipient Sec. of Def. Civilian Svc. award, 1968, Outstanding Alumni award U. Ill. Coll. Engring., 1970, Alumni Profl. Achievement award Iowa State U., 1972, President's medallion U. Fla., 1973; Disting. Achievement citation Iowa State U. Alumni Assn., 1980, Glenn Murphy award Am. Soc. for Engring. Edn., 1992; Named to Hall Disting. Alumni, Aerospace Dept., Iowa State U., 2005. Fellow ASME (life, Richards Meml. award 1969, ASME medal, 2005), AAAS, Am. Nuc. Soc. life, chmn. edn. com. 1962-64, chmn. tech. group for edn. 1964-66, bd. dirs. 1965-68, exec. com. bd. 1966-68); mem. Am. Soc. Engring. Edn. (pres. S.E. sect. 1972-73, chmn. nuc. engring. divsn. 1966-67, 88-89, rsch. award S.E. sect. 1962), John Henry Newman Honor Soc., Sigma Xi, Tau Beta Pi, Phi Mu Epsilon, Pi Tau Sigma, Phi Kappa Phi (Disting. Mem. award 1997). Home and Office: 5221 NW 44th Pl Gainesville FL 32606-4328 Personal E-mail: reuhrig@gmail.com. Business E-Mail: ruhrig@utk.edu.

UKROP, JAMES E., retail executive; b. 1937; Vice chmn., CEO Ukrop's Super Markets Inc., 1958—, chmn. Office: Ukrop's Super Markets Inc 600 Southlake Blvd Richmond VA 23236-3922

ULISSEY, MICHAEL J., diagnostic radiologist, educator; MD, Tex. A&M Health Sci. Ctr., 1991. Diplomate Am. Bd. Radiology-diagnostic radiology, 1998. Resident diagnostic radiology Univ. of Okla. Health Ctr., 1994—98; fellow radiology Univ. Tex. Southwestern Clin. Breast Radiology, Dallas, 1998—99; assoc. prof. radiology Univ. Tex. Southwestern, Dallas; fellow magnetic resonance imaging Univ. Tex. Southwestern Med. Ctr., Dallas, 2003—04, hosp. affiliation includes. Office: University of Texas Southwestern Medical Center Ste 300 5701 Maple Dr Dallas TX 75235 Office Phone: 214-266-3300.

ULLMAN, MYRON EDWARD, III, (MIKE ULLMAN), retail executive; b. Youngstown, Ohio, Nov. 26, 1946; s. Myron Edward Jr. and June (Cunningham) U.; m. Cathy Emmons, June 20, 1969; children: Myron Cayce, Denver Tryan, Peter Brynt, Benjamin Kyrk, Kathryn Kwynn, Madylin Ming Yan. BS in Indsl. Mgmt., U. Cin., 1969; postgrad. Inst. Ednl. Mgmt., Harvard U., 1977; D (hon.), U. Cin., 2006. Internat. account mgr. IBM Corp., Cin., 1969-76; v.p. bus. affairs U. Cin., 1976-81; exec. asst. to US Trade Rep. Office US Trade Rep., Exec. Office of the Pres., Washington, 1981-82; exec. v.p. Sanger Harris divsn. Federated Stores, Dallas, 1982-86; group mng. dir., chief oper. officer Wharf Holdings Ltd., Hong Kong, 1986-88; chmn., CEO R.H. Macy & Co. Inc., NYC, 1988-95; dir., deputy chmn. Federated Dept. Stores, Inc.; chmn., CEO DFS Group Ltd., San Francisco, 1995-98, group chmn., 1999-2000; dir. gen., group mng. dir. LVMH Louis Vuitton Moet Hennessy, Paris, 1999—2002; chmn. DeBeers-LV, 2000—02; chmn., CEO J.C. Penney Co., Inc., Plano, Tex., 2004—11, exec. chmn., 2011—12, CEO, 2013—. Mng. dir. Lane Crawford Ltd., Hong Kong, 1986-88; chmn. Omni Hotels, Hampton, N.H., 1988, Mercy Ships Internat., 1992-; co-chmn. Global Crossing, Ltd., 2002-04; bd. dirs. Polo Ralph Lauren Corp., 2004-06, Taubman Centers Inc., 2002-04, Kendall Jackson Wine Estates, 2001-04, Lucille Packard Found. Children's Health, 2001-04, Segway LLC, 2003-05, Starbuck's Corp., 2003-, Saks Corp., 2013, COFRA Holdings, A.G., 2012-13, J.C. Penney Co., Inc., 2004-12, CEO, 2013-, Fed. Res. Bank Dallas, 2008-, chmn., 2010-11. Internat. v.p. U. Cin. Alumni Assn., 1980—; bd. dirs. Nat. Multiple Sclerosis Soc., NYC; bd. dirs. Brunswick Sch., Greenwich, Conn., U. Cin. Found., Lincoln Ctr. Devel., Deafness Rsch. Found., 1997-01, Stanford U. Children's Med. Ctr., 2004-04; chmn. exec. coun. U. Calif. Med. Ctr. Found., San Francisco, 2002, bd. dirs., 1998—. Mem. White House Fellow Alumni Assn., Econ. Club N.Y.C. (bd. dirs., exec. com.), Nat. Retail Fedn. (chmn., bd. dirs., exec. com. 1993—2010, 13-, bd. dirs. Retail Industry largest assn. 2010-), Pzena Investment Mgmt. (bd. dirs. 2007-08). Republican. Office: JC Penney Co Inc 6501 Legacy Dr Plano TX 75024-3698 Business E-Mail: mike@meullman.com.

ULLYOT, TED (THEODORE WARREN ULLYOT), lawyer, former social networking company executive; b. 1967; BA, Harvard U., 1990; JD, U. Chgo., 1994; student, Institut d'Etudes Politiques, 1990—91. Law clk. to Hon. J. Michael Luttig US Ct. Appeals (4th cir.), 1994—95; law clk. to Justice Antonin Scalia US Supreme Ct., Washington, 1995—96; assoc. Kirkland & Ellis, LLP, Washington, 1996—2000; atty. Legal Dept. American Online, 2000—01; v.p., assoc. gen. counsel AOL Time Warner, 2001—03; gen. counsel AOL Time Warner Europe, 2002—03; dep. asst. to pres., assoc. counsel to Pres. The White House, Washington, 2003—05; chief staff to Atty. Gen. Alberto R. Gonzales US Dept. Justice, Washington, 2005; exec. v.p., gen. counsel ESL Investments, 2005—08; v.p., gen. counsel Facebook, Inc., Palo Alto, Calif., 2008—13; exec. v.p., gen. counsel RBS Partners, L.P., Greenwich, Conn., 2013—. Bd. dirs. AutoZone, Inc., 2006—11. Named one of The Most Influential Lawyers, The Nat. Law Jour., 2011. Republican. Office: RBS Partners LP 1170 Kane Concourse Ste 200 Miami FL 33154*

ULMER, DOUGLAS L., mathematics professor; b. 1960; AB in Math., Princeton U., 1978—82; PhD in Math., Brown U., 1983—87. C.L.E. Moore instr. MIT, 1987—89; Bateman rsch. instr. Calif. Inst. Tech., 1989—91; asst. prof. U. Ariz., 1991, assoc. prof., prof., Ga. Inst. Tech., 2009—, chair math. dept., 2009—. Recipient Eller BPA Student Coun. Faculty award, 1999. Office: Sch Math Ga Inst Tech Atlanta GA 30332-0160 Office Phone: 404-894-2747. Business E-Mail: ulmer@math.gatech.edu.

UMENYIORA, OSI, professional football player; b. London, Nov. 16, 1980; Grad., Troy State U., Ala. Defensive end NY Giants, 2003—12, Atlanta Falcons, 2013—. Named First Team All-Pro, NFL, 2005; named to Nat. Football Conf. Pro Bowl Team, 2005, 2007. Achievements include member of Super Bowl XLII and XLVI winning New York Giants. Office: Atlanta Falcons 4400 Falcon Pky Flowery Branch GA 30542*

UMHOLTZ, CLYDE ALLAN, financial analyst; b. Du Quoin, Ill., Dec. 20, 1947; s. Frederick Louis and Opal Kathleen (Beard) U. BS, U. Ill., 1969; MS, U. Miss., 1972; MBA, Memphis State U., 1983, PhD, 1986; Dr of Higher Learning (hon.), London Sch. Econs., 2002; PhD in Natural Philosophy (hon.), U. Frankfurt, Germany, 2010. CFA; cert. systems profl., tax practitioner; registered profl. engr.; cert. data processor. Supr. quality control Champion Internat. Corp., Oxford, Miss., 1971-72; mgr. divsn. quality control Cook Industries, Memphis, 1973; engring. planner Northwest Industries and subs., Memphis, 1974-75; long range planning and analysis W.R. Grace and Co. and subs., Memphis, 1975-78; mgr. planning and analysis Ctr. Nuc. Studies Memphis State U., 1979-83; data processing mgr. Shelby County (Tenn.) Govt., 1983-87, dep. adminstr., 1987—2005, spl. asst. to county exec., 1989—2005, vice chancellor higher edn. commn., 2005—. Adj. prof. U. Tenn., Memphis, 1985—; ptnr. Custom Data Systems Inc., Memphis, 1987—, Western Techs. Inc., Memphis, 1988—; bd. dir. Am. Tech. Inst., Memphis, Am. Info. Cons., Atlanta, Eastgate Corp., Anaheim, Calif., CIPCO Corp., Chgo., Sanford Cons. Group, London, Paris; bd. underwriters Lloyd's of London; diplomate edtl. adv. bd. Brent's Peerage, London, Memphis-Amsterdam Gateway Com., Holland, 1997; Goodwill Amb. Am. Ukrainian Trade Alliance, Kiev, 1997—, Asian Econ. Recovery Coun., Tokyo, 1998—; elected to U.S. China Bd. of Trade, 2002; adv. bd. Fed. Res. Bank, Memphis, 1998—; mem. Am.-Japanese Tire Safety Adv. Bd., 2000, Tenn. Commn. on Homeland Security, 2002—; diplomate Multi-Country Healthcare Exch., 2003, Medicare Nat. Study Com., 2003; oversight com. Internat. Energy Prodn. Alliance, 2003, 06; adv. com. OPEC Price Stblzn. Coop., 2004, 06; mem. Internat. Symposium Strategic Energy Resources, 2005, 06, Congressional Com. Social Security Reform, 2005, 06, Citizens' Congl. Ethics Coun., 2006, Emergency Mgmt. Comms. Coordinating Com., 2006, Accreditation Com., Internat. Baccalaureate Edn. Program, 2006, Mid-East Stabilization Planning Conf., 2006; mem. Govt. Ethics Reform Task Force, 2007; internat. bus. cons. McKinsey Co., 2007; bd. Am. Mideast Ednl. and Training Sys.,2008-;Tennessee Task Force Job Creation, 2009; US Congressional Commn. Economic Stimulation & Global Recovery Planning, 2009, Haiti Earthquake Recovery Commn., 2010; sci. cons. Royal Soc. Rsch. Coun., London, 2011, Delta Med. Ctr. North Miss., 2014; bd. recovery, Internat. Economic Alliance European Debt Crisis, 2011-12; co-chair Ctr. US Egyptian Arts Exch., 2013; edtl. advisor Fgn. Affairs, 2013; sponsor, Tenn. Task Force One, Disaster Relief, 2013; mem. adv. coun. Midsouth Cmty. Found. Charitable Trusts, 2014-; cons. in field. Author: Prototyping of Computerized Financial Systems, 3d edit., 1997, Context Analysis in System Design, 2d edit., 1999, The Family Partnership-An Estate Planning Model, 3d edit., 2000, The Use of Chemical Molecules as Computer Switches, 2002, The Science of Plastics, 2007, Foreign Investing, 2010, Materials Failure Analysis, 2011, The Engineering Basis Medical Diagnosis, 2012, Effects of Quantum Physics on Super Fast Computing, 2014; contbr. articles to profl. jours.; inventor angle trisector. Active presdl. election campaigns, 1968-72, 80-2004, 08, 12; del. Rep. Nat. Conv., 1996-2004, 08, 12; mem. Rep. Nat. Com., 2002—; active mayoral campaign, Memphis, 1975, 83, 87, 91, Shelby County, 1990, 94, sheriff's campaign Shelby County, 1990, 94, Mid-South Billy Graham Crusade, 1978; del. So. Govs.' Conf., 1992-93; gov. staff State of Tenn., 1993-94; mem. Mayor's Adv. Com., Memphis, 1991; steering com. Future Memphis, 1992, Arena Football League, Memphis, 1994; active Houston Oilers Relocation Com., 1996, Task Force Athletic Devel., Memphis-FedEx Forum, 2013; adv. coun. Kordes' Gardens, Hamburg, Germany; study com. Nat. Electoral Coll., 2001; co-chmn. 27th Ann. Pres.'s Dinner, 2002; oversight com. Fin. Acctg. Stds. Bd., 2002—; bd. dirs. West Tenn. Cmty. Found., 2006—, Memphis Biomed. Rsch. Found., 2007—, Resources for the Future, Washington, 2007-; bd. dirs. Internat Commn on Global Warming, 2008-; mem. adv. bd. Arbitron Media Cons., 2010-, Pres.'s Adv. Panel Sci. & Tech. Policy, Washington, 2011-. Recipient Oratorical award Optimist Club, 1963, Leadership and Human Rels. award Dale Carnegie Inst., 1977, Disting. Svc. award State of Tenn., 1991; Humanist award Internat. Ethical Union, 2008; NSF fellow, 1970-72. Fellow NAS, Australian Acad. Scis., NY Acad. Scis., Am. Acad. Info. Tech., Nat. Acad. U. Adminstr.; Internat. Enterprise Inst. (hon.); mem. AAAS, AIChE, Am. Mgmt. Assn., Fin. Execs. Inst., Am. Chem. Soc., Assn. MBA Execs., Data Processing Mgmt. Assn., Planning Execs. Inst., Am. Assn. Investment Advisors, U. Ill. Alumni Assn., U. Miss. Alumni Assn., Memphis State U. Alumni Assn., Am. Rose Soc. (accredited life rose judge 1990), Am. Iris Soc., Am. Hemerocallis Soc., Elvis Presley Meml. Soc., Am. Hort. Soc., Internat. Soc. Clin. Investigation, Internat. Platform Assn., Gt. Am. Pyramid Boosters Memphis, Mensa, Admirals Club, Oxford Club, London Club, Exec. Club Memphis, Petroleum Club Memphis, Olympic Soc. Atlanta, Order of De Molay, Phi Beta Kappa. Baptist. Achievements include patent on fiber optic router; patents for wireless digital x-ray, electrically heated footware. Home: 3580 Hanna Dr Memphis TN 38128-3451 Office: 100 N Main St Memphis TN 38103-5011 Office Phone: 901-388-3997. Business E-Mail: cau@memphis.gov. E-mail: cau@hannamem.gov.

UMMINGER, BRUCE LYNN, government agency administrator, research scientist, educator, consultant; b. Dayton, Ohio, Apr. 10, 1941; s. Frederick William and Elnora Mae Umminger; m. Judith Lackey Bryant, Dec. 17, 1966; children: Alison Grace, April Lynn. BS in Biology magna cum laude with honors, Yale U., 1963, MS, 1966, MPhil, 1968, PhD, 1969; postgrad., U. Calif., Berkeley, 1963—64; cert. univ. adminstrv./mgmt. tng. program, U. Cin., 1975; cert., Fed. Exec. Inst., 1984. Asst. prof. biol. scis. U. Cin., 1969-73, assoc. prof. dept. biol. scis., 1973-75, acting head dept. biol. scis., 1973-75, prof. dept. biol. scis., 1975-81, dir. grad. affairs, 1978-79; program dir. regulatory biology program NSF, Washington, 1979-84, dept. dir. cellular bioscis. divsn., 1984-89, mem. sr. exec. svc., 1984—2006, acting divsn. dir., 1985-87, 88-89, divsn. dir. cellular bioscis. divsn., 1989-91, divsn. dir. integrative biology and neurosci., 1991—99, sr. scientist office integrative activities, office of dir., 1999—2006, cons., 2006—09, The Implementation Group, Washington, 2006—, U. Nebr., 2006—; sr. advisor on health policy Office of Internat. Health Policy Dept. State, Washington, 1988; sr. advisor on biodiversity Smithsonian Instn., Washington, 1993-94. Exec. sec. Nat. Sci. Bd. Com. on Ctrs. and Individual Investigator Awards, 1986-88; rev. panel expl. program to stimulate competitive rsch. NSF, 1989, Rsch. Improvement in Minority Instns., 1986-87, US-India Coop. Rsch. Program, 1981-82, U.S.-India Exch. of Scholars Program, 1979-81; vice chmn. biotech. rsch. subcom. Fed. Coord. Coun. on Sci. Engring. and Tech., Office Sci. and Tech. Policy, 1991-94; exec. sec. subcom. biodiversity and ecosystem dynamics, com. on environment and natural resources Nat. Sci. and Tech. Coun., 1994, interagy. working group on rsch. misconduct policy implementation, 2000-06; group nat. experts on safety in biotech. OECD, 1988-89; sr. exec. panel Exec. Potential Program, Office Pers. Mgmt., 1988-89; space shuttle proposal rev. panel in life scis. NASA, 1978, rsch. assocs. in space biology award com., 1985-91, chmn. cell and devel. biology discipline working group, space biology program, 1990-91, chmn. gravitational biology panel, NASA Specialized Ctrs. Rsch. and Tng., 1990, chmn. specialized ctrs. rsch. and tng. peer rev. panel NASA, 1995, exec. steering com. in life scis., 1991, gravitational biology facility sci. working group, 1992-95, space sta. biol. rsch. project sci. working group, 1995-96, neurolab. steering com., 1993; panel study biol. diversity, Bd. Sci. and Tech. Internat. Devel. NRC, 1989; exec. sec. adv. planning bd. Nat. Biodiversity Info. Ctr., Smithsonian Instn., 1993-94; adv. screening com. in life scis. Coun. for Internat. Exch. of Scholars, 1978-81; liaison rep. nat. heart, lung and blood adv. coun. NIH, 1979-87, nat. adv. child health and human devel. coun., 1990-99; recombinant DNA adv. com., 1988; liaison rep. agrl. biotech. Rsch.

Adv. com., USDA, 1989-94; animal com. Interagy. Rsch., 1984-88; Interagy. working group on Internat. Biotech., 1988-94; chmn. proposal panel in biology Sci. Found. Ireland, 2002, Human Proteomics Site Visit, 2003; cons. U. Nebr., 2007-. Author book chpts. and contbr. articles to profl. jours.; assoc. editor Jour. Exptl. Zoology, 1977-79; editl. adv. bd. Gen. and Comparative Endocrinology, 1982. World mission com. Ch. of the Redeemer, New Haven, 1967-68; Sunday Sch. steering com. Calvary Episcopal Ch., Cin., 1972-73, sr. acolyte, 1972-77, adult edn. com., 1975-76; deacon Faith Presbyn. Ch., Springfield, Va., 1996-99; adv. com. Wakefield H.S., 1991-92, PTA exec. bd., 1991-92; sci. adv. com. Arlington Pub. Schs., 1987-92, adv. coun. on instrn., 1991-92; adv. bd. Campbell Comml. Coll., Cin., 1977-79. Recipient George Rieveschl, Jr. Rsch. award U. Cin., 1973, Presdl. Rank Meritorious Exec. award NSF, 1992; U. Cin. Grad. Sch. fellow 1977—, NSF fellow 1964; Rsch. grant NSF 1971-79. Fellow AAAS (coun. 1980-83, 89-90, program com. for 1989 ann. meeting 1988, chmn.-elect sect. G-Biol. Scis. 1987-88, chair 1988-89, ret. 1989-90); mem. Assn. of Yale Alumni (del. 1990-93), Mory's Assn., Sigma Xi (Disting. Rsch. award U. Cin. chpt. 1973, pres. U. Cin. chpt. 1977-79), Mensa. Home: 205 Helmsdale Dr Chapel Hill NC 27517 Personal E-mail: bruce.u@hotmail.com.

UMPHENOUR, RUSSELL V., JR., food services executive; Pres., CEO RTM Restaurant Group, Atlanta. Office: Arbys Restaurant Group 1155 Perimeter Ctr W Atlanta GA 30338-5463

UNDERHILL, KIM, consumer products company executive; b. Evansville, Ind. B in Chem. Engring., Purdue U.; M in Engring. Mgmt., Milwaukee Sch. Engring. Joined Kimberly-Clark Corp., 1988, v.p., North Am. Group Brands, positions, North Am. consumer bus., 1994—97, positions, Feminine Care, 1997—99, positions, chid care, 1999—2004, mktg. dir., North Am. Infant Care, 2004—06, pres., Family Care Mktg., N.Am., 2006, v.p., Ireland, 2009—, v.p., England, 2009—. Office: Kimberly Clark Corp 351 Phelps Dr Irving TX 75038 Office Phone: 972-281-1200. Office Fax: 972-281-1490. Business E-Mail: kim.underhill@kcc.com.

UNDERWOOD, CARRIE MARIE, singer; b. Muskogee, Okla., Mar. 10, 1983; d. Stephen and Carol Underwood; m. Michael Andrew Fisher, July 10, 2010. BA magna cum laude, Northeastern State U., Tahlequah, Okla., 2006. Recording artist RCA Music Group, NYC, 2005—. Singer: (albums) Some Hearts, 2005 (Album of Yr., Country Album of Yr., Billboard Music Awards, 2006, Album of Yr., Acad. Country Music Awards, 2007, Favorite Country Album, American Music Awards, 2007, Top Country Album of Decade, Billboard Music Awards, 2009), Carnival Ride, 2007 (Favorite Country Album, American Music Awards, 2008), Play On, 2009 (Favorite Country Album, American Music Awards, 2010, Album of Yr., American Country Awards, 2010), Blown Away, 2012 (Favorite Country Album, American Music Awards, 2012), (songs) Inside Your Heaven, 2005, Jesus, Take the Wheel, 2005 (Country Recorded Song of Yr., Gospel Music Assn. Awards, 2006, Female Video of Yr., Breakthrough Video of Yr., CMT Music Awards, 2006, Song of Yr., Nashville Songwriters Assn. Internat. Awards, 2006, Single Record of Yr., Acad. Country Music Awards, 2006, Best Female Country Vocal Performance, Best Country Song, Grammy Awards, 2007), Some Hearts, 2005, Before He Cheats, 2006 (Favorite Country Song, People's Choice Awards, 2007, Video of Yr., Female Video of Yr., CMT Music Awards, 2007, Video of Yr., Acad. Country Music Awards, 2007, Single of Yr., Country Music Assn. Awards, 2007, Best Female Country Vocal Performance, Best Country Song, Grammy Awards, 2008), Last Name, 2007 (Favorite Country Song, People's Choice Awards, 2009, Best Female Country Vocal Performance, Grammy Awards, 2009), (with Randy Travis) I Told You So, 2009 (Best Country Collaboration with Vocals, Grammy Awards, 2010), Cowboy Casanova, 2009 (Video of Yr., CMT Music Awards, 2010), Temporary Home, 2009, (with Brad Paisley) Remind Me, 2011 (Collaborative Video of Yr., CMT Music Awards, 2012), Good Girl, 2012 (Video of Yr., CMT Music Awards, 2012), Blown Away, 2012 (Best Country Solo Performance, Best Country Song, Grammy Awards, 2013, Video of Yr., CMT Music Awards, 2013); actress: (films) Soul Surfer, 2011; (TV films) The Sound of Music, 2013; TV appearances How I Met Your Mother, 2010, Blue Bloods, 2011. Recipient Horizon award, Country Music Assn., 2006, Red Carpet Fashion Icon award, Teen Choice Awards, 2008, Harmony award, Nashville Symphony, 2009, Spl. Achievement award, Acad. Country Music, 2011; named Rising Star of Yr., Okla. Music Hall of Fame, 2005, Oklahoman of Yr., Okla. Today, 2005, Country Single Sales Artist of Yr., Billboard Music Awards, 2005, Female Country Artist of Yr., 2006, Top New Female Vocalist of Yr., Acad. Country Music Awards, 2006, Female Vocalist of Yr., 2007, 2008, 2009, Entertainer of Yr., 2009, 2010, Female Vocalist of Yr., Country Music Assn. Awards, 2006, 2007, 2008, Favorite New Breakthrough Artist, American Music Awards, 2006, Favorite Female Country Artist, 2007, Favorite Female Singer, People's Choice Awards, 2007, 2009, Favorite Star Under 35, 2009, Favorite Country Artist, 2010; named one of Top 25 Entertainers of Yr., Entertainment Weekly, 2007, The 100 Most Powerful Celebrities, Forbes.com, 2008; named to Okla. Hall of Fame, 2009. Baptist. Achievements include winning the fourth season of American Idol on May 25, 2005; inducted into the Grand Ole Opry, 2008. Office: c/o Jeff Frasco Creative Artists Agency 2000 Avenue of the Stars Los Angeles CA 90067*

UNDERWOOD, PAUL BENJAMIN, gynecologist, oncologist, educator; b. Greer, SC, Aug. 8, 1934; s. Paul Benjamin and Gladys (Guest) Underwood; m. Peggy Joyce Outen, July 7, 1957; children: Paul Benjamin III, Mary Barton. MD, Med. U. S.C., 1959. Diplomate Am. Bd. Ob-gyn., Am. Bd. Gynecol. Oncology. Intern Med. U. S.C., Charleston, 1959—60, resident, 1960—64; fellow M.D. Anderson Hosp. and Tumor Inst., Houston, 1966—67; asst. prof. U. S.C., Charleston, 1967—70, assoc. prof., 1970—74, prof., 1974—99, staff, dir. gynecology, assoc. dean admissions Med. Sch., 1999—, dir. divsn. gynecol. oncology, 2002; chmn. dept. ob-gyn. U. Va. Sch. Medicine, Charlottesville, 1979-99. Contbr. articles to profl. jours. With USN, 1964—66. Recipient Alumni of Yr. award, Med. U. S.C., 1989. Mem.: Thegos Soc., S.C. Ob-Gyn. Soc., Charlottesville Med. Soc., So. Med. Soc., Felix Rutledge Soc. (pres. 1977), Am. Assn. Ob-Gyn. (sec. 1992—95, pres. 1999—), Soc. Gynecol. Oncologists (mem. coun. 1972—75, v.p. 1977—78, pres. 1983), Am. Coll. Ob-Gyn., Am. Gynecol. Club (pres. 1996), Alpha Omega Alpha. Office: 171 Ashley Ave Charleston SC 29425-0001 Office Phone: 843-792-4026. Business E-Mail: underwp@musc.edu.

UNGARO-BENAGES, URSULA MANCUSI, federal judge; b. Miami Beach, Fla., Jan. 29, 1951; d. Ludivico Mancusi-Ungaro and Ursula Berliner; m. Michael A. Benages, Mar., 1988. Student, Smith Coll., 1968-70; BA in English Lit., U. Miami, 1973; JD, U. Fla., 1975. Bar: Fla. 1975. Assoc. Frates, Floyd, Pearson et al, Miami, 1976-78, Blackwell, Walker, Gray et al, Miami, 1978-80, Finley, Kumble, Heine et al, Miami, 1980-85, Sparber, Shevin, Shapo et al, Miami, 1985-87; cir. judge State of Fla., Miami, 1987-92; judge US Dist. Ct. (so. dist.) Fla., Miami, 1992—. Mem. Fla. Supreme Ct. Race & Ethnic & Racial Bias Study Commn., Fla., 1989-92, St. Thomas U. Inns of Ct., Miami, 1991-92; mem. Jud. Resources Com. Jud. Conf. U.S.; chmn. Ct. Svcs. Com. So. Dist. Fla., chmn. Magistrate Judge Com.; mem. personnel com. 11th Cir. Jud. Coun. U.S. Bd. dirs. United Family & Children's Svcs., Miami, 1981-82; mem. City of Miami Task Force, 1991-92. Mem. ABA, Fed. Judges Assn., Fla. Assn. Women Lawyers, Dade County Bar Assn., Eugene Spellman Inns of Ct. U. Miami. Office: US Dist Ct Ferguson US Courthouse 400 N Miami Ave Rm 12-4 Miami FL 33128 Office Phone: 305-523-5550.

UNGER, JOHN R., II, state legislator; b. Martinsburg, W.Va., Jan. 24, 1969; BA, W.Va. U., 1993; BA, MA, U. Oxford, 2004. Coord., founder W.Va. U. Office of Svc. Learning Programs, 1991—93; chief of staff to Councilor Simon Ip Hong Kong Legis. Coun., 1994—95; v.p. cmty. and econ. devel. Van Wyk Enterprises, 1996—98; dir. comm. Save the Children Internat., Iraq, 2003; prodr., host WEPM Panhandle Live Talk Show, 1998—; sr. advisor homeland security and econ. devel. Edgerton, Germeshausen and Grier, Inc. / United Rsch. Svcs., Nat. Energy Tech. Lab., 2003—; mem. Dist. 16 W.Va. State Senate, 1999—, chair Transp. and Infrastructure Com., vice chair Econ. Devel. Com., mem. Agr. Com., Edn. Com., Fin. Com., Health and Human Resources Com. & Natural Resources Com. Asst. logistical coord. Internat. Rescue Com. UN Operation Provide Comfort, 1991; founder, pres. W.Va. Internat. Trade Devel. Coun., 1996—2000; mem. Berkeley County Devel. Authority, 1996—; dep. dir. disaster svcs. Office of Emergency Svcs., Berkeley County, 1998—; chair Homeland Security Econ. Devel. Commn., 2004—. Democrat. Mailing: PO Box 2415 Martinsburg WV 25402 Office: State Capitol Rm 216W, Bldg 1 1900 Kanawha Blvd E Charleston WV 25305 Office Phone: 304-263-5488, 304-357-7933. E-mail: john.unger@wvsenate.gov.

UNGER, PAUL WALTER, retired soil scientist; b. Winchester, Tex., Sept. 10, 1931; s. Edwin Herman and Elsie Anna U.; m. Barbara Charlene Dutton Steelman, Sept. 13, 1960; children: Gary Robert, Paula Dianne. BS in Agrl. Edn., Tex. A&M U., Coll. Sta., 1961; MS in Soil Sci., Colo. State U., Ft. Collins, 1963, PhD in Soil Sci., 1966. Soil scientist USDA Agrl. Rsch. Svc., Bushland, Tex., 1965-81, soil scientist/rsch. leader, 1981-87, supervisory soil scientist/rsch. leader, 1987-93, soil scientist, 1993-2000; ret., 2000. Cons. Food and Agrl. Orgn. UN, Rome, 1986. Author and co-author bulls. and articles; co-editor conf. proc., Agronomy Monograph, other publs.; editor Managing Agricultural Residues, 1994; author Soil and Water Conservation Handbook-Policies, Pratices, Conditions, and Terms, 2006, Tillage Systems For Soil and Water Conservation, 1984. With US Army, 1952—55. Recipient Disting. Svc. award Great Plains Agrl. Coun., 1984; named Scientist of Yr., USDA-Agrl. Rsch. Svc., So. Plains Area, 1987. Fellow Am. Soc. Agronomy (emeritus, selection com. 1988-89), Soil Sci. Soc. Am. (emeritus, assoc. editor 1977-82, divsn. chmn. 1986, mem. selection com. 1994-95, Applied Rsch. award 1991, Soil Sci. Disting. Svc. award 2009), Soil and Water Conservation Soc. (various local and state offices, photography awards 1990-92); mem. Internat. Soil Tillage Rsch. Orgn., World Assn. Soil and Water Conservation. Lutheran. Avocations: woodworking, gardening, photography. Personal E-mail: pwunger@suddenlink.net.

UNGRANGSEE, BUNDIT, conductor; b. Thailand, Dec. 7, 1970; M in Conducting, U. Mich. Worked with world-class artists including Maxim Vengerov, Julia Migenes, Joseph Alessi, the LaBeque Sisters, Paula Robison, and more; conducted more than 500 symphonic and operatic performances with more than 40 orchestras worldwide; condr. St. Luke Orch., NYC, LA Philharm. Orch., La Fenice Theatre, Venice, Italy, Pomeriggi Musicali, Milan, Orch. Sinfonica Siciliana, Palermo, Auckland Philharmonia, New Zealand, Orch. Internazionale d'Italia, Malaysian Philharm., Canada, Cukurova Symphony, Turkey, Seoul and Busan Philharm. Orch., Republic of Korea, Orch. di Roma e del Lazio, Rome; cover condr. NY Philharm.; apprentice condr. Oregon Symphony; asst. condr. Santa Rosa Symphony; prin. guest condr. Charleston Symphony; music dir. and condr. Young Musicians Found.; assoc. condr. Utah Symphony; prin. guest condr. Seoul Philharm. Orch., 2005. Operatic condr. (prodn.) Donizetti's L'Elisir d'Amore, Ascoli Piceno, La Traviat, South Korea Tour, Puccini's Il Trittico, Australia, Strauss' Die Fledermaus, US, Verdi's Aida, France, (rec.) Mozart flute concertos, Charleston Symphony Orch., 2004. Recipient Leonard Bernstein Conducting Fellowship award, 1998, 4th among 37 conductors from over 20 nations, Hungarian TV-Radio Internat. Conducting Competition; named Laureate, Maazel-Vilar Internat. Conductors' Competition. Office: c/o Charleston Symphony Orchestra Ste 100 756 Saint Andrews Blvd Charleston SC 29407-7169 Office Phone: 843-723-7528. Office Fax: 843-722-3463.

UNTERMAN, RENEE S., state legislator; children: Zachariah Albert & Rachel Elizabeth. BA, Univ. Ga.; RN, Ga. State Univ. Former critical care nurse; ins. co. exec.; mayor Loganville, Ga., 1986—90, 1996—98; commr. Gwinnett County, 1990—94; mem. Dist. 84 Ga. House Reps., 1999—2002; mem. Dist. 45 Ga. State Senate, 2003—. Republican. Office: 421-B State Capitol Atlanta GA 30334 Mailing: PO Box 508 Buford GA 30518 Office Phone: 770-945-1887, 404-463-1368. Office Fax: 404-651-6768. Business E-Mail: renee.unterman@senate.ga.gov.

UNTERMEYER, CHARLES GRAVES (CHASE UNTERMEYER), international business consultant; b. Long Branch, NJ, Mar. 7, 1946; s. Dewitt Edward and Marguerite Alonza (Graves) U.; m. Diana Cumming Kendrick, Oct. 6, 1990; 1 child, Ellyson Chase. AB, Harvard Coll., 1968. Polit. reporter Houston Chronicle, 1971-74; exec. asst. County Judge of Harris County, Houston, 1974-76; state rep. Tex. Ho. of Reps., Austin, 1977-81; exec. asst. V.P. George H.W. Bush, Washington, 1981-83; dep. asst. sec. installations & facilities Navy Dept., Washington, 1983—84, asst. sec. manpower & reserve affairs, 1984—88; asst. to the pres. White House, Washington, 1989-91; dir. Voice of Am., Washington, 1991-93; dir. govt. affairs Compaq Computer Corp., Houston, 1993—2002; v.p. prof. pub. policy U. Tex. Health Sci. Ctr., Houston, 2002—04; U.S. amb. to Qatar US Dept. State, 2004—07, vice chmn., strategic real estate advisors, 2007—09, mem. def., health bd., 2008—09, coun. foreign rels., 2009—; mem. Tex. Ethics Commn., 2010—. Bd. visitors U.S. Naval Acad., Annapolis, Md., 1993-96, chmn., 1995; mem. Tex. State Bd. Edn., 1999-2003, chmn., 1999-2001. Author: Houston Survival Handbook, 1980. Commnr. Port of Houston, 1995-98; bd. dirs. Nat. Pub. Radio, 1996-98. Lt. USNR, 1968-70. Inst. Politics fellow Harvard U., 1980; recipient George Washington Honor medal Freedoms Found., 1969. Republican. Episcopalian. Home and Office: 10000 Memorial Dr Ste 920 Houston TX 77024 Office Phone: 974-488-4101 ext. 6055, 713-683-9885. E-mail: chase@untermeyer.com.

UPADHIAYA, UMESH CHANDRA, engineer, consultant; b. Dabha, India, July 11, 1927; arrived in US, 1977; s. Bhagwati Prashad and Shri Devi Upadhiaya; m. Susila Devi, Nov. 7, 1954; children: Anita, Amit. Diploma in Elec. and Mech. Engring., Tech. Coll., Dayalbagh, India, 1948; MSME, Fla. Internat. U., 1991. Registered profl. engr., Fla. Asst. engr. Hindusthan Sugar, Gola, India, 1954—60; mech. engr. Bagpat Sugar, India, 1960—61; erection engr. Dhampur Sugar, India, 1961—62; cons. Mehta Group, Uganda, 1962—73; project mgr. KCP Ltd., Madras, India, 1973—74; design engr. Joint Sugar Project Unit, Surabaya, Indonesia, 1974—77; cons. engr. Tate & Lyle Enterprises Inc., Miami, Fla., 1977—85, ATV Projects, Bombay, 1990—93; ind. cons. Davie, Fla., 1993—. Contbr. articles to profl. jours. Home and Office: 6510 Sedgewyck Cir W Davie FL 33331-3455 Personal E-mail: ravay2k@bellsouth.net.

UPADHYAY, JYOTI J., urologist, educator; married. BA, U. Mich., Ann Arbor, 1990; MD, Wayne State U., Mich., 1994. Lic. Mich., 1999, Ont., Can., 2002, NY, Va., 2007, diplomate Am. Bd. Urology, 2008. Surgery resident Wayne State U., 1994—96, urology resident, 1996—2000; rsch. fellow, urology Hosp. Sick Children, Toronto, Canada, 2000—02; asst. prof. Dept. Urology and Pediat. SUNY, 2002—05, assoc. prof., 2006—08; assoc. prof., dept. urology and pediat. Eastern Va. Med. Sch., 2008—; chief, sect. pediat. urology SUNY, 2002—08, dir., pediat. urology, 2004—08; urologist, children's surg. splty. group Children's Hosp. of The King's Daughters, 2008—, Sentara Norfolk Gen. Hosp., 2008—, Sentara Leigh Hosp.; with Crouse Irving Meml. Hosp., 2002—08. Com. mem. for numerous orgnl. coms.; spkr. in field. Contbr. numerous articles and sci. papers to profl. publs. Peace physician, Morocco, Africa, 2010; lectr., tchr. GU Health 4th Grade Boys Norfolk Acad., Va., 2011—12. Recipient Hinman Jr. Pediatric Rsch. award, 2001; named one of Top Urologist of Norfolk, Internat. Assn. Healthcare Profls., 2012, Top Drs. of Hampton Rd., 2012, 2013; grant, Am. Found. Urologic Disease, 2001—02, Oceana Therapeutics Inc., 2009—10. Fellow: ACS, Am. Acad. Pediat.; mem.: AMA, Tidewater Pediatric Soc. Va., Tidewater Urol. Soc. Va., Soc. Pediatric Urology, Soc. Fetal Urology, Physicians for Peace, NY State Urol. Soc., European Soc. Paediatric Urology, Endourologic Soc., Assn. Women Surgeons, Am. Urol. Assn., Am. Coll. Physician Execs., Am. Bd. Urology, AOA Academic Fraternity. Office: Children's Hosp The King's Daughters Children's Surgical Specialty Group 601 Children's Ln 5th Fl Norfolk VA 23507 Office Fax: 757-668-7883. Business E-Mail: jyoti.upadhyay@chkd.org.*

UPBIN, HAL J., consumer products company executive; b. Bronx, NY, Jan. 15, 1939; s. David and Evelyn (Sloan) U.; m. Shari Kiesler, May 29, 1960; children: Edward, Elyse, Danielle. BBA, Pace Coll., 1961. CPA, NY. Tax sr. Peat, Marwick, Mitchell & Co., NYC, 1961-65; tax mgr. Price Waterhouse & Co., NYC, 1965-71; dir. taxes Wheelabrator-Frye Inc., NYC, 1971-72, treas., 1972-74; pres. Wheelabrator Fin. Corp., NYC, 1974-75; v.p., chief fin. officer Chase Manhattan Mortgage and Realty Trust (became Triton Group Ltd. 1980), NYC, 1975-76, pres., 1976-78, pres., chmn., 1978-83, also dir.; chmn., pres., dir. Isomedics, 1983-85; chmn., pres. Fifth Ave. Cards, Inc., Fifth Retail Corp., Ashley's Stores, Ashley's Outlet Stores, 1984-88; bd. dirs. Stacy Industries, 1984-88; vice chmn. Am. Recreation Products, St. Louis, 1985-88; vice chmn., pres. American Recreation Products, St. Louis, 1988—, chmn., 1992; v.p. corp. devel., chmn. acquistion com. Kellwood Co., Chesterfield, Mo., 1990, exec. v.p. corp. devel., chmn. acquisition com., 1992, pres., COO, 1994, pres., COO, dir., 1995-97, pres., CEO, 1997—2005, chmn., 1999—2006, chmn. emeritus, 2006—. Bd. dirs. First Banks, Inc., Regional Bus. Coun., Coun. Nat. Trustees, Nat. Jewish Med. and Rsch. Ctr., Nat. Coun. Wash. U. Olin Sch. Bus.; bd. mem. Brown Shoe; trustee Pace U. Past pres. Jewish Temple. Mem. AICPA, NY State Soc. CPA's, Franklin Jaycees (v.p.). Home: 3740 S Ocean Blvd Apt 801 Highland Beach FL 33487-3403 Home Phone: 561-276-4101.

UPBIN, SHARI, theater producer, director; m. Hal J. Upbin; children: Edward, Elyse, Danielle. Master tap instr. Talent mgr. Goldstar Talent Mgmt., Inc., NYC, 1989-91; theatre prodr., dir. Faculty Nat. Shakespeare Conservatory, N.Y., dir. Confessions of Jewish Shiksha, Dancing on Hitlers Grave, Kravis Theater West Palm Beach, Fla., 2009 Asst. dir.: (plays, 1st Black-Hispanic Shakespeare prodn.) Julius Ceasar, 1979; dir.(choreographer): (plays) Matter of Opinion, 1980, Side by Side, 1981; prodr.(dir.): Vincent, The Passions of Van Gogh, 1981,; (Broadway plays) Bojangles, The Life of Bill Robinson, 1984; dir.: Captain America, 1996; dir., choreographer (plays) Fiddler of the Roof, Cabaret, Life with Father, Roar of the Grease Paint, 1979—82; dir.: (plays) Feminist Movements, 1997, Danny Kaye and Sylvia, 2005; co-prodr.: One Mo' Time; prodr., dir.: Flypaper, 1991—92; Women on Their Own, Things My Mother Never Told Me; How Could Cupid Be So Stupid!, 1999; Timeless Divas, 2003, 2005; prodr., dir. (plays) Divas in Divaland, 2007; prodr.: (plays) Vintage 2001, Timeless Divas! Salute to Women in Cabaret, Broadway Over 40, Timeless Divas! Musical Stars of The Silver Screen, 2004, Dames in Divaland, 2007, Timeless Divas, Broadway Divas at Crest Theatre, 2008; dir.: Women's Minyan, 2011, Art of the Solo, South Fla. Dance Competition, Nat. Soc. Arts and Letters, 2011, Mus. Theatre Competition Lynn U. Nsal, 2012. Pres. NSAL Boca Raton-East Fla. Chpt., founder Queens Playhouse, N.Y., Children's Theatre, Flushing, N.Y.; mem. Willy Mays' Found. Drug Abused Children. Recipient Jaycees Svc. award Jr. Miss Pageants Franklin Twp., N.J., 1976. Mem. League Profl. Theatre Women (past pres.), Soc. Stage Dirs. and Choreographers, Nat. Soc. Arts and Letters (bd. mem.), Coalition of Women in Arts & Media (bd. dirs.), Actors Equity Assn., Villagers Barn Theatre (1st woman pres.), N.Y. Womens Agenda (bd. dirs.). Personal E-mail: shariupbin@aol.com.

UPDEGROVE, MARK K., library director; b. Phila. m. Evelyn Updegrove; children: Charlie, Tallie. BA in Economics, U. Md., 1984. Writer and LA mgr. TIME mag.; pres. Time Canada, Toronto; pub. Newsweek, NYC; pub. Nickelodeon and MTV magazines MTV Networks, NYC; v.p. sales and operations Yahoo! Canada; dir. Lyndon Baines Johnson Libr. and Mus., 2009—. Author: Second Acts: Presidential Lives and Legacies After the White House, 2006, Baptism By Fire: Eight Presidents Who Took Office in Times of Crisis, 2009, Indomitable Will: LBJ in the Presidency, 2012; contbr. articles to magazines including National Geographic, Worth, The Nation and American Heritage. Office: Lyndon Baines Johnson Library & Museum 2313 Red River St Austin TX 78705 Office Phone: 512-721-0158.

UPHAM, STEADMAN, academic administrator, anthropologist, educator; b. Denver, Apr. 4, 1949; s. Albert Tyler and Jane Catherine (Steadman) U; m. Margaret Anne Cooper, Aug. 21, 1971; children: Erin Cooper, Nathan Steadman. BA in English Lit and Spanish, U. Redlands, Calif., 1971; MA in Anthropology, Ariz. State U., 1977, PhD in Anthropology, 1980. Dist. sales mgr. Ind. News Co. Inc., LA, 1971-72; regional sales mgr. Petersen Pub. Co, LA, 1972-74; archeologist, researcher Bur. Land Mgmt., Phoenix, 1979; research asst. Ariz. State U., Tempe, 1979-80; chief archeologist Soil Sytems Inc., Phoenix, 1980-81, N.Mex. State U., Las Cruces, N.Mex., 1981-85, asst. prof. to assoc. prof., 1982-87, assoc. dean, 1987-90; prof. anthropology, vice provost for rsch., grad. dean U. Oreg., Eugene, 1990—98; pres. Claremont Grad. U., Calif., 1998—2004, U. Tulsa, Okla., 2004—12, 2012—. Interim dir. Cultural Resources Mgmt. divsn. N.Mex. State U., Las Cruces, 1988; mem. exec. com. Assn. Grad. Schs., 1994—2004; bd. dirs. Coun. Grad. Schs., 1995—2004. Author: Polities and Power, 1982, A Hopi Social History, 1992; editor: Computer Graphics in Archaeology, 1979, Mogollon Variability, 1986, The Sociopolitical Structure of Prehistoric Southwest Societies, 1989, The Evolution of Political Systems, 1990; also articles. Advanced seminar grantee Sch. of Am. Rsch., 1987, research grantee NSF, 1979, 1984-85, Hist. Preservation grantee State of N.Mex., 1982-84, 1991, 92, Ford Found. 1991-92, U.S. Dept. Edn. 1991-93.

Fellow Am. Anthropol. Assn.; mem. Nat. Phys. Sci. Consortium (pres. 1992-95), We. Assn. Grad. Schs. (pres. 1994-95), Assn. Grad. Schs. (exec. com. 1995—), Coun. Grad. Schs. (bd. dirs. 1995—). Office: University of Tulsa / Office of President Collins Hall, 2nd Floor 600 S College Ave Tulsa OK 74104*

UPRIGHT, DIANE WARNER, art dealer; b. Cleve. d. Rodney Upright and Shirley (Warner) Lavine. Student, Wellesley Coll., 1965-67; BA, U. Pitts., 1969; MA, U. Mich., 1973, PhD, 1976. Asst. prof. U. Va., Charlottesville, 1976-78; assoc. prof. Harvard U., Cambridge, Mass., 1978-83; sr. curator Ft. Worth Art Mus., 1984-86; dir. Jan Krugier Gallery, NYC, 1986-90; sr. v.p., head contemporary art dept. Christie's, NYC, 1990-95; pres. Diane Upright Fine Arts, NYC, 1995—. Author: Morris Louis: The Complete Paintings, 1979, Ellsworth Kelly: Works on Paper, 1987, various exhbn. catalogues; contbr. articles to art jours. Home: 404 S Beach Rd Hobe Sound FL 33455 Office Phone: 772-645-1230. Business E-Mail: diane@dufinearts.com.

UPSHAW, ANTHONY N., lawyer; b. Washington, July 3, 1960; BS, US Coast Guard Acad., 1982; JD, Univ. Miami, 1990. Bar: Fla. 1990, US Dist. Ct. (so., mid. dists.) Fla. 1991, US Dist. Ct. (ea. dist.) Wis., US Ct. Appeals, 11th cir. Ptnr., admiralty, maritime law, products liability def., litig. Adorno & Yoss, Miami, Fla. Former bd. dirs. Univ. Miami Sch. Law Alumni Assn. Lt. USCG, 1982—87. Mem.: Fla. Bar Assn., Dade County Bar Assn. (pres., young lawyers sect. 1995—96), ABA (bd. govs. 2006—09). Office: Adorno & Yoss Ste 400 PO Box 144008 Coral Gables FL 33114-4008 Office Phone: 305-460-1052. Office Fax: 305-460-1422. Business E-Mail: anu@adorno.com.

UPTON, B.J. (MELVIN EMANUEL UPTON), professional baseball player; b. Norfolk, Va., Aug. 21, 1984; d. Manny and Yvonne Upton. Shortstop Tampa Bay Rays (formerly Tampa Bay Devil Rays), 2004—05, third baseman, 2006—07, outfielder, 2007—12, Atlanta Braves, 2013—. Office: Atlanta Braves PO Box 4064 Atlanta GA 30302-4064

UPTON, DAVID M., finance educator, board member; b. England, 1959; BS in Engring. with honors, Cambridge U., MS in Mfg. Engring.; PhD in Indsl. Engring., Purdue U. Formerly with Unilever, IBM Corp., Deloitte & Touche Solutions; with Tube Investments Ltd., 1979—84; faculty mfg. sys. rsch. group Cambridge U., 1984—86; faculty, Albert J. Weatherhead III prof. bus. adminstrn. Harvard Business School, 1989—2009; American Std. Companies prof. ops. mgmt. Oxford U., 2009—. Bd. dirs. Tech Data Corp., 1997—. Contbr. chapters to books. Office: Tech Data Corp Bd Directors 5350 Tech Data Dr Clearwater FL 33760 Office Phone: 727-539-7429. Office Fax: 727-538-7803. Business E-Mail: david@upton.com.

UPTON, JUSTIN IRVIN, professional baseball player; b. Norfolk, Va., Aug. 25, 1987; s. Manny and Yvonne Upton. Outfielder Ariz. Diamondbacks, 2007—12, Atlanta Braves, 2013—. Recipient Nat. League Silver Slugger award, Maj. League Baseball, 2011; named to The Nat. League All-Star Team, 2009, 2011. Achievements include being the first overall pick of Major League Baseball's Amateur Draft, 2005. Office: Atlanta Braves PO Box 4064 Atlanta GA 30302

URBACH, ADAM ROBERT, chemistry professor; 1 child. BS in Chemistry, U. Tex., Austin, 1996; PhD in Chemistry, Calif. Inst. Tech., Pasadena, 2002. Postdoc. rsch. fellow Harvard U., Cambridge, Mass., 2002—04. Faculty adviser Am. Chem. Soc. Student Affiliates, Trinity U., San Antonio, 2004—; asst. prof. chemistry Trinity U., San Antonio, 2004—; vis. prof. Calif. Inst. Tech., 2011—12; vis. assoc. Calif. Tech., 2011—12. Contbr. articles to sci. jours. Recipient Dean's Honored Grad. award, Coll. Natural Sci., U. Tex., Austin, 1996, Nat. Rsch. Svc. award, NIH, 2003—04, Cottrell Coll. Sci. award, Rsch. Corp., 2006—08, Disting. Jr. Faculty award, Trinity U., 2007, NSF Career award, 2008; grad. fellowship, NSF, 1996—99, Henry Dreyfus Tchr. scholar, 2009. Mem.: Project Kaleidoscope, Coun. on Undergrad. Rsch., Am. Chem. Soc. (Outstanding Sr. award cen. Tex. divsn. 1996, student affiliate scholarship 1995), Phi Beta Kappa. Achievements include research in bioorganic chemistry and molecular recognition; artificial receptors and sensors for proteins. Avocations: snowboarding, skiing, rock climbing. Office: Trinity University Department Chemistry One Trinity Pl San Antonio TX 78212 Office Phone: 210-999-7660. Business E-Mail: adam.urbach@trinity.edu.

URBAN, JIM, metal products executive; B, LaSalle U., 1979. Sales & mgmt. positions Interstate Steel Supply Co., 1979—99; v.p. sales & mktg., Plates & Shapes group Metals USA Holding Corp., 1999—2001; regional v.p. Plates & Shapes group, gen. mgr. Langhorne Svc. Ctr. Metals USA Holdings Corp., 2001—10, v.p., Plates and Shapes Northeast, 2010—. Office: Metals USA Holdings Corp Ste 1100 1Riverway Houston TX 77056 Office Phone: 713-965-0990. Office Fax: 713-965-0067. Business E-Mail: jurban@metalsusa.com.

URBAN, KEITH, musician; b. Whangarei, New Zealand, Oct. 26, 1967; m. Nicole Kidman, June 25, 2006; children: Sunday Rose, Faith Margaret Kidman Urban. Band mem. The Ranch, Nashville, 1997—98; solo career, 1999—. Musician: (albums with The Ranch) The Ranch, 1997, (albums) Keith Urban, 1991, Keith Urban in the Ranch, 1997, Keith Urban, 1999, Golden Road, 2002, Be Here, 2004 (Album of Yr., Acad. Country Music Awards, 2005), Days Go By, 2005, Love, Pain & the Whole Crazy Thing, 2006, Greatest Hits: 18 Kids, 2007, Defying Gravity, 2009, Get Closer, 2010, The Story So Far, 2012, Fuse, 2013, (songs) Days Go By, 2004 (Video of Yr., Country Music TV Awards, 2005), You'll Think of Me, 2004 (Best Male Country Vocal Performance, Grammy Awards, 2006), Better Life, 2004 (Video of Yr., Country Music TV Awards, 2006), Stupid Boy, 2007 (Best Male Country Vocal Performance, Grammy Awards, 2008), Til Summer Comes Around, 2009 (Male Video of Yr., CMT Music Awards, 2010, Best Male County Vocal Performance, Grammy Awards, 2011), (song with Brad Paisley) Start a Band, 2008 (Vocal Event of Yr., Acad. Country Music Awards, 2009), (song with Miranda Lambert) We Were Us, 2013 (Vocal Event of Yr., Acad. Country Music Awards, 2014), (featured musician on Tim McGraw's track) Highway Don't Care, 2013 (Musical Event of Yr., Music Video of Yr., Country Music Assn. Awards, 2013, Video of Yr., Acad. Country Music Awards, 2014); judge American Idol, 2013—. Recipient ARIA award for outstanding achievement, Australian Record Industry Assn., 2001, Horizon award, Country Music Assn., 2001, Favorite County Male Artist award, Am. Music Awards, 2009, Best Male Country Vocal Performance, Grammy Awards, 2010; named Top New Male Vocalist, Acad. Country Music, 2001, 2005, Top Male Vocalist, 2006, Male Vocalist of Yr., Country Music Assn., 2004—06, Entertainer of Yr., 2005, Country Artist Yr., Radio Music Awards, 2005, Best-Selling Australian Artist, World Music Awards, 2007, Favorite Male Artist, People's Choice Awards, 2010. Office: Capital Records 3322 W End Ave Nashville TN 37203*

URBANIK, THOMAS, II, civil engineering educator, researcher; b. Oceanside, NY, Feb. 15, 1946; s. John George and Helen Rita (Waterhouse) U.; m. Cynthia Ellen Myers, Feb. 23, 1948; children: Michael T., Steven J. BS, N.Y. State Coll. Forestry, 1968; BSCE, Syracuse U., 1969; MSCE, Purdue U., 1971; PhD, Tex. A&M U., 1982. Registered profl. engr., Mich., Tex., Tenn. Traffic engr. City of Ann Arbor (Mich.), 1971-76; rsch. engr. Tex. A&M U., College Station, 1977—2001; prof., Goodrich chair of excellence in transp. U. Tenn., Knoxville, 2001—. Cons. Battelle Pacific N.W. Labs., Richland, Wash., Fed. Hwy. Adminstrn., Washington, Kittelson and Assocs., Portland, Oreg., Entergy, Buchanan, NY. Mem. ASCE, Inst. Transp. Engrs., Transp. Rsch. Bd. (assoc.). Republican. Lutheran. Office Phone: 865-974-7709, 512-535-5245. Personal E-mail: tom.urbanik@gmail.com. Business E-Mail: turbanik@utk.edu.

URBAN-KARR, JILL, insurance agent; Exec. v.p. Stewart Information Services Corp., 2010—. Office: Stewart Information Services 1980 Post Oak Blvd Ste 800 Houston TX 77056 Office Phone: 713-627-1310. Office Fax: 713-629-2244. Business E-Mail: jurban-karr@stewart.com.

URBANSKI, MICHAEL FRANCIS, federal judge; b. Livorno, Italy, Nov. 1, 1956; BA with high honors, Coll. William & Mary, 1978; JD, U. Va., 1981. Bar: Va. 1981, DC 1981, US Dist. Ct. (eastern dist.) Va. 1981, US Dist. Ct. (western dist.) Va. 1981, US Ct. Appeals, DC 1981, US Ct. Appeals (4th cir.) 1981. Law clk. to Hon. James Clinton Turk US Dist. Ct. (western dist.) Va., 1981—82; assoc. Vinson & Elkins, Washington, 1982—84, Woods Rogers, Roanoke, Va., 1984—88, prin., 1989—2004; magistrate judge US Dist. Ct. (western dist.) Va., 2004—11, judge, 2011—. Contbr. articles to law jours. Mem.: ABA (mem. Sections of Antitrust Law and Litig.), Def. Rsch. Inst., Roanoke Bar Assn., Va. Bar Assn. (mem. Civil Ligit. Sect. Coun. 1999—, Fellows Award, Young Lawyers Sect. 1992), Phi Beta Kappa. Office: US Court House PO Box 38 Roanoke VA 24038-0002 Office Phone: 540-857-5124.

URCAREY, DUANE GENE (DIGGER), astronaut; b. St. Paul, Apr. 30, 1957; m. Cheryl Ann Tobritzhofer. BSc in Aerospace Engring. & Mechanics, U. Minn., 1981, MSc in Aerospace Engring., 1982. Commn. lt. USAF, 1981, advanced through grades to lt. col., 1998; stationed at Torrejon Air Base, Spain, 1988—91; student USAF Test Pilot Sch., Edwards AFB, Calif., 1991—92; experimental test pilot Edwards AFB, 1992—96; astronaut candidate NASA, Houston, 1996—98, with spacecraft sys./ops. branch, 1998—. Pilot STS-109 Hubble Space Telescope Svc. Mission, 2002. Mem.: Air Force Assn., Nat. Space Soc., Am. Motorcyclist Assn. Avocations: motorcycling, travel, racing motocross, camping, reading science fiction. Office: Astronaut Office NASA Johnson Space Center Houston TX 77058

URESTI, CARLOS I., state legislator; b. Sept. 12, 1963; m. Yolanda Uresti; children: Carlos Jr., Michael. BA, JD, St. Mary's U. Former ptnr. Gonzales Hoblit; pvt. practice Uresti Law Firm, San Antonio; mem. Dist. 118 Tex. House of Representatives, 1997—2006; mem. Dist. 19 Tex. State Senate, 2006—. Active Southside United Against a Violent Environment, USMC Toys Tots; founding chmn. Blue Ribbon Task Force; bd. mem. South San Antonio Window Youth Found. Capt. USMC. Decorated Navy Achievement medal; recipient Patient Advocacy award, Tex. Acad. Family Physicians, 1999, San Antonio Found. Leadership award, 2005, several other awards and honors; named Legislator of Yr., Sr. Coalition Advocacy, 2003. Mem.: PiVOT, Alamo Silver Wings Airborne Assn., Am. Legion, USMC League, Family Alliance Coun. (chmn.), VFW Manuel Alvarado Post 9186 (life). Democrat. Office: Falcon International Bank 2530 SW Military Dr Ste 103 San Antonio TX 78224 also: PO Box 12068 Capitol Station Austin TX 78711 also: Maverick County Courthouse 501 Main St Ste 114 Eagle Pass TX 78852 also: 312 S Cedar Pecos TX 79772 Office Phone: 210-932-2568, 512-463-0119, 830-758-0294, 432-447-0270.

URSERY, FREDERICK STANLEY, lawyer; b. Pine Bluff, Ark., Mar. 5, 1942; s. William Stanley and Mary Charles (Lee) U.; m. Sharon Lee Davidson, Jan. 30, 1971; children: Stephen, Catherine. BA, Vanderbilt U., 1964; LLB, Columbia U., 1967. Bar: Ark. 1967, US Dist. Ct. (ea. and we. dists.) Ark. 1970, US Ct. Appeals (8th cir.) 1970. Atty. Friday, Eldredge & Clark, Little Rock, 1969—. Chmn. Pulaski County Red Cross, Little Rock, 1989-90; bd. dirs. Ouachita Girl Scout Coun., Little Rock, 1987-93, Ctrl. Ark. Libr. Bd. With arty. US Army, 1968—69, Vietnam. Fellow Am. Coll. Trial Lawyers, Am. Bar Found.; mem. State Bd. Law Examiners 1979-82, Am. Bd. Trial Advocates, Ark. Bar Assn. (exec. coun. chmn. 1989-90, pres. 2004, Outstanding Lawyer award 1996), Pulaski County Bar Assn. (pres. 1987-88), Downtown Kiwanis Club (pres. 1991-92), William R. Overton Inn of Ct. (pres. 1990-91). Democrat. Methodist. Home: 2804 N Taylor St Little Rock AR 72207-2837 Office: Friday Eldredge & Clark 2000 Regions Ctr 400 W Capitol Ave Little Rock AR 72201-3436 Office Phone: 501-370-1555. Business E-Mail: ursery@fridayfirm.com.

USEINOV, VYACHESLAV (YURI USEINOV), painter; b. Fergana, Uzbekistan, 1962; Grad., Bobruisk Coll. of Fine Arts, 1985. Numerous local and internat. exhbns., paintings and tapestries, Uzbekistan Nat. Mus. of Fine Arts, Art museums of Fergana, Samarkand, pvt. collections, France, Italy, Japan, Australia, Israel, Russia, US. Mailing: c/o Silka Gallery 7117 Enterprise Ave Mc Lean VA 22101

USHER, THOMAS JAMES, oil industry executive, former metal products executive; b. Reading, Pa., Sept. 11, 1942; s. Paul T. and Mary (Leonard) Usher; m. Sandra L. Mort, Aug. 14, 1965; children: Leanne, Jimmy, Lauren. BS in Indsl. Engring., U. Pitts., 1964, MS in Ops. and Rsch., 1965, PhD in Systems Engring., 1971. Indsl. engr. U. S. Steel Corp., Pitts., 1966—76, asst. gen. supt., 1975—78, asst. div. supt. Gary, Ind., 1978—81, asst. to pres., mng. dir. facility planning and engring. Pitts., 1982—83, v.p. engring., 1982—83, pres., 1991, US Steel Mining Co., Inc., Pitts., 1983—84, v.p. engring. steel, 1984—, sr. v.p. steel ops., 1984—, exec. v.p. heavy products steel divsn., 1986—89, pres. steel divsn., 1990; pres., COO USX Corp., Pitts., 1994—95, chmn., CEO, 1995—2001; chmn. US Steel Corp., Pitts., 2001—06. Bd. dir. PNC Fin. Svcs.; bd. dirs. PPG Industries, H.J. Heinz Co.; bd. dir., non-exec. chmn. Marathon Oil Corp., 2007—. Mem. Leadership Pitts., 1984; trustee Multiple Sclerosis, Pitts., 1985; chmn. Allegheny Trails coun. Boy Scouts Am., Pitts, 1985, United Way, Pitts., 1985, U.S.-Korea Bus. Coun., 1993—; U.S.-Japan Bus. Coun.; trustee U. Pitts., 1994—, The Bus. Roundtable Nat. Found., 1995; vice chmn. Internat. Iron and Steel Inst. Bus. Coun., 1997. Mem.: Am. Iron and Steel Engrs. (bd. dirs. 1984—85), Dinamo/Ovia (bd. dirs. 1985), Am. Iron and Steel Inst., The Club at Nevillewood, Augusta Nat. Golf Club, Burning Tree Club, Oakmont Club, Dougle Eagle Club, Laurel Valley Club, Duquesne Club, Rolling Rock Club. Avocations: golf, tennis, racquetball, scuba diving, swimming. Mailing: Marathon Oil Corp Bd Directors 5555 San Felipe Rd Houston TX 77056-2723

USHER, (USHER TERRENCE RAYMOND, IV), singer, actor; b. Dallas, Oct. 14, 1978; s. Usher Raymond III and Jonnetta (O'Neal) Patton; m. Tameka Foster, Aug. 3, 2007 (div. Nov. 4, 2009); children: Usher V, Naviyd Ely. Co-owner Cleve. Cavaliers NBA team. Singer: (albums) Usher, 1994, My Way, 1997, Live, 1999, All About U, 2000, 8701, 2001 (Best Male R&B/Soul Album, Soul Train Music Awards, 2002), Confessions, 2004 (Favorite Pop/Rock Album, Favorite Soul/R&B Album, American Music Awards, 2004, R&B/Hip Hop Album of Yr., Billboard Music Awards, 2004, Best Contemporary R&B Album, Grammy Awards, 2005, Best Male R&B/Soul Album, Soul Train Music Awards, 2005), Here I Stand, 2008, Raymond v. Raymond, 2010 (Album of Yr., Soul Train Music Awards, 2010, Favorite Soul/R&B Album, American Music Awards, 2010, Best Contemporary R&B Album,Grammy Awards, 2011, Top R&B Album, Billboard Music Awards, 2011), Looking 4 Myself, 2012, (songs) You Make Me Wanna, 1997 (Best R&B/Soul Single, Soul Train Music Awards, 1998), U Remind Me, 2001 (Best Male R&B Vocal Performance, Grammy Awards, 2002), U Don't Have to Call, 2002 (Best Male R&B Vocal Performance, Grammy Awards, 2003), (featuring Lil Jon & Ludacris) Yeah!, 2004 (BET Viewer's Choice award, 2004, Best Rap/Sung Collaboration,Grammy Awards, 2004), (with Alicia Keys) My Boo, 2004 (Best R&B/Soul Single, Group, Band or Duo, Soul Train Music Awards, 2005, Best R&B Vocal Performance By a Duo/Group, Grammy Awards, 2005, Best Collaboration, BET Awards, 2005), There Goes My Baby, 2010 (Best Male R&B Vocal Performance, Grammy Awards, 2011), (featuring will.i.am) OMG, 2010 (Top R&B Song, Billboard Music Awards, 2011), Climax, 2012 (Best R&B Performance, Grammy Awards, 2013); actor: (films) The Faculty, 1998, She's All That, 1999, Light It Up, 1999, Texas Rangers, 2001, In the Mix, 2005, Killers, 2010, Scary Movie 5, 2013, Muppets Most Wanted, 2014, Hands of Stone, 2014; featured in documentaries, prodr. Justin Bieber: Never Say Never, 2011, Justin Bieber's Believe, 2013, Undroppable, 2014; actor: (TV films) Gepetto, 2000; (TV series) Moesha, 1997—98, The Bold and the Beautiful, 1998; (Broadway plays) Chicago, 2006, (TV guest appearances) The Famous Jett Jackson, 2000, Sabrina the Teenage Witch, 2002, The Twilight Zone, 2002, American Dreams, 2002, 7th Heaven, 2002, Soul Food, 2003; vocal coach, judge (TV series) The Voice, 2013. Founder New Look. Recipient Favorite Soul/R&B Male Artist, Favorite Pop/Rock Male Artist, American Music Awards, 2004, Favorite Soul/R&B Male Artist, 2012; named Best Male R&B Artist, BET Awards, 2002, 2004, 2005, Favorite Male Singer, Nickelodeon Kids' Choice Awards, 2002, Artist of Yr., American Music Awards, 2004, Favorite Soul/R&B Male Artist, Favorite Pop/Rock Male Artist, 2008, 2011, Favorite Soul/R&B Male Artist, 2010, Artist of Yr., Billboard Music Awards, 2004, R&B/Hip-Hop Artist of Yr., 2004, Top R&B Artist, 2011, Artist of Yr., Radio Music Awards, 2004, Outstanding Male Artist, NAACP Image Awards, 2005, 2011, 2013, Favorite Male Peformer, People Choice Awards, 2005, Favorite R&B Artist, 2011, Entertainer of Yr., Soul Train Music Awards, 2005, Best Male R&B/Soul Artist, 2010. Achievements include finishing first place on the Star Search TV talent series, 1992. Mailing: c/o JPat Management 3996 Pleasantdale Rd # 104A Atlanta GA 30340*

USSERY, TERDEMA L., II, professional sports team executive; b. Watts, Calif. B in Pub. and Internat. Affairs, Princeton U., 1981; M in Govt., Harvard U., 1984; degree in law, U. Calif., Berkeley, 1987. Bus. and entertainment atty. Morrison & Foerster, LA; dep. commr., gen. counsel Continental Basketball Assn., 1990—91, commr., 1991—93; pres. Nike Sports Mgmt., 1993—97; pres., CEO Dallas Mavericks, 1997—; CEO HDNet, 2001—. Bd. dirs. Timberland Co., 2005—, TreeHouse Food, Inc., 2005—; alt. gov. NBA. Bd. trustees Princeton U., 2004—, Presbyn. Healthcare Found. Named Corp. Exec. of Yr., Black Enterprise mag., 2003; named one of Top 100 Most Powerful People in Sports, Sporting News, Top 101 Most Influential Minorities in Sports, Sports Illus. Office: Dallas Mavericks The Pavilion 2909 Taylor St Dallas TX 75226-1909 E-mail: terdema.ussery@dallasmavs.com.

UTT, WILLIAM P. (BILL UTT), construction executive; B in Mech. Engring., U. Va., 1979, M in Mech. Engring., 1980, MBA, 1984. With CRS Sirrine Engrs., Inc., 1984; various sr. mgmt. & exec. positions CRSS, Inc., 1984—95; pres., CEO North Am. Energy businesses Tractebel, 1995—2000; pres., CEO SUEZ Energy N.Am., 2000—06, KBR, Inc., 2006—, chmn., 2007—. Chmn. Electric Power Supply Assn.; mem. Nat. Petroleum Coun. Trustee Sch. Engring. and Applied Sci. U. Va.; trustee Episcopal HS, Houston. Office: KBR 601 Jefferson St Houston TX 77002 Office Phone: 713-753-2000. Office Fax: 713-753-5353.

UYS, JURGEN PETER BRINKER, securities analyst; s. Johannes Marthinus and Reinette McKay (Weidemann) U. BS, U. Pa., 1974; MBA, Columbia U., 1978. CFA. Securities analyst Equibank, N.A., Pitts., 1974-76; fin. analyst Amax Inc., Greenwich, Conn., 1978-80; v.p. Equitable Investment Mgmt., NYC, 1980-85; securities analyst Swiss Am. Securities, NYC, 1986-91; gen. ptnr. PBU Ptnrs. L.P. Ltd., Atlanta, 1991—; mng. mem. J.P. Brinker Uys & Co. LLC, Atlanta, 2004—. Mem.: CFA Inst., Huguenot Soc. Am. (treas. 1991—92), U. Club Chgo. Episcopalian.

UZAN, BERNARD, artistic director; b. Tunis, Tunisia, Dec. 5, 1944; arrived in Can., 1988; s. Henri and Elise Gabrielle (Pansieri) Uzan; m. Diana Soviero, Nov. 9, 1984. PhD, Paris U., 1968. Gen. & artistic dir. Théâtre français d'Amérique, Boston, 1973-83, Tulsa Opera, 1987-88, L'Opéra de Montreal, 1988—2001; stage dir. Palm Beach Opera, Fla., 2003—. Adminstr., exec. dir. Alliance français de Boston, 1974—83; stage dir. U.S., San Francisco, Fla., Phila., New Orleans, Portland, Dallas; stage dir. Can., Montreal, Toronto, Vancouver, Quebec City, Edmonton, Calgary; stage dir. europe, Monte-Carlo, Zurich, Palermo, Turin; stage dir. in charge internat. affairs Eurolyrica, 1997—; bd. dirs. Opera Am. Address: PO Box 8143 Englewood NJ 07631 Office: Palm Beach Opera 415 S Olive Ave West Palm Beach FL 33401 E-mail: odm@total.net.

UZMAN, BETTY BEN GEREN, retired pathologist; b. Ft. Smith, Ark., Nov. 17, 1922; d. Benton Asbury and Myra Estelle (Petty) Geren; m. L. Lahut Uzman, Dec. 17, 1955 (dec.); 1 dau., Betty Tuba. Student, Ft. Smith Jr. Coll., 1939—40; BS, U. Ark., 1942; MD, Washington U., 1945; postgrad., MIT, 1948—50; MA (hon.), Harvard U., 1968. Intern Childrens Hosp., Boston, 1945—46; resident pathology Barnes Hosp., St. Louis, 1946—48; Am. Cancer Soc. rsrch. fellow MIT, Cambridge, 1948—50; chief biol. ultra structure and exptl. pathology Children's Cancer Rsch. Found., Boston, 1950—71; instr. Harvard Med. Sch., Boston, 1949—53, assoc., 1953—56, rsch. assoc., 1956—67, assoc. prof., 1967—71, prof., 1971-72; head rsch. dept. Sparks Regional Med. Ctr., Ft. Smith, 1972—74; prof. pathology La. State U., Shreveport, 1974—77, U. Tenn., Memphis, 1978—89, ret., 1989. Assoc. chief staff rsch. VA, Shreveport, 1974-77; staff pathologist VA, Memphis, 1978-89, chief lab. svc., 1986-87; chief field ops., spl. asst. to dir. VA Ctrl. Office, Washington, 1978-79, dir. med. rsch. svcs., 1979-80; chmn. pathology A Study sect. NIH, 1973-76; cons. to sci. dir. Children's Cancer Rsch. Found., Boston, 1971-73; mem. adv. com. on prevention, diagnosis and treatment Am. Cancer Soc., 1970-73, 77-80; mem. adv. bd. Office Regeneration Rsch., VA, 1985-89; disting. vis. investigator Inst. Venezolano Investigation Cientificas, Caracas, 1972-74 Decorated Order Andres Bello 1st class Venezuela; recipient Weinstein award United Cerebral Palsy, 1964 Mem. AAAS, Am. Soc. Cell Biology (emerita), Microscopy Soc. Am. (emerita, Diatome poster award 1985), Internat. Acad. Pathology (emerita), Am. Assn. Neuropathology (emerita, assoc.), Soc. Neurosci. (emerita), Am. Assn. Cancer Rsch. (emerita). Home and Office: Geren Farm 16048 E State Hwy 197 Scranton AR 72863-0048 Personal E-mail: bettyguzman@centurytel.net.

UZOIGWE, GODFREY NWANORUO, history professor, consultant, researcher; b. Owerri, Nigeria, Sept. 25, 1938; came to U.S., 1970; s. Thompson and Esther U.; m. Patricia Marie Josephine Cahill, Feb. 15, 1964; children: Emeka Anthony, Amaechi Charles, Jaja Ndidi. BA in History with honors, Univ. Coll., Dublin, Ireland, 1963; higher diploma edn., Trinity Coll., Dublin, 1964; DPhil in Modern History, Christ Church, Oxford U., Eng., 1967. Lectr. history Makerere U., Kampala, Uganda, 1967-70; from asst. prof. history to prof. U. Mich., Ann Arbor, Mich., 1970—75, prof. history, 1975—84; prof., head history U. Calabar, Nigeria, 1981—87, dean Faculty of Arts, 1984—87; dean Coll. Humanities and Social Studies Imo State U., 1987—99; head, dept. history Miss. State U., 1999—2005. Acad. humanist Guardians Inc., Detroit, 1979-81, 99-2005; dir. African Inst. for Study of Human Values, Accra, Ghana, 1980—87; vis. prof. history U. Nigeria, Nsaukka, 1976-77, Tulano U., 1988-99, Cornell U., 1989-90, Lincoln U., 1997-98. Author: Revolution and Revolt in Bunyoro Kitara, 1970, Britain and the Conquest of Africa, 1974, Uganda: The Dilemma of Nationhood, 1982, Africa: Historical Essays, 1984, A Short History of South Africa, 1988, History and Democracy in Nigeria, 1990, Visions of Nationhood: Prelude to the Nigerian Civil War, 1960-1967; editor: Anatomy of An African Kingdom, 1973, International Ethnic and Religious Conflict Resolution in Nigeria, 1999, Foundations of Nigerian Federals, Vol. 2, 1996, Troubled Journey: Nigeria Since the Civil War, 2004. Chief Ezeugoma of Umunoha Nigeria, 1976, Chief Ugochinyere of Ubomini, 1995. Fellow Royal African Soc., Hist. Soc. Nigeria, Hist. Soc. Ghana, Hist. Soc. Kenya, African Studies Assn., Am. Hist. Assn., Smithsonian Instn., Oxford Union Soc. Clubs: Research of Mich. (Ann Arbor); Nigerian U. Staff Sports (chmn. 1982-83). Roman Catholic. Home: 203 Williamsburg Dr Starkville MS 39759 Office: Mississippi State U Dept of History PO Box H Mississippi State MS 39762 Home Phone: 662-323-8475; Office Phone: 662-325-3604. Business E-Mail: guzoigwe@history.msstate.edu.

VACA, NINA G. (XIMENA G. HUMRICHOUSE), management consultant, lawyer; b. 1971; Attended, Northwestern U.; BA in Speech Comm. & Bus. Adminstrn., Tex. State U.; LLD (hon.), Northwood U.; Corp. Governance Exec. Program, Harvard U.; Advanced Mgmt. Edn. Program, Dartmouth Coll. Founder Pinnacle Technologies Resources, Inc., 1996, chmn. CEO, 1996—; chmn., CEO Vaca Industries, Inc., 1999—. Bd. dirs. Comerica Inc., 2008—, Kohl's Corp., 2010—. Mem. Brit.-Am. Project, Youth President's Orgn., Dallas Summit. Named Youngest Disting. Alumna, Tex. State U.; recipient Entrepreneur of the Yr. award, Ernst & Young, 2005; named one of The 50 Most Important Hispanics in Bus. & Tech., Hispanic Engring. Technology Mag., The 100 Most Influential Hispanics in America, Latino Leaders Mag., Top 25 Women Bus. Builders, Fast Co. Mag. Office: Pinnacle Technical Resources Inc Ste 215 1230 River Bend Dr Dallas TX 75247 Office Phone: 214-740-2424. Business E-Mail: nina@pinnacle1.com.

VACAR, RICHARD M., airport executive; BS, MBA, Calif. State U.; JD, Loyola Marymount U. Dir. Dept. Aviation Houston Airport Sys.; also dir. aviation Ellington Field, Bush Intercontinental Airport (Houston), William P. Hobby Airport. Office: Houston Airport Sys 16930 JFK Blvd Houston TX 77032

VACHON, REGINALD IRENEE, mechanical engineer; b. Norfolk, Va., Jan. 29, 1937; s. Rene Albert Vachon and Regina (Galvin) Radcliffe; m. Mary Eleanor Grigg, Jan. 16, 1960; children: Reginald Irenee, Eleanor Marie. Student, U.S. Naval Acad., 1954-55; BME, Auburn U., 1958, MS, 1960; PhD, Okla. State U., 1963; LLB, Jones Law Sch., 1969. Registered profl. engr., Ala., Ga., Miss., La., Wis., Tex., chartered engr., U.K., cert. d'Iugenieur Mecanicien, France, lic. engr., European Fedn. Nat. Engring. Assns.; bar: Ala. 1971. Engr. Hayes Internat., 1958; instr., rsch. asst. Auburn U., 1958-60, rsch. assoc., 1961, assoc., prof., 1963-78; R&D engr. E.I. DuPont, 1960; aerospace engr., technologist NASA Marshall Space Flight Ctr., summers, 1964, 65; pres. Vachon Nix & Assoc., 1977—, VNA Sys. Inc., 1982—. COO Thacker Constrn. Co., Thacker Orgn., Inc., 1981—90, United Info. Techs., Inc., Global Interated Techs. Inc.; pres., CEO Compris Tech., Inc., 1991—92; chmn. Global Risk Mgr., Inc., 1992—, Direct Measurements, Inc., 2002—; prin. Gipco Holdings Internat., Ltd., 1994—2008; mem. sci. tech. adv. com. U.S. Dept. Homeland Security. Contbr. articles to profl. jours. With US Army, 1960—61. Fellow: ASCE, AIAA (assoc.), Singapore Instn. Engrs., Hong Kong Instn. Engrs., Instn. Mech. Engrs. U.K.; mem.: NSPE, ABA, ASME (hon.; pres. 2003—04), UN Rels. Com. for World Fedn. Engring. Orgn. (chair), Am. Assn. Engring. Socs. (chair 2010—12), N. Am. Pan Am. Assn. Engring. Socs. (v.p.), Soc. Frances des Mecaniciens, Ala. Bar Assn., Pan Am. Acad. Engring. (treas.), Phoenix Soc. Atlanta, Peachtree Racket Club, N.Y. Yacht Club, Cosmos Club. Roman Catholic. Achievements include patents in field. Home: 1414 Epping Forest Dr NE Atlanta GA 30319-2539 Office: PO Box 190093 Atlanta GA 31119-0093 Office Phone: 404-388-6588. Business E-Mail: vachonr@asme.org, rvachon@directheascre.com.

VACIK, STEPHEN M., dean; b. Fargo, ND, Dec. 31, 1968; s. James P. and Dorothy Nobles Vacik; m. Candace L. Fleming; children: Walter P., Michael C. PhD, U. Ala., Tuscaloosa, 1997. Assoc. dean Bevill State CC, Fayette, Ala., 1996—2004; academic dean East Miss. CC, Mayhew, 2004—. County chair Am. Cancer Soc., Fayette, 2002—03; bd. mem. C. of C., Fayette, 2002—04; com. mem. Fayette Area Econ. Planning, 2002—04. Named Bd. Mem. of Yr., Fayette Area C. of C., 2002. Office: East MS CC 8731 South Frontage Rd PO Box 100 Mayhew MS 39753

VADEN, WILLIAM R., oil industry executive, councilman; b. Grapeland, Tex., Apr. 7, 1948; Attended, Del Mar Coll., 1973. Asst. warehouse mgr. Texaco Inc., 1969—74; sr. field supr. SGS Control Svcs., 1978—87; CEO, pres. VIP Cargo Surveys, Inc., 1987—; councilman City of Ingleside, 1999—2000, 2006—, mayor, 2000—04. Voting mem. Am. Petroleum Inst., 1988—2006. Cpl. USMC, 1965—69. Mem.: Disabled Am. Veterans, Veterans Fgn. Wars, Am. Soc. Testing and Measurement, Navy League, Am. Legion. Republican. Office: 2043 La Quinta Ingleside TX 78362

VAHIDI, VIRASB, air transportation executive; b. Tehran, Iran, Feb. 24, 1967; s. Manouchehr and Delara (Sarafi) V. BS, U. Calif., San Diego, 1988; MBA, Ecole Nationale des Ponts et Chaussées, 1994. Engr. Eastman Kodak Co., San Diego, 1989; joined American Airlines, Inc., 1994, mng. dir. internat. planning, 1998—2000, mng. dir. airline profitability & fin. analysis, 2000—02, sr. v.p. planning, 2009, chief comml. officer, 2009—; v.p. corp. planning and investor rels. to sr. v.p. corp. strategy and development AT&T Inc. (merger of SBC Communications & AT&T Corp.), 2002—06; COO, bd. dirs. Phorm. Mem. Persian Club, L'Alliance Francaise, Biomed. Engring. Soc. Avocations: travel, skiing, reading, computers. Office: American Airlines Inc 4333 Amon Carter Blvd Fort Worth TX 76155 Office Phone: 817-963-1234. Office Fax: 817-967-4162.

VAIL, CHARLES STEWART, retail executive, lawyer; BS, Miss. State U., 1964; JD, U. Miss., 1966. Bar: Miss. 1966. Joined Fred's, Inc., 1968, sec., v.p. legal svcs. Memphis, 1973, gen. counsel, 1973—, corp. sec., 1975—, sr. v.p., legal svcs., 2006—. Office: Fred's Inc 4300 New Getwell Rd Memphis TN 38118 also: 4300 New Getwell Rd Memphis TN 38118 Office Phone: 901-365-8880. Office Fax: 901-328-0354. Business E-Mail: cvail@fredsinc.com.

VAIO, BRUCE A., construction executive; BA in Polit. Sci., U. Denver; MBA, U. Phoenix. V.p. regional mgr. Western Mobile Inc., Denver, 1994—96; pres., CEO Redland Stone Products Co., 1996—98, pres. S.W. divsn., 1999—2006; sr. v.p. Martin Marietta Materials, Inc., 2005, pres. S.W. divsn., 2005—06, exec. v.p., 2005—, pres. Martin Marietta Materials West San Antonio, 2006—. Office: Martin Marietta Materials Inc 2710 Wycliff Rd Raleigh NC 27607 Office Phone: 919-781-4550. Office Fax: 919-783-4695.

VALCÁRCEL, MARTA IRIS, pediatric educator; b. Santurce, P.R., Mar. 26, 1931; d. Jose and Solveida (Teruel) V. BS, U. P.R., 1951, MD, 1955. Diplomate Am. Bd. Pediatrics. Intern, then resident Kings County Hosp., NYC, 1955-58; fellow in neonatology Columbia Presbyn. Med. Ctr., 1968; chief perental neonatal sects. and neonatal ICU U. P.R. Sch. Medicine, San Juan, 1968—2014, pediat. dept. chmn., 1977—96; prof., chmn. dept. pediatrics U. P.R. Sch. Medicine Neonatal Care Unit, San Juan, 1977—2011; assoc. dean for clin. affairs U. P.R. Sch. Medicine, San Juan, 1976-77; exec. dir. Univ. Children's Hosp., San Juan, 1980-86; dir. newborn svcs. U. Dist. Hosp., San Juan, 1967-78, 91, pres. med. staff, 1975-76. Mem. Am. Pediatric Soc., Am. Acad. Pediatrics, So. Soc. Pediatric Rsch., PR Med. Assn. Roman Catholic.

VALE, FERNANDO LUIS, medical educator; b. San Juan, San Juan, PR, Dec. 8, 1965; s. Jose Luis Vale and Carmen Dalila Diaz; m. Lynda M. Vale, June 8, 1991; children: Gabriela, Fernando. BS with magna cum laude, U. P.R., 1987, MD, 1991. Cert. bd. cert. neurosurgery. Intern U. Ala. Hosps., Birmingham, 1991—92, resident in neurosurgery, 1992—97; asst. prof. U. South Fla., Tampa, 1997—2004, assoc. prof., 2004—10, prof., 2010—, prof. neurosurgery, 2011—. Residency program dir., neurosurgery U. of South Fla. Contbr. articles to profl. jours. Recipient Thompson Best Tchr. award, Dept Neurosurgery, U. South Fla., 2008—09, Honor's Dean List; named Best Doctors in America; Clin. fellowship, Congress Neurol. Surgeons, 1997. Mem.: AMA, Southern Neurol. Soc., Tampa Bay L.Am. Med. Soc., Am. Epilepsy Soc., Congress Neurol. Surgeons Stereotactic and Functional Neurosurgery, Am. Assn. Neurol. Surgeons, America's Registry Outstanding Profls., Alpha Omega Alpha. Office: USF Health 7th Fl 2 Tampa Gen Cir Tampa FL 33606 Office Phone: 813-259-0605. Business E-Mail: fvale@health.usf.edu.*

VALENTINE, ALAN DARRELL, performing company executive, conductor; b. San Antonio, July 18, 1958; s. Lonnie Darrell Jr. and Marjorie (Childs) V.; m. Jari Ann Ruhl, Aug. 10, 1979 (div. 1987); children: Brandon Darrell, Chelsea Michelle; m. Karen Kay Bingham, Oct. 21, 1989 (div. 2001); 1 child, Nathan Lee; m. Connie Linsler, July 21, 2002. MusB, U. Houston, 1981. Orch. mgr. U. Houston Symphony, 1977-81; gen. mgr. Mid-Columbia Symphony Soc., Richland, Wash., 1981-83, Greensboro (N.C.) Symphony Soc., 1983-85; orch. mgr. Symphony Soc. San Antonio, 1985-87; mng. dir. Chattanooga Symphony and Opera, 1987-88; exec. dir. Okla. Philharm. Soc., Oklahoma City, 1988-98, Nashville Symphony, 1998—. Mem. adj. faculty Arts Administrn., Oklahoma City U., 1992— Recs. include Best of Greensboro Symphony Orchestra Silver Season, 1983, A Christmas Festival-San Antonio Symphony, 1986, A Time of Healing-Oklahoma City Philharmonic, 1995; (CD) Howard Hanson The Nashville Symphony, 2000, Charles Ives The Nashville Symphony, 2000, George Whitefield Chadwick-Nashville Symphony, 2002, Bernstein's West Side Story, Nashville Symphonyh, 2002, Amy Beach Gaelic Symphony, Nashville Symphony, 2003, Beethoven's Missa Solemnis, 2004, Elliott Carter: Piano Concerto, 2004; TV prodns. include Music of the Americas-Placido Domingo with San Antonio Symphony, 1986, Perry Como Christmas Special-San Antonio Symphony, 1986, Sagebrush Symphony-Oklahoma City Philharmonic with Michael Martin Murphey, 1996, Kathie Lee: Just In Time for Christmas-Okla. City Philharmonic & Guests, 1996, Martina McBride Christmas Special Nashville, Symphony and Guests, 1998. Bd. dirs. Classen Sch. for Artistically and Academically Gifted, 1995-98, Arts Festival Okla., 1991-. Mem. NARAS (bd. dirs. 2002-), Am. Symphony Orch. League (bd. dirs. Cmty. and Urban Symphony Orch. divsn. 1981-83, policy com. A 1995-98, chmn. group III mgrs. 1996-98, vice chmn. group III mgr. 2003), Rotary, Phi Mu Alpha. Presbyterian. Avocations: computers, racquetball, reading. Office: Nashville Symphony 1 Symphony Pl Nashville TN 37201-2031 Personal E-mail: alandv@aol.com. Business E-Mail: alandv@nashvillesymphony.org.

VALENTINE, KENNETH T., energy and services company executive; Various mgmt. positions in supply planning & transp. svcs. Piedmont Natural Gas Co., Inc., 1996—, dir. fed. regulatory & transp. svcs., then mng. dir. planning & project mgmt., 2006—09, v.p. bus. devel. & carbon mgmt. strategies, 2009—. Office: Piedmont Natural Gas PO Box 33068 4720 Piedmont Row Dr Charlotte NC 28210 Office Phone: 704-364-3120. Office Fax: 704-365-3849.

VALK, HENRY S(NOWDEN), physicist, researcher; b. Washington, Jan. 26, 1929; s. Henry Snowden and Dorothy (Blencowe) V.; m. Gillian Wedderburn; children: Alison, Diana, Robert, Richard. BS, George Washington U., 1953, MS (Agnes and Eugene Meyer scholar), 1954; postgrad., Johns Hopkins, 1953-54; PhD (Shell fellow), Washington U., St. Louis, 1957. Profl. asst. NSF, 1957, asst. program dir. physics, 1959-60; asst. prof. physics U. Oreg., 1957-59; mem. faculty U. Nebr., 1960-70, prof. physics, 1964-70, chmn. dept., 1966-70; prof. physics Coll. Scis. and Liberal Studies, Ga. Inst. Tech., Atlanta, 1970—, acting dir. physics, 1991-96, dean, 1970-82. Cons. physics sect. NSF, 1961-62, program dir. theoretical physics, 1965-66; vis. prof. U. Frankfurt/Main, Germany, 1970, Rensselaer Poly. Inst., 1982, 88, Cath. U. Am., 1982-83, 88-89. Author: (with M. Alonso) Quantum Mechanics: Principles and Applications, 1973; contbr. articles to profl. jours. Decorated Most Excellent Order Brit. Empire. Fellow Am. Phys. Soc.; mem. Am. Math. Soc., Am. Assn. Physics Tchrs., Math. Assn. Am., Cosmos Club (Washington), Phi Beta Kappa, Sigma Xi. Office: Sch Physics Ga Inst Tech Atlanta GA 30332-0430 Business E-Mail: henry.valk@physics.gatech.edu.

VALLAS, PAUL G., school system administrator; b. June 10, 1953; m. Sharon Vallas; children: Paul, Gus, Mark. BA in Polit. Sci. & History, We. Ill. U., 1976, MA in Polit. Sci., 1980. Policy adv. to Elementary & Secondary Edn. & Appropriations Com. Ill. State Senate; exec. dir. Ill. Econ. Fiscal Com., 1985—90; revenue dir. City of Chgo., 1990—93, budget dir., 1993—95; CEO Chgo. Pub. Schools Sys., 1995—2001, Phila. Pub. Schools Sys., 2002—07; supt. Recovery Sch. Dist., New Orleans, 2007—. Office: La Dept Edn Recovery Sch Dist PO Box 94064 Baton Rouge LA 70804

VALLEJO, FRANCES M., oil industry executive; b. Pueblo, Colo. BS in Mineral Engring. Math., Colo. Sch. Mines, 1987; MBA in Fin. and Internat. Mgmt., Rice U., Houston, 1996. Geophysicist Exploration & Prodn. Phillips Petroleum Co., Bartlesville, Okla., 1987—91, with seismic interpretation Bellaire, Tex., 1991—93, with gas supply reporting, 1993—94, fin. assoc. treasury Bartlesville, 1996—99, mgr. strategic transactions, 1999—2001; asst. treas. ConocoPhillips, 2001—04, v.p. upstream planning & portfolio mgmt., 2004—07, gen. mgr. corp. planning and budgets, 2007—08, v.p., treas., 2008—. Chmn. bd. dirs. 66 Fed. Credit Union, mem. bd. dirs.; grad. Ctr. for Houston's Future Leadership Forum, 2007. Office: ConocoPhillips 600 North Dairy Ashford Rd PO Box 2197 Houston TX 77079

VALOIS, ROBERT ARTHUR, lawyer; b. NYC, May 13, 1938; s. Frank Jacob and Harriet Frances (LaCroix) V.; m. Ruth Emilie Skacil, Dec. 23, 1961; children: Marguerite Jeannette, Robert Arthur Jr. BBA, U. Miami, 1962; JD, Wake Forest U., 1972. Bar: N.C. 1972, Fla. 1972, U.S. Ct. Appeals (4th cir.) 1973, U.S. Dist. Ct. (ea. and mid. dists.) 1974, U.S. Supreme Ct. 1975, U.S. Ct. Appeals (6th cir.) 1986. Field examiner NLRB, Winston-Salem, NC, 1962-70; from assoc. to ptnr. Maupin, Taylor & Ellis, P.A., Raleigh, NC, 1972—, chmn. labor and employment sect., 1972-97, chmn. bd. dirs., pres., 1997—2002. Vice chmn. Legal Svcs. Corp., Washington, 1984-90, bd. dirs. Served with USN, 1956-59. Mem. Greater Raleigh C. of C. (chmn. fed. govt. com. 1991—). Democrat. Presbyterian. Home: 3952 Bentley Bridge Rd Raleigh NC 27612 Office: Williams Mullen Maupin Taylor PA PO Box 1000 Raleigh NC 27602-1000 Office Phone: 919-981-4000. E-mail: rvalois@maupintaylor.com.

VALVO, BARBARA-ANN, lawyer, surgeon; b. Elizabeth, NJ, June 7, 1949; d. Robert Richad and Vera (Kovach) V. BA in Biology, Hofsta U., 1971; MD, Pa. State U., 1975; JD, Loyola Sch. Law, New Orleans, 1993. Bar: La. 1993; diplomate Am. Bd. Surgery. Surg. intern Nassau County Med. Ctr., East Meadow, NY, 1975-76; resident gen. surgery Allentown-Sacred Heart Med. Ctr., Pa., 1976-80; asst. chief surgery USPHS, New Orleans, 1980-81; pvt. practice gen. surgery New Orleans, 1981-89; pvt. practice med. malpractice law, 1995—. Upjohn scholar, 1975. Fellow ACS; mem. ABA, Fed. Bar Assn., La. Bar Assn., La. Trial Lawyers Assn. Republican. Avocations: computers, raising animals. Office: 41 Harley Pl Willow Spring NC 27592 Personal E-mail: bavalvo@nc.rr.com.

VAN AKEN, JOHN HENRY, retired marine engineer; b. Haarlem, Netherlands, Sept. 26, 1922; arrived in U.S., 1952; s. Antony and Maria Petronella (Renzen) van Aken; m. Hendrika A. Bonneur, Sept. 25, 1947 (div. Feb. 1960); 1 child, Antony Laurens; m. Helen Jemison Waterman, July 17, 1962 (dec. Feb. 1978); m. Marilyn McDaniel, July 13, 1980 (dec. Sept. 2001). Marine Engr., Acad. Tech. Sci. and Arts of Design, 1940. Asst. mgr. repair dept. Wilton-Feyenoord Dockyards, Schiedam, Netherlands, 1945—52; supt. machinery Ala. Dry Dock & Shipbldg. Co., Mobile, 1958—60; mgr. project Kerr-McGee Oil Industries, Oklahoma City, 1954—58, 1960—63; insp. George Sharp Co., Naval Architects, Newport News, Va., 1960; pres. John H. van Aken Co. Inc., Marine Surveyors and Cons. Inc., Mobile, 1963—99; ret., 2002. Non-exclusive surveyor Panama Bur. Shipping, Internat. Cargo Gear Bur., Registr. Italiano Navale, Lloyd's Register of Shipping, Westminister Village Found., Inc., dir. Decorated comdr. Order Good Hope, South Africa; Paul Harris fellow Rotary. Mem. Soc. Naval Architects and Marine Engrs., Nat. Assn. Marine Surveyors, Netherlands Soc. Marine Technologists, Rotary Home: 302 S Georgia Ave Mobile AL 36604-2300 Personal E-mail: jhvanaken@wvsf.org.

VAN ANTWERP, ROBERT L., JR., retired military officer; b. Benton Harbor, Mich., Jan. 27, 1950; m. Paula Eberly; children: Jeff, Luke, Rob, Julia, Kathryn. BS, US Mil. Acad., 1972; MME, U. Mich.; MBA, LI U. Registered Profl. Engr., Va. Commd. 2d. lt. US Army, 1972, advanced through grades to lt. gen., 2007, platoon leader, 76th Engr. Battalion Fort Meade, Md., 1973—74; exec. officer 65th Engr. Battalion, 25th Infantry Div. Schofield Barracks, Hawaii, 1975—76, asst. div. engr. Hawaii, 1976—79, exec. officer 84th Engr. Battalion, 45th Gen. Support Group Hawaii, 1985—87; chief mil. construction US Army Western Command, Fort Shafter, Hawaii, 1987—88; exec. officer Office of Chief of Engrs. US Army, Washington, 1988—89; comdr. 326th Engr. Battalion, 101st Airborne Div., Fort Campbell, Ky., 1989—91; dist. comdr. LA Dist. US Army CE, LA, 1992—94, chief of staff Washington, 1994—95, comdr. South Atlantic Div. Atlanta, 1996—98; exec. asst. to vice chmn. Joint Chiefs of Staff US Dept. Def., Washington, 1995—96; dir. Office of Competitive Sourcing, Office of Asst. Sec. of Army US Army, Washington, 1998—99, asst. chief staff installation mgmt., 1999—2002; comdr. US Army Maneuver Support Ctr., 2002—04; chief US Army Accessions Command, Fort Knox, Ky., 2004—07; chief engineers, commdg. gen. US Army CE, Washington, 2007—11. Instr., mech. engring. US Mil. Acad., West Point, NY, 1981—82, asst. prof., exec. officer, 1982—84; commdg. gen. US Army Engr. Sch., Fort Leonard Wood, Mo. Pres. Officers' Christian Fellowship. Decorated Defense Superior Svc. Medal, Legion of Merit, Bronze Star Medal, Meritorious Svc. Medal.

VAN ARSDALE, CORBIN, state legislator; b. Dec. 17; m. Jacqueline Van Arsdale. Vice chmn. Urban Affairs Com.; mem. Ins. Com., Tex. State House, 2000; state rep. Dist. 130 Tex., 2002—. Republican. Office: State Capitol Rm EXT E1-412 PO Box 2910 Austin TX 78768 Mailing: 12777 Jones Rd Ste 175 Houston TX 77070 Office Phone: 512-463-0661. Fax: 512-463-5896.

VANATTA, BOB, athletic administrator; b. Columbia, Mo., July 7, 1918; s. Claude W. and Viola (Toler) V.; m. Lois A. Williams; children: Robert, Thomas, Timothy. BA, Ctrl. Meth. Coll., 1942; MEd, U. Mo., 1949. Tchr., coach Boonville (Mo.) High Sch., 1942-43, Kemper Mil. Sch., Boonville, 1943-44, Springfield (Mo.) High Sch., 1944-47; tchr., dir. athletics, coach Ctrl. Meth. Coll., Fayette, Mo., 1947-50, S.W. Mo. State U., Springfield, 1950-53, coach two NAIA champions, 1950—53; coach U.S. Mil. Acad., West Point, NY, 1953-54; dir. athletics, coach Bradley U., Peoria, Ill., 1954—56; tchr., coach Memphis State U., 1956-62, U. Mo., Columbia, 1962-68; bank mktg. officer Empire Bank, Springfield, 1968-71; profl. basketball exec. dir. Memphis Pros, 1971-72; tchr., coach Delta State U., Cleve., 1972-73; dir. athletics Oral Roberts U., Tulsa, 1973-77; commr. Ohio Valley Athletic Conf., Nashville, 1977-80, Trans Am. Athletic Conf., Shreveport, La., 1980-83; dir. athletics La. Tech. U., Rustin, 1983-86; commr. Sunshine State Athletic Conf., Jupiter, Fla., 1986-94. Assoc. dir athletics Fla. Atlantic U., coach basketball Ctrl. Meth. Coll., 1942, adv. com. mem., Roger Dean Stadium, 2000-. Author: Coaching Pattern Play Basketball, 1959; contbr. articles to profl. jours. Mem. Nat. Football Found. Hall of Fame Chpt., bd. mem., 2008 Named to Ctrl. Meth. Coll. Hall of Fame, S.W. Mo. State U. Hall of Fame, Nat. Athletic Intercollegiate Assn. Hall of Fame, Greater Springfield Hall of Fame, John Q. Hammons Mo. Sports Hall of Fame, U. Memphis Hall of Fame, Nat. Assn. Collegiate Dir. of Athletics, Nat. Assn. Collegiate Dir. of Athletics Hall of Fame, 1997, Helms Hall of Fame, Palm Beach Athletes Hall of Fame, 2007; recipient Lifetime Achievement award in football All-Am. Football Found., 1997, NCAA Divsn. II Commrs. award Merit, 1999, Champions of Character award NAIA, 2002, Coach of Yr., 1952, 53, Italian Am. Coach of Yr. 1953, numerous others. Mem. Nat. Assn. Basketball Coaches, Am. Football Coaches Assn., Nat. Assn. Collegiate Dirs. Athletics, All Am. Football Found. (Bud Dudley Outstanding Exec. award in Football, 2000, Asa Bushnell Commr. award 2001), Palm Beach County Sports Commn., Lou Groza, PBCS (mem. Hall of Fame Com.). Office: 300 N Highway A/A Bldg #F Unit #403 Jupiter FL 33477 Office Phone: 561-743-9763.

VANATTA, JASON MICHAEL, physician, educator; MD, MCP Hahnemann U., Phila., 2000. Diplomate Am. Bd. Surgery, 2006. Transplant surgeon, asst. prof., surgery Meth. U. Hosp. Transplant Inst., U. Tenn., Memphis, 2007—. Office: Methodist University Hosp Transplant Inst 1211 Union Ave Ste 340 Memphis TN 38104 Office Fax: 901-516-8993.*

VAN BEBBER, DAVID L., food products executive, lawyer; b. Hiawatha, Kans., May 10, 1956; m. Sue Van Bebber; 4 children. BA, U. Ark., 1978, JD, 1981. Bar: Ark. 1982. Sr. v.p., dir. legal svcs., dep. gen. counsel Tyson Foods, Inc., Springdale, Ark., 1998—2008, exec. v.p., gen. counsel, 2008—. Pres. Ark. Bd. Edn., Springdale; active St. Thomas Episcopal Ch., Springdale. Mem.: ABA, Ark. Bar Assn. Office: Tyson Foods Inc 2210 W Oakland Dr Springdale AR 72762-6999*

VANBUTSEL, MICHAEL R., real estate broker, construction executive; b. Alma, Nebr., Dec. 7, 1952; s. Julius and Margaret (McCorkle) VanB.; m. Susan Parsons; children: Krysta, Alexis. BArch, U. Nebr., 1975. Lic. real estate broker Fla. V.p. devel. J.C. Nichols Co. Real Estate, St. Petersburg, Fla., 1987-96; pres. North Star Devel., St. Petersburg, 1996—; real estate mgr., designated broker Danka Office Imaging, 1998-99; v.p., project exec. Beers Skanska USA Bldg. Co., Tampa, Fla., 1999—2004; project mgr. Tower divsn. Taylor Woodrow Cmtys., 2004—06; v.p. The Beach Residences Condominiums The Ritz Carlton Beach Club, 2004—06; sr. project mgr. tower divsn. WCI Cmtys. Inc., Palm Beach Gardens, Fla., 2006—08, sr. project mgr., resort singer island one bal harbour resort Rybovich Marina; project dir. BE&K Bldg. Group, Ft. Lauderdale, 2008—11; project exec. DPR Constrn. Sci. & Tech. Builder. Chair Environ. Devel. Commn., St. Petersburg, 2003-04; chair cmty. advancement coun. U. So. Fla., St. Petersburg, 1998—2004, Co-Chair of BioFlorida Tampa Bay, Chief of Staff, Regional Rsch. Coun. Tampa Bay, St Pete Chamber Govt. Affairs Com., BioFla. Govt. Affairs Com. Housing commr. City of Phoenix; mem. Paradise Valley Planning Com.; bd. dirs. Cmty. Water Leadership Program; chmn. facilities and strategic planning com. U. South Fla., St. Petersburg, 1999—2002, chmn. acad. planning com.; bd. dirs. Pinellas Econ. Devel. Coun.; vice-chair environ. adv. com. S.W. Fla. Water Mgmt. Dist., 2002—; Pinellas adv. bd. ARC; allocations com. United Way, 1998—2000; mem. Real Estate Investment Coun., St. Petersburg USA and Russia Birthday Commemoration, 2002—03, Pinellas County Transp. Task Force, Pinellas Redevel. Task Force; mem. CEO search com. U. South Fla., St. Petersburg; chair legis. affairs com. devel. coun. All Children's Hosp.; life sci. task force Tampa Hillsborough EDC; with Pinellas County Economic Devel. Coun.; co-chair Bio Fla. Tampa Bay regional rsch. Coun.; pres. Mariners for Sen. John McCain, Ariz.; surrogate spkr. for Congressman Eldon Rudd; mem. Senate roundtable Sen. Connie Mack, Fla.; Westside campaign chair Rick Baker for Mayor, 2001; mem. Ivory Club Pinellas County Rep. Party, 2001—05, Pinellas County Assembly, 2002; bd. dirs. Gran Prix St. Petersburg 2003 Found. Mem. Fla. Gulfcoast Comml. Assn. Realtors, Pinellas Leadership (mem. selection com. 2003), Leadership Tampa Bay, St. Petersburg C. of C. (chair environ. com., chair transp. com.), Valley Leadership (Phoenix), Precinct Com., Martin County, Fla., 2007, Martin Crossings (pres. 2007-), Hoa, Stuart, Fla., Country Meadows HOA Security Com., COAA Fla., Real Estate Investment Coun. Conservative. Protestant. Avocations: geo-political books, tai chi, languages. Office: DPR Constrn Ste 820 One North Dale herby Hwy Tampa FL 33609 Home Phone: 941-776-9648. Personal E-mail: michaelvb4@yahoo.com.

VANCE, C. GIBSON, lawyer; b. Troy, Ala. m. Kate Vance; children: Carter, Andrew. BS, Troy State U., Ala., 1987; JD, Jones Sch. Law, 1992. Bar: Ala. 1993, US Dist. Ct. (mid. dist.) Ala. 1993. Ptnr. Hawthorne, Hawthorne and Vance, Montgomery, Ala.; shareholder Beasley, Allen, Crow, Methvin, Portis & Miles PC, Montgomery. TV talk-show host, Law Call Sta WSFA-TV, Ala., regular host, Beasley Allen Report, Ala.; former mem. bd. dirs. Trial Lawyers Pub. Justice; spkr. in field. Contbr. articles to law jours. Apptd. mem. Ala. Jud. Compensation Com.; mem. Ala. Dem. Adv. Com., St. James United Meth. Ch.; bd. trustee Troy U., 2012—. Mem.: Nat. Bar Assn., Ala. State Bar Assn., Montgomery County Bar Assn. (mem. bd. dirs., former v.p.), American Assn. for Justice (pres. 2010—11, Joe Tonahill award), Ala. Assn. Justice (former pres., Spirit sword/President's award), Montgomery Trial Lawyers Assn. (former pres.), Ala. Trial Lawyers Assn. (former treas.), So. Trial Lawyers Assn., Inns. of Ct, Ala. Civil Justice Found. (former pres.), Pub. Justice Found. Office: Beasley Allen Crow Methvin Portis & Miles PC 218 Commerce St Montgomery AL 36104 Office Phone: 800-898-2034. Office Fax: 334-954-7555. Business E-Mail: gibson.vance@beasleyallen.com.*

VANCE, J. RANDALL, corporate financial executive; BBA in Fin. with distinction, U. Mo., 1985, MBA in Fin. with honors, 1988. Comml. banking officer Commerce Bank, 1988—91; v.p., treas. Farmland Industries, Inc., 1991—2003; sr. v.p., fin., treas. Hostess Brands, Inc. (formerly Interstate Bakeries Corp.), 2004—, CFO, 2007—. Office: Hostess Brands Inc 6031 Connection Dr Irving TX 75039 Office Phone: 972-532-4500. Office Fax: 972-892-7694. Business E-Mail: vance_randall@hostessbrands.com.

VANCE, JOYCE WHITE, federal prosecutor; b. 1960; m. Bob Vance; children: Robert Smith III, Edward Rodman, Eleanor Rainey, William Oliver. BA in Polit. Sci., Bates Coll., 1982; JD, U. Va. Sch. Law, 1985. Assoc. Bradley Arant Rose & White, Birmingham, Ala., 1988—91; asst. US atty. criminal divsn. US Dept. Justice, Birmingham, Ala., 1991—2002, asst. US atty. appellate divsn., 2002—09, US atty. (northern dist.) Ala., 2009—. Office: US Attorneys Office 1801 Fourth Ave Birmingham AL 35203 Office Phone: 205-244-2001. Office Fax: 205-244-2171.*

VANCE, KIM, lawyer; BA with highest honors, U. Ctrl. Ark.; JD with honors, U. Ark. Ptnr. King & Ballow, Nashville; gen. counsel, corp. sec. Tractor Supply Co., Brentwood, Tenn., 2003; shareholder Baker Donelson. Spkr. in field. Bd. dirs. Ctr. Nonprofit Mgmt. Mem.: ABA (mem. labor sect., employment law sect.), Lawyers' Assn. for Women. Office: Baker Donelson First Tennessee Bldg 165 Madison Ave Memphis TN 38103 Office Phone: 901-526-2000. Office Fax: 901-577-2303. Business E-Mail: kvance@bakerdonelson.com.

VANCE, LESLEY, state legislator; b. Oct. 23, 1939; m. Patricia Vance; children: Leslie, Carmen, Chris. Student in advanced bus. courses, Mortuary Coll. Coroner Russell County, Ala., commr.; owner, operator Vance Meml. Chapel; mem. Dist. 80 Ala. House of Rep., Montgomery, 1994—. Democrat. Baptist. Office: 3738 US 431 N Phenix City AL 36868 also: Ala House of Reps Ala State House 11 S Union St Rm 630-E Montgomery AL 36130 Office Phone: 334-298-0668, 334-242-7687.

VANCE, RALPH BROOKS, SR., oncologist, educator; b. Jackson, Miss., Dec. 4, 1945; s. Brooks C. and Chrystine G. (Gober) V.; m. Mary Douglas Allen, June 18, 1979; children: Brooks, Barrett. BA in Biology and German, U. Miss., 1968, MD, 1972. Asst. prof. medicine U. Miss., Jackson, 1978—86, assoc. prof. medicine, 1986—93, prof. medicine, 1993—. Chief of staff U. Miss. Hosp. and Clinics, Jackson, 1989-90; pres. faculty senate Univ. Med. Ctr., Jackson, 1986-87, univ. clin. assoc., pres., 1987-89. Author (with others) Development in Molecular Virology: Herpes Virus DNA, 1982; contbr. numerous articles and abstracts to profl. jours. Nat. pres. Am. Cancer Soc., 2003—04, bd. dirs. Atlanta, nat. pres., exec. com.; bd. dirs. ARC, Jackson; bd. Blue Cross/Blue Shield Miss., Jackson, 1989—92. Named to Hall of Fame, U. Miss., 1968. Fellow ACP; mem. Am. Assn. for Cancer Edn., Am. Fedn. for Clin. Rsch., Am. Soc. Clin. Oncology, Am. Assn. for Cancer Rsch., Miss. Acad. Scis., S.W. Oncology Group, U. Miss. Alumni Assn.(bd.dirs. 2009-), Sigma Xi. Office: University Miss Sch Medicine 2500 N State St Jackson MS 39216-4505 Home: 2105 Old Taylor Rd Oxford MS 38655 Office Phone: 601-984-5600. Business E-Mail: rvance@umc.edu.

VANCE, SARAH S., federal judge; b. Donaldsonville, La., 1950; BA, La. State U., 1971; JD, Tulane U., 1978. With Stone, Pigman, Walther, Wittmann & Hutchinson, New Orleans, 1978-94; judge US Dist. Ct. (ea. dist.) La., New Orleans, 1994—2008, chief judge, 2008—. Recipient Phi Beta Kappa Faculty Group award. Mem. ABA, Am. Law Inst., Fed. Judges Assn., Nat. Assn. Women Judges, La. State Bar Assn., Fed. Bar Assn., New Orleans Bar Assn., Bar Assn. of the Fed. Fifth Circuit, Order of Coif. Office: US Dist Ct 500 Poydras St Rm C255 New Orleans LA 70130

VAN CLEVE, RUTH GILL, retired lawyer; b. Mpls., July 28, 1925; d. Raymond S. and Ruth (Sevon) Gill; m. Harry R. Van Cleve, Jr., May 16, 1952 (dec. Oct. 2001); children: John Gill, Elizabeth Webster, David Hamilton Livingston. Student, U. Minn., 1943; AB magna cum laude, Mt. Holyoke Coll., 1946, LLD, 1976; LLB, Yale U., 1950. Bar: DC 1950, Minn. 1950. Intern Nat. Inst. Pub. Affairs, 1946-47; atty. Dept. Interior, 1950-54, asst. solicitor, 1954-64; dir. Office Territorial Affairs, 1964-69, 1977-80, dep. asst. sec., 1980-81, acting asst. sec., 1993; atty. Solicitor's Office, 1981-93, FPC, 1969-75, asst. gen. counsel, 1975-77. Author: The Office of Territorial Affairs, 1974, The Application of Federal Laws to the Territories, 1993. Mem. Guam War Claims Rev. Commn., 2003—04. Recipient Fed. Woman's award, 1966, Disting. Svc. award Dept. Interior, 1968, Presdl. Rank award, Pres. U.S., 1989. Mem.: Phi Beta Kappa. Unitarian. Home: 3440 S Jefferson St Apt 1015 Falls Church VA 22041

VANDEHEI, JIM (JAMES W. VANDEHEI), editor; b. 1971; m. Autumn Hanna VandeHei; children: Sophie, James. BA in Journalism & Polit. Sci., U. Wis., Oshkosh, 1995. Journalist Brillion News, Wis., 1993; sports reporter Oshkosh Northwestern; intern to Sen. Herb Kohl US Senate, 1994; with Inside Washington Publishers, 1995—96, Inside the New Congress, 1996—97, Roll Call, 1997—2000; White House & Congressional reporter The Wall Street Journal, 1998—2002; nat. polit. reporter, White House corr. The Washington Post, 2002—06; exec. editor The Politico, Arlington, Va., 2006—; co-founder, exec. editor Politico.com, Arlington, Va., 2007—; CEO Politico & Capital NY, 2013—. Guest appearances Face the Nation, CNN-Inside Politics, Hardball, analyst of politics Washington Post Radio, biweekly chats about politics Washingtonpost.com. Hoover Institution Media Fellow, 2005, 2006. Avocations: fishing, football. Office: The Politico 1000 Wilson Blvd Ste 601 Arlington VA 22209 Office Phone: 202-289-1155. Business E-Mail: jvandehei@politico.com.*

VANDEMARK, ROBERT GOODYEAR, retired retail executive; b. Youngstown, Ohio, Sept. 1, 1921; s. Arthur Glenn and Lola (Goodyear) V.; m. Jean Chapman, Sept. 19, 1943; children: Ann (Mrs. William K. Butler), Peggy Lynn (Mrs. Michael Murray). BSc, Ohio U., 1943. Dept. mgr. F. & R. Lazarus, Columbus, Ohio, 1947-54; asst. controller Boston Store, Milw., 1954-57; v.p., treas. Cleland Simpson Co., Scranton, Pa., 1957-65; asst. to exec. v.p. Bergdorf Goodman, NYC, 1965-68; treas. Garfinckel, Brooks Bros., Miller & Rhoads, Inc., Washington, 1968-69, v.p., 1969-73, exec. v.p., 1973-79, vice chmn., 1979-83; chmn., chief exec. officer Garfinckel's, 1983-87. Head dept. and specialty stores div. United Fund, Scranton, Pa., 1960-65; bd. dirs. Goodwill Industries, 1964-65; treas. Washington Nat. Cathedral. Served to 1st lt. AUS, 1943-46; col. Res. Decorated Bronze Star with V and cluster, Mil. Order of Wilheim. Mem. Fin. Execs. Inst., Nat. Retail Mchts. Assn. (sec., treas., 1st v.p., pres., dir., mem. exec. com. fin. exec. divsn.), Delta Tau Delta, City Club Washington, Washington Golf and Country Club, Army-Navy Club, Burning Tree Golf Club, Laurel Oak Country Club (Fla.), Masons (32d degree), Kiwanis (Fla.), Tower Club. Home: 933 Woburn Ct Mc Lean VA 22102

VANDEN BOUT, PAUL ADRIAN, astronomer, physicist, educator; b. Grand Rapids, Mich., June 16, 1939; s. Adrian and Cornelia (Peterson) Vanden B.; m. Rachel Ann Eggebeen, Sept. 1, 1961; children: Thomas Adrian, David Anton AB, Calvin Coll., 1961; PhD, U. Calif.-Berkeley, 1966. Postdoctoral fellow U. Calif., Berkeley, 1966-67, Columbia U., NYC, 1967-68, instr., 1968-69, asst. prof., 1969-70, U. Tex., Austin, 1970-74, assoc. prof., 1974-79, prof., 1979-84; dir. Nat. Radio Astronomy Obs., Charlottesville, Va., 1985—2002, sr. sci., 2003—; dir. Atacama Large Millimeter Array, Charlottesville, Va., 2002—03. Cons. NSF, NASA, NRC. Fellow Fulbright Found., Heidelberg, Fed. Republic Germany, 1961-62, Leiden, Netherlands, 1977 Fellow AAAS, Am. Phys. Soc.; mem. Am. Astron. Soc., Internat. Astron. Union, Internat. Radio Sci. Union. Office: Nat Radio Astronomy Obs 520 Edgemont Rd Charlottesville VA 22903-2454 Office Phone: 434-296-0231. Business E-Mail: pvandenb@nrao.edu.

VAN DE PUTTE, LETICIA, state legislator; b. Tacoma, Dec. 6, 1954; m. Pete Van De Putte; children: Nichole, Vanessa, Henry, Gregory, Isabella, Paul. BS, U. Tex., Austin. Pharmacist, Tex.; mem. Dist. 115 Tex. House of Representatives, 1991—99; mem. Dist. 26 Tex. State Senate, 1999—. Co-chair Dem. Nat. Conv., 2008. Recipient of several awards and honors; Kellogg fellow, Harvard U. John F. Kennedy Sch. Govt., 1993. Mem.: Nat. Hispanic Caucus State Legislators (pres. 2003—05), Nat. Conf. State Legislatures (pres. 2006—07). Democrat. Roman Catholic. Office: PO Box 12068 Capitol Station Austin TX 78711 also: 101 W Nueva Ste 809 San Antonio TX 78205-3445 Office Phone: 210-733-6604, 512-463-0126.

VANDERBROEK, MARK S., lawyer; b. Royal Oak, Mich., 1959; BBA with honors, Univ. Mich., 1981; JD, Univ. Chgo., 1984. Bar: Ga. 1985. Law clerk, Hon. James C. Hill. US Ct. Appeals (11th cir.), 1984—85; assoc. Troutman Sanders LLP, Atlanta, 1985—92, ptnr., 1993—. Office: Troutman Sanders LLP Bank of Am Plz Ste 5200 600 Peachtree St NE Atlanta GA 30308-2216 Office Phone: 404-885-3432. Office Fax: 404-962-6707. Business E-Mail: mark.vanderbroek@troutmansanders.com.

VANDERPLOEG, JAMES M., preventive medicine physician; b. Upland, Calif., Nov. 22, 1950; BS, Calvin Coll., 1972; MD, U. Iowa Coll. Medicine, 1975; MPH, U. Texas Sch. Public Health, 1980. Cert. Aerospace Medicine and Occupational Medicine. Intern U. Hosp./U. Calif., San Diego, 1975-76; resident in otolaryngoloty U. Iowa Hosps., Iowa City, 1978-79; resident in occupational medicine U. Tex. Sch. Pub. Health, Houston, 1980-82, assoc. prof. occupational health; mem. staff St. John Hosp., Nassau Bay, Tex.; pres., partner Ctr. Aerospace & Occupl. Medicine, Houston; assoc. prof. preventive medicine and community health, divsn. clinical preventive medicine U. Texas Medical Branch, assoc. prof. family medicine. Bd. mem. Am. Bd. Preventive Medicine, Schiller Park, Ill., 1993—98, exec. dir., 1998—. Mem. Am. Coll. Occupational Medicine, ACPrM-AerosMA. Office: U Texas Medical Branch 301 University Blvd Galveston TX 77555-0144

VANDERSLICE, MARA LOUISE, religious organization executive; b. 1975; BA, Earlham Coll., Richmond, IN, 1997. Worked Sojourners, Call to Renewal, Jubilee 2000 campaign for debt-relief, Howard Dean Campaign, Cmty. and Faith Outreach, 2004; dir. Religious Outreach for the Kerry-Edwards 2004 campaign, 2004; founder, sr. ptnr. Common Good Strategies. Named a Maverick, Details mag., 2007. Evangelical. Office: Common Good Strategies 949 N Pitt St Alexandria VA 22314

VAN DE VEN, MICHAEL GERARD, air transportation company executive; b. 1961; m. Cindy Van de Ven; children: Kyle, Garrett. BBA, U. Tex. Sr. audit mgr. Ernst & Young; joined Southwest Airlines Co., sr. dir., fin. planning & analysis, dir., internal audit, v.p., financial planning & analysis, 2001—04, sr. v.p., planning, 2004—05, exec. v.p., aircraft ops., 2005—06, chief, ops., 2006—08, exec. v.p., 2006—08, exec. v.p., COO, 2008—. Office: Southwest Airlines Co 2702 Love Field Dr Dallas TX 75235 Office Phone: 214-792-5015. Office Fax: 214-792-4000. Business E-Mail: michael.vandeven@southwest.com.

VAN DYKE, GENE, oil industry executive; b. Normal, Ill, Nov. 5, 1926; BS in Geol. Engring., U. Okla., 1950. Geologist Kerr-McGee, Oklahoma City, 1950; chief geologist S.D. Johnson Co., Wichita Falls, Tex., 1950-51; ind. geologist, oil operator Wichita Falls, Tex., 1951-58; ptnr. Van Dyke and Mejlaender, Houston, 1958-62; founder, owner, chmn. Van Dyke Energy Co. (formerly Vanco Energy Co.), Houston, 1962—. Bd. dirs. Van Dyke Netherlands, Inc. Compiler index of geol. articles to South La. With AC US Army, 1945. Named Living Legend in Wildcatting, Houston Geol. Soc., 2000; named to Hall of Fame, Dutch Am. Heritage Soc., 2001. Mem.: Am. Assn. Petroleum Geologists, Ind. Petroleum Assn., Houstonian Club, Houston Petroleum Club, Houston Club (pres.). Republican. Episcopalian. Gene Van Dyke sold controlling interest in Vanco Energy Company to an affiliate of LUKOIL in 2007 and is now concentrating on onshore Latin America with an emphasis on Colombia. When he owned Vanco Energy Company it was the largest license holder in deepwater West Africa with over 20 million acres in water depths between 1,000 and 10,000 feet; Vanco was also awarded the Prykerchenska Block in southeast Ukraine Black Sea, being 3.2 million acres wtih water depths from 150 meters to 2,200 meters. Office: Van Dyke Energy Co 11 Greenway Plz Ste 2010 Houston TX 77046 Office Phone: 713-457-8100. Office Fax: 713-457-8099.

VANE, TERENCE G., JR., finance company executive, lawyer; b. Elgin, Ill., Jan. 17, 1942; s. Terence Gregory and Velma Mary (Mersman) V.; m. Patricia Bryant, Aug. 29, 1964; children: Terence Gregory III, Lourdene DeLynne, Christopher Theodore. BA, Ind. U., 1964, JD, 1967. Bar: Ind. 1967, Tex. 1977, N.C. 1992, Fla. 2002. Staff atty. Assocs. Discount Corp., South Bend, Ind., 1967-69; asst. gen. counsel Assocs. Mgmt. Corp., South Bend, 1969-74, Assocs. Comml. Corp., South Bend, 1974-76, Assocs. Ins. Group, Inc., Dallas, 1976-77; gen. counsel, v.p. ins. ops. Assocs. Corp. N.Am., Dallas, 1977-80, gen. counsel, sr. v.p. ins. ops., 1981-82, gen. counsel, sr. v.p. consumer fin. and ins. ops., 1982-86, gen. counsel, sr. v.p. diversified consumer fin. svcs. and credit card ops., 1986-88; exec. v.p., gen. counsel, sec., dir. Barclays Am. Corp., Charlotte, NC, 1988-91; pres. Vector Fin. Svcs., Inc., Charlotte, 1991-95, bd. dirs.; sr. v.p., assoc. gen. counsel EquiCredit Corp., Jacksonville, Fla., 1996-97; sr. v.p., gen. counsel, sec. First Street Mortgage Corp., Jacksonville, 1997-98, Home Alliance Mortgage Co., Jacksonville, 1998-2000, Alliance Capital Ptnrs. Group, Jacksonville, 2000—02, Slott & Barker, Jacksonville, 2002—04; pvt. practice Jacksonville, 2005—. Chmn. bd. dirs., sec. Youth Concert Found. for Promotion Creative Arts, 1981—; bd. dirs. N.C. Bus. Com. Edn., 1988-91. Mem. ABA (com. on consumer fin. svcs. law), Fla. Bar Assn., Ind. Bar Assn., Tex. Bar Assn., N.C. Bar Assn., Nat. Assn. Ind. Insurers (laws com. 1978-86), Consumer Credit Ins. Assn. (chmn. property ins. legis. com. 1979-85), Am. Fin. Svcs. Assn. (law com., chmn. environ. law subcom.), Conf. Consumer Fin. Law (governing com.), Nat. Home Equity Mortgage Assn., Lawyers Round Table, Safari Club Internat. (pres., dir. North Fla. chpt.), River City Rep. Club (pres.), Duval County Fla. Rep. Party (exec. com. mem.). Conservative. Episcopalian. Office: Terence G Vane Jr PA 233 E Bay St Ste 620 Jacksonville FL 32202-3447 Office Phone: 904-353-8285. Business E-Mail: tvane@tvanelaw.com.

VAN FLEET, CONNIE JEAN, library and information scientist, educator; b. New Orleans, La., Oct. 3, 1950; d. Cornelius and Elizabeth Fisher Van Fleet; m. Danny Paul Wallace; children: Robyn Solomon, Elizabeth Wallace. BA, U. of Okla., 1972; M of Libr. Info. Sci., La. State U., 1987; PhD, Ind. U., 1990. Libr. assoc. New Orleans Pub. Libr., 1982—85; instr. La. State U., Baton Rouge, 1989—90, asst. prof., 1990—94, assoc. prof., 1994—96; adj. assoc. prof. Kent (Ohio) State U., 1996—98, assoc. prof., 1998—2000, U. of Okla., Norman, 2000—03, prof., 2003—. Panelist, proposal evaluator NEH, Washington, 1999; participant forum on libr. and info. svcs. policy Nat. Ctr. for Edn. Stats. and U.S. Nat. Commn. on Librs. and Info. Sci., Washington, 1996; panelist White House conf. on aging mini-conf. on the arts, the humanities, and older adults NEH/ Nat. Coun. on the Aging, Washington, 1995; co-investigator on grant project Okla. Dept. of Librs./U. of Okla., Oklahoma City, 2001—02, Inst. for Mus. and Libr. Svcs., USDE, Washington, 1999—2001; project cons. Ohio Libr. Coun. and State Libr. of Ohio, Columbus, 1998—99; co-investigator on grant Libr. Edn. and Human Resource Devel. Program, USDE, Washington, 1997—98; project cons. Ohio Libr. Coun., Columbus, 1996—98; inst. co-organizer Libr. Career Tng. and Devel. Program Inst. Awards, USDE, Washington, 1995—96, Libr. Career Tng. Program, USDE, Washington, 1994—95; project supr., grant adminstr. Libr. Career Tng. Program Fellowship Awards, USDE, Washington, 1992—94; project cons. Nat. Coun. on the Aging, Inc., Washington, 1990—91; guest instr. Mo. State Libr., Jefferson City, 1999. Editor: (jour.) Reference & User Svcs. Quar., 2000; co-editor: RQ, 1997, (book) Library Evaluation: A Casebook for Managers, 2001; co-author: Preparing Staff to Serve People with Disabilities, 1995; co-editor: A Service Profession, a Service Commitment: A Festschrift in Honor of Charles D. Patterson, 1992; co-author: (book chpt.) The Readers' Advisor's Companion, 2001, Research Issues in Public Librarianship: Trends for the Future, 1994; author: Adult Services: An Enduring Focus for Public Libraries, 1990, (procs.) Public Libraries and Community-Based Education for Lifelong Learning, 1995; co-author: Proceedings of Philosophical, Ethical and Practical Aspects of Refereed Science Journals; contbr. articles to profl. jours. Pres. Patrons of the Pub. Libr., East Baton Rouge Parish, Baton Rouge, 1994—96. Recipient John Edwards fellowship, Ind. U., 1988—89, grant Seminar: Ohio Libr. Evaluation, Libr. Edn. & Human Resource Devel. Program, U.S. Dept of Edn., 1997—98, grant for Rural Econ. Devel. Inst., Libr. Career Tng. and Devel. Program, U.S. Dept. of Edn., 1995—96, grant La. Pub. Librs. Electronic Access Seminar, 1994—95, scholarship support for interest in svcs. to people with disabilities, Libr. Career Tng. Program, U.S. Dept of Edn., 1993—94, 1992—93. Mem.: ALA (steering com., conf. on profl. edn.

1988—99, chair rsch. com. 1989—91, editl. adv. bd. co-chair Reference and Adult Svcs. Divsn. 1991—96, mem. (ex officio) bd. dirs. Reference and Adult Svcs. Divsn. 1991—97, Resolution of Appreciation Reference & User Services Assn. 1997, mem. task force on fgn. credentialing 1997—2000, chair, com. on edn. 1998—99, steering com. Congress on Profl. Edn. 1998—99, councilor at large 1998—2002, mem. (ex officio) bd. dirs. Reference and Users Svcs. Assn. 2000—06, reference & user svcs. quar. editl. adv. bd. co-chair 2000—06, planning and budget assembly 2001—02, nominating com. 2006, Pub. Libr. Assn., Intellectual Freedom Round Table, Assn. Specialized and Coop. Libr. Agys., Margaret E. Monroe Libr. Adult Svcs. award Reference and Adult Services Divsn. 1996), White House Conf. on the Aging Task Force, Assn. Libr. & Info. Sci. Edn. (pres. 2007—08, Tchg. Excellence award 2004, Svc. award 2010), La. Libr. Assn. (mem. com. on paraprofl. continuing edn. 1989—91, co-founder/mem. minority recruitment and profl. concerns group 1989—92, mem. scholarship com. 1989—92, mem. pub. libr. stds.com. 1993—95), Okla. Libr. Assn. (intellectual freedom com. 2001—10), Beta Phi Mu (chpt. advisor 1992—94, Rho chpt. advisor 1998—2000). Democrat. Avocations: reading, watercolor, needlecrafts. Office: U Oklahoma SLIS Rm 120 401 W Brooks Norman OK 73019-6032 Business E-Mail: cvanfleet@ou.edu.

VAN HORN, HUGH M., physicist, astronomer, educator; b. Williamsport, Pa., Mar. 5, 1938; s. Robert Dix and Virginia Elizabeth (Moody) Van H.; m. Mary Susan Boon, Sept. 17, 1960; children: Kathleen Susan, Mary Margaret, Michael Hugh George. BSc, Case Inst. Tech., 1960; PhD, Cornell U., 1965. NASA predoctoral trainee Cornell U., Ithaca, 1963-65; rsch. assoc. U. Rochester, 1965-67, asst. prof., 1967-73, assoc. prof., 1973-77, prof., 1977-96, chmn. dept. physics and astronomy, 1980-86, acting assoc. dean Coll. Arts and Scis., 1987-89, acting chmn. dept. physics and astronomy, 1992-93, adj. prof., 1996—2005, prof. emeritus, 2005—; Shapley lectr. Am. Astron. Soc., 1981-95; dir. divsn. astron. sci. NSF, Arlington, Va., 1993-2000, sr. sci. advisor Directorate Math. Phys. Sci., 2000—02, dir. nat. facilities divsn. materials rsch., 2002—04; ret., 2004. Vis. fellow Joint Inst. Lab. Astrophysics, 1973—74; sr. scientist Lab. Laser Energetics, 1985—96; vis. prof. U. Tex., 1987; vis. investigator dept. terr. magnetism Carnegie Inst. Washington, 2000—02; prin. investigator NASA and NSF grants. Editor: (with V. Weidemann) White Dwarfs and Variable Degenerate Stars, 1979, (with S. Ichimaru) Strongly Coupled Plasma Physics, 1993; contbr. articles on white dwarfs, neutron stars and dense matter to profl. jours. Fellow AAAS; mem. Internat. Astron. Union. E-mail: vanhorns1@verizon.net.

VAN HORN, MICHAEL D., oil and gas company executive; BS in Geologic Engring., U. Nev.; MS in Geology, Colo. Sch. Mines. With British Gas E&P, Inc.; dir. internat. exploration EOG Resources, Inc., v.p. internat. exploration; with Tenneco Oil Co.; sr. v.p. exploration Newfield Exploration Co., 2006, v.p. geoscience. Office: Newfield Exploration Co Ste 100 363 N Sam Houston Pky E Houston TX 77060 Office Phone: 281-847-6000. Office Fax: 281-405-4242.

VAN HOY, PHILIP MARSHALL, lawyer; b. Washington, Nov. 8, 1947; s. Joe Milton and Helen Virginia (Spangler) V.; m. Sylvia Kathryn Smith, Dec. 30, 1972; children: Marshall, Travis. AB, Duke U., Durham, NC, 1970; JD, U. NC, 1973. Bar: NC 1973, US Dist. Ct. (ea., we. and mid. dists.) NC 1974, US Ct. Appeals (4th cir.) 1974, US Supreme Ct. 1978. Labor counsel Duke Power Co., Charlotte, NC, 1973—80; assoc. Siegel, O'Connor & Kainen, Charlotte, 1980—83; ptnr. Mullins & Van Hoy, Charlotte, 1983—89, Van Hoy, Reutlinger, Adams & Dunn, Charlotte, 1989—. Mem. NC OSHA Rev. Commn., 1985—92, Mecklenburg County, NC Personnel Commn., 1985—92, NC Leadership Coun. Co-state chmn. Gardner for Lt. Gov., 1988, alt. del. Rep. Nat. Conv., Detroit, 1980; chmn. Mecklenburg County Young Rep. Com., 1979, vice chmn., 1980-83; Duke U. Athletics Coun., 1999-02. 1st lt. US Army, 1973-81. Recipient Salute to Am.'s Best Lawyers, Forbes mag. and Am. Airlines Sky Radio, 2005, Lawyer of the Yr., Employment Law Charlotte NC, 2012—; named Top Employment Lawyer NC, Bus. NC mag., 2002, Best Lawyers; named to Best Lawyers in Am., 2001—, Outstanding Lawyers of Am., 2003, NC Super Lawyers, 2006—. Mem. NC Bar Assn. (councillor labor and employment law sect. 1985-88, chmn. EEOC com. 1983-92), NC State Bar, 4th Cir. Jud. Conf., Rotary, Charlotte Cotillion Club (pres. 1979-80), City Club, Myers Park Country Club (dir. 1994-96, 2000-03). Republican. Methodist. Office: Van Hoy Reutlinger Adams & Dunn 737 East Blvd Charlotte NC 28203-5113 Home: 16631 Harbor View Rd Charlotte NC 28278

VAN KLEEF, WILLIAM T., oil industry executive; BA in Acctg., U. Tex. CPA. Various fin. & acctg. positions, including sr. v.p., CFO Damson Oil; various exec. mgmt. positions, including pres., refining & mktg. Tesoro Corp. (formerly Tesoro Petroleum Corp.), sr. v.p., CFO, exec. v.p., COO, exec. v.p., ops. & devel., treas., 1993. Bd. dirs. Noble Energy, Oil States Internat., Inc., 2006—. Office: Oil States International Inc Bd Directors 3 Allen Ctr 333 Clay St Ste 4620 Houston TX 77002 Office Phone: 713-652-0582. Office Fax: 713-652-0499. Business E-Mail: william.vankleef@oilstatesintl.com.

VANMETER, VANDELIA L., retired library director; b. Seibert, Colo., July 17, 1934; d. G.W. and A. Pearl Klockenteger; m. Victor M. VanMeter, Jan. 21, 1954; children: Allison C., Kristopher C. BA, Kansas Wesleyan U., 1957; MLS, Emporia State U., 1970; PhD, Tex. Woman's U., 1986. Cert. libr. media specialist. Tchr. Ottawa County Rural Sch., Kans., 1954-55; social scis. tchr. McClave (Colo.) High Sch., 1957-58, Ellsworth (Kans.) Jr. High Sch., 1959-68; libr., media specialist Ellsworth (Kans.) High Sch., 1968-84; asst. prof. libr. sci. U. So. Miss., Hattiesburg, 1986-90; chair dept. libr./info. sci. Spalding U., Louisville, 1990-96, libr. dir., 1991-99, prof., 1991—99. Cons. to sch., pub. and spl. librs., Kans., Miss., Ky., 1970-99; mem. Ky. NCATE Bd. Examiners. Author: American History for Children and Young Adults, 1990, World History for Children and Young Adults, 1992, America in Historical Fiction, 1997; editor: Mississippi Library Media Specialist Staff Development Modules, 1988, Library Lane Newsletter, 1991-99; contbr. chpts. to books; contbr. articles to profl. jours. Active City Coun., Ellsworth, Kans., 1975-79, Park Bd., Ellsworth, 1975-79; bd. dirs. Robbins Meml. Libr., 1977-79. Grantee Kans. Demonstration Sch. Libr., 1970-72, Miss. Power Found., 1989, Project Technology Enhances Curriculur Instrn., 1996-97; named Women of Yr. Bus. and Profl. Women of Ellsworth, Kans., 1976. Mem. ALA, Assn. Coll. and Rsch. Librs., Ky. Libr. Assn., Assn. for Libr. and Info. Sci. Educators.

VAN METRE, MARGARET CHERYL, performing company executive, dancer, educator; b. Maryville, Tenn., Nov. 24, 1938; d. Robert Fillers and Margaret Elizabeth (Goddard) Raulston; m. Mitchell Robert Van Metre II, Aug. 25, 1956; 1 child, Mitchell Robert. Elem., intermediate and advanced tchg. certs. Dir. Van Metre Sch. of Dance, Maryville, 1958-96; artistic dir. Appalachian Ballet Co., Maryville Coll., 1972-96; founding dir. Appalachian Ballet Co., 1972; dir. Van Metre Arts Mgmt., SC, 1996—. Chmn. dance panel Tenn. Arts Commn., 1973-74; chmn. Bicentennial Ballet Project, Tenn., 1975-76; mem. Nat. Bd. Regional Dance Am., 1997-2000; owner Van Metre Arts Mgmt., Edisto Island, S.C., 1996—. Choreographer ballets: Delusion, 1965, Hill Heritage Suite, 1972, Dancing Princesses, 1983. Mem. Tenn. Assn. of Dance (pres. 1972), Southeast Regional Ballet Assn. (pres. 1996, 97, 98, 99, 2003-2007). Democrat. Episcopalian. Home: 2103 Myrtle St Edisto Island SC 29438-3437

VAN MIDDLESWORTH, LESTER, physiology, biophysics and medicine educator, internist; b. Washington, Jan. 13, 1919; s. Lester and Hazel Lucile (Brandt) VanM.; m. Nellie Rue Franklin, June 29, 1948; children: Linda V. Anderson, Jane V. Norman, Frank L., Paul E. BS in Chemistry, U. Va., 1940, MS in Chemistry, 1942, MS in Physiology, 1944; PhD in Physiology, U. Calif., Berkeley, 1946; MD, U. Tenn., 1951, DSc (hon.), 2008. Teaching asst. dept. physiology U. Va., 1944, U. Calif., Berkeley, 1944—45; instr. U. Tenn. Med. Units, Memphis, 1946—52, instr. in medicine, 1953—57, asst. prof. physiology, 1952—54, assoc. prof., 1954—59, prof., 1959—89, prof. emeritus physiology and biophysics, 1989—, asst. prof. medicine, 1957—61, assoc. prof., 1961—72, prof. medicine, 1972—89, prof. medicine emeritus, 1989, Disting. prof. physiology and medicine, 1986—; U. disting. prof., 2007. Rotating intern City of Memphis Hosps., 1951-52; cons. chief chemist Piedmont Apple Products Corp., Charlottesville, Va., 1940-46, Crocker Radiation Lab., U. Calif., Berkeley, 1946-47, Oak Ridge Inst. Nuclear Studies, 1950-54; guest co-investigator Endocrine Labs. Tufts Med. Coll., Boston, summers 1954, 55, 56, 59, 61, 64, 66, 69, Scripps Clinic and Rsch. Found., La Jolla, Calif., 1957; guest investigator in endocrinology Harbor Gen. Hosp., UCLA, 1971, Frederick Joliot Hosp., Orsay, France, 1972, Lawrence Livermore Radiation Lab. U. Calif., 1970; staff mem. clinic for med. thyroid disease patients, City of Memphis and U., Tenn., 1951—; mem. internat. com., 1990-2002. Author 153 publs. in profl. jours., 192 abstracts and oral presentations; work on permanent display Smithsonian Nat. Mus. Am. History, Washington, D.C. Recipient Disting. Svc. award, 1985, Disting. Alumnus award, U. Tenn. Coll. Medicine, 1989, USPHS career rsch. grantee, 1962-89; nominee Prince Mahidol award, U. Tenn. Health Sci. Com., 2007. Mem. Am. Chem. Soc., Am. Physiol. Soc., AAAS, Soc. Exptl. Biology and Medicine, Am. Soc. Clin. Investigation, So. Soc. Clin. Investigation, Health Physics Soc., Endocrine Soc., Am. Thyroid Assn. (Disting. Svc. award 1988), Sigma Xi (rsch. award 1944, 86, nat. lectr. 1989-91), Alpha Chi Sigma. Achievements include research in audiogenic siezures and worldwide radioiodine fallout, and radium in normal human thyroid glands; first to observe and report worldwide spread of radioiodine fallout in animal thyroid glands. Office: U Tenn Health Sci Ctr 894 Union Ave Memphis TN 38163-3514 Home: 648 Des Moines Dr Hermitage TN 37076-1557 Office Phone: 901-448-5837. Personal E-mail: vanruehonve@gmail.com.

VAN MOL, LOUIS JOHN, JR., public relations executive; b. Knoxville, Tenn., Oct. 7, 1943; s. Louis John and Evelyn (Ramsay) Van M.; m. Deborah Ruth Boyd, Nov. 1, 1969; children: Derek, Millicent. BS, U. Tenn., 1966. Staff writer, editor AP, Knoxville and Nashville, 1963-66, 69; account exec. to exec. v.p. Holder, Kennedy & Co., Nashville, 1970-74, exec. v.p., 1978-79; dir. info. TVA, Knoxville, 1974-78; co-founder, ptnr. DVL Pub Rels & Advertising, Nashville, 1980—; CEO Dye, Van Mol & Lawrence, 2003—. Bd. dirs. East Tenn. Children's Hosp., Knoxville, 1977-78, Martha O'Bryan Ctr., Nashville, 1985-87, Crime Stoppers Nashville, 1986-92, Alcohol and Drug Coun. Mid. Tenn., Nashville, 1991-93, Martha O'Bryan Found., 1998-2000, Pencil Found., 2003—, Nashville Songwriters Found., 2004—, chmn. 2011, Tenn. C. of C. and Industry, 2005-, chmn. bd. dirs., 2008; bd. trustees Cumberland U., 2008-; chmn. bd. dirs. Nashville Downtown Partnership, 1999-2000, bd. dirs., 2006—; bd. govs., exec. com. Nashville C. of C., 1999-2000; chmn. Goodwill Industries Mid. Tenn., 1996-97, mem. exec. com., 1996-. Lt. U.S. Army, 1966-68. Lt. US Army, 1966—68, Ft. Eustis, Va.; Bien Hoa & Long Binh, Vietnam. Decorated Army Commendation medal, Bronze Star. Mem. Richland Country Club (bd. dirs. 1997-99, pres. 1999), Soc. Profl. Journalists. Presbyterian. Home: 2836 Wellesley Trace Nashville TN 37215-1049 Office: DVL Pub Rels & Advertising 700 12th Ave S Nashville TN 37203-1802

VANN, KEVIN WILLIAM, bishop; b. Springfield, Ill., May 10, 1951; s. William M. Vann, Jr. and Theresa (Jones) Vann. BS, Millikin Univ.; Licentiate in Canon Law, Pontifical U. St. Thomas Aquinas, Rome, D in Canon Law, 1985. Ordained priest Diocese of Springfield, 1981, parochial vicar, Blessed Sacrament Parish, Springfield, 1985—90; pastor St. Benedict Ch., Auburn, Ind., 1990—92, Our Lady of Lourdes Ch., Decatur, Ill., 1992—2001, Blessed Sacrament Parish, Springfield, 2001—05; ordained bishop, 2005; coadjutor bishop Diocese of Fort Worth, 2005, bishop, 2005—. Instr. canon law Kenrick Sem., St. Louis. Roman Catholic. Office: Diocese of Fort Worth 800 West Loop 820 S Fort Worth TX 76108 Office Phone: 817-560-3300. Office Fax: 817-244-8839.

VAN NAGELL, JOHN RENSSELAER, oncologist, gynecologist; b. NYC, Sept. 16, 1939; s. John Rensselaer and Rosamond Musgrave Van Nagell; m. Elizabeth Gay, June 10, 1977; children: John R Van Nagell III, Elizabeth Knox Pfister, Lucy Tepper. MD, U. Pa., 1967. Diplomate Am. Bd. Ob/Gyn. Prof., dir. divsn. gynecol. oncology U. Ky. Med. Ctr., Lexington, 1973—, Am. Cancer Soc prof. clin. oncology. Cons. NCI - PLCO Trial, Bethesda, Md., 1992—. Author: Modern Concepts of Gynecologic Oncology. Lt. USN, 1971—77. Named one of Top Doctors for Women, Ladies Home Jour., 2001—08, Ams. Top Doctors, Castle Connolly, 2002—12. Mem.: Masters of Foxhounds Assn. (bd.dirs. 2005, v.p. 2008), Soc. Gynecol. Oncologists (pres. 1994—95). Avocations: horseback riding, fox hunting. Business E-Mail: jrvann2@email.uky.edu.

VAN ORDEN, PHYLLIS JEANNE, librarian, educator; b. Adrian, Mich., July 7, 1932; d. Warren Philip and Mabel A. Nancy (Russell) Van O. BS, Ea. Mich. U., 1954; AMLS, U. Mich., 1958; EdD, Wayne State U., 1970. Cert. in elem. edn., lib. sci. Sch. librarian East Detroit (Mich.) Pub. Schs., 1954-57; librarian San Diego Pub. Library, 1958-60; media specialist Royal Oak (Mich.) Pub. Schs., 1960-64; librarian Oakland U., Rochester, Mich., 1964-66; instr. Wayne State U., Detroit, 1966-70; asst. prof. Rutgers U., New Brunswick, NJ, 1970-76; prof. library science Fla. State U., Tallahassee, 1977-91, assoc. dean for instrn., 1988-91; prof. libr. sci. program Wayne State U., Detroit, 1991-93; dir. Grad. Sch. of Libr. and Info. Sci. U. Wash., Seattle, 1993-96; cons. in field, 1996—. Author: Collection Program in Schools, 2001, Library Service to Children, 2005, Selecting Books for the Elementary School Library Media Center, 2000, Children's Books and Stamps: Studies in Design, 2005—, Children's Books: A Practical Guide to Selection, 2007; editor: Elementary School Library Collection, 1974—77; contbr. articles to profl. jours. Fla. State Libr. grantee, 1984, 86, 88; Lillian Bradshaw scholar Tex. Woman's U., 1993. Mem.: ALA (libr. resources and tech. svcs. divsn., Blackwell/N.Am. scholarship award 1983), Assn. for Libr. and Info. Sci. Edn. (pres. 1990, Svc. award 1997), Assn. Libr. Svc. to Children (pres. 1984—85, Dist. Svc. award 2002), Pi Lambda Theta. Avocations: music, physical fitness, cooking, travel, stamp collecting/philately.

VAN PELT, BO, professional golfer; b. Richmond, Ind., May 16, 1975; BA in Gen. Bus., Oklahoma State U., 1998. Mem. PGA Tour, 2006—. Achievements include winner Nationwide Tour event: Omaha Classic, 2003; winner PGA Tour event: US Bank Championship, 2009; winner Asian Tour event: CIMB Asia Pacific Classic Malaysia, 2011. Mailing: 100 PGA TOUR Blvd Ponte Vedra Beach FL 32082

VAN RIPER, PAUL PRITCHARD, retired political science professor; b. Laporte, Ind., July 29, 1916; s. Paul and Margaret (Pritchard) Van R.; m. Dorothy Ann Dodd Samuelson, May 11, 1964; 1 child, Michael Scott Samuelson. AB, DePauw U., 1938; PhD, U. Chgo., 1947. Instr. Northwestern U., 1947-49, asst. prof. polit. sci., 1949-51; mgmt. analyst Office Comptroller Dept. Army, 1951-52; mem. faculty Cornell U., 1952-70, prof., 1957-70; chmn. gov. bd., exec. com. Cornell Social Sci. Research Center, 1956-58; prof., head dept. polit. sci. Tex. A&M U., 1970-77, prof., 1977-81, prof. emeritus, 1981—, coordinator M.P.A. program, 1979-81, named prof. Bush Sch. Govt. and Pub. Svc., 1997—2008; ret., 2008. Vis. prof. U. Chgo., 1958, Ind. U., 1961, U. Strathclyde, Scotland, 1964, U. Mich., 1965, U. Okla., 1969-97, U. Utah, 1979. Author: History of the United States Civil Service, 1958, Some Educational and Social Aspects of Fraternity Life, 1961, (with others) The American Federal Executive, 1963, Handbook of Practical Politics, 3d edit., 1967; editor and co-author: the Wilson Influence on Public Administration, 1990. Exec. com. Civil Svc. Reform Assn., NY, 1960-64, hist. adv. com. NASA, 1964-66; bd. dir. Brazos Valley Cmty. Action Agy., 1975-79, Brazos County Hist. Commn., 1976-2006; charter mem. Brazos Heritage Soc., pres. 1977-79. Maj. AUS, 1942-46; lt. col. USAR ret. Decorated Croix de Guerre (France). Mem. Am. Polit. Sci. Assn., Am. Soc. Pub. Adminstrn. (nat adv. com. 1957-60, Dimock award 1984, Waldo award 1990, Van Riper award created in his honor 2002), Rotary (pres. Bryan club 1991-92, Rotary Dist., Roll of Fame award 2008), Phi Beta Kappa, Beta Theta Pi (v.p. 1962, gen. sec. 1963-65), Pi Alpha Alpha, Pi Sigma Alpha, Phi Kappa Phi, Sigma Delta Chi. Republican. Baptist.

VANRYCKEGHEM, MARTINE, speech language professional, educator; b. Gent, East Flanders, Belgium, Aug. 14, 1955; arrived in U.S., 1989; d. Roger Vanryckeghem and Juliette Vleeshouwers; m. Gene J. Brutten, Oct. 8, 1993. Grad. in Logopedics, Higher Inst. of Paramed. Professions, Gent, 1977; MS, So. Ill. U., Carbondale, 1991, PhD, 1994. Speech-lang. pathologist Clin. Ctr., Gent, Belgium, 1977—89; prof. U. Cen. Fla., Orlando, 1994—, U. Utrecht, 2006—09; vis. prof. U. Gent, 2006—. Cons. U. Zagreb, Croatia, 1998—2012, Artevelde Hogeschool, Gent, Belgium, 1994—2005, U. Gent, 1994—; fellow American Speech Lang. & Heaning Assoc. Mng. editor: Journal Fluency Disorders, 1990—2000; author: Behavior Assessment Battery: A Multi-dimensional and Evidence-based Approach to Diagnostic and Therapeutic Decision Making for Children and Adults who Stutter, 2003, Behavior Assessment Battery for School-Age Children who Stutter, 2007, KiddyCAT: Communication Attitude Test for Preschool and Kindergarten Children Who Stutter, 2007; contbr. articles to profl. jours. Recipient award. Mem.: Orgn. for Integration Handicapped People (sci. bd. mem. 1995—), Internat. Fluency Assn., American Speech-Lang.-Hearing Assn. (clin. competence in speech-lang. pathology, fluency specialist, fluency mentor). Achievements include research in Behavior Assessment Battery for Adults; Behavior Assessment Battery for Children; The KiddyCAT: A test investigating speech-associated attitude in preschoolers. Avocations: travel, cooking, hiking. Office: University Central Florida HPA-2 Ste 101 4000 Central Florida Blvd Orlando FL 32816-2215 Business E-Mail: martinev@ucf.edu.

VAN TATENHOVE, GREGORY FREDERICK, federal judge; b. LA, 1960; BA, Asbury Coll., 1982; JD, U. Ky., 1989. Aide to Senator Mitch McConnell US Senate, Ky.; law clerk US Dist. Ct., Ky.; trial atty. US Dept. Justice, DC, US atty. (ea. dist.) Ky, 2001—06; chief of staff, legal counsel to Congressman Ron Lewis US Congress; judge US Dist. Ct. (ea. dist.) Ky, London, 2006—. Office: US Dist Ct 310 S Main St Ste 434 London KY 40741

VANVLEET, EDWARD S., oceanographer, educator; b. Panama Canal, Panama, Apr. 7, 1948; s. Gerald E. and Janet Sutton VanVleet; children: Stacey Alison, Amanda Michelle. BS, U. Wash., Seattle, 1971; BA, U. Wash., 1971; MS, Old Dominion U., Norfolk, Va., 1974; PhD, U. RI, Naragansett, 1978. Prof. oceanography Coll. Marine Sci., U. S.Fla., St. Petersburg, 1979—. Office: Univ S Fla Dept Marine Sci 140 7th Ave S Saint Petersburg FL 33701 Business E-Mail: vanvleet@marine.usf.edu.

VAN VLIET, CAROLYNE MARINA, physicist, researcher; b. Dordrecht, Netherlands, Dec. 27, 1929; arrived in U.S., 1960, naturalized, 1967; d. Marinus and Jacoba (de Lange) Van V.; m. A.J. Cappon, Dec. 29, 1953 (div. 1983); children: Elsa Marianne, Mark Edward, Cynthia Joyce, Renata Annette Carolina. BS, Free U. Amsterdam, Netherlands, 1949, MA, 1953, PhD in Physics, 1956. Rsch. fellow Free U. Amsterdam, 1950-54, rsch. assoc., 1954-56, conservator, 1958-60; fullbright fellow U. Minn., Mpls., 1956-57, faculty, 1957-58, 60-70, prof. elec. engring. and physics, 1965-70; prof. theoretical physics U. Montreal, Que., Can., 1969-95, sr. rschr. math. rsch. ctr. Que., 1969-2000, prof. emerita, 1998—. Vis. prof. U. Fla., 1974, 78-88; prof. elec. and computer engring. Fla. Internat. U., 1992-2000; adj. prof. physics U. Miami, 2001—. Contbg. author: Fluctuation Phenomena in Solids, 1965; author Equilibrium and Non-Equilibrium Statistical Mechanics, 2008, rev. edit., 2010; contbr. articles to profl. jours. Rsch. grantee, NSF, Air Force OSR, Wright Patterson AFB, Nat. Sci. and Engring. Rsch. Coun., Ottawa. Fellow IEEE (life), Am. Phys. Soc.; mem. Am. Math. Soc., NY Acad. Scis. Office: University Miami James L Knight Physics Bldg 1320 Campo Sano Ave Coral Gables FL 33146 Office Phone: 305-284-7137. Business E-Mail: vanvliet@physics.miami.edu.

VAN WAGENEN, PAUL G., gas industry executive; BA, Brigham Young U., 1970; JD, U. Washington, 1973. With Exxon Corp.; mgmt. positions Pogo Producing Co., 1979—90, chmn., pres., CEO, 1991—. Bd. dirs. Domestic Petroleum Coun.; mem., exec. com. U.S. Oil & Gas Assn. Mem. Greater Houston Round Table, Greater Houston Partnership; mem. exec. com. Greater Houston YMCA. Mem.: Ctr. Strategic and Internat. Studies-Houston Roundtable, Royalty Owners Assn., Texas Independent Producers, Nat. Ocean Industries Assn. (exec. com., bd. dir.), Nat. Petroleum Coun., All-American Wildcatters. Home: PO Box 27984 Houston TX 77227-7984 Office: Pogo Producing Co 700 Milam St Ste 3100 Houston TX 77002-2764 Office Phone: 713-297-5000. Business E-Mail: paul_wagenen@pogoproducing.com.

VAN WYCK, GEORGE RICHARD, insurance company executive; b. Wilmington, Vt., Feb. 6, 1928; s. Harold Wait Van Wyck and Ruth Anna Learnard; m. Jeanne Mildred Anderson, Apr. 17, 1948; children: Diana Lee Van Wyck Jenkins, Beryl Jeanne. BS in Math. cum laude, St. Lawrence U., 1953. Actuarial clk. Aetna Life Ins. Co., Hartford, Conn., 1953-55; with Am. Bankers Ins. Group, Miami, Fla., 1955-91, sec., bd. dirs., 1983-89, ret., 1991. Bd. dirs. Jr. Achievement of Greater Miami, 1966-83, pres., 1975-76; bd. dirs. Epworth Village Retirement Complex, Miami, 1966-2000, v.p., 1998-99, chmn. investment com. 1995-99; founding dir., pres. Brickel Children's Ctr., Miami, 1980-82; mem. pers. adv. bd., vice chmn. Dade County, Miami, 1987-89. With USAF, 1946-49. Fellow Life Office Mgmt.

Inst.; mem. 1st United Meth. Ch. So. Miami, Phi Beta Kappa. Democrat. Methodist. Avocations: photography, golf, bridge, writing. Home: 8455 SW 44th St Miami FL 33155-4126 Personal E-mail: gvanwyck@cs.com.

VAN ZANT, CHARLES E., state legislator; b. Jacksonville, Fla., Nov. 24, 1943; m. Katherine Van Zant; 8 children. BA Architecture & Bldg Design, U. Fla., 1968; MDiv, Southern Bapt. Theol. Sem., 1974; DTh, Western Bapt. Theol. Sem., 2001. Owner Van Zant Assocs., 1972—; arch. Bruce McCarty & Assocs., Kemp, Bunch, & Jackson, Reynolds, Smith & Hills, Richmond Construction Co., Tafel-Schickli Assocs.; mem. Dist. 21 Fla. House of Reps., 2008—, vice chair health care regulation policy com., mem. energy and utilities policy com., joint legis. auditing com., mil. and local affairs policy com., natural resources appropriations com. Mem. Clay County Sch. Bd., 2007—, former vice chmn., Clay County Fla. Code Bd. Mem.: NRA, Am. Inst. Arch., Gospel Lighthouse Internat. Republican. Office: Capitol Office 402 S Monroe St Rm 1101 Tallahassee FL 32399-1300 also: 3841 Reid St Ste 5 Palatka FL 32177-2509 Office Phone: 850-488-0665, 386-312-2272. Business E-Mail: charles.vanzant@myfloridahouse.gov.

VAN ZWEDEN, JAAP, conductor, music director; b. Amsterdam, Dec. 12, 1960; m. Aaltje van Buuren, 1983; children: Anna-Sophie, Daniel, Benjamin, Alexander. Student, Julliard Sch., NYC. Violinist, concertmaster Royal Concertgebouw Orch., 1979—95; chief condr. Netherlands Symphony Orch., Enschede, 1996—2000, Residentie Orch., The Hague, Netherlands, 2000—05; chief condr., artistic dir. Netherlands Radio Philharm., Hilversum, 2005—12; music dir. designate Dallas Symphony Orch., 2007—08, music dir., 2008—; chief condr. Royal Flemish Philharm., Antwerp, Belgium, 2008—12; music dir. Hong Kong Philharm. Orch., 2012—. Guest condr. St. Louis Symphony Orch., Orchestre National de France, Munich Philharm., Rotterdam Philharm., Oslo Philharm., St. Petersburg Philharm., Tokyo Philharm., Hong Kong Philharm., London Philharm., City of Birmingham Symphony Orch., West German Radio Symphony Orch. Cologne, Danish Radio Orch. Co-founder found. for autistic children Papageno Found., Netherlands. Named Condr. of Yr., Musical America, 2012. Office: Dallas Symphony Orch 2301 Flora St Dallas TX 75201 Office Phone: 214-871-4000.

VARELLAS, SANDRA MOTTE, lawyer; d. James E. and Helen Lucille (Gilliam) Motte; m. James John Varellas, July 3, 1971; children: James John III, David Todd. BA, Winthrop U., 1968; MA, U. Ky., 1970, JD, 1975. Bar: Ky. 1975, Fla. 1976, U.S. Dist. Ct. (ea. dist.) Ky. 1975, U.S. Ct. Appeals (6th cir.) 1976, U.S. Supreme Ct. 1978. Instr. Midway Coll., Ky., 1970-72; adj. prof. U. Ky. Coll. Law, Lexington, 1976-78; instr. dept. bus. adminstrn. U. Ky., Lexington, 1976-78; ptnr. Varellas, Pratt & Cooley, Lexington, 1975-93, Varellas & Pratt, Lexington, 1993-97, Varellas & Varellas, Lexington, 1998—. Fayette County judge exec., Ky., 1980-2010; hearing officer Ky. Natural Resources and Environ. Protection Cabinet, Frankfort, 1984-88; bd. trustees Lexington Network 1994-98, 2002-2004, sec., 1994-98. Committeewoman Ky. Young Dems., Frankfort, 1977-80; pres. Fayette County Young Dems., Lexington, 1977; bd. dirs. Ky. Dem. Women's Club, Frankfort, 1980-84, bd. dirs., Bluegrass Estate Planning Coun., 1995-98; grad. Leadership Lexington, 1981; chairwoman Profl. Women's Forum, Lexington, Ky., 1985-86, bd. dirs., 1984-87, Aequum award com., 1989-92; mem. devel. coun. Midway Coll., 1990-92; co-chair Gift Club Com., 1992; mem. pub. svc. sector com. United Way of Bluegrass, 2004. Named Outstanding Young Dem. Woman, Ky. Young Dems., Frankfort, 1977, Outstanding Former Young Dem., Ky. Young Dems., 1983. Mem. Ky. Bar Assn. (treas. young lawyers divsn. 1978-79, long range planning com. 1988-89), Fla. Bar, Fayette County Bar Assn. (treas. 1977-78, bd. govs. 1978-80), LWV (nominating com. 1984-85), Greater Lexington C. of C. (legis. affairs com. 1994-95, bd.d irs. coun. smaller enterprises 1992-95), The Lexington Forum (bd. dirs. 1996-99), Lexington Philharm. Guild (bd. dirs. 1979-81, 86-2006), Nat. Assn. Women Bus. Owners (chmn. cmty. liaison/govtl. affairs com. 1992-93); Clubs: Creative Camera Club (bd. dirs. 2008-10). Office: Varellas & Varellas 249 W Short St Ste 201 Lexington KY 40507-1245 Home Phone: 859-268-7307; Office Phone: 859-252-4473. Business E-Mail: svarellas@varellaslaw.com.

VARGA, PAUL C., beverage products executive; b. Louisville, 1964; m. Melissa Varga; 2 children. BA business administration, finance, U Ky.; MBA, Purdue U. Various marketing positions Brown-Forman Corp., 1987—96, sr. v.p., 1996—2003, global chief mktg. officer, Brown-Forman Spirits, 2000—03, pres., CEO, Brown-Forman Beverages, 2003—05, pres., CEO, 2005—07, CEO, 2005—, chmn., 2007—. Office: Brown-Forman Corp 850 Dixie Hwy Louisville KY 40210 Office Phone: 502-585-1100. Office Fax: 502-774-6633. Business E-Mail: paul_varga@b-f.com.

VARGAS, JOE FLORES, insurance adjuster; b. Corpus Christi, Tex., Dec. 18, 1940; s. Jose Arispe Vargas and Francisca (Flores) V.; m. Anita Munoz, Feb. 16, 1963; children: Joseph Dean, Bernice Ann Vargas Burns. AA in Police Sci., Del Mar Jr. Coll., 1973; BS in Criminal Justice, Tex. A&M at Corpus Christi, Corpus Christi, 1979. Life ins. underwriter Am. Nat. Ins. Co., 1962—65; ct. interpreter Nueces County, Corpus Christi, Tex., 1966—70, dep. sheriff, ct. bailiff, 1970—78; ins. adjuster Greene Claims Svc., Corpus Christi, Tex., 1978; pvt. investigator Equifax, Corpus Christi, Tex., 1978—79; ins. claims rep. Crum & Forster Comml. Ins., Corpus Christi, Tex., 1979—86; owner, pres., ins. claims adjuster South Tex. Claims Svc. Inc., Corpus Christi, Tex., 1986—2012. Avocation: hunting. Office: South Tex Claims Svc Inc PO Box 270276 Corpus Christi TX 78427-0276 Office Phone: 361-855-5913.

VARGAS-LAND, VANESSA, wholesale distribution executive, lawyer; BA in English, U. Ill., Urbana, 1987, JD, 1991. Mem. Compliance and Ethics Leadership Council; counsel III, litigation Abbott Laboratory, Inc., 2000—04, dir., ethics, compliance, 2004—05; divsn. ethics officer, divsn. compliance officer Abbott Internat., 2005—06, Abbott Nutrition Internat., 2006—07, Abbott Laboratory, Inc., 2000—07; v.p., chief compliance officer Chiquita Brands International, Inc., 2007—. Mem. Ethics & Compliance Officers Assn., Soc. of Corp. Compliance and Ethics; mem., adv. bd. Cintas Inst. for Bus. Ethics. Mem.: Chgo. Bar Assn. Avocations: reading, gardening. Office: Chiquita Brands International Inc 550 S Caldwell St Ste 1010 Charlotte NC 28202-2681 Office Fax: 513-784-8030. Business E-Mail: vvargas-land@chiquita.com.

VARGHA, REBECCA BROGDEN, librarian, library association executive; BA, U. NC, Chapel Hill, 1979; MLS, NC Ctrl. U., 1980. Libr. asst. Nat. Humanities Ctr., Rsch. Triangle Park, NC, 1979—80, asst. libr., 1980—87, assoc. libr., 1987—94; info. analyst SAS Inst. Inc., Cary, NC, 1994; sr. rsch. specialist Nortel Networks; adj. faculty U. NC, Chapel Hill, 1996—98; libr. U. NC Sch. Info. & Libr. Sci., Chapel Hill, 2001—. Mem.: ALA, Spl. Librs. Assn. (chair conf. com. 1993, chair elect & chair divsn. cabinet 1996—98, pres. 2006—07, NC ch. archivist, chair networking com., chair scholarships com., chair student & academic rels. com., NC ch. Meritorious Achievement award 1994), Beta Phi Mu. Office: U NC Manning Hall CB #3360 Chapel Hill NC 27599-3360 Office Phone: 919-962-8361. Office Fax: 919-962-8071. Business E-Mail: vargha@ils.unc.edu.

VARGO, RONALD PAUL, information technology executive; b. Painesville, Ohio, Mar. 26, 1954; s. Anton M. and Ingrid E. (Olson) V.; m. Kathleen M. Martell, Nov. 20, 1976; children: Mary Christine, Kevin Matthew. BA in Econs., Dartmouth Coll., 1976; MBA, Stanford U., 1981. Various fin. positions GE, Stamford, Conn., 1976-79, Standard Oil Co., Cleve., 1981-87, dir. corp. fin., 1986-87; comml. mgr. BP Exploration, Houston, 1987-89; gen. mgr. crude oil trading BP Oil Supply Co., 1989—91; joined TRW, 1991, v.p. bus. devel. automotive electronics, v.p., treas., corp. treas., v.p. investor relations, 2001—04; v.p., treas. Electronic Data Systems Corp., 2004, co-interim CFO, 2006, exec. v.p., CFO, 2006—. Office: EDS Corp 5400 Legacy Dr Plano TX 75024

VARIAN, MICHELE A., food service executive; m. Dave Varian; children: Angela, David. BBA in Mktg., U. North Tex., Denton; MBA in Internat. Mgmt., U. Tex., Dallas. Purchasing mgr. Campbell Taggart Inc., 1986—93, Maybelline Cosmetics, 1993—96, Lyrick Corp., 1996—97; bus. mgr. Brinker International Inc., 1997—2005, Chili's Grill & Bar, 2000—05; dir. purchasing Cracker Barrel Old Country Store, Inc., 2005—09, v.p. strategic sourcing, 2009—. Office: Cracker Barrel Old Country Store Inc 305 Hartmann Dr Lebanon TN 37088-0787 Office Phone: 615-444-5533. Office Fax: 615-443-9818.

VARLAN, THOMAS A., federal judge; b. Oak Ridge, Tenn., 1956; BA, U. Tenn., 1978; JD, Vanderbilt U., Nashville, 1981. Pvt. practice atty., Atlanta, 1981—87, Knoxville, 1998—2003; law dir. City of Knoxville, 1988—98; judge US Dist. Ct. (ea. dist.) Tenn., Knoxville, 2003—. Office: US Dist Ct 800 Market St Ste 143 Knoxville TN 37902 Office Phone: 865-545-4762.

VARMA, ABHAY K., neurosurgeon, educator; s. Sudershan and Ramesh Varma; m. Deepa Khullar, Feb. 19, 1992; children: Bhavya, Prachi. MBBS, All India Inst. Med. Scis., New Delhi, 1985, MCh, 1992; MSCR, Med. U. SC, Charleston, 2007. Assoc. prof., neurosurgery Med. U. SC, 2012—. Mem.: SC. Assn. Neurol. Surgery, North Am. Spine Soc., Soc. Neurooncology, Congress Neurol. Surgeons. Hindu. Avocations: photography, reading, travel. Office: Med University SC 96 Jonathan Lucas St Ste 301 CSB Charleston SC 29425*

VARNER, CHILTON DAVIS, lawyer; b. Opelika, Ala., Mar. 12, 1943; d. William Cole and Frances (Thornton) Davis; m. K. Morgan Varner, III, June 19, 1965; 1 child, Ashley Elizabeth. AB with distinction, Smith Coll., 1965; JD with distinction, Emory U., 1976. Assoc. King & Spalding, Atlanta, 1976-83, ptnr., 1983—, mem. mgmt. com., 1996—98. Bd. dirs. Wesley Woods Healthcare, 1997—2007, 11th Cir. Ct. Appeals Hist. Soc.; trustee Emory U., Atlanta, 1995—, Product Liability Adv. Coun., 1987—; mem. Adv. Com. Fed. Civil Rules, 2004—. Author: Appellate Handbook for Georgia Lawyers, 1995. Mem. Leadership Atlanta, 1984—85; mem. exec. com. Atlanta Arts Alliance, 1981—85; mem. Atlanta Symphony Chorus, 1970—74; asst. clk., elder, bd. elders Trinity Presbyn. Ch., Atlanta, 1975—78. Recipient Disting. Alumna award, Emory U. Law Sch., 1998; named one of Top 10 Women Litigators, Nat. Law Jour., 2001. Fellow: Am. Coll. Trial Lawyers; mem.: ABA, Atlanta Bar Assn., Ga. Bar Assn., Phi Beta Kappa, Order of Coif. Office: King & Spalding 1180 Peachtree St NE 37th Fl Atlanta GA 30309-3521 Office Phone: 404-572-4789, 404-572-4789. Office Fax: 404-572-5100. E-mail: cvarner@kslaw.com.

VARNER, DAVID EUGENE, lawyer; b. Dallas, Oct. 9, 1937; s. E.C. and D. Evelyn (Bauguss) V.; m. Joan Paula Oransky, Aug. 13, 1962; children: Michael A., Kevin E., Cheryl L. BA, So. Meth. U., Dallas, 1958, JD, 1961. Bar: Tex. 1961, Fla. 1974, Okla., 1977, U.S. Supreme Ct. 1978. Assoc. Eldridge, Goggans, Davidson & Silverberg, Dallas, 1962-65; atty., asst. sec. Redman Industries, Inc., Dallas, 1965-66; assoc. gen. atty. Tex. Instruments, Inc., Dallas, 1966-73; sr. atty., asst. sec. Fla. Gas Co., Winter Park, 1973-76; v.p., gen. counsel, sec. Facet Enterprises, Inc., Tulsa, 1976-78, Summa Corp., Las Vegas, Nev., 1978-82; sr. v.p., gen. counsel, sec. Transco Energy Co., Houston, 1982-95; pres. The MKC Group, Houston, 1995—. Mem. royalty mgmt. adv. com. U.S. Minerals Mgmt. Svc., 1985—87. Mng. editor Southwestern Law Jour., 1960-61 Mem.: Fla. Bar Assn., Tex. Bar Assn. Office: PO Box 79571 Houston TX 77279-9571

VASLEF, STEVEN NICHOLAS, surgeon; b. Colorado Springs, Colo., Aug. 16, 1958; s. Nicholas P. and Irene I. (Koncz) V.; m. Maria E. Vaslef, July 11, 1988. BS, MIT, 1980; MD, U. Va., 1984; PhD, Northwestern U., 1990. Diplomate Am. Bd. Surgery with subspecialty in surg. critical care. Intern U. Ill., Chgo., 1984-85, resident in gen. surgery, 1985-92; mem. staff Evanston/Glenbrook Hosps., 1992-94; asst. prof. surgery, asst. pro. bio-med. engring. Northwestern U. Med. Sch., Chgo., 1992-94; asst. prof. surgery Duke U. Med. Ctr., Durham, N.C., 1994-2000, assoc. prof., 2000—, asst. prof. bio-med. engring., 1994—97, asst. prof. anesthesiology, 1996—. Mem. ACS; mem. Soc. Critical Care Medicine, Am. Soc. Artificial Internal Organs, Soc. for Surgery of Alimentary Tract, Am. Assn. Surgery of Trauma, Ea. Assn. for Surgery of Trauma. Office: Duke Univ Med Ctr Dept Surgery Box 2837 Durham NC 27715-2601 Home Phone: 919-382-8208. E-mail: vasle001@mc.duke.edu.

VÁSQUEZ, JOSÉ STEPHEN, bishop; b. Stamford, Tex., July 9, 1957; s. Juan and Elvira Vásquez. B in Theology, U. St. Thomas, 1980. Ordained priest Diocese of San Angelo, Tex., 1984; parochial vicar St. Joseph Ch., Odessa, Tex., 1985—87, pastor, 1997—2002, St. Joseph's Ch., Ft. Stockton, Tex., 1987—97; ordained bishop, 2002; aux. bishop Archdiocese of Galveston-Houston, Tex., 2002—10; bishop Diocese of Austin, Tex., 2010—. Roman Catholic. Office: Diocese of Austin PO Box 13327 1600 N Congress Austin TX 78711 Office Phone: 512-476-4888. Office Fax: 512-469-9537.

VASQUEZ, WILLIAM LEROY, business educator, consultant; b. Austin, Tex., Mar. 9, 1944; s. Eliseo M. and Janie (Garcia) V. BS with distinction, Nova Southeastern U., 1983, MBA, 1985, DBA, 1992. Cert. Inst. Cert. Profl. Mgrs., 1990, Inst. Cert. Computing Profls., 1993. Svc. mgr. Data Gen. Corp., various, Latin Am., 1972-80; product mgr. Gould, Inc., Ft. Lauderdale, Fla., 1980—84, Tektronix Inc., Portland, Oreg., 1984—86, Racal-Milgo, Ft. Lauderdale, 1988—90, Citibank Internat., Ft. Lauderdale, 1991—2001; ret., 2001. Instr. City U., Portland campus, 1987-88; Maryhurst Coll., 1985-88, Nova Southeastern U. (domestic and internat.), 1988—, pres. internat. alumni assn.; instr. St. Thomas U., 1989—, Fla. Atlantic U., 1993—. Mem. VFW, Nat. Bus. Edn. Assn., U.S. Submarine Vets., Inc., Mensa. Republican. Avocations: guitar, model trains, fine arts. Home: 9788 NW 18th St Coral Springs FL 33071-5824 Office Phone: 954-309-3507. E-mail: vasquezw@bellsouth.net.

VASSER, ALBERT GLENN, lawyer; b. Pine Bluff, Ark., July 20, 1947; s. Albert P. Vasser and Bobbie Ann (Nipper) Hogan; m. Judith Jackson, Aug. 16, 1969; 1 child, Vicki Suzanne. BSBA with honors, U. Ark., 1969, JD, 1972. Bar: Ark., 1972, US Dist. Ct. Ark., Fed., 1972, US Ct. Appeals (8th cir.), US Supreme Ct. From assoc. to ptnr. McKenzie, Vasser and Barber, PLLC, Prescott, Ark., 1972—. Served US Mil., 1972. Pres. Prescott (Ark.) Sch. Bd., 1985; mcpl. judge City of Prescott, Ark.; bd. dirs. SW Ark. Regional Health Ctr., El Dorado; bd. trustees, adminstr. Bd. First United Meth. Ch. 1st lt. US Army. Recipient Spl. Justice award Ark. Supreme Ct., 1991. Fellow American Coll. Mortgage Attys., Ark. Bar Found. (bd. mem., pres.); mem. Ark. Bar Assn. (del. and com. chmn., pres.-elect 2004, Golden Gavel award 1984), Nev. County Bar Assn. (pres., com. mem.). Avocations: tennis, golf. Office: McKenzie McRae & Vasser 122 E 2nd St PO Box 599 Prescott AR 71857-0599

VASSILOPOULOU-SELLIN, RENA, researcher; b. Dec. 29, 1949; MD, Albert Einstein Coll. Medicine, 1974. Resident Montefiore Hosp., Bronx, 1974-77; fellow Northwestern U., Chgo., 1977-80; prof. Univ. Tex., Houston, 1980—. Fellow ACP, Am. Assn. Clin. Endocrinol.; mem. AAAS, AMA, Am. Soc. Bone and Mineral Rsch., Am. Diabetes Assn., Am. Soc. Clin. Oncology, Endo Soc. Office: Anderson Cancer Ctr 1515 Holcombe Blvd # 15 Houston TX 77030-4009

VAUGHAN, DONALD RAY, state legislator, lawyer, mayor pro tem, municipal official; b. Greensboro, NC, Sept. 13, 1952; s. Rowland G. and Catherine (Braswell) V. BA with highest honors, U. N.C., 1974; MA in Pub. Adminstrn., Am. U., 1976; JD, Wake Forest U., 1979. Bar: N.C., U.S. Dist. Ct. (mid. dist.) N.C., U.S. Ct. Appeals (4th cir.), D.C. Legis. aide U.S. Senator Robert Morgan, Washington, 1975-76; cons. R.J. Reynolds Industries, Winston-Salem, N.C., 1976-79; atty., econ. advisor Office of the Gov., Raleigh, N.C., 1979-81; v.p. govt. affairs Stedman Corp., Asheboro, N.C., 1981-86; v.p. Stedman Found., Asheboro, N.C., 1987—; mem. Dist. 27 NC State Senate, 2008—. Lectr. Am. U., Washington, 1975, 76; adj. prof. Master of Pub. Affairs Program, U. N.C. Mem. staff Wake Forest U. Law Review; contbr. articles to profl jours. Gen. counsel Found. Am. and Found. for Civic Literacy, 1988—; legal counsel Gov.'s Efficiency Study Commn., Raleigh, 1985; city councilman City of Greensboro, 1992-94, mayor pro tem, 1994. Fellow N.C. Inst. Politics; mem. ABA, N.C. Bar Assn., N.C. Acad. of Trial Lawyers, Greensboro Bar Assn. Democrat. Office: NC Senate 300 N Salisbury St Rm 515 Raleigh NC 27603-5925 also: 612 W Friendly Ave Greensboro NC 27401 also: PO Box 265 Greensboro NC 27402-0265 Office Phone: 919-733-5856, 336-273-1415. Office Fax: 919-715-5815. Business E-Mail: Don.Vaughan@ncleg.net.

VAUGHAN, EUGENE H., investment company executive; b. Brownsville, Tenn., Oct. 5, 1933; s. Eugene H. Sr. and Margaret (Musgrave) V.; m. Susan Bolinger Westbrook, May 11, 1963; children: Margaret Corbin, Richard Bolinger. BA, Vanderbilt U., 1955; MBA, Harvard U., 1961. CFA, 1967. Security analyst Putnam Mgmt. Co., Boston, 1961-64; dir., dir. rsch. Underwood, Neuhaus & Co., Inc., Houston, 1964-70; pres., chief exec. officer Vaughan, Nelson & Boston, Inc., Houston, 1970-77, Vaughan, Nelson, Scarborough & McCullough, L.P., Houston, 1970—. Chmn. bd. dirs. Dreyfus Founders Asset Mgmt. Co., Denver, 1970—. Chair Fin. Analyst Fedn., N.Y.C., 1973-74, bd. dirs., 1969-76; dir. U. Tex. Health Sci. Ctr., Houston, 2002—; pres. Houston Soc. Fin. Analysts, 1967-68; trustee exec. com. Vanderbilt U., Nashville, 1972—, St. John's Sch., Houston, 1980-85, Goodwill Industries, Houston, 1978—, United Way of Tex. Gulf Coast, 1994—; elder First Presbyn. Ch., 1976—; founding chmn., trustee Presbyn. Sch., Houston, 1986-90. Lt. USN, 1955-58. Recipient Disting. Svc. award Fin. Analyst Fedn., 1978, Humanitarian award Am. Jewish Com., 1993, Bus. Leader of Yr. award U. St. Thomas, 1996. Mem. Inst. Chartered Fin. Analysts (trustee 1986-93, chmn. 1989), Assn. for Investment Mgmt. and Rsch. (founding chmn. 1990-91, gov. 1990-93), Greater Houston Partnership (bd. dirs. 1990—, exec. com. 1993—, chair Ctr. Houston's Future 1999—), Houston Club (pres. 1983-84, bd. dirs. 1979-85, chair centennial celebration, 1992-94), Houston Country Club, Coronado Club (Houston), Houston Forum (pres. 1991-92, chmn. 1992-93), Harvard U. Bus. Sch. Club Houston (pres. 1968-69, bd. dirs. 1966-71, 86-90), Vanderbilt Club Houston (chmn. 1984—, pres. 1966-68, Disting. Svc. award 1994), Conferie des Chevaliers du Tastevin, Belle Meade Country Club (Nashville). Republican. Avocations: travel, sailing. Home: 3465 Inwood Dr Houston TX 77019-3129 Office: 4400 Post Oak Pkwy Ste 2500 Houston TX 77027-3455

VAUGHAN, JOSEPH LEE, JR., entrepreneur, educational consultant; s. Joseph Lee and Ann (Doner) Vaughan; m. Mary Linda De Silva; children: Leigh Ann, Kelley, Stephen, Kathleen. BA, U. Va., 1964, MEd, 1968, EdD, 1974. Real estate lic. Tex. Assn. Realtors, 1999, cert. entrepreneur bus. Southern Meth. U., Dallas, 2007. Tchr. Madison HS, Va., 1965-67, Darlington Sch., Rome, Ga., 1967-69, Woodberry Forest Sch., Va., 1969-74; asst. prof. edn. U. Ariz., Tucson, 1974-80; prof. Tex. A&M U.-Commerce, Mesquite, 1980—2006, dir. grad. programs in reading edn., 1980—86, 1991—92, 2000—06; real estate agent Adleta & Poston, Dallas, 1999—2000, RE/MAXLandmark, 2007—08, Network Realtors, Royse City, 2008—10. Dir. Tex. Ctr. Learning Styles, 1989—95; exec. dir. Children's Inst. Literacy Devel., Inc., 1995—2004, The Ctr. Acad. Progress, Inc., 2004—05; cons. faculty in humanities St. Alban's Episcopal Sch., 2000—07; assoc. faculty devel. reading Mountain View Coll., Dallas; CEO Learning and Literary Sys., 2006—, Head Sch. Union Valley Acad., 2011—. Co-author: Reading and Learning in Content Classrooms, 1978, 2d rev. edit., 1985, Reading and Reasoning Beyond The Primary Grades, 1986. Bd. govs. Sancta Sophia Sem., 1991—98, Royse City Rotary Club, 2007—09, Royse City C. of C., 2007—. Mem. Internat. Reading Assn. Methodist. Avocations: golf, travel. Home: 447 Ridgemont Dr Heathridge TX 75126 Office: 9424 Fm35 Royse City TX 75189

VAUGHAN, KEITH W., lawyer; b. Bluefield, W.Va., Oct. 1, 1950; BA cum laude, Wake Forest U., 1972; JD cum laude, U. Ga., 1975. Bar: Ga. 1975, NC 1975, US Dist. Ct. (ea., mid. & we. dists.) NC, NC Supreme Ct., US Ct. Appeals (4th cir.), US Supreme Ct. Ptnr. Womble Carlyle Sandridge & Rice PLLC, Winston-Salem, NC, former litig. practice group leader, chmn. mgmt. com., mng. mem., 2002—. Bd. dir. NC Assn. Def. Attys., 1985—88. Editor-in-chief Ga. Law Rev., 1974-75. Chmn. NC Partnership Econ. Devel., 2008—09; chmn. bd. dirs. Piedmont Triad Partnership, 2006—09; mem. exec. bd., mem. bd. dirs United Way Forsyth County; mem. bd. visitors of coll. and grad. sch. Wake Forest U.; mem. bd. dirs. Winston-Salem Alliance; mem. exec. com., mem. bd. dirs. Winston-Salem C. of C., chmn., 2010; pres. Winston-Salem Downtown Rotary Club, 2006—07; mem. exec. com., bd. trustees Winston-Salem State U.; chmn. Smith-Shaver Law Sch. Scholarship Fund. Named to Bus. North Carolina's Legal Elite (Litigation). Fellow Am. Coll. of Trial Lawyers; mem. ABA, NC Bar Assn., Forsyth County Bar Assn., Ga. Bar Assn., Forsyth County Young Lawyers Assn. (pres., 1981), Am. Inns of Ct. (Master of Bench), Omicron Delta Kappa, Delta Sigma Rho, Tau Kappa Alpha. Office: Womble Carlyle Sandridge & Rice PLLC One W 4th St Winston Salem NC 27101 Office Phone: 336-721-3600. Office Fax: 336-733-8417. Business E-Mail: kvaughan@wcsr.com.

VAUGHAN, NANCY, Mayor, Greensboro, North Carolina; m. Don Vaughan; children: John Mincello, Michael Mincello, Catherine. Student, Fairfield U., Conn., 1979—81. Mktg. coord. York Wastewater Consultants, 1985—88; ops. mgr. Talley Machinery, 1989—2006; mem. Dist. 4 Greensboro City Coun., 1997—2001, at-large rep.,

2009—13; mayor City of Greensboro, 2013—. Bd. mem. Piedmont Triad Internat. Airport Authority, 2003—09; with Greensboro Housing Devel. Partnership. Mem. Jr. League Greensboro, 2000—04; bd. mem. Greensboro Beautiful, 2005—08; Brownie leader Girls Scouts, 2008—; mem. bd. trustees Greensboro Day Sch., 2009—13; mem. Westminster Presbyn. Ch. Office: Office of the Mayor PO Box 3136 Greensboro NC 27402-3136 Home: 902 Sunset Dr Greensboro NC 27408 Office Phone: 336-373-2396. Office Fax: 336-574-4003.

VAUGHAN, WILLIAM WALTON, atmospheric scientist; b. Clearwater, Fla., Sept. 7, 1930; s. William Walton and Ella Vermelle (Warr) Vaughan; m. Wilma Geraldine Stapleton, Dec. 23, 1951; children: Stephen W., David A., William D., Robert T. BS with honors, U. Fla., 1951; grad. cert., USAF Inst. Tech./Fla. State U., 1952; PhD, U. Tenn., 1976. AMS cert. cons. meteorologist. Sci. asst. Air Force Armament Ctr., Eglin AFB, Fla., 1955-58, Army Ballistic Missile Agy., Huntsville, Ala., 1958-60; chief aerospace environ. div. Marshall Space Flight Center, NASA, Huntsville, 1960-76, chief atmospheric scis. div., 1976-86; rsch. prof. atmospheric sci. U. Ala., Huntsville, 1986—, dir. Rsch. Inst., 1986-94; ret., 1994. Cons. atmospheric sci., applied meteorlogy and tech. stds.; mem. adv. com. NASA Nat. & Internat. Sci. Tech. Com.; assoc. editor Jour. Advanced Tech. and Mgmt. Contbr. articles to profl. jours. Served to capt. USAF, 1951—55. Recipient Exceptional Svc. medal, NASA, 1971. Fellow: AIAA (standard exec. coun., atmospheric & space environment tech. com., space ops. tech. com., Losey Atmospheric Scis. award 1980, Excellence in Aerospace Stds. award 2003, disting. Svc. award 2007), Am. Meteorol. Soc. (aviation, range & aerospace meteorlogy tech. com.); mem.: AAAS, Am. Geophys. Union, Stds. Engring. Soc., Sigma Xi. Office: Univ Ala Atmospheric Sci Dept Huntsville AL 35899-0001 Business E-Mail: vaughan@nsstc.uah.edu.

VAUGHN, JACQUE, professional basketball coach; b. LA, Feb. 11, 1975; m. Laura Vaughn; children: Jalen, Jeremiah. BBA, U. Kans., Lawrence, 1997. Guard Utah Jazz, 1997—2001, Atlanta Hawks, 2001—02, 2003—04, Orlando Magic, 2002—03, head coach, 2012—; guard NJ Nets, 2004—06, San Antonio Spurs, 2006—09, asst. coach, 2010—12. Named Big 8 Conf. Player of Yr., 1996. Achievements include member of NBA Finals championship winning San Antonio Spurs, 2007. Office: Orlando Magic 8701 Maitland Summit Blvd Orlando FL 32810*

VAUGHN, LEWIS R., state legislator; b. Greenville, SC, Mar. 18, 1934; s. William Randolph and Sally Allen Vaughn; m. Lila Mae Waldrop, 1955; 1 child, R. Keith. Former mem. Hazardous Disabilities Coun. Transition Task Force, Employee Security Commn. Screening Com.; former vice chmn. House Bus. Caucus, Agy. Head Salary Rev. Commn., Joint Legislature Screening Com. Employee Security Commn.; former chmn. House Operating & Mgmt. Com., Greenville County Legislature Del., Sales & Income Tax Subcom. of House, Ways & Means Com.; house rep. SC; project mgr. Greenville, SC, 1976—85; dept. mgr. St. Louis, 1985—86; state interagency coord. Coun. Edn. of Handicapped, 1989—90; state rep. Dist. 18 SC, 1989—2006; mem. State Devel. Disabilities Coun. Transition Task Force; state senator Dist. 5 SC; ret. businessman. Mem.: Scottish Rite Mason, Hejaz Shrine Temple, Blue Ridge Ruritan Club, Taylors Masonic Lodge 345. Republican. Baptist. Office: 501 Gressette Bldg Columbia SC 29202 Address: 623 Ashley Commons Ct Greer SC 29651 Home Phone: 864-848-0368; Office Phone: 803-212-6100. Business E-Mail: LRV@scsenate.org.

VAUGHN, MICHAEL S., law educator; s. Harley (Bud) Dewitt and Judith Ann Vaughn; m. Tzu-Hsiu Nancy Vaughn, Dec. 2, 1989; 1 child, Rachel. PhD in Criminal Justice, Sam Houston State U., Huntsville, Tex., 1990—93. Prof. Ga. State U., Atlanta, 1993—2006, chmn. dept. criminal justice, 2002—05; prof. Sam Houston State U., Huntsville, Tex., 2006—; co-dir. Inst. Legal Studies Criminal Justice, 2006—; asst. dean grad. studies, dir. criminal justice PhD program SHSU, 2009—12. Editor: Internat. Criminal Justice Rev., Criminal Justice Rev., Ga. State U., 2001-05; book rev. editor Jour. Criminal Justice Edn. Acad. Criminal Justice Scis., Greenbelt, Md., 1993—1996, editor, police forum police sect., Md., 1996—2001; contbr. correctional health care report Civic Rsch. Inst., NYC, 1999—2006, articles to profl. jours. and publs. Recipient Outstanding Service award, Police Section, Acad. of Criminal Justice Sciences, 1998, Outstanding Paper, Acad. of Criminal Justice Scis., 1996, Outstanding Faculty Achievement award, Ga. State U., 2004; named Outstanding Alumnus, Coll. of Criminal Justice, Sam Houston State U., 2002. Mem.: ABA (criminal justice sect. mem.), Am. Assn. Univ. Profs., Am. Judicature Soc., Am. Soc. Criminology, Acad. Criminal Justice Scis. Democrat. Methodist. Avocation: reading. Office: Sam Houston State Univ Criminal Justice PO Box 2296 Huntsville TX 77341-2296 Office Phone: 936-294-1349. Business E-Mail: mvaughn@shsu.edu.

VAUGHN, ROBERT CANDLER, JR., lawyer; b. Winston Salem, NC, Sept. 6, 1931; s. Robert Candler and Douglas Arthur V.; m. Carolyn (Hartford), May 2, 1959; children: Patricia Anne, Robert Candler III. BS in Bus. Adminstrn., U. N.C., 1953, JD, 1955. Bar: N.C., 1955, U.S. Dist. Ct. (mid. dist.), 1959, U.S. Tax Ct., 1981. Assoc. Petree, Stockton, Robinson, and predecessor firms, Winston Salem, 1959-65, ptnr., 1965-2000. Bd. dirs. Forsyth Bank & Trust Co., Winston-Salem. Pres. United Way Forsyth County, Winston Salem, 1970-71, Forsyth County Bar Assn.; chmn. Winston Salem Coliseum and Conv. Ctr. Commn., 1974-78; bd. adv.U. NC Tax Inst., Chapel Hill; bd. dirs. Leadership Winston Salem; chmn. Winston Salem Found., 2003,chmn, Forsyth Med. Ctr. Found., 1999-01; chmn. Forsyth Tech. Coll. Found., 2006-. Lt. USN, 1955-58. Fellow Am. Bar Found., Am. Coll. Trusts and Estates Counsel (N.C.chmn. 1990-1995); mem. N.C. Bar Assn. (pres. 1985-86, bd. dirs.), U. N.C. Law Alumni Assn. (pres. 1974-75), Am. Coll. Tax Counsel, Old Town Club, Piedmont Club, Rotary. Republican. Methodist. Office: Vaughn Perkinson Ehlinger & Moxley PO Box 25715 Winston Salem NC 27114 Home: 1244 Arbor Rd Apt A411 Winston Salem NC 27104-1144 Home Phone: 336-722-8068; Office Phone: 336-794-6001. E-mail: bob.vaughn@vpems.com.

VEACH, ROBERT RAYMOND, JR., lawyer; b. Charleston, SC, Nov. 28, 1950; s. Robert Raymond and Evelyn; m. Lori Sue Erickson, May 27, 1989. Student, St. Olaf Coll., 1968-70; BS in Acctg., Ariz. State U., 1972; JD, So. Meth. U., 1975. Bar: Tex. 1975, Nebr. 1975, US Dist. Ct. Nebr. 1975, US Dist. Ct. (no. dist.) Tex. 1975, Temporary Emergency Ct. Appeals 1975. Acctg. instr. Sch. Bus. So. Meth. U., Dallas, 1973-74; law clk. to Hon. Joe E. Estes US Dist. Ct. No. Dist. Tex.-Temp. Emergency Ct. Appeals, Dallas, 1975-76; assoc. Locke Purnell Boren Laney & Neely, Dallas, 1976-80; v.p. The Lomas & Nettleton Co., Dallas, 1980-83, Rauscher Pierce Refsnes, Inc., Dallas, 1983-87; pres. RPR Mortgage Fin. Corp., Dallas, 1985-87; sr. shareholder Locke Purnell Rain Harrell, Dallas, 1987-97; exec. v.p. gen. counsel Precision Document Solutions, Inc., Dallas, 1998—; pvt. practice Dallas, 1998—. Allied mem. NY Stock Exch., 1985-87; lectr. securities and banking confs.; bd. dirs. pvt. corps.; trustee CentraCore Properties Trust (NYSE-CPV), chmn. audit and fin. com., 1998-2002, 05-07, chmn. bd., 2002-07, chmn. corp. gov. and nominating com., 2003-07. Author legal articles. Dir. North Tex. affiliate Am. Diabetes Assn., Dallas, 1978-81; mem. Gov.'s Task Force Wash. State Housing Commn., 1982-83. Fellow Nebr. State Bar Found.; mem. ABA, State Bar of Tex., Nebr. State Bar Assn., Fed. Bar Assn., Dallas Bar Assn. Avocation: golf. Home: 4223 Brookview Dr Dallas TX 75220-3801 Office: 2911 Turtle Creek Blvd Ste 1240 Dallas TX 75219-6277 Office Phone: 214-520-7544. Business E-Mail: bob@veachlaw.com.

VEASEY, MARC, United States Representative from Texas, former state legislator; b. Tarrant County, Tex., Jan. 3, 1971; s. Joseph and Corinne Veasey; m. Tonya Veasey; 1 child, Adam Clayton. BS in Mass Comm., Tex. Wesleyan U., 1995. Staff mem. US House of Representatives; mem. Dist. 95 Tex. House of Reps., 2005—13; mem. US Congress from 33rd Tex. Dist., Washington, 2013—, US House Armed Services Com., 2013—, US House Sci., Space & Technology Com., 2013—. Democrat. Christian. Office: US House of Representatives 414 Cannon House Office Bldg Washington DC 20515 also: 1881 Sylvan Ave Ste 108 Dallas TX 75208 Office Phone: 202-225-9897, 202-225-9702, 214-741-1387. Office Fax: 214-741-2026.*

VEGA RAMOS, LUIS R., territorial legislator; b. June 11; s. Luis Fertile and Olga E. Branches Creek. Pres. PROELA, 1995—2003; dir. PR Office of Advisers, 2001—03; at-large rep. PR Legislature, 2006—, mem. Consumer Affairs, Ethics, Judiciary and Pub. Security, Natural Resources, Conservation and Environ., Work and Labor Rels. Coms. Author: The Nation in Association, 2000, Between Fraud and History: An Election in History, 2005, Bread, Earth and Freedom: History and Philosophy of the Democratic Popular Party, 2006. Popular Democratic Party. Office: PR Legislature PO Box 922228 San Juan PR 00902-2228 Office Phone: 787-722-2494. Office Fax: 787-724-7025. Business E-Mail: lvega@camaraderepresentantes.org.

VELA, FILEMON BARTOLOME, JR., United States Representative from Texas, lawyer; b. Harllingen, Tex., Feb. 13, 1963; s. Filemon Bartolome and Blanca Vela; m. Rose Vela. BA, Georgetown U., 1985; JD, U. Tex. Sch. Law, 1987. Pvt. law practice, 1988—2012; mem. US Congress from 34th Tex. Dist., Washington, 2013—, US House Agrl. Com., 2013—, US House Homeland Security Com., 2013—. Democrat. Roman Catholic. Office: US House of Representatives 437 Cannon House Office Bldg Washington DC 20515 also: 333 Ebony Ave Brownsville TX 78520 Office Phone: 202-225-9901, 202-225-9770, 956-544-8352.*

VELÁSQUEZ, JENNIFER, librarian; BA in Art History, Edinboro U., Pa., 1987; MLS, Rutgers U., NJ, 1991. Children services libr. I Manatee County pub. Libr. Sys., Bradenton, Fla., 1991—95; young adult services libr. II San Antonio Pub. Libr., Tex., 1995—97, youth dept. mgr., libr. III, 1999—2000, teen services coord., 2000—. Part-time online lectr. San José State U., Calif. Recipient La Promesa award, Nat. Latino Children's Inst., 1996, Excellence in Libr. Svc. to Young Adults award, Young Adult Libr. Services Assn., 1996, 1999, Innovator award, Tutor.com, 2005, Librarian award, NY Times, 2005; named to Movers & Shakers, Libr. Jour., 2011. Office: San Antonio Public Library 600 Soledad San Antonio TX 78205 Office Phone: 210-207-2678.

VENINGA, JAMES FRANK, humanities educator, editor, writer; b. Milw., Aug. 26, 1944; s. Frank and Otila Ann (Mauch) V.; m. Catherine M. Williams, Apr. 5, 1969; 1 child, Jennifer Elisa. BA, Baylor U., 1966; MTheol Studies, Harvard U., 1968; MA, Rice U., 1973, PhD, 1974. Instr. U. St. Thomas, Houston, 1971-73, asst. prof., 1974; asst. dir. Tex. Coun. for Humanities, Austin, 1975, exec. dir., 1976-97; pres., dir. Inst. for the Humanities at Salado, 1997—2000; CEO, campus dean U. Wis.-Marathon County, Wausau, 2000—07, assoc. prof. religious studies, 2000—10; exec. dir. emeritus Humanities Tex.; prof. emeritus U. Wis. Colls. Dir. Nat. Fedn. State Humanities Couns., Washington, 1980-83; trustee Inst. for Humanities at Salado, Tex., 1980-85; vis. prof. Am. studies U. Tex., Austin, 1984, sr. lectr. Am. studies, 1986; vis. prof. Am. studies Baylor U., 1999; bd. dirs. Wisc. Humanities Coun., 2007-09; chair Wisc. Inst. Pub. Policy and Svc., 2007-09. Author: The Humanities and Civic Imagination, 1999; editor: The Biographer's Gift, 1983, Vietnam in Remission, 1985, Standing with the Public, 1997; editor-in-chief Tex. Jour. Ideas, History and Culture, 1982-97. Recipient Baylor Man of Merit award, Baylor U., 1985. Home: PO Box 1838 Bastrop TX 78602 Office Phone: 715-551-1851. Business E-Mail: james.veninga@uwc.edu.

VENIT, WILLIAM BENNETT, electrical products company executive, consultant; b. Chgo., May 28, 1931; s. George Bernard and Ida (Schaffel) V.; m. Nancy Jean Carlson, Jan. 28, 1956; children: Steven Louis, Aprilann. Student, U. Ill., Champaign, 1949; degree, Am. Coaching Acad., 2011. Sales mgr. Coronet, Inc., Chgo., 1952-63, pres., chmn. bd. dirs., 1963-74, Roma Wire Inc., Chgo., 1971-74; chmn. bd. dirs. Swing Time #2, Chgo., 1988-89; pres. Wm. Allen Inc., Chgo., 1972-74; pres., chmn. bd. dirs. Wraprama Inc., 1988-95, Swag Lite, Inc., 1989—92. Pres. William Lamp Co., Inc., 1993, 97, William Wire Co., Inc., 1974-76; chmn. bd. dirs. MSWV, Inc., 1978—, pres. bd. dirs. 1985—; pres. Trio Steel Inc., Chgo., 1987-90; chmn. bd. Chgo. Lamp Works LLB, 1995, 98, chair 1996, 98; CEO Chgo. Chair Works, 1998, 2000, 2001; pres. MSWV Inc. Mobile Home Divsn., 2001, spl. cons. Roto Products, 1998-2002, DMSI Inc., 2002-2008; cons. Nu Style Lamp Shade, 2002-08. Patentee Printed-Cir., 1964. With QMC AUS, 1949-52, dir. Timber Oaks, 2000-08. Avocations: bicycling, golf. Home and Office: 323 Suwanee Ave Sarasota FL 34243-1930 Home Phone: 941-351-5265; Office Phone: 847-477-9997. Personal E-mail: lampbill@aol.com.

VENKATARAMAN, KUMAR, finance professor; MMS, Birla Inst. Tech. and Sci., India, 1994; PhD in Finance, Ariz. State U., 2000. Asst. prof. finance Cox Sch. Bus., Southern Meth. U., 2000—06, assoc. prof., 2006—, Fabacher endowed prof. in alternative assets mgmt., 2009—11, academic dir. ENCAP Investments & LCL Group Alternative Asset Mgmt. Ctr., 2009—, James M. Collins chair finance, 2011—. Spkr. in field. Mem.: Tex. Hedge Fund Assn., Financial Intermediation Rsch. Soc., Soc. for Promotion of Financial Studies, Financial Mgmt. Assn., Western Finance Assn., American Finance Assn. Office: Department of Finance, Cox School of Business Southern Methodist University 330A Fincher Dallas TX 75275 Office Phone: 214-768-7005. Office Fax: 214-768-4099. E-mail: kumar@mail.cox.smu.edu.

VENKATESAN, RAJKUMAR, business administration professor; B in Computer Sci., U. Madras, 1997; PhD in Mktg., U. Houston, 2002. Instr.-in-residence U. Conn., 2001—02, asst. prof., 2002—06; assoc. prof. Darden Sch. Bus., U. Va., 2006—09, Bank of America rsch. assoc. prof., 2009—. Contbr. articles to profl. jours. Office: University of Virginia Darden Graduate School of Business FOB 191B Charlottesville VA 22903 Office Phone: 434-924-6916. E-mail: venkatesanr@darden.virginia.edu.

VENTERS, DANIEL JOSEPH, state supreme court justice; b. Charleston, W.Va., Apr. 13, 1950; s. Joseph Coleman and Mary Delores (Brand) Venters; married; 3 children; 2 stepchildren. BS, Ohio State U., 1972; JD, U. Ky., 1975. Bar: Ky. 1975, US Dist. Ct. (ea. dist.) Ky. 1977, US Supreme Ct, 2001, US Dist. Ct. (western dist.) Ky., 2004. Ptnr. Rogers & Venters, Somerset, Ky., 1975-79; pros. atty. Office of Commonwealth's Atty., Somerset, 1975-79; dist. ct. judge 28th Jud. Dist. Ky., Somerset, 1979-84; cir. ct. judge 28th Jud. Cir. Ct. Ky., Somerset; venters law officer Somerset, Ky., 2003—08; assoc. justice Ky. State Supreme Ct., 2008—. Mem. Ky. Bd. Bar Examiners. Recipient Outstanding Trial Judge award Ky. Acad. Trial Lawyers, 1986. Mem. ABA, Nat. Conf. State Trial Judges, Ky. Bar Assn., Pulaski County Bar Assn. (sec.-treas. 1975-76, pres., 03-04). Republican. Methodist. Office: Ky State Supreme Ct Rm 235 Ky State Capital 700 Capitol Ave Frankfort KY 40601 Office Phone: 606-677-4248. Business E-Mail: danielventers@kycourts.net.*

VENTO, M. THÉRÈSE, lawyer; b. NYC, June 30, 1951; d. Anthony Joseph and Margaret (Stechert) V.; m. Peter Michael MacNamara, Dec. 23, 1977; children: David Miles, Elyse Anne. BS, U. Fla., 1974, JD, 1976. Bar: Fla. 1977, U.S. Dist. Ct. (so. and mid. dists.) Fla. 1982, U.S. Ct. Appeals (5th and 11th cirs.) 1981, U.S. Supreme Ct. 1985. Clk. to presiding justice U.S. Dist. Ct. (so. dist.) Fla., Miami, 1976-78; assoc. Mahoney, Hadlow & Adams, 1978-79, Shutts & Bowen LLP, 1979-84, ptnr., 1985-95; founding ptnr. Gallwey Gillman Curtis & Vento, P.A., 1995—2004; ptnr. Shutts & Bowen, LLP, 2004—. Trustee Miami Art Mus., 1988—, v.p., 1999—2010,sec., 2010-; trustee The Beacon Coun., 1995-97, Law Sch. Alumni Coun., U. Fla., 1994-2004. Named Leading Am. Attorney, 2002, Florida Super Lawyer, 2006. Fellow Am. Bar Found.; mem. Dade County Bar Assn. (dir. young lawyers sect. 1978-83, editor newsletter 1981-83), Fla. Assn. for Women Lawyers, Fla. Bar Assn. (bd. govs., young lawyers div. 1983-85, civil procedure rules com. 1983-90, exec. coun. trial lawyers sect. 1996-2004), The Miami Forum (v.p. 1987-88, bd. dirs. 1989-91, co-pres. 2001-2002). Home: 3908 Main Hwy Miami FL 33133-6513 Office: Shutts & Bowen LLP 201 S Biscayne Blvd Ste 1500 Miami FL 33131 Office Phone: 305-347-7318. Business E-Mail: TVento@shutts.com.

VERBURG, EDWIN ARNOLD, retired management consultant; b. Lakehurst, NJ, Oct. 6, 1945; s. Edwin Donald Verburg and Dorothy (Orrell) Hoodless; m. Joyce Elaine Majack, Sept. 14, 1968; children: Adelle Kristine, Wendi Elizabeth. BS, Calif. Poly. U., 1968; M in City Planning, U. Calif., Berkeley, 1970; D in Pub. Adminstrn., George Washington U., 1975. Planner City of Glendale, Calif., 1971-72; asst. planner City of Inglewood, Calif., 1970-71; grad. assoc. U.S. Army Corps Engrs., Washington, 1974-75; mgr. fiscal analysis Met. Washington Coun. Govt., 1975-77; sr. program analyst U.S. Fish and Wildlife Svc., Washington, 1977-79, asst. divsn. chief, 1979-80, divsn. chief, 1980-82, asst. dir. planning and budget, 1982-86, dep. asst. dir. policy budget and adminstrn., 1986-87; dir. office of fin. U.S. Dept. Treas., Washington, 1987-88, dir. fin. svc. directorate, 1988-91, dep. CFO, 1991-95; assoc. adminstr. adminstrn. FAA, 1995-98; prin. ptnr. Avant Mgmt. Group, Inc., 1998-99; prin., fedn. govt. svc. Kelly, Anderson & Assocs., 1999—2007, v.p., 2003—08, trustee, bd. dirs., 2005—07, sr. assoc., 2008—14; ret. Author: Local State and Federal Fiscal Flows, 5 Vols., 1976; contbr. articles to profl. jours. Recipient Disting. Pub. Svc. award George Washington U., Sch. Bus. and Pub. Mgmt., 1994, Sec. of Treasury Disting Svc. award, 1995, Fin. Mgmt. Svc. Commr. award, 1996. Mem. Am. Inst. Cert. Planners, Am. Planning Assn. (Merit award Calif. chpt. 1973, First award Nat. Capital area chpt. 1980, Peer award for pub. svc. Dept. of Treasury 1990, sec. of treas. cert. appreciation 1991, Pres.'s Meritorious Svc. award 1991, Commr. Citation Fin. Mgmt. Svc. 1996, Pres. award Combined Fed. Campaign 1997), Kiwanis (Arlington chpt. bd. dirs. 1999-2001, v.p. 2001-02, pres.-elect 2002-03, disting. pres. 2003-04, Capitol dist. disting. lt. gov. 20th divsn. capitol dist. Kiwanis Internat. 2005-06, Tucson-de Amigos chpt. bd. dirs. 2009-, v.p. 2009-10, pres. elect 2010-11, pres. 2011-12, treas. 2012-, lt. gov. 9th divsn., SW Dist., 2014-, Hixson award 2004), Tucson Mountains Assn. (v.p. 2010-11, pres. 2011-12, chair Cmty. Water Coalition 2012-14), Assn. Govt. Accountants (cert. govt. fin. mgr.). Home: 5555 W Lazy C Dr Tucson AZ 85745-9055 Personal E-mail: eaverburg@yahoo.com.

VERCELLOTTI, JOHN RAYMOND, chemist, researcher; b. Joliet, Ill., May 2, 1933; s. Joseph Francis and Mary Teresa (Walowski) V.; m. Sharon Cecile Vergez, Sept. 3, 1966; children: Ellen Theresa, Paul Auguste. BA, St. Bonaventure U., 1955; MS, Marquette U., 1960; PhD, Ohio State U., 1963. Lectr., rsch. assoc. Ohio State U., Columbus, 1963-64; asst. prof. Marquette U., Milw., 1964-67; assoc. prof. U. Tenn., Knoxville, 1967-70; prof. Va. Poly. Inst. & State U., Blacksburg, 1970-79; vis. prof. Inst. G. Ronzoni, Milan, 1977-78; sr. scientist Gulf South Res. Inst., New Orleans, 1980-85; rsch. chemist, rsch. leader So. Regional Rsch. Ctr. USDA, New Orleans, 1985-96, collaborator, 1999—. V.p. and sr. chemist V-Labs Inc., Covington, La., 1980-85, 96—; sr. rsch. advisor Sugar Processing Rsch. Inst., Inc., New Orleans, 1996-99, 2001--; adj. prof. chemistry and physics S.E. La. U., Hammond, 1986—. Contbr. articles to profl. jours., chapters to books. U. Tenn. minority colls. grantee, 1968-70, NSF grantee, 1964—. Fellow Sigma Xi; mem. Am. Chem. Soc. (sec. 1968-90, Melville L. Wolfrom award 1994), Inst. Food Technologists. Democrat. Roman Catholic. Achievements include research on food flavor quality and agricultural commodity utilization, origin of flavor from carbohydrates, lipid oxidation products, and peptides. Home: 113 E 25th Ave Covington LA 70433-2819 Office: V-Labs Inc 423 N Theard St Covington LA 70433-2837 Office Phone: 985-893-0533. Business E-Mail: v-labs@v-labs.com.

VERDASCO, FERNANDO, professional tennis player; b. Madrid, Nov. 15, 1983; s. Jose and Olga Verdasco. Profl. tennis player ATP, 2001—. Achievements include patents pending in field of winner (singles) Valencia Open 500, 2004, ATP Studena Croatia Open, 2008, Pilot Pen Tennis, 2009, Barcelona, 2010, San Jose, 2010; winner (doubles) Stockholm Open, 2004. Office: c/o ATP Tour 201 ATP Tour Blvd Ponte Vedra Beach FL 32082

VERDIN, DANIEL B., III, state legislator; b. Alexandria, La., May 9, 1964; s. Daniel B. and Eloise Watts Verdin; m. Kimberlee Diane Owens, 1987; children: Annamarie, Daniel, David Whitson, Whitson. BA, Bob Jones U., 1986. Owner Verdin'S Farm & Garden Ctr.; agr. and natural resources advisor Office of Gov., SC, 1987—89; mem. Dist. 9 SC State Senate, 2000—, chair Agr. and Natural Resources Com. Mem.: Mountville Grange, Hickory Tavern Young Farmer, Laurens County Cattlemen's Assn., Sons Confederate Vets. (SC divsn. comdr. 1998—2000). Republican. Presbyterian. Office: 404 Gressette Bldg PO Box 142 Columbia SC 29201 Mailing: PO Box 272 Laurens SC 29360 Home Phone: 864-682-8914; Office Phone: 803-212-6230, 864-984-4129. E-mail: DBV@scsenate.org.

VEREB, TERESA B., psychiatrist; b. Poland; d. Joseph and Henryka Biskup; m. Bartholomew Vereb, Aug. 3, 1968; children: Bartholomew Jr., Teresa Tilden. MD, Acad. Medicine, Warsaw, 1966. Cert. stress mgmt. Am. Acad. Experts in Traumatic Stress, 2005. Resident psychiatry Hosp. Wolsky, Warsaw, 1966—68, Med. Sch. Safarik U., Kosice, Czech Republic, 1968—70, staff psychiatry, 1971—72; resident psychiatry SUNY, Buffalo, 1977—78; clin. instr. psychiatry Meyer Meml. Hosp., Buffalo, 1977—78; resident psychiatry U. Fla., Gainesville, 1978—80; pvt. practice gen. psychiatry Bradenton, Fla., 1980—; staff psychiatrist Blake Hosp., Bradenton, 1980—, Manatee Meml. Hosp., Bradenton, 1980—, chief psychiatry, sectional chief psychiatry, 1981—85, 1987—91, chairperson psychiat. sect., 2000. Active Sacred Heart Cath. Ch., Bradenton, 1980—. Recipient Disting. Physician award, Fla. Med. Assn., 2005; named Profl. of Yr., 2008; named to Am. Top Psychiatrists, Consumer's Rsch. Coun. Am., 2006,

2007. Mem.: AMA (Physician Recognition award 1995—2002, 2005—06), Am. Acad. Experts in Traumatic Stress, Manatee County Med. Soc., Fla. Psychiat. Assn., Fla. Med. Assn. (Physician Recognition award 1995—2005, Rogeriem Pfizer Re-Commn. 1999, Am. Top Rate Physician 1999, Top Psychiatrist 2004—08, Boar Cert. for stress mgmt. 2005, Am. Top Rate Physician 2008), Am. Psychiat. Assn. Achievements include successfully climbed Mount Kilimanjaro, 1997. Avocations: water-skiing, skiing, swimming, hiking, mountain climbing. Office: Vereb and Vereb MDs PA 5015 Manatee Ave West Bradenton FL 34209

VERENES, J. CHRIS, bank executive; Various mgmt. positions Wash. Group Internat.; contr., dir., Control Data and Bus. and Tech. Ctr. Riegel Textile Corp.; dep. mgr., bus. devel. Wash. Group Internat., 1996—2000, dir., strategic programs, bus. unit, 2000—01, chief staff, 2001, dir., Planning and Adminstrn., 2001—04; bd. dirs. Security Federal Corp., pres., 2004—; bd. dirs. Security Federal Bank (subs. of Security Federal Corp.), pres., 2004—. Exec. dir SC Dem. Party. Office: Security Federal Corp 238 Richland Ave W Aiken SC 29801 Office Phone: 803-641-3000. Office Fax: 803-641-3046. Business E-Mail: cverenes@securityfederalbank.com.

VERITY, WILLIAM W., investment company executive; b. 1959; BA in Economics, U. Va., 1981; MBA, Harvard U., 1985. Investment banker Alex Brown Inc.; chmn. & CEO ENCOR Holdings Inc.; ptnr. Pathway Guidance LLC, 2000—02; mng. dir. Thomas Ptnrs. Inc.; pres. Verity & Verity Investment Management, 2002—. Former bd. dirs. Peritus Software Svcs.; bd. dirs. Chiquita Brands, 1994—2002, Am. Fin. Group Inc., 2002—. Office: Verity Investment Ptnrs Ste 315 2015 Boundary St Beaufort SC 29902 Office Phone: 843-379-6661. Office Fax: 843-379-6664. Business E-Mail: will@verityvip.com.

VERMA, ARUN K., mathematician, educator; b. Dibrugarh, India, June 1955; 3 children. MSc, Dibrugarh U., India, 1977; Diploma, PhD, Indian Inst. of Tech., Kharagpur, 1984. Lectr. in math. Regional Engring. Coll., Silchar, Assam, India, 1984—89; rsch. assoc. Hampton U., Hampton, Va., 1989—89, vis. lectr. in math., 1989—92, asst. prof. of math., 1992—93, assoc. prof. of math., 1993—2001, prof. of math., 2001—, chair dept. math., 2011. Reader for AP calculus Ednl. Testing Svcs., Princeton, NJ, 1998—2004; ASEE summer faculty fellow NASA Langley Rsch. Ctr., Hampton, Va., 2000; US EdD project cons. Ala. State U., Montgomery, Ala., 2002—03; Schev project cons. Norfolk State U., Norfolk, Va., 2002—03; faculty summer rsch. participant Oak Ridge Inst. for Sci. and Rsch., Oak Ridge, Tenn., 1993—93; lead tchr. Thompson Learning Brooks Coll., Inc., 2004—09; coord. Math. Counts Peninsula Chpt., Va., 2005—; project dir. various grants. Treas. Yorktown 4th July Committe, Yorktown, Va., 2003—; elected com. mem. Internat. Baccalaureate Adv. Coun., Yorktown, Va., 2000—04; nominated com. mem. New Horizon Governors Sci. & Tech. Adv. Com., Hampton, Va., 2000—07; bd. mem. Yorktown Hist. Mus. Corp., 2013; sec. exec. com. Hindu Temple of Hampton Roads, Chesapeake, Va., 2006—. Recipient William C. Lowry Outstanding Math. Tchr. award, coll. level, Va. Coun. of Teachers of Math., 2001, 2002 QEM (Quality Edn. for Minorities) Excellence in Math. and/or Sci. Tchg. award, 2002; named Leader in Edn., Hewlett-Packard Inc., 2000. Mem.: Yorktown Hist. Mus. Corp. (bd. mem.), Va. Acad. Sci. (elect. fellow 2010), Nat. Tech. Assn., Va. Coun. of Teachers of Math., Math. Assn. of Am., Sigma Xi. Office: Hampton U E Queen St Hampton VA 23668 Business E-Mail: arun.verma@hamptonu.edu.

VERMUND, STEN HALVOR, epidemiologist, educator; b. Mpls., Jan. 31, 1954; s. Halvor and Karen (Bergfjord) V.; m. Pilar Vargas, Apr. 8, 1978; children: Julian, Gabriel. BA, Stanford U., 1974; MD, Albert Einstein Coll. Medicine, 1977; MSc, London Sch. Hygiene and Tropical Medicine, 1981; PhD, Columbia U., 1990. Diplomate Am. Bd. Pediatrics, Am. Bd. Preventive Medicine. Intern Presbyn. Hosp., NYC, 1977-78, resident in pediat., 1978-80; asst. prof. Columbia U., NYC, 1982-85, Albert Einstein Coll. Medicine, Bronx, NY, 1985-88; chief epidemiology br. divsn. AIDS Nat. Inst. Allergy and Infectious Diseases, Bethesda, Md., 1988-92, chief vaccine trials and epidemiology br. divsn. AIDS, 1992-94; prof. epidemiology, internat. health, medicine & pediat. U. Ala., Birmingham, 1994—2005, chmn. dept. epidemiology, 1994-98, dir. divsn. geog. medicine, 1994—2005, sr. scientist Comprehensive Cancer Ctr., 1994—2005, assoc. dir. Ctr. for AIDS Rsch., 1994—2003, pres. Gorgas Meml. Inst., 1995—2005, dir. John J. Sparkman Ctr. for Internat. Pub. Health Edn., 1999—2005; prof. pediat., medicine, preventive medicine and ob/gyn Vanderbilt U., Nashville, 2005—, dir., inst. for global health, 2005—, Amos Christie chair in global health, 2005—. Cons. NYC Dept. Environ. Protection, 1986-88, Med. Bd. Nat. Coun. Chs., NYC, 1984-85, CDC, Atlanta, 1989—, FDA, Rockville, Md., 1991-94, NIH, 1994—; mem. Inst. Medicine Panel on Perinatal Transmission of HIV, 1997-98, mem. Inst. Medicine Panel on HIV Prevention, 1999-2000. Contbg. author: AIDS Epidemiology, 1993, Until the Cure: Caregiving for Women with HIV, 1993, Parasitic Protozoa, 2d edit., vol. 6, 1993, HIV in Women, 1995, AIDS, 4th edit., 1997; co-editor, contbg. author: Preventing HIV Infection in Developing Countries, 1999; contbr. articles to profl. jours. Mem. adv. bd. health rsch. tng. program N.Y.C. Dept. Health, 1986—88; mem. sci. adv. bd. World AIDS Found., 1994—95; mem. adv. com. Office AIDS Rsch., NIH, 2000—. Recipient Curnan award Babies Hosp., NYC, 1980, Lalcaca medal U. London, 1981, Commrs. Spl. Svc. award NYC Dept. Health, 1988, Merit award USPHS, Bethesda, 1989, Cert. of Appreciation, U.S. Surgeon Gen., 1993, Superior Svc. award USPHS, 1994; med. rsch. grantee Ctrs. for Disease Control, Nat. Cancer Inst., Nat. Inst. Allergy Infectious Diseases, Nat. Inst. Child Health and Devel., others, 1986-88, 94—. Fellow Am. Acad. Pediatrics (sec., founding mem. regional com. on homeless children 1986-88), Am. Coll. Epidemiology, Soc. Adolescent Medicine, Royal Soc. Tropical Medicine and Hygiene, Infectious Disease Soc. Am.; mem. APHA, Internat. AIDS Soc., Internat. Epidemiologic Assn., Am. Soc. Tropical Medicine and Hygiene. Avocations: hiking, tennis, violin, ping pong/table tennis. Office: Vanderbilt U Inst Global Health Light Hall 319 0242 Nashville TN 37232 E-mail: sten.vermund@vanderbilt.edu.

VERNAVA, ANTHONY M., III, colon and rectal surgeon; MD, St. Louis U., Mo., 1982. Diplomate Am. Bd. Surgery, 1988, Am. Bd. Surgery, 2007, Am. Bd. Colon and Rectal Surgery, 1989, lic. Fla. Intern St Louis Univ. Med. Ctr., Mo., 1982—83, resident in surgery, 1983—87; resident in colon and rectal surgery Univ. Minn. Med. Ctr., Mpls., 1988—89; fellow in colon and rectal surgery Nat. Cancer Ctr., Japan, 1989, St. Marks Hosp., England, 1989—90; hosp. affiliation includes Physicians Regional Med. Group, Naples, Fla., 2005—. Office: Physicians Regional Medical Group 6101 Pine Ridge Rd Naples FL 34119 Office Phone: 232-348-4001.

VERPLANK, SCOTT RACHAL, professional golfer; b. Dallas, July 9, 1964; m. Kim Verplank; children: Scottie, Hannah, Emma, Heidi. BS in Bus., Okla. State U., 1986. Profl. golfer PGA Tour, 1986—; US Amateur champion, 1984; NCAA champion, 1986; winner Western Open, 1985, Buick Open, 1988, World Cup of Golf (individual), 1998, Reno-Tahoe Open, 2000, Bell Can. Open, 2001, EDS Byron Nelson Championship, 2007. Mem. Walker Cup team, 1985, World Cup team, 1998, 2004, Ryder Cup team, 2002, 2006, Presidents Cup team, 2005. Recipient Ben Hogan award, 2002. Avocations: reading, kids, sports, quail hunting. Office: PGA 100 Ave of Champions Palm Beach Gardens FL 33418

VERST, CYNTHIA L., pharmaceutical executive; BS in Biology and Chemistry, No. Ky. U.; MS in Structural and Cellular Biology, U. Ill.; BS in Pharmacy, U. Cin., PharmD. Sect. head N.Am. med. & tech. affairs P&G Pharmaceuticals, Cin., 1994—2002; v.p. late phase Kendle Internat. Inc., Cin., 2002—07; sr. v.p. late phase rsch. i3 Innovus Inc., Medford, Mass., 2007—11; global head late phase ops. Quintiles, Durham, NC, 2011—. Office: Quintiles 4820 Emperor Blvd Durham NC 27703 Office Phone: 919-998-2000. Office Fax: 919-998-2003.

VESEY, ANDREW M., electric power industry executive; BA in Economics, Union Coll., Schenectady, NY, BS in Mech. Engring.; MS, NYU. CEO, mng. dir. Citipower Pty Ltd., Melbourne, Australia; ptnr., Energy, Chemicals and Utilities Ernst & Young LLP; mng. dir., Utility Fin. and Regulatory Adv. Practice FTI Consulting Inc.; v.p., Integrated Utilities Devel. Group AES Corp., 2004—05, v.p., Global Bus. Transformation Group, 2005—06, v.p., group mgr., L.Am., 2006—07, COO, L.Am., 2007—08, regional pres., L.Am., 2008—09, exec. v.p., 2008—, regional pres., L.Am. and Africa, 2009—. Office: The AES Corp 11th Fl 4300 Wilson Blvd Arlington VA 22203 Office Phone: 703-522-1315. Office Fax: 703-528-4510. Business E-Mail: Andrew.Vesey@aes.com.

VEST, CHRISTINA WEAVER, private equity firm executive; b. 1971; BA, Harvard U., 1993; MBA, Harvard Bus. Sch., 1999. Policy dir. for US Senate candidate Richard Fisher; prin. analyst Hicks, Muse, Tate & Furst Inc., 1995—2005; sr. v.p. Hicks Holdings, LLC, 2005—07; mng. dir., ptnr. Hicks Equity Partners LLC, 2007—10; sr. v.p., CFO Hicks Acquisition Co. II, Inc., Dallas, 2010—. Bd. dirs. Ocular LCD, Inc., Greatwide Logistics Svcs., Sturm Foods, Inc., iParty Corp., Fox Pan Am. Sports, Claxson Interactive Group, Inc., Digital Latin America LLC. Office: Hicks Acquisition Co II Inc 100 Crescent Ct Ste 1200 Dallas TX 75201

VEST, GAYLE SOUTHWORTH, obstetrician, gynecologist; b. Duluth, Minn., Apr. 7, 1948; d. Russell Eugene and Brandon (Young) Southworth; m. Steven Lee Vest, Nov. 27, 1971; 1 child, Matthew Steven. BS, U. Mich., 1970. Diplomate Am. Bd. Ob-Gyn. Intern in ob-gyn. Milw. County Gen. Hosp., 1974-75, So. Ill. U. Sch. Medicine, 1975-78; pvt. practice Chapel Hill (N.C.) Ob-Gyn., 1978-80; asst. attending physician dept. ob-gyn. U. N.C. Sch. Medicine, Chapel Hill, 1978-80; clin. assoc. dept. ob-gyn. Duke U. Med. Ctr., Durham, NC, 1978-80; pvt. practice Big Stone Gap (Va.) Clinic, 1980-88, Norwise Ob-Gyn. Assocs., Norton, Va., 1988—. Fellow: ACOG; mem.: Med. Soc. Va., Christian Med. and Dental Assn. Avocations: skiing, kayaking, travel.

VETROVEC, GEORGE WAYNE, cardiologist, medical researcher, educator; b. Akron, Ohio, Aug. 12, 1943; MD, U. Va., 1970. Diplomate Am. Bd. Internal Medicine, Am. Bd. Cardiovascular Medicine. Intern, medicine Med. Coll. Va., Richmond, 1970-71, resident, cardiology, 1971-74, fellow in cardiology, 1974-76; faculty mem. Va. Commonwealth U., Richmond, 1976—, chmn., prof. med. cardiology, 1986—, chmn. divsn. cardiology, Pauley Heart Ctr., dir. Adult Cardiac Catheterization Lab., assoc. chmn. of medicine for clin. affairs, Dept. Internal Medicine, Martha M. and Harold W. Kimmerling, M.D. chair cardiology. Mem. staff Med. Coll. Va.; mem. VCUHS Authority Bd. Dirs. Contbr. several articles to journals, chapters to books; mem. of several editl. bds. Recipient W. Robert Irby Philanthropic Leadership Award, MCV Found.; named Clinician of Yr., 1997; named one of Best Doctors in Am., Best Doctors Inc.; named to AOA Med. Honor Soc. Fellow: ACP, European Soc. Cardiology, Royal Coll. Physicians of Thailand, Soc. Cardiac Angiography and Interventions (past pres.), Am. Coll. Cardiology, Am. Coll. Chest Physicians; mem.: Irish Cardiac Soc., Assn. Univ. Cardiologists (past pres.), Assn. Profs. Cardiology (past pres.), Physician Workforce Adv. Com. (former chmn. bd. trustees), Am. Heart Assn. (former pres. Richmond Coun. and Va. Affiliate, chmn. Mid Atlantic Regi, chmn. Catheterization Com, Coun. Clin. Cardiology, Nat. Award of Merit 1991, Richmond Golden Heart Award 1997). Office: Divsn Cardiology Virginia Commonwealth U Health Sys PO Box 980036 Richmond VA 23298-0036 Office Phone: 804-828-8885. Business E-Mail: gvetrovec@mcvh-vcu.edu.

VETTER, DAVID R., lawyer; b. Balt., Apr. 3, 1959; BA in English and Econs., Bucknell U., 1981; JD, U. Fla., 1984. Bar: Fla. 1984, US Dist. Ct. (mid. dist. Fla.) 1985. Atty. Robbins, Gaynor and Bronstein, Tampa, Fla., 1984—93, ptnr., 1991—93; v.p., gen. counsel Tech Data Corp., Clearwater, Fla., 1993—2000, corp. v.p., gen. counsel, 2000—03, sr. v.p., gen. counsel, sec., 2003—. Mem.: ABA, Assn. Corp. Counsel, Fla. Bar Assn. Office: Tech Data Corp 5350 Tech Data Dr Clearwater FL 33760-3122*

VEZINA, ANN, data processing executive; BSBA cum laude, Ctrl. Mich. U. With EDS; mng. dir., Bus. Process Solutions Affiliated Computer Services, Inc. (ACS) (acquired by Xerox Corp.), exec. v.p., 2006—, group pres., comml. solutions, 2007—. Office: Affiliated Computer Services Inc 2828 N Haskell Ave Dallas TX 75204 Office Phone: 214-841-6111. Office Fax: 214-821-8315. Business E-Mail: Ann.Vezina@acs-inc.com.

VEZIROGLU, TURHAN NEJAT, mechanical engineering educator, researcher; b. Istanbul, Turkey, Jan. 24, 1924; came to U.S., 1962; s. Abdul Kadir and Ferruh (Bürün) V.; m. Bengi Isikli, Mar. 17, 1961; children: Emre Alp, Oya Sureyya. A.C.G.I., City and Guilds Coll., London, 1946; B.Sc. with honors, U. London, 1947; D.I.C., Imperial Coll., London, 1948; PhD, U. London, 1951. Engring. apprentice Alfred Herbert Ltd., Coventry, U.K., 1945; project engr. Office of Soil Products, Ankara, Turkey, 1953-56; tech. dir. M.K.V. Constrn. Co, Istanbul, 1957-61; assoc. prof. mech. engring. U. Miami, Coral Gables, Fla., 1962-65, prof. Coral Fables, Fla., 1966—, dir. grad. studies mech. engring. Coral Gables, Fla., 1965-71, chmn. dept. mech. engring., 1971-75, assoc. dean research Coll. Engring., 1975-79, dir. Clean Energy Research Inst., 1974—. UNESCO cons., Paris; vis. prof. Middle East Tech. U., Ankara, 1969 Editor-in-chief: Internat. Jour. Hydrogen Energy, 1976—. Pres. Learning Disabilities Found., Miami, 1972-73, advisor, 1974-80. Recipient Turkish Presdl. sci. award Turkish Sci. and Tech. Research Found., 1975; named hon. prof. Xian Jiaotong U., China, 1982 Fellow AAAS, ASME, Instn. Mech. Engrs.; mem. Internat. Assn. Hydrogen Energy (pres. 1975), AIAA, Assn. Energy Engrs., Am. Nuclear Soc., Am. Soc. Engring. Edn., AAUP, Internat. Soc. Solar Energy, Systems Engring. Soc., Sigma Xi Home: 5783 SW 40th St # 303 Miami FL 33155 Home Phone: 305-442-4540; Office Phone: 305-284-4666. Business E-Mail: veziroglu@iahe.org.

VICE, CHARLES A., state banking agency administrator; BS in Fin., U. Southern Miss., Hattiesburg; grad. from Grad. Sch. Banking program, La. State U., Baton Rouge. Bank examiner FDIC, Lexington, Ky.; commr. Ky. Dept. Fin. Instns., Frankfort, 2008—. Vice chmn. Dist. II region Conf. State Bank Suprs., mem. Fed. Fin. Instn. Exam. Coun. State Liaison Com., 2009—, mem. bd. trustees Ednl. Found. State Banking Suprs., 2009. Office: Kentucky Department Financial Institutions 1025 Capital Center Dr Ste 200 Frankfort KY 40601 Office Phone: 502-573-3390. Office Fax: 502-573-8787. E-mail: charles.vice@ky.gov.

VICK, COLUMBUS EDWIN, JR., retired civil engineering design firm executive; b. Jacksonville, Fla., Nov. 8, 1934; s. Columbus Edwin Sr. and Lucretia (Dean) V.; m. Laura Anne McGowan, Mar. 28, 1964; children: Jennifer, Carolyn, Elizabeth. BSCE, N.C. State U., 1956, MSCE, 1960. Registered profl. engr., 15 states. Rsch. asst. N.C. State Civil Engring. Dept., Raleigh, 1958-60; transp. planning engr. Harland Bartholomew & Assocs., Memphis, 1960-64, office and project mgr. Raleigh, 1964-67; prin., co-founder Kimley-Horn and Assocs. Inc., Raleigh, 1967-72, pres., 1972-92; chmn., 1992-2000. Bd. dirs. Wachovia Bank, Design Profls. Coalition Am. Cons. Engrs. Coun. Co-author: North Carolina Atlas; contbr. articles to profl. jours. Past pres., bd. dirs. NC State U. Engring. Found.; past pres. bd. assocs. Meredith Coll.; past dir. NC State U. Alumni Assn.; bd. visitors NC State U.; past 2d v.p. Bapt. State Conv. of NC; bd. dirs. Assoc. Bapt. Press, past chmn.; bd. dirs. Bibl. Recorder; trustee Kenan Inst. for Engring. Tech. and Sci., Gardner Webb U., Meredith Coll.; bd. advisors Wake Forest U. Sch. Divinity; bd. trustees Cooperative Bapt. Fellowship Found., past chmn. Recipient Meritorious Svc. award, NC State U., 2006; named Disting. Engring. alumnus, 1991. Fellow ASCE (Outstanding Young Engr. award ea. br. NC sect. 1966), Inst. Transp. Engrs. (Oustanding Individual Activity award so. sect. 1978, Disting. Svc. award so. sect. 1981, Lifetime Svc. award N.C. sect. 1995); mem. NSPE (Disting. Svc. award), Am. Con. Engrs. Coun., Am. Inst. Cert. Planners, Profl. Svcs. Mgmt. Assn. (Coll. of Fellow, Leonardo da Vinci award 2005), NC Soc. Engrs. (Outstanding Engring Achievement award 1992, NC Transp. Hall of Fame 2007), Good Old Boys Club (Raleigh, NC), Raleigh Host Lions Club. Baptist. Home: 2205 Nancy Ann Dr Raleigh NC 27607-3318 Office: Kimley-Horn and Assocs Inc 3001 Weston Pky Cary NC 27513-2301 Home Phone: 919-787-8859; Office Phone: 919-677-2002. E-mail: ed.vick@kimley-horn.com.

VICK, TED MARTIN, state legislator; b. Cheraw, SC, Nov. 14, 1975; m. Melissa Gainey Vick; children: Willow Grace, Laurel Faith. BA, The Citadel, 1995; MEd, U. SC, 1997. Pres. MTV Properties, LLC, 2002—; CEO Ted Vick Motor Co., Inc., 2003—; pres. V and B Properties, Inc., 2003—; mem. Dist. 53 SC House of Reps., 2004—, sec. Agr., Natural Resources and Environ. Affairs Com. Democrat. Mailing: 333A Blatt Bldg Columbia SC 29211 Home: 929 Shag Rd Chesterfield SC 29709 Office Phone: 803-734-2999. Business E-Mail: VickT@scstatehouse.net.

VICTORY, JEFFREY PAUL, state supreme court justice; b. Shreveport, La., Jan. 29, 1946; s. Thomas Edward and Esther (Horton) V.; m. Nancy Clark Victory, Jan. 20, 1973; children: Paul Bradford, William Peter, Christopher Thomas, Mary Katherine. BA in History and Govt., Centenary Coll., 1967; JD, Tulane U., 1971. Bar: La. 1971. Ptnr. Tucker, Jeter, Jackson & Victory, Shreveport, 1971-82; dist. ct. judge 1st Jud. Dist. Ct., Shreveport, 1982-90; appellate judge 2d Circuit Ct. of Appeal, Shreveport, 1991-95; assoc. justice Supreme Ct. La., 1995—. Bd. dirs. La. Judicial Coll. Bd. dirs. CODAC Drug Abuse, Shreveport; mem. La. Sentencing Commn. La. NG, 1969-75. Mem. ABA, Shreveport Bar Assn., La. Bar Assn. Republican. Baptist. Avocations: tennis, motorcycles, classic cars. Office: Supreme Ct 400 Royal St New Orleans LA 70130*

VIERCK, CHARLES JOHN, JR., retired neuroscience educator; b. Columbus, Ohio, July 6, 1936; s. Charles John and Esther (Amadon) V.; m. Cheryl Stogner; children: Kenneth Christopher, Karl Frederick. BSc, U. Fla., Gainesville, 1959, MSc, 1961, PhD, 1963. Postdoctoral fellow U. Pa., Phila., 1963-65; asst. prof. U. Fla., Gainesville, 1965-71, assoc. prof., 1971-77, prof., 1977—2004, prof. emeritus, 2004. Adj. prof. U. NC, Chapel Hill, 1977—2007; dir. Ctr. Neurobiol. Scis. U. Fla., 1975-2005. Mem. editorial bd. Somatosensory Motor Research, Am. Pain Soc. Jour., Jour. Neurosci.; contbr. articles to profl. jours., chpts. to books Grantee NIH, NIMH, NSF, VA, 1966—. Mem. Soc. Neurosci., Internat. Assn. Study Pain Democrat. Avocations: jazz, golf. Home: 6519 SW 37th Way Gainesville FL 32608-5146 Personal E-mail: vierck@mbi.ufl.edu.

VIERLING, JOHN MOORE, physician; b. Bellflower, Calif., Nov. 20, 1945; s. Lester Howard and Ruth Ann (Moore) V.; m. Gayle Aileen Vandermast, June 30, 1968 (div. 1984); children: Jeffrey M., Janet A; m. Donna Marie Sheps, May 4, 1985; children: Matthew R., Mark L. (dec.). BA in Biology with great distinction, Stanford U., 1967, MD, 1972. Intern then resident Strong Meml. Hosp. U. Rochester, N.Y., 1972-74; clin. assoc. liver unit NIH, Bethesda, Md., 1974-77; gastroenterology fellow U. Calif., San Francisco, 1977-78, instr. medicine, 1978-79; from asst. to assoc. U. Colo. Sch. Medicine, Denver, 1979-90, med. dir. liver transplantation, 1987—90; dir. hepatology, med dir. liver transplantation Cedars-Sinai Med. Ctr., LA, 1990—96, prof. medicine, 1996—2004; prin. Clin. Rsch. Ctrs. America LLC, 2012—. Assoc. prof. medicine UCLA, 1990-96, prof. medicine, 2005-; prof. medicine & surgery, chief hepatology, Baylor Coll. Med., Houston, 2005-. Assoc. editor: Prinicples and Practice of Gastroenterology and Hepatology, 1992; editorial bd. Hepatology, 1985-90, Gastroenterology, 1993-98, Liver Transplantation, 2004-; co-editor Liver Immunology, 2002, 2007-; co-patentee in hybridization assay for hepatitis virus, 1992; mouse model for hepatitis C, 1997. Fellow ACP; mem. Am. Assn. Study Liver Diseases (pres. 2006), Am. Clin. and Climatol. Assn., Am. Gastroenterolog. Assn., Internat. Assn. for Study Liver, European Assn. for Study Liver, Am. Liver Found. (chmn. bd. dirs. 1994—2000, sec. treas., Digestive Disease Week 2008-13). Avocations: photography, tennis, hiking. Office: 6620 Main St Ste 1425 Houston TX 77030*

VIERS, THAD T., state legislator; b. Grundy, Va., Mar. 13, 1978; s. Bill and Brenda Viers; m. Natalie Ann McKelvey, June 29, 2002. BA, The Citadel, 1999; JD, U. SC, 2007. Exec. dir. Horry County Rep. Party, 1999—2000; mem. Myrtle Beach Chamber Govt. Affairs Com., 2001—02, Conway Chamber Govt. & Econ Affairs Com., 2002; mem. Dist. 68 SC House of Reps., 2003—; mem. Agr. Com., Natural Res. Com., Environ. Affairs Com. Mem.: Polit. Sci. & Inst. Studies Honor Socs., Socastee Neighborhood Coalition, Sons of Confederate Vets., Sons Confederate Vets., Grand Strand Baptist Ch., Boys Nation, Palmetto Boys State, Myrtle Beach Rotary Club, Socastee Lions Club. Republican. Mailing: PO Box 31231 Myrtle Beach SC 29588 Office: 327B Blatt Bldg PO Box 11867 Columbia SC 29201 Office Phone: 803-734-3064. E-mail: ViersT@scstatehouse.net.

VIETS, ELAINE FRANCES, writer; b. St. Louis, Feb. 5, 1950; d. Henry Frederick and Elaine Viets; m. Don Crinklaw, Aug. 6, 1971. BJ, U. Mo., 1972. Columnist St. Louis Post-Dispatch, 1979-95, United Media, NYC, 1996-2000. Tchr. writing seminars Broward Libr., Fla. Ctr. for the Book, 1998-99, St. Louis Pub. Libr., 1999. Author: (Francesca Vierling Series) Backstab, 1997, Rubout, 1998, Pink Flamingo Murders, 1999, Doc in the Box, 2000, (Dead-end Job Mystery Series) Stop Till You Drop, 2003, Murder Between the Covers, 2003, Dying to Call You, 2004, Just Murdered, 2005, Murder Unleashed, 2007, Murder With Reservations, 2007, Clubbed to Death, 2008, Killer Cuts, 2009, Half-Price Homicide, 2010, Pumped For

Murder, 2011, Final Sail, 2012, Board Stiff, 2013, (Josie Marcus Mystery Shopper Series) Dying In Style, 2005, High Heels Are Murder, 2006, Accessory to Murder, 2007, Murder With All the Trimmings, 2008, The Fashion Hound Murders, 2009, An Uplifting Murder, 2010, Death on a Platter, 2011, Murder Is a Piece of Cake, 2012, Fixing to Die, 2013, Catnapped?!, 2014; (short stories) Red Meat, 2004, Blonde Moment, 2004, Wedding Knife, 2004, Killer Blonde, 2005; host (talk show) Dead-end Job Show. Recipient Emmy award St. Louis chpt. NATAS, 1989, 90; named Fla. Au. of Yr., Pompano Beach Friends of the Libr., 2000. Mem. Mystery Writers of Am. (bd. dirs., sec. Fla. chpt. 1999-00, pres. Fla. chpt. 2000, dir.-at-large 2002, Edgar com. best novel 1999, chair Edgar com. best first novel 2002), Sisters in Crime (bd. dirs.). Avocations: reading, walking. E-mail: eviets@aol.com.

VIG, BART F., food service executive; Regional v.p. restaurant ops. Cracker Barrel Old Country Store, Inc. Office: Cracker Barrel Old Country Store Inc 305 Hartmann Dr Lebanon TN 37087 Office Phone: 615-444-5533. Office Fax: 615-443-9476.

VIGUERIE, RICHARD ART, advertising and direct mail executive; b. Golden Acres, Tex., Sept. 23, 1933; s. Arthur Camile and Elizabeth Mary (Stoufflet) V.; m. Elaine Adele O'Leary, Feb. 17, 1962; children: Renée Elaine, Michelle Marie, Richard Ryan Student, Tex. A&I U., 1952-56; BS in Polit. Sci., U. Houston, 1958. Exec. dir. Young Americans for Freedom, 1961-63; pres. Viguerie Co., Falls Church, Va., 1965; chmn. Am. Target Advt., Inc.; pres., chmn. Conservative-HQ.com; co-founder Am. Freedom Agenda, 2007. Chmn. bd. Am. Mailing List Corp., Falls Church, 1972; founder Conservative Digest, Falls Church, 1975-85. Author: The New Right: We're Ready To Lead, 1980, The Establishment vs. The People, 1983, America's Right Turn: How Conservatives Used New and Alternative Media to Take Power, 2004, Conservatives Betrayed: How George W. Bush and Other Big Government Republicans Hijacked the Conservative Cause, 2006. With N.G., 1957. Named one of 50 Future Leaders of America, Time mag., 1979, 25 Most Intriguing People of Yr., People mag., 1981, 25 Most Influential Republicans, Newsmax mag., 2008. Republican. Roman Catholic. Office: Am Target Advertising 12500 Fair Lakes Cir Ste 155 Fairfax VA 22033-3863

VILA, ADIS MARIA, academic administrator; b. Guines Habana, Cuba, Aug. 1, 1953; d. Calixto Vila and Adis C. Fernandez. BA with distinction, Rollins Coll., Winter Park, Fla., 1974; JD with honors, U. Fla., Gainesville, 1978; LLM with high honors, Institut Universitaire de Hautes Estudes Internationales, Geneva, 1981; MBA, U Chgo., 1997. Bar: Fla. 1979, DC 1984. Assoc. Paul & Thomson, 1979-82; White House fellow Office Pub. Liaison, Washington, 1982-83; spl. asst. to asst. sec. for inter-American affairs US Dept. State, Washington, 1983-86; dir. Office Mex. & Caribbean Basin US Dept. Commerce, Washington, 1986-87; sec. adminstrn. State of Fla., Tallahassee, 1987-89; asst. sec. for adminstrn. USDA, Washington, 1989-91; vis. fellow Nat. Def. U., Washington, 1992-93; v.p. internat. devel. Vigoro Corp., Chgo., 1994-95; v.p. govt. affairs regulatory policy, Carribean & Latin America Nortel Networks, 1997-2000; pres., CEO Vila & Associates, 2001—; chief diversity officer USAF Acad., Colo. Springs, 2010—. Vis. asst. prof. Fla. Internat. U., 1993—94; mem. adv. bd. Americas Global Asset Mgmt. Fund, 1999—; v.p. external affairs Miami Dade C.C., 2002—03; adj. faculty bus. law various not-for-profit, for profit institutions, 2002—; vis. prof. Internat. Bus. & Mgmt. Dickinson Coll., 2007—09; prof., scholar in residence Winter Park Inst., Rollins Coll., 2009—10. Trustee So. Ctr. Internat. Studies, 1987—. Paul Harris fellow, Rotary Internat., 1983, US-Japan Leadership fellow, 1991—92, Eisenhower Exch. fellow, Beca Fiore, Argentina, 1992. Mem.: Women Execs. in State Govt. (bd. dirs. 1987—89), American Coun. Young Polit. Leaders (bd. dirs. 1984—), Internat. Women's Forum, Coun. Fgn. Rels. (term mem. 1987—92), Dade County Bar Assn. (bd. dirs. young and lawyers sect. 1979—87). Republican. Roman Catholic. Avocations: tennis, skiing, golf, theater, art. Office: US Air Force Academy 2304 Cadet Dr Ste 3300 U S A F Academy CO 80840

VILASUSO, ALEJANDRO J., critical care medicine; MD, Grenada, 1982. Cert. internal medicine 1985, critical care medicine 2005. Resident in internal medicine Univ. Miami- Jackson Meml. Hosp., Miami, 1983—85; hosp. affiliations include Mercy Hosp., Univ. Miami Hosp. Office: University of Miami Hospital 1400 NW 12th Ave Ste No 1 Miami FL 33143 Office Phone: 305-325-0913.

VILLANUEVA, RON A., state legislator; b. Phila., Mar. 30, 1970; m. Catherine Montemayor Caragan; children: Matthew, Elise, Cole, Kate. BA in Polit. Sci., Old Dominion U., Norfolk, Va., 1992; grad., CIVIC Leadership Inst., 1999. Owner, operator marine ship repair and indsl. svc. firm; exec. v.p., prin. SEK Solutions LLC, Va.; at-large dist. mem. Va. Beach City Coun., 2002—09; mem. Dist. 21 Va. House of Delegates, Richmond, Va., 2010—. Active Operation Smile, New Castle Elem Sch. PTA, Green Run HS PTA, Cox Comm. Charitable Found. Reservist USCG, 1987—95. Recipient Va. Beach Human Rights Commn. award, 1994, Operation Smile Vol. award, 2008, Va. Beach Minority Bus. Coun. award, 2009; named one of Top Forty Under 40, Inside Bus. Weekly, 2006. Republican. Roman Catholic. Office: Va House of Dels Gen Assembly Bldg Rm 721 PO Box 406 Richmond VA 23218 also: PO Box 61005 Virginia Beach VA 23466 also: SEK Solutions Hdqs Pinehurst Ctr 477 Viking Dr Ste 350 Virginia Beach VA 23452 Office Phone: 804-698-1021, 757-216-3883, 757-416-7524. Office Fax: 804-698-6721, 757-216-3885. Business E-Mail: delrvillanueva@house.virginia.gov.

VILLARREAL, LORA JEAN, information technology executive, human resources specialist; b. LA, Mar. 14, 1944; d. Carlos L. and Estella M. (Marquez) Licon; m. Lorenzo Villarreal; children: Michelle Villarreal Price, Christopher J. BS in Human Resource Mgmt., Bellevue U., Nebr.; MS in Adminstrn. and Mgmt., Ctrl. Mich. U.; PhD in Philosophy and Mgmt., Calif. Coast U. Pers. mgr. Omaha World-Herald, 1977—81; pers. specialist Youth for Understanding, Washington, 1981—82; spl. asst. EEOC, Washington, 1982—83; employment mgr. United Hosp., Grand Forks, ND, 1984—85; pers. mgr. Rapid Printing & Mailing, Omaha, 1985—86; v.p. adminstrn. First Data Resources Inc., Mexico City; v.p. human resources Transamerica Real Estate Info. Companies; pres. Human Resources Group, Inc.; sr. v.p., chief people officer Affiliated Computer Services, Inc. (ACS) (acquired by Xerox Corp.), Dallas, 1998—2007, exec. v.p., chief people officer, 2007—. Bd. dirs. Buck Consultants, LLC, 2005—, Better Bus. Bur. Met. Dallas, Inc.; pres. ACS Philanthropic Found. Bd. dirs. Dallas County Cmty. Coll. Dist. Found., Tex. Diversity Coun. Recipient Ogletree Deakins Human Resources Profl. of Yr. award, Latina Style mag./North Dallas C. of C., 2008, Minority Bus. Leaders award, Dallas Bus. Jour.; named one of Outstanding Young Women in America, US Jaycees, 1975, 80 Elite Hispanic Women in Bus., Hispanic Bus. Mag., 2005, Most Outstanding Women to Watch, 2008. Mem.: Nat. Assn. Female Execs., Hispanic Women's Coun., American Soc. Tng. & Devel., American Soc. Pers. Adminstrs. Roman Catholic. Achievements include being selected as one of 25 Hispanic women from throughout the US to attend the National Hispanic Leadership Institute, a program designed to prepare women for positions of national impact and to influence public policy. Avocations: jogging, reading, jazzercise. Office: ACS Corp Hdqs 2828 N Haskell Ave Dallas TX 75204-2909 Business E-Mail: Lora.Villarreal@acs-inc.com.

VILLARREAL, MICHAEL (MIKE VILLARREAL), state legislator; b. San Antonio, 1971; m. Jeanne Russell; children: Bella, Marcos. Attended, San Antonio Coll.; degree in Economics, Tex. A&M U.; M in Pub. Policy, Harvard U.; PhD in Pub. Policy, U. Tex., Austin. With Fed. Reserve Bd. Governors, JP Morgan Securities; mcpl. fin. profl. SAMCO Capital Markets, San Antonio; mem. Dist. 123 Tex. House of Representatives, 2003—. Democrat. Office: 1114 S St Marys Ste 110 San Antonio TX 78210 also: Room E1.506 Capitol Extension PO Box 2910 Austin TX 78768 Office Phone: 210-734-8937, 512-463-0532.

VILLARRUBIA, TODD M., lawyer; b. New Orleans, Aug. 13, 1966; BA, U. New Orleans, 1988; JD, La. State U., 1992; LLM in Taxation, Emory U., 1993. Bar: La. 1992, US Tax Ct., cert.: La. State Bar Assn. (estate planning and adminstrn.). Atty. Steeg & O'Connor; ptnr. Livaccari, Villarrubia & Lemmon, LLC, Blue Williams, LLP, Metairie, La., 2005—08. Contbr. articles to profl. publs. Estate planner Nat. Assn. Estate Planning Couns. Named one of Top 100 Attys., Worth mag., 2005—07. Mem.: New Orleans Estate Planning Coun., ABA, La. Bar Assn., New Orleans Bar Assn. Office: Wealth Planning Law Group 101 West Robert E LEe Blvd Ste #404 New Orleans LA 70124 Office Phone: 504-212-3440. Office Fax: 504-837-1182. Business E-Mail: todd@lawealthplan.com.

VILLEGAS, CAMILO, professional golfer; b. Medellin, Colombia, Jan. 7, 1982; Grad. in bus., U. Fla., Gainesville, 2004. Profl. golfer, 2004—, PGA Tour, 2006—. Mem. internat. team President's Cup, 2009; mem. Colombian team World Cup of Golf, 2006, 2011. Named First Team All-Am., NCAA, 2001, 2002, 2004, First Team All Conf., Southeast Conf., 2001, 2002, 2004, Player of Yr., 2002, 2004, Most Improved Player, PGA Tour, Golf Digest, 2008. Achievements include winning PGA Tour events: BMW Championship, Tour Championship, 2008; Honda Classic, 2010; other professional golf wins include: Colombian Open, 2001; Coca-Cola Tokai Classic, 2007; TELUS World Skins Game, CVS Caremark Charity Clasic, Notah Begay III Foundation Challenge, 2008; World Golf Salutes King Bhumibol Skins Tournament, 2010. Office: PGA Tour 100 PGA Tour Blvd Ponte Vedra Beach FL 32082

VILLERE, ROGER FRANCIS, JR., political organization administrator; b. New Orleans, Aug. 16, 1949; s. Roger Sr. and Ursula (Wattigny) Villere; m. Donna Gunckel; children: Roger III, Mark Charles, Jacques Philip. Night clk. Ill. Ctrl. Railroad; owner, pres. Villere's Florist, Metairie, La., 1978—; chmn. Rep. Party East Jefferson, 1989—92, Rep. Party Jefferson Parish, La., 1993, La. Rep. Party, 2004—. Fellow La. State U. Acad. Politics, 1989, Loyola Inst. Politics, 1990, bd. mem., 2004—; fellow U. New Orleans Govt. Leadership Inst., 1991. Mem. Rep. State Ctrl. Com., 1992—2000; mem. rules com. Rep. Nat. Com., 1997—2000; vol. Rep. Nat. Com. Conv., New Orleans, 1988, del. Phila., 2000; charter mem., parliamentarian Jefferson Parish Young Republicans, 1991; bd. dirs. East Jefferson Hosp. Found., Woman's New Life Ctr. Mem.: NRA, Am. Acad. Florists, La. State Florist Assn. (pres.), Alliance for Good Govt. (pres. 2002—04), Pelican State Pachyderms (founder, charter mem., bd. mem. 2002—), Metairie Jaycees (pres.), La. Jaycees (v.p.), Lafreniere Kiwanis (pres.). Republican. Office: Rep Party Of LA PO Box 3557 Baton Rouge LA 70821-3557 E-mail: villerejr@villeresflorist.com.*

VILMA, JONATHAN POLYNICE, professional football player; b. Coral Gables, Fla., Apr. 16, 1982; BS in Fin., U. Miami, 2004. Linebacker NY Jets, 2004—07, New Orleans Saints, 2008—. Recipient Ed Block Courage award, 2008; named NFL Defensive Rookie of Yr., 2004; named to Am. Football Conf. Pro Bowl Team, NFL, 2005, Nat. Football Conf. Pro Bowl Team, 2009. Achievements include member of Super Bowl XLIV championship winning New Orleans Saints, 2010. Office: New Orleans Saints 5800 Airline Dr Metairie LA 70003

VIÑAS, LUIS A., plastic surgeon; Attended, U. Puerto Rico, 1977—78, U. Mass., 1978—79; MD, Universidad Central del Caribe, 1980—83. Diplomate Am. Bd. of Plastic Surgery, 1993, lic. Puerto Rico, Fla., 1990, Nev. State Bd. of Med. Examiners, 2004. Resident in gen. surgery Nassau County Med. Ctr., East Meadow, NY, 1984—87, fellow in burn care, 1987—88, resident in plastic surgery, 1988—90; surg. asst. Hosp. Gen. San Carlos, 1984—84; med. spa dir. Alesandra Salon and Spa, Boynton Beach, Fla., 2009—; hosp. affiliations include St. Mary's Med. Ctr., JFK Med. Ctr., Good Samaritan Med. Ctr. Cons. & faculty ethicon endo-surgery Johnson & Johnson, Cincinnati, Ohio, 2008—; cons. TEI Biosciences, Boston, 2008—. Recipient Susan G. Komen Breast Cancer Found. Appreciation award, Messenger of Peace & Hope award, 2004, Physician Hero award, Heroes in Medicine award, 2005. Mem.: AMA, Fla. Med. Assn., Palm Beach. Med. Soc., Fla. Soc. of Plastic and Reconstructive Surgeons, Am. Bd. of Plastic Surgery, Am. Soc. of Plastic Surgeons, Am. Soc. for Aesthetic Plastic Surgery. Office: LA Viñas Plastic Surgery & Med Spa 550 South Quadrille Blvd West Palm Beach FL 33401 Office Phone: 561-655-3305. Office Fax: 561-655-3951.

VINCENT, CHARLES EAGAR, JR., sportswriter; b. Beaumont, Tex., Mar. 24, 1940; s. Charles Eagar and Hazel Ruth (Balston) V.; m. Mary Jacquelyn Bertman, Aug. 8, 1959 (div. Jan. 1969); children: Lisa Marie, Dixie Ann, Charles Joseph, John Patrick; m. Patricia Helene Skinner, Mar. 28, 1970 (div. Apr. 1985); 1 child, Susanna Lee; m. Karen Judith Peterson, Aug. 17, 1985. Student, Victoria Coll., 1958-59. Reporter Victoria (Tex.) Mirror, 1958-59, Taylor (Tex.) Daily Press, 1959-60; sports writer Beaumont (Tex.) Jour., 1960-62; sports editor Galveston (Tex.) Tribune, 1962-63; sports writer San Antonio Express-News, 1963-69, Sandusky (Ohio) Register, 1969-70, Detroit Free Press, 1970-85, sports columnist, 1985-99. Author: Welcome to My World, 1994, Broken Wings, 1998, Men of Courage; Women of Strength, 2004; co-author: (with Richard Bak) The Corner, A Century of Memories at Michigan and Trumbull, 1999. Recipient 4th Pl. award Nat. AP Sports Editors, 1981, 5th Pl., 1989, 92, Sister Mary Leila Meml. award, 1991, Mich. Columnist of Yr. award, 1991, 97; Afro-Am. Night honoree, 1991, Mich. Writer of the Yr. Nat. Sportscasters and Sportswriters, 1998. Mem.: Baseball Writers Assn. Am. Avocations: travel, cooking, genealogy. Personal E-mail: cev1940@gmail.com.

VINES, JOHN T., state legislator; m. Elizabeth Vines; children: Reese Catherine, Ellie Justice. BA in Fin. & Banking, U. Ark., 1996, JD, 1999. Bar: US Ct. Appeals (8th cir.). Mem. Ark. State Bar Assn., Am. Bar Assn., Garland Bar Assn., Garland County Habitat for Humanity, Hot Springs Boys and Girls Club, Hot Springs Nat. Park Rotary Club; pres., class XIV Leadership Hot Springs; chmn., bd. govs. Nat. Park Cmty. Coll. Found.; mem. Oaklawn Found., Small Claims Magistrate, Hot Springs Dist., US Dist. Ct. Bar, Eastern Dist. of Ark.; pres. Garland County Chpt., Ark. Alumni Assn., 2003—04; chmn. Greater Hot Springs C. of C., 2007; atty. Wood, Smith, Schnipper, Clay and Vines; mem. Dist. 25 Ark. House of Representatives, 2011—. Democrat. Office: 123 Market St Hot Springs AR 71901 Office Phone: 501-624-1252. Business E-Mail: jtvines13@sbcglobal.net.

VINIK, JEFFREY N., hedge fund manager, professional sports team executive; m. Penny Vinik; 4 children. BS in Civil Engring., Duke U., 1981; MBA, Harvard U. Portfolio mgr. growth & income fund Fidelity Investments, Boston, 1992, portfolio mgr. Magellan Fund, 1992—96; founder, chmn., pres., CEO Vinik Asset Mgmt. LP, Boston, 1996—. Minority owner Boston Red Sox; owner Tampa Bay Sports and Entertainment LLC, Tampa Bay Lightning, 2010—. Office: Vinik Asset Mgmt 260 Franklin St, Ste 1900 Boston MA 02110 also: Tampa Bay Lightning St Pete Times Forum 401 Channelside Dr Tampa FL 33602 Office Phone: 617-204-5400.

VINIKAS, VINCENT, historian, educator; b. Erie, Pa., Mar. 29, 1951; s. Matthias Vytautas Vinikas and Eva Aldona Damarodas. BA magna cum laude, Pa. State U., 1972; MA, Columbia U., 1974, PhD, 1983. Asst. prof. U. Ark., Little Rock, 1983—89, assoc. prof., 1989—98, prof., 1998—. Inst. fellow NEH, Ariz. State U., Tempe, 1984; conferee Newberry Libr., Smithsonian Instn., Washington, 1985; inst. fellow NEH, U. N.C., 1993; vis. prof. Karl Franzens U., Graz, Styria, Austria, 1994; inst. fellow NEH, Columbia U., NY, 1998; referee/cons. St. Martin's Press, Prentice-Hall, McGraw-Hill, Houghton-Mifflin, Wadsworth. Author: (monograph) Soft Soap Hard Sell: American Hygiene in an Age of Advertisement; reviewer: Am. Hist. Rev., Jour. So. History, Jour. Social History, Jour. Econ. History, The Historian, Tech. and Culture, Ark. Hist. Quar., Jour. Am. History; contbr. articles to profl. jours.; conferee Sandage Symposium, U. Ill, 2000. Mem. ACLU, Gurdjieff Found. of Ark., Little Rock. Recipient Rsch. award, U. Ark., 1984, 1996; Pres.'s fellow, Columbia U., 1974-1975. Mem.: Am. Hist. Assn., Ark. Assn. of Coll. History Tchrs. (Biennial Essay Award 1993), Phi Alpha Theta (advisor Iota Zeta chpt.), Phi Kappa Phi (exec. bd. chpt. 134 1989—92), Phi Beta Kappa. Avocations: boating, bridge. Home: 3312 W Capitol Ave Little Rock AR 72205 Office: Univ Ark History Dept 2801 S University Ave Little Rock AR 72204 Office Fax: 501-569-3059. Business E-Mail: vxvinikas@ualr.edu.

VINING, ROBERT LUKE, JR., federal judge; b. Chatsworth, Ga., Mar. 30, 1931; m. Martha Sue Cates; 1 child, Laura Orr. BA, U. Ga., Athens, 1959, JD, 1959. With Mitchell & Mitchell, 1958-60; ptnr. McCamy, Miner & Vining, Dalton, 1960-69; solicitor gen. Conasauga Judicial Cir., 1963-68; judge Whitfield County Superior Ct., Dalton, 1969-79, US Dist. Ct. (no. dist.) Ga., 1979—95, chief judge, 1995—96, sr. judge, 1996—. Served to staff sgt. USAF, 1951-59. Office: 600 E First St Ste 345 Rome GA 30162-6226 Office Phone: 706-378-4070.

VINROOT, RICHARD ALLEN, lawyer, mayor; b. Charlotte, NC, Apr. 14, 1941; s. Gustav Edgar and Vera Frances (Pickett) V.; m. Judith Lee Allen, Dec. 29, 1964; children: Richard A., Laura Tabor, Kathryn Pickett. BS in Bus. Adminstrn., U. N.C., 1963, JD, 1966. Bar: N.C. 1966, U.S. Dist. Ct. (ea., mid. and we. dists.) N.C. 1969, U.S. Ct. Appeals (4th cir.) 1969. Ptnr. Robinson, Bradshaw & Hinson, P.A., Charlotte, 1969—. Mayor City of Charlotte, 1991-95; bd. dirs. Martin-Marietta Materials Inc. Tchr. sr. h.s. sunday sch. Myers Park Presbyn. Ch., 1970—, ruling elder, 1970-76, 1978-84, 1996-2000, chmn. of session, 1984; mem. Charlotte City Coun., 1983-91. With U.S. Army, 1967-68, Vietnam. Recipient Bronze Star, 1968; named Mcpl. Leader of the Yr. Am. City & County Mag., 1995. Mem. ABA, VFW, N.C. Bar Assn., Mecklenburg County Bar Assn. (sec. 1976, bd. dir. 1970-76), Mecklenburg County Vietnam Vets. Assn., Mecklenburg County Eagle Scouts Assn., Am. Legion, Phalanx Lodge Mason. Republican. Presbyterian. Office: Robinson Bradshaw & Hinson PA 1900 Independence Ctr 101 N Tryon St Ste 1900 Charlotte NC 28246-0103

VINSON, CLYDE ROGER (ROGER VINSON), federal judge; b. Cadiz, Ky., Feb. 19, 1940; BS, US Naval Acad., 1962; JD, Vanderbilt U., 1971. Bar: Fla. 1971. Commd. ensign USN, 1962, advanced through grades to lt., 1963, naval aviator, until 1968, resigned, 1968; assoc. to ptnr. Beggs & Lane, Pensacola, Fla., 1971-83; judge US Dist. Ct. (no. dist.) Fla., Pensacola, 1983—97, 2004—05, chief judge, 1997—2004, sr. judge, 2005—; judge Fgn. Intelligence Surveillance Ct. (FISC), 2006—. Mem. Jud. Conf. Adv. Com. on Civil Rules, 1993-99; mem. 11th Cir. Pattern Instrn. Com. Contbr. articles to profl. jours. Divsn. chair, area chair United Way of Escambia County; bd. dirs. Pensacola Arts Coun., also treas.; mem. corp. bd. Bapt. Hosp. of Pensacola, 1977-82; co-founder, v.p., charter bd. dirs. Escambia County Epilepsy Soc.; trustee, sec., chair Fellows Meml. Fund Found.; trustee Fla. Bapt. Found., 1979-83; Sunday sch. tchr., bd. dires. First Bapt. Ch. Pensacola. Recipient J. Nixon Daniel Leadership award, 1976, Rinehardt Holm Disting. Svc. award, 1976, Pensacola Action '76 Achievement award, 1976; Wilson Merit scholar, 1968-71. Mem. Am. Judicature Soc., Fla. Bar, Escambia-Santa Rosa Bar Assn., Soc. Bar of 1st Jud. Cir., N.W. Fla. Fed. Bar Assn. (co-founder), Rotary Club of Pensacola (bd. dirs. 1997—, pres. 1998-99), Panhandle Tiger Bay Club (co-founder, pres. 2002-03). Office: US Courthouse 5th fl 1 N Palafox St # 32501 Pensacola FL 32501-5665

VINSON, LAURENCE DUNCAN, JR., lawyer; b. Gadsden, Ala., Mar. 17, 1947; BS with hons., U. Ala., Tuscaloosa, 1969; JD, U. Ala., 1973. Bar: Ala., U.S. Dist. Ct. (no., mid. and so. dists.) Ala., U.S. Ct. Appeals (11th cir.), U.S. Supreme Ct. Assoc. Bradley Arant Boult Cummings, LLP, Birmingham, Ala., 1973—79, ptnr., 1979—. Bar: Ala. 1973, U.S. Dist. Ct. (no. dist.) Ala. 1973, U.S. Supreme Ct. 1977, U.S. Ct. Appeals (11th cir.) 1981, U.S. Dist. Ct. (so. dist.) Ala. 1989, U.S. Dist. Ct. (mid. dist.) Ala. 1991. Chmn. Ala. Uniform Comml. Code Revisions Coms., 1991-2011 Mem. ABA, Birmingham Bar Assn., Ala. State Bar, Ala. Law Inst., Order of Coif, Phi Beta Kappa, Omicron Delta Kappa. Office: Bradley Arant Boult Cummings LLP One Federal Pl 1819 5th Ave N Birmingham AL 35203-2104 Office Phone: 205-521-8000. Business E-Mail: lvinson@babc.com.*

VIOLA, VINCENT, corporate financial executive, professional sports team executive; m. Teresa Viola; children: John, Michael, Travis. Degree, US Mil. Acad., West Point, NY, 1977, US Army Airborne, Infantry and Ranger Schs.; JD, NY Law Sch., 1983. Adv. CMEG NYMEX Holdings Inc. (Nymex Holdings Inc.), CEO, 1985—, chmn., 2001—04; dir. NY Mercantile Exch. (NYMEX), 1987—90, vice chmn., 1993—96, chmn., 2001—04; founder, chmn., CEO Virtu Financial LLC, 2008—; ptnr. Virtu Financial Capital Markets LLC; chmn., owner. gov. Sunrise Sports & Entertainment / Fla. Panthers (NHL), 2013—. Dir. Nat. Italian American Found.; founder, dir. Pioneer Futures. Founder Combating Terrorism Ctr., West Point, 2003. Recipient Ellis Island Medal of Honor; named to Energy Risk Mgmt. Hall of Fame, 2004, Futures Hall of Fame, 2009. Office: c/o Florida Panthers One Panthers Parkway Sunrise FL 33323 also: Virtu Financial LLC 645 Madison Ave New York NY 10022*

VIRKHAUS, TAAVO, symphony orchestra conductor; b. Tartu, Estonia, June 29, 1934; arrived in US, 1949; s. Adalbert August and Helene Marie (Sild) Virkhaus; m. Nancy Ellen Herman Virkhaus, Mar. 29, 1969. MusB, U. Miami, 1955; MusM, Eastman Sch. Music,

Rochester, 1957; DMA, Eastman Sch. Music, 1967. Dir. music U. Rochester, NY; assoc. prof. Eastman Sch., Rochester, 1967—77; music dir., condr. Duluth Superior Symphony Orch., Minn., 1977—94; guest condr. Rochester Philharm, Minn. Orch., Balt. Symphony, Vancouver Symphony, 1972—, Tallinn, Estonia, 1978, 1988, 1990, 1992, 1993, 1994, 1999, 2004; music dir., condr. Hunstville Symphony Orch., Ala., 1989—2003, condr. emertius, 2003—; lectr. U. Minn., Duluth, U. Wis.-Superior. Composer: Violin Concerto, 1966, Symphony No. 1, 1976, Symphony No. 2, 1979, Symphony No. 3, 1984, Symphony No. 4, 1989, Symphony No. 5, 1994, Violin Concerto No. 2, 1995, Symphony No. 6, 2008. With US Army, 1957—58, with USAR, 1957—61. Recipient Howard Hanson Composition award, 1966, Am. Heritage award, JFK Libr. Minorities, 1974; Fulbright scholar, Musickhochschule, Cologne, 1963. Mem.: Am. Fedn. Musicians, Am. Symphony Orch. League. Lutheran. Personal E-mail: taavo@knology.net.

VIRMANI, SANT SINGH, agronomist, researcher; arrived in USA, 2006, permanent resident, 2006; s. Mani Singh and Jeewan Kaur (Muniyal) V.; m. Inderjeet Kaur Narula, Aug. 10, 1969; children: Raminder K., Jusmeet S. BS in Agr., Vikram U., Ujjain, India, 1961, MS in Agrl. Botany, 1963; PhD in Plant Breeding, Punjab Agrl. U., Ludhiana, India, 1969. Rsch. asst. plant breeding Madhya Pradesh Dept. Agriculture, Pawarkheda, India, 1963-64, Punjab Argl. U., 1964-66; sr. rsch. fellow univ. grants com. Punjab Agrl. U., 1966-69, asst. geneticist legumes, 1972-73; rice breeder Internat. Inst. Tropical Agriculture, Ibadan, Nigeria, 1973-79; post doctoral rsch. fellow Internat. Rice Rsch. Inst., Manila, Philippines, 1970-72, vis. scientist, 1979-80, plant breeder, 1980—2004, dep. head plant breeding, genetics, biochemistry div., 1990—2005, prin. scientist, 2004—05; cons. Virmani Internat., Plano, Tex., 2005—. Cons. Internat. Inst. Tropical Agr., Ibadan, 1979, Food and Agr. Orgn., Rome, 1988, 91, 92, 93 Mem. editorial bd. Internat. Jour. Plant Breeding, Euphytica, 1987—; contbr. chpts. to books, and papers and abstracts to jours. Dir. Rotary Club, Los Banos, Philippines, active mem. dist. 3820, 1987—2005, active mem. dist. 5820 Frisco, Tex., 2007—, dir. Recipient Commendation Letter, Govt. Liberia, 1977, Paul Harris fellow Rotary, 2003, Third World Network Sci. Orgn. (TWNSO) award, 2000; The Internat. Svc. in Crpp Sci. award Crop Sci. Soc. America, 2002, Agr. and Rural Devel. medal Ministry Agr., Vietnam, 2002, The Koshihikari Internat. Rice prize, 2005; Monsanto Crop Sci. Disting. Career award, 2005, Pravasi Bhartiya award Pres. India, 2005; Padma Shri award, Pres. India, 2008. Fellow Indian Soc. Genetics and Plant Breeding, Indian Acad. Agrl. Scis., Am. Soc. Agronomy, Crop Sci. Soc. Philippines, Crop Sci. Soc. America, Crop Improvement Soc. India (Life), Assn. Rice Rsch. Workers in India. Progressive. Achievements include research leadership in hybrid rice outside china. Avocations: tennis, indian music, bridge. Home and Office: Virmani Consulting Internat 4425 Partney Ct Plano TX 75024 Office Phone: 469-682-8710. Business E-Mail: santvirmani@gmail.com.

VISCUSI, W(ILLIAM) GREGORY KIP, law and economics educator; b. Trenton, NJ, Oct. 3, 1949; s. William Edward and Evelyn (Martin) V.; m. Catherine Makdisi, Sep. 26, 1972 (div.); children: Kira Margaret, Michael Kip; m. Joni Hersch, Jan. 18, 1998. AB summa cum laude, Harvard U., Cambridge, Mass., 1971, MPP, 1973, AM, 1974, PhD, 1976. Prof. econs. Northwestern U., Evanston, Ill., 1976-80, 85-88; dep. dir. White House Council on Wage and Price Stability, Washington, 1979-81; prof. econs. Duke U., Durham, NC, 1981-85; John M. Olin prof. econs. U. Chgo., 1985-86; George G. Allen prof. econs. Duke U., Durham, NC, 1988-96; John M. Olin vis. prof. law and econs. Harvard Law Sch., Cambridge, Mass., 1995, John F. Cogan Jr. prof. law and econs., 1996—2006; univ. disting. prof. law, econs., mgmt. Law Sch. Vanderbilt U., Nashville, 2006—. Rsch. assoc. Nat. Bur. Econ. Rsch., 1978—, Nat. Commn. for Employment Policy, 1981; mem. EPA Sci. Adv. Bd., 1986—, econs. bd., 1992—, Clean Air Act, 1992—, Nat. Acad. Sci. Panel, 1978-79; cons. US Gen. Acctg. Office, 1981-85, Dept. Justice, 1986-87, 89-91, U.S. Office Mgmt. and Budget, 1983; assoc. reporter Am. Law Inst., 1986-91; adj. fellow in civil justice Manhattan Inst., 1987—; inaugural spkr. Geneva Risk Econ. Lectrs., Geneva Assn. Risk and Ins., 1989; John R. Commons lectr. U. Wis., 1990; Ayne Ryde lectr. Lund U., Sweden. Author: Employment Hazards, 1979 (Wells prize 1977), Risk by Choice, 1983, Reforming Products Liability, 1991, Fatal Tradeoffs, 1992, Smoking, 1992, Rational Risk Policy, 1998, Smoke-filled Rooms: A Post-mortem on the Tobacco Deal, 2002; founding editor Jour. Risk and Uncertainty; contbg. editor Regulation mag.; assoc. editor Internat. Rev. of Law Econs., Geneva Papers on Risk and Ins. Theory, Jour. Regulatory Econs., Jour. Environ. Econs. and Mgmt., J Risk and Ins., Rev. Econs. and Stats., Am. Econ. Rev., Managerial and Decision Econs., Contemporary Econ. Policy. Recipient Article of the Yr. award Econ. Inquiry, 1988, Royal Econ. Soc., 1999; Book of the Yr. awards Am. Risk and Ins. Assn., 1992, 93, 94, 2000, Article award Am. Risk and Ins. Assn., 1999, Coase prize, 2006. Mem. Am. Econs. Assn., Econometric Soc., Assn. Environ. and Resource Economists, Assn. for Pub. Policy Analysis and Mgmt., So. Econs. Assn. We. Econs. Assn., Managerial and Decision Econs. Roman Catholic. Office: Vanderbilt Univ Law Sch 131 21st Ave South Nashville TN 37203-1181

VISH, DONALD H., lawyer, writer, photographer, educator; b. Ft. Benning, Ga., Jan. 18, 1945; s. D. H., Jr. and Dorris (Parrish) Vish; m. Catherine Pence Hamilton, Aug. 20, 1966 (div. 1986); children: Donald Hamilton, Daphne Mershon Sullivan. BA in English, Bellarmine Coll., 1968; JD cum laude, U. Louisville, 1971. Bar: Ky. 1971, Fla. 1972. Sec., gen. counsel Gen. Energy Corp., Lexington, Ky., 1978-83; ptnr. Wyatt, Tarrant & Combs, Lexington, 1980-88, Frost Brown Todd, Lexington, 1988-89, 1991-98; gen. counsel Ky. Coal Producers' Self-Ins. Fund, 1992-98; sec., gen. counsel AIK Workers Compensation Fund, 1998—2004, exec. v.p., 2002—04, Middleton, Reutlinger, 2004—; exec. dir. & bd. mem. The J & L Found., 2008—; dir. advocacy Ky. Coalition Against The Death Penalty, 2009—. Adj. prof. Law & Lit. Brandeis Sch. Law, 2010—; apptd. assoc. solicitor U.S. Dept. Interior, 1989—91; adj. assoc. prof. mineral law U. Ky., Lexington, 1979—85. Author: Poems and Musings, 2001; contbr.; contbg. author: American Law of Mining, 2d edit., 1984, co-editor, contbg. author: Coal Law and Regulation, 1983—93, Kentucky Election Law, 1995. Trustee Sayre Sch., Lexington, 1980—88, chmn. bd. dir., 1986—88; mem. Blue Grass coun. Boy Scouts Am., 1988—93; bd. mem. Ctr. Non-Profit Excellene, 2010—, Ky. Sch. Art, 2010; apptd. gov. Ky. Registry Election Fin., 1991—93; bd. dir. Highlands Cmty. Ministries, 2001—04; bd. dirs. Ky. Shakespeare Festival, 2005—08, Interfaith Paths to Peace, 2006—, Louisville Bar Assn., 2007—; pres. Interfaith Paths to Peace, 2007—10. Recipient Disting. Alumnus award, Brandeis Sch. Law, 2011; named to Gallery of Disting. Grads., Bellarmine Coll., 2008. Fellow: Am. Bar Found. (life); mem.: ABA (chmn. coal com., natural resources sect. 1987), LBA, Louisville Bar Assn. Com. Judicial Integrity & Independence (bd. mem. 2009—), Ky. Bar Assn. (mem. ethics com. 1983—85, chair residency com. 1998—2002), Fla. Bar, Energy and Mineral Law Found. (mem. exec. com. 1979—82, trustee 1979—91, trustee emeritus 1998), Louisville Bar Found. (life), Am. Law Inst. (life), Ky. Bar Found. (life). Office: Middleton Reutlinger 2500 Brown and Williamson Tower Louisville KY 40202 Home: 521 Zorn Ave D-6 Louisville KY 40206 Home Phone: 502-299-0155; Office Phone: 502-299-0155, 502-584-1135. Personal E-mail: donaldvish@gmail.com.

VISITANTE, EL (EDUARDO CABRA), singer, musician; b. Santurce, PR, Sept. 10, 1978; Co-founder, pianist & singer Calle 13; signed to White Lion Records Inc., Santurce, PR. Musician: (albums) Calle 13, 2005 (Latin Grammy award for Best Urban Music Album, 2006), Residante O Visitante, 2007 (Best Urban Music album, Latin Grammy Awards, 2007, Grammy award, Best Latin Urban Album, 2008), Los de Atrás Vienen Conmigo, 2008, (songs) Atrévete Te, Te!, 2005 (Latin Grammy award for Best Short Form Music Video, 2006), Pal Norte, 2007 (Best Urban song, Latin Grammy Awards, 2007). Recipient Best New Artist award, also Best Urban Music Album & Best Short Music Video awards, Latin Grammy Awards, 2006. Office: White Lion Records Inc Urb Ocean Park 2072 Calle Cacique Santurce PR 00911-1514

VISSCHER, PIETER BERNARD, physicist, researcher; b. Mpls., Dec. 11, 1945; s. Maurice B. and Janet Gertrude (Pieters) V.; m. Helga Bjarney Björnson, June 17, 1972; children: Kristina Maria, Paul Jon. BA, Harvard U., 1967; MA, U. Calif., Berkeley, 1968, PhD, 1971. Rsch. assoc. U. Ill., Urbana, 1971-73; rsch. physicist U. Calif., San Diego, 1973-75; asst. prof. physics U. Oreg., Eugene, 1975-78; from asst. prof. to assoc. prof. physics U. Ala., Tuscaloosa, 1978-84, prof. physics, 1984—2011, coord., tricampus materials sci. program, 2005—08; emeritus prof., 2011—. Cons. Los Alamos (N.Mex.) Nat Lab., 1985-86, Sci. and Engring. Rsch. Coun. fellow U. Surrey, Britain, 1992-93, Seagate Rsch. Inc. 2011-. Samsung Inc. 2011-. Author: Fields and Electrodynamics, 1988, simulation software for electrodynamics, 1991; contbr. articles to profl. jours. Sec. West Ala. Group of Sierra Club, 2000—11. Recipient grants Cottrell Rsch. Corp., 1979, NSF, 1979, 81, 92, 94, 98, 2000, 02, 08, Dept. Energy, 1994-98, 2001-06. Mem. AAUP (chpt. v.p. 1983, 84), Am. Phys. Soc., IEEE Magnetics Soc. Home: 4301 Kendlewood Ln Northport AL 35473-1625 Office: University Ala MINT Center Tuscaloosa AL 35487-0209*

VITERISI, JOHN E., tax specialist; B in Economics, Ind. U., Bloomington, 1984, B in Acctg., 1993. Tax acct., tax mgr., dir., tax Arthur Andersen LLP, 1992—2000; dir., v.p., tax, sr. tax mgr. Stryker Corp., 2000—04; dir., v.p., tax Cintas Corp., 2004—07; v.p., tax Scripps Networks Interactive, Inc., sr. v.p., tax, 2007—; v.p., tax E.W. Scripps Co., 2007. Office: Scripps Networks Interactive Inc 9721 Sherrill Blvd Knoxville TN 37932 Office Phone: 865-694-2700. Office Fax: 865-985-7778. Business E-Mail: jviterisi@scrippsnetworks.com.

VITT, JOE, professional football coach; b. Syracuse, NY; m. Linda Vitt; children: Joe, Jennifer. B, Towson U., Md., 1978. Strength/quality control coach Balt. Colts, 1979—81; defensive quality control coach, asst. strength & conditioning coach Seattle Seahawks, 1982, quality control/asst. linebackers coach, 1983—87, safeties coach, 1988—91; asst. head coach, defensive backs coach LA Rams, 1992—94; linebackers coach Phila. Eagles, 1995—98; defensive backs coach Green Bay Packers, 1999; linebackers coach Kansas City Chiefs, 2000—03; asst. head coach, linebackers coach St. Louis Rams, 2004—05, interim head coach, 2005; asst. head coach, linebackers coach New Orleans Saints, 2006—, interim head coach, 2012. Named to Towson Univ. Hall of Fame. Achievements include member of NFL Super Bowl XLVI championship winning New Orleans Saints. Office: New Orleans Saints 5800 Airline Dr Metairie LA 70003

VITTER, DAVID BRUCE, United States Senator from Louisiana; b. New Orleans, May 3, 1961; s. Al and Audrey Vitter; m. Wendy Baldwin, 1991; children: Sophie, Lise, Airey, Jack BA magna cum laude, Harvard U., 1983; BA/MA in History/Econs. with highest honors, Oxford U., 1985; JD with honors, Tulane U. Sch. Law, 1988. Bar: La. 1988. Bus. atty., La., 1988—99; assoc. Golden, Kingsmill and Riess, New Orleans, Duplass, Witman, Zwain and Williams, Metairie, La., Duplass, Zwain and Bourgeois, Metairie, La.; mem. La. House of Reps., 1991—99, US Congress from 1st. La. Dist., 1999—2005; US Senator from La., 2005—. Adj. prof. law Tulane U., 1993—99, Loyola U., 1993—99. Articles editor Tulane Law Rev., 1987-88. Lector, St. Francis Xavier Cath. Ch., Metairie, La.; Mem. Coastal Conservation Assn., Ducks Unlimited. Rhodes scholar; Recipient Legis. of Yr., Alliance for Good Govt., Lifetime Achievement award Victims & Citizens Against Crime, Republican of Yr. award Northshore Republican Men's Club, 2005. Mem. ABA, New Orleans Bar Assn., Phi Beta Kappa, Nat. Rifle Assn.; former mem. La. Bar Assn. Republican. Roman Catholic. Office: US Senate 516 Hart Senate Office Bldg Washington DC 20510 also: District Office Ste 201 2800 Veterans Blvd Metairie LA 70002 Office Phone: 504-589-2753, 202-224-4623. Office Fax: 504-589-2607, 202-228-5061.*

VITTER, JEFFREY SCOTT, academic administrator, computer science educator, researcher; b. New Orleans, Nov. 13, 1955; s. Albert Leopold Jr. and Audrey Malvina (St. Raymond) V.; m. Sharon Louise Weaver, Aug. 14, 1982; children: Jillian St. Raymond, J. Scott Jr., Audrey Louise. BS in Math. with highest honors, U. Notre Dame, 1977; PhD in Computer Sci., Stanford U., 1980; AM (hon.), Brown U., 1986; MBA, Duke U., 2002. Asst. computer performance analyst Standard Oil Co. Calif., San Francisco, 1976—77; rsch. and tchg. asst. Stanford (Calif.) U., 1977—80, tchg. fellow, 1979; asst. prof. computer sci. Brown U., Providence, 1980—85, assoc. prof. computer sci., 1985—88, prof. computer sci., 1988—93; Gilbert, Louis and Edward Lehrman prof. computer sci. Duke U., Durham, NC, 1993—2002, chmn. dept., 1993—2001, co-dir. Ctr. for Geometric and Biol. Computing, 1997—2002; prof. computer sci. Purdue U., 2002—08, Frederick L. Hovde dean Coll. of Science, 2002—08; provost and exec. v.p. acads. Tex. A&M U., College Station, 2008—, prof. computer sci. and engring., 2008—. Cons. IBM, 1981-86, Inst. for Def. Analyses, 1986, Ctr. for Computing Scis., 1992-94, Lucent Technologies, Bell Labs., 1997; mem. rsch. staff Math. Scis. Rsch. Inst., Berkeley, 1986, Inst. Recherche en Informatique et en Automatique, Roquencourt, France, 1986-87, Inst. Recherche en Informatique et en Automatique, Sophia Antipolis, France, 1998-1999; vis. prof. Ecole Normale Superieure, Paris, 1986-89; vis. and adj. prof. Tulane U., 1990-2006, mem. bd. advisors Sch. Sci. and Engring., 2006—; lectr. Asian Sch. on Computer Sci., Bangkok, 1987; assoc. mem. Ctr. Excellence in Space Data and Info. Scis. Author: The Design and Analysis of Coalesced Hashing, 1987, Efficient Algorithms for MPEG Video Compression, 2002, Algorithms and Data Structers for External Memory, 2008; editor Algorithmica, 1994—, guest editor, 1988, 94; editor Math. Sys. Theory: Internat. Jour. on Math. Computing Theory, 1991—, Soc. for Indsl. and Applied Math. Jour. on Computing, 1989-1997, Algorithm Engineering, 1999, External Memory Algorithms, 1999; contbr. articles to profl. jours.; patentee in field. Recipient Faculty Devel. award IBM, 1984, NSF Presdl. Young Investigator award, 1985, Test of Time award ACM Sigmod, 2009; NSF grad. fellow, 1977-80; Guggenheim fellow, N.Y.C., 1986-87. Fellow IEEE (editor Trans. on Computers 1985, 87-91), Assn. for Computing Machinery (editor Comms. 1988-95, Jour. Exptl. Algorithmics, 2000; mem.-at-large spl. interest group on automata and computability theory 1987-91, vice chair spl. interest group on algorithms and computation theory 1991-1997, chair 1997-2001, exec. com. 2001-05, Recognition of Svc. award 1997, 2001); mem. Computing Rsch. Assn. (bd. dirs. 2000-, co-chair govt. affairs com. 2001-), Phi Beta Kappa, Sigma Xi. Avocations: reading, golf, basketball, football, genealogy. Office: Office Provost and Exec VP Acads Tex A&M Univ 1248 Tamu College Station TX 77843-1248 Office Phone: 979-845-4016. Business E-Mail: jsv@tamu.edu.

VITTI, NIKOLAI PAUL-CARLO, school system administrator; m. Rachel Burke Thomas, June 29, 2001; children: Lorenzo Carlo, Cecila Nikoletta. BA in History, Wake Forest U., Winston-Salem, NC, 2000, EdM, 2001; EdD in Edn. and Adminstrn., Harvard U., Cambridge, 2006, EdD candidate in Edn., Adminstrn. and Social Policy. Social studies tchr. Parkland HS, Winston-Salem, 2001, Carver HS, Winston-Salem, 2001—02; mid. sch. social studies tchr. Pub. Sch. 117 Wade Acad., Bronx, 2002—03; HS dean students Pub. Sch. 438 Fordham Leadership, Bronx, 2003—05; asst. supt. of edn. transformation office Miami-Dade County Pub. Schs., prin. Homestead Mid. Sch., chief academic officer; dep. chancellor, sch. improvement and student achievement Fla. Dept. Edn.; supt. Duval County Pub. Schools, Jacksonville, Fla., 2012—. Office: Duval County Public Schools 1701 Prudential Dr Jacksonville FL 32207 Office Phone: 904-390-2000.*

VITTORI, ROBERTO, astronaut; b. Viterbo, Italy, Oct. 15, 1964; m. Valeria Nardi; 3 children. Grad., Italian Air Force Acad., 1989; grad. undergrad. pilot tng., Reese AFB, Tex., 1989; grad., U.S. Navy Test Pilot Sch., 1995; attended, U.S. Air Force Flight Safety Sch., 1997—98. Flew Tornado GR1 aircraft 155th Squadron, 50th Wing, Piacenza, Italy, 1991—94; project pilot for devel. of European aircraft EF2000 Italian Test Ctr., 1995—98; nat. rep. Beyond Visual Range Air-to-Air Missile R&D Program, 1996—98; wing flight safety officer Italian Test Ctr., 1997; tchr. aerodynamics accident investigation course Italian Air Force; astronaut Italian Space Agy. in cooperation with ESA, 1998; joined European Astronaut Corp., ESA European Astronaut Ctr., Cologne, Germany, 1998; mission specialist candidate astronaut NASA Johnson Space Ctr., Houston, 1998—, with Astronaut Office New Generation Space Vehicles Br., 2002; tng. as bd. engr. Yuri Gagarin Cosmonaut Tng. Ctr., Star City near Moscow, 2001; participated in a taxi-flight to Internat. Space Station, 2002; mem. of crew with Salizhan Sharipov and Leroy Chiao Expedition 11, 2005. Spaceflight participant Internat. Space Station-Marco Polo Mission, 2002, Internat. Space Station-Eneide Mission, 2005; mission specialist STS-134 Mission-Final Flight of Endeavour, 2011. Maj. Italian Air Force. Avocations: soccer, running, swimming, reading. Office: NASA Johnson Space Ctr Astronaut Office/CB Houston TX 77058

VITZ, PAUL CLAYTON, psychologist, educator; b. Toledo, Aug. 27, 1935; m. Evelyn Birge; 6 children. BA high honors in Psychology, U. Mich., 1953; PhD, Stanford U., 1962. Instr. psychology Pomona (Calif.) Coll., 1962-64; asst. prof. NYU, 1965-70, assoc. prof., 1970-85, dir. psychology dept. undergrad. program, 1973-79, prof., 1985—2004, prof. emeritus, 2004—. Adj. prof. John Paul II Inst. on Marriage and Family, Washington, 1990-2003, Internat. Acad. Philosophy, 1994-98; prof./sr. scholar Inst. for Psychol. Scis., 2000—; lectr. in field. Author: Psychology as Religion: The Cult of Self-Worship, 1977, 2d edit., 1994, (with A.B. Glimcher) Modern Art and Modern Science: The Parallel Analysis of Vision, 1984, Censorship: Evidence of Bias in Our Children's Textbooks, 1986, Sigmund Freud's Christian Unconscious, 1988, Faith of the Fatherless: The Psychology of Atheism, 1999; editor: (with S. Krason) Defending the Family: A Sourcebook, 1998, (with S. Felch) The Self: Beyond the Postmodern Crisis, 2006; contbr. articles to profl. jours., chpts. to books. Grantee Nat. Inst. Mental Health, 1963-64, 64-66, 66-67, Nat. Inst. Neurol. Diseases and Blindness grantee, 1970-73, 73-74, Nat. Inst. Edn., 1983, 84-85, Dept. Edn., 1986-87. Office: Inst for the Psychol Scis Ste 511 2001 Jefferson Davis Hwy Arlington VA 22202

VIVIAN, C.T. (CORDY TINDELL VIVIAN), retired civil rights organization administrator; b. Booneville, Mo., July 28, 1924; s. Robert Cordie and Euzetta Tindell Vivian; m. Octavia Vivian. Attended, Western Ill. U., Macomb, American Bapt. Theol. Sem., Nashville. Asst. boy's dir. Carver Cmty Ctr., Peoria, Ill., 1942; co-founder Nashville Christian Leadership Conf., 1955; joined Student Nonviolent Coordinating Com., 1961; nat. dir. affiliates Southern Christian Leadership Conf. (SCLC), 1963—66, interim pres. Atlanta, 2012; dir. Christian Missions Urban Tng. Ctr., Chgo., 1966; coord. Coalition for United Cmty. Action; dir. Sem. Without Walls at Shaw U. Divinity Sch., Raleigh, NC, 1972; founder Black Strategies and Info. Ctr., Nat. Ctr. Human Rights Edn., Ctr. Democratic Renewal (formerly Nat. Anti-Klan Network); co-founder Capital City Bank, Atlanta. Bd. dirs. Ctr. Democratic Renewal, Nat. Voting Rights Mus. Recipient Presdl. Medal of Freedom, The White House, 2013. Office: SCLC National Headquarters 320 Auburn Ave NE Atlanta GA 30303*

VIVIANI, TANIOS E., food products executive; Studied Economics, Brazil; MBA, U. Akron. Asst. brand mgr. Procter & Gamble Co., Puerto Rico, various mktg., sales, advt. & gen. mgmt. positions, 1989, Belize, 1989, China, 1989, mgr., Global Consortium, 2003—04; pres. Fresh Express Group (acquired by Chiquita Brands Internat., Inc.), 2006—07; v.p., Fresh Cut Fruit Chiquita Brands International, Inc., 2004—05, pres., Fresh Express Group, 2005—07, chief mktg. officer, pres., global innovation & emerging markets, 2007—. Recipient Exec. Scholar, Northwestern University. Office: Chiquita Brands International Inc 550 S Caldwell St Ste 1010 Charlotte NC 28202-2681 Office Phone: 513-784-8000. Office Fax: 513-784-8030. Business E-Mail: tviviani@chiquita.com.

VLADIMIROVICH, VINOGRADOV PAVEL, cosmonaut; b. Magadan, Russia, Aug. 31, 1953; married; 3 children. Grad. in Dept. Airborne Vehicles, Moscow Aviation Inst., 1977. Pilot-cosmonaut, 3rd class cosmonaut Russian Fedn.; specialized in software develop for automated interactive designing systems of recoverable vehicles, develop. aerodynamics and aerodyne arrangement design models, computer graphics, 1977—83; with Head Design Bur. Rocket Space Corp., Energia, 1983; joined Energia cosmonaut corp, 1992; completed generic space tng. Yu. A. Gagarin Cosmonaut Tng. Ctr., 1992—94, complete advance test-cosmonaut tng., 1994—95; flight engr. tng. of Mir-20 and EuroMir-95 back-up crew Soyuz TM and Mir Space Station, 1995; trained for Spaceflight on Soyuz TM vehicle and Mir spac e station as flight engr. Mir-22/NASA-3 and Cassiopeia programs, 1995—96; trained as flight engr. Mir-24 prime crew, 1996—97; flight engr. Soyuz TM and Mir Station, Expedition 24 (Mir-24/NASA 5. 6), 1997—98; trained for spaceflight as back-up flight engr. Mir-28, 1999—2000; trained as flight engr. Mir-29, 2000; completed tng. as test cosmonaut Internat. Space Station group, 2001—02; trained as flight engr. Internat. Space Station Taxi Back-up crew 5, 2002—03; crew comdr. Internat. Space Station, Expedition-13, Soyuz TMA-8, 2006. Avocations: game sports, astronomy, history of avaiation and cosmonautics. Office: Astronaut office CB NASA Johnson Space Center Houston TX 77058

VO, HURBERT, state legislator; b. May 30, 1956; m. Kathy Vo. BS in Mech. Engring., U. Houston. Former machinist Hughes Tool Co.; businessman, entrepreneur, real estate developer; mem. Dist. 149 Tex.

House of Reps., 2004—. Democrat. Office: 7474 S Kirkwood St Ste 106 Houston TX 77072 also: Room E2.208 Capitol Extension PO Box 2910 Austin TX 78768 Office Phone: 281-988-0212, 512-463-0568.

VOEGELI, VICTOR JACQUE, historian, educator, dean; b. Jackson, Tenn., Dec. 21, 1934; s. Victor Jacque Voegeli and Winnie Lassiter; m. Anna Jean King, Oct. 14, 1956; children: Victor Jacque, Charles Lassiter. BS, Murray State Coll., Murray, Kentucky, 1956; MA, Tulane U., New Orleans, 1961, PhD, 1965. Instr. history Tulane U., 1963-65, asst. prof., 1965-67; asst. prof. history Vanderbilt U., 1967-69, assoc. prof., 1969-73, prof. history, 1973-98, chmn. history dept., 1973-76, dean Coll. Arts and Sci., 1976-92, acting dean Coll. Arts and Sci., 1996-97, prof. emeritus, dean emeritus, 1998—. Author: Free But Not Equal: The Midwest and the Negro During the Civil War, 1967. Served with US Army, 1956-58. Nat. Endowment Humanities grantee, 1969-70, 72. Mem. So. Hist. Assn. Address: 2110 Golf Club Ln Nashville TN 37215-1224

VOGEL, JILL HOLTZMAN, state legislator; b. Roanoke, Va., July 6, 1970; m. Alex Vogel; 4 children. BA, Coll. William & Mary; JD, DePaul U. Atty.; mem. Dist. 27 Va. State Senate, 2008—. Republican. Office: 117 East Picadilly St Winchester VA 22601 also: Senate of Virginia PO Box 396 Richmond VA 23218 Office Phone: 540-662-4551, 804-698-7527. Office Fax: 540-341-8809, 804-698-7651. E-mail: district27@senate.virginia.gov.

VOGEL, JON, political media firm executive, political strategist; b. 1975; m. Kate Kumpuris; 1 child, Anya. BA in Internat. Relations, Conn. Coll., 1997. Finance dir. to Rep. Mike Forbes, campaign mgr. to Va. Del. Robert Hull, 1997—2000; finance dir. Steve Israel for Congress, 2000, dep. chief of staff Washington, 2001—03; Midwest fin. dir. Dick Gephardt for Pres. Campaign, 2004; v.p. Winning Directions, Inc., 2004—05; joined as fin. asst. Democratic Congressional Campaign Com. (DCCC), Washington, 2005, NE/Fla. regional dir., 2006, polit. dir., 2007—08, dir. Ind. Expenditure Program, 2008—09, exec. dir., 2009—10, adviser, 2010—11; ptnr. Global Strategy Group, LLC, Washington, 2009; mng. ptnr. Murphy Vogel Askew Reilly, Alexandria, Va., 2011—. Named one of The Fabulous 50, Roll Call, 2009. Democrat. Office: Murphy Vogel Askew Reilly 1199 N Fairfax St Ste 220 Alexandria VA 22314-1437 Office Phone: 703-549-4181. Office Fax: 703-549-2976.

VOGEL, STEVEN, biologist, educator; b. Beacon, NY, Apr. 7, 1940; s. Max and Jeanette Rachel (Zucker) V.; m. Mariette Seeley Booth, June 3, 1963 (div. Jan. 1974); 1 child, Roger Booth; m. Jane Gregory, Dec. 13, 1974. BS, Tufts U., 1961; AM, Harvard U., 1963, PhD, 1966. 01. Instr. Tufts U., Medford, Mass., 1962; from asst. prof. to prof. Duke U., Durham, NC, 1966-93, James B. Duke prof., 1993—2006, prof. emeritus, 2006—. Instr. U. Wash., Friday Harbor, summer, 1979, 81, 83; cons. in field. Author: Life in Moving Fluids, 1981, Life's Devices, 1988, Vital Circuits, 1991, Cats' Paws and Catapults, 1998, The Life of a Leaf, 2012, Comparative Biomechanics, 2013; contbr. articles to profl. jours. Jr. fellow Harvard U., 1964; recipient Stone prize for sci. writing L.A. County Museum, 1990. Fellow AAAS. Achievements include findings concerning the interrelationships between the shapes of organisms (from algae to mammals) and the fluid mech. phenomena around and within them. Office: Duke University Dept Biology PO Box 90338 Durham NC 27708-0338 Home: 6 Aldersgate Ct Durham NC 27705-1310 Office Phone: 919-684-3791. Business E-Mail: svogel@duke.edu.

VOGT-LOWELL, ROBERT W., pediatric cardiologist; b. Havana, Cuba, Aug. 28, 1959; B, Univ. Miami; MD, Univ. Puerto Rico, 1986. Diplomate Am. Bd. Pediatrics, 1989, in pediatric cardiology Am. Bd. Pediatrics, 1996. Intern in pediatrics, resident in pediatric cardiology Miami Children's Hosp., 1986—89; fellow in pediatric cardiology LI Jewish Med. Ctr., Albert Einstein Med. Ctr., NY, 1989—92, asst. prof., 1992—94; pediatric cardiologist Single Source Pediatric Heart Ctr., Miami, Fla., 1994, Miami Children's Hosp., 1998—. Office: Miami Children's Hosp Ste 110 7765 SW 87th Ave Miami FL 33173 Office Phone: 305-595-1833, 866-756-9355. Office Fax: 305-595-2024.

VOGUS, TIMOTHY J., management professor; BA in Polit. Economy and Spanish with high honors, Mich. State U., 1995; PhD in Mgmt. and Organizations, U. Mich., Ann Arbor, 2004. Asst. prof. mgmt. and organization studies Owen Grad. Sch. Mgmt., Vanderbilt U., 2004—. Affiliate Ctr. for Catastrophic Risk Mgmt., U. Calif., Berkeley. Contbr. articles to profl. jours. Recipient Thomas William Leabo Meml. Award for Academic Excellence, 2001; Hicks Fellowship, 1999—2003. Mem.: Phi Beta Kappa. Office: Owen Graduate School of Management Vanderbilt University 401 21st Avenue South Nashville TN 37221 Home: 9161 Sydney Lane Brentwood TN 37027 Office Phone: 615-343-8094. E-mail: timothy.vogus@owen.vanderbilt.edu.

VOITIER, DORIS, school system administrator; b. New Orleans, June 2, 1949; BA, U. New Orleans, 1971. Math tchr. Chalmette HS, La.; supt. St. Bernard Parish Pub. Sch. Dist., 2004—. Recipient Woman of Yr. award, St. Bernard Bus. and Professional Women's Club, Profile in Courage award, John F. Kennedy Libr. Found., 2007. Office: St Bernard Parish Pub Sch Dist 200 E St Bernard Highway Chalmette LA 70043 Office Phone: 504-301-2000.

VOLANAKIS, JOHN EMMANUEL, immunologist, rheumatologist; b. Thessaloniki, Greece, Mar. 17, 1938; arrived in US, 1968, naturalized, 1978; s. Emmanuel (Manolis) John and Cleo (Agathonos) Volanakis; children: Emmanuel (Manolis) John, Marina Cleo. MD, Aristotle U., Thessaloniki, 1962; DMed, Nat. U. Athens, Greece, 1968, PhD (hon.), 2003. Cert. Bd. Internal Medicine Ministry Health, Greece, 1967. Fellow rheumatology Cleve. Met. Gen. Hosp., 1968—71; instr. dept. medicine U. Ala., Birmingham, 1971—73, asst. prof. dept. medicine, 1973—77, assoc. prof. dept. medicine, 1977—83, prof. dept. medicine, 1983—2003; pres., sci. dir. Biomedical Sciences Rsch. Ctr. Alexander Fleming, Vari, Greece, 1997—2003. Dir., rsch. component Multipurpose Arthritis Ctr., Birmingham, Ala., 1984—97. Editor: The Human Complement System in Health and Disease; contbr. articles to profl. jours. Cadet Mil. Med. Sch., 1956—61, Thessaloniki, Greece. Recipient Alexander von Humbolt, Rsch. award for Sr. U.S. Scientists, Alexander von Humbolt Stiftung, 1996—97; named Anna Lois Waters Chair of Medicine in Rheumatology, U. Ala., 1989—97; Robert M. Stecher fellow, Arthritis Found. Ohio, 1969—71, Fogarty Sr. Internat. Rsch. fellow, NIH, 1978—79. Mem.: Assn. Am. Physicians. Achievements include patents for crystals of human factor D. Avocation: literature. Office: University Alabama 1530 3rd Ave S Shel 411 Birmingham AL 35294-0012 Office Phone: 205-934-5235. Business E-Mail: volanaki@uab.edu.

VOLENTINE, RICHARD J., JR., lawyer; b. Tampa, Fla., Apr. 2, 1955; s. Richard J. Sr. and Mary Francis (Shaw) V.; m. Lisa Dennis Volentine; children: Rachel Elizabeth, Scott Thomas, Melissa Mary. BS, Spring Hill Coll., 1977; JD, U. Ala., 1980. Bar: Ala. 1980, Mo. 1982, Fla. 1984, Ga. 2005. Staff atty. Ala. Jud. Coll., Tuscaloosa, 1980-81; staff counsel Citicorp Person-to-Person, Inc., St. Louis, 1982; regional counsel Citicorp Person-to-Person Corp., Tampa, 1982-84; asst. gen. counsel Citicorp Savs. Fla., Miami, 1984-85; assoc. counsel Home Fed./Capital Corp., Atlanta, 1985-86; regional atty. FDIC, Atlanta, 1986-88; gen. counsel, v.p. Altus Bank, Mobile, Ala., 1988-90; v.p., assoc. gen. counsel Chase Home Mortgage Corp., Tampa, Fla., 1990-91; sr. v.p., chief legal officer Prudential Bank, Atlanta, 1991—2000; assoc. gen. counsel Fannie Mae, Atlanta, 2010; gen. counsel Prommis Solutions LLC, Atlanta, 2010—. Mem. ABA, Assn. Corp. Counsel, Ala. Jud. Coll. Faculty Assn. (hon.). Republican. Roman Catholic. Avocations: playing golf, basketball, and other sports, photography, writing. Office: 400 Northridge Rd Ste 700 Atlanta GA 30350 Home: 4217 Hardy Ave Smyrna GA 30082-4702 Home Phone: 770-953-3157; Office Phone: 678-280-1804. Business E-Mail: dick.volentine@prommis.com.

VOLICER, LADISLAV, physician, educator; b. Prague, Czechoslovakia, May 21, 1935; came to U.S., 1969, naturalized, 1977; s. Ladislav and Vilma (Molnarova) V.; m. Olga Holeckova, July 14, 1959 (div. 1970); children: Irena, Katerina; m. Beverly J. Beers, May 20, 1972 (div. 1998); children: Zuzka, Marika, Nadine, m. Joyce Simard, Jan. 1, 2009. MD, Charles U., 1959; PhD of Pharmacology, Czechoslovak Acad. Scis., 1964. Rsch. assoc. Czechoslovak Acad. Sci., Prague, 1966—68; rsch. asst. prof. U. Munich, 1968—69; from asst. prof. to assoc. prof. pharmacology Boston U. Sch. Medicine, 1969—77, asst. prof. medicine, 1975—2004, prof. pharmacology, 1977—2004, prof. psychiatry, 1985—2004, mem. inst. rev. bd., 1975—78; courtesy prof. Sch. Aging Studies U. South Fla., Tampa, 2004—; external prof., 3d med. faculty Charles U., Prague, Czech Republic, 1995—; adj. prof. Sch. Nursing Midwif U. Westerd Sydney, Australia. Clin. pharmacologist E.N. Rogers Meml. Vets. Hosp., Bedford, Mass., 1980-87, dep. dir. Geriatric Research Edn. Clin. Ctr., 1987-92, clin. dir., 1992-2004; mem. drug formulary com. State Mass., Boston, 1977-83; mem. inst. rev. bd. McLean Hosp., Belmont, Mass., 1980-2000, rsch. psychiatrist, 1997-2004 Editor: Clinical Aspects of Cyclic Nucleotides, 1977, Clinical Management of Alzheimer's Disease, 1988, Hospice Care for Patients with Advanced Progressive Dementia, 1998; Enhancing Quality of Life in Advanced Dementia, 1999, Management of Challenging Behaviors in Dementia, 2000; contbr. papers to profl. publs. Grantee Nat. Inst. Aging, 1986-2004, Nat. Inst. Alcoholism and Alcohol Abuse, 1972-79, Nat. Inst. Drug Abuse, 1973-78, Merck, Sharp & Dohme, 1971; recipient Alcoholism Research award VA, 1979-85. Fellow: Am. Acad. Nursing, Gerontol. Soc. America; mem.: Am. Med. Dirs. Assn. Democrat. Unitarian Universalist. Office: U South Fla Sch Aging Studies 4202 E Fowler Ave MHC 1342 Tampa FL 33620 Home: 2337 Dekan Ln Land O Lakes FL 34639 Office Phone: 813-909-0539. Business E-Mail: lvolicer@cas.usf.edu.

VOLK, WILLIAM R., lawyer; b. Corpus Christi, Tex., Aug. 11, 1950; BA, Vanderbilt U., 1972; JD with honors, U. Tex., 1975. Bar: Tex. 1975. Ptnr., mng. ptnr. Vinson & Elkins LLP, Austin, Tex. Fellow: Texas Bar Found. (life); mem.: ABA, Austin Bar Assn. Office: Vinson & Elkins LLP 2801 Via Fortuna, Ste 100 Austin TX 78746 Business E-Mail: wvolk@velaw.com.

VOLKHARDT, JOHN MALCOLM, retired food products executive; b. Chester, Pa., Apr. 13, 1917; s. George Thomas and Evelyn (Mitchell) V.; m. Linda J. Volkhardt; children: Michael, Jacqueline, Janet, Dana. AB cum laude, Brown U., 1939. Product mgr. Vick Chem. Co., NYC, 1939-48; gen. mgr. Northam Warren Co., Stamford, Conn., 1948-56, Rit div. Best Foods Co., NYC, 1956-58; with Best Foods div. CPC Internat. Inc., Englewood Cliffs, N.J., 1958-78, exec. v.p., 1968-71, pres., 1971-78; pres. North Am. div. CPC Internat. and exec. v.p. CPC Internat., 1978-82, group v.p., 1979; v.p. CPC, 1971-78, dir., 1977-82; pres., chmn. Full Circle Corp., Moss Creek, 1985-91; pres. Water Oak Utility, 1985-91. Dir. Storm Eye Inst., 2002—05. Chmn. bd. Keep Am. Beautiful, Inc., 1979-82, chmn. bd. trustees, 1982. Recipient Herbert Hoover award Nat. Assn. Wholesale Grocers Am.; honoree Nat. Jewish Hosp., 1976. Mem. Phi Beta Kappa.

VOLLER, RANDY, political organization administrator; b. Grand Forks, ND, Jan. 8, 1969; s. Lothar A. and Viktoria Danning Voller; m. Lesley Love Russell Landis, Aug. 1998; 1 child, Lily McCoy (dec.). BA in History, Ind. U., 1991. Mayor Town of Pittsboro, NC, 2005—13; chair NC Dem. Party, Raleigh, 2013—. Mem. Chatham County C. of C. Mem.: Nat. Assn. Realtors. Democrat. Office: NC Democratic Party 220 Hillsborough St Raleigh NC 27603 Office Phone: 919-821-2777. Office Fax: 919-821-4778. E-mail: RandyVoller@ncdp.org.

VOLLKOMMER, MICHAEL T., credit reporting company executive; CFO, v.p. Alumax Inc., Atlanta; corp. v.p., contr. Equifax, Inc., Atlanta. Office: Equifax Inc 1550 Peachtree St NW Atlanta GA 30309

VOLLMER, JOHN E., III, corporate financial executive; BA in Acctg., Mich. State U. Various positions, including sr. v.p., fin., CFO, music divsn. Blockbuster Entertainment, 1992—97; sr. v.p., corp. devel., CFO, treas., sec. Patterson-UTI Energy Inc., 1998—2001; sr. v.p., corp. devel. Patterson-UTI Energy, Inc., 2001—; sec. Patterson-UTI Energy Inc., 2005—07; CFO, treas. Patterson-UTI Energy, Inc., 2005—, sr. v.p., corp. devel., CFO, treas., 2007—. Office: Patterson UTI Energy Inc 450 Gears Rd Ste 500 Houston TX 77067 Office Phone: 281-765-7100. Office Fax: 281-765-7175.

VOLPE, ANGELO ANTHONY, retired academic administrator, chemist, educator; b. Nov. 8, 1938; s. Bernard Charles and Serafina (Martorana) V.; m. Jennette Murray, May 15, 1965. BS, Bklyn. Coll., 1959; MS, U. Md., 1962, PhD, 1966; M in Engring. (hons.), Stevens Inst. Tech., 1975; DSc (hon.), Tusculum Coll., 2008. Rsch. chemist USN Ordnance Lab., Silver Spring, Md., 1961-66; from asst. prof. to prof. chemistry Stevens Inst. Tech., Hoboken, NJ, 1966-77; chmn. dept. chemistry East Carolina U., Greenville, NC, 1977-80, dean Coll. Arts and Scis., 1980-83, vice chancellor for acad. affairs, 1983-87; pres. Tenn. Technol. U., Cookeville, 1987-2000, ret., 2000, pres. emeritus, 2000—; mem. bd. of trustee Tusculum Coll., 2005—, acting pres., 2007. Adj. prof. textile chem. N.C. State U., Raleigh, 1978-82; guest lect. Plastics Inst. Am., Hoboken, 1967-82. Contbr. articles to profl. jours. Recipient Ednl. Svc. award Plastics Inst. Am., 1973; named Freygang Outstanding Tchr., Stevens Inst. Tech., 1975. Mem. Am. Chem. Soc., Tenn. Acad. Scis., Sigma Xi, Phi Kappa Phi. Democrat. Roman Catholic. Avocations: golf, reading. Home: 734 Loweland Rd Cookeville TN 38501-2888 Home Phone: 931-526-9543. Personal E-mail: avolpe@tntech.edu.

VOLPE, VINCENT R., JR., manufacturing executive; BA in German Lit., Lehigh U., BS in Mech. Engring. Joined Dresser-Rand Group, Inc., 1981, various engring., mktg. and ops. positions, v.p., mktg. and engring, Steam & Turbo Products, European ops., v.p., applications engr. Caracas, Venezuela, exec. v.p., European ops. Le Havre, France, 1992—93, v.p., gen. mgr.Turbo Products divsn., European ops., 1993—96, pres., Europe, 1996—97, pres., Turbo Products divsn., 1997—99, COO, 1999—2000, CEO, pres., 2000—. Bd. dirs. FMC Corp., 2007—. Bd. dirs. Archbishop Walsh High Sch., Olean, NY, NY State Bus. Coun.; trustee St. Bonaventure U. Office: Dresser-Rand Group Inc West8 Tower Ste 1000 10205 Westheimer Rd Houston TX 77042 Office Phone: 713-354-6100. Office Fax: 713-354-6110. Business E-Mail: vrvolpe@dresser-rand.com.

VONA, DANIELLE M., marketing executive; b. 1968; m. Jeffrey M. Vona; 3 children. BA, Hofstra U., Hempstead, NY. Group account supr. TracyLocke Advt. Agy., NYC, 1997—99; various positions from dir. juice & juice drinks to v.p. mktg. PepsiCo, Inc., Purchase, NY, 1999—2010; chief mktg. officer Sonic Corp., Oklahoma City, 2010—. Office: Sonic Corp Hdqs 300 Johnny Beach Dr Oklahoma City OK 73104

VON ALLMEN, DANIEL, pediatric surgeon; b. Boston, June 4, 1958; BA, Williams Coll., Mass., 1980; MD, U. Vt. Coll. Medicine, 1986. Diplomate Am. Bd. Surgery, cert. in pediatric surgery. Intern U. Cin., 1986—87, resident, 1987—93; fellow Children's Hosp. Med. Ctr., Cin., 1993—95; asst. prof. surgery & pediat. U. NC Sch. Med., Chapel Hill, 1995—96, assoc. prof. then prof. surgery, divsn. chief pediatric surgery, 2003—; surgeon in chief NC Children's Hosp.; asst. prof. surgery U. Pa. Sch. Med., Phila., 1996—2003. Contbr. articles to profl. jours. Named a Top Doc. for Kids, Phila. Mag., 2001. Office: UNC Dept Surgery Divsn Pediatric Surgery 170 Manning Dr CB 7223 Chapel Hill NC 27599 Office Phone: 919-966-4643. Office Fax: 919-843-2497.

VON ARX, DOLPH WILLIAM, food products executive; b. St. Louis, Aug. 30, 1934; s. Adolph William and Margaret Louise (Linderer) von A.; m. Sharon Joy Landolt, Dec. 21, 1957; children: Vanessa von Arx Gilvarg, Eric S., Valerie L. BSBA, Washington U., St. Louis, 1961; LHD, St. Augustine Coll., 1988. Account exec. Compton Advt., NYC, 1961-64; v.p. mktg. Ralston Purina Co., St. Louis, 1964-69; exec. v.p. mktg. Gillette Personal Care Div., Chgo., 1969-72; exec. v.p. gen. mgmt. group T.J. Lipton Inc., Englewood Cliffs, NJ, 1973-87; pres., chief exec. officer R.J. Reynold Tobacco Co., Winston-Salem, NC, 1987-88; chmn., chief exec. officer Planters LifeSavers Co., Winston-Salem, 1988-91. Bd. dirs. Internat. Multi Food, Mpls., Hosp. Ptnrs. Am., Charlotte, N.C., No. Trust Fla. Corp., Miami, Cree Rsch. Inc., Durham, N.C., Ruby Tuesday Inc., BMC Fund Inc., Hosp. Ptnrs. Am., Charlotte, NC, Aquascent, Inc.; chmn. Morrison's Restaurant Atlanta, 1996-98, Juice Techs., Columbus, Ohio, Sanibel Captiva Trust Co., Fla. Bd. visitors U. NC, 1988-92; chmn. bd. trustees Wake Forest U. Grad. Sch. Mgmt., 1988-96; pres. bd. trustees NC Dance Theater, Winston-Salem, 1989-90; bd. dirs. Forsyth Meml. Hosp., 1988-92, Naples Conservancy, Naples Philharm. Ctr. for Arts, 1994-2009, Fla. Arts Coun., Reynolds Mus. Am. Art, Naples Cmty. Hosp., chmn., 1994-99, Health Care Sys., chmn., 1995-2005; chmn. Regional Bus. Alliance SW Fla., Naples, Fla., 2004—09; bd. mem. Everglades Found., 2011-14; chmn. Conservancy SW Fla.; mem. bd. Fla. Gulf Coast U. Found., Bir Medial Leadership. Mem. Belle Haven Club (Greenwich) (bd. dirs. 1983-87), Naples Yacht Club, Univ. Club (N.Y.C.), Linville Ridge Country Club (Linville, N.C.), Royal Poinciana Club (Naples, Fla.), Port Royal Club (Naples). Avocation: tennis. Home: 3663 Rum Row Naples FL 34102 Personal E-mail: dvonarx@comcast.net.

VON DER MEHDEN, FRED R., political science professor; b. San Francisco, Dec. 1, 1927; s. Fred G. and Margaret (de Valasco) von der M.; m. Audrey Eleanor Whitehead, Dec. 27, 1954; children: Laura Davis, Victoria Margaret Fredrickson. BA, U. of Pacific, 1948; MA, Claremont Grad. Sch., 1950; PhD, U. Calif., Berkeley, 1957. Mem. faculty U. Wis. Madison, 1957-68; chmn. East Asian studies U. Wis.-Madison, 1963-65, 67-68; Albert Thomas prof. polit. sci. Rice U., 1968—2000, dir. Center for Research, 1969-70, chmn. dept., 1975-78, dir. program devel. studies, 1978-83; editor Rice U. Press, 1982-95; Albert Thomas prof. emeritus Rice U., 2000—. Cons. AID, 1967-78 Author: Politics of the Developing Nations, 1964, 2d edit., 1969, Religion and Nationalism in Southeast Asia, 1963, Comparative Political Violence, 1973; co-author: Issues of Political Development, 1967, The Military and Politics of Five Developing Nations, 1970, Southeast Asia 1930-1970, 1974, Religion and Modernization in Southeast Asia, 1986, Two Worlds of Islam, 1993; editor: (with R. Soligo) Issues on Income Distribution, 1975, Ethnic Groups of Houston, 1984, Radical Islam in Southeast Asia, 2006. Mem. Mid-West Conf. Asian Affairs (pres. 1968-69), Assn. Asian Studies, Am. Polit. Sci. Assn., SW Conf. Asian Affairs (pres. 1976-77) Home: 12530 Mossycup Dr Houston TX 77024-4937

VON DREHLE, RAMON ARNOLD, lawyer; b. St. Louis, Mar. 12, 1930; s. Arnold Henry and Sylvia E. (Ahrens) Von D.; m. Gillian Margaret Turner, Sept. 13, 1980; children by previous marriage: Carin L., Lisa A., Courtney A. BS, Washington U., St. Louis, 1952; JD, U. Tex., Austin, 1957; postgrad, Parker Sch. Internat. Law, Columbia U., 1965. Bar: Tex. 1956, Mich. 1957, U.S. Supreme Ct. 1981. Sr. atty. Ford Motor Co., Dearborn, Mich., 1957-67; assoc., asst. gen. counsel Ford of Europe, Inc., Brentwood, Essex, Eng., 1967-75, v.p., gen. counsel, 1975-79; v.p. legal Ford Motor Credit Co., Dearborn, 1979-87; v.p., gen. counsel Am. Road Ins. Co., Dearborn, 1979-87; exec. dir. legal affairs Ford Fin. Services Group, Dearborn, 1987-91; leader in residence Walsh Coll., Mich., 1992. Panelist large complex case program Am. Arbitration Assn., 1993—; advisor to Czech Republic Ministry of Privatization, Prague, 1993-94; leader Russian Def. Conversion Project, 1995-96; lectr. in Ea. Europe, 1995; pres. Focus Internat. LLC, 1995—. Article editor: Tex. Law Rev, 1956-57. Trustee Birmingham Unitarian Ch., 1966-67. Served to 1st lt. AUS, 1952-54, Korea. Mem. ABA, Mich. Bar Assn., Tex. Bar Assn., Internat. Bar Assn., Am. Fin. Svcs. Assn. (chmn. 1990-91, bd. dirs. 1981-91), Fin. Svcs. Coun. (bd. dirs. 1987-91), Washington U. Alumni Club Detroit (past pres.), Order of Coif, Tower Club (Tysons, Va.), Confrérie des Chevaliers du Tastevin (France, Washington), Royal Automobile Club (London), Cosmos Club (Washington). Mem. Christ Ch. Home and Office: 519 Princess St Alexandria VA 22314-2332 E-mail: rvond2@aol.com.

VON HAGGE, ROBERT, design company executive; Pres. von Hagge Design Assocs.; now pres./CEO von Hagge Smelek and Baril. Office: 2906 Cedar Placid Cir Houston TX 77068-1421

VON HOLDEN, MARTIN HARVEY, psychologist; b. Bronx, NY, May 29, 1942; s. Leon and Gertrude (Fishbein) Von H.; m. Virginia T. Brown, Dec. 17, 1971; 1 child, Mark Walter; children by previous marriage: Sandi Gwen Bitton, David Lawrence; 1 stepchild, Theresa Ann Brilli BA, NYU, 1964; MA, U. Toledo, 1965; D Pub. Adminstrn., NYU, 1981. Sr. psychologist N.Y. State Dept. Mental Hygiene, Rockland State Hosp., Orangeberg, 1966-67, team leader, 1970-71, dir. interdisciplinary tng. team, 1971-73; chief of service Metro Unit Harlem Valley Psychiat. Ctr., Wingdale, NY, 1973-74, dep. dir. programs, 1974-75; dep. dir. treatment svcs. Pilgrim Psychiat. Ctr., West Brentwood, NY, 1975-76; dir. Matteawan State Hosp., Beacon, NY, 1977, Ctrl. N.Y. Psychiat. Ctr., Marcy, NY, 1977-82; exec. dir. Rochester (N.Y.) Psychiat. Ctr., 1982-97; privatization project mgr. Fla. Dept. Children & Families, Tallahassee, 1997-98; from svc. team coord. to adminstr. G. Pierce Wood Meml. Hosp., Arcadia, Fla., 1998-2000; adminstr. G. Pierce Wood Meml., Arcadia, Fla., 2000—02; ops. mgmt. cons. mgr. DeSoto Juvenile Correctional Facility, 2002—06; cons. mental health Fla. Dept. Juvenile Justice, 2006—, sr. psychologist, Detention North Region, 2008—10, sr.

behavioral analyst, 2013; dir., Dr. Martin H. Von Holden assoc. cons. Mental Health & Forensic Mental Health. Assoc. dir. Inst. Motivation Rsch., Croton-on-Hudson, N.Y., 1965-73; dir. Martin H. Von Holden Assocs., motivation rsch., Fairlawn, N.J., 1970-74; cons. psychologist, group therapist Green Haven Correctional Facility, Stormville, N.Y., 1970-77; cons. psychologist, group therapist Auburn (N.Y.) Correctional Facility, 1977-94, Butler Correctional Facility, 1994-96, Willard Drug Treatment Ctr., 1997; clin. assoc. prof. dept. psychiatry Sch. Medicine, U. Rochester, 1983-97; cons. in field; spkr. in field. Contbr. articles to profl. jours. Mem. adv. coun. N.Y. State Commn. Quality Care to Mentally Disabled, 1989-97. Capt. MSC US Army, 1967—70. Recipient James Gordon Bennett prize NYU, 1964, Outstanding Achievement award United Way of N.Y. State, 1994. Fellow Am. Assn. Mental Health Adminstrs. (cert. mental health adminstr.); mem. Am. Psychol. Assn., Am. Correctional Assn., Am. Assn. Correctional Psychologists, Assn. Facility Dirs. N.Y. State Office Mental Health (pres. 1984-85), Order of Arrow, Psi Chi, Fla. Suicide Prevention Coun. Jewish. Avocation: bowling. Home: 1250 Peppertree Ln Port Charlotte FL 33952-1357 Personal E-mail: vonholden@comcast.net.

VOORHEES, RICHARD LESLEY, federal judge; b. Syracuse, NY, June 5, 1941; s. Henry Austin and Catherine Adeline (Fait) V.; m. Barbara Holway Humphries, 1968; children: Martha Northrop, Steven Coerte. BA, Davidson Coll., 1963; JD, U. N.C., Chapel Hill, 1968. Bar: N.C. 1968, U.S. Dist. Ct. (we. dist.) N.C. 1969, U.S. Tax Ct. 1969, U.S. Ct. Appeals (4th cir.) 1978, U.S. Dist. Ct. (mid. dist.) N.C. 1981. Mem., ptnr. Garland, Alala, Bradley & Gray, Gastonia, NC, 1968-80; pvt. practice Gastonia, NC, 1980-88; judge US Dist. Ct. (we. dist.) NC, Charlotte, 1988—91, 1998—, chief judge, 1991—98; mem. com. on adminstrn. of magistrate judges sys. U.S. Dist. Ct., Charlotte, 2005—. Mem. N.C. State Rep. Exec. Com., Gaston County Rep. Com., chmn., 1979-83, U.S. Jud. Conf. Com., 1993—, case mgmt. and ct. adminstrn. com., 4th Cir. Ct. Appeals Jud. Coun., 1992-93; chmn. Gaston County Bd. Elections, Gastonia, 1985-86; alt. del. Rep. Nat. Conv., Kansas City, Kans., 1976. 1st lt. U.S. Army, 1963-65, U.S. Army Res., 1963-69. Mem. N.C. Bar Assn., Fed. Judges Assn., Dist. Judges Assn. Avocation: boating. Office: US Dist Ct WDNC 250 Fed Bldg 401 W Trade St Charlotte NC 28202-1619

VOORHEES, STEVEN C., packaging manufacturing executive; BA in Economics & Math., Northwestern U.; MBA, U. Va. Various positions including exec. v.p., mktg. Sonat Inc., 1980—99; mng. ptnr. Kinetic Ptnrs., LLC, Birmingham, Ala., 1999—2000; exec. v.p., CFO Rock-Tenn Co., Norcross, Ga., 2000—, chief adminstrv. officer, 2008—. Office: Rock-Tenn Co 504 Thrasher St Norcross GA 30071 Business E-Mail: svoorhees@rocktenn.com.

VOORHESS, MARY LOUISE, pediatric endocrinologist; b. Livingston Manor, NY, June 2, 1926; d. Harry William and Helen Grace (Schwartz) V. RN, City Hosp. Sch. Nursing, Binghamton, NY, 1946; BA in Zoology, U. Tex., 1952; MD, Baylor Coll., Houston, 1956. Diplomate Am. Bd. Pediatrics and Pediatric Endocrinology. Rotating intern Albany (N.Y.) Med. Ctr., 1956-57, asst. resident pediatrics, 1957-58, chief resident pediatrics, 1958-59; rsch. fellow pediatric endocrinology and genetics SUNY Health Sci. Ctr., Syracuse, 1959-61, asst. prof. pediatrics, 1961-65, assoc. prof. pediatrics, 1965-70, prof. pediatrics, 1970-76, acting chmn. dept. pediat., 1970—72, SUNY Sch. Medicine and Biomed. Scis., Buffalo, prof. pediatrics, 1976-91, prof. pediatrics emeritus, 1991—; co-chief div. endocrinology Children's Hosp. Buffalo, 1976-91; retired, 1997; acting chmn. SUNY Sch. Medicines & Biomed. Scis., Buffalo, 1988—89. Mem. nat. adv. environ. health scis. coun. NIH, 1980-83. Ad hoc reviewer Jour. Pediat., Pediat., Am. Jour. Diseases Children, others, 1960-97; contbr. sci. articles to profl. jours., chpts. to books. Mem. adv. bd. Interim Healthcare inc., 1991-97; mem. devel. coun. Children's Hosp. Buffalo Found., 1991-97; med. dir. Children's Growth Found., Buffalo, 1976-97; cmty. advisor Assn. for Rsch. Childhood Cancer, Buffalo, 1990-97. Recipient rsch. career devel. award Nat. Cancer Inst., 1961-71, Dean's award SUNY Sch. Medicine and Biomed. Scis., 1991. Fellow Am. Acad. Pediatrics, AAAS; mem. Soc. Pediatric Rsch. (emeritus), Am. Pediatric Soc. (emeritus), Endocrine Soc. (emeritus), Pediatric Endocrine Soc. (emeritus), Phi Beta Kappa, Alpha Omega Alpha. Presbyterian. Home: Apt 33 5707 Williamsburg Landing Dr Williamsburg VA 23185-8008 E-mail: mvoorhess@cox.net.

VORHOFF, DAVID C., investment company executive; b. 1955; BA in Interdisciplinary Studies & Polit. Economies phi beta kappa, U. NC, Chapel Hill, 1977, MBA, 1981. Mng. dir., mergers and acquisitions group NationsBank Capital Markets, Charlotte; mng. dir., Health Care Group NationsBanc Montgomery Securities, Banc of America Securities; co-founding ptnr., mng. dir. McColl Partners, LLC, 2001—. Bd. dirs. Star Scientific, 2005—07, Sonic Automotive, Inc., 2007—. Mem. Beta Gamma Sigma Honor Soc. Office: McColl Partners LLC 54th Fl 100 North Tryon St Charlotte NC 28202 Office Phone: 704-333-0525. Office Fax: 704-333-0118. Business E-Mail: dvorhoff@mccollpartners.com.

VORNBERG, JAMES ALVIN, education educator; b. Corpus Christi, Tex., Nov. 23, 1943; s. Hadley F. and Gladys O. (Smith) V.; children: Scott, Mark. BS in Edn., S.E. Mo. State U., 1965; MEd, U. Ariz., 1969, PhD, 1973. Cert. tchr., prin., supt., Mo., Tex., Ariz. Tchr. Pattonville Schs., St. Ann, Mo., 1965-66; asst. to supt. Am. Sch., São Paulo, Brazil, 1971-73; asst. prof. U. Ariz., Tucson, 1973-74; from. asst. prof. to assoc. prof. Tex. A&M U., Commerce, 1974-81, prof., 1981—2011, prof. emeritus, 2011—, head dept., 2001—06, interim dean coll. edn. and human svcs., 2006—07. Co-author: The New School Leader for 21st Century: The Principal, 2002; co-author, editor: Texas Public School Organization and Administration, 13th edit., 2012. Lt. col. USAFR, 1967-94. Office: Tex A&M U-Commerce Edn Leadership Commerce TX 75429 Office Phone: 903-886-5520.

VOSBECK, WILLIAM FREDERICK, JR., architect; b. Mankato, Minn., May 13, 1924; s. William Frederick and Gladys (Anderson) V.; m. Elizabeth Just, Aug. 2, 1947; children: Lee, William Frederick III, Lynn, James Stephen. Student, U. Notre Dame, 1943, Cornell U., 1945; BArch, U. Minn., 1947. Ptnr. Vosbeck & Ward, Alexandria, Va., 1957-62, Vosbeck Vosbeck & Assos. (changed to Vosbeck Vosbeck Kendrick Redinger, Architects, Engrs., Planners), Alexandria, 1962-68; chmn. bd. dirs. VVKR, Inc., merged with Suter & Suter, Basel, Switzerland. Bd. dirs. Dominion Resources Va. Power, Crestar Fin. Corp. Prin. works include Nat. Automobile Dealers Assn. Hdqs., Am. Trucking Assn. Hdqs., Woodrow Wilson Rehab. Bldgs. and campus planning. Mem. Gov.'s Com. Employment Handicapped, 1973; trustee Va. Found. Ind. Colls., Va. Mus. Fine Arts, Va. C. of C.; vis. design critique, U. Va. Architecture; mem. Alexandra Hosp. Bd., pres., 1970, Mt. Vernon Presbyn. Ch. With USMCR, 1943—50. Recipient Wash. Acad. Sci. Nat. Capital award for achievement in arch., Nat. Rehab. Assn. citation tech. svcs., Gargoyle award, T. David Fitz-Gibbon Archt. Firm awrd, numerous honor and merit awards Va. Soc. AIA, Va. Mus. Fine Arts, Outstanding Achievement award Engring. News Record, 1977. Fellow AIA (pres. Va. chpt. 1971), Sigma Alpha Epsilon Found., Belle Haven Country Club, Cosmos Club, Rotary. Home: 7512 Fort Hunt Rd Alexandria VA 22307-1924 Office: Vosbeck Assocs 211 N Union St Alexandria VA 22314-2643 Office Phone: 703-765-5526. Personal E-mail: wfvosbeck@gmail.com.

VOSE, KATHRYN KAHLER, marketing and communications executive; b. Denton, Tex., Aug. 18, 1953; d. James and Martha Kahler; m. William O. Vose, June 1, 1996. BA in Sociology, Sophie Newcomb Coll. Tulane U., 1975; MA in Mass Communications, U. Minn., 1977. Health/scis. reporter The Jour.-News, Nyack, NY, 1977—83; nat. corr. Newhouse Newspapers, Washington, 1983—93; comm. dir. U.S. Dept. Edn., Washington, 1993—96; dir. comm. and mktg. Campaign for Tobacco-Free Kids, Washington, 1996—99, v.p. comm. and mktg., 1999—2000; sr. v.p., worldwide dir. anti-tobacco group Porter Novelli, Washington, 2001—02, exec. v.p., 2002—07, dir. health and social mktg. practice, 2002—07; exec. mng. dir. Yellow Brick Rd., NYC, 2007—; with Healthy Schs. Expert Panel. Panelist Washington Week In Review; vis. fellow Woodrow Wilson Nat. Fellowship Found; adviser World Health Orgn.; bd. mem., chair mktg. com. Nat. Partnership for Women and Families; mem. steering com. for the women, tobacco and cancer initiative Nat. Cancer Inst.; mem. program and comm. coms., chmn. subcom. on comm. 11th World Conf. on Tobacco and Health; contbr. Nat. Acad. Scis. Recipient Crystal Medallion award AMA, Clarion award Assn. Women Comm., Silver Inkwell award Internat. Assn. Bus. Communicators, Mercury Grand award MerComm Internat., Thoth (2) awards Pub. Rels. Soc. Am., Assoc. Press Mng. Editors Pub. Svc. award. Mem. Nat. Press Club (pres. 1991, bd. govs.), Pub. Rels. Soc. Am. Home: 112 The Pt White Stone VA 22578-2911 Home Phone: 804-435-0948. Business E-Mail: kayvose@kayvose.com.

VOSEVICH, KATHI ANN, writer, editor; b. St. Louis, Oct. 12, 1957; d. William and Catherine V. AB with honors, St. Louis U., 1980, MA, 1983; PhD, U. Denver, 1988. Tchg. fellow St. Louis U., 1980-83, acad. advising fellow, 1983-84; tchg. fellow U. Denver, 1985-87; prof. ESL BNM Talensch., Uden, Netherlands, 1988-91; instr. English, mentor U. Ga., Athens, 1992-94; vis. asst. prof. Colo. Coll., Colorado Springs, 1994; sr. tech. writer and editor Titan Client/Server Techs., Colorado Springs, 1994-96, head documentation, libr., 1996-97; documentation mgr. Beechwood, Colorado Springs, 1997-98, tech. mgr., 1998-99; tech. writer Microsoft, Redmond, Wash., 1999-2000; documentation and process mgr. Sprint, Denver, 2000; practice and group mgr. e-bus. Sprint Corp., Denver, 2000—02, svc. launch mgr. Mobile Computing Svcs., 2002—03, strategic market mgr., 2003—05, strategic alliances mgr., 2005, lead bus. strategist, 2005—06, sr. comm. mgr., 2006—07; pres. The Dufallu Group, Summerville, 2007—, CEO, 2007—; asst. prof. & asst. dir. honors program Shorter Coll., 2008—; chair dept. liberal arts Shorter U., 2009—; sponsor Alpha Chi Faculty, 2009—; sr. telecom analyst Faulkner Info., 2008—. Forensic judge USAF Acad., Colo., 1987-88; edn. officer Volkel (The Netherlands) Air Base, 1988-91; instr. English European divsn. U. Md., The Netherlands and Belgium, 1989-91, chair liberal arts Shorter U., 2009- Author: Customer Care User's Guide, 1996, Interview with Joseph Heller, 1999, Conversations with Joseph Heller in Understanding the Literature of World War II, 1999, Office Update, 1999-2000, Tutoring the Tudors, 2000, Sprint Takes Messaging into the Future, 2003; editor: Subscription Services System Documentation, 1996, Titan Process Documentation, 1994-96; copy editor: Language, Ideas, and American Culture; War, Literature and the Arts; contbr. over 100 electronic texts and articles to profl. jours. Colo. scholar U. Denver, 1985-86, grad. dean scholar, 1988; NEH fellow U. Md., 1994 Mem. MLA, Phi Beta Kappa, Alpha Sigma Nu, Alpha Chi, Sigma Tau Delta. Roman Catholic. Avocations: writing, drawing.

VOTH, DOUGLAS W., physician, health facility administrator; MD, U. Kans., 1959. Diplomate Am. Bd. Internal Medicine, 1966. Intern U. Kans. Sch. Medicine, Kansas City, 1959—60, resident in internal medicine, 1960—61, 1964—65, assoc. prof. medicine, 1971—73, prof. medicine, chair dept. and dir. residency program, 1974—84, pres. corp., 1978—84; fellow in infectious diseases Upstate Med. Ctr., Syracuse, NY, 1961—64; mem. sect. infectious diseases Kans. U. Med. Ctr., 1965—73; prof. medicine U. Okla. Sch. Medicine, 1973—74; med. dir., chief med. svc. King Fahad Hosp, Al Baha, Saudi Arabia, 1985—86; overseas advisor Royal Coll. Physicians, England, 1987—; prof. medicine U. Okla. Coll. Medicine, Oklahoma City, 1987—, acting chair dept. neurology, 1990—92, exec. dean, 1992—96; dean Faculty of Medicine and Health Scis., United Arab Emirates, 1996—2000; dir. med. edn. Sheikh Zayed Hosp., Abu Dhabi, 2000—01; dir. alumni and devel. U. Okla. Health Scis. Ctr., 2001—02, 2007—10; dean U. Okla. Coll. Pharmacy, Oklahoma City, 2002—07. Trustee U. Presbyn. Neurol. Inst., Oklahoma City, 1994—96. Recipient Delp award, 2006; named Regents' Prof., 2010. Fellow: ACP, Infectious Diseases Soc. Am. Office: Univ Okla Health Sci Ctr 1000 Stanton L Young Blvd Ste 162 Oklahoma City OK 73190 Home Phone: 405-340-6267; Office Phone: 405-271-2300. Business E-Mail: douglas-voth@ouhsc.edu.

VOUGHT, MICHEAL, insurance company executive; Mng. dir., Markel Excess and Umbrella Markel Corp., 2009—. Office: Markel Corp 4521 Highwoods Pky Glen Allen VA 23060 Office Phone: 804-747-0136. Office Fax: 804-965-1600. Business E-Mail: mvought@markelcorp.com.

VREDENBURGH, JAMES JOSEPH, medical educator; b. Mt. Kisco, NY, Feb. 17, 1957; BA in Psychology, U. Va., Charlottesville, 1979; MD, U. Vt., 1983. Lic. Conn., NH, Vt., NC, cert. Med. Oncology, Hematology. Resident St. Francis Hosp. and Med. Ctr., Hartford, Conn., 1983—86; fellow Dartmouth-Hitchcock Med. Ctr., Hanover, NH, 1986—90; instr., medicine Dartmouth Med. Sch., Hanover, NH, 1986—90, assoc. medicine, 1990; asst. prof. Duke U. Med. Ctr., Durham, NC, 1990—96, assoc. prof. medicine, dept. medicine, dept. surgery, divsn. neurosurgery, 1996—2003, prof. medicine, 2003—, med. dir., adult clin. services. Med. dir. stem cell cryopreservation lab., 1990—2002; med. dir. Hillandale Clin. Lab., 1992—2002; interim dir. bone marrow transplant program, 1995; mem. cancer protocol review com., 1991—2001, 2004—; med. dir., pharmacology lab., 1995—; mem. clin. microbiology users com., 1998—; mem. cancer ctr. users exec. com., 2000—; med. dir. clin. ops., 2005—. Contbr. several articles to profl. jours.; refereed journals. Mem.: Soc. Neuro-Oncology, Internat. Soc. for Hematotherapy and Graft Engring., Am. Soc. Blood & Marrow Transplantation, Am. Soc. Hematology, Am. Soc. Clin. Oncology, Phi Beta Kappa, Sigma Xi, Alpha Omega Alpha. Office: Duke U Med Ctr DUMC Box 3624 Durham NC 27710 Office Phone: 919-668-2993. Office Fax: 919-684-6674. Business E-Mail: vrede001@mc.duke.edu.

VUCINIC, ZORAN A., soft drink manufacturing executive; B, European Bus. Sch., Germany, Middlesex Bus. Sch., London; MBA in Mgmt., MIT, Cambridge, 2002. Pres. Dukat (LURA Group); positions, consumer goods Egon Zehnder Internat.; mktg. & sales idr. Coca-Cola Amatil Europe; cons. Coca-Cola Hellenic, Austria, 2006; mktg. dir. Coca-Cola Co., Warsaw, Va., dep divsn. pres., Southeast West Asia Divsn. Bangkok, region mgr. Malaysia, Singapore, Austria, regiona mgr. Switzerland, mktg. svc. mgr., 1988, pres., Bus. Unit, Belarus, 2008—, pres., Bus. Unit, Russia, 2008—, pres., Bus. Unit, Ukraine, 2008—. Office: The Coca-Cola Co 1 Coca-Cola Plz Atlanta GA 30313 Office Phone: 404-676-2121. Office Fax: 404-676-6792. Business E-Mail: zvucinic@na.ko.com.

VUONO, CARL E., communications systems company executive, retired military officer; b. Monongahela, Pa., Oct. 18, 1934; BS in Engring., US Mil. Acad., West Point, NY, 1957; grad., Field Artillary Sch., USMC Command and Staff Coll., US Army War Coll.; MS in Pub. Adminstrn., Shippensburg State Coll., Pa., 1973; D in Pub. Adminstrn. (hon.), Shippensburg U. Commd. 2nd lt. US Army, 1957, advanced through grades to gen., 1986, dep. chief. of staff Ops. and Plans Washington, chief of staff, 1987-91; with MPRI, Alexandria, Va., 1993, pres., 1999; sr. v.p., pres. L-3 Svcs. Group L-3 Comm. Holdings, Inc. Roman Catholic. Office: L-3 Comm Holdings Inc 1215 S Clark St Ste 1205 Arlington VA 22202

WADDELL, DOUGLAS HOWARD, family physician; b. Bluff City, TN, May 6, 1943; s. Cecil Howard and France Daisy (Boling) W.; m. Luz Isabel Garza, Jan 2, 1971; children: Amy, Christopher, Brandon. BS in Biology, Chemistry, Carson-Newman Coll., Jefferson City, Tenn., 1965; MD, U. Tenn., 1969. Diplomate Am. Bd. Family Practice. Intern Baylor U. Med. Ctr., Dallas, 1970; physician, owner Launey Med. Clinic, Dallas, 1971-82, Beltline North Med. Clinic, Dallas, 1983-85, Atrium Med. Clinic, Dallas, 1985—. Fellow Am. Acad. Family Physicians; mem. Tex. Med. Assn., Dallas County Med. Soc., Tex. Acad. Family Physicians (bd. dirs. state assn., past sec., treas., v.p., pres. Dallas chpt.), Am. Coll. Occupational and Environ. Medicine. Republican. Baptist. Avocations: gardening, cooking. Home: 10473 Epping Ln Dallas TX 75229-6310 Office: 10473 Epping Ln Dallas TX 75229-6310 Home Phone: 214-350-2370; Office Phone: 972-247-6900. Personal E-mail: dhwaddell@yahoo.com.

WADDELL, WAYNE, museum director, former state legislator; m. Susan Simpson. With art gallery, 1970—; moulding supply businessman, 1980—; parish commr., 1992; with plastics industry, 1995—; justice peace, 1996—97; mem. Dist. 5 La. House of Reps., 1998—2010, chair legis. bur., house exec. com., house com. on enrollment, vice chair commerce com., mem. house and govtl. affairs com.; dir. La. State Exhibit Mus., Shreveport, 2010—. Mem.: Rotary, Shreveport Symphony Bd. Republican. Mailing: PO Box 6772 Shreveport LA 71136 Office: Louisiana State Exhibit Museum 3015 Greenwood Rd Shreveport LA 71109 Office Phone: 318-632-2020. Office Fax: 318-632-2056.

WADDELL, WILLIAM JOSEPH, pharmacologist, toxicologist; b. Commerce, Ga., Mar. 16, 1929; s. Daniel and Lillian Marie (Vollrath) Waddell; m. Grace Carolyn Marlowe, Oct. 19, 1974; children: William Joseph, James Glenn, Martin Christie, Amy Allison. AB in Chemistry, U. N.C., 1951, MD, 1955. Postdoctoral rsch. fellow U. N.C. Sch. Medicine, 1955-58, asst. prof. pharmacology, 1958-62, asso. prof., 1962-72, assoc. prof. oral biology Dental Rsch. Ctr., 1967-69, prof., 1969-72, assoc. dir., 1968-72; prof. pharmacology U. Ky. Coll. Medicine, Lexington, 1972-77; prof., chmn. dept. pharmacology and toxicology U. Louisville, 1977-97, emeritus chmn., 1997—, prof. emeritus, 1998—. Centennial Alumni Disting. vis. prof. U. N.C. Sch. Medicine, 1979. Contbr. articles to profl. jours. Fellow: Acad. Toxicological Scis.; mem.: Soc. Toxicology, Soc. Exptl. Biology and Medicine, Internat. Soc. Study Xenobiotics, Am. Teratology Soc., Am. Physiol. Soc., Am. Soc. Pharmacology and Exptl. Therapeutics, Sigma Xi. Home: 14300 Rose Wycombe Rd Prospect KY 40059-9024 Office: U Louisville Dept Pharmacology Louisville KY 40292-0001 Office Phone: 502-228-4220. E-mail: bwaddell36@gmail.com.

WADE, DWYANE (DWYANE TYRONE WADE JR.), professional basketball player; b. Chgo., Jan. 17, 1982; s. Dwyane and Jolinda Wade; m. Siohvaughn Funches, 2002; children: Zaire Blessing, Zion Malachi Airamis. Attended, Marquette U., Milw., 2000—03. Guard Miami Heat, 2003—. Mem. US Men's Sr. Nat. Basketball Team, Athens, Greece, 2004, Beijing, 2008. Author: A Father First: How My Life Became Bigger Than Basketball, 2012. Recipient Bronze medal, men's basketball, Athens Olympic Games, 2004, Gold medal, men's basketball, Beijing Olympic Games, 2008, Best Breakthrough Athlete, ESPY awards, 2005, Best NBA Player, 2006; named Sportsman of Yr., Sports Illus., 2006, NBA Finals MVP, 2006, NBA All-Star Game MVP, 2010; named to NBA All-Rookie 1st Team, 2004, All-NBA 2nd Team, 2005, 2006, Ea. Conf. All-Star Team, NBA, 2005—13, All-NBA 1st Team, 2009, 2010. Achievements include winner of the NBA All-Star Weekend Skills Challenge, 2005, 2006; member of the NBA Championship winning Miami Heat, 2006, 2012, 2013; leading the NBA in: scoring, 2009. Office: c/o Miami Heat American Airlines Arena 601 Biscayne Blvd Miami FL 33132*

WADE, GARY R., state supreme court justice; b. Tenn., May 31, 1948; married; 3 children. BS, U. Tenn., 1970; JD, U Tenn. Coll. Law, 1973. Pvt. practice, 1973—87; judge Tenn. Ct. Criminal Appeals, 1987—2006; assoc. justice Tenn. Supreme Ct., 2006—. Mem. Chancellor's Assocs. U. Tenn., 1988—91, bd. visitors Coll. Arts & Sciences, mem. Coll. Law Dean's Cir., mem. devel. coun.; bd. trustees Walters State Cmty. Coll. Found.; pres. assoc. Pellissippi State Tech. Cmty. Coll.; mem. Tenn. Sentencing Commn., 1990—94. Mayor City of Sevierville, Tenn., 1977—87; pres. Friends of the Great Smoky Mountains Nat. Park; bd. dirs. East Tenn. Found.; hon. chmn. Boys & Girls Club of the Smoky Mountains; bd. dirs. AAA East Tenn., Tenn.'s Resource Valley. Recipient Presdl. award, Am. Heart Assn., 1987, Key to the City of Sevierville, 1987, Sevierville C. of C. award, 1987; named Mover & Shaker of Yr., Mountain Press, 1983—85, 1997. Fellow: Tenn. Bar Found.; mem.: Tenn. Jud. Conf. (exec. com. 1990—97, pres. 1995—96), Am. Inns of Ct., Tenn. Assn. Criminal Def. Lawyers, Tenn. Trial Lawyers Assn., Tenn. Bar Assn., Sevier County Heart Assn., Sevierville Lions, Phi Delta Theta (pres. Eta S. Province 1990—97). Methodist. Office: 505 Main St Ste 200 Knoxville TN 37902 Office Phone: 865-549-6121.*

WADE, J. LANKFORD, healthcare company executive; Attended, Princeton U. Assoc. Morgan Stanley; sr. assoc. Gen. Atlantic Ptnrs.; sr. v.p. corp. devel. HealthSpring, Inc., Franklin, Tenn., sr. v.p. corp. devel., treas., 2009—. Office: HealthSpring Inc Bd Directors 9009 Carothers Pky Ste 501 Franklin TN 37067 Office Phone: 615-291-7000. Office Fax: 615-401-4566.

WADE, JIM L. (JIMMIE L. WADE), automotive executive; m. Ellen E. Wade. B in Acctg., Va. Tech. CPA. V.p. fin. Am. Motor Inns, 1979—87; v.p. fin. and ops. S.H. Heironimus, 1987—93; joined Advance Auto Parts, Inc., Roanoke, Va., 1994, sec., 2000—01, CFO, 2000—03, exec. v.p. bus. devel., 2005—08, exec. v.p. customer devel. officer-commercial, 2008—09, pres., 2009—. Bd. dirs. Advance Auto Parts, Inc., 1999—. Established Jimmie L. Wade Acctg. Fellowship Va. Tech. Office: Advance Auto Parts Inc 5008 Airport Rd Roanoke VA 24012 Office Phone: 877-238-2623.

WADLINGTON, WALTER JAMES, law educator; b. Biloxi, Miss., Jan. 17, 1931; s. Walter and Bernice (Taylor) Wadlington; m. Ruth Miller Hardie, Aug. 20, 1955; children: Claire, Charlotte, Ian(dec.), Susan, Derek Alan. AB, Duke U., 1951; LLB, Tulane U., 1954. Bar: La. 1954, Va. 1965. Pvt. practice, New Orleans, 1954—55, 1958—59;

asst. prof. Tulane U., 1960—62; mem. faculty U. Va., 1962—, prof law, 1964—, James Madison prof., 1970—2002, James Madison prof. emeritus, 2002—, prof. legal medicine Med. Sch., 1979—2002, Harrison Found. rsch. prof., 1990—92. Tutor civil law U. Edinburgh, Scotland, 1959—60; vis. Tazewell Taylor prof. law Coll. William and Mary, 1986; dir. med. malpractice program Robert Wood Johnson, 1985—91, mem. adv. com. clin. scholars program, 1989—97; chmn. nat. adv. bd. Improving Malpractice Prevention and Compensation Sys., 1994—98; disting. health law tchr. Am. Soc. Law, Medicine and Ethics, 1988; trustee-at-large Edn. Commn. Fgn. Med. Grads., 1995—2003. Author (with O. Brien): Cases and Materials on Domestic Relations, 1970, 6th edit., 2007, Family Law in Perspective, 2001; author: 2d edit., 2007; author: (with Waltz and Dworkin) Cases and Materials on Law and Medicine, 1980; editor-in-chief: Tulane U. Law Rev., 1953—54; author (with Davis, Scott, and Whitebread): Children in the Legal System, 3rd edit., 2004; author: 4th edit., 2009. Fulbright scholar, U. Edinburgh, 1959—60. Home: 1620 Keith Valley Rd Charlottesville VA 22901-3018 Office: U Va Sch Law 580 Massie Rd Charlottesville VA 22903-1738 Office Phone: 434-293-5261. Personal E-mail: wjwadlington@gmail.com. Business E-Mail: wjw@virginia.edu.

WADSWORTH, DYER SEYMOUR, minerals executive; b. NYC, June 16, 1936; s. Seymour and Phoebe Armistead (Helmer) Wadsworth; m. Beverley Allen Dunn Barringer, Feb. 2, 1963; children: Sophia, Jennifer. BA, Yale U., 1959; JD, Harvard U., 1962. Bar: N.Y. 1963, Pa. 1979. Assoc. Humes, Andrews & Botzow, NYC, 1962-64; with Inco Ltd. and subs., NYC, 1964-96; asst. gen. counsel Inco Ltd., NYC, 1982-96; pres. Inco US, Inc., NYC, 1993-96; chmn., CEO, treas., dir. Cass County Iron Co., Linden, Tex., 1992—; chmn. Barringer Crater Co., Flagstaff, Ariz., 1996—. Gen. counsel Sailors Snug Harbor, Sea Level, NC, 1987—2000, Baseline Fin. Svcs., Inc., NYC, 1997—2000. Trustee Isaac Tuttle Fund for Aged, NYC, 1968—96; bd. dirs. Frenchman Bay Conservancy, Hancock, Maine, 1997—; bd. trustees Pierre Monteux Mus. Sch., Hancock, Maine, 2009—, sec., 2012—13, treas., 2014—; bd. dirs. Amsterdam Nursing Home Corp., NYC, 1982—2013, chmn. bd. dirs., 1986—2000. Named Trustee of the Yr., N.Y. Assn. Homes and Svcs. for Aging, 1995. Mem.: Meteoritical Soc., Yale Club Suncoast (bd. dirs. 2001—, pres. 2002—04), Union Club (N.Y.C.), Ivy League Club (Sarasota, Fla.) (bd. dirs. 2005—07), Pilgrims Soc. (N.Y.C.). Home: 8466 Lockwood Ridge Rd PMB 304 Sarasota FL 34243-2951

WAGER, MICHAEL, manufacturing executive; Pres. Robert H. Wager Co. Address: Robert H Wager Co 570 Montroyal Rd Rural Hall NC 27045-9550

WAGGONER, J.T. (JABO WAGGONER), state legislator; b. Birmingham, Ala., Jan. 8, 1937; m. Marilyn; children: Mark, Scott (dec.), Lyn Waggoner Kilpatrick, Jay. BA, Birmingham So. Coll.; JD, Birmingham Sch. Law. Rep., Jefferson County & dist. 51 Ala. House of Reps., Montgomery, 1966—83; v.p. Healthsouth Corp.; mem. Dist. 16 Ala. State Senate, Montgomery, 1990—, minority leader; pres. Birmingham Bus. Consultants, LLC. Bd. dris. United Cerebral Palsy, Ala. Sports Hall of Fame, Faulkner U., Gtr. Birmingham Conventionand Visitors Bur. Mem. Vestavia Hills Civitan Club, Birmingham Touchdown Club, Birmingham Tip Off Club, Zamora Shrine. Republican. Mem. Ch. of Christ. Avocations: golf, boating. Office: PO Box 660609 Vestavia Hills AL 35266-0609 also: Ala State Senate Ala State House 11 S Union St Rm 737 Montgomery AL 36130-2103 Office Phone: 334-242-7892, 205-978-7405. Business E-Mail: jabo.waggoner@alsenate.gov.

WAGNER, AUREEN PINTO, psychologist, educator; d. Baptist and Winifred Pinto; m. Scott C. Wagner, June 25, 1994; 2 children. BA, St. Agnes Coll., Mangalore, India, 1981; MA, Mysore U., India, 1983; PhD, U. Iowa, 1989. Lic. psychologist NY. Clin. intern Yale U. Child Study Ctr., New Haven, 1988—89; postdoctoral fellow Brown U., Providence, 1989—91; asst. prof. psychiatry/psychology U. Rochester (NY) Sch. Medicine and Dentistry, 1991—98; founder, dir. Lighthouse Press, Inc., Rochester, 1998—2006; clin. assoc. prof. neurology U. Rochester, Sch. Medicine and Dentistry, NY, 2003—10. Mem. profl. adv. bd. Tourette Syndrome Assn. Rochester, 1997—; dir. The Anxiety Wellness Ctr., Rochester, 2006—10, Cary, NC, 2010—; mem. sci. adv. bd. Obsessive Compulsive Found., Boston, 2005—; internat. spkr. in field. Author: Up and Down the Worry Hill: A Children's Book about Obsessive-Compulsive Disorder and its Treatment, 2000 (Reader's Preference Editors' Choice Award, 2003), What to Do When Your Child Has Obsessive-Compulsive Disorder: Strategies and Solutions, 2002, (manual) Treatment of OCD in Children and Adolescents, 2003, Worried No More: Help and Hope for Anxious Children, 2002, 2d edit., 2005. Grantee J.N. Tata scholar, Tata Found., Bombay, India, 1984—88; Lady Meherbai Tata scholar, Lady Meherbai Tata Edn. Trust, Bombay, India, 1984—88, Robert J. Haggerty Rsch. scholar, U. Rochester Sch. of Medicine, 1995, Nat. Merit scholar, Govt. of the State of Karnataka, India, 1981—83. Mem.: APA, Genesee Valley Psychol. Assn. (chmn. newsletter com. 2005—), Anxiety Disorders Assn. Am., Obsessive Compulsive Found. Roman Catholic. Achievements include development of conceptual framework to explain treatment of OCD to children. Avocations: travel, gardening, choral music, walking. Office: 2000 Regency Pky # 204 Cary NC 27518 Office Phone: 919-371-8230. Office Fax: 919-469-8639. E-mail: awagner@anxietywellness.com.

WAGNER, CHAROLETTE, state legislator; b. Monette, Ark., Aug. 12, 1946; m. Wayne Wagner; children: Tommy, Wes. BSE, Ark. State Univ., 1967; MA, Univ. Ky., 1975. Cert. Ark. Sch. adminstr., Ark. Gifted & Talented Edn. Supt. Etowah Sch. Dist., 1986—87; coord. Fed. programs Manila Pub. Schools, 1987—2001, supt., 2001—04; sales rep. Rigby Steck-Vaughn Book Pub. Co., 2004—08; mem. Dist. 77 Ark. House of Reps., 2007—. Mem. exec. com. Econs. Ark.; mem. Blytheville Gosnell C. of C., Osceola South Mississippi County C. of C., Manila Bus. & Profl. Women, Miss. County Retired Tchrs. Assn.; hon. mem. Ark. Northeastern Coll. Found. Bd. Recipient Outstanding Young Woman America, 1979. Democrat. Methodist. Address: PO Box 909 Manila AR 72442 Office Phone: 870-561-4600. Office Fax: 870-561-4601. Business E-Mail: wagnerc@arkleg.state.ar.us.

WAGNER, DONALD BERT, health facility administrator; b. York, Pa., July 27, 1930; s. Bert Daniel and Mary Elizabeth (Roelke) W.; m. Janet Louise Bankert, July 12, 1952; children: Kimberly, Susan, David, John. Student, Franklin & Marshall, 1948-50; BS in Phys. Therapy, Columbia U., 1952; MHA, Baylor U., 1960. Commd. 2d lt. USAF, 1952, advanced through grades to brig. gen., 1982; physical therapist Randolph AFB, San Antonio, 1952-55; asst. adminstr. USAF/RAF S. Ruislip, London; adminstr. USAF/RAF Bentwaters, Ipswich, England, 1955-58; various adminstrv. roles USAF Hosps. and Commands, Europe and U.S., 1958-73; dep. comdr. USAF Sch. Health Care Sci., Wichita Falls, Tex., 1973-75; adminstr. Wilford Hall Med. Ctr., San Antonio, 1975-79; chief med. svc. corps Office Surgeon Gen. USAF, San Antonio, 1979-82; dep. surgeon gen. USAF Med. Svc. Ctr., San Antonio, 1981-82, ret., 1982; adminstr., assoc. v.p. M. D. Anderson/U. Tex. Cancer Ctr., Houston, 1982-85; chief exec. officer Meml. Southwest Hosp., Houston, 1985-91; v.p. Meml. Hosp. System, Houston, 1985-91, internal cons., interim hosp. CEO, 1991—2005; mem. adv. bd. Grad. Program in Healthcare Adminstrn. Texas Women's U., Houston. Adj. prof. Baylor and Trinity U., San Antonio, 1975-82; assoc. prof. U. Houston, St. Louis U., 1982-88; CEO Woodlands Hosp., Angleton-Danbury Hosp., Prevention and Recovery Ctr., Bellville Hosp., MHHS Long Term Acute Care Hosp., MH S.E. Hosp.; chief operating officer St. Joseph Med. Ctr.; cons., El Salvador, Nicaragua, China, Saudi Arabia, Japan, Korea, 1991-02, mem. gov. bd., St. Lukes Sugar Land Hosp., Tex., 2012-. Bd. dirs. Hospice at the Med. Ctr., 1982-2001, Child Advocates, Houston, 1985-89, Kidney Found., Houston, 1985-88, Westland YMCA, Houston, 1985-88, 90-94, Ft. Bend County YMCA, 1998-03, Greater Houston Hosp. Coun., 1983-87, Sam Houston area Alzheimer's Assn. 1990-94; mem.n. external adv. bd. Sch. Allied Health, U. Tex. Med. Br.; mem. adv. bd. gradrogram healthcare adminstrn. Tex. Women's U., Houston; bd. mem. Vet. Adminstrn. Rsch. & Edn. Found. Named Disting. Alumnus Baylor U. Program in Healthcare Adminstrn., 1993. Fellow Am. Coll. Healthcare Execs. (life fellow, edn. com., ethics com., comm. com.), Royal Soc. Health; mem. Am. Hosp. Assn. (bd. dirs. hosp. rsch. and edn. found. 1990—), Tex. Hosp. Assn., Assn. Mil. Surgeons U.S. (Am. coll. healthcare exec. Ray E. Brown award 1982, Lifetime Achievement award, 2009, Outstanding Sr. Level Healthcare Exec. Regents award 1991, Regents Lifetime Achievement award 2004), Am. Mgmt. Soc. Republican. Methodist. Avocation: music. Home and Office: 1746 Carriage Way Sugar Land TX 77478-4201 Home Phone: 281-980-5613.

WAGNER, ELLYN SANTI, retired mathematics educator; BS, No. Ariz. U., 1971, MA, 1974; postgrad., George Mason U., 1980-82. Cert. tchr., Va. Tchr. math. Flagstaff (Ariz.) Pub. Schs., 1972-76, head math. dept., 1974-76; asst. prof. math. No. Va. C.C., Annandale, Va., 1976—2004. Participant Writing Across the Curriculum Workshops, Annandale, 1992-93. Recipient recognition for outstanding contbns. to edn. No. Va. C.C. Alumni Fedn., 1993. Mem. Am. Math. Assn. Two-Yr. Colls., Va. Math. Assn. Two-Yr. Colls. (regional v.p. 1989-91, coord. spring conf. 1992), Phi Kappa Phi. Avocations: classical piano, ballroom dancing.

WAGNER, FRANK W., state legislator; b. Ruislip, Eng., Dec. 18, 1955; m. Susan O'Rourke; 1 child, Sara; children: Cynthia, Victoria, Tessa. Shipyard owner & engrng. cons.; state del. Dist. 21 Va., 1992—2002; mem. Edn. Com., Gen. Laws Com., Fin. Com., Corp. Com., Ins. & Banking & Militia & Police Com.; state senator Dist. 7 Va., 2003—. Mem.: Am. Coun Young Polit Leaders, Optimist Club, Naval Acad. Alumni Assn. Republican. Methodist. Mailing: PO Box 396 Richmond VA 23218 also: PO Box 68008 Virginia Beach VA 23471 Office Phone: 757-671-2250. E-mail: district07@sov.state.va.us.

WAGNER, FREDERICK WILLIAM (BILL WAGNER), lawyer; b. Daytona Beach, Fla., Apr. 13, 1933; s. Adam A. and Nella (Schroeder) W.; m. Ruth Whetstone; children: Alan Frederick, Darryl William, Thomas Adam. BA, U. Fla., 1955, LLB with honors, 1960. Bar: Fla. 1960, U.S. Supreme Ct. 1967, D.C. 1989; cert. civil trial lawyer, Fla. Bar; cert. aviation lawyer, Fla. Bar. Pvt. practice law, Miami, Fla., 1960-63, Orlando, Fla., 1963-65, Tampa, Fla., 1965—; ptnr. Nichols, Gaither, Beckham, Colson, Spence & Hicks, Tampa, 1965-67; ptnr., shareholder Wagner, Vaughan & McLaughlin, P.A., 1967—. Mem. Gov.'s Jud. Nominations Commn., 1971-72, Constnl. Jud. Nominations Commn., 1972-75; mem. Fla. Bd. Bar Examiners, 1974-77, emeritus mem., 1995—; chmn. Civil Procedure Rules Com. Fla. Bar, 1977-78; bd. govs. Fla. Bar, 1978-83; trustee Roscoe Pound Inst., 1984-92; mem. civil jury instrn. com. Fla. Supreme Ct., 1985-2003. Contbr. articles to profl. jours. 1st lt. USAF, 1955-57. Fellow Am. Bar Found., Am. Coll. Trial Lawyers, Internat. Acad. Trial Lawyers, Am. Bd. Trial Advs.; mem. Am. Assn. for Justice (formerly known as ATLA; bd. govs. 1973-80, 84-89, chmn. pub. affairs dept. 1984-89, treas. 1982-84, v.p. 1986-87, pres.-elect 1987-88, pres. 1988-89), Am. Inns of Ct. Found. (trustee 1996-2000), Fla. Justice Assn. (formerly known as Acad. Fla. Trial Lawyers; bd. dirs. 1965-84, pres. 1972-73), Bay Area Trial Lawyers Assn. (v.p. 1966-68), Am. Law Inst. (coun. 1993—), Lawyer-Pilots Bar Assn., Fla. Bar Found., U. Fla. Alumni Assn., Nat. Bd. Trial Advocacy (cert. civil), Assn. Personal Injury Lawyers, Australian Lawyers Alliance, Pan European Orgn. Personal Injury Lawyers, So. Trial Lawyers Assn., Tampa Bay Trial Lawyers Assn. Democrat. Methodist. Avocations: travel, boating. Home: 901 Mariner Way Tampa FL 33602-5759 Office: Wagner Vaughan & McLaughlin 601 Bayshore Blvd Ste 910 Tampa FL 33606-2786 Office Phone: 813-225-4000. Business E-Mail: billwagner@ragnerlaw.com.

WAGNER, JAMES WARREN, academic administrator, engineering educator; b. Washington, July 12, 1953; s. Robert Earl and Bernice (Bittner) W.; m. Debbie Kelley, July 31, 1976; children: Kimberly Renee, Christine Kelley. BSEE, U. Del., 1975; MS in Clinical Engrng., Johns Hopkins U., 1978, PhD in Materials Sci. & Engrng., 1984. Electronics engr. U.S. FDA, Washington, 1975-84; asst. prof. Johns Hopkins U., Balt., 1984-88, assoc. prof., 1988-93, prof., 1993-97, chmn. dept. materials scis. and engrng., 1993-97; provost Case Western Res. U., Cleve., 2000-01, interim pres., 2001—02, dean, prof. materials sci. & engrng., Case Sch. Engrng., 1998—2000; pres. Emory U., Atlanta, 2003—. Vice chmn. Presdl Commn. for the Study of Bioethical Issues, 2009—. Contbr. articles to profl. jours. Elder Presbyn. Ch. U.S.A.; bd. mem. Carter Ctr., Ga. Rsch. Alliance, SunTrust Banks, Metro Atlanta C. of C. Fellow, AAAS, 2009. Mem. IEEE, Optical Soc. Am., Laser & Electro-Optics Soc. Presbyterian. Achievements include scientific contributions to the field of optical metrology applied to materials characterization, especially advanced holographic and laser-based ultrasonic methods. Office: Emory University Office of President Mail Stop #1000/001/1AP Atlanta GA 30322 Office Phone: 404-727-6013. Office Fax: 404-727-6013. E-mail: wagner@emory.edu.*

WAGNER, PAUL ANTHONY, JR., education educator; b. Pitts., Aug. 28, 1947; s. Paul A. and Mary K. Wagner; m. Jeanene H. Wagner; children: Nicole S., Eric P., Jason G., Emily Ryann. BS, N.E. Mo. State U., 1969; MEd, U. Mo., 1972; MA in Philosophy, 1976, PhD in Philosophy of Edn., 1978. Internal expeditor electromotive div. GM, La Grange, Ill., 1970-71; instr. Moberly Jr. Coll., Mo., 1972-73, U. Mo., Columbia, 1973-78, acting dir. instl. rsch. and planning, 1990-92, dir. univ. self study, 1991-92; instr. Mo. Mil. Acad., 1978-79; prof. edn., philosophy U. Houston-Clear Lake, Atrium Cir. disting. rsch. prof., 1980, dir., Inst. Logical and Cognitive Studies, 1980—, chancellor's disting. svc. prof., 1985, dir., project in profl. ethics, 1989—, chmn., dept. edn. found., 2003—, founding doctoral faculty mem., 2006—; rsch. prof. Pres. U., 2009—10, Pres. Disting., 2009—10; univ. fellow, 2010—; bd. dirs. SOBR DBA Lifeway & Three Oaks Acad. Judge Sears Intercollegiate Ethics Bowl, Dallas, 1998; pres. Wagner & Assoc. Ednl. Consulting, 1988-93; dir. Tex. Ctr. for Study Profl. Ethics in Tchg., 1988-95; rsch. assoc. Ctr. for Moral Devel., Harvard U., 1985-86; vis. scholar Stanford U., Palo Alto, Calif., 1981; cons. total quality mgmt. Golden Gate U., 1992-93, M.D. Anderson Cancer Ctr. and Hosp., 1992-93, U. Houston-Victoria, 1993; cons. strategic planning Houston Chronicle Newspaper, 1997; chair So. Accreditation of Coll. and Sch. steering com. U. Houston, Clear Lake, 1990-93, pres. faculty senate, 1999-2001; chair planning and budgeting com., 1996-98, Univ. Life com., 2003-2007, Houston Tenneco Marathon, 1992-94; dir. U. Gifted Acad.; steering com. Trilateral Conf. and Supershow Greater Human Partnership, 1994-95; cons., ethics trainer Am. Leadership Forum, 1995-98; chair Tchr. Cert. Coun. 2000-; planning com. Tex. Ethics in Govt. Ann. Conf., 1995-98;; adj. prof. ethical theory U. Houston, 2000—; faculty exec. com. U. Houston Sys., 1999-2001, chair univ. life com., 2003—, faculty senate exec. comm., 1999— dept. chair Ednl. Found., 2003—, mem. doctoral faculty, 2005—, chair, doctoral curriculum and develop., 2012-, mem. grad. faculty, 1990—; adj. prof. bus. mgmt. U. Houston, Victoria, chmn. edn. dept., 2003—, chair economics day Fed. Res. Bank, pres. rsch. professor, edtl. bd. mem. Jour. Psych., 2010-; cons. in field Author: (with F. Kierstead) The Ethical Legal and Multicultural Founds. of Teaching, 1992, Understanding Professional Ethics, 1996, Wagner-Disting. Moral Self-Assessment Protocol, 2d edit., 2002. 3rd, 4th, 5th edit., Meml. Self assessment Protocol 6th edit; co-author: Educational Leadership as Moral Architecture, 2009; contbr. articles to profl. jours. on sci. edn., mgmt. theory and philosophy of edn.; mem. editl. bd. Jour. of Thought, 1981-85, Focus on Learning, 1982-85; editl. cons. Instrnl. Scis., 1981-83; editl. assoc. Brain and Behavioral Scis., 1985. Vice-chmn. Human Rights Com., Columbia, Mo., 1978-79; Sunday sch. tchr. Mary Queen Cath. Ch., Friendswood, Tex., 1979-85; founding bd. dir. Bay Area Symphony Soc., 1983-85; capital campaign com. Soc. Prevention Cruelty to Animals, 1989-91; publicity com. Am. Cancer Soc., Houston chpt., 1989-92; cons. in strategic planning M.D. Anderson Cancer Ctr. vol. divsn., 1992-93; steering com. City of Houston Emerging Bus. Conf., 1994-95, Trilateral Conf., Greater Houston Partnership, 1994-95; active Houston Bus. Promise; chair strategic planning com. Leadership Houston, 1996-98; bd. dirs. Houston Vol. Ctr., Leanna Spraianno Dance Co., 1999-2002, Baker Inst., 1998-2001, chair, 1999-2001; bd. dirs. Hope Village Friendswood, Tex.; ann. leadership briefing com. Rice U., 2001-03; mem. Linda Lorelle Scholarship Com., 1995—, Project Grad Coordinating Coun., 1994-96, pres., 1995-96; emcee, expert commentator for pub. TV, Channel 8, Houston, 1989-2002. Sgt. Mo. N.G., 1970-76; mem. choir Queen of Angels Cath. Ch., Dickinson, Tex., 2003—10, with keynote Inst. Profls. Taxation, bd. dirs. John Cates Found., 2011-14, Three Oaks Acad., Sugarland, Tex., bd. dir., Lifeway Internat., 2012-, bd. dirs., Three Oaks Acad. Recipient Cert. of Appreciation, City of Columbia, 1978; K.E. Graessle scholar, 1968, Mo. Peace Studies Inst. grantee, 1971, U. Career Reward, 2009. Mem. AAUP, Assn. Applied and Profl. Ethics, Am. Assn. Pub. Adminstrs. (ethics com.), Am. Philos. Assn., Assn. Philosophers in Edn. (exec. bd., v.p.), Philosophy of Edn. Soc. (exec. sec.-treas., hospitality chair 1995-96), Am. Ednl. Studies Assn., Philosophy Sci. Assn., S.W. Philosophy Edn. Soc., Tex. Network for Tchr. Tng. in Philosophy for Children (bd. dirs. 1983-90), Tex. Ctr. for Ethics in Edn. (bd. dirs. 1990-98), Tex. Ednl. Found. Soc. (pres. 1995-98), Tex. Assn. Coll. Tchrs., So. Assn. Colls. Coord., Houston Bar Assn. (steering com. NAFTA Conf. 1993-94), Informal Logic Assn., Leadership Houston, Friends Hermann Pk., Clearlake Cir. (chair 1979-85), Phi Delta Kappa, Kappa Delta Pi. Roman Catholic. Avocations: running, reading, opera, ballet. Office: U Houston 2700 Bay Area Blvd Rm 338 Houston TX 77058-1002 Home: 19850 Clements Ln Navasota TX 77868-9413 Office Phone: 281-283-3571. Business E-Mail: wagner@cl.uh.edu.

WAGNER, RICHARD E., economist, educator; b. Jamestown, ND, Apr. 28, 1941; s. Herbert and Dorothy Mae King; m. Barbara Helen (Westgate) W., June 9, 1962; children: Stephanie Wagner Tice, Valerie Wagner Smith. AA, Fullerton CC, Calif., 1961; BS, U. So. Calif., 1963; PhD, U. Va., 1966. Asst. prof. econs. U. Calif., Irvine, 1966-68, Tulane U., New Orleans, 1968-73; prof. econs. Va. Poly. Inst. and State U., Blacksburg, 1973-79, Auburn (Ala.) U., 1979-81, Fla. State U., Talahassee, 1981-88; Holbert L. Harris prof. econs. George Mason U., Fairfax, Va., 1988—. Sr. fellow, chmn. acad. adv. bd. Pub. Interest Inst., Mt. Pleasant, Iowa, 1995—. Author: Democracy in Deficit, 1977, To Promote the General Welfare, 1989, The Economics of Smoking, 1991, Trade Protection in the United States, 1995, Fiscal Sociology and the Theory of Public Finance, 2007; editor: Public Choice and Constitutional Economics, 1988, Charging for Government, 1991, Limiting Leviathan, 1999, Federalist Government in Principle and Practice, 2001, Politics, Taxation, and The Rule of Law, 2002, Fiscal Sociology and the Theory of Public Finance, 2007, Mind, Society, and Human Action, 2010. Mem. Am. Econ. Assn., So. Econ. Assn. (exec. com. 1987-88), Pub. Choice Soc. Home: 11845 Clara Way Fairfax Station VA 22039 Office: George Mason U Dept Econs Fairfax VA 22030 Office Phone: 703-993-1132. Business E-Mail: rwagner@gmu.edu.

WAGNER, ROBERT F., consumer products company executive; V.p., info. tech. Tupperware Brands Corp., 2001—02, v.p., chief tech. officer, 2002—. Office: Tupperware Brands Corp 14901 S Orange Blossom Trail Orlando FL 32837 Office Phone: 407-826-5050.

WAGNER, ROY, anthropology educator, researcher; b. Cleve., Oct. 2, 1938; s. Richard Robert and Florence Helen (Mueller) W.; m. Brenda Sue Geilhausen, June 14, 1968 (div. Dec. 1994); children: Erika Susan, Jonathan Richard. AB, Harvard U., 1961; AM, U. Chgo., 1962, PhD, 1966. Asst. prof. anthropology So. Ill. U., Carbondale, 1966-68; assoc. prof. Northwestern U., Evanston, Ill., 1969-74; prof. U. Va., Charlottesville, 1974—, chmn. dept., 1974-79. Mem. cultural anthropology panel NSF, Washington, 1981-82. Author: Habu, 1972, The Invention fo Culture, 1975, Lethal Speech, 1978, Symbols That Stand for Themselves, 1986, An Anthropology of the Subject, 2001. Social Sci. Research Council faculty research grantee, 1968; NSF postdoctoral research grantee, 1979. Fellow Am. Anthropol. Assn. Avocation: flying hot air balloons. Home: 726 Cargil Ln Charlottesville VA 22902-4302

WAGNER, TODD, Internet company executive; Grad., Ind. U., U. Va. CPA Tex. Co-founder, CEO broadcast.com. (now Yahoo! Broadcast), 1995—; co-owner, CEO 2929 Entertainment. Founder Todd Wagner Found., 2000—; founder, co-chmn. Content Partners, LLC; bd. trustees Am. Film Inst., Tribeca Film Inst.; spkr. in field. Guest appearances on CNBC and CNN, featured in Wall Street Journal, Fortune, NY Times, Business Week and Variety, actor, exec. prodr. (films) Akeelah and the Bee, 2006; exec. prodr.: (TV series) Star Search, 1983, The Benefactor, 2004; (films) Searching for Debra Winger, 2002; exec. prodr.: (films) Godsend, 2004; exec. prodr.: (films) Criminal, 2004, Enron: The Smartest Guys in the Room, 2005, The Jacket, 2005, Good Night, and Good Luck, 2005; exec. prodr.: (films) One Last Thing..., 2005; exec. prodr.: (films) The War Within, 2005, Herbie Hancock: Possibilities, 2006, The Architect, 2006, Diggers, 2006; exec. prodr.: (films) Fay Grim, 2006. Bd. dir. After-School All Stars Dallas. Recipient Trailblazer Award, Dallas Film Festival, 2004, Dallas CASA's Champion of Kids, 2005, First Star Visionary award; named Man of Yr., 2000, Social Entrepreneur of Yr., Dallas Ctr. for Nonprofit Mgmt., 2002, Kappa Sigma Man of Yr., 2003; named one of Forbes 400: Richest Americans, 2006—. Office: Yahoo Broadcast 2914 Taylor St Dallas TX 75226-1908 also: Todd Wagner Found 3008 Taylor St Dallas TX 75226 E-mail: twagner@2929entertainment.com.

WAGONER, ANNA MILLS, former prosecutor; b. 1949; BA, Agnes Scott Coll.; JD, Wake Forest U. Assoc. Woodson, Linn, Sayers, Lawther, Short and Wagoner, 1985—87, ptnr., 1987—90; chief dist. ct. judge Dist. 19-C, NC, 1994—2001; US atty. (mid. dist.) NC US Dept. Justice, 2001—10.

WAGONER, GERALDINE VANDER POL, music educator; b. Kankakee, Ill., Sept. 16, 1931; d. Ralph and Josie (Mieras) VanderPol; children: Joel Timothy, Stephanie Anne. BA, Central U. Of Iowa, 1954; MA, Montclair U., 1968; postgrad., Juilliard Sch. Music, 1955-56, 66-67, NYU, Royal Conservatory, Toronto, 1971, Mozarteum, Salzburg, Austria, 1972. Music specialist Bd. Edn., Edison, NJ, 1954—56, Ridgewood, NJ, 1975—95; dir. Musical Spheres Co., 1995—. Mem. Amb. to Amb. program Russian Conservatories, 1998. Trustee, Hudson Symphony Orch., 1965-71; mem. Met. Mus. of Art, Teaching fellow NYU, 1990-91; adj. prof. music William Paterson Coll., Wayne, N.J. Mem. Profl. Music Tchrs. Guild (cert. for highest goals and achievements 1966), Nat. Music Tchrs. Nat. Assn., N.J. Music Tchrs. Assn., Am. Orff Schulwerk Assn., NEA, Music Educators Nat. Conf. (Recognition and Appreciation award 2005), Nat. Guild Piano Tchrs. (judge 2003—), Met. Opera Guild, Netherland-Am. Found., Collegiate Chorale N.Y.C. 1995—, Netherland Club. Office Phone: 201-961-3203. E-mail: grazioso@cox.net.

WAGUESPACK, STEVEN G., endocrinologist, educator; BS in Biology summa cum laude, Loyola U., 1990; MD with honors, U. Tex., 1994. Diplomate Am. Bd. Internal Medicine-endocrinology, diabetes and metabolism, 2002, Am. Bd. Pediatrics-pediatric endocrinology, 2003. Intern and resident internal medicine/pediatrics Ind. Univ. Med. Ctr., Indpls., 1994—98, fellow, adult and pediatric endocrinology, 1998—2002; asst. prof., dept. endocrine neoplasia and hormonal disorders and dept. pediatrics Univ. of Tex. MD Anderson Cancer Ctr., Houston, 2002, assoc. prof., dept. endocrine neoplasia and hormonal disorders, divsn. internal medicine, 2007—, dep. chair, dept. endocrine neoplasia and hormonal disorders, 2010—. Co-author: (publs.) Inhibition of the Ras/Raf/MEK/ERK and RET Kinase Pathways with the Combination of the Multikinase Inhibitor Sorafenib and the Farnesyltransferase Inhibitor Tipifarnib in Medullary and Differentiated Thyroid Malignancies, 2011, Cushing syndrome secondary to ectopic adrenocorticotropic hormone secretion: The University of Texas MD Anderson Cancer Center Experience, 2011, Acute-Onset Ectopic Adrenocorticotropic Hormone Syndrome Secondary to Metastatic Endometrioid Carcinoma of the Ovaries As a Fatal Complication, 2011, and numerous other publs. Recipient The Ruth and Lee Faust award, Loyola Univ., 1990, Walter G. Sterling award, Univ. of Tex.-Houston Med. Sch., 1994, Richard B. Schnute award, Ind. Univ. Sch. of Medicine, 2002, Teacher of the Year, 2005; named one of The Leading Physicians of the World, Internat. Assn. of Healthcare Profls., 2010, America's Top Doctors for Cancer, Castle Connolly, 2010, America's Top Pediatricians, Consumers Rsch. Coun. of America, 2010, Best Doctors in America, Best Doctors, Inc., 2010—12. Fellow: Am. Coll. of Endocrinology, Am. Acad. of Pediatrics; mem.: ThyCa: Thyroid Cancer Survivors' Assn., Inc. (med. adv. coun. 2010—12), The Pituitary Soc., The Lawson Wilkins Pediatric Endocrine Soc. (drug and therapeutics com. 2009—), The Endocrine Soc., Nat. Cancer Comprehensive Network (thyroid carcinoma panel 2007—), Am. Thyroid Assn., Am. Assn. of Clin. Endocrinologists, Alpha Omega Alpha. Office: The University of Texas MD Anderson Cancer Center Unit No 1461 Rm FCT12 5030 1400 Pressler St Houston TX 77030-3722 Office Phone: 713-792-2841. Office Fax: 793-714-4065.*

WAH, ROBERT M., reproductive endocrinologist, obstetrician, gynecologist; b. Oreg., July 10, 1957; m. Debra Ann Wah; 1 child, Renee Megan. BA in Chemistry, U. Oreg.; MD, Oreg. Health Scis. U. Diplomate American Bd. Ob-gyn., cert. in reproductive endocrinology/infertility. Resident ob-gyn. Nat. Navel Med. Ctr., Bethesda, Md.; reproductive endocrinology fellowship Harvard Med. Sch./Brigham & Womens Med. Ctr., Boston; physician, instr. Nat. Naval Med. Ctr. in Md., Bethesda, Walter Reed Army Med. Ctr., Washington; assoc. chief info. officer Military Health Sys., US Dept. Def.; dep. nat. coord. for health info. tech. US Dept. Health & Human Svcs., Washington, 2005—06; v.p. pub. sector, chief med. officer Computer Scis. Corp. (CSC), Falls Church, Va., 2007—. Faculty Uniformed Svcs. U.Health Scis., Harvard Med. Sch., U. Calif., San Diego. Capt, USN Med. Corps. Named one of 50 Most Powerful Physician Execs. in US, Modern Physician/Modern Healthcare mags., 2008, 2009. Mem.: AMA (bd. trustees 2005—, chair bd. trustees 2011—), American Congress Ob-gyn., American Soc. Reproductive Medicine, Assn. Mil. Surgeons US (exec. adv. coun.), Oreg. Med. Assn., Med. Soc. Va. Office: CSC 3170 Fairview Park Dr Falls Church VA 22042

WAHL, FLOYD MICHAEL, geologist; b. Hebron, Ind., July 7, 1931; s. Floyd Milford and Ann Pearl (DeCook) W.; m. Dorothy W. Daniel, July 4, 1953; children: Timothy, David, Jeffrey, Kathryn. AB, DePauw U., 1953; MS, U. Ill., 1957, PhD, 1958. Cert. profl. geologist. Prof. geology U. Fla., Gainesville, 1969-82, assoc. dean Grad. Sch., 1974-80, acting dean, 1980-81; exec. dir. Geol Soc Am., Boulder, Colo., 1982-94; ret., 1994. Contbr. articles to profl. jours. Served to cpl. U.S. Army, 1953-55. Recipient Outstanding Tchr. award U. Ill., 1967 Fellow Geol. Soc. Am. (Outstanding Svc. award 1994); mem. Am. Inst. Profl. Geologists (chpt. pres.), Sigma Xi

WAHL, ROSEMARIE, biologist, educator; d. Arnold Spencer and Rosemary Doyle Wahl; m. Michael Leroy Tumlinson, May 31, 1992; m. Miroslav Synek (div.); children: Mary Rose Synek, Thomas Robert Synek. BS, MIT, 1956; MS, U. Chgo., 1961, PhD, 1967. Instr. U. Ill., Chgo., 1965—66; asst. prof. Tex. Christian U., Ft. Worth, 1967—72; assoc. prof. St. Mary's U., San Antonio, 1976—83, prof., 1983—, chair dept. biol. scis., 1979—2004. Vis. asst. prof. U. Tex., Austin, 1972—75; chief advisor health professions St. Mary's U., 1979—2004, chair premed./predental adv. com., 1979—2004. Mentor, advisor on biotechnology, mayor, city ofcl. City of San Antonio, 1984—95. Recipient Disting. Faculty award, St. Mary's U. Sch. Sci., Engring and Tech., 1986, Alice Wright Franzke Feminist award, Selection Com., St. Mary's U., 2013. Mem.: MIT Class 1956 (v.p. 2001—), Tex. Genetics Soc., Tex. Assn. Advisors for Health Professions (exec. com.), Am. Soc. Microbiology, Sigma Xi. Avocation: travel. Office: St Marys U Dept Biol Scis 1 Camino Santa Maria San Antonio TX 78228 Office Phone: 210-431-8064. Business E-Mail: rwahl@stmarytx.edu.

WAHLQUIST, ANDREW FOLKMAN, government affairs executive; b. Ogden, Utah, Jan. 29, 1940; s. Keith Campbell and Ruth (Folkman) W.; m. Myrna Helen Kasparek, July 13, 1962; children: Kristin Diane, Andrea Katherine. BS in Comm., U. Utah, 1963. Asst. news dir. KCPX-TV & Radio, Salt Lake City, 1959-67; pub. relations asst. U.S. Steel, Pitts., 1967-72; nat. coord., Let's Clean Up Am. Office Sec. Interior, Washington; spl. asst. The White House, Washington, 1973-74; deputy asst. adminstr. Am. Revolution Bicentennial Adminstrn., Washington, 1974—76; pres. Commemorative Mktg., Washington, 1976; chief of staff to Senator John Warner US Congress, Washington, 1979-86; v.p. govt. relations, v.p. corp. relations Greenwich Air Services, Miami; v.p. bus. devel. Kellstrom Industries; ptnr. Alcalde & Fay, Arlington, Va., 2002—; dir. Insolutions, Crofton, Md., Tasm, Fairfax, Va., 2013—; sr. advisor Introlink Capital Strategies, 2013—. Dir. Wolf Trap Assocs., Vienna, Va., 1995; mem., Salt Lake City C. of C.; commr. Va. Port Authority, Norfolk, 1994-97; guest lectr. U. Va., George Mason U., Am. U. Producer, writer (documentary) Utah Hoover Commission, 1970 (Utah Broadcasters award 1970), Scrapbook of a Grand Old Lady, 1968 (1st pl. award Utah Broadcasting 1968). Dir. Claude Moore Colonial Farm, McLean, Va., 1980—; dir. emeritus Fairfax (Va.) Symphony, 1980—; adminstr. Am. Revolution Bicentennial. Recipient George Washington medal Freedoms Found., Valley Forge, Pa., 1972, Man of Yr. award Utah Jaycees, Salt Lake City, 1966. Mem. Pub. Rels. Soc. Am., Soc. Profl. Journalists, Army and Navy Club Washington, Am. League Lobbyists. Republican. Mem. Lds Ch. Office: Alcalde & Fay 2111 Wilson Blvd Ste 850 Arlington VA 22201-3058 Office Phone: 703-841-0626. Office Fax: 703-243-2874. Business E-Mail: wahlquist@alcalde-fay.com.

WAID, THOMAS HENRY, physician, researcher, educator; b. Ashtabula, Ohio, May 21, 1949; s. Carl Thomas and Ruth Agusta Waid; m. Nancee Ann Bartlett; children: Ashley Nicole, Andrew McClellan. BS in Pharm., U. Cin.; MS; MD, U. Ky., Lexington. Cert. internal medicine, nephrology Am. Bd. Internal Medicine, 1985. Med. dir. kidney transplantation U. Ky. Med. Ctr., 1985—; prof. medicine U. Ky., 2000—. Med. dir. heart transplantation U. Ky. Med. Ctr., 1992—, med. dir. lung transplantation, 1992—, med. dir. pancreas transplantation, 1994—, med. dir. dialysis, 1996—2007. Recipient Lifetime Achievement award, Harbor HS, Chief Residents Faculty award, 1991, 1994—95. Mem.: Rho Chi Soc., Lexington Med. Soc. (svc. coun. chair. elect 2005—). Republican. Methodist. Achievements include research in immunosuppression. Avocations: golf, fishing, travel, ballroom dancing, water-skiing, antiques.

WAIDE, BEN, state legislator; b. May 17, 1963; BA in Health Sci., U. Louisville. Ptnr., phys. therapist Liberty Rehab.; mem. Dist. 10 Ky. House of Reps., Frankfort, 2011—. Republican. Office: Liberty Rehab 100 YMCA Dr Ste 5 Madisonville KY 42431 also: Kentucky House of Reps Annex Room 429A 702 Capitol Ave Frankfort KY 40601 Office Phone: 270-824-9227, 502-564-8100 ext. 704.

WAINWRIGHT, DALE V., lawyer, former state supreme court justice; b. Tenn. m. Debbie Wainwright; 3 children. Studied, London Sch. of Economics, 1981; BA, Howard U., 1983; JD, U. Chgo. Law Sch., 1988. With Andrews & Kurth, Houston, Haynes & Boone, Houston; dist. judge. Harris County, 1999—2002; justice Tex. Supreme Ct., Austin, 2002—12; ptnr. Bracewell & Giuliani, Austin, Tex., 2012—. Mem. Am. Law Inst., Tex. Commn. on Jud. Efficiency. Co-founder Aspiring Youth Program; bd. mem. Houston Volunteer Lawyers Program, Texas Young Lawyers Assn.; former pres. Houston Young Lawyers Assn. Recipient Legal Excellence award, NAACP, 2000. Fellow: Houston Bar Found., Tex. Bar Found.; mem.: ABA, Houston Bar Assn., State Bar Tex. Office: Bracewell & Giuliani 111 Congress Ave Ste 2300 Austin TX 78701-4061 Office Phone: 512-494-3610. Office Fax: 800-404-3970. E-mail: dale.wainwright@bgllp.com.

WAKATA, KOICHI, astronaut; b. Saitama, Japan, Aug. 1, 1963; s. Nobutaka and Takayo Wakata; m. Stefanie von Sachsen-Altenburg; 1 child. BS in Aero. Engring., Kyushu U., 1987, MS in Applied Mechanics, 1989, D in Aerospace Engring., 2004. Structural engr. Japan Airlines, Narita, Japan, 1989—91, with engring. dept. airframe group, systems engring. office, 1991—92; astronaut Nat. Space Devel. Agy. Japan, NASA Johnson Space Ctr., Houston, 1992—, payload sci. support staff Astronaut Office Mission Devel. Br., 1993—95, with Space Shuttle flight software verification testing, Shuttle Avionics Integration Lab (SAIL), 1994, with Space Shuttle and Space Sta. Robotics, Astronaut Office Robotics Br. Houston, 1996—2006, with Extravehicular Activities (EVA) develop., Astronaut Office EVA Br., 2001—06, mission specialist STS-72 Endeavor (first Japanese mission specialist) Houston, 1996, asst. payload ops. dir. for manipulator flight demonstration (STS-85 mission), 1997, mem. STS-92 Discovery flight (first Japanese to work on the Internat. Space Station assembly), 2000; NASA robotics instructor astronaut, 2000—; comdr. NASA Extreme Environment Mission Ops. (NEEMO) mission, 2006; crew mem., mission specialist STS-119 and become the first resident station crew mem. from Japanese Aerospace Exploration Agy. (JAXA), 2009; flight engr. to Internat. Space Station Expedition 18, 2007; crew mem. STS-127 Mission (Endeavour), 2009. NASA robotics instr. astronaut, 2000—; flight engring. tng. for Russian Soyuz spacecraft, 2006; flight engr. to Internat. Space Station Expedition 18, 2007. Recipient commendation, Min. of State for Sci. and Tech., 1996, Spl. award, Saitama Prefecture, 1996, Omiya City, 1996, Outstanding Svc. award, Nat. Space Devel. Agy. Japan, 1996, Diplome pilote-cosmonaute, URSS V.M. Komarov, 1997, 2001, Exceptional Svc. medal, NASA, 2001, Fgn. Min.'s Cert. of Commendation, 2004, Japanese Prime Minister's Certificate of Commendation, 2009, Russian Medal of Merit for Space Exploration, 2011. Mem.: AIAA, Japanese Soc. Biol. Scis. in Space (Disting. Svc. award 2001), Robotics Soc. Japan, Japan Soc. Aero. and Space Scis. Avocations: flying, hang-gliding, baseball, tennis, skiing. Office: NASA Johnson Space Ctr Astronaut Office/CB 1601 NASA Pky Houston TX 77058

WAKE, CAMERON (DEREK CAMERON WAKE), professional football player; b. Beltsville, Md., Jan. 30, 1982; B in Sociology, Pa. State U., 2005. Draftee NY Giants, 2005; mortgage broker Castle Point Mortgage, Elkridge, Md., 2006; defensive end BC Lions, Can. Football League, 2007—08; linebacker Miami Dolphins, 2009—. Recipient Jackie Parker trophy, Can. Football League, We. Divsn., 2007, Norm Fieldgate trophy, 2007, 2008; named Most Outstanding Rookie, Can. Football League, 2007, Most Outstanding Defensive Player, 2007, 2008; named to We. Divsn. All-Star Team, 2007, 2008, American Football Conf. Pro Bowl Team, NFL, 2010, 2012. Office: Miami Dolphins 7500 SW 30 St Davie FL 33314

WAKEMAN, GLEN R., bank executive; BS in Economics & Fin., U. Scranton, 1981; MBA, U. Chgo., 1993. CEO, Consumer Fin. L.Am. General Electric Co., 1999—2006; COO Doral Financial Corp., 2006, bd. dirs., pres. and CEO, 2006—; pres., CEO Doral Bank (subs. of Doral Financial Corp.), Puerto Rico, 2008—. Office: Doral Financial Corp 1451 Franklin D Roosevelt Ave San Juan PR 00920-2717 Office Phone: 787-474-6700. Business E-Mail: gwakeman@doralbankny.com.

WAKIMOTO, ROGER MASAO, meteorology educator, researcher, aerospace scientist; b. San Jose, Dec. 11, 1953; s. Tsutomu and Magarita rose (Kurokawa) Wakimoto; m. Jina Choi, Mar. 7, 1981; children: Paul, Sean. BS in Meteorology, San Jose State U., Calif., 1976; PhD in Geophysical Sci., U. Chgo., 1981. Rsch. assoc. dept. geophysical sciences U. Chgo., 1981-83; asst. prof. dept. atmospheric sciences UCLA, 1983-89, assoc. prof. dept. atmospheric sciences, 1989—93, prof. dept. atmospheric sciences, 1993—95, vice chair dept. atmospheric sciences, 1993—96, chair dept. atmospheric sciences, 1996—2000; assoc. dir. Earth Observing Lab. Nat. Ctr. Atmospheric Rsch., 2005—10, dir., 2010—13; asst. dir. Directorate for Geosciences Nat. Sci. Found., 2013—. Contbr. several articles to peer-reviewed publications; assoc. editor Monthly Weather Review, 1999—2004. Recipient Nat. Weather Svc. award, 1984, Scientific and Technological Achievement award, EPA, 1988. Fellow American Meteorol. Soc. (chmn. undergrad. awards com. 1987-88, severe local storms com. 1988-91, councilor, 1997-2000, chair com. on radar meterology, 2001-04, other committeeships, Meisinger award 1992), Univ. Corp. for Atmospheric Rsch. (chmn. univ. rels. com. 1991-92, bd. trustee, 1993-96) Office: National Science Foundation Directorate for Geosciences 4201 Wilson Blvd Rm 705N Arlington VA 22230 Office Phone: 703-292-8500. Office Fax: 703-292-9042. Business E-Mail: rwakimot@nsf.gov.*

WALBESSER, HENRY HERMAN, computer science educator; b. Buffalo, May 9, 1935; s. Henry Herman and Florence (Schoenl) W.; m. Diane L. Walker, Aug. 16, 1958; children: Henry, Kathleen, James. BS, SUNY, Buffalo, 1958; MA, U. Md., 1960, PhD, 1965; DSc, U. of the Republic, Uruguay, 1976. Asst. prof. U. Tex., Austin, 1961-63; assoc. dir. AAAS, Washington, 1963-68; assoc. prof. U. Md., College Park, 1968-76, assoc. dean/assoc. provost, 1971-76, prof., chair Catonsville, 1976-92, prof. emeritus, 1992—; prof. Baylor U., Waco, Tex., 1992—, dean, 1992—96; COO, provost Henry Cogswell Coll., Everett, Wash., 2005—06; dir. Human-Computer Interaction Rsch. Lab., Hewitt, Tex., 2006—. Author: Evaluation Model, 1965, Integrity and Higher Education, 2001, A Brief Primer on Teaching: For New University Personnel, 2002, Imagination, 2003, An Introduction to Data Analysis for Computer Scientists and Engineers, 2003; co-author: Descriptive Data Analysis, 1991, Inferential Data Analysis, 1994; contbr. articles to profl. jours. Active adv. bd. Gov.'s Econ. Devel. Office, Annapolis, Md., 1988-91, Strecker Mus., Waco, 1992-2006, Lyric Opera of Waco, 1997-2006; worker Habitat for Humanity, Waco, 1996—. Fulbright-Hays fellow, 1967, 68, SEAMEO fellow, 1981, 82, OECD fellow, 1988. Fellow: AAAS; mem.: Nat. Hist. Soc. Democrat. Baptist. Avocation: gardening. Office: PO Box 1428 Hewitt TX 76643 Home: 400 Shadow Mt Waco TX 76712 Office Phone: 254-644-0841. Personal E-mail: hhwalbesser@aol.com.

WALCHER, GREG E., small business owner; s. Wendell Barge and Adeline Delilah Walcher; m. Diana Schlauger, July 12, 1992; 1 child, Amber Duncan. BA in Polit. Sci. and History, Mesa State Coll., Grand Junction, Colo., 1979. Senate staff US Senator William Armstrong, Washington, 1979—89; pres., CEO Club 20, Grand Junction, 1989—99; exec. dir. Colo. Dept. Natural Resources, Denver, 1999—2004; owner, CEO Natural Resources Group LLC, Washington, 2005—. Owner Walcher Orchards, Palisade, Colo., 1992—; sr. assoc. Stillwell Group, Washington, 2006—; sr. advisor Dawson and Assocs., Washington, 2006—. Exec. com. mem. Aspinall Meml. Commn., Palisade, 1998—2007; commr. Colo. Wildlife Commn., Denver, 1999—2004; bd. mem. Colo. Water Conservation Bd., Denver, 1999—2004, Gt. Outdoors Colo. Trust Fund, Denver, 1999—2004, Colo. Commn. of Indian Affairs, Denver, 1999—2004; GOP nominee US Congress, Colo., 2004—04; bd. mem. Pinchot Inst. for Conservation, Millford, Pa., 2000—04. Recipient John Vanderhoof award, Club 20, 1999. Mem.: Grand Junction Rotary Club. Conservative. Methodist. Home: PO Box 1393 Palisade CO 81526 Office: Natural Resources Group 9028 Armendown Dr Springfield VA 22152-2140 Personal E-mail: gregwalcher@aol.com.

WALDEN, JAMES WILLIAM, accountant, educator; b. Jellico, Tenn., Mar. 5, 1936; s. William Evert and Bertha L. (Faulkner) Walden; m. Eva June Selvia, Jan. 16, 1957 (dec. Aug. 1988); 1 child, James William; m. Hattie Nan Lamb, Jan. 6, 1990 (div. June 1992); m. Janet Faulkner, Aug. 12, 1993 (div. May 2001); m. Louise Davis, Apr. 28, 2004. BS, Miami U., Oxford, Ohio, 1963; MBA, Xavier U., Cin., 1966. CPA Ohio. Tchr. math. Middletown (Ohio) City Sch. Dist., 1963-67, Fairfield (Ohio) High Sch., 1967-69; instr. accounting Sinclair Community Coll., Dayton, Ohio, 1969-72, asst. prof., 1972-75, assoc. prof., 1975-78, prof., 1978-89, prof. emeritus, 1991—. Cons., public acct.; mem. adj. faculty in acctg. Capital U., 1980—. Group comdr., fin. officer and chief staff Ohio wing CAP; bd. dirs. Frankin Cmty. Svcs.; bd. dir. Franklin Food Pantry. With USAF, 1954—59. Mem.: Campbell County Libr. Bd., Ohio Soc. CPAs, Greater Hamilton Estate Planning Coun., Nat. Soc. Pub. Accts., Pub. Accts. Soc. Ohio (pres. S.W. chpt. 1985—86), Springboro C. of C. (bd. dirs., treas.), Kiwanis (pres. Springboro chpt.), Lions, Rotary, Butler County Torch Club, Am. Legion (life), Beta Alpha Psi. Office: Sinclair CC 251 Siler St Jellico TN 37762 Office Phone: 423-784-1502. Personal E-mail: waldenjames@gmail.com.

WALDMAN, JAMES W., state legislator; b. Washington, Mar. 21, 1958; children: Jacquelyn, Steven. Attended, U. Conn.; BS in Fin., U. Fla., 1980; JD, Nova U. Law Sch., 1985. Bar: US Supreme Ct., Fla., Va. Atty.; commr. City of Coconut Creek, Fla., vice mayor, mayor; gen. counsel Keiser U.; mem. Dist. 95 Fla. House of Reps., Tallahassee, 2006—, Dem. whip, 2006—08, ranking mem. rules and calendar coun., mem. criminal and civil justice policy coun., fin. and tax coun., joint com. on pub. counsel oversight, pub. safety and domestic security policy com. Mem. adv. coun. Aging and Disability Resource Ctr.; bd. dirs. Temple Beth Israel, Endowment Fund. Mem. Wynmoor Dem. Club, Palm-Aire Dem. Club, Margate Dem. Club, Coconut Creek Dem. Club, Jewish Nat. Fund. Democrat. Jewish. Office: 4800 W Copans Rd Coconut Creek FL 33063-3879 also: 313 House Office Bldg 402 S Monroe St Tallahassee FL 32399-1300 Office Phone: 954-956-5600, 850-488-3164.

WALDRON, ROBERT LEROY, II, radiologist, educator; b. Carbondale, Ill., Feb. 6, 1936; s. Robert Leroy and Violet Mae (Thompson) W.; m. Sandra Sellers; children: Richard, Robert Leroy III, Ryan, Burton Johnson. AB, Princeton U., 1958; MD, Harvard U., 1962. Diplomate in radiology and neuroradiology Am. Bd. Radiology. Intern Mass. Gen. Hosp., Boston, 1962-63; resident radiology Columbia-Presbyn. Med. Ctr., NYC, 1965-68; instr. radiology Coll. Physicians and Surgeons Columbia U., NYC, 1968-69, assoc. prof. clin. radiology Coll. Physicians and Surgeons, 1971-73, spl. fellow neuroradiology Neurol. Inst., 1968-69; clin. asst. radiology Harvard Med. Sch., Cambridge, Mass., 1969-71; asst. radiologist Mt. Auburn Hosp., MIT, Cambridge, 1969-71; dir. radiology French Hosp., French Med. Clinic, San Luis Obispo, Calif., 1973-80, v.p., dir., 1976-77; assoc. clin. prof. radiology Loma Linda (Calif.) U. Sch. Medicine, 1977-80; dir. radiology Richland Meml. Hosp., Columbia, SC, 1980-90, trustee, 1990-98; clin. prof. radiology U. SC Sch. Medicine, Columbia, 1985—. Mng. ptnr. Richland Radiol. Assocs., Columbia, 1988-90; founder Chilean N.Am. Hosp. Corp., 1989; pres. MedBill, 1994-95. Contbr. articles to profl. jours. Bd. dirs. Am. Cancer Soc., San Luis Obispo. With USPHS, 1963-65. Recipient grants James Picker Found., Am. Cancer Soc., NRC, NAS, Nat. Cancer Inst. Fellow Am. Coll. Radiology, Soc. Internat. Med. Sci. Cooperation; mem. AMA, Am. Roentgen Ray Soc., Radiol. Soc. N.Am., Am. Soc. Neuroradiology, San Luis Obispo County Med. Soc. (pres. 1979), Columbia Med. Soc., Sierra-Cascade Trauma Soc. (pres. 1983-84), S.C. Radiol. Soc. (pres. 1992-93), Ivy Club of Princeton, Mems. Club Woodcreek & Wildewood, Govs. Club (Kiawah Island). Republican. Methodist. Home: 1420 Adger Rd Columbia SC 29205-1406 Office: Richland Meml Hosp 5 Medical Park Rd Columbia SC 29203-6873

WALEND, TRUDI M., state legislator; b. Atlanta, June 25, 1943; m. Ken Walend. Commr. Transylvania County, 1996—98; state rep. Dist. 68 NC, 1999—2002; state rep. Dist. 113 NC, 2003—08, NC, 2012—; businessperson MacIntosh Computer Services. Recipient Legislature fo Yr., Antism Soc. & Found. NC., 2000, Legislature Baby Bootie award, 2003, March of Dimes Saving Babies Together award, 2003,

Appreciation award, NC. Assoc. of Cmty. Coll. Pres. award, 2004; named Outstanding Legislature, NC. Acad. Trial Lawyer, 2001. Republican. Roman Catholic. Office Phone: 828-883-3790, 919-715-4460. Fax: 919-754-3228. E-mail: Trudi.Walend@ncleg.net.

WALHEIM, REX J., astronaut, military officer; b. Redwood City, Calif., Oct. 10, 1962; s. Lawrence M. Walheim, Jr. and Avis L. Walheim; m. Margie Dotson; 2 children. BS in Mech. Engring., U. Calif., Berkeley, 1984; MS in Indsl. Engring., U. Houston, 1989. Commd. 2nd lt. USAF, 1984, advanced through grades to lt. col.; missile warning ops. crew cmmdr. USAF Cavalier (N.D.) Air Force Sta., 1984—86; mech. systems flight engr., lead ops. engr. for Space Shuttle landing gear, brakes and emergency runway barrier. NASA, Houston, 1986—89; mgr. upgrading missile warning radar USAF Hdqtrs. Air Force Space Command, Colo. Springs, Colo., 1989—91; flight test engr. course USAF Test Pilot Sch., 1991; attended course Edwards AFB, Calif., 1992; project mgr. to comdr. avionics and armament flight F-16 Combined Test Force, Edwards AFB, Calif., 1993—96; astronaut NASA Johnson Space Ctr., Houston, 1996—. Served on EVA (extravehicular activity) crew STS-110 Atlantis Mission, 2002; astronaut office rep. for the Extra Vehicular Mobility Unit (EVA spacesuit) NASA; crew mem. STS-122 Atlantis Mission to deliver the European Space Agency's Columbus Lab. to the Internat. Space Station, 2008; mission specialist STS-135-Atlantis-The Final Space Shuttle Mission, 2011. Named Disting. grad and top flight engr., USAF Test Pilot Sch. 92A. Avocations: football, hiking, skiing, softball. Office: Astronaut Office/CB Johnson Space Ctr Houston TX 77058

WALKER, AL (R.A. WALKER, ROBERT A. WALKER JR.), oil industry executive; b. 1957; m. Stephanie Walker; 2 children. BS, U. Tulsa, 1979, MBA, 1984. Various mcht. banking positions up to sr. mng. dir, co-head Prudential Capital Group, 1987—2000; pres., CEO, CFO 3TEC Energy Corp., 2000—03; mng. dir. Global Energy Group UBS Investment Bank, 2003—05; sr. v.p. finance, CFO Anadarko Petroleum Corp., Houston, 2005—09, COO, 2009—10, pres., COO, 2010—12, pres., CEO, 2012—13, chmn., pres., CEO, 2013—; gen. ptnr., chmn. Western Gas Partners, LP, 2007—09. Bd. dirs. Maxus Energy Corp., 1994—, Western Gas Partners, LP, 2007—, Temple-Inland Inc., 2008—, CenterPoint Energy, Inc., 2010—, Anadarko Petroleum Corp., 2012—. Bd. trustees United Way Greater Houston, Houston Mus. Natural Sci., treas., 2007. Office: Anadarko Petroleum Corp 1201 Lake Robbins Dr The Woodlands TX 77380-1046 Office Phone: 832-636-1000. Office Fax: 832-636-8220. Business E-Mail: rwalker@anadarko.com.*

WALKER, DAVID A., state legislator; b. Charleston, W.Va., Jan. 16, 1952; s. Dorothy Whit Scarbo; m. Darleen Walker; children: Angie, Stephanie, Darlinda, David Jr. Pastor Procious Com. Church; exec. bd. mem. IUOE Local #132; mem. Dist. 33 W.Va. House of Delegates, 2008—, mem. Edn. Com., Energy, Industry and Labor/Econ. Devel. and Small Bus. Com. & Roads and Transp. Com. W.Va. National Guard US Army. Democrat. Christian. Office: State Capitol Complex Rm 230E, Bldg 1 Charleston WV 25305 Mailing: 1056 Elk River Rd Clendenin WV 25045 Home Phone: 304-548-6765; Office Phone: 304-340-3135. E-mail: dwalker@mail.wvnet.edu.

WALKER, DAVID G., telecommunications industry executive; children: Carl Walkey. BS in Engring., Tex. A&M U.; PhD in Elec. Engring., U. Calgary, 1987. With GTE Mobilnet, 1987—95; regional dir. engring. & ops. PrimeCo PCS, v.p. gen. mgr., 1999—2000; regional dir. engring. AT&T Wireless, 2000—05; staff v.p., network ops. MetroPCS Communications, Inc., regional v.p. network ops. DFW, 2005, v.p. network ops., 2007—. Mem. Inst. of Elec. and Electronics Engrs. Office: MetroPCS Communications Inc 2250 Lakeside Blvd Richardson TX 75082 Office Phone: 214-570-5800. Office Fax: 214-570-5859. Business E-Mail: David.Walkerdwalker@ieee.org.

WALKER, DAVID H., medical educator; b. Nashville, May 31, 1943; s. William and Sarah Huddleston Walker; m. Marjorie B. Walker, May 31, 1968. BA, Davidson Coll., 1965; MD, Vanderbilt U. Sch. Medicine, 1969; Docteur Honoris Causae (hon.), U. Mediterranee, Marseille, France, 1999. Asst. surgeon USPHS, 1973—75; rsch. med. officer CDC, Atlanta, 1973—75; clin. asst. prof. Emory U., 1974—75; asst. prof. U. NC, Chapel Hill, 1975—80, assoc. prof., 1980—86, prof., 1986—87; prof., chmn. U. Tex. Med. Br., Galveston, 1987—; com. mem. Def. Health Bd., 2006—11; with, nat. rsch. coun. standing com. US Dept. Def., 2007—10. Com. mem. Nat. Biodefense Network, 2003—; mem. sci. adv. bd. Armed Forces Inst. Pathology, 1996—2004. Editor: (book) Tropical Infectious Diseases: Principles, Pathogens, and Practice, 8 books; contbr. articles to profl. jours., chapters to books. Grantee, NIH, 1980—2011. Mem.: Am. Soc. Rickettsiology, Am. Soc. Tropical Medicine and Hygiene (pres. 2012—13), US-Can. Acad. Pathology. Achievements include patents for ehrlichia Disulfide Bond Formatiopn (DSB) proteins and uses thereof; an immunoreactive ferric binding protein of ehrlichia canis and uses thereof; p153 and p156 antigens for the immunodiagnosis of canine and human ehrlichioses; immunoreactive 38-kda ferric binding protein of ehrlichia canis and uses thereof; Rickettsia felis outer membrane protein; 28-kda immunoreactive protein gene of ehrlichia canis and uses thereof; p43 antigen for the immunodiagnosis of canine ehrlichiosis and uses thereof; ehrlichia canis 120-kda immunodominant antigenic protein and gene; immunodominant 120 kda surface-exposed adhesion protein genes of ehrlichia chaffeensis. Office Phone: 409-772-3989.

WALKER, DIANNE, human resources specialist; V.p., bus. adminstrn., Maintenance & Tech. Support Svcs. divsn. Field Tech. Svcs., Inc.; joined DynCorp Internat. Inc., 1979, various positions, v.p., human resources, Maintenance & Tech. Support Svcs. divsn., v.p., bus. adminstrn., Maintenance & Tech. Support Svcs. divsn.; sr. v.p., human resources DynCorp International, Inc., 2007—. Office: DynCorp International Inc 3190 Fairview Park Dr Ste 700 Falls Church VA 22042 Office Phone: 571-722-0210. Office Fax: 571-722-0252.

WALKER, EDWARD KEITH, JR., retired management consultant, military officer; b. Annapolis, Md., Jan. 23, 1933; s. Edward Keith and Miriam (Whitmore) W.; m. Carol Ann Turner, June 12, 1954 (dec. June 14, 2002); children: Lynn Walker Streett, Wendy Louise. BS, U.S. Naval Acad., Annapolis, Md., 1954; postgrad., Armed Forces Staff Coll., Norfolk, Va., 1966; MBA in Fin. Mgmt., George Washington U., Washington, 1970. Commd. ensign U.S. Navy, 1954, advanced through grades to rear admiral, 1981; force supply officer COMSUBLANT Norfolk, Va., 1975—78; exec. officer SPCC Mechanicsburg, Pa., 1978—80; comdr. Naval Supply Ctr., Puget Sound, Bremerton, Wash., 1980—81; Atlantic Fleet supply officer CINCLANTFLT Norfolk, 1981—83; asst. comptroller Navy Dept., Washington, 1983—84; comdr. Naval Supply Systems Command and 35th Chief Supply Corps Washington, 1984—88; v.p. adminstrn. and corp. strategy Resource Cons. Inc., Vienna, Va., 1989—2000, v.p. emeritus, 2000—. Vice chmn. bd. dirs. Herley Industries, 1997-10; bd. visitors Elon U. Decorated D.S.M., Legion of Merit (3 awards); recipient Def. Superior Service medal, 1983 Mem. Vinson Hall Corp. (bd. dirs., chmn. 2003-11), Naval Acad. Found. (trustee), US Navy Meml. Found. (pres.& CEO, 2009-11, bd. dirs., treas.), Supply Corps Found. (past pres.), Supply Corps Assn. (past pres.), U.S. Naval Inst. (golden life), Naval Submarine League (life), Naval Order U.S. (life), Surface Navy Assn. (life), Navy League U.S. (life), Naval Acad. Alumni Assn. (life), Mil. Officers Assn. (life), N.Y. Yacht Club, Chesapeake Yacht Club. Republican. Episcopalian. Home: 3520 Saylor Pl Alexandria VA 22304-1831

WALKER, GEORGE KONTZ, law educator; b. Tuscaloosa, Ala., July 8, 1938; s. Joseph Henry and Catherine Louise (Indorf) W.; m. Phyllis Ann Sherman, July 30, 1966; children: Charles Edward, Mary Neel. BA, U. Ala., 1959; LLB, Vanderbilt U., 1966; AM, Duke U., 1968; LLM, U. Va., 1972; postgrad. (Sterling fellow), Law Sch. Yale U., 1975-76. Bar: Va. 1967, NC 1976. Law clk. US Dist. Ct., Richmond, Va., 1966—67; assoc. Hunton, Williams, Gay, Powell & Gibson, Richmond, 1967—70; pvt. practice Charlottesville, Va., 1970-71; asst. prof. Law Sch. Wake Forest U., Winston-Salem, NC, 1972-73, assoc. prof. Law Sch., 1974-77, prof. law, 1977—2012, dean's rsch. prof. admiralty & internat. law, 2012—, mem. bd. advisors Divinity Sch., 1991-94; Charles H. Stockton prof. internat. law US Naval War Coll., 1992—93. Vis. prof. Marshall-Wythe Sch. Law, Coll. William and Mary, Williamsburg, Va., 1979-80, U. Ala. Law Sch., 1985; cons. Naval War Coll., 1976—, Nat. Def. Exec. Res., 1991—, Naval War Coll., Internat. Law Dept. Adv. Bd., 1993—. Author: The Tanker War, 1980-88, 2000, Definitions for the Law of the Sea, 2012; contbr. articles to profl. jours. With USN, 1959-62, capt. USNR, ret. Woodrow Wilson fellow, 1962-63; decorated Order of the long Leaf Pine; recipient Joseph Branch Alumni Svc. award, Wake Forest, 1988, Meritorious Unit Commendation, USN, 1992-93; named Hon. Atty. Gen. NC, 1986. Mem.: ABA, Joseph Br. Am. Inns Ct. (master of bench), Internat. Inst. Humanitarian Law, Maritime Law Assn. (proctor), Am. Law Inst., Am. Judicature Soc., Internat. Law Assn. (exec. com. Am. br. 2001—), Am. Soc. Internat. Law (exec. coun. 1988—91), N.C. Bar Assn. (v.p. 1997—98), Va. Bar Assn., Order of Barristers (hon.), Piedmont Club, Phi Delta Phi, Sigma Alpha Epsilon, Phi Beta Kappa, Order of the Coif (hon.). Democrat. Episcopalian. Home: 3321 Pennington Ln Winston Salem NC 27106-5439 Office: Wake Forest U Sch Law PO Box 7206 Winston Salem NC 27109-7206

WALKER, GEORGE W. C., bishop; b. Oct. 11, 1940; m. Geraldine J. Walker; 4 children. AB, Benedict Coll., Columbia, SC, 1970; MDiv., Hood Theol. Sem., 1971. Bishop African Meth. Episcopal Zion Ch., Charlotte, NC, 1988—2004, sr. bishop, 2004—. Mem. Publishing House Bd., Harriet Tubman Found., Restructuring Com., Balm in Gilead. Named one of 100 Most Influential Black Americans, Ebony mag., 2006; named to Power 150, 2008. Office: AME Zion Hdqs 3225 Suqar Creek Rd Charlotte NC 28262

WALKER, GLORIA LEE, training services executive; b. Okla. City, Dec. 31, 1942; d. Russell Holland and Ethel Wanita (Kierig) Walker; m. Thomas William Rupprath, June 3, 1966 (div. Feb. 1995); children: Robert Rupprath, John Rupprath. BA in Sociology, U.S.C., 1965; MS in Elem. Edn., U. Nebr., 1971; EdD in Adminstrn., Fla. Atlantic U., 1986. Ops. rsch. analyst U.S. Bur. Mines, Washington, 1988-90; employment devel. specialist IRS, Dallas, 1991-92; pres. AMERITRAIN, Dallas/Lubbock, Tex., 1992—. Author: Training a Diversified Workforce, 1993, Developing Training Materials, 1995, Instructing Diversified Employee, 1995, Seminars in Training, 1995, The Educated Instructor, 2008. E-mail: walker@omega.net.

WALKER, IAN DAVID, engineering educator; BSc in Math., U. Hull, Eng., 1983; MS in Elec. and Computer Engring., U. Tex., Austin, 1985, PhD in Elec. and Computer Engring., 1989. Asst. prof., elec. and computer engring. Rice U., Houston, 1989-95, assoc. prof. dept. elec. and computer engring., 1995-97, Clemson U., SC, 1997—2001, prof., dept. elec. and computer engring. SC, 2001—. Contbr. articles to profl. jours.; assoc. editor Internat. Jour. Robotics and Automation, Internat. Jour. Environmentally Conscious Design and Mfg.; sr. editor IEEE Trans. on Robotics and Automation; mem. editl. bd. IEEE Transactions on Robotics, the IEEE Transactions on Robotics and Automation, the International Journal of Robotics and Automation, the IEEE Robotics and Automation Magazine, and the International Journal of Environmentally Conscious Design and Manufacturing. Fellow IEEE (program com., v.p. fin. activities Robotics and Automation Soc.), AIAA (chair, tech. com. on space automation and robotics)., Am. Nuclear Soc. Achievements include research in robotics, biologically inspired continuum robots, multifingered robot hands, cooperating manipulators, trunk and tentacle robots, robot reliability and safety. Office: Clemson U 320 Flour Daniel Engring Innovation Bldg Dept Electrical & Computer Engring Clemson SC 29634 Office Fax: 864-656-7220. Business E-Mail: ianw@ces.clemson.edu.

WALKER, JOHN E. (NED WALKER), air transportation executive; married. B in Mass Comm., U. Colo., Boulder. News dir. KLMO Radio, Colo.; various positions including reporter, weekend anchor and asst. news dir. KWGN-TV, Denver; dir. corp. comm. Frontier Horizon Frontier Airlines; with Continental Airlines, Inc., Houston, 1987—, sr. dir. comm. dept., staff v.p. corp. comm., v.p. corp. comm., 1995—2000, sr. v.p. worldwide corp. comm., 2000—. Bd. dirs. Theater Under the Stars, Houston. Named an Employee Comm. All-Star, Inside PR, 1996. Office: Continental Airlines Inc PO Box 4607 Houston TX 77210 Office Phone: 713-324-5000. Office Fax: 713-324-2637. E-mail: ned.walker@coair.com.

WALKER, JOHN W., SR., state legislator; B, U. Ark., Pine Bluff; MEd, NYU, NYC; JD, Yale U., New Haven. Pvt. practice atty.; mem. Dist. 34 Ark. House of Representatives, 2011—. Democrat. Methodist. Office: 1723 Broadway St Little Rock AR 72206 Office Phone: 501-614-9772. Personal E-mail: johnwalkeratty@aol.com.

WALKER, JULIE WHITE, librarian; B in Polit. Sci., U. NC, Chapel Hill, M in Libr. Sci. Mgmt. positions NC Pub. Librs.; assoc. dir. Athens Regional Libr. Sys., Ga., 1990—2003; program dir. Pub. Info. Network Electronic Svcs. (PINES) to asst. state libr. support svcs./strategic initiatives Ga. Pub. Libr. Svc., 2003—08, dep. state libr., 2008—. Cons. PINES, 1998—. Assoc. editor Georgia Library Quarterly. Mem.: Ga. Libr. Assn. (past pres.). Office: Ga Pub Libr Svc 1800 Century Pl Ste 150 Atlanta GA 30345 Office Phone: 404-235-7200.

WALKER, KENNETH LYNN, lawyer; b. New Haven, Nov. 22, 1948; s. John Charles and Virginia Clare (Lovett) Walker; m. Suzanne Kay Thompson, Jan. 27, 1979; children: Katherine Leslie, Caroline Leigh, Christine Lynn. BA, Coe Coll., 1969; MA, New Sch. Social Rsch., 1973; JD, U. Iowa, 1975. Bar: Ohio. Assoc. Baker & Hostetler, Cleve., 1975—79; atty. Cole Nat. Corp., Cleve., 1979—84; sr. group counsel TRW, Inc., Cleve., 1984—91; v.p., gen. coun. sec. Varity Corp., 1991—97; v.p. gen coun. sec. Sealy Corp., 1997—2000, sr. v.p., gen. counsel, sec., 2000—09, v.p. legal, 2009—. Editor Jour. Corp. Law, 1974. Mem.: ABA, Cleve. Bar Assn., Ohio Bar Assn. Office: Sealy One Office Parkway at Sealy Dr Trinity NC 27370 Business E-Mail: kwalker@sealy.com.

WALKER, LEN, minister, former state legislator; m. Marilyn Walker. Assoc. min. Norcross First United Meth. Ch., Ga.; sr. min. Trinity Ch., Loganville, Loganville First United Meth. Ch., Ga., Jasper First United Meth. Ch., Ga.; mem. Dist. 107 Ga. House of Reps., 1995—2011; sr. chaplain Big Canoe Chapel, Ga., 2011—. Republican. Office: Big Canoe Chapel 10455 Big Canoe Jasper GA 30143-5125 Office Phone: 706-268-3203.

WALKER, MARK EATON, federal judge; b. Winter Garden, Fla., 1967; BA, U. Fla., 1989; JD, U. Fla. Fredric G. Levin Coll. Law, 1992. Law clk. to Hon. Emmett Ripley Cox US Ct. Appeals (11th Cir.), 1993—94; law clk. to Justice Stephen H. Grimes Fla. Supreme Ct., 1994—96; pvt. law practice Tallahassee, 1996, 1997, 1999—2008; law clk. to Hon. Robert Lewis Hinkle US Dist. Ct. (northern dist.) Fla., 1996—97, judge, 2012—; asst. public defender Fla. Second Judicial Cir., 1997—99. Office: US District Court 111 North Adams St Tallahassee FL 32301

WALKER, PURCY D., state legislator; b. Chickasha, Okla., Nov. 11, 1951; s. L. Purcy and Carolyn (Smith) Walker; m. Tonya Pinkston; children: Brandon, Crystal, Candace. Grad., Southwestern Okla. State Univ., 1975. Small business owner; county commr. Beckham County, 1991—2000; mem. Dist. 60 Okla. House of Representatives, 2001—. Mem.: Gideons, Elk City C. of C., Syre City C. of C., Erick City C. of C., Kiwanis City C. of C., West Ctrl. Oklahoma Red Cross. Democrat. Office: 2300 N Lincoln Blvd Rm 541 Oklahoma City OK 73105 Mailing: PO Box 461 Elk City OK 73648 Office Phone: 405-557-7311, 580-225-5207. Business E-Mail: purcywalker@okhouse.gov.

WALKER, RICHARD HAROLD, pathologist, educator; b. Cleve., Dec. 2, 1928; s. Harold Deford and Bernice Margaret (Wright) W.; m. Carolyn Franklin, Sept. 28, 1954; children: Bruce, Lynn, Cara, Leah. BS, Emory U., 1950, MD, 1953. Intern City of Memphis Hosps., 1953-54; resident in pathology Coll. Medicine U. Tenn., Memphis, 1954-55, 57-59, prof. pathology, 1966-70; Am. Cancer Soc. clin. fellow U. Tenn. Coll. Medicine, 1957-59; med. dir. blood bank and transfusion svc. City of Memphis Hosps., Memphis, 1961-70; chief of blood bank and transfusion service William Beaumont Hosp., Royal Oak, Mich., 1970-95, med. dir. Sch. Med. Tech., 1970-91. Clin. prof. pathology Sch. Medicine Wayne State U., Detroit, 1982-95. Contbr. articles on blood transfusion, blood group genetics and transfusion medicine to med. jours. Capt. USNR ret. Recipient Murray Thelin Humanitarian award Memphis chpt. Nat. Hemophilia Found., 1968. Mem. AMA, Coll. Am. Pathologists, Am. Soc. Clin. Pathologists (Disting. Svc. award 1977, Ward Burdick award 1992), Am. Assn. Blood Banks (pres. 1976-77, John Elliott Meml. award 1986), Tenn. Assn. Blood Banks (L.W. Diggs award 1986), Internat. Soc. Blood Transfusion, Am. Soc. for Histocompatibility and Immunogenetics. Republican. Presbyterian. Home: 4204 Fleet Landing Blvd Atlantic Beach FL 32233-4590

WALKER, RONALD TRACY, retired personnel director; b. North Wilkesboro, NC, July 27, 1937; m. Nena Watkins; 2 children. Student, Wilkes C.C., Wake Forest U. Ret.; with CMI Industries Inc., Elkin, NC, 1967-99, plant human resource mgr.; former mem. NC House of Reps., 1999—2008. Commr. Wilkes County, 1978-96, past mem. region "D" coun. govts., regional econ. devel. coun., indsl. park com., chmn. regional transp. com., mem. regional adv. com. to WNCREDC, liaison Advantage West and region "D" coun. govts.; past chmn. region"D" coun. govts. Wilkes County, northwestern housing authority, past mem. bd. edn., 1972-76, airport authority; past vice-chmn., chmn. Wilkes County Commrs.; past bd. dirs. Blue Ridge Water Assn.; pres. Northwestern Devel. Assn.; trustee Health Ins. N.C. Assn. County Commrs.; mem. N.C. Regional Econ. Devel. Commn.; apptd. mem. N.C. Adv. Coun. Vocat. and Technical Edn., 1972-76, N.C. Dept. Correction, 1984-92; Rep. candidate for N.C. Commr. of Labor, 1996; candidate N.C. House, 1998, 2000, N.C. House of Rep., 2001-, With USAF, 1955-59. Recipient Leadership award Western N.C., 1996. Office Phone: 919-733-5935. Personal E-mail: tracyw@ncleg.net.

WALKER, THOMAS GRAY, federal prosecutor; b. Atlanta, 1964; BA, Baylor U., Waco, Tex., 1986; JD, Campbell U. Sch. Law, Buies Creek, NC, 1990. Office asst. Tracy, Crumley & Holland, Ft. Worth, 1986—87; clk. Law Office Mr Whitney E. Fanning, Waco, 1988, Van Winkle, Buck, Wall, Starnes & Davis, P.A., Asheville, NC, 1989; asst. dist. atty. Mecklenburg County Dist. Atty.'s Office, Charlotte, NC, 1990—94; asst. US atty. (western dist.) NC US Dept. Justice, Charlotte, 1994—2001, US atty. (eastern dist.) NC Raleigh, 2011—; spl. counsel to atty. gen. State of NC, Raleigh, 2001—03; ptnr. litig. & trial practice group Alston & Bird, LLP, Charlotte, 2003—11. Instr. American Inst. Paralegal Studies, 1992—93. Office: US Attorney's Office Fed Bldg Ste 800 310 New Bern Ave Raleigh NC 27601 Office Phone: 919-856-4530. Office Fax: 919-856-4487.*

WALKER, WILLIAM EASTON, surgeon, educator, lawyer; b. Glasgow, Scotland, Aug. 7, 1945; came to U.S., 1969; s. William Telfer and Josephine Blair (Easton) W.; m. Mary Fraley Cooley, June 23, 1973; children— Sarah Cooley, Blair Easton, Denton Arthur Cooley, William Easton, II MD, Glasgow U., Scotland, 1968; PhD, Johns Hopkins U., 1975; JD, South Tex. Coll Law, 1993. Diplomate Am. Bd. Surgery, Am. Bd. Thoracic Surgery, Am. Bd. Vascular Surgery. Intern, resident Johns Hopkins U., Balt., 1969-75; resident Vanderbilt U., Nashville, 1975-79; assoc. prof., dir. div. thoracic and cardiovascular surgery U. Tex. Med. Sch., Houston, 1979-94. Cons. M.D. Anderson Hosp., Houston, 1979—. Recipient Harwell Wilson award Vanderbilt U., Nashville, 1979 Fellow ACS, So. Surg. Assn., Royal Coll. Surgeons, Am. Coll. Cardiology; mem. Am. Assn. Thoracic Surgery, Coun. Fgn. Rels., Houston Country Club, Belle Meade Country Club, Cosmos Club (Washington), Krewe of Endymion (New Orleans), Phi Beta Kappa, Sigma Xi. Republican. Presbyterian. Avocations: law, bridge, Wagner, World War I history, cooking. Home and Office: 2831 Sackett St Houston TX 77098-1125 Home Phone: 713-204-4267; Office Phone: 713-520-0021. E-mail: ww19@comcast.net.

WALKER, WILLIAM OLIVER, JR., retired humanities educator, dean; b. Sweetwater, Tex., Dec. 6, 1930; s. William Oliver and Frances Baker (White) W.; m. Mary Scott Daugherty, Dec. 22, 1955 (div. Dec. 29, 1978); children: William Scott, Mary Evan, Michael Neal. BA, Austin Coll., 1953; MDiv, Austin Presbyn. Sem., 1957; MA, U. Tex., 1958; PhD, Duke U., 1962. Instr. greek religion Austin Coll., Sherman, Tex., 1954—55, Duke U., 1960—62; from asst. to prof. religion Trinity U., San Antonio, 1962—2000, Jennie Farris Railey King prof. religion, 2000—02; ret., 2002. Chair dept., 1980-88, acting dean divsn. Humanities and Arts, 1988-89, dean, 1989-1999. Author: Interpolations in the Pauline Letters, 2001; editor: The Relationships, 1978, The HarperCollins Bible Pronunciation Guide, 1994; assoc. editor HarperCollins Bible Dictionary, 1996. Mem. Studiorum Novi Testamenti Soc., Soc. Bibl. Lit. (regional sec.-treas. 1980-86, pres. 1999-2000), Cath. Bibl. Assn. Am. Democrat. Presbyterian. Avocations: tennis, travel, photography. Home: 315 Cloverleaf Ave San Antonio TX 78209-3822 Office Phone: 210-999-8325.

WALKOWIAK, VINCENT STEVEN, lawyer; b. Apr. 22, 1946; s. Vincent Albert and Elizabeth (Modla) W.; m. Linda Kae Schweigert, Aug., 1968; children: Jenifer, Steven. BA, U. Ill., 1968, JD, 1971. Bar: Ill. 1971, Minn. 1971, Tex. 1981, U.S. Ct. Appeals (8th cir.) 1971, (5th cir.) 1982, U.S. Dist. Ct. (ea., we., so., and no. dists.) Tex. 1982. Assoc. Dorsey, Marquart, Windhorst, West & Halladay, Mpls., 1971-74; ptnr. Fulbright & Jaworski LLP, Dallas, 1982—2010, ret. Prof. Fla. State U., Tallahassee, 1974-76, So. Meth. U., Dallas, 1976-84. Editor: Uniform Product Liability Act, 1980, Trial of a Product Liability Case, vol. 1, 1981, vol. 2, 1982, Preparation and Presentation of Product Liability, 1983, Attorney Client Privilege in Civil Litigation, 5th edit., 2012. Office: Fulbright & Jaworski LLP 2200 Ross Ave Ste 2800 Dallas TX 75201-2784 Home Phone: 214-692-6046; Office Phone: 214-855-8037. Business E-Mail: vincent.walkowiak@nortonrosefulbright.com.

WALL, JERRY LEON, retired management educator, university administrator, dean; s. Claude Leon and Beulah Dollie (Widney) W.; m. Katharine Hoffmann, Sept. 4, 1965; children: Christopher, Stephan, Alison. BA, Okla. State U., 1964; MBA, East Carolina U., 1968; PhD, U. Mo., 1974. Cert. sr. profl. human resources; accredited pers. diplomate. From asst. to full prof. mgmt. Western Ill. U., Macomb, 1972-81, prof. mgmt., 1982; prof. mgmt. scis. U. Iowa, Iowa City, 1981-82; dir. Ctr. Bus. and Econ. Rsch. N.E. La. U., Monroe, 1983—2005; dean Coll. Bus. Northwestern State U., Natchitoches, La., 2007—11. Pres., prin. JKW Assocs., West Monroe, 1972—; adj. prof. law enforcement Western Ill. U., Macomb, 1979-81; owner/mgr. Wall-Baird Family Farms. Editor Jour. of Behavioral Economics, 1975-81, Northeast La. Bus. Rev., 1983-89, Delta Bus. Rev., 1989-91; contbr. over 200 articles to profl. jours., papers and books. Mem. joint legis. com. on alt. econ. strategy La., Baton Rouge, 1986-87; grad. Leadership La.; mem. La. Data Base Commn., 1996-04, La. Tax Commn., 1995-03., lt. col. civil air patrol Ret. col. US Army. Mem. Rotary Internat. (dist. gov. elect.), Mil. Officers Assn. America (nat. bd. dirs. 1999-2004), Beta Gamma Sigma, Phi Kappa Phi. Avocations: scuba diving, magic.

WALL, PHIL, information technology executive; B in mech. engring., Imperial Coll., London Univ.; MBA, Brookes Univ., Oxford. Chartered Acct. Fin. mgmt. positions Schlumberger Inc., Equifax Inc.; v.p. fin. internat. fin. ops. First Data Corp.; exec. v.p., CFO Bank of America, Merchanton Svcs., 2008—. Office: 5565 Glenridge Connector NE Atlanta GA 30342

WALL, TARA J., healthcare company executive; Attended, Fla. A&M U., 1988; BS in Comm., Law & Govt., Eastern Mich. U., 1989. Edn. reporter WOOD-TV, 1996—99; assoc. dir., governor's office State of Mich., 1999—2000; reporter KDNL-TV, St. Louis, 2000—01; dir., pub. affairs, host producer, reporter WWJ-TV & WKBD-TV, 2001—04; polit. contbr. CNN, 2008; dep. editl. page editor columnist, news anchor, analyst The Wash. Times, 2008—09; sr. v.p., corp. comm. Amerigroup Corp., 2009—. Sr. adviser outreach comm. Rep. Nat. Com., 2004-07; dir., comm. US Dpt. of Homeland Security, 2007-08; dir., pub. affairs Adminstrn. for Children and Families, 2007, US Dpt. of Health and Human Svcs., 2007. Office: Amerigroup Corp 4425 Corporation Lane Virginia Beach VA 23462 Office Phone: 757-490-6900. Office Fax: 757-518-3600. Business E-Mail: twall01@amerigroupcorp.com.

WALLACE, BARBARA BROOKS, writer; b. Soochow, China, Dec. 3, 1922; arrived in U.S., 1938; d. Otis Frank and Nicia Brooks; m. James Wallace, Jr., Feb. 27, 1954; 1 child, James V. BA, UCLA, 1945. Script sec. Foote, Cone & Belding, Hollywood, Calif., 1946-49; tchr. Wright MacMahon Secretarial Sch., Beverly Hills, Calif., 1949-50; head fund drive Commerce and Industry Divsn. ARC, San Francisco, 1950-52. Author: Claudia, 1969 (Nat. League Am. Pen Women Juvenile Book award, 1970), Andrew the Big Deal, 1970, The Trouble with Miss Switch, 1971, Victoria, 1973, Can Do, Missy Charlie, 1974, The Secret Summer of L.E.B. (Nat. League Am. Pen Women Juvenile Book award, 1974), Julia and the Third Bad Thing, 1975, Palmer Patch, 1976, Hawkins, 1977, Peppermints in the Parlor, 1980 (William Allen White award, 1983), The Contest Kid Strikes Again, 1980, Hawkins and the Soccer Solution, 1981, Miss Switch to the Rescue, 1981, Hello, Claudia, 1982, Claudia and Duffy, 1982, The Barrel in the Basement, 1985, Argyle, 1987, 1992, Perfect Acres, Inc., 1988, The Twin in the Tavern, 1993 (Edgar award Mystery Writers Am., 1994), Cousins in the Castle, 1996, Sparrows in the Scullery, 1997 (Edgar award, 1998), Ghosts in the Gallery, 2000, Secret in St. Something, 2001, Miss Switch Online, 2002, The Perils of Peppermints, 2003, Have Dragon, Will Travel, 2009, Anastasia Florence Nightingale and I, A Nurse's Story, 2009, Small Footsteps: In the Land of The Dragon, Growing up in China, 2009, Diary of A Little Devil, 2012, Miss Switch and the Vile Villains, 2012, Miss Switch's Bathsheba & The Cat Caper. Mem.: Authors Guild, Children's Book Guild of Washington, Alpha Phi. Episcopalian. Home: 5000 Fairbanks Ave Apt 221 Alexandria VA 22311-1231 Office Phone: 703-797-3870. Personal E-mail: bubb16.wallace@gmail.com. E-mail: bbwallace@cox.net.

WALLACE, BARRON F., lawyer; b. Beaumont, Tex., 1964; BA in History, U. Tex., Austin, 1986; JD, U. Mich., 1989. Bar: Tex. 1990. Ptnr., co-head, pub. fin. sect. Vinson & Elkins LLP, Houston. Bd. dirs. Tex. Lyceum Assn., Fourth Ward Redevelopment Authority; mem. Tex. C-Bar Adv. Bd. Mem. Ctr. for Houston's Future, 2004 Edn. Policy Com. Greater Houston Partnership, Tex. Rising Stars 2004; bd. dirs. Park People. Recipient Tex. Rising Star, Tex. Super Lawyers Rising Stars Edn. mag., 2004, Outstanding Texan award, Black Leg. Caucus, 1999, 2001; named one of Am. Top Black Lawyers, Black Enterprise mag., 2003. Mem.: Tex. Bar Found., Nat. Assn. Bond Lawyers (vice chair gen. law com.), State Bar Tex. (mem. adminstrv. and pub. law section). Office: Vinson & Elkins LLP Ste 2300 First City Tower 1001 Fannin St Houston TX 77002-6760 Office Phone: 713-758-4810. Office Fax: 713-615-5076. Business E-Mail: bwallace@velaw.com.

WALLACE, BETTY JEAN, retired elementary school educator, lay minister; b. Denison, Tex., Dec. 5, 1927; d. Claude Herman and Pearl Victoria (Freels) Moore; m. Billy Dean McKneely, Sept. 2, 1950 (div. Nov. 1964); children: Rebecca Lynn, Paul King, David Freels, John Walker, Philip Andrew McKneely. Student, Tulane U., New Orleans, 1947; BA, Baylor U., Waco, Tex., 1949; postgrad., U. Houston, Tex., 1949-50, 74, 81, Rocky Mountain Bible Inst., 1959, U. Colo., 1969-70, U. No. Colo., Greeley, 1965, 68, 72, U. St. Thomas, 1992, Autonomous U. Guadalajara, summer 1993; MEd, Houston Bapt. U., Tex., 1985. Cert. life profl. elem., high sch., life profl. reading specialist, secondary field ESL tchr., Tex. Tchr. Galena Park Ind. Sch. Dist., Tex., 1949-50, 52-53, 72-98, Corpus Christi Ind. Sch. Dist., Tex., 1950-51, Denver Pub. Schs., 1953-54, 63-72, Wackenhut Cleveland Correctional Ctr., Tex., 1999—2003; ret. Author: The Holy Spirit Today, 1989, Our God of Infinite Variety, 1991, God Speaks in a Variety of Ways, 1991, Messages from the Lord Given in Dreams, 2010, (stories) Meeting Walt Disney, Two Clouds That Followed Above Me. Sunday sch. tchr. So. Bapt. Conv. chs., Tex., 1946-50, Denver, 1952-56; tchr. kindergarten Emmanuel Bapt. Ch., Denver, 1956-63; missionary, Queretaro, Mex., 1977-78; active Rep. Senatorial Inner Circle, Washington, 1989-91, 2002, Round Table for Ronald Reagan, Washington, 1989-90, Round Table for Pres. Bush, 2004; founding mem. RNC Presdl. Trust; helper Feed the Poor, Houston, 1983-85; active Suicide Prevention, Houston, 1973-76, Literacy, Houston, 1978-81; rep. NEA, Denver, 1966-72; mem. Retirement Com., Denver, 1970-72; bd. adv. Oliver North, 1994; mem. Rep. Presdl. Task Force, 2006. Recipient Rep. Senatorial medal of freedom, 1994, Rep. Senatorial medal of Victory, Justice, Freedom and Liberty, 2002, Congl. Order of Merit, 2003; grantee, NSF, 1969—70. Mem. Tex. Classroom Tchrs. Assn. (officer rep., pres. Galena Park chpt. 1988-91), Pres.'s Club, Delta Alpha Pi (pres. Waco chpt. 1948-49), Alpha Epsilon Delta. Republican. Avocations: writing, archaeology, gardening, reading. Home: 14831 Anoka Dr Channelview TX 77530-3201

WALLACE, BEVERLY B., hospital administrator; b. Jan. 14, 1951; B in Acctg. with honors, U. West Fla. Various positions, including CFO, hosp., market & divsn. Humana, Inc., Fla., 1983—93; various positions Galen (merged with HCA Inc.); joined HCA, Inc., 1993, CFO, Mid-America Divsn., 1994—96, CFO, 1996—97, pres., Homecare Divsn., 1997—98, v.p., Managed Care, 1998—99, sr. v.p., Revenue Cycle Ops. Mgmt., 1999—2003, pres., Fin. Svcs. Group, 2003—06, pres., Shared Svcs. Group, 2006—. Former bd. dirs., mem., Governance Com. Healthcare Fin. Mgmt. Assn. (HFMA); bd. dirs. Fedn. of Am. Hosps. Office: HCA Inc 1 Park Plz Nashville TN 37203 Office Phone: 615-344-9551. Office Fax: 615-344-2266. Business E-Mail: beverly.wallace@hcahealthcare.com.

WALLACE, CHARLES ALAN, plastic surgeon; b. Ft. Worth, Tex., Feb. 13, 1957; MD, U. Tex. Southwestern Med. Sch., 1982. Cert. Am. Bd. Plastic Surgery. Intern, gen. surgery U. Hawaii, Honolulu, 1982—83; resident Baylor U. Med. Ctr., Dallas, 1984—87, resident, plastic surgery, 1986—87; resident St. Joseph-MD Anderson, Houston, 1987—89; private practice Dallas, 1989—. Fellow: ACS; mem.: Tex. Soc. Plastic and Reconstructive Surgeons, Dallas Soc. Plastic Surgeons, Cronin and Brauer Soc., AMA, Tex. Med. Assn., Dallas County Med. Assn., Am. Soc. Plastic Surgeons, Soc. Baylor Surgeons. Avocations: riding motorcycles, fixing cars, boats & airplanes. Office: 17110 Dallas Pky Ste 100 Dallas TX 75248 Office Phone: 972-380-7090. Office Fax: 972-380-7016.

WALLACE, CHRIS, professional sports team executive; m. Debby Wallace; 1 child, Truman. Founder Blue Ribbon Coll. Basketball Yearbook, 1981; draft cons. US Basketball League; with NY Knicks, LA Clippers, Denver Nuggets, Portland Trail Blazers; scout Miami Heat, dir. player pers.; gen. mgr. Boston Celtics, 1997—2007; v.p. basketball ops., gen. mgr. Memphis Grizzlies, 2007—. Mem. NBA Basketball Without Borders Africa Camp, Johannesburg. Named one of Most Influential Members of Coll. Basketball Media, Sports Illus., 1991. Office: Memphis Grizzlies 191 Beale St Memphis TN 38103

WALLACE, DANIEL, writer; b. Birmingham, Ala., 1959; m. Laura Kellison; children: Henry, Lillian Bayley Hoover. Attended, Emory U., USC. With trading co., Nagoya, Japan; bookstore mgr. Chapel Hill, NC; illustrator; contributing editor Garden and Gun Magazine; J. Ross MacDonald Disting. Prof. of English U. NC, Chapel Hill. Author: Big Fish: A Novel of Mythic Proportions, 1998, Ray in Reverse, 2000, Watermelon King, 2003, Crossroads, 2004, Mr. Sebastian and the Negro Magician, 2007, The Kings and Queens of Roam, 2013, (children's book) Elynora, 2008, O Great Rosenfeld!; contbr. stories to magazines; illustrations have appeared in Los Angeles Times, Italian Vanity Fair and many other magazines and books. Big Fish adapted to film by Tim Burton. Office: Department of English and Comparative Literature Greenlaw Hall CB #3520 University of North Carolina at Chapel H Chapel Hill NC 27599-3520 E-mail: daniel@danielwallace.org.*

WALLACE, KURT, state legislator; b. Maplesville, Ala., July 17, 1957; m. Connie Wallace; children: Terri Wallace, Jennifer Wallace, Jeremy Wallace. BSBA, Faulkner U., 2001, MBS in Mgmt., 2005. Dir. distbn. Bush Hog, 1984—2009; mem. Maplesville City Coun., Ala., 1999—2007, mayor, 2008—10; mem. Dist. 42 Ala. House of Representatives, 2011—. Republican. Baptist. Office: Ala House of Reps Rm 522-C 11 S Union St Montgomery AL 36130 Office Phone: 334-242-7772. Business E-Mail: representativewallace@gmail.com.

WALLACE, MARK ALLEN, hospital administrator; b. Oklahoma City, Apr. 24, 1953; s. William Howell and Mollie Marie (Godsy) W.; children: Emily, Benjamin. BS, Okla. Bapt. U., 1975; MS, Washington U., St. Louis, 1978. Adminstrv. asst. Bapt. Med. Ctr., Oklahoma City, 1975-77; administrv. resident Meth. Hosp., Houston, 1977-78; asst. v.p. Tex. Meth. Hosp., Houston, 1978-80, v.p., 1980-83, sr. v.p., 1983-89; pres., CEO Tex. Children's Hosp., Houston, 1989—. Adj. instr. Washington U., 1984—; adj. asst. prof. Tex. Womans U., Houston, 1983—; bd. dirs., chmn. fin. com., treas. Greater Houston Hosp. Svc. Corp., 1986-90; bd. trustees, Nat. Assn of Children's Hospitals and Related Institutions Contbr. articles to profl. jours. Chmn. campaign drives United Way, Houston, 1984, 86, corporate walk for Juvenile Diabetes Found. Walk to Cure Diabetes, 2000; class chmn. alumni vision for excellence and growth for future campaigns Okla. Bapt. U., 1982; bd. dirs. Tex. Gulf Coast chpt. March of Dimes Birth Defects Found., 1985-91, Zoological Society of Houston, Sam Houston Area Coun. of the Boy Scouts, World Health & Golf Assn., Greater Houston Partnership (vice-chair Flood Control Task Force), Greater Houston Community Found.; bd. governors, Houston Forum; active mem. Second Baptist Ch., Houston, Young Presidents' Orgn., and Houston Country Club Recipient Emerging Leaders in Health Care award Healthcare Forum Mag. and Korn/Ferry Internat., 1987. Fellow Am. Coll. Healthcare Execs. (com. on membership, subcom. on recruitment 1990—, Robert S. Hudgens Meml. award, 1992, Young Healthcare Exec. of Yr., 1992); mem. Am. Heart Assn. (med. adv. com. 1990-91), Healthcare Forum (pres. emerging leaders alumni group 1988-91), Am. Hosp. Assn., Tex. Hosp. Assn. (bd. dirs., bd. dirs. polit. action com. 1988—, chmn. bd. trustees, 1998-1999), Greater Houston Hosp. Coun. (bd. dirs. 1991—, chmn. 1993-1994), Houston Area Health Care Coalition, Childrens Hosp. Assn. Tex. (pres. 1992—, chmn. 2002-2003), Tex. Gulf Coast Arthritis Found. (bd. dirs. 1990-91). Republican. Baptist. Office: Tex Children's Hosp 6621 Fannin St Houston TX 77030 also: PO Box 300630 Houston TX 77230-0630

WALLACE, MIKE (BURNELL MICHEAL WALLACE), professional football player; b. New Orleans, Aug. 1, 1986; s. Burnell and Sonjia Wallace. BA in African American Studies, U. Miss., Oxford, 2009. Wide receiver Pitts. Steelers, 2009—12, Miami Dolphins, 2013—. Recipient Joe Greene Great Performance award, Pro Football Writers America, Pitts Chpt., 2009; named to The American Football Conf. Pro Bowl Team, NFL, 2011. Achievements include leading the NFL in: yards per reception, 2009. Office: Miami Dolphins 7500 SW 30 St Davie FL 33314

WALLACE, PETER MARSDEN, radio personality and producer, commentator, writer; b. Parkersburg, W.Va., Aug. 15, 1954; s. Aldred Pruden and Margaret Anne (Yoak) Wallace; m. Bonita Lucille Shock, Oct. 15, 1977 (div. 2005); children: Meredith Anne, Matthew Edward. AB in journalism/advt., Marshall U., 1976; ThM, Dallas Theol. Sem., 1984. Editor W.Va. Hillbilly, Richwood, W.Va., 1976-79; editl. asst. Dallas Theol. Sem., 1981-84; editl. mgr. Walk Thru the Bible Ministries, Atlanta, 1984-85, editl. dir., 1985-90; sr. copywriter & broadcast prodr. Larry Smith & Associates, Atlanta, 1990—2001; exec. prodr. Day 1 radio program (formerly The Protestant Hour), Atlanta, 2001—, host, 2005—; v.p. Alliance for Christian Media. Mem. Faith & Values Media Mem. Coun. Author: What Jesus Is Saying to You Today, 1994, What the Psalmist is Saying to You Today, 1994, What God Is Saying to You Today, 1995, Psalms for Today, 2001, TruthQuest Devotional Journal, 2002, Old Testament for Today, 2003, Out of the Quiet: Responding to God's Whispered Invitations, 2004, Living Loved: Knowing Jesus as the Lover of Your Soul, 2007; co-author: The West Virginia Picture Book, 1979; contbr. articles to religious magazines; editor: The Daily Walk Bible, 1987. Recipient Outstanding Young Men Am. Award, US Jaycees, 1984. Democrat. Avocations: reading, camping, travel. Home: 3972 Briarcliff Rd NE Atlanta GA 30345-2648 Office: Day 1 Ste 300 2715 Peachtree Rd NE Atlanta GA 30305-2907 Office Phone: 404-815-9110. Office Fax: 404-815-0495. E-mail: pwallace@day1.net.

WALLACE, ROGER WINDHAM, oil and gas company executive; B, Washington and Lee U.; MBA, Fletcher Sch. Law and Diplomacy. Dep. dir. Tex. Dept. of Commerce; dep. under sec. for internat. trade US Dept. of Commerce, 1989—91; min. counselor comml. affairs US Embassy, Mexico City, 1991—93; co-founder Investamex, 1993, pres., CFO; v.p. govt. affairs Pioneer Natural Resources Co., 2005—. Mem. Coun. of Fgn. Rels.; co-chair Woodrow Wilson Ctr.'s Mex. Inst. Adv. Bd.; chair Inter-Am. Found. Office: Pioneer Natural Resources Co Ste 200 5205 N O Connor Blvd Irving TX 75039 Office Phone: 972-444-9001. Office Fax: 972-969-3576.

WALLACE, STEVEN R., college president; m. Amelia Wallace; children: Devon, Michael. AA, Chaffey C.C., 1972; BS in Psychology, MS in Psychology, Calif. State U., San Bernardino; D in Higher Edn. Adminstrn., Claremont Grad. U., 1989. V.p. adminstrv. svcs. Lakeland CC, Ohio, 1981-90; pres. Austin CC, Minn., 1990-92, Inver Hills CC, Minn., 1992-97, Fla. CC, 1997—. Adj. faculty Chaffey CC, faculty Innovative Learning Ctr., dist. dir. learning disabilities, dir. mktg. and legis. affairs. Bd. dirs. Communities in Schs. and Enterprise North Florida. Mem. C. of C. (bd. dirs.), Jacksonville Symphony Assn. (bd. dirs.). Office: Fla Cmty Coll 501 W State St Jacksonville FL 32202-4086

WALLACE, TIMOTHY R., manufacturing executive; b. 1954; Grad., So. Meth. U., 1975. Joined Trinity Industries, Inc., 1975, v.p., 1984, sr. v.p., 1989, COO railcars and containers segment, chmn., pres., CEO, 1996—. Bd. dirs. VIAD Corp., Phoenix. Office: Trinity Industries 2525 Stemmon Freeway Dallas TX 75207

WALLACH, ALAN, art historian, educator; b. Bklyn., June 8, 1942; s. Israel and Vivian (Esner) W.; m. Phyllis Rosenzweig, Jan. 3, 1988. BA in Math., Columbia U., 1963, MA, 1965, PhD, 1973. Assoc. prof. Kean Coll., Union, NJ, 1974-89; Ralph H. Wark prof. art and art history, prof. Am. studies Coll. William and Mary, Williamsburg, Va., 1989—. Vis. prof. UCLA, 1982-83, Stanford (Calif.) U., 1987, CUNY, 1988, U. Mich., 1989; disting. vis. prof. U. Del., 2006; disting vice prof., Clark Instn. and Williams Coll. FACC, 2008, co-curator Nat. Mus. Am. Art, Washington, 1991-94. Author: (with William Truettner) Thomas Cole: Landscape into History, 1994; Exhibiting Contradiction: Essays on the Art Museum in the United States, 1998; mem. editl. bd. Am. Quar., 2000-03; contbr. articles to profl. jours. Mem. Am. Studies Assn. (bd. mng. editors, 2000-03), Coll. Art Assn. (bd. dirs. 1996-2000, Disting. Tng. Art History award, 2007), Assn. Art Historians. Office: Coll William and Mary Dept Art and Art History Williamsburg VA 23187-8795 Office Phone: 757-221-2530. Business E-Mail: axwall@wm.edu.

WALLE, ARMANDO LUCIO, state legislator; b. Houston, Mar. 7, 1978; m. Debbie Dimas Walle; 1 child, Armando Pedro Walle. BS in Polit. Sci., U. Houston. Former asst. to assoc. dir. Ctr. Mex.-Am. Studies Program U. Houston; former intern, liason to Hispanic cmty. to councilwoman Carol Mims Galloway Houston City Coun.; former staff mem. to rep. Gene Green Tex. House of Representatives, mem. Dist. 140, 2008—. Democrat. Roman Catholic. Office: 150 W Parker Rd Ste 700 Houston TX 77076 also: Room EXT E1.220 Capitol Extension PO Box 2910 Austin TX 78768 Office Phone: 713-694-8620, 512-463-0924.

WALLENBY, ROBERT, professional golfer; b. Melbourne, Australia, July 12, 1971; Australian rep. World Amateur Team Championship, 1990, Dunhill Cup, 1993; winner as amateur Victorian Open, Australia, 1991; winner PGA European Tour Honda Open, Germany, 1994, Marconi Pennsylvania Classic, 2001. Led Australasian Order of Merit, 1992; mem. Pres. Cup Team, 1994, 2003. Office: care PGA Tour 112 Tpc Blvd Ponte Vedra Beach FL 32082-3046

WALLER, EDWARD MARTIN, JR., lawyer; b. Memphis, July 2, 1942; s. Edward Martin and Freda (Lazarov) W.; m. Laura Jayne Rhodes, June 18, 1982; children: Lauren, Jonathan, Melissa. BA, Columbia U., 1964; JD, U. Chgo., 1967. Bar: Fla. 1967. Assoc. Fowler, White, Boggs, P.A., Tampa, Fla., 1967-72, ptnr., 1972—. Mem.: ABA (chmn. 1995—97, standing com. professionalism, lit. sec. budget officer 1996—2000), Am. Inns Ct. (bd. trustees 2011—), Bay Area Legal Svcs. (bd. dir. 2003—09, pres. 2006—07, bd. dir. 2011—), Hillsborough County Bar Assn., Fla. Bar Assn., Fla. Supreme Ct. Commn. on Professionalism. Democrat. Jewish. Office: Fowler White Boggs PO Box 1438 Tampa FL 33601-1438 Office Phone: 813-222-1137.

WALLER, JOHN HENRY, JR., retired state supreme court justice; b. Mullins, SC, Oct. 31, 1937; s. John Henry and Elnita (Rabon) Waller; m. Jane McLaurin Cooper, Nov. 16, 1963 (div.); children: John Henry III, Melissa McLaurin; m. Debra Ann Meares, May 9, 1981; children: Ryan Meares, Rand Ellis. AB in Psychology, Wofford Coll., Spartanburg, SC, 1959; LLB, JD, U. SC, 1963. Mem. SC Ho. of Reps., 1967—77, asst. majority leader, 1973—74, majority leader, 1975—76; mem. SC Senate, 1977—80; judge SC Cir. Ct., 1980—94; justice SC Supreme Ct., 1994—2009. Capt. US Army, 1959—60. Recipient Disting. Svc. award, Municipal Assn. SC, 1968. Mem.: Millins Rotary Club (1st pres.), Shriners, Masons. Avocations: woodworking, golf, water sports, skiing.

WALLER, JOHN LOUIS, anesthesiologist, educator; b. Loma Linda, Calif., Dec. 1, 1944; s. Louis Clinton and Sue (Bruce) W.; m. Jo Lynn Marie Haas, Aug. 4, 1968; children: Kristina, Karla, David. BA, So. Coll., Collegedale, Tenn., 1967; MD, Loma Linda U., 1971. Diplomate Am. Bd. Anesthesiology. Intern Hartford (Conn.) Hosp., 1971—72; resident in anesthesiology Harvard U. Med. Sch.-Mass. Gen. Hosp., Boston, 1972—74, fellow, 1974—75; asst. prof. anesthesiology Emory U. Sch. Medicine, Atlanta, 1977—80, assoc. prof., 1980—86, chmn. dept. anesthesiology, 1986—2000, prof., 1986—2001, prof. emeritus, 2001—; chief anesthesiology Emory U. Hosp., Atlanta, 1986-94, med. dir., 1993-95; assoc. v.p. info. svcs. Woodruff Health Scis. Ctr., 1995-97; chief info. officer Emory U. System Healthcare, Atlanta, 1995-97; prof. anesthesiology Med. U. S.C., Charleston, 2002—, chmn. dept. anesthesia and perioperative medicine, 2002—05, dir. med. informatics, 2005—. Cons. Arrow

Internat., Inc., Reading, Pa., 1988—; mem. adv. com. on anesthetic and life support drugs FDA, Washington, 1986—92; numerous vis. professorships and lectures. Contbr. articles to med. jours. Bd. dir. Picis Inc., 2006—. Maj. MC USAF, 1975—77. Recipient cert. of appreciation Office Sec. Def., 1983. Fellow: Am. Coll. Chest Physicians, Am. Coll. Anesthesiologists; mem.: Assn. Cardiac Anesthesiologists, Soc. Acad. Anesthesia Chmn. (councillor 1989—), Assn. Univ. Anesthesiologists, Internat. Anesthesia Rsch. Soc. (trustee 1984—2002, sec. 1996—98, chair 1998—2000), Soc. Cardiovascular Anesthesiologists (pres. 1991—93), Am. Soc. Anesthesiologists. Avocations: fishing, sailing, swimming. Office: Med Univ SC Dept Anes and Perioperative Medicine 167 Ashley Ave Ste 301 Charleston SC 29425 Business E-Mail: wallerj@musc.edu.

WALLER, KATHY NADINE, beverage company executive; b. Atlanta, Ga., 1958; BA in History, U. Rochester, NY, 1980; MBA in Acctg. & Finance, U. Rochester William E. Simon Graduate Sch. Bus., NY, 1983. CPA. Sr. acct. Deloitte Haskins & Sells, Rochester, NY & Atlanta; sr. acct., acctg. rsch. dept. The Coca-Cola Co., 1987, prin. acct., Northeast Europe & Africa Group, mktg. contr., McDonald's Group, 1991, dir., financial reporting, 1998—2004, v.p., chief internal audit, 2004—09, v.p., contr., 2009—13, v.p. finance, contr., 2013—14, exec. v.p., CFO, 2014—; financial services mgr., Africa Group The Minute Maid Co., 1996—98. Chair The Coca-Cola Co. Women's Leadership Coun.; bd. advisors Catalyst. Bd. dirs. YWCA Greater Atlanta; pres. U. Rochester Atlanta Regional Alumni Coun., U. Rochester Alumni Nat. Coun.; trustee U. Rochester, Spelman Coll.; mem. AICPA, Ga. Soc. Cert. Pub. Accountants. Recipient Career Achievement award, U. Rochester, 2005, Disting. Alumna award, U. Rochester William E. Simon Graduate Sch. Bus., 2007; named one of The 100 Most Influential People in Finance, Treasury & Risk mag., 2007. Office: The Coca Cola Co One Coca Cola Plz Atlanta GA 30313 Office Phone: 404-676-2121. Business E-Mail: kwaller@na.ko.com.*

WALLER, ROBERT ALFRED, retired college administrator; b. Sublette, Ill., July 1, 1931; s. Benonia and Martha Gertrude (Mueller) W.; m. Joan Ann Sodaro, Aug. 16, 1952; children: Margaret Ann, Thomas Edward, James Joseph. BA in History, Lake Forest Coll., 1953; MA in History, U. Ill., 1958, PhD in History, 1963. High sch. tchr. New London (Wis.) pub. schs., 1955-57, Urbana (Ill.) community schs., 1958-62; prof. U. Ill., Urbana, 1963-67, prof., adminstr., 1967-81; adminstr. Clemson U., SC, 1981—94, prof., 1994—2000, The Village Coll., 2003—14. Cons. Ednl. Testing Svc., Princeton, N.J., 1964-76, U.S. Office Edn., 1965-68; reviewer NEH, Washington, 1986-89. Author: Rainey of Illinois, 1977 (Merit award 1978), (with others) These United States, 1981. Contbr. numerous articles and book reviews to mags. Mem. Urbana Sch. Bd., 1972-73. With US Army, 1953—55, Germany. Grantee Carnegie Corp., 1962-63, NEH, 1985-89; fellow U. Ill., 1957-58, 62-63. Mem. Ill. Hist. Soc., Orgn. Am. History, Acad. Affairs Adminstrs., Coun. Colls. Arts and Scis. Democrat. Roman Catholic. Avocations: stamp-collecting, golf, water volleyball. Home: 1550 El Camino Real Apt 236 The Villages FL 32159-1007 Personal E-mail: robertwaller31@yahoo.com.

WALLER, STEPHEN, air transportation executive; b. 1949; Student, New Zealand U., 1970-74. Courier, country mgr., european mktg. mgr. DHL Airways, Inc., London, 1975-80, Tehran, Iran, 1975-80, v.p. field svcs. Redwood City, Calif., 1980-93, sr. v.p. Network Trans. divsn., 1994—. Office: DHL 1200 S Pine Island Rd Ste 170 Plantation FL 33324-4469

WALLER, WILLIAM LOWE, JR., state supreme court chief justice; b. Miss., Feb. 9, 1952; s. Bill and Carroll (Overton) Waller; m. Charlotte Brawner, Aug. 4, 1979; children: William, Jeannie, Clayton. BA in Bus., Miss. State U., 1974; JD, U. Miss., 1977; grad., U.S. Army War Coll. Bar: Miss. 1977. Ptnr. Waller and Waller, 1977-97; judge City of Jackson, Miss., 1995-96; justice Miss. Supreme Ct., Jackson, 1998—, presiding justice, 2004—08, chief justice, 2009—. Chmn. Miss. Pub. Defenders Task Force, 2000-05; mem. Study Commn. on the Miss. Jud. Sys.; chmn. Supreme Ct. Rules Com., 2001-. Deacon First Bapt. Ch., Jackson, Miss. Recipient Chief Justice award, 2005. Mem. ABA, Miss. Bar Assn. (chmn. Lawyer Referral Service 1987-89), Miss. Trial Lawyers Assn. (bd. mem. 1979-82), Hinds County Bar Assn. (Jud. Innovation award 2003-04), Jackson Young Lawyers Assn., Christian Legal Soc., Am. Legion, Miss. Army Nat. Guard. Office: Mississippi Supreme Ct PO Box 117 Jackson MS 39205-0117 Office Phone: 601-359-2139.*

WALLIN, LELAND DEAN, artist, educator; b. Sioux Falls, SD, Oct. 14, 1942; s. Clarence Forrest and Leona Mae (McInnis) W.; m. Meredith Maria Hawkins, Mar. 26, 1977; 1 child, Jessica Wallin Mace. Student, Columbus Coll. Art and Design, 1961-62; BFA in Painting, Kans. City Art Inst., Mo., 1965; MFA in Painting, U. Cin. with Cin. Art Acad., 1967. Prof. drawing, painting, sculpture St. Cloud State U., Minn., 1967-86; prof. Queens Coll., CUNY, Flushing, NY, 1983-84; prof., coord. MFA painting Marywood U., Scranton, Pa., 1985-90; prof. painting and drawing East Carolina U., Greenville, 1992—2008, prof. emeritus, 2006. Lectr. Rutgers U. NJ, 1981, Carnegie-Mellon U., Pitts., 1988; curator Philip Pearlstein Retrospective Exhibit, Scranton, 1988; juror Belin Arts Grant Com., Waverly, Pa., 1986-89; judge, juror No. Nat. Art Competition, 1993. One-man shows include Mpls. Coll. Art and Design, 1977—78, Harold Reed Gallery, NYC, 1983, Gallery Henoch, 1991, Greenville Mus. Art, NC, 2007, exhibited in group shows at Bklyn. Mus., 1979, Greenville County Mus. Art, SC, 1983, Huntsville Mus. Art, 1994, San Bernardino County Mus. Internat., Calif., 1995, Contemporary Realism, Phila., 1996, Ctr. Arts, Laredo, Tex., 1997 (Internat. First Pl. award, 1997), Downey Mus. Art, Calif., 1998, Ctr. Arts, Laredo, Tex., 1999 (Internat. First Pl. award, 1999), Palm Springs Desert Mus., 1999, Fine Arts Ctr., Sacramento, 1999, Bellevue Art Mus., Wash., 2001, Morris Mus. Art, Ga., 2001, Huntsville Mus. Art, Ala., 2002, Miss. Mus. Art, 2002, Barret Art Ctr., Poughkeepsie, NY, 2003, Myth, Magic & Metaphor, Chgo., Union St. Gallery, 2004, Fayetteville Mus. Art, NC, 2008, Contemporary Realism Biennial Fort Wayne Mus. of Art, Ind., 2010, Art Elements, 2011; contbr. articles to profl. jours. Recipient Scholar-Tchr. award for Coll. Fine Arts and Comm., East Carolina U. Sch. Art and Design, 2005, numerous rsch. awards, East Carolina U., 1994—2005; named Outstanding Tchr., 1994, 1995. Home and Office: 159 West Hills Dr Stroudsburg PA 18360

WALLINGFORD, JOHN, science educator, researcher; BA in Biology and Biochemsitry, Wesleyan U.; PhD in Biology, U. Tex., Austin, 1998. Asst. prof. U. Tex., Austin. Howard Hughes Med. Inst. Early Career Scientist U. Tex., Austin, 2009—. Contbr. of articles to profl. journals. Recipient Career award in Biomedical Sciences, Burroughs Wellcome Fund, Early Career Excellence award, Sandler Program for Asthma Rsch. Office: U Tex Austin Molecular Cell & Developmental Biology PAT 222 1 University Station 214 Patterson Labs Austin TX 78712 Office Phone: 512-232-2784. Business E-Mail: wallingford@mail.utexas.edu.

WALLIS, CARLTON LAMAR, librarian; b. Blue Springs, Miss., Oct. 15, 1915; s. William Ralph and Tellie (Jones) W.; m. Mary Elizabeth Cooper, Feb. 22, 1944; 1 child, Carlton Lamar. BA with spl. distinction, Miss. Coll., 1936; MA, Tulane U., 1946; B.L.S., U. Chgo., 1947; L.H.D., Rhodes Coll., Memphis, 1980. English tchr., coach Miss. Pub. Schs., 1936-41; teaching fellow Miss. Coll. and Tulane U., 1941-42; chief librarian Rosenberg Library, Galveston, Tex., 1947-55; city librarian Richmond, Va., 1955-58; dir. Memphis Pub. Library, 1958-80, ret., 1980. Author: Libraries in the Golden Triangle, 1966; contbr. articles to library jours. Trustee Belhaven Coll., 1978-82, Nat. Ornamental Metal Mus., 1989—. Served as chief warrant officer AUS, 1942-46. Decorated Bronze Star. Mem. ALA (chmn. library mgmt. sect. 1969-71), Pub. Library Assn. (dir. 1973-77), Tex. Library Assn. (pres. 1952-53), Va. Library Assn., Southwestern Library Assn. (exec. bd. 1950-55), Southeastern Library Assn. (chmn. pub. library sect. 1960-62), Tenn. Library Assn. (pres. 1969-70, Distinguished Service award 1979, Intellectual Freedom award 1998). Presbyterian (elder). Club: Egyptian (pres. 1973-74). Home: 3597 Oakley Ave Memphis TN 38111-6141

WALLIS, OLNEY GRAY, lawyer; b. Llano, Tex., July 27, 1940; s. Ben Alton and Jessie Ella (Longbotham) W.; m. Linda Lee Johnson, June 29, 1963; children: Anne, Brett. BA, U. Tex., 1962, JD, 1965. Bar: Tex. 1965, U.S. Dist. Ct. (so. dist.) Tex. 1966, U.S. Ct. Mil. Appeals 1968, U.S. Surpeme Ct. 1970, U.S. dist. Ct. (we. dist.) Tex. 1976, U.S. Ct. Appeals (5th cir.) 1977, U.S. Tax Ct. 1980, U.S. Ct. Appeals (10th cir.) 1981, U.S. Ct. Appeals (11th cir.) 1983, U.S. Dist. Ct. (no. dist.) Tex. 1985, U.S. Dist. Ct. (ea. and we. dists.) Ark. 1985, U.S. Ct. Appeals (8th cir.) 1985. Assoc. Brown & Cecil, Houston, 1965-66; asst. U.S. atty. Dept. Justice, Houston, 1971-74; mem. Jefferson, Wallis & Sherman, Houston, 1975-81, Wallis & Pruitt, Houston, 1981-87, Wallis and Short, Houston, 1987—. Instr. U. Md., Keflauik, Iceland, 1968-69; mem. faculty continuing legal edn. U. Houston, 1981-84. Capt. USAF, 1966-70. Decorated Air Force Commendation medal. Mem. Assn. Trial Lawyers Am., Am. Judicature Soc., Tex. Trial Lawyers Assn., Houston Bar Found., Phi Delta Phi, Phi Kappa Tau. Office: Wallis & Short 9535 S Hwy 16 Llano TX 78643 Office Phone: 325-248-0111. Personal E-mail: ogwlawyer@earthlink.net.

WALLIS, QUVENZHANÉ, actress; b. Houma, La., Aug. 28, 2003; d. Venjie Sr. and Qulyndreia Wallis. Actress: (films) Beasts of the Southern Wild, 2012 (Best Breakthrough Performance-Female, Nat. Bd. Review, 2012, Best Breakout Performance, African American Film Critics Assn., 2012, Best Young Actor/Actress, Critics Choice Awards, 2013, youngest actress to ever receive an Academy Award nomination, 2013), Twelve Years a Slave, 2013, The Prophet (voice), 2014, Annie, 2014.*

WALLMAN, AMY, retail executive; b. 1950; m. Richard F. Wallman. MBA, U. Chgo., 1975. Audit ptnr. Ernst & Young Internat., 1984—2001, health care industry leader, 1995—2001. Bd. dirs. Omnicare, Inc., 2004—. Office: Omnicare Inc 1600 RiverCenter II 100 E RiverCenter Blvd Covington KY 41011 Office Phone: 859-392-3300. Office Fax: 859-392-3333. Business E-Mail: amy.wallman@omgi.com.

WALLS, GEORGE HILTON, JR., manufacturing executive; b. Coatesville, Pa., Nov. 30, 1942; s. Philip Robert and Elizabeth (Walls) Gibson; m. Portia Diane Hall, July 12, 1977; children: George III, Steven, Kevin. BS in Edn., West Chester U., Pa., 1964; MA in Edn., NC Ctrl. U., 1975; DHL, Va. Union U., 1993. Rep. U.S. Army Engr. Sch., Ft. Belvoir, 1980-82; commdg. officer, prof., Naval Sci. NROTC unit U. N.C., 1989-91; commd. 2d lt. USMC, 1965, comdr. Wing Engr. Squadron-17, 1983-84, spl. asst. and marine aide to Asst. Sec. of Navy, 1984-87, head engr., Motor Transport, Gen. Supply Br. Washington, 1987-89, comdr., 2d Force Svc. Support Group, 1991, brig. gen., 1993; commdg. gen., Joint Task Force for Ops. GTMO, Guantanamo Naval Base, Cuba, 1991-93; spl. asst. to chancellor NC Ctrl. U., Durham, 1993—; chief dep. auditor NC, 2001—04. Bd. dirs. Lincoln Electric Holdings Inc. Decorated D.S.M., Legion of Merit, Navy Commendation Medal with Combat "V", Navy Achievement Medal, Meritorious Svc. Medal; recipient Meritorious Svc. award NAACP, 1993, Humanitarian award Chapel of the Four Chaplains, Valley Forge, Pa., 1993. Avocations: running, basketball, hunting, fishing, boating. Home: 100 Canberra Ct Cary NC 27513-2923 Office: Lincoln Electric Holdings Inc Bd Directors 22801 St Clair Ave Cleveland OH 44117 Office Phone: 216-481-8100. Office Fax: 216-486-1751. E-mail: george_walls@lincolnelectric.com.

WALLS, JOHNNIE E., judge, former state legislator; b. Clarksdale, Miss., Apr. 25, 1945; m. Dorothy L. Sanders; children: Sdahri Ayanna, Nzinga Niambi, Kwasi Kefentse, Christopher, Anika Shacora. Atty.; mem. Dist. 12 Miss. State Senate, 1993—2010; chmn. Miss. State Dem. Party; judge 11th Jud. Dist. Ct. Pl. 2, Miss., 2011—. Mem.: NAACP, Miss. Trial Lawyers Assn., Miss. Nat. & Magnolia Bar Assn., 100 Black Men of Delta. Democrat. Methodist. Office: 11th Jud Dist Court Pl 2 Greenville MS 38702

WALLS, MARTHA ANN WILLIAMS (MRS. B. CARMAGE WALLS), publishing executive; b. Gadsden, Ala., Apr. 21, 1927; d. Aubrey Joseph and Inez (Cooper) Williams; m. B. Carmage Walls, Jan. 2, 1954; children: Byrd Cooper, Lissa Walls Vahldiek. Student pub. schs., Gadsden. Pres., dir. Walls Newspapers, Inc., 1969-70; sec., treas., dir. Summer Camps, Inc., Guntersville, Ala., 1954-69; CEO, pres., dir. So. Newspapers, Inc., Houston, 1970—; pres., dir. So. Newspapers of Ala., Inc., Scottsboro. V.p., dir. Ft. Payne (Ala.) Newspapers, Inc., Galveston Newspapers, Inc.; dir. Monroe (Ga.) Newspapers, Inc.; bd. dirs. Jefferson Pilot Corp., Greensboro, N.C., 1990-98, Jefferson-Pilot Life Ins. Co., 1990-98, Jefferson Pilot Comm., 1990-98. Bd. dirs. Montgomery Acad., 1970-74. Mem.: Soc. Profl. Journalists. Episcopalian. Office: 5701 Woodway Ste 131 Houston TX 77057 Office Phone: 713-266-5481.

WALLS, ROBERT HAMILTON, JR., lawyer; b. Austin, Tex., May 19, 1960; s. Robert Hamilton Sr. and Anita L. (Hoffman) W.; m. Nancy R. Ghormley, Aug. 11, 1984. BBA in Petroleum, U. Tex., 1983, JD, 1985. Bar: Tex. 1985. Atty. Vinson & Elkins LLP, Houston, 1985—92; sr. v.p., gen. counsel for subsidiary domestic power & internat. energy bus. Enron Corp., Houston, 1992—99, dep. gen. counsel, mng. dir. global assets & services, 1999—2002, exec. v.p. & gen. coun., 2002—05; founding ptnr. Post Oak Energy Capital, 2006—09; exec. v.p., gen. counsel Clear Channel Communications, Inc., San Antonio, 2010—. Mem. ABA, Tex. Bar Assn., Houston Bar Assn. Office: Clear Channel Comm 200 E Basse Rd San Antonio TX 78209-8328

WALMER, EDWIN FITCH, retired lawyer; b. Chgo., Mar. 24, 1930; s. Hillard Wentz and Anna C. (Fitch) W.; m. Florence Poling, June 17, 1952; children: Linda Diane Walmer Dennis, Fred Fitch. BS with distinction, Ind. U., 1952, JD with high distinction, 1957. Bar: Wis. 1957, U.S. Dist. Ct. (ea. dist.) Wis. 1957. Assoc. Foley & Lardner, Milw., 1957-65, ptnr., 1965-90, ret., 1990. Served to 1st lt. U.S. Army, 1952-54. Recipient Cal. C. Chambers award Culver (Ind.) Mil. Acad., 1948. Fellow Am. Coll. Trust and Estate Counsel; mem. Order of Coif, Dairymen's Country Club (Boulder Junction, Wis.), Vineyards Country Club (Naples, Fla.), Phi Eta Sigma, Beta Gamma Sigma. Republican. Congregationalist. Avocations: golf, fishing.

WALSH, DAVID JOSEPH, pediatric neurologist, educator; b. St. Louis, Oct. 5, 1946; s. Joseph Lloyd and Dorothy Ann Walsh. BS, Georgetown U., Washington, DC, 1968; MD, Med. U. SC, 1973. Diplomate Am. Bd. Psychiatry and Neurology, Am. Bd. Pediat. Asst. prof. neurology and pediat. Jacksonville Health Edn. Program, U. Fla., Jacksonville, 1981—82; asst. prof. pediat. and neurology U. Kans., Kansas City, 1982—88; pvt. practice Allegheny Neurol. Assoc., Pitts., 1988—90; asst. prof. neurology Med. Coll. Wis., Milw., 1990—2004; assoc. prof. neurology St. Louis U., St. Louis, 2004—11, prof. neurology psychiatry, 2011—12; prof. neuroscis. Med. U. SC, 2012—, chief divsn. child neurology. Program dir. pediat. residency U. Kans., Kansas City, 1982—87; program dir. pediat. neurology residency program Med. Coll. Wis., Milw., 2001—03; chief med. staff, divsn. neurology Children's Hosp. Wis., Milw., 2001—04; chief sect. child neurology St. Louis U., St. Louis, 2004—11. Author: (short story) Upping the Ritalin. Chair profl. adv. bd. Epilepsy Found. S.E. Wis., Milw., 1992—2004, pres., 1994—2004; sec. profl. adv. bd. Epilepsy Found., 2006—11; pres. profl. adv. bd. Epilepsy Found. Greater St. Louis area, 2008—11. Lt. USNR, 1974—76. Fellow: Am. Acad. Neurology; mem.: Assn. U. Profs. Neurology, Harvard Med. Alumni Assn., Med. U. SC Alumni Assn., Child Neurology Soc. Independent. Roman Catholic. Avocations: Aikido, opera, travel. Office: Divsn Pediat Neurology 96 Jonathan Luins St Ste 301 CSB MSC 606 Charleston SC 29425-6060 Office Phone: 843-792-4858. Personal E-mail: walsh1312@comcast.net. Business E-Mail: walshdj@musc.edu.*

WALSH, JAMES ANTHONY (TONY WALSH), theater and film educator; b. Bklyn., Aug. 21, 1947; s. Henry Michael and Clara (Nappi) Walsh. BA in Theater, Hofstra U., 1968; MA in Theater, Adelphi U., 1976. Tchr., dir. theater N.C. Sch. of Arts, Winston-Salem, 1976-81; artistic dir. Cross and Sword/State Play of Fla., St. Augustine, 1982-91; dean Fla. Sch. of Arts, Palatka, 1982-91; dir. Inst. of Entertainment Technologies Valencia C.C., Orlando, Fla., 1992-93, dir. Ctr. Profl. Devel., 1993-96; producing dir. TV and video prodn. Valencia Coll., Orlando, 1996-2001; mng. dir. The Performing and Visual Arts Ctr. St. Johns River C.C., Orange Park, Fla., 01—, exec. dir. The Thrasher-Horne Ctr. for Arts, 2003—; v.p. Fla. Profl. Presenters Consortium, 2007—. Freelance theater dir., acting coach, NYC, 1973-76; cons. Network of Performing and Visual Arts Schs., Washington, 1980—, Inst. Outdoor Drama, Chapel Hill, NC, 1989—, Univ. Film and Video Assn., Sarasota, Fla., 1992, Internat. Film Workshops, Rockport, Maine, 1992, Dir. Guild Am. Educators Workshop, LA, 1993, Dir.'s Workshop, 1996, Acad. TV Arts and Scis. Educators Seminar, LA, 1995; writer, dir. LifeMap, 2000. Writer PBS documentary World of Family, NCCJ, 1995; exptl. theater playwright; lyricist (off-Broadway mus.) Sugar Hill, 1990. Bd. dirs. Enzian Film Theatre, Concert on the Green, Maitland Art Ctr.; mem. adv. coun. Fla. Film Festival. NEH grant, 1978; recipient playwriting fellowships Atlantic Ctr. for Arts, 1983, Fla. Divsn. Cultural Affairs, 1983; named Winner Fla. Playwrite Competition, 1994, Winner Best Video, Fla. Assn. C.C., 1996. Mem. Assn. Theater in Higher Edn., Fla. Motion Picture and TV Assn. (bd. dirs., v.p.), Ctrl. Fla. Film Commn. (bd. dirs.), Fla. Inst. for Film Edn. (bd. dirs.) Actors Equity Assn., Dramatists Guild N.Y.C., Players Club (N.Y.C.). Home: 2375 Coleen Lane Fleming Island FL 32003 Office: Thrasher-Home Ctr Arts St Johns River State Coll 283 College Dr Orange Park FL 32065 Personal E-mail: twalsh@aol.com, twalshwpk@aol.com.

WALSH, JAMES HAMILTON, lawyer; b. NYC, May 20, 1947; s. Edward James and Helen Smith (Hamilton) W.; m. Janice Ausherman, Aug. 3, 1967; children: Tracy, Courtney, Eric. BA in Psychology, Bridgewater Coll., Va., 1968; JD, U. Va., Charlottesville, 1975. Bar: Va. 1975, US Dist. Ct. (ea. and we. dists.) Va. 1975, US Ct. Appeals (4th cir.) 1976, US Supreme Ct. 1982, US Ct. Appeals (3d cir.). Assoc. McGuire, Woods LLP, Richmond, Va., 1975-82; ptnr. McGuire, Woods, Battle & Boothe (and predecessor firms), Richmond, Va., 1982—. Instr. Nat. Inst. Trial Adv.; adj. prof. U. Richmond, 1992, 93; spl. prosecutor US Dist. Ct. (ea. dist.) Va., 1979, 84. Contbr. articles to profl. jours. Mem. bd. trustees Bridgewater Coll., mem. exec. com.; mem. staff Va. Law Rev. With US Army, 1969-72. Named Best Lawyers in Am., 2003—, Va. Legal Elite, 2002—, Va. Super Lawyers. Mem. ABA (mem. antitrust sect. health care com., litigation sect.), Fedn. Def. and Corp. Counsel, Va. State Bar (bd. govs. antitrust sect. 1984-90, chmn. 1986), Va. Bar Assn. (chmn. criminal law sect. 1997, 98), Richmond Bar Assn., Willow Oaks, Order Coif, Phi Delta Phi, County Club of Va. Episcopalian. Home: 113 Adingham Ct Richmond VA 23229-7761 Office: McGuire Woods LLP 1 James Ctr 901 E Cary St Richmond VA 23219-4004 Office Phone: 804-775-4356. Business E-Mail: jwalsh@mcguirewoods.com.

WALSH, JENNIFER FITZGERALD, former legislative staff member; b. Lancaster, Pa., Aug. 14, 1973; BA, U. Md., College Park, 1995. Dep. campaign mgr., field rep. to Rep. Vic Fazio US House of Representatives, 1995—98; chief of staff for to Assemblyman Thomas Calderon Calif. State Assemblyman, 1999—2002; dep. chief of staff to Rep. Dennis Cardoza, US House of Reps., 2003—05, chief of staff, 2005—11. Mem.: Omicron Delta Kappa, Alpha Omicron Pi.

WALSH, JOHN BREFFNI, aerospace consultant; b. Bklyn., Aug. 20, 1927; s. George and Margaret Mary (Rigney) W.; m. Marie Louise Leclerc, June 18, 1955; children: George Breffni, John Leclerc, Darina Louise. BEE, Manhattan Coll., 1948; MS, Columbia U., 1950; postgrad., NYU, 1954-62. Asst., instr. Columbia U., NYC, 1948-51, asst. prof., asst. dir. Electronics Rsch. Labs., 1953-66; various positions through tech. dir. Intelligence and Reconnaissance Div., Rome Air Devel. Center, NY, 1951-53; dep. for rsch. to asst. sec. Air Force, 1966-71; sr. staff mem. Nat. Security Council, 1971-72, asst. to Pres.'s sci. advisor, 1971-72; dep. dir. Def. Research and Engring., 1972-77; asst. sec. gen. for def. support NATO, 1977-80; chmn. Trisvc. Navigation Satellite Exec. Group, (GPS), to devise architecture for navigation satellite system to reconcile competing incompatible Air Force and Navy proposals, 1969—71; holder chair in systems acquisition mgmt., dean exec. inst. Def. Systems Mgmt. Coll., Ft. Belvoir, Va., 1981-82, prof. emeritus, 1982—; v.p., chief scientist Boeing Mil. Airplane Co., Wichita, Kans., 1982-89; v.p. rsch. and engring. programs Boeing Aerospace and Electronics div., Seattle, 1990-92; v.p. strategic analysis Boeing Defense and Space Group, Seattle, 1992-93; prin. John B. Walsh Assocs., 1993—. Mem. aeros. adv. com. NASA; mem. Congl. Adv. Com. on Aeros., 1984-85; assoc. Def. Sci. Bd.; mem. indsl. adv. bd. Wichita State U. Coll. Engring., adj. prof. elec. engring., 1989-90; chmn. tech. working group Def. Trade Adv. Group Dept. State, 1992-95; chmn. com. on adv. group on aeronautics R & D, NATO, 1981-82; cons. Def. Sci. Bd., 2003-. Author: Electromagnetic Theory and Engineering Applications, 1960; (with K.S. Miller): Introductory Electric Circuits, 1960, Elementary and Advanced Trigonometry, 1977; contbr. tech. papers to publs.; patentee in field. Mem. planning bd., Cresskill, N.J., 1964-66; commr. Kans. Advanced Tech. Commn., 1985-86; bd. dirs. Kans. Inc., 1986-90; mem. math. scis. edn. bd. NRC, 1989-92. Served with U.S. Army, 1946-47, USAR, 1947-52. Recipient Air Force Exceptional Civilian Service award, 1969; recipient Dept. Def. Meritorious Civilian Service award, 1971, Disting. Civilian Service award, 1977, Air Force Assn. citation of honor as outstanding Air Force civilian employee of year, 1971, Theodore von Karman award Air Force Assn., 1977. Fellow IEEE (life), AIAA (v.p. tech. 1987-89); mem.

Internat. Inst. for Strategic Studies, N.Y. Acad. Scis., GPS Internat. Assn., Electromagnetics Acad., Sigma Xi, Eta Kappa Nu. Roman Catholic. Office: 8800 Prestwould Pl Mc Lean VA 22102-2231 Home Phone: 703-893-3610.*

WALSH, NICOLAS EUGENE, rehabilitation services professional, educator; b. Mpls., July 1, 1947; s. Leonard Cyril and June Alice Walsh; m. Wendy Sarah Allnutt, June 1, 1973; children: Meghan, Rorey, Katlin, Alaine. BS, USAF Acad., 1969; MS, Marquette U., 1974; MD, U. Colo., 1979. Asst. prof. naval sci. Marquette U., Milw., 1972—74; from asst. prof. to assoc. prof. rehab. medicine U. Tex. Health Sci. Ctr., San Antonio, 1982—89, prof., chmn. rehab. medicine, 1989—, exec. assoc. dean Sch. Medicine, 1999—2000, disting. prof., 2001—. Dir. Am. Bd. Phys. Medicine and Rehab., Rochester, Minn., 1994—2006, sec., 1996—98, chmn., 1998—2005; pres., CEO Univ. Physician Group, 1998—2001. Author book chpts.; editor: Rehabilitation of Chronic Pain, 1991; editor-in-chief Archives of Phys. Medicine and Rehab., Chgo., 1994—2000; mng. editor: Rehabilitation Medicine: Principles and Practices, 2005. Recipient Excellence in Rsch. award, Am. Jour. Phys. Medicine and Rehab., 1991; named Health Care Profl. of Yr., Gov.'s Com. for Disabled Persons, 1989. Fellow: Am. Acad. Phys. Medicine and Rehab. (Richard and Hinda Rosenthal Found. award 1991, Zieter lectr. 2003), Am. Bd. Pain Medicine (v.p. 1993—94, sec. 1994—96); mem.: Phys. Medicine and Rehab. Edn. and Rsch. Found. (pres. 1993—2000, Excellence in Rsch. award 1991), Assn. Acad. Physiatrists (v.p. 1993—95, pres. 1996—98). Office: U Tex Health Sci Ctr Mail Code 7872 7703 Floyd Curl Dr San Antonio TX 78229-3900 Home Phone: 210-493-1174; Office Phone: 210-567-5350. Business E-Mail: walshn@uthscsa.edu.

WALSH, ROBERT K., law educator, former dean; m. Kathie Walsh; 4 children. AB, Providence Coll., 1964; JD, Harvard U., 1967. Bar: Calif. 1967, Ark. 1979. Assoc. McCatchen, Black, Verleger & Shea, LA, 1967-70; asst. prof. Villanova U., Phila., 1970-71, assoc. prof., 1971-73, prof., 1973-76; dean U. Ark., Little Rock Sch. Law; ptnr. Friday, Eldredge & Clark, Little Rock, 1981-89; prof. law Wake Forest Sch. Law, Winston-Salem, NC, 1989—, dean, 1989—2007, dean emeritus. Bd. trustees Nat. Assn. Law Placement Found., Am. Inns of Ct. Found. Mem. ABA (chair Accreditation Com. 1984-86, chair Standards Rev. Com. Sect. Legal Edn. 1991—, Central European and Eurasian Law Initiative Adv. Coun.), N.C. Bar Assn. (chair bar bench and law schs. com. 1990-92, v.p., bd. govs. 1994-95). Office: Wake Forest Sch Law 1834 Wake Forest Rd Winston Salem NC 27109 Office Phone: 336-758-5770. Business E-Mail: walshrk@wfu.edu.

WALSH, W. TERENCE, lawyer; b. Toledo, Nov. 18, 1943; s. Walter James and Ann (Gifford) W.; m. Patricia Jane Walker, Dec. 17, 1966; children: Christopher O'Brien, Ryan Kerrick, Ann Elisabeth. AB, Brown U., 1965; JD, Emory U., 1970. Bar: Ga., 1971, U.S. Dist. Ct. (no. dist.) Ga., 1971, U.S. Ct. Appeals (11th cir.), 1971, U.S. Supreme Ct., 2003. Assoc. Alston, Miller & Gaines, Atlanta, 1970-76, ptnr., 1976-83; ptnr., litig. trial practice group Alston & Bird LLP, Atlanta, 1983—. Lectr. various seminars on bus. litig., appellate procedure, juvenile law, ethics, and professionalism. Contbr. articles to profl. jours. Co-founder Truancy Intervention Project, 1991—; chmn. Kids In Need of Dreams, Inc., 1993-; bd. dirs. Family Connection Partnership, 2000-, Georgians for Children, 1993-2003, The Bridge, 1994-99, Ga. Justice Project, 1987-97, Juvenile Justice Fund, 2000—, Ga. Acad., 1999-2002; bd. dirs. Atlanta Legal Aid Soc., Inc., 1976-98, pres., 1987; chmn. Capital Area Mosaic, 1994-96; chmn. sch. bd. Christ the King Sch., 1982-84; alumni trustee Brown U., 1994-2001; chmn. State Bar Com. on Children and the Cts., 1996—; bd. dirs. Justice for Children Adv. Bd. Supreme Ct. Ga., 2000—. Recipient cmty. svc. award Martin Luther King, Jr. Ctr. for Nonviolent Social Change, 1995. Fellow: Ga. Bar Found.; mem.: ABA (Livingston Hall Juvenile Justice award 1999, John Minor Wisdom award, litigation sec. 2007), Atlanta Bar Assn. (Leadership award 2005), Gate City Bar Assn., Atlanta Bar Assn. (bd. dirs. 1987—93, pres. 1991—92, Charles E. Watkins award 1994, S. Phillip Heiner award 1994, David Pollard award 1995), State Bar Ga. (bd. govs. 1979—99, pres. YLD 1980—81, H. Sol Clark award 1987, Chief Justice's award for cmty. svc. 1998), Emory Law Alumni Assn. (exec. com. 1990—98, Disting. Law Alumnus award 2000). Avocations: sports, gardening, reading. Office: Alston & Bird LLP One Atlantic Ctr 1201 W Peachtree St NW Ste 4200 Atlanta GA 30309-3449 Home Phone: 404-351-5916; Office Phone: 404-881-7161. Office Fax: 404-253-8884. Business E-Mail: twalsh@alston.com.

WALSH, WILLIAM ARTHUR, JR., lawyer; b. Washington, Mar. 17, 1949; children: Jesse Walsh, Patrick McKay. BS in Econs. and Fin., U. Md., 1972; JD, U. Richmond, 1977. Bar: Va. Ptnr. Hunton & Williams LLP, Richmond, Va., 1985—. Guest lectr. Greater Richard Assn. Comml. Real Estate. Trustee, bd. dirs. Va. Commonwealth U. Real Estate Found.; mem. Va. Commonwealth U. Real Estate Circle of Excellence. Mem. Va. Bar Assn., Am. Coll. Real Estate Lawyers. Home: 4705 Leonard Pky Richmond VA 23226-1337 Office: Hunton & Williams LLP Riverfront Plz East Tower 951 E Byrd St Richmond VA 23219-4074 Office Phone: 804-788-8378. Business E-Mail: wwalsh@hunton.com.

WALSWORTH, MICHAEL (MIKE) A., state legislator; b. Mar. 27, 1956; m. Deanne Breedlove. Mem. Dist. 15 La. House of Reps., 1996—2007; mem. Dist. 33 La. State Senate, 2008—, vice chair agr., forestry, aquaculture and rural devel. com., mem. fin. com., labor and indsl. rels. com., senate and govtl. affairs com., chair select com. on homeland security. Republican. Address: 210 Breckenridge West Monroe LA 71292 Office: Dist Off 4007 Whites Ferry Rd Ste A West Monroe LA 71291 Home Phone: 318-396-2491; Office Phone: 318-340-6453. Fax: 318-340-0480. Business E-Mail: walsworthm@legis.state.la.us.

WALTER, DONALD ELLSWORTH, federal judge; b. Jennings, La., Mar. 15, 1936; s. Robert R. and Ada (Lafleur) D'Aquin; m. Charlotte Sevier Donald, Jan. 5, 1942; children: Laura Ney, Robert Ellsworth, Susannah Brooks. BA, La. State U., 1961, JD, 1964. Bar: La. 1964, U.S. Supreme Ct. 1969. Assoc. Cavanaugh, Brame, Holt & Woodley, 1964-66, Holt & Woodley, Lake Charles, La., 1966-69; U.S. atty. U.S. Dept. Justice, Shreveport, La., 1969-77; lawyer Hargrove, Guyton, Ramey & Barlow, Shreveport, La., 1977-85; judge US Dist. Ct. (we. dist.) La., Monroe, 1985—92, Shreveport, La., 1993—2001, sr. judge, 2001—. Served with AUS, 1957-58. Office: US Dist Ct 300 Fannin St Ste 4200 Shreveport LA 71101-3122

WALTER, PAUL HERMANN LAWRENCE, chemistry professor; b. Jersey City, Sept. 22, 1934; s. Helmuth Justus and Adelaide C. J. (Twardy) W.; m. Grace Louise Carpenter, Aug. 25, 1956; children: Katherine Elizabeth Walter Bousquet, Marjorie Allison Walter Moran. BS, MIT, 1956; PhD, U. Kans., 1960. Rsch. scientist DuPont Cen. Rsch. Dept., Wilmington, Del., 1960-67; prof. chemistry Skidmore Coll., Saratoga Springs, NY, 1967-96, chair chemistry and physics, 1975-85, prof. emeritus, 1996—. Translator: (book) Foundations of Crystal Chemistry, 1968; contbr. articles to profl. jours. Named Wall of Fame, Stamford Ct. HS Conn., 2009. Fellow Chem. Inst. Can., Am. Chemical Soc.; mem. AAAS, AAUP (pres. 1984-86), Am. Chem. Soc. (bd. dirs. 1991-99, chmn. 1993-95, pres.-elect 1997, pres. 1998, Radding award 2002), Soc. Quimica de Mexico (hon.), Malta Conf. Found. (v.p. 2011-). Presbyterian. Achievements include patents in field. Home: 95 Skidaway Island Park Rd Apt 121 Savannah GA 31411-1112 E-mail: phlw@alum.mit.edu.

WALTER, VIRGINIA LEE, psychologist, educator; b. Temple, Tex., Oct. 30, 1937; d. Luther Patterson and Virginia Lafayette (Wilkins) W.; m. Glen Ellis, 1958 (div.); children: Glen Edward, David Walter; m. Robert Reinehr, 1963 (div.); 1 son, Charles Allen; m. Robert Bruininks, 1975 (div.). BS, U. Tex., Austin, 1959, MEd, 1967; postgrad. internship program in spl. Edn. Adminstrn., 1970; EdD, U. Houston, 1973. Prof. ednl. psychology dept. ednl. psychology U. Minn., Mpls., 1973-85; pres. Sch. Resource Ctr., Austin, Tex., 1985-90; tchr. Llano Pub. Schs., 1988-97; dir. Walter Resources, 1998—. Chmn. State Adv. Coun. for Inservice Tng. Regular Classroom Tchrs., 1977-79; cons. spl. ednl. various sch. dists., state depts. and agys. Editl. cons.: Jour. Ednl. Psychology, 1979, Reading Rsch. Quar., 1982; assoc. editor: Exceptional Children, 1979-84; assoc. editor Teaching Exceptional Children, 1985-89; contbr. articles to profl. jours., papers to profl. confs. Named Minn. Spl. Educator of Yr., 1978; recipient Svc. award Internat. Coun. Exceptional Children, 1978; HEW Office of Human Devel. Svcs. grantee, 1976-80; Dept. Edn. contractee, 1980-83 Mem. Coun. for Exceptional Children, Nat. Assn. Children with Learning Disabilities (dir. Minn. chpt. 1978-80), Nat. Assn. Retarded Citizens, AAUP, Assn. Supervision and Curriculum Devel. Home and Office: 7108 Running Rope Austin TX 78731-2128

WALTERS, ARTHUR SCOTT, neurologist, educator, clinical research scientist; b. Balt., Feb. 20, 1943; s. Charles Henry and Jean Vivian (Scott) W.; m. Bokyun Kim, May 18, 1985 (div. Oct. 1992); m. Lesley J. Gill, Dec. 19, 1992. BA, Kalamazoo Coll., 1965; MS, Northwestern U., 1967; MD, Wayne State U., 1972. Diplomate Am. Bd. Psychiatry and Neurology; diplomate Am. Bd. Sleep Medicine. Intern Oakwood Hosp., Dearborn, Mich., 1972-73; resident in neurology SUNY Downstate Med. Ctr., Bklyn., 1976-79; movement disorder fellow Neurol. Inst., NYC, 1982-84; asst. prof. neurology Robert Wood Johnson Med. Sch., U. Medicine & Dentistry NJ, New Brunswick, 1984-91, assoc. prof. neurology, 1991-99, clin. prof. neurology, 1999—2008; asst. chief divsn. neurology Lyons VA Med. Ctr., NJ, 1985-89, neurology cons., 1984-99; prof. neurosci. Seton Hall U. Sch. Grad. Med. Edn., South Orange, NJ, 1999—2008, NJ Neurosci. Inst., Edison, 1999—2008; prof. neurology Vanderbilt U. Sch. Medicine, Nashville, 2008—. Nat. chmn. med. adv. bd. Restless Legs Syndrome Found., 1992-98; chair Internat. Restless Legs Study Group, 1992-2007; head Restless Legs Syndrome and Periodic Limb Movement Coun. for the Nat. Sleep Found., 1994-96; neurology cons. Coney Island Hosp., Bklyn., Bklyn. Jewish Hosp., 1980-81; presenter in field. Contbr. articles to profl. publs., chpts. to books; organizer symposia. Named Rschr. of Yr. in medicine Seton Hall U. Sch. Grad. Med. Edn., 2003-04, Michael S. Aldrich hon. lectr. in sleep medicine for outstanding contbns. to patient care, rsch. and edn. U. Mich., 2006, Best Vol. neurology faculty member UMDNJ-Robert Wood Johnson Med. Sch., 2007; recipient Disting. Svc, award Internat. Restless Legs Syndrome Study Group, 2007, Tchg. award, Sleep Fellows and Cmty. Sleep Physicians NJ Neurosci. Inst. JFK Med. Ctr., 2008; grantee UMDNJ, 1984-86, VA RAG, 1985-86, Sandoz Corp., 1985-88, VA Merit Rev., 1989-98, Clemente Found., 1994-95, Purdue Pharma, 2000—, NIH, 2002-07, EKBOM award, Disting. Svc. award Restless Legs Syndrome Found., 1998, Bronze Oak LEAF Disting. Svc. award, Lyons Va. Med. Ctr, 1998, Disting. Faculty Medical License, Tenn., 2008, Excellence in Sleep Resch., Am. Acad. Neurology Sleep Sci. award, 2010, Vice Chairperson Speciality Com. Sleep Medicine, World Pediat. Chinese Medicine Socs., 2011-. Fellow Am. Acad. Neurology, Am. Acad. Sleep Medicine; editl. bd., (journal) Sleep, Sleep Medicine; mem. AAAS, Am. Neurol. Assn., Sleep Rsch. Soc., Movement Disorder Soc., NY Acad. Scis., NJ Sleep Soc. (sec. 1995-96, treas. 1996-97, v.p. 1998-99). Achievements include Formed the first med. advisory bd. of the Restless Legs Syndrome Found; formed the Int. RLS study group compriseed of 130 physicians & scientists from 17 countries dedicated to resch on RLS & Periodic Limb Movements in sleep. Office: Dept Neurology Vanderbilt Univ Sch Medicine MCN A-0118 1161 21st Ave S Nashville TN 37232-2551 Office Phone: 615-322-0283. Personal E-mail: artumdnj@aol.com. Business E-Mail: arthur.walters@vanderbilt.edu.

WALTERS, JOHNNIE MCKEIVER, lawyer; b. Hartsville, SC, Dec. 20, 1919; s. Tommie Ellis and Lizzie Lee (Grantham) W.; m. Donna Lucile Hall, Sept. 1, 1947; children: Donna Dianne Walters Gent, Lizbeth Kathern Walters Kukorowski, Hilton Horace, John Roy. AB, Furman U., 1942, LLD (hon.), 1973; LLB, U. Mich., 1948. Bar: Mich. 1948, N.Y. 1955, S.C. 1961, D.C. 1973. Atty. office chief counsel IRS, Washington, 1949-53; asst. mgr. tax div. law dept. Texaco, Inc., NYC, 1953-61; ptnr. firm Geer, Walters & Demo, Greenville, SC, 1961-69; asst. atty. gen. tax div. Dept. Justice, Washington, 1969-71; commr. IRS, 1971-73; ptnr. firm Hunton & Williams, Washington, 1973-79, Leatherwood Walker Todd & Mann, P.C., Greenville, 1979-95; exec. v.p., gen. counsel Colonial Trust Co., Greenville, 1996—2005; ret., 2006. Bd. dirs. Textile Hall Corp., Greenville, Colonial Trust Co. Mem. S.C. Coun. on Competitiveness, 1987—91, S.C. Ethics Commn., 2005—08. With USAF, 1942—45. Fellow Am. Coll. Tax Counsel (founding regent), Am. Coll. Trust and Estate Counsel, Am. Bar Found., S.C. Bar Found. (bd. dirs. 1988-92); mem. ABA (taxation sect.), S.C. Bar (chmn. taxation sect. 1983-84), Rotary (pres. local club 1968-69, Frances Legion of Honor medal, 2012). Republican. Baptist. Home: 50 Arboretum Ln Apt 215 Greenville SC 29617

WALTERS, LYNDA HENLEY, family and human development professor; b. St. Louis, Nov. 23, 1942; d. Fred Louis and Bernice Chilton Henley; m. Walters James, May 25, 1975; children: Connor Maithe Walters-Dutton, Chris Meyers, Anna Walters Morgan. BS in Christian Edn., Presbyn. Sch. Edn., Richmond, Va., 1964; MS, Okla. State U., Stillwater, 1972; PhD in Child and Family Devel., U. Ga., Athens, 1978. Lectr. U. Guelph, Ontario, Canada, 1972—74; staff devel. specialist Coop. Edn. Svc. Agy., Atlanta, 1974—75; assoc. dean, prof. U. Ga., Athens, 1982—. Contbr. articles to profl. jours. Recipient Tchg. award, Coll. Family and Consumer Scis., U. Ga., 1985, 1990, Disting. Svc. to Families award, Southeastern Coun. Family Rels., 1995, Family & Consumer Scis. Alumni Award, Coll. Family and Consumer Scis. Alumna Assn., 1996, Creswell award, 1996, Disting. Alumna award, Okla. State U., 1998, Commemorative Lectr. award, Am. Assn. Family and Consumer Scis., 1999, Top Three Paper award, Internat. Comm. Assn., 2001, sr. tchg. fellow, U. Ga., 2001—02. Mem.: Internat. Sociol. Assn., European Sociol. Assn., Soc. Rsch. Adolescence, Nat. Coun. Family Rels. (pres. 1990—91). D-Liberal. Avocations: photography, poetry. Office: Univ Ga Dawson Hall Athens GA 30602

WALTERS, MICHAEL P., state legislator; Grad., NC State U. Sec., treas. Claybourn Walters Logging Co., 1978—2002, pres., 2003—; farmer; state senator Dist. 13 NC, 2009—. Bd. dirs. NC State U. Wolfpack Club. Democrat. Office: NC Senate 16 W Jones St Rm 1118 Raleigh NC 27601-2808 Address: PO Box 26 Proctorville NC 28375 Office Phone: 919-733-5651. E-mail: Michael.Walters@ncleg.net.

WALTERS, ROBERT C., electric power industry executive, lawyer; b. Gene Autry, Okla., Mar. 28, 1958; BA, U. Tex., 1980, JD, 1983. Bar: Tex. 1983, U.S. Supreme Ct., U.S. Ct. Appeals, Fifth and Ninth Cir., U.S. Dist. Ct., No., So., and Ea. Dist. Tex. Sr. ptnr. Vinson & Elkins LLP, Dallas, 2008; exec. v.p., gen. counsel Energy Future Holdings Corp., 2008—. Adj. prof. Southern Meth. U.; mem. Dallas Citizens Coun., Dallas Assembly, Woodall Rodgers Park Found. Office: Energy Future Holdings Corp 1601 Bryan St Dallas TX 75201 Office Phone: 214-812-4600. Business E-Mail: robert.walters@energyfutureholdings.com.

WALTERS, SUE FOX, broadcast executive, accountant; b. Louisville, June 9, 1941; d. Thomas Burke and Reva Crick Fox; m. Hugh Alexander Walters (dec. 2001); children: Thomas Wade Walters, Alexandra Walters Ebling. Student, N.C. State U., Ky. Wesleyan Coll. Acct., paralegal for fin. instns. and firms; ct. adminstr. 45th Jud. Cir. Ct., Ky.; v.p., treas. Alexander and Assocs., CATV cons. firm, Greenville, Ky.; corp. adminstr., pub. corp. Bellevue, Wash.; sr. acctg. specialist Japanese/Am. Automotive Mfg. Co., Bowling Green, Ky.; land developer. Pres., Jr. Woman's Club Greenville, 1964-65, Woman's Club of Greenville, 1976-78; vice gov. 2d dist. Ky. Fedn. Women's Clubs, 1980. Avocations: interior decorating, flying, antiques. Home: 151 N Main St Greenville KY 42345-1503

WALTERS, THOMAS R., gas and power company executive; b. Hammond, Ind. B in Mech. Engring., Vanderbilt U.; M in Ocean Engring., Tex. A&M U. Joined Exxon U.S.A., LA, 1978; v.p., Africa ExxonMobil Develop. Co., 1999, exec. v.p., 2007—09; v.p., US Exxon Prod. Co., 2002; pres. ExxonMobil Global Services Co., 2005; v.p. & pres. Exxon Gas & Power Marketing Co., 2009—. Office: Exxon Mobil 5959 Las Colinas Blvd Irving TX 75039-2298

WALTHER, BARBARA ANN LANE, judge, former lawyer; b. San Angelo, Tex., Oct. 6, 1952; d. James Franklin and Dorothy Ann (Watson) Lane; m. Stevem Milton Walther, June 15, 1974; children: Katherine Ann, Stewart Lane. AA, Stephens Coll., 1972; BA, U. Tex., 1975; JD, Southern Meth. U., 1977. Bar: Tex. 1977, US Dist. Ct. (no. dist.) Tex. 1977. Law clk. Regional Atty. HEW, Dallas, 1976-77; pvt. law practice Dallas, 1977-83, San Angelo, Tex., 1985-87; assoc. Davis, Wardlas & Hay, San Angelo, 1983-85; family law master Tom Green County, San Angelo, 1987—92; dist. judge Tex. 51st Dist. Ct., 1992—. Mem. San Angelo Lake Bd., 1985-87; bd. dirs. San Angelo Nature Ctr., 1991—; v.p. El Camino Girl Scouts, San Angelo, 1988, Acad. Excellence Found., San Angelo, 1990. Mem. State Bar of Tex. (family law sect., litigation sect., Coll. of State Bar 1990), Carrolton Farmers Br. Lawyers Assn. (pres. 1982), Tom Green County Bar Assn. (sec.-treas. 1990), San Angelo Jr. League. Republican. Methodist. Avocation: scuba diving. Office: Tex 51st Dist Ct 112 W Beauregard San Angelo TX 76903-5850 Office Phone: 325-659-6571. Office Fax: 325-658-8046.

WALTON, ALICE LOUISE, philanthropist, art collector; b. Newport, Ark., Oct. 7, 1949; d. Samuel Moore and Helen (Robson) Walton. BBA, Trinity U., 1971; D in Bus. Adminstrn. (hon.), S.W. Bapt. U., 1988. Investment analyst First Commerce Corp., New Orleans, 1972-75; dir., v.p. investments Walton Enterprises, Bentonville, Ark., 1975—; retail & investment broker E.F. Hutton Co., New Orleans, 1975-79; vice chair, investment dir. Walton Bank Group, Bentonville, Ark., 1982-88; founder, former pres., chair, CEO Llama Co./Llama Asset Mgmt. Co., Fayetteville, Ark. Mem. dean's adv. coun. U. Ark. Coll. Bus. Adminstrn., Fayetteville, 1989—90. Bd. trustees Amon Carter Mus., Ft. Worth. Named Arkansan of Yr., Ark. Easter Seals Soc., 1990; named a Disting. Bus. Lectr., Ctrl. State U., Edmond, Okla., 1989; named one of The Top 100 Women in Ark., Ark. Bus., 1995, The Top 200 Collectors, ARTnews mag., 2006—, The Forbes 400: Richest Americans, 1999—, The World's Richest People, Forbes mag., 2001—, The 100 Most Powerful Women, Forbes Mag., 2011, The 100 Most Influential People in the World, TIME mag., 2012. Mem.: N.W. Ark. Coun. (first chairperson 1990). Republican. Avocations: horse racing, art collector.

WALTON, ANDREW SCOTT, medical products executive; Ptnr. Subsidium Health Advisors, 2002—05; v.p., strategic planning Laboratory Corp. of America Holdings, 2005—06, chief info. officer, 2006—08, exec. v.p., strategic planning, corp. devel., 2007, exec. v.p., esoteric businesses (Nat. Genetics Inst., Colo. Coagulation, Viro-Med, Endocrine Sciences). Office: Laboratory Corp of America Holdings 358 S Main St Burlington NC 27215 Office Phone: 336-229-1127. Office Fax: 336-436-1205. Business E-Mail: waltona@labcorp.com.

WALTON, CHARLES MICHAEL, civil engineering educator; b. Hickory, NC, July 28, 1941; s. Charles O. and Virginia Ruth (Hart) W.; m. Betty Grey Hughes; children: Susan, Camila, Michael, Gantt. BS, Va. Mil. Inst., 1963; MCE, N.C. State U., 1969, PhD, 1971. Research asst. N.C. State U., Raleigh, 1967-71; transp. planning engr. N.C. Hwy. Commn., Raleigh, 1970-71; asst. prof. civil engring. U. Tex., Austin, 1971-76, assoc. prof., 1976-83, prof., 1983—, Bess Harris Jones Centennial prof. natural resource policy studies, 1987-91, Paul D. and Betty Robertson Meek Centennial prof. engring., 1991-93, Ernest H. Cockrell Centennial chair engring., 1993—, chmn. dept. civil engring., 1988-96. Transp. cons., 1970—; assoc. dir. Ctr. for Transp. Rsch. U. Tex., 1980-88; chmn., exec. com. Transp. Rsch. Bd., NRC, 1991, Disting. Lectr., 1994. Contbr. articles to profl. jours. Past chmn. Urban Transp. Commn., Austin. Recipient Disting. Engring. award N.C. State U., 1995, Joe J. King Profl. Engring. Achievement award U. Tex. at Austin, 1995-96, W.N. Carey Jr. Disting. Svc. award Transp. Rsch. Bd., 1998, George S. Bartlett award AASHTO, Transp. Rsch. Bd., ARTBA, 2000, Disting. Contbns. to Univ. Transp. Edn. and Rsch. award Coun. Univ. Transp. Ctrs., 2005; named to Am.'s Top 100 Pvt. Sector Transp. Design and Constrn. Profls. of 20th Century, 2004, Am. Rd. and Transp. Builders Assn., 2005. Fellow ASCE (Harland Bartholomew urban planning award 1987, Frank M. Masters transp. engring. award 1987, James Laurie prize 1992, Francis C. Turner lectr. 1999, Outstanding Projects and Leaders award, 2005), Inst. Transp. Engrs.; mem. NSPE, NAE, Intelligent Transp. Soc. Am. (tech. coord. coun., past chair bd. dirs., past chair tech. coord. coun.), Am. Rd. and Transp. Assn. (western v.p., past pres. edn. divsn., 1st vice chair, named to Am.'s Top 100 Pvt. Sector Transp. Design and Constrn. Profls. of 20th Century), Am. Rd. and Transp. Builders Assn. (chmn.), Soc. Automotive Engrs., Urban Land Inst., Inst. for Ops. Rsch. and Mgmt. Scis., Soc. Am. Mil. Engrs., Internat. Rd. Fedn. (bd. dirs.), Internat. Rd. Ednl. Found. (bd. dirs.), Austin C. of C. (Leadership Austin program). Democrat. Methodist. Home: 3404 River Rd Austin TX 78703-1031 Office: U Tex Dept Civil Engring Dept Civil Engring ECJ Hall Ste 6 3 Austin TX 78712 Home Phone: 512-477-9258; Office Phone: 512-471-1414. Business E-Mail: cmwalton@mail.utexas.edu.

WALTON, GIB (DAN GIBSON WALTON), lawyer; b. Houston, Mar. 26, 1950; s. Dan Edward and Lucy Frances (Gibson) Walton; m. Martha Sandlin, June 24, 1972; children: Cole Gibson, Emily Wyatt. BA with honors, U. Va., 1972; JD with honors, U. Tex. Sch. Law, 1975. Bar: Tex. 1975, US Supreme Ct. 2001, US Dist. Ct. (no., so., ea. and we. dists.) Tex., US Ct. Appeals (2d, 4th, 5th, 7th and DC cirs.); cert. specialist civil trial law Tex. Bd. Legal Specialization, 1982. Law clk. to hon. Malcolm R. Wilkey US Ct. Appeals (DC cir.), 1975-76;

assoc. Vinson & Elkins LLP, Houston, 1976-82, ptnr., 1982—2009; ptnr. litig. practice Hogan Lovells US LLP, Houston, 2009—. Mem. admissions com. US Dist. Ct. (so. dist.) Tex., 1999—2005, chair US Magistrate Judge selection com., 2003. Bd. dirs. Brookwood Cmty. & Briarwood Sch., Brookshire, Tex., 1991—, Tex. Equal Access to Justice Found., 2000—06; bd. dirs., sec. Meth. Hosp., Houston. Recipient Karen H. Susman Jurisprudence award, Anti-Defamation League, 2009; named a Tex. Super Lawyer, Law & Politics mag., 2003—10. Fellow: American Bar Found., Tex. Bar Found. (chair-elect 2010—11), Houston Bar Found. (chair 1994—95), American Coll. Trial Lawyers, Internat. Soc. Barristers; mem.: Tex. Assn. Appellate & Civil Trial Specialists, Garland Walker American Inn of Ct., Internat. Assn. Def. Counsel, Houston Bar Assn. (pres. 1998—99), State Bar Tex. (bd. dirs. 1999—2002, pres. 2007—08, Michael J. Crowley award 2002, Judge Sam Williams Leadership award 2003, President's award 2003), American Bd. Trial Advocates, Phi Beta Kappa (Outstanding Alumnus award 2007). Avocations: golf, skiing. Office: Hogan Lovells US LLP 700 Louisiana St Ste 4300 Houston TX 77002 Office Phone: 713-758-2026, 713-632-1435. Office Fax: 713-632-1401. E-mail: gib.walton@hoganlovells.com.

WALTON, JIM CARR, bank executive; b. 1948; s. Sam Moore and Helen Walton; m. Lynne Walton; 4 children. Grad., U. Ark. Pres., chmn., CEO Arvest Bank, Bentonville, Ark. At-large exec. com. mem. Ark. Coun. Econ. Edn.; mem. dean's exec. adv. bd. Sam M. Walton Coll. Bus. Mem. nat. bd. advs. Children's Scholarship Fund. Named one of World's Richest People, Forbes Mag., 2001—, Forbes 400: Richest Americans, 2006—. Office: 125 W Central Ste 218 Bentonville AR 72712

WALTON, ROB (SAMUEL ROBSON WALTON), retail executive; b. Tulsa, Oct. 28, 1944; s. Sam Moore and Helen Walton; m. Carolyn Walton (div.); 3 children. Student, Wooster Coll.; BA in Acctg., U. Ark., 1966; JD, Columbia Law Sch., 1969. Atty. Conner, Winters, Ballaine, Barry & McGowen; with Wal-Mart Stores Inc., Bentonville, Ark., 1969, sr. v.p., 1978-82, vice chmn., 1982-92; chmn. Wal-Mart Stores, Inc., Bentonville, Ark., 1992—. Bd. dirs. Wal-Mart Stores, Inc., 1978—. Trustee Wooster Coll.; bd. dirs. Walton Family Found. Inc., Enterprise Corp. of the Delta. Named one of The World's Richest People, Forbes Mag., 2005—, The Forbes 400: Richest Americans, 2006—. Avocations: bicycling, pheasant hunting. Office: Wal-Mart Stores Inc 702 SW 8th St Bentonville AR 72716-0299*

WALTRIP, ROBERT L., funeral company executive; b. Austin, Tex., 1931; BBA in Mgmt., U. Houston, 1954. With Heights Funeral Home, 1954—62; founder, chmn. bd. Service Corp. International, Houston, 1962—; CEO Service Corp. Internat., Houston, 1962—2005; founder, chmn. bd. dirs. Waltrip Enterprises, Inc., Houston, 1982—; with Tanknology Corp. Internat., Houston, 1988, Tanknology Environ. Inc., Houston, 1989. Office: Service Corp International 1929 Allen Pky Houston TX 77019-2507 also: Tanknology Environ Inc 5225 Hollister St Houston TX 77040-6205

WALTRIP, W. BLAIR, financial consultant; b. 1955; s. R.L. Waltrip. Various positions including v.p., corp. devel., sr. v.p. funeral ops. & exec. v.p. real estate divsn. Svc. Corp. Internat., 1977—2000, chmn., pres. Svc. Corp. Internat. Ltd. Canada, 1990—99. Bd. dirs. Svc. Corp. Internat., 1986—, TEI, Inc., 1988—99, Sanders Morris Harris Group Inc., 1999—. Mailing: c/o Svc Corp Internat 1929 Allen Pky Houston TX 77019 Office Phone: 206-575-7547.

WALZ, CARL E., manufacturing executive; b. Cleve., Sept. 6, 1955; m. Pamela J. Glady; 2 children. BS in Physics, Ky. State U., 1977; MS in Solid State Physics, John Carroll U., 1979. Advanced through grades to col. USAF, commd. 2d lt., 1977; with Atomic Energy Detection Sys. 1155th Tech. Ops. Squadron, McClellan AFB, Calif., 1979—82; flight test engr. USAF Test Pilot Sch., Edwards AFB, Calif., 1983—84, F-16 Combined Test Force, Edwards AFB, Calif., 1984—87; flight test mgr. Detachment 3 Air Force Flight Test Ctr., 1987—90; mission specialist STS-108 Endeavour, Internat. Space Sta., 2001—02; now mgr., Life Support and Habitation program, Exploration Systems Mission Directorate NASA, Washington, astronaut Houston, 1990—2003, dir., Advanced Capabilities Divsn., 2005—08; v.p., Human Space Flight Operation Orbital Sciences Corp., 2008—. Recipient Disting. Alumnus award, Kent State U., 1997, Carroll Univ., 2002, Gagarin award, Nat. Aeronautic Assn., 2003; named to, Ohio Vets. Hall of Fame. Mem.: Kent State U. Alumni Assn., Am. Legion. Achievements include logged over 231 days in space; mission specialist STS-51 Discovery (1993); Orbiter flight engr. STS-65 Columbia (1994); U.S. record for 196 days in space; mission specialist STS-79 Atlantis (1996). Avocations: piano, vocal music, sports, lead singer MAX-Q (rock-n-roll band). Office: Orbital Sciences Corp 21839 Atlantic Blvd Sterling VA 20166 Office Phone: 703-406-5000. Office Fax: 703-406-3506. Business E-Mail: walz.carl@orbital.com.

WALZ, JEFF (JEFFREY J. WALZ), women's college basketball coach; b. 1971; s. Roger and Janine Walz; m. Kim Kumfer, May 17, 2003; children: Kaeley Thöney, Jacob Joseph. BS in Secondary Edn. and Bus., No. Ky. U., 1995; MEd, Western Ky. U. Adminstrv. asst. Western Ky. U., asst. coach, 1995—97, U. Nebr., 1997—2001, U. Minn., 2001—02, U. Md., 2002—06, assoc. head coach, 2006—07; head coach U. Louisville, 2007—. Office: Univ Louisville Athletic Dept Womens Basketball 2100 S Floyd St Louisville KY 40292

WAMPLER, KEVIN S., corporate financial executive; BSBA in Acctg., Mich. Technol. Inst., 1986. CPA. Audit mgr., nat. acctg. Ernst & Young LLP, 1986—93; corp. contr. The Finish Line, 1997—2001, asst. sec., 1997—2008, sr.v.p., chief acctg. officer, 2000—03, chief acctg. officer, 2001—03, exec. v.p., CFO, 2003—08; CFO, prin. fin. & acctg. officer Dollar Tree Stores, Inc., 2008—. Office: Dollar Tree Inc 500 Volvo Pky Chesapeake VA 23320 Office Phone: 757-321-5000. Office Fax: 757-321-5111. Business E-Mail: kevin.wampler@dollartree.com.

WAMUTOMBO, DIKEMBE MUTOMBO MPOLONDO MUKAMBA JEAN JACQUE See MUTOMBO, DIKEMBE

WANDERS, HANS WALTER, banker; b. Aachen, Germany, Apr. 3, 1925; came to US, 1929, naturalized, 1943; s. Herbert and Anna Maria (Kusters) W.; m. Elizabeth Knox Kimball, Apr. 2, 1949; children: Crayton Kimball, David Gillette. BS, Yale U., 1947, Ga. Inst. Tech., 1945; postgrad., Rutgers U., 1961—64. With GE, 1947-48, Libbey-Owens-Ford Glass Co., 1948-53, Allied Chem. Co., 1953-55, McKinsey & Co., Inc., 1955-57; from asst. cashier to v.p. No. Trust Co., Chgo., 1957-65; v.p. Nat. Blvd. Bank, Chgo., 1965-66, pres., 1966-70; exec. v.p. Wachovia Bank & Trust Co., N.A., Winston-Salem, NC, 1970-74, chmn., 1977-85, vice chmn., 1985-88, also bd. dirs.; pres. Wachovia Corp., Winston-Salem, 1974-76, 85-87, chmn., 1977-85, vice chmn., 1987-88, also bd. dirs.; pres., chief exec. officer 1st Wachovia Corp. Services, Inc., Winston-Salem, 1986-88; dir. Exxon Supply Co., 1989-94, Goody's Mfg. Corp., 1989-94, Gulf Resources, Inc., 1989-92, Turnpike Properties, Inc., 2001—. Chmn. Winston-Salem Found. Com., 1981-82; bd. dirs. NC Textile Found., NC Engring. Found., Inc., 1971-88; trustee, mem. exec. com. Salem Coll. and Acad., 1986-91, Tax Found., 1982—, vice chmn., 1984-86, chmn., 1986-88, chmn. exec. com., 1989; mem. bd. visitors Fuqua Sch. Bus., Duke U., 1978-89, NC Japan Ctr., 1982—; mem. nat. corps. com. United Negro Coll. Fund; mem., chmn. NC Bd. Econ. Devel., 1989-93; corporator Belmont Hill Sch., 1996—. Lt. USNR, 1943-46, 51-53. Mem. Am. Bankers Assn. (chmn. mktg. divsn. 1979-80, dir. 1971-73), Assn. Res. City Bankers, Conf. Bd. (So. regional adv. coun.), Assn. Bank Holding Cos. (bd. dirs., exec. com. 1981-83), Chgo. Club, Commonwealth Club Chgo., Twin-City Club Winston Salem, Old Town Club Winston-Salem Home: 10 Graylyn Pl Winston Salem NC 27106 Office: Wachovia Corp 420 W 4th St Ste 202-A Winston Salem NC 27101-2837 Home Phone: 336-816-5080; Office Phone: 336-761-5016. Personal E-mail: hwander98@yahoo.com.

WANG, TAYLOR GUNJIN, science administrator, educator, astronaut; b. Shanghai, June 16, 1940; came to U.S., 1963; m. Beverly Fung, 1966; children: Kenneth, Eric. BS, UCLA, 1967, MS, 1968, PhD, 1971. Mgr. microgravity sci. and applications program Jet Propulsion Lab., Pasadena, Calif., 1972-88, cons., 1987-89; Space Shuttle astronaut-scientist NASA, 1983-85; Centennial prof., dir. Ctr. for Microgravity Rsch. and Applications Vanderbilt U., Nashville, 1988—, Centennial Prof. of Mechanical Engring. emeritus, Centennial Prof. of Materials Sci. and Engring. emeritus. Crew mem. STS-51B Mission (Challenger)-first operational Spacelab Mission, 1985. Contbr. of several articles to profl. jours. Bd. dirs. Com. of 100. Fellow Acoustical Soc. Am.; mem. AIAA, Am. Phys. Soc., Assn. Space Explorers-USA (pres. 1988), Sigma Xi. Achievements include first person of Chinese descent to travel in space; invention of acoustic levitation and manipulation chamber for the DDM; patents in field. Business E-Mail: taylor.wang@vanderbilt.edu.

WANG, XIAODONG, biomedical researcher, educator; b. 1963; BS in Biology, Beijing Normal U., 1984; PhD in Biochemistry, U. Tex. Southwestern Med. Ctr., Dallas, 1991. Fellow Damon Runyon-Walter Winchell Cancer Rsch. Fund, 1991; George L. MacGregor disting. chair, prof. biomedical sci. U. Tex. Southwestern Med. Ctr., Dallas, 1991—; investigator Howard Hughes Med. Inst., 1997—. Contbr. article to profl. jours. Recipient Wilson S. Stone Meml. award, Anderson Cancer Ctr., Eli Lilly award, Am. Chem. Soc., 2000, Paul Marks prize, Meml. Sloan-Kettering Cancer Ctr., 2001, Norman Hackerman award in Chemical Rsch., Welch Found., 2002, Shaw prize in Life Sci. and Medicine, Shaw Found., Hong Kong, 2006. Mem.: NAS (Award in Molecular Biology 2004, Richard Lounsbery award 2007), Soc. Chinese Biomed. Scientists in Am. (Young Investigator award 1999), Ray Wu Soc., Am. Soc. Cell Biology, Am. Soc. Biochemistry and Molecular Biology (Schering-Plough award 2000), Am. Assn. Cancer Rsch. (Outstanding Achievement in Cancer Rsch. 2004). Office: Univ Tex Southwestern Med Ctr Dallas/Biomed Sci 5323 Harry Hines Blvd Dallas TX 75390-9038

WANI, MANSUKHLAL CHHAGANLAL, chemist; b. Nandurbar, Maharastra, India, Feb. 20, 1925; came to U.S., 1958, naturalized, 1977; s. Chhagnalal Kikabhai and Maniben Chhanganlal (Shah) W.; m. Ramila Mansukhlal Dalal, Dec. 4, 1954; 1 child, Bankim M. BS with honors, St. Xavier's Coll., Bombay U., 1947, MS, 1950; PhD, Ind. U., 1962. Lectr. chemistry Bhavan's Coll., Bombay, 1951-58; rsch. asst. Ind. U., Bloomington, 1958-61; rsch. assoc. U. Wis., Madison, 1961-62; prin. scientist Rsch. Triangle Inst., Rsch. Triangle Park, NC, 1962—. Inventor anticancer drugs. Recipient B.F. Cain Meml. award Am. Assn. Cancer Rsch., 1994, City of Medicine award Durham, N.C., 1994, Award of Recognition Nat. Cancer Inst., 1996, Charles E. Kettering prize GM Cancer Rsch. Found., 2000, Ranbaxy Rsch. award. Mem. AAAS, Am. Chem. Soc., Am. Soc. Pharmacognosy, N.Y. Acad. Scis., India Assn. (pres. 1970-72), Hindu Soc. (dir. 1976-81), Assn. Indians in Am., Indo-Am. Forum, Sigma Xi, Phi Lambda Upsilon. Democrat. Avocations: reading, travel, sports. Home: 2801 Legion Ave Durham NC 27707-1921 Office: Rsch Triangle Inst 3040 W Cornwallis Rd Research Triangle Park NC 27709-2194 Home Phone: 919-489-2573; Office Phone: 919-541-6685. Business E-Mail: mcw@rti.org.

WANNER, ADAM, medical educator; b. Budapest, Apr. 16, 1940; MD, U. Basel, Switzerland, 1966. Diplomate Am. Bd. Internal Medicine. Prof. medicine U. Miami, 1985—. Mem.: Am. Thoracic Soc. (pres.). Office: 1600 NW 10 Ave # 7052 Miami FL 33136 Office Phone: 305-243-3045. Office Fax: 305-243-6992. Business E-Mail: awanner@miami.edu.

WANNSTEDT, DAVID RAYMOND, professional football coach, former college football coach; b. Pitts., May 21, 1952; m. Jan Wannstedt; children: Keri, Jami. Grad., U. Pitts., 1974. Player Green Bay Packers, 1974; grad. asst. U. Pitts. Panthers, 1975—76, receivers & spl. teams coach, 1977—78, head coach, 2004—10; defensive line coach Okla. State U. Cowboys, 1979-82, U. So. Calif. Trojans, 1983-85; defensive. coord. U. Miami Hurricanes, 1986-89; def. coord. Dallas Cowboys, 1989-93; head coach Chgo. Bears, 1993-98; asst. head coach Miami Dolphins, 1999-2000, head coach, 2000—04; spl. asst. to the athletic dir. U. Pitts., 2010—11; assoc. head coach, inside linebackers coach Buffalo Bills, 2011, defensive coord., 2012; spl. teams coord. Tampa Bay Buccaneers, 2013—. Named to NCAA 2nd team All-East, NFL Coach of the Year UPI, Football News, 1994; inducted into Western Pa. Hall of Fame, 1990. Office: Tampa Bay Buccaneers One Buccaneer Pl Tampa FL 33607

WANTLAND, WILLIAM CHARLES, retired bishop, lawyer; b. Edmond, Okla., Apr. 14, 1934; s. William Lindsay and Edna Louise (Yost) W. BA, U. Hawaii, 1957; JD, Okla. City U., 1967; D in Religion, Geneva Theol. Coll., Knoxville, Tenn., 1976; DD (hon.), Nashotah House, Wis., 1983, Seabury-Western Sem., Evanston, Ill., 1983. With FBI, various locations, 1954-59, Ins. Co. of N.Am., Oklahoma City, 1960-62; law clk.-atty. Bishop & Wantland, Seminole, Okla., 1962-77; vicar St. Mark's Ch., Seminole, 1963-77, St. Paul's Ch., Holdenville, Okla., 1974-77; presiding judge Seminole Mcpl. Ct., 1970-77; atty. gen. Seminole Nation of Okla., 1969-72, 75-77; exec. dir. Okla. Indian Rights Assn., Norman, 1972-73; rector St. John's Ch., Oklahoma City, 1977-80; bishop Episcopal Diocese of Eau Claire, Wis., 1980-99; interim bishop of Navajoland, 1993-94; ret., 1999. Adj. prof. Law Sch. U. Okla., Norman, 1970-78; instr. canon law Nashotah House, 1983-97, 2004-09; nat. coun. Evang. and Cath. Mission, Chgo., 1977-90; mem. Episcopal Commn. on Racism, 1990-92, Episcopal Coun. Indian Ministries, 1990-95, Standing Commn. on Constn. and Canons, 1992-95; assisting bishop Diocese of Dallas, 2002—04, of Ft. Worth, 2000—. Author: Foundations of the Faith, 1982, Canon Law of the Episcopal Church, 1984, The Prayer Book and the Catholic Faith, 1994; The Catholic Faith, The Episcopal Church and the Ordination of Women, 1997; co-author: Oklahoma Probate Forms, 1971; contbr. articles to profl. jours. Pres. Okla. Conf. Mcpl. Judges, 1973; v.p. South African Ch. Union, 1985-95; trustee Nashotah House, Wis., 1981—, chmn., 1992-98; bd. dirs. SPEAK, Eureka Springs, Ark., 1983-89; Wis. adv. com. US Civil Rights Commn., 1990-91; support com. Native Am. Rights Fund, 1990—; coun. mem. City of Seminole, Okla., 2002—, vice mayor, 2003—; co-chmn. Luth.-Anglican-Roman Cath. Commn. of Wis., 1989-95; pres. Wis. Episc. Conf., 1995-97, Wis. Coun. Chs., 1985-86; active Living Ch. Found., 1981-02; bd. dirs. Seminole Nation Hist. Soc., 1999—, pres., 2006—; adv. bd. Seminole Hist. Soc., 2003—. Recipient Most Outstanding Contbn. to Law and Order award Okla. Supreme Ct., 1975, Outstanding Alumnus award Okla. City U., 1980, Wis. Equal Rights Coun. award, 1986, Manitou Ikwe award Indian Alcoholism Coun., 1988, Episcopal Synod Pres.'s award, 1995, 2004. Mem. Okla. Bar Assn., Okla. Indian Bar Assn., Oklahoma City Law Sch. Alumni Assn. (pres. 1968), Ct. Indian Offenses Seminole Nation Okla. (chief magistrate 2006—). Democrat. Anglican. Avocations: canoeing, skin-diving, cross country skiing. Personal E-mail: puca382@mbo.net, puca382@suddenlink.net.

WARD, AARON, sportscaster, retired professional hockey player; b. Windsor, Ont., Canada, Jan. 17, 1973; Student in comm., U. Mich., Ann Arbor, 1990—93. Defenseman Detroit Red Wings, 1993—2001, Carolina Hurricanes, 2001—06, 2009—10, NY Rangers, 2006—07, Boston Bruins, 2007—09, Anaheim Ducks, 2010; NHL studio analyst TSN, 2010—; founding ptnr. CanAm Global Energy Solutions, LLC, 2010—. Investor BioLumix, Inc., 2006—. Achievements include being a member of Stanley Cup Champion Detroit Red Wings, 1997, 1998, Carolina Hurricanes, 2006. Office: CanAm Globales Inc 8450 Chapel Hill Rd Ste 203 Cary NC 27513

WARD, CAM, professional hockey player; b. Sherwood Park, Atla., Canada, Feb. 29, 1984; s. Ken and Laurel Ward; m. Cody Ward; 1 child, Nolan. Goalie Lowell Lock Monsters (AHL), 2004—05, Carolina Hurricanes, 2005—. Recipient Conn Smythe Trophy, 2006. Achievements include being a member of Stanley Cup Champion Carolina Hurricanes, 2006; tying the record for playoff wins by a rookie goalie, 2006. Office: Carolina Hurricanes RBC Ctr 1400 Edwards Mill Rd Raleigh NC 27607

WARD, CAMERON (ROBERT CAMERON WARD, CAM WARD), state legislator; b. Milton, Fla., Mar. 24, 1971; m. Julie Ward; 1 child, Riley. BS in Internat. Rels. & Polit. Sci., Troy State U., 1993; JD, Samford U., 1996. Polit. staff asst. Ala. Republicam Party Headquarters, Birmingham, 1994-96; dep. atty. gen. State of Ala., Montgomery, 1996-97, confidential asst. to sec. state, 1998; dist. dir. to Rep. Spencer Bachus US House of Representatives, Birmingham, 1998—2001; exec. dir. Indsl. Devel. Bd., Alabaster, Ala., 2001—; mem. Dist. 49 Ala. House of Reps., Montgomery, 2002—10; mem. Dist. 14 Ala. State Senate, Montgomery, 2010—. Mem. Westwood Bapt. Ch., Hoover, Ala.; bd. mem. Leadership Shelby County, Greater Edn. Found. Shelby County, The American Village, CASA Shelby County. Mem. Ala. Bar Assn., Shelby County Rep. Exec. Com. (fin. chmn.), Shelby County Young Reps. (officer), Shelby County GOP Club (chmn.), Republican State Exec. Com., Alabaster Rotary Club, North Shelby County C. of C. Republican. Baptist. Office: Alabama State Senate Ala State House 11 S Union St Rm 625-C Montgomery AL 36130 also: 201 1st St N Alabaster AL 35007 Office Phone: 205-664-6848, 334-242-7750. Business E-Mail: camjulward@aol.com.

WARD, DONALD PATRICK, obstetrician, gynecologist; MD, Baylor U., 1980. Lic. Tex., 1980, diplomate American Bd. Ob-Gyn, 2006. Resident ob-gyn. Baylor Coll. of Medicine, 1980—84; hosp. affiliations include St. David's Med. Ctr., South Austin Hosp., Univ. Med. Ctr. Brackenridge, St. David's South Austin Med. Ctr. Fellow: American Congress of Obstetricians and Gynecologists. Office: St David's South Austin Medical Center 901 W Ben White Blvd Austin TX 78704-6903 Office Phone: 512-447-2211.*

WARD, FELKER W., JR., investment company executive; Grad., Tuskegee Inst.; JD, Emory U. Bus. and fin. lawyer; civilian aide emeritus to sec. of army; co-founder, vice chmn. & pres. Concessions Internat., Inc., 1979—; pres. Ward & Associates, Inc., 1988—; chmn. Ward Bradford & Co. LP, 1992—96, Pinnacle Investment Advisors, LLC, 1994—2004, CEO, mng. mem., 1994—. Former bd. dirs. Bank South NA; bd. dirs. Bank South Corp., 1982, Servidyne Inc. (formerly Abrams Industries Inc.), 1992—2006, Fidelity Nat. Corp, 1997—2001, Smith Garden Products Inc., 1997—, AGL Resources Inc., 1988—, Shoney's Inc., 1998—, Atlanta Gas Light Co., Atlanta Life Ins. Co., Servidyne, Inc. (formerly Abrams Industries, Inc.), 1992—2006, The AeroClinic. Bd. advisors Atlanta Falcons Football Club LLC; trustee emeritus Emory U., Tuskegee U., Ga. Cancer Coalition, Morehouse School Medicine, Ga. Rsch. Alliance Inc., Herndon Found. Lt. Col. and Airfield Comdr. US Army, 1974. Decorated Vietnamese Cross of Gallantry with Bronze Star. Mem.: Rotary Club Atlanta (former pres., chmn.), 100 Black Men Atlanta. Office: Pinnacle Investment Advisors 233 S Detroit Ave Ste 100 Tulsa OK 74120-2406 Office Phone: 918-582-6864. Office Fax: 918-587-6502. E-mail: dpoarch@pinnacleholdings.net.

WARD, GEORGE FRANK, JR., international programs executive, ambassador; b. Jamaica, NY, Apr. 9, 1945; s. George Frank and Hildegard Louisa (Evans) W.; m. Peggy Elizabeth Coote, June 12, 1965; 1 child, Pamela Ward Priester. BA, U. Rochester, 1965; MPA, Harvard U., 1980. U.S. vice consul Am. Consulate, Hamburg, Germany, 1970-72; ops. officer Office Sec. State, Washington, 1972-74; U.S. consul Am. Consulate Gen., Genoa, Italy, 1974-76; polit. officer Am. Embassy, Rome, 1976-77, exec. asst., 1977-79, polit. officer Bonn, Germany, 1984—85, dep. chief mission, 1989—92; polit.-mil. officer US Dept. State, Washington, 1980-84, 1985—88, prin. dep. asst. sec. Bur. Internat. Orgn., 1992-96, US amb. to Namibia, 1996-99, US coord. for humanitarian assistance to Iraq, 2003; v.p., dir. profl. tng. program US Inst. Peace, Washington, 1999—2005; sr. v.p. internat. programs World Vision, 2005—11; dir. Africa Program Inst. Def. Analyses, 2011—. Capt. USMC, 1965—69, maj. USMCR, 1969—78. Decorated Vietnamese Cross Gallantry, Navy Commendation medal with combat V; recipient Presdl. Meritorious Svc. award, 1992, 1994, Disting. Honor award, U.S. State Dept., 1992. Fellow: Phi Beta Kappa; mem.: Am. Fgn. Svc. Assn., Washington Inst. Fgn. Affairs, Cosmos Club. Anglican. Office: Institute Defense Analyses 4850 Mark Center Dr Alexandria VA 22311-1882 Business E-Mail: gward@ida.org.

WARD, GEORGE TRUMAN, architect; b. Washington, July 24, 1927; s. Truman and Gladys Anna (Nutt) W.; m. Margaret Ann Hall, Sept. 10, 1949; children: Carol Ann Ward Dickson, Donna Lynne Ward Solomon, George Truman, Robert Stephen. BS, Va. Poly. Inst., 1951, MS, 1952; postgrad., George Washington U., 1966. Registered profl. arch., Va., Md., D.C., W.Va., N.C. Archtl. draftsman Charles A. Pearson, Radford, Va., 1950; head archtl. sect. Hayes, Seay, Mattern & Mattern, Radford and Roanoke, 1951-52; with Joseph Saunders & Assocs., Alexandria, Va., 1952-57, assoc. arch., 1955-57; ptnr. Vosbeck-Ward & Assocs., Alexandria, 1957-64, Ward/Hall Assocs., Fairfax, 1964—2008, emeritus, 2008. Dir. Crestar Bank/Greater Washington Region, 1967-99. Pres. PTA Burke (Va.) Sch., 1970-71; mem. bd. mgrs. Fairfax (Va.) County YMCA, 1964-76; chmn. adv. com. Coll. Arch., Va. Poly. Inst., 1984-90; bd. dirs., mem. investment com. Va. Tech. Found., Inc., 1986-91, 93-98; pres. Springfield Rotary Found. 1978-79; chmn. county adv. bd. Salvation Army, 1978-79, 89-95, co-chmn. Fairfax County Salvation Army Capital Campaign, 1991-95; mem. Gen. Bd. Va. Bapts., deacon, moderator; mem. bd. vis. Va. Poly. Inst. & State U., 1984-87; trustee Fairfax County Pub. Schs. Edn. Found., Inc. With AUS, 1946-47. Paul Harris fellow; recipient Disting. Svc. award Va. Tech. Alumni Assn., 1988; recipient William H. Ruffner medal Va. Tech., 1996, VSAIA William C. Noland award, 1998, Va. Tech. Coll. Arch. and Urban Studies Lifetime Contbn.

award, 1998, 2007. Fellow Coll. AIA; mem. AIA (corp., charter Octagon Soc.), No. Va. Soc. AIA (chmn. polit. action com. 1991-93, Disting. Svc. award 1990, treas. Va. soc. 1994-98, Outstanding Achievement award 1996), Rowe Fellowship (charter mem. 1988), Alumni Assn. Va. Poly. Inst. & State U. (bd. dirs., v.p. 1992, pres. 1994), Interfaith Forum on Religion, Art and Arch., Va. Found. for Arch. (trustee), Va. Assn. Professions, Va. C. of C., No. Va. Angus Assn. (pres. 1987-88), Va. Tech. Alumni Assn. (hon., life, bd. dirs. Disting. Svc. award 1988), Masons, Shriners, KT, Rotary (charter mem., pres. Springfield 1973-74, Disting. Svc. award dist. 7610 1995), Tau Sigma Delta, Omicron Delta Kappa, Phi Kappa Phi, Pi Delta Epsilon, Ut Prosim. Baptist. Business E-Mail: gtward@wardhall.com.

WARD, GILES, state legislator; b. Mar. 6, 1948; m. Kay Burrage; children: Laura S. Harris, Jeremy. Attended, Miss. State U., U. Southern Miss. Ret. regional mgr. Georgia-Pacific Corp.; mem. Dist. 18 Miss. State Senate, 2008—. Republican. Methodist. Home: 114 Jordan Cir Louisville MS 39339 Office: PO Box 1018 Jackson MS 39215 Home Phone: 662-773-8391; Office Phone: 601-359-3172. E-mail: gkward@senate.ms.gov.

WARD, HORACE TALIAFERRO, federal judge; b. LaGrange, Ga., July 29, 1927; m. Ruth LeFlore (dec.); 1 son (dec.). AB, Morehouse Coll., 1949; MA, Atlanta U., 1950; JD, Northwestern U., 1959. Bar: Ga. 1960. Instr. polit. sci. Ark. A.M. and N. Coll., 1950-51, Ala. State Coll., 1951-53, 55-56; claims authorizer US Social Security Adminstrn., 1959-60; assoc. Hollowell Ward Moore & Alexander (and successors), Atlanta, 1960-69; individual practice law Atlanta, 1971-74; judge Civil Ct. of Fulton County, 1974-77, Fulton Superior Ct., 1977-79, US Dist. Ct. (no. dist.) Ga., Atlanta, 1979—93, sr. judge, 1993—. Lectr. bus. and sch. law Atlanta U., 1965-70; dep. city atty., Atlanta, 1969-70, asst. county atty., Fulton County, 1971-74 Former Trustee Friendship Baptist Ch., Atlanta; mem. Ga. adv. com. U.S. Civil Rights Commn., 1963-65; assisting lawyer NAACP Legal Def. and Edn. Fund, Inc., 1960-70; mem. Jud. Selection Commn., Atlanta, 1972-74, Charter Commn., 1971-72; mem. Ga. Senate, 1964-74, jud. com., rules com., county and urban affairs com.; mem. State Democratic Exec. com., 1966-74; former bd. dirs. Atlanta Legal Aid Soc.; bd. dirs. Atlanta Urban League, Fed. Defender Program, No. Dist. Ga.; trustee Met. Atlanta Commn. on Crime and Delinquency, Atlanta U., Fledgling Found. Mem. Am. Bar Assn., Nat. Bar Assn. (chmn. jud. council 1978-79), State Bar Ga., Atlanta Bar Assn., Gate City Bar Assn. (pres. 1972-74), Atlanta Lawyers Club, Phi Beta Kappa, Alpha Phi Alpha, Phi Alpha Delta, Sigma Pi Phi. Office: US Dist Court 1252 US Courthouse 75 Spring St SW Atlanta GA 30303-3309 Home Phone: 404-588-0641.

WARD, JACQUELINE ANN BEAS, nurse, healthcare administrator, legal nurse consultant; b. Somerset, Pa., Oct. 23, 1945; d. Donald C. and Thelma R. (Wable) Beas; divorced; children: Charles L. Jr., Shawn M. BSN, U. Pitts., 1966; MA in Counseling and Guidance, W.Va. Coll. Grad. Studies, 1976; MBA, Columbus Coll., 1983; AS in Health Svcs. Mgmt./Nursing Home Adminstrn., St. Petersburg Jr. Coll., 1997. Cert. advanced nursing adminstrn., legal nurse cons., 2007; adult living facility adminstr., nursing home adminstr. preceptor. Staff nurse W.Va. U. Hosp., Morgantown, 1966—67; staff nurse, head nurse Meml. Hosp, Charleston, W.Va., 1967—69; staff nurse Santa Rosa Hosp., San Antonio, 1969; staff nurse, supr. Bexar County Hosp., San Antonio, 1970; charge and staff nurse Rocky Mountain Osteo. Hosp., Denver, 1971; from staff nurse to asst. DON Charleston Area Med. Ctr., 1971—82; DON H.D. Cobb Meml. Hosp., Phenix City, Ala., 1982—84; v.p. nursing Venice Hosp., Fla., 1984—90, v.p. ops., 1990—94; exec. dir., v.p. Life Counseling Ctr., Osprey, Fla., 1994—95; dir. skilled unit and spl. projects Bon Secours/Venice Hosp., 1995—97; adj. clin. nursing faculty Manatee CC, Bradenton, 1998—99; interim adminstr. DON Contracting, Sarasota, 1999—2000; adminstr. Ctrs. for Long Term Care Venice Beach, 2000—01, Lake Towers-Sun Terrace Health Care Ctr., Sun City Center, Fla., 2002—05, Tandem Health Care Sarasota, 2005—07; exec. dir. Beneva Park Club, Sarasota, 2005. Clin. instr. Chattahoochie Valley C.C., Phenix City, 1982—84; support svcs. cons. Bon Secours Healthcare, Venice, 1996—97; support svcs. cons., interim adminstrn. Long Term Care, 1997—98; legal nurse cons., 2007—.

WARD, JEION A., state legislator; b. Newport News, Va., Jan. 6, 1954; m. James Addrill Ward; children: James A. Jr., Jason A., Jeremy A. State del. Dist. 92, Va., 2004—. Mem.: Va. AFL-CIO (exec. com.), Hampton Fedn. Tchrs. (pres.), NAACP, Nat. Coun. Negro Women, Dem. Women's Club. Democrat. Mailing: Dist Off PO Box 7310 Hampton VA 23666 Office Phone: 804-698-1092. Fax: 804-786-6310. E-mail: Del_Ward@house.state.va.us.

WARD, JESMYN, writer, educator; Degree in English, Stanford U., Master's in Media Studies and Communication; MFA in Fiction, U. Mich., 2005. John and Renee Grisham Vis. Writer-In-Residence U. Miss., 2010—11; asst. prof. creative writing U. of South Alabama, 2011—. Author: (novels) Where the Line Bleeds, 2008 (Black Caucus of the American Libr. Assn. Honor award, Essence Mag. Book Club Selection), Salvage the Bones, 2011 (National Book award (Fiction), National Book Found., 2011, Oprah.com selected as Book of the Week, 2011), (short stories) Barefoot, 2011. Finalist Virginia Commonwealth U. Cabell First Novelist award, Hurston/Wright Legacy award; Wallace Stegner Fellow, Stanford U., 2008—10. Office: University of South Alabama HUMB 259 Mobile AL 36688 Office Phone: 251-460-6146. Business E-Mail: jward@usouthal.edu.

WARD, JEWELL C., clinical geneticist, educator; MD, Indiana U., 1971. Cert. Am. Bd. Clin. Genetics-Med. Genetics, 1982, Am. Bd. Clin. Biochemical Genetics-Med. Genetics, 1982. Intern Children's Hosp., Ohio, 1973, resident pediat. Ohio, 1972—74; fellow Indiana Univ. Hosp., 1972, fellow med. genetics, 1974—75, Johns Hopkins Univ. Hosp., 1975—79; prof. pediat. Univ. Tenn.; physician Methodist Hosp. Office: Methodist Hospital 777 Washington Ave Ste 400 Memphis TN 38103 Office Phone: 901-866-8818.

WARD, LLEWELLYN ORCUTT, III, oil industry executive; b. Oklahoma City, July 24, 1930; s. Llewellyn Orcutt II and Addie (Reisdorph) W.; m. Myra Beth Gungoll, Oct. 29, 1955; children: Casidy Ann, William Carlton. Student, Okla. Mil. Acad., 1948—50; BS, U. Okla., 1953; postgrad., Harvard U., 1986. Registered profl. engr., Okla. Dist. engr. Delhi-Taylor Oil Corp., Tulsa, 1955-56; ptnr. Ward-Gungoll Oil Investments, Enid, Okla., 1956—; owner L.O. Ward Oil Ops., Enid, 1963—; chmn. bd. Ward Petroleum Corp. Mem. Okla. Gov.'s Adv. Coun. Energy; rep. to Interstate Oil Compact Commn.; dir. Hydril Corp; chmn. Chmn. Indsl. Devel. Commn., Enid, 1968—; active YMCA; mem. bd. visitors Coll. Engring., U. Okla.; mem. adv. coun. Sch. Bus., trustee Phillips U., Enid, Univ. Bd., Pepperdine, Calif.; Okla. chmn. U.S. Olympic Com., 1986—; Rep. nat. committeeman from Okla., 1982-88; mem. Pres.'s adv. com. on arts Kennedy Ctr. Served with C.E., U.S. Army, 1953-55. Recipient Gov's. Arts award, 2006, Trailblazer award, U. Okla., 2009, Pillar of Plains award, 2007, Seed Sower award, 2008, Legends award, Okla. Geol. Found., 2012, Lifetime Achievement award, Okla. Ctr., 2013; named Chief Roughneck of Yr., Lone Star Steel, 1999, Disting. Alumnus, Okla. Mil. Acad., 1993; named to Hall of Fame, Enid Pub. Sch. Found., 2006, Energy Header of Yr., NARO, 1996, Okla. Hall. of Fame, 2010. Mem. Ind. Petroleum Assn. Am. (chmn. 1996-98), Okla. Ind. Petroleum Assn. Am. (pres., bd. dirs.), Nat. Petroleum Coun., Enid C. of C. (Businessman of Yr. 1988, Citizen of Yr. 2006), U. Okla. Coll. Engring. Disting. Grads. Soc., Am. Bus. Club (pres. 1964), Masons, Shriners, Rotary (pres. Enid 1990-91), Alpha Tau Omega. Methodist. Home: 900 Brookside Dr Enid OK 73703-6941 Office: 502 S Fillmore St Enid OK 73703-5703 Home Phone: 580-234-8779; Office Phone: 580-234-3229.

WARD, MICHAEL JOHN, rail transportation executive; b. Balt., Sept. 2, 1950; BS, U. Md., 1972; MBA, Harvard U., 1976. Rsch. analyst Chessie Sys., Balt., 1977—80, mgr., coord. analysis-finance, 1980—81, mgr. bus. rsch. Cleve., 1981—82, dir. nat. accts., 1982—84, asst. v.p. coal mktg., 1984—86; v.p. coal mktg. CSX Distbn. Services, Balt., 1986—88; v.p. coal CSX Transp., Jacksonville, 1988—94, gen. mgr. C&O Bus. Unit, v.p. coal Huntington, W.Va., 1994—95, sr. v.p. finance Jacksonville, 1995—96, CFO, 1995—98, exec. v.p. finance, 1996—98, exec. v.p. coal & merger planning, 1998—99, exec. v.p. coal svc. group, 1999—2000, exec. v.p. ops., 2000, pres., 2000—02, pres., CEO, 2002—03; pres. CSX Corp., Jacksonville, 2002—03, chmn., pres., CEO, 2003—. Bd. dirs. Ashland, Inc., 2001—, CSX Corp., 2002—, Ky. Coal Coun., American Assn. Clean Coal Electricity. Bd. dirs. Ctr. Energy Econ. Devel., Take Stock in Children. Mem.: Fla. Coun. 100, Assn. American Railroads (bd. dirs.), Phi Kappa Phi, Beta Gamma Sigma. Republican. Office: CSX Corp 500 Water St C 900 Jacksonville FL 32202

WARD, RICK, III, state legislator; m. Dawn White; children: Reese, Hayes. B, La. State U.; JD, So. U. Law Sch. Counsel Iberville Parish Coun., La., West Baton Rogue Parish Sheriff's Office, La.; juvenile prosecutor City of Plaquemine, La., 2009—; atty. Clayton and Fruge, Port Allen, La.; mem. Dist. 17 La. State Senate, Baton Rogue, 2012—. Mem.: NRA, ABA, La. Bar Assn., Lottie Wildlife Protective Assn., Quality Deer Mgmt. Assn., Nat. Wild Turkey Fedn. Democrat. Office: 3741 Hwy 1 Port Allen LA 70767 also: La State Senate 900 N 3rd St Baton Rouge LA 70804 Office Phone: 225-246-8838. Business E-Mail: wardr@legis.la.gov.

WARD, T. JOHN, lawyer, former federal judge; b. Bonham, Tex., Apr. 17, 1943; BA in Chemistry, Tex. Tech U., 1964; LLB, Baylor Law Sch., 1967. Bar: Tex. 1967, US Supreme Ct. 1985. Asst. county atty. Lubbock County, Tex., 1968; atty. Ward & Ross, 1969—70, Sharp Ward, 1971—90; ptnr. Brown McCarroll & Oaks Hartline, Houston, 1991—99; judge US Dist. Ct. (eastern dist.) Tex., Marshall, Tex., 1999—2011; ptnr. Ward & Smith, Longview, Tex., 2011—. Named Baylor Lawyer of Yr., Baylor U. Law Sch., 2004, Trial Judge of Yr. (Tex. chapter), American Bd. Trial Advocates, 2009. Fellow Tex. Bar Found., American Coll. Trial Lawyers, 1986-99, 2011-; mem. ABA, State Bar Tex. (mem. grievance com. dist. 2A 1973-85, mem. disciplinary rev. com. 1986—), Tex. Assn. Def. Counsel, Gregg County Bar Assn. (treas. 1972), 5th Cir. Bar Assn. (bd. govs. 1987-91, 96-99). Office: Ward & Smith 111 West Tyler St Longview TX 75601 Office Phone: 903-757-6400. Office Fax: 903-757-2323.

WARD, WILLIAM E., mayor; b. Lunenburg County, Va., 1933; BA, Va. State Coll., Petersburg, Va., 1957, MA, 1960; PhD, Clark Univ., Worchester, Mass., 1972; studied, Hampton, African History Inst., 1963, Norfolk State Coll., Am. History Inst., 1967, Carnegie-Mellon Univ., Afro-Am. History Inst., 1969, Am. Forum Internat. Study, Ghana, West Africa, 1972, Univ. West Indies, Kingston, Jamaica, 1977. Mayor City of Chesapeake, Chesapeake, VA., 1990—; tchr. I.C. Norcom H.S., Portsmouth, Va., 1958—62, P.S. 181, Baltimore, Md., 1962—63; asst. prof. Norfolk State Coll., 1968—70; TTT fellow Clark Univ.; assoc. prof. Norfolk State Coll., 1973—79; prof. Norfolk State Univ., 1980—98, chair, history dept., 1997—2000; ret., 2000; part-time tchr., 2000—. Course instr. Clark Univ., 1972; co-dir. In-Svc. Workshop, 1971; cons. Norfolk State Coll., 1971—72, Norfolk Com., 1970—78; participated Econ. Trade Cultural Missions to Japan, Brazil, Taiwan, Israel, Europe, Japan, 1990—99; former host PRIDE, WAVY-TV; chmn., insurance com. Norfolk State Univ., chmn., faculty senate Va. benefits com., chmn., senate grievance com., chmn., black history com., mem., coll. wide coun. tchr. ed., coll. exe. coun., 1971—82, pres. faculty senate, 1975—77. Bd. dir. Norfolk Chesapeake Va. Beach United Way, Tidewater Va. Urban League; mem. Chesapeake City Coun., 1978—, mayor, 1990—; mem. U.S. Conf. Mayors, Chesapeake Forward Civic Orgn.; past pres. Chesapeake Men Progress Civic Orgn., Fernwood Farms Civic League; mem. Hampton Rds. Military Diplomats; chmn. Fourth Congl. Voters League; mem. Va. State Dem. Ctr. Com., WAVY-TV Minority Adv. Bd.; delegate Nat. Dem. Conv., NYC, 1976, San Francisco, 1984; chmn. Hampton Rds. Mayors Chair Caucus, 1995—96; elected to joint subcom. study use of incentives for joint activities by localities appointed by Va. Senate Com. Privileges, 1996; appointed Va. Municipal League Legislative Com., 1997; exe. bd. Tidewater Coun. Boy Scouts Am., 1997—2000; delegate 17th Ann. Jerusalm Conf. Mayors, 1997; 2nd vice chmn. Hampton Rds. Partnership, 1997; bd. dirs. Hampton Rds. Econ. Alliance, 1997; appointed Internat. Task Force, Nat. League Cities, 1998, U.S. Conf. Mayors Task Force Electronic Commerce Internet Tech., 1999. Recipient cmty. svc. award, Kappa Alpha Psi Fraternity, 1970, three yr. acad. fellowship award, Clark Univ., brotherhood award, Christians and Jews, outstanding alumni award, Va. State Univ., 1993, chamber of commerce commendation award, 1994, various cmty. awards, Martin Luther King, Jr. memorial award, Old Dominion Univ., 1995; grantee study in Africa, Clark Univ., 1972. Mem.: Va. Soc. Sci. Assn., Am. Historical Assn., Southern Historical Assn., Assn. Study Negro Life History, Va. Soc. History Tchrs., Nat. Fatherhood Initiative (co-chair mayor 2001—02), Great Bridge Battlefield Waterways History Found. (pres.), Tidewater Regional Health Coun., Va. World Tech. Fair Commn., Internat. Torch Club, Kappa Alpha Psi. Democrat. Office: Office of Mayor 306 Cedar Rd Chesapeake VA 23322 E-mail: wward@council.chesapeakeva.net.

WARDEN, WILLIAM C., JR., board member; Gen. counsel, sec. Lowe's Companies, Inc., North Wilkesboro, NC, 1996—99, exec. v.p., chief adminstrn. officer, 1999—2001, exec. v.p., adminstrn., 1996—2003. Bd. dirs. Ruddick Corp., 2008—. Office: Ruddick Corp Bd Directors 301 S Tryon St Ste 1800 Charlotte NC 28202 Office Phone: 704-372-5404. Office Fax: 704-372-6409. Business E-Mail: wwarden@ruddickcorp.com.

WARDLAW, JEFF R., state legislator; b. Hermitage, Ark. m. Brittany Wardlaw; children: Mason Wardlaw, Reid Wardlaw, Paisleigh Wardlaw. BS in Agr., U. Ark., Monticello, 2002. Bd. dirs. Hermitage Sch. Dist.; mgr. Med. Necessities; owner, mgr. Wardlaw Farms; mem. Dist. 8 Ark. House of Representative, 2011—. Democrat. Office: 801 E Church St Warren AR 71671 Office Phone: 870-226-9501. Business E-Mail: jeff@jeffwardlaw.com.

WARE, CARL, bottling company executive; b. Newnan, Ga., Sept. 30, 1943; s. U.B. and Lois (Wimberly) W.; m. Mary Clark, Jan. 1 1966; 1 son, Timothy Alexander. BA, Clark Coll., 1965; M.P.A., U. Pitts., 1968; postgrad., Carnegie Mellon U., 1965-66. Dir. Atlanta Housing Authority, 1970-73; pres. city council City of Atlanta, 1974-79; v.p. Coca-Cola Co., Atlanta, 1974-86, sr. v.p., 1986-2000, exec. v.p., 2000; councilman, Atlanta; councilman Georgia; exec. Coca-Cola. Bd. dirs. Ga. Power Co., Cummins Inc., Chevron Corp., 2001—. Mem. adv. council U.S. Civil Rights Commn., 1983; bd. dirs. Nat. Council Black Agencies, 1983—, United Way of Met. Atlanta, 1983—; trustee Clark Coll. Mem. Gammon Theol. Sem. (trustee), Ga. State U. Found. (trustee), Sigma Pi Phi Democrat. Methodist. Office: Cummins Inc 500 Jackson St Columbus IN 47201 Office Phone: 812-377-5000. Office Fax: 812-377-3334. Business E-Mail: cware@na.ko.com.

WARE, JOHN DAVID, retired valve and hydrant company executive; b. Beaumont, Tex., Feb. 2, 1947; s. Clarence David Ware and Lois Pearl (Coffey) Hardy; m. Dorothy Ann Jones, Mar. 27, 1986. Cert. in mgmt., James Madison U. Announcer Stas. KAYC and KAYD-FM, Beaumont, 1966-71, 1971-77; asst. supr. Am. Valve & Hydrant, Beaumont. Mem. Am. Soc. for Quality Control (chmn. SE Tex. 1989-90), Nat. Mgmt. Assn., Inst. Cert. Profl. Mgrs. (cert. mgr.). Baptist. Avocations: coin collecting/numismatics, painting. Home: PO Box 1390 Mauriceville TX 77626-1390

WARE, ONZLEE, state legislator; b. Greensboro, NC, Jan. 4, 1954; Mem. Dist. 11 Va. House of Delegates, 2004—. Mem.: Roanoke City Pks. & Recreation Adv. Bd. (chmn.), NAACP, Va. State Bar Assn. Democrat. Presbyterian. Office: Capitol Office Gen Assembly Bldg PO Box 406 Richmond VA 23218 also: 325 N Jefferson St Roanoke VA 24016 Office Phone: 804-698-1011, 540-344-7410. Office Fax: 804-698-6711, 540-344-7980. Business E-Mail: DelOWare@house.virginia.gov.

WARE, ROBERT LEE, state legislator; b. Fitchburg, Mass., Aug. 20, 1952; m. Kathleen Annette Nulton Ware; children: Karen Chandler, Robby, Thomas, Jeb Stuart. House del., Va.; bd. supr. Powhatan County, 1988—95; mem. Va. State Bd. Edn., 1995—97; state del. Dist. 65 Va., 1998—; mem. Fin. Com., Militia Com., Police & Urban Safety Com., Agr. Com., Natural Resources & Chesapeake Bay Com., Commerce & Labor Com. Recipient Excellence Tchg. US Constrn. award, John Marshall Found. Republican. Presbyterian. Mailing: Gen Assembly Bldg Off 409 PO Box 406 Richmond VA 23218 E-mail: Del_LWare@house.state.va.us.

WARFIELD, RANELLE Q., gas industry executive; Grad., Va. Polytechnic Inst. and St. Univ., 1978. Various mgmt. positions Piedmont Natural Gas Co., 1981—2004, v.p. sales and mktg., 2004—09; v.p. customer svc. Piedmont Natural Gas Co., Inc., 2009—. Office: Piedmont Natural Gas Co Inc 4720 Piedmont Row Dr Charlotte NC 28210 Mailing: Piedmont Natural Gas Co Inc PO Box 33068 Charlotte NC 28233 Office Phone: 704-364-3120. Office Fax: 704-365-3849.

WARING, BRADISH J., lawyer; b. New Orleans, Mar. 6, 1952; s. Simons Vanderhorst and Mary Barnwell (Rhett) W.; m. Amelia B., May 27, 1978; children: Amelia S., Mary B.R., Louisa V. BA, U. S.C., 1975, JD, 1977. Bar: SC 1978, US Dist. Ct. (Dist. SC) 1978, US Ct. Appeals (4th Cir.) 1978, US Supreme Ct. 1978. Assoc. Young, Clement, Rivers & Tisdale, Charleston, SC, 1978—81, ptnr., 1981—2003, Nexsen Prue & Adams Kleemeier, Charleston, SC, 2003—. Corp. counsel Town of Sullivan's Island, SC, 1979-81; chair emeritus Am. Law Firm Assn. Sch. Law., LA, 1998—; mem. U. SC Law Sch. Assn.; bd. dirs. U. SC Law Sch. Partnership. Bd. dirs., treas. Charleston Day Sch., 1996, chmn. bd.; vestry mem., sec. St. James Episcopal Ch., Goose Creek, SC, 1991; apptd. chair Commrs. Plottage Charleston Br., 1993-94. Fellow SC Bar Found.; mem. ABA, SC Bar Assn. (bd. govs. 1997—, house dels. 1985—, pres. 2007), Fedn. Ins. & Corp. Counsel, Am. Judicature Soc., Charleston County Bar Assn., Def. Rsch. Inst., Historic Charleston Found. (v.p.), Port of Charleston Pilotage Commn., SC Def. Trial Attys. Assn. Avocations: sailing, golf, hunting, travel. Office: Nexsen Prue & Adams Kleemeier PO Box 486 Charleston SC 29402 Office Phone: 843-577-9440. Office Fax: 843-720-1777. E-mail: bwaring@nexsenpruet.com.

WARING, GEORGE ORAL, III, ophthalmologist, surgeon; b. Buffalo, Feb. 21, 1941; s. George Oral Waring and Mary Jane Fitzpatrick-Waring; children from previous marriage: George Oral IV, John Timothy, Joy Waring-Harty, Matthew. BS cum laude, Wheaton Coll., Ill., 1963; MD, Baylor Med. Coll., Houston, 1967. Diplomate Am. Bd. Ophthalmology (assoc. examiner, 1980, 89). Rotating intern Ben Taub Gen. Hosp., Houston, 1967—68; resident Wills Eye Hosp. and Rsch. Inst., Phila., 1970—73, Heed fellow in corneal and external disease, 1973—74; staff physician Hosp. Ship Hope, Natal, Brazil, 1973; asst. prof. U. Calif., Davis, 1974—79, assoc. prof., 1979; surg. dir. Sacramento Valley Eye Bank, 1976—79; staff physician Emory Clinic, Inc., Atlanta, 1979—82, clinic ptnr., 1982—2002, with, 2002—04; mng. dir. Emory Vision Correction Ctr., 1994—2001; founding surgeon InView Vision (formerly Emory Vision), 2001—; pvt. practice Atlanta, 2004—. Affiliate scientist Yerkes Regional Primate Rsch. Ctr. Emory U. Sch. Medicine, Atlanta, 1982—92, assoc. prof., 1979—83, prof., dir. refractive surgery, 1983—2004, clin. prof., 2006—; rsch. assoc. French Ministry Rsch. & Tech., 1992; Fogarty sr. internat. fellow US NIH, 1992; vis. prof. Ain Shams U., Cairo, 1992—93; chmn. dept. ophthalmology, dir. rsch. dept. El-Magrabi Eye Hosp. and Med. Ctr., Jeddah, Saudi Arabia, 1992—95; cons. Summit Tech., 1990—95, Chiron Corp., 1993—2000, Nidek, Inc., 2001—, Bausch and Lomb, 2001—05, Advanced Med. Optics, 2005—, Schwind Corp., 2006—08; mem. sci. adv. bd. Calhoun Vision, 2002—; mem. sci. adv. bd., clin. investigator AcuFocus, 2005—; lectr. in field. Author 2 textbooks; mem. editl. bd.: Am. Jour. Ophthalmology, 1981—87, mem. consultative bd.:, 1987—97; mem. editl. bd. Jour. Refractive Surgery, 1985—87; assoc. editor: Jour. Refractive Surgery, 1987—88, editor-in-chief:, 1989—, mem. editl. bd.: numerous jours.; contbr. more than 50 chpts. to books, more than 500 articles to profl. jours. Lt. USPHS, 1968—70. Recipient Hon. medal, Ain Shams U., Ceiro, 1989, Barraquer prize, Internat. Soc. Refractive Keratoplasty, 1992, Gold medal, Pan Arab Coun. Ophthalmology, 1993, 1997, Gregg medal, Royal Assn. Coll. Ophthalmology, 1996, Buasch and Lomb Visionary award, 2004, Kritzinger medal, South Africa Cataract Refraction Surgery; co-recipient Emmy award, NATAS, 1977; grantee, NIH, 1978—81, 1980—, 1980—91, others, U. Calif., Davis, 1973—76, 1982—83, 1987—88, others, various industries; Pew Found. scholar, 1971—72, Training grantee, NIH, 1971. Fellow: ACS (mem. com. applicants 1991), Eye Bank Assn. Am. (mem. constitution and by-laws com. 1984—86, mem. program com. 1985, mem. adv. bd.), Royal Coll. Ophthalmologists, Am. Acad. Ophthalmology (mem. interprofessional edn. com. 1978—81, mem. instrn. adv. com. 1978—81, cons. 1983—, Honor, Sr. Honor and Life Achievement awards 2004), Explorer's Club; mem.: AMA (mem. ophthalmology program com. 1975—79, Physician's Recognition award 1989—95), Wills Eye Hosp. Ex-Resident's Soc., Soc. Heed Fellows (mem. Heed award nomination com. 1983—84, 2000—04, chmn. 2004, Outstanding Ophthalmologist 1978), Saudi Ophthal. Soc., Paton Corneal Transplant Soc., Internat. Soc. Refractive Surgery of Am. Acad. Ophthalmology (trustee 1981—89, editor Jour. Refractive Surgery 1989—, Lans award 1986, Berraguer award 1992, Lifetime Achievement award in Refractive Surgery 1997, Kvitzinger award 2003), Egyptian Soc. Ocular Implants and Refractive Surgery (hon.), Internat. Ophthalmic Microsurgery Study Group, Ga. Soc. Ophthalmology (mem. pub. edn. com. 1981—84, mem. govtl. com.

1988—89, mem. laser com. 1991—92), Dekalb Med. Soc., Coun. Refractive Surgery Quality Assurance, Castroviejo Cornea Soc. (mem. exec. com. 1981—85, program chmn. 1983—85, Castroviejo medal 2004), Assn. Rsch. Vision and Ophtalmology (mem. cornea sect. com. 1985—88, chmn. cornea sect. com. 1987—88, Weisenfeld award 2008), Am. Ophthal. Soc., Commd. Officers Assn. USPHS, Am. Eye Study Club (emeritus mem. 1988—). Avocations: art, kayaking, mountain climbing, scuba diving, sailing. Home: 36 Willow Glen Atlanta GA 30342 Office Phone: 404-642-2848. Office Fax: 404-250-9006.

WARING, SUMNER J., III, funeral and cemetery services company executive; Degree in mortuary sci., Mt. Ida Coll., Newton Centre, Mass.; BBA, Stetson U., DeLand, Fla.; MBA, U. Mass., Dartmouth. Lic. funeral dir. Area v.p. Svc. Corp. Internat., 1996—99, regional pres. Northeast region, 1999—2001, regional pres. Pacific region, 2001—03, v.p. Western ops., 2002—04, v.p. major market ops., 2003—05; sr. v.p. major market ops. Service Corp. International, 2005—. Office: Service Corporation International 1929 Allen Pky Houston TX 77019 Office Phone: 713-522-5141. Office Fax: 713-525-5586.

WARLICK, HOLLY, women's college basketball coach; b. June 11, 1958; BS in Mktg., U. Tenn., 1981; MS in Athletic Adminstrn., Va. Tech. U., 1983. Asst. coach Va. Tech U. Hokies, Blacksburg, Va., 1981—83; asst. head coach U. Nebr. Cornhuskers, Lincoln, 1983—85; asst. coach U. Tenn. Lady Volunteers, Knoxville, 1985—2003, assoc. head coach, 2003—12, head coach, 2012—. Mem. US Olympic Women's Basketball Team, 1980; co-founder Champions For A Cause Found., 2007—. Named Asst. Coach of Yr., Women's Basketball Coaches Assn., 2007, Southeastern Conf. Coach of Yr., 2013; named to The Knoxville Sports Hall of Fame, 1994, The Women's Basketball Hall of Fame, 2001, The U. Tenn. Lady Vol Hall of Fame, 2002, The Tenn. Sports Hall of Fame, 2004. Office: University Tennessee 207 Thompson-Boling Ctr and Arena 1600 Phillip Fulmer Way Knoxville TN 37996

WARNATH, MAXINE AMMER, psychologist, arbitrator; b. NYC, Dec. 3, 1928; d. Philip and Jeanette Ammer; m. Charles Frederick Warnath, Aug. 20, 1952; children: Stephen Charles, Cindy Ruth. BA, Bklyn. Coll., 1949; MA, Columbia U., 1951, EdD, 1982. Lic. psychologist Oreg. Various profl. positions Hunter Coll., U. Minn., U. Nebr., U. Oreg., 1951-62; asst. prof. psychology Oreg. Coll. Edn., Monmouth, 1962-77; assoc. prof. psychology, chmn. dept. psychology & spl. edn. Western Oreg. U., Monmouth, 1978-83, prof., 1983—96, prof. emeritus, 1996—. Dir. organizational psychology program, 1983—96; pres. Profl. Perspective Internat., Salem, Oreg., 1987—; cons., dir. Orgn. R&D, Salem, Oreg., 1983—87; seminar leader Endeavors for Excellence program. Author: Power Dynamism, 1987. Mem.: APA (com. pre-coll. psychology 1970—74), Western Psychol. Assn., Oreg. Psychol. Assn. (pres. 1980—81, pres.-elect 1979—80, legis. liaison 1977—78), Oreg. Acad. Sci., N.Y. Acad. Scis., Am. Psychol. Soc. Home and Office: 658 Village Dr Pompano Beach FL 33060-7767 Office Phone: 954-786-3108, 954-707-0199. Business E-Mail: warnathm@wou.edu.

WARNE, WILLIAM ROBERT, economist; b. Washington, Nov. 30, 1937; BA, Princeton U., N.J., 1960; MA, Johns Hopkins U., Balt., 1974. Provincial advisor U.S. Mission, Vinh Binh, Vinh Long, Vietnam, 1962-64; officer in charge trade, devel. and fin. policy U.S. Mission to European Communities, Brussels, 1974-77; dep. dir. E. Asian Econ. Policy, 1977-79; dir. Caribbean affairs U.S. Dept. State, Kingston, Jamaica, 1979-81, chargé d'affaires, dep. chief mission, 1981-84, dir. Latin Am. Econ. Policy Washington, 1984-86; counselor for trade, energy, social affairs and agr. U.S. Delegation OECD, Paris, 1986-88; v.p. Midwest Ctr. Exec. Coun. Fgn. Diplomats, Indpls., 1988-89; pres. Korea Econ. Inst. Am., Washington, 1990-99; instr. Fgn. Svc. Inst., U.S. Dept. State, Washington, 2000—; prof. internat. studies Ewha Woman's U., Seoul, Republic of Korea, 2000—01; instr. Fgn. Svc. Inst. U.S. Dept. State, Washington, 2001—03. Prof. internat. studies Korea U., Seoul, Republic of Korea, 2003; instr. fgn. svc. Inst. U.S. Dept. State, Washington, 2004—. With US Army, 1960—62.

WARNER, DOUGLAS ALEXANDER, III, (SANDY WARNER), retired diversified financial services company executive; b. Cin., June 9, 1946; s. Douglas Alexander Jr. and Eleanor (Wright) W.; m. Patricia A. Grant, May 13, 1977; children: Alexander, Katherine, Michael, Alice. BA, Yale U., 1968. Officer's asst. J.P. Morgan & Co. Inc., NYC, 1968-70; asst. treas. J.P. Morgan & Co., Inc., NYC, 1970-72, asst. v.p., 1972-75; v.p. Morgan Guaranty Trust Co., NYC, 1975-85, sr. v.p., 1983-87; exec. v.p. J.P. Morgan & Co., Inc. (formerly Morgan Guaranty Trust Co. N.Y.), NYC, 1987-89, mng. dir., 1989-90, pres., 1990-95, chmn., pres., CEO, 1995—2000; chmn. J.P. Morgan Chase & Co., NYC, 2000—01; financial adv. Pres. George H.W. Bush Transition Team, 2000. Bd. counselors Bechtel Group, Inc., 1995-2009; bd. dirs. J.P. Morgan & Co., Inc. 1990-2000, General Electric Co., 1992-, Anheuser-Busch Companies, Inc., 1992-2008, J.P. Morgan Chase & Co., 2000-01, Motorola, Inc., 2002-; chmn. bd. of overseers and mgrs. Meml. Sloan-Kettering Cancer Ctr.; mem. The Bus. Coun. Trustee Yale U., 2008-; chmn. Yale Investment Com., 2008-. Mem. Meadowbrook Club (LI). Republican. Avocations: golf, skiing, shooting. Office Phone: 212-270-2323. Business E-Mail: warner_d_a@jpmorgan.com.

WARNER, ISIAH MANUEL, chemistry professor; b. DeQuincy, La., July 20, 1946; s. Humphrey and Irma (St. Romain) W.; m. Della Blount, June 1, 1968; children: Isiah Jr., Chideha, Edward. BS chemistry, Southern U., 1968; PhD, U. Wash., 1977. Teaching asst. U. Wash., Seattle, 1973-75, rsch. asst., 1975-77; asst. prof. Tex. A&M U., College Station, Tex., 1977-82; assoc. prof. Emory U., Atlanta, 1982-86, prof., 1986, 1987-92; Philip W. West prof., analytical and environ. chem. La. State U., Baton Rouge, 1992—, chair, dept. chem., 1994—97, Boyd prof., chem., 2000—, vice chancellor, strategic initiatives, 2001—. Cons. Nat. Sci. Found., 1980—, Coca Cola, Atlanta, 1984-92, NIH, Bethesda, Md., 1979—, Eli Lilly & Co., Indpls., 1988, 89; rsch. prof., Howard Hughes Med. Inst., 2002-. Contbr. articles to profl. jours. Recipient Charles Holmes Herty award, 1992, Benedetti Pichler award, 1994, NY SAS Gold medal, 1991, Presdl. Young Investigator award, 1984, Outstanding Tchr. award, 1993, AAAS Lifetime Mentor award, Banneker Legacy award, 2006, AnaChem award, Assn. Analytical Chemists, 2007, Banneker Legacy award, 2006, Divsn. Aanalytical Chemistry award in Spectrochem. Analysis, Am. Chem. Soc., 2008; grantee, Howard Hughes Med. Inst., 2002; Fulbright fellow for rsch., tchg. in Kenya. Mem.: Internat. Chemometrics Soc. (N.Am. chpt.), Soc. Applied Spectroscopy, Nat. Orgn. Black Chemists and Chem. Engrs., Am. Chem. Soc. (So. Chemist award 2006, award for encouraging disadvantaged students into the scis. 2003), Sigma Xi. Avocations: racquetball, chess, cards. Office: La State Univ Dept Chemistry Baton Rouge LA 70803-0001 Office Phone: 225-578-2829. Office Fax: 225-578-3971. Business E-Mail: iwarner@lsu.edu.

WARNER, KENNETH WILSON, JR., editor, publishing executive; b. Chgo., Dec. 22, 1928; s. Kenneth Wilson and Ann S. (Knapp) W.; m. Deborah Ann Bollo, Dec. 28, 1982 (div. Apr. 1995); 1 child, Joseph; children by previous marriages: Sara, Seth, Katharin. BS Ed., No. Ill. State Teachers Coll., 1950. Staff editor Bldg. Supply News, Chgo., 1953-56; staff editor Elec. Merchandising, 1956-60; free-lance writer Sarasota, Fla., 1960-66; editor Gunsport Mag., Alexandria and Falls Church, Va., 1966-67, Gunfacts Mag., Arlington, Va., 1968-70, pub., 1968-70; exec. editor Am. Rifleman, Nat. Rifle Assn., Washington, 1971-78, asst. dir. publs. div., 1972-78; founding editor Am. Hunter, 1973-78, Am. Rifleman, 1976-78; dir. publs. NRA, Washington, 1977-78; editor in chief Gun Digest, Knives Annual-Krause Publs., Inc., Greenville, W.Va., 1979-99; editor, pub. Knives Digest Two Knife Guys Pub., Inc., Chattanooga, 2000—01; pres. Knifeware, Inc., Greenville, W.Va. Cons. firearms and cutlery cos.; co-founder Am. Knife and Tool Inst., 1997. Author: The Practical Book of Knives. 1976; The Practical Book of Guns, 1978. Editor: The Bolt Action, 1976. Contbr. articles to profl. jours. Cpl. U.S. Army. 1951-53. Recipient Cutlery Hall of Fame; inducted into Am. Bladesmith Soc. Hall of Fame, 1999. Mem.: NRA (life), Knifemaker's Guild Am. (assoc.). Office: Prin Office PO Box 52 Greenville WV 24945-0052 Office Phone: 304-832-6878. Personal E-mail: kenwarner@frontier.com.

WARNER, KRIS, political organization administrator; Vice chmn. Rep. Party W.Va., 1998—2002, chmn., 2002—. Republican. Achievements include raising more than $100,000 for the Republican party; getting 94 Republican candidates to file to run for the House of Delegates and the State Senate.

WARNER, M. RICHARD, paper and forest products company executive; b. Lufkin, Tex., Nov. 8, 1951; s. M.L. and Gladys (Hester) W.; m. Elizabeth Denman, July 28, 1973; children: Virginia Lee, Richard Denman. BBA, Baylor U., 1974, JD, 1975. Cons. Cerberus; with Lufkin, 1976—83; gen. counsel Temple-Eastex Inc., Diboll, Tex., 1983—84; treas., v.p., gen. coun. & chief adminstrv. officer Temple-Inland, Inc., Austin, 1986, pres., 2003—05, sr. advisor, 2006; interim CFO Hilco Receivables, LLC, 2009. Bd. dirs. Peoples Nat. Bank, Lufkin, Lumbermans Investment Corp., Austin, Tex., Guaranty Fed. Savs. Bank, Dallas. Bd. dirs. Diboll Booster Club, 1986—; pres. Temple-Inland Found., Diboll, 1986—. Mem. State Bar of Tex., Angelina County Bar Assn. (sec.-treas. 1976), Angelina County Young Lawyers Assn. (pres. 1980), Baylor Law Alumni Assn. (bd. dirs. 1985—). Avocations: hunting, fishing, golf. Office: BlueLinx Holdings Inc Bd Directors 4300 Wildwood Pkwy Atlanta GA 30339 Office Phone: 770-953-7000. Office Fax: 770-221-8902. Business E-Mail: m.warner@bluelinxco.com.

WARNER, MARK ROBERT, United States Senator from Virginia, former Governor of Virginia; b. Indpls., Ind., Dec. 15, 1954; s. Robert and Margaret Warner; m. Lisa Collis; children: Madison, Gillian, Eliza. BA, George Washington U., 1977; JD, Harvard Law Sch., 1980. Founding ptnr. Columbia Capital Corp., Alexandria, Va., 1989; gov. State of Va., Richmond, 2001—06; US Senator from Va., 2009—. Chmn. Va. State Democratic Party, 1993—95; mem. Democratic Nat. Com., 1993—95; chmn. Nat. Governors Assn., 2004—05, Edn. Commn. of the States, Southern Tech. Coun. Founding chmn. Va. Health Care Found.; creator SeniorNavigator.com; founder TechRiders, Va. High-Tech Partnership; co-chmn. Va. Cmtys. in Schs. Found.; mem. Old Presbyn. Meeting House; past bd. dirs. Va. Union U., George Washington U., Appalachian Sch. Law, Va. Found. for Ind. Colls., Va. Math and Sci. Coalition. Mem.: Southern Govs. Assn. (1st vice chmn.), Dem. Govs. Assn. (recruitment chmn.). Democrat. Presbyn. Office: US Senate 475 Russell Senate Office Bldg Washington DC 20510 Home: #116 611 Pennsylvania Ave SE Washington DC 20003-4303 Office Phone: 202-224-2023.*

WARNER, SETH L., mathematician, educator; b. Muskegon, Mich., July 11, 1927; s. Seth LeMoyne and Agnes (Brustad) W.; m. Susan Emily Rose, June 16, 1962; children: Susan Emily, Sarah Southall, Lawrence Warner. BS, Yale U., 1950; MA, Harvard U., 1951, PhD, 1955. Rsch. instr. Duke U., 1955-57, asst. prof., 1957-61, asso. prof., 1961-65, prof. math., 1965-95, dir. grad. studies math., 1960-68; prof. emeritus math., 1995—; chmn. Duke U., 1968-70, 73-82; visitor Inst. Advanced Studies, 1959-60; vis. disting. prof. math. Reed Coll., 1970-71; visitor U. Paris, 1964-65, U. Oslo, 1982-83. Author: Modern Algebra, vols. I and II, 1965, re-issued, 1990, Classical Modern Algebra, 1971, Topological Fields, 1989, Topological Rings, 1993. Served with Med. Service Corps AUS, 1946-48. Mem. Phi Beta Kappa, Sigma Xi. Episcopalian. Office: Duke U Math Dept Box 90320 Durham NC 27708-0320 Home: 2708 Circle Dr Durham NC 27705-5727

WARNER, STANLEY T., food service executive; BA in Psychology, Sociology, Hiram Coll., Ohio, 1975; attended exec. devel. program, U. Tenn., 1997; attended, Belmont U. Scarlett Leadership Inst., Nashville, 2008—09. Regional v.p. restaurant ops. Cracker Barrel Old Country Store, Inc. Named Regional V.P. of Yr., 2002, 2008. Mem.: Nat. Social Sci. Honor Soc. Office: Cracker Barrel Old Country Store Inc 305 Hartmann Dr Lebanon TN 37087 Office Phone: 615-444-5533. Office Fax: 615-443-9476.

WARNER, TIMOTHY C., movie theater company executive; Pres., CEO Nat. Assn. Theatre Owners of Calif./Nev.; gen. chmn. Nat. Assn. Theatre Owners/Show West; pres. Cinemark Internat., LLC, 1996—2006, sr. v.p., 2002—06; pres., COO Cinemark Holdings, Inc., 2006—12, CEO, 2012—. Office: Cinemark Holdings Inc 3900 Dallas Pky Ste 500 Plano TX 75093-7865 Office Phone: 972-665-1000. Office Fax: 972-665-1004. Business E-Mail: twarner@cinemark.com.*

WARNER, TOM, lawyer, former state legislator, mediator; b. Rochester, NY, Feb. 6, 1948; m. Martha C. Warner. BS in Bus. Adminstrn., U. Fla., 1970, JD cum laude, 1973. Bar: Fla. 1973. Practiced law, to 1992; mem. Fla. Ho. of Reps., 1992-99; solicitor gen. Office of Atty. Gen., Tallahassee, 1999—2002; with firm Carlton Fields, West Palm Beach, Fla., 2002—. City atty., Stuart, Fla., 1984-88; chmn. Jud. Nominating Commn., 19th Cir., 1990-92; mem. City of Stuart Bd. of Adjustment, 1978. Mem., pres. Martin County Coun. for the Arts, 1989-91; bd. dirs. Tri County TEC, Fla. Taxwatch; mem. choir Palm City Presbyn. Ch. Mem. Martin County Bar Assn. (past pres.). Republican. Presbyterian. Avocations: fishing, NASCAR, camping, skiing, hunting. Office: Carlton Fields Pa 525 Okeechobee Blvd Ste 1200 West Palm Beach FL 33401-6350 Business E-Mail: twarner@carltonfields.com.

WARREN, CHARLES DAVID, library consultant; b. Martin, Tenn., June 12, 1944; s. Charles Alton and Evelyn (Bell) W.; children: Aaron David, Meredith Hild, Julia Myers. BS, U. Tenn., 1967; MS, U. Ill., Urbana, 1969. cert. pub. library adminstr. Dir. Shiloh Regional Library, Jackson, Tenn., 1969-72, Cumberland County Pub. Library, Fayetteville, NC, 1973-79; exec. dir. Richland County Pub. Library, Columbia, SC, 1979—2009, exec. dir. emeritus, 2009—. Bd. dirs. Civic Music Assn., Fayetteville, N.C., 1973-79, Fayetteville Symphony, 1973-78, Fayetteville Arts Commn., 1975; v.p. Friends of Librs. U.S.A., 1994—2009; mem. Columbia Coord. Coun., 1987-88; chmn. Richland County History Commn., 1987-93; mem. John Cotton Dana Awards Commn., 1994-99. Recipient Lucy Hampton Bostick award, 1993, S.C. Pub. Adminstr. Yr. award, 1993; named Young Man of Yr., Fayetteville Jaycees, 1977, S.C. Libr. of Yr., 1991, Internat. Fedn. Librs., 1997-2001, Order of Silver Crescent, 1999. Mem. ALA (pres. Jr. Member Roundtable 1977, chmn. awards com. 1984), Southeastern Libr. Assn. (pres. pub. libr. sect. 1978), S.C. Libr. Assn. (bd. dirs. 1980), Friends Libraries USA (bd. dirs. 1992-2007), Southeastern Libr. Network (bd. dirs. 2002-), Rotary, Kiwanis, Beta Phi Mu. Democrat. Episcopalian. Home: 7 West St C Charleston SC 29401 Personal E-mail: cdwarrenlll@yahoo.com.

WARREN, DANIEL CHURCHMAN, health facility administrator; b. Washington, Sept. 23, 1939; s. Walter Thomas and Laura Katherine W.; m. C. Frederica Lescure, June 5, 1958(dec. Mar. 7, 2007), Elaina Gianatasio, Apr. 5, 2008; 1 child, Christopher C. BS, Roanoke Coll., 1960; MD, Med. Coll. Va., 1964; MPH, U. N.C., 1971; MMAS, U.S. Army Command & Gen. Coll., 1974. Diplomate Nat. Bd. Med. Examiners, Am. Bd. Preventive Medicine, lic. physician VA; ordained Anglican Cath. priest 2002. Intern Georgetown U. Hosp., 1964-65; resident in surgery Med. Coll. Va., 1967-68, William Beaumont Gen. Hosp., 1968-69; resident in preventive medicine Walter Reed Army Inst. Rsch., 1971-73; commd. 2d lt. U.S. Army, 1965, advanced through grades to col., 1986; asst. med. dir. HealthAm. Va., 1986; pvt. practice travel, 1987-89; dir. Peninsula Health Dist., Newport News, Va., 1990—2001; warden Holyrood Sem., 2001—03; rector St. Matthews Anglican Cath. Ch., 2002—09; priest-in-charge All Saints ACC, 2007—; warden Scott Sch. Theology, 2003—. Clin. asst. prof. family and cmty. medicine Ea. Va. Med. Sch., Norfolk; cons. Riverside Regional Med Ctr., Newport News. Active Gloucester County Rep. Com., 1987-96, chmn. 1992-95, Gloucester County Redistricting Adv. Com., 1991, 2001; hon. chmn. Combined Va. Campaign United Way the Va. Peninsula, 1992. Fellow: Am. Coll. Preventive Medicine; mem.: Knight of the Order St. Lazarus Jerusalem, Order Founders Patriots America, Jamestowne Soc., Med. Soc. Va. Republican. Anglican. Avocation: English and Virginia history. Business E-Mail: dwarrenmd@cox.net.

WARREN, DONALD WILLIAM, medical and dental educator; b. Bklyn., Mar. 22, 1935; s. Sol B. and Frances W.; m. Priscilla Girardi, June 10, 1956; children: Donald W. Jr., Michael C. BS, U. N.C., 1956, DDS, 1959; MS, U. Pa., 1961, PhD, 1963; D in Odontology (hon.), U. Kuopio, Finland, 1991. Asst. prof. dentistry U. N.C., Chapel Hill, 1963-65, dir. Craniofacial Ctr., 1963-2000, assoc. prof., 1965-69, prof., 1969-80, chmn. dept. dental ecology, 1970-85, Kenan prof., 1980—2004, Kenan prof. emeritus, 2004—, rsch. prof. otolaryngology, 1985—2004; ret. Cons. NIH, Bethesda, Md., 1967-2000, R. J. Reynolds-Nabisco, Winston-Salem, N.C., 1986-99; owner Cabin Banch Tack Shop, 1995-. Contbr. articles to profl. jours. Recipient Honor award Am. Cleft Palate Assn./Craniofacial Assn., 1992, O. Max Garner award U. N.C. Bd. Govs., 1993, honors award Angle Orthodontic Soc., 1998. Fellow AAAS, Internat. Coll. Dentists, Am. Speech and Hearing Lang. Assn. (Editors award 1998, Honors award 2003), Internat. Assn. Dental Rsch., Acoustical Soc. Am., Am. Cleft Palate Assn. (pres. 1981-82, Disting. Svc. award 1984), Am. Cleft Palate Edn. Found. (pres. 1976-77), Am. Equest Trade Assn. (treas. 2008-, pres. 2010). Avocations: horse related activities, running, farming. Home: PO Box 1356 Southern Pines NC 28388-1356

WARREN, EDITH D., state legislator; b. Jan. 29, 1937; m. Billy Warren. State rep. Dist. 8, NC, 1999—; small bus. owner; ret. educator. Mem. Agrl. com., Commerce, Small Bus. and Entrepreneurship com., Edn. com.; vice chmn. Appropriations com., Edn. Subcom. on Pre-School, Elementary and Secondary Sch. com. Democrat. Baptist. Address: PO Box 448 Farmville NC 27828 Office: North Carolina House of Representatives 16 W Jones St Rm 1323 Raleigh NC 27601-5406 Fax: 252-753-5603. Business E-Mail: Edith.Warren@ncleg.net. E-mail: edithw@ms.ncga.state.nc.us.

WARREN, HARRY JOSEPH, state legislator; b. East Liverpool, Ohio, May 31, 1950; m. Catherine Warren; children: Jason Warren, Adam Warren, Emily Warren, Alexandra Warren, Morgan Warren, Joshua Warren. BS in Polit. Sci., Kent State U., 1972. Human resource specialist Tar Heal Capital Corp., 1999—; mem. Youth+Minority Outreach Com., 2009; del. Dist. 12 NCCCA, 2009—; del. State Conv., 2010; mem. Dist. 77 NC House of Representatives, 2011—. Republican. Methodist. Mailing: 401 Kingsbridge Rd Salisbury NC 28144 Office: North Carolina House of Representatives 300 N Salisbury St Room 533 Raleigh NC 27603-5925 Office Phone: 704-603-8898, 919-733-5784. Office Fax: 704-603-8898. Business E-Mail: harry@harrywarrennc77.com, Harry.Warren@ncleg.net.

WARREN, JERRY LEE, conductor, educator; b. Montgomery, Ala., Jan. 12, 1935; s. H.L. and Lula B. (Dowdy) Warren; m. Dorothy Glen Floyd Warren, Aug. 17, 1955; children: Dorothy Lee, Laura Ellen, John Floyd. BM, Samford U., 1955; MCM, Sch. Ch. Music, Southern Bapt. Theol. Sem., 1959, DMA, 1967. Min. music First Bapt. Ch., Cartersville, Ga., 1956—57, Auburn, Ala., 1959—63; asst. prof. music Shorter Coll., Rome, Ga., 1966—69; chmn. dept. music Belmont U., Nashville, 1969—83; dean Sch. Music, 1983—91, acting v.p. acad. affairs, 1991—92, provost, 1992—99, acting pres., 1999—2000, prof., 2000—; choral performer Broadman Singers Rec. Group, Nashville, 1972—80. Clinician sch. & ch. choral groups Tenor Soloist 1st Presbyn. Ch., Nashville, 1970—75, 1977—79; founder, music dir. Bella Voci, 1997—. Mem.: Nat. Assn. Tchrs. Singing (local pres. 1974—76), Coll. Music Soc., Mid. Tenn. Vocal Assn. (coll. rep. 1976—88), Tenn. Music Educators Assn. (state bd. 1976—88), Music Educators Nat. Conf., Am. Choral Dirs. Assn. (state pres. 1979—81, editor so. div. newsletter 1987—93, edtl. bd. Choral Jour. 1987—94, program chair nat. conv. 1989, so. divsn. conv. 1994, pres. so. divsn. 2003—05), Pi Kappa Lambda. Republican. Baptist. Avocations: golf, reading. Home: 7103 Sunrise Cir Franklin TN 37067 Office: Belmont U 1900 Belmont Blvd Nashville TN 37212-3757 Office Fax: 615-460-6678. Personal E-mail: jwarren202@aol.com. Business E-Mail: Warrenj@mail.belmont.edu.

WARREN, JOE D., computer science educator; BA in Math. and Computer Sci., with honors, Rice U., Houston, 1983; MS in Computer Sci., Cornell U., NYC, 1985, PhD, 1986. Faculty Rice U., 1986—, prof. computer sci., chair dept. computer sci., 2008—. Co-author: Subdivision Methods for Geometric Design, 1995; contbr. articles to profl. jours. Office: Rice U Dept Computer Sci 3114 Duncan 6100 S Main St Houston TX 77251 Office Phone: 743-348-5728. Office Fax: 743-348-5930. E-mail: jwarren@cs.rice.edu.

WARREN, JOSEPH LAWRENCE (JOE), state legislator; b. Magee, Miss., May 31, 1952; m. Susan Duckworth; children: Joseph, Lott, Anna Lee. Lic. in real estate. Mem. Dist. 90 Miss. House of Reps., 1980—; atty.; farmer; salesman. Mem.: Covington County Cattleman's Assn., Covington County Landowner's Assn., Miss. Trial Lawyers Assn., Covington County Forestry Assn., Farm Bur., C. of C., Miss. Bar Assn., Am. Bar Assn., Lions. Democrat. Presbyterian. Mailing: PO Box 42 Mount Olive MS 39119 Home Phone: 601-797-4702. E-mail: jwarren@house.ms.gov.

WARREN, KELCY L., energy executive; b. Gladewater, Tex., Nov. 9, 1955; s. Hugh Brinson and Bertie (Robinson) W. BSCE, U. Tex., Arlington, 1978. Pipeline design engr. Lone Star Gas Co., Dallas, 1978-81; pres., chief oper. officer Cornerstone Natural Gas, Inc.,

Dallas, 1993—96; pres. Energy Transfer Partners, Energy Transfer Equity, Dallas, 1996—2004, co-chmn., co-CEO, 2004—07, chmn., CEO, 2007—. Named one of Forbes 400: Richest Americans, 2009. Mem. Natural Gas Transp. Assn., Natural Gas Soc. North Tex. (pres. 1981—), Energy Club Dallas (bd. dirs. 1985—). Office: Energy Transfer Company 3738 Oak Lawn Ave Dallas TX 75219-4333

WARREN, PEBBLIN W., state legislator; b. Burke County, Ga. d. Joe H. & Annie G. (dec.) Walker; m. David M. Warren; children: Sharon DaShun & Pebblin Davida. BS in Bus. Adminstrn., Tuskegee U., MEd. Staff mem., sch. veterinary medicine dean's office Tuskegee U., 1974—79, work-study officer, 1979—82, asst. dir., office fin. aid, 1982—89; dir. student services Ala. Dept. Postsecondary Edn., 1989—; mem. Dist. 82 Ala. House of Reps., Montgomery, 2005—. Mem. Tuskegee Area C. of C.; v.p. Democrats of 82nd Dist., Ala.; elder Westminster Presbyn. Ch.; bd. dirs. Aid to Inmate Mothers, Macon-Russell Cmty. Action. Recipient John H. Buchanan Jr. Disting. Svc. award. Mem.: Delta Sigma Theta. Democrat. Presbyterian. Office: PO Box 1328 Tuskegee Institute AL 36087 also: One Technology Ct Montgomery AL 36116 also: Ala House of Reps Ala State House 11 S Union St Rm 517-C Montgomery AL 36130 Office Phone: 334-727-2213, 334-242-7734. Business E-Mail: pwarren@alhouse.gov.

WARREN, ROY G., non-alcoholic manufacturing company executive; m. Martha Warren; 3 children. Chmn. China Premium Food Corp. Co Ltd. (subs. Bravo! Brands Inc.); exec. officer, prin., securities broker and ptnr. Laffer Warren and Co., Alex Brown and Sons, Kemper Fin. Companies; sec. Bravo! Brands Inc. (formerly Bravo! Foods Internat. Corp.), founder, 1996, day-to-day ops. positons, 1997—2000, bd. dirs., 1997—2007, CEO Florida, 1999—2007, pres., COO, 2000—07; compliance officer, acting CFO Attitude Drink Co., Inc. (subs. of Attitude Drinks, Inc.), bd. dirs., founder, 2007, CEO, 2007—, chmn., pres., sec. and CEO, 2007—. Office: Attitude Drinks Inc Ste 101 712 US Highway 1 Ste 200 North Palm Beach FL 33408-4521 Office Phone: 561-799-5053. Office Fax: 561-799-5039. Business E-Mail: roy@attitudedrinks.com.

WARREN, RUSSELL GLEN, educational consultant; b. Balt., Apr. 29, 1942; s. Clarence N. and Kathryn (Butler) W. BBA, U. Richmond, 1964; PhD, Tulane U., 1968. Asst. prof. to assoc. prof. U. Richmond, Va., 1971—74, dean, 1974—76, asst. to pres. for acad. affairs, 1976—78; v.p. acad. affairs U. Montevallo, Ala., 1978-84, James Madison U., Harrisonburg, Va., 1984-90, v.p. acad. affairs, acting pres., 1986—87; pres. N.E. Mo. State U., Kirksville, 1990—94; disting. prof. econs., mgmt. Hardin-Simmons U., Abilene, Tex., 1995-97, dir. Ctr. for Rsch. Tchg. and Learning, 1995-97; exec. v.p., provost Mercer U., Macon, Ga., 1997—2002; prof. econs. So. Wesleyan U., 2003—06; pvt. practice cons.; provost Fla. Southern Coll., 2009—. Chmn. adv. bd. Coll. Humanities, Social Sci. Coll. Charleston, SC, 1999—2007. Author: Antitrust in Theory and Practice, 1976, Carpe Diem, 1995. Bd. dirs. Va. Rural Devel. Corp., Richmond, 1975-78, Am. Coll. Bldg. Arts, 2005-08; v.p. Kiawah Island Cmty. Assn., 2006-07, chmn. bd., 2007-08. Capt. US Army, 1969—71. Named One of Outstanding Young Men of Va., Va. Jaycees, 1976. Mem.: Am. Coun. on Edn. (coun. of fellows), Am. Assn. Colls. and Univs. (bd. dirs. 1994—95). Methodist. Avocations: golf, collecting cars. Home and Office: 175 Marsh Island Dr Kiawah Island SC 29455 Personal E-mail: russwarr@bellsouth.net.

WARREN, STEPHEN THEODORE, geneticist, educator; b. Grosse Point, Mich., Nov. 30, 1953; s. Theodore Stephen and Frances (Fedo) W.; m. Karen Lee Pierce, Aug. 27, 1978; 1 child, Thomas. BS, Mich. State U., 1976, PhD, 1981. Diplomate American Bd. Med. Genetics. Grad. asst. Mich. State U., East Lansing, 1976-81; rsch. assoc. U. Ill., Chgo., 1981-83, instr., 1983-85; asst. prof. Emory U. Sch. Medicine, Atlanta, 1985-91, assoc. prof., 1991-93, William Patterson Timmie prof. human genetics, 1993—, chmn. dept. human genetics, 2001—; investigator Howard Hughes Med. Inst., 1992—2002. Vis. scientist European Molecular Biol. Lab., Heidelberg, Germany, 1984.; cons. Ctrs. for Disease Control, Atlanta, 1988-89, NIH, Bethesda, Md., 1989—; collaborator Ctr. D'Etude du Polymorphysme Humain, Paris, 1989—. Editor-in-chief Am. Jour. Human Genetics, 2000-2005; mem. editl. bd. Human Molecular Genetics, Am. Jour. Human Genetics, Cytogenetics, Cell Genetics, Mammalian Genome, others; contbr. chpts. to books and more than 200 articles to profl. jorus. Recipient Sigma Xi prize Mich. State Sigma Xi, East Lansing, 1981, NIH fellowship NIH, Bethesda, 1982, Basil O'Connor award March of Dimes, N.Y.C., 1986, Albert E. Levy award Emory U., Atlanta, 1987, William Rosen Rsch. award Nat. Fragile X Found., 1996, Mich. State U. Outstandinf Alumni award, 2007, Brandwein award in Genetic Rsch., "Champion for Babies" award March of Dimes, 2008, Jacob's Ladder Internat. Rsch. prize, 2009, American Acad. Neurology "Frontiers in Clinical Neuroscience" award, 2009; inductee Nat. Inst. Child Health & Human Devel. Hall of Fame Honor, 2003. Fellow American Coll. Med. Genetics; mem. American Soc. Human Genetics (nominating com. 1991, awards con. 1992—, bd. dirs. 1997—, William Allan award 1999), American Soc. Biochemistry and Molecular Biology, American Soc. Microbiology, Genetics Soc. America, American Soc. Human Genetics (pres., 2005), Human Genome Orgn., Inst. Medicine., NAS Achievements include research on molecular genetic studies of the fragile X syndrome and other human genetic diseases. Office: Emory University School Medicine 301 Whitehead Bldg 615 Michael St Atlanta GA 30322-4218 Office Phone: 404-727-5979. E-mail: swarren@emory.edu.

WARREN, WILLIAM MICHAEL, JR., hospital administrator, lawyer; b. Bryan, Tex., June 8, 1947; s. William Michael and Rebecca Carolyn (Glass) W.; m. Anne Candler McLeod, June 5, 1968; children: William Powers, Laura Anne, Amy Lynn. BA, Auburn U., 1968; JD, Duke U., 1971. Bar: Ala. 1971. Assoc. Bradley, Arant, Rose & White, Birmingham, Ala., 1971-77, ptnr., 1977-83; v.p., gen. counsel Ala. Gas Corp., Birmingham, 1983-84, pres., COO, 1984; pres, COO Energen Corp., Birmingham, 1987-91; pres., CEO Children's Health System, bd. trustees, 1988—. Bd. dirs. AmSouth Bank Birmingham N.A., Energen Corp., Ala. Gas Corp., So. Gas Assn., Inst. Gas Tech., Protective Life Corp., 2001-. Contbr. articles to periodicals. Bd. dirs. Ala. Symphony Assn., 1988-90, pres., 1990—, chmn., 1991-92; chmn. Met. Devel. Bd., 1989-90; trustee Ala. Inst. for Deaf and Blind, 1988—, 1st lt. USAF, 1971-72. Mem. Ala. State Bar, ABA, Am. Gas Assn. (edn. 2000 com. 1991—), So. Gas Assn. (bd. dirs. 1989—), Inst. Gas Tech. (bd. trustees 1989—), Birmingham Area C. of C. (bd. dirs. 1986—, v.p. 1989), Summit Club (bd. dirs. 1989). Lodges: Rotary. Democrat. Methodist. Home: 3533 Mill Springs Rd Birmingham AL 35223-1637 Office: Childrens Health System 1600 7th Ave S Birmingham AL 35233 Office Phone: 205-939-9100. Business E-Mail: mike.warren@chsys.org.

WARTHEN, HARRY JUSTICE, III, lawyer; b. Richmond, Va., July 8, 1939; s. Harry Justice Jr. and Martha Winston (Alsop) W.; m. Sally Berkeley Trapnell, Sept. 7, 1968; children: Martha Alsop, William Trapnell. BA, U. Va., 1961, LLB, 1967. Bar: Va. 1967, U.S. Ct. Appeals (4th cir.) 1967, U.S. Dist. Ct. (ea. dist.) Va. 1969. Law clk. to judge US Ct. Appeals (4th cir.), Richmond, Va., 1967-68; assoc. Hunton & Williams, Richmond, 1968—2005, sr. counsel, 2005—. Lectr. in field U. Va. Law Sch., Charlottesville, 1975—77. Trustee exec. com. Hist. Richmond Found., 1986-95, 96—08, pres., 2000-02; trustee Woodrow Wilson Presdl. Libr., 1997-2003, 05-11; dir. exec. com. Preservation Alliance of Va. (now part of Preservation Va.), 1991-97, pres., 1994-96; Va. rep. bd. advisors The Nat. Trust for Historic Preservation, 2003-11; dir. The Corp. for Thomas Jefferson's Poplar Forest, 2005—; elder, trustee endowment fund Grace Covenant Presbyn. Ch.; moderator Hanover Presbytery, Presbyn. Ch. (USA), 1988. Lt. US Army, 1962—64. Fellow Am. Coll. Trust and Estate Counsel, Va. Law Found.; mem. Va. Bar Assn. (chmn. sect. on wills, trusts and estates 1981-89), Antiquarian Soc. Richmond (pres. 1977-78, 98-99), Country Club Va., Deep Run Hunt Club. Home: 1319 Shallow Well Rd Manakin Sabot VA 23103-2305 Office: Hunton & Williams Riverfront Plz E Tower 951 E Byrd St Richmond VA 23219 Home Phone: 804-784-5245; Office Phone: 804-788-8414. Business E-Mail: hwarthen@hunton.com.

WASHBURN, JOHN ROSSER, entrepreneur; b. Hopewell, Va., July 24, 1943; s. Winthrop Doane and Mary Virginia (Overstreet) W.; m. Rebecca m. Wells, Sept. 1991; 1 child, Amanda Ashley Washburn; stepchildren: Eric Joseph Harrison, Leo M. Cicone, Suzann R. Weldon. Student, Louisburg Jr. Coll., 1963-64, U. Richmond Ext., 1967-69, Williams Coll., 1985, Stanford U., 1986-87. Asst. mgr. Liberty Loan Corp., Richmond, Va., 1965-67; loan interviewer Ctrl. Fidelity Bank, Richmond, Va., 1967-69; regional credit/sales supr. Moores Bldg Supplies, Inc., Roanoke, Va., 1969-74; corp. credit mgt. Owens & Minor, Inc., Richmond, 1974-88; fin., investment cons. JA-GO Enterprises, Richmond, 1982-98; prin. agt., owner Washburn Ins. and Fin. Svcs. Group, Richmond, 1996—2005. Instr., lectr. investment fin., credit mgmt., retail pharmacy cons. & Brokerage Washburn Enterprises, 1970—; sec.-treas. Multi-Enterprises, Inc., Richmond, 1988-98; ind. agt. N.Y. Life Ins. Co., Richmond, 1994-98; dir., v.p. Forbes Clin. Rsch. Group, Richmond, 1995-2005; exec. sr. v.p. E-Com Cons., Inc., Richmond, 1998—; charter mem., ptnr. Nations Bus. Cons. Group, Tysons Corner, Va., 1998-2003; pres., CEO Washburn & Assocs., 2003—; sr. v.p. Am. Wellness Alliance Immune Health Mgmt. Group LLC, 2005—; bd. mem. Greenwoods State Bank, Pharmacy Adv. Bd., 2007-, DaneVest Capital LLC, Pharmacy Adv. Bd., 2007-; vessel examiner officer Dept. Homeland Security US Coast Guard Aux., 2007—; flotilla comdr., 2009-11, divsn. pub. affairs officer, 2011-. Active YMCA, 1979—, Am. Mus. Nat. History, 1982—, Nat. Rep. Congl. Com., 1980—, U.S. Def. Com., 1981—; mem. Credit Rsch. Found. Mem. Internat. Platform Assn., Nat. Assn. Credit Mgmt. (Appreciation cert. for outstanding svc. 1980-81, pres. ctrl. Va. sect. 1979-80, chmn. legis. com. 1977-79, dir. 1983—), Am. Mgmt. Assn., Nat. Wildlife Fedn., Nat. Assn. Life Underwriters (Nat. Quality award 1996, 97), Va. Assn. Life Underwriters, Am. Pharmacists Assn., Congressional Club, Hopewell Yacht Club, Mathews Yacht Club, Classic Yacht Club America. Episcopalian. Office: Washburn Enterprises PO Box 477 Dutton VA 23050-0477 Home Phone: 804-725-1790; Office Phone: 804-725-2614. Business E-Mail: jack@washburnandassociates.com. E-mail: jrwashburn@wildblue.net.

WASHINGTON, DONALD W., lawyer, former prosecutor; b. 1955; m. Yvonna Malonson; children: Tiffany, Greg, Donny. BS in Mech. Engring., U.S. Mil. Acad., 1977; JD, S. Tex. Coll. Law, 1989. Assoc. Alexander & McEvily, Houston, 1990—91; gen. litig. counsel Conoco Inc., 1993—96, chief counsel, Gulf of Mex. divsn., 1993—96; ptnr. Jeansonne and Redmondet, Lafayette, La., 1996—2001; US atty. (we. dist.) La. US Dept. Justice, Shreveport, La., 2001—10; ptnr. Jones Walker, Lafayette, La., 2010—. With US Army, 1977—82, with USAR, 1983—87. Office: Jones Walker 600 Jefferson St Ste 1600 Lafayette LA 70501 Office Phone: 337-262-9014. Office Fax: 337-262-9001. Business E-Mail: dwashington@joneswalker.com.

WASHINGTON, KELVIN CORNELIUS, US marshal; b. 1969; Attended, SC State U.; BS in Criminal Justice, Am. Intercontinental U., Atlanta, 2006; MS in Criminal Justice, Troy U., Ala. Various positions including patrolman, narcotics agent & investigator City of Florence Police Dept., SC, 1990—93; chief investigator, then chief dep. Williamsburg County Sheriff's Office, Kingstree, SC, 1993—98, interim-sheriff, 1998—99, sheriff Williamsburg County, 1999—2010; US Marshal for Dist. SC US Marshals Svc., US Dept. Justice, Columbia, SC, 2010—. Adj. faculty Horry-Georgetown Tech. Coll., Myrtle Beach, SC, 2007—, Charleston Southern U., 2008—. Mem.: SC Sheriff's Assn. (pres. 2007—08), Palmetto State Law Enforcement Officers' Assn., Kingstree Rotary Club. Office: US Courthouse 901 Richland St Ste 1300 Columbia SC 29201

WASHINGTON, RON, professional baseball manager; b. New Orleans, Apr. 29, 1952; m. Gerry Washington, Sept. 16, 1972. Attended, Manatee Jr. Coll., Bradenton, Fla. Infielder LA Dodgers, 1977, Minn. Twins, 1981—86, Balt. Orioles, 1987, Cleve. Indians, 1988, Houston Astros, 1989; minor league coach Tidewater Tides, Internat. League, 1991—92; minor league mgr. Capital City Bombers, South Atlantic League, SC, 1993—94; minor league coach Norfolk Tides, Internat. League, 1995; first base coach Oakland Athletics, 1996, infield coach, third base coach, 1997—2006; mgr. Tex. Rangers, 2006—. Office: Texas Rangers Baseball Club 1000 Ballpark Way Arlington TX 76011 Office Fax: 817-273-5174.

WASIELE, HARRY W., JR., diversified electrical manufacturing company executive; b. Chgo., June 29, 1926; s. Harry W. and Antoinette (Tuleja) W.; m. Loretta K. Anderson, Jan. 3, 1948; children: Kathleen Ann Wasiele Bach, Brian David, Larry Scott, Mark Thomas. Grad. high sch. Asst. sales mgr. Drake Mfg. Co., Chgo., 1950—55; sales engr. AMP, Inc., Chgo., 1955, Detroit, 1956—57, product mgr. Harrisburg, Pa., 1958—61, industry mgr., 1961—67, dir. marketing, 1967—68; gen. mgr. Brand-Rex divsn. Am. Enka Corp., Willimantic, Conn., 1968—70; pres. Brand-Rex Co., subs. Akzona Inc., 1967—83; ret., 1983. Chmn. Brand-Rex Ltd., Glenrothes, Scotland, 1974-83, Electronics SA, Iserables, Switzerland, Decollatage SA, Saint-Maurice, Switzerland, 1972-83, Pyle Nat. Ltd., Nottingham, Eng., 1974-83; v.p. sales and corp. devel. Cablec Corp., New City, N.Y., 1985—; bd. dirs. Berkel Inc.; chmn., pres. Tarpon Springs (Fla.) Internat. Tannery, Inc., 1990—. Bd. dirs. Ea. Conn. State Coll. Found., 1972-83; trustee Windham Cmty. Hosp., Willimantic, 1969-83, trustee emeritus, 1983—, pres. bd. trustees, 1981-83; trustee YMCA of Martin County Found. Served USN Air Corps., 1944-46. With air corps USN, 1944—46. Mem. Nat. Elec. Mfrs. Assn. (chmn. wire and cable div., bd. govs. 1982-84), Conn. Bus. and Industry Assn. (emeritus dir.), New Seabury Country Club, PGA Country Club. Republican. Roman Catholic. Home (Summer): PO Box 826 Mashpee MA 02649-0826 Home: 10774 Stony Creek Way Port Saint Lucie FL 34987 Home Phone: 508-477-1992, 772-345-4221. Personal E-mail: wasieles@aol.com.

WASIK, BARBARA HANNA, psychologist, educator; b. Douglas, Ga., May 29, 1942; d. Frank Joseph and Josephine (Nahoom) Hanna; m. John L. Wasik, June 24, 1966; children— John Gregory, Mark Timothy, Jeffrey Joseph AB, U. Ga., 1963; MA, Fla. State U., 1965, PhD, 1967. Lic. psychologist, N.C. Postdoctoral research fellow Duke U., Durham, NC, 1967-68; dir. research Ford Found. grant, Durham, NC, 1968-69; from asst. prof. to assoc. prof. U. N.C., Chapel Hill, 1969-77, prof., 1977—, William R. Kenan Jr. disting. prof., 2003—, assoc. dean Grad. Sch., 1972-75, chmn. div. human devel. and psychol. services, 1975-77, assoc. dean Sch. Edn., 1977-83, 1988—92, sr. investigator Child Devel. Ctr., 1972—. Mem. commn. NAS, 1998—2000; co-facilitator Nat. Forum Home Visiting, 1999—2006. Assoc. editor Jour. Applied Behavior Analysis, 1972; mem. editorial bd. Behavioral Assessment, 1984-85; contbr. chpts. to books and articles to profl. jours.; author 5 books Mem. N.C. Psychological Assn. (sec. 1982-85, pres. 1988-89), Am. Psychol. Assn. (divsn. 25 sec-treas. 1983-86, coun. rep. 1994-99, bd. edn. affairs 1999-2001, chair bd edn. affairs 2001), Soc. Research in Child Development, Southeastern Psychol. Assn., Assn. Advancement Behavior Therapy. Democrat. Roman Catholic. Home: 609 Brookview Dr Chapel Hill NC 27514-1402

WASON, ROBERT A., IV, building products manufacturing executive; JD, U. Va. Sch. Law, 1977. Various sr. mgmt. positions including gen. counsel Vulcan Materials Co., 1988—, sr. v.p. corp. devel., 1998—2008, sr. v.p., gen. counsel, 2008—, asst. sec., 2009—. Trustee, pres. Vulcan Materials Co. Found. Office: Vulcan Materials Co 1200 Urban Ctr Dr Birmingham AL 35242 Office Phone: 205-298-3000. Office Fax: 205-298-2911. Business E-Mail: robert.wason@vul.com.

WASSELL, STEPHEN ROBERT, mathematics professor, researcher; b. Santa Monica, Calif., Jan. 17, 1963; s. Desmond Anthony and Catherine Ann (Stephens) W. BS in Arch., U. Va., Charlottesville, 1984, MS in Math, 1987, PhD in Math, 1990, M in Computer Sci., 1999. Programmer, analyst UNISYS, McLean, Va., 1984-85, graphics artist, 1986; tutor summer transition program U. Va., Charlottesville, 1987-88, tchg. asst., 1986-90; asst. prof. math. Sweet Briar (Va.) Coll., 1990-96, assoc. prof. math., 1996—2002, prof. math., 2002—, dept. chmn., 1996—97, 1999—2002, 2004—05, 2009—. Prof. of record Ctr. for the Liberal Arts, U. Va., 1991; vis. asst. prof. math., U. Va., Charlottesville, 1992, vis. assoc. prof. computer sci., 1998-99; doctoral cons., Charlottesville, 1989-90. Author: (with Kim Williams) On Ratio and Proportion, 2002, (with Branko Mitrovic) Villa Cornaro, 2006, (with Kim Williams and Lionel March) Mathematical Works of Leon Battista Alberti, 2010; editor: The Golden Section, 2003, (with Kim Williams) Andrea Palladio, 2008. Recipient Grad. assistantship award U. Va., 1986-90; Gordon T. Whyburn fellow, 1985-86. Mem. AAUP (Sweet Briar chpt. sec.-treas. 1993-99), Am. Math. Soc., Math. Assn. Am., Am. Solar Energy Soc., Soc. Arch. Historians, Sigma Nu. Achievements include patents for solar powered lawnmover, solar shed, ear muffs. Office: Sweet Briar Coll Dept Math Scis Sweet Briar VA 24595 Home: PO BOX 1112 Sweet Briar VA 24595 Office Phone: 434-381-6214. Business E-Mail: wassell@sbc.edu.

WASSERMAN, MARK D., lawyer; BS summa cum laude, Clemson U., SC, 1982, MA, 1983; JD, Emory U., Ga., 1986. Bar: Ga. Ptnr. Sutherland Asbill & Brennan LLP, Atlanta, former co-chmn. corp. transactional team and mem. exec. com., mng. ptnr., 2005—. Bd. dirs. Atlanta Symphony Orch., American-Israeli C. of C., Boys & Girls Clubs Metro Atlanta, Clemson U. Rsch. Found., Equal Justice Works, Metro Atlanta C. of C.; mem. adv. bd. Georgetown U. Law Ctr. Pro Bono Inst., Best Lawyers; grad. Leadership Cobb, Leadership Ga. Named one of The Best Lawyers in America, Corp. Law, 2005—11; named to Ga. Super Lawyers, 2004—11. Office: Sutherland Asbill & Brennan LLP 999 Peachtree St NE Atlanta GA 30309-3996 Office Phone: 404-853-8398. Office Fax: 404-853-8806. Business E-Mail: mark.wasserman@sutherland.com.

WASSERMAN-SCHULTZ, DEBBIE (DEBORAH WASSERMAN-SCHULTZ), United States Representative from Florida; b. Forest Hills, NY, Sept. 27, 1966; BA in Polit. Sci., U. Fla., 1988, MA in Polit. Sci., 1990. Legis. aide office to Rep. Peter Deutsch US House of Representatives, Washington, 1989—92; mem. Dist. 97 Fla. House of Reps., 1993—2001, Democratic floor leader, 1998—99, Democratic leader pro tempore, 2000; mem. Dist. 32 Fla. State Senate, 2001—03, mem. Dist. 34, 2003—04; mem. US Congress from 20th Fla. Dist., 2005—13, US Congress from 23rd Fla. Dist., 2013—; sr. whip, 2005—06; chief dep. whip, 2008—; mem. US House Budget Com., US House Judiciary Com., 2005—06, 2011, US House Appropriations Com., 2006—; vice chair Democratic Nat. Com. (DNC), 2009—11, chair, 2011—; vice chair incumbent retention Democratic Congressional Campaign Com. (DCCC), 2009—11. Mem. Classrooms First Task Force, 1993, Fla. Edn. Facilities Study Com., 1994, Governor's Commn. Edn., 1995—97, Fla. Supreme Ct. Gender Bias Study Implementation Commn., 1992—; second v.p. Gwen Cherry Women's Polit. Caucus, 1992—; mem. legis. adv. coun. Southern Regional Edn. Bd., 1995—; chair South Fla. Democratic Caucus, 1998—. Sec. young leadership coun. Jewish Fedn. Greater Ft. Lauderdale, 1989—90; sec., v.p. Broward County Young Democrats, 1990—92; bd. trustees Westside Regional Med. Ctr., Plantation, Fla., 1993—; bd. dirs. Fla. Distance Learning Network, 1995—97, South Fla. chpt. Nat. Safety Coun., Nat. Jewish Democratic Coun., S.E. Region American Jewish Congress. Recipient Giraffe award, Women's Advocacy Majority Minority (WAMM), 1993, Outstanding Family Advocacy award, Dade County Psychol. Assn., 1993, Rosemary Barkett award, Acad. Fla. Trial Lawyers, 1995; named Woman of Yr., AMIT, 1994, Outstanding Legislator of Yr., Fla. Fedn. Bus. & Profl. Women, 1994; named a Quality Floridian, Fla. League of Cities, 1994, Woman of Vision, Weizmann Inst. Sci.; named one of The Six Most Unstoppable Women, South Fla. Mag., 1994. Mem.: NOW, Nat. Coun. Jewish Women, Hawkes Bluff Panel & Homeowner's Assn. (sec.), Weston C. of C., Pembroke Pines C. of C., Miramar C. of C., Omicron Delta Kappa. Democrat. Jewish. Avocations: bowling, golf, politics, old houses. Office: US House of Representatives 118 Cannon House Office Bldg Washington DC 20515-0920 also: 10100 Pines Blvd Pembroke Pines FL 33026 Office Phone: 202-225-7931, 954-437-3936. Office Fax: 202-226-2052, 954-437-4776.*

WASSERSTEIN, RONALD L., statistics organization director; BA in Math., Washburn U., Topeka; MS in Stats., PhD in Stats., Kans. State U., Manhattan. Faculty mem. Washburn U., 1984—96, prof. stats., 1996—2007, v.p. acad. affairs, 2001—07; exec. dir. Am. Statis. Assn., Alexandria, Va., 2007—. Mem. Kans. Ratio Study Tech. Adv. Com., 1994. Fellow: Am. Statis. Assn. Office: Am Statis Assn 732 N Washington St Alexandria VA 22314-1943 Office Phone: 703-684-1221 ext. 1859. E-mail: ron@amstat.org.

WASTAWY, SOHAIR F., library dean, consultant; b. Cairo, Nov. 7, 1954; came to U.S., 1981; d. Fahmy Elsayed Wastawy and Alia Ahmed Shaffie; children: Kareim. BA, Cairo U., 1975, MA, 1978; MLS, Cath. U., 1983; PhD, Simmons Coll., 1987. Micrographics specialist Cairo U., 1975-83; asst. prof. Inst. Pub. Adminstrn., Riyadh, Saudi Arabia, 1984-85; info. specialist, mktg. dir. Data Processing Services, Cairo, 1983-87; info. researcher Ill. Inst. Tech., Chgo., 1988-91, dir. libr., 1991—. Cons. UN, 1989—. Mem. Egyptian Soc. Info. Sci., Ill. Libr. Assn. Republican. Office: Florida Institute of Technology Dean of Libraries 150 West University Blvd Melbourne FL 32901*

WATABE, NORIMITSU, marine biologist, educator; b. Kure, Hiroshima, Japan, Nov. 29, 1922; came to U.S., 1957; s. Isamu and Matsuko (Takamatsu) W.; m. Sakuko Kobayashi, Dec. 12, 1952 (dec.); children: Shoichi, Sachiko. BS, 1st Nat. High Sch., Tokyo, 1945; MS, Tohoku U., Sendai, Japan, 1948, DSc, 1960. Rsch. investigator Fuji Pearl Co., Mie-ken, Japan, 1948-52; instr. Prefect U. Mie, Tsu, Mie-ken, 1952-55, asst. prof., 1955-59; rsch. assoc. Duke U., Durham, N.C., 1957-70; assoc. prof. U. S.C., Columbia, 1970-72, prof. biology and marine sci., 1972-93, disting. prof., 1993-94, disting. prof. emeritus, 1994—. Cons. Ford Found., 1968; vis. prof. U. Bonn, Germany, 1976-77; dir. Electron Microscipy Ctr., 19770-95; cons. in field. Author: Studies on Pearls, 1959; editor: Mechanisms of Mineralization, 1976, Mechanisms of Biomineralization, 1980, Hard Tissue Mineralization and Demineralization, 1991; assoc. editor, Jour. Morphology, 1999—; contbr. articles to profl. jours. Recipient Pearl Rsch. award Elmer W. Ellsworth, 1952, Alexander Von Humboldt award Govt. of Germany, Russel award U. SC, 1981; grantee NIH, 1971-76, NSF, 1973-95. Fellow AAAS; mem. Am. Micros. Soc. (life). Avocation: music.

WATERMAN, ROBERT A., lawyer; b. LA, Jan. 4, 1954; m. Leslie Waterman; children: Brandon, Zachary. B in English summa cum laude, Calif. State U., Long Beach, 1976; JD, U. Calif., Berkeley, 1979. Bar: Calif. 1979. Mem. McCutchen, Doyle, Brown & Enersen; ptnr. Latham & Watkins, 1993—97; sr. v.p., gen. counsel HCA, Inc., 1997—, chief labor rels. officer, 2009—. Assoc. editor Calif. Law Rev., 1977-78, note and comment editor, 1978-79. Bd. dirs. U. Sch. of Nashville; bd. editors Calif. Law Rev. Mem. State Bar Calif. Office: HCA Inc 1 Park Plz Nashville TN 37203 Office Phone: 615-344-9551. Business E-Mail: robert.waterman@hcahealthcare.com.

WATERS, JOHN B., lawyer; b. Sevierville, Tenn., July 15, 1929; s. J. B. and Myrtle (Paine) W.; m. Patsy Temple, Apr. 8, 1953; children: John B., Cynthia Beth BS, U. Tenn., 1952, JD, 1961; D in Environ. Sci. (hon.), Milligan Coll., 1993. Bar: Tenn. 1961, U.S. Dist. Ct. (ea. dist.) Tenn. 1961, U.S. Supreme Ct. 1969, U.S. Dist. Ct. D.C. 1970. Of counsel Long, Ragsdale & Waters, P.C., Knoxville, Tenn.; mng. ptnr. Waters and Co. Investment Mgmt., 1993—. Mem. hearing com. Bd. Profl. Responsibility Supreme Ct., 1974—80, 1995—2001, Fed. co-chmn. Appalachian Regional Commn., 1968—71; chmn. Sevier County Indsl. Bd., Sevierville Libr. Found.; mem. Gov.'s Com. Econ. Devel.; Tenn. rep. to So. Growth Policies Bd., 1970—74; appointed dir. by Pres. Reagan TVA, Knoxville, 1984, appointed chmn. bd. dirs. by Pres. Bush, 1992; bd. dirs. Inst. Nuc. Power Ops., 1985—93; trustee East Tenn. Bapt. Hosp., Knoxville; mem. Tenn.-Tombigbee Waterway Authority, 1993—2000; bd. dirs. East Tenn. Found.; chmn. Leadership Sevier, 1996—2001. Author: Downbound, The Memoirs of John B. Waters, Jr., 2004. Dir. Friends of Great Smoky Mountain Nat. Pk., 1993—2006. Lt. USN, 1952—55. Fellow Am. Bar Found.; mem. Tenn. Bar Assn. (pres. 1983-84), Sevier County Bar Assn. (past pres.). Republican. Baptist. Home: Waters Edge 405 Burridge Dr Sevierville TN 37862-3202 107 Joy St Sevierville TN 37862-3524 Home Phone: 865-453-3913; Office Phone: 865-453-1051. Business E-Mail: jbwaters@esper.com.

WATERS, JOHN W., minister, educator; b. Atlanta, Feb. 5, 1936; s. Henry and Mary Annie (Randall) W. Cert., U. Geneva, Switzerland, 1962; BA, Fisk U., Nashville, 1957; STB, Boston U., 1967, PhD, 1970; DD, St. Thomas Christian Coll., Jacksonville, Fla., 2006. Ordained to ministry Bapt. Ch., 1967. Min. religious edn. Ebenezer Bapt. Ch., Boston, 1965-67, assoc. min., 1967-69; min. Myrtle Bapt. Ch., West Newton, Mass., 1969, Greater Solid Rock Bapt. Ch., Atlanta, 1980—2005, sr. min. emeritus, 2005—; interim min. Friendship Baptist Ch., Atlanta, 2007—08, Fellowship Missionary Bapt. Ch., Mpls., 2008—09. Prof. Interdenominational Theol. Ctr., Atlanta, 1976-86, trustee, 1980-83, adj. prof., 2005-; bd. dirs. Habitat for Humanities, Atlanta, 1984-90; chmn. South Atlanta Joint Urban Ministries, 1983-93; chairperson Coun. Overseers New Era Bapt. Conv. Ctr., 1996-2001; pres. Clayton County Ministers Conf., 2000 Contbr. articles to profl. jours. Mem. Va. Highlands Neighborhood Assn., Atlanta, 1977-87, Butler St. YMCA, 1980-86, South Atlanta Civic League, 1983, others; treas. Prison Ministries with Women, Inc.; v.p. South Met. Ministries Fellowahip, Atlanta, 1990-94; mem. bd. overseers Sch. Theology, Boston U., 2006—. Fund for Theol. Edn. fellow, 1965-67, Nat. Fellowship Fund fellow, 1968-70, Rockefeller doctoral fellow, 1969. Mem. AAUP (chpt. pres. 1971-72), Am. Acad. Religion, Soc. Bibl. Lit., Blacks in Bibl. Studies, New Era Missionary Bapt. Conf. Ga., So. Bapt. Conv., Am. Legion Address: PO Box 310416 Atlanta GA 30331 Home: 4725 Walton Xing SW Apt 1203 Atlanta GA 30331-6282 Personal E-mail: jwwatersphd@yahoo.com.

WATERS, MICHAEL DEE, consultant; s. Dee Howard and Mary Elizabeth Waters. PhD, U. NC Sch. Medicine, Chapel Hill, 1969. Dir., Genetic Toxicology Divsn. EPA, Health Effects Rsch. Lab., Research Triangle Park, NC, 1979—92, asst. nat. lab. dir., 1992—2002; asst. dir. NIEHS, Nat. Ctr. Toxicogenomics, 2002—07; chief sci. officer Integrated Lab. Systems, Inc., 2007—13. Capt. USAR, 1969—71, Edgewood Arsenal. MD. Recipient Alexander Hollaender award sci. achievement, Environ. Mutagen Soc., 1996, Lifetime Achievement award, Genotoxicity and Environ. Mutagen Soc., 2000, Merit award, NIH, 2004, Bronze Commendable Svc. medal, EPA, 1980, 1987, 1997, 2001. Mem.: Rotary Club RTP (pres. 2008). Office: Integrated Lab Systems Inc PO Box 13501 Research Triangle Park NC 27709 Office Fax: 919-281-1118. Business E-Mail: mwaters@ils-inc.com. E-mail: mdwaters@centurylink.net.

WATJEN, THOMAS ROS, insurance company executive, board member; Attended Va. Mil. Insti., B in Economics, 1976; MBA, U. Va., 1981. With investment and corp. fin. depts. Aetna Life and Casualty, 1981-84; ptnr. Conning and Co., 1984-87; mng. dir., ins. practice group Morgan Stanley & Co., 1987-94; exec. v.p., CFO Provident Cos., Inc., Chattanooga, 1994—97, vice chmn., dir., 1997—99; exec. v.p., fin. UnumProvident Corp., Chattanooga, 1999—2002; vice chmn., COO UnumProvident Corp. (now Unum Group), Chattanooga, 2002—03; pres., CEO and dir. Unum Group, Chattanooga, 2003—. Bd. dirs. SunTrust Banks Inc., Americas Health Ins. Plans, 2004—08, Fin. Svcs. Roundtable, 2005, Am. Coun. of Life Insurers, 2007. Mem. VMI Found., 2003—. Office: Unum Group One Fountain Sq Chattanooga TN 37402 Office Phone: 423-294-1011. E-mail: twatjen@unumprovident.com.

WATKINS, CRAIG, prosecutor; b. Dallas, Nov. 16, 1967; m. Tanya Watkins; children: Taryn Michelle, Cale Marcus, Chad Marcus. BA, Prairie View A&M U., 1990; JD, Texas Wesleyan U., 1994. Dist. atty. intern. Tarrant County Dist. Atty., Tex.; prosecutor City Atty. Office, Dallas; atty. Dallas County Pub. Defender's Office; founder, prin. Craig Watkins Atty. at Law, Dallas, 1997—2007; dist. atty. Dallas, 2007—. Instr. El Centro Jr. Coll., Univ. Tex., Arlington. In numerous TV shows. Recipient Promenade Disting. award, 2009, Trumpet award, 2009; named Texan of Yr., Dallas Morning, 2008; named to Power 150, Ebony mag., 2008. Democrat. Office: Dallas Districy Atty Frank Crowley Courts Bldg LB19 133 N Industrial Blvd Dallas TX 75207-4399 Office Phone: 214-653-3600. Office Fax: 214-653-5774.

WATKINS, GEORGE DANIELS, physics professor; b. Evanston, Ill., Apr. 28, 1924; s. Paul F. and Lois V. (Daniels) W.; m. Carolyn Lenore Nevin, June 19, 1949; children: Lois Roberta, Paul Brent, Ann Romaine. BS, Randolph-Macon Coll., 1943; D.Sc. (hon.), 1976; MA, Harvard U., 1947, PhD, 1952. Research physicist Gen. Electric Research Lab., Schenectady, 1952-75; adj. prof. Rensselaer Poly. Inst., 1962-65, SUNY-Albany, 1969-72; Sherman Fairchild prof. physics Lehigh U., Bethlehem, Pa., 1975-95, prof. emeritus, 1995—; chmn. Gordon Research Conf. on Defects in Semiconductors, 1981; mem. solid state adv. com. Oak Ridge Nat. Lab., 1980-85. Mem. editl. bd. Phys. Rev. B, 1978-82; contbr. articles to profl. jours. Served to lt. (j.g.) USNR, 1943-46. NSF fellow, 1966-67; named Virginian of Yr. Va. Press Assn., 1980; recipient Alexander von Humboldt sr. U.S. Scientist award, 1983, 91. Fellow Am. Phys. Soc. (Oliver E. Buckley award 1978), AAAS, Nat. Acad. Scis. Democrat. Unitarian Universalist. Home Phone: 804-474-8654. Business E-Mail: gdw0@lehigh.edu.

WATKINS, HAYS THOMAS, retired railroad executive; b. Fern Creek, Ky., Jan. 26, 1926; s. Hays Thomas Sr. and Minnie Catherine (Whiteley) W.; m. Betty Jean Wright, Apr. 15, 1950; 1 son, Hays Thomas III. BS in Acctg., Western Ky. U., 1947; MBA, Northwestern U., 1948; LLD (hon.), Baldwin Wallace Coll., 1975, Alderson Broaddus Coll., 1980, Coll. of William and Mary, 1982, Va. Union U., 1987. CPA, Ill., Ohio. With C. & O. Ry. Cleve., 1949-80, v.p. fin., 1964-67, v.p. adminstrv. group, 1967-71, pres., CEO, 1971—73, chmn. bd., CEO, 1973—80; with B. & O. R.R., 1964-80, v.p. finance, 1964-71, pres., CEO, 1971—73, vice chmn. bd., CEO, 1973—80; chmn., CEO Chessie System, Inc., 1973—80; pres. and co-CEO CSX Corp. (merger of Chessie System, Inc. and Seaboard Coast Line Industries, Inc.), Richmond, Va., 1980—82, chmn. bd., CEO, 1982—89, chmn. bd., 1989-91; chmn. emeritus, 1991—. Vice-rector bd. visitors Coll. William & Mary, 1984-87, rector, 1987-93. With AUS, 1945-47. Named Man of Yr., Modern R.R. mag., 1984; recipient Excellence in Mgmt. award Industry Week mag., 1982. Mem. Nat. Assn. Accts., Am. Inst. C.P.A.'s. Clubs: Commonwealth (Richmond, Va.). Home: 2111 Cedarfield Ln Richmond VA 23233-1937

WATKINS, JOAN MARIE, osteopath, physician; b. Anderson, Ind., Mar. 9, 1943; d. Curtis David and Dorothy Ruth (Beckett) W.; m. Stanley G. Nodvik, Dec. 25, 1969 (div. Apr. 1974). BS, West Liberty State Coll., 1965; Cert. of Grad. Phys. Therapy, Ohio State U., 1966; DO, Phila. Coll. Osteo., 1972; M of Health Professions Edn., U. Ill., Chgo., 1986; MPH, U. Ill., 1989. Diplomate Osteo. Nat. Bds., Am. Bd. Preventive Medicine, Am. Bd. Occupl. and Environ. Medicine, Am. Bd. Emergency Medicine. Resident in phys. medicine and rehab. U. Pa., 1973—74; emergency osteo. physician Cooper Med. Ctr., Camden, 1974-79, Shore Meml. Hosp., Somers Point, NJ, 1979-81, St. Francis Hosp., Blue Island, Ill., 1981-82, Mercy Hosp. and Med. Ctr., Chgo., 1982-90, dir. emergency ctr., 1984-88; resident in occupl. and preventive medicine U. Ill., 1988-90; corp. med. dir. occupl. health svc. Univ. Cmty. Hosp., Tampa, 1992—2006; assoc. prof. environ. & occupl. health Coll. Pub. Health, USF; cons. in field, 2006—; with Tampa Occupl. Health Svcs. Fellow Am. Coll. Occupl. and Environ. Medicine, Am. Soc. Preventive Medicine, Fla. Assn. Occupl. and Environ. Medicine (pres. 1999-2001). Avocations: sailing, needlecrafts, swimming. Home: 4306 Harbor House Dr Tampa FL 33615-5408 Office: 2919 Swann Ave 102 Tampa FL 33609 Office Phone: 813-414-9400. Business E-Mail: ywatkin9@tampabay.rr.com, jwatkins@health.usf.edu.

WATKINS, JOHN CHEWNING, state legislator; b. Petersburg, Va., Mar. 1, 1947; s. Benjamin Chewning Watkins and Margaret Bowman W.; m. Kathryn Clawson, 1967; children: John Michael, Robert Schoefield, Thomas Ryan. Pres. Watkins Nurseries, Inc., 1971—; adj. faculty J. Sargeant Reynolds CC, 1972—80; mem. & Midlothian rep. Chesterfield County Bd. of Zoning Appeals, 1977—81; Va. state del. Dist. 34, 1982—83; former mem. Privileges & Election Com., Corps. Com., Ins & Banking, Fin. Com., Agr. Com.; Va. state senator, Dist. 10, 1999—; mem. Agr., Conservation & Natural Resources Com., Va. State Senate, Local Govt. & Transp. Com., Va. State Senate. Bd. dir. Sovran Bank, Richmond. Named Outstanding Young Nurseryman of South, Southern Nurseryman's Assn., 1978, Outstanding Young Man of Yr., Chesterfield County, 1982, Va. Nurseryman of Yr., 1987. Mem.: Va. Tech. Alumni Assn. Bd., Richmond Metro Chamber, Va. & Southern Nurserymen's Assn., America Assn. Nurseymen, Richmond Nurserymen's Assn. (pres. 1972), America Soc. Landscape Archs., America Nurserymen's Assn. (gov. 1983), Chesterfield Hist. Soc., America Legion Post 186, Midlothian Rotary, Va. Jaycees (life). Republican. Luth. Mailing: PO Box 159 Midlothian VA 23113-0159 Office Phone: 804-379-2063, 804-698-7510. Business E-Mail: district10@sov.state.va.us. E-mail: jnwatkins@aol.com.

WATKINS, JOHN CUMMING, JR., law educator; b. Mobile, Ala., Apr. 2, 1935; s. John Cumming and Myrtle Lisette (van Devender) W.; m. Nancy Lee Parham, Sept. 24, 1964 (div. Oct. 1971); 1 child, Scott Christopher; m. Sallie Ann Wilson, Aug. 12, 1972; children: Alicia Anne, Melissa Renee, John Cumming V. BS, U. Ala., Tuscaloosa, 1957; JD, U. Ala., 1962; MS, Fla. State U., 1964; LLM, Northwestern U., 1968. Bar: Ala. 1962, U.S. Dist Ct. (no. dist.) Ala. 1968, U.S. Ct. Appeals (5th cir.) 1970, U.S. Supreme Ct. 1973. Law clk. to assoc. justice Supreme Ct. Ala., Montgomery, 1962-63; law clk. to presiding justice U.S. Ct. Appeals (5th cir.), Tuscaloosa, Ala., 1965-66; asst. prof. bus. law Coll. Commerce U. Ala., Tuscaloosa, 1965-69, chmn. dept. criminal justice Coll. Arts and Scis., 1971-77, prof., 1975—2003, prof. emeritus criminal justice Coll. Art and Scis., 2003, acting dept. chair dept. criminal justice Coll. Arts & Scis., summer 1995; assoc. prof. criminology Sam Houston State U., Huntsville, Tex., 1969-71; adj. prof. U. Ala. Honors Coll., Tuscaloosa, Ala., 2006—. Cons. Am. Correctional Assn., 1969-71, W.K. Kellogg Found., 1976, Kresge Found., 1979-80, CHOICE, 1980—; acting dept. chmn. dept. criminal justice Coll. Arts & Scis., summer 1996—. Author: The Juvenile Justice Century, 1998, Selected Cases on Juvenile Justice in the Twentieth Century, 1999, Centennial Sourcebook on Juvenile Justice Literature: 1900-1999, 2001, War Crimes and War Crime Trials: From Leipzig to the ICC and Beyond, Cases, Materials and Comments, 2006; co-author: Introduction to Criminal Justice, 1982. Mem. adv. bd. Tuscaloosa County Juvenile Ct., 1984-88. 1st lt. U.S. Army, 1958-60. Mem. Ala. Bar Assn. (chmn. com. correctional instns. and procedures 1984-86, mem. com. on citizenship edn. 1995-96). Democrat. Episcopalian. Avocations: mil. history, model trains. Home: 2324 Trenton Dr Tuscaloosa AL 35406-1623 Personal E-mail: watkins86@comcast.net.

WATKINS, PAUL B., academic administrator, medical educator; b. Schenectady, NY, Feb. 17, 1953; s. George Daniels and Carolyn Lenore (Nevin) W.; m. Joanne Carol Spalty, July 4, 1981; children: Andrew James, Melanie Ann. BA, Cornell U., 1975; MD, Cornell Med. Sch., 1979. Intern NY Hosp.-Cornell Med. Ctr., 1979-80, resident, 1980-82; fellow Med. Coll. Va., 1982-84, from instr. to asst. prof., 1984-86; physician admission ward Khao-I-Dang Cambodian Refuge Camp, Thailand, 1982; asst. prof. U. Mich., Ann Arbor, 1986-91, assoc. prof. medicine, 1991-97, prof. medicine, 1997-99, prof. pharmacology, 1997—99, assoc. dir., Gen. Clin. Rsch. Ctr., 1991, dir., Gen. Clin. Rsch. Ctr., 1992—99; Verne S. Caviness Disting. prof. medicine U. NC, Chapel Hill, 1999—, prof. pharmacotherapy, 1999—, prof. toxicology, prof. exptl. therapeutics; dir., Gen. Clin. Rsch. Ctr. U. NC Hospitals, 1999—; dir., Inst. for Drug Safety Sciences Hamner Inst. and U. NC, Rsch. Triangle Park, 2009—. Advisor toxic waste orgn. Inst. Medicine, Washington, 1993-96; mem. toxicology study sect. NIH, Bethesda, Md., 1992-96; mem. steering com. for the Pharmacogenetics Network, Nat. Inst. Gen. Med. Sciences; steering com. chair, Drug Induced Liver Injury Network; sci. cons. Parke-Davis Pharm., Organon Internat., Wyeth-Ayerst, Proctor and Gamble, Abbott Labs., Bristol-Meyers Squibb, Severe Adverse Events Consortium, Preclinical Safety Testing Consortium; FDA cons., 1997—. Contbr. articles to profl. jours. Mem. St. Andrews Ch., Ann Arbor, 1990—. Recipient VA Career Devel. Associate Investigator award, 1984-86, Rsch. Assoc. award, 1987-91, Annual Therapeutic Frontiers' award Am. Coll. Clin. Pharmacy, 1998, NIH Merit award, 1998. Fellow ACP; mem. AAAS, Am. Soc. Clin. Investigation (elected), Am. Assn. Study Liver Disease, Am. Gastroent. Assn., Am. Fedn. Clin. Rsch., Midwest Gut Club, Ctrl. Soc. Clin. Rsch., Internat. Assn. Study Liver, Internat. Soc. Study Xenobiotics. Avocations: jogging, skiing, wind surfing, tennis, scuba diving. Home: 116 Carolina Ave Chapel Hill NC 27514-3200 Office: U NC 3312 Kerr Hall CB#7360 Chapel Hill NC 27599-7360 Address: Hamner Inst for Health Sciences 6 Davis Dr PO Box 12137 Research Triangle Park NC 27709-2137 Office Phone: 919-966-1435. Business E-Mail: pbwatkins@med.unc.edu.

WATKINS, W(ILLIAM) KEITH, federal judge; b. Troy, Ala., July 5, 1951; s. William Harold and Emily Joanne (Davis) W.; m. Teresa Marie Madigan, Sept. 11, 1976; children: William Scott, Emily Anne. BS, Auburn U., 1973; JD, U. Ala., 1976. Bar: Ala. 1976, US Dist. Ct. (no., mid., and so. dists.) Ala. Ptnr. Studwick & Watkins, Troy, Ala., 1976—78, Clower & Watkins, 1978—85, Clower, Watkins & Douglas, 1985—86, Calhoun, Watkins & Clower, 1987—90, Calhoun, Faulk, Watkins, Clower & Cox, 1990—94, Calhoun, Faulk, Watkins & Faircloth, LLC, 1994—2006; judge US Dist. Ct. (mid. dist.) Ala., 2005—. Baptist. Office: US Dist Ct E300 Fed Courthouse Annex One Church St Montgomery AL 36104

WATSON, ARTHUR DENNIS, federal official; b. Brownsville, Pa., May 11, 1950; s. Arthur Francis and Margaret Teresa (Mastile) Puglia, John Leslie Watson (Stepfather); m. Kathleen Frances Zaccardo, July 16, 1983; 1 child, Fiona Kathleen. BSBA, U. Richmond, 1972; MS in Bus.-Govt. Rels., Am. U., 1977, MA in Lit., 1979; PhD in English Lang. and Lit., Cath. U., 1987. Statis. asst. U.S. Postal Svc. Hdqrs., Washington, 1972—73, economist assoc., 1973—74, staff economist, 1974—77, mktg. analyst, 1977; rate analyst U.S. Postal Rate Commn., Washington, 1977—79, dir. pub. affairs, 1979—82; pub. affairs officer ICC, Washington, 1982—89, dep. dir. pub. affairs, 1989—93, assoc. dir. congl. and pub. affairs, 1993—95; dir. media affairs Dept. Transp., Washington, 1996—2008, dir. comm. surface transp., 2008—. Pres. Arthur D. Watson and Co., Clifton, Va., 1983—; Washington corr. Linn's Stamp News, Sidney, Ohio, 1983—84. Contbr. articles to profl. jours. With USCG, 1972—78. Recipient Meritorious Svc. medal, USCG Res., Pub. Svc. award, ICC, 1989, Spl. Achievement award, Surface Transp. Bd., 1999, Merger Response Team Performance award, 2000, Performance award for media and pub. affairs, 2000, Second Pl. award, Internat. Plastic Modelers Soc. (No. Va. divsn.), 2000, Merger Response Team Performance award, Surface Transp. Bd., 2001, Agy. Performance award Merger team, 2001, Performance award for website enhancements, 2002, Performance award for media and pub. affairs, 2002, award, Fed. Govt., 2011, Spl. Performance award, 2008, Unique Contribution award, 2012. Mem.: Nat. Assn. Govt. Communicators, Assn. Transp. Law Profls., Nat. Assn. RR Passengers, E. Clairborne Robins Sch. Bus. Alumni Assn. Avocations: classical music, reading, writing, model building, travel. Home: 6521 Rockland Dr Clifton VA 20124-2415 Office: Surface Transp Bd 395 E St SW Ste 1208 Washington DC 20423-0001 Office Phone: 202-245-0234.

WATSON, BARBARA, state legislator; b. Miami, Fla. m. Alvin Watson; 6 children. Former owner Watson Antique and Classic Cars; councilwoman Miami Gardens City Coun., Fla., 2003—10, vice mayor, 2007—09; mem. Dist. 103 Fla. House of Reps., Tallahassee, 2011—. Founder Jr. Coun., Miami Gardens, Young Progressive Adults, Miami Gardens, World Care, Inc.; mem. Dade County Limousine Adv. Bd., North Dade Mcpl. Adv. Com., Miami-Dade County North Task Force, Com. to Inc. Miami; mem. Dist. 1 Miami-Dade Task Force; coun. mem. Nat. State and County League of Cities. Mem.: CIND, Fla. Limousine Assn. South Fla., Andover Civic Assn. Democrat. Office: 610 NW 183rd St Ste 204 Miami FL 33169-4472 also: Fla House of Reps 1401 The Capitol 402 S Monroe St Tallahassee FL 32399-1300 Office Phone: 305-654-7100, 850-488-0766.

WATSON, BEN, state legislator; b. July 27; m. Bernice Watson; 3 children. B, U. Ga.; MD, Med. Coll. Ga. Primary care physician, Savannah, Ga., 1988—; mem. Dist. 163 Ga. House of Representatives, 2011—. Republican. Office: 1326 Eisenhower Dr #2 Savannah GA 31406 also: Georgia House of Reps 404 Coverdell Legis Office Bldg Atlanta GA 30334 Office Phone: 404-656-0109. Business E-Mail: ben.watson@haouse.ga.gov.

WATSON, BUBBA (GERRY LESTER WATSON JR.), professional golfer; b. Bagdad, Fla., Nov. 5, 1978; s. Gerry Lester and Molly Marie Watson; m. Angela P. Ball; 1 adopted child, Caleb. Grad., U. Ga., 2008. Mem. Nationwide Tour, 2003—05, PGA Tour, 2006—. Mem. US team Ryder Cup, 2010, 2012, Presidents Cup, 2011. Christian. Achievements include winner PGA Tour events: Travelers Championship, 2010; Farmers Insurance Open, Zurich Classic, 2011, Northern Trust Open, 2014; winner PGA Tour major championships: Masters Tournament, 2012, 2014. Office: 100 PGA TOUR Blvd Ponte Vedra Beach FL 32082*

WATSON, CAROL A., law librarian; BA in Comparative Lit., U. Ga., 1981, MEd, JD cum laude, 1987; MSLS, Atlanta U., 1990. Joined Alexander Campbell King Law Library, U. Ga. Sch. Law, Athens, 1987, assoc. dir. info. tech., dir. Co-author (with James Donovan): Behind a Law School's Decision to Implement an Institutional Repository; contbr. articles to law jours. Mem.: ABA, Ga. Bar Assn., American Assn. Law Libraries. Office: University of Georgia School Law Law Library 225 Herty Dr Athens GA 30602-6012 Office Phone: 706-542-5078. Office Fax: 706-542-5001. E-mail: cwatson@uga.edu.

WATSON, CHUCK, oil industry executive; m. Kim Watson; 3 children. Chmn., CEO NGC Corp.; with Conoco Inc.; pres. Natural Gas Clearinghouse (predecessor Dynegy), 1985-89; predecessor Dynegy, 1989, chmn., CEO, 1989—2002; chmn. Wincrest Ventures, LP, 1994—, Eagle Energy Ptnrs., 2003—09, Collegiate Zone LP, 2004, Sigma Chi Found., 2005; mng. dir. Lehman Bros., 2007—08; sr. advisor EDF Trading N. Am. LLC, 2008, Electricite de France, 2008; chmn. CLW Investments, Inc., 2009—. Bd. dirs. Nat. Petroleum Coun., Ind. Prodrs. Assn. of Am. Bd. dirs. Make-a-Wish Found., Houston, Arts Fund, Theatre Under the Stars; chmn. Alexis de Tocqueville Soc. 1997-98 campaigns for United Way of Texas Gulf Coast; chmn., trustee, gov. Ohio State U. Found. Named (with family) Family of Yr., Child Advocates. Mem. Nat. Petroleum Coun., Interstate Natural Gas Assn. (bd. dirs.), Natural Gas Coun. (founding mem.), Tex. Gov.'s Bus. Coun., Houston Forum (bd. govs.). Office: 1000 Louisiana St Houston TX 77002-5000 also: CLW Investments Inc 223 S Hillcrest Dr Goldsboro NC 27534-7540 Office Phone: 919-922-9980. Business E-Mail: charles.watson@bakerhughes.com.

WATSON, DAVID H., physician; BS, Baylor U., Waco, Tex.; MD, Baylor Coll. Medicine, Houston, 1957. Rotating gen. internship Hermann Hosp., Houston; with Yoakum Med. Clinic, Tex., 1958—. Recipient Country Doctor of Yr., Staff Care, 2008. Avocations: crossword puzzles, reading, history. Office: Yoakum Medical Clinic 402 Hubbard St Yoakum TX 77995 Office Phone: 361-293-2371.

WATSON, DONALD CHARLES, JR., cardiothoracic surgeon, educator; b. Fairfield, Ohio, Mar. 15, 1945; s. Donald Charles and Pricilla H. Watson; m. Susan Robertson Prince, June 23, 1973; children: Kea Huntington, Katherine Anne, Kirsten Prince. BA in Applied Sci., Lehigh U., 1968, BSME, 1969; MSME, Stanford U., 1969; MD, Duke U., 1972; MBA, Vanderbilt U., 1992. Diplomate Am. Bd. Thoracic Surgery, Am. Bd. Surgery. Intern Stanford U. Med. Ctr., Calif., 1972-73, resident in cardiovasc. surgery Calif., 1973-74, resident in surgery Calif., 1976-78, chief resident in heart transplant Calif., 1978-79, chief resident in cardiovasc. and gen. surgery Calif., 1978-80; clin. assoc. surgery br. Nat. Heart and Lung Inst., 1974-76, acting sr. surgeon, 1976; assoc. cardiovasc. surgeon dept. child health and devel. George Washington U., Washington, 1980-84, asst. prof. surgery, asst. prof. child health and devel., 1980-84, attending cardiovasc. surgeon dept. child health and devel., 1984-89, assoc. prof. surgery, 1984-89; assoc. prof. pediats. U. Tenn.-Memphis, 1984-90, prof. surgery, 1990—2006, prof. pediats., 1990—2006, chmn. cardiothoracic surgery, 1984-99, assoc. chief med. officer, 1999—2001. Mem. staff Le Bonheur Children's Med. Ctr., Memphis, 1984—2006, chmn. cardiothoracic surgery, 1984-99; cons. in field; instr. advanced trauma life support; profl. cons., program reviewer HHS. Contbr. chpts., numerous articles, revs. to profl. publs. Bd. dirs. Airlift Hope Am., Internat. Children's Heart Found., Child Health Alliance Mid-South. Served to lt. comdr. USPHS, 1974-76. Smith Kline & French fellow Lehigh U., 1967; NSF fellow Lehigh U., 1968; univ. interdepartmental scholar and univ. scholar Lehigh U., 1968. Fellow Am. Coll. Cardiology, ACS; mem. Am. Assn. Thoracic Surgery, Soc. Thoracic Surgeons, So. Thoracic Surg. Assn., Andrew G. Morrow Soc., Norman E. Shumway Soc. (multiple bd. dirs.), NIH Alumni Assn., Stanford U. Med. Alumni Assn., Stanford U. Alumni Assn., Lehigh U. Alumni Assn., Smithsonian Assocs., U. Tenn. Pres.'s Club, LeBonheur Pres' Club, Pilots Internat. Assn., Nat. Assn. Flight Instrs., Aircraft Owners and Pilots Assn., Biltmore Forest Country Club, Phi Beta Kappa, Tau Beta Pi, Pi Tau Sigma, Phi Gamma Delta. Republican. Presbyterian. Achievements include established a regional referral center for the treatment of congenital heart disease. Avocations: golf, sailing, mountain climbing, flying.

WATSON, ERIC, state legislator; b. Sept. 14, 1973; Former police officer Bradley County Sheriff'S Office; promoted to lt., 2006; mem. Eric Watson & Tenn. Harmony, 1998—2005; mem. Dist. 22 Tenn. House of Reps., 2006—; mem. Judiciary Com., Transp. Com., Task Force, Immigration & Citizenship. Recipient Excellence Award, Tenn. Govt., 1998, Bradley County Life Saving award, 2001, Officer of Month, Bradley County Sheriff's Office, 2001, Bradley County Pub. Svc. award, 2003. Mem.: NRA, Tenn. Warrant Officers Assn., Nat. Wild Turkey Fedn., Fraternal Order Police, Southern Gospel Music Assn. Republican. Baptist. Office: 605 Ocoee Hills Cir Cleveland TN 37323-8771 also: 205 War Memorial Bldg Nashville TN 37243-0122 Office Phone: 423-339-0939, 615-741-7799. Office Fax: 615-532-8221. Business E-Mail: rep.eric.watson@capitol.tn.gov.

WATSON, FOY W. (BO WATSON), state legislator; b. Oct. 20, 1960; married; 1 child. Former mem. Health & Human Resources Com., Govt. Oper. Com.; state rep. Dist. 31 Tenn., 2005—07; house rep. Tenn.; state senator Dist. 11 Tenn., 2007—. Mem.: U. Tenn. Nat. Alumni Assn., America Cancer Soc. Relay Life, Pachyderm Club. Republican. Methodist. Office: 1607 Gunston Hall Rd Hixson TN 37343 also: 6A Legislative Plz Nashville TN 37243-0211 Office Phone: 615-741-3227. Office Fax: 615-253-0280. Business E-Mail: sen.bo.watson@capitol.tn.gov.

WATSON, JACK CROZIER, retired state supreme court justice; b. Jonesville, La., Sept. 17, 1928; s. Jesse Crozier and Gladys Lucille (Talbot) W.; m. Henrietta Sue Carter, Dec. 26, 1958; children: Carter Crozier (dec.), Wells Talbot. BA, U. Southwestern La., 1949; JD, La. State U., 1956; completed with honor, Appellate Judges Seminar, NYU, 1974, Sr. Appellate Judges Seminar, 1980. Bar: La. 1956. Atty. King, Anderson & Swift, Lake Charles, La., 1956—58; prosecutor City of Lake Charles, 1960; asst. dist. atty. Calcasieu Parish, La., 1961—64; ptnr. Watson & Watson, Lake Charles, 1961—64; judge 14th Jud. Dist., La., 1964—72; judge ad hoc Ct. Appeals, 1st Cir., Baton Rouge, 1972—73; judge Ct. Appeals, 3d Cir., Lake Charles, 1973—79; assoc. justice La. Supreme Ct., New Orleans, 1979—96, ret., 1996; of counsel Baggett, McCall, Burgess, Watson & Gaughan, Lake Charles, 2004—. Faculty advisor Nat. Coll. State Judiciary, Reno, 1970, 73; adj. prof. law admiralty summer sch. program in Greece, Tulane U., 1988-2000, 2005-11; adj. prof. law So. U., Baton Rouge, 1998-99; del. NEH Seminar, 1976; La. del to Internat. Conf. Appellate Magistrates, The Philippines, 1977; mem. La. Jud. Coun., 1986-92. 1st lt. USAF, 1950-54. Mem. ABA, La. Bar Assn., S.W. La. Bar Assn. (pres. 1963), Law Inst. State of La., La. Coun. Juvenile Ct. Judges (pres. 1969-70), Am. Judicature Soc., S.W. La. Camellia Soc. (pres. 1973-74), Am. Legion (post comdr. 1963), Lake Charles Yacht Club (commodore 1974), Blue Key, Sigma Alpha Epsilon, Phi Delta Phi, Pi Kappa Delta. Democrat. Baptist. Office Phone: 337-478-8888.

WATSON, JAMES RAYMOND, philosopher; b. Blue Island, Ill., July 29, 1938; s. William James Henry Watson and Edna Mae Stucker; m. Suzette Marie Gehant, July 8, 1969. AB, Marquette Univ., Milw., 1966; MA, Univ. Wisc., Milw., 1969; PhD, So. Ill. Univ., Carbondale, Ill., 1973. Data analyst Clark Oil & Refining, Blue Island, Ill., 1958—59; photographic asst. Waltersheffer's Studio of Photography, Milw., 1960—61; photography instr. Layton Sch. of Art, Milw., 1960—61; asst. prof. Loyola Univ., New Orleans, 1973—77, assoc. prof., 1977—94, prof., 1994—2009, prof. emeritus, 2009—. Pres. SPSGH, 1996—; rsch. assoc. Pic. Univ. of Binghamton, NY, 2002—; assoc. editor Routledge Contintential Phila. Series, NY, 2001—; editor Rodopi Genocide & Holocaust Studies, 2009—. Author: Between Auschwitz and Tradition, 1994, Continental Philosophers in America, 1999, Contemporary Portrayals of Auschwitz, 2000, Metacide, 2010. Exec. com. ACLU Miss., Jackson, 2002—06; bd. dirs. Picayune on Stage, Picayune, Miss., 2001—06. Pvt.1st. class US Army, 1961—63. Vis. scholar Max-Planck-Gesellschaft, Berlin, Germany, 1994. Mem.: Soc. Phenomenology and Existential Philosophy, Soc. for Philos. Study of Genocide and the Holocaust (pres.), Am. Philos. Assn. Avocations: photography, theater, painting. Home: 7 Pertusa Way Hot Springs Village AR 71909-8140 Personal E-mail: profjrwatson@me.com.

WATSON, JIM ALBERT, gas industry executive, lawyer; b. Rotan, Tex., Feb. 1, 1939; s. Morris Gilbert and Mae (Montgomery) W.; m. Paula Gayle Hickman, June 3, 1962; children: Michael Montgomery, Jennifer Ruth. BA, U. Tex., 1962, JD with Honors, 1964. Bar: Tex. 1964. Ptnr. Johnson & Gibbs, Dallas, 1975-95, Vinson & Elkins L.L.P., Dallas, 1995; sr. counsel Carrington, Coleman, Sloman, & Blumenthal, L.L.P, Dallas, 2003. Adj. prof. law U. Tex., 2000-2004; chmn. adv. bd. legal history Southern. Meth. U., 1989, bd. dirs., Pioneer Natural Resources Co., 2004-, Johnson & Gibbs, Dallas, Tex. Mem. exec. council The Tex. State Hist. Assn., 1992—. Office: Pioneer Natural Resources Co Bd Directors 5205 N O'Connor Blvd Ste 200 Irving TX 75039 Office Phone: 972-444-9001. Office Fax: 972-969-3576. Business E-Mail: watsonj@pioneernrc.com.

WATSON, JOHN, retail executive; BA in Economics, Georgetown U.; MBA, Dartmouth Coll. Various positions Espirit De Corp., Germany; pres., gen. mgr. Fairwinds Gourmet Coffee Co., New Hampshire; mgmt. cons. McKinsey & Co. Inc.; various positions Mexx Group B.V., Holland; sr. v.p., strategic mktg. Reebok International Ltd.; pres., CEO Sunglass Hut Internat.; COO HSN, Inc., 2003, COO, HSN US, 2003—. Office: HSN Inc 1 HSN Dr Saint Petersburg FL 33729 Office Phone: 727-872-1000. Business E-Mail: john.watson@hsn.net.

WATSON, KIRK, state legislator; b. Oklahoma City, 1958; m. Liz McDaniel; children: Preston, Cooper. JD cum laude with highest honors, Baylor U., 1981. Bar: Tex., U.S. Dist. Ct. (wc., ea. and no. dists.) Tex., U.S. Ct. Appeals (5th and 11th cirs.), U.S. Claims Ct., U.S. Supreme Ct. Law clk. to Hon. Sam D. Johnson US Ct. Appeals (5th cir.), 1981-82; assoc. Scott, Douglass & Luton, 1982-84, ptnr., 1985-86; assoc. Kidd, Whitehurst & Harkness, 1986-87; ptnr. Whitehurst, Harkness, Watson, London, Ozmun & Galow (formerly Kidd, Whitehurst, Harkness & Watson and Whitehurst, Harkness & Watson), 1987-97; mng. ptnr. Watson, Bishop, London & Galow, Austin, Tex., 1997; mayor City of Austin, 1997—2001; ptnr. Hughes & Luce LLP, 1997—; mem. Dist. 14 Tex. State Sentate, 2007—. Chair Tex. Air Control Bd., 1991-93; vice-chair Gov.'s Environ. Agys. Transition Com., 1993; bd. dirs. Leadership Austin, 1994-96; lectr. in field. Contbr. articles to profl. jours. Bd. dirs. Austin chpt. Am. Diabetes Assn., Am. Cancer Soc., 1995-97; mem. govtl. affairs com. Am. Lung Assn., 1993-97; bd. dirs. Downtown Austin Alliance, Tex. Mcpl. League, Austin Fire Fighters' Relief and Ret. Fund, Lance Armstrong Found.; treas., bd. dirs. Environ. Def. Fund Tex.; bd. dirs. Tex. Lyceum Assn., 1993-97; mem. instnl. rev. bd. Tex. Cancer Ctr., Brackenridge, 1994-96; chair CLEAN AIR Force Ctrl. Tex., Welfare-to-Work Oversight Com., Homeless Stakeholder's Com., Audit and Finance Sub-Com.; vice chair govtl. rels. Greater Austin C. of C., 1996; pres. Austin Dem. Forum, 1989-93; chair com. legal svcs. to poor in civil matters State Bar Tex., 1991—; CEO HIV Planning Coun.; mem. U.S. Conf. Mayors, task force electric utility restructuring; chair Dem. Precinct, 1982-83, mem. exec. coun. Travis County, 1982-83, chair, 1994-96; pres. North Austin Dems., 1984; vice chair New Tex. Found., 1991. Recipient Presdl. citation State Bar Tex., 1991, 93, Advocacy award Am. Lung Assn. Tex., 1993, Spl. Svc. award Lone Star chpt. Sierra Club, 1994, Excellence in Pub. Interest award Tex. Law Fellowship, 1997, Cmty. Trusteeship award Leadership Austin, 1998, Impact award Downtown Austin Alliance, 1998, Bravo award Ballet Austin, 1998; named Outstanding Young Lawyer of Tex., Tex. Young Lawyers Assn., 1994, one of Baylor U. Sesquicentennial Men and Women of Merit, Baylor U., 1995, Outstanding Young Alumni, 1996, Young Baylor Lawyer of Yr., 1997, Pub. Adminstr. of Yr., Am. Soc. Pub. Adminstrs., 1998, Cmty. Person of Yr., S.M.A.R.T., 1998. Fellow Am. Bar Found., Tex. Bar Found. (life); mem. Assn. Trial Lawyers Am., Tex. Trial Lawyers Assn. (assoc. dir. 1988—), Trial Lawyers for Pub. Justice. Democrat. Office: PO Box 12068 Capitol Station Austin TX 78711 Office Phone: 512-463-0114.

WATSON, MICHAEL, state legislator; b. Pasagula, MS, Dec. 22, 1977; Attended, U. Miss. Atty.; mem. Dist. 51 Miss. State Senate, 2008—, vice chair judiciary B com. Republican. Assembly Of God. Home: 5402 Hilltop St Pascagoula MS 39567 Office: PO Box 1018 Jackson MS 39215 Office Phone: 228-762-2272, 601-359-3234. E-mail: mwatson@senate.ms.gov.

WATSON, MICHAEL B., state legislator; b. Hopewell, Va., Sept. 19, 1961; m. Amy Michelle Bourbonais; children: Thomas, Adam, Taylor. AAS in Instrumentation Tech., New River CC, 1983. Pres., CEO Control Automation Technologies Corp.; mem. Dist. 93 Va. House of Delegates, 2012—, mem. Gen. Laws Com. & Sci. and Tech. Com. Mem.: Internat. Soc. Automation (sr.). Republican. Office: General Assembly Building PO Box 406 Richmond VA 23218 also: PO Box 6628 Williamsburg VA 23188 Office Phone: 804-698-1093. Office Fax: 804-698-6793. E-mail: DelMWatson@house.virginia.gov.

WATSON, PERCY WILLIS, state legislator; b. Hattiesburg, Miss., June 5, 1951; m. Dianne Davis; children: Ayanna, Kobie, Anika Nina, Megan, Mallori. Mem. Dist. 103 Miss. House of Reps., 1980—; advisor bd. mem. Deposit Guaranty Nat. Bank; atty. Mem.: NAACP, Miss. Legal Svc., Optimist, Am. Judicature Soc., Hattiesburg C. of C., Miss. Trial Lawyers Assn., Hattiesburg Advisor Bd., Forrest Colo. Chap., Am. Bar Assn., Nat. Bar Assn., Alaska Bar Assn., Iowa Bar Assn., Miss. Bar Assn., Jesse Brown Lodge. Democrat. Baptist. Mailing: PO Box 1767 Hattiesburg MS 39403 Home Phone: 601-544-6490; Office Phone: 601-359-3343, 601-545-1051. E-mail: pwatson@house.ms.gov.

WATSON, RAYMOND COKE, JR., engineering executive, consultant, academic administrator; b. Anniston, Ala., Aug. 31, 1926; BS, Jacksonville State U.; MSE, U. Ala.; MS, U. Fla.; MBA and PhD in Engring. Sci., Calif. Coast U. Chief engr. Dixie Svc. Co., 1948-54; head dept. physics and engring. Jacksonville State U., 1954-60; v.p. engring. and rsch. Teledyne Brown Engring., 1960-70, chief engr., chief scientist, 1990—2001; dir. continuing edn., engring. and math. U. Ala., Huntsville, 1970-76; pres., prof. engring. and math. Southeastern Inst. Tech., Huntsville, 1976—; owner RC Watson & Assocs., 1980—; pres., CEO Vision Techs. Kinetics, 2000—03. Adj. assoc. prof. U. Ala., Huntsville, 1961-70. Contbr. more than 450 articles and reports to profl. jours. Chmn. elec. engring. adv. bd. Ala. A&M U. Recipient NASA Pub. Svc. award; NSF Sci. Faculty Fellow. Mem. IEEE, AIAA, Optical Soc. Am., Ops. Rsch. Soc. Am., Inst. Mgmt. Sci., Internat. Soc. Optical Engrs., Inst. Indsl. Engrs. Achievements include research in defense systems, space systems and electro-optics. Home: 1801 Inspiration Ln SE Huntsville AL 35801-1150 Office: RC Watson & Assocs PO Box 1485 Huntsville AL 35807 Office Phone: 256-651-1834. Business E-Mail: rcw-assoc@comcast.net.

WATSON, ROBERT FRANCIS, lawyer; b. Houston, Jan. 9, 1936; s. Louis Leon and Lora Elizabeth (Hodges) W.; m. Marietta Kiser, Nov. 24, 1961; children: Julia, Melissa, Rebecca. BA, Vanderbilt U., 1957; JD, U. Denver, 1959. Bar: Colo. 1959, U.S. Dist. Ct. (no. dist.) Tex. 1967, U.S. Supreme Ct. 1968, Tex. 1973, U.S. Ct. Appeals (5th cir.) 1973, U.S. Dist. Ct. (so. dist.) Tex. 1980, U.S. Ct. Appeals (11th cir.) 1981. Law clk. U.S. Dist. Ct. Colo., 1960-61; trial atty. SEC, Denver, 1961-67, asst. regional adminstr. Ft. Worth, 1967-72, regional adminstr., 1972-75; ptnr. Law, Snakard & Gambill, P.C., Ft. Worth, 1975-98, of counsel, 1998—2005, shareholder, 2005—12, of counsel, 2012—; exec. v.p., gen. counsel First Command Fin. Svcs., Inc., Ft. Worth, 1998—2005. Counsel City of Ft. Worth Police Investigation Commn., 1975; spl. counsel Office Atty. Gen. State Ariz., 1977-78. Contbr. articles to profl. jours. Mem. Ft. Worth Crime Commn., 1987-93. Honoree 27th Ann. Rocky Mountain State-Fed.-Provincial Securities Conf. Fellow: Coll. of State Bar Tex., U. Denver Law Sch. Alumni Coun., Colo. Bar Assn., Tex. Bar Found. (life), Tarrant County Bar Assn., Ft. Worth Club; mem.: ABA, Tarrant County Bar Found. (charter), Tex. Bus. Law Found. (bd.dirs. 1988—93), State Bar Tex., Fed. Bar Assn., Shady Oaks Country Club (Ft. Worth), Phi Delta Phi. Republican. Presbyterian. Office: Law Snakard & Gambill PC 4055 International Plz Fort Worth TX 76109-4874 Office Phone: 817-878-6374. Business E-Mail: bwatson@lawsnakard.com.*

WATSON, ROBERT JOE, retired health facility administrator, retired career officer; b. Wellington, Kans., Nov. 12, 1934; s. Charles Bruce and Marguerite B. (Scholes) W.; m. Ursula Eschenroeder, Dec. 26, 1983; children: Stephanie Watson-Zollinger, Stacy Watson Bruce, Susannah Watson Gold; stepchildren: Jurgen Wanke, Claudia Beeck. MS in Edn., Kans. State Tchrs. Coll., 1963; MBA, U. Hawaii, 1969; MHA, George Washington U., 1973, EdD, 1976; student, Command-Gen. Staff Coll., 1973, U.S. Army War Coll., 1986. Commd. 2nd lt. U.S. Army, 1963, advanced through grades to col., 1989; stationed at Tripler Army Med. Ctr., Honolulu, 1967-69, USARV Surgeons Office, Long Binh, Vietnam, 1969-70, Surgeon Gen.'s Office, Washington, 1970-74, Walter Reed Med. Ctr., Washington, 1974-76, Acad. Health Svcs., Ft. Sam Houston, Tex., 1976—80, 68th Med. Group, Ziegenberg, Germany, 1980-82, U.S. Army Hosp., Ft. Riley, Kans., 1982-84, 34th Gen. Hosp., Augsburg, Germany, 1984-87; assoc. dean USA Med. Field Svc. Sch., Ft. Sam Houston, Tex., 1987—89; assoc. dir. Student Health Ctr. U. Fla., Gainesville, 1989—2005; ret., 2005. Fellow Am. Coll. Healthcare Execs. (adv., regent 1982-84). Episcopalian. Avocations: tennis, golf, gardening.

WATSON, ROBERT WINTHROP, poet; b. Passaic, NJ, Dec. 26, 1925; s. Winthrop and Laura Berdan (Trimble) W.; m. Elizabeth Ann Rean, Jan. 12, 1952; children: Winthrop, Caroline. BA, Williams Coll., 1946; postgrad., U. Zurich, 1947; MA, Johns Hopkins, 1950, PhD in English, 1955. Instr. English Williams Coll., 1946, 47-48, 52-53, Johns Hopkins, 1950-52; mem. faculty U. NC, Greensboro, 1953—, prof. English, 1963-90. Vis. poet, prof. English Calif. State U., Northridge, 1968-69 Author: (poetry) A Paper Horse, 1962, Advantages of Dark, 1966 (Runner-up, Pulitzer prize), Christmas in Las Vegas, 1971, Selected Poems, 1974, Island of Bones, 1977, Night Blooming Cactus, 1980, The Pendulum: New and Selected Poems, 1995, Complete Poems, 2011; (novels) Three Sides of the Mirror, 1966, Lily Lang, 1977, (art book) Betty Watson Paintings, 1999; co-founder The Greensboro Rev., 1966. Swiss-Am. exch. fellow, 1947; grantee Nat. Endowment for Arts, 1973; recipient Am. Scholar Poetry prize, 1959, Lit. award Am. Acad. Inst. Arts Letters, 1977. Home: 4321 Galax Trail Greensboro NC 27410

WATSON, STEVEN L., chemicals executive; Pres., bd. dirs. Contran, 1998—, Valhi Corp., 1998—, CEO, 2002—, Titanium Metals Corp., 2006—09, vice chmn., 2005—, Kronos Worldwide, 2004—, CEO, 2009—. Bd. dirs. Keystone Consolidated Industries, Inc., NL Industries Inc., 2000—, CompX Internat. Inc., 2000. Vice chmn. bd. Kronos Worldwide, 2004—; bd. dir. CompX, Keystone, TIMET. Office: Valhi Inc 5430 Lyndon B Johnson Fwy Ste 1700 Dallas TX 75240 Office Phone: 972-233-1700. Office Fax: 972-448-1445. Business E-Mail: swatson@valhi.net.

WATSON, WELDON, state legislator; Mem. Dist. 79 Okla. House of Representatives, 2007—. Republican. Address: PO Box 35692 Tulsa OK 74153 Office: Oklahoma House of Representatives 2300 N Lincoln Blvd Rm 302 Oklahoma City OK 73105 Office Phone: 405-557-7330. E-mail: weldon.watson@okhouse.gov.

WATT, J.J. (JUSTIN JAMES WATT), professional football player; b. Pewaukee, Wis., Mar. 22, 1989; s. John and Connie Watt. Attended, Ctrl. Mich. U., Mount Pleasant, 2007, U. Wis., Madison, 2008—11. Defensive end Houston Texans, 2011—. Founder, bd. dirs. Justin J. Watt Found. Recipient Lott IMPACT award, Pacific Club IMPACT Found., 2010; named NFL Defensive Player of Yr., AP, 2012, Defensive Player of Yr., Pro Football Writers America (PFWA), 2012, 1st Team All-Pro, AP, 2012; named to The American Football Conf. Pro Bowl Team, NFL, 2012. Achievements include leading the NFL in: sacks, 2012. Office: The Houston Texans Two Reliant Pk Houston TX 77054 also: Justin J Watt Foundation PO Box 530 Pewaukee WI 53072*

WATT, JOSEPH MICHAEL, state supreme court justice; b. Austin, Tex., Mar. 8, 1947; m. Cathy Watt; children: Justin, Christopher, Jennifer, Michael. BA in Hist., Tex. Tech U., 1969; JD, U. Tex. Law Sch., 1972. Bar: Tex. 1972, Okla. 1974. Pvt. practice, Altus, Okla., 1972-85; judge Dist. Trial Ct., 1985-91; gen. counsel to gov. State of Okla., Oklahoma City, 1991-92; justice Okla. Supreme Ct., Okahoma City, 1992—, vice-chief justice, 2001—02, chief justice Okahoma City, 2003—04. Liaison to Okla. Bar Assn. Okla. Supreme Ct., 1997—98; mem. Appellate Divsn. Ct. on Judiciary, 1997—98, Truth in Sentencing Commn., Supreme Ct. Long Range Planning Commn.; chmn. Supreme Ct. Com. Time Standards. Mem.: Okla. Bar Assn. Office: Oklahoma Supreme Ct Okla Judicial Ctr 2100 N Lincoln Blvd Ste 4 Oklahoma City OK 73105-4907 Office Phone: 405-521-3848. Fax: 405-521-6982. E-mail: joseph.watt@oscn.net.*

WATT, WILLIAM STEWART, retired physical chemist; b. Perth, Scotland, Feb. 25, 1937; BSc, U. St. Andrews, Scotland, 1959; PhD in Phys. Chemistry, U. Leeds, 1962. Fellow Cornell U., 1962-64; rsch. chemist Cornell Aeronautics Lab., Buffalo, 1964-71; head chem. laser sect. Naval Rsch. Lab., 1971-73, dep. head laser physics br., 1973-76, head laser physics br. optical sci. divsn., 1976-79; gen. mgr. wash ops. W. J. Schafer Assoc., Arlington, Va., 1979-80, v.p. program devel., 1980-90, sr. v.p., dir. programs, 1991-94; CEO Lawrence Assocs., Inc., Arlington, 1994-95; pres. WSW Consulting Inc., 1996—2002. Active U.S. Army Sci. Bd., 1992-98. Recipient J. B. Cohen Rsch. prize, 1962. Mem. IEEE (assoc. editor Jour. Quantum Electronics), Am. Phys. Soc., Combustion Inst., Sigma Xi. Achievements include research in laser physics and development, laser-induced chemistry, energy transfer and reaction rate measurements, optical diagnostics. E-mail: billswatt@bellsouth.net.

WATTS, ANTHONY LEE, bank executive; b. Griffin, Ga., Jan. 24, 1947; s. Edgar Lee and Eula Mae (Benton) W.; m. Barbara Malinda Harp, Oct. 11, 1969; children: Natalie Paige, Barbara Leigh, Melanie Marie. AA, Gordon Mil. Coll., 1967; ABJ, U. Ga., Atlanta, 1969. Conventional loan rep. Fed. Nat. Mortgage Assn., Atlanta, from 1971, asst. regional appraiser, quality control and property mgr., to 1976; v.p., dir. ins. svcs. Ticor Mortgage Ins. Co., Atlanta, 1976-82; v.p., regional sales and exec. v.p. Ticor Indemnity Co., 1982-85; sr. v.p., regional mgr. Ticor Mortgage Ins. Co., Atlanta, 1984, sr. v.p., ea. divsn. mgr., 1984-85; pres. Mt. Vernon Fed. Savs. Bank, Dunwoody, Ga., 1985-95, Mt Vernon Fin. Corp., 1993-95; prin., dir. Banc Mortgage Fin. Corp., 1996-99, vice chmn., co-CEO, 1999—2002, co-pres., 2003—04; ret., 2004. Lectr. to trade assns. Founder, pres, co. registered Watts Family Enterprises, Inc., 1995; elder, bd. Peachtree Christian Ch.; former bd. dirs. Ga. Spl. Olympics, 2006—09, hon. bd., 2010—. With US Army, 1969—71. Recipient Bronze Star. Mem.: Phoenix Soc. (former bd. dirs.), Gridiron Club, Rotary Club (Paul Harris fellow 1987).

WATTS, CLAUDIUS ELMER, III, retired military officer; b. Bennettsville, SC, Sept. 22, 1936; s. Claudius Elmer and Blanche Robey (Wannamaker) Watts; m. Patricia Jane Sims, July 23, 1960;

children: Claudius Elmer IV, Patricia Watts Heck. AB in Polit. Sci., The Citadel, 1958; postgrad. (Fulbright scholar), London Sch. Econs. and Polit. Sci., 1958-59; MBA, Stanford U., 1967; PhD, Citadel, Charleston,SC, 1996. Commd. officer USAF, 1958, advanced through grades to lt. gen., 1986, comdr. 438th Mil. Airlift Group McGuire AFB, NJ, 1979-80, comdr. 63d Mil. Airlift Wing Norton AFB, Calif., 1980-82, asst. dep. chief staff plans Mil. Airlift Command Scott AFB, Ill., 1982-83, dep. chief staff plans Mil. Airlift Command, 1983-84; dir. budget Hdqrs. U.S. Air Force, Washington, 1984-85; sr. mil. asst. to dep. sec. def. U.S. Dept. Def., Washington, 1985-86; compt. USAF, Washington, 1986-89; pres. Citadel, Charleston, SC, 1989-96; ret., 2000. Former adv. coun. grad. sch. bus. Stanford U.; former bd. visitors Air U.; former chmn. peer rev. teams, mem. coun. NCAA Coun.; former trustee Aerospace Edn. Found.; bd. dirs., chair audit com. Cmty. First Bank S.C.; former bd. dirs. Crescent Mortgage Co.; chmn. Carolina Fin. Corp. Past trustee Palmetto Partnership; past chmn. Marion Sq. Commn.; former bd. dirs., mem. fin. com. Air Force Aid Soc.; mem. bd. advisors Am. Leadership Found. Decorated Def. Disting. Svc. medal, USAF Disting. Svc. medal, Legion of Merit with oak leaf cluster, DFC with two oak leaf clusters, Air medal with 10 oak leaf clusters, Gallantry Cross with Palm, Vietnamese Svc. medal with 2 svc. stars Vietnam; Paul Harris fellow, Rotary. Mem.: VFW, Mil. Officers Assn. Am., Am. Soc. Mil. Comptrs., Airlift Assn., Air Force Sgts. Assn., Air Force Assn., Am. Legion, Order of Daedalians, Mil. Order World Wars. Methodist. Avocations: golf, reading. Office: 229 Country Club Ln Charleston SC 29412-2208 Business E-Mail: wattsc@citadel.edu.

WATTS, D. WAYNE, telecommunications industry executive, lawyer; b. Abilene, Tex. BBA, U. Tex., Austin, 1976; JD, So. Meth. U., Dallas, 1980. Bar: US Dist. Ct. (no. dist. Tex.), US Dist. Ct. (ea. dist. Tex.), US Ct. Appeals (5th cir.), US Ct. Appeals (8th cir.). Atty. Southwestern Bell Telephone Co., Dallas, 1983—86, mergers and acquisitions staff, legal dept. St. Louis, 1988—89, v.p., asst. gen. counsel; gen. atty. Southwestern Bell Publs., St. Louis, 1986—88; v.p., gen. atty., sec. Southwestern Bell Mobile Systems, Dallas, 1989—95; gen. atty., asst. gen. counsel SBC Comm. Inc., counsel, mergers and acquisitions, wireless ops.; v.p., assoc. gen. counsel AT&T Inc. (merger of SBC Communications & AT&T Corp.), sr. exec. v.p., gen. counsel, 2007—. Mem.: ABA, Mo. Bar Assn., State Bar Tex. Office: AT&T Inc 175 E Houston St San Antonio TX 78299 Office Phone: 210-821-4105.

WATTS, RAY L., dean, neurologist, educator; b. Birmingham, Ala. BS in Engring., U. Ala., Birmingham, 1976; MD, Wash. U., St. Louis, 1980. Internship, residency in neurology Mass. Gen. Hosp., Boston; clin. fellowship Harvard U. Med. Sch., Mass.; fellowship in motor control and movement disorders NIH, 1984—86; mem. neurology faculty Emory U., Atlanta, 1986—2003, prof., vice chmn. neurology dept., 1998—2003; John N. Whitaker prof. and chmn. neurology U. Ala., Birmingham, 2003—10, sr. v.p. medicine, dean sch. medicine, 2010—, James C. Lee endowed chmn., prof. neurology, 2010—; pres. U. Ala. Health Services Found., 2005—; interim CEO U. Ala. Birmingham Health Sys., 2008; chief neurology U. Ala. Hosp. Co-editor: Movement Disorders: Neurologic Principles and Practice, 1997—. Office: University Ala Birmingham Office of Sr VP and Dean of Sch Medicine 1530 3d Ave S FOT 1203 Birmingham AL 35294-3412 Office Phone: 205-934-1111. Office Fax: 205-996-4039. Business E-Mail: rlwatts@uab.edu.*

WATTS, VIVIAN E., state legislator; b. Detroit, June 7, 1940; BA cum laude, U. Mich., 1962. Dir. rsch. & legis. Fairfax C. of C., 1977—79; legis. aide to Joseph L. Fisher US House of Representatives, 1979—80; mem. Dist. 39 Va. House of Delegates, 1982—86, 1996—; rsch. cons. Arthur Young & Co., 1985—86; exec. dir. Fairfax Ct. Apptd. Spl. Advocates, 1993; mem. Cts. Justice Com., Sci. & Tech. Com., Fin. Com. Author: (book) The Role of General Government Elected Officials in Criminal Justice, 1993, Guide to the Criminal Justice System for General Government Elected Officials, 1993; contbr. articles. Recipient Grand Cross Color, Supreme Assembly Order Rainbow, 1959, Fairfax Citizen of Yr., Washington Star, 1978, America Soc. of Civil Engr. Svc. award, 1989; named Most Promising Freshman, Va. Gen. Assembly Leadership, 1982, Woman of Yr., Network Bus. & Profl. Women, 1982, Citizen of Yr., Annadale C. of C., 1986. Mem.: Fairfax Com. 100 (foundong mem. 1977), Women Exec. in State Govt. (nat. bd. mem. 1987—), League Women Voters (pres. 1975—77), Nat. Capital Area United Way (bd. mem. 1977—). Democrat. Unitarian Universalist. Office: 8717 Mary Lee Ln Annandale VA 22003 Office Phone: 703-978-2989. Office Fax: 703-978-5762. Business E-Mail: DelVWatts@house.virginia.gov.

WATTS, WENDY HAZEL, wine consultant; b. York, Pa., Oct. 9, 1952; d. Alphonso Irving and Daphne Jean (Gainsford) Watts; m. Frederic Joseph Bonnie, (div. 1986); m. Kenneth Scott Herron, Feb. 14, 1987 (div. Jan. 1992). BS, U. Cin., 1975. Store mgr. The Grapevine, Inc., Birmingham, Ala., 1978-81; sales rep. Supreme Beverage Co., Birmingham, 1981-84, Internat. Wines Co., Birmingham, 1984-90; nat. sales exec. Kermit Lynch Wine Mcht., Berkeley, Calif., 1990-91; on-premise mgr., fine wine mgr. Premier Beverage Co., Birmingham, 1991-94; key accounts mgr. Ala. Crown Distbg. Co., Birmingham, 1994-95; dir. of wine Mountain Brook location Western Supermarkets, 1995—2001; dist. mgr. Winebow Italian Imports, 2001—05, state mgr., 2005—07; creative dir. Vintage Wine Shoppe, 2007—09; wine buyer Whole Foods Market, Mountain Brook, 2009—. Instr. ednl. wine tasting classes, 1996—; spkr., instr. various groups, Birmingham; co-chmn. Sonoma Wine Tour of Birmingham, 1987—88, chmn., 1989—90, Wine Tour of France, Birmingham, 1988—89; mem. exec. com. Taste of the Nation, 1992—98; exec. com. Alabama Chpt. Internat. Wine and Food Soc., 2004—06, 2013—; mem. Tuesday Group, Pvt. Wine Tasting Group, 1978—; founding mem. Monday Group, 2012—; wine instr. Farmhouse in Trussville; wine columnist Birmingham Weekly, 2011—12. Wine radio show host, 1992, Wine Edn. Videos, 2009—. Co-chmn. Multiple Sclerosis Wine Auction, 1992—93, mem. exec. com., 1997-2011; co-chair Share Our Strength Taste of the Nation, Birmingham, 1996-98; bd. dirs. Magic City Harvest, 1999-2009, vice chair, 2005-2008; mem. com. So. Environ. Ctr. Democrat. Avocations: films, hiking, travel, jewelry making. Office Phone: 205-912-8400 ext 196. Personal E-mail: winewench@windstream.net.

WAUD, ROGER NEIL, economist, educator; b. Detroit, Mar. 26, 1938; s. Othneil Stockwell and Mary Josephine (Gough) Waud; children: Heather, Neil. BA magna cum laude, Harvard U., 1956—60; MA in Applied Stats., U. Calif., Berkeley, 1960—62; PhD in Economics (Ford Found. fellow), U. Calif., Berekley, 1962—64. Asst. prof. bus. econs. Grad. Sch. Bus. U. Chgo., 1964-69; assoc. prof. econs. U. N.C., Chapel Hill, 1969-72, prof., 1972-97, prof. emeritus, 1997—; sr. economist, bd. govs. Fed. Res. Sys., Washington, 1973-75; prof., dir. grad. econs. program Va. Tech., 1997—2002. Cons. Dept. Labor; mem. adv. bd. Taxpayers Ednl. Coalition, 1981; rsch. assoc. Nat. Bur. Econ. Rsch., 1982—92; vis. scholar Cambridge U., 1983; mem. N.C. Energy Policy Coun., 1986—92; vis. prof. Duke U., 1992—94. Author: Macroeconomics, 5th edit., 1992, Microeconomics, 5th edit., 1992; mem. editl. bd. So. Econ. Jour., 1970—73, Studies Econs. and Fin., 1995—97; contbr. articles to profl. jours., anthologies to poems. Mem.: Potomac River Generating Sta. Monitoring Group, Urban Design Adv. Com., AGENDA Alexandria (bd. mem.), North Old Town Ind. Citizens Assn. (pres. 2003—10), Alexandria Fedn. Civic Assn. (co-chair 2010—12), So. Econ. Assn. (exec. com. 1977—79), Am. Econ. Assn.

WAUN, ROGER, small business owner, minister; b. Mount Clemens, Mich., Oct. 20, 1944; m. Vicki Waun; 5 children. BS, Eastern Mich. U., 1966, MA, 1968; attended, Pitts. Theol. Sem. Strategic intelligence officer US Army Reserves; co-owner regional wholesale distributorship bus.; pastor First Presbyn. Ch., Childress, Tex., Quanah. Democrat. Office: One Surrey Cir Wichita Falls TX 76309 Business E-Mail: roger@rogerwaun.com.

WAX, GEORGE LOUIS, lawyer; b. New Orleans, Dec. 6, 1928; s. John Edward and Theresa (Schaff) W.; m. Patricia Ann Delaney, Feb. 20, 1965; children: Louis Jude, Joann Olga, Therese Marie. LLB, Loyola U. South, 1952, BCS, 1960. Bar: La. 1952. Law practice, New Orleans, 1954—. With USNR, 1952—54. Mem.: New Orleans Bar Assn., La. Bar Assn., Southern Yacht Club, Suburban Gun and Rod Club, New Orleans Athletic Club, Kiwanis, Am. Legion. Roman Catholic. Office: 3228 6th St Ste 100 Metairie LA 70002 Home: 4609 Chateau Dr Metairie LA 70002 Home Phone: 504-456-0772; Office Phone: 504-837-3428. Personal E-mail: gwax2@cox.net.

WAY, BARBARA HAIGHT, retired dermatologist; b. Franklin, NJ, Dec. 27, 1941; d. Charles Padley and Alice Barbara (Haight) Shoemaker; m. Anthony Biden Way; children: Matthew Shoemaker Way, Sarah Shoemaker Way. AB in Music cum laude, Bryn Mawr Coll., 1962, postgrad., 1963-64; MD, U. Pa., 1968. Diplomate Am. Bd. Dermatology. Systems engr. IBM, Balt., 1962—63; mem. dean's staff Bryn Mawr (Pa.) Coll., 1963—64; med. intern U. Wis. Hosps., Madison, 1968—69, resident in dermatology, 1969—72; physician emergency rm. St. Francis Hosp., La Crosse, Wis., 1969—72, founder dept. dermatology, 1972; asst. prof. dept. dermatology Tex. Tech U. Sch. Medicine, Lubbock, 1972—73, from asst. clin. to assoc. clin. prof., 1973—74, asst. prof., assoc. chair, 1974—76, assoc. prof., chair, 1976—81, assoc. clin. prof., 1981—92; clin. prof. Tex. Tech. U. Health Scis. Ctr., Lubbock, 1995—2005, founder, dir. dermatology residency tng. program, 1978—81, pvt. practice, 1973—74, 1981—2006; acting dir. Lubbock City Health Dept., 1982—83; ret., 2006. Mem. credentials com. Covenant Hosp., Lubbock, 1990, 92, 94, 95, founding dir. phototherapy unit, 1990-91, 93, exec. com., 1991, 93, 98, chief dermatology sect., 1991, 93, 98, subsect. chief, 1992, 94. Alumna admissions rep. Bryn Mawr Coll., 1972-75, 87-96; mem. selection com. outstanding physician Lubbock chpt. Am. Cancer Soc., 1991-94, chmn., 1991; bd. dirs. Tex. Tech. U. Med. Found., 1987-89, Double T. Connection, 1988-90. Fellow Am. Acad. Dermatology (reviewer jour.); mem. Tex. Dermatol. Soc. (chmn. roster com. 1980), Tex. Med. Assn. (mem. sexually transmitted diseases com. 1986-90, mem. coun. pub. health 1990-92, vice councillor dist. III 1992-98, councillor dist. III 1998-2000, chmn. reference com. fin. and orgnl. affairs ann. session 1992), Lubbock County-Garza County Med. Soc. (mem. various coms. 1980-2000, chmn. sch. and pub. health com. 1983, mem. bd. censors 1983-85, chair 1985, sec. 1986, v.p. 1987, liaison with Tex. Tech. U. Health Scis. Ctr. com. 1988-91, co-chmn. pub. rels. com. 1988-89, alt. Tex. Med. Assn. del. 1988-89, del. 1990-95, 98-2000, pres.-elect 1989, pres. 1990, chmn. ad hoc bylaws com. 1991-94, chmn. Hippocratic award 1991), Women's Dermatologic Soc. (founding sec.), Dallas County Medical Res. Corp. Personal E-mail: anthony.way@ttuhsc.edu.

WAY, JACOB EDSON, III, museum director; b. Chgo., May 18, 1947; s. Jacob Edson Jr. and Amelia (Evans) W.; m. Jean Ellwood Chappell, Sept. 6, 1969; children: Sarah Chappell Quiroga, Rebecca Stoddard, Jacob Edson IV. BA, Beloit Coll., 1968; MA, U. Toronto, 1971, PhD, 1978; MDiv, Episcopal Theol. Sem. S.W., 2008. From instr. to assoc. prof. Beloit (Wis.) Coll., 1972—85; dir. Logan Mus. Anthropology, Beloit, 1980-85, Wheelwright Mus. Am. Indian, Santa Fe, 1985-89; interim dir. N.Mex. Mus. Natural History, Albuquerque, 1990-91; exec. dir. Space Ctr. Internat. Space Hall of Fame, Alamogordo, N.Mex., 1991-94; dir. N.Mex. Farm and Ranch Heritage Mus., 1994-99; cultural affairs officer State of N.Mex., Santa Fe, 1997—2003; realtor Margo Cutler, Ltd., Santa Fe, 2003—05; rector St. Christopher Episcopal Ch., Lubbock, Tex., 2008—. Evaluator Nat. Park Service, Denver, 1986. Contbr. articles to profl. jours. Mem. Nuke Watch, Beloit, 1983-84; cultural affairs officer State of N.Mex., 1997-2003. Research grants Wis. Humanities Com., 1984, NSF, 1981; grantee Cullister Found., 1978-84; fellow U. Toronto, 1971. Mem. Am. Assn. Mus., Am. Assn. Phys. Anthropology, Can. Assn. for Phys. Anthropology, N.Mex. Assn. Mus. (pres. 1994-96), Soc. Am. Archaeology, Wis. Fedn. Mus. (adv. bd. 1982-85). Avocations: camping, skiing, fishing, reading, horseback riding. Office Phone: 806-799-8208. Personal E-mail: jeway@earthlink.net.

WAYNE, DONALD CHARLES, lawyer; b. Ala., 1967; m. Robin Wayne; children: Sophia, Natalie. BS, Tufts U., 1989; JD, St. Louis Sch. Law, 1994; MBA, Washington U. Atty. Akin, Gump, Strauss, Hauer & Feld, LLP, 1994—99; v.p., gen. counsel, sec. US Concrete, Inc., 1999—2006, Universal, 2006—07; v.p., sec. Exterran GP, LLC, sr. v.p., gen. counsel, 2006—08; sr. v.p., gen. counsel, sec. Exterran Holdings, Inc., 2008—. Office: Exterran Holdings Inc 16666 Northchase Dr Houston TX 77060 Office Phone: 281-836-7000.

WAYNE, JIM, state legislator; b. May 21, 1948; Psychotherapist & president Wayne & Assoc. Inc.; mem. Dist. 35 Ky. House of Reps., 1991—; mem. Smith Coll. Sch. Social Work, Louisville Coalition Homeless Bd. Mem.: Governor's Advisor Coun. Cmty. Svcs., Beargrass Creek Task Force, Ky. Soc. Clin. Social Work (former pres.), Jefferson Co. Advisor Coun. Women, Louisville Forum. Democrat. Roman Catholic. Mailing: 1280 Royal Ave Louisville KY 40204 Home Phone: 502-456-4856; Office Phone: 502-564-8100 ext. 616.

WEAKLEY, CLARE GEORGE, JR., insurance company executive, theologian, entrepreneur; b. Dallas, Apr. 14, 1928; s. Clare George and Louise (Cunningham) Weakley; m. Jean C. Burrow, July 20, 1962; children from previous marriage: Clare George III, Carol J.(dec.), Charles E. BBA, So. Meth. U., 1948, ThM, 1967. Ordained to ministry Christian Cmty., 1977. With Employers Ins., Dallas, 1948-52; owner Weakley & Co., Dallas, 1952-2001. Founder, pres. Am. Svc. Found., Inc., 1967—, Cornerstone Ministries, 1982—, Small Bus. Assn., Inc., 1988—; founder Christian Cmty., 1977—, leader; vis. prof. western bus. theory and Christian ethics St. Petersburg (Russia) Internat. Mgmt. Inst. (formerly Leningrad Internat. Mgmt. Inst.), 1990—. Author: In God We Trust, 1997, God 101, 1998; author, editor: The Wesley Library Series for Today's Reader, The Nature of the Kingdom, 1976, The Nature of Spiritual Growth, 1977, The Nature of Revival, 1987, The Nature of Salvation, 1988, The Nature Holiness, 1988; editor: John Wesley's Commentary on the Sermon on the Mount. Republican. Home: 13731 Goldmark Dr Apt 1207 Dallas TX 75240-4220 Office: Christian Cmty 13731 Goldmark Dr #1207 Dallas TX 75240 E-mail: clare@christian-community.org, cweaklty1@tx.rr.com.

WEATHERFORD, WILL W., state legislator; b. Dallas, Nov. 14, 1979; m. Courtney Weatherford; 1 child, Ella Kate. BS, Jacksonville U., Fla., 2002. Businessman; mem. Dist. 61 Fla. House of Reps., Tallahassee, 2006—, chair edn. policy coun., mem. preK-12 appropriations com., rules and calendar coun., select policy coun. on strategic and econ. planning. Mem. Commn. on Open Govt., Big Brothers Big Sisters; Fund for Am. Studies; Wesley Chapel C. of C. Republican. Christian. Office: 28963 State Rd 54 Ste A Wesley Chapel FL 33544 also: 222 The Capitol 402 S Monroe St Tallahassee FL 32399-1300 Office Phone: 813-558-5115, 850-488-5744.

WEATHERSBY, CECIL JERRY, accounting and finance manager; b. Birmingham, Ala., Oct. 28, 1952; s. E.W. and Dorothy M. (Zuiderhoek) W.; m. Julia Diane Harris, Feb. 26, 1976; children: Matthew, Blake, Nathan. BBA, St. Bernard Coll., 1975; MS in Adminstrv. Sci., U. Ala., Huntsville, 1988. Acct. City of Cullman, 1977; asst. plant acct. Cullman (Ala.) Electric Coop., 1977-82, contr., 1982-88, mgr. acctg. and fin., 1988-95; chief fin. officer Hired Hand Mfg., Inc., 1995—. Bd. dirs. HessAire Products, Inc., Cullman, Hired Hand Mfg., Inc.; mem. adj. faculty Wallace State C.C., Hanceville, Ala. Bd. dirs. Cullman Regional Med. Ctr., 1994—, sec. 1997, vice chmn. 1998, chmn. bd. dirs., 2001-03; bd. dirs. Cullman Area C. of C., 1999-2002, Leadership Cullman County, 1999; moderator Cullman Presbytery, 2000; trustee Cullman Regional Med. Ctr. Found., 2001. Recipient Founders award, Cullman Family Recreation Complex, 1990. Mem. Nat. Inst. Mgmt. Accts., North Ala. Power Accts. Assn. (chmn. 1986-87), Tenn. Valley Pub. Power Assn. (pres. acctg. sect. 1989), Kiwanis (bd. dirs. 1994-95). Presbyterian. Office: Hired Hand Mfg Inc PO Box 99 Bremen AL 35033-0099

WEATHERSBY, MICHAEL NELSON, lawyer; b. Columbus, Ga., Oct. 20, 1956; s. Nelson Jennings and Erma (Spann) W.; m. Phyllis Solomon, Nov. 30, 1973 (div. Dec. 1980); 1 child, James Michael; m. Risë Hegwood, Mar. 21, 1982; children, Alexander Hegwood, John Thomas. Lang. cert. Turkish, Presidio of Monterey (Calif.), 1976; BA summa cum laude, Ga. SW Coll., 1981; JD cum laude, U. Ga., 1984. Bar: Ga., D.C, Fla., Tex. Retail mgr. Benson Wholesale Co., Geneva, Ala., 1973-75; translater Ft. Meade, Md., 1976—79; sales mgr. Williams Office Equipment Co., Americus, Ga., 1980-81; law clk. Ga. Gov.'s Office, Atlanta, 1982; assoc. Neely & Player, Atlanta, 1984-87, Glass, McCullough, Sherrill & Harrold, Atlanta, 1987-89; ptnr. Evert Weathersby Houff, Atlanta, 1989—. Gen. counsel HDX-USA, Inc., Atlanta. Mem. and elder Intown Comty. Presbyterian Church. With USAF, 1975—79. Fellow Bryant T. Castellow Found., 1981-84. Mem. ABA, State Bar of Ga., D.C. Bar, Tex. Bar, Ga. Trial Lawyers Assn., Assn. Trial Lawyers Am., Druid Hills Golf Club, Sigma Tau Delta. Office: Evert Weathersby Houff Ste 200 3405 Piedmont Rd Atlanta GA 30305 Office Phone: 678-651-1222. Office Fax: 678-651-1201. Business E-Mail: mnweathersby@ewhlaw.com.

WEATHERSBY, THOMAS CABE (TOM WEATHERSBY), state legislator; b. Jackson, Miss., Aug. 24, 1944; m. Beverly Cook; children: Tommy, Clay, Bradley. Mem. Dist. 62 Miss. House of Reps., 1992—; businessman. Mem.: Nat. Rifle Assn., Miss. Cattleman's Assn., Rankin & Copiah County C. of C., Rankin County Livestock Assn. (bd. mem.), Kiwanis, Florence Lions Club, Mason. Republican. Baptist. Mailing: 3806 Hwy 49 S Florence MS 39073 Home Phone: 601-845-2017; Office Phone: 601-359-4076, 601-845-2017. Business E-Mail: tweathersby@house.ms.gov.

WEATHERSON, DONALD, information technology executive; Grad., US Naval Acad.; MS in Petroleum Mgmt., U. Kansas. Pres. Compaq Can., Compaq Fed., Wash., DC; various sr. exec. positions Compaq Computer Corp., 1993—2002; CEO Navy Exch. System, 1990—93; v.p., N.Am. ops & strategy Hewlett-Packard Co., 2000—02; interim CEO, chmn., pres. GovConnection, Inc., 2003—04; chmn. Enliven Mktg. Technologies Corp. (acquired by DG FastChannel, Inc.). Bd. dirs. GovConnection, Inc., 2003—05, PC Connection, Inc., 2005—. CEO Navy Exch. System, USN, 1990-93; former rear admiral USN, 1993. Rear admiral USN, 1993. Office: DG FastChannel Inc Ste 700 750 W John Carpenter Fwy Irving TX 75039 also: Enliven Marketing Technologies Corp 205 W 39th St Fl 16 New York NY 10018 Office Phone: 212-201-0800. Office Fax: 212-201-0801. Business E-Mail: dweatherson@pcconnection.com.

WEATHERSPOON, TERESA GAYE, women's college basketball coach, retired professional basketball player; b. Jasper, Tex., Dec. 8, 1965; Grad., La. Tech. Inst., 1988. Guard Blusto, Italy, 1988—89, 1990—93, Magenta, Italy, 1989—90, Como, Italy, 1996—97, CSKA, Russia, 1993—95, NY Liberty, NYC, 1997—2003, LA Sparks, 2004; head coach Westchester Phantoms, 2007—08; assoc. head coach La. Tech. U. Lady Techsters, 2008—09, head basketball coach, 2009—. Recipient Gold medal, World Championship, 1986, Goodwill Games, 1986, World Univ. Games, 1987, Olympic Games, Seoul, 1988, Bronze medal, Olympic Games, Barcelona, 1992, Broderick Cup, Wade Trophy; named La. State Player of Yr., 1988, Kodak All-Am., 1987, 1988, WNBA Defensive Player of Yr., 1997, 1998; named a WNBA All-Star, 1999—2002; named to NCAA Women's Basketball Team Decade, 1980, La. Tech Athletics Hall of Fame, 1996, Women's Basketball Hall of Fame, 2010, La. Sports Hall of Fame, 2010, NY Liberty Ring of Honor, 2011. Office: La Tech Athletics PO Box 3046 Ruston LA 71272 Office Phone: 318-257-4111. Business E-Mail: tspoon@latech.edu.

WEAVER, APRIL C., state legislator; married. BBA, U. Ala., 1993; MBA, 2006. Registered nurse, 1997; cert. legal nurse. Joined Bibb Med. Ctr., 1999, dir. pub., cmty. & govt. rels.; joined Shelby Baptist Med. Ctr., 2002, dir. bus. devel.; mem. Dist. 49 Ala. House of Representatives, 2011—. Mem. Statewide Healthcare Coordinating Coun., Ala. State Rep. Exec. Com., Bibb County Rep. Party, Shelby County Rep. Party, Westwood Baptist Ch. Mem.: Ala. Hosp. Assn. (hon. chmn.), Ala. Healthcare Public Rels. & Mktg. Soc. (hon. chmn.). Republican. Office: Ala House of Reps Rm 522-B 11 S Union St Montgomery AL 36130 Office Phone: 334-242-7731.

WEAVER, DIANNE JAY, lawyer; b. Kansas City, Mo., June 28, 1944; d. Thomas G. and Anna Jeanette Jay; m. Benjamin J. Weaver, Sept. 16, 1970; children: Jay, Jenny, Scott, Elizabeth. BS, U. Kans., 1965; JD, Ind. U., 1970. Bar: Ind., Fla., Colo.; bd. cert. trial lawyer. Ptnr. Weaver & Weaver, P.A., Ft. Lauderdale, Fla.; of counsel Krupnick Campbell Malone Roselli Buser Slama & Hancock P.A., Ft. Lauderdale; ptnr. Harrell & Narrel, P.A., Jacksonville, 2002—. Speaker in field. Contbr. articles to profl. jours. Trustee Civil Justice Found.; bd. dirs. Trial Lawyers for Pub. Justice; chmn. publicity com. Civil Justice Found. Fellow Roscoe Pound Found. (life); mem. ATLA (bd. govs., sec.), Acad. Fla. Trial Lawyers (bd. dirs.), So. Trial Lawyers Assn. (bd. govs.), Fla. Bar Assn. (chair trial advocacy com.). Fed. Bar Assn., Broward County Women Lawyers Assn. (founding pres.). Office: Harrell & Harrell PA 4735 Sunbeam Rd Jacksonville FL 32257 Business E-Mail: dweaver@forjustice.com.

WEAVER, JANET See COATS, JANET

WEAVER, LISA, information technology executive; BSBA, Wayne State U., Detroit, Mich. Dir. fin. retail products divsn. Fruit of the Loom's; ops. contr. N.Am. Sitel Corp., v.p. global fin. planning & analysis, CFO, Recall N.Am. Office: Recall North America One Recall Center 180 Technology Pky Norcross GA 30092 Office Phone: 888-732-2556.

WEAVER, LYNN EDWARD, academic administrator, consultant, editor; b. St. Louis, Jan. 12, 1930; s. Lienous E. and Estelle F. (Laspe) W.; m. JoAnn D., 1951 (div. 1981); children: Terry Sollenberger, Gwen, Bart, Stephen, Wes; m. Anita G. Gomez, Oct. 27, 1983. BSEE, U. Mo., 1951; MSEE, So. Meth. U., 1955; PhD, Purdue U., 1958. Devel. engr. McDonnell Aircraft, St. Louis, 1952-53; aerophysics engr. Convair Corp., Ft. Worth, 1953-55; instr. elec. engring. Purdue U., Lafayette, Ind., 1955-58; assoc. prof., then prof., dept. head U. Ariz., Tucson, 1959-69; assoc. dean coll. engring. U. Okla., Norman, 1969-70; exec. asst. to pres. Argonne Univs., Chgo., 1970-72; dir. sch. nuclear engring. and health physics Ga. Inst. Tech., 1972-82; dean engring., disting. prof. Auburn (Ala.) U., 1982-87; pres. Fla. Inst. Tech., Melbourne, 1987—2002, pres. emeritus, prof. elec. engring., 2002—. Cons. Ga. Power; bd. dirs. DBA Systems, Inc., Melbourne, Fla.; chmn. pub. affairs coun. Am. Assn. Engring. Soc., Washington, 1984-87; bd. adv. Ctr. for Sci., Tech. and Media, Washington; chmn. Ind. Colls. and Univs. Fla., 1999-2001. Author: (textbook) Reactor Dynamics & Control, State Space Techniques, 1968; exec. editor Annals of Nuclear Energy; contbr. numerous articles to tech. jours. U.S. rep. World Fedn., Engring. Orgn. Energy Com., 1981-86; bd. dirs. myregion.org, 2001-. Served to lt. USAF, 1951-53. Recipient U. Mo. Honors award for disting. svc. in engring., 1996. Fellow Am. Nuclear Soc.; mem. IEEE (sr.), Am. Soc. Engring. Edn., Sigma Xi, Eau Gallie Yacht Club. Republican. Roman Catholic. Avocations: tennis, jogging. Office: Fla Inst Tech 150 W University Blvd Melbourne FL 32901-6975 Office Phone: 321-674-8099. Business E-Mail: lweaver@fit.edu.

WEAVER, PAMELA ANN, education educator; b. Little Falls, NY, July 7, 1947; d. Floyd Aron Weaver and Norma May (Putnam) Hoyer; m. Ken Ward McCleary, Mar. 2, 1947; children: Brian Wilson, Blake McCleary, Ryan McCleary. AA, Fulton Montgomery C.C., Amsterdam, NY, 1968; BA, SUNY, 1970; MA, U. South Fla., 1973; PhD, Mich. State U., East Lansing, 1978. Mem. math. dept. Riviera Jr. H.S., Miami, Fla., 1970-72; grad. asst. Office Med., Edn. R & D Mich. State U., East Lansing, 1973-74, grad. asst. dept. mktg., 1974-75, instr. mktg.; asst. prof. mktg., hospitality svcs. administrn. Ctrl. Mich. State U., Mt. Pleasant, 1978-79, 1982-86, chair acad. senate, 1985-86, prof. mktg., hospitality svcs. administrn., 1986-89; prof., undergrad. program coord. dept. hospitality and tourism mgmt. Va. Poly. Inst. and State U., Blacksburg, 1989—, undergrad. program coord., 2005—. Contbr. over 100 articles to profl. jours. Mem. Coun. on Hotel, Restaurant and Instl. Edn. (John Wiley & Sons, Inc. award for Lifetime Achievement to Hospitality Industry 1994). Office: Va Poly Inst and State U Wallace Hall Blacksburg VA 24061-0429 Business E-Mail: weaver@vt.edu.

WEAVER, PAUL E., board member; BS, Elizabethtown Coll.; MBA, U. of Mich. CPA. Joined PricewaterhouseCoopers, LLP, 1972, global ptnr., vice chmn., 1994—99, chmn., global tech. practice group, 1999—2006. Bd. dirs. Gateway Inc., 2006, Idearc, Inc., 2006—09, Unisys Corp., AMN Healthcare Services, Inc., 2006—, WellCare Health Plans, Inc., 2010—. Bd. dirs. Ellis Island/Statue of Liberty Found.; corp. advisory bd. U. of Mich. Bus. Sch. Office: WellCare Health Plans Inc Bd Directors 8725 Henderson Rd Tampa FL 33634 Office Phone: 813-290-6200. Office Fax: 813-262-2802. Business E-Mail: paul.weaver@wellcare.com.

WEAVER, TERRI LYNN, state legislator; b. Mansfield, Ohio, Sept. 19, 1957; m. Mike Weaver; 1 child, Justin. Singer; songwriter; small bus. owner; co-chmn. Rep. Party Smith Co.; pres. Women's Rep. Party; mem. Dist. 40 Tenn. House of Reps., 2008—. Republican. Mailing: 100 Seabowisha Ln Lancaster TN 38569 Office: 105 War Memorial Bldg Nashville TN 37243 Office Phone: 615-741-2192. Office Fax: 615-253-0378. Business E-Mail: rep.terri.lynn.weaver@capitol.tn.gov.

WEAVER, WILLIAM CHARLES, manufacturing executive; b. Nov. 10, 1941; s. Curtis D. and Mary (Yahres) W.; m. Karla Lee Kottas, June 13, 1964; children: Michael, Kelli. BS in Bus. Edn., Indiana U. of Pa., 1963; postgrad. in acctg., Tex. Christian U., 1964-65. CPA, Pa. With Price Waterhouse & Co., Pitts., 1965-73, audit mgr., 1970-73; corp. contr. Kennametal Inc., Latrobe, Pa., 1973-78, v.p., contr., 1978-83, v.p., treas., 1983-86, v.p., CFO, 1987-89; sr. v.p., CFO Oak Industries, Inc., Waltham, Mass., 1990-95; ret., 1995. Bd. dirs. Gemini Precision Products, 1987—; chmn. bd. dirs. Weaver Enterprises, Inc., 1996—, Weaver Properties, LLC. Pres. Mountain View Parent Tchrs. Orgn., 1976—77; bd. dirs. East High Acres Civic Assn., 1976—77; treas. Greater Latrobe Hockey Club, 1982—87; chmn. bd. dirs., mem. adv. coun. Jr. Achievement, Latrobe, 1982—85; chmn. bd. trustees Latrobe United Way, 1988—89; trustee Hampton United Presbyn. Ch., 1972—73. 1st lt. US Army, 1963—65. Mem.: Fin. Execs. Inst., Palmetto Dunes Club Inc. (pres. 1998—2001). Home Phone: 843-785-2218. Personal E-mail: kbweaver@roadrunner.com.

WEAVER, WILLIAM E., JR., corporate financial executive; BS in Acctg., M in Acctg., U. Miss. CPA. Various acctg. positions, ptnr. Arthur Andersen LLP, 1984—2002; ptnr. KPMG LLP, 2002—06; v.p., CFO, Home Loans MetLife, 2006—08; v.p., contr. Thomas & Betts Corp., 2008—09, sr. v.p., CFO, 2009—. Office: Thomas & Betts Corp 8155 T&B Blvd Memphis TN 38125 Office Phone: 901-252-8000. Office Fax: 901-680-5112. Business E-Mail: william.weaver@tnb.com.

WEBB, DOYLE L., political organization administrator, former state legislator; b. Little Rock, Dec. 3, 1955; BA in Hist., U. Ark., Little Rock; JD, U. Ark. Sch. Law. Atty., Benton, Ark.; justice of the peace Saline County, Ark., 1986—92; mem. Dist. 14 Ark. State Senate, 1994—2002; chief of staff to lt. gov. Win Rockefeller, Office of Lt. Gov., Ark., 2002—07; chmn. Rep. Party of Ark., 2008—, gen. counsel, mem. exec. com. Mem.: ABA, Benton Civitan Club, Saline County Bar Assn., Ark. Bar Assn., Benton-Bauxite Rotary Club, Benton Lodge. Republican. Presbyterian. Office: Rep Party of Ark Rockefeller Republican Ctr 1201 W 6th St Little Rock AR 72201 Office Phone: 501-372-7301. Office Fax: 501-372-1656.*

WEBB, JACK D., lawyer, former councilman; b. 1962; m. Elizabeth Webb; children: Michael, Eamon, Maura. BA in Hist., Iona Coll., 1984; MBA, U. Fla., 1987, JD, 1994. With Mahoney, Adams & Criser; dir. Labor & Employee Rels. CEVA Logistics, Inc.; former councilman Dist. 6 Jacksonville City Coun., Fla.; of counsel Brennan, Manna & Diamond, P.L. Chmn. Dist. 6 Duval County Rep. Com.; mem. Land Use & Zoning Com.; chmn. Rules Com.; mem. Jacksonville Juvenile Justice Comprehensive Strategy Steering Com.; coun. liaison Jacksonville Transp. Authority; vice chmn. Jacksonville Waterways Commn.; mem. Personnel Com., Post-Employment Appeals Com. Bd. dirs. Divine Mercy House; vol. Jacksonville Basketball League; parish leader St. Joseph's Ch. Mem.: Mandarin Hist. Soc., St. Joseph's Men's Club (former pres.), Mandarin Cmty. Club. Republican. Office: Brennan, Manna & Diamond 800 W Monroe St Jacksonville FL 32202 Office Phone: 904-630-1386, 904-630-1388. Business E-Mail: webb@coj.net.

WEBB, KARRIE, professional golfer; b. Ayr, Queensland, Australia, Dec. 21, 1974; Profl. golfer, 1994—; mem. LPGA Tour, 1996—; mem. Australian Team Women's World Cup of Golf, 2005. Recipient Vare Trophy, LPGA, 1997, 1999, 2000, Crowne Plaza Achievement award, 2000; named Rookie of Yr., Women Profl. Golfers' European Tour, 1995, Rolex Rookie of Yr., LPGA, 1996, Rolex Player of Yr., 1999, 2000, Outstanding Women's Golf Performer of Yr., ESPN Espy awards, 1997, 2001, Female Player of Yr., Golf Writers Assn. Am., 2000, Queensland Sportswomen of Yr., 2000—02, 2001, 2002. Achievements include winning LPGA Tour events including the Weetabix Women's Brit. Open, 1995, 97, 2002, Healthsouth Inaugural, 1996, Sprint Titleholders Championship, 1996, SAFECO Classic, 1996, 1997, ITT LPGA Tour Championship, 1996, Susan G. Koman Internat., 1997, Australian Ladies Masters, 1998, 99, 2000; winner, LPGA Tour events including the City of Hope Myrtle Beach Classic, 1998, Wegmans Rochester Internat., 1999, Mercury Titleholders Championship, 1999, Standard Register PING, 1999, The Office Depot, 1999, 2000; winner, LPGA Tour events including the du Maurier Classic, 1999, Nabisco Championship, 2000, Oldsmobile Classic, 2000, LPGA Takefuji Classic, 2000, AFLAC Champions presented by Southern Living, 2000, US Women's Open, 2000, 01; winner, LPGA Tour events including the McDonald's LPGA Championship presented by AIG, 2001, Tyco/ADT Championship, 2001, Wegmans Rochester LPGA, 2002, John Q. Hammons Hotel Classic, 2003, Kellogg-Keebler Classic, 2004, Kraft Nabisco Championship, 2006, Michelob Ultra Open, 2006, Evian Masters, 2006; winner, international events including the Women's Australian Open, 2000, 02, 07, ANZ Ladies Masters on the Robe di Kappa Ladies European Tour, 2005; inducted into World Golf Hall of Fame, 2005; first LPGA player to achieve the Super Career Grand Slam by winning all 5 majors available in her career, 2002. Avocations: reading, basketball, fishing. Office: c/o LPGA 100 Internat Golf Dr Daytona Beach FL 32124-1092

WEBB, KATHY, state legislator; b. Blytheville, Ark. BA, Randolph-Macon Women's Coll. Regional v.p. Bruegger's Bakeries; owner Lilly's Dim Sum, Then Some; mem. Dist. 37 Ark. House of Reps., 2007—. Mem.: Nat. Org. Women (Pulaski County pres. 1980—82, nat. sec. 1981—87). Democrat. United Methodist. Address: PO Box 251018 Little Rock AR 72225 Office Phone: 501-412-6443. Office Fax: 501-716-2701. Business E-Mail: webbk@arkleg.state.ar.us.

WEBB, MARK O., lawyer; Grad., Texas Christian U.; JD, U. Va. Assoc. Andrews & Kurth, Houston, 1993—95, Hunton & Williams, Richmond, 1995—97; asst. gen. counsel Dominion Resources. Inc., Richmond, Va., 1997—2004, dep. gen. counsel, 2004—13, v.p., gen. counsel, 2013—, chief risk officer, 2014—. Bd. mem. Historic Richmond Found., Preservation Virginia. Office: Dominion Resource PO Box 26532 Richmond VA 23261-6532*

WEBB, MARTY FOX, principal; b. Des Moines, July 15, 1942; d. Joseph John and Jean (Way) Fox; m. Andrew H. Rudolph, Aug. 17, 1963 (div. Jan. 1988); children: Kristen Ann, Kevin Andrew; m. Eugene J. Webb, Nov. 23, 1991. BS, U. Mich., 1964; MEd, Houston Bapt. U., 1982; EdD, U. San Francisco, 1993. Cert. adminstr., Tex., elem. and spl. edn. educator, Mich., Tex. Tchr. spl. edn. Hawthorn Ctr., Northville, Mich., 1964-70; tchr. Bellaire (Tex.) Sch. for Children, 1977-80; prin. Corpus Christi Sch., Houston, 1980-97; founder, head of sch. The Monarch Sch., Houston, 1997—. Spkr. in field. Bd. dirs. DeBusk Found. Recipient Elem. Sch. Recognition award U.S. Dept. Edn., 1989-90, Blue Ribbon Sch. award, 1990, Outstanding Doctoral Student award, 1994. Mem. ASCD, U. Mich. Alumni Assn. Avocations: reading, fly fishing, camping, hiking, bodybuilding. Home: 3531 Sun Valley Dr Houston TX 77025-4148 Office: 2815 Rasefield Dr Houston TX 77080 Office Phone: 713-479-0800. Business E-Mail: mwebb@monarchschool.org.

WEBB, PAULA, school librarian; AA in Mass. Comm., James H. Faulkner State CC, Bay Minette, Ala., 1994; BA in English, Judson Coll., Marion, Ala., 1996; MLIS, U. Ala., Tuscaloosa, 2002. Law libr. asst. Balch & Bingham, LLP, Birmingham, Ala., 1997—2003; serials/interlibrary loan librarian Delta State U., Cleveland, Miss., 2003—07; reference and electronic resources govt. documents librarian U. South Ala., Mobile, 2007—. Named to Movers & Shakers, Libr. Jour., 2011. Mem.: ALA. Office: University South Ala Library 5901 USA Dr N Mobile AL 36688 Office Phone: 251-460-7021. Business E-Mail: pwebb@jaguar1.usouthal.edu.

WEBB, ROBERT J., information technology executive; b. Toronto, Canada; m. Noriko Webb; 2 children. Grad., Univ. We. Ontario; MBA, European Sch. Mgmt., Paris. Cons. EDS, Andersen Consulting; chief info. officer GE Power Systems General Electric Co., chief info. officer GE global consumer fin., chief info. officer GE Capital mid-market fin., mng. dir. Canadian vendor fin., chief info. officer, GE Comml. Fin., GE Global Consumer Fin. and GE Energy Svcs.; chief tech. officer Equifax, Inc., Atlanta, 2004—, chief info. officer, 2004—09, Hilton Hotels Corp, 2009—. Office: Hilton Hotels Corp 7930 Jones Branch Dr Ste 100 Mc Lean VA 22102-3389 Office Phone: 310-278-4321. Office Fax: 310-205-7678. Business E-Mail: robert_webb@equifax.com.

WEBB, ROBERT W., JR., lawyer; b. Thomasville, Ga., Mar. 16, 1950; BA magna cum laude, Vanderbilt Univ., 1972; JD, Univ. Va., 1975. Bar: Ga. 1975, US Dist. Ct. (no. dist.) Ga., Us Ct. Appeals (11th cir.), US Supreme Ct. Assoc. Troutman Sanders LLP, Atlanta, 1975—80, ptnr., 1981—, mng. ptnr. & chmn., 1992—2011, mem. exec. com., chmn., 2011—. Mem.: ABA, State Bar Ga., Atlanta Bar Assn., Phi Beta Kappa. Office: Troutman Sanders LLP One Logan Sq Ste 5200 600 Peachtree St NE Atlanta GA 30308-2216 Office Phone: 404-885-3240. Office Fax: 404-962-6716. Business E-Mail: robert.webb@troutmansanders.com.

WEBB, ROBIN L., state legislator, lawyer; b. Sept. 6, 1960; AAS, BS, Morehead State U.; JD, Chase Coll. Law. Pvt. practice atty., Grayson, Ky.; rep. Dist. 96 Ky. Legislature, 1999—2009, state senator Dist. 18, 2009—; alumni assoc., v.p. Morehead State U.; sec. Nat. Assembly Sportsmen's Caucuses. Mem.: NRA (life), Ky. Young Dem. (former pres., sec. & treas.), Grayson C. of C., Ky. Bar Assn., Nat. Wild Turkey Fedn., Ducks Unlimited. Democrat. Baptist. Mailing: 404 W Main St Grayson KY 41143 Office: Capitol Annex Rm 229 702 Capitol Ave Frankfort KY 40601 Office Phone: 502-564-8100 ext. 676. Business E-Mail: robin.webb@lrc.ky.gov.

WEBB, WATTS RANKIN, surgeon; b. Columbia, Ky., Sept. 8, 1922; s. Frank Elbert and Susie Josephine (Rankin) W.; m. Frances Luella Cooke, Aug. 19, 1944; children: Michael Andrew, Paul Alan, Harvey Elbert, Gordon Lewis. BA, U. Miss., 1942; MD, Johns Hopkins U., 1945. Diplomate Am. Bd. Surgery, Am. Bd. Thoracic Surgery, Am. Bd. Surg. Critical Care. Intern Barnes Hosp., St. Louis, 1945-46; resident in surgery VA Hosp., Biloxi, Miss., 1946-48; resident in gen. and thoracic surgery Barnes Hosp., 1948-52; chief surgeon Miss. State Sanatorium, 1952-63; instr. surgery U. Miss., 1955-56, asst. prof. surgery, 1956-58, prof., 1958-63; prof., chmn. div. thoracic and cardiovascular surgery U. Tex. Southwestern Med. Sch., Dallas, 1964-70; prof., chmn. dept. surgery SUNY Upstate Med. Center, Syracuse, 1970-77; chmn. dept. Tulane U., New Orleans, 1977-89, prof. surgery, 1977-93, La. State U., New Orleans, 1993—, Shreveport, 2007—, Huey P. Long Hosp., Alexandria, 2007—. Author: Pulmonary Problems in Surgery, 1974, Surgery in Acute Coronary Problems, 1974, Aneurysms, 1983, Cardiovascular Emergencies, 1986, Atlas of Pulmonary Resections, 1988, (with others) Surgical Management for Chest Injuries, Vol. VII, 1990; mem. editl. bd.: Annals of Thoracic Surgery, 1968-79, Surg. Rounds, 1978-82, Surgery Clinics, 1980-82, Microcirculation, 1983-84, Brit. Jour. Surgery, 1981-89; contbr. articles to profl. jours. Recipient award Hadassah, 1965, Knockers Soc. Outstanding Tchr. award SUNY Upstate Med. Ctr., 1972, Owl Club Clin. Tchr. of Yr. award Tulane U. Med. Sch., 1978, 86, 88-93, Gloria P. Walsh award for best tchr. in Med. Sch., 1992, Aesculapian Tchr. of Yr. award La. State U., 1995, 96. Fellow ACS, Am. Coll. Chest Physicians; mem. AMA, Am. Assn. Thoracic Surgery, Am. Coll. Cardiology, Am. Fedn. Clin. Research, Am. Heart Assn. (Silver medal 1963), Am. Physiol. Soc., Am. Surg. Assn., Am. Thoracic Soc., Halsted Soc., La. Med. Soc., Orleans Parish Med. Soc., New Orleans Surg. Soc., Societe International de Chirurgie, Soc. Cryobiology, Soc. Thoracic Surgeons, Soc. Univ. Surgeons, Southeastern Surg. Congress, So. Med. Assn., So. Soc. Clin. Research, So. Surg. Assn. (Shipley medal 1961), So. Thoracic Soc., So. Thoracic Surg. Assn., Surg. Assn. La., Surg. Biology Club II, Internat. Soc. Heart Transplantation, Gulf Coast Vascular Soc., Sigma Xi, Alpha Omega Alpha, Pi Kappa Pi, Beta Beta Beta, Alpha Epsilon Delta. Methodist. Office: La State U Huey P Long Hosp PO Box 5352 Pineville LA 71361-5352 Office Phone: 318-448-0811. Personal E-mail: webbwatts@yahoo.com.

WEBB-EDGINGTON, ALECIA, state legislator; b. Aug. 23, 1966; m. Ted Webb-Edgington; 1 child. BA in Sociology & Criminology, Western Ky. U.; MA in Criminal Justice, Eastern Ky. U. Former chief info. officer Ky. State Police, ret. major; former exec. dir. Ky. Office Homeland Security; mem. Dist. 63 Ky. House of Reps., 2009—. Republican. Baptist. Office: 702 Capitol Ave Rm 405A Frankfort KY 40601 also: 1650 Chestnut Ct Covington KY 41011 Office Phone: 502-564-8100 Ext. 701, 859-426-7322.

WEBBER, CHRIS (MAYCE EDWARD CHRISTOPHER WEBBER III), sportscaster, retired professional basketball player; b. Detroit, Mar. 1, 1973; s. Mayce and Doris Webber. Student, U. Mich., 1991—93. Drafted Orlando Magic, Fla., 1993; forward Golden State Warriors, San Francisco, 1993—94, Washington Bullets, 1994—98, Sacramento Kings, 1998—2005, Phila. 76ers, 2005—07, Detroit Pistons, 2007, Golden State Warriors, Calif., 2008; ret., 2008; studio analyst NBA TV, 2008—. Rap album, 2 Much Drama, 1999. Founder Timeout Found. Named Nat. H.S. Player of Yr., 1990—91, Mr. Basketball, State of Mich., 1991, Coca-Cola Classic NBA Player of Yr., 1994, Brut Bullets Player of Yr., 1994—95; named to NBA All-Rookie 1st team, 1994, NBA All-Interview Team, 1999—2003, All-NBA First Team, 2001, All-NBA Second Team, 1999, 2002—03, All-NBA Third Team, 2000. Achievements include being drafted 1st round Orlando Magic, 1993; five-time NBA All-Star, 1997, 2000-03. Avocations: collecting signed historical documents of prominent African-Americans, water sports. Office: NBA TV 1065 Williams St NW Atlanta GA 30309

WEBER, DONALD B., advertising executive, marketing professional; s. John William and Rose Ann (Saroshi) Weber; m. Ann McDermaid, 1955 (div. 1975); children: Martha Elizabeth, Margaret Ann; m. Jean Host, 1980; children: Kimberly Elizabeth, Kristen Ann. BA, Rollins Coll., Winter Park, Fla.; MBA, Kellog/Northwestern U., Evanston, Ill. Account exec. Leo Burnett Co., Inc., Chgo., 1958-63; sr. v.p., mgmt. supr. Foote, Cone & Belding, Chgo., 1963-76; pres. Blau Bishop Assocs., 1976-79; v.p. Russell Reynolds Assocs., Chgo., 1979-82; sr. v.p., regional mgr. MSL Internat., Chgo., 1982-85; exec. v.p. Rumrill-Hoyt, Inc., Rochester, N.Y., 1985-88; sr. v.p. D'Arcy Masius Benton & Bowles, Chgo., 1988-95; sr. v.p., group mgmt. dir. Cramer-Krasselt, Chgo., 1996-99; pres. Intact, Inc., 1999—. Lectr. Northwestern U. Chmn. bd. Am. Cancer Soc., Chgo., 1996—99, pres., cons.; bd. dirs., chmn. comm. exec. com. Ill. divsn. Am. Cancer Soc., 1999—2001; bd. dirs. Am. Inst. Wine and Food, 1995—97; chmn. Chgo. coun. Boy Scouts Am., 1991—95. Lt. comdr. USNR, 1955—63. Mem.: Chgo. Advt. Fedn. (bd. dirs. 1988—93), Meadows Country Club. Home: 3891 Chatsworth Greene Ct Sarasota FL 34235 Personal E-mail: intactdbw@aol.com.

WEBER, FREDRIC ALAN, lawyer; b. Paterson, NJ, July 31, 1948; s. Frederick Edward and Alida (Hessels) W.; m. Mary Elizabeth Cook, June 18, 1983. BA in History, Rice U., 1970; JD, Yale U., 1976. Bar: Tex. 1976, U.S. Dist. Ct. (so. dist.) Tex. Assoc. Fulbright & Jaworski LLP, Houston, 1976-80, participating assoc., 1980-83, ptnr., 1983—. Dir. Houston Symphony Soc., 1993—, v.p. devel., 2001-03, 2005-07. Mem. ABA, Am. Coll. Bond Counsel (treas. 2003-04, v.p. 2004-06, pres. 2006-08), Nat. Assn. Bond Lawyers (bd. dirs. 1988-89, treas. 1989-90, pres.-elect 1991, pres. 1991-92), Houston Bar Assn. Office: Fulbright & Jaworski LLP 1301 McKinney St Ste 5100 Houston TX 77010-3095 Office Phone: 713-651-5151, 713-651-3628. Office Fax: 713-651-5246. Business E-Mail: fweber@fulbright.com.

WEBER, HANS JÜRGEN, physics professor; b. Berlin, May 3, 1939; came to U.S., 1966; naturalized, 1993; s. Hans Gustav Wilhelm and Hedwig Bertha Elisabeth (Angermann) W.; m. Edith E. Enzian, Aug. 19, 1966; 1 child, Chris H. MS in Math., U. Frankfurt, Fed. Republic Germany, 1961, PhD in Physics, 1965. Postdoctoral rsch. assoc. U. Frankfurt, 1965-66, Duke U., Durham, NC, 1966-67, U. Va., Charlottesville, 1967, asst. prof. physics, 1968-71, assoc. prof., 1971-77, prof., 1977—2003. Vis. scientist U. Mainz, Fed. Republic Germany, 1972, 77, 91, U. Paris-Sud, Orsay, France, 1979; vis. prof. U. Lyon, France, 1978. Co-author: Mathematical Methods for Physicists, 1995, 2001, 2005, Essentials of Math Methods for Physicists, 2003; contbr. to Physics Reports, Springer Tracts, Phys. Letters, Phys. Rev. Rsch. grantee NSF, 1971-95. Mem. Am. Phys. Soc., Am. Assn. Physics Tchrs., Sigma Xi. Lutheran. Achievements include development of a nuclear force (NN interaction) from quark models and a possible connection between quantum chromodynamics and meson dynamics; rsch. on isobars in nuclei. Office: U Va Inst Nuclear and Particle Physics McCormick Rd Charlottesville VA 22904-0001 Business E-Mail: hw@virginia.edu.

WEBER, JANICE ANN, library director, grant writer; b. Baytown, Tex., Aug. 28, 1952; d. James Thelmer Jr. and Doris Geraldine (Bush) Foster; m. Louis Haldane Weber, Feb. 1, 1983; 5 stepchildren. BS, Tex. Woman's U., Denton, 1982, MLS, 1985. Cert. county libr. Tex. Libr. dir. Dimmit County Libr., Carrilo Springs, Tex., 1985, Val Verde County Libr., Del Rio, Tex., 1986—89, Laredo Pub. Libr., Tex., 1989—. Sec., bd. dirs. Lit. Vol. Am., Laredo, 1989-95, bd. dirs. Webb County Heritage Found., Laredo, 1990-94; chmn. Webb County Hist. Commn., 1989-94; mem. Tuesday Music & Lit. Club, Laredo, 1997—, past pres. Mem. ALA, Nonprofit Mgmt. Assn., Tex. Libr. Assn., Tex. Mcpl. Libr. Dirs. Assn. (Libr. of Yr. 1999), Pub. Libr. Assn., Tex. City Mgrs. Assn., Reforma, Nat. Hispanic Network, AARP (pres. Laredo chpt. 965 2004-, Woman of Yr. 2001). Avocations: gourmet cooking, weaving, book making, scrapbooks, genealogy, gardening. Office: Laredo Pub Libr 1120 E Calton Rd Laredo TX 78041-7328 E-mail: janice@laredolibrary.org.

WEBER, JEFFREY S., medical oncologist, educator; PhD in Molecular Cell Biology, Rockefeller U., 1979; MD, NYU, 1980. Diplomate American Bd. Internal Medicine, 1983, American Bd. Internal Medicine-med. oncology, 1987. Intern medicine Univ. Calif., 1981; resident internal medicine Univ. Calif. San Diego Med. Ctr., 1981—83; fellow medicine branch Nat. Cancer Inst., Bethesda, Md., 1986, fellow surgery branch tumor immunology, 1988—90; sr. mem. H. Lee Moffitt Cancer Ctr. & Rsch. Isnt., dir. Donald A. Adam Comprehensive Melanoma Rsch. Ctr.; assoc. prof. medicine Univ. Southern Calif.; prof. internal medicine Univ. South Fla., prof. oncologic sciences. Contbr. articles to profl. publs. Office: H Lee Moffitt Cancer Center & 12902 Magnolia Dr Tampa FL 33612 Office Phone: 813-745-2007.*

WEBER, JENNIFER L., energy executive; m. Eric Weber; 3 children. B cum laude, Miami U., Ohio; M, Carnegie Mellon U., Pitts. Ptnr., mng. dir. Towers Perrin, Cin., 1993—2005; sr. v.p. human resources Scripps Networks Interactive, Inc., 2005—08; group exec. human resources and corp. rels. Duke Energy Corp., 2008—. Former bd. mem. Dan Beard Boy Scout Coun. Greater Cin., Salvation Army; mem. bus. adv. com. Miami U. Farmer Sch. Bus.; mem. bd. advisors U. NC Belk Coll. Bus., Charlotte; bd. dirs. United Way Ctrl. Carolinas. Mem.: Phi Beta Kappa. Office: Duke Energy Corp 526 S Church St Charlotte NC 28202-1904

WEBER, JEROME CHARLES, human relations educator, retired academic administrator; b. Bklyn., Sept. 1, 1938; s. Meyer and Ethel (Shier) W.; m. Elizabeth Lynn Wiley, July 18, 1975; children: Amy Elizabeth, Jeffrey Glenn. BS, Bklyn. Coll., 1960; MA, Mich. State U., 1961, PhD, 1966. Mem. faculty U. Okla., Norman, 1964—, prof. edn., phys. edn., human rels. and social work, 1973—, Regents' prof. edn. and human rels., 1991—, asst. and acting dean, 1969-72, dean Univ. Coll., 1973-91, vice provost instructional svcs., 1979-91; chmn. ednl. leadership and policy studies, 1991-93. Author: (with D.R. Lamb) Statistics and Research in Physical Education, 1970, (with G. Henderson) College Survival for Student-Athletes, 1985, (with R. Cintron) Enduring Enigmas: Issues in Adult and Higher Education, 1997; contbr. chpts. to books; contbr. articles to profl. jours. Bd. dirs. Univ. div. United Way, 1970; pres. Norman Kindergarten Assn., 1968; commr. Norman Bd. Parks, 1971-79. Recipient Outstanding Faculty award, Okla. U., 2007; named to Higher Edn. Hall Fame, Okla., 2005. Fellow Am. Coun. Sports Medicine; mem. Am. Assn. Higher Edn., Coun. Sports Psychology, Am. Coun. on Edn. Democrat. Jewish. Home: 5 Pebble Creek Rd Norman OK 73072-2822 Office: 630 Parrington Oval Norman OK 73069-8813 Office Phone: 405-325-3629. E-mail: jcweber@ou.edu.

WEBER, RANDY, United States Representative from Texas, former state legislator; b. Pearland, Tex., July 2, 1953; m. Brenda Weber; 3 children. Attended, Alvin Cmty. Coll., Tex., 1971—74; BA in Public Affairs, U. Houston, Clear Lake, 1977. Owner Webers Air & Heat Air-Conditioning Co., 1981—; city councilman City of Pearland, Tex., 1990—96; mem. Dist. 29 Tex. House of Representatives, 2009—13; mem. US Congress from 14th Tex. Dist., Washington, 2013—, US House Fgn. Affairs Com., 2013—, US House Space, Sci., & Technology Com., 2013—. Republican. Baptist. Office: US House of Representatives 510 Cannon House Office Bldg Washington DC 20515 also: 174 Calder Rd League City TX 77573 Office Phone: 202-225-2831, 281-316-0231. Office Fax: 202-225-0271, 281-316-0271.*

WEBER, SAMUEL C. (SAM WEBER), otolaryngologist, educator; Attended, Emory U., 1959—60, U. of Chattanooga, Tenn., 1960—62; MD, U. Tenn., 1962—65. Diplomate Am. Bd. Otolaryngology, 1972. Intern gen. surgery Univ. of Tenn. Coll. of Medicine, Memphis, 1966; resident otolaryngology head and neck surgery Baylor Coll. of Medicine, Houston, 1967—71; assoc. clin. prof. dept. of otolaryngology head and neck surgery Baylor Coll. of Medicine; current chief olaryngology, past pres. med. staff St. Luke's Episcopal Hosp., chief med. staff, 2004; clin. prof. otolaryngology, head and neck surgery Univ. of Tex., Houston, Galveston; lt. comdr. with letter of commendation Navy Med. Ctr., San Diego, 1971—73, dir. otolaryngology rsch.; hosp. affiliations include Tex. Children's Hosp., The Meth. Hosp. Co-author: (publs.) Neurophysiology of Facial Nerve Testing, 1973, Temporal Bone Findings in Cryptococcal Meningitis, 1975, Fracture of the Frontal Sinus in Children, 1977, Clinical Restoration of Voice Junction After Loss of Vagus Nerve, 1985, and numerous others. Recipient Guide to Top Doctors, 1st pl. Houston, Tex. for Otolaryngology, 1999; named Top Doc, H Tex. Mag., 2007, 2009; named one of the Best Doctors in America, Woodward and White, 1996—97, 1998—99, 1999—2007, 2001—02, 2003, 2004, 2005, 2007, 2008, America's Top Doctors for Cancer, A Castle Connolly Guide, 2007—09, America's Top Physicians, Consumers Rsch. Coun. of America, 2003—06, 2008, 2009, Houston Top Docs, Inside Houston Mag., Houston's Top M.D.s, Met. Houston, Texas Super Docs, Tex. Monthly Mag., 2004—09. Fellow: ACS; mem.: Assn. of Mil. Surgeons of the US, Centurion Club, Doctors Club of Houston (past pres.), Am. Thyroid Assn., Hous. Surg. Soc., Thyroid Soc. for Edn. and Rsch. (bd. 1992—2000, v.p. 1997), Houston Otolaryngological Head and Neck Soc. (pres. 1990), Harris County Med. Soc., Tex. Assn. of Otolaryngology, Head and Neck Surgery, Tex. Soc. of Ophthalmology and Otolaryngology, Tex. Med. Assn., Am. Acad. of Sleep Medicine, Am. Assn. of Head and Neck Surgeons, Am. Acad. of Otolaryngology Head and Neck Surgery. Office: St Lukes Episcopal Hospital 6720 Bertner Houston TX 77030 Office Phone: 832-355-1000.

WEBER, SHEA, professional hockey player; b. Sicamous, BC, Canada, Aug. 14, 1985; s. James and Tracy Weber. Defenseman Nashville Predators, 2006—, capt., 2010—. Mem. Team Canada, World Jr. Championships, Grand Forks, ND, 2005, Team Canada, Olympic Games, Vancouver, 2010, Sochi, Russia, 2014. Named to NHL YoungStars Game, 2007, NHL All-Star Game, 2009, 2011, 2012, All-Star Team, Winter Olympic Games, 2010, First All-Star Team, NHL, 2011. Achievements include being a member of gold medal winning Team Canada, World Junior Championships, 2005; being a member of gold medal winning Canadian Hockey Team, Vancouver Olympics, 2010, Sochi Olympics, 2014. Office: Nashville Predators Sommet Ctr 501 Broadway Nashville TN 37203*

WEBER, YVONNE ROEBUCK, research administrator, educator; b. McKeesport, Pa. d. Raymond Henry and Clara Maria (Roberts) Roebuck; m. William Frederick Weber, June 16, 1961; children: Laurel, Wendy. BA, U. Pitts., 1947, MLitt, 1952, PhD, 1973; postgrad., Kent State U., 1950, Ecole Normale, Paris, 1953, Goethe Institut, 1960. Tchr. French, German, English, history Carrollton HS, 1947—51, Canton, Ohio, 1951—52, Munhall HS, 1952—58, Wilkinsburg HS, 1958—61, Upper St. Clair HS, 1963—65; asst. prof. French and German Calif. State Coll., 1965—66, Point Park Coll., 1968—72; asst. prof., supr. edn. Washington and Jefferson Coll., 1976—79; scholar/discussion leader Pa. Humanities Coun., 1993. With internat. rsch. project, 1979—82. Author: A Beacon to the Future: Charting a Course for Advancement; contbr. articles to profl. jours. Recipient Good Citizenship award, DAR, 1943, Doctoral Assn. Outstanding Svc. award, U. Pitts., 1989, Disting. Alumni award, 1985, 1993; Fulbright Grant, 1960. Mem.: U.Pitts. Alumni Coun., Pa. Assn. Tchr. Educators, Pa. State Modern Lang. Assn., Doctoral Assn. Educators, Modern Lang. Assn., Delta Kappa Gamma, Zeta Tau Alpha, Phi Delta Gamma, Pi Lambda Theta, Mensa Internat., Delta Kappa Gamma Soc. Internat.

WEBERT, MICHAEL J., state legislator; b. Denver, Colo., Sept. 24, 1979; m. Rebecca Funkhouser. BA in Comm., George Mason U., 2010. Mem. Dist. 18 Va. House of Delegates, 2012—, mem. Agr. Chesapeake and Natural Resources Com. & Militia Police and Pub. Safety Com. Recipient John Marshall Soil and Water Conservation Farm Award, 2010. Mem.: Blue Ridge Cattlemen's Assn., Fauquier Livestock Exchange (bd. mem.), County Farm Bur. (bd. mem.), Northern Va. Angus Assn., Va. Forage and Grassland Coun. Republican. Office: General Assembly Building PO Box 406 Richmond VA 23218 also: PO Box 631 Marshall VA 20116 Office Phone: 804-698-1018. Office Fax: 804-698-6718. E-mail: DelMWebert@house.virginia.gov.

WEBSTER, CARRIE LEE, judge, former state legislator; b. Fairfax, Va., Jan. 17, 1966; d. Buddy Lewis and Ada Katherine (Bean) Webster; m. Greg Skinner; 1 child, Katherine. BA in Polit. Sci., W.Va. U., 1988, JD, 1997. Bar: W.Va. Asst., press. sec. W.Va. Atty. Gen.'s Office; law clk. W.Va. Legal Svcs. Corp.; asst. pub. defender Kanawha County Pub. Defender's Office, 1997—2000; assoc. Bucci, Bailey & Javins; mem. Dist. 31 W.Va. House of Delegates, 2001—09, chair Judiciary Com., 1996—2009; cir. judge Kanawha County, 2009—. Bd. govs. W.Va. Assn. Justice. Fellowship, Judith A. Herndon fellowship program, 1986. Mem.: Am. Assn. Justice, Nat. Orgn. Women, Nat. Assn. Female Exec., W.Va. Polit. Sci. Alumni Advisor Bd. (bd. dir. 1992—), W.Va. Kanawha Valley Alumni Assn. (bd. dir. 1992—). Democrat. Methodist. Office: Kanawha County Cir Ct 111 Court St Charleston WV 25301

WEBSTER, DANIEL ALAN, United States Representative from Florida, former state legislator; b. Charleston, W.Va., Apr. 27, 1949; m. Sandy Jordan; children: David Lee, Brent Alan, Jordan Daniel, Elizabeth Anne, John Elliott, Victoria Suzanna. BS in Electrical Engring., Ga. Inst. Tech., 1971. Owner Webster-Air Conditioning & Heating Inc.; mem. Dist. 41 Fla. House of Reps., spkr., minority fl. leader, 1982—84, vice chmn., minority policy com., 1985—88, minority whip, 1988—90, Republican leader pro tem, 1992—94, Republican leader, 1994—96; mem. Dist. 12 Fla. State Senate, 1999—2002, mem. Dist. 9, 2003—08, majority leader, 2006—08; mem. US Congress from 8th Fla. Dist., Washington, 2011—13, US Congress from 10th Fla. Dist., 2013—, US House Rules Com., 2011—, US House Transp. & Infrastructure Com., 2013—. Recipient Legislature Leadership award, Fla. Med. Soc., 1993, D.I. Rainey award, Fla. Chiropractic Assn., 1994, Legislature award, Bd. Regents, 1995, Fla. Farm Bur., 1995, Quality Floridian award, Fla. League Cities, 1995, Spl. Recognition award, Fla. Hotel & Motel Assn., 1995, Award, Fla. Banking Assn., 1995, Leadership award, Fla. Assn. State Toppers, 1996; named Legislator of Yr., Fla. Chamber of Commerce, 1995, Fla. Statesman of Yr., Fla. Republican Party, 1995. Mem.: United Cmty. Action for Israel, Farm Bur., West Orange & Winter Garden Chamber of Commerce, Nat. Fedn. Ind. Bus., Air Conditioning Contractors Assn., Assn. Bldg. Contractors, Sertoma. Republican. Baptist. Office: US House of Representatives 1039 Longworth House Office Bldg Washington DC 20515 also: 300 West Plant St Winter Garden FL 34787 Office Phone: 202-225-2176, 407-654-5705. Office Fax: 202-225-0999, 407-654-5814.*

WEBSTER, DOUGLAS WAYNE, federal agency administrator, management consultant; b. Huntington Park, Calif., Aug. 11, 1948; s. William Mac and Lorraine Marie (Browner) Webster; m. Concepcion Tumulak Bingco, Apr. 12, 1975; children: Kathy, Dawn. Grad., Air War Coll., Maxwell AFB, Ala., 1987; BS in Engring., UCLA, 1972; MS in Systems Mgmt., U. So. Calif., 1983; DBA, U.S. Internat. U., San Diego, 1991. Cert. credit union devel. educator; govt. fin. mgr., project mgmt. profl., Info. Tech. Infrastructure Libr. Commd. 2d lt. USAF, 1972, advanced through grades to lt. col., 1988, C-130 navigator Clark Air Base Philippines, 1973-77, C-130 instr. navigator McChord AFB Wash., 1977-79, chief ops. br. space divsn. LA, 1979-84, comdr. airlift control element 374th Tactical Airlift Wing Clark Air Base, 1984-87, dir. systems engring. space divsn. LA, 1987-90, ret., 1993; dep. concurrent engring. US Dept. Def., Washington, 1990-93; prin. American Mgmt. Systems, Fairfax, Va., 1992-97; dir. pub. sector cost mgmt. svcs. Price Waterhouse, Arlington, Va., 1997—2004; prin. fin. adv. Ministry Transp. Coalition Provisional Authority, Baghdad, Iraq, 2004; sr. mgr. Grant Thornton LLP, 2004—08; CFO US Dept. Labor, Washington, 2008—09; dep. dir. Bus. Transformation Agy. (BTA) US Dept. Def., Washington, 2009—. Mgmt. cons. US Dept. Def., 1993—, NASA, 1994—; bd. dirs. Pentagon Fed. Credit Union, 2004—. Author: Activity-Based Costing and Performance, 1994; co-author: Chasing Change: Building Organizational Capacity in a Turbulent Environment, 2008; mem. editl. adv. com. Concurrent Engring., 1992—, Quality Observer, 1992—. Decorated Defense Supr. Svc. medal, Meritorious Svc. medal (3), Air Force Commendation medal (3). Mem.: Am. Def. Preparedness Assn., Am. Soc. Quality Control (sr.). Avocations: genealogy, amateur radio, flying, teaching flying.

WEBSTER, HUGH B., accountant, former state legislator; b. Caswell County, NC, Aug. 6, 1943; m. Patricia Webster; 2 children. BS, U. NC, 1968, postgrad., 1969, U. Ill., 1970. CPA NC. Farmer, NC, 1953-62; CPA, 1967—2003; constrn. project auditor; auditor, tax specialist Big Six Cert. Pub. Accountant Firms; auditor Dept. Def., Dept. Labor; mem., dist. 21 NC State Senate, Raleigh, 1995—2002, mem., dist. 24, 2003—06; accountant, 2003—. Mem. agr., environ. and natural resources com., fin. com., ins. com., ways and means com.; ranking minority mem. state and local govt. com. Former bd. mem. Caswell C. of C.; founding mem. Leasburg Vol. Fire Dept., former bd. pres. Mem.: Leasburg Ruritan Club. Republican. Methodist. Home: 700 Plum Tree Ln Yanceyville NC 27379-9272

WEBSTER, MURRAY ALEXANDER, JR., sociologist, educator; b. Manila, Philippines, Dec. 10, 1941; s. M.A. and Patricia (Morse) W. AB, Stanford U., 1963, MA, 1966, PhD, 1968. Asst. prof. social rels. Johns Hopkins U., Balt., 1968-74, assoc. prof., 1974-76; prof. sociology, adj. prof. psychology U. S.C., Columbia, 1976-86; vis. prof. sociology Stanford U., 1981-82, 85, 88-89; sr. lectr. San Jose State U., 1987-89; dir. sociology program NSF, 1989-91,99-2000; prof. sociology U. N.C., Charlotte, 1993—. Author (with Barbara Sobieszek): Sources of Self-Evaluation, 1974; author: Actions and Actors, 1975; author: (with Martha Foschi) Status Generalization: New Theory and Research, 1988; author: (with Jane Sell) Laboratory Experiments in the Social Sciences, 2007. Recipient First Citizens Bank Scholars award, 2003; NIH fellow, 1966-68; grantee NSF, Nat. Inst. Edn. Mem.: Internat. Sociol. Assn., Sociol. Rsch. Assn., So. Sociol. Soc., Am. Sociol. Assn. Office: Univ NC Dept Sociology Charlotte NC 28223 Office Phone: 704-687-7806. Business E-Mail: mawebste@uncc.edu.

WEBSTER, PETER DAVID, lawyer; b. Framingham, Mass., Feb. 12, 1949; s. Waldo John and Helen Anne (Borovek) W.; m. Michele Page Hernandez, Jan. 13, 1989; 1 stepchild, Alana Perryman. BS, Georgetown U., 1971; JD, Duke U., 1974; LLM, U. Va., 1995. Bar: Fla. 1974, US Dist. Ct. (mid. dist.) Fla. 1975, US Ct. Appeals (5th cir.) 1975, US Dist. Ct. (so. dist.) Fla. 1977, US Dist. Ct. (no. dist.) Fla. 1978, US Supreme Ct. 1978, US Ct. Appeals (11th cir.) 1981. Law clk. U.S. Dist. Judge, Jacksonville, Fla., 1974-75; assoc. Bedell, Bedell, Dittmar, Smith & Zehmer, Jacksonville, 1975-78; ptnr. Bedell, Bedell, Dittmar & Zehmer, Jacksonville, 1978-85; cir. judge State Fla., Jacksonville, 1986-91; judge Dist. Ct. of Appeal, First Dist., State of Fla., Tallahassee, 1991—2011; shareholder Carlton Fields Jorden Burt, Tallahassee, 2011—. Master of bench Chester Bedell Am. Inn Ct., 1988-91, Tallahassee Am. Inn Ct., 1992-2002, pres. 1999-2000; master of bench E. Robert Williams Am. Inn Ct., 2007, 1st Dist. Appellate Am. Inn. Ct., 2008-, pres., 2012-13; adj. prof. Fla. Coastal Sch. Law, 1997-2006; Fla. Supreme Ct.: mem. com. standard jury instrns. civil cases, 1979-2001, chmn. 1999-2000; mem. com. trial ct. info. sys., 1986-91; mem. com. confidentiality records jud. br., 1993-95; mem. task force on complex litig., 2006-08, mem., Fla. bd. bar examiners testing com., 2008-09, mem. professionalism commn., 2010-; mem. jud. mgmt. coun. Fla., 2006-08; chmn. com. jud.,evaluations, 2006-07, chmn. court rep. cert. planning com., 1995-99. Contbg. author: Sanctions: Rule 11 and Other Powers, 1986, Florida Criminal Rules and Practice Manual, 1990. Bd. dirs. Jacksonville Area Legal Aid, Inc., 1978-82, River Region Human Svcs., Inc., Jacksonville, 1986-88; mem. adv. bd. P.A.C.E. Ctr. for Girls, Inc., Jacksonville, 1986-91; com. mem. Shawnee Dist. North Fla. Coun. Boy Scouts Am., 1974-78; mem. delinquency task force Mayor's Commn. on Children and Youth, City of Jacksonville, 1988-91; officer, mem. exec. bd. Suwanee River Area Coun. Boy Scouts, 1991-96, trustee Am. Inns. Ct. Found., 2009-13. Named one of Fla. Super Lawyers, 2012, 2013—14. Mem. ABA (exec. com. Jud. Divsn. Lawyers' Conf., 2013-, fellow Am. Bar Found.), Am. Judicature Soc. (bd. dirs. 2002—, sec. 2008-09, v.p., 2009-10, pres.-elect, 2010-11, pres. 2011-12), Fla. Conf. Appellate Judges, Jacksonville Bar Assn., Tallahassee Bar Assn., Phi Beta Kappa, Phi Alpha Theta, Phi Eta Sigma. Office: 215 S Monroe St Ste 500 Tallahassee FL 32301-1866 Home Phone: 850-668-0079; Office Phone: 850-224-1585.

WEBSTER, RUSTON, professional sports team executive; b. Madison, Wis. m. Gayle Webster; children: Hannah, Jacob, Drew. B, U. Miss. Grad. asst. coach U. SW La. Ragin' Cajuns, 1985, U. Ala. Crimson Tide, 1986, Tulsa U. Golden Hurricane, 1987; NE regional coll. scout Tampa Bay Buccaneers, 1988, dir. pro pers., 1989—91, south regional coll. scout, 1992, MW regional coll. scout, 1993, SW regional coll. scout, 1995—2000, dir. coll. scouting, 2001—04, dir. player pers., 2005; v.p. player pers. Seattle Seahawks, 2006—10, interim gen. mgr., 2009—10; v.p. player pers. Tenn. Titans, 2011, exec. v.p., gen. mgr., 2012—. Office: Tenn Titans One Titans Way Nashville TN 37213

WEBSTER, TODD, legislative staff member, communications executive; BA in Govt., Bowdoin Coll., 1994; MA in Polit. Mgmt., George Washington U., 1996. Dep. comm. dir. Gore/Lieberman 2000, 1999—2000; comm. dir., chief spokesman to Senator Patty Murray US Senate, 2001—03, comm. dir., chief spokesman to Senator Tom Daschle, 2003—05, chief of staff to Senator Christopher Coons, 2011—; prin. Webster Strategies, 2005—; founding ptnr. WebStrong Group, 2007—. Spokesman Mid-Atlantic Sports Network, 2006—; assoc. prof. comm. strategy Grad. Sch. Polit. Mgmt. George Washington U. Assoc. prodr. Equal Time with Paul Begala and Oliver North, MSNBC. Named one of Fabulous Fifty: Movers and Shakers Behind the Scenes on Capitol Hill, Roll Call, the Rising Star in American Politics, Campaigns & Elections mag. Democrat. Office: Office of Senator Christopher Coons 383 Russell Senate Office Bldg Washington DC 20510 also: Webster Strategies Suite 200 101 N Columbus St Alexandria VA 22314 Office Phone: 703-837-1110, 202-224-5042. E-mail: todd@toddwebster.com, todd_webster@coons.senate.gov.

WEBSTER, WILLIAM G., JR., career military officer; b. Baton Rouge, July 3, 1951; married; 3 children. BS, U.S. Mil. Acad., 1974. Commd. 2d lt. U.S. Army, 1974, advanced through grades to lt. gen., 2007, tank co. comdr. Fort Polk, La., 1974—78, ops. and plans officer Seventh Army Combined Arms Tng. Ctr., 1979—82, ops. officer 3-64 Armor, 3d Inf. Divsn. Germany, 1979—82, asst. G-3 and brigade ops. officer 24th Inf. Divsn. Ft. Stewart, Ga., 1984—87, joint staff War Plans Divsn. Washington, 1988—91, comdr. 3d bn., 77th armor in 4th inf. divsn., 1991-93; sr. armor observer contr. Cobra Team Nat. Tng. Ctr., Ft. Irwin, Calif., 1993-94; comdr. 1st brigade, 1st cavalry divsn. Ft. Hood, 1995-97; asst.divsn. comdr. 3d Inf. Divsn., Ft. Stewart, Ga., 1997-98; comdr. Ft. Irwin and Nat. Tng. Ctr., 1998—2000; deployed Ops. Desert Thunder U.S. Army, 1998, Army's dir. tng. Office Dep. Chief of Staff (G-3), 2000—01, dep. (J-3) U.S. Ctrl. Command Operation Enduring Freedom Afghanistan, 2001—02; dep. comdg. gen. for ops. Third U.S. Army, Combined Forces Land Component Command, Operation Iraqi Freedom Third U.S. Army, Combined Forces Land Component Command (CLCC), Operation Iraqi Freedom, Kuwait, 2002—03; comdg. gen. 3rd Inf. Divsn. U.S. Army, Ft. Stewart and Hunter Army Airfield, 2003—06; comdr. Multi-Nat. Divsn. Baghdad, Task Force Baghdad, 2005—06; dir. ops. US Northern Command (USNORTHCOM), 2006—07, dep. comdr., 2007—; vice comdr. US Element North American Aerospace Def. Command (NORAD), Peterson AFB, Colo., 2007—09; commdg. gen. US Army Ctrl. (USARCENT), Coalition Forces Land Component Command (CFLCC), Ft. McPherson, Ga., 2009—. Decorated Def. Disting. Svc. medal, Def. Superior Svc. medal, Disting. Svc. medal, Legion of Merit with 4 oak leaf clusters, Air Assault badge, Bronze Star (2), Armed Forces Expeditionary medal, Parachutist badge. Office: US Army Central (USARCENT) Atlanta GA 30330

WEDDING, CHARLES RANDOLPH, architect; b. St. Petersburg, Fla., Nov. 16, 1934; s. Charles Reid and L. Marion (Whitaker) W.; m. Audrey Whitsel, Aug. 18, 1956 (div. Apr. 1979); children: Daryl L., Douglas R., Dorian B.; m. Vonnie Sue Hayes, June 22, 1984 (div. Dec. 1991); stepchildren: Stephanie W., Brian E.; m. June A. Free, Mar. 31, 1993; stepchildren: Gregory, Kristine. BArch, U. Fla., 1957. Registered arch., Fla., Ga., N.C., S.C., Del., Va., Tex., Ill., Ind., Kans., La., Mo., Okla., Tenn. Arch. in tng. Harvard & Jolly AIA, St. Petersburg, 1957-60; arch., prin., pres. Wedding & Assocs., St. Petersburg, 1960—. Mayor City of St. Petersburg, 1973-75; past chmn. Pinellas County Com. of 100, Bldg. Dept. Survey Team, City of St. Petersburg; trustee All Children's Hosp., 1968-70; sect. leader St. Petersburg United Fund, 1965-70; mem. city coun. Action Team for Pier Redevel., 1967-68; mem. exec. com. Goals for City of St. Petersburg, 1970-72; den leader Webelos, Boy Scouts Am., 1971-72; chmn., trustee Canterbury Sch. YMCA, 1968-72; mem. adv. com. Tomlinson Vocat. Sch., 1969-79; past trustee Mus. Fine Arts; past bd. dirs. Neighborly Ctr., Jr. Achievement Pinellas County; chair Downtown Partnership, 2001—, Mcpl. Pier Task Force, City of Petersburg, 2009-; chair Pinelles County Local PLanning Agy., 2010-. Served to 1st lt. U.S. Army, 1958-60. Fellow AIA (5 Silver Spike awards, Merit of Honor, Medal of Honor); mem. Am. Soc. Landscape Archs., St. Petersburg Assn. Archs. (past pres.), Fla. Assn. Archs. (8 Merit Design awards), St. Petersburg Yacht Club, Suncoasters Club. Republican. Episcopalian. Avocations: sailing, hunting, golf, tennis. Home: 6900

10th Ave N Saint Petersburg FL 33710-6152 Office: Wedding & Stephenson Archs Inc 42 First St SE Saint Petersburg FL 33701-4209 Office Phone: 727-821-6610. Business E-Mail: randy@weddingarchitects.com.

WEDDINGTON, SARAH RAGLE, lawyer, educator; b. Abilene, Tex., Feb. 5, 1945; d. Herbert Doyle and Lena Catherine Ragle. BS magna cum laude, McMurry Coll., 1965, PhD (hon.), 1979; JD, U. Tex., 1967; PhD (hon.), Hamilton Coll., 1979, Southwestern U., 1989, Austin Coll., 1993, Nova Southeastern U., 1999; PhD in Human Letters (hon.), Fitchburg State Coll., 2004. Bar: Tex. 1967, D.C. 1979, U.S. Dist. Ct. (we., no. and ea. dists.) Tex., U.S. Ct. Appeals (5th cir.), U.S. Supreme Ct. Pvt. practice law, Austin, Tex., 1967-77, 1985—; gen. counsel USDA, Washington, 1977-78; spl. asst. to Pres. The White House, Washington, 1978—79, asst. to Pres., 1979—81; chmn. Interdepartmental Task Force on Women, 1978-81; mem. Pres.'s Commn. on Exec. Exchange, 1981; Carl Hatch prof. law and pub. adminstrn. U. N.Mex., Albuquerque, 1982-83; dir. Tex. Office State-Fed. Rels., Austin, Washington, 1983-85; founder The Weddington Ctr., Austin. Vis. prof. govt. Wheaton Coll., Norton, Mass., 1981-83; sr. lectr. Tex. Woman's U., Denton, 1981-90, 93, U. Tex., Austin, 1986-1989, adj. assoc. prof. 1989-2001, adj. prof., 2001-. Author: A Question of Choice, 1992; contbr. articles to various mags.; contbg. editor Glamour mag., 1981-83. Mem. Tex. Ho. of Reps., 1973-77; named hon. chair San Francisco Bar Assn. Breast Cancer Hotline/Network, 2001, named hon. chair ann. benefit for Breast Cancer Rsch. Ctr., Austin, 2002, named lecture showcase presenter Nat. Assn. Campus Activities, 2003. Recipient Woman of Yr. award, Tex. Women's Polit. Caucus, 1973, Outstanding Young Am. Leaders, Time Mag., 1979, Leadership award, Ladies Home Jour., 1980, Spl. Recognition award, Esquire mag., 1984, Elizabeth (Betty) Boyer award, Equity Action League, 1992, Woman Who Dares award, Nat. Coun. Jewish Women, 1993, Woman of Distinction award, Nat. Conf. for Coll. Women Student Leaders, 1993, Colby award for Pub. Svc., Sigma Kappa, 1996, Hummingbird award, Leadership Am., 1998, Tallest Texan award, Houston Chronicle, 2000, Speaking Out for Justice award, AAUW Legal Advocacy Fund, 2001, AAUW Ednl. Found., 2001, Ally award, Possible Woman Leadership Conf., 2001, Sarah Weddington Leadership Conf. named in her honor, Tex. Woman's U., 2001, Humanitarian of Yr. award, Planned Parenthood, Tex., 2003, Courage award, Women Lawyers LA, 2004, Reproductive Equity award, Lilith Orgn., 2005, Knowledge is Power award, Tex. Women Lawyers, 2007, Margaret Brent Women Lawyers of Achievement award, ABA, 2008; named Lectr. of Yr., Nat. Assn. Coll. Activities, 1990, Tex. Woman of Century, Tex. Women's C. of C., 1999, Face of Century, San Antonio Express News, 1999, 2000, Outstanding Alumnus, McMurry U., 2004, Nat. Pub. Health Hero, U. Calif., Berkeley, 2005, Keynote Spkr., China's Women Fedn., U.S. Conf. on Women in Leadership, Beijing, 2004; named one of Most Influential Lawyers of the 20th Century, Tex. Lawyer, 2000. Mem. Tex. Bar Assn. Office: The Weddington Ctr 709 W 14th St Austin TX 78701-1707 Business E-Mail: sw@weddingtoncenter.com.

WEDEL-COWGILL, MILLIE REDMOND, secondary school educator, journalism and performing arts, communication; b. Harrisburg, Pa., Aug. 18, 1939; d. Clair L. and Florence (Heiges) Aungst; m. T.S. Redmond, 1956 (div. 1967); children: T.S. Redmond II; m. Frederick L. Wedel, Jr., 1974 (div. 1986); m. Paul R. Cowgill, May 19, 2001. BA, Alaska Meth. U., 1966; MEd, U. Alaska, Anchorage, 1972; postgrad. in comm., Stanford U., Calif., 1975-76. Lic. third class broadcasting, FCC. Profl. actress Charming Models & Models Guild of Phila., 1954-61; asst. dir. devel. in charge pub. rels. Alaska Meth. U., Anchorage, 1966, part-time lectr., 1966, 73; comm. tchr. Anchorage Sch. Dist., 1967-96; owner Wedel Prodns., Anchorage, 1976-86; cons. comms., media and edn., owner Cowgill Cons., 2003—. Pub. rels. staff Alaska Purchase Centennial Exhibit, U.S. Dept. Commerce, 1967; writer gubernatorial campaign, 1971; instr. Chapman Coll., 1990-93; adj. instr. U. Alaska, Anchorage, 1972, 77-79, 89-2001; cons. Cook Inlet Native Assn., 1978, No. Inst., 1979; judge Ark. Press Women's Writing Contest, 1990-91; sec. exec. bd. Alaska Dept. Edn. Profl. Tchg. Practices Commn., 1993-94. Bd. dirs. Sta. KAKM, Alaska Pub. TV, membership chmn., 1978-80, nat. lay rep. to Pub. Broadcasting Svc. and Nat. Assn. Pub. TV Stas., 1979; bd. dirs. Ednl. Telecom. Consortium for Alaska, 1979, Mid-Hillside Cmty. Coun., Municipality of Anchorage, 1979-80, 83-88, Hillside East Cmty. Coun., 1984-88, pres., 1984-85; rsch. writer, legal asst. Vinson & Elkins, Houston, 1981; v.p., bd. dirs. Inlet View ASD Cmty. Sch., 1994-95, pres., 1995-97; Valley Forge Freedoms Found., Murdoch Scholarships; bd. dirs. Rev. Richard Gay Trust, Alaska and Pa., 1992-2000. Recipient awards for newspapers, lit. mags.; award Nat. Scholastic Press Assn., 1981, 82, 83, 84; Alaska Coun. Econs., 1982, Merits award Alaska Dept. Edn., 1982-93, Legis. commendation State of Alaska, Nat. Blue Ribbon Outstanding Sch. award, 1993. Mem. NEA (AEA bldg. rep., state del. 70s, 80s, 94-95), Assn. Pub. Broadcasting (charter mem., nat. lay del. 1980), Indsl. TV Assn. (San Francisco and Houston 1975-81), Alaska Press Club (chmn. high sch. journalism workshops, 1968-69, 73, awards for sch. newspapers 1972, 74, 77), Alaska Fedn. Press Women (dir. 1978-86, 94-95, pres. 1995-96, h.s. journalism competition youth projects dir., award for brochures 1978, chair youth writing contest 1994-95), Chugach Electric (chair 1990, nomination com. for bd. dirs. 1988-90), English Speaking Union, Hood Coll. Alaska Alumni Assn., Stanford U. Alumni Club (Alaska pres. 1982-84, 90-92, 99-2000, v.p. 1998-99), UAA Alumni & AMU, APU Alumni Anchorage, Rotary Club of Naples (photographer and asst. program chair 2003), Philharm. League (bd. dirs., 2006), Naples Fla. U. Pa. Club, Naples Press Club (Fla.), Pelican Bay Women's League (Naples), Imperial Golf Club (Naples). Presbyterian. Home: PO Box 111489 Anchorage AK 99511-1489 Office: Cowgill Cons PO Box 770662 Naples FL 34107-0662 Home Phone: 907-345-7793; Office Phone: 239-598-3770.

WEEKLEY, BOO (THOMAS BRENT WEEKLEY), professional golfer; b. Milton, Fla., July 23, 1973; m. Karyn Weekley; 1 child, Thomas Parker. Attended, Abraham Baldwin Agrl. Coll., Tilton, Ga., 1992—93. Laborer Monsanto chemical plant, Pensacola, Fla.; profl. golfer, 1997—; mem. Ryder Cup team, 2008. Achievements include winning Verizon Heritage, 2007, 2008, Ryder Cup, 2008. Avocations: hunting, fishing. Office: PGA Tour 100 PGA Tour Blvd Ponte Vedra FL 32082

WEEKLEY, FREDERICK CLAY, JR., lawyer; b. San Antonio, Aug. 29, 1939; s. F. Clay and Topsy (Stevens) W.; m. Lynda Freeman; children: Amber Lee Carothers, Caroline Karazissis. BBA, Baylor U., 1962, LLB, 1963; LLM, NYU, 1969. Bar: Tex. 1963. Ptnr. Bracewell & Patterson, Houston, 1974-90; atty. Bank One, Tex., N.A., 1990-98; ptnr./counsel Shannon, Gracey, Ratliff & Miller, LLP, Ft. Worth, 1999—. Mem. coun. real property, probate and trust law sect., State Bar of Tex., 1987-90; mem. adminstrv. coun. trust divsn. Tex. Bankers Assn., 1992-95, chmn. legis. com., 1992-95. Mem. Commn. Probate Law Examiners, Tex. Bd. Legal Specialization, 1978-82. Fellow Am. Coll. Trust and Estate Counsel. Home: 1821 Mossy Oak St Arlington TX 76012-5619

WEEKS, ALBERT LOREN, writer, educator, journalist; b. Highland Park, Mich., Mar. 28, 1923; s. Albert Loren and Vera Grace (Jarvis) W. Student, U. Mich., 1942-43; MA, U. Chgo., 1949; PhD, Columbia U., 1965; cert., Russian Inst., 1960. Reporter Chgo. City News Bur., 1946; polit. analyst U.S. Dept. State, 1950-53, Free Europe Com., Inc., 1953-56; editorial asst. Newsweek mag., 1957-58; Russian tech. glossary compiler McGraw-Hill Book Co., 1960-61; prof. continuing edn. NYU, 1959-89. Lectr. U.S. diplomatic history and soviet govt. Columbia U., 1951-52; mem. adv. coun. Nat. Strategy Info. Ctr., 1979-89; instr. Ringling Sch. Art and Design, 1991—; pub. spkr. S.W. Fla. Host: A Week's View of Red Press, Sta. WNBC, 1965-68; series Myths That Rule America, NBC-TV, 1979-82; author: Reading American History, 1963, The First Bolshevik: A Political Biography of Peter Tkachev, 1968, The Other Side of Coexistence: An Analysis of Russian Foreign Policy, 1970, Richard Hofstadter's The American Political Tradition and the Age of Reform, 1973, Andrei Sakharov and the Soviet Dissidents, 1975, The Troubled Detente, 1976, Solzhenitsyn's One Day in the Life of Ivan Denisovich, 1976, Myths That Rule America, 1980, War and Peace: Soviet Russia Speaks, 1983; editor/compiler Brassey's Soviet and Communist Quotations, 1987, The Soviet Nomenklatura, 1987-1991, Stalin's Other War: Soviet Grand Strategy 1939-1941, 2002, Russia's Life-Saver: Lend-Lease Aid to the USSR in World War II, The Choice of War, Assured Victory How Stalin Won the War But Lost the Peace; internat. affairs editor Def. Sci. mag., 1982-85; columnist Def. Report, 1982-90; contbr. articles to N.Y. Times, New Republic, New Leader, Annals, Russian, Slavic revs., Christian Sci. Monitor, Problems of Communism, Survey, Mil. Intelligence, Strategic Rev., World War II mag., Air Univ. Rev., L.A. Times, Washington Times, Orbis, Global Affairs, Panorama, Sarasota Herald-Tribune, Bradenton Herald, Defense and Diplomacy, Am. Intelligence Jour., USA Today, Rossiiskiye Vesti, Vechernii Vladimir, CityTempo mag., Modern Age mag. Home: 4884 Kestral Park Cir Sarasota FL 34231-3369 Personal E-mail: aweeks1@compuserve.com.

WEEKS, CHARLES THOMAS, II, federal marshal; b. 1959; BA, Southwestern Okla. State U., 1982. Various positions of increasing responsibility including comdr., exec. sec., then maj. Okla. Hwy. Patrol, Okla. Dept. Pub. Safety, 1985—2010; US marshal (western dist.) Okla. US Marshals Svc., US Dept. Justice, Oklahoma City, 2010—. Office: US Courthouse 200 NW 4th St Rm 2418 Oklahoma City OK 73102 Office Phone: 405-231-4206.

WEEKS, J. DAVID, state legislator, lawyer; b. Sumter, SC, Sept. 24, 1953; s. Goliath Brunson Sr. and Eartha Lee Weeks Brunson; m. Cheryl Elaine Hannibal, July 31, 1985; children: Lynette, Davida. BA, Morris Coll., 1975; JD, U. S.C., 1989; MEd, Howard U., 1996. Mcpl. ct. judge City of Timmonsville, SC, 1996—2000; mem. Dist. 51 SC House of Reps., 2001—, mem. Judiciary Com. Bd. trustees Morris Coll., 2001—. Mcpl. ct. judge, Timmonsville, SC, 1996—2000; chmn. Sumter County Voter Registration Bd., 1994, Sumter City-County Planning Commn., 1998—2000; deacon Jehovah Missionary Bapt. Ch., ch. sch. tchr. Democrat. Office: State Capitol 330C Blatt Bldg Columbia SC 29211 Home: 2 Marlborough Ct Sumter SC 29154 E-mail: JDW@scstatehouse.net.

WEEKS, ROBERT ANDREW, materials science researcher, educator; b. Birmingham, Ala., Aug. 23, 1924; s. William Andrew and Annie Bell (Hammond) W.; m. Jane Sutherland, Mar. 20, 1948; children: Kevin Dale, Robin Dee, Loren Hammond, Kerry Andrew. BS, Birmingham-So. Coll., 1947; MS, U. Tenn., 1951; PhD, Brown U., 1966. Sr. physicist Union Carbide Corp., Oak Ridge, Tenn., 1951-84; rsch. prof. material sci. Vanderbilt U., 1984-99, prof. emeritus, 1999—. Disting. vis. prof. Am. U. in Cairo, 1970-71; invited prof. Ecole Poly. Fed. de Lausanne, Switzerland, 1981; vis. prof. Cath. U., Leuven, Belgium, 1983; cons. numerous pvt. corps. and fed. agys.; prin. investigator lunar materials, 1968-74; co-prin. investigator expdn. Western desert of Egypt to desert glass site, 1981; CEO Oak Ridge Cons., 1993—. Co-editor: Effects of Modes of Formation on Structure of Glass, 1985, 88, Editing the Refereed Scientific Journal, 1994; assoc. editor Jour. Geophys. Rsch., 1968-74; editor Jour. Noncrystalline Solids, 1988-98; conf. editor Jour. Non-Crystalline Solids, 1998-2000, editl. bd. mem., 2000-; contbr. numerous articles to profl. jours. Served with U.S. Army, 1943-46. Union Carbide fellow, 1964; Fulbright lectr., 1980, Rsch. fellow Reading U., 1971, USIA Am. participant Egypt, India, Nepal and Sri Lanka, 1986; Sir Neville Mott award, Jour. Non-Crystalline Solids, 2006. Fellow Am. Ceramic Soc. (SiO_2, advanced dielectrics and related devices conf. hon. chmn. 2004, 06, 08, R. A. Weeks Symposium named in his honor, Honolulu 1993, 2004, George W. Morey award 1998); mem. AAAS, Am. Phys. Soc., Sigma Xi. Avocation: photography. Home: 804 Shannondale Way # 120 Maryville TN 37803-5970 Personal E-mail: e1e2e4@bellsouth.net.

WEGNER, ARTHUR EDUARD, aerospace company executive; b. Madison, Wis., June 23, 1937; s. Arthur Eduard and Elynore (Bell) W.; m. Patricia J. Vining, Oct. 21, 1960; children: Meleda A., Elisabeth K. BS in Marine Engring., U.S. Naval Acad., 1960; MBA, Harvard U., 1969. Comdr. USNR, 1969; v.p., planning Rust-Litton Industries, Birmingham, Ala., 1970—73; exec. v.p., mfg. div. Pratt & Whitney, East Hartford, Conn., 1976—81, pres., 1983—91; with United Technologies Corp., sr. v.p. power div. Hartford, Conn., 1986—89, pres. aerospace and def., exec. v.p., 1989; joined Raytheon Co., 1993, exec. v.p., 1995—2000; chmn. Raytheon Aircraft, 2000; chmn., CEO Raytheon's Beech Aircraft Corp.; sr. v.p. Raytheon Co. Bd. dirs. BE Aerospace, Inc., 2007—. Trustee Conn. Pub. Broadcasting, Hartford, Hartford Grad. Ctr. Avocation: farming. Office: BE Aerospace Inc 1400 Corporate Ctr Way Wellington FL 33414 Office Phone: 561-791-5000. Office Fax: 561-791-7900. Business E-Mail: arthur_wegner@beaerospace.com.

WEGNER, JUDITH WELCH, lawyer, educator, dean; b. Hartford, Conn., Feb. 14, 1950; d. John Raymond and Ruth (Thulen) Welch; m. Warren W. Wegner, Oct. 13, 1972. BA with honors, U. Wis., 1972; JD, UCLA, 1976. Bar: Calif. 1976, D.C. 1977, N.C. 1988, U.S. Supreme Ct. 1980, U.S. Ct. Appeals. Law clk. to Judge Warren Ferguson, U.S. Dist. Ct. for So. Dist. Calif., LA, 1976-77; atty. Office Legal Counsel and Land & Natural Resources Divsn. U.S. Dept. Justice, Washington, 1977-79; spl. asst. to sec. U.S. Dept. Edn., Washington, 1979-80; vis. assoc. prof. U. Iowa Coll. Law, Iowa City, 1981; asst. prof. U. NC Sch. Law, Chapel Hill, 1981-84, assoc. prof., 1984-88, assoc. dean, 1986-88, prof., 1988—2007, dean, 1989-99, Burton Craige prof., 2007—; sr. scholar Carnegie Found. for Advancement of Tchg., 1999—2001; chmn. faculty U. NC, 2003—06. Spkr. in field. Chief comment editor UCLA Law Rev., 1975-76; co-author Educating Lawyers, 2007, State and Loval Government in a Federal System, 6th edit., 2007; contbr. articles to legal publs. Mem. Bd. Alderman, Carrboro, NC, 1984—89; mem. planning bd. Orange County, NC, 2006—. Recipient Ernest Bell award, NC Assn. Mcpl. Attys. Mem.: ABA, Assn. Am. Law Schs. (pres. 1995), Internat. Mcpl. Lawyers Assn., Women's Internat. Forum, NC Assn. Women Attys., NC State Bar Assn., Order of the Coif, Phi Beta Kappa. Democrat. Office: U NC Sch Law Van Hecke Wettach Hall Campus Box 3380 Chapel Hill NC 27599-3380 Home Phone: 919-929-5024; Office Phone: 919-962-4113. Business E-Mail: judith_wegner@unc.edu.

WEHRING, BERNARD WILLIAM, nuclear engineering educator; b. Monroe, Mich, Aug. 3, 1937; s. Bernard Albert and Alma Christina (Graf) W.; m. Margaret Mary Robinson, Sept. 5, 1959; children: Mary Ann, James, Susan, Barbara. BSE. in Physics, U. Mich., 1959, BSE. in Math, 1959; MS in Physics, U. Ill., 1961, PhD in Nuclear Engring, 1966. Asst. prof. nuc. engring. U. Ill., Urbana, 1966-70, assoc. prof., 1970-77, prof., 1977-84, asst. dean engring., 1981-82; prof. nuc. engring. N.C. State U., Raleigh, 1984-89; dir. nuc. reactor program NC State U., Raleigh, 1984-89; prof. mech. engring. U. Tex., Austin, 1989-2000, dir. Nuc. Engring. Tchg. Lab., 1989-2000; adj. prof. nuc. engring. NC State U., Raleigh, 2000—. Cons. Argonne and Los Alamos nat. labs.; mem. crosssect. evaluation working group Brookhaven Nat. Lab. Contbr. sects. to books, articles to profl. publs. AEC fellow, 1963-65; NSF grantee, 1968— Fellow Am. Nuc. Soc.; mem. Am. Nuclear Soc. (standards com.), Am. Phys. Soc. Achievements include contributing in the generation of basic nuc. data and develop. of new instruments and exptl. techniques. Home: 516 Westbrook Dr Raleigh NC 27615-7321 Business E-Mail: bwwehrin@ncsu.edu.

WEI, JEANNE Y., geriatrician, educator; PhD, U. Ill., MD, 1975. Diplomate Am. Bd. Internal Medicine, Am. Bd. Internal Medicine-cardiology, Am. Bd. Internal Medicine-geriatrics. Intern Johns Hopkins Hosp., 1976, resident in internal medicine, 1997, fellow in cardiology, 1980; joined faculty Harvard Med. Sch., dir. divsn. on aging; joined faculty Beth Israel Med. Ctr., chief gerontology; Dillard prof. of geriat. coll. of medicine Univ. Ark. Med. Sciences, chmn. Reynolds dept. of geriat., dir. Reynolds inst. on aging. Recipient Outstanding Clin. Educator award, Harvard Med. Sch., 2000, Outstanding Woman Faculty award, UAMS Coll. of Medicine, 2005, Willie Birmingham Medal. in Geriat., Irish Gerontol. Soc., 1998, Spl. award of Appreciation, Gerontol. Soc. of Taiwan, 2005. Mem.: Soc. of Geriatric Cardiology (pres.), Assn. of Dirs. of Geriatric Academic Programs (pres.). Office: University of Arkansas for Medical Sciences 4301 W Markham St Little Rock AR 72205 Office Phone: 501-686-7000.

WEIDMAN, SHEILA, marketing professional; b. Bradenton, Fla., July 11, 1961; BS in sci., Journalism and Comm., U. Fla., 1983. Mgr., comm. ASHRAE, 1983—88; mgr., corp. comm. Georgia-Pacific Corp., 1988—90, dir., external comm. and corp. advt., 1990—98, dir., spl. asst. to chmn. and CEO, 1998—2000, sr. dir., corp. mktg. and sales excellence, 2000—01, v.p., corp. mktg., 2001—02, v.p., corp. comm. and mktg. Atlanta, 2002—. Com. mem. Am. Heart Assn., Atlanta Hist. Soc.; mem. Leadership Atlanta, Class of 2004. Recipient Women of Achievement awards, YWCA, 1995. Mem.: Atlanta Sports Coun. (bd. dirs., chmn. mktg. com.), Atlanta CMO Roundtable, CMO Group of N.Am., Ga. Press Assn., Ga. State CMO Roundtable, Met. Atlanta C. of C. (vice chair chmn.'s campaign 2003), Mktg. Leadership Coun. (vice chair chmn.'s campaign 2004), Pub. Rels. Soc. Am., Sales and Mktg. Execs., Atlanta Press Club. Office: Georgia-Pacific Corp 133 Peachtree St NE Atlanta GA 30303 Office Phone: 404-652-4000. Office Fax: 404-230-7052. Business E-Mail: sweidman@gapac.com.

WEIDNER, DONALD J., dean, law educator; BS, Fordham U., 1966; JD, U. Tex., Austin, 1969. Bar: SC, U.S. Tax Ct., U.S. Dist. Cts. for No. Dist. Ohio and Dist. SC, Supreme Ct. U.S. Assoc. Willkie Farr & Gallagher, New York, NY, 1969—70; Bigelow fellow U. Chgo. Law Sch., 1970—71; asst. prof. U. SC Sch. Law, 1971—74; assoc. prof. Cleveland State U., 1974—76, Fla. State U. Coll. Law, 1976—78, prof., 1978—, assoc. dean, 1984—85, dean, 1991—97, interim dean, 1998—2000, dean, Alumni Centennial prof., 2000—. Vis. prof. U. Tex. Sch. Law, 1978, U. N.Mex, 1979, Stanford Law Sch., 1981, U. NC Sch. Law, 1991; prof in residence Ruden McClosky Smith Schuster & Russell, PA, 1997; reporter Uniform Partnership Act (1994) Nat. Conf. Commrs. on Uniform State Laws, 1987—94. Co-author: Real Estate: Taxation and Bankruptcy, 1979, General and Limited Liability Partnerships Under the Revised Uniform Partnership Act, 1996, The Revised Uniform Partnership Act, 1998—2009. Order of Coif. Mem.: Am. Law Inst., Assoc. Am. Law Schs. (mem. Membership Review (Accrediation) Com. 2001—03), Fla. Supreme Ct. Hist. Soc. (Bd. Trustees), Fla. Supreme Ct. Commn. on Professionalism. Avocations: boating, fishing, scuba diving, reading, exercise. Office: Florida State University College of Law Advocacy Center Room A301 Tallahassee FL 32306-1601 Office Phone: 850-644-3071. Office Fax: 850-644-5487. E-mail: dweidner@law.fsu.edu.*

WEIGEL, PAUL HENRY, biochemistry educator, researcher, consultant; b. NYC, Aug. 11, 1946; s. Helmut and Jeanne Weigel; m. Nancy Shulman, June 15, 1968 (div. Dec. 1987); 1 child, Dana J.; m. Janet Oka, May 17, 1992 BA in Chemistry, Cornell U., 1968; MS in Biochemistry, Johns Hopkins U., Balt., 1969, PhD in Biochemistry, 1975. NIH postdoctoral fellow Johns Hopkins U., Balt., 1975-78; asst. prof. U. Tex. Med. Br., Galveston, Tex., 1978-82, assoc. prof., 1982—87, prof. biochemistry and cell biology, 1987-94, vice chmn. dept. human biol. chemistry and genetics, 1990-93, acting chmn. dept. human biology, chemistry and genetics, 1992-93; prof., chmn. dept. biochemistry and molecular biology U. Okla. Health Scis. Ctr., Oklahoma City, 1994—, George Lynn Cross rsch. prof., 2004—, Ed Miller chair in molecular biology, 2006—; co-founder Hyalose LLC, 2000—. Mem. NIH Pathobiochemistry Study Sect., Washington, 1985-87; cons. Teltech, Mpls., 1985—, Hyalose LLC 2000—. Contbr. articles to profl. jours. Treas. Bayou Chateau Neighborhood Assn., Dickinson, Tex., 1981-83, v.p., 1983-84, pres., 1984-86. With U.S. Army, 1969-71. Grantee NIH, 1979—, Office Naval Rsch., 1983-87, Tex. Biotech., 1989-94, Okla. Ctr. Advancement Sci. and Tech., 2000-03, 2010-, Dept. Def., 2010-2012; recipient Disting. Tchr. award U. Tex. Med. Br., 1989, Disting. Rsch. award, 1989, OUHSC Innovator award, 2011. Mem.: Internat. Soc. for Hyaluronan Scis. (founding mem. 2004, sec. 2004—08, acting pres. 2007, treas. 2009—11, pres. 2012—), Soc. for Glycobiology (mem. nominations com. 2004—08), Assn. Med. and Grad. Depts. Biochemistry (webmaster 2002—07, bd. dirs. 2002—10, pres. 2007), Am. Soc. Biochemistry and Molecular Biology (mem. pub. affairs adv. com. 2000—03), Am. Soc. Cell Biology, Am. Chem. Soc. Democrat. Lutheran. Achievements include 26 US, 16 foreign patents in field. Avocations: basketball, poetry, camping, basketball card collecting. Home: 817 Hollowdale Edmond OK 73003-3022 Office: U Okla Health Scis Ctr Dept Biochem & Mol Biology Bmsb Rm 860 Oklahoma City OK 73190-0001 Office Phone: 405-271-2227. Business E-Mail: paul-weigel@ouhsc.edu.

WEIL, RICHARD, III, surgeon, medical educator; b. NYC, Feb. 22, 1936; s. Richard Jr. and Allene (Hall) W.; m. Polly Edgar, Aug. 22, 1959; children: Wendy, Richard. AB, Princeton U., 1957; MD, Columbia U. Coll. Physicians and Surgeons, 1961. Diplomate Am. Bd. Surgery, Nat. Bd. Med. Examiners. Intern in surgery Presbyn. Hosp., 1961-62, asst. resident in surgery, 1962-63, 65-67, chief resident in gen. surgery, 1968; chief resident in pediat. surgery Babies Hosp., 1969, chief resident in vasc. surgery, 1969, asst. attending surgeon, chmn. surg. house staff com., 1970-74, dir. kidney transplantation, 1973-74; asst. in surgery Columbia U. Coll. Physicians and Surgeons, 1967-68, instr. surgery, 1969, asst. prof. surgery, 1970-74; fellow in transplantation surgery U. Minn., 1970; assoc. prof. surgery U. Colo., 1974-79, prof. surgery, 1979-87, dir. transplantation, 1980-87; prof. surgery, dir. transplantation NYU, 1987-93; assoc. dean medicine, prof. surgery Brown U., Providence, 1993-98. Cons.

surgeon Manhattan VA Hosp., 1989-92, Denver VA Hosp., 1980-87, Denver Gen. Hosp., 1980-87, St. Anthony-Ctrl. Hosp. Denver, 1980-87; attending surgeon Bellevue Hosp. Ctr., 1989-93 Contbr. more than 130 articles to profl. jours. including Surg. Forum, Am. Jour. Surgery, Transplantation, Surgery, Jour. Pediat. Surgery, Surgery, Gynecology & Obstets., among others. Bd. dirs. 2002-12, chmn. 2009-12, Indian River Med. Ctr., Vero Beach, Fla., capt. U.S. Army Med. Corps, 1963-65, Germany. Capt. US Army Med. Corps, 1963—65, Germany. Mem. Am. Assn. Tissue Banks, ACS, Am. Fedn. Clin. Rsch., Am. Soc. Transplant Surgeons, Am. Soc. for Artificial Internal Organs, Am. Surg. Assn., Assn. for Acad. Surgery, Allen O. Whipple Surg. Soc. (recorder 1976-78), Ctrl. Surg. Assn., Clin. Immunology Soc., Denver Acad. Surgery, Harvey Soc., Intermountain End-Stage Renal Disease Network (exec. com. 1975-79), Internat. Cardiovasc. Soc., N.Y. Ctr. for Liver Transplantation, N.Y. Clin. Soc., N.Y. Regional Transplant Program (pres. 1991-92), N.Y. Surg. Soc., Rocky Mountain Vasc. Surg. Soc., Soc. Internat. de Chirurgie, Soc. Vascular Surgery, Soc. U. Surgeons, Transplantation Soc., Western Assn. Transplant Surgeons, United Network for Organ Sharing (councilor for Colo., Wyo., Nebr., Kans., Iowa, Mo. 1986-87). Personal E-mail: rweiliii@msn.com.

WEIL, THOMAS P., retired health services consultant; b. Mount Vernon, NY, Oct. 2, 1932; s. H.M. and Alice (Franc) W.; m. Janet Whalen, Feb. 13, 1965. BA, Union Coll., 1954; MPH, Yale U., 1958; PhD, U. Mich., 1964. S.S. Goldwater fellow Mount Sinai Med. Ctr., NYC, 1957-58; assoc. cons. J.G. Steinle Assocs., Garden City, NY, 1958-61; asst. prof. UCLA, 1962-65; assoc. dir. Touro Infirmary, New Orleans, 1964-66; prof., dir. U. Mo., 1966—71; v.p. E.D. Rosenfeld Assocs., NYC, 1971-75; pres. Bedford Health Assocs. Inc., NY, NC, 1975-2000; ret. Chmn. Health Edn. & Applied Rsch. Found., Washington, 1981-83; bd. dirs. Albany Med. Ctr., Inc., NY, 1974-77; cons. to numerous hosps., med. schs., health related orgs., 1958-2000. Contbr. articles profl. jours. Named vis. prof. W.K. Kellogg Found., Sydney, Australia, 1969; recipient svc. award Am. Assn. Healthcare Cons., 1982; Weil Disting. Prof. in Health Svcs. Mgmt., U. Mo., 1991-2001. Fellow APHA (emeritus), Am. Assn. Healthcare Cons. (emeritus), Am. Coll. Healthcare Execs. (emeritus). Jewish. Personal E-mail: tpweil@aol.com.

WEILAND, JESSICA, apparel executive; BA in English Literature, U. Tex., Austin; MBA in Fin., Am. U., Wash., DC. Mktg. sys. mgr. AMRE; various positions, media dir. Time-Life Books, Alexandria, Va.; circulation dir., Horchow Mail Order The Neiman Marcus Group, Inc, 1987—99, v.p., 1999—2000, sr. v.p., 2000—07; sr. v.p., mktg., customer care, Neiman Marcus Direct Neiman Marcus Group, Inc., 2007—. Bd. adv. CMO Coun. Office: The Neiman Marcus Group Inc 1618 Main St Dallas TX 75201 Office Phone: 214-743-7600. Office Fax: 214-573-5320. Business E-Mail: jessica_weiland@neimanmarcus.com.

WEIMER, JOHN L., state supreme court justice; b. Thibodaux, La., Oct. 2, 1954; m. Penny Hymel; 3 children. BS (with honors), Nicholls State U., 1976; JD, La. State U., 1980. Pvt. practice law, 1980—95; judge 17th Judicial Dist. Ct., 1995—98, 1st Cir. Ct. of Appeal, Dist. 1, Divsn. B, 1998—2001; assoc. justice La. Supreme Ct., 2001—. Adj. prof. law Nicholls State U., 1982—97; regional co-chmn. Citizens' Summit for Justice Reform, 1997. Mem. Thibodaux Vol. Fire Dept., Rotary Club, Nicholls State U. Alumni Bd., Thibodaux Chamber of Commerce, Houma-Terrebonne Chamber of Commerce, Assumption Chamber of Commerce; established Lafourche Parish Student Govt. Day Program. Recipient Crimefighter's Outstanding Jurist award, Outstanding Jud. award, Victims & Citizens Against Crime. Mem.: Lafourche Parish Bar Assn., La. State Bar Assn. (delegate). Achievements include development of Lafourche Parish Drug Treatment Court. Office: La Supreme Ct 400 Royal St New Orleans LA 70130*

WEINBERG, GERHARD LUDWIG, history professor, writer; b. Hannover, Germany, Jan. 1, 1928; arrived in UK, 1938, arrived in US, 1940, naturalized, 1949; s. Max Bendix and Kate Sarah (Gruenebaum) Weinberg; m. Janet Kabler White, Apr. 29, 1989. BA in Social Studies, SUNY, Albany, 1948, LHD (hon.), 1989; MA, U. Chgo., 1949, PhD in History, 1951; PhD (hon.), U. Hannover, 2001. Rsch. analyst, war documentation project Columbia U., NYC, 1951-54; vis. lectr. history U. Chgo., 1954-55, U. Ky., Lexington, 1955-56, asst. prof., 1957-59; faculty U. Mich., Ann Arbor, 1959—63, prof. history, 1963-74, chmn. history dept., 1972-73; William Rand Kenan, Jr. prof. history U. NC, Chapel Hill, 1974-99, prof. emeritus, 1999—, acting chmn. history dept., 1989-90. Vis. prof. U. Bonn, Germany, 1983, USAF Acad., 1990—91; Shapiro sr. scholar-in-residence US Holocaust Meml. Mus., Washington, 2001—02. Author: Guide to Captured German Documents, 1952, Germany and the Soviet Union, 1939-1941, 1954, The Foreign Policy of Hitler's Germany: Diplomatic Revolution in Europe, 1933-36, 1970, The Foreign Policy of Hitler's Germany: Starting World War II, 1937-1939, 1980, World in the Balance: Behind the Scenes of World War II, 1981, A World at Arms: A Global History of World War II, 1994, Germany, Hitler, and World War II: Essays in Modern German and World History, 1995, Visions of Victory: The Hopes of Eight World War II Leaders, 2005; editor, translator Hitler's Second Book: The Unpublished Sequel to Mein Kampf, 2003; contbr. numerous articles to various hist. jours., chapters to books; mem. bd. editors Jour. Modern Hist., 1970—72, Ctrl. European Hist., 1970—72, Internat. Hist. Rev., 1990—2000, Jour. Intelligence Hist., 2001. Chmn. Ann Arbor Dem. Com., 1961—63; mem. Mich. Dem. Ctrl. Com., 1963—67. Served with US Army, 1946—47. Recipient Pritzker Mil. Libr. Lit. award for lifetime achievement in mil. writing, Tawani Found., Chgo., 2009; fellow Am. Coun. Learned Societies, 1965—66, John Simon Guggenheim Meml. Found., 1971—72, NEH, 1978—79. Mem.: Soc. Mil. History, Am. Acad. Arts & Scis., WW II Studies Assn. (bd. dirs.), German Studies Assn. (exec. com. 1989—92, v.p. 1994—96, pres. 1996—98, Halverson prize 1981), So. Hist. Assn. (chmn. European sect. 1989), Am. Hist. Assn. (v.p. rsch. 1982—84, George Louis Beer prize 1971, 1995), Phi Beta Kappa. Jewish. E-mail: gweinber@email.unc.edu.

WEINBERG, JERROLD G., lawyer; b. Norfolk, Va., Apr. 5, 1928; s. Charles Paul and Reba Gladstone Weinberg; m. Marcia Ellen Moress (dec.); children: Ellen Jane(dec.), Nancy Louise von Auersperg, Andrew Steven; m. Ruth A. Hofheimer, Feb. 6, 1999. BS in Comm., U. Va., Charlottesville, 1947, LLB, 1950. Bar: Va. 1949. Atty. pvt. practice, Norfolk, 1950—78; pres. Weinberg & Stein PC, Norfolk, 1978—. Lectr. law William & Mary Law Sch., Williamsburg, Va., 1980; mem. Jud. Conf. US Ct. Appeals (4th cir.). With US Army, 1951—53. Master: James Kent Am. Inn Ct. (pres. 1996—97); fellow: Va. Law Found., Am. Bar Found., Am. Coll. Trial Lawyers; mem.: ABA, Norfolk and Portsmouth Bar Assn. (pres. 1973—74), Va. Bar Assn. Republican. Jewish. Office: Weinberg Stein Pc 999 Waterside Dr Ste 2202 Norfolk VA 23510-3320 Home: 1 Colley Ave Apt 809 Norfolk VA 23510

WEINBERG, LOUISE, law educator, writer; b. NYC; m. Steven Weinberg; 1 child, Elizabeth. AB summa cum laude, Cornell U.; JD, Harvard U., 1969, LLM, 1974. Bar: Mass. Sr. law clk. Hon. Chas. E. Wyzanski, Jr., Boston, 1971-72; assoc. in law Bingham, McCutchen (formerly Bingham, Dana & Gould), Boston, 1969—72; teaching fellow Harvard Law Sch., Boston, 1972-74; lectr. law Brandeis U., Waltham, Mass., 1974; assoc. prof. law Suffolk U., Boston, 1974-76, prof., 1977-80; vis. assoc. prof. law Stanford U., Palo Alto, Calif., 1976-77; vis. prof. law Sch. Law, U. Tex., Austin, 1979, prof. law, 1980-84, Thompson prof. law, 1984-90, Andrews and Kurth prof. law, 1990-92, Fulbright and Jaworski regents rsch. prof., 1991-92, Angus G. Wynne, Sr. prof., 1992-97, Fondren chair faculty excellence, 1995—, Eugene R. Smith Centennial rsch. prof. law, 1993-97, holder William B. Bates chair, 1997—. Vis. scholar Hebrew U., Jerusalem, 1989; Forum fellow World Econ. Forum, Davos, Switzerland, 1995—; cons. PBS; pub. spkr., lectr. in field. Author: Federal Courts: Judicial Federalism and Judicial Power, 1994; co-author: Conflict of Laws, 1990, 2d edit., 2002; contbr. chpts. to books and encyclopedias, articles to profl. jours. Bd. dirs. Ballet Austin, 1986-88, Austin Coun. on Fgn. Affairs, 1985—, Austin Civil War Round Table, 1998—. Recipient Disting. Educator award Tex. Exes Assn., 1996, fellow Charles Alan Wright Chair., 2010- Mem.: Soc. Am. Legis. History, Supreme Ct. Hist. Soc., Am. Constn. Soc., Assn. Am. Law Schs. (chair sect. on conflict of laws 1991—93, chair sect. on fed. cts. 2003—05, chair sect. admiralty 2005—06, chair sect. on conflict of laws 2013—), The Philos. Soc. Tex., Am. Law Inst. (life; consultative com. complex litigation 1989—93, consultative com. enterprise liability 1990—95, adv. group fed. judicial code revision project 1996—2001, mems.' consultative group, intellectual property 2004—, internat. jurisdiction and judgments 2004—, aggregate litigation 2006—), Phi Kappa Phi, Phi Beta Kappa. Office: U Tex Sch Law 727 Dean Keeton St Austin TX 78705-3224 Business E-Mail: lweinberg@law.utexas.edu.

WEINBERG, MORRIS, JR., (SANDY WEINBERG), lawyer; b. Chattanooga, Tenn., June 4, 1950; s. Morris Sr. and Jamie May (Stokely) Weinberg; m. Rosemary Armstrong, Aug. 11, 1979; children: Stokely, Lilly, Antonio. BA magna cum laude, Woodrow Wilson Sch. Internat. & Urban Affairs, Princeton U., NJ, 1972; JD, Vanderbilt U. Law Sch., Nashville, 1975. Bar: Ga. 1975, DC 1979, Fla. 1985, US Dist. Ct. (no., so. and mid. dists.) Fla., US Ct. Appeals (11th cir.). Assoc. Powell & Goldstein, Atlanta, 1975-79; asst. US atty. (so. dist.) NY US Dept. Justice, NYC, 1979-85; sr. ptnr. Carlton & Fields, Tampa, Fla., 1985-91; mng. ptnr. Zuckerman Spaeder LLP (formerly Zuckerman, Spaeder, Taylor & Evans), Tampa, 1991—. Mem.: ABA (co-chair White Collar Crime com.), Nat. Assn. Criminal Def. Lawyers, Fla. Assn. Criminal Def. Lawyers, Fla. Bar Assn. Avocation: running. Office: Zuckerman Spaeder LLP 101 E Kennedy Blvd Ste 1200 Tampa FL 33602-5838 Office Phone: 813-221-1010. E-mail: sweinberg@zuckerman.com.

WEINBERG, ROBERT LESTER, lawyer, law educator; b. NYC, May 23, 1931; s. Abraham Matthew and Beatrice (Kohn) Weinberg; m. Patricia Wendy Yates, Aug. 19, 1956; children: Susan Clare, David Hal, Jeremy Michael. BA, Yale U., 1953, LLB, 1960; PhD in Econs., U. London, 1960. Bar: DC 1961, Conn. 60, US Supreme Ct. 63. Assoc. Law Offices of Edward Bennett Williams and successor firms, 1960—66; founding ptnr. Williams & Connolly, 1967—96; vis. lectr. U. Va. Sch. Law, Charlottesville, 1965; adj. prof. U. Tex. Sch. Law, 1986, George Washington U. Law Sch., 1999—; chmn. standing com. on pro bono matters DC Cir. Jud. Conf., 1980—96; mem. Found. Bar Assn. DC, 1999—2004. Contbr. articles to profl. jours. Pres. No. Va. Fair Housing, Inc., 1968—69; chmn. Arlington Pub. Utilities Commn., Va., 1968. Served with US Army, 1957—59. Recipient Servant of Justice award, Legal Aid Soc. of DC, 1996; named Outstanding Citizen of Yr., Washington Evening Star and Arlington County Civic Fedn., 1975. Mem.: ABA, Nat. Jewish Dem. Coun., Internat. Assn. Jewish Lawyers and Jurists, Am. Assn. Jewish Lawyers and Jurists, DC Bar Found, DC Bar, Conn. Bar Assn., Bar Assn. DC. Home: 30 Passfield Ln Sperryville VA 22740 Office: 5171 37th Rd N Arlington VA 22207-1825

WEINBERG, STEVEN, physicist, educator; b. NYC, May 3, 1933; s. Fred and Eva (Israel) Weinberg; m. Louise Goldwasser, July 6, 1954; 1 child, Elizabeth. BA, Cornell U., Ithaca, NY, 1954; PhD, Princeton U., NJ, 1957; AM (hon.), Harvard U., 1973; ScD (hon.), Knox Coll., 1978, U. Chgo., 1978, U. Rochester, 1979, Yale U., 1979, CUNY, 1980, Clark U., 1982, Dartmouth Coll., 1984, Columbia U., 1990, U. Salamanca, 1992, U. Padua, 1992, Bates Coll., 2002, McGill U., 2003, U. Waterloo, 2004; D (hon.), U. Barcelona, 1996; PhD (hon.), Weizmann Inst., 1985; DLitt (hon.), Washington Coll., 1985. Rsch. assoc., instr. Columbia U., NYC, 1957-59; rsch. physicist Lawrence Radiation Lab., Berkeley, Calif., 1959-60; faculty U. Calif., Berkeley, 1960-69, prof. physics, 1964-69; vis. prof. MIT, 1967-69, prof. physics, 1969-73; Higgins prof. physics Harvard U., 1973—82, Morris Loeb vis. prof. physics, 1983—; Jack S. Josey-Welch Found. chair in sci., Regental prof. U. Tex., Austin, 1982—, founder Theory Group, dept. physics. Cons. Inst. Def. Analyses, Washington, 1960—73; chair in physics Coll. France, 1971; sr. scientist Smithsonian Astrophysical Lab., Cambridge, Mass., 1973—82; Scott lectr. Cavendish Lab., Cambridge U., 1975; Silliman lectr. Yale U., 1977; Lauritsen Meml. lectr. Calif. Inst. Tech., 1979; Bethe lectr. Cornell U., 1979; de Shalit lectr. Weizmann Inst., 1979; mem. Pres.'s Com. Nat. Medal Sci., 1979—82, NRC Com. Internat. Security & Arms Control, 1981; Cherwell-Simon lectr. Oxford U., 1983; Bampton lectr. Columbia U., 1983; mem. Coun. Scholars, Libr. of Congress, 1983—85; Einstein lectr. Israel Acad. Arts and Sciences, 1984; Hilldale lectr. U. Wis., 1985; Clark lectr. U. Tex., Dallas, 1986; Dirac lectr. U. Cambridge, 1986; Klein lectr. U. Stockholm, 1989; Brittin lectr. U. Colo., 1994; Sackler lectr. U. Copenhagen, 1994; Gibbs lectr. Am. Math. Soc., 1996; Bochner lectr. Rice U., 1997; Sanchez lectr. Tex. A&M Internat. U., 1998; Witherspoon lectr. Washington U., 2001; bd. dirs. Fedn. Am. Scientists. Author: Principles and Application of the General Theory of Relativity, 1972, The First Three Minutes: A Modern View of the Origin of the Universe, 1977, The Discovery of Subatomic Particles, 1982, Dreams of a Final Theory, 1992, The Quantum Theory of Fields - Vol. I: Foundations, 1995, Modern Applications, Vol. II, 1996, Supersymmetry, Vol. III, 2000, Facing Up: Science and Its Cultural Adversaries, 2001, revised edit., 2003, Glory and Terror: The Growing Nuclear Danger, 2004, Cosmology, 2008, Lake Views: This World and the Universe, 2009; co-author (with R. Feynman): Elementary Particles and the Laws of Physics; mem. adv. bd. Issues in Sci. and Tech., 1984—87, mem. editl. bd. Jour. Math. Physics, 1986—88, mem. bd. editors Daedalus, 1990—, Jour. Math. Physics, 1998—; contbr. articles to profl. jours. Bd. advisors Santa Barbara Inst. Theoretical Physics, 1983—86. Recipient J. Robert Oppenheimer Meml. prize, 1973, Dannie Heineman prize in math. physics, 1977, Nobel prize in physics, 1979, Elliott Cresson medal, Franklin Inst., 1979, Madison medal, Princeton U., 1991, Nat. Medal Sci., 1991, Andrew Gemant prize, Am. Inst. Physics, 1997, Piazzi prize, Sicily/Palermo, Italy, 1998, Lewis Thomas prize, Rockefeller U., 1999, Trotter prize, Tex. A&M U., 2008, James Joyce award, Literacy & Hist. Soc., Univ. Coll., Dublin, 2009; named an Hon. Citizen, Padua, Italy, 2007. Mem.: NAS, Royal Irish Acad. (Hamilton lectr. 2005), Tex. Inst. Letters, Philos. Soc. Tex., Royal Soc. London, Am. Philos. Soc. (Benjamin Franklin medal 2004), Coun. Fgn. Rels., Internat. Astron. Union, Am. Phys. Soc., Am. Acad. Arts & Scis., Cambridge Sci. Soc., Headliners Club (Austin), Saturday Club (Boston), Tuesday Club (Austin), Phi Beta Kappa. Office: U Tex Dept Physics 1 Univ Station C1600 Austin TX 78712 Business E-Mail: weinberg@physics.utexas.edu.

WEINBERG, THOMAS, commissioner, former legislative staff member; b. July 1949; m. Linda Weinberg; 5 children. AA, Brevard CC, 1969; BS in Criminology, Fla. State U., 1971. Sr. mgmt. positions Dept. Health & Rehabilitative Services, Fla.; dep. county adminstr. Orange County, Fla.; Fla. state dir., dep. chief of staff, Senator Mel Martinez US Senate, Washington, 2007—08, chief of staff to Senator Mel Martinez, 2008—09; commr. Dist. 5 Canaveral Port Authority Bd., Fla., 2011—. Adj. prof. criminal justice Brevard CC. Republican. Office: Canaveral Port Authority 445 Challenger Rd Ste 301 Cape Canaveral FL 32920-4100 Office Phone: 321-783-7831. Office Fax: 321-783-4651.

WEINER, HOWARD MARC, physician; b. Feb. 25, 1946; BSc, Marietta Coll., 1967; MD, U. Cin., 1971; MPH, Med. Coll. Wis., 1994. Diplomate Am.Bd. Allergy, Asthma and Immunology, Am. Bd. Preventive Medicine/Occupl. Medicine. Intern medicine Temple U. Hosp., Phila., 1971—72, resident internal medicine, 1972—74; fellow allergy and clin. immunology Hosp. U. Pa., Phila., 1974—76; pres., physician Allergy & Asthma Assocs. West Boca, Boca Raton, Fla., 1988—; pres., med. dir. Med. Assessment Inst. Inc., Boca Raton, Fla., 1997—; adv. bd. mem. Florida Altantic U. Dorothy F Scumidt Coll. Arts & Letters, 2012—13. Chmn. ethics com. Palm Beach County Med. Soc., West Palm Beach, Fla., 1994-97; bd. dirs. Primus Physicians Svcs., Inc., So. Fla. Mem. Omicron Delta Kappa Soc., Pi Kappa Epsilon. Office: Med Assessment Inst Inc 2385 NW Executive Ctr Dr Ste 100 Boca Raton FL 33431 Office Phone: 561-451-0200.

WEINER, IRVING BERNARD, psychologist; b. Grand Rapids, Mich., Aug. 16, 1933; s. Jacob H. and Mollie Jean (Laevin) W.; m. Frances Shair, June 9, 1963; children: Jeremy Harris, Seth Howard. BA, U. Mich., Ann Arbor, 1955, MA, 1957, PhD, 1959. Diplomate Am. Bd. Profl. Psychology. From instr. to prof. psychiatry and pediat. U. Rochester, NY, 1959-72; head divsn. psychology U. Rochester Med. Center, 1968-72; prof. psychology, chmn. dept. Case Western Res. U., 1972-77, dean grad. studies, 1976-79; vice chancellor for acad. affairs U. Denver, 1979-83, prof. psychology, 1979-85; v.p. for acad. affairs Fairleigh Dickinson U., Teaneck, NJ, 1985-89, prof. psychology, 1985-89; prof. psychiatry U. South Fla., Tampa, 1989—. Adv. editor John Wiley & Sons, 1967-93, 99—, Lawrence Erlbaum Assocs., 1993-99; psychology edn. rev. com. NIMH, 1977-81. Author: Psychodiagnosis in Schizophrenia, 1966, Psychological Disturbance in Adolescence, 1970, rev. edit., 1992, Rorschach Handbook, 1971, Child Development, 1972, Principles of Psychotherapy, 1975, rev. edit., 1998, 2009, Development of the Child, 1978, Child and Adolescent Psychopathology, 1982, Rorschach Assessment of Children and Adolescents, 1982, rev. edit., 1995, Adolescence, 1985, rev. edit., 1995, Handbook of Forensic Psychology, 1987, rev. edit., 1999, 2006, 2014, Principles of Rorschach Interpretation, 1998, rev. edit., 2003, Handbook of Psychology, 2003, Revised Edit., 2013, Handbook of Personality Assessment, 2008; editor: Readings in Child Development, 1972, Clinical Methods in Psychology, 1976, 83, Adult Psychopathology Case Studies, 2004, Corsini Encyclopedia of Psychology, 4th Edit., 2010, Jour. Personality Assessment, 1985-93, Rorschachiana, 1989-96; mem. editl. bd. Profl. Psychology, 1971-76, Jour. Adolescent Health Care, 1979-87, Children and Youth Svcs. Rev., 1979-91, Jour. Pediat. Psychology, 1981-87, Devel. and Behavioral Pediat., 1985-96, Studi Rorschachiani, 1985-1996, European Jour. Psychol. Assessment, 1985—2011, Jour. Adolescent Rsch., 1986-91, Jour. Personality Disorders, 1986-92, Psychol. Assessment, 1994—2003, Jour. Personality Assessment, 2003—, Assessment, 2004—, Jour. Child Custody, 2005-. Recipient Disting. Profl. Achievement award Genesee Psychol. Assn., 1974, Disting. Profl. Contbr. award, Soc. Clin. Psychology, 2010 Fellow: APA (Reps. coun., 2011-2014), Assn. Psychol. Sci., Acad. Clin. Psychology, Acad. Forensic Psychology, Acad. of Assessment Psychology (Lifetime Achievement awrd 2001); mem. Assn. Advancement Psychology, Soc. Personality Assessment (pres. 1976-78, 2005-07, Disting. Contbn. award 1983), Assn. Internship Ctrs. (exec. com. 1971-76), Soc. Rsch. in Adolescence, Soc. for Rsch. in Child and Adolescent Psychopathology, Soc. for Exploration Psychotherapy Integration, Soc. Pediat. Psychology, Am. Psychol. Law Soc., Internat. Rorschach Soc. (pres. 1999-2005), Soc. Clin. Psychology (pres. 2008-09), Phi Beta Kappa, Sigma Xi, Phi Kappa Phi. Avocation: clarinet. Home and Office: 13716 Halliford Dr Tampa FL 33624-6903 Office Phone: 813-960-4772. Business E-Mail: iweiner@health.usf.edu.

WEINER, RICHARD, public relations executive; b. Bklyn., May 10, 1927; s. George M. and Sally (Kosover) W.; m. Florence Chaiken, Dec. 9, 1956; children: Jessica Weiner Lampert, Stephanie Weiner Iosbaker. BS, U. Wis., 1949, MS, 1950. Pres. Creative Radio Assocs., Madison, Wis., 1951-52, Weiner-Morton Assocs., Madison, 1952-53; sr. v.p. Ruder & Finn, Inc., NYC, 1953-68; pres. Richard Weiner, Inc., NYC, 1968-86; pres. N.Y. divsn. Porter/Novelli, NYC, 1987-88, sr. counselor, 1988—. Author: Professional's Guide to Public Relations Services, 1968, News Bureaus in the U.S., 1970, Syndicated Columnists, 1972, Professional's Guide to Publicity, 1979, Military Publications, 1979, College Alumni Publications, 1980, Investment Newsletters, 1981, Webster's New World Dictionary of Media and Communications, 1996, The Skinny About Best Boys: Dollies, Green Rooms, Leads and other Media Lingo, 2006, contbr. articles to profl. jours. Fellow Pub. Rels. Soc. Am. (accredited counselor, Silver Anvil award 1965, 84, 86, 87, John Hill award 1984, Gold Anvil award 1990). Jewish. Home Phone: 305-865-3262. Personal E-mail: rweiner522@aol.com.

WEINER, SANFORD ALAN, lawyer; b. Houston, Aug. 21, 1946; s. Abe I. and Zelda C. (Caplan) Weiner; m. Leslie Eve Grenadier, Aug. 16, 1970; children: Edward, David, Evan, Rebecca. BA, U. Tex., 1968; JD, Harvard U., 1971. Bar: Tex. 1971. Of counsel Vinson & Elkins, Ltd. Liability Partnership, Houston, 1971—. Pres. Am. Coll. Real Estate Lawyers, 2003. Mem. Houston Bar Assn., Tex. Bar Assn. (Property, Probate and Trust Sect. Lifetime Achievement award, 2007), Houston Real Estate Lawyers Council, Anglo-Am. Real Property Inst. Jewish. Office: Vinson & Elkins LLP 1001 Fannin St Ste 2500 Houston TX 77002-6760 Office Phone: 713-758-2558. Business E-Mail: sweiner@velaw.com.*

WEINER, TIMOTHY M., pediatric surgeon; b. Bethesda, Md., Jan. 9, 1961; BA in biology, Oberlin Coll., 1983; MD, Georgetown Univ., 1989. Cert. Am. Bd. Surgery, 1997, in Pediatric Surgery Am. Bd. Surgery, 2000. Intern in pediatric surgery Univ. NC Sch. Med., Chapel Hill, 1989—90, resident in pediatric surgery, 1990—93; rsch. fellow Lineberger Comprehensive Cancer Ctr., Univ NC, Chapel Hill, 1991—93; sr. resident pediatric surgery Univ. NC Sch. Med., Chapel Hill, 1993—95; fellow in pediatric surgery Children's Hosp. Pitts., Pa., 1995—97; asst. prof. pediatric surgery Univ. NC Sch. Med., Chapel Hill, 1997—2004, assoc. prof. pediatric surgery, 2004—. Contbr. articles to profl. jours. Recipient Nat. Rsch. Svc. award, 1992—93, James Ewing Travel award, Soc. Surgical Oncology, 1993. Office: UNC Sch Med Dept Surgery CB#7210 3010 Old Clinic Bldg Chapel Hill NC 27599-7210 Office Phone: 919-966-4220. Office Fax: 919-966-8806.

WEINGARTEN, JORDAN STEWART, critical care specialist; MD, Baylor U., 1980. Cert. internal medicine 1984, pulmonary disease 1988, critical care medicine 1999. Resident in internal medicine Univ. Tex. Southwestern Hosps., Dallas, 1982—85, fellow in pulmonary disease, 1985—87; hosp. affiliation includes Seton Med. Ctr. Office: Seton Medical Center 1201 W 38th St Austin TX 78705-1006 Office Phone: 512-324-1000.

WEINGARTNER, H(ANS) MARTIN, finance educator; b. Heidelberg, Germany, Apr. 4, 1929; came to U.S., 1939, naturalized, 1944; s. Jacob and Grete Weingartner; m. Joyce Trellis, June 12, 1955; children— Steven M., Susan C. De La Paz, Eric H., Kenneth L. AB, SB, U. Chgo., 1950, AM, 1951; MS, Carnegie Mellon U., 1956, PhD, 1962. Economist Dept. Commerce, 1951—53; instr. Grad. Sch. Indsl. Adminstrn., Carnegie Mellon U., 1956—57; instr., then asst. prof. Grad. Sch. Bus., U. Chgo., 1957—63; assoc. prof. fin. Alfred P. Sloan Sch. Mgmt., Mass. Inst. Tech., 1963—66; prof. Grad. Sch. Mgmt., U. Rochester, Rochester, 1966—77; Brownlee O. Currey prof. fin. Owen Grad. Sch. Mgmt., Vanderbilt U., Nashville, 1977—98, Brownlee O. Currey Prof. of Fin., emeritus, 1998—; dir. Computer Consoles, Inc., 1974—89. Cons. to industry. Author: Mathematical Programming and the Analysis of Capital Budgeting Problems, 3d edit, 1974, (with George Benston and Dan Horsky) An Empirical Study of Mortgage Redlining, 1978; also articles.; Deptl. editor: Mgmt. Sci, 1967-73. With US Army, 1953—54. Mellon fellow, 1954-55; Ford Found. fellow, 1955-56. Fellow: Inst. for Ops. Rsch. and the Mgmt. Scis.; mem.: Coun. Sci. Soc. Pres. (alumni mem.), Inst. Mgmt. Scis. (v.p. fin. 1978—84, pres. elect, pres., past pres. 1985—88), Harbor Island Yacht Club (bd. mem. 2005—08), Beta Gamma Sigma. Home: 1616 Ash Valley Dr Nashville TN 37215-4202 Office: Vanderbilt U Owen Grad Sch Mgmt 401 21st Ave S Nashville TN 37203

WEINSTEIN, ALAN EDWARD, lawyer; b. Bklyn., Apr. 20, 1945; s. John and Matilda W.; m. Patti Kantor, Dec. 18, 1965; children: Steven R., David A. AA, U. Fla., 1964; BBA, U. Miami, Fla., 1965, JD cum laude, 1968. Bar: Fla. 1968, U.S. Dist. Ct. (so. dist.) Fla. 1968, U.S. Ct. Appeals (5th cir.) 1969, U.S. Supreme Ct. 1973, U.S. Ct. Appeals (4th and 11th cirs.) 1981. Assoc. Cohen & Hogan, Miami Beach, Fla., 1968-71; pvt. practice Miami Beach, 1972-81; sr. ptnr. Weinstein & Preira, Miami Beach, 1981-92; prin. Law Offices of Alan E. Weinstein LLC, Miami, 1992—. Lectr. in field. Mem. ABA (criminal and family law sect. 1968—, white collar crime commn. 1986—), Nat. Assn. Criminal Def. Lawyers, 1st Family Law Am. Inn of Court, Fla. Bar Assn. (criminal and family law sect. 1968—, ethics com. 1987-88, bench/bar com. 1988-89, grievance com. 1999-2002, chmn. 2002, unlicensed practice of law com. 2002-05), Fla. Criminal Def. Attys. Assn. (pres. 1978-79), Fla. Assn. Criminal Def. Lawyers (treas. 1989-90), Miami Beach Bar Assn., Soc. Wig and Robe, Phi Kappa Phi. Avocations: marlin fishing, reading, travel. Office: 4500 Biscayne Blvd Ste 203 Miami FL 33137 Office Phone: 305-576-8666. Personal E-mail: defense1@bellsouth.net.

WEINSTEIN, ANDREW H., lawyer; b. Pitts., Oct. 5, 1943; m. Susan Balber, Aug. 11, 1968; children: Jodi L., Matt T., Jamie M. BSBA, Duquesne U., 1965; JD, U. Pitts., 1968; LLM in Taxation, NYU, NYC, 2008. Bar: Pa. 1969, US Tax Ct. 1969, Fla. 1970, US Dist. Ct. (so. dist.) Fla., U.S. Ct. Fed. Claims. Trial atty. IRS, LA, 1969-70, Miami, Fla., 1970-73; ptnr. Glass, Schultz, Weinstein & Moss, Coral Gables, Fla., 1973-80, Holland & Knight, Miami, 1980—. Contbr. articles to profl. jours. Bd. dirs. Zool. Soc. Fla. Fellow Am. Coll. Tax Counsel, Am. Coll. Trusts and Estates Counsel; mem. ABA (tax sect., bd. cert. tax law), Fla. Bar. (Best Lawyers in America). Avocations: golf, travel. Office: Holland & Knight 701 Brickell Ave Ste 3000 Miami FL 33131-2898 Office Phone: 305-789-7755. Business E-Mail: andrew.weinstein@hklaw.com.

WEINSTEIN, DAVID F., state agency administrator, former state legislator; b. Charlotte, NC, June 17, 1936; m. Karen Weinstein. BS, N.C. State U., 1958. Retail, 1959-91; mayor City of Lumberton, N.C., 1987-91; real estate agt., 1994—; mem. Dist. 13 NC State Senate, 1996—2009; dir. Gov Hwy Safety Program State of NC, 2009—. Mem. Lumberton Bd. Realtors; dir. Wesley Pines Meth. Retirement Home; bd. dirs. First Union Nat. Bank; chmn. bd. trustees Pembroke State U. With USAR, 1959-65. Mem. Rotary. Democrat.

WEINSTEIN, JAY A., social sciences educator, researcher; b. Chgo., Feb. 23, 1942; s. Lawrence E. and Jacqueline L. (Caplan) W.; m. Lauren R. Braun, July 16, 2011; children Liza, Bennett. AB, U. Ill., 1963, PhD, 1973; MA, Washington U., St. Louis, 1965. Teaching fellow U. Ill., Urbana, 1963-64; teaching asst. McGill U., Montreal, Que., Canada, 1966-68; instr. Sir George Williams U., Montreal, Que., Canada, 1967-68; lectr. Simon Fraser U., Vancouver, B.C., Canada, 1968; asst. prof. North Central Coll., Naperville, Ill., 1970-71, U. Iowa, 1973-77; prof. social sci. Ga. Inst. Tech., Atlanta, 1977-86; head dept. sociology Eastern Mich. U., 1986-90, 2004—06, faculty rsch. fellow, 1990-91; grantee ednl. devel. project USIA-Soros Found., Albania, 1992—; dir. Applied Rsch. Unit, 1996—; vis. faculty, sociology U. North Fla., 2007—. Cons. World Bank Study Social and Econ. Vulnerability in Albania, 1997, World Bank Study on Closing the Vulnerability Gap, Albania, 1997—98; project dir. Ea. Mich.-U-Ypsilanti Cmty. Outreach Partnership Ctr.; cons. pvt. and pub. agencies; rschr. in field. Author: Madras: An Analysis of Urban Ecological Structure in India, 1974, Demographic Transition and Social Change, 1976, Sociology-Technology: Foundations of Postacademic Social Science, 1982, The Grammar of Social Relations: The Major Essays of Louis Schneider, 1984; editor: Paradox and Society, 1986; (with Vinod Tewari and V.L.S. Prakash Rao) Indian Cities: Ecological Perspectives, Social and Cultural Change: Social Science for a Dynamic World, 1997, 2005, The Holocaust: A Sociological Analysis, 1997, Demography: The Science of Population, 2000, Social Change, 3rd edit., Applying Social Statistics, 2010; Studies in Comparative International Development, 1978-88; mem. editorial bd. Social Development Issues, 1977-85; specialized contbr. Calcutta Mcpl. Gazette, 1979—; editor: Social and Cultural Change, 1974-75; editor Mich. Soc. Rev., 1997-2003, Jour. Applied Sociology, 2004—06; Applied Social Sci., 2006-, editl. reviewer Jour. Asian Studies, Social Devel. Issues, Tech. and Culture, Am. Sociologist, Technol. Forecasting and Social Change; contbr. chpts. to book, articles to profl. jours. Recipient Charles Horton Cooley award for outstanding contbns. to sociology in Mich., 1998, Alex Boros award, 2005; Fulbright prof. Ahmedabad, India, 1975-76, Hyderabad, India, 1981-82; grantee Ga. Tech. Found., 1981-82, World Order Studies Course, 1994-97, State of Mich. Rsch. Excellence Fund; Steinberg fellow, 1967. Mem. Am. Sociol. Assn. (pres. 2002-03), Soc. for Applied Sociology (v.p. 1998-99, chair sociol. practice sect., 2004-05), mem. exec. bd. 2000, pres. 2002-03), Mich. Sociol. Assn. (pres. 1988-89, v.p. 1994-95), North Ctrl. Sociol. Assn. (pres. 2007-08, John F. Schnabel award for tchg. excellence), Sigma Xi, Phi Kappa Phi. Jewish. Home Phone: 313-563-5292; Office Phone: 912-634-0799. Personal E-mail: jay.weinstein@emich.edu.

WEINSTEIN, MARTIN, aerospace transportation and manufacturing executive, materials scientist; b. Mar. 3, 1936; s. Benjamin and Dora (Lemo) Weinstein; m. Sandra Rebecca Yaffie, June 5, 1961; children: Hilary Ann, Sarah Elizabeth, Joshua Aaron. BS in Metals Engring., Rensselaer Poly. Inst., Troy, NY, 1957; MS, MIT, Cambridge, 1960, PhD, 1961. Mgr. materials sci. Tycolabs., Waltham, Mass., 1961-69; tech. dir. turbine support divsn. Chromalloy Am. Corp., San Antonio, 1968-71, v.p., asst. gen. mgr., 1971-74, pres., 1975-79, Chromalloy Compressor Techs., San Antonio, 1979-82; group pres. Chromalloy Gas Turbine, San Antonio, 1982-86, chmn., CEO NYC, 1986—2004; vice chmn., exec. officer SEQUA Corp., NYC, 2004—05, vice chmn., CEO, 2005—09; CEO, owner Sheffield Sci., Houston, 2010—. Supervisory mng. dir. Turbine Support Europe, Tilburg, Netherlands, 1975—2009; bd. dirs. Sequa Corp., NYC, 1999—2009, vice chmn., CEO, 2004; bd. dirs. Turbine Support Thailand, Bangkok, Chromalloy UK, Nottingham, England, Malichaud Orleans, France. Contbr. articles to profl. jours. Bd. dirs. Chamber Players San Antonio, 1979—83, NCCJ, 1982—85, Jewish Fedn., 1981—85; mem. vis. com. dept. metallurgy and materials sci. MIT, 1992—2001. Recipient Turner Meml. award, Electrochem. Soc., 1963, Achievement award, NASA, 1963, Fellows award, Rensselaer Alumni Assn., 2006, Davies medal, RPI, 2010, RPI, 2010; Am. Iron and Steel Inst. fellow, 1960. Mem.: NY Acad. Sci., Am. Inst. Metall. Engrs., Am. Soc. Metals, Sigma Xi. Achievements include patents for diffusion coating of jet engine materials. Home: 111 Sheffield San Antonio TX 78213-2626 Office: Sheffield Sci 3100 S Gessner Ste Houston TX 77063 Home Phone: 210-344-0028. Personal E-mail: martin.weinsteintx@gmail.com.

WEINSTEIN, MICHAEL B., state legislator; b. Livingston, NJ, Feb. 6, 1949; m. Sara Weinstein; children: Daryl, Scott, Danielle. BA in Polit. Sci., Hartwick Coll., NY; MS in Criminal Justice Adminstrn., Calif. State U., Long Beach; ABD in Criminology, Fla. State U.; JD, U. Fla. Dir. adminstrn & fin. dept. Mayor Ed Austin & Mayor John Delaney; former atty. 4th Jud. Circuit Ct. State Atty. Office; mem. Dist. 19 Fla. House of Reps., 2008—, vice chair civil justice and courts policy com., mem. criminal and civil justice policy coun., fin. and tax coun., preK-12 appropriations com., preK-12 policy com. Exec. dir. Jacksonville Econ. Devel. Commn.; pres. & CEO Jacksonville Super Bowl Host Com.; bd. trustees Fla. Cmty. Coll., Jacksonville, Fla. First Coast Crime Stoppers; former mem. Jacksonville Cmty. Coun. Mem.: Nat. Multiple Sclerosis Soc. North Fla. Chpt., Leadership Jacksonville, Police Athletic League (bd. trustees), Downtown Rotary. Republican. Office: House Office Bldg 402 S Monroe St Rm 417 Tallahassee FL 32399-1300 also: 155 Blanding Blvd Ste 10 Orange Park FL 32073-3005 Office Phone: 850-488-1304, 904-213-3005. Business E-Mail: mike.weinstein@myfloridahouse.gov.

WEINSTEIN, ROY, physics professor; b. NYC, Apr. 21, 1927; s. Harry and Lillian (Ehrenberg) W.; m. Janet E. Spiller, Mar. 26, 1954 (dec. 1995); children: Lee Davis, Sara Lynn; m. Gail A. Birdsell, July 26, 1996. BS, MIT, 1951, PhD, 1954; ScD (hon.), Lycoming Coll., 1981. Rsch. asst. Mass. Inst. Tech., 1951-54, asst. prof., 1956—59, Brandeis U., Waltham, Mass., 1954-56; assoc. prof. Northeastern U., Boston, 1960-63, prof. physics, 1963-82, exec. officer, chmn. grad. div. of physics dept., 1967-69, chmn. physics dept., 1974-81; spokesman MAC Detector Stanford U., 1981-82; dean Coll. Natural Scis. and Math. U. Houston, 1982-88, prof. physics, 1982—2007, rsch. prof. physics, emeritus prof., 2007—; assoc. dir., spokesman Tex. Ctr. for Superconductivity, 1987-89; dir. Inst. Beam Particle Dynamics U. Houston, 1985-95, prin. investigator., Beam Particle Dynamics Lab., 1995—. Vis. scholar and physicist Stanford (Calif.) U., 1966-67, 1968-69, 81-82, Harvard, 1969-70; bd. dirs. Perception Tech., Inc., Winchester, Mass., Omniwave Inc., Gloucester, Mass., Wincom Inc., Woburn, Mass., Houston Area Rsch. Ctr., Exec. Comm.; cons. ret. Visidyne Inc., Burlington, Mass., Hodotector Inc., Houston, Park Square Engring., Marietta, Ga., Harvard U., Cambridge, Mass., Cambridge Electron Accelerator, Harvard mem. adv. com., 1967-69, rsch. physicist, 1970-71; adv. com. and portfolio evaluation com. Houston Venture Ptnrs., 1990-99; chmn. bd. dirs. Xytron Corp., 1986-91; dir., mem. exec. com. Houston Area Rsch. Ctr., 1984-87; chmn. organizing com. Internat. Conf. on Meson Spectroscopy, 1974, chmn. program com., 1977, mem. organizing com., 1980; chmn. mgmt. group Tex. Accelerator Ctr., Woodlands, 1985-90; chmn. Tex. High Energy Physicists, 1989-91; keynote spkr. MIT Alumni series, 1988; permanent mem. exec. com. Large Vol. Detector (Underground Neutrino Telescope, Italy), 1988—; organizer session High Temperature Superconducting Magnets 3d and 4th World Congress on Superconductivity, Munich, 1993, Orlando, 1994; CEO Roxxyguest Magnetics Corp., 2009-. Author: Atomic Physics, 1964, Nuclear Physics, 1964, Interactions of Radiation and Matter, 1964; editor: Nuclear Reactor Theory, 1964, Nuclear Materials, 1964; editor procs.: Proceedings of the 5th Internat. Conf. on Mesons, 1977; contbr. over 200 articles to profl. jours. Mem. Lexington (Mass.) Town Meeting, 1973-84; vice chmn. Lexington Coun. on Aging, 1977-83. With USNR, 1945-46. Recipient Founders award World Congress Superconductivity, 1988, Materials/Devices award Internat. Superconductivity Technology Ctr., Japan, and Materials Rsch. Soc., 1995, High Current award, 1997, Award of Execellence, 1999, Internat. Program Com. Processing and Applications of Large Superconducting Rare Earth Large Grains Worshop, 1999, NSF Rsch. awards, 1961-96, Tex. Rsch. award, 1986-87, 90-94, 96-98, Tex. Ctr. Superconductivity award, 1988-, US Dept. Energy award 1974, 77, 87-97, NASA award, 1990-98, 2004-2006, ARO award, 1994-2010, Elec. Power Rsch. Inst. award, 1990-95, Welch Found. award, 1997—2012, Nat. Cancer Inst. award, 2000-04, Office Naval Rsch. award 2010-12, Nat. Oilwell Varco grant, 2012-; NSF fellow Bohr Inst., Copenhagen, 1959-60, Stanford U. 1969-70, Guggenheim fellow Harvard U., 1970-71. Fellow Am. Phys. Soc. (organizer session SSC and High Energy Physics 1984); mem. Am. Assn. Physics Tchrs., Masons, Sigma Xi, Phi Kappa Phi (chpt. pres. 1977-79, Nat. Triennial Disting. Scholar prize 1980-83), Pi Lambda Phi (pres. Theta chpt. 1949-50). Unitarian Universalist. Achievements include measurement of fine structure of positronium; first measurement of rho meson coupling to gamma rays, of phi meson decay to two muons; rho-omega meson interference, early observation of break down in SU3 symmetry; demonstration of electron-muon universality, discovery of non-applicability of Lorentz contraction to length measured by a single observer; disproof of splitting of A2 meson; independent discovery of upsilon meson (bottom quark); achievement of highest magnetic field for any permanent magnet in YBaCu307, 10.1 Tesla; achievement of highest current density in textured superconductor, 0.8 megA/cm2 & coated conductor 0.7 megA/cm2 at 1 Tesla; development of MILD pinning centers for high temperature superconductor; successful flux pumping activation of bulk trapped field magnets; 5 patents for high temperaturesuper conductivity. Home: 4368 Fiesta Ln Houston TX 77004-6603 Office: U Houston IBPD 632 SR1 Houston TX 77204-5005 Business E-Mail: weinstein@uh.edu.

WEIR, MIKE, professional golfer; b. Sarnia, Ont., May 12, 1970; m. Bricia Weir; children: Elle Marisa, Lili. BS, Brigham Young U., 1993. Winner Air Canada Championships, 1999, WGC-Am. Express Championships, 2000, The Tour Championships, 2001, Bob Hope Chrysler Classic, 2003, Nissan Open, 2003, Masters Tournament, 2003, Nissan Open, 2004, Fry's Electronics Open, 2007. Mem. internat. team Presidents Cup, 2000, 2003, 2005, 2007, 2009. Recipient The Canadian Press Male Athlete of Yr., 2000, 2001, 2003. Avocations: hockey, skiing, fly fishing. Office: c/o PGA Tour 112 PGA Tour Blvd Ponte Vedra Beach FL 32082

WEIRICH, AMY P., prosecutor; married; 4 children. B, Univ. Tenn., Martin; JD, Univ. Memphis. Bar: Tenn. Prosecutor through dep. dist. atty. gen. Shelby County, Tenn., 1991—2011; chief prosecutor gang & narcotic unit; divsn. leader spl. prosecution unit; dist. atty. gen. Shelby County, Tenn., 2011—. Mem.: Leo Bearman Sr. Am. Inn of Ct. Roman Catholic. Office: Shelby County Dist Atty Gen 3rd Fl 201 Poplar Ave Memphis TN 38103 Office Phone: 901-545-5900.

WEISBERG, LYNNE WILLING, psychiatrist, consultant; b. NYC, Apr. 11, 1948; d. Stanley S. and Pearl R. Willing. BA, Barnard Coll., 1969; PhD, U. Mich., 1972; MD, SUNY, Downstate, 1978. Diplomate Am. Bd. Psychiatry and Neurology, Am. Bd. Adolescent Psychiatry. Intern NYU Med. Ctr., 1978-79; resident in adult psychiatry Mt. Sinai Hosp., NYC, 1979-81; fellow in child psychiatry Columbia Med. Ctr., 1981-83; staff psychiatrist Fair Oaks Hosp., Summit, N.J., 1983-85, asst. dir. child and adolescent psychiatry, 1985-88, assoc. dir. child and adolescent psychiatry, 1988-92; dir. child and adolescent outpatient psychiat. svcs. Psychiat. Assocs. N.J. at Fair Oaks Hosp., Summit, 1992—; pvt. practice Morris County, 1993—2013. Cons. Bonnie Brae Sch., Millington, N.J., 1984-92. Author: When Acting Out Isn't Acting, 1991. Horace Rackham Prize fellow, 1972. Mem. AMA, Med. Soc. N.J., Am. Soc. Clin. Psychopharmacology. Office Phone: 908-850-7141.*

WEISENBURGER, RANDALL J., advertising executive; b. 1958; With Coopers & Lybrand, 1980-85, First Boston Corp., 1987-88; mng. dir. to pres. & CEO Wasserstein Perella & Co., 1988-99; CEO Wickes Mfg. Co., Inc., Southfield, Mich., 1990-93; co-chmn. Collins & Aikman Corp., Charlotte, NC, 1993-99; exec. v.p. & CFO Omnicom Group, Inc., NYC, 1999—. Vice-chmn. Maybelline, Inc.; chmn. Yardley of London; bd. dirs. Alliance Entertainment Corp., CTS Corp. Office: Omnicom Group Inc 437 Madison Ave New York NY 10022 also: 701 Mccullough Dr Charlotte NC 28262-3318 Office Phone: 212-415-3600. Office Fax: 212-817-6551. E-mail: ir@omnicomgroup.com.

WEISER, SHERWOOD MANUEL, hotel and corporation executive, lawyer; b. Cleve., Mar. 9, 1931; s. Aaron A. and Helen (Scheiner) W.; m. Judith A. Zirkin, July 31, 1955; children: Douglas J., Warren P., Bradley A. BS, Ohio State U., 1952; LLB, Case Western Res. U., 1955. Bar: Ohio 1955. Ptnr. Weiser & Weiser, Attys., Cleve., 1955-65, Weiser & Lefton, Attys., Cleve., 1965-69; chmn., chief exec. officer TCC, Miami, Fla., 1970—. Bd. dirs. Mellon United Bank, Miami, Interstate Hotels, Watsco. Trustee Fla. Internat. U. Found., Miami, 1984-94, U. Miami, 1988—, New World Symphony, Miami, 1987—; trustee, chmn. bd. Ransom-Everglades Sch., Miami, 1974-84; co-chmn. bd. advisors Coconut Grove Playhouse, 1986-90; chmn. Performing Arts Ctr. Found., 1994—. Mem. Cleve. Bar Assn., Soc. of Benchers, Order of Coif. Jewish. Avocations: tennis, sailing, art. Office: The Continental Companies LLC 2665 S Bayshore Dr Ste 1206 Miami FL 33133-5468 Home Phone: 305-663-5766; Office Phone: 305-445-4220. E-mail: weiser@tcchotels.com.

WEISFELD, SHELDON, lawyer; b. McAllen, Tex., Feb. 20, 1946; s. Morris and Pauline (Horwitz) W.; m. Eve F. Weisfeld, Jan. 23, 1994; 1 child, Raquel Paolina. BBA, U. Tex., 1967; postgrad., Nat. U. Mex., 1969; JD, U. Houston, 1970. Bar: Tex. 1971, U.S. Dist. Ct. (so. dist.) Tex. 1978, U.S. Dist. Ct. (we. dist.) Tex. 1995, U.S. Dist. Ct. (ea. dist.) Tex. 2001, U.S. Ct. Appeals (5th cir.) 1978, U.S. Ct. Appeals (11th cir.) 1981, U.S. Supreme Ct. 1982. Pvt. practice, Austin, Tex., 1973—77; pvt. practice law Brownsville, Tex., 1980—. Asst. fed. pub. defender U.S. Dist. Ct. (so. dist.) Tex., Brownsville, 1977-80. Fellow Tex. Bar Found. (life); mem. ABA, Nat. Assn. Criminal Def. Lawyers (life), Tex. Criminal Def. Lawyers (dir.), Fed. Bar Assn., State Bar Tex., Cameron County Bar Assn., Hidalgo County Bar Assn., B'nai B'rith. Democrat. Office: 855 E Harrison St Brownsville TX 78520-7173 Office Phone: 956-546-2727. Fax: 956-544-7446. Personal E-mail: isweisfeld@aol.com.

WEISHAR, GREGORY S., pharmaceutical executive; B in biology & econ., Northwest Mo. State Univ.; M in econ., Univ. Mo., Kansas City. Founder, v.p. Argus Health Systems Inc., 1984—88; sr. mgmt. positions PCS Inc., 1988—92; exec. v.p. sales & mktg. Diagnostek Inc., 1992—94; founder PharmaCare Mgmt. Services (CVS subs.), 1994, pres., CEO, 1994—2007; v.p. CVS Caremark Corp., 2002—07; CEO Capstone Pharmacy Services, 2007, Pharmerica Corp., 2007—. Bd. dirs. PharMerica Corp., Long Term Care Pharmacy Alliance. Office: PharMerica Corp 1901 Campus Pl Louisville KY 40299 Office Phone: 502-627-7000. Business E-Mail: g.weishar@pharmerica.com.

WEISMAN, R(OBERT) BRUCE, physical chemist, educator, entrepreneur; b. Balt., Nov. 23, 1950; s. Samuel and Eva (Abramson) W.; m. Kathleen Mary Beckingham, July 25, 1986; 1 child, Caroline Mary. BA, Johns Hopkins U., 1971; PhD, U. Chgo., 1977. Postdoctoral fellow U. Pa., Phila., 1977-79; asst. prof. Rice U., Houston, 1979-84, assoc. prof., 1984-93, prof., 1993—. Founder, pres. Applied Nano Fluorescence, LLC. Mem. editl. bd. Rev. Sci. Instruments, 1991-93; co-editor Applied Physics A, 2004-12; contbr. more than 145 articles to profl. and sci. jours. Grad. fellow Fannie and John Hertz Found., 1973-76, NSF, 1971-73; postdoctoral fellow NSF, 1977-78; rsch. fellow Alfred P. Sloan Found., 1985-89, fellow Am. Physical Soc., 2008, Electrochemical Soc., 2012, Am. Chem. Soc. GHS award, 2012. Fellow Electrochem. Soc.; mem. AAAS, Am. Chem. Soc., Am. Phys. Soc., Electrochem. Soc. (sec. Fullerenes Divsn. 2004-08, vice chair 2008—12, chair 2012-), Sigma Xi. Office: Rice U Dept Chemistry Houston TX 77005 Home Phone: 713-665-8845; Office Phone: 713-348-3709. Business E-Mail: weisman@rice.edu.

WEISS, ARMAND BERL, economist, association management executive; b. Richmond, Va., Apr. 2, 1931; s. Maurice Herbert and Henrietta (Shapiro) W.; m. Judith Bernstein, May 18, 1957; children: Jo Ann Michele, Rhett Louis. BS in Econs., Wharton Sch. Fin., U. Pa., 1953, MBA, 1954; DBA, George Washington U., 1971. Cert. assn. exec. Officer USN, 1954—65; spl. asst. to auditor gen. Dept. Navy, 1964—65; sr. economist Ctr. for Naval Analyses, Arlington, Va., 1965—68; project dir. Logistics Mgmt. Inst., Washington, 1966—74; dir. sys. integration Fed. Energy Adminstrn., Washington, 1974—76; sr. economist Nat. Commn. Supplies and Shortages, 1976—77; project dir. and tech. asst. to v.p. Sys. Planning Corp., 1977—78; chmn. bd., pres., CEO Assns. Internat. Inc., 1978—; chmn. bd. dirs., CFO Rail Digital Corp., 1988—91; v.p., treas. Tech. Frontiers, Inc., 1978—80; sr. v.p. Weiss Pub. Co., Inc., Richmond, 1960—2013, pres., 2013—; co-founder US Strategic Petroleum Res.; adj. prof. Am. U., 1979—81, 1989—91. Treas. Nat. Jewish Youth Conf., 1948—52; v.p. Condo News Internat., Inc., 1981; v.p., bd. dirs. Leaders Digest inc., 1987—88; sec., bd. dirs. Mgmt. Svcs. Internat. Inc., 1987—88, 1989—90; vis. lectr. George Washington U., 1971; assoc. prof. George Mason U., 1984; mem. Dranesville (Va.) Dist. Dem. Com., 1974—, treas., 1989—93, 2003—06, Fairfax County (Va.) Dem. Com., 1992—; assisted Pres. Clinton, v.p. Gore transition at White Ho., 1993; mem. Fairfax County(Va.) Budget Task Force Dranesville Dist., 2008—, chmn., 2013—; pres. Washington Mgmt. and Bus. Assn., 1993—; chmn. US del., session chmn. NATO Symposium on Cost-Benefit Analysis, The Hague, Netherlands, 1969, NATO Conf. on Operational Rsch. in Indsl. Sys., St. Louis, France, 1970; pres. Nat. Coun. Assns. Policy Scis., 1971—77; chmn. adv. group Def. Econ. Adv. Coun. Dept. Def., 1970—74; resident assoc. Smithsonian Instn., 1973—; expert cons. Dept. State, GAO; undercover agt. FBI, 3 yrs.; del. conf. UN, 2004; bd. dirs. Fairfax County Water Authority, Va., 2010—, treas., chair fin. and audit com., 2012—; treas. Friends of

McLean(Va.) Cmty. Ctr., 2010—12, McLean(Va.) Citizen's Assn.; chair membership com. Budget & Taxation Comm., 2009—13, v.p., 2013—; mem. McLean Planning Com., Va., 2012—, Dranesville Budget Task Force, 2009—, chmn., 2013—. Co-editor: Systems Analysis for Social Problems, 1970, The Relevance of Economic Analysis to Decision Making in the Department of Defense, 1972, Toward More Effective Public Programs: The Role of Analysis and Evaluation, 1975; editor: Cost-Effectiveness Newsletter, 1966-70, Operations Rsch./Systems Analysis Today, 1971-73, Operation Rsch./Mgmt. Sci. Today, 1974-87, Feedback, 1969-93, Condo World, 1981, The Democrat, 1997-2000; assoc. editor Ops. Rsch., 1971-75; pub. IEEE Scanner, 1983-89, Spl. and Individual Needs Tech. (SAINT) Newsletter, 1987-88, Jour. Parametrics, 1984-88. Del. Pres.'s Mid-Century White House Conf. on Children and Youth, 1950; scoutmaster Japan, U.S.; leader World Jamborees, France, Can., U.S., 1945-61; Eagle scout, 1947; mem., Nat. Eagle Scout Assn., 1970-, U.S. del. Internat. Conf. on Ops. Rsch., Dublin, Ireland, 1972; organizing com. Internat. Cost-Effectiveness Symposium, Washington, 1970; spkr. Internat. Conf. Inst. Mgmt. Scis., Tel Aviv, 1973, del., Mexico City, 1967; mem. bus. com. Nat. Symphony Orch., 1968-70, Washington Performing Arts Soc., 1974-88; bus. mgr. Nat. Lyric Opera Co., 1983—2008, Internat. Assn. Med. Sci. Educators, 1997-98, Data Adminstrv. Mgmt. Assn. Nat. Capital, 1992-2001, Potomac Pedalers Touring Club, 1990-2001, Am. Friends of London Sch. Econs., 1988-97; mem. mktg. com. Fairfax Symphony Orch., 1984-91; bd. dirs. McLean (Va.) Orch., 1992-94; exec. com. Mid Atlantic coun. Union Am. Hebrew Congregations, 1970-79, treas., 1974-79, mem. nat. MUM com., 1974-79; mem. dist. com. Boy Scouts Am., 1972-75, steering com. Eagle Scout 100th Anniversary, Boy Scouts America, 2009-10; bd. dirs. Nat. Coun. Career Women, 1975-79; pres. Temple Rodef Shalom, Falls Church, 1970-72, bd. dirs. 1966-, chmn. Archives Com., 2009-; adminstr. Daniel Heumann Fund for Spinal Cord Rsch., 2000-07; treas. Quest for the Cure, 2000-07; mem. Coalition for Advancement of Med. Rsch., 2002-09; del. UN Sci. Conf., 2004; mem. adv. bd. U. Pa. Mid. Atlantic Region, 2003-, U. Pa. Emeritus Soc., 2003-, George Washington U. Emeritus Soc., 2009-. Recipient Silver medal 50-yard free style and half mile swimming meet, No. Va. Sr. Olympics, 1990, Gold, 2 Silver, 3 Bronze medals, 2001; named Hero of Hope, Rutgers U. Rally for Cure, 2004. Fellow AAAS, Washington Acad. Scis. (gov. 1981-92, v.p. 1987-88, pres.-elect 1989-90, pres. 1990-91, past pres. 1991-92), Va. Acad. Scis., Nat. Assn. Acad. Sci. (del. 1991-93), Ops. Rsch. Soc. Am. (chmn. meetings com. 1969-71, chmn. cost-effectiveness sect. 1969-70), Washington Ops. Rsch./Mgmt. Sci. Coun. (editor newsletter 1969-93, sec. 1971-72, pres. 1973-74, trustee 1975-77, bus. mgr. 1976-93, Moving Spirit award 1994), Internat. Inst. Strategic Studies (London), Am. Soc. Assn. Execs. (membership com. 1981-82, assn. mgmt. co. sect. com. 1995-98, cert.), Inst. Ops. Rsch. and Mgmt. Scis., Am. Econ. Assn., Wharton Grad. Sch. Alumni Assn. (exec. com. 1970-73), Nat. Eagle Scout Assn., VFW, Am. Legion, Navy League US, Jewish War Vets., Greater Washington Soc. Assn. Execs. (new ventures com. 1995-97), Alumni Assn. George Washington U. (governing bd. 1974-82, chmn. univ. publs. com. 1976-78, Alumni Svc. award 1980), Alumni Assn. George Washington U. Sch. Govt. and Bus. Adminstrn. (exec. v.p. 1977-78, pres. 1978-79), George Washington U. Doctoral Assn. (sr. v.p. 1968-69), Wharton Sch. Washington (sec. 1967-69, pres. 1969-70, exec. dir. 1987-2001, Joseph Wharton award 1991, Lifetime Svc. award 2000, Founder's award, 2008). Home: 6516 Truman Ln Falls Church VA 22043-1821 Office Phone: 703-241-0333. Personal E-mail: aiboss@aol.com.

WEISS, CHRISTOPHER JOHN, lawyer; b. Oswego, NY, Sept. 1, 1952; s. Robert Leo and Flora Elizabeth Weiss; children: Allison Ardis, Natalie Elizabeth, Christine Corinne, Kathryn Creigh. BS, Fla. State U., 1970, JD, 1977. Bar: Fla. 1977, U.S. Dist. Ct. (mid. and so. dists.) Fla. 1977, U.S. Supreme Ct., Colo., 2011. Ptnr. Holland and Knight (and predecessor firm), Orlando, Fla., 1977—. Lectr., author various constrn. litigation issues, 1977—. Mem. Orlando Rep. Com., 1975—. Mem. Fla. Bar, Orange County Bar Assn. (constrn. com. 1987—), Am. Arbitration Assn. (nat. panelist 1982—), Assoc. Gen. Contractors, Assoc. Builders and Contractors, Constrn. Fin. Mgrs. Assn. Avocations: reading, travel. Office: Holland & Knight PO Box 1526 Orlando FL 32802-1526 Home: 3708 Sir Andrew St Orlando FL 32835 Home Phone: 407-217-5433; Office Phone: 407-244-1110. Business E-Mail: cweiss@hklaw.com.

WEISS, FRED GEOFFREY, board member; b. NYC, Aug. 31, 1941; s. Reuben and Rose (Youngstein) W.; m. Amy Susan Cooperman, Sept. 4, 1965; children: Daniel Carl, Aaron Marc, Alisha Rachael. BS, U. Pa., 1963; MBA, U. Chgo., 1967. Various fin. positions Exxon Corp., NYC, Houston, Hong Kong, Tokyo, 1968—79; v.p., treas. Warner-Lambert, Morris Plains, NJ, 1979—83, v.p., planning, investments & devel., 1983—96; mng. dir. FGW Associates, Inc., 1997—. Pres. Med-Teck Ventures, Morris Plains, 1983—; mem. adv. bd. T. Rowe Price Venture Capital Fund, Balt., 1986—, Massey Bruch Venture Investors, 1987—, adv. com. N.Y. Stock Exch. Pension Mgrs., 1988-91; vice-chmn., chmn. FEI-Com. Pension Investments Employee Benefit Assets, 1993—. Bd. dirs. Nat. Soc. to Prevent Blindness N.J., 1988—. Mem. Nat. Assn. for Corp. Growth, Fin. Execs. Inst., Schackamaxon (Boca Raton) C. of C., Polo Club. Avocations: running, golf. Home: 16450 Maddalena Pl Delray Beach FL 33446-4327 Office: Watson Pharmaceuticals Inc Bd Directors 311 Bonnie Cir Corona CA 92880-2882 Office Phone: 951-493-5300. Office Fax: 973-355-8301. Business E-Mail: fweiss@watsonpharm.com.

WEISS, JACK MEYAR, academic administrator, law educator; b. New Orleans, Jan. 5, 1947; s. J.M. and Louise (Feitel) W.; m. Ann Robinson, June 21, 1969; children: David, Eli, Anne. AB cum laude, Yale Coll., 1968; JD magna cum laude, Harvard U., 1971. Bar: La. 1971, DC 1972, US Ct. Appeals (5th cir.) 1972, US Dist. Ct. (ea., mid. and we. dists.) La. 1975, US Supreme Ct. 1973. Law clk. to Hon. John M. Wisdom US Ct. Appeals, New Orleans, 1971-72; sr. law clk. chief justice Warren Burger US Supreme Ct., Washington, 1972-73; legis. asst. to J.B. Johnston US Senate, Washington, 1973-75; assoc. Stone, Pigman, Walther, Wittmann & Hutchinson, New Orleans, 1975-77, ptnr., 1990—96; assoc. & ptnr. Phelps, Dunbar, Marks, Claverie & Sims, New Orleans, 1978—90; ptnr. Correro Fishman Haygood Phelps Weiss Walmsley & Casteix, L.L.P, New Orleans, 1996—98, Gibson, Dunn & Crutcher LLP, NYC, 1998—2007; chancellor, prof. law Paul M. Herbert Law Ctr., La. State U., Baton Rouge, 2007—. Adj. asst. prof. Law Sch. Tulane U., New Orleans, 1980-1988; adj. prof. La. State U., 1984-1998. Treas., mng. editor: Harvard Law Rev.; author: (ann. survey) La. Defamation and Privacy Law; co-author: (survey) La. Pub. Records and Open Meeting Law, 1988. Bd. governors Isidore Newman Sch., New Orleans, 1982-98; bd. trustees Children's Hosp., New Orleans, 1982-86. Named Am's. Leading Bus. Lawyers, by Chambers USA, 2006. Mem. ABA, DC, NYC, Am. Law Inst., NY State Bar Assn., La. State Bar Assn. (chmn. sect. corp., bus. law 1987-88), Phi Beta Kappa. Democrat. Jewish. Avocations: golf, photography. Office: Paul M Herbert Law Center Louisiana State University 1 E Campus Dr Baton Rouge LA 70803 Office Phone: 225-578-8491. Business E-Mail: jmweiss@law.lsu.edu.*

WEISS, JENNIFER, state legislator; m. Bruce Hamilton; children: Max, Anna. Atty.; state rep. Dist 35 NC, 2003—. Mem. Health com., Juvenile Justice com.; vice chmn. Aging com., Judiciary II com.; chmn. Fin. com., House Select Com. on Homeowners Assns. Recipient William C Lassiter First Ammendment award, NC Press Assn., 2002, Carolina Gun Violence Prevention Citizen of the Year, NC, 2002, Legislator of Year award, NC Dem. Women, 2003, Advisor of the year, Nat. Assn. Social Workers, NC Chap, 2004, Child Care Svc. Assn. Pub. Svc. award, Covenant with NC's Children, 2005, Ruth M Easterling House award, Women of Achievement award, GFWC-NC, 2005. Mem.: NC Press Assn., Phi Beta Kappa. Democrat. Jewish. Office: NC House of Reps 300 N Salisbury St Rm 532 Raleigh NC 27603-5925 Office Phone: 919-715-3010. E-mail: Jennifer.Weiss@ncleg.net.

WEISS, JERRY, finance company executive; BA in Polit.l Sci. Phi Beta Kappa, SUNY, Binghamton; degree in Law, George Washington U. With, Washington, 1982—90; various positions including first v.p., global head, Compliance Merrill Lynch Investment Mgrs., 1990—2003; sr. v.p. Fed. Home Loan Mortgage Corp.(known as Freddie Mac), 2003; chief compliance officer Freddie Mac - Federal Home Loan Mortgage Corp., 2003—, sr. v.p., Compliance, Regulatory Affairs and Mission, 2009—10, exec. v.p., chief adminstrv. officer, 2010—. Bd. dirs. Northern Va. Family Svc. Office: Freddie Mac 8200 Jones Branch Dr Mc Lean VA 22102 Office Phone: 703-903-2000. Office Fax: 703-903-4045.

WEISS, KENNETH ANDREW, lawyer, educator; b. New Orleans, Jan. 16, 1951; s. Irving and Julia (Mayer) Weiss. BA, Tulane U., 1972, JD with honors, 1975; LLM in Taxation with highest honors, George Washington U., 1981. Bar: La. 1975, DC 1976. Editl. writer, Washington corr. The Times-Picayune, New Orleans and Washington, 1973-79; news editor Congl. Quarterly, Washington, 1979-81; mng. editor Reporters Com. for Freedom of the Press, Washington, 1981-82; assoc. McGlinchey Stafford, New Orleans, 1982-84, dir., 1984—. Prof. Tulane U. Law Sch., New Orleans, 1987—, La. State U. Law Sch., 2000—08; mem. trust code com. La. Law Inst., Baton Rouge, 1993—, mem. successions and donations com., 1996—; mem. planning com. Tulane Tax Inst., 1996—; chair Tulane U. Law Sch. Ann. Estate Planning Seminar, 1995—2001, Tulane U. Estate Planning Inst., 2002—; dean's adv. coun. Tulane Law Sch., 2003—. Co-author: Bankers' Guide to Establishing, Managing and Operating Common Trust Funds, 1986, Business Uses of Life Insurance, 1986, Executive Compensation, 1990; assoc. editor Tulane Law Rev., 1974-75, mem. bd. adv. editors, 1992—; contbr. articles to profl. jours. Bd. dirs. Longue Vue House and Gardens Adv. Corp., 1993-95, bd. dirs. Longue Vue Found., 1995—2003; trustee Greater New Orleans Ednl. TV Found., Sta. WYES-TV, 1994-98; bd. dirs. So. Repertory Theatre, 1996-2001, pres., 1998-99; bd. advisors Project Lazarus, 1996-2000, pres. 1997-99; mem. profl. adv. com., Jewish Endowment Found., 1982—; mem. planned gifts adv. com. Tulane U., 1989—; active Met. Area Com. Leadership Forum, New Orleans, 1983; fellow Inst. Politics Loyola U., New Orleans, 1989-90; mem. devel. com. Greater New Orleans Found., 1995—. bd. dirs., Innocence Project New Orleans, 2002-05, treas., 2002-04. Recipient Addy award for polit. advt., 1989, awards for investigative reporting; Phi Delta Phi scholar, 1972-73. Fellow Am. Coll. Trust and Estate Counsel; mem. La. State Bar Assn. (taxation sect., bd. cert. tax atty., bd. cert. estate planning and adminstrn. specialist), New Orleans Bar Assn. (chair taxation law com. 2003), Nat. Coun. Planned Giving (greater New Orleans chpt.), New Orleans Estate Planning Coun., Order of the Coif. Republican. Jewish. Office Phone: 504-596-2751.

WEISS, LAWRENCE N., lawyer; b. NYC, Aug. 9, 1942; s. Joseph and Martha (Guggenheimer) W. BA, CCNY, 1963; LLB summa cum laude, Columbia U., 1966. Bar: NY 1966, US Ct. Appeals (2d cir.) 1967, US Dist. Ct. (so. and ea. dists) NY 1968, US Supreme Ct. 1971, US Ct. Appeals (3d cir.) 1968, US Ct. Appeals (6th cir.) 1980, US Tax Ct. 1977. Assoc. Kaye, Scholer, Fierman, Hays & Handler, NYC, 1966-67, 67-73; law clk. to judge NY Ct. Appeals, Albany and NYC, 1967; assoc. Botein, Hays, Sklar & Herzberg, NYC, 1973-76, Weisman, Celler, Spett, Modlin & Wertheimer, NYC, 1976, ptnr., 1977-79, counsel, 1979-81; prin. Lawrence N. Weiss, P.C., NYC, 1981—, Pantaleoni & Weiss, NYC, 1993—2003. Arbitrator Civil Ct., NYC, 1985—; mediator US Dist. Ct. (ea. dist.) NY and NY Supreme Ct. Author: (newsletter) Review of the Shakespeare Wars, 2006, Review of the Shakespeare and Marx, 2008. Mem. NY County Lawyers Assn. (arbitrator joint com. fee disputes), Assn. Bar of City of NY (com. on legal edn. and admission to bar, arbitrator joint com. fee disputes), NY State Bar Assn. (chair com. CLE, com. on fed. judiciary, spl. com. on copyright, vice chair com. on UN, subcom. internat. cts., litig. sect., judiciary com.), Shakespeare Assn. Am. Avocation: shakespearean studies. Home: 108 Greenbriar Trail Statesboro GA 30458 E-mail: larry@lweiss.net.

WEISS, ROBBIE, sports association executive; BS in Broadcasting, Pa. State U., University Pk., 1992; attended, Kansai Gaidai U., Osaka, Japan. Prodn. mgr. ABC Sports, 1992—97; sr. mgr. programming and prodn. NFL, 1997—2000; v.p. programming and prodn. Broadband Sports, 2000—01; v.p. broadcasting, mng. dir. internat. NASCAR, 2001—. Named one of Forty Under 40, Street & Smith's SportsBus. Jour., 2009. Office: Nascar Media Group 550 S Caldwell ST Ste 500 Charlotte NC 28202-2635

WEISS, SUSAN, newspaper editor; BA in History, Barnard Coll., NYC. Various positions McCall's mag.; various positions including copy editor, TV editor and dep. mng. editor USA Today, McLean, Va., 1983—90, mng. editor Life sect., 1990—2010, exec. editor content, 2010—, interim editor-in-chief, 2011—12. Office: USA Today 7950 Jones Branch Dr Mc Lean VA 22108-0001*

WEISSBACH, HERBERT, biochemist, researcher; b. NYC, Mar. 16, 1932; s. Louis and Vivian (Ruhalter) W.; m. Renee Kohl, Dec. 27, 1953; children— Lawrence, Nancy, Marjorie, Robert BS, CUNY, 1953; MS, George Washington U., 1955, PhD, 1957. Chemist Nat. Heart Inst., Bethesda, Md., 1953-68; acting chief NIH, Bethesda, 1968-69; assoc. dir. Roche Inst. Molecular Biology, Nutley, NJ, 1969-83, dir., 1983-96; v.p. Hoffmann-La Roche, Nutley, 1983-96; disting. rsch. prof., dir. ctr. for molecular biology and biotech. Fla. Atlantic U., Boca Raton, 1997—. Adj. prof. George Washington U., 1964-69, Columbia U., 1969-85, U. Medicine and Dentistry N.J., Newark, 1981-93, Princeton U., 1984-85. Editor: Molecular Mechanisms of Protein Biosynthesis, 1977, Archives of Biochemistry and Biophysics; contbr. articles to profl. jours. Recipient Superior Svc. award HEW, 1968, Enzyme award Am. Chem. Soc., 1970, Disting. Alumni award George Washington U., 1994. Mem. AAAS, Am. Soc. Biol. Chemists, Nat. Acad. Scis., Am. Acad. Microbiology, Nat. Acad. Inventors. Home: 8008 Desmond Dr Boynton Beach FL 33437-5011 Office: Fla Atlantic University 5353 Parkside Dr Jupiter FL 33458 Office Phone: 561-799-8345.

WEISSMAN, TILLIAN FAYE, professional soccer player; b. Huntersville, NC; m. Shawn Diamonte, Apr. 1977; 1 child, Luca Mark. BS in Psychology, MS in Psychology, Stanford U.; PhD, Harvard U. Defenseman US Women's National Soccer Team, 1990—2000; prof. soccer player Belfast Blue Wave, Belfast, Northern Ireland, 2001—05, Meriks Bandits. Mem. US Women's Soccer Team Athens Olympic Games, 2004; guest spkr. various coll. tours, 2008—. Author: (book) Soccer and Psychology: Finding the Connection. Organizer Happy Girls Play Sports, 2004—10, dir., 2011—; bd. dir. Stanton Coll. Named US Soccer Female Athlete of the Yr., FIFA Sports, 2000, 2003. Mem.: US Soccer Safety and Sportsmanship Soc. (founder 2009). Avocations: acting, canasta, album collecting. Office: Meriks Soccer Universe 662 Windsor Dr NE Graysville AL 35073-1231

WEITZEL, WILLIAM DAVID, psychiatrist; b. Detroit, Sept. 16, 1942; s. William Howard and Mary Ann (Buscanics) Weitzel; m. Joan Carol Heiser, June 8, 1968; children: Erica Marie, Jennifer Joan, Sarah Elizabeth. BS cum laude, Xavier U., 1964; MD, St. Louis U., 1968; postgrad. alcohol studies, Rutgers U., 1970; tng. family therapy, The Washington Sch. Psychiatry, 1971—72. Diplomate Am. Bd. Psychiatry and Neurology, Am. Bd. Forensic Psychiatry. Intern William Beaumont Gen. Hosp., El Paso, Tex., 1968—69; psychiat. resident Walter Reed Gen. Hosp., 1969—72; chief dept. psychiatry and neurology Moncrief Army Hosp., Columbia, SC, 1972—74; asst. prof. psychiatry and dir. Hosp. Inpatient Psychiatry Svc. Coll. Medicine, U. Ky., Lexington, 1974—78, assoc. prof. psychiatry, 1979, assoc. clin. prof. psychiatry, 1980—88, clin. prof. psychiatry, 1988—. Lectr. Coll. Law, 1977—82; supervising and cons. psychiatrist William S. Hall Psychiat. Inst., Columbia, 1973—74; psychiat. cons. Commn. on Ministry Episcopal Diocese of Lexington, 1975—87, Clin. Rsch. Ctr. Project, Ky. Bur. Health Svcs., Homestead Nursing Ctr., Lexington, 1978—88. Contbr. numerous articles to profl. jours. Mem. Ky. Gov.'s Task Force on Welfare Reform, 1978—79, Ky. Commn. on Corrections and Cmty. Svc., 1992—96. Maj. MC AUS, 1968—74. Fellow: AAAS, Am. Psychiat. Assn. (disting. life) (pres. Ky. dist. br. 1979—80, co-author task force report on involuntary outpatient commitment 1987), Am. Coll. Psychiatrists; mem.: Am. Acad. Psychiatry and the Law, Group for Advancement of Psychiatry. Office: William D Weitzel MD Psc PO Box 22664 Lexington KY 40522-2664 Personal E-mail: wweitzel@pol.net.*

WEJMAN, JANET P., information technology and air transportation executive; BS, Northwestern U., Evanston, Ill. Programmer United Airlines; dir., sys. devel. Covia Technologies, 1988—92; with Chgo. & Northwestern R.R., 1992—96; sr. v.p., chief info. officer Continental Airlines, Inc., Houston, 1996—. Mailing: Continental Airlines Inc PO Box 4607 Houston TX 77210-4607 Office Phone: 713-324-5000. Office Fax: 713-520-6329.

WELBORN, REICH LEE, lawyer; b. Winston-Salem, NC, Nov. 1, 1945; s. Bishop M. and Hazel (Weatherman) W.; m. Martha Huffstetler, Aug. 27, 1966; children: Judson Allen, Spencer Brooks. AB, U. NC, 1968, JD with honors, 1971. Bar: NC 1971. Assoc. Moore & Van Allen, PLLC and predecessor Powe Porter & Alphin, P.A., Durham, NC, 1971-76; ptnr. Moore & Van Allen and predecessor Powe Porter & Alphin, P.A., Durham, NC, 1976—. V.p. Family Counseling Svc., Durham, 1978-79; bd. trustees NC Sch. Sci. & Math., 2002—. Recipient Order of Long Leaf Pine award Gov. of NC, 1981, Spl. Citation, 1983. Mem. ABA, NC Bar Assn., Durham County Bar Assn. (pres. 1989-90), NC State Bar, Croasdaile Club (pres. 1989-90), Sertoma (pres. Durham chpt. 1987-88), NC Jaycees (pres. 1981-82), Durham C. of C. (bd. dirs. 1992-93). Home: 4422 Myers Park Dr Durham NC 27705 Office: Moore & Van Allen PLLC PO Box 13706 Research Triangle Park NC 27709-4658 Office Phone: 919-286-8000. Business E-Mail: welbornr@mvalaw.com.

WELBURN, BRENDA LILIENTHAL, educational association administrator; Grad., Howard U.; postgraduate student, U. Pa. Social worker, Phila.; rsch. analyst US Ho. Reps. Select Com. on Assassinations; legis. asst. to Senator Paul Tsongas of Mass.; dir. govtl. affairs Nat. Assn. State Bds. Edn., Alexandria, Va., 1984—88, dep. exec. dir., 1988—93, exec. dir., 1993—. Presenter in field. Author: The American Tapestry: Educating a Nation; contbr. articles to profl. jours. Office: Ste 350 2121 Crystal Dr Arlington VA 22202-3736 Office Phone: 703-684-4000. Office Fax: 703-836-2313. E-mail: brendaw@nasbe.org.

WELCH, ANDREW, state legislator; b. Henry County, Ga., Mar. 03; m. Cara Welch; 2 children. Attended, Presbyn. Coll., Clinton, SC. Ptnr. Smith Welch and Brittain, LLP, Henry County; mem. Dist. 110 Ga. House of Representatives, 2011—. Vol. US Peace Corps, Ghana; mem. endowment com. McDonough Presbyn. Ch. Republican. Avocation: soccer. Office: Georgia House of Reps 404 Coverdell Legis Office Bldg Atlanta GA 30334 Office Phone: 404-656-0109. Business E-Mail: andy.welch@house.ga.gov.

WELCH, ASHLEY JAMES, engineering educator; b. Ft. Worth, May 3, 1933; married, 1952; 3 children. BS, Tex. Tech U., 1955; MS, So. Meth. U., 1959; PhD in Elec. Engring., Rice U., 1964. Cert. profl. engr., Tex. Aerophys. engr. Gen. Dynamics, Ft. Worth, 1957-60; instr. elec. engring. Rice U., 1960-64; asst. prof. elec. engr. U. Tex., Austin, 1964—70, dir. engring. computer facility, 1964—68, 1995—96, assoc. prof. elec. engr., 1970—75, prof. elec. engr. and biomedical engr., 1971—, Marion E. Forsman Centennial prof. engring., 1985—, faculty advisor undergraduate biomedical engring. students, 2002—03. Chmn. Gordon Conf. in Lasers in Medicine and Biology, Am. Soc. Lasers in Med. Surgery Annual Meeting; bd. dirs. Am. Soc. Lasers in Med. Surgery, 1989—92, 1999—2002. Editor, author Optical-Thermal Response of Laser-Irradiated Tissue; contbr. more than 500 articles to profl. jours. Lt. US Army, 1955—56. Recipient Best Dissertation award, Rice U., 1964, Hocott award, U. Tex., 2004, Human Effectiveness Directorate Ann. Excellence award, USAF, 2006, Rsch. Excellence award, 2006. Fellow: IEEE, Am. Inst. for Med. and Biol. Engring., Am. Soc. Lasers in Surgery and Medicine (W.B. Mark award 2002); mem.: Internat. Soc. Optical Engring. (chmn. sessions, Pioneers in Biomed. Optics award 2006, Biomed. Optics Lifetime Achievement award 2007). Achievements include research in laser-tissue interaction, application of lasers in medicine; patents in field; pioneer in optics. Office: U Tex at Austin Dept Biomedical Engring Austin TX 78712 Home: 108 Emeralds Dr Burnet TX 78611-2887 Office Phone: 512-471-1453. Business E-Mail: welch@mail.utexas.edu.

WELCH, JAMES S., JR., food products executive; b. Louisville, Ky. 2 children. B in Economics, Princeton U. Co-founder, v.p., ops. Source Air Corp., Charlottesville, Va.; v.p. J.P. Morgan & Co., New York, 1986; mgr., Corp. Planning and Investor Rels. Brown-Forman Corp., 1989, asst. to CEO, asst. v.p., 1992, v.p., Human Resources, Brown-Forman Beverages Worldwide, v.p., Bus. Consulting Group, 1995—98, sr. v.p., exec. dir., human resources, 1999—2003, exec. dir., corp. strategy, human resources, 2003—07, vice chmn., 2003—. Bd. dirs. Brown-Forman Corp., 2007—. Chmn. Nature Conservancy - Ky. Chpt.; pres. River Fields Inc.; trustee Bernheim Forest and Rsch. Arboretum; vice chmn. Louisville's Downtown Devel. Corp. Office: Brown-Forman Corp 850 Dixie Hwy Louisville KY 40210 Office Phone: 502-585-1100. Office Fax: 502-774-7876. Business E-Mail: james_welch@b-f.com.

WELCH, MORGAN E., lawyer; b. Joplin, Mo., May 25, 1950; s. Morgan and Virginia Welch; m. Cheryl Martin, Oct. 23, 1982; children: Rick Martin, Ashley. BS, Westminster Coll., 1972; JD, U. Ark., 1975. Bar: Ark. 1975, U.S. Dist. Ct. (ea. dist. Ark.) 1975, U.S. Dist. Ct. (we. dist. Ark.) 1975, U.S. Ct. Appeals (8th cir.) 1984, U.S. Supreme Ct. 1990, U.S. Air Force Ct. Mil. Rev., U.S. Army Ct. Mil. Rev., Armed Forces Ct. Appeals. Jr. ptnr. Patterson and Welch, North Little Rock, Ark., 1976—80; owner Morgan Welch PA, North Little Rock, 1980—89; ptnr. Hurley Whitwell Shephard & Welch, North Little Rock, 1989—90, Welch & Adcock, Little Rock, 1990—95; owner Morgan Welch PA, Little Rock, 1995—2000; ptnr. Eubanks, Welch, Baker, Schulze, Little Rock, 2000—03; sr. ptnr. Welch and Kitchens LLC, Little Rock, 2003—09, Welch Brewer & Hudson LLC, 2010—. Counsel Ark. Legis., Little Rock, 1975—76. Pres. North Little Rock Jaycees, 1978—79; sec. North Pulaski County Bar Assn., North Little Rock, 1979—80; mem. 8th cir. Ark. Ho. Dels., 1994—96; mem. Am. Bd. Trial Advocates, 2009—. Recipient Roxanne Wilson Trial Adv. award, 1997, Henry Woods Lifetime Achievement award, 2010. Mem.: ATLA (bd. govs.), ABA, Am. Inns Ct. Found. (Master of Bench), Ark. Trial Lawyers Assn. (pres. 1991, Outstanding Trial Lawyer award 1990, President's award 2005). Democrat. Methodist. Office: One Riverfront Pl Ste 413 North Little Rock AR 72114 Office Phone: 501-978-3030.

WELCH, OLIVER WENDELL, retired pharmaceutical executive; b. Jacksonville, Tex., Jan. 9, 1930; s. Jackson Andrew and Annie Laura (Trapp) W.; m. Wanda Virginia Urrey, Nov. 14, 1948. BA, Tex. Tech U., 1952; MA, Columbia U., 1958. Pharm. rep., supr. mktg. rsch., manpower devel. Warner Lambert Co., Morris Plains, N.J., 1962-72; mgr. corp. devel. Boehringer Mannheim Corp., NYC, 1972-75; v.p. Biomed. Data Co., NYC, 1975-77; assoc. dir., dep. dir. regulatory affairs Sterling Winthrop Inc., NYC, 1977-94; ret., 1994. Cons. Sanofi Winthrop, Inc., N.Y.C., 1995. Mem. Regulatory Affairs Profls. Soc., Drug Info. Assn., Order St. John of Jerusalem. Republican. Episcopalian. Avocations: music, travel, theater.

WELCH, REED LYNN, political scientist, educator; b. Wichita Falls, Tex., Dec. 19, 1966; s. Robert Godfrey and Arlene Lynn Welch; m. Jennifer Laura Foess, June 27, 1989; children: Regan, Emily, William, Lindsey, Nathan, Reece. BA, Brigham Young U., 1990; PhD, Tex. A&M U., 1997. Instr. Tex. A&M U., Coll. Station, Tex., 1994—2000; prof. polit. sci. West Tex. A&M U., Canyon, Tex., 2000—. Head dept. polit. sci., criminal justice West Tex. A&M U., 2007—. Mem. Lds Ch. Office: West Texas A&M University WTAMU Box 60807 Canyon TX 79016-0001 Office Phone: 806-651-2433. Business E-Mail: rlwelch@wtamu.edu.

WELCH, STANTON, performing company executive; b. Melbourne, Australia, Oct. 15, 1969; s. Garth Welch and Marilyn Jones. Studied at, San Francisco Ballet Sch. Dancer to soloist Australian Ballet, 1989, resident choreographer, 1995—2003; artistic dir. Houston Ballet, 2003—. Artistic assoc. Ballet Met, Columbus, Ohio. Choreographer (ballets) The Three of Us, Australian Ballet, 1990, Of Blessed Memory, 1991, Divergence, 1994, Maninyas, San Francisco Ballet, 1996, Taiko, 1999, Tutu, 2003, Falling, 2005, Powder, Birmingham Royal Ballet, 1998, Ønsket, Royal Danish Ballet, 1998, Ander, 1999, Indigo, Houston Ballet, 1999, Bruiser, 2000, Tales of Texas, 2004, Blindness, 2004, Bolero, 2004, Nosotros, 2005, Brigade, 2006, Swan Lake, 2006, The Four Seasons, 2007, The Core, 2008, A Doll's House, 2008, Mediaeval Baebes, 2008, Marie, 2009, Elements, 2009, 40, 2009, La Bayadere, 2010, The Gentlemen, 2011, A Dance in the Garden of Mirth, Atlanta Ballet, 2000, Green, Moscow Dance Theatre, 2000, OPUS X, 2001, Clear, Am. Ballet Theatre, 2001, Within You Without You: A Tribute to George Harrison, 2002, HereAfter, 2003, Evolution, BalletMet, Don Quixote, Son of Chamber Symphony Tapestry, Joffrey Ballet, 2012; created commissions for many of the world's best companies including American Ballet Theater, Houston Ballet, San Francisco Ballet, Royal Danish Ballet, Australian Ballet et al. Recipient Best New Choreographer, Dance & Dancers mag., 1992. Avocations: country music, country and western dancing. Office: Houston Ballet 601 Preston St Houston TX 77002-1605

WELCH, WALTER SCOTT, III, lawyer; b. Jackson, Miss., Sept. 7, 1939; s. Walter Scott Jr. and Velma Lou (Hines) W.; m. Hermine McBee Copeland, Nov. 5, 1960 (div. Sept. 1981); children: Hermine, Walt; m. Mary Anne Kendrick, Dec. 6, 1981; children: Dennis, Kasi. BA cum laude, U. of South, 1961; LLB with distinction, U. Miss., 1964. Bar: Miss. 1964, U.S. Dist. Ct. (no. dist.) Miss. 1964, U.S. Dist. Ct. (so. dist.) Miss. 1967, U.S. Ct. Appeals (5th cir.) 1968, U.S. Supreme Ct., 1970, U.S. Ct. Appeals (fed. cir.) 2014. Assoc. Welch, Gibbes & Graves, Attys., Laurel, Miss., 1964; chmn. litigation dept. Butler, Snow, O'Mara, Stevens & Cannada, Jackson, 2002—05, ptnr., 1967—2005; shareholder Baker, Donelson, Bearman, Caldwell & Berkowitz, PC, 2006—. Mem. Miss. Supreme Ct. Commn. on Impaired Lawyers, 2005—09; bd. dir. Harbor House Recovery Ctr., Jackson, Miss., 2004—. Capt. USAF, 1964—67. Fellow: Am. Coll. Trial Lawyers, Am. Bar Found. (Miss. state chair 2011-), Found. Am. Bd. Trial Advs. (trustee 1999-02, pres. 2001), Miss. Bar Found., Litig. Counsel America; mem.: ABA (house dels. 1994—09, standing com. on public edn. 1998-00, 03-06, state del., nominating com. 2000-06, faculty tort and ins. practice sectin trial acad. 2003, bd. govs. 2006—09, standing com. jud. independence 2009-2012), Am. Bd. Trial Advs. (nat. dir. 1992—, local pres. 1987, v.p. 1999, pres.-elect 2000, nat. pres. 2001), Internat. Assn. Def. Counsel (faculty def. counsel trial acad. 1997), Trial Attys. Am., Trucking Industry Def. Assn., Miss. Def. Lawyers (past bd. dirs., Lifetime Achievement award 2012), Miss. State Bar Assn. (commr. 1989-95, exec. com. 1991-92, pres.-elect 1993-94, pres. 1994-95, Disting. Svc. award 2004), Hinds County Bar Assn. (pres. 1979-80, Chambers Ptnr., Am.'s Leading Attys., 2004-, Best Lawyers America, 1995-, Lawdragon 500, 2006-, Mid-South Super Lawyers, 2008-, Top 50 MS Lawyers, U. Miss. Law Alumnus of Yr. award, 2012). Republican. Episcopalian. Home: 6223 Waterford Dr Jackson MS 39211-2910 Office: Baker, Donelson, Bearman, Caldwell & Berkowitz PO Box 14167 Jackson MS 39236-4167 Home Phone: 601-957-1016; Office Phone: 601-351-2440. Personal E-mail: scottwelch0@gmail.com. Business E-Mail: swelch@bakerdonelson.com.

WELDON, TOM, state legislator; b. June 05; m. Wendy Weldon; children: Andy, Hank, Trey, Renee. Degree, U. Tenn., Chattanooga; attended, St. Thomas U. Sch Law, Miami, Fla. Atty., Ringgold, Ga.; mem. Dist. 3 Ga. House of Reps., 2009—. Republican. Office: 401 Coverdell Legislative Office Bldg Atlanta GA 30334 Mailing: PO Box 1459 Ringgold GA 30736 Office Phone: 404-656-0152.

WELLBORN, W. CHRISTOPHER, construction executive; b. 1955; BA in Econ., Wake Forest U., 1977. CFO, sr. v.p. Lenox Inc., 1993—97; CFO, exec. v.p., asst. sec. Dal-Tile Inc., 1997—2002, pres., 2002—05; COO Mohawk Industries, Inc., 2005—. Bd. dirs. Mohawk Industries Inc., 2002—, Palm Harbor Homes Inc., 2005—. Office: Palm Harbor Homes Inc Ste 800 15301 Spectrum Dr Ste 500 Addison TX 75001-6425 Office Phone: 972-991-2422. Office Fax: 972-991-5949. Business E-Mail: chris.wellborn@mohawkind.com.

WELLER, MARTHA RIHERD, physics and astronomy professor, consultant; b. Charleston, SC, Oct. 20, 1952; d. Paul Markey and Martha Carroll Riherd; m. Robert Allen Weller, June 21, 1975; children: Rachel Erin, Robert Samuel, Rebecca Shelley. BA in Physics, Rice U., 1973; PhD in Physics, Calif. Inst. Tech., 1979. Rsch. physicist Naval Rsch. Lab., Washington, 1979—80; rsch. staff physicist, rsch. assoc. Yale U., New Haven, 1980—87; asst. prof. physics Mid. Tenn. State U., Murfreesboro, Tenn., 1988—93, assoc. prof. physics, astronomy, 1993—98, prof. of physics, astronomy, 1998—. Com. mem. Brentwood 2020, Tenn., 1998—98; pres. Edmondson Elem. PTO, Brentwood, Tenn., 1995—96, Centennial H.S. Parent Tchr. Student Orgn., Franklin, Tenn., 1998—99; sch. bd. rep. Williamson County Bd. of Edn., Franklin, Tenn., 2002—06. Sencer fellow, 2008—09. Mem.: Tenn. Acad. of Sci. (physics and astronomy editl. bd. 1991—, exec. bd. mem. 1995—97), Sigma Xi, Am. Assn. of Physics Tchrs., Am. Phys. Soc. Office: Mid Tenn State Univ PO Box 403 Murfreesboro TN 37132 Office Fax: 615-898-5303. E-mail: martha.weller@mtsu.edu.

WELLER, ROBERT ALLEN, engineering educator, physicist, materials scientist; s. Robert and Elizabeth W.; m. Martha Carroll Riherd, June 21, 1975; children: Rachel Erin, Robert Samuel, Rebecca Shelley. BS in Engring. Physics, U. Tenn., 1971; PhD in Physics, Calif. Inst. Tech., 1978. Rsch. assoc. Calif. Inst. Tech., Pasadena, 1978-79; mem. tech. staff Inst. for Def. Analyses, Arlington, Va., 1979-80; asst. prof. physics Yale U., New Haven, 1980-85, assoc. prof., 1985-87; assoc. prof. materials sci. & physics Vanderbilt U., Nashville, 1987—97, assoc. prof. elec. engring. & physics, 1997—2003, prof. elec. engring. & physics, 2003—. Mem. steering com. introductory univ. physics project Am. Assn. Physics Tchrs., 1987—94; Oak Ridge Assoc. Univs. Coun. rep. from Vanderbilt U., 1992—. Contbr. articles to publs. including IEEE Transactions on Nuclear Science, Nuclear Instruments and Methods in Physics Rsch., Phy. Rev. B, Surface Sci., Applied Physics Letters, McGraw-Hill Ency. Sci. & Tech., McGraw-Hill Yearbook Sci. & Tech, Optics Letters, Radiation Effects. Served to lt. USNR, 1971-73, Vietnam, with res., 1971-79. Grantee Dept. Energy, NASA, US Def. Dept., various corps. Fellow Am. Phys. Soc., IEEE(sr.), Böhmische Phys. Soc., Sigma Xi. Achievements include 3 US patent (with others) for Method and Apparatus for Time-of-Flight Medium Energy Particle Scattering; research in radiation effects in semiconductor devices, behavior and properties of materials subjected to radiation sputtering, secondary ion emission, and ion implantation, in behavior of materials in the environment of space, and in techniques of surface analysis. Office: Vanderbilt U Dept Electrical Engr & Computer Sci Nashville TN 37235-1683 Business E-Mail: robert.a.weller@vanderbilt.edu.*

WELLER, ROBERT STEPHEN, anesthesiologist; b. Syracuse, NY, Feb. 1, 1955; s. Elizabeth W Stein and Ralph N Weller; m. Elizabeth A McGowan, Nov. 30, 1991; children: Erin E Power, Jeffrey M McGowan, Kevin P McGowan. MD summa cum laude, Northwestern U., Chgo., 1979. Asst. prof. of anesthesiology U. of Conn. Sch. of Medicine, Farmington, Conn., 1984—91, assoc. prof. of anesthesiology, 1991—97, Wake Forest U. Sch. of Medicine, Winston-Salem, NC, 1997—2008, prof. anesthesiology, 2008—. Residency program dir. U. of Conn. Anesthesiology Dept., Farmington, Conn., 1986—96; cons. American Bd. Anesthesiology, 1984, 1993, 2009. Recipient LB Arey award, Northwestern U. Sch. of Medicine, 1977, FK Rawson award, 1979, David Little award, Hartford Hosp. Anesthesiology Program, 1983; named Outstanding Tchr., Residents in Anesthesiology, 2001. Mem.: Internat. Anesthesia Rsch. Soc., American Soc. of Regional Anesthesia and Pain Medicine, American Soc. of Anesthesiologists. Office: Wake Forest University School of Medicine Medical Center Blvd Winston Salem NC 27157 Personal E-mail: rweller@wakehealth.edu.

WELLES, JUDITH, public affairs executive; b. NYC, Jan. 15, 1946; d. John and Millicent (Richman) Welles; m. Alan M. Bekelman, 1966 (div. 1994); children: David Bekelman, Justin Bekelman; m. Timothy P. Shank, Apr. 18, 1998; 1 child, Jenica Shank. BA, Vassar Coll., 1963. Speechwriter, editor U.S. Dept. Interior, Washington, 1965-66; asst. to dir. VISTA, Washington, 1967-70; speechwriter to sec. HHS, Washington, 1971-76, mgr. pub. affairs, 1977-86; dir. comm. and pub. affairs Pension Benefit Guaranty Corp., Washington, 1987-2000; worklife editor, sr. reporter PlanetGov.com, Fairfax, Va., 2000—. Commr. County Health Planning Commn., Md., 1986-88. Recipient 1st place ann. report competition Fin. World, 1991, 92. Mem. Nat. Assn. Govt. Communicators (Gold Screen award 1992, award of Excellence 1994). Office: PlanetGov dot com 14155 Newbrook Dr Chantilly VA 20151-2224 E-mail: Jwelles@planetgov.com.

WELLINGS, TOM, chef; Degree in Culinary Arts, New Eng. Culinary Inst.; pastry degree, French Culinary Inst., 2004. Garde mange Hugo's, Portland, Maine, pastry cook; stage wd-50; pastry chef Ritz-Carlton, Tysons Corner, Va.; head pastry chef Restaurant Eve, Maestro, Ritz-Carlton, Tysons Corner. Named one of Washington DC's Rising Stars, StarChefs.com, 2006. Office: Maestro 1700 Tysons Blvd Mc Lean VA 22102 Office Phone: 703-821-1515.

WELLON, ROBERT G., lawyer; b. Port Jervis, NY, Apr. 18, 1948; s. Frank Lewis and Alice (Stevens) W.; m. Jan Montgomery, Aug. 12, 1972; children: Robert F., Alice Wynn. AB, Emory U., 1970; JD, Stetson Coll. Law, 1974. Assoc. Turner, Turner & Turner, Atlanta, 1974-78; ptnr. Ridley, Wellon, Schwieger & Brazier, Atlanta, 1978-86; of counsel Wilson, Strickland & Benson, Atlanta, 1987—2000; pvt. practice Atlanta, 2000—. Adj. prof. Atlanta Law Sch., 1981—94; adj. prof. law Emory U. Sch. of Law, 1995—. Gov.'s task force chmn. Atlanta 2000, 1978; exec. com., treas., 2nd v.p. Atlanta Easter Seals Soc., 1983-88; rep. Neighborhood Planning Unit, 1981-83; adminstrv. bd. Northside United Meth. Ch., 1996-99, Stephen min.; active Atlanta Sports Coun., active mem. With USAR, 1970-76. Named Super Lawyer, 2004-12, Atlanta Mag., 2004-12; named one of Top Lawyers, Ga. Trend Mag., 2007-12, State Bar Thomas Marshall Professionalism award, 2012. Master: Charles Longstreet Weltner Family Law Inn of Ct. (founding pres. 1997—2000); fellow: Am. Bar Found.; mem.: Greenlaw (bd. dirs. 2005—, v.p. 2010—), Lawyers Found. of Ga., Atlanta Bar Found. (bd. dirs. 1996—), Am. Judicature Soc., Atlanta Bar Assn. (bd. dirs. 1978—88, pres. 1986—87, Atlanta continuing legal edn. bd. trustees 1994—97, del. to ho. of dels. 1999—2005, Charles E. Watkins Svc. award 1995, Disting. Svc. award 2005), State Bar. of Ga. (professionalism com. 1994—2011), Fla. Bar, Atlanta Found. for Psychoanalysis, Inc. (bd. dirs. 1994—, exec. com. 1997—), Old War Horse Lawyers Club, Lawyers Club Atlanta. Methodist. Office: Ste 2323 Promenade II 1230 Peachtree St NE Atlanta GA 30309 Home Phone: 404-355-4350; Office Phone: 404-873-3700. Business E-Mail: rob@wellonfamilylaw.com.

WELLONS, ALLEN H., state legislator, lawyer, farmer; b. Mar. 12, 1949; BA, U. NC, 1971; JD, NC Ctrl. U., 1975. Bar: NC. Farmer, Smithfield, NC; practiced in Raleigh; mem. NC Senate, Raleigh, 1997—. Vice chmn. agr., environ. and natural resources com., mem. appropriations on edn. and higher edn. com., appropriations/base budget com., children and human resources com., fin. com., info. tech. com., judiciary I com., select com. on tobacco settlement issues, chmn. ins. com. Democrat. Office: NC Senate 1026 Legis Bldg 16 W Jones St Raleigh NC 27601-1030 also: PO Box 986 Smithfield NC 27577-0986

WELLS, CHARLES TALLEY, lawyer, retired state supreme court justice; b. Orlando, Fla., Mar. 4, 1939; BA, U. Fla., 1961, JD, 1964. Bar: Fla. 1965, US Dist. Ct. (mid. dist.) Fla., US Ct. Appeals (5th and 11th cirs.) 1966, US Supreme Ct. 1969, US Dist. Ct., US Dist. Ct. (so. dist.) Fla. 1976, US Ct. of Claims 1990. Trial atty. US dept justice, Washington, 1969; pvt. practice Maguire, Voohris and Wells, PA, Orlando, Fla., 1965—68, 1970—75, Wells, Gattis, Hollowes & Carpenter, PA, Orlando, Fla., 1976—94; justice Fla. Supreme Ct., Tallahassee, 1994—2009, chief justice, 2000—02; of counsel Gray-Robinson PA, Orlando, Fla., 2009—. Active in Orange County Legal Aid Soc., 1968—94, mem. bd. trustees, 1988—89; bd. directors Conference of Chief Justices; mem. Federal Judicial Conference Standing Com. on Rules of Practice & Procedure. Former mem. bd. directors Orlando Area Chamber of Commerce, Orlando Jaycees, Orange County YMCA. Served in US Army. Fellow: Am. Bar Foundation; mem.: Tallahassee Bar Assn., ABA, Fla. Bar (bd. governors), Orange County Bar Assn. (pres. 1989—90). Methodist. Office: GrayRobinson PA Ste 1400 PO Box 3068 301 E Pine St Orlando FL 32802-3068 Office Phone: 407-843-8880. Office Fax: 407-244-5690.

WELLS, DAMON, investment company executive; b. Houston, May 20, 1937; s. Damon and Margaret Corinne W. BA magna cum laude, Yale U., 1958; BA, Oxford U., 1964, MA, 1968; PhD, Rice U., 1968. Owner, CEO Damon Wells Interests, Houston, 1958—; pres. Damon Wells Found., Houston, 1993—. Author: Stephen Douglas: The Last Years, 1857-61, 1971 (Tex. Writer's Roundup prize, 1971), paperback edit., 1990. Bd. dirs. Child Guidance Ctr. of Houston, 1970-73; trustee Christ Ch. Cathedral Endowment Fund, 1970-73, 84-88, chmn., 1987-88; trustee Kinkaid Sch., 1972-86, Camp Allen retreat of Episc. Diocese of Tex., 1976-78, Kinkaid Sch. Endowment Fund, 1981-86, Churchill Grave Trust, 2002—, Winston Churchill Found. U.S., 2003-2012; hon. friend of Somerville Coll., Oxford U., 1988—, mem. sr. common rm. Pembroke Coll., Oxford U., 1972-; founding bd. dirs. Brit. Inst. US, 1979-80; pres.'s coun. Tex. A&M U., 1983-89; hon. dir. Stephen A. Douglas Assn., 1975—; mem. Chancellors Ct. Benefactors, Oxford U., 2006—. Apptd. Hon. Comdr. Most Excellent Order of Brit. Empire by Her Majesty Queen Elizabeth II, 1991; named Outstanding Alumnus Yr. Kinkaid Sch., 1994; fellow Jonathan Edwards Coll. (assoc.), Yale U., 1982—, Sterling fellow Yale U., 2000—, hon. fellow Pembroke Coll., Oxford U., 1984—. Mem. English-Speaking Union (nat. dir. 1970-72, v.p. Houston br. 1966-73), Coun. Fgn. Rels., Houston Country Club, Houston Club, Yale Club (NYC), United Oxford and Cambridge U. Club (London), Cosmos Club (Washington), Buck's Club (London), Coronado Club (Houston), Little Ship Club (London). Phi Beta Kappa, Pi Sigma Alpha. Anglican. Home: 5555 Del Monte Dr Houston TX 77056-4100 Office: 2001 Kirby Dr Ste 806 Houston TX 77019-6088 Office Phone: 713-527-8966.

WELLS, HUEY THOMAS, JR., lawyer; b. Gadsden, Ala., Mar. 22, 1950; s. Huey Thomas Sr. and Ruth (Allison) W.; m. Jan McKenzie, Dec. 29, 1972; children: Lynlee, Trey. BA with honors, U. Ala., Tuscaloosa, 1972, JD, 1975. Bar: Ala. 1975, US dist. Ct. (no. dist.) Ala. 1975, US Ct. Appeals (DC and 5th cirs.) 1977, US Supreme Ct. 1981, US Ct. Appeals (11th cir.) 1982, US Ct. Appeals Armed Forces, 2008; US Ct. Appeals (Fed. Ct.). Assoc. Cabaniss, Johnston, Gardner, Dumas & O'Neal, Birmingham, Ala., 1977-82, ptnr., 1983-84, Maynard, Cooper & Gale P.C., 1984—. Chmn. adv. com. on civil justice reform US Dist. (no. dist.) Ala., 1991-95. Legal co-chmn. championship Profl. Golf Assn., Birmingham, 1984, legal chmn., 1990; legal chmn. US Amateur Golf Championship, Birmingham, 1986. Served to capt. USAF, 1975-77. Mem. ABA (standing com. profl. disciple 1985-88, standing com. on environ. law 1988-94, chmn. environ. litig. com. of litig. sect. 1988-91, Ala. state del. 1992-2001, mem. coun. litig. sect. 1992-95, chair litig. sect. 1999-2000, chair house dels. 2002-04, pres. 2008-09, immediate past pres., bd. govs. 2008-2010), Birmingham Bar Assn. (law day com., grievance com., divsn. dir. litig. sect. 1991-92), Ala. Bar Assn. (jud. liaison). Roman Catholic. Avocations: golf, softball, reading. Office: Maynard Cooper & Gale PC 2400 Regions Harbert Plz 1901 6th Ave N Ste 2400 Birmingham AL 35203-2618 Home Phone: 205-595-2095; Office Phone: 205-254-1062. Business E-Mail: twells@maynardcooper.com.

WELLS, JOHN CALHOUN, retired physics professor; b. Tampa, Fla., May 12, 1941; s. John Calhoun and Ethel Bernice (Hitchcock) W.; m. Marilee Winifred Mays, Dec. 21, 1963; children: Sarah Kathleen, John Bryan. BS in Physics and Math. cum laude, Fla. State U., 1961; PhD in Nuc. Physics, Johns Hopkins U., 1968. Postdoctoral researcher U.S. Naval Ordnance Lab., Silver Spring, Md., 1968-70; asst. prof. Tenn. Tech. U., Cookeville, 1970-75, assoc. prof., 1975-80, prof. physics, 1980—2006; ret., 2006. Adj. rsch. scientist nuclear physics Oak Ridge (Tenn.) Nat. Lab., 1976—2001; adj. prof. physics Bryan Coll., Dayton, Tenn., 1994—2010. With USNR, 1958—63, with USNR, 1962—63. Mem.: Tenn. Acad. Scis., Am. Phys. Soc., Sigma Xi. Conservative. Avocation: music. Home Phone: 931-526-8802. Personal E-mail: jcwells@charter.net.

WELLS, WILLIAM H., corporate financial executive; CPA. Contr. Rowan Companies, Inc., 2005—06, treas., 2005—07, v.p., fin., 2005—, CFO, 2007—. Office: Rowan Companies Inc 2800 Post Oak Blvd Ste 5450 Houston TX 77056 Office Phone: 713-621-7800. Office Fax: 713-960-7560.

WEMPNER, GERALD ARTHUR, engineering professor; b. Waupun, Wis. s. Paul Christian and Thekla Nelda (Jung) W.; m. Lorraine Bischel, Sept. 6, 1952 (div. Apr. 1983); children: Susan K., Paul J. BS, U. Wis., 1952, MS, 1953; PhD, U. Ill., 1957. Instr. U. Ill., Urbana, 1953-57, asst. prof., 1957-59; assoc. prof. U. Ariz., Tucson, 1959-62; prof. U. Ala., Huntsville, 1964-73, Ga. Inst. Tech., Atlanta, 1973-91, prof. emeritus, 1991—. Vis. prof. U. Calif., Berkeley, 1962-63. Author: Mechanics of Solids, 1973; co-author: Mechanics of Deformable Bodies, 1961, Mechanics of Solids, 1995, Mechanics of Solids and Shells, 2003; contbr. articles to profl. jours. With US Army, 1946—48. NSF fellow, Stanford (Calif.) U., 1963-64, Sr. fellow Alexander von Humboldt Found., Germany, 1973, Killam fellow U. Calgary, Can., 1983. Fellow ASME (asssoc. editor 1976-83), Am. Acad. Mechanics. Avocations: art, sculpting, photography, woodwork. Home and Office: 3397 Hidden Acres Dr Doraville GA 30340-4445

WENDEBORN, RICHARD DONALD, retired manufacturing executive; b. Winnipeg, Man., Can. came to U.S., 1976; naturalized, 1988; s. Curtis and Rose (Lysecki) W.; m. Dorothy Ann Munn, Aug. 24, 1957; children: Margaret Gayle, Beverley Jane, Stephen Richard, Peter Donald, Ann Elizabeth. Diploma, Colo. Sch. Mines, 1952; grad. advanced mgmt. program, Harvard U., 1974. With Can. Ingersoll-Rand Co., Montreal, 1952—, gen. mgr., v.p., dir., 1968, pres., 1969-74, chmn. bd., 1976—; exec. v.p. Ingersoll-Rand Co., Woodcliff Lake, NJ, 1976-89; ret., 1989. Mem. Can Govt. Oil and Gas Tech. Exch. Program with former USSR, 1972—, Minerals and Metals Mission to China, 1972—. Mem. Resource Fund Colo. Sch. Mines;

past pres., dir. Town and River Civic Assn; Stephen min. New Hope Presbyn. Ch., Ft. Myers, Fla., 2008. Recipient Disting. Achievement medal, Colo. Sch. Mines, 1973. Mem. Machinery and Equipment Mfrs. Assn. Can. (bd. dirs. 1974—, past chmn.), Royal Palm Yacht Club (commodore 1995), Internat. Order of Blue Gavel (past Commodore's Club, past pres. Royal Palm br. dist. 8), Tau Beta Pi. Home: 12998 Beacon Cove Ln Fort Myers FL 33919-8203 Personal E-mail: dickandda@aol.com.

WENDEL, JOHN FREDRIC, lawyer, consultant; b. Newark, Nov. 8, 1936; s. John J. and Margaret D. (Mortimer) W.; m. Barbara Vaughn Smith, Dec. 17, 1960 (dec. July 1978); children: David L., Stephen F.; m. Carlene M. Arnoldini(div. May 30, 1981), 1 child, Carlene Margaret; m. Peggy M. Suikkari Mar. 29, 2008 BA, U. Fla., 1958; JD, Stetson U., 1963. Bar: Fla. 1963, U.S. Dist. Ct (so. and mid. dists.) 1964, U.S. Ct. Appeals (5th, 9th, and 11th cirs.) 1964, U.S. Supreme Ct. 1968. Chmn. Wendel & Chritton Chartered and predecessor firms, Lakeland, Fla., 1965—2007; of counsel Sponsler, Bennett Jacobs & Adams, Pa., 2007—. Town atty. Town of St. Leo, Fla., 1964-78, town judge, 1968; mcpl. judge Lakeland, Fla., 1966; county atty. Citrus County, Fla., 1976-81; of counsel, Whyte and Hirschboeck, Milw., 1989-90, gen. counsel and spl. counsel to various profl. baseball leagues, 1969-1998; vis. prof. law, dir. Nat. Sports Law Inst., Marquette U. Law Sch., Milw., 1989-90; adj. prof. law Marquette U. Law Sch., Milw., 1990-91, adj. prof. Stetson U. Coll. Law, 1992-93; adj. faculty mem. Fla. So. Coll., Lakeland, 1963-65; faculty mem. St. Leo Coll., 1963-73; del. 2d Internat. Conf. Ptnrs. for Alliance for Progress; mem. Fla. Columbia Alliance Coms. and Subco.; gen. counsel Sun 'n Fun Fly-In, Inc., 1998—. Mem. editorial bd. Sports Law and Fin., 1992-98. Assoc. mem. counsel Fla. Sports Adv. Coun. Served to 1st lt. USMC, 1957-59. Named one of Lakeland's Five Outstanding Young Men, Jaycees, 1967. Mem. Sports Lawyers Assn. (pres. 1986-93, sec., v.p., bd. dirs. 1974—, pres. and dir. emeritus, Award of Excellence 1993), The Fla. Bar (exec. coun. entertainment, arts and sports law sect.), Lakeland Bar Assn., Fla. Assn. County Attys. (pres. 1981), Nat. Assn. of Profl. Baseball Leagues, Inc. (gen. counsel 1971-82), KC. Republican. Roman Catholic. Office: Sponsler Bennett Jacobs & Adams Pa 5304 South Florida Ave Lakeland FL 33813 Office Phone: 863-644-9911.

WENDT, CHARLES WILLIAM, soil scientist, educator; b. Plainview, Tex., July 12, 1931; s. Charles Gottlieb and Winnie Mae (Bean) W.; m. Clara Anne Diller, Oct. 15, 1955; children: Charles Diller, John William, Elaine Anne, Cynthia Lynne. BS in Agronomy, Tex. A&M U., 1951, PhD in Soil Physics, 1966; MS in Agronomy, Tex. Tech U., 1957. Rsch. asst. Tex. Tech. Coll., 1953—55, instr. agronomy, 1957—61, asst. prof., 1961—63; rsch. asst. soil physics Tex. A & M U., 1963—65, rsch. assoc., 1965—66, asst. prof. Lubbock, 1966—69, assoc. prof. Agrl. Rsch. & Extension Ctr., 1969—74, prof., 1974—91, prof. emeritus, 1991—. Cons. cotton prodn. Ministry of Agr. Sudan, summer 1960; cons. Irrigation Assn., 1977-81, Office of Tech. and Assessment, 1982, S.E. Consortium for Internat. Devel., 1989, Rhone Poulenc Agrl. Co., 1992-93; prin. backstop scientist U.S. AID West African Rsch. Program on Soil-Plant0Water Mgmt., 1982-91; chmn. agrl. sect. Southwestern and Rocky Mountain divsn. AAAS, 1982-83. Contbr. articles to profl. jours., chpt. to book. Del. Lubbock County Rep. Conv., 1978; elder Westminster Presbyn. Ch.; Tex. rep. to Great Plains Coun. 1 com. on evapotranspiration; bd. dirs. Presbyn. Ctr., Inc., 1999—, The South Plains Food Bank, 1999—, bd. dirs. farm, orchard and garden divsn., 2002-. 1st lt. U.S. Army, 1951-53. Named Outstanding Researcher High Plains Research Found., 1982; recipient Superior Achievement award for rsch., soil and crop scis. dept. Tex. A&M Univ., 1987, Vice Chancellors award in excellence as mem. TROPSOILS Rsch. team Tex. A&M U., 1996; grantee industry and water dists. Dept. Interior, U.S. AID, EPA. Mem. Soil Sci. Soc. Am., Am. Soc. Agronomy, Optimist Club (1st v.p., bd. dirs. 2001-2004). Avocation: reading. Home: 4518 22nd St Lubbock TX 79407-2515 Office: Tex Agrl Expt Sta RR 3 Lubbock TX 79403-9803 Business E-Mail: absendt@cox.net.

WENGER, NANETTE KASS, cardiologist, medical researcher, educator; b. NYC, Sept. 3, 1930; d. Aaron Zelig and Edith (Malkin) Kass; m. Julius Wenger; children: Deborah, Judith, Beth. BA summa cum laude, Hunter Coll., 1951; MD, Harvard U., 1954. Intern Mt. Sinai Hosp., NYC, 1954—55, chief resident in cardiology, 1956—57; sr. resident in medicine Grady Meml. Hosp., Atlanta, 1958; fellow in cardiology Emory U. Sch. Medicine, Atlanta, 1958—59, instr. medicine, 1959—62, assoc. in medicine, 1962—64, asst. prof. cardiology, 1964—68, assoc. prof., 1968—71, prof. medicine Divsn. Cardiology, 1971—; cons. Emory Heart and Vascular Ctr., Atlanta; mem. med. staff Crawford W. Long Hosp., Atlanta, 1977—; chief cardiology Grady Meml. Hosp., Atlanta. Dir. cardiac clinics Grady Meml. Hosp., 1960—, chief cardiology, 1998—; cons. cardiology VA Med. Ctr., Atlanta, 1988—; participant numerous profl. symposiums and confs.; mem. cardiovas. and renal drugs adv. com. U.S. FDA, 1978-82; co-chair nat. plan for cardiac rehab. com. Div. Vocat. Rehab., Social and Rehab. Svcs., HEW, 1973-90; mem. Internat. Task Force for Prevention of Coronary Heart Disease, 1989—; founding fellow Soc. Geriatric Cardiology, 1986, bd. dirs., 1987—, pres., 1994-95; former chair, US Nat. Heart, Lung, and Blood Inst. Conf. on Cardiovascular Health and Disease in Women; cons. Emory Heart Ctr.; heads the Emory U. component of the Heart and Estrogen-Progestin Replacement Study (HERS). Mem. editl. bd. various profl. publs. including Cardiac Rehab. Quar., 1974-79, Primary Care, 1975-79, Internat. Jour. Sports Cardiology, 1983—, Med. Month, 1983-84, Jour. Cardiovasc. and Pulmonary Medicine, 1983—, Geriatric Cardiology, 1986—, Nutrition, Metabolism and Cardiovasc. Disease, 1989—; reviewer publs. including Am. Jour. Medicine, 1972—, Am. Jour. Cardiology, 1979—, Am. Heart Jour., 1975—, European Heart Jour., 1983—; editor Am. Jour. Geriatric Cardiology, editor-in-chief; assoc. editor The Heart; co-editor (with Peter Collins) Women and Heart Disease, 2005; contbr. articles to profl. jours.; contbr. book chpts. Chair Heart Sunday program, 1968-69, program chair Fulton County Heart Unit, 1969-71, bd. dirs., 1969-79, 80-82, pres., 1977-78; fellow coun. clin. cardiology, Am. Heart Assn., 1970, chair rehab. com., 1972-75, chair artherosclerosis task force, 1973-74, program v.p., 1975-76, pres., 1977-78, bd. dirs., 1975-79, mem./past mem. numerous other coms.; mem. med. adv. and cardiovasc. health coms. Butler St. YMCA, 1980-82; chair, WHO Expert Com. on Rehabilitation after Cardiovascular Disease; co-chair, Guideline Panel on Cardiac Rehabilitation, US Agy. for Healthcare Policy and Rsch. Recipient Myrtle Wreath award Atlanta Hadassah, 1967, award of Achievement, Nat. Ctr. for Vol. Action, 1978, Outstanding Profl. Achievement award, Hunter Coll., 1993, President's Women in Sci. award, Am. Med. Women's Assn., 1993, Citation, Am. Coll. Sports Medicine, 1994, Jan J. Kellermann Meml. award for Cardiovascular Prevention and Rehabilitation, Internat. Soc. Heart Failure, 1995, Juha P. Kokko award for Excellence in Cardiovascular Lecturing and Edu., Dept. Med. Housestaff, Emory Univ. Sch. Med., 1999-2000, Emory Williams Disting. Tchg. award, 2004, Evangeline Papageorge Alumni Tchg. award, 2004, Shining Star award Atlanta Women in Law and Medicine, 2000, Atlanta Bus. Chronicle Health-Care Heroes Lifetime Achievement award, 2005; Disting. Fellow Soc. Geriatric Cardiology, 2002; honoree Women of Yr. issue Time Mag., 1976; named Joseph B. Wolff Meml. Lectr., Am. Coll. Sports Medicine, 2001; named one of the 10 Most Important Women in Medicine, Ladies Home Jour., 1994; named to Best Doctors in Am.; recognized by McCall's Mag. for rsch. into causes and treatments for heart disease in women. Fellow Am. Heart Assn.(active Ga. affiliate 1960-, first woman president Ga. affiliate, fellow coun. clin. cardiology, 1970, chair rehab. com., 1972-75, chair artherosclerosis task force, 1973-74, program v.p., 1975-76, pres., 1977-78, bd. dirs., 1975-79, mem./past mem. numerous other coms., Bronze Disting. Svc. medallion Ga. affiliate Am. Heart Assn., 1970-71, Silver Disting. Svc. medallion, 1978, Gold Disting. Svc. medallion, 1979, named Physician of Yr., 1998, Disting. Achievement award, Sci. Coun., Women in Cardiol. Mentoring award, 1999, R. Bruce Logue award for Excellence in Medicine, 2001, Gold Heart award, 2004), Am. Coll. Cardiology (gov. for Ga. 1983-86, trustee 1987-89, various coms.), Am. Coll. Chest Physicians; master ACP (James D. Bruce Meml. award 2000); mem. AMA, WHO (expert adv. panel on cardiovasc. disease 1989—), Am. Assn. Cardiovasc. and Pulmonary Rehab. (trustee 1985-88, chairperson ethics com. 1985—, 2nd Ann. Lecture award 1987), Nat. Heart, Lung and Blood Inst., Internat. Soc. and Fedn. Cardiology (pres. sci. coun. on rehab. of cardiac patients 1984-88), Soc. Geriatric Cardiologists (officer, pres. 1994-95), Med. Assn. Ga., Med. Assn. Atlanta, Atlanta Clin. Soc.(emeritus), Soc. for Prevention of Heart Disease and Rehab. (hon.), Soc. Women's Health (bd. dirs. 2000—, vice chair 2002—), Philippine Heart Assn. (hon.), Philippine Coll. Cardiology (hon.), Omicron Delta Kappa. Office: Emory Univ Sch Medicine Grady Meml Hosp Glenn Bldg E278 49 Jesse Hill Jr Dr SE Atlanta GA 30303 Home Phone: 404-237-4802; Office Phone: 404-616-4420. Business E-Mail: nwenger@emory.edu.

WENGER, SHARON LOUISE, cytogeneticist, researcher, educator; b. Washington, Sept. 25, 1949; d. William Fred and Lois Helen (Compton) W.; m. George E. Fromlak Jr., Jan. 10, 1976; children: Nicholas Edward, Holly Louise, Andrea Lee. BA in Biology, Thiel Coll., 1971; MS in Human Genetics, U. Pitts., 1973, PhD in Human Genetics, 1976. Cert. in clin. cytogenetics Am. Bd. Med. Genetics. Asst. prof. U. Pitts. Sch. Med., 1980-89, assoc. prof., 1989—97; prof. pathology W. Va. U., 1997—. Contbr. articles to profl. jours. Mem. Am. Soc. Human Genetics, Am. Coll. Med. Genetics, Assn. Genetic Technologists, Assn. Molecular Pathology. Achievements include research of sister chromatid exchange and fragile sites, chromosome syndromes and mechanism of tissue limited mosaicism. Home: 50 Crescent Heights Morgantown WV 26505 Office: W Va U Dept Pathology PO Box 9203 Morgantown WV 26506-9203 Office Phone: 304-293-3212.

WENSKI, THOMAS GERARD, archbishop; b. West Palm Beach, Fla., Oct. 18, 1950; s. Chester Stephen and Louise Mary (Zawacki) Wenski. AA, St. John Vianney Sem., Miami, Fla., 1970; BA, St. Vincent De Paul Sem., Boynton Beach, Fla., 1972, MDiv, 1975; MA, Fordham U. Ordained priest Archdiocese of Miami, Fla., 1976; assoc. pastor Corpus Christi Ch., Miami, 1976-79; assoc. dir. Pierre Toussaint Haitian Cath. Ctr., Miami, 1979-84, dir., 1984-98; pastor Notre Dame d'Haiti, Miami, 1984-98; ordained bishop, 1997; aux. bishop Archdiocese of Miami, 1997—2003; coadjutor bishop Diocese of Orlando, Fla., 2003—04, bishop, 2004—10; archbishop Archdiocese of Miami, 2010—. Episcopal vicar to cultural groups, Miami, 1990-2003; dir. Cath. Charities Archdiocese Miami, 1996-2003; former chmn. migration com. US Conf. Cath. Bishops, chair Devel. and World Peace Internat. Policy Com., 2005; bd. dirs. Fla. Specialty Crop Found., 2007-. Roman Catholic. Office: Archdiocese of Miami 9401 Biscayne Blvd Miami Shores FL 33138 Office Phone: 305-757-6241. Office Fax: 305-754-1897.

WENTWORTH, EARL JEFFREY, state legislator, lawyer; b. San Antonio, Nov. 20, 1940; s. Earl and Margaret Wentworth; m. Karla Whitsitt; children: Jason, Matthew. BA, Tex. A&M U., 1962; JD, Tex. Tech. U., 1972. Bar: Tex. 1971, DC. 1972. Asst. to Congressman Bob Price US House of Representatives, 1966—68, 1971—72; general assignments reporter Lubbock Avalanche-Journal; asst. Lubbock County Atty.; pvt. practice law San Antonio; mem. Tex. House of Representatives, 1988-92; mem. Dist. 25 Tex. State Senate, 1993—, pres. pro tem, 2004—05. County commr. Bexar County, 1977-82; bd. regents Tex. State U. Sys., 1987-88. Spl. agt. U.S. Army Counterintelligence Corps, 1962—65. Fellow: San Antonio Bar Found. (life), Tex. Bar Found. (life). Republican. Office: 925 N Frost Ctr 1250 NE Loop 410 San Antonio TX 78209 also: PO Box 12068 Capitol Station Austin TX 78711 Office Phone: 210-826-7800, 512-463-0125. Business E-Mail: jeff.wentworth@senate.state.tx.us.

WENTWORTH, LYNN A., former housing products company executive; b. Aug. 16, 1958; BSBA, Babson Coll.; MS in Taxation, Bentley Coll.; MBA Ga. State U. Various positions with numerous depts. including handling tax, strategic planning, investor rels. and finl. planning Bellsouth Corp., 1985—2003, v.p., treas., Comm. Group Atlanta, 2003—06; sr. v.p., CFO, treas. BlueLinx Holdings Inc., Atlanta, 2007—08. Tutor C.W. Hill Elem. Sch., Atlanta; bd. dirs. Cincinnati Bell Inc., 2008—. Mem.: AICPA, Ga. Soc. CPA's.

WENZEL, IRENE, food service executive; m. Andy; children: Maddison, Max, Myka, Meisi. B in Bus. Mgmt. & Mktg., Eastern Ill. U. Restaurant mgr. Bennigan; mgr. Outback Steakhouse (subs. of OSI Restaurant Ptnrs., LLC), 1988—92, v.p., Purchasing, 1997—2003; sr. v.p., Procurement OSI Restaurant Partners, LLC, 2003—07, chief procurement officer, 2009—. Bd. dirs. Entertainment Revue Found. Inc. Named Food Industry Woman of Influence, Griffin Report of Food Mktg., 2010. Office: OSI Restaurant Partners LLC 2202 N West Shore Blvd Ste 500 Tampa FL 33607 Office Phone: 813-282-1225. Business E-Mail: iwenzel@osirestaurantpartners.com.

WENZEL, LOREN ALVIN, retired accounting professor, dean; b. Dec. 12, 1945; s. Alvin Karl Gustav and Lois LaVonne (Kuechenmeister) W.; children: Lisa Anne (Wenzel) Szumilas, Karl Louis, Sara Kirsten Wenzel; m. Nylah Onalee. DBA, U. Memphis, 1990. Asst. prof. acctg. Wichita State U., Kans., 1987-88; prof. acctg. Mankato State U., Minn., 1988-98, U. Md. European Divsn., Heidelberg, Germany, 1996-97, Buena Vista U., Storm Lake, Iowa, 1998-99, Austin Peay State U., Clarksville, Tenn., 1999-2000; prof., head divsn. accountancy and legal environment Marshall U., 2000—09, Elizabeth McDowell Lewis endowed chair Lewis Coll. Bus., 2000—09, prof., 2005—09; prof. acctg., dean, Gary E. West Coll. Bus. West Liberty U., 2009—13; prof. Bharatiya Vidya Bhavan, Bangalore, India, 2005, 2006. Founder, pres. W.Va. Acctg. Educators, 2003—05; dean Coll. Bus., West Liberty U., W.Va., Gary E. West Coll. Bus. Contbr. articles to profl. publs. Named W.Va. Outstanding Acctg. Educator of Yr., W.Va. Soc. CPAs, 2004. Office: Main Hall LSC 123 West Liberty WV 26074 Personal E-mail: loren.wenzel@gmail.com.

WERBNER, MARK S., lawyer; b. San Antonio, Oct. 8, 1954; BA with high honors, U. Tex., Austin, 1975; JD cum laude, So. Meth. U., Dallas, 1978. Bar: Tex. 1978, US Dist. Ct. (all dists. Tex.) 1978, US Ct. Appeals (5th cir.) 1978, US Supreme Ct. Atty. Carrington, Coleman, Sloman & Blumenthal, Dallas; founder, ptnr. Sayles Werbner, P.C., Dallas, 1994—. Named one of Best Lawyers in Dallas, D Mag., 2001, 2003, 2005, 2007, The Nation's Top Litigators, The Nat. Law Jour., 2001, 2007. Master: Patrick E. Higginbotham Inn Ct.; fellow: Internat. Soc. Barristers, Am. Coll. Trial Lawyers; mem.: Dallas Bar Assn. (bd. dir. 2003), Am. Bd. Trial Lawyers. Office: Sayles Werbner PC 4400 Renaissance Tower 1201 Elm Street Dallas TX 75270 Office Phone: 214-939-8711. Office Fax: 214-939-8787. E-mail: mwerbner@swtriallaw.com.

WERLE, ROBERT GEARY, academic administrator; b. Washington, Mar. 28, 1944; s. Francis Bernard and Evelyn Mae (Case) W. BA, Christian Bros. Coll., 1970; MEd, U. Toronto, Ont., Can., 1976. Cert. Ednl. Adminstr. Tchr. La Salle H.S., Cin., 1970-73; tchr., adminstr. Roncalli H.S., Omaha, 1973-77; asst. prin. O'Hara H.S., Kansas City, Mo., 1977-79; dir. Stritch Retreat Ctr., Memphis, 1979-82; vocation dir. La Salle Inst., St. Louis, 1982-84; admissions counselor Christian Bros. U., Memphis, 1984-85, dir. campus ministry, 1985-86, dir. campus activities, 1986-91, assoc. dir. Stritch Conf. Ctr., 1991-94; archives and exhbn. cons., 1995—. Archivist Christian Bros. U., C.B. Midwest Dist.; curator of art Christian Bros.; archival cons. Mem. Soc. Am. Archivists, Religious Archives Assn., De La Salle Regional Archivist Assn. (founder, chair USA-Toronto region 1989—), Art Today (sec. 1997-98, treas. 1998-2000, membership chair 2000-01, archives cons. 1995—), Memphis/Shelby Urban Art Commn., Pi Kappa Phi (adv. 1986-89, 94-96, Founder's Svc. award 1989, Alumni award 1995), Memphis in May Archives Com. (Founders award 1994), Records Mgr. Assn. Democrat. Roman Catholic. Avocations: reading, graphic design, writing. Office: Christian Bros Univ O Donnell Archives 2455 Avery Ave Memphis TN 38112-4824 Office Phone: 901-321-3243. Business E-Mail: rwerle@cbu.edu.

WERLEIN, EWING, JR., federal judge; b. Houston, Sept. 14, 1936; s. Ewing and Ruth (Storey) W.; m. Kay McGibbon Werlein, June 29, 1963; children: Ewing Kenneth, Emily Kay. BA, Southern Meth. U., 1958; LLB, U. Tex., 1961. Bar: Tex. 1961, US Dist. Ct. (so. dist.) Tex. 1965, US Dist. Ct. (ea. dist.) Tex. 1990, US Ct. Appeals (5th cir.) 1970, US Ct. Appeals (10th cir.) 1980, US Claims Ct. 1985, US Tax Ct. 1985, US Supreme Ct. 1983. Ptnr. Vinson & Elkins, Houston, 1964-92; judge US Dist. Ct. (so. dist.) Tex., 1992—2006, sr. judge, 2006—. Trustee So. Meth. U., Dallas, 1976-92, Asbury Theol. Sem., Wilmore, Ky., 1989—; mem. gen. bd. pub. United Meth. Ch., Nashville, 1974-84, chmn., 1980-84, chancellor Tex. ann. conf., 1977-2004; mem. exec. com. World Meth. Coun., 1981-96, treas., 1991-93; mem. bd. dirs. The Meth. Hosp., 1990-, chmn. 2007-. Capt. USAF, 1961-64. Fellow Am. Coll. Trial Lawyers, 1984, Internat. Soc. Barristers, 1987; recipient Disting. Alumni award SMU Alumni Assn., 1994; Samuel Passarra Outstanding Jurist award, 2011 Fellow Am. Bar Found., Tex. Bar Found., Houston Bar Found.; mem. State Bar Tex. (dir. 1990-93), Nat. Conf. Bar Pres., Houston Bar Assn. (pres. 1988-89), Houston C. of C. (life), SAR, Order of Coif, Petroleum Club, Houston Club, Phi Beta Kappa. Office: US District Court Texas US Courthouse 515 Rusk Ave Ste 11521 Houston TX 77002-2605

WERNER, DAWN HETERICK, elementary school educator; b. Va. BA in Office Adminstrn., Va. Intermont Coll; MA in Edn., Eastern Tenn. State U., PhD in Edn., 2005. Worked in banking; Title I tchr., parent involvement coord., corrective reading dir. Fairmount Elem. Sch., Bristol, Tenn. Recipient E. Tenn. E. Grand Divsn. Tchr. of Yr., 2005; named Tenn. Tchr. of Yr., 2006. Office: Fairmount Elem Sch 500 Cypress St Bristol TN 37620 Business E-Mail: wernerd@btcs.org.

WERNER, ROBERT JOSEPH, dean, music educator; b. Lackawanna, NY, Feb. 13, 1932; s. Edward Joseph and Marian L. (Gerringer) W.; m. Sharon Lynne Mohrfeld, June 22, 1957; children: Mark J., Kurt M., Erik J. BME, Northwestern U., 1953, MusM, 1954, PhD, 1967. Dir. instrumental music Evanston (Ill.) Twp. H.S., 1956-66; assoc. prof. mus. Harpur Coll. SUNY, Binghamton, 1966-68, dir. Contemporary Music Project, 1968-73; dir. Sch. Mus. U. Ariz., Tucson, 1973-85, dean fine arts, 1981-82; dean Coll.-Conservatory of Music U. Cin., 1985-2000, dean emeritus, 2000—. Editor: Comprehensive Musicianship: An Anthology of Evolving Thought, 1971; author, editor: Musical Chairs: A Handbook for Music Executives in Higher Education, 2006; contbtr. articles to profl. internat. and nat. jours. Mem. exec. bd. Tucson Symphony Orch., 1974-85; bd. dirs. Cultural Commn. Tucson, 1974-75, Cin. Symphony Orch., 1985-2000, Cin. Opera, 1985-2000, Cin. Ballet, 1985-2000, Roanoke Symphony Orchestra, 2010-; mem. artistic directorate Am. Classical Music Hall of Fame; v.p., pres. bd. dirs. The Coll. Music Soc. Fund, 2002-08, pres., 2000-08. With U.S. Army, 1954-56. Mem. Nat. Assn. Schs. Music (pres. 1989-91), Coll. Music Soc. (pres. 1977-78), Internat. Soc. for Music Edn. (pres. 1984-86, treas. 1986-97), Music Educators Nat. Conf., McDowell Soc., Psi Upsilon, Phi Mu Alpha Sinfonia, Sigma Alpha Iota, Mu Phi Epsilon. E-mail: wernerrj@uc.edu.

WERTHER, WILLIAM B., JR., finance educator, consultant; b. NYC, Apr. 11, 1947; s. William B. Werther Sr. and Thea C. Werther; 1 child, William B. III. BA, U. Fla., Gainesville, 1968, BS, MA, 1969, PhD, 1971. Cert. arbitrator Am. Arbitration Assn., FMCS, 1976. Prof. Ariz. State U., Tempe, 1971—85, U. Miami, Coral Gables, 1985—; advisor Werther and Assocs., Miami, 1971—. Author: (book) Labor Rels. in the Health Professions (Book of Yr. award, 1976), Strategic Corporate Social Responsibility. Dir. Ctr. Nonprofit Mgmt., Coral Gables, Fla., 1997—. NDEA Title IV fellow, US Dept. Edn., 1968—71. Fellow: Internat. Soc. Productivity and Quality Rsch. (pres. 1998—99). Avocations: sailing, travel, writing. Office: Univ Miami 414 Jenkins Bldg Miami FL 33124 Office Fax: 305-284-3655.

WESELIN, MARY LOU, interior designer; b. Salem, Ohio, Nov. 15, 1946; d. Andrew Herbert and Wilma Gertrude (Bauman) Herbert Berry; m. Robert Pross, May 29, 1966 (div. 1978); m. Dietmar Weselin, Apr. 27, 1979; 1 child, Adrian. Cert., N.Y. Sch. Interior Design, NYC, 1968. Self-employed interior designer, Jamaica Estates, N.Y., 1968-78; prin. Mary Lou Weselin, Interior Design, Fredericksburg, Va., 1981—. Designer mag. cover Better Homes & Gardens, Decorating, 1986, Fredericksburg Decorator's Showhouse, 1997; mag. articles Decorating, 1986-87, Window & Wall Ideas, 1989; books: In Fredericksburg, 1984, Expression of Style, 1990. Co-chair fundraising Rappahannock Hospice-In-Motion, Fredericksburg, 1987, chairperson benefit, 1990; co-chair benefit auction Mary Washington Hosp., Fredericksburg, 1989; co-chmn. entertainment Fredericksburg Polo Classic, 1997; bd. dir. Mary Washington Hosp. Found., 1989-92, Fredericksburg Festival of Arts, 1996-2005, regent George Wash. Found., 2011-. Lutheran. Avocations: travel, cooking, entertaining, sailing, reading. Home and Office: 212 Lake Shore Dr Fredericksburg VA 22405

WESLEY, DAVID, professional basketball coach, retired professional basketball player; b. San Antonio, Tex., Nov. 14, 1970; Attended, Temple Coll., Tex., Baylor U., Waco, Tex. Guard NJ Nets, 1993—94, Boston Celtics, 1994—97, Charlotte/New Orleans Hornets, 1997—2004, Houston Rockets, 2004—06, Cleve. Cavaliers, 2006—07; asst. coach Tex. Legends, NBA Devel. League, 2010—. Host youth basketball camp, 1998. Avocations: bowling, golf, playing video games. Office: Texas Legends 2601 Avenue of the Stars Ste 300 Frisco TX 75034

WESLEY, GLEN, retired professional hockey player; b. Red Deer, Alta., Can., Oct. 2, 1968; m. Barb Wesley; children: Amanda, Josh, Matthew. Defenseman Boston Bruins, 1987—94, Hartford Whalers,

1994—97, Carolina Hurricanes, 1997—2003, 2003—08, Toronto Maple Leafs, 2003; dir. defenseman devel. Carolina Hurricanes, 2008—. Player NHL All-Star Game, 1989. Achievements include being a member of Stanley Cup Champion Carolina Hurricanes, 2006. Office: Carolina Hurricanes RBC Ctr 1400 Edwards Mill Rd Raleigh NC 27607

WESSELHOFT, PAUL, state legislator; b. Okla. City, Aug. 16, 1947; s. Billy J. and Virgie Trumbly Wesselhoft; m. Judy Albright; children: Justin, Holly. BA, Univ. Ctrl. Okla., 1972; MA in Religion, So. Nazarene Univ., 1976; MA, MDiv, Gordon-Conwell Theol. Sem., 1979. Ordained Southern Baptist Minister; pastor Community Chapel, Vincenza, Italy; state coordinator of Okla. abstinence sex edn. for teens Okla. Health Dept.; mem. Dist. 54 Okla. House of Representatives, 2005—. Served from pvt. to maj. as Airborne Ranger chaplain US Army, served front line combat liberating Kuwait in the first Persian Gulf War. Decorated Nat. Def. medal, Army Commendation medal with third oak leaf cluster, Meritorious Svc. medal with third oak leaf cluster, Good Conduct medal, St. Barbara Artillery medal, Armed Forces Reserve medal, Southwest Asia Svc. medal. Republican. Baptist. Mailing: 1105 NE 29th St Oklahoma City OK 73160 Office: 2300 N Lincoln Blvd Rm 332 Oklahoma City OK 73105 Office Phone: 405-557-7343. Business E-Mail: paulwesselhoft@okhouse.gov.

WESSELMANN, GLENN ALLEN, retired health facility administrator; b. Cleve., Mar. 21, 1932; s. Roy Arthur and Dorothy (Oakes) W.; m. Genevieve De Witt, Sept. 6, 1958; children: Debbie, Scott, Janet. AB, Dartmouth, 1954; MBA with distinction, Cornell U., 1959. Research aide Cornell U., Ithaca, NY, 1958-59; adminstrv. resident Meml. Hosp., NYC, 1957-58, adminstrv. asst., 1959-61, asst. adminstr., 1961-65, asst. v.p., 1965-68; v.p. for adminstrn. Meml. Hosp. for Cancer and Allied Diseases, NYC, 1968-79; exec. v.p., chief operating officer St. John Hosp., Detroit, 1979-84; pres., CEO St. John Health System, 1984-95, vice chmn., 1995-97; chmn., pres., CEO St. John Hosp. & Med. Ctr., 1984-94, ret., 1995. Mem. bus. adv. bd. City of Detroit, 1991-95, chmn., 1993-94; mem. exec. com. Greater Detroit Area Health Coun.; bd. dirs. Caymich Ins. Co. Ltd., Mich. Health Care Alliance, SelectCare, Detroit Econ. Growth Corp. Trustee Sisters of St. Joseph Health System 1981-94, Sisters of St. Joseph Health Svc., 1983-95, St. John Hosp. and Med. Ctr., 1979-95, St. John Health System, 1984-95, The Oxford Inst., 1984-95, Eastwood Clinics, 1992-95; pres. Providence Ch. Corp., Hilton Head Island, S.C., chmn. ch. fin. ocm., corp. pres. session; mem. bus. adv. bd.! City of Detroit, 1991-95, chmn. 1993-94. Served with MC AUS, 1955-57. Fellow ACHE; mem. Am. Hosp. Assn., Internat. Hosp. Fedn., Mich. Hosp. Assn. (trustee, chmn. 1994-95, mem. exec. com.), Assn. Am. Med. Colls. (Coth rep.), Am. Cancer Soc. (regional adv. bd. 1994-95), Med. Group Mgmt. Assn., Soc. Health Service Adminstrs., Sigma Phi Epsilon. Home: 63 Big Woods Dr Hilton Head Island SC 29926-2604 Personal E-mail: glengen@hargray.com.

WEST, ALLEN BERNARD, former United States Representative from Florida, retired military officer; b. Atlanta, Feb. 7, 1961; m. Angela West; children: Aubrey, Austen. BS in Polit. Sci., U. Tenn., Knoxville, 1983; MS in Polit. Sci., Kansas State U., Manhattan, 1996; MS in Polit. Theory/ Mil. Hist. and Ops., US Command & Gen. Staff Officer Coll., Ft. Leavenworth, Kans., 1997. Served in US Army, 1982—2004, ret. as lt. col., 2004; tchr., track coach Deerfield Beach HS, Fla., 2004—05; sr. support adv. US Ctrl. Command (USCENTCOM), 2005—07; sr. analyst, chief ops. planner US Army Installation Mgmt. Command, 2007—09; mem. US Congress from 22nd Fla. Dist., Washington, 2011—13, US House Armed Services Com., Washington, 2011—13, US House Small Bus. Com., Washington, 2011—13; dir. programming Next Generation Today, 2013; founder Allen West Found.; contributor FOX News Channel, 2013—. Decorated Bronze Star, 3 Meritorious Svc. medals, 3 Army Commendation medals, Valorous Unit award US Army; named Instr. of Yr., US Army ROTC, 1993. Republican. Christian.*

WEST, BOB, pharmaceutical executive; b. Ellenville, NY, Mar. 7, 1931; s. Harry and Elsie May Wicentowsky; m. Betty Parker, May 9, 1957 (div.); children: Debra Ellen, Elizabeth Ann, Sharon Lynn; m. Jacqueline Cutler, Jan. 3, 1982. BS, Union U., 1952; MS, Purdue U., 1954, PhD, 1956; postgrad. mgmt. seminar, U. Chgo., 1972. Pres., dir. research Food, Drug, Chem. Svcs., Stamford, Conn., 1975—; pres., dir. research Bob West Assocs., Inc., Stamford, 1975—. Pres. Drug Info. Assn., Phila., 1974-75; sci. adv. bd. Fountain Pharms., Inc., Largo, Fla., 1993—, Dovetail Techs., Inc., College Park, Md., 1996—, Phytopede, Inc., Sarasota, Fla., 1999—. Mem. editl. bd. Drug Info. Assn. Jour., Phila., 1977-85; contbr. articles to profl. jours. Mem. ASPET, Soc. Toxicology, Acad. Pharm. Scis., Assn. Rsch. Dirs., Drug Info. Assn., Assn. Univ. Tech. Mgrs. Home and Office: Food Drug Chem Svcs 7925 Meadow Rush Loop Sarasota FL 34238-4319 Office Phone: 941-925-8958. Personal E-mail: bjwest22@verizon.net.

WEST, LEE ROY, federal judge; b. Clayton, Okla., Nov. 26, 1929; s. Calvin and Nicie (Hill) W.; m. MaryAnn Ellis, Aug. 29, 1952; children: Kimberly Ellis, Jennifer Lee. BA, U. Okla., 1952, JD, 1956; LL.M. (Ford Found. fellow), Harvard U., 1963. Bar: Okla. 1956. Individual practice law, Ada, Okla., 1956-61, 63-65; faculty U. Okla. Coll. Law, 1961-62; Ford Found. fellow in law teaching Harvard U., Cambridge, Mass., 1962-63; judge 22d Jud. Dist. Okla., Ada, 1965-73; mem. CAB, Washington, 1973-78, acting chmn., 1977; practice law Tulsa, 1978-79; spl. justice Okla. Supreme Ct., 1965; judge US Dist. Ct. (we. dist.) Okla., 1979—93, chief judge, 1993—94, sr. judge Okla., 1994—. Editor: Okla. Law Rev. Served to capt. USMC, 1952-54. Named to Field Trial Hall of Fame, 2005; recipient Humanitarian award Nat. Conf. Cmty. and Justice, 2000, Jud. Excellence award Okla. Bar Assn., 2000, E.T. Dunlap medal and Lectureship award, 2006, Constn. Day award Rogers State U., 2006, Jour. Record award, Okla. County Bar Assn. and Jour. Record, 2010. Mem. U. Okla. Alumni Assn. (dir.), Phi Delta Phi (pres. 1956), Phi Eta Sigma, Order of Coif. Home: 6500 E Danforth Rd Edmond OK 73034-7601 Office: US Dist Ct 3001 US Courthouse 200 NW 4th St Oklahoma City OK 73102-3027 Office Phone: 405-609-5140. Business E-Mail: judgeleerwest@okwd.uscourts.gov.

WEST, REXFORD LEON, retired bank executive; b. Syracuse, NY, Feb. 18, 1938; s. Rexford A. and Nina (Crysler) W.; children: Lisa, Julie, Gregory, Kristen AAS, Auburn C.C., NY, 1957; BS magna cum laude, Syracuse U., NY, 1972; Advanced Mgmt. Program, Harvard Bus. Sch., Boston, 1984. Accountant Marine Midland Bank, Syracuse, NY, 1959-67, v.p., asst. treas., 1967-72; v.p., contr. Marine Midland Services Corp., Buffalo, 1972-76; v.p. ops. divsn. Marine Midland Bank, N.A., Buffalo, 1976-77, sr. v.p., sr. ops. officer, 1977-79, exec. v.p., sr. ops. officer, 1979-85, divsn. exec. ops., 1985-87, sector exec. ops. and fin. mgmt., 1987-90, sr. exec. v.p. corp. engring., 1990-92; exec. v.p. adminstrv. svc. Fleet Bank, Melville, NY, 1992-94; exec. v.p. loan servicing Fleet Mortgage Group, Columbia, SC, 1994-96; ret., 1996. Served with U.S. Army, 1957-61

WEST, ROGER, state legislator; Contractor; former state rep. Dist. 53 NC; state rep. Dist. 120 NC, 2003—. Mem. Appropriations com., Appropriations Subcom. on Natural and Econ. Resources, Environ. and Natural Resources com., Fed. Rels. and Indian Affairs com., House Select Com. on High Speed Internet Access in Rural and Urban Areas, House Select Com. on Small Bus., House Select Com. on Use of 911 Funds, Judiciary I com.; vice chmn. Wildlife Resources com. With USN, 1968—70. Republican. Office: North Carolina House of Representatives 16 W Jones St Rm 1229 Raleigh NC 27601-1096 Home Phone: 828-837-5246; Office Phone: 919-733-5859. E-mail: Roger.West@ncleg.net.

WEST, ROYCE, state legislator; b. Sept. 26, 1952; m. Carol R. West. BA, MA, U. Tex., Arlington; JD, U. Houston. Former ptnr. Robinson, West & Gooden, PC; mng. ptnr. West & Associates, LLP; mem. Dist. 23 Tex. State Senate, 1993—. Recipient Exceptional Cmty. Involvement award, Holyland Found., Tex. Hero award, NAACP, Valued Cmty. Svc. award, Oak Cliff Devel. Corp., Nat Alumni award, Prairie View A&M U., Appreciation award, Lancaster Kiest Neighborhood Assn., Black Dance Theater, Environ. Justice award, Sierra Club, Cmty Svc. award, Dallas Black C. of C., and several others. Democrat. Baptist. Office: 5787 S Hampton Rd Ste 385 Dallas TX 75232 also: Tex State Senate Capitol Sta PO Box 12068 Austin TX 78711 Office Phone: 214-467-0123, 512-463-0123. Office Fax: 214-467-0050, 512-463-0299.

WEST, TERESA (TERRI) L. (TERRI WEST), electronics executive; BA in Journalism, U. North Tex., 1982. Student intern Texas Instruments, Inc., 1978, mgr. media rels., v.p., mgr. strategic comm., sr. v.p. comm. and investor rels. Dallas. Dir. Dallas Pub. Broadcasting Sys. affiliate, KERA-TV; mem. Nat. Investor Rels. Inst. and Conf. Bd.; founding mem. Women of Tex. Instruments Fund; v.p. Tex. Instruments Found.; chair comm. com. (during renewal of US-Japan Semiconductor Trade Arrangement) Semiconductor Industry Assn., 1992, 1996. Mem. chancellor's leadership coun. U. North Tex. Office: Tex Instruments Inc PO Box 660199 Dallas TX 75266-0199 Office Phone: 972-995-2011, 972-995-4360.

WESTBROOK, JAY LAWRENCE, law educator; b. Morristown, NJ, Dec. 11, 1943; s. Joel W. and Elaine Frances (Summers) W.; m. Pauline June Travis, Feb. 15, 1969; 1 child, Joel Mastin. BA in Polit. Sci./Philosophy, U. Tex., 1965, JD, 1968. Bar: Tex. 1968, DC 1969, US Ct. Appeals (DC cir.) 1969, US Supreme Ct. 1976, US Ct. Appeals (4th cir.) 1978, US Ct. Appeals (2d cir.) 1979. Assoc. Surrey & Morse (now Jones, Day, Reavis & Pogue), Washington, 1969-74; ptnr. Surrey & Morse (now Jones, Day & Reavis), Washington, 1974-80; mem. law faculty U. Tex., Austin, 1980—, Benno C. Schmidt Chair Bus. Law, 1991—. Vis. prof. U. London, 1990, Harvard Law Sch., 1991-92; advisor Tex. Internat. Law Jour., 1985-91; reporter Am. Law Inst. Transnat. Insolvency Project, 1994-2000; co-leader US delegation to UN Commn. on Internat. Trade Law Working Group on Model Law Internat. Insolvency, 1995-97, 99; sr. advisor Nat. Bankruptcy Rev. Com., 1997; mem. State Dept. Adv. Com. on Pvt. Internat. Law, 1997-2000; vis. scholar Humboldt U., Berlin, 2002, 10. Co-author: As We Forgive Our Debtors: Bankruptcy and Consumer Credit in America, 1989 (Silver Gavel award ABA 1989), The Law of Debtors and Creditors: Text, Cases and Problems, 6th edit., 2009, Teacher's Manual, The Law of Debtors and Creditors, 6th edit., 2009, The Fragile Middle Class: Americans in Debt(Ann. Writing award Am. Coll. Consumer Fin. Svcs. Lawyers), 2000, A Global of of Business Insolvency Systems (Martinus Nijhoff 2010); contbr. articles to profl. jours. Grantee U. Tex. Law Sch. Found., 1982, U. Rsch. Inst., 1982-83, NSF, 1983-86, Policy Rsch. Inst., Lyndon Johnson Sch. Pub. Affairs, 1984, Tex. Bar Found., 1985, Nat. Inst. Child Health and Human Devel., 1986, Nat. Conf. Bankruptcy Judges, 1991, 93, Am. Coll. Banker, 2004. Mem. ABA (bus. bankruptcy com., vice chair internat. bankruptcy subcom. 1999—, Meyer rsch. grant 1986), Am. Law Inst., Am. Coll. Bankruptcy, Nat. Bankruptcy Conf., State Bar Tex. (governing coun. internat. sect. 1987-89), Internat. Insolvency Inst. (bd. dirs. 2000—), Internat. Acad. Comml. and Consumer Law (pres. 2008—10), Order of Coif. Office: U Tex Sch Law 727 E Dean Keeton St Austin TX 78705-3224

WESTBROOK, JIMI, singer; b. Ark., Oct. 20, 1971; m. Karen Fairchild, May 31, 2006; 1 child, Elijah Dylan. Co-founder Little Big Town, 1999. Singer: (albums) (with Little Big Town) Little Big Town, 2002, The Road to Here, 2005, A Place to Land, 2007, The Reason Why, 2010, Tornado, 2012, (songs) Pontoon, 2012 (Single of Yr., Country Music Assn. Awards, 2012, Best Country Duo/Group Performance, Grammy Awards, 2013), Tornado, 2012 (Video of Yr., Acad. Country Music Awards, 2013). Named Top New Duo/Vocal Group, Acad. Country Music Awards, 2012, Vocal Group of Yr., Country Music Assn. Awards, 2012, 2013, Acad. Country Music Awards, 2013. Office: c/o Sandbox Entertainment 54 Music Square East Suite 200 Nashville TN 37203*

WESTBROOK, RUSSELL, professional basketball player; b. Long Beach, Calif., Nov. 12, 1988; s. Russell Westbrook and Shannon Horton. Attended, UCLA, 2006—08. Guard Oklahoma City Thunder, 2008—. Mem US nat. team FIBA World Championships, Turkey, 2010, Summer Olympic Games, London, 2012. Recipient Gold medal, FIBA World Championship, 2010, Gold medal, men's basketball, Summer Olympic Games, 2012; named 1st Team All-Rookie, NBA, 2009; named to Western Conf. All-Star Team, 2011—13. Office: Oklahoma City Thunder 100 W Reno Rd Oklahoma City OK 73102

WESTEN, DREW, psychology professor; b. 1959; married; 2 children. BA, Harvard U.; MA in Social & Polit. Thought, U. Sussex, Eng.; PhD in Clin. Psychology, U. Mich. Tchr. U. Mich.; chief psychologist Cambridge Hosp., Mass.; assoc. prof. psychiatry Harvard Med. Sch.; rsch. assoc. prof. Boston U., psychologist, Ctr. Anxiety and Related Disorders; prof. Emory U., 2002—, dir. Lab. Personality and Psychopathology, prof. Dept. Psychology, prof. Dept. Psychiatry and Behavioral Sciences. Founder Westen Strategies, LLC; advised a range of candidates & organizations, from presdl. & congl. campaigns to major progressive organizations, to Fortune 500 companies. Performer: (albums) I'm a Professor: Songs for Mediocre Guitar and Inadequate Vocals, (songs) Oy, to be a Goy on Christmas; author: Self and Society: Narcissism, Collectivism, and the Development of Morals, The Political Brain: The Role of Emotion in Deciding the Fate of the Nation, 2007; co-author: Psychology, Study Guide, 2004; occassional commentator All Things Considered, Nat. Pub. Radio, 1998—; contbr. several articles to profl. jours.; author of several scholarly articles. Recipient Theodore Millon award, Am. Psychol. Found., 2004. Office: Emory U 308 Psychology Bldg 532 Kilgo Cir Atlanta GA 30322 Office Phone: 404-727-7407. Office Fax: 404-727-0372. E-mail: dwesten@emory.edu.

WESTENBERGER, RICHARD F., corporate financial executive; Attended, U. Chgo., U. Notre Dame. CPA. Sr. fin. analyst Kraft Foods, Inc.; sr. v.p., CFO Lands' End, Inc. (divsn. of Sears Holdings Corp.); sr. acct. Price Waterhouse LLP; various sr. fin. mgmt. positions, v.p., Corporate Planning & Analysis, v.p., Investor Rels. Sears Holdings Corp.; v.p., Corp. Fin., treas. Hewitt Associates, Inc., 2006—08; exec. v.p., CFO Carter's, Inc., 2009—. Office: Carter's Inc 1170 Peachtree St NE Ste 900 Atlanta GA 30309 Office Phone: 404-745-2700. Office Fax: 404-892-0968. Business E-Mail: richard.westenberger@carters.com.

WESTERHOFF, JOHN HENRY, III, priest, theologian, educator; b. Paterson, NJ, June 28, 1933; s. John Henry and Nona Celia (Walsh) W.; m. Alberta Louise Barnhart, Dec. 27, 1955 (div. 1991); children: Jill Louise, John Jeffrey, Beth Anne; m. Caroline Askew Hughes, Oct. 27, 1991. BS, Ursinus Coll., 1955; STB, Harvard U., 1958; EdD, Columbia U., 1974; DD, Ursinus Coll., 1990. Ordained to ministry United Ch. of Christ, 1958, Episcopal Ch., 1978; pastor Congl. Ch., Presque Isle, Maine, 1958-60, assoc. pastor Needham, Mass., 1960-64; pastor 1st Congl. Ch., Williamstown, Mass., 1964-66; edn. sec., editor Colloquy (United Ch. Bd. for Homeland Ministries), NYC, 1966-73; Lentz lectr. Harvard U. Div. Sch., 1973-74; prof. Duke U. Div. Sch., Durham, NC, 1974-94; dir. Inst. Pastoral Studies, Atlanta, 1992—2003; interim rector St. Bartholomew Episcopal Ch., Atlanta, 1993-94; theologian in residence St. Lukes Episcopal Ch., Atlanta, 1994—2004; vis. prof. Gen. Theol. Sem., NYC, 2004—05; priest assoc., resident theologian St. Anne's Episc. Ch., Atlanta, 2005—. Author: Values for Tomorrows Children, 1970, A Colloquy on Christian Education, 1972, Generation to Generation, 1974, Tomorrow's Church, 1976, Will Our Children Have Faith?, 1976, McGuffey and His Readers, 1978, Who Are We?, 1978, Learning Through Liturgy, 1978, Inner Growth-Outer Change, 1979, The Church's Ministry in Higher Education, 1979, Liturgy and Learning Through the Life Cycle, 1980, Christian Believing, 1980, Bringing Up Children in The Christian Church, 1980, A Faithful Church, 1981, The Spiritual Life: Learning East and West, 1981, Building God's People, 1983, A Pilgrim People, 1984, Living the Faith Community, 1985, On the Threshold of God's Future, 1986, Living Into Our Baptism, 1990, Schooling Christians, 1992, The Spiritual Life: Foundation for Preaching and Teaching, 1994; A People Called Episcopalians, 1995, Holy Baptism: A Guide for Parents and Godparents, 1996, Grateful and Generous Hearts, 1997, To Love and to Cherich Till Death Do Us Part, 1998, Sensing Beauty, 1998, A Pilgrim People, 1999, Will Our Children Have Faith?, 2000, Living Faithfully as a Prayer Book People, 2005; editor: Religious Edn, 1979-89. Mem. Assn. Profs. and Researchers in Religious Edn., Religious Edn. Assn. Democrat. Episcopalian. Personal E-mail: johnwest33@bellsouth.net.

WESTERLING, RICHARD (DICK), movie theater company executive; Formerly with AMC Entertainment, Inc.; sr. v.p. mktg. & advt. Regal Entertainment Group, 2000—. Office: Regal Entertainment Group Corp Hdqs 7132 Regal Ln Knoxville TN 37918 Office Phone: 865-922-1123. Business E-Mail: richard.westerling@regalcinemas.com. E-mail: dick.westerling@REGmovies.com.

WESTERMAN, BRUCE, state legislator; b. Hot Springs, Ark., Nov. 18, 1967; m. Sharon Westerman; children: Eli Westerman, Asa Westerman, Amie Westerman, Ethan Westerman. BS in Biol. & Agrl. Engring., U. Ark., 1990; MF, Yale U., 2001. Plant engr. Riceland Foods, 1990—92; engr., forester Mid-South Engring. Co., 1992—; mem. Dist. 30 Ark. House of Representatives, 2011—. Republican. Baptist. Office: PO Box 1399 Hot Springs AR 71902 Office Phone: 501-321-2276. Business E-Mail: bwforarkansas@hughes.net.

WESTERMANN, EDWARD BURTON, military officer, analyst, educator; b. Temple, Tex., Nov. 18, 1961; s. Francis X. and Suzann Westermann; m. Brigitte Angelika Engel, Dec. 16, 1991; children: Sarah E, Marie-Louise. BS, USAF Acad., 1984; MA in European History, Fla. State U., 1992; MA, Sch. Advanced Airpower Studies, Maxwell AFB, 1997; PhD in European History, U. N.C., 2000. Helicopter Pilot USAF, 1985. Commd. 2d lt. USAF, 1984, advanced through grades to col.; exch. instr. pilot with German air force Hubschraubertransportgeschwader 64, Ahlhorn, Germany, 1988—91; asst. prof. history U.S. Air Force Acad., Colorado Springs, 1992—95; strategy devel. officer Hdqs. European Command, Stuttgart, Germany, 2000—02; prof. comparative mil. theory Sch. Advance Air and Space Studies, Maxwell AFB, Ala., 2002—; sr. mil. prof. USAF Acad., 2006—08; comdr. USAF, Basic Mil. Training, 2008—; prof. hist Tex. A & M, San Antonio. Selected mem. internat. adv. panel Royal Air force Ctr. for Air Power Studies, 2007; apptd. disting. scholar Holocust Meml. Mus. San Antonio. Author: (historical work) Hitler's Police Battalions: Enforcing Racial War in the East, Flak: German Anti-Aircraft Defenses, 1918-1945. Decorated Ehrenkreuz der Bundeswehr in Bronze Fed. Rep. Germany; recipient John L. Snell prize, 1998, League of WWI Aviation Historians Nat. award, 1999; named Legion of Merit; fellow, German Academic Exch. Svc., U. Calif. Berkeley, 1993, Fulbright fellow, U.S. Govt., 1994—95, U.S. Holocaust Meml. Mus., 1999, German Academic Exch. Svc., 1999, 2003—04. Mem.: Soc. Mil. History (Mancado prize 2002), Am. Hist. Assn., German Studies Assn., Daedalians (life), Phi Alpha Theta. Independent. Roman Catholic. Office: Tex A & M University Dept History San Antonio TX 78236 Home: 1426 Summit Crk San Antonio TX 78258-1916 Personal E-mail: bawebw4@aol.com. Business E-Mail: edward.westermann@yahoo.com.

WESTFALL, LYNN D., oil industry executive; B in Chem. Engring., U. Tex.; MBA, U. Houston. Process engr. Amoco Chems. Corp., 1975; v.p. strategy and strategic issues Ultramar Diamond Shamrock, San Antonio; v.p. devel. and bus. analysis Tesoro Corp., San Antonio, 2002—05, v.p., chief economist, 2005—06, sr. v.p. external affairs, chief economist, 2006—. Office: Tesoro Corp 300 Concord Plz San Antonio TX 78216-6999 Office Phone: 210-283-2000.

WESTFIELD, FRED MEINHARD, economics professor; b. Essen, Germany, Nov. 7, 1926; came to U.S., 1940; s. Dietrich and Grete (Stern) W.; m. Joyce A. Horwitz Nochlin Westfield, Nov. 15, 1968; stepchildren: Steven Nochlin, Keith Nochlin. BA magna cum laude, Vanderbilt U., 1950; PhD in Indsl. Econs., MIT, 1957. Teaching asst., instr. MIT, Cambridge, 1952-53; lectr. Northwestern U., Evanston, Ill., 1953-57, asst. prof., 1957-60, assoc. prof., 1960-65; prof. econs. Vanderbilt U., Nashville, 1965-98, mem. faculty coun. Coll. Arts and Sci., 1974-76, mem. faculty senate, 1979-82, 94-95, dir. undergrad. studies dept. econs. and bus. adminstrn., 1984-87, mem. grad. faculty coun., 1991, prof. econs. emeritus, 1998—. Vis. prof. U. Colo., summers 1973-74; condr. seminars, lectr., participant univs. and rsch. orgns.; Fulbright sr. lectr. U. Nac. del Sur, Argentina, 1986; cons. Coun. Econ. Advisers, Exec. Office Pres., 1968, World Bank and Water and Power Devel. Authority, Pakistan, 1970-72, World Bank and East African Power and Light Co., Kenya, 1975, NSF, 1975, FTC, 1976-78, World Bank, UN Devel. Program and Econ. Planning Bd. South Korea, 1975-76; expert witness Tenn. Pub. Svc. Commn., 1980-89, Consumer Advocate Tenn. Atty. Gen., 1994; also others. Mem. editl. bd. Utilities Policy, 1990—2002, mem. bd. editors So. Econ. Jour., 1973—75, editl. referee Am. Econ. Rev., Jour. Polit. Economy, Econometrica, So. Econ. Jour., Econ. Inquiry; contbr. articles and book revs. to profl. jours. With US Army, 1945—46. Fellow Gen. Edn. Bd., MIT, Ford Found., 1958-59. Mem. Am. Econ. Assn., Econometric Soc. (program com. 1967, chmn. conf. sessions), So. Econ. Assn. (v.p. 1976-77, chmn. conf. sessions), Phi Beta Kappa. Home: 1097 Lynnwood Blvd Nashville TN 37215-4540

WESTHAUSER, KARL E., historian; b. NYC, July 27, 1961; s. Karl Edwin and Margaret Marie Westhauser. BA, Cornell U., 1983; MA, Brown U., 1985, PhD, 1994. Prof. history Ala. State U., Montgomery, Ala., 1993—. Cons. Montgomery City-County Pub. Schs., Ala., 2006. Editor: Creating Community, 2005; mem. editl. bd.: Griot: Jour.

African.-Am. Studies, 2005—. Docent Montgomery (Ala.) Mus. Fine Arts, 1996—2001. Mem.: So. Conf. African-American Studies, Am. Hist. Assn., Montgomery (Ala.) County Hist. Soc. Office: Campus Box 25 Alabama State U 915 S Jackson St Montgomery AL 36101 Home Phone: 334-265-9954; Office Phone: 334-229-4365.

WESTLING, JOHN T., retail executive; m. Donna Westling. With Nash Finch Co.; assoc. Wal-Mart Stores, Inc, 1988, dept. mgr., asst. mgr., asst. buyer, buyer, merchandise mgr., v.p. divisional merchandising mgr. household chemicals and papergoods, 1998—2001, sr. v.p. gen. merchandising mgr. consumables, 2001, sr. v.p. replenishment, pricing, & planning, now exec. v.p. replenishment, pricing, & planning. Bd. mem. Children's Miracle Network, Will Golf for Kids, 1st Tee, Global 20/20 program. Office: Wal-Mart Stores, Inc 702 SW 8th St Bentonville AR 72716-8611

WESTMAN, CARL EDWARD, lawyer; b. Youngstown, Ohio, Dec. 12, 1943; s. Carl H. and Mary Lillis (Powell) W.; m. Carolyn J., July 17, 1965; children: C. Forrest, Stephanie A. BBA, Sam Houston State U., 1966; JD, U. Miami, 1969, LLM in Taxation, 1972. Bar: Fla. 1969. Ptnr. Frost & Jacobs, 1983-93, Roetzel & Andress, 1993-98; adminstrv. ptnr. Steel, Hector & Davis, Naples, Fla., 1999—2004, Cohen & Grigsby, 2004—08, GaryRobinson, 2009—. Trustee David Lawrence Found. for Mental Health, Inc., 1976-86, chmn., 1985-86; trustee Pikeville Coll., 1993-2005; trustee, 1991, chmn. NCH Healthcare Sys. Inc., 2005-10; trustee, chmn. Naples Cmty. Hosp., 2001-10; past pres. bd. trustees, elder Moorings Presbyn. Ch.; bd. govs. Sr. Friendship Ctrs., 2011-; chmn., bd. dirs. Friendship Health Clinic, 2011-. Master lic. capt. USCG. Recipient Legacy award, Am. Red Cross, 2011; named Person of Yr., Estero C. of C., 2009. Mem.: Fla. Bar Assn. (Real Property, Probate & Trust Law Sect.), Collier County Bar Assn. (Trusts & Estates Sect.), Estate Planning Coun. Republican. Presbyterian. Home: 1952 Crayton Rd Naples FL 34102-5070 Office: GrayRobinson Pelican Bay Financial Ctr 8889 Pelican Bay Blvd Naples FL 34108 Office Phone: 239-598-3601 ext. 4801. Business E-Mail: carl.westman@gray-robinson.com.

WESTMORELAND, ANDREW, academic administrator; m. Jeanna Westmoreland; 1 child, Riley. BA, Ouachita Baptist U., 1979; MA in Polit. Sci., U. Ark., Fayetteville; PhD in Higher Edn. Adminstrn., U. Ark., Little Rock. With Ouachita Baptist U., 1979—2006, prof. polit. sci. and edn., exec. v.p., v.p. devel., pres., 1998—2006, Samford U., Birmingham, Ala., 2006—. Cons., evaluator Higher Learning Commn. Author: Leading by Design, 2005. Office: Samford University Office of President 800 Lakeshore Dr Birmingham AL 35229 Office Phone: 205-726-2727.*

WESTMORELAND, LYNN A., United States Representative from Georgia; b. Atlanta, Apr. 2, 1950; m. Joan Eskew; children: Heather, Marcy, Trae. Attended, Ga. State U. Mem. Ga. House of Reps., Atlanta, 1992—2004, US Congress from 8th Ga. Dist., 2005—07, US Congress from 3rd Ga. Dist., 2007—; dep. chmn. Nat. Republican Congressional Com. (NRCC), 2013—. Mem. Fayette Bd. Realtors, Ga., Nat. Bd. Realtors. Mem.: Midwest Ga. Homebuilders Assn. Republican. Baptist. Office: US House of Representatives 2433 Rayburn House Office Bldg Washington DC 20515-1008 also: 1601-B E Highway 34 Newnan GA 30265 Office Phone: 202-225-5901. Office Fax: 202-225-2515.*

WESTON, CHARLES HINTON, retired law educator; b. Americus, Ga., Feb. 23, 1946; AB, Mercer U., 1968; JD, Mercer U. Sch. Law, 1971. Adj. prof., GA criminal practice and procedure Sch. Law Mercer U., 1984—2000, sr. lectr., Coll. Liberal Arts, 2002—; chief asst. dist. atty., asst. dist. atty. Macon Jud. Cir., State of Ga., 1972—93, dist. atty., 1994—2000; dist. atty. emeritus State of Ga., 2001—03. Recipient Outstanding Svc. award, Pros. Attys. Coun. Ga., 1983, J. Roger Thompson Disting. Svc. award, 2000. Home: 861 Windsor Rd Macon GA 31204 Office Phone: 478-301-2410. Business E-Mail: weston_ch@mercer.edu.

WESTON, GEORGE W., plastic surgeon; b. Aug. 14, 1953; married. Attended, U. Ala., 1971—75, Samford U., 1975—77, U.South Ala., 1977—81. Diplomate Am. Bd. Plastic Surgery, 1990. Resident gen. surgery and plastic surgery Wake Forest Univ. Med. Ctr., 1981—86; fellow plastic surgery Charlotte Plastic Surgery Ctr., 1986, Univ. of Ala. Med. Ctr., 1986; hosp. appointment Fairfax Hosp.; joined Austin-Weston Ctr. for Cosmetic Surgery, 1987, pres. Invited panelist Aesthetic Surgery Jour., 1999; invited faculty perspectives and advances in plastic surgery, Vail, Colo., 2000, 2004; invited faculty Perioral Plastic Surgery Symposium, 2003, Australian Sci. and Math. Sch. Mid-Face Symposium, 2004; invited spkr. NC Soc. of Plastic Surgeons, 2006; invited panelist Am. Soc. of Aesthetic Plastic Surgery, 2006. Author: (publs.) Rejuvenating the Aging Mouth, 1993—2007. Named one of Top Plastic Surgeons, Washingtonian Mag., 1989, Am. Rsch. Coun., 2007—10, Northern Va. Mag., 2010. Mem.: Nat. Capital Soc. of Plastic Surgeons, Va. Soc. of Plastic Surgery, AMA, Am. Soc. of Plastic Surgeons. Office: Austin-Weston Center for Cosmetic Surgery 1825 Samuel Morse Dr Reston VA 20190 Office Phone: 703-893-6168.

WESTON, J. DAVID (DAVE WESTON), political organization administrator; m. Tyra Weston; children: Tanner, Savana, Sela. BS in agrl. econs., Okla. State U., 1990. Fin. dir. Okla. Rep. Party, Oklahoma City, 2005—06, chmn., 2013—; grassroots coord. Okla. Divsn. Huckabee's Army, 2007—08; with campaign mgmt. team Staff of Congressman James Lankford, 2009—10, Staff of Congressman Jim Bridenstine, 2011—12. At-large alt. del. Rep. Nat. Conv., 2008; mem. Emmanuel Bapt. Ch., Purcell, Okla. Republican. Office: Oklahoma Republican Party 4031 N Lincoln Blvd Oklahoma City OK 73105 Office Phone: 405-528-3501.

WESTPHAL, ROGER ALLEN, electrical engineer; b. Waterloo, Iowa, Feb. 17, 1946; s. Clifford Henry and Pauline Vere (Kleinow) Westphal; foster children: Puja-kumari Ram, Sudha Radh children: Deuwmi Sathsara, Iddamaldeniya. BSEE, U. Fla., 1981, MSEE, 1990. Registered profl. engr., Fla. Instrumentation technician Gen. Dynamics, Ft. Worth, 1966-68, Gen. Dynamics/Convair, Edwards AFB, Calif., 1968-72; electronics technician Lockheed Calif. Co., Burbank, Calif., 1973-74, field svc. rep., 1974-78; engring. technician engring. scis. dept. U. Fla., Gainesville, 1980-84, instr. elec. engring. dept., 1984-86, 90; engr. elec. utility Gainesville Regional Utilities, 1987—. Mem. Friends of Classic 89, Gainesville, Friends of Five, Gainesville; supporting mem. Smithsonian, Washington. With USN, 1968-71. Mem. IEEE, Am. Solar Energy Soc., Internat. Solar Energy Soc., Phi Kappa Phi, Eta Kappa Nu, Tau Beta Phi. Republican. Methodist. Avocations: carpentry, winemaking. Office: Gainesville Regl Utilities # A 132 PO Box 147117 Gainesville FL 32614-7117 Office Phone: 352-393-1289. Business E-Mail: westphalra@gru.net.

WESTROM, SUSAN, state legislator; b. May 15, 1952; BA, MA, U. Ky. Dir. advocacy & mktg. Buckhorn Children's Home; realtor Keller Williams; mem. Dist. 79 Ky. House of Reps., Ky., 1999—; chairwoman Ky. State Dem. Party, 2003—05. Mem.: Bluegrass ADD Regional Coun. (chair), Profl. Women's Forum, Leadership Ky. (chair 1995). Democrat. Baptist. Mailing: PO Box 22778 Lexington KY 40522-2778 Office: Capitol Annex Rm 352 702 Capitol Ave Frankfort KY 40601 Office Phone: 859-266-7581, 502-564-8100 ext. 740.

WESTWOOD, JACK (JACK WESTWOOD), state legislator; b. Covington, Ky., Mar. 6, 1944; m. Kelley Kay. BA, U. Ky., 1966; MEd, No. Ky. U., 1980. Former mem. Erlanger-Elsmere Bd. Edn.; state senator Dist.23 Ky., 1997—; mem. Edn. Com., Health & Welfare Com., Judiciary Com., Vet Affairs Com., Mil. Affairs & Pub. Safety Com., Ky. State Senate; hardware salesman. Mem. Erlanger-Elsmere Bd. Edn., 1995-96. Mem. Ky. Retired Tchrs. Assn., No. Ky. Retired Tchrs. Assn., Ky. Coun. Edn. Journalism, Erlanger-Elsmere Edn. Assn., Lloyd High Sch. Alumni Assn. Republican. Church Of Christ. Address: 36 Forest Ave Erlanger KY 41018 Office: Capitol Annex Rm 230 Frankfort KY 40601 Home: 209 Graves Ave Erlanger KY 41018-1616 Home Phone: 859-344-6154; Office Phone: 502-564-8100 ext 615. E-mail: jack.westwood@lrc.state.ky.us.

WETHERELL, THOMAS KENT, former academic administrator; b. Daytona Beach, Fla., Dec. 22, 1945; m. Virginia B. Wetherell; children: Kent, Blakely, Page. BS in Social Studies, Fla. State U., 1967, MS in Social Studies, 1968, PhD in Adminstrn., 1974. Pres. Wetherell Enterprises, Inc.; dir. housing and adminstrn., asst. v.p., asst. dean housing U. Ctrl. Fla.; assoc. prof. Bethune-Cookman Coll.; exec. asst. to pres. to dean of instrn. Daytona Beach CC, v.p., provost acad. and univ. transfer programs, dist. v.p., planning and devel.; pres. First Am. Mortgage and Investments, Inc., Tallahassee CC, 1975, Fla. State U., Tallahassee, 2003—09. Mem. Fla. Ho. of Reps., 1980-92, spkr. 1990-92, chair appropriations com., 1989-90, chair appropriations edn. com., 1986-88, chair higher edn. com., 1984-86, majority fl. leader, 1982-84, chair Volusia county legis. delegation, 1981-83, 86-87. Bd. dirs. Econ. Devel. Coun., ARC, Canaveral Nat. Seashore Park, Southern Scholarship Found., United Way. Mem. Tallahassee C. of C. (bd. dirs.), Lions, Kiwanis, Blue Lodge, Shriners, Bahia Temple. Office Phone: 850-644-1085. E-mail: wetherell@mailer.fsu.edu.

WETZEL, CARROLL ROBBINS, JR., manufacturing executive; b. Phila., June 10, 1943; s. Carroll and Phoebe Francine (Meade) W.; m. Berta C. Schreiber, Feb. 28, 1982; children: William, Evan. BA, Stanford U., 1965; MA, George Washington U., 1967, PhD, 1971. Asst. v.p. Phila. Nat. Bank, 1971-76; corp. fin. officer Dillon Read & Co., Inc., v.p., 1976-81; corp. fin. officer Smith Barney, mng. dir., 1981-88; mng. dir., head M&A Chem. Bank, 1988; co-head, Merger & Acquisition Group Chase Manhattan Bank, 1988—96; chmn. Safety Components Internat., Inc., 2000—05; vice chmn. Arch Wireless, 2001—02. Bd. dirs. Brinks Co., Exide Technologies, 2005—. Mem. exec. bd. Westchester and Putnam Counties area Boy Scouts Am., 1988—. Mem. Links Club, Larchmont Yacht Club. Office: Exide Technologies Bd Directors 13000 Deerfield Pky Bldg 200 Milton GA 30004 Office Phone: 678-566-9000. Office Fax: 678-566-9188. Business E-Mail: carroll.wetzel@exide.com.

WETZEL, KATHRYN C., mathematics and engineering professor; BS in Nuclear Engring., Tex. A&M U., College Station, 1979; ME, Tex. Tech U., Lubbock, 1990, PhD in Interdisciplinary Engring., 1995. Prof. math. and engring. Amarillo Coll., chair Dept. Math., Sciences and Engring., 2004—. Author: (nonfiction) Mind Games The Aging Brain and How to Keep It Healthy, 1999. Recipient John F. Mead Award, 2002, Phi Theta Kappa Apple Award, 2005, Educator of Yr. Award, Tex. Alliance for Minorities in Engring. (Amarillo Chapter), 2010, Outstanding Cmty. Colleges Prof. of Yr. award, Carnegie Found. for Advancement of Tchg. & the Coun. for the Advancement & Support of Edn., 2011, Minnie Stevens Piper Prof. State Award, 2007. Office: Amarillo College Engineering 214 2201 S Washington St Amarillo TX 79109 Office Phone: 806-371-5097. E-mail: wetzel-kc@actx.edu.

WEXLER, DAVID B., law educator; b. NYC, Apr. 4, 1941; s. Irving Wexler and Lillian Heiden; m. Ghislaine Laraque, Nov. 13, 2004; children: Nancy, Douglas. BA, Binghamton U., NY, 1961; JD, NYU, NY, 1964. Atty., criminal divsn. US Dept. Justice, Washington, 1965—67; disting. rsch. prof. law and psychology U. Ariz., Tucson, 1967—2007. Dir. Internat. Network Therapeutic Jurisprudence, San Juan, 1997—; prof. law U. PR, San Juan, 1997—; disting. rsch. prof. law U. Ariz., Tuscon, 2007—; cons. in field. Author: Mental Health Law: Major Issues, 1981, Essays in Therapeutic Jurisprudence, 1991; author: (editor) Therapeutic Jurisprudence: The Law as a Therapeutic Agent, 1990, Law in a Therapeutic Key, 1996, Practicing Therapeutic Jurisprudence: Law as a Helping Profession, 2000, Judging in a Therapeutic Key: Therapeutic Jurisprudence and the Courts, 2003, Rehabilitating Lawyers: Principles of Therapeutic Jurisprudence for Criminal Law Practice, 2008. Mem. legal task panel Pres.'s Commn. Mental Health, Washington, 1977—88; mem. rsch. network mental health and law MacArthur Found., Chco., 1987—97. Recipient Guttmacher Forensic Psychiatry award, Am. Psychiat. Assn., 1972, Outstanding Svc. award, Nat. Assn. for Mental Health, 1974, Creative Tchg. award, U. Ariz. Pres.'s Club, 1975, Disting. Tchg. Scholarship award, NYU Sch. Law, 1989, Disting. Svc. award, Nat. Ctr. State Cts., 2000; fellow, Fulbright Found., Australia, 2002. Mem.: Iberoam. Assn. Therapeutic Jurisprudence (hon. pres. 2012), Am. Psychology-Law Soc. (disting.). Achievements include development of the field of therapeutic jurisprudence. Office: PO Box 23349 San Juan PR 00931-3349 Personal E-mail: davidbwexler@yahoo.com.

WHALEN, ANDREW P., political organization administrator, former legislative staff member; BA in History, Denison U., Granville, Ohio, 2003. Comm. dir. Jon Jennings for Congress, 2003—04; campaign mgr. David Cox for Va. House of Delegates, 2005—06, John Montgomery for Va. House of Delegates, 2005—06; comm. dir. and dep. campaign mgr. Heath Shuler for Congress, 2006, campaign mgr., 2008; comm. dir. to Rep. Heath Shuler US House of Representatives, 2007—08; exec. dir. NC Democratic Party, 2009—. Democrat. Office: North Carolina Democratic Party PO Box 1926 Raleigh NC 27602-1926 Office Phone: 919-821-2777 218. E-mail: awhalen@ncdemocraticparty.org.

WHALEN, JAMES W., energy executive; BS in Fin., U. Ill.; M in Fin., St. Louis U. Sr. v.p., fin. Coastal Corp., 1981—92; CFO Tejas Gas Corp., 1992—98; chief comml. officer Coral Energy, 1998—2000; CFO Diversified Diagnostic Products, Inc, 2002; sr. v.p., CFO Parker Drilling Co., 2002—05, bd. dirs., Targa Resources Partners, LP, 2004—, pres. fin. & adminstrn., 2005—10, exec. chmn., 2010—11, advisor to the chmn. and CEO, 2012—. Bd. dirs. Equitable Resources, Inc. Office: Targa Resources Partners LP 1000 Louisiana St Ste 4300 Houston TX 77002 Office Phone: 713-584-1000. Office Fax: 713-584-1100. Business E-Mail: JWhalen@targaresources.com.

WHALEY, STEVEN P., retail executive; BBA, U. Okla., Norman, 1981. CPA 1985. Assoc. KPMG; v.p., controller Southwest Airlines Co., 2001—05; v.p., asst. controller Wal-Mart Stores, Inc., Bentonville, Ark., 2005—06, v.p., controller, 2006—07, sr. v.p., controller, prin. acctg. officer, 2007—. Mem.: Fin. Execs. Internat., Am. Inst. Cert. Pub. Accts. Office: Wal-Mart Stores Inc 702 SW 8th St Bentonville AR 72716-8611

WHAN, MICHAEL, Ladies Professional Golf Association commissioner, former apparel executive; b. Feb. 10, 1965; m. Meg Whan; children: Austin, Wesley, Connor. B, Miami U., Ohio, 1987. Brand asst., brand mgr., dir. mktg. Oral Care Proctor & Gamble Co., 1987—94; v.p., gen. mgr. Wilson Sporting Goods Co., 1994—95; v.p. mktg., v.p. sales and mktg. TaylorMade Golf Co., 1995—96, exec. v.p. & gen. mgr. N.Am. TaylorMade-Adidas Golf, 1996—99; pres., chief mktg. officer Britesmile, Inc., 1999—2002; CEO Mission Hockey, 2002—04; pres., CEO Mission ITECH Hockey, 2004—09; commr. LPGA, 2010—. Bd. dirs. World Golf Found., 2010—, LPGA, 2010—. Office: LPGA 100 Internat Golf Dr Daytona Beach FL 32124-1092 Office Phone: 386-274-6200. Office Fax: 386-274-1099.

WHARTON, A.C., JR., mayor, Memphis, Tennessee; b. Lebanon, Tenn. m. Ruby Wharton; 6 children. B in Polit. Sci., Tenn. State U., Nashville, 1966; JD, U. Miss., 1971. Adj. prof. law U. Miss.; ptnr. Wharton & Wharton & Assocs.; atty. Lawyer's Com. for Civil Rights under Law; investigator Equal Opportunity Employment Commn., Washington; chief pub. defender Shelby County, mayor, 2002—09, City of Memphis, 2009—. Office: City Hall 125 N Main St Rm 700 Memphis TN 38103 Office Phone: 901-576-6000. Business E-Mail: mayor@memphistn.gov.*

WHATLEY, JACQUELINE BELTRAM, lawyer; b. West Orange, NJ, Sept. 26, 1944; d. Quirino and Eliane (Gruet) Beltram; m. John W. Whatley, June 25, 1966 (dec. July 1998). BA, U. Tampa, 1966; JD, Stetson U., 1969. Bar: Fla. 1969, Alaska 1971, cert.: (real estate law specialist). Assoc. Tucker, McEwen, Smith & Cofer, Tampa, Fla., 1969-71; pvt. practice Anchorage, Alaska, 1971-73; ptnr. Gibbons, Tucker, Miller, Whatley & Stein, P.A., Tampa, 1973—; pres., 1981—. Bd. dirs. Travelers Aid Soc., 1982-94; trustee Humana Women's Hosp., Tampa, 1987-93, Keystone United Meth. Ch., 1986-89, 99—. Mem. ABA, Fla. Bar Assn. (real estate cert. com. 1993-95), Alaska Bar Assn., Tenn. Walking Horse Breeders and Exhibitors Assn. (v.p. 1984-87, dir. Fla. 1981-87, 90-93, 97-99, adv. com. Tenn. Walking Horse Celebrateion 1994-97), Fla. Walking and Racking Horse Assn. (bd. dirs. 1988-89, pres. 1980-82), Athena Soc. Republican. Methodist. Office: 8108 Old Hixon Rd Ste 101 Tampa FL 33626 Home: 9006 Hixon Rd Tampa FL 33626 Office Phone: 813-228-7841.

WHATLEY, TOM, state legislator; b. Lee County, Ala. BA in Pub. Adminstrn., Auburn U., Ala., 1994; JD, Faulkner U., Montgomery, Ala., 1998. Chief staff to the chief justice Ala. Supreme Ct.; pvt. practice atty.; mem. Dist. 27 Ala. State Senate, 2011—. Mem. Ala. Pub. Svc. Commn. Serves with Ala. Army Nat. Guard, 1988—. Republican. Methodist. Office: 337 E Magnolia Dr Auburn AL 36830 also: Alabama State Senate State House Rm 733 11 S Union St Montgomery AL 36130 Office Phone: 334-209-0831, 334-242-7865. Business E-Mail: tom.whatley@alsenate.gov.

WHEAT, BILL W., construction executive; BBA in Acctg. and Fin., Baylor U., Waco, Tex. CPA. Auditor Price Waterhouse LLP (now PricewaterhouseCoopers LLP); various positions including fin. planning mgr. and asst. contr. The Bombay Co., 1991—98; acctg. mgr. D.R. Horton, Inc., Fort Worth, 1998—2000, sr. v.p., contr., 2000—03, exec. v.p., CFO, bd. dirs., 2003—. Office: DR Horton Inc DR Horton Tower 301 Commerce St Ste 500 Fort Worth TX 76102

WHEAT, DOUGLAS, publishing executive; Various positions sr. mgmt. Donaldson Lufkin & Jenrette Securities Corp., Grauer & Wheat; pres. Haas Wheat & Partners, 1992—2006; co-founder, chmn. Foxbridge Partners, 2006—07; chmn. AMN Healthcare Svcs., Inc., SuperMedia, LLC. Bd. dirs. Dr. Pepper/Seven-Up Companies, Inc., Thermadyne Industries Inc., Sybron Internat. Corp., Smarte Carte Corp., Nebraska Book Corp., ALC Comm.Corp.; chmn. Playtex Products Inc., 2004—06, bd. dirs., 1995—2007; mng. ptnr. Southlake Equity Group (formerly Challenger Equity Group), 2008. Office: SuperMedia LLC 2200 W Airfield Dr Dallas TX 75261 Office Phone: 972-453-7000. Office Fax: 972-453-3969. Business E-Mail: douglas.wheat@supermedia.com.

WHEATLEY, ARTHUR EDWIN, JR., security firm executive; b. Chester, Pa., Jan. 19, 1943; s. Arthur E. Sr. and Kathryn (Scott) W.; m. Linda Susan Ponsitory, July 31, 1973; children: Scott Arthur, Ryan Barry. BA in Economics, Davis & Elkins Coll., 1965. Assoc., Risk Mgmt. Conn. Claims; supr. Liberty Mutual Insurance Co., Charlotte, NC, 1971—74, Atlanta, 1971—74, East Orange, 1971—74; ins. coord. Becton-Dickinson & Co., Rutherford, 1974—78; mgr. property and liability ins. Scovill, Inc., Waterbury, Conn., 1978—85; v.p., dir. risk mgmt. The Pittston Co., Greenwich, Conn., 1985; v.p. risk mgmt. & ins. Brink's Co. (formerly Pittston Co.), 1988—. With USAF, 1967-71. Mem. Risk and Ins. Mgmt. Soc., Woodbury-Bethew Youth Soccer (bd. dirs. 1987—, Woodbury, Conn.). Avocations: youth soccer coach, reading, children. Office: The Brink's Co 1801 Bayberry Ct Richmond VA 23226 Office Phone: 804-289-9600. Office Fax: 804-289-9746. E-mail: arthur.wheatley@brinksinc.com.

WHEELER, CARRIE A., investment company executive; b. 1970; Positions in mergers and acquisitions dept. Goldman Sachs & Co., 1993—96; ptnr. TPG Capital, LP, 1996—. Former bd. dirs. Interlink Group, Inc.; bd. dirs. Metro-Goldwyn-Mayer, Inc., Petco Animal Supplies, Inc., Denbury Resources Inc., 2000—, Neiman Marcus, Inc., 2005—. Office: TPG Capital LP Ste 3300 301 Commerce St Fort Worth TX 76102 Office Phone: 817-871-4000. Office Fax: 817-871-4010.

WHEELER, CASS (M. CASS. WHEELER), healthcare consultant, former health science association administrator; b. Tex. BA in Bus., U. Texas, Austin, 1963. Stockbroker NY Stock Exch. firm, Dallas, 1969—73; with Am. Heart Assn., Austin, Tex., 1973—82, COO Dallas, 1982—96, sr. v.p., field ops., 1996—97, CEO, 1997—2008, ret., 2008. Guest lectr. Harvard U. Sch. Bus. & Pub. Health, U. Texas Sch. Mgmt., Dallas, U. Texas Lyndon B. Johnson Sch. Pub. Affairs, Austin; former bd. chmn. Nat. Health Coun.; bd. mem. Partnership for Prevention, Research! America, Nat. Ctr. Tobacco-Free Kids, Nat. Assembly Health & Human Svc. Organizations; advisory bd. mem. Discovery Health Media, Inc.; former mem. President's Commn. Improving Econ. Opportunity in Communities Dependent on Tobacco Production While Protecting Pub. Health; bd. dirs. Am. Legacy Found. Avocations: running, skiing, bicycling.

WHEELER, HOYT NOLAND, management educator, arbitrator; b. Ravenswood, W.Va., Jan. 21, 1937; s. Harold Lee and Virginia Laura Wheeler; m. Elizabeth Dawson Scrivener, May 30, 1996; children: Jeffrey Smith, Jonathan Philip. BA cum laude, Marshall U., Huntington, W.Va., 1958; JD, U. Va., Charlottesville, 1961; PhD, U. Wis., 1974. Bar: W.Va. 1961. Assoc. Kay, Casto & Chaney, Charleston, W.Va., 1961—65, ptnr., 1966—70; instr. in bus. adminstrn. U. Wyo., Laramie, 1973—74, asst. prof. of bus. adminstrn., 1974—76; assoc. prof. of indsl. rels. U. Minn., Mpls., 1976—81; prof. of mgmt. U. SC, Columbia, 1981—2009, dist. prof. emeritus, 2009—. Labor arbitrator, Columbia, SC, 1974—. Author: (scholarly book) Workplace Justice Without Unions, (scholarly/trade book) The Future of the American Labor Movement, (scholarly book) Workplace Justice: Employment Obligations in International Perspective, Industrial Conflict: An Integrative Theory. Fellow: Labour & Employment Rels. Assn.; mem.:

Internat. Labor and Employment Rels. Assn. (exec. bd. 2006—12), Internat. Soc. for Labor Law and Social Security (exec. bd. 2003—04), Nat. Acad. of Arbitrators (bd. govs. 2009—12), Indsl. Rels. Rsch. Assn. (pres. 1996—97). Episcopalian. Avocations: tennis, reading, swimming. Home: 109 Saluda View Ct West Columbia SC 29169 Office: 109 Saluda View Ct West Columbia SC 29169 Business E-Mail: hwheeler@sc.rr.com.

WHEELER, JOHN WATSON, lawyer; b. Murfreesboro, Tenn., Sept. 11, 1938; s. James William and Grace (Fann) W.; m. Dorothy Anita Pressgrove, Aug. 5, 1959; children: Jeffrey William, John Harold. BS in Journalism, U. Tenn., 1960, JD, 1968. Bar: Tenn. 1968, U.S. Dist. Ct. (ea. dist.) Tenn. 1968, U.S. Dist. Ct. (mid. dist.) Tenn., U.S. Dist. Ct. (we. dist.) Tenn., U.S. Supreme Ct. 1974, U.S. Ct. Appeals (6th cir.) 1975. Editor The Covington (Tenn.) Leader, 1963-65; adminstrv. asst. to lab. dir. UT-AEC Rsch. Lab., Oak Ridge, Tenn., 1965-68; assoc. Hodges, Doughty & Carson, Knoxville, Tenn., 1968-72, ptnr., 1972—2005, of counsel, 2005—. Mem. commn. to study Applellate Cts. in Tenn.; chair U.S. magistrate merit selection panel, U.S. Dist. Ct. (ea. dist.) Tenn., 1991, 2002, 03, mem. bankruptcy judge merit selection panel, 1992-94; chmn. hist. soc., U.S. Dist. Ct. (ea. dist.) Tenn., 1993-2004. Mem. organizing com. Tenn. Supreme Ct. Hist. Soc. Lt. U.S. Army, 1961-63, capt. Res. Fellow Am. Bar Found. (life, Tenn. chair 1999-2008), Tenn. Bar Found. (life); mem. ABA (ho. of dels. 1986-2000), Tenn. Bar Assn. (pres. 1989-90, bd. govs. 1981-91), Nat. Conf. Bar Pres., Am. Inns. of Ct. (master of bench, emeritus), Internat. Assn. Def. Counsel, So. Conf. Bar Pres., 6th Cir. Jud. Conf. (life), Fox Den Country Club (bd. dirs. 2001-04), Fox Hollow Golf Club Trinity, Fla. Republican. Lutheran. Avocations: golf, travel. Office: Hodges Doughty & Carson PO Box 869 Knoxville TN 37901-0869 Home: 12009 N Fox Den Dr Knoxville TN 37934-2540 Home Phone: 865-966-5323; Office Phone: 865-546-9611. Business E-Mail: jwheeler911@yahoo.com.

WHEELER, MARY FANNETT, aerospace engineering and engineering mechanics professor, petroleum and geosystems engineering, mathematics professor; BS in Social Sciences, U. Tex., 1960, BA in Math., 1960, MA in Math., 1963; PhD in Math., Rice U., 1971; hon. doc., Colo. Sch. Mines, 2008. Registered profl. engr., Tex., 1999. Instr., dept. Math. Rice Univ., Houston, 1971—73, asst. prof., dept. Math. Sciences, 1973—77, assoc. prof., dept. Math. Sciences, 1977—80, prof., dept. Math. Sciences, 1980—88, Noah Harding prof. Computational and Applied Math. (formerly Math. Sciences), 1988—95; affiliated sr. scientist Univ. Houston, 1990—; The Ernest and Virginia Cockrell chair in engring. Univ. Tex., Austin, 1995—, prof., dept. Math., 1995—, prof., Aerospace Engring. and Engring. Mechanics, 1995—, prof., Petroleum and Geosystems Engring., 1995—; dir. Ctr. for Subsurface Modeling. Editor: Numerical Algorithms, Numerical Methods in Partial Differential Equations, SIAM Multiscale and Simulation, Concurrency and Computation: Practice and Experience; adv. editor Computer Methods in Applied Mechanics and Engring., editl. bd. Springer, SIAM Computational Sci. and Engring. Book Series, authored/co-authored, editor/co-editor various publs. Recipient Educator award, Am. Women in Aerospace, 1997, Joe J. King award, Univ. of Tex. at Austin, 2006, Faculty Recognition award, IBM, 2006, 2007, 2008; fellow Internat. Assn. for Computational Mechanics. Fellow: American Acad. of Arts and Sciences, Internat. Assn. for Computational Mechanics; mem.: Am. Women in Math., Soc. of Petroleum Engrs., Soc. of Indsl. and Applied Math., Am. Geophys. Union, Math. Assn. of America, Phi Beta Kappa, Sigma Xi. Office: The University of Texas at Austin Institute for Computational Engineering 201 East 24th St Austin TX 78712 Office Phone: 512-475-8625. Office Fax: 512-232-2445. E-mail: mfw@ices.utexas.edu.

WHEELER, STEVE DEREAL, neurologist; b. Chgo., Sept. 15, 1951; s. Clarence and Tommie L. (Andrews) W.; m. Debra B. Buckingham; children: Winter N., Ryan S., Gabrielle S. Student, Mich. State U., 1973; MD, Dartmouth Coll., 1976. Diplomate Am. Bd. Psychiatry and Neurology, Nat. Bd. Med. Examiners; lic. Mich., Ohio, Fla. Intern Thomas Jefferson U., Phila., 1976—77; emergency physician River Dist. Hosp. Emergency Cons., Inc., St. Clair, Mich., 1977—78; fellow Dartmouth Med. Sch., 1978; resident U. Miami, Fla., 1978—81; fellow Washington U., St. Louis, 1981—82; instr., neurology Med. Coll. Pa., Phila., 1982—83; electroencephalograph reader, attending neurologist VA Med. Ctr., Phila., 1982—83; asst. neurologist, attending neurologist Muscle Clinic U. Hosps. Cleve., 1983—86; electromyographer Rainbow Babies and Children's Hosp., U. Hosps. Cleve., 1983—86; chief neuromuscular diseases divsn., asst. prof. neurology Case Western Res. U., Cleve., 1983—86, co-dir. muscle disease ctr. and lab., 1985—86; clin. assoc. prof. of neurology U. Miami, 1987—89; pvt. practice Miami, 1987—; dir., co-founder Ryan Wheeler Headache Treatment Ctr., 2001—. Lectr. Myasthenia Gravis Found., Cleve., 1983—86, Vermillion, 1984; vol. assoc. prof. U. Miami Sch., 1992—97, 2004—, vis. lectr., 1993—2001; chief headache divsn. Neurologic Ctr. for South Fla.; neurology cons. Low Back Pain Team U. Hosps. Cleve., 1984—86; mem. quality assurance com. Coral Reef Hosp., Miami, 1987—88; cons. dir. planning Bapt. Headache Clinic Bapt. Hosp., 1993—95; mem. adminstrv. com. Deering Hosp. Pain Mgmt. Ctr., 1993—94; mem. sleep diagnostic ctr. com. Bapt. Hosp., 1990—92, 1994—98, advisor to headache support group, 1995—; lectr. in field; co-founder, dir. Ryan Wheeler Headache Treatment Ctr.; mem. AAN Found. Minority Scholars Program Subcom., 2010; mem. editl. bd., 2001—02; with Jour. Nat. Med. Assn., 2001—. Contbr. chapters to books. Named Internat. Man Yr., 1991-92; recipient Celebration Excellence Black Achiever award Family Christian Assn. Am., 1992. Fellow Am. Acad. Neurology, Am. Headache Soc. (Com. for Headache Edn.); mem. ACP, So. Med. Assn. (chmn. psychiatry and neurology sect. 2000-02), Nat. Headache Found., Internat. Headache Soc., Fla. Soc. Neurology, Muscular Disease Soc. Northeastern Ohio (trustee 1984-86), Dade County Med. Assn. Achievements include research in plasmaphereses in treatment of acute Guillain-Barre Syndrome; repeat neuroimaging in headache when first study normal, migraine with cluster features, hemicrania continua, migraine-associated gluten sensitivity, secondary headaches, novel phenotype-driven strategies for headache and migraine prevention; nutritional features associated with migraine. Office: Ryan Wheeler Headache Treatment Ctr 7800 SW 57th Ave Ste 229 South Miami FL 33143-5523 Office Phone: 305-661-2022. Office Fax: 305-661-2133.

WHEELER, SUSAN HAWKES, legislative staff member, communications executive; b. Preston, Idaho, Jan. 29, 1961; d. Vaughn Thomas and Frances Arlene (Anderson) Hawkes; m. Joseph Farris Wheeler, Aug. 27, 1994; 1 child, Daniel. BA, Brigham Young U., 1985. Assignment editor, gen. assignment reporter Sta. KIFI-TV, Idaho Falls, Idaho, 1985-89; gen. assignment reporter Sta. KBCI-TV, Boise, 1989-90, assignment editor, 1990-92; comm. dir. to Rep. Mike Crapo US House of Representatives, Washington, 1992-99; comm. dir. to Senator Mike Crapo US Senate, Washington, 1999—. Office: Office of Senator Michael Crapo 239 Senate Dirksen Bldg Washington DC 20510-1205 Office Phone: 202-224-6142. E-mail: susan_wheeler@crapo.senate.gov.

WHEELING, ROBERT FRANKLIN, computer consultant; b. Springboro, Pa., Sept. 10, 1923; s. Alfred Abraham and Louwaive Letty (Hollabaugh) W.; m. Luella Mae Race, June 2, 1951; 1 child, Eric Wayne. BSEE, Pa. State Coll., 1944; MS in Math., U. Rochester, 1949; postgrad., Brown U., 1947—51. Project engr. Eastman Kodak Co., Rochester, NY, 1944—47; mathematician Mobil R&D Corp., Paulsboro, NJ, 1952—70; mgr. computer technology Mobil Oil Corp., NYC, 1971—72; engring. cons. Mobil R&D Corp., Princeton, NJ, 1973—84; pvt. practice computer cons. Naples, Fla., 1985—. Contbr. chpt. to book Optimizers, 1964; contbr. articles to profl. jours.; patentee in field. Mem. Math. Assn. Am., Assn. for Computing Machinery (lectr. 1963). Avocations: robotics, carpentry. Home and Office: 37602 Lilly Bea Ave Zephyrhills FL 33541 E-mail: luellaw@msn.com.

WHELAN, KAREN MAE LEPPO, manufacturing executive; b. Lancaster, Pa., Mar. 20, 1947; children: Katherine, John. BA, U. Pitts., 1967; MS in Bus., Va. Commonwealth U., 1977. Sr. acct. Arthur Young, Richmond, Va., 1977-80; various positions, advanced to v.p. fin. reporting James River Corp., Richmond, 1980-92; v.p., treas. Universal Corp., Richmond, 1993—. Mem. AICPA (Elijah Watts Sells award 1976), Nat. Investor Rels. Inst., Fin. Execs. Inst., Va. Soc. CPAs (cert. CPA, gold medal award 1976). Mailing: Universal Corp PO Box 25099 Richmond VA 23260-5099 Office: Universal Corp 1501 N Hamilton St Richmond VA 23230 Office Phone: 804-359-9311. Office Fax: 804-254-3582.

WHETSELL, PAUL W., hotel executive; BA in History, Davidson Coll. Various positions, including v.p., franchise Quality Inns (now Choice Hotels Internat.); various devel. & operating positions, including v.p. devel. Lincoln Hotels; chmn., CEO MeriStar Hotels & Resorts, Inc., MeriStar Hospitality Corp., Washington, 1998—2006; CEO Interstate Hotels & Resorts, Inc., 1998—2003, chmn., 1998—2009; founder, chmn. CapStar Hotel Co. (merged with American Gen. Hospitality Corp.), Washington, 1987—98, pres., CEO, 2006—. Bd. dirs. NVR, Inc., 2007—. Bd. trustees, mem., governing coun. Cystic Fibrosis Found., Washington; bd. govs. NAREIT; mem., industry real estate & financing adv. coun. Am. Hotel & Lodging Assn.; mem. Urban Land Inst., Travel Bus. Roundtable. Office: CapStar Hotel Co 4501 N Fairfax Dr Ste 600 Arlington VA 22203 Office Phone: 703-387-3800. Office Fax: 703-387-3844. Business E-Mail: paul.whetsell@capstar.com.

WHETZEL, CHARLES E., JR., apparel executive; With Health-Tex, Inc., Mast Industries, Inc., Wellmade Industries, Inc.; v.p., mfg. The HD Lee Co., Inc.; v.p., apparel Aileen, Inc., 1971; with Bassett-Walker, Inc., 1988; exec. v.p., ops. William Carter Co. (formerly Carter William Co.), 1992—97, exec. v.p., mfg., 1997, exec. v.p., global sourcing, 2000; exec. v.p., ops. Carter's, Inc., 1992—97, exec. v.p., mfg., 1997—2000, exec. v.p., global sourcing, 2000—05, chief sourcing officer, 2005—10, exec. v.p., 2005—, chief supply chain officer, 2010—. Office: Carter's Inc 1170 Peachtree St NE Ste 900 Atlanta GA 30309 Office Phone: 404-745-2700. Office Fax: 404-892-0968. Business E-Mail: charlie.whetzel@carters.com.

WHICHARD, WILLIS PADGETT, lawyer, retired educator, judge; b. Durham, NC, May 24, 1940; s. Willis Guilford and Beulah (Padgett) W.; m. Leona Irene Paschal, June 4, 1961; children: Jennifer Diane, Ida Gilbert. AB, U. N.C., 1962, JD, 1965; LLM, U. Va., 1984, SJD, 1994. Bar: N.C. 1965. Law clk. NC Supreme Ct., Raleigh, 1965-66, assoc. justice, 1986-98; assoc. judge NC Ct. Appeals, Raleigh, 1980-86; ptnr. Powe, Porter, Alphin & Whichard, Durham, 1966-80; dean, prof. law Campbell U., 1999—2006, Moore and Van Allen Law Firm, 2006—. Instr. grad. sch. bus. adminstrn. Duke U., 1978; vis. lectr. U. N.C. Sch. Law, 1986-98. Contbr. articles to profl. jours. Rep. N.C. Ho. of Reps., Raleigh, 1970-74; senator N.C. Senate, 1974-80, chair numerous coms. and commns.; N.C. legis. rsch. commn., 1971-73, 75-77, land policy coun., 1975-79; bd. dirs. Sr. Citizens Coordinating Coun., 1972-74; chair local crusade Am. Cancer Soc., 1977, state crusade chair, 1980, chair pub. issues com., 1980-84; pres., bd. chmn. Downtown Durham Devel. Corp., 1980-84; bd. dirs. Durham County chpt. ARC, 1971-79; Durham county campaign dir. March of Dimes, 1968, 69, chmn., 1969-74, bd. dirs. Triangle chpt., 1974-79; bd. advisors Duke Hosp., 1982-85, U. N.C. Sch. Pub. Health, 1985-96, U. N.C. Sch. Social Work, 1989—; bd. visitors N.C. Ctrl. U. Sch. Law, 1987—; mem. law sch. dean search com. U. N.C., 1978-79, 88-89, self-study com., 1985-86; pres. N.C. Inst. Justice, 1984-94; bd. dirs. N.C. Ctr. Crime and Punishment, 1984-94. Staff sgt. N.C. Army NG, 1966-72. Recipient Disting. Service award Durham Jaycees, 1971, Outstanding Legis. award N.C. Acad. Trial Lawyers, 1975, Outstanding Youth Svc. award N.C. Juvenile Correctional Assn., 1975, named Citizen of Yr. Eno Valley Civitan Club, Durham, 1982, Faith Active in Pub. Life award N.C. Coun. of Churches, 1983, Outstanding Appellate Judge award N.C. Acad. Trial Lawyers, 1983; named to Durham H.S. Hall of Fame, 1987. Mem. ABA, N.C. Bar Assn. (v.p. 1983-84, 2001-02), Durham County Bar Assn., U. N.C. Law Alumni Assn. (pres. 1978-79, bd. dirs. 1979-82), Nat. Guard Assn. (judge adv. 1972-73, legis. com. 1974-76), Order of Golden Fleece, Order of Grail, Order of Old Well, Amphoterothen Soc., Order of Coif, Phi Alpha Theta, Phi Kappa Alpha, Durham-Chapel Hill Torch Club (pres. 1984-85), Watauga Club (Raleigh, pres. 1994-95). Democrat. Baptist. Home: 84402 Winslow Chapel Hill NC 27517 Office: Moore and Van Allen Attys PO Box 13076 Research Triangle Park NC 27709 Office Phone: 919-286-8054. Business E-Mail: williswhichard@mvalaw.com.

WHIDDON, SHELLEY E., finance company executive; Attended, U. N. Tex., Southern Meth. U. Mgr., external comm. Alliance Data Sys. Corp., 2005; dir., external comm. Alliance Data Systems Corp., 2005—. Office: Alliance Data Systems Corp 7500 Dallas Pkwy Ste 700 Plano TX 75024-4006 Office Phone: 972-348-5100. Office Fax: 972-348-5335.

WHIDDON, THOMAS E., board member; BS in Acctg. magna cum laude, U. Ala., 1974. Tax ptnr. KPMG Peat Marwick, Tampa, Fla.; various positions, v.p. & treas. Eckerd Corp.; treas. Zale Corp., 1994-95, sr. v.p., 1994—96, CFO, 1995-96; exec. v.p., CFO Lowe's Companies, Inc., North Wilkesboro, NC, 1996-2000, exec. v.p., logistics & tech., 2000—03. Bd. dirs. Sonoco Products Co., 2001—; bd. adv. Berkshire Ptnrs. LLC, 2005—. Office: Sonoco Products Co Bd Directors 1 N 2nd St Hartsville SC 29550-3305 Office Phone: 843-383-7000. Office Fax: 843-383-7008. Business E-Mail: thomas.whiddon@sonoco.com.

WHIGHAM, MARK ANTHONY, computer scientist; b. Mobile, Ala., Jan. 14, 1959; s. Tommie Lee Sr. and Callie Mae (Molette) W. BS in Computer Sci., Ala. A&M U., 1983, MS in Computer Sci., 1990; postgrad., Ala. A&M Univ., 1995; student in Religious Edn., Andersonville Theological Sem., Camilla, GA, 2003—; cert., Am. C.C. Leadership Acad., U. Ala., 2005. Cert. Microsoft cert. profl., A+ cert CompTIA, i-Net+ cert. profl. CompTIA, network + cert. profl. CompTIA, Microsoft Office specialist cert. 2003, trainer Microsoft, Application Specialist; cert. profl. instr. Computer programmer U.S. Army Corps of Engrs., Huntsville, Ala., 1985-88; programmer analyst, coord. acad. computing Ala. A&M U., Normal, Ala., 1988-89, programmer analyst II, DEC systems coord., instr. part-time computer sci. dept., 1989-91; systems engr. Advanced Bus. Cons. Inc. Dow Chem. Co., 1991-93; owner Whigham's Computer Cons., 1990—; sys. engr. DOW Chem. Co.-USA La. Divsn., Plaquemine, La., 1991-93; network specialist/cons. Ala. A&M U., Normal, 1994—; computer info. sys. instr. Calhoun C.C., Decatur, Ala., 1994—; mgmt. info. sys. dir., CIO J.F. Drake Tech. Coll., Huntsville, Ala., 1997-98; software engr. Colsa Corp., Huntsville, Ala., 1998—99; dir. info. tech. Lane Coll., 1999—2000; instr. computer sci. Lawson State CC, 2000—10, microsoft office specialist, 2007. Instr. computer sci. dept. Ala. A&M U., 1989-91. Active Huntsville Interdenominational Ministerial Fellowship, Huntsville, 1984, adv. com. mem. Comp TIA Edn Careers, 2009- Mem. Nat. Assn. Sys. Programmers, Computer Sci. Tchrs. Assn., Ala. Info. Tech. Assn. (adv.com.), Ala. Coun. for Computer Edn., Assn. for Computing Machinery, Huntsville Jaycees, Nat. Soc. Black Engrs., Assn. Info. Tech. Profls., So. Poetry Assn., Nat. Arts Soc., Internat. Black Writers and Artists Assn., Optimists, U.S. Chess Fedn. (cert. chess coach), Future Bus. Leaders of Am.-Phi Beta Lambda, Sigma Tau Epsilon, Alpha Phi Omega. Democrat. Baptist. Avocations: chess, skating, reading, playing piano. Home: 7900 Old Madison Pike Apt 3016 Madison AL 35758 Office: Calhoun CC 102B Wynn Dr Huntsville AL 35805 Office Phone: 256-713-4814. Business E-Mail: mark_whigham@msn.com, mwhigham@lawsonstate.edu, maw@callhoun.edu.

WHINERY, MICHAEL ALBERT, physician; b. Herts Watsford, Eng., June 30, 1951; s. Leo Howard and Doris Eileene Whinery and Alma Piper; m. Tatijana Dunnebier, 1976 (dec. Jan. 1981); m. Judy Renee Wright, Apr. 30, 1982; children: Rhiannon Daire Eileene, Terron Rae Lee. BS, Okla. U., 1976; D of Osteopathy, Okla. State U., 1980. Diplomate Am. Bd. Family Practice. Intern Hillcrest Health Ctr., Oklahoma City, 1980-81; with McLoud Clinic, McLoud, Okla., 1981-98; staff physician Okla. Vets. Ctr., Claremore, 2000—. House physician McLoud Nursing Ctr., 1988—; med. examiner Pottawatomie County Health, McLoud, 1983–. Author: Poetic Voices of America, 1991; composer lyrics and music at Stella Gospel Rec. Studio, 2000, A Soldier Last Prayer. Mem. Presdl. Order Merit Nat. Repub. Senatorial Com., Washington, 1991, Presdl. Task Force, 1983—, Senatorial Commn. Repub. Senatorial Inner Circle, Washington, 1991; mem. U.S. Congrl. Adv. Bd., 1993. Served with USMC, Vietnam era. Recipient Acknowledgement of Outstanding Contbn. in Clin. Rsch. award SANDOZ Labs., 1992, Rep. Presdl. Legion of Merit, 1994, Rep. Majority medal, U.S. Senate, 1997, Rep. Task Force medal of merit, 1997. Mem. Am. Legion, C. of C., Jr. C. of C., U.S. Senatorial Club (preferred mem.), U.S. Congressional Act Bd. (state advisor 1990-91). Baptist. Avocations: fishing, music, composing songs, poetry and writing lyrics. Office: PO Box 2745 3001 W Bluestarr Claremore OK 74018-2745 Office Phone: 918-342-5432 ext. 217, 918-720-8770. Personal E-mail: mwdocstar@yahoo.com. Business E-Mail: mwhinery@odva.state.ok.us.

WHIPPER, J. SETH, state legislator, lawyer; b. Charleston, SC, June 27, 1949; s. Benjamin J. and Lucille S. Whipper; m. Carrie Ophelia Fulse, July 18, 1984; children: Jasiri L.K., Subira N.K. BA, U. SC, 1972; JD, NC Ctrl. U., 1984. Atty.; mem. Dist. 113 SC House of Reps., 1995—. Gen. counsel Citizens Patrol Against Drugs; founding mem. Charleston County Coalition for Black Voter Participation; sr. bd. trustees St. Matthew Bapt. Ch.; bd. dirs. Neighborhood Legal Assistance Program, Father to Father; mem. SC Fair Share, SC United Action. Fleming fellow, 2000. Mem.: SC Legis. Black Caucus, SC Black Lawyers Assn., Charleston County Bar Assn., SC Bar Assn., NAACP (NC pariamentarian 1988—94), Liberty Hill Athletic Club. Democrat. Office: State Capitol 328C Blatt Bldg Columbia SC 29211 Home: 4592 Durant Ave North Charleston SC 29405 E-mail: JSW@scstatehouse.net.

WHISENANT, BERT ROY, JR., insurance company executive; b. Brownsville, Tex., Oct. 10, 1950; s. Bert R. and Jimmie Lee (Tallon) W.; m. Margaret Elizabeth Bugge, Aug. 21, 1970; children: Michelle, Bert III, Bryan, Monette. BBA in Ins., S.W. Tex. State U., 1972. Owner Bert Whisenant Ins., McAllen, Tex., 1972—. Pres. BRW Properties, Inc. Contbr. articles to Tex. Insuror, 1984. Recipient Blue Ribbon Honors award Aetna Life and Casualty, Co., 1974, Charter Pacesetter award West Coast Life Ins. Co., 1982. Mem. Ind. Ins. Agts. Am. (bd. dirs. 1984—), Ind. Ins. Agts. Tex. (com. person 1986—), Ind. Ins. Agts. McAllen (pres. 1985-86), Associated Risk Mgrs. of Tex., Upper Valley Life Underwriters (sec.-treas. 1978), Jaycees (bd. dirs., chaplain 1974). Lodges: Optimists (pres. McAllen club 1986), Rotary. Republican. Avocations: surfing, piloting, golf, fishing, skiing, water-skiing, surfing. Office: 816 E Hackberry Ave Mcallen TX 78501-5739

WHISENHUNT, KEN (KENNETH MOORE WHISENHUNT), professional football coach; b. Atlanta, Feb. 28, 1962; m. Alice Whisenhunt; children: Kenneth Jr., Mary Ashley. BS in Civil Engring., Ga. Tech. U., 1990. Tight end Atlanta Falcons, 1985—88, Washington Redskins, 1989—90, NY Jets, 1991—93; spl. teams, half backs, & tight ends coach Vanderbilt U. Commodores, 1995—96; tight ends coach Balt. Ravens, 1997—98; spl. teams coach Cleve. Browns, 1999; tight ends coach NY Jets, 2000, Pitts. Steelers, 2001—03, offensive coord., 2004—06, San Diego Chargers, 2013; head coach Ariz. Cardinals, Tempe, 2007—12, Tenn. Titans, Nashville, 2014—. Achievements include being the offensive coordinator for Super Bowl XL winning Pittsburgh Steelers, 2006. Office: Tennessee Titans One Titans Way Nashville TN 37213*

WHITACRE, EDWARD E., JR., retired automotive executive; b. Ennis, Tex., Nov. 4, 1941; m. Linda Whitacre; 2 children. BS in Indsl. Engring., Tex. Tech U., 1964. Various positions ops. dept. Southwestern Bell Tel. Co., 1963-85, pres. Kans. divsn. Topeka, 1982-85; group pres. Southwestern Bell Corp., 1985-86, v.p. revenues/pub. affairs, vice-chmn., CFO St. Louis, 1986-88, pres., COO, 1988-89; chmn., CEO SBC Comm. (now AT&T, Inc.), San Antonio, 1990—2007; chmn. General Motors Co., Detroit, 2009—10, 2010, interim CEO, 2009—10, chmn., CEO, 2010. Bd. dirs. Anheuser Busch, Inc., 1988—2008, May Dept. Stores, 1989—2004, Emerson Electric Co., 1990—2004, Burlington Northern Santa Fe, Inc., 1993—2007, ExxonMobil Corp., 2008—, Gen. Motors Co., 2009—10. Author (with Leslie Cauley): American Turnaround: Reinventing AT&T and GM and the Way We Do Business in the USA, 2013. Nat. pres. Boy Scouts of America, 1999—2000; campaign chmn. United Way, San Antonio, 1998; mem. gov. bus. coun. State of Tex.; chmn. bd. regents Tex. Tech U. Health Sci. Ctr., Lubbock, Tex., 1992—98; bd. govs. S.W. Found. Bio Med. Rsch. Recipient Internat. Citizen of Yr. award, World Affairs Coun., San Antonio, 1997, Freeman award, San Antonio C. of C., 1997, Spirit of Achievement award, Nat. Jewish Med. & Rsch. Ctr., 1998; named one of The 50 Who Matter Now, CNNMoney.com Bus. 2.0, 2006; named to The Tex. Bus. Hall of Fame, 1997. Presbyterian. Avocations: golf, hunting, cooking, reading.

WHITAKER, DARLA, electronics executive; BSEE, So. Meth. U., 1989; MBA, U. Dallas, 1997. Joined Texas Instruments, Inc., 1984, compensation mgr. Asia region Taipei and Singapore, human resources mgr. ASIC orgn., dir. human resources for application specific products bus. unit, v.p., mgr. compensation and human resource systems and svcs., sr. v.p., dir. worldwide human resources, mem. strategy leadership team. Office: Tex Instruments Inc PO Box 660199 Dallas TX 75266-0199 Office Phone: 972-995-2011. Office Fax: 972-995-4360.

WHITAKER, RUTH REED, state legislator, retired publishing executive; b. Blytheville, Ark., Dec. 13, 1936; d. Lawrence Neill and Ruth Shipton (Weidemeyer) Reed; m. Thomas Jefferson Whitaker, dec. 29, 1961; children: Steven Bryan, Alicia Morrow. BA, Hendrix Coll., 1958. Copywriter, weather person KTVE TV, El Dorado, Ark., 1958-59; nat. bridal cons. Treasure House, El Dorado, 1959; bridal cons. Pfeifers of Ark., Little Rock, 1959-60; dir. of continuity S. M. Brooks Advt. Agy., Little Rock, 1960-61; layout artist C. V. Mosby Co., St. Louis, 1961-62; editor, owner Razorback Am. Newspaper, Ft. Smith, Ark., 1979-81; ret., 1981; mem. Dist. 3 Ark. State Senate, 2001—. Host Crawford Conversations TV show; contbr. author indsl. catalog, 1979 (Addy award). State sec. Rep. Party of Ark., 1992-94, mem. Ark. Electoral Coll., 1996, del. Rep. Nat. Conv., 1996;; mem. Ben Geren Regional Park Commn., Sebastian County, Ark., 1984-89, pres., 1990; past pres. Jr. Civic League; mem. Ft. Smith Orchid Com.; mem. com. of 21 United Way; publicity chmn. Sebastian County Rep. Com., 1983-84; state press officer Reagan-Bush Campaign, 1984; exec. dir. Ark. Dole for Pres., 1995-96; pres. Women's Aux. Sebastian County Med. Soc., 1974; mem. Razorback Scholarship Fund; class agt. alumni fund Hendrix Coll., 1990, 91, 92; mem. Sparks Woman's Bd.; 1st vice chmn. 3d Dist. Rep. Party; state committeewoman Rep. Party Ark.; chmn. Crawford County Rep. Com.; apptd. by Gov. of Ark. to Commr. Ark. Ednl. TV Network Commn., sec. 1998-99; mem. city coun. City of Cedarville, Ark., 1998; dist. panelist NOW in Bux., 2003. Recipient Disting. Vol. Leadership award Nat. Found. March of Dimes, 1973, Appreciation award Ft. Smith Advt. Fedn., 1977, 78, Recognition award United Cerebral Palsy, 1980, Hon. Parents of Yr. award U. Ark., 1984, Firekeeper award Sparks Hosp. Women's Ctr., 2003. Mem. AAUW, Alden Soc. Am. (life), Ft. Smith C. of C., Ark. Nature Conservancy, Am. Legion Aux., Frontier Rschrs. Soc. (pres. 1995-96), Daus. Union Vets. Republican. Presbyterian. Avocations: philanthropy, genealogy, writing, photography, ornithology. Mailing: PO Box 349 Cedarville AR 72932-0349 Office Phone: 479-474-0911. Business E-Mail: whitakerr@arkleg.state.ar.us.

WHITAKER, THOMAS PATRICK, lawyer; s. Thomas J. and Mary K. (Finn) W.; m. Donna Mae Brenish, Feb. 16, 1974; children: Laura, Kevin. BA, George Washington U., 1966, MPA, 1973, JD, 1979; postgrad., Naval War Coll., 1984, Nat. Def. U., 2005. Bar: Va. 1979. Analyst Adminstrn. Office of U.S. Cts., Washington, 1975-77, Planning Research Corp., McLean, Va., 1973—75; program mgr. Social Security Adminstrn., Falls Church, Va., 1982—; US house rep. aide Rep. Abercrombie, 2005; legislative bill mgr. Atomic Veterans Relief Act, 2005. Author: Hexagon Annual Volunteer Political Satire Revue, 2006—12. Ret. capt. USNR, 1997, Vietnam, Iceland, Egypt, Malaysia. Avocation: running. Home: 9817 Days Farm Dr Vienna VA 22182-7306 Office Phone: 703-605-8292. Personal E-mail: thomas.whitaker44@gmail.com.

WHITBREAD, THOMAS BACON, language educator, writer; b. Bronxville, NY, Aug. 22, 1931; s. Thomas Francis and Caroline Nancy (Bacon) W. BA, Amherst Coll., 1952; A.M., Harvard U., 1953, PhD, 1959. Instr. English, U. Tex. at Austin, 1959-62, asst. prof., 1962-65, asso. prof., 1965-71, prof., 1971—. Vis. asso. prof. Rice U., 1969-70; mem. lit. adv. panel Tex. Commn. on Arts and Humanities, 1972-76 Author (poetry): Four Infinitives, 1964, Whomp and Moonshiver, 1982, The Structures Minds Erect, 2007; co-author: Prize Stories, 1962, The O. Henry Awards, 1962; editor: Seven Contemporary Authors, 1966. Recipient third Aga Khan prize for fiction Paris Rev., 1960, Lit. Anthology Program award Nat. Endowment for Arts, 1968, Outstanding Freshman Tchr. award Phi Eta Sigma, 1972-73 Mem. AAUP, Tex. Inst. Letters (Poetry award 1965, 83), Nat., Am. amateur press assns., Phi Beta Kappa. Democrat. Home: 1014 E 38th St Austin TX 78705-1835 Office: University Tex Dept English 208 W 21st St B5000 Austin TX 78712 Business E-Mail: whitbread@austin.utexas.edu.

WHITCHURCH, CHARLES R., retired information technology executive, board member; BA in Economics, Beloit Coll.; MBA, Stanford U., 1973. CFO Resinoid Engring. Corp.; corp. svcs. officer Harris Bank; v.p., fin. Corcom Inc., 1981—91; CFO, treas., prin. acctg. officer Zebra Technologies Corp., 1991—2008. Bd. dirs. SPSS Inc., 2003—, Landmark Aviation, 2008—, ScanSource Inc., 2009—. Office: ScanSource Inc Bd Directors 6 Logue Ct Greenville SC 29615 Office Phone: 864-288-2432. Office Fax: 864-288-1165.

WHITCOMB, JAMES HALL, geophysicist, foundation administrator; b. Sterling, Colo., Dec. 10, 1940; s. Clay Thane and Julia Melvina Whitcomb; m. Sandra Lynn McMurdo, July 13, 1965 (div. 1978); m. Teresa R. Idoni, Feb. 3, 1989; children: Lisa Michelle, Marisa Giulia, Sabina Maria. Geophysics engring. degree, Colo. Sch. of Mines, 1962; MS in Oceanography, Geophysics, Oreg. State U., 1964; PhD in Geophysics, Calif. Inst. Tech., 1973. Grad. rsch. asst. dept. oceanography Oreg. State U., Corvallis, 1962-64; geophysicist Ctr. Astrogeology U.S. Geol. Survey, Flagstaff, Ariz., 1964-66; Fulbright-Hayes program rsch. fellow Seismol. Inst. U. Uppsala, Sweden, 1966-67; grad. rsch. asst. seismol. lab. Calif. Inst. Tech., Pasadena, 1967-73, sr. rsch. fellow seismol. lab., 1973-79; assoc. prof. attendant rank dept. geol. scis. U. Colo., Boulder, 1979-82, fellow Coop. Inst. Rsch. in Environ. Scis., 1979-84; v.p. technical applications and mktg. ISTAC, Inc., Pasadena, 1984-88; program dir. seismology NSF, Washington, 1989-99, acting dep. divsn. dir., 1999—2002, sect. head, 2002—07, acting divsn. dir., 2008—. Expert witness U.S. Ho. Reps. Com. on Sci. and Tech., 1977; mem. geodynamics rev. bd. Jet Propulsion Lab., 1980-82, com. on geodesy Nat. Acad. Scis., 1982-85; pres. Boulder Systems, Inc., Pasadena, 1987-88. Recipient Outstanding Achievement award U.S. Geol. Survey, 1964, Dir.'s award for mgmt. excellence NSF, 1995, 2003; scholar State of Colo., 1958-62, Mobil Oil Co., 1960; fellow Sweden-Am. Found., 1966. Mem. AAAS, Am. Geophysical Union, Seismol. Soc. Am., Soc. Exploration Geophysicists (scholar 1963), Tau Beta Pi, Phi Kappa Phi, Sigma Xi. Office: Nat Sci Found Geosciences 4201 Wilson Blvd Arlington VA 22230-0002

WHITCOMB, R. STEVEN, career officer; Grad., U. Va., 1970; MEd, Calif. State Coll. Commd. 2d. lt. US Army, 1970, advanced through grades to brigadier gen.; various assignments 82d Airborne Divsn.; stationed at Fed. Rep. Germany; asst. prof. military sci. Calif. State Coll.; served in Rep. Korea; various assignments Fort Hood, Tex.; staff leader Fort Leavenworth; served in Operation Desert Shield/Desert Storm, Germany; chief western hemisphere current ops. Office the Dep. Chief Staff; stationed at Fort Stewart, Ga.; chief combat manuever divsn. Force Devel.; asst. divsn. comdr. 1st Cavalry Divsn. Decorated Legion of Merit with one oak leaf, Bronze Star medal with V device and oak leaf, Meritorious Svc. medal with three oak leaf clusters.

WHITE, BILL (WILLIAM HOWARD WHITE), former mayor, Houston; b. San Antonio, June 16, 1954; m. Andrea White; 3 children. BS in Econs. magna cum laude, Harvard U., 1976; JD, U. Tex., 1979. Atty. Susaman Godfrey LLP, Houston, 1979—93; instr. antitrust law and voting rights U. Tex., Austin; dep. sec., COO US Dept. Energy, Washington, 1993—95; chmn. Howe-Baker Internat., Tyler, Tex., 1997—2000; pres., CEO The Wedge Group, Houston, 1997—2003; mayor City of Houston, 2004—10. Recipient Profile in Courage award, John F. Kennedy Libr. Found., 2007. Office: PO Box 1562 Houston TX 77251 Office Phone: 713-247-2200.

WHITE, CHARLES SIDNEY JOHN, retired humanities educator; b. New Richmond, Wis., Sept. 25, 1929; s. Ferne Rosemary Holt. BA in English with honors, U. Wis., Madison, 1951; MA magna cum laude, U. de las Am. Mexico City Coll., Mexico City, 1957; MA, U. Chgo., 1962, PhD with distinction, 1964. Staff pub. rels. and advt. Wallace Supplies Mfg. Co., Chgo., 1957—61; asst. prof. Indian studies U. Wis., Madison, 1965—66; asst. prof. religious thought U. Pa., 1966—71; assoc. prof. philosophy and religion Am. U., Washington, 1971—78, prof. philosophy and religion, 1978—94, prof. emeritus philosophy and religion, 1995—, dir. Asia Ctr. Sch. Internat. Svc., 1976—78, chmn. dept. philosophy and religion, 1984—87, 1988—94. Vis. lectr. history of religions Princeton (N.J.) U., 1968; vis. prof. world religions Lakehead U., Thunder Bay, Ont., Canada, 1974—88; vis. prof. Wesley Seminary, 1985, 1986; lectr. in field; vis. prof. Hindu studies faculty theology Oxford U., England, 2002; mem. program adv. com. diploma in Buddhist studies U. Hyderabad, 2006. Author: The Caurāsī Pad of Śrī Hit Harivaṃś, 1977, Ramakrishna's Americans, 1979, The Adyar Library, The Institute for Vaisnava Studies and The American University Microfilm Collection of Vaisnava Literature, 2001, Teaching Saranagati: A Dialogue with HH Sri Sathguru Swami Gnanananda Sarasvathi, 2002, Catalogue of Vaisnava Literature, 2004, The Garden of Loneliness, Jay Shankar Prasad's Tears, 2006, Roses from the Desert of my Heart, A Book of Poetry, 2007; co-author: The Religious Quest, 1983, 2d edit., 1985, Joseph Campbell: Transformations of Myth Through Time, 1990; contbr. chapters to books, articles to profl. jours. and encyclopedias, numerous book reviews. With USN, 1951—55. Decorated Nat. Def. Svc. medal; grantee, Smithsonian Instn., India, 1982—83; fellow, Hindi-Urdu U., Chgo., 1961—64, Am. Inst. Indian Studies, India, 1964, 1968, 1974, 1978, 1995. Mem.: Am. Inst. Indian Studies (exec. com. 1988—90). Office Phone: 202-885-2925. Business E-Mail: philrel@american.edu.

WHITE, CHRISTOPHER W., air transportation executive; b. St. Petersburg, Fla. BS in Pub. Rels., U. Fla. Spokesman FAA; dep. asst. adminstr. Strategic Comm. & Pub. Affairs Office, pub. affairs mgr. SE Transp. Security Adminstrn.; sr. account exec. pub. rels. Cohn & Wolfe, Gainesville, Fla., pub. info. officer Fire Rescue Dept.; dir. pub. rels. AirTran Airways, Inc., 2009—. Air traffic contr., trainer USAF. Office: AirTran Airway Inc 2702 Love Field Dr Dallas TX 75235-1908 Office Phone: 407-318-5600. Office Fax: 407-251-5727. Business E-Mail: Christopher.white@airtran.com.

WHITE, DALE ANDREW, journalist; b. Jacksonville, Fla., Feb. 17, 1958; s. John Andrew and Jeannelle Corinne White. B in Journalism, U. Fla., 1983. Reporter UPI, Miami, Fla., 1980, Orlando (Fla.) Sentinel Star, 1981; corr. Fla. Times-Union, Gainesville, 1982; reporter, columnist, editl. writer, editor Sarasota Herald-Tribune, Fla., 1983—. Contbr. short stories to profl. publs. Recipient Chmn.'s award N.Y. Times, 1987, 2004, 3d place Editorial Writing award Fla. Soc. Newspaper Editors, 1993, 1st place Ind. Reporter Media award Fla. Sch. Bds. Assn., 1996. Office: PO Box 1695 Bradenton FL 34206-1695

WHITE, DANIEL BOWMAN, lawyer; b. Charlotte, NC, Apr. 12, 1948; s. William Garner and Elizabeth (Bowman) W.; m. Sarah de Saussure Peterson, May 29, 1976; children: Bentley Parker, Sarah de Saussure. AB, Davidson Coll., 1970; JD, U. S.C., 1976. Bar: S.C. 1976, U.S. Dist. Ct. S.C. 1976, U.S. Ct. Appeals (4th cir.) 1978, U.S. Ct. Appeals (fed. cir.) 1990. Ptnr. Gallivan, White & Boyd P.A., Greenville, SC, 1976—. Mem. Fed. Cir. Jud. Conf. Comments editor U. S.C. Law Rev., 1975-76. Commr. Greenville Zoning Commn., 1980-85; mem. Supreme Ct. Bd. Commrs. on Grievances and Discipline, 1988-91. 1st lt. U.S. Army, 1971-73, bd. of advisors, Charleston Sch. Law; gen. counsel, Artisphere; Leadership in Law, 2013 1st lt. US Army, South Vietnam. Decorated Bronze Star; Dana scholar Davidson Coll., N.C., 1966-70, Named one of Best Lawyers in Am., SC Super Lawyers; State Co-chair & Charter fellow Litig. Counsel Am., named Leading Lawyers Chambers USA. Mem.: ABA (house of dels.), Assn. Def. Trial Attys., Internat. Assn. Def. Counsel, Nat. Assn. R.R. Trial Counsel, S.C. Bar (ho. dels. 1986—, bd. govs. 1992—95, chmn. ho. dels. 2000—02, bd. govs. 2000—, sec. 2002—03, treas. 2003—04, pres.-elect 2004—05, pres. 2005—06, del. ABA house), Def. Rsch. Inst., Greenville Young Lawyers Club (pres. 1981). Episcopalian. Office: Gallivan White & Boyd PO Box 10589 Greenville SC 29603-2804 Office Phone: 864-271-5342. Business E-Mail: dwhite@gwblawfirm.com.

WHITE, GEORGE, US marshal; BS, Alcorn State U., Miss., 2009. With Miss. Dept. Pub. Safety, 1980—2010, numerous positions including dir. driver records divsn., examiner Driver's Lic. Bur., enforcement divsn. trooper, dir. comml. driver's lic. divsn. & motor carrier safety divsn.; US marshal (so. dist) Miss. US Dept. Justice, 2010—. Named Miss. Trooper of Yr., 1988. Office: James O Eastland Courthouse Bldg 245 E Capitol St Ste 305 Jackson MS 39201 Office Phone: 601-965-4444.

WHITE, GEORGE EDWARD, lawyer, educator; b. Northampton, Mass., Mar. 19, 1941; s. George LeRoy and Frances Dorothy (McCafferty) W.; m. Susan Valre Davis, Dec. 31, 1966; children: Alexandra V., Elisabeth MD. BA, Amherst Coll., Mass., 1963; MA, Yale U., New Haven, Conn., 1964, PhD, 1967; JD, Harvard U., Cambridge, Mass., 1970. Bar: DC 1970, Va. 1975, US Supreme Ct. 1973. Vis. scholar Am. Bar Found., 1970—71; law clk., chief justice Warren US Supreme Ct., 1971—72; asst. prof. law U. Va., 1972—74, assoc. prof., 1974—77, prof., 1977—86, John B. Minor prof. law and history, 1987—2003, David and Mary Harrison disting. prof. law, 2003—. Vis. prof. Marshall-Wythe Law Sch. spring 1988, NY Law Sch., fall 1988, London Sch. Economics and Polit. Sci., 2005, Harvard Law Sch., 2010, U. Auckland, 2012. Author: The Eastern Establishment and The Western Experience, 1968, Rev. Edit., 1989, The American Judicial Tradition, 1976, 3d edit., 2007, Patterns of American Legal Thought, 1978 (Gavel award ABA, 1979), Tort Law in America: An Intellectual History, 1980 (Gavel award ABA, 1981), 2nd edit., 2003, Earl Warren: A Public Life, 1982 (Gavel award ABA, 1983), The Marshall Court and Cultural Change, 1988, 2nd edit., 1991 (James Willard Hurst prize, 1990), Justice Oliver Wendell Holmes: Law and the Inner Self, 1993 (Gavel award ABA, 1994, Scribes award, 1994, Littleton-Griswold prize, 1994, Triennial Order of the Coif award, 1996), Intervention and Detachment: Essays in Legal History and Jurisprudence, 1994, Creating the National Pastime: Baseball Transforms Itself, 1903-1953, 1996, The Constitution and the New Deal, 2000, Alger Hiss's Looking-Glass Wars, 2004, Oliver Wendell Holmes Jr., 2006 (Green bag award, 2007), History and the Constitution, 2007, Law in American History: Volume One, From the Colonial Years Through the Civil War, 2012, American Legal History: A Very Short Introduction, 2014; editor: Studies in Legal History, 1980—86; editor: (Oliver Wendell Holmes) The Common Law, 2009 (Green Bag award, 2010). Mem. AAAS, Am. Law Inst., Soc. Am. Historians. Office: Law Sch U Va 580 Massie Rd Charlottesville VA 22903-1789 Office Phone: 434-924-3455. Business E-Mail: gew@virginia.edu.

WHITE, GORDON ELIOT, historian, writer; b. Glen Ridge, NJ, Oct. 25, 1933; s. Maurice Brewster and Sarah Fullilove (Gordon) W.; m. Nancy Johnson, 1955 (div. 1957); m. Mary Joan Briggs, Aug. 6, 1960 (dec. Nov. 1987); children: Sarah Elizabeth and Gordon O'Neal Brewster (twins), David McIntyre; m. Francis C. Barrineau, 1989 (div. 1996); m. Angela Tyler, Mar. 27, 1999 (dec. Mar., 2009). BA, Cornell U., 1955; MS in Journalism, Columbia U., 1957. Lic. master mariner USCG; lic. pilot FAA. Stringer Nassau Daily Rev.-Star, Rockville Centre, L.I., NY, 1948-50, Freeport (N.Y.) Leader, 1949-50; sports writer Morris County (N.J.) Citizen, 1950-51; stringer Ithaca (N.Y.) Evening News, 1951-55; photo editor, editl. writer Cornell Daily Sun, 1951-55; copy editor Am. Banker, NYC, 1958; Washington corr. Chgo. Am., 1958-61; chief Washington bur. Deseret News, Salt Lake City, 1961-88. Also corr. in Europe, U.S. and Antarctic for WJR, Detroit; KSL-KSL-TV, Salt Lake City, also KGMB, Honolulu; free lance writer with U.S. Navy, Army and Air Force, 1959; cons. Nat. Air and Space Mus.; auto racing, mil. aviation electronics historian. Author: Offenhauser, the Legendary American Racing Engine and the Men Who Built It, 1996, The Indianapolis Racing Cars of Frank Kurtis, 1940-1963, 2000, Kurtis-Kraft: Masterworks of Speed & Style, 2001, Lost Race Tracks, 2003, The Marvelous Mechanical Designs of Harry A. Miller, 2004, Ab and Marvin Jenkins and the Mormon Meteors, 2006, Leader Card Racers, Three Times Winners at Indianapolis, A History of Moore's Creek Middlesex Country, 1608—2008. Advisor auto racing Nat. Mus. Am. History, Smithsonian Instn., 1989—; curator Miller-Offenhauser Archive of historic race engine blueprints. Recipient Raymond Clapper Meml. award White House Corrs. Assn., 1978; award for excellence in reporting Exec. Dept. and White House; Roy W. Howard award for outstanding pub. svc. by a newspaper corr., 1979; award for disting. investigative reporting Investigative Reporters and Editors, 1980, Reser-Tuthill award for writing on history of automobile racing, Indpls., 1985. Mem. Nat. Press Club (Washington, Excellence in Reporting award 1979), Sigma Delta Chi (1st prize for newsphoto, 1954, Nat. award 1979), Pi Kappa Phi, Pi Delta Epsilon Episcopalian. Home and Office: PO Box 129 Hardyville VA 23070 Office Phone: 804-695-4628. Personal E-mail: gewhite@crosslink.net.

WHITE, JACK (JOHN ANTHONY GILLIS), guitarist, singer, record label owner; b. Detroit, July 9, 1975; m. Meg White, Sept. 21, 1996 (div. Mar. 24, 2000); m. Karen Elson, June 1, 2005 (separated 2011); children: Scarlett Teresa, Henry Lee. Drummer Goober and the Peas, The Go, The Upholsterers, Jack White and The Bricks; singer, guitarist The White Stripes, 1997—2011, The Raconteurs, 2005—, The Dead Weather, 2009—; founder, owner Third Man Records, Detroit, 2001—09, Nashville, 2009—. Singer: (albums with The White Stripes) The White Stripes, 1999, De Stijl, 2000, White Blood Cells, 2001, Elephant, 2003 (Grammy award for Best Alternative Music Album, 2003, Grammy award for Best Rock Song, 2003), Get Behind Me Satan, 2005, Icky Thump, 2007 (Grammy award for Best Alternative Music Album, 2008, Grammy award for Best Duo Rock Performance with Vocals, 2008), (album with The White Stripes) Under Great White Northern Lights, 2010, (songs with The Whites Stripes) Conquest, 2007 (Best Cinematography, MTV Video Music Awards, 2008), (albums with The Raconteurs) Broken Boy Soldiers, 2006, Consolers of the Lonely, 2008 (Grammy award for Best Engineered Non-Classical Album, 2009), (albums with The Dead Weather) Horehound, 2009, (solo album) Blunderbuss, 2012; prodr.: (albums with The Von Bondies) Lack of Communication, 2001, (albums by Whirlwind Heat) Do Rabbits Wonder?, 2003; prodr.: (albums with Loretta Lynn) Van Lear Rose, 2004 (Grammy award for Best Country Album, 2004); actor, composer (films) Cold Mountain, 2003; actor: (films) Coffee and Cigarettes, 2003, Walk Hard: The Dewey Cox Story, 2007; appeared in (documentaries) Shine a Light, 2008, It Might Get Loud, 2009. Named one of The 100 Agents of Change, Rolling Stone mag., 2009. Office: Press Here Publicity 138 W 25th St New York NY 10001 also: Third Man Records 623 7th Ave S Nashville TN 37203 Office Phone: 615-891-4393.

WHITE, JAMES RICHARD, lawyer; b. McKinney, Tex., Jan. 22, 1948; s. James Ray and Maxine (Brown) White; children: Nicole Olivia, Mandi Leigh, James Derek. BBA, So. Meth. U., 1969, MBA, 1970, JD, 1973, LLM, 1977. Bar: Tex. 1973, US Tax Ct. 1975, US Supreme Ct. 1989, US Ct. Appeals (5th cir.) 1989); cert. Comml. Real Estate Law Tex. Bd. Legal Specialization. Assoc. Elliot, Meer, Vetter, Denton & Bates, Dallas, 1973-74, Atwell, Cain & Davenport, Dallas, 1974-75; atty. Sabine Corp., Dallas, 1975-77; assoc. Brice & Barron, Dallas, 1977-79; ptnr. Millard & Olson, Dallas, 1979-82, Johnson & Swanson, Dallas, 1982-83, Winstead P.C., Dallas, 1983—, hiring ptnr., 1987-2001, exec. com., 2000-01. Mem. staff Southwestern Law Jour., Dallas, 1971-73; mem. So. Meth. U. Moot Ct. Bd., Order Barristers, Dallas, 1972-73; prof. North Lake Coll., Dallas, 1985; bd. dirs. Tex. Assn. Young Lawyers, Austin, 1980-82; sec. bd. dirs. Dallas Assn. Young Lawyers, 1976-80; adv. bd. Sports Source Inc., 2007-. Contbr. articles to profl. jours. Chmn. bd. dir. Tex. Lawyers Credit Union, Austin, 1980-82; pres. North Tex. Premier Soccer Assn., Dallas, 1979-81; v.p. Lake Highlands Soccer Assn., 1995-96, pres., 1996—; North Tex. State Soccer Assn., Volunteer of the Year, 2003; mem., Adult Com., 2013-; mem. regional mobility task force Real Estate Coun., City of Dallas, 1991-92, mem. downtown revitalization com., 1995-97; mem. Dallas Indsl. Devel. Bd., 1992-93, Dallas Higher Edn. Authority Bd., 1994-96; spkr.'s bur. and accreditation divsn. World Cup USA '94; mem. exec. coun. Recreational Interleague Assn. Dallas, 2002—; pres. Storm Soccer Club, 2003-05; founding mem. Premiere Acad. League, 2004-10, founder & pres. Dallas Invitational Acad. League, 2011; mem. outstanding sr. man selection com. Dad's Club So. Meth. U., 2007-10, bd. mem., 2007-10, pres. 2009-10, mem. Southern Meth. U. Presdl. Commn. Alcohol & Substance Abuse, 2010-13, mem., Audit & Budget comm. N Tex. State Soccer Assoc., 2013-. Staff sgt. 49th Armored Divsn. Tex. Nat. Guard, 1969—75. Named Vol. of the Yr., North Tex. State Soccer Assn., 2003, Honoree of Yr., Sport Source, 2010; named a Texas Super Lawyer, 2003—; named to Best Lawyers in Am., 2003—. Mem. ABA (mem. title ins. and survey, mortgage loan origination and structure com., mortgage financing and opinion, non-traditional comml. real estate fin. coms.), Tex. Bar Assn. (cert. 1973, mem. mortgage loan opinion com.), Tex. Coll. Real Estate Attys., Coll. State Bar Tex., Storm Soccer Club (pres. 2003-05). Methodist. Avocations: soccer, golf, skiing, racquetball, guitar. Home: 8003 Hundley Ct Dallas TX 75231-4728 Office: Winstead PC 500 Winstead Bldg 2728 N Harwood St Dallas TX 75201 Office Phone: 214-745-5126. Business E-Mail: jrwhite@winstead.com.

WHITE, JASON, state legislator; m. Jolynn McLellon. B, JD, Miss. Coll., Clinton. Atty., Miss.; mem. Dist. 48 Miss. House of Reps., Jackson, 2012—. Mem.: Miss. Bar Assn., Attala County Bar Assn., Attala County Forestry Assn., Attala County Farmers Co-op, West Hist. & Preservation Soc. Democrat. Baptist. Office: Miss House of Reps PO Box 1018 Jackson MS 39215 Business E-Mail: jwhite@house.ms.gov.

WHITE, JOHN AUSTIN, JR., engineering educator, retired academic administrator; b. Portland, Ark., Dec. 5, 1939; s. John Austin and Ella Mae (McDermott) W.; m. Mary Elizabeth Quarles, Apr. 13, 1963; children: Kimberly Elizabeth White Brakmann, John Austin III. BS in Indsl. Engring., U. Ark., 1962; MS in Indsl. Engring., Va. Poly. Inst., 1966; PhD, Ohio State U., 1970; PhD (hon.), Cath. U. of Leuven, Belgium, 1985, George Washington U., 1991. Registered profl. engr., Va. Indsl. engr. Tenn. Eastman Co., Kingsport, 1961-63, Ethyl Corp., Baton Rouge, 1965; tchg. assoc. Ohio State U., Columbus, 1966-70; instr. Va. Poly. Inst. and State U., Blacksburg, 1963-66, asst. prof., 1970-72, assoc. prof., 1972-75, Ga. Inst. Tech., Atlanta, 1975-77, prof., 1977-84, Regents' prof., 1984-97, Gwaltney prof., 1988-97, dean engring., 1991-97; disting. prof. indsl. engring. University of Arkansas, Fayetteville, 1997—, chancellor, 1997—2008. Asst. dir. engring. NSF, 1988-90, acting dep. dir., 1990-91; founder, chmn. SysteCon Inc., Duluth, Ga., 1977-84; exec. cons. Coopers & Lybrand, N.Y.C., 1984-93; mem. mfg. studies bd. NRC, Washington, 1986-88; bd. dirs. Russell Corp., 1992-2006, Eastman Chem. Co., 1994-2004, Motorola Corp., 1995-, Logility Inc., 1997-2009, J.B. Hunt Transport Svcs., Inc., 1998-, Nat. Sci. Bd., 1995-2006, Malcolm Baldrige Nat Quality Award Found., 1999-2008; pres, Southeastern U. Rsch. Assn., 2003-04, chair coun. presidents 2004; pres. Nat. Consortium for Grad. Degrees for Minorities in Engring. and Sci., Inc., 1993-95; bd. dirs. Nat. Collegiate Athletic Assn.; mem. exec. com. NCAA, 2002—05; apptd. U.S. del. to the Internat. Steering Com. of the Intelligent Mfg. System, 1995-97; dir. Ark. Sci. and Tech. Authority, 2002-08, chair, 2004-05; dir. Ark. Biosciences Inst. 2002-08; pres. S.E. Conf., 2002—04, pres. NW Ark. Regional Airport Authority, 2005-08; co-chair NW Ark. Coun., 2005-08. Co-author: Facility Layout and Location: An Analytical Approach, 1974 (Book of Yr. award Inst. Indsl. Engrs. 1974), 2d edit., 1991, Analysis of Queueing Systems, 1975, Principles of Engineering Economic Analysis, 4th edit., 1998, Capital Investment Decision Analysis for Management and Engineering, 1980, 3d edit., 2005, Facilities Planning, 1984 (Book of Yr. award Inst. Indsl. Engrs. 1984), 3rd edit., 2003; editor: Production Handbook, 1987; co-editor: Progress in Materials Handling and Logistics, Vol. 1, 1989; also numerous articles to profl. jours., chpts. to books and handbooks in field, conf. procs. Recipient Outstanding Tchr. award Ga. Inst. Tech., 1982, Disting. Alumnus award Ohio State U. Coll. Engring., 1984, Disting. Indsl. Engring. alumnus award Va. Polytech. Inst. and State U., 1993, Reed-Apple award Material Handling Edn. Found., 1985, Disting. Svc. award NSF, 1991, Rodney D. Chipp Meml. award Soc. Women Engrs., 1994, Disting. Alumnus award U. Ark. Alumni Assn., 2005, Humanitarian of Yr. award NW Ark. chpt. Nat. Coalition for Cmty. and Justice, 2005. Fellow Am. Inst. Indsl. Engrs. (pres. 1983-84, facilities planning and design award 1980, outstanding indsl. engr. award region III 1974, region IV 1984, Albert G. Holzman disting. educator award 1988, outstanding pub. award 1988, David F. Baker disting. rsch. award 1990, Frank and Lillian Gilbreth award 1994), Am. Soc. Engring. Edn. (Donald E. Marlowe award 1994), Inst. Ops. Rsch. & Mgmt. Scis., 2002, Nat. Soc. Profl. Engrs. Inst. for Ops. Rsch. and the Mgmt. Scis. (hon.), Am. Assn. Engring. Socs. (bd. govs., chmn. 1986, Kenneth Andrew Roe award 1989); mem. Nat. Acad. Engring., Ark. Acad. Indsl. Engring. (ASEE award 2006), Internat. Material Mgmt. Soc. (material mgr. of yr. 1989), Soc. Mfg. Engrs. (mfg. educator award 1990), Golden Key, Sigma Nu (Regent's medallion of Merit 2005), Sigma Xi, Alpha Pi Mu, Omicron Delta Kappa, Phi Kappa Phi, Tau Beta Pi, Omega Rho. Baptist. Avocations: reading, golf, writing. Office: U Ark Engr 308 Fayetteville AR 72701 Office Phone: 479-575-2773. E-mail: jawhite@uark.edu.

WHITE, LONNIE JOE, retired history educator; b. Knox City, Tex., Feb. 12, 1931; s. John Alexander and Fannie Coates White; m. Nancy Louella Evans, June 23, 1951; children: John Evans, Brenda Jo White Holman. BA in History, W. Tex. State Coll., 1950; MA in History, Tex. Tech. Coll., 1955; PhD in History, U. Tex., Austin, 1961. Tchg. asst. history U. Tex., Austin, 1957—61; prof. history Memphis State Univ. (now U. Memphis), 1961—89; prof. emeritus U. Memphis, 1989—. Editl. adv. bd. Jour. of the West, Manhattan, Kans., 1963—88; assoc. edit. Military History of Texas and the Southwest, Austin, Tex., 1977—88. Author: Politics on the Southwestern Frontier: Arkansas Territory, 1819-1836, 1964, Panthers to Arrowheads: The 36th (Texas-Oklahoma) Division in World War I, 1984, The 90th Division in World War I: The Texas-Oklahoma Draft Division in the Great War, 1996; co-author: Hostiles and Horse Soldiers: Indian Battles and Campaigns In the West, 1972; co-editor: By Sea to San Francisco, 1849-50: The Journal of Dr. James Morison, 1977, 2nd edit., 2000; editor: Old Mobeetie, 1877-1885: Texas Panhandle News Items from the Dodge City Times, 1967, The Miles Expedition of 1874-1875: An Eyewitness Account of the Red River War, 1971, Chronicle of a Congressional Journey: The Doolittle Committee in the Southwest, 1865, 1975; contbr. more than 45 articles to profl. jour., book reviews over 97 pub. to prof. jour. Sgt. US Army, 1951—53. Grantee Rsch. Grant, Am. Philos. Soc., 1963. Mem.: So. Hist. Assn., Am. Hist. Assn. Republican. Baptist. Avocations: history, writing, travel, flying, genealogy. Personal E-mail: ljwhiteside@cableone.net.

WHITE, MACK (BODI) A., state legislator; Mem. Dist. 64 La. House of Reps., 2004—12; mem. Dist. 6 La. State Senate, 2012—. Republican. Office: 808 O'Neal Ln Baton Rouge LA 70816 Office Phone: 225-272-1324. Business E-Mail: whitem@legis.la.gov.

WHITE, MARK, state legislator; b. Union City, Tenn., Mar. 11, 1950; Grad., U. Memphis, 1974. Prin. Harding Acad., Memphis; mem. Dist. 83 Tenn. House of Reps., 2010—. Republican. Office: 301 6th Ave N Nashville TN 37243 Office Phone: 615-741-4415. Office Fax: 615-253-0349. Business E-Mail: rep.mark.white@capitol.tn.gov.

WHITE, MARTIN CHRISTOPHER, academic administrator; b. Anderson, SC, Oct. 16, 1943; s. Jesse Martin and Christine Freida (Powell) W.; m. Linda Ann Fleming, July 31, 1965; children: Martin Lynn, Andrew Christopher. AB, Mercer U., 1965; MDiv, So. Bapt. Theol. Sem., 1968; PhD, Emory U., 1972. Prof. Elon Coll. (N.C.), 1972-76, dean acad. affairs, 1976-82, v.p. for acad. and student affairs, 1982-86; pres. Gardner-Webb U., Boiling Springs, NC, 1986—2002, Chowan U., Murfreesboro, NC, 2002—. Cons. So. Assn. Colls. and Schs., Atlanta, 1982—. Contbr. articles in field. Bd. dirs. United Way, Shelby, N.C., 1987. Woodrow Wilson fellow, 1971. Mem. Soc. Bibl. Lit., Nat. Assn. Bapt. Profs. of Religion, N.C. Ind. Coll. Assn., Alpha Chi, Omicron Delta Kappa. Lodges: Rotary (bd. dirs. Burlington, N.C. chpt. 1986). Democrat. Baptist. Avocations: golf, tennis, music, travel. Home: 100 Jones Dr Murfreesboro NC 27855-1800 Office: One University Dr Murfreesboro NC 27855 Home Phone: 252-398-5266; Office Phone: 252-398-6221. E-mail: whitec@chowan.edu.

WHITE, PATRICIA DENISE, dean, law educator; b. Syracuse, NY, July 8, 1949; d. Theodore C. and Kathleen (Cowles) Denise; m. Nicholas P. White, Feb. 20, 1971 (div. 1997); children: Olivia Lawrence, Alexander Cowles; m. James W. Nickel, Sept. 15, 2005. BA, U. Mich., 1971, MA, 1974, JD cum laude, 1974. Bar: DC 1975, Mich. 1988, Utah 1995. Assoc. Steptoe & Johnson LLP, Washington, 1975-76; vis. asst. prof. Coll. of Law U. Toledo, 1976-77; assoc. Caplin & Drysdale, Washington, 1977-79; vis. assoc. prof. Law Ctr. Georgetown U., 1979—80, asst. prof., 1980—84, assoc. prof. Law Ctr., 1985-88; vis. prof. Law Sch. U. Mich., Ann Arbor, 1988-94; counsel Bodman, Longley and Dahling, Detroit, Ann Arbor, 1990—95; prof. U. Utah, Salt Lake City, 1994-98; counsel Parsons, Behle and Latimer, Salt Lake City, 1995—98; dean, prof. Sandra Day O'Connor Coll. Law, Ariz. State U., 1999—2008, Jack Brown prof., 2008—09, dean emeritus, 2008—; spl. counsel Steptoe & Johnson LLP, Wash., 2008—09; vis. prof. Georgetown U. Law Ctr., 2008—09; dean, prof. U. Miami Sch. Law, 2009—. Affiliated prof, Dept. Philosophy Ariz. State U., faculty fellow, Ctr. Study of Law, Sci., & Tech.; founder Legal Corps. Contbr. articles to profl. jours. Recipient Judge Learned Hand award for Disting. Pub. Svc., American Jewish Com., 2009, Equal Justice Leadership award, Legal Services of Greater Miami, 2012; named one of The Most Influential People in Legal Edn., The National Jurist, 2013. Fellow: Am. Coll. Tax Coun.; mem.: Mich. Bar Assn., Utah Bar Assn., Law Sch. Admission Coun. (bd. dirs. 2003—07), Am. Law Deans Assn. (bd. dirs. 2001—). Office: University of Miami School of Law 1311 Miller Dr Room C225 Coral Gables FL 33146 Home Phone: 480-838-6550; Office Phone: 305-284-2394. Office Fax: 305-284-3210. Business E-Mail: pwhite@law.miami.edu.

WHITE, PERRY MERRILL, JR., orthopedic surgeon; b. Texarkana, Ark., Oct. 11, 1925; s. Perry Merrill and Mary Gladys (Shelton) W.; m. Lucy Katherine Freeman, Dec. 23, 1947; children: Perry Merrill III, MD., Georgia Lynette, Katherine Landis White Long, John David. BS, Baylor U., 1948, MD, 1953; postgrad., Vanderbilt U., 1948-49. Diplomate Am. Bd. Orthopedic Surgery. Intern VA Hosp., Houston, 1953-54; gen. practice medicine Spearman, Tex., 1955-57; resident orthopedic surgery Eugene Talmadge Meml. Hosp., Augusta, Ga., 1957-61; pvt. practice orthopedic surgery Atlanta, 1961-83; chief Ga. Adult Amputee Clinic, 1965-79; active staff Scottish Rite Hosp. for Crippled Children, Decatur, Ga., 1965-73; instr. orthopedic surgery residency program Ga. Bapt. Hosp., 1965-83; orthopedic panelist Ga. Dept. Vocat. Rehab. Cons. Ga. Crippled Children's Service, 1965-76 Former mem. bd. dirs. Haggai Inst., Atlanta, London, Singapore. Served with USNR, 1944-46. Fellow ACS, Am. Acad. Orthopedic Surgeons; mem. So., Ga., Atlanta med. assns., Eastern Orthopedic Assn., Ga., Atlanta orthopedic socs., Alpha Kappa Kappa. Republican. Baptist (deacon). Home: 1547 Cave Rd NW Atlanta GA 30327-3119 E-mail: kaper1947@bellsouth.net.

WHITE, RANDALL WAYNE, educational association administrator; b. Keystone, Okla., Jan. 11, 1942; s. Wiley and Helen (Ottinger) W.; m. Carol L. Thompson, Feb. 1, 1964; children: Craig M., Todd R. BS, Okla. State U., 1963. Acctg. mgr. Mapco, Tulsa, 1963-69; controller CCI Corp., Tulsa, 1969-71, PepsiCo., Tulsa, 1971-74; pres. Arctic Express, Tulsa, 1975-80; CFO Nicor Drilling Co., Tulsa, Okla., 1980—83; pres. Educational Developmental Corp., Tulsa, 1983—, treas., 1984—, chmn., 1986—. Bd. dirs. Okla. Osteopathic Hosp. Tulsa, 1987—, Original Chili Bowl, Inc., 1986—. Mem. Shadow Mountain Racquet Club, Kiwanis (bd. dirs. Tulsa club 1988). Republican. Methodist. Office: Ednl Devel Corp 10302 E 55th Pl Tulsa OK 74146-6507 Home: 11598 S 69th East Ave Bixby OK 74008-2047

WHITE, RAYMOND PETRIE, JR., dentist, educator, dean; b. NYC, Feb. 13, 1937; s. Raymond Petrie and Mabel Sarah (Shutze) White; m. Betty Pritchett, Dec. 27, 1961; children: Karen Elizabeth, Michael Wood. Student, Washington and Lee U., 1955—58; DDS, Med. Coll. Va., 1962, PhD, 1967. Diplomate Am. Bd. Oral and Maxillofacial Surgery. Postdoctoral fellow anatomy Med. Coll. Va., Richmond, 1962—67, resident in oral surgery, 1964—67; asst. prof. U. Ky., Lexington, 1967—70, assoc. prof., 1970—71, chmn. dept. oral surgery, 1969—71; prof., asst. dean adminstrn. Va. Commonwealth U., Richmond, 1971—74; prof. Sch. Dentistry U. N.C., Chapel Hill, 1974—, Dalton L. McMichael disting. prof., 1993—, dean Sch. Dentistry, 1974—81, assoc. dean Sch. Medicine, Sch. Dentistry, 1981—92. Mem. staff U. N.C. Hosps., mem. exec. com., 1974—98, sec., 1977—78, assoc. chief staff, 1981—92; mem. adv. panel on dentistry U.S. Pharmacopial Conv., 1985—; sr. program cons. The Robert Wood Johnson Found., 1982—90. Author (with E.R. Costich): Fundamentals of Oral Surgery, 1971; author: (with Bell and Proffit) Surgical Correction of Dentofacial Deformities, 1980; author: (with W.R. Proffit) Surgical Orthodontic Treatment, 1990; author: (with M.R. Tucker, B.C. Terry, J.E. Van Sickels) Rigid Fixations for Maxillofacial Surgery, 1991; co-editor: Internat. Jour. Adult Orthodontics and Orthodontic Surgery, 1985—2002; asst. editor: Jour. Oral and Maxillofacial Surgery, 1993—; author (with W.R. Profit, R.P. Jr., and D. Sarver): Contemporary Treatment of Dentofacial Deformity, 2002; contbr. sci. articles to profl. jours. Bd. dirs. Am. Fund for Dental Health, 1978—86, v.p., 1982—85. Recipient Disting. Svc. award, Am. Fund Dental Health, 1987, Dental Found. N.C., 1981, John C. Brauer award for acad. distinction, U. N.C. Alumni Assn., 2000, Daniel M. Laskin award, 2002, Rsch. Excellence award, Oral and Maxillofacial Surgery Found., 2003. Mem.: AAAS, ADA, N.C. Assn. Oral and Maxillofacial Surgeons, Am. Assn. Oral and Maxillofacial Surgeons (gen. chmn. sci. sessions com. 1974—76, chmn. strategic planning com. 1990—96, Outstanding Svc. award as committeeman 1976, William Gies award 2000, Disting. Svc. award 2003), Chalmers J. Lyons Acad. Oral Surgery, Inst. Medicine of NAS, Internat. Assn. Dental Rsch. (pres. Ky. sect. 1970), N.C. Dental Soc., Sigma Xi, Omicron Kappa Upsilon, Sigma Zeta, Alpha Sigma Chi, Delta Tau Delta, Psi Omega. Roman Catholic. Home: 1506 Velma Rd Chapel Hill NC 27514-7601 Office: U NC Sch Dentistry Dept Oral/Maxillofacial Surgery Chapel Hill NC 27599-7450 Office Phone: 919-966-1126. Business E-Mail: ray_white@dentistry.unc.edu.

WHITE, REBECCA HANNER, dean, law educator; BA, Ea. Ky. U.; JD, U. Ky. Jud. law clerk to Chief Judge George C. Edwards US Ct. Appeals (6th cir.); atty. Dinsmore & Shohl, Cincinnati; prof. U. Ga. Sch. Law, 1989—, assoc. provost and assoc. v.p. academic affairs, interim dean, 2003—04, dean, 2004—, J. Alton Hosch prof. law. Co-author: Employment Discrimination, 2002, Cases and Materials on Employment Discrimination, 2003; editl. bd. The Labor Law Jour. Recipient Josiah Meigs Award, 2000, John C. O'Byrne Award, Woman of Distinction award, State Bar Ga. Younger Lawyers Div., 2004, Faculty Book Award for Excellence in Teaching. Fellow: Foundation Fellows, U. Ga. (sr.); mem.: Teaching Acad., U. Ga. Office: University of Georgia Law School Office of the Dean Athens GA 30602 Office Phone: 706-542-7140. Office Fax: 706-542-5556. E-mail: rhwhite@uga.edu.*

WHITE, RICHARD D., diagnostic radiology, educator; MD, Duke U., 1981. Diplomate Am. Bd. Radiology-diagnostic radiology, 1986. Resident diagnostic radiology Univ. Calif. San Francisco Med. Ctr., 1983—85, fellow cardiovasc. radiology, 1985—87; prof. Coll. of Medicine Univ. of Fla.; hosp. affiliation includes Shands Jacksonville Med. Ctr. Office: Shands Jacksonville Medical Center Box C-90 Fl 2 655 W 8th St Jacksonville FL 32209 Office Phone: 904-244-4888.

WHITE, RICHARD L., management consultant; Attended, Fla. State U. Various devel. & mgmt. positions AMRDS, 1982—95, American Airlines, Inc., 1982—95, SABRE, 1982—95; v.p., chief info. officer Cellstar Corp., 1996—2000; chief info. officer MPS (Modis Professional Services) Group, Inc. (acquired by Adecco), 2000—08, sr. v.p., 2002—08; pres. Employer Svcs. Corp. (acquired by Beeline), Beeline (subs. of MPS Group, Inc.), 2002—. Bd. dirs. BSG Alliance, IT, 1995—96. Office: Beeline 12724 Gran Bay Pky W Ste 200 Jacksonville FL 32258-4467 Office Phone: 904-527-5700.

WHITE, RODDY (SHAROD LAMOR WHITE), professional football player; b. James Island, SC, Nov. 2, 1981; s. Joenethia White; children: Roddy Jr., Milan. B in Sociology, U. Ala., Birmingham, 2005. Wide receiver Atlanta Falcons, 2005—. Founder Playmaker Found., 2005—. Named 1st Team NFL All-Pro, AP, 2010; named to Nat. Football Conf. Pro Bowl Team, NFL, 2008—11. Achievements include leading the NFL in: receptions (115), 2010. Office: Atlanta Falcons 4400 Falcons Pky Flowery Branch GA 30542

WHITE, RONALD A., federal judge; b. Sapulpa, Okla., 1961; BA, U. Okla., 1983, JD, 1986. Pvt. practice atty., Tulsa, Okla., 1986—2003; judge US Dist. Ct. (ea. dist.) Okla., Muskogee, 2003—. Office: US Dist Ct PO Box 1009 Muskogee OK 74402 Office Phone: 918-684-7965.

WHITE, ROY BERNARD, performing arts association administrator; b. Cin. s. Maurice and Anna (Rudin) W.; m. Margaret White; children: Maurice, Barbara Dee, Daniel Robert. BA, U. Cin., 1949. Sales staff Twentieth Century Fox Films, Cin.; pres. Mid-States Theatres; dir. Nat. Assn. Theatre Owners, nat. pres., exec. com., chmn. bd. Mem. film adv. panel Ohio Arts Coun.; bd. dirs. Will Rogers Meml. Fund, Found. Motion Picture Pioneers, Inc.; mem. media arts panel Nat. Endowment for Arts. Served with USAAF, 1944-45. Named Exhibitor of Year Internat. Film Importers and Distbrs. Am. Mem. Nat. Assn. Theater Owners (pres.), Am. Film Inst. (trustee 1972-75, exec. com. 1972-75, trustee emeritus), Fedn. Motion Picture Pioneers (v.p.), Masons, Queen City Racquet, Amberley Village (Ohio) Tennis Club (pres. 1972-73), Bankers Club, Quail Creek Country Club, Bay Colony Country Club, Bay Colony Golf Club, Morrings Country Club, Forum Club (Naples, Southwest Fla.)(dir.), SW Fla. Edn. Found. (selection com. mem.). Home: 1274 Waggle Way Naples FL 34108-1994 Personal E-mail: royb3140@aol.com.

WHITE, STAN, state legislator; children: Vicki, Caroline. Grad., East Carolina U. Part owner Basnight's Lone Cedar Cafe; owner Stan White Realty and Construction; former director Outer Banks Chamber of Commerce; former director emeritus Outer Banks Cmty. Found.; mem. Dist. 1 NC State Senate, 2011—. Democrat. Office: PO Box 1447 Nags Head NC 27959 also: NC Senate 16 W Jones St Room 1121 Raleigh NC 27601-2808 Office Phone: 919-715-8293, 252-441-1515. Business E-Mail: Stan.white@ncleg.net.

WHITE, TERESA LYNNE, insurance company executive; married; 2 children. BBA, U. Tex., Arlington; M in Mgmt., Troy U., Ala. Second v.p. policy/payroll account svcs. AFLAC, Inc., Columbus, Ga., 1998—2000, v.p. client svcs., 2000—04, sr. v.p. sales support and adminstrn., 2004—07, sr. v.p., dep. chief adminstrv. officer, 2007—08, exec. v.p., chief adminstrv. officer, 2008—. Bd. dirs. Communicorp, Columbus. Bd. mem. Columbus Housing Initiative; mem. bd. pensions South Ga. Conf. of United Meth. Ch. Named one of Top 77 Women in Exec. Leadership Worth Watching in 2006, Profiles in Diversity Jour.; named to 2006 Divas List, Bus.-to-Bus. mag. Fellow: Life Mgmt. Inst. Office: AFLAC Inc 1932 Wynnton Rd Columbus GA 31999 Office Phone: 706-323-3431.

WHITE, W. BRIAN, state legislator; b. Anderson, Nov. 20, 1967; s. Earl and Sara White; m. Courtney Simmons Bell White, Apr. 17, 1992; 1 child, Amelia Grace. Mem. Dist. 6 SC House of Reps., 2000—; v.p. White's Aviation; ins. agent Capstone Ins. Services LLC. Mem.: Anderson Rotary Club (sgt. at arms). Republican. Mailing: 525 Blatt Bldg Columbia SC 29201 Address: PO Box 970 Anderson SC 29622 Office Phone: 803-734-3144, 864-260-4025. E-mail: WBW@scstatehouse.net.

WHITE, WILL WALTER, III, public relations consultant, writer; b. Glen Ridge, NJ, July 3, 1930; s. Will Walter and Miriam Chandler (Milburn) W.; m. Phyllis Marcia DuFlocq, Dec. 28, 1951 (div. 1971); children: Will Walter IV, Scott, Alan; m. Anne Elizabeth Levenson, Nov. 21, 1971 (div. 1992); children: Duncan, Christopher; stepchildren: Michael, Susan; m. Catherine Laur, Aug. 26, 1992. BA, Cornell U., 1952. Supr. Union Carbide Corp., NYC, 1954-59; account exec. Ketchum, MacLeod & Grove, NYC, 1959-62; sr. v.p. Wilson, Haight & Welch, Hartford, Conn., 1962-72; chmn., chief exec. officer Lowengard & Brotherhood, Hartford, 1972-83; pres., chief exec. officer Harland & Tine & White, Hartford, 1983-87; chmn. Donahue Inc., Hartford, 1987-89; ptnr. Laur White & White, Heathsville, Va., 1992—2000; owner Omega Cubed Press, 1996—. Exec. com. Conn. Dist. Export Council, 1979-88. Author: The Sunfish Book, 1983, 96; contbg. editor Mid-Gulf Sailing mag., 1994-95; sailing columnist, Waterline Mag., 2007-10. Mem. exec. com. Hartford Stage Co., 1982-86; pres. Vis. Nurse Assn., Hartford, 1979; fin. chmn. Vis. Nurse and Home Care, Inc., Hartford and Waterbury, 1982-91; mem. pub. rels. com. Fairfield County Rep. Com., 1961; chmn. S.W. Fla. Regional Harbor Bd., 1995-2000. 1st lt. U.S. Army, 1952-54, bd. dirs. Charlotte Harbor Regatta Inc., 2009- Nat. champion Sunfish Racing Class, 1966, 68 Mem. Pub. Rels. Soc. Am. (accredited, chmn. investor rels. sect. 1983, charter mem. Hall of Fame 1990), Bus. Profl. Advt. Assn. (cert. bus. communicator), Nat. Investor Rels. Inst., U.S. Sunfish Class Assn. (pres. 1985-88, charter mem. Hall of Fame 1991), Boaters Action and Info. League (exec. v.p. 1992-2000), Hist. Soc. Sarasota County (bd. dirs. 1995-2000). Address: 3220 S E Hansel Ave Arcadia FL 34266-3143 Personal E-mail: omegacubedone@yahoo.com.

WHITEHEAD, KENNETH DEAN, writer, translator, retired federal agency administrator, editor; b. Rupert, Idaho, Dec. 14, 1930; s. Clarence Christian and May Bell (Allen) W.; m. Margaret Mary O'Donohue, Aug. 2, 1958; children: Paul Daniel, Steven Francis, Matthew Patrick, David Joseph. BA in French, U. Utah, 1955; postgrad., U. Paris, 1956-57; cert. in Arabic and Middle East studies, Fgn. Service Inst., Beirut, 1962; LittD (hon.), Franciscan U., Steubenville, Oho, 2003. Instr. English U. Utah, Salt Lake City, 1955-56; fgn. service officer Dept. State, Rome, Beirut and Tripoli, Libya, 1957-65; chief Arabic service Voice of Am., Washington, 1965-67; dep. dir. fgn. currency program Smithsonian Instn., Washington, 1967-72; exec. v.p. Caths. United for Faith Inc., New Rochelle, NY, 1972-81; dir. Ctr. for Internat. Edn. U.S. Dept. Edn., Washington, 1982-86, dep. asst. sec. for higher edn. programs, 1986-88, asst. sec. for postsecondary edn., 1988-89. Author: Respectable Killing: The New Abortion Imperative, 1972, Agenda for the Sexual Revolution, 1981, Catholic Colleges and Federal Funding, 1988, DOA: The Ambush of the Universal Catechism, 1993, Political Orphan? The Prolife Cause after 25 Years of Roe v. Wade, 1998, One, Holy, Catholic, and Apostolic: The Early Church Was the Catholic Church, 2000, The New Ecumenism, 2009, Mass Misunderstandings: The Mixed Legacy of the Vatican II Liturgicul Reforms, 2009, The Renewed Church, 2009, Affirming Religious Freedom, 2010; co-author: The Pope, The Council and the Mass, 1981, rev. edit., 2006, Flawed Expectations: The Reception of the Catechism of the Catholic Church, 1996; sr. editor: World Almanac Book of Dates, 1982, Macmillan Concise Dictionary of World History, 1983; editor: Marriage and the Common Good, 2001, Pope John Paul II--Witness to Truth, 2001, The Catholic

Imagination, 2003, Voices of the New Springtime, 2004, The Catholic Citizen: Debating the Issues of Justice, 2004, The Church, Marriage, and the Family, 2007, Vatican Council II's Diverse Legacy, 2007, Sacrosanctum Concilium & the Reform of the Liturgy, 2009, The Idea of the Catholic University, 2009, Conscience, Cooperation And Complicity, 2010, The Thought of Joseph Ratzinger Pope Benedict XVI, 2010; co-editor: The Battle for the Catholic Mind, 2001, The Second Vaticurs Ecumenical Coun., 2010; translator 20 books from French, German, Italian, 1980—. Bd. dir. Notre Dame Inst. for Advanced Study, Arlington, Va., 1986-95, Philosophy Edn. Soc., 1995—, Christas Magister Found., 1997-2001. Fulbright scholar U.S. Dept. State, 1956-57. Mem. Fellowship Cath. Scholars (bd. dir. 1990-2000, 2004-10), Brent Soc. Cath. Profls. (bd. dir. 1992-98), Cath. League for Religious and Civil Rights (bd. dir. 1992—), KC. Republican. Home: 809 Ridge Pl Falls Church VA 22046-3631 E-mail: whiteheadz@msn.com.

WHITEHORN, HENRY LEE, US marshal; b. 1954; BA, La. State U., Shreveport, 1986; MA in Criminal Justice, Grambling State U., La., 1989. Patrolman Mo. Police Dept., St. Louis, 1977—78; various positions including narcotics trooper & dep. sec. pub. safety svcs. La. State Police, 1978—2007, rose through ranks to state police supt., 2007—10; US marshal (we. dist.) La. US Dept. Justice, Shreveport, 2010—. Sgt. USAF, 1973—77. Office: US Courthouse 300 Fannin St Ste 1202 Shreveport LA 71101 Office Phone: 318-676-4200.

WHITEHURST, BROOKS MORRIS, chemical engineer; b. Apr. 9, 1930; s. David Brooks and Bessie Ann (Lowry) W.; m. Carolyn Sue Boyer, July 4, 1951; children: Garnett, Anita, Robert. BS, Va. Poly. Inst. and State U., 1951; DSc (hon.), Roanoke Coll., 2012; LittD (hon.), Internat. Biog. Ctr., Cambridge, 2013. Registered profl. engr., NC. Sr. process asst. Am. Enka Corp., Lowland, Tenn., 1951-56; sr. process devel. engr. Va.-Carolina Chem. Corp., Richmond, Va., 1956-63; project engr. Texaco Inc., Richmond, 1963-66; mgr. engring. svcs. Texasgulf, Inc., Aurora, NC, 1967-80, mgr. spl. projects, long range planning, 1980-81; pres. Whitehurst Assocs., Inc., New Bern, NC, 1981—. Instr., lectr., cons. alt. sources of energy comty. colls. and univs.; presenter paper Solar World Forum, Brighton, Eng., 1981. Co-chmn. NC state supt. task force on secondary edn., 1974—; mem. NC state adv. com. on trade and indsl. edn, 1971-77; chmn. Gov.'s Task Force Vols. in Workplace, 1981; chmn. State Adv. Coun. Career Edn., 1977—; gov.'s liaison for edn. and bus., 1978-79. Recipient commendation Pres. US, 1981, Gold medal Internat. Biog. Ctr. Mem. AIChE, Am. Inst. Chemists (cert., bd. dirs. 1980-84), NC Inst. Chemists (pres. 1975-77), Nat. Soc. Profl. Engrs., NC Soc. Profl. Engrs., Royal Soc. Chemistry. Achievements include patents and current work on biodegradable chelate systems, municipal yard waste disposal, micronutrients for agriculture, waste rubber recycling, conversion of industrial by-products containing manganese and phosphorous to useful non-toxic materials for use in agriculture for environmental clean-up; development of environmentally friendly products for forest fertilization and chelates for organic agriculture, and a process for purification of impure phosphoric acid, patent for the development of products and processes to minimize ammonia volatilization from urea, products for applications of micronutrient coatings on solid fertilizer substrates. Home: 1983 Hoods Creek Rd New Bern NC 28562-9103 Office: PO Box 3335 New Bern NC 28564-3335

WHITEHURST, JIM (JAMES M. WHITEHURST), former air transportation executive; b. Columbus, Ga., 1967; m. Lauren N.; 2 children. BS in Computer Sci. and Econs., Rice U., Houston, 1989; student, Friedrich-Alexander U., Erlangen, Germany, London Sch. Econs.; MBA, Harvard Bus. Sch. V.p., dir. Boston Consulting Group, Inc., 2001; sr. v.p. fin., treasury & bus. devel. Delta Air Lines, Inc., Atlanta, 2002—04, sr. v.p., chief network and planning officer, 2004—05, COO, 2005—07; pres., CEO Red Hat, Inc., 2008—. Bd. dirs. Red Hat, Inc., 2008—. Office: Red Hat Inc 100 E Davie St Raleigh NC 27601-2088 Office Phone: 919-754-3700. Office Fax: 919-547-0024. Business E-Mail: jim.whitehurst@redhat.com.

WHITEHURST, WILLIAM OSCAR, lawyer; b. Ardmore, Okla., Oct. 23, 1945; s. William Oscar and Freddie Elizabeth (Ormsby) W.; m. Stephanie Anne Evans, June 22, 1968; children: Emilee Dawn, Rebecca Danielle. BS in Pharmacy, U. Okla., 1968; JD, U. Tex., 1970. Bar: Tex. 1971, U.S. Dist. Ct. (we. dist.) Tex. 1971, U.S. Ct. Mil. Appeals 1971, U.S. Ct. Appeals (5th cir.) 1971, U.S. Supreme Ct. 1971; bd. cert. in personal injury trial law, Tex.; bd. cert. civil trial adv. Assoc. Fulbright & Jaworski, Houston, 1971; counsel, staff dir. jud. affairs com. Tex. Ho. Reps., Austin, 1975; sr. shareholder Whitehurst, Harkness & Brees Cheng & Imhoff, P.C., Austin, 1975—. Mem. Senate-House Select Com. on the Judiciary, 1983-84, subcom. on Svc. Delivery, subcom. on Jurisdicition; faculty law U. Tex., 1979-86, 88, Tex. Coll. Trial Adv., 1984—. Served to capt. JAGC, USAF, 1971-75. Fellow Am. Bar Found., Tex. Bar Found. (chmn. bd. trustees 1992-93), Am. Coll Trial Lawyers, Internat. Acad. Trial Lawyers (pres. 2008-09); mem. ABA (chmn. standing com. legal aid and indigent defendants 2003-06), Nat. Conf. Bar Pres. (exec. coun. 1992-95), Tex. Bar Assn. (pres. 1986-87, exec. com. 1981-84, 85-88, bd. dirs. 1981-84, active various coms.), Travis County Bar Assn. (sec. 1980-81, bd. dirs. 1979-81), Am. Bd. Trial Advs., Tex. Young Lawyers Assn. (pres. 1982-83, bd. dirs. 1979-84), Austin Young Lawyers Assn. (pres. 1978-79), Tex. Trial Lawyers Assn. (pres. 1995), Am. Soc. Pharmacy Law, Am. Soc. Law and Medicine, Order of Barristers, Univ. Club, Austin Country Club. Democrat. Presbyterian. Avocations: flying, skiing, travel. Home: 2703 Westlake Dr Austin TX 78746-1909 Office: Whitehurst Harkness et al 5113 Southwest Pky Ste 150 Austin TX 78735 Office Phone: 512-476-4346. Business E-Mail: bwhitehurst@austintriallaw.com.

WHITENER, CAROLYN RAYE, artist; b. Corpus Christi, Texas, Feb. 2, 1941; d. Rayburn N. and Alice G. Hamilton; children: Mark Dwain, Rynn Rayna. Student, Okla. State U., 1970, U. Sci. and Arts Okla., 1981-85. Co-owner Honk'n'Holler's, Stillwater, Okla., 1962-75; owner Clynn's Designs, Okla. City, 1969—; co-owner W&W Cattle Ranch, Okla., 1973—2007; comml. artist, co-owner Colorvision, Inc., Okla. and Tex., 1979—2007; coll. & univs. students nat. spkr. women's groups Motivational Speaking, 2011. Cons. Tele-Weight, Buena Vista, Colo., 1985-92, Craig Versus Boren, 1972-76; comml. design cons. for one and two dimensional rendering drawings Rynn's Lawncare & Landscaping, Oklahoma City, 1997—; dir. staging and backdrops, NY, Stillwater, Okla., 1973-74; mem. adv. coun. Status of Okla. Woman, 2001—. Active Grady County Environ. Coalition, 1991—92; adv. mem. Gov.'s Okla. Commn. on Status of Women, 2000—. Recipient Outstanding Cmty. Svc. award Ninnekah, Oka., 1992, One Person Who Made a Difference League Women Voters, 1997, Pres. Prestigious award Okla. State U., 1996, Okla.'s First Person Okla. Commn. on Status of Women, 2001, Gov. Commendation award Gov. Frank Keating, 2001, State of Okla. Citation award Rep. Richard Phillips and Sen. Mike Fair, 2001; named Woman of Yr. Okla. City Coun. of Beta Sigma Phi, 1997-98, Okla. Woman Hall of Fame Gov. Brad Henry, 2009; named to Chickasha HS Students Hall of Fame, 2009. Mem. Okla. Assn. Family Cmty. and Edn., Grady County Ext. Homemakers, Oklahoma City Newcomer's Club, Beta Sigma Phi (Woman of Yr. award 1997-98, Outstanding Svc. award 1992, Evening Lions Homecoming Window Design awards, 1966-68), All 50's and 60's Chickesha Okla. HS Alumni Class (decorations com. 1989—), Motivation Speaking Coll. Students and Orgns., Sr. River Loving Life, Rockport Art Ctr. and Dosent, Phi Alpha Delta (award, 2012), Rockport Women's Club. Democrat. Methodist. Avocations: art, sewing, cooking, travel. Business E-Mail: leqrights@gmail.com.

WHITESIDE, CHARLES B., III, investment company executive; b. Ft. Smith, Ark., Mar. 17, 1941; s. Charles B. Jr. and R. Evelyn cindy Whiteside; m. Catherine Ware, Jan. 29, 1966; children: Carrie H., Charles B. IV. BSBA, U. Ark., Fayetteville, 1963. 1st v.p. Merrill Lynch & Co., Little Rock, 1965—. Trustee Ark. Children's Hosp., 1974—, chmn., treas., 1985—88; vice chmn. bd. dirs. Ark. Children's Hosp. Found., 1983—; trustee Ark. Children's Rsch. Inst., 1989—2000, chmn., 1990—; trustee, treas. Lyon Coll., Batesville, Ark., 1992—; bd. advisors U. Ark., Fayettville, 2006. 1st lt. US Army, 1963—65. Recipient Outstanding Vol. Fundraising award for State of Ark., Nat. Soc. Fund Raising Execs., 2000; Sr. Paul Harris fellow, Rotary. Mem.: Kappa Sigma Alumni Assn. (pres. bd. dirs. 1974—). Episcopalian. Avocations: hunting, fishing. Office: Merrill Lynch 2200 Rodney Parham Ste 300 Little Rock AR 72212 Office Phone: 501-312-7285.

WHITFIELD, EDWARD (WAYNE), United States Representative from Kentucky; b. Hopkinsville, Ky., May 25, 1943; m. Constance Harriman; 1 child, Kate. BS in Bus., U. Ky., 1965; JD, U. Ky. Coll. of Law, 1969. Mem. Ky. Ho. of Reps., 1974-75; pvt. practice law, 1970-79; govt. affairs counsel Seaboard Sys. R.R. subs. CSX Corp., 1979-83, counsel to pres., 1983-85; v.p. state rels. CSX Corp., 1986-88, v.p. fed. r.r. affairs, 1988-91; legal counsel to chmn. Interstate Commerce Commn., 1991-93; mem. US Congress from 1st Ky. dist., 1995—; mem. energy and commerce com. 1st lt. USAR. Republican. Office: US House of Representatives 2184 Rayburn House Office Bldg Washington DC 20515 also: 1403 S Main St Hopkinsville KY 42240 Office Phone: 202-225-3115.*

WHITFIELD, FRED, JR., professional sports team executive; s. Fred Whitfield; m. Mary Whitfield. BBA in Econs., Campbell U., Buies Creek, NC, 1980, MBA in Mktg.; JD, NC Ctrl. U., Durham. Pvt. practice lawyer, Greensboro, NC; dir. Carolinas region Falk Assocs. Mgmt. Enterprises; dir. player devel. basketball divsn. Nike, dir. bus. and legal affairs Brand Jordan divsn., 2003—06; dir. player pers., asst. legal counsel Washington Wizards, 2000—03; pres., COO Bobcats Sports & Entertainment, Charlotte, NC, 2006—. Founder, dir. Achievements Unlimited Basketball Sch., Greensboro, NC, 1985—. Named to Campbell U. Sports Hall of Fame, 1995. Office: Charlotte Bobcats 333 E Trade St Charlotte NC 28202

WHITFIELD, GRAHAM FRANK, orthopedic surgeon; b. Eng., 1942; arrived in U.S., 1969, naturalized, 1975; BSc, King's Coll., U. London, 1963; PhD, Queen Mary Coll., U. London, 1969; MD, NY Med. Coll., 1976. Rsch. scientist Unilever Rsch. Lab., England, 1963-66; postdoctoral fellow dept. chemistry Temple U., 1969-71, instr., 1971-72, asst. prof., 1972-73; resident in surgery NY Med. Coll. Affiliated Hosps., NYC, 1976-78, resident in orthopedics, 1978-79, sr. resident in orthop. surgery, 1979-80, chief resident, 1980-81; attending orthop. surgeon Good Samaritan Hosp., West Palm Beach, Fla., 1981-87, St. Mary's Hosp., West Palm Beach, 1981—82, JFK Med. Ctr., Lake Worth, Fla., 1981—, Palms Wellington Surg. Ctr., West Palm Beach, 1994-96, Wellington Regional Med. Ctr., West Palm Beach, 1996—, Bethesda Health City, Boynton Beach, Fla., 1996—2009, Palms West Hosp., Loxahatchee, Fla., 1997—2004, Columbia Hosp., West Palm Beach, 1997—2002. Instr. health professions divsn. Nova Southeastern U., North Miami, Fla., 1994-95, clin. asst. prof. dept. surgery, Coll. Osteo. Medicine, Nova Southeastern U., Ft. Lauderdale, Fla., 1995—, expert med. advisor, Divsn. Managed Care & Health Quality, Bureau Managed Health Care Workers Compensation Unit Agy. Health Care Administrn. & Judges Compensation Claims, 1996-2008 Author: (with Joseph Cohn and Louis Del Guercio) Critical Care Readings, 1981; editl. bd., contbg. editor Hosp. Physician, 1978-82; cons. editor Physician Asst. and Health Practitioner, 1979-82; orthop. cons. Conv. Reporter, 1980-82; assoc. editor-in-chief Critical Care Monitor, 1980-82; editl. bd. Complications in Orthopedics, 1986-96; practice panel cons. in orthop. surgery Complications in Surgery, 1982-96. Vol. with med. mission Orthop. Splty. Med. Care to the indigenous population, Andes Mountains Ecuador, 2007—08. Recipient N.Y. Med. Coll. Surg. Soc. award, 1976, Rotarian of Yr. award, Palm Beach Flagler Rotary Club, 1998, 2011—12. Fellow: Internat. Coll. Surgeons; mem.: AMA, Fla. Orthop. Soc., So. Orthop. Assn., Royal Inst. Chemistry (Eng.), Palm Beach County Med. Soc., Fla. Med. Assn., Soc. the Four Arts, Princeton Club (NYC), Rotary, Explorer's Club (N.Y.C.), Brit. Schs. and Univs. Club, Soc. Sons of St. George (N.Y.C.), Sigma Xi. Avocation: travel. Office: 2150 S Congress Ave West Palm Beach FL 33406-7604 Office Phone: 561-965-5200. Business E-Mail: doctorwhitfield@aol.com.

WHITING, RICHARD ALBERT, lawyer; b. Cambridge, Mass., Dec. 2, 1922; s. Albert S. and Jessie (Coleman) W.; m. Marvelene Nash, Feb. 22, 1948 (div. 1984); children— Richard A. Jr., Stephen C., Jeffrey D., Gary S., Kimberly G.; m. Joanne Sherry, Oct. 14, 1984 (div., 2007). AB, Dartmouth Coll., 1944; JD, Yale U., 1949. Bar: D.C. 1949. Assoc. Steptoe & Johnson, Washington, 1949-55, ptnr., 1956-86, of counsel, 1987—. Adj. prof. Vt. Law Sch., South Royalton, 1985-90; mem. exec. com. Yale Law Sch. Assn., New Haven, 1985-88; mem. adv. bd. The Antitrust Bull., N.Y.C., 1975-99. Contbr. articles to profl. jours. Trustee Colby-Sawyer Coll., 1987-97. 1st lt. U.S. Army, 1945-46. Mem. ABA (council mem. Antitrust Law sect. 1977-85, del. to Ho. Dels. 1982-83, chmn. 1984-85) Presbyterian. Office: 1550 Pantobs ME Pl Apt 109 Charlottesville VA 22911 Office Phone: 202-429-8080.

WHITLEY, JOE DALLY (JOE DALLY WHITLEY), lawyer; s. Thomas Youngie and Mary Jo (Dally) W.; m. Kathleen Pinion, Sept. 27, 1975; children: Lauren Jacqueline, Thomas McMillan. BA, U. Ga., 1972, JD, 1975. Bar: Ga. 1975, DC, 1990, US Supreme Ct. 1989. Assoc. Kelly, Denney, Pease & Allison, Columbus, Ga., 1975-78; asst. dist. atty. Chattahoochee Jud. Cir., Columbus, 1978-79; assoc. Hirsch, Beil & Partin, P.C., Columbus, 1979-81; US atty. (mid. dist.) GA US Dept. Justice, Macon, 1981-87, dep. asst. atty. gen., criminal divsn. Washington, 1987-88, dep. assoc. atty. gen., 1988-89, acting assoc. atty. gen., 1989; ptnr. Smith, Gambrell & Russell, Atlanta, 1989-90; US atty. (no. dist.) GA US Dept. Justice, Atlanta, 1990-93; ptnr. Kilpatrick Stockton, Atlanta, 1993-97, Alston & Bird, Atlanta, 1997—2003, 2005—08; gen. counsel US Dept. Homeland Security, Washington, 2003—05; shareholder Greenberg Traurig LLP, Atlanta, 2008; shareholder, chair Atlanta White Collar Practice Group. Mem. Atty. Gen.'s adv. com. dept. justice, Washington, 1982-85; chmn. organized crime and violent crime subcom. Atty. Gen.'s adv. com., 1990-93; mem. investigative subcom.; chmn. white collar crime subcom., 1993-99; adj. prof. U. Ga. Law Sch., 1994, Am. U., Washington Coll. Law, 2005, George Washington U. Law Sch., 2006; program chmn. Ga. Inst. Continuing Legal Edn. Programs, 6th Ann. Homeland Security Law Inst., Washington, 2011; co-chair Ga. ICLE Southeastern Health Care Fraud Inst., 2010; moderator 21st Ann. Nat. Inst. Health Care Fraud, Miami Beach, Fla., 2011; lectr. in field. Co-author: Global Settlements, Indictments and trials in FCPA Cases: Increasing Protection, 2010; contbr. articles to numerous profl. jours., chapters to books. Treas. Muscogee County Young Reps., Columbus, 1979-80. Named one of Best Lawyers in America, 2001—10, Super Lawyers Mag., Ga. Super Lawyers Mag., 2010, Ga.'s Legal Elite, Ga. Trend, 2008—10. Fellow Am. Bar Found.; mem. ABA (sect. litig., antitrust litig. com. mem. criminal justice dect. voun., vice-chmn. govt. affairs 2002-03, co-chmn., co. homeland security & nat. def., fundraising com. chair, adminstrv. law & regulatory practice, coun. mem., named Vol. of Yr.), DC Bar Assn., Fed. Bar Assn. (adv. bd. mem., Atlanta chpt.), Ga. State Bar Assn., Macon Bar Assn., Nat. Assn. Former US Attys., Nat. Dist. Atty. Assn., Nat. Coll. Dist. Attys. (past bd. mem.), Young Lawyers Club (pres. Columbus chpt. 1980-81), Lawyers Club of Atlanta. Republican. Presbyterian. Office: Greenberg Traurig LLP 3290 Northside Pky Ste 400 Atlanta GA 30327 also: Greenberg Traurig LLP 2101 L St NW Ste 1000 Washington DC 20037 Office Phone: 678-553-7339, 202-331-3131. Business E-Mail: whitleyj@gtlaw.com.

WHITLEY, MARK D., energy executive; B in Chem. Engring., Worcester Poly. Inst.; M in Chem. Engring., U. Ky., 1975. Prodn., operation mgr. Devon Energy Corp.; prodn. & reservoir engr. Shell Oil Co.; v.p., ops. Quicksilver Resources Inc.; with Mitchell Energy & Devel. Corp. (acquired by Devon Energy Corp.), 1982—2002; sr. v.p., southwest and engring. tech. Range Resources Corp., 2005—. Office: Range Resources Corp 100 Throckmorton St Ste 1200 Fort Worth TX 76102 Office Phone: 817-870-2601. Office Fax: 817-870-2316. Business E-Mail: MWhitley@rangeresources.com.

WHITLEY, RICHARD JAMES, pediatrician, educator; b. Nutley, NJ, Sept. 15, 1945; s. Robert Jackson and Helen (Sigemund) W.; m. Sally Bendroth, Apr. 11, 1973; children: Kevin, Christopher, Catherine, Jennifer BA, Duke U., 1967; MD, George Washington U., 1971. Diplomate Am. Bd. Pediatrics. Intern in pediatrics U. Ala., Birmingham, 1971-72, resident in pediatrics, 1972-73, fellow dept. pediatrics, 1973-76, asst. prof. pediatrics, 1976-77, asst. prof. pediatrics and microbiology, assoc. scientist Cancer Research and Tng. Ctr., 1977-78, assoc. prof. pediatrics, asst. prof. microbiology, 1978-80, scientist Cancer Research and Tng. Ctr., dir. clin. research unit Univ. Hosp., 1978-80, assoc. prof., vice chmn. dept. pediatrics, asst. prof. microbiology, 1980-81, scientist Cancer Research and Tng. Ctr., dir. clin. research unit Univ. Hosp., 1980-81, prof., vice chmn. dept., assoc. prof. microbiology, 1981-83, scientist Cancer Research and Tng. Ctr., dir. clin. research unit, Univ. Hosp., 1981-83, prof., acting chmn. dept. pediatrics, assoc. prof. microbiology, 1983-84, scientist Cancer Rsch. and Tng. Ctr., dir. clin. rsch. unit, Univ. Hosp., 1983-84, prof. pediatrics and microbiology, 1985-87, prof. medicine, 1988—, vice chmn. dept. pediatrics, 1989—, acting dir. div. perinatal medicine, 1989-91, scientist Cancer Rsch. and Tng. Ctr., dir. clin. rsch. unit, Univ. Hosp., 1984-88, Loeb eminent scholar chair in pediatrics, 1992; staff physician U. Ala. in Birmingham Hosps. and Clinics, Children's Hosp., Birmingham. Cons. in field; mem. virology sect. NIH, 1985-89, chmn. Nat. Inst. Allergies and Infectious Diseases Data Safety and Monitoring Bd., 1986—, reviewer, site visitor; pres. IDSA, 2009-10. Sect. editor Intervirology, 1986—; editor Antiviral Rsch., 1987—; mem. editorial bd. Jour. Infectious Diseases, 1988—, Sexually Transmitted Diseases, 1989—; contbr. numerous articles to profl. jours. Bd. dirs. Ala. Sch. of Fine Arts, Birmingham, 1982-90 Recipient award of Commendation U. Ala. in Birmingham, 1977, Pres.'s medal, 2007, named Disting. Prof., 2009. Mem. Am. Soc. Virology (bd. dirs. 1988—), Internat. Soc. Antiviral Rsch. (pres. 1988-90), Soc. for Health and Human Values, Transplantation Soc., Infectious Diseases Soc. (past pres. 2010-11), Soc. for Pediatric Rsch., Alpha Omega Alpha Home: 216 Shades Crest Cir Birmingham AL 35216-1316 Office: U Ala Dept Pediatrics 1600 7th Ave S Birmingham AL 35233-1711

WHITLEY-TAYLOR, LINDA K., healthcare company executive, human resources specialist; m. David Taylor; children: Whitley, Harrison. BA in Psychology, Radford U., 1986. cert. six sigma master black belt. Various positions in ops., quality, and human resources Gen. Elec.; sr. v.p. human resources Genworth Financial, Inc., Richmond, Va., sr. v.p. human resources ops.; exec. v.p. assoc. services Amerigroup Corp., 2008—. Guest spkr. Soc. Human Resource Mgmt. Past vol. Tuckahoe Jr. Women's Club, Fan Free Clinic, United Way, Habitat for Humanity; bd. visitors Radford U.; chair nominating com. Radford U. Found. Mem.: Corp. Edn. Coun. Office: Amerigroup Corp National Support Ctr 1330 Amerigroup Way Virginia Beach VA 23464 Office Phone: 757-518-3673. Office Fax: 757-518-3600.

WHITLOCK, GARY L., energy executive; b. Houston, 1950; B in Bus. Adminstrn. Acctg., Sam Houston State U., 1972. CPA. Joined Dow Chemical Co., 1972, responsible for worldwide fin. consolidation and mgmt. reporting, 1981, fin. dir. UK and Ireland, 1984; v.p. fin., CFO Dow AgroScis. subs. Dow Chem. Co., 1998—2001; exec. v.p., CFO delivery group Reliant Energy, Inc., 2001—02; exec. v.p., CFO CenterPoint Energy, Inc., Houston, 2002—. Mem.: AICPA, Tex. Soc. CPAs, Inst. Mgmt. Accts. Office: CenterPoint Energy PO Box 1700 Houston TX 77251-1700

WHITMAN, BURKE WILLIAM, health services executive; b. Newport, RI, Feb. 26, 1956; s. Homer William and Anne (Sarran) W. BA cum laude, Dartmouth Coll., 1978; MBA, Harvard U., 1984. Project mgr. HCB Contractors/Barker Interests Ltd., Atlanta, Houston, 1979-85; investment banker Morgan Stanley & Co. Inc., NYC, 1988-92; v.p. fin./devel. Almost Family Inc., Balt., 1992-94; pres., CFO Deerfield Healthcare Corp., Balt., 1994-99; CFO Triad Hosps., Inc., Plano, Tex., 1999—2005; pres., COO Health Mgmt. Assocs., Inc., Naples, Fla., 2005—07, pres., CEO, 2007—08. Bd. dirs. Fedn. Am. Hosps., chmn. audit com., 2005—06. Former bd. dirs. Outward Bound, Police Athletic League; bd. advisors Marine Corps U.; mem. Founders Group, Nat. Mus. Marine Corps. With USMC, 1985—2005, lt. col. USMCR, 1988—. Mem.: Fedn. Am. Hosps. (bd. dirs.), Piedmont Driving Club. Episcopalian. Avocations: hiking, bicycling, outdoor sports.

WHITMER, W. CARL, hospital administrator; BS, Western Ky. U. Sr. mgr. KPMG LLP, 1986—94; v.p., fin., treas. & CFO PhyCor Inc., 1994—2000; v.p., treas. IASIS Healthcare LLC, 2000—01, CFO, 2001—10, pres., CEO, 2010—. Bd. dirs. Fenwall Inc. Office: IASIS Healthcare LLC 117 Seaboard Ln Bldg E Franklin TN 37067 Office Phone: 615-844-2747. Office Fax: 615-846-3006. Business E-Mail: wwhitmer@iasishealthcare.com.

WHITMIRE, JOHN, oil industry executive; Various sr. mgmt. positions Phillips Petroleum Co., exec. v.p. exploration & prodn., 1987-91; chmn. E & P Forum, London, 1993-95; chmn., CEO Union Tex. Petroleum, 1995-99; dir., exec. v.p. Global Marine, Inc., Houston, 1999—, also bd. dirs. Office: 8080 NH Central Expwy Ste 1440 LB 4 Dallas TX 75206-4493 Office Phone: 214-378-5751.

WHITMIRE, JOHN, state legislator; b. Hillsboro, Tex., Aug. 13, 1949; s. James M. and Ruth Bennett Whitmire; children: Whitney, Sarah. BA, JD, U. Houston. Bar: Tex. 1981. Atty. Locke, Liddell & Sapp, Houston; of counsel Locke, Lord, Bissell & Liddell, LLP; mem. Tex. House of Representatives, 1973—82; mem. Dist. 15 Tex. State

Senate, 1983—; apptd. mem. State Pension Rev. Bd., Tex., 1996—. Mem.: Heights Assn., Timbergrove Manor Civic Club, Mason. Democrat. Office: 803 Yale St Houston TX 77007 also: PO Box 12068 Capitol Station Austin TX 78711 Office Phone: 713-864-8701, 512-463-0115. Office Fax: 713-864-5287.

WHITMIRE, MARK ALEXANDER, music educator, conductor; b. Dallas, Nov. 29, 1951; s. Charles Alexander and Bettye Marilyn Whitmire; m. Virginia Ann Ewing; children: Kathryn Brie, Elizabeth Jane. MusB in Edn., Abilene Christian U., Tex., 1977; MusM, U. Tex., San Antonio, 1980; DMA, U. Md., Coll. Pk., Md., 1991. Prof. music No. Va. Cmty. Coll., Alexandria, 1984—; adj. prof. music and liturgy Va. Theol. Sem., Alexandria, 1989—; music dir. St. James's Episcopal Ch., Richmond, Va., 1995—. Composer: (chorus and orchestra) Magnificat and Nunc dimittis, 2003; conductor, Gloucester Cathedral, Canterbury Cathedral. Recipient Pres. Sabbatical award, No.Va. Cmty. Coll., 2005; named Tchr. of Yr., 1993. Mem.: Coll. Music Soc., Am. Guild Organists, Am. Choral Dirs. Assn. Office: No Va Cmty Coll 3001 N Beauregard St Alexandria VA 22311 Office Fax: 703-845-6060. Business E-Mail: mwhitmire@nvcc.edu.

WHITMIRE, WILLIAM R., state legislator; b. Seneca, Aug. 24, 1948; s. Ramsey and Marie Fagan Whitmire; m. Kathy Lynn Pittard Whitmire, June 26, 1975; children: Ashley Aven, Alanya Brianne, Trevor Ramsey. Ret. educator Oconee County Sch. District; owner S&W Farms; mayor pro tempore City of Walhalla, SC, 1998—99, mayor SC, 2000—02; mem. Dist. 1 SC House of Reps., SC, 2003—. Republican. Office: 436D Blatt Bldg Columbia SC 29201 Office Phone: 803-734-3068. E-mail: whitmirew@scstatehouse.net.

WHITMORE, DOUGLAS MICHAEL, physician; b. Cambridge, Mass., Oct. 30, 1947; s. Donald Herbert and Marcela (Klein) W.; m. Ana Maria Lopez. BS, MS in Physics, U. Ill., Champaign-Urbana, 1969; MS in Physics, Stanford U., 1970, PhD in Physics, 1975; MD, U. Miami, 1978. Diplomate Am. Bd. Internal Medicine, Am. Bd. Pulmonary Disease, Am. Bd. Critical Care Medicine, Am. Bd. Geriatric Medicine. Physician Holy Cross Hosp., Ft. Lauderdale, Fla., 1983—. Pres. med. staff Holy Cross Hosp., 1996-97, chief of medicine, 1995-98. Trustee Holy Cross Hosp., 1995-98. Fellow ACP, Am. Coll. Chest Physicians; mem. Caducean Med. Soc. (pres. 1996-97), Am. Thoracic Soc. Office: Med Complex West 1930 NE 47th St Ste 205 Fort Lauderdale FL 33308-7728

WHITNEY, FRANK DEARMON, federal judge; b. Charlotte, NC, Nov. 22, 1959; s. A. Grant and Lillian (DeArmon) Whitney; m. Catherine Whitney; children: Anne Stone, Frances Hunter. BA, Wake Forest U., 1982; MBA, JD, U. NC, 1987. Bar: NC 1987, DC 1988. Assoc. McKenna Conner Cuneo, Washington, 1987—90; law clk. to Hon. David B. Sentelle US Ct. Appeals (DC Cir.), 1988—89; asst. US atty. (we. dist.) NC US Dept. Justice, Charlotte, 1990—2001, US atty. (ea. dist.) NC Raleigh, 2002—06; counsel Kilpatrick Stockton LLP, Charlotte, 2001—02; judge US Dist. Ct. (we. dist.) NC, 2006—. Col., military judge Judge Advocate Corps. Serves in USAR, 1982—2012, paratrooper USAR, military intelligence officer USAR. Presbyterian. Office: US Dist Ct 195 Charles R Jonas Bldg 401 W Trade St Charlotte NC 28202 Office Phone: 704-350-7480.

WHITNEY, LENAR L., state legislator; Assoc. bus. degree, Nicholls State U., Thibodaux, La. Account exec. AccessCom; owner Studio 371; mem. Dist. 53 La. House of Reps., Baton Rogue, 2012—. Republican. Office: La House of Reps 900 N 3rd St PO Box 94062 Baton Rouge LA 70804 Business E-Mail: whitneyl@legis.la.gov.

WHITNEY, RAY, professional hockey player; b. Saskatchewan, Alta., Can., May 8, 1972; s. Floyd and Wendy Whitney; m. Brijet Whitney, June 4, 2000; children: Hanna, Harper, Hudson. Left wing San Jose Sharks, 1991—97, Edmonton Oilers, 1997, Fla. Panthers, 1998—2001, Columbus Blue Jackets, 2001—03, Detroit Red Wings, 2003—04, Carolina Hurricanes, 2005—10, Phoenix Coyotes, 2010—12, Dallas Stars, 2012—. Named to NHL All-Star Game, 2000, 2003. Achievements include being a member of Stanley Cup Champion Carolina Hurricanes, 2006. Avocation: golf. Office: Dallas Stars American Airlines Ctr 2500 Victory Ave Dallas TX 75201

WHITTAKER, BILL DOUGLAS, minister; b. Bowling Green, Ky., June 14, 1943; s. Ewing A. and Lois (Jenkins) W.; m. Rebecca Kaye Howard, June 18, 1966; children: John, Karen, Mary. BA, Western Ky. U., 1965; MDiv, So. Bapt. Theol. Sem., Louisville, 1969, D of Ministry, 1974; MA, Union Coll., 2004. Ordained to ministry So. Bapt. Conv., 1964. Pastor 1st Bapt. Ch., Sturgis, Ky., 1969-76, Murray, Ky., 1976-82; missionary Internat. Mission Bd., So. Bapt. Conv., The Philippines, 1983-86; pastor Downtown Bapt. Ch., Orlando, Fla., 1986-88; pres. Clear Creek Bapt. Bible Coll., Pineville, Ky., 1988—2007; pastor Glasgow Bapt. Ch., Ky., 2007—. Author: Preparing to Preach, 1999, Korean edit. 2002; columnist Western Recorder newspaper, 1988—07; editor: Ky. Bapt. Heritage, 2001—. Bd. dirs. Coalition for the Homeless, Cen. Fla. YMCA, Orlando, 1986-88; mem. Ky. Bapt. Archives Adv. Bd. Mem. Assn. Bible Colls. (accredited, del. 1988—07), Assn. So. Bapt. Colls. and Schs. (del. 1988—07), So. Assn. Coll. and Schs. (del. 1999-06), Kiwanis (pres. Pineville chpt. 1994-95, dist. 6 lt. gov. 1997-98), Ky. Bapt. Conv. (pres. 1980). Baptist. Home: 105 Terrace Manor Glasgow KY 42141 Office Phone: 270-651-2186. Business E-Mail: bill@glasgowbaptist.org.

WHITTEMORE, ANNE MARIE, lawyer; b. Southampton, Eng., Mar. 19, 1946; d. Rober R. and Vera (McMullen) Grimes; m. F. Case Whittemore, June 22, 1968; 1 child, Robert Pendleton. AB, Vassar Coll., 1967; LLB, Yale U., 1970. Bar: Va. 1970. Law clk. to presiding judge US Ct. Appeals (4th cir.), Alexandria, Va., 1970-71; assoc. McGuireWoods LLP (formerly McGuire, Woods, Battle & Boothe), Richmond, Va., 1971-77; ptnr. McGuireWoods, LLP, Richmond, Va., 1977—. Bd. dirs. Fed. Res. Bank of Richmond., Owens & Minor, Inc., 1991-, Albemarle Corp., 1996-, T. Rowe Price Group, Inc., 1995-. Bd. of govs. Greater Richmond Comm. Found., 1978—; bd. advisors Va. Commonwealth U., Richmond, 1981—; trustee Confederate Meml. Libr. Soc., Richmond, 1988—. Named one of Best Lawyers in Am., Woodward/White, Inc., The 50 Most Influential Women Lawyers in Am., Nat. Law Jour., 2007; named to Leading Lawyers in Am. list, Lawdragon 3000, 2006. Mem. Richmond Bar Assn. (exec. com. 1986—), Va. Law Found. (bd. of govs. 1986—), Downtown Club (bd. dirs.). Republican. Roman Catholic. Office: McGuireWoods LLP 1 James Ctr 6th Fl 901 E Cary St Richmond VA 23219 Office Phone: 804-775-4359. Office Fax: 804-698-2206. Business E-Mail: awhittemore@mcguirewoods.com.

WHITTEMORE, JAMES D., federal judge; b. Walterboro, SC, 1952; BSBA, U. Fla., 1974; JD, Stetson U., 1977. Pvt. practice atty., Fla., 1977, Fla., 1981—90; asst. fed. pub. defender Office Fed. Pub. Defender, 1978—81; judge 13th Jud. Cir. Ct., Fla., 1990—2000, US Dist. Ct. (mid. dist.) Fla., Tampa, 2000—. Office: US Dist Ct Gibbons US Courthouse 801 N Florida Ave Tampa FL 33602 Office Phone: 813-301-5880.

WHITTEN, JERRY LYNN, chemistry professor; b. Bartow, Fla., Aug. 13, 1937; s. John Graves and Dorothy Iola (Jordan) W.; m. Mary Hill (div. Sept. 1977); 1 child, Jerrard John; m. Adela Chrzeszczyk, June 21, 1980; 1 child, Christina. BS in Chemistry, Ga. Inst. Tech., 1960, PhD, 1964. Cert. chemist. Rsch. assoc. to instr. Princeton (N.J.) U., 1963-65; asst. prof. chemistry Mich. State U., East Lansing, 1965-67, SUNY, Stony Brook, 1967-68, assoc. prof., 1968-73, prof., 1973-89, chmn. chemistry dept., 1985-89; prof. chemistry, dean Coll. Phys. and Math. Scis. N.C. State U., Raleigh, 1989-99. Vis. prof. Centre Europèen de Calcul Atomique et Molèculaire, Orsay, France, 1974-75, Univ. Bonn and Wuppertal, Fed. Republic Germany, 1979-80, Eidgenossische Technische Hochschule, Zurich, Switzerland, 1984, U. Wuppertel, 2005 Contbr. more than 200 articles to profl. jours. Bd. dirs. N.C. Sch. Sci. and Math Found., chair; bd. dirs. Burroughs Wellcome Fund. Recipient Alexander von Humboldt U.S. Sr. Scientist award, 1979; grantee Petroleum Rsch. Fund, 1966-67, 74-76, 77-81, NSF, 1967-72, U.S. Dept. Energy, 1977—; SDIO/ONR grantee, 1991-92; Alfred P. Sloan fellow, 1969-71. Mem. AAAS, Am. Phys. Soc., Am. Chem. Soc., N.Y. Acad. Scis., Sigma Xi (pres. N.C. chpt.), Phi Beta Kappa, Phi Kappa Phi. Episcopalian. Avocations: boating, tennis, skiing. Office: NC State U Coll Dept Chemistry PO Box 8204 Raleigh NC 27695-0001 Office Phone: 919-515-7960. E-mail: j_whitten@ncsu.edu.

WHITTINGTON, CHRISTOPHER L., lawyer, former political organization administrator; b. 1965; children: Lauren, Lucy. BS in Fin., La. Tech. U., 1987; JD, Southern U. Law Ctr., Baton Rouge, 1992. Ptnr. Whittington & Reynolds, Baton Rouge, The Whittington Law Firm. Legal counsel La. Dem. Party, chmn., 2006—09. Mem.: ABA, Am. Assn. Justice, La. Assn. Justice (bd. govs.), Baton Rouge Bar Assn., La. Bar Assn., Am. Assn. Trial Lawyers, La. Assn. Trials Lawyers. Democrat. Avocations: reading, golf, trivia, hunting. Office: Whittington Law Group PO Box 3035 Baton Rouge LA 70821 Office Phone: 225-346-8777, 225-336-4155. Office Fax: 225-346-0009. Business E-Mail: cwhittington@lademo.org. E-mail: chris@whittingtonlawfirm.com.

WHITTINGTON, JOHN P., lawyer; b. Kannapolis, NC, Apr. 17, 1947; BA, Guilford Coll., 1969; JD, Samford U., 1972. Bar: Ala. 1972. Ptnr. Bradley, Arant, Rose & White LLP, Birmingham, chair Restructuring and Reorganization Practice Group, 1990—2005; gen. counsel, corp. sec. HealthSouth Corp., Birmingham, 2006, exec. v.p., gen. counsel, corp. sec., 2006—. Adj. prof. Cumberland Sch. Law, Samford U., Birmingham, Ala., 1990—. Mem. ABA (mem. bus. law sect.), Am. Coll. of Bankruptcy, Birmingham Bar Assn., Ala. State Bar. Office: HealthSouth Corp 3660 Grandview Pky Ste 200 Birmingham AL 35243 Business E-Mail: john.whittington@healthsouth.com.

WHITTINGTON, LINDA, state legislator; b. Altus Oklahoma; Mem. Dist. 34 Miss. House of Reps., 2007—, vice chair constn. com., mem. agr. com., corrections com., edn. com., juvenile justice com. Democrat. Episcopal. Mailing: PO Box 185 Schlater MS 38952 E-mail: lwhittington@house.ms.gov.

WHITTINGTON, STEPHEN LUNN, museum director; b. Washington, Jan. 31, 1956; s. Charles Lunn and Alice Marie (Doyle) W.; m. Christine Ann Carlson, Aug. 18, 1979; children: Daniel, Joseph. AB in Anthropology, U. Chgo., 1977; MA, Pa. State U., 1981, PhD, 1989. Dir. Proyecto Arqueologico Ostuman, Copan, Honduras, 1989, U. Maine Hudson Mus., 1991—2002, Teozacoalco Archaeol. Project, 2002, Iximche Osteological Project, 1992—95; asst. curator collections Wyo. Hist. and Geol. Soc., Wilkes-Barre, Pa., 1989-90; cooperating assoc. prof. dept. anthropology, dir. Hudson Mus., U. Maine, 1991—2002. Adj. assoc. prof. dept. anthropology Wake Forest U., dir. Mus. Anthropology, 2002—. Author: Archaeology and Ethnohistory of Iximche, 2003; editor: Bones of the Maya, 1997; contbr. articles to profl. jours. Active Maine State Mus. Commn., 1998—2002; treas. Southeastern Mus. Conf., 2006—08; chair Hispanic Arts Initiative Steering Com., 2005; bd. dirs. Assn. Coll. & U. Mus. & Galleries, 2009—. Grantee Wenner-Gren Found. for Anthrop. Rsch., 1992-93, NSF, 1989, Inst. Internat. Edn., 1988, Found. for the Advancement of Mesoamerican Studies, 1995, 99, 2002, NEH, 1997, 2005, Inst. Mus. and Lib. Svcs., 1991, 94, 96-98, 2001, 04, 06, 08, 09, Dumbarton Oaks, 2009. Mem. Am. Assn. Mus., N.C. Mus. Coun., Soc. for Am. Archaeology, Southeastern Mus. Conf. Avocations: jogging, fencing, bicycling. Home: 1307 Brookwood Dr Winston Salem NC 27106 Office: Wake Forest Univ Mus Anthropology PO Box 7267 Winston Salem NC 27109 Office Phone: 336-758-5827. E-mail: whittisl@wfu.edu.

WHITWORTH, HALL BAKER, forest products company executive; b. St. Paul, NC, Feb. 15, 1919; s. A. Frederick and Maude Ethel (Baker) W.; m. Mary Margaret Mease, May 18, 1946; children: Hall Baker, Laura Ellen, David Allen. Student, Miss. So. Coll., 1942, U. N.C., 1957. With Champion Internat., Canton, NC, 1936-62, mgr. materials, 1956-62, dir. materials packages div. Chgo., 1962-65, dir. purchase U.S. Plywood-Champion Papers, Inc. (now champion Internat. Corp.) Hamilton, Ohio, 1965-68, dep. dir. corporate materials services, 1966, v.p., dir. purchase, 1968-75, v.p. materials Stamford, Conn., 1975—, dir., 1975—, now ret.; v.p., dir. So. Agrl. Co., 1985—; pres., dir. H. Whitworth Enterprises, Cin., 1985—. Bd. dirs. Pathfork-Harlan Coal Co., Elmac Corp. Served with U.S. Army, 1942-46. Recipient Thomas award Carolina-Va. Purchasing Agts. Assn., 1963 Mem. Am. Paper Inst. (chmn. energy subcom.), Am. Mgmt. Assn. (v.p. purchasing, transp. and phys. distbn. div. council) Clubs: Canton Toastmasters (founder, 1st pres.). Lodges: Elks. Methodist. Home and Office: 7230 Southport Dr Boynton Beach FL 33472-2978 Personal E-mail: hall_whitworth@msn.com.

WHITWORTH, KATHRYNNE ANN, professional golfer; b. Monahans, Tex., Sept. 27, 1939; d. Morris Clark and Dama Ann (Robinson) W. Student, Odessa Jr. Coll., tex., 1958. Joined tour Ladies Profl. Golf Assn., 1959—. Named to Hall of Fame Ladies Profl. Golf Assn., Tex. Sports Hall of Fame, Tex. Golf Hall of Fame, World Golf Hall of Fame; Capt. of Solheim Cup, 1990-92. Mem. Ladies Profl. Golf Assn. (sec. 1962-63, v.p. 1965, 73, 88, pres. 1967, 68, 71, 89, 1st mem. to win over $1,000,000). Office: care Ladies Profl Golf Assn 2570 Volusia Ave Daytona Beach FL 32114-8144

WHYBARK, DAVID CLAY, business educator, researcher; b. Tacoma, Sept. 18, 1935; s. Clay Alfred and Irene (Stanton) W.; m. Neva Jo Richardson, July 6, 1957; children: Michael David, Suzanne Marie (dec.). BS, U. Wash., 1957; MBA, Cornell U., 1960; PhD, Stanford U., 1967; PhD (hon.), Corvinus U., Budapest, Hungary, 2010. Rsch. assoc. Stanford (Calif.) U., 1962-67; asst. prof. Ariz. State U., Tempe, 1965-66; assoc. prof. Purdue U., West Lafayette, Ind., 1967-76; prof. Ind. U., Bloomington, 1976—90; Macon G. Patton disting. prof. U. NC, Chapel Hill, 1990—2008, emeritus prof., 2008—; academic advisor Inst. Defense & Bus., 2005—. Vis. prof. Shanghai Inst. Mech. Engring., 1986-87, Chinese U. of Hong Kong, 1996, Victoria U., New Zealand, 1996, Canterbury U., New Zealand, 1996; adj. prof. Inst. for Mgmt. Devel., Lausanne, Switzerland, 1981-82, 85-90; dir., founder Global Mfg. Rsch. Group, 1990—; cons. in field. Author: Master Production Scheduling: Theory and Practice, 1979, Manufacturing Planning Control Systems, 1984, International Operations Management, 1989, Integrated Production and Inventory Management, 1993, Why ERP?, 2000, Manufacturing Planning and Control Systems for Supply Chain Management, 2004; editor: Internat. Jour. Prodn. Econs., 1991-95, Global Manufacturing Practices, 1993. Recipient Lilly Alumni MBA Tchg. Excellence award, 1990, Disting. Rsch. award, Kenan-Flagler Sch., 1998. Fellow: Pan Pacific Bus. Assn. (mem. coun., Disting. Global Leadership award 2007), Ops. Mgmt. Assn. (pres. 1992—93), Internat. Soc. Inventory Rsch. (mem. coun., pres. 2000—02), Decision Scis. Inst. (past pres., Disting. Svc. award 1984). Avocations: travel, winemaking. Office: U NC Kenan-Flagler Sch Chapel Hill NC 27599-3490 Office Phone: 919-962-3206, 919-969-8008. Business E-Mail: clay_whybark@unc.edu.

WI, CHARLIE, professional golfer; b. Seoul, Republic of Korea, Jan. 3, 1972; m. Cathy Wi; 1 child. Attended, U. Nev., Reno, U. Calif., Berkeley. Profl. golfer Asian Tour, 1995—2007, Nationwide Tour, 1996—2005, European Tour, 2003—07, PGA Tour, 2007—. Mem. Asian team Dynasty Cup, 2003, Royal Trophy, 2009, 2010; mem. South Korean team World Cup, 2006, 2009. Achievements include winning Asian Tour events: Mild Seven Kuala Lumpur Open, 1997, Volvo China Open, Sinhan Donghae Open, 2001, SK Telecom Open, 2001, 2002, Taiwan Open, 2004, Maybank Malaysian Open, 2006; member of Dynasty Cup winning Asian Team, 2003; winning European Tour event: Maybank Malaysian Open, 2006; member of Royal Trophy winning Asian Team, 2009. Office: c/o PGA Tour 112 PGA TOUR Blvd Ponte Vedra Beach FL 32082

WIANT, SARAH KIRSTEN, law educator, law librarian, educator; b. Waverly, Iowa, Nov. 20, 1946; d. James Allen and Eva (Jorgensen) Wiant; m. Robert E. Akins (dec.). BA, Western State Coll., 1968; MLS, U. North Tex., 1970; JD, Washington & Lee U., 1978. Asst. law libr. Tex. Tech. U., 1970—72, Washington & Lee U., Lexington, Va., 1972—78, dir. Law Libr., 1978—2009, asst. prof. law, 1978-83, assoc. prof. law, 1984-92, prof. law, 1993—. Participant Conf. on Fair Use, NII, 1995—98; visitor U. Melbourne, Monash U., 2001. Co-author: Copyright Handbook, 1984, Libraries and Copyright: A Guide to Copyright Law in the 1990s, 1994, UCITA Encyclopedia of Lib. and Information Science, 2010; co-author: (Va. sect.) Legal Research in the District of Columbia, Maryland and Virginia, 2005; co-author: (admiralty chpt.) Specialized Legal Research, 2009; co-author: Developments on Copyright Law, Bowker Annual, 2009; mem. adv. bd. Westlaw, 1988—93, 2003—; contbr. chapters to books. Mem.: ABA (com. on librs. 1987—93), U.S. Trademark Assn., Maritime Law Assn., Spl. Librs. Assn. (chair copyright com. 1990—96, John Cotton Dana award 1997), Am. Assn. Law Schs. (chmn. sec. on librs. 1990—92, accreditation com. 1991—94), Am. Assn. Law Librs. (mem. exec. bd. 1981—84, mem. copyright com. 1990—94, chmn. 2003—04, copyright office rep., Pres.' award 2001, Spl. Dist. Svc. award Southeastern chpt. 1997). Office: Washington and Lee University 425 Sydney Lewis Hall 1 Denny Circle Lexington VA 24450 Office Phone: 540-458-8543. Business E-Mail: wiants@wlu.edu.

WICHERN, DEAN WILLIAM, business educator; b. Medford, Wis., Apr. 29, 1942; s. Arthur William and Rebecca Ann (Ambler) W.; m. Dorothy Jean Rutkowski, Dec. 7, 1968; children: Michael, Andrew. BS in Math., U. Wis., 1964, MS in Stats., 1965, PhD in Stats., 1969. Instr. Sch. Bus. U. Wis., Madison, 1967-69, asst. prof., 1969-72, assoc. prof., 1972-76, prof., 1976-84, chmn. quantitative analysis dept., 1975-78; prof. Mays Bus. Sch. Tex. A&M U., 1984—2006, head info. and ops. mgmt. dept., 1984—88, 1997—98, 2004—06, assoc. dean, 1988-95, John E. Pearson prof. bus. adminstrn., 1985—2006, prof. emeritus, 2006—. Vis. prof. Math. Rsch. Ctr., 1978-79. Co-author: Intermediate Business Statistics, 1977, Applied Multivariate Statistical Analysis, 6th edit., 2007, Business Statistics: Decision Making With Data, 1997, Business Forecasting, 9th edit., 2008; mem. editl. bd. Jour. Bus. and Econ. Stats., 1983—91. Mem. Beta Gamma Sigma, Phi Kappa Phi. Office: Tex A&M U Mays Bus Sch 4217 TAMU College Station TX 77843-4217 Home: 4782 Stonebriar Cir College Station TX 77845-8987 Business E-Mail: d-wichern@tamu.edu.

WICK, RANDALL W., retail executive; V.p., Music, Movies, and Car Stereo Best Buy Co., Inc.; exec. merchandising positions Petters Group Worldwide; v.p. Best Buy Co., Inc., 1996—2004; exec. v.p., Sales & Mktg. Polaroid Consumer Electronics, 2003—04; sr. v.p., gen. mdse. mgr., Consumer Electronics Circuit City Stores, Inc., 2005—07; v.p., Merchandising, Strategy, and Svcs. Office Depot, Inc., 2007—. Office: Office Depot Inc 6600 N Military Trail Boca Raton FL 33496 Office Phone: 561-438-4800. Office Fax: 561-438-4001. Business E-Mail: Randy.Wick@officedepot.com.

WICKER, ROGER FREDERICK, United States Senator from Mississippi; b. Pontotoc, Miss., July 5, 1951; s. Fred and Wordna Wicker; m. Gayle Long; children: Margaret, Caroline, McDaniel. BA in Polit. Sci. & Journalism, U. Miss., 1973; JD, Ole Miss Law Sch., 1975. Judge adv. USAF, 1976—80; staff me. to Rep. Trent Lott US House of Representatives, Washington, 1980-82; ptnr. Sparks, Wicker, & Colburn, 1982—94; pub. defender Lee County, Miss., 1984—87; judge pro tem Mcpl. Ct. City of Tupelo, 1986—87; mem. Miss. State Senate, 1987—94, US Congress from 1st Miss. Dist., 1995—2007, US House Appropriations Com., 1995—2007, US House Budget Com., 2003—07; US Senator from Miss., 2007—. Mem. Cmty. Devel. Found., Lions Club, Tupelo First Baptist Church, Miss. With USAF, 1976—80, positions up to lt. col. USAFR, 1980—2004. Recipient Nat. Pub. Svc. award, Am. Heart Assn., 1998, Capitol Dome award, Am. Cancer Soc., 2003, Award, Mfg. Excellence, NAM, 2003. Republican. Baptist. Office: US Senate 555 Dirksen Senate Office Bldg Washington DC 20510*

WICKER, WILLIAM WALTER, librarian; b. Canaan, Miss., Sept. 11, 1930; s. Richard Fenton and Willie Thomas (Dunn) W.; m. Nella Ruth Harris, Sept. 5, 1954; children: Carolyn, William W. Jr., Deborah Lynne. BA, U. Miss., 1951; MLS, La. State U., 1955; AM, Fla. State U., 1970, PhD, 1977. Libr. dir. Capital Area Regional Libr., Raymond, Miss., 1955-57, Sch. of Ozarks, Point Lookout, Mo., 1957-61; head serials dept. Memphis State U., 1961-62, assoc. dir., 1966-73; libr. dir. Frederick Coll., Portsmouth, Va., 1962-65; head circulation dept. Miss. State U., Starkville, 1965-66; dir. learning resources U. Houston-Clear Lake, 1973-86, interim dean Sch. Edn., 1984-85; libr. dir. La. Tech. U., Ruston, 1986—. Capt. USAF, 1951-53. Mem. La. Libr. Assn. (pres. 1994-95), Space City Rotary Club (bd. dirs. 1980-83, Paul Harris fellow 1981), Ruston Rotary Club (bd. dirs. 1988-89). Republican. Methodist. Office: Prescott Meml Libr La Tech Univ Ruston LA 71272-0001

WICKLIFFE, CHARLES WALTON, cardiologist; b. Gaffney, SC, Mar. 17, 1943; s. Charles Walton and Maude W. Badgett; m. Melody Anne Craig, Mar. 25, 1965; children: Charles, Andrew. MD cum laude, Emory U., 1967. Cert. Am. Bd. Internal Med., 1973, Am. Bd. Cardiovascular Diseases, 1975. Fellow cardiology Emory U. Sch. of Medicine, Atlanta, 1973-75, asst. prof. medicine, cardiology faculty, 1975-76; co-dir. cardiac cath lab. Grady Meml., Atlanta, 1975—76; clin. asst. prof. of medicine, cardiology Emory U. Sch. of Medicine, Atlanta, 1976-87, clin. assoc. prof., 1987—; pvt. practice internal med., cardiovascular diseases Cardiology of Ga., P.C., Atlanta, 1976—. Chmn., bd. trustees West Paces Ferry Hosp., Atlanta, 1984, bd. trustees, 1981—84; chmn. credentials Piedmont Hosp., Atlanta, 1995, pres. elect-med. staff, 1996—97, pres. med. staff, 1998—2000, trustee, bd. dirs., 1996—; chmn. Specialty Physician Orgn. Piedmont Clin.; chmn. bd. dirs. Piedmont Healthcare, 2002—. Editor: (of profl. jours.) Med. Assn., 1985—89. Venue med. officer ACOG; com. Olympic games, 1995—96. Flight surgeon USN, 1969, lt. comdr., flight surgeon USN, 1969—72. Fellow: Am. Coll. Clinical Cardiology, Am. Heart Assn., Atlanta Diabetes Assn., Am. Coll. Cardiology; mem.: Med. Assn. Atlanta, Med. Assn. Ga., Am. Med. Assn., Atlanta Clinical Soc., Atlanta Cardiology Forum. Democrat. Methodist. Avocations: reading, horseback riding, golf, fishing. Office: 275 Collier Rd NW Ste 500 Atlanta GA 30309-1749 Office Phone: 404-605-2800. Personal E-mail: docwickliffe@aol.com.

WIDMAN, RUDOLPH PAUL, college administrator; b. Abington, Pa., Sept. 19, 1940; s. Rudolph Paul and Sara (Brinker) Widman; m. Alberta Elanora Sabino, May 20, 1963; children: Rudi Paul, Karl Albert. BA, Eastern Nazarene Coll., Wollaston, Mass., 1963; MS, Northeastern U., 1965, PhD, 1971; MBA, Fla. Inst. Tech., Jensen Beach, 1982. Tchr. Plymouth-Carver HS, Mass., 1964—66; prof. chemistry Curry Coll., Milton, Mass., 1966—68; rsch. fellow U. Va., Charlottesville, 1971—73; adminstrv. asst. Piedmont Va. CC, Charlottesville, 1974—2003; dean of librs. Indian River CC, Ft. Pierce, Fla., 1974—2003. Pres. bd. dirs. Sun Grove Montessori Sch., Ft. Pierce, 1975—; bd. dirs. St. Michael's Sch., Stuart, Fla., 1977—. Contbr. articles to profl. jours. Bd. dirs. Cmty. Gainesville., Ft. Pierce, 1975—78, Fla. Found. Future Scientists, Gainesville, 1977—. Recipient 4th Annual award, Soc. Applied Spectroscopy, 1970. Mem.: Fla. Assn. Cmty. Colls., St. Lucie County Libr., Fla. Atlantic U., Phi Delta Kappa, Phi Kappa Phi, Sigma Xi.

WIE, MICHELLE SUNG, professional golfer; b. Honolulu, Oct. 11, 1989; d. Byung-Wook and Hyun-Kyong Sung Wie. Student, Stanford U., Calif. Profl. golfer, 2005—, LPGA Tour, 2009—. Mem. US nat. team Solheim Cup, 2009. Named one of The 100 Most Influential People in the World, TIME mag., 2006. Mem.: Hawaii State Jr. Golf Assn. Achievements include winner amatuer tournaments: Hawaii State Women's Stroke Play Championship, 2001, USGA Women's Amateur Pub. Links Championship, 2003, Jennie K. Wilson Invitational 2004; youngest player to make a LPGA major cut (13 years old), playing in the Kraft Nabisco Championship, 2003; member of Solheim Cup winning US national team, 2009; winner LPGA Tour events: Lorena Ochoa Invitational, 2009; CN Canadian Women's Open, 2010. Avocations: reading, drawing, computers. Office: c/o LPGA 100 Internat Golf Dr Daytona Beach FL 32124-1092

WIEGNER, EDWARD ALEX, financial and energy executive; b. Waukesha, Wis., Dec. 13, 1939; s. Roy Edward and Margaret (Kuehnlein) Wiegner; m. Cathryn J. Mullens, Oct. 16, 1970; children: Carlin, Ryan, Christine. BBA, U. Wis., Madison, 1961, MS in Econs., 1965, PhD in Econs., 1969. Asst. prof. bus. adminstrn. Marquette U., Milw., 1965-71; assoc. prof U. Wis., Madison, 1972-73; sec. Wis. Dept. Revenue, Madison, 1971-74; sr. v.p. fin., bd. dirs. Wis. Power and Light Co., Madison, 1974-76, sr. v.p. consumer, pub. and fin. affairs, dir., 1976-80, exec. v.p., bd. dirs., 1980-82; sr. v.p., CFO, bd. dirs. Am. Natural Resources Co., 1982-85, exec. v.p., chief adminstrv. officer, bd. dirs., 1985-86; sr. v.p. Coastal Corp., 1985-86; sr. v.p., chief fin. officer Household Internat., Inc., 1986-88; exec. v.p., CFO Progressive Corp., Mayfield Heights, Ohio, 1988-91, pres. fin. svcs. div., 1989-93; vice chmn. 1st Am. Ins. Co., Kansas City, Mo., 1994-97; chmn., CEO First Am. Fin. Corp., 1997-98; chmn. Geologix, Inc., Placerville, Calif., 1998—2012, Ins. Distbn. Solutions, LLC, Jacksonville, Fla., 1999—2009; dir. Mogul Energy, LLC and Big Mogul Coal and Energy, LLC, 2010—14; vice chmn. Western Res. Energy Svcs. LLC., Akron, Ohio, 2012—. Contbr. articles to profl. jours. Mem.: Grand Harbor Country Club. Home and Office: 151 Shores Dr Indian River Shores FL 32963

WIELAND, GILBERT DARRYL, medical researcher, anthropologist, gerontologist; b. Hagerstown, Md., Oct. 31, 1951; s. Gilbert Hugh and Joan Kanaga Wieland; m. Manhal A. Wieland, Apr. 26, 1980; 1 child, Christopher. BA cum laude in Anthropology, Am. U., Washington, DC, 1972; PhD in Anthropology, U. Rochester, NY, 1982; MPH in Health Svcs., UCLA, 1983. Sr. rsch. scientist VA Geriatric Rsch., Edn. and Clin. Ctr., Sepulveda, Calif., 1982—96; rsch. dir. Beverly Found., Pasadena, Calif., 1987—90; assoc. rsch. prof. divsn. geriat. UCLA, 1991—96; rsch. dir. geriat. Palmetto Health Richland, Columbia, 1998—2014. Prof., divsn. geriat., dept. medicine USC Sch. Medicine, 1996—2014; dep. editor Jour. Gerontology A Med. Scis., 2005—11; sr. rsch. scientist Duke U. Ctr., 2014—; assoc. bd. mem. J. Gerantology A Med. Sci., 2012—. Assoc. editor Aging: Clinical and Experimental Research, 2004—, mem. editl. bd., reviewer 47 med. and sci. jours., —; editor: Geriatric Assessment Technology, 1995, Cultural Diversity & Geriatric Care, 1994, Case-Based Geriatrics, 2011. Recipient Spl. Recognition award, Am. Geriat. Soc., 2011. Fellow: Soc. Applied Anthropology, Gerontol. Soc. Am. (chair pub. policy com. 2000—02, chair rsch. task force), Am. Geriatrics Soc. (mem. rsch. com. 2000—05, mem. publ. ed. com. 2008—14). Office Fax: 803-434-4331. Business E-Mail: darryl.wieland@palmettohealth.org.

WIELAND, PAUL OTTO, environmental control systems engineer; b. Louisville, Apr. 9, 1954; s. Otto George and Flora Carolyn (Wolf) W. BS in Botany, U. Louisville, 1982, BS in Applied Sci., 1985, M. in Engring., 1987. Lic. profl. engr.; cert. indoor air quality profl. Assn. of Energy Engrs. LEED AP. Paper carrier Courier-Jour., Louisville, 1976-77; youth program dir. UNICORN, Louisville, 1978; recreation worker Met. Parks Dept., Louisville, 1978-80; retail sales clk. Lose Bros. Lawn and Garden, Louisville, 1980-82; trainee engr. Sealand Svc., Inc., Elizabeth, NJ, 1982; engr. NASA Marshall Space Flight Ctr., Huntsville, Ala., 1983—2005; pres. Wiseland Svcs., Huntsville, 1996—. Author: Designing for Human Presence in Space: An Introduction to Environmental Control and Life Support Systems, 1994, Living Together in Space: The Design and Operation of the Life Support Systems on the International Space Station, 1996, rev. edit., 1998, A Guidebook to a Healthier House, 1999, Living Together in Space: The International Space Station Internal Active Thermal Control System Issues and Solutions - Sustaining Engineering Activities at the Marshall Space Flight Center from 1998 to 2005, 2007, Crossing The Threshold Advancing into Space to Benefit the Earth, 2010 (Ind. Pub. Book award, 2011, Gold medal); contbg. author: Space Launch and Transportation Systems, 2005; contbr. articles to profl. jours. Vol. advocate R.A.P.E. Relief Ctr., Louisville, 1977-80; vol. tutor Adult Basic Edn. Program, Huntsville, 1988-89; vol. projectionist Film Co-op., Huntsville, 1990-91; vol. tech. advisor Am. Lung Assn. Health House '96, Huntsville. Recipient Gold medal, Independent Publisher Book, 2011. Mem. ASME, ASHRAE, AIAA (chmn. student chpt. 1984-85), NSPE, Inst. Advanced Studies Life Support (treas. 1990-92), Huntsville ArtsCoun. (panel mem.). Avocations: nature, art, dance. Home and Office: 4212 9th Ave SW Huntsville AL 35805-3408 Office Phone: 256-426-4325.

WIENER, ALAN H., mortgage company executive, former real estate company executive; married; 2 children. Asst. to mayor, NYC, 1976—78; NY dir. US Dept. Housing and Urban Devel., 1978—81; exec. v.p. Integrated Resources; founder, chmn., CEO Am. Property Financing, Inc., NYC, 1991—2006; co-head, multifamily lending group Wachovia Corp., NYC, 2006—, mng. dir., Wachovia Multifamily Capital Inc., 2006—. Bd. trustees Phipps Houses Svcs. Inc.; bd. dirs. Grand Ctrl. Partnership Inc. Recipient Achievement award, Integrated Resources. Mem.: Real Estate Bd. NY (Harry B. Helmsley Disting. New Yorker award 2008). Office: Wachovia Corp 301 S College St Ste 4000 One Wachovia Ctr Charlotte NC 28288

WIENER, JACQUES LOEB, JR., federal judge; b. Shreveport, La., Oct. 2, 1934; s. Jacques L. and Betty (Eichenbaum) Wiener; m. Sandra Mills Feingerts; children: Patricia Wiener Shifke, Jacques L. III, Betty Ellen Wiener Spomer, Donald B. BA, Tulane U., 1956, JD, 1961. Bar: La. 1961, US Dist. Ct. (we. dist.) La. 1961. Ptnr. Wiener, Weiss & Madison, Shreveport, 1961—90; judge US Ct. Appeals (5th cir.), New Orleans, 1990—2010, sr. judge, 2010—. Mem. coun. La. State Law Inst., 1963—; master of the bench Am. Inn of Ct., 1990—98. Pres. United Way N.W. La., 1975, Shreveport Jewish Fedn., 1969—70. Fellow: La. Bar Found., Am. Bar Found., Am. Coll. Trust and Estates Counsel; mem.: ABA, Am. Law Inst., Shreveport Bar Assn. (pres. 1982), La. Bar Assn., Internat. Acad. Estate and Trust Law (academician). Avocations: fly fishing, upland game bird hunting, photography, travel. Office: Court of Appeals Building 600 Camp St Rm 244 New Orleans LA 70130-3425

WIGGINS, BRICE, state legislator; b. Irving, Tex., Aug. 8, 1971; m. Heather Boyd; children: Landen, Grace. Attended, Tulane U., New Orleans, Miss. Coll. Atty.; mem. Dist. 52 Miss. State Senate, Jackson, 2012—. Pres. Singing River Soccer Club; chmn. Excel By 5, Pascagoula, Miss. Mem.: Miss. Bar Assn., Jackson County Bar Assn., EMERGE Pascagoula, Rotary. Republican. Methodist. Office: Miss State Senate PO Box 1018 Jackson MS 39215 Business E-Mail: bwiggins@senate.ms.gov.

WIGGINS, MICHAEL R., human resources specialist; B, State U. West Georgia, Carrollton. Mayor, Ranburne, Ala.; steel stranding machine operator, Carrollton Utility Products Plant Southwire Co., 1969—79, quality mgr., 1979—85, dir., quality, 1985—88, dir., human resources, 1988—95, asst. v.p., 1995—99, v.p., 1999—2005, exec. v.p., human resources, 2005—. Mem.: Ala. League of Municipalities, Soc. of Human Resource Mgmt. Office: Southwire Co 1 Southwire Dr Carrollton GA 30119 Office Phone: 770-832-4242. Business E-Mail: mike_wiggins@southwire.com.

WIGGS, SHIRLEY JOANN, retired secondary school educator; b. Johnston County, NC, Nov. 6, 1940; d. William H. and Sallie P. (Barden) Wiggs. BA, Atlantic Christian Coll., 1963; postgrad., Duke U., 1966, East Carolina U., 1979-80; grad., Newspaper Inst. Am. Tchr. pub. schs., South Hill, Va., 1963-64; tchr. lang. arts and social studies Glendale Chapel HS, Kenly, NC, 1964-65, Benson HS, NC, 1965-69; tchr. advanced placement English, lang. arts, journalism South Johnston HS, Four Oaks, NC, 1969-96, chairperson dept. lang. arts, 1971-83; ret., 1996; historian, 2003—04. Evaluator profl. books Allyn and Bacon, Inc., 1974, 79; yearbook judge Columbia Scholastic Press Assn., 1986-92, yearbook advisor, 1980-94. Sunday Sch. tchr. 1st Bapt. Ch., Smithfield, NC, 1964-66, assoc. supt. young people's dept., 1964-67, scholarship chair, 1987-91, ch. libr., 1992, tutor, 2000, Clothes' Closet dir., 2004, discipleship tng., 2005-2013, summer music camp, 2011, Mission Friends, 2010-13; dir. WMU, 2004-08, 2013-14, JBA WMU, 2008-10; chmn. Keep Johnston County Beautiful, 1979-81. Named Woman of Yr., Atlantic Christian Coll., 1962; recipient Internat. Cheerleading Found. award 1972, Acad. Booster Club award, 1986, Living Legend award Johnson County Bd. Edn., 2011. Mem. NEA, Nat. Coun. Tchrs. English, Assn. Supervision and Curriculum Devel., NC Assn. Educators), NC English Tchrs. Assn. (dir. dist. 12, 1980-85), Johnston County Assn. Educators (pres. 1979), Johnston Co. Ret. Sch. Pers. (historian 2003—08, treas. 2006-12, pres. 2012-, Vol. award 2009). Home: 102 E Sanders St Smithfield NC 27577-4211

WIGINTON, JAY SPENCER, sales executive; b. Lubbock, Tex., Sept. 21, 1941; s. Clarence Elbert and Faye (George) W.; m. Billye Kay Freitag, Nov. 28, 1968 (div. Feb. 1993); children: Lauren, Lindsay; m. Laverne Shook, June 18, 1993. BS, Tex. Tech. U., 1963, MS, 1968. Sales rep. West Tex. ter. Syntex Labs., Lubbock, 1968-70, regional sales rep., 1970-72, Far East regional mgr. Des Moines, 1972-73, dir. mtkg., 1973-74; regional sales mgr. Zoecon Corp., Dallas, 1974-76; nat. account mgr. Custom divsn., 1976-78; gen. mgr. V.A. Snell & Co. divsn. Gt. Plains Chem. Co., San Antonio, 1978-83, Southwest regional mgr., 1983-84, dir. field devel., 1984-85; dist. mgr. Agri-Sales Assocs., Inc., San Antonio, 1985-87; sales mgr. western region Allflex U.S.A., Inc., 1987-91; gen. mgr. Pro. Vet. S., 1991-93; equine sales specialist Merial Ltd., 1993—2009; ind. indsl. cons. With AUS, 1964-66, Vietnam. Mem. Tex. Grain and Feed Assn., Tex. Cattle Feeders Assn., Tex. Chem. Assn., Kappa Sigma. Mem. Christian Ch. (Disciples Of Christ).

WIGNER, PRESTON DOUGLAS, lawyer, tobacco company executive; b. Mountainhouse, Idaho, Sept. 11, 1968; BBA, James Madison U., 1990; JD cum laude, U. Richmond, 1997. Assoc. Hunton & Williams; assoc. Capital Formation Sect. and Corp. and Securities Law Groups Williams, Mullen, Clark & Dobbins, PC, 2000—03; counsel Universal Leaf, 2003—04, sr. counsel, 2004—05; gen. counsel, sec. Universal Corp., Richmond, Va., 2005—, v.p., chief compliance officer, 2007—. Former atty., bd. mem. Richmond Recreation and Parks Found. Editor (in chief): Univ. Richmond Law Review, 1996—97. Office: Universal Corp 1501 N Hamilton St Richmond VA 23230 Mailing: Universal Corp PO Box 25099 Richmond VA 23260 Office Phone: 804-359-9311. Office Fax: 804-254-3582.

WIKE, D. ELAINE, small business owner; b. Ridgecrest, Calif., Sept. 26, 1954; d. Robert G. and Jimmie Mae (Sallee) Field; m. Mike Wike, Oct. 14, 1978 (dec.); children: Mike II, Angelina Elaine, William Willy, Danielle Elizabeth, Edward Lawrence, Windy Gale. Student, U. Houston, 1975—77. Legal sec. Morgan, Lewis & Bockius, Washington, 1977—78; legal asst. Alfred C. Schlosser & Co., Houston, 1972—77, 1978—81, Jerry Sadler, atty., Houston, 1982—83; founder, owner DEW Profl. & Bus. Svcs., Houston, 1979—; office mgr. Law Offices Mike Wike, Houston, 1983—2010. Contbr. poetry to publs. including Internat. Libr. of Poetry, 2001. Treas. Wilhelm Schole Parents Orgn, 1981—82; mem. Free, Inc.; vol. campaign worker Ron Paul for Congress and Reagan for Pres., 1975, 1976. Recipient 3d place, Nassau Bay Tex. Christmas Boat Lane Parade First Ann. Photography Contest, 1990. Mem.: Nat. Paralegal Assn., Am. Soc. Notaries, Nat. Assn. Female Execs., Nat. Notary Assn., Young Ams. for Freedom. Republican. Libertarian. Mem. Christian Ch.

WILBANKS, CODY, attorney; B in History, U. Tex., Arlington; JD with high honors, Southern Methodist U., 1981. Assoc. atty. Vinson & Elkins LLP, Austin, Tex., 1984—87; worked GTE Inc., Verizon Communications, Inc., 1987—2006; v.p., assoc. gen. counsel Verizon Info. Svcs. Inc., 2006, SuperMedia, Inc., 2006—08, apptd. exec. gen. counsel and corp. sec., 2008—. Bd. dirs. Captain Hope's Kids Inc. army officer Med. Svc. Corps, 1975-81, Regular army captain, 1975-1984, criminal prosecutor US Army Judge Adv. Gen. (JAG) Corps., 1981-84 Office: SuperMedia Inc 2200 W Airfield Dr Dallas TX 75261 Office Phone: 972-453-7000. Office Fax: 972-453-6829. Business E-Mail: cody.wilbanks@desmedia.com.*

WILBUR, KIRBY ALLEN, foundation administrator, former political organization administrator; b. Washington, Nov. 11, 1953; m. Trina Wilbur; children: Nathan, Adam. BA in History, U. Wash., Seattle; attended, Hillsdale Coll., Mich., Georgetown U., Washington. Real estate appraiser, owner Liberty Consultants; radio show host Sta. KVI-AM, Seattle, 1993—2009; home sch. coop history, govt. and economics tchr.; sub. radio host Sta. KTTH 770 and Sta. KIRO 97.3; chmn. Wash. State Republican Party, 2011—13; exec. dir. Nat. Journalism Ctr. Young America's Foundation (YAF), 2013—. Assoc. Hillsdale Coll. Co-author (with Floyd Brown): Say the Right Thing: Talk Radio's Favorite Conservative Quotes, Notes, and Gloats, 1999. Bd. dirs. Young America's Found., Second Amendment Found.; mem. Civil Svc. Commn., Duvall, Wash. Mem.: NRA (life), Club for Growth, Tailhook Assn., Internat. Churchill Soc. (life). Republican. Office: Young America's Foundation (YAF) 110 Elden St Herndon VA 20170 Office Phone: 703-318-9608. Office Fax: 703-318-9122.*

WILCHER, LARRY K., lawyer; b. Lebanon, Ky., July 19, 1950; s. Dwain LaRue and Juanita (Tungate) W.; m. Mary Jo Hayden, Aug. 21, 1971; children: Emily Jane, Joseph Keith. BS in Pharmacy, St. Louis Coll. Pharmacy, 1973; JD, No. Ky. U., 1984; program of instrn. for lawyers, Harvard U., 1987, 91, 94. Dir. real estate SuperX Drugs Corp., Cin., 1975-84; dir. real estate, real estate counsel Dollar Gen. Corp., Goodlettsville, Tenn., 1984-85, gen. counsel, corp. sec., 1985—2002; pres. Nations Title Co., Inc., 1999—2002; ptnr. Wyatt, Tarrant & Combs LLP, 2002—07; group v.p., sec., gen. counsel Bass Pro Group, LLC, Springfield, Mo., 2007—. Dir. Ky. Auth. for Ednl. TV, chmn. fin. com. Contbg. author: Kentucky Business Organizations, 1989, Corporate Governance and Compliance Strategies, 2007; presenter in field. Sec., dir. Scottsville-Allen County Indsl. Devel. Authority, Inc., 1991—2006; dir. Leadership Ky., 1994—2000, mem. exec. com., 1997—2000; dir. Bowling Green-We. Ky. U. Symphony Orch., 1998—2000; chmn. Warren County Young Reps, Bowling Green, Ky., 1979, Scottsville-Allen County Planning Commn., 1997—. Named to Hon. Order Ky. Cols., 1968, One of Outstanding Young Men of Am., U.S. Jaycees, 1978; recipient Johnson & Johnson award St. Louis Coll. Pharmacy, 1973, Thurston B. Morton Leadership award Ky. Young Rep. Fedn., 1979. Mem. ABA, Nat. Assn. Corp. Dirs., Ky. Bar Assn. (recognition award 1987), Def. Rsch. Inst. Republican. Baptist. Office: Bass Pro Group LLC 2500 E Kearney Springfield MO 65803

WILCOX, DAVID ERIC, electrical engineering, educator, consultant, business owner; b. Cortland, NY, Sept. 4, 1939; s. James A. and Lucille (Fiske) C.; m. Phillipa Ann Wilcox, Jan. 23, 1977; children: Terri L., Cindy A., Jana L. 0postgrad., Syracuse U., 1965; BSEE, U. Buffalo, 1961; 0postgrad., Marist Coll., Rutgers U.; MS, U. Bridgeport, 1977. Registered profl. engr., N.Y. Rsch. engring. mgr. input/output devices Rome (NY) Air Devel. Ctr., 1966—70; dir. sales Mercom Inc., Winsooki, Vt., 1970-73; pres. Wilcox Tng. Sys., Newburgh, NY, 1973—98; pres., CEO Global Skills Exch., Alexandria, Va., 2003—. Exec. dep. dir., Nat. Skill Stds. Bd., 1998-2003, bd. dirs.; prin. Exec. Effectiveness, Inc., NYC; instr. Dale Carnegie courses. Author: Information System Sciences, 1965; contbr. articles to profl. jours.; patentee in field. Pres. N.Y. State Jaycees, 1972-73, chmn., 1973-74; dir. U.S. Jaycees, 1970-71; bd. dirs., v.p. N.Y. State Spl. Olympics, 1972-73; bd. dirs., treas. Family Counseling Svc., Inc.; mem. Orange County Pvt. Industry Coun., N.Y. State Excelsior Examiner, 1995. Lt. USAF, 1961-65. Mem. IEEE, Soc. Info. Display, N.Y. State Soc. Profl. Engrs., Internat. Transactional Analysis Assn., Internat. Platform Assn., Am. Soc. Quality Control. Methodist. also: 30 W 60th St New York NY 10023-7902 Office: Global Skills Exch 1410 King St Alexandria VA 22314 Home: 413 N Fairfax St Alexandria VA 22314-2321 Office Phone: 703-684-5067. Business E-Mail: dwilcox@gskillsxchange.com, dwilcox@skillsdmo.com.

WILCOX, HARRY WILBUR, JR., retired manufacturing executive; b. Phila., Feb. 13, 1925; s. Harry Wilbur and Justine Elizabeth (Doolittle) Wilcox; m. Colleen Ann Cerra, Apr. 6, 1946 (dec. 2004); children: Justine, Harry Wilbur III; m. Elizabeth W. Crowther, 2006. BS, Yale U., New Haven, Conn., 1949. With GE Co., NYC, 1949-50; mfg. supt. Sylvania Electric Products, 1951-67; v.p., gen. mgr. Granger Assocs., Palo Alto, Calif., 1967-70; gen. mgr. ITT-Cannon Electric Co., Phoenix, 1970-72; pres. Hills McCanna Co., Carpentersville, Ill., 1972-75, VSI, and group v.p. IU Internat. Corp., 1975-78; exec. v.p. ITT-Grinnell, 1978-85; pres. ITT Indsl. and Constrn. Divsn., Lancaster, Pa., 1985-88; ret., 1988. Bd. dirs. Meyer Industries, Nat. Temperature Control Ctrs., Paul N. Howard Co.; former chmn. VSI, VSI-UK. Mem. adv. com. Town of Sherborn, Mass. With US Army, 1943—46. Decorated Bronze Star. Mem.: Madison Beach Club (Conn.), Grand Harbor Golf and Beach Club (Vero Beach), Yale Club of Treasure Coast. Achievements include patents in field of electroluminescence. Home: 1135 Harbor Links Cir Vero Beach FL 32967 Personal E-mail: harcon13@comcast.net.

WILCOX, RAYMOND I., oil industry executive; b. Mar. 19; BSME cum laude, U. Mich., 1968; postgrad., London Bus. Sch., 1994. Design & constrn. engr. Chevron, 1968—81, mem., fgn. ops. staff, 1981—86, ops. supt. Lafayette, La., 1986—90; mng. dir. Chevron Asiatic, Melbourne, Australia, 1990—96; v.p., gen. mgr., marine transp. Chevron Shipping Co., San Ramon, Calif., 1996—99; gen. mgr., asset mgmt. Chevron Nigeria Ltd., 1999—2000, chmn., mng. dir., 2000—01; mng. dir., Nigeria/Mid-Africa strategic bus. unit ChevronTexaco Corp., 2001—02; pres. ChevronTexaco Exploration and Prodn. Co., 2002—06; v.p. ChevronTexaco Corp., Houston; pres., CEO Chevron Phillips Chemical Co., LLC, 2006—11. Bd. dirs. Dynergy Inc., 2003—. Bd. dirs. Spindletop Charities, Greater Houston Partnership; chmn. Century divsn. United Way of Tex. Gulf Coast, 2003. Mem.: Am. Petroleum Inst. (mem. upstream com.). Office: Chevron Phillips Chemical Co LLC 10001 Six Pines Dr The Woodlands TX 77380 Office Phone: 832-813-4100.

WILCOX, SHIRLEY JEAN LANGDON, genealogist; b. Arcata, Calif., Dec. 10, 1942; d. Elmore Harold and Alberta May (Starkey) Langdon; m. Wayne Kent Wilcox, June 22, 1963; 1 child, Harold Bonner. BS, U. Md., 1964. Cert. Bd. for Certification of Genealogists. Tchr. Prince George's County (Md.) Sch. System, 1964-67, substitute tchr., 1968-73; profl. genealogist Lanham, Md., Arlington, Va., 1973—; genealogy tchr. Fairfax County Pub. Schs., 1995-99. Level II coord. Mid-Atlantic Genealogy and History Inst., George Mason U., Fairfax, Va., 1986; trustee Bd. for Certification of Genealogists, 2000—09. Editor: A Bibliography of Published Genealogical Source Records, Prince George's County, Maryland, 1975, Prince George's County Land Records, Vol. A, 1696-1702, 1976, 1850 Census Prince George's County, Maryland, 1978, 1828 Tax List Prince George's County, Maryland, 1985; author: The National Genealogical Society: A Look at Its First One Hundred Years, 2003. Elder Presbyn. Ch., 1970-73, 95-98. Fellow: Nat. Geneal. Soc. (chmn. conf. program subcom. 1990, 2d v.p. 1990—94, councilor 1994—96, pres. 1996—2000); mem.: DAR (libr. Gov. Robert Bowie chpt. 1985—, Outstanding Jr. Mem. award 1979), Fairfax Geneal. Soc. (pres. 1986—89), Prince George's County Geneal. Soc. (pres. 1973,

1975—76, book rev. editor 1976—96, Jane Roush McCafferty award of excellence 1985), Va. Geneal. Soc. (gov. 2001—07, pres. 2007—), Assn. Profl. Genealogists (pres. 1991—93, pres. Nat. Capital area chpt. 1994—96, dir. region 3 2004—06, Grahame Thomas Smallwood Jr. award of merit 1995), Clay Family Soc. (dir. 2002—06, 2010—), Soc. Mayflower Descs. in DC (bd. assts. 2007—), Paperweight Collectors Assn. (pres. Md.-DC-Va. chpt. 1988—90), numerous others. Avocation: collecting paperweights. Home: 1500 23rd St S Arlington VA 22202-1523

WILCOX, TRE, chef; Corp. trainer Eatzi's; chef Toscana; grill cook Abacus Restaurant, Dallas, 1999, sous chef, exec. sous chef, 2003, chef de cuisine. Menu cons. KRLD Restaurant Week, Dallas, 2003. Guest appearances include Tex. Cable News Network, Good Morning Tex., ABC, Good Day Dallas, Metro, Fox News. Recipient Best Food & Wine Pairings award, KRLD Restaurant Week, 2003, First Place, Rising Star Chef contest, Dallas Morning News, 2004, James Beard award; named one of Top Young Guns in Dallas, D Mag., Dallas' Rising Stars, StarChefs.com, 2007, Top Chef. Home: PO Box 4015 Cedar Hill TX 75106

WILD, JAMES ROBERT, biochemistry and genetics professor; b. Sedalia, Mo., Nov. 24, 1945; s. Robert Lee and Frances Elleta (Wheeler) W.; m. Ann Lynn Brenner, Aug. 1, 1973; 1 child, Kalli Ann. BA in Zoology, U. Calif., Davis, 1967; PhD in Cell Biology, U. Calif., Riverside, 1971, post doctoral fellow, 1972. From asst. to assoc. prof. genetics and biochemistry Tex. A&M U., Coll. Sta., Tex., 1975-84, prof., chair genetics faculty, 1984—, prof. biochemistry & genetics, 1984—2000, head biochemistry and biophysics dept., 1986-90, exec. assoc. dean Coll. Agr. and Life Scis., 1987—92, prof., head dept. biochemistry and biophysics Coll. Agr. and Life Scis., 1994—2000, chmn. faculty genetics. Fellow faculty Tex. Agrl. Experiment Sta., 1999. With USN, 1972-75. Recipient So. Regional award for excellence in coll. anduniv. tchg. in food and agrl. scis., Higher Edn. program USDA, 1992. Fellow AAAS. Methodist. Office: Tex A&M U 2128 Biochemistry Bldg Rm 332 College Station TX 77843-2128 Office Phone: 979-845-6539. Business E-Mail: j-wild@tamu.edu.

WILDE, DANIEL UNDERWOOD, computer engineering educator; b. Wilmington, Ohio, Dec. 27, 1937; s. Arthur John and Ruby Dale (Underwood) Wilde. BSEE, U. Ill., 1960; MS, M.I.T., 1962, PhD, 1966. Rsch. instr. medicine Boston U. Med. Sch., 1964-66; asst. prof. info. adminstrn. U. Conn., 1966-69, assoc. prof., 1970-75, prof., 1976-85; assoc. dir. New Eng. Rsch. Application Ctr., Storrs, Conn., 1966-72, dir., 1973-85, NASA Indsl. Application Ctr., 1972-91; pres. NERAC, Inc., Tolland, Conn., 1985-99. Cons. NERAC Inc., 1999-2004; trustee Engring. Index, Inc.; cons. Am. Soc. Metals, 1973-76; bd. dirs. Internat. Coun. Sci. Info. Author: Author: Introduction to Computing: Problem Solving, Algorithms and Data Structures, 1973; contbr. articles to profl. jours. With USAF. Recipient NASA Public Service award, 1975 Fellow Nat. Fedn. Abstracting and Indexing Svcs. (hon.), Internat. Coun. Sci. Info. (hon.); mem. IEEE, Am. Soc. Info. Sci., Assn. Computing Machinery, Assn. Info. and Dissemination Centers (sec.-treas. 1976-79, pres. 1979-81).

WILDE, EDWIN FREDERICK, retired mathematics professor; b. Lombard, Ill., Jan. 14, 1931; s. Edwin Frederick and Carrie Belle (Hammond) W.; m. Connie Mae Rawlings, Aug. 23, 1952 (dec. July 2002); children— Brad Alan, Bruce Ramon, Elizabeth Lynn; m. Kathleen Wright, Sept. 25, 2004. BS, Ill. State U., Normal, 1952, MS, 1953; MA, U. Ill., Champaign-Urbana, 1955, PhD, 1959; postgrad., U. Wis., Madison, part time, 1955-58, Stanford U., Calif., 1964-65; PhD in Edn. (hon.), Roger Williams Coll., 1980. With Beloit Coll., Wis., 1955-76, prof. math., dean faculty Wis., 1969-71, v.p. for planning Wis., 1971-75; dean Roger Williams Coll., Bristol, RI, 1976-80; provost, dean of faculty U. Tampa, Fla., 1980-86; vice chancellor U. S.C., Spartanburg, 1986-91, prof. math., 1991-99; ret., 1999. Cons. AID insts., India, 1964, Insts. Internat. Edn., East Pakistan, 1969 Recipient Disting. Svc. award, U. SC, 2010; NSF Sr. Sci. Faculty fellow, 1964—65, Endowed Professorship in his honor, Beloit Coll., 2008. Mem. Math. Assn. Am. (bd. govs. 1968-69, 72-75). Home: 409 Summit Lake Ct Spartanburg SC 29307 Personal E-mail: efw1931@yahoo.com.

WILDE, WILLIAM KEY, lawyer; b. Houston, May 3, 1933; s. Henry Dayton and Louise (Key) W.; m. Ann Jeannine Austin, Aug. 3, 1957; children— William Key, Austin, Adrienne, Michael Degree, Coll. William and Mary, Williamsburg, Va., 1955; JD, U. Tex., Austin, 1958. Bar: Tex. 1958. Assoc. Bracewell & Patterson, Houston, 1958-61, ptnr., 1961—. Bd. trustees Montreat Coll. Bd. dirs. Goodwill Industries Houston, 1972—; elder 1st Presbyn. Ch.; trustee Presbyn. Found. U.S.A., Ky., 1983-91; chmn. bd. trustees Schriener Coll., 1991-2000. Fellow ABA, Am. Bar Found., Am. Coll. Trial Lawyers; mem. Tex. Bar Assn. (bd. dirs. 1984-87), Houston Bar Assn. (pres. 1982-83), Houston Club (pres. 1981-82), Houston Country Club (bd. dirs., pres. 1989-90). Republican. Avocations: golf, skiing, scuba diving. Home: 6206 Woods Bridge Way Houston TX 77007-7041 Office: Bracewell & Giuliani 2900 S Tower Pennzoil Pl Houston TX 77002 Office Phone: 713-221-1128. Business E-Mail: william.wilde@bgllp.com, williamwilde@sbcglobal.net.

WILDEMUTH, BARBARA M., education educator; BMus in Edn., North Ctrl. Coll., Naperville, Ill., 1971; MLS, U. Ill., Urbana, 1976; MEd, Rutgers U., New Brunswick, NJ, 1982; PhD, Drexel U., Phila., 1989. Indexer, abstractor, user serv, ERIC Clearinghouse, Ednl. Testing Svc., Princeton, NJ, 1976—78, assoc. dir., 1979—85; head, test collection Ednl. Testing Svc., 1978—79; asst. assoc. prof. U. NC, Chapel Hill, 1989—2000, prof., 2000—. Recipient Outstanding Alumna award, North Ctrl. Coll., Naperville, 2001. Mem.: Am. Soc. for Info. Sci. & Tech. (bd. at-large 2007—, ISI Outstanding Info. Sci. Tchr. award 2000). Office: Sch of Information & Library Science Univ of North Carolina CB #3360 Chapel Hill NC 27599-3360

WILDENTHAL, CLAUD KERN, physician, educator; b. San Marcos, Tex., July 1, 1941; s. Bryan and Doris (Kellam) W.; m. Margaret Dehlinger, Oct. 15, 1964; children: Pamela, Catharine. BA, Sul Ross Coll., 1960; MD, U. Tex. Southwestern Med. Ctr., Dallas, 1964; PhD, U. Cambridge, Eng., 1970; DSc (hon.), Southern Meth. U., Austin Coll., 2010. Intern Bellevue Hosp., NYC, 1964-65; resident in medicine, fellow cardiology Parkland Hosp., Dallas, 1965-67; rsch. fellow Nat. Heart Inst., Bethesda, Md., 1967-68; vis. rsch. fellow Strangeways Rsch. Lab., Cambridge, 1968-70; asst. prof. to prof. internal medicine and physiology U. Tex. Southwestern Med. Ctr., Dallas, 1970-76, prof., dean grad. sch., 1976-80, prof., dean Southwestern Med. Sch., 1980-86, prof., pres., 1986—2008, prof., 2008—13; pres. Southwestern Med. Found., 2008—12; pres. emeritus Children's Med. Ctr. Found., 2013—; prof. emeritus and pres. emeritus, 2013—. Hon. fellow Hughes Hall, U. Cambridge, 1994—. Author: Regulation of Cardiac Metabolism, 1976, Degradative Processes in Heart and Skeletal Muscle, 1980; contbr. articles to profl. jours. Bd. dirs. Southwestern Med. Found, Dallas Ctr. Performing Arts, Dallas Symphony, Dallas Opera, Dallas Mus. Art, Dallas Citizen's Coun., Dallas Regional C. of C., Cambridge in Am., Hoblitzelle Found., Reves Found., Hamon Found., Moncrief Cancer Found., Kronos Worldwide Inc. Recipient rsch. career devel. award NIH, 1972; spl. rsch. fellow USPHS, 1968-70; Guggenheim fellow, 1975-76. Mem. AMA, Inst. Medicine/NAS, Am. Soc. Clin. Investigation, Royal Soc. Medicine Gt. Britain, Am. Physiol. Soc., Internat. Soc. Heart Rsch. (past pres. Am. sect.), Am. Fedn. Clin. Rsch., Assn. Am. Physicians, Am. Heart Assn. (past chmn. sci. policy com.), Assn. Acad. Health Ctrs. (past chmn. sci. policy com.). Home: 4001 Hanover Ave Dallas TX 75225-7010 Office: 2777 Stemmons Freeway Ste 700 Dallas TX 75219 Office Phone: 214-456-5335.

WILDER, CHARLES DAVID, lawyer; b. Orlando, Fla., Aug. 6, 1948; s. Thomas Vaughn and Virginia (McKinney) W. BA, U. South Fla., 1970; JD cum laude, Nova Southeastern U. Ctr. for Study of Law, 1980; LLM in Taxation, U. Fla., 1981. Bar: Fla. 1980, US Dist. Ct. (mid. dist. Fla.) 1980, US Supreme Ct., 2007; cert. Fla. Bar (wills, trusts and estates). Mgr. So. Bell Tel. Co., Miami, Fla., 1970-77; assoc. Broad & Cassel, Orlando, Fla., 1981-84; pvt. practice Orlando, 1984-85; ptnr. Johnson & Wilder, Orlando, 1985-88, Dittmer & Wilder, Maitland, Fla., 1988-92, Wilder & Culton, Maitland, Fla., 1992-94, Wilder & Assocs., Winter Park, Fla., 1994-95, Wilder & Berkson, Winter Park, Fla., 1995; founder, sr. atty. Estate Planning & Legacy Law Ctr., Maitland, Fla. Recipient Lexis Nexis Maritindale Hubble Av Peer Review Rated award, 2007; named Fla. Super Lawyers, 2007—13, Orlando's Top Legal Profl., 2009—12; named one of Top 100 Attys., Worth mag., 2005, Best Attys. in Central Fla., 2009—13, Best Attys. in Fla., 2010—13, Best Attys. in Am., 2011—13. Mem. Fla. Bar Assn. (exec. coun. real property probate & trust law sect. 1994-2013), Estate Planning Discussion Grp. (chmn. 1985-2007). Republican. Avocations: travel, photography. Office: Estate Planning and Legacy Law Ctr PLC 159 Lookout Pl Ste 101 Maitland FL 32751 Office Phone: 407-647-7526. Office Fax: 407-644-2194. Business E-Mail: cwilder@epllc-plc.com.

WILDER, LINDA MASONE, rehabilitation nurse, healthcare company executive; b. Jersey City, Jan. 26, 1957; d. Steve Aldo Masone and Tommie Linda (Moody) Covert; m. Charles Austin Wilder, Nov. 14, 1987. Student, Wagner Coll., U. London; BSN, U. Ala., Birmingham; MBA, Ala. A&M U., 1993. RN, Ala.; bd. cert. rehab. RN. Patient care asst. Shelby Meml. Hosp., Alabaster, Ala., 1977-79; staff RN Univ. Hosp., Birmingham, 1979-80, asst. head nurse, 1980-81; dir. staff devel. Lakeshore Birmingham, 1981-82, dir. nursing, 1982-87; adminstrv. dir., patient care svcs. ReLife North Ala. Rehab. Hosp., 1987—94; adminstr., regional dir., ops., area mgr., regional v.p. & v.p. HealthSouth Corp., asst. adminstr. Dothan, Ala., 1994, pres., South-east Region. Faculty Rehab. Nursing Found. Mem. curriculum adv. bd. Samford U., U. Ala. Birmingham, Bessemer State Coll.; past pres. Birmingham Orgn. Nurse Execs. Mem. Assn. Rehab. Nurses, Rehab. Constituency (pres.), Ala. Hosp. Assn., Dothan C. of C. (bd. dirs.), Rotary. Home: 2335 Ridge Trl Birmingham AL 35242-3759 Office: HealthSouth Corp 3660 Grandview Pky Ste 200 Birmingham AL 35243 Office Phone: 205-967-7116. Office Fax: 205-969-3543. Business E-Mail: linda.wilder@healthsouth.com.

WILDHACK, WILLIAM AUGUST, JR., lawyer; b. Takoma Park, Md., Nov. 28, 1935; s. William August and Martha Elizabeth (Parks) W.; m. Martha Moore Allston, Aug. 1, 1959; children: William A. III, Elizabeth L. BS, Miami U., Oxford, Ohio, 1957; JD, George Washington U., 1963. Bar: Va. 1963, D.C. 1965, Md. 1983, U.S. Supreme Ct. 1967. Agt. IRS, Va., 1957-65; pvt. prac. Washington, 1965—69; v.p., corp. counsel B.F. Saul Co. and affiliates, Chevy Chase, Md., 1969-87, Chevy Chase Bank, F.S.B. and affiliates, 1987-90; atty. pvt. practice, Arlington, Va., 1990—. Sec. B.F. Saul Real Estate Investment Trust, Chevy Chase, 1972-87. Named AV peer review rating, Martindale-Hubbell, 2008—. Mem. ABA, Va. Bar, Arlington County Bar Assn. (chmn. trusts and estates sect. 2002—), Nat. Acad. Elder Law Attys., Soc. Corp. Secretaries and Governance Profls. Home: 3440 S Jefferson St Ste 470 Falls Church VA 22041-3150 Office: 6045 Wilson Blvd # 101 Arlington VA 22205 Business E-Mail: waw@wildhacklaw.com.

WILDING, DIANE, computer scientist, consultant; b. Chgo. Heights, Nov. 7, 1942; d. Michael Edward and Katherine Surian; m. Manfred Georg Wilding, May 7, 1975 (div. 1980). BSBA in Acctg. magna cum laude, No. Ill. U., DeKalb, 1963; postgrad., U. Chgo., 1972—74; cert. in German lang., Goethe Inst., Rothenburg, Germany, 1984; cert. in internat. bus. German, Goethe Inst., Atlanta, 1994; cert. in Web page design, Kennesaw State U., Ga., 2000. Lic. cosmetologist. Sys. engr. IBM, Chgo., 1963-68; data processing mgr. Am. Res. Corp., Chgo., 1969-72; system R & D project mgr. Continental Bank, Chgo., 1972-75; fin. industry mktg. rep. IBM Can., Ltd., Toronto, Ont., 1976-79; regional telecom. mktg. exec. Control Data Corp., Atlanta, 1980-84; gen. mgr. The Plant Plant, Atlanta, 1985-92; SAP cons. IBM Global Svcs., Atlanta, 1993—. Pioneer installer on-line automatic teller machines Pos Equipment. Author: The Canadian Payment System: An International Perspective, 1977. Mem. Chgo. Coun. Fgn. Rels.; bd. dirs. Easter House Adoption Agy., Chgo., 1974—76. Mem.: Internat. Brass Soc., Mensa, Goethe Inst., Libertyville Racquet Club, Royal Ont. Yacht Club, Ponte Verde Club (Fla.). Avocations: travel, languages, antiques. Personal E-mail: diane.wilding@gmail.com.

WILEMON, JP, JR., state legislator; b. Prentiss County, Miss., Sept. 10, 1940; m. Bobbie Johnson Wilemon; children: Mark, Gina. Mem. Dist. 5 Miss. State Senate, 2004—. Democrat. Baptist. Address: PO Box 82 Belmont MS 38827 Home Phone: 662-454-7585; Office Phone: 610-359-3232. Fax: 601-359-2166. E-mail: jwilemon@senate.ms.gov.

WILEY, JOHN EDWIN, cytogeneticist; b. Roanoke, Va., Mar. 2, 1951; s. James Edwin and Marie Rita (Cassell) W. BA, U. N.C., Greensboro, 1973, MA, 1976; PhD, N.C. State U., 1981. Diplomate Am. Bd. Med. Genetics-Clin. Cytogenetics. Biomed. rschr. St. Paul's Coll., Lawrenceville, Va., 1981-82; postdoctoral trainee U. Wis., Madison, 1982-84; mem. faculty East Carolina U. Sch. Medicine, Greenville, NC, 1984—. Contbr. articles to profl. jours. Biomed. rsch. support grantee United Way, Greenville, 1986-87, USPHS, Washington, 1987-90. Mem. AAAS, Am. Soc. Human Genetics, Am. Soc. Zoologists, Am. Soc. Ichthyologists and Herpetologists. Democrat. Achievements include observation that certain genes on frog chromosomes seem to move frequently around, that chromosome constitution in many breast cancer tumors seems normal, that in some patients with ring X chromosomes the ring may not be turned off, that the addition of tumor promoting agents helps white blood cells in many vertebrates to divide, and that DNA sequences on ends of frog chromosomes are the same as those on the ends of human chromosomes. Office: East Carolina U Brody Sch Medicine 600 Moye Blvd Greenville NC 27834-4300 Home: 206 Ravenwood Dr Greenville NC 27834-6737 Home Phone: 252-758-0621; Office Phone: 252-744-2525. E-mail: wileyj@ecu.edu.

WILFERT-KATZ, CATHERINE M., medical association administrator, pediatrician, epidemiologist, educator; b. LA, July 26, 1936; m. Samuel L. Katz; children: Rachel, Catherine stepchildren: John, David, William, Deborah, Susan, Penelope. BA with distinction, Stanford Coll., 1958; MD cum laude, Harvard U., 1962. Med. intern Boston City Hosp., 1962—63; resident in pediat. Children's Hosp., Boston, 1964—66, fellow in infectious diseases, 1966—68; asst. prof. pediat. and virology Duke U., 1969—73, assoc. prof. pediat., 1974—79, prof. pediat. and microbiology, chief pediatric infectious diseases, 1980—96, prof. emeritus; sci. dir. Elizabeth Glaser Pediat. AIDS Found., Santa Monica, Calif., 1997—2009. Chair Adv. Com. on Immunization Practices, 1980, Perinatal Working Group of Prevention Trials Network, NIH; mem. adv. com. Office of AIDS Rsch., 1999—2005. Recipient Christopher award, Am. Acad. Pediat., 2007. Mem.: NIH AIDS Coms., Inst. Medicine, Infectious Diseases Soc. Am. (pres. 2000). Home Fax: 919-968-0447. Personal E-mail: wilfert@mindspring.com.

WILFONG, JOHN SCOTT, banker; b. Balt., June 6, 1950; s. Francis Xavier and Helen (Loughman) W.; m. Susan Regina Burns, Aug. 7, 1971; children: Scott, Julie, Sarah. BS in Econs., Mt. St. Mary's Coll., 1972; MBA in Fin., Loyola Coll., Balt., 1978. Mgmt. trainee Equitable Bank N. A., Balt., 1972-73, comml. lender, 1973-76, v.p., 1976-78; sr. v.p. First Nat. Bank Md. (now M&T Bank), Balt., 1982-89, group sr. v.p., 1989; pres., CEO, SunTrust Bank, Greater Washington and Md. Region SunTrust Banks, Inc., 2005—. Bd. dirs. Devel. Credit Fund, Balt., 1986-89; mem. econ. devel. com. Greater Balt. Com., 1989—. Com. mem. Archdiocese Balt. Parish Coun., 1986—, Jewish Nat. Fund, Balt., 1987—, Cath. Charities, Balt., 1989; bd. dirs. United Way of Met. Atlanta, Ctrl Atlanta Progress, Atlanta Symphony Orchestra, Atlanta Police Found., The Cmty. Found., One Ninety One Club of Atlanta, Buckhead Coalition, Inc., Marcus Inst. and St. Joseph's Hosp; chmn., econ. devel. com. Met. Atlanta C. of C.; trustee Mt. St. Mary's Coll., Agnes Scott Coll. Recipient Humanitarian award Community Chest Md., 1986. Mem. Robert Morris Assocs., Balt. Coun. Fgn. Affairs, Center Club, Balt., Hillendale Country Club, Balt. Republican. Roman Catholic. Avocations: golf, tennis. Office: SunTrust Banks Inc 303 Peachtree St NE Atlanta GA 30308 Office Phone: 404-588-7711. Office Fax: 404-332-3875. Business E-Mail: john.wilfong@suntrust.com.

WILHOIT, HENRY RUPERT, JR., federal judge; b. Ashland, Ky., Feb. 11, 1935; s. H. Rupert and Kathryn (Reynolds) W.; m. Jane Horton, Apr. 7, 1956; children: Mary Jane, H. Rupert, William. LLB, U. Ky., 1960. Ptnr. Wilhoit & Wilhoit, 1960-81; city atty. City of Grayson, Ky., 1962-66; county atty. Carter County, Ky., 1966-70; judge US Dist. Ct. (ea. dist.) Ky., 1981—98, chief judge, 1998—2000, sr. judge, 2000—. Recipient Disting. Service award U. Ky. Alumni Assn., 1980 Mem. ABA, Ky. Bar Assn. Office: US Dist Ct 320 Fed Bldg 1405 Greenup Ave Ashland KY 41101-7542

WILKERSON, DAVID, state legislator; b. Fort Dix, NJ, Jan. 06; s. Richard and Helen Wilkerson; m. Penny Wilkerson; children: Olivia, David Jr. Degree in Acctg., NC Agrl. and Tech. State U., Greensboro. CPA 1991. Acct. Deloitte & Touche LLP; project cons. Resources Global Profls.; mem. Dist. 33 Ga. House of Representatives, 2011—. Democrat. Office: 909 Tranquil Dr Austell GA 30106 also: Georgia House of Reps 409 Coverdell Legis Office Bldg Atlanta GA 30334 Office Phone: 404-656-0116. Business E-Mail: david.wilkerson@house.ga.gov.

WILKERSON, LAWRENCE B., former federal official, retired military officer; b. Gaffney, SC, Jan. 28, 1945; m. Barbara Wilkerson; 2 children. Attended, Bucknell U., Lewisburg, Pa.; MA in Internat. Rels., US Naval War Coll., Newport, RI, MS in Nat. Security Studies; degree, Savina Regina U., Newport RI. Col. US Army, Vietnam, Korea, Japan and Hawaii, ret., 1997; exec. asst. US Navy Admiral Stewart A. Ring, Dir. Strategy and Policy, 1984—87; dep. exec. officer US Army Forces Command, Atlanta, 1989; spl. asst. to Gen. Colin Powell Chmn. the Joint Chiefs of Staff, 1989—93; dep. dir., and dir. USMC War Coll., Quantico, Va., 1993—97; cons. and advisor to Gen. Colin L. Powell, 1997—2000; mem. transition office US Dept. State, Washington, 2000—01, policy planning staff mem., East Asia and the Pacific and legis. and polit.-mil. affairs, 2001—02, assoc. dir. policy planning, 2002, chief of staff, 2002—05; from co-chmn. to chmn., US-Cuba Policy Initiative New America Found., Washington. Faculty mem. US Naval War Coll.; vis. Pamela C. Harriman prof. govt. and pub. policy College of William & Mary, Williamsburg, Va.; professorial lectr., honors program George Wash. U., Washington. Contbr. articles to profl. jours. including Proceedings, The Naval War Coll. Rev., Mil. Rev., Joint Force Quar. Office: Coll William & Mary Govt Dept Morton Hall Rm 10 100 Campus Dr Williamsburg VA 23185 also: George Wash U Honors Program 714 21st St NW Washington DC 20006

WILKERSON, PATRICIA HELEN, retired director; b. Victoria, Tex., Aug. 2, 1936; d. Milo Andrew and Gertrude H. (Nichols) Beeman; children: Cheryl Lynn, Susan Leigh, Debra Ann, Jon Craig. Student, U. Corpus Christi, Tex., 1954—56, Del Mar Coll., 1970—71, student, 1986—88. Cert. moo tcr. 2013, esl tchr. 2013. Tax clk. Nueces County Tax Assessor, Corpus Christi, Tex., 1956—57; corr. sec. Boy Scouts of American Gulf Coast Coun., Corpus Christi, 1957—58; elem. dir, nursery sch. coord. First Bapt. Ch., Corpus Christi, 1972—73, pre-K tchr., sec., 1975—85; dir. child devel. ctr. 2d Bapt. Ch., Corpus Christi, 1985—99, Northway Bapt. Ch., Dallas, 1999—2007; tchr. Mothers Day Out, 2008—12, ESL tchr., 2008—12. ASSIST pre-sch. leader Corpus Christi Bapt. Assn., 1967—99; conf. leader, cons. Bapt. Gen. Conv., Dallas, 1967—2005; mem. early childhood adv. bd. Del Mar Coll., Corpus Christi, 1981—86; mem. adv. com. Tex. Bapt. Weekday Assn., Dallas, 1995—98, Gulf Coast Tng. coalition. Writer Presch. Sunday Sch. Curriculum, 1992-99, Southern Bapt. Conv. Tchr. adult ESL Plymouth Pk. Baptist Ch., 2008—12, MDO tchr., 2008—12; Sunday sch. tchr., 1959—2012, various Tex. Bapt. chs., 1959—2009; conf. leader Dallas Bapt. Assn., 2000—02. Mem. Bay Area Assn. Edn. Young Children (sec. 1981-82, co-chair conf. 1991). Avocations: reading, sewing. Home: 2323 Anderson Irving TX 75062

WILKINS, BARRATT (GEORGE WILKINS), librarian; b. Atlanta, Nov. 6, 1943; s. George Barratt and Mabel Blanche (Brooks) W. BA, Emory U., 1965; MA, Ga. State U., 1968, U. Wis., 1969. Reference libr. SC State Libr., Columbia, 1969-71; instl. libr. cons. Mo. State Libr., Jefferson City, 1971-73; asst. state libr. State Libr. Fla., Tallahassee, 1973-77, state libr., 1977—2003; dir. div. Libr. and Info. Svcs. State Fla., Tallahassee, 1986—2003; acting asst. sec. state Fla. Dept. of State, 1987. Abstractor Hist. Abstracts, 1967—71; dir. survey project Nat. Ctr. Edn. Stats., 1976—77, chmn. state libr. agys. survey steering coun., 2003—09; bd. dirs. S.E. Libr. Network, Inc., 1979—82, treas., 1980—81, vice chmn., 1981—82; mem. adv. coun. US Pub. Printer, 1983—86, S.E. Atlantic Regional Med. Libr. Svcs., 1986—89; mem. planning com. Fla. Automated Edn. Commn., 1989—94; del The White House Conf., Libr., Info Svcs., 1991; mem. steering com. pub., state libr. surveys Nat. Ctr. Edn. Stats., 1992—2009; mem. adv. coun. Fla. State Bd. Ind. Colleges, Universities, 1995—98, Fla. State U. Sch. Info. Studies, 1999—2000; mem. pub. libr. surveys Nat. Ctr. Ednl. Stats., 1997—2003; mem. privacy, tech. task force State Fla., 2000—01; mem. Speakers Legis. Hist. Preservation Com., 2000—03; mem. libr. stats. revision com. Nat. Info. Stds. Orgn., 2001—03; del The White House Conf. Sch. Librs., 2002; bd. dirs. First Am. Found., Inc., Fla. Distance Learning Network, Inc.; mem. planning com. Fla. Gov.'s Conf. Libraries, Info. svcs.; cons. in field. Contbr. articles profl. jours. Mem. adv. com. statewide jail project Mo. Assn. Social Welfare, 1971-73, bd. dirs. ctrl divsn., 1971-73; mem. State Univ. System Interinstl. Lib. Com.,

1977-2003; bd. dirs. Fla. Ctr. Libr. Automation, 1984-2003, Fla. Ctr. for the Book, 1984—, Fla. Coll. Ctr. for Libr. Automation, 1990-2003, Coun. for Fla. Librs., 1981—; pres. Rose Hollow Homeowners Assn., 2004-05, 2009-; patron Atlanta Hist. Soc. Recipient Leadership Achievement award Assn. Specialized and Coop. Libr. Agys., 1991, Outstanding Pub. Svc. award Gov. of Fla., 1991, Keppel award and Lorenz award Nat. Ctr. Edn. Stats., 1995—2003, Profl. Achievement award Assn. Specialized and Coop. Libr. Agencies, 2003, Disting. Alumni award U. Wis. Sch. Libr. and Info. Studies, 2003; U. Wis. fellow, 1969. Mem. ALA (coun. 1981-85, legis. com. 1982-86, com. on orgn. 1988-90, planning com., 1993-95, standards, 1996-98, legis. honor roll 1996, legis. com. subcom. LSTA reauthorization 2006-), Assn. State Libr. Agys. (pres. 1976-77), Assn. Hosp. Instl. Librs. (bd. dirs. 1973-74), Am. Correctional Assn. (chair instn. libr. com. 1975-80), Southeastern Libr. Assn. (pres. 1982-84), Assn. Specialized and Coop. Libr. Agys. (bd. dirs. 1981-85, 87-89, stds. rev. 1997—2003, chair awards com., 2003-05, chair legis. com., 2005-), Fla. Libr. Assn. (hon. life mem.), Libr. Adminstrn. and Mgmt. Assn. (chair govt. affair com. 1984-86), Chief Officers of State Libr. Agys. (bd. dirs. 1980-82, pres. 1990-92, chair legis. com. 1992-96, chair rsch. & stats. com. 1998-2003), Univ. Club, Gov.'s Club, Beta Phi Mu, Phi Alpha Theta. Episcopalian. E-mail: barratt.wilkins@mac.com.

WILKINS, BUTCH, state legislator; Mem. Dist. 74 Ark. House of Reps., 2009—. Democrat. Baptist. Office: State Capitol Rm 350 Little Rock AR 72201 also: 2639 Country Rd 333 Bono AR 72416 Office Phone: 501-682-6211, 501-682-7771, 870-972-5503. Business E-Mail: wilkinsb@akleg.state.ar.us.

WILKINS, CHARLES L., chemist, educator; s. Richard and Lenore M. Wilkins; m. Ingrid Fritsch, 1997; children: Mark R., Connor W. Fritsch, Eric. BS, Chapman Coll., 1961; PhD, U. Oreg., 1966. Prof. chemistry U. Nebr., Lincoln, 1967-81; prof. U. Calif., Riverside, 1981-98; disting. prof. U. Ark., Fayetteville, 1998—. Recipient Frank H. Field and Joe L. Franklin award for Outstanding Achievement in mass spectrometry, Am. Chem. Soc., 1997, Eastern Analytical Symposium award in the fields of Analytical Chemistry, 2002, Alumni Disting. Achievement award, Ark. U., 2003, Alumni Achievement award, U. Oreg. Dept. Chemistry, 2004—05, Fulbright Coll. Master Rschr.; award, 2006. Fellow: Am. Chem. Soc. (life), Soc. Applied Spectroscopy (life). Office: U Ark Dept Chem & Biochem Fayetteville AR 72701 E-mail: cwilkins@uark.edu.

WILKINS, DAVID HORTON, lawyer, former ambassador; b. Greenville, SC, Oct. 12, 1946; m. Susan Clary; children: James, Robert. BA, Clemson U., 1968; JD, U. SC, 1971; degree (hon.), Med. U. SC, Citadel; HHD (hon.), Clemson U., 2003. Bar: SC. Mem. SC House of Reps., 1980—2005, chmn. judiciary com., 1986—92, spkr. pro tempore, 1992-95, spkr., 1995—2005; US amb. to Can. US Dept. State, Ottawa, 2005—09; ptnr., chair pub. policy & internat. law practice Nelson Mullins Riley & Scarborough LLP, Greenville, SC, 2010—. Adj. prof. Greenville Tech. Coll., 1972—94; chmn. Greenville County Legis. Del., 1985—86; pres. Nat. Spkrs. Assn., 1998—2005; fellow Am. Acad. Matrimonial Lawyers. Bd. visitors US Mil. Acad., 2002—05; bd. trustees Clemson U., 2007—, chmn., 2009—. With US Army, 1971, with USAR, 1973—76. Recipient Friend of the Taxpayer award SC Assn. Taxpayers, others; named Outstanding Legislator of Yr. by SC C. of C., Dept. Probation of Parole, SC Sch. Bds. Assn., SC Troopers Assn., others, Nat. Rep. Legislator of Yr. Nat. Rep. Legis. Assn. Republican. Baptist. Office: Nelson Mullins Riley & Scarborough LLP Ponsett Plz Ste 900 104 S Main St Greenville SC 29601 Office Phone: 864-250-2231. Office Fax: 864-250-2925.

WILKINS, DOMINIQUE (JACQUES DOMINIQUE WILKINS), professional sports team executive, retired professional basketball player; b. Orléans, France, Jan. 12, 1960; came to US, 1964; s. John and Geraldine Wilkins; m. Nicole Berry, Sept. 26, 1992 (div.); m. Robin Wilkins; 6 children. BBA, U. Ga., 1982. Player Atlanta Hawks, 1982—94, LA Clippers, 1994, Boston Celtics, 1994—95, Panathinaikos-Athens, Greece, 1995—96, San Antonio Spurs, 1996—97, Teamsystem, Bologna, Italy, 1997—98, Orlando Magic, 1998—99, Anaheim Roadrunners, 2000; spl. asst. to the exec. v.p., player devel. asst. to v.p. basketball Atlanta Spirit, LLC (parent co. of NBA Atlanta Hawks, NHL Atlanta Thrashers and Philips Arena), 2000—04, v.p. basketball, 2004—, TV analyst. Named to NBA All-Rookie Team, 1983, NBA All-Star Team, 1986-94, All-NBA First Team, 1986, Ga. Sports Hall of Fame, 2004, Atlanta Sports Hall of Fame, 2005, Naismith Basketball Hall of Fame, 2006 Achievements include holding a single game record for most free throws without a miss (23), 1992; 9th all-time leading scorer in NBA history; NBA scoring leader, 1986; NBA slam dunk champion NBA, 1985, 90; won European Championship as a member of Panathinaikos-Athens, 1996. Office: Atlanta Spirit LLC 101 Marietta St NW Ste 1900 Atlanta GA 30303 Office Phone: 404-878-3800.

WILKINS, HENRY (HANK), IV, state legislator; b. Pine Bluff, Ark., Dec. 13, 1954; m. Phyllis Wilkins; 2 children. BA, Univ. Mich., 1975; MDiv, St. Paul Sch. Theology, Kansas City, Mo., 1981; LHD, Philander Smith Coll., Little Rock, 1998. Pastor St. James Meth. Ch., Pine Bluff, Ark., 1994—; mem. Ark. House of Reps., 1999—2000, mem. Dist. 17, 2011—; mem. Dist. 5 Ark. State Senate, 2001—10, asst. pres. pro tempore, 2007—11. Author: Faith in Public Service, 2010. Founding mem., past pres. Ark. Legis. Black Caucus Found. Recipient Disting. Grad. award, St. Paul Sch. Theology, 2000, Cmty. Champions award, MADD, 2009, Rebirth award, Martin Luther King Commn., 2009, Pub. Health Hero award, 2009. Mem.: Black Methodists for Ch. Renewal (mem. nat. bd. dirs.). Democrat. Methodist. Mailing: Dist Address 717 W 2nd Ave Pine Bluff AR 71601 Office: St James Methodist Ch 900 North University Pine Bluff AR 71601 Office Phone: 870-536-6366. Office Fax: 870-536-6327. Business E-Mail: hwilkins@arkleg.state.ar.us.

WILKINS, RAYFORD, JR., telecommunications industry executive; b. Waco, Tex. m. Lorena Wilkins; 1 child. BBA, U. Tex., Austin, 1974. Comml. asst. Southwestern Bell Tel., Houston, 1974; with SBC Comm., 1983—2005, pres. Kans. & western Mo. area, pres. Pacific Bell Bus. Comm. Svcs., 1997, pres. SBC Comm. Svc., 1997—99, pres. CEO Southwestern Bell Tel., pres. SBC bus. comm. svcs., 1999—2000, pres., CEO Pacific Bell, 2000, grp. pres. SBC mktg. & sales, 2000, grp. pres., CEO SBC enterprise bus. svcs.; CEO diversified businesses AT&T Inc. (merger of SBC Communications & AT&T Corp.), San Antonio, 2005—. Chmn. bd. Cingular Wireless; bd. mem. H&R Block, Telefonos de Mexico, Am. Movil. Bd. mem. AT&T Found., Tiger Woods Found., Tiger Woods Learning Ctr.; mem. adv. coun. U. Tex. McCombs Sch. Bus., Austin. Recipient Eagle award, Nat. Eagles Leadership Inst., 1997; named CEO of Yr., Minority Supplier Coun., 1997; named one of Top 50 African Ams., Black Enterprise mag., 1999, Nation's 50 Most Powerful Black Execs., Fortune mag., 2002, 50 Most Important African Ams. in Tech., eAccess Corp., 2002, 2005, 75 Most Powerful African Ams. in Corp. Am., Black Enterprise mag., 2005, 100 Most Important Blacks in Tech., US Black Engr. & Info. Tech. mag., 2006, Top 100 Blacks in Corp. Am., Black Profl. mag., 2006. Office: AT&T Inc 208 S Akard St Dallas TX 75202 Office Phone: 210-821-4105.

WILKINS, ROBERT HENRY, neurosurgeon, editor, educator; b. Pitts., Aug. 18, 1934; s. George H. and Mary M. (Lemon) W.; m. Gloria A. Kohl, Dec. 28, 1957; children: Michael L., Jeffrey K., Elizabeth A. BS, U. Pitts., 1955, MD, 1959. Diplomate Am. Bd. Neurol. Surgery. Intern, resident gen. surgery Duke U. Med. Ctr., Durham, NC, 1959-61, resident in neurosurgery, 1963-68, asst. prof. neurosurgery, 1968-72, prof. neurosurgery, 1976—2004, chief divsn. neurosurgery, 1976-96, emeritus prof. neurosurgery, 2005—; clin. assoc. surgery br. Nat. Cancer Inst., Bethesda, Md., 1961-63; chmn. dept. neurosurgery Scott and White Clinic, Temple, Tex., 1972-75; assoc. prof. neurosurgery U. Pitts., 1975-76. Lectr. Cook County Grad. Sch. Medicine, Chgo., 1976-96; attending neurosurgeon Durham VA Hosp., 1968-72, 78-98; mem. Nat. Adv. Coun. Nat. Inst. Neurol. Disorders and Stroke, 1989-92. Co-editor: Neurosurgery, 2d edit., 3 vols., 1996, Neurosurgery Updates I and II, 1990, 91, Neurosurgical Operative Atlas, 1991-2000, Principles of Neurosurgery, 1994; editor Clin. Neurosurgery, 1972-75; assoc. editor Surg. Neurology, 1975-76; founding editor Neurosurgery, 1977-82, mem. editl. rev. bd., 1997-2001; mem. editl. bd. Jour. Neurosurgery, 1987-96, chmn., 1996-97, mem. adv. bd., 1997—; neurosurgery editor Key Neurology and Neurosurgery, 1993-96, Yr. Book of Neurology and Neurosurgery, 1994-97. Recipient Travel award Copenhagen, Nat. Inst. Neurol. Diseases and Blindness, 1965, Royal Australasian Coll. Surgeons, Found. lectr. Adelaide 1986. Fellow ACS (gov. 1996); mem. Congress Neurol. Surgeons (pres. 1979-80), Am. Assn. Neurol. Surgeons (treas. 1989-92), So. Neurosurg. Soc. (sec. 1988-91, pres. 1992-93), Soc. Neurol. Surgeons (v.p. 1995-96), Am. Bd. Neurol. Surgery (dir. 1991-97, chmn. 1996-97), Phi Beta Kappa, Alpha Omega Alpha. Democrat. Avocation: medical writing and editing. Office: Duke U Med Ctr PO Box 3807 Durham NC 27710-0001 Personal E-mail: rhwilkins@aol.com.

WILKINS, W.A. (WINKIE), state legislator; b. Roxboro, NC, Jan. 31, 1941; m. Frances Wilkins; children: Wyn, Mac. Former newspaper writer, editor; state rep. Dist. 55 NC, 2005—. With US Army and USAR, 1962—68. Recipient award, 23 NC Pres.'s Assn. Democrat. Baptist. Office: NC House of Reps 16 W Jones St Rm 1301 Raleigh NC 27601-1096 Office Phone: 919-715-0850. E-mail: Winkie.Wilkins@ncleg.net.

WILKINSON, CLAUDE HENRY, writer, artist, English literature educator; b. Memphis, Dec. 17, 1959; s. Henry Bridgforth and Lula (Moncrief) W. BSc, U. Miss., 1981; cert. d'excellence, Alliance Française, Memphis, 1991; MA, U. Memphis, 1992. Instr. English McNeese State U., Lake Charles, La., 1990-91, U. Memphis, 1991-92, Lane Coll., Jackson, Tenn., 1992-94, LeMoyne-Owen Coll., Memphis, 1998; owner Claude Wilkinson Fine Art Studio, Nesbit, Miss., 1984—; editl. asst. River City, Memphis, 1991; asst. editor Jour. Ethnic Am. Lit., Itta Bena, 2011—. Assoc. editor Valley Voices, Itta Bena, 2007-, assoc. editor Poetry South, Itta Bena, 2009-; John and Renée Grisham So. writer in residence U. Miss., 2000-01, provost scholar, 2006; asst. prof. English Miss. Valley State U., Itta Bena, 2007-. Author: Reading the Earth, 1998 (Naomi Long Madgett Poetry award, 1998), Joy in the Morning, 2004; author poetry; contbr. articles to profl. jours. Recipient New Poets award, Ursus Press, 1984, Grand prize, Miss. Poetry Soc., 1985, W.M. Whittington Jr. Purchase award, Cottonlandia Mus. Juried Exhbn., 1993, 1st prize in painting, Carnegie Ctr. for Arts and History, 1994, Pioneer Br. Poetry award, Ark. Writers' Conf., 1995, Kenneth Beaudoin Meml. award, Mid-South Poetry Festival, 1995, Paul Laurence Dunbar Poetry award, Detroit Black Writers Guild, 1998, Whiting Writer's award, Mrs. Giles Whiting Found., 2000; Provost Scholar, U. Miss., 2006, Walter E. Dakin fellow, Sewanee Writers' Conf., 1999. Avocations: music, mythology, nature study. Office Phone: 662-429-4935.

WILKINSON, DORIS, medical family sociology educator; b. Lexington, Ky., June 13, 1936; d. Howard Thomas and Regina Wilkinson. BA, U. Ky., 1958; MA, Case Western Res. U., 1960, PhD, 1968; MPH, Johns Hopkins U., 1985; postgrad., Harvard U., summer 1991. Asst. prof. U. Ky., Lexington, 1968-70; assoc. prof., then prof. Macalester Coll., St. Paul, 1970-77; exec. assoc. Am. Sociol. Assn., Washington, 1977-80; prof. med. sociology Howard U., Washington, 1980-84; vis. prof. U. Va., 1984-85; prof. sociology U. Ky., Lexington, 1985—. Chmn. panel women in sci. program NSF, Washington, 1976; rev. panelist Nat. Inst. Drug Abuse, Washington, 1978—79; mem. bd. sci. counselors Nat. Cancer Inst., Bethesda, Md., 1980—84; vis. scholar Harvard U., Cambridge, Mass., 1989—90, vis. prof. (summers), 1992, 1993, 1994, 1997; Rapoport vis. prof. social theory (summers) Smith Coll., 1995, 1996; bd. dirs. Nat. Conf. for Cmty. Justice, 1992—96; dir. Heritage Project, 2000—. Author: Workbook for Introductory Sociology, 1968; editor: Black Revolt: Strategies of Protest, 1969; editor: The Black Male in America, 1977, co-editor: Alternative Health Maintenance and Healing Systems, 1987, Race, Gender and the Life Cycle, 1991, Race, co-editor, Class and Gender, 1996; social history photographic exhbn. "The African American Presence in Medicine" Harvard Med. Libr., 1991, Pearson Mus.-Southern Ill. U. Med. Sch., 1992, NJ Coll. Medicine and Dentistry, 1993, Louisville Mus. History and Sci., 1994, U. Cin. Med. Sch. Libr., 1994, Albert Einstein Coll. of Medicine, 1995, Midway Coll., 1996; contbr. articles to profl. jours. Bd. overseers Case Western Res. U., Cleve., 1982-87; apptd. Ky. Commn. on Women, 1993-96. Named to Hall of Disting. Alumni, U. Ky.,1989; recipient Pub. Humanities award U. Ky., 1990, Midway Coll. Women's History Month award, 1991, Gt. Tchr. award Nat. Alumni Assn. U. Ky., 1992, Disting. Scholar award Assn. Black Sociologists, 1993, Cmty. Svc. award Frankfort-Lexington Links, Inc., 2005-, Cmty. Svc. award Girl Scout Wilderness Road Coun., Lexington, Ky., 2005, Ida Lee Willis Mem. award Ky. Heritage Found., 2006 Coretta Scott King award Alpha Kappa Alpha, 2007; fellow Woodrow Wilson Found., 1959-61, Ford Found., 1989-90; grantee Social Sci. Rsch. Coun., 1975, Nat. Inst. Edn., 1978-80, Nat. Cancer Inst., 1986-88, Ky. Humanities Coun., 1988, 2001, 2008, Am. Coun. Learned Soc., 1989-90, NEH, 1991; Disting. Prof. in Coll. Arts and Scis., U. Ky., 1992-93, Coll. of Social Work Hall of Fame, U. Ky., 1999; Disting. Lectureship named in her honor African Am. Studies Rsch. Program, 2000; Endowed Professorship Created in the name of Doris Wilkinson, 2007, Lifetime Achievement award Women Leading Ky., 2009, Inspiring Tchr. award, 2009; grant, Ky. Humanities Coun., 2008-., award, ASA, 2010, Idn Lee Willis Meml. award, Frankport, Ky., 2006-, Ky. Women Mem. Portrait in State Capital, 2009, Lifetime Achievement award, Women Leading Ky., 2009 Mem.: Ky. Women Remembered, Organized Social Sci. Rsch. Writing Inst., Ea. Sociol. Soc. (v.p. 1983—84, pres. 1992—93, I. Peter Gellman award 1987), Soc. Study Social Problems (v.p. 1984—85, pres. 1987—88), DC Sociol. Soc. (pres. 1982—83), So. Sociol. Soc. (honors com. 1993—94), Am. Sociol. Assn. (exec. assoc. 1977—80, budget com. 1985—88, v.p. 1991—92, mem. coun. 1994—97, elected v.p. 1990—91, Dubois-Johnson-Frazier award 1988, Pub. Understanding Sociology award 2010), Phi Beta Kappa.

WILKINSON, EDWARD ANDERSON, JR., retired military officer, manufacturing executive; b. Selma, Ala., Sept. 21, 1933; s. Edward Anderson and Alice Margaret (Moorer) W.; m. Barbara Anne Parker, June 4, 1955 (dec. June 1991); children: Daryl Edward, Daniel Bryan, Edward Anderson III, David Park; m. Sondra Marie Moore, Oct. 2, 1994. BS, U.S. Naval Acad., 1955; MS in Mech. Engring., 1964; grad., Nat. War Coll., 1972. Commd. ensign U.S. Navy, 1955, advanced through grades to rear adm., 1979; dir. Anti-Submarine Warfare Systems Program Office, Washington, 1978-79; dep. dir. Def. Mapping Agy., Washington, 1979-81; cmdr. Patrol Wings, U.S. Atlanta Fleet, Brunswick, Maine, 1981-83; dir. Def. Mapping Agy., Washington, 1983-85; ret., 1985; exec. v.p. Internat. Fed. Systems Intergraph Corp., Reston, Va. Recipient Decorated Legion of Merit, Dept. Def., Disting. Svc. medal. Methodist. Home and Office: 9680 Perdido Vista Dr Perdido Beach AL 36530-6028 Home Phone: 251-961-1314. Business E-Mail: andson@gulftel.com.

WILKINSON, J(AMES) HARVIE, III, federal judge; b. NYC, Sept. 29, 1944; s. James Harvie and Letitia (Nelson) W.; m. Lossie Grist Noell, June 30, 1973; children: James Nelson, Porter Noell. BA, Yale U., 1963-67; JD, U. Va., 1972; JD (hon.), U. Richmond, 1997, U. SC, 1998; LLD (hon.), Christopher Newport U., 2003. Bar: Va. 1972. Law clk. to Hon. Lewis F. Powell, Jr. US Supreme Ct., Washington DC, 1972-73; asst. prof. law U. Va., 1973-75, assoc. prof., 1975-78, prof. law, 1981-82, 83-84; editor Norfolk Virginian-Pilot, 1978—81; dep. asst. atty. gen. Civil Rights divsn. US Dept. Justice, 1982-83; judge US Ct. Appeals (4th Cir.), 1984—, chief judge, 1996—2003. Author: Harry Byrd and the Changing Face of Virginia Politics, 1968, Serving Justice: A Supreme Court Clerk's View, 1974, From Brown to Bakke: The Supreme Court and School Integration, 1979, One Nation Indivisible: How Ethnic Separatism Threatens America, 1997. Bd. Visitors U. Va., 1970-73; Republican candidate for Congress from 3d Dist. Va., 1970; bd. dirs. Fed. Jud. Ctr., 1992-96, James Madison Meml. Found., 2003-. Served with US Army, 1968-69. Recipient Thomas Jefferson Found. medal Law, U. Va., 2004, Medal, Lawrenceville Sch., 2008. Mem. Va. State Bar, Va. Bar Assn., Am. Law Inst. Episcopalian. Office: US Ct Appeals 255 W Main St Ste 230 Charlottesville VA 22902-5058 Office Phone: 434-296-7063.

WILKINSON, JOHN K., state legislator; m. Debbie Wilkinson; children: Terrell, Tara. BS in Agr., U. Ga., MEd. Tchr. Forsyth County HS, 1977—80, Banks County HS, 1980—83; exec. sec. Ga. Future Farmers America, 1983—; mem. Dist. 50 Ga. State Seante, 2011—. State agrl. edn. program mgr. Ga. Dept. Edn., state FFA advisor; state young farmer advisor, chmn. Ga. FFA-FCCLA. Mem. Ga. FFA Alumni Coun.; vice chmn. Stephens County Rep. Party; Sunday sch. tchr., supt., deacon, ch. pianist Tates Creek Bapt. Ch.; bd. dirs. Ga. FFA Found., Nat. FFA; bd. trustees Nat. FFA Found. Named to Ga. Agrl. Edn. Hall of Fame. Mem.: NRA, Atlanta Farmers Club (past pres.), Masonic Lodge #309. Republican. Office: PO Box 2227 Toccoa GA 30577 also: Ga State Senate Coverdell Legis Office Bldg Atlanta GA 30334

WILKINSON, JOSEPH B., state legislator; Former state rep. Dist. 43, Ga.; former mem. Health & Ecology, Ins. Com., Econ. Devel. & Tourism Com.; state rep. Dist. 52 Ga., 2004—. Republican. Home: 200 River Vista Dr Unit 203 Atlanta GA 30339-7604 Office Phone: 404-656-0325. Office Fax: 404-705-8310. Business E-Mail: joe@joewilkinson.org.

WILKINSON, KEITH D., biochemist, educator; BA in Chemistry cum laude, Albion Coll., 1972; MS, Univ. Mich., PhD in Biochemistry, 1977; postdoctoral study, Inst. Cancer Rsch., Fox Chase Cancer Ctr. Prof. biochemistry and dir., divsn. biol. & biomed. sci. Emory Univ., Atlanta. Vis. prof., doctoral programme in experimental biology and biomedicine Univ. Coimbra, Portugal. Recipient Albion Coll. Presdl. award, Alfred P. Sloan Meml. Scholarship, NIH postdoctoral fellowship. Mem.: Am. Com. on Proteolysis, Am. Soc. Biol. Chemistry and Molecular Biol., Am. Chem. Soc. Office: Biol and Biomed Sci Emory Univ--Ste 314 1462 Clifton Rd Atlanta GA 30322 also: Biochem Dept--Emory Univ 4017 Rollins Rsch Bldg 1510 Clifton Rd Atlanta GA 30322 Office Phone: 404-727-2545, 404-727-5980. Business E-Mail: genekdw@emory.edu.

WILKINSON, STANLEY RALPH, retired agronomist; b. West Amboy, NY, Mar. 28, 1931; s. Ralph Ward and Eva Goldie (Perkins) W.; m. Jean Saye; children: Rachael, Stanley Ralph., Augusta J. BS, Cornell U., 1954; MS, Purdue U., 1956, PhD, 1961. Soil scientist U.S. Regional Pasture Rsch. Lab., University Park, Pa., 1960-64, So. Piedmont Conservation Rsch. Ctr., Watkinsville, Ga., 1965-98, ret., 1998. Contbr. more than 22 chpts. to books, more than 145 articles to tech. jours. Past advance chmn. Boy Scouts Am. Served to capt. USAF, 1955-57. Recipient 3d prize Freedoms Found., 1956. Fellow Soil and Water Conservation Soc. Am., Am. Soc. Agronomy; mem. Agronomy Soc., Soil & Water Cons. Soc. Methodist. Personal E-mail: stanleywilkinson@att.net.

WILKS, LARRY DEAN, lawyer; b. Columbia, SC, Jan. 8, 1955; s. Ray Dean and Jean (Garrett) W.; m. Jan Elizabeth McIllwain, May 2,1981; children: John Ray, Adam Garrett. BS, U. Tenn., 1977, JD, 1980. Bar: Tenn. 1981, U.S. Dist. Ct. (mid. dist.) Tenn. 1981, U.S. Supreme Ct. 1986, U.S. Ct. Appeals (6th cir.) 1993, U.S. Dist. Ct. (we. dist.) Tenn. 1996, US Dist. Ct. (ea. dist.) 2006. Assoc. Mayo & Norris, Nashville, 1981-82; sole practice Springfield, Tenn., 1982-84; ptnr. Walton, Jones & Wilks, 1984, Jones & Wilks, 1984-89; pvt. practice Springfield, Tenn., 1989—. Chmn. Dem. Orgn. Robertson County Tenn., 1986-93. Fellow Tenn. Bar Found., Am. Bar Found., Nashville Bar Found.; mem. ABA, ATLA, Tenn. Bar Assn. (assoc. gen. counsel 1991-94, gen. counsel 1994-99, bd. profl. responsibility 1993-98, bd. govs. 1991—2008, young lawyers divsn. lifetime fellow, asst. treas. 1999-2000, treas. 2000—03, co-chair leadership law 2003-04, 2008-10, v.p. 2004-2005, pres. elect 2005-06, pres. 2006-07, immediate past pres. 2007-08), Tenn. Assn. Criminal Def. Lawyers, Tenn. Trial Lawyers Assn. (bd. govs. 2002—), Robertson County Bar Assn. (pres. 1993-96), Nat. Assn. Criminal Def. Laywers, Tenn. Young Lawyers Conf. (bd. dirs. 1987, editor quar. newsletter 1987-88, Mid. Tenn. v.p. 1988-89, v.p. 1989-90, pres.-elect 1990-91, pres. 1991-92), Robertson County U. Tenn. Alumni Assn. (pres. 2003-04). Methodist. Office: Atty at Law 509 W Court Sq Springfield TN 37172-2413 Office Phone: 615-384-8444.

WILLARD, HOWARD A., III, food products executive; With Salomon Brothers, Inc., Bain & Co., Inc.; various positions in fin., sales, info. services and corp. responsibility Philip Morris USA Altria Group, Inc., 1992—2008, exec. v.p. strategy and bus. devel., 2008—10, exec. v.p., CFO, 2011—. Bd. mem. YMCA Greater Richmond, Va., Communities in Schools Va. Office: Altria Group Inc 6601 W Broad St Richmond VA 23230 Office Phone: 804-274-2200.

WILLARD, LOUIS CHARLES, retired librarian; b. Tallahassee, Sept. 28, 1937; s. Bert and Rose (De Milly) W.; m. Nancy Booth, June 22, 1963. BA, U. Fla., 1959; BD, Yale, 1965, MA, 1967, PhD, 1970. Tchr. Tripoli (Lebanon) Boys' Sch., 1959-62; ordained to ministry Presbyn. Ch., 1965; acting librarian Princeton Theol. Sem., 1968-69, librarian, 1969-86; librarian, mem. faculty Harvard Div. Sch., 1986-99; dir. accreditation and instnl. evaluation Assn. Theol. Schs., 1999—2008. Mem. A.L.A., Theol. Library Assn., Soc. Bibl. Lit., Am. Acad. Religion, Phi Beta Kappa, Chi Phi. Home: 1010 American Eagle Blvd 302 Sun City Center FL 33573 Office Phone: 813-634-7047. Business E-Mail: charles@willard.cc.

WILLARD, WENDELL, state legislator; Former state rep. Dist. 44, Ga.; former mem. Ins. Coms., Judiciay Coms., State Planning & Cmty. Affairs Coms.; mem. Dist. 49, 2004—. Republican. Office: 755 River Gate Dr Atlanta GA 30350 Office Phone: 770-392-0676. E-mail: wkwillard@hotmail.com.

WILLE, ROSANNE LOUISE, educational consultant; b. Hackensack, NJ, Aug. 4, 1941; d. Albert Wille and Rose Marie (Rock) Eberhardt; m. George B. Jacobs, Mar. 12, 1980; children: Leigh, Steven, Alexander, Jeffrey. M Pub. Adminstrn., Rutgers U., 1986; PhD, N.Y.U., 1980. Dept. chair Rutgers U., Newark, 1978-84, Lehman Coll., Bronx, NY, 1984-87, dean, 1987-92, provost, sr. v.p., 1992—2002; cons. for higher edn., 2002—. Contbr. articles to profl. jours. Bd. dirs. Family Support Svcs., Bronx, N.Y., 1994-2002, bd. dirs. South Bronx Overall Economic Devel., Inc., Bronx, 1991-2002. Recipient Vision award Family Support Svcs., Bronx, 1996, Thousand Points of Light award Pres. George Bush, Washington, 1991. Mem. N.Y. Acad. Scis., N.Y. Acad. Medicine, Am. Assn. Higher Edn. Avocations: aviation, golf. Address: 5506 Harbour Preserve Cir Cape Coral FL 33914 Personal E-mail: rlwille@earthlink.net.

WILLENBRINK, ROSE ANN, retired lawyer; b. Louisville, Ky., Apr. 20, 1950; d. J.L. Jr. and Mary Margaret (Williams) W.; m. William I. Cornett Jr. Student, U. Chgo., 1968-70; BA in Anthropology with highest honors, U. Louisville, 1973, JD, 1975. Bar: Ky. 1976, Ind. 1976, U.S. Dist. Ct. (we. dist.) Ky. 1976, Ohio 1999. Atty. Mapother & Mapother, Louisville, 1976-79; v.p., counsel Nat. City Bank, Louisville, 1980-99, v.p., sr. atty. Cleve., 1999—2004, Louisville, 2004—05, ret., 2005. Mem. Ky. Bar Assn., Phi Kappa Phi. Home: 6803 Chadworth Pl Prospect KY 40059 Home Phone: 502-292-2857. Personal E-mail: willenbrink@yahoo.com.

WILLERSON, JAMES THORNTON, cardiologist, researcher, medical educator; b. Lampasas, Tex., Nov. 16, 1939; m. Nancy Beamer; 2 children. BS, U. Tex., Austin, 1961; MD, Baylor Coll. Medicine, 1965. Diplomate Internal Medicine 1972, Cardiovascular Disease 1974. Intern, internal medicine Mass. Gen Hosp., Boston, 1965—66, resident, cardiology, 1966—67, fellow, 1969—72; clin. assoc. NIH, Bethesda, Md.; former chief, cardiology St. Luke's Episcopal Hosp.; former chief, med. svcs. Meml. Hermann Hosp.; joined faculty, held positions including prof. medicine and dir., cardiovascular divsn. U. Tex. Southwestern Med. Sch., Dallas, 1972—89; chair, dept. medicine U. Tex. Med. Sch., Houston, 1989—2001, Edward Randall II Chair, dept. internal medicine, 1989—; prof. medicine U. Tex. Health Sci. Ctr., Houston, 1976—, Alkek/Williams Disting. Prof., 1989—, interim pres., 2000—01, pres., 2001—08; med. dir., chief cardiology rsch., co-dir. Cullen Cardiovascular Rsch. Lab. Tex. Heart Inst., St. Luke's Episcopal Hosp., 1993—, pres.-elect, 2004—07, pres., 2007—. Adj. prof. medicine Baylor Coll. Medicine, U. Tex. MD Anderson Cancer Ctr.; invited lectr. in field. Editor-in-chief Circulation, 1993—2004; contbr. several articles to profl. jours.; editl. bd. mem. of several peer-reviewed jours., author and co-author of several textbooks; co-editor: Cardiovascular Medicine, 3rd edit., 2007. Recipient James B. Herrick award, Am. Heart Assn., 1993, Disting. Svc. award, Coun. Clin. Cardiology, Am. Heart Assn., 2002, Merit medal, Internat. Acad. Cardiovascular Scis., 2004, Career Achievement award, Transcatheter Cardiovascular Therapeutics Mtg., 2005, Ignacio Chavez Medallion, Nat. Autonomous U. Mex., 2008; named Disting. Alumnus, U. Tex. Austin, 1999, Disting. Scientist, Am. Coll. Cardiology, 2000, Outstanding Cardiologist, Shanghai Internat. Symposium Cardiology, 2006, Lewis Katz Vis. Prof. in Cardiovascular Rsch. and Katz prize in Cardiovascular Rsch., Columbia U. Med. Ctr., 2007. Fellow: Royal Soc. Medicine; mem.: Nat. Am. Heart Assn. (former chmn. rsch. com. & NIH Cardiovascular & Renal Study Sect., bd. dirs. and steering com.), Inst. Med., Alpha Omega Alpha, Phi Beta Kappa. Achievements include creation of the Brown Foundation Institute of Molecular Medicine for the Prevention of Human Diseases; being honored as an international honorary member of the Japanese Circulation Soc. Among the first 7 physicians outside of Japan to be inducted & one of only 2 Americans to receive this honor in 2006. Home: 6601 Westchester Ave Houston TX 77005 Office: Texas Heart Inst 6770 Bertner MC 3-116 Houston TX 77030

WILLETT, DON R., state supreme court justice; BBA, Baylor U.; JD, MA in Polit. Sci., Duke U. Law clk. to Honorable Jerre S. Williams US Ct. Appeals (5th cir.), Tex.; atty. Haynes and Boone, LLP, 1993—96; legal adv. to gov. Tex., 1996—2000; dep. atty. gen. for legal counsel Tex., 2000—04; justice Tex. Supreme Ct., 2005—. Served on Bush-Cheney 2000 Presidential Campaign and Transition Team; supreme ct. liaison Tex. Ctr. for Legal Ethics and Professionalism. Former mem. Tex. Commn. on Volunteerism & Cmty. Svc.; bd. mem. Nat. Fatherhood Initiative, Big Brothers Big Sisters Ctrl. Tex., SafePlace, Tex. Lyceum Assn. Recipient Austin Under 40 award for Govt./Polit. Affairs, 2006. Fellow: Tex. Bar Found.; mem.: Tex. Assn. for Ct. Administration (judicial adv. bd.), Am. Law Inst. Office: Tex Supreme Ct PO Box 12248 Austin TX 78711 Office Phone: 512-463-1312. Office Fax: 512-463-1365.*

WILLEY, FRANK PATRICK, financial company executive, lawyer; b. Albany, NY, July 15, 1953; BS in Acctg., LeMoyne Coll., 1975; JD, Union U., 1978. Bar: Ariz. 1978. Assoc. T. M. Shumway, Scottsdale, Ariz., 1978-80, Foley, Clark & Nye, Phoenix, 1980-83; gen. counsel, v.p. Land Resources Corp., Scottsdale, 1983-84; gen. counsel, exec. v.p. Fidelity National Financial, Inc., Irvine, Calif., 1984—94, pres., 1995—2000, vice chmn., 2005—. Former bd. dirs. DriveTime Automotive, Inc., Santa Barbara Restaurant Group; bd. dirs. CKE Restaurants, Inc., PennyMac Mortgage Investment Trust. Office: Fidelity National Financial Inc 601 Riverside Ave Jacksonville FL 32204 Office Phone: 904-854-8100. Office Fax: 904-357-1007. Business E-Mail: frank.willey@fnf.com.

WILLIAM, BOB (ROBERT LYNN WILLIAMS), state legislator; b. Clarksburg, WV, Sept. 10, 1951; s. Thomas and Betty; m. Jennifer William. BS, Fairmont State coll.; MS, W.Va. U. Mem. Dist. 14 W.Va. State Senate, 2008—, vice chair Agr. Com. & Labor Com., mem. Econ. Devel. Com., Energy, Industry and Mining Com., Govt. Orgn. Com., Judiciary Com. & Mil. Com. Mem.: W.Va. Cattlemen's Assn. (former bd. mem.), W.Va. Coll. of Agriculture & Forestry & Consumer Sci. Alumni assn. (past pres.). Democrat. Methodist. Office: State Capitol Complex Rm 209W, Bldg 1 1900 Kanawha Blvd E Charleston WV 25305 Mailing: PO Box 562 Grafton WV 26354 Office Phone: 304-357-7995. E-mail: bob.williams@wvsenate.gov.

WILLIAMS, AL, state legislator; Former state rep. Dist. 128, Ga.; mem. Econ. Devel. & Tourism Com., State Insts & Property Com.; sec. Game, Fish & Pks. Com.; state rep. Dist. 165 Ga., 2004—. Democrat. Office: 9041 E Oglethorpe Hwy Midway GA 31320 Mailing: 511 Legislative Office Bldg Atlanta GA 30334 Office Phone: 912-368-4982, 404-656-6372. E-mail: coachewilliams2002@msn.com, caw@coastalnow.net.

WILLIAMS, ALAN B., state legislator; b. Tallahassee, Fla., Mar. 22, 1975; m. Opal McKinney-Williams; children: Adrianna, Alan-Louis. BS, Fla. A&M U., 1998, MBA, 2003. Sales Sprint Co.; cmty. rels. aide Mayor John Marks; mem. Dist. 8 Fla. House of Reps., 2008—, ranking mem. govt. ops. appropriations com., energy and utilities policy com., gen. govt. policy coun., joint selet com. on collective bargaining. Mem. Tallahassee Airport Adv. Bd., Fla. Selective Svc. Bd., US Commn. on Civil Rights Fla. Adv. Com. Bd. govs. & chmn. Leadership Tallahassee; coun. adv. Leadership Fla.; bd. dirs. Challenger Learning Ctr. Recipient Rattler Pride award, 2007; named Brother of Yr., Kappa Alpha Psi Frat.; named one of 30 Future Leaders under 30, Ebony Mag., 2003. Mem.: Nat. Forum for Black Pub. Adminstrs., League Women Voters Fla., United Way Big Bend (bd. dirs.), Tallahassee Boys Choir (bd. mem.), FAMU Alumni Assn. (life; chpt. pres.). Democrat. Baptist. Office: The Capitol 402 S Monroe St Rm 1001 Tallahassee FL 32399-1300 Office Phone: 850-488-1798. Business E-Mail: alan.williams@myfloridahouse.gov.

WILLIAMS, ALFRED C., state legislator; 5 children. BA, So. U., Baton Rogue, 1972, JD, 1977. Pvt. practice atty., La.; mem. Office of Atty. Gen. of 19th Jud. Dist.; chief adminstrv. officer to Melvin Holden Office of Mayor-Pres., East Baton Rogue, La.; COO The Conrad Group, LLC; mem. Dist. 61 La. House of Reps., Baton Rogue, 2012—. Bd. dirs. Coun. on Aging, Melrose Pl. Crime Prevention Dist. Mem.: La. Bar Assn. (bd. mem.), Capitol HS Alumni Assn. (bd. mem.). Democrat. Office: 701 S Acadian Thruway Baton Rouge LA 70806 also: La House of Reps 900 N 3rd St Baton Rouge LA 70804 Office Phone: 225-382-3243. Business E-Mail: williamsa@legis.la.gov.

WILLIAMS, BILL, energy and services company executive; Attended, Washington & Jefferson Coll., Pa. Gen. mgr. gas supply & sales Pub. Svc. Co. of NC, Inc. (PSNC); mng. dir. transp. & major account svcs. Piedmont Natural Gas Co., Inc., 2006—09, v.p. sales & delivery svcs., 2009—. Office: Piedmont Natural Gas Co Inc PO Box 33068 4720 Piedmont Row Dr Charlotte NC 28210 Office Phone: 704-364-3120. Office Fax: 704-365-8515.

WILLIAMS, BOB, professional sports team executive; married; 2 children. Grad., U. Ga., Athens. Various positions in ticket sales, concerts and entertainment Omni Coliseum, Atlanta, 1975—94, pres., 1994—97, Philips Arena, 1997—2010; pres. Atlanta Hawks and Philips Arena, exec. v.p. Atlanta Spirit, LLC, 2010—. Bd. mem. Ga. Alliance Children, Atlanta Convention & Visitors Bur., Atlanta Sports Coun., Hawks Found., Ctrl. Atlanta Progress. Mem.: Rotary Club Atlanta. Office: Atlanta Spirit LLC Philips Arena 1 Philips Dr Atlanta GA 30303

WILLIAMS, BRENT (BUZZ WILLIAMS), men's college basketball coach; b. Tex., Sept. 1, 1972; m. Corey Norman; children: Zera, Calvin, Mason. BS in Kinesiology, Okla. City U., 1994; MS in Kinesiology, Texas A&M U., Kingsville, 1999. Student asst. coach Navarro Coll. Bulldogs, 1990—92, Okla. City U. Stars, 1992—94; asst. coach U. Tex.-Arlington Mavericks, 1994—98, Tex. A&M-Kingsville Javelinas, 1998—99, Northwestern State U. Demons, 1999—2000, Colo. State U. Rams, 2000—03, assoc. head coach, 2003—04; asst. coach, recruiting coord. Tex. A&M U. Aggies, 2004—06; head coach U. New Orleans Privateers, 2006—07; asst. coach Marquette U. Golden Eagles, 2007—08, head coach, 2008—14, Va. Tech Hokies, Blacksburg, Va., 2014—. Office: Virginia Tech Okies Hahn Hurst Basketball Practice Blacksburg VA 24061*

WILLIAMS, CECILIA LEE PURSEL, optometrist; b. Lewisburg, Pa., Nov. 15, 1948; d. Lee LaVerne and Geraldine May (Steininger) Pursel; m. Richard Lee Williams, May 17, 1975; 1 son, Kent Lee. Student, Lycoming Coll., 1966—68; BS, Pa. Coll. Optometry, 1970, OD, 1972. Lic. and/or cert. optometrist, D.C., Pa., N.Y., N.J., Va. Rsch. optometrist in soft lens materials Gumpelmayer Optik, Vienna, Austria, 1973; optometrist Sterling Optical Co. Contact Lens Ctr., Washington, 1974-79; pvt. practice optometry Springfield, Va., 1980—. Recipient Clin. Efficiency award Pa. Coll. Optometry, 1972; Women's Aux. of Pa. Optometrists scholar, 1968-70, 70-72; Pa. State grantee, 1968-70, 70-72. Mem. Optometric Ctr. of Nation's Capital (dir. 1977-80), Am. Optometric Assn., Va. Optometric Assn., No. Va. Optometric Soc., Nat. Honor Soc. for Optometry, Omega Delta. Home: 3600 Wilton Hall Ct Alexandria VA 22310-2176 Office: 7241 Commerce St Springfield VA 22150-3411 Office Phone: 703-866-9364.

WILLIAMS, CHARLES, state legislator; b. Aug. 22; m. Beth Williams. Tree farmer; mem. Dist. 113 Ga. House of Reps., Atlanta, 2011—. Republican. Office: PO Box 206 Watkinsville GA 30677 also: Ga House of Reps 601-E Coverdell Legis Office Bldg Atlanta GA 30334 Office Phone: 404-656-0254. Business E-Mail: chuck.williams@house.ga.gov.

WILLIAMS, CLAY C., oil industry executive; BS in Civil & Geol. Engring., Princeton U.; MBA, U. Tex., Austin. Engr. Shell Oil Co, 1985—92; assoc. SCF Ptnrs., 1994—96; dir., corp. develop. National Oilwell Varco, Inc., Houston, 1996—97, v.p., corp. develop., 1997—2002, v.p., pipeline svcs., 1999—2001, v.p., fin. & corp. develop., 2002—03, CFO, 2003—, v.p., 2003—05, sr. v.p., 2005—09, exec. v.p., 2009—. Bd. dirs. Benchmark Electronics Inc., 2008—. Office: National Oilwell Varco Inc 7909 Parkwood Cir Dr Houston TX 77036-6565 Office Phone: 713-375-3700. Business E-Mail: clay.williams@bench.com.

WILLIAMS, CORY T., state legislator; b. Stillwater, Okla. m. Shannon Jacobson; 1 child, Kase. BS in Polit. Sci., Okla. State U., 2001, MS in Internat. Trade and Development, 2003; JD, Okla. City U. Sch. Law, 2006. Atty. Williams Law Firm; mem. Dist. 34 Okla. House of Representatives, 2008—. Mem.: ABA, Okla. Bar Assn., Payne County Bar Assn. Democrat. Office: 2300 N Lincoln Blvd Rm 316 Oklahoma City OK 73105 also: 621 S Husband St Stillwater OK 74074-4033 Office Phone: 405-557-7411. Business E-Mail: cory.williams@okhouse.gov.

WILLIAMS, DAN, state legislator; Grad., Auburn U., Ala. Mem. Athens City Bd. of Edn., Ala., 1979—84, Athens City Coun., 1984—92; mayor City of Athens, 1992—2010; mem. Dist. 5 Ala. House of Representatives, 2011—. First sgt., 1343rd engr. bn. Ala. Army Nat. Guard. Republican. Office: Ala House of Reps Rm 527-B 11 S Union St Montgomery AL 36130 Office Phone: 334-242-7741. Business E-Mail: dan.williams@alhouse.gov.

WILLIAMS, DANNY CHAPPELLE, federal prosecutor; b. 1966; married; 2 children. BA, Dillard U., 1988; JD, U. Tulsa Sch. Law, 1991. Asst. dist. atty. Tulsa County, 1991—93; assoc., shareholder Riggs, Abney, Neal, Turpin, Orbison, & Lewis, 1993—2000; ptnr. Bodenheimer & Levinson, 2000—03; sr. ptnr., pres. Charney, Buss, & Williams, 2003—12; US atty. (northern dist.) Okla. US Dept. Justice, 2012—. Office: US Attorney's Office 110 W 7th St Ste 300 Tulsa OK 74119 Office Phone: 918-382-2700. Office Fax: 918-560-7938.*

WILLIAMS, DARRIN L., state legislator; m. Nicole Williams; 2 children. BA in Hist., Hendrix Coll.; JD, Vanderbilt U. Sch. Law; LLM in Securities & Fin. Regulation, Georgetown U. Law Ctr. Chief dep. atty. gen. & chief of staff Atty. Gen. Mark Pryor; gen. counsel US Securities & Exchange Commn.; admin. aide US Senator David Pryor; mem. Dist. 36 Ark. House of Reps., 2008—. Mem. Nat. Lawyer's Steering Com. Dem. Nat. Com., dep. dir., 1995—99; dir. Ark. Coordinated Campaign, 1998; commr. Little Rock's Planning Commn., 2003—. Vol. Ark. Commitment Program; bd. chmn. & founding bd. mem. Jack Stephens Youth Golf Acad.; bd. mem. Little Rock Central High Visitor's Ctr. & Mus.; chmn. Jud. Forums Com. Little Rock Central High Sch. 50th Anniversary Commemoration, 2008; deacon Central Ch. Christ. Recipient Disting. Alumnus award, Hendrix Coll. Students for Black Culture; named Citizen of Yr., Sch. Religious Studies, Outstanding Govt. Lawyer, Harold Flowers Law Soc.; named one of 40 under 40, Ark. Bus. Mem.: 100 Black Men of Greater Little Rock (founding bd. mem.). Democrat. Church Of Christ. Office: State Capitol Rm 350 Little Rock AR 72201 also: 11311 Arcade Dr Ste 200 Little Rock AR 72212 Office Phone: 501-682-6211, 501-682-7771, 501-312-8500. Business E-Mail: williamsd@arkleg.state.ar.us.

WILLIAMS, DAVID, history professor; b. Columbus, Ga., June 5, 1959; s. Harold Otha and Anita Daniels Williams; m. Teresa Crisp, Aug. 29, 1981. PhD, Auburn U., Ala., 1988. Prof. history Valdosta State U., Ga., 1988—. Author: (book) A People's History of the Civil War: Struggles for the Meaning of Freedom, Bitterly Divided: The South's Inner Civil War, Plain Folk in a Rich Man's War: Class and Dissent in Confederate Georgia, Johnny Reb's War: Battlefield and Homefront, Rich Man's War: Class, Caste, and Confederate Defeat in the Lower Chattahoochee Valley, The Georgia Gold Rush: Twenty-niners, Cherokees, and Gold Fever, Gold Fever: America's First Gold Rush. Avocations: bicycling, music. Office: Valdosta State Univ Dept History Valdosta GA 31698 Business E-Mail: david.williams@valdosta.edu.

WILLIAMS, DAVID C., federal agency administrator; BA, Southern Ill. U.; MA, U. Ill., 1975; attended, US Mil. Intelligence Acad., Fed. Law Enforcement Tng. Ctr., US Secret Svc. Tng. Acad. Spl. agent US Secret Svc., 1979; with Office of Inspector Gen. Office of Labor Racketeering US Dept. Labor, spl. agent in charge Cleve., NYC, with Pres. Reagan's Commn. on Organized Crime, field dir. Office of Labor Racketeering, dir. Office Spl. Investigations Gen. Acctg. Office; inspector gen. Nuclear Regulatory Commn., 1989—96, Social Security Adminstrn., 1996—98, US Dept. Treasury, Washington, 1998—99, inspector gen. for tax adminstrn., 1999—2001; acting inspector gen. US Dept. Housing & Urban Devel. (HUD), Washington, 2001—02; dep. asst. adminstr. for aviation ops. Transp. Security Adminstrn. (TSA), Washington, 2002—03; insp. gen. US Postal Svc. (USPS), Arlington, 2003—. Active mem. Treasury Task Force. Decorated Bronze star, Vietnamese Medal of Honor. Office: US Postal Service (USPS) 1735 N Lynn St Arlington VA 22209 Office Phone: 703-248-2100.*

WILLIAMS, DAVID L., state legislator; b. May 28, 1953; m. Elaine G. State rep., Ky., 1985—86; rep. nominee US Senate, 1992; former rep. fl. leader Ky.; atty.; chmn., Corp. Subcomt. Const. Rev. Cmty., 1987; mem. Ky. State Senate, Judiciary State & Local Govt. Com.; senate pres., 2000—; mem. Dist. 16, 1987—. Mem.: Ky. Bar Assn. Republican. Methodist. Mailing: PO Box 666 Burkesville KY 42717 Office: 702 Capitol Ave Annex Rm 236 Frankfort KY 40601 also: 700 Capitol Ave Capitol Rm 324 Frankfort KY 40601 Home Phone: 270-433-7777; Office Phone: 270-864-5636, 502-564-3120.

WILLIAMS, DEANGELO, professional football player; b. Little Rock, Apr. 25, 1983; B in Mktg., U. Memphis, 2006. Running back Carolina Panthers, 2006—. Named Offensive Player of Yr., Conf. USA, 2003—05, First Team All-Conf., 2003—05; named to Nat. Football Conf. Pro Bowl Team, NFL, 2009. Achievements include leading the NFL in: rushing touchdowns (18), total touchdowns (20), 2008. Office: Carolina Panthers 800 S Mint St Charlotte NC 28202

WILLIAMS, DON R., singer, songwriter; b. Floydada, Tex., May 27, 1939; s. James and Loveta M. W.; m. Joy Bucher, Apr. 10, 1960; children: Gary, Timmy. Grad. high sch. Mem. Grand Ole Opry. Played guitar and sang with group in high sch. years; formed trio, Pozo Seco Singers, 1964-71; entered bus., Tex.; wrote country songs for, Jack Clement Pub.; rec. artist, formerly with, JMI and ABC, now with, MCA; albums include You're My Best Friend (Brit. Country Music Assn. Album of Year 1975), Visions (Brit. Country Music Assn. Album of Year and Best Mktg. award 1977), Images (Brit. Phonographic Inst. Double Platinum award 1979), 20 Of My Best (K-Tel Internat., Ltd. Platinum award 1979), Portrait, Listen to the Radio, Cafe Carolina, New Moves, Love Stories, Don Williams, vol. I; singles include I Recall A Gypsy Woman (Brit. Country Music Assn. Single of Year 1976), You're My Best Friend (Country Music, People Mag., and BBC Radio-2 Country Club program All-Time Favorite Country Record 1977), Tulsa Time (Acad. Country Music Single of Year 1979); numerous concert appearances; appeared in: films W.W. and The Dixie Dance Kings, 20th Century Fox, Smokey & The Bandit II; TV appearances include Tonight Show, NBC telecast of 14th Acad. of Country Music Awards. Served with Security Agy. U.S. Army, 4 years. Recipient 6 gold albums in U.K.; recipient Top Male Records Sales award Music Week mag., U.K., 1978, Cliffie Stone Pioneer award, Acad. Country Music, 2008; Named Male Vocalist of Yr., Brit. Country Music Assn., 1975; named Internat. Male Vocalist of Yr., U.K. Internat. Country Music Awards, 1977; Named Vocalist of Yr. in Ireland, 1980; Winner N.Y. Sta. WHN spl. poll. and Radio and Records poll. Mem. Country Music Assn. (Male Vocalist of Year 1978) Mem. Christian Ch. (Disciples Of Christ). Office: care Jim Halsey Co Inc PO Box 40703 Nashville TN 37204-0703

WILLIAMS, DREW DAVIS, surgeon; b. San Augustine, Tex., Jan. 18, 1935; s. Floyd Everett and Villamae (Morehead) W.; m. Marilyn Raus, June 27, 1958; children: Leslie, Cynthia, Matthew, Jennifer, Amelia. BS, Tex. A&M Coll., 1957; MD, U. Tex., 1960; grad., naval flight surgeon, U.S. Naval Sch. Aviation Medicine, 1963. Diplomate Am. Bd. Surgery, Am. Bd. Quality Assurance and Utilization Rev. Physicians. Intern USPHS Hosp., Seattle, 1960-61; resident in gen. surgery U. Tex. Med. Br., Galveston, 1961-62, 64-68; resident in pulmonary svc. M.D. Anderson Hosp., Houston, 1968; pvt. practice Baytown, Tex., 1968—. Active staff San Jacinto (Tex.) Meth. Hosp., 1968-95, chief of surgery, 1972, 73, pres. med. staff, 1976; mem. courtesy staff Bay Coast Hosp., Baytown, 1968-95; cons. staff Baytown Med. Ctr. Hosp., 1972-95; 1st chmn. dept. surgery in devel. of family practice residency program affiliated with Tex. Med. Sch., Houston, 1977; mem. Tex. State Bd. Med. Examiners, 1983-89, sec.-treas., 1984-88, pres., 1988-89; unit med. dir., clin. instr. dept. preventive medicine and cmty. health U. Tex. Med. Br., Galveston, 1995-99. Contbr. chpt. to book and articles to profl. jours. Mem. Baytown Area Citizen's Adv. Panel. Flight surgeon USN, 1962—64, lt. comdr. USNR, ret., 1967. Clin. fellow, Am. Cancer Soc., 1966—67. Mem.: SAR (past pres. local chpt.), AMA (Physicians Recognition award), ACS, Ret. Physicians Orgn. (med. reserve com.), Houston Surg. Soc. (past pres.), Baytown Surg. Soc., East Harris County Med. Soc. (pres. 1982), Harris County Med. Soc. (exec. bd. 1994, chmn. coun. med. splty., co-chmn. disaster response com. of ret. physician orgn.), Singleton Surg. Soc. (past pres.), Tex. Surg. Soc., Tex. Med. Assn., Sovereign Colonial Soc.-Am. of Royal Descent, Colonial Order of the Crown, Soc. Descendents of Colonial Clergy, Sir William Osler Soc., Sons of Republic of Tex. (at large life), Magna Carta Barons, Am. Cancer Soc. (pres. Baytown chpt. 1970—71), Knights

Templar, Shriners, Masons (32 degree). Democrat. Mem. Ch. of Christ. Avocations: hunting, fishing, genealogy, painting, gardening. Home and Office: 1217 Kilgore Rd Baytown TX 77520-3912 Office Phone: 281-422-7969. Business E-Mail: ddw@hal-pc.org.

WILLIAMS, DWIGHT M., security firm executive; Grad., FBI Nat. Acad., 1994; BA in Law Enforcement, U. Md., 1979; MS in Mgmt. & Leadership, Johns Hopkins U., 1998. Officer Met. Police Dept., Washington, 1979—2000; dir. security programs, Customs and Border Protection US Dept. Homeland Security, 2002—04, chief security officer, 2004—07; v.p., security DynCorp International, LLC, 2007—. Recipient Commr. Award, US Dept. Homeland Security, 2002. Office: DynCorp International LLC 3190 Fairview Park Dr Ste 700 Falls Church VA 22042 Office Phone: 571-722-0210. Office Fax: 571-722-0252.

WILLIAMS, EARNEST, state legislator; b. Newton, Ga., June 14; m. Rubie Tobert Williams; children: Earnest Lydell, Erin Lynett. Former state rep. Dist. 61, Ga.; state rep. Dist. 89 Ga., 2004—; mem. Edn. & Pub. Utilities Coms.; sec. Retirement Com. Democrat. Baptist. Mailing: 611 Legis Office Bldg Atlanta GA 30334 Office: 5044 Club Vista Point Stone Mountain GA 30088 Office Phone: 404-656-0314. Business E-Mail: ewilliam@legis.state.ga.us.

WILLIAMS, EDWARD EARL, JR., entrepreneur, educator; b. Houston, Aug. 21, 1945; s. Edward Earl and Doris Jewel (Jones) W.; m. Susan M. Warren, June 28, 1983; children: Laura Michelle, David Brian. BS, U. Pa., 1966; PhD, U. Tex., 1968. Asst. prof. econs. Rutgers U., New Brunswick, NJ, 1968-70; assoc. prof. fin. McGill U., Montreal, Que., Canada, 1970-73; v.p. Svc. Corp. Internat., Houston, 1973-77; prof. adminstrv. sci. Rice University, Houston, 1978-82, Henry Gardiner Symonds prof., 1982—, prof. stats., 1995—. Chmn. bd. dirs. Edward E. Williams & Co., Houston, 1976-92; chmn. bd., pres. Tex. Capital Investment Co., 1979-95; chmn. bd. First Tex. Venture Capital Corp., 1983-92; mng. dir. First Tex. Venture Capital, LLC, 1992-2000, Svc. Corp. Internat., Simugram Sys., Inc.; adv. dir. Frost Nat. Bank Author: Prospects for the Savings and Loan Industry, 1968, An Integrated Analysis for Managerial Finance, 1970, Investment Analysis, 1974, Business Planning for the Entrepreneur, 1983, The Economics of Production and Productivity: A Modeling Approach, 1996, Entrepreneurship and Productivity, 1998, The N.Y. Times Pocket MBA Series: Business Planning, 1999, Models for Investors in Real World Markets, 2003, Preparing an Entrepreneurial Business Plan, 2004, Essentials of Entrepreneurship, 2010; contbr. articles to profl. jours. Benjamin Franklin scholar, Jesse Jones scholar U. Pa., 1966; fellow Tex. Savs. and Loan League, fellow NDEA U. Tex., 1968. Mem. So. Pacific Hist. and Tech. Soc., Santa Fe Rlwy. Hist. and Modeling Soc., Carlton Woods County Club, Jewish Comm. North, Beta Gamma Sigma, Alpha Kappa Psi. Republican. Office: Rice U Jesse H Jones Grad Sch Mgmt Houston TX 77251 Home: 51 N Lamerie Way The Woodlands TX 77382 Office Phone: 713-348-5381. Business E-Mail: jinkeynes@rice.edu.

WILLIAMS, ELLEN C., lobbyist, political organization worker; children: Sam, Joey. BA, U. Ky., 1980. Staff asst. Congressman Larry Hopkins, 1982; exec. dir. Young Rep. Fedn., 1983; staff Senator Bob Kasten, 1986—88; mem. Bush Quayle Campaign, 1988, Reagan Bush Campaign, 1984, Dole Kemp campaign, 1996, Bush Cheney campaign, 2000; staff Nat. Republican Senate Committee, 1988—89; regional polit. dir. Nat. Rep. Com.; exec. dir. Rep. Party of Ky., 1990—92, chmn., 1999—2004; vice chmn. Ky. Public Service Commission, 2004—05; commissioner for local devel. Gov. Kentucky, 2004—05; founder, lobbyist Capital Network LLC, Frankfort, Ky., 2006—; apptd. to Bd. Gov. by US Pres. George W. Bush USPS, 2006—. Cons. Lexington Bluegrass Bd. of Realtors; active Anderson County United Way Bd., Ch. of Lawrenceburg. Office: PO Box 4618 Frankfort KY 40604-4618 Office Phone: 502-227-1065.

WILLIAMS, GREG, women's college basketball coach; m. Suzanne Williams. BS in Phys. Edn., Rice U., Houston, 1970. Asst. men's basketball coach Rice U. Owls, 1970—75, head women's basketball coach, 2005—; asst. coach WBL Houston Angels, 1979—80; coach WBA Dallas Diamonds, 1981—82, WABA Dallas Diamonds, 1994; head women's basketball coach Colo. State U. Rams, 1990—97; asst. coach Detroit Shock, 1989—2000, head coach, dir. player pers., 2000—02; asst. coach U. Dayton Flyers, 2003—05. Named Coach of Yr., WBL, 1980—81, 1984, Southwest Conf., 1988, Western Athletic Conf., 1995—96. Office: Rice Univ Womens Basketball MS 548 PO Box 1892 Houston TX 77251-1892

WILLIAMS, GREGG E., former professional football coach; b. July 15, 1958; m. Leigh Ann Williams; children: Blake, Chase, Amy. BS, Northeast Mo. State U. (now Truman State U.), Kirksville; MEd, Ctrl. Mo. State, Warrensburg. Asst. football coach Excelsior Springs HS, Mo.; head football coach Belton HS, Mo., 1984—87; grad. asst. U. Houston Cougars, 1988—89; 1st quality control coach Houston Oilers, 1990, spl. team coach, 1993, linebackers coach, 1994—96; defensive coord. Tenn. Titans, 1997—2000; head coach Buffalo Bills, 2001—03; defensive coord., asst. head coach Washington Redskins, 2004—07, Jacksonville Jaguars, 2008; defensive coord. New Orleans Saints, 2009—12.

WILLIAMS, H. THOMAS (TOM WILLIAMS), academic administrator, physicist, educator; b. Hampton, Va. BS in Physics, U. Va., 1965, PhD in Physics, 1967. NSF post-doctoral rsch. fellow Nat. Bur. Stds., 1967—69; rschr. Inst. for Theoretical Physics, U. Erlangen-Nuernberg, Germany, 1970—71; staff scientist Kaman Scis. Corp., Colorado Springs, Colo., 1971—73; mem. faculty Washington and Lee U., Lexington, Va., 1974—, assoc. dean, 1986—89, chair dept. physics, 1989—2000, physics prof., 2007—, Edwin A. Morris prof. physics, 1994—, chief acad. officer, provost, 2003—07. Cons. Nat. Bur. Stds., 1974—86, Los Alamos Sci. Lab., 1987—93. Office: Washington and Lee Univ Lexington VA 24450 Business E-Mail: williamsh@wlu.edu.

WILLIAMS, IFOR R., immunologist, director; b. Wallingford, England, June 10, 1960; s. Thomas Ffrancon and Astra Silvia Williams; m. Kimber Poffenberger, May 29, 2011; children: Grant Martin, Austin Heath. BS, Davidson Coll., NC, 1980; MD, PhD, Emory U., Atlanta, 1986. Cert. in anatomic pathology Am. Bd. Pathology, 1989, lic. Physician Ga., 1997. Pathology internship and residency Wash. U. Sch. Medicine, St. Louis, 1986—91, rsch. assoc., 1991—92; instr. dermatology Harvard Med. Sch., Boston, 1992—95, asst. prof. dermatology, 1995—97; asst. prof. pathology Emory U., 1997—2006, assoc. prof. pathology, 2006—. Assoc. dir., clin. immunology lab. Emory U. Hosp., Atlanta, 1997—2004, dir., clin. immunology lab., 2004—. Contbr. articles to profl. jours. Recipient Thomas B. Fitzpatrick Rsch. award, 1994, Career Devel. award, Dermatology Found., 1994, Janet and Elvin Price award, Crohn's and Colitis Found. Am., 2002. Fellow: Assn. Med. Lab. Immunologists, Coll. Am. Pathologists; mem.: Am. Soc. Investigative Pathology, Soc. Mucosal Immunology (bd. councilors 2011, sec.-treas. 2012), Am. Gastroenterology Assn., Soc. Investigative Dermatology, Am. Assn. Immunologists, Pi Kappa Alpha, Davidson Coll. (sec. 1978—79). Methodist. Achievements include discovery of lymphotoxin and its receptor are required for the development of cryptopatches and isolated lymhoid follicles in the small intestine; that RANKL protein and Spi-B transcription factor critical for the development of specialized epithelial cells called M cells involved in antigen uptake into intestinal Peyer's patches. Avocations: running, skiing, racquetball. Office: Emory Univ 615 Michael St Whitehead 105D Atlanta GA 30322

WILLIAMS, ISHAN CANTY, researcher, educator; d. Mary Ann and Tyrone Canty; m. Derick Javon Williams, June 10, 2000; 1 child, Daylan Jeriah. PhD in Human Devel. and Family Studies, U. NC, Greensboro, 2003. Rsch. asst. Bowman Gray Sch. Medicine, Winston-Salem, 1996—97, data collector; grad. rsch. asst. U. NC, 1997—2003, postdoc. rsch. fellow Chapel Hill, 2003—05; rsch. assoc. NC Agrl. and Tech. State U., Greensboro, 2005; rsch. asst. prof. U. Va., Charlottesville, 2005—. Mem.: APHA, So. Gerontol. Assn., Gerontol. Soc. Am. Office: Univ Virginia 202 Jeanette Lancaster Way Charlottesville VA 22903-3388 Office Fax: 434-982-3275. Business E-Mail: icw8t@virginia.edu.

WILLIAMS, JACK, state legislator; b. Sept. 7, 1957; m. Glenda Cantrell; children: Regan, Jordan. BA, Southeastern Bible Coll., Birmingham, Ala. Tax collector Jefferson County, Ala.; real estate cons.; mem. Dist. 47 Ala. House of Reps., Montgomery, 2004—. Past chmn. Dept. Human Resources' Quality Assurance Com., Greater Birmingham Young Republicans; mem. Fullness Christian Fellowship; bd. chmn. Greater Birmingham Habitat for Humanity. Republican. Office: 2100 Southbridge Pky Ste 650 Birmingham AL 35209 also: Ala House of Reps Ala State House 11 S Union St Rm 536-D Montgomery AL 36130 also: 2501 Glendmere Pl Vestavia AL 35216-2603 Office Phone: 205-414-7539, 334-242-7600. Office Fax: 205-414-7531. Business E-Mail: jack@jackwilliams.org.

WILLIAMS, JAMES A., software company executive, former federal agency administrator; b. Nov. 24, 1954; B in Bus. Adminstrn., Va. Commonwealth U., 1979; M in Bus. Adminstrn., George Washington U., 1986. Exec. dir. FTC; dir. telecommunications procurement divsn. US Gen. Services Adminstrn. (GSA); dep. asst. commr. procurement IRS, US Dept. Treasury, 1991—99, dir. procurement, 1999—2001, dep. assoc. commr. prog. mgmt., 2001—03; dir. US Visitor and Immigrant Status Indicator Tech. (US-VISIT) US Dept. Homeland Security, 2003—06; commr. Fed. Acquisition Svc. US Gen. Services Adminstrn. (GSA), 2006—08, 2009—10, acting adminstr., 2008—09; sr. v.p. global profl. services Daon, 2010—. Mem. US Interagency Coun. on Homelessness, Nat. Capital Planning Commn. Mem. bus. industry coun. Radford U., Va.; mem. pres. com. Nat. Found. Arts & Humanities. Recipient Presdl. Meritorious Exec. award, 1985, FTC Disting. Svc. award, 1986, Adminstr. Meritorious Svc. award, Gen. Services Adminstrn. (GSA), 1996, 1999. Mem.: Sr. Execs. Assn. (bd. dirs.), Nat. Contract Mgmt. Assoc. (bd. advs.), Project Mgmt. Inst. Office: Daon 11325 Random Hills Rd Fairfax VA 22030-6051

WILLIAMS, JAMES ARTHUR, retired military officer, information technology executive; b. Paterson, NJ, Mar. 29, 1932; s. Charles M. and Elsie (Kretszchmar) W.; m. Barbara Widnall, June 26, 1959; children: Steven, Karen. BS, U.S. Mil. Acad.; MA in Latin Am. Studies, U. N.Mex. Commd. 2d lt. U.S. Army, 1954, advanced through grades to lt. gen.; asst. army attache U.S. Def. Attache Office, Caracas, Venezuela, 1966-72; exch. officer State-Def. Exch. Program Office of Sec. Def., Washington, 1972-74; comdr. 650th MI Group, Shape, 1974-76; dep. dir. estimates Def. Intelligence Agy., Washington, 1977-80; dep. chief staff for intelligence U.S. Army, Europe, 1980-81; dir. Def. Intelligence Agy., Washington, 1981-85; ret., 1985; v.p. PSC Corp., 1986; pres. Direct Info. Access Corp., Annandale, Va., 1987—2008; chmn. bd. dirs. Info. Ops. Inc., 2000—04; pres. Info Assure, Inc., Arnold, Md., 2004—12. Sr. fellow Joint Forces Staff Coll., 1998; intelligence advisor Dept. Homeland Security, 2004; pres. Washington Inst. Foreign Affairs, 2007. Bd. visitors Joint Mil. Intelligence Coll., 1996—2010. Decorated Legion of Merit, Bronze Star with oak leaf cluster, Air medals, D.S.M., Nat. Intelligence D.S.M.; Legion of Honor (France); named Disting. Mem. Mil. Intelligence Hall of Fame. Mem. Assn. US Army, Nat. Mil. Intelligence Assn. (chmn. bd. 1986—), Wash. Inst. Fgn. Affairs(pres., 2009); fellow Nat. Mil. Intelligence Found. Methodist.

WILLIAMS, JAMES B., private equity firm executive; b. 1957; BA in Bus. Adminstrn., with honors, U. So. Calif., 1978, MBA, 1980. Various sr. exec. positions Kaiser Permanente, 1994—98; ptnr. TPG Capital (formerly Texas Pacific Group), 1999—. Bd. dirs. Magellan Health Svcs., Inc., 1999—2003, GMP Companies Inc., 2000—, MEMC Electronic Materials, Inc., 2003—, Genesis Health Ventures, Inc. Mem. exec. com. US Golf Assn., 2010—. Office: TPG Capital Ste 3300 301 Commerce St Fort Worth TX 76102 Office Phone: 817-871-4000. Office Fax: 817-871-4010.

WILLIAMS, JAMES KENDRICK, bishop emeritus; b. Athertonville, Ky., Sept. 5, 1936; Student, St. Mary's Coll., Ky., St. Maur's Sch. Theology, South Union, Ky. Ordained priest Archdiocese of Louisville, 1963; pastor Holy Trinity Parish, Louisville, 1983—84; ordained bishop, 1984; aux. bishop Diocese of Covington, Ky., 1984—88; bishop Diocese of Lexington, Ky., 1988—2002, bishop emeritus Ky., 2002—08. Roman Catholic. Office: Diocese of Lexington 1310 W Main St Lexington KY 40508-2048

WILLIAMS, JAMES LEE, finance company executive; b. Tampa, Fla., Nov. 5, 1941; s. Donald Clark and Nell (Medlin) W.; m. Linda Taylor, Dec. 28, 1968; children: Donald Clark II, Taylor Lee. AA, St. Petersburg Jr. Coll., Fla., 1965; BS, Fla. State U., 1967. Mgmt. Ryder Truck Lines, Jacksonville, Fla., 1967—69; dist. mgr. underwriting divsn. U.S. Leasing Corp., Dallas, 1969—73; area v.p. Mfrs. Hanover Leasing Corp., Houston and London, 1973—79; v.p. corp. fin. Underwood Neuhause & Co. Inc., Houston, 1979—81; chmn., CEO 1st City Leasing Corp., Houston, 1981—85; mng. dir. capital markets 1st City Bancorp., Houston, 1985—89; mng. dir. fin. svcs. M.P.S.I. Sys. Inc., Dallas, 1989—90; pres., CEO Strategic Decisions Holdings Corp., Dallas, 1990—92; sr. mng. dir. Williams and Assocs., 1992; pres. Global Svcs. Capital Corp., Houston, 1993—96; v.p., dist. CFO Ikon Hou Adminstrv. Svc. Ctr., Houston, 1997—98; CFO Insync Internet Svcs., Houston, 1998—99, Walkabout Software, 1999—2001; pres. BancLeasing, Inc., 2001—03; mng. dir. Global Svcs., Houston, 2003—04; exec. dir. SIRE-Therapeutic Equestrian Ctrs., 2004—11; sr. mng. dir. Williams Assoc., 2011—. Served with USN, 1959-62. Mem. Equipment Leasing Assn. (fed. govt. rels. com. 1984-88, 95—), Tex. Assn. Equipment Lessors (bd. dirs. 1985-89), Greater Houston Partnership (Arabian horse and Announcer's com. 1994-, chmn. Horse Show Announcers com. 2009-11, Houston Livestock Show and Rodeo), Spcl. Commn. Harris Co. Ct., Houston Ctr. Club (bd. dirs. 1985-89), Lakeside Racquet Club (athletic com. 1986-89), Forum Club Houston. Republican. Presbyterian. Avocations: golf, jogging, swimming. Home: 289 Sarah Canyon Lake TX 78133

WILLIAMS, JENNIFER R., lawyer; BS with honors, Univ. Tenn., Knoxville, 1989; JD, Washington Univ., St. Louis, 1994. Chief counsel labor & employment to gen. counsel Unisource Worldwide, Inc., Norcross, Ga., 2003—. Office: Unisource Worldwide Inc 6600 Governors Lake Pkwy Norcross GA 30071 Office Phone: 770-447-9000.

WILLIAMS, JODY, political organization administrator; b. Brattleboro, Vt., Oct. 9, 1950; BA, U. Vt., Burlington, 1972; MA in Tchg., Sch. Internat. Tng., Vt., 1974; MA in Internat. Rels., Johns Hopkins U., Balt., 1984; PhD (hon.), Briar Cliff Coll., Marlboro Coll., U. Vt., Williams Coll., Pa. State U., Royal Mil. Coll. Canada, Wesleyan U., Franklin Pierce Coll., Regis U., Shensu U., Rockhurst U., Gustaus Adolphus Coll., Lehman Coll., Smith Coll. Co-coord. Nicaragua-Honduras Edn. Project, Washington, 1984—86; assoc. dir. Med. Aid for El Salvador, LA, 1986—92; founding coord. Internat. Campaign to Ban Landmines, 1992—98, campaign amb., 1998—. Disting. vis. prof. social work & global justice U. Houston, 2003—07, Sam & Cele Keeper endowed prof. in peace & social justice, 2007—; head of mission on Darfur UN Human Rights Coun., 2007. Author: Banning Landmines: Disarmament, Citizen Diplomacy and Human Security, 2008; co-author: After the Guns Fall: The Enduring Legacy of Landmines, 1995; sr. editor Landmine Monitor Report, 1999—2004; contbr. articles to profl. jours. Mem. Human Rights Watch Arms Adv. Com., 1998—; mem. adv. com. Women for World Peace Fund, 2003—; co-founder Nobel Women's Initiative, 2006; bd. dirs. Roots of Peace, Calif., 2001—. Recipient Nobel Peace prize, 1997, Disting. Peace Leadership award, Nuc. Age Peace Found., 1998, Hollywood Humanitarian award, 2002, Fiat Lux award, Clark U.; named one of 100 Most Powerful Women in the World, Forbes mag., 2004. Office: University of Houston College of Social Work 4800 Calhoun Rd Houston TX 77004 Business E-Mail: williams@icbl.org.

WILLIAMS, JOHN EDWARD, lawyer; b. Atlanta, May 21, 1946; s. Edward Carl and Mary E. (Griffin) W.; m. Kristin Forsberg, May 22, 1976; children: Alexandra, Courtney, Charles. BA, Yale U., 1968; JD, U. Va., 1974; LLM in Taxation, Georgetown U., 1977. Bar: Va. 1974, D.C. 1975, U.S. Dist. Ct. D.C. 1975, U.S. Tax Ct. 1975, U.S. Ct. Appeals (D.C. cir.) 1975, U.S. Supreme Ct. 1977. Law clk. to Judge Charles R. Richey U.S. Dist. Ct. (D.C. dist.), 1974-75; assoc. Patton, Boggs & Blow, Washington, 1975-78, Cadwalader, Wickersham & Taft, Washington, 1978-81; asst. to the commr. IRS, Washington, 1981-84; tax counsel Ropes & Gray, Washington, 1984-86; ptnr. David & Hagner, P.C., Washington, 1986-90, Winston & Strawn, Washington, 1990-2000; atty. Law Offices of John E. Williams, 2000—. Editl. bd. U. Va. Law Review, 1972-74; mem. Jud. Conf. of D.C. Cir., 1978, 82, 85, 87, 92. With USAR, 1968—74. Recipient IRS Commissioner's award, 1984. Mem. ABA (tax sect., chmn. tech. subcom., adminstrv. practice com. 1986-88), Met. Club, Yale Club N.Y.C., Heritage Hunt Club. Office: 3213 Duke St Ste 601 Alexandria VA 22314 Office Phone: 703-838-2939. Business E-Mail: johnedwardwilliams@earthlink.net.

WILLIAMS, JOHN LEE, lawyer; b. Nashville, Dec. 23, 1942; s. Leslie Elwood and Gladys Mae (Ridings) W.; m. Norma Jean Givens, May 27, 1967; 1 child, Jacob Andrew. BA, Tenn. Technol. U., 1964; JD, U. Tenn., 1967. Bar: Tenn 1967. Ptnr. Porch, Peeler & Williams, Waverly, Tenn., 1967-78, Porch, Peeler, Williams & Thomason, Waverly, 1978—; asst. dist. atty. 23d Jud. Cir. Ct. Tenn., 1972-74; judge Ct. Gen. Sessions of Humphreys County, Tenn., 1978-82; county exec. Humphreys County, 2010. County atty. Humphreys County, 1968—72, 1982—86, 1994—; city atty. City of Waverly, 1978—, City of McEwen, Tenn., 1978—, City of Lobelville, Tenn., 1985—89; gen. counsel Meriwether Lewis Elec. Coop., Centerville, Tenn., 1980—. State legal counsel Tenn. Jaycees, 1970; treas., sec. Humphreys County Dem. Exec. Com., 1978-2001; chmn. Humphreys County Election Commn., 1968-72. Col. U.S. Army ret. Mem.: Humphreys County Bar Assn. (pres. 1978—), Masons (master 1985, 1999, 2005). Home: 1739 Ogden Rd Mc Ewen TN 37101 Home Phone: 931-296-1369; Office Phone: 931-296-7741. Business E-Mail: john.williams@porchpeeler.com.*

WILLIAMS, JOHN N., dean, dental educator; BA with honors, Transylvania U., Lexington, KY, 1974; DMD, U. Louisville, 1980, MBA, 1987. Asst. u. provost U. Louisville, 1988—91; dean U. Louisville Sch. Dentistry, 1999—2005; assoc. dean for ednl. programs U. of Louisville Sch. of Dentistry, 1991—98; prof. dept. periodontics, endontics and dental hygiene U. Louisville Sch. Dentistry; dean U. N.C. Sch. Dentistry, Chapel Hill, NC, 2005—. Mem. editl. bd. Jour. Contemporary Dental Practice. Mem.: Am. Acad. Devel. Medicine and Dentistry. Avocations: boating, classical & choral singing. Office: Sch Dentistry NC Univ CB #7450 1090 Old Dental Bldg Chapel Hill NC 27599-7450 Office Phone: 919-966-2731. Business E-Mail: john_williams@dentistry.unc.edu.

WILLIAMS, JONATHAN L., pediatric radiologist, educator; MD, Thomas Jefferson U., Phila., 1967. Diplomate Am. Bd. Radiology-diagnostic radiology, 1974. Resident diagnostic radiology Temple Univ. Hosp., Phila., 1970—73; fellow pediatric radiology St. Christopher's Hosp. for Children, Phila., 1973—74; prof. diagnostic radiology Coll. of Medicine Univ. of Fla.; hospital affiliation includes Shands at the Univ. of Fla. Office: PO Box 100374 1600 SW Archer Rd Gainesville FL 32610-0374 Office Phone: 352-395-0102.

WILLIAMS, KAREN JOHNSON, retired federal judge; b. Orangeburg, SC, Aug. 4, 1951; d. James G. Johnson and Marcia Johnson (Reynolds) Dantzler; m. Charles H. Williams, Dec. 27, 1968; children: Marian, Ashley, Charlie, David. BA, Columbia Coll., 1972; postgrad., U. SC, 1973, JD cum laude, 1980. Bar: SC 1980, US Dist. Ct. SC 1980, US Ct. Appeals (4th cir.) 1981. Tchr. Irmo (SC) Mid. Sch., 1972—74, O-W H.S., Orangeburg, 1974—76; assoc. Charles H. Williams PA, Orangeburg, 1980—92; judge US Ct. Appeals (4th Cir.), 1992—2009, chief judge, 2007—09. Exec. bd. grievance commn. SC Supreme Ct., Columbia, 1983—92. Child devel. bd. First Bapt. Ch., Orangeburg; bd. dirs. Orangeburg County Mental Retardation Bd., 1986—94, Orangeburg-Calhoun Hosp. Found., Columbia Coll., 1988—92, Reg. Med. Ctr. Hosp. Found., 1988—92; adv. bd. Orangeburg-Calhoun Tech. Coll., SC, 1987—92. Mem.: ABA, Nat. Assn. of Women Judges, Bus. and profl. Women Assn., SC Trial Lawyers Assn., Orangeburg County Bar Assn. (co-chair Law Day 1981), SC Bar Assn., Fed. Judges Assn., Am. Judicature Soc., Rotary, Order of Coif, Order of Wig and Robe.

WILLIAMS, KATHLEEN MARY, federal judge; b. Derby, Conn., Dec. 4, 1956; BA, Duke U., 1978; JD, U. Miami, 1982. Law. clk. Colson & Hicks, P.A., Miami, 1980—82; assoc. Fowler, White, Burnett, Hurley, Banick & Strickroot, 1982—84; asst. US atty. (southern dist.) Fla. US Dept. Justice, 1984—88; assoc. Morgan, Lewis & Bockius, Miami, 1988—90; chief asst. pub. defender Fed. Pub. Defender's Office (southern dist.) Fla., 1990—95; fed. pub. defender Fed. Pub. Defender's Office. (southern dist.) Fla., 1995—2011; acting pub. defender Fed. Pub. Defender's Office. (middle dist.) Fla., 1999—2000; judge US Dist. Ct. (southern dist.) Fla., 2011—. Office: US District Courthouse 701 Clematis St West Palm Beach FL 33401-5196 Office Phone: 561-803-3450.

WILLIAMS, KENT, state legislator; b. Marion, SC, Sept. 15, 1960; AS, Florence Darlington Tech. Coll., 1981; BS, SC State U., 1987. Mem. Dist. 30 SC State Senate, 2004—, mem. Agr. and Natural Resources Com., Corrections and Penology Com., Fish Game and Forestry Com., Judiciary Com. & Labor, Commerce and Industry Com. Democrat. Office: 602 Gressette Bldg Columbia SC 29201 Mailing: 4205 Stirk Pl Marion SC 29571 Office Phone: 803-212-6008. Business E-Mail: williamsk@scsenate.org.

WILLIAMS, LANCE LAMONT, legislative assistant; b. Jacksonville, Fla., Aug. 17, 1962; s. Nathaniel and Earnestine Burley (Jackson) W. BS, Fla. State U., 1985. Adminstrv. aide to city mgr. City Tallahassee, Fla., 1985; sales assoc. Ivey's Dept. Store, Jacksonville, 1986; sec. to dean Columbia U., Kings Coll., Ivey League, NYC, 1990; driver HRS Jax Juvenile Detention Ctr., Jacksonville, 1991; congl. intern U.S. Congress, Jacksonville, Fla., 1995—; grad. senator Fla. A & M U., U. North Fla. US HUD Team Captain Surveyors; US senator Bill Nelson Camp; team capt. of surveyor U. North Fla.; subs. tchr. K.E.S. D.C.P. s/d C.P.S. Duval County Pub. Schs.; v.p. Black Student Union Fla. State U.; congl. intern U.S. Congresswoman Corrine Brown; homecoming ct. mem. Wm. M. Raines Sr. HS. Pk. supr. Jax Youth Employment Program; subs. tchr. Kelly Ednl. Staff & Duval Co. Public Schools, Jacksonville, Fla. Dir. newspaper B.S.U. Awareness, 1982. Dir., pres. Black Student Union Fla. State U., Tallahassee, 1982-83; legis. intern Fla. Ho. Reps., Tallahassee, 1985, Fla. Senate, Tallahassee, 1983. Recipient Outstanding Leadership award Operation PUSH, Chgo., V.P. Student Affairs award for Outstandign Leadership, Fla. State U. Mem. Omega Psi Psi (v.p.). Democrat. Baptist. Home: 2645 Edgewood Ave W Jacksonville FL 32209-2430 Office: US Congress 1248 Edgewood Ave W Jacksonville FL 32208-2768

WILLIAMS, MARSHA RHEA, computer scientist, educator, researcher, consultant; b. Memphis, Aug. 4, 1948; d. James Edward and Velma Lee W. Cert., Schiller Coll., West Berlin, Germany, 1968; BS in Physics, Beloit Coll., 1969; MS in Physics, U. Mich., 1971; MS in Sys. and Info. Sci., Vanderbilt U., 1976, PhD in Computer Sci., 1982. Cert. data processor. Engring. coop. student Lockheed Missiles & Space Co., Sunnyvale, Calif., 1967-68; asst. transmission engr. Ind. Bell Tel. Co., Indpls., 1971-72; sys. analyst, instr. physics Memphis State U., 1972-74; computer-assisted instrn. project programmer Fisk U., 1974-76; mem. tech. staff Hughes Rsch. Labs., Malibu, Calif., 1976-78; assoc. sys. engr. IBM, Nashville, 1978-80; rsch. and tchg. asst. Vanderbilt U., Nashville, 1980-82, spl. asst. to dean Grad. Sch., spring 1981, minority engr. advisor, 1975-76; cons. computer-assisted instrn. project Meharry Med. Coll., Nashville, summer 1982; assoc. prof. computer sci. Tenn. State U., Nashville, 1982-83, 84-90, full tenured prof., 1990—2013, univ. marshal, 1992-97. Assoc. prof. U. Miss., Oxford, 1983-84, faculty senator; assoc. program dir. Applications of Advanced Techs. Sci. and Engring. Edn., NSF, 1987-88, apptd. USRA Sci. and Engring. Edn. Coun., Advanced Design Program, 1992-94; cons. on minority scientists and engrs. Univ. Space Rsch. Assn., Washington, 1988; vis. scientist CSNET-Minority Instn. Networking Project Bolt, Beranek & Newman, Cambridge, Mass., 1989; mem. tech. staff Bell Comm. Rsch., Red Bank, N.J., 1990; prin. investigator NSF Computer Sci., Engring. & Math. Scholarships Project, 2002-03; presenter papers profl. meetings. Editor-in-chief newspaper Pilgrim Emanuel Bapt. Ch., 1975-76. Advisr Chi Rho Youth Fellowship, Temple Bapt. Ch., 1975-81, adv. com. Golden Outreach Sr. Citizens Fellowship, 1979-80, 86-87, 89-93, Women's Day spkr., 1979-81, Ebenezer Missionary Bapt. Ch., 1993; adviser Nat. Soc. Black Engring. Students, 1983-84; founder, coord. Tenn. State U. Assn. for Excellence in Computer Sci., Math. and Physics (AE-COMP), 1986-87, coord. Tech. Opportunities Fair, 1986, 87; dir. Tenn. State U. Minorities in Sci., Engring. and Tech. Rsch. Project-MISET, 1989-1992; child sponsor World Vision, 1981—; mem., newsletter staff Lake Providence Missionary Bapt. Ch., 1997; mem. Miss. Blvd. Christian Ch., 2000-. Recipient Disting. Instr. award, 1984, Disting. Svc. citation Beloit Coll. Alumni Assn., 1994; grantee Digital Equipment Corp., 1989-92; rsch. grantee Tenn. State U., 1993, 94, NSF, 2002-03. Mem. NAACP (nat. judge ACT-SO sci. olympics 1992), Assn. Computing Machinery, Assn. Info. Tech. Profls. (edn. chmn., bd. dirs. 1986), Tenn. Acad. Sci., Info. Sys. Audit & Control Assn., Phi Kappa Phi. Home: PO Box 281946 Nashville TN 37228

WILLIAMS, MARTHA SPRING, psychologist; b. Dallas, Oct. 5, 1951; d. Thomas Ayers and Emma Martha (Felmet) Spring; m. James Walter Williams, June 30, 1979; children: Dane Ayers, Jake Austin BA, Tex. A&M Commerce, 1972, MEd, 1974, EdD, 1978. Cert. and lic. psychologist, Tex.; lic. profl. counselor, marriage and family therapist. Tchr. Dallas Ind. Sch.; grad. asst. to dean Coll. Edn. East Tex. State U., 1975—77; intern Terrell State Hosp. Outreach Clinic and Hunt County Clinic, Greenville, Tex., 1975—76; intern Counseling Ctr. East Tex. State U., 1976—77; learning dir. Man and His Environ. Program, 1978—85; pvt. practice psychology Dallas, 1981—. Adolescent group therapist in-patient psychiat. facility, 1986-91; mem. staff Baylor/Richardson (Tex.) Med. Ctr., clin. dir. allied mental health profls., 1992-94; v.p. for provider rels. Advanced Behavioral Health Care Sys., Inc., 1995—2000; mem. staff Lake Pointe Hosp., credentials mem., Com. Nat. Dem. Convention Charotte, NC, 2012 Author: (with others) The Role Innovative Woman and Her Positive Impact on Family Functioning, 1981, Women and Intimacy, 1982, Premenstral Syndrome: A Family Affair, 1984, The Expanding Horizons of Traditional Private Practice: High Tech High/Touch, 1986, Adolescent Suicide: Consequences of an Anti-Child Society, 1986, Therapist as a Partner, 1987 Nat. del. Dem. Conv., San Francisco, 1984, LA, 2000, Boston, 04; Dem. county chair Kaufman County, 1990-95; mem. state Dem. Exec. Com. 1993—2010, nat. del., Dem. Com. LA, 2000, Boston LA, 2004-. Mem.: Tex. State Soc. Lutheran. Avocations: skiing, travel, politics, tap dancing. Home: PO Box 1119 Terrell TX 75160-7144 Office: 12840 Hillcrest Rd Ste E-101 Dallas TX 75230-1599 Office Fax: 972-386-6558.

WILLIAMS, MICHAEL EDWARD, SR., history professor; b. Mobile, Ala., July 30, 1960; s. Charles Edward and Ollie Jo (Hayes) Williams; m. Roberta Jean Norton, Nov. 28, 1987; children: Michael Edward Jr., Joshua Cody, Carey Alan. BS in Secondary Edn. Hist., Troy State U., 1982; MACT in Hist., Auburn U., 1984; MDiv, Souwestern Bapt. Theological Sem., 1987, PhD in Ch. Hist., 1993. Grad. tchg. asst. Auburn (Ala.) U., 1982—84; pastor Trinity Hills Bapt. Ch., Benbrook, Tex., 1987—94; tchg. fellow ch. hist. Southwestern Bapt. Theological Sem., Fort Worth, Tex., 1991, adj. prof. ch. hist., 1994; adj. prof. hist. Dallas (Tex.) Bapt. U., 1991—94, asst. prof. hist., 1995—96, prof. hist., 1996—, dean coll. humanities and social scis., 1996—2011. Edtl. bd. Bap. Hist. Heritage Jour., 1997—, Jour. Tex. Bapt. Hist., Dallas, 1998—; editor Tex. Bapt. History Jour., 2008—; academic book review editor Bapt. Hist. Heritage Jour., Nashville, 2003—. Co-author: Presdl. Praise: Our Pres. & Their Hymns, 2008, co-editor Turning Points in Baptist History; author: Isaac Taylor Tichenor: The Creation of the Baptist New South, 2005, To God Be The Glory: The Centennial History of DBU, 1998 (Tex. Bapt. Hist. Soc. Ch. Hist. award, 1998), Victory Thru Faith: A History of the Rosen Heights Baptist Church, 1996 (Tex. Bapt. Hist. Soc. Ch. Hist. award, 1996); contbr. articles various profl. jours. Recipient Hon. Alumnus award, Decatur Bapt. Coll., 1999, Disting. Svc. award, Bapt. History & Heritage Soc., 2013; named Prof. of Yr., Dallas Bapt. U., 1999—2000, 2012—13, Educator of Yr., Oak Cliff C. of C., 2013. Mem.: Am. Soc. Ch. History, Tex. Baptist History Soc., So. Hist. Assn., Fellowship Bapt. Historians, Bapt. Hist. and Heritage Soc. (v.p. 2007—09, pres. 2009—11). Independent. Bapt. Avocations: sports, jogging, swimming, movies, reading. Home: 169 Deer Creek Dr Aledo TX 76008 Office: Dallas Bapt U 3000 Mt Creek Pkwy Dallas TX 75211 Office Phone: 214-333-5276. Business E-Mail: mikew@dbu.edu.

WILLIAMS, MONTY (TAVARES MONTGOMERY WILLIAMS JR.), professional basketball coach, retired professional basketball player; b. Fredericksburg, Va., Oct. 8, 1971; s. Tavares and Joyce; m. Ingrid Williams; 5 children. BA in Comm. & Theatre, U. Notre Dame, Ind. Forward NY Knicks, 1994—96, San Antonio Spurs, 1996—99, coaching intern, 2004—05; forward Denver Nuggets, 1999, Orlando Magic, 1999—2002, 2003, Phila. 76ers, 2002—03; asst. coach Portland Trail Blazers, 2005—10; head coach New Orleans Pelicans (formerly New Orleans Hornets), 2010—. Summer league head coach San Antonio Spurs, 2005, Portland Trail Blazers, 2007, 2008. Office: New Orleans Pelicans 5800 Airline Dr Metairie LA 70003*

WILLIAMS, NOEL BROWN, hospital administrator; b. Pasadena, Tex., Mar. 15, 1955; 2 children. B Engring. in Computer Sci. & Math., Vanderbilt U., 1977; MS in Healthcare Fin. Mgmt., U. SC, 1987. Chief info. officer Am. Svc. Group, Brentwood, Tenn., Prison Health Svcs., Inc., 1996—97; various positions HCA, Inc., 1979—93, various info. svcs. dept. positions, including v.p., info. svcs., 1994—95; pres. HCA Info. Tech. & Svcs., Inc. (subs. HCA, Inc.); sr. v.p., chief info. officer HCA, Inc., 1997—. Office: HCA Inc One Park Plz Nashville TN 37203 Office Phone: 615-344-9551. Office Fax: 615-320-2266. Business E-Mail: noel.williams@hcahealthcare.com.

WILLIAMS, PAT, professional sports team executive; b. Phila., May 3, 1940; m. Ruth Williams; 19 children. B in Phys. Edn., Wake Forest U.; MS in Phys. Edn., Ind. U., 1964. Bus. mgr. Fla. State League Miami Marlins Class A Baseball Club, 1964—65; gen. mgr. West Carolina League Spartanburg Phillies, SC, 1965—67, pres., 1967—68, Orlando Double-A So. League Baseball Team, 1990—93; bus. mgr. Phila. 76ers, 1968—69, gen. mgr., v.p., 1974—86; gen. mgr. Chgo. Bulls, 1969—73, Atlanta Hawks, 1973—74; gen. mgr., COO Orlando Magic, 1986—96, sr. v.p., 1996—. Author: Making Magic, Coaching Your Kids to be Leaders: The Keys to Unlocking Their Potential, 2005, Who Wants to Be a Champion, How to Be Like Coach Wooden. Recipient John W. Bunn Lifetime Achievement award, Naismith Meml. Basketball Hall of Fame, 2012; named Minor League Exec. of Yr., The Sporting News, 1967; named to Del. Sports Hall of Fame, 2001, Wake Forest Sports Hall of Fame. Mem.: Fellowship of Christian Athletes. Office: Orlando Magic 8701 Maitland Summit Blvd Orlando FL 32810-5915 Office Phone: 407-916-2401. Office Fax: 407-916-2986. E-mail: pwilliams@patwilliamsmotivate.com.

WILLIAMS, PATRICK C., state legislator; BA in Architecture, Southern U.; MBA, Centenary Coll.; attending in Decision Sci. Mgmt. Orgnl. Leadership, Walden U., Pa., 2007—. Arch. cons.; mem. Dist. 4 La. House Reps., 2008—; mem. appropriations com. La. House of Reps.; chmn. Sub-Committee of Appropriations- Corrections and Safety, Health & Welfare, Labor & Industry, Joint Legislative. Com. Budget. Mem.: MLK Cmty., NRA (life). Democrat. Office: State Capitol PO Box 44486 Baton Rouge LA 70804 also: 1500 N Market St Ste B106 Shreveport LA 71107-6553 Office Phone: 318-676-5990, 225-342-6945. Office Fax: 318-676-5992. Business E-Mail: larep004@legis.state.la.us.

WILLIAMS, PHIL, state legislator; b. Ala. m. Lisa Williams; 1 child. BS in Internat. Bus., U. Ala., Huntsville. Small bus. econ. and devel. recruiter, Ala.; contract specialist US Army Small Bus. and Contract Office; co-founder 3D Rsch. Corp., Synapse Wireless, Soldier 1 Corp.; mem. Dist. 6 Ala. House of Reps., Montgomery, 2009—. Pro bono small bus. mentor; participant Madison County/Huntsville Leadership Program; dir. Ala. Archives Bd. Ala. History; bd. mem. Huntsville Heritage Found. Republican. Office: 2185 Old Monrovia Rd Huntsville AL 35806 also: Ala House of Reps Rm 536-C 11 S Union St Montgomery AL 36130 Office Phone: 256-489-5471, 334-353-3507.

WILLIAMS, PHIL, state legislator; b. Fort Monmouth, NJ, May 20, 1965; m. Charlene Williams; children: Caitlin Williams, Josh Williams. BS, U. South Ala.; JD, Birmingham U.; grad., Combined Arms and Svcs. Staff Sch., US Army Command and Gen. Staff Coll. Mng. ptnr., atty. Brunson and Assocs.; COO, chief counsel TaxBreak Limited Liability Co.; mem. Dist. 10 Ala. State Senate, 2011—. Mem. Etowah County Rep. Party; area dir. YoungLife. Lt. col. USAR. Mem.: Nat. Assn. of Profl. Employer Orgns., Alabama Bar Association. Republican. Office: Alabama State Senate State House Rm 733 11 S Union St Montgomery AL 36130 Office Phone: 334-242-7857. Business E-Mail: philw.williams@alsenate.gov.

WILLIAMS, REDFORD BROWN, medical educator, researcher, medical geneticist, internist; b. Raleigh, NC, Dec. 14, 1940; s. Redford Brown Sr. and Annie Virginia (Betts) W.; m. Virginia Carter Parrott, August 9, 1940; children: Jennifer Betts, Lloyd Carter. AB, Harvard U., 1963; MD, Yale U., 1967. Diplomate Am. Bd. Internal Medicine. Intern, then resident Yale-New Haven Med. Ctr., 1967-70; sr. surgeon USPHS, Bethesda, Md., 1970-72; asst. prof. Duke U. Med. Ctr., Durham, NC, 1972, prof. psychiatry, 1977—, prof. psychology, 1990—, dir. behavioral medicine rsch. ctr., 1985—; CEO Williams LifeSkills, Inc., 1997—. Cons. NIH rev. coms., Bethesda, 1977—. Author: The Trusting Heart, 1989, Anger Kills, 1993, Lifeskills, 1998, In Control, 2006; contbr. articles to profl. jours. Dir. NC Heart Assn., Chapel Hill, 1980-83. Recipient Rsch. Scientist award NIMH, 1974—; NIH grantee, 1976—. Fellow Soc. Behavioral Medicine (pres. 1984-85, Upjohn Disting. Scientist award 1992), Acad. Behavioral Medicine Rsch. (pres. 1995—); mem. Am. Psychosomatic Soc. (bd. dirs. 1978-81, pres. 1992), Internat. Soc. Behavioral Medicine (pres.-elect 2004-06, pres. 2006-08). Unitarian Universalist. Achievements include identification of hostility as the toxic component of the Type A (coronary-prone) behavior pattern, genetic variants that increase expression of cardiovascular disease risk factors in persons exposed to chronic stress. Avocation: tennis. Office: Duke U Med Ctr PO Box 3926 Durham NC 27710-0001 Office Phone: 919-684-3863. Business E-Mail: redfordw@duke.edu.

WILLIAMS, REED (W. REED WILLIAMS), councilman, retired oil industry executive; m. Joan Williams; children: Carter, Kate. BA, U. Tex., Austin, 1969. Joined Tesoro Petroleum Corp., San Antonio, 1973, group v.p. refining, mktg. and supply; with Diamond Shamrock, 1993—2000; exec. v.p. refining and mktg. Frontier Oil Corp., Denver, 2000—06; councilman, Dist. 8 San Antonio City Coun., 2009—. Dir. HMT Inc., 2008—. Co-author: Activities and Resources of Galveston Bay. Mem.: Nat. Petrochemical and Refining Assn. (bd. mem. 1989—92, 2000—06), Sons of the Am. Revolution. Office: Colonnade Centre Bldg 9830 Colonnade Blvd Ste 460 San Antonio TX 78230 also: City Hall PO Box 839966 San Antonio TX 78283 Office Phone: 210-207-0943. E-mail: district8@sanantonio.gov.

WILLIAMS, RICKY (ERRICK LYNNE WILLIAMS), retired professional football player; b. San Diego, May 21, 1977; s. Errick and Sandy Williams; m. Kristin Barnes, Sept. 4, 2009; children: Prince, Asha; children: Marley, Blaze. Grad., U. Tex., Austin. Running back New Orleans Saints, 1999—2001, Miami Dolphins, 2002—03, 2005, 2007—10, Toronto Argonauts, 2006, Balt. Ravens, 2011. Founder The Ricky Williams Found. Actor: (films) Stuck On You, 2003; appeared in (documentaries) Run, Ricky, Run, 2009. Founder Run Ricky Run Found. Recipient Jim Brown Trophy, 1997, 1998, Heisman Meml. Trophy, Heisman Trophy Trust, 1998, Maxwell award, Maxwell Football Club, 1998, Doak Walker award, 1997, 1998, Walter Camp award, 1998; named First Team All-Pro, NFL, 2002, Coll. Player of Yr., AP, 1998; named to The American Football Conf. Pro Bowl Team, NFL, 2002. Achievements include leading the NFL in: rushing attempts, 2002, 2003, rushing yards, 2002, rushing yards per game, 2002, touches, 2003; setting a NFL record for longest span between 1,000 rushing yards seasons (6), 2009. Office: The Ricky Williams Foundation 2805 East Oakland Park Ste 247 Fort Lauderdale FL 33306 Office Phone: 954-701-8539. Office Fax: 954-563-3256.*

WILLIAMS, RITA TUCKER, lawyer; b. Atlanta, Jan. 26, 1950; d. Claude Edward and Lillian Bernice (Barber) Tucker; m. Raymond Williams, Jr., Jan. 1, 1973; children: Monet Danielle, Brandon Raynard, Blake Hassan. BA, Spelman Coll., 1972; MA, U. Mich., 1976; JD, Emory U., 1987. Bar: Ga. 1987. Tchr. pub. schs., Suisun, Calif., 1977-82; assoc. Alston & Bird, Atlanta, 1987-89, Bernard & Assocs., Decatur, Ga., 1989-90; prin. Williams & Assocs., Decatur, Ga., 1990—. Instr. seminar Nat. Inst. Trial Advocacy, Emory U., Atlanta, spring 1992-95, tutor 1st yr. law students, 1996. Named Outstanding Alumna, Emory U. Law Sch., 1996. Mem. ABA, State Bar Ga. Assn., Omicron Delta Kappa. Democrat. Office: 220 Church St Decatur GA 30030-3328 Office Phone: 404-370-3783. Personal E-mail: ritw@atlonline.com. Business E-Mail: rtwilliams@williamsandassoc.com.

WILLIAMS, ROBERT HENRY, oil industry executive; b. El Paso, Jan. 12, 1946; s. William Frederick and Mary (Page) W.; m. Joanne Marie Mudd, Oct. 22, 1967; children: Lara, Michael, Suzanne, Jennifer. BS in Physics, U. Tex., El Paso, 1968; PhD in Physics, U. Tex., Austin, 1973; MS in Physics, Va. Poly. Inst., 1971. Dir. Gulf Oil R&D, Houston, 1978-81; tech. mgr. Gulf Oil Internat., Houston, 1981-83; exploration mgr. Gulf Oil Co., Houston, 1983-85; mgr. geophys. rsch. Tenneco Oil Co., Houston, 1985-87, mgr., chief geophysicist, 1987-88; founder, mng. dir. Dover Energy, Houston, 1988—; exec. v.p. Tatham Offshore Inc, Houston, 1989-95, also bd. dirs.; chmn., CEO Dover Tech. Inc., Houston, 1989—. Cons. Tenneco Inc., Houston, 1989—; DeepTech Internat., 1992-95; Ukraine Acad. Sci., 1993; bd. dirs., exec. v.p. DeepTech Inc., 1991-95; founder, pres. Westway tech. Assocs., 1986—; co-founder, chmn. CEO Castaway Graphite Rods, Inc., 1990—2011; Bulldog Lures, Inc., 1994—2011; founder, CEO Houston Books Inc., 1994—; founder, CEO, chmn. Dover Energy Exploration, 1995—; pres. Westway Interests; chmn., CEO, bd. dirs. W.B. Oil & Gas Inc., 1997-2001, Dover (Belize), 1996-2002; bd. dirs. Tatham Offshore, Swep, Inc.; CEO Norman Lures, 1997—2010; founder, bd. dirs., CEO Win Leisure Products, 1997—; dir./founder William Found., 1998—; CEO, chmn. bd. dirs. Airrus Fishing Products, 2003-11. Contbr. articles to profl. jours. Coun. mem. Boy Scouts Am., Houston, 1989—; leader Girl Scouts U.S., Houston, 1989—. Mem. Soc. Exploration Geophysics, Am. Assn. Petroleum Geologists, Am. Geophys. Union. Republican. Avocations: scuba diving, book collecting, fishing. Office: Dover Tech 14420 Westway Ln Houston TX 77077

WILLIAMS, ROBERT Q., state legislator; b. Darlington, July 12, 1964; s. James Jim and Robbie Mae Williams; m. Janice Ham Williams; children: Jacobie, Rodrick, Jarell. BS, Voorhees Coll., 1984; MPA, Troy State U., 2003. Security officer Burns Int. Security, 1989—90; addiction counselor Correctional Med. Svc., 1997—99; dir. fatherhood program Telamon Corp., 1999—2003; mem. Fatherhood and Families Engagement Program, 2003—; mem. Dist. 62 SC House of Reps., 2007—, mem. Med., Mil., Pub. and Mcpl. Affairs Com. Recipient Humanitarian award, Florence C. of C., 2002, Trailblazer award, SC Fatherhood Practitioners Network, 2003, Cert of Recognition, SC Dept. Corrections, 2004, Army Achievement medal, 2002, 2004, Army Commendation medal, 2005; named Man of Yr., Round O Missionary Baptist Ch., 2001. Mem.: VFW, Tifton Cmty. Assn., Florence County Mental Health Assn., Darlington County Coord. Coun., Darlington County First Steps, Nat. Practitioners Fathers & Families, Alston Wilkes Soc., Nat. Mental Health Prevention & Children's Mental Health Svc. Commn., SC Network Fathers & Families, Phi Beta Sigma. Democrat. Home: 2512 Holly Circle Darlington SC 29532 Office: 309D Blatt Building Columbia SC 29201 Home Phone: 843-395-9408; Office Phone: 843-679-5350. Business E-Mail: WilliamsR@schouse.org.

WILLIAMS, ROBERT SANDERS (SANDY WILLIAMS), health facility administrator; b. Athens, Ga. m. Jennifer Williams; children: Molly, Nicholas, Owen. Degree, Princeton U., 1970; MD, Duke U., 1974. Internship, residency, Internal Medicine Mass. Gen. Hosp., 1974—76; fellowship, Cardiology Duke U. Med. Ctr., 1977—80; vis. prof., Biochemistry Dept. Oxford U., 1984—85; chief, Cardiology, prof., Internal Medicine, Biochemistry, & Molecular Biology, dir., Ryburn Ctr. for Molecular Cardiology U. Tex. Southwestern Med. Ctr., 1990—2001; vis. scientist Cold Spring Harbor Lab., NY, 1995—96; asst. prof., Medicine, Physiology & Cell Biology Duke U. Sch. medicine, 1980—84; assoc. prof., Medicine & Microbiology Duke University School Medicine, 1986—90, dean, vice chancellor, Acad. Affairs, 2001—07, sr. vice chancellor, Acad. Affairs, 2007—. Bd. advisor Nat. Heart, Lung and Blood Inst.; bd. dirs. NIH, Laboratory Corp. of America Holdings, 2007—. Contbr. more than 150 scholarly articles to biomed. jours., Proceedings of the Nat. Acad. Scis. Mem. Inst. of Medicine of the Nat. Acad. of Sciences; fellow Am. Assn. for the Advancement of Science; pres. Assn. of U. Cardiologists; chmn., Rsch. Com. Am. Heart Assn. Recipient Disting. Alumnus Award, Duke U. Sch. Medicine, 2000. Fellow: AAAS; mem.: NAS, Inst. of Medicine, Assn. Univ. Cardiologists, Am. Heart Assn. Achievements include being the leader of the Dallas Heart Disease Prevention Project, an innovative program of research in the genetic epidemiology of cardiovascular disease. Office: Laboratory Corp of America Holdings Bd Directors 531 S Spring St Burlington NC 27215 Office Phone: 336-436-5274. Office Fax: 336-436-1569. E-mail: williamsr@labcorp.com.

WILLIAMS, ROGER (JOHN ROGER WILLIAMS), United States Representative from Texas, former state official; b. Evanston, Ill., Sept. 13, 1949; m. Patty Williams; children: Jaclyn, Sabrina. B, Tex Christian U., 1972. Pres., CEO Roger Williams Automall, 1974—95; profl. baseball player Atlanta Braves farm team, 1971—74; baseball coach Tex. Christian U., 1974—76; sec. of state State of Tex., Austin, 2004—07; mem. US Congress from 25th Tex. Dist., Washington, 2013—, US House Budget Com., 2013—, US House Transp. & Infrastructure Com., 2013—. Regional finance chmn. George W. Bush Gubernatorial Campaign, 1994, 1998; north Tex. chmn. Bush/Cheney 2000 Campaign, 2000; north Tex. finance chmn., nat. grassroots fundraising chmn. Bush/Cheney 2004 Campaign, 2004;

chmn. Republican Nat. Committee's Eagles Program, 2001, Tex. Republican Victory 2008 Coordinated Campaign, 2007—08; state finance chair John Cornyn for US Senate, 2002; chair Tex. Base Realignment & Closure Response Strike Force, 2005. Republican. Christian. Office: US House of Representatives 1122 Longworth House Office Bldg Washington DC 20515 also: 1005 Congress Ave Ste 925 Austin TX 78701 Office Phone: 202-225-9896, 512-473-8910. Office Fax: 512-473-8946.*

WILLIAMS, ROGER, state legislator; m. Joann Williams; children: Michael, Kathleen, William, Allyson. State rep. Dist. 6, Ga., 1977—86; state rep. Dist. 4 Ga., 2001—. Democrat. Episcopal. Office: 409 Legis Office Bldg Atlanta GA 30334 also: Po Box 2125 Dalton GA 30722

WILLIAMS, ROY, men's college basketball coach; b. Spruce Pine, NC, Aug. 1, 1950; m. Wanda; children: Scott, Kimberly. BA in Edn., U. NC, 1972, MAT, 1973. Basketball & golf coach Charles D. Owen HS, NC; asst. coach U. NC Tarheels, 1978—88, head coach, 2003—, U. Kans. Jayhawks, 1988—2003. Asst. coach U.S.A. Sr. Men's Nat. Basketball Team, 2003, US Olympic Men's Basketball Team, Athens, Greece, 2004. Co-author (with Tim Crothers): Hard Work: My Life On and Off the Court, 2009. Named Nat. Rookie Coach of Yr. Basketball Times, 1989, Nat. Coach of Yr. 1990-92, 1997, 2006, Big 8 Coach of Yr. (7 times), Coach of Yr. AP, 1992, 2006, ACC Coach of Yr., 2006, 2011, Dist. III Coach of Yr. US Basketball Writers Assn., 2011; recipient John R. Wooden Legends of Coaching award LA Athletic Club, 2003, Nat. Coach of Yr. award NY Athletic Club, 2005; named to Naismith Meml. Basketball Hall of Fame, 2007. Achievements include head coach of the NCAA Men's Basketball National Championship winning University of North Carolina Tarheels, 2005, 2009. Office: U NC Athletic Dept Men's Basketball PO Box 2126 Chapel Hill NC 27514 Office Phone: 919-962-6000. E-mail: williara@email.unc.edu.

WILLIAMS, SUE DARDEN, library director; b. Miami, Fla., Aug. 13, 1943; d. Archie Yelverton and Bobbie (Jones) Eagles; m. Richard Williams, Sept. 30, 1989. BA, Barton Coll., Wilson, NC, 1965; M.L.S., U. Tex., Austin, 1970. Cert. librarian, N.C., Va. Instr. Chowan Coll., Murfreesboro, NC, 1966-68; libr.'s asst. Albemarle Regional Libr., Winston, NC, 1968-69; br. libr. Multnomah County Pub. Libr., Portland, Oreg., 1971-72; asst. dir. Stanly County Pub. Libr., Albemarle, NC, 1973-76, dir., 1976-80; asst. dir. Norfolk (Va.) Pub. Libr., 1980-83, dir., 1983-94, Rockingham County Pub. Libr., Eden, NC, 1996—2004, Albemarle Regional Libr., Winton, NC, 2004—08. Mem. ALA (coun. 1987-91, orientation com. 1990-92, chair 1991), Libr. Adminstrv. and Mgmt. Assn. (pub. rels. sec. 1985-87bd. dirs. 2004—), Southeastern Libr. Assn. (staff devel. com. 1986-88, Rothrock award com. 1984-86, sec. pub. libr. sect. 1982-84), Va. Libr. Assn. (SELA rep. 1993-96, coun. 1984, 88-91, 93-96, ad hoc conf. guidelines com. 1985-86, chmn. conf. program 1984, awards and recognition com. 1983, mem. SELA outstanding libr. program award com. 2002), Pub. Libr. Assn. (bd. dirs.-at-large Met. area 1986-89), Va. State Libr. (coop edn. com. 88-89), N.C. Libr. Assn. (scholarship com. 1999-2005, chair 2001-2005), LAMS. Home: 105 Hunters Trl E Elizabeth City NC 27909-3218 Personal E-mail: swilliams13@roadrunner.com.

WILLIAMS, SUNITA L., astronaut; b. Euclid, Ohio, Sept. 19, 1965; d. Deepak N. and Ursaline B. Pandya; m. Michael J. Williams. BS in Physical Sci., U.S. Naval Acad., 1987; MS in Engring. Mgmt., Fla. Inst. Tech., 1995. Commn. ensign USN, 1987, advanced through grades to lt. comdr., various assignments, 1987—89, overseas combat, 1989—92; officer in charge Hurrican Andrew Relief Ops. USS Sylvania, 1992—93; various assignments USN, 1993—95; served on USS Saipan, Norfolk, Va., 1995—98; astronaut NASA, Houston, 1998—, dep. chief, Astronaut Office. Worked with Russian Space Agy. on Russian contbn. to Internat. Space Station (ISS) and with first Expedition Crew to ISS; worked within Robotics branch of ISS Robotic Arm and the follow on Spl. Purpose Dexterous Manipulator; NEEM02 crewmember; flight engr. Expedition-14(after traveling to the International Space Station (ISS) with the crew aboard STS-116)/Expedition 15 (Return to Earth with STS-117 Crew), 2006—07; will perform spacewalks Expedition-14, 2006; flight engineer Expedition 32, 2012—13; ISS commander Expedition 33, 2012—13. Decorated Commendation medal USN, Achievement medal USN & USMC, Humanitarian Svc. medal USN. Mem.: Soc. Flight Test Engrs., Soc. Exptl. Test Pilots, American Helicopter Assn. Sets women's spacewalk record of 22 hours and 27 minutes on Expedition-14 mission (record includes the following spacewalks-one in December, 2006 & two in February, 2007). Spacewalks marked the first time three spacewalks have been conducted in such a short period without a space shuttle docked to it. Total time spent in space on Expedition-14 mission was 29 hours and 17 minutes of walking in space. Will run Boston Marathon aboard international space station using a treadmill and bungee cords to keep from floating away. On astronaut time, so start time will differ from Boston, Massachusetts race in 2007 (finished, unofficially, 4 hours, 23 minutes and 46 seconds). Set an endurance record for the longest single spaceflight by a woman at 195 days in 2007. Established a world record for females with four spacewalks totaling 29 hours and 17 minutes of Extravehicular Activity (EVA). First person ever to complete a triathlon in space (swimming, biking & running events aboard the ISS using exercise equipment specialized for space in 2012. Office: Astronaut Office CB NASA Johnson Space Center Houston TX 77058

WILLIAMS, THOMAS (TOMMY), state legislator; b. Dec. 17, 1956; m. Marsha Williams; 2 children. BBA, Tex. A&M U., 1978. Industry and pub. acctg. profl., 1978—83; ins. and fin. services profl., 1983—; pres. Woodforest Fin. Services; mem. Dist. 15 Tex. House of Representatives, 1997—2002; mem. Dist. 4 Tex. State Senate, 2003—. Mem.: Tex. Soc. CPA's. Republican. Office: PO Box 5819 Beaumont TX 77726-5819 also: PO Box 12068 Capitol Station Austin TX 78711 also: 2825 IH-10 East Ste 100 Beaumont TX 77702 also: 2441 High Timbers Ste 400 The Woodlands TX 77380 Mailing: PO Box 8069 The Woodlands TX 77387-8069 Office Phone: 512-463-0104. Office Fax: 409-896-2350.

WILLIAMS, THOMAS EUGENE, pediatric hematologist and oncologist, pharmaceutical executive; b. Texarkana, Ark., May 13, 1936; s. Thomas Earle and Frankie Jo (Garner) W.; m. Peggy Jane O'Neill, May 31, 1958; children: Thomas Eugene, Elizabeth Anne, James David. BA, Yale U., 1958; MD, U. Tex. Southwestern Med. Sch., 1962. Rotating intern Hermann Hosp., Houston, 1962-63; pediat. resident Children's Med. Ctr., Dallas, 1963-65; fellow pediat. hematology-oncology U. Va. Hosp., Charlottesville, 1967-68; rsch. assoc. Cancer Rsch. Lab., U. Va. Hosp., Charlottesville, 1968-69; clin. fellow bone marrow transplantation program Johns Hopkins U. Sch. Medicine, Balt., 1985; asst. prof. pediat. and pathology U. Tex. Health Sci. Ctr., San Antonio, 1969-72, assoc. prof. pediat., asst. prof. pathology, 1972-73, assoc. prof. pediat. and pathology, 1973-79, assoc. prof. pediat., 1985-94; sr. clin. rsch. scientist Burroughs Wellcome Co., 1979—85; dir. new drug devel. Orphan Med., Inc., 1994—96; dir. med. affairs ILEX Oncology Svcs., Inc., 1997—98, ILEX Oncology Products, Inc., 1998—2002; sr. dir., divsn. oncology ICON Clin. Rsch., Inc., 2002—07; pres. Thistle Advisors Internat. Inc., 2007—; chief med. officer Amplimed Corp., 2008; assoc. med. dir. Cetero, San Antonio, 2008—09; med. dir. ONYX Pharm. Inc., 2009—11. Med. dir. Santa Rosa Children's Hosp. Cancer Rsch. and Treatment Ctr., 1974—79, South Tex. Comprehensive Hemophilia Ctr., San Antonio, 1977—79; pres. Bexar Co. Chpt., Am. Cancer Soc., 1978—79; med. dir. Santa Rosa Children's Hosp. Bone Marrow Transp. Ctr., San Antonio, 1985—94, Corpus Christi City Employees Health's Wellness Clinic, 2013, Vis. Physician Assn., 2013—, New Braunfels Rural Health Clinic, 2010—12, N. Tex. State Hosp., 2012; instl. med. dir. Nat. Marrow Donor Program, 1990—94. Contbr. articles to profl. jours. Exec. dir. Episcopal Med. Missions Found., 1997—. Lt. comdr. US Naval Hosp. USNR, 1965—67, Corpus Christi. Recipient travel award Am. Soc. Pharmacology and Exptl. Therapeutics, 1968; Am. Cancer Soc. advanced clin. fellow, 1968-69, 70-72. Mem. Am. Soc. Clin. Oncology, Am. Soc. Hematology, Am. Assn. for Cancer Rsch. Anglican. Office: 84 NE Loop 410 Ste 195 San Antonio TX 78216 Office Phone: 210-979-8400. Business E-Mail: twilliams@thistleoncology.com.

WILLIAMS, THOMAS FFRANCON, chemist, educator; b. Colwyn Bay, Wales, Jan. 30, 1928; came to U.S., 1961; s. David and Margaret (Williams) W.; m. Astra Silvia Birins, Jan. 31, 1959; children: Ifor Rainis, Gwyn David. BSc, U. Coll., London, 1949; PhD, U. London, 1960. Sci. officer U.K. Atomic Energy Authority, Harwell, Eng., 1949-55, sr. sci. officer, 1955-61, prin. sci. officer, 1961; rsch. scientist Ill. Inst. Tech. Research Inst., Chgo., 1961; asst. prof. chemistry U. Tenn., Knoxville, 1961-63, assoc. prof., 1963-67, prof., 1967-74, Alumni Distinguished Service prof., 1974—. Tchg. and rsch. assoc. Northwestern U., Evanston, Ill., 1957-58; NSF vis. scientist Kyoto (Japan) U., 1965-66; coord. U.S.-Japan Sci. Sem., Hakone, Japan, 1969; chmn. Gordon Rsch. Conf. on Radiation Chemistry, New Hampton, N.H., 1971, Gordon Rsch. Conf. Radical Ions, Wolfeboro, N.H., 1984; John Simon Guggenheim Meml. Found. fellow, Swedish Rsch. Coun. Lab., Studsvik, Nykoping, 1972-73; vis. scientist Royal Inst. Tech., Stockholm, Sweden, 1972-73; chmn. 10th Southeastern Magnetic Resonance Conf., 1978; mem. chemistry div. rev. com. Argonne (Ill.) Nat. Lab., 1988, 91, 95; cons. Pacific N.W. Nat. Lab., 1996-97. Contbg. author: Fundamental Processes in Radiation Chemistry, 1968, Radiation Chemistry of Macromolecules, 1972; mem. editl. bd. Radiation Rsch., 1993-2000, assoc. editor, 1993-97, cons. editor, 1997-2000; contbr. numerous articles on free radicals, radical ions, and chem. effects of high energy radiation to profl. jours. AEC, ERDA, Dept. Energy grantee, 1962-99. Mem. Am. Chem. Soc. (program chmn. sect. 1968-69, exec. com. 1986-88), (life) Royal Soc. Chemistry, Radiation Rsch. Soc., Phi Beta Kappa (hon.), Sigma Xi (pres. U. Tenn. chpt. 1993-94). Home: 3117 Montlake Dr Knoxville TN 37920-2836 Office: University Tenn Dept Chemistry Knoxville TN 37996-1600 Office Phone: 865-974-3468. Business E-Mail: fwilliam@utk.edu, williams@ion.chem.utk.edu.

WILLIAMS, THOMAS L., recreational facility executive; b. 1947; Degree, Calif. State U., Fresno, 1970. Various leading mgmt. roles MCA Recreation Svcs. Group, Hollywood, Calif., 1970-87; with Universal City Fla. Ptnr., Orlando, 1987—, pres., 1990; chmn., CEO Universal Parks and Resorts, Orlando, 1999—. Bd. dirs. NBC. Bd. dirs. Emeril Lagasse Found.; founding trustee World Class Schools, United Arts of Central Fla. Office: Universal City Fl Ptnr 1000 Universal Studios Plz Orlando FL 32819-7601

WILLIAMS, TIMOTHY A., security firm executive, former federal agency administrator; BA in Criminal Justice, Moravian Coll., 1985; grad., Police Exec. Rsch. Forum, Law Enforcement Mgmt. Inst. of Tex. Joined US Marshals Service (USMS), 1986, dep. marshal, supr. fugitive ops. Dist. of NJ, inspector/instr. Fed. Law Enforcement Training Ctr., inspector Spl. Ops. Group, comdr. NY/NJ Regional Fugitive Task Force, chief Tech. Ops. Group (TOG); dep. dir. US Nat. Ctrl. Bur. INTERPOL, US Dept. Justice, 2006—09, dir., 2009—12; sr. adv. Internat. Assn. Chiefs of Police, Alexandria, Va., 2012—13; gen. mgr. G4S Secure Solutions (USA) Inc., Washington, 2013—. Mem. Interagency Coun. for Applied Homeland Security Tech., INTERPOL Fin. Adv. Group, Lyon, France. Mem.: Nat. Ctr. for Missing and Exploited Children (NCMEC) (mem. Law Enforcement Com.), Fed. Law Enforcement Officers Assn., Internat. Chiefs of Police (mem. Internat. Organized Crime Com. and Internat. Police Steering Com.). Office: G4S Secure Solutions (USA) Inc 1395 University Blvd Jupiter FL 33458*

WILLIAMS, TIMOTHY L., lawyer; BBA, Univ. Mich., JD, 1993. Sr. dir. labor & employment law Winn-Dixie Stores, Jacksonville, Fla., 2003—08, asst. gen. counsel, 2008—10, sr. v.p., sec., gen. counsel, 2010—. Office: Winn-Dixie Stores 5050 Edgewood Ct Jacksonville FL 32254-3699 Office Phone: 904-783-5000.

WILLIAMS, TOMMIE, state legislator; b. Dec. 04; m. Stephanie Williams; children: Emma, Jack 1 stepchild, Madison. B, U. Ga.; MA in Edn., Ga. Southern U. Founder, owner Ga. Pine Straw, Inc., Lyons; mem. Dist. 6 Ga. State Senate, 1999—2002, mem. Dist. 19, 2003—, majority leader, 2005—09, pres. pro tempore, 2009—. Active HOPE (Helping Outstanding Pupils Educationally); deacon First Bapt. Ch. Vidalia; bd. dirs. Toombs County Health Dept.; bd. trustees Brewton Parker Coll.; past bd. dirs. Altamaha Bank Vidalia. Named one of 100 Most Influential Georgians, Ga. Trend Mag., 2007. Mem.: Toombs County C. of C. (past pres.), Toombs/Montgomery Vidalia Onion Growers Assn. (sec./treas.). Republican. Baptist. Office: 148 Williams Ave Lyons GA 30436 Office Phone: 912-526-7444. Business E-Mail: tommie.williams@senate.ga.gov.

WILLIAMS, TRUDI K., state legislator, engineering company executive; b. Ottawa, Can., Oct. 22, 1953; m. Don Williams; children: Ryan, Kristen, Shannen. BSCE, Fla. Internat. U., Miami. Civil, environ. engr.; founder, CEO TKW Consulting Engrs., Inc., Ft. Meyers, Fla., 1989—; mem. Dist. 75 Fla. House of Reps., Tallahassee, 2004—, chair agr. and natural resources policy com., mem. gen. govt. policy coun., health care svcs. policy com., natural resources appropriations com. Mem. small bus., agr. and labor adv. coun. Fed. Res. Bank, Atlanta; dir., founding shareholder Fla. Gulf Bank, 2001—; environ. dir. Fla. Inst. Consulting Engrs., 2003—04. Mem. exec. bd. Am. Red Cross, 1997—; trustee Corkscrew Regional Ecosystem Watershed, 1999—, Babcock Preservation Partnership, Inc., 2004—. Recipient Gov. A.W. Gilchrist award, Fla. Inst. Consulting Engrs., 2005. Republican. Baptist. Office: 12811 Kenwood Ln Ste 212 Fort Myers FL 33907 also: 303 House Office Bldg 402 S Monroe St Tallahassee FL 32399 Office Phone: 239-433-6775, 850-488-2047.

WILLIAMS, WAYMON KENT, state legislator; b. Elizabethton, Tenn., June 23, 1949; m. Gayle Williams; 4 children. Mem. Rep. Caucus Crime Task Force Com., Edn. Oversight Com, Fin. Com., Ways & Means Com., Health & Human Resources Com.; house reps. mem. Dist. 4 Tenn., 2007—; spkr., 2009—. Mem.: NRA, Tenn. Restaurant Assn., Carter County Rep. Party, Elizabethton-Carter County Hunting & Fishing Club. Republican. Southern Baptist. Office: 126 South Main St Elizabethton TN 37643 also: 19 Legislative Plz Nashville TN 37243-0104 Office Phone: 615-741-7450, 423-768-3431. Office Fax: 615-253-0310. Business E-Mail: speaker.kent.williams@capitol.tn.gov.

WILLIAMS-BARNES, SONYA, state legislator; Attended, Bishop State CC, Mobile, Ala., Jackson State U., Miss. Funeral dir.; mem. Dist. 119 Miss. House of Reps., Jackson, 2012—. Active Saving Our Sisters-Teen Pregnancy Prevention; mem. adv. bd. Youth Coun.; mem. Morning Star M.B. Ch. Mem.: NAACP, AKA Sorority, Inc. Democrat. Baptist. Office: Miss House of Reps PO Box 1018 Jackson MS 39215 Business E-Mail: swilliamsbarnes@house.ms.gov.

WILLIAMSON, BRUCE, state legislator; b. Apr. 17; m. Vickie Williamson; 4 children. BA in Bus. Adminstrn., Furman U., 1976; grad. student in risk mgmt. and ins., U. Ga. Co-founder Walton Bank & Trust Co., Liberty First Bank, Monroe, Ga.; owner Williamson Ins. Agy., Inc.; mem. Dist. 111 Ga. House of Representatives, 2011—. Republican. Office: PO Box 430 Monroe GA 30655 also: Georgia House of Reps 512 Coverdell Legis Office Bldg Atlanta GA 30334 Office Phone: 770-267-2566, 404-656-7859. Business E-Mail: bruce.williamson@house.ga.gov.

WILLIAMSON, BRUCE A., retired energy executive; b. Great Falls, Mont., 1959; BS in Finance, U. Mont., 1981; MBA, U. Houston, 1995. With Royal Dutch/Shell Group, 1981—95; sr. v.p. finance, bus. develop. & risk mgmt. PanEnergy Corp., v.p. finance, 1995—97; pres., CEO Duke Energy Internat., 1997—2001, Duke Energy Global Markets, 2001—02; CEO Dynegy Inc., Houston, 2002—04, chmn., CEO, 2004—07, chmn., pres., CEO, 2007—11, pres., CEO, 2011. Bd. dirs. Dynegy, Inc., 2002—11, Questar Corp., 2006—. Chancellor's nat. adv coun. U. Houston, Dean's adv. bd., C.T. Bauer Coll. Bus.; bd. dir. Greater Houston Partnership.

WILLIAMSON, DENNIS ARTHUR, former federal marshal; b. Fla. BS in Criminology, Fla. State U., Tallahassee; grad. student, U. Va.; grad., FBI Nat. Acad., Fla. Criminal Justice Exec. Inst., FBI Fla. Command Coll. Officer in the uniform, detective and narcotics divisions Sarasota County Sheriff's Dept., Fla., 1973—77; spl. agent Fla. Dept. Law Enforcement, Miami, 1977—80, spl. agent supr. through the ranks to dep. commr. Tallahassee, 1980—2000, dep. commr., 2000—03; US Marshal (northern dist.) Fla. US Marshals Svc., US Dept. Justice, Tallahassee, 2003—11. Mem.: State Law Enforcement Chiefs Assn. (past pres.), FBI Nat. Acad. Assn., Assn. State Criminal Investigative Agencies, Internat. Assn. Police Chiefs.

WILLIAMSON, DONALD ELLIS, state agency administrator, public health service officer; b. Louisville, Miss., June 17, 1955; m. Anita Hudspeth; 1 child, Jonathan Stuart. Student, East Miss. Jr. Coll., 1972-73, Miss. State U., 1973-75; MD cum laude, U. Miss., 1979. Diplomate Am. Bd. Internal Medicine. Intern, resident in internal medicine U. Va. Hosp., Charlottesville, 1979-82; with East Miss. State Hosp., Meridian, 1979; state TB control officer Miss. State Dept. Health, 1982-86; dir. divsn. disease control Ala. Dept. Pub. Health, 1986-88, dir. bur. preventive health svcs., 1988-92, state health officer, 1992—. Faculty mem. Injury Control Rsch. Ctr. U. Ala., Birmingham; clin. assoc. prof. dept. internal medicine U. South Ala.; presenter in field. Contbr. articles to profl. jours. Chmn. Ala. Pub. Health Care Authority, Ala. Radiation Adv. Bd. Health; mem. Ala. Commn. Aging, State Bldg. Commn., Statewide Health Coordinating Coun., Ala. Youth Svcs. Bd., Ala. Child Abuse & Neglect Prevention Bd., Ala. Resource Devel. Com., Ala. Anat. Bd., Planning and Adv. Coun. Devel. Disabilities, Ala. Bd. Med. Scholarship Awards, Pesticides Adv. Com., Gov.'s Interagy. Coordinating Coun., Ala. Juvenile Justice Coordinating Coun., Emergency Med. Svcs. Adv. Coun., 1986-92, Legis. Adv. Com. AIDS, 1988-90, Atty. Gen.'s Task Force Med-.Waste, 1989, Water Resources Adv. Coun., exec. coun. Ala. Children's Svcs. Facilitation Team, 1993—; mem. med. adv. com. ARC. Recipient Mosby Book award, 1979, Dr. Robert Ramsey award, 1995; Pub. Health Leadership Inst. scholar, 1996. Mem. APHA, Assn. State and Territorial Health Ofcls. (exec. com. 1995-2000, pres. 1997-98), Am. Acad. of Pediatrics (Child Health Advocate of the Yr. award 1999), Pub. Health Found. (Theodore R. Ervin award 1999), Med. Assn. State Ala., Ala. Pub. Health Assn. (bd. dirs. 1991—, chmn. disease control and epidemiology sect. 1991-92, D.G. Gill award 1997), Pub. Health Found. (bd. dirs. 1995-99, treas. 1997—), Phi Theta Kappa, Phi Kappa Phi, Alpha Omega Alpha. Home: 8113 Lichfield Ct Montgomery AL 36117-5124 Office: Ala Dept Pub Health PO Box 303017 201 Monroe St Montgomery AL 36104-3735

WILLIAMSON, DONALD RAY, retired military officer; b. Amarillo, Tex., Oct. 13, 1943; s. Floy Edwin and Dorothy Lorene (Orr) W.; m. Beverly Ann Howard, Aug. 31, 1963; children: Rebecca Ann, Catherine Paige. BS in Econs., W. Tex. State U., 1966; MA in Bus., Cen. Mich. U., 1977; degree, Dept. Def. Program Mgrs., 1982, U.S. Army Command and Gen. Staff Coll., 1980. Commd. 2d lt. U.S. Army, 1966, advanced through grades to lt. col., 1982, retired, 1986, comdg. officer combat support co. Ft. Hood, Tex., 1973-74, comdg. officer 2d aviation co., 1974-75, dep. insp. gen. Ft. Leavenworth, Kans., 1975-78, comdg. officer 213th aviation co. Rep. of Korea, 1978-79, asst. program mgr. advanced scout helicopter program, 1981-86; owner Witan Group, Chesterfield, Mo., 1986—; pres., owner Sys. Test Evaluation Inc., Huntsville, Ala., 1988-99; gen. mgr. LESCO, Huntsville, Ala., 1999-2000. Contbr. articles to profl. jours. Decorated Bronze Star, 37 Air medals with "V" device, D.F.C. with oak leaf cluster, Legion of Merit. Mem. Army Aviation Assn. Am., Assn. U.S. Army, Lansing Jaycees (past pres.), Mensa. Avocations: flying, reading, tennis. Home: 2110 Greenslope Trl NE Huntsville AL 35811-2608

WILLIAMSON, DOUGLAS FRANKLIN, JR., lawyer; b. Anniston, Ala., Mar. 23, 1930; s. Douglas Franklin and Elizabeth Louise (Connor) W.; m. Barbara Tuerk, Dec. 28, 1957; children: Mary Leyden, Douglas Franklin III, Bruce Reynolds. AB summa cum laude, Amherst Coll., 1952; LLB, Yale U., 1955. Bar: NY 1958, Fla. 1976. Assoc. Breed, Abbott & Morgan, NYC, 1957-63, ptnr., 1963-72, Williamson & Hess and predecessor firm, NYC, 1972-79; of counsel Winthrop, Stimson, Putnam & Roberts, NYC, 1979-81, ptnr., 1982-95, sr. counsel, 1996-2000, Pillsbury Winthrop Shaw Pittman LLP and predessors, NYC, 2001—. Bd. dirs. World Wildlife Fund, Washington, 1979-88, treas., 1986-88, mem. nat. coun., 1988-2006; bd. dirs. Conservation Found., Washington, 1985-88, treas., 1986-88; bd. dirs. Ea. N.Y. chpt. Nature Conservancy, Mt. Kisco, N.Y., 1976-87, 93-97, sec., 1976-87, hon. dir., 1987—, chmn., 1993-94; bd. dirs. Oblong Land Conservancy, Pawling, N.Y., 1990-98, chmn. 1996-98; bd. dirs. Quaker Hill Civic Assn., Pawling, 1974-2000, past pres.; chmn. Pawling Assessment Rev. Bd., 1976-2001. With U.S. Army, 1955-57. Fellow: NY State Bar Found.; mem.: Assn. Bar City NY (life), Soc. Colonial Wars, Everglades Club, Quaker Hill Country Club (pres. 1980—81), Phi Beta Kappa, Phi Beta Kappa Soc. (sec. 1975—77, v.p. 1977—79).

WILLIAMSON, GLORIA, state legislator; Chairwoman Miss. State Dem. Party, 1998—; mem. Dem. Nat. Com., 1998—; state senator Dist. 18 Miss., 2001—. Democrat. Mailing: Miss Dem Party PO Box 1583 Jackson MS 39215 Address: 521 Holland Ave Philadelphia MS 39350 Office Phone: 601-359-2220, 601-656-5634. Office Fax: 601-947-8804.

WILLIAMSON, JAMES ALLEN, state legislator; b. Fort Riley, Kans., May 27, 1951; s. Dwight Allen Williamson and Shirley Lee Hahn W.; m. Sandra Joan D'Amario, 1979; children: Joshua, Angela, Kenn, Andrew. Former atty. Parks, Beard & Williamson; tchr. Tulsa Pub. Sch., 1972—75; precinct chmn. Okla. State Rep. Party, 1972—79; Okla. state rep. Dist. 76, 1980—86; dir. Metro Tulsa Planning Commn.; house rep. Okla.; asst. minority floor leader, 1982—86; mem. Okla. State Rep. Exec. Com., 1989—96; asst. Rep. floor leader Oklahoma State Senate, 1998—99; mem. appropriations subcom. human Svc. Okla. State Senate, mem. econ. devel., edn., rules, judiciary & sunset rev. coms.; Okla. state senator Dist. 35, 1996—2008. Named Outstanding Local Pres., Oklahoma Jaycees, 1979, One of Ten Outstanding State Legislators, NRLA, 1983. Mem.: C. of C. Tulsa (hon. dir.), Oklahoma Bar Assn., Tulsa Bus. Connection, Hugh O'Brian Youth Found. (dir. 1979—), Jaycees (former pres.). Republican. Address: 1605 E 63rd St Tulsa OK 74136 Mailing: State Capitol Rm 530 2300 N Lincoln Blvd Oklahoma City OK 73105-4808 also: 6111 South Trenton Tulsa OK 74136 Office Phone: 918-744-6050. Business E-Mail: williamson@lsb.state.ok.us.

WILLIAMSON, JOEL RUDOLPH, humanities educator, writer; b. Anderson County, SC, Oct. 27, 1929; s. James Henry and Carrie Mae (Swaney) W.; m. Marie Ahearn, Nov. 17, 1953 (div. May 1983); children: Joelle, William, Alethea; m. Anna Woodson, Oct. 18, 1986. AB, U. S.C., 1948, MA, 1951; PhD, U. Calif., 1964. Instr. dept. history U. N.C., Chapel Hill, 1960-64, asst. prof., 1964-66, assoc. prof., 1966-69, prof., 1969-85, Lineberger prof. in humanities, 1985—. Resident fellow Rockefeller Ctr., Bellagio, Italy, 1988; Eudora Welty prof. in so. studies Millsaps Coll., 1984; disting. vis. prof. Rhodes Coll., 1984; vis. prof. dept. history, assoc. Lowell House Harvard U., 1981-82. Author: After Slavery: The Negro in South Carolina During Reconstruction, 1861-1877, 1965, The Origins of Segregation, 1968, New People: Miscegenation and Mulattoes in the United States, 1980, The Crucible of Race, 1984 (Francis Parkman prize Soc. Am. Historians, Ralph Waldo Emerson award Phi Beta Kappa, Mayflower Cup, Frank L. and Harriet C. Owsley award 1985, Robert Francis Kennedy Book award, Pulitzer prize in History nomination 1985), A Rage for Order, 1986, William Faulkner and Southern History, 1993 (Pulitzer prize in History nomination 1994, Mayflower Cup), also articles. Lt. USN, 1951-55. Fellow Guggenheim Found., 1970-71, NEH, 1987-88, Ctr. for Advanced Study in Behavioral Scis., Stanford, Calif., 1977-78, summer 1979, 80, 81, So. fellow, 1961-62, Charles Warren Ctr., 1981-82. Mem. Soc. Am. Historians, Orgn. Am. Historians, Am. Hist. Assn., So. Hist. Assn., So. Assn. for Women Historians. Achievements include having two books (The Crucible of Race, 1984, William Faulkner and Southern History, 1993) that were among three finalists for the Pulitzer Prize in History. Avocation: travel. Home: 129 Essex Dr Chapel Hill NC 27514-1583 Personal E-mail: annaleoww@aol.com.

WILLIAMSON, MARVEL, dean, nursing administrator, sexologist, educator; b. Holton, Kans., Nov. 4, 1953; d. Thomas Arthur and Lois M. (Ihrig) Ansley; m. Paul Williamson, May 12, 1973; children: Marcus W., Sean W. BS in Nursing, Wichita State U., 1976; MS in Nursing, U. Ky., 1978; PhD, U. Iowa, 1987. Cert. sex educator, nurse educator. Fellow Acad. Nursing Edn. Prof. U. Iowa, Iowa City, 1980-89; dir. patient svcs. Ransom Meml. Hosp., Ottawa, Kans., 1989-91; dir. schs. nursing at Rolla, Sikeston and Kansas City Park Coll., Parkville, Mo., 1991-97; prof. Albany (Ga.) State U., 1997-99; sexologist Silver Spring, Md., 1999—2001; dean Kramer Sch. Nursing, Oklahoma City U., 2001—. Contbr. articles to profl. jours. Mem. ANA, Am. Assn. Sex Educators, Counselors and Therapists, Sigma Theta Tau. Office: Oklahoma City U 2501 N Blackwelder Oklahoma City OK 73106 Home: 4112 NW 22nd St Oklahoma City OK 73107-2620 Office Phone: 405-208-5900.

WILLIAMSON, PETER DAVID, lawyer; b. Houston, Oct. 13, 1944; s. Sam and Sophie Ann (Kaplan) W.; m. Patricia Golemon; children: Heather, Amber, Asia, Ginger, Anna, Alison, Aaron. BA, U. Ill., 1966; JD, U. Tex., 1969. Bar: Tex. 1969, US Supreme Ct. 1974, US Ct. Appeals (4th, 5th, 6th, 8th, 9th, 10th, 11th and DC cirs.); lic. comml. pilot. Pvt. practice, Houston, 1971—. Founder IMMLAW, The Nat. Consortium of Immigration Law Firms. Mem. Am. Immigration Lawyers Assn. (pres. 1994-95). Home: 1522 Park St Houston TX 77019-5324 Office: Chamberlain Hrdlicka White Williams & Aughtry 2 Allen Ctr 1200 Smith St # 1400 Houston TX 77002 Office Phone: 713-658-2508. Business E-Mail: peter.williamson@chamberlainlaw.com.

WILLIAMSON, SAMUEL RUTHVEN, JR., historian, educator; b. Bogalusa, La., Nov. 10, 1935; s. Samuel Ruthven and Frances Mitchell (Page) Williamson; m. Joan Chaffe Andress, Dec. 30, 1961; children: George Samuel, Treeby Andress, Thaddeus Miller. BA, Tulane U., 1958; AM, Harvard U., 1960, PhD, 1966, grad. in Advanced Mgmt., 1986; degree (hon.), Furman U., Va. Theol. Sem., Centre Coll., The U. of the South, 2006. Asst. prof. U.S. Mil. Acad., 1963—66; from instr. history to asst. dean Harvard U., 1966—69, asst. to dean of Harvard Coll., 1969—70; rsch. assoc. Inst. Politics, faculty assoc. Ctr. for Internat. Affairs, 1971—72; mem. faculty J.F. Kennedy Sch. Govt., 1971—72; from assoc. prof. history to provost U. N.C., Chapel Hill, 1972—84, provost univ., 1984—88; pres., vice chancellor U. of South, Sewanee, Tenn., 1988—2000, vice chancellor emeritus, prof. history, 2000—05, Robert M. Ayres Jr. disting. univ. prof., 2001—05; historiographer U. South, 2008. Cons. historian's office Office of Sec. Def., 1974—76; vis. fellow Churchill Coll., 1976—77; mem. vis. com. Harvard Coll., 1986—92; dir. Rsch. Triangle Inst., 1984—88; mem. bd. visitors Air U., 1994—2002. Author: The Politics of Grand Strategy: Britain and France Prepare for War 1904-1914, 1969, 1990; co-author: The Origins of U.S. Nuclear Strategy, 1945-53, 1993, July 1914: Soldiers, Statesmen, and the Coming of the Great War, 2003; editor: The Origins of a Tragedy, July 1914, 1981, War and Soc. Newsletter, 1973—88; co-editor: Essays on World War I: Origins and Prisoners of War, 1983, Austria-Hungary and the Origins of the First World War, 1991, Sewanee Sesgivesentenniel History: In Making University south, 2008, Perspecture on the History of University South, 2009. Mem. cen. com. Morehead Found., 1978—93; vice chmn. bd. visitors Air U., 1996—98, chmn. bd. visitors, 1998—2000. Capt. US Army, 1963—66. Grantee, Ford Found., 1976; fellow, NEH, 1976—77, Nat. Humanities Ctr., 1983; Fulbright scholar, U. Edinburgh, 1958—59, Woodrow Wilson Ctr. scholar, Washington, 2002, Woodrow Wilson fellow, 1958—63, Danforth fellow, 1958—63. Mem.: Nat. Assn. Colls. and Univs. (vice chmn., chmn. bd. dirs. 1993—95), Internat. Inst. Strategic Studies, Am. Hist. Assn. (George Louis Beer prize 1970). Democrat. Episcopalian. Office: U of South duPont Libr Sewanee TN 37383-1000 Home: 47 Speyside Cir Pittsboro NC 27312-8638 Business E-Mail: swilliam@sewanee.edu.

WILLIAMSON, SANDRA CRAWFORD, marketing executive; BA in Comm., La. State U.; MBA in Global Mgmt., U. Pune, 2001, PhD in Orgnl. Mgmt. COO, chief global officer True.com; mktg. and sales positions Procter & Gamble Co., 1990—95, Coca-Cola Co., 1995—96, Nabisco, 1996—98; v.p., mktg. and sales Universal Studios, Inc., 1998—2000; pres., gen. mgr. Zapf Creation, Germany, 2000—04; COO HDVMS, 2004—09; founder, CEO Crawford Consulting, 2009—10; exec. v.p., chief mktg. officer SuperMedia, LLC, 2010—. Office: SuperMedia Inc 2200 W Airfield Dr Dallas TX 75261 Office Phone: 972-453-7000. Office Fax: 972-453-3969. Business E-Mail: sandra.crawford-williamson@supermedia.com.

WILLIAMSON, THOMAS ARNOLD, retired publishing executive; b. Sagamore, Pa., Oct. 4, 1939; s. Thomas and Mabel (Kennedy) Williamson; m. Kathryn Steiner White, Mar. 1, 1980; 1 child, Thomas J. Grad., Phillips Exeter Acad., 1957; AB, Harvard U., 1961. From sales person to sr. v.p. Harcourt Brace & Co., NYC, 1962—88, sr. v.p., 1988—95; pres. Psychol. Corp., San Antonio, 1982—88; v.p. Holt Rinehart & Winston Harcourt Brace, 1989—95; pres. Harcourt Sch. Publishers, 1989—93, Learning Initiative, Austin, Tex., 1994—, T. Williamson Assocs., Inc., Austin, 1995—2005, Focused Learning, Ltd., Austin, 1998—2005; exec. v.p. Kathryn Williamson Real Estate Inc., Austin, 2003—. Bd. dirs. Lesson Lab, 2001—03, The Austin Project, 2000—08, adv. bd. mem., 2010—. Co-chmn. vis. com. to psychology dept. U. Tex., Austin, 1986—89, 1995—98; vol., chair chpt. 249 SCORE, 2003—04. Mem.: Hills Country Club, Town and Gown Club, Harvard Club N.Y.C. Office Phone: 512-731-4649. Personal E-mail: tawilliamson@austin.rr.com.

WILLIAMSON, WILLIAM PAUL, JR., journalist; b. Des Moines, Mar. 30, 1929; s. William Paul and Florence Alice (Dawson) W.; m. Vania Torres Nogueira, Nov. 27, 1959; children: Mary Liz, Jon Thadeus, Margaret Ann Student, Mexico City Coll., 1952, U. Havana, 1955; BA, U. No. Iowa, 1953; MA, U. Iowa, 1954. Editor Brazilian Bus., Rio de Janeiro, 1958-60; mng. ptnr. Editora Mory Ltd., Rio de Janeiro, 1960-79; editor Brazil Herald, Rio de Janeiro, 1960-80; exec. dir. Inter Am. Press Assn., Miami, Fla., 1981-94, hon. life mem., mem. adv. coun., 1994—, dir., 1966-80, chmn. awards com., 1975-80. Solo navigator 1st passage Madeira Island, Portugal-Madeira Island, Brazil, 1994-95. Editor for Brazil, Fodor's South America, 1970-79; contbr. articles to various newspapers and mags. Pres. Am. Soc., Rio de Janeiro, 1968; bd. dirs. Instituto Brasil-Estados Unidos, Rio de Janeiro, 1977-80, Am. C. of C. for Brazil, Rio de Janeiro, 1964-68; rear commodore Seven Seas Cruising Assn., 2000—. With USMC, 1946—48, with USMCR, 1948—51. Decorated Order of Rio Branco (Brazil); recipient Citizen of Rio de Janeiro award State Legislature, 1975; Hon. Carioca award O Globo Newspaper, Rio de Janeiro, 1972; Ralph Greenberg award Am. Soc. Rio de Janeiro, 1977; Outstanding Svc. to Freedom of Expression and Newspapers awards Internat. Fedn. of Newspaper Pubs. and Internat. Assn. of Broadcasting, 1994; Benemeritous Citizen award Mcpl. Legislature, Itaguai, Brazil, 1995. Mem. Am. Soc. Assn. Execs., South Fla. Soc. Assn. Execs. (pres. 1987), Soc. Profl. Journalists, Overseas Press Club Am., Brazil Fgn. Corr. Assn. (founder, mem. honor), Rio Yacht Club, Ilha da Madeira Yacht Club, Kappa Tau Alpha. Home: 1418 NE 57th Pl Fort Lauderdale FL 33334-6120 Personal E-mail: bill.williamson2011@gmail.com.

WILLINGHAM, CLARK SUTTLES, lawyer; b. Houston, Nov. 29, 1944; s. Paul Suttles and Elsie Dell (Clark) W.; m. Jane Joyce Hitch, Aug. 16, 1969; children: Meredith Moores, James Barrett. BBA, Tex. Tech U., 1967; JD, So. Meth. U., 1971, LLM, 1984. Bar: Tex. 1971. Ptnr. Kasmir, Willingham & Krage, Dallas, 1972—86, Finley, Kumble et al, Dallas, 1986—87, Brice & Mankoff, Dallas, 1988—98, Moseley Law PC, Dallas, 1999—2008, Key Harrington Barnes PC, Dallas, 2008—. Contbr. articles to profl. jours. Bd. dirs. Dallas Summer Musicals, 1971—2010, exec. com., 1979-93, 97-2003, pres. 1994. Mem. ABA (chmn. agrl. com. tax sect. 1984-86), State Bar Tex. (chmn. agrl. tax com. 1985-87), Dallas Bar Assn., Am. Law Inst., Tex. Rangers Law Enforcement Assn.(bd. dirs.), Nat. Cattlemen's Beef Assn. (bd. dirs., pres. 1998), U.S. Meat Export Fedn. (exec. com. 1991-93), Beef Industry Coun. (exec. com. 1990-91, promotion chmn. 1992-94), Tex. Cattle Feeders Assn. (bd. dirs., pres. 1988), Tex. Bd. Vet. Med. Examiners (pres. 1994), Tex. Beef Coun. (bd. dirs., pres. 1989), Nat. Cattlemen's Found. (trustee 2004-), Tex. Agrl. Land Trust (trustee 2006-), State Fair Tex. (bd. dirs. 2010-), Dallas Country Club. Republican. Episcopalian. Office: Key Harrington Barnes PC 3710 Rawlings St Ste 950 Dallas TX 75219 Home: 3525 Turtle Creek Blvd 18A Dallas TX 75219 Office Phone: 214-525-3940. E-mail: clarkw@airmail.net.

WILLINGHAM, JEANNE MAGGART, retired performing company executive, educator; b. Fresno, Calif., May 8, 1923; d. Harold F. and Gladys (Ellis) Maggart. Student, Tex. Woman's U., 1942; student profl. dancing schs. worldwide. Ret. Studio Channel, 2010. Mem. Tex. Arts and Humanities Coun., Tex. Arts Alliance, Pampa C. of C. (fine arts com.), Pampa Fine Arts Assn.

WILLINGHAM, MARY MAXINE, fashion retailer; b. Childress, Tex., Sept. 12, 1928; d. Charles Bryan and Mary (Bohannon) McCollum; m. Welborn Kiefer Willingham, Aug. 14, 1950; children: Sharon, Douglas, Sheila. BA, Tex. Tech U., 1949. Interviewer Univ. Placement Svc., Tex. Tech U., Lubbock, 1964-69; owner, mgr. buyer Maxine's Accent, Lubbock, 1969—. Speaker in field. Leader Campfire Girls, Lubbock, 1964-65; sec. Cmty. Theatre, Lubbock, 1962-64. Recipient Golden Sun award Dallas Market, 1985, Woman of Excellence award in Bus., YWCA, 2001; named Outstanding Mcht., Fashion Retailer Mag., 1971, also Outstanding Retailer. Mem. Federated Clubs (Temple, Tex.) Personal E-mail: maxinewil@ccnlink.net.

WILLIS, CLAYTON, broadcaster, government official, educator, arts consultant; b. Washington, Aug. 11, 1933; s. William H. and Elizabeth Carl (Keferstein) W. Student, Sorbonne, Paris, 1953-54; BA, George Washington U., 1957; student, U. Oslo, 1953; grad., NY Inst. Fin., 1966, Assn. Commodities Exch. Firms Inc., 1966. Spl. assignment Am. Embassy, London, 1957; writer NBC Network radio show Tex and Jinx, 1958; spl. corr. NBC News, La Paz, Bolivia, 1959; spl. Washington corr. Fin. News TV Network (now CNBC), NYC, 1988; contbr., anchor, TV prodr., corr. Saudi Arabian TV, Newsweek mag., Phillips News Svc. Hope (Ark.) Star; contbr., corr. Christian Sci. Monitor, LA Times-Mirror Syndicate, Greenwich (Conn.) Time, Fin. News TV Network, New York, Mainichi, Tokyo, China Post, Taipei, Taiwan, Chattanooga Times, Nashville Tennesseean, Daily Nation of Kenya, Khartoum Echo, Sudan, The Washington Daily News, Washington Post, Cape Argus of Capetown, South Africa, Bangkok Post, Irish Times, Dublin; reporter, movie, art critic Albuquerque Tribune, 1959-61; asst. editor Newsweek Mag., NYC, 1961-62; TV broadcaster-writer UPI Newsfilm, NYC, 1962; White House corr., chief bur., anchor World Radio News, Houston; White House, Washington corr. WAVA Radio Sta., Washington, 1963-65; editorial writer, corr. Hearst Newspapers, NYC, 1965; press officer UN, NYC, 1965-66; spl. assignment Am. Embassy, Reykjavik, Iceland, 1967; editorial writer, critic, corr. NY Amsterdam News, NYC, 1967-68; cons. govt., law, and ethics programs Ford Found., NYC, 1968-69; dir. pub. affairs US EEOC, Washington, 1969-70; cons. OEO, Washington, 1970, Pres.'s Nat. Coun. on Indian Opportunity, Washington, 1970-71, Cmty. Rels. Svc., US Dept. Justice, Washington, 1970-73, Cabinet Com. on Opportunities for Spanish-Speaking People, 1971-72, Fed. Energy Adminstrn., Washington, 1973-74; dir. pub. affairs Office of Petroleum Allocation, U.S. Dept. Interior, 1973-74; dir. Congl. rels., dir. pub. affairs Pres.'s Nat. Commn. on Fire Prevention and Control, 1971-73; pub., editor, owner Four Corners Chieftain, Ignacio and Durango, Colo., 1972-73; lectr. Sch. of Bus., U. DC, Washington, 1973-74; owner, White House corr., photojournalist Willis News Svc., Washington, 1974—; pub. affairs dir. Inaugural Vets. Com., 1976-77. Adviser to Fernando E.C. de Baca, spl. asst. to the Pres., White House, 1974-76; lectr. nat., internat. affairs, Haiti, art, communications, energy; corr.-broadcaster Sta. KTEN-TV, Ada, Okla., 1985; mem. staff presdl. transition office US Pres. Bush, 1988-89, 90; dir. and curator L. Clayton Willis Art Collection, Palm Beach, Fla.; pres., White House corr., congressional corr., photojournalist, The Evening News Broadcasting Co., Willis News Service; prodr., anchor documentary programs Saudi Arabian TV, 1992—; exec. prodr., anchor Glimpses of the World documentaries, 1993; White House corr., photojournalist Hope Star, Ark., 1994—; dir., curator L. Clayton Willis Art Collection, Palm Beach; chmn. emeritus Haitian Art Mus., Delray Beach, Fla.; White House corr., exec. prod., host, commentator, critic The Clayton Willis Talk Show, WPBR, Palm Beach, Fla, 2000-. Co-author: Capital Fare, 1977, Lott-Willis Pictorial Digest of US Presidential Elections and Inaugurations, 1997; host/exec. prodr., commentator The Clayton Willis Talk Show, WPBR, 1998-; pres.'s White House corr. Evening News Broadcasting Co., Washington, 2000; contbr. articles to Daily Mail, London, London Sunday Express, Umtali Post, Zimbabwe, Gwelo (Zimbabwe) Times, To the Point news mag., Johannesburg, The Citizen, Johannesburg, Hartford Courant, Sacramento Union, Chattanooga Times, UPI Radio Networks, The Hope Star, Phillips News Svc. Broadcaster with Bush/Quayle Nat. Campaign Hdqrs., Washington, 1988; adviser Presdl. Transition Office of Pres. George Bush, 1988-89; loaned Haitian paintings for spl. exhbn. to Haitian Embassy, Washington, 1991, Milw. Art Mus., 1992, Hypoluxo Town Hall, Fla., 2005, Grace Gallery, Dania Beach, Fla. Recipient Outstanding Svc. award Harlem Prep. Sch., Johannes Gutenberg medal (Mainz, Germany), 1984, Letters of Cert. Appreciation Pres. of US, 1989. Covered Vietnam, Congo, Mid. East, Rhodesian and South African wars; covered Clarence Thomas and Robert Gates US Senate confirmation hearings, 1991; covered 2000 presdl. election and re-count, Palm Beach, Fla.; covered Haitian rebellion and fall of Pres. Aristide, Haiti, 2004; covered the 2004 Kerry-Bush Presidential Campaign, 2008 Obama-McCain Presidential Campaign. Office: Clinton Willis Take Show 1711 5th Ave S Lake Worth FL 33460 Personal E-mail: lclaytonwillis@aol.com.*

WILLIS, GLADDEN WILLIAMS, retired pathologist, scientific photographer, tree farmer; b. Minden, La., Mar. 26, 1939; s. John Stillmon and Virgie Williams Willis; m. Lydia Hall, May 14, 1966; children: Charles Austin, Loye Stillmon. BS, Centenary Coll., 1960; MD, Tulane U., 1964. Intern La. State U. Med. Ctr., Shreveport, 1964-65, resident, 1965-69; fellow Meml. Sloan-Kettering Med. Ctr., NYC, 1969-71; pathologist St. Luke's Hosp., Houston, 1971-72, St. Mary's Hosp., Roswell, N.Mex., 1972-73, Ochsner Clinic Found., New Orleans, 1973—2005, dir. anat. pathology, 1976—2003, vice chmn. lab. medicine, 1996—2003. Contbr. articles to profl. jours., 3490 sci. photographs to encys. and books. Past pres. Jefferson Performing Arts Soc., Metarie, La. Capt. USAF, 1966—72. Recipient George Washington Honor medal, Valley Forge Found., 1996. Fellow Arthur Purdy Stout Soc., Royal Microscopical Soc.; mem. Assn. Dirs. of Anatomic Pathology, Internat. Acad. Pathology, Am. Soc. Media Photographers, NY Acad. Scis., Found. Preservation of Caroline Dormoy Nature Preserve (chair). Republican. Methodist. Avocation: photography. Home and Office: PO Box 719 Doyline LA 71023 Personal E-mail: gladdenandlydia@gmail.com.

WILLIS, MARK NYE, state legislator; b. Greenville, SC, Sept. 1, 1963; s. Jack and Gerry Willis; m. Tracy Langston, June 4, 1988; children: Mary, Elledge, Reeves. BA, Erskine Coll., 1986. Long term care adminstr.; mem. Dist. 16 SC House of Reps., SC, 2008—, mem. Med., Mil., Pub. and Mcpl. Affairs Com. Republican. Office: Dist/Home Office 201 Quillen Ave Fountain Inn SC 29644 also: Capitol Office 326B Blatt Bldg Columbia SC 29201 Office Phone: 864-369-2000, 864-862-6179, 803-212-6882. E-mail: markwillis@schouse.org.

WILLIS, PAUL ALLEN, retired librarian, dean; b. Floyd County, Ind., Oct. 1, 1941; s. Clarence Charles and Dorothy Jane (Harritt) Willis; m. Barbara Marcum, June 15, 1963; children: Mark, Sally. AB, U. Ky., 1963, JD, 1969; MLS, U. Md., 1966. Cataloger Libr. Congress, Washington, 1963; head descriptive cataloging br. Sci. and Tech. Info. Facility NASA, College Park, Md., 1963-66; law libr., prof. law U. Ky., Lexington, 1966-73, dir. librs., 1973—2002, acting dean Coll. Libr. Sci., 1975-76, 88; dean librs. U. SC, Columbia, 2002—07; ret. Exec. sec. Ky. Jud. Retirement and Removal Commn., 1977-81; adv. com. Ctr. Jud. Conduct Orgns., Am. Judicature Soc., Chgo., 1979-81; chmn. Southeastern Libr. Network, Atlanta, 1998-99; exec. com. Ky. Hist. Soc., 1984-88; mem. Ky. Adv. Coun. on Librs., 1985-2002, adv. com. Online Computer Libr. Ctr., 1986-90; cons. SE Consortium Internat. Devel., U. Sriwijaya, Palembang, Sumatera, Indonesia, 1987-88, Hanoi U. Tech., 1999, 2001, Vietnam Nat. U., Ho Chi Minh City, 1999 Sr. fellow, UCLA, 1982. Mem. Assn. Southeastern Rsch. Librs. (chair 1986-88, bd. dirs. 2002-), Assn. Rsch. Librs. (bd. dirs. 2002—05). Personal E-mail: willis@sccoast.net.

WILLIS, RALPH HOUSTON, retired mathematics professor; b. McMinnville, Tenn., Dec. 26, 1942; s. Carl Houston and Carrie Lee (Hill) Willis; m. Gayle Catherine Celestin, June 29, 1973 (div. Apr. 1985); m. Velma Inez Church, Aug. 10, 1985; 1 stepchild, Bobbie Lynn White Buckner. BS in Math., Mid. Tenn. State U., 1964, MA in Math., 1966. Cert. secondary edn. tchr. Instr. depts. math. and computer sci. Western Carolina U., Cullowhee, NC, 1968-73, asst. prof., 1973-83, assoc. prof., 1983—2010, prof. emeritus. Co-founder State Math Contest Com., 1977—78, mem. western regional rep. exec. steering com., recording sec., 1978—2010; co-founder NC Math. League, 1981—82, mem. problem writing com., 1981—84. Editor: (newsletter) Abelian Grapevine-Secondary Math., 1970—88, The Child of Math.-Elem.-Mid. Grade Math., 1972—78; mem. editl. bd. The Centroid, 1995—2000; contbr. articles to profl. jours. Coord. state road paving project Univ. Heights Cmty. Devel. Orgn., 1974—76, chmn. founder cmty. watch, 1978—79, coord. pub. water sys. upgrade project, 1980—84; founder, coord., bd. dirs., trustee Hunerwadle Cmty. Cemetery Assn., Beersheba, Tenn., 1983—; co-founder NC State Math. Contest and Contest Network, 1977—78; founder., dir., coord. HS Math. Contest, founder., coord. math. dept. student awards program Western Carolina U., 1970—2010, solicitor-coord. Math. Contest Scholarship Program, 1971—82, initiator-coord. math. dept.'s vis. spkr. program, 1974—77, founder., faculty sponsor NC Coun. Tchrs. Math. Student Affiliate, 1990—2010. Recipient Hon. Mention NC Gov.'s award for Excellence, 1991, Exeplary Site award, State Math. Contest Com., 1990, Paul A. Reid Disting. Svc. award for Faculty, 1991, W.W. Rankin award, 2001, Coll. Arts and Scis. Disting. Career Svc. award, 2003; named Tchrs. Math. Innovator award, N. C. Coun., 1994. Mem.: NC Coun. Tchrs. Math. (state bd. dirs., historian 1993—98, mem. editl. bd. Centroid 1995—2000, W. W. Rankin award 2001, Innovator award 1994), Nat. Coun. Tchrs. Math., Kappa Mu Epsilon, Phi Kappa Phi. Avocations: gardening, military history, model building, die cast model collector, carpentry.

WILLIS, WILLIAM DARRELL, JR., neuroscientist, educator; b. Dallas, July 19, 1934; s. William Darrell and Dorcas (Chamberlain) W.; m. Jean Colette Schini, May 28, 1960 (dec. Jan. 1, 2006); 1 child, Thomas Darrell. BS, BA, Tex. A&M U., 1956; MD, U. Tex.

Southwestern Med. Sch., 1960; PhD, Australian Nat. U., 1963. Postdoctoral research fellow Nat. Inst. Neurol. Diseases and Blindness, Australian Nat. U., 1960-62, Istituto di Fisiologia, U. Pisa, Italy, 1962-63; from asst. prof. to prof. anatomy, chmn. dept. U. Tex. Southwestern Med. Sch., Dallas, 1963-70; chief lab. comparative neurobiology Marine Biomed. Inst., prof. anatomy and physiology U. Tex. Med. Br., Galveston, 1970—, dir. Marine Biomed. Inst., 1978—2004, chmn. dept. anatomy and neurosci., 1986—2004, Ashbel Smith prof., 1986-95, Cecil and Ida Green prof., 1995—. Mem. neurology B study sect. NIH, 1968-72, chmn., 1970-72, mem. neurol. disorders Program Project rev. com., 1972-76, Nat. Adv. Neurol. and Communicative Disorders and Stroke Coun., 1987-90; tng. grant com. Nat. Inst. of Neurol. Disorders and Stroke, 1994-98. Mem. editl. bd. Neurosci., Exptl. Neurology, 1970-90, Archives Italienne Biologie, Neurosci. Letters, 1976-92; chief editor Jour. Neurophysiology, 1978-83, Pain, 1986-89; assoc. editor Jour. Neurosci., 1986-89, editor-in-chief, 1993-94; sect. editor Exptl. Brain Rsch., 1990-92, 1995-2004. Mem. AAAS, Am. Assn. Anatomists (exec. com. 1980-86), Am. Pain Soc. (pres. 1982-83), Internat. Assn. Study Pain (coun. 1984-90), Am. Physiol. Soc., Soc. Exptl. Biol. Medicine, Soc. Neurosci. (pres. 1984-85), Internat. Brain Rsch. Orgn., Cajal Club, Sigma Xi, Alpha Omega Alpha. Office: U Tex Med Br 301 University Blvd Galveston TX 77555-1069 Home: 7312 Seawall Blvd Apt 109 Galveston TX 77551-1994 Business E-Mail: wdwillis@utmb.edu.

WILLITS, TIM, computer game company executive; BS in Computer Sci., Bus., U. Minn., 1995. Lead designer, creative dir. id Software, LLC, Mesquite, Tex., 1995—, co-owner, 2004—. Credited (computer games) The Ultimate Doom, Quake, Quake II, Quake III Arena, Quake III: Team Arena, lead designer Doom 3; exec. prodr.: (computer games) Quake 4. Office: id Software 1500 N Greenville Ave Ste 700 Richardson TX 75081-2271 Office Phone: 972-613-3589. Office Fax: 972-686-9288. Business E-Mail: twillits@idsoftware.com.

WILLMANN, DONNIE GLENN, safety executive; b. Waco, Tex., Aug. 25, 1955; s. Robert and Marie Louise (Schraeder) W.; m. Susan Lynn Martin, June 14, 1975. Student, Tarleton State U., 1973-75; BS in Indsl. Tech., Tex. A & M U., 1978. Cert. safety profl. Mfg. ops. devel. trainee Sii Drilco, Houston, 1978-80, loss control rep., 1980-81; safety mgr. Weatherford/Lamb U.S. Inc., Houston, 1981-83; corp. safety mgr. Weatherford Internat., Houston, 1983-86; loss control specialist CNA Ins., Houston, 1986-88; sr. safety adminstr. Enron Ops. Corp., Houston, 1988-96; mgr. safety/environ. Enron Internat., Houston, 1996-99, dir. environ. health and safety, 2000—01; sr. health, safety and environment coord. ABB Vetco Gray, Houston, 2002—04; mgr. health safety, environ. Vetco Gray, Houston, 2004—. Mem. Am. Soc. Safety Engrs. (membership chmn. 1989-90, treas. 1990-91, v.p. membership 1991-92, program chmn. 1992-94, pres.-elect. 1994-95, pres. 1995-96, named Gulf Coast chpt. Safety Profl. of Yr. 1994-95, asst. v.p. region III 1995-96), Nat. Safety Mgmt. Soc. Lutheran. Avocations: fishing, hunting, raquetball, woodworking. Office: Vetco Gray 12221 N Houston Rosslyn Rd Houston TX 77086 Home: 13101 Willow Tree Ct Haslet TX 76052-6232 Office Phone: 281-405-3572. E-mail: dwillmann@msn.com.

WILLMOTT, THOMAS P., state legislator; Grad., Jefferson Parish Sheriff's Office Tng. Acad.; ADN, La. State U.; BA in Govt., Southeastern La. U.; JD, So. U. Law Ctr. Atty.; registered nurse; mem. Dist. 92 La. House of Reps., 2008—, mem. civil law and procedure com., health and welfare com. Republican. Office: 2002 20th St Ste 204A Kenner LA 70062 also: Capitol Office PO Box 44486 Baton Rouge LA 70804 Office Phone: 504-465-3479, 225-342-6945. Office Fax: 504-465-3481. E-mail: willmott@legis.state.la.us.

WILLNER, EUGENE BURTON, food and liquor company executive; b. Chgo., July 27, 1934; s. Fred and Mae (Goodhartz) W.; m. Karen Nell Kaye, Feb. 22, 1962; children: Tracy Fran, Kelly Kaye. BA, Northwestern U., 1956. Pres. World Wide Fisheries Inc., Chgo., 1956—60; merchandiser Edison Bros. Stores Inc., St. Louis, 1960—66; v.p. Mo. Supreme Life Ins. Co., St. Louis, 1966—67; exec. v.p. Exec. Agys., Inc., St. Louis, 1966—67; pres. Bluff Creek Industries, Inc., Ocean Springs, Miss., 1967—69, Purse String Stores, Inc., Miami, Fla., 1969—73, World Wide Fisheries, Miami, 1969—73, Renwill Seafoods, Inc., 1979—. Chmn. bd. Astral Liquors, Inc., Foxy Laidy Lounges, Prime Universal Seafood Corp., Miami, also Key West, Fla., Caracas, Venezuela, San Juan del Sur, Nicaragua, Quito, Ecuador; pres., chmn. bd. Common Markets, Inc., Miami, London and Moscow, 1980— Mem. Deering Bay Country Club, Turnberry Club, Grove Isle Club, Fisher Island Club, Palm Beach Country Club. Office: 29000 S Dixie Hwy Homestead FL 33033-2302 Office Phone: 305-251-0087. Personal E-mail: asiamoon@att.net.

WILLS, ELANA CUNNINGHAM, commissioner, former state supreme court justice; BS, Ark. State Univ., 1984; JD with honors, Univ. Ark., 1987. Bar: Ark. 1987. Assoc. Rose Law Firm, 1987—88; asst. atty. gen. State of Ark., 1988—93, dep. atty. gen., 1993—99, sr. asst. atty. gen., 1999—2003, dep. atty. gen., 2003—08; assoc. justice Ark. Supreme Ct., 2008—10; commr. Ark. Pub. Svc. Commn., 2011—. Contbr. articles to law jours. Mem.: ABA, Ark. Bar Assn., Pulaski County Bar Assn. Office: Arkansas Public Service Commission PO Box 400 Little Rock AR 72203-0400 Office Phone: 501-682-2051.

WILLS, WILLIAM RIDLEY, II, retired insurance company executive, historian; b. Nashville, June 19, 1934; s. Jesse Ely and Ellen (Buckner) W.; m. Irene Weaver Jackson, July 21, 1962; children: William Ridley III, Morgan Jackson, Thomas Weaver. BA, Vanderbilt U., 1956. Agt., staff mgr. Nat. Life & Accident Ins. Co., Nashville, 1958-62, supr., 1962-64, asst. sec., 1964-67, asst. v.p., 1967-70, 2d v.p., 1970-75, v.p., 1975-81, sr. v.p., 1981-83, Am. General Services Co., 1982-83; dir. Nat. Life & Accident Ins. Co., Nashville, 1976-83; pres. Tenn. Hist. Soc., 1985-87; bd. dirs. Nat. Trust for Hist. Preservation, 1988-91; chmn. campaign Land Trust Tenn., 2011—13. Author: History of Belle Meade: Mansion, Plantation and Stud, 1991, Old Enough to Die, 1996, Touring Tennessee: A Post Card Panorama, 1989-1955, 1996, Tennessee Governors at Home, 1999, Belle Meade Country Club: The First One Hundred Years, 2001, Gentleman, Scholar, Athlete: The History of Montgomery Bell Academy, 2005, Elizabeth and Matt: A Love Story, 2006, Yours to Count On-A Nashville Banker Extraordinaire, Sam M. Fleming, Jr., 2007, (book) Jessie and Ridley: They Made a Difference, 2008, The Hermitage at One Hundred: Nashville's First Million Dollar Hotel, 2009, Heritage, Highballs & Hijinks:Colorful Characters I've known, 2010, The YMCA of Middle Tennessee: Three Centuries of Service, 2011, Nashville Streets and Their Stories, 2011. Nat. chmn. Living Endowment Drive Vanderbilt U., 1974; pres. Cumberland Mus. and Sci. Ctr., Nashville, 1977; gen. chmn. campaign United Way, Nashville, 1978; pres. YMCA of Met. Nashville, 1984; trustee Ladies Hermitage Assn., 1981—90; mem. Tenn. Hist. Commn.; chmn. YMCA Found. Mid. Tenn., 1998—99; chmn. bd. Montgomery Bell Acad., 1988—97, gen. chmn. $43 million capital campaign, 1999—2000; mem. adv. bd. Pub. Libr. Nashville and Davidson County, 2002—08; trustee Tenn. Hist. Soc., 2007—; pres. Monteagle Sundy Sch. Assembly, 2002—04; bd. dirs. Vanderbilt U., 1988—. Lt. USN, 1956—58. Recipient awards YMCA, 1977, 1983, United Way De Tocqueville award, 1989, Tenn. History Book award Tenn. Libr. Assn. and Tenn. Hist. Commn., 1991, Disting. Alumnus award Montgomery Bell Acad., 1996, H.G. Hill award YMCA of Mid. Tenn., 2003. Fellow Life Office Mgmt. Assn.; mem. Assn. Preservation Tenn. Antiquities (pres. Nashville chpt. 1987-89), Belle Meade Country Club, Coffee House Club, Round Table Literary Club. Presbyterian. Home Phone: 615-269-5429.

WILLSON, C. GRANT, chemical engineering and chemistry professor; b. Vallejo, Calif., Mar. 30, 1939; s. Carlton P. and Margaret Ann (Cosner) Willson; m. Deborah Jeanne Merritt, Dec. 13, 1975; children: William, Andrew. BS in Chemistry, U. Calif., Berkeley, 1962, PhD in Organic Chemistry, 1973; MS in Organic Chemistry, San Diego State U., 1969. With propellent rsch. Aeroject Gen. Corp., Sacramento, 1962-64; tchr., coach Fairfax H.S., LA, 1964-67; prof. Calif. State U., Long Beach, 1973-74, U. Calif., San Diego, 1974-78; mgr. polymer sci. and tech. IBM Almaden Rsch. Ctr., San Jose, Calif., 1978-93; prof. chemistry, chem. engring. U. Tex., Austin, 1993—. Contbr. articles to profl. jours.; patentee in field. Recipient Kosar award, Soc. Imaging Sci. and Tech., 1998, Aristotle award, Semicondr. Rsch. Corp., Photopolymer Sci. award, Japan, 2003, 2007 Nat. Medal Technology and Innovation. Fellow SPIE; m.Mem. NAE, AAAS, Soc. Photog. and Instrumentation Engrs., Am. Phys. Soc., ACS, (Arthur K. Doolittle award 1986, ACS Chemistry of Materials 1991, Carothers award 1992, Coop. Rsch. award in Polymer Sci. 1993, Applied Polymer Sci. Award, 2004, Heroes of Chemistry award, Arthur Dehon Little award 2005, SEMI North America award), NAS (award for chem. in svc. to soc. 1999), Coun. for Chem. Rsch. (Malcom Pruitt award 1997, Gordon Moore medal, Nat. Tech. and Innovation medal 2007), St. Francis Yacht Club, Sigma Xi. Avocations: sailing, skiing. Office: Univ Texas Dept Chem and Chem Engring Austin TX 78712 Business E-Mail: willson@che.utexas.edu.

WILMOTH, WILLIAM DAVID, lawyer; b. Elkins, W.Va., July 11, 1950; s. Stark Amasa and Goldie (Johnson) W.; m. Rebecca Weaver, Aug. 21, 1971; children: Charles, Anne, Samuel, Peter. BS in Fin. cum laude, W. Va. U., 1972; JD, W.Va. U., 1975. Bar: W.Va. 1975, US Dist. Ct. (so. dist.) W.Va. 1975, US Dist. Ct. (no. dist.) W.Va. 1976, US Ct. Appeals (4th cir.) 1977, US Supreme Ct. 1981, Pa. 1986. Law clk. to presiding judge U.S. Dist. Ct. (no. dist.) W.Va., Elkins, 1975—76; assoc. Bachmann, Hess, Bachmann & Garden, Wheeling, W.Va., 1976—77; asst. U.S. atty. U.S. Dept. Justice, Wheeling, 1977—80; ptnr. Schrader, Byrd, Byrum & Companion, Wheeling, 1980—93; U.S. atty. U.S. Dist. Ct. (no. dist.) W.Va., Wheeling, 1993—99; ptnr. Steptoe & Johnson, Wheeling, 1999—; vice chair Litigation Dept. Vice chair bd. dir. Nat. Civil War Meml. Commn.; past pres. and chmn. bd. dir. Nat. Trail coun. Boy Scouts Am., Wheeling, W.Va.; past chmn. bd. dir. Wheeling Nat. Heritage Area Corp., Wheeling, W.Va., Wheeling YMCA, State Coll. Sys. W.Va., past bd. dir.; dir., past chmn. Edn. Alliance, Inc.; bd. dir. W.Va. Ind. Colls. and Univs., Inc., 2006. Recipient Silver Antelope award, Boy Scouts Am., 2006; named one of Best Lawyers in Am. Mem. Def. Rsch. Inst., Def. Trial Counsel W.Va., Rotary Club Wheeling (past pres.). Democrat. Home: 258 Arborland Rd Wheeling WV 26003-9314 Office: Steptoe & Johnson PO Box 751 Wheeling WV 26003-0751 Office Phone: 304-231-0456. E-mail: wilmotw@steptoe-johnson.com.

WILSON, ALAN MCCRORY, state attorney general; b. July 16, 1973; s. Joe and Roxanne (Dusenberry) Wilson; m. Jennifer Wilson; children: Michael, Anna Grace. B, Francis Marion U., Florence, SC, 1996; JD, U. SC Sch. Law, 2002. Law clk. to Hon. Marc H. Westbrook 11th Jud. Cir., SC; asst. solicitor, asst. atty. gen. State of SC, Columbia, atty. gen., 2011—; atty. Willoughby & Hoefer, Columbia, SC, 2009—10. Maj. SC Nat. Guard, 1996—. Decorated Combat Action Badge. Republican. Office: Office of the Attorney General Rembert C Dennis Office Building PO Box 11549 Columbia SC 29211-1549 Office Phone: 803-734-3970.*

WILSON, BLAKE SHAW, electrical engineer, researcher; b. Orlando, Fla., Mar. 7, 1948; s. Joseph Richard Hoyle and Jacqueline Lucy (Jones) W.; m. Doris Jane Rouse, Jan. 6, 1974; children: Nadia Jacqueline, Blair Elizabeth. BSEE, Duke U., 1974. Rsch. engr. Rsch. Triangle Inst., Research Triangle Park, NC, 1974-78, sr. rsch. engr., 1978-83, sr. rsch. scientist, 1979-83, head neurosci. program, 1983-94, dir. Ctr. for Auditory Prosthesis Rsch., 1994—2002; sr. fellow, 2002—06; emeritus sr. fellow, 2007—. Guest scientist Coleman Meml. Lab., U. Calif., San Francisco, 1983-86; adj. asst. prof. otolaryngology Duke U. Med. Ctr., 1984-94, assoc. prof., 1994-2002, prof., 2002—; sci. adv. coun., Internat. Ctr. Hearing and Speech, Kajetany, Poland, 2003—; oversight com. cochlear implants Kresge Hearing Rsch. Inst., U. Mich., 1987—, U. Iowa, 1994—; sci. adv. coun. House Ear Inst., L.A., 1990; gen. chair Conf. Implantable Auditory Prostheses, Pacific Grove, Calif., 1991; co-chair Hearing Preservation Workshop, Indpls., 2002; spl. panel hearing aids NIDCD, 1992, ad hoc adv. com. hearing aid R & D, 1993—; guest of honor numerous internat. confs.; reviewer grant applications NIH, NSF, VA and Med. Rsch. Coun., Can.; cons. cochlear implants NIH; mem. faculty various continuing edn. courses; prin. investigator numerous projects, chief strategy advisor MED EL Med. Electronics GmbH, Innsbruck, Austria, 2007, co-dir. Duke Hearing Ctr., 2008-, chair Hearing Preservation Workshop, Res, Traingle Pk., 2005; presenter in field, expert Marie Curie Project, 2007-. Reviewer numerous jours. in field; contbr. numerous articles to profl. jours. Recipient Discover award for tech. innovation, 1996, Presdl. citation for major contbns. to restoration of hearing in profoundly deaf persons Am. Otologic Soc., Disting. Alumnus award Pratt Sch. Engring. Duke U., 2007, Neel Disting. Rsch. Leadership award Am. Acad. Otolaryngology-Head & Neel Surgery Found., 2008; co-recipient Lasker-Debakey Clinical Medical Research award, Albert and Mary Lasker Found., 2013 Mem.: Brit. Cochlear Implant Group (hon.). Home: 2410 Wrightwood Ave Durham NC 27705-5802

WILSON, BRENT LAWRENCE, lawyer, mediator; b. New Orleans, Jan. 9, 1952; s. Commodore Waddell and Mildred Louise (Quave) W.; m. Trojanell Theresa Bordenave, June 22, 1974. BA, Morehouse Coll., 1973; postgrad., U. Ga., 1973-74; JD, SUNY, Buffalo, 1976. Bar: La. 1976, Ga. 1979, U.S. Dist. Ct. (no. dist.) Ga. 1979, U.S. Ct. Appeals (5th and 11th cirs.) 1979, U.S. Ct. Appeals (3d cir.) 1982, U.S. Ct. Appeals (6th cir.) 1986. Field atty. NLRB, Atlanta, 1976-80; assoc. Elarbee, Thompson & Trapnell, Atlanta, 1980-87; ptnr. Elarbee, Thompson, Sapp & Wilson, Atlanta, 1987—. Lectr. Atlanta U., 1984; adj. prof. law Emory U., Atlanta, 1984-85; mem. Study Commn. on Employment Laws, 1997-98. Contbr. articles to profl. jours. Mem. Fulton County Bd. Ethics 1991, Homelessness Task Force United Way of Metropolitan Atlanta, 2005; exec. bd. dirs. Boys and Girls Clubs of Metro Atlanta, 1999—, exec. com., 2005; bd. dirs. St. Judes Recovery Ctr., Inc., 1989—, bd. chair, 2005; active Christ our Hope Cath. Ch. Recipient Am.'s Top Black Lawyers, Ga. Legal Elite, 2003, 2006, Best Lawyers for Bus., Chambers USA, 2005, 2006; named one of Top 100 Ga. Super Lawyers, 2004, 2005, 2006; named to Am.'s Top Black Lawyers, Black Enterprise Mag., 2003. Mem.: Labors and Employment Rels. Assn., ABA (mem. labor and employment law mgmt. com.), NAACP (life), Coll. Labor and Employment Lawyers, Atlanta Soc. African Am. Human Resources, Soc. Human Resource Mgmt. (legis. com. co-chmn. 1987—88, 1990—91), Nat. Employment Law Coun., Nat. Assn. Securities Dealers (arbitrator), State Bar Ga. (co-chair Ga. Diversity Prog. 1998—99), Nat. Bar Assn. (mem. comml., labor and arbitration sect.), Gate City Bar Assn., Atlanta Bar Assn. (sec., treas. labor and employment law sect. 1985, vice chmn. labor and employment law sect. 1986, chmn. labor and employment law sect. 1987), 100 Blackmen of Atlanta, Atlanta Morehouse, Lawyers Club Atlanta, 191 Club, Atlanta Bus. League, Am. Inns. Ct., Phi Alpha Delta, Omega Psi Phi. Avocations: spectator sports, racquetball, reading, travel. Office: Elarbee Thompson Sapp & Wilson LLP 800 Internat Tower 229 Peachtree St NE Atlanta GA 30303-1614 Office Phone: 404-659-6700, 404-582-8427. Business E-Mail: bwilson@elarbeethompson.com.

WILSON, CECIL BRUCE, internist; b. Columbus, Ga., 1935; m. Betty Jane Wilson; 3 children. BA in History, Emory U., Atlanta; MD, Emory U. Sch. Medicine, 1961. Diplomate American Bd. Internal Medicine. Intern US Naval Hosp., Portsmouth, Va., 1961—62; resident internal medicine US Naval Hosp., San Diego, 1966—69; internal medicine pvt. practice Winter Park, Fla. Past pres. med. staff Winter Park Meml. Hosp., Fla. Hosp. Med. Ctr., Orlando. Nat. fellow, advisor Ctr. Global Health & Med. Diplomacy, U. North Fla.; past pres. Fla. Statewide Health Coun.; past chair Local Health Coun. East Ctrl. Fla. Flight surgeon, comdr. USN. Master: ACP (past chair bd. regents); mem.: World Med. Assn. (coun. mem.), American Soc. Internal Medicine, AMA (House of Delegates 1992—, bd. trustees 2002—, chair bd. trustees 2006—07, pres. 2010—11, immediate past pres. 2011—), Orange County Med. Soc. (past pres.), Fla. Med. Assn. (past pres., Cert. of Merit 2003). Office: Cecil B Wilson MD 263 Salvador Sq Winter Park FL 32789-5618 Office Phone: 407-647-2122. Office Fax: 407-647-6701.

WILSON, CHARLES REGINALD, federal judge; b. Pensacola, Fla., 1954; BS, U. Notre Dame, 1976, JD, 1979. Bar: Fla. 1979. Law clk. to Hon. Joseph W. Hatchett US Ct. Appeals (11th cir.), 1979—80; asst. county atty. Hillsborough county, Fla., 1980—81; county judge 13th Jud. Cir. of Fla., 1986—90; pvt. practice Fla., 1981—86; US magistrate judge US Dist. Ct. (mid. dist.) Fla., 1990—94, US atty., 1994—99; judge US Ct. Appeals (11th cir.), Tampa, Fla., 1999—. Mem.: Ferguson-White Inn of Am. Inn of Ct., Fed. Bar Assn., Am. Law Inst. Office: 11th Cir Ct Appeals 801 N Florida Ave Ste 14B Tampa FL 33602-3849

WILSON, CLARK R., geophysicist, educator; BA with high honors in Physics, U. Calif. San Diego Revelle Coll., 1970; MS in Earth Sci., U. Calif. San Diego Scripps Instn. Oceanography, 1973, PhD in Earth Sci., 1975. Asst. prof. to assoc. prof. U. Tex., Austin, 1976—89, prof., 1989—, Wallace Pratt prof. geophysics, 1992—. Chmn. dept. geol. scis. U. Tex., Austin, 1990—94, 2004—; geodynamics and geopotential fields prog. specialist NASA, Washington, 1996—99; head Geophys. Fluids Ctr. Hydrology, 1999—2004; mem. directing bd. Internat. Earth Rotation Svc., 2000—. Contbr. articles to sci. jours.; assoc. editor geodesy: Jour. Geophys. Rsch., 1993—99. Office: Geol Scis Dept U Tex 1 Univ Sta C1100 Austin TX 78712-0254 E-mail: crwilson@mail.utexas.edu.

WILSON, CLAUDE RAYMOND, JR., lawyer; b. Dallas, Feb. 22, 1933; s. Claude Raymond and Lottie (Watts) W.; m. Emilynn Wilson; children: Deidra Wilson Graves, Melissa Woodard Utley, Michele Woodard Dunn. BBA, So. Meth. U., Dallas, 1954, JD, 1956. Bar: Tex. 1956; CPA, Calif., Tex. With Cervin & Melton, Dallas, 1956-58, Tex. & Pacific R.R. Co., Dallas, 1958-60; atty. office regional counsel IRS, San Francisco, 1960-63, sr. trial atty. office chief counsel Washington, 1963-65; ptnr. Wilson & White, LLP, Dallas, 1965—98, Vial, Hamilton, Koch & Knox LLP, Dallas, 1998—2007, Looper Reed & McGraw, Dallas, 2007—. Chmn., Dallas dist. dir. IRS Adv. Commn., 1990-91. Chmn. Dallas Hist. Soc., 2000-01; mem. fin. com. Dallas Arboretum and Bot. Gardens, 2003-08, mem. policy bd., 2012-, City of University Park, 2004-; bd. govs., mem. fin. com., mem. ethics com. Dallas Symphony Orch., 2004-08. Mem.: AICPA (coun. 1989—93, tax exec. com. 1998—2001), ABA, Head Start Greater Dallas (bd. dirs. 2012—), Tex. Soc. CPAs (pres. Dallas chpt. 1983—84, pres. 1989—90), Dallas Bar Assn. (pres. sect. taxation 1969—70), State Bar Tex., Greater Dallas C. of C. (chmn. appropriations and tax com. 1990—91), Dallas Petroleum Club, Masons, Delta Theta Phi., Delta Sigma Phi. Republican. Episcopalian. Office: Looper Reed & McGraw 4600 Thanksgiving Tower 1601 Elm St Dallas TX 75201 Office Phone: 214-237-6335. Business E-Mail: cwilson@lrmlaw.com.

WILSON, DAVE, editor; Joined The Miami Herald, 1986, mng. editor, Broward Bur., sr. editor, adminstrn., mng. news editor, 2006. Office: The Miami Herald 1 Herald Plz Miami FL 33132 Office Phone: 305-305-2111. Office Fax: 305-376-5287. Business E-Mail: dwilson@miamiherald.com.

WILSON, EDWARD CONVERSE, JR., oil and natural gas production company executive; b. Cambridge, Mass., Jan. 1, 1928; s. Edward Converse and Jean (McLean) W.; m. Patricia Ann Cairns, Sept. 10, 1953; children—Amy Cairns, Sarah Converse. AB, Harvard U., 1949. Brokerage trainee Estabrook & Co., Boston, 1951; Midwest Stock Exch. clk. Paul H. Davis & Co., Chgo., 1951-52; mem. Chgo. Bd. Trade, 1952-78, dir., 1966-67, chmn., 1970-71; ptnr. Nolan & Wilson Co. (specialists on Midwest Stock Exchange), 1965-72; sr. ptnr. Wilson Prodn. Co., Ft. Smith, Ark., 1972-74. Mem. devel. com. Chgo. chpt. Nat. Multiple Sclerosis Soc., 1970; mem. vis. com. on univ. resources Harvard, 1971-74, 76-81; Bd. dirs. Franklin Blvd. Community Hosp., 1970-74. Served with USAAF, 1946-47. Home: 11114 Wickwood Dr Houston TX 77024-7523

WILSON, FLOYD C., oil industry executive; children: Christopher, Andrew. Ptnr. Wilson Group Companies; founder, chmn., pres., CEO Hugoton Energy Corp., 1987—98; chmn., CEO 3TEC Energy Corp., 1999—2003; owner, pres., CEO PHAWK, LLC (formerly Petrohawk Energy, LLC), 2003—04; pres. Petrohawk Energy Corp., Houston, 2004—09, chmn., CEO, 2004—. Office: Petrohawk Energy Corp 1000 Louisiana St Ste 5600 Houston TX 77002-5038 Office Phone: 832-204-2700. Office Fax: 832-204-2827. Business E-Mail: fwilson@petrohawk.com.

WILSON, FREDERICA SMITH, United States Representative from Florida, former state legislator; b. Miami, Fla., Nov. 5, 1942; d. Thirlee and Beulah (Finley) Smith; children: Nicole Wilson-St. Hilaire, Lakesha Wilson-Rochelle, Paul Jr. BS, Fisk U., 1963; MA, U. Miami, 1972; LHD (hon.), Fla. Meml. U. Mem. Miami-Dade County Sch. Bd., Fla., 1992—98; founder, exec. dir. 5000 Role Models of Excellence Project, 1993—; exec. dir. Office Alternative Edn. & Dropout Prevention, Miami; mem. Dist. 104 Fla. House of Reps., Tallahassee, 1998—2002; mem. Dist. 33 Fla. State Senate, Tallahassee, 2003—10, minority leader pro tempore, 2006—08, minority whip, 2008—10; mem. US Congress from 17th Fla. Dist., Washington, 2011—13, US Congress from 24th Fla. Dist., 2013—, US House Fgn. Affairs Com., 2011—13, US House Space, Science, & Tech. Com., 2011—, US House Edn. & the Workforce Com., 2013—. Mem.: Nat. Assn. Black Sch. Educators, The Links, Inc., Alpha Kappa Alpha. Democrat. Episcopalian. Office: US House of Representatives

208 Cannon House Office Bldg Washington DC 20515 also: 18425 NW 2nd Ave Ste 355 Miami FL 33169 Office Phone: 202-225-4506, 305-690-5905. Office Fax: 202-226-0777.*

WILSON, GRETCHEN, musician; b. Granite City, Ill., June 26, 1973; 1 child, Grace. Signed by Epic Records, 2003—. Singer: (singles) Redneck Woman, 2004 (Breakthrough Video of Yr., Country Music Television Music award, 2005), When I Think About Cheatin, 2004 (Female Video of Yr., Country Music Television Music award, 2005), (five singles) 5-Mo-Fo-Ya, 2005, (albums) Here for the Party, 2004, All Jacked Up, 2005, One of the Boys, 2007, I Got Your Country Right Here, 2010; TV appearances include: In The Moment, 2004; co-author (with Allen Rucker): Redneck Women: Stories from My Life, 2006. Recipient Horizon award, Country Music Assn., 2004, Favorite New Artist, Am. Music Awards, 2004, Favorite Female Country Artist, 2005, Female Country Artist of Yr., Billboard Music Awards, 2004, New Country Artist of Yr., 2004, Top New Artist, Acad. Country Music Awards, 2005, Top Female Vocalist, 2005; named Female Vocalist of Yr., Country Music Assn., 2005. Achievements include first new artist to debut at #1 on Billboard's Country LP chart.

WILSON, HAROLD STACY, history professor, writer; b. Neva, Tenn., June 22, 1935; s. Joseph Hooker Wilson and Bertie Hazel Reece; m. Henrietta Sheppard Fair, June 21, 1968; children: Katherine McColl, Kyle Stacy. BA, King Coll., 1957; MA, Johns Hopkins U., 1959; PhD, Emory U., 1966. Asst. prof. Wesleyan Coll., Macon, Ga., 1962—66, Old Dominion U., Norfolk, Va., 1966—68, assoc. prof., 1968—2003, chair, history dept., 1991—98, mem. faculty senate, 1999—2008, vice-chair faculty senate, 2001—03, prof. history, 2003—09, dir., Rsch. Integrity Office, 2008—, emeritus history prof., 2009—. Fulbright prof. Fu Ren U., Taipei, Taiwan, 1971—72, Tamkang U., Taipei, 1971—72, Nat. U. Singapore, 1978—80; exch. prof. Kitakyushu U., Japan, 1995. Author: (history book) McClure's Magazine and the Muckrakers, 1970, Confederate Industry: Manufacturers and Quartermasters in the Civil War, 2002; editor: Textile History Rev., 1963—66; assoc. editor: Wesleyan Quar. Rev., 1964—66, editl. asst.: The Great American and The Blue and the Gray; contbr. scholarly articles and book revs. in field. Supporter Union Mission, Norfolk, Va., 1966—, Salvation Army, Norfolk, 1966—, Young Life, Norfolk, 1966—, Stas. WHRO-TV, WHRV-TV, Norfolk, 1966—, Norfolk Pub. Libr., 1966—; founder, Patrick scholarship King Coll., Bristol, Tenn., 1996—; short-term missioner South Am. Missionary Soc., Honduras, 2002—; founding mem. Christ the Redeemer Anglican Ch., Norfolk, 2005—. Nominee Peter Seaborg award, 2002; grantee Tech. and Tchg. grant, U. 21st Century, 1992; Rsch. grant, Nat. Found. Arts and Humanities, 1968, Faculty Field Rsch. grant, US Mil. Acad., 1987. Mem.: So. Hist. Assn. (chair arrangements com. 1987—88), Friends of Old Dominion U. Perry Libr. (life). Independent-Republican. Baptist. Avocations: hiking, swimming, travel. Home: 626 W Princess Anne Rd Norfolk VA 23517-1806 Office: Old Dominion Univ Hampton Blvd Norfolk VA 23529 Business E-Mail: hwilson@odu.edu.

WILSON, JAMES CHARLES, JR., lawyer; b. Birmingham, Ala., Sept. 13, 1947; s. James C. and Angelina (Serio) W.; m. Ann Bullock, Mar. 1, 1975; children: Brent Trammell, Lucy Bullock. BA, Tulane U., New Orleans, 1969, JD, 1972; MBA, Samford U., Birmingham, Ala., 1995. Ptnr. Bradley, Arant, Rose & White, Birmingham, 1972-90, Lange, Simpson, Robinson & Somerville, Birmingham, 1990-93, Sirote & Permutt, P.C., Birmingham, 1993-96; v.p. and gen. counsel Shop-A-Snak Food Mart, Inc., Birmingham, 1996; pres. Lucent Holdings, Inc., Golden, Miss., 1997-98; ptnr. Baker, Johnston & Wilson LLP, Birmingham, Ala., 1999—2002; shareholder Baker Donelson, Bearman, Caldwell & Berkowitz, PC, Birmingham, 2003—13; mem. Wilson Resha LLC, 2013—. Adj. prof. internat. bus. transactions and internat. law U. Ala., Tuscaloosa, 1983-85, 89-96, adj. prof. transactional drafting healthcare, 2013-; internat. bus. transactions Cumberland Sch. Law, 1990-95, adj. prof. corp. fin., 2001—, adj. prof. securities regulation, 2003-08. Author: Alabama Business Corporation Law, 1980; co-author: Corporate Law for the Healthcare Provider: Organization, Operation, Merger and Bankruptcy, 1993, Alabama Business Corporation Law Guide, 1995, International Trade Settlements and Negotiations, 2006. Adv. bd. Jr. League of Birmingham, 1984; bd. dirs. Ala. chpt. Am. Liver Found., 1993-97, sec., 1994-95; trustee The Altamont Sch., 1995-2001, v.p., 1996-98, pres., 1998-2000. With U.S. Army, 1972-76. Mem.: ABA (sect. internat. law, tax and corp., banking and bus. law), Am. Resources Ins. Co., Inc. (bd. dirs.), Birmingham Bar Assn. (chmn. pub. rels. com. 1990, chmn. spl. projects com. 2002, chmn. membership benefits com. 2003), Ala. Law Inst., Ala. Bar Assn., Am. Law Inst., Birmingham Golf Assn. (pres., v.p., treas. 1982—84), Rotary (pres. Birmingham-Sunrise club 1986—87, bd. dirs. 2006—08). Office: PO Box 43181 Birmingham AL 35243 Business E-Mail: jcw@wilsonresha.com.

WILSON, JAMES LAURENCE, real estate development executive, financial services consultant, educator; s. William Henry and Beulah (Baylis) Wilson; m. Marilyn Murray, June 13, 1981; children: Leigh William, Robin Steele, Brennen Julian, Daniel Laurence. BS, Union Coll., 1968. Dir. World Assocs., Inc., Ft. Lauderdale, Fla., 1970—77; comml. loan divsn. head Royal Trust Bank, Miami, Fla., 1976—81; sr. real estate lending officer Southeast Bank, Tampa, 1982—85; pres. Bayshore Investments, Investors and Cons. Shopping Ctr. Developing Co., Tampa, 1986—90; exec. v.p. & sr. lending officer Boca Bank, Boca Raton, Fla., 1990—92; CEO & organizing dir., vice chmn. Southern Security Bank Corp., 1993—2001; adj. faculty mem. Fla. Atlantic U., Charles E. Schmidt Coll. Sci., 2000—; sr. v.p. & sr. real estate lending officer Fla. Capital Bank, 2004—07; chief credit officer Security Bank, 2007—10, South Coast Advisors, LLC, DelRay Beach, Fla.; ptnr. Real Estate Developer, & Comml. Lending Consulting Group Major Banking entities in Fla. Contbr. articles to profl. jours. Mem.: ICSC, Internat. Coun. Shopping Ctrs., Am. Inst. Banking, Econ. Soc. South Fla., Am. Bankers Assn., Mortgage Bankers Assn. Republican. Office Phone: 561-416-1100. Office Fax: 561-892-2681. Business E-Mail: 416.1100@gmail.com, jim.wilson.ISAGENIX@gmail.com.

WILSON, JEAN DONALD, endocrinologist, educator; b. Wellington, Tex., Aug. 26, 1932; s. J. D. and Maggie E. (Hill) Wilson. BA in Chemistry, U. Tex., 1951, MD, 1955. Diplomate Am. Bd. Internal Medicine. Intern, then resident in internal medicine Parkland Meml. Hosp., Dallas, 1955—58; clin. assoc. Nat. Heart Inst., Bethesda, Md., 1958—60; instr. internal medicine U. Tex. Southwestern Med. Sch., Dallas, 1960—61, prof., 1968—. Editor: Jour. Clin. Investigation, 1972—77. Sr. asst. surgeon USPHS, 1958—60. Recipient Fuller prize, Am. Urol. Assn., 1983, Lita Annenberg Hazen award, 1986, Dale medal, Soc. for Endocrinology, 1991, Pincus medal, Worchester Found., 1992. Fellow: Royal Coll. Physicians; mem.: NAS, Endocrine Soc. (Oppenheimer award 1972, Koch award 1993), Am. Soc. Biochemistry and Molecular Biology, Soc. Exptl. Biology and Medicine, Am. Philos. Soc., Assn. Am. Physicians (Kober medal 1999), Am. Soc. Clin. Investigation, Inst. Medicine, Am. Acad. Arts and Scis. (Amory prize 1977). Office: U Tex Southwestern Med Ctr Dept Internal Medicine 5323 Harry Hines Blvd Dallas TX 75390-8857 Home Phone: 214-351-1837; Office Phone: 214-648-3469. Office Fax: 214-648-8917. Business E-Mail: jwils1@mednet.swmed.edu.

WILSON, JIM, state legislator; b. Madison, Wis., Mar. 9, 1947; s. Joel and Mary McCammon W.; m. Connie Thompson; children: David, Kim, Jamie. BS in Math., Okla. State Univ. With Okla. Crime Commission, Okla. City; bd. dirs. Thompson House; business owner; mem. Dist. 4 Okla. House of Representatives, 2000—04; mem. Dist. 3 Okla. State Senate, 2005—. With USMC, Vietnam War. Mem.: American Legion, Talequa C. of C., Kiwanis Club of Tahlequah. Democrat. Mailing: 2300 N Lincoln Blvd Rm 533C Oklahoma City OK 73105 also: 708 W Shawnee Tahlequah OK 74464 Office Phone: 405-557-7408, 918-456-4036, 405-521-5574. Business E-Mail: wilson@oksenate.gov.

WILSON, JOE (ADDISON GRAVES WILSON), United States Representative from South Carolina; b. Charleston, SC, July 31, 1947; s. Hugh deVeaux and Wray Smart (Graves) Wilson; m. Roxanne Dusenbury McCrory, Dec. 30, 1977; children: Michael Alan, Addison Graves, Julian Dusenbury, Hunter Taylor. BA, Washington & Lee U., Lexington, Va., 1969; JD, U. SC, Columbia, 1972. Bar: SC 1972. Staff mem. to rep. Strom Thurmond US Senator Strom Thurmond, Washington, 1967; staff mem. US Rep. Floyd Spence, Columbia, SC, 1970-72; ptnr. Kirkland, Wilson, Moore, Taylor & Thomas, West Columbia, 1972—2001; mem. US Congress from 2nd SC dist., 2001—. Dep. gen. counsel to sec. Jim Edwards US Dept. Energy, Washington, 1981—82; mem. SC State Senate, 1984—2001; presdl. appointee Intergovernmental Adv. Coun. Edn., 1990—91; bd. dirs. Bank of America, Lexington, SC. Vice chmn. SC Rep. Party, 1972—74; campaign mgr. Staff US Rep. Floyd Spence, 1974, 1978, 1980, 1982, 1998, Columbia. Served in USAR, 1972—75, positions to col. SC Army N.G., 1975—2003. Republican. Presbyterian. Office: US House of Representatives 2229 Rayburn House Office Bldg Washington DC 20515 Office Phone: 202-225-2452. Office Fax: 202-225-2455. E-mail: joe.wilson@mail.house.gov.*

WILSON, JOHN H., corporate financial executive; Grad., Southern Meth. U.; BBA in Econ. & Fin., Baylor U. Pres. US Equity Corp., 1983—. Bd. dirs. Capital Southwest Corp., 1988—, Encore Wire Corp., 1994—, Palm Harbor Homes Inc., 1994—. Office: Encore Wire Corp 1329 Millwood Rd Mc Kinney TX 75069 Office Phone: 972-562-9473. Office Fax: 972-562-3644. Business E-Mail: John.Wilson@encorewire.com.

WILSON, JOHN SILVANUS, JR., academic administrator, former federal agency administrator; b. 1957; BA, Morehouse Coll., 1979; MA in Theological Studies, Harvard U., MA, PhD in Ednl. Adminstrn., Planning and Social Policy. Prof. Afro-American Studies Dept. Harvard U.; dir. found. rels. and asst. provost MIT, Cambridge, Mass.; joined George Washington U., 2001, exec. dean Va. campus, 2002—06, assoc. prof. higher edn., 2006—09; exec. dir. White House's Initiative on Historically Black Colleges & Universities US Dept. Edn., Washington, 2009—12; pres. Morehouse Coll., Atlanta, 2013—. Chmn. Alumni Coun. Harvard Grad. Sch. Bus., 1996—2000; advocate, advisor Kresge Found., Mott Found., United Negro Coll. Fund; bd. mem. Spelman Coll., Atlanta, Independent Fed. Savings Bank, Washington. Office: Office of the President Morehouse Coll 830 Westview Dr SW Atlanta GA 30314

WILSON, JOHN T., pediatrics and pharmacology educator; children from previous marriage: Mary Laurence, Anne Abigail, John Tyler. BS, Tulane U., 1960, MS, MD, Tulane U., 1963. Diplomate Am. Bd. Pediatrics, Am. Bd. Clin. Pharmacology (charter cert.). Pediatric intern Palo Alto (Calif.)-Stanford Med. Ctr., 1963-64, pediatric resident, 1964-65; rsch. assoc. dept. pharmacology U. Iowa, Iowa City, 1965-66; rsch. assoc. sect. on endocrinology Nat. Inst. Child Health Devel., Bethesda, Md., 1966-68; fellow in pediatrics, attending pediatrician and dir. Children's Hosp. of San Francisco, 1968-69, 69-70; rsch. assoc. George Peabody Coll. for Tchrs., Kennedy Ctr., Nashville, 1970-78; assoc. prof. pediatrics and pharmacology Vanderbilt U. Med. Ctr., Nashville, 1970-78; attending physician gen. pediatrics Vanderbilt Hosp. and Nashville Gen. Hosp., 1970-78; prof. pediatric medicine dir. La. State U. Med. Ctr., Child Clin. Rsch. Ctr., Shreveport, 1978—. Mem. Am. Acad. Pediat. Com. on Drugs, 1995—99. Contbr. numerous articles to profl. jours. Lt. comdr. USPHS, 1965—68. Recipient The Paracelsus award U. Amsterdam, 1985, Pharm. Mfrs. Assn. Found. award for Clin. Pharmacology Units, 1979, NIH Rsch. Career Devel. award, 1969, 72, The John T. Halsey award Tulane U., 1963, Tulane Med. Alumni Lifetime Achievement award, 2013; grantee NIH Pediat. Pharmacology Rsch. Unit, 1993-2003. Fellow: Am. Coll. Clin. Pharmacology, Am. Acad. Pediat.; mem.: Shreveport Med. Soc., Soc. Pediat. Rsch., La. State Med. Soc., Am. Pediat. Soc., Am. Soc. Clin. Pharmacology and Therapeutics, Stanford Med. Alumni Assn. Office: La State U Med Ctr 1501 Kings Hwy Shreveport LA 71103-4228 Office Phone: 318-675-5080.

WILSON, LLOYD LEE, registrar, educator; b. Elkton, Md., Sept. 14, 1947; s. Clifton Laws and Betty Raye (Bare) W.; m. Susan Sieg Wilson, 1992; children: Asa, Ryan, Morgan, Daniel. BS in Mgmt., MIT, 1969, MS in Mgmt., 1977; MA in Religion, Earlham Sch. Religion, 2009. Bus. mgr. med. clinics Mass. Gen. Hosp., Boston, 1970-73; ptnr. Willow Co., mgmt. cons., Cambridge, Mass., 1974-77; dir. community relations Wilson Neuropsychiat. Hosp., Charlottesville, Va., 1977-78; exec. dir. Jefferson Area United Transp. Inc., Charlottesville, Va., 1978-80, Va. Mountain Housing Inc., Blacksburg, 1980-82; gen. sec. Friends Gen. Conf. Religious Soc. Friends, Phila., 1982-85; dir. rsch. and devel. Va. Mountain Housing, Inc., Christiansburg, 1985-88, dir. multifamily housing, 1989-91, regional dir., 1991-92; pres. Friendly Mgmt. Svcs. Corp., Norfolk, Va., 1992-95, Not-for-Profit Mgmt., Inc., Norfolk, Va., 1995—2004; asst. prof. religion Chowan U., 2006—10, registrar, 2002—10, registrar emeritus, 2010—. Treas. NC Yearly Meeting of Friends, 2011-; dir. instnl. rsch. Chowan U., Murfreesboro, N.C., 2000—10; asst. prof. of acctg., 2001—10; pres., dir. Va. Housing Coalition, Inc., 1981-82; treas., bd. dirs., Cedar Grove Consulting, LLC, 2004—06, Fiddle Hill Farm, Inc., Barboursville, Va., 1982-89; bd. mgrs. Bible Assn. Friends in Am., Phila., 1983-85; mem. com. rec. ministers Balt. Yearly Meeting Friends, Sandy Spring, Md., 1984-86; asst. sec.-treas. Friends Meeting House Fund, Inc., Phila., 1984-85; asst. presiding clk. Comm. Commn. of Friends United Meeting, Richmond, Ind., 1987-88; recorded min. of gospel, Soc. of Friends, 1989— (presiding clk. Va. Beach monthly meeting 1990-92); dir. coordinating cabinet Va. Coun. Chs., 1988; presiding clk. N.C. Yearly Meeting of Friends, 1991-92. Author: Essays on the Quaker Vision of Gospel Order, 1993, Why Do You Still Read That Old Thing?, 1996, Wrestling with Our Faith Tradition, 2005, Holy Surrender, 2007, Change and Preservation in the Same Current, 2011, Radical Hospitality, 2014; contbr. articles to profl. jours. Treas., bd. dirs. Norfolk (Va.) Quaker House, Inc., 1995-2000; bd. dirs. New Dominion Housing, Inc., Norfolk, 1992-94; vice chmn. Montgomery County Cmty. Svc. Commn., Christianburg, Va., 1980-82; mem. ednl. coun. MIT, 1977-89; bd. dirs. Am. Friends Svc. Com., Inc., Phila., 1980-83; bd. dirs. Interfaith Housing Corp. Cambridge, Inc., 1975-77, treas., 1976-77, also numerous others. Conservative Quaker. Home and Office: 4117 W Greensboro-Chapel Hill Rd Liberty NC 27298-9070 Personal E-mail: lloydleewilson@gmail.com. Business E-Mail: llwilson@alum.mit.edu.

WILSON, MIKE, state legislator; b. New Albany, Miss., Dec. 4, 1951; m. Deanna Wilson; children: Michael, Dawn, Sam, Grace, Jessie. AA, Fullerton Coll., Calif.; BA in Bus. Adminstrn. Mgmt., Calif. State U., 1986. Sales agent, sales mgr. & br. mgr. Calvary Chapel of South Bay; promotions dir., bus. partnership dir. Sta. WCVK Christian Family Radio, 1994—97, gen. mgr., 1997—; mem. Dist. 32 Ky. State Senate, Frankfort, 2011—. Served with USMC. Republican. Baptist. Office: Kentucky State Senate Annex Rm 203 702 Capitol Ave Frankfort KY 40601 Office Phone: 502-564-8100 ext. 717.

WILSON, PATRICIA POTTER, author, educator, agriculture business owner; b. Jennings, La., May 3, 1946; d. Ralph Harold and Wilda Ruth (Smith) Potter; m. Wendell Merlin Wilson, Aug. 24, 1968. BS, La. State U., 1967; MS, U. Houston-Clear Lake, 1979; EdD, U. Houston, 1985. Cert. tchr., learning resources specialist (libr.), Tex. Tchr. England AFB Elem. Sch., La., 1967-68, Edward White Elem. Sch./Clear Creek Ind. Schs., Seabrook, Tex., 1972-77; libr. C.D. Landolt Elem. Sch., Friendswood, Tex., 1979-81; instr./lectr. children's lit. U. Houston, 1983-86; with U. Houston/Clear Lake, 1984-87, asst. prof. libr. sci. and reading, 1988-94, assoc. prof. learning resources and reading edn., 1994—2001, assoc. prof. emerita, 2001—. Cons. Hermann Hosp., Baywood Hosp., 1986-87, Bedford Meadows Hosp., 1989-90, Wetcher Clinic, 1989; co-owner, v.p. Potter Farms, Inc.; pres. cabinet U. Houston Ctrl., Clear Lake; mem. cmtys. in schs. World Affairs Coun. Houston. Author: Happenings: Developing Successful Programs for School Libraries, 1987, The Professional Collection for Elementary Educators, 1996, Premiere Events: Library Programs That Inspire Elementary Patrons, 2001, Leadership for Today's School Library, 2001, Igniting the Spark: Library Programs that Inspire High School Patrons, 2001, Center Stage: Library Programs That Inspire Middle School Patrons, 2002, Eagle on Ice: Eagle Scout Paul Siple's Antaractic Adventures With Commander Byrd, 2008; editor: A Review Sampler, 1985—86, 1989—90; contbg. editor: Tex. Libr. Jour., 1988—94; contbr. articles to profl. jours. Trustee Freeman Meml. Libr., Houston, 1982—87, v.p., 1985—86, pres., 1986—87; trustee Evelyn Meador Libr., 1993—94, adv. bd., 1994—, Houston Symphony League-Bay Area, 1996—, bd., chair ann. fund campaign, 2005; founder Friends of Neumann Libr., 1998—2001; chmn. hospitality com. Lunar Rendevous Festival, 1998—2001; gen. chmn. Lunar Rendezvous Festival, 2002, mem. adv. bd., 2002—07; mem. Assistance League of the Bay Area, 1997—; vol. Houston: A Visit from St. Nicholas Com., 2004—, co-chmn. kick-off event, 2005; donar Quiet Rm. Meada Libr., Seabrook, Tex.; with Meador Libr., Seabrook, Tex., 2011; mem. adv. bd. Bay Area Soc. Prevention Cruelty Animals, 1994—98, Bay Area Turning Point, 1998—2007; bd. dirs. Sta. KUHT-TV, 1984—87, Bay Area Houston Ballet and Theatre, 2001—04, vice chair bd. dirs., 2003—04, chmn. kickoff event, 2003; dir. Learning Resources Book Rev. Ctr., 1989—90; bd. dirs. Armand Bayou Nature Ctr., Houston, 1989—94; mem. Bay Area Houston Econ. Partnership, 2002—, mem. banquet com., 2002—; mem. Longhorn devel. bd. NASA and Clear Creek Ind. Sch. Dist., 2005—09; mem. devel. and adv. coun. U. Houston Clear Lake, 2006—09, mem. cmty. ptnrs. coun.; mem. UHCL Cmty. Ptnrs. Coun. Recipient Rsch. award, Tex. State Reading Assn., 1993, Pres. award, Tex. Coun. Tchrs. English, Disting. Tchg. award, Enron Corp., 1996, Disting. Alumni award, U. Houston-Clear Lake, 1998, Disting. Alumna award, U. Houston, Coll. Edn., 2002, Disting. Alumni award, U. Houston Ctrl., 2005, Bravo award, Bay Area Houston Ballet & Theater, 2006, Kay Burnett Outstanding Friend of the Arts Award, Arts Alliance Ctr. at Clear Lake, 2008, Philanthropy award, U. Houston-Clear Lake Pres.'s Cabinet, 2009, UHCL Cmty. Ptnrs. Coun., 2010—; named Outstanding Vol. of Yr., Houston's Nat. Philanthropy Day, 1999; named one of 10 Men and Women of Heart, Bay Area Turning Point, 2001; grantee, Tex. Libr. Assn., 1993. Mem. Nat. Coun. Tchrs. English (Books for You rev. com. 1985-88, 97-98, Your Reading rev. com. 1993-96), Tex. Coun. Tchrs. English, Antarctican Soc., Clear Lake Panhellenic Assn., Travelers' Century Club, Phi Kappa Phi (sec. 1997-98, pres. 1998-99).

WILSON, RHYS THADDEUS, lawyer; b. Albany, Ga., May 9, 1955; s. Joseph Farr Jr. and Betty Ann W.; m. Carolyn Reid Saffold, June 2, 1984. AB, Duke U., 1976; JD, U. Ga., 1979; LLM, Emory U., 1985. Bar: Ga. 1979. Pvt. practice law, Atlanta, 1979-89; sr. v.p., gen. counsel Monarch Capital Group, Inc., Atlanta, 1989-92, Jackson & Coker, Inc., Atlanta, 1992-93; pres. Jackson & Coker Locum Tenens, Inc., Atlanta, 1993-95; ptnr. Robins, Kaplan, Miller & Ciresi, Atlanta, 1995—2005, Nelson Mullins Riley & Scarborough LLP, 2006—; adv. bd. Cure Childhood Cancer. Spkr. CLE seminars. Contbr. articles to profl. jours. Bd. dirs, treas. Atlanta Opera Co. Named Ga. Super Lawyer, Mergers & Acquisitions, 2004—; named to Georgia Trend's Legal Elite, 2013—. Mem. ABA, Ga. Bar Assn. (chmn. internat. law sect. 1987-88, exec. com. corp. and banking law sect. 1987-89, editl. bd. Ga. State Bar Jour. 1986-89), Atlanta Bar Assn. (editor newsletter 1984-86, Outstanding Svc. award 1986), Assn. for Corp. Growth, Atlanta Tech. Angels (bd. dirs. 2001-08), Vistage Internat., Capital City Club. Episcopalian.

WILSON, RICHARD LEE, political science professor; b. Worthington, Minn., Dec. 20, 1944; s. G. Roy and Dorothy Eileen (Johnson) W.; m. Carolyn Ann Dirks, Aug. 24, 1968 (div.); 1 child, Kevin Richard. BA, U. Chgo., 1966, postgrad., 1966-67; PhD, Johns Hopkins U., 1971; postgrad., Columbia U., 1988, Stanford U., 1992. Congl. aide 4th Congl. Dist. Md., 1971; asst. prof. polit. sci. U. Tenn., Chattanooga, 1971-76, assoc. prof., 1976-87, prof., 1988—. Registrar-at-large Hamilton County Election Commn., 1977-84; lectr. Robert A. Taft Inst. Govt., U. Tenn., Nashville, 1978, 79, 81; supr. state legis. and met. internship program U. Chattanooga, 1972-86; vis. prof. Govt. Fgn. Affairs Coll., Beijing, 1986-87; Fulbright prof. govt. Beijing U., 1988-89, Samford U., Birmingham, Ala., 1991-93. Author: Tennessee Politics, 1976, American Government, 1993, 2d edit., 1995, American Political Leaders, 2002; editor: Encyclopedia of American Government, 2001, (Choice award 2009), Historical Encyclopedia of Am. Bus., 2009(choice award, 2009); co-editor: Ready Reference: Censorship, 1997 (named Outstanding Ref. Source 1998 ALA), Encyclopedia of the Supreme Court, 2000 (named OUtstanding Ref. Scouce 2002 ALA); contbr. chpts. to books. Chmn. Hamilton County Health Planning Adv. Council, 1975-79; bd. dirs. Ga.-Tenn. Regional Health Commn., 1978-82; active Tenn. State Health Coordinating Council, 1977-81; exec. com. State Health Coordinating Council, 1979-81. Named Outstanding Educator of Yr., Signal Mountain (Tenn.) Jaycees, 1973, Outstanding Prof. of Yr., SGA, 1985-86, Oustanding Reference Source ALA, 2002; recipient Polit. Edn. award NAACP, 1980, Excellent Prof. award Fgn. Affairs Coll., Beijing, 1987, UTC Exceptional Merit award, 1990, 94; NEH grantee, 1988, 92. Mem. So. Polit. Sci. Assn., Midwest Polit. Sci. Assn., Am. Polit. Sci. Assn. (nat. rsch. grant 1995), Nat. Soc. Internships and Exptl. Edn., SAR, China People's Friendship Assn., Aircraft Owners and

Pilots Assn. Methodist. Office: Univ of Tenn Dept Political Sci Fletcher Hall 414 Chattanooga TN 37403 Office Phone: 423-425-4281. Business E-Mail: richard-wilson@utc.edu.

WILSON, ROBLEY CONANT, JR., language educator, editor, writer; b. Brunswick, Maine, June 15, 1930; s. Robley Conant and Dorothy May (Stimpson) W.; m. Charlotte A. Lehon, Aug. 20, 1955 (div. 1991); children: Stephen, Philip; m. Susan Hubbard, June 17, 1995. BA, Bowdoin Coll., 1957, D.Litt (hon.), 1987; M.F.A., U. Iowa, 1968. Reporter Raymondville Chronicle, Tex., 1950-1951; asst. publicity dir. N.Y. State Fair Syracuse, 1956; instr. Valparaiso U., Ind., 1958-63; asst. prof. English U. No. Iowa, Cedar Falls, 1963-69, assoc. prof., 1969-75, prof., 1975-2000, prof. emeritus, 2000—, editor N.Am. Rev. Cedar Falls, 1969-2000. Author: The Pleasures of Manhood, 1977, Living Alone, 1978, Dancing for Men, 1983 (Drue Heinz Lit. prize, 1982), Kingdoms of the Ordinary (Agnes Lynch Starrett award, 1986), Terrible Kisses, 1989, A Pleasure Tree, 1990 (Soc. Midland Authors Poetry award, 1990), The Victim's Daughter, 1991, A Walk Through the Human Heart, 1996, Everything Paid For, 1999, The Book of Lost Fathers, 2001, Splendid Omens, 2004, The World Still Melting, 2005, Who will Hear Your Secrets?, 2012; co-editor: 100% Pure Florida Fiction, 2000. Bd. dirs. Associated Writing Programs, Norfolk, Va., 1983-86; pres. Iowa Woman Endeavors, Inc., 1986-90. With USAF, 1951-55. Guggenheim fellow, 1983-84, Nicholl Screenwriting fellow, 1995-96. Mem.: Authors' Guild. Home: PO Box 4009 Winter Park FL 32793-4009

WILSON, RONALD LAWRENCE, former professional hockey coach, retired professional hockey player; b. Windsor, Ont., Canada, May 28, 1955; BA in Econs., Providence Coll., 1977. Defenseman Toronto Maple Leafs, 1975—80, Minn. North Stars, 1985—88; asst. coach Moncton Hawks, 1988—90, Vancouver Canucks, 1990—93; head coach Anaheim Mighty Ducks, 1993—97, Washington Capitals, 1997—2002, San Jose Sharks, 2002—08, Toronto Maple Leafs, 2008—12. Head coach Team USA, World Cup of Hockey, 1996, 2004, Team USA, Olympic Games, Nagano, Japan, 1998, Vancouver, 2010. Named to NCAA All-Am. East 1st Team, 1974—76, Providence Hall of Fame. Avocation: golf.

WILSON, SAMUEL H., biologist, researcher, former federal agency administrator; married; 2 children. AB, U. Denver, 1961; MD, Harvard U., 1968. Grad. fellow Dept. Chemistry Denver Rsch. Inst., U. Denver, 1961—62; rsch. assoc. Dept. Bacteriology and Immunology Harvard Med. Sch., 1964—66; postdoctoral fellow Dept. Biochemistry Dartmouth Med. Sch., 1967—68; rsch. assoc. Lab. Biochemical Genetics Nat. Heart Inst., NIH, 1968—70; rsch. sci. Lab. Biochemistry Nat. Cancer Inst., NIH, 1970—92, chief Nucleic Acid Enzymology Sect., 1986—92; founding dir. Sealy Ctr. Molecular Sci. U. Tex. Med. Branch, 1991—96, dir. Centennial Ctr. Environ. Toxicology, 1991—96; interim assoc. Nat. Inst. Environ. Health Scis., NIH, 1998—2000, dep. dir., 1996—2007, chief DNA repair and nucleic acid enzymology sect., Lab Structural Biology, 1996—, acting dir., 2007—09; dep. dir. Nat. Toxicology Program, 1996—2007, acting dir., 2007—09. Lectr. biochemistry George Washington U., 1975—78; prof. Dept. Human Biological Chemistry & Genetics U. Tex. Med. Branch, 1991—96, Mary G. Jones disting. chair environ. toxicology, 1994—96; spkr. in field. Editor: Eukaryotic Nucleus, 1990, Cancer Biology and Biosynthesis, 1991; co-editor: Base Excision Repair, 2001, Biomarkers of Environmentally Associated Disease: Technologies, Concepts, and Perspectives, 2002. Office: NIEHS PO Box 12233 Mail Drop B2-06 Research Triangle Park NC 27709 Office Phone: 919-541-3201. Office Fax: 919-541-3592. E-mail: wilson5@niehs.nih.gov.

WILSON, STEPHANIE D., astronaut; b. Boston, 1966; m. Julius B.J. McCurdy. BS in Engring., Harvard U., Divsn. Engring. and Applied Sciences, 1988; MS in Aerospace Engring., U. Tex., 1992. Loads and dynamic engr. astronautics group Martin Marietta, Denver, 1988—90; mem. attitude and articulation control subsystem for Galileo spacecraft Jet Propulsion Lab., Pasadena, Calif., 1992—96; astronaut NASA, Johnson Space Ctr., Houston, 1996—. Lead CAPCOM (capsule communicator) Columbia Mission, 2003; mission specialist, load master, operating robotic arm STS-121, Return-to-Flight test mission and assembly flight to Internat. Space Station, 2006; mission specialist STS-120 Discovery Mission to Internat. Space Station, 2007, STS131 Discovery Mission, 2010. Mem.: AIAA. Achievements include research in control and modeling of large, flexible space structures; second African-American women in space. Avocations: skiing, music, astronomy, stamp collecting/philately, travel. Office: Astronaut Office/CB NASA Johnson Space Ctr Houston TX 77058

WILSON, THOMAS LEON, physicist, researcher; b. Alpine, Tex., May 21, 1942; s. Homer Marvin and Ogarita Maude (Bailey) W.; m. Joyce Ann Krevosky, May 7, 1978; children: Kenneth Edward Byron, Bailey Elizabeth Victoria. BA, Rice U., 1964, BS, 1965, MA, 1974, PhD, 1976. With NASA, Houston, 1965—2011, astronaut instr., 1965-74, high-energy theoretical physicist, 1969—2012. Author 3 books; contbr. articles to profl. jours. Recipient Hugo Gernsback award, IEEE, 1964; fellow, NASA, 1969—76. Mem.: AAAS, Am. Nuc. Soc., Am. Assn. Physicists in Medicine, NY Acad. Scis., Am. Phys. Soc. Achievements include research on grand unified field theory, relativistic quantum field theory, quantum chromodynamics, quantum probability theory, supergravity, quantum cosmology, astrophysics, deep inelastic scattering, neutrino astronomy, neutrino tomography; discoverer classical uncertainity principle; subspeciality: relativity and gravitation; patentee in field; contributor to design of NASA's proposed lunar base; originator olive branch as symbol of man's 1st landing on moon (on Susan B. Anthony and Eisenhower dollars); and manual Saturn takeover for Apollo Moon program. Home: 206 Woodcombe Dr Houston TX 77062-2538 Home Phone: 281-480-2194. Personal E-mail: thomas.l.wilson@att.net. Business E-Mail: Thomas.Wilson@cern.ch.

WILSON, TROY MICHAEL (T. MICHAEL WILSON), lawyer; b. San Diego, Aug. 13, 1945; BBA, U. Tex., 1967, JD, 1969. Bar: Tex. 1969. Atty. Jackson Walker LLP, Dallas, mng. ptnr. of firm, 1992—2010, mng. ptnr. emeritus, 2010—. Fellow Tex. Bar Found. (life), Dallas Bar Found. (life); mem. Tex. Bar Assn., Dallas Bar Assn., Tex. Assn. Def. Counsel, Dallas Assn. Def. Counsel., Fedn. Def. and Corp. Counsel. Office: Jackson Walker LLP 901 Main St Ste 6000 Dallas TX 75202-3797 Office Phone: 214-953-6020. Office Fax: 214-661-6620. Business E-Mail: mwilson@jw.com.

WILSON, WALTER CLINTON, retired oil and gas industry executive; b. Brownwood, Tex., Sept. 21, 1942; s. Henry Eliga and Lottie Mae (Palmore) Wilson; m. Debra M. Thompson, Aug. 26, 1965; children: Walter Scott, Aimée Renee. BS cum laude, Howard Payne U., 1965, HHD (hon.), 2009, PhD (hon.) in Humanities, 2009. Fin. mgmt. Exxon Co. USA, Kingsville, Corpus Christi, Houston, Tex., 1965-81; asst. contr. Superior Oil Co., Houston, 1982-85, fin. cons., 1985-87; v.p. contr. EOG Resources, Inc. (formerly Enron Oil and Gas Co.), Houston, 1987-88, sr. v.p., CFO, 1988-2000; ret., 2000. Mem. adv. bd. H. S. Grace & Co., Houston, 2001—. Trustee Fin. Exec. Rsch. Found., 1998—2001; chmn. pers. com. 1st Bapt. Ch., Houston, 1985—87, chmn. deacons, 1994—96; trustee Howard Payne U., Brownwood, 1999—2008, 2010—, chmn., 2002—04; bd. dirs. Lyric Performing Arts Co., Brownwood, 2004—, chmn., 2004—. Lt. USNR, 1966—69, Vietnam. Mem.: Kingwood Country Club, Club Corp. Am.-Houston Soc. Republican.

WILSON, WILLIAM BERRY, lawyer; b. Cape Girardeau, Mo., June 17, 1947; s. Charles F. and Anita (Bartlum) Wilson; m. Suzanne T. Wilson; children: Matthew James, Sarah Talbot. BA summa cum laude, Westminster Coll., 1969; JD, U. Mich., 1972. Bar: Fla. 1972, U.S. Dist. Ct. (mid. dist.) Fla. 1972, U.S. Ct. Appeals (11th cir.) 1972, U.S. Supreme Ct. 1976, bd. cert.: Civil Trial Lawyer 1983. Ptnr. Maguire, Voorhis & Wells P.A., Orlando, Fla., 1977-98, pres., 1984-97, chmn., 1997-98; ptnr. Holland & Knight LLP, Orlando, 1998—, dir., 1999—, exec. ptnr., 2003—. Bd. dirs. SunTrust Bank Ctrl. Fla., 1990—. Bd. overseers Crummer Sch. Bus., Rollins Coll., 1994—2002; mem. Fla. Fed. Jud. Nominating Commn., 2001—; bd. dirs. Orlando Regional C. of C., 1997—2004, chmn., 2002—03; bd. dirs. Fla. Symphony, Orlando, 1983—93, Jr. Achievement, 1998—, chmn., 2007—08; bd. dirs. Fla. TaxWatch, Inc., 1992—98; trustee Orlando Mus. Art, 1993—2003, pres., 1997—99, chmn., 1999—2001; trustee U. Ctrl. Fla. Found., 1996—2004; bd. dir. Heart of Fla. United Way, 2004—, chmn., 2008—09. Mem.: Am. Arbitration Assn. (mem. panel arbitrators), Fla. Bar (mem. com. civil procedure rules 1974—77, chmn. code and rules of evidence com. 1982—92, mem. rules of jud. adminstrn. 1985—88, chmn. 1986—88, mem. exec. coun., trial lawyers sect. 1987—97, chmn. 1996), Am. Bd. Trial Advocates, Orange County Bar Assn. (mem. jud. rels. com. 1989—90, chmn. professionalism com. 1997—99, mem. civil justice commn. 1998—99), ABA, Citrus Club (bd. dirs. 1994—2002, chmn. 1998—2002), Country Club of Orlando, Rotary. Republican. Presbyterian. Avocations: tennis, scuba diving. Office: Holland & Knight LLP PO Box 1526 200 S Orange Ave Ste 2600 Orlando FL 32801-3453 Office Phone: 407-244-1115. Business E-Mail: bill.wilson@hklaw.com.

WILSON, WILLIAM J., language educator; b. Oxford, Ind., Sept. 18, 1932; s. William Woodward Wilson and Esta Ella (Burton) Dilley; m. Edith Lucille McElhaney, June 1, 1955 (dec. Mar. 1969); children: Susan Wilson Siener, Maura A., Kyle A. BS summa cum laude, Ill. State U., 1959; MA, Peabody-Vanderbilt U., Nashville, 1968; EdD, Nova U., Ft. Lauderdale, Fla., 1983. Tchr. Manteno (Ill.) High Sch., 1959-60; teaching asst. U. Ill., Urbana, 1960-61; tchr. Wheaton (Ill.) Central High Sch., 1961-67; editor Laidlaw Pubs., Chgo., 1968-69; asst. prof. Ball State U., Muncie, Ind., 1969-70; assoc. prof. English Palm Beach State Coll. (formerly Palm Beach C.C.), Lake Worth, Fla., 1970—. Test reader Ednl. Testing Svc., Princeton, N.J., 1965-96; pres. Am. Lang. Rsch. Found., Lake Worth, 1976—. Editor: New Approaches to Language and Composition, 1969; author children's mus. Winter Comes to Florida, 1974, children's mus. play A Cruise on the S.S. Eternal, 1975, Arnold's Answering Apparatus, 1976. Bd. dirs. Village Green Condominiums, Palm Springs, 1985-86. With USN, 1951-55. No. Ill. U. fellow in linguistics, DeKalb, 1965—66, humanities fellow, Peabody-Vanderbilt U., Nashville, 1967. Mem. VFW, NEA, Am. Legion, Nat. Assn. Tchrs. English., Faculty Assn. Palm Beach C.C. (pres. emeritus 1999—), Palm Beach State Lodge, Kappa Delta Pi, Sigma Tau Delta. Democrat. Episcopalian. Avocations: kairos prison ministry, sports, square dancing, travel, collecting timepieces. Home: 2100 Springdale Blvd Apt 216Y Palm Springs FL 33461-6366 Office: Palm Beach State Coll 4200 Congress Ave Lake Worth FL 33461-6366 Personal E-mail: wilson_william54@yahoo.com.

WILSON, WILLIAM PRESTON, retired psychiatrist and seminary professor; b. Fayetteville, NC, Nov. 6, 1922; s. Preston Puckett and Rosa Mae (VanHook) W.; m. Dorothy Elizabeth Taylor, Aug. 21, 1950; children: William Preston, Benjamin V., Karen E., Tammy E., Robert E. BS, Duke U., 1943, MD, 1947; DD, Carolina Grad. Sch. Div., Greensboro, NC, 2012. Diplomate Am. Bd. Psychiatry and Neurology (examiner). Intern Gorgas Hosp., Ancon, Panama; from resident psychiatry to prof. emeritus Duke U. Med. Ctr., Durham, NC, emeritus prof. psychiatry, 1985—; assoc. prof. psychiatry, dir. psychiat. rsch. U. Tex. Med. Br., Galveston, 1958-60; dir. Inst. Christian Growth, Durham, NC, 1985—; dist. prof. counseling Carolina Grad. Sch. Divinity, Greenshore, NC, 1996—2007; ret., 2007. Chief neurophysiol. labs. VA Hosp., Durham, N.C., 1961-76; sec. Am. Bd. Qualification in Electroencephalography, 1971-77; mem. N.C. Gov.'s Task force on Diagnosis and Treatment; mem. med. adv. com. N.C. Found. Mental Health Rsch.; bd. dirs. nat. divsn. Contact Teleminstry USA, also mem. internat. commn. healing; cons. numerous area hosps.; Finch lectr. Fuller Theol. Sem., Pasadena, Calif., 1974; vis. prof. psychiatry Marshall U. Sch. Medicine, Huntington, W.Va., 1985-89. Author: The Nuts and Bolts of discipleship; co-author: The Grace to Grow; editor: Applications of Electroencephalography in Psychiatry; co-editor: EEG and Evoked Potentials in Psychiatry and Behavioral Neurology; contbr. articles to med. jours.; contbr. articles to 166 sci. and religious jours. Mem. ofcl. bd. Asbury United Meth. Ch., Durham; mem. program and curriculum com. United Meth. Ch., 1973-81; trustee Meth. Retirement Home, Durham; pres. United Meth. Renewal Svcs., Inc., 1978-82; scout master BSA. Served with AUS, 1943-46. Recipient Ephraim McDowell award Christian Med. Found., 1982, Pioneer in Christian Psychiatry award Congress on Christian Counseling, 1988; named Educator of Yr., Christian Med. and Dental Assn., 1996, Pres. Heritage award, 2011; EEG Montreal Neurol. Inst. fellow, 1954-55, postdoctoral fellow NIMH. Mem. Am. Psychiat. Assn., So. Psychiat. Assn. (pres. 1977-78), AMA, So. Med. Assn. (chmn. sect. neurology and psychiatry 1970), Med. Soc. N.C., Durham-Orange County Med. Soc. (chmn. student recruitment com. 1965), Soc. Biol. Psychiatry, Am. EEG Soc. (councillor), So. EEG Soc. (pres. 1964), Assn. Rsch. Nervous and Mental Diseases, Am. Epilepsy Soc., AAAS, Am. Acad. Neurology, Sigma Xi, Alpha Omega Alpha, U.S. Power Squadron Club (comdr. Durham 1971), AACC Republican. Methodist. Avocations: fishing, sailing, gardening, camping, hiking, travel. Personal E-mail: williamwilson622@gmail.com.

WILSON, WILLIAM ROY, JR., federal judge; b. Little Rock, 1939; Student, U. Ark., 1957—58; BA, Hendrix Coll., 1962; JD, Vanderbilt U., 1965. Atty. Autrey & Goodson, Texarkana, Ark., 1965-66, Wright, Lindsey & Jennings, Little Rock, 1969-72, Wilson & Hodge, Little Rock, 1972-74; prin. William R. Wilson Jr., P.A., Little Rock, 1974-80, Wilson & Engstrom, Little Rock, 1980-83, Wilson, Engstrom & Vowell, Little Rock, 1984, Wilson, Engstrom, Corum & Dudley, Little Rock, 1984-93; judge US Dist. Ct. (ea. dist.) Ark., Little Rock, 1993—2008, sr. judge, 2008—. Chair Ark. Supreme Ct. Com. on Model Criminal Jury Instrns., 1978—; active Ark. Supreme Ct. Com. on Civil Practice, 1982—. Lt. USN, 1966-69. Named Disting. Alumnus, Hendrix Coll., 1993, Outstanding Lawyer, Pulaski County Bar Assn., 1993. Mem. ABA, ATLA, American Bd. Trial Advocates (Nat. Civil Justice award 1992), American Coll. Trial Lawyers, Internat. Acad. Trial Lawyers, Internat. Soc. Barristers, Ark. Bar Assn. (Outstanding Lawyer 1991), S.W. Ark. Bar Assn., Ark. Trial Lawyers Assn. (pres. 1982, Outstanding Trial Lawyer 1988-89), Pulaski County Bar Assn. (Outstanding Lawyer 1993). Office: US Dist Ct Ea Dist Ark 500 W Capitol Ave Ste 423 Little Rock AR 72201-3320

WILSON-MCELREATH, VICKI W. (VICKI W. MCELREATH), board member, retired accountant; BSBA, Ga. State U. Acct. Price-Waterhouse Coopers LLP, Savannah, Ga., 1979—90; ptnr., audit practice PriceWaterhouseCoopers LLP, Savannah, Ga., 1990—99, mng. ptnr. Carolinas, 1999—2006. Bd. dirs. RBC Bank, 2006—, Piedmont Natural Gas Co., 2006—. Mem. bus. adv. coun. Univ. NC, Charlotte; mem. president's com. on efficiency & effectiveness Univ. NC Sys.; mem. Inst. Social Capital. Named Charlotte Bus. Woman of the Yr. award, 2001, Women in Bus. Achievement award, 2000. Office: Piedmont Natural Gas Co Bd Directors 4720 Piedmont Row Dr Charlotte NC 28233 Office Phone: 704-364-3120. Office Fax: 704-365-3849. Business E-Mail: vicki.wilson-mcElreath@piedmontng.com.

WIMAN, THOMAS M., healthcare services company executive; Cert. FACHE. Exec. dir. Rankin Med. Ctr., Brandon; joined Health Management Associates, Inc., 1997, dir., hosp. and physician svcs. Jackson, regional v.p. Miss., 2004—. Mem., selection com. HCC Sports Hall of Fame; mem. HCC Devel. Found., HCC Athletic Alumni Chpt. Recipient Alumnus of the Yr., Hinds Cmty. Coll. (HCC), 2003. Office: Health Management Associates Inc 5811 Pelican Bay Blvd Ste 500 Naples FL 34108-2710 Office Phone: 239-598-3131. Office Fax: 239-598-2705. Business E-Mail: Thomas.Wiman@hma.com.

WIMBERLY, KENNETH W., air transportation executive, corporate financial executive; b. Lake Charles, La. BA, Tulane U., 1986, grad., 1989. Assoc. Fulbright & Jaworski LLP, Gardere Wynne Sewell LLP; atty., legal dept. Am. Airlines, Inc. (subs. of AMR Corp.), 1995—2000, sr. atty., 2000—01, asst. corp. sec., 2001—06; corp. sec. American Airlines, Inc., 2006—; asst. corp. sec. AMR Training Group, Inc. (subs. of AMR Corp.), 2001—06, corp. sec., 2006—; asst. corp. sec. AMR Corp., 2001—06, corp. sec., 2006—. Office: AMR Corp 4333 Amon Carter Blvd Fort Worth TX 76155 Office Phone: 817-963-1234. Office Fax: 817-967-4162. Business E-Mail: Kenneth.Wimberly@aa.com.

WIMPRESS, GORDON DUNCAN, JR., management consultant, foundation administrator; b. Riverside, Calif., Apr. 10, 1922; s. Gordon Duncan and Maude A. (Waldo) Wimpress; m. Jean Margaret Skerry, Nov. 30, 1946; children: Wendy Jo, Victoria Jean, Gordon Duncan III. BA, U. Oreg., 1946, MA, 1951; PhD, U. Denver, 1958; LLD (hon.), Monmouth Coll., Ill., 1970; LHD (hon.), Tusculum Coll., Greenville, Tenn., 1971. Lic. comml. pilot. Dir. pub. rels., instr. journalism Whittier Coll., Calif., 1946-51; asst. to pres. Colo. Sch. Mines, Golden, 1951-59; pres. Monticello Coll., Alton, Ill., 1959-64, Monmouth Coll., Ill., 1964-70, Trinity U., San Antonio, 1970-77; vice chmn. S.W. Found. Biomed. Rsch., San Antonio, 1977-82, pres., 1982-92, also bd. govs.; pres. Duncan Wimpress & Assocs., Inc., San Antonio, 1992—. Chmn. scholarship commn. Valero Energy Corp.; bd. dirs. SW Rsch. Inst. Author: American Journalism Comes of Age, 1950. Mem. adv. bd. Alamo Area chpt. Am. Diabetes Assn.; ruling elder United Presbyn. Ch., U.S.A.; bd. dirs. ARC, Am. Heart Assn.; trustee San Antonio Med. Found. 1st lt. US Army, 1942—45, ETO. Decorated Bronze Star Vator. Mem.: Pilots Internat. Assn., Nat. Pilots Assn., Am. Assn. Higher Edn., Am. Acad. Polit. and Social Sci., Newcomen Soc. N.Am., North San Antonio C. of C., Mensa, Greater San Antonio C. of C., Assn. Former Intelligence Officers, Confederate Air Force, Aircraft Owners and Pilots Assn., San Antonio Golf Assn., Ptz. Club, Argyle Club, Rotary (dist. gov. San Antonio club 1983—84), Quiet Birdmen, Sigma Upsilon, Sigma Phi Epsilon (trustee found.), Sigma Delta Pi, Sigma Delta Chi, Pi Gamma Mu. Presbyterian. Avocations: golf, skiing, flying. Home and Office: 455 Pecan Way San Antonio TX 78240 Personal E-mail: dwimpress@satx.rr.com.

WINANS, BEBE (BENJAMIN WINANS), gospel and R&B vocalist; b. Sept. 17, 1962; Host BeBe Winans Radio Show; host, Sirius XM Radio Show The BeBe Experience. Performer: (Broadway plays) The Color Purple, (films) The Manchurian Candidate, 2003; judge Sunday Best, BET; co-prodr.: (song for Motion Picture The Bodyguard) Jesus Loves Me; singer: (solo albums) BeBe Winans, 1997, Love & Freedom, 2000, Live and Up Close, 2002, My Christmas Prayer, 2003, Dream, 2004, Cherch, 2007, America America, 2012, (albums with CeCe Winans) Lord Lift Us Up, 1984, BeBe & CeCe Winans, 1987, Heaven, 1988 (with CeCe Winans) Dove award for Pop/Contemporary Album of Yr., 1990, (with CeCe Winans) Dove award for Pop/Contemporary Gospel Recorded Song of the Yr.-Heaven, 1990, (with CeCe Winans) Soul Train award for Best Gospel Album, 1990, (with CeCe Winans) Stellar award for Album of the Year-Contemporary, 1990, (with CeCe Winans) Stellar award for Song of the Year-Contemporary, 1990), Different Lifestyles, 1991 (Best Contemporary Soul Gospel Album, 1991, (with CeCe Winans) Soul Train award for Best Gospel Album, 1992), First Christmas, 1993, Relationships, 1994, BeBe and CeCe Winans Greatest Hits, 1996, Count on Me, 1996, The Best of BeBe and CeCe, 2006, Still, 2009, (songs) All of Me, 1996, In Harm's Way, 1997, Thank You, 1997, Stay, 1997, Coming Back Home, 2000, Jesus Children of America, 2000, Tonight Tonight, 2000, Do You Know Him, 2002, I Have A Dream, 2005, Safe From Harm, 2005, Love Me Anyway, 2005; author: The Whitney I Knew, 2012. Recipient Grammy award for Best Soul Gospel Performance, Male-Abundant Life, 1988, Grammy award for Best Gospel Vocal Performance-Male-Meantime, 1989, Grammy award-Album of Yr.-The Bodyguard, 1993, Stellar award for Best New Gospel Artist, 1988, Stellar award for Best Inspirational Gospel Performance, 1990, Three NAACP awards, (with CeCe Winans) Star on Hollywood Walk of Fame; co-recipient (with CeCe Winans) Dove award-New Artist of Yr., 1988, (with CeCe Winans) Dove award-Group of the Yr., 1990, (with CeCe Winans) Dove award-Contemporary Gospel Recorded Song of the Yr.-With My Whole Heart, 1990, (with CeCe Winans) Dove award-Group of Yr., 1992, (with CeCe Winans) Dove award-Contemporary Gospel Recorded Song of the Yr.-Addictive Love, 1992, (with CeCe Winas) Dove award for Contemporary Gospel Recorded Song of the Yr.-Up Where We Belong, 1998, (with CeCe Winas) Stellar award for Best Performance by Group or Duo, 1990. Address: My Destiny Productions Attn: Toni Noble PO Box 1976 Brentwood TN 37024-1976

WINANS, CECE, gospel vocalist; b. Detroit, Oct. 8, 1964; d. David and Delores; m. Alvin Love; children: Ashley, Alvin III. Albums: (with Bebe Winans) Lord Lift Us Up, 1985, Bebe and Cece Winans, 1987, Heaven, 1988 (Dove award Pop/Contemporary Album, 1990, Dove award Pop/Contemporary Recorded Song-Heaven, 1990, Soul Train award for Best Gospel Album, 1990), Different Lifestyles, 1991 (Grammy award for Best Contemporary Soul Gospel Album, 1991, Soul Train for Best Gospel Album, 1992), First Christmas, 1993, Relationships, 1994, Bebe & Cece Winans Greatest Hits, 1996, Count on Me, 1996, The Best of Bebe & Cece Winans, 2006, Still, 2009; (solo albums) For Always (1987 Grammy award for Best Female Gospel Performance), Don't Cry (Grammy award for Best Female Gospel Vocal Performance, 1989), Alone In His Presence, 1995 (Grammy award for Best Soul Gospel Album, 1995), Everlasting Love, 1998, His Gift, 1998(Best Gospel Album, 1999), Alabaster Box, 1999 (Dove award for Contemporary Gospel Recorded Song-Alabaster Box, 2001), CeCe Winans, 2001(Grammy award for Best Pop/Contemporary Gospel Album, 2001, Dove award for Contemporary Gospel Album, 2002), Throne Room, 2003, Purified, 2005 (2 Grammy awards), Thy Kingdom Come, 2008 (Grammy award for Best Pop/Contemporary Gospel Album, 2008, Contemporary Female Artist of the Yr, 2009), Songs of Emotional Healing, 2010, For Always: The Best of Cece Winans, 2010; other albums The Born Again Church Choir, 2003, Kingdom Kidz, 2007, Pure Worship, 2008,; actress: (films) White Men Can't Jump, 1992, Waiting to Exhale, 1995, The Prince of Egypt, 1998; (TV appearances) Sesame Street, Martin, Living Single, Touched By an Angel, 7th Heaven, All My Children, Christmas in Washington, Nat. Meml. Day Concert; host (TV program) Cece's Place, (radio program) On A Positive Note; author: Feel the Spirit, 1998, On A Positive Note, 2000, Throne Room: Ushered Into the Presence of God, 2004; co-author Always Sisters: becoming the Princess You Were Created to Be, 2007; featured on the covers of Essence, Jet, Women's World, Black Enterprise, Aspire, Los Angeles Times Magazine, Charisma, Planet, CCM and Today's Christian Woman and others; guest appearances on the following talk-shows The Today Show, Early Show, CNN-Showbiz Today, BET, Good Day New York, Oxygen Network, Lifetime Live, Bloomberg TV, Rosie, Entertainment Tonight, Good Morning America, Oprah, Live with Regis & Kathie Lee and others. Recipient Grammy award for Best Pop Contemporary Gospel Album, Andrae Crouch (Various Artists), 1996, NAACP Image awards, Stellar award-Chevrolet Most Notable Achievement award, 2007, Lifetime Achievement award-Trumpet honoree, 2007; Dove awards include: New Artist of the Yr., BeBe and CeCe, 1988, Group of the Yr. BeBe and CeCe, 1990, Contemporary Gospel Recorded Song -With My Whole Heart (with BeBe), 1990, Group of the Yr. BeBe and CeCe Winans, 1992, Contemporary Gospel Recorded Song-Addictive Love (with BeBe), 1992, Praise and Worship Album-Coram Deo II (Various Artists), 1995, Female Vocalist of Yr., 1996, Traditional Gospel Recorded Song-Great is Thy Faithfulness (with mother), 1996, Female Vocalist of Yr., 1997, Contemporary Gospel Recorded Song-Take Me Back, 1997, Special Event Album-Tribute: The Songs of Andrae Church (Various Artists), 1997, Special Event Album-God With Us: A Celebration of Christmas Carols (Various Artists), 1998, Contemporary Gospel Recorded Song-Anybody Wanna Play?, 2002, Traditional Gospel Album of the Yr.-CeCe Winans Presents: The Born Again Choir, 2004, Contemporary Gospel Recorded Song of the Yr.-Hallelujah Praise, 2004, Urban Recorded Song of the Yr.-Close to You (with BeBe), 2010; honored with Star on Hollywood Walk of Fame with BeBe Winans Office: CeCe Winans Ste 300-377 115 Penn Warren Dr Brentwood TN 37027

WINBORNE, RAYMOND E., corporate financial executive; BSBA, Troy U., 1990. Sr. mgr., audit PricewaterhouseCoopers, 1990—99; v.p., contr. & chief acctg. officer BellSouth Corp. (acquired by AT&T), 1999—2007; sr. v.p., CFO, Southeast Region AT&T Inc. (merger of SBC Communications & AT&T Corp.), 2007; v.p., fin., chief acctg. officer Delta Air Lines, Inc., 2007—08, sr. v.p., fin., contr., 2008—09; sr. v.p., contr. First Data Corp., 2009—10, CFO, 2010—. Pres. Mortar Bd., Sigma Alpha Eplison Fraternity. Office: First Data Corp 5565 Glenridge Connector NE Ste 2000 Atlanta GA 30342 Office Phone: 303-967-8000. Office Fax: 303-967-7000. Business E-Mail: Raymond.Winborne@firstdata.com.

WINCHESTER, JAMES R., state supreme court justice; b. Clinton, Okla., Mar. 23, 1952; m. Susan Winchester; 1 child, Davis. BA, U. Okla.; JD, Okla. City U. Pvt. practice, Weatherford, Okla., Hinton, Okla.; assoc. dist. judge Caddo County, Okla., 1983; dist. judge 6th Jud. Dist. Okla., 1983—97; U.S. adminstrv. law judge, 1997—2000; justice Okla. Supreme Ct., 2000—, vice chief justice, 2005—06, chief justice, 2007—08. Mem. exec. bd. Okla. Jud. Conf., 1992—96, pres., 1995. Named Outstanding State Trial Ct. Judge, Okla. Trial Lawyers Assn., 1986. Office: Oklahoma Supreme Ct Admin Office 2100 N Lincoln Blvd Ste 3 Oklahoma City OK 73105-4923*

WINDHAM, JOHN FRANKLIN, lawyer, educator; b. Fayette, Ala., Jan. 21, 1948; s. Grover B. Windham Jr. and Nancy Katherine (McAdams) Haynie; 1 child, John Franklin Jr.; m. Denise Roche McNair, Apr. 6, 1999; 1 stepchild, Brittany Danielle McNair. BA, U. West Fla., 1970; JD, U. N.C., 1975. Bar: Fla. 1975, U.S. Dist. Ct. (no. dist.) Fla. 1976, U.S. Ct. Appeals (11th cir.) 1983, U.S. Supreme Ct. 1984. Acctg. supr. Monsanto Co., Research Triangle Park, N.C., 1970-72; law clk. to U.S. Atty Pensacola, Fla., 1974; assoc. Beggs & Lane, Pensacola, 1975-79, ptnr., 1979—. Adj. asst. prof. bus. law Troy State U., Pensacola, 1983-90. Mem. bd. dirs. Am. Cancer Soc., 1980-06, exec. com. Fla. divsn., 1982-93, 95-2000, chmn. legacies and planned giving, 1984-88, chmn. income devel., 1980-91, chmn. ad hoc adv. com., 1991-05, mem. risk adv. subcom., 1991-97, chmn. 1996-97, legal advisor, 1992—, vol. and staff devel. com., 1994-95, planning com., 1994-98, spokesperson tobacco media, 1995-96, mem. cause mktg. work group, 1995-96, mem. scholarship com., 1995-98, chmn. dist. VII steering com., 1995-96, v.p, 1996-97, mem. Winn Dixie adv. com., 1996-99, field ops. com. 1995-98, chmn. field ops. com., 1996-98, mem. task force volunteerism, 1996-97, call ctr. work group, 1996-98, mktg. and comms. com., 1997-2000, divsn. chartering com., 1997-98, chmn.-elect bd. 1997-98, chmn. bd. 1998-99, personnel subcom., 1998-99, patient svc. ctr. work group, 1998-99, audit com., 1999-00, nominating com., 1999—, evaluation adv. com., 2001-03, 05—08, bylaws com. chmn., 1990-96, triple 5 ad hoc com., 1995-95, cancer control com., 1994-96, stewardship com., 1996-02; mem. Nat. Assembly, 2002—, mem. budget and fin. com., nom. ad hoc com., bd. governance task force, 1990—2004, chmn. bylaws com., 2002—, stewardship com., 2006—, bd. governance com. 07-; chmn. bd. Escambia Christian Sch., Pensacola, 1976-86; deacon Ch. of Christ, 1985-95, 99-02; adminstrv. team First City Ch., 2002-04, mem. adv. bd.; elder First City Ch., 2004—; mem. adv. bd. Interim Healthcare, 1993-96, Panhandle Rehab. Injury Mgmt. and Evaluation, 1993-96; mem. found. bd. East Hill Christian Sch., 1995-97; bd. govs. Pensacola chpt. Order Granaderos e Dames de Galvez, 1990-98, pres. 1995-98; mem. U. West Fla. Found., 1983-85. Mem. Fla. Bar (workers compensation rules com. 1995-01, drafting subcom. 2000-01), Fla. Def. Lawyers Assn., Fla. Workers Compensation Inst., Southeastern Admiralty Law Inst. (bd. dirs. 1986-89), Northwest Fla. Blood Ctr. Found. (treas. 2002-04, pres. 2006-08), N.W. Fla. Blood Ctr. (bd. dirs. 2006—08), Fla. Blood Svc. (bd. dirs. 2008-), Northwest. Fla. Blood Svcs. Found. (pres. 2008-), U. West Fla. Nat. Alumni Assn. (bd. dirs.), Kiwanis (pres. Pensacola 1978-79, 88-89). Republican. Avocation: church activities. Office: Beggs & Lane PO Box 12950 Pensacola FL 32591-2950

WINDLE, JOHN MARK, state legislator; b. May 21, 1962; Atty.; mem. Dist. 41 Tenn. House of Reps., 1991—. Democrat. Christian. Mailing: PO Box 707 Livingston TN 38570 Office: 108 War Memorial Bldg Nashville TN 37243-0141 Office Phone: 615-741-1260, 931-823-3970. Business E-Mail: rep.john.windle@capitol.tn.gov.

WINEMILLER, ALBERT E., information technology executive; m. Debra Winemiller. BS in Math. & Stats., MS in Math. & Stats., U. Mo.; MBA in Fin., Harvard U. Sys. engr., software developer IBM Corp.; sr. v.p. Automatic Data Processing; pres., CEO InfoUSA (formerly Am. Bus. Info. Inc.), 1993—96, Rsch. Ltd., 1996—97; pres. Albert Winemiller, Inc.; pres., CEO Pros Holdings, Inc., 1999—, chmn., 2000—; pres., CEO, chmn. Pros Revenue Mgmt. Inc.; CEO, chmn. Pros Pricing Solutions. Former bd. dirs. Ultralink LLC; bd. dirs. Newgen Results Corp., 1997, eIntelligence Inc. Pres. strategic adv. bd. U. Mo. Office: Pros Holdings Inc 3100 Main St Ste 900 Houston TX 77002 Office Phone: 713-335-5151. Office Fax: 713-335-8144. Business E-Mail: awinemiller@prosrm.com.

WINER, WARD OTIS, mechanical engineer, educator; b. Grand Rapids, Mich., June 27, 1936; s. Mervin Augustus and Ina Katherine (Wood) W.; m. Mary Jo Wielinga, June 15, 1957; children: Mathew Owen, James Edward, Paul Andrew, Mary Margaret. Asso., Grand Rapids Jr. Coll., Mich., 1956; BS, U. Mich., Ann Arbor, 1958; MS, U. Mich., 1959, PhD, 1962; PhD (Cavendish Lab. fellow), Cambridge U., Eng., 1964. Asst. prof. dept. mech. engring. U. Mich., Ann Arbor, 1963-66, assoc. prof., 1966-69; assoc. prof. mech. engring. Ga. Inst. Tech., 1969-71, prof., 1971-84, regents' prof., 1984—2007, mem. exec. bd., 1983-88, chmn., 1984-86, dir. and chmn. Sch. Mech. Engring., 1988—2007, Eugene C. Gwaltney jr. chair George W. Woodruff Sch. Mech. Engring., 2001—07, Eugene C. Gwaltney jr. sch. chair emeritus, 2007—; interim chair Sch. Civil & Environ. Engring., 2011—12. Chmn. Gordon Research Conf. on Friction, Lubrication and Wear, 1980; mem. NRC, 1980-88; chmn. Com. on Recommendations for U.S. Army Basic Sci. Research, 1985-87; chair, Engring. Applied Sci. and Math. Pannel NRC Assoc. Program, 2007-; mem. div. mech., structural, materials engring. adv. bd. NSF Engring. Directorate, 1984-89; bd. dirs. Taiho Tribology Rsch. Found. Co-editor: Wear Control Handbook, 1980; tech. editor: Jour. Lubrication Tech., 1980-84, Jour. of Tribology, 1984-87; contbr. articles to profl. jours. Democratic precinct chmn., 1967-68; Mem. exec. bd. Horace H. Rackham Sch. Grad. Studies, U. Mich., 1968. Recipient Disting. Faculty Svc. award Coll. Engring. U. Mich., 1967, Alumni Merit award, 1998, Cert. Recognition, NASA, 1977, Clarence E. Earle Meml. award Nat. Grease Lubricating Inst., 1979, Disting. Prof. award Ga. Inst. Tech., 1987; named Hon. Alumni, Ga. Tech., 2003. Fellow: AAAS, ASME (hon.; bd. comms. 1987-91, v.p. rsch. 1989-93, found. trustee 2006-, vice chair, 2009-11, chair 2011-13, bd. dir., Melville medal 1975, Centennial medallion 1980, Mayor D. Hersey award 1986, Charles Russ Richards Meml. award 1988), Soc. Tribologists and Lubrication Engrs. (bd. dirs. 1983-86, Internat. award 1997), Brit. Tribology Trust (gold medal 1987), Am. Soc. Engring. Educators (Benjamin Garver Lamme award 1995, Donald Marlowe award 1996); mem. NAE, Metro Atlanta Engring. Soc. (Engr. of Yr. 1989), Rheology, Soc. Engring. Sci. (dir. 1980-84), AAUP (pres. Ga. Tech. chpt. 1972-74, v.p. state conf. 1973-75), Sigma Xi (chpt. pres. 1982-83, Sustained Rsch. in Engring. award 1975), Tau Beta Pi, Pi Tau Sigma, Phi Kappa Phi. Home: 1025 Mountain Creek Trl NW Atlanta GA 30328-3535 Business E-Mail: ward.winer@me.gatech.edu.

WINES, LYNNE, bank executive; BS in Bus. Adminstrn., Nova Southeastern U., 1989. Pres., CEO Union Bank Fin. Corp., Sunrise, Fla., 1986—2005; pres., CEO, comml. banking, South Fla. Colonial Bank NA, mem., exec. mgmt. team, 2004; CEO, South Fla. divsn. CNL Bank, 2008—09, pres., COO, 2008—10; pres. First Southern Bank, Boca Raton, Fla., 2010—12, pres., CEO, 2012—. Bd. mem. Fla. Bankers Assn.; bd. dirs. Eras JV LLP, ERAS Diebold, LLC, Union Bank Of Fla. Chair United Way Broward County. Recipient Diamond CEO & Bus. Woman of the Yr. award, South Fla. Bus. Journal; named Bus. Women of Yr., South Fla. Bus. Jour., 2002; named one of The Top 25 Women to Watch, US Banker mag., 2004. Office: First Southern Bank 900 North Federal Highway Boca Raton FL 33432 Office Phone: 561-479-2100. Office Fax: 561-338-6445.

WINESKI, LAWRENCE E., medical educator, biomedical researcher; b. Fort Dix, NJ, June 29, 1949; s. Max E. and Irene R. Wineski; m. Lynn E. Comerford, Aug. 16, 1980; children: Matthew C., Benjamin C. BA, Calif. State U., Fullerton, 1972; MA, San Francisco State U., 1978; PhD, U. of Ill., Chgo., 1981. Sci. officer State U. of Groningen, Netherlands, 1980—81; postdoctoral scholar U. Mich., Ann Arbor, 1981—82; rsch. assoc. U. Ill., Chgo., 1982—83; asst. prof., assoc. prof. Morehouse Sch. Medicine, Atlanta, 1983—. Vis. prof. Emory U. Sch. Medicine, Atlanta, 1999—2000; mem. anatomy adv. bd. Lippincott Williams & Wilkins Publishers, Balt., 2005—; reviewer in field. Author: (educational CD-ROMs) TIPS/Temporal Infratemporal and Pteygopalatine Study Guide, 2002, Introduction to the Face and Scalp, 2005, Introduction to Dissection, 2006; contbr. scientific papers to profl. jours., chapters to books. Grantee Rsch. Grants, NIH, 1986—98, NASA, 1995—2005. Mem.: Am. Soc. Mammalogists, Anatomical Bd. Ga., Am. Assn. Advancement Sci., Am. Assn. Clinical Anatomists, Am. Assn. Anatomists, Soc. for Neuroscience; Soc. for Integrative and Comparative Biology. Avocations: soccer, travel. Office: Morehouse Sch of Medicine 720 Westview Dr SW Atlanta GA 30310-1495 Business E-Mail: lwineski@msm.edu.

WINFIELD, JOHN BUCKNER, rheumatologist, educator; b. Kentfield, Calif., Mar. 19, 1942; s. R. Buckner and Margaret G. (Katterfelt) Winfield; m. Patricia Nichols (div. 1968); 1 child, Ann Gibson; m. Teresa Lee McGrath, 1969 (div. 2000); children: John Buckner III, Virginia Lee; m. Leigh Fleming Callahan, 2001. BA, Williams Coll., 1964; MD, Cornell U., 1968. Diplomate Am. Bd. Internal Medicine. Intern in medicine N.Y. Hosp., NYC, 1968-69; staff assoc. LI/Nat. Inst. Allergy and Infectious Diseases NIH, Bethesda, Md., 1969-71; resident in medicine, fellow in rheumatology U. Va. Sch. Medicine, Charlottesville, 1971-73; fellow in immunology Rockefeller U., NYC, 1973-75; asst. prof. medicine U. Va. Sch. Medicine, Charlottesville, 1975-76, assoc. prof. medicine, 1976-78, U. N.C., Chapel Hill, 1978-81, prof. medicine, 1981—2006, chief div. rheumatology and immunology, 1978-99; dir. Thurston Arthritis Rsch. Ctr., U. N.C. Sch. Medicine, Chapel Hill, 1982—2001; dir Daughtridge Arthritis Ctr., Lenoir, NC, 2002—07; consulting rheumatologist Appalachian Regional Rheumatology, 2007—; Smith prof. medicine U. NC Sch. Med., Chapel Hill, 1987—2006, emeritus, 2006—, adj. prof. exercise sports physiology, 2003—; adj. prof. endodontics Neurosensory Disorders Ctr., UNC Sch. Dentistry, sr. mem.; owner Winfield Medical, L.L.C., 2004—. Adv. coun. Nat. Inst. Arthritis and Musculoskeletal and Skin Diseases, NIH, 1988-92; chmn. edn. com. Am. Rheumatism Assn., Atlanta, 1980-84; immunol. scis. study sect. NIH, 1979-83, Arthritis Musculoskeletal and Skin study sect., 1992-96; vice-chair fellowship com. Arthritis Found., 1982; med. coun. Lupus Found. Am., 1987-96. Author more than 150 med. and sci. articles in peer reviewed rheumatology and immunology jours.; mem. editl. bd. Arthritis and Rheumatism, Bull. Rheumatic Diseases, Rheumatology Internat., Clin. Exptl. Rheumatology, Am. Jour. Medicine, Clin. Immunology, Current Rev. Rheumatology. Sr. asst. surgeon with USPHS, NIH, Bethesda, Md., 1968-71. Recipient Borden prize Cornell U. Med. Coll., 1964, numerous rsch. grants NIH and Arthritis Found., 1975—, Sr. Investigator award Arthritis Found., 1976-79, Kenan award U. NC, 1985, NIH merit award, 1992. Fellow ACP; mem. Am. Assn. Immunologists, Am. Fedn. Clin. Rsch., Am. Soc. Clin. Investigation, Assn. Am. Physicians, Am. Clin. Climatol. Assn., Nat. Soc. Clin. Rheumatologists (treas. 1997-02), Henry Kunkel Soc. (councilor 2000-02), Chapel Hill Country Club; master, Am. Coll. Rheumatology. Democrat. Episcopalian. Avocations: golf, on and off-road motorcycling, scuba diving instructor, skiing. Home: 102 Greenwood Ln Chapel Hill NC 27514-5957 Business E-Mail: john_winfield@med.unc.edu.

WINFIELD, RICHARD DIEN, humanities educator; b. NYC, Apr. 7, 1950; s. Sidney Lincoln and Lillian Winfield; m. Sujata Gupta, Apr. 28, 1983; children: Kalindi, Manas Samuel, Rasik Sidd. BA in Philosophy, Yale Coll., New Haven, Conn., 1972; MA in Philosophy, U. Heidelberg, Germany, 1973; PhD in Philosophy, Yale U., New Haven, Conn., 1977. Asst. prof. U. Ga., Athens, 1982—87, assoc. prof., 1987—93, prof., 1993—2001, disting. rsch. prof., 2001—. Author: (books) Reason and Justice, 1988, The Just Economy, 1988, Overcoming Foundations: Studies in Systematic Philosophy, 1989, Freedom and Modernity, 1991, Law in Civil Society, 1995, Systematic Aesthetics, 1995, Stylistics: Rethinking the Artforms After Hegel, 1996, The Just Family, 1998, Autonomy and Normativity: Investigations of Truth, Right, and Beauty, 2001, The Just State: Rethinking Self-Government, 2005, From Concept to Objectivity: Thinking Through Hegel's Subjective Logic, 2006, Modernity, Religion, and the War on Terror, 2007. Mem.: Soc. Systematic Philosophy (pres. 1986—), Hegel Soc. Am. (pres. 2002—04). Office: Univ Ga Dept Philosophy 103 Peabody Hall Athens GA 30602-1627 Business E-Mail: winfield@uga.edu.

WINFREY, JOHN CRAWFORD, economist, educator; b. Somerville, Tenn., July 2, 1935; s. Arthur Peter and Frances (Crawford) W.; m. Barbara Ann Strickland, July 20, 1957; 1 child, Mae Millicent. AB, Davidson Coll., 1957; PhD, Duke U., 1965. Asst. dir. data processing Hanes Hosiery, Winston Salem, NC, 1959-62; rsch. asst. in econs. Duke U., Durham, NC, 1963-64; asst. prof. econs. Washington and Lee U., Lexington, Va., 1965-68, assoc. prof., 1969-73, prof., 1974—. Vis. prof. Vanderbilt U., Nashville, 1966, Tufts U., Boston, 1975, UCLA, 1978, U. Ill., 1982, U. Va., 1986, Duke U., 1989, 95, U. Calif., Berkeley, 1993, U. Utrecht, Netherlands, 1995; adj. prof. Southern Va. U., 2009. Co-author: The Motion Commotion, 1972; author: Public Finance, Public Choice and the Public Sector, 1973, Social Issues, The Ethics and Economics of Taxes and Public Programs, 1997. Bd. dirs. Lexington Tennis Clinic, 1968-72, Rockbridge Area Conservation Coun., 1982-84, Rockbridge Area Social Svc., 2002—, Lexington Family Mentoring Program; mem. Rockbridge Area Behavioral Health Adv. Bd., 2001—, Nelson Fine Art Gallery, Lexington, Va.; pres. Rockbridge Arts Guild, 1986-88, 2001-02. Recipient Cmty. Svc. award Lexington Jaycees, 1971; NEH fellow, 1975, 78, 82, 86, 89, 93; vis. fellow U. Coll. Oxford U., Eng., 1979, 95. Fellow Soc. for Values in Higher Edn.; mem. Am. Econ. Assn., So. Econ. Assn., History of Econs. Soc., Eastern Econ. Assn., High Wheelers Club (Lexington), Sunrise Rotary Club. Democrat. Presbyterian. Home: 160 Kendal Dr #1035 Lexington VA 24450 Office: Washington and Lee U Dept Econs Lexington VA 24450 Business E-Mail: winfreyj@wlu.edu.

WINFREY, TIMOTHY J., manufacturing executive; Various project mgmt. positions Brit. Petroleum, 1990—94; mgr. strategic planning, assoc. dir. corp. devel. Eaton Corp., 1995—96; dir. corp. devel., gen. mgr. joint ventures and svcs. bus. Owens Corning, Inc., 1996—99; v.p., gen. mgr. reciprocating compressor divsn. Ingersoll Rand Co., 1999—2001, pres. comml. and retail air solutions bus., 2001—02; group v.p. energy sys. and controls Roper Industries, Inc., 2002—. Office: Roper Industries Inc Ste 200 6901 Professional Pky E Sarasota FL 34240 Office Phone: 941-556-2601. Office Fax: 941-556-2670.

WING, ELIZABETH SCHWARZ, museum curator, educator; b. Cambridge, Mass., Mar. 5, 1932; d. Henry F. and Maria Lisa Schwarz; m. James E. Wing, Apr. 18, 1957; children: Mary Elizabeth Wing-Berman, Stephen R. BA, Mt. Holyoke Coll., 1955; MS, U. Fla., 1957, PhD, 1962. Interim asst. curator Fla. Mus. Natural History, U. Fla., Gainesville, 1961-69, asst. curator, 1969-73, assoc. curator, 1973-78, curator, 1978—2001, curator emeritus, 2001—; prof. anthropology dept. U. Fla., 1979—2001, prof. zoology dept., 1988—2001. US rep. Internat. Congress Archaeozoology, 1981—2001. Author: (with A.B. Brown) Paleonutrition, 1979, (with E.J. Reitz) Zooarcheology, 1999, 2nd edit., 2008, (with Lee A. Newsom) On Land and Sea, 2004; editor (with J.C. Wheeler) Economic Prehistory of the Central Andes, 1988; contbr. articles to profl. jours. Recipient Fryxell award Soc. Am. Archaeology, 1996; NSF grantee, 1961-64, 68-73, 79-80, 84-85, 89-91, 95-96. Mem. NAS, Soc. Ethnobiology (pres. 1989-91, trustee 1991-). Office: U Fla Dickinson Hall/Fla Mus Natural History PO Box 117800 Gainesville FL 32611-7800

WING, JAMES DAVID, lawyer; b. Milw., May 4, 1943; s. William H. and Elaine E. (Koehler) W.; m. Colleen Clifton Wing; children: Benjamin, Tracy, Nathaniel, John. BA, Beloit Coll., Wis., 1965; MA, U. Chgo., 1966, JD, 1969. Bar: Wis. 1969, Fla. 1975, U.S. Ct. Appeals (7th cir.) 1973, U.S. Dist. Ct. (mid. dist.) Fla. 1975, U.S. Ct. Appeals (5th cir.) 1978, U.S. Dist. Ct. (so. dist.) Fla. 1981, U.S. Ct. Appeals (11th cir.) 1981, U.S. Supreme Ct. 1979. Assoc. Whyte, Hirschboeck, Minahan, Harding & Harland, Milw., 1969-75, Carlton, Fields, Ward, Emmanuel, Smith & Cutler, Tampa, Fla., 1975-85, Myers, Kenin, Levinson, Frank & Richards/Shea & Gould, Miami, Fla., 1985-88, Fine, Jacobson, Schwartz, Nash, Block & England, Miami, 1988-94, Holland & Knight, Miami, 1994—. Mem. Internat. Bar Assn., ABA (chmn. bus. sect. subcom. director officer liability ins.), Phi Beta Kappa, Phi Eta Sigma, Omicron Delta Kappa. Avocations: germanistics, tennis. Office: Holland & Knight LLP 701 Brickell Ave Ste 3000 Miami FL 33131 Office Phone: 305-374-8500, 305-789-7768. Fax: 305 789 7799. E-mail: james.wing@hklaw.com.

WINGARD, JOHN REID, medical educator; b. Charleston, SC, Jan. 30, 1947; m. Frances Diane Phillips, 1974; children: Ellen, Emily, Sally, Benjamin. BA in English, Yale U., 1969; MD, The Johns Hopkins U., 1973. Diplomate Am. Bd. Internal Medicine, subspecialty of Med. Oncology. Intern City of Memphis Hosp./U. Tenn. Ctr. for Health Scis., 1973-74, resident, 1974-76; chief resident V.A. Hosp., Memphis, 1976-77; instr. in medicine U. Tenn. Ctr. for Health Scis., Memphis, 1976-77; fellow in oncology and internal medicine The Johns Hopkins U. Sch. Medicine, Balt., 1977-79, various to asst. prof. oncology, 1977-87, assoc. prof. oncology, 1987-91, assoc. prof. medicine, 1990-91; prof. medicine Emory U. Sch. Medicine, Atlanta, 1991-96, prof. Winship Cancer Ctr., 1992-96; dir. bone marrow transplant program, prof. medicine U. Fla., Gainesville, 1996—; dep. dir. U. Fla. Shands Cancer Ctr., 2011—. Dir. bone marrow transplant program Emory U. Sch. Medicine, 1991-96; dir. Bone Marrow Transplant Outpatient Clinic, Johns Hopkins Oncology Ctr., 1984-91; cons. Office of Disability Programs, Social Security Adminstrn., Balt., 1981-91; study group Nat. Inst. Allergy and Infectious Diseases, 1988—; adv. com. Internat. Bone Marrow Transplant Registry, 1989-91, 95—, sec.-treas., 1998—; chair, steering com. Blood and Marrow Transplant Clin. Trials Network, 2001—; bd. dirs. Found. Cellular Therapies, 2005-, Nat. Marrow Donor Program, 2007-2013. Contbr. articles to profl. jours.; contbr. chpts. to books; assoc. editor: Biology of Blood and Marrow Transplantation. Mem. Am. Soc. Microbiology, Am. Soc. Clin. Oncology, Am. Soc. Hematology, Am. Soc. Blood and Marrow Transplantation (pres. 2002-2003). Office: U Fla Coll Medicine PO Box 100277 Gainesville FL 32610-0277 Home: 9297 SW 31st Pl Gainesville FL 32608-7936 Office Phone: 352-273-7760, 352-273-8010. Business E-Mail: wingajr@medicine.ufl.edu, wingajr@ufl.edu.

WINGATE, HENRY TRAVILLION, federal judge; b. Jackson, Jan. 6, 1947; s. J.T. and Eloise (Anderson) Wingate; m. Turner Arnita Ward, Aug. 10, 1974. BA, Grinnell Coll., 1969; JD, Yale U., 1972; LLD (hon.), Grinnell Coll., 1986. Bar: Miss. 1973, admitted to practice: US Dist. Ct. (So. Dist.) Miss. 1973, US Ct. Appeals (5th Cir.) 1973, US Mil. Ct. 1973. Law clk. New Haven (Conn.) Legal Assistance, 1971-72, Community Legal Aid, Jackson, 1972-73; spl. asst. atty. gen. State of Miss., Jackson, 1976-80; asst. dist. atty. (7th cir.), Jackson, 1980-84; asst. U.S. atty. US Dist. Ct. (So. Dist.) Miss., Jackson, 1984-85, judge, 1985—2003, 2010—, chief judge, 2003—10. Lectr. Miss. Prosecutors Coll., 1980—84, Law Enforcement Tng. Acad., Pearl, Miss., 1980—84, Miss. Jud. Coll., 1980—84, Nat. Coll. Dist. Attys., 1984—85; adj. prof. law Golden Gate U., Norfolk, Va., 1975—76, Tidewater Community Coll., 1976, Miss. Coll. Sch. Law, 1978—84. Former mem. adv. bd. Jackson Parks and Recreation Dept.; former mem. bd. dirs. SCAN Am. of Miss., Inc., Jackson Arts Alliance, Drug Rsch. and Edn. Assn. in Miss., Inc., United Way Jackson; mem. exec. com. Yale U. Law sch., 1989—; chmn. bd. dirs. YMCA, 1978-80. Racquetball State Singles Champion Jr. Vets. Div., 1981, State Singles Champion Srs. Div., 1982, Outstanding Legal Service award NAACP (Jackson br. and Miss. br.), 1982, Civil Liberties award Elks, 1983, Community Service award Women for Progress Orgn., 1984. Mem.: Fed. Bar Assn., Hinds County Bar Assn., Miss. Bar Assn., ABA, Yale Club Miss. Avocations: reading, theater, racquetball, jogging, bowling. Home: 6018 Huntview Dr Jackson MS 39206-2130 Office: James O Eastland Courthouse 245 E Capitol St Ste 430 Jackson MS 39201-2414 Office Phone: 601-965-4042.

WINGO, CHARLES, medical educator; MD, LSU New Orleans Sch. Med., 1975. Prof. medicine, physiology, functional genomics U. Fla., 1990—. Mem. Am. Physiol. Soc., 1983, Am. Soc. Clin. Invest, 1990. Fellow: ACP. Office: University Fla Div Nephrology PO Box 100224 Gainesville FL 32610 Business E-Mail: cswingo@ufl.edu.*

WINKEL, RAYMOND NORMAN, aerospace scientist, consultant, retired military officer; b. Flint, Mich., Dec. 8, 1928; s. Norman Martin and Evelyn Matilda (Hylen) W.; m. Ellen Stefula, Dec. 29, 1955 (dec. Feb. 2006); children: Raymond Norman, Ann, Maryellen. BS, U.S. Naval Postgrad. Sch., Monterey, Calif., 1964; MS, Villanova U., Pa., 1967; grad. advanced mgmt. program, Harvard U., 1973. Enlisted in USN, 1948, commd. ensign, designated naval aviator, 1951, advanced through grades to rear adm., 1979; service in Far East; comdg. officer Naval Electronics Systems Test and Evaluation Facility St. Inigoes, Md., 1969-71; dir. avionics U.S. Navy, 1973-76; project mgr. Navy/Marine Corps heavy lift helicopter, 1976-78; gen. mgr. Navy/industry team to develop new ship/aircraft weapon system for anti-submarine warfare LAMPS Mark III, 1978-81; ret. USN, 1981; v.p. Washington ops. Telephonics Corp., Huntington, NY, 1981-82; v.p. programs and contracts Astronautics Corp. Am., Milw., 1982-94; aerospace industry cons. Heathsville, Va., 1994-95. Decorated Legion of Merit, Air medal, Navy Achievement medal. Mem. NRA, Exptl. Aircraft Assn., U.S. Naval Inst., Assn. Naval Aviation, Mil. Officers Assn. Am., Kiwanis, Indian Creek Yacht and Country Club, U.S. Power Squadron, Experimental Aircraft Assn., Am. Legion. Republican. Roman Catholic. Home: 1860 Island Point Rd Heathsville VA 22473-3729 Personal E-mail: radm@raywinkel.com.

WINKLER, KATHERINE MAURINE, retired management consultant, educator; b. Louisville, Nov. 29, 1940; d. Myrick and Maurine (Holland) W. Cert. in foreign studies, Inst. for Am. Univs., 1961; BA, Transylvania U., 1963. Market rsch. field supr. Procter & Gamble, Cin., 1963-65; Eng. tchr. Louisville Ky. Sch. System, 1967-68; mgmt. and staff positions in sales, mktg., human resources, total quality mgmt. and edn. IBM, Louisville, Lexington, Ky., Mpls., Cin., and Westchester, NY, 1968-93; pvt. practice NYC, Richmond, Va., 1993—2005; ret., 2005. Adj. prof. NYU. Author: Leadership, 1982, Across the Board, Executive Excellence, Westchester Historian, The Scarsdale Inquirer; contbr. articles to publs. Com. mem. Mpls. Cultural Affairs Com., 1970, Village of Tarrytown (N.Y.) Main St. com., 1981—82; bd. dirs., chair trustee affairs com. Westchester County Hist. Soc., Elmsford, NY, 1989—99; mem. mgmt., bus., econs. study group NYU, 1995—97; vol. cons. White Plains Hosp. Ctr., 1998—2000; vice chair Friends of Monroe Park, Richmond, 2005—06. Named Outstanding Young Woman of Am., 1972. Mem. Ky. Col., Fan Dist. Assn. (bd. dirs., chair pub. rels. com. 2003-05, v.p. 2004-05, historian 2005—09), Fan Woman's Club (bd. dirs. 2002-05, pres. 2005- 06), Libr. Va. Found. (vol. cons. 2007-08, Named Vol. of Yr. award, 2008), Fan Town House & Garden Club (v.p. 2008-09, pres., 2009-10, chair projects com., 2010-12), Women's Health at Retreat Hosp. (bd. mem. 2011-). Home: 642 Valencia Ave Unit 406 Coral Gables FL 33134-5649 E-mail: kittywink@attglobal.net.

WINOGRAD, AUDREY LESSER, retired advertising executive; b. NYC, Oct. 6, 1933; d. Jack J. and Theresa Lorraine (Elkind) Lesser; m. Melvin H. Winograd, Apr. 29, 1956; 1 child, Hope Elise. BA, U. Conn., 1953. Asst. advt. mgr. T. Baumritter Co., Inc., NYC, 1953-54; asst. dir. pub. rels. and creative merchandising Kirby, Block & Co., Inc., NYC, 1954-56; divsn. mdse. mgr., dir. advt. and sales promotion Winograd's Dept. Store, Inc., Point Pleasant, NJ, 1956-73, v.p., 1960-73, exec. v.p., 1973-86; pres., CEO AMW Assocs., Atlanta, 1976—2002, ret., 2002—. Editor: bus. newsletters. Active Alley Cat Allies, Fund for Animals; bd. dirs. Temple Beth Am, Lakewood, NJ, 1970—72, Temple Emanuel, Atlanta, 1999—2001. Mem.: LWV, NAFE, Noah's Lost Ark, Retail Advt. Conf., Am. Soc. Advt. and Promotion, NJ Assn. Women Bus. Owners, Monmouth County Bus. Assn. (bd. dirs. 1985—97, pres. 1988—90, Woman of the Yr. 1992—93, Person of the Yr. 1995), Monmouth Ocean Devel. Coun., Retail Advt. and Mktg. Assn. Internat., Jersey Pub. Rels. and Advt. Assn. (pres. 1982—83, bd. dirs.), Greenpeace (mem. Physicians Com. for Responsible Medicine, mem. Grey 2K), Environ. Defense, Wilderness Soc., Best Friends, Humane Soc. US, Delta Rescue, People Ethical Treatment Animals, In Defense of Animals, Ocean C. of C. (bd. dirs. 1994—97, Career Achievements and Contbns. to Soc. award 1993), Soc. Prevention Cruelty to Animals, Animal Protection Inst. Am., Humane Soc., Internat. Fund Animal Welfare, World Wildlife Fund, Friends of Animals, Defenders of Wildlife, Nat. Humane Edn. Soc., Atlanta Humane Soc., Natural Resources Def. Coun., Last Chance for Animals, United Animal Nat., Lifesavers Wild Horse Rescue, Audobon, Sierra Club. Avocations: collecting animal collectibles, gourmet cooking, environmental protection, exercise. Office: AMW Assocs 5304 Vernon Lake Dr Atlanta GA 30338-3527 Personal E-mail: audwin@fastmail.fm.

WINSLETT, STONER, artistic director; b. Jacksonville, Fla., Aug. 17, 1958; m. Donald Paulding Irwin; children: Louise Gray Irwin, Elizabeth Irwin, Alexander Pankoff, Caroline Irwin. Attended, Am. Ballet Theatre Sch., NC Sch. Arts; BFA summa cum laude, Smith Coll., 1980. Artistic dir. Richmond Ballet, 1980—. Cadmus leader-in-residence U. Richmond Jepson Sch.; pres. John Butler Found.; vice-chmn DanceUSA. Panel mem. Nat. Endowment for the Arts. Recipient Smith Coll. Medal, Smith Coll., 2005, Gov.'s award for Arts, 2008; named Woman of Yr., YWCA; named one of 100 Most Influential Richmonders of 20th Cent., Style mag. Mem.: Phi Beta Kappa. Office: Richmond Ballet 407 E Canal St Richmond VA 23219-3811 Office Phone: 804-344-0906.

WINSTEAD, DANIEL KEITH, psychiatrist; b. Cin., Dec. 30, 1944; s. Daniel Sebastian and Betty Jane (Kirsch) W.; m. Jennifer Reiner, June 15, 1968; children: Laura Suzanne, Nathaniel Scott. BA, U. Cin., 1966; MD, Vanderbilt U., 1970. Diplomate Am. Bd. Psychiatry and Neurology. Resident U. Cin., 1970-72, fellow, 1972-73; chief VA Med. Ctr. psychiat. svc. Tulane U., New Orleans, 1976-79, dir., consultation/liaison psychiat. tng., 1979-83, dir. psychiatric edn. and residency tng., 1983-87, assoc. prof., 1979-84, prof., 1984—, chmn. dept. psychiatry and neurology, 1987—; chief psychiat. svc. VA Med. Ctr., New Orleans, 1976-80; assoc. chief staff for edn. VA Med Ctr., New Orleans, 1979-87; staff psychiatrist VA Med. Ctr., New Orleans, 1987—. Med. dir. Jefferson Parish Substance Abuse Clinic, 1980-81; cons. E.R. Squibb and Sons, 1985-86; vis. physician psychiatry Charity Hosp., New Orleans, 1979-90. Contbr. articles to profl. jours. Maj. U.S. Army, 1973-76. Mem. AMA, Am. Bd. Psychait. and Neurology (pres. bd. dirs. 2006), Am. Coll. Psychiatrists, Am. Acad. Psychiatry and Law, Am. Psychiat. Assn., La. State Med. Soc., So. Assn. for Rsch. in Psychiatry, Acad. Psychosomatic Medicine (pres.), Am. Assn. Chairmen Depts. Psychiatry (pres.-elect), Am. Assn. Dirs. Psychiat. Residency Tng., Assn. Acad. Psychiatry, La. Psychiat. Assn. (pres. 1991-92, 2009-2010), Soc. Biol. Psychiatry, New Orleans Area Psychiat. Assn., New Orleans Neurol. Soc., Orleans Parish Med. Soc. Republican. Presbyterian. Avocations: oenology, travel. Office: Tulane Med Sch 1440 Canal St Ste 1000 New Orleans LA 70112-2703 Home: 5348 Bellaire Dr New Orleans LA 70124-1033 E-mail: winstead@tulane.edu.

WINSTON, JAMEIS, student athlete; b. Hueytown, Ala., Jan. 6, 1994; s. Antonor and Loretta Winston. Student in exploratory, Fla. State U., Tallahassee, 2012—. Quarterback Fla. State U. Seminoles, 2013—. Recipient Davey O'Brien award, Davey O'Brien Found., 2013, Walter Camp award, Walter Camp Football Found., 2013, Heisman Meml. Trophy award, The Heisman Trust, 2013; named First Team All-Conf., Rookie of Yr., Offensive Player of Yr. & Player of Yr., Atlantic Coast Conf., 2013, First Team All-American, AP, 2013, Player of Yr., 2013, Sporting News Player of Yr., 2013. Achievements include becoming the youngest recipient of the Heisman Memorial Trophy Award, 2013, a member of the BCS National Championship winning Florida State University Seminoles, 2013. Office: Florida State University Football Program c/o FSU Athletics Dept PO Box 2195 Tallahassee FL 32316*

WINSTON, JULIA L., geriatric psychiatrist; MD, Columbia U., 1984. Diplomate Am. Bd. Psychiatry & Neurology, 1990, Am. Bd. Psychiatry & Neurology-geriatric psychiatry, 2006. Intern St. Luke's Roosevelt Hosp., 1985; resident in psychiatry Presbyn. Hosp., 1985—88; hosp. affiliation includes: James A. Haley Veterans Hosp. Office: James A Haley Veterans Hospital 13000 Bruce B Downs Blvd Tampa FL 33612 Office Phone: 813-972-2000, 888-811-0107.*

WINSTON, MARY ANN, retail executive; b. 1961; BS in Acctg. & Info. Sys., U. Wis., 1983; MBA in Internat. Bus., Finance & Mktg., Northwestern U., 1991. Sr. auditor Arthur Andersen & Co., 1983—87; various positions Ameritech, 1987—91; dir., bus. devel. & strategy Biotech Divsn. Baxter International, Inc., 1991—95; sr. mgmt. positions Warner-Lambert, 1995—2002; v.p. Visteon Corp., 2002—04, treas., 2002—03, controller, 2003—04; exec. v.p., CFO Scholastic Corp., 2004—07; founder, pres. WinsCo Financial, LLC, 2007—08; sr. v.p., CFO Giant Eagle, Inc., 2008—12; exec. v.p., CFO Family Dollar Stores, Inc., Matthews, NC, 2012—. Bd. dirs. Dover Corp., 2005—, Plexus Corp., 2008—. Office: Family Dollar Stores Inc 10401 Monroe Rd Matthews NC 28105

WINTER, LARRY EUGENE, accountant; b. Williamsport, Pa., Jan. 17, 1950; s. Robert Schrader and Betty Irene (Foresman) Winter; m. Constance Dianne Snyder, June 2, 1973; children: John, Matthew, Noël, James. A in Bus. Adminstrn., Palm Beach Jr. Coll., 1969; BSBA, U. Fla., Gainesville, 1971; cert. in bus., U. Pa., Phila., 1977. Cert. valuation analyst, fraud examiner, CPA Fla., Ga.; cert. fin. planning specialist. Audit supr. Touche Ross & Co., Atlanta, 1971-74; chief. fin. officer Hawthorne Industries, Dalton, Ga., 1974-79; pvt. practice acctg. Dalton, 1979-89; mng. ptnr. Winter & Scoggins, CPAs, Dalton, 1990—. Mem. White House Conf. Small Bus., Atlanta, 1979; instr. W. Ga. Coll., Carollton, 1985, Eastern European Bus. Coll., Budapest, Hungary, 1995; cons. Christian Businessman's Com. Internat., 1986—2003; acct. in residence Ga. Coll., Milledgeville, 1989. Author: The American Free Enterprise System and the Ethics that Make it Work, 1991. Trustee Dalton Jr. Coll. Found., 1974—77; chair Whitfield County/Dalton Day Care Ctrs., 1987—92; mem. N.W. Ga. Healthcare Partnership, 1994—2004, 2006—, chair, 2001—03; mem. Downtown Dalton Devel. Authority, 2001—04; adv. coun. Ga. State Bd. Workers Compensation, 1991—2003; fee arbitration panel State Bar Ga., 1987—; mem. Dalton-Whitfield Planning Commn., 2004—; mem. target tomorrow leadership team, edn. alliance chair Leadership Dalton-Whitfield; elder Fellowship Bible Ch., 1985—; mem. Ga. State Bd. Edn., 2006—. Mem.: SAR, AICPA, Ga. Sheriffs Assn. (Disting. Humanitarian award), Ga. Soc. CPAs (pres. 1983—84), Nat. Assn. Cert. Valuation Analysts, Assn. Cert. Fraud Examiners, Dalton-Whitfield C. of C. (treas. 1992—94), Rotary, Kiwanis (life; pres. 1978—79, lt. gov. 1981—84, George Hixson fellow 2000). Avocations: cooking, credit and financial counseling. Office: PO Box 2644 Dalton GA 30722-2644

WINTER, RICHARD LAWRENCE, diversified financial services company executive; b. St. Louis, Dec. 17, 1945; s. Melvin Lawrence and Kathleen Jane (O'Leary) Winter; m. Kathryn Ann Geppert, Dec. 4, 1993; children: Leigh Ellen, Jessica Marie, George Bradford stepchildren: Jason N. Geppert, Jamie L. Girouard. BS in Math., St. Louis U., 1967, MS in Math. (fellow), 1969; MBA, U. Mo., St. Louis, 1976. Rsch. analyst Mo. Pacific R.R., St. Louis, 1971-73; dir. fin. rels. Linclay Corp., St. Louis, 1973-74; asst. v.p. 1st Nat. Bank in St. Louis (now Centerre Bank, NA) subs. Boatmen's Nat. Bank, 1974-79; v.p. fin. UDE Corp., St. Louis, 1979-81; pres. Health Care Investments, Ltd., St. Louis, 1981—, Larus Corp., St. Louis, 1981—, Garden View Care Ctr., Inc., O'Fallon, Mo., 1987—, Garden View Care Ctr. of Chesterfield, Inc., 1990—, Garden View Care Ctr. of St. Louis, Inc., Valley Park, Mo., 1998—. Exec. bd. Duchesne Bank, St. Peters, Mo., 1989—97; lectr. math. U. Mo., St. Louis, 1972—74, St. Louis U., 1982—90. Chmn. Mo. State Coun. Arts, 2005—06; cmty. adv. bd. Coll. Fine Arts and Comm. U. Mo., St. Louis, 2003—09; bd. dirs. Dance St. Louis, 1998—2004, 2006—, pres. bd. dirs., 2008—10, chmn. bd. dirs., 2010—; bd. dirs. Mid-Am. Arts Alliance, 2005—06, Jazz St. Louis, 2006—; mem. fundraising staff St. Louis Symphony; mem. bd. dirs. Mo. Health Care Assn., 2010—; exec. adv. bd. St. Louis U. Coll. Arts and Scis., 2000—; mem. fundraising staff Jr. Achievement; fundraising staff United Way St. Louis, Arts and Edn. Fund, St. Louis, 1974—79. With US Army, 1969—71. Mem.: Nat. Health Lawyers Assn., Mo. Athletic Club (St. Louis), Pi Mu Epsilon. Roman Catholic. Office: Ste 170 12444 Powerscourt Dr Saint Louis MO 63131-3659 Home: 2700 N Ocean Dr Unit 2501B Singer Island FL 33404 Office Phone: 314-965-1991. Business E-Mail: richard-l-winter@gvcc.com.

WINTER, WILLIAM L., retired professional society administrator; PhD in Higher Edn. Adminstrn. Newspaper and wire svc. writer, editor; bur. chief AP, Ky.; exec. sports editor Courier Jour., Louisville Times; asst. mng. editor Akron Beacon Jour.; exec. editor Pasadena (Calif.) Star-News; pres., exec. dir. Am. Press Inst., Reston, Va., 1987—2003; ret., 2003. Bd. dirs. World Editors Forum. Mem.: ASNE. Avocations: golf, classic rock, modern country, cats, Oreo cookies. Office: Am Press Inst 11690 Sunrise Valley Dr Reston VA 20191-1498

WINTERHALTER, GARY G., cosmetics executive; b. 1952; BS, MBA, U. Akron. Various oper. positions Alberto-Culver, 1987—96; pres. Sally USA, 1996—2004, BSG No. America, 2004—05, Sally Beauty Supply, 2004—05, Sally Beauty Holdings, Inc., 2005—, CEO, 2006—. Bd. dirs. Sally Beauty Holdings, Inc., 2006—. Office: Sally Beauty Holdings Inc 3001 Colorado Blvd Denton TX 76210 Office Phone: 940-898-7500. Office Fax: 940-898-7927. Business E-Mail: GWinterhalter@sallybeauty.com.*

WINTERS, BRIAN JOSEPH, professional basketball coach; b. Rockaway, NY, Mar. 1, 1952; m. Julie Winters; children: Cara, Keelin, Meghan, Brendan, Kevin, Ryan. Grad., U. SC, 1974. Profl. basketball player LA Lakers, 1974—75, Milw. Bucks, 1975—83; asst. coach Princeton U. Tigers, 1984—86, Cleve. Cavaliers, 1986—93, Atlanta Hawks, 1993—95, Denver Nuggets, 1997—98, Golden State Warriors, 1999—2001, head coach, 2001—02, Vancouver Grizzlies, 1995—97, Ind. Fever, WNBA, 2003—07; scout Ind. Pacers; asst. coach Charlotte Bobcats, 2012—. Named to NBA All-Rookie Team, 1974, NBA All-Star Team, 1976, 1978. Office: Charlotte Bobcats 333 E Trade St Charlotte NC 28202*

WINTERS, DAVID DOUGLAS, lawyer; s. Frederick Douglas and Wanda Mae Hudson Winters; m. Debbie Elaine Tipton, Apr. 23, 1977; children: Charity, Patience, Ian. BS, US Naval Acad., Annapolis, Md., 1976; MS, U. So. Miss., Gulfport, 1987; diploma in Law, Oxford Brookes, UK, 1996; JD, So. Ill. U., Carbondale, 2002. Bar: US Patent Office 2001, Tenn. 2002, US Supreme Ct. 2003. With US Navy, 1971—94; internat. cons. group mng. dir. London, 1994—96; internat. bus. cons., negotiator Nagasaki, Japan, 1996—99; patent atty. Clarksville and Nashville, Tenn., 2002—. Standing city judge pro tem, Clarksville, 2004—; judge Brit. Inventor Show, 2008—10. Author: The Boat Officer's Handbook, 1981, 1991, The Pirates Guide to Patents Trademarks and Copyrights, 2012. Founder Charles M. Hudson Grant for Excellence in Patent Law So. Ill. U., Sch. Law, 2005. Named Author of Yr., Nashville Bar Jour., 2008. Mem.: Civil Air Patrol (maj.), Fed. Bar Assn., Tenn. Bar Assn. (del. 2007), Nashville Bar Assn., US Naval Inst., Brit. Spl. Forces Club, Mensa, Phi Delta Phi. Avocations: flying, yachting, scuba diving. Office: Winters Patent Law 2277 Wilma Rudolph Blvd Ste C Clarksville TN 37040-6161*

WINTERS, KENNETH W., state legislator; b. June 27, 1934; State senator Dist. 1, Ky., 2005—; mem. Vet. Com., Military Affairs & Pub. Protection Com., Econ. Devel. Com., Tourism Com., Labor Com.; chmn. Edn. Com. Mem.: NRA, Experimental Aircraft Assn., Lions Club. Republican. Baptist. Address: 1500 Glendale Rd Murray KY 42071 Office: 209 Capitol Annex Frankfort KY 40601 Office Phone: 270-759-5751, 502-564-8100 870. Fax: 270-759-5751.

WINTERS, SAM, lawyer; b. Tex. BA, U. Tex., 1944, JD, 1948. Bar: Tex. 1948. Shareholder Clark, Thomas & Winters, Austin, Tex.; bd. govs. U.S. Postal Svc., Washington, 1991—2000, vice chair, 1996-97, chmn. bd. govs., 1994-95, 98. Chmn. Tex. Rsch. League, 1990, 91; past mem. Nat. Hwy. Safety Adv. Com.; mem. devel. bd. U. Tex., Austin. With USN, World War II. Mem. ABA (past chair sect. pub. utilities, comm. and transp.), Am. Law Inst. (life), State Bar Tex. Office: Clark, Thomas & Winters PO Box 1148 Austin TX 78767

WINTERSHEIMER, DONALD CARL, retired state supreme court justice; b. Covington, Ky., Apr. 21, 1931; s. Carl E. and Marie A. (Kohl) W.; m. Alice T. Rabe, June 24, 1961; children: Mark D., Lisa Ann, Craig P., Amy T., Blaise Q. BA, Thomas More Coll., 1953; MA, Xavier U., 1956; JD, U. Cin., 1959; LHD (hon.), No. Ky. U., 1999. Pvt. practice, Covington, 1960-76; city solicitor City of Covington, 1962-76; judge Ky. Ct. Appeals, Frankfort, 1976-83; justice Ky. Supreme Ct., Frankfort, 1983—2007. Chmn. Ky. Supreme Ct. Criminal Rules Com., 1988-94, Continuing Jud. Edn. Com., 1983—2007, Rules Com., 1994—2007; del. Foster Parent Rev. Bd., 1985-2002; mem. adv. bd. Sta. WNKU-FM, 1984-94, Am. Soc. Writers on Legal Subjects. Published articles in Law Jour. of Nat. Legal Ctr. for Medically Disabled, Issues in Law & Medicine, Albany Law Review, Quinnipiac Law Review, Temple Law Review, No. Ky. U. Chase Law Rev., NYU Annual Survey of Am. Law. Trustee Sta. WNKU-FM. Recipient Cmty. Svc. award Thomas More Coll., 1968, Disting. Alumnus award, 1982, Monsignor Murphy award, 2007, Disting. Alumni award Coll. Law/U.Cin., 1998, Lincoln award No. Ky. U., 2007; named Disting. Jurist Chase Coll. Law, 1983, Outstanding Jurist Phi Alpha Delta Law Frat., 1990, Murphy award, Thomas More Coll., 2006, Lincoln award Northern Ky. U., 2007. Mem. ABA, Am. Judicature Soc., Ky. Bar Assn., Ohio Bar Assn., Cin. Bar Assn., Inst. Jud. Adminstrn., Am. Inns of Ct. (founder Chase chpt.). Democrat. Roman Catholic. Home Phone: 859-581-8781.

WINZER, P.J., lawyer; b. Shreveport, La., June 7, 1947; d. C.W. Winzer and Pearlene Hall Winzer Tobin. BA in Polit. Sci., So. U., Baton Rouge, 1968; JD, UCLA, 1971. Bar: Bar: Calif. 1972, U.S. Supreme Ct. 1986. Staff atty. Office of Gen. Counsel, U.S. HEW, Washington, 1971-80; asst. spl. counsel U.S. Office of Spl. Counsel Merit Systems Protection Bd., Dallas, 1980-82; regional dir. U.S. Merit Systems Protection Bd., Alexandria, Va., 1982—. Mem. Calif. Bar Assn., Fed. Cir. Bar Assn., Delta Sigma Theta. Office: US Merit System Protection 1800 Diagnol Rd Ste 205 Alexandria VA 22314-2840

WIORKOWSKI, JOHN JAMES, mathematics professor; b. Chgo., Sept. 30, 1943; BS, U. Chgo., 1965, MS, 1966, PhD, 1972. Rsch. assoc. U. Chgo., 1972; asst. prof. Pa. State U., University Park, 1973-74; assoc. prof. U. Tex. at Dallas, Richardson, 1975, assoc. prof. and program head Math. Scis. Program, 1979-81, prof., 1981—, asst. to v.p. acad. affairs, 1980-85, asst. v.p. acad. affairs, 1985-94, assoc. provost, 1994-2001, vice-provost, 2001—, head math. scis. program, 1996-98. Cons. to Fed. Energy Adminstrn., 1975, Tex. Instruments, 1977, Frito-Lay Inc., 1977-78, Republic Nat. Bank, 1979; mem. panel studying 55 mile per hour speed limit Nat. Acad. Sci. Contbr. articles to profl. jours. Served to capt. U.S. Army, 1968-71. Decorated Army Commendation medal, NSF grantee, 1975—; Am. Coun. Edn. fellow, 1981-82. Mem. Am. Statis. Assn. (chpt. pres. 1974, v.p. 1977, chpt. pres. 1978), AAAS, Inst. Math. Stats., Biometric Soc., Sigma Xi. Unitarian Universalist. Home: 9922 Lincolnshire Ct Rockwall TX 75087-4509 Office: U Tex at Dallas PO Box 830688 Richardson TX 75083-0688 Office Phone: 972-883-2274. Personal E-mail: wiorkow@msn.com. Business E-Mail: wiorkow@utdallas.edu.

WIRTH, FREMONT PHILIP, JR., neurosurgeon, educator; b. Nashville, July 23, 1940; s. Fremont P. and Willa (Dean) W.; children: Fremont Philip III, Andrew Simpson, Carolyn Howe. BA with honors in History, Williams Coll., 1962; MD, Vanderbilt U., 1966. Diplomate Am. Bd. Neurol. Surgery (guest examiner 1989, bd. dirs. 1992-98, vice chmn. 1997-98), Nat. Bd. Med. Examiners; cert. advanced trauma life support ACS. Surg. intern Johns Hopkins Hosp., Balt.,

1966-67, resident and fellow in surgery, 1967-68; asst. resident in neurosurgery Barnes Hosp., Washington U., St. Louis, 1970-72, fellow in neurosurgery, 1972-74; pvt. practice, Savannah, Ga., 1974—. Asst. clin. prof. neurosurgery Med. Coll. Ga., Augusta, 1991—, vis. prof., 1978, 79, 86, 87; mem. staff, neurosurg. ICU, St. Joseph's Hosp., 1974—, dir. neurosurg. ICU, 1978—; mem. staff Meml. Med. Ctr., 1974-75, dir. rehab., 1983; mem. staff Candler Gen. Hosp., 1974—; med. dir. Head and Spinal Cord Injury Prevention Project for Ga., 1984-96; presenter in field, 1970—; vis. prof. U. Md., Balt., 1981, Tufts New Eng. Med. Ctr., Boston, 1982. Series editor (with R.A. Ratcheson) Concepts in Neurosurgery, 1986-93; editor: (with Ratcheson) Neurosurgical Critical Care, Concepts in Neurological Surgery, Vol. 1, 1987, Ruptured Cerebral Aneurysms, Concepts in Neurological Surgery, Vol. 6, 1994; contbr. articles and book revs. to med. jours., chpts. to books. Elder Skidaway Island Presbyn. Ch., 1981-83; mem. pack 57 com. Cub Scouts Am., Savannah, 1979-84; mem. troop 57 com. Boy Scouts Am., Savannah, 1980-85, mem. fin. com. Coastal Empire coun., 1987-90, mem. adv. bd., 1990-96; chmn. physicians' solicitation United Way Coastal Empire, 1987; bd. dirs. Think First Found., 1990-95. With USPHS, 1968-70. Fellow ACS (bd. govs. 1984-90, sr. mem. trauma com. 1991-93); mem. AMA (physician's recognition award 1973-76, 77-79, 80-82, 83-85, 88-91, 91-94, 95-98, 98—), Congress Neurol. Surgeons (profl. conduct com. 1989-93, v.p. 1985-86, Disting. Svc. award 1989), Am. Acad. Neurol. Surgeons, Neurosurg. Soc. Am., Am. Assn. Neurologic Surgeons (nominating com. 1994-96, bd. dirs. 1998-2001, v.p. 2002-03, pres. 2005-06), Brain Surgery Soc., Ga. Med. Soc. (pres. 1995, bd. trustees 1996-2001, chmn. 2000-01), Med. Assn. Ga. (editl. bd. 1987-93), Ga. Neurosurg. Soc. (exec. com. 1981-88, pres. 1988-89), So. Neurosurg. Soc. (exec. com. 1982-91, pres. 1988-89, Semmes lectr. 1997), N.Am. Skull Base Soc., Am. Heart Assn. (fellow stroke coun.). Avocations: golf, fly fishing, hunting. Office: Neurol Inst Savannah 4 E Jackson Blvd Savannah GA 31405-5810

WISDOM, PAIGE, bank executive; BS in Math. and Computer Sci., U. Ill., Chgo.; MBA, U. Chgo. Various mgmt. positions Swiss Bank Corp., Salomon Smith Barney, Citibank, Warburg Dillon Read; CFO, corp. bank JPMorgan Chase (merged with Bank One Corp.), 2000—04; bus. unit CFO Bank of America Corp., 2004—07; CFO, Bus. Unit Freddie Mac - Federal Home Loan Mortgage Corp., 2008—10, sr. v.p., chief enterprise risk officer, 2010, exec. v.p., chief enterprise risk officer, 2010—. Office: Federal Home Loan Mortgage Corp 8200 Jones Branch Dr Mc Lean VA 22102-3110 Office Phone: 703-903-2000. Office Fax: 703-903-4045. Business E-Mail: paige_wisdom@freddiemac.com.

WISE, ALISA KELLI, state supreme court justice; b. Geneva, Ala. d. Bobby W. and Betty Mathis Wise; m. Arthur Ray; 1 child, Hanah-Mathis. BS in Biology, Auburn U., 1985; JD, Jones Sch. Law, 1994; MPA, Auburn U. Montgomery, 2000. With Gov.'s Legis. Office State of Ala.; legal counsel ProStaff HRM, Inc.; atty. John Taber & Assocs., Pittman, Pittman, Carwie & Fuquay; staff atty. Ct. Criminal Appeals Supreme Ct. Ala.; judge Ala. Ct. Criminal Appeals, 2001—11, presiding judge, 2008—11; assoc. justice Supreme Ct. Ala., 2011—. Mem. Ala. Coun. on Juvenile Justice and Delinquency Prevention, 2003—; mem. Criminal Code Com. Ala. Law Inst. Bd. dirs. Family Sunshine Ctr., Disting. Young Women of Ala., Max Credit Union. Named Outstanding Student, Auburn U. Montgomery Dept. Polit. Sci. and Pub. Adminstrn., 2005. Mem.: Capital City Rep. Women, Ala. State Bar Assn., Montgomery Symphony League, Ala. Wildlife Fedn. Office: Supreme Court of Alabama 300 Dexter Ave Montgomery AL 36104 Office Phone: 334-229-0700.*

WISE, CHARLA KAMM, aeronautics company executive; m. Michael Wise; 3 children. B in Aero. and Aerospace Engring., U. Mich., Ann Arbor, 1975. Assoc. engr. Gen. Dynamics, Ft. Worth, prog. dir. F-16 USAF progs., 1987; v.p., prog. dir. F-22 prog. Lockheed Martin Corp., Ft. Worth, v.p., dep. co. ops., v.p. engring. home dept., 1998—2003; v.p. bus. ops. Lockheed Martin Aeronautics Co., Ft. Worth. Pres. Lockheed Martin Aeronautics Employees' Reaching Out Club, Ft. Worth; pres. bd. dirs. Goodwill Industries Ft. Worth. Recipient Upward Mobility award, Soc. Women Engrs., 1996, Henry Laurence Gantt medal, ASME, 2006. Mem.: Women in Aerospace, Soc. Aerospace Engrs., Rotary Internat. Office: Lockheed Martin Aeronautics Lockheed Blvd Fort Worth TX 76108

WISE, GARY LAMAR, electrical engineering and mathematics educator, investment researcher; b. Tex. City, July 29, 1945; s. Calder Lamar and Ruby Lavon (Strom) Wise; m. Mary Estella Warren Wise, Dec. 28, 1974; 1 child, Tanna Estella. BA summa cum laude, Rice U., 1971; MSE, MA, Princeton U., 1973, PhD, 1974. Postdoc. rsch. assoc. Princeton U., NJ, 1974; asst. prof. Tex. Tech U., Lubbock, 1975—76, U. Tex., Austin, 1976—80, assoc. prof., 1980—84, prof. elec. & computer engring. & math., 1984—; rsch. assoc. stats. U. Calif. Berkeley, 1989; tech. reviewer Rsch. Office US Army, Durham, NC, 1976; office sci. rsch. USAF, Washington, 1980—83, Harper & Row Pu., NYC, 1982—83, NSF, 1984, 1987, 1989—90, Springer-Verlog Pubs., NYC, 1987—88, John Wiley & Sons Pubs., NYC, 1988, PWS-Kent Pubs., Boston, 1990; cons. Baylor Coll. Medicine, Houston, 1972; mem. control group League City Nat. Bank, 1978—82; spkr. at numerous tech. confs. Contbr. chapters to books, articles to profl. publs. Recipient Outstanding Contbns. award, Coll. Engring., U. Tex. Engring. Found., 1979, 1981; vis. scholar grantee, Office Naval Rsch., 1990—; Sci. Rsch. grantee, USAF, 1976—90, grantee, Rsch. Contracts E-Sys. Inc., 1983—85, Simmons Centennial Tchg. fellow, U. Tex., Austin, 1982—84. Mem.: IEEE, Math. Assn. America, Inst. Math. Stats., Am. Math. Soc., Soc. Indsl. & Applied Math., Tau Beta Pi, Phi Beta Kappa, Eta Kappa Nu. Methodist. Home: 10031 Childress Dr Austin TX 78753-4348

WISE, SCOTT W., financial services executive; BA in Economics, Rice U., Houston; MA in Acctg., U. Tex. Various positions including contr., assoc. treas., v.p. investments & treas. Rice University, 1979—89, chief investment officer, 1989—2010; chief investment officer new bus. Teachers Insurance & Annuity Association-College Retirement Equities Fund (TIAA-CREF), Houston, 2010—. Bd. dirs. HCC Ins. Holdings, Inc., 2008—10. Mailing: TIAA CREF Hdqs 730 Third Ave New York NY 10007 Office: TIAA CREF 6400 Fannin St Ste 2450 Houston TX 77030-1509 Office Phone: 713-348-2514. Office Fax: 713-348-5479.

WISE, STEPHEN R., state legislator; b. Canton, Ohio, Dec. 11, 1941; m. Kathryn Beeman; children: Kelly Anne Legg, Tara Elizabeth Thompson. BS, Fla. So. Coll., 1963; MEd, Mid. Tenn. State U., 1968; EdD, U. Ala., 1970. Educator, cons.; v.p. devel. Fla. CC Jacksonville Campus; mem. Dist. 14 Fla. House of Reps., Tallahassee, 1988—93, mem. Dist. 13, 1993—2001; mem. Dist. 5 Fla. State Senate, Tallahassee, 2003—, chair edn. preK-12 appropriations com., mem. children, families and elder affairs com., cmty. affairs com., regulated industries com., rules com., joint legis. auditing com. Chmn. Gov. Coun. on Handicapped Concerns, 1984; mem. Jacksonville Landmarks Commn., 1985-87, State Job Tng. Coord. Coun., 1989-95, Nat. Coun. Resource Devel. Bd., Coun. Advancement & Support Edn. Two Yr. Coll. Adv. Bd.; v.p. Arthritis Found., 1987-88, Jacksonville CC Inst. Advancement; pres. Fla. Coun. Resource Devel., Opportunity Devel. Inc., 1986-95. Named Legis. of Yr. Fla. Alcohol & Drug Abuse Assn., Inc., 1991-93. Mem.: Save-a-Child. Republican. Baptist. Office: 1460 Cassat Ave Ste B Jacksonville FL 32205 also: 410 Senate Office Bldg 404 S Monroe St Tallahassee FL 32399-1100 Office Phone: 904-381-6000, 850-487-5027. Business E-Mail: wise.stephen@flsenate.gov.

WISE, THERESA, air transportation executive; BA in Math. and Chemistry, St. Olaf Coll., Northfield, Minn.; MS in Ops. Rsch. and Applied Math., PhD in Ops. Rsch. and Applied Math., Cornell U., Ithaca, NY. Joined NW Airlines Corp., Minn., 1993, mng. dir. info. svcs., v.p. Info. Svcs. Group, 2001—07; sr. v.p., chief info. officer NW Airlines Corp. & Delta Air Lines, 2007—. Mailing: Delta Air Lines 1030 Delta Blvd Atlanta GA 30320-6001 Office Phone: 612-726-2111.

WISEHART, MARY RUTH, retired religious organization administrator; b. Myrtle, Mo., Nov. 2, 1932; d. William Henry and Ora (Harbison) W. BA, Free Will Bapt. Bible Coll., 1955, George Peabody Coll. Tchrs., 1959, MA, 1960, PhD, 1976. Tchr. Free Will Bapt. Bible Coll., Nashville, 1956-60, chmn. English dept., 1961-85; exec. sec.-treas. Free Will Bapt. Women Nat. Active for Christ, 1985-98. Author: Sparks Into Flame, 1985, Beyond the Gate, 1998; contbr. poetry to jours. Mem. Scribbler's Club. Free Will Baptist. Avocations: photography, music, drama. Personal E-mail: wisemrw@aol.com, wisemyw@att.net.

WISEMAN, ERIC C., apparel executive; b. 1955; BS, Wake Forest U., 1977, MBA, 1988. Exec. v.p. JanSport VF Corp., Greensboro, NC, 1995—98, pres. Bestform Intimates, 1998—2000, v.p. & chmn. global intimate apparel, 2000—03, v.p. & chmn. sportswear coalition, 2003—04, v.p. & chmn. outdoor & sportswear coalitions, 2004—05, exec. v.p. global brands, 2005—06, pres., COO, 2006—07, pres., CEO, 2008, chmn., pres., CEO, 2008—. Bd. dirs. V.F. Corp., 2006—, Cigna Corp., 2007—. Bd. visitors Babcock Grad. Sch. Mgmt., Wake Forest U. Office: VF Corp 105 Corporate Ctr Blvd Greensboro NC 27408 Mailing: VF Corp PO Box 21488 Greensboro NC 27420-1488 E-mail: eric_wiseman@vfc.com.

WISEMAN, FRANK L., JR., chemistry professor; Prof., chair chemistry dept. Georgetown Coll., Ky. Recipient US Prof. of Yr. award, Carnegie Found. for Advancement of Tchg. and Coun. for Advancement and Support of Edn., 2006. Avocations: painting, hunting. Office: Chemistry Dept Georgetown Coll 400 E College St Georgetown KY 40324 Office Phone: 502-863-8103. E-mail: Frank_Wiseman@georgetowncollege.edu.

WISEMAN, THOMAS ANDERTON, JR., federal judge; b. Tullahoma, Tenn., Nov. 3, 1930; s. Thomas Anderton and Vera Seleta (Poe) W.; m. Emily Barbara Matlack, Mar. 30, 1957; children: Thomas Anderton III, Mary Alice, Sarah Emily. BA, Vanderbilt U., 1952, LL.B., 1954; LLM, U. Va., 1990. Bar: Tenn. Pvt. practice, Tullahoma, 1956-63; ptnr. Haynes, Wiseman & Hull, Tullahoma and Winchester, Tenn., 1963-71; treas. Tenn., 1971-74; ptnr. Chambers & Wiseman, 1974-78; judge US Dist. Ct. (mid. dist.) Tenn., Nashville, 1978—84, 1991—95, chief judge, 1984—91, sr. judge, 1995—; 6th cir. rep. Jud. Conf. of the U.S., 1996—2001, chair dist. judges conf., 1998-99; mem. Bankruptcy Adv. Rules Com., Jud. Conf., 1984—89. Mem. Tenn. Ho. of Reps., 1964-68; adj. prof. law Vanderbilt U. Sch. Law; cons. to judiciary of Brcko, Bosnia, 2002; mem. pattern jury instrn. com. 6th cir., 1988—. Asso. editor: Vanderbilt Law Rev, 1953-54. Democratic candidate for gov., Tenn., 1974; Chmn. Tenn. Heart Fund, 1973, Middle Tenn. Heart Fund, 1972. Served with U.S. Army, 1954-56. Fellow Tenn. Bar Found.; mem. Fed. Judges Assn. (bd. dirs. 1982-87, v.p. 1982-91, 87-91), Masons (33 deg.), Shriners, Amateur Chefs Soc. Presbyterian. Office: US Dist Ct 777 US Courthouse 801 Broadway Nashville TN 37203-3816 Office Phone: 615-736-7013.

WISH, LESLIEBETH BERGER, psychotherapist, writer, management consultant; d. Irving L. and Miriam Solomon Berger; m. Peter A. Wish, Nov. 16, 1984; 1 stepchild, Carly Sidra. AB in History & English, Carnegie Mellon U., 1970; MA in English, Ohio U., 1971; MA in Social Svc. Mgmt., Byrn Mawr Coll., 1976; EdD in Human Devel., U. Mass., 1996. Lic. clin. social worker Md., 1980, Mass., 1982, Fla., 2003, diplomate clin. social work Bd. Examiners, 1988; cert. aquatics fitness instr. 2005. Post doctoral tng. in marriage & family therapy sys. Georgetown U. Med. Sch., DC, 1979—82; dir. social work & families The Linwood Sch., Ellicott City, Md., 1980—81; dir. human resource devel. & clin. svcs. The New England Inst. Family Rels., Framingham, Mass., 1982—94; faculty coord., admissions acad. advisor Grad. Ctr. Bus. & Counseling Webster U., Sarasota, 2001—04; v.p. Gulfcoast Healthstyle, Sarasota, Fla., 1994—. Girls' career workshop developer Girls, Inc., Sarasota, Fla., 2006—07; lectr., cons. in field; founder lovevictory.com; adv. bd. mem., expert Qualityhealth.com; feature writer itsallaboutwomen-.com, 2014—. Author: Incest, Women & Work, 1998; author, contbg. editor: Trafalgar Publs., 2001—06; author: The Love Adventures of Almost Smart Cookie, 2013, Smart Relationships, 2013; contbr. articles to popular mags., websites;, author numerous poems; contbr. columns in newspapers. Chair Sarasota Women's Advisory Commn., 1994—2001; pres. coun. Easter Seals, 2002—; co-coord. counseling network, spl. ops. Warrior Found., 2006—; co-coord. counselor network Spl. Ops. Warrior Found.; co-coord. Child Abuse Task Force, Sarasota, 2006—07; program and workshop devel. The Women's Resource Ctr., Sarasota, 2007—, bd. mem., 2009—; active bd. mem. Womens Resource, Sarasota, Fla., 2009, U. South Fla., Acad. Lifelong Learning Faculty, 2008—; adv. bd. mem. & writer qualityhealth.com, 2009—. Recipient Md.'s Best Small Press award, Md. Arts Commn., 1981; named one of The Fifty, NASW, 2011—. Mem.: Am. Biog. Inst. (Woman Yr. 2006), Women's Leadership & Acad. Honor Society (mortar bd. 1970), Phi Kappa Phi. Achievements include first to expand sex education and awareness of sexual issues at work and home for The New England Institute of Family Relations; research in the connection between childhood sexual abuse and its impact on work and career in women; on career-family history inventory. Avocations: travel, opera, writing, painting.

WISLER, DARLA LEE, pastor; b. Balt., May 14, 1940; d. Hugh Charles Douglas and Angela Rita (Poffel) Mayer; m. Norman Marvin Wisler, Dec. 26, 1960; children: David Paul, Diane Lynn. A in Biblical Studies, Christian Internat. U., 1982, BTh, 1984, MDiv, 1990, D in Ministry, 1993. Asst. pastor Anderson Christian Assembly, SC, 1978-80; founder, sr. apostle Living Water Ch., Anderson, 1981—; on call chaplain Anderson Area Medical Center, 2003—; sr. apostle, dean Living Water Ministry Tng. Ctr., 2006—, Living Water Network Ministries, 2011. Mid-week devotion min. NHC Healthcare of Anderson, 1980—, pres. adv. bd., 1988—; dean Living Water Bible Coll., Anderson, 1982—; prin. Living Water Christian Sch., Anderson, 1983-88; apostle, dean Living Water Ministry Tng. Ctr., 2006—; regular host and co-host Dove Broadcasting TV-16, Greenville, S.C., 1984—; coord. Christian Internat. Network of Chs. Mid-East Region, 1994-96. Author: Basic Christian Teaching Made Plain and Clear, 1994, Advanced Christian Teaching Made Plain and Clear, 1995, Bible Lessons for Children, 2003, Tremendous Teens, 2004. Pres. clergy staff exec. com. Anderson Area Med. Ctr., 1993-94, on-call chaplain, 2003—; sec. Anderson County Sheriff's Dept. Chaplaincy, Anderson, 1996-98; chaplain Anderson County Sheriff's Dept., 1996-2004, 2010-, bd. dirs., 1996-2004, vice chair bd. dirs., 2001-02, chair, 2002-04. Republican. Avocations: walking, reading, crocheting, cooking. Office: Living Water Ch PO Box 1823 Anderson SC 29622-1823 Office Phone: 864-224-9315. Personal E-mail: dr_wisler@charter.net.

WISNICKI, JEFFREY LEONARD, plastic surgeon; b. NYC, May 15, 1957; s. Joseph and Lorraine (Justman) Wisnicki; m. Rebecca Lynn O'Shields, Feb. 2, 1997; children: Justin Robert, Brandon Lawrence. BS summa cum laude, Rensselaer Poly. Inst., 1976; MD cum laude with honors, Union U., 1980. Diplomate Am. Bd. Plastic Surgery. Intern in surgery Stanford (Calif.) U. Med. Ctr., 1980-81, resident in gen., plastic and reconstructive surgery, 1981-84, chief resident in plastic and reconstructive surgery, 1985-86; fellow in plastic and reconstructive surgery Dartmouth-Hitchcock Med. Ctr., Hanover, NH, 1984; active staff Good Samaritan Hosp., West Palm Beach, Fla., 1986—, Wellington Regional Hosp., West Palm Beach, 1986—; chief divsn. plastic surgery John F. Kennedy Meml. Hosp., West Palm Beach, 1990-93; chmn. dept. surgery Palms West Hosp., West Palm Beach, 1991-93, chief med. staff, 1994-97, 2014—, chmn. bd. trustees, 1997—2002, trustee, 2002—03; chief divsn. plastic surgery Good Samaritan and St. Mary's Hosp., West Palm Beach, 1997—2001, Good Samaritan Hosp., 2001—04. Clin. instr. surgery U. Calif., San Francisco, 1985; bd. dirs. Interplast, 1985-86, clin. faculty, 1986—90; presenter in field. Contbr. chpts. to books and articles to profl. jours. Named Best Plastic Surgeon, Palm Beach Mag., 1998. Fellow ACS; mem. Am. Soc. Plastic & Reconstructive Surgeons, Alpha Omega Alpha. Office: 13005 Southern Blvd Ste 133 Loxahatchee FL 33470 Office Phone: 561-798-1400. Business E-Mail: info@drwisnicki.com.

WISSINGER, JOHN, retail executive; Dir., area ops. RadioShack Corp., area v.p., mng. dir., Caribbean, v.p., Caribbean ops., 2008—. Office: RadioShack Corp Mail Stop CF3-201 300 RadioShack Cir Fort Worth TX 76102 Office Phone: 817-415-3011. Office Fax: 817-415-2647. Business E-Mail: john.wissinger@radioshack.com.

WITCHER, MICHAEL H., homeland and national security expert; b. Birmingham, Ala., Apr. 27, 1970; s. Pam Grass and James S. Witcher. BS in Bus. Adminstrn., Birmingham-Southern Coll., Ala., 1993. Bus. account exec. GTE Wireless, Birmingham, Ala., 1998—99; dir. sales, mktg. and pub. rels. Vazda Studios, Birmingham, 1999—2001; west coast IT/control systems sales mgr. Prophet Systems Innovations, Denver, 2001—02; EVP Homeland Security; dir. BSI2000, Washington, DC, 2002—04, Praetorian Sys., Birmingham, Ala., 2006—; CEO & homeland and nat. security expert Omega Force, 2004—. Capt. Mountain Brook Police Dept., Explorers, Mountain Brook, Ala., 1985—88; co-chairman Pub. Rels. Com., Operation New Birmingham, Ala., 1995—97; fundraiser Ala. Symphonic Assn., Birmingham, 1995—97; govtl. affairs com. Chamber of Commerce, Birmingham, 1997—, law enforcement com., 1997—; fin. com. mem. Colo. State Rep. Party, Denver, 2002—05; program mem. Infraguard, Washington, 2006—; citizen's acad. grad. FBI, Birmingham, 2006—, steering com., P.U.S.H. Homeland Sec. Program, 2006—; dir. ALPS LLC, 2010—; advisor US Congress, Bush White House, Pentagon, CIA, NSA. Author: (poetry) Over 300 poems, 6 published poems (Top 50 Poetic Works award, 2006); dir.: (wrote, directed, and edited video) Rebuilding a City Center;, author multiple marketing pieces and op-eds. Eagle scout; campaign mgr. multiple polit. campaigns, Birmingham, 1996—2000; founder, chmn. Omega Polit. Action Com., Birmingham, 1996—2004; bd. mem., treas. Birmingham Advt. Fedn., Birmingham, 1999—2001; bd. mem., exec. com. Ala. Zool. Soc., Birmingham Zoo, Ala., 1999—2005; bd. mem. Rocky Mountain Butterfly Consortium, Denver, 2002—03. Mem.: Birmingham Mus. of Art (assoc.), Alpha Tau Omega (life). Achievements include listing in Top 40 Under 40, Birmingham Business Journal. Avocations: horseback riding, soccer, Karate, sailing, travel. Office Phone: 205-603-3450. Personal E-mail: mhwitcher@ymail.com.

WITEK, JAMES EUGENE, retired public relations executive; b. LaPorte, Ind., Sept. 14, 1932; s. Stanley and Victoria (Peret) W.; m. Mary Carolyn Hood, June 18, 1955; children: James Jay, Janet Marie, Jeffrey Patrick, Jean Theresa. AB, Ind. U., 1954; MA, U. Mo., 1970. Joined U.S. Army, 1954, commd. 2d lt., 1954, advanced through grades to lt. col., 1968; editor, pub. Infantry Mag., Fort Benning, Ga., 1968-70; advisor to Vietnamese Mil. Region IV Ranger Comdr., 1970-71; plans officer CINCPAC, Hawaii, 1971-75; exec. editor Soldiers, Washington, 1975-77, editor in chief, 1977-79; dir. public affairs Nat. Com. for Employer Support Guard and Res., Arlington, Va., 1979-82, ret., 1982; dep. dir. pub. relations Am. Legion, Washington, 1982-86; mgr. pub. rels. Dowty Aerospace, Sterling, Va., 1986-99; ret. Decorated Legion of Merit, Bronze Star, Air Medal, Purple Heart, Vietnamese Cross of Gallantry with Silver Star. Mem. Am. Legion, Ret. Officers Assn., Disabled Am. Vets., Phi Beta Kappa, Tau Kappa Alpha, Pi Kappa Phi. Roman Catholic. Home: 3240 Atlanta St Fairfax VA 22030-2128

WITHERSPOON, CAROLYN BRACK, lawyer; b. Little Rock, Mar. 29, 1950; d. Gordon Paisley and Mildred Louise (Lemon) Brack; m. Joseph Roger Armbrust, July 25, 1970 (div. 1976); 1 child, Catherine Paisley Armbrust; m. John Leslie Witherspoon, June 15, 1979. Student, So. Meth. U., 1970; BA, U. Ark., 1974, JD with honors, 1978. Bar: Ark. 1978, U.S. Dist. Ct. (ea. and we. dists.) Ark. 1978, U.S. Ct. Appeals (8th cir.) 1979, U.S. Supreme Ct. 1981. Asst. atty. City of Little Rock, 1978, chief dep. atty., acting city atty., 1984—85; assoc. House, Wallace & Jewell, Little Rock, 1985—87, ptnr., 1987—90; dir. McGlinchey Stafford Lang, Little Rock, 1990—97, Cross, Gunter, Witherspoon & Galchus, Little Rock, 1997—. Mem. com. Fed. Ct. Practice, 1988—91; mem. civil practice com. Ark. Supreme Ct., 1989—97, mem. continuing legal edn. bd., 1998—2001; chair adv. com. Civil Justice Reform Act, 1993—95; chair State Bd. Bar Examiners, 2001—05. Contbr. articles to profl. jours. Commr. Ark. Real Estate Commn., 1978—81; past chmn. Little Rock Housing Authority Bd. Commn.; past pres., bd. dirs. Advs. for Battered Women; past pres. Women's Found. Ark., Ark. Women's History Inst. Recipient Labor Law award, Am. Jurisprudence, 1977. Fellow: Coll. Labor and Employment Lawyers, Am. Bar Found. (Ark. Fellows Past chair); mem.: ABA (ho. dels. 1997—, equal employment opportunity com.), Am. Employment Law Coun., William R. Overton Inn of Ct. (pres. 1992—93), Nat. Inst. Mcpl. Law Officers (state chmn. 1985—87, v.p. 1987—89), Pulaski County Bar Assn. (pres. 1989—90), Ark. Assn. Women Lawyers (pres. 1982—83), Ark. Bar Assn. (pres. 1995—96, Golden Gavel award 1989, Ark. Inst. Cont. Legal Edn. award 1991, Golden Gavel award 1993, Charles L. Carpenter award 2005), Transp. Lawyers Assn. (mem. exec. com. 1997—99), Nat. Conf. Bar Pres. (mem. exec. coun. 1996—99), Am. Jur Soc., Am. Law Inst. Avocations: hunting, fishing, reading, travel. Office: Cross Gunter Witherspoon and Galchus 500 President Clinton Ave Ste 200 Little Rock AR 72201-1747 Office Phone: 501-371-9999. Business E-Mail: cspoon@cgwg.com.

WITHERSPOON, LYNN RALPH, physician, information technology executive; b. Mt. Pleasant, Mich., Nov. 11, 1942; m. Glory Ann Smith, Jan. 27, 1980; children: Eric W., Kevin B., Heather A. BA, Fla. State U., 1964; MD, U. Wis., 1968. Diplomate Am. Bd. Nuclear Medicine, Am. Bd. Internal Medicine. With Ochsner Clinic/Alton

Ochsner Med. Found., New Orleans, 1974—, dir. radioimmunology lab., 1975-95, chmn., dir. med. informatics, 1994-96; chief info. officer Ochsner Clinic, 1997—2001; chief info. officer, v.p. Ochsner Clinic Found., 2001—06; intern, then resident in internal medicine Ochsner, New Orleans, 1968-70; fellow in nuclear medicine Duke U., Durham, N.C., 1972-74, chief resident in nuclear medicine, 1973-74; chief info. officer, system v.p. Ochsner Health System, 2006—09; chief med. info. officer, system v.p. Ochsner Health Sys., 2009—. Contbr. numerous articles to profl. jours. Elder Jefferson (La.) Presbyn. Ch., 1982—; mem. adv. bd. Sta. WWNO, New Orleans, 1985—2005. Lt. comdr. USNR, 1970-72. Fellow ACP; mem. Soc. Nuclear Medicine, Southwestern Soc. Nuclear Medicine (v.p. 1980-81, sec. 1983-86, pres. 1988-89), Soc. Nuclear Medicine (trustee 1988-89), La. Healthcare Quality Farm Health Info. Tech. Com., 2008-. Presbyterian. Avocations: violin, swimming. Office: Ochsner Clinic 1514 Jefferson Hwy New Orleans LA 70121-2483 Office Phone: 504-842-4033. E-mail: lwitherspoon@ochsner.org.

WITHERSPOON, WALTER PENNINGTON, JR., orthodontist; b. Sept. 3, 1938; s. Walter P. and Florence Evelyn (Jones) W.; m. Joyce Ann Smith, Sept. 6, 1970; 1 child, Annie Melissa. BS, U. S.C., 1960; DDS, U. N.C., 1964, MSO, 1969. Pvt. practice, Columbia, 1969—. Med. staff Bapt. Med. Ctr., Columbia, 1970—, Lexington County Hosp., West Columbia, 1974—. Host Nite Line Broadcasting Co. Adv. bd. 1st Palmetto Bank and Trust, West Columbia, 1982; mem. adv. bd. 1st Citizens Bank; candidate S.C. Ho. of Reps., 1994; del. S.C. Rep. Com., 1989—; mem. platform com. S.C. Rep. Party Conv., poll com., 1992; del. Rep. Nat. Conv., Houston, 1992, rules com., task force on edn.; Rep. nat. committeeman, 1996-2008, rules com., rep. nat. com.; pres. Rep. Electoral Coll., 1996, 2000-04; bd. dirs. Southeastern Coll. Assemblies of God, Lakeland, Fla., 1984, Brookland Plantation Home for Boys, Orangeburg, S.C.; pres. Friends of Irmo Libr.; chmn. Lexington County Rep. Party; commr. Richland/Lexington Counties Commn. for Tech. Edn., S.C. Commn. on Alcohol and Drug Abuse; bd. dirs. Centerplace for Homeless; mem. Presdl. Visit-Ticket Com.; amb. Irmo C. of C.; vol. lockup telethon Muscular Dystrophy Assn. Lt. USN, 1964-66; candidate US Senate, 2008; treas. Fin. Devel. Champions For Life, Columbia, SC. Recipient Century Mem. award Boy Scouts Am., 1984. Mem. ADA, Greater Columbia Dental Assn. (pres. 1975-76), U. NC Dental Alumni Assn. (bd. dirs.), SC Dental Assn. (ho. of dels. 1971-73, 91-96, legis. com. 1993), SC Orthodontic Assn. (ctrl. dist. dir., state rep.), Am. Assn. Orthodontists, (polit. action com.), Sertoma (pres. 1975-76), Am. Legion (mem. baseball com.), Come for Boys and Girls State, So. Assn. Orthodontists (SC rep. Am. Assn. Orthodontists polit. action com.), Cen. Dist. Dental Soc., 1st Founds. Inc. (bd. dirs.). Home: 250 Lancer Dr Columbia SC 29212-1216

WITOWSKI, GERALD T., aerospace and defense manufacturing company executive; BS, US Naval Acad., Annapolis, MD; MA in Mgmt. & Human Rels., Webster U. Mktg. engr., sensor sys. divsn. Goodrich Corp., 1978—88, v.p., mktg. & sales, 1988—97, v.p., gen. mgr., comml. transport & test sys. bus., 1997—2001, v.p., gen. mgr., sensor sys., 2001—06, pres., segment pres., electronic sys., 2006—07, exec. v.p., operational excellence & tech., 2007—. Commd. officer, pilot USN. Office: Goodrich Corp Four Coliseum Ctr 2730 W Tyvola Rd Charlotte NC 28217 Office Phone: 704-423-7000. Office Fax: 704-423-7127. Business E-Mail: g_w@goodrich.com.

WITSCHEY, WALTER ROBERT THURMOND, anthropologist, educator, former museum director; b. Charleston, W.Va., June 19, 1941; s. Robert E. and Sarah Elizabeth (Thurmond) W.; m. Joan DuRelle Vincent, July 19, 1980; children: Anne Elizabeth, Schon Roberts Parris, Sarah C. Brauner, Walter Robert Thurmond II, Benjamin Hart Vincent. BA in Physics, Princeton U., 1963; MBA in Ops. Rsch., U. Va., 1965; MA in Anthropology-Maya Archaeology, Tulane U., 1989, PhD in Anthropology-Maya Archaeology, 1993. Systems engr. IBM Corp., Richmond, Va., 1965-67, mktg. rep., 1967-69; v.p. The Computer Co., Richmond, Va., 1969-70, pres., CEO, 1970-84; cons., pub., proprietorship Gatewood Co., Richmond, Va., 1978—; dir., CEO Sci. Mus. Va., Richmond, Va., 1992—2007, dir. emeritus, 2007—; prof. anthropology and sci. edn. Cook-Cole Coll. Arts and Scis., Longwood U., Farmville, Va., 2007—. Bd. dirs. Highland Data Svcs., 1982-85; vis. instr. computer systems U. Va., 1985-86; instr. word processing, Delgado Community Coll., 1989; lectr. microcomputer applications, Our Lady Of Holy Cross Coll., 1989-92; lectr. dept. Anthropology, Tulane U., 1987-92, asst. to the dir., 1987-88, lectr., curriculum cons., 1988-92, adj. instr. A.B. Freeman Sch., 1991; adj. faculty dept. Sociology, Anthropology and Mathematical Scis., Va. Commonwealth U., 1992—2007, rsch. fellow Middle Am. Rsch. Inst., Tulane U. Contbr. articles to profl. jours. Dir. Assn. Sci.-Tech. Ctrs., 1995—2006, pres. 2001-03, Sci. Mus. Va. Found., Richmond, 1981-90, La. Sci. Ctr., New Orleans, 1985-90; pres., dir. Richmond-on-the-James, 1984-85; sec., dir. Richmond Cmty. H.S. Policy Bd.; cons. Federated Arts Coun., Richmond; pres. Va. Rail Policy Inst., 2008-2011. Tinker Found. archaeol. rsch. grantee (3), Middle Am. Rsch. Inst. archaeol. grantee, Mesoam. Ecology Inst. archaeol. rsch. grantee (3), Middle Am. Rsch. Inst. archaeol. rsch. grantee (3), pvt. archaeol. rsch. grantee. Mem. AAAS, Soc. Am. Archaeology, Va. Acad. Sci. (pres. 2003-04), Sigma Xi. Presbyterian. Office: Longwood U 201 High St Farmville VA 23909 Business E-Mail: witscheywr@longwood.edu.

WITT, HUGH ERNEST, manufacturing executive, consultant; b. Winchester, Ky., Nov. 18, 1921; s. Hugh E. and Louella (Milliken) W.; m. Janie Bryan (dec. Oct. 1990); m. Evelyn Chapman, Apr. 22, 1993 (dec. 2011). Student, Transylvania U., 1941-43; BS, U. Ky., 1945; MS, MIT, 1957. Asst. to dep. asst. sec. Dept. of Air Force, Washington, 1954-61, dep. asst. sec., 1961-70, Dept. of Navy, Washington, 1970-73; prin. dep. asst. sec. of Def., Washington, 1973-74; fed. procurement policy adminstr. Office Mgmt. and Budget, Washington, 1974-77; dir., govt. liaison United Techs. Corp., Washington, 1977-81, v.p., govt. liaison, 1981-87, cons. to United Techs. Corp., 1987—. Pres. Old Town Civic Assn., Alexandria, Va., 1961-63; bd. dirs. Alexandria Hist. Found.; mem. Alexandria Bd. Archtl. Rev., 1964-77; trustee Alexandria Hosp. Found., 1992-94. Alfred P. Sloan fellow MIT, Cambridge, Mass., 1956-57. Fellow Nat. Contract Mgmt. Assn.; mem. Aerospace Industries Assn., Nat. Security Indsl. Assn., MIT Alumni Assn., Soc. Sloan Fellows, Kappa Alpha.

WITT, JIM, newspaper editor; Grad., Tex. State U., San Marcos, 1974. Asst. mng. editor news Star-Telegram, Arlington, Tex., 1986—92, editor, 1992—95, pub. Northeast Tarrant County edit., 1995; sr. v.p., exec. editor Ft. Worth Star-Telegram, 1996—. Named to University Star Hall of Fame, Tex. State U.-San Marcos, 2007. Mem.: Tex. AP Mng. Editors, American Soc. Newspaper Editors. Office: Ft Worth Star-Telegram 808 Throckmorton St PO Box 1870 Fort Worth TX 76101 Office Phone: 817-390-7704. E-mail: jwitt@star-telegram.com.

WITT, ROBERT E., academic administrator; b. Sept. 16, 1940; m. Anne Witt; children: Peter, Karen. BA in Econs., Bates Coll., 1962; MBA, Dartmouth Coll., 1964; PhD in Bus. Adminstrn., Pa. State U., 1968. Rsch. asst. Amos Tuck Sch., Dartmouth Coll., Hanover, N.H., 1964-65; instr. mktg. Pa. State U., 1967-68; asst. prof. Coll. and Grad. Sch. Bus., U. Tex., Austin, 1968-71, assoc. prof., 1971-75, chmn. dept. mktg., 1973-83, prof., 1975-83, Zale Corp. centennial prof. bus., 1983-85, Betty and Glenn Mortimer centennial prof. bus., 1985-95, centennial chairperson bus. edn. leadership, 1986-95, acting dean, then dean, 1985—95; interim pres. U. Tex., Arlington, 1995-96, pres., 1996—2003, U. Ala., Tuscaloosa, 2003—12; chancellor U. Ala. Sys., 2012—. Mem. budget coun. dept. mktg. adminstrn. U. Tex., Austin, mem. faculty exec. devel. program, mem. dean's coun.; mem. athletes adv. com. NCAA; mem. acad. adv. bd. World Mgmt. Coun., 1988; mem. future directions coun. U. Tex. Ex-Students Assn., 1978-88, mem. exec. coun., 1981-83, 87-89; mem. adv. bd. dirs. Post Oak Bank, Frost Nat. Bank; mem. Acctg. Edn. Change Commn.; bd. dirs. Life Ptnrs. Group. Assoc. editor Social Sci. Quar., 1970-72; mem. editl. rev. bd. Jour. Mktg., 1971-73, 82-85; contbr. articles to profl. jours. Bd. dirs. Austin Symphony, Univ. Coop. Soc., 1978-82. Recipient Top Hand award U. Tex. Ex-Students Assn., 1988. Mem. Am. Mktg. Assn. (fellow doctoral consortium 1967, progran chmn. doctoral consortium 1972, reviewer, presenter), Assn. for Consumer Rsch. (treas. 1976, mem. exec. com. 1975-76, reviewer, conf. session chmn.), Am. Assembly Collegiate Schs. of Bus. (bd. dirs. 1991—, mem. visitation com. 1991, mem. govtl. rels. com. 1986-89, chmn. govtl. rels. com. 1987-89), So. Mktg. Assn. (conf. trach chmn., presenter), Beta Gamma Sigma (v.p. U. Tex. chpt. 1973-74, pres. chpt. 1974-75), Phi Kappa Phi. Office: Office of the Chancellor University of Alabama 401 Queen City Ave Tuscaloosa AL 35401-1551 Office Phone: 205-348-9731. Office Fax: 205-348-9788.*

WITT, WALTER FRANCIS, JR., lawyer; b. Richmond, Va., Feb. 18, 1933; s. Walter Francis and Evelyn Virginia (Riggleman) W.; m. Rosemary Winter, Sept. 5, 1964; children: Leslie Anne Millman, Walter Francis III. BS, U. Richmond, 1954, JD, 1966. Bar: Va. 1966, DC 1974. Assoc. Hunton and Williams, Richmond, 1966-74, ptnr., 1974—. Contbr. articles to profl. jours. 1st lt. US Army, 1955-57. Mem. ABA (chmn. real property com. sect. gen. practice 1995-2000, Va. Bar Assn., Richmond Bar Assn., DC Bar Assn., Phi Beta Kappa, Phi Delta Phi. Home: 8901 Tresco Rd Richmond VA 23229-7725 Home Phone: 804-740-8420; Office Phone: 804-788-8391. Personal E-mail: wittwf@aol.com.

WITTEN, JASON (CHRISTOPHER JASON WITTEN), professional football player; b. Elizabethton, Tenn., May 6, 1982; Attended, U. Tenn., 2000—02. TE Dallas Cowboys, 2003—. Founder Jason Witten SCORE Found. Named 1st Team All-Pro, AP, 2007, 2010; named to Nat. Football Conf. Pro-Bowl Team, NFL, 2004—10, 2012. Achievements include tying the NFL record for receptions by a tight end in a single game (15), 2007. Office: Dallas Cowboys One Cowboys Pkwy Irving TX 75063-4999

WITTENBORG, KARIN, university librarian; m. Michael B. Sullivan. BA, Brown U., 1969; MLS, SUNY Buffalo, 1976. Various positions SUNY Buffalo, 1976—79; libr. mgmt. intern MIT, 1981—82; chief gen. reference dept. and curator social sci. collections Stanford U., 1979—85; assoc. univ. libr. collections UCLA, 1985—93; univ. libr. U. Va., 1993—. Adv. coun. Academic Computing and Libr. Stanford U.; mem. com. info. resources Brown U.; exec. com. Digital Libr. Fedn. Recipient Zintl Leadership award, U. Va., 2005. Avocations: cooking, running, gardening. Office: Univ Virginia Library PO Box 400113 Charlottesville VA 22904 Office Phone: 434-924-7849. Fax: 434-924-1431. E-mail: kw7g@virginia.edu.

WITTICH, WESLEY E., corporate financial executive; BBA in Acctg., Armstrong State Coll.; MA in Acctg., U. Ga., 1978. Joined Lithonia Lighting, 1980, v.p., fin., 1994—98, v.p., CFO, 1998—2001; exec. v.p., CFO Acuity Brands Lighting; sr. v.p., audit and risk mgmt. Acuity Brands, Inc., 2004—. Office: Acuity Brands Inc 1170 Peachtree St NE Ste 2300 Atlanta GA 30309-7676 Office Phone: 404-853-1400. Office Fax: 404-853-1411.

WITTMAN, ROBERT J., United States Representative from Virginia, former state legislator; b. Washington, Feb. 3, 1959; m. Kathryn Jane Sisson; children: Devon, Josh. BS in Biology, Va. Poly. Inst., 1981; MPH, U. NC, Chapel Hill, 1990; PhD in Pub. Policy and Adminstrn., Va. Commonwealth U., 2002. Environ. health specialist Va. Dept. Health, dir. divsn. shellfish sanitation, 1992—2007; mem. Dist. 99 Va. House of Delegates, 2006—07; mem. US Congress from 1st Va. dist., 2007—. Councilman Montross Town Coun., 1986—96, mayor, Town of Montross, 1992—96; mem. Westmoreland County Bd. Supervisors, 1996—2005, chmn., 2003—05. Bd. visitors US Naval Acad., 2009—; mem. Northern Neck Planning Dist. Commn., 2003, Montross Fall and Spring Festival Com.; chmn. Montross-Westmoreland Sewer Authority, Rappahannock River Basin Commn., Interstate Shellfish Sanitation Conf. Mem.: Pi Alpha Alpha. Republican. Episcopalian. Office: US House of Representatives 2454 Rayburn House Office Bldg Washington DC 20515 also: 3504 Plank Rd Ste 203 Fredericksburg VA 22407*

WITTMER, JAMES FREDERICK, preventive medicine physician, educator; b. Carlinville, Ill., Dec. 30, 1932; s. Franklin Benjamin and Eva Caroline (Zihlman) W.; m. Juanita Lou Wilkey, June 29, 1962; children: Ellen, Carol, Nancy. MD, Washington U., St. Louis, 1957; MPH, Harvard U., 1961. Diplomate Am. Bd. Preventive Medicine. Intern U. Va. Hosp., Charlottesville, 1857-58; commd. capt. USAF, 1958, advanced through grades to col., 1971; ret., 1979; dean allied health U. Tex. Health Sci. Ctr., San Antonio, 1979-80; asst. med. dir. Conoco Oil Co., Ponca City, Okla., 1980-81; assoc. med. dir. Mobil Oil Corp., NYC, 1981-83; dir. health, environ. and safety ITT, NYC, 1983-95, corp. v.p., 1990-95. Clin. prof. medicine Cornell U. Med. Coll., NYC, 1984—; lectr. environ. medicine NYU, NYC, 1984—; adj. prof. U. Tex. Sch. Pub. Health, Houston, 1987—, prof. occupl. health, 1996—97; nat. coord. com. on clin. preventive svcs. USPHS, 1994—97; cons. office hearings and appeals U.S. Social Security Adminstrn., 1997—2003; cons. Met. Health Dist., San Antonio, 2002—08. Mem. Pres.'s Com. on Employment People with Disabilities, Washington, 1986-2000, chmn. med. and ins. com., 1986-90. Fellow ACP, Am. Coll. Occupational and Environ. Medicine (bd. dirs. 1990-97, sec. 1992-94), Am. Coll. Preventive Medicine, Aerospace Med. Assn., N.Y. Acad. Medicine; mem. AMA. Home: 159 Sabine Rd Boerne TX 78006-6217 Home Phone: 830-537-4782; Office Phone: 830-537-4782. Business E-Mail: wittmer@gvtc.com.

WITWER, BRUCE, retired editor; b. St. Petersburg, Fla., Nov. 4, 1940; Mng. editor Tampa Tribune, 1996-99, ret., 1999. Office: Tampa Tribune 202 S Parker St Tampa FL 33606-2395

WODLINGER, MARK LOUIS, broadcast executive; b. Jacksonville, Fla., July 13, 1922; s. Mark H. and Beatrice Mae (Boney) W.; m. Marilyn Stone-Birk; children: Kevin, Michael, Stephen, Mark. BS, U. Fla., 1943. Salesman Sta. WQUA, Moline, Ill., 1948; mgr. Sta. WOC-AM-FM-TV, Davenport, Iowa, 1949-58; v.p. Sta. WMBD-TV, Peoria, Ill., 1959-61; v.p., gen. mgr. Sta. WZZM-TV, Grand Rapids, Mich., 1962-63, Sta. KMBC-TV, Kansas City, Mo., 1963-69; pres. Intermedia, Kansas City, 1969-73; builder, owner comml. radio stas. Swaziland, Africa; operator Radio Malawi, Blantyre, and Marknews TV and Radio News Bur., Nairobe, Kenya, 1971-74; owner, pres. Sta. KBEQ, Kansas City, 1973-77; owner Sta. WCJX-FM, Miami, 1985-86, Sta. WPWR WIXI-FM, Naples and Ft. Myers, Fla., 1986-95, Sta. KKLO-AM, Leavenworth, Kans., 1982-92, Sta. KCWV, Kansas City, Mo., 1982-90, TV-5, Hit Video USA, Satellite Music Network, Houston, 1985-88, SMR-2-way radio/telephone, Naples, Fla., 1993—95, San Francisco, 1993—; cons. Radio Hirszolgalat, Roxy Radio, Budapest, Hungary, 2007—08, Roxy Advt. Network, 2007—08. Mem. Wodlinger Broadcasting Co., Naples, 1978—; ptnr. Wireless Cable, Naples, 1990—; cons. KABELTEL KFT (Hungary), Budapest, Sopron, Nagykanizsa, Szombathely, 1991-96; comml. FM Radio Ikva, Sopron, 1993—2008, FM Radio Zalaegerszeg, 1995—, comml. FM Reflex Radio 99.2 MHz, Szekesfehervar, Hungary, 1996—2001, FM Love Radio 97.8, Tallinn, Paide, Rakvere, Tartu, Sindi, Viliandi and marjamaa, Estonia, 1993—2007; with wireless cable TV Ukrainian-Am. Broadcasting, Kiev, Ukraine, 1990—95, comml. TV Channel 7, 1990—95, comml. FM Radio 69.89, Kiev, 1992—95; with FM Radiocentras, Vilnius, Lithuania, 1992-96; with comml. FM Radiola 99.70 MHz, 1996—, European HiT Radio; with joint mktg. AT&T Paradyne, Largo, Fla., 1992-94; with real estate devel., Croatia, 1991—95; owner outdoor advt. billboards, Tallinn, Estonia, 1993-95; with real estate devel., Hungary, 1991—. Bd. dirs. Kansas City Philharm., Kansas City Civic Coun., Naples YMCA, Budapest Festival Orch., 2000; mem. Conservancy, Naples Civic Assn. Served to lt. USN, Air 1941-45. Mem. Nat. Assn. Broadcasters, Mo. Assn. Broadcasters, Broadcast Pioneers. Clubs: Kansas City, Univ., Vanguard, Carriage, Port Royal, Naples Yacht, Houston Yacht, White Lake Yacht (Whitehall, Mich.), Haile Plantation Country Club. Lodges: Rotary, Reynolds Plantation Country Club, Lake Oconee, Ga. Republican. Episcopalian.

WOLCOTT, HUGH DIXON, obstetrics and gynecology educator; b. NYC, Jan. 12, 1946; s. Charles Edmund and Joan Degrau (Loveland) W.; m. Jane Jarrell Smith; children: Allison, James. BS, U.S. Naval Acad., 1967; MSE, Princeton U., 1969; MD, Northwestern U., 1979. Diplomate Am. Bd. Ob-Gyn, Am. Bd. Med. Examiners. Commd. ensign USN, 1967, advanced through grades to capt., 1990; aviator, Fighter Squadron 14 Naval Air Station, Oceana, Va., 1971-74; test pilot Naval Air Test Ctr., Patuxent River, Md., 1974-76; staff physician Naval Hosp., Portsmouth, Va., 1984, Jacksonville, Fla., 1984-86, dir. colposcopy and laser clins. Portsmouth, Va., 1986-89, dir. ob-gyn. residency program, 1989-91, acting chmn. dept. ob-gyn., 1990-91; ret., 1991; asst. prof. Med. Coll. Hampton Roads, Norfolk, Va., 1991—. Chmn. dept. ob-gyn. Sentara Hosps, Norfolk, 1996—2001; ob-gyn. splty. advisor Sentara Health Mgmt. Corp., 2000—09; chmn. bd. mgrs. Mid-Atlantic Women's Care, LLC, 2005—08; mem. Congl. Adv. Com. Healthcare, 2006—09; program chmn. MAWC Patient Safety Conf., 2010. Contbr. articles profl. jours. Mem. steering com. Sentara ObRight Patient Safety Initiative, 2005—11; mem. Senatara Clin. Effectiveness Com. Obsteric Simulation Team, VHMA Team Stepps Faculty, 2013—14. Awarded 1st prize scientific paper by resident physician Am. Coll. Obstetricans and Gynecologists; recipient Guggenheim fellowship Princeton U., 1967-68, MVP award Am. Coll. Ob-gyn. PAC, 2010; Trident scholar U.S. Naval Acad., 1966-67, named one of Most Valuable Player, Am. Coll. Ob-Gyn., 2010, named Super Drs., Hampton Rds., Va., 2011, Castle Connoly Top Drs., 2013. Fellow Am. Coll. Ob.-Gyns. (chmn. Navy sect. armed forces dist. 1989-91), Assn. Profs. Ob.-Gyns. (assoc.); mem. Am. Assn. Gynecol. Laparoscopists. Episcopalian. Office: Woman Care Ctrs 100 Kingsley Ln Ste 400 Norfolk VA 23505 Home: 1202 Yancey Cir Virginia Beach VA 23454 Home Phone: 757-481-5670.

WOLF, FRANK RUDOLPH, United States Representative from Virginia; b. Phila., Jan. 30, 1939; m. Carolyn Stover; children: Frank, Virginia, Anne, Brenda, Rebecca. Attended, U. Miss., Oxford; BA, Pa. State U., 1961; LLB, Georgetown U. Sch. Law, 1965. Bar: Va., DC. Legislative asst. to Rep. Edward G. Biester, Jr. US House of Representatives, 1968-71; asst. to Sec. Rogers C.B. Morton US Dept. Interior, Washington, 1971-74, dep. asst. sec. for congressional & legislative affairs, 1974-75; mem. US Congress from 10th Va. dist., 1981—; chmn. US House Transp. Appropriations Subcommittee, 1995—2000, US House Sci.-State-Justice-Commerce Appropriations Subcommittee, 2001—06. Served in US Army, 1962—63, served in USAR, 1963—67. Recipient Edwin C. Whitehead award for Medical Rsch. Advocacy, 2014. Republican. Presbyterian. Office: US House of Representatives 233 Cannon House Office Bldg Washington DC 20515 also: 13873 Park Center Rd Ste130 Herndon VA 20171 Office Phone: 202-225-5136. Office Fax: 202-225-0437.*

WOLF, GARY WICKERT, retired lawyer; b. Slinger, Wis., Apr. 19, 1938; s. Leonard A. and Cleo C. (Wickert) W.; m. Jacqueline Weltzin, Dec. 17, 1960; children: Gary, Jonathan. BBA, U. Minn., 1960, JD cum laude, 1963. Bar: N.Y. 1964, U.S. Ct. Appeals (2d cir.) 1969, U.S. Dist. Ct. (so. dist.) N.Y. 1969, U.S. Supreme Ct. 1971. Assoc. Cahill, Gordon & Reindel, NYC, 1963—70, ptnr., 1970—2003, counsel, 2004—09; bd. dirs. Southwestern Pub. Svc. Co., 1980—93. Bd. dirs. N.J. Resources Corp., 1995—2008, N.J. Natural Gas Co., 1995—2007. Mem. Anglers Club (N.Y.C.), Henryville Conservation Club, Mashomack Fish and Game Club. Personal E-mail: garywwolf@msn.com.

WOLF, HENRY C., retired corporate financial executive, board member; m. Dixie Wolf. BA in Econ., Coll. of William and Mary, 1964, JD, 1966; MBA in Bus., La. State U., 1970; LLM, Georgetown U., 1973; attended Advanced Mgmt. Program, Harvard U., 1992. Held various positions, fin. divsn. Norfolk Southern Corp., 1973—91, v.p., taxation, 1991—93, exec. v. p., fin., 1993—98, vice chmn., CFO, 1998—2007. Bd. dirs. AGL Resources Inc., 2004—; bd.dirs. Hertz Global Holdings Inc., 2006—. Mem Bd. of Visitors Coll. William and Mary, 2003—, vice rector Bd. of Visitors, 2006—09, rector Bd. of Visitors, 2009—; trustee Colonial Williamsburg Found. Served four years to rank of captain Judge Advocate General's Corps US Army. Mem.: Order of the Coif (hon.). Office: AGL Resources Inc Ten Peachtree Pl Atlanta GA 30309 Office Phone: 404-584-4000. Office Fax: 404-584-3945. Business E-Mail: hwolf@hertz.com.

WOLF, JACQUELYN HVIZDOS, human resources specialist; b. Youngstown, Ohio, Apr. 19, 1961; d. John Andrew and Joyce Dale (McWhorter) Hvizdos; m. Dan William Wolf, Aug. 27, 1988. BA in Orgnl. Commun., Youngstown State U., Ohio, 1984; MA in Mgmt., Baker U., Overland Park, Kans., 1990; M in Orgnl. & Human Sys., PhD in Orgnl. & Human Sys., Fielding Grad. U., Santa Barbara, Calif. V.p., human resources, Aerospace Market Segments Honeywell (previously AlliedSignal), v.p., human resources, Truck Brakes divsn.; employee rels. trainee GE Co., Warren, Ohio, 1982-85, employee rels. specialist, 1985, area rels. mgr. Overland Park, Kans., 1985-88, human resources mgr. Merriam, Kans., 1989; pers. mgr. Hallmark Cards, Kansas City, Mo., 1988-89; various positions in info. sys. & svcs. GM Corp., 2000—02, global human resources dir., fin., asset mgmt., econ. devel. & enterprise svcs. orgns., 2002; exec. v.p., chief human resources officer Comerica Inc., 2006—09; sr. v.p., human resources Celanese Corp., 2009—. Freelance writer, Youngstown, 1984-85, Kansas City, 1985—. Mem. Pers. Mgmt. Assn. (legis. affairs com.). Avocations: writing, photography, travel. Home: 9098 N 114th Pl Scottsdale AZ 85259-5814 Office: Celanese Corp 1601 W LBJ Freeway Dallas TX 75234-6034 Office Phone: 972-443-4000. Office Fax: 972-443-8555. Business E-Mail: jackie.wolf@celanese.com.

WOLF, JEFFREY STEPHEN, physician; b. Hartford, Conn., July 30, 1946; s. Abraham and Norma Wolf; m. Nina Loving Lockridge; children: Sarah Loving, Lawren Hiley. BS, McGill U., 1968; MD, Med. Coll. Va., 1972, MS, 1973. Diplomate Am. Bd. Colon and Rectal Surgery. Intern in surgery Mt. Sinai Hosp., NYC, 1972-73, resident, 1973-75, N.Y. Med. Coll.-Met. Hosp., NYC, 1975-77; chief resident in surgery Met. Hosp., NYC, 1977-78; fellow colon-rectal surgery Grtr. Balt. Med. Ctr., 1978-79; colon-rectal surgeon Portsmouth, Va., 1979—. Fellow ACS, Am. Soc. Colon and Rectal Surgery; mem. AMA, Portsmouth Acad. Medicine, Med. Soc. Va., Am. Soc. Colon and Rectal Surgeons, So. Med. Assn., Chesapeake Colon-Rectal Soc., S.E. Va. Soc. Colon-Rectal Surgeons. Office: 3235 Academy Ave Ste 200 Portsmouth VA 23703-3200 Office Phone: 757-484-9653.

WOLF, JEROME L., lawyer; BA, George Washington U., 1970; JD, Duquesne U. Sch. Law, 1973. Bar: NY 1974, Fla. 1984, cert.: Fla. Bd. Legal Specialization and Edn. (wills, trusts and estates). Ptnr. Berger Singerman, Boca Raton, Fla., Duane Morris LLP, Boca Raton. Contbr. articles to law jours. Named one of Top 100 Attys., Worth mag., 2005—06, Top South Fla. Lawyers in Tax and Estate Law, South Fla. Legal Guide, 2007. Mem.: ABA, South Palm Beach County Bar Assn., Fla. Bar (mem. real property and probate and trust law sects., chmn. trust law com. 1991—95, chmn., lectr. bi-ann. will and trust drafting seminar, recipient Ann. Svc. award from real property, probate and trust law sect. 1993), NY State Bar Assn. (mem. trusts and estates sect., mem. com. on estate planning, chmn. subcommittee on fin. planning 1983—84, chmn. subcommittee on cmty. property 1979—82, mem. com. on estate planning for the disabled), Palm Beach County Bar Assn. (mem. estate and probate continuing legal edn. com. 1986—, lectr. ann. probate and guardianship law seminar 1987—89, 1993). Office: Duane Morris LLP Ste 300 5100 Town Center Cir Ste 650 Boca Raton FL 33486-1070 Office Phone: 561-962-2111. Office Fax: 561-516-6317. E-mail: jwolf@duanemorris.com.

WOLF, MICHAEL, mathematics professor; b. Phila., Jan. 29, 1960; BS in Math. and Philosophy, Yale U., 1981; PhD, Stanford U., 1986. C.L.E. Moore instr. MIT, 1986—88; asst. prof. Rice U., 1988—93, assoc. prof., 1993—99, prof., 1999—, chair dept. math., 2005—09. Math. scis. postdoctoral rsch. fellow NSF, 1987—91, mem. adv. panels, 2003—04, 2005—06; rsch. prof. Math. Scis. Rsch. Inst., 1993—94. Contbr. articles to profl. jours. Alfred P. Sloan Rsch. fellow, 1991—95. Office: Rice Univ Dept Math MS-136 PO Box 1892 Houston TX 77251 Office Phone: 713-348-6293.

WOLF, STEVEN E., surgeon, educator; b. Balt., Oct. 16, 1964; s. Gerald Wayne and Margaret Louise (Melcher) W.; m. Kristin Steele, Dec. 2, 1989; children: Travis O., Hailey E. BS in Zoology cum laude, U. Tex., 1986; MD, U. Tex. Med. Br., Galveston, 1990. Diplomate Am. Bd. Surgery, Tex. State Bd. Med. Examiners, Mo. State Bd. Healing Arts. Resident in surgery U. Mo., Kansas City, 1990-95; rsch. fellow in trauma and burns Shriners Hosp. for Children, Galveston, 1995-96, staff surgeon, 1996, clin. fellow in critical care and burns, 1996—97; asst. prof. surgery U. Tex., Galveston, 1996; vice-chair for rsch., dept. surgery U. Tex. Health Sci. Ctr., San Antonio, Betty and Bob Kelso Disting. Chair in Burn and Trauma Surgery, 2007—; dir., US Army Inst. Surgical Rsch. Burn Ctr. Brooke Army Med. Ctr., Fort Sam Houston, Tex. Chmn. info. sys. steering Shriners Burns Inst., 1996-97; mem. pharmacy and therapeutics com. U. Tex., 1997; mem. burn adv. bd. Beiersdorf-Jobst Internat., 1997. Co-author (chpt.) Baillere's Clinical Endocrinology, 1996; contbr. several articles to profl. jours. Mem. ACS (assoc.), Soc. Parenteral & Enteral Nutrition, Am. Burn Assn., Assn. Acad. Surgery, AMA, Am. Soc. for Parenteral and Enteral Nutrition, Assn.for Academic Surgery, AAAS, J. Bradley Aust Surgical Soc., Shock Soc., Singleton Surgical Soc., Soc. for Critical Care Medicine; elected to Am. Assn. for the Surgery of Trauma, Eastern Assn. for the Surgery of Trauma, Soc. U. Surgeons, So. Surgical Assn., Surgical Infection Soc., Tex. Surgical Soc. Republican. Methodist. Achievements include work with mortality determinants in massive pediatric burns; team member that developed an adaptable arm sling for military burn patients. Office: U Tex Health Sci Ctr Dept Surgery 7703 Floyd Curl Dr San Antonio TX 78229-3900 Business E-Mail: wolfs@uthscsa.edu.

WOLFBERG, MELVIN DONALD, optometrist, educational association administrator, consultant; b. Altoona, Pa., June 24, 1926; s. Max Alex and Claire (Schiffman) Wolfberg; m. Audrey Iris Koch, Apr. 26, 1952; children: Debra Lynn, Michael Alex, Daniel Ben; m. Linda Diane Machesic, Dec. 4, 1979. OD, Pa. Coll. Optometry, Phila., 1951; D of Ocular Sci. (hon.), New England Coll. Optometry, 1989, Ill. Coll. Optometry, 1990; LHD (hon.), Pa. Coll. Optometry, 1998. Lic. optometrist, Pa. Pvt. practice and ptnr. optometric practice, Selinsgrove, Pa., 1951-79; pres. Pa. Coll. Optometry, Phila., 1979-89, chmn. bd., 1976-79; v.p. profl. rels. Bausch and Lomb, Rochester, NY, 1991-95; pres. In Vision Inst., Boston, 1991-95; ptnr., dir. Sylvan Learning Ctr., Vero Beach, Fla., 1996—2009. Cons. to sec. HEW, Washington, 1970-77; dir. Better Vision Inst., N.Y.C., 1960-80. Mem. Selinsgrove City Coun., 1961-62; pres. Selinsgrove Community Chest, 1957; chmn. Optometrists Rep. Nat. Com., 1972, 76; chmn. Nat. Inter-Profl. Health Coun., Washington, 1972-77; dir. Univ. City Sci. Ctr., Phila., 1980-87; adv. com. Coun. Higher Edn., Commonwealth Pa., 1980-89. Served with U.S. Army, 1944-46, ETO. Decorated Purple Heart, Bronze Star, Silver Star; named Man of Yr. Central Pa. Optometric Soc., 1964, Alumnus of Yr. Pa. Coll. Optometry, 1970; recipient Carel C. Koch Meml. medal, 1989. Fellow Am. Acad. Optometry (pres. 1985-86, Eminent Svc. award, 2005); mem. Pa. Assn. Colls. and Univs. (exec. com. 1982-89, sec.-treas. 1985-88, vice chmn. 1988-89), Pa. Optometric Assn. (pres. 1959-61, Optometrist of Yr., Ewalt Meritorious Svc. award 2003), Am. Optometric Assn. (pres. 1969-70, Disting. Svc. award 1994, named to Nat. Optometry Hall Fame 2004), Pa. Coll. Optometry Alumni Assn. (pres. 1957), Beta Sigma Kappa. Personal E-mail: machesic@msn.com.

WOLFE, MARGARET RIPLEY, historian, educator, consultant; b. Kingsport, Tenn., Feb. 3, 1947; d. Clarence Estill and Gertrude Blessing Ripley; m. David Early Wolfe, Dec. 17, 1966; 1 child, Stephanie Ripley. BS magna cum laude, East Tenn. State U., 1967, MA, 1969; PhD, U. Ky., 1974. Instr. history East Tenn. State U., 1969-73, asst. prof., 1973-77, assoc. prof., 1977-80, prof., 1980—, prof. history emerita, 2004—, sr. rsch. prof. history, 1999—2004, prof. history emerita, sr. faculty affiliate, 2004—06. Disting. vis. prof. in history Washington and Lee U., 2006. Author: Lucius Polk Brown and Progressive Food and Drug Control, Tennessee and New York City, 1908-1920, 1978, An Industrial History of Hawkins County, Tennessee, 1983, Kingsport, Tennessee: A Planned American City, 1987, Daughters of Canaan: A Saga of Southern Women, 1995; gen. editor: Women in Southern Culture Series, 1995-2004; contbg. author to books, also introductions to books; contbr. articles to profl. jours. Mem. Tenn. Com. for Humanities, 1983-85, exec. coun. mem., 1984-85; mem. Women's Symphony Com., Kingsport, 1990-95; exec. com. Tenn. Commemorative Woman's Suffrage Commn., 1994-95; mem. state rev. bd. Tenn. Hist. Commn., 1995—2005. Haggin fellow U. Ky., 1972-73; recipient Disting. Faculty award East Tenn. State U., 1977, East Tenn. State U. Found. rsch. award, 1979, Alumni cert. merit, 1984. Mem. AAUP, ACLU (exec. com. Tenn. 1991-92), NOW, Tenn. State Employees Assn., Am. Studies Assn. (John Hope Franklin Prize com. 1992), Am. Hist. Assn., Orgn. Am. Historians, So. Assn. Women Historians (pres. 1983-84, exec. com. 1984-86), So. Hist. Assn. (com. on status of women 1987, program com. 1988, interim chair program com. 1988, mem. com. 1993, 94, 95, nominating com. 1994, chair nominating com. 1995, chmn. mem. com. 1997, exec. coun. 1998-2000), Smithsonian Assocs, Tenn. Hist Commn. (state rev. bd. 1995-2005), Tenn. Hist. Soc. (editl. bd. 1995—2004), Coordinating Com. for Women in History, East Tenn. Hist. Soc. (mem. editl. bd. Jour. East Tenn. History 1995-2004), Phi Kappa Phi. Democrat. Methodist. Avocations: travel, reading, walking.

WOLFENDEN, RICHARD VANCE, biochemistry educator; b. Oxford, Eng., May 17, 1935; s. John Hulton and Josephine (Vance) W.; m. Anita Gaunitz, June 25, 1965; children: Peter, John. BA, MA, Exeter Coll., Oxford U., Eng., 1958; PhD, Rockefeller Inst., 1964. Asst. prof. chemistry Princeton U., NJ, 1964-70; assoc. prof. biochemistry U. N.C., Chapel Hill, 1970-73, prof. biochemistry, 1973-83, alumni disting. prof., 1983—. Vis. fellow Exeter Coll., Oxford, 1969; vis. prof. U. Montpellier, France, 1976; mem. molecular biology panel NSF, Washington, 1973-76; mem. bio-organic and natural products study sect. NIH, Washington, 1981-86. Mem. editl. bd. Bioorganic Chemistry, 1983—, Biomed. Chem. Letters, 1993—. Fellow AAAS, Am. Acad. Arts and Scis.; mem. NAS, Am. Chem. Soc. (chair biol. divsn. 2000-02), Am. Soc. Biol. Chemists. Democrat. Home: 104 Jolyn Place Chapel Hill NC 27517 Office: U North Carolina Dept Biochemistry Chapel Hill NC 27514

WOLFENSON, AZI U., electrical, mechanical and industrial engineer, consultant; b. Rumania, Aug. 1, 1933; arrived in Peru, 1937; s. Samuel G. and Polea S. (Ulanowski) Wolfenson; m. Rebeca Sterental, Jan. 10, 1983; 1 child, Michael Ben;children from previous marriage: Ida, Jeannette, Ruth, Moises, Alex. Mech., Elec. Engr., U. Nacional de Ingenieria, Peru, 1955; Indsl. Engr., U. Nacional de Ingenieria, 1967; MSc in Indsl. Engring., U. Mich., 1966; PhD in Engring. Mgmt., Pacific Western U., 1983; PhD in Engring. Energy, Century U., 1985; D in Philosophy of Engring. (hon.), World U. Roundtable, Ariz., 1987. Power engr. Peruvian Trading Co., 1956-57; gen. mgr. AMSA ingenieros S.A., 1957-60; prof. U. Nacional de Ingenieria, Peru, 1956-72, dean mech. and elec. engring., 1964-66, dean indsl. engring., 1967-72; dir. SWSA Automotive Parts, Peru, 1954-77; project mgr. Nat. Fin. Corp., Cofide, 1971-73; Peruvian dir. Corporacion Andina de Fomento, CAF, 1971-73; rep. in Peru CAF, 1973-74; pres. DESPRO cons. firm, 1973-76; exec. pres. Electroperu, 1976-80. Cons. engr., 1964—; dir. Tech. Transference Studies, 1971—72. Author: (book) Work Communications, 1966, Programmed Learning, 1966, Production Planning and Control, 1968, Transfer of Technology, 1971, National Electrical Development, 1977, Energy and Development, 1979, El Gran Desafio, 1981, Hacia una politica economica alternativa, 1982, The Power of Communications: The Media, 1987, Festividades y Celebraciones de Mi Pueblo, 2010, 2nd edit, 2012; contbr. articles to newspapers and jours. Mem. Nat. Coun. Fgn. Investment and Tech. Transfer, 1972—73, Superior Coun. Electricity, 1964—66; metal mech. expert for andean group, 1970—71; promoter, cofounder, gen. mgr. La Republica Newspaper, Peru, 1981; pres. PROA Project promotion AG, Switzerland, 1982—; chmn. Inst. for the Devel. of the Ams., Inc., Fla., 1993—; co-founder El Popular, 1983, El Nacional, 1985, Todo Sport, 1993, El Chino, 1994, La Reforma, 1997, El Men, 1999, La Razon, 2001; pres. bd. dirs., newspapers; v.p. bd. dirs. Island Way Cmty. Assn., 1995—97; mem. exec. bd. dirs. Miami State Israel Bonds, 1997; mem. consultative coun. Instituto Peruano de Deportes, 1999; mem. consultive coun. Min. Econ. and Fin., 1973—74; councilman at the Concejo Provincial De Lima, 1969—75; pres. Peruvian Jewish Cmty., 1966—70, Peruvian Hebrew Sch., 1976—78. Recipient Recognition award, Israel Govt., 1967, Disting. Contbn. award, City of Lima, 1970, 1971, Disting. award, Trujillo, 1978, Huaral, 1979, City Coun. Huancayo, 1980, Piura, 1980, Disting. Contbn. to Elec. Devel. in Peru, 1979, Disting. Svc. awards, Order Merit, Peru, 1980, Disting. Comision Integracion Electrica Regional medal, CIER, 1984, El Sol Radiante, City Hall of Magdalena, Peru, 1995, Medal of Honor, Electrical Engring. Colegio de Ingenieros del Peru, 2003, Spl. award, Gente mag., 2006; named Exec., Gente Mag., 1979. Fellow: Brit. Inst. Mgmt., Inst. Prodn. Engrs.; mem.: J.C.C. Fla., FCL, AIIE (sr.), ASME, MTM Assn., AAAS, World Assn. Newspapers (exec. mem. 2003), Asociacion Periodistas Peru, Circulo Periodistas Peru, Swiss sect. PEN Club INternat., Swiss Soc. Writers, United Writers Assn., Assn. Energy Engrs., Am. Nuc. Soc. (vice chmn. 1988, 1990, chmn. Swiss sect. 1991—93, Significant Contbn. to Advancement of Nuc. Sci. award 1995), Inst. Adminstrv. Mgmt., Asociacion Peruana Avance Ciencia, Assn. Mgmt. Sci. (dir. 1968), Am. Inst. Mgmt. Sci., Am. Soc. Engring. Edn., Asociacion Electrotechnica del Peru, Inst. Peruano Ingenieros Mecanicos (pres. 1965—66, v.p. 1967, dir. 1969, 1970, 1976), Colegio Ingenieros Peru (medal of honor award 2003), Alumni Assn. Mich., Pacific Western and Century U., Hebraica Club, Club dr 2000. Office: 20533 Biscayne Blvd Ste 4 Aventura FL 33180-1501 Personal E-mail: aziwolfenson@aol.com.

WOLFF, CANDIDA PEROTTI (CANDI WOLFF), lobbyist, former federal official; b. Sharon, Conn., June 9, 1964; m. Mark Roger Wolff; 2 children. BA in Math & Polit. Sci., Mount Holyoke Coll., 1986; JD, George Washington U., 1989. Pub. policy lobbyist Akin, Gump, Strauss, Hauer & Feld, LLP, 1989—93; tax counsel to Senator Malcolm Wallop US Senate, 1993—95; legis. counsel US Senate Steering Com., 1995—96; dep. staff dir. US Senate Republican Policy Com., 1997—2000; dep. asst. to Vice Pres. for legis. affairs The White House, 2001—02, asst. to Vice Pres. for legis. affairs., 2002—04, asst. to Pres., dir. legis. affairs, 2005—07; ptnr. Washington Coun. Ernst & Young, 2004, Hogan Lovells US LLP, Washington, 2008—11; exec. v.p. for global govt. affairs Citigroup Inc., Washington, 2011—. Republican. Office: Citigroup Inc 399 Park Ave New York NY 10043

WOLFF, EDWARD ALVIN, electronics engineer; b. Chgo., Oct. 31, 1929; s. Samuel S. and Lillian P. Wolff; m. Anna Lee Tishk, June 19, 1951; children: David Steven, Eliot Marvin, Susan Toby. BSEE, U. Ill., 1951, MS, 1953; PhD, U. Md., 1961. Electronic scientist Naval Research Lab., Washington, 1951-54; project engr. Md. Electronic Mfg. Corp., Litton Industries, College Park, Md., 1956-59, Electromagnetic Research Corp., College Park, Md., 1959-61; engring. mgr. Aero Geo Astro-Keltec Industries/Aiken Industries, Alexandria, Va., 1961-67; v.p. Geotronics, Inc., Falls Church, Va., 1967-71; supervisory electronics engr. NASA Goddard Space Flight Ctr., Greenbelt, Md., 1971—; system mgr. Network TDRS System, 1981-89, MRJ, Inc., Oakton, Va., 1989-98; cons. in field, 1998—. Instr. Tex. A&M U., 1962. Author: Spacecraft Technology, 1962, Antenna Analysis, 1966, 2d edit., 1988, Geoscience Instrumentation, 1974, Urban Alternatives, 1975, Microwave Engineering and Systems Applications, 1988. Mem. Md. Gov.'s Sci. Resources Adv. Bd., 1963—67; pres. U.S. Environment and Resources Coun., 1972—75; treas. World Environment and Resources Coun., 1975—81. With US Army, 1954—56. Fellow: IEEE (life; bd. dirs. 1971—72), Washington Acad. Scis.; mem.: NSPE, AIAA, Phi Eta Sigma, Sigma Tau, Eta Kappa Nu. Home: 16870 Island Cove Dr Apt 130 Jupiter FL 33477-2356 Personal E-mail: ewolff@bigfoot.com.

WOLFSON, AARON HOWARD, radiation oncologist, educator; b. Nashville, May 13, 1955; s. Sorrell Louis and Jacqueline Adele (Falis) W.; m. Adrienne Sue Mates, Dec. 16, 1979; children: Alexis Ellyn, Andrew Lane. BA, U. Fla., 1978, MD, 1982. Diplomate Am. Bd. Radiology. Intern internal medicine Jackson Meml. Hosp., Miami, Fla., 1982—83; staff physician Pub. Health Svc., Miami, 1983—85; pvt. practice Palm Beach Gardens, Fla., 1985—86; resident in radiation oncology Med. Coll. Va., Richmond, 1986—89; from instr. to assoc. prof. radiation oncology U. Miami, Miller Sch. Medicine, 1989—2003, prof., 2003—, vice chair dept. radiation oncology, 2005—12. Co-dir. Gynecology Site dis. group Sylvester Cancer Ctr., 2001—. Contbr. articles to profl. jours. Bd. dirs. Children's Home Soc., Ft. Lauderdale, Fla., 1993—, Temple Beth Israel, Sunrise, Fla., 1994—2004; mem. spkrs. bur. U. Miami, 1993—; vol. spkr. Broward County Schs., 1990—1999; exec. v.p. Temple Beth Israel, 1996-98, pres., 1998-99. Sylvester Cancer Ctr. grantee, 1992. Fellow Am. Coll. Radiology; mem. Gynecologic Oncology Group (bd. dir. 2007-11), Radiation Therapy Oncology Group, Am. Soc. Therapeutic Radiology and Oncology. Jewish. Achievements include research on malignant tumors of the female genital tract; patent for radiation implant for gynecologic cancer. Office: Univ Miami 1475 NW 12th Ave # D-31 Miami FL 33136-1002 Home Phone: 954-370-8038; Office Phone: 305-243-4210. Business E-Mail: awolfson@med.miami.edu.

WOLIN, HARRY A., lawyer, electronics company executive; m. Tracy Wolin; 3 children. BS in Chemistry, U. Ariz.; JD, Ariz. State U. Bar: Ariz., Tex., US Patent and Trademark Office. V.p., dir. legal affairs Semiconductor Products Sector Motorola; joined Advanced Micro Devices, Inc. (AMD), 2000, v.p. intellectual property, mgr. Tech. Law Dept., sr. v.p., gen. counsel, 2003—, sec., 2010—. Bd. dirs. GlobalFoundries Inc., 2011—. Bd. dirs. Lifeworks, Austin. Recipient Magna Stella award, Tex. Gen. Counsel Forum, 2008. Office: AMD Austin, Lone Star Advanced Micro Devices 7171 Southwest Pkwy Austin TX 78735 Office Phone: 512-602-1000.

WOLRAICH, MARK LEE, pediatrician, educator; BA, SUNY, Binghamton, 1966; MD, SUNY, Syracuse, 1970. Diplomate Am. Bd. Pediat. Pediatric intern SUNY, Syracuse, 1970-71; pediatric resident U. Okla. Health Scis. Ctr., Oklahoma City, 1973-74; pediatric fellowship U. Oreg. Health Scis. Ctr., 1974-76; asst. prof. U. Iowa, 1976-81, assoc. prof., 1981-86, prof., 1986-90, Vanderbilt U., 1990-2001, dir. divsn. child devel., dir. child devel. ctr., 1990-99, dir. ctr. for chronic illnesses and disabilities in children, 1990-2000; investigator J.F. Kennedy Ctr. for Rsch. on Edn. and Human Devel., 1990-2001; prof. pediat., dir. Child Study Ctr. Okla. U. Health Scis. Ctr., 2001—, Edith Kinney Gaylord presdl. prof., 2010. Med. supr. U. Iowa Divsn. of Devel. Disabilities, 1980-90; vis. prof. Great Ormond St. Hosp. for Sick Children, London, 1983, U. Cape Town, Rondebosch Cape, South Africa, 1986, Columbus Children's Hosp., Ohio State U., Dept. Pediat., 1988; mem. Iowa State Foster Care Rev. Bd. Co-editor Advances in Developmental and Behavioral Pediatrics, 1981-92; cons. editor Am. Jour. on Mental Deficiency; editl. adv. bd. A Guide to Parent Counseling; editor The Classification of Child and Adolescent Mental Disorders in Primary Care-Diagnostic and Statistical Manual for Mental Disorders in Primary Care Child and Adolescent Version, 1996; cons. reviewer Developmental Medicine and Child Neurology, Pediatrics, Nutrition and Behavior, Jour. Pediatrics, Jour. of Social and Personal Relationships, Applied Rsch. in Mental Retardation, Jour. of Clin. Psychology, Jour. Developmental and Behavioral Pediatrics, Clin. Pediatrics, others; contbr. numerous articles to profl. publs. Mem. Children and Adults with Attention Deficit, 2003—. Recipient Disting. and Dedicated Svc. award Spina Bifida Assn. Iowa, 1979, Lou Holloway award Health Scis. Edn., Presdl. Professorship award U. Okla. Health Scis. ctr., 2010; grantee NIMH, 1987-90, 98-2001, Nat. Inst. on Disability and Rehab. Rsch., 1987-89, NIH, 1988-91, Iowa Dept. Human Svcs., 1986-89, U. Iowa, 1979-87, United Cerebral Palsy Rsch. and Endl. Found., Inc., 1978-87, Iowa March of Dimes, 1980, Sugar Assn., Inc., 1983, Internat. Life Scis. Inst., 1988-91, W.T. Grant Found., 1989; MCH Lend grant, 1999—, CDC grant, 2002; named to Children and Adults with Attention-Deficit/Hyperactivity Disorder Hall of Fame, 2003. Fellow Am. Acad. Pediat. (com. 1992-2000, chair com. on psychosocial aspects child and family health 1997-2000, chair child and adolescent health action group 2000-04, chair-elect mgmt. com., 2004-, chmn. mgmt. com. 2006—, Aldrich award, Sect. Devel. and Behavioral Pediats. 2011), Am. Acad. Cerebral Palsy and Devel. Medicine; mem. Soc. for Devel. and Behavioral Pediat. (pres. 1994-95, program dir. 1990-93), Soc. Pediatric Psychology Assn. (assoc., Lee Salk award for disting. svc.), Soc. for Pediatric Rsch. (sr.), Am. Acad. on Comm. in Healthcare (charter), Am. Pediatric Soc., Ctr. Diseases Control & Prevention (mem. bd. sci. counsellors). Office: Okla U Health Scis Ctr 1100 NE 13th St Oklahoma City OK 73117

WOLTZ, HOWARD OSLER, III, metal products executive; b. Mount Airy, NC, Aug. 23, 1956; s. Howard Osler Jr. and Joan (Moore) W.; m. Agnes Parker, Mar. 7, 1981; children: Louise, Parker, Charlotte, Reddin. BBA, U. N.C., 1978. Salesman Expo Wire Co., Mount Airy, 1978-80; pres. Rappahannock Wire Co. (subs. of Insteel Industries, Inc.), Mount Airy, 1981—89, Florida Wire and Cable, Inc. (merged with Insteel Wire Products Co.); bd. dirs. Insteel Wire Products Co. (subs. of Insteel Wire Industries, Inc.), 1986, pres.; COO Insteel Industries, Inc., 1989—91, pres. Mount Airy, 1989—, CEO, 1991—, chmn., 2009—. Chmn. Surry County com. of 100, Mount Airy, 1992; bd. dirs Piedmont Triad, Partnership, 1992. Mem. Am. Wire Producers Assn. (bd. dirs. 1990—), Wire Reinforcement Inst. (bd. dirs. 1991—). Republican. Methodist. Office: Insteel Industries Inc 1373 Boggs Dr Mount Airy NC 27030-2145 Office Fax: 336-786-2144. Business E-Mail: hwoltz@insteel.com.

WOMACK, BAXTER FRANK, electrical and computer engineering educator, researcher; b. Charleston, Ark, Sept. 5, 1930; s. Clifford F. and Dena Arzela (Goff) W.; m. Wanda Lois Raney, Jan. 26, 1952; children: Carey Bruce, David Frank. AA, Ft. Smith Jr. Coll., 1950; BSEE, U. Ark., 1956, MSEE, 1958; PhD, Purdue U., 1963. Registered profl. engr., Tex. From instr. to asst. prof. U. Ark., Fayetteville, 1956-59; asst. prof. elec. engring. U. Tex., Austin, 1961-66, assoc. prof. elec. engring., 1966-71, prof. elec. and computer engring., 1971—. Cons. numerous cos., 1961—. Contbr. over 100 articles to profl. jour. Served to 1st lt. US Army, 1950-53. Recipient Award of Excellence, Haliburton Ednl. Found., 1980; elected to Ark. Acad. Elec. Engring., 1981. Fellow Am. Soc. for Engring. Edn.; mem. IEEE (Centennial medal and cert. 1984), Kiwanis (Austin pres. 1970—). Avocations: ranching, raising purebred cattle. Home: 4900 Beverly Skyline Austin TX 78731-4707 Office: Univ Tex Dept ECE CO 803 Austin TX 78712 Home Phone: 512-452-6916; Office Phone: 512-471-3732. E-mail: womack@ece.utexas.edu.

WOMACK, CHRISTOPHER C., utilities executive; b. Greenville, Ala, 1958; Attended Exec. Program, 2001—01; B, Western Mich. U.; M in Pub. Adminstrn., American U. Sr. v.p., sr. prodn. officer Southern Co. (Southern Co. Generation); legis. aide to Leon Panetta US House of Representatives, staff dir., subcommittee on pers. & police (com. house on adminstr.); govtl. affairs rep. (Alabama Power) Southern Co., 1988, chief people officer, sr. v.p., human resources, 1998, exec. v.p., external affairs (Georgia Power), dir., cmty. rels. & sr. v.p., pub. rels. & corp. svcs. (Alabama Power), exec. v.p., pres., external affairs,

2009—. Office: Southern Co 30 Ivan Allen Jr Blvd NW Atlanta GA 30308 Office Phone: 404-506-5000. Office Fax: 404-506-0455. Business E-Mail: cwomack@southernco.com.

WOMACK, JAMES E., veterinary pathobiology educator; BS in Math. Edn., Abilene Christian Coll., 1964; PhD in Genetics, Oreg. State U., 1968. Asst. prof. Abilene Christian Coll., 1968—71, assoc. prof., 1971—73; vis. scientist The Jackson Lab., 1973—75, staff scientist, 1975—77; assoc. prof. Tex. A&M U., 1977—83, prof. vet. pathology, 1983—, W.P. Luse prof., 1987—, interim asst. dept. head, Dept. Vet. Pathology, 1990—93, disting. prof., 2001—, dir. Ctr. Animal Biotechnology and Genomics, 2001—; dir. Ctr. Animal Genetics Inst. Biosciences and Tech., 1989—96. Recipient Beecham award rsch. excellence, 1986, Carrington award rsch. in cell biology, 1990, CIBA prize rsch. in animal health, 1993, Wolf prize in agr., Wolf Found., Israel, 2001; named Outstanding Tex. Geneticist, Tex. Genetics Soc., 1996; McMaster fellow, CSIRO (Commonwealth Sci. and Indsl. Rsch. Orgn.), Australia, 1990. Fellow: AAAS; mem.: Nat. Acad. Sci. Office: Dept Veterinary Pathobiology Tex A&M Univ Coll Vet Medicine 4467 TAMU College Station TX 77843-4467 Office Phone: 979-845-9810. Office Fax: 979-845-9972. E-mail: jwomack@cvm.tamu.edu.

WOMACK, JERRY T., construction executive; m. Alice Womack. Pres., CEO Suburban Grading & Utilities, Inc., Norfolk, Va. Bd. dirs. Gateway Fin. Holdings, Inc., 2000—08, Hampton Roads Bankshares, Inc., 2008—. Office: Suburban Grading & Utilities Inc 6330 N Center Dr Ste 125 Norfolk VA 23502-4008 Office Phone: 757-461-1800. Office Fax: 757-461-0989. Business E-Mail: jerrywomack@gwfh.com.

WOMACK, LEE ANN, country musician; b. Jacksonville, TX, Aug. 19, 1966; married; 2 children. Singer: (albums) Lee Ann Womack, 1997, Some Things I Know, 1998, I Hope You Dance, 2000, The Season for Romance, 2002, Something Worth Leaving Behind, 2002, Greatest Hits, 2004, There's More Where That Came From, 2005 (Album of Yr., Country Music Assn., 2005), Call Me Crazy, 2008, (singles) The Fool, 1997, Does My Ring Burn Your Finger, 2000 (USA Today song of yr., 2001), I Hope You Dance, 2000, I May Hate Myself in the Morning, 2005 (Single of Yr., Country Music Assn., 2005); with Willie Nelson (duet) Mendonceno County Line, 2002 (Country Music Assn. Vocal Event of Yr.). Office: Richard De la Font Agency Inc Ste 505 4845 S Sheridan Rd Tulsa OK 74145 Office Phone: 615-244-8944, 918-665-6200.

WOMACK, STEVE, United States Representative from Arkansas, former mayor; b. Russellville, Ark., Feb. 18, 1957; m. Terri Williams; 3 children. B, Ark. Tech U., Russelville, 1979. Mgr. Sta. KURM Radio, Rogers, Ark., 1979—90; exec. officer US Army ROTC program U. Ark., Fayetteville, 1990—96; fin. cons. Merrill Lynch, Rogers, 1997; mayor City of Rogers, 1998—2010; mem. US Congress from 3rdd Ark. Dist., Washington, 2011—, US House Appropriations Com., Washington, 2011—. Former councilman Rogers City Coun.; chmn. NW Ark. Regional Planning Commn., 2003—05. Apptd. mem. Ark. Commn. on Nat. and Cmty. Svc., 1999, chmn., 2001; mem. Ch. at Pinnacle Hills, Rogers; former pres. Rogers-Lowell United Fund; former mem. NW Ark. CC Task Force, St. Mary's Hosp. Found., Rogers Pk. Commn. Ret. col. Ark. Army Nat. Guard, 1979—2009. Decorated Legion of Merit, Meritorious Svc. medal with Oak Leaf Cluster, Army Commendation medal, Army Achievement medal, Global War on Terrorism Expeditionary and Svc. medals; named Citizen of Yr., March of Dimes; Paul Harris fellow. Mem.: Ret. Res. of Army. Republican. Baptist. Office: US House of Representatives 1508 Longworth House Office Bldg Washington DC 20515 Office Phone: 202-225-4301. Office Fax: 202-225-5713.

WOMBLE, LARRY W., state legislator; b. Winston-Salem, NC, June 6, 1941; s. Luchion Owen and Dorothy Gwyn Womble. BS, Winston-Salem State U., 1963; attended, U. NC, Appalachian State U. Ret. educator; former state rep. Dist. 66 NC; state rep. Dist. 71 NC, 1995—. Mem. Winston-Salem Bd. of Aldermen, 1981—93. Recipient Young Ned of Yr., Winston-Salem Forsyth Sch. Sys., 1964; named Asst. Prin. Yr., NC Assn. Edn., 1980—81; scholarship, RJ Reynolds Tobacco Co., 1972. Mem.: Urban Laegue, NC Assn. Edn., Nat. Edn. Assn., NAACP (v.p., Winston-Salem Chap 1985), Winston-Salem State U. Alumni Assn. Democrat. Baptist. Office: NC House of Reps 300 N Salisbury St Rm 514 Raleigh NC 27603-5925 Office Phone: 919-733-5777. E-mail: Larry.Womble@ncleg.net.

WOMBLE, WILLIAM FLETCHER, retired lawyer; b. Winston-Salem, NC, Oct. 29, 1916; s. Bunyan Snipes and Edith (Willingham) Womble; m. Jane Payne Gilbert, Oct. 11, 1941 (dec. Mar. 16, 2010); children: William Fletcher, Jr., Jane Womble Haver, Russell G., Ann Womble Strader; m. Allan Clements Hollan Womble, Sept. 8, 2012. Student, U. NC Law Sch., Chapel hill, Summer Sch., 1938; AB, Duke U., 1937, JD, 1939; LHT (hon.), High Point U., 2000. Bar: NC 1939, US Supreme Ct. 1950. Assoc. Womble Carlyle Sandridge & Rice P.L.L.C. and predecessors, Winston-Salem, 1939-47; mem. Womble Carlyle Sandridge & Rice PLLC and predecessors, Winston-Salem, 1947—. Permanent mem. 4th Cir. Jud. Conf. Campaign chmn. Forsyth County Cmty. Chest, 1949; mem. NC Gen. Statutes Commn., 1953—55, NC Bd. Higher Edn., 1955—57, 1960—63, NC Adv. Budget Commn., 1957—58; trustee, past chmn., life trustee High Point U., 1950—; trustee Winston-Salem State U., 1953—55, Children's Home, 1959—75, pres., 1969—75, Winston Salem C. of C., 1960—61; bd. dirs. Triad United Meth. Home (now Arbor Acres United Meth. Retirement Cmty.), 1976—87, 1989—97, treas., 1975—79, pres., 1979—85; hon. chair United Way, Forsyth County, 1998; mem. People-to-People Citizen Amb. Program, 1981, 1986, NC House of Reps., 1953—58, chmn. com. higher edn., vice chmn. fin. com., 1957; chmn. adminstrv. bd. Centenary United Meth. Ch., 1961—63, chmn. bd. trustees, 1983—85; bd. mem. Sr. Svcs., Inc., 1998—2005, chair ann. fund., 2004—05; bd. dirs. Children's Ctr. Assn. Physically Disabled, 1952—56, pres., 1952—53; hon. bd. mem. Children's Ctr. for Physically Disabled, 1998—; bd. dirs., pres. Experiment in Self-Reliance, Inc., 1964—65. Served to maj. USAF, 1941—46. Recipient Fifty Yr. award, Fellows Am. Bar Found., ABA, 1995; named Trustee of the Yr., Gen. Bd. Global Mins. of United Meth. Ch., Health and Wlfare Minst. Dept., 1989. Fellow: Am. Bar Found. (state chmn. 1984—89, life benefactor fellow); mem.: ABA (ho. dels. 1978—87, bd. govs. 1982—85, exec. coun. Nat. Conf. Bar Pres. 1985—88, ethics com. 1985—91, chmn. jud. code subcom. 1988—91, chair affiliate outreach com. 1994—97, coun. mem. sr. lawyers divsn. 1995—97), Forsyth County Bar Assn. (pres. 1962), Am. Judicature Soc., NC State Bar (trustee Interest on Lawyers Trust Accounts 1983—91, vice chmn. 1989—91, Chief Justice's Professionalism award 2001), NC Bar Assn. (pres. 1966—67, chmn. endowment founders campaign 1986—87, chair sr. lawyers divsn. 1994—95, Judge John J. Parker award 1984), Soc. Cin., Old Town Club, Rotary (local pres. 1964). Democrat. Methodist. Home: 1244 Arbor Rd 441 Winston Salem NC 27104-1139 Personal E-mail: billwomble1@gmail.com.

WONG, FAYE LING, public health service officer; BS in Dietetics, U. Wash., 1972; MPH, U. Calif.-Berkeley, 1973. Registered dietitian, lic. Ga. Relief dietary supr. Va. Mason Hosp., Seattle, 1968—72; chief Bur. of Nutrition Coconino County Dept. Pub. Health, Flagstaff, Ariz., 1974—76; nutrition cons. Office of Cmty. Health Svcs., Oreg. State Health Divsn., Portland, 1976—81; dir. Sentinel Site project Detroit Health Dept., 1981—83; pub. health nutritionist field svcs. br. Ctr. for Health Promotion and Edn. CDC, Atlanta, 1983—89, program analyst Ctr. for Chronic Disease Prevention and Health Promotion, 1988—89, chief field svcs. br. divsn. nutrition, 1989—92, chief program ops., program svcs. br., 1992—94, asst. chief divsn. cancer prevention and control, 1994—95, asst. chief policy and devel., 1995—96, assoc. dir. diabetes edn., dir. nat. diabetes edn. program, 1996—2000, dir. Youth Media Campaign, 2001—. Contbr. numerous articles, abstracts to profl. jours., to resource manuals. Recipient Award for Disting. Svc., Dept. Health and Human Svcs., 2000, Questar Internat. award, 2000, Thoth award., Pub. Rels. Assn. Am., 2000, Aesculapius Awards for Excellence, Nat. Diabetes Edn. Program, 1999, 1998, Award for Excellence in recognition of outstanding leaderhsip and dedicated svc., Assn. of State and Territorial Pub. Health Nutrition Dirs., 1991. Mem.: Am. Diabetes Assn. (mem. health profls. sect. 1996—), Am. Assn. Diabetes Educators (mem. pub. health specialty practice group 1996—), Am. Dietetic Assn. (mem. diabetes care and edn. practice group 1996—, mem. nominating com. 1999—), APHA (mem. food and nutrition sect. 1975—, mem. exec. bd. pub. policy rev. and devel. com. 1995—97, chair editl. bd. Am. Jour. Pub. Health 1997—2000, pres. 2001—02, co-chair task force on aging 2001—03, chair, exec. dir. search com. 2001—, Apple award 1991). Office: 4770 Buford Hwy NE lc 94 Atlanta GA 30341 Business E-Mail: fwong@cdc.gov.

WONG, MARTHA J., state legislator; b. Houston, Jan. 20, 1939; m. Kimberly B. Wong; children: Bill Ben, Troy Jim. Prin. Kolter Elementary Sch., 1978—82; adminstr. Houston Independent Sch. Dist., 1982—84; assoc. supt., 1985—87; assoc. prof. Baylor U., 1986—87; dir. staff devel. Houston Cmty. Coll. System, 1989—92; dir. Cnty. Devel.; city councilwoman Dust. C house Tex., 1994—2001; former chairwoman Competitive Serv & Edn. Coms.; mem. Parks, CATV Pub. Access, Redevelopment & Revitalization Com., Bus. & Tourism Com., Ethics Com., Taxicabs Com., Human Rels., Youth Violence & Gangs, Houston City Coun.; former mem. Minority Women Owned Bus Enterprise Coms.; house rep. Tex.; state rep. Dist. 134 Tex., 2003—. Recipient America Leadership Forum award, 1991, Woman Yr. Edn. award, YWCA, 1992, Woman Excellence, Tex. Women's Hall Fame, Gov. Tex., 1994, Fabulous Femme award, Greater Houston Women's Found, 1994, Disting. Alumni, U. Houston Coll. Edn., 1995. Mem.: Tex. Arthritis Found (v.p. 2005—), Holocaust Bd., Tex. Cmty. Sch., Greater Houston Women's Found (govt. v.p. 1992—94), Md. Cmty. Improvement Assn. (pres. 1993), Tex. Lion's Eye Bank (bd. mem. 1993—95), America Red Cross-(Hoston) (bd. mem. 1993—95), River Oaks Women's Bus. Exchange Club (v.p. social 1994). Republican. Office: State Capitol EXT E1 406 PO Box 2910 Austin TX 78768 Mailing: 15 E Greenway Plz 16F Houston TX 77046-1505 Office Phone: 713-247-2676.

WOOD, ANDELYS, literature and language professor; b. Randolph, Vt., Jan. 10, 1947; d. Robert and Lyndell Wood. AB, Middlebury Coll.; PhD, Ind. U. Prof. English Union Coll., Barbourville, Ky., 1977—, interim v.p., academic affairs, 2012—13. Recipient Exemplary Tchr. award, Gen. Bd. Higher Edn. and Ministry United Meth. Ch., 1997, 2007—08, Excellence Tchg. award, Union Coll., 1998, Excellence Rsch. award, 1994, 1996, 2000, 2005, 2009. Mem.: MLA, Lit. London Soc., Children's Lit. Assn., Ky. Philol. Assn. (v.p. to pres. 1989—91). Office: Union Coll CPO 809 310 College St Barbourville KY 40906 Business E-Mail: acwood@unionky.edu.*

WOOD, FRANK MAXWELL (MAX WOOD), judge, former federal prosecutor; b. Forest Park, Ga., 1959; m. Suzanne Brunson; children: Frank, Sydney, James. BA, LaGrange Coll., 1981; JD, U. Ga., 1985. Law clk. Floyd County Superior Ct., 1985—87; staff atty. Pros. Attys.' Coun. Ga., 1992—94; asst. dist. atty. Ocmulgee Dist. Atty.'s Office, 1994—97; pvt. law practice Macon, Ga.; US atty. (middle dist.) Ga. US Dept. Justice, Macon, Ga., 2001—09; chief state adminstrv. law judge Ga. Office State Adminstrv. Hearings, Atlanta, 2010—. Mem. Martha Bowman Meml. United Meth. Ch. With USAF, col. Ga. Air Nat. Guard. Office: Office State Administrative Hearings 230 Peachtree St NW Ste 850 Atlanta GA 30303 Office Phone: 404-657-2800.

WOOD, JAMES JERRY, judge; b. Rockford, Ala., Aug. 13, 1940; s. James Ronald and Ada Love Wood; m. Earline Luckie, Aug. 9, 1959; children: James Jerry, William Gregory, Diana Lynn. AB, Samford U., 1964, JD, 1969. Bar: Ala. 1969, U.S. Supreme Ct. 1976. Dir. legal affairs Med. Assn. State of Ala., Montgomery, 1969-70; asst. atty. gen. State of Ala., Montgomery, 1970-72; asst. U.S. atty. Middle Dist. Ala., Montgomery, 1972-76; pvt. practice, 1977-78; pres. Wood & Parnell, P.A., Montgomery, Ala., 1979-89; pvt. practice Montgomery, 1990—2011. Chmn. character and fitness com. Ala. State Bar, 1981-84, 86-89, chair task force on quality of life, 1990-92, chair task force on mem. svcs., 1994-96, admin law judge, State Al Personnel Dept., 2011-, gen. counsel, Home Bldg. Assoc., Ala. Home Bldg. Self Insoners Fund, Constrn. Claws Mgmt, 1978-2011. Capt. USAR, 1974-79. Fellow: Ala. Law Found., Am. Bar Found.; mem.: FBA (pres. Montgomery chpt. 1974—75), ABA (ho. of dels. 1990—98), Ala. Coun. Assn. Execs. (pres. 2001), Ala. Bar Assn., Ala. Assn. Workers Compensation Group Self-Insured Funds (chmn. 1994—2011), Am. Soc. Assn. Execs., Am. Nat. Inns of Ct., Rotary (pres. Montgomery Capital chpt. 1986—87, 1996—97). Republican. Baptist. Home Phone: 334-356-0573. Business E-Mail: Jameswood5903@att.net.

WOOD, JOAN, retired chemist; b. Bklyn., May 19, 1934; d. Harry Christian Nintzel and Helen Pauline (Diviak) Levesen; m. Randall Leroy Field Sr., Nov. 15, 1952 (div. Feb. 1972); children: Randall Leroy Jr., Roland, Gary, Brian, Lorraine, Thomas; m. Bransford Wayne Almond, Dec. 9, 1986 (div. Apr. 1993); m. Roy Allen Wood, Sr., Oct. 9, 1999 (dec. Dec. 23, 2012). Grad. high sch., Bklyn. Sec. Fulton Savs. Bank, Bklyn., 1952-53; mgr. reprodn. Air Pre-heater Corp., Wellsville, N.Y., 1958; chemistry technician fibers div. Allied Chem., Hopewell, Va., 1963-76; chemistry technician Va. Power Co.-North Anna Power Sta., Mineral, 1976-86, assoc. instr., 1987-92, sr. chemistry technician, 1992-94, sr. chemistry technician shift leader, 1992-94; ret., 1994; craft shop owner Stuffed Stuff and Other Stuff, Bumpass, Va., 1994-99. Recipient cert. of achievement, Nat. Acad. for Nuclear Tng., 1988. Mem.: Women of Moose (com. chmn. Moosehart Hopewell 1971). Roman Catholic.

WOOD, JOHN, state legislator; b. Lakeland, Fla., Dec. 7, 1952; children: Malloy, Johanna. Attended, U. Fla, 1971—72; BA in Econ., Columbia U., 1974; JD, Fla. State U., 1977. Atty. pvt. practice; CEO John Wood Enterprises; mem. Dist 65 Fla. House of Reps., 2008—, mem. govt. ops. appropriations com., health care svcs. policy com., ins., bus. and fin. affairs policy com., mil. and local affairs policy com. Mem.: Polk County Builders Assn., Lakeland Bar Assn., East Polk Assn. Realtors, Boy Scouts of America Gulf Ridge Coun. (exec. bd. mem. 2001—, v.p. endowment 2008). Republican. Episcopal. Office: House Office Bldg 402 S Monroe St Rm 210 Tallahassee FL 32399-1300 Home: 702 E Main St Haines City FL 33844-4226 Office Phone: 850-488-2721, 863-419-3470. Business E-Mail: john.wood@myfloridahouse.gov.

WOOD, JOHN MARTIN, lawyer; b. Detroit, Mar. 29, 1944; s. John Francis and Margaret Kathleen (Lynch) Wood; m. Judith Anne Messer; children: Timothy Peter, Meagan Anne. BA, Boston Coll., 1966; JD, Cath. U. Am., 1969. Bar: D.C. 1970, Va. 2001, U.S. Dist. Ct. D.C. 1970, U.S. Dist. Ct. Va. 2001, U.S. Ct. Appeals (D.C. cir.) 1973, U.S. Ct. Appeals (3d cir.) 1973, U.S. Ct. Appeals (4th cir.) 1973, U.S. Supreme Ct. 1973. Trial atty, tax divsn. Dept. Justice, Washington, 1969-73; assoc. Reed Smith LLP, Washington, 1973-80, ptnr., 1980—2009, mng. ptnr., 1989-95, dir. legal pers., 1995-98. Dir. adv. bd. Salvation Army, Va. and Met. Washington, Leadership Washington, 1993—. Mem.: The Currituck Club N.C., River Bend Golf and Country Club, Barristers Club Washington, Delta Sigma Pi, Phi Alpha Delta. Home: 9490 Oak Falls Ct Great Falls VA 22066-4143 Office Phone: 703-759-1995. Business E-Mail: jmwood@jmwoodlaw.com.

WOOD, JOSEPH GEORGE, neuroscientist, educator; b. Victoria, Tex., Dec. 8, 1928; s. Harold Robert and Frances Josephine (Marcak) W.; m. Jane L. Andrews; 1 dau., Marian. BS, U. Houston, 1954, MS, 1958; PhD, U. Tex., Galveston, 1962. Teaching asst. biology, U. Houston, 1956-58; instr. anatomy U. Tex. Dental Br., Houston, 1961, Yale U., 1962-63; asst. prof. U. Ark. Med. Sch., Little Rock, 1963-66; assoc. prof. U. Tex., San Antonio, 1966-70, asst. dean acad. devel., 1967-69, prof. and chmn. dept. neurobiology and anatomy Houston, 1970—84, prof. neurobiology and anatomy, 1984—88; prof., chmn. dept. anat. sci. U. Okla. Coll. Medicine, 1988-93; dir. Okla. Ctr. Neurosci., 1990-95. Guest prof. dept. pathobiology, cell biology and neuroanatomy U. Minn., 1993—96; sr. lectr. molecular and cell biology U. Tex., Dallas, 1997—2007, asst. dean pre-health professions, 1998—2002, assoc. dean pre-health edn., 2002—07, clin. prof. human devel., 2002—07; vis. prof. Philips U., Marburg, Germany, 1984. Served with AUS, 1954-56. Recipient Basic Sci. Tchg. award U. Ark. Med. Ctr., 1963, U. Tex. Houston, 1972, 75, 86, Disting. Alumnus award U. Tex. Med. Br., 1976 Mem.: Tex. Assn. Advisors for the Health Professions (chair), Tex. Soc. Electron Microscopy (pres. 1970—71, exec. coun. 1971—79), Assn. Anatomy Chmn., Histochem. Soc., Assn. Am. Med. Colls., Soc. Neurosci. (exec. com. Houston chpt. 1971—77, pres. 1973—77, rsch. award 1962), Am. Assn. Anatomists (exec. com. 1974—78), Cajal Club, Alpha Omega Alpha, Sigma Xi, Golden Key, Phi Kappa Phi.

WOOD, L. LIN, JR., lawyer; b. Raleigh, NC, Oct. 19, 1952; s. Lucian Lincoln and Josephien (Currin) Wood; m. Deborah Anne Jamison, July 25, 1987; children: Elizabeth, Ashley, Matthew Carlton. BA cum laude, Mercer U., 1974, JD cum laude, 1977. Bar: Ga. 1977, US Dist. Ct. (No. Dist.) Ga. 1977, US Dist. Ct. (Mid. Dist.) Ga. 1977, US Dist. Ct. (Dist. Colo.), US Ct. Appeals (5th Cir.) 1977, US Ct. Appeals (11th Cir.) 1981, US Supreme Ct. Assoc. Jones, Cork, Miller & Benton, Macon, Ga., 1977—80, Freeman & Hawkins, Atlanta, 1980—83; ptnr. Wood & Grant, Atlanta, 1983, Bryan Cave LLP (formerly Powell Goldstein LLP), Atlanta. Staff mem. Mercer Law Rev., 1975—77; numerous appearances on various TV networks including NBC, CBS, ABC, CNN, MSNBC, Court TV; spkr. in field. Recipient Am. Jurisprudence award, 1976, 1977, US Law Week award, 1977; named Ga. Super Lawyer, 2008, 2009; named one of Top 100 Ga. Super Lawyers, Law and Politics mag., 2006, 2007, 2008, Georgia's Elite Lawyers, 2008. Mem.: Atlanta City Club, Ga. Trial Lawyers Assn., Lawyers Club Atlanta, Atlanta Bar Assn., State Bar Ga., Assn. Trial Lawyers Am., ABA (vice-chmn. media law & defamation torts com.). Republican. Methodist. Office: Bryan Cave LLP One Atlanta Ctr 14th Floor 1201 W Peachtree St NW Atlanta GA 30309 Office Phone: 404-572-6633. Office Fax: 404-572-0633. E-mail: lin.wood@bryancave.com.

WOOD, LISA GODBEY, federal judge; b. Lexington, Ky., Jan. 28, 1963; married; 2 children. BA summa cum laude, U. Ga., Athens, 1985, JD summa cum laude, 1990. Bar: Ga. 1990. Law clk. to Hon. Anthony A. Alaimo US Dist. Ct. (so. dist.) Ga., 1990; assoc. Gilbert, Harrell, Summerford & Martin, Brunswick, Ga., 1991—2004, ptnr., 1995—2004; US atty. (so. dist.) Ga. US Dept. Justice, Savannah, Ga., 2004—07; judge US Dist. Ct. (so. dist.) Ga., 2007—10, chief judge, 2010—. Adv. com. US Dist. Ct.; disciplinary review panel State Bar Ga.; mem. Ga. Bd. Pub. Safety. Mem.: ABA, Def. Rsch. Inst. Office: US Dist Ct PO Box 1636 Brunswick GA 31521

WOOD, MAURICE, medical educator; b. Pelton, Eng., June 28, 1922; came to U.S., 1971; s. Joseph and Eugenie (Lumley) W.; m. Erica Joan Noble, May 1, 1948; children: Roger Lumley, Ashley Michael, Frances Jane. MB BS, U. Durham, Eng., 1945. Diplomate Am. Bd. Family Practice. Sr. ptnr. med. practice South Shields County, Durham, 1950-71; gen. practice teaching group U. Newcastle, Newcastle-on-Tyne, Eng., 1969-71; gen. clin. asst. dept. psychology-medicine South Shields Gen. Hosp., 1966-71; assoc. prof., dir. rsch. in family practice Med. Coll. Va.-Va. Commonwealth U., Richmond, 1971-73, prof., dir. rsch. in family practice, 1973-87, prof. emeritus, 1987—. Cons. advisor WHO, Geneva, 1979-90, chmn. working party to develop a classification for primary care, 1979-90; founding mem. exec. dir. N.Am. Primary Care Rsch. Group, Richmond, 1972-92, past pres., pres. emeritus, 1993—; chmn. com. on cmty. oriented primary care Insts. of Medicine, 1982-84. Assoc. editor Jour. Family Practice, 1976-83. Recipient award for meritorious svc. Va. Acad. Family Physicians, 1976; Maurice Wood award for career achievement in primary care rsch. founded in his honor, 1995. Fellow Royal Coll. Gen. Practitioners, Am. Acad. Family Physicians, World Orgn. Famaly Drs. (WONCA); mem. Inst. Medicine-Nat. Acad. Sci., Soc. Tchrs. Family Medicine (Curtis Hames Career Research award 1984), Ambulatory Sentinel Practice Network, Internat. Primary Care Network (treas., bd. dirs.), N.Am. Primary Care Rsch. Group (treas., bd. dirs., exec. dir., 1982-92), Rotary. Episcopalian. Personal E-mail: wood150w@verizon.net.

WOOD, MICHAEL W., lawyer; b. Austin, Tex. B, Rice Univ., Houston, 1967; JD, Univ. Tex., 1970. Bar: Tex. 1971, US Supreme Ct., US Ct. of Appeals (5th cir.), US Tax Ct. Co-founder Wood Campbell Moody & Gibbs, 1971; ptnr. Nathan Wood Sommers & Lippman; sr. v.p. and CEO Azurix Water Resources; co-ptnr. in charge of Houston office Akin Gump Strauss Hauer & Feld LLP, Houston, 2002—. Bd. trustees Houston Grand Opera; former bd. dir. Houston Ballet Found. and Wortham Theater Ctr. Mem.: ABA, Houston Bar Assn. Office: Akin Gump Strauss Hauer & Feld LLP 44th Fl 1111 Louisiana St Houston TX 77002-5200 Office Phone: 713-220-8111. Office Fax: 713-236-0822. Business E-Mail: mwood@akingump.com.

WOOD, PATRICK HENRY, III, energy executive, lawyer; b. Port Arthur, Tex., July 4, 1962; m. Kathleen Ryder; 4 children. BS in Civil Engring., Tex. A&M U.; JD, Harvard U. Atty. Baker & Botts LLP, Washington; engr. Arco Indonesia; legal counsel to chmn. Tex. Railroad Commn.; advisor to Commr. Jerry Langdon Fed. Energy Regulatory Commn. (FERC), Washington, staff mem., 1991—93, chmn., 2001—05, Pub. Utility Commn. of Tex., 1995—2001; prin. Wood3 Resources, 2005—. Bd. dirs. SunPower Corp., 2005—; chmn. advisory bd. Airtricity N.Am., 2006—; bd. dirs. Quanta Svcs., Inc., 2006—. Office: Wood3 Resources 5847 San Felipe Ste 1700 Houston TX 77057 Office Phone: 713-821-1345. Business E-Mail: pat@wood3resources.com.

WOOD, RANDY, state legislator; b. Tift County, Ga., Mar. 25, 1947; m. Linda Wood; 1 child, Allison. Grad., So. Union Coll. Owner Wood's Auto Body Shop, Anniston, Ala.; commr. Calhoun County, Ala., 1998—2002; mem. Dist. 36 Ala. House of Reps., Montgomery, 2002—. Served with Ala. Nat. Guard. Mem.: Fraternal Order Police, Weaver Lions, Saks Civitan Club. Republican. Office: PO Box 4432 Anniston AL 36204 also: 4422 Sprague Ave Anniston AL 36206 also: Ala House of Reps Ala State House 11 S Union St Rm 524-E Montgomery AL 36130 Office Phone: 256-237-8114, 334-242-7700.

WOOD, RICHARD COURTNEY, library director, educator; b. Spartanburg, SC, Aug. 8, 1943; s. Herman Alva and Mildred Eloise (Porter) W. BA, U. Tex., 1966; MLS, U. S.C., 1977. Head cataloging Wofford Coll. Libr., Spartanburg, 1969-78; hosp. libr. John Peter Smith Hosp., Ft. Worth, 1978-80; reference libr. Tex. Coll. Osteo. Medicine, Ft. Worth, 1980-82, assoc. dir. libr., 1982-91; exec. dir. librs., assoc. prof. Sch. Medicine, chair HCOM dept. Tex. Tech U. Health Scis. Ctr., Lubbock, 1991—. Cons. Tarrant County Med. Libr. Assn., Fort Worth, 1978-82, 84, Med. Plaza Hosp., Fort Worth, 1979-82, Grand Prairie (Tex.) Community Hosp., 1980-81, Cook-Fort Worth Children's Hosp., 1988-91. Contbr. scientific papers. Patron Kimball Art Mus. Fort Worth, 1987—; spokesman Neighborhood Assn., Fort Worth, 1989; vis. exec. United Way, Fort Worth, 1990; session mem. Grace Presby. Ch., Lubbock, 2010, bd. mem. Neurosci. Board, Covenant Hosp., 2010; co-chair El Paso Campus Transition Com., 2013-. Recipient Dean's award Sch. Nursing, Tex. Tech U. Health Sci. Ctr., 1998. Mem. Dallas-Tarrant County Consortium (chmn. 1980-81), Metroplex Consortium Health Scis. (chmn. 1980-81), South Cen. Regional Group, Med. Libr. Assn. (chmn. osteo. librs. sect. 1986-87), South Cen. Acad. Med. Librs. (bd. dirs. 1991—, past chair), Nat. Network Librs. Medicine (bd. dirs. South Cen. region 1991-93, chair regional adv. coun., 2008-), Tex. Assn. Academic Health Scis. Ctrs. (chair 2009-), Deutsche Gesellschaft für Heereskunde, LIS Users Group (chair exec. bd.), Sigma Tau Delta. Republican. Presbyterian. Avocations: languages, travel, history, gardening, music. Office: Preston Smith Libr Health Scis 3601 4th St Lubbock TX 79430-0001 Home Phone: 806-791-2724; Office Phone: 806-743-2203. Office Fax: 806-743-2218. Business E-Mail: richard.wood@ttuhsc.edu.

WOOD, R(OBERT) CRAIG, lawyer, educator; b. Charlottesville, Va., May 31, 1951; s. Robert Aldine and Julia Ann (Heflin) Wood; m. Lisa Lynn Browne, June 20, 1981; children: Rudy, Robert, Emily, Ashley, Marshall. BA, U. Va., 1973, MEd, 1975; JD magna cum laude, Washington & Lee U., 1984. Bar: Va. 1984, DC, 1985, US Dist. Ct. We. Dist. Va. 1984, US Dist. Ct. Ea. Dist. Va., US Ct. Appeals 4th Cir. 1984, US Supreme Ct. 1991. Ptnr. McGuireWoods LLP, Charlottesville, Va., 1984—, head Charlottesville litig. dept., 1991—, mng. ptnr. Charlottesville office, 2001—09. Adj. prof. U. Va. Law Sch., 1992—, Washington & Lee Law Sch., 2009-; bd. dirs. Albemarle 1st Bank, 1999-2007. Chmn. bd. dirs. Va. Found. for Law and Citizenship Studies, 1985-91, The Covenant Sch., 1989-96, 97—; session bd. dirs. Trinity Presbyn. Ch., 1987—, Charlottesville Housing Improvement Program, 1990-92; chmn. Va. Coun. Sch. Attorneys, 1995-96. Mem. Edn. Law Assn. (bd. dirs. 1996-2003, pres. 2001-02), Va. Bar Assn., Va. State Bar (bd. governors litigation sect. 1990-97, chmn. 1996-97), Thomas Jefferson Inn of Ct. (pres. 1992-93). Presbyterian. Avocations: golf, tennis, travel, reading. Office: McGuireWoods LLP Court Sq Bldg Ste 300 310 Fourth St NE Charlottesville VA 22902-1288 Office Phone: 434-977-2558. Office Fax: 434-980-2274. Business E-Mail: cwood@mcguirewoods.com.

WOOD, ROBERT E., philosopher, educator; b. Racine, Wis., Oct. 20, 1934; s. Earl J. and Cathryn M. Wood; m. Marjorie M. Simanek; children: Robert L., Gregory T., Mary T. Kubala, David J., Mark C. BA, Marquette U., Milw., 1958, MA, 1961, PhD, 1967. From assoc. to prof. St. Joseph's Coll., Rensselaer, Ind., 1961—76; assoc. prof. St. Joseph's U., Phila., 1976—79; from asst. to prof. U. Dallas, Irving, 1979—. Vis. assoc. Cath. U. Am., Washington, 1968—69, Duquesne U., Pitts., 1974; vis. prof. Marquette U., 1995; chmn. dept. philosophy St. Joseph's Coll., 1969—77, U. Dallas, 1984—96, grad. dean, 1987—90, acting provost, dean Constantin Coll., 1988, interim provost, dean Constantin Coll., 1990—91, chair acad. senate, 1996. Author: Martin Buber's Ontology, 1969, A Path Into Metaphysics, 1991, Placing Aesthetics, 1999; editor: The Future of Metaphysics, 1970; contbr. more than 70 articles to profl. jours. Fulbright grantee, Tübingen, Germany, 1989. Mem.: Am. Cath. Philos. Assn. (editor Am. Cath. Philosophy Quar. 1989—2009, pres. 1993—94). Democrat. Roman Catholic. Avocations: sculpting, gardening. Home: 209 E Scotland Dr Irving TX 75062 Office: U Dallas Dept Philosophy 1845 E Northgate Dr Irving TX 75062 Personal E-mail: woodr348@aol.com.

WOOD, SHELTON EUGENE, JR., education educator, minister, consultant; b. Douglas, Ga., May 20, 1943; s. Shelton and Mae Lillie (Pheil) Wood; m. Louise Wood, Aug. 25, 1961; children: Shelton John, Deirdre Louise. AA, St. John's U., 1958; BA, U. Nebr., 1959; MEd, Coll. William and Mary, Williamsburg, Va., 1971; PhD, Sussex U., 1973; EdD, Southeastern U., Washington, DC, 1975; MBA, Ctrl. Mich. U., Mount Pleasant, 1977; MA, U. Okla., Norman, 1980; D in Ministry, Wesleyan Bible Coll., 1999; Cert. in Internt. Rels., Fgn. Svc. Inst., 1971; Cert. in Mgmt., Indsl. Coll. Armed Forces, 1970. Area mgr. Marshall Fields Corp., Fla., 1957-58; transp. supr. Greyhound Corp., Jacksonville, Fla., 1959-62; officer US Army, 1963, advanced through grades to inf. col., 1996; with Redstone Readiness Group, 1977-80; chief studies and analysis divsn. Korean Inst. for Def. Analysis, 1981-83; faculty St. John River C.C., 1984-90; nat. and internat. bus. and mgmt. cons., 1995—; sr. pastor Fellowship Wesleyan Ch., Spring Hill, Fla., 1998—2005, asst. dist. supt. Fla., 2005—. Faculty Wesleyan Bible U., 1997—; pres. Georgetown Wesleyan U., 2005-. Author: Strategic for Implementing A Family Life Ministry Ctr., 1997; contbr. articles to profl. jours. Active Boy Scouts Am., 1977—90; lay leader United Meth. Ch., Falls Ch., Va., 1977—79, St. James United Meth. Ch., 1986—90; mem. dist. bd. ministerial develop. Fla. Dist. of Wesleyan Ch., 1999, chair evangelism and ch. growth com., 1999—, supt., 2009—; bd. dirs. Baby Love. Decorated Bronze Star with 2 oak leaf clusters, Air medal with 3 oak leaf clusters, Purple Heart with 2 oak leaf clusters; Sussex Coll. fellow, 1969-70. Mem. NEA, Am. Soc. Trainers and Developers (pres. S.E. chpt. 1974-75), Am. Def. Preparedness Assn., Putnam County C. of C. (pres. 1990-91), Toastmasters Internat. (Disting. Toastmaster 1989), Kiwanis (pres. 1989-90), Assn. Christian Counselor, Rotary, Phi Delta Kappa. Address: 8485 Chatsworth St Spring Hill FL 34608 Personal E-mail: ewood11@tampabay.rr.com.

WOOD, STEPHEN WRAY, minister, educator, legislator, singer, writer; b. Winston Salem, NC, Oct. 6, 1948; s. D.W. and Annie Lee (Harris) W.; m. Starr Smith, June 18, 1978; children: Allyson, Joshua. BTh., John Wesley Coll., 1970; BA, Asbury U., 1973; MA, UNC, Greensboro, 1979; DMin, Luther Rice U., Ga., 1980; MDiv, Houston Grad. Sch. Theology, 1990. Asst. dean, asst. prof. John Wesley Coll., High Point, NC, 1975-81; min. Soc. of Friends, 1980—. Adj. prof. Luther Rice U.; assoc. prof. Houston Grad. Sch. Theology; pres. Triad Christian Counseling, Greensboro, 1979. Contbr. articles to hist., ednl. and religious jours., Dictionary of NC Biography, Oxford Internat. Roundtable, 1997—; composer, singer religious music. Trustee John Wesley Coll., High Point, 1981—; bd. dirs. Friends Ctr.-Guilford Coll., Greensboro, 1982-89; vice chmn. Guilford County Rep. Party, NC, 1981-85; mem. NC State Ho. Reps., 1985-86, 89-90, 91-92, 93-94, 95-96, 97-98, 99-2000, 2003-05, spkr. pro tem, 1997—; apptd. mem. Selective Svc. Commn., 2001—; chaplain High Point Jaycees. With US Army, 1970-71; capt. NC State Militia. Mem. BMI (affiliate songwriter 1978—). Avocations: golf, book collecting, reading, cowboy boots. Office: PO Box 55 Tobaccoville NC 27050 Personal E-mail: repstevewood@juno.com.

WOOD, VIVIAN POATES, retired mezzo soprano, writer, educator; b. Washington, Aug. 19, 1923; d. Harold Poates and Mildred Georgette (Patterson) W. Studies with Walter Anderson, Antioch Coll., 1953-55; studies with Denise Restout, Saint-Leu-A-Forêt, France and Lakeville, Conn., 1960—62, studies with Denise Restout, 1964—70; studies with Paul A. Pisk, 1968—71; studies with Paul Ulanowsky, NYC, 1958—68; Elemer Nagy, 1965-68, Vyautas Marijosius, 1967-68; MusB, Hartt Coll. Music, 1968; postgrad. (fellow), Yale U., 1968; MusM (fellow), Washington U., St. Louis, 1971, PhD (fellow), 1973. Debut in recital series Internat. Jeunesse Musicals Arts Festival, 1953; solo fellowship Boston Symphony Orch., Berkshire Music Ctr., Tanglewood, 1964, St. Louis Symphony Orch., 1969, Washington Orch., 1949, Bach Cantata Series Berkshire Chamber Orch., 1964, Yale Symphony Orch., 1968. Appearances in U.S. and European recitals, oratorios, operas, radio and TV, 1953-68; soloist Landowska Ctr., Lakeville, 1969, Internat. Harpsichord Festival, Westminister Choir Coll., Princeton, N.J., 1973; prof. voice, head voice area Sch. of Music, U. So. Miss., Hattiesburg, 1971-2000, ret. 2000, prof. emerita, 2000—; asst. dean Coll. Fine Arts, 1974-76, acting dean, 1976-77; guest prof. Hochschüle für Musik, Munich, 1978-79; prof. Italian Internat. Studies Program, Rome, 1986; Miss. coord. Alliance for Arts Edn., Kennedy Ctr. Performing Arts, 1974—; mem. Miss. Gov.'s Adv. Panel for Gifted and Talented Children, 1974—, 1st Miss. Gov.'s Conf. on the Arts, 1974—. Author: Poulenc's Songs: An Analysis of Style, 1979. Recipient Young Am. Artists Concert award N.Y.C., 1955; Wanda Landowska fellow 1961-68. Mem. Miss. Music Tchrs. Assn., Nat. Assn. Tchrs. of Singing, Music Tchrs. Nat. Assn., Am. Musicology Soc., Golden Key, Delta Kappa Gamma, Tau Beta Kappa (hon.), Pi Kappa Lambda. Democrat. Episcopalian.

WOODALL, JAMES C., insurance company executive; b. Columbus, Ga. BBA, Columbus State U. Pres., CEO The Print House, Inc.; CEO AFLAC, Inc., 1988; v.p., Ops. and Mktg. Communicorp (subs. of Aflac, Inc.), 1991, pres., bd. dirs., CEO, 2005—. Bd. dirs. Aflac Credit Union, Columbus State U. Friends of Art, Printing and Imaging Assn. of Ga., Youth Orchestra of Greater Columbus; bd. adv. Muscogee County Juvenile Drug Court. Office: Communicorp 1001 Lockwood Ave Columbus GA 31999 Office Phone: 706-324-1182. Office Fax: 706-321-3100.

WOODALL, ROBERT, United States Representative from Georgia; b. Athens, Ga., Feb. 11, 1970; Grad., Furman U., Greenville, SC, 1992; JD, U. Ga., Athens, 1998. Law clk. Balch & Bingham, 1993—94; legis. corr., legis. asst., legis. dir. to Rep John Linder, US House of Reps., Washington, 1994—2000, chief of staff, 2000—10; mem. US Congress from 7th Ga. Dist., Washington, 2011—, US House Rules Com., Washington, 2011—. Co-author: FairTax: The Truth, 2008. Republican. Methodist. Office: US House of Representatives 1725 Longworth House Office Bldg Washington DC 20515 Office Phone: 202-225-4272. Office Fax: 202-225-4696.*

WOODALL, THOMAS A., lawyer, former state supreme court justice; b. Meridian, Miss., July 14, 1950; m. Debbie Bogan, 1972; children: Scott, Matthew, Claire. BA in History, Millsaps Coll., 1972; JD, U. Va., 1975. Former legal editor Michie Co.; with Rives and Peterson, Birmingham, Ala., 1975—91; ptnr. Woodall and Maddox, Birmingham, 1991—96; circuit judge Jefferson County, 1996—2001; assoc. justice Ala. Supreme Ct., 2001—13; shareholder Sirote, Birmingham, 2013—. Mem. Ala. Pattern Jury Instrn.-Civil Com., 1985—2001, vice chmn., 1992—2001; chair appellate practice group Sirote. Mem.: Birmingham Bar Assn. (chair com. on grievance, civil ct. procedures and membership). Republican. Methodist. Office: Sirote 2311 Highland Ave South Birmingham AL 35205 Office Phone: 205-930-5319. Office Fax: 205-212-2897. E-mail: twoodall@sirote.com.

WOODARD, JOSEPH LAMAR, law librarian, emeritus professor; s. Wilbur Allen and Florence Virginia (Ladd) Woodard; m. Eleanor Eugenia Cummings, Aug. 7, 1964; children: Robert Edward, James Frederick. BA, U. Fla., 1959, JD, 1962; MLS, Columbia U., 1964. Bar: Fla. 1962, U.S. Dist. Ct. (mid. dist.) Fla. 1970. Asst. reference libr. Columbia U., NYC, 1962—64; asst. libr. Cahill, Gordon, Reindel and Ohl, NYC, 1964—65; law libr. Tulane U., 1965—69; ptnr. Schuh, Schuh and Woodard, St. Petersburg, Fla., 1969—71; law libr. Stetson U., 1971—2001, prof. law, 1979—2001, law libr., prof. emeritus, 2001—. Pres. Tampa Bay Libr. Consortium, 1981, 1988—89. Stated clk. Presbytery Tampa Bay, 2005—06. With USAR, 1957—63. Named to Hall of Fame, Stetson U. Coll. Law, 2006. Mem.: Pinellas Pub. Libr. Coop. (sec.-treas. 1993—94, pres. 1994—95), Am. Assn. Law Librs. (sec.-treas. SE chpt. 1975—78), Fla. Bar Assn. Republican. Personal E-mail: lamar@woodardfamily.org.

WOODBURY, EDWINA DOWDY, controller; b. Rocky Mount, NC, Aug. 9, 1951; d. John Horton Dowdy and Elizabeth Gerald (Duke) Holt; m. Thomas Meares Woodbury, Sept. 23, 1969. BSBA in Acctg., U. NC, 1972. CPA N.C., N.Y. Auditor Peat Marwick Mitchell & Co., Raleigh, N.C., 1973-74, sr. auditor, 1974-75, audit supr. sr., 1975-77; exec. v.p., CFO Avon Cosmetics Inc., 1977—98; supr. acctg. Avon Products, Inc., NYC, 1977-79, exec. v.p., CFO and chief adminstrv. officer, 1977—98, mgr. acctg. NYC, 1979-82, group mgr. U.S. planning, 1982-83, dir. U.S. planning, 1983-84, asst. contr., 1984-86, contr., 1986; pres., CEO Chapel Hill Press, Inc., 1999—. Bd. dirs. RadioShack Corp., 1997—, Click Commerce, Inc., 2000—05, R H Donnelley Corp., 2005—10. Active Inwood House Maternity Shelter, N.Y.C., 1983—. Mem. Nat. Assn. Accts., N.C. Assn. N.Y. Democrat. Episcopalian. Avocation: choral music. Office: Chapel Hill Press Inc 976 Martin Luther King Jr Blvd Ste 250 Chapel Hill NC 27514-2611 Office Phone: 919-942-8389. Office Fax: 919-933-9233. Business E-Mail: edwina.woodbury@chapelhillpress.com.

WOODCOCK, DAVID GEOFFREY, architect, educator; b. Manchester, Eng., May 28, 1937; s. Herbert Edwin and Constance Mary (Bristol) Woodcock; m. Kathleen Mary Bishop, Oct. 1, 1960 (dec. 1964); 1 child, Jonathan Alfred; m. Valerie Frances Gubbins, July 4, 1964; children: Frances Mary, Penelope Jane. BA in Architecture with 1st class honors, U. Manchester, 1960, D in Town Planning, 1966. Arch. emeritus, Tex. Lectr. U. Manchester, 1961; asst. prof. Tex. A&M U., College Station, 1962-66; sr. lectr. Kent. Coll. Art & Design, Canterbury, England, 1966—70; assoc. prof. Tex. A&M U., College Station, 1970—76, prof., 1976—; dir. Ctr. Heritage Conservation, 1991—2007. Pvt. practice, Canterbury, 1966—70, College Station, 1980—. Bd. dirs. Opera and Performing Arts Soc., Tex. A&M U., 1980—83, 1988—91, pres., 1993—94; peer reviewer U.S. Gen. Svc. Adminstrn., 2004—; active Episc. Diocese Tex. Archtl. Commn., 1987—95; mem. adv. bd. Hammons Sch. Architecture Drury Coll., Mo., 1990—93, Savannah (Ga.) Coll. Arts and Design/Architecture, 1987—93. Recipient Rsch. Excellence award, Tex. Hist. Commn., 1991, Romieniec award for Archtl. Edn., Tex. Soc. Archs., 1995, Truett Latimer Profl. award, Preservation Tex., Inc., 1998, J. M. Fitch award, Nat. Coun. Preservation Edn., 2010. Fellow: AIA (hist. resource com. adv. group 2005—09, chair 2009), Assn. Collegiate Schs. Architecture (regional dir. 1981—84, Disting. prof. 1991), Assn. Preservation Tech. Internat. (bd. dirs. 1990—, v.p. 1998—99, pres. 1999—2001, Harley J. McKee award 2003), Soc. Antiquaries London. Avocations: drawing, cross disciplinary education. Office: Tex A&M U Dept Architecture College Station TX 77843-3137 Office Phone: 979-845-7850. Business E-Mail: d-woodcock@tamu.edu.

WOODHOUSE, MICHAEL A., restaurant chain company executive; b. 1945; BS, MS in Natural Sciences, Queen's Coll., Cambridge, Eng. Exec. v.p., CFO S&A Restaurant Corp., T.G.I. Friday's Inc., 1987; CFO Tia's Inc.; v.p. fin. Daka Internat. Inc., 1993—94, sr. v.p., CFO, 1994—95; sr. v.p. finance, CFO Cracker Barrel Old Country Store, Inc., Lebanon, Tenn., 1995—99, exec. v.p., CFO, 1999—2000, pres., COO, 2000—01, pres., CEO, 2001—04, chmn., CEO, 2004—11, exec. chmn., 2011—. Bd. dirs. Cracker Barrel Old Country Store, Inc., 1999—. Office: Cracker Barrel Old Country Store Inc 307 Hartmann Dr Lebanon TN 37087 Office Phone: 615-444-5533. Office Fax: 615-443-9818. Business E-Mail: mwoodhouse@crackerbarrel.com.

WOODHURST, ROBERT STANFORD, JR., architect; b. Abbeville, SC, July 12, 1921; s. Robert Stanford and Eva (Ferguson) W.; m. Dorothy Ann Carwile, Aug. 4, 1945; 1 son: Robert Stanford III. BS in Architecture, Clemson U., 1942. Registered arch., S.C., Ga., NCARB. Designer Harold Woodward, Arch., Spartanburg, SC, 1946-47; assoc. arch. F. Arthur Hazard, Arch., Augusta, Ga., 1947-54; ptnr. Woodhurst & O'Brien, Architects, Augusta, Ga., 1954-83, Woodhurst Partnership, Augusta, Ga., 1983—. V.p. Southeastern Architects and Engrs., Inc., Augusta, 1964-83; lectr. history architecture N. Augusta Community Coll.; mem. nat. exam. com. Nat. Council Arch tl. Regis. Bds.; pres. Ga. State Bd. Archs. Chmn. Augusta-richmond County Planning Commn., 1966-68; trustee Hist. Augusta, Inc., active Mayor's Adv. Com., 1965-68; mem. Augusta Bldg. Code Bd. Appeals, 1955-58. Served to capt. U.S. Army, 1942-45. Decorated Air medal with 7 oak leaf clusters; Croix de Guerre avec palms (France); prisoner of war, Germany. Fellow AIA (Bronze medal 1942); mem. Ga. Assn. AIA (pres. 1977, Bronze medal 1977, Rothchild Silver Medal 1987), Soc. Archtl. Historians, Nat. Coun. Archtl. Registration Bds., Augusta Country Club, Pinnacle Club. Democrat. Baptist. Achievements include designed and built: 1st Bapt. Ch., Augusta, Univ. Hosp. Med Ctr., Augusta, Peabody Apts. and Irvin Towers, Augusta, W. Lake Country Club, Augusta, Med. Libr., Med. Coll. Ga., Libr. Voorhees Coll., Denmark, S.C., Ambulatory Care Ctr. Univ. Hosp. Augusta, Married Students Apts., Med. Coll. Ga., Covenant Presbyn. Ch., Augusta, Student Ctr. Voorhees Coll., Pres.' Home Voorhees Coll., others. Home: 810 Dogwood Ln Augusta GA 30909-2704 Office: Woodhurst Partnership 607 15th St Augusta GA 30901-2601 Office Phone: 706-724-4343. Personal E-mail: twparch@aol.com.

WOODLIEF, JOHN B., supermarket chain executive; b. 1950; Joined Price Waterhouse, 1972; mng. ptnr. PricewaterhouseCoopers, Charlotte, 1997—99, ptnr., 1998, Price Waterhouse, 1985—98, mng. ptnr., 1997—98; v.p. finance, CFO Ruddick Corp., 1999—2012; exec. v.p., CFO Harris Teeter Supermarkets, Inc. (formerly Ruddick Corp.), Matthews, NC, 2012—. Office: Harris Teeter Supermarkets Inc 701 Crestdale St Matthews NC 28105

WOODRING, DEWAYNE STANLEY, religious association executive; b. Gary, Ind., Nov. 10, 1931; s. J. Stanley and Vera Luella (Brown) Woodring; m. Donna Jean Wishart, June 15, 1957; children: Judith Lynn Bigelow, Beth Ellen Carey. BS in Speech with distinction, Northwestern U., Evanston, Ill., 1954; postgrad., Northwestern U., 1954—57; MDiv, Garrett Theol. Sem., 1957; LHD, Mt. Union Coll., 1967; DD, Salem Coll., 1970. Ordained to ministry Meth. Ch., 1955. Assoc. dir. youth Gary YMCA, 1950—55; min. edn. Griffith Meth. Ch., Ind., 1955—57; min. adminstrn. and program 1st Meth. Ch., Eugene, Oreg., 1957—59; dir. pub. rels. Dakotas area Meth. Ch., 1959—60, dir. pub. rels. Ohio area, 1960—64; adminstrv. exec. to bishop Ohio East area United Meth. Ch., Canton, 1964—77, asst. gen. sec. Gen. Coun. Fin. and Adminstr. Evanston, Ill., 1977—79, assoc. gen. sec., 1979—84; exec. dir., CEO Religious Conf. Mgmt. Assn., Indpls., 1982—2012. Staff dept. radio svcs. 2d Assembly World Coun. Chs., Evanston, 1954; chmn. comm. commn. Ohio Coun. Chs., 1961—65; v.p. Ohio East Area United Meth. Found., 1967—77; exec. com. Nat. Assn. United Meth. Found., 1968—72, World Meth. Coun., 1986—2001; vice-chmn. commn. entertainment and program North Ctrl. Jurisdictional Conf., 1968—72, chmn., 1972—76; mem. divsn. interpretation United Meth. Ch., 1969—72, mem. commn. gen. conf., 1972—93, mgr., exec. dir., 1976—93; chmn. bd. mgrs. United Meth. Bldg., Evanston, 1977—84; mem. adv. bd. Nassau/Paradise Island, 1997—99, Red Lion Hotels and Inns, PR Conv. Ctr.; lectr., cons. in field; del. White House Travel and Tourism Conf., 1995. Creator (radio series) The Word and Music, prodr., dir. (TV series) Parables in Miniature, 1957—59. Adviser East Ohio Conf. Comm. Commn., 1968—76; bd. dirs. First Internat. Summit Edn., 1989; trustee, 1st v.p. Copeland Oaks Retirement Ctr., Sebring, Ohio, 1969—76; pres. Guild Assocs., 1971—. Recipient Cert. Meeting Profl. award, 1985, Cert. Expt. Mgr. award, 1988, Sagamore of Wabash award, State Ind., 2007; named one of 25 Leaders Who Shaped The Industry, Convention South Mag., 2008; named to, Ky. Cols., 1989, Hall of Leaders, Conv. Liaison Coun., 1994. Mem.: ISAE (Meeting Planner of the Yr. award 1990), Marriott Customer Leadership Forum (mem. customer adv. bd.), Found. Internat. Meetings (bd. dirs.), Cert. Meeting Profls. (bd. dirs. 1983—92), Ind. Conv. Visitors Assn. (bd. dirs. 1996—2000, bd. advisors), Conv. Industry Coun. (bd. dirs., past chmn.), Am. Soc. Assn. Execs. Home: 1309 Noble Way Flower Mound TX 75022

WOODRUFF, JUDY CARLINE, broadcast journalist; b. Tulsa, Nov. 20, 1946; d. William Henry and Anna Lee (Payne) W.; m. Albert R. Hunt, Jr., Apr. 5, 1980; children: Jeffrey Woodruff, Benjamin Woodruff, Lauren Ann Lee. Student, Meredith Coll., 1964-66; BA, Duke U., 1968. News announcer, reporter Sta. WAGA-TV, Atlanta, 1970-75; news corr. NBC News, Atlanta, 1975-76, White House corr. Washington, 1977-83; anchor Frontline, PBS documentary series, 1984—90; corr. MacNeil-Lehrer News Hour, PBS, Washington, 1983-93; anchor, sr. corr. CNN, Washington, 1993—2005; moderator Vice Presidential Debate, 1988, America Votes, 2003, 2004; sr. corr., polit. editor The News Hour With Jim Lehrer, 2007—09; co-anchor, sr. corr. PBS News Hour, 2009—, co-anchor, mng. dir., 2013—. Bd. advisors Henry Grady Sch. Journalism, U. Ga., 1979-82, Benton Fellowship in Broadcast Journalism, U. Chgo., 1984-90, Knight Fellowship in Journalism, Stanford U., 1985-99; bd. visitors Wake Forest U., 1982-89; trustee Duke U., 1985-97, emerita; founding co-chair, bd. dirs. Internat. Women's Media Found.; vis. fellow, Joan Shorenstein Ctr. on the Press, Politics and Pub. Policy, Harvard U., 2005—; vis. prof. media and politics Duke U., 2006. Author: This is Judy Woodruff at the White House, 1982; corr: PBS Special Generation Next, 2006. Active Commn. on Women's Health, The Commonwealth Fund., 1993-98, Duke Endowment; bd. trustee Freedom Forum, Urban Inst.; trustee Nat. Mus. Am. History, 2005—11; mem. Knight Commn. on Intercollegiate Athletics, 2008-, trustee, Duke

Endowment, 2013-, bd. trustee Carnegie Corp. NY, 2013- Recipient award Leadership Atlanta, Class of 1974, Atlanta chpt. Women in Comms., 1975, Edward Weintal award for excellence in fgn. policy reporting, 1987, Joan Shorenstein Barone award for series on def. issues, 1987, Helen Bernstein award for excellence in journalism N.Y. Pub. Libr., 1989, Pres.'s 21st Century award Nat. Women's Hall of Fame, 1994, CableAce award for best newscaster, 1995, CableAce Best Anchor Team award, 1996, Allen H. Neuharth award for excellence in journalism, 1995, News and Documentary Emmy award, 1997, Internat. Matrix award, Assn. for Women in Comm., 2003, Leonard Zeidenberg First Amendment award, Radio-Television News Directors Assn. and Found., 2003; named to Ga. Assn. of Broadcasters Hall of Fame, 2003, Edward R. Murrow Excellence in Broadcasting award, Wash. State U., 2010, Walter Cronkite Journalism Excellence award, U. Southern Calif., 2011; grantee Pew Charitable Trusts, 2006—. Mem. NATAS (Atlanta chpt. Emmy award 1975), White House Corrs. Assn. Address: JudyWoodruff 3620 South 27th St Arlington VA 22206 Office Phone: 703-998-2497.

WOODS, JAMES DUDLEY, energy executive; b. Falmouth, Ky., July 24, 1931; s. Alva L. and Mabel L. (Miller) W.; m. Darlene Mae Petersen, Nov. 8, 1962; children: Linda, Debbie, Jeffrey, Jamie. AA, Long Beach City Coll., 1958; BA, Calif. State U., Fullerton, 1967, postgrad., 1970. Pres. Baker Packers, Houston, 1976-77, Baker Oil Tools, Orange, Calif., 1977-87; pres., CEO Baker Internat. Corp., Houston, mgr., planning and control, 1965-68, v.p., fin. and adminstrn., Baker div., 1968-73, corp. v.p., group fin. officer, 1973-76, exec. v.p., 1977—85, bd. dirs., 1987—97; CEO Baker Hughes, Inc., 1987—97, chmn. Houston, 1989—97. Bd. dirs. ESCO Technologies, Foster Wheeler Ltd, Nat. Oilwell Varco, Inc., 1988—2005, OMI Corp., 1998—2007, Integrated Prodn. Svcs., Inc., 2001—05, USEC Inc., 2001—07, Complete Prodn. Svcs., Inc., 2001—. Trustee Nat. Boys and Girls Club of America; bd. dirs. Petroleum Equipment Supplier's Assn., Nat. Ocean Industries Assn., The Greater Houston YMCA, U. Tex. Health Sci. Ctr., Houston. With USAF, 1951—55. Republican. Lutheran. Office: Complete Production Services Inc 1001 Louisiana St Houston TX 77002-5089 Office Phone: 281-372-2300. Office Fax: 281-372-2301. Business E-Mail: jwoods@completeproduction.com.

WOODS, JON, state legislator; b. Charlotte, Ark., Aug. 23, 1977; BA, Univ. Ark., 2002. Bank officer; mem. Dist. 93 Ark. House of Reps., 2007—. Republican. Roman Catholic. Address: PO Box 8082 Springdale AR 72766 Office Phone: 479-445-6678. Office Fax: 479-756-7655. Business E-Mail: woodsj@arkleg.state.ar.us.

WOODS, PHYLLIS MICHALIK, librarian; b. New Orleans, Sept. 12, 1937; d. Philip John and Thelma Alice (Carey) Michalik; 1 child, Tara Woods Knowles. BA, Southea. La. U., 1967. Cert. in speech and English, libr. sci., secondary edn., La. Tchr. speech, English and drama St. Charles Parish Pub. Schs., Luling, La., elem. tchr., secondary tchr. remedial reading, Chpt. 1 reading specialist, Wicat tchr. coord., elem. sch. libr.; media specialist Jefferson Parish Pub. Sch. System. Tchr. cons. St. Charles parish writing project La. State U. Writing Project; tchr. gifted writing students in a summer writing workshop. Author: Egbert, the Egret, Egbert's Picnic, Egbert Visits Sammy, Angel Without Wings, The Necklace and Egbert's Calf, The Hurricane, The Cleanup Day, The Rainbow, The Fair, The Tornado, The Farm Baby Sitting The Argument Mickey Mocking Bird; songwriter; musical compositions include The Fruits of the Spirit, Father's Day Song, Mother's Day Song; contbr. articles and poems to River Parish Guide, St. Charles Herald; Actor: Our Town, The Curious Savage. Sch. rep. United Fund, St. Charles Parish Reading Assn.; parish com. mem. Young Authors, Tchrs. Who Write; active 4-H leader; bd. trustees Michalik Scholarship Trust. Mem. ASCD, Internat. Platform Assn., Internat. Reading Assn., Am. Fedn. Tchrs., St. Charles Parish Reading Coun., Newspaper in Edn. (chmn., historian), La. Assn. Newspapers in Edn. (state com.), Jefferson Parish Libr. Assn., Jefferson Parish Reading Assn., Jefferson Parish Tchrs. Union, Nat. Assn. Profl. Women.

WOODS, RONALD G., lawyer, former prosecutor; b. Moab, Utah, Jan. 1, 1938; LLB, U. Tex. Law Sch., 1964. Bar: Tex. 1964, US Supreme Ct. 1967, US Ct. Appeals (5th cir.) 1976, US Dist. Ct. (no., so., ea. and we. dists.) Tex. 1997, US Ct. Appeals (10th cir.). Spl. agent, legal advisor FBI, 1965—68; asst. dist. atty. Harris County Dist. Atty.'s Office, Tex., 1969—76, chief prosecutor Special Crimes divsn. Tex., 1972—76; asst. US atty. (so. dist.) Tex. US Dept. Justice, Houston, 1976—85, chief Narcotics divsn., 1976—78, chief Pub. Integrity divsn., 1978—80, chief Fraud divsn., sr. litig. counsel, 1980—85, US atty. (so. dist.) Tex., 1990—93; pvt. practice Houston, 1993—. Adj. faculty Trial Advocacy seminars U. Tex. Law Sch., 1985—94, 2002—. Recipient Director's award for superior performance, Exec. Office US Attorneys, 1985; named Best Atty. in Houston, Houston Press, 1999; named a Tex. Super Lawyer in White Collar Crime, Tex. Monthly, 2003—11. Mem.: ABA, Nat. Assn. Former US Attorneys, Coll. State Bar Tex., Nat. Criminal Def. Lawyers Assn., Tex. Criminal Def. Lawyers Assn., Fed. Bar Assn., Houston Bar Assn. (chair Fed. Practice sect. 1992—93). Office: Ronald G Woods 5300 Memorial Ste 1000 Houston TX 77077 Office Phone: 713-862-9600. Office Fax: 713-864-8738. E-mail: ron@ronwoodslaw.com.

WOODS, THOMAS (TOMMY) LAMAR, state legislator; b. Byhalia, Miss., Dec. 6, 1933; m. Jan Dickinson; children: Prentis, Pat, Ray, Jeana. Former mem. Co. Affairs Fees & Salaries Pub. Officers; mem. Dist. 52 Miss. House of Reps.; mem. Adv. Bd. NW Jr. Coll.; cotton farmer & ginner; owner, farm supply. Mem.: Automotive Occupant Protection Assn., Cotton Ginners Assn., Marshall County Soil & Water Conservation, Farm Bur., Shriner, Mason, Gideon. Republican. Methodist. Mailing: PO Box 388 Byhalia MS 38611 Home Phone: 601-838-6201. Business E-Mail: twoods@house.ms.gov.

WOODS, TIGER (ELDRICK WOODS), professional golfer; b. Cypress, Calif., Dec. 30, 1975; s. Earl Dennison (died May 5, 2006) & Kultida Woods, m. Elin Nordegren, Oct. 5, 2004 (div. Aug. 23, 2010); children: Sam Alexis Woods, Charlie Axel Woods. Student, Stanford U., Calif., 1994—96. Profl. golfer, 1996—; winner Optimist Internat. Jr. World Championship, 1984, 1985, 1988, 1989, 1990, 1991, Ins. Youth Golf Classic (youngest ever to win), 1990, Ins. Youth Golf Classic, 1992, CIF-Southern Calif. HS Invitational Championship, 1991, Southern Calif. Jr. Championship, 1991, PING/Phoenix Jr. Championship, 1991, 1992, Edgewood Tahoe Jr. Classic, 1991, L.A. City Jr. Championship, 1991, Orange Bowl Jr. Internat. Championship, 1991, US Jr. Amateur Championship (youngest ever to win), 1991, US Jr. Amateur Championship, 1992, US Jr. Amateur Championship (only golfer to win three times), 1993, Nabisco Mission Hills Desert Jr. Championship, 1992, Pro Gear San Antonio Shootout, 1992, Southern Calif. Jr. Best Ball Championship, 1993, US Amateur Championship (youngest ever to win, largest comeback ever), 1994, US Amateur Championship, 1995, 1996, Western Amateur Championship, 1994, Southern Calif. Golf Assn. Amateur Championship, 1994, Pacific Northwest Amateur Championship, 1994, William Tucker Invitational, 1994, Jerry Pate Invitational, 1994, Stanford Invitational, 1995, Walt Disney World/Oldsmobile Classic, 1996, Las Vegas Invitational, 1996, NCAA Championship, 1996, John A. Burns Invitational, 1996, Cleve. Golf Championship, 1996, Tri-Match Championship (Stanford U., Ariz. State U., U. Ariz.), 1996, Cougar Classic, 1996, Pac-10 Championship (shot course record 61), 1996, NCAA West Regional, 1996, Masters Tournament, 1997, 2001, 2002, 2005, Mercedes Championships, 1997, 2000, Asian Honda Classic, 1997, GTE Byron Nelson Classic, 1997, Motorola Western Open, 1997, 1999, Johnnie Walker Classic, 1998, 2000, BellSouth Classic, 1998, PGA Grand Slam, 1998, 1999, 2000, 2001, 2002, 2005, 2006, Meml. Tournament, 1999, 2000, 2001, 2009, 2012, PGA Championship, 1999, 2000, 2006, 2007, Buick Invitational, 1999, 2003, 2005, 2006, 2007, 2008, Deutsche Bank-SAP Open, 1999, 2001, 2002, WGC NEC Invitational, 1999, 2000, 2001, 2005, Nat. Car Rental Classic, 1999, Tour Championship, 1999, WGC American Express Championship, 1999, 2002, 2003, 2005, 2006, WGC American CA Championship (formerly WGC American Express Championship), 2007, WGC-Cadillac Championship, 2013, World Cup individual and team titles (with Mark O'Meara), 1999, AT&T Pebble Beach Pro-Am, 2000, Bay Hill Invitational, 2000, 2001, 2002, 2003, Arnold Palmer Invitational, 2008, 2009, 2012, 2013, US Open Championship, 2000, 2002, 2008, Brit. Open Championship, 2000, 2005, 2006, Bell Canadian Open, 2000, World Cup (with David Duval), 2000, The Players Championship, 2001, 2013, Williams World Challenge, 2001, Buick Open, 2002, 2006, 2009, WGC Accenture Match Play Championship, 2003, 2004, 2008, Western Open, 2003, Ford Championship, 2005, 2006, WGC Bridgestone Invitational, 2006, 2007, 2009, 2013, Deutsche Bank Championship, 2006, Target World Challenge, 2006, 2007, Wachovia Championship, 2007, BMW Championship, 2007, 2009, Dubai Desert Classic, 2008, AT&T National, 2009, 2012, Farmers Ins. Open, 2013. Mem. US Team World Amateur Team Championships, Versailles, France, 1994, Walker Cup Match, Porthcawl, Wales, 1995, Ryder Cup, 1997, 1999, 2002, 2004, 2006, 2010, 2012, Dunhill Cup, 1998, Presidents Cup, 1998, 2000, 2003, 2005, 2007, 2009, 2011; founder, chmn. Tiger Woods Design, 2006—. Co-founder (with father, Earl) Tiger Woods Found. 1996-; With the Tiger Woods Foundation, initiated and supported community-based programs that promote the health, education and welfare to America's children (programs include: Tiger Woods Learning Center, Southern California, started in 2006, Start Something (partners with Target Corporation), started in 2000, Tiger Woods Foundation National Junior Golf Team, Target World Challenge (also host), Tiger Jam (AT&T-sponsored event) (also host) and various grant/scholarship programs). Recipient Dial award, 1993, Jack Nicklaus Trophy, PGA America, Golf Writers Assn. America, 1997, 1999, 2000, 2001, 2002, 2003, 2005, 2006, ESPY award, Best Male Athlete, ESPN, 1998, 2000, 2001, 2002, 2008, ESPY award, Best Golfer, 2005, 2006, 2007, 2008, ESPY award, Best Championship Performance, 2008, Mark H. McCormack award as No. 1 player on world ranking, 1998—2010, Byron Nelson award, PGA Tour, 1999—2003, 2005—07, 2009, Vardon Trophy, PGA of America, 1999, 2000—03, 2005, 2007, 2009, Charlie Bartlett award, Golf Writers Assn. America, 2007, FedEx Cup, PGA, 2007, 2009; named Player of Yr., American Jr. Golf Assn., 1991, Golf Digest, 1991, 1992, Golf World, 1993, 1994, L.A. Times, 1994, Orange County, 1994, PGA Tour Player of Yr., 1997, 1999, 2000, 2001, 2002, 2003, 2005, 2006, 2007, 2009, 2013, Player of Yr., Golf Writers Assn. America, 2006, Southern Calif. Player of Yr., 1991, 1992, 1993, Nat. Amateur of Yr., Titleist-Golfweek, 1991, 1992, Orange County League MVP, 1994, Pac-10 Player of Yr., 1995, 1996, First Team All-American, 1995, 1996, Sportsman of Yr., Sports Illustrated, 1996, 2000, Reuters, 2000, PGA Tour Rookie of Yr., 1996, Fred Haskins Coll. Player of Yr., 1996, Jack Nicklaus Coll. Player of Yr., 1996, Male Athlete of Yr., AP, 1997, 1999, 2000, 2006, World Sportsman of Yr., World Sports Acad., 1999, Most Powerful Person in Sports, Sporting News, 2000, World Champion of Champions, L'Equipe, France, 2000, Athlete of the Decade, AP, 2009; named one of The Most Influential People in the World of Sports, Bus. Week, 2007, 2008, The 100 Most Powerful Celebrities, Forbes.com, 2008, The World's Most Influential People, TIME mag., 2009, The 40 Under 40 Rising Stars, Fortune mag., 2009; named to First Team Rolex Jr. All American, 1991, 1992, The Calif. Hall of Fame, 2007, Power 150, Ebony mag., 2008, Stanford U. Athletics Hall of Fame, 2009. Achievements include winning 14 major PGA Tour events including Masters Tournament, 1997, 2001, 2002, 2005, PGA Championship, 1999, 2000, 2006, 2007; US Open Championship, 2000, 2002, 2008, Brit. Open Championship, 2000, 2005, 2006; youngest player, first African Am., first Asian Am., and having largest margin of victory (12 strokes) to win Masters Tournament, 1997; first player ever to win US Open, Brit. Open and PGA Championship in same yr., 2000; first player ever to hold all 4 major golf championships at the same time, 2001; ranked number 1 by the Official World Golf Ranking for a record 281 consecutive weeks, 2005-2010; youngest to win 50 PGA Tour titles with victory at Buick Open, 2006; winner for the 7th time of the Farmers Insurance Open at Torrey Pines, also marked the milestone of the 75th time winning a PGA Tour event in 2013. Office: PGA PO Box 109601 186 Atlantis Blvd Lake Worth FL 33462-1111*

WOODSON, JAMIE, educational association administrator, former state legislator; b. Mar. 6, 1972; m. Jeff Woodson. Mem. Tenn. House of Reps., 1999—2005; mem. Dist. 6 Tenn. State Senate, 2005—11; pres., CEO State Collaborative on Reforming Education (SCORE), 2011—. Mem.: United Way, Knoxville Symphony League, Knoxville & Tenn. Bar Assns., Epilepsy Found. East Tenn. (bd. mem.), South Knox & West Knox Rep. Clubs, Knoxville Quarterback Club (bd. mem., past exec. dir.). Republican. Baptist. Home: SCORE Suite 326 1207 18th Ave South Nashville TN 37212 Office Phone: 865-523-8683, 615-741-1648. Office Fax: 615-253-0270. Business E-Mail: sen.jamie.woodson@capitol.tn.gov.

WOODSON, RANDY (WILLIAM RANDOLPH WOODSON), academic administrator; m. Susan Woodson; 3 children. BS, MS, U. Ark.; PhD in Horticulture, Cornell U. Tchr. La. State U., 1983—85; prof. Dept. Horticulture Purdue U., 1985, head Dept. Horticulture and Landscape Architecture, assoc. dean agr., dir. Office Agr. Rsch. Programs, 1998—2004, Glenn W. Sample dean agr., exec. v.p. academic affairs, provost, 2008—10; chancellor NC State U., Raleigh, 2010—. Vis. scholar École Nationale Supérieure Agronomique de Toulouse, France. Recipient Am. Soc. for Horticultural Sci. Outstanding Rschr. Career Award, B.Y. Morrison Medal, USDA-Agr. Rsch. Svc. Fellow: Am. Soc. Horticultural Sci. Office: North Carolina State University Office of Chancellor Box 7001 Raleigh NC 27695 Office Phone: 919-515-2191. Office Fax: 919-831-3545. E-mail: randy_woodson@ncsu.edu.*

WOODWARD, JAMES HOYT, engineering educator, former academic administrator; b. Sanford, Fla., Nov. 24, 1939; s. James Hoyt and Edith Pearl (Breeden) Woodward; m. Martha Ruth Hill, Oct. 13, 1956; children: Connie, Tracey, Wade. BS in Aero. Engring. with honors, Ga. Tech. Inst., 1962, MS in Aero. Engring., 1963, PhD in Engring. Mechanics, 1967; MBA, U. Ala.-Birmingham, 1973. Asst. prof. engring. mechanics USAF Acad., Colo., 1965-67, assoc. prof. Colo., 1967-68; asst. prof. NC State U., 1968-69; assoc. prof. engring. U. Ala., Birmingham, 1969-70, assoc. prof., 1973-77, prof. civil engring., 1977-89, asst. v.p., 1973-78, dean engring., 1978-84, acad. v.p., 1984-89; chancellor U. NC, Charlotte, 1989—2005, chancellor emeritus, prof. engring., 2005—; interim chancellor NC State U., Raleigh, 2009—10. Dir. tech. devel. Rust Engring. Co., Birmingham, 1970—73; cons. in field. Contbr. articles to profl. jours. With USAF, 1965—68. Mem.: Am. Soc. Engring. Edn., Sigma Xi. Methodist. Office: University NC Charlotte Chancellors Emeriti Office 9201 University City Blvd Charlotte NC 28223-0002 Office Phone: 704-687-2484, 919-515-2191. Business E-Mail: etdeese@uncc.edu. E-mail: chancellor@ncsu.edu.

WOODWARD, LAWRENCE H., JR., lawyer; b. Radford, Va., May 29, 1957; married; 2 children. BA, Hampden-Sydney Coll., Va., 1979; JD, T.C. Williams Sch. Law, U. Richmond, Va., 1982. Bar: Va. 1982, US Dist. Ct. (ea. dist.) Va. 1984, US Ct. Appeals Armed Forces 1984, US Ct. Fed. Claims 1984, US Supreme Ct. 1984. Shareholder Shuttleworth, Ruloff, Swain, Haddad & Morecock, PC, Virginia Beach. Served with USAF, 1983—92, maj., Cir. Def. Counsel, 1985—91. Mem.: ABA, Va. State Bar, Portsmouth Bar Assn. Achievements include obtaining multi-million dollar negligence and malpractice jury verdicts; aquittals in criminal defense cases ranging from murder, fraud, conspiracy and drug offenses; sucessfully negotiating multi-million dollar endorsement deals and team contracts for NFL and NBA players. Office: Shuttleworth Ruloff Swain Haddad & Morecock PC 4525 S Blvd Suite 300 Virginia Beach VA 23452 Office Phone: 757-671-6047. Office Fax: 757-671-6004. Business E-Mail: lwoodward@srgslaw.com.

WOOLDRIDGE, TIM L., state legislator, academic administrator; b. Paragould, Ark., May 5, 1960; s. Winston H. and Shirley (Riggs) W.; m. Lisa Woodson, June 5, 1981; children: Jeremy M., Tiffany N. BS in Pub. Rels., Comm., Ark. State U., 1982. Dir. coll. affairs Crowleys Ridge Coll., Paragould, 1983-86, with ins., 1987-88, v.p. for Instl. Advancement, 1988—; mem. Ark. Ho. of Reps. from 20th dist., Little Rock, 1991-98, Ark. Senate from 30th dist., Little Rock, 1998—2002, Ark. Senate from 11th dist., 2003—07; exec. dir. Ark. Assn. Public Universities, 2007—. Councilman City of Paragould, 1985-90; active Pargould 2000, Pargould Indsl. Devel. Corp. Mem. Paragould C. of C., Exchange Club (pres. 1985, Exchangite of the Yr. 1984, 85). Democrat. Mem. Ch.Of Christ. Avocations: hunting, fishing, baseball. Office: AAPU 111 Center St Ste 1140 Little Rock AR 72201

WOOLEY, JEFFREY I., automotive executive; b. 1945; Grad., U. Okla. Ptnr. Lexus of Tampa Bay, 1990; pres., CEO Asbury Automotive Tampa G.P. LLC (subs. of Asbury Automotive Group, Inc.), 1998—2005, chmn., 2005—; bd. dirs. Asbury Automotive Group, Inc., 2003—. Pres. Pontiac Nat. Dealer Coun; mem. Berkeley Prep. Sch., The Children's Hosp., St. Joseph; bd. dirs., Gulf Ridge Coun. Boy Scouts of America. Office: Asbury Automotive Group Inc Bd Directors 2905 Premiere Pky NW Ste 300 Duluth GA 30097 Office Phone: 770-418-8200. Business E-Mail: jwooley@asburyauto.com.

WOOLEY, MICHAEL W., retired military officer; b. 1950; BS in Bus. Adminstrn., Northeast La. State U., 1972; MS, Webster U., 1981; Grad., Air Command & Staff Coll., Maxwell AFB, 1983, Air War Coll., 1985, Indsl. Coll. Armed Forces, Ft. Lesley J. McNair, 1992, Exec. Program Gen. Officers of the Russian Fedn. & US, John F. Kennedy Sch. Govt. Harvard U., 1999; Grad, Black Sea Security Program, John F. Kennedy Sch. Govt. Harvard U., 2003. Commd. 2d lt. USAF, 1972, advanced through grades to lt. gen., 2004; pilot, instr., aide-de-camp 20th Mil. Aircraft Squadron, Scott AFB, Ill., 1974-79; analyst Headquarters Mil. Airlift Command, Scott AFB, Ill., 1979-82; pilot 41st Mil. Airlift Squadron, Charleston AFB, S.C., 1983-84, chief airlift dir. br. current ops., 1985-87; comdr. 17th Mil. Airlift Squadron, Charleston AFB, 1987-89; sec. Joint Chiefs Staff & Nat. Security Matters, Pentagon, 1990-91; chief strategy & policy U.S. Forces Korea Yongsan Army Garrison, Seoul, Republic of Korea, 1992-94; chief inspections divsn. Air Mobility Command (AMC), Scott AFB, Ill., 1994-95; comdr. 375th Airlift Wing, Scott AFB, Ill., 1995-97; vice comdr. Air Force Spl. Ops. Command (AFSOC), Hurlburt Field, Fla., 1997-98; comdr. 86th Airlift Wing & Kaiserslautern Mil. Cmty., Ramstein Air Base, Germany, 1998—99, Tanker Airlift Control Ctr., Scott AFB, Ill., 2000—02, 3rd Air Force, RAF Mildenhall, England, 2002—04, Air Force Spl. Ops. Command (AFSOC), Hurlburt Field, Fla., 2004—08. Decorated Disting. Svc. medal, Def. Superior Svc. medal, Legion of Merit, Def. Meritorious Svc. medal, Meritorious Svc. medal with three oak leaf clusters, Air medal with oak leaf cluster, Bronze Star; recipient Joint Svc. Commendation medal, Rep. of Korea Order Nat. Security Merit (Samil medal).

WOOLF, KENNETH HOWARD, architect; b. NYC, Aug. 19, 1938; s. Howard Walter and Elizabeth Ann (Levy) W.; m. Elizabeth Adair Rainwater, July 3, 1965; children: Robert Gregg, Susan Adair, Jennifer Adair. BArch, Cornell U., 1961. Staff arch. Look & Morrison, Archs., Pensacola, Fla., 1965-72; pvt. practice arch. Pensacola, Fla., 1972—. Instr. architecture Pensacola Jr. Coll., part-time 1967-76; chmn. Pensacola Archtl. Rev. Bd., 1970-81; mem. Gulf Breeze Planning Bd., 1976-78; chmn. Pensacola City Bd. Adjustment and Appeals, 1995—. Prin. works include Coca-Cola Bottling Co. Plant, Pensacola, 1974, 3 profl. office bldgs. towers, Pensacola, 1976, 1984, 1992, Bapt. Hosp. addition, 1977, The Village, Housing for Elderly, 1978, 1981, 1998, 2006, 09, Azalea Trace Ret. Cmty. Complex, 1980, 1999, Northview Cmty., 1981, Coca-Cola Bottling Plant, Beaumont, Tex., 1983, Episcopal Day Sch., Pensacola, 1993, 6 oncology ctrs., 1990, 1994, 1996, 1999, 2002, 2003, 2005. With USN, 1961-65. Named Jaycee of Yr., 1970. Mem. AIA (sec. N.W. Fla. chpt. 1976-77, 77-78, pres. 1979-81, Comml. Design Hon. award 1975), Rotary. Episcopalian. Home: 15 N Sunset Blvd Gulf Breeze FL 32561-4051 Office: 100 W Gadsden St Pensacola FL 32501-3910 Office Phone: 850-438-3653. Business E-Mail: khwarch@caytel.net.

WOOLLEY, BEVERLY, state legislator; b. July 25, 1939; m. Lynn Woolley; 3 children. Grad. cum laude, U. Houston. Former owner Houston Armature Works, Inc.; mem. Dist. 136 Tex. House of Representatives, 1995—. Bd. mem. Ct. Apptd. Spl. Advocates; mem. allied health adv. bd. U. Tex. Recipient Leader Excellence award, Free Enterprise PAC, 1995. Mem.: Mental Health Assn. (bd. mem.), Magic Cir. Rep. Women's Club (former pres.). Republican. Office: 2400 Augusta Dr Ste 266 Houston TX 77057 also: Room CAP GS.02 Capitol PO Box 2910 Austin TX 78768 Office Phone: 713-629-6313, 512-463-0696.

WOOLWORTH, ERIC S., professional sports team executive; m. Jocelyn Woolworth; 1 child, Cassidy. Grad. cum laude, Georgetown U.; JD cum laude, Georgetown U. Law Ctr. Gen. counsel Miami Heat, Fla., 1995—2001, interim pres., 2000—01, pres. bus. ops., 2001—. Bd. mem. Big Bros. Big Sisters, Children's Craniofacial Assn. Office: Miami Heat AmericanAirlines Arena 601 Biscayne Blvd Miami FL 33132

WOOSTER, ROBERT, history professor; b. Beaumont, Tex., Aug. 27, 1956; s. Ralph Ancil and Edna Lee (Jones) W.; m. Catherine Cox, 1992. BA, Lamar U., 1977, MA, 1979; PhD, U. Tex., 1985. Scholar in residence Tex. State Hist. Assn., Liberty, 1985-86; asst. prof. Tex. A&M U., Corpus Christi, 1986-90, assoc. prof., 1990-95, prof., 1995—, chmn. dept. humanities, 1997—2000, Piper prof., 1998, Frantz prof. history, 2001—04, regent's prof., 2008. Author: Soldiers, Sutlers and Settlers (Bates award 1987), U.S. Military and Indian Policy, 1988, History of Fort Davis, 1990, Nelson A. Miles and The

Twilight of the Frontier Army, 1993, The Civil War 100, 1998, The Civil War Bookshelf, 2001, Frontier Crossroads: Fort Davis and the West, 2006; editor: Soldier, Surgeon, Scholar: The Memoirs of William Henry Corbusier, 2003; co-editor: (with William Kessel) Encyclopedia of Native American Wars & Warfare, 2005, The American Military Frontrers, 1983-1903, 2009; editl. adv. bd. Southwestern Hist. Quar., Austin, Tex., 1989—, Military History of the West, 1995—, Jour. of the West, 1996-2000. Dep. dir. U.S. Mil. Acad./ROTC fellowship U.S. Mil. Acad., West Point, N.Y., 1990. Fellow Tex. State Hist. Assn. (pres. 2005—06); mem. Orgn. Am. Historians. Democrat. Home: 4600 Ocean Dr Apt 708 Corpus Christi TX 78412-2543 Office: Texas A&M Univ 6300 Ocean Dr Corpus Christi TX 78412-5599 Office Phone: 361-825-2402. Business E-Mail: robert.wooster@tamucc.edu.

WOOTAN, GERALD DON, osteopathic physician, educator; b. Oklahoma City, Nov. 19, 1944; s. Ralph George and Corrinne (Loafman) W. BA, Ctrl. State U., Edmond, Okla., 1970, BS, 1971, MEd, 1974; MB, U. Okla., Oklahoma City, 1978; DO, Okla. State U., 1985. Dir. mfg. engring. lab. GE, Oklahoma City, 1965-70; counseling psychologist VA Hosp., Oklahoma City, 1970-76; physician asst. Thomas (Okla.) Med. Clin., 1978-81; pvt. practice, Jenks, Okla., 1986—; intern Tulsa Regional Med. Ctr., 1985-86; assoc. prof. Okla. State U. Coll. Osteo. Medicine, 1986—, with Springer Clinic, 1995-98; owner Jenks (Okla.) Health Team LLC, 1998—. Chmn. gen. practice quality assurance Tulsa Regional Med. Ctr., 1989-91; v.p. New Horizons Counseling Ctr., Clinton, Okla., 1977-81; sr. aviation med. examiner FAA, Tulsa, 1991—; pres. S.W. Diagnostics, Inc., Tulsa, 1989-91, Okla. Edn. Found. Osteo. Medicine, Tulsa, 1988-89, 96, trustee Tulsa Long Term Care Authority; med. dir. Grace Living Ctr. Contbr. articles to profl. jours.; patentee for human restraint. Advancement chmn., chmn. Eagle bd. rev. Boy Scouts Am., Tulsa, 1987-88; trustee Tulsa Long Term Care Authority, 1988-91; trustee Tulsa Community Found. for Indigent Health Care, Inc., 1988-91. With USN, 1962-64. Named Clin. Preceptor of Yr., U. Okla., 1980, Outstanding Alumni award Okla. State U. Coll. Osteo. Medicine, 1990. Mem.: Am. Coll. Osteo. Family Physicians (cert. of added qualification in geriatrics 1982, bd. cert. 1993, pres. Okla. chpt. 1993—94, qualified hyperbaric oxygen therapy 2001, med. dir. Narconon Drug Treatment Ctr.), Okla. Acad. Gen. Practitioners (pres.), Am. Coll. Gen. Practitioners, Am. Acad. Physician Assts., Tulsa Dist. Osteo. Soc. (pres. 1991—92), Okla. Osteo. Assn. (legis. bur. 1986—2001, trustee 1998—2001, membership bur. 1998—2001, bur. on membership benefits 1998—2001), Am. Osteo. Assn., Okla. State U. Coll. Osteo. Medicine Alumni Assn. (pres. 1988—89). Avocations: scuba diving, aviation medicine. Address: 715 W Main St Ste S Jenks OK 74037-3553 Office: Ste S 715 W Main St Jenks OK 74037-3553 Home: 6649 E 88th Pl Tulsa OK 74133-5039 Office Phone: 918-299-9447.

WOOTEN, CECIL AARON, retired religious organization administrator; b. Laurel, Miss., June 3, 1924; s. Cecil A. and Alice (Cox) W.; m. Helen Moss, Apr. 4, 1947; children: Michael, Margaret, Martin, Marsha, Mark. BS in Mech. Engring. U. Ala., 1949. With CBI Industries, 1941—83, bd. dirs., 1965-83, mng. dir. CBI Constructors Ltd., London, 1957-62, mgr. Houston sales dist., 1962-64, v.p. engring., 1964—68, v.p., mgr. corp. svcs. Oak Brook, Ill., 1968-69, sr. v.p.-gen. sales mgr., 1969-78; sr. v.p. comml. devel. Chgo. Bridge & Iron Co. (subs. CBI Industries), 1978-79; sr. v.p. corp. adminstrn. CBI Industries, Oak Brook, 1980-83; dir. devel. Christian Family Services, Gainesville, Fla., 1983-86, Denver Ch. of Christ, 1986-88, Boston Ch. of Christ, 1988-92; pres. Internat. Chs. of Christ, Inc., LA, 1994-99; chair Internat. Chs. Christ, LA, 1999—2000, retired, 2002. Bd. dirs. Oak Brook (Ill.) Bank. Former trustee Elmhurst (Ill.) Coll.; former bd. sponsors Good Samaritan Hosp., Downers Grove, Ill. Served to 1st lt. AUS, 1943-46. Mem. ASME, NSPE, Rotary. Personal E-mail: cecilwooten@hotmail.com.

WOOTEN, JOEL ORBA, JR., lawyer; b. Hazlehurst, Ga., June 4, 1950; s. Joel Orba and Mary Eleanor (Whitlock) W.; m. Sybrina G. Franklin; children: Joel III, Katherine, Frank. BBA, U. Ga., 1972, JD, 1975. Bar: Ga. 1975, U.S. Dist. Ct. (mid. dist.) Ga. 1976, U.S. Ct. Appeals (11th cir.) 1981. Ptnr. Kelly, Denney, Pease & Allison, Columbus, Ga., 1975-88, Butler, Wooten, Overby & Cheeley, Columbus, Ga., 1988—2006, Butler, Wooten, Fryhofer, LLP, 2006—. Bd. regents Univ. Sys. of Ga., 1999-2006, chair, 2004-05; mem. bd. Ga. Ports Authority, 2013-. With U.S. Army, 1972. Mem. AAJ, Am. Bar Assn., Fed. Bar Assn., Ga. Trial Lawyers Assn., State Bar Ga. (chmn. gen. practice & trial sect. 1990-91), Columbus Lawyers Club (pres 1988-89), Columbus Younger Lawyers (pres. 1983-84), U. Ga. Alumni Soc. (bd. dirs. 1981-83, 89-91). Office: Butler Wooten & Fryhofer LLP PO Box 2766 Columbus GA 31902 Office Phone: 706-322-1990.

WOOTEN, TERRY L., federal judge; b. Louisville, 1954; BA, U. SC, 1976, JD, 1980. Pvt. practice atty., SC, 1980—82; asst. solicitor Richland County, SC, 1982—86; chief counsel US Senate Judiciary Com., 1986—91; asst. US atty. US Atty.'s Office (dist. SC), 1992—99; magistrate judge US Dist. Ct. SC, 1999—2001, judge, 2001—. Office: US Dist Ct PO Box 2557 Florence SC 29503 Office Phone: 843-676-3812.

WOOTON, ADRIENNE, state legislator; b. Mar. 7, 1970; m. Dewayne Wooton. BA, Alcorn State U.; JD, U. Miss. Atty.; mem. Dist. 71 Miss. House of Reps., vice chair apportionment and elections com., congl. redistricting com., legis. reapportionment com. Democrat. Baptist. Home: PO Box 665 Canton MS 39046 Office: PO Box 1018 Jackson MS 39215 Home Phone: 601-502-2444; Office Phone: 601-859-1567. E-mail: awooten@house.ms.gov.

WORD, JAMES, state legislator; Mem. Dist. 16 Ark. House of Reps., 2009—. Democrat. Baptist. Office: State Capitol Rm 350 Little Rock AR 72201 also: 6503 Little Dove Dr Pine Bluff AR 71603 Office Phone: 501-682-6211, 870-543-6891. Office Fax: 501-682-7771. Business E-Mail: jword@aaasea.org.

WORDSWORTH, JERRY L., wholesale distribution executive; b. Charlotte, NC, Sept. 22, 1945; BS, N.C. State U., 1963. With MBM, Rocky Mount, NC, 1966—, CEO, pres. & chmn. Co-owner Carolina Panthers. Office: MBM 2641 Mountainbrook Rd Rocky Mount NC 27802 Home: PO Box 800 Rocky Mount NC 27802-0800 Office Fax: 252-985-7241.

WORELL, JUDITH P., psychologist, educator; b. NYC; d. Moses and Dorothy Goldfarb; m. Leonard Worell, Aug. 11, 1947 (div.); children: Amy, Beth, Wendy; m. H.A. Smith, Mar. 23, 1985 BS magna cum laude, Queens Coll., 1950; MA, Ohio State U., 1952, PhD in Clin. Psychology, 1954; DHL (hon.), Colby-Sawyer Coll., 1993. Research assoc. Iowa Psychopathic Hosp., Iowa City, 1957-59; research assoc. Okla. State U., 1960-66; asst. prof. U. Ky., Lexington, 1969-71, assoc. prof., 1971-75, prof. ednl. and counseling psychology, 1976—, dir. counseling psychology tng. program, 1980-93, chairperson dept. ednl. and counseling psychology, 1993-97, prof. emerita, 1999—. Author: (with C.M. Nelson) Managing Instructional Problems, 1974; (with W.E. Stilwell) Psychology for Teachers and Students, 1981; Psychological Development in the Elementary Years, 1982; (with Fred Danner) The Adolescent as Decision-maker: Applications to Development and Education, 1989; (with Pam Remer) Feminist Perspectives in Therapy: An Empowerment Model for Women, 1992; (with N. Johnson) Shaping the Future of Feminist Psychology: Education, Research, and Practice, 1997, (with Norine Johnson & Michael Roberts) Beyond Appearance: A New Look at Adolescent Girls, 1999, Encyclopedia of Women and Gender: Sex Similarities and Differences and the Impact of Society on Gender, 2001, (with Pam Remer) Feminist Perspectives in Therapy: Empowering Diverse Women, 2003, (with Carol Goodheart) Oxford Handbook of Girls' and Women's Psychological Health, 2006; assoc. editor Jour. Cons. and Clin. Psychology, 1976-79, mem. editl. bd., 1984-89; assoc. editor Psychol. Women Quar., 1984-89, editor, 1989-95; mem. editorial bd. Sex Roles, 1984-2000, Psychol. Assessment, 1991-97, Clin. Psychology Rev., 1991-97, Women and Therapy, 1992-2000; cons., reviewer 10 jours.; contbr. articles to profl. jours. Named U. Ky. Campus Woman of Yr., 1976, Outstanding Univ. Grad. prof., 1991, Disting. Ky. psychologist, 1990; USPHS fellow, 1953; NIMH rsch. grantee, 1962-69; recipient: APF Gold Medal, 2010 Fellow APA (pres. Clin. Psychology of Women 1986-88, chmn. com. state assn. rels. 1982-83, fellow selection divsn. 35 com. 1983-84, policy and planning bd. 1989-92, publs. and comm. bd. 1992-99, chair 1996-98, chair jours. com., pres. divsn. psychology of women 1997-98, Disting. Leader for Women in Psychology 1990, Carolyn Wood Sherif award, 2001, Psychology of Women Heritage award 2004, coun. rep. 2000-02, chair women's caucus 2002) Soc. Psychol. Study of Social Issues (chmn. fellow com. 2005-), Ky. Psychol. Assn. (pres. 1981-82, rep. at large 1995-97), Southeastern Psychol. Assn. (exec. coun. mem.-at-large, pres.-elect 1993-94 pres. 1994-95), Am. Women in Psychology, Phi Beta Kappa. Home: 3892 Gloucester Dr Lexington KY 40510-9729 Personal E-mail: jworell02@gmail.com.

WORK, JANE MAGRUDER, retired professional society administrator; b. Owensboro, Ky., Mar. 30, 1927; d. Orion Noel and Willie May (Stallings) Magruder; m. William Work, Nov. 26, 1960; children: Paul MacGregor, Jeffrey William. BA, Furman U., 1947; MA, U. Wis., 1948; PhD, Ohio State U., 1959. Dir. radio U. South Miss., Hattisburg, 1948-51; pub. rels. assoc. Ohio Fuel Gas Co./Columbia Gas, Columbus, 1952-62; adj. prof. comm. Pace U., NYC, 1963-75; dir. speechmodule ERIC, Washington, 1975-76; mgr. orgn. liaison, dir. legis. analysis Nat. Assn. Mfgs., Washington, 1977-84, asst. v.p. legis. analysis, 1984-87, v.p. legis. analysis, 1987-93, v.p. mem. comm., 1993-2001, ret., 2001. Adv. bd. pub. affairs NYU Grad. Bus. Sch., 1983-87; adv. bd. Prodn. Mag., 1984-87; cons. IBM, Xerox, 1963-77. Contbr. articles to profl. jours. Mem. transition team Consumer Product Safety Commn., Washington, 1979—80; chair No. Va. Pvt. Industry Coun., Fairfax County, 1979—85; co-chair Va. Gov.'s Employment & Tng. Task Force, Richmond, 1983; bd. dirs. Alzheimer's Assn. Nat. Capital Area, 2002—08; bd. govs. Arts Club Washington, 2009—12; vol. info. specialist Smithsonian Instn., 2001—; co-leader Alzheimer's Support Group, 2008—; bd. dirs. Arlington Philharmonie Orch., 2012. Named to Acad. Women Achievers YWCA, 1987. Mem.: World Future Soc. (steering network 1993 Gen. Assembly), The Planning Forum (bd. dirs. Capital chpt. 1990—93), Speech Comm. Assn. (sect. chmn. 1980—82), Am. Soc. Assn. Execs. (rsch. adv. com. 1989—97), Nat. Assn. Industry-Edn. Coop. (bd. dirs. 1983—2001), Issue Mgmt. Assn. (bd. dirs. 1985—88), Future Homemakers of Am. (bd. dirs. 1985—88), Pi Kappa Delta (hon.), Alpha Psi Omega (hon.). Independent. Unitarian Universalist. Avocations: volunteering, travel. Home: 900 N Stuart St Apt 815 Arlington VA 22203-4106

WORKMAN, JOHN L., corporate financial executive; B in acctg., Ind. U.; MBA, U. Chgo. CPA. Ptnr. KPMG; various positions including contr., CFO and chief restructuring officer Montgomery Ward & Co., Inc., gen. auditor, 1984; CFO U.S. Can Corp., 1998—2002, various sr. exec. positions, 1998—2004, COO, 2002—03, CEO, 2003—04; exec. v.p., CFO HealthSouth Corp., 2004—09, Omnicare, Inc., 2009—11, pres., CFO, 2011—, interim CEO, 2012—. Bd. dirs. APAC Customer Svcs., Inc., 2008—. Office: Omnicare Inc 1600 RiverCenter II 100 E RiverCenter Blvd Covington KY 41011 Office Phone: 859-392-3300. Office Fax: 859-392-3333. Business E-Mail: jworkman@omnicare.com.

WORKMAN, MARGARET LEE, state supreme court justice, lawyer; b. May 22, 1947; d. Frank Eugene and Mary Emma (Thomas) W.; m. Edward T. Gardner III; children: Lindsay Elizabeth, Christopher Workman, Edward Earnshaw. AB in Polit. Sci., W.Va. U., 1969, JD, 1974. Bar: W.Va. 1974. Asst. counsel Pub. Works Com. US Senate, Washington, 1974-75; law clk. 13th Judicial Cir., Charleston, W.Va., 1975-76, judge, 1981-88; pvt. practice Charleston, 1976—81, 1999—2009; justice W.Va. Supreme Ct. of Appeals, Charleston, 1989-99, 2009—, chief justice, 1993, 97, 2011. Advance person for Rosalyn Carter, Carter Presdl. Campaign, Atlanta, 1976. Democrat. Episcopalian. Office: WVa Supreme Ct Appeals Capitol Complex Bldg 1 Rm E-307 Charleston WV 25305*

WORKMAN, RITCH, state legislator; b. Bellville, Can., May 3, 1973; m. Tiffanie Workman; children: Bailey, Sofia. BS, Appalachian State U., 1995; grad. 2nd lt., NC Mil. Acad., 1995. Co-owner Workman Group Inc., 1992—; mem. Dist. 30 Fla. House of Reps., 2008—, vice chair roads, bridges and ports policy com., mem. elder and family svcs. policy com., govt. ops. appropriations com., ins., bus. & fin. affairs policy com., joint com. on public counsel oversight. Mem. Home Ownership Promotes the Economy Task Force, 2008, Fin. Action Team, 2008—. With Nat. Guard US Army, 1990—2005. Recipient Small Bus. of Yr., 2004, Innovative Bus. of Yr., 2006. Mem.: Fla. Assn. Mortgage Brokers (pres. 2006—08), Rockledge Rotary Club. Republican. Office: House Office Bldg 402 S Monroe St Rm 308 Tallahassee FL 32399-1300 also: 33 Suntree Pl Ste D Melbourne FL 32940-7602 Office Phone: 850-488-9720, 321-757-7019. Business E-Mail: ritch.workman@myfloridahouse.gov.

WORKMAN, WILLIAM DOUGLAS, III, retired town manager, mayor, gas industry executive; b. Charleston, SC, July 3, 1940; s. William Douglas Jr. and Rhea (Thomas) W.; m. Marcia Mae Moorhead, Apr. 23, 1966 (div. Dec. 1995); children: William Douglas IV, Frank Moorhead; m. Patti Gage Fishburne Marks, June 22, 1996; stepchildren: Gage Russell Marks Beerer, Barnwell Johnson Marks, Kemp Fishburne Bouvia. BA, The Citadel, 1961; grad., U. S.C., 1962. Reporter Charleston News & Courier, 1965-66, Greenville (S.C.) News, 1966-70; tchr., adminstr., dean allied health scis. Greenville Tech. Coll., 1967-75; exec. asst. to gov. State of S.C., Columbia, 1975-78; mktg. exec. Daniel Internat. Corp., Greenville, 1978-90, dir. facilities Fluor Daniel, 1991-93; v.p. S.C. ops. Piedmont Natural Gas, Greenville, 1994—2004; pres., bd. dirs. Greenville County Rsch. & Tech. Devel. Corp., 1999—2006; mayor City of Greenville, 1983-95. Chmn. bd. dirs. Greenville Area Devel. Corp., 2002—05. Chmn. Greenville County Rep. Conv., 1980, 82, 87, 89, 91, S.C. 4th Congl. Dist. Rep. Conv., 1980, 82, 84; chmn. S.C. Rep. Conv., 1984, 89, vice chmn., 1982, 87; Rep. nominee for U.S. Ho. of Reps. from 4th Dist. S.C., 1986; mem. S.C. Adv. Commn. on Intergovtl. Rels., 1990-96; bd. dirs. S.C. Appalachian Coun. Govts., 1991-95, Mcpl. Assn. S.C., 1990-95, pres., 1993-94; trustee Sch. Dist. Greenville County, 1969-75, vice-chmn.; bd. dirs. YMCA Camp Greenville, 1973-83, 90-95, chmn., 1975; chmn. S.C. Health Coordinating Coun., 1976-78; founder S.C. Literacy Assn., treas., 1969-73; bd. dirs.; Greenville City Coun., 1981-83, So. Growth Policies Bd., 1992-95. With U.S. Army, 1962-64; ret. lt. col. USAR. Named Outstanding State Chmn., S.C. Jaycees, 1969, Order of Palmetto, 1978; named 2000 Bus. Person of Yr., Greenville Mag., Vol. of Yr., S.C. Econ. Devel. Assn., 2000, Disting. Svc. award, SC Econ. Devel. Assn., 2003, Wiseman Vision award, Devel. Dists. Appalachia Assn., 2004. Mem. Savanna River Maritime Commn., 2009, Res. Officers Assn., Assn. U.S. Army, Am. Legion, Nat. Mgmt. Assn. (Mgr. of Yr. award Greenville chpt. 1985), SC Downtown Devel. Assn. (bd. dirs., 1985-1995), Beaufort Citadel Club, Dogwood Hills Country. Club, Carolina Yacht Club, VFW. Home: 3985 Charleston Hwy Walterboro SC 29488 Personal E-mail: bill@billworkman.com.

WORLEY, NANCY L., political organization administrator; b. Madison County, Ala., Nov. 7, 1951; d. Leonard O. and Lillian (Smith) W. BA magna cum laude, U. Montevallo, Ala., 1973; MA, Jacksonville State U., Ala., 1974; postgrad., U. Ala., Tuscaloosa and Huntsville, 1974, U. Edinburgh, Scotland, 1975. Cert. English, speech and Latin tchr., Ala. Instr. English, NE State Jr. Coll., Rainsville, Ala., Calhoun Community Coll., Decatur, Ala.; tchr. lang. arts Decatur City Schs.; sec. state State of Ala., Montgomery, 2003—07; vice chair Ala. Dem. Party, chair, 2013—. Former mem. Governor's Task Force on Welfare Reform, Governor's Task Force on Education Reform. Contbr. articles to profl. jours. Named Ala.'s Outstanding Young Educator, Dist. Tchr. of Yr., Decatur City Schs.; grantee grantee UN. Mem. NEA, Ala. Edn. Assn. (pres., 1983-84, 95-97, legis. com.), Ala. Fgn. Lang. Tchrs. Assn. (past pres.), Ala. Classroom Tchrs. Assn. (past pres., bd. dirs.), Sigma Tau Delta, Kappa Delta Pi, Lambda Sigma Chi, Omicron Delta Kappa. Democrat. Office: Alabam Democratic Party PO Box 950 Montgomery AL 36101*

WORLEY, ROBERT BRUCE, JR., lawyer; b. Mobile, Ala., Mar. 9, 1960; s. Robert Bruce and Linda (Knight) Worley; m. Catherine Anna Steck, Nov. 14, 1987; children: Nancy Jane, Catherine Turner. BBA with honors and distinction, U. Ky., 1982; JD, Tulane U., 1985. Bar: La. 1985, Tex. 2003, US Dist. Ct. (ea. dist. La.) 1985, US Dist. Ct. (mid. dist. La.) 1986, US Dist. Ct. (we. dist. La.) 1988, US Dist. Ct. (ea. dist. Ark.) 1996, US Dist. Ct. (we. dist. Ark.) 1996, US Dist. Ct. (cen. dist. Ill.) 1997, US Dist. Ct. (so. dist. Tex.) 2001, US Dist. Ct. (ea. dist. Tex.) 2001, US Ct. Appeals (5th cir.) 1990, US Ct. Appeals (4th cir.) 1990, US Ct. Appeals (6th cir.) 1996, US Ct. Appeals (7th cir.) 1997, US Ct. Appeals (11th cir.) 1998, US Ct. Appeals (8th cir.) 1999, US Supreme Ct. 1999. Assoc. Gelpi, Sullivan, Carroll and Laborde, New Orleans, 1985—88; ptnr. Kullman Firm, New Orleans, 1988—99; ptnr. mem. bd. dirs. Jones, Walker, Waechter, Poitevent, Carrere & Denegre, New Orleans, 1999—2011; exec. v.p. and gen. counsel, corp. sec. Iberia Bank Corp., New Orleans, 2011—. Chmn. profl. employment com. Jones Walker et al, New Orleans, 2001—04, chmn. United Way, 2000—, mem. bd. dirs., 2009—. Mem., pres. New Orleans Area Habitat for Humanity Bd., 2006—08; chair lawyers com. New Orleans United Way Campaign, 2003; chmn. La. Jr. Tennis Coun., 2004—11; exec. v.p. La. Tennis Assn.; bd. trustees, former pres. ch. coun. Rayne Meml. United Meth. Ch.; chmn. Southern Tennis Assn. Constitution & Rules Com. Recipient Leadership in Law award, City Business, 2006; named One of Best Labor and Employment Lawyers, New Orleans Mag., 2005, 2006, 2007, 2008—11. Mem.: ABA, US Tennis Assn. Constrn. & Rules Com., Am. Inns Ct., Coll. Master Adv. and Barristers, New Orleans Bar Assn., La. State Bar Assn. Avocations: tennis, swimming, fishing. Mailing: 601 Poydras St Ste 2075 New Orleans LA 70130 Office Phone: 504-582-8192. Business E-Mail: rworley@joneswalker.com, robert.worley@iberiabank.com.

WORRELL, ANNE EVERETTE ROWELL, newspaper publisher; b. Surry, Va., Mar. 7, 1920; d. Charles Gray and Ethel (Roache) Rowell; m. Thomas Eugene Worrell, Sept. 12, 1941; 1 child, Thomas Eugene. Student, Va. Intermont Coll., 1939, LittD (hon.), 1991; student, U. Richmond, 1965. Founding stockholder Worrell Newspapers Inc., 1949, v.p., dir., 1969-73; v.p., sec. Worrell Investment Co., Charlottesville, Va.; pres. The Genan Co. (formerly Bristol Newspapers). Pres. Bristol Jr. League, 1959; bd. dirs. The Corp. for Thomas Jefferson's Poplar Forest Found., Va. Hist. Soc., Va. Intermont Coll., Antiquities; active Monticello Cabinet. Named Outstanding Alumna, Va. Intermont Coll., 1981. Mem.: Nat. Trust for Hist. Preservation, Greencroft Club, Farmington Country Club, Contemporary Club. Episcopalian. Office: Pantops PO Box 5386 Charlottesville VA 22905-5386

WORTEL, GARY G., publishing executive; b. Ottawa, Can., 1956; m. Patti C. Wortel; children: Erin, Garrett, Elise, Patrick. BA, San Jose State U., Calif. Various mktg. & sales exec. positions San Jose Mercury News, 1978—93; display advt. mgr., then advt. dir. The Tennessean, Nashville, 1993—2001; v.p. advt. & mktg. St. Paul Pioneer Press, Minn., 2001—05; pres., pub. Sun News, Myrtle Beach, SC, 2005—07, Ft. Worth Star-Telegram, Tex., 2007—. Office: Ft Worth Star-Telegram 808 Throckmorton St PO Box 1870 Fort Worth TX 76101 Office Phone: 817-390-7454. E-mail: gwortel@star-telegram.com.

WORTH, MELVIN H., surgeon, educator; b. Norwich, Conn., July 14, 1930; s. Melvin H. and Stella E. (Cline) W.; m. Alice Tenzer, May 17, 1953; children: Nancy, David. AB, Clark U., 1950; MD, NYU, 1954. Diplomate Am. Bd. Surgery. Intern Bellevue Hosp., NYC, 1954-55, resident, 1957-61, dir. trauma svc., 1966-79; dir. surgery S.I. U. Hosp., NYC, 1979-96; assoc. prof. NYU, NYC, 1968-69; prof. clin. surgery SUNY, Bklyn., 1979—96, Uniformed Svc. U. Health Sci. Ctr., 1996—. Chmn. trauma designation com. N.Y.C. Emergency Med. Svc., 1990; mem. Office of Profl. Med. Conduct of N.Y. State, 1983-98. Vice chmn. N.Y. State Health Rev. and Planning Coun., 1988-94, chair, 1995. Capt. USMC, 1955-57. Scholar-in-residence Inst. Medicine, 1996—. Fellow ACS, Am. Coll. Gastroenterology; mem. Internat. Soc. Surgery, Soc. Am. Gastrointestinal Endoscopic Surgeons, Am. Assn. for Surgery of Trauma, Assn. Acad. Surgery, Soc. Critical Care Medicine, Assn. Surg. Edn., N.Y. Surg. Soc. (pres. 1989), Alpha Omega Alpha. Home: 817 Freedom Plaza Cir Apt 104 Sun City Center FL 33573-7210 Personal E-mail: alicemelworth@msn.com.

WORTHINGTON, MELVIN LEROY, minister, writer; b. Greenville, NC, June 17, 1937; s. Wilbur Leroy and Alma Lee (Braxton) W.; m. Anne Katherine Wilson, Sept. 12, 1959; children: Daniel Edward, Lydia Anne. Diploma, Imperial Detective Acad., Cin., 1965; B.Bi-bl.Edn., Columbia Bible Coll., SC, 1959; B.Th., Luther Rice Sem., Jacksonville, Fla., 1967, B.Div., 1969, M.Th., 1970, D.Th., 1974; M.Ed., Ga. State U.-Atlanta, 1979; EdD, Vanderbilt U., 1998. Ordained to ministry, Central Conf. Free Will Baptists, 1957. Pastor Union Chapel Free Will Bapt. Ch., Chocowinity, NC, 1959-62, Palmetto Free Will Bapt. Ch., Vanceboro, NC, 1959-62, First Free Will Bapt. Ch., Darlington, SC, 1962-66, Wesconnett Free Will Bapt. Ch., Jacksonville, Fla., 1967, First Free Will Bapt. Ch., Amory, Miss., 1967-72, Albany, Ga., 1972-79; exec. sec. Nat. Assn. Free Will Bapt., Inc., Antioch, 1979—2002, chmn. Sunday Sch. bd., 1975-77, asst. moderator, 1977-79, chmn. grad. study com., 1976-77, exec. sec. emeritus, 2002—; pastor Liberty Free Will Bapt. Ch., Ayden, NC, 2003—. Clk. S.C. State Assn. Free Will Bapt., Florence, 1966-67;

asst. moderator Ga. State Assn. Free Will Bapt., Moultrie, 1973-74, moderator, 1975-79; pres. Ga. Bible Inst., Albany, 1978 Editor in chief: Contact mag., 1979—2002, author editorial, 1980—2002; contbr. articles to profl. jours. Adv. bd. Nat. Fedn. Decency, 1985; nat. bd. dirs. Christian Leaders for Responsible TV, 1986 Mem. Evang. Press Assn., Religious Conf. Mgmt. Assn. (dir. 1983, v.p. 1986, pres. 1989-92, 2009-13), Nashville C. of C., Future Farmers Am. (N.C. Farmer degree 1955, Am. Farmer degree 1957). Democrat. Mem. Free Will Baptist Ch. Office: Nat Assn Free Will Bapt Inc 5233 Mount View Rd Antioch TN 37013-2306 Office Phone: 252-746-3132.

WORTHINGTON, ROBERT FLETCHER, JR., lawyer; b. Knoxville, Tenn., July 17, 1931; s. Robert Fletcher Worthington and Rachel Ann Boggs; m. Julia McCrary (dec.); children: Julia Elizabeth Worthington Farry, Katherine Louisa Worthington Kinnard; m. Carole Lynch Worthington. LLD, U. Tenn., 1957. Bar: Tenn. 1957, DC 1957. Assoc. Baker & Baker, Knoxville, 1957—59; ptnr. Baker, Young, Young & Baker, Knoxville, 1959—63, Baker Worthington, Knoxville, 1963—94; of counsel Baker, Donelson, Bearman, Caldwell & Berkowitz, Knoxville, 1994—. Gen. counsel Tenn. Valley indsl. com. Tenn. Gas Assn. and NeWire, Inc. Mem. past pres. coun. Tenn. Bus. Roundtable; past vice chmn. Tenn. Higher Edn. Commn.; gen. counsel World's Fair, Knoxville, 1982; mem. adv. bd. conf. Cumberland Trail; mem. adv. bd. Florence Crittenton Agy., Inc. Devel. Coun., Cmty. Sch. Arts; former chmn. bd. govs. Club LeConte; bd. dirs. Boathouse Benevolent Soc., Inc., Knoxville Zoo Soc., East Tenn. Hist. Soc. 1st lt. inf. US Army, 1953—56. Named to Dean's Cir., U. Tenn. Coll. Law-, Best Lawyers in Am., 1991—. Mem.: ABA, D.C. Bar Assn., Tenn. Bar Assn., Phi Delta Phi. Office: Baker Donelson Bearman Caldwell & Berkowitz 265 Brookview Ctr Way Ste 600 Knoxville TN 37919 Office Phone: 865-549-7000. Office Fax: 865-633-7200. Business E-Mail: rworthington@bakerdonelson.com.

WORTHINGTON, WILLIAM ALBERT, III, lawyer; b. June 26, 1950; s. William Albert Jr. and Patricia Lou (Reynolds) W.; children: Elizabeth Clark, Emily Robin, Katherine Anne, William Jackson. BS, U. Utah, 1972; JD, Washington and Lee U., 1976. Bar: Tex. 1976, U.S. Dist. Ct. (so. dist.) Tex. 1977, U.S. Ct. Appeals (5th cir.) 1977, U.S. Ct. Appeals (11th cir.) 1981, U.S. Supreme Ct. 1981, U.S. Dist. Ct. (we. dist.) Tex. 1982, U.S. Dist. Ct. (ea. dist.) Tex. 1986, U.S. Dist. Ct. (no. dist.) Tex. 1993. Assoc. Sewell & Riggs, Houston, 1976—82, ptnr., 1982—89, shareholder, 1990—94; ptnr. Strasburger & Price, LLP, Houston, 1994—. Exec. editor Washington and Lee Law Rev., 1976; contbr. articles to law jours. Active Houston YMCA, Amnesty Internat. U.S.A., ARC; del. state bar of Tex. to Rep. Cuba, 2001. Mem. Am. Law Inst., Am. Judicature Soc., Product Liability Adv. Coun., Houston Bar Found., Tex. Bar Found., Tex. Bd. Legal Specialization (cert. civil trial lawyer, personal injury trial lawyer), US Cycling Fedn., Sierra Club. Office: Strasburger & Price LLP 909 Fannin St Ste 230 Houston TX 77010-1036 Home Phone: 713-661-2977; Office Phone: 713-951-5600. Business E-Mail: william.worthington@strasburger.com.

WORTHY, JAMES AGER, entrepreneur, retired professional basketball player; b. Gastonia, NC, Feb. 27, 1961; m. Angela Wilder, 1984 (div. 1996); children: Sable, Sierra. B, U. NC, Chapel Hill, 1985. Forward LA Lakers, 1982-94; ret. NBA, 1994; CEO James Worthy Enterprises (and subs. Worthy Partners, Worthy Devel. and the James Worthy Found.); NBA analyst WCBS 2 Sports Ctrl.; co-host LTV. Named NCAA Divsn. I Tournament MVP, 1982, NBA Playoffs MVP, 1988; named to Sporting News All-Am. First Team, 1982, NBA All-Rookie Team, 1983, We. Conf. All-Star Team, 1986-92, Naismith Meml. Basketball Hall of Fame, 2003, Nat. Collegiate Basketball Hall of Fame, 2011. Achievements include member of NCAA men's basketball national championship winning University of North Carolina Tar Heels, 1982; being the first overall selection in the NBA Draft, 1982; member of NBA Finals championship winning Los Angeles Lakers, 1985, 1987, 1988. Office: James Worthy Found 2212 Union Rd Ste 700-408 Gastonia NC 28054 Office Phone: 704-671-2620.

WOZNIACKI, CAROLINE, professional tennis player; b. Odense, Denmark, July 11, 1990; d. Piotr and Anna Wozniacki. Profl. tennis player WTA Tour, 2005—. Named Newcomer of Yr., Sony Ericsson WTA Tour, 2008. Achievements include winner 4 career singles titles, ITF; winner 7 career singles titles, 2 career doubles titles, WTA; winner (singles) Japan Open, 2008, New Haven, 2008, 2009, Stockholm, 2008, Ponte Vedra Beach, 2009, Eastbourne, 2009. Avocations: handball, swimming, soccer, piano. Office: c/o WTA Tour Ste 1500 One Progress Plaza Saint Petersburg FL 33701

WRAY, BETTY BEASLEY, allergist, immunologist, pediatrician; b. Ga., 1935; MD, Med Coll. Ga., 1960. Diplomate Am. Bd. Allergy and Immunology, Am. Bd. Clin. Lab. Immunology. Intern Talmadge Meml. Hosp., Augusta, Ga., 1960-61, resident in pediatrics, 1962, 64-65, fellow in pediatric allergy, 1966-68; staff mem. Med. Coll. Ga., Augusta, 1979—, prof. pediat. medicine, interim dean Sch. Medicine, v.p. clin. activities, 2000—02, prof. emeritus, 2002—; vol. physician David Pk. Comm. Health Ctr., 2007—. Mem.: Am. Coll. Allergy, Asthma and Immunology, Am. Acad. Pediat., Am. Acad. Allergy and Immunology, Am. Pediatric Soc. Office: Med Coll Ga Ga Regents University BG 1009 Augusta GA 30912

WRAY, MICHAEL H., state legislator; b. Roanoke Rapids, NC, Apr. 06; s. Harold W. and Shilrey Clary Wray. State bd. CPA examiners, NC, 1994—2003; former commr. Gaston; state rep. Dist. 27 NC, 2005—; sec. Wj Wray Contractors, treas. Mem.: Ducks Unlimited, Nat Wildlife Turkey Fed., Rotary Club, Lions Club. Democrat. Methodist. Mailing: PO Box 904 Gaston NC 27832 Office: North Carolina House of Representatives 300 N Salisbury St Rm 502 Raleigh NC 27603-5925 Office Phone: 919-733-5662. Business E-Mail: Michael.Wray@ncleg.net.

WRAY, THOMAS JEFFERSON, lawyer; b. Nashville, July 17, 1949; s. William Esker and Imogene (Cushman) W.; m. Susan Elizabeth Wells, Aug. 19, 1972; children: William Clark, Caroline Kell. BA, Emory U., 1971; JD, U. Va., 1974. Bar: Tex. 1974, U.S. Dist. Ct. (so., no. and ea. dists.) Tex. 1976, U.S. Ct. Appeals (5th and 11th cirs.) 1976, U.S. Supreme Ct. 1987. Assoc. Fulbright & Jaworski, L.L.P., Houston, 1974-82; ptnr. Fulbright & Jaworski, Houston, 1982—. Editor (assoc.): Tex. Employment Law Handbook, 2005—09; contbr. chapters to books. Mem. ABA, Coll. Labor and Employment Lawyers, Houston Bar Assn., Houston Mgmt. Lawyers Forum (chmn. 1981-82), Briar Club, Phi Beta Kappa. Republican. Episcopalian. Home: 3662 Ella Lee Ln Houston TX 77027-4105 Office: Fulbright & Jaworski 1301 Mckinney St Ste 5100 Houston TX 77010-3095 Office Phone: 713-651-5585. Business E-Mail: tjwray@fulbright.com.

WREN, FRANK, professional baseball team executive; b. Hamilton, Ohio; m. Teri Wren; children: Kyle, Colby, Jordan. Outfielder Montreal Expos minor league sys., Canada, 1976-81, coach, 1981-84; gen. mgr. Montreal Expos Class A affiliate, Jamestown, NY, 1985-86; asst. dir. scouting Montreal Expos, 1986-91, dir. Latin Am. scouting and ops., 1989-91; asst. gen. mgr. Fla. Marlins, 1991-97; gen. mgr. Balt. Orioles, 1998-99; asst. gen. mgr. Atlanta Braves, 1999—2007, exec. v.p., gen. mgr., 2007—. Office: Atlanta Braves Turner Field 755 Hank Aaron Dr Atlanta GA 30315

WREN, GREG, state legislator; b. Jan. 21, 1955; m. Susan Anderson; children: Rachael Wren Lindmark, Christa, Catherine. BA, U. Ala. Chartered fin. cons. Legis. analyst Legislative Fiscal Office; staff asst. US Senate; govtl. affairs dir. Ala. Assn. REALTORS; owner Wren and Associates; mem. Dist. 75 Ala. House of Reps., Montgomery, 1994—2002, 2005—. Chmn. state-fed. affairs com. Nat. Conf. Ins. Legislators; vice chmn. commerce, fin. services and comm. com. Nat. Conf. State Legislatures; mem. commerce, ins. and econ. devel. task force Am. Legis. Exch. Coun.; mem. Coun. State Govts. Club advisor YMCA Tri-Hi-Y; chmn. emeritus Hugh O'Brian Youth Found.; apptd. Rep. Nat. Com. Bus. Adv. Coun.; mem. First Bapt. Ch. Disaster Relief and Resource Ctr. Team; bd. mem. Montgomery YMCA, Family Guidance Ctr., YMCA Camp Chandler, Cmty. Intensive Treatment for Youth, Envision 2020, Ala. Asthma and Allergy Found.; mem. Auburn Montgomery Adv. Bd. Dirs., Ala. Mental Illness Planning Coun. Recipient Congl. Medal Distinction Nat. Rep. Congl. Com.; named Lawmaker of Yr. Ind. Agents Assn. Ala., Ala. State Employees Assn., Montgomery YMCA Man of Yr., 2005. Republican. Baptist. Office: 4213 Carmichael Rd Montgomery AL 36106 also: Ala House of Reps Ala State House 11 S Union St Rm 517-B Montgomery AL 36130 Office Phone: 334-395-0123, 334-242-7764. Business E-Mail: repgregwren@yahoo.com.

WREN, HAROLD GWYN, arbitrator, educator; b. Big Stone Gap, Va., May 19, 1921; s. James H. and Jessie M. (Reeve) W.; m. Beryl E. Bird, Nov. 20, 1948; children: James H., II, Geoffrey G. AB, Columbia U., 1942, LL.B., 1948; J.S.D., Yale U., 1957. Bar: N.Y. 1948, Okla. 1956, Tex. 1959, Ky. 1983. Capt. USNR, 1942—80; assoc. firm Willkie Farr & Gallagher, NYC, 1948-49; assoc. prof. law U. Miss., Oxford, 1949-54; prof. law U. Okla., Norman, 1954-57, So. Meth. U., Dallas, 1957-65, Boston Coll., 1965-69; dean, prof. law Lewis and Clark Law Sch., Portland, Oreg., 1969-72, U. Richmond, Va., 1972-76; prof. law U. Louisville, 1976-91, dean, 1976-81; arbitrator Am. Arbitration Assn., 1958—, Fed. Mediation and Conciliation Service, 1958—, FINRA, 2002—. Bd. dirs. Q-Mark, Inc., 2002—06. Author: Creative Estate Planning, 1970, Problems in Corporate Changes, 1958, Problems in Texas Estates, 1961, (with Gabinet and Carrad) Tax Aspects of Marital Dissolution, 1987, 2d edit., 1997, (with Glascock) The Of Counsel Agreement, 1991, 3d edit., 2005. Served to capt. USNR, 1942-80. USNR, 1942—80. Fulbright scholar, 1953-54 Fellow Am. Coll. Trust and Estate Counsel, Am. Coll. Tax Counsel, Am. Bar Found. (life); mem. ABA, Louisville Bar Assn., Conversation Club, Order of Coif, Phi Beta Kappa, Phi Kappa Phi. Democrat. Episcopalian. Avocation: coin collecting/numismatics. Home: 5944 Ashwood Bluff Dr Louisville KY 40207-1269 Office: 6006 Brownsboro Park Blvd Ste C Louisville KY 40207-1296 Office Phone: 502-893-2719. Personal E-mail: haroldgwren@gmail.com.

WREN, TOMMY, state legislator; b. Aug. 4, 1976; m. Ann Wilson Wren. Rep. Ark. State House of Representatives, 2010—; mem. Dist. 71 Ark. House of Representatives, 2011—. Democrat. Baptist. Office: PO Box 943 Melbourne AR 72556 Office Phone: 870-613-7585. Business E-Mail: wrenappraisals@centurytel.net.

WRENN, CHRISTOPHER JAY, physician; b. Margarita, Panama Canal Zone, July 16, 1947; s. Earl Walton and Maxine Elizabeth (Luther) Wrenn; m. Nancy Margaret Bowie, June 27, 1970; children: Kristina Elizabeth, Courtney Bowie. BS, Baylor U., 1969; MD, U. Nebr., 1973. Diplomate Am. Bd. Pediatrics, Am. Bd. Allergy and Immunology. Intern pediatrics Children's Med. Ctr., Dallas, 1973-74, resident pediatrics, 1974-76, chief resident pediatrics, 1976-77; staff pediatrician Los Barrios Unidos Community Clinic, Dallas, 1977-78; fellow allergy and immunology Med. Br. U. Tex., Galveston, Tex., 1978-80; practice medicine specializing in allergy Graves-Gilbert Clinic, Bowling Green, Ky., 1980-83, Wichita Clinic, 1983-84, Allergy Clinic, Tyler, Tex., 1984—. Staff pediatrician Dallas County Juvenile Detention Ctr., 1975—78, Buckner Bapt. Children's Home, 1977—78. Co-author: Pediatrics by Self Instruction, 1982. Fellow: Am. Coll. Allergists, Am. Acad. Pediat.; mem.: Am. Acad. Allergy and Immunology. Presbyterian. Avocation: writing fiction and poetry. Office: Allergy Clinic PA 1128 Medical Dr Tyler TX 75701

WRIGHT, BETH SEGAL, art historian, educator; b. NYC, July 23, 1949; d. Ben and Ella (Litvack) Segal; m. Woodring Erik J. Wright, Sept. 5, 1971; children: Benjamin, Joshua. AB cum laude, Brandeis U., 1970; MA, U. Calif., Berkeley, 1972, PhD, 1978. Instr. Mountain View Coll., Dallas, 1978—82; lectr. U. Tex., Dallas, 1980—81, Tex. Christian U., Ft. Worth, 1981; asst. prof. U. Tex., Arlington, 1984—88, assoc. prof., 1988—98, prof., 1998—, interim dean liberal arts, 2003—04, dean liberal arts, 2004—. Adj. and vis. asst. prof. art history U. Tex., Arlington, 1981-84. Author: Painting and History During the French Restoration. Abandoned by the Past, 1997; author, editor: The Cambridge Companion to Delacroix, 2001; contbr. articles to Art Bull., Arts Mag., Word & Image, Oxford Art Jour., Nineteenth-Century French Studies, Nouvelles de l'Estampe, Clio, others; contbr. chapters to books. U. Calif., Berkeley hon. traveling fellow, 1975-76; NEH Travel to Collections grantee, Paris, 1987, 93; U. Tex. Arlington Rsch. Enhancement grantee, Paris, 1990, 93, 99, Coll. Art Assoc. Meiss grant, 1996; recipient Dallas Mus. Art Vasari award Painting and History, 1998; named Woman of Influence for excellence in edn. Fort Worth Bus. Press, 2006; YWCA Tribute to Women in Bus. honoree, 2004; Robert R. Palmer Travel Fund award Am. Soc. Eighteenth-Century Studies; U. Tex., Arlington Outstanding Rsch. Achievement award 1998. Mem. Soc. Histoire Art Français (contbr. articles to bull.), Am. Soc. 18th-Century Studies (bd. dirs. 2005-07), Coll. Art Assn., Internat. Assn. Word & Image Studies Assn., Historians Nineteenth-Century Art, Midwest Art History Soc. (bd. dirs. 1990-93).

WRIGHT, BRUCE A., military officer; BS, USAF Acad., 1973; grad., Squadron Officer Sch., 1976, USAF Fighter Weapons Sch., 1982; M of Pub. Adminstrn., Golden Gate U., 1984; grad., Armed Forces Staff Coll., 1984, Air War Coll., 1992; grad. program sr. ofcls. nat. security, Syracuse U., 1996; grad. Capstone, Nat. Def. U., 1998. Commd. 2d lt. U.S. Army, 1973, advanced through grades to brigadier gen., 1998; F-4E instr. pilot 68th Tactical Flight Squadron Moody AFB, Ga., 1976-78; F-4C Wild Weasel instr. pilot 67th Tactical Fighter Squadron Kadena Air Base, Japan, 1978-79; F-4G Wild Weasel instr. pilot 90th Tactical Fighter Squadron Clark Air Base, The Philippines, 1979-80; air ops. officer air staff tng. program Hdqs. USAF, Washington, 1980-81; F-4E instr. pilot 422d Test and Evaluation squadron Nellis AFB, Nev., 1981-84; ops. officer The Joint Staff J3, Washington, 1985-88; F-16C ops. officer, squadron comdr. 614th Fighter Squadron Torrejon Air Base, Spain, 1988-91; comdr. 52 Support Group Spangdahlem Air Base, Germany, 1992-93; comdr. 86th Ops. Group Ramstein Air Base, Germany, 1993-94; dir. of ops. J3 U.S. Forces Japan, Yokota Air Base, Japan, 1994-97; comdr. 35th Fighter Wing Misawa Air Base, Japan, 1997-98; dep. dir. info. ops. J39 The Joint Staff, Washington, 1998—; gen. comdr. Air Intelligence Agy., San Antonio. Decorated Def. Superior Svc. medal, Legion of Merit, DFC, Bronze Star, Def. Meritorious Svc. medal, Meritorious Svc. medal with 3 oak leaf clusters, Air medal with 5 oak leaf clusters. Office: ACC/CV 200 Dodd Blvd Ste 207 Langley AFB VA 23665-2788

WRIGHT, C(ARROLL) LEE, JR., architecture educator; m. Beverly Ann Carroll, 1980; children: Benjamin Carroll, Alexander Lee. BArch, U. Tex., 1963, MArch, 1969. With Hirsch and Cassetti, Elmira, NY, 1964—65, Claude Pendley, Austin, Brook, Barr, Graeber and White, Austin, Pierce/Lacey Assocs., Dallas, 1965; mem. faculty U. Tex., Arlington, 1968—, assoc. prof. arch., 1972—, assoc. dean, 1975—77, dir. arch. program, 1978—79, undergrad. advisor, 1989—99, interim dean Sch. Arch., 1999—2001, assoc. dean Sch. Arch., 1993—99, dir. arch., 2002—04; pvt. practice Lee Wright Assocs., 1968—. Mem. univ. curriculum com. U. Tex., Arlington; bd. dirs. Dallas Arch. Found., 1999—2002; acad. and career counselor Sch. Arch., 2004—. With USMC, 1954—56. Named Outstanding Advisor, U. Tex. Arlington, 1993, Tchr. of Yr., Sch. Architecture, UTA, 1981. Mem.: Tex. Soc. Architects, Am. Inst. Architects. Avocations: architecture, painting, sculpting, art, sailing. Home: 904 Blue Lakke Dr Fort Worth TX 76103

WRIGHT, CHARLES PENZEL, JR., writer, educator; b. Pickwick Dam, Tenn., Aug. 25, 1935; s. Charles Penzel and Mary Castleman (Winter) Wright; m. Holly McIntire, Apr. 6, 1969; 1 child, Luke Savin Herrick. BA, Davidson Coll., 1957; MFA, U. Iowa, 1963; postgrad., U. Rome, 1963—64. Mem. faculty U. Calif., Irvine, Calif., 1966—83, prof. English, 1976—83; Souder Family Prof. Poetry U. Va., Charlottesville, 1983—. Vis. prof. N.Am. Lit. U., Padua, Italy, 1968—69; disting. vis. prof. U. Degli Studi, Florence, Italy, 1992. Translator: The Storm and Other Poems (Eugenio Montale), 1978 (PEN Translation prize, 1979), Orphic Songs (Dino Campana), 1984; author: (books) The Grave of the Right Hand, 1970, Hard Freight, 1973, Bloodlines, 1975, China Trace, 1977, The Southern Cross, 1981, Country Music - Selected Early Poems, 1982, The Other Side of the River, 1984, Halflife, 1988, Zone Journals, 1988, Xionia, 1990, The World of the Ten Thousand Things, 1990, Quarter Notes, 1995, Chickamauga, 1995 (Lenore Marshall Poetry prize Acad. Am. Poets, 1996), Black Zodiac, 1997 (Pulitzer prize poetry, 1998), Appalachia, 1998, North American Bear, 1999, Negative Blue, 2000, A Short History of the Shadow, 2002, Buffalo Yoga, 2004, Scar Tissue, 2006 (Griffin Poetry prize (internat.), 2007), Littlefoot, 2007, Sestets, 2009. With AUS, 1957—61. Recipient Nat Book award for Poetry, 1983, citation in poetry, Brandeis U. Creative Arts Awards, 1987, L.A. Times Book prize, 1997, award, Nat. Book Critics Circle, 1997, Amb. Book award, 1998, Preano AnTicho Fattore, Italy, 1999, Poetry prize, Griffen Internat., Can., 2007, Bobbitt Nat. Poetry prize, Libr. Congress, 2008, Premio Internat. Mario Luzi, Italy, 2008; fellow Guggeheim fellow, 1976, Ingram Merrill fellow, 1980, 1993; scholar, Fulbright Found., 1963—65. Mem.: Acad. Am. Poets (chancellor), Am. Acad. Arts and Sci., Am. Acad. Arts and Letters, Fellowship of So. Writers. Home: 940 Locust Ave Charlottesville VA 22901-4030 Office: English Dept Univ Va Charlottesville VA 22901

WRIGHT, DOREEN A., retired food products executive; b. Feb. 27, 1957; BA, U. Pa., 1979. Mgr. retail client svc. & processing units Merrill Lynch & Co., Inc.; v.p. instl. trust & custody mktg. to various positions in defined contbn. asset svcs., instl. trust ops. and global assets defined benefit sys. Bankers Trust Co., 1984—91, mng. dir., 1991—94; sr. v.p. ops. & systems Prudential Investment Group, Prudential Ins. Co., 1995—98; exec. v.p., chief info. officer Nabisco, Inc., 1999—2001; sr. v.p., chief info. officer Campbell Soup Co., 2001—08, interim chief human resources officer, 2002, ret., 2008. Bd. dirs. Conseco, Inc., 2007—, Dean Foods Co., 2009—, Oriental Trading Co., Crocs, Inc., 2011—; former bd. dirs. Alphanet Solutions, Inc., Yankee Candle Co., Inc. Bd. trustees Am. Repertory Ballet; bd. dirs. Riverside Symphonia, Lambertville, NJ. Office: Conseco Inc 11825 N Pennsylvania St Carmel IN 46032 Mailing: Dean Foods Co Ste 1200 2515 McKinney Ave Dallas TX 75201 Business E-Mail: Doreen_Wright@conseco.com.

WRIGHT, FREDERICK LEWIS, II, lawyer; b. Roanoke, Va., Sept. 17, 1951; s. Frederick Lewis and Dorothy Marie (Trent) W.; m. Margaret Suzanne Rey, Oct. 16, 1982; children: Lauren Elizabeth, Emily Trent. BA, Ga. State U., 1978; JD, U. Ga., 1981. Bar: Ga. 1982, US Dist. Ct. (no. dist.) Ga. 1984, US Ct. Appeals (11th, 8th and 4th cirs.) 1984, US Supreme Ct. 1990. Law clk. to presiding justice US Ct. Appeals, Atlanta, 1981-82; ptnr. Smith, Currie and Hancock, Atlanta, 1982-96, Vaughn, Wright and Boyer, Atlanta, 1997—. Articles editor Ga. Law Rev., 1980—81. Mem.: ABA (forum com. constrn. industry), Ga. Def. Lawyers Assn., Fed. Bar Assn., Def. Rsch. Inst., Order of Coif. Methodist. Office Phone: 770-402-5434. Personal E-mail: fwright@mindspring.com.

WRIGHT, G. HAROLD, JR., state legislator; m. Carol Wright; children: Angela, Heston. BA in Speech, Southwestern Okla. State U., 1971. Programming & sales KWEY Radio, Weatherford; sales mgr. WMBR Radio, Jacksonville, Fla.; part owner & gen. mgr. KRPT Radio, Anadarko, Okla., 1975; mayor Anadarko, 1985—87; pres. Okla. Assn. Broadcasters, 1986; former pres. Anadarko Rotary, Anadarko C of C; owner & mgr. Wright Wradio, Weatherford, 1991—; mem. Dist. 57 Okla. House of Representatives, 2008—. Republican. Methodist. Office: 2300 N Lincoln Blvd Rm 400-B Oklahoma City OK 73105 Mailing: 10132 State Hwy 54 Weatherford OK 73096 Office Phone: 405-557-7325. Personal E-mail: harold.wright@okhouse.gov.

WRIGHT, GERALD (GED WRIGHT), state senator, lawyer, pilot; b. Wagoner, Okla., July 7, 1942; s. Norman and Evelyn Wright; m. Linda Quimby; children: Brian, Brent, Janna. BS, Okla. State U.; JD, U. Tulsa. Bar: Okla. Practiced law; mem. Okla. Senate, 1983—, minority whip, 1991-92, minority floor leader, 1995-96. Past bd. dirs. Tulsa Mental Health Assn.; bd. dirs. Gateway Found., Broken Arrow. With USAF, 5 yrs., Minn. N.G., 2 yrs. Mem. Okla. Bar Assn., Tulsa County Bar Assn., Masons, Shriners (crippled children's com.). Republican. Episcopalian. Avocations: golf, skiing, flying, racquetball.

WRIGHT, GREGORY A., oil industry executive; BBA, Ohio State U., 1971; MBA, U. Del., 1979. With Columbia Gas Systems Inc., 1972—81; positions through v.p. Valero Energy Corp., 1981—95; v.p. corp. comm. Tesoro Corp., San Antonio, 1995—2001, sr. v.p., CFO, 2001—03, exec. v.p., CFO, 2003—07, 2008—, exec. v.p., Chief Adminstrv. Officer, 2007—08. Office: Tesoro Petroleum 300 Concord Plz San Antonio TX 78216-6999

WRIGHT, HARRY HERCULES, psychiatrist; b. Charleston, SC, Jan. 4, 1948; s. Harry Vernon and Agnes Lucile (Simmons) W. BS, U. S.C., 1970; MD, MBA, U. Pa., 1976. Resident in psychiatry Wm. S. Hall Psychiat. Inst., Columbia, SC, 1977—79; adminstrv. fellow in psychiatry NIMH, Rockville, Md., 1979; fellow in child psychiatry William S. Hall Psychiat. Inst., 1979—81, instr. child psychiatrist, 1981—; instr. dept. neuropsychiatry and behavioral sci. U. S.C. Sch. Medicine, 1981—82, asst. prof., 1982—86, assoc. prof., 1986—90, prof., 1990—. Contbr. articles to profl. jours. Bd. dirs. Carolina Children's Home, 1992—, Zero to Three, 1997—; bd. trustees, First Steps to Sch. Readiness, 1999-2003; mem. landmarks commn. City of Columbia, 1986-98. Recipient Freed award, Hall Psychiat. Inst., 1978, Outstanding Svc. award, Sickle Cell Found., Clin. Sci. Rsch. award, 1998, Am.'s Top Doctors award, 2001—, Rsch. Advancement award, U. SC, 2002, 2004, 2006, 2008; grantee Falk fellow, 1977—79,

Laughlin fellow, 1979. Mem.: Am. Coll. Psychiatrists, Am. Soc. Human Genetics, Soc. Study Psychiatry and Culture, Acad. Orgnl. and Occupl. Psychiatry, So. Med. Assn., Am. Soc. Adolescent Psychiatry, World Assn. Infant Mental Health, World Psychiat. Assn., Am. Acad. Child Psychiatry, Am. Physiatry Assn., Autism Soc. Am., Riverbank Zool. Soc., Sigma Xi, Omicron Delta Kappa. Home: PO Box 12474 Columbia SC 29211-2474 Office: 3555 Harden St Ext Ste 301 Columbia SC 29203-6894 Office Phone: 803-434-4250, 803-261-9316. Business E-Mail: harry.wright@uscmed.sc.edu.

WRIGHT, JAMES F., agricultural products executive; Sr. level positions K-Mart Corp., 1974—88, Western Auto Supply Co., 1988—96; pres., CEO Tire Kingdom, 1997—2000; pres., COO Tractor Supply Co., Brentwood, Tenn., 2000—04, pres., CEO, 2004—07, chmn., pres., CEO, 2007—09, chmn., CEO, 2009—. Bd. dir. Spartan Stores Inc. Mem.: Automotive Parts and Accessories Assn. (past chmn.). Office: Tractor Supply Co 200 Powell Pl Brentwood TN 37027

WRIGHT, JESSE HARTZELL, psychiatrist, educator; b. Altoona, Pa., Sept. 21, 1943; s. Jesse H. and Marion (Stone) W.; m. Susanne Judy Wright, July 9, 1967; children: Andrew, Laura. BS, Juniata Coll., 1965; MD, Jefferson Med. Coll., 1969; PhD, U. Louisville, 1976. Diplomate Am. Bd. Psychiatry and Neurology, Am. Bd. Med. Examiners; lic. psychiatrist, Ky. Asst. prof. U. Louisville, 1975-79, assoc. prof., 1979-87, prof., 1987—; clin. dir. Norton Psychiat. Clinic, Louisville, 1975-83, med. dir., 1983—2009; chief adult psychiatry U. Louisville, 2000—09, vice-chmn academic affairs, dir. depression ctr., dept. psychiat., 2009—; resident in psychiatry U. Mich., Ann Arbor, 1970-73. Author: first multimedia computer program for psychotherapy, Good Days Ahead, author: (self help book for depression) Breaking Free from Depression, (textbooks with DVD) Learning Cognitive-Behavior Therapy, Cognitive-Behavior Therapy for Severe Mental Illness, High-Yield Cognitive-Behavior Therapy for Brief Sessions (Health Book of Yr. Brit. Med. Soc., 2009), others; chpts. to books; contbr. articles to prof. jours. Fellow Am.Psychiat. Assn., Am. Coll. Psychiatrists; mem. Ky. Psychiat. Assn. (sec. 1979-80, v.p. 1980-81, pres. 1982-83), Acad. Cognitive Therapy (founding pres.), Alpha Omega Alpha. Avocations: gardening, bicycling, fly fishing. Home: 15 Indian Hills Trl Louisville KY 40207-1532 Office: Univ Psychiatric Group 401 E Chestnut St Louisville KY 40202

WRIGHT, JOHN COLLINS, retired chemistry professor; b. Oak Hill, W.Va., Aug. 5, 1927; s. John C. and Irene (Collins) W.; m. Margaret Ann Cyphers, Sept. 11, 1949; children: Jeffrey Cyphers, John Timothy, Curtis Scott, Keith Alexander. BS, W.Va. Wesleyan Coll., 1948, LLD, 1974; PhD, U. Ill., 1951; DSc (hon.), U. Ala., 1979, W.Va. Inst. Tech., 1979. Research chemist Hercules, Inc., 1951-57; mem. faculty W.Va. Wesleyan Coll., 1957-64; asst. program dir. NSF, 1964-65; dean Coll. Arts and Scis., No. Ariz. U., 1966-70, W.Va. U., Morgantown, 1970-74; vice chancellor W.Va. Bd. Regents, Charleston, 1974-78; pres. U. Ala., Huntsville, 1978-88, prof. chemistry, 1988-95, prof. emeritus, 1995—; interim pres. W.Va. Coll. Grad. Studies, Institute, 1975-76. Hon. rsch. assoc. Univ. Coll., London, 1962-63; cons. NSF, 1965—, Army Sci. Bd., U.S. Army, 1979-82, Nat. Sci. Resources Ctr. Served with USNR, 1945-46. Mich. fellow Center Study Higher Edn., U. Mich., 1965-66 Mem. AAAS, NSTA. Home: 4724 Panorama Dr SE Huntsville AL 35801-1215 Office Phone: 256-883-2272. E-mail: johnhasp@aol.com.

WRIGHT, LAURA H., air transportation executive; m. Randy Wright; children: Lindsay, Jeffrey. BS in Accounting, U. North Tex., MS in Accounting, 1982. CPA. Tax mgr. Arthur Young & Co., Dallas; dir. corp. taxation SW Airlines Co., 1988—90, dir. corp. fin., 1990—95, asst. treas., 1995—98, treas., 1998—2004, v.p., fin., 2001—04; sr. v.p., fin., CFO Southwest Airlines Co., 2004—. Office: Southwest Airlines Co 2702 Love Field Dr Dallas TX 75235 Office Phone: 214-792-4000. Office Fax: 214-792-5015.

WRIGHT, MARK, telecommunications industry executive; BA, U. Tenn., Knoxville, 1987. Various positions with in-house media and sponsorship divsn. including v.p. corp. media Anheuser-Busch Companies, Inc., 1991—2009, v.p. media, sponsorship & activation, 2009—11; v.p. media svcs. AT&T Inc., 2011—. Named a Media Maven, Advt. Age, 2011; named one of 50 Most Influential People in Sports Bus., Street & Smith's SportsBus. Jour., 2009. Mailing: AT&T Corp Hdqs 208 S Akard St Dallas TX 75202

WRIGHT, MARSHALL, state legislator; b. LA; m. Kristen Wright; children: Collier Wright, Syble Wright. BSBA, JD, U. Ark. Tchr., legal environment of bus. East Ark. CC; pro bono atty., pub. defender First Jud. Dist. Ark.; ptnr. Sharpe Beavers Cline and Wright; mem. Dist. 51 Ark. House of Representatives, 2011—. Mem.: St. Francis County Bar Assn., Ark. Bar Assn. (vol. atty., mem. House Dels.), Rotary (treas.). Democrat. Office: 117 S Washington St Forrest City AR 72335 Office Phone: 870-633-3141. Business E-Mail: marshall.wright@arkansashouse.org.

WRIGHT, MURRAY, information technology executive; B, Clarkson U., Potsdam, NY. Pres., gen. mgr. Lenovo Can.; various info. tech., sales and mgmt. positions Xerox Can. Inc. (subs. Xerox Can. Ltd.), 1980—90; sales and mgmt. positions, v.p. Triathlon Leasing, 1990—94; gen. mgr. Sharp Electronics of Can., Ltd., 1994—98; gen. mgr., info. tech. distributor, v.p., sales Ingram Micro Can., 1998—2005; sr. v.p., sales Tech Data Corp., 2006—10, pres., Americas, 2010—. Office: Tech Data Corp 5350 Tech Data Dr Clearwater FL 33760 Office Phone: 727-539-7429. Office Fax: 727-538-7803. Business E-Mail: Murray.Wright@techdata.com.

WRIGHT, ROBERT PAYTON, lawyer; b. Beaumont, Tex., Feb. 15, 1951; s. Vernon Gerald and Huberta Read (Nunn) W.; m. Sallie Chesnutt Smith, July 16, 1977; children: Payton Cullen, Elizabeth Risher. AB, Princeton U., 1972; JD, Columbia U., 1975. Bar: Tex. 1975. Ptnr. Baker Botts L.L.P., Houston, 1975—. Author: The Texas Homebuyer's Manual, 1986. Mem. Am. Coll. Real Estate Lawyers (bd. govs. 2002-05), Anglo-Am. Real Property Inst., State Bar Tex. (chmn. coun. real estate, probate, trust law sect. 1994-95), Houston Bar Assn. (chmn. real estate sect. 1989-90), Tex. Coll. Real Estate Lawyers, Houston Real Estate Lawyers Coun., Houston Club. Episcopalian. Office Phone: 713-229-1237.

WRIGHT, ROBERT THOMAS, JR., lawyer; b. Detroit, Oct. 4, 1946; s. Robert Thomas and Jane Ellen (Blandin) W.; m. Diana Feltman, June 8, 1994; children: Sarah Allison, Jonathan Brian. BA in History and Polit. Sci., U. N.C., 1968; JD, Columbia U., 1974. Bar: Fla. 1974. Assoc. Paul & Thomson, Miami, Fla., 1974-77, Mershon, Sawyer, Johnston, Dunwoody & Cole, Miami, 1977-81, ptnr., 1981-95, Shutts & Bowen, Miami, 1995-98; shareholder, dir. Verner, Liipfert, Bernhard, McPherson & Hand, Miami, 1998—2001; founding ptnr. Coffey & Wright, L.L.P., Miami, 2002—06, Coffey, Burlington, Wright et al, 2007—08; ptnr. Stroock & Stroock & Lavan LLP, 2008—. 1st lt. US Army, 1968—71. Mem. ABA, Fla. Bar, Dade County Bar Assn. Avocations: golf, rugby, African cichlids. Home: 140 Jefferson Ave Apt 14010 Miami Beach FL 33139 Office: Stroock & Stroock & Lavan LLP 200 S Biscayne Blvd Ste 3100 Miami FL 33131 Home Phone: 305-397-8644; Office Phone: 305-358-9900. Personal E-mail: RTWJr1@yahoo.com. Business E-Mail: RWright@Stroock.com.

WRIGHT, THEODORE ROBERT FAIRBANK, biologist, educator; b. Kodaikanal, Tamil Nadu, India, Apr. 10, 1928; s. Horace Kepler and Adelaide Caskey (Fairbank) Wright; m. Eileen Marie Yongen, Jan. 6, 1951 (dec. Jan. 2002). AB in Biology, Princeton U., 1949; MA in Biology, Wesleyan U., 1954; PhD in Zoology, Yale U., 1959. Asst. professor biology Johns Hopkins U., Balt., 1959-65; assoc. prof. biology U. Va., Charlottesville, 1965-75, prof. biology, 1975-95; prof. emeritus, 1995—. Vis. scientist Max Planck Inst. for Biology, Tubingen, 1975-76, Devel. Biology Ctr., U. Calif., Irvine, 1982. Editor: The Genetics and Biology of Drosophila, vol. 2a-c, 1978, vol. 2d, 1980, Genetic Regulatory Hierarchies in Development, 1990; co-editor: Advances in Genetics, 1988-92. With U.S. Army, 1950-52. NIH postdoctoral fellow Max Planck Inst. for Biology, Tubingen, Fed. Republic Germany, 1958-59; NSF grantee, 1967-72, 90-93; NIH grantee, 1972-93; Am. Cancer Soc. grantee, 1988-90. Fellow AAAS; mem. AAUP, Genetics Soc. Am., Soc. for Devel. Biology, Va. Acad. Sci., Sigma Xi.

WRIGHT, THOMAS C., JR., state legislator; b. Richmond, Va., Apr. 27, 1948; m. Frances Rose Abernathy. BA in Polit. Sci., Old Dominion U., 1970. Ret. grocer; mem. Dist. 61 Va. House of Delegates, 2001—. Mem. Lunenburg County Bd. Supr., 1993—2000, chmn., 1995—97; mem. Regional Econ. Devel. Adv. Coun.; bus. rep. Work Force Investment Bd., 2000; county rep. Ft. Picket Local Reuse Authority; mem. Southside Bus. Edn. Commn., Crossroads Cmty. Svcs. Bd., 2000; trustee Victoria Christian Ch., elder; bd. dirs. Victoria H.S. Preservation Found. Mem.: Victoria C. of C., Lunenburg Crime Solvers Assn., Rotary. Republican. Office: Capitol Office Gen Assembly Bldg Rm 410 PO Box 406 Richmond VA 23218 also: PO Box 1323 Victoria VA 23974 Office Phone: 434-696-3061. Office Fax: 804-698-6761, 434-696-4061. Business E-Mail: DelTWright@house.virginia.gov.

WRIGHT, WILEY REED, JR., lawyer, retired judge, mediator; b. Seattle, Jan. 31, 1932; s. Wiley Reed and Gertrude Ellen (Datson) W.; m. Sally Harrison Clarke, 1955 (div. 1963); children: Wiley III, Margaret, Andrew; m. Roberta Hostinsky, Oct. 18, 1963; children: Cathryn, Amy, Susan. BS in Commerce, Washington and Lee U., 1954, LLB, 1956. Bar: Va. 1956, U.S. Dist. Ct. (ea. dist.) Va. 1956, U.S. Ct. Appeals (4th cir.) 1956, U.S. Supreme Ct. 1993. Law clk. to hon. judge U.S. Dist. Ct., Alexandria, Va., 1958-59; ptnr. Clarke, Richard, Moncure & Whitehead, Alexandria, 1959-68; judge corp. and cir. cts. Alexandria, 1968-79; chief judge cir. ct., 1979-84; ptnr. Hazel & Thomas P.C., Alexandria, 1984-96; mediator McCammon Mediation Group Ltd., Richmond, Va., 1998—2013. Mem. at large Va. State Bar Coun., 1984-90; mem. Jud. Coun. Va., 1982-84, vice chmn. jud. conf. Va., 1980-82. Assoc. editor: Virginia Circuit Judges Benchbook, 1987. Legal counsel to Alexandria C. of C., 1984-88. 1st lt. U.S. Army, 1956-58. Fellow: Va. Law Found., Am. Bar Found.; mem.: Va. Bar Assn., Omicron Delta Kappa, Phi Delta Phi. Avocations: boating, fishing. Home: 579 Lovers Ln Lancaster VA 22503

WRIGHT, WILLIAM EVAN, physician, consultant; b. NYC, Aug. 1, 1946; s. Samuel and Frances Elnora (Perpente) W.; m. Diana Claire Dryer, Aug. 15, 1970; children: Jason William, Elizabeth Garland, Edwin Samuel. BA in Music, U. Rochester, 1968; MD, U. Pa., 1972; MSPH, U. Utah, 1979; MS in Physiology, Harvard U., 1980. Diplomate Am. Bd Internal Medicine, Am. Bd. Preventive Medicine, Occupl. Medicine, Am. Bd. Ind. Med. Examiners; ACOEM cert. med. rev. officer; cert. FAA med. examiner, Am. Bd. Disability Analysts. Intern LDS Hosp., Salt Lake City, 1972-73, resident, 1973-75, U. Utah Med. Ctr., Salt Lake City, 1978-79, Harvard Sch. Pub. Health, Boston, 1979-80; asst. prof. U. So. Calif., LA, 1980-86; med. dir. U.S. DEA, Arlington, Va., 1986-96; program mgr., site med. dir. DynCorp, Reston, Va., 1991-96; med. dir. Md. Office, CORE, Inc., Irvine, Calif., 1996—2003; cons. Office of Worker Advocacy, U.S. Dept. Energy, Washington, 2003—05; pres. WorkWright, Inc., 2005—. Cons. Westwood Group, 2003—05; dist. med. cons. U.S. Dept. Labor, 2006—12; med. dir. Reliable Review Svcs., Boca Raton, Fla., 2007—. Author, editor: (med. textbook) Couturier's Occupational and Environmental Infectious Diseases, 2009; Contbr. articles to profl. jours. Maj. M.C., U.S. Army, 1975-77. Fellow ACP, Am. Coll. Occupl. and Environ. Medicine, mem. Cosmos Club (Washington), Alpha Omega Alpha. Avocation: music. Home: 6801 Wemberly Way Mc Lean VA 22101-1532 E-mail: 1wc_wright@post.harvard.edu.

WRIGHT ALLEN, ARENDA L., federal judge; b. Phila., 1960; m. Delroy Anthony Allen; children: Yanni Anthony, Nyle Anthony. BS, Kutztown U., 1982; JD, NC Ctrl. U., 1985. Asst. US atty. (western dist.) Va. US Dept. Justice, 1990—91, asst. US atty. (eastern dist.) Va., 1991—2005; supervisory asst. fed. pub. defender Federal Pub. Defender's Office (eastern dist.) Va., Norfolk, 2005—11; judge US Dist. Ct. (eastern dist.) Va., 2011—. JAG officer USN, 1985—90, JAG officer USNR, 1992—2005. Mem.: ABA. Office: Walter E Hoffman United States Courthouse 600 Granby St Norfolk VA 23510 Office Phone: 757-222-7499.

WRINKLE, JOHN NEWTON, lawyer; b. Chattanooga, July 31, 1929; s. John Stuart and Anne (Ownbey) W.; m. Louise Rucker Agee, Feb. 1, 1958; children: Anne Blair, Margaret Rucker. BA, Vanderbilt U., 1951; LLB, Yale U., 1955. Bar: Ala. 1955, U.S. Dist. Ct. (no. dist.) Ala. 1956, U.S. Ct. Appeals (5th cir.) 1958, U.S. Ct. Appeals (11th cir.) 1981, U.S. Tax Ct. 1957. Assoc. White, Bradley, Arant, All & Rose, Birmingham, Ala., 1955-63; ptnr. Bradley Arant Boult Cummings LLP (formerly Bradley Arant Rose & White LLP), 1963—92, counsel, 1993—. Coord. pre-law students Birmingham So. Coll., 1989—. Trustee Birmingham Symphony Assn., 1970-79, 80-83, Episcopal Found. Jefferson County, 1994-2000; bd. dirs. Yale Law Sch. Fund, 2005—11. With USAF, 1951-52. Disting. fellow Birmingham-Southern Coll., 1995—. Fellow Am. Coll. Trust and Estate Counsel; mem. ABA, So. Employee Benefits Conf. (steering com. 1970-73), Birmingham Bar Assn., Assn. of Bar of City of N.Y., Birmingham Com. Fgn. Rels., Redstone Club, Mountain Brook Club, Knickerbocker Club (N.Y.C.), Yale Club (N.Y.C.), Phi Beta Kappa, Phi Alpha Delta. Episcopalian. Home: 2 Beechwood Rd Birmingham AL 35213-3914 Office: Bradley Arant Boult Cummings LLP 1819 5th Ave N Birmingham AL 35203 Office Phone: 205-521-8000. Business E-Mail: jwrinkle@babc.com.

WROBLE, ARTHUR GERARD, retired former judge; s. Arthur Stanley and Sophia P. Wroble; m. Mary Ellen Sheehan, Nov. 19, 1977; children: Sophia Ann, Sarah Jean, Stacey Margaret. BSBA with honors, U. Fla., Gainesville, 1970, MBA, 1971, JD, 1973. Bar: Fla. 1973, US Ct. Appeals (5th cir.) 1974, US Dist. Ct. (so. dist.) Fla. 1974, US Supreme Ct. 1976, US Ct. Appeals (11th cir.) 1981, US Dist. Ct. (mid. dist.) 1982, US Dist. Ct. (no. dist.) Fla. 1986, US Army Ct. Mil. Rev. 1989, US Ct. Mil. Appeals 1990, Fla. Supreme Ct. Cir./County Mediator 2007. Ptnr. Burns, Middleton, Farrell & Faust, Palm Beach, Fla., 1973—80, Steel, Hector, Davis, Burns, Middleton, et al (merger), Palm Beach, 1980—82, Wolf, Block, Schorr & Solis-Cohen, Phila. & West Palm Beach, 1982-87, Scott, Royce, Harris & Bryan, PA, Palm Beach, Fla., 1987-89, Grantham and Wroble, PA, Lake Worth, Fla., 1989-92; prin. Arthur G. Wroble, PA, West Palm Beach, 1992—2001; cir. judge 15th Jud. Ct. Fla., Palm Beach, 2001—07. Mem. 15th Jud. Cir. Ct. Nominating Commn., 1979-83; mem. U. Fla. Law Ctr. Coun., 1981-84, 99—, US Magistrate Merit Selection Panel, so. dist. Fla., 1987; adv. bd. alternative sentencing program Palm Beach County Pub. Defender's Office; adj. instr. bus. law Coll. Boca Raton (now Lynn U.), 1988; 16th Dist. Screening Com. US Svc. Acad., Fla., 2001-07, 22nd Dist. US Svc. Acad. Screening Com., Fla., 2011-13. Contbr. articles to profl. jours. Bd. dirs. Palm Glades Girl Scout Coun., 1996—2006, 2006—08; co-chmn. profl. devel. United Way, 1984—85; dir. Leadership Palm Beach County, 1990—92. Served to lt. col. JAG, USAR. Named Eagle Scout, Boy Scouts Am., 1962; named to Athletic Hall Fame, Bishop Moore HS, Orlando, Fla., 1997; recipient AV Preeminent, Martindale-Hubbell, 2011 Mem. ABA, Fla. Acad. Profl. Mediators, Fla. Bar (bd. govs. young lawyers sect. 1979-83, bd. govs. 1985-89), Palm Beach County Bar Assn. (pres. young lawyers sect. 1978-79, bd. dirs. 1979-81, sec. treas. 1981-83, pres. 1984-85), Fla. Bar Found. (bd. dirs. 1990-93), Fla. Assn. Women Lawyers, Fla. Coun. Bar Assn. Pres. (bd. dirs. 1986-92), Hispanic Bar Assn. of Palm Beach County, F.M. Cunningham Sr. Bar Assn., Guild Cath. Lawyers Diocese Palm Beach, Inc. (pres. 1980-81, bd. dirs. 1981-2001, Monsignor Jeremiah P. O'Mahoney Outstanding Lawyer award 1993), Legal Aid Soc. Palm Beach County, Inc. (bd. dirs. 1981-2000), Univ. Fla. Alumni Assn., Palm Beach County Gator Club (pres. 1983-84), West Palm Beach, Fla., Kiwanis Club (pres. 1980-81, pres. West Palm Beach found. 1989-2000, dir. 1991-2007, Citizen of Yr. 1994, George F. Hixon fellowship 1999), KC (grand knight, Council 2075, 1978-79), Am. Inns of Ct. LIV (West Palm Beach chpt. pres. 1999-2000, bd. dirs. 1995-2000, emeritus 2000), Am. Legion, Knights of Columbus (life). Roman Catholic. Achievements include 87% of decisions as circuit judge reviewed on appeal were affirmed; rated AV preeminent, the highest possible peer review in Legal Ability & Ethical Standards by Martindale-Hubbell for 25 years in 2011.

WROTEN, DAVID, medical association administrator; BA in Fin., Ark. State U., MBA, 1983. Bus. cons. officer Small Bus. Devel. Ctr., Ark. State U., Jonesboro; profl. rels. coord. Ark. Med. Soc., Little Rock, 1983—86, asst. exec. v.p., 1986—2005, exec. v.p., 2005—. Pres., CEO AMS Benefits Inc.; mem. Gov.'s Medicaid Adv. Com. Named to The Power List, ArkansasBusiness.com, 2009. Mem.: Ark Soc. Assn. Executives (pres. 2002—03), Am. Assn. Med. Soc. Executives, Am. Soc. Assn. Executives. Office: Ark Med Soc PO Box 55088 #10 Corporate Hill Dr Ste 300 Little Rock AR 72215 Office Phone: 501-224-8967. Office Fax: 501-224-6489. Business E-Mail: dwroten@arkmed.org.

WROTH, JAMES MELVIN, retired military officer; b. Lincoln, Nebr., Feb. 2, 1929; s. Charles M. and Reba (Sharp) Wroth; m. Donna Mae Benson, June 4, 1951 (dec.); children: Mark, David S., Mary E.; m. Molly B. Mullan, June 15, 1975; stepchildren: Edward H. Mullan(dec.), Philip C. Mullan. BS, U. Nebr., 1951; postgrad., F.A. Sch., 1955—56, Command and Gen. Staff Coll., 1962—63; MBA, Syracuse U., 1963; with, Armed Forces Staff Coll., 1967; postgrad., Army War Coll., 1968, Harvard U., 1972. Commd. 2d lt. US Army, 1951, advanced through grades to brig. gen., 1973, U.S. Army, Republic of Korea, 1952-53; instr. A.A.A. Sch., Ft. Bliss, Tex., 1954-56; with 3d Inf. Div., Ft. Benning, Ga., also Germany, 1957-61; with Office Chief of Staff US Army, 1963-66; comdg. officer 1st Bn. 31st Arty., Republic of Korea, 1967; exec. asst. to asst. sec. US Army, 1968-70; exec. officer I Field Force Vietnam Arty., 1970; comdg. officer 52d Arty. Group, Vietnam, 1971; with Office Dep. Chief Staff for Personnel, Dept. Army, 1972-75; comdg. gen. VII Corps Arty. and Augsburg Germany Mil. Community, 1975-77; comdr. 2d ROTC region, Ft. Knox, Ky., 1977-79; ret., 1979; v.p., dir. mgmt. scis. ops. Gen. Research Corp., McLean, Va., 1979-82; group v.p Info. Systems & Network Corp., Bethesda, Md., 1982-93; pres. J-Tech, Inc., 1993—96. Trustee Washington Adventist Hosp. Found., 1989—93. Decorated D.S.M., Legion of Merit, Bronze Star, Air Medal with V device, Army Commendation medal, Vietnamese Gallantry Cross with palm; recipient F. A. Assn. award, 1950, John J. Pershing award, 1951, 40 and 8 award, 1951, Presdl. Unit Citation, US Coast Guard, 2005. Mem.: U.S. Coast Guard Aux. (past flotilla comdr.), Mil. Officers Assn. (past chpt. pres.), Nat Soc. Pershing Rifles (past nat. comdr.), Indian Creek Yacht and Country Club (dir. 2000—03), Indian Creek Yacht Club (past commodore), Beta Gamma Sigma, Alpha Kappa Psi. Personal E-mail: jim.wroth@us.army.mil.

WRUBLE, BRIAN FREDERICK, investor; b. Kalamazoo, Apr. 18, 1943; s. Milton and Rose Muriel (Nathanson) W.; m. Susan Roberta Shifrin, June 23, 1968 (div. Oct. 1984); children: Amy Carolyn, Jordan Todd; m. Kathleen Wilson Bratton, Apr. 20, 1985; 1 child, Henrietta Zane Bratton. BEE, Cornell U., 1965, MEE, 1966; MBA with distinction, NYU, 1976. Field engr. Sperry Gyroscope Corp., Lake Success, NY, 1966—70; v.p. Alliance One Instl. Svcs., Inc., NYC, 1970—76, H. C. Wainwright and Co., Inc., NYC, 1976-77, Wainwright Securities, Inc., NYC, 1977; v.p., co-mgr. fundamental equities rsch. Smith Barney, Harris Upham & Co., NYC, 1977-79; exec. v.p. chief fin. ops. Equitable Life Assurance Soc. U.S., NYC, 1979-92; chmn., pres., CEO Equitable Capital Mgmt. Corp., NYC, 1985-92; chief investment officer Equitable Life Assurance Soc. U.S., NYC, 1991-92; pres., COO, dir. Delaware Mgmt. Holdings, Inc., 1992-95; pres., CEO The Delaware Group, 1992-95; pres., COO Delaware Mgmt. Co., 1992-95; chmn. Delaware Distributors, Inc., 1992-95; chmn., CEO Delaware Svc. Co., Inc., 1992—95; gen. ptnr. Odyssey Ptnrs., L.P., NYC, 1995—2007; mng. prin. Odyssey Investment Ptnrs., LLC, NYC, 1997—98, spl. ltd. ptnr., 1999—2004. Chmn., pres. Equitable Realty Assets Corp., Atlanta, 1983—92; v.p., dir. TELMARI, Inc., NYC, 1982—83, Equitable Variable Life Ins. Co., 1987—92; chmn. Equico Capital Corp., NYC, 1984—92; CEO Equitable Gen. of Okla., Oklahoma City, 1985—86; trustee Equitable Retirement Plans, NYC, 1980—86; trustee bd. III Oppenheimer Funds, 2001—, trustee bd. I, 2005—, chmn. bd. I, 2006—; pres. Hudson River Trust, 1991—92, Equitable Funds, 1991—92, The Jackson Lab., 1999—2007, chmn., 2007—11; mem. investment adv. bd. Zurich Fin. Svc. Group, 2004—07, mem. investment mgmt. adv. coun., 2008—; dir. Spl. Value Opportunities Fund LLC, 2004—. Vice-chmn. Boys Choir of Harlem, NYC, 1984—92; vice chmn. Corp. Ptnrs. Phila. Art Mus., 1993—95; bd. govs. Jerome Levy Econ. Inst., 1990—2001; bd. dirs. Harlem Youth Devel. Found., 1989—92, Corp. Ptnrs. Phila. Art Mus., 1992—95, The Jackson Lab. Corp., 1991—99, Inst. for Advanced Study, 1992—, treas., 2006—. Recipient Heroes award Boys Choir Harlem, 1990, Founders award, 1993. Mem.: IEEE, Phila. C. of C. (bd. dirs. 1992—95, mem. exec. com. 1993—95), Inst. CFAs (CFA, bd. trustees 1992—98, vice chmn. 1993—94, chmn. 1994—95, bd. trustees rsch. found. 1994—95, 2000—02, assoc. editor CFA Digest 1983—), N.Y. Soc. Security Analysts, Assn. Investment Mgmt. and Rsch. (gov. 1992—98, C. Steward Sheppard award 2000). Republican. Jewish. Avocations: skiing, amateur radio. Home: 1107 Key Pl Box 447 Key West FL 33040-4077

WU, GUOYAO, animal scientist, nutritionist, educator; b. China, July 28, 1962; s. Fanjiu Wu and Meixiao Huang; m. Yan Chen, Aug. 7, 1995; 1 child, Neil David. BS in Animal Sci., South China Agrl. U., 1982; MS in Animal Nutrition, Beijing Agrl. U., 1984; MS in Animal

Biochemistry, U. Alta., Can., 1986, PhD in Animal Biochemistry, 1989; postgrad. in metabolism/diabetes, McGill U., Mont., Can., 1989-91; postgrad. in biochemistry, Meml. U. Nfld., Can., 1991. Grad. tchg. asst. U. Alta., 1985-88; postdoctoral rschr. Royal Victoria Hosp., McGill U., 1989-91, Meml. U. Nfld., 1991; asst. prof. dept. animal sci. and faculty nutrition Tex. A&M U., College Station, 1991-96, assoc. prof., 1996—. Reviewer Amino Acids, Am. Jour. Clin. Nutrition, Am. Jour. Physiology, Analytical Biochemistry, Biochimica et Biophysica Acta, Can. Jour. Physiology and Pharmacology, Diabetes, Diabetologia, Gastroenterology, Gene, Hormone and Metabolic Rsch., Jour. Animal Sci., Jour. Nutrition, Jour. Nutritional Biochemistry, Jour. Cellular Physiology, Metabolism, Poultry Sci., Reproduction-Nutrition-Devel., Can. Diabetes Assn., Med. Rsch. Coun. Can., U. Toronto Banting and Best Ctr., Can.; editl. advisor Biochem. Jour., 1993—; mem. editl. bd. Jour. Nutrition, 1997—; contbr. articles to profl. jours. Grantee Tex. A&M U., 1992—, Ajinomoto Inc., Japan, 1992, USDA, 1992—, Houston Livestock Show and Rodeo, 1992-95, Am. Heart Assn., 1995—; nat. scholarship for grad. studies abroad Ministry Edn. China, 1984-86, grad. tchg. assistantship U. Alta., 1985-88, dissertation fellowship, 1989, Ctr. Rsch. Fund award, 1988, Andrew Stewart Grad. prize, 1989, U. Alberta, Can. Rsch. Inst. fellowship Royal Victoria Hosp., 1988, fellowship Can. Diabetes Assn., 1989, Med. Rsch. Coun. Can. fellow, 1989-91; established investigator Am. Heart Assn., 1998—. Mem. AAAS, Am. Diabetes Assn., Am. Heart Assn., Am. Soc. for Nutritional Scis., Am. Heart Assn., Am. Physiol. Soc., Am. Soc. Animal Sci., Biochem. Soc. U.K., Can. Soc. Nutritional Scis., Juv. Diabetes Found. Internat. (grantee 1992-94), Soc. for the Study of Reproduction. Home: 4707 Shoal Creek Dr College Station TX 77845-4410 Office: Tex A&M Univ Dept Animal Sci College Station TX 77843-0001

WU, HSIU KWANG, economist, educator; b. Hankow, China, Dec. 14, 1935; came to U.S., 1952, naturalized, 1963; s. Kao Cheng and Edith (Huang) W.; m. Kathleen Gibbs Johnson, Aug. 17, 1968. Grad., Lawrenceville Sch., 1954; AB, Princeton U., 1958; MBA, U. Pa., 1960, PhD, 1963. Prof., group coordinator fin., econs. and internat. bus. Boston U., 1968-72; prof., chmn. fin., econs. and legal studies faculty U. Ala., 1972-81, Lee Bidgood prof. fin. and econs., 1978-97, Ala. Banker Edn. Found. Banking Chair prof., 1973-78, prof. emeritus fin., 1997—; econ. adviser Office of Comptroller of Currency, U.S. Treasury, 1966-69, 75-80; dir. Ala. Fed., 1984-88, SECOR Bank FSB, 1988-93, chmn. bd., 1992-93. Cons. instl. investor study SEC, 1969-70; mem. com. examiners undergrad. program for counseling and evaluation test in bus. Ednl. Testing Service, 1971, 77 Co-editor: Elements of Investments, 2d rev. edit, 1972; Contbr. articles to law and econ. jours. Sloan Faculty fellow Sloan Sch. Mgmt., Mass. Inst. Tech., 1965-66 Mem. Am. Fin. Assn., Fin. Mgmt. Assn. Home: 3201 Old Barn Ct Ponte Vedra Beach FL 32082-3713

WU, JIE, electronics engineer, educator; d. Fu Chen Wu and Zheng Chen Yu; life ptnr. Michael Heinz Stoiber. B in Engring., Hefei U. Tech., Hefei, Anhui Prov., China, 1993; MS in Engring., Hefei U. Tech., 1996; PhD, Chinese Acad. of Scis., Shanghai, P.R. China, 1999, U. Notre Dame, Notre Dame, Ind., 2004. Rsch. assoc. U. Notre Dame, Ind., 2003—04; asst. prof. U. Tenn., Knoxville, 2004—. Contbr. articles to profl. jour. Recipient Faculty Early Career Devel. Award, NSF, 2005, Ralph E. Powe Jr. Faculty Award, Oak Ridge Associated Univ., 2006; grantee Rate-Based Sensor Devel. for Advancing Heat Transfer Measurements, NSF. Achievements include patents pending for method and apparatus for AC micropump; method and apparatus for enhancing microbial detection; parallel plate electrodes for particle concentrate or removal; rate-based sensors for advanced real-time analysis and diagnosis; patents for AC electrothermal techniques for microfluidics maniplulation. Office: U Tenn 1508 Middle Dr Knoxville TN 37996 Office Fax: 865-974-5483. Personal E-mail: jaynewu@utk.edu.

WU, LI-TZY, alcohol and drug abuse services professional, researcher; d. Yu-Tsai and Yu-Chi Wu; m. Hsin-Hsong Tseng, Apr. 20, 1992; children: Jonathan Tseng, Harrison Tseng. DSc, Johns Hopkins U., 1998. RN N.J., 1993. Psychiat. epidemiologist RTI Internat., Research Triangle Park, NC, 1999—2005; assoc. prof. Sch. Medicine Duke U., Durham, NC, 2005—. Recipient Nat. Inst. on Drug Abuse Women and Gender Jr. Investigator Travel award, 2001; grantee, Nat. Inst. Drug Abuse, 2000—, Nat. Inst. Alcohol Abuse and Alcoholism, 2001—03; fellow, NIH, 1997—99. Mem.: Coll. on Problems of Drug Dependence, Delta Omega (Alpha chpt.).

WUBBENA, JAN HELMUT, music professor; b. Dover, Del., July 11, 1947; s. Wyatt Jan and Erika Luise Wubbena; m. Teresa Lee Roper, May 17, 1980; children: Robert, Mary. BA, Lebanon Valley Coll., Annville, Pa., 1969; MusM, U. Colo., Boulder, 1970, D of Mus. Arts, 1975. Asst. prof. music Ferrum Coll., Va., 1975—77; prof. music John Brown U., Siloam Springs, Ark., 1977—. Organist, choirmaster Grace Episcopal Ch., Siloam Springs, 1977—. Composer: (choral work) With Every Power for Good, 1980, There is a Land of Pure Delight, 1999, Guide Us Waking Lord, 2002. Fellow: Am. Guild Organists (assoc.; chpt. dean 1982—84, coord. for edn. in Region VII 1984—88, chair nat. com. on ednl. resources 1988—90, dist. convenor for Ark. 2006—); mem.: Assn. Anglican Musicians. Episcopalian. Home: 410 E Jefferson St Siloam Springs AR 72761 Office: John Brown Univ 2000 W University Ave Siloam Springs AR 72761 Office Phone: 479-524-7159. Personal E-mail: wubbenark@cox.net. Business E-Mail: jwubbena@jbu.edu.

WUCHNER, ADDIA KATHRYN, state legislator; b. June 8, 1955; Ret. hosp. adminstr.; mem. Dist. 66 Ky. House of Reps., 2005—; mem. Banking & Ins. Com., Edn. Com., Health & Welfare Com. Republican. Roman Catholic. Address: PO Box 911 Burlington KY 41005 Office: 424A Capitol Annex Frankfort KY 40601 Office Phone: 859-525-6698, 502-564-8100 ext. 707.

WUERKER, MATT, cartoonist, illustrator; Editorial cartoonist, illustrator The Politico, Washington, 2006—. Mem. Sarah Thaves' CartoonistGroup. Work published in Funny Times, New York Times, The Nation, The American Prospect, and Z Magazine, Los Angeles Times, Washington Post, Christian Science Monitor, Time, Smithsonian and others, staff artists Jim Hightower's Lowdown, collections of works published in Standing Tall in Deep Doo Doo, A Cartoon Chronicle of the Bush Quayle Years, 1991, Meanwhile in Other News...A Graphic Look at Politics in the Empire of Money, Sex and Scandal, 1998; co-author: The Madness of King George, 2003. Recipient Herblock prize, 2010, Nat. Press Found. Berryman award, 2010, Pulitzer Prize in Editorial Cartooning, 2012; finalist, 2009, 2010. Mem.: Assn. of American Editorial Cartoonists. Office: POLITICO 1100 Wilson Blvd Ste 610 Arlington VA 22209

WULF, WILLIAM ALLAN, engineering educator; b. Chgo., Dec. 8, 1939; s. Otto H. and Helen W. (Westermeier) Wulf; m. Anita K. Jones, July 1, 1977; children: Karin, Ellen. BS, U. Ill., 1961, MSEE, 1963; PhD in Computer Sci., U. Va., 1968. Prof. computer sci. Carnegie-Mellon Univ., Pitts., 1968—81; chmn., CEO Tartan Labs., Pitts., 1981—87; univ. prof., AT&T prof. engring. U. Va., Charlottesville, Va., 1988—. Bd. dir. Inst. Women; asst. dir. NSF, Washington, 1988—90; cons. various computer mfrs. Author: Fundamental Structures of Computer Science, 1981. Bd. dirs. Pitts. High Tech. Coun., 1982—88. Recipient Kenneth Andrew Roe award, Am. Assn. Engring. Socs., 2001, Chair's award, 2007. Fellow: AAAS, IEEE (IEEE-U.S.A. award for Disting. Pub. Svc. 2009), Assn. Women in Sci., Assn. Computing Machinery, Venezuelian Acad. Engring., Am. Philos. Soc.; mem.: NAE (pres. 1996—2007, councillor), Chinese Acad. Engring., Japanese Acad. Engring., Russian Acad. Sci., Spanish Acad. Engring., Am. Acad. Arts and Scis. Avocations: woodworking, photography. Office: Dept Computer Sci Univ Va Thornton Hall Charlottesville VA 22901

WUORI, STEPHEN J., energy executive; BS in Civil Engring., Mich. Technol. U., Houghton. Pres. Enbridge Pipelines Inc. and Enbridge Energy Ptnrs., L.P. Enbridge, Inc., 1997—2000, group v.p. planning and devel., 2001—03, group v.p., CFO, 2003—06, exec. v.p., CFO & corp. devel., 2006—08, exec. v.p. liquid pipelines, 2008—. Office: Enbridge Energy Ptnrs LP 1100 Louisiana Ste 3300 Houston TX 77002 Office Phone: 713-821-2000.

WÜRSIG, BERND GERHARD, marine biology educator; b. Barsinghausen, Germany, Nov. 9, 1948; s. Gerhard Paul and Charlotte Annemarie (Yorkowski) Würsig; m. Melany Anne Carballeira, Nov. 19, 1969; children: Kim Wuersig, Paul Wuersig. BS, Ohio State U., 1971; PhD, SUNY, Stony Brook, 1978. Postdoct. rschr. U. Calif., Santa Cruz, 1978-81; prof. Moss Landing (Calif.) Marine Labs., 1981-89; prof. marine biology, dir. Marine Mammal Lab. Tex. A&M U., Galveston, 1989—, Regents prof., 2006—, dir. The Inst. of Marine Life Scis., 1996—2012, chair, inter disciplinary program grad. studies marine biology, 2008—10, disting. prof., 2013—. Govt. cons. Minerals Mgmt. Svc., Washington, 1980—; George P. Mitchell academic chair. Contbr. articles to profl. jours., 7-part miniseries to TV on lives of dolphins, dolphin problems induced by humans, also Discovery Channel show on Life of B Würsig; co-author: The Hawaiian Spinner Dolphin, 1994, Whales, Dolphins and Porpoises, 1995; sr. advisor (IMAX film) Dolphins, 2000 (nominee Acad. award best spl. category nature movie), sr. author The Marine Mammals of the Gulf of Mexico, 2000; co-editor: The Encyclopedia of Marine Mammals, 2002, 2nd edit., 2009, The Dusky Dolphin: Master Acrobat Off Different Shores, 2010. Recipient Chmn.'s award for rsch. and exploration, Nat. Geog. Soc., 1998, Alban-Heiser award for excellence in Tex. conservation rsch., Zool. Soc. Houston, 1991, Regents Professorship award, Tex. A&M U., 2006, Disting. Achievement award, 2008, Disting. Prof. award, 2013, Elected Piper Prof. award, 2010, George Mitchell Chair award, Sustainable Fisheries, 2012; Fulbright Found. scholar, 2001—03. Mem. Marine Mammal Soc. (pres. 1991-93), N.Y. Acad. Scis., Soc. Cryptozoology, Am. Behavior Soc., Am. Mus. Natural History, Soc. Archimedes. Clubs: Explorers (N.Y.C.) (fellow of research). Avocations: photography, diving, skiing, hiking, aviation. Home: 2402 Creekridge Dr Pearland TX 77581-5728 Office Phone: 409-740-4413. Business E-Mail: wursigb@tamug.edu.

WURTZ, GEORGE W., III, consumer products company executive; b. LI, NY, June 19, 1956; BS in Indsl. Arts & Tech., SUNY, Oswego, 1978. Various mfg. positions Miller Brewing Co. (divsn. Phillip Morris), 1978—87; dir., logistics James River Corp., Norwalk, Conn., 1987—90, sr. v.p., ops., 1987—95, dir., mfg. planning Norwalk, Conn., 1990—91, plant mgr. Berlin Gorham, NH, 1991—94; v.p., procurement Fort James, Norwalk, 1994—97, sr. v.p., ops., 1995—2001, sr. v.p. logistics and procurement Deerfield, Ill., 1997—98, sr. v.p. mfg., 1998—2001; sr. v.p., consumer products mfg. control Georgia-Pacific LLC, Green Bay, Wis., 2001, pres., paper, bleached bd. & kraft Atlanta, 2001—03, exec. v.p., pres., pulp & paper, 2002—06; owner WinCup; pres., CEO New WinCup Holdings, 2007—. Mem.: Am. Prodn. Inventory Control Soc., Coun. Logistics Mgmt., Paper Distbn. Coun., Nat. Paper Trade Assn., Am. Forest & Paper Assn., Brotherhood Eagles. Office: WinCup 4640 Lewis Rd Stone Mountain GA 30083 Office Phone: 770-938-5281. Office Fax: 770-493-8884. Business E-Mail: georgewurtz@wincup.com.

WYATT, DAVID W., state legislator; Farmer; judge Independence County, Ark.; mem. Dist. 72 Ark. House of Reps., 2005—08; mem. Dist. 12 Ark. State Senate, 2009—. Democrat. Baptist. Mailing: 159 Wyatt Ln Batesville AR 72501 Office Phone: 870-613-3014. Business E-Mail: wyattd@arkleg.state.ar.us.

WYATT, FRANK B., II, lawyer; Atty. Bell, Seltzer, Park & Gibson, P.A. (now Alston & Bird LLP); gen. counsel, sec. CommScope, Inc., 1996—, sr. v.p., 2000—, corp. compliance and ethics officer. Office: CommScope Inc 1100 CommScope Pl SE Hickory NC 28602 Office Phone: 828-324-2200. Office Fax: 828-982-1708. Business E-Mail: frank.wyatt@andrew.com.

WYCHE, CYRIL THOMAS, lawyer; b. Greenville, SC, Jan. 28, 1926; C. Granville and Mary (Wheeler) W.; m. Harriet Smith, June 19, 1948; children: Sara McCall, Bradford Wheeler, Mary Frances. BE, Yale U., 1946; LLB, U. Va., 1949; LLD (hon.), Clemson U., 1997, Furman U., 1997; HLD (hon.), Wofford Coll. Bar: S.C. 1948, U.S. Dist. Ct. S.C. 1950, U.S. Ct. Appeals (4th cir.) 1952, U.S. Ct. Claims 1964, U.S. Supreme Ct. 1970. Ptnr. Wyche, Burgess, Freeman & Parham, P.A., Greenville, SC, 1948—. Pres., bd. dirs. YMCA, Greenville, 1960; pres. Greenville Little Theatre, 1965, Arts Festival Assn., Greenville, 1970, Greenville Community Corp., 1976—; bd. dirs. Greater Greenville C. of C., 1980. Served with USN, 1943-46. Named Environmentalist of Yr., State of S.C., 1979; recipient Conservation award Gulf Oil Corp., 1983, Alexander Calder award, 1996, Garden Clubs Am., 1999, Oak Leaf award The Nature Conservancy, 1996, Order of the Palmetto award S.C. Gov., 1996. Mem. ABA (Environ. award 2002), S.C. Bar Assn., Greenville County Bar Assn., Am. Judicature Soc., Nat. Wildlife Fedn. (Spl. Conservation Achievement award 2003). Presbyterian. Avocations: skiing, scuba diving, piano, tennis, white water canoeing. Office: Wyche Burgess Freeman & Parham 44 E Camperdown Way PO Box 728 Greenville SC 29602-0728 Home Phone: 864-288-6049; Office Phone: 864-242-8213. E-mail: twyche@wyche.com.

WYCHE, MADISON BAKER, III, lawyer; b. Albany, Ga., Aug. 11, 1947; s. Madison Baker Jr. and Merle (McKemie) W.; m. Marguerite Jernigan Ramage, Aug. 7, 1971; children: Madison Baker IV, James Ramage. BA, Vanderbilt U., 1969, JD, 1972. Bar: Ga. 1972, U.S. Dist. Ct. (mid. dist.) Ga. 1972, U.S. Ct. Appeals (5th cir.) 1973, S.C. 1976, U.S. Dist. Ct. S.C. 1977, U.S. Ct. Appeals (4th cir.) 1977, U.S. Supreme Ct. 1980, U.S. Ct. Appeals (11th cir.) 1981, U.S. Dist. Ct. (no. dist.) Ga. 1995. Assoc. Perry, Walters, Lippitt & Custer, Albany, 1972-76, Thompson, Ogletree & Deakins, Greenville, SC, 1976-77, Ogletree, Deakins, Smoak & Stewart, Greenville, 1977-80; shareholder Ogletree, Deakins, Nash, Smoak & Stewart P.C., Greenville, 1980—. Bd. dirs. Happy Ho., Inc., Albany, 1975. Co-editor Labor and Employment Law for South Carolina Lawyers, 1999, 4th edit., 2011. Co-incorporator, sec. Tenn. Intercollegiate State Legislature, Nashville, 1967-69; mem. employer and employee rels. com., legal issues & workplace policy com. N.C. Citizens for Bus. and Industry, Raleigh, 1984—2009; mem. Greenville C. of C., gen. counsel, 2003-06, bd. dirs., 2003-06; mem. Advantage Greenville, Greenville Chamber Found., 2003-06; United Way Greenville; bd. dirs. Palmetto Soc. of the United Way, 1992-2004; mem. vestry Christ Episcopal Ch., Greenville, 1981-85; treas. All Saints Episcopal Ch., Linville, NC 2001-05; mem. bd. visitors Clemson U., 1998-2001, mem. profl. advancement and continuing edn. bd., 2003—; bd. dirs. Blue Ridge coun. Boy Scouts Am., 1999-2000; bd. dirs. Internat. Arts Festival, ARTISPHERE, Greenville, 2003—, gen. counsel, 2006—09. Capt. US Army, 1969—77. Recipient Eagle Scouts award Boy Scouts Am., 1961, God and Country award, 1961, named One Hundred Most Powerful Employment Lawyers in America, 2009-10, named one of Best Lawyers in America, 2008-11, SC Super Lawyers, 2008-10. Mem. ABA, Coll. Labor and Employment Lawyers, SC Bar Assn. (unauthorized practice of law com. 1977-95, chmn. 1982-92, ho. of dels. 1991-98, 2004—, nominating com. 1992-95, CLE divsn., chmn., 1997-98, exec. com. 1995-99, chmn. seminars subcom. 1995-97), Ga. Bar Assn., Atlanta Bar Assn., S.C. Def. Trial Lawyers Assn., St. Andrews Soc. Upper S.C. (bd. dirs. 1979-81, v.p. 1986-87, pres. 1988-90, heritage com. chmn. 1998—), Vanderbilt U. Alumni Assn. (pres. S.C. chpt. 1990-95, bd. dirs. 1994—), The Poinsett Club (v.p., bd. dirs., 2000-02, 09-, pres., 2010, v.p. 2011) (Greenville, S.C.), Rotary (bd. dirs. 1982-84, Paul Harris fellow 1986), Commerce Club of Greenville (bd. dirs. 1990-2007), Phi Delta Phi. Office: Ogletree Deakins Nash Smoak & Stewart PO Box 2757 Greenville SC 29602-2757 Office Phone: 864-271-1300.

WYLIE, FORREST E., energy executive; BBA, U. Houston; MBA, U. Tex., Austin. Mgmt. positions American Exploration Co.; sr. mgmt. positions Transocean Sedco Forex, 1993—97; sr. v.p. nat. gas trading Coastal Corp. & Engage Energy, 1997—2000; pres., CFO NuCoastal Corp., 2002—05; chmn., CEO Buckeye Partners, LP, 2007—12, non-exec. chmn., 2012—. Vice chmn. Pacific Energy Mgmt. LLC, 2005—06; bd. dirs. The Cross Group, Inc., Coastal Energy Co., 2006—11, Eagle Bulk Shipping Inc., 2007—10. Office: Buckeye Partners LP One Greenway Plz Houston TX 77046

WYLLY, BARBARA BENTLEY, volunteer; b. Bala-Cynwyd, Pa., June 10, 1924; d. William Henry and Virginia (Barclay) Bentley; m. William Beck Wylly, Apr. 26, 1947; children: Virginia Wylly Johnson, Barbara Wylly Klausman, Thomas C. II. A, Briarcliff Jr. Coll., 1943. Pres. bd. dirs. Hillside Hosp. Inc., Atlanta, 1982, mem. adv. coun., 1982—; pres. Atlanta Symphony Assocs., 1975—76, mem. adv. bd., 1976—; chmn. bd. dirs. Ctr. Puppetry Arts, Atlanta, 1988—2004, mem. exec. com., 1988—. Bd. dirs. Mountain Conservation Trust, 1996—, Atlanta Opera Guild, 1999—2012; mem. bd. sponsors Georgian Chamber Players, 2000—11. Republican. Episcopalian. Avocations: walking, reading, music. Office: Ctr Puppetry Arts 1404 Spring St NW Atlanta GA 30309-2820 Home: 1223 Lenbrook 3747 Peachtree Rd Atlanta GA 30319

WYLY, SAMUEL E., entrepreneur; b. La., 1934; married; 6 children. Founder University Computing Co., 1963-79; co-owner, chmn. Bonanza Steakhouse, 1967-89; founder Datran, Inc., 1968; co-founder, mem. exec. com. Earth Resources Co., 1968-80; co-founder, chmn. Sterling Software, Inc., 1981—; chmn. Michaels Stores Inc., Irving, Tex., 1984—. Founder Sam Wyly Found., 1968—. Author: 1,000 Dollars and an Idea: Entrepreneur to Billionaire, 2008. Recipient Murphy award for Lifetime Entrepreneurial Achievement, Murphy Ctr., U. North Tex., 2003; named one of Forbes 400: Richest Americans, 2006—.

WYMAN, RICHARD THOMAS, retired information technology manager, researcher; b. Wilmington, Del., June 4, 1951; s. William Harper and Marian Kathryn (Bode) W., Pa. State U., 1969-71, Def. Language Inst., 1974-75, Control Data Inst., Dallas, 1979. Enlisted U.S. Army, 1971, served to staff sgt., 1979; data ctr. mgr. thrift svcs. divsn. ADP Inc., Dallas, 1979-80; support mgr. Electronic Data Sys., Inc., Dallas, 1980-85, info. modeling analyst, 1985-90; pres. Strategic InfoSource, Plano, Tex., 1991-93; sr. cons. The SABRE Group, Ft. Worth, 1993-97; assoc. Perot Sys. Corp., Richardson, Tex., 1997-98; info. architect The Technical Resource Connection, Inc., Tampa, Fla., 1998—2005; enterprise architect Perot Sys. Corp., Plano, Tex., 2005—10. Rep. 101st Airborne Divsn. Nat. Conf. Skill Maintenance, Ft. Meade, Md., 1977. Author: (spl. course) U.S. Army Intelligence, 1978-79. Co-chmn. sub-com. City Bond Referendum Com., Plano, 1990; mem. City of Plano Hist. Landmark Com., 1993-97, vice chmn. 1996, chmn. 1996-97, mem. Vols. Plano, 2010-. Recipient Army Commendation medal, 1978, 79, Vol. Svc. award, Office of Mayor, Plano, 1990. Achievements include patents pending for computer system and process for aiding in an outsourcing environment. Home: 3608 Trailview Dr Plano TX 75074

WYNGAARDEN, JAMES BARNES, retired physician; b. East Grand Rapids, Mich., Oct. 19, 1924; s. Martin Jacob and Johanna (Kempers) W.; m. Ethel Vredevoogd, June 20, 1946 (div. 1977); children: Patricia Wyngaarden Fitzpatrick, Joanna Wyngaarden Gandy, Martha Wyngaarden Krauss, Lisa Wyngaarden, James Barnes Jr. Student, Calvin Coll., 1942—43, Western Mich. U., 1943—44; MD, U. Mich., 1948; DSc (hon.), U. Mich., Med. Coll. of Ohio, 1984, U. Ill., 1985, George Washington U., 1986, U. SC, West Mich. U., 1989, Duke U., 2006; PhD (hon.), Tel Aviv U., 1987. Diplomate Am. Bd. Internal Medicine. Intern Mass. Gen. Hosp., Boston, 1948-49, resident, 1949-51; vis. investigator Pub. Health Rsch. Inst., NYC, 1952-53; investigator NIH, USPHS, Bethesda, Md., 1953-56; asso. prof. medicine and biochemistry Duke U. Med. Sch., 1956-61, prof., 1961-65; vis. scientist Inst. Biologie-Physiochemique, Paris, 1963-64; prof., chmn. U. Pa. Med. Sch., 1965-67; physician-in-chief Med. Svc. Hosp. U. PA., Phila., 1965-67; Frederic M. Hanes prof., chmn. dept. medicine Duke U. Sch. of Medicine, Durham, NC, 1967-82; physician-in-chief Med. Svc. Duke U. Hosp., Durham, 1967-82; chief of staff Duke U. Hosp., Durham, 1981-82; dir. NIH, Bethesda, MD, 1982-89; assoc. dir. life scis. Office of Sci. and Tech. Policy, Exec. Office of Pres., The White House, 1989-90; dir. Human Genome Orgn., 1990-91; fgn. sec. NAS, 1990-94; prof. medicine, assoc. vice chancellor for health affairs Duke U., Durham, NC, 1990-94, ret., 1994; mem. staff VA, Durham County Hosps.; sr. assoc. dean internat. med. programs U. Pa., Phila., 1995-97. Cons. Office Sci. and Tech. Exec. Office of Pres., 1966-72; Mem. Pres.'s Sci. Adv. Com., 1972-73; mem. Pres.'s Com. for Nat. Medal of Sci., 1977-80; mem. adv. com. biology and medicine AEC, 1966-68; mem. bd. sci. counselors NIH, 1971-74; mem. adv. bd. Howard Hughes Med. Inst., 1969-82; mem. adv. council Life Ins. Med. Research Fund, 1967-70; adv. bd. Sci. Yr., 1977-81; vice-chmn. Com. on Study Nat. Needs for Biomed. and Behavioral Rsch. Personnel, NRC, 1977-81; bd. dirs. Idera Pharm., prin. Wash. Adv. Group, 1995-02. Author: (with W.N. Kelley) Gout and Hyperuricemia, 1976; mem. editorial bd. Jour. Biol. Chemistry, 1971-74, Arthritis and Rheumatism, 1959-66, Jour. Clin. Investigation, 1962-66, Ann. Internal Medicine, 1964-74, Medicine, 1963-90; editor: (with J.B. Stanbury, D.S. Fredrickson) The Metabolic Basis of Inherited Disease, 1960, 66, 72, 78, 83, (with O. Sperling and A. DeVries) Purine Metabolism in Man, 1974, (with L.H. Smith, Jr.) Cecil Textbook of Medicine, 16th edit., 1982, 19th edit., 1992. Bd. dirs. Royal Soc. Medicine Found., 1971-76, The Robert Wood Johnson Found. Clin. Scholar Program, 1973-78. Ensign USNR, 1943-46; sr. surgeon USPHS, 1951-56, rear adm. USPHS, 1982-90. Recipient Borden Undergrad. Research award, U. Mich., 1948, NC Gov.'s award for sci., 1974, Disting. Alumnus award We. Mich. U., 1984, Robert Williams award Assn. Profs. Medicine, 1985, Dalton scholar in medicine, Mass. Gen. Hosp., 1950, Richard Schweiker Excellence in Govt. award, 1985, Fedn. of Am. Socs. of Exptl. Biology Pub. Svc. award, 1989, Humanitarian award Nat. Orgn. for

Rare Diseases, 1990; Royal Coll. Physicians fellow, 1984. Mem. Am. Rheumatism Assn., Am. Fedn. Clin. Rsch., So. Soc. Clin. Investigation (pres. 1974, founder's medal 1978), ACP (John Phillips Meml. award 1980), Am. Soc. Clin. Investigation, AAAS, Am. Soc. Biol. Chemists, Assn. Am. Physicians (councillor 1973-77, pres. 1978, Kober medal 1991), Endocrine Soc., Nat. Acad. Scis., Royal Acad. Scis. Sweden, Am. Acad. Arts and Sci., Inst. Medicine, Sigma Xi. Clubs: Interurban Clinical (Balt.). Democrat. Presbyterian. Avocations: tennis, skiing, painting.

WYNN, JAMES ANDREW, JR., federal judge; b. Robersonville, NC, Mar. 17, 1954; BA in Journalism, U. N.C., 1975; JD, Marquette U., 1979; LLM, U. Va., 1995. Capt. JAG Corp., USN, Norfolk, 1979-83, reserve capt., 1983—2009; asst. appellate defender State of NC, 1983-84; ptnr. Fitch, Wynn & Associates, 1984-90; judge NC Ct. of Appeals, 1990-98, 1999—2010; assoc. justice NC Supreme Ct., 1998—99; judge US Ct. Appeals (4th Cir.), 2010—. Office: US Court Appeals 1100 East Main St Richmond VA 23219

WYNN, JOHN THOMAS, retired academic administrator, farming executive, economic consultant, oil and gas producer; b. Corsicana, Tex., May 4, 1938; s. Sam Grady and Marjorie (Reese) W.; m. Sally Ruth Adams, Mar. 19, 1958 (div. 1975); children: Martha Maria, Catherine Clarissa, Lorraine Lemae; m. Myra Louise Alexander, Oct. 30, 1976; 1 child, John Thomas. AA, Wharton County Jr. Coll., 1960; BBA in Gen. Bus., Agrl. and Mech. Coll. Tex., 1962; MBA, Tex. A&M U., 1965; PhD in Higher Edn. Mgmt., U. So. Miss., 1973. Asst. registrar, then. instr. Tex. A&M U., College Station, 1962—67; exec. dean Delgado C.C., New Orleans, 1967—74, program dir., 1977—78; asst. exec. sec. So. Assn. Colls and Schs., Atlanta, 1974—77; pres. emeritus Williamsburg Tech. Coll., Kingstree, SC, 1978—94; pres., CEO econ. cons. M&W Farm & Ranch, Egypt, Tex., 1994—. Cons. AID, Dominican Republic, 1966; bd. govs. Coastal Edn. Consortium, Conway, S.C., 1982-90; mem. exec. com. pres.'s coun. S.C. Tech. Edn. Coll., Columbia, 1985-86. Vestryman St. Thomas Episc. Ch., College Station, 1962-67, St. George Episc. Ch., New Orleans, 1969-72; vestryman St. Thomas' Episc. Ch., Wharton, Tex., 1998-2001, 06—, sr. warden, 1999-2000; Rep. precinct 2 chmn., Wharton County, Tex., 1998-2000, 2008-10, 2012-14. Served as sgt. USAR, 1955-62. Recipient Order of the Palmetto S.C. Gen. Assembly, 1994; named Hon. Order of Ky. Cols.; col. Aide-de-Camp, La., col. Aide-de-Camp, Ala.; col. Aide-de-Camp, N.Mex. Mem. Future Farmers Assn. (hon.), S.C. Tech. Edn. Assn. (bd. dirs. 1985-88), Kingstree C. of C. (bd. dirs. 1981-84), Kiwanis, Masons (32 degree), Shriners (hon.), Phi Delta Kappa, Kappa Delta Pi. Avocations: chess, camping, music composition, reading. Home and Office: PO Box 307 Egypt TX 77436 Office Phone: 979-677-3572. Personal E-mail: johnthomaswynn@gmail.com, mwfr.egypt@gmail.com.

WYNN, WILL, former Mayor, Austin, Texas; b. Beaumont, Tex. m. Anne Elizabeth Wynn, 1992; 2 children. B in Environ. Design cum laude, Tex. A&M U., 1984. Founder CIVITAS Investments, Inc., 1997; mayor City of Austin, Tex., 2003—09. With Hill Country Conservancy, St. David's Found., Women and their Work, KLRU, Blanton Mus., Austin Poetry Slam, Austin Film Soc.; chmn. Downtown Austin Alliance; dir. Children's Mus. and Heritage Soc. Recipient Scenic Hero award, Scenic Austin; named Austinite of Yr., Austin Under Forty. Mem.: Urban Land Inst. Avocations: listening to music, canoeing, bicycling. Mailing: PO Box 1088 Austin TX 78767

WYNNE, DIANA S., food service executive; b. Dayton, Ohio, 1955; B in Acctg. & Pre-Law, Spelman Coll., Atlanta; M in Bus. Adminstrn. & Fin., Wright State U., Ohio. CPA Ohio. Acct. Price Waterhouse-Coopers, Deloitte & Touche, Ponderosa, Inc.; various positions including treas. and sr. v.p. Metromedia Restaurant Group; v.p., treas. Blockbuster, Inc.; sr. v.p. corp. affairs Cracker Barrel Old Country Store, Inc., 2006—. Former chairwoman Women's Foodservice Forum. Office: Cracker Barrel Old Country Store Inc Hartmann Dr Lebanon TN 37088-0787 Office Phone: 615-444-5533. Business E-Mail: Diana.wynne@crackerbarrel.com.

WYNNE, TERRY LYNNE, career counselor, writer; b. Ridgeland, SC, Mar. 28, 1951; d. Herbert Ray and Carolyne (Taylor) W. BA, Ga. State U., 1972, MEd, 1974, EdS, 1977. Lic. profl. counselor, Ga.; nat. cert. counselor; nat. cert. career counselor, bd. cert. coach; master career counselor; master career devel. profl.; qualified to administer Myers-Briggs Type Indicator; bd. cert. coach; cert. laughter yoga leader. Asst. Ernest L. Robinson, PhD, Atlanta, 1976—77; various SunTrust Bank, Atlanta, 1971—75, 1977—84; trainer, spkr., writer Atlanta, 1980—; product info. specialist Unisys Corp., Atlanta, 1984—87; career counselor Emory U., Atlanta, 1987—96, 1997—2004, Charter Behavioral Health Sys., Atlanta, 1995—2000; owner, sole propr. Profl. Edge, Tucker, Ga., 1990—; freelance writer, 1980—. Ice skating instr. Omni Internat. Ice Skating, 1980—82; career counselor, tng. cons. grad. sch. USDA, Atlanta, 1996—2002; radio talk show host and guest; spkr. trainer Nat. and State Convs., Cruise Ships. Exhibitions include Ballroom Dance Competitor (Amateur and Pro-Am). Model for fund raising events, 2005—06. Recipient 3d pl. Maupintour Travel Photography Contest, 1991, Sullivan award Furman U., 1969, 2 Exemplary Action awards Unisys Corp., 1985, Appreciation award US Dept. Edn. Region IV, 1999, Civil Rights Southern Divn.; Ednl. Opportunity grantee Furman U., 1968. Mem. ACA, MENSA, Nat. Career Devel. Assn., Lic. Profl. Counselors Ga. Assn., Ga. Career Devel. Assn. Avocations: ballroom dance, writing, travel, photography. Personal E-mail: tlwynne@bellsouth.net.

WYRICK, CHARLES, state legislator; Bd. dirs. of several state, regional and nat. dairying promotion organizations, 1996—2003; representative Southeast Council of Dairy Farmers of America, 1998—2006; mem. Dist. 1 Okla. State Senator, Okla., 2004—. Democrat. Mailing: 58500 E 155 Rd Fairland OK 74343 Office: 2300 N Lincoln Blvd Rm 521 Oklahoma City OK 73105 Office Phone: 405-521-5561. Business E-Mail: wyrick@oksenate.gov.

WYRICK, CHARLES LLOYD, JR., editor, writer; b. Greensboro, NC, May 5, 1939; s. Charles Lloyd and Edythe Ellen (Ellis) W.; m. Constance Michelle Hooper, Aug. 22, 1964; 1 child, Charles Lloyd, III; m. Katherine Harrison, Apr. 26, 1997; 1 child, Christopher Conrad; m Sandi Turner, Jul 30, 2005 BA, Davidson Coll., NC, 1961; MFA, U. NC, 1967. Instr. Stephens Coll., Columbia, Mo., 1964—66; asst. head programs div. Va. Museum, Richmond, 1966-68; exec. dir. Assn. Preservation Va. Antiquities, Richmond, 1968-70; pres. Research & Restoration, Inc., Richmond, 1970-73; dir. Del. Art Mus., Wilmington, 1973-79, Gibbes Mus. Art, Charleston, S.C., 1980-86; pres. Wyrick & Co., Charleston, 1986—, Dixie Media, Inc., Charleston, 1989—; sr. editor Gibbs Smith, Pub., 2005—09; editor, pub. "Omnibus", 1989-94. Mem. Richmond Commn. Archt. Rev., 1969-72, New Castle County Hist. Rev. Bd., Del., 1975-88, also vice chmn.; mem. Bd. Archtl. Rev. City of Charleston, 1988-94, chmn., 1992-94; mem. Charleston Consortium on Higher Edn.; cons. in field. Author: "The 17th Street Market", 1972; contbr. articles to profl. jours. Bd. visitors Davison Coll., 1974-77; chmn. Econs. of Amenities City of Charleston, 1978; chmn. bd. dirs. SC Coastal Conservation League, 1989-94, Charleston Area Arts Coun., 1989-91, Friends of Charleston County Courthouse, 1989-94, Pub. Art Trust, 1988-90; adv. com. SC Dept. Natural Resources, 1992-2004, Halsey Inst., 2008, Arts History Comm. City Charleston, 2007-, Gibbes Mus. Art, 2010- 1st lt. US Army, 1961—63. Recipient 1st award spl. column writing Va. Press Assn., 1973 Mem. Assn. Am. Pubs., Pubs. Assn. of South (bd. dirs. 1990-92, pres. 1991-92), SC Acad. Authors (bd. dirs. 1990-92), Carolina Yacht Club, Yeamans Hall Club, Cedar Creek Racquet Club. Office: PO Box 89 Charleston SC 29402-0089 Home: 3 Chisolm St Unit 201 Charleston SC 29401-1838 Office Phone: 843-795-9946.

WYSOCKI, ANNETTE B., nurse scientist, educator; b. Raleigh, NC, Dec. 31, 1954; d. Robert Joseph and Frances (Overton) W.; m. John Nussbaum, May 2, 1987. BSN, East Carolina U., 1978, MSN, 1980; PhD, U. Tex., 1986. Staff nurse U. Va., Charlottesville, 1978-79, Seton Med. Ctr., Austin, Tex., 1981-86; rsch. and tchg. asst. U. Tex., Austin, 1982-84; sr. rsch. assoc. U. Tex. Southwestern Med. Ctr., Dallas, 1986-87; NIH postdoctoral rsch. fellow U. Tex., Dallas, 1987-89, Cornell U. Med. Coll., NYC, 1989-91; adj. asst. prof. NYU, NYC, 1991-97; rsch. asst. prof., dir. nursing rsch. NYU Med. Ctr., NYC, 1991-97; sci. dir., dir. intramural rsch. program Nat. Inst. Nursing Rsch., NIH, Bethesda, Md., 1997—2000; chief wound healing lab. NINR/NIH, 1997—2000; prof. Sch. Nursing and Medicine, U. Mo. Med. Ctr., 2002—. Bd. dirs. Wound Healing Soc., chair publs. com. Mem. editl. bd. Wounds: A Compendium of Clin. Rsch. and Practice; contbr. articles to profl. jours. Vol. Girl Scouts U.S.A.; bd. govs. Warren Grant Magnuson Clin. Ctr., NIH, 1999—2000. Recipient Outstanding Alumni award East Carolina U., 1999; Am. Nurses Found. scholar; grantee NIH, 1988-91, 93-97, Nat. Inst. Nursing Rsch., Am. Nurses Found., 1984-85. Fellow Am. Acad. Nursing; mem. AAAS, Am. Soc. Cell Biology, N.Y. Acad. Scis., Wound Healing Soc. (bd. dirs., chair jour. com. 1999—2002), Soc. Investigative Dermatology, Assn. Oper. Rm. Nurses, Sigma Theta Tau. Avocations: hiking, camping, gardening, sailing. Office: University Miss Med Ctr 2500 North State St Jackson MS 39216 Office Fax: 601-984-5127. Business E-Mail: awysocki@umc.edu.

WYVILL, J. CRAIG, retired research engineer, program director; s. Andrew J. and Rach. C. Wyvill; m. Peggy T. Wyvill. BSME, Ga. Tech, 1973; MBA, Ga. State U., 1981. Registered profl. engr., Ga., Va. Energy sys. engr. Union Carbide Corp., Charleston, W.Va., 1973-75; project officer EPA, Washington, 1975-79; rsch. engr. Ga. Tech Rsch. Inst., Atlanta, 1979—2009, dir., agrl. tech. rsch. program, 1982—2009, dir. office food industry programs, 1994-99, chief, food processing divsn., 1999—2009, ret., 2009. Recipient Lamplighter award, US Poultry and Egg Assn., 2010. Office: Ga Tech Rsch Inst Food Processing Tech Bldg Atlanta GA 30332-0823 Home Phone: 404-894-3412. E-mail: craig.wyvill@gtri.gatech.edu.*

YAGER, KEN, state legislator; b. Jan. 5, 1947; married; 2 children. BA, U. Tenn, Martin, 1969, MS, 1972; JD, U. Memphis, 1977. Asst. prof. history & law Roane State Cmty. Coll.; asst. broker Roane Realty, Rockwood; pres. elect Civitan Internat.; bd. mem. & former chmn. Cmty. Reuse Orgn. East Tenn., Mideast Cmty. Action Agy.; bd. mem. Roane Co. Rescue Squad, Roane Co. Heritage Commn.; mem. Dist. 12 Tenn. State Senate, 2008—. Republican. Baptist. Mailing: 111 McNew Dr Harriman TN 37748 Office: 3 Legislative Plaza Nashville TN 37243 Office Phone: 615-741-1449. Office Fax: 615-253-0237. Business E-Mail: sen.ken.yager@capitol.tn.gov.

YAJNIK, SANJIV, corporate financial executive; Completed Exec. Mgmt. Program, Stanford U., 2003; MBA, U. Western Ont. Chief engr. Mobile Oil; market mgr. PepsiCo, Inc., Canada; gen. mgr. Circuit City Stores; dir., credit risk mgmt. Capital One Europe, exec. v.p., prin. mng. dir.; pres. fin. services Capital One Auto Financial, Inc. (subs. of Capital One Financial Corp.), 2007—09; pres., fin. services Capital One Financial, Inc., 2009—. Office: Capital One Financial Corp 1680 Capital One Dr Mc Lean VA 22102 Office Phone: 703-720-1000. Office Fax: 703-720-2306. Business E-Mail: sanjiv.yajnik@capitalone.co.uk.

YAMANE, STANLEY JOEL, retired optometrist, consultant; b. Lihue, Kauai, Hawaii, Mar. 13, 1943; s. Tooru and Yukiko (Miura) Y.; m. Joyce Mitsuko Tamura; children— Stanley Tooru Aiichi, Karen Margaret BS in Optometry, Pacific U., 1966, O.D., 1966, LHD (hon.); DS (hon.), Pa. Coll. Optometry. Diplomate Am. Acad. Optometry. Practice optometry, Waipahu, Hawaii, 1967-73; ptnr. with Dr. Dennis M. Kuwabara, 1973-81; ptnr. Drs. Kuwabara & Yamane, Optometrists, Inc., Waipahu, 1981-91, with br. office Honolulu; with DBA Eye Care Assocs. of Hawaii, Honolulu, 1989-91; dir. profl. affairs Vistakon, Inc., 1991-92; v.p. profl. affairs Vistakon Inc., 1992—2004, chair global profl. affairs coun., 1996-99; ret., 2004—05; v.p. profl. rels. VisionWeb, Inc., 2005—08; ret., 2008. Lectr., cons. in field; sec.-treas. Hawaii Bd. Examiners in Optometry, 1975-76, v.p., 1976-78, pres., 1978-80; mem. adj. faculty Coll. Optometry, Pacific U., 1977-91, Pa. Coll. Optometry, 1981-91, So. Coll. Optometry, 1982-91, U. Mo., St. Louis, 1990-91; bd. dirs. Hawaii Vision Svc. Plan, 1984-91. Cons. editor Optometric Mgmt. Jour., 1981-91, Contact Lens Forum Jour., 1987-91, editor, 1991; contbr. articles to profl. jours. Bd. mgrs. Leeward Oahu Br. YMCA, 1967-70, Hi-Y advisor, 1967-71, mem. Century Club, 1967-91, bd. mgrs. West Oahu Br., 1971-78, gen. chmn. sustaining membership, 1976; 2d v.p. August Ahrens Elem. Sch. PTA, 1969; mem. Leeward Mental Health Adv. Council, 1975-76, Friends of Waipahu Cultural Garden Park Found., 1976—, Aloha council Boy Scouts Am., 1976-91; mem. bus. adv. council Waipahu High Sch., 1976-81, Parent-Tchr.-Community Adv. Council, 1978-80; bd. dirs. Central/Leeward unit Am. Cancer Soc., 1977-80, pub. edn. dir., 1978-79, v.p., 1979-80, founder, chmn. Celebrity Auction, 1980, dir. Oahu Baseline Survey, 1978; bd. dirs. Barbers Point council Navy League Am., 1981-85; profl. bd. advisors U. Houston Inst. for Contact Lens Research. Recipient Merit award Nat. Eye Research Found., 1974, Disting. Service award, 1976, Founder's award Pacific U., 1996, Heart of Am. Contact Lens Soc. Vision Svc. award, 1998, Lifetime Achievement award, 2004. Fellow Am. Acad. Optometry (cornea and contact lens diplomate, vice chair cornea and contact lens sect. 1992-94, chair cornea and contact lens sect. 1994-96, immediate past chair, 1997-99, sec., 1990-92, vice chair ethics com. 1991-92, corp. support for Jour. com. 1981, chair diplomate awards com. 1988-90), AAAS, Asian Optometric Soc. (Legends award, 2012)), Am. Optometric Assn. (ann. congress del. 1978, pub. health com. 19738, optometric paraoptometric personnel com. 1978-79, contact lens project team 1979-80, task force on R&D 1984-87, contact lens sect. coun. 1988-92, sec., 1989-90, vice chair 1990-91, chair elect 1991-92, numerous coms.), Leeward Oahu Jaycees (Disting. Service award 1969, Top Outstanding Young Man award 1975), Hawaii State Jaycees, Am. Optometric Found. (bd. dirs. 1981-91, chmn. task force clin. research 1981-83, nominations com. 1982, treas. 1985-86, sec., 1987-88, pres.-elect, 1988-89, pres. 1989-90), Am. Pub. Health Assn. (recipient Disting. Svc. award, Vision Care Section, 2003), Better Vision Inst., Coll. Optometrists in Vision Devel., Hawaii Optometric Assn. (corr. sec. 1968-70, state newsletter editor 1968-70, rec. sec. 1971, 2d v.p. 1972, pres. 1974-75; Man of Yr. 1975, Optometrist of Yr. 1979), Internat. Optometric & Optical League, Internat. Soc. Contact Lens Rsch., Brit. Contact Lens Assn., Japan Contact Lens Acad., Nat. Assn. of the Professions, Nat. Eye Research Found. (fellow Internat. Orthokeratology sect.; editorial bd. Contacto Jour. 1979, contact lens cert. com. 1981-85), Nat. Fedn. Ind. Bus., Optometric Cons. in Contact Lens Optometric Extension Program Found. (chmn. study group 1969-70, state dir. 1971-73), Optometric Hist. Soc., Optometric Polit. Action Coms., Soc. Contact Lens Specialists, Hawaii Assn. Children with Learning Disabilities, Hawaii Assn. Intellectually Gifted Children (pub. relations chmn. 1st Ann. State Conf. 1975, legis. lobbyist 1975-76), Waipahu Bus. Assn. (bd. dirs. 1974-78, chmn. pub. relations 1974-75, legis. lobbyist 1974-75, pres. 1974-75), Nat. Acad. Practice in Optometry (mem.-at-large on exec. com., disting. practitioner in optometry) Democrat. Baptist. Home: 8609 Autumn Green Dr Jacksonville FL 32256-9560 E-mail: sjyamane@comcast.net.

YANCEY, ASA G., SR., physician, educator; b. Atlanta, Aug. 19, 1916; s. Arthur H. and Daisy L. (Sherard) Yancey; m. Carolyn E. Dunbar, Dec. 28, 1944; children: Arthur H. II, Carolyn L., Caren L., Asa Greenwood Jr. BS, Morehouse Coll., Atlanta, 1937, ScD (hon.), 1991; MD, U. Mich., 1941; ScD (hon.), Howard U., Washington, DC, 1991. Diplomate Am. Bd. Surgery. Intern City Hosp., Cleve., 1941-42; resident Freedmen's Hosp., Washington, 1942-45, U.S. Marine Hosp., Boston, 1945; instr. surgery Meharry Med. Coll., 1946-48; chief surgery VA Hosp., Tuskegee, Ala., 1948-58; chief surgery of Hughes Spalding Pavilion, 1958-72; pvt. practice specializing in surgery Atlanta, 1958-86; from asst. prof. to assoc. prof. surgery Emory U., 1958—75, prof., 1975-86, prof. emeritus, 1986—, assoc. dean Sch. Medicine, 1972-89; med. dir. Grady Meml. Hosp., Atlanta, 1972-89, trustee, 1989—93; clin. prof. surgery Morehouse Sch. Medicine, 1985—; mem. staff Hughes Spalding Hosp., St. Joseph Hosp., Emory U. Hosp., 1986—88. Contbr. articles to profl. jours. Mem. Atlanta Bd. Edn., 1967—77, Fulton-De Kalb Hosp. Authority. 1st lt. M.C. US Army, 1942. Fellow: ACS, Am. Surg. Assn.; mem.: So. Surg. Assn., Inst. Medicine of NAS, Nat. Med. Assn. (1st v.p. 1988—89, trustee 1960—66, mem. editl. bd. jour. 1964—80). Baptist. Home and Office: 2845 Engle Rd NW Atlanta GA 30318-7216 Office Phone: 404-799-5045.

YANCEY, DAVID E., state legislator; b. Newport News, Va., Apr. 6, 1972; BA in Polit. Sci. and History, U. Ga., 1995. Mem. Dist. 94 Va. House of Delegates, 2012—, mem. Edn. Com. & Transp. Com. Mem.: Va. Peninsula C. of C., Newport News Rugby Football Club, Rotary Internat. Republican. Roman Catholic. Office: General Assembly Building PO Box 406 Richmond VA 23218 also: PO Box 1163 Newport News VA 23601 Office Phone: 804-698-1094. Office Fax: 804-698-6794. E-mail: DelDYancey@house.virginia.gov.

YANCEY, JAMES D., bank executive; b. July 12, 1941; Grad., La. State U., Rutgers U.; AS, Columbus State U., Ga., 1964; D (hon.), Columbus State U., 1997. Teller Columbus Bank & Trust Co. (Divsn. Synovus Bank), 1959—83, pres., 1983—90, chmn.; pres. Synovus, 1990, vice chmn., 1992—98, pres., COO, 1998—2003, chmn., 2003. Bd. dirs. Synovus Finl. Corp., Columbus Bank & Trust Co., Total System Svcs., Inc., Shoney's Inc. Former mem. Bus. Coun. Ga.; former campaign chmn. United Way; former pres. Met. Boys Club; former dir. YMCA; former vice chmn. Southern Open; former pres. Historic Columbus Found.; former bd. trustee Brookstone Sch.; former chmn. bd. trustees Columbus State U. Recipient Thomas Y. Whitley Dist. Alumnus award, Columbus State U. Alumni Assn., 1987. Mem.: Ga. C. of C. (former bd. dirs.). Office: Columbus Bank & Trust Co 1148 Broadway Columbus GA 31901 Office Phone: 706-649-4900. Business E-Mail: jyancey@tsys.com.

YANCY, CLYDE WARREN, JR., cardiologist, educator; b. Baton Rouge, Jan. 2, 1958; MD, Tulane U. Sch. Medicine, 1982. Diplomate Am. Bd. Internal Medicine, Sub-specialty Cardiovascular Disease. Intern, internal medicine Parkland Meml. Hosp. and U. Tex. Southwestern Med. Ctr., Dallas, 1982—83, resident, internal medicine, 1983, dir., cardiology clinics, 1990—96; clin. rsch. assoc., dept. cardiovascular rsch. Tulane U. Sch. Medicine, New Orleans, 1985—86; staff physician, dept. internal medicine and ambulatory care New Orleans Vet. Adminstrn. Hosp., New Orleans, 1985—86; staff physician Gen. Hosp. Lakewood, Dallas, 1987—89; attending cardiologist, coronary care unit Parkland Meml. Hosp., Dallas, 1989, assoc. dir., cardiac rehabilitation program, 1990—93, cons. cardiologist, renal transplant program, 1990—92, acting med. dir., coronary care unit, 1992—93; attending cardiologist, coronary care unit Dallas Vet. Adminstrn. Hosp., Dallas, 1989; clin. cardiologist Zale-Lipshy U. Hosp., Dallas, 1989; assoc. attending staff, dept. medicine, divsn. cardiology St. Paul Med. Ctr., Dallas, 1993; fellow, cardiology U. Tex. Southwestern Med. Ctr., Dallas, 1986—89, attending cardiologist, 1989, asst. prof. medicine, divsn. cardiology, 1989—95, assoc. prof. medicine, divsn. cardiology, 1995—2004, prof. medicine, divsn. cardiology, 2004—06, Carl Westcott Disting. Chair, med. rsch., 1996, med. dir., Heart Failure/Heart Transplant Program, 1991—2006, assoc. dean, clin. affairs, 2002—06; med. dir., Baylor Heart & Vascular Inst. Baylor U. Med. Ctr., Dallas, 2006—, chief, cardiothoracic transplantation, 2006—. Rsch. asst., biomedical scis. dept. So. U., Baton Rouge, 1976; rsch. chemist Merck, Sharpe and Dohme Rsch. Lab., Rahway, NJ, 1978; camp counselor Am. Diabetes Assn., 1979; vis. tchg. staff dept., sect. medicine, cardiology St. Paul Med. Ctr., Dallas, 1989; advanced cardiac life support instr., 1990—93; cons. Ctr. for Disease Control, Vet. Affairs Med. Ctrs., NIH; mem., cardiovascular device panel Ctr. for Devices and Radiological Health; FDA; Integrity-Com. and Conf. Mgmt. Br., 2003—; mem., Nat. Immunization Program Adv. Com. Ctr. for Disease Control; FDA, 2003—05; mem., Circulatory Sys. Devices Panel of the Med. Devices Adv. Com., Dept. HHS, FDA, 2005—08; mem., physician health and recovery com. U. Tex. Southwestern Med. Ctr., Dallas, 2006; mem. scientific adv. bd. Internat. Acad. Cardiology and the World Congress, 2006—07; Newall Powell Vis. professorship Scott & White Clinic, Temple, Tex., 2004; invited lectr. in field. Contbr. chapters to books, several articles to profl. jours., web-based ednl. media, to several CD-Roms; assoc. editor Am. Jour. Cardiology, Congestive Heart Failure, mem. editl. bd., 2002—, Am. Heart Jour., Cardiology Review, Urban Cardiology, Jour. Cardiovascular Pharmacology and Therapeutics & Circulation, Progress in Transplantation, 2002—, Jour. Cardiac Failure, 2002—04, Current Heart Failure Reports, 2003—, Jour. Acute Cardiac Care, 2006—07, reviewer for major cardiovascular jours. Bd. dirs. Family Place. Named one of Top Doctors, D Mag., 1992, Top 330 Doctors in 2001, Top 381 Doctors in 2002 (Featured Top Doctor), Best Doctors, 2003—04, Top 572 Doctors of 2003 (Featured Top Doctor), Top 638 Doctors of 2004 (Featured Top Doctor), Best Doctors, 2005, Best Doctors in Am., 1998, 2000, America's Leading Physicians, Black Enterprise Mag., 2001, Tex. Super Docs, Tex. Monthly, 2004, Tex. Super Doctors 2005, America's Top Physicians, Guide to America's Top Physicians, e-book, 2006. Fellow: Internat. Soc. on Hypertension in Blacks (Outstanding Rsch. award 2001), ACP, Am. Heart Assn. (first v.p., Dallas Divsn. 1993—94, pres.-elect, Dallas Divsn 1994—95, pres., Dallas Divsn. 1995—96, first v.p., Tex. affiliate 1996—97, pres.-elect, Tex. affiliate 1997—98, pres., Tex. affiliate 1998—99, bd. dir., Tex. affiliate 2001—02, coun. clin. cardiology's heart failure and transplantation sub-com., mem. nat. bd. dirs. 2000—02, nat. spokesperson, bd. dirs. Dallas Divsn. and Tex. Affiliate, chmn., hypertension task force, Dallas Divsn., Douglas Perry Vol. Yr. award, Dallas Divsn. 1996, Walter M. Kirkendall award for Outstanding Scientist/Educator Vol., Tex. affiliate 1996, Physician Vol. Yr., Tex. Affiliate 2001, Nat. Physician of Yr. 2003), ACS, Am. Coll. Cardiology (sec.-treas., Tex. chpt. 1993—95); mem.: Dallas County Med. Soc., Tex. Med. Assn., Tex. Transplatation Soc., Tex. Acad. Physician Assts. (hon.), Am. Soc.

Transplantation, Am. Diabetes Assn. (minority initiative com., bd. dirs. 1990—92), Assn. Black Cardiologists, Inc. (chmn., organ transplatation com. 2002—03, heart failure com. chair 2002—03, editl. bd. Digest of Urban Cardiology 2002—04, Daniel Savage award for Scientific Merit 2002, Cardiologists-In-Tng. Hero award 2006), Heart Failure Soc. Am. (mem. exec. com., ex-officio 2001—03), Am. Soc. Hypertension, Internat. Soc. Heart and Lung Transplantation, Alpha Omega Alpha. Office: Baylor Heart & Vascular Inst Baylor U Med Ctr 3500 Gaston Ave Ste H-030 Dallas TX 75246 Office Phone: 214-820-7357. Office Fax: 214-820-7533. Business E-Mail: clydey@baylorhealth.edu.

YANG, CHAO YUH, biochemistry professor, medical educator; b. Pingtung, Taiwan, May 8, 1939; came to U.S., 1982; s. Shang-Sheng and Kuei-Mei (Lee) Y.; m. Manlan Lou Yang; children: Tseming, Tseliang, Thomas. BS, Tamkang U., Taipei, Taiwan, 1962; MS, Georg-August U., Goettingen, Germany, 1970, PhD, 1973. Tchr. Chiatung Agr. High Sch., Pingtung, Taiwan, 1963-64; chemist Kuantu Glass Plant, Taipei, 1964-68; postdoctoral fellow dept. molecular biology Max-Planck Inst. for Exptl. Medicine, Goettingen, 1973-75, scientist dept. immunochemistry, 1975-82; asst. prof. biochemistry Baylor Coll. Medicine, Houston, 1982-89, asst. prof. dept. medicine, 1983-86, rsch. assoc. prof. dept. medicine, 1986-90, rsch. assoc. prof. dept. biochemistry, 1989-91, rsch. prof. medicine, 1990-95; rsch. prof. biochemistry, 1991-95; prof. medicine and biochemistry, 1995—2009; emeritus prof. Baylor Coll. Medicine, 2009—. Dir. peptide core Nat. Rsch. and Demonstration Ctr. in Arteriosclerosis, Baylor Coll. Medicine, 1984-96, internal adv. com., 1986-96; organizing com. 10th Internat. Conf. on Methods in Protein Structure Analysis, Snowbird, Utah, 1994; sci. com. Internat. Conf. on Methods in Protein Sequence Analysis, Berlin, 1988, Sweden, 1990; reviewer grants Biomed. Rsch. rev. Com., Nat. Inst. on Drug Abuse, NSF, Washington; lectr. in field. Reviewer papers for Jour. Chromatography, Jour. Lipid Rsch., Jour. Protein Chemistry, Molecular and Cellular Biochemistry, Biochemistry, Arteriosclerosis, Circulation; contbr. articles to profl. jours. Pres. Taiwanese Am. Citizens League of Houston, 1988-90, Taiwanese Am. Assn. Houston, 1985-86. Grantee BRSG Funds, 1982-83, NIH, 1986-96, 2001-2006, AHA, 1985-90, 97-99, Meth. Hosp. Found., 1988-91, AHA Tex., 1997-2001, ADA, 2003-06. Home: 4102 Levonshire Dr Houston TX 77025-3915 Office: Acad Bio-Med Co 1417 Kress St Houston TX 77020 Office Phone: 713-675-4040. Business E-Mail: cyang@academybiomed.com.

YANG, EMELINE, lawyer; b. Oxford, Miss. BA in Econs. and Managerial Studies, Rice U., Houston, 1992; JD, U. Pa. Law Sch., 1995. Bar: Tex. 1995. Assoc. Hughes & Luce, LLP, Tex., 1995—97, Winstead, Sechrest & Minick, P.C., Dallas, 1997—2002, shareholder, 2003—. Co-worker Formosan Christian Ch. Dallas, 1997—2011; bd. dir. Asian Am. Forum, Inc., Dallas, 2001—08, Women's Fin. Exch. Inc., Dallas, 2001—02. Named Tex. Super Lawyer, Tex. Monthly, 2005—06; named a Tex. Rising Star, 2004—05; named one of Best Lawyers in Dallas, D Mag., 2002, 2004, 2005, 2007—09, 2010. Fellow: Dallas Assn. Young Lawyers Found., Dallas Bar Assn. (bd. dir. 2000), Tex. Bar Found. (life); mem.: ABA, Tex. Assn. Bank Counsel, Dallas Asian Am. Bar Assn. (pres. and bd. dir. 2000), Dallas Women Lawyers Assn. (historian 2001, bd. dir. 2001—02), Nat. Asian Pacific Am. Bar Assn. (S.W. regional gov. 2004—05). Office: Winstead PC 5400 Renaissance Tower 2728 N Harwood St Ste 500 Dallas TX 75201-1743 Office Phone: 214-745-5687. Office Fax: 214-745-5390. E-mail: eyang@winstead.com.

YANG, KICHOON, educational association administrator, mathematics educator; b. Pusan, Republic of Korea, Apr. 12, 1955; came to US, 1972; s. Mooyong and Kyungsik (Lee) Y.; m. Heejin Kim; 1 child, Eli. BS, U. NC, 1977; PhD, Washington U., St. Louis, 1982. Asst. prof. Ark. State U., Jonesboro, 1982-86, assoc. prof. math., 1986-91, prof. math., 1991—94; program dir. geometric analysis program, divsn. math. sciences NSF, 1994—97; dept. chmn., prof. math. U. Tex. Pan Am., 1997—99, asst. v.p. undergraduate studies, 1999—2001; dean, prof. U. No. Iowa Coll. Natural Sciences, 2001—04; provost, prof. NW Mo. State U., 2005—09; exec. dir. Nat. Coun. Teachers Mathmatics, 2009—. Reviewer NSF, 1984—, Math. Revs., Ann Arbor, Mich., 1988—; invited spkr. at profl. confs. Author: Almost Complex Homogeneous Spaces and Their Submanifolds, 1987, Compact Riemann Surfaces and Algebraic Curves, 1988, Complete and Compact Minimal Surface, 1989, Complex Algebraic Geometry, 1991, Exterior Differential Systems and Equivalence Problems, 1992, Complete Minimal Surfaces of Finite Total Curvature, 1994, Meromorphic Functions and Projective Curves, 1998; contbr. articles to numerous profl. jours. Grantee NSF 1983-86, 2002-04, US Dept. Edn. 1998-2001, NASA, 2002-07, US Dept.Energy, Verizon Found—. Mem. Am. Math. Soc., Math. Assn. Am., Korean Math. Soc., AAAS Sci. and Human Rights Commn., Coun. Sci. Soc. Presidents. Office: Nat Coun Teachers of Mathematics 1906 Association Dr Reston VA 20191-1502 Office Phone: 703-620-9840. Office Fax: 703-476-2970.

YANG, PHILIP Q., sociologist; arrived in US, 1986, naturalized, 2005; m. Jianling Li, Dec. 20, 1984; children: Ming, William Zeus. PhB, Zhongshan U., Guangzhou, China, 1982; MA, 1988; PhD, UCLA, 1993. Asst. prof. Zhongshan U., Guangzhou, 1982—86; lectr. UCLA, 1994—95; from asst. prof. to assoc. prof. Calif. Poly. State U., San Luis Obispo, 1995—2001; from assoc. prof. to prof. Tex. Woman's U., Denton, 1999—. Book review editor Jour. Asian Am. Studies, 2008—. Author: Post-1965 Immigration to the United States: Structural Determinants, 1995, Ethnic Studies: Issues and Approaches, 2000, Asian Immigration to the US, 2011; editor: Introduction to Ethnic Studies: A Reader, 1999; contbr. articles to profl. jours., chapters to books. Grantee, NSF, 2002—04; fellow, UN, 1986—87; Chancellor's Rsch. fellow, Tex. Woman's U., 2001—02, 2002—03. Mem.: Population Assn. Am., N.Am. Chinese Sociologists' Assn. (bd. dirs. 2001—03), Nat. Assn. for Ethnic Studies, Assn. for Asian Am. Studies (bd. dirs. 2001—03), Southwestern Social Sci. Assn., Assn. Chinese Profs. Social Scis. in the US, Am. Sociol. Assn. (Book award Internat. Migration Sect. 1998, Rsch. award, Asia and Asian America Sect. 2011), Alpha Kappa Delta. Office: Texas Womans Univ PO Box 425887 Denton TX 76204 Office Fax: 940-898-2067. Business E-Mail: pyang@mail.twu.edu.

YANG, Y.E. (YONG-EUN YANG), professional golfer; b. Jeju-do, Republic of Korea, Jan. 15, 1972; m. Ju Pak Young, 1999; children: Hyeonwoo, Isu, Kyungmin. Profl. golfer Korean PGA Tour, Japan Golf Tour, European Tour, 2006—, PGA Tour, 2008—. Mem. Asian team Royal Trophy, 2007; mem. internat. team Presidents Cup, 2009, 2011. Served with South Korean Army. Named Rookie of Yr., Korean PGA Tour, 1997. Achievements include winning Korean Tour events: SBS Championship, 2002, Kolon-Hana Bank Korea Open, 2006, Kolon Korea Open, 2010; winning Japan Golf Tour events: Sun Chlorella Classic, 2004, Asahi Ryokuken Yomiuri Asolizuka, 2004, Coca-Cola Tokai Classic, 2005, Suntory Open, 2006; winning European Tour event: HSBC Champions, 2006; winning PGA Tour events: The Honda Classic, 2009, PGA Championship, 2009. Office: PGA Tour 100 PGA Tour Blvd Ponte Vedra Beach FL 32082

YANG, YUANQING, computer company executive; MS, Inst. Computer Sci., Univ. Sci. & Tech., China, 1989. With Lenovo Group Ltd., Beijing, 1989—2001, pres., CEO, 2001—05, chmn. Beijing & Purchase, NY, 2005—. Prof. Univ. Sci. & Tech., China; dir. China Entrepreneur Assn.; mem. internat. advisory com. NY Stock Exch. Mem. Nat. Youth Com., China. Named Man of Year, CCTV, 2004; named one of Stars of Asia, BusinessWeek mag., China's Ten Star Entrepreneurs, Ten Most Valuable Managers. Office: Lenovo 1009 Think Pl Morrisville NC 27560-9002

YANTA, JOHN WALTER, bishop emeritus; b. Runge, Tex., Oct. 2, 1931; s. John and Mary Pollok Yanta. Ordained priest Archdiocese of San Antonio, 1956; second asst. pastor St. Ann's Parish, San Antonio, 1956—62; pastor Sacred Heart Ch., San Antonio, 1973—81, St. James Ch., San Antonio, 1983—96; ordained bishop, 1994; aux. bishop Archdiocese of San Antonio, 1994—97; bishop Diocese of Amarillo, Tex., 1997—2008, bishop emeritus, 2008—. Dir. Cath. Youth Orgn., San Antonio, 1962—63, youth dir., 1963—65; founder, exec. dir. San Antonio Neighborhood Youth Org., 1965—71; founder, pres. Polish Am. Congress Tex., 1971—73; pres. Tex. Cath. Conf. Priest Senates, 1978—82; editor Today's Cath., San Antonio, 1981—83; founder, exec. dir. Cath. TV San Antonio, 1981—83; founder Polish Am. Priests Assn., 1990; bd. dirs. Cath. Relief Svc., 2000—, Kenedy Meml. Found., St. Joseph & St. Peter Sem., Brownsville, Tex.; treas. Tex. Conf. Churches, 2003—. Roman Catholic. Office: Diocese of Amarillo PO Box 5644 Amarillo TX 79117-5644 Office Phone: 806-383-2243.

YARBOROUGH, CLAY, councilman; BA in Bus. Mgmt., U. North Fla. Recruiter UPS; mem. Duval Soil & Water Conservation Bd., 2000, Greater Arlington-Beaches Citizens Planning Adv. Com., 2001; councilman, Dist. 1 Jacksonville City Coun., Fla. Mem. Sheriff's Adv. Coun., Greater Arlington Civic Coun.; chmn. Pub. Health & Safety Com.; mem. Rules Com., Fin. Com.; coun. liaison Mil. & Veterans Affairs. Mem.: Arlington Rotary Club (hon.). Republican. Office: 117 W Duval St Ste 425 Jacksonville FL 32202 Office Phone: 904-630-1386, 904-630-1389. Business E-Mail: clay@coj.net.

YARBOROUGH, WILLIAM GLENN, JR., military officer, forester, international business executive; b. Rock Hill, SC, June 21, 1940; s. William Glenn and Bessie (Rainsford) Y.; m. Betsy Gibson, Jan. 24, 1969; children: Bill, Clinton, Frank, Elizabeth. BS, U. S.C., 1961, MBA, 1969; postgrad., Command and Gen. Staff Coll., 1970, Naval War Coll., 1979, U. Va., 1983. Commd. to U.S. Army, advanced through grades to col., 1980, co. and troop comdr., squadron staff officer Vietnam and Europe, 1961-71, strategist Washington, 1971-73; chief of assignments Office Pers. Mgmt. Mil. Pers. Ctr., Washington, 1973-76; comdr. 1st Squadron 1st Cavalry, Europe, 1976-78; chief of staff, spl. asst. to chief of staff 1st Armored Divsn., Europe, 1978; br. chief Office of Chief of Staff, Washington, 1979-80; exec. to dep. comdg. gen. Material Devel. and Readiness Command, Washington, 1980-81; mil. dep. for asst. sec. for rsch., devel. and acquisition Washington, 1981-85; dir. ops. Ford Aerospace, Washington, 1986—89; army mktg. dir. Grumman Corp., Bethpage, NY, 1990-93; pres., CEO Allied Rsch. Corp., Vienna, Va., 1993—2001; founder & prin. WGY & Assocs. Bd. dirs. Carleton Techs., EADS N.Am., Valentec Inc. Trustee Patton Mus.; treas. US Cavalry Assn.; bd. dirs. So Others Might Eat (Some); treas. Easter Seals; bd. dirs. Moore Sch. Bus. U. S.C. Decorated Silver Star, Bronze Star medal with 4 oak leaf clusters and V device, Purple Heart, Legion of Merit. Mem. VFW, SAR, KC, Assn. U.S. Army (George Washington chpt., v.p. membership), Am. Legion (comdr., post 270), Armed Forces Comms. and Electronics Assn., U.S. Army Armor Assn., Nat. Def. Indsl. Assn. (bd. dirs. N.Y. chpt. trustee), Rotary Internat., McLean Rotary (pres.), Mil. Order of the World Wars, N.G. Assn., Res. Officers Assn., Soc. of the Purple Heart, Army-Navy Club, Army Navy Country Club, Belle-Meade Country Club, Tower Club, Sigma Chi. Republican. Roman Catholic. Home: Box 115 Thomson GA 30824-0115 Office: Box 828 Mc Lean VA 22101 Office Phone: 703-748-1717. Office Fax: 928-222-5742. Personal E-mail: wgyarc@aol.com.

YARBROUGH, EDWARD MEACHAM, lawyer, former prosecutor; b. Nashville, Dec. 17, 1943; s. Gurley McTyeire and Miriam (Mefford) Y. BA, Rhodes Coll., 1967; JD, Vanderbilt U., 1973. Bar: Tenn. 1973. Asst. dist. atty. Davidson County, Nashville, 1973-76; ptnr. Hollins, Wagster & Yarbrough, Nashville, 1976—2007; US atty. (mid. dist.) Tenn. US Dept. Justice, Nashville, 2007—10; ptnr. Walker Tipps & Malone PLC, Nashville, 2010—13, Bone McAllester Norton PLLC, 2013—. Chmn. com. Crime Commn., Nashville, 1981-82; mem. task force House Judiciary Com., Nashville, 1984; chmn. Crimestoppers Inc., Nashville, 1983-86; trustee United Way, Nashville, 1983-86, Belmont U., 1993-99, Cumberland Sci. Mus., 1996-98; bd. dirs. Big Bros. Inc., Nashville, 1983-85; mem. nat. devel. bd. Lipscomb U., 2000-03; chmn. deacons Elder Forest Hills Bapt. Ch. Served to 1st lt. U.S. Army, 1969-71, Vietnam. Decorated Bronze Star; named Best Criminal Def. Atty., Bus. Nashville mag., 1999. Fellow Nat. Speleological Soc. (bd. dirs. 1960—), American Coll. Trial Lawyers; mem. ABA, Tenn. Bar Assn. (Svc. award 2011), Nashville Bar Assn. (bd. mem., 1981-83, 2007-09, pres. 1983, Jack C. Norman award 2010), Tenn. Criminal Def. Lawyers, Nashville Kiwanis (pres. 1992), Am. Legion, City Club (Nashville). Baptist. Avocations: cave exploring, photography, skiing, golf. Office: Bone McAllester Norton PLLC 1600 City Ctr 511 Union St Nashville TN 37219 Office Phone: 615-313-6031, 615-313-6000. Office Fax: 615-313-6001. E-mail: eyarbrough@walkertipps.com.

YARBROUGH, REBECCA K., electronics executive; Degree in Bus. Adminstrn., Huntingdon Coll., 1959. Former bd. dirs. Universal Bank; bd. dirs. Total System Svcs., Inc., 1999—. Former bd. dirs. Brookstone Sch., Columbus Mus., Downtown YMCA, Historic Columbus Found.; mem. Columbus Symphony Women's Assn., Daus. of the Am. Revolution, Jr. League of Columbus, Muscogee County Med. Aux. Office: Total System Services Inc One TSYS Way Columbus GA 31901 Office Phone: 706-649-2310. Office Fax: 706-649-5740. Business E-Mail: ryarbrough@tsys.com.

YARMUTH, JOHN ALLAN, United States Representative from Kentucky; b. Louisville, Nov. 4, 1947; s. Stanley Robert and Edna Elaine (Klein) Yarmuth; m. Catherine Elizabeth Creedon, 1981; 1 child, Stanley Aaron. BA in Am. Studies, Yale U., 1969; student, Georgetown U. Sch. Law. Stockbroker Stein Bros. & Boyce, Louisville, 1969-70; legis. asst. to Senator Marlow Cook US Senate, Washington, 1971-75; pub. Louisville Today mag., 1976-82; asst. v.p. univ. rels. U. Louisville, 1983-86; worked in pub. rels. and mktg. Caretenders Healthcorp, 1986—90; founder, exec. editor Louisville Eccentric Observer Newsweekly, 1990—2003; mem. US Congress from 3rd Ky. Dist., 2007—, US House Ethics Com., 2011—. Founder, pres. Ctr. Ky. Progress. Host (radio talk shows) Yarmuth & Ziegler, WAVE 3 TV, 2003, guest appearances Hot Button, 2004—05, editor, owner (publications) Kentucky Golfer. Bd. regents No. Ky. U., Highland Heights, 1980—83, Jewish Cmty. Ctr., Planned Parenthood Louisville Forum; bd. dirs. Better Bus. Bur., Louisville, 1979—85, Louisville Sch. Art, 1980—83, Sta. WKPC-TV, Louisville, 1983—88. Recipient editorial and column writing awards, Metro Louisville Journalism; named Person of Yr., Louisville Chpt. Alzheimer's Assn., 2004; named to Atherton High Sch. Hall of Fame, 2002. Mem.: Soc. Profl. Journalists, Ky. Golf Assn., SC Melrose Club, Valhalla Golf Club. Democrat. Jewish. Avocation: golf. Office: 319 Cannon House Office Bldg Washington DC 20515 also: Romano Mazzoli Fed Bldg Ste 216 600 Martin Luther King Dr Louisville KY 40202

YARNO, WENDY, pharmaceutical executive; BS in Mktg., Portland State U., 1982; MBA in Bus. & Mktg., Temple U., 1988. Profl. rep. U.S. Human Health, 1983—85, mktg. analyst, 1985—87, product mgr., pediatric vaccines, 1988, assoc. dir., econ. affairs, 1989, sr. dir. mktg. planning, 1990—91, nat. account exec., 1991—92, sr. dir., managed health care affairs, 1992, project leader, U.S. Health Care Reform, 1992—93; v.p. ctrl. region Merck-Medco, 1994; v.p., hypertension and heart failure therapeutic bus. group U.S. Human Health, 1994—97; v.p., Women's Health Care Franchise Johnson & Johnson, 1997—98; v.p., Cholesterol Reducers, Worldwide Human Health Mktg. Merck & Co., Inc. (formerly Schering-Plough Corp.), Whitehouse Station, NJ, 1999, v.p. human resources, 1999—2000, sr. v.p. human resources, 2000—02, exec. v.p. worldwide human health mktg., 2002—05, gen. mgr., bus. unit, Cardiovascular & Metabolic U.S, 2005—06, chief mktg. officer, 2006—08; halsey prof. U.Va. Sch. Engring. and Applied Sci., 2009—10. Bd. dir. St. Jude Med. Inc., 2002—; bd. advisors HemoShear, 2009—, openQ, 2009—; bd. dirs. ADial Pharmaceuticals, 2009—. Bd. dirs. St. Jude Med. Ctr.; pres. bd. trustees Women's Health and Counseling Ctr., Somerville. Office: ADial Pharmaceuticals Bd Directors 3445 Seminole Trail Ste 103 Charlottesville VA 22911 Office Phone: 434-249-2544.

YATES, DANIEL J., energy efficiency services company executive; b. 1977; m. Tobie E. Whitman. AB in Computer Sci. summa cum laude, Harvard U., 1999. Co-founder Echo Networks, 1999—2000; founder, CEO Edusoft, 2000—05; divsn. pres. Houghton Mifflin Co., Boston, 2004—05; co-founder, CEO Opower, Arlington, Va., 2007—. Recipient Ernst & Young Entrepreneur of Yr. Greater Washington Award, 2011; named a Tech Titan, Washingtonian mag., 2009, 2010, 2011; named one of The 40 Under 40, Fortune mag., 2011. Office: Opower 1515 N Courthouse Rd, 8th Floor Arlington VA 22201 Office Phone: 703-778-4544. Office Fax: 703-778-4547.

YATES, JOHN P., state legislator; b. Nov. 24, 1921; m. Annie Yates; children: Peggy, Linda, John Jr. Former state rep. Dist. 85, Ga.; former mgr. Distbn. Ctr.; city councilman Suny Side, Ga., 1948—54; state rep. Dist. 75 Ga., 1989—90; state rep. Dist. 106, 1993—2002; state rep. Dist. 73, 2004—; mem. appropriations com.; mem. legislature & congressional reapportionment com.; mem. Motor Vehicles Com.; house rep. Ga. Mem.: Gordon Col. Found., Griffin-Spaulding C. of C. Republican. Methodist. Mailing: 961 Birdie Rd Griffin GA 30223-6310 Office: 411 Legislative Office Bldg Atlanta GA 30334

YATES, JOHN THOMAS, JR., chemistry professor, research scientist; b. Winchester, Va., Aug. 3, 1935; s. John Thomas and Kathryn (Barnett) Y.; m. Kerin Joyce Narbut, Oct. 18, 1958; children: Geoffrey, Nathan. BS, Juniata Coll., 1956; PhD, MIT, 1960. Asst. prof. chemistry Antioch Coll., Yellow Springs, Ohio, 1960-63; NRC fellow, rsch. chemist Nat. Bur. Standards (now Nat. Inst. Standards and Tech.), Washington, 1963—65, rsch. staff, sect. chief, surface chemistry, 1965—82; R.K. Mellon prof. chemistry and physics U. Pitts., 1982—2006, founding dir., Surface Sci. Ctr., 1982—2006; prof. chem. U. Va., 2007—, Shannon fellow, 2007—. Sr. vis. scholar, U. East Anglia, 1970-71; Gwathmey vis. prof. U. Va., 2002-03 Author: Experimental Innovations in Surface Science, 1997; co-author: The Surface Scientist's Guide to Organometallic Chemistry, 1987, Molecular Physical Chemistry for Engineers, 2007; co-editor: Vibrational Spectroscopy of Molecules on Surfaces, 1987, Chemical Perspectives of Microelectronic Materials, Vol. 131; assoc. editor: Studies in Surface Science and Catalysis, 1986; series editor: Methods of Surface Characterization, 1987; bd. editors Ann. Rev. Phys. Chemistry, 1983-85, Jour. Phys. Chemistry, 1983-88, Jour. Chem. Physics, 1984-87, Jour. Catalysis, 1987-91, Chem. Revs., Langmuir, Surface Sci., Applications of Surface Sci., Accounts Chem. Rsch., Chem. Phys. letters, 1997-; assoc. editor Langmuir, 1991-98; mem. adv. bd. Chemical & Engineering News, 2001-2003; contbr. revs. and articles to profl. jours.; inventor desorption spectrometer, 1981. Sherman Fairchild Disting. scholar Calif. Inst. Tech., 1977-78; recipient Silver medal Dept. Commerce-Nat. Bur. Stds., 1973, Stratton award for Disting. Rsch., 1978, Gold medal Dept. Commerce Nat. Bur. Stds., 1981, Pres.'s Disting. Rsch. award U. Pitts., 1989, Procter & Gamble award, 1989, Alexander von Humboldt Sr. Rsch. award, 1995, 1997, Pitts.-Cleve. Catalysis Soc. award, 1998, J.W. Linnett lectr. Cambridge U., 2000, Outstanding Alumnus Juniata Coll., 2000, named Among 100 Most Highly Cited Chemists in World 1984—, G.N. Lewis lectr. U. Calif.-Berkeley, 2002; fellow Sidney Sussex Coll., 2000, Japan Soc. Promotion of Sci., 2002, Inst. Physics, 2004 Fellow Am. Phys. Soc. (bd. dirs. divsn. chem. physics 1991—, chmn. divsn. chem. physics 1989), Am. Vacuum Soc. (chmn. surface sci. divsn. 1973, 92, trustee 1975, bd. dirs. 1982-85, Medard Welch award 1994, fellow 1994); mem. NAS, Am. Chem. Soc. (chmn. divsn. colloid and surface chemistry, Langmuir lectr. 1979, Kendall award in colloid of surface chemistry 1986, E.W. Morley prize Cleve. chpt. 1990, Peter Debye lectr. Cornell U. 1993, Pitts. award 1998, Arthur W. Adamson award for Disting. Svc. in the Advancement of Surface Chemistry, 1999, Peter Debye Phys. Chemistry award, 2007), Pitts.-Cleve. Catalysis Soc. Office: Univ Va Dept Chemistry Charlottesville VA 22904-4319 Home: Po Box 124 Free Union VA 22940 Business E-Mail: johnt@virginia.edu.

YATES, LEIGHTON DELEVAN, JR., lawyer; b. Atlanta, Sept. 4, 1946; s. Leighton Delevan and Stella Louise (Hill) Y.; m. Phyllis Jeanne Hummer, Dec. 22, 1968; children: Leighton Delevan III, Lauren Jeanne. BA, Hampden-Sydney Coll., Va., 1968; JD with high honors, U. Fla., 1973. Bar: Fla. 1974, U.S. Dist. Ct. (middle dist.) Fla. 1975. Assoc. Maguire, Voorhis & Wells, P.A., Orlando, Fla., 1974-77, shareholder, 1978-98, dept. chmn., 1985-90; ptnr. Holland & Knight LLP, Orlando, Fla., 1998—, nat. practice group leader, 2005—. Bd. dirs. Hubbard Constrn. Co., Winter Park, Fla., 1985—2004, Blythe Constrn., Inc., Charlotte, NC, 1999—2004; adminstrv, dir. SunTrust Bank, Orlando, Fla., 1990—. Exec. editor U. Fla. Law Rev., 1973. Mem. Fla. Bd. Bar Examiners, 1992-97, 2002-05, vice chmn., 1995-96, chmn. 1996-97; chmn. Fla.'s Blood Ctrs., 1995-2010, vice chmn., 1980-95; chmn. Orlando Opera Co., 1994, pres., 1993; bd. dirs. Metro Orlando Econ. Devel. Commn., 2007-. Fellow Am. Bar Found.; mem. ABA, Fla. Bar Assn., Orange County Bar Assn., Univ. Club of Orlando, Country Club of Orlando, Order of the Coif, Omicron Delta Kappa, Phi Kappa Phi. Republican. Presbyterian. Avocations: bicycling, music, reading. Home: 3218 S Osceola Ave Orlando FL 32806-6251 Office: Holland & Knight LLP 200 S Orange Ave Ste 2600 Orlando FL 32801-3453 Office Phone: 407-425-8500. Personal E-mail: lyates@cfl.rr.com. Business E-Mail: leighton.yates@hklaw.com.

YATES, SALLY QUILLIAN, federal prosecutor; b. Atlanta, Aug. 20, 1960; m. J. Comer Yates. BA in Journalism, U. Ga., 1982; JD, U. Ga. Sch. Law, 1986. Staff asst. to rep. Jack Brinkley US House of Representatives, Washington, 1981—82; assoc. Swift, Currie, McGhee & Hiers LLP, Atlanta, 1984, Troutman, Sanders, Lockerman & Ashmore, Atlanta, 1985, King & Spalding LLP, Atlanta, 1985—89; asst. US atty. (northern dist.) Ga. US Dept. Justice, 1989—94, chief fraud & pub. corruption unit, 1994—2002, 1st asst. US atty., 2002—09, acting US atty., 2004, 2009—10, US atty., 2010—. Named one of 40 Under 40, Ga. Trend Mag., 1997. Office: US Attorneys Office Richard B Russell Federal Bldg 75 Spring St SW Ste 600 Atlanta GA 30303*

YATSENKO, YURI PETROVICH, business professor, mathematician; b. Kiev, Ukraine, Oct. 15, 1955; arrived in US, 2000, permanent resident, 2001; s. Petr Yatsenko and Nadiya Betina; m. Natali Hritonenko; children: Oleg, Victoria, Olga. BS in Physics, Kiev State U., Ukraine, 1977, MS, 1977, PhD, 1981; DSc, Presidium Acad. Scis. USSR, 1988. Lic. prof. Edn. Ministry Ukraine, 1995. Sr. rschr., dept. head Cybernetics Inst. Ukrainian Acad. Scis., Kiev, 1983—96; prof. Kiev State U., 1991—93, Acad. Tech. & Agr., Bydgoszcz, Poland, 1993—95; sr. analyst Electric Submersible Pumps, Inc., Okla. City, Okla., 1997—99; adj. prof. U. Alta., Edmonton, Alberta, Canada, 1999—99; sr. sys. analyst Netherland, Sewell & Assoc., Inc., Dallas, 2000—01; prof. Houston Bapt. U., 2002—. Owner Cybernetics Cons. Inc., Edmonton, Alberta, Canada, 1996—2000; lectr. in field; mem. editl. bd. Internat. Jour. Applications and Applied Maths., United States, 2005—, Internat. Jour. Ecology and Devel., India, 2006—, Jour. Computational and Applied Maths., Ukraine, 2006—; assoc. editor Internat. Jour. Ecological Econs. and Stats., India, 2006—; mem. program & organizing coms. at confs. in field. Author: 7 Books; contbr. scientific papers to profl. jours. Rsch. grants, Sorros Internat. Sci. Found. & Edn. Ministry Ukraine, 1992—95, Rsch. grant, NATO, 2006—08. Russian Orthodox. Achievements include research in mathematical modeling and optimization of economic and industrial development, technological change, innovation processes, and technology replacement. Home: 15434 Tysor Park Ln Houston TX 77095 Office: Houston Bapt Univ 7502 Fondren Houston TX 77074 Office Fax: 281-649-3436. Business E-Mail: yyatsenko@hbu.edu.

YEAKEL, EARL LEROY, III, (LEE YEAKEL), federal judge; b. Oklahoma City, Apr. 18, 1945; BA, U. Tex., 1966, JD, 1969. Bar: Tex. 1969, U.S. Ct. Appeals (5th and 11th cirs.), U.S. Supreme Ct. Mem. Clark, Thomas & Winters, Austin, Tex.; judge US Dist. Ct. (we. dist.) Tex., 2003—. Fellow Tex. Bar Found.; mem. ABA, State Bar Tex., Tex. Young Lawyers Assn. (chmn. legis. com. 1976-78, dir. 1978-79), Tex. Assn. Def. Counsel, Travis County Bar Assn. (bd. dirs. 1976-78), Austin Young Lawyers Assn. (pres. 1977-78), Delta Theta Phi. Office: Clark Thomas & Winters Tex Commerce Bldg POB 1148 700 Lavaca St Fl 21 Austin TX 78701-3109 also: 200 West 8th St Austin TX 78701

YEARGIN-ALLSOPP, MARSHALYN, medical epidemiologist, pediatrician; b. Greenville, SC, May 17, 1948; d. Grady Andrew and Willie Mae (Blocker) Yeargin; m. Ralph Norman Allsopp, Apr. 5, 1975; children: Timothy Chandler, Whitney Marisha. Student, Bennett Coll., 1964—66; BA, Sweet Briar Coll., 1968; MD, Emory U., 1972. Diplomate Am. Bd. Pediatrics. Intern Montefiore Hosp., Bronx, NY, 1972—73, resident, 1973—75; instr. pediatrics Albert Einstein Coll. Medicine, Bronx, 1975—77, asst. prof. pediatrics, 1977—78, 1980—81; pediatrician Montefiore-Morrisania Comprehensive Health Care Ctr., Bronx, 1975—78, Louise Wise Adoption Agy., NYC, 1975—80, Children's Evaluation and Rehab. Ctr., Rose F. Kennedy Ctr., Bronx, 1980—81; officer USPHS, 1981—, comdr., 1983—; epidemiologic intelligence surveillance officer birth defects br. Ctrs. Disease Control, Atlanta, 1981—83, preventive medicine resident, 1982—84, med. epidemiologist, 1984—; pediatric cons. Clayton County Early Intervention Program, Jonesboro, Ga., 1983—; med. dir. Easter Seal Presch. Program, Atlanta, 1981—83; physician Com. Handicapped, NYC, 1979—81, United Cerebral Palsy Program, Bronx, 1980—81. Bd. overseers Sweet Briar Coll., 1981—89; bd. dirs. Neighborhood Arts Ctr., Atlanta, 1984—87; mem. prevention edn. com. Retarded Citizens, Atlanta, 1984—96; mem. fundraising campaign Greater Atlanta YWCA, 1985; bd. trustees Pace Acad., 1986—; co-chmn. Minority Atlanta Families Ind. Schs., Inc., 1986—; chair, bd. dirs. profl. adv. com. Cerebral Palsey Ctr., REACH, Inc., Atlanta, 1988—; mem. State of Ga. Interagy. Coun. Edn. Handicapped Act., 1988—96; mem. sci. adv. bd. Nat. Alliance Autism Rsch. Recipient Disting. Alumna award, Sweet Briar Coll., 1992. Fellow: Am. Acad. Cerebral Palsy and Devel. Medicine, Am. Acad. Pediatrics; mem.: AMA, Jack and Jill Am., Atlanta Med. Assn., Delta Sigma Theta, Phi Beta Kappa. Office: Ctrs for Disease Control 4770 Buford Hwy NE Atlanta GA 30341-3717

YEATES, MARIE R., lawyer; b. New Orleans, Feb. 24, 1956; BS summa cum laude, La. State U., 1977, JD, 1980. Bar: La. 1980, U.S. Ct. Appeals (5th cir.) 1981, U.S. Ct. Appeals (11th cir.) 1981, Tex. 1982, Tex. Supreme Ct. 1982, U.S. Dist. Ct. (so. dist.) Tex. 1985, U.S. Supreme Ct. 1986, U.S. Ct. Appeals (9th cir.) 1998, U.S. Dist. Ct. (no. dist.) Tex. 2001, U.S. Ct. Appeals (10th cir.) 2002, U.S. Ct. Appeals (7th cir.) 2004. Ptnr., co-head Appellate Sect. Vinson & Elkins LLP, Houston, 1990—. Office: Vinson & Elkins LLP First City Tower 1001 Fannin St, Ste 2300 Houston TX 77002 Office Phone: 713-758-4576. E-mail: myeates@velaw.com.

YEATMAN, HARRY CLAY, biologist, educator; b. Ashwood, Tenn., June 22, 1916; s. Trezevant Player and Mary (Wharton) Y.; m. Jean Hansford Anderson, Nov. 24, 1949; children— Henry Clay, Jean Hansford. AB, U. NC, Chapel Hill, 1939, MA, 1942, PhD, 1953; student, Cornell U., Ithaca, NY, summer 1937. Asst. prof. biology U. of South, Sewanee, Tenn., 1950-54, assoc. prof., 1954-60, prof., 1960—, Kenan prof., 1980—, chmn. dept., 1972-76, elderhostel tchr., 1987-88. Vis. prof. marine biology Va. Inst. Marine Sci., Gloucester Point, summer 1967; cons. Smithsonian Instn., Sci. Applications, Inc., La Jolla, Calif., Ctrs. for Disease Control, Atlanta, WHO, Ecol. Analysts, Inc., Balt., Duke Power Co., Charlotte, N.C., Helminthic Disease Branch. Contbr. articles to profl. jours. Served with AUS, 1942-46. Gen. Edn. Bd. fellow, 1941-42; Brown Found. fellow, 1984, State Naturalist award Tenn. Dept. Environ. & Concervation. Fellow AAAS; mem. Soc. Systematic Biology (charter), Soc. Limnology and Oceanography (charter), Soc. Ichthyology and Herpetology, Tenn. Acad. Sci., Am. Micros. Soc., Am. Ornithologists Union, Tenn. Ornithol. Soc., Tenn. Archeol. Soc., Nat. Speleological Soc., Blue Key, Phi Beta Kappa, Sigma Xi, Omicron Delta Kappa, Sigma Nu. Republican. Episcopalian. Home: PO Box 356 199 Cloudcroft Pl Jumpoff Rd Sewanee TN 37375 Office: 735 University Ave Sewanee TN 37383-1000 Office Fax: 931-598-1145.

YELICH, NOLAN T., library director; b. Wis. BS, U. Wis., Oshkosh; MS, U. Wis., Madison. Dir. pub. svcs. Earl Gregg Swem Libr., Coll. William & Mary, Williamsburg, Va., 1968—73; dir. libr. svcs. Libr. Va., Richmond, 1973—94, acting state libr., 1994—95, state libr., 1994—. Recipient John Phillip Immroth Meml. award for Intellectual Freedom, ALA Intellectual Freedom Round Table, 2005. Mem.: Va. Sch. Boards Assn., Va. Libr. Assn. (past pres.), Chief Officers of State Libr. Agys. (Libr. of Congress liason 2004—06). Office: Libr of Va 800 E Broad St Richmond VA 23219 Office Phone: 804-692-3535. Office Fax: 804-692-3594. E-mail: nyelich@lva.lib.va.us.

YELLEN, BENJAMIN, engineering educator; BS in Chemistry, Emory U., Atlanta, Ga., 1998; PhD in Electrical Engring., Drexel U., Phila., Pa., 2004. Grad. rsch. asst., dept. electrical and computer engring. Drexel U., Phila., 2001—04, Nat. Def. Sci. and Engring. Graduate fellow, dept. electrical and computer engring., 2002—05; postdoctoral researcher Children's Hosp. of Phila., Divsn. Cardiology, U. Pa., 2004—05; mem., Ctr. for Bioinspired Materials and Materials Systems Duke U., Durham, NC, 2005—, asst. prof., dept. mechanical engring. and materials sci., 2005—. Invited presenter in field. Contbr. of articles to several publications, chapters to books; ad hoc reviewer. Recipient Benjamin Franklin Key award, Phila., Pa., 2005. Achievements include patents in field; patents pending in field. Office: Duke Univ Dept Mechanical Engring & Materials Sci Box 90300 Hudson Hall CIEMAS Rm 3389 Durham NC 27708-0300 Office Phone: 919-660-8261. Office Fax: 919-660-8963. Business E-Mail: yellon@duke.edu.

YELTON, JEFFREY E., wholesale distribution executive; BS in Bus Adminstrn., U. NC, Chapel Hill, 1981. Various positions including mktg. mgr. & sys. integration mgr. IBM Corp., 1983—95; various positions including dir. sales, v.p. sales & mktg. and exec. v.p. strategy & bus. devel. Kyrus Corp., 1995—2002; CEO N.Am., exec. v.p. acquisitions & bus. devel. Retalix Ltd, 2002—05; v.p. merchandising ScanSource, Inc., 2005—08, pres. POS & barcoding sales unit, 2008—. Office: ScanSource Inc 6 Logue Ct Greenville SC 29615 Office Phone: 864-288-2432. Office Fax: 864-288-1165.

YERRID, C. STEVEN, lawyer; b. Charleston, W.Va., Sept. 30, 1949; s. Charles George and Audrey Faye Yerrid. BA in History and Polit. Sci., La. State U., 1971; JD, Georgetown U., 1975. Bar: Fla. 1975, Va. 1975, U.S. Supreme Ct. 1979, D.C. 1984; cert. civil trial advocate Nat. Bd. Trial Advocacy. Aide U.S. Senator Ellender, Washington, 1971-73; ptnr. Holland & Knight, Tampa, Fla., 1975-86; pres. Stagg, Hardy & Yerrid, Tampa, 1986-89, Yerrid, Knopik & Krieger PA, Tampa, 1990-2000, The Yerrid Law Firm, Tampa, 2000—. Mediator and Cir. Ct. arbitrator Fla. and Fed. Cts. Mem. ABA, Va. Bar Assn., D.C. Bar Assn., Fla. Bar Assn. (chmn. admiralty law com. 1984-85, bd. cert. com. 1988-91, vice chmn. 1990-91, chmn. 1994-95, bd. cert. civil trial lawyer), Southeastern Admiralty Law Inst., Am. Judicature Soc., ATLA (sustaining), Am. Bd. Trial Advocates (advocate), Maritime Law Assn. (proctor), Tex. Trial Lawyers Assn., Acad. Fla. Trial Lawyer (designated continuing legal edn. speaker 1982—, bd. dirs. 1989-97, 2000-01), Inner Cir. Advocates, Internat. Soc. Barristers, Am. Inns. of Ct. (supporting fellow), Cousteau Soc., Tampa Club, Univ. Club, Grand Havana Club, Old Memorial Golf Club. Democrat. Avocations: fishing, tennis, boxing. Office: The Yerrid Law Firm Bank of America Plz Ste 3910 101 E Kennedy Blvd Tampa FL 33602-5192 Office Phone: 813-222-8222. E-mail: syerrid@yerridlaw.com.*

YERVES, KEN, information technology executive; B, Dowling Coll., Oakdale, NY; MBA, Jacksonville Univ., Fla. Cert. computer Programming Grumman Data Sys. Inst., NY. System cons. Todd Travel Promotions, Micro Cons. Co. Inc.; sr. v.p., asst. v.p., remarketing applications devel. JM Family Enterprises, Inc., Deerfield Beach, Fla., asst. v.p., tech. arch., planning and control, v.p., tech. delivery, 2001, exec. v.p., chief adminstrv. officer & chief info. officer; pres. JM Service Ctr. LLC (subs. of JM Family Enterprises, Inc.). Office: JM Family Enterprises Inc 100 Jim Moran Blvd Deerfield Beach FL 33442 Office Phone: 954-429-2000. Office Fax: 954-429-2300. Business E-Mail: ken.yerves@jmfamily.com.

YESAWICH, PETER CHARLES, advertising executive; b. Ithaca, NY, Oct. 28, 1950; s. Paul Joseph Jr. and Elizabeth (Larkin) Y.; m. Paris Pyne; children: Peter Charles, Paul Christopher, Logan Baker. BS, Cornell U., 1972, MS, 1974, PhD, 1976; AMP, Yale U., 1994. Dir. rsch. Robinsons, Inc., Orlando, Fla., 1976-78, v.p., 1978-81, exec. v.p., 1981-83; pres., CEO Ypartnership, Orlando, 1983—. Vis. assoc. prof. Cornell U., Ithaca, 1977—, U. Ctrl. Fla., Orlando, 1988—; chmn. Pope Tourism Inst., Orlando, 1988-90. Co-author: Marketing, Leadership in Hospitality, 2006; contbr. articles to profl. jours. Recipient World Travel award Am. Assn. Travel Editors, 1985, Silver Medal award Am. Assn. Advt. Agys., 1992, Adrian award Hospitality Sales and Mktg. Assn. Internat., 1993; named Author of Yr. Cornell Quar., 1986. Mem. Cornell Hotel Soc., Am. Hotel & Motel Assn., Caribbean Hotel Assn., Hotel Sales Mktg. Assn., Am. Mktg. Assn. Avocations: jogging, writing. Office: Ypartnership 423 S Keller Rd # 100 Orlando FL 32810-6102 Office Phone: 407-875-1111. Business E-Mail: peter.yesawich@ypartnership.com.

YETTER, R. PAUL, lawyer; b. Milw., Aug. 5, 1958; s. Richard and Lobelia (Gutierrez) Y.; m. Patricia D. Yetter, May 6, 1983; children: Chris, Mark, Michael, Joseph, Thomas, Andrew, Daniel. BA in Bus., U. Tex., El Paso, 1980; JD, Columbia U., 1983. Bar: Tex. 1983, US Dist. Ct. (all dists. Tex.), US Ct. Appeals (3rd cir., 5th cir., 11th cir.); bd. cert. in civil trial law Tex. Bd. Legal Specialization. Law clk. to Hon. John R. Brown US Ct. Appeals (5th cir.), Houston, 1983-84; assoc. Baker & Botts, LLP, Houston, 1984-89, ptnr., 1990-97, Yetter Coleman LLP, Houston, 1997—. Chair state judiciary rels. com. State Bar, 1995-96; mem. Funding Parity Task Force, 1995-97; mem. ex officio Jud. Selection Task Force, 1995-97; chair Alliance for Jud. Funding, Inc., 1996—; mem. ex officio contbns. com. Tex. Ctr. for the Judiciary; mem. com. on admissions, So. Dist., Tex., 2000—; mem. Tex. Jud. Found., 2008-. Contbr. articles to profl. jours. Recipient Presdl. citation State Bar Tex., 1996, Disting. alumnus U. Tex., El Paso, 2008; rsch. fellow Southwestern Legal Found., Am. Bd. Trial Advs., Internat. Soc. Barristers; named one of Top 10 Trial Lawyers in Am., Nat. Law Jour., 2004, Tex. Super Lawyer Bus. Litig., Tex. Monthly, 2003-11. Fellow Tex. Bar Foun., Houston Bar Found. Office: Yetter Coleman LLP 2 Houston Ctr 909 Fannin Ste 3600 Houston TX 77010 Office Phone: 713-632-8000. Business E-Mail: pyetter@yettercoleman.com.

YEUNG, CECIL S.T., plastic surgeon; Grad., U. of Toronto, Med. Sch. U. Toronto. Intern Toronto Gen. Hosp.; resident otolaryngology head & neck surgery Univ. of Toronto; fellow head & neck plastic & microvascular reconstructive surgery Washington Univ.; asst. prof. otolaryngology Univ. of Texas Health Sci. Ctr., 1986—90, clin. asst. prof. otolaryngology, 1991; mem. ent collaborative com. St. Luke's Episcopal Hosp., 1996—; mem. msrdp quality assurance com. Univ. of Texas. Recipient Scholastic award, 1987, Residents award, 1987; grantee Biomedical Research Support grant. Mem.: ACS, Harris County Med. Assn., Texas Med. Assn., Am. Assn. of Advance Sci., Am. Acad. of Otolaryngology, Am. Acad. of Facial & Reconstructive Surgery. Office: Yeung Institute 1103 Banks St Houston TX 77006 Office Phone: 713-795-4885.

YI, DONNA, psychiatrist, educator; MD, Meharry Med. Coll., 1983. Diplomate Am. Bd. Psychiatry and Neurology-psychiatry, 1989, Am. Bd. Psychiatry and Neurology-addiction psychiatry, 2004, lic. Tex., 2000. Resident psychiatry LA County - Univ. South Calif. Med. Ctr., 1984—86; resident addiction psychiatry UCLA Neuropsychiatric Inst, 1986—87; faculty Cornell Univ., Univ. South Calif., Baylor Univ.; dir. profl. assessments Menninger Clinic, assoc. chief of staff, eating disorders program med. dir.; psychiatrist Donna Yi MD PA, Houston. Office: Donna Yi MD PA Ste 950 3701 Kirby Dr Ste 790 Houston TX 77098-3923 Office Phone: 832-900-2548. Office Fax: 832-582-8656.

YIELDING, K. LEMONE, physician; b. Auburn, Ala., Mar. 25, 1931; s. Riley Lafayette and Bertie (Dees) Y.; m. Lerena Wade Hauge, Dec. 8, 1973; children: K. Lemone, Michael Lafon, Teresa Louise, Riley Lafayette, Katrina Elizabeth, Elaine Louise Blodgett, Laura Carlen Blodgett. BS, Ala. Poly. Inst., 1949; MS, U. Ala., 1952, MD, 1954. Intern U. Ala. Med. Center, 1954-55; clin. assoc. Nat. Inst. Arthritis and Metabolic Diseases, NIH, 1955-57, sr. investigator, 1958-64; resident med. service USPHS Hosp., Balt., 1957-58; physician in practice of oncology and emergency medicine, 1995—. Adj. asst. prof. medicine Georgetown U. Med. Sch., 1958-64; cons. USPHS, 1964-68, 75—; prof. biochemistry, assoc. prof. medicine, chief lab. molecular biology U. Ala. Med. Ctr., Birmingham, 1964-80; prof., chmn. dept. anatomy, prof. medicine U. So. Ala. Coll. Medicine, Mobile, 1980-87; dean grad. sch. U. Tex. Med. Br., Galveston, 1987-95, dean emeritus, 1995—, v.p. for rsch., 1987-94; cons. Am. Heart Assn., Arthritis Found., NIH, NASA, EPA, FDA, NIOSH. Contbr. to profl. jours., books. Served with USPHS, 1955-64. Grantee USPHS, Am. Cancer Soc., Nat. Found.-March of Dimes, U.S. Army, Am. Inst. Cancer Research. Mem. Am. Soc. Biol. Chemistry, Am. Assn. Cancer Research, Am. Assn. Photobiology, Assn. Research Vision and Ophthalmology, Soc. Exptl. Biology and Medicine, Am. Soc. Pharm. and Exptl. Therapeutics, Am. Assn. Pathologists, So. Soc. Clin. Investigation, Am. Assn. Anatomy, Soc. Toxicology, Sigma Xi. Personal E-mail: k.yielding@yahoo.com.

YING, ANITA K., pediatric endocrinologist, educator; BA in Sociology cum laude, Rice U., 1994; MD, Duke U., 1999. Diplomate American Bd. Internal Medicine, 2003, American Bd. Pediatrics, 2003, American Bd. Internal Medicine-endocrinology, diabetes and metabolism, 2008, American Bd. Pediatrics-pediatric endocrinology, 2009. Clin. intern medicine/pediat. Duke Univ. Med. Ctr., Durham, NC, 1999—2000, clin. resident medicine/pediat., 2000—03; clin. fellow adult and pediatric endocrinology Baylor Coll. of Medicine/The Univ. of Tex. M.D. Anderson Cancer Ctr., Houston, 2004—08; asst. prof., divsn. pediat. The Univ. of Tex. M.D. Anderson Cancer Ctr., Houston, asst. prof., dept. endocrine neoplasia and hormonal disorders, divsn. internal medicine. Office: The University of Texas MD Anderson Cancer Center Unit No 1461 1515 Holcombe Blvd Houston TX 77030 Office Phone: 713-792-2841. Office Fax: 713-794-4065.*

YOAKAM, DWIGHT, musician; b. Pikeville, Ky., Oct. 23, 1956; s. David and Ruth Ann Yoakam. Ph.D (hon.), Ohio Valley Coll., 2005. Founder Bakersfield Biscuits. Musician: (albums) Guitars, Cadillacs, Etc. Etc., 1985, Hillbilly Deluxe, 1987, Buenas Noches From A Lonely Room, 1988, Just Lookin' for a Hit, 1989, If There Was a Way, 1990, This Time, 1993, Dwight Live, 1995, Gone, 1996, Under the Covers, 1997, Come on Christmas, 1997, A Long Way Home, 1998, La Croix d'Amour, 1999, dwightyoakamacoustic.net, 2000, Tomorrow's Sounds Today, 2000, South of Heaven, West of Hell, 2001, Reprise, Please, Baby, 2002, In Others' Words 2003, Population Me, 2003, Dwight's Used Records, 2004, The Very Best of Dwight Yoakam, 2004, Blame the Vain, 2005, Live from Austin, TX, 2005, Dwight Sings Buck, 2007, 3 Pears, 2012; duet with Buck Owens Streets of Bakersfield, 1988 (No. 1 single); co-prodr. stage appearance Southern Rapture, 1993; actor: (films) Red Rock West, 1992, The Little Death, 1995, Sling Blade, 1996, Painted Hero, 1997, The Newton Boys, 1998, Ozzie and Harriet: The Adventures of America's Favorite Family, 1998, The Minus Man, 1999, South of Heaven, West of Hell, 2000, Panic Room, 2002, Hollywood Homicide, 2003, 3-Way, 2004, The Three Burials of Melquiades Estrada, 2005, Wedding Crashers, 2005, Bandidas, 2006, Crank, 2006, Four Christmases, 2008, 2:13, 2009, Crank: High Voltage, 2009, Bloodworth, 2010, The Last Rites of Ransom Pride, 2010, Dirty Girl, 2010, (TV films) Roswell, 1994, Don't Look Back, 1996, When Trumpets Fade, 1998, (TV appearances) Ellen, 1997, (voice) King of the Hill, 1998, Wilfred, 2011. Named Top Male Vocalist Acad. Country Music, 1986; recipient Grammy award for Best Country Vocal Performance by Male for Ain't That Lonely Yet, 1993, Grammy award for Best Country Collaboration with Vocals for Same Old Train, 1998, Premiere Performance acting award Motion Picture Club, 1996, Internat. Touring Artist award CMT Europe, 2007, Pioneer award Acad. Country Music Awards, 2012. Office: c/o Fitzgerald Hartley 1908 Wedgewood Ave Nashville TN 37212

YODER, EDWIN MILTON, JR., columnist, educator, editor, writer; b. Greensboro, NC, July 18, 1934; s. Edwin M. and Mytrice M. (Logue) Y.; m. Mary Jane Warwick, Nov. 1, 1958; children: Anne Daphne, Edwin Warwick. BA, U. N.C., 1956; BA, MA (Rhodes scholar), Oxford U., Eng., 1958; D.H.L. (hon.), Grinnell Coll., 1980, Elon Coll., 1986; DLitt (hon.), U. N.C., 1993, Richmond Coll., London. Editorial writer Charlotte (N.C.) News, 1958-61; editorial editor Greensboro Daily News, 1961—64, assoc. editor, 1965-75; asst. prof. history U. N.C., Greensboro, 1964-65; assoc. editor & editorial page editor Washington Star, 1975—81; syndicated columnist Washington Post Writers Group, 1982-97; prof. journalism and humanities Washington and Lee U., 1992—2002, prof. emeritus, 2002—, novelist and historian, 2002—. Hon. fellow Jesus Coll., Oxford, Eng., 1998—. Author: Night of the Old South Ball, 1984, The Unmaking of a Whig, 1990, Joe Alsop's Cold War, 1995, The Historical Present, 1997, Telling Others What to Think: Recollections of a Pundit, 2004, (novel) Lions at Lamb House, 2007, Vacancy, 2010; contbr. articles to periodicals. Trustee Inst. Early Am. History and Culture, Nat. Humanities Ctr., U. NC, 1990-96. Recipient awards editorial writing N.C. Press Assn., 1958, 61, 66, Walker Stone award Scripps-Howard Found., 1978, Pulitzer prize editorial writing, 1979; Disting. Alumnus award U. N.C., Chapel Hill, 1980 Mem. Nat. Conf. Editorial Writers, Am. Soc. Newspaper Editors, Army Navy Country Club, 1925 F Street Club. Democrat. Episcopalian. Home: 4001 Harris Pl Alexandria VA 22304-1720 Office Phone: 703-751-9022. E-mail: yoderem@aol.com.

YODER, PATRICIA DOHERTY, public relations executive; b. Pitts., Oct. 30, 1939; d. John Addison and Carmella Grace (Conti) Doherty; children: Shari Lynn, Wendy Ann; m. James Ronald Wolfe, Oct. 30, 1999. BA, Duquesne U., 1961. Press sec. US House of Representatives, 1965-69; dir. Office of Pub. Info., City of Ft. Wayne, 1973-76; asst. mgr. pub. and corp. comm. Mellon Bank N.A., Pitts., 1977-79; v.p. pub. affairs Am. Waterways Operators Inc., Washington, 1980-83, sr. v.p., 1983-86, exec. v.p., dir. banking, 1989-91; exec. v.p., dir. internat. banking Hill and Knowlton Inc., Pitts.; sr. v.p. corp. and pub. affairs PNC Fin. Svcs. Group, Pitts., 1987-89; v.p., corp. pub. rels. and advt. GE Capital Svcs. Corp., Stamford, Conn., 1991-95; corp. v.p. pub. affairs and comm. GTE Corp., Stamford, 1995-96; sr. v.p. corp. comm. Avis Group Holdings, Garden City, NY, 1996-99; prin. PDY Assocs., 1999—. Trustee, exec. com. Duquesne U., Shadyside Hosp., Pressley Ridge Sch., Pitts., Ellis Sch.; bd. dirs. Children's Mus., Civic Light Opera, Pitts. Ballet Theatre, Jr. League of City of N.Y. Recipient Outstanding Woman Bus. and Industry, 1988, Disting. Alumni award Duquesne U., 1996, McAnulty Svc. award, 2006. Mem. Pitts. Field Club, Duquesne Club, Indian Harbor Yacht Club, Boca Raton (Fla.) Resort and Country Club, Gardiner's Bay Country Club, Miznergrand Condominium Assn. (pres. bd. dirs.). Roman Catholic. Home and Office: 500 SE 5th Ave Apt 601 Boca Raton FL 33432-5510 Personal E-mail: pdyoder@mac.com.

YODER-WISE, PATRICIA SNYDER, nursing educator; d. Belford Grant and Leona Cora (Mohler) Snyder; m. Robert Thomas Wise, Feb. 17, 1973; children: Doreen Ellen Wise, Deborah Ann Wise. BSN,

Ohio State U., 1963; MSN, Wayne State U., 1968; EdD, Tex. Tech. U., 1984. RN Tex., CNAA-BC. Interim assoc. dean practice program Tex. Tech. U. Health Sci. Ctr. Sch. Nursing, Lubbock, 1979—, interim dean, prof., 1991-93, dean, prof., 1993-2000; clin. prof. U. Tex. Health Sci. Ctr., San Antonio, 1993—2000; prof. Tex. Woman's U., 2004—. Mem. rev. panel Nursing Outlook, 1993—; mem. adv. com. GlaxoWellcome, 1996—2000; mem. Nat. Quality Forum Health Profls. Provide and Health Plans Panel, 2001—06. Author, editor: Leading and Managing in Nursing, 1994 (Book of Yr. award, 1996, 2003), 1998, 2002; co-author: Beyond Leading and Managing, 2006 (Book of Yr. award, 2007); peer reviewer Jour. Profl. Nursing, 1984—2003, mem. editl. bd. Jour. Continuing Edn. Nursing, 1978—; editor: Jour. Continuing Edn. Nursing, 1988—2007; editor-in-chief Jour. Continuing Edn. Nursing, 2008—. Mem. Leadership Am., 1999—2000; participant Leadership Tex.-Found. Women's Resources, 1997—98; mem. Leadership Tex., 1998—99. Recipient Women of Excellence in Medicine, YWCA, Lubbock, 1996, Woman of Excellence in Medicine, 1996, Nurse of Yr. Fellow: Acad. Nursing Edn. (treasurer 2007—), Am. Acad. Nursing (chair Inst. for Nursing Leadership 1999—2002, mem. planning com. 2004); mem.: ANCC (pres. 2005—07), ANA (del. 1995—2000, chair constituent assembly 1998—2000, sec. 2000—02, 1st v.p. 2002—05), Wise Group (pres.), Tex. Nurses Assn. (pres. 1995—99). Home: 7309 93d St Lubbock TX 79424 Office Phone: 806-559-5957, 806-790-4600. Personal E-mail: psywrn@aol.com.

YOHO, FRANKLIN H., gas industry executive; BA in Economics, Wash. & Jefferson Coll.; MBA, Ohio State U. Sr. v.p., mktg. and gas supply Pub. Svc. Co. of NC; v.p., bus. devel. CT Comm., Inc., 2000—02; sr. v.p., comm. ops. Piedmont Natural Gas Co., Inc., 2002—. Bd. mem. Southern Gas Assn.; past v.p. Southeastern Gas Assn.; past trustee Inst. Gas Tech. Bd. dirs. Charlotte Regional Sports Commn., CTN. Office: Piedmont Natural Gas 4720 Piedmont Row Dr Charlotte NC 28210 Mailing: Piedmont Natural Gas PO Box 33068 Charlotte NC 28233 Office Phone: 704-364-3120. Office Fax: 704-365-8515.

YOHO, TED (THEODORE SCOTT YOHO), United States Representative from Florida, veterinarian; b. Mpls., Apr. 13, 1955; m. Carolyn Yoho; children: Katie, Lauren, Tyler. AA, Broward Cmty. Coll., 1977; BS in Animal Sci., U. Fla., 1979; D in Veterinary Medicine, Fla. Coll. Veterinary Medicine, 1983. Pvt. veterinary practice, 1983—2010; mem. US Congress from 3rd Fla. Dist., Washington, 2013—, US House Agrl. Com, 2013—, US House Fgn. Affairs Com, 2013—. Serves in USCG. Mem.: NRA, Fla. Cattleman's Assn., Fla. Assn. Equine Practicioners, Fla. Veterinary Medical Assn., American Veterinary Medical Assn. Republican. Christian. Office: US House of Representatives 511 Cannon House Office Bldg Washington DC 20515 also: 5000 NW 27th Court Ste E Gainesville FL 32606 Office Phone: 202-225-5744, 352-505-0838.*

YOKUBAITIS, ROGER T., lawyer; b. Wharton, Tex., Jan. 9, 1945; Student, St. Louis U.; BA, JD, U. Houston, 1969. Bar: Tex. 1969, U.S. Dist. Ct. (so., we., ea. and no. dists.) Tex., U.S. Ct. Appeals (5th, 9th, 11 cirs.), U.S. Supreme Ct. Ptnr. Carmody & Yokubaitis, L.L.P., Houston, 1995—99; prin. Roger T. Yokubaitis, P.L.L.C., Houston, 2000—. Mem. ABA, Houston Bar Assn., State Bar of Tex., Am. Bankruptcy Inst., Fed. Bar Assn., Federalist Soc. Office Phone: 713-227-9000. Business E-Mail: Yokubaitis@msn.com.

YONTS, BRENT LARRY, state legislator; b. Greenville, Ky., Mar. 21, 1949; s. Larry Ray and Dorothy Nell (Sweeney) Yonts; m. Janice Faye Covington, Nov. 20, 1976; children: Emily, Ellen, Harrison. BS, Murray State U., Ky., 1971; JD, U. Ky., 1975. Bar: Ky. 1976. Assoc. Streets & Cisney, Greenville, 1976—78; pvt. practice atty., 1978—; mem. Greenville Bd. Edn., 1978—83; mem. Dist. 15 Ky. House of Reps., 1997—, chmn. govt. contact rev. com., mem. state govt. com., energy com., judiciary com., labor & indsl. com., tobacco task force. Bd. dirs. Muhlenberg County Indsl. Bd. Treas. First Baptist Ch., 1993—, deacon, 1995—. 1st lt. US Army, 1971—77. Mem.: Ky. Bar. Assn., Kiwanis (former pres.). Democrat. Baptist. Mailing: 232 Norman Circle Greenville KY 42345 Home Phone: 270-338-6790; Office Phone: 270-338-0816, 502-564-8100 ext 686. Fax: 270-338-1639. Business E-Mail: brent.yonts@lrc.ky.gov.

YORK, ANDREW JUSTIN, legislative staff member; b. 1977; m. Mary Claire Butt, Dec. 13, 2008. BA, MA in Polit. Sci., U. Ark., Fayetteville, 1999. Profl. staff mem. US Senate Commerce, Sci. & Transp. Com.; staff Office Atty. Gen. State of Ark., Little Rock; legis. dir. to Senator Mark Pryor, US Senate, Washington, 2003—10, chief of staff, 2010—. Office: Office Senator Mark Pryor 255 Dirksen Senate Office Bldg Washington DC 20510 also: The River Market 500 Clinton Ave Ste 401 Little Rock AR 72201 Office Phone: 202-224-2353. Business E-Mail: andy_york@pryor.senate.gov.

YORK, CAROLYN PLEASANTS STEARNS, language educator; b. High Point, NC, Aug. 23, 1949; d. Frank Ellis and Jessie May (Pleasants) Stearns; m. Guy Aaron York, July 11, 1970; children: Adam Landon, Emily Pleasants, Jonathan Aaron. BA, U. N.C., Greensboro, 1971; MEd, U. N.C., Chapel Hill, 1985. Project Head Start asst. Forsyth County Schs., Winston-Salem, N.C., 1968; publicity dir. House in the Horseshoe Outdoor Drama, Southern Pines, N.C., 1975-76; chpt. I reading tchr. Lee County Schs., Sanford, N.C., 1977-86, English instr., 1987—2012. Reading instr. Ctrl. Carolina C.C., Sanford, 1985; reading chmn. So. Assn., Sanford, 1978; workshop dir., conf. spkr. N.C. Assn. Compensatory Educators, Raleigh, 1983; advisor, Internat. Thespian Soc., 2002-2003; writer-in-residence Peace Coll EDS Prog., 2003; diplay artis, Artists Colony Artists Loft, 2008-12; judge Fields Earth Poetry Symposium, 2010. Author: (poetry) Pleasantries, 1996, Weaver of Destiny, 1999, (novel) Dream Within a Dream, 2011; editor newsletter Creations, 1976; appeared on Friday Noon Poets Assn. Pub. TV Program, 1997, 2004-05, Sanford Centennial Adv. Com., 2007; photographer Lee High Rev. lit. mag., 1998-99, Tarheel Tapestry, 2004, 10; author numerous poems. Founding mem. Lee County Arts Coun., Sanford, 1975, v.p. 2004-05, pres., 2005-10; sec. Footlight Players, Lee County Recreation Dept., 2002, pres. 2005—; Sunday Sch. tchr., Bible sch. tchr. First Presbyn. Ch., Sanford, 1982, 86-89; bd. dir. Child Devel. Ctr., Sanford, 1980-82; adv. coun. Cmty. Playhouse of the Temple Theater, 1997-99; Builders Club sponsor Kiwanis Club of Lee County, Sanford, 1978-80. Recipient local and state prize, N.C. Reading Assn., 1995, 1st prize, Fields of Earth Poetry Symposium, 1996, Am. Scholastic Press Assn., 2000, Golden Pen award, Writers' Ink Guild, 2005. Mem. NC Poetry Soc. (bd. dir., 3d v.p. 1997-2010, workshop dir. 1993, 2d prize 1993, 1st prize 1999), San-Lee Writers (pres. 1993—, co-founder), Tri County English Alliance (coord., English Fair rep. 1995-2001), Lee County Reading Assn. (young authors' chmn. 1996-97; advisor lit. mag. Lee High Rev. 1998-2005), Guild Am. Papercutters, Poetry Coun. NC (contest judge 2003, First prize, 2013), Artists Loft (vol.), Boys and Girls Club (vol. mentor). Avocation: snorkeling. Home: 315 N Steele St Sanford NC 27330-3956 E-mail: yorkshome@wave-net.net.

YORK, JAMES WESLEY, JR., retired theoretical physicist, educator; b. Raleigh, NC, July 3, 1939; s. James Wesley and Mary Smedes (Poyner) York; m. Betty Louise Mattern, Aug. 19, 1961 (div. Apr. 2002); m. Sarah Williams Wolf, June 13, 2002; children: Virginia York Setzer, Guilford Mattern. BS with high honors in Physics, N.C. State U., Raleigh, 1962, PhD in Physics, 1966. Asst. prof. N.C. State U., Raleigh, 1965-68; rsch. assoc. Princeton U., 1968-69, lectr., 1969-70, asst. prof., 1970-73; assoc. prof. U. N.C., Chapel Hill, 1973-77, prof. dept. physics, 1977-89, Agnew H. Bahnson, Jr. disting. prof. physics, 1989—2001, dir. Inst. Field Physics, 1984-90; vis. asst. prof. U. Md., College Park, 1972; prof. associe U. Paris, 1976; vis. scientist ctr. astrophysics Harvard, Smithsonian, Cambridge, 1977; vis. prof. U. Tex., Austin, 1979, 87; prof. physics Cornell U., 2002—07; rsch. prof. NC State U., 2007—12. Spkr. Internat. Symposium on Methods of Differential Geometry in Physics and Mechanics, Warsaw, 1976; spr. in field; Alfred Schild Meml. lectr. U. Tex., 1979; del. Seventh Internat. Congress on Math. Physics, Boulder, Colo., 1983, Tex. Symposium on Relativistic Astrophysics, Jerusalem, 1984, Marcel Grossman Meeting, Rome, 1985, Jerusalem, 1997, Rio de Janeiro, 2003, Paris, 2009, NATO Advanced Study Inst., Les Houches, France, 1982, Huelva, Spain, 1992, Paris, 1992, Banff, Canada, 1992, other internat. and nat. meetings; co-organizer sci. meetings including Neutron stars and pulsars, Princeton, 1969; Spacetime dynamics Aspen Ctr. for Theoretical Physics, 1981, Classical Problems in Gravitation, 1990, Cosmic Censorship, 1992; coord. lectr. Inst. Theoretical Physics U. Calif., Santa Barbara, 2000; mem. com. of visitors physics divsn NSF, 1991; plenary lectr. Fifth Can. Conf. on Gen. Relativity and Astrophysics, Waterloo, 1993, Directions in Gen. Relativity, College Park, Md., 1993, Pacific Coast Gravity Mtg., Salt Lake City, 1996, 2d Samos meeting, Greece, 1998; plenary lectr. 50 Years of the Cauchy Problem, Cargese, Corsica, 2002; hon. physics chmn. Cornelius Lanczos Internat. Centenary, Raleigh, NC, 1993; vis. prof. dept. physics N.C. State U., 1998—99, Inter-Instl. Disting. prof. physics, 2001—02. Mem. editl. bd. Jour. Math. Physics, 1989-92; contbr. chpts. to books, articles to sci. jours. Decorated Companion of St. Patrick, 1960; Ford Found. fellow, 1962-65, NSF postdoctoral fellow, 1969-70; Battelle Found. grantee, 1967, Nat. Rsch. Com. France grantee, 1976, NSF grantee, 1974—2007, travel grantee, 1971, 76, 83, 84; U.S.A.-Israel Binat. Sci. Found. grantee, 1987-90, 90-93, Kenan Found. grantee, 1990, W.N. Reynolds Found. grantee, 1998; recipient Disting. Alumnus award, 1997, Marcel Grossmann prize, Rio de Janeiro, 2003; co-winner Dannie Heineman prize for math. physics Am. Phys. Soc., 2003. Fellow Am. Phys. Soc.; mem. AAAS, Internat. Soc. Gen. Relativity and Gravitation, Phi Beta Kappa, Sigma Xi, Phi Kappa Phi, Tau Beta Pi, Sigma Pi Sigma, Pi Mu Epsilon, Phi Eta Sigma. Avocations: literature, reading. Personal E-mail: jaswyork1@mac.com.

YORK, JILL, state legislator, small business owner; b. Oct. 21, 1966; d. James H. and Sally (Hunter) York. BA in Psychology, Transylvania U., Lexington, Ky., 1988; grad. student in journalism, Marshall U. W. Page Pitt Sch. Journalism, Huntington, W.Va., 1990—92. Owner, operator Printworks Unlimited, Inc., Grayson, Ky., 1993—; mem. Dist. 96 Ky. House of Reps., 2009—. Asst. advisor Venture Crew 160; mem. Bayless Meml. Presbyn. Ch., Grayson; mem., pres., media chair Carter County Fair Bd. Named to Hon. Order of Ky. Colonels. Mem.: NRA, Grayson Area C. of C. (past pres., mem. bd. dirs., S.V. Pratt Cmty. Svc. award), Grayson Jaycees (past pres.), Delta Theta of Phi Mu. Republican. Presbyterian. Mailing: PO Box 591 Grayson KY 41143 Office: Ky Legislature Annex Rm 451D 702 Capitol Ave Frankfort KY 40601 Office Phone: 606-474-7263, 502-564-8100 ext. 602. Office Fax: 606-474-7638. Business E-Mail: jill.york@lrc.ky.gov.

YORK, JOHN LYNDAL, medical educator; b. Morton, Tex., Aug. 14, 1936; s. James Lee and Jewell Fern (Breedin) Y.; m. Cynthia Carolyn Giles, June 29, 1958; children: John Lee, Michelle Annette. BS in Chemistry and Math., Harding Coll., 1958; PhD in Physiol. Chemistry, Johns Hopkins U., 1962. NIH predoctoral rsch. fellow Johns Hopkins U., Balt., 1958-62, fellow dept. physiol. chemistry Sch. Medicine, 1962-64; biochemist Stanford Rsch. Inst., Menlo Park, Calif., 1964-65; asst. prof. dept. biochemistry Coll. Basic Med. Sci. U. Tenn., Memphis, 1965-68; assoc. prof. dept. biochemistry Coll. Medicine U. Ark., Little Rock, 1968-76, prof. dept. biochemistry, 1977—2002, prof. emeritus, 2002; prof. dept. chemistry Hendrix Coll. Conway, 2006—07. Mem. faculty-student liason com. U. Ark., 1969-70, co-chair edn. bldg. II wet lab. design com., 1973-74, computer aided instrn. com., 1972-74, rep. to univ. senate coun., 1973-74, animal care com., 1975-76, chmn. grad. com., 1976-80, rep. to pres.'s grad. adv. coun., 1976-78, subcom. on curriculum, 1976-77, program evaluation com., 1976-78, search com. for pharmacology chmn., 1976-77, chmn. biochemistry grad. student admissions, 1975-79, med. biochemistry cirriculum com., 1975-80, 89—, grad. biochemistry com., 1981-85, coll. med. appeals bd., 1980-2002, com. on ednl. devel. Acad. Senate, 1979-80, com. on ednl. resources, 1979-80, chmn. com. on acad. affairs., 1980-81, search com. for assoc. dean grad. sch., 1982, dir. grad. program dept. biochemistry, 1983-85, dir. seminar program dept. biochemistry, 1986-95, chmn. biochemistry faculty recruitment com., 1982-86, 90-92, exec. com. dept. biochemistry, 1982—, chmn. faculty senate, 1987, handbook com., 1988-89, com. on assessment instrn., 1991-92, chair grad. assessment com. grad. sch., 2000-02; vis. prof. dept. coagulation rsch. Karolinska Inst., Stockholm, 1974-75; vis. prof. Hendrix Coll., Conway, Ark., 2006; judge biochemistry divsn. Ark. State Sci. Fair, 1985—2007; mem. River Mountain Park adv. com. Little Rock Parks Dept., 1991; mem. Gov's Mercury Adv. Com., 1993—98; bd. dirs. Ark. Audobon Soc., 2004-; mem. adv. bd. Ark. Wildlife Observation or Trails Program, 2012-. Author: The Porphyrias, 1972, (with N.S. Sloan) Review of Biochemistry, 1969, translated into German, 1972; contbr. numerous articles and abstracts to profl. and sci. jours. Grantee NIH, 1966-69, 76-78, 80-84, 89-91, 91-94, NSF, 1969-74, Swedish Med. Rsch. Coun., 1974-75, Am. Cancer Soc., 1986-88. Fellow Swedish Med. Rsch. Coun.; mem. AAAS, AAUP (Ark. conf. exec. com. 1994, co-chair Ark. Conf. com. 1995-97, chair 1998-2002), Am. Chem. Soc. (vice chmn. ctrl. Ark. sect. 1971-72, chmn. 1972-73, program chmn. 33rd Southwest regional meeting 1977, 43rd Southwest regional meeting 1987, Disting. Svc. award 1989), Soc. Biol. Chemists, Johns Hopkins Med. and Surg. Assn., Sigma Xi., Alpha Chi. Home: 42 Pine Manor Dr Little Rock AR 72207-5137

YORK, TINA, painter; b. Germany, Feb. 9, 1951; Student, Sch. Mus. Fine Arts, Boston, 1967-71; studied with, George Dergalis, Wayland, Mass., 1967-75; BA cum laude, Brandeis U., 1978; postgrad., N.Y. Med. Coll., 1980-83. Contbr. works to numerous publs., 1987-2003; columns in newspapers; one woman shows include Gallery Contemporary Art, Provincetown, Mass., 1969, Springfield (Mass.) Art Assn., 1971, Copley Soc., Boston, 1972-73, Boston U., 1974, Mendler Gallery, Rockport, Mass., 1974, Cambridge (Mass.) Art Assn., 1975, Ames Gallery, N.Y.C., 1976, Gallery Seven, Boston, 1977, Brandeis U., Waltham, Mass., 1978, Rue Oker Gallery of Art, Sturbridge, Mass., 1979, Art Collectors Gallery, N.Y.C., 1981, 153 Gallery, Inc., N.Y.C., 1982, Creative Concepts, L.A., 1984, Alpha Contemporary Exhibits, L.A., 1985, Darraby Gallery, L.A., 1986, 8th St. Gallery, L.A., 1986, Koplin Gallery, L.A., 1987, Galerie Beverly Hills, Calif., 1988, Conv. Ctr., Rome, 1988, Merck, Sharpe & Dohme, Rahway, N.J., 1988, Erlgangen Kultur Borse, Germany, 1989, Arwell Gallery, Laguna, Calif., 1989, Deutsch-Amerikanisches Inst., Regensburg, Germany, 1990, Art in Pub. Bldgs., Nuremberg, Germany, 1990, Art Expo, N.Y.C., 1990, Amerikahaus, Nuremberg, 1990, Art 5, Nuremberg, 1990, Dresdner Bank, Nuremberg, 1990, Amer. Hosp. Assn., Washington, 1990, So. Med. Assn., Nashville, 1990, 94-95, Studio Gallery, North Hollywood, Calif., 1991-92, Galerie Lehman, Germany, Galerie Sud, Studio la Citta, Italy, Studio Gallery, Calif., 1991 La Foire Internat. d'Art Contemporain, Paris, 1992, 94, Med. Heritage Gall., Waco, Tex., 1991, Herbstmesse, Frankfurt, Germany, 1992-93, Kunstforum Internat., Aachen, Germany, 1993, Kunstlerhaus, Germany, 1993, Ambiente, Frankfurt, 2003-07, ART/LA, 1993-95, Internat. Art Fair, Czechoslovakia, 2003-2007, Art Fair, Seattle, 1993-94, Art Expo, Chgo., 1993-94, Art Expo, N.Y.C., 1993-96, Chgo. Trade Show, 1993, 95, 97, Toronto Trade Show, 1993, Art Cologne, Germany, 1993-94, 96, Centre d'Art Contemporain, Switzerland, Dresdner Bank, Germany, Galerie Littmann, Switzerland, Galerie Fischer, 1994, Art Asia, Hong Kong, 1994-96, Art Expo, Calif., 1994, 96, PPFA Toronto Trade Show, 1994-95, Limited Edit. Expo, New Orleans, 1994-95, Frankfurt Book Fair, 1994, 97-98, 2000, 03, Internat. Spring Fair, Birmingham, Eng., 1994, 95, Art Miami, 1994-95, Exposition of Art, Sydney, Australia, 1993, Art Taipei, Taiwan, 1993, 94, 95, Art Santa Fe, 1993-95, NASA Ames Rsch. Ctr., Moffett Field, Calif., 1994, NASA Johnson Space Ctr., Houston, 1995, Galerie Rudelko, Germany, Scheffler Galerie, Germany, 1995, Studio Gall., Ariz., 1996, Jahns House, Germany, 1996, Internat. Contemporary Art Fair, Madrid, 1995, West Valley Mus. Art, Phoenix, 1998, Las Vegas Art Mus., 2000, Paul Joseph Galleries, Las Vegas, 2002, Rio Decor, 2003, Tina York Studio, Naples, Fla., 2003, Marco Island Art Assn., Fla. 2004, Studio Gallery, Naples, 2004, 06, Area Arts Gallery, Naples, Fla., 2005, I.C. Fine Art 2000 Gallery, Las Vegas, 2005, Waterways Studios, Naples, 2007, Arsenault Gallery, 2007, South Dennis Art Gallery, NJ, 2009-10, Cape May Ct. Hoouse, 2009-10; group shows include Area Arts Gallery, Mag., Naples, Floridaand article and painting, NASA Art Programs, Washington, 2007, Mus. Fine Arts, Salt Lake City, Mus. Art, Las Vegas, Regional Mus. Art, Bautzen, Germany, 2007, Mus. Art, Downey, Calif., 2007, Carter Ctr., Atlanta, 2008, Shakespeare Theatre, NJ, 2007, Las Vegas Art Mus., Nev., 2007, Washigton, 2007; represented in permanent collections, Rio Decor, Mus. of Art, Las Vegas, 2009, Downey (Calif.) Mus. Art, 2010, Mus. Fine Arts, Salt Lake City, Mcpl. Art Mus., Osaka, Japan, Regional Mus. Art, Bautzen, Germany, Carter Ctr., Atlanta, Kennedy Space Ctr., Fla., New Zealand Space Adminstrn., Auckland, NASA, Internat. Peace Acad., NY, USIA, BBC (Brit. Broadcasting Co.), Lagan Jute, Ltd., India, NIH, Universitet Kliment Orchridski, Bulgaria, Hiatt Internat., Beverly Hills, Calif., Paris, Gallery Dmovrosek, Yugoslavia, Columbia U., Nat. Cancer Inst., Md., Kulturamt der Stadt Nurnberg, Germany, Planetary Soc., Calif., Mayo Clin., Ariz., Nat. Air and Space Mus., Washington, Nat. Air and Space Mus., others; represented on Artrain USA; pub. NASA/Exploration of Space, 2004; contbr. various articles and paintings in journals, to profl. publs. First prize painting Arts Fest., Scituate, MA, 1969, Internatl. Show, Fall River, MA, 1971; third prize mixed media painting, De Cordova Mus., Lincoln, MA, 1972; second prize painting, Amer. Artists in Paris, Paris, 1975; first prize mixed media painting Inst. Contemporary Art, 1979; Gold medal painting, Spring Arts Fest., LA, 1985; first prize mixed media painting, One Fifty Three Gall., Inc., 1987. Mem.: Top One Percent Soc., Internat. High IQ Soc. Home: 754 Waterloo Ct Naples FL 34120-0495 Office Phone: 239-455-2164. Business E-Mail: tinayorkstudio@aol.com.

YORK, VERMELLE CARDWELL, retired real estate broker and developer; b. Evergreen, Ala., Jan. 30, 1925; d. Frederick Lofton and Emmie Mildred (Pitts) Cardwell; m. E. Travis York, Jr., Dec. 26, 1946; children: Lisa, Travis. BS, Auburn U., Ala., 1946. Pres. Tralisa Corp., Gainesville, Fla., 1966—87, sec., treas., 1988—94, Caret Corp., Gainesville, Fla., 1979—86, pres., 1987—2004; ret., 2004. Mem. devel. com. Harn Mus., Gainesville, 1990-96, Hospice House, Gainesville, 1992-96; co-chair March of Dimes, Gainesville, 1995, Red Ribbon Campaign, 1989, 90; bd. dirs. Keep Alachua County Beautiful, Phillips Ctr. Performing Arts U. Fla.; bd. Gainesville Cmty. Found. Recipient Pres.'s Medallion, U. Fla., 1980; named Woman of Distinction, Santa Fe C.C., Gainesville, Fla., 1988, Vam York Theatre at Gainesville Cmty. Playhouse 05 dedicated in her honor; named one of Women Who Make a Difference, Girl Scouts Am., 2005 Mem. Gainesville Builders Assn. (bd. dirs. 1997—), The Heritage Club (mem. amb. com. 1991-96), P.E.O. (pres. 1989-90), Surfside N. Club, (dir. 1988-91), Gainesville Women's Forum (membership chair 1994-96), Altrusa, Rotary, DAR, Phi Kappa Phi. Avocation: genealogy. Home: 5200 SW 25th Blvd #4216 Gainesville FL 32608-8925

YORMARK, MICHAEL, professional sports team executive; b. Sept. 28, 1966; s. Arlene Sloan; m. Dana Yormark; 1 child, Sophia. Attended, U. Md.; MA in Sports Mgmt., Ohio U., 1989. Corp. sponsorship sales NY Yankees, Katz Comm., NYC; v.p. sales Front Row Comm.; v.p. integrated sales and broadcasting Columbus Blue Jackets; exec. v.p. Palace Sports & Entertainment, Tampa Bay Lightning; joined Sunrise Sports & Entertainment, 2003, pres., COO, 2007—, Fla. Panthers, 2007—13, pres., CEO, 2013—. Alt. gov. NHL Bd. Govs. Pres. bd. City of Sunrise Found.; bd. mem. Broward Health, Boys & Girls Club of Broward County. Recipient City of Sunrise Bus. Leader Award; named one of 40 Under 40, Tampa Bay Bus. Jour., SportsBusiness Jour. Mem.: Young Pres. Orgn. Office: Florida Panthers One Panther Parkway Sunrise FL 33323*

YOST, JOSEPH R., state legislator; b. Pearisburg, Va., Oct. 9, 1986; m. Lisa Michelle Robinson. BS, Radford U., 2006, MA, 2008. Mem. Dist. 12 Va. House of Delegates, 2012—, mem. Edn. Com. & Health Welfare and Institutions Com. Mem. New River Cmty. Criminal Justice Bd. Mem.: Sons. of the American Revolution. Republican. Office: General Assembly Building PO Box 406 Richmond VA 23218 also: PO Box 621 Blacksburg VA 24063 Office Phone: 804-698-1012. Office Fax: 804-698-6712. E-mail: DelJYost@House.virginia.gov.

YOSTE, CHARLES TODD, lawyer; b. Vicksburg, Miss., Nov. 11, 1948; s. Harry M. and Charlene (Todd) Y. BS, Miss. State U., 1971; JD, U. Miss., 1976. Bar: Miss. 1976, U.S. Dist. Ct. Miss. 1976, U.S. Ct. Appeals, 1982, U.S. Supreme Ct. 2002. Sole practice, Starkville, Miss., 1976—; city atty., 1979-85; pros. atty., 1977-79; city judge, 1981-82. Candidate for Congress 2d dist., Miss., 1980. Served to capt. U.S. Army, 1971-73. Recipient Outstanding Young Man award Starkville Jaycees, 1980. Mem. ABA, Miss. Bar Assn., Am. Trial Lawyers Assn., Miss. Trial Lawyers Assn. (bd. govs. 1988-94), Starkville C. of C. (pres. 1982), Am. Legion, Rotary, Am. Coll. Barristers, Internat. Acad. Litigators. Republican. Roman Catholic. Office: PO Box 80288 Starkville MS 39759-0288 Home: PO Box 488 Starkville MS 39760-0488 Office Phone: 662-323-1233. Business E-Mail: cyoste@yostelaw.com.

YOUNA, GERARD, information technology executive; Degree in Info. Tech. Engring., Inst. Informatique d'Entreprise, Paris. Various positions, including consulting engr., dir., IS Divsn. McDonnell Douglas Corp.; regional mng. dir. Tech Data Corp., France, Switzerland, gen. mgr., sales & mktg. France, 1989, regional mng. dir. Israel, 1989—99, France, 1989—2000, sr. v.p. Southern Europe Clearwater, Fla., 2000—04, v.p., Southern Europe, 2000, pres., Europe, 2004. Office: Tech Data Corp 5350 Tech Data Dr Clearwater FL 33760-3122 Office Fax: 727-538-7803. Business E-Mail: gyouna@techdata.com.

YOUNG, ALFRED BYRON, retired neurosurgeon; b. Nov. 6, 1939; s. Carlos Young and Margaret Louise (Rayburn) Stout; m. Judith Floy Gaines, Aug. 26, 1961; children: John Kevin, Alexander Bryce. BA, Transylvania U., 1961, D (hon.), 2006; MD, U. Ky., 1965; DSc honoris causa, Transylvania U., 2006. Diplomate Am. Bd. Neurol. Surgery (guest examiner 1980, 84, 94, 2005). Intern Vanderbilt U., Nashville, 1965-66, asst. resident in surgery, 1966-67, resident in neurosurgery, 1967-71; clin. instr. U. Ky., Lexington, Ky., 1973-74; pvt. practice Lexington, Ky., 1973-74; asst. prof. divsn. neurosurgery, dept. surgery U. Ky. Med. Ctr., Lexington, Ky., 1974—, prof., 1982—2011, acting chief, 1974-75, chief neurosurgery, 1977—2008; chief of staff U. Hosp., 2000—05, assoc. dean clin. affairs, 2000—05, sr. assoc. dean for clin. affairs, 2005—06, founding chair dept. neurosurgery, 2008—09; dir. Ky. Neurosci. Inst., 2000—11. Chmn. dept. surgery U. Ky., 1986-96, chmn. operating rm. comm. 1986-96, hosp. clin. bd., 1986-96, VA dean's comm. 1986-96, press comm., 1991-96, hosp. bd. elected faculty rep., 1994-96, chmn. managed care comm., 1994-96, coun. clin. chair, 1995-96; vis. prof. U. Cin., 1981, U. Louisville, 1988, Vanderbilt U., 1988; chmn. Johnston-Wright Endowed chair, 1988-2007, chair dept. neurosurg., 2008-09; dir. Ky. Neuroscience Inst., 2004—; past bd. dirs. Ky. Organ Donor Affiliates; mem. exec. com., bd. trustees Transylvania U., bd. mem. North America Gaumma Knife Constorium, exec. com. mem., Tronsylvania U., chair Strategic Planning Com.; presenter in field. Contbr. articles to profl. jours. Adv. bd. Ctrl. Bank & Trust, 1999—2005; mem. liaison com. Shriner's Hosp., 1999—2005; bd. mem. North American Gamma Knife Consortium. Maj. US Army, 1971—73, Korea. Recipient Disting. Outstanding Alumnus award, Transylvania U., 2001, Disting. Alumnus award, 2001, Morrison Medallion awards, 2001, Irving E. Lunger award, 2011, Mahaley Clin. Rsch. award, Congress Neurol. Surgeons, Assn. Neurol Surgeons, 1998, William R Willard Deoris award, UK Coll Med., 2004, Disting. Alumni award, 2001, Irwin Elunger award, Tronsylvania U., 2011; named one of Am.'s Best Drs., 2005—11, Am.'s Top Drs. for Cancer, 2005, 2006—11; grantee NIH, 1987—95, 1988—99, Bowman Gray/Pfizer, 1992—96, Upjohn Pharm., 1992—94, Sterling Winthrop, 1992—95, Ciba-Geigy, 1993—97. Mem. ACS, AMA, NIH (advisory comm. 1991-95, monitoring comm. 1994—, com. mem.), Nat. Inst. Neurol. Disorders, Acad. Neurological Surgeons, Am. Surgical Assn., Soc. Neurological Surgeons, Neurosurgical Soc. Am., Am. Assn. Neurological Surgeons (bylaws comm. 1979-83, chmn. bylaws comm. 1982-83, rep. to Nat. Inst. Neurol and Comm. Disorders and Stroke 1987-2010), Congress Neurological Surgeons (rep. to NIH 1987—2010), Ky. Med. Assn., Fayette County Med. Soc., Southern Neurosurgical Soc. (pres. 1991-92, pres.-elect 1990, exec. coun. 1986-94, treas. 1986-89, chmn. fin. comm. 1986-89, long range planning comm. 1990—, chmn. long range planning comm. 1992-93, constn. and bylaws comm. 1989-90, comm. disting. practioner award, 1992—, chmn. comm. disting. practioner award, 1992-93, nominating comm. 1992—, chmn. nominating comm. 1992-93, residents award comm. 1981-82), Am. Soc. Stereotactic and Functional Neurosurgery, Ky. Neurosurgical Soc. (pres. 1990-91), Soc. Internat. Surgery, Internat. Stereotactic Radiosurgery Soc., Leksell Gamma Knife Soc., Neurotrauma Soc Achievements include patent (with others) in Multiple Function Intubation Apparatus and Method, 5,836,935 Implantable refillable controlled release device to deliver drugs directly to an internal portion of the body; research in zinc supplementation associated with improved neurologic recovery rate and visceral protein levels of patients with severe closed head-injury, nutritional and metabolic mgmt. of the head-injury patient, demographics of brain metastasis, neurosurgical diseases of aging patients, brain metastases, nutritional and metabolic variables correlate with amino acid forearm flux in patients with severe head injury, effect of lovastatin on early carotid atherosclerosis and cardiovascular events, cyclosporins- severe head injury, stereotactic surgery for brain tumors and numerous others.

YOUNG, AUSTIN PRENTISS, III, retired communications executive; b. Houston, Nov. 11, 1940; s. Austin P. Jr. and Gracemary (Barbato) Crenshaw; m. Jacklyn Joy Goodroe (div. Oct. 1982); m. Susan Critendon Roach Bailey, Apr. 13, 1985; children: Lisa Lee Jilek, Adam Edward Young, Kathryn Bennet Bailey, Charles William Bailey III. BBA, U. Tex., 1962. CPA, Tex., N.Y. Chmn., bd. dirs. Tower Group, Inc., Amerisafe, Inc.; chmn., Fin., Risk Mgmt. and Audit Com. Administaff Inc.; profl. staff KPMG Peat Marwick, Houston, 1962—74, ptnr. NYC, 1974—77, Houston, 1977—86; CFO Sun Resorts Ltd., N.A., St. Maarten, 1986—87; sr. v.p. gen. auditor American General Corp., Houston, 1987—88, sr. v.p., CFO, 1988—; exec. v.p., fin. & adminstrn. Metamor Worldwide, Inc., 1996—99; sr. v.p., CFO & treas. CellStar Corp., 1999—2001. Bd. dirs. Administaff Inc., 2003—, chmn. Finance, Risk Mgmt. and Audit Com. Bd. dirs. Alley Theatre, 1990—, Houston Ballet Found., 1984—, treas., 1990-90. Capt. Q.M., U.S. Army, 1962-70., mem. Houston and State Chpts. of the Tex. Soc. of CPA, mem. AICPA, mem. Fin. Execs. Inst. Mem. Zool. Soc. Houston (v.p. 1978-86, bd. dirs. 1977—), Escape Ctr., Inc. (bd. dirs. 1988—), Exchange Club (pres. 1984-85, 90-91). Avocation: hot air ballooning. Office: Administaff Inc Bd Directors 19001 Crescent Springs Dr Kingwood TX 77339-3802 also: Am Gen Corp 2929 Allen Pkwy Houston TX 77019-7100 Office Phone: 281-358-8986. E-mail: austin_young@administaff.com.

YOUNG, BARNEY THORNTON, lawyer; b. Chillicothe, Tex., Aug. 10, 1934; s. Bayne and Helen Irene (Thornton) Y.; m. Sarah Elizabeth Taylor, Aug. 31, 1957; children: Jay Thornton, Sarah Elizabeth, Serena Taylor. BA, Yale U., 1955; LLB, U. Tex., 1958. Bar: Tex. 1958. Assoc. Thompson, Knight, Wright & Simmons, Dallas, 1958-65; ptnr. Rain, Harrell, Emery, Young & Doke, Dallas, 1965-87; shareholder Locke Purnell Rain Harrell (A Profl. Corp.), 1987-98; of counsel Locke, Lord, LLP, 1999—. Bd. dirs. Mental Health Assn. Dallas County, Inc., 1969-72, Trammell Crow Family Found., 1984-87, Hockaday Sch., Dallas, 1971-77, 90—, chmn., 1994-96, Dallas Zool. Soc., 1986-92, Lamplighter Sch., Dallas, 1976-99, 2006—, chmn., 1983-86, St. Mark's Sch., Dallas, 1970—, pres., 1976-78, The Found. for Callier Ctr. and Comm. Disorders, 1988-99, Friends of Ctr. for Human Nutrition, 1988-2005, Dallas Hist. Soc., 1993-2001, Susan G. Komen Breast Cancer Found., 2000-06, Nat. Assn. Ind. Schs., 2000-04; mem. Yale Devel. Bd., 1984-91, 98—2011, Yale U. Coun. Com. on Devel. Rev., 1988-93. Recipient Yale U. medal, 1999. Fellow Tex. Bar Found., Dallas Bar Found.; mem. ABA, Tex. Bar Assn., Dallas Bar Assn., Am. Judicature Soc., Order of Coif, Philos. Soc. Tex., Phi Beta Kappa, Pi Sigma Alpha, Phi Gamma Delta, Phi Delta Phi, Dallas Country Club., Petroleum Club (Dallas), Yale Club (Dallas, NYC, medal 2001), Quail Run Club (Santa Fe). Office Phone: 214-740-8402. Business E-Mail: byoung3@me.com.

YOUNG, BILL, lawyer, former health products executive; m. Jane Young; 1 child, Beth. B, JD, Vanderbilt U., Nashville. Law clk. to Hon. George Paine US Bankruptcy Ct.; with FDIC, Washington; pvt. practice atty. Nashville, Washington, DC; former asst. atty. gen., sr. counsel Office of Atty. Gen., Tenn., 1987—95; dep. commr. of TennCare divsn. Tenn. Dept. Commerce and Ins., 1995—99; pres. The Hosp. Alliance Tenn.; sr. v.p., gen. counsel Tenn. Hosp. Assn.; univ. counsel Vanderbilt U., Nashville; sr. v.p., gen. counsel, chief compliance officer Blue Cross Blue Shield Tenn., 2003—11; solicitor gen. Office of Atty. Gen., Tenn., 2011—. Office: Tenn Atty Generals Office PO Box 20207 Nashville TN 37202-4015

YOUNG, BRYANT COLBY, college football coach, retired professional football player; b. Chicago Heights, Ill., Jan. 27, 1972; m. Kristen Young; children: Kai, Colby, Kennedy, Bryce, Kamille. B in Mktg., U. Notre Dame, Ind., 1994. Defensive tackle San Francisco 49ers, 1994—2007; grad. asst. U. Notre Dame Fighting Irish, 2009; defensive line coach San Jose State U. Spartans, 2010, U. Fla. Gators, 2011—. Named 1st Team NFL All-Pro, 1996, NFL Comeback Player of Yr., AP, 1999; named to Nat. Football Conf. Pro Bowl Team, NFL, 1996, 1999, 2001, 2002. Achievements include member of NFL Super Bowl XXIX championship winning San Francisco 49ers; leading the NFL in: safeties, 1996, 1999. Office: University of Florida Football Program c/o Univeristy Athletic Assn PO Box 14485 Gainesville FL 32604*

YOUNG, CHARLES, JR., state legislator; Attended, Meridian CC, Miss., Tougaloo Coll., Miss. State U., Meridian. Cosmetics salesman E.F. Young, Jr. Mfg. Co.; mem. Dist. 82 Miss. House of Reps., Jackson, 2012—. Mem. Newell Chapel C.M.E. Ch. Mem.: Masons. Democrat. Methodist. Office: Miss House of Reps PO Box 1018 Jackson MS 39215 Home Phone: 601-693-1961. Business E-Mail: cyoung@house.ms.gov.

YOUNG, CHARLES B., energy executive; Grad., U.S. Naval Acad., 1970; MS in Civil Engring., U. Del., 1971. Commd. ensign USN, advanced through grades to rear adm., submarine officer, RADM, 1970—2006, various assignments, 1972-86, dir., strategic sys. programs, 2002—06, assoc. mem., NRAC, 2008—; commdg. officer USS San Juan (SSN 751), 1986-89; dep. comdr. for readiness and tng. Submarine Squadron 2, 1989-90; undersea warfare asst. office dir. Def. Advanced Rsch. Projects Agy., Washington, 1990-92; commdg. officer USS Holland, 1992-94; dir. resources and evaluation Office Asst. Sec. of Navy for Rsch., Devel. and Acquisition, Washington, 1994-95; program mgr. Unmanned Underseas Vehicles Program Office, 1995-97; comdr. Naval Undersea Warfare Ctr., 1998—2000; dir., Submarine Tech. Office Naval Sea Sys. Command, vice comdr., 2001—02; v.p., strategic bus. planning Oceaneering International, Inc., 2006—. Decorated Def. Superior Svc. medal, Legion of Merit, Meritorious Svc. medal with Gold star. Office: Oceaneering International Inc 11911 FM 529 Houston TX 77041 Office Phone: 713-329-4500. Office Fax: 713-329-4951. Business E-Mail: cyoung@oceaneering.com.

YOUNG, CHARLES EDWARD, former academic administrator; b. San Bernardino, Calif., Dec. 30, 1931; s. Clayton Charles and Eula May (Walters) Young. AA, San Bernardino Coll., 1954; AB, U. Calif., Riverside, 1955; MA, UCLA, 1957, PhD, 1960; DHL (hon.), U. Judaism, LA, 1969; DHL (hon.), Occidental Coll., LA, 1997. Congl. fellow, Washington, 1958—59; adminstrv. analyst Office of the Pres., U. Calif., Berkeley, 1959—60; asst. prof. polit. sci. University of California, Davis, 1960, UCLA, 1960—66, assoc. prof., 1966—69, prof., 1969—97, asst. to chancellor, 1960—62, asst. chancellor, 1962—63, vice chancellor, adminstrn., 1963—68, chancellor, 1968—97, chancellor emeritus, 1997; pres. U. Fla., Gainesville, 1999—2003. Cons. Peace Corps., 1961—62, Ford Found. on Latin Am. Activities, 1964—66; mem. bd. dirs. Intel Corp., Acad. TV Arts and Sci. Found., L.A. Met. Project, I-Mark Inc., AAFL Enterprises, Nicholas-Applegate Growth Equity Fund Inc., Fiberspace Inc., Student Advantage Inc., Perma-Fix Environ. Svcs. Inc., 2003—. Mem. Nat. Com. on U.S.-China Rels.; adminstrv. bd. Internat. Assn. Univs; mem. Knight Found. Commn. on Intercollegiate Athletics, Calif. Coun. on Sci. and Tech., Town Hall of Calif., Carnegie Comm. Task Force on Sci. and Tech. and the States, Pacific Coun. on Internat. Policy, NCAA Pres.'s Commn., Coun. for Govt.-Univ.-Industry Rsch. Roundtable and the Nat. Rsch. Coun. Adv. Bd.-Issues in Sci. and Tech.; chancellor's assocs. UCLA; coun. trustees L.A. Ednl. Alliance for Restructuring Now; past chair. Assn. Am. Univs., Nat. Assn. State Univs. and Land-Grant Colls.; past co-chair Calif. Campus Compact; trustee UCLA Found.; CEO Los Angeles Mus. of Contemporary Art, 2009—; bd. dirs. Found. Internat. Exchange Sci. and Cultural Info. by Telecom., L.A. Internat. Visitors Coun., Greater L.A. Energy Coalition, L.A. World Affairs Coun. With USAF, 1951—52. Recipient Inter-Am. U. Cooperaton award, Inter-Am. Orgn. Higher Edn., Neil H. Jacoby Internat. award, UCLA Student Ctr., 1987, Edward A. Dickson Alumnus of Yr. award, UCLA Alumni Assn., 1994, Disting. Svc. award, U. Calif. Riverside Alumni Assn., 1996, Treasure of L.A. award, L.A. Ctrl. City Assn., 1996, Albert Schweitzer Leadership award, Hugh O'Brien Youth Found., 1996; named Young Man of Year, Westwood Jr. C. of C., 1962; fellow, UCLA Coll. Letters and Sci., 1996. Fellow: AAAS; mem.: Nat. Collegiate Athletic Assn. Pres. Commn. Office: Perma-Fix Environmental Services Inc Ste 250 8302 Dunwoody Pl Atlanta GA 30350 Office Phone: 770-587-9898. Office Fax: 770-587-9937. Business E-Mail: cyoung@perma-fix.com.

YOUNG, DANA D., state legislator; b. Tallahassee, Nov. 9, 1964; m. Matt Young; children: Alexandra, Carson. BS in Polit. Sci., Fla. State U., 1985; JD in Law, U. Va., 1993. Intern to Don Fuqua US Congress; law clk. US Dept. Justice; lawyer Fowler White Boggs PA; mem. Dist. 57 Fla. House Of Representatives, 2011—. Republican. Office: 2909 W Bay to Bay Blvd Ste 202 Tampa FL 33629-8175 also: Fla House of Reps 1101 The Capitol 402 S Monroe St Tallahassee FL 32399-1300 Office Phone: 813-835-2270, 850-488-2770.

YOUNG, DONALD ALLEN, writer, consultant; b. Columbus, Ohio, June 11, 1931; s. Clyde Allen and Helen Edith (Johnston) Y.; m. Rosemary Buchholz, Feb. 26, 1955 (div. Nov. 1976); children: Kent Allen, Kelly Ann; m. Marjorie Claire Kirkel, Aug. 20, 1977; stepchildren: Jo Alene, Andrea Lynn, Beth Ellen. Student, Ohio State U., 1949-51, Columbia Coll., 1952, North Cen. Coll., Naperville, Ill., 1956, Coll. DuPage, 1978. Editor various newspapers, mags., Detroit, Chgo., Columbus, 1946-63, 1973-74, 1978-79; v.p. Frydenlund Assocs., Chgo., 1963; pub. rels. mgr. info. sys. divsn. Gen. Electric Co., Phoenix, 1963-70; publs. dir. Data Processing Mgmt. Assn., Park Ridge, Ill., 1970-72; pub. rels. mgr. Addressograph-Multigraph Corp., Arlington Heights, Ill., 1975-76; acct. exec. John Ripley & Assocs., Glenview, Ill., 1977-78; editl. dir. Radiology/Nuc. Medicine mag., Des Plaines, Ill., 1979-81; pres. Young Byrum Inc., Hinsdale, Ill., 1982-83; writer, cons. Tucson, 1983—2010. Cons. in field; sports reporter, Copley newspapers, 1975-83; mem. adv. coun. Oakton C.C., 1970-75. Author: (books) Principles of Automatic Data Processing, 1965, Data Processing, 1967, Rate Yourself as a Mgr., 1985, Nobody Gets Rich Working for Somebody Else, 1987, 1993, 2001, Adventure Guide to Iceland, 2008, Rate Your Exec. Potential, 1988, 2001, If They Can.You Can, 1989, The Entrepreneurial Family, 1990, How to Export, 1990, Women in Balance, 1991, Sleep Disorders: America's Hidden Nightmare, 1992, Small Bus. Troubleshooter, 1994, 2000, Crime Wave: Am. Needs a New Get-Tough Policy, 1996, Popcorn Publications, 1996, Adventure Guide to So. Calif., 1997, Romantic Weekends: America's S.W., 1998, Adventure Guide to the Pacific N.W., 1998, Momentum: How to Get It-How to Keep It, 1999, Don't Get Mad-Get Rich, 1999, Walking Places in Wash. D.C., 2000, 100 Ways to Bring Out Your Best, 2002, Louisiana, An Adventurer's Guide, 2004, Travel Adventures Iceland, 2009, Improve Your Life-Work to Win, Inside Advantage, 2010, Global Golfer North American Edition, 1992, Fast Track, 1999, Bounce Back and Win, 1999, Stand and Deliver or Step Aside, 2008. Arbitrator Better Bus. Bur., Tucson, 1987-92; docent Ariz. Sonora Desert Mus., 1988-92, Tucson/Pima Arts Coun., 1993-94. With USAF, 1952-56. Recipient Jesse Neal award Assn. of Bus. Pub., 1959, 61, Silver Anvil award Pub. Rels. Soc. of Am., 1976. Mem. Publicity Club of Chgo. (pres. 1978-79). Soc. Southwestern Authors (pres. 1992), Glen Ellyn (Ill.) Jaycees (bd. dirs., SPOKE award 1959, Outstanding Jaycee 1960), Young Reps. Club (v.p. 1960). Avocations: photography, travel, hiking, fishing. Home: 12429 Scofield Farms Dr Austin TX 78758

YOUNG, GEORGE CRESSLER, federal judge; b. Cin., Aug. 4, 1916; s. George Philip and Gladys (Cressler) Y.; m. Iris June Hart, Oct. 6, 1951; children: George Cressler, Barbara Ann. AB, U. Fla., 1938, LLB, 1940; postgrad., Harvard Law Sch., 1947. Bar: Fla. 1940. Practice in, Winter Haven, 1940-41; assoc. Smathers, Thompson, Maxwell & Dyer, Miami, 1947; adminstrv., legis. asst. to Senator Smathers of Fla., 1948-52; asst. US atty. Jacksonville, 1952; ptnr. Knight, Kincaid, Young & Harris, Jacksonville, 1953-61; judge US Dist. Ct. (so. and no. dists.) Fla., 1961—66, US Dist. Ct. (mid. dist.) Fla., Orlando, 1962—73, chief judge, 1973—81, sr. judge, 1981—. Mem. com. on adminstrn. fed. magistrates system Jud. Conf. U.S., 1973-80 Bd. dirs. Jacksonville United Cerebral Palsy Assn., 1953-60. Served to lt. (s.g.) USNR, 1942-46. Mem. Rollins Coll. Alumni Assn. (pres. 1968-69), ABA (spl. com. for adminstrn. criminal justice), Fla. Bar Assn. (gov. 1960-61), Jacksonville Bar Assn. (past pres.), Order of Coif, Fla. Blue Key, Phi Beta Kappa, Phi Kappa Phi, Phi Delta Phi, Sigma Alpha Epsilon. Office: US Dist Ct US Courthouse 401 W Central Blvd Rm 3600 Orlando FL 32801 Office Phone: 407-835-4280.

YOUNG, HENRY E., tissue engineering medical educator; b. Dayton, Ohio, Dec. 5, 1951; s. Henry O. and Lucille M. Y.; m. Valerie E. Achorn, May 16, 1976; 1 child, Katherine. BS in Biology, Ohio State U., 1974; MSc in Zoology, U. Ark., 1977; PhD, Tex. Tech. U., 1983; postdoc. in Carbohydrate Biochemistry, Case Western Res. U., Cleave. Instr.biochemistry Rush-Presbyn.-St. Luke's Med. Ctr., Chgo., 1987—88; asst. prof. anatomy Mercer U. Sch. Medicine, Macon, Ga., 1988—95, asst. prof. surgery, 1988—94, assoc. prof. anatomy, pediat., 1995—2004, prof. anatomy, pediat., 2004—; prof. ob/gyn, 2007—; prof. anesthesiology, 2009—. Inventor in field. Recipient Hooding award for excellence in tchg. and rsch., Mercer U. Med. Sch., 1993, Merit award, 1993, Hooding award for excellence in tchg. and rsch., 1994, Gender Equity award, Am. Med. Women's Assn., 1997, Humanism in Medicine award, Arnold P. Gold Found., 2005, Internat. Einstein Iconic Achievement award, 2009, Tchg. award, 1993—94, Men Achievement award, 1996; nominee Man of Yr. award, 2010; NIH Postdoctoral fellow in biochemistry, Case We. Res. U., Cleve., 1983—85, postdoctoral fellow, Muscular Dystrophy Assn., 1985—87. Mem.: Internat. Cellular Medicine Soc., Am. Soc. Cell Biology, Stem Cells and Regen Medicine, Tissue Culture Soc., Am. Assn. Anatomists, Arnold P. Gold Found., Humanism Hon. Soc. Achievements include discovery of adult germ layer lineage stem cells, adult pluripotent stem cells, and adult near totipotent stem cells; invention of muscle morphogenetic protein and scar inhibitory factor; research in basic mechanisms of fetal alcohol syndrome, tissue regeneration and stem cell biology. Avocation: reading. Office: 1550 College Str Macon GA 31207 Office Phone: 478-301-4034, 478-301-4088. Office Fax: 478-301-5487. Personal E-mail: young.he@yahoo.com. Business E-Mail: young_he@mercer.edu.

YOUNG, JAMES E., banker; BS in Bus. Adminstrn., Tenn. State U., 1971. Mgmt. trainee Chase Manhttan Bank, 1971-72, lending officer, from 1972, various lending position, v.p., team mgr., credit audit divsn., human resource specialist; v.p., chief comml. loan officer City Nat. Bank N.J., 1989-90, sr. v.p., gen. adminstrn. and comml. loans, 1990-93; pres., CEO & bd. dirs. 1st So. Bancshares, 1993; bd. dirs. Citizens Trust Bank, pres., CEO, 1998—. Mem. regional adv. bd. Fannie Mae; pres., CEO, bd. dirs. Citizens Bancshare Corp., Atlanta, Citizens Trust Bank Mortgage Svcs., Inc., Atlanta. Bd. dirs. Metro tlanta YMCA, Atlanta Neighborhood Devel. Partnership, DeKalb Conv. and Visitors Bur. Mem. Nat. Bankers Assn., DeKalb C. of C. Office: Citizens Trust Bank 75 Piedmont Ave Ste C Atlanta GA 30303-2569 Office Phone: 404-659-5959. Office Fax: 404-653-2877. Business E-Mail: jyoung@ctbconnect.com.

YOUNG, JAMES JULIUS, academic administrator, retired military officer; b. Ft. Ringgold, Tex., Nov. 28, 1926; s. John Cooper and Violet Thelma (Ohl) Y.; m. June Agnes Hillstead, Dec. 17, 1948; children: Robert Michael, Steven Andrew, Patrick James, Mary Frances. BS, U. Md., 1960; M.H.A., Baylor U., 1962; PhD in Hosp. and Health Adminstrn, U. Iowa, 1969. Commd. 2d lt. U.S. Army, 1947, advanced through grades to brig. gen., 1977, comdr., med. ops. officer, dir. tng. field med. units in European Command, 1949-53; comdr. Mil. Med. Leadership Sch., 1953-54; med. advisor (Nationalist Army of China), 1955-57; asst. adminstr. Fitzsimons Army Med. Center, 1957-60; med. plans and ops. officer (US Forces), Korea, 1962-63; sr. field med. instr., chief field med. service Med. Field Service Sch., 1963-66; dir. health care orgn. and mgmt. analysis Office of Surgeon Gen., 1969-71; dir. med. plans and ops. directorate Office of the Surgeon, Military Assistance Command, Vietnam, 1971-72; exec. officer, chief adminstrv. services Silas Hays Army Hosp., 1973-74; military health analyst, military health care study OMB, Exec. Office of Pres., 1974-76; dep. dir. resources mgmt. and cons. for health care adminstrn. Office of Surgeon Gen., 1976-77; chief med. svcs. corps U.S. Army, 1977-81; dir. resources mgmt. Office of Surgeon Gen., 1977-81; ret., 1981; instr. U. Iowa, 1967-69; asst. prof., preceptor Baylor U., 1973-74; vice chancellor for health affairs W.Va. Bd. Regents, Charleston, 1982-87; dean sch. of allied health scis. U. Tex. Health Sci. Ctr., San Antonio, 1987-90, interim dean Sch. Medicine, 1988-89, dean Sch. Medicine, 1989—, dean emeritus, 2000—. Cons. to Min. of Health, Republic of Vietnam, 1971-72, 1989-2000; adj. prof. Baylor U., 1977-81, George Washington U., 1975-76, W.Va. U., 1986; prof. U. Tex. health Sci. Ctr., San Antonio, 1989-2000. Contbr. articles to profl. jours. Decorated D.S.M., Legion of Merit, Meritorious Service medal, others; recipient Walter Reed medal, 1981; Army Med. Dept. medal for contbn. to health service, 1981, Order of Mil. Med. Merit, 1981, U. Tex. Health Scis. Ctr. Hon. medallion Fountains of Progress, 2000; recipient Humanism in Medicine medallion Health Care Foun. NJ, 2000; named to Hall of Fame, Infantry Sch. Officer Cand. Roman Catholic. Home: 1610 Anchor Dr San Antonio TX 78213-1943 Personal E-mail: jyoung51@satx.rr.com.

YOUNG, JOHN F., electric power industry executive, energy executive; b. 1956; m. Julie Young; children: Jack, Will. BS in Mech. Engring., US Naval Acad., Annapolis, Md., 1978. Sr. v.p. Sierra Pacific Resources Corp.; various positions, comml. sales rep., wholesale and retail mktg., fuel planning and procurement, head fin. and investor rels. office Southern Co., 1983—2000, exec. v.p., southern generation, 1983—2000; pres., COO Exelon Power, 2003—04; pres. Exelon Generation Co., LLC, 2004—05; exec. v.p., fin. & markets Exelon Corp., 2005—08; pres., CEO Energy Future Holdings Corp. (formerly TXU Corp.), Dallas, 2008—. Bd. dirs. Assn. Edison Illuminating Cos., Utility Bus. Edn. Coalition, Electric Power Research Inst. Engring. officer USS Ticonderoga USN. Office: Energy Future Holdings Corp Energy Plz 1601 Bryan St Dallas TX 75201-3411 Office Phone: 214-812-4600. Business E-Mail: john.young@energyfutureholdings.com.

YOUNG, LARRY D., beverage company executive; m. Colette Young. Exec. v.p. corp. affairs PepsiAmericas Inc., 1997—2005; pres., COO Peps-Cola Gen. Bottlers, 1997—2005; pres., CEO Dr. Pepper Seven Up Bottling Group, 2005—07, Dr. Pepper Snapple Group (divsn. Cadbury Schweppes plc), 2007—08, Dr. Pepper Snapple Group Inc. (formerly Cadbury Schweppes Americas Beverages), Plano, Tex., 2008—. Chmn. Am. Beverage Assn. Office: Dr Pepper Snapple Group 5301 Legacy Dr Plano TX 75024 Office Phone: 972-673-7000.

YOUNG, LUCY CLEAVER, retired physician; b. Aug. 8, 1943; d. Oliver B. and Ada (Smith) Cleaver; m. Lynn H. Young, Feb. 4, 1968 (div. 1977); m. Lynn H. Young, Apr. 2, 1986; 1 child, Clinton Oliver. BS in Chemistry, Wheaton Coll., Ill., 1965; MD, Ohio State U., 1969. Diplomate Am. Bd. Family Practice, Bd. Ins. Medicine. Rotating intern Riverside Meth. Hosp., Columbus, Ohio, 1969—70; resident Trumbull Meml. Hosp., Warren, Ohio, 1970—71; practice medicine specializing in family practice West Chicago, Ill., 1971—73, Paw Paw and Mendota, Ill., 1973—78; co-founder, med. dir. Wholistic Health Ctr. of Mendota, 1976—78; asst. med. dir. Gt. Lakes head office Met. Life Ins. Co., Aurora, Ill., 1979—80; med. dir. Commonwealth Life Ins. Co., Louisville, 1980—85; locum tenens family practice Kron Med. Corp. of Chapel Hill, NC, 1986—89; physician Red Bird Mission & Med. Ctr., Beverly, Ky., 1989—90; family practice floater Ochsner Clinic satellites, New Orleans, 1990—2006; ret. Assoc. prof. U. Ill. Abraham Lincoln Sch. Medicine, 1976-79; faculty monitor MacNeal Meml. Hosp. Family Practice Ctr. (Ill.), 1979-80; faculty preceptor U. Louisville Family Practice Dept., 1981-85; clin. faculty preceptor La. State U. Sch. Medicine, 1992-2006; mem. staffs Ctrl. DuPage Hosp., Winfield, Ill., 1971-73, Mendota Cmty. Hosp., 1973-80, Ochsner Found. Hosp., New Orleans, 1991-2006; musician La. Via de Cristo, 2003-05. Vol. Red Bird Med. Ctr., 1985—2006; part-time worship coord. Hosanna Luth. Ch., Mandeville, La., 1996-97; musician, lay preacher, nursing home visitor, 1990—2006; musician, lay preacher, coun. mem., bible class tchr. St. Matthew, Lake Luth. Ch., Benton, Ky., 2006-; vol. H.P.O.E. Clinic Crisis Pregnancy Ctr., Benton, 2007-. Fellow Am. Acad. Family Practice; mem. Christian Med. and Dental Assns. (del. to Ho. 1995-2000). Lutheran. Home: PO Box 187 239 Jetty Dr #6-27 Grand Rivers KY 42045-0187

YOUNG, MARK PHILIP, allergist; b. NYC, May 30, 1954; MD, U. Ctrl. Del Caribe, 1982. Cert. Am. Bd. Allergy/Immunology. Resident pediat. Miami Children's Hosp., 1983—86, former assoc. dir. Department of Allergy/Immunology; fellowship allergy and immunology Emory U., Atlanta, 1986—87, Georgetown U., 1987—88; pvt. practice Asthma & Allergy Assocs. of Fla., PA, Miami. Fellow: Am. Coll. Allergy, Asthma and Immunology; mem.: Fla. Allergy Asthma and Immunology Soc. Office: Asthma & Allergy Assocs of Fla, PA 7800 SW 87th Ave, Ste C-340 Miami FL 33173 Office Phone: 305-595-0109. Office Fax: 305-595-7092.

YOUNG, MIKE, men's college basketball coach; m. Margaret Young, Aug. 13, 1994; children: Cooper, Davis. B, Emory & Henry Coll., Va., 1986. Asst. coach Emory & Henry Coll. Wasps, 1986—88; grad. asst. Radford U. Highlanders, 1988—89; asst. coach Wofford Coll. Terriers, 1989—98, assoc. head coach, 1998—2002, head basketball coach, 2002—. Recipient Hugh Durham Mid-Major Coach of Yr. award, 2010; named Coach of Yr., Southern Conf., 2010, Dist. 22 Coach of Yr., Nat. Assn. Basketball Coaches, 2010. Office: Wofford Coll Basketball c/o Dept Athletics 429 N Church St Spartanburg SC 29303 Office Phone: 864-597-4117. Business E-Mail: youngmk@wofford.edu.

YOUNG, PAUL RAY, medical association administrator, physician; b. Fairfield, Nebr., June 27, 1932; s. Earl Edward and Louisa May (Saunders) Young; m. Irene Marie Gray (div. 1971); children: Michael, Susan, Jean, James; m. Faye Elizabeth Hall, Oct. 28, 1972. BA, U. Nebr., Lincoln, 1953; MD, U. Nebr., Omaha, 1958. Diplomate Am. Bd. Family Practice. Intern Rsch. Hosp., Kansas City, Mo., 1958—59, dir. continuing med. edn., 1967—71; pvt. practice Raytown, Mo., 1961—67; assoc. prof. family practice U. Mo. Coll. Medicine, Columbia, 1971—75; chmn. dept. U. Nebr. Coll. Medicine, 1975—80, U. Tex. Med. Br., Galveston, 1980—88; dep. dir. Am. Bd. Family Practice, Lexington, Ky., 1988—90, exec. dir., 1990—97, sr. exec., 1998—2003, emeritus exec. dir., 2003—. Chmn. RRC for Family Practice, Chgo., 1979—87. Founding editor: Family Practice Recert, 1979, Jour. Am. Bd. Family Practice, 1987. Pres. Nicholas J. Piscano Meml. Found., 1990—97. Capt. M.C. USAF, 1959—61. Fellow: Am. Acad. Family Physicians; mem.: Soc. Tchrs. Family Medicine (bd. dirs. 1970—72), Alpha Omega Alpha. Office: Am Bd Family Medicine Inc 1648 McGrathiana Pkwy Fl5 Lexington KY 40511-1338 Office Phone: 859-269-5626. Business E-Mail: pyoung@theabfm.org.

YOUNG, PHYLLIS CASSELMAN, music educator; b. Milan, Kans., Oct. 20, 1925; d. Phillip James and Velma (Stewart) Casselman; m. James M. Young, July 14, 1945 (dec. Sept. 1991). MusB with high honors, U. Tex., 1949, MusM, 1950. Tchr. string instruments Kansas City (Kans.) Pub. Schs., 1951-52; prof. cello and string pedagogy U. Tex., Austin, 1953—2007; dir. U. Tex. String Project, Austin, 1958-93; Parker C. Fielder Regents prof. music U. Tex., Austin, 1991—2007. Presenter numerous workshops and master classes, 1976—. Author: Playing the String Game, 1978, The String Play, 1986; also articles. Recipient Phyllis Young Outstanding Studio Tchr. award, 2006, Paul Rolland Lifetime Achievement award, 2002, Eva Janzer Cello award, Ind. U., 2000, award, U. Tex. String Project Fiftieth Anniversary Celebration, 1998, Outstanding Collegiate Tchg. Achievement award, 1987, Disting. Svc. award, Am. String Tchrs. Assn., 1984. Mem. Am. String Tchrs. Assn. (state pres. 1972-74, nat. pres. 1978-80, Nat. citation 1974, 82, Disting. Svc. award 1984, Paul Rolland Lifetime Achievement award 2002), European String Tchrs. Assn. (hon. mem. Brit. br.), Music Educators Nat. Conf., Suzuki Assn. Ams., Tex. Music Educators Assn., European String Tchrs. Assn. (hon. 1997). Home: 4200 Jackson Ave Apt 4010 Austin TX 78731 Business E-Mail: phyllis@utexas.edu.

YOUNG, ROBERT A., III, freight systems executive; b. Ft. Smith, Ark., Sept. 23, 1940; s. Robert A. and Vivian (Curtis) Y.; m. Mary Carleton McRae; children: Tracy, Christy, Robert A. IV (dec.), Stephen BA in Econs., Washington and Lee U., 1963. V.p., gen. mgr. Data-Tronics Inc, Ft. Smith, 1965-67; sr. v.p. Nat. Bank of Commerce, Dallas, 1967-70; v.p. fin., exec. v.p. Arkansas Best Corp., Ft. Smith, 1970-73, exec. v.p., 1973, COO, 1973-88, pres., 1973—2004, CEO, 1988—2006, chmn., 2004—; supr. terminal ops. Ark. Best Freight, Ft. Smith, 1964-65; pres. ABF Freight Systems, Inc., Ft. Smith, 1979-94. Bd. dirs. First Nat. Bank, Ft. Smith, Treadco, Inc., 1991-1999 Pres. United Way, Ft. Smith, 1981; bd. dirs. ATA Found., Inc., Ft. Smith Boys and Girls Club; chmn. bd. trustees Lyon Coll., Sparks Regional Med. Ctr., Ft. Smith, 1995-2004. Recipient Silver Beaver award Boy Scouts Am. Mem. Am. Trucking Assn. (v.p. at large), Phi Delta Theta. Presbyterian. Office: Arkansas Best Corp 3801 Old Greenwood Rd Fort Smith AR 72903-5937 Office Fax: 479-785-6004. Business E-Mail: robertyoung@arkansastrucking.com.

YOUNG, RONALD FARIS, commodities trader; b. Schenectady, Dec. 17, 1939; s. James Vernon and Dorothy (Girod) Y.; m. Anne Randolph Kendig, Feb. 23, 1963; children: Margaret Randolph Reynolds, Anne Corbin Gray. BA, U. Va., 1962; MBA, Harvard U., 1966. Grain trader Continental Grain Co., 1966-70; pres. Conti-Commodities, Chgo., 1970; v.p. commodity sales DuPont, Glore Forgan, Chgo., 1971-72; self-employed commodity trader Chgo. Bd. Trade, 1972-78; ind. trader Va. Trading Co., 1978-90, pres., 1978-84, dep. chmn., 1984-89; pres. Randolph Ptnrs., Ltd., 1983-91. Chmn. bd. Chgo. Bd. Trade, 1978, dir., 1975—77, 1980, 2003. Bd. dirs. Princeton Fund, 1981-82, Lake Forest Hosp., 1981-84, Lake Forest Country Day Sch., 1981-86. Served with USMCR, 1959-65. Mem. Racquet Club (bd. dirs. 1989-97), Onwentsia Club (Lake Forest, Ill., bd. dirs. 1981-90, pres. 1991-93), Everglades Club (Palm Beach, Fla.), Bath and Tennis Club of Palm Beach (bd. dirs. 2007—). Republican. Episcopalian.

YOUNG, SOPHIA YVONNE, professional basketball player; b. St. Vincent and The Grenadines, Dec. 15, 1983; d. Denniston Young and Annie Christopher. BEd, Baylor U., Waco, Tex., 2006. Forward San Antonio Silver Stars, 2006—, Gambrinus, Brno, Czech Republic, Galatasaray, Istanbul, Turkey. Named All. Am., Kodak, US Basketball Writers Assn., First Team All-Am., AP, 2005—06, Player of Yr., Big 12 Conf., 2006; named to We. Conf. All-Star Team, WNBA, 2006, 2007, Turkish League All-Star Team, 2007. Achievements include being a member of the NCAA Women's National Championship winning Baylor University Bears, 2005. Office: San Antonio Silver Stars One AT&T Ctr San Antonio TX 78219

YOUNG, THOMAS LEE, medical educator; b. Farmville, Va., Apr. 2, 1950; s. Ruth Vining Young; m. Teresa Tucker Young; children: Travis Aaron, Tara Dawn. BS, U. Ky., Lexington, 1997; MPH, U. Pitts., 1980; MD, U. Louisville, Ky., 1976. Fellow Am. Acad. Pediats. Pediatrician Lexington Clinic, Ky., 1984—94; prof. pediat. U. Ky., 1994—. Contbr. articles to profl. jours. Bd. dirs., chair Ky. Child Now, Frankfort, Ky., 2001—07; bd. chair Success by Six, Lexington, 2006—07; sch. health com. me. Am. Acad. Pediat., Chgo., 1999—2006; founder Shoulder to Shoulder, Ecuador. Recipient Doane Fischer Cmty. Svc. award, U. Ky., 1998, 2000, 2007, Health Hero, 1998. Fellow: AAP (licentiate; pres. Ky. chpt. 1996—98). Office: Univ Ky Ky Clinic Lexington KY 40536 Business E-Mail: tyoung@uky.edu.

YOUNG, THOMAS R., JR., state legislator; b. Aiken, SC, Oct. 8, 1971; s. Thomas R. Young Sr. and Delly O. Young; m. Heather Winkles, Aug. 4, 2001; children: Hailey Elizabeth, Ashley Caroline. BA, U. SC, 1993, JD, 1996. Mem. Dist. 81 SC House of Reps., SC, 2008—, mem. Subcommittee on Criminal Laws. Mem.: Kappa Sigma. Republican. Methodist. Mailing: 1017 Westcliff Dr Aiken SC 29801 Office: Capitol Office 416B Blatt Bldg Columbia SC 29201 Home Phone: 803-649-1030; Office Phone: 803-649-0000, 803-212-6884. E-mail: tomyoung@schouse.org.

YOUNT, MICHAEL H., gas industry executive; B in Mech. Engring. with honors, Ga. Inst. Tech., 1976. Various mgmt. positions in project devel., sales and mktg., customer svc. Williams/Transco (formerly Transcontinental Gas Pipe Line Corp.); v.p., cons. Senn-Delaney Leadership Consulting Group, 1996—2006; sr. v.p., utility ops. Piedmont Natural Gas Co., Inc., 2006—. Bd. mem. Knoxville YMCA. Office: Piedmont Natural Gas 4720 Piedmont Row Dr Charlotte NC 28210 Mailing: Piedmont Natural Gas PO Box 33068 Charlotte NC 28233 Office Phone: 704-364-3120. Office Fax: 704-365-8515.

YOUZHNY, MIKHAIL, professional tennis player; b. Moscow, June 25, 1982; s. Mikhail and Lubov Youzhny; m. Yulia Youzhny, Nov. 22, 2008; 1 child, Maxim. Profl. tennis player ATP, 1999—. Achievements include winning 6 career singles titles, 7 career doubles titles, ATP; winning (singles) Stuttgart, 2002, St. Petersburg, 2004, Rotterdam, 2007, Chennai, 2008, Moscow, 2009, Munich, 2010; winning (doubles) Moscow, 2005, Munich, 2007, Tokyo, 2008, London, 2009, Halle, 2010. Office: c/o ATP Tour Inc 201 Atp Tour Blvd Ponte Vedra Beach FL 32082-3211

YOW, DEBORAH A., athletic director; b. Gibsonville, NC, 1949; m. William W. Bowden. Grad. in English, Elon Coll., 1974; M in Counseling, Liberty U.; PhD, Baptist Christian U., 1993. Basketball coach U. Ky., 1976—80, Oral Roberts, 1980—83, U. Fla., 1983—85, asst. dir. Gator boosters, 1985—87; assoc. athletic dir. U. NC, Greensboro, 1987—90; dir. athletics St. Louis U., 1990—94, U. Md., College Pk., 1994—2010, NC State U., Raleigh, 2010—. Contbr. articles to profl. jours. Recipient Carl Maddox Sport Mgmt. award, US Sports Acad.; named one of 20 Most Influential People in Intercollegiate Athletics, 10 Most Powerful People in Coll. Sports, 2007, The 100 Most Powerful Women in DC, Washingtonian mag., 2009; named to Md. Women's Hall of Fame, 2003, NC Sports Hall of Fame, 2006. Mem.: Nat. Assn. Collegiate Dirs. of Athletics (pres. 2001). Achievements include being the only Division I coach to take three previously unranked teams to the Top 20. Office: North Carolina State Univ Athletics 2500 Warren Carroll Dr PO Box 8502 Raleigh NC 27695 Office Phone: 919-515-2109. Business E-Mail: d_yow@ncsu.edu.

YU, ROBERT KUAN-JEN, biochemistry professor; b. Chungking, China, Jan. 27, 1938; came to U.S., 1962; m. Helen Chow, July 1, 1972; children: David S., Jennifer S. BS, Tunghai U., Taiwan, 1960; PhD, U. Ill., 1967; Med.ScD. (hon.), Tokyo, 1980; MA (hon.), Yale U., 1985. Rsch. assoc., instr. Albert Einstein Coll. Medicine, Bronx, 1967-72; asst. prof. Yale U., New Haven, 1973-75, assoc. prof., 1975-82, prof., 1983-88; prof. biochemistry, chmn. dept. Med. Coll. Va. Va. Commonwealth U., Richmond, 1988-2000; dir. Inst. Mol. Med. Genetics, Ga. Regents U., Augusta, 2000—09; prof. Inst. Mol. Med. Genetics Med. Coll. Ga, 2009—; dir. inst. neurosci. Ga. Regents U., Med. Coll. Ga., Augusta, 2005; biologist VH Med. Ctr., Augusta, Ga., 2011—. Mem. study sect. NIH, Washington, 1980-84, 96—; mem. Bd. Lab. Svcs., Va., 1994-98, Acadmician, Acad. Sinica, Taiwan, 2004-, Ga. Comm. saving and Cure, 2007-, Editor: Gangioside Structure Function and Biomedical Potential, 1984, New Trends in Ganglioside Research, 1988; contbr. over 500 articles to profl. publs. Josiah Macy scholar, 1979; grantee NIH, 1975—, 84-91; recipient Va. Outstanding Scientist of Yr. award, 1995, Alexander von Humboldt award, 1990, GRA Eminent scholar, 2000, Dist. Alumnus award Tunghai U., 2003, Achievement award Chinese Assn. Engrs. and Scientists So. Calif., 2004, Outstanding Faculty award Sch. Medicine, Med. Coll. Ga., 2006, 2009, Lifetime Achievement award, Va. Merit award 2010-. Mem. AAAS, Am. Soc. Cell Biology, Am. Soc. Neurochemistry (mem. coun. 1983-86, 91-95, pres. 2001-03), Internat. Soc. Neurochemistry, Soc. Neurosci., Am. Soc. Biochemistry and Molecular Biology, Am. Chem. Soc., N.Y. Acad. Sci., Soc. Glybiol, Am. Soc. Cell Biol. Office Phone: 706-721-0699. Business E-Mail: ryu@gru.edu.

YU, SIMON SHYI-JIAN, entomologist, educator; b. Ilan, Taiwan, Republic of China, Sept. 11, 1935; arrived in Can. 1963, U.S. in 1968; s. Son-Wei and Ah-So (Liao) Yu; m. Rachel R.C. Yeh, Setp. 16, 1967; children: Robert Yu, Edmund Yu. BS, Nat. Taiwan U., 1959; MS, McGill U., Montreal, Can., 1965, PhD, 1968; postdoctoral, Cornell U. and Oreg. State U., 1968-74. Rsch. entomologist Taiwan Sugar Co., Kuohsiung, Taiwan, 1961-62; rsch. asst. McGill U., Montreal, 1963-68; postdoctoral fellow Cornell U., Ithaca, N.Y., 1968-69; rsch. assoc. Oreg. State U., Corvallis, 1969-74, asst. prof., 1974-79; asst. prof. U. Fla., Gainesville, 1980-82, assoc. prof., 1982-86, prof., 1986—2006, prof. emeritus, 2006—. Contbr. articles to profl. jours., chapters to books; author: (text book) The Toxicology and Biochemistry of Insecticides, 2008. 2nd lt. Chinese infantry, 1959-61. Rsch. grantee NIH, 1979, USDA, 1980, 82, 85, 90, 91, EPA, 1981, 2005, NSF, 1988, 90. Mem. Entomol. Soc. Am., AAAS, Am. Chem. Soc., The Soc. Sigma Xi, Fla. Entomol. Soc. Avocations: classical music, fishing, bicycling. Office: U Fla Dept Entomology and Nematology Gainesville FL 32611 Home: 5205 NW 43rd Rd Gainesville FL 32606-4323 Office Phone: 352-273-3953. Business E-Mail: yusj@ufl.edu.

YURA, JOSEPH ANDREW, structural engineer, educator; b. Hazelton, Pa., Apr. 11, 1938; s. Michael and Anna (Sokol) Y.; m. Joan Marie Seman, Aug. 22, 1964; children: Thomas, Christine, Paul, Elizabeth. BS, Duke U., 1959; MS, Cornell U., 1961; PhD, Lehigh U., 1965. Registered profl. engr., Tex., Pa., Fla. Asst. prof. Lehigh U., Bethlehem, Pa., 1965-66, U. Tex., Austin, 1966-70, assoc. prof., 1970-75, prof., 1975-82, Warren Bellows prof., 1982-2000; chair Cockrell Family, 1982-2000. Recipient Gen. dynamics Teaching award U. Tex., 1972; recipient T.R. Higgins Lectureship award Am. Inst. Steel Constrn., 1974, Hussein M. Alharthy Centennial Professorship award U. Tex., Austin, 1987. Mem. NAE, ASCE (Raymond C. Reese Rsch. prize 1991, Shortridge Hardesty Awd., 1997), Structural Stability Rsch. Coun., Rsch. Coun. on Structural Connections, Structural Engrs. Assn. Tex., Phi Beta Kappa, Tau Beta Pi. Democrat. Roman Catholic. Home: 5308 Bull Run Austin TX 78727-6608 Office: U Tex Dept Civil Engring Austin TX 78715

YURCHIKHIN, FYODOR NIKOLAYEVICH, cosmonaut; b. Batumi, Georgia, Jan. 3, 1959; s. Nikolai Fyodorovich Yurchikhin and Mikrula Sofoklevna; m. Larisa Anatolievna Yurshikina; 2 children. Degree in mech. engring., Moscow Aviation Inst., 1983; PhD in Econs., Moscow Svc. State U., 2001. Engr., sr. engr., lead engr. Russian Space Corp. Energia, 1983—97, cosmonaut candidate, 1997—99, test cosmonaut, 2000—. Started tng. for Shuttle mission (STS-112) Johnson Space Ctr., NASA, 2001; mission specialist Atlantis STS-112 Mission, 2002; trained as ISS-13 backup crew mem. (Soyuz TMA and ISS flight engr., 2004—05; trained as ISS-13 crew mem. (Soyuz TMA flight engr. and ISS comdr., 2005—06; trained as ISS-13 crewmember (ISS comdr. and Soyuz TMA flight engr., 2006—07; trained as ISS-15 prime crewmember (ISS comdr. and Soyuz TMA flight engr., 2006—07; trained as ISS-24/25 (ISS flight engr. and Soyuz TMA comdr.), 2009—10; comdr., flight engr. Expedition-15 Mission, Soyuz TMA10, 2007; ISS-24 flight engr., comdr. Soyuz TMA-19, 2010. Avocations: reading history, science fiction and classics, collecting stamps and space logos. Office: NASA/Johnson Space Ctr c/o Astronaut Office/CB Houston TX 77058

YUSPEH, ALAN RALPH, lawyer, hospital executive; b. New Orleans, June 13, 1949; s. Michel and Rose Fay (Rabenovitz) Y.; m. Janet Horn, June 8, 1975. BA in Polit. Sci. and Econ. magna cum laude with honors, Yale U., 1971; MBA with distinction, Harvard U., 1973; JD, Georgetown U., 1978. Bar: DC 1978. Mgmt. cons. McKinsey & Co., Washington, 1973-74; adminstrv. asst., legis. asst. to senator J. Bennett Johnston La., 1974-78; atty. Shaw, Pittman, Potts & Trowbridge, Washington, 1978-79, Ginsburg, Feldman, Weil & Bress, Washington, 1979-82; gen. counsel US Senate Com. on Armed Svcs., Washington, 1982-85; ptnr. Preston, Thorgrimson, Ellis & Holman, Washington, 1985-88, Miller & Chevalier, Washington, 1988-91, Howrey & Simon, Washington, 1991-97; sr. v.p., ethics, compliance & corp. responsibility HCA, Inc., 1997—2007, sr. v.p., chief ethics officer & chief compliance officer, 2007—. Coord. Def. Industry Initiative on Bus., Ethics and Conduct, 1987-97; pres. Health Care Compliance Assn., 2002. Editor Law and Policy in Internat. Bus. Jour., 1978-79, Nat. Contract Mgmt. Jour., 1988-92; assoc. editor Pub. Contract Law Jour., 1987-91. Chmn. bd. ethics, City of Balt., 1988-96, planning commn., 1996-97; chmn. bd. dirs. Tenn. Repertory Theater, 2002-05; bd. dirs. Balt. Housing Authority, 1996-97, Ethics Officer Assn., 2001-04, YMCA Mid. Tenn. Camp, 2002-09, Tenn. Performing Arts Ctr., 2003-09, Nashville Pub. Libr. Found., 2005-11. 1st lt. USAR, 1971-77, nat. pres. Health Care Compliance Assn., 2004, bd. dirs. United Way of Nashville, 2007-10, Urban League of Middle Tenn., St. Timothy's Sch., 2007-10, Nashville Pub. Edn. Found., Nashville Opera, chmn., Ctr., Bus. Ethics Belmont U., bd. adv. Vanderbilt Inst. for Global Health, 2007-11, Montgomery Bell Acad.Adv. Bd., mem., Citizens Adv. Comm. on Ethics Recipient Health Care Compliance Profl. of the Yr., Health Care Compliance Assn., 1999. Office: HCA Inc 1 Park Plz Nashville TN 37203 Home: 126 Third Ave N Franklin TN 37064 Office Phone: 615-344-9551. Business E-Mail: alan.yuspeh@hcahealthcare.com.

YZERMAN, STEVE (STEPHEN GREGORY YZERMAN), professional sports team executive, retired professional hockey player; b. Cranbrook, BC, Canada, May 9, 1965; m. Lisa Brennan; children: Isabella Katherine, Maria Charlotte, Sophia Rose. Center Detroit Red Wings, 1983—2006, captain, 1986—2006, v.p., alt. gov., 2006—10; v.p., gen. mgr. Tampa Bay Lightning, 2010—. Mem. Team Canada, Olympic Games, Nagano, Japan, 1998, Salt Lake City, 2002, exec. dir., Vancouver, 2008—10; gen. mgr. Team Canada, IIHF World Championship, Moscow, 2007. Recipient Lester B. Pearson award, 1989, Conn Smythe Trophy, 1998, Frank J. Selke Trophy, 2000, Bill Masterton Trophy, 2003, Lester Patrick Award, 2006; named NHL Rookie of Yr., Sporting News, 1984; named to All-Rookie Team, NHL, 1984, First All-Star Team, 2000, NHL All-Star Game, 1984, 1988—93, 1997, 1999, 2000. Achievements include being the youngest person ever to play in the NHL All-Star game, 1984; being a member of Stanley Cup Champion Detroit Red Wings, 1997, 1998, 2002; being a member of gold medal winning Canadian Hockey Team, Salt Lake City Olympics, 2002; being the longest serving captain in NHL history; having his number, 19, retired by Detroit Red Wings, 2007; being inducted into the Canadian Sports Hall of Fame, 2008; being inducted into the Hockey Hall of Fame, 2009. Office: Tampa Bay Lightning Hockey Club St Pete Times Forum 401 Channelside Dr Tampa FL 33602

ZABETAKIS, PAUL MICHAEL, nephrologist, educator; b. Washington, Pa., July 30, 1947; s. Michael G. and Rebecca A. (Banakas) Z.; m. Martha Robinson, Oct. 3, 1970; 1 child, Amy Shannon. BA, Washington & Jefferson Coll., 1969; mD, U. Tenn., 1972. Diplomate Am. Bd. Internal Medicine, Am. Bd. Nephrology. Intern in medicine U. Pitts., 1972-73, resident in medicine, 1973-75; fellow in nephrology Yale U., New Haven, 1975-77; asst. chief nephrology-hypertension Lenox Hill Hosp., NYC, 1977-82, assoc. chief nephrology-hypertension, 1978-99, dir. home peritoneal dialysis, 1985-99; asst. prof. clin. medicine NY Med. Coll., Valhalla, 1980-88, assoc. prof. clin. medicine, 1988-92; clin. asst. prof. medicine Cornell U., NYC, 1992-93; clin. assoc. prof. medicine NYU, 1993-99; exec. v.p., COO Everest Healthcare Svc., Oak Park, Ill., 1999-2001; CEO Extracorporeal Alliance Fresenius Med. Care, N.Am., 2001—06; pres. Renal Rsch. Inst., 2006—. Mem. editl. bd. Clinical Nephrology, 1979—, Clinical and Experimental Dialysis and Apheresis, 1983-86,

Geriatric Nephrology and Urology, 1995—, Advances in Renal Replacement Therapy, 1999—; nephrology cons. Nicholas Inst. Sports Medicine and Athletic Trauma Lenox Hill Hosp., N.Y.C., 1978-99, rsch. physician, 1982-99; mem. hypertension svc. adv. com. ARC, N.Y.C., 1981-99; mem. exec. com. End Stage Renal Disease Network N.Y. Inc., 1986-99, treas., 1992-93, chmn. long-range planning com., 1994; bd. dirs. Physician Hosp. Orgn. Lenox Hill Hosp., chmn. bd. dirs., 1996-99, v.p. med. bd., 1997-99; vice-chmn. quality improvement, med. dir. Everest Healthcare Svcs., Chgo., 1996-99. Contbr. numerous chpts. to books; patentee in field; lectr. in field; contbr. articles to profl. jours. Fellow ACP, Am. Coll. Preventive Medicine, Am. Coll. Sports Medicine; mem. N.Y. County Med. Soc., Med. Soc. of State of N.Y., Am. Heart Assn., Westchester Heart Assn., N.Y. Soc. Nephrology, Am. Soc. Nephrology, Internat. Soc. Nephrology, N.Y. Acad. Scis., N.Y. State Fedn. Profl. Health Educators, Am. Fedn. Clin. Sch., Internat. Soc. Peritoneal Dialysis, Am. Soc. Artificial Internal Organs (program com. 1995-99), Soc. Critical Care Medicine, Am. Coll. Nutrition, Internat. Soc. for Renal Nutrition and Metabolism, Internat. Soc. Geriatric Nephrology and Urology (founding mem., sec-treas. 1994-99). Avocation: sailboat racing. Business E-Mail: paul.zabetakis@fmc-na.com.

ZACHERT, MARTHA JANE, retired librarian; b. York, Pa., Feb. 7, 1920; d. Paul Rodes and Elizabeth Agnes (Lau) Koontz; m. Edward G. Zachert, Aug. 25, 1946; 1 child, Lillian Elizabeth. AB, Lebanon Valley Coll., 1941; MLS, Emory U., 1953; DLS, Columbia U., 1968. Asst. Enoch Pratt Free Library, Balt., 1941-46; head librarian Wood Research Inst., Atlanta, 1947; sch. librarian DeKalb (Ga.) County Schs., 1950-52; head librarian, prof. history of pharmacy So. Coll. Pharmacy, Mercer U., Atlanta, 1952-63; instr. Ga. State Coll., 1962-63, Emory U., summers 1955-59, 1956-57, 59-60; mem. faculty Library Sch., Fla. State U., 1963-78, prof., 1973-78, Coll. Librarianship U. S.C., Columbia, 1973-74, 78-84. Vis. fellow Brit. Library, 1980; cons. So. Regional Med. Library, Emory U., 1976-77, Nat. Library Medicine, 1977, others. Author: Fine Printing in Georgia, 1950s-1990, 1994; assoc. editor Jour. Libr. History, 1966-71, 73-76; mng. editor, 1971-73; cons. editor Jour. Libr. Adminstrn., 1979-86; contbr. numerous articles to profl. jours. Fellow Med. Libr. Assn. (named among 100 Most Notables 1998); mem. ALA, Spl. Librs. Assn. (past pres. Fla. chpt., spl. citation 1977, Hall of Fame 1985), Am. Printing History Assn., Beta Phi Mu (pres. 1974-75). Home and Office: 4436 Meandering Way #108AG Tallahassee FL 32308-8705 Business E-Mail: mjzachert@earthlink.net.

ZACHRY, HENRY BARTELL, JR., construction executive; b. Laredo, Texas; m. Mollie Zachry; children: John, David, Anne Rochelle, Ellen Carrie. BS in Civil Engring., Tex. A&M, 1954. Joined H.B. Zachry Co. (now Zachry Constrn. Corp.), 1957; pres. Zachry Constrn. Corp., 1965, CEO San Antonio, 1984—2004, chmn., 1984—. Pilot USAF, 1954—57. Recipient Texas A&M Disting. Alumnus, 1997, Texas A&M Engineering's Outstanding Alumni Honor award, 2005, Sterling C. Evans medal, Texas A&M Found. Bd. Trustees, 2008; named a Texas Bus. Hall of Fame inductee. Office: Zachry Construction Corp 12625 Wetmore Rd Ste 301 PO Box 33240 San Antonio TX 78247-3611 Office Phone: 210-871-2700. Office Fax: 210-475-8060.

ZACK, STEPHEN NEAL, lawyer; b. Detroit, Dec. 2, 1947; s. Benn Zack and Anita (Rabinovich) Petluck; children: Jason, Tracey. BA, U. Fla., 1969, JD, 1971. Bar: Fla. 1972, NY 1982, DC 1986, US Dist. Ct. (no. and so. dists.) Fla. 1986, U.S. Ct. Appeals (5th and 11th cirs.)1986. Sr. ptnr. Floyd, Pearson, Richman, Greer, Weil, Zack & Brumbaugh P.A., Miami, Fla., 1972-91, Zack, Hanzman & Ponce P.A., Miami, 1991—95, Zack Kosnitzky P.A., 1995—2002, Boies, Schiller & Flexner LLP, Miami, 2002—. Legis. aide to Congressman Claude Pepper, 1971-72; chmn. environ. rev. bd. City of Miami, 1978-79, Fla. law ctr. coun. U. Fla., 1982; mem. Speakers Adv. Com. on Future, Jud. Nomination Commn. for 11th Cir.; spl. counsel to Gov. Bob Graham, 1986; bd. dirs. Jewish Family Services, 1984-; chmn. State Fla. Ethics Comm.; former pres. Nat. Conf. Bar Presidents. Named to Hall of Fame, U. Fla. Mem. ABA (life fellow, chmn. House Del. 2004—2006, mem. bd. govs., pres.-elect 2009-10, pres., 2010-), ALTA, Fla. Bar Assn. (pres. young lawyers sect. 1975-76, bd. govs. 1977-88, chmn. internat. law sect. 1981-82, pres. 1989-90), Acad. Fla. Trial Lawyers (bd. dirs. 1982-86), Dade County Bar Assn. (bd. dirs. & pres. young lawyers sect. 1975-76), Cuban-Am. Lawyers Assn., Federacion Interamericana de Abogados, Blue Key (pres. Fla. chpt.), Omicron Delta Kappa. Office: Boies Schiller & Flexner LLP Bank of Amer Tower 100 SE 2nd St Ste 2800 Miami FL 33131-2115 Office Phone: 305-539-8400. E-mail: szack@bsfllp.com.

ZADEH, JAVAD HAMADANI, mathematics professor; b. Kerman, Iran, Oct. 2, 1940; arrived in U.S., 1964; s. Bagher Hamadani Zadeh and Fatemeh Asadi; children: Neda, Mina. BA, The Am. U. Beirut, Lebanon, 1963; MS, Purdue U., West Lafayette, Ind., 1966; PhD, MPhil, Columbia U., NYC, 1976. Cert. tchr. Ga. Profl. Standards Commn., 1988. Instr. math. Shiraz U., Iran, 1963—64, Ctr. Coll. Ky., Danville, Ky., 1966—67, Bowling Green State U., Ohio, 1969—70; from instr. to asst. prof. Sharif U. Tech., Tehran, Iran, 1970—82, chmn. dept. math. and computer sci., 1979—81, assoc. prof., 1982—86; vis. prof. math. U. Ga., Athens, 1986—87; tchr. math. Ga. Pub. Schs., Alamo, 1990—92; asst. prof. math. Mid. Ga. Coll., Cochran, Ga., 1992—93; assoc. prof. Brewton-Parker Coll., Mt. Vernon, Ga., 1993—97, prof., 1997—2006; asst. prof. math. Dalton State Coll., Ga., 2006—. Postdoctoral rsch. fellow dept. math. U. Calif., 1976—77. Author: Shenidi Che-Gaft, 1970, 2d edit., 2000; editor: Bull. Iranian Math. Soc., 1979—81; contbr. articles to profl. jours. Home: 8740 Roswell Rd 9D Atlanta GA 30350 Office Phone: 706-272-2580.

ZADEH, MANSOUR T., food products executive; Sr. info. tech. leader PepsiCo, Inc.; head info. tech. Miller Brewing Co.; chief tech. officer Kraft Foods; chief info. officer Smithfield Foods, Inc., Va., 2002—. Named one of 25 Most Influential Consumer Goods Execs. That Make a Difference, Consumer Goods Tech. mag., 2004. Office: Smithfield Foods Inc 200 Commerce St Smithfield VA 23430 Office Phone: 757-365-3000.

ZAFFIRINI, JUDITH, state legislator; b. Laredo, Tex., Feb. 13, 1946; d. George and Nieves Mogas Pappas; m. Carlos M. Zaffirini; 1 child, Carlos Jr. Attended, U. Houston, Laredo Jr. Coll.; BS, MA, PhD, U. Tex., Austin. Former tchr.; mem. Dist. 21 Tex. State Senate, Tex., 1987—; owner, comm. specialist Zaffirini Comm., 1997—. Pub. rels. dir., mem. bd. dir. Laredo Civic Music Assn., 1968—; chairwoman govt. affairs com. Laredo C. of C. Co-author: Cross-Cultural Communication of Emotions via Facial Expressions and Content-free Language, 1974; author: Publicity Planner, Or How To Get Publicity In Laredo News Media, 1975. Former mem. Dem. Nat. Com.; del. Dem. Nat. Conv., 1980, 1984; sec., conv. del. Webb County Dem. Com., 1976—; vice chairwoman Tex. State Dem. Com., 1984—86. Recipient Outstanding Women award, Tex. Mex. Am. Polit. Caucus, Tex. Herione & Friend of Bus. award, Tex. C. of C., Merit award, Jose Maria Morelos y Pavon, 1987, award, Children's Trust Fund Tex., 1996, Tex. for a Day award, Office of Gov., 1997, and several others. Mem.: Tex. Press Women (Achievement award), Nat. Fedn. Press Women, Tex. Pub. Rels. Assn., Nat. Coun. Cmty. Rels., Assn. Edn. Jour., Internat. Comm. Assn., Tex. Philos. Soc., Phi Kappa Phi. Democrat. Roman Catholic. Office: 1407 Washington St Laredo TX 78042 also: PO Box 12068 Capitol Station Austin TX 78711 also: 12702 Toepperwein Rd Ste 214 San Antonio TX 78233 Office Phone: 956-722-2293, 512-463-0121, 210-657-0095.

ZAGORIA, SAM D(AVID), reporter, educator, federal agency administrator; b. Somerville, NJ, Apr. 9, 1919; s. Nathan and Rebecca (Shapiro) Z.; m. Sylvia Bomse, Dec. 21, 1941; children: Paul, Marjorie Zagoria Isacks, Ronald. BL in Journalism, Rutgers U., 1941. With New Brunswick (N.J.) Daily Home News, 1940-41, N.J. Def. Coun., Trenton, 1941-42, Fed. Office Govt. Reports, Newark, 1942; reporter Washington Post, 1946-55; adminstrv. asst. to Senator Clifford P. Case, Washington, 1955-65; pres. Washington Newspaper Guild, 1953; mem. NLRB, Washington, 1965-69; dir. Labor-Mgmt. Rels. Svc. U.S. Conf. of Mayors, Washington, 1970-78; mem. U.S. Consumer Product Safety Commn., 1978-84; ombudsman Washington Post, 1984-86; arbitrator, 1986—. Fulbright lectr., Copenhagen, 1987; vis. prof. Fla. Atlantic U., Boca Raton, 1988—91; adj. prof. Wake Forest U., Winston-Salem, NC, 1993—2001. Author: Public Workers, Public Unions, 1972, The Ombudsman: How Good Governments Handle Citizens' Grievances, 1988. Campaign mgr. reelection Senator Case, 1960; campaign mgr. race for gov., former Sec. of Labor James P. Mitchell, 1961. With USAAF, 1942-45. Nieman fellow Harvard U., 1954. Mem. Common Cause, Nat. Consumers League, Rutgers U. Alumni Assn. Jewish. also: 2864 Wynfield Crossing Ln Winston Salem NC 27103-6597 Address: 3101 S Ocean Blvd 622 Boca Raton FL 33487 Office Phone: 561-274-6376.

ZAHN, CARL FREDERICK, museum program director, photographer, graphics designer; b. Louisville, Mar. 9, 1928; s. Fred Joseph and Myrtle (Fulks) Z.; m. Betty Jane Woodrow, Nov. 18, 1950 (div. July 1977); children: Lisa, Karen, Richard; m. Felicitas Magdalena Fuhlrott, July 30, 1979 (dec. Mar. 1999). BA, Harvard Coll., 1948. Asst. in conservation Fogg Art Mus., Cambridge, Mass., 1949-50; with art dept. Benton & Bowles Inc., NYC, 1950-51; design asst. Inst. Contemporary Art, Boston, 1951-56; dir. publs. Mus. Fine Arts, Boston, 1956—; also dir. exhbns., 1995-96; ret., 1997; co-founder Mus. Pub. Ptnrs., 2000. Exhibitions include: Addison Gallery Am. Art, Andover, Mass., 1959, Am. Inst. Graphic Arts, N.Y.C., 1960—, Rose Art Mus. Brandeis U., Waltham, Mass., 1969; author: Introduction to Hermann Zapf and His Design Philosophy, 1987, Books and Such Designed by Carl Zahn at the Museum of Fine Arts, Boston, 1956-97, 1997; co-author Weston's Westons: Portraits and Nudes, 1989; co-editor: Eye of the Beholder: Masterpieces from the Isabella Stewart Gardner Museum, 2003. Mem. Soc. Printers, Bund Deutscher Buchkünstler, East Chop Tennis Club (bd. dirs. 1970-72), Longwood Cricket Club. Home: 2030 E Leewynn Dr Sarasota FL 34240-9637 E-mail: czbird@verizon.net.

ZAINEY, JAY C., federal judge; b. New Orleans, 1951; BS, U. New Orleans, 1972; JD, La. State U., 1975. Law clk. in pvt. practice, La., 1974—75; pvt. practice atty. La., 1976—2002; judge US Dist. Ct. (ea. dist.) La., New Orleans, 2002—. Mem. USAFR, 1970—76. Office: US Dist Ct 500 Poydras St Rm C455 New Orleans LA 70130 Office Phone: 504-589-7590.

ZAISER, KENT AMES, lawyer; b. St. Petersburg, Fla., June 10, 1945; s. Robert Alan and Marion (Brown) Z. AB, Duke U., 1967; postgrad., U. Calif., Berkeley, 1971; JD, U. Fla., 1972. Bar: Fla. 1973, U.S. Dist. Ct. (no. dist.) Fla. 1974, U.S. Supreme Ct. 1978, U.S. Dist. Ct. (so. dist.) Fla. 1980, U.S. Dist. Ct. (mid. dist.) Fla. 1981, U.S. Ct. Appeals (11th cir.) 1981. Rsch. aide Fla. Supreme Ct., Tallahassee, 1973-75, adminstrv. asst. to chief justice, 1975-76; asst. gen. counsel Fla. Dept. Natural Resources, Tallahassee, 1976-80; asst. atty. gen. Fla. Dept. Legal Affairs, Tallahassee, 1980-85; dep. gen. counsel S.W. Fla. Water Mgmt. Dist., Brooksville, 1985-89, gen. counsel, 1989-92; ptnr. Foley and Lardner, Tallahassee, 1992-93; prin. Kent A. Zaiser, P.A., Tallahassee, 1994—. Cons. Fla. State Cts. Adminstr., Tallahassee, 1975; mem. Fla. New Motor Vehicle Arbitration Bd., 1998-99. Contbg. author: Environmental Regulation and Litigation in Florida, 1980-84. Campaign chmn. Vince Fechtel for State Rep. of Fla., Leesburg, 1972. Mem. Jefferson County Bar Assn., Govs. Club. Democrat. Episcopalian. Home: 3286 Longleaf Rd Tallahassee FL 32310-6406 Office: PO Box 6045 Tallahassee FL 32314-6045 Home Phone: 850-576-2464; Office Phone: 850-576-7600.

ZAK, LEOCADIA IRINE, federal agency administrator, lawyer; b. 1957; BA, Mt. Holyoke Coll., 1979; JD, Northeastern U., 1982. Ptnr. bus. and fin. sect. Mintz, Levin, Cohn, Ferris, Glovsky and Popeo, PC, Washington, Boston; gen. counsel US Trade and Devel. Agency (USTDA), Arlington, 2000—05, dep. dir., 2006—09, acting dir., 2007—08, 2009—10, dir., 2010—. Adj. prof. law Boston U. Sch. Law, Morin Ctr. Banking and Fin. Law Studies, Georgetown U. Law Ctr. Office: US Trade and Development Agency 100 Wilson Blvd, Ste 1600 Arlington VA 22209 Office Phone: 703-875-4357. Office Fax: 703-875-4009.*

ZAKHEIM, DOV SOLOMON, economist, former federal agency administrator; b. Bklyn., Dec. 18, 1948; s. Zvi Hirsh and Bella (Rabinowitz) Zakheim; m. Barbara Jane Portnoi, Aug. 20, 1972 (div. 1990); children: Keith Samuel, Roger Israel, Scott Elisha; m. Deborah Bing Lowy, May 26, 1991. Student, London Sch. Econs., 1968—69; BA summa cum laude, Columbia U., NYC, 1970; DPhil, Oxford U., Eng., 1974. Rsch. fellow St. Antony's Coll. Oxford U., 1974; asst. to mng. dir. U.K. br. Internat. Credit Bank Geneva, 1974-75; assoc. analyst Nat. Security and Internat. Affairs Congl. Budget Office (CBO), Washington, 1975-78, prin. analyst, 1978-81; spl. asst. to asst. sec. for internat. security policy US Dept. Def., Washington, 1981-82, spl. asst. to under sec., 1982-83, asst. under sec. for policy & resources, 1983-85, dep. under sec. for planning & resources, 1985-87; exec. v.p. Sys. Planning Corp., Arlington, Va., 1987-90, corp. v.p., 1990-2001; CEO SPC Internat. Inc, 1998—2001; under-sec. (comptr.), CFO US Dept. Def., Washington, 2001—04; sr. v.p. Booz Allen Hamilton, McLean, Va., 2004—10; sr. adv. Ctr. for Strategic & Internat. Studies (CSIS), Washington, 2007—; sr. fellow Ctr. for Naval Analyses, 2010—. Cons. to sec. def. and undersec. def., 1987—2000, 2004—; adj. scholar Heritage Found., 1988—2001; adj. prof. Nat. Def. U., 1992, Columbia U., 1995—96, Yeshiva U., 1995—96; adj prof., presdl. fellow Trinity Coll., Conn., 1998; adj. sr. fellow Coun. on Fgn. Rels., 2000—01; commr. US Comm. on Wartime Contracting in Iraq & Afghanistan (CWC), 2009—11; adj. prof. Georgetown U., 2012. Author: Flight of the Lavi: Inside a U.S.-Israeli Crisis, 1996, A Vulcan's Tale: How the Bush Administration Mismanaged the Reconstruction of Afghanistan, 2011. Mem US Commn. Preservation America's Heritage Abroad, 1991—95; mem. Dept. Def. Bus. Bd., 2004—10, 2013—, Chief Naval Ops. Exec. Panel, 2004—; mem. bd. visitors Dept. Def. Overseas Regulatory Centers, 1998—2001; sr. fellow DBB Chief Naval Ops. Exec. Panel, 2010—; mem US Dept. Def. Task Force on Def. Reform, 1997; bd deputies Brit Jews, 1971—72; mem Chief Rabbi's Chaplaincy Bd, England, 1971—72; bd. dirs. Friends of Jewish Chapel, US Naval Acad, 1997—; mem. Sec. Navy Advisory Bd., 2008; commr. Mil. Compensation and Ret. Modernization Commn., 2013—. Recipient Disting. Pub. Svc. medal, US Dept. Def., 1986, 1987, 2004, Medal for Outstanding Pub. Svc., Dept. Navy, 2004; fellow, NSF, 1970—73, Kellet, Columbia Col, 1974. Mem.: Royal Swedish Acad. War Scis., Royal Inst Int Affairs (UK), Int Inst Strategic Studies, Coun Foreign Relations, Cosmos Club, United Oxford and Cambridge Univ Club, Columbia Club, Phi Beta Kappa. Office: CNA 4825 Mark Center Dr Alexandria VA 22311-1850 Office Phone: 703-819-4315, 703-824-2420.

ZALL, ROBERT ROUBEN, food scientist, educator; b. Lowell, Mass., Dec. 6, 1925; s. Samuel and Sarah (Cohen) Z.; m. Mollie Leah Wiseblood, June 8, 1949; children— Linda Zall Sheffield, Judy Zall Kusek, Jonathan J. BS, U. Mass., 1949, MS, 1950; PhD, Cornell U., 1968. Gen. mgr. Grandview Dairies, Bklyn. and Arkport, N.Y., 1950-66; dairy industry cons. Ithaca, N.Y., 1966-68; dir. research prodn. Crowley Foods Co., Binghamton, N.Y., 1968-71; prof. food sci. Cornell U., 1971-92; prof. emeritus, 1992—. Past trustee Milk Industry Pension and Welfare Fund; dairy industry cons., project dir. EPA-Industry demonstration whey processing plant. Author: (with Bela G. Liptak) Environmental Engineers Handbook, 1972, Managing Food Industry Waste: Common Sense Methods for Food Processors, 2004; co-contbr. to Food Processing Waste Management, 1979, Food Processing, 15 vols., 1979, Dairy Microbiology, 1981, rev. edit., 1990; contbr. numerous articles to profl. jours., popular mags.; patentee automatic cleaning apparatus, stabilization of milk and improved cheese yield, Rennin-like enzymes from clams, a process for preserving fish and microbial production of acetaldeyde. Served with AUS, 1944-46. Recipient Cert. Appreciation EPA, 1975, 79; Howard B. Marlott award N.Y. State Milk and Food Sanitarians Mem. Internat. Assn. Milk, Food and Environ. Sanitarians, Internat. Dairy Fedn., Inst. Food Technologists, Am. Soc. Agrl. Engrs., Masons, Phi Kappa Phi. Office: 1120 SW 22nd Ave V12-4 Delray Beach FL 33445

ZALLEN, HAROLD, academic administrator, chemist; b. Boston, Apr. 7, 1926; s. Joseph and Lillian L. (Stahl) Z.; m. Eugenia Malone, Aug. 23, 1959. BS in Pharmacy, Northeastern U., Boston, 1951; EdM in Sci. and Math. Statistics, Psychology, Boston U., 1954; MS in Organic Synthetic Medicinal Chemistry and Biochemistry, Purdue U., West Lafayette, Ind., 1958; PhD in Analytical Medicinal Chemistry and Nucleonics, Purdue U., 1960. Registered pharmacist, Mass., Ind. With USAAF, 1943-46, combat flier, sgt. 487th bomb group H Twelve O Clock High, 839th bomb squadron; commd. 1st lt. Med. Svc. U.S. Army, 1955, advanced through grades to col., nuclear perfects officer effects, 1986; ret.; mgr. Shoppers World Pharmacy, Inc., Framingham, Mass., 1951—55; asst. prof. phys. sci. Portia Law Sch. Calvin Coolidge Coll., Boston, 1952-54; tchr. physics and chemistry Natick (Mass.) High Sch., 1955-56; asst. prof. microbiology Lowell Gen. Hosp. Sch. Nursing, Mass., 1955-56; grad. instr., asst. radiol. control officer Purdue U., West Lafayette, Ind., 1957-58; assoc. prof. chemistry Coll. Pharmacy Mercer U., Atlanta, 1960-61; assoc. prof. to prof., head dept. radiol. scis., dir. Office Radiol. Safety Auburn U., Ala., 1961-66; specialist phys. sci. rsch. div. higher edn. rsch. Bur. Rsch., U.S. Office Edn., 1966-67, head curriculum higher edn. rsch., 1967; head instructional sci. equipment program, assoc. program dir., then dir. spl. projects program NSF, Washington, 1967-72; asst. dean, dir. rsch. and grad. studies Okla. State U., Stillwater, 1972-73, prof. chemistry, 1972-73, rsch. prof. biochemistry and molecular biology, 1973-75; assoc. v.p. for adminstrn. and fin., CEO Health Scis. Ctr. Campus U. Okla., Oklahoma City and Tulsa, 1973-75, assoc. v.p. for systems planning, procedure devel. and spl. projects, cen. adminstrn. Norman, 1975—; exec. v.p. Acad. World Inc., 1975—; pres., CEO Malone, Zallen & Assocs. div. AcaWorld Corp., Greenville, NC; v.p., dir. nuclear divsn. Vachon, Nix & Assocs., Atlanta; pres., CEO Computer Profls. Inc., Computer Distbrs. Corp., Malone Group Internat., Columbus, Ga.; sci. advisor Litton Corp./Army Rsch. Inst., 1991, Omega Tng. Group Inc./GIAT Industries, France, 1992—, Wetzel Internat., Inc., 1994—; chmn. bd. dirs. Cons. Unltd., Columbus, Ga.; rsch. dir., joint project Malone Group Internat. and Auburn U.; with NE Field Track Assn. Boston Marathon, 1954—56. Analytical chemist Communicable Diseases Ctr. USPHS, Atlanta, 1962; spl. lectr. NSF Radiobiology Inst., Tuskegee U., 1963-64, head instrnl. sci. equipment program, assoc. program dir., dir. spl. projects program, 1967-72; pres. Pres.'s Sci. and Technol. Adv. Commn., Washington; v.p. Okla. Coll. Osteo. Medicine and Surgery, Tulsa; Gov. NC primary alt. to So. States Energy Bd., 1984-90, exec. com. bd., 1986; bd. vis. Tex. Christian U., Ft. Worth, 1973-76, bd. visitors, Dartmouth Coll., 1973-74; leadership coun. Coll. Sci. and Math. Auburn U., 2003—; cons. in field; rsch. dir., joint project Auburn U. COB Aviation Mgmt.-CLA COE Aerospace Engring., Audiology Divsn-COSAM Math. & Stats.-Auburn-Auburn U. Airport & Malone Group Internat., Head Tilt & Pilot Fatigue Measured By Flight Simulation, Engring. & Aerospace Engering. Internat. Jour., 2012, Aircraft Surgical Aerospace Technology. Editor, pub. Jour. Internat 6800 Computer Ctr.; contbr. articles to profl. jours. Hon. chmn. bus. adv. coun., Ala., 2003; rep. candidate NC Gen. Assembly, 1986; mem. nat. rep. congl. com. Recipient Mayoralty cert. of merit and Key to City, City of New Orleans, 1973, Most Outstanding Alumni award Northeastern U., 1996, Comdg. Gen. award U.S. Army Inf. Ctr., 1998; GE sci. fellow Union U., Schenectady, NY., 1955, fellow Purdue Rsch. Found., 1958, Elks Cancer Soc., 1959, Am. Cancer Soc., 1960; named Disting. Vis. Rsch. Prof., Dept. Aerospace Engring. Auburn U., 2009-. Mem. Am. Chem. Soc. (bd. dirs., chmn. Auburn sect. 1966), Am. Soc. Engring. Edn. (long range planning com.), Nat. Coun. Univ. Adminstrs., Soc. Rsch. Adminstrs. (pres. So. sect. from 1974, chmn. publs. com.), Health Physics Soc., Greenville (NC) Area C. of C. (chmn. rsch.), Columbus Club, Rotary (chmn. bull. com. Auburn 1963, bd. dirs. Auburn 1964, bd. dirs. Stillwater 1972-73, Greenville 1981-86, charter pres. Greenville, N.C. Morning Club 1986, 91, 94, Paul Harris fellow, (5) R.I. Svc. Above Self award 1986), Rotary Club (Auburn Chmn. Classification Ctr. mem. 2000-), Masons (32 degree), Shriners, Sigma Xi, Phi Lambda Upsilon, Rho Chi, Phi Delta Kappa, Delta Sigma Theta, Beta Phi (past nat. sec.) Baptist. Office: Malone Group International PO Box 3682 Auburn AL 36831-3682 Office Phone: 334-887-2085.

ZAMAN, PATRICK, telecommunications industry executive; Grad., Solvay Bus. Sch., Brussels. Mktg. mgr. Belgacom S.A., Belgium, 1998—2002, sr. sales account mgr., 2002—05, unit sales mgr. small, medium & large enterprises market, 2005—07, sales dir. large enterprises South, 2007—09; mng. dir. ScanSource Communications Europe, 2009—. Office: ScanSource Inc 6 Logue Court Greenville SC 29615 Office Phone: 864-288-2432. Office Fax: 864-288-1165.

ZAMIR, IGAL, consumer products company executive; BS in Indsl. Engring., Tel Aviv U., 1989; MBA in Mktg., Bar-Ilan U., 1994. CEO Rostam Ltd., 1998—2004; ind. venture ptnr. Israel, 2004—06; CEO Metrolight, Ltd., 2006—09; pres. MAPCO Express, Inc., 2009—. Office: MAPCO Express Inc 7102 Commerce Way Brentwood TN 37027 Office Phone: 615-771-6701. Business E-Mail: Igal.Zamir@mantech.com.

ZAMKA, GEORGE D., astronaut; b. Jersey City, June 29, 1962; s. Conrad P. and Sofia Zamka; m. Elisa P. Walker; 2 children. BS in Math., U.S. Naval Acad., 1984; MS in Engring. Mgmt., Fla. Inst. Tech., 1997. Commd. 2d lt. USMC, 1984, advanced through grades to lt. col.; with Navy Attack Squadron, Marine All Weather Attack Squadron, VMA, El Toro, Calif.; squadron weapons and tactics instr.; with Marine All Weather Fighter Attack Squadron VMFA, El Toro;

forward air contr. 1st Bn., 5th Marines, Camp Pendleton, Calif.; with 31st Marine Expeditionary Unit, USS Belleau Wood, Western Pacific; test pilot/project officer Naval Strike Aircraft Test Squadron; aircraft maintenance officer VMFA, 1998; astronaut (pilot) NASA, Houston, 1998—, various duties with Astronaut Office. Comdr. STS-120 Discovery Mission to Internat. Space Station, 2007, STS-130 Endeavour Mission, 2010. Decorated 6 Navy Strike Air medals, Navy Commendation medal with Combat V; recipient Superior Accomplishment award, NASA, GEM award. Mem.: Soc. Exptl. Test Pilots, Marine Corps Assn., U.S. Naval Acad. Alumni Assn. Achievements include logged over 3,000 flight hours in over 30 different aircraft. Avocations: weightlifting, running, bicycling, scuba diving, boating. Office: Astronaut Office /CB NASA Johnson Space Ctr Houston TX 77058

ZAMORA, EDDIE, JR., communications executive; b. Mission, Tex., Oct. 8, 1962; children: Joshua, Jared, Timothy. Grad., Southwest Sch. Electronics, US Navy Electronics Technician "A" Sch. Qualified Reactor Operator S1C Navy Nuclear Prototype Tng. Unit, 1985, cert. Welder Piedmont Cmty. Coll., 1996. Min. Abundant Grace Cmty. Ch.; engring. technician Fed. Aviation Adminstrn. - Raleigh-Durham Airport, 1991—95; sales cons. Toyota of Durham, 2001—02, What's On Hold Prodns., 2003—04; sr. sales cons. Rioplex Broadband, 2004—. Permanent committeeman, Permanent Rules Com. Tex. Rep. Conv., San Antonio, 2006, temp. committeeman, Temp. Rules Com., 2006. Leader, tchr. singles' bible study group Abundant Grace Ch., 2004—; vol. umpire Christian Youth Athletics, 1986—87. Republican. Office: 5111 N 10th St #191 Mcallen TX 78504 Business E-Mail: ezamora@rioplexwireless.com.

ZARAMA, LUIS RAFAEL, bishop; b. Pasto, Colombia, Nov. 28, 1958; arrived in USA, 1991, naturalized, 2000; Licentiate in philos. & theol., Pasto Sem., Universidad Mariana, Colombia, 1982—87; licentiate in canon law, Universidad Javeriana, Bogota, Colombia, 1987—91. Ordained priest Archdiocese of Atlanta, 1993; parochial vicar Sacred Heart parish, Atlanta, 1993—96; adminstr. St. Helena mission, Clayton, Ga., 1996—2006; pastor St. Mark parish, Clarkesville, Ga., 1996—2006; vicar gen. Archdiocese of Atlanta, 2006—; ordained bishop, 2009; aux. bishop Archdiocese of Atlanta, 2009—. Advocate, Ct. Appeals Ecclesiastical Province Atlanta, 1993—97, Defender of the Bond, Ct. Appeals, 1997—; asst. dir. vocations Archdiocese of Atlanta, 2000—. Roman Catholic. Office: Archdiocese of Atlanta Catholic Ctr 2401 Lake Park Dr SE Ste 100 Smyrna GA 30080-8859 Office Phone: 404-888-7805. Office Fax: 404-888-7230.

ZARWYN, BERTHOLD, physicist, consultant; b. Vienna, Aug. 22, 1921; came to US, 1949, naturalized, 1955; s. Joseph and Bronislawa Regina (Unger) Zarwyn. ME, Gliwice, Poland, 1946; ScD, UN Univ., Munich, 1947; PhD, NYU, 1954; ScD in Engring., Columbia U., NYC, 1963. Project engr. Curtiss-Wright Corp., Woodridge, NJ, 1951-55; staff scientist AMF Corp., NYC, 1955-57; chief scientist Link Aviation Co., Binghamton, NY, 1957-58; head rsch. staff Am. Bosch-Arma Corp., Garden City, NY, 1958-63; corp. cons. Cutler-Hammer Corp., Deer Park, NY, 1963-65; chief engr. Bell Aerosystems Corp., Niagara Falls, NY, 1965-66; sr. cons. Mitre Corp., Bedford, Mass., 1966-68; spl. asst. to commdg. gen., acting chief engr. Hdqs. US Army Materiel Command, Arlington, Va., 1968-71; chief phys. scis. br. US Army Devel. and Readiness Command, Alexandria, Va., 1971-75; phys. scientist US Army Harry Diamond Labs., Washington, 1975-78; chief sys. analysis br. US Army Elec. Rsch. and Devel. Command, Adelphi, Md., 1978-79, chief tech. divsn., 1979-81, asst. tech. dir., 1981-85; spl. asst. to dep. chief of staff for tech. & program mgmt. US Army Lab. Command, Adelphi, Md., 1985-87; pres. Pan-Tech. Corp., Delray Beach, Fla., 1987—. Adj. faculty U. Conn., lectr., cons. in field; dir. Film Microelectronics Co. Inc., Burlington, Mass., 1965-67. Mem. editl. bd. Bavarian Soc. Engrs., 1947-49, transl. panel Russian Jour. Applied Math. and Mechanics with Pergamon Inst., 1956-57; inventor nuc. gyroscope, microwave holography, other items. Mem. IEEE, Am. Phys. Soc., NY Acad. Scis., Sigma Xi. Home and Office: Pan-Tech Corp 7589 Mansfield Hollow Rd Delray Beach FL 33446-3314 Office Phone: 561-637-9387. Personal E-mail: zarwyn22@comcast.net.

ZEALEY, SHARON JANINE, lawyer; b. St. Paul, Aug. 30, 1959; d. Marion Edward and Freddie Zealey. BS, Xavier U. of La., 1981; JD, U. Cin., 1984. Bar: Ohio 1984; U.S. Dist. Ct. (so. dist.) Ohio 1985; U.S. Ct. Appeals (6th cir.) 1990; U.S. Supreme Ct. 1990. Law clk. US Atty. S. Dist. Ohio, Cin., 1982; trust adminstr. US Bank (formerly First Nat. Bank), Cin., 1984-86; atty. UAW Legal Svcs., Cin., 1986-88; assoc. Manley, Burke, Lipton & Fischer, Cin., 1988-91; mng. atty. and dep. atty. gen. Ohio Atty. Gen. Office, Cin., 1991-95; asst. US atty. criminal div. for So. Dist. Ohio US Attys. Office, Cin., 1995-97; United States atty. So. Dist. Ohio, Cin., 1997—2001; ptnr. Blank Rome LLP, 2001—06; sr. litig. counsel Coca-Cola Co., Atlanta, 2006—. Adj. instr. Coll. Law U. Cin., 1997—; mem. U.S. Atty. Gen.'s Adv. Com., 1999—2001, chair civil rights subcom., 2001; mem. merit selection com. Sixth Cir. Ct. of Appeals Bankruptcy Ct., 1992—96, 2003. Mem. commn. Cin. Cmty. Action Now, 2001—; commr. Tall Stacks Commn., City of Cin., 1990—94, Mayor's Commn. on Children, City of Cin., 1992—94; mem. equal employment adv. rev. panel City of Cin., 1989—91; trustee, bd. visitors U. Cin. Coll. Law, 1992—2006; trustee Legal Aid Soc. Cin., 1987—92; bd. dirs. Freestore Foodbank, 2003—, Playhouse in the Park, 2002—06, Nat. Inst. for Law and Equity, 2002—; co-chair Greater Cin. Minority Counsel Program, 2005—06; mem. exec. bd. Cin. Youth Collaborative, 2005—06. Recipient Disting. Alumni award, Friends of Women's Studies, U. Cin., 2001, Theodore M. Berry award for outstanding achievement in politics and in svc. to cmty., Cin. chpt. NACCP, 1998, Nicholas Longworth III Alumni Achievement award for disting. pub. svc., U. Cin. Coll. Law, 1997; named Career Woman of Achievement, Cin. YWCA, 1988; named one of Top Ten Women Attys., Women's Bus. Cin., 2005; named to Super Lawyers, Ohio, 2006. Mem. Black Lawyers Assn. of Cin. (pres. 1989-91, round table 1988-), Legal Aid Soc. (sec. 1991-92), ABA, Fed. Bar Assn., Ohio Bar Assn., Nat. Bar Assn. (bd. govs. 1988-1990, Mem. of Yr. region VI 1990), Cin. Bar Assn. (trustee 1989-94), Cin. CAN Commn. Democrat. Episcopalian. Office: Coca-Cola Co One Coca-Cola Plz NAT 2062 PO Box 1734 Atlanta GA 30301 Office Phone: 404-676-2121. Business E-Mail: zealey@blankRome.com.

ZEDLER, WILLIAM, state legislator; b. Aug. 19, 1943; m. Ellen Zedler; 3 children. BBA, Sam Houston State U., Huntsville, Tex., MBA, 1967. Ret. healthcare profl.; mem. Dist. 96 Tex. House of Representatives, 2002—08, 2011—. Mem. Tarrant County Rep. Assembly. Chmn. bd. elders Pk. Springs Bible Ch.; mem. adv. bd. Arlington Pregnancu Ctr. 1st lt., hosp. pers. officer US Army. Mem.: Arlington C. of C., Rep. Forum, Arlington Rep. Club (sec.), Arlington Kiwanis Club, Rep. Women Arlington Club (assoc.). Republican. Office: Room E1.302 Capitol Extension PO Box 2910 Austin TX 78768 Address: 5840 W Interstate 20 Ste 110 Arlington TX 76017 Office Phone: 512-463-0374, 817-483-1885. Office Fax: 512-463-0364.

ZEDLITZ, ANN C., dermatologist; Grad., U. New Orleans; MD with honors, La. State U. Med. Ctr., 1996. Diplomate Am. Bd. Dermatology. Intern, emergency medicine La. State Univ., resident, dermatology, resident, emergency medicine, chief resident, 2009—10, asst. clin. prof. dermatology; diplomat Am. Bd. Dermatology, Am. Bd. Emergency Medicine; joined Dermatology Clinic, 2010—. Mem.: Our Lady of the Lake Hosp., Am. Soc. of Dermatologic Surgery, Women's Dermatol. Soc., Am. Soc. for Laser Medicine and Surgery, Alpha Omega Alpha Med. Honor Soc. Office: Dermatology Clinic 5326 O'Donovan Dr Baton Rouge LA 70808 Office Phone: 225-769-7546.

ZEITHAML, CARL PAUL, dean, educator; b. 1950; BA in Economics, U. Notre Dame, 1971; MBA in Health & Hosp. Adminstrn., U. Fla., 1974; DBA in Strategic Mgmt., U. Md., 1980. Faculty mem. U. NC Kenan-Flagler Sch. Bus., Chapel Hill, 1986—97; dean, prof., mgmt. area U. Va. McIntire Sch. Commerce, 1997—. Bd. dirs. Dollar Tree, Inc., 2007—. Author: Strategic Mgmt. Jour., Measuring Orgnl. Knowledge: A Conceptual and Methodological Framework, Asia Pacific Jour. of Mgmt., The International Expansion Process of MNEs from Developing Countries: A Case Study of Thailand's CP Group, Orgn. Sci., Garbage Cans and Advancing Hypercompetition: The Creation and Exploitation of New Capabilities and Strategic Flexibility in Two Regional Bell Oper. Companies, Strategic Mgmt. Jour., Competencies and Firm Performance: Exam. the Causal Ambiguity Paradox, Acad.of Mgmt. Exec., Mng. Orgnl. Competencies for Competitive Advantage: The Mid. Mgmt. Edge; co-author: cases on global strategy issues. Office: McIntire Sch Commerce UniversityVa PO Box 400173 Rouss & Robertson Halls Charlottesville VA 22904 Office Phone: 434-924-0311. Office Fax: 434-982-4378. Business E-Mail: czeithaml@virginia.edu.

ZELBY, LEON WOLF, retired electrical engineer, educator, consultant; b. Sosnowiec, Poland, Mar. 26, 1925; came to U.S., 1946, naturalized, 1951; s. Herszel and Helen (Wajnryb) Zylberberg; m. Rachel Kupfermintz, Dec. 28, 1954; children: Laurie Susan, Andrew Stephen. BSEE, Moore Sch. Elec. Engring., 1956; MS, Calif. Inst. Tech., 1957; PhD, U. Pa., 1961. Registered profl. engr., Pa., Okla. Mem. staff RCA, Hughes R & D Labs., Lincoln Lab., MIT, Sandia Corp., Argonne (Ill.) Nat. Labs., Inst. for Energy Analysis; mem. faculty U. Pa., 1959-67, assoc. prof., 1964-67; assoc. dir. plasma engring. Inst. Direct Energy Conversion, 1962-67; prof. U. Okla., Norman, 1967-95, dir. Sch. Elec. Engring., 1967-71; ret., 1995. Cons. RCA, 1961-67, Moore Sch. Elec. Engring., 1967-68, also pvt. firms. Editor Tech. and Soc. mag., 1990-93; contbr. articles on energy-associated problems and issues to profl. jours. With AUS, 1946-47. Cons. Electrodynamic Corp. fellow Calif. Inst. Tech., 1957, Mpls.-Honeywell fellow U. Pa., 1957-58, Harrison fellow, 1958. Mem. IEEE, Franklin Inst., Sigma Xi, Tau Beta Pi, Eta Kappa Nu, Pi Mu Epsilon, Sigma Tau, Phi Kappa Phi. Business E-Mail: zelby@ou.edu.

ZELEK, MARK EDWARD, lawyer; b. Nov. 6, 1955; m. Alicia Margarita Castilla, Mar. 10, 1984. BA, Yale U., New Haven, 1977; JD, Columbia U. Law Sch., NYC, 1982. Bar: Fla. 1979. Assoc. Finley, Kumble, Wagner, Heine, Underberg, Manley & Casey; mng. ptnr., mem. labor & employment law practice group Morgan Lewis & Bockius LLP, Miami, Fla., 2002—. Co-author: Miami-Dade & Broward County Employment Law Handbook; contbr. articles to profl. jours. Office: Morgan Lewis & Bockius LLP 5300 Southeast Financial Ctr 200 S Biscayne Blvd Miami FL 33131-2339 Office Phone: 305-415-3303. Office Fax: 305-415-3001. Business E-Mail: mzelek@morganlewis.com.

ZELIKOW, PHILIP DAVID, public policy educator, professor former federal official; b. NYC, Sept. 21, 1954; s. Nate and Lee (Landsman) Z.; m. Paige Ellen Partain, May 30, 1982; children: Alexander, Carolyn. BA, U. Redlands, 1977; JD, U. Houston, 1981; MA, Tufts U., 1984, PhD, 1995. Bar: Tex. 1979. Briefing atty. Tex. Ct. Criminal Appeals, Austin, 1979-80; assoc. David Berg and Assocs., P.C., Houston, 1980-84; adj. prof. Naval Postgrad. Sch., Monterey, Calif., 1984-85; fgn. svc. officer US Dept. State, Washington and overseas, 1985-89; dir. European security NSC, Washington, 1989-91; assoc. prof. pub. policy John F. Kennedy Sch. Govt. Harvard U., Cambridge, Mass., 1991-98; Burkett Miller prof. history U. Va., Charlottesville, 1998—, dir. Miller Ctr. Pub. Affairs, 1998—2005; counselor US Dept. State, Washington, 2005—07. Mem. Presdl. Fgn. Intelligence Advisory Bd., 2001—03; exec. dir. Nat. Commn. on Terrorist Attacks Upon U.S. (The 9-11 Commn.), 2003—04. Author: American Military Strategy: Memos to a President, 2001; co-author: (with Condoleeza Rice) Germany United and Europe Transformed: A Study in Statecraft, 1995, (with Ernest R. May) The Kennedy Tapes: Inside the White House During the Cuban Missile Crisis, 1997, (with Graham T. Allison) Essence of Decision: Explaiing the Cuban Missile Crisis, 1999; editor: Why People Don't Trust Government, 1997; commentator newspapers, TV and radio programs, 1991—. Recipient 1st Pl. in Nation award Moot Ct. Competition, ABA, 1979. Mem. Am. Hist. Assn., Org. Am. Historians, Internat. Inst. for Strategic Studies, Coun. Fgn. Rels., State Bar Tex., Soc. for Historians of Am. Fgn. Rels. Avocations: hiking, skiing, tennis. Office: Corcoran Dept History U Va PO Box 400180 Randall Hall Charlottesville VA 22904 E-mail: pdz6n@Virginia.edu.

ZELNICK, RONALD STUART, surgeon; b. NYC, Dec. 6, 1958; BS, George Washington U., 1980; MD, Albany Med. Coll., 1984. Diplomate Am. Bd. Surgery, Am. Bd. Colon Rectal Surgery. Resident gen. surgery L.I. Jewish Hosp., New Hyde Park, N.Y., 1984-89; fellowship colon and rectal surgery Henry Ford Hosp., Detroit, 1989-90; pvt. practice Jupiter, Fla., 1991—. Fellow ACS, Am. Soc. Colon Rectal Surgeons; mem. Fla. Surg. Soc., Fla. Colon Rectal Surgery Soc. Office: Ste 105 210 Jupiter Lakes Blvd #3105 Jupiter FL 33458 Office Phone: 561-575-7875.

ZEMANICK, SUE, chef; Grad., Culinary Inst. America, Hyde Park, NY. Fellow seafood dept. Culinary Inst. America; cook Commander's Palace, New Orleans; sous chef Gautreau's, New Orleans, 2003—05, exec. chef, 2005—. Named one of Seven Chefs to Watch, Times-Picayune, 2007, Chefs to Watch, La. Cookin' Mag., 2008, America's Best New Chefs, Food & Wine Mag., 2008. Office: Gautreaus Restaurant 1728 Soniat St New Orleans LA 70115

ZENN, MICHAEL ROBERT, plastic and reconstructive surgeon; b. NYC, Feb. 28, 1962; s. Renee Schwam; m. Susan Speer; children: Andrew, Erica. BA summa cum laude, U. Pa., 1984; MD, Cornell U., 1988. Diplomate Am. Bd. Gen. Surgery, 1994, Am. Bd. Plastic Surgery, 1998. Resident in gen. surgery NY Hosp. Cornell Med. Ctr., NYC, 1988—92, chief surgical resident, 1992—93; resident in plastic surgery Mass. Gen. Hosp., Boston, 1993-95; fellow in microsurgery Meml. Sloan-Kettering Cancer Ctr., NYC, 1995; asst. prof. plastic surgery U. N.C., Chapel Hill, 1996-2000, Duke Univ. Med. Ctr., Durham, NC, 2000—05, assoc. prof. plastic surgery, program dir. plastic surgery residency, 2005—. Contbr. articles to profl. jours. Named a Best Doctor for Women-Southeast Region, Ladies Home Jour., 2002, Best Doctor, Redbook mag., 2001; recipient NC Med. Soc. Tobacco Control award, 1999; named Best Cosmetic Surgeon in the Triangle, News and Observer, 1997. Fellow ACS (assoc.); mem. AMA, Am. Soc. Plastic Surgeons, Am. Soc. Reconstructive Microsurgery, World Soc. Reconstructive Microsurgery, Plastic Surgery Rsch. Coun., NC Med. Soc., NC Soc. Plastic and Reconstructive Surgeons (v.p., 2001-02, pres., 2002-03), Nathan A. Womack Surg. Soc., Alpha Omega Alpha Avocations: painting, golf. Office: Plastic Surgery 3358 Duke Univ Med Ctr Durham NC 27710 Office Fax: 919-684-4954. Business E-Mail: michael.zenn@duke.edu.

ZENTALL, THOMAS R., psychologist, educator; b. Bezier, Herault, France, Sept. 29, 1940; came to the US, 1942; s. Robert Sigmund and Elizabeth Aigner Zentall; m. Sydney Snider, Aug. 29, 1965 (div.); m. Melodie Rae, June 4, 1988; children: Gabriel Clay, Shannon Rae. BA, BSEE, Union Coll., 1963; PhD, U. Calif., Berkeley, 1969. Asst. prof. U. Pitts., 1969-75; prof. U. Ky., Lexington, 1975—. Editor: Social Learning, 1988, Animal Cognition, 1993, 2006, Stimulus Class Formation, 1996; assoc. editor Psychonomic Bull. and Rev., 1998-2002, Animal Learning & Behavior, 2002-08, Comparative Cognition, 2006. Fellow APA (exec. com. divsn. 6 1998-2001, pres. 2005-06, exec. com. divsn. 3 1999—2002, pres. 2005-06, exec. com. divsn. 25 2006-), Am. Psychol. Soc., Midwestern Psychol. Assn. (sec.-treas. 1998-2001, pres. 2002-03), Ea. Psychol. Assn. (bd. dirs. 2006—), Psychonomic Soc. (governing bd. 2001—, chair 2006-07), Comparative Cognition Soc. (pres. 2004-06). Office: Dept Psychology Univ Ky Lexington KY 40506-0044 Business E-Mail: zentall@uky.edu.

ZEPPOS, NICHOLAS S., academic administrator; BA, U. Wis., 1976, JD, 1979. Atty., Washington; joined faculty Vanderbilt U., Nashville, 1987, assoc. dean rsch. Law Sch., assoc. provost, 1999, vice chancellor for instnl. planning and advancement, 2000, provost, vice chancellor for acad. affairs, prof. law, 2001—, interim chancellor, 2007—08, chancellor, 2008—. Contbr. articles to publs. Office: Vanderbilt University Chancellor's Office 211 Kirkland Hall Nashville TN 37240 Office Phone: 615-322-1813. Office Fax: 615-322-6060. E-mail: nick.zeppos@vanderbilt.edu, chancellor@vanderbilt.edu.*

ZERNELL, JAMES T., oil and gas company executive; BS in Petroleum Engring., Pa. State U. With Tenneco Oil E&P, ARCO Alaska; joined Newfield Exploration Co., 1997, mgr. prodn. and H.S. & E, v.p. prodn., 2005—. Chmn. exec. sub-com. Offshore Operators; chmn. Offshore Issues Task Group, Domestic Petroleum Coun. Office: Newfield Exploration Co Ste 100 363 N Sam Houston Pky E Houston TX 77060 Office Phone: 281-847-6000. Office Fax: 281-405-4242.

ZERWAS, JOHN, state legislator; m. Cindy Zerwas, 1978; children: John Jr., Joseph, Brandon, Sherry. Grad., U. Houston; MD, Baylor U. Coll. Medicine, 1980. Pvt. practice physician, 1985—; chief med. officer Meml. Hermann Hosp. Sys.; former pres. Meml. Hermann Health Network Providers; anesthesiologist Greater Houston Anesthesiology; mem. Dist. 28 Tex. House of Representatives, 2007—. Republican. Office: PO Box 434 Simonton TX 77476 also: Room EXT E2.310 Capital Extension PO Box 2910 Austin TX 78768 Address: 9315 F.M. 1489 Ste C Simonton TX 77476 Office Phone: 281-533-9042, 512-463-0657.

ZESCH, HAL, energy executive; BBA in Acctg., U. Tex., Austin. CPA. Audit and consulting mgr. Deloitte & Touche; various positions including v.p. best bus. practices, asst. corp. contr., contr. natural gas ops., and dir. corp. acctg. Valero Energy Corp., San Antonio, v.p. SAP systems integration, v.p., chief info. officer, 2003. Office: Valero Energy Corpn PO Box 696000 San Antonio TX 78269-6000

ZEVNIK-SAWATZKY, DONNA DEE, retired litigation coordinator; b. Tulsa, Dec. 15, 1946; d. Robert Joseph and Dorothy Dee (Robertson) Zink; m. Kenneth Sawatzky, May 30, 1965; children: K. Brian Sawatzky, Kaira D. Sawatzky. Student, U. Ctrl. Okla., Edmond, 1977, Okla. State U., Oklahoma City, 1984. Cert. AIDS educator Okla. Sec. Farmers Ins. Co., Oklahoma City, 1974-80; office mgr. S.A.F.E., Inc., Oklahoma City, 1980-83; jr. acct. Southeast Exploration Corp., Oklahoma City, 1983-84; acct. Young Bros., Inc., Oklahoma City, 1984-88, The Denman Co., Inc., Oklahoma City, 1988-89; litig. coord. ACLU Okla., Oklahoma City, 1994—2003; ret., 2011. Founder, owner, CEO Otherwhere Arts, 1994—. Author, illustrator: That Place--Otherwhere, 1994, Something for Otherwhere, 1995; author: At Our House, 1979—83; columnist: Putnam City-N.W. News, 1979—83; designer stage sets: Miss Warr Acres Pageant, 1971—88. Treas. ACLU Okla., 1995—2004, bd. dirs., 1994—2004, vol., bookkeeper, 1994—2011; bd. dirs. ACLU Okla. Found., 2005—09; child welfare adv. Okla. State Dept. Human Svcs., Oklahoma City, 1987—89; coord. AIDS Clinic Triangle Assn., Oklahoma City, 1994—97; founder Cir. Friends with Arachnoiditis World Wide Web Chronic Pain Support Group, 1997; bd. dirs. Miss Warr Acres Pageant, 1984—88, Warr Acres C. of C., 1981—85. Recipient Outstanding Vol., Okla. State Dept. Human Svcs., 1988, Svc. award, Warr Acres C. of C., 1979, Legis. commendation, State of Okla., 1988, numerous Okla. Newspaper Column of the Month awards, Okla. Press Assn., 1981—82, Ten Yr. Vol. Svc. award, ACLU of Okla., 2005; named Hon. Mayor of Warr Acres, 1971, Super Citizen, 1973. Mem.: ACLU (Exec. Dir. Vol. Svc. award 1996, Vol. Svc. award 2011, Okla. Fedn. Vol. Svc. award 2010), NAFE, Am. Inst. Profl. Bookkeepers, Nat. Notary Assn., Okla. Coalition to Abolish the Death Penalty, Amnesty Internat., Human Rights Campaign, Interfaith Alliance, Pflag. Democrat. Methodist. Avocations: painting, writing, photography, crafts.

ZHENG, QI, statistician, biomathematician; b. Lanxi, Zhejiang, China, July 8, 1958; arrived in U.S., 1988; s. Huanming Zheng and Sulan Zhuge; m. Huiping Hu, May 12, 1987; children: Yan, Eric Hugh. BS in math., Zhejiang U., 1978—82; PhD in stats., Tex. A&M U., 1988—93, postgrad., 1993. Cert. independent Mathematica trainer. Post-doc Nat. Ctr. Toxicological Rsch., Jefferson, Ark., 1994—96, staff fellow, 1996—2002; rsch. scientist Tex. A&M U., College Station, 2002—03, assoc. prof. dept. epidemiology and biostats. Sch. Rural Pub. Health, 2003—. Contbr. articles to jour. Recipient Achievement award, Nat. Ctr. Toxicological Rsch., 1995, Commendable Svc. award, FDA, 1997; grantee Mathematica Vis. Scholar Grant, Wolfram Rsch. Inc., 1995, 1997. Mem.: Am. Statis. Assn., Phi Kappa Phi. Achievements include research in directed mutation hypothesis; stochastic modeling of carcinogenesis; development of algorithms and first comprehensive computer software SALVADOR for estimating mutation rates using data from fluctuation experiments. Avocations: reading, mountain hiking, music. Office: Tex A&M U Health Sci Ctr Sch Rural Pub Health Dept Epidemiology and Biostats College Station TX 77843 E-mail: qzheng@srph.tamhsc.edu.

ZHENG, SHUANG-CAI, physics educator, researcher; b. Shen-Ze County, He-Bei, China, Sept. 19, 1939; s. Quan-De Zheng and Jun-Mei Cao; m. Wen-Li Hu, May 1, 1969; children: Yue, Hui. BS, Nan-Kai U., Tian-Jin, China, 1966. Asst. Beijing Inst. Tech., 1966-80, lectr., 1980-94, prof., 1994—. Contbr. articles to profl. journals Mem. AAAS. Home and Office: 12701 Little Dipper Path Austin TX 78732 Office Phone: 86 10 68918496. Personal E-mail: sc_zheng@hotmail.com.

ZIBART, MICHAEL ALAN, wholesale book company executive; b. Nashville, Mar. 12, 1947; s. Alan Walter and Joy (Hughes) Z.; m. Margaret Anne Boyd, Dec. 27, 1976; children: Emily Joy, Mary Claire. BA, Vanderbilt U., 1969. Mgmt. trainee Zibart Bros. Books, Nashville, 1961-69; property mgr. Pollack Co., Nashville, 1966-69;

buyer Ingram Book Co., Nashville, 1970-75, mgr. trade dept., 1976, v.p., 1976-85, exec. v.p., 1985-88; founder, pres. ProMotion, Inc., Nashville, 1988—. Author: Almanac on Bookselling, 3d edit., 1980; pub. (monthly book review) BookPage, 1988—. Office: ProMotion Inc 2143 Belcourt Ave Nashville TN 37212-3503 Office Phone: 615-292-8926. Business E-Mail: michael@bookpage.com.

ZIEGLER, CHARLES EDWARD, political science professor, university scholar; b. Plymouth, Ind., Oct. 17, 1953; s. Charles A. and Justine D. Ziegler; m. Janna Shakhmuratovna Tajibaeva, Oct. 14, 1995; 1 child, Alan Taj. PhD, U. Ill., 1979, AM, 1975—77; BA, Purdue U., 1975. Asst. prof. St. Leo Coll., St. Leo, Fla., 1979—80, U. Louisville, Ky., 1980—86, prof., 1993—, prof., chair, dept. of polit. sci., 1998—2007, scholar, 2007—12, disting. scholar, 2012—, assoc. prof., 1986—93, dir. Grawemeyer Award Ideas Improving World Order, 2011—, founder Ctr. Asian Dem., 2006; legislative asst. U.S. Senate, Washington, 1989. Exec. dir. Louisville Com. on Fgn. Rels., Louisville, 1990—; pres. Ky. Polit. Sci. Assn., Ky., 1997—98. Author: (book) Environmental Policy in the USSR, 1987, Foreign Policy and East Asia, 1993, The History of Russia, 1999, 2nd edit., 2009; editor: (book) The Russian Far East, 2002. Mem., exec. com. Am. Committees on Fgn. Rels., Washington, 1995—98; mem., bd. trustees Chance Sch., Louisville, 2010—12. Sr. Fulbright scholar Pusan Nat. U., Republic of Korea, 1995, Nat. fellow Hoover Instn., 1985-86, Internat. Affairs fellow Coun. on Fgn. Rels., 1987-88. Mem.: Internat. Studies Assn., So. Conf. on Slavic Studies, Internat. Inst. for Strategic Studies, Nat. Com. on United States-China Rels., Am. Assn. for the Advancement of Slavic Studies, Am. Polit. Sci. Assn. Avocation: Tae Kwon Do. Office: U Louisville Dept Polit Sci Louisville KY 40292-0001 Business E-Mail: ceziegler@louisville.edu.

ZIEGLER, JAN L., dentist; Dentist Miami Cosmetic Ctr. for Cosmetic and Implant Dentistry. Mem.: South Fla. Dist. Dental Assn., Fla Dental Assn., Dental Orgn. for Conscious Sedation, Fla. Acad. of Cosmetic Dentistry, Am. Acad. of Cosmetic Dentistry, ADA. Office: Miami Center for Cosmetic and Implant Dentistry 13840 SW 56th St Miami FL 33175 Office Phone: 305-387-6453.

ZIEGLER, JOHN ALAN, historian, political scientist, educator, short story writer; b. Belleville, Ill., Jan. 28, 1933; s. John Wendell and Georgia Elizabeth (Reppel) Z.; children: Nathaniel, Robin; m. Iris Butler Scales, July 21, 2012. BS, So. Ill. U., 1955, MS, 1956; Rotary Found. fellow, St. Andrews U., Scotland, 1956-57; PhD, Syracuse U., 1970. Asst. prof. polit. sci. and social sci. Calif. State U., East Bay, 1966-72; lectr. Am. civilization Calif. State Poly. U., Pomona, 1972-74; assoc. prof. polit. sci. Hendrix Coll., Conway, Ark., 1974-84, prof., 1984-91, Harold and Lucy Cabe Disting. prof. history and politics, 1991-98, emeritus prof., 1998—, legendary lectr., 1998. Coord. and founder Hendrix-Oxford program, 1979-98, head social sci. area, 1978-82, chmn. dept. polit. sci. and history, 1974-83; guest lectr. St. Peter's Coll., Oxford U., 1983, 90, 94, Clare Coll., Cambridge U., 1988, 89, Dundee U., 1994; Churchill life fellow Westminster Coll., Fulton, Mo.; participant Wilton Pk. Confs., Wiston House Internat. Conf. Ctr., Sussex, England, 1979—. Author: Experimentalism and Institutional Change, 1994, 2014, In Search of the Special Relationship with Britain, 2000, Special Relationships: Six Stories, 2013, The John Ziegler London Collection, Hendrix Coll. Archives. With AUS, 1957-60. Mem. AAUP, Friends Churchill Meml. (life), ACLU, Royal Oak Found., South Downs Soc. (life), Dundee (Scotland) Curling Club. Mem. United Ch. of Christ. Home: PO Box 1045 Conway AR 72033-1045

ZIEGLER, PENELOPE, psychiatrist, educator; MD, George Wash. U., Washington, DC, 1978. Diplomate Am. Bd. Psychiatry and Neurology-psychiatry, 1986, Am. Bd. Psychiatry and Neurology-addiction psychiatry, 2003. Resident psychiatry Sheppard Enoch Pratt Hosp., Balt., 1978—82; assoc. prof. dept. psychiatry Virginia Commonwealth Univ., dir. health practitioners' intervention program dept. psychiatry. Office: Virginia Commonwealth University PO Box 980109 Richmond VA 23298-0109 Office Phone: 757-565-0106. E-mail: ppziegle@vcu.edu.

ZIEGLER, STEVE, healthcare company executive; CPA. Acct. Pearlman, Nebben & Assocs.; regional contr., reimbursement mgr. Life Care Ctrs. of America, Cleveland, Tenn., v.p., 1996, CFO Cleveland, Tenn., 1996—. Office: Life care centers of America 3570 Keith St NW Cleveland TN 37312 Office Phone: 423-472-9585. Office Fax: 423-476-5974. Business E-Mail: steve_ziegler@lcca.com.

ZIEMBA, LARRY (LAWRENCE MICHAEL ZIEMBA), oil industry executive; b. 1955; BS in Mech. Engring., U. Ill.-Champaign, 1977; MBA, U. Chgo., 1985. Plant mgr. Avon refinery Tosco Corp., Calif.; gen. mgr. US refinery services ConocoPhillips, pres. ctrl/West coast refining, 2003, pres. US refining Houston, 2003—10, pres. global refining, 2010—12; exec. v.p. refining Phillips 66, Houston, 2012—. Mem.: Nat. Petrochemical & Refiners Assn. Office: Phillips 66 3010 Briarpark Dr Houston TX 77042*

ZILVETI, CARLOS BENJAMIN, preventive medicine physician, pediatrician; b. Sucre, Bolivia, June 14, 1928; arrived in USA, 1956; s. Carlos and Marina (De La Reza) Z.; m. Halina J. Daszewski, Sept. 8, 1957 (div. Sept. 1976); 1 child: Carlos Joseph III; m. Vita Palazzolo, Sept. 5, 1987. BS, Sacred Heart Coll., Sucre, Bolivia, 1946; MD, U. San Francisco Xavier, Sucre, Bolivia, 1954; MPH, Yale U., New Haven, Conn., 1966. Physician in rural medicine Bolivian Power Co., La Paz, 1955; intern Hosp. Obrero Victor Paz Estenssoro, La Paz, 1956; asst. resident in pediats. St. Luke's Hosp., Meml. Cancer Ctr., Woman's Hosp., NYC, 1957-58; resident and chief resident in pediats. Hosp. of St. Raphael, New Haven, 1958-59; pvt. practice New Haven and Branford, Conn., 1960-63; dir. maternal-child health New Haven Dept. Health, 1964-74; regional med. officer South and Ctrl. Am. Peace Corps, Bogota, Colombia, 1975-76; regional med. officer, sci. attache in West Africa U.S. Dept. of State, Liberia, Ghana, Togo, Sierra Leone, 1976-79; reserve appt. of maj., advanced to col. USAF, San Antonio, 1979-91, chief environ. medicine Wilford Hall Med. Ctr., 1979-83, cons. preventive and occupl. medicine, 1983-91, cons. aerospace-preventive medicine Wilford Hall Med. Ctr. Lackland AFB, Tex., 1984-91, ret. col., 1991. Cons. FDA, HEW, Washington, 1966-75; cons. to Headstart Am. Acad. Pediats., Stanford-Norwalk, Conn., 1968-75; regional med. officer, sci. attache West Africa U.S. Dept. State. Contbr. articles to profl. jours. Chmn. gov.'s task force Conn. State Dept. Health, Hartford, 1969-75. Fellow Am. Acad. Pediats. (emeritus), Am. Coll. Preventive Medicine (emeritus); mem. APHA, AMA, New Eng. Pub. Health Assn., Conn. Acad. Preventive Medicine, Am. Occupl. Med. Assn. Avocations: swimming, tennis, golf, travel, classical music. Home: 9222 Dover Rdg San Antonio TX 78250-3557

ZIMMERMAN, JORDAN B., advertising executive; b. Newark, 1956; m. Denise Zimmerman; children: Chase, Cara, Jett, Jordana. BA, MBA, U. South Fla. Founder, chmn., CEO Zimmerman Advt., Ft. Lauderdale, Fla., 1984—. Pres., co-owner Fla. Panthers, 2001—. Bd. mem Take Stock in Children, Pine Crest Sch., Boca Raton, Fla., Cleve. Clinic, Fla. Recipient Alumni Entrepreneur of the Year, U. South Fla., 1991, Diamond award, South Fla. Bus. Jour., 2004; named one of 100 Most Powerful People, South Fla. CEO Mag. Republican. Achievements include named Mr. Florida as a onetime competitive body-builder; led Just Say No marketing initiative during the Carter administration which is one of the most recognizable anti-drug campaigns to date. Office: 2200 W Commercial Blvd Fort Lauderdale FL 33309

ZIMMERMAN, RAND, insurance company executive; BA Western Ill. U. Cert. Title Ins. Specialist, Land Title Assn.of Colorado. Joined Stewart Title Guaranty Co. (subs. Stewart Info. Svcs. Corp), 1977, pres., with Netherlands, 1985, assoc. region f mgr., 1997—99, region f mgr., 1999, group pres., region prodn. centers. Office: Stewart Title Guaranty Co 1980 Post Oak Blvd Ste 800 Houston TX 77056 Office Phone: 713-625-8100. Business E-Mail: rzimmerman@stewart.com.

ZIMMERMANN, THOMAS CALLANDER PRICE, retired historian, educator; b. Bryn Mawr, Pa., Aug. 22, 1934; s. R.Z. and Susan (Goodman) Z.; m. Margaret Upham Ferris. BA, Williams Coll., 1956, Oxford U., 1958, MA, 1964; AM, Harvard U., 1960, PhD, 1964. Asst. prof. Reed Coll., Portland, Oreg., 1964-67, assoc. prof., 1967-73, prof. history, 1973-77, chmn. dept. history, 1973-75; v.p. acad. affairs Davidson (N.C.) Coll., 1977-86, Charles A. Dana prof. History, 1986-99, Charles A. Dana prof. history emeritus, 1999-2000, ret., 2000. Mem. Oreg. Com. for Humanities NEH, 1971—77; mem. Region 14 selection com. Woodrow Wilson Nat. Fellowship Found., Princeton, NJ, 1967—70. Author: Paolo Giovio: The Historian and the Crisis of Sixteenth-Century Italy, 1995 (Helen and Howard R. Marraro Book prize Am. Hist. Assn. 1996, Presdl. Book award Am. Assn. for Italian Studies 1997, Italian Translation Milan 2012); co-editor of collected works of Paolo Giovio, 1985; contbr. articles to profl. jours. Pres. Am. Alpine Club, NYC, 1979-82, bd. dirs., 1975-83; bd. dirs. Charlotte Opera Assn., NC, 1980-82, NC Outward Bound Sch., Morgantown, 1978-81; bd. advisors Lowell Obs., 1988-93; mem. Rome Prize Jury (Post-Classical Humanistic Studies) Am. Acad. in Rome, 1993; adv. coun. bot. gardens U. NC, Charlotte, 2007-08. Danforth fellow, 1956-62, Fulbright fellow, Italy, 1962-64, Villa "I Tatti" fellow Harvard U. Ctr., 1970-71; Am. Council of Learned Socs. fellow, N.Y.C., 1975-76. Mem. Renaissance Soc. Am., Soc. Italian Hist. Studies, Am. Assn. Italian Studies, Phi Beta Kappa, Opera Carolina Endowment (bd. advisors, 2008-).

ZINK, CHARLIE, sports association executive; Grad. in Fin., Bus. Mgmt., U. Md., 1971, grad., 1975. With Price Waterhouse and Cooper, Lybrand; CFO PGA Tour, Inc., Ponte Vedra Beach, Fla., exec. v.p. co-COO. Lt. USN. Office: PGA Tour Inc 100 PGA Tour Blvd Ponte Vedra Beach FL 32082

ZINKLE, STEVEN JOHN, engineer, researcher; s. Aloysius Peter and Katherine Edith (Brownlee) Z.; m. Teresa Allen Medford, May 26, 1990; children: Austin Chase, Allen Peter. BS in Nuc. Engring., U. Wis., Madison, 1980, MS in Nuc. Engring., 1982, PhD in Nuc. Engring., 1985, MS in Materials Sci., 1985. Wigner fellow, 1985—87; rsch. staff Oak Ridge Nat. Lab., Tenn., 1985—2006, corp. fellow, 2004—13, dir. materials sci. and tech. divsn., 2006—10; chief scientist Nuc. Sci. and Engring. Directorate, 2010—13; govs. chair U. Tenn., 2013—. Vis. scientist Forschungszentrum Jülich, Germany, 1991-92, Risø Nat. Lab., Roskilde, 1991-92. Assoc. editor: Jour. ASTM Internat., 2003—06; editor: Metallurgical & Materials Transactions E: Materials for Energy Systems, 2013—. Recipient Rsch. Publ. award Martin Marietta Energy Systems, Oak Ridge, 1991, David Rose Excellence in Fusion Engring. award Fusion Power Assocs., Gaithersburg, Md., 1992, Oak Ridge Nat. Lab. Tech. Achievement award, 1997, 99, 2002, Ernest Orlando Lawrence award in Nuc. Tech. Dept. Energy, 2006, Fusion Technol. award IEEE Nuc. Plasma Sci. Soc. 2006, Disting. Achievement award, U. Wis. Coll. Engring., 2010, Elsevier Robert W. Cahn award, 2010. Fellow Am. Assn. Advancement Sci. (physics sect., 2010), Am. Ceramic Soc. (Nuc. and Environ. Techs. Best Paper award 1994-95, 2007), Am. Soc. Metals Internat. (nominating com., 2007, awards policy com. 2009—, chair nuc. material com. 2003-05), Am. Nuc. Soc. (hons. and awards com., 2009—, materials sci. and tech. exec. com. 2003-09, Best Paper award 1996, 2006, Materials Sci. & Tech. Divsn. Outstanding Achievement award 2005, Mishima award 2007), Materials Rsch. Soc., The Minerals, Metals and Materials Soc., Am. Phys. Soc.; mem. US Dept. Energy Fusion Energy Scis. Adv. Com., Nat. Acad. Engring. (elected mem., 2012), Sigma Xi, Phi Kappa Phi, Tau Beta Pi. Office: University Tenn 306 Pasqua Engineering Bldg Knoxville TN 37996-2300 Home Phone: 865-748-1083; Office Phone: 865-974-4589. Business E-Mail: szinkle@utk.edu.

ZIPF, ROBERT EUGENE, JR., medical laboratory director, legal medicine consultant, pathologist; b. Sept. 18, 1940; s. Robert Eugene and Meriam (Murr) Z.; m. Nancy J. Gaskell, Sept. 11, 1965; children: Karin Lorene, Marjorie Kristine. BA, DePauw U., 1962; MD, Ohio State U., 1966. Diplomate Am. Bd. Pathology. Intern Miami Valley Hosp., Dayton, Ohio, 1966-67; dir. forensic pathology Duke U. Med. Ctr., Durham, NC, 1967-72; dir. radioisotope pathology Riverside Meth. Hosp., Columbus, 1974-78; dep. coroner, forensic pathologist Franklin County, Columbus, 1974-78; regional forensic pathologist State of N.C., Rocky Mount, 1978—; pres. R.E. Zipf, PA, Pathology Assocs., Rocky Mount, NC, 1978—2005. Clin. asst. prof. East Carolina U. Med. Sch., Greenville, N.C., 1979—; bd. dirs. Rocky Mt. Kiwanis, 1980-; adj. prof. Atlantic Christian Coll., Wilson, N.C., 1980-89, dir. Sch. Med. Tech., 1983-89; dir. clin. and diagnostic labs., chief patholgy Nash Gen. Hosp., Rocky Mount, 1978-2006; dir. forensic toxicology lab. Nash Health Care Sys., Rocky Mount, 1990-2000; cons. in field, v.p. Computerized Office Sys., 1986-2000, Founder Clintrac Pathology Computers, adv. bd. mem., NC Forensic Sci. Adv. Bd., 2012-. Contbr. articles to profl. jours. Trustee United Fund, 1979-84; active Mayor's Com. on Drug and Substance Abuse, 1987—; bd. dirs. NC Wesleyan Coll. Found., 2005—, Nash C.C., 2005—; advisor Zipf Charitable Trust and Fund, 1999—; mentor Nash-Rocky Mount Pub. Schs., 1980—; mem. adv. bd. NC Forensic Sci, eagle scout leader, supporter, Boys Scout America. Maj. USAF, 1967—74, chief anatomic pathologist, maj. Med. Ctr. USAF, 1972, cons., surgeon gen. USAF, 1972—74. Fellow Am. Soc. Clin. Pathologist, Am. Acad. Forensic Scientists; mem. SMS (clin. adv. bd. 1988-91, lab. advisors bd. 1989-91, pres. advisor bd. 1990), Assn. Clin. Scientists, Am. Coll. Nuc. Medicine, N.C. Med. Soc., N.Y. Acad. Scis. (pres. Lab. Users Group 1988-90, 92), Nash County Med. Soc. (pres. 1995). Achievements include providing medical legal and medical information service for attorneys, law enforcement agencies, hospitals and healthcare information corporations. Home: 120 Newby Ct Rocky Mount NC 27804-3322 Personal E-mail: rezpath@hotmail.com.

ZIRKLE, WILLIAM VERNON, not-for-profit consultant; b. Berlin, Feb. 5, 1959; (parents Am. citizens); s. Michael Neale and Nancy (Behrend) Z. AAS in Electronics, No. Va. C.C., 1980; BA in Humanities, U. Va., 1984. Cert. ETS Praxis I, 1997, ETS Praxis II, 2008, Va. Comm. and Literacy Assesment., 2008. Cons. designer audio sys. Uno's Pizzeria, Washington, 1989; cons. crises mgmt. APC, Merrifield, Va., 1993-99; electronics tech. WESCO, Falls Church, Va., 1977—2010; propr. Circle Enterprises, Arlington, Va., 1984—, Allco Fin., 1998—; ptnr. Homestead Builders, 2000—03; software specialist Dok Klaus Computer Care, 2011—. Canvass Children's Def. Fund, Washington, 1991, 92; specializer Md. Sherriff's Youth Ranch, 1991, 92; chair Adult Religious Edn., Falls Church, St. Antony Parish, 1986. Mem. Park Springs Condo Assn. (bd. mem., dir. 1991), Cath. Alumni Club (internat. chair 1990, v.p. 1991, 92, social justice com., 1992), Cath. Young Adults Club (religion com. 1988-89, parliamentarian 1987-88), U. Va. Alumni Club. Independent. Avocations: travel, camping, computers, the arts. Home: PO Box 222051 Chantilly VA 20153-2051 Personal E-mail: zirkle1@gmail.com.

ZLOCH, WILLIAM J., federal judge; b. Ft. Lauderdale, Fla., 1944; BA, U. Notre Dame, 1966, JD, 1974. Pvt. practice atty., Ft. Lauderdale, 1974—85; judge US Dist. Ct. (so. dist.) Fla., Ft. Lauderdale, 1985—2000, 2007—, chief judge, 2000—07. Lt. USN, 1967—69. Office: US Dist Ct 299 E Broward Blvd Fort Lauderdale FL 33301-1944

ZLOTKY, JEFFREY A., lawyer; AB magna cum laude, Princeton U., NJ, 1982; JD, U. Tex., 1985. Bar: Tex. Ptnr. Thomson & Knight LLP, Dallas, global mng. ptnr., mem. mgmt. com. Mem. Thomson & Knight LLP Found. Named one of The Best Lawyers in America, Corp. Law, 2001—, Best Lawyers in Dallas, D Mag., 2005, 2007—, Leading Lawyers in America, Lawdragon 500, 2007; named to Tex. Super Lawyers, Securities & Corp. Fin., Mergers & Acquisitions, Bus./Corp., Thomson Reuters, 2003—, Best Lawyers, Corp., Mergers & Acquisitions and Securities Law, Corp. Counsel, 2004. Mem.: ABA (mem. bus. law and natural resources, energy and environ. law sections), Dallas Bar Assn. Office: Thompson & Knight LLP One Arts Plz 1722 Routh St Ste 1500 Dallas TX 75201 Office Phone: 214-969-1384. Office Fax: 214-880-3131. Business E-Mail: jeffrey.zlotky@tklaw.com.

ZOCCHI, LOUIS JOSEPH, product designer, game company executive; b. Chgo., Feb. 16, 1935; s. Louis Alexander and Martha (Adams) Z.; m. Elissa Lorelei Scott, June 8, 1959 (Sept. 1976); children: David, Suzanne, LaRee, Lisa; m. Sharon Annette Olson, May 25, 1985; 1 child, Heidi Olson. Cert. air traffic controller, 1955, air traffic control instr., 1964. Commd. USAF, 1954, advanced through grades to tech. sgt., air traffic contr. Offut AFB, Nebr., 1954, Lincoln AFB, Nebr., 1955-59, Misawa AFB, Japan, 1959-63, Holloman AFB, N.Mex., 1963-64, air traffic control instr. Keesler AFB, Miss., 1964-70, air traffic contr. Mather AFB, Calif., 1970-71, Kimpo AFB, Korea, 1971-72, George AFB, Calif., 1972-73, Biloxi, Miss., 1973-75, ret., 1975; commd. 1st lt. Miss. State Guard, 1991, advanced through grades to capt., 1993; owner Zocchi Distbrs., Victorville, Calif., 1972—; pres. Gamescience, Inc., Cedarhurst, N.Y., 1974—. Cruise dir. Europa Star cruise ship, 1988; cons. Dupuy Inst., 1995. Designer (games) Battle of Britain, 1968, Star Fleet Battle Manual, 1977 (Gamesday award 1981), Basic and Advanced Fighter Combat, 1980 (H.G. Wells award 1981); inventor Zocchihedron 100-sided dice, 1985, inventor 16 sided die, 5-sided die, 3-sided die, 14 Sided Die, D-Total Die, 2008. Major Ala. State Guard, 1997—, col., 2003. Recipient Hobbyist award Metro Detroit Gamers, 1979, Spl. Svc. award Strategists Club, 1982, Charles Roberts Adventure Gaming Hall of Fame award, 1987, Gama Honor of Svc. award 1991, George award Coastcon, 2005, The D-Total Die, 2009. Mem. Game Mfrs. Assn. (chmn. membership com. 1978-84, v.p. 1978-84, bd. dirs. 1985), Internat. Brotherhood Magicians (Order of Merlin 2000, Order of Merlin with Shield 2011), Hobby Industry Assn. (pres. gaming div. 1981), Gulf Coast Jazz Soc. (pres.), Soc. Am. Magicians (pres.). Avocations: playing jazz music, ventriloquism, magic. Home and Office: Gamescience Inc 7604 Newton Dr Biloxi MS 39532-2830 Home Phone: 228-392-4177; Office Phone: 228-392-4177.

ZOGHBI, WILLIAM ANTOINE, cardiologist, educator; b. Beirut, Oct. 28, 1955; arrived in US, 1977; m. Huda El Hibri, Sept. 17, 1983; children: Roula Maya, Anthony William. BS, Am. U., Beirut, 1975; postgrad., Am. U., 1975-77; MD, Meharry Med. Coll., 1979. Diplomate Internal Medicine 1982, Cardiovascular Diseases Am. Bd. Internal Medicine, 1985. Intern, internal med. U. Tex. Med. Br. Hosps., Galveston, 1979-80; resident, cardiology Baylor Coll. Affiliated Hosps., Houston, 1980-82; fellow, electrocardiogram Baylor Coll. Medicine, Houston, 1982-85, instr., asst. prof., 1985-91, assoc. prof., 1991-98, prof. medicine, 1998—, dir., echocardiography rsch.; assoc. dir., echocardiography lab. Methodist DeBakey Heart Ctr., Tex., dir., Cardiovascular Imaging Inst. Tex.; William Williams Chair in Cardiovascular Imaging Methodist Hosp., Tex. Dir. medicine Meth Hosp., Houston, 1990—. Contbr. articles to profl. jours.; reviewer (of sci. jours.). Fellow: Coun. on Clin. Cardiology, Am. Coll. Cardiology (chmn. scientific sessions 2000, bd. trustee (five-year) 2002—07, bd. trustee 2008—09, treas., v.p. 2010); mem.: Harris County Med. Soc., Tex. Med. Assn., Am. Heart Assn. (prog. com. 1991—94), Am. Soc. Echocardiography (v.p. 2006—07, pres.-elect 2007—08, pres. 2008—, bd. dirs.), Alpha Omega Alpha. Home: 6618 Sewanee St Houston TX 77005-3750 Office: Methodist Hosp 6550 Fannin St SM 677 Houston TX 77030-2717 also: Methodist Hosp 6550 Fannin Ste 1901 Smith Tower Houston TX 77030 Office Phone: 713-441-4342, 713-441-1100.

ZOLLAR, JAWOLE WILLA JO, artist, choreographer; b. Kansas City, Kans., Dec. 21, 1950; d. Alfred Jr. and Dorothy Delores Zollar; 1 child, Elizabeth Herron. BA in Dance, U. Mo., Kansas City, 1975; MFA in Dance, Fla. State U., 1979; PhD (hon.), Columbia Coll., Chgo., 2002. Faculty Fla. State U., Tallahassee, 1977-80, Nancy Smith Fichter prof. dance, 1997—; founding artistic dir. Urban Bush Women, Bklyn., 1984—; Worlds of Thought Resident Scholar Mankato State Univ., 1993—94; regents lectr., dept. dance, world arts and culture UCLA, 1995—96; vis. artist Ohio State Univ., 1996; Abramowitz Meml. lectr. MIT, 1998. Recipient NY Dance Performance award, 1992, 2006, Capezio award for outstanding achievement in dance, 1994, Doris Duke awad, Am. Dance Festival, 1997; named Outstanding Alumni, U. Mo., 1993, Regent's lectr. dept. dance and worlds culture, UCLA, 1995—96, Alumna of Yr., U. Mo., 1993, Fla. State U., Tallahassee, 1997; fellow John Simon Guggenheim Meml. Found., 2009; Choreography fellow, NEA, 1992, 1993, 1994, Wynn fellow in dance, US Artists, 2008. Mem.: Internat. Assn. Blacks in Dance, Assn. Am. Cultures. Office: Florida State Univ Dept of Dance PO Box 3062120 130 Collegiate Loop Tallahassee FL 32306-2120 also: Urban Bush Women # 4B 138 S Oxford St Brooklyn NY 11217 also: c/o IMG Artists 420 W 45th St Fl 6 New York NY 10036-3503 Office Phone: 850-644-2525. E-mail: info@urbanbushwomen.org, jwjzollar@mac.com.

ZOLLER, MICHAEL, otolaryngologist, head and neck surgeon, educator; b. New Orleans, July 21, 1947; s. Harry and Mildred (Daitch) Z.; m. Linda Kramer, Dec. 21, 1974; children: Rebecca, Jonathan. BS, U. New Orleans, 1971; MD, Tulane U., 1972. Resident in gen. surgery Jewish Hosp., St. Louis, Washington U. Sch. Medicine, 1972—74; resident in otolaryngology Mass. Eye and Ear Infirmary, Harvard U. Med. Sch., Boston, 1974—77; pres. Ear, Nose and Throat Assocs., Savannah, Ga., 1977—; chmn. eye, ear, nose and throat dept. Candler Hosp., 1996—98; clin. prof. otolaryngology, head neck surgery Med. Coll. Ga., Augusta, 2009—. Asst. clin. prof. otolaryngology, head and neck surgery Med. Coll. Ga., Augusta, 1982—96, assoc. clin. prof. otolaryngology, head and neck surgery, 1996—2009; assoc. prof. surgery Mercer Med. Sch., 2000—09, clin. prof. surgery, 2009—; dir. otology otoneurology dept. St. Joseph's Hosp., Savannah, 1994—; bd. dirs. Darby Bank and Trust, 2007—10.

Chmn. med. divsn. United Way, Savannah, 1990, chmn. profl. divsn., 1991, 94-2001, vice chmn. campaign, 2002, chmn. campaign, 2003, bd. dirs., 2002-07, vice chmn. bd. dirs., 2004-05, chmn. bd. dirs., 2005-2006; allocation panel, 1997-2002; bd. dirs. Am. Cancer Soc., Savannah, 1993-2000, pres. Chatham County unit, 1996-97, chmn. bd., 1997-98; bd. dirs. Savannah Country Day Sch., 1993-97, chmn. ann. campaign, 1995-96; bd. dirs. St. Joseph's Candler Found., 2001-; pres. Savannah Jewish Fedn., 1991-93; active Savannah Jewish Fedn. Endowment Bd., 1995-99; mem. med. adv. bd. South Coll., 1996-2000; mem. parents coun. Washington U., St. Louis, 1997-2001, Tulane U., 2002-05, Tulane Med. Sch., 2005-06, Tulane Med. Alumni Assn, 2007-2010; bd. dirs. Leadership Savannah, 1996-98. Recipient Young Leadership award Savannah Jewish Fedn., 1985, Boss of Yr. award Savannah Jaycees, 1993, Celebrate Savannah award for outstanding contbns. to Savannah, Ga. Guardian, 1996; Harvard U. Med. Sch. fellow, 1976-77, C.G. Taylor Alumnus award Tulane Med. Alumny, 2009. Fellow: ACS; mem.: Ga. Soc. Otolaryngology (pres. bd. trustees 1997—98, editor newsletter 1998—2001, Lester Brown Lifetime Achievement award 2005), Med. Assn. Ga. (mem. ho. of dels. 1990—2005, bd. dirs. 1995—2004, editl. bd. mem. 2001—, Ga. Cup award 1993, Ayest-Wyeth Cmty. Svc. award 1996, Cmty. Svc. award 2001), 1st Dist. Med. Assn. (pres. 1987—88), Ga. Med. Soc. (pres. 1992, chmn. bd. trustees 1997, chmn. endowment fund 2004—, John B. Rabun Cmty. Svc. award 1995, Hero's award 2001, Cmty. Star award 2012), Am. Neurotology Soc., Am. Soc. Head and Neck Surgery, Am. Acad. Otolaryngology and Head and Neck Surgery (tonsils and adenoids com. 1996—99, sleep disorders com. 1996—2002, pediat. otolaryngology com. 2003—09, equilibrium com. 2005—12, edn. com. mem. 2013—). Office: Ear Nose and Throat Assocs Savannah 5201 Frederick St Savannah GA 31405-4501 Personal E-mail: MZ47ent@aol.com.

ZORETIC, RICHARD C., medical insurance company executive; Degree in Fin., Penn. State U. Leadership positions United Healthcare, 1994—2000; sr. v.p., network ops. and distbn. CIGNA Dental Health, 2003—03; sr. v.p. Amerigroup, Corp., 2003; chief mktg. officer Amerigroup Corp., 2003—05, exec. v.p., Health Plan Ops., 2005—07, exec. v.p., COO, 2008—. Office: Amerigroup Corp 4425 Corporation Ln Virginia Beach VA 23462 Office Phone: 757-490-6900. Office Fax: 757-518-3600. Business E-Mail: rzoretic@amerigroupcorp.com.

ZORN, ERIC STUART, retail executive; b. Newark, Oct. 2, 1948; s. Arthur and Evelyn (Bernstein) Z.; m. Lois Karen Green, Nov. 29, 1979. Student, Fairleigh Dickinson Coll., Wayne, NJ, Upsala Coll., East Orange, NJ. Cash ops. supr. Vornado Inc., Garfield, N.J., 1966-69; corp. auditor Mangel Stores Corp., NYC, 1969-70; sr. v.p. Jamesway Corp., Secaucus, NJ, 1970; pres. Omnia Protective Services Inc., Ft. Lee, NJ, 1979, 1530 Owners Corp. (coop. bldg.), Ft. Lee; regional v.p. Wal-Mart Stores Inc., 1993—97, v.p. realty, 1997—99, sr. v.p. realty, 1999, pres. realty, 2003—05; exec. v.p. Wal-Mart Realty Wal-Mart Stores, Inc., 2005—. Mem. Internat. Mass Retailing Inst. (chmn. loss prevention group 1979-82), NJ Retail Mchts. Assn. (chmn.), Internat. Soc. Stress Analysts, Soc. Strategic Planning, Internat. Coun. Shopping Centers (trustee). Republican. Jewish. Office: Wal-Mart Realty 2001 SE 10th St Bentonville AR 72712-6489

ZOROWSKI, CARL FRANK, engineering educator, academic administrator; b. Pitts., July 14, 1930; s. Stanley and Mary Josephine (Kozuch) Z.; m. Sarah Jane Crossley, Aug. 7, 1954 (dec. 1983); children: Kathleen Ann, Karl Alan, Kristine Alaine; m. Louise Parrish Lockwood, Apr. 13, 1985. BSME, Carnegie Inst. Tech., 1952, MSME, 1953, PhD, 1956. Instr. Carnegie Inst. Tech., Pitts., 1952-56, asst. prof., 1956-61, assoc. prof., 1961-62; prof. dept. mech. and aero. engring. NC State U., Raleigh, 1964-66; R.J. Reynolds Industries prof., 1966-97; assoc. dept. head, 1964-72; dept. head, 1972-79; assoc. dean acad. affairs Sch. Engring., 1979-85; dir. Integrated Mfg. Sys. Inst., 1986-92; dept. head, 1992-93; dir. Succeed/NSF Coalition, 1993-97; assoc. dean acad. affairs, 1993-94; R.J. Reynolds Industries emeritus prof., 1997—. Contbr. articles to profl. jours.; patentee in field. 2d lt. USAR, 1952-58. Recipient Rsch. award Sigma Xi, 1967. Fellow ASME (Richards Meml. award 1975), Fellow Am. Soc. Engring. Edn. (We. Electric award 1968); mem. Fiber Soc. (Achievement award 1970). Home: 103 Windyrush Ln Cary NC 27511-9758 Office: NC State University Page Hall Rm 245 PO Box 7901 Raleigh NC 27695-0001 Home Phone: 919-851-3145; Office Phone: 919-515-6597. Personal E-mail: zorowski@att.net. Business E-Mail: zorowski@ncsu.edu.

ZOU, YUE, medical educator; arrived in US, 1985, naturalized, 2004; s. Shaoming Zou and Ming Lee; m. Zhiping Dong, June 20, 1985; children: Charley, Daniel. BS, Chengdu U. Tech. and Scis., China, 1982; MS, Dalian Inst. Chem. Physics, China, 1985; PhD, Clark U., Worcester, Mass., 1991. Postdoc. fellow Carnegie-Mellon U., Pitts., 1991—92, U. Vt. Cancer Ctr., Burlington, 1992—93, Va. Commonwealth U. Cancer Ctr., Richmond, 1993—94, U. Tex. Med. Br., Galveston, 1994—96, asst. scientist, 1996—98, asst. prof., 1998—2001; assoc. prof. Quillen Coll. Medicine, East Tenn. State U., Johnson City, 2001—07, prof., 2007—. Contbr. over 47 articles to profl. pubs. including rsch. work on Bio-Chemistry. Deacon Galveston Chinese Ch., 1998—2001, Chinese Ch. Great Tri-City, 2005—. Recipient Dir.'s Bridge award, NIH, 2007—08, Acad. Rsch. Enhancement award, 2008—; grantee, 1999—2007, 2000—06; scholar, Dalian Inst. Chem. Physics, 1982—85. Mem.: AAAS, Am. Soc. for Biochemistry and Molecular Biology. Baptist. Achievements include breakthroughs in DNA damage and repair research. Avocations: basketball, hiking, computers. Office: East Tennessee State Univ 100 CR DR Campus Box 70581 Johnson City TN 37614 Business E-Mail: zouy@etsu.edu.

ZSCHAU, JULIUS JAMES, lawyer; b. Peoria, Ill., Apr. 1, 1940; s. Raymond Johann Ernst and Rosamond Lillian Z.; m. Leila Joan Krueger, Aug. 7, 1971; children: Kristen Elisabeth, Kimberly Erna, Kira Jamie White, Karla Johanna. BS, U. Ill., Champaign, 1964, JD, 1966; LLM, John Marshall Law Sch., 1978. Bar: Ill. 1966, Fla. 1975. Atty. Ill. Central Gulf R.R. Co., Chgo., 1966-68; assoc. Coin & Sheerin, Chgo., 1968-70, Snyder, Clarke et al, Waukegan, Ill., 1970-72; counsel Ill. Ctr. Corp., Chgo., 1972-74; v.p., gen. counsel, sec. Am. Agronomics Corp., Tampa, Fla., 1974-76; pres. Sorota & Zschau, Clearwater, Fla., 1976-90; shareholder Baynard, Harrell, Ostow & Ulrich PA, 1990-94, Johnson, Blakely, Pope, Bokor, Ruppel and Burns, Clearwater, 1994—2002, Pennington Moore Wilkinson Bell & Dunbar PA, 2002—. Bd. dirs. Attys. Title Ins. Fund, Inc., chmn. bd. dirs., 1994—95; chmn. com. on land trusts Fla. Bar, past chmn. Real Property, Probate and Trust Law sect., vice chair grievance com., 1985—87, chair leadership conf., 1987; chmn. Jud. Nominating Commn. of 6th Jud. Dist., 1991—94; past chmn. jud. nominating com. Ct. Appeals (2d dist.). Mem. Pinellas County Exec. Com., Tampa Regional Planning Coun., 1988-92. Served to capt. USNR, 1962-92. Fellow: Am. Bar Found. (life); mem.: ABA (chmn. standing com. lawyers title guaranty funds 1991, chmn. land trust com., chmn. standing com. lawyers title guaranty funds 2004—07), Fla. Bar Found. (chmn. jud. nominations procedures com. 1992—93, legal aid to poor com.), Fla. Coun. Bar Assn. (past pres., past chmn. vol. bar liaison com.), Clearwater Bar Assn. (past pres.), Chgo. Bar Assn., Ill. Bar Assn., Am. Coll. Real Estate Lawyers (past chmn. condominium com.), Clearwater C. of C. (bd. govs., exec. com., past v.p.), Countryside Country Club. Republican. Home: 1910 Saddlehill Rd N Dunedin FL 34698-2437 Office: Julius J Zschau 1247 S Myrtle Ave Clearwater FL 33756-3469 Home Phone: 727-784-8490. Business E-Mail: jayz@penningtonlaw.com.

ZUBER, HENRY B., III, (HANK ZUBER), state legislator; b. Covington, La., June 11, 1966; s. Patricia and Barry Zuber. BA in Finance, Millsaps Coll.; JD, U. Miss. Law Sch. Mem. Dist. 113 Miss. House of Reps., 2000—; atty. Zuber Law Firm, Ocean Springs, Miss. Mem. Transp., Fees & Salaries of Pub. Officers, Games & Fish, Investigative State Offices & Mcpl. coms. Mem. bd. dirs. YMCA. Mem.: K. of C. Republican. Roman Catholic. Office: Zuber Law Firm 2336 Government St Ocean Springs MS 39564 also: PO Box 1018 Jackson MS 39215 Office Phone: 228-875-1097. Business E-Mail: hzuber@house.ms.gov.

ZUBIETA, ALBERTO ALEMAN, construction executive; b. Panama City, Panama; Degree in Indsl. Engring., Civil Engring., Tex. A & M U. Adminstr. Panama Canal Commn., 1996—98, Panama Canal Authority, 1998—, CEO, bd. dirs., 2005—. Recipient Fed. Engr. of Yr. award, ASCE, 1998, Personality 2001 award, Seatrade Orgn., William Ross medal, 1992, Florencio Icaza award, 1998, Fed. Engr. of Yr. award, 1998, Maritime Personality award, 2001, Friendship award, 2002, Order of Rio Branco award, 2003, Meritorious Son of City of Panama, 2003, Govt. Oficial of Yr., 2003, Outstanding Internat. Alumnus award, Tex. A & M U., 2003, Disting. Grad. award, 2009, Silver Bell award, 2009, Lifetime Achievement award, 2009, Honorary Mention-Abel Bravo medal, 2009, International Maritime prize, 2008—09; named Businessman of Yr., 2002, Nat. Order of the Legion of Honor, 2006, Maritime Personality, 2009; Hon. fellow, 1997, Maritime International Hall of Fame, 1997. Mem.: Young Profls. Assn. (Panama Chpt.), Panama Architects and Engrs. Assn., Panamanian Chamber of Constrn. (William Ross Medal 1992). Mailing: Panama Canal Authority PO Box 526725 Miami FL 33152-6725 Office Phone: 507-272-1400.

ZUBIZARRETA, JOHN, English professor; b. NYC, Sept. 1, 1950; s. Juan and Consuelo (Romero) Zubizarreta; m. Margaret Elizabeth Carlisle, Aug. 2, 1980; children: Anna Ruth, Maria Elizabeth. AA, Miami-Dade Jr. Coll., 1971; BA, Fla. Internat. U., 1973; MA, U. S.C., 1975, PhD, 1983. Instr. Western Carolina U., Cullowhee, NC, 1979-82, 85-86; tchr. Ashley Hall Upper Sch., Charleston, SC, 1986-87; vis. asst. prof. Coll. of Charleston, 1986-88; prof. Columbia Coll., SC, 1988—, dir. Honors and Faculty Devel. Program, 1989—. Contbr. articles to profl. jours. Mem. SC Humanities Coun. Speakers Bur., 1989—, SC Libr. Let's Talk About It Program, 1990—. Recipient Outstanding Tchr. award, South Atlantic MLA, 1993, Gov.'s Disting. Prof. award, SC Commn. on Higher End., 1992, Exemplary Tchr. award, Nat. United Meth. Bd. Higher Edn., 1992, Outstanding Faculty award, Columbia Coll., 1991, Sears-Roebuk Found. Tchg. Excellence and Campus Leadership award, 1991, Outstanding Faculty Citizen and Exemplary Tchr. Recognition, Am. Assn. for Higher Edn., 1994, Outstanding Baccalaureate Colleges Prof. of Yr. award, Carnegie Found. for Advancement of Tchg. & the Coun. for the Advancement & Support of Edn., 2010; named CASE US Prof. of Yr. for SC, Carnegie Found. for Advancement of Tchg., 1994. Mem.: Conf. on Christianity and Lit. (Michael K. Maher prize for Outstanding Essay 1999), Nat. Collegiate Honors Coun., Am. Lit. Assn., Modern Lang. Assn. Avocations: telemark skiing, whitewater canoe and kayak, fishing. Office Phone: 803-786-3014. E-mail: jzubizarreta@columbiasc.edu.

ZUCKER, ALEXANDER, physicist, researcher; b. Zagreb, Croatia, Aug. 1, 1924; came to U.S., 1939; s. William and Bertha (Klopfer) Z.; m. Joan-Ellen Jamieson, Nov. 28, 1953; children: Rebecca, Claire, Susannah. BA, U. Vt., Burlington, 1947; MS, Yale U., New Haven, 1948, PhD, 1950. Physicist Oak Ridge Nat. Lab., 1950-60, assoc. dir. electro-nuclear div., 1960—70, dir. heavy ion project, 1972—74, assoc. dir. phys. scis., 1973-88, acting lab. dir., 1988, assoc. dir. for nuclear techs., 1989-93; exec. dir., environ. studies bd. NAS-NAE, Washington, 1970-72; prof. physics U. Tenn., 1996—. Mem. U.S. del. to USSR on Peaceful Uses of Atomic Energy, 1963; Ford prof. physics U. Tenn., Knoxville, 1968-73; U.S. del. to Pugwash Conf., 1971; research coordination council Gas Research Inst., Chgo., 1978-85; com. Army manpower Nat. Research Council, Washington, 1982-83; adv. panel on technologies to reduce U.S. materials import vulnerability Office of Technology Assessment, Washington, 1982-85; council on energy engring. research Dept. of Energy, Washington, 1983—; industry, nat. lab. steel initiative White House, Washington, 1984 Editor Internat. Jour. Nuclear Sci. Applications, 1980—; cons. editor Ency. and Yearbook of Sci. and Tech. McGraw-Hill Pub. Co., 1989; mem. editorial bd. Science, 1981-82; contbr. articles to profl. jours. Pres. Oak Ridge Civic Music Assn., Oak Ridge Arts Coun.; bd. chair Ridgeview Psychiatric Hosp. Guggenheim fellow, 1966-67; Fulbright-Hays Research scholar, 1966-67 Fellow Am. Phys. Soc., AAAS, Sigma Xi; mem. ASME, Nat. Acad. Scis. (nuclear physics del. to People's Republic of China 1979), Internat. Union Pure and Applied Physics (mem.-at-large U.S. nat. com. 1976-78) Achievements include research in nuclear physics with heavy ions and protons; accelerators, especially cyclotrons; materials research programs, especially high-temperature materials and surfaces; nuclear power reactors, especially gas-cooled reactors; research reactor with ultra high neutron flux.

ZUCKER, ANITA, plastics company executive; BA in Edn., 1972; MEd in Adminstrn. and Supervision, U. North Fla., 1978. Owner Tristan Restaurant; chmn., CEO InterTech Group, Inc., dir., cmty. rels., 1982; gov. Hudson's Bay Co., 2008. Office: InterTech Group Inc 4838 Jenkins Ave North Charleston SC 29405 Office Phone: 843-744-5174. Office Fax: 843-747-4092. Business E-Mail: zuckera@intertechsc.com.

ZUCKER, JEFFREY A., broadcast executive; b. Homestead, Fla., Apr. 9, 1965; m. Caryn Stephanie Nathanson, 1996; children: Andrew, Elizabeth, Peter. BA in American History, Harvard Coll., 1986. Rschr., 1988 Olympic Games, Seoul, Korea NBC Sports, 1986—88; field prodr. NBC News, 1989; exec. prodr. Today, 1992—93, Now with Tom Brokaw and Katie Couric, 1992, NBC Nightly News with Tom Brokaw, 1993, Today, 1994—2000; pres. NBC Entertainment, 2000—03, NBC Entertainment, News and Cable Group, 2003—05; CEO NBC Universal TV, 2005—07; pres., CEO NBC Universal, Inc., 2007—10; pres. CNN Worldwide, 2013—. Exec. prodr.: (news segments) Russian coup, 1991, Persian Gulf War, 1991, 1993 and 1997 presdl. inaugurations, the bombing of Centennial Olympic Pk., 1996, 1996 and 2000 polit. conventions, Decision 2000; writer: The Games of the XXIV Olympiad (Emmy award, outstanding writing, 1988); supervising prodr.: "Senator Edward Kennedy" Today (Emmy award, outstanding interview, 1991); exec. prodr.: "California Fire" Now with Tom Brokaw and Katie Couric (Emmy award, outstanding coverage of a single breaking news story, 1993), "Tragedy in Rwanda" Now with Tom Brokaw and Katie Couric (Emmy award, outstanding background/analysis of a single current story, 1994), "The Brain" Now with Tom Brokaw and Katie Couric (Emmy award, outstanding informational or cultural program, 1994); exec. prodr.: (daytime talk show) Katie, 2011—12. Jewish. Office: CNN Worldwide 1 CNN Ctr NW Atlanta GA 30303*

ZUHDI, NABIL (BILL), lawyer, litigator, consultant, producer, film professional boxing and concerts; b. NYC, June 8, 1955; s. Nazih and Lamya Zuhdi; child from previous marriage: Noah; m. Darla L. Boyd, May 19, 1984. BS, U. Ctrl. Okla., 1979; JD, U. Okla., 1982. Bar: Okla. 1982, U.S. Dist. Ct. (we. dist.) Okla. 1982, U.S. Ct. Appeals (10th cir.) 1989, U.S. Supreme Ct. 1990, Tex. 1991, U.S. Dist. Ct. (no. dist.) Tex. 1998, US Ct. Appeals (5th Cir), 1991. Assoc. Linn & Helms, Oklahoma City, 1982-85; ptnr. Zuhdi & Denum, Oklahoma City, 1985-87; assoc. Law Firm Darrell Keith, Ft. Worth, 1994; pvt. practice Oklahoma City, 1987—; pres. Cat Box Entertainment Inc. Film Concert And Boxing Promotion Co., 2007—. Pres. Zuhdi Entertainment Group, Inc., Okla. City, 1986—, Amerisphere, Inc., Okla. City, 1996—, criminal justice act panel We. Dist. Okla., 1985—, spl. death penalty habeas corpus panel, 1998, criminal justice act voluntary panel No. Dist. Tex., 1998. Producer: (concerts) Frank Sinatra, Julio Iglesias, Darla Z Live From Las Vegas TV Music Special; promoter: WBU World Lightweight Title Championship, Appearances ABC World News, Wall St. Jour. & NY Times, Trial Distortion and the End of Innocence in Federal Criminal Justice, Wake Forest U. Patron Okla. Heart Ctr., Oklahoma City, 1994—, bd. dirs., Friend Okla. History Ctr. Mem. ABA, ATLA, State Bar Tex., Oklahoma Bar Assn., Oklahoma County Bar Assn., Phi Alpha Delta, Alpha Chi. Democrat. Avocations: boxing, films, music. Office: PO Box 1077 Oklahoma City OK 73101-1077

ZUHDI, NAZIH, surgeon scientist retired; b. Beirut, May 19, 1925; arrived in US, 1950, naturalized, 1960; s. Omar and Lutfiye (Atef) Z.; children by previous marriage: Omar, Nabil; m. Annette McMichael; children: Adam, Leyla, Zachariah BA, Am. U., Beirut, 1946, MD, 1950. Diplomate Am. Bd. Surgery, Am. Bd. Thoracic Surgery. Intern St. Vincent's Hosp., SI, NY, 1950-51, Presbyn.-Columbia Med. Ctr., NYC, 1951-52; resident Kings County SUNY Med. Ctr., NYC, 1952-56; fellow SUNY Downstate Med. Ctr., Bklyn., 1953-54; resident Univ. Hosp., Mpls., 1956, Okla. City, 1957-58, practice surgery specializing in cardiovasc. and thoracic, 1958-87, Nazih Zuhdi Transplant Inst. founder and adminstr., 1984—99, ret., 1999; co-founder, chmn. labs. Mercy Heart and Rsch. Inst., 1958—65. Founder, chmn., dir., surgeon-in-chief Oklahoma Transplantation Inst. (renamed Nazih Zuhdi Transplant Inst., Aug., 1999) Bapt. Med. Ctr., 1984-99, chmn. dept. transplantation, Baptist Hosp., Okla. City, 1994-99; co-founder, chmn. Okla. Cardiovasc. Inst., Okla. City, 1983-84, Okla. Heart Ctr., Okla. City, 1984-85 Contbg. author Cardiac Surgery, 1967, 2d edit., 1972; contbr. articles to profl. jour.; developer numerous med. devices, techniques, rsch. and publs. on cardiopulmonary bypass, internal hypothermia, assisted circulation, heart surgery and transplantation of thoracic organs; developer heart-lung machines; designer, use of exptl. plastic bypass hearts; originator of clin. non-hemic primes of heart-lung machines producing total intentional hemodilution, at present, the universally accepted principle of cardiopulmonary bypass for partial and total body perfusion, use of banked citrated blood for surgical field blood loss replacement if needed beyond the cell-saver during open heart surgery, heart transplantation, and lung transplantation; researcher in cardiovasc. studies. Founder Islamic Ctr., Inc., Oklahoma City, 1985-1986; Internat. Bd. Vis., U. Okla., 1996-. Named to Okla. Hall of Fame, 1994. Fellow ACS; mem. AMA, NCCJ (Humanitarian award 1996), Am. Thoracic Soc., Okla. Thoracic Soc., So. Med. Assn., Okla. Med. Assn., Internat. Coll. Angiology, Am. Coll. Chest Physicians, Oklahoma City C. of C., Oklahoma County Med. Soc., Oklahoma City Clin. Soc., Okla. Surg. Assn., Oklahoma City Surg. Soc., Southwestern Surg. Congress, Am. Coll. Cardiology, Am. Soc. Artificial Internal Organs, Soc. Thoracic Surgeons (founding mem.), Am. Assn. for Thoracic Surgery, Internat. Cardiovasc. Soc., Okla. State Heart Assn., Osler Soc., So. Thoracic Surg. Assn., Lillehei Surg. Soc., Internat. Soc. Heart Transplantation, Dwight Harken's Founder's Group Cardiac Surgery, Westaby's Pioneers in Cardiac Surgery, Am. Soc. Transplant Surgeons, Milestones of Cardiovas. Medicine of Am. Coll. Cardiology, Okla. City Golf and Country Club, Okla. Hall of Fame. Moslem. Achievements include first to use banked citrated blood for cardiopulmonary bypass for open heart surgery; origination and completion of experiments leading to and first clinical non-hemic primes of heart-lung machines producing total intentional hemodilution, laid the foundation and opened the gateway for bloodless surgery for all patients, biography by Brooks Barr "The Life of Nazih Zuhdi Uncharted Voyage of a heart", 2005, Oklahoma History Center, 2006; naming Nazih Zuhdi Drive to become official address of Oklahoma History Center, 2009. Personal E-mail: anz70@aol.com.

ZUMBRUNNEN, DAVID ARNOLD, engineering educator; b. Salt Lake City, Sept. 3, 1955; m. Elizabeth. B in Mech. Engring., U. Minn., 1977; MS in Mech. Engring., Purdue U., 1984, PhD in Mech. Engring., 1988. Registered profl. engr., Ind., SC. Co-founder NSF Ctr. Advanced Engring. Fibers and Films; asst. prof. mech. engring. Clemson U., SC, 1988—93, assoc. prof. mech. engring., 1993—97, prof. mech. engring., 1997—2003, Warren H. Owen-Duke Energy disting. prof. mech. engring., 2003—. Lt. USN, 1977—82. Presdl. Faculty Fellow The White House/NSF, 1992-97. Fellow: ASME; mem.: Am. Nuclear Soc., Polymer Processing Soc., SPE, AIChemE. Achievements include invention of structured materials formed by chaotic advection, and smart blending machinery & processes. Office: Dept Mech Engring Clemson Univ Clemson SC 29634-0921 Business E-Mail: zdavid@clemson.edu.

ZUNZ, OLIVIER JEAN, history professor; b. Paris, July 19, 1946; s. Jean R. and Monique M. (Blin) Z.; m. Christine M. Crommen, July 3, 1970; children: Emmanuel, Sophie. Licence in history and geography, U. Paris X, 1968, M in History, 1969; Doctorat-ès-Lettres, U. Paris I, Panthéon-Sorbonne, 1982. Scientist Ctr. Nat. de la Recherche Scientifique, Paris, 1976-78; asst. prof. dept. history U. Va., Charlottesville, 1978-83, assoc. prof., 1983-88, prof., 1988-99, Commonwealth prof., 1999—. Vis. prof. Ecole des Hautes Etudes en Scis., Sociales, Paris, 1985—2011, Coll. France, 1997; dir. seminar for Coll. Tchrs. NEH, 1989, 92. Author: The Changing Face of Inequality: Urbanization, Industrial Development, and Immigrants in Detroit, 1980-1920, 1982, Making America Corporate, 1870-1920, 1990, Why the American Century?, 1998, Philanthropy in America: A History, 2012; editor, co-author: Reliving the Past: The Worlds of Social History, 1985; editor: Alexis de Tocqueville, Democracy in America (transl. A. Goldhammer), 2004, Alexis de Tocqueville and Gustave de Beaumont in America: Their Friendship and Their Travels, 2010; co-editor: (with David Ward) The Landscape of Modernity: Essays on New York City, 1900-1940, 1992, (with Leonard Schoppa and Nobuhiro Hiwatari): Social Contracts under Stress: The Middle Classes of America, Europe, and Japan at the Turn of the Century, 2002, (with Alan S. Kahan): The Tocqueville Reader: A Life in Letters and Politics, 2002; mem. editl. bd. Revs. in Am. History, 1990-98; contbr. articles, book revs. to profl. jours. Jr. fellow Mich. Soc. Fellows, 1973-76, John Simon Guggenheim Meml. Found. fellow, 1986-87; grantee U. Mich.-Ford Found. Population Devel. Fund, 1974-76, NSF, 1976-78, NEH, 1979-81, 84-87, Ford Found., 2004-07; named Officer L'Ordre Nat. du Mérite, French Govt., 2011; also recipient numerous rsch. grants. Mem. Am. Hist. Assn., Orgn. Am. Historians, The Tocqueville Soc. (pres. 2001–06). Home: 1368 Hilltop Rd Charlottesville VA 22903-1225 Office: U Va Corcoran Dept of History PO Box 400180 Randall Hall Charlottesville VA 22904-4180 Business E-Mail: oz@virginia.edu.

ZUREK, PATRICK JAMES, bishop; b. Wallis, Tex., Aug. 17, 1948; s. Arnold and Victoria Zurek. BS in Math. magna cum laude, U. St. Thomas, Houston; STB in Theology magna cum laude, U. St. Thomas, 1974; STL in Moral Theology magna cum laude, Inst. of Lateran U., 1976. Ordained priest Diocese of Austin, Tex., 1975; assoc. pastor St. Mary's Cath. Ch., Temple, Tex., 1976–79, St. Joseph's Cath. Ch., Bryan, Tex., 1979–82; founding pastor St. Thomas Aquinas Cath. Ch., College Station, 1982–92; pastor St. John Neumann Cath Ch., Austin, 1992–98; ordained bishop, 1998; aux. bishop Archdiocese of San Antonio, 1998—2008; bishop Diocese of Amarillo, Tex., 2008—. Mem.: Czech Am. Priests Assn. (pres., CEO 2002—), US Conf. Cath. Bishops. Roman Catholic. Office: Diocese of Amarillo Chancery Office 1800 N Spring St Amarillo TX 79117 Office Phone: 806-383-2243. Office Fax: 806-383-8452.

ZWIENER, DAVID KENNETH, bank executive; b. 1954; BA, Duke U., Durham, NC; MBA in Fin. and Mktg., Northwestern U. Asst. treas. internat. ops. Kimberly Clark Corp., 1984—87; sr. v.p., treas. to exec. v.p. capital markets Heller Internat. Corp., 1987—93; CFO, exec. v.p. ITT Fin. Corp., 1993—95; exec. v.p., CFO Hartford Fin. Svcs. Group, Inc., 1995—2001, pres., COO property & casualty ops., 2000—07; mng. dir., co-head fin. inst. group The Carlyle Group, Washington, 2007—08; sr. exec. v.p., CFO Wachovia Corp., Charlotte, NC, 2008—. Office: Wachovia Corp 301 S Coll St Ste 4000 Charlotte NC 28288 Office Phone: 704-590-0000. Office Fax: 704-374-3425.

ZWILICH, ELLEN TAAFFE, composer; b. Miami, Fla., Apr. 30, 1939; d. Edward Porter and Ruth (Howard) Taaffe; m. Joseph Zwilich, June 22, 1969 (dec. June 1979). MusB, Fla. State U., 1960, MusM, 1962; D Mus. Arts, Juilliard Sch., 1975; studies with Roger Sessions and Elliott Carter; MusD (hon.), Oberlin Coll., 1987, Converse Coll., 1994; LHD (hon.), Manhattanville Coll., 1991, Marymount Manhattan Coll., 1994, N.Y. New Sch., Mannes, 1995, Mich. State U., 2006.

Francis Eppes disting. prof. Fla. State U., Tallahassee, 1999—. Composer in residence Santa Fe Chamber Music Festival, 1990, Am. Acad. Rome, 1990; first Composer's Chair, Carnegie Hall, 1995-99, Saratoga Chamber Music Festival, 2004. Premiere, Symposium for Orch., Pierre Boulez, N.Y.C., 1975, Chamber Symphony and Passages, Boston Musica Viva, Richard Pittman, 1979, 82. Symphony 1, Gunther Schuller, Am. Composers Orch., 1982; violinist Am. Symphony, N.Y.C., 1965-73; composer: Sonata in Three Movements, 1973-74; String Quartet, 1974; Clarino Quartet, 1977; Chamber Symphony, 1979; Passages (for Soprano and Chamber Ensemble), 1981; String Trio, 1982; Symphony 1:3 Movements for Orch., 1982 (Grammy nomination New World Records, 1987); Divertimento, 1983; Einsame Nacht, 1971; Emlekezet, 1978; Im Nebel, 1972; Passages for Soprano and Orch., 1982; Trompeten, 1974; Fantasy for Harpsichord, 1983; Intrada, 1983; Prologue and Variations, 1983; Double Quartet for Strings, Chamber Music Soc. of Lincoln Ctr., 1984; Celebration for Orch., Indpls. Symphony, John Nelson, 1984; Symphony #2 (Cello Symphony) San Francisco Symphony, Edo De Waart, 1985, Symphony #2 Louisville Orch. recording, L.L. Smith (Grammy nomination 1991); Concerto Grosso 1985, Handel Festival Orch., Steven Simon, 1986; Concerto for Piano and orch., Detroit Symphony, Gunther Herbig, Marc-André Hamelin, 1986; Images for 2 Pianos and orch., Nat. Symphony Orch., F. Machetti, 1987; Tanzspiel, Peter Martins N.Y.C. Ballet, 1987; Praeludium Boston chpt. AGO, 1987; Trio for piano, violin and cello; Kalichstein, Laredo, Robinson trio, 1987; Symbolon, Zubin Mehta and the N.Y. Philharm., Leningrad and Moscow (USSR), N.Y.C. (Koussevitsky Internat. Rec. award nominee 1990), 1988; concerto for trombone and orch. J. Friedman, Sir Georg Solti, Chgo. Symphony, 1989, concerto for trombone and orch. Christian Lindberg, James De Priest, Malmö Symphony, concerto for flute and orch. D.A. Dwyer, Seija Ozawa, Boston Symphony, 1990, quintet for clarinet and string quartet David Schifrin, Chamber Music N.W., Lincoln Ctr. Chamber Mus. Soc., 1990; concerto for oboe and orch. John Mack, Christoph von Dohnanyi, Cleve. Orch., 1991; concerto for bass trombone strings, timpani and cymbals Chgo. Symphony Orch. Ch. Vernon, Daniel Barenboim, 1991; concerto for violin, violoncello and orch. Jaime Laredo, Sharon Robinson, Louisville Orch., L. Smith, 1991; Immigrant Voices Peter Leonard, St. Lukes Orch., N.Y. Internat. Festival ot the Arts Chorus, Ellis Island, 1991, concerto for flute and orch, D.A. Dwyer, J. Sedares, London Symphony Orch., 1992, Symphony # 3

(Grammy nominee 1993), J. Ling, N.Y. Philharmonic, 1993, concerto for bassoon and orch., Nancy Goeres, Lorin Maazel, Pitts. Symphony, 1993, concerto for horn and string Orch., David Jolley, Rochester Philharm., L.L. Smith., 1993, Fantasy for Orch., JoAnn Falletta, Long Beach Symphony Orch., 1994, American Concerto Doc Severinsen, J. Falletta San Diego Symphony, 1994, A Simple Magnificat, 1994, Triple Concerto Kalichstein, Laredo, Robinson Trio Zdenek Macal, Minn. Orch., 1995, for piano and orch., Peanuts Gallery, 1996, violin concerto, Pamela Frank, H. Wolff, 1997; String Quartet # 2, 1998, Emerson Quartet; Upbeat! 1998, Nat. Symphony Orch., conducted by Anthony Aibel, Symphony # 4 (orch., chorus, children's chorus) Mich. State U., L. Gregorian 2000, Lament for solo piano Carnegie Hall, 2000, Millenium Fantasy for Piano & Orch., J. Biegel, J. Cobos-Lopez, Cin. Symphony, 2000, Lament for Cello & Piano, Met. Mus., N.Y.C., 2000, Partita for Violin & String Orch., Carnegie Hall, 2001, One Nation, 2002, Openings for Orch., 2002 JoAnn Falletta Va. Symphony, Clarinet Concerto, D. Shifrin, Chamber Music Soc. of Lincoln Ctr., Buffalo Philharm, 2002, Episodes for Violin & Piano, Itzhak Perlman, 2003, Quartet for Oboe & Strings, Saratoga Festival, 2004, Rituals for 5 Percussionists and Orchestra, Iris Orchestra, Nexus, 2004, LUVN BLM, Calif. Ear Unit, 2005, Naxos Am. Classics, Violin Concerto and Rituals, M.Stern, Frank, 2005; New World Records: Music By Ellen Taaffe Zwilich; N.Y. Philharm. conducted by Zubin Mehta. Bd. dir. Copland Fund. Recipient Elizabeth Sprague Coolidge Chamber Music prize, 1974, Gold medal, G.B. Viotti, Vercelli, Italy, 1975, citation, Ernst von Dohnanyi, 1981, Pulitzer prize for music, 1983, Composers award, Lancaster Symphony Orch., Arturo Toscanini Music Critics award, 1987, Alfred I. DuPont award, 1991, Performing Arts award, Miami Ctr. Performing Arts, 2000, named, Musical Am. Composer of Yr., 1999, Key to the City Cinn., 2001; named Martha Baird Rockefeller Fund rec. grantee, 1977, 1979, 1982, Guggenheim fellow, 1981; named to, Fla. Artists Hall of Fame, 1994. Fellow: Am. Acad. Arts & Sci.; mem.: AAAL (Acad. award 1984), Guggenheim Found. (bd. dirs.), MacDowell Colony (bd. dirs.), Am. Fedn. Musicians (hon.; life), BMI Found. (bd. dirs.), Am. Music Ctr. (v.p. 1982—84, bd. dirs.). Office: Coll Music Fla State Univ Tallahassee FL 32306-1180 Office Phone: 850-644-4744. Office Fax: 850-644-2033.

ZWINGE, RANDALL JAMES HAMILTON See RANDI, JAMES

Professional Index

AGRICULTURE

UNITED STATES

ALABAMA

Auburn University
Mosjidis, Jorge *agricultural studies educator, researcher*

Tuskegee Institute
Hill, Walter A. *agricultural sciences and chemistry educator, researcher, chemistry educator, researcher*

ARKANSAS

Fayetteville
Kellogg, David Wayne *agricultural studies educator, researcher*

KENTUCKY

Midway
Clay, Robert N. *thoroughbred breeder*

TEXAS

College Station
Christiansen, James Edward *agricultural educator*
Gan, Jianbang *agricultural studies educator, economist*
Murano, Elsa A. *agricultural studies educator, former academic administrator*

Industry
Huitt, Jimmie L. *rancher, oil and gas industry executive, real estate developer*

Ingram
Hughes, David Michael *rancher*

ADDRESS UNPUBLISHED

Stimpert, Michael Alan *retired agricultural products company executive*

ARCHITECTURE & DESIGN

UNITED STATES

ALABAMA

Auburn
Millman, Richard George *architect, educator*

ARKANSAS

Little Rock
Burruss, Terry Gene *architect*
Truemper, John James, Jr. *retired architect*

FLORIDA

Atlantic Beach
Morgan, William Newton *architect, educator*

Daytona Beach
Amick, William Walker *golf course architect*

Fort Lauderdale
Coolman, C. Douglas *landscape architectural firm executive*

Fort Myers
Sappenfield, Charles Madison *architect, educator*
Trudnak, Stephen Joseph *landscape architect*

Miami
Feito, Jose *architect*
Hampton, Mark Garrison *architect*
Shulman, Allan T. *architect, architectural firm*

Naples
Bradley, Charles MacArthur *retired architect*
Lewis, Gordon Gilmer *golf course architect*

Lickhalter, Merlin *architect, consultant*

Palm Beach
Smith, Jeffery W. *architect*

Pensacola
Bullock, Ellis Way, Jr. *architect*
Torgersen, Torwald Harold *architect, consultant*
Woolf, Kenneth Howard *architect*

Plant City
Burns, Arthur Lee *architect*

Saint Petersburg
Ginn, Ronn *architect, environmental planner, general contractor*
Wedding, Charles Randolph *architect*

Tallahassee
Lewis, Tom E., Jr. *architect, architectural firm executive*

Tampa
Howey, John Richard *architect, writer*
Jennewein, James Joseph *architect*

West Palm Beach
Marshall, Elizabeth Libby *landscape architect*
Ross, Edward Joseph *architect*

GEORGIA

Atlanta
Bainbridge, Frederick Freeman III *architect*
Diedrich, Richard Joseph *architect*
Elam, Merrill L. *architectural firm executive*
Harrison, Philip *architect*
Hatch, Helen Davis *architect*
Pulgram, William Leopold *architect, space designer*
Scogin, Mack *architect, educator*
Sizemore, Michael Maynard *architectural firm executive*

Augusta
Woodhurst, Robert Stanford, Jr. *architect*

Decatur
Mc Intosh, James Eugene, Jr. *interior designer*

Macon
Dunwody, Eugene Cox *architect*

Norcross
Greene, Don Howard *product designer*

Savannah
Engle, Reed Laurence *landscape architect*
Johnson, Eric *architect, former state legislator*

Valdosta
McCall, John Clark, Jr. *interior designer, writer, theatre organist*

KENTUCKY

Lexington
Co, Angela *architect, educator*
Romanowitz, Byron Foster *architect, engineer*

LOUISIANA

New Orleans
Bookhardt, Fred Barringer, Jr. *architect*
Klingman, John Philip *architect, educator*
Steinmetz, Deborah Susan *interior designer*

MISSISSIPPI

Biloxi
Zocchi, Louis Joseph *product designer, game company executive*

NORTH CAROLINA

Asheville
Latta, Diana Lennox *retired interior designer*

Black Mountain
Martin, Edward Curtis, Jr. *landscape architect, educator*

Chapel Hill
Dixon, Frederick Dail *architect*
Godschalk, David Robinson *architect, urban development planner, educator*

Charlotte
Huberman, Jeffrey Allen *architect*

Raleigh
Clarke, Lewis James *landscape architect*

Flournoy, William Louis, Jr. *retired landscape architect*
Malecha, Marvin John *architect, academic administrator*

OKLAHOMA

Norman
Henderson, Arnold Glenn *architect, educator*

Tulsa
Broach, David E. *architectural firm executive*

SOUTH CAROLINA

Clemson
Barker, Jim (James Frazier Barker) *architecture educator, retired academic administrator*
Halfacre, Robert Gordon *ombudsman, landscape architect, horticulturist, educator*

Greenville
Hultstrand, Charles John *architect*

TENNESSEE

Chattanooga
Derthick, Alan Wendell *architect, firm executive*

Knoxville
Poole, Scott *architect, educator*

Nashville
Swensson, Earl Simcox *architect*

TEXAS

Arlington
Ferrier, Richard Brooks *architect, educator*

Austin
Aloisin, Anthony *architect, art historian, writer, educator, artist*
Lawrence, Mell *architect*

Bellaire
Lundy, Victor Alfred *architect, educator*

College Station
Shepley, Mardelle McCuskey *architect, educator*
Woodcock, David Geoffrey *architect, educator*

Dallas
Landry, Jane Lorenz *architect*
Stacy, Dennis William *architect*

Fort Worth
Wright, C(arroll) Lee, Jr. *architecture educator*

Houston
Bair, Royden Stanley *retired architect*
Blackstone, W. C. *architectural firm executive*
Farrell, John Marshall *architect*
Lerup, Lars G. *architecture educator, dean*
Stubbs, William W. *interior designer*

Irving
Rees, Frank William, Jr. *architect*

San Antonio
Munoz, Henry R. III *architectural firm executive*

VIRGINIA

Alexandria
Gurney, Robert M. *architectural firm executive*
Vosbeck, William Frederick, Jr. *architect*

Arlington
Hellmuth, George William *architect*
Tarpgaard, Peter Thorvald *naval architect*

Blacksburg
Rodriguez-Camilloni, Humberto Leonardo *architect, historian, educator*

Charlottesville
Beatley, Timothy *architecture educator*
Bednar, Michael John *architecture educator*
McDonough, William Andrews *architect, former dean*
Root, James Benjamin *landscape architect*
Swofford, Donald Anthony *architect*

Falls Church
Barkley, Paul Haley, Jr. *architect*

Fredericksburg
Weselin, Mary Lou *interior designer*

Reston
Scheeler, James Arthur *architect*

Richmond
Joel, William Lee, II, *interior and lighting designer*

Staunton
Mortensen, Robert Henry *landscape and golf course architect*

Woodbridge
Peck, Dianne Kawecki *architect*

WEST VIRGINIA

Summit Point
Taylor, Harold Allen, Jr. *industrial minerals consultant*

ADDRESS UNPUBLISHED

Bull, Frank James *retired architect*
Cross, Eason, Jr. *architect*
Gantz, Carroll Melvin *industrial design consultant, consumer product designer*
Gui, James Edmund *architect*
McGee, Humphrey Glenn *retired architect*
Mc Ginty, John Milton *architect, consultant*
Mumma, Albert Girard, Jr. *architect*
Muncey, James Arthur, Jr. *architect*
Murray, David George *retired architect*
Ward, George Truman *architect*

ARTS: LITERARY See also COMMUNICATIONS MEDIA

UNITED STATES

ALABAMA

Mobile
Ward, Jesmyn *writer, educator*

CALIFORNIA

San Francisco
Garner, Douglas Russell *scientific & medical analyst, writer, editor*

FLORIDA

Beverly Hills
Bilir, Ali F. *poet*

Boca Raton
Keyes, Daniel *author*

Bradenton
Blanchard, Leonard Albert *writer, consultant, educator*

Cape Coral
Hopkins, Lee Bennett *writer, educator*

Gainesville
Leavitt, David Adam *writer, English educator*

Jacksonville
Moses, Daniel *writer, singer*

Miami
Alperin, Stanley I. *writer, editor, consultant*

Palm Coast
Dandy, Roscoe Greer *author, psychotherapist, educator, retired public health service analyst*

Panama City
Schafer, John Stephen *poet*

Sarasota
Stevens, Elisabeth Goss (Mrs. Robert Schleussner Jr.) *writer, graphic artist*
Weeks, Albert Loren *writer, educator, journalist*

Tallahassee
Butler, Robert Olen *writer, educator*
Fielding, Raymond Edwin *writer, communications educator*

Tampa
Jones, Franklin Ross *writer, educator*

West Palm Beach
Passy, Charles *writer*

GEORGIA

Atlanta
Rushdie, Sir Salman (Ahmed Salman Rushdie) *writer, educator*
Trethewey, Natasha *poet, literature educator*

Marietta
Aebersold, Carol *writer*

Savannah
Coffey, Thomas Francis, Jr. *retired writer*

ILLINOIS

Oak Lawn
Laird, Jean Elouise Rydeski (Mrs. Jack E. Laird) *author, adult education educator*

KENTUCKY

Lexington
Finney, Nikky *poet, educator*

LOUISIANA

Baton Rouge
Owen, Sue Ann *retired poet*

Lafayette
Gaines, Ernest James *writer*

New Orleans
Dunbar, Leslie Wallace *writer, consultant*
Pizer, Donald *author, educator*

MINNESOTA

Stillwater
Cardozo, Arlene Rossen *writer*

MISSISSIPPI

University
Ford, Richard *writer*

NEW YORK

Bronxville
Conroy, Pat (Donald Patrick Conroy) *writer*

Catskill
Philp, Richard Nilson *writer, editor, journalist, historian*

New York
Card, Orson Scott *writer*
Grisham, John Ray, Jr. *writer*
Leamer, Laurence Allen *writer*

NORTH CAROLINA

Bostic
Hooper, Kay *writer*

Chapel Hill
Wallace, Daniel *writer*

Charlotte
Finley, Glenna *writer*

Cullowhee
Rash, Ron Vincent *writer, educator*

Greensboro
Watson, Robert Winthrop *poet*

Winston Salem
Ehle, John Marsden, Jr. *writer*

OKLAHOMA

Oklahoma City
Carr, Robyn *writer*
Macomber, Debbie *writer*

Pawhuska
Drummond, Ree (Ann Marie Drummond) *writer, television personality, photographer, food writer*

RHODE ISLAND

Charlestown
Huetteman, Susan Ann Bice *writer, reviewer*

SOUTH CAROLINA

Fort Mill
Bristow, Robert O'Neil *writer, educator*

TENNESSEE

Brentwood
Bolton, Martha O. *writer*

Kingsport
Kiss, Mary Catherine Clement *writer*

Knoxville
Thomas, Joyce Carol *author, educator*

Nashville
López, Lorraine M. *writer, literature and language professor*

Sevierville
Koff, Shirley Irene *writer*

TEXAS

Amarillo
Mojtabai, Ann Grace *author, educator*

Arlington
Brown, Sandra Lynn *writer*

Austin
Young, Donald Allen *writer, consultant*

Boerne
Price, John Randolph *writer*

Cedar Hill
Stowers, Carlton Eugene *writer*

Dallas
Phillips, Betty Lou (Elizabeth Louise Phillips) *writer, interior designer*

Houston
Cronin, Justin *writer, English professor*
Mallia, Marianne *medical writer*
Plunkett, Jack William *writer, publisher*
Sarwar, Sehba *writer*
Sidhwa, Bapsi *writer*

VIRGINIA

Alexandria
Wallace, Barbara Brooks *writer*

Arlington
Timperlake, Edward Thomas *writer*

Blacksburg
Falco, Edward *writer, English educator*

Bristol
Cooper, Carlotta Arlene *writer, animal breeder*

Charlottesville
Casey, John Dudley *writer, language educator*
Dove, Rita Frances *poet, language educator*
Eisenberg, Deborah *writer*
Wright, Charles Penzel, Jr. *writer, educator*

Falls Church
Orben, Robert *writer*
Whitehead, Kenneth Dean *writer, translator, retired federal agency administrator, editor*

Lexington
Stuart, Dabney *poet, language educator*

Meadowview
Kingsolver, Barbara Ellen *writer*

Reston
Smith, Ralph Lee *writer, musician*

Williamsburg
McLennan, Barbara Nancy *writer, historic site interpreter, tax specialist*

ADDRESS UNPUBLISHED

Bartlett, Bruce Reeves *writer*
Bonura, Larry Samuel *writer*
Bova, Benjamin William *writer, editor*
Danticat, Edwidge *writer, educator*
Desjardins, Daniel D. *poet, composer, translator, playwright*
Friedman, Kinky (Richard S. Friedman) *writer, musician*
Griffith, W.E.B. (William Edmund Butterworth III) *writer*
Hairston, William *author, poet, playwright, former actor*
Haldeman, Joe William *writer*
Horsman, David A. Elliott *writer, finance company executive, educator*
Lee, Harper (Nelle Harper Lee) *writer*
Madden, David *author*
Meltzer, Brad *writer*
Moore, Robert Henry *writer, editor, communications consultant*
Murphy, Randall Kent *writer, educator, consultant*
North, Marjorie Mary *writer*
Nova, Craig *writer*
Oliver, Mary *poet*
Perrin, Robert *writer, consultant*
Polsgrove, Carol Claxon *writer, retired communications educator*
Portis, Charles McColl *writer*
Powell, Alma Johnson *writer, advocate, foundation administrator*
Siddons, Anne Rivers *writer*
Viets, Elaine Frances *writer*
Vosevich, Kathi Ann *writer, editor*

Wilkinson, Claude Henry *writer, artist, English literature educator*

ARTS: PERFORMING

UNITED STATES

ALABAMA

Birmingham
Sanchez, Fabian *dancer*

Huntsville
Kruja, Mira *concert pianist, presenter, professor, clinician*

Mobile
Guerra, Juan Luis *musician*

ARKANSAS

Fort Smith
Bailey, Donald Keith *music educator, composer, musician*

Rogers
Soderquist, Donald G. *entertainment company executive*

Siloam Springs
Wubbena, Jan Helmut *music professor*

CALIFORNIA

Culver City
Kaufman, Richard Stuart *conductor*

Los Angeles
Ashforth, Alden *composer, educator*
Underwood, Carrie Marie *singer*

San Francisco
Gockley, David (Richard David Gockley) *opera company director*

West Hollywood
Campbell, Glen *musician*

FLORIDA

Bushnell
Cobb, Terri Reamer (Ceci Cobb) *film and video producer*

Coral Gables
Sandoval, Arturo *jazz musician*

Cutler Bay
Catanzaro, Tony *dancer*

Fort Lauderdale
LeRoy, Miss Joy *model, apparel designer*
Randi, James (Randall James Hamilton Zwinge) *magician, educator*

Fort Pierce
Norton, Robert Howard *entertainer, writer, music arranger*

Gainesville
Jaeger, Ina Claire *music educator, violinist*

Miami
Juanes, (Juan Esteban Aristizábal Vásquez) *musician*
Kahn, Jack Merrill *television producer*

Miami Beach
Lopez, Lourdes *performing company executive, choreographer*
Minaj, Nicki (Onika Tanya Maraj) *rap artist*
Rosenhaus, Drew *professional sports agent*

Naples
Chang, Marian S. *filmmaker, composer*
White, Roy Bernard *performing arts association administrator*

Orange Park
Walsh, James Anthony (Tony Walsh) *theater and film educator*

Orlando
Rosene, Paul Earl *music educator*

Palm Harbor
Katzen-Guthrie, Joy *performance artist, engineering executive*

Pembroke Pines
Gibbons, Leeza Kim *television and radio talk show host, writer, journalist*

Sarasota
Faron, Sally Rogers *performing arts association administrator, consultant*
McCollum, John Morris *tenor*

Stuart
Amos, Tori *musician, singer, composer*

Tallahassee
Corzine, Jennifer Jean *music educator*

Delp, Roy Edward *music educator, singer*
Madsen, Clifford Kimball *music educator, therapist*
Zwilich, Ellen Taaffe *composer*

Tampa
Hankenson, E(dward) Craig, Jr. *performing arts executive*
Moore, Janet L.S. *music educator, dean*

West Palm Beach
Hale, Marie Stoner *performing company executive*
Uzan, Bernard *artistic director*

GEORGIA

Athens
Buck, Peter *musician*
Mills, Mike *musician*

Atlanta
Harris, Clifford Joseph, Jr., (T.I., Tip Harris) *rap artist*
Jacobus, Arthur *performing company executive*
McFall, John *performing company executive*
O'Brien, Conan *talk show host, writer*
Pink, (Alecia Beth Moore) *singer*
Ray, Amy *vocalist, guitarist*
Saliers, Emily *singer, musician*
Spano, Robert *conductor, music director*
Tullis, Bill *sound recording engineer, music company executive*
Usher, (Usher Terrence Raymond, IV) *singer, actor*
Wallace, Peter Marsden *radio personality and producer, commentator, writer*

Columbus
Smith, Roland C. *movie theatre company executive, former food service company executive*

Duluth
Moss, Shad Gregory (Bow Wow, Lil' Bow Wow) *rap artist, actor*

East Point
Bridgewater, Herbert Jeremiah, Jr. *radio personality*

Roswell
Ludacris, (Christopher Brian Bridges) *musician, actor*

Saint Simons Island
Cedel, Melinda Irene *music educator, violinist*

Sandy Springs
Richardson, Rey, Jr. *dancer*

Savannah
Deen, Paula H. *television personality, restaurant owner, chef*

KENTUCKY

Frankfort
Fletcher, Winona Lee *retired theater educator*

Louisville
Lin, Stephen Houng Tze *music educator*
Tofteland, Curt L. *producer, director*

LOUISIANA

Baton Rouge
Buchmann, Molly O'Banion *choreographer, educator*
Mathews, Sharon Walker *performing company executive, secondary school educator*
McCoy, Wesley Lawrence *musician, educator, conductor*

New Orleans
Blanchard, Terence *musician, composer*
Hebert, Bobby Joseph, Jr. *radio personality, retired professional football player*

NEW YORK

Ithaca
Husa, Karel *composer, conductor, educator*

New York
Milsap, Ronnie *singer*
White, Jack (John Anthony Gillis) *guitarist, singer, record label owner*

NORTH CAROLINA

Chapel Hill
Moeser, James Charles *music educator, former academic administrator*
Neff, Severine *music educator*

Charlotte
Bonnefoux, Jean-Pierre *choreographer, dancer*

Cullowhee
Beam, Richard Squires *theater educator*

Durham
Jang, Na Ra *singer*

Greensboro
Hammond, David Alan *stage director, educator*
Middleton, Herman David, Sr. *retired theater educator*

Salisbury
Hagy, David Lee *conductor*

Todd
Cole, Susan Stockbridge *retired theater educator*

Wake Forest
Johnson, Ben Sigel *music educator*

Winston Salem
Holmes, Anna-Marie *ballerina*

OKLAHOMA

Ada
Shelton, Blake Tolison *musician*

Lawton
Klein, Scott Richard *acting and directing educator*

Oklahoma City
Jackson, Wanda Lavonne *country western musician*
Schimek, John Bradley *music educator, musician*

Tulsa
Angelini, Marcello *performing company executive*
Womack, Lee Ann *country musician*

SOUTH CAROLINA

Charleston
Cantwell, Don *artistic director*
Ungrangsee, Bundit *conductor*

Columbia
Nakahara, Morihiko *conductor*

Edisto Island
Van Metre, Margaret Cheryl *performing company executive, dancer, educator*

Hilton Head Island
Brock, Karena Diane *dancer, educator*

Lexington
Robinson, Raymond Edwin *conductor, music educator, writer*

Simpsonville
Selvy, Barbara *dance instructor*

TENNESSEE

Brentwood
Winans, BeBe (Benjamin Winans) *gospel and R&B vocalist*
Winans, CeCe *gospel vocalist*

Charlotte
Lambert, Miranda Leigh *musician*

Clarksville
Gotcher, Sara Elizabeth *theater educator*

Cordova
Pugh, Dorothy Gunther *performing company executive*

Goodlettsville
Haggard, Merle Ronald *musician*
Tyminski, Dan *musician*

Hendersonville
Rogers, Kenny (Kenneth Donald Rogers) *entertainer, recording artist*
Skaggs, Ricky *musician*

Hurricane Mills
Lynn, Loretta Webb *singer*

Johnson City
Jenrette, Thomas Shepard, Jr. *music educator, choral director*

Knoxville
De Laria, Donald A. *theatre company executive*
Westerling, Richard (Dick) *movie theater company executive*

Lawrenceburg
Hayes, Sylvia Richmond *music educator*

Memphis
Green, Al *soul and gospel singer*
Presley, Lisa Marie *singer*

Nashville
Adams, Ryan (David Ryan Adams) *musician*
Adkins, Trace (Tracy Darrell Adkins) *musician*
Aldean, Jason (Jason Aldean Williams) *musician*
Atkins, Rodney *musician*
Bentley, Dierks *singer*
Bice, Bo (Harold Elwin "Bo" Bice Jr.) *singer, musician*
Brice, Lee *singer*
Brooks, Garth (Troyal Garth Brooks) *musician*
Brooks, Kix (Leon Eric Brooks) *musician*
Bryan, Luke (Thomas Luther Bryan) *musician*
Caillat, Colbie Marie *singer*
Chesney, Kenny *musician*
Church, Eric (Kenneth Eric Church) *musician*
Clarkson, Kelly Brianne *singer, songwriter*
Douglas, Jerry *bluegrass musician, dobro player*
Dunn, Ronnie Gene *musician*
Fairchild, Karen *singer*
Foglesong, James Staton (Jim) *music educator*
Gentry, Judy Fenton *choreographer, educator*
Gill, Vince *country musician, singer*
Harris, Emmylou *singer*
Haywood, Dave *musician*
Hubbard, Tyler *musician*
Ingram, Jack *musician*
Jackson, Alan *musician*

Judd, Wynonna Ellen (Christina Claire Ciminella) *musician*
Keith, Toby (Toby Keith Covel) *musician, producer*
Kelley, Brian *musician*
Kelley, Charles *singer, musician*
Kesha, (Kesha Rose Sebert) *singer*
Krauss, Alison *country musician*
Kwami, Paul T. *musical director and educator*
Mayer, John *musician*
McAnally, Mac (Lyman Corbitt McAnally Jr.) *musician*
McBride, Martina *singer*
McCreery, Scott Cooke (Scotty McCreery) *singer*
McEntire, Reba Nell *musician, actress*
McGraw, Tim *musician, actor*
Midler, Bette *singer, actress*
Moore, Justin Cole *musician*
Moore, Sam *singer*
Musgraves, Kacey Lee *musician*
Owen, Randy Yeuell *country musician, cattle rancher*
Paisley, Brad *musician*
Perry, Kimberly *musician*
Perry, Neil *musician*
Perry, Reid *musician*
Pickler, Kellie Dawn *singer*
Rich, John *musician, songwriter*
Robison, Emily Burns *musician*
Rucker, Darius *musician*
Schlapman, Kimberly Roads *singer*
Scott, Hillary *singer*
Sheik, Duncan *singer, songwriter*
Sweet, Phillip *singer*
Swift, Taylor *singer, songwriter*
Taylor, Nicole Renée (Niki Taylor) *model, shop owner*
Thompson, Keifer *musician*
Thompson, Shawna *singer*
Tritt, Travis *musician*
Twain, Shania (Eilleen Regina Edwards) *singer, musician*
Urban, Keith *musician*
Valentine, Alan Darrell *performing company executive, conductor*
Warren, Jerry Lee *conductor, educator*
Westbrook, Jimi *singer*
Williams, Don R. *singer, songwriter*
Yoakam, Dwight *musician*

Pigeon Forge
Parton, Dolly *singer, composer, actress*

TEXAS

Aubrey
Pizzamiglio, Albert Theodore (Al Pierson) *conductor*

Austin
Antokoletz, Elliott Maxim *music educator*
Holmes, Michael *performing arts company executive, educator*
Kurkul, Wen Wang *musician, educator, administrator*
Mills, Stephen *performing company executive*
Robbins, Mary *concert pianist, mozart specialist*
Young, Phyllis Casselman *music educator*

Borger
Allen, Bessie Malvina *music educator, organist*

Dallas
Cerny, Keith *performing arts association administrator*
Dederich-Pejovich, Susan *musician, educator*
Franklin, Kirk *singer*
Holcomb, Stephen Norris *music educator*
Horchow, S. Roger *theater producer*
Joyner, Tom *radio personality*
Palmer, Larry Garland *music educator, writer, musician*
Pell, Jonathan Laurence *performing company executive*
Sargon, Simon A. *composer, music educator*
van Zweden, Jaap *conductor, music director*

El Paso
Gladstein, Mimi Reisel *theater and literature educator*

Fort Worth
Crawford, Julie *nonprofit arts administrator*
Stevenson, Ben *performing company executive*

Houston
Ballas, Mark, Jr. *dancer*
Brown, Glenda Ann Walters *ballet director*
Fiese, Richard Kelly *music educator*
Gladden, Dean Robert *arts administrator, educator, consultant*
Graf, Hans *conductor, music director*
Hough, Derek *dancer, choreographer, musician, actor*
Knowles, Beyoncé Giselle *singer, actress*
Knowles, Solange *singer, model*
Krajewski, Michael *conductor*
Norris, Chuck (Carlos Ray Norris) *actor*
Snyder, John L. *music educator*
Welch, Stanton *performing company executive*

Pasadena
Gilley, Mickey Leroy *musician*

Plano
Warner, Timothy C. *movie theater company executive*

Round Rock
Ruiz, Brian Patrick *former radio producer*

San Antonio
Oppenheim, Martha Kunkel *pianist, educator*
Strait, George *musician*

Wichita Falls
Henschel, Donald Francis, Jr. *theater educator, artist, designer*

VIRGINIA

Alexandria
Whitmire, Mark Alexander *music educator, conductor*

Arlington
Hamilton, Anthony *singer*
Schaeffer, Eric D. *theater director, performing company executive*

Fairfax
Hudson, William L. *conductor*
Loveless, Patty (Patty Ramey) *country music singer*
Miller, Patricia A. *music educator, opera and concert artist*

Harrisonburg
Arthur, Thomas Hahn *theater educator, director*

Leesburg
Kutner, Lawrence Alan *executive director*
Levin, Mark Reed *radio personality, legal foundation administrator*

Lexington
Rader, Angela Nichole *music educator*

Richmond
Winslett, Stoner *artistic director*

Staunton
Balsley, Philip Elwood *entertainer*

Virginia Beach
Dixon, John Spencer *performing arts association administrator*

Williamsburg
Gavaler, Joan Susan *dance educator, choreographer, performer*

Winchester
Aiosa, Charlotte Nelson *music educator*

WEST VIRGINIA

Charleston
Cooper, Grant *composer, conductor, educator*

Inwood
Rizzetta, Carolyn Teresa *sound recording entrepreneur*

Salem
Raad, Virginia *pianist, educator*

TERRITORIES OF THE UNITED STATES

PUERTO RICO

Santurce
Residante, El (René Pérez) *singer, composer*
Visitante, El (Eduardo Cabra) *singer, musician*

VIRGIN ISLANDS

Kingshill
Bryson, Valrica *music educator*

ADDRESS UNPUBLISHED

Aiken, Clay (Clayton Holmes Aiken) *singer*
Asman, Bub (Henry B. Asman) *sound editor*
Bays, Yvonne Mary Erbe *music educator, marketing specialist, guidance counselor*
Bencini, Sara Haltiwanger *concert pianist*
Boehle, William Randall *music educator emeritus*
Borkowski, Francis Thomas *music educator*
Christopher, Russell Lewis *baritone*
Cooper, Judith Kase *retired theater educator, playwright*
Costa, Mary *soprano*
Feek, Joey Martin *singer*
Feek, Rory Lee *musician, songwriter*
Flannery, James William *performing arts educator, scholar, theater director and producer, singer*
Galt, John William *actor, writer*
Gordon, Marjorie *lyric-coloratura soprano, opera producer, educator*
Graves, Lorraine Elizabeth *dancer, educator, coach*
Herson, Arlene *television host producer, journalist, television personality, radio commentator*
Heuer, Robert Maynard, II, *retired opera company executive*
Hodges, Ann *retired television editor, columnist*
Jackson, Barbara Ann Garvey *music educator, publisher*
Kaskinen, Barbara Kay *composer, musician, educator*
Kavanaugh, Frank James *film producer, educator*
Klein, Stephen Thomas *performing arts executive*
Lebon, Rachel L. *musician, educator*
Maguire, Martie (Martha Elenor Erwin Maguire) *musician*
Marcy, Kevin Michael *film producer, lawyer*
Marks, Bruce *performing company executive, choreographer*
Moffatt, Joyce Anne *performing company executive*
Morelan, Paula Kay *choreographer*
Newton, Wayne (Carson Wayne Newton) *entertainer, actor, recording industry executive*
Olenchak, Frank Richard *retired music educator, musician*
Ostrow, Stuart *theatrical producer, educator, author*

Prince, Anna Lou *composer, music publisher, construction executive*
Scarwid, Diana Elizabeth *actress*
Smith, Charlotte Reed *retired music educator*
Sorrell, Rozlyn *singer, actress, theater director, educator*
Stanley, Margaret King *performing arts administrator, educator, designer*
Suzuki, Hidetaro *violinist*
Topham, Shari *theater producer, director*
Trythall, Harry Gilbert *music educator, composer*
Upbin, Shari *theater producer, director*
Virkhaus, Taavo *symphony orchestra conductor*
Wagoner, Geraldine Vander Pol *music educator*
Wallis, Quvenzhané *actress*
Willingham, Jeanne Maggart *retired performing company executive, educator*
Wilson, Gretchen *musician*
Wood, Vivian Poates *retired mezzo soprano, writer, educator*

ARTS: VISUAL

UNITED STATES

ALABAMA

Huntsville
Benzle, Curtis Munhall *artist, educator*

Montevallo
Stephens, Scott *art educator*

Tuscaloosa
Hopkins, Martha Ann Markline *artist*

ARKANSAS

Dover
Royal, Rey *apparel designer*

Little Rock
Martin, Floyd W. *art educator*

DISTRICT OF COLUMBIA

Washington
DiPerna, Frank Paul *photographer, educator*

FLORIDA

Cape Coral
Hunsperger, Elizabeth Jane *educator*

Clearwater
Slade, Roy *artist, college president, museum director*

Fort Myers
Schwartz, Carl Edward *artist, printmaker*

Hobe Sound
Upright, Diane Warner *art dealer*

Hollywood
Sadowski, Carol Johnson *artist*

Key Largo
Fundora, Thomas *art director, artist*

Lake Mary
Bachmann, Bill *photographer*

Miami
Bannard, Walter Darby *artist, critic*
Dignac, Geny (Eugenia M. Bermudez) *sculptor*
Farrell, Patrick *photographer, photojournalist*
Steinbaum, Bernice *art dealer*

Naples
Eldridge, David Carlton *art and antique appraiser*
Hebald, Milton Elting *sculptor*
York, Tina *painter*

Osprey
Gross, Marilyn Agnes *artist, audiologist, small business owner*

Sarasota
Lengyel, Alfonz *art history, archeology and museology educator*

Tallahassee
Zollar, Jawole Willa Jo *artist, choreographer*

Tampa
de Lama, Alberto *artist*
Kashdin, Gladys Shafran *painter, educator, volunteer*

GEORGIA

Albany
Ferrell, Lee *artist*

Athens
Herbert, James Arthur *retired art educator, artist, filmmaker*
Kaufman, Glen Frank *retired art educator*
Olsen, Richard James *artist, educator*
Paul, William Dewitt, Jr., (Bill Paul) *retired art educator, collector, artist*

Cumming
Pirkle, George Emory *photographer, instructional media producer*

Villa Rica
McKibbin, William Alex *artist*

KENTUCKY

Lexington
Sandoval, Arturo Alonzo *artist, educator*

LOUISIANA

Folsom
Golden, Rolland Harve *artist*

New Orleans
Thornell, Jack Randolph *photographer*

MARYLAND

Columbia
Blackwell-Taifel, Camellia Ann *art educator, consultant*

MISSISSIPPI

Meridian
Marshall, John Steven *artist, educator, museum administrator*

NORTH CAROLINA

Asheville
Tynes, Robert Dick *artist, educator*

Chapel Hill
Grabowski, Beth *artist, educator*
Lowman, Robert Paul *photographer, small business owner, retired academic administrator*

Cullowhee
Fariello, M. Anna *art educator, project manager, curatorial consultant, museum director*

Davidson
Grosch, Laura Dudley *artist, educator*

Lexington
Frontz, Leslie Kay *art educator*

Pittsboro
Kachergis, Joyce W. *book designer*

Winston Salem
Faccinto, Victor Paul *artist, director*
Tilford, Joseph P. *scenic and lighting designer, educator*

Zebulon
Ruffing, Anne Elizabeth *artist*

OHIO

Gahanna
Kobeck, Jo Karen *artist, writer*

OKLAHOMA

Tishomingo
Coulter, Lisa June *art educator*

PENNSYLVANIA

Stroudsburg
Wallin, Leland Dean *artist, educator*

SOUTH CAROLINA

Camden
Blackwell, Patton *artist*

Columbia
Elkins, Toni Marcus *artist, association administrator*

TENNESSEE

Chattanooga
Mills, Olan, II, *photography company executive*

TEXAS

Austin
Garriott, Richard Allen *game software designer*
Hatgil, Paul Peter *artist, sculptor, educator*
Smith, Jeffrey Chipps *art educator*

College Station
Martin, Carol Jacquelyn *artist, educator*

Denton
Gough, Georgia Belle *art educator*

Houston
Kagle, Joseph Louis, Jr. *artist, administrator, historian*
Reid, Katherine Louise *artist, educator, writer*

Stockholder, Jessica *sculptor*
von Hagge, Robert *design company executive*

Huntsville
Lea, Stanley E. *artist, educator*

Plano
Cotter-Smith, Cathleen Marie *artist, educator*

VERMONT

Charlotte
Robinson, Sally Winston *artist*

VIRGINIA

Arlington
Dunlap, William *artist, critic, educator*

Charlottesville
Everson, Kevin Jerome *artist, filmmaker, educator*

Clifton
Hennesy, Gerald Craft *artist*

Fredericksburg
Schmutzhart, Berthold Josef *sculptor, educator*

Henrico
Kevorkian, Richard *artist*

Mc Lean
Kohelet, Gregory *painter*
Safer, John *sculptor*
Useinov, Vyacheslav (Yuri Useinov) *painter*

Mclean
Puchkovsky, Vladimir *painter*

Norfolk
Nicholson, Myreen Moore *artist, researcher*

Williamsburg
Coleman, Henry Edwin *artist, educator*

Woodbridge
Gallick, Rosemary *art educator*

WEST VIRGINIA

Wheeling
Peace, Bernie Kinzel *art educator, artist*

ADDRESS UNPUBLISHED

Gordon, Lonny Joseph *artist, educator, dean*
Han, Nong *artist, sculptor, painter*
Huffington, Anita *sculptor*
Lee, Catherine *sculptor, painter*
Manuella, Frank *retired art and design educator*
Marks, Roberta Barbara *artist, educator*
Mayer, Susan Martin *art educator*
Rivo, Shirley Winthrope *artist*
Roberts, Marilyn Gottlieb *artist, educator*
Rogers, James Gordon, Jr. *retired art educator*
Rush, Julia Ann Halloran (Mrs. Richard Henry Rush) *artist, writer*
Saks, Judith-Ann *artist*
Sennema, David Carl *arts consultant*
Whitener, Carolyn Raye *artist*

ASSOCIATIONS AND ORGANIZATIONS *See also specific fields*

UNITED STATES

ALABAMA

Birmingham
Armistead, William Cole, Jr. *political organization administrator*
Carroll, Philip Joseph, Jr. *board member*
Carter, Frances Tunnell (Fran Carter) *fraternal organization administrator*
Farmer, Phillip W. *board member*
Franklin, H. Allen *retired board member*

Dothan
Biggs, Jeffery Ladon *social welfare administrator*

Montgomery
Worley, Nancy L. *political organization administrator*

ARKANSAS

Bentonville
Bartlett, Dan (Daniel Joseph Bartlett) *lobbyist, former federal official*

Fayetteville
Malone, David Roy *public fund consultant retired educational association administrator, director*

Little Rock
Insalaco, Vincent *political organization administrator*
Webb, Doyle L. *political organization administrator, former state legislator*

CALIFORNIA

Corona
Weiss, Fred Geoffrey *board member*

CONNECTICUT

Danbury
Edwards, James D. *board member*

DISTRICT OF COLUMBIA

Washington
Boaz, David Douglas *foundation executive*
Conner, Chuck (Charles F. Conner) *trade association administrator, former federal agency administrator*
Davis, Lance Alan *foundation administrator, research and development executive, metallurgical engineer*
Evans, Donald Louis *think-tank executive, former United States Secretary of Commerce*
Everett, Ralph Bernard *think-tank executive*
Feulner, Edwin John, Jr. *retired think-tank executive*
Finkle, Jeffrey Alan *professional association executive*
Gibson, Thomas James *professional society executive, former naval architect*
Hills, John Merrill *educational association administrator, consultant, public relations executive, researcher*
Hofmeister, John D. *not-for-profit organization executive, retired oil industry executive*
Kolb, Charles Chester *foundation administrator*
Marvel, Kevin Boyd *professional society administrator, astronomer*
McElveen-Hunter, Bonnie *international relief organization executive*
Rademaker, Stephen Geoffrey *lobbyist, former federal agency administrator*
Santora, Kathleen Curry *lobbyist, lawyer*
Saunders, Harold Henry *foundation administrator*
Simmons, Kyle *lobbyist, former legislative staff member*

FLORIDA

Boca Raton
Leary, William James *educational association administrator, educator*

Bonita Springs
Cooperman, Saul *retired educational administrator*

Bradenton
Bloch, Ralph Jay *professional association executive, marketing consultant*

Coral Springs
Burg, Ralph *art association executive*

Delray Beach
Stewart, Patricia Carry *foundation administrator*

Fort Lauderdale
Calhoun, Peggy Joan *fundraising executive*
Crowley, William C. *board member, investment company executive*
Ivey, Susan M. *corporate board member, retired tobacco company executive*
Stone, Roger Jason, Jr. *political consultant*

Fort Myers
Ball, Armand Baer *former association executive, consultant*

Jacksonville
Curry, Leonard B. *political organization administrator, management consultant*

Jacksonville Beach
Soderberg, Nancy *foundation administrator, former ambassador*

Miami
Arison, Marilyn Barbara (Lin Arison) *art foundation executive*
Elwes, Timothy *board member*
Fontanals-Cisneros, Ella *art association administrator, information systems specialist*
Ibarguen, Alberto *foundation administrator, former publishing executive*

Naples
Mayberry, William Eugene *retired foundation administrator, board member*

Okeechobee
Bishop, Sid Glenwood *union official*

Orlando
Murray, Robert J. *retired board member*

Palm Beach
Daly, Charles Ulick *foundation executive*
Elson, Suzanne Goodman *social services administrator*

Ponte Vedra Beach
Slayton, Gus *foundation administrator*

Port Orange
Collyer, Robert B. *retired trade association administrator*

Saint Petersburg
Fulp, James Alan *board member, finance company executive, securities firm executive*

Sarasota
Devonshire, David W. *board member*
Johnson, Robert D. *board member*

Prezzano, Wilbur John *board member*

Sebring
Maire, Barbara Jean *volunteer*

Tallahassee
Stipanovich, John McKager (Mac Stipanovich) *lobbyist, lawyer*
Tant, Allison (Allison Tant Richard) *political organization administrator*
Turnbull, Marjorie Reitz *educational consultant, state legislator*

Tampa
Weaver, Paul E. *board member*

Tarpon Springs
Callan, Joseph Patrick *social service administrator*

GEORGIA

Atlanta
Bankoff, Joseph R. *art center president*
Codina, Armando M. *board member*
Copenhaver, John Barns *not-for-profit executive, lawyer*
Dotson, Albert *not-for-profit fundraiser*
Gayle, Helene Doris *humanitarian organization administrator, pediatrician*
Hardin, P. Russell *foundation administrator*
Hardman, Laura Jones *volunteer, board member*
Kidd, Jane V. *former political organization administrator, state legislator*
Levato, Joseph Anthony *board member*
McTier, Charles Harvey *former foundation administrator*
Miller, Joseph (Buzz) *lobbyist, nuclear energy industry executive*
Padgett, John *political organization administrator*
Porter, Dubose *political organization administrator, former state legislator*
Wylly, Barbara Bentley *volunteer*

Augusta
Knox, Wyck Austin, Jr. *board member, lawyer*

Buford
Martin, Jenny Beth *political organization worker, consultant*

Decatur
Goldstein, Barry David *educational association administrator, pharmacology educator*
Higgins, Bradford Robert *humanitarian organization executive, former federal agency administrator*

Fayetteville
De Revere, David Wilsen *retired professional society administrator*

Marietta
Kelly, William Watkins *retired educational foundation executive*

Peachtree City
Nix, Kemie Richards *educational association administrator, editor*

Saint Simons Island
Bell, Ronald Mack *university foundation administrator, consultant*

KENTUCKY

Bowling Green
Algeo, John Thomas *association executive, retired educator*

Corbin
Barton-Collings, Nelda Ann *retired political organization worker, bank executive, entrepreneur*

Florence
Durbin, Dean D. *educational association administrator*

Frankfort
Logsdon, Daniel *political organization administrator*
Robertson, Steve *political organization administrator*
Williams, Ellen C. *lobbyist, political organization worker*

Lexington
Hardymon, James Franklin *board member*
Simon, Lisa *travel association executive*

Louisville
Early, Jack Jones *foundation executive*

Paducah
Ryan, Heather A. *former not-for-profit company executive*

LOUISIANA

Baton Rouge
Capps, Thomas E. *board member*
Davis, Carol *educational association administrator, educator*
Villere, Roger Francis, Jr. *political organization administrator*

New Orleans
Sullivan, Daniel Edmond *fundraising executive*

MICHIGAN

Dearborn
Ojakli, Ziad S. *lobbyist, automotive executive*

MISSISSIPPI

Jackson
Cole, Rickey L. *political organization administrator*
Hiatt, Jane Crater *arts agency administrator*
Nosef, Joseph D. III *political organization administrator, lawyer*
Risley, Rod Alan *educational association administrator*

NEW YORK

New York
Wolff, Candida Perotti (Candi Wolff) *lobbyist, former federal official*

Stony Brook
Brandwein, Ruth Ann *social welfare educator, professor, dean emeritus, social services administrator, writer*

NORTH CAROLINA

Asheville
Dickens, Charles Henderson *advocate, retired social sciences educator*
Miller, Tyson *environmental advocate*

Cary
Bryant, Mynora Joyce *not-for-profit fundraiser*
Martin, William Royall, Jr. *retired technical society administrator*

Chapel Hill
Krasno, Richard Michael *foundation executive, educator*
Morgan, G. Kenneth *association executive*

Charlotte
Anderson, Kerrii B. *board member, former food service executive*
Bohn, Robert G. *board member, retired manufacturing executive*
Burton, E. James *board member, business school dean*
Cochrane, Eugene W., Jr. *foundation administrator*
Locke, Elizabeth Hughes *retired foundation administrator*
Shaw, Minor Mickel *board member, investment company executive*
Sheubrooks, Muriel W. *board member, gas industry executive, retired real estate company executive*
Warden, William C., Jr. *board member*
Wilson-McElreath, Vicki W. (Vicki W. McElreath) *board member, retired accountant*

Greensboron
McCollough, W. Alan *retired board member*

Raleigh
Allen, Barbara Kirkman *political organization administrator*
Holding, Frank B., Jr. *board member, bank executive*
Pope, Claude E., Jr. *political organization administrator*
Voller, Randy *political organization administrator*
Whalen, Andrew P. *political organization administrator, former legislative staff member*

Wilson
McCain, Betty Landon Ray *retired political party and state official*

OHIO

Cleveland
Blackburn, Richard Wallace *retired board member, lawyer*

OKLAHOMA

Binger
Goodman, Todd *former political organization administrator*

Norman
Mooneyham, Bobby R. *educational association administrator*

Oklahoma City
Collins, Wallace *political organization administrator, former state legislator*
Jones, Gary *former political organization administrator*
Pinnell, Matt *political organization worker*
Weston, J. David (Dave Weston) *political organization administrator*

Tulsa
Hinshaw, Juanita H. *board member*
Schusterman, Lynn *foundation administrator*
White, Randall Wayne *educational association administrator*

SOUTH CAROLINA

Columbia
Harrison, Jaime R. *political organization administrator, communications executive*
Moore, Matt *political organization administrator*
Sherrer, John M. III *cultural organization administrator*

Greenville
Grainger, Michael J. *board member*

Hartsville
Mullin, John Hatchman III *board member*
Whiddon, Thomas E. *board member*

Hilton Head Island
Ostergard, Paul Michael *retired foundation executive*

Lancaster
Bundy, Charles Alan *retired foundation executive*

Orangeburg
Johnson, I.S. Leevy *social services administrator*

Woodruff
Childers, Bob Eugene *educational association executive*

TENNESSEE

Athens
Brown, Sandra Lee *art association administrator, consultant, artist*

Brentwood
Adams, John C., Jr. *board member*

Chattanooga
Caulfield, E. Michael *board member*
Godwin, Pamela June *board member, investment company executive*
Goldsberry, Ronald E. *board member*
Smith, Robin *former political organization administrator*

Goodlettsville
Brophy, Stephen Jeremiah *lobbyist, former legislative staff member*

Hollow Rock
Coffman, Michael S. *international organization official, ecologist*

Knoxville
Froula, James DeWayne *honor society administrator*
Taylor, Jackie A. *educational association administrator*

Memphis
Stevens, David D. *board member*

Nashville
Benson, Edwin Welburn, Jr. *retired trade association executive*
Devaney, Chris *political organization administrator*
Faris, Jack *association executive*
Henderson, Milton Arnold *professional society administrator*
Herron, Roy Brasfield *political organization administrator, former state legislator*
Woodson, Jamie *educational association administrator, former state legislator*

TEXAS

Austin
Barr, Ronald E. *educational association administrator*
Dougherty, Molly Ireland *organization executive*
Hinojosa, Gilberto *political organization administrator*
Mackowiak, Matthew *lobbyist, former legislative staff member*
Mountain, Janet M. *foundation administrator, former computer company executive*
Munisteri, Stephen P. *political organization administrator, lawyer*
Qunell, Kerri Wynn *educational association administrator*

College Station
Davis, Eddie Joe *foundation administrator*

Corpus Christi
Steinhart, Ronald G. *board member, retired bank executive*

Dallas
Best, Rhys John *board member*
Brinker, Nancy Goodman *foundation administrator, former ambassador*
Cockerham, Sidney Joe *professional society administrator*
Cregg, Roger A. *board member, retired construction executive*
Echols, Leldon E. *board member*
Evans, Linda Perryman *foundation administrator*
Haddock, Ronald Wayne *board member*
Lane, John Rodger *art association administrator, retired museum director*
Loeffler, Nancy B. *volunteer, board member*
Martinez Tucker, Sara (Sara Alicia Tucker) *educational initiative administrator, former federal agency administrator*
McLaren, Brian D. *advocate, writer*
Mulford, Clay (Ross Clayton Mulford) *think-tank executive, lawyer*
O'Donnell, Peter, Jr. *foundation administrator*
Piergallini, Alfred A. *board member*
Salerno, Judith Alyce *foundation administrator, former health science association administrator*

Fredericksburg
Hagee, Michael W. *foundation administrator, retired military officer*

Houston
Adams, John Lewis *board member, retired transportation executive*
Bischoff, Susan Ann *foundation executive*
Faulkner, Larry Ray *foundation administrator, retired academic administrator*
Kramek, Robert E. *board member*
Williams, Jody *political organization administrator*

Irving
Birch, Glynn R. *non-profit organization administrator*

Liberty Hill
Lujan, Manuel, Jr. *think-tank executive, former United States Secretary of the Interior*

Mc Kinney
Daley, Tom *not-for-profit foundation executive*
Newton, Lloyd Warren *board member*

Plano
Roberts, Leonard H. *board member*
Sanders, Wayne R. *board member, retired paper products manufacturing executive*

San Antonio
Brown, Stephen H. *lobbyist*
Burzik, Catherine M. *corporate board member, retired medical products executive*
Choate, Jerry D. *retired board member*
Cisneros, Mary Alice P. *not-for-profit executive, former councilwoman*
Crichton, Flora Cameron *volunteer, foundation administrator*
McKone, Timothy P. *lobbyist, telecommunications industry executive*
Robinson, David Maurice *philanthropist, retired professional basketball player*

Seguin
Tillman, Mary Norman *urban affairs consultant*

Spring
Bartlow, Gene Steven *professional society executive, retired military officer*

The Woodlands
Jorden, Yon Yoon *board member*

VIRGINIA

Afton
Rhett, Haskell Emery Smith *educational association administrator*

Alexandria
Anderson, Steven C. *pharmacy association executive*
Bailey, Paul *lobbyist*
Baker, Brent Harold *foundation executive, blogger*
Bartels, Teresa Hall *non-profit organization administrator*
Castellanos, Alex (Alejandro Castellanos) *lobbyist, media consultant*
Chu, David S.C. *think-tank executive, former federal agency administrator*
Connaughton, Sean Thomas *lobbyist, former federal agency administrator*
Connelly, Gail *educational association administrator*
Davis, Margaret Bergan *foundation administrator*
Foster, Serrin Marie *non-profit organization executive*
Gallagher, Brian A. *foundation administrator*
Hirt, Jim (James R. Hirt) *professional society administrator*
Jacobson, Lawrence Albert *professional society administrator, lawyer*
Kratovil, Jane Lindley *think tank associate, not-for-profit developer*
Kruse, Dennis K. *professional society administrator, retired military officer*
Lachance, Janice Rachel *professional association and federal agency administrator, lawyer*
Lenz, Edward Arnold *trade association administrator, lawyer*
Rabun, John Brewton, Jr. *criminal justice agency administrator*
Roberts, William A. *relief organization administrator*
Ryan, John D. *not-for-profit organization administrator*

Arlington
Ashcroft, John David *lobbyist, law educator, former United States Attorney General*
Berger, Dan (Brian Daniel Berger) *lobbyist*
Blakey, Marion Clifton *aerospace association executive, former federal agency administrator*
Emerson, Jo Ann H. *electric power association executive, former United States Representative from Missouri*
Fulgham, Alonzo L. *not-for-profit organization administrator*
Fulton, Michael (C. Michael Fulton) *lobbyist*
Futrell, John William *environmental agency executive, lawyer*
Herbst, Robert LeRoy *organization executive*
Huband, Frank Louis *corporate officer, general counsel, electrical engineer, lawyer*
Hughes, Bill *lobbyist, former legislative staff member*
Kaplan, Robert N. *foundation administrator*
Langworthy, Everett Walter *professional society administrator, natural gas exploration company executive*
Little, Caroline H. *trade association administrator*
Maehara, Paulette V. *fundraising executive*
Meltsner, Jim *lobbyist*
O'Day, Paul Thomas *trade association executive*
Roy, Manik *lobbyist*
Shapiro, Gary Joel *trade association administrator*
Stanton, Michael J. *lobbyist*
Welburn, Brenda Lilienthal *educational association administrator*
Work, Jane Magruder *retired professional society administrator*

Ashburn
Do Canto, Licy M. *lobbyist*

Baskerville
Boyd, John Wesley, Jr. *trade association administrator, farmer*

Blacksburg
Nowak, Jerzy *educational association administrator, horticulture professor, director*

Boston
Fisher, John Morris *association official, business executive, educator*

Chantilly
Zirkle, William Vernon *not-for-profit consultant*

Charlottesville
Handler, Richard *educational association administrator, anthropologist*
Jordan, Daniel Porter, Jr. *foundation administrator, historian, educator*

Chincoteague Island
Chagnon, Lucille Tessier *owner, literacy acceleration consultant*

Fairfax
Cox, Chris W. *lobbyist*
Hollans, Irby Noah, Jr. *retired trade association administrator*
LaPierre, Wayne R., Jr. *advocacy group executive*
Porter, Jim (James W. Porter II) *advocacy group executive, lawyer*
Robinson, Kayne B. *lobbyist, former political organization officer*

Falls Church
Chavez, Linda *think-tank executive, author, columnist*
David, Ruth A. *public service research institute executive*
Harper, Diane *lobbyist*

Flint Hill
Dietel, William Moore *former foundation executive*

Garrisonville
Emely, Charles Harry *trade association executive, consultant*

Gloucester
James, Kay Coles *think-tank executive, former federal agency administrator*

Herndon
Adcock, Samuel Denton *lobbyist, former legislative director*
Kilberg, Bobbie Greene *trade association administrator*
Wilbur, Kirby Allen *foundation administrator, former political organization administrator*

Lake Ridge
Rector, John Michael *pharmaceutical association executive, lawyer*

Leesburg
De Barbieri, Mary Ann *not-for-profit management consultant*

Louisa
Small, William Edwin, Jr. *association and recreation executive*

Mc Lean
Hillen, John Francis *think-tank executive, former federal agency administrator*
Rose, Mitch (Mitchell Franklin Rose) *lobbyist*
Schubert, Richard Francis *social services administrator, consultant*

Middleburg
Sodolski, John *retired professional society administrator*

Norfolk
Bowyer, E. Carlton *board member*
Magee, Kathleen S. *foundation executive*
Newkirk, Ingrid *animal rights organization administrator*

Orange
Sass, Arthur Harold *educational training administrator*

Reston
Brennan, Norma Jean *retired professional society administrator*
Gates, James David *retired professional society administrator*
Natale, Patrick J. *professional society administrator*
Reeve, Deborah B. *art association administrator, educator*
Terracciano, Anthony Patrick *board member, consumer products company executive, finance company executive*
Winter, William L. *retired professional society administrator*
Yang, Kichoon *educational association administrator, mathematics educator*

Richmond
Carlock, Margo *museum association administrator*
Mullins, Pat *political organization administrator, insurance company executive*
Sterling, Anne D. *not-for-profit developer*

Springfield
Larson, Reed Eugene *foundation administrator*

Triangle
Roberts, Cecil Edward, Jr. *labor union administrator*

Virginia Beach
Fullwood, Emerson U. *board member*

Williamsburg
Campbell, Colin Goetze *foundation president*

WEST VIRGINIA

Charleston
Lucas, Conrad G., II, *political organization administrator*

Puccio, Larry *political organization administrator*

TERRITORIES OF THE UNITED STATES

PUERTO RICO

Aguadilla
Méndez, Carlos (Don Carlos Méndez Martínez) *political organization administrator, mayor*

Hato Rey
de Las Heras, Gonzalo *board member, banker*

San Juan
Prats Palerm, Roberto L. *political organization administrator*

VIRGIN ISLANDS

Christiansted
Canegata, John Michael *political organization administrator*

St Croix
Benjamin, Cecil *political organization administrator*

ADDRESS UNPUBLISHED

Archey, William T. *retired trade association administrator*
Ayers, Nick (James Nicholas Ayers) *political organization executive*
Beals, Loren Alan *association executive*
Berger, Joyce Muriel *foundation administrator, writer, editor*
Breakiron-Evans, Maureen *corporate board member, accountant*
Brim, Orville Gilbert, Jr. *former foundation administrator, writer*
Burki, Fred Albert *labor union official*
Butcher, Harry William *workplace learning development executive, educator, writer, teacher*
Carter, Henry Moore, Jr. *retired foundation executive*
Carter, Hodding, III, (William) *educator, retired foundation executive, retired journalist, commentator and public official*
Chattman, Raymond Christopher *association executive*
Dawson, Katon Edwards *former political organization administrator*
Drennen, William Miller, Jr. *cultural organization administrator, film producer, writer*
Duncan, Mike (Robert Michael Duncan) *political organization administrator*
Elsenhans, Lynn Laverty *corporate board member, former oil industry executive*
Fields, Jan (Janice Lynn Fields) *corporate board member, retired food service executive*
Fiorina, Carly (Cara Carleton Sneed Fiorina) *not-for-profit executive, former computer company executive*
Glasgow, Agnes Jackie *social welfare administrator, therapist*
Glassick, Charles Etzweiler *foundation administrator*
Hager, John Henry *former lieutenant governor and homeland security director, former federal agency administrator*
Harlow, Larry (Bryce Larimore Harlow) *lobbyist, former federal official*
Harrison, John Raymond *foundation administrator, retired publishing executive*
Helm, DeWitt Frederick, Jr. *professional society administrator, consultant*
Henry, Janice K. *corporate board member, retired construction materials company executive*
Hohlt, Richard Frederick *lobbyist*
Kruesi, Frank Eugene *lobbyist, former government executive*
Krull, Michael *political consultant*
Kussrow, Nancy Esther *educational association administrator*
Lancaster, Sally Rhodus *retired non-profit executive, consultant*
Ledwig, Donald Eugene *election official, association executive, retired broadcast executive, military officer*
Lenhart, Cynthia Rae *conservation organization executive*
Lincoln, Blanche Lambert *lobbyist, former United States Senator from Arkansas*
Lorch, George A. *corporate board member, retired manufacturing executive*
Lyles, Lester Lawrence *corporate board member, retired military officer*
Malek, Marlene Anne *foundation administrator*
McEntee, Gerald W. (Gerry McEntee) *retired labor union administrator*
McWethy, Patricia Joan *educational association administrator*
Mulva, James Joseph (Jim Mulva) *corporate board member, retired oil industry executive*
Munro, Donald William, Jr. *non-profit organization executive*
Nelson, David Daniel *lobbyist, former ambassador*
O'Connor, Doris Julia *not-for-profit fundraiser, consultant*
Pascoe, B. Lynn (Burton Lynn Pascoe) *former international organization official, former ambassador*
Peiser, Robert Alan *board member*
Rathke, Wade (Stephen Wade Rathke) *social services administrator*
Roberson, James O. *foundation executive*
Sampson, Robert Neil *professional society administrator, consultant*
Sanford, Jenny (Jennifer Sullivan Sanford) *not-for-profit fundraiser, former investment banker*
Stearns, Stewart Warren *charitable association executive*
Steele, Charles, Jr. *retired civil rights association executive, former state legislator*
Steinhauser, Brendan Michael *political campaign administrator*
Sutton, Johnny Keane *lobbyist, former prosecutor*
Thurman, Karen L. *lobbyist, former United States Representative from Florida*
Transou, Lynda Lou *advertising art administrator*
Walton, Alice Louise *philanthropist, art collector*
Warner, Kris *political organization administrator*

ATHLETICS

UNITED STATES

ALABAMA

Auburn
Barbee, Tony *men's college basketball coach*
Housel, David *emeritus athletic director*
Malzahn, Gus (Arthur Gustav Malzahn) *college football coach*

Birmingham
Slive, Michael Lawrence *sports association executive, lawyer*

Graysville
Weissman, Tillian Faye *professional soccer player*

Montgomery
Hester, Hortense *retired physical education educator*

Tuscaloosa
Grant, Anthony *men's college basketball coach*
Kiffin, Lane *college football coach*
Saban, Nick (Nicholas Lou Saban) *college football coach, former professional football coach*

ARKANSAS

Fayetteville
Anderson, Mike *men's college basketball coach*
Bielema, Bret Arnold *college football coach*
Collen, Tom *women's college basketball coach*

Hot Springs
Pelton, Elois Bleidt *retired physical education educator*

DISTRICT OF COLUMBIA

Washington
Backstrom, Nicklas (Lars Nicklas Backstrom) *professional hockey player*
Green, Mike *professional hockey player*
Ovechkin, Alexander *professional hockey player*

FLORIDA

Boca Raton
Jarvis, Mike *men's college basketball coach*
Roddick, Andy Stephen *retired professional tennis player*

Coral Gables
Golden, Al *college football coach*

Coral Springs
Erlich, Jonathan Dario *professional tennis player*
Ram, Andy *professional tennis player*

Davie
Philbin, Joe (Joseph A. Philbin) *professional football coach*
Wake, Cameron (Derek Cameron Wake) *professional football player*
Wallace, Mike (Burnell Micheal Wallace) *professional football player*

Daytona Beach
Ahn, Shi Hyun *professional golfer*
Creamer, Paula *professional golfer*
Duncan, Mariano *professional baseball coach, retired professional baseball player*
Helton, Mike (Michael Gregory Helton) *sports association executive*
Jang, Jeong *professional golfer*
Kang, Jimin *professional golfer*
Kerr, Cristie *professional golfer*
Kim, In-Kyung *professional golfer*
Kim, Mi Hyun *professional golfer*
Lee, Jee Young *professional golfer*
Lee, Meena *professional golfer*
Lee, Seon-Hwa *professional golfer*
Mears, Casey *race car driver*
Miyazato, Ai *professional golfer*
Moromizato, Shinobu *professional golfer*
Pak, Se Ri *professional golfer*
Park, Hee-Jung (Gloria Park) *professional golfer*
Park, Inbee *professional golfer*
Pressel, Morgan *professional golfer*
Tseng, Yani *professional golfer*
Webb, Karrie *professional golfer*
Whan, Michael *Ladies Professional Golf Association commissioner, former apparel executive*
Whitworth, Kathrynne Ann *professional golfer*
Wie, Michelle Sung *professional golfer*

Fort Lauderdale
Williams, Ricky (Errick Lynne Williams) *retired professional football player*

Gainesville
Butler, Amanda *women's college basketball coach*
Donovan, Billy (William John) *men's college basketball coach*
Muschamp, Will *college football coach*
Roberts, Norm *men's college basketball coach*
Young, Bryant Colby *college football coach, retired professional football player*

Jacksonville
Bradley, Gus (Paul Casey Bradley) *professional football coach*
Caldwell, David *professional sports team executive*
Croom, Sylvester *professional football coach*
Lamping, Mark C. *professional sports team executive*

Jupiter
Vanatta, Bob *athletic administrator*

Lake Worth
Woods, Tiger (Eldrick Woods) *professional golfer*

Miami
Allen, Ray (Walter Ray Allen) *professional basketball player*
Battier, Shane *professional basketball player*
Beasley, Michael Paul *professional basketball player*
Bosh, Chris *professional basketball player*
Coghlan, Chris (Christopher B. Coghlan) *professional baseball player*
Conine, Jeffrey Guy *professional sports team executive, retired professional baseball player*
Dawson, Andre Nolan *professional sports team executive, retired professional baseball player*
Hill, Michael *professional sports team executive*
James, LeBron Raymone *professional basketball player*
Larranaga, Jim *men's college basketball coach*
Lewis, Rashard Quovon *professional basketball player*
Loria, Jeffrey H. *professional sports team executive*
Martinez, Tino *professional baseball coach, retired professional baseball player*
McAdoo, Bob (Robert Allen McAdoo Jr.) *professional basketball coach, retired professional basketball player*
Mourning, Alonzo *professional sports team executive, retired professional basketball player*
Oden, Greg *professional basketball player*
Perez, Tony (Atanasio Perez) *professional sports team executive, retired professional baseball player*
Pierre, Juan *professional baseball player*
Redmond, Mike *professional baseball coach, retired professional baseball player*
Riley, Patrick James *professional sports team executive*
Rothstein, Ronald *professional basketball coach*
Slice, Kimbo (Kevin Ferguson) *boxer*
Spoelstra, Erik *professional basketball coach*
Turner, Ron *college football coach*
Wade, Dwyane (Dwyane Tyrone Wade Jr.) *professional basketball player*
Woolworth, Eric S. *professional sports team executive*

Naples
Frazer, John Howard *tennis association and retired manufacturing executive*

Oldsmar
Gaston, Clarence Edwin (Cito Gaston) *retired professional baseball coach*

Orlando
Fritz, Jim *professional sports team executive*
Hennigan, Rob *professional sports team executive*
Jones, Donnie *men's college basketball coach*
Martins, Alex *professional sports team executive*
Nelson, Jameer *professional basketball player*
O'Leary, George Joseph *college football coach*
Starkey, Bob (Robert G. Starkey) *women's college basketball coach*
Turkoglu, Hedo (Hidayet) *professional basketball player*
Vaughn, Jacque *professional basketball coach*
Williams, Pat *professional sports team executive*

Palm Beach Gardens
Choi, K.J. (Kyung-ju Choi) *professional golfer*
Couples, Frederick Steven *professional golfer*
Furyk, Jim (James Michael Furyk) *professional golfer*
Leonard, Justin (Justin Charles Garret Leonard) *professional golfer*
Mickelson, Phil (Philip Alfred Mickelson Jr.) *professional golfer*
Toms, David *professional golfer*
Verplank, Scott Rachal *professional golfer*

Ponte Vedra
Hart, Dudley *professional golfer*
O'Hair, Sean *professional golfer*
Perry, Kenny (James Kenneth Perry) *professional golfer*
Pettersson, Carl *professional golfer*
Weekley, Boo (Thomas Brent Weekley) *professional golfer*

Ponte Vedra Beach
Atwal, Arjun *professional golfer*
Austin, Woody *professional golfer*
Azinger, Paul *professional golfer*
Baddeley, Aaron John *professional golfer*
Bjorkman, Jonas *professional tennis player*
Campbell, Chad *professional golfer*
Cink, Stewart *professional golfer*
Clark, Tim (Timothy Henry Clark) *professional golfer*
Crane, Benjamin McCully *professional golfer*
Day, Jason *professional golfer*
Djokovic, Novak *professional tennis player*
Donald, Luke *professional golfer*
Ferrer, David *professional tennis player*
Finchem, Tim *PGA Tour commissioner, lawyer*
Fowler, Rickie *professional golfer*
Garcia, Sergio *professional golfer*
Ginepri, Robby (Robert Louis Ginepri) *professional tennis player*
Glover, Lucas Hendley *professional golfer*
González, Fernando Francisco *professional tennis player*
Granollers, Marcel *professional tennis player*
Johnson, Zach (Zachary Harris Johnson) *professional golfer*
Kim, Anthony *professional golfer*
Knowles, Mark *professional tennis player*
Kubot, Lukasz *professional tennis player*
Mahan, Hunter *professional golfer*
Marach, Oliver *professional tennis player*
Melzer, Jurgen *professional tennis player*
Mirnyi, Max *professional tennis player*
Montgomerie, Colin Stuart *professional golfer*
Moore, Ryan *professional golfer*
Nalbandian, David *professional tennis player*
Nestor, Daniel Mark *professional tennis player*
Overton, Jeffrey Laurence *professional golfer*
Paes, Leander *professional tennis player*
Querrey, Sam *professional tennis player*
Sabbatini, Rory *professional golfer*
Singh, Vijay *professional golfer*
Snedeker, Brandt *professional golfer*
Soderling, Robin *professional tennis player*
Stricker, Steve *professional golfer*
Tsonga, Jo-Wilfried *professional tennis player*
Van Pelt, Bo *professional golfer*
Verdasco, Fernando *professional tennis player*
Villegas, Camilo *professional golfer*
Wallenby, Robert *professional golfer*
Watson, Bubba (Gerry Lester Watson Jr.) *professional golfer*
Weir, Mike *professional golfer*
Wi, Charlie *professional golfer*
Yang, Y.E. (Yong-Eun Yang) *professional golfer*
Youzhny, Mikhail *professional tennis player*
Zink, Charlie *sports association executive*

Saint Petersburg
Allaster, Stacey *sports association executive*
Alstott, Michael Joseph (Mike Alstott) *high school football coach, retired professional football player*
Azarenka, Victoria *professional tennis player*
Bell, Heath Justin *professional baseball player*
Dementieva, Elena Vyacheslavovna (Yelena Dementyeva) *professional tennis player*
Friedman, Andrew *professional sports team executive*
Huber, Liezel *professional tennis player*
Jankovic, Jelena *professional tennis player*
King, Vania *professional tennis player*
Kuznetsova, Svetlana *professional tennis player*
Longoria, Evan Michael *professional baseball player*
Maddon, Joe (Joseph John Maddon) *professional baseball manager*
Pennetta, Flavia *professional tennis player*
Price, David Taylor *professional baseball player*
Raymond, Lisa *professional tennis player*
Safina, Dinara Mikhailovna *professional tennis player*
Sharapova, Maria *professional tennis player*
Shvedova, Yaroslava *professional tennis player*
Silverman, Matthew *professional sports team executive*
Stephens, Sloane *professional tennis player*
Sternberg, Stuart L. *professional sports team executive, retired finance company executive*
Stosur, Samantha *professional tennis player*
Wozniacki, Caroline *professional tennis player*

Sunrise
Campbell, Brian Wesley *professional hockey player*
Huberdeau, Jonathan *professional hockey player*
Jovanovski, Ed *professional hockey player*
Luongo, Roberto *professional hockey player*
Ramsay, Craig *professional hockey coach, retired professional hockey player*
Stillman, Cory *professional hockey player*
Tallon, Dale *professional sports team executive, former professional hockey player*
Theodore, Jose *professional hockey player*
Yormark, Michael *professional sports team executive*

Tallahassee
Fisher, Jimbo (John James Fisher) *college football coach*
Hamilton, Leonard *men's college basketball coach*
Semrau, Sue *women's college basketball coach*
Winston, Jameis *student athlete*

Tampa
Byner, Earnest Alexander *professional football coach, retired professional football player*
Callahan, Ryan *professional hockey player*
Campbell, Ron *professional sports team executive*
Carle, Matt *professional hockey player*
Commodore, Mike *professional hockey player*
Cooper, Jon *professional hockey coach*
Cox, Bryan Keith *professional football coach*
Davis, Butch (Paul Hilton Davis) *former college football coach*
Filppula, Valtteri *professional hockey player*
Frazier, Leslie *professional football coach, retired professional football player*
Glazer, Malcolm *professional sports team owner*
Heath, Stan *men's college basketball coach*
Hedman, Victor (Victor Erik Olof Hedman) *professional hockey player*
Jackson, Vincent *professional football player*
Kurvers, Tom (Thomas James Kurvers) *professional sports team executive, former professional hockey player*
Messick, Andrew *sports association executive*
Roloson, Dwayne *professional hockey player*
Smith, Lovie *professional football coach*
Stamkos, Steven *professional hockey player*
Tedford, Jeff (Jeffrey R. Tedford) *professional football coach, former college football coach*
Wannstedt, David Raymond *professional football coach, former college football coach*
Yzerman, Steve (Stephen Gregory Yzerman) *professional sports team executive, retired professional hockey player*

Vero Beach
Fish, Mardy *professional tennis player*

West Palm Beach
Floyd, Raymond Loran professional golfer
Massimino, Roland V. (Rollie Massimino) men's college basketball coach

GEORGIA

Athens
Fox, Mark men's college basketball coach

Atlanta
Aaron, Hank (Henry Louis Aaron) professional sports team executive, retired professional baseball player, entrepreneur
Brand, Elton Tyron professional basketball player
Budenholzer, Mike professional basketball coach
Butcher, Richard O., II, sports association administrator, former legislative staff member
Curry, Bill (William Alexander Curry) college football coach, retired professional football player
Dimitroff, Thomas G., Jr. professional sports team executive
Enstrom, Tobias professional hockey player
Ferry, Danny professional sports team executive, retired professional basketball player
Gonzalez, Fredi Jesus professional baseball manager
Gregory, Brian men's college basketball coach
Horford Reynoso, Alfred Joel (Al Horford) professional basketball player
Hudson, Tim professional baseball player
Johnson, Paul college football coach
Jurrjens, Jair F. professional baseball player
Kuchar, Matt G. professional golfer
McCoughtry, Angel professional basketball player
Meadors, Marynell professional basketball coach
Mutombo, Dikembe (Dikembe Mutombo Mpolondo Mukamba Jean Jacque Wamutombo) retired professional basketball player
Pendleton, Terry Lee professional baseball coach, retired professional baseball player
Pioli, Scott professional sports team executive
Sund, Rick (Richard W. Sund) professional sports team executive
Tosca, Carlos professional baseball coach
Upton, B.J. (Melvin Emanuel Upton) professional baseball player
Upton, Justin Irvin professional baseball player
Wilkins, Dominique (Jacques Dominique Wilkins) professional sports team executive, retired professional basketball player
Williams, Bob professional sports team executive
Wren, Frank professional baseball team executive

Augusta
Payne, Billy Porter (William Porter Payne) golf course and tournament executive

Flowery Branch
Blank, Arthur M. professional sports team executive, retired retail executive
Jackson, Steven Rashad professional football player
Koetter, Dirk J. professional football coach
McKay, Richard James professional sports team executive
Nolan, Mike professional football coach
Ryan, Matt (Matthew Thomas Ryan) professional football player
Scelfo, Chris professional football coach
Smith, Mike professional football coach
Turner, Michael professional football player
Umenyiora, Osi professional football player
White, Roddy (Sharod Lamor White) professional football player

Kennesaw
Dooley, Vincent Joseph college athletics administrator, retired college football coach

ILLINOIS

Chicago
Bowman, Scotty (William Scott Bowman) professional sports team executive, retired professional hockey coach

KENTUCKY

Bowling Green
Harper, Ray men's college basketball coach

Lexington
Calipari, John Vincent men's college basketball coach
Stoops, Mark college football coach
Strickland, Rod (Rodney Strickland) men's college basketball coach, retired professional basketball player

Louisville
Borel, Calvin H. jockey
Petrino, Bobby (Robert Patrick Petrino) college football coach
Pitino, Rick men's college basketball coach
Riggleman, Jim (James David Riggleman) professional baseball coach
Walz, Jeff (Jeffrey J. Walz) women's college basketball coach

Murray
Prohm, Steve men's college basketball coach

LOUISIANA

Baton Rouge
Caldwell, Nikki women's college basketball coach
Cameron, Cam (Malcolm G. Cameron III) college football coach
Jones, Johnny men's college basketball coach
Mainieri, Paul college baseball coach
Miles, Les (Leslie Edwin Miles) college football coach
Reeve, Thomas Gilmour physical education educator

Metairie
Ayers, Randy professional basketball coach
Benson, Tom (Thomas Benson) professional sports team owner
Benson LeBlanc, Rita professional sports team executive
Brees, Drew (Andrew Christopher Brees) professional football player
Colston, Marques professional football player
Davis, Anthony, Jr. professional basketball player
Demps, Dell professional sports team executive
Ellard, Henry Austin professional football coach, retired professional football player
Evans, Tyreke Jamir professional basketball player
Gordon, Eric professional basketball player
Ingram, Mark, Jr. professional football player
Loomis, Mickey professional sports team executive
Payton, Sean (Patrick Sean Payton) professional football coach
Ryan, Rob professional football coach
Vilma, Jonathan Polynice professional football player
Vitt, Joe professional football coach
Williams, Monty (Tavares Montgomery Williams Jr.) professional basketball coach, retired professional basketball player

Ruston
Holtz, Skip (Louis Leo Holtz Jr.) college football coach
Weatherspoon, Teresa Gaye women's college basketball coach, retired professional basketball player

MICHIGAN

Bloomfield Hills
Keselowski, Brad race car driver

MISSISSIPPI

Ellisville
Perkins, Ray college football coach, former professional football coach

Mississippi State
Mullen, Dan college football coach
Ray, Rick men's college basketball coach

University
Freeze, Hugh college football coach
Kennedy, Andy men's college basketball coach

NEW JERSEY

Newark
Robinson, Larry Clark professional hockey coach, retired professional hockey player

Somerville
Evans, Philip G. sports association executive, media consultant

NEW YORK

Brooklyn
Terry, Jason Eugene professional basketball player

NORTH CAROLINA

Chapel Hill
Fedora, Larry college football coach
Fox, Mike college baseball coach
Hatchell, Sylvia R. women's college basketball coach
Smith, Dean Edwards retired men's college basketball coach
Williams, Roy men's college basketball coach

Charlotte
Carlson, Marshall professional sports team executive
Cho, Richard professional sports team executive
Clifford, Steve professional basketball coach
Earnhardt, Dale, Jr. race car driver
Ewing, Patrick Aloysius professional basketball coach, retired professional basketball player
Gettleman, Dave professional sports team executive
Gordon, Ben professional basketball player
Gordon, Jeff race car driver
Guelli, Pete professional sports team executive
Hendrick, Joseph Riddick, III, (Rick Hendrick) race team owner
Higgins, Rod (Roderick Dwayne Higgins) professional sports team executive, retired professional basketball player
Jefferson, Al professional basketball player
Johnson, Jimmie Kenneth (James Kenneth Johnson) race car driver
Jordan, Michael Jeffrey professional sports team executive, retired professional basketball player
Kuechly, Luke August professional football player
Newton, Cam (Cameron Jerrell Newton) professional football player
Proehl, Ricky professional football coach, sports complex owner, retired professional football player
Richardson, Jerry professional sports team executive
Rivera, Ron (Ronald Eugene Rivera) professional football coach
Shula, Mike (Michael John Shula) professional football coach, former college football coach
Weiss, Robbie sports association executive
Whitfield, Fred, Jr. professional sports team executive
Williams, DeAngelo professional football player
Winters, Brian Joseph professional basketball coach

Concord
Biffle, Greg race car driver
Edwards, Carl race car driver
Franchitti, Dario race car driver
Kenseth, Matt Roy race car driver
McMurray, Jamie race car driver
Montoya, Juan Pablo professional race car driver

Durham
Capel, Jeff III men's college basketball coach
Case, Richard W. sports association executive
Cutcliffe, David college football coach
Krzyzewski, Mike (Michael William Krzyzewski) men's college basketball coach
McCallie, Joanne P. women's college basketball coach

Greensboro
Swofford, John sports association executive

Greenville
Lebo, Jeff men's college basketball coach

Huntersville
Busch, Kyle race car driver
Gibbs, Joe Jackson professional sports team executive, former professional football coach
Hamlin, Denny race car driver

Kannapolis
Newman, Ryan Joseph race car driver
Stewart, Tony (Anthony Wayne Stewart) professional race car driver

Leland
Carr, Bonnie Jean professional ice skater

Mooresville
Benson, Johnny professional race car driver
Busch, Kurt Thomas professional race car driver
Castroneves, Hélio race car driver
Earnhardt, Teresa race team owner
Johnson, Robert Louis professional sports team owner, former broadcast executive
Kahne, Kasey (Kenneth) race car driver

Raleigh
Barrasso, Tom professional hockey coach, retired professional hockey player
Boucher, Brian professional hockey player
Brind'Amour, Rod professional hockey coach, retired professional hockey player
Francis, Ron professional sports team executive, retired professional hockey player
Gottfried, Mark Fredrick men's college basketball coach
Komisarek, Mike professional hockey player
Lewis, Dave professional hockey coach, retired professional hockey player
MacLean, John professional hockey coach, retired professional hockey player
Muller, Kirk professional hockey coach, former professional hockey player
Rutherford, Jim professional sports team executive
Semin, Alexander professional hockey player
Skinner, Jeff professional hockey player
Staal, Eric professional hockey player
Staal, Jordan professional hockey player
Ward, Cam professional hockey player
Wesley, Glen retired professional hockey player
Yow, Deborah A. athletic director

Trinity
Labonte, Bobby race car driver

Welcome
Burton, Jeff Brian race car driver
Harvick, Kevin race car driver

Wilmington
Cooper-Dyke, Cynthia women's college basketball coach, retired professional basketball player
Peterson, Buzz (Robert Bower Peterson) men's college basketball coach

Winston Salem
Manning, Danny (Daniel Ricardo Manning) men's college basketball coach, retired professional basketball player

OKLAHOMA

Norman
Coale, Sherri women's college basketball coach
Kruger, Lon men's college basketball coach
Stoops, Bob college football coach
Stoops, Mike (Michael J. Stoops) college football coach

Oklahoma City
Barth, Danny professional sports team executive
Bennett, Clayton Ike professional sports team owner
Brooks, Scott William professional basketball coach
Durant, Kevin Wayne professional basketball player
Fisher, Derek Lamar professional basketball player
Ibaka, Serge (Serge Jonas Ibaka Ngobila) professional basketball player
Presti, Sam professional sports team executive
Westbrook, Russell professional basketball player

Stillwater
Ford, Travis men's college basketball coach
Gundy, Mike college football coach

Tulsa
Edwards, Teresa professional sports team executive, professional basketball coach, retired professional basketball player

SOUTH CAROLINA

Charleston
McClain, Katrina retired professional basketball player

Clemson
Brownell, Bradley Robert men's college basketball coach
Swinney, Dabo college football coach

Columbia
Martin, Frank (Francisco J. Martin) men's college basketball coach
McCray, Nikki Kesangame women's college basketball coach, former professional basketball player
McGhee, Carla Renee women's college basketball coach, retired professional basketball player
Spurrier, Steve (Steven Orr Spurrier) college football coach
Staley, Dawn Michelle women's college basketball coach, retired professional basketball player
Tanner, Ray (Donald Ray Tanner Jr.) college baseball coach

Conway
Moglia, Joseph H. college football coach, brokerage house executive

Gaffney
Spencer, Albert Franklin physical education educator

Spartanburg
Young, Mike men's college basketball coach

TENNESSEE

Johnson City
Bartow, Murray men's college basketball coach

Knoxville
Jones, Butch (Lynn Allen Jones) college football coach
Martin, Cuonzo LaMar men's college basketball coach
Serrano, Dave (David Scott Serrano) college baseball coach
Summitt, Pat (Patricia Sue Summitt) retired women's college basketball coach
Warlick, Holly women's college basketball coach

Memphis
Allen, Tony professional basketball player
Barone, Tony, Sr. professional sports team executive
Bibby, Henry (Charles Henry Bibby) professional basketball coach
Fuente, Justin college football coach
Joerger, David professional basketball coach
Pastner, Josh men's college basketball coach
Prince, Tayshaun Durell professional basketball player
Randolph, Zach professional basketball player
Stoudamire, Damon Lamon men's college basketball coach, retired professional basketball player
Wallace, Chris professional sports team executive

Nashville
Balcomb, Melanie S. women's college basketball coach
Britt, Kenny (Kenneth Lawrence Britt) professional football player
Byrd, Rick men's college basketball coach
Duckett, Rick men's college basketball coach
Fisher, Mike professional hockey player
Matthews, Bruce Rankin professional football coach, retired professional football player
Palmer, Chris professional football coach
Poile, David Robert professional sports team executive
Rinne, Pekka professional hockey player
Stallings, Kevin men's college basketball coach
Weber, Shea professional hockey player
Webster, Ruston professional sports team executive
Whisenhunt, Ken (Kenneth Moore Whisenhunt) professional football coach

TEXAS

Amarillo
Thomas, Zach Michael (Zachary Michael Thomas) retired professional football player

Arlington
Beltre, Adrian professional baseball player
Berkman, Lance professional baseball player
Cruz, Nelson Ramon professional baseball player
Daniels, Jon professional sports team executive
Darvish, Yu professional baseball player
Feliz, Neftali Antonio professional baseball player
Fernandez, Tony (Octavio Antonio Castro Fernandez) professional baseball coach, retired professional baseball player
Fielder, Prince Semien professional baseball player
Maddux, Greg (Gregory Alan Maddux) professional sports team executive, retired professional baseball player
Magadan, David Joseph professional baseball coach, retired professional baseball player
Nathan, Joe (Joseph Michael Nathan) professional baseball player
Ryan, Nolan professional baseball team executive, former professional baseball player
Soria, Joakim Agustin professional baseball player
Soto, Geovany professional baseball player
Uehara, Koji professional baseball player
Washington, Ron professional baseball manager

Austin
Barnes, Rick (Richard Dale Barnes) men's college basketball coach
Ford, Terrence Jerod (T.J. Ford) professional basketball coach, retired professional basketball player
Garrido, Augie (August Edmun Garrido Jr.) college baseball coach
Strong, Charlie (Charles R. Strong) college football coach

Beaumont
Knight, Pat (Patrick Knight) *men's college basketball coach*

College Station
Blair, Gary *women's college basketball coach*
Kennedy, Billy *men's college basketball coach*
Manziel, Johnny (Johnathan Paul Manziel) *student athlete*
Stallings, Gene (Eugene Clifton Stallings Jr.) *retired college football coach*
Sumlin, Kevin *college football coach*

Corpus Christi
Schmitt, Patricia Ann *health and physical education educator*

Dallas
Blackman, Rolando Antonio *professional sports team executive, retired professional basketball player*
Brown, Larry (Lawrence Harvey Brown) *men's college basketball coach*
Calderon, Jose *professional basketball player*
Carlisle, Rick (Richard Preston Carlisle) *professional basketball coach, retired professional basketball player*
Carter, Vince *professional basketball player*
Cole, Erik *professional hockey player*
Cuban, Mark *professional sports team owner, Internet company executive*
Dalembert, Samuel Davis *professional basketball player*
Ellis, Monta *professional basketball player*
Gonchar, Sergei *professional hockey player*
Harris, Devin Lamar *professional basketball player*
Hicks, Tom (Thomas Ollis Hicks Sr.) *professional sports team executive, real estate developer*
Horcoff, Shawn *professional hockey player*
Jones, June Sheldon III *college football coach*
Marion, Shawn *professional basketball player*
Nelson, Donnie *professional sports team executive*
Nill, James *professional sports team executive, former professional hockey player*
Nowitzki, Dirk Werner *professional basketball player*
O'Brien, Jim *professional basketball coach*
Peverley, Rich *professional hockey player*
Seguin, Tyler *professional hockey player*
Thomas, Tim *professional hockey player*
Ussery, Terdema L., II, *professional sports team executive*
Whitney, Ray *professional hockey player*

El Paso
Floyd, Tim *men's college basketball coach*

Fort Worth
Johnson, Trent *men's college basketball coach*
Patterson, Gary *college football coach*

Frisco
Benn, Jamie *professional hockey player*
Cogen, Jeffrey David *professional sports team executive*
Harris, Del William *professional sports team executive, professional basketball coach*
Jackson, Les *professional sports team executive*
Lieberman-Cline, Nancy *professional sports team executive, retired professional basketball player*
Roberts, Gary *retired professional hockey player*
Robidas, Stephane *professional hockey player*
Ruff, Lindy *professional hockey coach*
Wesley, David *professional basketball coach, retired professional basketball player*

Galveston
Foster, William Edwin (Bill Foster) *retired men's college basketball coach*

Houston
Alexander, Leslie Lee *professional sports team owner*
Bedard, Erik Joseph *professional baseball player*
Biggio, Craig (Alan) *baseball coach, retired professional baseball player*
Brown, Thaddeus B. *professional sports team executive*
Casspi, Omri *professional basketball player*
Clemens, Roger (William Roger Clemens) *retired professional baseball player*
Cushing, Brian *professional football player*
Davis, Mike *men's college basketball coach*
Dickey, James Allen *men's college basketball coach*
Donie, Scott *Olympic athlete*
Dorrell, Karl James *professional football coach, former college football coach*
Foster, Arian *professional football player*
Gardner, Pamela J. *sports association executive*
Harden, James E., Jr. *professional basketball player*
Howard, Dwight David, II, *professional basketball player*
Johnson, Andre Lamont *professional football player*
Jolibois, Marcus *professional sports team executive*
Levine, Tony *college football coach*
Lin, Jeremy Shuhao *professional basketball player*
Luhnow, Jeff *professional sports team executive*
McHale, Kevin Edward *professional basketball coach, retired professional basketball player*
McNair, Robert C. *professional sports team executive, energy executive, entrepreneur*
Morey, Daryl R. *professional sports team executive*
O'Brien, Bill *professional football coach, former college football coach*
Olajuwon, Hakeem Abdul *retired professional basketball player*
Phillips, Wade *professional football coach*
Porter, Bo (Marquis Donnell Porter) *professional baseball coach*
Postolos, George *professional sports team executive*
Sampson, Kelvin Dale *professional basketball coach, former college basketball coach*
Schaub, Matt (Matthew Rutledge Schaub) *professional football player*
Smith, Rick *professional sports team executive*
Trembley, Dave *professional baseball coach*
Watt, J.J. (Justin James Watt) *professional football player*
Williams, Greg *women's college basketball coach*

Irving
Austin, Miles J. *professional football player*
Bowlsby, Bob *sports association executive*
Callahan, Bill (William E. Callahan) *professional football coach*
Garrett, Jason Calvin *professional football coach, retired professional football player*
Jones, Jerry (Jerral Wayne Jones) *professional sports team owner*
Jones, Jerry, Jr. *professional sports team executive*
Jones, Stephen *professional sports team executive*
Linehan, Scott Thomas *professional football coach*
Marinelli, Rod *professional football coach*
Orton, Kyle *professional football player*
Romo, Tony (Antonio Ramiro Romo) *professional football player*
Witten, Jason (Christopher Jason Witten) *professional football player*

Lubbock
Kingsbury, Kliff *college football coach*
Smith, Tubby (Orlando Smith) *men's college basketball coach*

Plano
Kirkendall, Bill *professional golfer*
Liukin, Nastia *former Olympic gymnast*

San Antonio
Boylen, Jim *professional basketball coach*
Buford, R.C. *professional sports team executive*
Coker, Larry E. *college football coach*
Diaw, Boris (Boris Diaw-Riffiod) *professional basketball player*
Duncan, Tim (Timothy Theodore Duncan) *professional basketball player*
Ginobili, Manu *professional basketball player*
Holt, Peter M. *professional sports team owner, agricultural products executive*
Hughes, Dan *professional basketball coach*
Layden, Scott *professional sports team executive*
Parker, Tony (William Anthony Parker II) *professional basketball player*
Popovich, Gregg *professional basketball coach*
Pych, Rick *professional sports team executive*
Young, Sophia Yvonne *professional basketball player*

Temple
McLane, Drayton, Jr. *former professional sports team executive*

Waco
Briles, Art (Arthur Ray Briles) *college football coach*
Drew, Scott *men's college basketball coach*
Mulkey, Kim *women's college basketball coach*
Teaff, Grant *sports association administrator*

VIRGINIA

Ashburn
Fletcher, London Levi *professional football player*
Griffin, Robert Lee III *professional football player*
Grossman, Rex *professional football player*
Gruden, Jay *professional football coach*
Hall, DeAngelo *professional football player*
Haslett, Jim (James Donald Haslett) *professional football coach*
Jackson, DeSean William *professional football player*
Morris, Raheem *professional football coach*
Moss, Santana Terrell *professional football player*
Smith, A.J. (Albert J. Smith) *professional sports team executive*
Snyder, Daniel *professional sports team owner*

Blacksburg
Beamer, Frank *college football coach*
Williams, Brent (Buzz Williams) *men's college basketball coach*

Charlottesville
Bennett, Tony (Anthony G. Bennett) *men's college basketball coach*
Boyle, Joanne *women's college basketball coach*
London, Mike *college football coach*
O'Connor, Brian *college baseball coach*

Fairfax
Hewitt, Paul Harrington *men's college basketball coach*

Lynchburg
Gill, Turner *college football coach*

Mc Lean
Hewitt, Lleyton Glynn *professional tennis player*

Norfolk
Jones, Jeffrey Allen (Jeff Jones) *men's college basketball coach*

Richmond
Smart, Shaka *men's college basketball coach*

Sterling
Green, Darrell *retired professional football player*

The Plains
O'Connor, Karen Lende *Olympic athlete, sports association administrator*

Virginia Beach
Schottenheimer, Marty (Martin Edward Scottenheimer) *professional football coach*

WEST VIRGINIA

Morgantown
Holgorsen, Dana *college football coach*
Hostetler, Jeff (William Jeffrey Hostetler) *high school football coach, retired professional football player*
Huggins, Bob *college basketball coach*

ADDRESS UNPUBLISHED

Ames, Stephen Michael *professional golfer*
Bowden, Bobby (Robert Cleckler Bowden) *retired college football coach*
Curtis, Joyce Mae *retired physical education educator*
Dawson, Carroll R. *retired professional sports team executive*
DePaoli, Lou *former professional sports team executive*
Freeman, David Scott *professional sports team executive, venture capitalist, lawyer*
Hart, James Warren *retired athletic administrator, professional football player*
Hurney, Marty (Martin Russell Hurney) *former professional sports team executive*
Jackson, Stephen Jesse *professional basketball player*
Kavalek, Lubomir *chess expert*
McPhee, George *former professional sports team executive*
Namath, Joe (Joseph William Namath) *retired professional football player*
Ochoa, Lorena *retired professional golfer*
Robredo, Tommy *professional tennis player*
Rutherford, John Sherman, III, (Johnny Rutherford) *retired professional race car driver*
Sanders, Barry *retired professional football player*
Tortorella, John *former professional hockey coach*
Williams, Gregg E. *former professional football coach*
Wilson, Ronald Lawrence *former professional hockey coach, retired professional hockey player*

BUSINESS *See* FINANCE: INDUSTRY

COMMUNICATIONS *See* COMMUNICATIONS MEDIA; INDUSTRY: SERVICE

UNITED STATES

NORTH CAROLINA

Cary
Gruskin, James *marketing services company executive*

COMMUNICATIONS MEDIA *See also* ARTS: LITERARY

UNITED STATES

ALABAMA

Birmingham
Blackledge, Brett J. *reporter*
Griffin, Eleanor *publishing executive*
Hanson, Victor Henry, II, *newspaper publisher*
Kennedy, Joe David, Jr., (Joey Kennedy) *editor*
Scarritt, Thomas Varnon *newspaper editor*
Schumann, Greg *publishing executive*
Seitz, Karl Raymond *editor*
Siddall, Pamela K. *publishing executive*

Vestavia
Smyth, Rich *publishing executive*

ARKANSAS

Fayetteville
Brady, Robert *communications educator*
Tomlinson, Abel *columnist*

Little Rock
Greenberg, Paul *editor*
Hussman, Walter E., Jr. *publishing executive*
Smith, Griffin *newspaper editor*

DISTRICT OF COLUMBIA

Washington
Abrams, Elliott *foreign policy analyst, former federal official*
Bandow, Douglas Leighton *editor, consultant, writer*
Donlan, Thomas Garrett *journalist*
Gerson, Michael John *columnist*
Leeds, Charles Alan *publishing executive*
Lewis, Charles Joseph *journalist*
Lutz, Theodore Compton *retired publishing executive*
Morano, Marc Peter *editor, former legislative staff member*
Parker, Kathleen *syndicated columnist*
Policinski, Eugene Francis *non-profit organization executive, syndicated columnist, editor, radio and television personality, producer*
Terzian, Philip Henry *journalist*

FLORIDA

Aventura
Bookspan, Martin *broadcaster, writer*

Boca Raton
Handel, Morton Emanuel *retired film company executive, management consultant*
Klein, Bernard *publishing executive*

Bonita Springs
Gillis, James R. *publishing executive*
Gustafson, Jim *broadcast executive*
Sullivan, Michael L. *publishing executive*
Tuchman, Alan *publishing executive*

Bradenton
Crouthamel, Thomas Grover, Sr. *editor, consultant*
Turner, Robert G., Jr. *publishing executive*
White, Dale Andrew *journalist*

Cocoa Beach
Quinn, John Collins *publishing executive, editor*

Dade City
Barnes, Andrew Earl *former newspaper executive*

Doral
Hiaasen, Carl *journalist, writer*
Landsberg, David A. *publishing executive*
Marqués Gonzalez, Aminda *newspaper editor*

Fort Lauderdale
Greenberg, Howard *publishing executive*
Marino, Dan (Daniel Constantino Marino Jr.) *sportscaster, retired professional football player*
Saltz, Howard Joel *newspaper editor*
Williamson, William Paul, Jr. *journalist*

Gainesville
Kaplan, John *photojournalist, educator, consultant*
Kelly, Kathleen S(ue) *communications educator*

Heathrow
Argirion, Michael *editor*

Hialeah
Arrarás, Maria Celeste *newscaster, journalist*
Romano, Emilio *broadcast executive*

Jacksonville
Hartmann, Frederick William *newspaper editor*

Key Biscayne
Pope, John Edwin *editor, columnist*

Lake Mary
Boyko, Alan *publishing executive*

Lake Worth
Willis, Clayton *broadcaster, government official, educator, arts consultant*

Lakewood Ranch
Marino, Eugene Louis *publishing executive, director*

Melbourne
Jenkins, Marshall *internet consultant, entrepreneur*

Miami
Barry, Dave *columnist, writer*
Fichtner, Margaria *journalist*
Lawrence, David, Jr. *journalist, early childhood advocate*
Lew, Salvador *radio station executive*
Russell, James Webster, Jr. *retired editor, columnist*
Savage, James Francis *retired editor*
Terilli, Samuel A., Jr. *newspaper publishing executive*
Wilson, Dave *editor*

Naples
Blevins, Charles Russell *publishing executive*
Clapp, Roger Howland *retired publishing executive*
Penniman, Nicholas Griffith, IV, *retired newspaper publisher*

North Bay Village
Ansin, Edmund *broadcast executive*

North Palm Beach
Evans, Thomas R. *magazine publisher*

Orlando
Dunn, William Bruna III *journalist*
Maupin, Elizabeth Thatcher *theater critic*
Pierce, Jerry Earl *publishing executive*

Ormond Beach
Campbell, Byron Chesser *newspaper publishing executive*

Pensacola
Bowden, Jesse Earle *editor, writer, cartoonist*
Ivey, Denise Hassell *retired publishing executive*

Ponte Vedra Beach
Bayat, Ehsan *broadcast executive*

Port Salerno
Kaat, Jim *sportscaster, retired professional baseball player*

Saint Petersburg
Belich, John Patrick, Sr. *journalist, private investigator*
Brown, Neil *publishing executive, newspaper editor*
Corty, Andrew P. *publishing executive*
DeGregory, Lane *journalist, features writer*
Dennis, Brady *journalist*
Grossman, Mindy Faye *broadcast executive*
Haiman, Robert James *editor, journalist, educator, media consultant, expert witness, critic*
Martinez, Arthur C. *broadcast executive*
Nickens, Tim *editor*
Ruben, Peter N. *broadcast executive*
Tash, Paul Clifford *publishing executive*

Sanford
Scott, Mellouise Jacqueline *retired media specialist*

Sanibel
Hilliard, Robert L. *emeritus communications professor, author, playwright*

Sarasota
Coats, Janet S. (Janet Weaver) *media consultant, former editor*
Proffitt, Waldo, Jr. *newspaper editor*
St. John, Paige *investigative reporter*
Sims, Edward Howell *editor, writer*

Tallahassee
Morgan, Lucy Ware *senior correspondent, journalist*
Sanchez, Robert Francis *journalist*

Tampa
Barker, Bill *publishing executive*
Friedlander, Edward Jay *journalist, educator*
Petty, Marty *publishing executive*
Witwer, Bruce *retired editor*

Tarpon Springs
Leisner, Anthony Baker *publishing company executive*

Valrico
Pearson, Walter Donald *editor, columnist*

West Palm Beach
Ford, John Bassett *broadcasting executive*
Johnson, Martin Allen *publishing executive, artist*
Rukeyser, M.S., Jr. *television consultant, writer*

Winter Haven
Benton, Obie Folsom *publishing executive, writer*

Winter Park
Federle, Michael *publishing executive*

GEORGIA

Athens
Soloski, John *journalism and communications educator*

Atlanta
Aldridge, David *sportscaster, journalist*
Armstrong, David G. *journalist*
Barkley, Charles Wade *sportscaster, retired professional basketball player*
Barry, Brent Robert *sportscaster, former professional basketball player*
Behrens, William Blade *television program syndication and professional sports team executive*
Berry, Dennis (G. Dennis Berry) *publishing executive*
Bisher, James Furman *journalist, writer*
Blackmon, Douglas A. *newspaper reporter, writer*
Chambers, Anne Cox *publishing executive, former diplomat*
Champion, Sam (Samuel James Champion) *weather anchor*
Connelly, Terrence John, Sr. *broadcast executive*
Dupri, Jermaine *recording industry executive, music producer*
Franklin, Douglas E. *publishing executive*
Fratello, Mike (Michael Robert Fratello) *sportscaster, former professional basketball coach*
Free, Vicky *media executive*
Freeman, Brenda *broadcast executive*
Glennon, Amy *publishing executive*
Johnson, Ernie, Jr. *sportscaster*
Joseph, Michael J. *media company executive*
Kelly, Michael J. *broadcast executive*
Kennedy, James Cox *publishing and media executive*
Kent, Phil (Philip I. Kent) *broadcast executive*
Kerr, Steve (Stephen Douglas Kerr) *sportscaster, retired professional basketball player, former professional sports team executive*
Kloer, Philip Baldwin *journalist*
Luckovich, Michael Edward *cartoonist*
Maddox, Tony *broadcast executive*
Malveaux, Suzanne *news correspondent*
Martin, John K. *broadcast executive*
Miller, Cheryl DeAnn *sportscaster, former professional basketball player and coach*
Miller, Reginald Wayne (Reggie Miller) *sportscaster, retired professional basketball player*
Mullin, Bernard James *sport management and marketing consultant*
O'Leary, Robert C. *publishing and media executive*
O'Neal, Shaquille Rashaun *sportscaster, retired professional basketball player*
Polk, James Ray *journalist*
Rock, Megan *broadcast executive*
Sams, Louise S. *broadcast executive, lawyer*
Schwartz, Sanford *publishing executive*
Smith, Steven Delano *sportscaster, retired professional basketball player*
Stockton, Dick *sportscaster*
Taylor, Susan L. *former magazine editor, philanthropist*
Teepen, Thomas Henry *editor, journalist*
Turner, Ted (Robert Edward Turner III) *retired broadcast company executive, philanthropist*
Webber, Chris (Mayce Edward Christopher Webber III) *sportscaster, retired professional basketball player*
Zucker, Jeffrey A. *broadcast executive*

Decatur
Knight, Walker Leigh *publishing executive, minister*

Savannah
McMullin, Ruth Roney *retired publishing executive*
Smith, David Lee *retired media executive*

Smyrna
Lowe, Mira *media consultant, educator, former editor-in-chief*

IOWA

Des Moines
Kerr, William T. *publishing and broadcast executive*

KENTUCKY

Fort Mitchell
Silvers, Gerald Thomas *retired publishing executive*

Greenville
Walters, Sue Fox *broadcast executive, accountant*

Latonia
Surber, David Francis *media consultant, syndicated television producer, journalist*

Lexington
Cross, Alvin Miller (Al Cross) *journalist*
Kelly, Timothy Michael *newspaper publisher*

Louisville
Ivory, Bennie L. *newspaper editor*
Jackson, Wesley *publishing executive*

LOUISIANA

Lafayette
Lincoln Michel, Karen *publishing executive*

New Orleans
Eckert, Michael Joseph *television and technology executive, early state private equity capital executive*
Pope, John Marvin *journalist*
Roesler, Robert Harry *media consultant*
Sharper, Darren Mallory *sportscaster, retired professional football player*

MASSACHUSETTS

Wellfleet
Limpitlaw, John Donald *publishing executive, clergyman*

MISSISSIPPI

Gulfport
Biffle, Tony *editor*

Hattiesburg
Hosman, Lawrence Andrew *communications educator*

Jackson
Mitchell, Jerry *investigative reporter*

Natchez
Kirk, Susanne Smith *editor*

NEW YORK

New York
Blatt, Gregory R. *broadcast executive, lawyer*
Cowher, Bill (William Laird Cowher) *sportscaster, former professional football coach*
Grace, Nancy Ann *news correspondent, former prosecutor*
Huckabee, Mike (Michael Dale Huckabee) *political commentator, former Governor of Arkansas*
Mathews, Tomas Goodwin *broadcast executive*
Meacham, Jon (Jonathan Ellis Meacham) *publishing executive, journalist, writer*

NORTH CAROLINA

Cary
Desotelle, James *publishing executive*
Grote, Gordon *publishing executive*
Ward, Aaron *sportscaster, retired professional hockey player*

Chapel Hill
Bowers, Thomas Arnold *journalism educator, dean*
Cole, Richard Ray *communications educator, former dean*
Cook, J. Montgomery (Monty Cook) *communications educator*
Montross, Eric Scott *sportscaster, retired professional basketball player*
Ravenel, Shannon *book publishing professional*

Charlotte
Caulkins, Ann *publishing executive*
Gray, Ann Maynard *broadcasting company executive*
Haines, Kenneth H. *sports television broadcasting and marketing executive*
Thames, Rick *newspaper editor*

Conover
Jarrett, Dale (Arnold) *commentator, retired professional race car driver*

Cornelius
Kohlmeier, Louis Martin, Jr. *newspaper reporter*

Davidson
Turner, Kathleen J. *communications educator, consultant*

Durham
Fiske, Edward B. *editor, journalist*
Harrell, Carlton (Benjamin Carlton Harrell) *retired editor, writer*
Pelham, Ann *publishing executive, department chairman*

Greensboro
Blackwell, William Ernest *broadcast executive*
Jellicorse, John Lee *communications and theatre educator*
Koons, Linda *publishing executive*

Hickory
Drendel, Frank Matthew *cable company executive*

Jefferson
Franklin, Robert McFarland *book publisher*

Raleigh
Fox, Matthew Ignatius *publishing executive*
Markus, Robert Michael *retired journalist*
McKinney, Donald Lee *magazine editor*
Pittman, James Morris (Jack Pittman) *cartoonist, illustrator, character designer, consultant*
Reeves, Ralph Bernard III *publishing executive*
Reis, Don *publishing executive*

Wilmington
Jones, David Meredith *retired communications educator*

Winston Salem
Becker, Ralph Edward *broadcast executive, consultant*
Price, Henry Escoe *broadcast executive*
Zagoria, Sam D(avid) *reporter, educator, federal agency administrator*

OHIO

Cincinnati
Peirce, Mary McCabe *publishing executive*

Dayton
Matheny, Ruth Ann *editor*

OKLAHOMA

Norman
Weber, Jerome Charles *human relations educator, retired academic administrator*

Oklahoma City
Fry, Kelly Dyer *newspaper editor*
Reen, Christopher P. *publishing executive*
Triplett, E. Eugene *editor*

Ponca City
Collins, Walter Lloyd George *editor*

Terlton
Bender, John Henry, Jr., (Jack Bender) *editor, cartoonist*

Tulsa
Haring, Robert Westing *newspaper editor*
Nyikos, Stacy Ann *publishing executive*

Wewoka
Trimble, Vance Henry *retired newspaper editor*

PENNSYLVANIA

Philadelphia
McSlarrow, Kyle E. *broadcast executive, former federal agency administrator*

West Chester
Costello, William F. *broadcast executive*

SOUTH CAROLINA

Beaufort
Borton, Sara Johnson *publishing executive*

Bennettsville
Kinney, William Light, Jr. *editor, publishing executive*

Charleston
Schreadley, Richard Lee *newswriter, retired editor*
Wyrick, Charles Lloyd, Jr. *editor, writer*

Georgetown
Howard, Thomas Joseph, Sr. *editor*

Greenville
Mebane, William deBerniere *newspaper publisher*

Hilton Head Island
Shaheen, Jack George *communications educator*

TENNESSEE

Franklin
Balaban, Anne R. *publishing executive*

Johnson City
Perry, Murvin Henry *communications educator*

Knoxville
De Heer, Sarah *online editor*
Doherty, Kate *editor*
Hartmann, Bruce *publishing executive*
Lowe, Kenneth W. *broadcast executive*
McElroy, Jack *editor*
Miles, Amy E. *film company executive*
Ong, Laureen E. *broadcast executive*
Rukeyser, William Simon *journalist*

Memphis
Peck, Christopher *newspaper editor*

Murfreesboro
Flanagan, Van Kent *journalist*

Nashville
Brewer, Clint *editor*
Green, Lisa Cannon *editor*
Ingram, Martha Rivers *publishing executive*
Russo, James Michael *political consultant*
Sepetys, Ruta Elizabeth *entertainment company executive, writer*
Shaw, Carole *editor, publisher*
Turk, Thomas Liebig *arts consultant*

Newport
Ball, Travis, Jr. *editor, retired school administrator*

TEXAS

Abilene
Armstrong, Randy Lee *communications educator*
Potter, Paul Eugene *communications educator, consultant*

Austin
Conine, Ernest *columnist*
Ellwood, Susie *publishing executive*
Inoue, Hiroshi *broadcast executive*
Knapp, Mark Lane *communications educator, consultant*
Mayes, Wendell Wise, Jr. *former broadcasting company executive*
Robertson, Pauline Durrett *publishing executive, writer, poet*

College Station
Rowse, Darren *blogger*

Colleyville
Turner, Janine *political commentator, radio personality, actress*

Conroe
Read, Michael Oscar *editor, consultant*

Dallas
Brown, Larry *sportscaster, retired professional football player*
Cantrell, Scott *newspaper music critic*
Dillon, David Anthony *editor, educator*
Glines, Carroll Vane, Jr. *magazine editor*
Holmes, Bert Otis E., Jr. *retired editor*
Mays, L(ester) Lowry *broadcast executive*
McDonald, Peter J. *publishing executive*
Mong, Robert William, Jr. *publishing executive, newspaper editor*
Moroney, James McQueen III *publishing executive*
Petrick, Michael Joseph *journalism educator*
Rather, Dan (Daniel Irvin Rather, Jr.) *news correspondent, former network news anchor*
Schembri, Chris *media marketing executive*
Wheat, Douglas *publishing executive*

Denton
Staples, Donald Edward *radio, film and television educator*

Fort Worth
Record, Phillip Julius *journalist*
Witt, Jim *newspaper editor*
Wortel, Gary G. *publishing executive*

Galveston
Perez-Polo, Jose Regino *editor-in-chief, educator*

Houston
Cohen, Jeff *publishing executive, newspaper editor*
Downing, Margaret Mary *newspaper editor*
Flood, Mary Anne *journalist, lawyer, legal media consultant*
George, Deveral D. *editor, journalist, advertising consultant*
Hawes, William Kenneth *communication educator, author*
Hobby, William Pettus *retired broadcast executive*
McDavid, George Eugene (Gene) *retired newspaper executive*
Riggenbach, Jeff *journalist, broadcaster*
Stephenson, Thomas A. *publishing executive*
Sweeney, Jack *publishing executive*
Taylor, Daniel J. *film company executive*
Walls, Martha Ann Williams (Mrs. B. Carmage Walls) *publishing executive*

Katy
Gray, Robert Steele *publishing executive, editor, writer*

Lockhart
Smith, Sue Frances Mueck (Mueck Smith) *retired newspaper editor*

Round Rock
Halter, Jon Charles *retired magazine editor, writer*

San Antonio
Goldberg, Wendy *broadcast executive*
Gwathmey, Joe Neil, Jr. *retired broadcast executive*
Lenke, Joanne Marie *publishing executive*
McKeon, John C. *publishing executive*

Southlake
Aikman, Troy Kenneth *sportscaster, retired professional football player*

Tyler
Brock, Dee Sala *television executive, writer, consultant, educator*

VIRGINIA

Alexandria
Arundel, John Howard *journalist, publisher*
Hobbs, Michael Edwin *retired broadcast executive*

Shosky, John Edwin *media consultant, speechwriter*
Stanton, John Jeffrey *editor, director, journalist, non profit administrator educator*
Vogel, Jon *political media firm executive, political strategist*
Yoder, Edwin Milton, Jr. *columnist, educator, editor, writer*

Arlington
Allen, Mike *political correspondent*
Arnold, Gary Howard *film critic*
Berke, Rick (Richard Leland Berke) *newspaper editor*
Butler, Patrick Harold *media executive*
Dillin, John Woodward, Jr. *retired editor, reporter*
Glass, Andrew James *newspaper editor*
Harris, John F. *editor-in-chief*
Ifill, Gwen *moderator, political reporter*
Jones, Boisfeuillet, Jr., (Bo Jones) *broadcast executive*
Kerger, Paula Arnold *broadcast executive*
MacDougall, William Lowell *magazine editor*
Morse, John B., Jr. *retired publishing executive*
Neikirk, William Robert *retired journalist*
Regnery, Alfred Scattergood *publishing executive*
Reiss, Susan Marie *editor, writer*
Rockefeller, Sharon Percy *broadcast executive*
VandeHei, Jim (James W. VandeHei) *editor*
Woodruff, Judy Carline *broadcast journalist*
Wuerker, Matt *cartoonist, illustrator*

Ashburn
Sanfelici, Arthur H(ugo) *editor, writer*

Basye
Amolsch, Arthur Lewis *publishing executive*

Charlottesville
Kaiserlian, Penelope Jane *publishing executive*
Prosser, Michael Hubert *communications educator*
Thornhill, Arthur H., Jr. *retired publishing executive*
Worrell, Anne Everette Rowell *newspaper publisher*

Dulles
North, Oliver Laurence (Ollie North) *syndicated columnist, retired military officer*

Fairfax
McAllister, William Howard III *newspaper reporter, columnist, public affairs consultant*

Fairfax Station
Randell, Cortes W. *news service executive*

Falls Church
Aukofer, Frank Alexander *journalist*
Rowlands, Sharon Theresa *publishing executive*

Great Falls
Garrett, Wilbur Bill (Bill) *magazine editor*

Herndon
Davis, Nathaniel (Nate) A. *broadcast executive*

Leesburg
Petranek, Stephen Lynn *editor*

Luray
Burzynski, Norman Stephen *editor*

Mc Lean
Beall, Lynn *broadcast executive*
Chu, Kathy *reporter*
Dickey, Robert J. *publishing executive*
Gallagher, Brian *editor*
Gendron, Teresa S. (Teri Gendron) *publishing executive*
Giallombardo, Leslie *publishing executive*
Harker, Victoria Dux *publishing executive*
Hasson, Janet *publishing executive*
Hillkirk, John M. *newspaper editor*
Kane, Michael G. *publishing executive*
Krans, Michelle M. *publishing executive*
Martore, Gracia C. *publishing company executive*
Mayman, Todd A. *publishing executive, lawyer*
McCorkindale, Douglas Hamilton *publishing executive*
Micek, Sandra Cordova *publishing executive*
Moreno, Karen R. *publishing executive*
Murcko, Mary *publishing executive*
Parshall, Gerald *journalist*
Tonning, Ken *broadcast executive*
Weiss, Susan *newspaper editor*

Midlothian
Chapman, Gilbert Whipple, Jr. *publishing executive*

Norfolk
Addis, Kay Tucker *newspaper editor*
Barry, Richard Francis III *retired media executive*
Ciara, Barbara *news anchor*
Sizemore, William Howard, Jr. *journalist*

Reston
Powell, Anne Elizabeth *editor-in-chief*

Richmond
Ashe, Reid (O. Reid Ashe) *publishing executive*
Bryan, John Stewart III *newspaper publisher*
FitzSimons, Dennis Joseph *former broadcast and publishing executive*

Round Hill
Hillis, John David *broadcast executive, television producer, newswriter*

Saint Paul
Gregory, Ann Young *editor*

Springfield
Hulbert, Mark J. *columnist*
Kieffer, Jarold Alan *publishing executive, writer*
Myers, Elissa Matulis *publishing executive, professional society administrator*
Turner, Douglas Laird *writer, editor, columnist*

Stanardsville
Anns, Arlene Eiserman *publishing company executive*

Vienna
Higginbotham, Wendy Jacobson *political advisor, freelance writer*
McElveen, Joseph James, Jr. *journalist, writer, newscaster, educator*

Virginia Beach
Robertson, Pat (Marion Gordon Robertson) *religious broadcasting executive, university president and chancellor*

WEST VIRGINIA

Charleston
Chilton, Elizabeth Easley Early *newspaper executive*
Haught, James Albert, Jr. *journalist, editor*

Clarksburg
Florio, Mike *sportswriter, lawyer*

Greenville
Warner, Kenneth Wilson, Jr. *editor, publishing executive*

TERRITORIES OF THE UNITED STATES

PUERTO RICO

San Juan
Angulo, Gerard Antonio *publishing executive*

ADDRESS UNPUBLISHED

Adelman, Kenneth Lee *journalist, former ambassador*
Andrisani, John Anthony *editor, writer*
Baggett, Donnis Gene *newspaper editor*
Barber, Charles Edward *publishing executive, journalist*
Barrows, Frank Clemence *journalist*
Brooks, Kathleen *communications professional*
Browne, Donald Victor *retired broadcast executive*
Buchanan, Pat (Patrick Joseph Buchanan) *journalist, author, political commentator*
Burleigh, William Robert *retired media executive*
Bynum, Richard Cary *author, former publisher*
Clark, James Covington *journalist, historian*
Colan, Joanne *video blogger, television personality*
Cooper, Charles Howard *retired photojournalist, publishing executive*
Corey, Orlin Russell *publishing executive*
Curley, Thomas (Tom Curley) *former publishing executive*
Curry, Dale Blair *retired journalist*
Dahlburg, John-Thor Theodore *news correspondent*
de Leon, Lidia Maria *magazine editor*
Dubow, Craig A. *former publishing executive*
Fenwick, James Henry *editor, writer, columnist*
Floyd, John Alex, Jr. *retired publishing executive*
French, Mary B. *editor, photographer, poet, retired literature educator*
Furnad, Bob (Vasil Robert Furnad) *retired broadcast executive*
Gulledge, Sandra Smith *publicist*
Hobbs, Landel C. *former broadcast executive*
Holtz, Lou (Louis Leo Holtz) *sportscaster, retired college football coach*
Hoyt, Clark Freeland *editor*
Huey, Ward L(igon), Jr. *retired media executive*
Jones, Joe Kenley *journalist*
Kessler, Ronald Borek *journalist, writer*
Keyes, James Willard (Jim Keyes) *film rental company executive*
Kiel, Jeff E. *former publishing executive*
Kissling, Fred Ralph, Jr. *publishing and insurance agency executive*
Kotz, Nathan Kallison (Nick Kotz) *news correspondent, author*
Langer, Ralph Ernest *journalist, retired editor*
Lauder, Valarie Anne *retired editor*
Lavine, Alan *columnist, writer*
Liberman, Gail Jeanne *editor*
Little, Christopher Mark *retired publishing executive*
Mears, Walter Robert *retired journalist*
Meyer, Philip Edward *journalism educator*
Michel, Daniel John *communications educator, writer, photographer, artist*
Mitrovgenis, James William, Jr. *retired journalist*
Moss, Madison Scott *retired editor*
Obermayer, Herman Joseph *newspaper publisher*
O'Brien, Soledad *broadcast executive, journalist*
Parkyn, John William *editor, writer, columnist*
Rankin, Robert Arthur *retired journalist*
Roberts, Delmar Lee *editor*
Roberts, Edwin Albert, Jr. *editor, journalist*
Roberts, Margaret Harold *editor, publisher*
Roberts, Samuel Smith *television news executive*
Rodriguez, Ray *retired broadcast executive*
Roth, Harvey Paul *retired publishing executive*
Salinas, Rodney Jay C. *media company executive*
Schulz, John Joseph *communications educator, journalist, book author*
Seals, Margaret Louise Crumrine *retired journalist*
Shales, Thomas William *former television and film critic, writer, journalist*
Smith, A. Robert *editor, author*
Soeteber, Ellen *journalist, editor*
Spence, James Robert, Jr. *television executive, educator, mediator*
Stanley, Scott, Jr. *editor*
Stiff, Robert Martin *newspaper editor*
Strothman, James Edward *editor-in-chief*
Tharpe, Frazier Eugene *journalist*
Thiessen, Marc A. *journalist, former federal official*
Vincent, Charles Eagar, Jr. *sportswriter*
Williamson, Thomas Arnold *retired publishing executive*
Wodlinger, Mark Louis *broadcast executive*

EDUCATION *See also* specific fields for postsecondary education

UNITED STATES

ALABAMA

Alabaster
Copes, Marvin Lee *academic administrator*
McChesney, Robert Michael, Sr. *retired academic administrator*

Athens
Glenn, Robert Kyle *academic administrator*

Auburn
Alderman, Charles Wayne *university dean*
Galbraith, Ruth Legg *retired dean, home economist*
Miller, Wilbur Randolph *academic administrator*
Zallen, Harold *academic administrator, chemist*

Auburn University
Gogue, Jay (G. Jay Gogue) *academic administrator*

Birmingham
Berte, Neal Richard *academic administrator*
Krulak, Charles Chandler *academic administrator, retired military officer*
Mc Callum, Charles Alexander *academic administrator*
Thomas, Huw Francis *dean, dental educator*
Watts, Ray L. *dean, neurologist, educator*
Westmoreland, Andrew *academic administrator*

Dothan
Flowers, V. Anne *retired academic administrator*

Florence
Cale, William Graham, Jr. *university administrator, environmental sciences educator, researcher*

Huntsville
Altenkirch, Robert A. *academic administrator*
Baird, James Kern *educator, consultant, academic administrator*
Lundquist, Charles Arthur *academic administrator*

Livingston
Green, Asa Norman *academic administrator*

Madison
Brannan, Eulie Ross *educational consultant*

Mobile
Copeland, Lewis *principal*
Franks, Ronald Dwyer *dean, psychiatrist, educator*
Strada, Samuel J. *dean, pharmacologist, educator*
Webb, Paula *school librarian*

Montgomery
May, Cecil Richard, Jr. *academic administrator*
Rogers, Betsy *elementary school educator*
Tracy, Mike *director*

Muscle Shoals
Sparkman, Brandon Buster *educator, consultant, writer*

Troy
Kline, John Alvin *distinguished professor of leadership*

Tuscaloosa
Bonner, Jo (Josiah Robins Bonner Jr.) *academic administrator, former United States Representative from Alabama*
Bonner, Judy L. *academic administrator*
McNealey, Ernest *college president*
Portera, Malcolm *academic administrator*
Randall, Kenneth C. *retired dean, retired law educator*
Witt, Robert E. *academic administrator*

ARIZONA

Phoenix
Koppell, Jonathan *dean, political science professor*

ARKANSAS

Arkadelphia
Dunn, Charles DeWitt *academic administrator*
Elrod, Ben Moody *academic administrator*
Grant, Daniel Ross *retired academic administrator*
Thomas, Herman L. *school system administrator*

Conway
Courtway, Thomas C. *academic administrator, former state legislator*
Meadors, Allen Coats *academic administrator, educator*
Spatz, Kenneth Chris(topher), Jr. *statistics educator*

Fayetteville
Gearhart, G. David *academic administrator, education educator*
Kohler, Peter Ogden *academic administrator, internist, educator*
Leeds, Stacy L. *dean, law educator*
Smith, Robert Victor *academic administrator, educator*

Hot Springs Village
Watson, James Raymond *philosopher*

Little Rock
Kimbrough, Walter Mark *academic administrator*

Pine Bluff
Davis, Lawrence A., Jr. *academic administrator*

COLORADO

Denver
Emmet, Thomas Addis, Jr. *college administrator, consultant*

U S A F Academy
Vila, Adis Maria *academic administrator*

CONNECTICUT

Fairfield
Miles, Leland Weber *retired academic administrator*

DISTRICT OF COLUMBIA

Washington
Keaney, Thomas Addis *academic administrator, management consultant, military officer*

FLORIDA

Atlantic Beach
Kinne, Frances Bartlett *academic administrator*
Kurth, Ronald James *retired academic administrator, military officer*

Boca Raton
Bjorkman, David Jess *dean, gastroenterologist, educator*
Friedland, Michael Lawrence *dean, medical educator*
Lichtstein, Daniel M. *dean, internist*
Tennies, Robert Hunter *headmaster*

Bonita Springs
Johnson, Franklyn Arthur *academic administrator*

Bradenton
Driscoll, Constance Fitzgerald *education educator, writer, consultant*

Cape Coral
Wille, Rosanne Louise *educational consultant*

Clearwater
Glasser, William Arnold *academic administrator*

Coral Gables
Shalala, Donna Edna *academic administrator, former United States Secretary of Health and Human Services*
Tien, James M. *dean, engineering educator, consultant*
White, Patricia Denise *dean, law educator*

Daytona Beach
Hartsell, Horace Ed *college president*

Deland
Dascher, Paul Edward *dean, accounting educator*
Libby, Wendy B. *academic administrator*

Destin
O'Brien, Gregory Michael St. Lawrence *academic administrator*

Fort Lauderdale
Carter-Miller, Jocelyn *educational services company executive, former retail executive*
Fischler, Abraham Saul *retired academic administrator, educator*
Hanbury, George Lafayette, II, *university president and professor*
Silvagni, Anthony Joseph *dean, osteopath*
Uchin, Robert Allen *dean, endodontist*

Fort Myers
Colgate, Doris Eleanor *sailing school owner, administrator*
Tinker, Thomas Eaton *retired headmaster*

Gainesville
Binford, Michael William *professor physical geography*
Bryan, Robert Armistead *academic administrator, educator*
Chambers, Robert Hunter III *academic administrator, consultant, historian, educator*
Dolan, Teresa A. *dean, educator, researcher*
Guzick, David S. *academic administrator, hospital administrator*
Jerry, Robert Howard, II, *dean, law educator*
Lowenstein, Ralph Lynn *university dean emeritus*
Machen, James Bernard (Bernie Machen) *academic administrator*
Mills, Jon *dean emeritus, law educator*
Phillips, Winfred Marshall *academic administrator, professor, mechanical engineer*

Graceville
Kinchen, Thomas Alexander *college president*

Highland Beach
Featherman, Sandra *retired academic administrator, political science professor*

New York
Marcuse, Adrian Gregory *academic administrator*

NORTH CAROLINA

Asheville
Brown, David G. *academic administrator*
Dowd, Kenneth Robert *elementary school educator*
Fernandes, Jane K. *academic administrator, sign language professional*
Ponder, Anne *academic administrator*

Banner Elk
Buxton, Barry Miller *academic administrator, writer, educator*

Boone
Hay, Fred J. *education educator, librarian, editor*

Cary
Krotee, Leslie Latshaw *special education educator*

Chapel Hill
Andrews, Richard Nigel Lyon *academic administrator, educator*
Campbell, Bobby Jack *academic administrator*
Carroll, Roy *retired academic administrator*
Cronenwett, Linda r. *dean, educator, hospital administrator*
Folkerts, Jean *dean, journalism educator*
Folt, Carol L. *academic administrator, environmental scientist*
Joyner, Leon Felix *retired university administrator*
King, Emily *school librarian*
Locke, Robert John *academic administrator*
Magill, Samuel Hays *academic administrator, consultant*
Michalak, Sarah C. *university librarian*
Rimer, Barbara K. *dean, healthcare educator*
Roper, William Lee *dean, preventive medicine physician, administrator*
Ross, Thomas Warren, Sr. *academic administrator, former judge*
Smith, Michael R. *dean, academic administrator*
Vargha, Rebecca Brogden *librarian, library association executive*
Watkins, Paul B. *academic administrator, medical educator*
Wildemuth, Barbara M. *education educator*
Williams, John N. *dean, dental educator*
Wolfenden, Richard Vance *biochemistry educator*

Charlotte
Bowles, Erskine Boyce *former academic administrator, former White House chief of staff*
Davies, Pamela L. *academic administrator*
Dubois, Philip Leon *academic administrator, political scientist, educator*
Morrison, Heath E. *school system administrator*
Smelser, Ronald E. *dean, mechanical engineer, educator*
Tyson, Cynthia Haldenby *academic administrator*

Davidson
Kuykendall, John Wells *retired academic administrator, theology studies educator*
Quillen, Carol E. *academic administrator, history professor*

Durham
Andrews, Nancy Catherine *dean, pediatrician, hematologist, educator*
Boulding, William *dean, business professor*
Brodhead, Richard H. *academic administrator*
Brownell, Kelly David *dean, psychologist, educator*
Feaver, Peter Douglas *political science educator, consultant, defense analyst*
Gilliss, Catherine Lynch *academic administrator, dean, nursing educator*
Jakubs, Deborah *university librarian*
Kuniholm, Bruce Robellet *academic administrator, educator*
Levi, David F. *dean, former federal judge*
Parker, William *education educator*

Elon
Tolley, Jerry Russell *academic administrator*

Fairview
Brown, Gregory Neil *academic administrator, forester, educator*

Glendale Springs
Carter, Roy *secondary school educator, coach*

Greensboro
Schunk, Dale Hansen *professor*

Greenville
Bearden, James Hudson *university official*
Leggett, Donald Yates *academic administrator*
Leggett, Nancy Porter *administrative assistant chief legal counsel*

Hickory
Beasley, Diana F. *biology educator*

High Point
Carter, Kathleen Sharp *educational consultant, appraiser, shop owner*

Kinston
Petteway, Samuel Bruce *college president*

Lake Junaluska
Martinson, Jacob Christian, Jr. *academic administrator*
Stanton, Donald Sheldon *retired academic administrator*

Laurinburg
Doubles, Malcolm Carroll *college administrator*

Liberty
Wilson, Lloyd Lee *registrar, educator*

Mount Olive
Raper, William Burkette *retired college president*

Murfreesboro
White, Martin Christopher *academic administrator*

Raleigh
Burris, Craven Allen *retired college administrator, professor*
Casden, Jason *school librarian*
Dolce, Carl John *education administration educator*
Nelson, Larry A. *statistics educator, consultant*
Parramore, Barbara Mitchell *education educator*
Phillips, Richard B. *education educator*
Woodson, Randy (William Randolph Woodson) *academic administrator*

Smithfield
Wiggs, Shirley JoAnn *retired secondary school educator*

Wilmington
Rorison, Margaret Lippitt *reading consultant*

Winston Salem
Abraham, Edward *dean, medical educator*
Collins, Jennifer *academic administrator, law educator*
Hatch, Nathan Orr *academic administrator*
Jaffe, Susan *dean, ballerina*
Morant, Blake *dean, law educator*
Reinemund, Steven S. *dean, educator, retired food products executive*

OKLAHOMA

Ada
Cheper, Nicholas J. *biology educator*

Disney
Hamilton, Carl Hulet *retired academic administrator*

Durant
Turner, Michael Dan *academic administrator*

Edmond
Betz, Donald *academic administrator*

Langston
Haysbert, JoAnn Wright *academic administrator*
Showalter, Betsy S. *mathematics educator*

Maramec
Blair, Marie Lenore *elementary school educator*

Norman
Boren, David Lyle *academic administrator, former United States Senator from Oklahoma*
Harroz, Joseph, Jr. *dean, law educator*
Pappas, James Pete *university administrator*

Oklahoma City
Kruschwitz, Walter Hillis *retired physics educator*
Springer, Karl *school system administrator*
Weigel, Paul Henry *biochemistry educator, researcher, consultant*
Williamson, Marvel *dean, nursing administrator, sexologist, educator*

Ponca City
Rice, Sue Ann *retired dean, psychologist*

Stillwater
Hargis, V. Burns (Burns Hargis) *academic administrator, lawyer*
Strathe, Marlene I. *academic administrator*

Tahlequah
Haskins, V. Lyle *retired academic administrator*
Howard, James Kenton *academic administrator, journalist*

Tulsa
Buthod, Mary Clare *school superintendent*
Donaldson, Robert Herschel *university administrator, educator*
Hill, Bryce Dale *school administrator*
Juneau, Ted *academic administrator*
Shrum, Kayse *dean, educator, pediatrician*
Upham, Steadman *academic administrator, anthropologist, educator*

SOUTH CAROLINA

Bluffton
Markwood, Stephen Ernest *educator, consultant, college president*

Central
Sinnamon, Walter Bruce *college administrator, biology educator, biologist, educator*

Charleston
Greenberg, Raymond Seth *academic and health facility administrator, educator*
Morris, Valerie Bonita *dean*
Rosa, John William *academic administrator, career military officer*
Strauch, Katina Parthemos *college librarian, publishing executive*

Clemson
Bennett, Archie Wayne *academic administrator*
Clements, James P. (Jim Clements) *academic administrator*
Kelly, John William, Jr. *academic administrator*
Reel, Jerome Vincent, Jr. *academic administrator, historian*

Columbia
Hoppmann, Richard Anthony *dean, physician, educator*
Palms, John Michael *academic administrator, physicist*
Pastides, Harris *academic administrator*
Sinclair, Linda Drumwright *educational consultant*
Torres, Raymond *professor*

Greenville
Payne, George Frederick *academic administrator*
Smith, Philip Daniel *academic administrator, education educator*
Smolla, Rodney Alan *academic administrator, law educator*

Greenwood
Jackson, Larry Artope *retired college president*

Hilton Head Island
Levy, Maurice *retired medical educator, researcher*

Kiawah Island
Warren, Russell Glen *educational consultant*

Mount Pleasant
Gilbert, James Eastham *academic administrator*

Myrtle Beach
Decenzo, David A. *academic administrator*

Orangeburg
Hill, Howard Darnell *professor, consultant*

Pawleys Island
Proefrock, C. Kenneth *academic medical administrator*

Rock Hill
Franklin, A. David *retired university dean, music educator, journalist*

Spartanburg
Corden, Paul H. *retired college program director, food service executive*
Dunlap, Benjamin Bernard *academic administrator*
Stephens, Bobby Gene *college administrator, consultant*

TENNESSEE

Bristol
Werner, Dawn Heterick *elementary school educator*

Cleveland
Harper, James Edward, Jr. *academic administrator*

Cookeville
Volpe, Angelo Anthony *retired academic administrator, chemist, educator*

Franklin
Daniel, Cathy Brooks *educational consultant*

Greeneville
Casteel, DiAnn Brown *education educator*

Jackson
Agee, Bob R. *academic administrator, minister, educator*
Barefoot, Hyran Euvene *academic administrator, educator, minister*

Johnson City
Bagnell, Philip C. *dean, pediatrician, educator*
Tollefson, Terrence Alfred *retired educator and consultant*

Knoxville
Blaze, Doug A. *dean, law educator*
Boling, Edward Joseph *retired academic administrator*
Cheek, Jimmy Geary *academic administrator, agricultural studies educator*
Creasia, Joan Catherine *dean, nursing educator*
DiPietro, Joseph A. *academic administrator, medical educator*
Mankel, Francis Xavier *retired principal, priest*

Memphis
Gourley, Dick R. *dean, pharmacy educator*
Ranta, Richard Robert *university dean*
Stern, David Mark *dean, medical educator*
Troutt, William Earl (Bill Troutt) *academic administrator*
Werle, Robert Geary *academic administrator*

Murfreesboro
Doyle, Delores Marie *retired principal*

Nashville
Balser, Jeffrey R. *dean, medical educator*
Benbow, Camilla Persson *dean, psychology professor*
Bradford, James Warren, Jr., (Jim Bradford) *dean, finance educator*
Cyrus, Cynthia J. *provost, music educator*
Guthrie, Chris *dean, law educator*
Meyer, Ellen L. *academic administrator*
Mouton, Charles Peter *dean, physician, educator*
O'Leary, Hazel Rollins *academic administrator, former United States Secretary of Energy, lawyer*
Register, Jesse *school system administrator*
Seligson, Mitchell A. *political science educator*
Swan, Patricia Brintnall *academic administrator, researcher*
Zeppos, Nicholas S. *academic administrator*

Pleasant Hill
Hull, Charles William *retired special education educator*

Sewanee
Croom, Frederick Hailey *academic administrator, mathematician, educator*
McCardell, John Malcolm, Jr. *academic administrator, history professor*
Patterson, William Brown *retired dean, history professor*

TEXAS

Abilene
McCaleb, Gary Day *university official*
Specht, Alice Wilson *university libraries dean*

Arlington
Butler, Donald Philip *educator*
Graca, Thomas John *education educator, lawyer*
Han, Chien-Pai *statistics educator*
Pomerantz, Martin *chemistry educator, researcher*

Austin
Carpenter, Delbert Stanley *educational administration educator*
Carstarphen, Meria Joel *school system administrator*
Cigarroa, Francisco Gonzalez *academic administrator, pediatric surgeon*
Cunningham, William Hughes *retired academic administrator, marketing professional, educator*
Doluisio, James Thomas *dean, pharmacy educator*
Ellis, Martha McCracken *academic administrator, psychology professor*
Farnsworth, Ward *dean, law educator*
Golden, Paula Englander *psychology, social work, addiction educator, consultant*
Graham, Lawrence Sherman *political science educator, management consultant*
Harris, Ben M. *education educator*
Hutchings, Robert L. *dean, former ambassador*
Johnston, Keith P. *professor of chemical engineering*
Lynn, Laurence Edwin, Jr. *academic administrator, educator*
Powers, William Charles, Jr. *academic administrator, law educator*
Roueche, John Edward, II, *education educator, director*
Shilling, Roy Bryant, Jr. *academic administrator*
Shine, Kenneth Irwin *academic administrator, cardiologist, educator*
Sussman, Harvey Martin *educator*

Blackwell
Davis, Thomas Pinkney *secondary school educator, department chairman*

Bonham
Swanson, Jacqueline V. *academic administrator, women's health nurse practitioner, educator*

Brownsville
Garcia, Juliet Villarreal *academic administrator*

Bryan
Sadoski, Mark Christian *education educator*
Shomaker, Sam (Thomas Samuel Shomaker) *dean, anesthesiologist, former lawyer*

Canyon
Long, Russell Charles *retired academic administrator*

Channelview
Wallace, Betty Jean *retired elementary school educator, lay minister*

College Station
Adkisson, Perry Lee *university system chancellor*
Bowen, Ray Morris *academic administrator, engineering educator*
Byrne, C. William, Jr. *athletics program director*
Cocanougher, Arthur Benton *retired academic administrator*
Crocker, Ryan Clark *dean, former ambassador*
Dickey, Nancy Wilson *chancellor, physician*
Erlandson, David Alan *education administration educator*
Flagg, James C. *educational administrative officer*
Loftin, Richard Bowen *academic administrator*
Monroe, Haskell Moorman, Jr. *chancellor emeritus, retired history professor, dean*
Strawser, Jerry R. *dean*
Vitter, Jeffrey Scott *academic administrator, computer science educator, researcher*

Commerce
Justice, Madeline Carol *education educator*
Scott, Joyce Alaine *academic administrator*
Vornberg, James Alvin *education educator*

Dallas
Cole, James S. *dean, dental educator*
Cook, Gary Raymond *academic administrator, minister*
Fitz, J. Gregory *dean, gastroenterologist, educator*
Green, Hubert Gordon *university professor, pediatrician*
King, Alan *school system administrator*
McTeer, Robert D., Jr. *former academic administrator, bank executive*
Miles, Mike *school system administrator*
Niemi, Albert William, Jr. *economics professor*
Podolsky, Daniel K. *university administrator, physician*
Richard, Debra Lynn *school librarian*
Shambaugh, Irvin Calvin, Jr. *aptitude test firm executive, consultant*
Turner, R. Gerald (Robert Gerald Turner) *academic administrator*

Denton
Greenlaw, Marilyn Jean *retired adult education educator*
McCaslin, Richard Bryan *history educator*
Rawlins, V. Lane *academic administrator, economics professor*
Smith, Howard Wellington *education educator, retired dean*

Totten, Herman Lavon *dean, library and information science educator*
Turner, Philip Michael *academic administrator, writer*

Edinburg
Nelsen, Robert Steven *academic administrator, literature and language professor*
Nevarez, Miguel A. *academic administrator*

Egypt
Wynn, John Thomas *retired academic administrator, farming executive, economic consultant, oil and gas producer*

El Paso
Boyd, Dana Kristin *elementary school educator*
Jarvis, Richard S. *academic administrator*
Natalicio, Diana Siedhoff *academic administrator*

Euless
Bielss, Otto William, Jr. *secondary school educator*

Fort Worth
Boschini, Victor John, Jr. *academic administrator*
Dansby, Walter *school system administrator*
Peska, Don N. *dean, surgeon, educator*
Tucker, William Edward *academic administrator, minister*

Gainesville
Dietz, David W. *elementary school educator*

Galveston
Stobo, John David *academic administrator, physician*

Georgetown
Inman, Marianne Elizabeth *retired academic administrator*
Schrum, Jake Bennett *academic administrator*

Granbury
Curl, Samuel Everett *retired dean, agriculturist, consultant*

Houston
Alfini, James Joseph *dean, lawyer, educator*
Anderson, Deborah Gail Cook *elementary school educator, special education educator*
Beckingham, Kathleen Mary *education educator, researcher*
Bradshaw, Major William *dean, medical educator*
Butler, William Thomas *academic administrator, physician, educator*
Caram, Dorothy Farrington *educational consultant*
Colasurdo, Giuseppe N. *dean, pulmonologist, educator*
Colby, Ira *dean, educator*
Djerejian, Edward Peter *academic administrator, retired ambassador*
Feinberg, Mike *school system administrator*
Flaitz, Catherine M. *former dean, dental educator*
Glick, William H. *dean, management educator*
Greenberg, Stephen Baruch *dean, medical educator*
Grier, Terry B. *school system administrator*
Khator, Renu *academic administrator, political science professor*
Klotman, Paul *academic administrator, physician*
Leebron, David Wayne *academic administrator, law educator*
Malki, Heidar A. *dean*
Mariotto, Marco Jerome *dean, psychology educator, researcher*
Matthews, Kathleen Shive *biochemistry educator*
McConnell, Charles DeWitt *academic administrator, former federal agency administrator*
Pickering, James Henry III *academic administrator, educator*
Prestage, James Jordan *consultant*
Rudley, John M. *academic administrator*
Sharp, Douglas Andrew *secondary school educator*
Sloan, Robert Bryan, Jr. *academic administrator*
Wagner, Paul Anthony, Jr. *education educator*
Webb, Marty Fox *principal*

Irving
Martin, Thomas Lyle, Jr. *academic administrator*
Wilkerson, Patricia Helen *retired director*

Kemp
Shugart, Jill *retired school administrator*

Kingsville
Tallant, Steven Hall *academic administrator, social worker*

Laredo
Black, Clifford Merwyn *academic administrator, sociologist, educator*

Lubbock
Bailey, Guy H. *academic administrator*
Berk, Steven Lee *dean, internist, educator*
Conover, William Jay *statistics educator*
Haragan, Donald Robert *academic administrator, geologist, educator*
River, Sandra A. *university librarian*
Strauss, Jon Calvert *academic administrator*

Midland
Bridges, Judy Cantrell *gifted and talented education educator*

New Braunfels
Ellis, John *retired school system administrator, writer*
Oestreich, Charles Henry *retired university president*

Pasadena
Blue, Monte Lynn *college president*

Plano
Gideon, Sharon Lee *secondary school educator*

Richardson
Daniel, David Edwin *academic administrator, civil engineer*

Rockwall
Dennison, Ramona Pollan *special education educator*

San Antonio
Cassidy, Jack *academic administrator, educator*
Henderson, Dwight Franklin *dean, educator*
Kalkwarf, Kenneth Lee *dean, dental educator*
Madrid, Olga Hilda Gonzalez *retired elementary school educator*
Perry, George *dean, neuroscientist, educator*
Purcell, Susan Kaufman *director*
Romo, Ricardo *academic administrator, history educator*
Young, James Julius *academic administrator, retired military officer*

The Woodlands
Beller, Stephen Mark *retired academic administrator*

Tyler
Davidson, Jack Leroy *academic administrator*

Waco
Belew, John Seymour *academic administrator, chemist*
Brooks, Roger Leon *retired academic administrator*
Garland, David Ellsworth *dean, theology studies educator*
Lindsey, Jonathan Asmel *retired academic administrator, academic librarian*
Starr, Kenneth Winston *academic administrator, law educator, lawyer*
Toben, Bradley J.B. *dean, law educator*

VIRGINIA

Arlington
Polsby, Daniel D. *dean, law educator*
Wakimoto, Roger Masao *meteorology educator, researcher, aerospace scientist*

Blacksburg
Steger, Charles William *academic administrator*
Tillar, Thomas Cato, Jr. *academic administrator, consultant*
Torgersen, Paul Ernest *academic administrator, educator*
Weaver, Pamela Ann *education educator*

Charlottesville
Biltonen, Rodney Lincoln *biochemistry and pharmacology educator*
Garson, Arthur, Jr. *academic administrator, medical educator*
Mahoney, Paul G. *dean, law educator*
Rappaport, Yvonne Kindinger *educator*
Sullivan, Teresa Ann *academic administrator, law and sociology educator*
Wittenborg, Karin *university librarian*
Zeithaml, Carl Paul *dean, educator*

Chester
Law, Thomas Melvin *academic administrator*

Fairfax
Cabrera, Ángel *academic administrator, finance educator*
Carty, Rita Mary *dean, emerita*

Falls Church
Boucouvalas, Marcie *adult development and learning educator, professor, researcher, author*

Farmville
Finnegan, Patrick *academic administrator, military officer, lawyer*

Fredericksburg
Hample, Judy G. *academic administrator*

Hampden Sydney
Bortz, Walter M. III *academic administrator*

Hampton
Goodson, Dorothy Moore *English educator, counselor*

Harrisonburg
Carrier, Ronald Edwin *academic administrator, director*

Lexington
Demleitner, Nora Verena *dean, law educator*
John, Lewis George *retired political science educator*
Peay, J.H. Binford III *academic administrator, retired career military officer*
Ruscio, Kenneth Patrick *academic administrator, political science professor*
Williams, H. Thomas (Tom Williams) *academic administrator, physicist, educator*

Lynchburg
Bowman, Kathleen Gill *academic administrator*
Klein, John E. *academic administrator*

Manassas
Archer, Chalmers, Jr. *retired education educator, military service force*

Norfolk
Baysal, Oktay *dean, educator*
Budd, Richard Wade *academic administrator, dean, priest*
Homan, Richard V. *dean, physician*
Koch, James Verch *academic administrator, economist*

Petersburg
Moore, Eddie N., Jr. *college president*

Radford
Carter, Fletcher Fairwick *university administrator, education educator retired*

Richmond
Ayers, Edward L. *academic administrator, history professor*
Boudinot, Frank Douglas *dean*
Cooper, William Edwin *professor, former academic administrator*
DeMary, Jo Lynne *academic administrator, retired school system administrator*
Epstein, David Stanley *educator, consultant*
Hunt, Ronald J. *dean, dental educator*
Jones, Jeanne Pitts *retired pre-school administrator*
McGee, Henry Alexander, Jr. *academic administrator*
Morrill, Richard Leslie *academic administrator, former foundation administrator*
Peart, Sandra Joan *dean*
Perdue, Wendy Collins *dean, law educator*
Rettig, James R. *university librarian, library association executive*
Stover, Jill S. *school librarian, writer*
Strauss, Jerome Frank III *dean, medical researcher, educator*

Roanoke
Gray, Nancy Ann Oliver *academic administrator*

Rockbridge Baths
Glidden, Robert Burr *academic administrator, music educator, consultant*

Salem
Day, John T. *academic administrator, dean*

Springfield
Lambert, Vickie Ann *retired dean, nursing consultant*

Vienna
Marx, Gary Dean *educational consultant, futurist, think-tank executive*

Virginia Beach
Selig, William George *academic administrator*

Williamsburg
Calver, Richard Allen *retired dean*
Douglas, Davison McDowell *dean, law educator*
Gates, Robert Michael (Bob Gates) *academic administrator, former United States Secretary of Defense*
Reveley, Taylor (Walter Taylor Reveley III) *academic administrator, former dean, law educator*

Winchester
Pleacher, David Henry *secondary school educator*

Wise
Smiddy, Joseph Charles *retired academic administrator*

Woodberry Forest
Campbell, Dennis Marion *academic administrator, theologian, educator*

WEST VIRGINIA

Bridgeport
McClure, Charles Richard *retired school system administrator*

Charles Town
Boston, Wallace Ellsworth, Jr. *academic administrator*

Charleston
Hansbarger, L. Clark *dean*
Richardson, Sally Keadle *academic administrator*

Clarksburg
Leuliette, Connie Jane *secondary school educator*

Dunbar
Russell, James Alvin, Jr. *college administrator*

Elkins
Smith, Godfrey Taylor (Buck Smith) *college president*

Huntington
Dennison, Corley Francis III *dean*
Hayes, Robert Bruce *former college president, educator*
Shapiro, Joseph Isaac *dean, nephrologist*

Lewisburg
Adelman, Michael D. *academic administrator*
Pence, Lorenzo L. *dean, osteopath, educator*

Morgantown
Bucklew, Neil S. *former academic administrator, educator*
Gee, Elwood Gordon (Gordon Gee) *academic administrator, corporate board member*
Hardway, Wendell Gary *retired academic administrator*
McConnell, Joyce E. *dean, law educator*

Philippi
Shearer, Richard Eugene *educational consultant*

TERRITORIES OF THE UNITED STATES

PUERTO RICO

Bayamon
Ginel Rodríguez, José *dean, physician, educator*

Fajardo
Fernós, Manuel J. *academic administrator*

San Juan
Carreras, Francisco José *retired academic and foundation administrator*
Matheu, Federico Manuel *university chancellor*
Santiago-Borrero, Pedro J. *dean, pediatrician, educator*

VIRGIN ISLANDS

Frederiksted
Birbahadur, Dindial *secondary school educator*

St Thomas
DePass-Creque, Linda Ann *educational consultant, association executive, former education commissioner*

ADDRESS UNPUBLISHED

Akanbi, Linda Barbara *education educator*
Alexander-Davis, Deborah Radford *retired principal, educational consultant*
Armacost, Mary-Linda Sorber Merriam *educational consultant*
Arnett, Edward McCollin *chemistry educator, researcher*
Baczko, Joseph Richard, Jr. *retired dean*
Bataille, Gretchen M. *former academic administrator, educator*
Bishop, Charles Edwin *academic administrator, economist, educator*
Bishop, Ina Sue Marquis *retired dean*
Bondi, Joseph Charles, Jr. *education educator, consultant*
Brooke, Francis John III *retired academic administrator*
Brown, Myra Suzanne *retired university librarian*
Brownlee, Paula Pimlott *higher education consultant*
Burnham, Tom *retired school system administrator*
Burris, John Edward *academic administrator, biologist, educator*
Cantrell Trusdell, Mary Louise *retired academic administrator*
Carleton, Don Edward *academic administrator, writer*
Carr, Bessie *retired elementary school educator*
Casteen, John Thomas III *retired academic administrator*
Clawson, Roxann Eloise *retired college administrator, computer company executive*
Cooper, James Michael *education educator*
Cooper, Kathleen Bell *senior fellow, dean, former federal agency administrator*
Copeland, Henry Jefferson, Jr. *former college president*
Cunningham, Alice Jeanne *chemistry educator, author, consultant*
Delahanty, Rebecca Ann *school system administrator*
Dobranski, Bernard *dean, law educator*
Dockery, J. Lee *retired medical school administrator*
Dodd, Emmeline Irwin *retired biology educator*
Evans, Richard Austin *education educator, consultant*
Forsyth, Ben Ralph *retired academic administrator, medical educator*
Foster, Martha Tyahla *pre-school administrator*
Franz, Frank Andrew *academic administrator, physicist, educator*
Gaddis, Paul Otto *university dean*
Garrett, Sandy Langley *former school system administrator*
Graham-Moore, Brian Edward *retired educator, consultant*
Gruberg, Cy *educational administrator*
Gunther, William David *retired academic administrator, economics professor*
Haborak, George Edward *retired academic administrator, educator*
Hall, Lawrence *secondary school educator*
Hamel, Dana Bertrand *retired academic administrator*
Harper, Sandra Stecher *academic administrator*
Heck, James Baker *retired education educator*
Hernandez, Kenneth J. *dean*
Hovland, Eric Jeffrey *retired dean, endodontics educator*
Hudson, Celeste Nutting *retired education educator, consultant, reading clinic administrator*
Huntley, Robert Edward Royall *retired academic administrator*
Ibanez, Manuel Luis *academic administrator, biologist, educator*
James, Allix Bledsoe *retired university president*
Janeway, Richard *retired academic administrator*
Kern, Ronald Paul *dean, consultant*
Knowles, Julie Nall *secondary school educator*
Krug, John Carleton (Tony Krug) *retired academic administrator, educator, library director, consultant*
Kukura, Rita Anne *pre-school educator, counselor*
Leather, Victoria Potts *college librarian*
Lick, Dale Wesley *educational leadership educator, mathematician*
Little, Peter D. *anthropology professor*
Lober, Irene Moss *educational consultant*
Long, Leland Timothy *retired geophysics educator, seismologist*
Main, Edna Dewey (June Main) *emeritus education professor*
Massey, Thomas Benjamin *retired university president*
Mathis, Luster Doyle *academic administrator, political scientist, educator*
Meyer, Richard W. *retired university librarian*
Monteith, Larry King *chancellor emeritus*
Morgan, Ruth Prouse *academic administrator, educator*
Morrow, Bruce William *retired military officer academic administrator, management consultant*
Musa, Samuel Albert *university executive*
Orr, Kenneth Bradley *academic administrator*
Patterson, Oscar III *retired academic administrator*
Patton, Carl Vernon *retired academic administrator*
Pennington, Jodie A. *education outreach educator*
Pewitt, James Dudley *retired academic administrator*
Pitman, Sharon Gail *retired middle school counselor*

Prokasy, William Frederick *academic administrator*
Rada, Ruth Byers *retired dean*
Reed, Leon Samuel *secondary school educator, photographer*
Reese, Clara Cook *retired educator*
Reid, Helen Veronica *provost*
Remley, Audrey Wright *retired academic administrator, psychologist*
Riggsby, Dutchie Sellers *retired education educator*
Ritvo, Roger Alan *research management professor, health management-policy educator*
Rorie, Nancy Catherine *retired secondary school educator*
Russell, Rob *academic administrator*
Ryan, Ione Jean Alohilani Rathburn *retired education educator, counselor*
Saenz, Michael *retired academic administrator*
Shapiro, Lee Tobey *mathematics educator, astronomer*
Springer, Marlene *retired academic administrator*
Stellar, Arthur Wayne *school system administrator*
Thomas, Beverly Irene *special education educator, counseling administrator, educational diagnostician*
Todd, Lee Trover, Jr. *retired academic administrator, electrical engineer*
Tomlinson, Carol Ann *education educator, writer*
Wagner, Ellyn Santi *retired mathematics educator*
Weber, Yvonne Roebuck *research administrator, educator*
Werner, Robert Joseph *dean, music educator*
Wetherell, Thomas Kent *former academic administrator*
White, Lonnie Joe *retired history educator*
Widman, Rudolph Paul *college administrator*
Wynne, Terry Lynne *career counselor, writer*

ENGINEERING

UNITED STATES

ALABAMA

Auburn
Cochran, John Euell, Jr. *aerospace engineer, lawyer, educator*
Cutchins, Malcolm Armstrong *aerospace engineer, educator, researcher*
Hanley, Thomas Richard *engineering educator*
Irwin, John David *electrical engineering educator*
Jaeger, Richard Charles *electrical engineer, educator, science association director*
Sforzini, Richard Henry *aerospace engineer, educator*

Auburn University
Choe, Song-yul *engineering educator*

Birmingham
Goldman, Jay *industrial engineer, educator, dean emeritus*
Goodrich, Thomas Michael *engineering and construction executive, lawyer*
Nash, David J. *engineering and construction company executive, retired military officer*

Florence
Badger, Phillip Charles *engineer, manager*

Hartselle
Johnson, Loyd *agricultural engineer, researcher*

Huntsville
Karbhari, Vistasp M. *engineering educator, researcher*
King, David A. *aerospace engineer*
Pittman, William Claude, Jr. *retired electrical engineer*
Sackheim, Robert Lewis *aerospace engineer, educator*
Watson, Raymond Coke, Jr. *engineering executive, consultant, academic administrator*
Wieland, Paul Otto *environmental control systems engineer*

Madison
Adams, Gary Lee *systems engineer*

Mobile
van Aken, John Henry *retired marine engineer*

Montgomery
Pan, Chai-Fu *engineering educator*

Mosul
Southern, Terry Keith *engineering executive*

Tuscaloosa
Moynihan, Gary Peter *industrial engineering educator*

ARKANSAS

Fayetteville
Gaddy, James Leoma *chemical engineer, educator*
Johnson, Michael R. *civil engineer, academic administrator, retired military officer*
White, John Austin, Jr. *engineering educator, retired academic administrator*

CALIFORNIA

La Jolla
Luo, Jian *engineering educator, researcher*

Pasadena
List, Ericson John *environmental engineering science educator, consultant*

DISTRICT OF COLUMBIA

Washington
Giallorenzi, Thomas Gaetano *optical engineer*
Pickholtz, Raymond Lee *electrical engineering educator, consultant*

FLORIDA

Aventura
Wolfenson, Azi U. *electrical, mechanical and industrial engineer, consultant*

Boca Grande
Marini, Robert Charles *environmental engineering executive*

Boca Raton
Lin, Yukweng M. *engineer, educator*

Coral Gables
Abdel-Mottaleb, Mohamed *electrical engineer, educator*
Mantell, Murray I. *engineering educator*

Davie
Upadhiaya, Umesh Chandra *engineer, consultant*

Daytona Beach
Helfrick, Albert Darlington *electronics engineering educator, consultant, department chairman*

Eglin AFB
Franzen, Larry William *aerospace electronics engineer*

Gainesville
Abernathy, Cammy R. *engineering professor, dean*
Anderson, Timothy J. *chemical engineering distinguished professor*
Capehart, Barney Lee *industrial and systems engineer, educator*
Cristescu, Nicolaie Dan *engineering educator*
Delfino, Joseph John *environmental engineering sciences educator*
Fossum, Jerry George *electrical engineering educator*
Hollien, Harry Francis *communications engineer*
Isaacs, Gerald William *retired agricultural engineering educator, consultant*
Khargonekar, Pramod Prabhakar *engineering professor, former dean*
Kurzweg, Ulrich Hermann *engineering science educator*
Sherif, S. A. *engineering educator*
Uhrig, Robert Eugene *nuclear engineer, educator*
Westphal, Roger Allen *electrical engineer*

Hillsboro Beach
Mandel, Herbert Maurice *retired civil engineer*

Indialantic
Preece, Betty P. *electrical engineer, educator*

Jacksonville
Joyce, Edward Rowen *retired chemical engineer, educator*
McGovern, Jay *aeronautical engineer, consultant*
Mueller, Edward Albert *retired transportation engineer*

Jupiter
Migliaro, Marco William *electrical engineer*
Wolff, Edward Alvin *electronics engineer*

Lady Lake
Granger, Robert Alan *mechanical and aerospace engineering educator*

Lighthouse Point
Farho, James Henry, Jr. *mechanical engineer, consultant*

Miami
Barthel, William Frederick, Jr. *electrical engineer*
Maidique, Modesto Alex *engineering educator, former academic administrator*
Veziroglu, Turhan Nejat *mechanical engineering educator, researcher*

Miami Beach
Milne, Edward Lawrence *biomedical engineer*

Naples
Corn, Morton *environmental engineer, educator*

North Venice
Anthony, Donald Barrett *engineering executive*

Orlando
DeMara, Ronald Francis *computer engineer, educator*
Simaan, Marwan *electrical engineering educator*

Palm Beach Gardens
Gillette, Frank C., Jr. *retired mechanical engineer*

Panama City
D'Arcy, Gerald Paul *engineering executive, consultant*

Pompano Beach
Roush, Robert Warren *electrical engineer, director*

Port Charlotte
Kok, Hans Gebhard *consulting engineer*

Riviera Beach
Cuschieri, Joseph M. *acoustical engineer, professional society administrator*

Santa Rosa Beach
Batchman, Theodore Earl *retired electrical engineering educator, researcher*

Sarasota
Long, Robert Radcliffe *fluid mechanics engineer, educator*

Satellite Beach
Potvin, Alfred Raoul *retired engineering executive*

Tallahassee
Coloney, Wayne Herndon *civil engineer*
De Forest, Sherwood Searle *agricultural engineer, products executive*

Tampa
Carnahan, Robert Paul *retired civil engineer, educator, researcher, consultant*
Kaw, Autar Krishen *mechanical engineer, educator*

The Villages
Dupies, Donald Albert *retired civil engineer*

West Palm Beach
Flescher, Harole Lee *retired engineering executive*
Holness, Gordon Victor Rix *engineering executive, mechanical engineer*

Winter Haven
Johnson, Gordon Selby *consulting electrical engineer*

GEORGIA

Athens
McCutcheon, Steven Clifton *ecological and environmental engineer, hydrologist*
Nelson, Stuart Owen *agricultural engineer, researcher, educator*

Atlanta
Abdel-Khalik, Said Ibrahim *nuclear and mechanical engineering educator*
Ayazi, Farrokh *engineering educator*
Bonaparte, Rudolph *engineering company executive*
Braun, Robert David *aerospace engineer, educator, former federal agency administrator*
Clements, Mark Andrew *electrical and computer engineering professor, entrepreneur*
Cressler, John David *electrical engineering educator*
Crittenden, John Charles *engineering educator*
Ellingwood, Bruce Russell *structural engineer, educator*
Giddens, Don Peyton *engineering educator, researcher*
Harrison, George Brooks *engineer, researcher, retired military officer*
Hess, Dennis William *chemical engineering educator*
Hodges, Dewey Harper *aerospace engineer, educator*
Howard, Ayanna MacCalla *electrical and robotics engineer, educator*
Johnson, Roger Warren *chemical engineer*
Kemp, Charles C. *engineering educator*
McDowell, David Lynn *mechanical engineering educator*
McIntire, Larry Vern *biomedical engineering educator*
Meindl, James Donald *electrical engineering educator, academic administrator*
Michaels, Jennifer Emmons *engineering educator*
Nemhauser, George L. *industrial engineer, systems engineer, educator, operations research specialist*
Rouhani, Shahrokh *civil engineering environmental educator, consultant*
Salant, Richard Frank *mechanical engineer, educator*
Shortal, Terence Michael *retired systems company executive*
Sokol, Joel S. *engineering educator*
Stacey, Weston Monroe, Jr. *nuclear engineer, physicist, educator*
Teja, Amyn Sadrudin *chemical engineering educator, consultant*
Thuesen, Gerald Jorgen *industrial engineer, educator*
Vachon, Reginald Irenee *mechanical engineer*
Winer, Ward Otis *mechanical engineer, educator*
Wyvill, J. Craig *retired research engineer, program director*

Big Canoe
Bendelius, Arthur George *engineering firm executive*

Columbus
Haneman, Vincent Siering, Jr. *consulting engineer, educator, dean*

Dillard
Aldridge, Melvin Dayne *engineering educator*

Doraville
Wempner, Gerald Arthur *engineering professor*

Duluth
Colwell, Gene Thomas *engineering educator*

Fort Valley
Hedden, Kenneth Forsythe *chemical engineer*

Fortson
Hanna, William Johnson *electrical engineering educator*

Macon
Leonard, Michael Steven *industrial engineering educator*

Savannah
Henne, Preston A. *engineering executive*
Hsu, Ming-Yu *engineering educator*

Stone Mountain
Nerem, Robert Michael *engineering educator, consultant*

Thomaston
Beohm, Richard Thomas *safety engineering consultant*

INDIANA

West Lafayette
Grace, Richard Edward *engineering educator*
Marshall, Francis Joseph *aerospace engineer*

KENTUCKY

Covington
Baker, Merl *engineering educator*

Georgetown
Caroland, William Bourne *structural engineer*

Lexington
Brock, Louis Milton, Jr. *engineering educator, researcher*
Drake, Vaughn Paris, Jr. *electrical engineer*
Holsapple, Clyde Warren *decision and information systems educator*

Louisville
Tran, Long Trieu *industrial engineer*

LOUISIANA

Amite
Parish, Richard Lee *engineer, consultant*

Baton Rouge
Bernhard, James M., Jr. *engineering executive*
Ferraioli, Brian K. *engineering executive*
Khonsari, Michael M. *mechanical engineering educator*
Lima, Marybeth *engineering educator*
Pike, Ralph Webster *chemical engineer, educator, academic administrator*
Tumay, Mehmet Taner *geotechnical engineering educator, researcher, consultant*

Lafayette
Marshak, Alan Howard *electrical engineer, educator*

Metairie
Nicoladis, Michael F. *engineering company executive*

New Orleans
Lannes, William Joseph III *electrical engineer*

Pearl River
Gernon, Clarke Joseph, Sr. *mechanical and forensic engineering consultant*

Ruston
Barron, Randall Franklin *mechanical engineer, educator, consultant*

Slidell
Stuart, Charles Edward *electrical engineer, oceanographer*
Tewell, Joseph Robert, Jr. *retired electrical engineer*

MICHIGAN

Ann Arbor
Gibala, Ronald *metallurgical engineering educator*

MISSISSIPPI

University
Cheng, Alexander Hung-Darh *engineering educator, consultant*
Sadana, Ajit *chemical engineer, educator*

Vaiden
Murphy, Ben Carroll *retired engineering company executive*

NEW HAMPSHIRE

Manchester
Murphy, William Parry, Jr. *mechanical engineer*

NORTH CAROLINA

Asheville
Hatch, Ross Riepert *weapon system engineering executive*

Cary
Vick, Columbus Edwin, Jr. *retired civil engineering design firm executive*

Chapel Hill
Marchionini, Gary Joseph *information science educator*
Prins, Jan F. *computer science and engineering educator*
Smith, Allie Maitland *retired engineering educator*

Charlotte
Merrifield, Jeffrey S. *engineering company executive, former commissioner*
Woodward, James Hoyt *engineering educator, former academic administrator*

PROFESSIONAL INDEX 943 ENGINEERING

Durham
Agarwal, Pankaj K. *computer engineering educator*
Casey, H(orace) Craig, Jr. *electrical engineering educator*
Dowell, Earl Hugh *aerospace and mechanical engineering educator*
Friedman, Morton Harold *engineering educator, department chairman*
Goodwin, Frank Erik *materials engineer*
New, William, Jr. *engineer, physician, investor*
Petroski, Henry *engineering educator, writer*
Plonsey, Robert *electrical and biomedical engineer*
Wilson, Blake Shaw *electrical engineer, researcher*
Yellen, Benjamin *engineering educator*

Granite Falls
Humphreys, Kenneth King *engineer, professional society administrator, educator, pastor*

Greensboro
Iyer, Shanthi *electrical engineering and nanoengineering educator, researcher*

New Bern
Painter, Jack Timberlake *civil engineer*
Whitehurst, Brooks Morris *chemical engineer*

Raleigh
Beatty, Kenneth Orion, Jr. *chemical engineer, educator*
Bernhard, Richard Harold *industrial engineer, educator*
Bitzer, Donald Lester *electrical engineer, educator, retired lab administrator*
Gardner, Robin Pierce *engineering educator*
Grimes, Dale Mills *physics and electrical engineering educator*
Hall, Carol K. *chemical engineering educator, researcher*
Havner, Kerry Shuford *civil engineering and solid mechanics educator, scientist*
Hawari, Ayman I. *engineering educator, director*
Holton, William Coffeen *electrical engineering executive*
Jameel, Hasan *chemical engineering professor*
Kolbas, Robert Michael *electrical engineering educator*
Sneed, Ronald Ernest *retired project engineer, educator*
Turinsky, Paul Josef *nuclear engineer, educator*
Wehring, Bernard William *nuclear engineering educator*
Zorowski, Carl Frank *engineering educator, academic administrator*

Salisbury
Cobb, Tyrus Raymond, Jr., (Ty Cobb) *retired engineer, retired military officer*

OHIO

Cincinnati
Hodge, Bobby Lynn *mechanical engineer, manufacturing executive*

OKLAHOMA

Medford
Robbins, Frankie *civil engineer*

Norman
Bert, Charles Wesley *mechanical and aerospace engineer, educator*
Campbell, John Morgan *retired chemical engineer*
Egle, Davis Max *mechanical engineering educator*
Gollahalli, Subramanyam Ramappa *engineering educator*
Lamb, Peter James *meteorology educator, researcher, consultant*
Meo, Mark *engineering educator*

Stillwater
Hoberock, Lawrence Linden *mechanical engineer, educator*
Mize, Joe Henry *industrial engineer, educator*
Thompson, David Russell *engineering educator, dean*

Tulsa
Azar, J. J. *engineering educator*
Prayson, Alex Stephen *design engineering educator*

SOUTH CAROLINA

Beaufort
Pinkerton, Robert Bruce *mechanical engineer*

Charleston
Fei, James Robert *engineering executive, consultant*
Haemmerich, Dieter *biomedical engineer*
Karakostas, Tasos *engineer, director*

Clemson
Greenstein, Joel Sandor *industrial engineering educator*
Gulari, Esin *chemical engineering educator, dean*
Kimbler, Delbert Lee, Jr. *retired industrial engineering educator*
Pursley, Michael Bader *engineering educator, communications systems researcher, consultant*
Singh, Rajendra *electrical engineering educator, researcher*
Walker, Ian David *engineering educator*
Zumbrunnen, David Arnold *engineering educator*

Greenville
Plumstead, William Charles, Sr. *quality engineer, consultant*

Hartsville
Menius, Espie Flynn, Jr. *electrical engineer*

Hilton Head Island
Huckins, Harold Aaron *engineering executive consultant*
Jerger, Edward William *engineering educator, dean*

Orangeburg
Hong, Jae-Dong *industrial engineering educator*

West Union
Klutz, Anthony Aloysius, Jr. *health, safety and environmental manager*

TENNESSEE

Cookeville
Chowdhuri, Pritindra *retired electrical engineer, educator*
Sissom, Leighton Esten *engineering educator, dean, consultant*

Crossville
Bell, Charles Eugene, Jr. *retired industrial engineer*

Greenbrier
Newell, Paul Haynes, Jr. *engineering educator*

Knoxville
Bose, Bimal Kumar *electrical engineering educator*
Brown, Donald Vaughn *retired engineer*
Prados, John William *retired engineering educator*
Richards, Stephen Harold *engineering educator*
Roth, John Reece *electrical engineer, educator, researcher, inventor*
Scott, Bob (Robert Scott) *retired chemical engineer, educator*
Wu, Jie *electronics engineer, educator*
Zinkle, Steven John *engineer, researcher*

Louisville
Nutt, Ronald *electrical engineer*

Nashville
Bodruzzaman, Mohammad *engineering educator*
Galloway, Kenneth Franklin *engineering professor, dean*
Gore, John Christopher *engineering professor*
Hahn, George Thomas *materials engineering educator, researcher*
LeVan, Martin Douglas *chemical engineering professor*
Parker, Frank Leon *environmental engineering educator, consultant*
Schnelle, Karl Benjamin, Jr. *chemical engineering professor, consultant, researcher*
Speece, Richard Eugene *civil engineer, educator*
Weller, Robert Allen *engineering educator, physicist, materials scientist*

Oak Ridge
Alexeff, Igor *retired electrical engineering educator*
DeHart, Mark David *nuclear engineer, researcher*

Soddy Daisy
Sunderland, Richard H. *electrical engineer, freelance/self-employed lawyer*

Tullahoma
Hill, Susan Sloan *safety engineer*

TEXAS

Addison
Lopus, Thomas Albert *petroleum engineer*

Allen
Biard, James Robert *retired electrical engineer, consultant*

Arlington
Clark, Dayle Meritt *civil engineer*
Stevens, Gladstone Taylor, Jr. *retired industrial engineer, retired educator*

Austin
Aggarwal, Jagdishkumar Keshoram *electrical and computer engineering educator, administrator, researcher*
Baker, Lee Edward *biomedical engineering educator*
Breen, John Edward *civil engineer, educator*
Bronaugh, Edwin Lee *retired electrical engineer*
Burns, Ned Hamilton *civil engineering educator*
Diller, Kenneth Ray *mechanical and biomedical engineer, educator*
Fenves, Gregory L. *engineering professor, dean*
Fowler, David Wayne *architectural engineering educator*
Freeman, Benny Dean *engineering educator*
Goodenough, John Bannister *engineering educator, physicist, researcher*
Harris, Richard Lee *engineering executive, retired military officer*
Hester, Phillip D. *engineering company executive*
Himmelblau, David Mautner *chemical engineer*
Hixson, Elmer L. *retired engineering educator*
Hughes, Thomas Joseph Robert *mechanical engineering educator, consultant*
Hull, David George *aerospace engineering educator, researcher*
Koen, Billy Vaughn *mechanical engineering educator*
Mc Ketta, John J., Jr. *chemical engineering professor*
Nichols, Steven Parks *mechanical engineer, educator, academic administrator, lawyer*
Oden, John Tinsley *engineering educator, mathematician, consultant*
Peppas, Nicholas Athanassiou *chemical and biomedical engineering educator, consultant*
Reible, Danny David *environmental chemical engineer, educator*
Reiter, David S. *engineering company executive, lawyer*
Sandberg, Irwin Walter *retired electrical and computer engineering educator*
Schechter, Robert Samuel *chemical engineer, educator*
Stice, James Edward *chemical engineer, educator*
Stokoe, Kenneth H., II, *civil engineer, educator*
Streetman, Ben Garland *engineering professor, former dean*
Swartzlander, Earl Eugene, Jr. *engineering educator, former electronics company executive*
Tapley, Byron Dean *aerospace engineer, educator*
Walton, Charles Michael *civil engineering educator*
Welch, Ashley James *engineering educator*
Wheeler, Mary Fannett *aerospace engineering and engineering mechanics professor, petroleum and geosystems engineering, mathematics professor*
Willson, C. Grant *chemical engineering and chemistry professor*
Wise, Gary Lamar *electrical engineering and mathematics educator, investment researcher*
Womack, Baxter Frank *electrical and computer engineering educator, researcher*
Yura, Joseph Andrew *structural engineer, educator*

Beaumont
Hopper, Jack Rudd *chemical engineering professor*

Big Spring
Fryrear, Donald William *agricultural engineer, researcher*

Bryan
Piper, Lloyd Llewellyn, II, *engineer, government and service industry executive*

Bushland
Howell, Terry Allen *agricultural engineer*

College Station
Bennett, G. Kemble (George Kemble Bennett) *engineering professor, dean*
Buchanan, Walter Woolwine *electrical engineer, educator, academic administrator*
Ehsani, Mehrdad (Mark) *electrical engineering educator, consultant*
Fletcher, Leroy Stevenson *mechanical engineer, educator*
Hall, Kenneth Richard *chemical engineering professor, consultant*
Hann, Roy William, Jr. *civil engineer, educator*
Holditch, Stephen Allen *petroleum engineering educator, consultant*
Lowery, Lee Leon, Jr. *civil engineer*
Lu, Mi *computer engineer, educator*
Lytton, Robert Leonard *civil engineer, educator*
Mathewson, Christopher Colville *engineer, geologist, educator*
Mercer, Melvin Ray *electrical engineer, educator*
Mukhtar, Saqib *agricultural engineer, educator*
Ntaimo, Lewis *engineering educator, researcher*
Patton, Alton DeWitt *electrical engineering consultant*
Radovic, Miladin *engineering educator, researcher*
Richardson, Herbert Heath *retired mechanical engineer, educator, dean, academic administrator*
Saric, William Samuel *aerospace engineering educator*
Savari, Serap Ayse *engineering educator, researcher*

Dallas
Eberhart, Robert Clyde *biomedical engineering educator, researcher*
Etter, Delores M. *engineering educator, former political appointee*
Jester, Guy Earlscourt *engineering consultant*
Schulze, Richard Hans *environmental engineering executive*
Szygenda, Stephen A. *electrical and computer engineering educator, researcher*

Denton
Needleman, Alan *mechanical engineering educator*

El Paso
Bartel, Herbert Herman, Jr. *retired engineering educator*
Grieves, Robert Belanger *engineering and language educator*

Fort Worth
Astrup, Jens Leo *retired civil engineer*
Cunningham, Atlee Marion, Jr. *aeronautical engineer*
Lewis, Frank Leroy *electrical engineer, educator, researcher*
Nichols, James Richard *civil engineer, consultant*
Wise, Charla Kamm *aeronautics company executive*

Frisco
Mihm, John Clifford *chemical engineer*

Granbury
Rodenberger, Charles Alvard *aerospace engineer, consultant*

Houston
Akers, William Walter *chemical engineering educator*
Burrus, Sidney (Charles Sidney Burrus) *engineering professor, dean*
Cooper, Keith D. *computer science and engineering educator*
Coskey, William A. *engineering company executive*
Duerr, David *civil engineer*
Edwards, Paul Beverly *retired science and engineering educator*
Henley, Ernest Justus *retired chemical engineering professor*
Horton, Thomas Edward, Jr. *mechanical engineering educator*
Hsu, Thomas Tseng-Chuang *civil engineer, educator*
Hunsaker, Barry, Jr. *aerospace engineer, lawyer*
Jackson, David R. *electrical engineer, educator*
Kavandi, Janet Lynn *astronaut aerospace power engineer, chemist*
Khachaturian, Jon *civil engineer, manufacturing executive*
Kim, Hyungjun *biomedical engineer, educator*
Lienhard, John Henry, IV, *mechanical engineer, educator*
Liu, Donald *mechanical engineer*
Luss, Dan *chemical engineering professor*
Miele, Angelo *engineering educator, researcher, consultant, author*
Morris, Owen Glenn *engineering corporation executive*
Moschetta, Robert P. *safety engineering administrator*
O'Geary, Dennis Traylor *retired engineering company executive*
Powell, Alan *engineering educator, research scientist*
Prats, Michael *petroleum engineer, educator*
Segner, Edmund Peter III *engineering professor, former natural gas company executive*

Humble
Brown, Samuel Joseph, Jr. *engineer, scientist*

Irving
Barnard, Ray F. *engineering and construction management company executive*
Boeckmann, Alan L. *engineering and construction management company executive*
Flowers, Garry W. *engineering and construction management company executive*
Gilbert, H. Steven *engineering and construction management company executive*
Hallgren, Wendy *engineering company executive*
Hopkins, John L. *engineering company executive*
Seaton, David T. *engineering company executive*

Lubbock
Kiesling, Ernst Willie *civil engineering educator*
Kristiansen, Magne *electrical engineer, educator*

Mc Kinney
Gill, David bRIAN *electrical engineer, educator*

Port Aransas
Lehmann, William Leonardo *electrical engineer, educator*

Rockport
Minor, Joseph Edward *civil engineer, educator*

San Antonio
Abramson, Hyman Norman *engineering and science research executive*
Agaian, Sos Suien *electrical engineer, researcher*

San Marcos
Asiabanpour, Bahram *engineering educator*

Stafford
Le, Duy-Loan *electrical engineer*

Sugar Land
Finch, Robert David *mechanical engineer, educator, consultant*
Swanberg, Christopher Gerard *environmental engineer*

Tyler
Sathyamoorthy, Muthukrishnan *engineering educator, associate provost*

Waco
Farison, James Blair *electrical and biomedical engineer, educator*
Kittlitz, Rudolf Gottlieb, Jr. *chemical engineer, researcher*

Wharton
Schulze, Arthur Edward *biomedical engineer, researcher*

VIRGINIA

Afton
Anderson, Donald Norton, Jr. *retired electrical engineer*

Alexandria
Mack, Carl B. *engineering executive*
Poehlein, Gary Wayne *retired chemical engineering professor*
Wilcox, David Eric *electrical engineering, educator, consultant, business owner*

Arlington
Cox, Henry *engineer, researcher*
Hall, Carl William *agricultural and mechanical engineer*
Hazelrigg, George Arthur, Jr. *systems engineer, educator*

Ashburn
Nickle, Dennis Edwin *electronics engineer, consultant, deacon*
Ramsey, Forrest Gladstone, Jr. *retired engineering company executive*

Blacksburg
Batra, Romesh Chander *engineering educator, researcher*
Benson, Richard Carter *mechanical engineering professor, dean*
Brown, Gary Sandy *electrical engineering educator*
Gray, Festus Gail *electrical engineer, educator, researcher*
Hong, Dennis Wonsuh *engineering educator, researcher*
Jones, James Beverly *retired mechanical engineering educator, consultant*
Lee, Fred C. *electrical engineering educator*
Meirovitch, Leonard *engineering educator, educator*
Mitchell, James Kenneth *civil engineer, educator*
Price, Dennis Lee *industrial engineer, educator*
Randall, Clifford Wendell *civil engineer, educator*
Squires, Arthur Morton *chemical engineer, educator*
Thorp, James Shelby *electrical engineering educator*

Chantilly
Austin, Wanda Murry *systems engineer*

Charlottesville
Aylor, James Hiram *engineering professor, dean*
Dorning, John Joseph *nuclear engineering, applied physics and applied mathematics educator*
Fink, Lester Harold *retired engineering company executive, educator*
Hudson, John Lester *chemical engineering professor*
Krzysztofowicz, Sir Roman *systems engineering and statistical science educator, consultant*
Soffa, Mary Lou *computer science and engineering educator*
Townsend, Miles Averill *aerospace and mechanical engineering educator*
Wulf, William Allan *engineering educator*

Elliston
Smith, Rodney Wike *retired engineering executive*

Fairfax
Chen, Chun-Hung *engineering educator*
Cook, Gerald *electrical engineering educator*
Gertler, Janos John *electrical engineer, educator*
Houck, Mark Hedrich *engineering educator*
Levis, Alexander Henry *systems engineer, educator, consultant*
Lott, Wayne Thomas *systems engineer*
Palmer, James Daniel *information technology educator*
Sage, Andrew Patrick *systems engineering and management educator*

Fairfax Station
Duff, William Grierson *electrical engineer, educator*

Falls Church
Jones, Russel Cameron *civil engineer, educator*

Hampton
Bangert, Linda S. *aeronautical engineer*
Cragg, Clinton H. *aerospace engineer, retired military officer*
Logan, Kathryn Vance *research engineer*
Meyers, James Frank *electronics engineer*
Noor, Ahmed Khairy *engineering educator, researcher*
Sobieski, Jaroslaw *aerospace engineer*

Mc Lean
Cambel, Ali B. *engineering educator*
Grasso, Alfred *engineering company executive, systems engineer*
Rosenbaum, David Mark *engineering executive, consultant, educator*
Walsh, John Breffni *aerospace consultant*

Montross
Fountain, Robert Roy, Jr. *retired engineering company executive, farmer, military officer*

Norfolk
Gheorghe, Adrian Velicu *safety, engineering management and system engineer, educator*
Karim, Mohammad Ataul *electrical engineering educator, researcher*

Petersburg
Nwoke, Ben U. *engineering educator, consultant*

Port Royal
Everett, Woodrow Wilson *electrical engineer, educator*

Reston
Kahn, Robert Elliot *engineer, computer scientist*

Richmond
Gad-el-Hak, Mohamed *aerospace and mechanical engineering educator, researcher*
Mattauch, Robert Joseph *retired electrical engineering educator, retired dean*

Springfield
Ochs, Walter J. *civil engineer, consultant*

Vienna
Keiser, Bernhard Edward *engineering executive, communications engineer, consultant*

Warrenton
Gullace, Marlene Frances *systems engineer*

Williamsburg
Lynn, Larry (Verne Lauriston Lynn) *engineering executive*

Woodbridge
Ren, Chiang H. *aerospace engineer, senior executive*

WEST VIRGINIA

Huntington
Fischer, Robert Lee *engineering executive, educator*

Morgantown
Eck, Ronald Warren *civil engineer, educator*
Halabe, Udaya Bhatta *civil engineering educator, researcher*
Peng, Syd S. *mining engineer, educator*

South Charleston
Nielsen, Kenneth Andrew *chemical engineer*

WISCONSIN

Milwaukee
Khachaturian, Mark Haig *systems engineer, consultant*

TERRITORIES OF THE UNITED STATES

PUERTO RICO

Gurabo
Kuruganty, Sastry Pratap *electrical engineering educator*

JORDAN

Amman
Nayfeh, Ali Hasan *engineering educator*

ADDRESS UNPUBLISHED

Bass, Steven Craig *electrical engineering educator, researcher*
Bhada, Rohinton Khurshed *chemical engineering educator*
Binkley, David Martin *electrical engineer, educator, musician*
Bowman, Bruce Alan *civil engineer*
Brennan, Lawrence Edward *retired electronics engineer*
Casazza, John Andrew *electrical engineer, energy executive*
Chou, Chung-Kwang *bio-engineer*
Coar, Richard John *mechanical engineer, aerospace transportation executive, consultant*
Cobbs, James Harold *engineer, retired engineering consultant*
Conway, Richard Ashley *environmental engineer*
Dally, James William *mechanical engineering educator, consultant*
Dobson, Donald Alfred *retired electrical engineer*
Eaglet, Robert Danton *electrical engineer, aerospace scientist, consultant, retired military officer, fighter pilot*
Edwards, Victor Henry *chemical engineer*
Evans, Gerald William *engineering educator, consultant*
Faw, Richard Earl *nuclear engineering educator*
Foley, Gary J. *chemical engineer, computer scientist, federal agency administrator, researcher*
Forney, Larry J. *chemical engineer, educator*
Fox, Joan Phyllis *environmental engineer, company executive*
Funk, Gary Lloyd *control engineer*
Ghovanloo, Maysam *engineer, educator*
Gouse, S. William, Jr. *mechanical engineering executive, researcher*
Gubbins, Keith Edmund *chemical engineering educator*
Hackney, James Acra III *industrial engineer, consultant, retired manufacturing executive*
Halpin, Daniel William *engineering educator, consultant, writer*
Hanneman, Rodney Elton *metallurgical engineer*
Harrison, Gordon Ray *retired engineering executive, consultant, research scientist*
Hiler, Edward Allan *agricultural and engineering educator*
Hootman, Harry Edward *retired educator, nuclear engineer, consultant*
Hornby, Sara Ann *metallurgical engineer, marketing professional*
Juricic, Davor *engineering educator*
Katona, Peter Geza *biomedical engineer, educator*
Kinsman, Frank Ellwood *engineering executive*
Kittelberger, Larry E. *retired engineering executive*
Kretschmer, Frank Frederick, Jr. *electrical engineer, researcher, consultant*
Kunze, Otto Robert *retired agricultural engineering educator*
Levitt, Gerald Steven *retired engineering executive*
Maksi, Gregory Earl *retired engineering educator*
Marple, Stanley Lawrence, Jr. *electrical engineer, educator and researcher*
McGinnis, Charles Irving *civil engineer*
McNair, John William, Jr. *civil engineer*
Miah, Abdul Malek *electrical engineer, educator*
Moeller, Dade William *environmental engineer, educator*
Moore, Fay Linda *systems engineer*
Morley, Lloyd Albert *electrical engineering educator*
Nguyen, Charles Cuong *engineering educator, researcher, dean*
Painter, John Hoyt *engineer*
Pastrick, Harold Lee *aeronautical engineer*
Peebles, Peyton Zimmermann, Jr. *retired electrical engineer, educator*
Pence, Ira Wilson, Jr. *engineering executive, researcher*
Robe, Thurlow Richard *retired engineering educator, dean*
Rose, James Turner *aerospace engineer, consultant*
Sah, Chih-Tang *electrical and computer engineering and physics educator*
Schuler, Theodore Anthony *retired civil engineer*
Sechrist, Chalmers Franklin, Jr. *electrical engineering educator*
Selwyn, Donald *retired engineering administrator, researcher, inventor, educator*
Shaffer, Bernard William *mechanical and aerospace engineering educator*
Shaw, Judy Browder *engineer*
Simpson, Murray *electrical engineer, consultant*
Skeen, David Ray *systems engineer, consultant, engineering executive, educator*
Skelland, Anthony Harold Peter *chemical engineering professor*
Sommerfeld, Jude Thomas *chemical engineer, educator*
Stancell, Arnold Francis *chemical engineering educator, retired oil industry executive*
Straughan, William Thomas *structural engineering consultant, educator*
Tether, Anthony John *aerospace executive*
Thackston, Edward Lee *civil engineering educator*
Urbanik, Thomas, II, *civil engineering educator, researcher*
Wilde, Daniel Underwood *computer engineering educator*
Zelby, Leon Wolf *retired electrical engineer, educator, consultant*

FINANCE: BANKING SERVICES
See also FINANCE: INVESTMENT SERVICES

UNITED STATES

ALABAMA

Birmingham
Brown, Shelaghmichael *bank executive*
Hall, O.B. Grayson, Jr., (Grayson Hall) *bank executive*
Northen, Charles Swift III *retired bank executive*
Owen, John B. *bank executive*
Padalino, Michael L. *mortgage company executive*

Dothan
Peterson, Roger *community bank executive, retired international investment banker, manufacturing executive, air force general*

Montgomery
Lowder, Robert E. *bank executive*

ARKANSAS

Bentonville
Walton, Jim Carr *bank executive*

Fayetteville
Brooks, Mary Elizabeth *bank executive*

Little Rock
Martin, R. Brad *bank executive*
Smith, Susan *bank executive*
Stephens, Warren A. *bank executive*

FLORIDA

Boca Raton
Wines, Lynne *bank executive*

Coral Gables
Brownell, Edwin Rowland *retired banker, civil engineer, land surveyor*

Fort Lauderdale
Freeman, Douglas K. *bank executive*

Jacksonville
Harris, Hugh R. *mortgage company executive*

Marco Island
Cooper, Thomas Astley *bank executive*

Miami Lakes
Kanas, John Adam *bank executive*

Naples
de Saint Phalle, Thibaut *investment banker, consultant*
Martinuzzi, Leo Sergio, Jr. *banker*

Palm Beach
Clifford, Stewart Burnett *banker, director*
Glickman, Carl David *banker*

Palm City
Thayer, Charles James *investment banker*

Pensacola
Stuart, Walter Bynum III *retired banker*

Ponte Vedra Beach
de Selding, Edward Bertrand *retired bank executive*

Punta Gorda
Haswell, Carleton Radley *banker*

Saint Petersburg
Godbold, Francis Stanley *investment banker, security firm executive*
Stewart, John Murray *retired bank executive*

Sarasota
Jennings, Christine Louise *retired bank executive*

Vero Beach
Sheehan, Charles Vincent *investment banker*

GEORGIA

Albany
Dorminey, O. Leonard *bank executive*

Alpharetta
Chau, Pin Pin *bank executive*

Athens
Douglas, J. William, Jr. *bank executive*

Atlanta
Abbott, Gay O. *bank executive*
Breeden, Mimi *bank executive*
Chancy, Mark A. *bank executive*
Dowling, Roderick Anthony *investment banker*
Freeman, Thomas E. *bank executive*
Gillani, Aleem *bank executive*
Guynn, Jack (George C. Guynn) *retired bank executive*
Henderson, Barry L. *bank executive*
Hollis, Timothy Martin *bank executive*
Humann, L. Phillip *retired bank executive*
Ivey, Michael Wayne *mortgage broker*
Joseph, Pamela A. *bank executive*
Kirby, C. Eugene, Jr. *bank executive*
Labarge, Suzanne B. *bank executive*
Lockhart, Dennis P. *bank executive*
Patterson, Dennis M. *bank executive*
Rogers, William H., Jr. *bank executive*
Spencer, Jill Wilemon *bank executive*
Sullivan, Timothy E. *bank executive*
Turtz, Steven *bank executive*
Wilfong, John Scott *banker*
Young, James E. *banker*

Chatsworth
Sarvis, Michael M. *bank executive*

Columbus
Blanchard, James Hubert *retired bank executive*
Carr, Leila S. *bank executive*
James, Elizabeth R. (Lee Lee James) *bank executive*
Stelling, Kessel D., Jr. *bank executive*
Yancey, James D. *bank executive*

Cumming
Knox, Boone A. *bank executive*

Hinesville
Smith, Barbara *bank executive*

Lagrange
McRae, William Frank *bank executive*

Macon
Ruddick, Linda S. *bank executive*

Milton
Aspbury, Herbert Francis *retired bank executive, board member*

Newnan
Carroll, J. Randall *bank executive*

KENTUCKY

Bowling Green
Kanipe, M. Todd *bank executive*

Lexington
Morrison, John M. *bank executive*

Louisville
Bouvette, Maria L. *bank executive*
Thompson, Kathy C. *bank executive*

Pikeville
Hale, Jean R. *bank executive*

LOUISIANA

Covington
Blossman, Alfred Rhody, Jr. *banker*

Lafayette
Bordelon, John *bank executive*
Byrd, Daryl Glynn *bank executive*
Cloutier, C. R. *bank executive*
Hail, Karen Lee *bank executive*
McLemore, James *bank executive*

New Orleans
Guerra, Donna T. *bank executive*
McDonald, Alden J., Jr. *bank executive*

MASSACHUSETTS

Boston
Bruce, Maryann *bank executive*

Westwood
Riley, Henry Charles *banker*

MISSISSIPPI

Biloxi
Swetman, Chevis *bank executive*

Gulfport
Chaney, Carl J. *bank executive*

Jackson
Hickson, Richard G. *bank executive*

Tupelo
Patterson, Aubrey Burns, Jr. *banker*

MISSOURI

Saint Louis
Perry, A. Michael *banker*

NEW JERSEY

Princeton
Gallagher, Thomas Joseph *investment banker*

NEW YORK

New York
Martinez, Melquiades R. (Melquiades Rafael Martinez) *bank executive, lawyer*
Tovey, Joseph *investment banker*

NORTH CAROLINA

Chapel Hill
Sewright, Charles William, Jr. *mortgage banking advisory services company executive*

Charlotte
Banks, Keith *bank executive*
Bednar, Ray *bank executive*
Bessant, Cathy (Catherine Pombier Bessant) *bank executive*
Bramble, Frank P. *bank executive*
Chance, Gloria A. *bank executive*
Cotty, Neil A. *bank executive*
Curl, Gregory L. *bank executive*
Darnell, David Clark *bank executive*
Davis, Jean E. *bank executive*
Dennard, Thomas S. *mortgage company executive*
Di Rita, Larry (Lawrence T.) *bank executive, former federal agency administrator*
Dixon, Georgette (Gigi) *bank executive*
Finucane, Anne Marie *bank executive*
Fox, William J. *bank executive, former federal official, lawyer*
Gifford, Charles K. *bank executive*
Hain, J. Travis *bank executive*
Hill, Jennifer *bank executive*
Holliday, Charles O. (Charles Otis Holliday Jr.) *bank executive*
Jenkins, Benjamin P. III *bank executive*
Jones, Milton H., Jr. *bank executive*
Kelly, Stanhope A. *bank executive*
Laughlin, Terry P. (Terrence P. Laughlin) *bank executive*
Lebda, Douglas R. *bank executive*
Mairone, Rebecca *mortgage company executive*
Montag, Tom (Thomas Kell Montag) *bank executive*
Moynihan, Brian Thomas *bank executive*
Nash, James E., Jr. *bank executive*
O'Connor, Bridget *bank executive*
O'Keefe, Edward Peter *bank executive, lawyer*
Rosato, Craig Richard *bank executive*
Smith, Andrea B. *bank executive*
Thompson, Bruce R. *bank executive*
Wiener, Alan H. *mortgage company executive, former real estate company executive*
Zwiener, David Kenneth *bank executive*

Huntersville
Abbott, James A. *bank executive*

Pinehurst
Rhody, Ronald Edward *bank executive, communications executive*

Raleigh
Hardin, Eugene Brooks, Jr. *bank executive*
Smith, Lanty Lloyd *bank executive, lawyer*

Wilson
Harton, Herbert Lynn *banker*

Winston Salem
Bible, Daryl N. *bank executive*
Henson, Christopher L. *bank executive*
King, Kelly S. *bank executive*
McMullen, Donald A., Jr. *bank executive*
Robertson, Walter S. III *bank executive*
Starnes, Clarke R. III *bank executive*
Wanders, Hans Walter *banker*

OKLAHOMA

Bartlesville
Doty, Donald D. *retired bank executive*

Oklahoma City
Fiegel, Jacque R. *bank executive*
Reich, Richard Allen *bank executive*

Wewoka
Rains, Mary Jo *banker*

SOUTH CAROLINA

Aiken
Verenes, J. Chris *bank executive*

Columbia
Boggs, Jack Aaron *retired banker, municipal government official, publisher*

North Myrtle Beach
Byrne, James Frederick *banker*

Spartanburg
Calvert, Jerry L. *bank executive*
Chapman, Martha Cloud *bank executive*

TENNESSEE

Memphis
Adams, Thomas C., Jr. *bank executive*
Cherry, Kim *bank executive*
Jordan, D. Bryan *bank executive*
Rose, Michael David *bank executive, lawyer*

Murfreesboro
Ford, William F. *banker*

Nashville
Bottorff, Dennis C. *banker*
Burch, John Christopher, Jr. *investment banker*
Daane, James Dewey *banker*
Shell, Owen Gladstone, Jr. *retired bank executive*

TEXAS

Abilene
Bentley, Clarence Edward *savings and loan association executive*

Bellaire
Martinez, George *bank executive*

Dallas
Babb, Ralph W., Jr. *bank executive*
Drago, Dana A. *bank executive*
Fisher, Richard Welton *bank executive*
Holland, James Richard, Jr. *bank executive*
Jacobs, Andrew F. *mortgage company executive*
Reid, Langhorne III *merchant banker*

Fort Worth
Minton, Jerry Davis *retired banker, lawyer*

Houston
Ball, George L. *investment banker*
Comper, Tony (F. Anthony) *retired bank executive*
Currie, John Thornton (Jack Currie) *retired investment banker*
Innes, Deborah *bank executive*
Jordan, Carmen Angelle *bank executive*
Moore, Preston *bank executive*

Laredo
Gonzalez, Eugene Robert *investment banker*

New Braunfels
Pharis, Ruth McCalister *retired bank executive*

Pasadena
Moon, John Henry, Sr. *banker*

Plano
Tankersley, Michael Wayne *bank executive*

San Antonio
Duncan, A. Baker *investment banker*

VIRGINIA

Alexandria
Smith, Phillips Guy *banker*
Tucker, Howard McKeldin *investment banker, consultant*

Arlington
Ochoa-Brillembourg, Hilda Margarita *investment banker*
Rogers, James Frederick *banker, management consultant*

Ashburn
Pavsek, Daniel Allan *banker, educator*

Chantilly
Pocalyko, Michael Nicholas *investment banker, corporate director, novelist*

Danville
Majors, Charles H. *bank executive*

Glen Allen
Akin, Thomas B. *mortgage company executive*

Mc Lean
Boyd, Ralph F., Jr. *mortgage company executive, former federal agency administrator*
Clineburg, Bernard H. *bank executive*
Fitzgerald, Peter Gosselin *bank executive, former United States Senator from Illinois*
George, Paul G. *mortgage company executive*
Hammett, Suzanne *bank executive*
Kari, Ross Jay *mortgage company executive*
Layton, Donald Harvey *mortgage company executive, retired investment company executive*
Lynch, Christopher S. *mortgage company executive, retired accounting executive*
May, Michael C. *mortgage company executive*
Morton, John Templeton *bank executive, former federal agency administrator*
Perlman, Mike *mortgage company executive*
Pike, Lynn A. *bank executive*
Renzi, Anthony *mortgage company executive*
Romano, Raymond G. *mortgage company executive*
Schneider, Ryan M. *bank executive*
Wisdom, Paige *bank executive*

Midlothian
Corsiglia, Nancy *bank executive*

Reston
Andersen, Shaza L. *bank executive*
Beckmann, Bill *mortgage company executive*

Richmond
Lacker, Jeffrey Malcolm *bank executive, economist*
Talley, Charles Richmond *retired bank executive*

Vienna
Blum, Edward Howard *investment banker*

TERRITORIES OF THE UNITED STATES

PUERTO RICO

Hato Rey
Moreno Blanco, Juan S. *bank executive*

San Juan
Carrion, Richard L. *bank executive*
Carrión Muñoz, Arturo L. *banker*
Chafey, David H., Jr. *bank holding company executive*
Wakeman, Glen R. *bank executive*

ENGLAND

London
Leland, Marc Ernest *trust company executive, consultant, lawyer*

ADDRESS UNPUBLISHED

Alphin, John Steele (Steele Alphin) *retired bank executive*
Blake, Gerald Rutherford *retired banker*
Boardman, William Penniman *retired bank executive*
Carpenter, Robert C. *retired banker, former state legislator*
Clifton, Russell B. *retired mortgage company executive, consultant*
Cook, Charles Wilkerson, Jr. *retired bank executive, municipal official*
Curry, John Michael *investment banker*
Czarnecki, Gerald Milton *investment banker, venture capitalist*
Dittenhafer, Brian Douglas *banker, economist*
Dodson, Samuel Robinette III *retired investment banker*
Fahringer, Catherine Hewson *retired savings and loan association executive*
Geithner, Paul Herman, Jr. *retired banker*
Greer, K. Gordon *banker*
Gundlach, Heinz Ludwig *investment banker*
Harris, Charles Edison *banker, lawyer*
Hickey, Joseph Michael *investment banker*
Hower, Frank Beard, Jr. *retired banker*
Jennings, Joseph Ashby *banker*
Jepson, Robert Scott, Jr. *bank executive*
Jones, Charles Hill, Jr. *banker*
Lewis, Kenneth D. *retired bank executive*
Mintz, Norman Nelson *investment banker, educator, retired academic administrator*
Moore, Jackson Watts *retired bank executive*
Moyse, Hermann III *banker*
Price, Joseph Lee, II, (Joe Price) *former bank executive*
Price, William James, IV, *investment banker*
Smith, Hilary Cranwell Bowen *investment banker*
Stone, Edmund Crispen III *banker*
Tyrrell, Gerald Gettys *banker*
Watts, Anthony Lee *bank executive*
West, Rexford Leon *retired bank executive*

FINANCE: FINANCIAL SERVICES

UNITED STATES

ALABAMA

Auburn
Park, Jung Chul *finance educator*

Birmingham
Godin, Barb *diversified financial services company executive*
Hendley, Dan Lunsford *retired bank executive*
Newton, Don Allen *economic development consultant*
Stilwell, John P. *mining company executive*
Turner, David J., Jr. *corporate financial executive*

Bremen
Weathersby, Cecil Jerry *accounting and finance manager*

Dothan
Lord, Jacqueline Ward *retired accountant, photographer, artist*

Tuscaloosa
Axel, Bernard *finance executive*

ARKANSAS

Bentonville
Smith, Catherine R. *corporate financial executive*

Conway
Horton, Joseph Julian, Jr. *economics and finance educator*
Mayor, Randy E. *corporate financial executive*
McNew, Bennie Banks *retired finance educator*

Little Rock
Massey, Richard N. *finance company executive, lawyer*

Springdale
Leatherby, Dennis *corporate financial executive*
Pless, Rodney S. *corporate financial executive*

FLORIDA

Atlantic Beach
Forrest, Allen Wright *tax consultant*

Aventura
Fishel, Peter Livingston *finance company executive, accountant*
Kliger, Milton Richard *diversified financial services company executive*

Boca Raton
Hecht, William David *retired accountant*
Miller, Eugene *business educator, consultant*
Peterson, Mark F. *business educator*
Sigel, Marshall Elliot *financial consultant*

Bradenton
Hashmi, Sajjad Ahmad *finance educator, dean*

Clearwater
Archbold, Thomas G. *corporate financial executive*
Finkenbrink, Ralph T. *corporate financial executive*
Gabos, Paul G. *corporate financial executive*
Upton, David M. *finance educator, board member*

Coral Springs
Vasquez, William Leroy *business educator, consultant*

Crystal River
Schlumberger, Robert Ernest *accountant*

Deerfield Beach
Armstrong, Frank *finance company executive*
Haeffner, Robert *corporate financial executive*
Siegel, Steven L. *finance company executive, consultant*

Fort Lauderdale
Callahan, Rebecca *corporate financial executive*
Grubbs, William J. *corporate financial executive*
McKay, Patricia A. *accounting firm executive*
Miller, Teri L. *corporate financial executive*
Shoemaker, William Edward *corporate financial executive*

Fort Myers
Adams, Todd Porter *financial and investment advisor*
Kleeberger, Kent A. *corporate financial executive*

Gainesville
Ritter, Jay Rial *finance educator*
Shugan, Steven Mark *business statistics and economics educator*

Jacksonville
Brenholt, John *corporate financial executive*
Bronson, David M. *corporate financial executive*
Carpenter, Alvin Rauso *finance company executive*
Cook, Ronald D. *diversified financial services company executive, lawyer*
Danzeisen, Marcia *corporate financial executive*
Ficarra, Anthony Michael *finance company executive*
Hayford, Michael D. *corporate financial executive*
Hollis, Charles Eugene, Jr. *finance company executive*
Hunt, James Kelso *finance company executive*
Jaffe, Barbara Gefen *finance company executive*
Kennedy, Lee A. *finance company executive*
Kersch, Michelle *finance company executive*
Martire, Frank R. *diversified financial services company executive*
Munoz, Oscar *corporate financial executive*
Murphy, Daniel Kennedy *corporate financial executive*
Norcross, Gary A. *diversified financial services company executive*
Park, Anthony J. *corporate financial executive*
Patch, Darcy L. *finance company executive*
Preslar, B. Clyde *corporate financial executive*
Sizemore, Carolyn T. *controller*
Tomlinson, William Holmes *management educator, retired military officer*
Vane, Terence G., Jr. *finance company executive, lawyer*

Lake Wales
Luing, Gary Alan *financial management educator*

Miami
Berkowitz, Bruce R. *equity fund manager*
Birns, Ira Michael *corporate financial executive*
Carlson, Gary E. *finance company executive*
Coton, Carlos David *finance manager*
DeHombre, Maria Cristina *accountant*
Garcia, Art A. *corporate financial executive*
Kirkland, James Bryant III *chief financial officer*
LeBow, Bennett S. *corporate financial executive*
Sanchez, Robert E. *corporate financial executive*
Werther, William B., Jr. *finance educator, consultant*

Miami Beach
Cohen, Philip Herman *accountant*
Howard, Melvin *financial executive*

Miami Shores
Diener, Betty Jane *business educator*

Naples
Madigan, Joseph Edward *financial executive, director, consultant*
Schoen, William Jack *finance company executive*

Niceville
Litke, Donald Paul *acquisition executive, retired military officer*

North Miami Beach
Castro, Ángel *accountant, author, educator*

North Palm Beach
Kee, Tommy *corporate financial executive*

Oldsmar
MacLeod, Donald Martin *corporate executive*

Orlando
Burchfield, Teresa C. *corporate financial executive*
Kellison, Stephen George *actuarial consultant*

Pompano Beach
Doery, Michelle *corporate financial executive*
Rosenbloom, Bruce S. *corporate financial executive*

Saint Petersburg
Ackart, Jennifer C. *corporate financial executive*
Allison, Paul D. *finance company executive*
Averitt, Richard Garland III *diversified financial services company executive*
Biever, Angela Mary *diversified financial services company executive*
Bryant, Timothy Clark *financial advisor*
Eitel, J. Timothy *finance company executive*
Freeman, Corinne *financial analyst, retired mayor*
Naimoli, Vincent Joseph *diversified financial services company executive*
Riess, Richard K. *finance company executive*
Saltzman, Robert Paul *retired diversified financial services company executive*
Schmeling, Judy *corporate financial executive*
Simmons, Hardwick *diversified financial services company executive*
Tremaine, Thomas R. *finance company executive*

Sarasota
Bailey, Robert Elliott *financial executive*
Culkin, Charles Walker, Jr. *certified Government financial manager, retired trade association administrator*
Humphrey, John *corporate financial executive*
Schmalzried, Marvin Eugene *financial consultant*
Soni, Paul J. *corporate financial executive*

Sunrise
Prygelski, Peter J. III *corporate financial executive*
Viola, Vincent *corporate financial executive, professional sports team executive*

Tampa
Alexander, William Olin *retired finance company executive*
Lebouitz, Martin Frederick *diversified financial services company executive, consultant*
Montgomery, Dirk A. *corporate financial executive*
Nord, Walter Robert *business administration educator, researcher, consultant*

Vero Beach
Conway, Earl Cranston *business educator, retired manufacturing company executive, educator*
McKane, David Bennett *business executive*
Riefler, Donald Brown *financial consultant*

Wellington
McCaffrey, Thomas P. *corporate financial executive*
Swisher, Stephen R. *corporate financial executive*

Wesley Chapel
Mendelsohn, Louis Benjamin *financial analyst*

West Palm Beach
Harper, Mary Sadler *wealth advisor and relationship manager*
Herrick, John Dennis *financial planner, consultant, retired food products executive*

Weston
Holtzman, Gary Yale *retired diversified financial services company executive*

Wimauma
Badalamenti, Anthony *financial planner*

Winter Park
Matulich, Serge *accounting educator, writer*
McMurtry, Nancey M. *finance company executive*
Starr, Martin Kenneth *management educator*

GEORGIA

Alpharetta
Corby, Francis Michael, Jr. *business executive*

Atlanta
Adrean, Lee *corporate financial executive*
Bane, Sandra N. *retired corporate financial executive, accountant*
Bartlett, Jerry *finance company executive*
Blaul, Frank *finance company executive*
Blum, Terry Christine *management educator, former dean*
Byrd, Carolyn H. *financial consultant*
Dyer, John M. *corporate financial executive*
Ferguson, Bradley A. *corporate financial executive*
Figuereo, Juan R. *corporate financial executive*
Forehand, Joseph W. *finance company executive*
Hamilton, Ryan *marketing professor*
Hill, Scott A. *stock exchange executive*
Holcom, Karen J. *corporate financial executive*
Kimball, Curtis Rollin *financial analyst*
Lienhard, Jerome T., II, *corporate financial executive*
Lobb, William Atkinson *financial services executive*
Malhotra, Naresh Kumar *marketing educator*
McCabe, Joseph, Jr. *corporate financial executive*
Naccarato, Ben *corporate financial executive*
Parsons, Leonard Jon *marketing educator, consultant*
Presby, J. Thomas *financial advisor, director*
Purcell, J. Neal *retired diversified financial services company executive*
Quick, Jeremy M. *corporate financial executive*
Reece, Richard Kent *corporate financial executive*
Sedlacek, Petr *finance company executive*
Shannon, Michael *finance company executive*
Smith, Richard F. *financial services company executive*
Troubh, Raymond Stanley *financial consultant*
Westenberger, Richard F. *corporate financial executive*
Winborne, Raymond E. *corporate financial executive*
Wittich, Wesley E. *corporate financial executive*
Wolf, Henry C. *retired corporate financial executive, board member*

Columbus
Dowe, Alison *finance company executive*
Jowers, Gaylon, Jr. *finance company executive*
Kennedy, LeAnne P. *diversified financial services company executive*
Prescott, Thomas J. *finance company executive*
Pruett, William A. *finance company executive*
Reynolds, Patrick A. *diversified financial services company executive*
Tomlinson, Philip W. *diversified financial services company executive*
Turner, John T. *finance company executive*

Conyers
Spearman, Maxie Ann *financial analyst, administrator*

Dalton
Winter, Larry Eugene *accountant*

Duluth
DeCoster, Gretchen *controller*
Fishman, Robert *corporate financial executive*
McColgan, Ellyn A. *former diversified financial services company executive*

Greensboro
Campbell, Charles Alton *private equity instructor, transportation executive*

Johns Creek
Cantrell, Wesley E. *retired finance company executive*

Kennesaw
Lapides, Paul Drew *business professor, board member*

Marietta
Aronoff, Craig Ellis *business educator, consultant*
Geminder, Philip H., II, *corporate finance and operations executive*

Milton
Martinez, Louis E. *corporate financial executive*

Norcross
Sills, John *corporate financial executive*
Stakel, John *corporate financial executive*

Statesboro
Murkison, Eugene Cox *finance educator*

Washington
Mansfield, Norman Connie *bookkeeper*

ILLINOIS

Chicago
Schweinhart, Richard Alexander *corporate financial executive*

KENTUCKY

Covington
Workman, John L. *corporate financial executive*

Highland Heights
Robinson, Brian J. *corporate financial executive*

Lexington
Gamble, John W., Jr. *corporate financial executive*
Stromquist, Gary D. *corporate financial executive*

Louisville
Lechleiter, Richard A. *corporate financial executive*
Linen, Jonathan S. *diversified financial services company executive*
McKim, Ruth Ann *financial planner*

Madisonville
Kington, Barry Clark *investor, consultant*

LOUISIANA

Baton Rouge
Bedeian, Arthur George *business educator*
Crumbley, Donald Larry *accounting educator, writer*

Covington
Doody, Louis Clarence, Jr. *retired accountant*

Kenner
Scherich, Edward Baptiste *retired diversified company executive*

Metairie
Gereighty, Andrea Saunders *diversified financial services company executive, poet*

New Orleans
Cook, Victor Joseph, Jr. *business educator, consultant*

Thibodaux
Fairchild, Joseph Virgil, Jr. *finance educator*

MARYLAND

Adelphi
Sutherland, Alan Roy *business educator*

MASSACHUSETTS

Boston
Hamermesh, Richard G. *management professor*

MICHIGAN

East Lansing
Luccock, Thomas Nelson *auditor, director*

MINNESOTA

Minneapolis
Avella, Joseph Ralph *university professor*

MISSISSIPPI

Natchez
Posey, Clyde Lee *business administration and accounting educator*

Tupelo
Nash, Henry Warren *marketing educator*

MISSOURI

Saint Louis
Winter, Richard Lawrence *diversified financial services company executive*

NEBRASKA

Elkhorn
Seymour, Harlan Francis *finance company executive*

NEW JERSEY

Florham Park
Bossen, Wendell John *retired financial planner*

NEW YORK

New York
Curd, Howard R. *financial consultant, textiles executive*
Daleo, Robert *corporate financial executive*
Hessels, Jan-Michiel *stock exchange executive*
Parker, David Raymond *finance company executive*

Pittsford
Snyder, Donald Edward, Sr. *finance company executive*

NORTH CAROLINA

Asheville
Letzig, Betty Jean *retired financial consultant*

Burlington
Hayes, William B. *corporate financial executive*

Cary
Blondy, Steven M. *corporate financial executive*
Ley, Peter D. *corporate financial executive*

Chapel Hill
Fragale, Alison R. *organizational behavior professor*
Jones, W. S. (Steve Jones) *management educator, former dean*
Perreault, William Daniel, Jr. *business administration educator*
Reed, Adam V. *finance professor*
Whybark, David Clay *business educator, researcher*
Woodbury, Edwina Dowdy *controller*

Charlotte
Almond, Giles Kevin *financial planner*
Anderson, Gerald Leslie *finance company executive*
Barker, Howard W., Jr. *accountant*
Frias, James D. *corporate financial executive*
Labardi, Jillian Gay *financial planner, insurance agent*
Linsz, Mark Douglas *diversified financial services company executive*
Ritchey, Lori A. *corporate financial executive*
Schnaper, Cara L. *diversified financial services company executive*
Schumaker-Kreig, Diane *diversified financial services company executive*
Sims, Michael B. *corporate financial executive*
Singh, Manjit Manmohan *corporate financial executive*
Taylor, Wendy Hall *auditor*
Thompson, Ronald L. *finance company executive, former manufacturing company executive*

Durham
Bettman, James Ross *management educator*
Breeden, Douglas Tower *finance educator, consultant, former dean*
Keller, Thomas Franklin *business administration educator*
Rosette, Ashleigh Shelby *management professor*
Sheppard, Blair H. *finance educator, former dean*
Staelin, Richard *business administration educator*
Sylver, Donna *accountant*

Greensboro
Englar, John David *finance educator, textiles executive, lawyer*
Petitt, Anthony B. *corporate financial executive*
Pickard, Frank Clemence III *corporate financial executive*
Shearer, Robert K. *corporate financial executive*
Taylor, David H. *corporate financial executive*

Hickory
Olson, Mark A. *corporate financial executive*

High Point
Saxon, Franklin N. *finance executive*

Morrisville
Finney, B. Lynne *corporate financial executive*

Nags Head
Roughton, Billy G. *diversified financial services company executive*

Raleigh
Jessen, David Wayne *retired accountant*
Lloyd, Anne H. *corporate financial executive*

Winston Salem
Gallo, Vincent John *financial planner*
Mounts, L. David *corporate financial executive*
Patel, Ajay *finance educator*

Yanceyville
Webster, Hugh B. *accountant, former state legislator*

OHIO

Cincinnati
Niehoff, Karl Richard Besuden *financial industry executive*

OKLAHOMA

Broken Arrow
Gaddis, Richard William *management educator*

Durant
England, Dan Benjamin *accountant*

Oklahoma City
Agosta, Jeffrey A. *corporate financial executive*
Cassel, John Elden *accountant*
LeBlanc, Eddie M. III *corporate financial executive*
Smith, Gregory Edward *finance company executive*

Tulsa
Helm, Gordon K. *controller*
Kaiser, George B. *corporate financial executive*
Monnet, Beverly C. *corporate financial executive*
Trennepohl, Gary Lee *finance educator, academic administrator*

SOUTH CAROLINA

Aiken
Thomas, Frank M., Jr. *corporate financial executive*

Anderson
Alewine, James William *financial executive*

Charleston
Donnem, Sarah Lund *financial analyst, non-profit and political organization consultant*
Factor, Mallory *independent merchant bank and financial relations consulting firm company executive*
Lader, Philip *corporate director, lawyer, academic administrator, diplomat*
Pritchett, Samuel Travis *finance and insurance educator, researcher, consultant*

Columbia
Monahan, Thomas Paul *accountant*

Greenville
Fischer, Steven R. *retired diversified financial services company executive*
Foody, James G. *retired corporate financial executive*
Lyons, Gerald *corporate financial executive*

Hartsville
Saunders, Barry L. *corporate financial executive*

Seneca
Hodges, Marlane Fairleigh *retired management educator*

Spartanburg
Adams, C. Dan *diversified financial services company executive*

West Columbia
Wheeler, Hoyt Noland *management educator, arbitrator*

TENNESSEE

Bristol
Brouillette, Frederick, Jr. *corporate financial executive*

Chattanooga
Harlin, Ray M. *corporate financial executive*

Cleveland
Rhodes, Arthur Delano *benefits administrator*

Franklin
Doyle, John M. *corporate financial executive*
Minissale, Joe *corporate financial executive*

Jellico
Walden, James William *accountant, educator*

Knoxville
Jones, David P. *corporate financial executive*
Viterisi, John E. *tax specialist*

Memphis
Brackett, Thomas G. *corporate financial executive*
Martin, David W. *corporate financial executive*

PROFESSIONAL INDEX 947 FINANCE: INSURANCE

Martin, Steven J. *corporate financial executive*
Pilon, Nathalie *corporate financial executive*
Umholtz, Clyde Allan *financial analyst*
Weaver, William E., Jr. *corporate financial executive*

Nashville
Brophy, Jeremiah Joseph *retired finance company executive, military officer*
Ford, Gerald J. (Jerry) *finance company executive*
Freudenthal, Ernest Guenter *technology and business educator*
Harms, Russell K. *corporate financial executive*
Hininger, Damon *private sector financial services company executive*
Johnson, R. Milton *corporate financial executive*
Laffer, Arthur Betz *finance company executive*
Marks, Mike A. *corporate financial executive*
Rutherford, William B. *corporate financial executive*
Tarleton, Jesse S. *retired business educator*
Vogus, Timothy J. *management professor*
Weingartner, H(ans) Martin *finance educator*

TEXAS

Addison
Gutierrez, Juan Restrepo *corporate financial executive*

Arlington
Swanson, Peggy Eubanks *retired finance educator*

Austin
Burke, William W. *corporate financial executive*
Gau, George W. *finance educator, former dean*
Granof, Michael H. *finance educator, department chairman*
Graydon, Frank Drake *retired accounting educator, administrator*
Kimberlin, Sam Owen, Jr. *financial consultant*
Larson, Kermit Dean *finance educator*

Beaumont
Andes, Joan Keenen *tax specialist*

Brownwood
DeHay, Jerry Marvin *business educator, small business owner*

Burton
Knauss, Robert Lynn *corporate financial executive*

Canyon Lake
Williams, James Lee *finance company executive*

College Station
Mahajan, Arvind *finance educator*
Wichern, Dean William *business educator*

Coppell
Fenstermacher, Stephen D. *corporate financial executive*

Cypress
Hlozek, Carole Diane Quast *finance company executive*

Dallas
Acton, Elizabeth S. *corporate financial executive*
Brooks, Carla Jo *financial services manager*
Buthman, Mark A. *corporate financial executive*
Cancelmi, Daniel J. *controller*
Constant, Guy J. *corporate financial executive*
Dawson, Edward Joseph *diversified financial services company executive*
Engel, Bryce *diversified financial services company executive*
Forte, Linda D. *finance company executive*
Garner, Paul Trantham *auditor*
Grant, Joseph Moorman *finance company executive*
Guthrie, M. Philip *corporate financial executive*
Hay, Jess Thomas *retired finance company executive*
Hinson, Jeffrey T. *corporate financial executive*
Jobe, Larry Alton *finance company executive*
Keglevic, Paul *corporate financial executive*
Lemaster, Arthur James *educator*
Martin, Gary L. *corporate financial executive*
Martin, Stacey *public accountant*
Mielke, Wayne J. *financial services company executive*
Morris, Tracy L. *corporate financial executive*
Ogden, Thomas D. *finance company executive*
Parkhill, Karen *diversified financial services company executive*
Pendergraft, Philip A. *diversified financial services company executive*
Porter, Biggs C. *corporate financial executive*
Pullen, Timothy L. *corporate financial executive*
Rossel, Cary *corporate financial executive*
Shirley, Stacie *corporate financial executive*
Skene-Stimac, Phyllis *corporate financial executive*
Sullivan, Patricia *corporate financial executive*
Venkataraman, Kumar *finance professor*

Denton
Brock, Horace Rhea *finance educator*
Newell, Charldean *public administration educator*

Duncanville
Trotter, Ide Peebles *financial planner, investment manager*

Fort Worth
Bass, Robert Muse *financier*
Berce, Daniel Eugene *financial services company executive, accountant*
Feehan, Daniel R. *finance company executive*
Jones, Kenneth H., Jr. *finance company executive*
Kniffen, Bennie G. *corporate financial executive*
Morris, Clifton H., Jr. *finance company executive*
Rogers, Dale Craig *finance company executive*

Grapevine
Lloyd, Robert A. *corporate financial executive*

Martin, Sandra J. (Sandy Martin) *corporate financial executive*

Houston
Arnold, Daniel Calmes *retired finance company executive, lawyer*
Baldwin, Mark E. *corporate financial executive*
Beason, Jeffrey I. *corporate financial executive*
Caruso, Nick J. *corporate financial executive*
Chan, Philip S. *corporate financial executive*
Collins, Patrick B. *retired corporate financial executive*
Crispin, Andre Arthur *diversified financial services company executive*
DeNicola, T. Kevin *corporate financial executive*
Driggers, Timothy K. *corporate financial executive*
Duer, Walter M. *retired corporate financial executive*
Faulk, John, Sr. *accountant*
Gish, Kathy Oates *treasurer*
Hajdik, Lloyd A. *corporate financial executive*
Hampton, Robert Wesley *corporate financial executive*
Hendrix, Mark D. *finance company executive*
Heusinkveld, Dick G. *corporate financial executive*
Karger, Howard Jacob *finance educator*
Klebe, Terry A. *corporate financial executive*
Kreidler, R. Chris (Robert C. Kreidler) *corporate financial executive*
Landry, Stephen J. *tax specialist*
Larkin, William Vincent, Jr. *corporate executive*
Loring, Harris E. III *financial services executive*
Maki, Mark A. *corporate financial executive*
McCollum, Mark A. *corporate financial executive*
McShane, Michael M. *corporate financial executive*
Pipkin, Gregory W. *corporate financial executive*
Quinn, Nancy K. *finance company executive*
Reed, John Boyd *tax specialist*
Rickmers, Brian L. *corporate financial executive*
Riordan, Stephen A. *corporate financial executive*
Saltarelli, Robert J. *corporate financial executive*
Schumann, William Henry III *corporate financial executive*
Shannon, Michael Edward *finance company executive*
Starkey, Elizabeth LaRuffa *accountant*
Sult, John R. *corporate financial executive*
Tanzberger, Eric D. *corporate financial executive*
Tisch, James Solomon *diversified holding company executive, energy executive*
Tripodo, Anthony *corporate financial executive*
Vollmer, John E. III *corporate financial executive*
Waltrip, W. Blair *financial consultant*
Wells, William H. *corporate financial executive*
Wise, Scott W. *financial services executive*

Irving
Appel, Matthew W. *corporate financial executive*
Freeman, Dean P. *corporate financial executive*
Gordon, Cynthia T. *corporate financial executive*
Guiltinan, Richard J. *corporate financial executive*
Sullivan, James E. *corporate financial executive*
Vance, J. Randall *corporate financial executive*

Laredo
Sagafi-Nejad, Tagi *business educator*
Sears, Robert Stephen *finance educator*

Mc Kinney
Wilson, John H. *corporate financial executive*

Plano
Carlton, Bob D. *corporate financial executive*
Carter, Barry R. *corporate financial executive*
Dastugue, Michael P. *corporate financial executive*
Ellen, Martin M. *corporate financial executive*
Heffernan, Edward J. *financial services company executive*
Horn, Charles L. *credit services company executive*
Kubic, Michael D. *corporate financial executive*
Rhoades, Alan *corporate financial executive*
Santillan, Laura *corporate financial executive*
Schumacher, Richard E., Jr. *tax specialist*
Szeftel, Ivan *corporate financial executive*
Whiddon, Shelley E. *finance company executive*

Richardson
Enthoven, Adolf Jan Henri *accounting educator*

Round Rock
Puri, Rajendra Kumar *business and tax specialist, consultant*

San Antonio
Biglari, Sardar *diversified financial services company executive*
Casey, Thomas W. *corporate financial executive*
Darling, John Rothburn *business educator*
Hannah, John Robert, Sr. *accountant*
Litoff, Robert *accountant*

Sherman
Avard, Stephen Lewis *retired finance educator*

Stephenville
Collier, Boyd Dean *finance educator, management consultant*

Sugar Land
Pici, Frank A. *corporate financial executive*

The Woodlands
Busmire, Bruce W. *corporate financial executive*

Tyler
Doty, Duane Harold *business educator*

Waco
Rose, John Thomas *finance educator*

Wimberley
Skaggs, Wayne Gerard *retired diversified financial services company executive*

VIRGINIA

Alexandria
Hammad, Alam E. *international business consultant, author, educator*
Norquist, David Lutz *financial services company executive, former federal agency administrator*

Arlington
Millay, Roger Foster *accountant*

Blacksburg
Brozovsky, John A. *accounting educator*
Moore, Laurence John *business educator*
Patterson, Douglas MacLennan *finance educator*

Chantilly
Carlson, Robert Charles *financial planner, writer*

Charlottesville
DeMong, Richard Francis *finance and investments educator*
Harris, Robert Shields *finance educator*
Lenox, Michael *business professor*
Shenkir, William Gary *business educator*
Sihler, William Wooding *finance educator*
Venkatesan, Ramkumar *business administration professor*

Chesapeake
McKee, Timothy Carlton *retired taxation educator*
Wampler, Kevin S. *corporate financial executive*

Falls Church
Phillips, Randy E. *corporate financial executive*

Herndon
Marion, Elaine D. *corporate financial executive*
Thomas, Laura W. *corporate financial executive*

Keswick
Pochick, Francis Edward *financial consultant*

Lexington
DeVogt, John Frederick *management science and business ethics educator, consultant*

Mc Lean
Blisk, Brenda Pack *financial consultant*
Clurman, Sally *tax specialist*
Cox, Heather *finance company executive*
Fairbank, Richard D. *diversified financial services company executive*
Goudet, Olivier *corporate financial executive*
Kennedy, Tom *corporate financial executive*
Milligan, Peter J. *corporate financial executive*
Perlin, Gary Laurence *diversified financial services company executive*
Strickland, Samuel Ray *corporate financial executive*
Weiss, Jerry *finance company executive*
Yajnik, Sanjiv *corporate financial executive*

Midlothian
King, Robert Leroy *business administration educator*

Mineral
Mayo, Louis Allen *policy management counseling company executive*

Norfolk
Petrovich, Neal A. *corporate financial executive*

Reston
Clark, Jonathan C. *finance company executive*
Famiglietti, Robin *finance company executive*
Franke, J. Lance *corporate financial executive*
Hemmady, Gokul V. *corporate financial executive*
Kotowski, Karen *finance company executive*
Lewy, Zachary *finance company executive*
Nickel, Richard *finance company executive*
Parkhill, Susan *finance company executive*
Polemitou, Olga Andrea *accountant*
Reich, Joni (Johnsine J. Reich) *finance company executive*
Remondi, John F. (Jack Remondi) *finance company executive*
Scherschel, Patricia *finance company executive*

Richmond
Faurot, Barbara S. *finance company executive*
Harris, Ruth Hortense Coles *retired accounting educator*
Lascu, Dana-Nicoleta *marketing educator*
Mann, Stephen Ashby *financial consultant*
Morton, Marshall Nay *finance executive*
Peters, Jean S. *diversified financial services company executive*
Rajkowski, E. Mark *corporate financial executive*
Reedy, Thomas W., Jr. *corporate financial executive*
Salomon, Dalal Maria *financial consultant*
Schneider, Kevin D. *diversified financial services company executive*

Virginia Beach
Anglin, Scott *corporate financial executive*
O'Brien, Robert James *financial consultant, small business owner*
Price, Alan Thomas *business and estate planner*
Roomsburg, Margaret M. *corporate financial executive*
Tagliareni, Joseph M. *corporate financial executive*
Truess, James W. *corporate financial executive*

Williamsburg
Holstein, William Kurt *business administration educator*
Kottas, John Frederick *business administration educator*
Montgomery, Joseph William *financial consultant*
O'Connell, William Edward, Jr. *retired finance educator*
Paige, Hilliard Wegner *corporate executive, consultant*
Pearson, Roy Laing *business administration educator*

WEST VIRGINIA

Harpers Ferry
Boucher, Wayne Irving *policy analyst*

TERRITORIES OF THE UNITED STATES

PUERTO RICO

Hatillo
Santos, Isabel Rodriguez *marketing educator*

San Juan
Roman, Juan Jose *corporate financial executive*

ADDRESS UNPUBLISHED

Aldridge, Adrienne Yingling *accountant, writer*
Baxter, Lawrence Gerald *financial analyst, law educator, consultant*
Bennett, Alan M. *retired finance company executive*
Berry, William Lee *business administration educator*
Broome, Oscar Whitfield, Jr. *finance educator*
Coates, Shirley Jean *finance educator*
Collette, Frances Madelyn *retired tax specialist, lawyer, consultant, advocate*
Connor, John Thomas, Jr. *portfolio manager*
Dozier, Glenn Joseph *diversified financial services company executive*
Estrin, Herbert Alvin *financial consultant, film company executive*
Furst, E. Kenneth *financial executive*
Gambrell, Luck Flanders *business executive*
Garcia-Granados, Sergio Eduardo *portfolio manager, writer, historian*
Gavagan, George R. *retired corporate financial executive*
Goodsell, Charles True *public administration educator, researcher*
Harper, Edwin Leland *corporate financial executive, manufacturing executive*
Hudak, Thomas F(rancis) *finance company executive*
Hughes, Ralph Eugene *management educator*
Kaplan, Leonard Eugene *accountant*
Kinney, Thomas J. John *finance educator*
Kolb, Jerry Wilbert *accountant*
Lamont, Alice *accountant, financial consultant*
LeMaster, Sherry Renee *financial advisor, foundation administrator*
Lewins, Steven *financial analyst, investment company executive, legislative staff member, retired military officer*
Livingstone, John Leslie *accountant, economist, management consultant, educator*
Malek, Frederic Vincent *finance company executive*
Martinez, Roman, IV, *retired diversified financial services company executive, board member*
Mayoras, Donald Eugene *corporate executive, writer, consultant, educator*
McClinton, Donald George *retired diversified holding company executive*
Messmer, Donald Joseph *business management educator, marketing consultant*
Mitchem, Cheryl E. *accounting educator*
Moyer, R. Charles *finance company executive, educator, dean emeritus*
Myers, Phillip Fenton *corporate financial and technology executive*
Noonan, Patrick Sutton *author management educator*
Osias, Richard Allen *corporate financial executive*
Prewitt, Lena Voncille Burrell *management educator*
Reiss, Dale Anne *corporate financial executive*
Robertson, Jack Clark *accounting educator*
Sayles, Leonard Robert *management educator, consultant*
Shultis, Robert Lynn *retired finance educator, professional society administrator, consultant, corporate financial executive*
Simon, Donald John *financial planner, theta healer, small business owner*
Starling, Larry Eugene *consultant*
Taylor, Francis Michael *auditor, municipal official*
Tew, E. James, Jr. *management services company executive*
Trent, Robert Harold *retired business educator*
Wall, Jerry Leon *retired management educator, university administrator, dean*
Warner, Douglas Alexander, III, (Sandy Warner) *retired diversified financial services company executive*

FINANCE: INSURANCE

UNITED STATES

ALABAMA

Birmingham
Johns, John D. *insurance company executive, lawyer*
Starnes, William Stancil *insurance company executive, lawyer*

Foley
Russell, Ralph Timothy *retired insurance company executive*

Mobile
Beville, Lewis E. *insurance company executive*
Robinson, Kenneth Larry *insurance company executive*

FLORIDA

Delray Beach
Richardson, R(oss) Fred(erick) *insurance company executive, consultant*

Gainesville
Boothroyd, Herbert *insurance company executive*

Jacksonville
Bickett, Brent B. *insurance company executive*
Carpi, Janice E. *insurance company executive, lawyer*
Foley, William Patrick, II, *insurance company executive*
Hughes, Keith William *insurance company executive*
Lyon, Wilford Charles, Jr. *insurance executive*
Quirk, Raymond R. (Randy Quirk) *insurance company executive*
Stinson, Alan Lynn *insurance company executive*
Willey, Frank Patrick *financial company executive, lawyer*

Jensen Beach
Keegan, Jane Ann *retired insurance executive, consultant*

Miami
Heggen, Arthur William *insurance company executive*
Shusterman, Nathan *underwriter, financial consultant*
Van Wyck, George Richard *insurance company executive*

Tallahassee
Gunter, William Dawson, Jr., (Bill Gunter) *insurance company executive, consultant*
Hunt, John Edwin *insurance company executive, consultant*

Tampa
Cooper, Walter W. *insurance company executive*

GEORGIA

Atlanta
Bowman, Jeffrey T. *insurance company executive*
Geneen, Lawrence I. *insurance company executive*
Karaoglan, Alain Maurice *insurance company executive*
Meyers, Archie L., Jr. *risk management consultant*
Mistretta, Paul L. *insurance company executive*
Steenbergen, Ewout *insurance company executive*

Columbus
Amos, Daniel Paul *insurance company executive*
Amos, Paul Shelby *insurance company executive*
Amos, Paul Shelby, II, *insurance company executive, lawyer*
Baker, Janet P. *insurance company executive*
Blanck, Susan R. *insurance company executive*
Davis, Rebecca C. *insurance company executive*
Friou, Phillip J. (Jack Friou) *insurance company executive*
Isonaka, Jun *insurance company executive*
Janke, Kenneth S., Jr. *insurance company executive*
Jeffery, William Jeremy *insurance company executive*
Matsui, Hidefumi *insurance company executive*
Moorefield, John A. *insurance company executive*
Ottman, Bob *insurance company executive*
Pringle, David L. *insurance company executive*
Rogers, Ralph A., Jr. *insurance company executive*
Shields, Gerald W. *insurance company executive*
Tillman, Audrey Boone *insurance company executive, lawyer*
White, Teresa Lynne *insurance company executive*
Woodall, James C. *insurance company executive*

Conyers
Lilley, Mili Della *insurance company executive, entertainment management consultant*

Kennesaw
Strusz, Daniel A. *insurance company executive*

Savannah
Dodge, William Douglas *risk management consultant*

ILLINOIS

Chicago
Bartholomay, William C. *insurance brokerage company and professional sports team executive*

Naperville
Dombeck, Harold Arthur *insurance company executive*

Northbrook
Mabe, Katherine *insurance company executive*

INDIANA

Carmel
Hilliard, Robert Glenn *insurance company executive, lawyer*

KANSAS

De Soto
Strubbe, Thomas R. *insurance industry executive*

KENTUCKY

Louisville
Goodman, Bruce *insurance company executive*
Kusserow, Paul B. *insurance company executive*
Liston, Thomas J. *insurance company executive*

Margulis, Heidi S. *insurance company executive*
McCallister, Mike (Michael B. McCallister) *insurance company executive*
Rosky, Theodore Samuel *insurance company executive*

LOUISIANA

Deridder
Bradley, C. Allen, Jr. *insurance company executive*

MICHIGAN

East Lansing
Byers, John R. *insurance company executive, lawyer*

NORTH CAROLINA

Camden
Hammond, Roy Joseph *reinsurance company executive*

Chapel Hill
Clark, Arthur Watts *insurance company executive*
Fine, J(ames) Allen *insurance company executive*

OKLAHOMA

Oklahoma City
Hamilton, Thomas Allen *financial planner insurance agent, securities representative*

Tulsa
Hoe, Richard March *securities consultant, writer*

TENNESSEE

Chattanooga
McKenney, Richard P. *insurance company executive*
Ring, Susan *medical insurance company executive*
Ryan, William J. *insurance company executive, retired bank executive*
Watjen, Thomas Ros *insurance company executive, board member*

Franklin
Fritch, Herbert A. *health insurance company executive*
Hailey, James R. *health insurance company executive, pharmacist*
Terry, David L., Jr. *health insurance company executive*

Memphis
Ascolese, Richard A. *insurance company executive*
Crawford, David J. *insurance company executive*

TEXAS

Austin
Mullen, Ron *insurance company executive, wealth manager*
Riley, Harold Eugene *insurance company executive*

Bedford
Blackburn, Wyatt Douglas *insurance company executive*

Corpus Christi
Vargas, Joe Flores *insurance adjuster*

Dallas
Ash, Darron *insurance company executive*
Cline, Bobby James *insurance company executive*
Weakley, Clare George, Jr. *insurance company executive, theologian, entrepreneur*

Galveston
McDaniel, Dixie N. *insurance company executive*
Moody, Robert Lee *insurance company executive*
Price, Ronald C. *insurance company executive*
Regini, Judith L. *insurance company executive*
Schouweiler, Steven Harvey *insurance company executive*

Grapevine
Gedwed, William J. *insurance company executive*

Houston
Benoit, Gary *insurance company executive*
Bramanti, Frank J. *insurance company executive*
Buechler, Mark Alan *insurance company executive*
Clements, Glenn H. *insurance company executive*
Couch, Jesse Wadsworth *retired insurance company executive*
Glitzsburg, Jacques *insurance company executive*
Kaiser, Thomas Griffeth *insurance company executive*
Lindsey, John H. *former insurance agency executive*
Molbeck, John N., Jr. *insurance company executive*
Morris, Matthew W. *insurance company executive*
Morris, Stewart, Jr. *title insurance company executive*
Oaas, Eric *insurance company executive*
Oesterreicher, James E. *insurance company executive*
Poulos, Michael James *insurance company executive*
Skalka, Michael B. *insurance company executive, lawyer*
Urban-Karr, Jill *insurance agent*
Zimmerman, Rand *insurance company executive*

Irving
Halbert, Jon S. *insurance company executive*
Phillips, T. Danny *insurance company executive*

Livingston
Stovall, Jerry Coleman *insurance company executive*

Mc Kinney
Coleman, Gary L. *insurance company executive*
Herbel, Vern D. *insurance company executive*
McAndrew, Mark S. *insurance company executive*
Tucker, Russell B. *insurance company executive*

Mcallen
Whisenant, Bert Roy, Jr. *insurance company executive*

North Richland Hills
Hildebrand, Phillip J. *insurance company executive*

San Antonio
Bergner, Kevin J. *insurance company executive*
Buckelew, John D. *insurance company executive*
Conklyn, Elizabeth D. *insurance company executive*
Matus, Kristi Ann *insurance company executive*
Robles, Josue, Jr. *insurance company executive*

Sugar Land
Clay, Jerrell G. *insurance company executive*

VIRGINIA

Charlottesville
Long, Charles Farrell *insurance company executive*

Glen Allen
Behymer, Christopher Glenn *insurance company executive*
Kay, Bruce A. *insurance company executive*
Kirshner, Alan I. *insurance company executive*
Latham, John K. *insurance company executive*
Vought, Micheal *insurance company executive*

Penhook
Hahn, John William *retired insurance company executive*

Richmond
Kelleher, Patrick B. *insurance company executive*
Klein, Martin P. *insurance company executive*
McInerney, Thomas J. *insurance company executive*
Schutz, Pamela S. *insurance company executive*

Roanoke
DeVries, James D. *insurance company executive*

Virginia Beach
Finley, John R. *medical insurance company executive*
Fletcher, Gary *medical insurance company executive*
Grden, Nancy L. *medical insurance company executive*
Locke, Julie *medical insurance company executive*
Pace, Nicholas Joseph *insurance company executive, lawyer*
Shirk, Richard D. *retired insurance company executive*
Sotunde, Tunde *medical insurance company executive, pediatrician*
Spillane, Timothy J. *medical insurance company executive*
Trudell, Julie Loftus *medical insurance company executive*
Zoretic, Richard C. *medical insurance company executive*

TERRITORIES OF THE UNITED STATES

PUERTO RICO

San Juan
Marini-Mir, Luis A. *insurance company executive*
Ruiz-Comas, Ramón M. *insurance company executive, lawyer*

ADDRESS UNPUBLISHED

Copeland, Floyd Dean *insurance company executive, lawyer*
Cox, Kermitt L. *former insurance company executive*
Driver, Joe Luther *insurance agent, consultant*
Fibiger, John Andrew *life insurance company executive*
Harrison, Gail L. *retired insurance company executive*
Hauenstein, George Carey *life insurance executive*
Kirkland, Ronald E. *retired insurance company executive*
Pearson, Paul Holding *insurance company executive*
Ryan, James *insurance company executive*
Schulte, James Allen *former insurance company executive*
Snyder, William Burton *insurance company executive*
Tringale, Anthony Rosario *insurance executive*

Wills, William Ridley, II, *retired insurance company executive, historian*

FINANCE: INVESTMENT SERVICES

UNITED STATES

ALABAMA

Birmingham
Aldag, Edward Karl, Jr. *investment company executive*
Tucker, Thomas James *retired investment company executive*

ARKANSAS

Fort Smith
Edelstein, Frank *retired investment company executive, board member*
Morris, John Harvey *retired investment company executive, board member*

Little Rock
Good, Mary Lowe *investment company executive, educator*
Whiteside, Charles B. III *investment company executive*

CALIFORNIA

Corona Del Mar
Ricks, Thomas G. *investment company executive*

COLORADO

Denver
Reiman, Scott J. *investment company executive*

DISTRICT OF COLUMBIA

Washington
Isaac, William Michael (Bill Isaac) *brokerage house executive, retired federal official*
McKinley, John *investment company executive*
Rabaut, Thomas W. *private equity firm executive*

FLORIDA

Boca Raton
Hampton, Benjamin Bertram *brokerage house executive*
Mischler, Harland Louis *investment company executive*

Bradenton
Nelson, Ralph Erwin *investment company executive*

Fort Lauderdale
Berrard, Steven R. *investment company and former automotive retail company executive*
Huizenga, Wayne (Harry Wayne Huizenga) *entrepreneur, professional sports team owner*
Levan, Alan B. *investment company executive*

Gainesville
Oliver, Robert Bruce *retired investment company executive*

Jacksonville
Thomas, Lee Muller *investment company executive, former government official*

Jupiter
Uhlmann, Frederick Godfrey *securities trader*

Key Largo
Hawkins, Frank Nelson, Jr. *investor relations and public relations/communications consultant, writer*

Key West
Wruble, Brian Frederick *investor*

Miami
Arison, Shari *investment company executive*
Newlin, Kimrey Dayton, Sr. *retired international trade and political consultant, personal computer analyst*

Miami Beach
Selin, Ivan *entrepreneur*

Palm Beach
McCarter, Thomas Nesbitt III *investment company executive, consultant*
Quick, Thomas Clarkson *brokerage house executive*

Palm Beach Gardens
Lagomasino, Maria Elena (Mel Lagomasino) *investment company executive*

Pensacola
Merkel Moran, Christa Ilse *investor, linguist, educator*

Pompano Beach
Rifenburgh, Richard Philip *retired investment company executive*

Ponte Vedra Beach
Abe, Valentin *entrepreneur*
Monsky, John Bertrand *investment company executive*

Punta Gorda
Presley, Brian *investment company executive*

Saint Petersburg
Emerson, William Allen *retired investment company executive*
Helck, Chester B. *investment company executive*
James, Thomas A. *investment company executive*
Julien, Jeffrey P. *investment company executive*
Raney, Steven M. *investment company executive*
Reilly, Paul C. *investment company executive*

Sarasota
Sullivan, Michael Evan *investment company executive*

Singer Island
Gad, Lance Stewart *investment advisor, lawyer, private investor*

Stuart
Mergler, H. Kent *investment counselor*

Tampa
Burton, Donald W. *venture capitalist*

Village Of Golf
Birle, James Robb *investor*

Wellington
Cowart, Jim Cash *investment company executive*

West Palm Beach
Garvy, Robert Andrew *investment company executive*
Kiely, Dan Ray *fund manager, real estate company executive, consultant*

Windermere
Lewis, Joseph *investor, real estate development company executive*

GEORGIA

Athens
Pittard, Patrick S. *investment company executive*

Atlanta
Christensen, Suzanne *investment company executive*
Durham, Michael Jonathan *investment professional*
Edmonds, Christopher S. *investment company executive*
Feidler, Mark L. *investment company executive*
Green, Holcombe Tucker, Jr. *investment company executive*
Hammond, Thomas J. *securities exchange company executive*
Johnson, Thomas H. *investment company executive*
Keough, Donald Raymond *investment company executive*
Lally, John Patrick *private equity investor*
Mitchell, Stephen Milton *investor and company executive*
Needham, Wendy Beale *retired investment company executive, board member*
Ridley, David A. *investment company executive*
Roach, William Henry, Jr. *investment company executive*
Smith, Catherine H. *investment company executive*
Sprecher, Jeffrey C. *stock exchange executive*

Clayton
Hartwell, Stephen *investment company executive*

Cleveland
Lewis, Richard, Sr. *securities broker, consultant*

Columbus
Camp, Elizabeth W. *investment company executive, lawyer*
Ogie, Elizabeth C. *investor*

Kennesaw
Petit, Parker Holmes *investment company executive*

Roswell
Handy, F. Philip *investment company executive, educational association administrator*
Huntley, William Thomas III *private investor, consultant*

Saint Simons Island
Turbidy, John Berry *investor, management consultant*

Stockbridge
Cain, Herman *entrepreneur*

ILLINOIS

Chicago
Oliver, Harry Maynard, Jr. *retired brokerage house executive*
Slansky, Jerry William *investment company executive*

KENTUCKY

Covington
Crotty, John T. *investment advisor*

Louisville
Jones, David A., Jr. *venture capital firm executive, former insurance company executive*

MASSACHUSETTS

Boston
Klessel, Lewis *investment company executive, retail executive*
Vinik, Jeffrey N. *hedge fund manager, professional sports team executive*

Siasconset
Albani, Thomas J. *investor*

Woods Hole
Adams, Rex *investment company executive*

NEW YORK

Hauppauge
Fogg, Joseph Graham III *investment company executive*

New York
Hance, James Henry, Jr., (Jim Hance) *private equity firm executive, retired bank executive*
Icahn, Carl Celian *investor*
Jensen, Kenneth R. *private equity firm executive*
McGovern, John Francis *investment company executive*
Michelini, Matthew R. *investment company executive*
Minicucci, Robert A. *investment company executive*
Schoellkopf, Wolfgang *investment company executive*
Solari, Larry Thomas *private equity firm executive*
Townsend, John L. III *private investor*

NORTH CAROLINA

Ararat
Marsh, Joseph Virgil *investment advisor, analyst, broker, consultant, research scientist*

Charlotte
Alexander, John W. *investment company executive*
Claxton, Philip A. *brokerage house executive*
Cummings, Stephen Emery *investment banking executive*
Desmond, Thomas A. *brokerage house executive*
Donovan, Roberto E. *brokerage house executive*
Grimaldi, James Thomas *private investor*
Hagen, Richard J., Jr. *brokerage house executive*
Madison, Thomas F. *investment company executive*
McColl, Hugh Leon, Jr. *investment company executive, retired bank executive*
Montanaro, Donato A., Jr. *brokerage house executive*
Muhammad, Muhsin, II, *investment company executive, retired professional football player*
Noujaim, Fares Dourid *investment company executive*
Ragan, Robert Allison *private investment executive, financial consultant*
Raju, Dan *brokerage house executive*
Stevens, Scott R. *investment company executive*
Stowe, Harold Crosby *investment company executive*
Vorhoff, David C. *investment company executive*

Gastonia
Worthy, James Ager *entrepreneur, retired professional basketball player*

Greensboro
Cole, Sue W. *investment company executive*
Johnson, Marshall Hardy *investment company executive*

Hickory
Krause, L. William *investment company executive*

High Point
Flavin, Patrick Brian *investment company executive, securities analyst*

Murphy
Pezzella, Jerry James, Jr. *investment and real estate company executive*

Raleigh
Gillfillan, Michael J. *investment company executive*

West End
Krallinger, Joseph Charles *entrepreneur, consultant, writer*

OKLAHOMA

Tulsa
Healey, David Lee *investment company executive*
Ward, Felker W., Jr. *investment company executive*

RHODE ISLAND

Woonsocket
Dorman, David W. *private equity firm executive, former telecommunications industry executive*

SOUTH CAROLINA

Beaufort
Verity, William W. *investment company executive*

Ridgeland
Cameron, Thomas William Lane *investment company executive*

TENNESSEE

Franklin
Andrews, William Frederick *private equity firm executive*

Memphis
Baird, Robert A. *investment company executive*
Carson, John C., Jr. *investment company executive*
Ferguson, Richard S. *investment company executive*
Giddis, Kevin H. *investment company executive*
Krausnick, E. Carl, Jr. *investment company executive*
Kruczek, R. Patrick *investment company executive*
Maxwell, Charles Darryl *investment company executive*

Murfreesboro
Hutchens, J. Justin *investment company executive*

Nashville
Byrd, Andrew Wayne *investment company executive*
George, Eddie (Edward Nathan George) *entrepreneur, retired professional football player*
Hanselman, Richard Wilson *entrepreneur*
Michelson, Michael W. *investment company executive, lawyer*
Nelson, Edward Gage *brokerage house and bank executive, consultant*

TEXAS

Addison
Carreker, James D. *investment company executive*

Austin
Marengi, Joseph Alexander *private equity firm executive, board member*
Meredith, Thomas J. *investment company executive*

Dallas
Bass, J. Kyle (Kyle Bass) *investment company executive*
Beal, Andrew *entrepreneur, bank executive*
Brown, Benjamin A. *investment advisor*
Buchholz, Donald Alden *stock brokerage company executive*
Carrozza, Vincent A. *investment company executive*
Casey, Brian O. *investment company executive*
Crockett, Dodee Frost *brokerage house executive*
Hegi, Frederick B., Jr. *investment company executive*
Hirsch, Laurence Eliot *private equity firm executive, lawyer*
Kriscunas, Suzanne B. (Suzy Kriscunas) *private equity firm executive*
Muse, John R. *investment company executive*
Parent, David Hill *investment company executive*
Pickens, T. Boone (Thomas Boone Pickens Jr.) *hedge fund manager, former oil industry executive*
Rachofsky, Howard *retired investor, art collector, patron*
Rose, Edward W., III, (Rusty Rose) *investment company executive, former professional sports team executive*
Smith, Cece *venture capitalist*
Stoffel, Paul T. *investment company executive*
Vest, Christina Weaver *private equity firm executive*

Fort Worth
Bass, Edward P. *venture capitalist*
Bass, Sid Richardson *investment company executive*
Bonderman, David *investment company executive, lawyer*
Boyce, Richard W. *investment company executive*
Coslet, Jonathan *investment company executive*
Coulter, James G. *investment company executive*
Kusin, Gary M. *investment advisor*
Ma (Xuezheng), Mary *investment company executive*
Moore, Darla Dee *investment company executive*
Rainwater, Richard Edward *retired investor*
Sisitsky, Todd B. *investment company executive*
Trujillo, David *investment company executive*
Wheeler, Carrie A. *investment company executive*
Williams, James B. *private equity firm executive*

Horseshoe Bay
Anderson, Kenneth Ward *investor, consultant*

Houston
Ansary, Hushang *oil industry entrepreneur, philanthropist, private global investment company executive, former diplomat*
Arnold, John Douglas *hedge fund manager*
Arpey, Gerard J. *private equity firm executive, retired air transportation executive*
Barth, Carin Marcy *private equity firm executive, former federal agency administrator*
Coneway, Peter Richard *private equity firm executive, former ambassador*
Duncan, Charles William, Jr. *investor, former United States Secretary of Energy*
Harte, Christopher M. *investor, former publishing executive*
Harvey, Robert W. *investment company executive*
Kellner, Larry (Lawrence Wesley Kellner) *private equity firm executive, retired air transportation executive*
Lovoi, John V. *investment company executive*
O'Connor, Ralph Sturges *investment company executive*
Ranck, Bruce E. *investment company executive*
Richards, Leonard Martin *investment executive, consultant, coach*
Rieman, Deborah D. *investment company executive*
Ryan, J. Stuart *investment company executive*
Sarofim, Fayez Shalaby *investment company executive*
Vaughan, Eugene H. *investment company executive*
Wells, Damon *investment company executive*
Williams, Edward Earl, Jr. *entrepreneur, educator*

Irving
Arthur, Thomas D. *investor*
Beckles, Ingrid *investment company executive*

Mont Belvieu
Neumann, David A. *investment company executive, former councilman*

Richardson
Richards, Frederick Francis, Jr. *investment company executive*

Royse City
Vaughan, Joseph Lee, Jr. *entrepreneur, educational consultant*

San Antonio
Terracina, Roy David *entrepreneur*

Sugar Land
Gaffney, James J. *investment advisor, board member*

Wichita Falls
Silverman, Gary William *investment company executive*

VIRGINIA

Arlington
Burns, Timothy H. *investment company executive*
Choksi, Mary Claire *investment company executive*
Drayton, Bill (William Drayton) *social entrepreneur, lawyer, management consultant*
Scarborough, Robert Henry, Jr. *entrepreneur*

Bedford
Rasoul, Sam *entrepreneur*

Charlottesville
Gunter, Bradley Hunt *capital management executive*

Dutton
Washburn, John Rosser *entrepreneur*

Mc Lean
Kercheval, John William III *vulture capitalist, philanthropist, finance professor, former aerospace and defense executive*

Middleburg
Johnson, Sheila Crump *entrepreneur*

Richmond
Riepe, James Sellers *investment company executive*

Springfield
Tian, Li *investment company executive, educator*

Stanardsville
Anns, Philip Harold *brokerage house and pharmaceutical executive*

Sterling
Reynolds, Catherine Brescia *entrepreneur, philanthropist*

Virginia Beach
Child, Jeffrey B. *investment company executive*
Melsheimer, Mel P(owell) *venture capitalist*

Williamsburg
Gordon, Baron Jack *stockbroker*

TERRITORIES OF THE UNITED STATES

PUERTO RICO

Hato Rey
Ferrer, Miguel Antonio *brokerage house executive*

ADDRESS UNPUBLISHED

Albers, Charles Edgar *retired investment company executive*
Cahill, John T. *former private equity firm executive*
Connelly, Sharon Rudolph *lawyer, financier and real estate investor*
Cunningham, Ronnie Walter *venture capitalist*
Dean, Edwin Becton *entrepreneur*
Drakeman, Donald Lee *venture capitalist, educator*
Fitts, Catherine Austin *investment advisor*
Lewis, Hunter *investment advisor, writer*
Malin, Robert Abernethy *retired investment company executive*
McClane, Robert Sanford *entrepreneur, bank executive*
Pardue, Dwight Edward *venture capitalist*
Pauken, Thomas Weir *venture capital executive, mediator*
Ridgway, Rozanne LeJeanne *corporate director, retired ambassador*
Robertson, Mark Wayne *investment specialist*
Sheskey, Susan E. *venture capitalist and technology executive*
Tarr, Kenneth J. *retired investment company executive*
Uys, Jurgen Peter Brinker *securities analyst*
Wyly, Samuel E. *entrepreneur*

Young, Ronald Faris *commodities trader*

GOVERNMENT: AGENCY ADMINISTRATION

UNITED STATES

ALABAMA

Montgomery
Canfield, Greg *state agency administrator, former state legislator*
Collier, Spencer *state agency administrator, former state legislator*
Harrison, John D. *state banking agency administrator*
Williamson, Donald Ellis *state agency administrator, public health service officer*

ARKANSAS

Little Rock
Franks, Candace Ann *state banking agency administrator*
Halverson, Paul Kenneth *state agency administrator, public health service officer*

FLORIDA

Indian Rocks Beach
DeLucia, Gene Anthony *government administrator, computer company executive*

Jacksonville
Rutherford, John *sheriff*

Jensen Beach
Peterson, David Frederick *retired government agency administrator*

Melbourne
Straub, Chester John, Jr. *state agency administrator, former federal agency administrator*

Miami
Paul-Noel, Karls *firefighter*

Orlando
Garavaglia, Jan C. *forensic pathologist, chief medical examiner*

Tallahassee
Charity, Linda B. *state banking agency administrator*

GEORGIA

Atlanta
Aiken, Vernoy Fred *government agency administrator*
Arias, Ileana *federal agency administrator, psychiatrist, educator*
Braswell, Robert M. *state banking agency administrator*
Cochran, Kelvin James *fire chief, former federal agency administrator*
Frieden, Thomas R. *federal agency administrator*
Khan, Ali S. *federal agency administrator*
Smith, Vance Carlton *state agency administrator, former state legislator*
True, Susan Jane *federal agency administrator*

Brunswick
Patrick, Connie L. *federal agency administrator*

KENTUCKY

Frankfort
Comer, James R. *state agency administrator, former state legislator*
Vice, Charles A. *state banking agency administrator*

Louisville
Adams, Robert Waugh *retired state agency administrator, economist, educator*

MISSISSIPPI

Jackson
Brady, Theresa L. *state banking agency administrator*
Hyde-Smith, Cindy *state agency administrator, former state legislator*

NORTH CAROLINA

Candler
Hunt, Earl Stephen *independent consultant*

Canton
Roberts, Bill Glen *retired protective services official*

Chapel Hill
Umminger, Bruce Lynn *government agency administrator, research scientist, educator, consultant*

Moyock
Prince, Erik D. *protective services company executive*

Raleigh
Engel, Jeffrey P. *state agency administrator*

Research Triangle Park
Birnbaum, Linda S. *federal agency administrator, toxicologist*

Wingate
McGuirt, William Franklin *county sheriff*

OKLAHOMA

Oklahoma City
Cline, Terry Lee *state agency administrator, public health service officer*
Thompson, Mick *state banking agency administrator*

SOUTH CAROLINA

Columbia
Jacobs, Louie A. *state banking agency administrator*
Lloyd, Reginald Ivan *state agency administrator, former prosecutor*
Templeton, Catherine B. *state agency administrator*

Swansea
Inabinet, George Walker, Jr. *retired state agency administrator*

TENNESSEE

Knoxville
Johnson, William Dean (Bill Johnson) *federal agency administrator, former energy executive*

Memphis
Armstrong, Toney *police director*

Nashville
Dreyzehner, John Joseph *state agency administrator, physician*
Godwin, Larry A. *state agency administrator, retired protective services official*
Gonzales, Greg *state banking agency administrator*

Oak Ridge
Ryneska, John Joseph *government agency employee*

TEXAS

Austin
Acevedo, Art *police chief*
Ashworth, Kenneth Hayden *public administrator*
Cooper, Charles G. *state banking agency administrator*

Dallas
Brown, David O. *police chief*
Kunkle, David M. *former police chief*

Houston
Korth, David H. *international space station flight director*
McClelland, Charles A., Jr. *police chief*

San Antonio
McManus, William Paul *police chief*

VIRGINIA

Alexandria
Borzino, Bruce Edward *federal agency administrator*
Brady, Thomas M. *federal agency administrator, educator*
Brockert, Joseph Paul *government executive, writer, designer*
Fryzel, Michael E. *federal agency administrator, lawyer*
Hughes, Grace-Flores *federal agency administrator*
Matz, Deborah (Debbie Matz) *federal agency administrator*
Modzeleski, William *former federal agency administrator*
Rymer, Jon Thomas *federal agency administrator*

Annandale
Christianson, Geryld B. *government agency administrator, consultant*

Arlington
Carr, Nevin P., Jr. *federal agency administrator*
Cox, Stephen A. *consumer agency administrator*
Kempf, Steven J. *federal agency administrator*
Main, Joseph A. *federal agency administrator*
McDonald, Bernard Robert *retired federal agency administrator*
Philbin, Peggy (Margaret M. Philbin) *federal agency administrator*
Pistole, John S. *federal agency administrator*
Prabhakar, Arati *federal agency administrator*
Romo, Lawrence G. *federal agency administrator*
Williams, David C. *federal agency administrator*
Zak, Leocadia Irine *federal agency administrator, lawyer*

Chantilly
Sapp, Betty Jean *federal agency administrator*

Chester
Nixon, Samuel Anthony, Jr. *state agency administrator, former state legislator*

Fairfax
Jones, George Fleming *international consultant*

Fort Belvoir
Harnitchek, Mark D. *federal agency administrator*

McFarland, Katrina (Katharina G. McFarland) *federal agency administrator*
Syring, James D. *federal agency administrator, military officer*

Fort Lee
Jeu, Joseph H. *federal agency administrator*

Hampton
Roe, Lesa B. *federal agency administrator*

Mc Lean
Mahan, Clarence *federal agency administrator, writer*
Spearman, Kenneth Albert *federal agency administrator*
Strom, Leland A. (Lee Strom) *federal agency administrator*
Thompson, Jill Lynette Long *federal agency administrator, former United States Representative from Indiana*

Richmond
Dozier, Therese Knecht *government agency consultant, former education association administrator*
Face, E. Joseph, Jr. *state banking agency administrator*
Lohr, Matthew J. *state agency administrator, former state legislator*

Springfield
Harrigan, Thomas Michael *federal agency administrator*
Kalder, Frank M., Jr. *federal agency administrator*
Leonhart, Michele Marie *federal agency administrator*
Long, Letitia A. *federal agency administrator*

Virginia Beach
Stolle, Kenneth W. *protective services official, former state legislator*

WEST VIRGINIA

Charleston
Cline, Sara McLaughlin *state banking agency administrator*

TERRITORIES OF THE UNITED STATES

PUERTO RICO

San Juan
Blanco, Rafael *territorial banking agency administrator*

VIRGIN ISLANDS

St Thomas
Dullum, Mercedes K.C. *territorial agency administrator*

ADDRESS UNPUBLISHED

Barnett, Patricia Ann *development professional*
Braswell, Jackie Boyd *state agency administrator*
Crowell, Craven H., Jr. *retired federal agency administrator*
Friday, Elbert Walter, Jr. *federal agency administrator, meteorologist*
Kaminski, Paul Garrett *former federal agency administrator, investment banker*
Kusserow, Richard Phillip *federal agency administrator, corporate financial executive*
Mainella, Fran (Frances P. Mainella) *educator, former federal agency administrator*
McCormick, Robert Junior *former federal agency administrator*
Mecke, William Moyn *public relations consultant*
Molholm, Kurt Nelson *retired federal agency administrator*
Padden, Anthony Aloysius, Jr. *retired federal government official, US immigration hearings and court policy and procedures advisor*
Saxon, Don B. *state agency administrator*
Sheridan, Diane Frances *public policy facilitator*
Simon, Sandra Ruth Waldman *retired state agency administrator*
Swoap, David Bruce *government and state agency administrator, consultant, art director*
Webster, Douglas Wayne *federal agency administrator, management consultant*
Weinstein, David F. *state agency administrator, former state legislator*

GOVERNMENT: EXECUTIVE ADMINISTRATION

UNITED STATES

ALABAMA

Birmingham
Bell, William A., Sr. *mayor, Birmingham, Alabama*
Boomershine, Donald Eugene *bureau executive, development official*
Keely, Chester Martin *federal marshal*

Huntsville
Battle, Thomas M., Jr. *Mayor, Huntsville, Alabama*

Mobile
Andrews, Charles Edward *federal marshal*
Stimpson, Sandy *Mayor, Mobile, Alabama, lumber company executive*

Montgomery
Baylor, Arthur Darrow *federal marshal*
Bennett, Jim (James Ronald Bennett) *state official*
Bentley, Robert Julian *Governor of Alabama, dermatologist, former state legislator*
Ivey, Kay Ellen *Lieutenant Governor of Alabama, former state treasurer*
Strange, Luther Johnson III *state attorney general*
Strange, Todd *mayor, Montgomery, Alabama*

ARKANSAS

Fort Smith
Oglesby, Harold Michael *federal marshal*

Little Rock
Beebe, Mike Dale *Governor of Arkansas, former state attorney general, lawyer*
Martin, Mark Russell *state official, former state legislator*
Massanelli, Clifton Timothy *US marshal*
McDaniel, Dustin *state attorney general*
Stodola, Mark Allen *mayor, Little Rock, Arkansas, former prosecutor*
Wills, Elana Cunningham *commissioner, former state supreme court justice*

COLORADO

Denver
Brown, Keith Lapham *retired ambassador*

DISTRICT OF COLUMBIA

Washington
Fry, Tom *federal official*
Krol, George Albert *United States ambassador to Uzbekistan*
Mikulak, Robert Peter *federal official*
Watson, Arthur Dennis *federal official*

FLORIDA

Amelia Island
Smeeton, Thomas Rooney *government affairs consultant*

Cape Canaveral
Weinberg, Thomas *commissioner, former legislative staff member*

Cape Coral
Burch, Jim *former mayor*
Sawicki, Marni L. *Mayor, Cape Coral, Florida*

Fort Lauderdale
Gunzburger, Suzanne Nathan *municipal official, social worker*
Seiler, Jack P. *mayor, Ft. Lauderdale, Florida, prosecutor*

Gainesville
Heflin, Martin Ganier *diplomat, political scientist*

Hialeah
Bovo, Esteban L., Jr. *county official, former state legislator*
Hernandez, Carlos *mayor, Hialeah, Florida*

Jacksonville
Brown, Alvin *mayor, Jacksonville, Florida*
Corrigan, Michael *county official, former councilman*
Goldhagen, Jeffrey Lee *city health department administrator*
Park, Christopher S. *city manager*
Peyton, John *former mayor, Jacksonville, Florida*

Miami
Gimenez, Carlos Antonio *Mayor, Miami-Dade County, Florida*
Regalado, Tomas Pedro *mayor, Miami*

Orlando
Dyer, John Hugh, Jr., (Buddy Dyer) *mayor, Orlando, Florida, lawyer*

Palm Bay
Anderson, Richard Edmund *city manager, consultant*

Ponte Vedra Beach
Jacobsen, Diane DeMell *foreign policy specialist*

Port Saint Lucie
Faiella, JoAnn *mayor, Port St. Lucie, Florida*

Saint Petersburg
Baker, Rick (Richard M. Baker) *former mayor, St. Petersburg, Florida*
Kriseman, Richard David (Rick Kriseman) *Mayor, St. Petersburg, Fla., former state legislator*
Mussett, Richard Earl *city official*

Tallahassee
Bondi, Pamela Jo *state attorney general*
Detzner, Kenneth William *state official*
López-Cantera, Carlos *Lieutenant Governor of Florida, former state legislator*
Marks, John R. III *mayor, Tallahassee, Florida, lawyer*
Scott, Rick (Richard Lynn Scott) *Governor of Florida, investment company executive*

Spooner, Edward M. *federal marshal*

Tampa
Berger, William Benedict, Sr. *federal marshal*
Buckhorn, Bob *mayor, Tampa, Florida*
Freedman, Sandra Warshaw *former mayor*
Platt, Jan Kaminis *former county official*

West Palm Beach
Taylor, Priscilla Ann *county official*

GEORGIA

Atlanta
Cagle, Casey (Lowell S. Cagle) *Lieutenant Governor of Georgia*
Carter, Jimmy (James Earl Carter Jr.) *39th President of the United States*
Carter, Rosalynn Smith (Eleanor Rosalynn Smith Carter) *former First Lady of the United States*
Deal, Nathan (John Nathan Deal) *Governor of Georgia, former United States Representative from Georgia, lawyer*
Glover, Renée Lewis *city official*
Harvard, Beverly Joyce Bailey *federal marshal*
Kemp, Brian Porter *state official*
Laney, James Thomas *former ambassador, educator*
Olens, Samuel Scott *state attorney general*
Reed, Kasim (Mohammed Kasim Reed) *Mayor, Atlanta, former state legislator*
Scott, Donald Lavern *city manager, librarian, former army officer*

Augusta
Copenhaver, Deke *mayor, Augusta-Richmond, Georgia*

Canton
Angulo, Charles Bonin *foreign service officer, lawyer*

Columbus
Douglas, William Ernest *retired commissioner*
Tomlinson, Teresa *mayor, Columbus, Georgia*

Conyers
Kelly, John Hubert *diplomat*

Macon
Richardson, Willie Lee, Jr. *federal marshal*

Savannah
Smith, Stephen James *federal marshal*

Tucker
Streeb, Gordon Lee *diplomat, economist*

KENTUCKY

Frankfort
Abramson, Jerry Edwin *Lieutenant Governor of Kentucky, former mayor*
Beshear, Steven Lynn *Governor of Kentucky, lawyer*
Conway, Jack (John William Conway) *state attorney general*
Lundergan Grimes, Alison *state official*

Lexington
Carl, Parker Loren *US marshal*
Gray, Jim *mayor, Lexington, Kentucky*
Miller, Pamela Gundersen *retired mayor*
Newberry, Jim *former mayor*

Louisville
Clark, James Edward *federal marshal*
Fischer, Greg *mayor, Louisville, Kentucky*

LOUISIANA

Baton Rouge
Alexander, Rodney McKinnie *state official, former United States Representative from Louisiana*
Caldwell, Buddy (James David Caldwell, Jr.) *state attorney general*
Dardenne, Jay (John Leigh Dardenne Jr.) *Lieutenant Governor of Louisiana*
Gautreaux, Nick *state commissioner, former state legislator*
Harrison, Kevin Charles *US marshal*
Hebert, Troy *state commissioner, former state legislator*
Holden, Melvin Lee *mayor-president, Baton Rouge, Louisiana*
Holloway, Clyde Cecil *state commissioner, former United States Representative from Louisiana*
Jindal, Bobby (Piyush Jindal) *Governor of Louisiana*
Schedler, Tom (John Thomas Schedler) *state official, former state legislator*

Gretna
Templet, Ricky James *county official, former state legislator*

New Orleans
Duplessis, Ann *city official, former state legislator*
Landrieu, Mitch (Mitchell Joseph Landrieu) *Mayor, New Orleans, former Lieutenant Governor of Louisiana*
May, Genny (Genevieve Lynn May) *US marshal*

Shreveport
Glover, Cedric Bradford *mayor, Shreveport, Louisiana*
Whitehorn, Henry Lee *US marshal*

MISSISSIPPI

Diberville
Janus, Michael W. *municipal official, former state legislator*

Jackson
Bryant, Phil *Governor of Mississippi*
Hood, Jim (James Matthew Hood) *state attorney general*
Hosemann, Delbert (Charles Delbert Hosemann Jr) *state official*
Reeves, Tate (Jonathon Tate Reeves) *Lieutenant Governor of Mississippi, former state treasurer*
White, George *US marshal*

Ridgeland
Dale, George *former state commissioner*

Southaven
Davis, Greg (Charles G. Davis) *mayor*

NEW YORK

New York
Eisenstadt, G. Michael *diplomat, author, educator, researcher*

NORTH CAROLINA

Chapel Hill
Schoonover, Brenda B. *ambassador*

Charlotte
Clodfelter, Daniel Gray *Mayor, Charlotte, former state legislator, lawyer*
Nesbit, Kelly McDade *US marshal*

Durham
Bell, William (Bill) V. *mayor, Durham, North Carolina*
Joseph, James Alfred *retired ambassador, political scientist, educator*

Fayetteville
Rand, Anthony Eden *former state commissioner, former state legislator, lawyer*
Robertson, Nat *Mayor, Fayetteville, North Carolina*

Greensboro
Stafford, Willie Ransome III *federal marshal*
Vaughan, Nancy *Mayor, Greensboro, North Carolina*

High Point
Pate, William Patrick *city manager*

Pittsboro
Cotter, Michael William *retired ambassador*

Raleigh
Cooper, Roy Asberry III *state attorney general*
Forest, Daniel J. *Lieutenant Governor of North Carolina*
Marshall, Elaine Folk *state official*
McCrory, Pat (Patrick Lloyd McCrory) *Governor of North Carolina, consulting firm executive, former mayor*
McFarlane, Nancy *mayor, Raleigh, North Carolina*
Parker, Scott Jerome *US marshal*

Winston Salem
Joines, Allen *mayor, Winston-Salem, North Carolina*

OKLAHOMA

Ada
Anoatubby, Bill *Governor of the Chickasaw Nation*
Keel, Jefferson *Native American tribal leader*

Durant
Pyle, Gregory E. *Chief of the Choctaw Nation of Oklahoma*

Norman
Corr, Edwin Gharst *ambassador*
Koch, Steven Edward *federal official, meteorologist*
Reynolds, Jim *county official, former state legislator*

Oklahoma City
Benge, Chris *state official, former state legislator*
Cornett, Mick *mayor, Oklahoma City*
Fallin, Mary Copeland *Governor of Oklahoma, former United States Representative from Oklahoma*
Lamb, Todd *Lieutenant Governor of Oklahoma, former state legislator, lawyer*
Parman, Larry Vance *state official, lawyer*
Pruitt, Scott (Edward Scott Pruitt) *state attorney general, former state legislator*
Weeks, Charles Thomas, II, *federal marshal*

Tahlequah
Baker, Bill John *Principal Chief of the Cherokee Nation*

Tulsa
Bartlett, Dewey F., Jr. *mayor, Tulsa, Oklahoma*

SOUTH CAROLINA

Charleston
Riley, Joseph P., Jr. *mayor*

Columbia
Haley, Nikki Randhawa *Governor of South Carolina, former state legislator*
Hammond, Mark *state official*
McConnell, Glenn Fant *Lieutenant Governor of South Carolina, former state legislator*
Washington, Kelvin Cornelius *US marshal*
Wilson, Alan McCrory *state attorney general*

Walterboro
Workman, William Douglas III *retired town manager, mayor, gas industry executive*

TENNESSEE

Chattanooga
Berke, Andy *mayor, Chattanooga, Tennessee*

Fayetteville
Matlock, Jack Foust, Jr. *diplomat*

Knoxville
Fowler, James Thomas *federal marshal*
Rogero, Madeline *mayor, Knoxville, Tennessee*

Memphis
Holt, Jeffrey Thomas *federal marshal*
Wharton, A.C., Jr. *mayor, Memphis, Tennessee*

Nashville
Cooper, Robert Elbert, Jr. *state attorney general*
Dean, Karl *Mayor, Nashville*
Gore, Tipper (Mary Elizabeth Gore) *wife of the former Vice President of the United States*
Hargett, Tre *state official*
Haslam, Bill (William Edward Haslam) *Governor of Tennessee, former mayor*
Herzog, Laura Lefler *state official, former legislative staff member*
Ramsey, Ronald Lynn *Lieutenant Governor of Tennessee*

TEXAS

Amarillo
Harpole, Paul *mayor, Amarillo, Texas*

Arlington
Cluck, Robert *Mayor, Arlington, Texas*

Austin
Abbott, Gregory W. *state attorney general, former state supreme court justice*
Andrade, Hope (Esperanza Andrade) *state commissioner*
Berry, Nandita Venkate *state official, lawyer*
Cooke, Carlton Lee, Jr. *mayor*
Dewhurst, David *Lieutenant Governor of Texas*
Franke, Wayne Thomas *political and marketing consultant, retired government affairs director, consultant*
Leffingwell, Lee *mayor, Austin, Texas*
Peacock, Penne Korth *ambassador*
Perry, Rick (James Richard Perry) *Governor of Texas*
Steen, John Thomas, Jr. *state official, lawyer*
Wynn, Will *former Mayor, Austin, Texas*

Beaumont
Lord, Evelyn Marlin *mayor*

Brenham
Pipes, Paul Ray *county commissioner*

Brownsville
Martinez, Tony *mayor, Brownsville, Texas*

College Station
Card, Andy (Andrew Hill Card Jr.) *former White House chief of staff, former United States Secretary of Transportation*

Corpus Christi
Martinez, Nelda *mayor, Corpus Christi, Texas*

Dallas
Ely, Randy *federal marshal*
Rawlings, Mike *mayor, Dallas, Texas*
Thompson, Zachary *city health department administrator*

El Paso
Leeser, Oscar *Mayor, El Paso, Texas*
Sandoval, Juan *municipal official, commissioner*

Fort Worth
Price, Betsy *mayor, Fort Worth, Texas*

Garland
Athas, Douglas *Mayor, Garland, Texas*

Grand Prairie
Jensen, Ron *mayor, Grand Prairie, Texas, manufacturing executive*

Harlingen
Matz, James Richard *municipal official*

Houston
Barnhill, John Herschel *retired government administrator, historian*
Bush, George Herbert Walker *41st President of the United States*
Marcotte, Michael Steven *municipal official*
Parker, Annise Danette *mayor, Houston*
Perry, Cynthia Norton Shepard *retired ambassador*
White, Bill (William Howard White) *former mayor, Houston*

Irving
Duyne, Beth Van *mayor, Irving, Texas*

Laredo
Salinas, Raul G. *mayor, Laredo, Texas*

Lubbock
Robertson, Glen *mayor, Lubbock, Texas*

New Braunfels
Krueger, Robert Charles *former ambassador, congressman, senator*

Plano
LaRosiliere, Harry *mayor, Plano, Texas*

San Antonio
Almonte, Robert R. *US marshal*
Castro, Julián *Mayor, San Antonio, Texas*
Hardberger, Phillip Duane *former Mayor, San Antonio, judge, lawyer, journalist*

VIRGINIA

Alexandria
Havens, Harry Stewart *retired federal official, management consultant*
Mathieson, Robert William (Bobby Mathieson) *federal marshal, former state legislator*
McNicol, David Leon *retired federal official, researcher*
Smith, Elaine Diana *foreign service officer*
Ward, George Frank, Jr. *international programs executive, ambassador*

Annandale
Rogers, Stephen Hitchcock *retired ambassador*

Arlington
Bowen, Stuart W., Jr. *federal official*
Córdova, France Anne-Dominic *federal official, astrophysicist*
Henke, Robert J. *federal commissioner, former federal agency administrator*
Krys, Sheldon Jack *retired diplomat*
Marrett, Cora B. *federal official, science educator*
McDonald, John Warlick *diplomat*
Pendleton, Mary Catherine *retired foreign service officer*
Pyatt, Everett Arno *federal official*
Sarros, P. Peter *diplomat, consultant*

Chesapeake
Krasnoff, Alan P. *mayor, Chesapeake, Virginia*
Myrick, Bismarck *diplomat, history professor*
Ward, William E. *mayor*

Dulles
Cunningham, James Blair *United States ambassador to Afghanistan*
La Lime, Helen R. Meagher *ambassador*

Fairfax
Bulova, Sharon *county official*
Scialabba, Lori L. *federal official, lawyer*

King George
Newhall, David III *retired federal official*

Lake Ridge
Stottlemyer, David Lee *federal official*

Lynchburg
Davenport, James Robert *vice mayor, city council, retired utilities executive*

Markham
Ojeda Eiseley, Jaime de *former Spanish ambassador, educator*

Mc Lean
Cahill, Harry Amory *diplomat, educator*
Russell, Theodore Emery *diplomat*
Thernstrom, Abigail *federal commissioner*
Trout, Maurice Elmore *diplomat*

Newport News
Price, McKinley *mayor, Newport News, Virginia, dentist*

Norfolk
Fraim, Paul D. *mayor, Norfolk, Virginia*
Moss, Thomas Warren, Jr. *county official*
Quillen, Michael J. *state commissioner, former energy executive*

Richmond
Herring, Mark Rankin *state attorney general, former state legislator*
Jones, Dwight Clinton *mayor, Richmond, Virginia*
McAuliffe, Terry (Terence Richard McAuliffe) *Governor of Virginia, former political organization administrator*
Moran, Brian J. *state official, former state legislator*
Northam, Ralph Shearer *Lieutenant Governor of Virginia, former state legislator*
Stoney, Levar M. *state official*

Roanoke
Holt, Gerald Sidney *US marshal*

Round Hill
Ewing, Raymond Charles *retired ambassador*

Spotsylvania
Hardy, Dorcas Ruth *business and government relations executive*

Vienna
Almaguer, Frank *ambassador*

Virginia Beach
Fraser, Ruth Hodges *city clerk*
Sessoms, William D., Jr. *mayor, Virginia Beach, Virginia, bank executive*

Williamsburg
Wilkerson, Lawrence B. *former federal official, retired military officer*

WEST VIRGINIA

Charleston
Clark, Hanley C. *state insurance commissioner*
Foster, John Dale *US marshal*
Morrisey, Patrick *state attorney general*
Tennant, Natalie E. *state official*

Tomblin, Earl Ray *Governor of West Virginia, former state legislator*

Clarksburg
Gaskins, Gary Michael *US marshal*

Wheeling
McKenzie, R. Andy *mayor*

TERRITORIES OF THE UNITED STATES

PUERTO RICO

Bayamon
Rivera Cruz, Ramon Luis, Jr., (Ramon Luis Rivera Jr) *Mayor, Bayamon, Puerto Rico*

San Juan
Bernier, David *state official, odontologist*
Cruz Soto, Carmen Yulin *mayor, San Juan, Puerto Rico, former territorial legislator*
García Padilla, Alejandro Javier *Governor of Puerto Rico*
Miranda-Rodriguez, Cesar R. *attorney general*

VIRGIN ISLANDS

St Croix
Francis, Gregory R. *Lieutenant Governor of US Virgin Islands*

St Thomas
de Jongh, John Percy, Jr. *Governor of the United States Virgin Islands, real estate company executive*
Frazer, Vincent F. *territorial attorney general*

ADDRESS UNPUBLISHED

Amato Chiaramonte Bordonaro, Baron Carlo Camillo *ambassador, consultant*
Arcos, Cresencio S. *ambassador*
Ashe, Victor Henderson *former ambassador*
Banks, Lisa Jean *government official*
Betti, John Anso *federal official, retired automotive executive*
Beyer, Don (Donald Sternoff Beyer Jr.) *former ambassador*
Boyatt, Thomas David *retired ambassador*
Brook, Scott Jonathan Bradley *mayor, lawyer*
Brown, Lee Patrick *retired mayor, former federal official*
Bush, Barbara Pierce *former First Lady of the United States, volunteer*
Bush, George Walker *43rd President of the United States*
Bush, Laura Welch *former First Lady of the United States*
Cabaniss, William Jelks, Jr. *former ambassador, machining company executive*
Cason, James Caldwell *retired ambassador*
Chopra, Aneesh Paul *former federal official*
Dillon, Robert Sherwood *retired diplomat*
Earp, Naomi Churchill *former federal official*
Eastham, Alan Walter, Jr. *retired ambassador, lawyer*
Elson, Edward Elliott *diplomat*
Evans, Pat *former mayor, Plano, Texas*
Evatt, Parker *retired commissioner, state legislator*
Garrett, Henry *former mayor*
Garza, Ed *former mayor*
Giulianti, Mara Selena *former mayor*
Hanmer, Stephen Read, Jr. *retired federal official*
Javits, Eric Moses *ambassador, lawyer*
Johnson, Yvonne J. *former Mayor, Greensboro, NC*
McClinton, James Leroy *city administrator*
McCormack, Richard Thomas Fox *former ambassador*
McDonnell, Bob (Robert Francis McDonnell) *former Governor of Virginia, former state attorney general*
Moncrief, Michael Joseph *former Mayor, Fort Worth, former state legislator*
Naugle, James (Jim) Thomas *former mayor, Ft. Lauderdale, Florida*
Oberndorf, Meyera E. *former mayor, Virginia Beach, Virginia*
Page, Randall *state official*
Reno, Janet *former United States Attorney General*
Shevardnadze, Eduard Amvrosiyevich *former President of Georgia*
Sink, Alex (Adelaide Alexander Sink) *former state treasurer, retired bank executive*
Swimmer, Ross Owen *former federal official*
Williamson, Dennis Arthur *former federal marshal*

GOVERNMENT: LEGISLATIVE ADMINISTRATION

UNITED STATES

ALABAMA

Alexander City
Tuggle, Mark M. *state legislator*

Aliceville
Harper, Alan *state legislator*

Anniston
Boyd, Barbara Bigsby *state legislator*
Marsh, Del C. *state legislator*

Nordgren, Becky *state legislator, marketing professional*
Wood, Randy *state legislator*

Auburn
Whatley, Tom *state legislator*

Bay Minette
McMillan, Stephen A. *state legislator*

Bessemer
Dunn, Priscilla *state legislator*

Birmingham
Carns, Jim *state legislator*
Coleman, Merika *state legislator*
Moore, Mary A. *state legislator*
Newton, Demetrius C. *state legislator*
Robinson, Oliver *state legislator*
Rogers, John W. *state legislator*
Scott, Roderick Hampton (Rod Scott) *state legislator*
Smitherman, Rodger Mell *state legislator*
Williams, Jack *state legislator*

Brewton
Baker, Alan *state legislator*

Centre
Lindsey, Richard J. *state legislator*

Chatom
Beech, Elaine *state legislator*

Clayton
Beasley, Billy *state legislator*
Forte, Grover Berry *state legislator*

Columbiana
Hill, Mike *state legislator*

Cullman
Bussman, Paul David *state legislator, dentist*

Daphne
Pittman, Trip *state legislator*

Decatur
Hammon, Micky *state legislator*
Henry, William Ed *state legislator*
Orr, Arthur Wooten *state legislator, lawyer*

Demopolis
McCampbell, Artis (A.J. McCampbell) *state legislator*

Enterprise
Moore, Barry *state legislator*

Eva
Oden, Jeremy H. *state legislator*

Fairhope
Faust, Teddy Joe, Sr., (Joe Faust) *state legislator*

Florence
Irons, Tammy *state legislator, lawyer*

Gadsden
Ford, Craig *state legislator*
Galliher, Blain *state legislator*

Geneva
Chesteen, Donnie *state legislator*

Grand Bay
Sessions, David *state legislator*

Greensboro
Howard, Ralph *state legislator*

Greenville
Newton, Charles Oliver *state legislator*

Guntersville
Long, Oliver Wesley (Wes Long) *state legislator, lawyer*

Huntsville
Ball, Mike A. *state legislator*
Hall, Laura *state legislator*
McCutcheon, Mac *state legislator*
Sanderford, Howard *state legislator*
Sanford, Paul *state legislator*
Williams, Phil *state legislator*

Mc Calla
Farley, Allen *state legislator*

Meridianville
Patterson, James M., Jr. *state legislator*

Mobile
Brooks, Ben *state legislator*
Buskey, James E. *state legislator*
Figures, Vivian Davis *state legislator*
Gaston, Henry Victor (Victor Gaston) *state legislator*
Ison, Jamie *state legislator*
Mitchell, Joseph *state legislator*

Montgomery
Barton, James E., Jr. *state legislator*
Baughn, Richard *state legislator*
Beason, Scott *state legislator*
Beckman, Paul *state legislator*
Bedford, Roger H., Jr. *state legislator*
Blackwell, Slade *state legislator*
Boman, Daniel H. *state legislator, lawyer*
Bracy, Napoleon, Jr. *state legislator*
Brewbaker, Dick Lansden *state legislator*
Bridges, DuWayne *state legislator*
Brown, Koven L. (K.L. Brown) *state legislator, funeral director*
Burdine, Greg *state legislator*
Buttram, Marvin *state legislator*

Clouse, James Steven (Steve Clouse) *state legislator*
Coleman, Linda F. *state legislator*
Collins, Terri *state legislator*
Colston, David Bernard *state legislator*
Davis, Randy *state legislator*
DeMarco, Paul J. *state legislator*
Dial, Gerald *state legislator*
Fielding, Jerry L. *state legislator*
Givan, Juandalynn Deleathia *state legislator, lawyer*
Greer, Lynn *state legislator*
Greeson, Todd *state legislator*
Grimsley, Dexter *state legislator*
Holley, Jimmy W. *state legislator*
Holmes, Alvin A. *state legislator*
Hubbard, Joseph Lister *state legislator, lawyer*
Hubbard, Mike *state legislator*
Jackson, Thomas E. *state legislator*
Jinright, Charles W. *councilman*
Johnson, Wayne *state legislator*
Jones, Mike, Jr. *state legislator*
Keahey, George M. (Marc Keahey) *state legislator*
Knight, John F. *state legislator*
Lee, Charles McDowell *legislative staff member*
Lee, Paul W. *state legislator*
Love, Jay *state legislator*
McAdory, Lawrence *state legislator, retired principal*
McClammy, Thad C. *state legislator*
McGill, Shadrack *state legislator*
Millican, Mike *state legislator*
Reed, Greg J. *state legislator*
Rich, Kerry *state legislator*
Roberts, Bill *state legislator*
Ross, Quinton T. *state legislator*
Schmitz, Sue *state legislator*
Scofield, Clay *state legislator*
Shiver, Harry *state legislator*
Singleton, Bobby *state legislator*
Taylor, Bryan *state legislator, lawyer*
Thomas, Elwyn *state legislator*
Todd, Patricia *state legislator*
Wallace, Kurt *state legislator*
Ward, Cameron (Robert Cameron Ward, Cam Ward) *state legislator*
Weaver, April C. *state legislator*
Williams, Dan *state legislator*
Williams, Phil *state legislator*
Wren, Greg *state legislator*

Morris
Treadaway, Benjamin (Allen Treadaway) *state legislator*

Moulton
Johnson, Ken *state legislator*

Munford
Hurst, Steve *state legislator*

Opelika
Bandy, George C. *state legislator*

Pelham
McClurkin, Mary Sue *state legislator*

Phenix City
Vance, Lesley *state legislator*

Red Bay
Morrow, Johnny M. *state legislator*

Roanoke
Laird, Richard Joel *state legislator*

Scottsboro
Robinson, John *state legislator*

Selma
Melton, Darrio Tramen *state legislator*
Sanders, Hank *state legislator*

Semmes
Fincher, Chad *state legislator*
Glover, Rusty *state legislator*

Slocomb
Smith, Harri Anne *state legislator*

Springville
McClendon, Jim *state legislator*

Sylacauga
Johnson, Ronald G. (Ron Johnson) *state legislator*

Troy
Boothe, Alan C. *state legislator*

Trussville
Payne, Arthur Lee *state legislator*

Tuscaloosa
Allen, Gerald *state legislator*
England, Chris (Christopher John England) *state legislator*
Lathram, Othni J. *state legislative agency administrator, lawyer*
Merrill, John H. *state legislator*
Poole, William Stitt III *state legislator, lawyer*

Tuscumbia
Black, Marcel *state legislator*

Tuskegee Institute
Warren, Pebblin W. *state legislator*

Vestavia Hills
Waggoner, J.T. (Jabo Waggoner) *state legislator*

Wetumpka
Mask, Barry *state legislator*

ARKANSAS

Altheimer
Elliott, Efrem *state legislator*

Arkadelphia
Malone, W. Percy *state legislator*

Arkansas City
Moore, Robert, Jr. *state legislator, lawyer*

Batesville
Wyatt, David W. *state legislator*

Bella Vista
Hutchinson, Donna *state legislator*

Benton
Hammer, Kim D. *state legislator*
Taylor, Jerry *state legislator*

Bismarck
Mauch, Loy *state legislator*

Branch
Stubblefield, Gary *state legislator*

Brookland
Lenderman, Homer *state legislator*

Cedarville
Whitaker, Ruth Reed *state legislator, retired publishing executive*

Conway
Baker, Gilbert R. *state legislator*
Meeks, David M. *state legislator*

Crossett
Cheatham, Eddie *state legislator*
Jeffress, Jimmy Lane *state legislator*

El Dorado
Shepherd, Matthew *state legislator*

El Paso
Dismang, Jonathan *state legislator*

Elkins
Pritchard, Bill *state legislator*

Fayetteville
Collins, Charles S. *state legislator*
Leding, Greg *state legislator*
Madison, Sue Wood *state legislator*

Foreman
Cowling, Larry *state legislator*

Forrest City
Wright, Marshall *state legislator*

Fort Smith
Altes, Robert Dennis *state legislator*
Pennartz, Tracy *state legislator*

Gravette
Hendren, Kim D. *state legislator*

Green Forest
King, Bryan *state legislator*

Greenbrier
McFarland, Deborah S. *alderman, nurse*
Meeks, Stephen A. *state legislator*

Greenwood
Holland, Bruce *state legislator*

Helena
Smith, Kevin Andrew *state legislator, non-profit corporation executive*

Hensley
Mayberry, Andy *state legislator*

Hot Springs
Cozart, Bruce *state legislator*
Sample, Bill *state legislator*
Vines, John T. *state legislator*
Westerman, Bruce *state legislator*

Imboden
Ratliff, James *state legislator*

Jasper
Laverty, Randy *state legislator*

Jonesboro
Bookout, Paul *state legislator*
Hubbard, Jon *state legislator*

Judsonia
Gillam, Jeremy *state legislator*

Kirby
Stewart, Randy *state legislator, high school teacher*

Lamar
Overbey, Betty *state legislator*

Little Rock
Allen, Fred *state legislator*
Anderson, Keven L. *former legislator*
Baird, Duncan *state legislator*
Barnett, Jonathan *state legislator*
Burris, John *state legislator*
Carter, Davy *state legislator*
Chesterfield, Linda Pondexter *state legislator*
Clemmer, Ann V. *state legislator*
Dale, Robert E. *state legislator*
Edwards, John *state legislator*
Elliott, Joyce *state legislator*
English, Jane *state legislator*
Hobbs, Debra *state legislator*
Hopper, Karen *state legislator*
Ingram, Keith *state legislator*
Jeffress, Harmon (Gene) *state legislator*

Johnson, David E. *state legislator, lawyer*
Kerr, Allen *state legislator*
Lea, Andrea *state legislator*
Lindsey, Uvalde *state legislator*
Lipton, John M. *state representative*
Love, Fredrick J. *state legislator*
Malone, Stephanie *state legislator*
McCrary, Walls *state legislator*
Mclean, James *state legislator*
Nickels, Jim *state legislator*
Perry, Mark *state legislator*
Rice, Terry *state legislator*
Sanders, David J. *state legislator*
Slinkard, Mary *state legislator*
Smith, Gary L. *state legislator*
Summers, Tim *state legislator*
Teague, Larry *state legislator*
Tyler, Linda *state legislator*
Walker, John W., Sr. *state legislator*
Webb, Kathy *state legislator*
Wilkins, Butch *state legislator*
Williams, Darrin L. *state legislator*
Wooldridge, Tim L. *state legislator, academic administrator*
Word, James *state legislator*

Magnolia
Fielding, David *state legislator*

Manila
Wagner, Charolette *state legislator*

Marianna
Murdock, Reginald *state legislator*

Marion
Hallum, Hudson *state legislator*

Marked Tree
Lovell, Larry D. (Buddy Lovell) *state legislator*

Marshall
Branscum, David L. *state legislator*

Marvell
Hall, Clark *state legislator*

Maumelle
Garner, Ed *state legislator*

Melbourne
Wren, Tommy *state legislator*

Mena
Bell, Jerry Nathan *state legislator*

Monticello
Lampkin, Sheila E. *state legislator*

Morrilton
Thompson, Tommy *state legislator*

Mountain Home
Key, Johnny R. *state legislator*

Nashville
Steel, Nate *state legislator*

Newport
Dickinson, Jody *state legislator*

North Little Rock
Hyde, Barry *state legislator*
Salmon, Mary Anne *state legislator*
Steele, Tracy *state legislator*

Osceola
Baker, Tommy Lee *state legislator*

Ozark
Post, Leslee Milam *state legislator*

Paragould
Thompson, Robert III *state legislator, lawyer*

Paris
Cleveland, Herschel *state representative*
Eubanks, Jon S. *state legislator*

Piggott
Patterson, Mike *state legislator*

Pine Bluff
Bradford, Toni C. *state legislator*
Flowers, Stephanie *state legislator, lawyer*
Wilkins, Henry (Hank), IV, *state legislator*

Pocahontas
Collins-Smith, Linda *state legislator*

Rogers
Bledsoe, Cecile H. *state legislator*
Carnine, Leslie V. *state legislator, retired school system administrator*

Rose Bud
Johnston, Josh *state legislator*

Rover
Catlett, John *state legislator*

Russellville
Trusty, Sharon *former state legislator*

Searcy
Biviano, Mark *state legislator*

Sheridan
Pierce, Bobby *state legislator*

Springdale
Woods, Jon *state legislator*

Sturkie
Benedict, Lori A. *state legislator*

Texarkana
Harrelson, Steve *state legislator, lawyer*

Van Buren
Deffenbaugh, Gary *state legislator*

Warren
Wardlaw, Jeff R. *state legislator*

West Fork
Harris, Justin T. *state legislator*

Widener
Crumbly, Jack *state legislator*

Wynne
Luker, James Charles *state legislator, lawyer, former mayor*

Yellville
Linck, Kelley *state legislator*

DISTRICT OF COLUMBIA

Washington
Aderholt, Robert Brown *United States Representative from Alabama, lawyer*
Alexander, Lamar (Andrew Lamar Alexander) *United States Senator from Tennessee, former United States Secretary of Education*
Bachus, Spencer Thomas III *United States Representative from Alabama, lawyer*
Barr, Andy (Garland Hale Barr IV) *United States Representative from Kentucky*
Barrow, John Jenkins *United States Representative from Georgia, lawyer*
Barton, Joseph Linus *United States Representative from Texas*
Bilirakis, Gus Michael *United States Representative from Florida, lawyer*
Bishop, Sanford Dixon, Jr. *United States Representative from Georgia, lawyer*
Black, Diane Lynn *United States Representative from Tennessee, former state legislator*
Blackburn, Marsha *United States Representative from Tennessee*
Boozman, John Nichols *United States Senator from Arkansas, former United States Representative from Arkansas*
Boustany, Charles William, Jr. *United States Representative from Louisiana, surgeon*
Brady, Kevin Patrick *United States Representative from Texas*
Bridenstine, Jim (James Frederick Bridenstein) *United States Representative from Oklahoma*
Brooks, Morris J. (Mo Brooks) *United States Representative from Alabama, lawyer*
Broun, Paul Collins, Jr. *United States Representative from Georgia, physician*
Brown, Corrine *United States Representative from Florida*
Buchanan, Vern (Vernon Gale Buchanan) *United States Representative from Florida*
Burgess, Michael Clifton *United States Representative from Texas*
Burr, Richard Mauze *United States Senator from North Carolina*
Butterfield, George Kenneth, Jr., (G.K. Butterfield) *United States Representative from North Carolina, former state supreme court justice*
Bybee, Stewart M. *legislative staff member*
Byrne, Bradley Roberts *United States Representative from Alabama, lawyer, former state legislator*
Cantor, Eric Ivan *United States Representative from Virginia, lawyer*
Capito, Shelley Moore *United States Representative from West Virginia*
Carbonell, Ana *legislative staff member*
Carter, John Rice *United States Representative from Texas, lawyer*
Cassidy, Bill (William Cassidy) *United States Representative from Louisiana, former state senator*
Castro, Joaquín *United States Representative from Texas, former state legislator*
Chambliss, Saxby (Clarence Saxby Chambliss) *United States Senator from Georgia*
Christensen, Donna Marie *Delegate to United States House Representative from Virgin Islands*
Clyburn, James Enos (Jim Clyburn) *United States Representative from South Carolina*
Coble, John Howard *United States Representative from North Carolina, lawyer*
Coburn, Tom (Thomas Allen Coburn) *United States Senator from Oklahoma*
Cochran, Thad (William Thad Cochran) *United States Senator from Mississippi*
Cohen, Steve (Stephen Ira Cohen) *United States Representative from Tennessee, former state legislator*
Cole, Tom (Thomas Jeffrey Cole) *United States Representative from Oklahoma*
Collins, Doug (Douglas A. Collins) *United States Representative from Georgia, former state legislator*
Conaway, Mike (Kenneth Michael Conaway) *United States Representative from Texas*
Connolly, Gerald E. *United States Representative from Virginia*
Cooper, James Hayes Shofner (Jim Cooper) *United States Representative from Tennessee, lawyer*
Corker, Bob (Robert Phillips Corker Jr.) *United States Senator from Tennessee*
Cornyn, John III *United States Senator from Texas*
Cotton, Tom (Thomas Bryant Cotton) *United States Representative from Arkansas*
Crawford, Rick (Eric Alan Crawford) *United States Representative from Arkansas*
Crenshaw, Ander *United States Representative from Florida, lawyer*
Cruz, Ted (Rafael Edward Cruz) *United States Senator from Texas, lawyer*
Cuellar, Henry Roberto *United States Representative from Texas, lawyer*
Culberson, John Abney *United States Representative from Texas, lawyer*
Czarnecki, Karen M. *legislative staff member, former federal agency administrator*
Davis, Kolan Leon *legislative staff member*
DeSantis, Ron (Ronald Dion DeSantis) *United States Representative from Florida, former federal prosecutor*
DesJarlais, Scott Eugene *United States Representative from Tennessee, physician*
Deutch, Ted (Theodore Eliot Deutch) *United States Representative from Florida, former state legislator*
Diaz-Balart, Mario *United States Representative from Florida*
Doggett, Lloyd Alton, II, *United States Representative from Texas, retired judge*
Duncan, Jeff (Jeffrey D. Duncan) *United States Representative from South Carolina, former state legislator*
Duncan, John James, Jr. *United States Representative from Tennessee*
Ellmers, Renee Jacisin *United States Representative from North Carolina, nurse*
Eskeland, Philip Douglas *legislative staff member*
Farenthold, Blake (Randolph Blake Farenthold) *United States Representative from Texas*
Fincher, Stephen Lee *United States Representative from Tennessee*
Fleischmann, Chuck (Charles J. Fleischmann) *United States Representative from Tennessee, lawyer*
Fleming, John Calvin, Jr. *United States Representative from Louisiana, physician*
Flores, Bill (William Hose Flores) *United States Representative from Texas, former oil industry executive*
Forbes, James Randy *United States Representative from Virginia*
Frankel, Lois Jane *United States Representative from Florida, former state legislator*
Gallego, Pete P. *United States Representative from Texas, former state legislator*
Garcia, Joe (Jose Antonio Garcia Jr.) *United States Representative from Florida, former federal agency administrator*
Gingrey, Phil (John Phillip Gingrey) *United States Representative from Georgia*
Gohmert, Louie (Louis Buller Gohmert Jr.) *United States Representative from Texas, former judge*
Goodlatte, Robert William (Bob Goodlatte) *United States Representative from Virginia, lawyer*
Gowdy, Trey (Harold W. Gowdy III) *United States Representative from South Carolina*
Graham, Lindsey Olin *United States Senator from South Carolina*
Granger, Kay *United States Representative from Texas*
Graves, Tom (John Thomas Graves Jr.) *United States Representative from Georgia, former state legislator*
Grayson, Alan Mark *United States Representative from Florida*
Green, Gene (Raymond Eugene Green) *United States Representative from Texas*
Griffin, Tim (John Timothy Griffin) *United States Representative from Arkansas, former federal prosecutor, lawyer*
Griffith, Howard Morgan (Morgan Griffith) *United States Representative from Virginia, former state legislator, lawyer*
Guthrie, Brett (Steven Brett Guthrie) *United States Representative from Kentucky, former state senator*
Hagan, Kay Ruthven *United States Senator from North Carolina*
Hall, Ralph Moody *United States Representative from Texas*
Harper, Gregg *United States Representative from Mississippi, lawyer*
Hastings, Alcee Lamar *United States Representative from Florida, former federal judge*
Heck, Patrick George *legislative staff member, lawyer*
Hensarling, Jeb *United States Representative from Texas*
Hinojosa, Rubén *United States Representative from Texas*
Holding, George E.B. (George Edward Bell Holding) *United States Representative from North Carolina, former federal prosecutor*
Hope, Patrick Alan *state legislator, lawyer, lobbyist*
Hudson, Richard Lane, Jr. *United States Representative from North Carolina, former legislative staff member*
Hurt, Robert (Bob Hurt) *United States Representative from Virginia, former state legislator*
Inhofe, Jim (James Mountain Inhofe) *United States Senator from Oklahoma*
Isakson, Johnny (John Hardy Isakson) *United States Senator from Georgia*
Jackson Lee, Sheila *United States Representative from Texas*
Johnson, Eddie Bernice *United States Representative from Texas*
Johnson, Henry C., Jr., (Hank Johnson) *United States Representative from Georgia, lawyer*
Johnson, Samuel Robert *United States Representative from Texas*
Jolly, David Wilson *United States Representative from Florida*
Jones, Walter Beaman, Jr. *United States Representative from North Carolina*
Kaine, Tim (Timothy Michael Kaine) *United States Senator from Virginia, former Governor of Virginia*
Kingston, Jack (John Heddens Kingston) *United States Representative from Georgia*
Landrieu, Mary Loretta *United States Senator from Louisiana*
Lankford, James (Jim Lankford) *United States Representative from Oklahoma*
Lanzone, Deborah von Hoffmann *legislative staff member*
LesStrang, David (Dave) Matthew *legislative staff member*
Lewis, John Robert *United States Representative from Georgia*
Lucas, Frank D. *United States Representative from Oklahoma*
Manchin, Joseph, III, (Joe Manchin) *United States Senator from West Virginia, former Governor of West Virginia*
Marchant, Kenny Ewell *United States Representative from Texas*
Massie, Thomas Harold *United States Representative from Kentucky, farmer*
Mays, Janice Ann *legislative staff member, lawyer*
McAllister, Vance Michael *United States Representative from Louisiana, entrepreneur*
McCaul, Michael Thomas *United States Representative from Texas*
McConnell, Mitch (Addison Mitchell McConnell) *United States Senator from Kentucky, lawyer*
McHenry, Patrick Timothy *United States Representative from North Carolina*
McIntyre, Mike (Douglas Carmichael McIntyre II) *United States Representative from North Carolina*
McKinley, David B. *United States Representative from West Virginia*
Meadows, Mark Randall *United States Representative from North Carolina, real estate developer*
Mica, John L. *United States Representative from Florida*
Miller, Jeff *United States Representative from Florida*
Moran, Jim (James Patrick Moran Jr.) *United States Representative from Virginia*
Mullin, Markwayne *United States Representative from Oklahoma, plumber, rancher*
Mulvaney, Mick (John Michael Mulvaney) *United States Representative from South Carolina, former state legislator*
Murphy, Patrick Erin *United States Representative from Florida, accountant*
Nelson, Bill (Clarence William Nelson) *United States Senator from Florida*
Neugebauer, Randy (Robert Randolph Neugebauer) *United States Representative from Texas*
Nugent, Richard Byron *United States Representative from Florida, former sheriff*
Nunnelee, Alan (Patrick Alan Nunnelee) *United States Representative from Mississippi, former state legislator*
Olson, Peter Graham (Pete Olson) *United States Representative from Texas*
O'Rourke, Beto (Robert Francis O'Rourke) *United States Representative from Texas, former city councilman*
Palazzo, Steven McCarty *United States Representative from Mississippi, former state legislator*
Paul, Rand (Randal Howard Paul) *United States Senator from Kentucky, ophthalmologist*
Perez, Dennise *legislative staff member*
Pfeifer, Thomas J. *legislative staff member*
Phelan, Andy *legislative staff member*
Pierluisi, Pedro R. *Resident Commissioner from Puerto Rico, United States House of Representatives*
Pittenger, Robert *United States Representative from North Carolina, former state legislator*
Pittman, Lisa Etta *legislative staff member, lawyer*
Poe, Ted *United States Representative from Texas, former judge*
Posey, Bill (William Joseph Posey) *United States Representative from Florida*
Price, David Eugene *United States Representative from North Carolina, education educator*
Price, Thomas Edmunds (Tom Price) *United States Representative from Georgia*
Pryor, Mark Lunsford *United States Senator from Arkansas*
Rahall, Nick Joe, II, (Nick Rahall) *United States Representative from West Virginia*
Rice, Tom (Hugh Thompson Rice Jr.) *United States Representative from South Carolina, lawyer*
Richmond, Cedric Levon *United States Representative from Louisiana, former state legislator*
Rigell, Scott (Edward Scott Rigell) *United States Representative from Virginia*
Roby, Martha D. *United States Representative from Alabama*
Rockefeller, Jay (John Davison Rockefeller IV) *United States Senator from West Virginia*
Roe, Phil (David Phillip Roe) *United States Representative from Tennessee*
Rogers, Harold Dallas (Hal Rogers) *United States Representative from Kentucky*
Rogers, Mike D. *United States Representative from Alabama*
Rooney, Tom (Thomas J. Rooney) *United States Representative from Florida, lawyer*
Rosen, Mike *legislative staff member*
Ros-Lehtinen, Ileana Carmen *United States Representative from Florida*
Ross, Dennis Alan *United States Representative from Florida, former state legislator*
Rubio, Marco Antonio *United States Senator from Florida, former state legislator*
Sanford, Mark (Marshall Clement Sanford Jr.) *United States Representative from South Carolina, former Governor of South Carolina*
Scalise, Steve (Stephen Joseph Scalise) *United States Representative from Louisiana, former state legislator*
Schloegel, Scott P. *legislative staff member*
Scott, Austin (James Austin Scott) *United States Representative from Georgia, former state legislator*
Scott, Bobby (Robert Cortez Scott) *United States Representative from Virginia, lawyer*
Scott, David Albert *United States Representative from Georgia*
Scott, Tim (Timothy Eugene Scott) *United States Senator from South Carolina, former United States Representative from South Carolina*
Sessions, Jeff (Jefferson Beauregard Sessions III) *United States Senator from Alabama, former state attorney general*
Sessions, Peter Anderson *United States Representative from Texas*
Sewell, Terri Andrea *United States Representative from Alabama, lawyer*

Sheiner, Jonathan Robert *legislative staff member, lawyer*
Shelby, Richard Craig *United States Senator from Alabama*
Smith, Lamar Seeligson *United States Representative from Texas*
Southerland, Steve (William Southerland II) *United States Representative from Florida*
Stockman, Steve (Stephen Ernest Stockman) *United States Representative from Texas*
Thompson, Bennie G. *United States Representative from Mississippi*
Thornberry, Mac (William McClellan Thornberry) *United States Representative from Texas*
Veasey, Marc *United States Representative from Texas, former state legislator*
Vela, Filemon Bartolome, Jr. *United States Representative from Texas, lawyer*
Vitter, David Bruce *United States Senator from Louisiana*
Warner, Mark Robert *United States Senator from Virginia, former Governor of Virginia*
Wasserman-Schultz, Debbie (Deborah Wasserman-Schultz) *United States Representative from Florida*
Weber, Randy *United States Representative from Texas, former state legislator*
Webster, Daniel Alan *United States Representative from Florida, former state legislator*
Webster, Todd *legislative staff member, communications executive*
Westmoreland, Lynn A. *United States Representative from Georgia*
Wheeler, Susan Hawkes *legislative staff member, communications executive*
Whitfield, Edward (Wayne) *United States Representative from Kentucky*
Wicker, Roger Frederick *United States Senator from Mississippi*
Williams, Roger (John Roger Williams) *United States Representative from Texas, former state official*
Wilson, Frederica Smith *United States Representative from Florida, former state legislator*
Wilson, Joe (Addison Graves Wilson) *United States Representative from South Carolina*
Wittman, Robert J. *United States Representative from Virginia, former state legislator*
Wolf, Frank Rudolph *United States Representative from Virginia*
Womack, Steve *United States Representative from Arkansas, former mayor*
Woodall, Robert *United States Representative from Georgia*
Yarmuth, John Allan *United States Representative from Kentucky*
Yoho, Ted (Theodore Scott Yoho) *United States Representative from Florida, veterinarian*
York, Andrew Justin *legislative staff member*

FLORIDA

Altamonte Springs
Simmons, David *state legislator*

Apalachicola
Montford, William J. III *state legislator*

Apopka
Nelson, Bryan *state legislator*

Bartow
Albritton, Ben *state legislator*

Belleair Bluffs
Frishe, Jim *state legislator*

Boca Raton
Hager, Bill *state legislator*
Perman, Steven M. *state legislator*
Slosberg, Irving *state legislator*

Bradenton
Boyd, Jim *state legislator*

Clearwater
Hooper, Ed *state legislator*

Coconut Creek
Waldman, James W. *state legislator*

Coral Springs
Porth, Ari Abraham *state legislator*

Crestview
Evers, Gregory *state legislator*

Daytona Beach
Lynn, Evelyn Joan *state legislator*

Delray Beach
Berman, Lori Beth *state legislator*

Dunedin
Kraus, Elizabeth *state legislator*

Eustis
Metz, Larry Edward *state legislator, lawyer*

Fort Lauderdale
Bogdanoff, Ellyn Setnor *state legislator*
Dawson, Muriel Amanda (Mandy Dawson) *state legislator*
Jenne, Evan *state legislator*
Moraitis, George R., Jr. *state legislator*

Fort Myers
Benacquisto, Lizbeth *state legislator*
Caldwell, Matthew H. *state legislator*
Williams, Trudi K. *state legislator, engineering company executive*

Fort Walton Beach
Gaetz, Donald Jay *state legislator*

Gainesville
Chestnut, Charles S., IV, *state legislator*
Perry, W. Keith *state legislator*

Gulf Breeze
Broxson, Douglas Vaughn *state legislator*

Hialeah
Gonzalez, Eduardo *state legislator*
Oliva, Jose *state legislator*

Hollywood
Gibbons, Joseph A. *state legislator*
Schwartz, Elaine J. *state legislator*

Inverness
Dean, Charles S., Sr. *state legislator*

Jacksonville
Anderson, Greg *councilman*
Bishop, William *councilman*
Boyer, Lori N. *councilwoman*
Brown, Reginald L. *councilman*
Carter, Doyle *councilman*
Clark, Richard *councilman*
Crescimbeni, John R. *councilman*
Daniels, Kimberly *councilwoman*
Davis, Daniel *state legislator*
Fullwood, Reginald *state legislator*
Gaffney, Johnny A. *councilman*
Gibson, Audrey L. *state legislator*
Gulliford, Bill *councilman*
Holt, Ray *councilman*
Jones, Mia L. *state legislator*
Jones, Warren A. *councilman*
Joost, Stephen C. *councilman*
Lee, E. Denise *councilwoman*
Love, Jim *councilman*
Lumb, Robin *councilman*
McBurney, Charles Walker, Jr. *state representative, lawyer*
Ray, Lake III *state legislator*
Redman, Don *councilman*
Schellenberg, Matthew M. *councilman*
Williams, Lance Lamont *legislative assistant*
Wise, Stephen R. *state legislator*
Yarborough, Clay *councilman*

Lake City
Porter, Elizabeth *state legislator*

Lake Worth
Clemens, Jeff *state legislator*

Lakeland
McKeel, Seth *state legislator*

Lecanto
Smith, Jimmie T. *state legislator*

Margate
Ring, Jeremy *state legislator*

Melbourne
Altman, Thad *state legislator*

Miami
Artiles, Frank *state legislator*
Diaz, Jose Felix *state legislator*
Diaz de la Portilla, Miguel A. *state legislator*
Flores, Anitere *state legislator*
Garcia, Luis R. *state legislator*
Logan, Ana Rivas *state legislator*
Margolis, Gwen *state legislator*
Nunez, Jeanette M. *state legislator*
Stafford, Cynthia A. *state legislator*
Trujillo, Carlos *state legislator*
Watson, Barbara *state legislator*

Miami Gardens
Braynon, Oscar, II, *state legislator*

Miami Shores
Campbell, Daphne *state legislator*

Monticello
Boyd, Janegale *former state legislator, lobbyist*

Naples
Passidomo, Kathleen C. *state legislator*
Richter, Garrett S. *state legislator*

New Port Richey
Fasano, Michael Benjamin *state legislator*

North Miami Beach
Julien, John Patrick *state legislator*

Ocala
Baxley, Dennis K. *state legislator*

Orlando
Gardiner, Andy *state legislator*
Randolph, Scott *state legislator*
Siplin, Gary Anthony *state legislator*
Thompson, Geraldine F. (Geri Thompson) *state legislator*

Palm Beach Gardens
Rooney, Patrick, Jr. *state legislator*

Palm City
Negron, Joseph, Jr. *state legislator*

Panama City
Patronis, Jimmy T. *state legislator*

Parkland
Kiar, Martin David (Marty Kiar) *state legislator*

Plant City
Glorioso, Richard *state legislator*

Plantation
Sands, Franklin *state legislator*

Ponte Vedra Beach
Renuart, Ronald Joseph *state legislator, osteopath*

Port Orange
Hukill, Dorothy L. *state legislator*

Port Richey
Legg, John *state legislator*

Saint Augustine
Proctor, William Lee *state legislator, academic administrator*

Saint Petersburg
Ahern, Lawrence T. *state legislator*
Brandes, Jeff Paul *state legislator*

Sanford
Brodeur, Jason *state legislator*

Sarasota
Fitzgerald, Keith *former state legislator, political science professor*
Holder, Doug *state legislator*
Pilon, Ray *state legislator*
Steube, Greg *state legislator*

Sebring
Grimsley, Denise *state legislator*

Shalimar
Gaetz, Matt *state legislator*

Stuart
Snyder, William D. *state legislator*

Sunrise
Rich, Nan H. *state legislator*

Tallahassee
Abruzzo, Joseph *state legislator*
Adkins, Janet H. *state legislator*
Argenziano, Nancy *state legislator*
Aubuchon, Gary *state legislator*
Bembry, Leonard L. *state legislator*
Bennett, Michael S. *state legislator*
Bernard, Mackenson *state legislator*
Bullard, Dwight *state legislator*
Burgin, Rachel V. *state legislator*
Cannon, Dean *state legislator*
Clarke-Reed, Gwyndolen *state legislator*
Corcoran, Richard *state legislator*
Costello, Fredrick W. *state legislator*
Crisafulli, Steve *state legislator*
Detert, Nancy C. *state legislator*
Dockery, Paula *state legislator*
Dorworth, Christopher E. *state legislator*
Drake, Brad *state legislator*
Eisnaugle, Eric *state legislator*
Fresen, Erik *state legislator*
Garcia, Rene *state legislator*
Haridopolos, Mike *state legislator*
Harrell, Gayle B. *state legislator*
Harrison, Shawn *state legislator*
Horner, Mike *state legislator*
Hudson, Matt *state legislator*
Ingram, Clay *state legislator*
Jones, Dennis L. *state legislator*
Kreegel, Paige *state legislator*
Latvala, Jack *state legislator*
Mayfield, Debbie *state legislator*
Oelrich, Steve *state legislator*
O'Toole, H. Marlene *state legislator*
Pafford, Mark S. *state legislator*
Phelps, John Bridges *legislative official*
Plakon, Scott *state legislator*
Precourt, Stephen L. *state legislator*
Rehwinkle Vasilinda, Michelle *state legislator*
Roberson, Kenneth L. *state legislator*
Rogers, Hazelle *state legislator*
Rouson, Darryl Ervin *state legislator*
Sachs, Maria Lorts *state legislator*
Schenck, Robert C. *state legislator*
Smith, Christopher L. *state legislator*
Sobel, Eleanor *state legislator*
Soto, Darren *state legislator*
Stargel, Kelli *state legislator*
Storms, Ronda *state legislator*
Taylor, Dwayne L. *state legislator*
Thrasher, John *state legislator, former political organization administrator*
Thurston, Perry E., Jr. *state legislator*
Tobia, John *state legislator*
Van Zant, Charles E. *state legislator*
Weinstein, Michael B. *state legislator*
Williams, Alan B. *state legislator*
Wood, John *state legislator*
Workman, Ritch *state legislator*

Tampa
Castor, Kathy (Katherine Anne Castor) *United States Representative from Florida*
Cruz, Janet *state legislator*
Davis, Helen Gordon *retired state senator*
Grant, James W. *state legislator*
Joyner, Arthenia Lee *state legislator, lawyer*
Norman, Jim *state legislator*
Reed, Betty *state legislator*
Young, Dana D. *state legislator*

Tarpon Springs
Nehr, Peter *state legislator*

Tavernier
Saunders, Ron *state legislator*

Temple Terrace
Homan, Edward S. *state legislator*

Titusville
Goodson, Tom *state legislator*

Wesley Chapel
Weatherford, Will W. *state legislator*

West Miami
Bileca, Michael *state legislator*

Youngstown
Coley, Marti *state legislator*

GEORGIA

Albany
Dukes, Winfred J. *state legislator*
Meyer Von Bremen, Michael S. *state legislator*

Alpharetta
Jones, Jan *state legislator*

Americus
Hooks, George Bardin *state legislator, insurance company executive*

Athens
Cowsert, William S. (Bill) *state legislator, lawyer*
Heard, Keith G. *state legislator*
McBee, Mary Louise *state legislator, academic administrator*
McKillip, Doug *state legislator*

Atlanta
Abdul-Salaam, Roberta *state legislator*
Abrams, Stacey *state legislator*
Allison, Stephen *state legislator*
Anderson, Lee *state legislator*
Ashe, Kathleen B. *state legislator*
Baker, Glenn *state legislator*
Battles, Paul *state legislator*
Beasley-Teague, Sharon *state legislator*
Bell, Simone *state legislator*
Benfield, Stephanie Stuckey *state legislator*
Benton, Thomas H. (Tommy Benton) *state legislator*
Beverly, James *state legislator*
Black, Ellis *state legislator*
Brooks, Tyrone L. *state legislator*
Brown, Jeffrey Warner *state legislator*
Bruce, Roger *state legislator*
Bryant, Robert *state legislator*
Buckner, Debbie G. *state legislator*
Burns, Jon G. *state legislator*
Butler, Gloria S. *state legislator*
Carter, Earl (Buddy Carter) *state legislator*
Channell, R. Mickey *state legislator*
Cheokas, Mike *state legislator*
Coleman, Brooks P. *state legislator*
Cooke, Kevin *state legislator*
Cooper, Sharon Meyer *state legislator*
Crosby, John Dickey *state legislator*
Davis, Hardie *state legislator*
Davis, Steve *state legislator*
Dix, Scott *state legislator*
Dobbs, Elly *state legislator*
Dollar, Matt *state legislator*
Dudgeon, Mike *state legislator*
Epps, James A. *state legislator*
Floyd, Hugh *state legislator*
Fort, Vincent D. *state legislator*
Fullerton, Carol *state legislator*
Gardner, Pat *state legislator*
Geisinger, Harry *state legislator*
Golick, Rich *state legislator*
Grant, Johnny *state legislator*
Greene, Gerald E. *state legislator*
Hamrick, William (Bill) III *state legislator*
Harden, Buddy *state legislator*
Harden, Michael *state legislator*
Hatfield, John Mark *state legislator*
Heckstall, Joe *state legislator*
Hembree, William A. *state legislator*
Henson, Michele *state legislator*
Hill, Calvin *state legislator*
Hill, Jack *state legislator*
Holcomb, Scott *state legislator*
Holmes, Robert Alexander *state legislator*
Holt, Douglas *state legislator*
Jackson, Mack *state legislator*
Jackson, William S. *state legislator*
Jacobs, Mike *state legislator*
James, Lynmore *state legislator*
Jerguson, Sean *state legislator*
Jones, Sheila *state legislator*
Knight, David *state legislator*
Ladd, Bart (Charles) *state legislator, pilot*
Lane, Roger Bert *state legislator*
Lindsey, Edward *state legislator*
Long, Ralph III *state legislator*
Maddox, Billy *state legislator*
Marin, Pedro *state legislator*
Maxwell, Howard R. *state legislator*
Mayo, Rahn *state legislator*
McBrayer, Tony *state legislator*
McCall, Tom *state legislator*
Meadows, John *state legislator*
Millar, Fran *state legislator*
Mitchell, William *state legislator*
Mosby, Howard *state legislator*
Neal, Yasmin *state legislator*
Oliver, Mary Margaret *state legislator, lawyer*
O'Neal, Larry E. *state legislator*
Orrock, Nancy (Nan) Grogan *state legislator*
Pak, B.J. *state legislator*
Parent, Elena C. *state legislator*
Parham, Bobby Eugene *state legislator*
Parrish, Larry J. (Butch) *state legislator*
Paul, Russell Kent (Rusty Paul) *state legislator, marketing executive*
Powell, Alan T. *state legislator*
Powell, Jay *state legislator*
Purcell, Ann Rushing *state legislator, human services manager*
Ramsey, Matt *state legislator*
Roberts, Jay *state legislator*
Rogers, Carl *state legislator*
Rynders, Ed *state legislator*
Scott, Martin *state legislator*
Scott, Sandra *state legislator*
Setzler, Ed *state legislator*

Sheldon, Donna *state legislator*
Sims, Charles Neil *state legislator*
Smith, Lynn *state legislator*
Smith, Richard H. *state legislator*
Smith, Tommy *state legislator*
Stanley-Turner, LaNett Lorraine *state legislator*
Starr, Wade *state legislator*
Stephens, Edward Mickey *state legislator*
Stephens, Ron *state legislator*
Talton, Willie L. *state legislator*
Tate, Horacena *state legislator*
Taylor, Rashad *state legislator*
Thomas, Brian W. *state legislator*
Unterman, Renee S. *state legislator*
Welch, Andrew *state legislator*
Weldon, Tom *state legislator*
Wilkinson, Joseph B. *state legislator*
Willard, Wendell *state legislator*
Williams, Roger *state legislator*
Yates, John P. *state legislator*

Auburn
England, Terry Lamar *state legislator*

Augusta
Harbin, Ben L. *state legislator*
Murphy, Quincy *state legislator*
Sims, Barbara *state legislator*
Smith, Earnest *state legislator, nuclear energy industry executive*

Austell
Morgan, Alisha Thomas *state representative*
Wilkerson, David *state legislator*

Avondale Estates
Drenner, Karla *state legislator*

Blackshear
Nimmer, Chad *state legislator*

Blue Ridge
Ralston, David Edmund *state legislator*

Bremen
Heath, Bill *state legislator*

Brooklet
Tankersley, Jan B. *state legislator*

Brunswick
Atwood, Alex *state legislator*
Ligon, William T., Jr. *state legislator*
Majette, Denise *former congresswoman, real estate broker*

Buford
Clark, Josh *state legislator*

Cartersville
Coomer, Christian *state legislator*

Cassville
Loudermilk, Barry Dean *state legislator*

Cedartown
Crawford, Rick *state legislator*

Chickamauga
Mullis, Jeff E. *state legislator*

Clarkesville
Rogers, Terry *state legislator*

Cohutta
Dickson, Tom S. *state legislator*

College Park
James, Donzella *state legislator*

Columbus
Harbison, Ed *state legislator, broadcast journalist, motivational speaker*
Hugley, Carolyn F. *state legislator*
McKoon, Joshua *state legislator*
Smith, Kip *state legislator*
Smyre, Calvin *state legislator*

Conyers
Dickerson, Pamela A. *state legislator*

Cumming
Hamilton, Mark *state legislator*
Murphy, Jack *state legislator*

Dahlonega
Amerson, Amos *state legislator*
Gooch, Steve *state legislator*

Dalton
Bethel, Charles Jones *state legislator*

Danielsville
Ginn, Frank *state legislator*

Dawson
Sims, Freddie Powell *state legislator*

Decatur
Carter, Jason *state legislator*
Hudson, Helen (Sistie) G. *state legislator*
Jones, Emanuel *state legislator, automotive executive*
Mobley, Barbara Jean *former state legislator, lawyer*
Ramsey, Ronald B., Sr. *state legislator*

Douglas
Goggans, Greg *state legislator, orthodontist*

Douglasville
Hightower, Dustin *state legislator, lawyer*

Dublin
Hatchett, Matt *state legislator*

Duluth
Shafer, David J. *state legislator*

Dunwoody
Taylor, Tom *state legislator*

Eastman
Pruett, Jimmy *state legislator*

Fayetteville
Fludd, Virgil *state legislator*

Gainesville
Dunahoo, Emory West, Jr. *state legislator*
Miller, Butch *state legislator*

Glennville
Dutton, Delvis *state legislator*

Hephzibah
Frazier, Gloria *state legislator*

Hogansville
Nix, Randy *state legislator*

Jasper
Jasperse, Rick *state legislator*

Johns Creek
Riley, Lynne *state legislator*

Jonesboro
Davenport, Gail *state legislator*

La Fayette
Neal, Jay *state legislator*

Lakeland
Shaw, Jason *state legislator*

Lawrenceville
Brockway, Buzz *state legislator*
Clark, Valerie *state legislator*

Lilburn
Casas, David *state legislator*

Lithonia
Dawkins-Haigler, Dee *state legislator*
Kendrick, Dar'shun *state legislator*
McKinney, Cynthia Ann *former United States Representative from Georgia*
Stephenson, Pam *state legislator*

Locust Grove
Jeffares, Rick *state legislator*

Lyons
Williams, Tommie *state legislator*

Macon
Paris, Miriam *state legislator*
Peake, Allen *state legislator*
Randall, Nikki *state legislator*
Staton, Cecil *state legislator*

Marietta
Carson, John *state legislator*
Hill, Judson *state legislator*
Johnson, Terry *state legislator*
Manning, Judith Hubert *state legislator, real estate company executive*
Parsons, Don L. *state legislator*
Teasley, Sam *state legislator*
Thompson, Steve *state legislator*
Tippins, Lindsey *state legislator*

Menlo
Reece, Barbara Massey *state legislator*

Midway
Williams, Al *state legislator*

Milledgeville
Kidd, Rusty (E. Culver Kidd) *state legislator*

Monroe
Williamson, Bruce *state legislator*

Monticello
Holmes, Susan D. *state legislator*

Musella
Dickey, Robert *state legislator*

Nashville
Houston, Penny *state legislator*

Newnan
Crane, Mike *state legislator*

Norcross
Rice, Thomas (Tom) R. *state legislator*

Ochlocknee
Bulloch, John D., Jr. *state legislator*

Parrott
Hanner, Bob *state legislator*

Perry
Tolleson, Thorborn Ross, Jr. *state legislator*

Powder Springs
Braddock, Paulette Rakestraw *state legislator*
Ehrhart, Earl *state legislator*

Riverdale
Jordan, Darryl *state legislator*
Seay, Valencia *state legislator*

Rome
Dempsey, Katie M. *state legislator*

Roswell
Albers, John *state legislator*

Savannah
Gordon, J. Craig *state legislator*
Jackson, Lester G. III *state legislator, dentist*
Thomas, Regina *state legislator*
Watson, Ben *state legislator*

Smyrna
Evans, Stacey Godfrey *state legislator*
Stoner, Doug *state legislator*

Snellville
Balfour, Don *state legislator*
Harrell, Brett Alexander *state legislator*

Stone Mountain
Williams, Earnest *state legislator*

Thomasville
Taylor, Darlene K. *state legislator*

Toccoa
Wilkinson, John K. *state legislator*

Tucker
Henson, Steve *state legislator*
Thompson, Curt B. *state legislator, lawyer*

Tyrone
Chance, Ronnie *state legislator*

Valdosta
Carter, Amy Alexander *state legislator*
Golden, Tim Robert *state legislator*

Vidalia
Morris, Greg *state legislator*

Watkinsville
Williams, Charles *state legislator*

Waynesboro
Stone, Jesse *state legislator*

Woodbine
Spencer, Jason *state legislator*

Woodstock
Rogers, Chip *state legislator*

KENTUCKY

Brandenburg
Greer, Jeff *state legislator*

Crestwood
Harris, Ernest Leo *state legislator*

Erlanger
Koenig, Adam *state legislator*

Frankfort
Adams, Julie Raque *state legislator*
Adams, Royce W. *state legislator*
Adkins, Rocky *state legislator, mining executive*
Arnold, John A. *state legislator*
Belcher, Carolyn R. *state legislator*
Belcher, Linda *state legislator*
Blevins, Walter *state legislator*
Bowen, Joe R. *state legislator*
Bratcher, Kevin *state legislator*
Buford, Tom *state legislator*
Butler, Dwight D. *state legislator*
Carney, John *state legislator*
Carpenter, Jared K. *state legislator*
Cherry, Mike *state legislator*
Clark, Larry *state legislator*
Clark, Perry B. *state legislator*
Collins, Hubert c *state legislator*
Combs, Leslie A. *state legislator*
Couch, Tim *state legislator*
Coursey, Will *state legislator*
Crenshaw, Jesse *state legislator*
Crimm, Ronald (Ron) E. *state legislator*
Damron, Robert R. *state legislator, investment banker*
DeCesare, Jim *state legislator*
Denham, Mitchel B. *state legislator*
Denton, Julie Carman Rose *state legislator*
DeWeese, Bob M. *state legislator, retired surgeon*
Edmonds, Ted *state legislator*
Embry, Carlos Brogdon *state legislator*
Farmer, William P. *state legislator*
Fischer, Joseph Michael *state legislator*
Flood, Kelly *state legislator*
Floyd, David *state legislator*
Ford, Danny R. *state legislator*
Gibson, Carroll *state legislator*
Givens, David P. *state legislator*
Graham, Derrick W. *state legislator*
Gregory, Sara Beth *state legislator*
Harmon, Mike *state legislator*
Harper Angel, Denise (Denise Harper Angel) *state legislator*
Henderson, Richard D. *state legislator*
Henley, Melvin B. *state legislator*
Higdon, Jimmy *state legislator*
Hoover, Jeffrey H. *state legislator, lawyer*
Horlander, Dennis *state legislator*
Hornback, Paul *state legislator*
Housman, Brent *state legislator*
Hurt, Wade *state legislator*
Jones, Ray S. *state legislator*
Keene, Dennis *state legislator*
Kerr, Alice Forgy *state legislator*
King, Kim *state legislator*
King, Martha Jane *state legislator*
Lee, Jimmie *state legislator*
Lee, Stan *state legislator*

Leeper, Robert (Bob) J. *state legislator*
Mayfield, Donna *state legislator*
McKee, Thomas Miles *state legislator*
Meeks, Reginald K. *state legislator*
Meredith, Michael Lee *state legislator*
Miller, Charles *state legislator*
Mills, Terry *state legislator*
Montell, Brad *state legislator*
Moore, Tim *state legislator*
Napier, Lonnie *state legislator*
Neal, Gerald A. *state legislator*
Nelson, Rick *state legislator*
Nemes, Michael J. *state legislator*
Nesler, Fred *state legislator*
Osborne, David *state legislator*
Overly, Sannie *state legislator*
Owens, Darryl T. *state legislator*
Palmer, R.J., II, *state legislator*
Palumbo, Ruth Ann *state legislator*
Parrett, Dennis L. *state legislator*
Pendleton, Joey *state legislator*
Pullin, Tanya *state legislator*
Quarles, Ryan *state legislator*
Rader, Marie L. *state legislator*
Rand, Rick W. *state legislator*
Rhoads, Jerry P. *state legislator, lawyer*
Richards, Jody *state legislator, communications educator, small business owner*
Ridley, J. Dorsey *state legislator*
Riggs, Steven Ray *state legislator*
Riner, Tom *state legislator*
Rollins, Carl P., II, *state legislator*
Rudy, Steven J. *state legislator*
Sanders, Richard (Richie) A. *state legislator*
Santoro, Sal *state legislator*
Schickel, John *state legislator*
Seum, Dan (Malano) *state legislator*
Shaughnessy, Timothy Thomas *state legislator*
Simpson, Arnold *state legislator*
Sinnette, Kevin *state legislator*
Smart, Rita H. *state legislator*
Smith, Brandon *state legislator*
Stacy, John Will *state legislator*
Steele, Fitz *state legislator*
Stein, Kathy W. *state legislator*
Stewart, Jim III *state legislator*
Stine, Katie Kratz *state legislator*
Stivers, Robert *state legislator*
Stone, Wilson *state legislator*
Thayer, Damon *state legislator*
Thompson, Tommy N. *state legislator*
Turner, Johnny Ray *state legislator*
Turner, Tommy *state legislator*
Webb, Robin L. *state legislator, lawyer*
Webb-Edgington, Alecia *state legislator*
Westrom, Susan *state legislator*
Westwood, Jack (Jack Westwood) *state legislator*
Williams, David L. *state legislator*
Wilson, Mike *state legislator*
Winters, Kenneth W. *state legislator*
Wuchner, Addia Kathryn *state legislator*
York, Jill *state legislator, small business owner*

Glasgow
Bell, Johnny W. *state legislator*

Greenville
Yonts, Brent Larry *state legislator*

Hindman
Short, John W. *state legislator*

Hopkinsville
Adams, John W. *former state legislator*

Louisville
Carmack, Terry Alan *legislative staff member*
Casebier, Lindy *state legislator*
Marzian, Mary Lou *state legislator*
Wayne, Jim *state legislator*

Madisonville
Waide, Ben *state legislator*

Owensboro
Glenn, James H., Jr., (Jim Glenn) *state legislator, business educator*

Pembroke
Dossett, Myron B. *state legislator*

Phelps
Hall, W. Keith *state legislator*

Russell Springs
McGaha, Vernie *state legislator*

Shively
Jenkins, Joni L. *state legislator*

LOUISIANA

Abbeville
Hensgens, Bob *state legislator*

Abita Springs
Simon, Scott M. *state legislator*

Alexandria
Dewitt, Charles W (Charlie) *state legislator*
Harris, Lance *state legislator*

Amite
Edwards, John Bel *state legislator*

Baton Rouge
Adley, Robert R. *state legislator*
Amedee, Jody *state legislator*
Armes, James K. III *state legislator*
Arnold, Jeffery J. *state legislator*
Badon, Austin J. *state legislator*
Barham, Robert Jocelyn *state legislator*
Barras, Taylor F. *state legislator*
Barrow, Regina Ashford *state legislator*

Billiot, Robert E. *state legislator*
Broome, Sharon Weston *state legislator*
Brown, Terry R. *state legislator*
Burford, Richard T. *state legislator*
Burns, Henry L. *state legislator*
Burns, Timothy G. *state legislator*
Carmody, Thomas G., Jr. *state legislator*
Carter, Stephen F. *state legislator*
Chabert, Norby *state legislator*
Chaney, Charles R. *state legislator*
Cheek, Sherri Smith *state legislator*
Claitor, Dan *state legislator*
Connick, Patrick *state legislator*
Cox, Kenny R. *state legislator*
Crowe, A. G. *state legislator*
Danahay, Michael E. *state legislator*
Daniel, William Buchanan, IV, *state legislator*
Dixon, Herbert B. *state legislator*
Dorsey, Yvonne *state legislator*
Dove, Gordon E., Sr. *state legislator*
Fields, Cleo *state legislator*
Foil, Franklin J. *state legislator*
Fontenot, Heulette (Clo) *state legislator*
Franklin, Albert B. *state legislator*
Gaines, Randal L. *state legislator*
Geymann, Brett F. *state legislator*
Greene, Hunter V. *state legislator*
Guillory, Mickey James *state legislator*
Guinn, John E. *state legislator*
Harrison, Joe *state legislator*
Hazel, Lowell C. *state legislator*
Heitmeier, David R. *state senator*
Hill, Dorothy Sue *state legislator*
Hoffmann, Frank A. *state legislator*
Honroé, Dalton W. *state legislator*
Howard, Frank A. *state legislator*
Hunter, Marcus L. *state legislator*
Jackson, Girod III *state legislator*
Jackson, Katrina R. *state legislator*
James, Edward C., II, (Ted James) *state legislator*
Johnson, Robert A. *state legislator*
Jones, Sam *state legislator*
Kostelka, Robert W. (Bob) *state legislator*
LaFleur, Eric *state legislator*
Lambert, Eddie J. *state legislator*
Landry, Nancy R. *state legislator*
LeBas, H. Bernard *state legislator*
Lentini, Arthur (Art) J. *state legislator*
Long, Gerald *state legislator*
Miller, Gregory A. *state legislator*
Mills, Fred H., Jr. *state legislator*
Montoucet, Jack *state legislator*
Morris, James H. *state legislator*
Norton, Barbara M. *state legislator*
Ortego, Stephen J. *state legislator*
Pearson, J. Kevin *state legislator*
Perry, Jonathan W. *state legislator*
Peterson, Karen Carter *state legislator, political organization administrator*
Pierre, Vincent J. *state legislator*
Ponti, Erich E. *state legislator*
Price, Edward J. *state legislator*
Richardson, Clifton R. *state legislator*
Ritchie, Harold L. *state legislator*
Seabaugh, Alan T. *state legislator, lawyer*
Smith, Patricia Haynes *state legislator*
Thibaut, Major *state legislator*
White, Mack (Bodi) A. *state legislator*
Whitney, Lenar L. *state legislator*
Williams, Alfred C. *state legislator*
Williams, Patrick C. *state legislator*

Belle Chasse
Leopold, Christopher J. *state legislator*

Bogalusa
Nevers, Ben W. *state legislator*

Bossier City
Peacock, Barrow *state legislator*
Thompson, Jeff R. *state legislator*

Breaux Bridge
Huval, Mike *state legislator*

Bunkie
Hines, Donald E. *state legislator*

Columbia
Riser, Neil *state legislator*

Covington
Hollis, Paul B. *state legislator*
Schroder, John M. *state legislator*

Delhi
Thompson, Francis C. *state legislator*

Denham Springs
Hodges, Valarie *state legislator*
Pope, J. Rogers *state legislator*

Dry Creek
Cain, James David *state legislator*

Franklin
Allain, R.L., II, (Bret Allain) *state legislator*

Gonzales
Berthelot, John A. *state legislator*

Gretna
Adams, Bryan *state legislator*

Hammond
Broadwater, Christopher *state legislator*

Homer
Jefferson, Patrick O'Neal *state legislator*

Jackson
Havard, Kenneth E. *state legislator*

Jeanerette
Champagne, Simone *state legislator*

Jennings
Morrish, Dan *state legislator*
Theunissen, Gerald (Joseph Theunissen) *state legislator*

Jonesboro
Fannin, James R. *state legislator*

Kenner
Willmott, Thomas P. *state legislator*

Lafayette
Bishop, Stuart J. *state legislator*
Cortez, Patrick Page *state legislator*
Cravins, Donald R., Jr. *state legislator*
Landry, Terry C., Sr. *state legislator, former protective services official*
Robideaux, Joel C. *state legislator*

Lake Charles
Johns, Ronnie *state legislator*
Kleckley, Charles E. (Chuck Kleckley) *state legislator*

Larose
Gisclair, Jerry *state legislator*

Leesville
Smith, John R. *state legislator*

Livingston
Erdey, Dale *state legislator*
Mack, Sherman Q. *state legislator, lawyer*

Mandeville
Donahue, Jack *state legislator*

Meraux
Garofalo, Raymond E. *state legislator*

Metairie
Appel, Conrad *state legislator*
Hollis, Jesse Kendrick (Ken) *state legislator*
Ligi, Anthony V., Jr. *state legislator*
Lopinto, Joseph P. III *state legislator*
Martiny, Daniel *state legislator*

Minden
Reynolds, H. Eugene (Gene Reynolds) *state legislator*

Monroe
Dimos, Jimmy *state representative*
Morris, John C. III *state legislator*

Napoleonville
Brown, Troy E. *state legislator*

New Iberia
Romero, Craig F. *state legislator*

New Orleans
Abramson, Neil C. *state legislator*
Bishop, Wesley T. *state legislator*
Brossett, Jared C. *state legislator*
Heitmeier, Francis C. *state legislator*
Henry, Cameron *state legislator*
Leger, Walt III *state legislator*
Lorusso, Nick *state legislator*
Morrell, Jean-Paul J. *state legislator*
Murray, Edwin Rene *state legislator*

Norco
Smith, Gary L., Jr. *state legislator*

Opelousas
Thierry, Ledricka Johnson *state legislator*

Parks
Durand, Sydnie Mae *state legislator*

Pineville
McPherson, William Joseph (Joe) *state legislator*

Plaquemine
St. Germain, Karen Gaudet *state legislator*

Ponchatoula
Pugh, Stephen Edmund, Sr. *state legislator*

Port Allen
Ward, Rick III *state legislator*

River Ridge
Talbot, Kirk *state legislator*

Ruston
Gallot, Richard, Jr. *state legislator*
Shadoin, Robert E. *state legislator*

Shreveport
Burrell, Roy A. *state legislator*
Malone, Max Tatum *state legislator*
Tarver, Gregory Williams, Sr. *state legislator*

Slidell
Cromer, George Gregory *state legislator*

Sorrento
Schexnayder, Clay *state legislator*

Thibodaux
Richard, Jerome *state legislator*

Vidalia
Anders, John F. *state legislator*

West Monroe
Walsworth, Michael (Mike) A. *state legislator*

Westwego
Alario, John A., Jr. *state legislator*

Winnfield
Smith, Kenneth Michael (Mike) *state legislator*

Winnsboro
Pylant, Steven E. *state legislator*

MISSISSIPPI

Baldwyn
Turner, Jerry R. *state legislator*

Batesville
Gardner, Joe C. *state legislator*

Belmont
Wilemon, JP, Jr. *state legislator*

Belzoni
Straughter, Rufus E (Pete) *state legislator*

Biloxi
Gollott, Thomas (Tommy) Arlin *state legislator*
Patterson, Randall H. *state legislator*

Bogue Chitto
Moak, Robert Warren (Bobby) *state legislator*

Brandon
Baker, Mark *state legislator*
Moore, John L. *state legislator*

Bruce
Beckett, Charles Jim *state legislator*

Byhalia
Woods, Thomas (Tommy) Lamar *state legislator*

Canton
Blackmon, Edward, Jr. *state legislator*

Carthage
Malone, Bennett *state legislator*
Smith, Ferr *state legislator*

Charleston
Reynolds, Thomas Upton, II, *state legislator*

Clarksdale
Espy, Henry (Chuck) William III *state legislator*

Cleveland
Simmons, Willie Lee *state legislator*

Clinton
Gunn, Philip *state legislator*

Columbus
Brown, Terry Wayne *state legislator*
Chism, Gary Alan *state legislator*
Harrison, Esther M. *state legislator*
Smith, Jeffrey C. *state legislator*

Ellisville
Shows, C. H. (Bobby) *state legislator*

Florence
Weathersby, Thomas Cabe (Tom Weathersby) *state legislator*

French Camp
Jackson, Gary *state legislator*

Greenville
Bailey, Willie L. *state legislator*

Greenwood
Jordan, David *state legislator*
Perkins, Willie J. *state legislator*

Hattiesburg
Lott, Michael A. *state legislator*
Watson, Percy Willis *state legislator*

Hazlehurst
Holloway, Gregory L. *state legislator*

Hollandale
Clarke, Eugene (Buck) S. *state legislator*

Holly Springs
Buck, Kelvin O. *state legislator*

Indianola
Thomas, Sara Richardson *state legislator*

Jackson
Alday, Gene *state legislator*
Arnold, William Tracy *state legislator*
Bain, Nick *state legislator*
Banks, Earle S. *state legislator*
Baria, David *state legislator*
Barker, Toby *state legislator*
Barnett, Lester H. *state legislator, furniture store executive*
Barton, Manly *state legislator*
Bell, Donnie *state legislator*
Bennett, Richard *state legislator*
Blount, David *state legislator*
Boyd, Randy P. *state legislator*
Brown, Cecil C. *state legislator*
Brown, Chris *state legislator*
Bryan, Wendell Hobdy, II, (Hob Bryan) *state legislator*
Buck, Kimberly Campbell *state legislator*
Busby, Charles *state legislator*
Butler, Albert *state legislator*
Butler, Kelvin E. *state legislator*
Byrd, Larry *state legislator*
Calhoun, Credell *state legislator*
Carmichael, Videt *state legislator*
Carpenter, Lester *state legislator*
Clark, Bryant W. *state legislator*
Clarke, Alyce Griffin *state legislator*
Coleman, Mary H. *state legislator*
Collins, Nancy Adams *state legislator*
Crawford, Carolyn *state legislator*
Currie, Becky *state legislator*
Dawkins, Deborah Jeanne *state legislator*
DeBar, Dennis *state legislator*
DeLano, Scott *state legislator*
Denny, William (Bill) C. *state legislator*
Dixon, Deborah Butler *state legislator*
Doty, Sally Burchfield *state legislator*
Eure, Casey *state legislator*
Evans, Bob *state legislator*
Evans, James (Jim) *state legislator*
Evans, Michael T. *state legislator*
Fleming, Erik R. *former state legislator, paralegal*
Flowers, Merle G. *state legislator*
Frazier, Hillman Terome *state legislator*
Gandy, Phillip A. *state legislator*
Gipson, Andy *state legislator*
Guice, Jeffrey S. *state legislator*
Hale, Steve *state legislator*
Haney, Greg *state legislator*
Harkins, Josh *state legislator*
Hill, Angela Burks *state legislator*
Hines, John W., Sr. *state legislator, private investigator*
Hood, Joey *state legislator*
Hopson, W. Briggs III *state legislator*
Horan, Kevin *state legislator*
Horhn, John *state legislator*
Huddleston, Mac *state legislator*
Hudson, Billy *state legislator*
Jolly, Russell *state legislator*
Jones, Kenneth Wayne *state legislator*
Ladner, Timmy *state legislator*
Lamar, John Thomas (Trey Lamar) *state legislator*
Longwitz, William *state legislator*
Lott, Hank *state legislator*
Martinson, Rita R. *state legislator*
Massengill, Steve *state legislator*
Massey, Chris *state legislator*
Mayo, Brad *state legislator*
McDaniel, Chris *state legislator*
McGee, Kevin *state legislator*
McLeod, Doug *state legislator*
Mettetal, Nolan *state legislator*
Miles, Tom *state legislator*
Monsour, Alex *state legislator*
Montgomery, Haskins *state legislator*
Moran, Philip *state legislator*
Myers, David W. *state legislator*
Nelson, Pat *state legislator*
Oberhousen, Brad A. *state legislator*
Pigott, Bill *state legislator*
Polk, John A. *state legislator*
Potts Parks, Rita *state legislator*
Read, John O. *state legislator*
Rushing, Randy *state legislator*
Shirley, William *state legislator*
Simmons, Derrick T. *state senator*
Smith, Tony *state legislator*
Sojourner, Melanie *state legislator*
Steverson, Jody *state legislator*
Stone, Bill *state legislator*
Taylor, Tommy *state legislator*
Tindell, Sean J. *state legislator*
Ward, Giles *state legislator*
Watson, Michael *state legislator*
White, Jason *state legislator*
Wiggins, Brice *state legislator*
Williams-Barnes, Sonya *state legislator*
Williamson, Gloria *state legislator*
Wooton, Adrienne *state legislator*
Young, Charles, Jr. *state legislator*

Kilmichael
Howell, Bobby B. *state legislator*

Laurel
Scott, Omeria McDonald *state legislator*
Staples, Gary Victor *state legislator*

Macon
Dickson, Reecy L. *state legislator*

Magnolia
Cockerham, Angela *state legislator*

Marks
Jackson, Robert L. *state legislator*

Mccomb
Mims, Sam C., V, *state legislator*

Meridian
Horne, Stephen (Steve) A. *state legislator*
Snowden, Greg (Elton Gregory Snowden) *state legislator*

Montrose
Stringer, Johnny William *state legislator*

Morgantown
Morgan, Ken *state legislator*

Moss Point
Broomfield, Billy Frank *state legislator*

Mound Bayou
Coleman, Linda F. *state legislator*

Mount Olive
Warren, Joseph Lawrence (Joe) *state legislator*

Natchez
Johnson, Robert L. III *state legislator*

New Albany
Rogers, Margaret Ellis *state legislator*

Newton
Burton, Terry C. *state legislator*

Ocean Springs
Zuber, Henry B., III, (Hank Zuber) *state legislator*

Bennettsville
Munnerlyn, Elizabeth Rogers *state legislator*

Bishopville
Brown, Grady A. *state legislator*

Chapin
Ballentine, Nathan *state legislator*

Charleston
Gilliard, Wendell G. *state legislator*

Columbia
Agnew, Paul L. *state legislator*
Alexander, Terry *state legislator*
Alexander, Thomas C. *state legislator*
Allen, Karl B. *state legislator*
Allison, Merita Ann *state legislator*
Anderson, Carl L. *state legislator*
Anderson, Ralph *state legislator*
Anthony, Michael A. *state legislator*
Atwater, Todd K. *state legislator*
Bales, Jimmy C. *state legislator*
Bannister, Bruce Wyche *state legislator*
Barfield, Liston Douglas *state legislator*
Battle, James A. *state legislator*
Bedingfield, Eric M. *state legislator*
Bowen, Don C. *state legislator*
Bowers, William K. *state legislator, accountant*
Brady, Joan B. *state legislator*
Branham, Lester P., Jr. *state legislator*
Brannon, Norman Doug *state legislator*
Brantley, Curtis *state legislator*
Bright, Lee *state legislator*
Brown, Robert L. *state legislator*
Bryant, Kevin L. *state legislator*
Campsen, George E. III *state legislator*
Ceips, Catherine C. *state legislator*
Chumley, William Rob *state legislator*
Cleary, Raymond E. III *state legislator*
Clemmons, Alan D. *state legislator*
Clyburn, William, Sr. *state legislator*
Coleman, Creighton B. *state legislator*
Corbin, Thomas D. *state legislator*
Courson, John Edward *state legislator, insurance company executive*
Crawford, Kristopher R. *state legislator*
Cromer, Ronnie W. *state legislator*
Crosby, William E. *state legislator*
Delleney, Francis Gregory *state legislator*
Edge, Tracy Russell *state legislator*
Elliott, Dick F. *state legislator*
Erickson, Shannon *state legislator*
Fair, Michael L. *state legislator, insurance company executive*
Ford, Robert *state legislator*
Frye, Marion *state legislator*
Funderburk, Laurie Slade *state legislator*
Gambrell, Michael W. *state legislator*
Garrick, Mia Butler *state legislator*
Govan, Jerry N., Jr. *state legislator*
Gregory, Chauncey Klugh *state legislator*
Grooms, Lawrence K. (Larry Grooms) *state legislator*
Hamilton, Daniel P. *state legislator*
Hardwick, Nelson L. *state legislator*
Harrell, Robert W., Jr. *state legislator*
Harrison, James Hodges *state legislator*
Hart, Christopher R. *state legislator*
Hawkins, John David *state legislator*
Hayes, Jackie E. *state legislator*
Hayes, Robert Wesley, Jr. *state legislator, lawyer*
Henderson, Phyllis *state legislator*
Herbkersman, William G. (Bill) *state legislator*
Hiott, David R. *state legislator*
Hixon, William M. *state legislator*
Hodges, Kenneth F. *state legislator*
Horne, Jenny Anderson *state legislator*
Hosey, Lonnie *state legislator*
Howard, Leon *state legislator*
Huggins, Chip *state legislator*
Hutto, Charles Bradley (Brad Hutto) *state legislator*
Jackson, Darrell *state legislator*
Jefferson, Joseph H. *state legislator*
Johnson, Christine A. *former state legislator*
Johnson, Kevin L. *state legislator*
Knight, Patsy G. *state legislator*
Knotts, John Milton, Jr., (Jake Knotts) *state legislator*
Land, John Calhoun III *state legislator, lawyer*
Leatherman, Hugh Kenneth, Sr. *state legislator, engineering executive*
Leventis, Phil Peter *state legislator*
Limehouse, Harry Bancroft, III, (Chip) *state legislator*
Loftis, Dwight A. *state legislator*
Lourie, Joel B. *state legislator*
Lowe, Phillip D. *state legislator*
Mack, David III *state legislator*
Malloy, Gerald *state legislator*
Martin, Larry A. *state legislator*
Martin, Shane *state legislator*
Massey, A. Shane *state legislator*
Matthews, John Wesley *state legislator*
McCoy, Peter M., Jr. *state legislator*
McEachern, Joseph A. *state legislator*
McGill, John Yancey *state legislator, real estate broker, homebuilder*
McLeod, Walton James III *state legislator, lawyer*
Merrill, James H. *state legislator*
Mitchell, Harold *state legislator*
Moss, Dennis Carroll *state legislator*
Moss, V. Stephen (Steve Moss) *state legislator*
Nanney, Wendy K. *state legislator*
Neal, James M. *state legislator, retired principal*
Neal, Joseph H. *state legislator, minister, computer company executive*
Neilson, Denny Woodall *state legislator*
Nicholson, Floyd *state legislator*
Norman, Ralph W. *state legislator*
O'Dell, William H. *state legislator*
Ott, Harry L. *state legislator*
Owens, Phillip Drayton *state legislator*
Parks, Julia Anne *state legislator*
Patrick, Andrew S. *state legislator*
Peeler, Harvey Smith, Jr. *state legislator*
Pinckney, Clementa Carlos *state legislator*
Pinson, Lewis Eugene *state legislator*
Pitts, Michael A. *state legislator*
Pope, Thomas E. *state legislator*
Putnam, Joshua A. *state legislator*
Quinn, Richard M., Jr. *state legislator, marketing professional*
Rankin, Luke A. *state legislator*
Reese, Glenn G. *state legislator*
Ritchie, James H. *state legislator*
Rutherford, James Todd *state legislator*
Ryan, Kevin *state legislator*
Ryberg, Walter Greg *state legislator*
Sandifer, William Edward III *state legislator*
Scarborough, Wallace Berry *state legislator*
Scott, John Lee, Jr. *state legislator*
Sellers, Bakari T. *state legislator*
Setzler, Nikki Giles *state legislator*
Sheheen, Vincent A. *state legislator*
Shoopman, Phillip W. *state legislator*
Simrill, Gary J. *state legislator*
Skelton, B. R. *state legislator*
Smith, Garry R. *state legislator*
Smith, James Emerson, Jr. *state legislator*
Smith, James Roland *state legislator*
Sottile, F. Michael *state legislator*
Southard, Edward L. *state legislator*
Spires, L. Kit *state legislator*
Stavrinakis, Leonides Emmanuel (Leon Stavrinakis) *state legislator*
Tallon, Edward R., Sr. *state legislator*
Thayer, Anne J. *state legislator*
Thomas, David L. *state legislator*
Toole, McLain R. *state legislator*
Tribble, David, Jr. *state legislator*
Trotter, Teddy N. *state representative, consumer products company executive*
Vaughn, Lewis R. *state legislator*
Verdin, Daniel B. III *state legislator*
Vick, Ted Martin *state legislator*
Viers, Thad T. *state legislator*
Weeks, J. David *state legislator, lawyer*
Whipper, J. Seth *state legislator, lawyer*
White, W. Brian *state legislator*
Whitmire, William R. *state legislator*
Williams, Kent *state legislator*
Williams, Robert Q. *state legislator*
Young, Thomas R., Jr. *state legislator*

Conway
Hearn, George M. *state legislator*

Florence
Hines, Mack T. *state legislator*

Fort Mill
Long, Deborah *state legislator*

Fountain Inn
Willis, Mark Nye *state legislator*

Goose Creek
Campbell, Paul Gladstone, Jr. *state legislator, chemical engineer*
Daning, Joseph *state legislator*

Greeleyville
Sabb, Ronnie A. *state legislator*

Greenville
Bikas, Eric J. *state legislator*
Dillard, Chandra Elisa *state legislator*

Hartsville
Lucas, James H. *state legislator*

Landrum
Stringer, Tommy *state legislator*

Orangeburg
Cobb-Hunter, Gilda *state legislator*

Rock Hill
King, John R. *state legislator*

Spartanburg
Cole, Derham, Jr. *state legislator*
Forrester, Mike *state legislator*
Parker, Steve *state legislator*

Summerville
Murphy, Chris J. *state legislator*
Rose, Michael Thomas *state legislator, lawyer*

West Columbia
Bingham, Kenneth A. *state legislator*

Winnsboro
Brown, H. Boyd *state legislator*

TENNESSEE

Bartlett
Coley, Jim *state legislator*
Lollar, Ron *state legislator*

Bolivar
Shaw, Johnny W. *state legislator*

Brentwood
Johnson, Jack C. *state legislator*

Chattanooga
Dean, Vince *state legislator*
Floyd, Richard *state legislator*

Church Hill
Faulk, Michael Anthony *state legislator, lawyer*

Clarksville
Johnson, Curtis *state legislator*
Kurita, Rosalind *state legislator*
Pitts, Joe *state legislator*

Cleveland
Watson, Eric *state legislator*

College Grove
Casada, Glen *state legislator*

Collierville
Todd, Curry *state legislator*

Cordova
McManus, Stephen *state legislator*

Dickson
Shepard, David A. *state legislator*

Dunlap
Harmon, Bill W. *state legislator*

Elizabethton
Williams, Waymon Kent *state legislator*

Franklin
Sargent, Charles M. *state legislator*

Goodlettsville
Haynes, Joe M. *state legislator*

Greeneville
Hawk, David B. *state legislator*

Hendersonville
Maggart, Debra Young *state legislator*

Hixson
Watson, Foy W. (Bo Watson) *state legislator*

Jackson
Eldridge, Jimmy A. *state legislator*
Finney, Lowe *state legislator*

Joelton
Moore, Gary W. *state legislator*

Johnson City
Crowe, Dewey (Rusty) E., II, *state legislator*

Jonesborough
Ford, Robert Dale (Dale Ford) *state legislator*
Hill, Matthew *state legislator*

Knoxville
Armstrong, Joseph E. *state legislator*
Brooks, Harry *state legislator*
Brown, Daniel T. *councilman*
Campfield, Stacey *state legislator*
Dunn, Bill *state legislator*

Lenoir City
Matlock, Jimmy C. *state legislator*

Maryville
Overbey, Doug *state legislator*

Memphis
Cooper, Barbara Lee Ward *state legislator*
DeBerry, John J. *state legislator*
Ford, Ophelia *state legislator*
Kelsey, Brian *state legislator*
Kernell, Michael Lynn *state legislator*
Marrero, Beverly *state legislator*
Miller, Larry J. *state legislator*

Monterey
Burks, Charlotte *state legislator*

Morristown
Southerland, Steve *state legislator*

Murfreesboro
Hood, John D. *state legislator*
Ketron, Bill *state legislator*

Nashville
Barnes, Tim *state legislator*
Beavers, Alma Mae (Mae Beavers) *state legislator*
Brooks, Kevin D. *state legislator*
Brown, Tommie Florence F. *state legislator, social work educator*
Camper, Karen D. *state legislator*
Carr, Joe *state legislator*
Dennis, Vance W. *state legislator*
Evans, Joshua G. *state legislator*
Favors, Joanne *state legislator*
Fitzhugh, Calvin Craig *state legislator, lawyer*
Gilmore, Brenda *state legislator*
Halford, Curtis *state legislator*
Hardaway, G. A. *state legislator*
Harper, Thelma Marie *state legislator*
Harwell, Beth Halteman *state legislator*
Haynes, Ryan A. *state legislator*
Henry, Shirley Ann *legislative audit manager*
Hensley, Joseph (Joey Hensley) *state legislator*
Johnson, Phillip (Max Phillip Johnson) *state legislator*
Jones, Sherry Stoner *state legislator*
Kilby, Tommy *state legislator*
Kyle, James F. *state legislator*
Lundberg, Jon Clark *state legislator, public relations executive, former newscaster, reporter*
Marsh, Pat *state legislator*
Matheny, Judd *state legislator*
McCormick, Gerald *state legislator*
McNally, James Randy III *state legislator*
Naifeh, James (Jimmy) O. *state legislator*
Odom, Gary *state legislator*
Pruitt, Mary *state legislator*
Ramsey, Bob (Robert L. Ramsey) *state legislator*
Rich, Barrett *state legislator*
Richardson, Jeanne D. *state legislator*
Shipley, Tony *state legislator*
Sontany, Janis Baird *state legislator*
Stewart, Eric *state legislator*
Stewart, Mike *state legislator*
Tate, Reginald *state legislator*
Tindell, Harry J. *state legislator*
Towns, Joe *state legislator*
Weaver, Terri Lynn *state legislator*
White, Mark *state legislator*
Windle, John Mark *state legislator*
Yager, Ken *state legislator*

New Johnsonville
Tidwell, John Charles *state legislator*

Old Hickory
Turner, Michael L. *state legislator*

Pickwick Dam
Rinks, Randy (Bear) S. *state legislator*

Portland
McDonald, Michael Ray (Mike) *state legislator*

Prospect
Bass, Eddie *state legislator*

Rogersville
Harrison, Michael *state legislator*

Rutledge
Roach, Dennis E. *state legislator*

Sevierville
Montgomery, Richard (Johnny) *state legislator*

Shelbyville
Cobb, Curt *former state legislator*
Tracy, Jim *state legislator*

Smartt
Cooper, Jerry W. *state legislator*

Somerville
Gresham, Dolores R. *state legislator*

Sparta
Curtiss, Charles *state legislator*

Spring City
Cobb, Jim *state legislator*

Strawberry Plains
Niceley, Frank S. *state legislator*

Union City
Pinion, Phillip E. *state legislator*

Wildersville
McDaniel, Steve K. *state legislator*

TEXAS

Abilene
King, Susan *state legislator*

Amarillo
Seliger, Kel *state legislator*
Smithee, John True *state legislator, lawyer*

Angleton
Bonnen, Dennis H. *state legislator*

Arlington
Harris, Christopher J. *state legislator, lawyer*
Patrick, Diane *state legislator*

Austin
Alonzo, Roberto R. *state legislator*
Armbrister, Kenneth L. *state legislator*
Aycock, Jimmie Don *state legislator*
Birdwell, Brian *state legislator*
Branch, Daniel Hugh *state legislator, lawyer*
Brimer, Kenneth Kimberlin, Jr. *state legislator*
Chisum, Warren D. *state legislator*
Cook, Byron *state legislator*
Dukes, Dawnna *state legislator*
Estes, Craig *state legislator*
Fletcher, Allen *state legislator*
Hochberg, Scott *state legislator*
Hopson, Chuck *state legislator*
Howard, Donna *state legislator*
Isaac, Jason *state legislator*
Jackson, Mike *state legislator*
Kleinschmidt, Tim *state legislator*
Kuempel, John *state legislator*
Laubenberg, Jodie *state legislator*
Lucio, Eddie III *state legislator*
Marquez, Marisa *state legislator*
Miles, Borris L. *state legislator*
Miller, Doug *state legislator*
Mowery, Anna Renshaw *state legislator*
Naishtat, Elliott *state legislator*
Noriega, Rick (Richard Joel Noriega) *state legislator*
Paxton, Ken *state legislator*
Raney, John *state legislator*
Rodriguez, Eddie *state legislator*
Smith, Wayne *state legislator*
Strama, Mark *state legislator*
Truitt, Vicki *state legislator*
Van Arsdale, Corbin *state legislator*
Van de Putte, Leticia *state legislator*
Watson, Kirk *state legislator*
Wong, Martha J. *state legislator*
Zedler, William *state legislator*

Beaumont
Williams, Thomas (Tommy) *state legislator*

Bedford
Smith, Todd *state legislator*

Belton
Fraser, Troy L. *state legislator*

Brenham
Kolkhorst, Lois W. *state legislator*

Brownsville
Lucio, Eduardo, Jr. *state legislator*
Oliveira, Rene Orlando *state legislator*

Bryan
Brown, Fred *former state legislator*
Ogden, Steve *state legislator*

Burleson
Orr, Rob *state legislator*

Canton
Flynn, Dan *state legislator*

Carrollton
Jackson, Jimmy Lee *state legislator*
Solomons, Burt R. *state legislator*

Conroe
Creighton, Charles Brandon (Brandon Creighton) *state legislator*
Nichols, Robert *state legislator*

Corpus Christi
Hunter, Todd Ames *state legislator*

Dallas
Allen, Jerry R. *councilman*
Alonzo, Monica R. *councilwoman*
Anchia, Rafael *state legislator*
Atkins, Tennell *councilman*
Caraway, Dwaine R. *councilman*
Carona, John *state legislator*
Davis, Carolyn R. *councilwoman*
Davis, Yvonne *state legislator*
Goolsby, Tony *state legislator*
Greyson, Sandy *councilwoman*
Griggs, Scott *councilman, lawyer*
Hill, Vonciel Jones *councilwoman*
Hunt, Angela *councilwoman*
Jasso, Delia D. *councilwoman*
Johnson, Eric *state legislator*
Kadane, Sheffield A. *councilman, investment company executive, real estate agent*
Koop, Linda *councilwoman*
Mallory Caraway, Barbara *state legislator*
Margolin, Ann *councilwoman, insurance company executive*
Medrano, Pauline *councilwoman, language educator*
Pietsch, Vonnie *state legislator*
West, Royce *state legislator*

Dayton
Otto, John C. *state legislator*

Desoto
Giddings, Helen *state legislator*

Eagle Pass
King, Tracy O. *state legislator*

Eastland
Keffer, James L. (Jim Keffer) *state legislator*
Miller, Sid *state legislator*

Edinburg
Peña, Aaron, Jr. *state legislator*

El Paso
Margo, Donald Rupert, II, *state legislator, insurance company executive*
Pickett, Joe C. *state legislator*
Quintanilla, Chente *state legislator*

Flower Mound
Parker, Tan *state legislator*

Fort Worth
Burnam, Lon *state legislator*
Davis, Wendy Jean Russell *state legislator, lawyer*
Hancock, Kelly *state legislator*
Shelton, Mark M. *state legislator*

Grapevine
Nelson, Jane Gray *state legislator*

Houston
Adams, Wanda *former city councilwoman*
Allen, Alma A. *state legislator*
Alvarado, Carol *state legislator*
Bohac, Dwayne A. *state legislator*
Bradford, C.O. (Brad Bradford) *councilman, former protective services official*
Brown, Helena *councilwoman*
Burks, Andrew Charlie, Jr. *councilman, communications consultant, minister*
Callegari, William (Bill) *state legislator*
Christie, Jack *councilman, chiropractor*
Cohen, Ellen *councilwoman, former state legislator*
Coleman, Garnet F. *state legislator*
Costello, Stephen C. *councilman, engineering company executive*
Davis, Jerry *councilman*
Davis, John *state legislator*
Dutton, Harold V., Jr. *state legislator*
Elkins, Gary *state legislator*
Ellis, Rodney G. *state legislator*
Farrar, Jessica *state legislator*
Gonzalez, Edward *councilman*
Green, Larry *councilman*
Hernandez Luna, Ana E. *state legislator*
Hoang, Al *councilman, lawyer*
Laste, Michael H. *councilman, lawyer*
Murphy, Jim *state legislator*
Noriega, Melissa *councilwoman, educator*
Ortiz, Alvaro *legislative staff member*
Patrick, Dan *state legislator*
Pennington, Oliver *councilman, lawyer*
Riddle, Debbie *state legislator*
Rodriguez, James G. *councilman*
Sullivan, Mike *councilman, small business owner*
Thompson, Senfronia *state legislator*
Turner, Sylvester *state legislator*
Vo, Hurbert *state legislator*
Walle, Armando Lucio *state legislator*
Whitmire, John *state legislator*
Woolley, Beverly *state legislator*

Irving
Harper-Brown, Linda *state legislator*

Katy
Hegar, Glenn *state legislator*

Kerrville
Hilderbran, Harvey *state legislator*

Lake Dallas
Crownover, Myra *state legislator*

Lake Jackson
Huffman, Joan *state legislator*

Laredo
Zaffirini, Judith *state legislator*

League City
Taylor, Larry *state legislator*

Lubbock
Duncan, Robert Lloyd *state legislator, lawyer*

Mauriceville
Hamilton, Mike (Tuffy) *state legislator*

Mcallen
Gonzales, Veronica *state legislator*
Hinojosa, Juan J. *state legislator*

Mesquite
Deuell, Robert (Bob) F. *state legislator*

Midland
Craddick, Thomas Russell *state legislator*

Mineola
Hughes, Bryan *state legislator*

Nacogdoches
Christian, Wayne *state legislator*

Nederland
Ritter, Allan B. *state legislator*

Odessa
Lewis, Tryon D. *state legislator*

Pasadena
Legler, Ken *state legislator*

Plano
Madden, Jerry Agnew *state legislator*
McCall, Brian *former state legislator*
Shapiro, Florence *state legislator*

Port Arthur
Deshotel, Joe D. *state legislator*

Rio Grande City
Guillen, Ryan *state legislator*

River Oaks
Geren, Charlie *state legislator*

San Angelo
Darby, Drew *state legislator*

San Antonio
Bernal, Diego M. *councilman*
Chan, Elisa *councilwoman, engineering company executive*
Farias, Joe *state legislator*
Gutierrez, Roland *state legislator*
Haass, Christopher (Chip) *city councilman*
Larson, Lyle Thomas *state legislator, commissioner*
Lopez, Raynaldo T. *councilman*
Martinez-Fischer, Trey *state legislator*
McClendon, Ruth Jones *state legislator*
Medina, Cris *councilman*
Medina, David L. *councilman*
Menendez, Jose *state legislator*
Ozuna, Leticia *councilwoman*
Rowe, Louis E. *former councilman*
Saldaña, Rey *councilman*
Soules, Carlton *councilman*
Straus, Joe III *state legislator*
Taylor, Ivy R. *councilwoman*
Uresti, Carlos I. *state legislator*
Villarreal, Michael (Mike Villarreal) *state legislator*
Wentworth, Earl Jeffrey *state legislator, lawyer*
Williams, Reed (W. Reed Williams) *councilman, retired oil industry executive*

Sherman
Phillips, Larry *state legislator*

Simonton
Zerwas, John *state legislator*

Spring
Harless, Patricia Fincher *state legislator*

Sugar Land
Howard, Charlie F. *state legislator*

Temple
Sheffield, Ralph *state legislator*

Texas City
Eiland, Craig *state legislator*

The Woodlands
Eissler, Rob *state legislator*

Tyler
Berman, Leo *state legislator*
Eltife, Kevin *state legislator*

Vernon
Hardcastle, Rick L. *state legislator*

Victoria
Morrison, Geanie W. *state legislator*

Waco
Anderson, Charles (Doc) *state legislator*

Waxahachie
Pitts, Jim *state legislator*

Weatherford
King, Phil S. *state legislator*

Weslaco
Martinez, Armando *state legislator*

VIRGINIA

Abingdon
Johnson, Joseph Pickett *state legislator*

Accomac
Lewis, Lynwood W. *state legislator*

Alexandria
Barker, George L. *state legislator*
Comstock, Barbara J. *state legislator, lawyer*
Englin, David L. *state legislator*
Herring, Charniele L. *state legislator, political organization administrator*
Sickles, Mark D. *state legislator*

Amherst
Cline, Benjamin L. *state legislator*

Annandale
Watts, Vivian E. *state legislator*

Arlington
Blankenbeker, Lynne Ferrari *state legislator*
Brink, Robert Hendricks *state legislator*

Bedford
Putney, Lacey Edward *state legislator*

Burke
Marsden, David W. *state legislator*

Centreville
Hugo, Timothy D. *state legislator*

Charlottesville
Deeds, Creigh (Robert Creigh Deeds) *state legislator*
Toscano, David J. *state legislator*

Chesapeake
Cosgrove, John A. *state legislator*
Spruill, Lionell *state legislator*

Chesterfield
Martin, Stephen Holiday *state legislator*

Clarksville
Ruff, Frank Miller *state legislator*

Clifton
O'Brien, James K. (Jay O'Brien) *state legislator*

Colonial Heights
Cox, Marvin Kirkland *state legislator*

Culpeper
Scott, Edward T. *state legislator*

Danville
Marshall, Daniel W. III *state legislator*
Merricks, Donald W. *state legislator*

Fairfax
Miller, Emilie F. *former state senator, consultant*
Petersen, Chap *state legislator*
Scott, James M. *state legislator*

Fairfax Station
Bulova, David L. *state legislator*

Forest
Newman, Stephen D. (Steve Newman) *state legislator*

Fredericksburg
Howell, William James *state legislator*

Gate City
Kilgore, Terry Gene *state legislator*

Glade Hill
Poindexter, Charles D. *state legislator*

Glen Allen
Stosch, Walter Allen *state legislator*

Hampton
Locke, Mamie E. *state legislator*
Ward, Jeion A. *state legislator*

Harrisonburg
Obenshain, Mark Dudley *state legislator*

Highland Springs
Morrissey, Joseph Dee *state legislator*

Hopewell
Ingram, Riley Edward *state legislator*

Jarratt
Tyler, Roslyn C. *state legislator*

Leesburg
May, Joe T. *state legislator*
Minchew, John Randall *state legislator, lawyer*

Lynchburg
Byron, Kathy J. *state legislator*

Manassas
Marshall, Robert G. *state legislator*
Miller, Jackson H. *state legislator*

Mechanicsville
Peace, Christopher Kilian *state legislator*

Midlothian
Watkins, John Chewning *state legislator*

Montross
Stuart, Richard H. *state legislator*

Mount Solon
Hanger, Emmett Wilson *state legislator*

Mount Vernon
Puller, Linda T. *state legislator*

Newport News
Miller, John C. *state legislator*

Occoquan
McQuigg, Michèle B. *state legislator*

Petersburg
Dance, Rosalyn *state legislator*

Poquoson
Helsel, Gordon C., Jr. *state legislator*

Portsmouth
Joannou, Johnny Savas *state legislator*
Lucas, L. Louise *state legislator*

Reston
Howell, Janet Denison *state legislator*
Plum, Kenneth Ray *state legislator*

Richmond
Alexander, Kenneth C. *state legislator*
Anderson, Richard L. *state legislator, retired military officer*
BaCote, Mamye E. *state legislator*
Bell, Richard P. (Dickie Bell) *state legislator*
Bell, Robert B. *state legislator*
Black, Richard Hayden *state legislator*
Blevins, Harry Burns *state legislator*
Carrico, Charles W., Sr., (Bill Carrico) *state legislator*
Cole, Mark L. *state legislator, systems analyst*
Colgan, Charles Joseph *state legislator*
Cox, John A. *state legislator, transportation executive*
Devolites-Davis, Jeannemarie Aragona *state legislator*
Dudenhefer, L. Mark *state legislator*
Ebbin, Adam P. *state legislator*
Edmunds, James E., II, *state legislator, farmer*
Fariss, C. Matthew *state legislator*
Farrell, Peter F. *state legislator*
Favola, Barbara A. *state legislator*
Garrett, T. Scott (Scott Garrett) *state legislator, surgeon*
Garrett, Thomas A. *state legislator*
Greason, Thomas A. *state legislator*
Head, Christopher T. *state legislator*
Hodges, M. Keith *state legislator*
James, Matthew *state legislator*
Jones, Steven Christopher *state legislator*
Keam, Mark Lee *state legislator, lawyer*
Kory, Kaye *state legislator*
LeMunyon, James M. *state legislator*
Lopez, Alfonso H. *state legislator*
Loupassi, G. Manoli *state legislator*
Marsh, Henry L. III *state legislator*
Massie, James P. III *state legislator*
McClellan, Jennifer L. *state legislator*
McDougle, Ryan T. *state legislator*
McEachin, Aston Donald *state legislator*
McQuinn, Delores L. *state legislator*
McWaters, Jeffrey L. *state legislator, retired healthcare executive*
Morefield, James W., Jr., (Will Morefield) *state legislator*
Morris, Richard L. *state legislator*
O'Bannon, John M. III *state legislator*
O'Quinn, Israel D. *state legislator*
Pogge, Brenda L. *state legislator*
Ramadan, David I. *state legislator*
Ransone, Margaret B. *state legislator*
Reeves, Bryce E. *state legislator*
Rush, Larry N. *state legislator*
Rust, Thomas Davis *state legislator*
Saslaw, Richard Lawrence *state legislator*
Schaar, Susan Clarke *legislative staff member*
Smith, Ralph K. *state legislator*
Stanley, William Martin, Jr. *state legislator, lawyer*
Stolle, Christopher P. *state legislator, physician*
Surovell, Scott A. *state legislator, lawyer*
Torian, Luke E. *state legislator, minister*
Villanueva, Ron A. *state legislator*
Wagner, Frank W. *state legislator*
Ware, Onzlee *state legislator*
Ware, Robert Lee *state legislator*
Watson, Michael B. *state legislator*
Webert, Michael J. *state legislator*
Wright, Thomas C., Jr. *state legislator*
Yancey, David E. *state legislator*
Yost, Joseph R. *state legislator*

Roanoke
Edwards, John Saul *state legislator, lawyer*

Springfield
Albo, David Barr *state legislator*

Thornburg
Orrock, Robert Dickson (Bobby Orrock) *state legislator*

Verona
Landes, R. Steven (Steve Landes) *state legislator*

Virginia Beach
Iaquinto, Salvatore R. *state legislator*
Knight, Barry D. *state legislator*
Purkey, Harry Robert *state legislator*
Tata, Robert *state legislator*

Williamsburg
Norment, Thomas K. *state legislator*

Winchester
Sherwood, Beverly J. *state legislator*
Vogel, Jill Holtzman *state legislator*

Woodbridge
Lingamfelter, L. Scott *state legislator*

Woodstock
Gilbert, C. Todd *state legislator*

Wytheville
Crockett-Stark, Anne B. *state legislator*

WEST VIRGINIA

Charleston
Bailey, Billy Wayne *state legislator*
Barth, Elizabeth Anne *former aide*
Boley, Donna Jean *state legislator*
Butcher, Greg *state legislator*
Campbell, Thomas W. *state legislator*
Chafin, H. Truman *state legislator*
Crosier, Gerald L. *state legislator*
Edgell, Larry J. *state legislator*
Facemire, Douglas E. *state legislator*
Fanning, John Patton *state legislator*
Ferro, Michael T. *state legislator*
Fleischauer, Barbara Evans *state legislator*
Frazier, John R. *state legislator*
Givens, Roy E. *state legislator*
Guthrie, Nancy Peoples *state legislator*
Hall, Daniel J. *state legislator*
Helmick, Walter Dolph *state legislator*
Hunt, Mark A. *state legislator*
Hunter, Jon Blair *state legislator*
Jenkins, Evan H. *state legislator*
Kessler, Jeffrey Vincent *state legislator, lawyer*
Klempa, Orphy M. *state legislator*
Kump, Larry D. *state legislator, political scientist, public ethics advocate*
Laird, William R., IV, *state legislator*
Lawrence, Tiffany Elizabeth *state legislator*
Manypenny, Mike, II. *state legislator*
McCabe, Brooks Fleming, Jr. *state legislator*
Overington, John *state legislator*
Phillips, Linda Goode *state legislator*
Plymale, Robert H. *state legislator*
Poling, Daniel *state legislator*
Shaver, Stan E. *state legislator*
Skaff, Doug, Jr. *state legislator*
Smith, Margaret Donaldson *state legislator*
Snyder, Herb *state legislator*
Sprouse, Vic *state legislator*
Stowers, Josh *state legislator*
Talbott, Joseph B. *state legislator*
Unger, John R., II, *state legislator*
Walker, David A. *state legislator*
William, Bob (Robert Lynn Williams) *state legislator*

Clarksburg
Minard, Joseph M. *state legislator*

Fairmont
Prezioso, Roman W., Jr. *state legislator*

Morgantown
Beach, Robert D. *state legislator*

Oak Hill
Love, Shirley Dean *state legislator*

Philippi
Poling, Mary Martha *state legislator, secondary school educator*

Shinnston
Spears, Jae *state legislator*

TERRITORIES OF THE UNITED STATES

PUERTO RICO

San Juan
Ramos Peña, Jorge L. *territorial legislator*
Vega Ramos, Luis R. *territorial legislator*

VIRGIN ISLANDS

St Thomas
Berry, Lorraine Ledee *state senator*

Brown-Waite, Virginia (Ginny Brown-Waite) *former United States Representative from Florida*
Callahan, Vincent Francis, Jr. *state legislator, retired publishing executive*
Cao, Joseph (Anh Quang Cao) *former United States Representative from Louisiana, lawyer*
Coleman, Linda *former state legislator*
Davis, Lula Johnson *retired legislative staff member*
Drake, Thelma Day *former United States Representative from Virginia*
Dupre, Reggie Paul *former state legislator*
Hammerschmidt, John Paul *former United States Representative from Arkansas, lumber company executive*
Kosmas, Suzanne M. *former United States Representative from Florida, former real estate company executive*
Lee, Perry *state legislator*
McClain, Edward B. (E.B. McClain) *former state senator*
Myrick, Sue Wilkins *former United States Representative from North Carolina, former mayor*
Patterson, Elizabeth Johnston *former United States representative, South Carolina*
Radel, Trey (Henry June Radel III) *former United States Representative from Florida*
Redwine, John Newland *state legislator, physician*
Rhyne, Johnathan, Jr. *former state legislator*
Robinson, Armstrong Matthews *former legislative staff member*
Saucier, Gene Duane *state legislator, import/export company executive*
Schexnayder, Charlotte Tillar *state legislator*
Snow, John J. *state legislator*
Walend, Trudi M. *state legislator*
Walsh, Jennifer Fitzgerald *former legislative staff member*
West, Allen Bernard *former United States Representative from Florida, retired military officer*
Wright, Gerald (Ged Wright) *state senator, lawyer, pilot*

HEALTHCARE: DENTISTRY

UNITED STATES

FLORIDA

Aventura
Rosenbluth, Morton *retired periodontist educator*

Boca Raton
Eckelson, Robert Alan *orthodontist*
Lerner, Theodore Raphael *dentist*

Gainesville
Mjor, Ivar Andreas *dental educator*

Longwood
McKean, Thomas Wayne *retired dentist, military officer*

Miami
Higley, Bruce Wadsworth *retired orthodontist*
Ziegler, Jan L. *dentist*

Sarasota
Back, Jenifer C. *dentist*

West Palm Beach
Sadati, Sam S. *dentist*

GEORGIA

Atlanta
Garber, David Alexander *dentist, educator*
Salama, Maurice A. *dentist*

Augusta
Baker, Philip Steven *dentist, educator*
Rogers, Michael Bruce *orthodontist*

Marietta
Hoskyns, William A. *dentist*

KENTUCKY

Lexington
Hartsfield, James Kennedy, Jr. *orthodontist, geneticist*

Louisville
Parkins, Frederick Milton *dental educator, dean*

LOUISIANA

Shreveport
Lloyd, Cecil Rhodes *pediatric dentist*

NORTH CAROLINA

Chapel Hill
Proffit, William Robert *orthodontics educator*
White, Raymond Petrie, Jr. *dentist, educator, dean*

Charlotte
Broome, Patrick J. *dentist*
Chadwick, Gregory D. *endodontist*
Misiek, Dale Joseph *oral and maxillofacial surgeon*

Huntersville
Nash, Ross W. *dentist, educator*

Matthews
Twisdale, Harold Winfred *dentist*

OKLAHOMA

Oklahoma City
Shillingburg, Herbert Thompson, Jr. *dental educator*

SOUTH CAROLINA

Columbia
Witherspoon, Walter Pennington, Jr. *orthodontist*

TENNESSEE

Johnson City
Cameron, Angela R. *dentist*
Cunningham, Jason *dentist*

Nashville
Martin, James Larence *dentist, educator*

TEXAS

Dallas
García, Elba *dentist, former city councilwoman*

Flower Mound
Kolodny, Stanley Charles *oral surgeon, retired military officer*

Houston
Eswaran, Sridhar *periodontist, educator*
Sweet, James Brooks *oral and maxillofacial surgeon*

Spring
Lewis, Guy M. *cosmetic dentist*

VIRGINIA

Richmond
Laskin, Daniel M. *oral and maxillofacial surgeon, educator*

HEALTHCARE: HEALTH SERVICES

UNITED STATES

ALABAMA

Auburn
Kleppinger, Erika L. *pharmacist, educator*

Birmingham
Blechschmidt, Edward Allan *healthcare industry executive*
Correll, Donald L. *healthcare industry executive*
Grinney, Jay *health facility company executive*
Kennon, Rozmond Herron *retired physical therapist*
Price, Andy *health facility company executive, accountant*
Warren, William Michael, Jr. *hospital administrator, lawyer*
Wilder, Linda Masone *rehabilitation nurse, healthcare company executive*

Daphne
Curreri, Peter William *health facility administrator, consultant*

Mobile
Clark, Jack *retired health facility administrator*

Montgomery
Grauer, Phyllis A. *pharmacist*

Tuskegee Institute
Cooley, Fannie Richardson *counselor, educator*

ARKANSAS

Little Rock
Boling, David Alan *health policy center executive, former legislative staff member*
Elders, Joycelyn (Minnie Jocelyn Elders, Minnie Joycelyn Lee) *public health service officer, endocrinologist, former Surgeon General of the United States*
Seto, Lynn *healthcare company executive*
Smith, G. Richard *psychiatry educator*

FLORIDA

Bradenton
Benfer, David William *hospital administrator*
Harris, Judith Ann White *occupational health nurse, educator*

Clearwater
Barry, Joyce Alice *dietician, consultant*

Schabel, Shawn S. *healthcare industry executive*

Deerfield Beach
Solomon, Barry J. *human services administrator, consultant*

Delray Beach
Rothberg-Blackman, June Simmonds *retired nursing educator, psychotherapist*

Deltona
Bondinell, Stephanie *counselor, academic administrator*

Fort Lauderdale
Friesecke, Raymond Francis *health company executive, president*
Sutton, Douglas Hoyt *nursing educator*

Gainesville
Bzoch, Kenneth Rudolph *speech and language educator, department chairman*

Inverness
Mavros, George S. *hospital administrator, director*

Jacksonville
Yamane, Stanley Joel *retired optometrist, consultant*

Lauderhill
Ellsweig, Phyllis Leah *retired psychotherapist*

Miami
Chisholm, Martha Maria *dietitian*
Estores, Irene Mison *physical medicine and rehabilitation physician*
Leon, Benjamin, Jr. *healthcare services company executive*
Schultz, Sandra L. *healthcare educator*

Miami Beach
Bredemeier, Mary Elizabeth *counselor, educator*
Poliakoff, Steven R. *human services administrator, gynecologic oncologist, director*

Naples
Curry, Kelly Edwin *hospital administrator*
Drews, Jürgen *pharmaceutical researcher*
Jones, Bradley E. *healthcare service company executive*
Levine, Alan *health facilities company executive*
Newsome, Gary D. *hospital operations company executive*
Riner, Ronald Nathan *healthcare company executive*
Seavey, Christopher Gordon *psychotherapist, alcohol and drug abuse services professional*

Oakland Park
Alpert, Martin Jeffrey *chiropractic physician*

Ocala
Kelly, Edward John, V, *counselor*

Orange Park
Rice, Ronald James *retired hospital administrator*

Orlando
Fottler, Myron David *health services educator*
Garrett, Roberta Kampschulte *nurse*
Jacinto, George Anthony *social worker, counselor, educator, consultant*

Ormond Beach
Gary, Lawrence Edward *social work educator*

Plantation
Gonshak, Isabelle Lee *nurse, volunteer*

Port Saint Lucie
Logue, Judith Felton *psychoanalyst, educator*

Seminole
Haumschild, Mark James *pharmacist*

Tallahassee
Farmer, Harry Frank, Jr. *public health service officer*
Ford, Ann Suter *retired family practice nurse practitioner*

Tampa
Dalton, William Steven *hospital administrator, oncologist, educator*

Venice
Barritt, Evelyn Ruth Berryman *nurse, educator, dean*

West Palm Beach
Bernhardt, Marcia Brenda *mental health counselor*
Koslow, Stephen Hugh *health science association administrator, pharmacologist, neuroscientist*

Winter Park
Jernigan, Donald *hospital administrator*

GEORGIA

Acworth
Foster, Jayne Lynn Ankrum *community health nurse*

Alpharetta
Creran, Heather *diagnostic laboratory executive*

Atlanta
Andruszkiewicz, Peter *healthcare company executive*
Barker, Michael Daniel *hospital administrator*
Bauer, Ursula E. *public health service officer*
Bell, Beth P. *public health service officer*
Boyle, Coleen A. *public health service officer*
Carroll, Sean *healthcare services company executive*
De Cock, Kevin *public health service officer*
Degutis, Linda Christine *public health service officer, epidemiologist, researcher*

Honaman, J. Craig *health facility administrator*
Ikeda, Robin M. *public health service officer*
Khabbaz, Rima *public health service officer*
Monroe, Judith Ann *public health service officer*
Polhamus, Barbara *behavioral scientist*
Portier, Christopher Jude *public health service officer, research scientist*
Satcher, David *public health service officer, former Surgeon General of the United States*
Seffrin, John Reese *health science association administrator, educator*
Strange, H. Anthony *healthcare company executive*
Thomas, Beverly D. *healthcare company executive*
Wong, Faye Ling *public health service officer*

Augusta
Gillespie, Edward Malcolm *hospital administrator*
Hefner, David Stuart *health facility administrator, academic administrator*
Herz, Nathan (Ben) *occupational therapy professor*

Cordele
Jordan, Randall Warren *optometrist*

Decatur
Ford, Sandra Elizabeth *public health service officer, state agency administrator*
Hinman, Alan Richard *public health physician, epidemiologist*

Norcross
Medows, Rhonda M. *healthcare company executive, former public health service officer*

Statesboro
Bartels, Jean Ellen *nursing educator*

INDIANA

Indianapolis
Davis, Edgar Glenn *healthcare executive, educator*

KENTUCKY

Edgewood
Kalos, Alan V. *health planning administrator*

Lexington
DeLuca, Patrick Phillip *pharmacist, pharmaceutical educator, humanitarian scientist*

Louisville
Abell, Kelley *healthcare company executive*
Battafarano, Frank J. *healthcare company executive*
Bilney, Jody Lynn *health care company executive*
Bird, Christopher M. *heath services company executive*
Bloem, James H. *managed health care executive*
Broussard, Bruce D. *health care company executive*
Hathcock, Bonita Catherine (Bonnie Hathcock) *managed health care company executive*
Kelley, Patrick G. *human services administrator*
Kuntz, Edward Lawrence *healthcare executive*
Mountz, Wade *retired healthcare executive*
Murray, James E. *managed health care company executive*
Musacchio, Marilyn Jean *nurse midwife, administrator, educator*

Murray
Keller, Randal Joseph *toxicology educator*

LOUISIANA

Mandeville
Pittman, Jacquelyn *retired mental health nurse, nursing educator*

New Orleans
Carlson, Robert Marshall *health facility administrator*
Culbertson, Richard Allen *healthcare educator, health facility administrator*
Hollier, Larry Harold *hospital administrator, vascular surgeon*
Kimball, Molly *dietician, nutritionist*

MISSISSIPPI

Centreville
Nelson, Janie Rish *health facility administrator*

Jackson
Currier, Mary Margaret *public health service officer*

NORTH CAROLINA

Burlington
Boyle, James T., Jr. *health services company executive*
Fonseca, Lidia L. *health services company executive*
King, David Paul *health services executive, lawyer*
Powell, James Bobbitt *health facility administrator, pathologist*
Williams, Robert Sanders (Sandy Williams) *health facility administrator*

Chapel Hill
Baker, Edward L., Jr. *public health physician*

Charlotte
Schorr, Alvin Louis *social worker, educator*

Durham
Dzau, Victor Joseph *healthcare executive, cardiologist, director, researcher*
Fulkerson, William *hospital administrator, pulmonologist*
Merson, Michael Howard *public health physician, epidemiologist, educator*

Fayetteville
Jansen, Michael John *health facility administrator*

Greensboro
Allen, Jesse Owen III *organizational behavior specialist*
Barry, Dennis Robert *hospital administrator*
Knesel, Ernest Arthur, Jr. *health facility administrator, chemicals executive*

Hendersonville
Steinmetz, Jon David *health facility administrator, psychologist*

Hickory
Osbahr, Albert J. *hospital administrator*

Raleigh
Gerald, Laura I. *public health service officer*
Hughes, Barbara Ann *dietitian, public health administrator, nutritionist*

Winston Salem
Deskin, William C. *healthcare educator*

OKLAHOMA

Broken Arrow
Muller, Patricia Ann *nursing administrator, educator*

Edmond
Lewis, Gladys Sherman *retired university professor*

Oklahoma City
Forni, Patricia Rose *nursing educator*
Resman-Targoff, Beth Holly *pharmacist, educator*

Tulsa
Carpenter, Nancy J. *health science association administrator*
Cherry, Andrew Lawrence, Jr. *social work educator, researcher*
McCall, Charles Barnard *retired health facility administrator*

SOUTH CAROLINA

Aiken
Madory, James Richard *hospital administrator, retired military officer*

Columbia
Amidon, Roger Lyman *public health service officer, educator*
Moskowitz, Jay *health science association administrator, educator, dean*
Seigler, Ruth Queen *college nursing administrator, educator, consultant*

Greenville
Riordan, Michael C. *hospital administrator*

Hardeeville
Kearney-Nunnery, Rose *nursing administrator, educator, consultant*

Hilton Head Island
Wesselmann, Glenn Allen *retired health facility administrator*

TENNESSEE

Brentwood
Carpenter, William F. III *hospital management company executive, lawyer*
Dill, David M. *hospital administrator*
Evans, Richard H. *hospital administrator*
Gilbert, Paul D. *healthcare service executive*
Hallworth, Richard *health services executive*
Kaestner, H. Todd *hospital and healthcare company executive*
Maupin, John E., Jr. *hospital administrator*
Sherman, Jeffrey Scott *hospital administrator, lawyer*

Centerville
Gonzalez, Raquel Maria *pharmacist*

Cleveland
Preston, Forrest L. *healthcare executive*
Ziegler, Steve *healthcare company executive*

Franklin
Cigarran, Thomas G. *healthcare services company executive, professional sports team executive*
Coyle, Frank A. *healthcare company executive, lawyer*
Fitts, Barry *healthcare company executive*
Galin, Tomi *healthcare company executive*
Huebner, Scott C. *health insurance company executive*
Jacobs, Joey A. *healthcare service company executive*
Majhail, Ruby *healthcare company executive*
Mansukani, Sharad *healthcare service company executive*
McRee, Sandra Kay *healthcare executive*
Miller, Dennis Edward *health medical executive*
Mirt, Michael G. *healthcare company executive*
Olsen, Kirk (George Kirk Olsen) *healthcare company executive*
Portacci, Michael T. *healthcare services company executive*
Rash, Martin S. *healthcare company executive*
Sawyer, Dorothy *healthcare company executive*
Schuler, Lizbeth R. *healthcare services company executive*
Seay, Joseph Gary *healthcare services company executive*
Smith, Wayne Thomas *healthcare company executive*
Stanos, Peter *healthcare company executive*
Tate, Tom *healthcare company executive*
Wade, J. Lankford *healthcare company executive*
Whitmer, W. Carl *hospital administrator*

Harrogate
McGuire, Sandra Lynn *nursing educator*

Hixson
Twitty, H. R. *hospital administrator*

Knoxville
Burkel, Lyschel *healthcare company executive*
Carman, Joseph B. *healthcare services executive company*
Cornette, Robert E. *pediatric nurse practitioner, educator*
Massingale, Lynn *healthcare staffing company executive*
Mc Hargue, Carl Jack *lab administrator, educator*
Roth, Greg *healthcare industry executive*
Rybak, James J. *healthcare industry executive*
Sherlin, Stephen *medical technician*
Trout, Monroe Eugene *health facility administrator*

La Follette
Heitzenrater, James F. *hospital administrator*

Memphis
Bargagliotti, Lillian Antoinette *nursing educator*
Bowles, Grover Cleveland, Jr. *pharmacist, educator*
Evans, William Edward *hospital administrator, pharmacist, researcher*

Murfreesboro
Adams, W. Andrew *healthcare executive*

Nashville
Ausman, Dan F. *healthcare executive*
Beck, Thomas Martin *health facility company executive, former federal agency administrator*
Binkley, William *healthcare industry executive*
Bochaton, Philippe *hospital administrator*
Bolian, George Clement *healthcare executive, psychiatrist*
Bracken, Richard M. *hospital administrator*
Broad, Aaron *healthcare service company executive*
Brukardt, Gary A. *health facility administrator*
Corbeil, Stephen E. *healthcare services company executive*
Dalton, James Edgar, Jr. *health facility administrator*
Dorsa, Paul T. *healthcare executive*
Frist, Thomas Fearn, Jr. *hospital management company executive*
Geringer, Steven I. *healthcare services company executive*
Goldberg, Larry M. *hospital administrator*
Hazen, Samuel N *hospital administrator*
Jacobson, Harry Rudolf *hospital administrator, physician*
Kaiser, Allen Bernard *health facility administrator*
Martin, Charles Neil, Jr. *surgical hospital company executive*
McKeel, Sheryl Wilson *pharmacist*
Montoney, Mark R. *medical officer*
Perkins, Bradley A. *surgical hospital company executive*
Perlin, Jonathan Brian *hospital administrator*
Pitts, Keith B. *surgical hospital company executive*
Roe, Phillip W. *surgical hospital company executive*
Shelton, Amy Elizabeth *health facility administrator*
Sowell, Joseph A. III *hospital administrator, lawyer*
Wallace, Beverly B. *hospital administrator*
Williams, Noel Brown *hospital administrator*

Oak Ridge
Jones, Virginia McClurkin *retired social worker*

Pikeville
Levenson, Maria Nijole *retired medical technologist, biologist, oceanographer*

TEXAS

Arlington
McCuistion, Robert Wiley *hospital administrator, management consultant, lawyer*

Austin
Crossno, Ronald J. *health services company executive, physician*
French, Douglas Dewitt *medical facility administrator*
Gimson, William H., III, (Bill Gimson) *health facility administrator*
Larkam, Beverley McCosham *clinical social worker, marriage and family therapist*
Rubin, Allen *social worker, educator*

Bulverde
Lamoureux, Gloria Kathleen *nurse, consultant, retired military officer*

College Station
Ory, Marcia Gail *public health researcher*

Dallas
Brown, Nancy A. *health science association administrator*
Brown, Stephen F. *health facility administrator*
Fetter, Trevor *healthcare industry executive*
Flocken, Jeffery *healthcare services company executive*
Kangas, Edward A. *healthcare company executive*
Lefton, Robert A. *healthcare service company executive*
Miller, Jo Carolyn Dendy *family and marriage counselor, educator*
Mullins, Kem M. *healthcare company executive*
Muntz, David S. *healthcare company executive*
Newman, Steven L. *healthcare executive*
Schecter, Arnold Joel *public health physician, researcher*
Taulbee, Thomas Lester *psychotherapist, educator*

Deport
Sawyer, Mary Catherine *retired hospital administrator*

El Paso
Mitchell, Paula Rae *nursing educator, dean*

Fort Worth
Adams, Lavonne Marilyn Beck *critical care nurse, educator*
Brockman, Leslie Richard *social worker*

Galveston
Lemon, Stanley M. *hospital administrator*
Rassin, David Keith *nutrition educator, researcher*
Stonestreet, Jana *nursing administrator*

Georgetown
Smitheram, Margaret Etheridge *health facility administrator, director*

Hereford
Fangman, Karen Walker *school nurse practitioner*

Houston
Battin, R. Ray (Rosabell Harriet Ray) *audiologist, neuropsychologist*
Boom, Marc L. *hospital administrator*
DePinho, Ronald A. *health facility administrator, research scientist, medical educator*
Fine, David Jeffrey *hospital administrator, educator*
Montgomery, Denise Karen *nurse*
Moore, Lois Jean *health science facility administrator*
Potluri, Venkateswara Rao *medical facility administrator*
Reed, Kathlyn Louise *occupational therapist, retired educator*
Robbins, Robert Clayton (Bobby Robbins) *hospital administrator, surgeon*
Shaffer, Anita Mohrland *counselor, educator*
Vassilopoulou-Sellin, Rena *researcher*
Wallace, Mark Allen *hospital administrator*

Lubbock
Yoder-Wise, Patricia Snyder *nursing educator*

Pasadena
Kenagy, Cheri Lynn *nurse*

Plano
Gilliland, Mary Margarett *healthcare consultant*
Shelton, James D. (Denny Shelton) *hospital investment company executive*

Richardson
Steinorth-Powel, Christina Enni *psychotherapist, author*

San Angelo
Chatfield, Mary Van Abshoven *independent researcher*

San Antonio
Barrera, Elvira Puig *retired counselor, academic administrator, educational program evaluator*
Gonzalez, Hector Hugo *nursing educator*
Walsh, Nicolas Eugene *rehabilitation services professional, educator*

Sugar Land
Wagner, Donald Bert *health facility administrator*

VIRGINIA

Alexandria
Pastin, Mark Joseph *health science association administrator, educator*
Shern, David L. *mental health services professional, former dean*

Ashburn
Clayton, David A. *lab administrator*

Charlottesville
Howell, Robert Edward *hospital administrator*
Williams, Ishan Canty *researcher, educator*

Crozet
Detmer, Don Eugene *health informatics, management and policy researcher*

Culpeper
Goddard, Frances Byrd *clinical social worker*

Duffield
Orr, Emma Jane *pharmacist, educator*

Lynchburg
Lennon, Jeffrey Lynne *healthcare educator*

Mc Lean
Filerman, Gary Lewis *healthcare educator*

Mechanicsville
Colpo, Charles C. *healthcare industry executive*

Purcellville
Grob, George Frederick *independent program evaluator*

Richmond
Balster, Robert Louis *alcohol/drug abuse educator researcher*
Gandy, Gerald Larmon *rehabilitation counseling educator, psychologist, writer*
Glasser, Wolfgang Gerhard *science researcher, educator*

Springfield
Dake, Marcia Allene *retired nursing educator, dean*
Williams, Cecilia Lee Pursel *optometrist*

Virginia Beach
Ancona, Vincent M. *healthcare company executive*
Behrens, Leann *public health service officer*
Blair, Patrick *healthcare company executive*
Carlson, James G. *healthcare services executive*
Fitzgerald, Timothy P. *public health service officer*
Hopkins, Laura *public health service officer*
Kinzig, Dennis R. *healthcare company executive*
McBride, William J. *healthcare company executive*
McCluskey, Mary T. *health insurance company executive*
McCormick, Aileen *healthcare company executive*
McHugh, William *healthcare company executive*
Muñoz, Calise Ileen *healthcare company executive, lawyer*
Riordan, Kevin *healthcare company executive*
Root, Leon A., Jr. *healthcare company executive*
Shipp, Brian *healthcare company executive*
Wall, Tara J. *healthcare company executive*
Whitley-Taylor, Linda K. *healthcare company executive, human resources specialist*

Williamsburg
Cappetta, Pamela Guyler *counselor*

Woodbridge
Flori, Anna Marie DiBlasi *health facility administrator, nurse, anesthesiologist*

WEST VIRGINIA

Charleston
Swinker, Marian Lea *public health service officer, state official*

Morgantown
Collins, James William *health science association administrator, epidemiologist, mechanical engineer*
Kershner, Ruth *healthcare educator*
Narsavage, Georgia Roberts *nursing educator, researcher*

TERRITORIES OF THE UNITED STATES

PUERTO RICO

San Juan
Clavell-Rodriguez, Luis A. *healthcare company executive*
Feliciano, Lorenzo Gonzalez *public health service officer*

VIRGIN ISLANDS

Charlotte Amalie
Garfield, Winifred L. *nursing administrator*

Christiansted
Christian, Cora L.E *health facility administrator, physician*

St Thomas
Sheen-Aaron, Julia *public health service officer*

ADDRESS UNPUBLISHED

Aehlert, Barbara June *health facility administrator*
Ball, John Robert *healthcare executive*
Bishop, Anne Hughes *retired nursing educator*
Buckley, John Joseph, Jr. *healthcare executive*
Callender, Norma Anne *counselor, public relations executive*
Carper, Barbara Anne *nursing educator*
Cason, Nica Virginia *retired nursing educator*
Chow, Rita Kathleen *nursing consultant*
Coleman, Jean Black *nurse, physician assistant*
Cooper, Eugene Bruce *speech pathology/audiology services professional, educator*
Davis, George A. *pharmacist, researcher*
Dowdell, Michael Francis *retired anesthesia nurse practitioner*
Dyer, Wayne Walter *psychologist, writer, radio and television personality*
Erenstein, Alan *emergency nurse, legal nurse consultant, staff educator*
Fischer, Carl Robert *retired health facility administrator*
Foege, William Herbert *retired public health administrator, educator*
Foldy, Seth Leonard *public health officer, physician, educator, informatician*
Fountain, Linda Kathleen *health science association executive*
Gambino, S(alvatore) Raymond *lab administrator, educator*
Gendzwill, Joyce Annette *retired health officer*
Ginsberg, Leon Herman *social work educator*
Goldmann, James Allen *healthcare consultant, author*
Hanrahan, Lawrence Martin *healthcare consultant*
Harmon, Robert Gerald *physician executive*
Hempfling, Linda Lee *retired nurse*
Hertz, Kenneth Theodore *healthcare executive*
Hickman, Elizabeth Podesta *retired counselor*
Houtz, Duane Talbott *hospital administrator*
Howe, John Prentice III *health foundation president, physician*
Johnson Effinger, Naomi Bowers *nursing and health facility administrator*
Jones, David Allen *retired health benefits company executive*
Kelly, Lucie Stirm Young *retired nursing educator*
Lancaster, Carroll Townes, Jr. *health services executive*
Lee, Jan Louise *nursing educator*
Mastej, J. Michael *retired hospital administrator*
McBride, Sandra Teague *psychiatric nurse*
McCuistion, Peg Orem *retired health facility administrator*
Milunas, J. Robert *health care organization executive*
Mitchell, Madeleine Enid *retired nutritionist*
Nolly, Robert J. *pharmacist, educator, health facility administrator*
Olson, Cheryl Kay *public health consultant, educator*
Peters, Douglas Alan *appeals nurse manager*
Raines, Deborah A. *neonatal/perinatal nurse specialist, educator, nursing researcher, consultant*
Rudacille, Sharon Victoria *retired technologist*
Sawyer-Morse, Mary Kaye *nutritionist, educator*
Schneider, Phillip Harry Leonard (Phil Schneider) *healthcare organization executive*
Shannon, Mary Lou *adult health nursing educator*
Simpson, Jack Benjamin *medical technologist, business executive*
Spinella, Judy Lynn *health care operations consultant*
Swanson, Shirley June *retired emergency room nurse*
Terry, Wayne Gilbert *retired healthcare educator, hospital administrator*
Tower, Alton G., Jr. *pharmacist*
Trybulski, JoAnn *adult nurse practitioner, educator*
Ward, Jacqueline Ann Beas *nurse, healthcare administrator, legal nurse consultant*
Warren, Daniel Churchman *health facility administrator*
Watson, Robert Joe *retired health facility administrator, retired career officer*
Weil, Thomas P. *retired health services consultant*
Wheeler, Cass (M. Cass. Wheeler) *healthcare consultant, former health science association administrator*
Whitman, Burke William *health services executive*
Wish, LeslieBeth Berger *psychotherapist, writer, management consultant*
Wolfberg, Melvin Donald *optometrist, educational association administrator, consultant*
Wu, Li-Tzy *alcohol and drug abuse services professional, researcher*

HEALTHCARE: MEDICINE

UNITED STATES

ALABAMA

Auburn
Parsons, Daniel Lankester *pharmaceutics educator*

Bayou La Batre
Benjamin, Regina Marcia *physician, former federal official*

Birmingham
Andrews, James Rheuben *orthopedic surgeon*
Bebin, E. Martina *neurologist, educator*
Bittner, Vera *cardiologist*
Bloomer, Joseph Robert *physician, educator*
Bonner, James Ryan *allergist, immunologist, educator*
Boyd, Gwendolyn Louise *anesthesiologist, educator*
Briggs, Dick Dowling, Jr. *physician, educator*
Caulfield, James Benjamin *pathologist, educator*
Diethelm, Arnold Gillespie *surgeon*
Finley, Wayne House *medical educator*
Flowers, Robert Swaim *medical educator, surgeon*
Foft, John William *physician, educator*
Freeman, Arthur Merrimon III *psychiatry professor, dean*
Huechtker, Edward Darrell *professor*
Hunt, Thomas R. III *hand surgeon, educator*
Iskandrian, Ami Edward *cardiologist*
Kimberly, Robert Parker *medical educator*
Nanda, Navin Chandar *cardiologist, educator*
Pasche, Boris Claude Roger *hematologist, oncologist, educator*
Pittman, Constance Shen *endocrinologist, educator*
Pittman, James Allen, Jr. *endocrinologist, educator*
Russell, Richard Olney, Jr. *retired cardiologist*
Siegal, Gene Philip *pathology educator*
Steinkampf, Michael P. *physician*
Strickler, Howard Martin *physician, director*
Swaid, Swaid N. *neurosurgeon, educator*
Volanakis, John Emmanuel *immunologist, rheumatologist*
Whitley, Richard James *pediatrician, educator*

Fairhope
Mozley, Paul David *retired obstetrics and gynecology educator*

Huntsville
Huber, Donald Simon *physician*

Mentone
Merrell, Ronald Clifton *surgeon, educator*

Mobile
Guarino, Anthony Michael *pharmacologist, educator, consultant, counselor*
Haynes, Johnson *internist, educator, pulmonologist*
Pitcock, James Kent *otolaryngologist*
Rodning, Charles Bernard *surgeon*

Tuscaloosa
Blum, Alan M. *family practice physician, educator*
Lumpkin, Thomas Riley *retired physician*
Pieroni, Robert Edward *internist, educator, military officer*
Sinclair, Robert Ewald *retired physician*

ARIZONA

Davis Monthan AFB
Files, Douglas Scott *aerospace medicine specialist*

ARKANSAS

Fayetteville
Parker, Lee Bryan *retired physician*

Fort Smith
Snider, James Rhodes *radiologist*

Hot Springs
Kamel, Hosam Kamal *medical educator, researcher, geriatrician*

Jonesboro
Jones, Kenneth Bruce *surgeon*

Little Rock
Anand, Kanwaljeet Singh *pediatrician, researcher*
Bates, Joseph Henry *internist, educator*
Bruce, Thomas Allen *physician, educator*
Campbell, Gilbert Sadler *surgeon, educator*
Carney, John M. *dermatologist*
Hart, Ronald Wilson *radiobiologist, educator, toxicologist, business adviser*
Kemp, Stephen Frank *pediatric endocrinologist, educator, composer*
Krisht, Ali *neurosurgeon, educator*
Lucy, Dennis Durwood, Jr. *neurologist, educator*
Mehta, Jawahar Lal *cardiologist*
Moreno, Niberto L. *cardiologist*
Nair, Ganesh Kumar Venugopalan *endocrinologist, internist*
O'Brien, Mark Stephen *pediatric neurosurgeon*
Wei, Jeanne Y. *geriatrician, educator*
Wroten, David *medical association administrator*
York, John Lyndal *medical educator*

North Little Rock
Sotomora-von Ahn, Ricardo Federico *pediatrician, educator*

Scranton
Uzman, Betty Ben Geren *retired pathologist*

CONNECTICUT

Woodbridge
Sanderson, Mary Louise *medical association administrator*

DISTRICT OF COLUMBIA

Washington
Ascensão, João Luis Afonso *physician, researcher, educator*
Barnet, Robert Joseph *cardiologist, philosopher*
Ferdinand, Keith C. *cardiologist*
Jaffee, Michael Scott *neurologist, military officer*
Levin, Warren Mayer *family practice physician*
Paulson, Jerome Avrom *pediatrician*

FLORIDA

Altamonte Springs
Albert, Matthew Ross *colon and rectal surgeon, educator*

Amelia Island
Schiebler, Gerold Ludwig *pediatrician, educator*

Atlantic Beach
Walker, Richard Harold *pathologist, educator*

Beverly Hills
Alugubelli, Venkat R. *family medicine physician*

Boca Raton
Davis, Barry *critical care specialist*
Fagien, Steven *ophthalmologist, consultant*
Fields, Constance *cardiologist*
Friedman, Stuart Andrew *allergist, immunologist*
Garrod, Kenneth J. *orthopedist, surgeon*
Krebsbach, Michael J. *hand surgeon*
Levine, Richard A. *physician*
Man, Daniel *plastic surgeon*
Pasternack, Stefan Alan *psychiatrist, psychoanalyst*
Pozner, Jason N. *plastic surgeon*
Sperry, Len Thomas *psychiatrist and preventive medicine educator*
Weiner, Howard Marc *physician*

Bonita Springs
Grekos, Zannos G. *cardiologist*
Kopf, George Michael *retired ophthalmologist*

Boynton Beach
Glickman, Franklin Sheldon *dermatologist, educator*
Mellman, Michael J. *endocrinologist*

Bradenton
Blackwood, Robert E. *family practice physician*
Cella, John Paul *allergist, immunologist*
McCollough, Newton Clark III *orthopaedic surgeon*
Vereb, Teresa B. *psychiatrist*

Cape Canaveral
Carrick, Frederick Robert *neurologist, researcher*

Cape Coral
Jacobs, George Braun *neurosurgeon*
Martin, Benjamin Gaufman *ophthalmologist*

Clearwater
Adan, Joseph I. *child and adolescent psychiatrist*
Jurka, Edith Mila *psychiatrist, researcher*

Clermont
Allyn, David L. *dermatologist*

Coconut Grove
Stuzin, James M. *plastic surgeon*

Coral Gables
Penalver, Manuel A. *gynecologic oncologist*
Perez, Josephine *psychiatrist, educator*

Coral Springs
Dorf, Lawrence E. *family practice physician*

Delray Beach
Fishel, Robert S. *cardiac electrophysiologist, educator*
Goldman, Daniel S. *cardiac electrophysiology*
Luskin, Brandon J. *hand surgeon*
Oliveri, Eugene Alfred *gastroenterologist*
Rosenfeld, Steven Ira *ophthalmologist*

Englewood
Sanders, W(illiam) Eugene, Jr. *retired internist*

Fernandina Beach
Barlow, Anne Louise *pediatrician, medical researcher*
Kuehl, Alexander Edward *physician, health facility administrator, educator, writer*

Fort Lauderdale
Aguilera, Shino Bay *dermatologist, educator, medical researcher*
Chizner, Michael A. *cardiologist, educator*
Dragovic, Dusan M. *nephrologist*
Glick, Richard Stephen *internist, rheumatologist*
Rubinson, Howard Alan *physician*
Sichewski, Vernon Roger *physician*
Thomas, David Lamarr *surgeon, educator*
Whitmore, Douglas Michael *physician*

Gainesville
Abbitt, Patricia L. *diagnostic radiologist, educator*
Allegra, Carmen J. *oncologist, educator*
Behnke, Marylou *pediatrician, educator*
Berger, Jerry J. *anesthesiologist, educator*
Berns, Kenneth Ira *physician*
Copeland, Edward Meadors III *surgeon, educator*
Driscoll, Daniel J. *medical geneticist, educator*
Drummond, Willa Hendricks *neonatologist, educator, information technology developer and executive*
Flowers, Franklin P. *dermatologist, educator*
Freund, Gerhard *retired medical educator*
Good, Michael Lowell *anesthesiologist, educator, dean*
Heft, Marc W. *medical educator, researcher*
Kennedy, Laurence *endocrinologist, educator*
Mancuso, Anthony A *diagnostic radiologist*
Modell, Jerome Herbert *anesthesiologist, educator*
Neims, Allen Howard *pediatrician, educator, dean, researcher*
Pfaff, William Wallace *medical educator*
Rhoton, Albert Loren, Jr. *neurosurgeon, educator*
Rosenbloom, Arlan Lee *pediatrician, educator*
Rubin, Melvin Lynne *ophthalmologist, educator*
Shanklin, Douglas Radford *physician*
Silverstein, Janet Hope *pediatrician, educator*
Small, Parker Adams, Jr. *pediatrician, educator*
Southwick, Frederick Seacrest *epidemiologist, internist, medical educator, medical researcher*
Suzuki, Howard Kazuro *retired anatomist, educator*
Tisher, Charles Craig *nephrologist, educator, former dean*
Toskes, Phillip Paul *gastroenterologist, educator, researcher*
Williams, Jonathan L. *pediatric radiologist, educator*
Wingard, John Reid *medical educator*
Wingo, Charles *medical educator*

Gulf Breeze
Baehr, John J. III *diagnostic radiologist*

Hallandale
Arena, Joseph *dermatologist*

Hollywood
Bacchelli, Sandro *family practice physician*
Braffman, Bruce *diagnostic radiologist*
Duffner, Lee R. *ophthalmologist*
Knapp, Richard David *psychiatrist, educator*
Sandberg, Joel S. *ophthalmologist*
Sobel, Stuart A. *dermatologist*

Inverness
Alibrahim, Ayman *allergist, immunologist*

Jacksonville
Altomare, Jeffrey *pediatrician*
Alvarez-Elcoro, Salvador *internist, infectious disease*
Argenio, Sandra L. *family practice physician, educator*
Arn, Pamela Hawks *clinical geneticist, educator*
Bartley, Donald Craig *internist, infectious disease specialist*
Beadling, Brent *family practice physician*
Booras, Charles H. *family practice physician*
Dajani, Lorraine Hollingsworth *endocrinologist*
Divertie, Gavin D. *critical care specialist*
Johnson, Douglas William *radiologist*
Johnson, Margaret M. *critical care specialist*
Karstaedt, Nolan *diagnostic radiologist*
Loper, Robert Michael *otolaryngologist*
Mason, William Gray *pediatric radiologist*
Mooradian, Arshag Dertad *internist, educator*
Nussbaum, Michael Scot *physician, medical educator*
Perdikis, Galen *plastic surgeon*
Perszyk, Anthony Andrew *clinical geneticist*
Schwartz, Jonathan E. *neonatalogist*
Talley, Nicholas Joseph *medical educator, research scientist, physician*
Thorsteinsson, Gudni *physiatrist*
Tucker, N(imrod) H(olt) III *physician*
White, Richard D. *diagnostic radiology, educator*

Jonesville
Tandon, Rajiv *psychiatrist, educator*

Jupiter
Crandall, Chauncey Warren, IV, *cardiologist, director*
Kapnick, S. Jason *oncologist, surgeon*
Pinelli, Donna M. *gynecologic oncologist, director, gynecologist*

Sakmann, Bert *physician, cell physiologist*
Sykes, Robin Alexis *plastic surgeon*
Zelnick, Ronald Stuart *surgeon*

Lakeland
Barden, Glen A. *orthopedic surgeon*
Bradshaw, John *diagnostic radiologist*

Lakewood Ranch
Ristow, George Edward *neurologist, educator*

Largo
Bowers, Ronald E. *critical care specialist*
Brown, Warren Joseph *physician*
Grove, Jeffrey Scott *family practice physician*

Leesburg
Goldberg, Paul Bernard *gastroenterologist, clinical researcher*
Moore, Wistar *cardiovascular surgeon*

Longboat Key
Mendels, Joseph *psychiatrist, educator*

Loxahatchee
Wisnicki, Jeffrey Leonard *plastic surgeon*

Maitland
Blake, Thomas Benjamin III *colon and rectal surgeon*
Stoltzfus, Dan P. *critical care medicine, educator*

Melbourne
Croft, Charles *cardiologist*

Miami
Abreu, Maria T. *gastroenterologist, educator*
Altman, Donald *pediatric radiologist, educator*
Bacallao, Manuel D. *family practice physician*
Baker, Richard *diagnostic radiologist*
Baker, Thomas J., Jr. *plastic surgeon*
Bancalari, Eduardo *pediatrician, educator*
Bandstra, Emmalee S. *physician, pediatrician, researcher, educator*
Bauer, Mislen Stol *clinical geneticist*
Beck, Morris *allergist*
Benenati, Susan Vento *allergist, immunologist*
Benyunes, Abraham Joseph *pediatrician*
Block, Norman Louis *oncologist, educator*
Bradley, Walter G. *neurologist, educator*
Brandt, Fredric S. *dermatologist*
Bregman, Arthur *child and adolescent psychiatrist*
Burke, Redmond Paul *cardiologist, surgeon*
Chiron, Harlan S. *orthopedic surgeon, educator*
Civantos, Francisco J. *otolaryngologist, plastic surgeon, educator*
Clarkson, John G. *ophthalmologist, educator, medical association administrator*
Cohen, Bernard H. *dermatologist, educator*
Colon, Ennio M. *pediatrician*
Cote, Richard James *pathologist, researcher*
Craft, Phillip R. *plastic surgeon*
De Armendi, Fernando J. *cardiologist*
DeChurch, Stephanie J. *pediatrician*
Ditkowsky, William A. *otolaryngologist*
Eftekhari, Nasser *physiatrist*
Epstein, Jeffrey S. *hair restoration, facial plastic surgeon, otolaryngologist, educator*
Espinoza, Luis Alberto *medical educator, researcher*
Feltman, Douglas S. *child and adolescent psychiatrist, educator*
Forteza, Alejandro Mario *neurologist*
Freshwater, Michael Felix *hand surgeon, educator*
Fridman, J. Arturo *colon and rectal surgeon, director*
Furst, Alex Julian *thoracic and cardiovascular surgeon*
Ginsberg, Myron David *neurologist*
Goldschmidt-Clermont, Pascal J. *medical educator, cardiologist, dean*
Grichnik, James Michael *dermatologist*
Hare, Joshua Michael *cardiologist, educator*
Harrison, Lynn Henry, Jr. *cardiovascular surgeon, educator*
Heros, Roberto Cosme C. *neurosurgeon*
Hershberger, Ray E. *cardiologist, educator*
Howell, Ralph Rodney *pediatrician, geneticist, educator*
Interian, Alberto, Jr. *cardiac electrophysiologist, educator*
Jayakar, Parul *clinical geneticist*
Krau, Ary *plastic surgeon*
Kurlansky, Paul Alan *cardiovascular and thoracic surgeon*
Labbie, Andrew Scott *pediatric urologist, surgeon*
Lemberg, Louis *cardiologist, educator*
Lima-Marobona, Janice *dermatologist, cosmetics executive*
Lippman, Marc Estes *oncologist, educator, medical researcher*
Lucci, Joseph A. III *gynecologic oncologist, educator, obstetrician, gynecologist*
Mayoral, Flor A. *dermatologist*
Medieta, Constantino *plastic surgeon*
Mintz, Daniel Harvey *endocrinologist, educator, academic administrator*
Nahmad, Michel Henry *thoracic surgeon*
Nimer, Stephen David *physician, leukemia researcher*
Page, Larry Keith *neurosurgeon, educator*
Persoff, Myron Mayer *plastic surgeon*
Pham, Si Mai *cardiothoracic surgeon*
Porter, Wayne Randolph *dermatologist*
Quartin, Andrew A. *critical care specialist, educator*
Raskin, Jeffrey B. *medical educator*
Razdan, Sanjay *urologist*
Richton, Samuel M. *pediatric endocrinologist*
Ricordi, Camillo *surgeon, researcher*
Schally, Andrew Victor *endocrine oncologist, researcher*
Schein, Roland M. *critical care medicine*
Sequeira, Rafael Francis *cardiologist, educator*
Skyler, Jay S. *medical educator, consultant*
Smith, Stanley Bertram *clinical and anatomic pathologist, allergist, immunologist*
Soloway, Mark Stephen *urologist, urologic oncologist*
Thaller, Seth Ray *plastic surgeon*
Vilasuso, Alejandro J. *critical care medicine*
Vogt-Lowell, Robert W. *pediatric cardiologist*
Wanner, Adam *medical educator*
Wolfson, Aaron Howard *radiation oncologist, educator*
Young, Mark Philip *allergist*

Miami Beach
Agatston, Arthur Stephen *cardiologist, educator*
Chestler, Carl M. *internist*
Florin, Todd J. *cardiac electrophysiologist, educator*
Mandy, Stephen Howard *dermatologist, educator*
Tachmes, Leonard *plastic surgeon*

Milton
Cleveland, Crawford Haralson *allergist, immunologist*
Counselman, Kenneth *family practice physician, educator*
Fountain, Jonathan Edwin *family practice physician, educator*

Naples
Bobruff, Jerome *physician*
Camisa, Charles *dermatologist, educator*
Cera, Susan Marie *colon and rectal surgeon, director*
Deeb, Ziad L. *neuroradiologist*
Eichler, Craig J. *dermatologist*
Flynn, Michael S. *cardiologist, educator*
Gaskins, William Darrell *ophthalmologist*
Gehring, David Austin *cardiologist, physician, health facility administrator*
Greene, David *surgeon, researcher*
Perlmutter, David *neurologist, writer*
Randall, Neil Warren *gastroenterologist*
Schwartz, Stephen Gregory *ophthalmologist*
Temple, Donald *retired allergist, dermatologist*
Vernava, Anthony M. III *colon and rectal surgeon*

North Palm Beach
Stein, Mark Rodger *allergist*

Opa Locka
Bien-Aime, Tony *family practice physician*

Orlando
Anderson, Robert E. *diagnostic radiologist*
Andriole, Joseph G. *diagnostic radiologist*
Baxley, Richard D. *family practice physician*
Berman, Stephen Alan *neurologist*
Curry, R. Charles, Jr. *cardiologist*
DeCampli, William Michael *surgeon, researcher*
Finkler, Neil J. *gynecologic oncologist*
Herrera, Guillermo Antonio *pathologist, educator, researcher*
Judge, Kathleen W. *dermatologist*
McReynolds, John W. *clinical geneticist, educator*
Nathanson, Ian Thomas *pediatric pulmonologist*
Nocero, Michael A. *cardiologist*
Peters, Calvin Ronald *plastic and reconstructive surgeon*
Pollack, Lynda C. *clinical geneticist*
Soto, Armando *plastic surgeon*

Palm Beach
Nisenbaum, Layne D. *dermatologist, educator*
Pottash, A. Carter *psychiatrist, hospital executive*
Simon, Harold *radiologist*

Palm Beach Gardens
Murphy, Mark R. *plastic surgeon*

Palm Coast
Duma, Richard Joseph *epidemiologist, writer, microbiologist, pathologist, physician, researcher, educator*

Pensacola
Benson, Robert Scott *child and adolescent psychiatrist*
Canady, Alexa Irene *pediatric neurosurgeon, educator*
Chicola, Jeffrey P. (Jeff Chicola) *pediatric otolaryngologist*
Ricketson, George Manning III *retired surgeon*
Stanton, Robert Page *orthopedic surgeon*

Placida
Prabhudesai, Mukund M. *physician, educator, health facility and academic administrator, researcher*

Plantation
Morris, James Bruce *internist*

Pompano Beach
Dennis, Jeffrey S. *cardiologist*

Port Saint Lucie
Borchelt, Mark D. *endocrinologist*

Punta Gorda
Chandrahasa, Usha *allergist, immunologist*
Hollinshead, Ariel Cahill *oncologist, educator, researcher*

Safety Harbor
Brecher, David B. *family practice physician*

Saint Augustine
Leake, Deirdre *plastic surgeon*
Marathe, Shriram S. *nephrologist*

Saint Cloud
Kraus, Helen *plastic surgeon*

Saint Petersburg
Baran, Gregg *diagnostic radiology*
Betzer, Susan Elizabeth Beers *physician, geriatrician*
Cavitt, Mark A. *child and adolescent psychiatrist, educator*
Desai, Pratibha Kirit *hematologist*
Diamond, Frank B. *pediatric endocrinologist, educator*
Feaster, Burnes Lynn III *critical care specialist*
MaCris, Jack Achilles *surgeon*
Root, Allen William *pediatrician, educator*
Rosenblum, Martin Jerome *ophthalmologist*

Sanford
Shub, Harvey Allen *surgeon*

Sarasota
Aull, Susan *physician*
Callahan, Elizabeth F. *dermatologist*
Chatard, Peter Ralph Noel, Jr. *retired plastic surgeon*
Fiorca, James V. *gynecologic oncologist, educator*
Golub, Richard W. *colon and rectal surgeon, director, educator*
Hepp, Walter R. *cardiac electrophysiologist*
Jelks, Mary Larson *retired pediatrician*
Pirodsky, Donald Max *psychiatrist, educator*
Runge, Paul Edgar *ophthalmologist, educator*
Sturtevant, Ruthann Patterson *anatomist, educator*

Sebastian
Cordner, Harold *pain management specialist*

South Miami
Ballen, Ann E. *ophthalmologist*
Owens, Michael Howard *otolaryngologist*
Wheeler, Steve Dereal *neurologist*

Stuart
Maldonado, Carlos Manuel *surgeon*
Sabol, Stuart J. *otolaryngologist*

Sun City Center
Crow, Harold Eugene *physician, educator*
Worth, Melvin H. *surgeon, educator*

Sunrise
Adams, Nelson L. III *obstetrician, gynecologist*

Tallahassee
Deeb, Larry Charles *pediatric endocrinologist, epidemiologist*
Maguire, Charlotte Edwards *retired pediatrician*

Tampa
Afield, Walter Edward *psychiatrist, health facility administrator, educator*
Anderson, Stephen C. *diagnostic radiology, educator*
Antonia, Scott J. *medical oncologist, educator*
Arasu, Thiru *pediatric gastroenterologist*
Arrington, John A. *diagnostic radiologist, educator*
Balducci, Lodovico *medical oncologist, educator*
Barness, Lewis Abraham *retired physician*
Baumann, Shelly *diagnostic radiologist, educator*
Betz, Randal R. *orthopedist*
Boyce, H. Worth *gastroenterologist, educator*
Boyd, William Pinckney *gastroenterologist*
Brady, Patrick George *gastroenterologist*
Brannan, Anthony Netterville *colon and rectal surgeon*
Declue, Terry Joe *pediatric endocrinologist*
Edgerton, Norman B., Jr. *gastroenterologist*
Eichberg, Rodolfo David *physiatrist, educator*
Estores, David S. *gastroenterologist*
Farrior, Edward H. *otolaryngologist, educator*
Farrior, Joseph Brown *otolaryngologist, educator*
Gerhard, H. John *orthopaedic surgeon, retired military officer*
Gilbert-Barness, Enid F. *pathologist, educator*
Greene, Thomas L. *hand surgeon*
Judson, Patricia Lynn *obstetrician, gynecologist, oncologist*
Kazem, Ismail *radiation oncologist, educator, health facility administrator*
Lancaster, Johnathan M. *gynecologic oncologist, educator*
Lockey, Richard Funk *allergist, immunologist, educator*
Marcet, Jorge E. *colon and rectal surgeon, educator*
McCaffrey, Judith C. *otolaryngologist, educator*
Miguel, Rafael *anesthesiologist*
Muroff, Lawrence Ross *nuclear medicine physician, educator*
Nagera, Humberto *psychiatrist, psychoanalyst, educator, writer*
Older, Jay Justin *ophthalmic plastic surgeon*
Olson, Robert Eugene *physician, biochemist, educator*
Powers, Pauline Smith *psychiatrist, educator, researcher*
Ried, Stephanie *physiatrist, educator*
Ross, Sharona B. *surgeon*
Sanberg, Paul Ronald *medical educator, research scientist, administrator*
Shenefelt, Philip David *dermatologist*
Silbiger, Martin L. *radiologist, educator, dean*
Sinnott, John Thomas *internist, educator*
Smith, David John, Jr. *plastic surgeon*
Spellacy, William Nelson *obstetrician, gynecologist, educator*
Sporn, Paul Andrew *obstetrician, gynecologist*
Sullebarger, John Thompson *internist, cardiologist, educator*
Vale, Fernando Luis *medical educator*
Volicer, Ladislav *physician, educator*
Watkins, Joan Marie *osteopath, physician*
Weber, Jeffrey S. *medical oncologist, educator*
Winston, Julia L. *geriatric psychiatrist*

Venice
Schwarz, Charles Michael *family practice physician*

Vero Beach
Becker, Ferdinand F. *facial plastic surgeon, otolaryngologist, educator*
Christopher, Robert Paul *retired physical medicine physician*
Schwarz, Berthold Eric *psychiatrist*

Viera
Duffy, John Charles *psychiatrist, educator, consultant*

West Palm Beach
Adams, Lawrence M. *pediatric gastroenterologist*
Beer, Kenneth Robert *dermatologist*
Burke, Robert D. *diagnostic radiologist*
Cucin, Robert Louis *plastic surgeon, lawyer*
Friedman, Lee S. *ophthalmologist*
Green, Howard A. *dermatologist*
Kaye, William A. *endocrinologist, educator*
Levin, Ronald Mitchell *geriatrician*
Most-Levin, Carol Lynn *physician, geriatrician*
Newmark, Emanuel *ophthalmologist*
Pasternac, André *cardiologist, educator*
Schwartz, Michael L. *plastic surgeon*
Sokoloff, Daniel O. *dermatologist*
Viñas, Luis A. *plastic surgeon*
Whitfield, Graham Frank *orthopedic surgeon*

Weston
Astor, Frank *otolaryngologist, educator*
Bonilla, Ernesto *family practice physician*
Ciocon, Jerry O. *geriatrician*
Malave, Andres *pharmacologist, educator*

Winter Haven
Okun, Neil Jeffrey *vitreoretinal surgeon*

Winter Park
Baker, James L., Jr. *plastic surgeon, educator*
Wilson, Cecil Bruce *internist*

GEORGIA

Acworth
Andrews, Catherine A. *family practice physician*
De Rosa, Christopher Thomas *biomedical researcher*

Alpharetta
Steinhaus, John Edward *retired anesthesiologist, educator*

Athens
Bowen, John Metcalf *pharmacologist, toxicologist, educator*

Atlanta
Ambroze, Wayne L., Jr. *colon and rectal surgeon*
Babaliaros, Vasilis C. *cardiologist, educator*
Barnett, Crawford Fannin, Jr. *internist, educator, cardiologist, travel medicine specialist*
Blumberg, Henry Michael *internist, infectious disease, educator*
Brandenburg, David Saul *gastroenterologist, educator*
Brawley, Otis Webb *oncologist, educator*
Brigham, Kenneth Larry *medical educator*
Brown, William Virgil *internal medicine educator*
Buffalo, Elizabeth A. *medical educator, researcher*
Butler, Jay C. *epidemiologist, former public health service officer*
Cardemil, Cristina *epidemiologist, pediatrician*
Clements, Stephen D., Jr. *cardiologist, educator*
Collins, Janet L. *psychiatrist*
Cooper-Ruspoli, Annie Nataf *psychiatrist, director*
Corrigan, Victor E. *cardiologist*
DeLong, Mahlon R. *neurologist, educator*
DeLurgio, David *cardiac electrophysiologist, educator*
Dietz, William Harry *pediatrician*
Din-Dzietham, Rebecca L.P. *cardiologist, educator*
Dingledine, Raymond J., Jr. *pharmacologist, educator*
Dobes, William Lamar, Jr. *dermatologist, educator*
D'Orsi, Carl Joseph *medical educator, radiologist, researcher*
Douglas, John Simonton, Jr. *cardiologist, educator*
Edelhauser, Henry F. *ophthalmologist, physiologist, educator*
Elliott, Lester Franklyn *plastic surgeon*
Elliott, Norman L. *gastroenterologist, educator*
Fenton, Kevin Andrew *epidemiologist, educator*
Flacker, Jonathan M. *geriatrician, educator*
Frias, Jaime Luis *retired pediatrician, clinical geneticist, educator*
Galambos, John Thomas *internist, medical educator*
Ganaway, George Kenneth *psychiatrist, psychoanalyst, educator, researcher*
Gandy, Winston H., Jr. *cardiologist*
Gordon, Frank Jeffrey *medical educator*
Gupta, Sanjay *neurosurgeon, medical correspondent, journalist*
Guyton, Robert A. *cardiothoracic surgeon, medical educator*
Harris, Patrice A. III *physician, public health service officer*
Harrison, David Glenn *medical educator, cardiologist*
Hatcher, Charles Ross, Jr. *surgeon, health facility administrator*
Hester, Thomas Roderick, Jr. *plastic surgeon, educator*
Hidron, Alicia *internist, medical educator*
Hogue, Carol Jane Rowland *epidemiologist, educator*
Hug, Carl Casimir, Jr. *pharmacology and anesthesiology educator, medical ethics educator*
Israili, Zafar Hasan *pharmacologist, educator*
Karp, Herbert Rubin *neurologist, educator, geriatrician*
Kauten, James Richard *cardiothoracic surgeon*
King, Spencer Bidwell III *cardiologist, educator, medical educator*
Klippel, John H. *medical association administrator, physician*
Kupke, Kenneth G. *neonatalogist*
Lubin, Michael Frederick *physician, educator*
Milner, Ross *surgeon, educator*
Morgan, Jean Elizabeth *plastic surgeon*
Morris, Douglas Claude *cardiologist, educator*
Morris, Steven *gastroenterologist, educator*
Murphy, Douglas A. *cardiothoracic surgeon*
Namnoum, James Daniel *plastic surgeon*
Ogbuanu, Ikechukwu Udo *physician*
Parks, John Scott *pediatric endocrinologist*
Pickering, Larry Kenneth *pediatrician, researcher*
Popovic, Tanja *physician, research scientist*
Reed, James Whitfield *internist, educator, endocrinologist*
Royal, Frank S. *physician, board member*
Sands, Jeff Michael *medical educator*
Saslow, Debbie L. *cancer control specialist, director*
Schreiner, Rob *pulmonologist*
Sobol, Steven E. *otolaryngologist*
Spann, Cyril O., Jr. *gynecologic oncologist, educator*

Stillwagon, Gary Bouldin *radiation oncologist*
Sullivan, Louis Wade *medical educator, former United States Secretary of Health & Human Services*
Sullivan, Timothy John *allergist, immunologist, educator*
Thacker, Stephen Brady *medical association administrator, epidemiologist*
Thomas, Cheryll C. *epidemiologist, federal agency administrator*
Tsegaye, Theodros Solomon *biomedical researcher, medical doctor, educator*
Tune, Larry E. *geriatric psychiatrist, educator*
Udoff, Eric Joel *diagnostic radiologist*
Waring, George Oral III *ophthalmologist, surgeon*
Wenger, Nanette Kass *cardiologist, medical researcher, educator*
White, Perry Merrill, Jr. *orthopedic surgeon*
Wickliffe, Charles Walton *cardiologist*
Williams, Ilor R. *immunologist, director*
Wineski, Lawrence E. *medical educator, biomedical researcher*
Yancey, Asa G., Sr. *physician, educator*
Yeargin-Allsopp, Marshalyn *medical epidemiologist, pediatrician*

Auburn
Hutchinson, Leslie Julian *preventive medicine physician*

Augusta
Betts, Eugene Kohler *pediatric anesthesiologist*
Carroll, James Edwin *child neurologist, researcher*
Chandler, Arthur Bleakley *pathologist, educator*
Dodani, Sunita *physician, educator*
Fincher, Ruth Marie Edla *medical educator, dean*
Ghamande, Sharad A. *gynecologic oncologist, educator*
Given, Kenna Sidney *surgeon, educator*
Hooks, Vendie Hudson III *surgeon*
Horuzsko, Anatolij *medical researcher*
Hsu, Stephen De *medical educator*
Lee, Gregory Price *neuropsychology educator*
Luxenberg, Malcolm Neuwahl *ophthalmologist, educator*
Miller, D. Douglas *cardiologist, educator*
Nesbit, Robert Raymond, Jr. *surgeon*
Ownby, Dennis Randall *pediatrician, allergist, educator, researcher*
Rojiani, Amyn M. *pathologist, educator*
Ryan, James Walter *physician, researcher*
Talledo, Oscar Eduardo *medical educator*
Wray, Betty Beasley *allergist, immunologist, pediatrician*

Austell
Halwig, J. Michael *allergist*
Tissue, Mike *medical educator, respiratory therapist*

Buckhead
Codner, Mark Allen *plastic surgeon*
McCord, Clinton D., Jr. *oculoplastic surgeon*
Nahai, Foad *plastic surgeon, educator*

Buford
Byrd, Larry Donald *behavioral pharmacologist*

Columbus
Chan, Philip *retired dermatologist, military officer*
Currie, John L. *gynecologic oncologist*

Cumming
Kakkar, Aman K. *cardiologist*
Singh, Narendra *cardiologist, researcher, medical educator*

Decatur
Rumbaugh, Jeffrey Arlin *neurologist, neuroscientist*

Dublin
Giannini, A. James *psychiatrist, educator, researcher, author*

Jonesboro
Honeycutt, Deborah Ann *physician*

Lagrange
Copeland, Robert Bodine *internist, cardiologist*

Macon
Robinson, Joe Sam *neurosurgeon, educator*
Young, Henry E. *tissue engineering medical educator*

Marietta
Ranu, Harcharan Singh *biomedical scientist, administrator, orthopaedic biomechanics educator*

Martinez
Colborn, Gene Louis *anatomy educator, researcher*

Ocilla
McMahan, Howard Cleveland *physician*

Riverdale
Cohen, Stephen Mark *colon and rectal surgeon, educator*

Roswell
McCloud, Melody T. *obstetrician, gynecologist, surgeon, media consultant, health care strategist*

Savannah
DeVaro, John Michael *ophthalmologist*
Kuhn, Frederick Adair *otolaryngologist, educator*
Namnoum, Anne Brawner *obstetrician, gynecologist*
Skelton, William Douglas *physician*
Wirth, Fremont Philip, Jr. *neurosurgeon, educator*
Zoller, Michael *otolaryngologist, head and neck surgeon, educator*

Stone Mountain
Gotlieb, Jaquelin Smith *pediatrician*

Thomasville
Lichtenfeld, Jay Leonard *internist, oncologist*

Tifton
Dorminey, Henry Clayton, Jr. *allergist*

Valdosta
Beal, John M. *surgeon, medical educator*

ILLINOIS

Alden
Tayloe, David T., Jr. *pediatrician*

KANSAS

Manhattan
Riviere, Jim Edmond *pharmacologist, toxicologist, educator*

KENTUCKY

Bromley
Kelly, John B. *pain management specialist*

Danville
Nickens, Harry Carl *medical association administrator*

Edgewood
Dick, Barry Lee *surgeon*

Grand Rivers
Young, Lucy Cleaver *retired physician*

La Grange
Kelley, Michael *internal medicine and pediatric physician*

Lexington
Beck, Sandra J. *colon and rectal surgeon, educator*
Chance, Kenneth Bernard, Sr. *endodontist educator, humanitarian, philanthropist, academic administrator*
Clawson, David Kay *orthopedic surgeon*
DePriest, Paul D. *gynecologic oncologist, educator*
Hagen, Michael Dale *family physician educator*
Holsinger, James Wilson, Jr. *cardiologist, physician*
Hoven, Ardis Dee *epidemiologist, medical educator*
Kibler, William Benjamin *orthopedist, surgeon*
Moliterno, David J. *cardiologist, educator*
Puffer, James C. *sports medicine physician, educator, medical association administrator*
Randall, David Clark *medical educator, researcher*
Ribes, Julie A. *physician*
Roberts, Kenneth Boyett *pharmacy educator, former dean*
Romond, Edward H. *medical oncologist, educator*
Stack, Steven Joseph *emergency physician*
Weitzel, William David *psychiatrist*
Young, Paul Ray *medical association administrator, physician*
Young, Thomas Lee *medical educator*

Louisville
Amin, Mohammad *urology educator*
Andrews, Billy Franklin *pediatrician, educator*
Aronoff, George Rodger *medicine and pharmacology educator*
Bertolone, Salvatore J. *pediatric medicine educator*
Bousamra, Michael, II, *cardiothoracic surgeon*
Breidenbach, Warren Conrad III *plastic surgeon, hand surgeon*
Callen, Jeffrey Phillip *dermatologist, educator*
Calobrace, M. Bradley *plastic surgeon, educator*
Danzl, Daniel Frank *emergency physician*
Elin, Ronald John *pathologist, educator*
Galandiuk, Susan *colon and rectal surgeon, educator*
Gall, Stanley Adolph *immunologist, researcher*
Gleis, Linda Hood *physician*
Ildstad, Suzanne T. *transplant surgeon, immunologist, educator*
Kaplan, Henry Jerrold *ophthalmologist, educator*
Lederer, Eleanor DeLand *nephrologist, educator*
Mizuguchi, Nana N. *plastic surgeon*
Polk, Hiram Carey, Jr. *surgeon, educator*
Richardson, James David *surgeon*
Syed, Ibrahim Bijli *medical educator, physicist, founder evidence based religion*
Waddell, William Joseph *pharmacologist, toxicologist*
Wright, Jesse Hartzell *psychiatrist, educator*

Prospect
Cassis, Tami Buss *dermatologist, educator*

LOUISIANA

Baton Rouge
Bray, George August *internist, researcher, educator*
Kastin, Abba Jeremiah *endocrinologist, researcher*
Zedlitz, Ann C. *dermatologist*

Covington
Metzner, David Mark *plastic and reconstructive surgeon*

Doyline
Willis, Gladden Williams *retired pathologist, scientific photographer, tree farmer*

Kenner
Anthony, Lowell B. *medical oncologist, educator*

Lafayette
Meza, Luis Alberto *internist, researcher*

Lake Charles
Drez, David Jacob, Jr. *orthopedic surgeon, educator*
Gunderson, Clark Alan *orthopedic surgeon*

Luling
Ramee, Stephen R. *cardiologist*

Mandeville
McNulty, John Petty *internist, consultant*

Marrero
Kushner, Frederick Gary *cardiologist, medical educator*

Metairie
Colon, Gustavo Alberto *plastic surgeon*
Jacobs, Benjamin Franklin *cardiologist*
Khoobehi, Kamran *plastic surgeon*
Palmisano, Donald J. *general and vascular surgeon, medical educator*

Monroe
Cooksey, John Charles *ophthalmologist, former United States Representative from Louisiana*

New Orleans
Abdalian, Sue Ellen (Susan Abdalian) *internist, educator*
Amedee, Ronald G. *otolaryngologist, educator*
Area, Leandro C. *family practice physician*
Balart, Luis Antonio, Jr. *gastroenterologist*
Beck, David Edward *surgeon*
Bennett, James Toliver *pediatric orthopedist*
Berenson, Gerald Sanders *physician*
Cohn, Isidore, Jr. *surgeon, educator*
DellaCroce, Frank J. *plastic surgeon, entrepreneur*
Easson, William McAlpine *psychiatrist, educator*
Fisher, James William *pharmacologist, medical educator*
Frohlich, Edward David *medical educator*
Fuselier, Harold Anthony, Jr. *urologist, director, educator*
Gould, Harry J. III *neurology educator*
Grace, Marcellus *pharmacy educator, retired dean*
Hicks, Terrell Cohlman *surgeon, educator, health facility and academic administrator*
Hyslop, Newton Everett, Jr. *infectious disease specialist*
Jenkins, James Stephen *internist*
Johnson, Calvin M. *otolaryngologist, educator, facial plastic surgeon*
Kaufman, Herbert Edward *ophthalmologist, educator*
Keats, Bronya Joy Beveridge *medical educator, department chairman*
Kolinsky, Michael Allen *emergency physician*
Krause, John R. *pathologist*
Martin, David Hubert *internist, epidemiologist, educator*
Millikan, Larry Edward *dermatologist*
Navar, Luis Gabriel *physiology educator, director, researcher*
Nicholl, Jeffrey Scott *neurologist, educator*
Nichols, Ronald Lee *surgeon, educator*
Ochsner, John Lockwood *thoracic-cardiovascular surgeon*
Pankey, George Atkinson *internist, educator, researcher*
Porter, George Homer III *physician, medical foundation executive*
Reisin, Efrain *nephrologist, researcher, educator*
Riddick, Frank Adams, Jr. *physician, healthcare administrator*
Risher, William Henry *cardiothoracic surgeon, educator*
Sachs, Benjamin Paul *medical educator, dean*
Sacks, Joel Gerald *ophthalmologist, educator*
Threefoot, Sam Abraham *physician, educator*
Timmcke, Alan Edward *colon and rectal surgeon*
Winstead, Daniel Keith *psychiatrist*
Witherspoon, Lynn Ralph *physician, information technology executive*

Opelousas
Lafleur, Kenneth Charles *ophthalmologist*

Pineville
Webb, Watts Rankin *surgeon*

Scott
Bergeron, Wilton Lee *physician*

Shreveport
Adegboyega, Patrick *physician, educator*
Conrad, Steven Allen *critical care and emergency physician, biomedical engineer, educator*
Jaffe, Stephen L. *neurologist, educator, researcher*
Jones, Kenneth B., Jr. *retired surgeon, ER physician*
Misra, Raghunath Prasad *physician, educator*
Shelby, James Stanford *surgeon, researcher*
Wilson, John T. *pediatrics and pharmacology educator*

Slidell
McBurney, Elizabeth Innes *dermatologist, physician, educator*

Sulphur
Toniette, Sallye Jean *physician*

MAINE

Oakland
Rutherford, Robert Barry *vascular surgeon*

MISSISSIPPI

Flowood
Das, Suman Kumar *plastic surgeon, researcher*

Jackson
Bigelow, Carolyn L. *hematologist, educator*
Cowan, Bryan D. *medical educator, department chairman*
Cruse, Julius Major, Jr. *pathologist, educator*
deShazo, Richard Denson *medical educator, academic administrator, public broadcasting health producer, anchor*
Freeland, Alan Edward *orthopedic surgery educator, physician*
Gay, Hannah Berry *pediatric infectious disease physician, educator*
Jordan, James Randall *plastic surgeon, educator*
Marshall, Gailen Daugherty, Jr. *allergist, educator*
Moll, George William *pediatrician, educator*
Thigpen, James Tate *oncologist, educator*
Vance, Ralph Brooks, Sr. *oncologist, educator*
Wysocki, Annette B. *nurse scientist, educator*

Laurel
Lindstrom, Eric Everett *ophthalmologist*

Long Beach
Conrad, Harold Theodore *psychiatrist*

Ocean Springs
Brundage, Gertrude Barnes *pediatrician*

MISSOURI

Saint Louis
Dykewicz, Mark Steven *physician*
Goodenberger, Daniel Marvin *medical educator*

NEW YORK

New York
Allen, Robert Johnson *plastic surgeon, educator*

NORTH CAROLINA

Advance
Guth, Caryl Joy *retired anesthesiologist*

Asheville
Harley, David H. *facial plastic surgeon*
Turcot, Marguerite Hogan *medical researcher*

Banner Elk
Hutcheson, James Sterling *retired physician, allergist*

Buies Creek
Kaprielian, Victoria Susan *medical educator*

Carrboro
Prather, Donna Lynn *psychiatrist*

Chapel Hill
Bailey, Donald B., Jr. *medical and special education educator*
Ballard, David Eugene *anesthesiologist*
Barrett, Stephen *psychiatrist, educator, consultant, swimmer*
Bennett, Peter Brian *medical researcher, educator*
Bernard, Stephen Alan *oncologist*
Calikoglu, Muge Gucsavas *clinical geneticist, educator*
Campion, Edmund Ronan *orthopedist, educator*
Carson, Culley Clyde III *urologist, educator*
Chahin, Nizar *neurologist, educator*
Collier, Albert M. *pediatrician, educator, director*
Drake, Amelia F. *otolaryngologist*
Earp, H. Shelton III *endocrinologist, educator*
Fletcher, Suzanne Wright *epidemiologist, medical educator, editor*
Fordham, Lynn Ansley *pediatric radiologist*
Franceschini, Nora *medical researcher*
Frantz, Elman G. *pediatric cardiologist, surgeon*
Gold, Stuart Harrison *pediatrician*
Goldsmith, Lowell Alan *medical educator*
Goyer, Robert Andrew *pathology educator*
Greenwood, Robert Samuel *pediatric neurologist*
Greganti, Mac Andrew *physician, educator*
Guskiewicz, Kevin M. *sports medicine researcher, educator*
Hadler, Nortin Marvin *rheumatologist, clinical investigator, educator*
Hamrick, Harvey J. *pediatrician*
Hanson, Laura C. *geriatrician, educator*
Henry, G. William *pediatrician*
Henson, O'Dell Williams, Jr. *retired anatomy educator*
Hirsch, Philip Francis *pharmacologist, educator*
Hulka, Jaroslav Fabian *obstetrician, gynecologist*
Hurwitz, Shepard Raphael *orthopaedic surgeon, educator, medical association administrator*
Kaufman, David Gordon *medical educator*
Knowles, Michael Ray *medical educator, researcher*
Lohr, Jacob Andrew *pediatrician, educator*
Margolis, David Michael *medical educator*
Monahan, Paul Edward *pediatrician*
Morrell, Dean Scott *pediatric dermatologist*
Muss, Hyman Bernard *oncologist, educator*
Peacock, Erle Ewart, Jr. *surgeon, lawyer, educator*
Pillsbury, Harold Crockett III *otolaryngologist*
Pisano, Etta D. *radiologist, educator*
Retsch-Bogart, George Z. *pediatric pulmonologist, surgeon*
Sheldon, George Frank *medical educator*
Simmons, Michael Anthony *pediatrician*
Simpson, Ross Joseph, Jr. *cardiologist, educator*
Smith, Sidney Crawle, Jr. *cardiologist, educator*
Spencer, Roger Felix *psychiatrist, educator*
Stockman, James Anthony III *medical association administrator, pediatrician*
Su, Lishan *medical educator*
Taft, Timothy Ned *orthopedist, surgeon, sports medicine physician*
Thomas, Colin Gordon, Jr. *surgeon, medical educator*
Thorp, John Mercer, Jr. *physician*
Tolley, Aubrey Granville *psychiatrist, health facility administrator*
von Allmen, Daniel *pediatric surgeon*
Weiner, Timothy M. *pediatric surgeon*
Winfield, John Buckner *rheumatologist, educator*

Charlotte
Alderman, James F. *pediatrician*
Bock, William C. *cardiac electrophysiologist*

Eaves, Felmont Farrell III *plastic surgeon*
Ferree, Charles Elliot *internist, educator*
Hunstad, Joseph Paul *plastic surgeon, educator*
Jacobs, Gordon Waldemar *surgeon, educator*
Kremers, Mark S. *cardiac electrophysiologist*
Munavalli, Girish S. (Gilly Munavalli) *dermatologist*
Schafermeyer, Robert William *emergency physician, educator, health policy consultant*
Thompson, John Albert, Jr. *dermatologist*

Durham
Addison, Winnifred Allen *gynecologist, educator*
Anderson, William Banks, Jr. *ophthalmology educator*
Anlyan, William George *surgeon, educator, academic administrator*
Baker, Jay A. *diagnostic radiologist*
Bashore, Thomas Michael *cardiologist, educator*
Berchuck, Andrew *gynecologic oncologist, educator*
Blackwell, Kimberly Lynn *oncologist, educator*
Blazer, Dan German, II, *psychiatrist, epidemiologist*
Bollinger, Ralph Randal *surgeon, researcher*
Bordley, William Clayton (Clay) *pediatrician, educator*
Bradford, William Dalton *pathologist, educator*
Bradley, Sterling Gaylen *microbiology and pharmacology researcher*
Bravender, Terrill (Terry) D. *pediatrician*
Brodie, Harlow Keith Hammond *psychiatrist, educator*
Buckley, Rebecca Hatcher *allergist, immunologist, pediatrician, educator*
Burton, Claude S. III *dermatologist, educator*
Califf, Robert McKinnon *cardiologist, educator*
Cohen, Harvey Jay *geriatrician, hematologist, oncologist, educator*
Colvin, O. Michael *medical association administrator, educator*
Cook, Jonathan L. *dermatologist, educator*
Cook-Deegan, Robert Mullan *physician, educator*
Coppridge, Alton James *urological surgeon*
Douglas, Pamela Susan *physician, researcher, educator*
Falletta, John Matthew *pediatrician, educator*
Fitch, Robert D. *orthopedic surgeon*
Foreman, John William *pediatrician, educator*
Frank, Michael M. *physician*
Freedland, Stephen Jay *urologist*
Freedman, Sharon Fridovich *ophthalmologist*
Friedman, Allan Howard *neurosurgeon*
Gainetdinov, Raul Radikovich *pharmacologist, researcher*
Garst, Jennifer *oncologist*
Goldstein, Larry Bruce *neurologist, educator*
Greenfield, Joseph Cholmondeley, Jr. *physician, educator*
Hammond, Charles Bessellieu *obstetrician, gynecologist, educator*
Harrison, J. Kevin *cardiologist, educator*
James, Sherman Athonia *epidemiologist, educator*
Jennings, Robert Burgess *experimental pathologist, medical educator*
Katz, Samuel Lawrence *pediatrician, researcher*
Kishnani, Priya Sunil *medical geneticist*
Krishnan, Krishnaswamy Ranga Rama R. *psychiatry educator*
Lefkowitz, Robert Joseph *biomedical researcher, educator*
Li, Ting-Kai *medical educator, researcher, former federal agency administrator*
Lyles, Kenneth W. *geriatrician, educator*
Marcom, Paul Kelly *oncologist*
Matchar, David B. *physician, researcher*
McKinnon, Stuart J. *ophthalmologist, educator*
Means, Anthony Ross *pharmacology educator*
Michener, James Lloyd *medical educator*
Murphy, Thomas Miles *pediatrician, educator*
Newgard, Christopher B. *medical educator*
O'Connor, Christopher M. *cardiologist*
Ohman, E. Magnus *cardiologist, educator*
Ostbye, Truls *medical and public health researcher, epidemiologist*
Parkerson, George Robert, Jr. *medical educator*
Patz, Edward F. *diagnostic radiologist, educator*
Phillips, Harry R. III *cardiologist*
Pizzo, Salvatore Vincent *pathologist*
Podgorny, George *emergency physician*
Prose, Neil Stuart *pediatric dermatologist*
Robboy, Stanley J. *pathologist, educator*
Rogers, Joseph Gordon *cardiologist, educator*
St. Geme, Joseph W. III *pediatric and infectious diseases physician, educator*
Shelburne, John Daniel *pathologist*
Silver, Donald *surgeon, educator*
Smith, Peter K. *cardiothoracic surgeon*
Stacy, Mark Allen *neurologist*
Tedder, Thomas Fletcher *immunology educator, researcher*
Vaslef, Steven Nicholas *surgeon*
Vredenburgh, James Joseph *medical educator*
Wilkins, Robert Henry *neurosurgeon, editor, educator*
Williams, Redford Brown *medical educator, researcher, medical geneticist, internist*
Zenn, Michael Robert *plastic and reconstructive surgeon*

Fayetteville
Greene, Walter Blair *pediatric orthopedist*

Garner
Ference-Valenta, Mary Jean *osteopath, health facility administrator*

Greensboro
Barber, Byron, II, *plastic surgeon*
Bratton, Teresa Sue *pediatrician*
Houston, Frank Matt *dermatologist*
Roberts, Kenneth Barry *pediatrician*

Greenville
Babb, Joseph Dolby *physician*
Brillant, Patrick T. *colon and rectal surgeon*
Ferguson, Thomas Bruce, Jr. *cardiothoracic surgeon*
Herman, David Christopher *ophthalmologist*
Lee, Kenneth Stuart *neurosurgeon, educator*
Perkin, Ronald Murray *pediatrician, educator*
Pories, Walter Julius *surgeon, educator*

Henderson
Serafin, Donald *plastic surgeon, educator*

Hendersonville
Reinhart, John Belvin *retired child and adolescent psychiatrist, educator*
Roberts, James Allen *retired urologist, educator*

Hickory
Lefler, Wade Hampton, Jr. *ophthalmologist*

High Point
Bardelas, Jose Antonio *allergist*
Draelos, Zoe Diana *dermatologist, consultant*
Kandt, Raymond S. *neurologist*

Morganton
Baden, Thomas James *dermatologist*

New Bern
McKee, Francis John *medical association consultant, lawyer*

Raleigh
Barish, Charles Franklin *internist, gastroenterologist, researcher*
Friedman, Nancy E. *pediatric endocrinologist, educator*
Gordon, Morris Aaron *medical mycologist*
Parsons, William Jonathan *cardiologist*
Speer, Kevin Paul *surgeon*

Research Triangle Park
Waters, Michael Dee *consultant*

Southern Pines
Warren, Donald William *medical and dental educator*

Thomasville
Sprinkle, Robert Lee, Jr. *podiatrist*

Wake Forest
Elliott, Larry Paul *radiologist, educator*

Wilmington
Gonzalez, Jorge Jose *medical educator*

Wilson
Kushner, Michael James *neurologist, consultant, educator*
Ladwig, Harold Allen *neurologist*

Winston Salem
Applegate, William Brown *medical educator, researcher*
Atala, Anthony John *surgeon*
Bechtold, Robert *diagnostic radiologist, educator*
Browne, James Dale *otolaryngologist, educator*
Cui, Zheng *oncologist, educator*
Curl, Walton W. *orthopedic surgeon, educator*
Dean, Richard Henry *surgeon, educator*
Dyer, Raymond B. *diagnostic radiology physician*
Eldridge, J. Charles *endocrinologist, educator, researcher*
Ellis, Thomas L. *neurosurgeon, educator*
Hammon, John William, Jr. *medical educator, thoracic surgeon*
Harle, Thomas Stanley *radiologist*
James, Francis Marshall III *anesthesiologist*
Jorizzo, Joseph L. *dermatology educator*
Kohut, Robert Irwin *otolaryngologist, educator*
Kritchevsky, Stephen Bennett *epidemiologist, educator*
Lentz, Samuel S. *gynecologic oncologist, educator*
May, John S. *pediatric otolaryngologist, educator*
Maynard, Charles Douglas *radiologist*
O'Donovan, Cormac A. *neurologist, educator*
O'Steen, Wendall Keith *anatomist, neurologist, educator*
Powell, Bayard Lowery *oncologist, educator*
Roy, Raymond Clyde *anesthesiologist*
Schwartz, Robert Paul *pediatric endocrinologist*
Sherertz, Elizabeth *dermatologist*
Stein, Barry Edward *medical educator*
Weller, Robert Stephen *anesthesiologist*

OKLAHOMA

Claremore
Whinery, Michael Albert *physician*

Edmond
Lester, Richard Garrison *radiologist, educator*

Jenks
Wootan, Gerald Don *osteopathic physician, educator*

Kingfisher
Buswell, Arthur Wilcox *physician, surgeon*

Muskogee
Kent, Bartis Milton *retired physician*

Norman
Dille, John Robert *retired physician*

Oklahoma City
Andrews, Mitchell Dewayne *internist, dean, educator*
Bharucha, Kersi J. *neurologist, educator*
Bogardus, Carl Robert, Jr. *radiologist, educator*
Bozalis, John Russell *physician*
Bradford, Reagan Howard, Jr. *ophthalmology educator*
Chung, Kyung Won *medical educator, biomedical researcher*
Claflin, James Robert *pediatrician, allergist*
Clark, Keith F. *otolaryngologist*
Collins, William Edward, Jr. *aeromedical administrator, psychologist, researcher*
Comp, Philip Cinnamon *medical researcher*
Couch, James Russell, Jr. *neurology educator*
Culkin, Daniel Joseph *urologist, educator, department chairman*
Filley, Warren Vernon *allergist*
George, James Noel *hematologist, oncologist, educator*
Gilchrist, John Mark *otolaryngologist*
Hampton, James Wilburn *hematologist, oncologist*
Harvey, Mark N. *cardiac electrophysiology*
Lazzara, Ralph *cardiologist*
McCaffree, Mary Anne Wight *pediatrician, neonatal-perinatal specialist, educator*
McKee, Patrick Allen *physician*
Oehlert, William Herbert, Jr. *cardiologist, administrator, educator*
Parke, David Wilkin, II, *ophthalmologist, educator, health facility administrator*
Rettig, Philip J. *pediatrician, adolescent medicine, educator*
Rhoades, Everett Ronald *retired medical educator*
Ruffin, Richard A. *orthopedic surgeon*
Skuta, Gregory Louis *ophthalmologist, educator*
Sughrue, Michael Edward *neurosurgeon*
Thadani, Udho *physician, cardiologist*
Tuggle, David W. *pediatric surgeon*
Voth, Douglas W. *physician, health facility administrator*
Wolraich, Mark Lee *pediatrician, educator*

Stillwater
Confer, Anthony Wayne *veterinary pathologist, educator*
Cooper, Donald Lee *physician*
Ewing, Sidney Alton *veterinary medical educator, parasitologist*

Tulsa
Adelson, David M. *dermatologist, educator*
Alexander, Jeff *dermatologist*
Kalbfleisch, John McDowell *retired cardiologist*
LaButti, Ronald Stephan *orthopedist*
Say, Burhan *retired physician*
Street, Daron G. *gynecologic oncologist*

SOUTH CAROLINA

Cayce
Gaffney, Thomas Edward *physician*

Charleston
Anton, Raymond F., Jr. *psychiatrist, educator*
Baliga, Prabhakar K. *surgeon*
Bell, Norman Howard *retired endocrinologist, educator*
Bowman, C. Michael *physician*
Brady, Kathleen T. *psychiatrist, educator*
Colwell, John Amory *physician*
Crawford, Fred Allen, Jr. *cardiothoracic surgeon, educator*
Creasman, William Thomas *obstetrician-gynecologist, educator*
Daniell, Herman Burch *pharmacologist*
Day, Terrence A. *otolaryngologist, educator*
Deas, Deborah V. *child and adolescent psychiatrist, educator*
Field, Larry *anesthesiologist, educator*
Garr, David Ross *physician, educator*
Geier, C. David, Jr. *orthopaedic surgeon*
Glassman, Armand Barry *physician, educator, scientist, administrator, pathologist*
Hahm, Thomas X. *plastic surgeon*
Hebra, Andre *surgeon*
Hulsey, Thomas C. *epidemiologist, researcher*
Khan, Mushfiquddin *neuropharmacologist, researcher*
Kohler, Matthew F. *gynecologic oncologist, educator*
Kraveka, Jacqueline Maria *pediatrician, oncologist, researcher, scientist*
McConnell, Bright III *orthopaedic surgeon*
McCurdy, Layton *medical educator*
Metcalf, John Stevenson *surgical pathologist, dermatopathologist*
Mohr, Lawrence Charles *physician*
Oates, James Caldwell *rheumatologist, physician, research scientist*
Osguthorpe, John David *medical educator*
Othersen, Henry Biemann, Jr. *surgeon, physician, educator*
Reves, Joseph Gerald (Jerry Reves) *anesthesiology educator, dean*
Sahn, Steven Alan *internist, educator, pulmonologist*
Solomon, Kerry D. *ophthalmologist, surgeon, consultant*
Stuart, Robert Kenneth *internist, hematologist, oncologist, educator*
Underwood, Paul Benjamin *gynecologist, oncologist, educator*
Varma, Abhay K. *neurosurgeon, educator*
Waller, John Louis *anesthesiologist, educator*
Walsh, David Joseph *pediatric neurologist, educator*

Columbia
Adcock, David Filmore *radiologist, educator*
Almond, Carl Herman *surgeon, physician, educator*
Barrett, O'Neill, Jr. *medical educator*
Bell, Richard M. *critical care surgeon, educator*
Bogan, Richard Keith *medical educator, director*
Bryan, Charles Stone *internist, educator*
Donald, Alexander Grant *psychiatrist, educator*
Flanagan, Clyde Harvey, Jr. *psychiatrist, psychoanalyst, educator*
Hebert, James R. *epidemiologist, educator*
Humphries, John O'Neal *cardiologist, educator, dean*
Park, Yong-Moon *preventive medicine physician, educator*
Sheppe, Joseph Andrew *surgeon*
Tripathi, Ramesh Chandra *ophthalmologist, researcher, educator*
Waldron, Robert Leroy, II, *radiologist, educator*
Wright, Harry Hercules *psychiatrist*

Florence
Imbeau, Stephen Alan *allergist*

Greenville
Boineau, Franklin Girard *pediatric nephrologist*
Bonner, Jack Wilbur III *psychiatrist, educator, administrator*

Hilton Head Island
Burns, C(harles) Patrick *hematologist, oncologist*
Engelman, Karl *physician*
Field, James Bernard *internist, educator*
Jarvis, William Robert *epidemiologist, educator*

Isle Of Palms
Horger, Edgar Olin III *retired obstetrics and gynecology educator*

Mount Pleasant
Maize, John Christopher *dermatologist, educator*

Myrtle Beach
Favaro, Mary Kaye Asperheim *pediatrician & family practice, writer*
Schwartz, Steve Wendelin *physician*

Orangeburg
Smoak, Randolph Duncan, Jr. *surgeon*

Sullivans Island
Selby, John Bayne, Sr. *retired radiologist, medical educator*

TENNESSEE

Brentwood
Bates, George William *obstetrician, gynecologist, educator*

Clarksville
Smolenski, Lisabeth Ann *physician*

Germantown
Beaty, James Harold *pediatric orthopaedic surgeon*
Blaiss, Michael S. *allergist, immunologist*

Hendersonville
Burt, Alvin Miller III *anatomist, cell biologist, writer, educator*

Hermitage
Anderson, James Wingo *physician*

Johnson City
Cupp, Horace Ballard *surgeon, educator*
Hamdy, Ronald Charles *geriatrician*
Means, Robert Taylor, Jr. *hematologist, educator, researcher*
Olsen, Martin E. *gynecologist, educator, inventor*
Zou, Yue *medical educator*

Knoxville
Bielak, Kenneth M. *medical educator*
Cohn, Richard A. *gastroenterologist*
Kliefoth, A. Bernhard III *neurosurgeon*
Matteson, Karla J. *medical geneticist, educator, former health science association administrator*

Maryville
Howard, Cecil Byron *retired pediatrician*
Hunt, James Calvin *physician, academic administrator*

Memphis
Allen, David Mark *psychiatrist, educator, director*
Chesney, Russell Wallace *pediatrician, educator*
Cohen, Harris L. *diagnostic radiologist, consultant*
Cox, Clair Edward, II, *urologist, medical educator*
Currey, Thomas Arthur *ophthalmologist*
Doherty, Peter Charles *immunologist*
Eason, James David *surgeon*
Gerald, Barry *retired radiology educator, neuroscientist*
Green, Daniel Michael *pediatric oncologist*
Heimberg, Murray *pharmacologist, biochemist, physician*
Herrod, Henry Grady III *pediatrics professor, allergist, immunologist*
Heston, Jerry D. *child and adolescent psychiatrist, educator*
Hughes, Walter Thompson *pediatrician, educator*
Johnson, Karen C. *physician, epidemiologist, researcher*
Korones, Sheldon Bernarr *retired pediatrician, educator*
Mansbach, Charles *gastroenterologist, researcher*
Morreim, E. Haavi *medical ethics educator*
Ovitt, Kimberly *medical researcher*
Phillips, Owen P. *clinical geneticist, educator*
Shochat, Stephen Jay *pediatrician, surgeon*
Shulkin, Barry *physician*
Thompson, Jerome Walter *otolaryngologist*
Tonkin, Ina Lynn Dyer *physician, cardiovascular radiologist, educator*
Vanatta, Jason Michael *physician, educator*
Van Middlesworth, Lester *physiology, biophysics and medicine educator, internist*
Ward, Jewell C. *clinical geneticist, educator*

Murfreesboro
Coleman, Jack Andrew, Jr. *otolaryngologist*

Nashville
Ahmad, Rashid M. *thoracic surgeon*
Allison, Fred, Jr. *internist, retired medical educator*
Arildsen, Ronald *diagnostic radiologist, educator*
Baldwin, Harold Scott *pediatrician, educator*
Barnett, Joey Victor *pharmacologist, research scientist, educator*
Bernard, Louis Joseph *surgeon, educator*
Brill, Aaron Bertrand *nuclear medicine educator*
Brock, John William III *surgeon, urologist, educator*
Byrne, John G. *surgeon*
Carroll, Frank Edward, Jr. *radiologist, researcher*
Chang, Sam S. *urologist, surgeon, educator*
Chari, Ravi S. *surgeon*
Clair, Walter K. *cardiac electrophysiologist, educator*
Creech, Clarence Buddy *pediatric epidemiologist, educator*
Crispens, Marta Ann *gynecologic oncologist, educator*
Dmochowski, Roger *urologist, educator*

Edwards, Kathryn Margaret physician, researcher, educator
Epps, Anna Cherrie immunologist, educator, dean interim president
Fields, James Perry dermatologist, dermatopathologist, allergist, pharmacologist, pharmacist
Fisher, Jack medical educator, plastic surgeon
Fleischer, Arthur C. medical educator, radiologist
Gingrass, Mary Katherine plastic surgeon
Harris, Raymond Clement nephrologist, educator
Haynes, David S. otolaryngologist, educator
Hays, Stephen Robert pediatrician, anesthesiologist
Hickson, Gerald Bennett pediatrician
Jennings, Henry Smith III cardiologist
Johnson, David Horton oncologist
Johnson, Kevin B. pediatrician, biomedical researcher
Kao, Changqing Chris medical educator, director
Lee, Donald Han surgeon, orthopedist
Lynch, John Brown plastic surgeon, educator
Marney, Samuel Rowe, Jr. retired allergist, immunologist, educator
Maron, David Joel cardiologist, educator
Martin, Peter Robert psychiatrist, pharmacologist
Masys, Daniel Richard medical educator, department chairman
McLeod, Alexander Canaday physician
Oates, John Alexander III medical educator and biomedical scientist
O'Day, Denis Michael ophthalmologist, educator
Pagnani, Michael Joseph orthopaedic surgeon
Partain, Clarence Leon radiologist, nuclear medicine physician, educator, health facility administrator
Pinson, Charles Wright surgeon, educator, academic administrator
Ray, Wayne Allen epidemiologist, educator
Robertson, David physician, pharmacologist, educator
Ross, Joseph Comer pulmonologist, educator, academic administrator
Schaffner, William medical educator
Shack, Robert Bruce (Bruce Shack) plastic surgeon, department chairman
Smith, Bradley E. anesthesiologist
Smith, Joseph A., Jr. urologic surgeon
Sternberg, Paul ophthalmologist, researcher
Stork, Travis Lane emergency physician
Thornton, Spencer P. ophthalmologist, educator
Vermund, Sten Halvor epidemiologist, educator
Walters, Arthur Scott neurologist, educator, clinical research scientist

Oak Ridge
Spray, Paul Ellsworth retired surgeon

Williamsport
Dysinger, Paul William preventive medicine physician, educator

TEXAS

Amarillo
Marupudi, Sambasiva Rao surgeon, educator
Parker, Gerald M. osteopath, researcher
Pratt, Donald George physician

Arlington
Awasthi, Sanjay medical oncologist
Tingley, F. Warren retired internist

Austin
Aldrich, Richard W. biomedical researcher, neurobiology professor
Annis, Joseph P. anesthesiologist, educator
Austin, John Riley surgeon, educator, medical expert consultant
Bartz, Mary E. family practice physician
Brender, Jean Diane epidemiologist, educator, nurse, university administrator
Cain, Harold D. critical care specialist
Cook, Robert D. allergist, immunologist
Crismon, Miles Lynn clinical psychopharmacologist, dean, educator
Edmond, Michael Toole internist
Fleeger, David Clark colon and rectal surgeon
Harden, Roger Arthur allergist, immunologist
Morrison, Robert J. critical care specialist
Neavel, Celia Beth medical association administrator
Painter, Theophilus Shickel, Jr. internist, allergist
Smith, David English pathologist, educator
Sutton, Beverly Jewell psychiatrist
Ward, Donald Patrick obstetrician, gynecologist
Weingarten, Jordan Stewart critical care specialist

Baytown
Williams, Drew Davis surgeon

Beaumont
Sooudi, Matthew M. retired surgeon

Bellaire
Haywood, Theodore Joseph physician, educator

Boerne
Wittmer, James Frederick preventive medicine physician, educator

Brownsville
Fisher-Hoch, Susan P. epidemiologist, educator

College Station
Carlton, Paul Kendall, Jr. physician
Kier, Ann B. pathology educator

Commerce
Lemanski, Larry Fredrick medical educator, academic administrator

Conroe
Conwell, Halford Roger physician
Lewis, Alvin Edward pathology educator

Corpus Christi
Cook, Kenneth Ray radiologist

Sisley, Nina Mae physician, public health service officer

Dallas
Adams, William Peter, Jr. plastic surgeon, educator
Barton, Fritz Engel, Jr. plastic surgeon, educator
Bateman, Cathleen P. dermatologist
Bergstresser, Paul Richard dermatologist, educator
Bidic, Sean Michael plastic surgeon, orthopedist
Bleakney, Dana A. family practice physician
Bonte, Frederick James radiologist, educator, physician
Buchanan, George R. oncologist, hematologist, educator
Byrd, Steve (Henry Stephenson Byrd) plastic surgeon, educator
Caetano, Raul psychiatrist, educator
Cavanagh, Harrison Dwight ophthalmologist, educator
Cox, Rody Powell internist, educator
Davis, Gary L. gastroenterologist, educator
Dees, Tom Moore, II, retired internist
Einspruch, Burton Cyril psychiatrist
Emslie, Graham J. child and adolescent psychiatrist, educator
Ezaki, Marybeth hand surgeon, educator
Flatt, Adrian Ede surgeon
Fordtran, John Satterfield physician
Fyfe, Alistair Ian cardiologist, scientist, educator
Gilman, Alfred Goodman pharmacologist, educator
Gross, Gary Neil allergist, physician
Guleserian, Kristine Jane surgeon, thoracic surgeon, educator
Gunter, Jack Pershing plastic surgeon, otolaryngologist
Hamra, Sameer T. plastic surgeon, educator
Hobar, P. Craig plastic surgeon, educator
Hobbs, Helen Haskell medical geneticist
Kenkel, Jeffrey Miller plastic surgeon, educator
Lewis, Jerry M. psychiatrist, educator
Lichliter, Warren Eugene surgeon, educator
Lister, George pediatrician
Maddrey, Willis Crocker medical educator, internist, academic administrator, consultant, researcher
McClelland, Robert Nelson surgeon, educator
Miklius, Audrey B. endocrinologist, educator
Mitchell, Teddy Lee physician
Moore, Hugh Leslie retired pediatrician
Odom, Floyd Clark surgeon
Porteus, Matthew H. pediatric hematologist, oncologist
Ram, Chitta Venkata physician
Raskin, Philip physician, educator
Ring, W(illiam) Steves thoracic and cardiovascular surgeon
Robertson, Rose Marie cardiologist, educator
Rohrich, Rod(ney) James plastic surgeon, educator
Rosenberg, Roger Newman neurologist, educator, department chair
Sachson, Richard A. endocrinologist, educator
Sagalowsky, Arthur I. urologist, educator
Schiller, Joan Hoff oncologist, educator
Schwarz, Roderich Egbert surgeon, oncologist
Sheeran, Paul W. anesthesiologist, pediatrician, educator
Stone, Marvin Jules hematologist, oncologist, educator
Sucato, Daniel J. orthopaedic surgeon
Tebbetts, John Beryl plastic surgeon
Thiele, Dwain Louis medical educator, department vice chairman
Ulissey, Michael J. diagnostic radiologist, educator
Waddell, Douglas Howard family physician
Wallace, Charles Alan plastic surgeon
Wang, Xiaodong biomedical researcher, educator
Wildenthal, Claud Kern physician, educator
Wilson, Jean Donald endocrinologist, educator
Yancy, Clyde Warren, Jr. cardiologist, educator

El Paso
Greenberg, Harvey gynecologic oncologist
Martinez-Lopez, Jorge Ignacio internist, educator, cardiologist, consultant
Plavsic, Branko Milenko radiologist, educator
Taber, David O. urological surgeon

Fort Worth
Bailey, Susan Rudd allergist, immunologist, pediatrician
Cox, James Sidney physician
Hey, Wayne Albert urologic surgeon, medical association executive
Jurgensen, Warren Peter retired psychiatrist, educator
Lichtman, David Michael orthopedist, health facility administrator, educator, retired military officer
Smith, Jesse E. facial plastic surgeon

Fredericksburg
Scharold, Mary Louise psychoanalyst, psychiatrist, educator

Frisco
Culpepper, Guy Lee physician

Galveston
Anderson, Garland D. obstetrician, gynecologist
Bailey, Byron James otolaryngologist, medical association administrator, educator
Diven, Dayna dermatologist, educator
Gonzalez, Emilio Bustamante rheumatologist, educator
Goodwin, Jean McClung psychiatrist
Hawkins, Hal Kenneth pathologist
Powell, Don Watson gastroenterologist, educator
Prough, Donald Sanderson anesthesiologist
Raimer, Ben G. pediatrician, public health service officer
Sandstead, Harold Hilton physician, researcher, educator, director
Vanderploeg, James M. preventive medicine physician

Holland
Dyck, Walter Peter gastroenterologist, educator, academic administrator

Houston
Alexanian, Raymond hematologist
Alford, Bobby Ray otolaryngologist, academic administrator, educator
Angelaki, Dora E. medical educator
Appel, Stanley Hersh neurologist, educator
Ashe, Herbert J. otolaryngologist, educator
Ayus, Juan Carlos nephrologist
Bailey, Harold Randolph surgeon, educator
Baldwin, Bonnie physician
Barrett, Bernard Morris, Jr. plastic and reconstructive surgeon
Bast, Robert Clinton, Jr. medical researcher, educator, physician
Beadle, Beth Michelle oncologist
Beaudet, Arthur L. medical genetics researcher
Beaver, Hilary A. medical educator, ophthalmologist
Berg, Stacey Lynn pediatric oncologist
Bodey, Gerald Paul retired medical educator
Brandt, Mary L. medical educator
Bresalier, Robert Scott gastroenterologist, educator
Brewer, Eileen D. (L. Eileen Doyle Brewer) nephrologist, educator
Buja, L. Maximilian pathologist, academic administrator, educator
Bungo, Michael William cardiologist, educator, administrator
Burton, Allen W. pain medicine specialist, educator
Burzynski, Stanislaw Rajmund internist
Buster, John Edmond obstetrician, researcher
Catlin, Francis Irving physician
Champlin, Richard Eugene (Dick Champlin) hematologist, oncologist, medical educator
Chiou-Tan, Faye physician, educator
Coleman, Robert L. obstetrician, gynecologic oncologist
Corriere, Joseph N., Jr. urologist, educator
Cortes, Jorge oncologist
Craigen, William James clinical geneticist, educator
Crow, Mary Kurtz hematologist
Davies, Mark G. vascular surgeon, scientist
Davila, Marta Ligia gastroenterologist, educator
Desjardins, Raoul medical association administrator, financial consultant
Dickey, Burton F. critical care specialist, educator
Dinney, Colin P. surgeon, urologist
Dodd, Gerald Dewey, Jr. radiologist, educator
Donovan, Donald T. otolaryngologist, educator
Doody, Rachelle neurologist, educator, researcher
Drutz, Jan Edwin pediatrics educator
DuBois, Raymond N. medical educator, researcher
Duncan, Newton O. otolaryngologist, educator
DuPont, Herbert Lancashire medical educator, researcher
Dyer, Carmel B. geriatrician
Engelhardt, Hugo Tristram, Jr. physician, educator
Erasmus, Jeremy John diagnostic radiologist, educator
Evans, Harry Launius pathology educator
Feigon, Judith Tova ophthalmologist, surgeon, educator
Ferrendelli, James Anthony neurologist, educator
Fishman, Marvin Allen pediatric neurologist, educator
Fornage, Bruno Denis radiologist, educator
Franklin, Daniel J. (Dan Franklin) otolaryngologist, surgeon
Freedman, Ralph Stuart obstetrician, gynecologist, educator
Freireich, Emil J hematologist, educator
Fromm, Geri-Lynn gynecologic oncologist, educator
Gabbard, Glen Owens psychiatrist, psychotherapist
Gardner, Donald F. endocrinologist
Geng, Yong-Jian medical educator, researcher
Gertzbein, Stanley David orthopedic surgeon
Giardino, Angelo Peter pediatrician, director
Gilbert, Mark R. neuro-oncologist, educator
Glezen, William Paul pediatrician, virologist, educator
Green, Mary T. ophthalmologist
Green, Maurice Richard retired neuropsychiatrist
Grossman, Herbert Barton urologist, researcher
Grossman, Robert George neurosurgeon, department chairman
Gunn, Albert Edward, Jr. internist, health facility administrator, lawyer, educator
Guynn, Robert William psychiatrist, educator
Hall, Robert Joseph internist, educator
Hamilton, Carlos Robert, Jr. endocrinologist, academic administrator, consultant
Hamilton, Steven M. plastic surgeon
Harati, Yadollah neurologist, educator
Haynie, Thomas Powell III physician
Heird, William Carroll pediatrician, educator
Hergenroeder, Albert C. pediatrician, educator
Herlihy, James P. critical care specialist, educator
Hollinger, F. Blaine physician, educator
Hsu, Sylvia dermatologist, educator
Huynh, Phan Tuong diagnostic radiologist, educator
Hwu, Patrick oncologist
Jankovic, Joseph neurologist, educator
Jemison, Mae Carol physician, engineer, entrepreneur, philanthropist, educator, former astronaut
Jneid, Hani interventional cardiologist, researcher
Jones, Dan Brigman ophthalmologist, educator
Jones, Edith Irby internist
Jordon, Robert Earl physician
Kaplan, Alan Leslie gynecology educator, oncologist, department chairman
Katrana, David John retired plastic and reconstructive surgeon
Kent, Thomas Andrew neurologist, educator
Killian, James M. medical educator
Kimyai-Asadi, Arash surgeon
Kone, Bruce C. medical educator, nephrologist, scientist, former dean
Kosten, Thomas Richard psychiatrist, educator
Krajcer, Zvonimir cardiologist, educator
Kunik, Mark Edwin geriatric psychiatrist, educator
Lawrie, Gerald Murray cardiovascular and thoracic surgeon, educator
Leonard, Tommy, Jr. neonatalogist, educator
Letsou, George Vasilios cardiothoracic surgeon
Levin, Victor A. neurologist, oncologist, educator
Lippman, Scott Michael oncologist, educator
Lupski, James R. medical geneticist, educator
Massin, Edward Krauss physician
Masud, Faisal cardiologist
Max, Ernest surgeon
Mayor, Heather Donald molecular biology educator
McCauley, Stephen R medical educator
McKechnie, John Charles gastroenterologist, educator
McPherson, Alice Ruth ophthalmologist, educator
Mendelsohn, John oncologist, hematologist, educator, medical researcher
Mentz, Henry A. III plastic surgeon
Milam, John Daniel pathologist, educator
Miles, Brian John urologist
Miller, Gary Evan psychiatrist, mental health services professional
Miller, Robert Harold medical association administrator, otolaryngologist, educator
Mintz-Hittner, Helen Ann physician, researcher
Mitch, William Evans nephrologist
Moody, Frank G. surgeon
Munk, Zev Moshe physician, researcher
Murphy, William Alexander, Jr. diagnostic radiologist, educator
Musher, Daniel Michael medical educator, researcher, epidemiologist, director
Nagueh, Sherif F. cardiologist, educator
Nichols, Buford Lee, Jr. pediatrician, nutritionist
Northrup, Hope A. clinical geneticist, pediatrician
Oldham, John Michael physician, psychiatrist, educator
Phung, Nguyen Dinh medical educator
Plon, Sharon E. clinical geneticist, educator
Quinones, Miguel A. cardiologist, educator
Raijman, Isaac gastroenterologist, educator
Rapini, Ronald Peter dermatology educator
Rappaport, Norman Harvey plastic surgeon
Ribble, John Charles medical educator
Riley, William John neurologist
Risin, Semyon Aaron pathologist, educator
Robb, Geoffrey Lawrence plastic surgeon
Rosales, Oscar R. cardiologist
Ross, Patti Jayne obstetrics and gynecology educator
Schoolar, Joseph Clayton psychiatrist, pharmacologist, educator
Shabot, Myron Michael hospital system administrator
Shulman, Robert Jay pediatrician, nutritionist, gastroenterologist, educator
Siller, Barry S. gynecologic oncologist, gynecologist, obstetrician
Smythe, Cheves McCord internist, geriatrician, educator, dean
Sood, Anil K. oncologist, researcher
Sostman, Dirk physician, clinical researcher, medical educator
Spiegel, Aldona J. plastic surgeon
Stasney, C. Richard otolaryngologist, director
Sutton, Jeffrey Paul physician, scientist, administrator
Traber, Peter George medical educator, former academic administrator
Tweardy, David John physician, scientist, educator
Vierling, John Moore physician
Waguespack, Steven G. endocrinologist, educator
Walker, William Easton surgeon, educator, lawyer
Weber, Samuel C. (Sam Weber) otolaryngologist, educator
Willerson, James Thornton cardiologist, researcher, medical educator
Yeung, Cecil S.T. plastic surgeon
Yi, Donna psychiatrist, educator
Ying, Anita K. pediatric endocrinologist, educator
Zoghbi, William Antoine cardiologist, educator

Humble
Trowbridge, John Parks physician

Irving
Crim, Randall W. colon and rectal surgeon, educator

Lubbock
Cobos, Everardo hematologist, educator
Kurtzman, Neil A. medical educator
May, Donald Robert Lee ophthalmologist, educator, academic administrator, farmer
Sabatini, Sandra physician

Marshall
Sudhivoraseth, Niphon pediatrician, immunologist, allergist

Nacogdoches
Bommanna, Vasudeva M. allergist, immunologist

Odessa
Becker, Bruce family practice physician

Rockwall
Kotas, Robert Vincent pediatrician, educator
Pascoe, Rana S. physician, family medicine, adolescent medicine

San Antonio
Baker, Floyd Wilmer surgeon, retired military officer
Becker, Quinn Henderson orthopedic surgeon, military officer
Blanchett, Michael G. family practice physician
Bode, William Ernest colon and rectal surgeon
Bucay, Vivian W. dermatologist
Cervantes, Charles R. geriatrician
Ciolli, Kenneth family practice physician
Croft, Harry Allen psychiatrist
Dumitru, Daniel physiatrist
Freeman, Gregory L. cardiologist, educator
Garcia-Holguin, Mary H. child and adolescent psychiatrist
Greene, Mark W. plastic surgeon
Guerra, Fernando A. pediatrician, health facility administrator
Kasinath, Balakuntalam S. medical researcher
Leon, Robert Leonard psychiatrist, educator
McFee, Arthur Storer physician
McGill, Henry Coleman, Jr. pathologist, educator, researcher
Menendez, Jorge plastic surgeon
O'Rourke, Robert A. cardiologist, educator
Otto, Pamela diagnostic radiologist, educator
Palmaz, Julio C. cardiologist, radiologist, educator
Persellin, Robert Harold physician
Pestana, Carlos surgeon, retired dean, educator
Pruitt, Basil Arthur, Jr. surgeon, retired military officer

Roeder, Elizabeth Rose *clinical geneticist, educator*
Rogers, James N. *anesthesiologist, educator*
Schenker, Steven *emeritus professor of medicine*
Thompson, Ian Murchie, Jr. *urologist, oncologist*
Williams, Thomas Eugene *pediatric hematologist and oncologist, pharmaceutical executive*
Wolf, Steven E. *surgeon, educator*
Zilveti, Carlos Benjamin *preventive medicine physician, pediatrician*

Southlake
Bogdan, Michael Andrew *plastic surgeon*

Sugar Land
Schulze, Keith E. *dermatologist, surgeon*

Temple
Buckley, Clifford James *surgeon, educator*
Dehmer, Gregory Joseph *cardiologist*
Hoffer, John Lee *anesthesiologist, medical educator and anesthesia, parioperative systems developer*
Rohack, John James *cardiologist*
Rosa, Robert H., Jr. *ophthalmologist, medical educator, researcher*

The Woodlands
Bethea, Louise Huffman *allergist*

Tyler
Kronenberg, Richard Samuel *physician, administrator*
Wrenn, Christopher Jay *physician*

Waco
Richie, Rodney Charles *critical care and pulmonary medicine physician*

West Lake Hills
Canada, William H. *plastic surgeon*

Willis
Rappaport, Martin Paul *internist, nephrologist, educator*

Yoakum
Watson, David H. *physician*

VIRGINIA

Afton
McCoy, Sue *retired surgeon, biochemist, bioethicist*

Alexandria
Adams, Thomas L. *medical association administrator*
Dorn, Jennifer Lynn *medical association administrator, former federal agency administrator*
Fisher, Donald Wayne *medical association administrator*
Kaplowitz, Lisa Glauser *physician, educator*
Leinweber, William F. *medical association administrator*
Lichter, Allen S. *oncologist, medical association administrator*

Annandale
Shamburek, Roland Howard *physician*

Arlington
Ferraz, Francisco Marconi *neurological surgeon*
Nirschl, Robert Phillip *orthopedic surgeon*
Sanz, Luis E. *gynecologist, educator*

Ashburn
Jaffe, Russell Merritt *pathologist, research director*

Blacksburg
Anthony, Evelyn Y. *diagnostic radiologist, educator*

Charlottesville
Aldrich, Clarence Knight *physician, educator*
Alexander, Eben *neurosurgeon*
Balogun, Rasheed Abiodun *physician and medical educator*
Barrett, Eugene Joseph *physician, educator, researcher*
Baum, Victor Curtis *anesthesiologist*
Beller, George A. *cardiologist, educator*
Bruns, David Eugene *medical educator, researcher*
Carey, Robert Munson *physician, educator*
Carter, Bruce Thomas *ophthalmologist*
Cherry, Kenneth Jerome, Jr. *surgeon*
Chevalier, Robert Louis *nephrologist, educator, medical researcher*
Dalkin, Alan C. *endocrinologist, educator*
DeKosky, Steven Trent *neurologist*
Epstein, Robert Marvin *anesthesiologist, educator*
Flickinger, Charles John *anatomist, educator*
Holroyd, Suzanne *geriatrician, psychiatrist, educator*
Hunt, William B. *pulmonologist*
Kattwinkel, John *pediatrician, educator*
Lin, Kant *plastic surgeon, educator*
Marshall, John Crook *internal medicine educator, researcher*
Matherne, G. Paul *medical educator*
Nolan, Stanton Peelle *surgeon, educator*
Owen, John Atkinson, Jr. *internist, educator*
Pearson, Richard Dale *internist, infectious disease specialist, educator*
Phillips, Clifford Douglas *radiologist, educator*
Platts-Mills, Thomas Alexander Evelyn *immunologist, educator, researcher*
Rehm, Patrice Koch *radiologist, educator*
Rich, Tyvin Andrew *radiation therapist*
Rowlingson, John Clyde *anesthesiologist, physician, educator*
Rust, Robert Stanley *pediatrician, educator*
Saulsbury, Frank T. *pediatric immunologist and rheumatologist*
Smith, Philip William *surgeon, educator*
Sutphen, James L. *pediatrician*
Thorner, Michael Oliver *medical educator*

Fairfax
Albert, Moses K. *dermatologist*
Lindsey, Jennifer H. *pediatrician*
Schulman, Joseph Daniel *physician, health facility administrator, medical geneticist, educator, reproductive biologist*

Falls Church
Bicher, Annette *gynecologic oncologist, director*
Kurtzke, John Francis, Sr. *neurologist, epidemiologist*
Lundeen, William Bruce *radiologist*
Niederhuber, John Edward *medical researcher, surgeon, former federal agency administrator*
Wah, Robert M. *reproductive endocrinologist, obstetrician, gynecologist*

Gainesville
Lee, Won Jay *radiologist*
McCawley, Austin *psychiatrist, educator*

Henrico
Call, Robert Somerville *allergist, immunologist, educator*

Herndon
Naderi, Shervin *plastic surgeon*

King George
Hudson, Steven J. *surgeon*

Lancaster
Kingsbury, Ellen Ann Dagon *anesthesiologist, general practitioner*

Leesburg
Chang, Phillip J. *plastic surgeon*

Manassas
Cooper, James Nelson *medical educator*

Manquin
Osgood, Nancy Jean *medical educator, writer*

Mc Lean
Tenen, S. Mark *endocrinologist, educator*
Wright, William Evan *physician, consultant*

Midlothian
Friedel, Robert Oliver *physician*

Monterey
Tabatznik, Bernard *retired cardiologist*

Norfolk
Bluestein, Daniel A. *family practice physician*
Ciccone, Alvin J. *family practice physician*
Darrow, David H. *pediatric otolaryngologist, educator*
Faulconer, Robert Jamieson *retired pathologist, educator*
Fisher, Randall G. *pediatrician, educator*
Pariser, David Michael *dermatologist, educator*
Platsoucas, Chris Dimitrios *immunologist*
Strasnick, Barry *otolaryngologist, health facility administrator, educator*
Upadhyay, Jyoti J. *urologist, educator*
Wolcott, Hugh Dixon *obstetrics and gynecology educator*

Portsmouth
Wolf, Jeffrey Stephen *physician*

Reston
Poindexter, Byron D. *plastic surgeon*
Sigal, Robert K. *plastic surgeon*
Weston, George W. *plastic surgeon*

Richmond
Akbari, Homayoon Mohammed *colon and rectal surgeon, educator*
Atkinson, Richard Lee, Jr. *internal medicine educator*
Bates, Hampton Robert, Jr. *pathologist*
Blumberg, Michael Zangwill *allergist*
Boling, Peter A. *geriatrician, educator*
Cardenosa, Gilda *diagnostic radiologist, educator*
Corey, Linda Ann *medical educator, researcher*
Desai, Sanjay S. *hand surgeon, educator*
Garrett, Algin B. *dermatologist, educator*
Godin, Michael S. *plastic surgeon*
Hardy, Richard Earl *rehabilitation counseling educator*
Hillelson, Ruth Leanna *plastic surgeon*
Kendler, Kenneth Seedman *psychiatrist, medical educator*
Lawrence, Walter, Jr. *surgeon, educator*
Miller, W. Greg *pathologist, educator*
Mollen, Edward Leigh *pediatrician, allergist, clinical immunologist*
Nestler, John Edwin *endocrinology educator*
Owen, Duncan Shaw, Jr. *internist, retired educator*
Pellock, John Michael *child neurologist*
Richardson, David Walthall *cardiologist, educator, consultant*
Vetrovec, George Wayne *cardiologist, medical researcher, educator*
Ziegler, Penelope *psychiatrist, educator*

Roanoke
Hutcheson, Jack Robert *hematologist, medical oncologist*
Johnson, Cynda Ann *physician, educator*
Rubio, Edmundo Raul *physician, educator*

Spotsylvania
Bourne, Peter Geoffrey *physician, educator, writer*

Springfield
Furst, Eric Jonathan *physician, surgeon*

Vienna
Heppner, Donald Gray, Jr. *medical consultant*
Schwartz, Richard Harvey *pediatrician*

Virginia Beach
Magee, William Preston, Jr. *plastic surgeon*
McDaniel, David Henry *physician*
Musci, Michael N., Jr. *pediatrician, healthcare company executive*
Onsanit, Tawachai *physician*
Schreiber, Mark Traudt *psychiatrist*
Taylor, Robert Brown *physician, educator, writer*

Ware Neck
Tabb, Waller Crockett *retired allergist, immunologist*

Williamsburg
Connell, Alastair McCrae *physician*
Taylor, Jimmy Lynn *retired family practice physician, administrator*
Voorhess, Mary Louise *pediatric endocrinologist*

Winchester
Bechamps, Gerald Joseph *surgeon*

WASHINGTON

Seattle
Lyman, Gary Herbert *epidemiologist, cancer researcher, educator*

WEST VIRGINIA

Bruceton Mills
Moyers, Sylvia Dean *retired medical librarian*

Charleston
Boland, James Pius *surgeon, educator*

Frametown
Gintautas, Jonas *physician, scientist, administrator*

Huntington
Cocke, William Marvin, Jr. *plastic surgeon, educator*
Mufson, Maurice Albert *infectious diseases physician, educator*
Nerhood, Robert Clarke *obstetrician, gynecologist*

Martinsburg
McMurry, James Finley, Jr. *endocrinologist, researcher*

Morgantown
Albrink, Margaret Joralemon *medical educator*
Bang, Ki Moon *epidemiologist, professor*
Fleming, William Wright, Jr. *retired pharmacology professor*
Glover, Douglas Dennis *obstetrics, gynecology and pharmacology educator*
Hurst, Michael Kenneth *otolaryngologist, educator*
Madhavan, Sundareswaran Suresh *pharmacy educator*
Murray, Pamela J. *pediatrician, educator*
Nugent, George Robert *neurosurgeon*
Ramadan, Hassan H. *medical educator*
Remick, Scot Clifton *oncologist, clinical investigator, educator*

TERRITORIES OF THE UNITED STATES

PUERTO RICO

Guaynabo
Ramirez-Rivera, Jose *physician*

Mayaguez
Sahai, Hardeo *medical statistics educator*

San Juan
Bird, Hector Ramón *child psychiatrist, psychoanalyst, educator*
Bonilla-Felix, Melvin A. *pediatrician, educator*
Cordero, Jose Fernando *pediatrician, dean*

VIRGIN ISLANDS

Frederiksted
Chaikin, Harry Louis *internist*

SWITZERLAND

Zurich
Runge, Val Murray *medical educator*

ADDRESS UNPUBLISHED

Abou-Khalil, Bassel William *neurologist, epileptologist*
Achord, James Lee *retired gastroenterologist*
Adams, Christine Beate Lieber *psychiatrist, educator*
Aduen, Javier Francisco *physician, researcher*
Altenburger, Karl Marion *allergist*
Altshuler, Kenneth Z. *psychiatrist, educator*
Baliga, Radhakrishna *pediatrician, educator, nephrologist*
Ball, Carroll Raybourne *anatomist, researcher, medical educator*
Banta, James Elmer *epidemiologist, educator, dean*
Barzilay, Joshua Israel *endocrinologist, educator*
Berkelhamer, Jay Ellis *pediatrician*
Blazina, Janice Fay *pathologist*
Blount, Benroe Wayne *physician, department chairman*
Blumencranz, Peter William *surgeon*
Boggs, Charles Harmon, Jr. *retired surgeon*
Boland, Clement Richard *gastroenterologist, educator*
Brasher, George Walter *physician, consultant*
Brott, Walter Howard *retired cardiac surgeon, educator, military officer*
Brownlee, Robert Calvin *pediatrician, educator*
Bubrick, Melvin Phillip *surgeon*
Buhain, Wilfrido Javier *medical educator*
Buratynski, Theresa Joan *physician*
Burk, Raymond Franklin, Jr. *internist, educator, researcher*
Calvert, William Preston *radiologist*
Campbell, Andrew William *immunotoxicology physician*
Carswell, Jane Triplett *retired family physician*
Chapman, Daniel P. *epidemiologist*
Coeytaux, Remy Rene *physician, researcher*
Conrad-England, Roberta Lee *pathologist*
Coogan, Philip Shields *pathologist*
Cooley, Denton Arthur *surgeon, educator*
Couch, Robert Barnard *physician, scientist, microbiologist, educator*
Cronce, Paul Calvin *retired dermatologist*
Dalton, Claudette Ellis Harloe *anesthesiologist, educator, dean*
David, Geldmacher Stephen *medical educator*
Davis, Lawrence William *radiation oncologist*
Dennis, Bradley M. *surgeon, educator*
DePalma, Ralph George *surgeon, educator, medical administrator*
De Rosa, Guy Paul *retired orthopedic surgery educator*
Desbiens, Norman A. *medical educator, researcher*
Diehl, Louis F. *hematologist*
Di Sessa, Thomas Gerald *medical educator*
Dobson, Richard Lawrence *dermatologist, educator*
Dow, David Sontag *retired ophthalmologist*
Draper, Edgar *psychiatrist*
Durell, Jack *psychiatrist*
DuRocher, Frances A. *retired physician, educator*
Dutt, Kamla *retired medical educator*
Dyar, Kathryn Wilkin *pediatrician*
Ehlers, Kathryn Hawes (Mrs. James D. Gabler) *physician*
Eichenwald, Heinz Felix *physician*
Ellison, Lois Taylor *internist, educator, medical association administrator*
Fariss, Bruce Lindsay *endocrinologist, consultant*
Farman, Allan George *radiologist, consultant, pathologist, educator*
Farr, Barry Miller *physician, epidemiologist*
Feinstein, Robert P. *dermatologist*
Feldman, Marc David *psychiatrist*
Filston, Howard Church *retired pediatric surgeon*
Fischer, Craig Leland *physician*
Franks, John Julian *anesthesiologist, educator*
Freeman, Theodore Monroe *physician*
Frenkel, Eugene Phillip *physician*
Fudenberg, Hugh *neuroimmunologist, educator*
Gardner, Bernard *surgeon, educator*
Gates, Steven Leon *physician*
Gigli, Irma *dermatologist, academic administrator, educator, immunologist*
Glass, Dorothea Daniels *physiatrist, educator*
Goldberg, Burton *pathologist, researcher, educator*
Golden, Gerald Samuel *retired national medical board executive*
Goldsmith, Jay Paul *pediatrician, neonatalogist, educator*
Goldstein, Burton Jack *psychiatrist*
Gonzalez-Scarano, Francisco Antonio *neurologist, virologist*
Green, Louis Harry *retired surgeon*
Greenfield, George B. *radiologist*
Gulbrandsen, Patricia Hughes *physician*
Gulya, Aina Julianna *otologist, neurotologist, skull base surgeon*
Halliday, William Ross *retired physician, speleologist, writer*
Halverstadt, Donald Bruce *urologist, educator*
Hancock, John C. *pharmacologist*
Harmel, Merel Hilber *anesthesiologist, educator*
Harper, Michael John Kennedy *obstetrics and gynecology educator*
Heestand Skinner, Diane Elissa *retired health professions educator*
Heggers, John Paul *retired surgery, immunology and microbiology educator*
Henson, Anna Miriam *retired otolaryngologist, retired medical educator*
Holman, James *allergist*
Howards, Stuart S. *urologist, educator*
Irwin, Peter John *orthopaedic surgeon*
Jarquin Valdivia, Adrian Alberto *internist, neurologist, researcher*
Jung, Rodney C. *internist, academic administrator*
Justiniani, Federico Roberto *retired internist, educator*
Kahan, Barry Donald *surgeon, educator*
Kaufman, Stephen Lawrence *radiologist, educator*
Kettelkamp, Donald Benjamin *retired orthopedist*
Khan, Shah-Naz Hayat *neurosurgeon*
Kindberg, Shirley Jane *pediatrician*
Klein, Gordon Leslie *pediatrician, educator*
Kones, Richard *cardiologist, medical services company executive*
Lane, Richard Allan *preventive medicine physician, educator*
Lawless, Michael Rhodes *pediatrics educator*
Lefeber, Edward James, Jr. *internist, educator*
LeMaistre, Charles Aubrey *internist, epidemiologist, educator*
Lester, Mark Charles *neurosurgeon*
Lohmann, George Young, Jr. *neurosurgeon, health facility administrator, artist*
Luce, Edward Andrew *plastic surgeon*
Madewell, John Edward *radiologist*
Mahesh, Virendra Bhushan *endocrinologist*
Malluche, Hartmut Horst *nephrologist, medical educator*
Mandell, Gerald Lee *internist, educator*
Mannino, J(oseph) Robert *retired medical educator*
Martin, Daniel C. *surgeon, gynecologist, educator*
May, Robert M. *retired obstetrician, gynecologist, educator*
McCullough, David Legarde *urologist*
McCullough, Laurence Bernard *medical educator, consultant*
Merrill, Joseph Melton *medical educator*

Millar, John Donald *physician, occupational & environmental health services consultant, musician*
Mitchell, William Marvin *pathology educator*
Mladick, Richard Anthony *plastic surgeon*
Mohamadi, Masoud *retired surgeon*
Montgomery, John Richard *pediatrician, educator*
Moody, Dixon McGuire *radiologist*
Mueller-Heubach, Eberhard *medical educator*
Murry, J. Warren *surgeon, educator*
Nicholson, Henry Hale, Jr. *retired surgeon*
Nieto, Juan Manuel *emergency medicine physician*
Noonan, Jacqueline Anne *pediatrician, educator*
Novello, Antonia Coello *pediatric nephrologist, former state health commissioner, former United States Surgeon General*
O'Malley, Thomas Anthony *gastroenterologist, retired internist*
Orth, David Nelson *endocrinologist, educator, sculptor, potter*
Ory, Steven Jay *physician, educator*
Osborn, June Elaine *pediatrician, microbiologist, educator, foundation administrator*
Ossoff, Robert Henry *otolaryngologist, surgeon*
Pacifico, Albert Dominick *cardiovascular surgeon*
Parmley, Richard Turner *pediatric hematologist, oncologist*
Patel, Uptal Dinesh *nephrologist, researcher*
Pauly, John Edward *retired anatomist*
Pecora, David Victor *retired surgeon*
Pederson, William Christopher *plastic surgeon*
Perry, William Brian *colorectal surgeon*
Petrie, William Marshall *psychiatrist*
Petty, Roy William *orthopedist*
Pfeiffer, Eric Armin *psychiatrist, gerentologist, author*
Poehling, Katherine *pediatrician*
Porayko, Michael K. *internist, educator*
Pritz, Michael Burton *neurological surgeon*
Pryor, Carol Graham *retired obstetrician, gynecologist*
Quencer, Robert M. *neuroradiologist, researcher*
Quillian, Warren Wilson, II, *pediatrician, educator*
Raines, Jeff *biomedical scientist, medical research director*
Ramilo, Octavio *pediatrician, educator*
Rausher, David Benjamin *internist, gastroenterologist*
Ravdin, Peter Marcus *internist, educator, oncologist*
Reading, Anthony John *retired psychiatrist, educator*
Reiling, Richard Bernard *physician*
Robbins, Richard James *endocrinologist, researcher*
Rock, John Aubrey *gynecologist, obstetrician, educator, administrator, emeritus chancellor*
Rubin, Bruce Kalman *medical professor, researcher*
Rudolph, Andrew Henry *retired dermatologist, educator*
Salyer, Kenneth E. *surgeon*
Schell, Catherine Louise *physician*
Schneider, George T. *obstetrician, gynecologist*
Schulman, Harold *obstetrician, gynecologist*
Segars, Kelly Scott, Sr. *physician, banker*
Sharp, Dan Steven *epidemiologist*
Shaw, Ronald Ahrend *physician, educator*
Shuster, Frederick *retired internist, gastroenterologist*
Sigmon, J. Lewis, Jr. *medical educator*
Sirica, Alphonse Eugene *pathology educator*
Smith, Thomas F. *immunologist*
Soltero-Harrington, Luis Rubén *retired surgeon, educator*
Spackman, Thomas James *radiologist*
Surawicz, Borys *physician, educator*
Taylor, Peyton Troy, Jr. *oncologist, educator*
Thornton, James F. *plastic surgeon, former military officer*
Troost, Bradley Todd *neurologist, educator*
Tropez-Sims, Susanne *pediatrician, educator*
Trunnell, Thomas Newton *dermatologist*
Turner, Harry Spencer *preventive medicine physician, educator*
Valcárcel, Marta Iris *pediatric educator*
van Nagell, John Rensselaer *oncologist, gynecologist*
Vest, Gayle Southworth *obstetrician, gynecologist*
Waid, Thomas Henry *physician, researcher, educator*
Walker, David H. *medical educator*
Watson, Donald Charles, Jr. *cardiothoracic surgeon, educator*
Way, Barbara Haight *retired dermatologist*
Weil, Richard III *surgeon, medical educator*
Weisberg, Lynne Willing *psychiatrist, consultant*
Wieland, Gilbert Darryl *medical researcher, anthropologist, gerontologist*
Wilfert-Katz, Catherine M. *medical association administrator, pediatrician, epidemiologist, educator*
Wilson, William Preston *retired psychiatrist and seminary professor*
Wood, Maurice *medical educator*
Wyngaarden, James Barnes *retired physician*
Yielding, K. Lemone *physician*
Young, Alfred Byron *retired neurosurgeon*
Zabetakis, Paul Michael *nephrologist, educator*
Zuhdi, Nazih *surgeon scientist retired*

HUMANITIES: LIBERAL STUDIES

UNITED STATES

ALABAMA

Auburn
Amacher, Richard Earl *retired literature educator*

Birmingham
Benditt, Theodore Matthew *humanities educator*
Keitt, Andrew Wannamaker *history professor*

Jacksonville
Spector, Daniel Earl *historian, educator*

Montgomery
Westhauser, Karl E. *historian*

Ramer
Napier, John Hawkins III *historian*

Troy
Mitchell, Norma Taylor *history professor*

Tuscaloosa
Crowley, John William *literature and language professor*
Hocutt, Max Oliver *retired philosophy educator*

ARKANSAS

Arkadelphia
Gibson, Herman *humanities educator, department chairman*
Graves, John William *historian*

Conway
Ziegler, John Alan *historian, political scientist, educator, short story writer*

Fayetteville
Levine, Daniel Blank *classical studies educator*

Little Rock
Vinikas, Vincent *historian, educator*

Mena
Eddleman, Floyd Eugene *retired language educator*

Monticello
Babin, Claude Hunter *history professor*

State University
Milner, Clyde A., II, *historian*

DISTRICT OF COLUMBIA

Washington
Bush Hager, Jenna (Jenna Welch Bush) *language educator, writer, volunteer, former first daughter*

FLORIDA

Altamonte Springs
Murphrey, Elizabeth Hobgood *retired history professor, librarian*

Boca Raton
Shusterman, Richard Marc *philosophy educator*

Daytona Beach
Duval, Cynthia *art historian, museum administrator, curator, consultant*

Fort Myers
Halloran, William Frank *English educator*

Gainesville
Kushner, David Zakeri *musicologist*

Jacksonville
Carpenter, JoAnn Deakin *history professor*

Lake Worth
Wilson, William J. *language educator*

Miami
Neu, Charles Eric *historian, educator*
Sicius, Francis Joseph *history professor, writer*
Taddeo, Annette *language services professional*

Naples
Butters, Ronald Richard *language educator*

North Palm Beach
Gaudieri, Alexander V.J. *art historian, museum director, educator*

Oldsmar
Thompson, Mack Eugene *historian, educator*

Orlando
Berry, Leonard L. *humanities educator, board member*
Vanryckeghem, Martine *speech language professional, educator*

Saint Petersburg
Reilly, Tracy Lynn *language educator*

Sanibel
Bannister, Robert Corwin, Jr. *historian, educator*
Helmreich, Jonathan Ernst *history professor*

Sarasota
Doenecke, Justus Drew *historian*
Taplin, Winn Lowell *historian, retired federal agency administrator*

Tallahassee
Bartlett, Richard Adams *historian, writer, retired history professor*
Golden, Leon *classicist, educator*
Halpern, Paul G. *retired history professor*
Laird, Doris Anne Marley *retired humanities educator, musician*
Ortiz-Taylor, Sheila *retired English language educator*
Thompson, Janet Ann *history professor*

Tampa
Anton, John Peter *philosopher, educator*
Loewe, Barbara *speech educator, theater educator, humanities educator*
Mitchell, Mozella Gordon *professor, scholar, writer*
Perry, James Frederic *philosophy educator, writer*
Turner, Stephen Park *philosopher, sociologist, educator*

Temple Terrace
Crispell, Brian Lewis *history professor, dean of students*

Wesley Chapel
Peck, Abraham Joseph *historian*

Winter Park
Seymour, Thaddeus *language educator*
Wilson, Robley Conant, Jr. *language educator, editor, writer*

GEORGIA

Americus
Isaacs, Harold *history professor*

Andersonville
Boyles, Frederick Holdren *historian*

Athens
Commeyras, Michelle *literature and language professor*
Kretzschmar, William Addison, Jr. *language educator*
Winfield, Richard Dien *humanities educator*

Atlanta
Benario, Herbert William *classicist, educator*
Brown, Lorene B(yron) *retired library educator*
Burns, Thomas Samuel *history professor*
Felman, Shoshana *literature and language professor*
Gilman, Sander Lawrence *liberal arts and sciences professor, historian, writer*
Hartle, Robert Wyman *retired literature and language professor*
Holifield, Brooks E. *history professor*
Reynolds, Douglas R. *history professor*
Rubin, Larry Jerome *retired literature educator*

Augusta
Dyer, James Harold, Jr. *language educator*

Decatur
Dillingham, William Byron *literature educator, author*

Griffin
Henderson, Gloria Mason *retired literature and language professor*

Macon
Huffman, Joan Brewer *history professor*

Marietta
Luce, Willard Ray *historian, director*

Tifton
McGruder, Larry *history professor*

Valdosta
Williams, David *history professor*

KENTUCKY

Barbourville
Wood, Andelys *literature and language professor*

Bowling Green
Jackson, Carlton Luther *history professor, writer*

Danville
Allen, John Jay *Spanish language educator*

Georgetown
Klotter, James C. *historian, educator*

Highland Heights
Ramage, James Alfred *history professor*

Lexington
Breazeale, James Daniel *philosopher, educator*
Coffman, Edward McKenzie *retired history professor*
Pickens, Rupert Tarpley III *French language educator*
Thelin, John Robert *historian, educator, researcher, sportsman*

Louisville
McLeod, John Edmond *history professor*

Richmond
Huch, Ronald Kind *historian, educator*

Southgate
Glenn, Jerry Hosmer, Jr. *retired language educator*

LOUISIANA

Baton Rouge
Arceneaux, William *historian, educator, foundation administrator*
Cooper, William James, Jr. *history professor*
Doty, Gresdna Ann *theatre historian, educator*
Ricapito, Joseph Virgil (Giuseppe Ricapito) *literature educator*

Lafayette
Raffel, Burton Nathan *novelist, poet, translator*

New Orleans
Brumfield, William Craft *Slavic studies educator, photographer, writer*
Reck, Andrew Joseph *philosopher*

MISSISSIPPI

Clinton
Bigelow, Martha Mitchell *retired historian*

Gulfport
Swetman, Glenn Robert *literature and language professor, poet*

Mississippi State
Lowery, Charles Douglas *historian, dean, educator*
Uzoigwe, Godfrey Nwanoruo *history professor, consultant, researcher*

Oxford
Landon, Michael de Laval *retired history professor*

Shelby
Moore, Renee Alma *English educator*

University
Skemp, Sheila L. *history professor*

NORTH CAROLINA

Chapel Hill
Baxter, Stephen Bartow *retired historian*
Browning, Christopher R. *historian, educator*
Cole, Richard Cargill *language educator*
Flora, Joseph M(artin) *language educator*
Grendler, Paul Frederick *historian, educator*
Gura, Philip Francis *English and American literature educator*
Pérez, Louis A., Jr. *history professor*
Rabil, Albert, Jr. *humanities educator*
Sherman, Daniel James *art history professor*
Stadter, Philip Austin *classicist, educator*
Strauss, Albrecht Benno *retired English professor, editor*
Williamson, Joel Rudolph *humanities educator, writer*

Charlotte
Myers, Robert Manson *language educator, writer*

Durham
Chafe, William Henry *history professor, historian*
Clay, Diskin *classical studies educator*
Davis, Calvin De Armond *historian, educator*
Holley, Irving Brinton, Jr. *historian, educator*
Randall, Dale Bertrand Jonas *English language educator*
Scott, Anne Byrd Firor *history professor*
Smith, Grover Cleveland, Jr. *language educator*

Greensboro
Nieman, Valerie Gail *writer, language educator, journalist*
Penninger, Frieda Elaine *retired literature educator*

Raleigh
Pritchard, Ruie Jane *English educator, director*
Rhodes, Donald Robert *musicologist, educator, retired electrical engineer*

Sanford
York, Carolyn Pleasants Stearns *language educator*

Weaverville
Johnson, Herbert Alan *historian, lawyer*

Winston Salem
Barnett, Richard Chambers *historian, educator*
Covey, Cyclone *history professor*
Shapere, Dudley *philosophy educator*

OKLAHOMA

Ada
Barton, Donald Scott *history professor*

Norman
Leitch, Vincent Barry *literary and cultural studies educator*
Levy, David William *history educator*
Savage, William Woodrow, Jr. *historian, consultant, social sciences educator*

Tulsa
Buckley, Thomas Hugh *historian, educator*

SOUTH CAROLINA

Aiken
Sykes, Richard Nesbit *retired history professor, department chairman*

Charleston
Barrett, Michael Baker *historian, educator*

Clemson
Cranston, Philip Edward *foreign language professional*

Columbia
Franklin, Benjamin, V, *English language educator*
Howard-Hill, Trevor Howard *language educator*
Long, Eugene Thomas III *philosophy educator, academic administrator*

Donalds
Carlock, John Bruce, Jr. *retired language educator*

Greenville
Schoolfield, Brenda Thompson *history professor*

Travelers Rest
Bailey, Helen McShane *historian, consultant*

Union
Colbert, Alice Taylor *history professor*

Whitmire
Kibler, James Everett, Jr. *naturalist, writer, preservationist*

TENNESSEE

Chattanooga
Gartman, Max Dillon *language educator*
Resnick, Irven Michael *philosophy educator*

Columbia
Gidcomb, Barry Doyle *history professor*

Cookeville
Campana, Phillip Joseph *German language educator*

Franklin
Lee, Douglas A. *musicologist*

Jefferson City
Baumgardner, James Lewis *history professor*

Knoxville
Allington, Richard Lloyd *literacy studies educator*
Ash, Stephen Vaughan *history professor, writer*

Memphis
Russell, Thomas Arthur *humanities educator, religious studies educator, researcher*

Nashville
Compton, John Joseph *philosophy educator*
Cook, Ann Jennalie *literature educator, cultural organization administrator*
Dickerson, Dennis Clark, Sr. *historian, educator*
Girgus, Sam B. *English literature educator*
Hassel, Rudolph Christopher *language educator*
Jarman, Mark Foster *language educator*
Lachs, John *philosopher, educator*
Purcell, Mary Hamilton *speech educator*
Voegeli, Victor Jacque *historian, educator, dean*

Sewanee
Poe, George Wilkinson *literature, culture and language professor*
Williamson, Samuel Ruthven, Jr. *historian, educator*

TEXAS

Austin
Arens, Katherine Marie *language educator*
Brown, Norman Donald *history professor*
Divine, Robert Alexander *history professor*
Farrell, Edmund James *retired English language educator, writer*
Flowers, Betty Sue *literature and language professor, former library director*
Freeman, Robert Schofield *musicologist, pianist, educator*
Friedman, Alan Warren *humanities educator*
Galinsky, Gotthard Karl *classicist, educator*
Hopkins, Antony Gerald *history professor*
Kane, Robert Hilary *philosophy educator*
Louis, William Roger *historian*
Middleton, Christopher *Germanic languages and literature educator*
Moag, Rodney Frank *language educator, country and bluegrass singer, musician, record producer*
Rich, John Martin *humanities educator, researcher*
Seung, Thomas Kaehao *philosophy educator*
Whitbread, Thomas Bacon *language educator, writer*

Bastrop
Veninga, James Frank *humanities educator, editor, writer*

Brownsville
Langerbein, Helmut *history professor, department chairman*
Stephenson, Mimosa Summers *literature and language professor*

Bryan
Bryant, Keith Lynn, Jr. *history professor*

College Station
Dethloff, Henry Clay *historian, educator*
Harner, James Lowell *language educator*

Corpus Christi
Wooster, Robert *history professor*

Cypress
Seymour, James B., Jr. *history professor, department chairman*

Dallas
Chavez, John Richard *historian, educator*
Comini, Alessandra *art historian, educator, musicologist*
Crain, John Walter *historian, educator*
Davis, Daisy Sidney *history professor*
Hurley, Alfred Francis *historian, academic administrator emeritus, retired air force officer*
Williams, Michael Edward, Sr. *history professor*

Denton
Kesterson, David Bert *language educator, academic administrator*

Edinburg
Anderson-Mejias, Pamela L. *applied linguistics professor*

Fort Worth
Boller, Paul Franklin, Jr. *retired American history educator, writer*
DeLotto, Jeffrey Daniel *language educator, writer*
Reuter, Frank Theodore *historian, educator*

Galveston
Chance, Jane *English literature scholar*

Georgetown
Browning, Grayson Douglas *philosophy educator*
Proctor, Claude Oliver *Russian language educator*

Houston
Achenbaum, Wilbert Andrew *historian, gerontologist*
Brinkley, Douglas G. *historian, writer, educator*
Brosman, Catharine Savage *retired language educator, poet*
Drew, Katherine Fischer *history professor*
Ehrmann, Susanna *language educator, photographer, writer*
Lamb, Sydney MacDonald *linguistics educator*
Martin, James Kirby *historian, educator*
Minter, David Lee *English literature educator*
Pryor, William Daniel Lee *humanities educator*
Schnoebelen, Anne Mary *musicologist, educator*
Sher, George Allen *philosophy educator*

Irving
Sommerfeldt, John Robert *historian, educator*
Wood, Robert E. *philosopher, educator*

Lancaster
Rolling, Lincoln Curtis *history professor*

Longview
Batts, Martin *literature and language professor*

Lubbock
Curzer, Howard Jay *philosophy professor*
Ketner, Kenneth Laine *philosopher, educator*

Mesquite
Budd, Rose Antoinette *language educator*

Pasadena
Shelton, Hal Terry *history professor*

Richardson
Redman, Timothy Paul *language educator, writer*

San Angelo
Ellery, Jon Christopher *literature and language professor*

San Antonio
Atlas, Jay David *philosopher, linguist, consultant, cognitive scientist, educator*
Cordova, Ruben Charles *art historian, curator, photographer*
Grimshaw, James Albert, Jr. *retired language educator*
Himelblau, Jack Joseph *Latin-American literature and culture educator*
Kellman, Steven G. *literature educator, author*
Myers, Ellen Howell *historian, educator*
Passty, Jeanette Nyda Mendelssohn *literature and language professor, writer, editor*
Salvucci, Linda *history professor*
Walker, William Oliver, Jr. *retired humanities educator, dean*

Sherman
Melancon, Glenn *history professor*

Stephenville
Christopher, Joe Randell *retired language educator*

VIRGINIA

Alexandria
Duncan, Richard Ray *history professor*

Arlington
Wilcox, Shirley Jean Langdon *genealogist*

Ashland
Inge, Milton Thomas *American literature and culture educator, author*

Blacksburg
Doswald, Herman Kenneth *language educator, retired academic administrator*

Charlottesville
Battestin, Martin Carey *retired literature and language professor*
Belanger, Terry *historian, educator*
Bond, Julian *history professor, former civil rights association executive*
Carlson, W. Bernard *historian, educator*
Colker, Marvin Leonard *classics educator*
Daugherty, Leo *literature and language educator*
Hart, Kevin John *poet, educator*
Hirsch, Eric Donald, Jr. *language educator*
Humphreys, Paul William *philosophy educator, consultant*
Lane, Ann Judith *history and women's studies educator, director*
Little, Wm. A. (William Alfred Little) *language educator, researcher, musicologist*
McGann, Jerome John *language educator*
Megill, Allan *historian*
Mikalson, Jon Dennis *classics educator*
Nohrnberg, James Carson *language educator*
Rubin, David Lee *humanities educator, critic, editor, book publisher, editorial consultant*
Schuker, Stephen Alan *historian, educator*
Sedgwick, Alexander *retired historian, educator*
Shaw, Donald Leslie *Spanish language educator*
Spearing, Anthony Colin *English literature educator*
Tucker, Herbert *English professor*
Zunz, Olivier Jean *history professor*

Emory
Denham, Robert Dayton *language educator*

Fairfax
Hutcheon, Wallace Schoonmaker *retired historian*

Falls Church
Allard, Dean Conrad *historian, retired historical center director*

Farmville
Etheridge, Elizabeth Williams *history professor*

Fredericksburg
Bradshaw, Kellie K. *history professor, department chairman*

Hardyville
White, Gordon Eliot *historian, writer*

Lexington
Koeniger, Alfred Cash *history professor*
Koons, Kenneth Edward *historian, educator, consultant*
Sessions, William Lad *philosophy educator, academic administrator*
Stephens, Laurence David, Jr. *linguist, investor, oil industry executive*

Lovettsville
Foard, Douglas W. *historian*

Lynchburg
Henderson, Horace Edward *World War II historian, peace advocate*
Snead, David L. *history professor*

Newport News
Hoaglund, John Arthur *philosophy educator, editor*

Norfolk
Wilson, Harold Stacy *history professor, writer*

Portsmouth
Paquette, William Arthur *historian, educator*

Richmond
Cornis-Pope, Marcel Horatiu *literature educator, literary critic, program director*
Hall, James H(errick), Jr. *philosophy educator, writer*
Levit, Héloïse B. (Ginger Levit) *art historian, art journalist, art dealer, consultant*
Rilling, John Robert *history professor*
Sterling, Keir Brooks *historian, educator*

Staunton
Arnold, Albert James *retired foreign language educator, consultant*

Sweet Briar
Piepho, Lee (Edward Lee Piepho) *humanities educator*

Williamsburg
Axtell, James Lewis *retired history professor*
Chappell, Miles Linwood, Jr. *art historian, educator*
Crapol, Edward P. *history professor*
Esler, Anthony James *historian, novelist, educator*
Goldman, Alan H. *philosophy educator*
Hoffman, Ronald *historian, educator*
Landen, Robert Geran *retired historian, academic administrator*
McGiffert, Michael *retired historian*
Nelson, Scott Reynolds *historian, educator*
Nettels, Elsa *English language educator*
Sherman, Richard Beatty *historian, educator*
Stamelman, Richard Howard *French and humanities educator*
Wallach, Alan *art historian, educator*

WEST VIRGINIA

Morgantown
Blaydes, Sophia Boyatzies *English language educator*

TERRITORIES OF THE UNITED STATES

PUERTO RICO

San Juan
Lockwood-Benet, Mildred M. *language educator*

ADDRESS UNPUBLISHED

Agan, Cami D. *literature and language professor*
Almond, Ian *literature educator*
Bader, William Banks *historian, former corporate executive, foundation executive*
Becker, Lawrence Carlyle *philosopher, educator, writer*
Bishop, Rand *retired humanities educator*
Bolsterli, Margaret Jones *English professor, writer*
Bounds, Sarah Etheline *historian*
Brown, Stephen Ira *mathematics and philosophy of education professor emeritus*
Bryant, Paul Thompson *language educator*
Buckner, Sally Beaver *literature and language professor, writer*
Chappell, Fred Davis *language educator, poet*
Chasteen, John Charles *history professor*
Cher-Killigan, Beatrice M. *history professor, art educator*
Collmer, Robert George *retired language educator*
Courtney, Edward *retired classics educator*
Crackel, Theodore Joseph *historian*
Der-Houssikian, Haig *retired linguist, educator*
Edgar, Walter Bellingrath *retired historian, educator*
Edson, Evelyn *history professor, writer*
Froberg, Brent Malcolm *classics educator*
Gatewood, Willard Badgett, Jr. *retired historian, writer*
Gruber, Ira Dempsey *historian, educator*
Hall, Jacquelyn Dowd *historian, educator*
Hallen, Barry *philosopher, educator*
Hamilton, Virginia Van der Veer *historian, educator*
Hardin, James Neal *language educator, publisher*
Hasselbach, Karlheinz *retired literature educator*
Heffernan, Thomas Carroll *English literature and American studies educator*
Kaufman, Janice Horner *French and ESL instructor, interpreter*
Kohn, Richard H. *historian, educator*
Kolb, Harold Hutchinson, Jr. *language educator*
Labor, Earle Gene *literature and language professor*
Langbaum, Robert Woodrow *language educator*
Lawhon, Tommie Collins Montgomery *retired humanities educator*
Lewis, Douglas *retired art historian*
Lyons, John David *literature and language professor*
Mauskopf, Seymour Harold *history professor*
Mc Fadden, Joseph Michael *historian, educator*
Midelfort, Hans Christian Erik *retired history professor*
Morrissey, Charles Thomas *historian, educator*
Napier, Cameron Mayson Freeman *historic preservationist*
Norden, Ernest Elwood *retired foreign language educator*
Palmer, Marilyn Joan *English composition educator*
Pauley, Bruce Frederick *retired history professor*
Perkowski, Jan Louis *language, literature and folklore educator*
Pierce, Susan Resneck *author, consultant, retired academic administrator*
Reed, Mark Lafayette III *retired humanities educator*
Richards, David Gleyre *German language educator*
Richardson, Robert Dale, Jr. *language educator*
Rosenberg, David Alan *military historian, strategic analyst*
Ryan, Marleigh Grayer *language educator*
Salter, Mark *speechwriter*
Schafer, Elizabeth Diane *historian, writer*
Shaw, Nancy Rivard *art historian, independent scholar*
Skinner, James Lister III *retired language educator*
Smith, Ellen Louise *retired language educator*
Smock, Raymond William *historian*
Snapp, Harry Franklin *historian, educator*
Staley, Thomas Fabian *literature and language professor, museum director*
Stiebing, William Henry, Jr. *retired history professor*
Stiritz, Marette McCauley *English language educator, consultant*
Toplin, Robert Brent *history professor, television producer*
Torres, David *retired Spanish language educator*
Trelease, Allen William *historian, educator*
Tyler, Ronnie Curtis *art historian, former museum director*
Weinberg, Gerhard Ludwig *history professor, writer*
White, Charles Sidney John *retired humanities educator*
Wolfe, Margaret Ripley *historian, educator, consultant*
Wright, Beth Segal *art historian, educator*
Zimmermann, Thomas Callander Price *retired historian, educator*
Zubizarreta, John *English professor*

HUMANITIES: LIBRARIES

UNITED STATES

ALABAMA

Auburn University
MacEwan, Bonnie *librarian, dean*

Birmingham
DeBrecht, Susan J. *librarian*
Spence, Paul Herbert *librarian*
Stephens, Jerry Wayne *librarian, director*

Huntsville
Lett, Rosalind Kimber *library director, library and information scientist*

Jacksonville
Hubbard, William James *library director*

Mobile
Parsley, Brantley Hamilton *librarian*

Tuscaloosa
Osburn, Charles Benjamin *retired librarian, dean*

ARKANSAS

Fayetteville
Thorup, Shawna Saavedra *librarian*

Little Rock
Garner, Terri *library and museum director*
Mulkey, Jack Clarendon *retired library director*

FLORIDA

Deland
Caccamise, Genevra Louise Ball (Mrs. Alfred E. Caccamise) *retired librarian*

Destin
Deel, Frances Quinn *retired librarian*

Fort Lauderdale
Acosta, Lydia M. *library director*
Beach, Cecil Prentice *librarian*
Cannon, Robert Eugene *library director*

Gainesville
Russell, Judith *librarian, dean*

Hialeah
Medvinsky, Nathalia *library director*

Hudson
Fredericks, Nancy *library director*

Jacksonville
Lee, Hwa-Wei *librarian, educator, consultant*

Jensen Beach
Lowrie, Jean Elizabeth *librarian, educator*

Lakeland
Reich, David Lee *library director*

Lighthouse Point
Gauthier, Doreen Ann *retired librarian*

Melbourne
Wastawy, Sohair F. *library dean, consultant*

Miami
Santiago, Raymond *library director, educator*

Orlando
Allison, Anne Marie *retired librarian*
Hodel, Mary Anne *library director*

Saint Petersburg
Stamatoplos, Anthony *librarian, educator*

Sarasota
De Gennaro, Richard *retired library director*

Sun City Center
Willard, Louis Charles *retired librarian*

Tallahassee
McClure, Charles Robert *library and information science educator, consultant*
Ring, Judith A. *state librarian*
Zachert, Martha Jane *retired librarian*

Venice
Asp, William George *librarian*

Winter Park
Murray, Susan Lyons *library director*
Rogers, Rutherford David *librarian*

GEORGIA

Atlanta
Hakes, Jay Edward *library director, former federal agency administrator*
Murray-Rust, Catherine *library director*
Thaxton, Mary Lynwood *librarian, researcher*
Walker, Julie White *librarian*

Evans
Rowland, Arthur Ray *librarian*

Statesboro
Mitchell, Wilfrid Bede *librarian, library association executive*

Thomasville
Tillinghast, Nancy *library director*

KENTUCKY

Frankfort
Gibbons, Judith A. *librarian*

Lexington
Birdwhistell, Terry L. *library director*
Mason, Ellsworth Goodwin *retired librarian*
Steensland, Ronald Paul *library consultant*

Louisville
Deering, Ronald Franklin *librarian, minister*

LOUISIANA

Baton Rouge
Cargill, Jennifer S. *library director, educator*
Lusk, Glenna Rae Knight *librarian*

Lake Charles
Sawyer, Michael E. *library director*

Napoleonville
Maggio, Theresa Griffin (Terri Maggio) *librarian*

Pineville
Martin, W. Terry *librarian*

Ruston
Wicker, William Walter *librarian*

MISSISSIPPI

Jackson
Smith, Sharman Bridges *state librarian*

NORTH CAROLINA

Chapel Hill
Haefele, Chad M. *library and information scientist*
Jones, Houston Gwynne *archivist, history professor*
Moran, Barbara Burns *librarian, educator*
Pruett, James Worrell *librarian, educator, musicologist*

Charlotte
Blowers, Helene *library and information scientist*

Cove City
Hawkins, Elinor Dixon (Mrs. Carroll Woodard Hawkins) *retired librarian*

Davidson
Park, Leland Madison *retired librarian*

Durham
Auld, Skip (Hampton Auld) *library director*
Canada, Mary Whitfield *retired librarian*

Elizabeth City
Williams, Sue Darden *library director*

Greensboro
Miller, Marilyn Lea *library and information scientist, educator*

Matthews
Jordahl, Ronald Ivan *librarian, educator*

Raleigh
Littleton, Isaac Thomas III *retired library director*
Nutter, Susan K. *librarian, academic administrator*

Winston Salem
Sutton, Lynn Sorensen *librarian*

OKLAHOMA

Lawton
Bonnell-Mihalis, Pamela Gay Scoggins *library director*

Muskogee
Hinshaw, Marilyn L. *retired library director*

Norman
Lester, June *library and information scientist, educator*
Luce, Richard *library director*
Masters, Anne *library director*
Sherman, Mary Angus *public library administrator*
Van Fleet, Connie Jean *library and information scientist, educator*

SOUTH CAROLINA

Charleston
Warren, Charles David *library consultant*

Columbia
Hamby, Rogan *library and information scientist, director*
McNally, Thomas F. *library director*
Newman, Bobbi *library and information scientist*

West Columbia
Rawlinson, Helen Ann *librarian*

TENNESSEE

Greeneville
Smith, Myron John, Jr. *librarian, author*

Hixson
Clapp, David Foster *retired librarian*

Knoxville
Smith, Steven Escar *library director*

Maryville
Tabor, Curtis Harold, Jr. *retired librarian, minister*

Memphis
Wallis, Carlton Lamar *librarian*

Nashville
Cheney, Frances Neel *librarian, educator*
Dowell, Connie Vinita *library director*
Dowell, David Ray *genealogist, ethicist, author, lecturer, library administrator*
Stewart, David Marshall *librarian*
Sugg, Jeanne D. *library director*

TEXAS

Abilene
Tucker, John Mark *librarian, educator*

Austin
Bintliff, Barbara Ann *library director, law educator*
Heath, Fred Milton *library director, educator*
Roy, Loriene *library and information scientist, association executive*
Smith, Patricia H. *library association director*
Updegrove, Mark K. *library director*

Cedar Hill
Hickman, Traphene Parramore *retired library director, consultant, storyteller*

College Station
Carlson, David Harold *library director, dean*
Finch, Warren Luenberg, Jr. *library and museum director, archivist*
Piscitelli, Felicia Ann *librarian, musician, musicologist*

Dallas
Bockstruck, Lloyd DeWitt *librarian*

Denton
Poole, Eva Duraine *librarian*
Snapp, Elizabeth *librarian, educator*

Swigger, Keith *library and information scientist, educator*

El Paso
Gardner, Kerry Ann *librarian*
Mack-Harvin, Dionne L. *library director*

Fort Worth
Ard, Harold Jacob *library administrator*
de Tonnancour, Paul Roger Godefroy *library administrator*

Houston
Bigwood, David P. *librarian, writer*
Henington, David Mead *retired library director*
Lawson, Rhea Brown *library director*
Lowman, Sara Allison *library director*

Laredo
Weber, Janice Ann *library director, grant writer*

Lubbock
Wood, Richard Courtney *library director, educator*

Mcallen
McGee, William Howard John *retired library director*

Missouri City
Mobley, Emily Ruth *library director, educator, retired dean*

San Antonio
Brewster, Olive Nesbitt *retired librarian*
Hasenyager, Richard L., Jr. *library director*
Newton, Virginia *archivist, historian, librarian*
Velásquez, Jennifer *librarian*

Tyler
Albertson, Christopher Adam *librarian*

Waco
Hair, William Bates III *librarian, dean*

VIRGINIA

Alexandria
Gernand, Bradley Elton *archivist, librarian*
Manson, Connie Jeane *librarian*

Fairfax
Clay, Edwin S. III *library director*

Glen Allen
Kozlowski, Ronald Stephan *retired librarian*

Harrisonburg
Gill, Gerald Lawson *librarian*
Palmer, Forrest Charles *librarian, educator*

Lexington
Gaines, James Edwin, Jr. *retired librarian*
Leach, Maurice Derby, Jr. *librarian, educator*

Rapidan
Grimm, Ben Emmet *library director, consultant*

Richmond
Coalter, Milton J., Jr. *library director, educator*
Yelich, Nolan T. *library director*

Williamsburg
Brooks, Philip Coolidge, Jr. *archivist, curator, historian, editor, writer*
Cooper, Carrie *library director*
Moorman, John A. *library administrator*

WEST VIRGINIA

Glenville
Tubesing, Richard Lee *library director*

Morgantown
Pyles, Rodney Allen *archivist, retired county official*

Parkersburg
Heiss, Harry Glen *archivist*

Shepherdstown
Elliott, Jean Ann *retired library director*

ADDRESS UNPUBLISHED

Billings, Harold Wayne *retired library director, editor, writer*
Burnette, Brandon R. *librarian*
Burson, Betsy Lee *librarian*
Daffron, MaryEllen *retired librarian*
Dickerson, Lon Richard *retired library administrator*
Drake, Miriam Anna *retired librarian, educator, journalist consultant*
Felder-Hoehne, Felicia Harris *retired librarian*
Frank, Larry James *library director, writer, consultant*
Fredeman, Betty Coley (Betty Coley) *retired librarian, editor*
Funk Koble, Vicki *librarian*
Hayden, Linda C. *librarian, educator*
Hoke, Sheila Wilder *retired librarian*
Hughes, Sue Margaret *retired librarian*
Imhoff, Kathleen Ruth Tostrud *library administrator*
Kovacs, Beatrice *retired library studies educator*
Lee, Sul Hi *retired library administrator, dean*
Martin, Robert Sidney *librarian, educator*
Muñoz-Solá, Haydeé Socorro *retired library administrator*
Pelton, James Rodger *retired library director*
Rickard, Margaret Lynn *library director, consultant*
Ricklefs, Dale Lynne *retired library director*
Rosenthal, Susan Barbara *retired librarian*

Rouse, Roscoe, Jr. *retired librarian, educator*
Stubbs, Kendon Lee *retired librarian*
Summers, Lorraine Dey Schaeffer *retired librarian*
VanMeter, Vandelia L. *retired library director*
Van Orden, Phyllis Jeanne *librarian, educator*
Wilkins, Barratt (George Wilkins) *librarian*
Willis, Paul Allen *retired librarian, dean*
Wilson, Patricia Potter *author, educator, agriculture business owner*
Woods, Phyllis Michalik *librarian*

HUMANITIES: MUSEUMS

UNITED STATES

ALABAMA

Birmingham
Pijeaux, Lawrence J., Jr. *museum director*

Huntsville
Bass, Clayton *museum director*

Mobile
Alsobrook, David Ernest *museum director, archivist, historian*
Richelson, Paul William *curator*
Schenk, Joseph Bernard *museum director*

Montgomery
Johnson, Mark Matthew *museum director, curator*

Tuscaloosa
Gaddy, Kenneth C. *museum director*

ARKANSAS

Bentonville
Bacigalupi, Donald *museum executive*

Little Rock
Selz, Nan *museum director*

State University
Allen, Marti Lu *museum director*

FLORIDA

Daytona Beach
Atherholt, Wayne David *museum director*
Libby, Gary Russell *museum director emeritus, writer, consultant*

Eglin AFB
Jones, George W. *museum director, military officer*

Fort Lauderdale
Cavendish, Kim L. Maher *museum administrator*
Lippman, Irvin M. *museum director*

Gainesville
Wing, Elizabeth Schwarz *museum curator, educator*

Jacksonville
Peter, Jack E. *museum administrator*

Miami
Buergel, Roger M. *curator, art historian, educator*

Miami Beach
Camber, Diane Woolfe *association president*
Cubiñá, Silvia Karman *museum director, curator*

Orlando
Morrisey, Marena Grant *museum director*

Palm Beach
Blades, John Michael *museum director*

Pensacola
Rasmussen, Robert L. *museum director, military officer*
Spencer, Vivian L. *gallery director*

Saint Augustine
Harper, Robert Walter III *museum director*

Saint Petersburg
Schloder, John E. *museum director*

Sarasota
Zahn, Carl Frederick *museum program director, photographer, graphics designer*

Tallahassee
Palladino-Craig, Allys *museum director, educator*

Valparaiso
Severino, Michelle A. *museum director*

Vero Beach
Gedeon, Lucinda Heyel *museum director*

West Palm Beach
Orr-Cahall, Anona Christina *museum director, art historian*

GEORGIA

Athens
Nosanow, Barbara Shissler *museum director, curator*

Atlanta
Shapiro, Michael Edward *museum director*

Fort Benning
Hanner, Z. Frank *museum director*

KENTUCKY

Lexington
Henrich, Sarah E. *museum director*

Louisville
Haas, Joanna E. *museum director*
O'Brien, Kevin James *museum director*

Owensboro
Hood, Mary Bryan *museum director, painter*

LOUISIANA

Baton Rouge
Gikas, Carol Sommerfeldt *museum director*

New Orleans
Bullard, Edgar John III *museum director*
Fagaly, William Arthur *curator*
Gruber, J. Richard *museum director*

Shreveport
Waddell, Wayne *museum director, former state legislator*

Slidell
Dearing, Reinhard Josef *curator, retired city official*

MISSISSIPPI

Biloxi
Gowdy, Marjorie E. *museum director*

Madison
Brown, Paul *curator*

NORTH CAROLINA

Asheville
Rickman, Ellen Erwin *museum administrator*

Davidson
Thomas, Brad *gallery director, curator*

Raleigh
Howard, Kenneth B. *museum director*

Winston Salem
Rauschenberg, Bradford Lee *retired museum program director*
Sanford, Beverly Shaw *museum director*
Whittington, Stephen Lunn *museum director*

OKLAHOMA

Oklahoma City
Granger, Brenda Ann *museum director*
Plummer, William Hamilton III *museum director, editor*

Shawnee
Pollei, Dane F. *museum director*

SOUTH CAROLINA

Greenville
Davis, Joan Carroll *retired museum director*

Mount Pleasant
Macdonald, Robert Rigg, Jr. *retired museum director*

Pawleys Island
Salmon, Robin Robertson *museum curator, editor*

TENNESSEE

Chattanooga
Kret, Robert A. *museum director*

Knoxville
Butler, David *museum director*

Memphis
Kitchin, Cameron (L. Cameron Kitchin) *museum director*
Lyons, Al(pha) L. *museum director, retired manufacturing executive*

Nashville
Duvenhage, Susan B. *museum administrator*

TEXAS

Austin
Friis-Hansen, Dana *museum director*

Dallas
Anderson, Maxwell L. *museum director*
Hoffman, Marguerite Steed *former art gallery director*
Meslay, Olivier *museum director, curator*
Pitman-Gelles, Bonnie Louise *former museum director*
Strick, Jeremy Adam *art museum director*

El Paso
Sipiora, Leonard Paul *retired museum director, art appraiser*

Fort Worth
Fortson, Kay Kimbell Carter *museum and foundation administrator*
Lee, Eric McCauley *museum director, art historian*
Scott, Janice Wilkie *museum director*

Houston
Arning, Bill *museum director*
Daderko, Dean *curator, critic*
Shearer, Linda *museum director*
Tinterow, Gary H. *museum director*
Tucker, Anne Wilkes *curator, historian, photographer, critic*

San Antonio
Barilleaux, Rene Paul *curator*
Chiego, William J. *museum director*
Oettinger, Marion, Jr. *museum director, anthropologist*
Rubin, David Stuart *curator, art critic, art historian, artist*

VIRGINIA

Alexandria
Lundeberg, Philip Karl Boraas *curator, historian*
Moynihan, William J. *retired museum executive*

Martinsville
Gette, Timothy J. *museum director*

Richmond
Christison, Muriel Branham *retired museum director, art history educator*
Nyerges, Alexander Lee *museum director*

Sterling
Friedheim, Jerry Warden *museum consultant*

Williamsburg
Emerson, Philip G. *historic site director*
Sullivan, Timothy Jackson *museum administrator, retired academic administrator, educator*

TERRITORIES OF THE UNITED STATES

PUERTO RICO

Ponce
Arteaga, Agustín *museum director, architect*

ADDRESS UNPUBLISHED

Becker, Gail Roselyn *museum director*
Bishop, Budd Harris *retired museum director*
Bolas, Gerald Douglas *museum director, art historian, educator*
Booker, Nana Laurel *art gallery owner, honorary consul*
Elson, James Martin *retired landmark director*
Furlong, George Morgan, Jr. *museum program director, retired military officer*
Montrose-Graem, Douglass *museum director, poet, painter, music maker*
Newman, Bruce Murray *retired antiques gallery owner, designer author*
Perrot, Paul Norman *museum director*
Rifkin, Ned *former museum director*
Schlageter, Robert William *museum administrator*
Way, Jacob Edson III *museum director*

INDUSTRY: MANUFACTURING
See also **FINANCE: FINANCIAL SERVICES**

UNITED STATES

ALABAMA

Albertville
Ainsworth, William P. *manufacturing executive*

Bessemer
Henriques, George L. *medical products executive, information technology executive*

Birmingham
Breitfeld, Philip Paul *pharmaceutical executive, oncologist*
Deavenport, Earnest W., Jr. *retired chemicals executive*
Gorrie, M. Miller *construction executive*
James, Donald M. *construction materials executive*
McMahon, John J., Jr. *manufacturing executive, lawyer*
Styslinger, Lee Joseph, Jr. *manufacturing executive*
Wason, Robert A., IV, *building products manufacturing executive*

Huntsville
Geveden, Rex D. *aerospace and defense manufacturing company executive*

Opelika
Jenkins, Richard Lee *manufacturing executive*

Phenix City
Murray, James J. *textiles executive*

ARKANSAS

Fort Smith
Breaux, Randall P. *manufacturing executive*
Bullock, Roger V. *motor and generator manufacturing company executive*
Cinquemani, Michael A. *motor and generator manufacturing company executive*
Johnston, Larry L., Jr. *motor and generator manufacturing company executive*
Long, Tracy L. *manufacturing executive*
Shackelford, Mark L. *motor and generator manufacturing company executive*

Springdale
Baker, Mike *food products executive*
Huett, Greg *food products executive*
Lochner, James Victor (Jim Lochner) *food products executive*
Quillin, Sue *food products executive*
Rose, Kenneth L. *food products executive*
Smith, Donnie *food products executive*
Tyson, John H. *food products executive*
Van Bebber, David L. *food products executive, lawyer*

CALIFORNIA

Pasadena
McDuffie, Harvey Thomas, Jr. *construction executive*

San Francisco
Castagna, Vanessa J. *apparel executive*

Sunnyvale
Seifert, Thomas J. *electronics company executive*

FLORIDA

Amelia Island
Adelman, Robert Paul *retired construction executive, lawyer*

Boca Grande
Huml, Donald Scott *manufacturing executive*

Boynton Beach
Goldenberg, George *retired pharmaceutical executive*
Whitworth, Hall Baker *forest products company executive*

Bradenton
Barnebey, Kenneth Alan *food products executive*
Carnes, James Edward *retired electronics executive*

Cape Coral
Stuart, Robert *container manufacturing executive*

Clearwater
Ardelt, Maximilian *electronics executive*
Byrnes, John P. *medical products executive*
Malpocher, Raymond V. *manufacturing executive*

Coconut Grove
Lewis, William Headley, Jr. *manufacturing executive*

Coral Gables
Mas, José Ramon *construction executive*

Deerfield Beach
Brown, Colin *automotive executive*
Heathcott, Forrest *automotive executive*
Norelid, Jan A. *construction materials company executive*

Deland
McNulty, Carrell Stewart, Jr. *retired manufacturing executive, architect*

Delray Beach
Himmelright, Robert John, Jr. *rubber company executive*
Marlowe, Edward *retired pharmaceutical executive*

Fort Lauderdale
Capper, Joseph H. *medical products executive*
Dawes, Alan S. *automotive company executive*
Gonçalves, C. Lourenço *metal products executive*
Gray, Hugh M. *metal products executive*
Henneke, Dan *metal products executive*
Jackson, Michael J. *automotive retail company executive*
Koci, Keith *metal products executive*
Krohn, Roger, Jr. *metal products executive*
Marshall, Mickey *metal products executive*
Martens, David A. *metal products executive*
McPherson, Robert C. III *metal products executive*
Short, Michael J. *automotive executive*

Fort Myers
Alexander, John David *food products executive*
Dyer, David F. *apparel company executive*
Edmonds, Scott A. *apparel executive*
Knous, Pamela K. *apparel executive, former food service company executive*
Wendeborn, Richard Donald *retired manufacturing executive*

Highland Beach
Featherman, Bernard *steel company executive*
Frager, Albert S. *retired food products executive*

Hollywood
Spencer, Richard Thomas III *health products executive*

Holmes Beach
Kaiser, Albert Farr *manufacturing executive*

Homestead
Willner, Eugene Burton *food and liquor company executive*

Indian Harbor Beach
Buchanan, Richard Kent *retired electronics company executive*

Islamorada
Gates, Richard Daniel *retired manufacturing executive*

Jacksonville
Halverson, Steven Thomas *construction executive, lawyer*
Nussbaum, Bennett L. *food products executive*

Jupiter
Feinberg, Herbert *wine company executive*

Lady Lake
Akins, Zane Vernon *agricultural products executive*

Lakeland
Douglas, Laurie Zeitlin *food products executive, information technology executive*
Mutz, Oscar Ulysses *manufacturing and distribution executive*

Melbourne
Dattilo, Thomas A. *retired manufacturing executive*
Pearson, Daniel R. *electronics executive*

Merritt Island
Roub, Bryan R(oger) *electronics executive*

Miami
Becker, Steven Richard *beverage corporation executive*
Beckwitt, Richard *construction executive*
Bessette, Diane J. *construction executive*
Bolotin, Irving *retired construction executive, board member*
Braman, Norman *automotive and former sports team executive*
Clark, Kevin D. *medical products executive*
Frost, Phillip *pharmaceutical executive, dermatologist*
Gorman, Michael Stephen *construction executive*
Gross, Bruce E. *construction executive*
Haddad, Emile *construction executive*
Hogan, Mark T. *automotive executive*
Jaffe, Jonathan M. *construction executive*
Kaiserman, David J. *construction executive*
Landon, Robert Kirkwood *construction executive*
Lapidus, Sidney *construction executive, lawyer*
Mendelson, Laurans Adam *manufacturing executive*
Miller, Stuart A. *construction executive*
Nahmad, Albert H. *manufacturing executive*
Preston, John R. *beverage products executive*
Rice, Thomas P. *health products executive*
Robins, Craig *construction executive*
Roos, Jeff *construction executive*
Sonnenfeld, Jeffrey Alan *construction executive*
Sparks, Sam *construction executive, lawyer*
Zubieta, Alberto Aleman *construction executive*

Miramar
Dreimann, Leonhard *manufacturing executive*

Mulberry
Badcock, Wogan Stanhope, Jr. *manufacturing executive*

Naples
Gade, Marvin Francis *retired paper company executive*
LaRusso, Anthony Carl *company executive, lecturer, consultant*
Manetta, Richard L. *chemicals executive, lawyer*
Romans, Donald Bishop *retired manufacturing executive*
Salentine, Thomas James *pharmaceutical executive*
Swanson, Donald Frederick *retired food company executive*
von Arx, Dolph William *food products executive*

North Palm Beach
Nicklaus, Jack William *sports apparel executive, retired professional golfer*
Warren, Roy G. *non-alcoholic manufacturing company executive*

Orlando
Adams, Kenneth Francis *automotive executive*
Brownlee, Thomas Marshall *manufacturing executive*
Chin-Lor, Daisy *cosmetics executive*
Grum, Clifford J. *retired manufacturing executive, board member*
Halversen, David T. *plastics company executive*
Keane, Peter J. *construction executive*

Palm Beach
Karman, James Anthony *retired manufacturing executive*
Pearlman, Jerry Kent *electronics company executive*

Palm Beach Gardens
Jaffe, Jeff Hugh *retired food products executive*
Staub, W. Arthur *health care products executive*

Pompano Beach
Akdag, Menderes *manufacturing executive*
Richardson, Emilie White *manufacturing, investment company executive, educator*

Saint Augustine
McKinney, James Clayton *electronics executive, electrical engineer*

Saint Petersburg
Alexander, Forbes I.J. *electronics executive*

Main, Timothy L. *electronics company executive*
Mills, William Harold, Jr. *construction executive*
Mondello, Mark T. *electronics executive*
Morean, William D. *manufacturing executive*

Sanford
Davis, Darrell L. *retired automotive executive*

Sarasota
Daoust, Donald Roger *pharmaceutical executive, microbiologist, cosmetics executive*
Jellison, Brian D. *manufacturing executive*
Miranda, Carlos Sa *food products company executive*
Mullane, John Francis *pharmaceutical executive*
Venit, William Bennett *electrical products company executive, consultant*
Wadsworth, Dyer Seymour *minerals executive*
West, Bob *pharmaceutical executive*
Winfrey, Timothy J. *manufacturing executive*

Tampa
Berg, Charles G. *health products executive, lawyer*
Cunningham, Alec R. *health products executive*
Flom, Edward Leonard *retired metal products executive*
Tran, Thomas L. *health products executive*

Terra Ceia
Gross, Paul Allan *health products executive*

The Villages
Graham, David Bolden *food products executive*

Vanderbilt Beach
Gadsby, Robin Edward *chemicals executive*

Vero Beach
Bright, Willard Mead *retired manufacturing executive, director*
Cameron, Nicholas Allen *manufacturing executive*
Janicki, Robert Stephen *retired pharmaceutical executive*
Reed, Sherman Kennedy *chemicals executive, consultant*
Wilcox, Harry Wilbur, Jr. *retired manufacturing executive*

Village Of Golf
Boer, F. Peter *chemical company executive*

Wellington
Baughan, Michael B. *aerospace product and parts manufacturing executive*
Khoury, Amin J. *aerospace product and parts manufacturing executive*
Landry, RJ *aerospace product and parts manufacturing executive*
Lieberherr, Werner *aerospace product and parts manufacturing executive*
Marchetti, Robert A. *aerospace product and parts manufacturing executive*
Schofield, Jonathan M. *aircraft manufacturing company executive*

Wesley Chapel
Revelle, Donald Gene *manufacturing and health care company executive, consultant*

West Palm Beach
Brown, Paul A. *medical services executive*
Fanjul, Alfie, Jr., (Alfonso Fanjul) *food products executive*
Furlaud, Richard Mortimer *pharmaceutical executive*
Jenkins, Ruben Lee *chemicals executive*
Lanzkron, Rolf Wolfgang *manufacturing executive*

GEORGIA

Alpharetta
Brands, James Edwin *retired medical products executive*
Souerwine, David A. *healthcare company executive*
Thompson, Peter J. *manufacturing executive*

Atlanta
Abate, Victor R. (Vic Abate) *manufacturing company executive*
Blakely, Sara *apparel executive*
Blount, Ben B., Jr. *administration and finance executive*
Bommier, Bernard *beverage company executive*
Boone, Merrill *healthcare management executive*
Borman, J. Richard *automotive executive*
Bozer, Ahmet C. *beverage company executive*
Brock, John F. *beverage company executive*
Brown, Treg S. *automotive executive*
Carrico, Paul D. *chemical company executive*
Cathy, S. Truett *food products executive*
Corr, James Vanis *furniture manufacturing executive, accountant*
Cummings, Alexander B., Jr. *food products executive*
de Cespedes, Jorge L. *pharmaceutical executive*
Douglas, Sandy (J. Alexander M. Douglas) *beverage company executive*
Douglas, William W. *food products executive*
Downey, Laurence *retired pharmaceutical executive*
Ergas, Jean-Pierre Maurice *packaging company executive*
Finan , Irial *beverage company executive*
Fitzgerald, Lisa A. *apparel executive*
Francis, Julie *beverage company executive*
Franklin, Shirley Clarke *community development firm executive, former mayor*
Fratto, Fred J. *construction executive*
Fritsch, Eric G. *automotive executive*
Furlow, Michael H. *construction company executive*
Gallagher, Thomas C. *diversified manufacturing executive*
Gibbons, Brendan M. *apparel executive*
Govaerts, Frank *beverage company executive, lawyer*
Grucza, Dan *manufacturing executive*
Hendrix, Daniel T. *textile manufacturing company executive*
Hoza, Jeffrey S. *construction executive*
Isdell, Neville (Edward Neville Isdell) *retired beverage company executive*
James, Kathi *construction executive*
Justice, Rocklen R. *automotive executive*
Kambury, Stuart A. *automotive executive*
Kent, Muhtar *beverage company executive*
Kimmet, Pamela O. *beverage company executive*
Lanier, John Hicks *apparel company executive*
Liebmann, Seymour W. *construction executive, consultant*
Lischer, Charles D. *beverage company executive*
Marks, Terrance M. (Terry Marks) *food products executive*
McMurtrie, M. Todd *automotive executive*
Merrill, Allan P. *construction executive*
Mildenhall, Jonathan *beverage company executive*
Molinas, Galya Frayman *soft drinks manufacturing company executive*
Morgan, John K. *chemicals executive*
Nagel, Vernon J. *chemicals and electronics executive*
Nix, Jerry W. *automotive executive*
North, Julia B. *manufacturing executive*
Parker, John R., Jr. *food products executive, lawyer*
Patricot, Hubert *beverage company executive*
Patterson, Suzanne D. *food products executive, accountant*
Pensec, John *manufacturing executive*
Reiniche, Dominique *food products executive*
Rogowski, Gregory S. *manufacturing executive*
Salomon, Robert L. *homebuilding company executive, accountant*
Satrum, Jerry R. *chemicals company executive*
Seal, Mark J. *manufacturing executive*
Simonelli, Lorenzo *diversified technology and services company executive*
Tennyson, Fionnuala *food products executive*
Tierney, Cindy B. *construction executive*
Tripodi, Joseph V. *beverage company executive*
Tuggle, Clyde Cebron *beverage company executive*
Vucinic, Zoran A. *soft drink manufacturing executive*
Waller, Kathy Nadine *beverage company executive*
Warner, M. Richard *paper and forest products company executive*
Whetzel, Charles E., Jr. *apparel executive*

Augusta
DiRico, Tony *aggregate and chemical products company executive*

Bainbridge
Poitevint, Alec Loyd, II, *mineral company executive, political organization administrator*

Buford
Jacobs, M. Christine (M. Christine Jacobs) *medical products company executive*

Calhoun
Boykin, Frank H. *textiles executive*
Lorberbaum, Jeffrey S. *textiles executive*
Lucke, James T. *textiles executive*
Swift, John D. *manufacturing executive*

Carrollton
Murrah, Charlie *manufacturing executive*
Richards, Roy, Jr. *wire and cable manufacturing company executive*

Columbus
Yarbrough, Rebecca K. *electronics executive*

Dalton
Swanson, Larry *manufacturing executive*

Duluth
Beck, Andrew H. *farm equipment manufacturing executive*
Belle, Gerald *pharmaceutical executive*
Brody, Aaron Leo *food and packaging consultant*
Collar, Gary L. *industrial manufacturing executive*
Dorsman, Peter A. *self service technologies company executive*
Lukacs, Frank C. *manufacturing executive*
Mauldin, Jean Ann *pharmaceutical executive*
Richenhagen, Martin H. *manufacturing executive*
Wooley, Jeffrey I. *automotive executive*

Kennesaw
Anderson, Steven Goodwin *medical products executive*

Macon
McFarland, Terry Lynn *retired construction company executive*

Marietta
Blount, Daniel J. *lumber company executive*
Scheible, David W. *paper company executive*

Milton
Bregman, Mitchell S. *manufacturing executive*
Dette, Franz Josef *electrical industry company executive*
Reilly, John Paul *manufacturing executive*
Wetzel, Carroll Robbins, Jr. *manufacturing executive*

Monroe
Felker, G(eorge) Stephen *textile company executive*

Norcross
Currey, Russell M. *packaging company executive*
Holland, Paul V. *medical products executive*
Rubright, James Alfred *manufacturing executive*
Voorhees, Steven C. *packaging manufacturing executive*

Peachtree City
Leader, Christopher Robert *manufacturing executive*

Roswell
Gottung, Lizanne C. *health products executive*
McAlpin, Teri *electronics executive*
Moreau, Jay Michael *manufacturing executive*

Savannah
Cartledge, Raymond Eugene *retired paper company executive*

Sea Island
Mc Swiney, James Wilmer *retired pulp and paper manufacturing company executive*

Thomasville
Deese, George E. *food products company executive*
Turner, Marta Jones *food products executive*

Woodstock
Hudson, Roy Davage *retired pharmaceutical executive*

ILLINOIS

Chicago
Flynn, Donald F. *automotive executive*

Highland Park
Rudo, Milton *retired manufacturing executive*

Lake Forest
McCoy, Dustan Elwood *manufacturing executive, lawyer*

INDIANA

Carmel
Wright, Doreen A. *retired food products executive*

Columbus
Ware, Carl *bottling company executive*

South Bend
Kern, Paul John *manufacturing executive, retired military officer*

KENTUCKY

Bellevue
Carpenter, Woodrow Wilson *retired manufacturing executive, ceramics engineer*

Bowling Green
Holland, John Ben *clothing manufacturing company executive*

Covington
Chambers, Lamar M. *chemical company executive*
O'Brien, James J. *manufacturing executive*
Stamps, Jeffrey M. *pharmaceutical executive*

Erlanger
Agata, Tetsuo *automotive executive*
Niimi, Atsushi *automotive executive*

Highland Heights
Kenny, Gregory B. *industrial equipment executive*
Sandoval, Mathias F. *electronics executive*

Lexington
Foresti, Ronaldo M. *electronics executive*
Holland, Robert, Jr. *retired food products executive*
Rooke, Paul A. *electronics executive*

Louisville
Aguera, Ralph D. *beverage company executive*
Berg, Donald Crowley *beverage company executive*
Blankenship, Charles P., Jr., (Chip Blankenship) *diversified technology and services company executive*
Brown, Geo. Garvin, IV, *food products executive*
Diaz, Paul J. *health products executive*
Eaton, Roger *food products executive*
Farrer, Marshall B. *wine and spirits company executive*
Geisler, James E. *manufacturing executive*
Gronefeld, Ralph G., Jr. *healthcare services executive*
Heiden, Charles Kenneth *metal products executive, consultant, retired military officer*
Keyes, Michael J. *food products executive*
Lynch, Philip J. *beverages manufacturing company executive*
Mac Mahon, Thomas P. *pharmaceutical executive*
Shield, Gene *health products executive*
Sirchio, John Kristin *food products executive*
Strange, Roy *agricultural cooperative executive*
Street, William May *retired beverage company executive*
Stubbs, Dace Brown *beverage manufacturing company executive*
Varga, Paul C. *beverage products executive*
Weishar, Gregory S. *pharmaceutical executive*
Welch, James S., Jr. *food products executive*

LOUISIANA

Baton Rouge
Calabrese, Michael Raphael *manufacturing executive, lawyer, consultant*
Daniel, Nicole C. *chemicals executive*
Fishman, Richard G. *chemicals executive, lawyer*
Gottwald, William M. *chemicals executive*
Stewart, Charles E. *chemicals executive*

Lafayette
Mallet, Alexis, Jr. *construction company executive*

New Orleans
Cospolich, James Donald *electrical electronics executive, consultant*

MARYLAND

Nottingham
Harman, John R. *construction executive*

MASSACHUSETTS

Mashpee
Wasiele, Harry W., Jr. *diversified electrical manufacturing company executive*

Wellesley
Gailius, Gilbert Keistutis *manufacturing executive*

MICHIGAN

Grand Rapids
Baker, Hollis MacLure *furniture manufacturing company executive*

Rochester Hills
Akeel, Hadi Abu *robotics executive*

MISSISSIPPI

Hattiesburg
Chain, Bobby Lee *electrical contractor, former mayor*

Laurel
Mooney, Dianne *food products executive*
Sanderson, Joe F., Jr. *food products executive*
Taylor, Rowan H. *food products executive*

MISSOURI

Kansas City
Bass, Lee Marshall *food products company executive*

Saint Louis
Bain, Lorne Donald *electronics executive*
Bender, Jane *furniture manufacturing company executive*

NEW JERSEY

Franklin Lakes
Durack, David Tulloch *medical products executive*

New Brunswick
Larsen, Ralph S(tanley) *retired pharmaceutical executive*

Princeton
Costley, Gary Edward *chemicals executive*

Whitehouse Station
Gerberding, Julie Louise *pharmaceutical company executive, former federal agency administrator*

NEW YORK

New York
Georgescu, Peter Andrew *manufacturing executive*
Monaghan, Craig Thomas *automotive executive*
Nie, Zenon Stanley *manufacturing executive*
Potamkin, Alan *automotive company executive*

NORTH CAROLINA

Arden
Stackhouse, David William, Jr. *retired furniture systems installation contractor*

Asheboro
Stedman, W. David *textile manufacturing company executive*

Belmont
O'Keefe, Patrick Shaw *retired manufacturing executive*
Stowe, Robert Lee III *textile company executive*

Burlington
Bonello, William B. *medical products executive*
Flagg, Raymond Osbourn *retired medical products executive*
Lindblom, Eric *medical products executive*
Walton, Andrew Scott *medical products executive*

Cary
Collard, Craig A. *pharmaceutical executive*

Charlotte
Barbalas, Michael *manufacturing executive*
Bottle, Lisa *aerospace and defense parts manufacturing company executive*
Brown, Edward J III *automotive executive*
Browning, Peter Crane *manufacturing executive*
Carmola, John J. *aerospace and defense parts manufacturing company executive*
DiMicco, Daniel R. *manufacturing executive*
Doolan, Victor H. *retired automotive executive, board member*
Everett, Malcolm E. III *medical products executive, retired bank executive*
Ferriola, John J. *manufacturing executive*
Fisher, Robert W. *retired food products executive*
Growcock, Terry D. *manufacturing executive*
Hagen, Veronica M. *textile manufacturing company executive*
Kearney, Christopher J. *manufacturing executive, lawyer*
Kleiderer, Karl *aerospace and defense parts manufacturing company executive*
Kocher, Brian W. *food products executive*
Kuechle, Scott E. *manufacturing executive*
Larsen, Marshall O. *manufacturing executive*
Lea, Scott Carter *retired packaging company executive*
Lisenby, Terry S. *manufacturing executive*

Loeb, Michel *food products executive*
Lott, Hamilton, Jr. *manufacturing executive*
Mepham, Tom *aerospace and defense manufacturing company executive*
Morgan, James H. *food services company executive, former investment company executive*
Nelson, Thomas C. *manufacturing executive*
O'Leary, Patrick J. *manufacturing executive*
Reusser, Curtis C. *aerospace and defense manufacturing company executive*
Roberts, David A. *manufacturing executive*
Rodriguez, Manuel, Jr. *food products executive, lawyer*
Rutkowski, Joseph A. *manufacturing executive*
Siegel, Samuel *metals company executive*
Singer, David Vincent *food products executive*
Smith, B. Scott *automotive executive*
Smith, O. Bruton *automotive company executive*
Spangler, Clemmie Dixon, Jr. *construction company executive*
Stephen, Craig A., Jr. *food products executive*
Viviani, Tanios E. *food products executive*
Witowski, Gerald T. *aerospace and defense manufacturing company executive*

Denver
Stewart, John Richard *manufacturing company executive*

Durham
Gillings, Dennis B. *medical products executive*
Ingram, Robert Alexander *pharmaceutical executive*
Sharma, Anand *manufacturing executive*
Verst, Cynthia L. *pharmaceutical executive*

Greensboro
Bruce, Steve *construction executive*
Moree, F. Scott *apparel executive*
Scabbia Guerrini, Martino *apparel executive*
Wiseman, Eric C. *apparel executive*

Hertford
Johnson, Donald Lee *retired agricultural materials company executive, bio-process and product consultant*

Hickory
Cato, Carson *manufacturing executive*
Hutton, George N., Jr. *wire and cable manufacturing company executive*
Manka, Roger *wire and cable manufacturing company executive*

High Point
Fenn, Ormon William, Jr. *furniture company executive*

Huntersville
Berry, William E. *automotive executive*

Madison
Nardelli, Robert Louis *firearms and ammunition manufacturing company executive*

Matthews
Dickson, Thomas Walter *supermarket chain executive*
Woodlief, John B. *supermarket chain executive*

Morganton
Acks, Judy *furniture manufacturing company executive*

Morrisville
Cox, Carrie S. *pharmaceutical executive*

Mount Airy
Woltz, Howard Osler III *metal products executive*

Raleigh
D'Appolonia, Michael R. *construction executive*
Dixit, Ajit Suresh *chemicals executive, research scientist*
Franco, Richard Anthony, Sr. *pharmaceutical company executive, pharmacist*
Guzzo, Dana F. *construction executive*
Hardy, R. Dean *construction executive*
Johnson, Mark *construction executive*
Maffucci, David G. *manufacturing executive*
McCook, Richard Paul *automotive parts manufacturing executive, grocery chain financial executive*
McNulty, James A. *pharmaceutical executive*
Nye, C. Howard (Ward) *construction executive, lawyer*
Shea, John J. *pharmaceutical executive*
Shepard, Robert C. *pharmaceutical executive*
Shephard, Daniel G. *construction executive*
Sloan, O. Temple, Jr., (Orris Temple Sloan Jr.) *automotive executive*
Stewart, Jonathan T. *construction executive*
Vaio, Bruce A. *construction executive*

Research Triangle Park
Holden, E. Wayne *research and development company executive, psychologist*

Rural Hall
Wager, Michael *manufacturing executive*

Trinity
Norris, Paul J. *retired manufacturing executive*

Warsaw
Godwin, Jerry H. *food products executive*

Weldon
Barringer, Paul Brandon, II, *lumber company executive*

Wilmington
Orlowsky, Martin L. *tobacco company executive*
Randall, Richard D. *medical products executive*

Winston Salem
Adams, Thomas R. *tobacco company executive*
Chaden, Lee A. *apparel and former food products executive*
Chambers, Dwayne *food products executive, marketing professional*
Delen, Daniel M. (Daan Delen) *tobacco company executive*
Gentry, Jeffery S. *tobacco company executive*
Hall, Kevin D. *apparel company executive*
Maselli, John Anthony *food products executive*
Noll, Richard A. *apparel executive*

OHIO

Canton
Stipanovich, Chuck *metal products executive*

Cleveland
Walls, George Hilton, Jr. *manufacturing executive*

OKLAHOMA

Oklahoma City
Jones, Gene Paul *food products executive*
Lopez, John C. *meat processing company executive*

Pryor
Snyder, Robert Alan *paper company executive*

Tulsa
Capo, Thomas P. *automotive executive*
Rooney, Francis (Laurence Francis Rooney III) *construction executive, former ambassador*
Thomas, Robert Eggleston *retired manufacturing executive*
Thompson, Scott L. *automotive executive*

OREGON

Portland
Pamplin, Robert Boisseau, Jr. *manufacturing company executive, minister, writer*

PENNSYLVANIA

Bethlehem
St. John, Anthony Paul *retired manufacturing executive*

York
Miles, John Carlen, II, *dental company executive*

RHODE ISLAND

Cranston
Papitto, Ralph Raymond *manufacturing executive*

SOUTH CAROLINA

Charleston
Torras, Joseph Hill *pulp and paper company executive*

Clemson
Petzel, Florence Eloise *textiles educator*

Clinton
Cornelson, George Henry, IV, *retired textile company executive*

Columbia
Duggan, Carol Cook *research and development company executive*

Hartsville
Bowen, Jimmie Carl *manufacturing executive*
Harrell, James A. III *manufacturing executive*

Hilton Head Island
Cunningham, William Henry *retired food products executive*
Lewis, Gene Evans *retired medical equipment company executive*
Rulis, Raymond Joseph *manufacturing executive, consultant*
Russell, Allen Stevenson *retired metal products executive*

Kiawah Island
Korb, William Brown, Jr. *retired manufacturing executive*

Myrtle Beach
Gilbertson, John S. *manufacturing executive*

North Charleston
Zucker, Anita *plastics company executive*

Prosperity
Leath, Charles Alexander, Jr. *construction company executive*

Sumter
Craib, Kenneth Bryden *research and development company executive, physicist, economist*

Trenton
Collinson, Judy *apparel executive*

TENNESSEE

Arlington
Silverman, Stanley Wayne *chemical company executive*

Bartlett
Huffman, Delton Cleon, Jr. *pharmacy association executive*

Brentwood
Jackson, Lawrence V. *manufacturing executive, former retail executive*
Wright, James F. *agricultural products executive*

Bristol
Andrzejewski, Stephen Joseph *pharmaceutical executive*
Rtbeillt, Jean-claude *pharmaceutical executive*

Chattanooga
Street, Gordon P., Jr. *iron foundry executive*

Collegedale
McKee, Ellsworth R. *food products executive*

Franklin
Bailo, Carla *automotive executive*
Carolin, Brian *automotive executive*
Diaz, Fred M., Jr. *automotive executive*
Goodspeed, Linda A. *automotive executive*
Hirsch, Steven Neal *pharmaceutical executive*
Lankford, Monty J. *medical products executive*
Moake, James *healthcare company executive*

Greeneville
Renner, Glenn Delmar *retired agricultural products executive*

Hendersonville
David, Phillip J. *biotechnology company executive*

Kingsport
Espeland, Curtis E. *chemicals executive*
Findley, Don Aaron *manufacturing executive*
Rogers, James P. *chemicals executive*
Rutstrom, Dante Joseph *chemicals executive*

Knoxville
Goltry, Thom *medical products executive*
Staley, John R., Jr. *health products executive*

La Vergne
Helmkamp, Katrina L. *manufacturing executive*

Memphis
Christopher, Gregory L. *metal products executive*
DiCianni, Joe *electronics executive*
Isakson, Michael M. *furniture manufacturing company executive*
Laschinger, Mary A. *paper company executive*
Locke, Stanley P. *electronics executive*
Morris, Herman, Jr. *pharmaceutical executive, lawyer*
Nicholls, Tim S. *paper company executive*
Pileggi, Dominic J. *electronics executive*
Rhodes, William C. III *automotive executive*
Roberts, Carol *paper company executive*
Stockdale, Bryan K. *tobacco manufacturing company executive*
Stout, John T. *milling company executive*
Sutton, Mark S. *paper company executive*
Treadway, Charles L. *electronics executive*

Morristown
Comer, Evan Philip *manufacturing executive*

Nashville
Bailey, Sallie Ballantine *construction materials company executive*
Cook, E. Gary *manufacturing executive*
Fitzgerald, Edmund Bacon *electronics executive*
Frost, Richard W. (Rick Frost) *manufacturing executive*
Hanshaw, John *health products executive*
Harris, J(acob) George *health products executive*
Hass, Joseph Monroe *automotive executive*
Nishiyama, Asahiko *tire manufacturing company executive*
Shallcross, Richard *medical products executive*
Stevens, Curtis *construction materials company executive*

Oak Ridge
Poutsma, Marvin L. *retired chemical research administrator*

Springfield
Slater, Gary *automotive executive*

Tullahoma
Jackson, William David *research and development company executive*

TEXAS

Addison
Keener, Larry H. *construction executive*
Meyer, Frederick Ray *retired manufacturing executive, board member*
Wellborn, W. Christopher *construction executive*

Angleton
Delly, Gayla J. *electronics executive*
Fu, Cary T. *electronics executive*
Nigbor, Donald E. *electronics executive*

Austin
Beyer, Richard Michael *manufacturing executive*
Derrickson, William Borden *manufacturing executive*
Divljakovic, Vojislav *manufacturing executive*
Flanagan, Glenda Jane (Glenda Jane Chamberlain) *food products executive*
Gallo, A.C. *food products executive*
Lang, Roberta Lynn *food products company executive, lawyer*
Mackey, John P. *food products executive*
Read, Rory Patrick *electronics company executive*
Simons, Doyle R. *lumber company executive, lawyer*
Sullivan, Jerry Stephen *electronics executive*
Sunahara, Yukio *electronics executive*
Thornton, Joseph Scott *research and development company executive, materials scientist*

Bryan
Deatherage, James *agricultural products executive*
Lusas, Edmund William *food processing research executive*

Carrollton
Hansen, Thomas C. *footwear manufacturing company executive*

Carthage
Cooke, Walta Pippen *automobile dealership owner*

Coppell
Edmonds, Ian Colin *electronics executive*
Tan, William W. *electronics executive*

Dallas
Albright, Michael *construction executive*
Bradford, William Edward *manufacturing executive*
Brekhus, Melvin G. *construction executive*
Carosella, Debra B. *food products executive*
D'Aloia, G(iambattista) Peter *manufacturing executive*
Delagi, Greg *electronics executive*
Eller, Timothy R. *construction and real estate company executive*
Engles, Gregg L. *food products executive*
Falk, Thomas J. *health products executive*
Fugger, Edward F., Jr. *food products executive*
Gafford, Ronald J. *construction executive*
Gaglardi, R. Thomas *beverage company and hotel executive, professional sports team executive*
Hames, Michael J. *electronics executive*
Heacock, David *electronics executive*
Jastrow, Kenneth M. *forest products, real estate and financial company executive*
Jenkins, Michael Austin *corporate executive*
Kading, Kelly *food products executive*
Kazor, Lisa *apparel executive*
Kroeker, Harrald F. *food products executive*
Lovett, Melendy Ewing *electronics executive*
Lowe, Gregg A. *electronics executive*
Madden, Douglas M. *chemicals executive*
Mara, Shaun *food products executive*
March, Kevin P. *electronics executive*
McCrummen, Ronald L. *food products executive*
Muckley, Ronald *aerospace and defense manufacturing company executive*
Murphy, John Joseph *manufacturing executive*
Palmer, Anthony J. *health products executive*
Quinn, David W. *building company executive*
Reeder, Ginger *apparel executive*
Ritchie, Kevin *electronics executive*
Roach, John D. *building products company executive*
Rosson, Glenn Richard *building products and furniture company executive*
Schwarz, Michael L. *aircraft manufacturing company executive*
Sherman, Floyd F. *construction executive*
Sliva, Chris *food products executive*
Smith, Barbara R. *metal products executive*
Sterin, Steven M. *chemicals executive*
Stewart, Robert S. *construction executive*
Templeton, Richard K. *electronics executive*
Tucker, J. Walter, Jr. *manufacturing executive*
Wallace, Timothy R. *manufacturing executive*
Watson, Steven L. *chemicals executive*
Weiland, Jessica *apparel executive*
West, Teresa (Terri) L. (Terri West) *electronics executive*
Whitaker, Darla *electronics executive*

Denton
Winterhalter, Gary G. *cosmetics executive*

Fort Worth
Dingus, David H. *manufacturing executive*
Dwyer, Stacey H. *construction executive*
Horton, Donald R. *construction executive*
Mc Keen, Chester M., Jr. *retired manufacturing executive*
Morrow, Joseph J. *metal products executive*
Rayment, Cary *retired pharmaceutical executive*
Tomnitz, Donald J. *construction executive*
Wheat, Bill W. *construction executive*

Georgetown
Gerding, Thomas Graham *medical products executive*

Granbury
Adams, Christopher Steve, Jr. *retired electronics executive, military officer*

Hempstead
Propst, Catherine Lamb *biotechnology and pharmaceutical company executive*

Houston
Blakely, Robert T. *chemicals executive*
Brumley, Elizabeth D. *construction company executive, accountant*
Cambre, Ronald C. *construction executive*
Carroll, Chuck (Charles A. Carroll) *manufacturing executive*
Carter, Susan K. *construction executive*
Chambers, Norman C. *construction executive*
Chao, Albert *chemicals executive*
Chao, James *chemicals executive*
David, George Alfred Lawrence *retired manufacturing executive, board member*
Delaney, William J. III *food products executive*
Ducey, Michael E. *chemicals executive*
Ewert, Douglas S. *apparel executive*
Friedkin, Thomas H. *automotive executive*
Giadrossi, Nicoletta *manufacturing company executive*
Helland, George Archibald, Jr. *manufacturing executive, federal official*
Hesterberg, Earl J. *automotive executive*
Hynes, Thomas N. (Toby) *automotive company executive*
Jenkins, Dorothy C. *chemicals executive*
Malecky, Robert A. *manufacturing executive*
McDonald, Patrick L. *electronics executive*

Menscher, Barnet Gary *steel company executive*
Moore, Daniel J. *health products executive*
Munisteri, Joseph George *construction executive*
Nichols, Michael Cooper *food products executive, lawyer*
Nishi, Masao *supply chain executive*
Planck, Robert Dempsey *food company executive*
Poccia, Claudia *cosmetics company executive*
Pulliam, Larry G. *food products executive*
Rickel, John C. *automotive executive*
Riedel, Alan Ellis *manufacturing executive, lawyer*
Riley, Harold John, Jr. *chemicals executive*
Rossi, Christopher *manufacturing executive*
Roth, Philip R. *manufacturing executive*
Sorrentino, Charles Alan *manufacturing executive*
Swift, David L. *manufacturing executive*
Urban, Jim *metal products executive*
Utt, William P. (Bill Utt) *construction executive*
Volpe, Vincent R., Jr. *manufacturing executive*

Irving
Abernathy, Robert E. *health products executive*
Alvarado, Joseph *metal products executive*
Blinn, Mark A. *manufacturing executive*
Braverman, Yuval *stone manufacturing company executive*
De Bedout, Juan Ernesto *paper company executive*
Gajdos, Ludovit *metal products executive*
Henry, Mitch *health products executive*
Kafoure, Michael D. *food products executive*
Kresa, Kent *retired manufacturing executive*
Massaro, Anthony A. *retired metal products executive*
McKeown, Mick *aerospace and defense manufacturing executive*
Orzel, Dennis J. *aerospace and defense parts manufacturing company executive*
Rampacek, Charles M. *manufacturing executive*
Rohr, Mark C. *chemicals executive*
Romero, Joyce E. *aerospace and defense manufacturing company executive*
Sarkis, Elias *aerospace and defense parts manufacturing company executive*
Spencer, Jan B. *health products executive*

Lewisville
Jones, Tom *construction executive*

Mauriceville
Ware, John David *retired valve and hydrant company executive*

Mc Kinney
Milinazzo, Alan W. *medical products executive*

Pittsburg
Pilgrim, Lonnie (Bo Pilgrim) *food products executive*

Plano
Blum, Kristen E. *apparel executive*
Carey, Albert P. *food products executive*
Naor, Daniel *food products executive*
Young, Larry D. *beverage company executive*

Richardson
Bedapudi, Prakash *manufacturing executive*
Bizios, Harry J. *electronics executive*
Bluedorn, Todd M. *manufacturing executive*
Henry, Charles L. *manufacturing executive*
Holmen, Orrie Jeffrey *electronics company executive*
Norris, John W. *manufacturing executive*
Rumbough, Roy Albert, Jr. *manufacturing executive*
Thompson, Richard L. *retired manufacturing executive*

Rockwall
Rosenberg, Steven P. *food products executive*

San Antonio
Cisneros, Henry Gabriel *construction executive, former United States Secretary of Housing and Urban Development*
Dollens, Ronald W. *medical products executive*
Kotecki, Kevin *beer company executive*
McCombs, Billy Joe (Red McCombs) *automotive executive, former professional sports team executive*
McGuire, William Dennis *healthcare consultant, corporate director*
Roberts, Larry J. *construction executive*
Simpson, David John *medical products executive*
Smith, C. Thomas, Jr. *medical products executive*
Zachry, Henry Bartell, Jr. *construction executive*

Seguin
Robinson, Ronald Alan *manufacturing executive*

Southlake
Guerin, Dean Patrick *metal products executive*

Sugar Land
Sheptor, John C. *sugar company executive*

The Woodlands
Barker, Sam L. *pharmaceutical executive*
Podolski, Joseph S. *pharmaceutical executive*
Sands, Arthur T. *biopharmaceutical executive, medical geneticist*
Stolle, Russell Robert *chemicals executive*

Whitewright
Burg, John Parker *construction panel executive*

VERMONT

Burlington
Pizzagalli, James *construction and real estate company executive*

VIRGINIA

Alexandria
Crundwell, Duncan James *electronics executive*
Slutsky, Bernice *agricultural products executive*

Arlington
Culligan, Thomas M. *electronics executive*
Junker, Bobby Ray *research and development company executive, physicist*

Bristol
Kielty, Thomas J. *manufacturing executive*

Charlottesville
Yarno, Wendy *pharmaceutical executive*

Chesapeake
Smith, Roland Carroll, Sr. *construction executive*

Deltaville
Koedel, John Gilbert, Jr. *retired metal products executive*

Dulles
Thompson, David Walker *manufacturing executive*

Fairfax
Nedzbala, Paul *health products executive*

Falls Church
Heebner, David K. *manufacturing executive, retired military officer*
Helm, Bob (Robert Wilbur Helm) *manufacturing executive, former federal official*
Lanese, Herbert J. *retired multi-industry executive*
Linton, David J. *aerospace and defense manufacturing executive*
Novakovic, Phebe N. *defense industry manufacturing executive*
Redd, L. Hugh *manufacturing executive*
Scheferman, Jeffrey E. *defense manufacturing company executive*
Schorer, Steven T. *manufacturing executive*
Smeraglinolo, Anthony *aerospace and defense manufacturing company executive*

Glen Allen
Morecroft, Michael John *housewares company executive*

Herndon
Browning, Jonathan *automotive executive*

Mc Lean
Davidson, Ann D. *defense industry executive, lawyer*
Dempsey, James Raymon *manufacturing executive*
Hake, Ralph F. *manufacturing executive*
Hoogendoorn, Benno *food products executive*
Laubies, Pierre *food products executive*
Mars, Forrest E., Jr. *candy company executive*
Mars, Jacqueline Badger *candy company executive*
Mars, John Franklyn *candy company executive*
Melcher, David F. *defense industry executive, retired military officer*
Michaels, Paul S. *food products executive*
Mora, Alberto J. *food products executive, lawyer*
Petrovich, Dushan *food products executive*
Radvan, Martin *food products executive*
Swallow, Edward M. *aerospace and defense manufacturing company executive*

Mechanicsville
Bierman, James L. *health products executive*
Minor, George Gilmer III *drug and hospital supply company executive*
Smith, Craig R. *health products executive*

Norfolk
Womack, Jerry T. *construction executive*

Powhatan
Eberle, Charles Edward *paper and consumer products executive*

Reston
Butler, Robert Clifton *retired construction executive*
Donahue, Timothy M. *retired construction executive*
Guyette, James M. *manufacturing executive*
Malzahn, Dan *construction executive*
Picard, Dennis J. *retired electronics company executive*
Saville, Paul C. *construction executive*
Schar, Dwight C. *construction executive*
Thompson, Warren M. *food franchise executive*

Richmond
Amadio, Julia M. *packaging and container manufacturing executive*
Barrington, Martin J. *tobacco company executive*
Beran, David R. *food products executive*
Browning, Keith D. *automotive executive*
Buzzard, James A. *paper, packaging and chemical company executive*
Folliard, Thomas J. *automotive executive*
Garnick, Murray R. *tobacco company executive*
Gilchrist, Ernie *food products executive*
Gottwald, Floyd Dewey, Jr. *chemicals executive, director*
Gottwald, Thomas E. *chemicals executive*
Greenberg, David I. *tobacco company executive*
Grubb, Edgar Harold *automotive executive*
Hearington, Joseph W., Jr. *tobacco company executive*
Holm, George L. *food products executive*
Hoskins, Craig *food products executive*
Johnson, Craig A. *tobacco company executive*
Kiefaber, Clay H. *pump and motor manufacturing company executive*
Luke, John Anderson, Jr. *paper, packaging and chemical company executive*
Mulligan, John J. *tobacco company executive*
Newsome, Kenneth R. *manufacturing executive, venture capitalist*
Scherger, Stephen R. *packaging and container manufacturing company executive*
Snead, Thomas G., Jr. *healthcare executive*
Steenland, Douglas M. *food products executive*
Teer, Diane *food packaging company executive*
Whelan, Karen Mae Leppo *manufacturing executive*
Willard, Howard A. III *food products executive*

Roanoke
Brouillard, Jack (John Charles Brouillard) *automotive parts company executive*
Freeland, Kevin Paul *automotive executive*
Jackson, Darren Richard *automotive parts company executive*
Norona, Mike *automotive parts company executive*
Wade, Jim L. (Jimmie L. Wade) *automotive executive*

Smithfield
Cole, Michael H. *food products executive, lawyer*
Luter, Joseph Williamson III *food products executive*
Manly, Robert W., IV, *food products executive*
Pope, C. Larry *food products executive*
Zadeh, Mansour T. *food products executive*

Springfield
Downes, Cynthia A. *construction executive*

Sterling
Walz, Carl E. *manufacturing executive*

Toano
Griffiths, Jeffrey W. *electronics executive*

Winchester
Gratz, Jay M. *metal products executive*
Holland, James Tulley *retired plastics company executive*

WISCONSIN

Mequon
Schaefer, Gordon Emory *food products executive*

TERRITORIES OF THE UNITED STATES

PUERTO RICO

San Juan
Carrion, Arturo *health products executive*

Vega Baja
Diaz, Heriberto *medical products executive*

ADDRESS UNPUBLISHED

Ackerman, Roy Alan *research and development company executive*
Bain, Travis Whitsett, II, *retired general business executive*
Beck, Albert *manufacturing executive*
Berkoff, Charles Edward *pharmaceutical and biotech consultant*
Biggs, Arthur Edward *retired chemicals executive, social services administrator*
Block, Ryan *consumer electronics media startup company executive, technology journalist and critic*
Bunzl, Rudolph Hans *retired manufacturing executive*
Bush, Norman *research and development company executive*
Cheek, Arthur Lee *construction executive, pilot*
Cicolani, Angelo George *research and development company executive, operating engineer*
Clawson, Curtis Jay *retired manufacturing executive*
Craft, Edmund Coleman *retired manufacturing executive*
Dent, Frederick Baily *retired textiles executive, former United States Secretary of Commerce*
Egloff, Fred Robert *manufacturers representative, writer, historian*
Engels, Lawrence Arthur *retired metal products executive*
England, Julie Spicer *former electronics company executive*
Gallman, Clarence Hunter *textile executive*
Habicht, Frank Henry *retired manufacturing executive*
Harrelson, Nancy *construction and real estate development company executive*
Heimbinder, Isaac *lawyer*
Heininger, S(amuel) Allen *retired chemical company executive*
Hester, Ross Wyatt *retired manufacturing executive, small business owner*
Keeler, James Leonard *food products executive*
Kellgren, George Lars *manufacturing executive*
Kelly, Anthony Odrian *textiles executive*
Kendle, Candace *pharmaceutical executive*
Killian, William Paul *manufacturing executive*
Laney, Michael L. *manufacturing executive*
MacAvoy, Thomas Coleman *manufacturing executive, educator*
Mason, Frank Henry III *automotive and rental company executive*
Mobley, Stacey J. *retired chemical company executive, lawyer*
Morris, G. Ronald *automotive executive*
Morton, James Carnes, Jr. *retired automotive executive*
Neal Blixt, Dianne M. *former tobacco company executive*
Powell, Thomas Edward III *biological supply company executive, physician*
Reitan, Bernt *retired metal products executive*
Reynolds, Randolph Nicklas *aluminum company executive*
Rock, Douglas Lawrence *former manufacturing executive*
Roorda, John Francis, Jr. *manufacturing executive, consultant*
Sapoff, Meyer *retired electronics executive*
Sargent, Charles Lee *manufacturing executive*
Sheehan, Jeremiah J. *former metal company executive*
Simpson, Michael *retired metals service center executive*
Sklenar, Herbert Anthony *industrial products manufacturing company executive*
Southerland, S. Duane *manufacturing executive*
Spector, Michael Joseph *agribusiness executive*
Stratton, Robert *retired electronics executive*
Tarrance, Vernon Lance, Jr. *research and development company executive*
Thorp, Benjamin A. III *retired paper company executive*
Uffelman, Malcolm Rucj *electronics executive*
Volkhardt, John Malcolm *retired food products executive*
Watts, Wendy Hazel *wine consultant*
Weaver, William Charles *manufacturing executive*
Welch, Oliver Wendell *retired pharmaceutical executive*
Whitacre, Edward E., Jr. *retired automotive executive*
Witt, Hugh Ernest *manufacturing executive, consultant*

INDUSTRY: SERVICE

UNITED STATES

ALABAMA

Birmingham
Harris, Aaron *management consultant*
Hunter, Justin *healthcare services company executive, lawyer*

Gadsden
Grimm, James R. (Ronald) *management consultant*

Huntsville
Ivy, Joan Carol *data processing executive*

Mobile
Hart, Eric Mullins *consumer products company executive*

Montgomery
Chapman, Beth Killough *political consultant, former state official*

ARIZONA

Tucson
Verburg, Edwin Arnold *retired management consultant*

ARKANSAS

Bentonville
Ohm, Seong K. *consumer products company executive*
Quinn, Stephen F. *marketing executive*

Cedarville
Pendergrass, Ewell Dean *retired communications executive*

Clarksville
Mooney, Robbi Gail *consumer products company executive*

Conway
Hatcher, Joe Branch *management consultant*

Lowell
Bergant, Paul R. *marketing executive*

Pine Bluff
Long, Edward Arlo *management consultant, retired manufacturing executive*

Springdale
Bacon, Craig *consumer products company executive*

DISTRICT OF COLUMBIA

Washington
Aguirre, Eduardo, Jr. *consulting firm executive, former ambassador*
Chertoff, Michael *consulting firm executive, lawyer, former United States Secretary of Homeland Security*
Clayton, Eva M. *consulting firm executive, former United States Representative from North Carolina*
Davis, Tom (Thomas Milburn Davis III) *consulting firm executive, former United States Representative from Virginia*
Gephardt, Dick (Richard Andrew Gephardt) *consulting company executive, lawyer*
Grossman, Marc Isaiah *consulting firm executive, former diplomat*
McClellan, Scott *consulting company executive, former White House press secretary*
Reed, Travis Dean *public relations executive*
Stepp, John R. *management executive*
Terzian, Grace Paine *communications executive*

FLORIDA

Arcadia
White, Will Walter III *public relations consultant, writer*

Aventura
Schwartz, Gerald *public relations and fundraising agency executive*

Lakeland
Roquemore, James W. *consumer products company executive*

Marietta
Marshall, Allen Wright III *communications executive, financial consultant*
Smith, Baker Armstrong *management executive, lawyer*
Spann, George William *management consultant*

Norcross
Mangum, Mylle H. *consumer products company executive*
Stubbs, Charles J. *internet company executive*

Roswell
Hill, Donald Dee *former managing director, management consultant, educator, writer, engineer*
Rogers, Richard Hilton *hotel executive*

Savannah
Deen, Bobby *chef, restaurateur, television personality*
Deen, Jamie *chef, restaurateur, television personality*
Steves, Gale C. *marketing professional, writer, editor-in-chief, publishing executive*

Stone Mountain
Wurtz, George W. III *consumer products company executive*

KENTUCKY

Covington
Esler, Susan B. *human resources specialist*

Henderson
Geary, Ronald G. *race track executive, retired human services company executive*

Lexington
Gomory, Ralph Edward *printing company executive*
Isbell, Jeri L. *human resources specialist*
Montupet, Jean-Paul Leon *printing company executive*
Sarvary, Mark A. *consumer products company executive*

Louisville
Blum, Jonathan D. *restaurant company executive, lawyer*
Brooks, Sally *healthcare service company executive*
Byerlein, Anne P. *human resources specialist, food products executive*
Chapman, Richard E. *healthcare services company executive*
Hamel, Matthew Edward *consumer products company executive, lawyer*
Miles, David W. *personal care industry executive*
Nolan, Kevin F. *consumer products company executive*
Novak, David C. *restaurant company executive*
Richards-Person, Melissa *marketing executive*
Schnatter, John H. *food service executive*
Spriggs, James *sales executive*
Su, Samuel (Jing-Shyh S. Su) *restaurant chain company executive*
Sutton, John Schuhmann, Jr. *retired purchasing consultant*
Taylor, Robert Lewis *management consultant*
Tinsley, Richard L. *personal care industry executive*

Mammoth Cave
Craighead, Sarah L. *parks director*

Paducah
Ragada, Rey Holtby *hotel executive*

Versailles
Troutt, Kenny *communications executive*

LOUISIANA

Baton Rouge
Davis, Hall L., IV, *funeral director*

Gonzales
Chestnut, E. Randall *consumer product company executive*

Lake Charles
Richard, Oliver G., III, (Rick Richard) *energy and management consultant, board member*

Metairie
Grimm, John Lloyd *marketing professional*

Monroe
Shern, Stephanie Marie *management consultant*

New Orleans
Besh, John *chef, television personality, restaurateur*
Brennan, Ella *restaurant manager*
Hinson, Robert William *advertising executive, consultant*
Lagasse, Emeril *chef, restaurant owner, television show host, writer*
Prudhomme, Paul *chef, restaurant owner*
Schnoebelen, Ian *chef*
Snyder, Sharon Veta *management consultant, educator*
Zemanick, Sue *chef*

Ruston
Hudnall, Jarrett, Jr. *management consultant, educator, marketing professional*

MARYLAND

Baltimore
Howes, James Guerdon *communication and transportation executive*

Bethesda
Cooper, Simon F. *hotel executive*

Hanover
Moylan, James E., Jr. *communications executive*

MINNESOTA

Bloomington
Andrews, Charles Elliott (Charles Elliot Andrews Jr.) *management consultant*

MISSISSIPPI

Columbus
Labensky, Sarah Ross *culinary educator*

Jackson
Strenglis, William A. *business services company executive*

Oxford
Currence, John *chef*

NEVADA

Las Vegas
Moran, John Arthur *hotel executive*

NEW JERSEY

Montvale
Avedon, Marcia J. *diversified industrial products company and former pharmaceutical executive*

NEW YORK

Armonk
Potvin, William Tracey *management consultant*

New York
Foley, Rita *consumer products executive*
O'Neill, Robert Edward (Bobby O'Neill) *consulting firm executive, former federal prosecutor*
Weisenburger, Randall J. *advertising executive*

NORTH CAROLINA

Arden
Baker, Kerry Allen *management consultant*

Asheville
Mundt, Barry Maynard *management consultant*

Burlington
Jones, Frankie T., Sr. *consulting firm executive*

Cary
Gronbach, Tyler D. *communications executive*
Mockett, Alfred T. *marketing company executive*

Charlotte
Eppes, Thomas Evans *advertising and public relations executive*
Hauser, David L. *communications executive*
Holland, Kevin R. *human resources specialist*
Huval, Tim *human resources specialist*
Lee, Joseph William *sales executive*

Davidson
Henkel, Herbert Ludwig *diversified industrial products company executive*

Durham
Barker, Ben *chef, restaurant owner*
Krivoruchka, Mark William *rental company executive*

Elon
Powell, William Council, Sr. *service company executive*

Flat Rock
Childress, Richard Thomas *international business consultant, author*

Greensboro
Bruggeworth, Robert A. *communications executive*
Hennighausen, Ned *consumer products company executive*
Kessler, Murray S. *tobacco manufacturing company executive*
Spears, Alexander White III *tobacco company executive*
Staab, Thomas Robert *consumer product company financial executive*

Hickory
Crenshaw, Randall W. *communications executive*
Hughes, James R. *marketing executive*
Knedlik, Ronald W. *retail grocery distributing executive*

High Point
Qubein, Nido R. *management consultant*

Mills River
Hancock, William Frank, Jr. *professor*

Mooresville
Allen, William Leroy *consumer products company executive*
Ausura, Maureen K. *human resources specialist*
Dally, Troy J. *consumer products company executive*
Dayton, Everett Britt *consumer products company executive*
Johnston, James Wesley *retired consumer products company executive*
Mabry, Joseph M.(Mike), Jr. *consumer products company executive*
Niblock, Robert A. *consumer home products company executive*

Morrisville
Lanier, Joseph Lamar, Jr. *consumer products company executive*
O'Sullivan, Frances K. *computer company executive*
Yang, Yuanqing *computer company executive*

Murphy
Turner, Lisa Phillips *human resources executive*

Pinehurst
Rees, Clifford Harcourt, Jr., (Ted Rees) *consulting company executive, retired trade association administrator, military officer*
Stevenson, Josiah, IV, *management consultant*

Raleigh
Burton, Troy *parks director, museum association administrator*
Leak, Robert Edwards *economic development consultant*
Lucht, John Charles *management consultant, writer*

Southern Pines
Owings, Malcolm William *retired management consultant*

Wilkesboro
Bridgeford, Gregory M. *consumer products company executive*
Hull, Robert F., Jr., (Bob Hull) *consumer products company executive*

Winston Salem
Evans, Lisbeth *management consultant, political organization worker, director*
Lalik, Janeen *marketing executive*
Muir, Douglas R. *food service executive*
Otterbourg, Robert Kenneth *public relations consultant, writer*
Riccio, Cindy *consumer products company executive*
Schindler, Andrew J. *marketing executive*
Uffindell, Colin M. *consumer products company executive*

OHIO

Cincinnati
Clement-Holmes, Linda W. *consumer products company executive*

Youngstown
Hudak, Cheryl C. *travel company executive*

OKLAHOMA

Midwest City
Craig, Harold Kent *mechanical contracting executive, systems analyst*

Oklahoma City
Greiner, Kenneth Donald, Jr. *retired management consultant, health facility administrator*
Hudson, J. Clifford *hotel executive, federal agency administrator*
Vona, Danielle M. *marketing executive*

Tulsa
Henry, Kathleen Marie *international marketing consultant*

PENNSYLVANIA

Greensburg
Freidheim, Cyrus F., Jr. *management consultant, board member*

Philadelphia
Palmer, Vicki R. *management consultant*

RHODE ISLAND

Providence
Szostak, (M.) Anne *consulting firm executive, former bank executive*

SOUTH CAROLINA

Charleston
Chardon, Marc d'Estournelles *software company executive*
Ketner, Linda *consulting company executive, civic worker*
Lata, Mike *chef*
Martin, Thomas Rhodes *communications executive, writer, educator*
Stehling, Robert *chef*

Columbia
Barnum, William Douglas *retired communications executive*

Greenville
Blackwell, Larry G. *computer company executive*
Miles, Laveda Ann *advertising executive*

Greer
Sundstrom, Harold Walter *public relations executive*

Hartsville
DeLoach, Harris E.(Eugene), Jr. *consumer products company executive, lawyer*
Hartley, Cynthia A. *human resources specialist*
Sanders, M. Jack *consumer products company executive*
Schrum, Roger P. *consumer products company executive*

Hilton Head Island
Conn, Margaret Elbow *human resources specialist*
McKeldin, William Evans *management consultant*
Patton, Joseph Donald, Jr. *management consultant*
Peterson, Coleman Hollis *consulting firm executive, retired retail executive*

Mount Pleasant
Blevins, William Edward *management consultant*

Pawleys Island
Grubb, William Francis Xavier *consumer products company executive, marketing professional*

Seneca
Strong-Tidman, Virginia Adele *marketing professional*

Spartanburg
Allen, Frances L. *marketing executive*
Chmiel, Mark E. *marketing professional*
Floyd, Karen Kanes *marketing executive, former political organization administrator*
Floyd, W. Russel, Jr. *funeral services company executive*
Marchioli, Nelson Jerome *restaurant chain executive*
Smithart-Oglesby, Debra Lynn *restaurant chain executive*

Sunset
Brodbeck, William Jan *marketing professional*

TENNESSEE

Brentwood
Byars, Leisa *marketing professional, music company executive*
Koford, Joné Law *healthcare services company executive*
Schulte, Mark J. *healthcare service company executive*
Zamir, Igal *consumer products company executive*

Bristol
Tuffy, Janet *human resources specialist*

Cordova
Gersappe, Sunil *business development director*

Franklin
Abunaser, Bashar *healthcare services company executive*
Bosshart, Andi *healthcare services company executive*
Gallivan, Matthew S. *healthcare services company executive*
Jenson, Paul Martin *healthcare services company executive*

Hermitage
Burke, Kieran E. *water park company executive*

Knoxville
Campbell, Michael L. *theatre company executive*
Parent, Ken *travel company executive*

Lebanon
Barber, Douglas E. *restaurant chain company executive*
Christman, Lisa P. *food service executive*
Ciavarra, Christopher A. *food service executive*
Cochran, Sandra Brophy *restaurant chain company executive*
Cool, Brenda L. *food service executive*
Couvillion, P. Doug *food service executive*
Crayton, William H. *food service executive*
Dilley, Kathleen A. *food service executive*
Doyle, Robert F. *food service executive*
Dozier, Alvin M. *food service executive*
Emery, Alan L. *food service executive*
Evans, Deborah M. *food service executive*
Eytchison, Brian R. *food service executive*
Flanagan, Nicholas V. *restaurant chain company executive*
Fratrik, Deborah A. *food service executive*
Greene, Edward A. *food service executive*
Hallums, Bruce A. *food service executive*
Harig, Robert J. *food service executive, human resources specialist*
Hayes, Sandra K. *food service executive*
Hyatt, Lawrence Eliot (Larry Hyatt) *restaurant chain company executive*
Jones, J. Larry *food service executive*
Keiser, Peter B. *food service executive*
Maxwell, Terry *food service executive*
McCarthy, Catherine J. *food service executive*
Mullen, Timothy W. *food service executive*
Pate, Thomas R. *food service executive*
Quinn, Beth J. *food service executive*
Rains, John W. *food service executive*
Romanko, Mark W. *food service executive*
Scott-Ramirez, Michelle R. *retail executive*
Scruggs, Patrick A. *food service executive*
Stinson, Stacy L. *food service executive*
Swartling, David R. *food service executive*
Torcivia, S. James *food service executive*
Varian, Michele A. *food service executive*
Vig, Bart F. *food service executive*
Warner, Stanley T. *food service executive*
Woodhouse, Michael A. *restaurant chain company executive*
Wynne, Diana S. *food service executive*

Brown, Paul J. *travel company executive*
Cantus, H. Hollister *marketing and government relations consultant*
Carter, Ian R. *hotel executive*
England, Gordon Richard *international business consulting firm executive*
Ford, Nelson M. *consulting firm executive*
Garner, Joseph E. *management consultant*
Harbach, Ed (Frank Edwin Harbach) *management and technology consulting executive*
Harding, Robert A. *security firm executive, retired military officer*
Harlan, Stephen Donald *personal care industry executive*
Henry, Francis J., Jr. *management consultant*
Howell, Lloyd W., Jr. *management consultant*
Klinkov, Ivo *hotel executive*
Kroskin, Philip *healthcare services company executive*
Laben, Nancy Jill *consulting firm executive, lawyer*
Mahaffee, Joseph W. *management consultant*
Marosky, Kurt *hotel executive*
Mayer, John D. *management consultant*
McConnell, John Michael *retired management consultant*
Michaelis, Lynn Otto *forest products industry executive*
Mongeau, Luc *consumer products company executive*
Nassetta, Christopher J. *hotel executive*
Ordan, Mark S. *personal care industry executive*
Peck, Patrick F. *management consultant*
Pedrazas, Ximo *hotel executive*
Pugliese, Luigi *management consultant*
Richards, Clifton Marc *personal care industry executive*
Rozanski, Horacio Daniel *business services executive*
Schneiderbauer, Dieter *staffing services executive*
Schuyler, Matthew W. *hotel executive*
Shrader, Ralph William *consulting firm executive*
Terzotis, Judi *advertising executive*
Wellings, Tom *chef*

Middleburg
McNichols, Gerald Robert *consulting company executive*

Norfolk
Miller, Christine Marie *sales, marketing and public relations executive*

Reston
Abraham, Magid M. *Internet company executive*
Fulgoni, Gian Marc *Internet research company executive*
Maher, David Willard *Internet company executive*
Montoni, Richard A. *management consultant*

Richmond
Breslawsky, Marc C. *retired security firm executive*
Brewer, W. Keith *tobacco company executive*
Coronado, William J. *tobacco company executive*
Dan, Michael T. *retired security firm executive*
Freeman, George C. III *tobacco company executive, lawyer*
Gulling, Mark V. *consumer products company executive*
Habenicht, Peter A. *advertising and marketing professional*
Hellyar, Mary Jane *film equipment company executive*
Hughes, Mike *advertising executive*
Jacobs, Harry Milburn, Jr. *advertising executive*
Joynes, Barbara Cole *marketing executive*
Kelson, Richard B. *consumer products company executive*
Krouskop, Dirk *packaging company executive*
Lennon, Frank Thomas *security firm executive*
Marshall, McAlister C., II, *security firm executive, lawyer*
McCormack, Robert Cornelius *consumer products company executive*
Tuszynski, Daniel J., Jr. *sales, management and marketing consultant*
Wheatley, Arthur Edwin, Jr. *security firm executive*

Springfield
Bruen, John Dermot *management consultant*

Vienna
Jones, James Logan, Jr. *consulting firm executive, former national security advisor, retired military officer*
Monroe, Robert Rawson *national security consultant*
Olson, Walter Justus, Jr. *management consultant*
Saylor, Michael J. *computer software company executive*

Virginia Beach
Alexander, William Powell *business advisor*
Hilgers, John Jack William *management, transportation and veterans consultant*
Jenkins, Kent, Jr. *communications executive*
McDonald, Timothy F. *marketing executive*
Mellon, William Daniel *communications executive*

White Stone
Vose, Kathryn Kahler *marketing and communications executive*

Williamsburg
Hoving, John Hannes Forester *consulting firm executive*

Winchester
Bonometti, Robert John *technology management and strategy executive*

Woodbridge
Duke, Elaine Costanzo *consulting firm executive, former federal agency administrator*

WEST VIRGINIA

Bluefield
Gearheart, Gary *sales executive*

Charleston
Mc Gee, John Frampton *communications company executive*

Chester
Delatore, Richard C. *hotel executive*

WISCONSIN

Neenah
Seifert, Kathi P. *printing company executive*

TERRITORIES OF THE UNITED STATES

PUERTO RICO

San Juan
Kunda, Dolores A. *advertising executive*

ENGLAND

Colchester
Evans, Peter Kenneth *advertising executive*

ADDRESS UNPUBLISHED

Ambrose, Charles Stuart *sales executive*
Anderson, Mary Ann Grasso *business executive*
Bachner, John Philip *business consultant*
Baker, Daniel Richard *computer company executive*
Bamberger, Gerald Francis *plastics marketing consultant*
Beers, Charlotte Lenore *retired advertising executive, former federal agency administrator*
Birk, John Richard *management consultant*
Blanchard, Townsend Eugene *retired service companies executive*
Bradley, Melvin LeRoy *communications executive*
Brooks, Jeffrey Martin *marketing and sales executive*
Browne, Ann April *purchasing manager*
Buck, Jennifer Cooney *consulting firm executive, former federal agency administrator*
Burge, John Wesley, Jr. *management consultant*
Burnham, J. V. *retired sales executive*
Carter, Jaine M(arie) *human resources specialist, director*
Carty, Donald J. *former computer company executive, former air transportation executive*
Clarke, Janet Morrison *marketing executive*
Cody, Richard Arthur *communications executive, retired military officer*
Coker, Donald William *bank management, expert witness, business valuation and economic consultant*
Cooper, Cynthia F. *consulting firm executive, accountant*
Diehl, Stephen Anthony *government representative*
Dirvin, Gerald Vincent *retired consumer products company executive*
Dobbs, George Albert *retired researcher*
Downey, Mortimer Leo III *consulting firm executive, former transportation executive*
Elliot, Jared *financial management consultant*
Erwin, Joseph Arnold *advertising executive, former political organization administrator*
Ethell, Judy A. *former consulting company executive*
Fay, Conner Martindale *retired marketing executive*
Fischer, Russell Leonard *public relations executive*
Gamble, Mary G(race) *organizational development professional*
Gianturco, Delio Emanuele *management consultant, educator, author*
Gibbs, Robert Lane *consulting firm executive, former White House press secretary*
Goldsmith, Jeff Charles *management consultant*
Goldstein, Burton Benjamin, Jr. *university professor*
Grunder, Fred Irwin *retired industrial hygienist, consultant*
Haas, Edward Lee *management consultant*
Hathaway, Melissa E. *consulting company executive, former federal official*
Hearl, Peter R. *former food service executive*
Houghtaling, Pamela Ann *strategic communications consultant, writer, public speaker*
James, Robert Leo *retired advertising executive*
Kellermanns, Franz Willi *management consultant, educator*
Kenne, Leslie Farr *consulting firm executive, retired military officer*
Kennedy, Karen Syence *advertising agency executive*
Klaes, James Graham III *advertising executive*
Krieger, Robert Lee, Jr. *government affairs, human resource management consultant, educator, writer, travel and meeting planner, political analyst, internet marketing consultant*
Layton, William George *consultant, retired human resources and import/export company executive*
Levy, Robert Edward *retired management consultant*
Littman, Earl *advertising and public relations executive*
Logan, Don *retired communications executive*
Malone, Claudine Berkeley *management consultant*
Massey, William Walter, Jr. *sales executive*
Matsdorf, Tyler R. *consulting firm executive, former legislative staff member*
Mitchell, John Charles *marketing professional*
Monroe, William Lewis *human resources executive*
Mustard, Lewis Williams *management consultant, educator*
Orender, Donna *marketing executive, former sports association executive*
Palumbo, Benjamin Lewis *public relations executive, consultant*
Paolillo, Joseph Guy Peter *management professor, researcher*
Paresky, David S. *travel company executive*
Parsons, Vinson Adair *retired computer company executive*
Passaro, Paul Charles *business executive, management consultant*
Polen-Dorn, Linda Frances *communications executive*
Poppel, Harvey Lee *management consultant, investment banker*
Puckett, Ruby Parker *food service executive, consultant, writer, dietician*
Ray, Paul Richard, Jr. *executive recruiter, consultant*
Reisman, Judith Ann Gelernter *media communications executive, educator*
Robinson, Hobart Krum *management consulting company executive*
Schramm, Bernard Charles, Jr. *retired advertising agency executive*
Sharp, William *retired advertising executive*
Shelton, Robert Warren *marketing professional*
Siegel, George Henry *management consultant*
Solymosy, Edmond Sigmond Albert *marketing professional, manager, retired military officer*
Starkweather, Frederick Thomas *retired data processing executive*
Stults, Walter Black *management consultant, trade association administrator*
Tarbutton, Lloyd T. *hotel executive, consultant*
Temerlin, Liener *advertising executive*
Walker, Gloria Lee *training services executive*
Walker, Ronald Tracy *retired personnel director*
Weiner, Richard *public relations executive*
Wentworth, Lynn A. *former housing products company executive*
Wiginton, Jay Spencer *sales executive*
Witcher, Michael H. *homeland and national security expert*

INDUSTRY: TRADE

UNITED STATES

ALABAMA

Birmingham
Anderson, Clyde B. *retail executive*
Demme, James *retail executive*

Mobile
Jones, Joseph Seymour *small business owner, poet*

ARKANSAS

Bentonville
Agwunobi, John Oderah *retail executive, former federal agency administrator*
Brewer, Rosalind Gates (Roz Brewer) *retail executive*
Chambers, Susan (Mary Susan Chambers, M. Susan Chambers) *retail executive*
Cheesewright, Dave *retail executive*
Dach, Leslie Alan *retail executive, former public relations company executive*
Davis, Cindy *retail executive*
Davis, Jeffrey A. *retail company executive*
Dobbs, Johnnie C., Jr. *retail executive*
Duke, Mike (Michael Terry Duke) *retired retail executive*
Ford, Rollin Lee *retail executive*
Gearhart, Jeffrey J. *retail executive, lawyer*
Holley, Charles Murphy, Jr. *retail company executive*
Kistler, Matt *retail executive*
Kolodzieski, Ed *retail executive*
Mac Naughton, Duncan *retail executive*
Martello, Wan Ling *retail executive*
McMillon, Doug (Carl Douglas McMillon) *retail executive*
Moore, Michael S. *retail executive*
Price, Scott *retail executive*
Roberts, Karen L. *retail executive, lawyer*
Ruiz, Gisel A. *retail executive*
Scott, Lee (Harold Lee Scott Jr.) *retired retail executive*
Simon, William Steven (Bill Simon) *retail executive*
Sinclair, Jack L. *retail executive*
Terrell, Karenann *retail executive*
Thomas, Andrea B. *retail executive*
Thompson, Jane Johnson *retail executive*
Walton, Rob (Samuel Robson Walton) *retail executive*
Westling, John T. *retail executive*
Whaley, Steven P. *retail executive*
Zorn, Eric Stuart *retail executive*

Little Rock
Bolte, Tony *retail executive*
Dillard, Alex *retail executive*
Dillard, William, II, *retail executive*
Freeman, James I. *retail department store company executive*
Hankins, Randal L. *retail executive*
Heil, Gene D. *retail executive*
Mahaffy, Denise *retail executive*
Matheny, Drue (Drue Dillard Corbusier) *retail executive*
Sanderford, Robin *retail executive*
Squires, Burt *retail executive*
Stockman, James D. *retail executive*

FLORIDA

Boca Raton
Colley, Gerald (Jerry) E. *retail executive*
Fuente, David I. *retail executive*
Mahurin, Steve *retail executive*
Wick, Randall W. *retail executive*

Bonita Springs
Mays, Gregory *retail executive, publishing executive*

Bradenton
Beall, Robert Matthews, II, *retail executive*
Rutstein, Stanley Harold *apparel retailing company executive*

Clearwater
Maxwell, Richard Anthony *retail executive*
Turley, Stewart *retired retail company executive*

Dunedin
Corey, Kay Janis *small business owner, apparel designer, nurse*

Fort Lauderdale
Baldwin, John T. *wholesale distribution executive*
Drury, John R. *retail executive*

Fort Myers
Mackenzie, Mori C. *retail executive*
Murray, Cynthia *retail executive*

Hialeah
Herran, Manuel A. *supermarket chain executive*

Jacksonville
Corless, Gary A. *wholesale distribution executive*
Follit, Evelyn V. *retired retail executive*
Grebe, Michael J. *wholesale distribution executive*
Kellmanson, Mary *retail executive*
Kleffner, Gregory William *retail executive, accountant*
Onstead, R. Randall Randall, Jr. *retail executive*
Peets, Terry R. *retail executive*

Lakeland
Jenkins, Charles H., Jr. *retail company executive*
Jones, Todd *retail executive*

Merritt Island
Smith, David Edward *small business owner, aerospace engineer, aerospace scientist*

Miami
Chaplin, Harvey R. *wine and liquor wholesale executive*
Dick, Melvin A. *wholesale distribution executive*
Lauber, Mark E. *wholesale distribution executive*
Rawl, Arthur Julian (Lord of Cursons) *corporate director, retail executive, consultant, accountant, writer*

Palm Beach Gardens
Day, Lawrence C. *auto parts executive*
Runge, Donald Edward *food wholesale company executive*

Pembroke Pines
Schaefer, Bonnie (E. Bonnie Schaefer) *retail executive*

Port Saint Lucie
LaHowchic, Nicholas John *consulting company executive*

Saint Petersburg
Anderson, Chuck *retail executive*
Bohnert, Brad C. *retail executive*
Bradley, Brian S. *retail executive*
Brand, Bill *retail executive*
Henry, Michael *retail executive*
Johnson, Gerard *retail executive*
Kissell, Felise Glantz *retail executive*
Letizio, Lisa *retail executive, human resources specialist*
Martin-Vachon, Anne *retail executive*
McDevitt, John *retail executive*
McLaughlin, Bethlee *retail executive*
Ronon, Barbara Lynne *retail executive*
Siegel, Matthew *retail executive*
Solomon, Rob *retail executive*
Watson, John *retail executive*

Tallahassee
Keough, Philip J., IV, *retail executive*

Vero Beach
Murphy, Susan (Jane Murphy) *small business owner, real estate broker*

Winter Park
Smetanka, Sally S. *small business owner*

GEORGIA

Atlanta
Boltz, Bill *retail executive*
Bowman, Giles *retail executive*
Cagle, James Douglas *retail executive*
Campbell, Ann-Marie *retail executive*
Casey, Michael D. *retail executive*
Davis, Jay M. *wholesale distribution executive*
Dayhoff, Diane *retail executive*
Ellison, Marvin *retail executive*
Holifield, Mark *retail executive*
Judd, George R. *wholesale distribution executive*
Kalafut, George Wendell *retired distribution company executive, retired naval officer*
Kane, Jim *retail executive*
Kinzey, Cara D. *retail executive*
McFarland, Joseph *retail executive*
Menear, Craig *retail executive*
Peterson, Eric V. *retail executive*
Petty, James C. *retail executive*
Powers, Marc D. *retail executive*
Ridley, Clarence Haverty *retail executive*
Saldívar, Ricardo E. *retail executive*

Lavonia
Raines, Stephen Samuel *franchising, consulting and development firm executive, lawyer*

Milton
Bolch, James R. *industrial electrical equipment company executive*

Norcross
Nelson, Dean B. *wholesale distribution executive*

Savannah
Alexander, R. David *retail executive*

Smyrna
Beacham, C. Wayne *wholesale distribution executive*

Valdosta
Halter, Henry James, Jr., (Diamond Jim Halter) *retail executive*

KENTUCKY

Bowling Green
Gipson, Jim *retail executive*

Covington
Wallman, Amy *retail executive*

Lancaster
Arnold, Cecil Benjamin *former small business owner*

Winchester
Book, John Kenneth (Kenny) *retail store owner*

LOUISIANA

Houma
Rhodes, Gene Paul *small business owner*

MICHIGAN

Ann Arbor
Floto, Ronald John *supermarket executive*

MISSISSIPPI

Greenwood
Jones, Carolyn Ellis *retired employment agency owner*

Jackson
McAllister, Deuce (Dulymus Jenod McAllister) *small business owner, retired professional football player*
Moore, Oscar Kenney *small business owner, state representative*

NORTH CAROLINA

Black Mountain
Ingle, Robert P., II, *retail executive*

Cary
Hatchell, Dennis G. *retail executive*
Holman, Edwin J. *retail executive*

Charlotte
Belk, H.W. McKay *retail executive*
Belk, Irwin *retail executive*
Belk, John R. *retail executive*
Belk, Thomas Milburn, Jr., (Tim) *retail executive*
Bloom, Michael K. *retail executive*
Bufano, Kathryn *retail executive*
Fiorucci, Marianne *retail executive*
Gambrell, Sarah Belk *retail executive*
Levine, Howard R. *retail executive*
Macadam, Stephen E. *wholesale distribution executive*
Marley, Brian Thomas *retail executive*
Masserang, Deverl *wholesale distribution executive*
Morganthall, Frederick S., II, *retail executive*
Vargas-Land, Vanessa *wholesale distribution executive, lawyer*

Durham
Lieberman, Rochelle Phyllis *small business owner*

Greensboro
Dimperio, Julie *retail executive*

Hendersonville
Heltman, Robert Fairchild *distribution executive*

Hickory
George, Boyd L. *wholesale distribution executive*

Highlands
Shaffner, Randolph Preston *retired educator, writer, publisher*

Matthews
Flur, Dorlisa K. *retail executive*
Winston, Mary Ann *retail executive*

Mooresville
Damron, Rick D. *retail executive*
Gfeller, Robert J., Jr. *retail executive*
Steed, John David *retail executive*

Morrisville
McDaniel, Michael K. *wholesale distribution executive, human resources specialist*
O'Quinn, William L., Jr. *wholesale distribution executive, lawyer*
Paren, Dennis A. *wholesale distribution executive*

Rocky Mount
Wordsworth, Jerry L. *wholesale distribution executive*

Sanford
Bierley, Mark Russell *retail executive*

Wilkesboro
Brown, Michael K. *retail executive*

Winston Salem
Strickland, Robert Louis *retired retail executive*

OHIO

Hudson
Perdue, David A., Jr. *retail executive*

OKLAHOMA

Oklahoma City
Green, David *retail executive*
Love, Tom *retail executive*
Peace, H. W., II, *small business owner, retired oil industry executive*

Tulsa
Cadieux, Chester *retail executive*
Carter, Terry *retail executive*

SOUTH CAROLINA

Florence
Griffith, Martha *retired small business owner, controller*

Greenville
Aguilar, Araceli *wholesale distribution executive*
Baker, Glen D. (Buck Baker) *wholesale distribution executive*
Benbenek, R. Scott *wholesale distribution executive*
Black, John K. *wholesale distribution executive*
Botbol, Elias *wholesale distribution executive*
Byars, Michael D. *retail executive*
Cartiaux, Xavier *wholesale distribution executive*
Cleys, Richard P. *wholesale distribution executive*
Constantine, Paul J. *wholesale distribution executive*
Davis, Linda B. *wholesale distribution executive*
Dixon, Gregory B. *wholesale distribution executive*
Elrod, P. Christopher *wholesale distribution executive*
Gaillard, John R. *wholesale distribution executive*
Madore, Marsha M. *wholesale distribution executive*
McCloud, Shelby L. *wholesale distribution executive*
McLain, Robert S., Jr. *wholesale distribution executive*
Meade, Andrea D. *wholesale distribution executive*
Meyer, Bruce C. *wholesale distribution executive*
Sommese, James *wholesale distribution executive*
Sorrentino, Tony *wholesale distribution executive*
Yelton, Jeffrey E. *wholesale distribution executive*

Ridgeway
Tovell, William *wholesale distribution executive*

TENNESSEE

Blountville
McGlothlin, James W. *wholesale distribution executive*

Brentwood
Teter, Clay *retail executive*

Gallatin
Ellis, Joseph Newlin *retired wholesale distribution executive*

Goodlettsville
Dreiling, Richard W. (Rick Dreiling) *retail executive*
Guion, Kathleen R. *retail executive*
Tehle, David M. *retail executive*

Jackson
Alderson, Robert E. *retail executive*

Knoxville
Haslam, James A. III *retail executive, professional sports team executive*
Sansom, William B. *wholesale distribution executive*

Memphis
Efird, Bruce A. *retail executive*
Giles, William (Bill) T. *retail executive*
Hayes, Michael Joseph *retail executive, investment banker*
Vail, Charles Stewart *retail executive, lawyer*

Nashville
Dennis, Robert J. *footwear retail company executive*
Kocher, Kenneth J. *retail executive*
Marcum, James A. *retail executive*
Orton, Jeff *retail executive*
Zibart, Michael Alan *wholesale book company executive*

Waynesboro
Morris, Randy G. *small business owner*

TEXAS

Arlington
Satterlee, Warren Sanford, II, *retired retail management professional, writer*

Austin
Minardi, Christina *retail executive*

Beaumont
Alter, Nelson Tobias *retail and wholesale distribution executive*

Brenham
Lubbock, Mildred Marcelle (Midge Lubbock) *former small business owner*

Corpus Christi
Finley, George Alvin III *wholesale and oil industry executive*

Mahany, Kevin J. *retail executive*

Dallas
Barnes, Gerald A. *retail executive*
Bush, Jack Eugene *retail executive*
Callahan, Rickey Don *business owner*
Downing, Ken *retail executive*
Gierhart, Wanda Marie *retail executive*
Glazer, Bennett J. *wholesale distribution executive*
Gold, James J. *retail executive*
Hall, Neva L. *retail executive*
Hussey, Wayne A. *retail executive*
Katz, Karen W. *retail executive*
Maxwell, Phillip L. *retail executive*
Patrick, Russ *retail executive*
Skinner, James E. *retail executive*
Stordahl, Ann M. *retail executive*
Tansky, Burton M. *retail executive*

Denton
Berges, James G. *retail executive*

Fort Worth
David, Catherine Anne *retail executive*
Hallam, Robert G. *wholesale distribution executive*
Smith, Alexander W. *retail executive*
Stufflebeme, Sharon S. *retail executive*
Wissinger, John *retail executive*

Grapevine
Mauler, Michael K. *retail executive*
Olivera, Chris *retail executive*

Horseshoe Bay
Simpson, H. Richard (Dick Simpson) *retail merchandiser*

Houston
Carson, Sandra G. *retail executive*
De Meritt, John *retail executive*
Levit, Max *wholesale distribution executive*
Mullany, Hank *retail executive*
Myung, Gigi L. *retail executive*
Nesbitt, DeEtte DuPree *small business owner, investor*

Irving
Acevedo, William *retail executive*
Adams, J. Glen *retail executive*
Barsam, Jeannie *retail executive*
Christopher, Eric *retail executive*
Crombie, Nicholas E. *retail executive*
DeCaro, Thomas C. *retail executive*
Hollander, Gilbert P. *retail executive*
Hornbaker, Renee Jean *wholesale distribution executive*
Killion, Theo *retail executive*
Lowe, John B., Jr. *retail executive*
Massanelli, Stephen C. *retail executive*
Mayo, Susann C. *retail executive*
Ogun, Toyin *retail executive*
Pappas, Philo T. *retail executive*
Sternblitz, David H. *retail executive*
Sullivan, Douglas Burns *retail executive*

McKinney
Fernandes, Gary Joe *retail executive*

Odessa
Brumelle, Kenneth Coy *retired business owner*

Plano
Davis, Robert D. *retail executive*
Engibous, Thomas James *retail executive, retired electronics executive*
McNaught, Clark *retail executive*
Samford, Karen Elaine *small business owner, consultant*
Ullman, Myron Edward, III, (Mike Ullman) *retail executive*

San Antonio
Bowers, Kim (Kimberly Smith Bowers) *retail executive, lawyer*

Selma
Kent, Jeff (Jeffrey Franklin Kent) *business owner, retired professional baseball player*

Wichita Falls
Waun, Roger *small business owner, minister*

VIRGINIA

Alexandria
Coster, John M. *retail executive, health science association administrator*

Bluefield
Garside, John W., Jr. *wholesale distribution executive*

Bristow
Schrock, Simon *wholesale executive*

Chesapeake
Barron, Arnold S. *retired retail executive*
Brock, Macon F., Jr. *retail company executive*
Philbin, Gary M. *retail executive*
Sasser, Robert *retail executive*

Fairfax
Pugh, Arthur James (Jay Pugh) *retired retail executive*

Falls Church
Bruck, Bill *business owner*

Mc Lean
Vandemark, Robert Goodyear *retired retail executive*

Midlothian
Cauthen, Charles Edward, Jr. *retired retail executive, management consultant*

Richmond
Ukrop, James E. *retail executive*

Roanoke
Kozikowski, Tami *retail executive*

Salem
Brand, Edward Cabell *retail executive*

Springfield
Walcher, Greg E. *small business owner*

Upperville
Gebhard Powell, Joy Lee (Bok Sin Lee) *small business owner*

ADDRESS UNPUBLISHED

Banks, Charles Augustus III *distribution executive*
Bishop, Claire DeArment *small business owner, retired librarian*
Cody, Thomas Gerald *retired retail executive, lawyer*
de la Cruz, Carlos *wholesale distribution executive*
Johnston, Gregory L. *retail executive*
McGeorge, Don W. *retired retail executive*
Mench, John William *retail executive, electrical engineer*
Moulton, James Roger *small business owner*
Rodbell, Clyde Armand *retired distribution executive*
Ryan, Thomas Michael (Tom Ryan) *retired retail executive*
Wike, D. Elaine *small business owner*
Willingham, Mary Maxine *fashion retailer*

INDUSTRY: TRANSPORTATION

UNITED STATES

ALABAMA

Birmingham
Leonard, Joseph B. *retired air transportation executive, board member*

Huntsville
Goldman, Arthur E. *aerospace transportation executive, civil engineer*
Tucker, Richard A. *airport terminal executive*

ARKANSAS

Fort Smith
Young, Robert A. III *freight systems executive*

Lowell
Cope, Donald Gene *transportation company executive, controller*
Roberts, John N. III *transportation executive*
Thompson, Kirk *transportation executive*

Rogers
Hunt, Johnelle *transportation executive*

FLORIDA

Fort Lauderdale
Baldanza, Ben (Basil Ben Baldanza) *air transportation executive*
Foley, Arthur James *law firm executive*

Jacksonville
Baker, John Daniel, II, *trucking executive, crushed stone company executive*
Drucker, Ronald Walter *rail transportation executive*
Fogarty, Andrew B. *rail transportation executive*
Gerkens, Henry H. *trucking executive*
Gooden, Clarence W. *rail transportation executive*
Kneller, Michael K. *transportation services executive*
Mancini, Lisa A. *rail transportation executive*
Mastrean, Michele *rail transportation executive*
Thomas, Larry S. *transportation executive*
Ward, Michael John *rail transportation executive*

Miami
Ames, Richard D. *cruise line company executive*
Bald, Gary M. *cruise line executive*
Buckelew, Alan B. *cruise line company executive*
Cahill, Gerald R. *cruise line company executive*
Dasburg, John Harold *air cargo and freight services executive*
Goldstein, Adam M. *cruise line executive*
Kenna, Thomas H. *rail transportation executive*
Roberts, Rusty (Russell Leon Roberts) *transportation executive, former legislative staff member*
Swienton, Gregory T. *transportation company executive*

Naples
Myers, Robert Jay *retired aerospace executive*

Orlando
Breazeale, Will *pilot, military officer*
Hutcheson, Tad *air transportation executive*

Plantation
Donaway, Carl D. *messenger service executive*
Fellows, John *delivery service executive*
Smartt, Bill *air courier company executive*
Waller, Stephen *air transportation executive*

Saint Petersburg Beach
Mason, Phillip Howard *aircraft company executive, retired military officer*

Sanibel
Hasselman, Richard B. *retired rail transportation executive*

Satellite Beach
Loney, Mary Rose *former airport administrator, aviation industry consultant*

Tallahassee
Snowden, Lawrence Fontaine *retired air transportation executive, retired military officer*

Vero Beach
Ingwersen, Martin Lewis *water transportation executive*

Wellington
Wegner, Arthur Eduard *aerospace company executive*

GEORGIA

Alpharetta
Sutthoff, John *delivery service executive*

Atlanta
Abney, David P. *delivery service executive*
Anderson, Richard H. *air transportation executive*
Barnes, David A. *delivery service executive*
Bastian, Edward H. *air transportation executive*
Becker, Michael J. *air transportation executive*
Blissit, Doug W. *air transportation executive*
Bornhorst, Donald T. *air transportation executive*
Boyce, Donald Nelson *water transportation executive*
Brutto, Daniel J. *delivery service executive*
Capers, Laynglyn M. *delivery service executive*
Carp, Daniel Allen *air transportation executive, former consumer products company executive*
Charaf, Anthony N. *air transportation executive*
Davis, D. Scott (D. Scott Davis) *delivery service executive*
Dube, Vinay *air transportation executive*
Duffy, Thomas M. *transportation services executive, lawyer*
Gershenhorn, Alan *delivery service executive*
Gorman, Stephen E. *air transportation executive*
Gray, Myron A. *delivery service executive*
Gutmann, Kate (Kathleen M. Gutmann) *delivery service executive*
Halter, Hank *air transportation executive*
Harvey, Patricia Kiko *air transportation executive*
Hauenstein, Glen W. *air transportation executive*
Hill, Allen Edward *delivery service executive*
Hyland, Gregory E. *water transportation executive*
Kirchner, Eric W. *delivery service executive*
Kuehn, Kurt P. *delivery service executive*
Laughter, John *air transportation executive*
Loewy, Robert Gustav *aerospace executive, engineering educator*
McDevitt, John *delivery service executive*
Newman, Andrea Fischer *air transportation executive*
Owens, Christine M. *delivery service executive*
Shah, Neel *air transportation executive*
Sternad, Ken *delivery service executive*
Stronach, Neil *air transportation executive*
Torok, Ken *delivery service executive*
Wise, Theresa *air transportation executive*

Calhoun
Bonanno, Phyllis O. *transportation executive*

Duluth
O'Dell, Richard *trucking executive, board member*

Savannah
Lombardo, Joseph T. *aerospace transportation executive*

Stone Mountain
Horne, Nathan E. *air transportation executive*
Larkins, Jamail *air transportation executive*
Leonora, Arnold B. *air transportation executive*

KENTUCKY

London
Holbert, Jim *pilot, retired military officer*

Louisville
Hayes, William Meredith *pilot, retired military officer*

LOUISIANA

Lafayette
Gonsoulin, Al A. *air transportation executive*

Madisonville
Jobe, Tony Bryson *air transportation executive, lawyer*

NORTH CAROLINA

Chapel Hill
Moellering, John Henry *aviation maintenance company executive*

Charlotte
Handy, John W. *shipping company executive, retired military officer*

Cherryville
Mayhew, Kenneth Edwin, Jr. *retired transportation executive*

Kannapolis
Thigpen, Alton Hill *transportation executive*

Raleigh
Brantley, John C. III *airport executive*
Whitehurst, Jim (James M. Whitehurst) *former air transportation executive*

Thomasville
Congdon, David S. *transportation executive*

OKLAHOMA

Burns Flat
Khourie, Bill *aerospace transportation executive*

Enid
Groendyke, John D. *transportation executive*

SOUTH CAROLINA

Columbia
Conrad, Paul Ernest *transportation consultant*

Easley
Dyer, Jane Ballard *pilot*

TENNESSEE

Chattanooga
Quinn, Patrick *transportation executive*

Cookeville
Sasser, Gary *trucking executive*

Memphis
Aaholm, Sherry A. *delivery service executive*
Bronczek, David J. *transportation executive*
Carter, Robert B. *delivery service executive*
Glenn, T. Michael *delivery service executive*
Graf, Alan B., Jr. *delivery service executive*
Logue, William J. *delivery service executive*
Richards, Christine P. *delivery service executive, lawyer*
Smith, Frederick Wallace *delivery service executive*

TEXAS

Dallas
Dayley, Darren *air transportation executive*
Jordan, Lewis H. *airline executive*
Jordan, Robert E. *air transportation executive*
Kelly, Gary Clayton *air transportation executive*
Kolski, Stephen J. *air transportation executive, lawyer*
McGlade, Peter Gerard *airline executive*
Osterberg, Mark William *air transportation executive*
Philips, Brian D. *delivery service executive*
Ricks, Ron *air transportation executive, lawyer*
Ridley, Davis S. *air transportation company executive*
Van de Ven, Michael Gerard *air transportation company executive*
White, Christopher W. *air transportation executive*
Wright, Laura H. *air transportation executive*

Fort Worth
Campbell, Jeffrey J. *rail transportation executive*
Dolara, Peter J. *air transportation executive*
Endres, Arthur P. (Skip Endres) *rail transportation executive*
Garton, Daniel P. *air transportation executive, marketing professional*
Goren, Isabella D. (Bella Goren) *air transportation executive*
Goulet, Beverly Kenyon *air transportation executive*
Hertog, John Herman *transportation executive*
Horton, Tom (Thomas W. Horton) *air transportation executive*
Hund, Thomas N. *rail transportation executive*
Ice, Carl R. *rail transportation executive*
Johnson, Stephen L. *air transportation executive*
Lanigan, John P., Jr. *rail transportation executive*
Nober, Roger Paul *rail transportation executive, lawyer*
Reding, Robert W. *air transportation executive*
Rose, Matt (Matthew K. Rose) *rail transportation executive*
Vahidi, Virasb *air transportation executive*
Wimberly, Kenneth W. *air transportation executive, corporate financial executive*

Harlingen
Farris, Robert Gene *transportation company executive*

Houston
Acaba, Joseph M. *astronaut*
Anderson, Clayton C. *astronaut*
Anderson-Lehman, Ron *air transportation executive*
Antonelli, Dominic A. *astronaut*
Archambault, Lee Joseph *astronaut*
Barratt, Michael Reed *astronaut, internal and aerospace medical doctor*
Behnken, Robert L. *astronaut*
Bloomfield, Michael J. *astronaut*
Boe, Eric A. *pilot, astronaut*
Bowen, Stephen G. *astronaut*
Caldwell Dyson, Tracy Ellen *astronaut, researcher*
Chamitoff, Gregory Errol *astronaut, aerospace engineer*
Chang-Diaz, Franklin R. *astronaut*
Chiao, Leroy *astronaut*
Chiles, William E. *air transportation executive*
Crane, James R. (Jim Crane) *delivery service executive, professional sports team owner*
Doi, Takao *astronaut*
Drew, Benjamin Alvin, Jr. *astronaut*
Erwin, Mark A. *air transportation executive*
Eyharts, Leopold *astronaut*
Ferguson, Christopher J. *astronaut*
Feustel, Andrew J. *astronaut*
Fincke, Edward Michael (Mike) *astronaut*
Foreman, Michael J. *astronaut*
Fossum, Michael E. *astronaut*
Frick, Stephen N. *astronaut*
Garan, Ronald J., Jr. *astronaut*
Gidzenko, Yuri Pavlovich *astronaut*
Gobillot, Lori Auray *air transportation executive*
Grunsfeld, John M. *astronaut, astronomer*
Ham, Kenneth T. *astronaut, military officer*
Hobaugh, Charles Owen *astronaut*
Hoshide, Akihiko *astronaut*
Hurley, Douglas G. *pilot*
Kadenyuk, Leonid K. *astronaut*
Kelly, Scott J. *astronaut, military officer*
Kimbrough, Robert S. *astronaut*
Kotov, Oleg Valerievich *cosmonaut*
Lawrence, Charles Berdon *exploration company executive*
Lindsey, Steven W. *astronaut, military officer*
Linnehan, Richard M. *astronaut, veterinarian*
Magnus, Sandra H. *astronaut*
Mastracchio, Richard A. (Rick) *astronaut*
Meehan, William A. *air transportation executive*
Melvin, Leland D. *astronaut*
Morukov, Boris V. *cosmonaut*
Nespoli, Paolo Angelo *astronaut*
Noguchi, Soichi *astronaut*
Nyberg, Karen L. *astronaut*
Ochoa, Ellen *astronaut*
Onufriyenko, Yuri *cosmonaut*
Passonno Stott, Nicole Marie *astronaut, engineer*
Pettit, Donald R. *astronaut, flight engineer, researcher*
Phillips, John L. *astronaut*
Ream, James B. (Jim Ream) *air transportation executive*
Schlegel, Hans *astronaut*
Sellers, Piers J. *astronaut*
Shannon, Holden E. *air transportation executive*
Sharipov, Salizhan Shakirovich *cosmonaut*
Skvortsov, Aleksandr Aleksandrovich *cosmonaut*
Stefanyshyn-Piper, Heidemarie M. *astronaut*
Stone, Robert G., Jr. *water transportation executive*
Surayev, Maxim *cosmonaut, pilot*
Swanson, Steven R. *astronaut*
Thirsk, Robert Brent *astronaut*
urCarey, Duane Gene (Digger) *astronaut*
Vacar, Richard M. *airport executive*
Vittori, Roberto *astronaut*
Vladimirovich, Vinogradov Pavel *cosmonaut*
Wakata, Koichi *astronaut*
Walheim, Rex J. *astronaut, military officer*
Walker, John E. (Ned Walker) *air transportation executive*
Weinstein, Martin *aerospace transportation and manufacturing executive, materials scientist*
Williams, Sunita L. *astronaut*
Wilson, Stephanie D. *astronaut*
Yurchikhin, Fyodor Nikolayevich *cosmonaut*
Zamka, George D. *astronaut*

Irving
Plaskett, Thomas George *transportation executive, director*

New Braunfels
Rush, W.M. (Rusty) *trucking executive, board member*

Southlake
Jackson, Jeffery M. *transportation executive*

VIRGINIA

Abingdon
Giftos, P. Michael *transportation company executive*

Alexandria
Crum, Richard *air transportation executive*

Arlington
Ellis, Andrew Kingsley (Andy Ellis) *aerospace defense company executive, former legislative staff member*
Fort, Randall Martin *aerospace defense company executive, former federal agency administrator*
O'Keefe, Sean Charles *aerospace transportation executive, former academic administrator*
Wahlquist, Andrew Folkman *government affairs executive*

Chesterfield
Congdon, John Rhodes *transportation executive*

Falls Church
Bush, Wesley G. *aerospace transportation executive*
Cheston, Sheila Carol *aerospace defense company executive, lawyer*
Ervin, Gary W. *aerospace transportation executive*
Flach, Gloria A. *aerospace transportation executive*
Livanos, Alexis C. *aerospace transportation executive*
McGarey, Jennifer Campbell *aerospace defense company executive*
Mills, Linda Anne *aerospace transportation executive*
Palmer, James F. *aerospace transportation executive*
Rosenkranz, Robert Bernard *aerospace transportation executive*

Herndon
Pastorek, Paul G. *aerospace company executive, lawyer*

Mc Lean
Fogleman, Ronald Robert *aerospace company executive, retired military officer*

Norfolk
Fox, John William, Jr. *rail transportation executive*
Goode, David Ronald *retired transportation company executive*
Manion, Mark D. *rail transportation executive*
Moorman, Charles W. *transportation executive*
Parker, Richard Wilson *retired rail transportation executive, lawyer*
Squires, James A. *rail transportation executive*

Poquoson
Holloway, Paul Fayette *retired aerospace transportation executive*

Potomac Falls
Levell, Edward, Jr. *retired jet fighter pilot, airport director, aviation consultant*

Richmond
Holmes, Jack A. *trucking executive*
Watkins, Hays Thomas *retired railroad executive*

Vienna
Anderson, Eric C. *aerospace transportation executive*
Rogers, Raymond Jesse *retired federal railroad associate administrator*

Williamsburg
Spitzer, Cary Redford *avionics consultant, electrical engineer*

ADDRESS UNPUBLISHED

Baddour, Anne Bridge *pilot*
Brandenstein, Daniel Charles *astronaut, retired military officer*
Carter, Thomas Smith, Jr. *retired rail transportation executive*
Collins, Eileen Marie *astronaut*
Gitner, Gerald L. *air transportation executive, investment banker*
Griffin, J. Timothy *air transportation executive*
Heckel, John Louis (Jack Heckel) *aerospace management executive*
Higginbottom, Samuel Logan *retired air transportation executive*
Keenan, Anthony Lee *trucking executive*
Kelleher, Herbert David *retired air transportation executive, board member*
Reitz, Douglas John Frank *airline captain, computer consultant*
Stonecipher, Harry Curtis *former aerospace transportation executive*
Swanson, Ralph William *aerospace executive, consultant, engineer*
Tyurin, Mikhail *cosmonaut*

INDUSTRY: UTILITIES, ENERGY, RESOURCES

UNITED STATES

ALABAMA

Birmingham
Crosswhite, Mark A. *utilities executive*
Drummond, Garry N. *mining company executive*
Jones, David *mining executive*
McAnnally, Robert Sidney *energy company executive, lawyer*

Foley
St. John, Henry Sewell, Jr. *utility company executive*

ARKANSAS

El Dorado
Compton, Walter Knox *oil industry executive, lawyer*
Deming, Claiborne Payne *oil industry executive*
Doerr, Harvey *oil industry executive*
Fitzgerald, Kevin Gerard *oil industry executive*
Jenkins, Roger W. *oil industry executive*
McKinlay, Thomas *energy executive*

Fort Smith
Qualls, Robert L. *electric power industry executive*
Rogstad, Barry Kent *electric power industry executive*

Little Rock
Ford, Joe Thomas *retired telephone company executive, former state senator, state legislator*
Gardner, Jeffrey R. *telecommunications industry executive*
Nelson, Edward Sheffield *retired utilities executive, lawyer*

DISTRICT OF COLUMBIA

Washington
McCormick, Walter Bernard, Jr. *telecommunications industry executive*
Teslik, Sarah Anna Ball *oil industry executive*

FLORIDA

Boca Raton
Gralla, Eugene *natural gas company executive*

Deerfield Beach
Laser, Charles, Jr. *oil company executive*

Delray Beach
Gardiner, Hobart Clive *retired petroleum company executive*
Kruger, Paula *telecommunications industry executive*

Fort Lauderdale
Camburn, Clyde *oil industry executive*

Fabrikant, Charles L. *transportation and energy services executive, lawyer*

Indian River Shores
Wiegner, Edward Alex *financial and energy executive*

Jacksonville
Frantz, Francis X. *telecommunications industry executive, lawyer*

Juno Beach
Charanjiva, Lakshman *electric power industry executive*
Hay, Lewis III *utilities executive*
Olivera, Armando J. *electric power industry executive*
Robo, James L. *utilities executive*

Melbourne
Brown, William M. *telecommunications industry executive*
McArthur, Gary L. *telecommunications industry executive*

Miami
Claure, R. Marcelo *telecommunications industry executive*
Cost, Mike *telecommunications industry executive*
Ianni, Mark *telecommunications industry executive*
Kasbar, Michael J. *energy executive*
Perez, Carmen M. *telecommunications industry executive*
Pimentel, Armando *energy executive*
Shea, Francis X. *energy executive*
Stebbins, Paul H. *energy executive*

Naples
Gelfand, Neal *oil industry executive*
Marienthal, George *telecommunications industry executive*
Marino, William Francis *telecommunications industry executive, consultant*

North Palm Beach
Bennett, Christopher A. *electric power industry executive*
Davidson, Mitch *utilities executive*
Dewhurst, Moray P. *utilities executive*
Sieving, Charles E. *energy executive, lawyer*

Palm Beach Gardens
Harnett, Joseph Durham *oil industry executive*

Saint Augustine
Houskamp, Melissa *energy executive*

Saint Petersburg
Buchan, Douglas Charles *gas industry executive, government agency administrator*

Saint Petersburg Beach
Garnett, Stanley Iredale, II, *utilities executive, lawyer*

Stuart
Riordan, James Quentin *retired oil industry executive, lawyer*

Tampa
Brown, Deirdre A. *energy executive*
Brown, Troy Anderson, Jr. *retired electric power industry executive*
Hudson, Sherrill W. *energy executive*
Ramil, John B. *energy executive*

Village Of Golf
Allen, Robert Eugene *retired telecommunications industry executive*

West Palm Beach
Koch, William I *energy executive*

GEORGIA

Atlanta
Arroyo, F. Thaddeus *telecommunications industry executive*
Beattie, Art P. *utilities executive*
Bierria, Myra Coleman *gas industry executive*
Bolch, Carl Edward, Jr. *oil industry executive, lawyer*
Bowers, W. Paul *utilities executive*
Bulich, Micaela Niven *energy executive*
Carbonell, Joaquin R. III *telecommunications industry executive, lawyer*
Carson, Candace F. *oil industry executive*
Carter, Donald F. *gas industry executive*
Carter, Scott A. *gas industry executive*
Caston, Moanica *electric power industry executive*
Cave, Steve *gas industry executive*
Cleveland, Ralph *gas industry company executive*
Cordoba, Ricardo *energy executive*
Crisp, Charles R. *retired gas industry executive, board member*
Dallas, Wendell *gas industry executive*
Dearman, Andrew J. III *utilities executive*
de la Vega, Ralph *telecommunications industry executive*
Dunn, Rebecca M. *telecommunications industry executive*
Duvall, Robert *gas industry executive*
Eisner, Dean H. *telecommunications industry executive*
Evans, Andrew W. *energy executive*
Fanning, Thomas Andrew (Tom Fanning) *utilities executive*
Gidley, Jodi *gas industry executive*
Gillis, James A. *gas industry executive*
Greene, Kimberly Scheibe *utilities executive*
Greene, Margaret H. *telecommunications industry executive*
Horsley, Donald R. *telecommunications industry executive*
Hubbell, Richard A. *oil industry executive*
Johnson, Arthur E. *gas industry executive*
Johnson, Marsha Sampson *utilities executive*
Leamer, Marybeth N. *telecommunications industry executive*
Lindsey, Steve *gas industry executive*
Linginfelter, Henry P. (Hank) *gas distribution company executive*
McCrary, Charles D. *utilities executive*
McIntyre, Connie *gas industry executive*
Pearl, Ira G. *gas industry executive*
Peeples, Donna N. *gas industry executive*
Rawson, Charles A. III *gas industry executive*
Reese, Elizabeth W. *gas industry executive*
Rimmer, Todd *gas industry executive*
Rinne, Kristin *telecommunications industry executive*
Rozgonyi, Eugene V., Jr. *gas industry executive*
Smith, Elmer *telecommunications industry executive*
Somerhalder, John W., II, *energy executive*
Stovern, Brett A. *gas industry executive*
Surber, Joseph A. III *gas industry executive*
Sutton, Jay *gas industry executive*
Tumminello, Peter I. *gas industry executive*
Womack, Christopher C. *utilities executive*

Carrollton
Adkins, Norman *electric power industry executive*

Gainesville
Alexander, J. *energy executive*

Lyons
Odom, Rod D., Jr. *telecommunications industry executive*

Savannah
Demere, Robert H., Jr. *energy executive*

KENTUCKY

Central City
Cardwell, Sue Poole *reclamation services company executive*

Crescent Springs
Chellgren, Paul Wilbur *energy industry executive*

Lexington
Boyd, James Robert *retired energy executive*

Louisville
Ronald, Peter *utilities executive*

LOUISIANA

Baton Rouge
Nokes, Jim W. *retired oil industry executive*

Houma
Chauvin, Kerry J. *energy executive*

Lacombe
Harlan, Jim *energy executive*

Monroe
Ewing, R. Stewart *telecommunications company executive*
Owens, William Arthur (Bill Owens) *telecommunications industry executive, retired military officer*
Post, Glen Fleming III *telecommunications industry executive*
Puckett, Karen Anne *telecommunications industry executive*
Strandjord, Mary Jeannine *telecommunications industry executive*

New Orleans
Beck, Tony *energy executive*
Boutte, Tracie L. *electric power industry executive*
Conley, Renae *energy executive*
Lind, Thomas Otto *barge transportation company executive*
Moffett, James Robert *mining executive*
Savoff, Mark T. *energy executive*

MISSISSIPPI

Gulfport
Topazi, Anthony J. *utilities executive*

Jackson
Denault, Leo P. *energy executive*
Leonard, J. Wayne *energy executive*
Smith, Richard J. *energy executive*

NORTH CAROLINA

Asheville
Haynes, John Mabin *retired utilities executive*

Charlotte
Dzuricky, David J. *gas industry executive*
Ennis, A. Leslie *gas industry executive*
Esamann, Douglas F. *utilities executive*
Good, Lynn Jones *energy executive*
Jamil, Dhiaa M. *energy executive*
Janson, Julia S. *energy executive*
McArthur, John R. *utilities executive, lawyer*
Moore, June B. *gas industry executive*
Mulhern, Mark F. *electric power company executive*
Mullinax, A. R. *energy executive*
O'Hara, Kevin M. *gas industry executive*
Pritchard, Robert O. *gas industry executive*
Reising, Ronald *utilities executive*
Roche, Cathy *energy executive*
Rogers, James Eugene, Jr., (Jim Rogers) *energy executive*
Rolfe, Christopher C. *energy executive*
Shi, David E. *gas industry executive, retired academic administrator, historian*
Simon, Jose M. *gas distribution company executive*
Skains, Thomas E. *gas industry executive*
Trusty, David L. *energy and services company executive*
Valentine, Kenneth T. *energy and services company executive*
Warfield, Ranelle Q. *gas industry executive*
Weber, Jennifer L. *energy executive*
Williams, Bill *energy and services company executive*
Yoho, Franklin H. *gas industry executive*
Yount, Michael H. *gas industry executive*

Hickory
Edwards, Marvin S., Jr., (Eddie Edwards) *telecommunications industry executive*

Raleigh
Corbett, Jeffrey A. *electric power industry executive*
McDonald, William E. *retired telecommunications industry executive*
Pinnix-Ragland, Hilda *electric power industry executive*
Sipling, Philip J. *mining executive*
Smith, Sherwood Hubbard, Jr. *retired electric utilities executive*

Southern Shores
Kegel, William George *mining company executive*

OKLAHOMA

Ada
Surgnier, David Heral *gas company executive*

Bartlesville
Berney, Rand C. *oil industry executive*
Silas, Cecil Jesse *retired petroleum company executive*

Enid
Ward, Llewellyn Orcutt III *oil industry executive*

Oklahoma City
Brunetti, Wayne Henry *energy executive*
Campbell, David Gwynne *retired petroleum executive, geologist*
Delaney, Peter B. *energy executive*
Dell'Osso, Nick (Domenic J. Dell'Osso Jr.) *energy company executive*
Dixon, Steven C. *energy company executive, geologist*
Hamm, Harold Glenn *oil industry executive*
Lawler, David C. *energy executive*
Lawler, Robert Douglas (Doug Lawler) *energy company executive, petroleum engineer*
McCormick, J. Philip *natural gas company executive*
Mitchell, Malone III *oil industry executive, venture capitalist*
Richels, John *energy executive, lawyer*

Tulsa
Armstrong, Alan S. *energy executive*
Chappel, Donald R. *petroleum pipeline company executive*
Clerico, John Anthony *oil industry executive, investment company executive*
Dinan, Curtis L. *gas industry executive*
Dotson, George Stephen *retired oil industry executive*
Foutch, Randy A. *oil industry executive*
Gibson, John W. *gas industry executive*
Helmerich, Hans Christian *oil industry executive*
Hill, Ralph A. *energy executive*
Horkey, William Richard *retired oil industry executive*
Ingram, Charles Clark, Jr. *energy executive*
Kivisto, Thomas L. *former energy executive*
Lawhorn, Caron A. *gas industry executive*
Lindsay, John W. *oil industry executive*
Martinovich, Robert F. *gas industry executive*
Nedom, H. Arthur *petroleum consultant*
Norton, Pierce H. *gas industry executive*
Orr, M. Alan *oil industry executive*
Petranova, Ludmila *electric power industry executive*

PENNSYLVANIA

Allentown
Hunt, Terry H. *fuel company executive*

Canonsburg
Fritz, Martin Andrew *gas industry executive, lawyer*

SOUTH CAROLINA

Cayce
Addison, James (Jimmy) E. *electric power industry executive*
Marsh, Kevin B. *energy executive*

Columbia
Archie, Jeffrey B. *electric power industry executive*

Greenville
Zaman, Patrick *telecommunications industry executive*

Jackson
Smith, Mark Eugene *nuclear engineering service company executive*

TENNESSEE

Brentwood
Leonard, Charles H. (Chuck Leonard) *energy executive*

TEXAS

Addison
Higgins, Vincent *mining executive*

Arlington
Harper, Trudy A. *electric power industry executive*

Austin
Brigham, Ben M. (Bud Brigham) *oil industry executive*
Coursen, Sam *telecommunications industry executive, electronics executive*
Galloway, Gale Lee *oil and gas executive, rancher*
Haas, Joseph Marshall *retired petroleum consultant*
Hansen, Ken *telecommunications industry executive, electronics executive*

Bellaire
Danburg, Jerome Samuel *retired oil industry executive*

Corpus Christi
Adnani, Amir *mining executive*
Anthony, Harry L. *mining executive*
Susser, Sam L. *oil industry and consumer products company executive*

Dallas
Akers, J. Kevin *energy executive*
Aron, Doug S. *oil industry executive*
Baker, Tom *utilities executive*
Best, Robert Wayne *gas transmission company executive, lawyer*
Biegler, David W. *energy executive*
Burlage, Peter J. *energy executive*
Campbell, David *electric power industry executive, lawyer, utilities executive*
Chapman, N. A. *telecommunications industry executive*
Clifton, Matthew P. *petroleum refining company executive*
Cocklin, Kim Roland *gas industry executive, lawyer*
Davis, Barry E. *energy executive*
Davis, Ray C. *energy executive*
Drummond, Jere A. *telecommunications company executive*
Ellison, Luther Frederick *oil industry executive*
Enze, Charles R. *energy executive*
Farell, Dan *utilities executive*
Fielder, Charles Robert *retired oil industry executive*
Gaut, C. Christopher *energy executive*
Hardgrave, J. Jeffrey *energy executive*
Headington, Timothy *oil industry executive*
Hillstrand, Kris W. *energy executive*
Hoglund, Forrest Eugene *retired petroleum company executive*
Hunt, Ray Lee *petroleum company executive*
Jennings, Michael C. *oil industry executive*
Kaplan, Joel D. *electric power industry executive, lawyer*
Lamp, David L. *energy executive*
Langdon, Jerry J. *energy executive*
Linquist, Roger D. *telecommunications industry executive*
MacDonald, Brian Patrick *oil industry executive*
MacGillivray, Robin G. *telecommunications industry executive*
McCrea, Marshall S. III *energy executive*
McFarland, Mac A. *energy executive*
Meisenheimer, Fred E. *gas industry company executive*
Rabun, Daniel W. *oil and gas industry executive*
Rees-Jones, Trevor D. *oil industry executive*
Risch, Frank A. *oil industry executive*
Salinas, Martin *energy executive*
Sell, Clay (Jeffrey Clay Sell) *energy company executive, former federal agency administrator*
Shaw, Bruce R. *gas industry executive*
Spears, Ronald E. *telecommunications industry executive*
Stankey, John T. *telecommunications industry executive*
Stephens, John J. *telecommunications industry executive*
Storey, Debbie *telecommunications industry executive*
Walters, Robert C. *electric power industry executive, lawyer*
Warren, Kelcy L. *energy executive*
Whitmire, John *oil industry executive*
Wilkins, Rayford, Jr. *telecommunications industry executive*
Wright, Mark *telecommunications industry executive*
Young, John F. *electric power industry executive, energy executive*

El Paso
Dalke, Gary R. *oil industry executive*
Foster, Paul L. *oil industry executive*
Miracle, Rocky Reed *electric power industry executive*
Stevens, Jeff A. *oil industry executive*

Fair Oaks
Regan, William Joseph, Jr. *retired energy company executive*

Fort Worth
Craddock, Delbert L. *energy executive*
Hutton, Keith A. *energy executive*
Moncrief, William Alvin, Jr. *oil and gas producer*
Simpson, Bob R. *energy executive*
Whitley, Mark D. *energy executive*

Gainesville
Leach, Ken *retired utilities executive*

Horseshoe Bay
Jorden, James Roy *oil industry executive, consultant*

Houston
Anderson, Robert J. *oil and gas industry executive*
Archibald, Lawrence E. (Larry Archibald) *oil industry executive*
Armstrong, Greg L. *oil industry executive*
Auchinleck, Richard H. *energy executive*
Bahorich, Michael S. *energy executive*
Bartling, Phyllis McGinness *oil company executive*
Batchelder, Gene (Eugene Lewis Batchelder) *oil industry executive*
Bay, Annell R. *oil industry executive, geologist*

Beck, Jeffrey S. *oil industry executive*
Bennett, Bob *energy executive*
Bernhardt, Mona Leigh *oil and gas company executive*
Blumenshine, W. Mark *oil and gas company executive*
Boothby, Lee K. *energy executive*
Bourgeois, Doss R. *oil and gas industry executive*
Bowen, William Jackson *retired gas industry executive*
Brown, David A.B. *oil industry executive*
Brown, Jay A. *telecommunications industry executive*
Bullock, William L., Jr. *oil industry executive*
Burguieres, Philip J. *energy executive*
Burke, Michael Donald *oil and gas company executive*
Cabell, Matthew D. *oil and gas industry executive*
Caliel, Michael J. *electric power industry executive*
Campbell, Eileen M. *oil industry executive*
Campbell, Stephen C. *oil and gas company executive*
Cancilla, Russell J. *oil and gas industry company executive*
Carmichael, David M. *energy executive*
Carne, John D. *oil industry executive*
Carney, Ray, Jr. *mining executive*
Carroll, Barbara A. *drilling company executive*
Carroll, Milton *oil industry executive*
Chalmers, David B. *petroleum executive*
Chambers, Thomas P. *energy executive*
Chiang, W.C.W (Willie Chiang) *oil industry executive*
Childers, D. Bradley *energy executive, lawyer*
Clark, Janet F. *oil industry executive*
Clayton, Benjamin J. *oil industry executive*
Collins, T. Jay *retired energy executive*
Colson, John R. *electric power industry executive*
Cook, Charles Clinton *energy executive*
Cragg, Christopher Eugene *oil industry executive*
Craighead, Martin S. *energy executive*
Creel, Michael Allen *energy executive*
Cunningham, Ralph Sanford *energy executive*
Dallas, Terry G. *electric power industry executive*
Dang, Kimberly Allen *energy executive*
Davidson, Charles D. *energy executive*
Deaton, Chad C. *oil and gas industry executive*
Dees, Jerry L. *retired oil industry executive*
DeVault, John Lee *oil industry executive, geophysicist*
Dice, Bruce Burton *gas industry executive*
Dickerson, Lawrence Richard *oil industry executive*
Dobson, Rick *energy executive*
Dodson, J. Marshall (John Marshall Dodson) *energy company executive*
Dreyfuss, Lawrence J. *energy executive*
Drury, Leonard Leroy *retired oil company executive*
Dudman, Bryan L. *energy executive*
Ebel, Gregory L. *energy executive*
Edelman, Thomas Jeffrey *energy executive*
Eichler, Rodney J. *energy executive*
Erikson, Sheldon R. *oil industry executive*
Esrey, William Todd *energy executive, former telecommunications company executive*
Farris, G. Steven *energy executive*
Fawaz, Jed *telecommunications industry executive*
Flesher, Robert G. *oil industry executive*
Flexon, Robert C. *energy executive*
Foshee, Douglas L. *gas industry executive*
Fowler, W. Randall *energy executive*
Fulwiler, Robert Neal *oil industry executive*
Garland, Gregory Cyril *oil industry executive*
Gerry, Robert L. III *energy executive*
Goodman, Herbert Irwin *petroleum company executive*
Gould, Andrew *oil industry executive*
Grams, Dana A. *gas industry executive*
Gremp, John T. *energy executive*
Grijalva Mosquera, Victor Elias *energy executive*
Harris, Alan N. *energy executive*
Hatfield, Gregory M. *drilling company executive*
Hedrick, Kirby L. *energy executive*
Heidt, Larry P. *energy executive*
Heim, Michael A. *energy executive*
Hendrix, Dennis Ralph *energy executive*
Herman, Robert A. (Bob Herman) *oil industry executive*
Hildebrand, Jeffrey D. *oil industry executive*
Hill, Gregory Paul *oil industry executive*
Hill, Thad (John B. Hill) *energy executive*
Hirshberg, Alan J. *oil industry executive*
Holden, John William III *utilities executive*
Holmes, Grace B. *energy executive*
Horn, J. Stacy *energy executive*
Houston, Ken *energy executive*
Huff, John Rossman *energy executive*
Hutchinson, Scott *energy executive*
Jackson, John E. *energy executive*
Jacobs, Mark M. *energy executive*
Jasek, John H. *oil and gas company executive*
Jeter, Frances *gas industry executive*
Johnson, Wayne D. *gas industry executive*
Jones, Darilyn *gas industry executive*
Joyce, Rene R. *energy executive*
Jum'ah, Abdallah *oil industry executive*
Kean, Steven J. *energy executive*
Kelly, Janet Langford *oil industry executive, lawyer*
Kibsgaard, Paal *oil industry executive*
Kinder, Richard Dan *natural gas pipeline, oil and gas company executive*
Knesek, Michael John *energy executive*
Knickel, Carin S. *oil industry executive*
Korell, Harold M. *energy executive*
Kramer, Phillip D. *oil industry executive*
Krohn, Tracy W. *energy executive*
Lance, Ryan Michael *oil industry executive*
Lentz, Henry E., Jr. *energy executive*
Lesar, David J. *oil industry executive*
Lie, Bernt Aage *energy executive*
Limbacher, Randy L. *oil industry executive*
Lodzinski, Frank A. *oil and gas industry executive*
Lollar, John Henry III *oil company executive*
Lowe, John E. *oil industry executive, accountant*
Lowrey, Bill *oil industry executive*
Luigs, Charles Russell *retired gas and oil drilling industry executive*
Maddox, Scott E. *gas industry executive*
McArdle, Janine J. *energy executive*
McClanahan, David M. *energy executive*
McDonald, Martin *oil industry executive*
McDonald, Rebecca Ann *natural gas company executive*
McEvoy, M. Kevin *energy executive*
McGee, Richard K. *energy executive*
McKay, Lamar *oil industry executive*
McLeod, Suzanne M. *drilling company executive*
McParland, Jeffrey J. *energy executive*
Meloy, Matt *gas industry executive*
Merrick, Aaron S.G. *energy executive*
Messier, Luc J. *oil industry executive*
Miller, Merrill Anthony, Jr. *energy executive*
Miller, Steven L. *oil industry executive*
Miller, W. Thaddeus *energy executive*
Mitchell, Kevin J. *energy executive*
Moore, Jack B. *oil industry executive*
Moreland, W. Benjamin *telecommunications industry executive*
Muchmore, Robert Charles, Jr. *oil industry executive*
Mueller, Steven L. *energy executive*
Muller, Edward Robert *energy executive, lawyer*
Murray, Robert Charles *retired electric power industry executive*
Muslih, Khalid A. *oil industry executive*
Myers, Hance *energy executive*
Nelson, S. James, Jr. *oil industry executive*
Netherland, Joseph H. *energy executive*
Neumann, Henry W., Jr. *energy executive*
Odum, Marvin E. *oil industry executive*
O'Neil, James F. III *telecommunications industry executive*
Ordemann, William *energy executive*
Packer, Gary D. *gas industry executive*
Papa, Mark Gary *oil and gas industry executive*
Paulson, Bernard Arthur *oil industry executive, consultant*
Payne, James L. *oil industry executive*
Peak, Kenneth Raymond *energy executive*
Peebler, Robert Paul *energy executive*
Pefanis, Harry N. *oil industry executive*
Perkins, Joe Bob *energy executive*
Phillips, Robert Glenn *gas industry executive, lawyer*
Pitts, James *gas industry executive*
Plank, Roger B. *energy executive*
Probert, Timothy J. *oil industry executive*
Ragauss, Peter A. *oil industry executive*
Ralls, W. Matthew *energy executive*
Raspino, Louis A. *energy executive*
Rauf, Zamir *energy executive*
Reasor, C.C. (Craig Clayton Reasor, Clayton Reasor) *oil industry executive*
Rebell, Arthur Leslie *energy executive*
Reddy, J. Patrick *energy executive*
Reilley, Dennis H. *oil industry executive*
Reinbolt, Paul C. *oil industry executive*
Restrepo, William J. *offshore drilling company executive*
Riggs, Susan G. *oil and gas company executive*
Roberts, David E., Jr. *oil industry executive*
Rodríguez, Félix M. *oil industry executive*
Roff, J(ohn) Hugh, Jr. *energy executive*
Rutherford, John R. *energy executive*
Schneider, William D. *oil and gas company executive*
Schwarz, Glenda M. *oil industry executive*
Seitz, Kimberly *audit executive*
Shaper, C. Park *energy executive*
Sheets, Jeff W. *oil industry executive*
Skelly, Michael *energy executive*
Sledge, Charles M. *oil industry executive*
Smith, Clark C. *energy executive*
Smith, Philip B. *gas industry executive*
Sneed, Thomas K. *oil industry executive*
Snider, Stephen A. *oil industry company executive*
Songer, Mark Anthony *energy executive*
Spicer, Mark J. *oil and gas company executive*
Stewart, J.W. *energy executive, lawyer*
Story, Leslie (Eric Story) *oil industry executive*
Sullenbarger, Daniel James *oil industry executive, lawyer*
Swanson, Al *oil industry executive*
Swanson, Douglas E. *retired oil industry executive*
Talbert, Winston M. *oil and gas industry executive*
Talbott, Cloyce A. *oil industry executive, retired energy executive*
Taylor, Cindy B. *oil industry executive*
Teague, A. James *energy executive*
Thill, Howard J. *energy executive*
Thompson, Jerry E. *gas industry executive, former oil industry executive*
Tillman, Lee Mark *oil industry executive*
Tschinkel, Victoria Jean *energy executive*
Tucker, David E. *energy executive*
Usher, Thomas James *oil industry executive, former metal products executive*
Vallejo, Frances M. *oil industry executive*
Van Dyke, Gene *oil industry executive*
Van Horn, Michael D. *oil and gas company executive*
Van Kleef, William T. *oil industry executive*
Van Wagenen, Paul G. *gas industry executive*
Watson, Chuck *oil industry executive*
Whalen, James W. *energy executive*
Whitlock, Gary L. *energy executive*
Williams, Clay C. *oil industry executive*
Williams, Robert Henry *oil industry executive*
Wilson, Edward Converse, Jr. *oil and natural gas production company executive*
Wilson, Floyd C. *oil industry executive*
Wood, Patrick Henry III *energy executive, lawyer*
Woods, James Dudley *energy executive*
Wuori, Stephen J. *energy executive*
Wylie, Forrest E. *energy executive*
Young, Charles B. *energy executive*
Zernell, James T. *oil and gas company executive*
Ziemba, Larry (Lawrence Michael Ziemba) *oil industry executive*

Ingleside

Vaden, William R. *oil industry executive, councilman*

Irving

Albers, Mark W. *oil industry executive*
Bazelides, Philip J. *utilities executive*
Bullard, Denny B. *oil and gas company executive*
Cavanaugh, Lucille J. *oil industry executive*
Cheatwood, Chris J. *oil and gas company executive*
Clevenger, Rex T. *utilities executive*
Cohen, Kenneth P. *oil industry executive, lawyer*
Colton, W. M. *energy executive*
Dealy, Richard P. *oil and gas company executive*
Dolan, Michael J. *oil industry executive*
Dove, Timothy L. *oil and gas company executive*
Duffin, Neil W. *oil industry executive*
Fariello, Theresa M. *energy executive*
Glass, Sherman J., Jr. *oil industry executive*
Halbouty, Thomas C. *oil and gas company executive*
Hall, Frank W. *oil and gas company executive*
Hannes, William F. *oil and gas company executive*
Hopkins, Frank E. *oil and gas company executive*
Humphreys, Donald D. *oil industry executive*
Kelly, Alan J. *oil industry executive*
King, Reatha Clark *retired energy executive*
Kleinman, Mark H. *oil and gas company executive, lawyer*
Kohlenberger, Gerald L. *energy executive*
Kruger, Richard M. *oil industry executive*
Luxbacher, Roberta *oil industry executive*
McManus, David *oil and gas company executive*
Mulva, Patrick T. *oil industry executive*
Nelson, Marilyn Carlson *energy executive*
Pisarczyk, Richard V. *oil industry executive*
Pryor, Stephen D. *oil industry executive*
Sheffield, Scott D. *oil industry executive*
Still, Jay P. *oil industry executive*
Stuewer, Sherri K. *oil industry executive*
Swiger, Andrew P. *oil industry executive*
Tillerson, Rex W. *oil company executive*
Wallace, Roger Windham *oil and gas company executive*
Walters, Thomas R. *gas and power company executive*
Watson, Jim Albert *gas industry executive, lawyer*

Lewisville

Kopplin, Ron *mining executive*

Lubbock

Fullingim, Dwight B. *former oil industry executive*

Midland

Grover, Rosalind Redfern *oil and gas company executive*
Klein, Michael L. *oil industry executive*

Plano

Benson, Robert L. *mining executive*
Brumley, Jon S. *oil industry executive*
Gregory, Michael J. *mining company executive, human resources specialist*
Schuh, Frank Joseph *oil industry executive, consultant*

Port Isabel

English, Floyd Leroy *telecommunications industry executive*

Richardson

Anderson, Richard A. *telecommunications industry executive*
Pendleton, Todd *telecommunications industry executive*
Walker, David G. *telecommunications industry executive*

Salado

Parks, Lloyd Lee *oil industry executive*

San Antonio

Anastasio, Curtis V. *energy executive*
Arthur, Gary L., Jr. *energy executive*
Barron, Bradley C. *energy executive*
Blank, Steven A. *energy executive*
Brown, Mary Rose *energy executive*
Browning, Jay D. *energy executive, lawyer*
Ciskowski, Michael S. *energy executive*
Coughlin, Catherine M. *telecommunications industry executive*
Crownover, Mike *energy executive*
Donovan, John *telecommunications industry executive*
Edwards, S. Eugene *energy executive*
Fisher, Eric A. *energy executive, lawyer*
Flagg, C.A. (Chuck Flagg) *oil industry executive*
Gilbert, Steve *energy executive, lawyer*
Goff, Gregory J. *oil industry executive*
Gorder, Joseph W. *energy executive*
Greehey, William Eugene (Bill Greehey) *energy executive*
Killinger, Clayton *energy executive*
Martine, Cathy *telecommunications industry executive*
McCoy, Joseph G. *oil industry executive*
Miller, Forrest E. *telecommunications industry executive*
Monroe, Joseph M. *oil industry executive*
Moreau, Claude P. *oil industry executive*
Porter, Daniel J. *oil industry executive*
Spendlove, G. Scott *energy executive*
Stankey, John T. *telecommunications industry executive*
Stephenson, Randall L. *telecommunications industry executive*
Titzman, Donna M. *energy executive*
Watts, D. Wayne *telecommunications industry executive, lawyer*
Westfall, Lynn D. *oil industry executive*
Wright, Gregory A. *oil industry executive*
Zesch, Hal *energy executive*

Sugar Land

Jernigan, Wyatt E. *energy executive*
Lipinski, John J. (Jack) *oil industry executive*
Morgan, Edward A. *oil industry executive*
Riemann, Stanley A. *oil industry executive*

The Woodlands

Abendschein, Robert D. *energy executive, petroleum engineer*
Brightman, Stuart M. *energy executive*
Corbett, Luke R. *energy executive*
Gwin, Robert G. *oil industry executive*
Walker, Al (R.A. Walker, Robert A. Walker Jr.) *oil industry executive*
Wilcox, Raymond I. *oil industry executive*

VIRGINIA

Abingdon

Crutchfield, Kevin S. *mining executive*
Neely, Eddie W. *mining executive*

Alexandria

Hirsch, Robert Louis *energy analyst, consultant*

Arlington

Gluski, Andrés R. *electric power industry executive*
Hackenson, Elizabeth *electric power industry executive*
Laskey, Alexander *energy efficiency services company executive*
Luraschi, William R. *utilities executive, lawyer*
McFarlane, Robert Carl (Bud) *energy company executive, former national security advisor*
Odeen, Philip A. *energy company executive*
Santoroski, Richard *electric power industry executive*
Vesey, Andrew M. *electric power industry executive*
Yates, Daniel J. *energy efficiency services company executive*

Bristol

Hendriksen, Roger S. *mining executive*
Phillips, Baxter Francis, Jr. *energy executive*

Fairfax

Cramer, H. R. (Hal Cramer) *oil industry executive*

Herndon

Aquino, Peter D. *telecommunications industry executive*
Grivner, Carl J. *telecommunications industry executive*
O'Connell, Matthew McGowan *telecommunications industry executive, lawyer*

Mc Lean

Singh, K. Paul *telecommunications industry executive*

Oakton

Kapoor, Kay *telecommunications industry executive*

Reston

Ahuja, Sanjiv *telecommunications industry executive*
Cowan, Keith O. *telecommunications industry executive*
Dussek, Steven P. *telecommunications industry executive*
Redden, Shelton Dennis *telecommunications industry executive*
Shindler, Steven M. *telecommunications industry executive*

Richmond

Christian, David A. *energy executive*
Doswell, Mary Cummings *energy executive*
Farrell, Thomas Francis, II, *energy executive*
Foglesong, Robert H. *mining executive*
Gillenwater, Jeffrey M. *mining company executive, human resources specialist*
Hetzer, G. Scott *energy executive*
Koonce, Paul D. *energy executive*
McGettrick, Mark F. *energy executive*
Norden, Mark *mining executive*
Poma, John M. *mining company executive, lawyer*
Rogers, Steven A. *energy executive*
Sanderlin, James L. *energy executive, lawyer*
Stallard, Hubert R. *retired telephone company executive*
Suboleski, Stanley C. *mining executive*
Sypolt, Gary L. *energy executive*
Tshudy, Doug *mining executive*

South Boston

Hardy, Eva Teig *retired energy executive*

Sterling

Ganek, Jeffrey E. *telecommunications industry executive*
Hook, Lisa A. *telecommunications industry executive*

Suffolk

Hines, Angus Irving, Jr. *petroleum marketing executive*

Vienna

Herron, Edwin Hunter, Jr. *energy consultant*

WEST VIRGINIA

Charleston

Farshchian, Nasser *gas industry executive*
Lane, Andrew *energy executive*

Martinsburg

Blair, Craig P. *utilities executive, former state legislator*

Scott Depot

Hatfield, Bennett K. *mining executive*

TERRITORIES OF THE UNITED STATES

PUERTO RICO

Guaynabo

Lambert, Christina *telecommunications executive*

VIRGIN ISLANDS

St Thomas

Prior, Cornelius Bernard, Jr. *utilities executive, financial consultant*

ADDRESS UNPUBLISHED

Andras, Oscar Sidney (O.S. Andras) *energy executive*
Barham, Charles Dewey, Jr. *electric power industry executive, lawyer*
Barrow, Thomas Davies *retired oil and mining company executive, consultant*
Berry, William Willis *retired utilities executive*
Bryan, J(ames) P(erry), Jr. *energy executive*
Burrow, Harold *retired gas industry executive*
Chewning, Thomas N. *retired energy executive*
Cox, Glenn Andrew, Jr. *retired energy executive*
Draper, E(rnest) Linn, Jr. *retired electric utility executive*
Farley, Claire Scobee *retired petroleum company executive*
Fleming, William Sloan *energy and computer company executive*
Foosaner, Robert Stephen *telecommunications industry executive, lawyer*
Gurian, Mal *telecommunications executive*
Hammick, Patricia A. *retired energy executive*
Hines, Andrew Hampton, Jr. *utilities executive*
Irwin, John Robert *retired public company executive, educator, director*
Jackson, Robert William *retired utilities executive*
Kinnear, Peter D. *retired energy executive*
Klesse, William R. (Bill Klesse) *energy executive*
Leet, Richard Hale *oil industry executive*
Lilly, Edward Guerrant, Jr. *retired utilities executive*
Loveland, Eugene Franklin *retired gas industry executive*
Mazanec, George L. *natural gas company executive*
Moler, Elizabeth Anne *retired utilities executive*
Munsey, Virdell Everard, Jr. *retired utilities executive*
Myers, Franklin *oil industry executive*
Nicholson, Leland Ross *retired utilities executive, energy consultant*
Nyberg, Donald Arvid *oil industry executive, educator*
O'Hare, James Raymond *energy executive*
Sanchez, Antonio Rodolfo, Jr. *oil industry executive*
Smith, Paul Vergon, Jr. *retired gas industry executive*
Thorn, Terence Hastings *energy executive, consultant, writer*
Timmerman, William B. *retired utilities executive, accountant*
Williamson, Bruce A. *retired energy executive*
Wilson, Walter Clinton *retired oil and gas industry executive*

INFORMATION TECHNOLOGY
See also SCIENCE: MATHEMATICS AND COMPUTER SCIENCE

UNITED STATES

ALABAMA

Florence
Foote, Avon Edward *web developer/producer, communications educator*

Huntsville
Borman, Michael J. *information technology executive*
Childs, Rand Hampton *information technology executive, consultant*
Hassell, Stephen C. *information technology executive*

CONNECTICUT

Stamford
Breakstone, Robert Albert *information technology and consumer products company executive, consultant*

DISTRICT OF COLUMBIA

Washington
McGervey, Teresa Ann *technical information specialist*

FLORIDA

Beverly Hills
Hill, Charlyn Ann *information systems specialist*

Clearwater
Tonnison, John *information technology executive*
Wright, Murray *information technology executive*
Youna, Gerard *information technology executive*

Coral Springs
Sanders, Marc Andrew *computer technical consultant*

Deerfield Beach
Yerves, Ken *information technology executive*

Fort Lauderdale
Bordone, Adrian *information technology executive*
Chiu, Harry *information technology executive*
Levine, Peter *information technology executive*
Templeton, Mark B. *information technology executive*

Jacksonville
Payne, Timothy D. *information technology executive*
Scanlon, George Patrick *insurance industry executive, accountant*
Schaffer, Gregory Paul *information technology executive, former federal agency administrator*

Swenson, Eric D., Sr. *information technology executive*

Melbourne
Meyerrose, Dale William *information technology company executive, retired military officer*

Miami
Medina, Manuel D. *information technology services company executive*

Newberry
Thornton, J. Ronald *technology consultant*

Punta Gorda
Ott, Walter Richard *information technology executive, writer*

Sanibel
Trevor, Alexander Bruen *information technology consultant*

GEORGIA

Albany
Mizuguchi, Tetsuya *video game designer*

Alpharetta
Adair, Charles E. *information technology executive*
Borchert, Robert *information technology executive*
Heyman, John H. *information technology executive*
Phillips, Charles E., Jr. *computer software company executive*

Atlanta
Blalock, Rebecca A. *information technology specialist*
Cronin, Caroline *information technology executive*
Edenfield, J. Michael *information technology executive*
Judge, Jonathan J. *information technology executive, former financial services company executive*
Klinges, Vincent C. *information technology executive*
Markopoulos, Jody A. *information technology executive*
Pate, William *information technology executive*
Raina, Robin *information technology executive*
Sinisgalli, Peter F. *information technology executive*
Wall, Phil *information technology executive*

Carrollton
Barnes, Justin T. *healthcare information technology executive*

Norcross
Weaver, Lisa *information technology executive*

KENTUCKY

Lexington
Canning, Martin S. *information technology executive*

Prospect
Kehlbeck, Joseph H. *software developer, consultant*

LOUISIANA

Monroe
Brown, Peter C. *information technology executive*

MARYLAND

Baltimore
Leatherwood, Richard L. *information technology executive*

NORTH CAROLINA

Cary
Goodnight, James H. *information technology executive*
Sall, John *information technology executive*

Raleigh
Pace, Andrew K. *information technology library director*
Szulik, Matthew J. *information technology executive*

Research Triangle Park
DeMarco, Robert *information technology manager*

Winston Salem
Hanes, Ralph Philip, Jr. *network technician*

OKLAHOMA

Tulsa
Oliver, Georgianna White *technology consulting company executive*

SOUTH CAROLINA

Clemson
Bodde, David Leo *technology educator*

Columbia
Duggan, Kevin *information technology professional*

Greenville
Baur, Michael L. *information technology executive*
Whitchurch, Charles R. *retired information technology executive, board member*

Rock Hill
Reichental, Abraham N. *information technology executive*

TENNESSEE

Cookeville
Guimaraes, Tor *IT researcher, professor*

TEXAS

Austin
Anderson, Edward R. *information technology executive*
Harris, Nancy L. *information technology executive*
Knowles, Harry Jay *Internet personality, blogger, film critic*
Lam, Simon Sin-Sing *computer science educator*
Nelson, Erin Mulligan *social commerce industry executive, marketing professional*
Stanley, Tim *information technology executive*

Conroe
Kramm, Deborah Ann *retired information technology executive*

Dallas
Blodgett, Lynn R. *information technology executive*
Blodgett, Tom *information technology executive*
Capellas, Michael D. *information technology executive*
Rexford, John H. *information technology company executive*
Tranquill, Chris *information technology executive*
Villarreal, Lora Jean *information technology executive, human resources specialist*

Denton
Garcia, Oscar Nicolas *computer science educator*

Houston
Beauchamp, Robert E. *information technology executive*
Chan, Chiu M. *information technology executive*
Fishback, Dennis *information technology executive*
Settle, Mark *information technology executive*
Stouse, Mark *information technology executive*
Wejman, Janet P. *information technology and air transportation executive*
Winemiller, Albert E. *information technology executive*

Irving
Weatherson, Donald *information technology executive*

Plano
Condit, K.C. *information technology executive*
Dougherty, F(rancis) Kelly *application developer*
Feld, Charles S. *information technology executive*
Fickenscher, Kevin Michael *information technology executive, health services administrator*
Griffiths, Karen *mobile data services company executive*
Lyon, John *information technology executive*
Musser, Cherri M. *information technology executive*
Sweeney, William Robert, Jr. *information technology executive*
Vargo, Ronald Paul *information technology executive*
Wyman, Richard Thomas *retired information technology manager, researcher*

Richardson
Ansari, Anousheh *digital home and multimedia management technology company executive, entrepreneur*

Round Rock
Marmonti, David A. *information technology executive*
Roman, Ray *information technology executive*

San Antonio
Napier, Lanham (A. Lanham Napier) *web services company executive*
Pierce, Angela *information technology executive*
Scoble, Robert *information technology executive*

Southlake
Brandmaier, Jeff *information technology executive*

VIRGINIA

Alexandria
Sheffield, Greg *media blogger*

Annandale
Khim, Jay Wook *information technology executive*

Arlington
Azmi, Zalmai *information technology executive*
Brown, Jody A. *information technology executive*
Buford, Ted *information technology executive*
Cofoni, Paul Michael *former information technology executive*
Dragics, David Lee *information technology executive*
Framke, Gregory A. *information technology executive*
Jacoby, Lowell Edwin (Jake Jacoby) *information technology executive*
London, J. Phillip (Jack London) *information technology executive*
Makrinos, Stephen T. *information technology executive*
Mutryn, Thomas A. *information technology executive*

Centreville
Kneuer, John M.R. *information technology executive, former federal agency administrator*

Chantilly
Higginbotham, John Burnell *information technology executive*

Fairfax
Ballhaus, William Louis *information technology executive*
Campbell, Barry G. *information technology executive*
Nietsch, Elisabeth *information technology executive*
O'Neill, Molly Ann *information technology executive, former federal agency administrator*
Peake, James Benjamin *information technology executive, former United States Secretary of Veterans Affairs*
Pedersen, George J. *information technology executive*
Resor, Bill *information technology executive*
Roman, Gregory A. *information technology executive*

Falls Church
Cantus, Charles H. *information technology executive*
Courtney, William Harrison *IT firm executive*
DeMuro, Gerard J *information technology executive*
Fuller, Aaron B. III *information technology executive*
Gaffney, Steven F. *information technology executive*
Lawrie, Mike *information technology executive*
Menendez, James N. *information technology executive*
Moore, Alisoun *information technology executive*
Pagalia, Constantino *information technology executive*
Pullin, Susan *information technology executive*
Reinhardt, Thomas T. *information technology executive*
Saleh, Paul N. *information technology company executive*
Schambach, Patrick *information technology executive*

Herndon
Dunbar, W. Roy *information technology executive*
Parker, Kevin T. *information technology executive*
Toups, John M. *information technology executive*

Manassas
Bruno, Irene Evelyn *application developer, educator*

Mc Lean
Webb, Robert J. *information technology executive*

Reston
Balleweg, David *information technology executive*
Sacks, Jeffrey D. *information technology executive*
Sheffield, Matthew *media blogger*

Richmond
McDermid, Margaret E. (Lyn McDermid) *information technology executive*
Stokely, John E. *information technology executive*

Springfield
Greer, Mark Francis *information technology executive*

ADDRESS UNPUBLISHED

Bleszinski, Cliff (Clifford Michael Bleszinski) *game designer*
DiPentima, Renato Anthony *information technology executive*
Kleinlein, Kathy Lynn *training and development executive*
Salisbury, Alan Blanchard *information technology officer*
Spector, Warren E. *console and personal computer game developer*

INTERNET *See* INFORMATION TECHNOLOGY

LAW: JUDICIAL ADMINISTRATION

UNITED STATES

ALABAMA

Ashland
Ingram, Kenneth Frank *retired state supreme court justice*

Birmingham
Acker, William Marsh, Jr. *federal judge*
Blackburn, Sharon Lovelace *federal judge*
Bowdre, Karon O. *federal judge*
Coogler, L. Scott *federal judge*
Guin, Junius Foy, Jr. *federal judge*
Haikala, Madeline Hughes *federal judge*
Hancock, James Hughes *federal judge*
Hopkins, Virginia Emerson *federal judge*
Houston, James Gorman, Jr. *retired state supreme court justice*
Johnson, Inge Prytz *federal judge*
Kallon, Abdul Karim *federal judge*
Nabers, Drayton, Jr. *retired state supreme court chief justice, insurance company executive*
Proctor, R. David *federal judge*
Propst, Robert Bruce *federal judge*
Pryor, William Holcombe, Jr., (Bill Pryor) *federal judge, former state attorney general, educator*
Smith, Charles Lynwood, Jr. *federal judge*

Mobile
Butler, Charles Randolph, Jr. *federal judge*

Cox, Emmett Ripley *federal judge*
DuBose, Kristi K. *federal judge*
Graddick, Charles Allen *judge*
Granade, Callie Virginia Smith *federal judge*
Howard, Alex T., Jr. *federal judge*
Steele, William H. *federal judge*

Montgomery

Bolin, Michael F. *state supreme court justice*
Bryan, Tommy Elias *state supreme court justice*
Carnes, Edward Earl *federal judge*
De Ment, Ira *federal judge*
Dubina, Joel Fredrick *federal judge*
Fuller, Mark Everett *federal judge*
Hobbs, Truman McGill *federal judge*
Maddox, Alva Hugh *retired state supreme court justice*
Main, James Allen *state supreme court justice*
Moore, Roy S. *state supreme court chief justice*
Murdock, Glenn *state supreme court justice*
Parker, Tom *state supreme court justice, lawyer*
Shaw, James Gregory (Greg) *state supreme court justice*
Steele, Rodney Redfearn *judge*
Stuart, Lyn (Jacquelyn Stuart) *state supreme court justice*
Thompson, Myron Herbert *federal judge*
Watkins, W(illiam) Keith *federal judge*
Wise, Alisa Kelli *state supreme court justice*

Tuscaloosa

Malone, Charles R. *circuit court judge*

ARKANSAS

Batesville

Harkey, John Norman *retired judge*

El Dorado

Barnes, Harry Francis *federal judge*
Hickey, Susan Owens *federal judge*

Fayetteville

Brooks, Timothy Lloyd *federal judge*
Hendren, Jimm Larry *federal judge*

Fort Smith

Dawson, Robert Toombs *federal judge*
Holmes, Paul Kinloch, III, (P.K. Holmes) *federal judge, former federal prosecutor*

Little Rock

Arnold, Morris Sheppard *federal judge*
Baker, Karen R. *state supreme court justice*
Baker, Kristine Gerhard *federal judge*
Carter, Susan Webber (Susan Webber Wright) *federal judge*
Corbin, Donald L. *state supreme court justice*
Danielson, Paul E. *state supreme court justice*
Eisele, Garnett Thomas *federal judge*
Goodson, Courtney Hudson *state supreme court justice*
Hannah, James *state supreme court chief justice*
Hart, Josephine L. *state supreme court justice*
Holmes, J(ames) Leon *federal judge*
Hoofman, Cliff *state supreme court justice, former state legislator*
Marshall, Denzil Price, Jr. *federal judge*
Miller, Brian Stacy *federal judge*
Moody, James Maxwell, Jr., (Jay Moody) *federal judge*
Wilson, William Roy, Jr. *federal judge*

Searcy

Hughes, Thomas Morgan III *circuit judge*

Texarkana

Stroud, John Fred, Jr. *judge*

FLORIDA

Fort Lauderdale

Cohn, James I. *federal judge*
Dimitrouleas, William Peter *federal judge*
Gonzalez, Jose Alejandro, Jr. *federal judge*
Ray, Raymond B. *federal judge*
Zloch, William J. *federal judge*

Fort Myers

Chappell, Sheri Polster *federal judge*
Honeywell, Charlene Vanessa Edwards *federal judge*
Steele, John E. *federal judge*

Gainesville

Mickle, Stephan P. *federal judge*
Paul, Maurice Mitchell *federal judge*

Jacksonville

Adams, Henry Lee, Jr. *federal judge*
Corrigan, Timothy J. *federal judge*
Dalton, Roy Bale, Jr. *federal judge*
Davis, Brian Jordan *federal judge*
Howard, Marcia Morales *federal judge*
Melton, Howell Webster, Sr. *federal judge*
Schlesinger, Harvey Erwin *federal judge*
Tjoflat, Gerald Bard *federal judge*

Longboat Key

Morse, Marvin Henry *retired judge*

Miami

Altonaga, Cecilia M. *federal judge*
Cooke, Marcia Gail *federal judge*
Cristol, A. Jay *federal judge*
Gold, Alan Stephen *federal judge*
Graham, Donald Lynn *federal judge*
Hoeveler, William Marcellin *federal judge*
Huck, Paul C. *federal judge*
Jordan, Adalberto Jose *federal judge*
King, James Lawrence *federal judge*
Lederman, Cindy S. *judge*
Lenard, Joan A. *federal judge*
Marcus, Stanley *federal judge*
Martinez, Jose E. *federal judge*
Moore, Kevin Michael *federal judge*
Rosenbaum, Robin Stacie *federal judge*
Seitz, Patricia Ann *federal judge*
Siegel, Paul *retired judge*
Ungaro-Benages, Ursula Mancusi *federal judge*

Ocala

Hodges, William Terrell *federal judge*

Orlando

Antoon, John, II, *federal judge*
Conway, Anne Callaghan *federal judge*
Fawsett, Patricia Combs *federal judge*
Presnell, Gregory A. *federal judge*
Scriven, Mary Stenson *federal judge*
Sharp, George Kendall *federal judge*
Young, George Cressler *federal judge*

Panama City

Patterson, Christopher Nida *circuit judge*
Smoak, John Richard, Jr., (Richard Smoak) *federal judge*

Pensacola

Collier, Lacey Alexander *federal judge*
Rodgers, Margaret Catharine *federal judge*
Vinson, Clyde Roger (Roger Vinson) *federal judge*

Saint Petersburg

Dail, Joseph Garner, Jr. *retired judge*

Tallahassee

Canady, Charles Terrence *state supreme court justice, former congressman*
Grimes, Stephen Henry *retired state supreme court justice*
Hinkle, Robert Lewis *federal judge*
Labarga, Jorge *state supreme court justice, lawyer*
Lewis, R. Fred *state supreme court justice*
Pariente, Barbara J. *state supreme court justice*
Perry, James E.C. *state supreme court justice*
Polston, Ricky L. *state supreme court chief justice*
Quince, Peggy A. *state supreme court justice*
Stafford, William Henry, Jr. *federal judge*
Walker, Mark Eaton *federal judge*

Tampa

Bucklew, Susan Cawthon *federal judge*
Covington, Virginia Maria Hernandez *federal judge*
Kovachevich, Elizabeth Anne *federal judge*
Lazzara, Richard Allen *federal judge*
Merryday, Steven Douglas *federal judge*
Moody, James Shelton, Jr. *federal judge*
Whittemore, James D. *federal judge*
Wilson, Charles Reginald *federal judge*

West Palm Beach

Hurley, Daniel T. K. *federal judge*
Marra, Kenneth A. *federal judge*
Middlebrooks, Donald M. *federal judge*
Ryskamp, Kenneth Lee *federal judge*
Williams, Kathleen Mary *federal judge*

GEORGIA

Albany

Sands, Willie Louis *federal judge*

Atlanta

Batten, Timothy C., Sr. *federal judge*
Benham, Robert *state supreme court justice*
Blackwell, Keith R. *state supreme court justice*
Carnes, Julie Elizabeth *federal judge*
Cooper, Clarence *federal judge*
Duffey, William Simon, Jr. *federal judge*
Edmondson, J.L. (James Larry Edmondson) *federal judge*
Evans, Orinda Dale *federal judge*
Forrester, J. Owen *federal judge*
Hines, Preston Harris *state supreme court justice*
Hull, Frank Mays *federal judge*
Hunstein, Carol *state supreme court justice*
Hunt, Willis B., Jr. *federal judge*
Jones, Steve CarMichael *federal judge*
Martin, Beverly Baldwin *federal judge*
Melton, Harold D. *state supreme court justice*
Nahmias, David Erich *state supreme court justice, former prosecutor*
O'Kelley, William Clark *federal judge*
Pannell, Charles A., Jr. *federal judge*
Shoob, Marvin Herman *federal judge*
Story, Richard Wayne *federal judge*
Thompson, Hugh P. *state supreme court chief justice*
Thrash, Thomas Woodrow, Jr. *federal judge*
Tidwell, George Ernest *federal judge*
Totenberg, Amy Mil *federal judge*
Ward, Horace Taliaferro *federal judge*
Wood, Frank Maxwell (Max Wood) *judge, former federal prosecutor*

Augusta

Bowen, Dudley Hollingsworth, Jr. *federal judge*
Hall, James Randal *federal judge*

Brunswick

Wood, Lisa Godbey *federal judge*

Columbus

Land, Clay D. *federal judge*
Laney, John Thomas III *federal judge*

Lawrenceville

Reeves, Gene *retired judge*

Macon

Anderson, Robert Lanier III *federal judge*
Hershner, Robert Franklin, Jr. *judge*
Lawson, Hugh *federal judge*
Royal, C. Ashley *federal judge*
Treadwell, Marc Thomas *federal judge*

Newnan

Drake, W. Homer, Jr. *federal judge*

Rome

Murphy, Harold Lloyd *federal judge*
Vining, Robert Luke, Jr. *federal judge*

Roswell

Feldman, Joel Martin *retired judge*

Savannah

Edenfield, Berry Avant *federal judge*
Moore, William Theodore, Jr. *federal judge*

KENTUCKY

Ashland

Wilhoit, Henry Rupert, Jr. *federal judge*

Covington

Bunning, David L. *federal judge*
Keller, Michelle M. *state supreme court justice*

Frankfort

Cunningham, Bill *state supreme court justice*
Minton, John Dean, Jr. *state supreme court chief justice*
Reeves, Danny C. *federal judge*
Scott, Will T. *state supreme court justice*
Venters, Daniel Joseph *state supreme court justice*

Lexington

Caldwell, Karen K. *federal judge*
Coffman, Jennifer Burcham *federal judge*
Hood, Joseph Martin *federal judge*
Noble, Mary C. *state supreme court justice*

London

Siler, Eugene Edward, Jr. *federal judge*
Thapar, Amul Roger *federal judge*
Van Tatenhove, Gregory Frederick *federal judge*

Louisville

Boggs, Danny Julian *federal judge*
Cowan, Frederic Joseph *judge*
Heyburn, John Gilpin, II, *federal judge*
Hughes Abramson, Lisabeth *state supreme court justice*
Simpson, Charles R. III *federal judge*

Owensboro

McKinley, Joseph H., Jr. *federal judge*

Paducah

Russell, Thomas B. *federal judge*

Richmond

Chenault, James Stouffer *judge*

Springfield

Kelly, Dan *judge, former state legislator*

LOUISIANA

Alexandria

Drell, Dee D. *federal judge*

Baton Rouge

Brady, James Joseph *federal judge*
Dick, Shelly Deckert (Rachelle Lynne Deckert Dick) *federal judge*
Jackson, Brian Anthony *federal judge*
Parker, John Victor *federal judge*
Riedlinger, Stephen C. *federal judge*

Lafayette

Davis, William Eugene *federal judge*
Doherty, Rebecca Feeney *federal judge*
Duhe, John Malcolm, Jr. *retired federal judge, lawyer*
Haik, Richard T., Sr. *federal judge*
Melançon, Tucker Lee *federal judge*

Lake Charles

Minaldi, Patricia Head *federal judge*
Trimble, James Travis, Jr. *federal judge*

Monroe

James, Robert Gillespie *federal judge*

New Orleans

Africk, Lance M. *federal judge*
Banks, Fred Lee, Jr. *former state supreme court justice, lawyer*
Barbier, Carl Joseph *federal judge*
Beer, Peter Hill *federal judge*
Berrigan, Helen Ginger *federal judge*
Brown, Jerry A. *federal judge*
Brown, Nannette Jolivette *federal judge*
Clark, Marcus R. *state supreme court justice*
Clement, Edith Brown *federal judge*
Dennis, James Leon *federal judge*
Duval, Stanwood Richardson, Jr. *federal judge*
Engelhardt, Kurt D. *federal judge*
Fallon, Eldon E. *federal judge*
Feldman, Martin Leach-Cross *federal judge*
Guidry, Greg G. *state supreme court justice*
Heebe, Frederick Jacob Reagan *federal judge*
Higginson, Stephen Andrew *federal judge, former federal prosecutor*
Hughes, Jefferson D. III *state supreme court justice*
Johnson, Bernette Joshua *state supreme court chief justice*
Knoll, Jeannette Theriot *state supreme court justice*
Lemelle, Ivan L. R. *federal judge*
Lemmon, Mary Ann Vial *federal judge*
McNamara, A. J. *federal judge*
Morgan, Susie (Donna Sue Morgan) *federal judge*
Triche-Milazzo, Jane Margaret *federal judge*
Vance, Sarah S. *federal judge*
Victory, Jeffrey Paul *state supreme court justice*
Weimer, John L. *state supreme court justice*
Wiener, Jacques Loeb, Jr. *federal judge*
Zainey, Jay C. *federal judge*

Shreveport

Foote, Elizabeth Erny *federal judge*
Hicks, S. Maurice, Jr. *federal judge*
Stagg, Thomas E., Jr. *federal judge*
Stewart, Carl E. *federal judge*
Walter, Donald Ellsworth *federal judge*

MISSISSIPPI

Aberdeen

Aycock, Sharion *federal judge*
Davidson, Glen Harris *federal judge*

Greenville

Brown, Debra Marie *federal judge*
Walls, Johnnie E. *judge, former state legislator*

Gulfport

Gex, Walter Joseph III *federal judge*
Guirola, Louis, Jr. *federal judge*

Hattiesburg

Starrett, Melvin Keith *federal judge*

Jackson

Barbour, William Henry, Jr. *federal judge*
Barksdale, Rhesa Hawkins *federal judge*
Chandler, David A. *state supreme court justice*
Coleman, Josiah Dennis *state supreme court justice*
Dickinson, Jess H. *state supreme court justice*
Graves, James Earl *federal judge, former state supreme court justice*
Jolly, E. Grady *federal judge*
Jordan, Daniel Porter III *federal judge*
King, Leslie D. *state supreme court justice*
Kitchens, James W. *state supreme court justice*
Lamar, Ann Hannaford *state supreme court justice*
Lee, Tom Stewart *federal judge*
Ozerden, Halil Suleyman (Sul) *federal judge*
Pierce, Randy G. *state supreme court justice*
Randolph, Michael K. *state supreme court justice*
Reeves, Carlton Wayne *federal judge*
Southwick, Leslie Harburd *federal judge, lawyer*
Waller, William Lowe, Jr. *state supreme court chief justice*
Wingate, Henry Travillion *federal judge*

Natchez

Bramlette, David C. III *federal judge*

Oxford

Biggers, Neal Brooks, Jr. *federal judge*
Mills, Michael Paul *federal judge*

NORTH CAROLINA

Asheville

Cogburn, Max Oliver, Jr. *federal judge*
Reidinger, Martin Karl *federal judge*

Charlotte

Conrad, Robert James, Jr. *federal judge*
Horn, Carl III *retired federal judge, lawyer, mediator, arbitrator, law educator*
Mullen, Graham Calder *federal judge*
Voorhees, Richard Lesley *federal judge*
Whitney, Frank DeArmon *federal judge*

Durham

Silliman, Scott Livingston *federal judge, law educator*

Elizabeth City

Boyle, Terrence William *federal judge*

Greensboro

Eagles, Catherine Caldwell *federal judge*
Osteen, William Lindsay, Jr. *federal judge*
Stocks, William L. *federal judge*
Tilley, Norwood Carlton, Jr. *federal judge*

Greenville

Howard, Malcolm Jones *federal judge*

New Bern

Flanagan, Louise W. *federal judge*

Raleigh

Beasley, Cheri *state supreme court justice*
Britt, William Earl *federal judge*
Dever, James Columcille III *federal judge*
Eagles, Sidney Smith, Jr. *lawyer and retired judge*
Edmunds, Robert Holt, Jr. *state supreme court justice*
Hudson, Robin E. *state supreme court justice*
Jackson, Barbara *state supreme court justice*
Martin, John Charles *judge*
Martin, Mark D. *state supreme court justice*
McGee, Linda Mace *judge, lawyer*
Newby, Paul Martin *state supreme court justice*
Parker, Sarah Elizabeth *state supreme court chief justice*

Wilmington

Fox, James Carroll *federal judge*

Winston Salem

Beaty, James Arthur, Jr. *federal judge*
Schroeder, Thomas D. *federal judge*

OHIO

Cincinnati

Rogers, John Marshall *federal judge*

OKLAHOMA

Lawton

Moore, Roy Dean *retired judge*

Muskogee
Payne, James Hardy *federal judge*
Seay, Frank Howell *federal judge*
White, Ronald A. *federal judge*

Norman
Trimble, Preston Albert *retired judge*

Oklahoma City
Bacharach, Robert Edwin *federal judge*
Bohanon, Richard Lee *federal bankruptcy judge*
Cauthron, Robin J. *federal judge*
Colbert, Tom *state supreme court chief justice*
Combs, Douglas L. *state supreme court justice*
DeGiusti, Timothy D. *federal judge*
Edmondson, James E. *state supreme court justice*
Friot, Stephen P. *federal judge*
Gurich, Noma Diane *state supreme court justice*
Heaton, Joe L. *district judge*
Kauger, Yvonne *state supreme court justice*
Lavender, Robert Eugene *former state supreme court justice*
Leonard, Timothy Dwight *federal judge*
Miles-LaGrange, Vicki *federal judge*
Reif, John F. *state supreme court justice*
Russell, David L. *federal judge*
Taylor, Steven W. *state supreme court justice*
Watt, Joseph Michael *state supreme court justice*
West, Lee Roy *federal judge*
Winchester, James R. *state supreme court justice*

Tulsa
Beasley, William Rex *retired judge*
Dowdell, John Edward *federal judge*
Eagan, Claire Veronica *federal judge*
Ellison, James Oliver *federal judge*
Frizzell, Gregory Kent *federal judge*
Goodman, Jerry L(ynn) *judge*
Holmes, Jerome A. *federal judge*
Kern, Terry C. (Terence C. Kern) *federal judge*
Seymour, Stephanie Kulp *federal judge*

SOUTH CAROLINA

Anderson
Anderson, George Ross, Jr. *federal judge*

Charleston
Blatt, Solomon, Jr. *federal judge*
Duffy, Patrick Michael *federal judge*
Gergel, Richard Mark *federal judge*
Norton, David C. *federal judge*

Columbia
Anderson, Joseph Fletcher, Jr. *federal judge*
Beatty, Donald W. *state supreme court justice*
Currie, Cameron McGowan *federal judge*
Hamilton, Clyde Henry *federal judge*
Hearn, Kaye Gorenflo *state supreme court justice*
Kittredge, John Williamson *state supreme court justice*
Lewis, Mary Geiger *federal judge, lawyer*
Pleicones, Costa M. *state supreme court justice*
Seymour, Margaret B. *federal judge*
Shedd, Dennis W. *federal judge*
Toal, Jean Hoefer *state supreme court chief justice*

Florence
Harwell, Robert Bryan *federal judge*
Houck, Charles Weston *federal judge*
Wooten, Terry L. *federal judge*

Greenville
Childs, Julianna Michelle *federal judge*
Simmons, Charles Bedford, Jr. *judge*
Traxler, William Byrd, Jr. *federal judge*

Greenwood
Moore, James E. *former state supreme court justice*

Pauline
Burnett, E. C. III *former state supreme court justice*

TENNESSEE

Chattanooga
Collier, Curtis Lynn *federal judge*
Mattice, Harry Sandlin, Jr. *federal judge*

Greeneville
Greer, J. Ronnie *federal judge*

Jackson
Breen, John Daniel *federal judge*
Todd, James Dale *federal judge*

Knoxville
Jordan, Robert Leon *federal judge*
Lee, Sharon Gail *state supreme court justice, lawyer*
Murrian, Robert Phillip *retired federal judge, educator*
Phillips, Thomas Wade *federal judge*
Reeves, Pamela Lynn *federal judge, lawyer*
Varlan, Thomas A. *federal judge*
Wade, Gary R. *state supreme court justice*

Memphis
Anderson, Stanley Thomas *federal judge*
Donald, Bernice Bouie *federal judge, legal association administrator*
Fowlkes, John Thomas, Jr. *federal judge*
Gibbons, Julia Smith *federal judge*
Gilman, Ronald Lee *federal judge*
Holder, Janice Marie *state supreme court justice*
Mays, Samuel H., Jr. *federal judge*
McCalla, Jon Phipps *federal judge*
Person, Curtis S., Jr. *judge, former state legislator, lawyer*

Nashville
Brown, Joe Blackburn *judge*
Clark, Cornelia A. *state supreme court chief justice*
Daughtrey, Martha Craig *federal judge*
Haynes, William Joseph, Jr. *federal judge*
Koch, William C., Jr. *state supreme court justice*
Merritt, Gilbert Stroud *federal judge*
Nixon, John Trice *federal judge*
Sharp, Kevin Hunter *federal judge, lawyer*
Stranch, Jane Branstetter *federal judge*
Trauger, Aleta Arthur *federal judge*
Wiseman, Thomas Anderton, Jr. *federal judge*

Signal Mountain
Cooper, Robert Elbert *state supreme court justice*
Franks, Herschel Pickens *judge*

TEXAS

Amarillo
Robinson, Mary Lou *federal judge*

Austin
Benavides, Fortunato Pedro (Pete Benavides) *federal judge*
Boyd, Jeffrey S. *state supreme court justice*
Brown, Jeff *state supreme court justice*
Devine, John Phillip *state supreme court justice*
Green, Paul Warren *state supreme court justice*
Guzman, Eva Martinez *state supreme court justice*
Hecht, Nathan Lincoln *state supreme court chief justice*
Higginbotham, Patrick Errol *federal judge*
Hudspeth, Harry Lee *federal judge*
Jefferson, Wallace B. *former state supreme court justice*
Johnson, Philip Wayne *state supreme court justice*
Lehrmann, Debra H. *state supreme court justice*
Nowlin, James Robertson *federal judge*
Owen, Priscilla Richman *federal judge, former state supreme court justice*
Pope, Andrew Jackson, Jr., (Jack Pope) *retired judge*
Ray, Cread L., Jr. *retired judge*
Sparks, Sam *federal judge*
Willett, Don R. *state supreme court justice*
Yeakel, Earl Leroy, III, (Lee Yeakel) *federal judge*

Beaumont
Clark, Ron *federal judge*
Crone, Marcia Ann *federal judge*
Heartfield, Thad *federal judge*

Brownsville
Hanen, Andrew Scott *federal judge*
Tagle, Hilda Gloria *federal judge*

Bryan
Smith, Steven Lee *judge*

Corpus Christi
Head, Hayden Wilson, Jr. *federal judge*
Jack, Janis Graham *federal judge*
Ramos, Nelva Gonzales *federal judge*

Dallas
Boyle, Jane J. *federal judge*
Fish, A. Joe *federal judge*
Fitzwater, Sidney Allen *federal judge*
Furgeson, William Royal, Jr. *federal judge*
Godbey, David Charles *federal judge*
Haynes, Catharina D. *federal judge, lawyer*
Kinkeade, James E. (Ed Kinkeade) *federal judge*
Lindsay, Sam A. *federal judge*
Lynn, Barbara Michele *judge, federal judge*
Maloney, Robert B. *federal judge*
McGuire, Robert C. *retired federal judge*
O'Connor, Reed Charles *federal judge*
Solis, Jorge Antonio *federal judge*

Del Rio
Ludlum, Alia Moses *federal judge*

El Paso
Briones, David *federal judge*
Cardone, Kathleen *federal judge*
Guaderrama, David Campos *federal judge*
Martinez, Philip Ray *federal judge*
Montalvo, Frank *judge*

Fort Worth
McBryde, John Henry *federal judge*
Means, Terry Robert *federal judge*

Galveston
Costa, Gregg Jeffrey *federal judge*

Houston
Atlas, Nancy Friedman *federal judge*
DeMoss, Harold Raymond, Jr. *federal judge*
Ellison, Keith P. *federal judge*
Gilmore, Vanessa D. *federal judge*
Harmon, Melinda Furche *federal judge*
Hittner, David *federal judge*
Hoyt, Kenneth M. *federal judge*
Hughes, Lynn Nettleton *federal judge*
Jones, Edith Hollan *federal judge*
King, Carolyn Dineen *federal judge*
Lake, Simeon Timothy III *federal judge*
Miller, Gray Hampton *federal judge*
Reavley, Thomas Morrow *federal judge*
Rosenthal, Lee Hyman *federal judge*
Smith, Jerry Edwin *federal judge*
Sondock, Ruby Kless *retired judge*
Werlein, Ewing, Jr. *federal judge*

Kaufman
Tygrett, Howard Volney, Jr. *judge, lawyer*

Laredo
Alvarez, Micaela *federal judge*
Kazen, George Philip *federal judge*
Saldaña, Diana *federal judge*

Lubbock
Cummings, Sam R. *federal judge*

Marshall
Gilstrap, James Rodney *federal judge, lawyer*

Mcallen
Crane, Randy *federal judge*
Hinojosa, Federico Gustavo, Jr. *retired judge*
Hinojosa, Ricardo H. *federal judge*

Plano
Schell, Richard A. *federal judge*

San Angelo
Walther, Barbara Ann Lane *judge, former lawyer*

San Antonio
Biery, Samuel Fred, Jr., (Fred Biery) *federal judge*
Clark, Leif Michael *federal judge*
Garcia, Orlando Luis *federal judge*
Garza, Emilio Miller *federal judge*
Rodriguez, Xavier *federal judge*

Texarkana
Folsom, David *federal judge*

Tyler
Davis, Leonard *federal judge*
Guthrie, Judith K. *federal judge*

Victoria
Rainey, John David *federal judge*

Waco
Patterson, Jan Powell *former judge*
Smith, Walter Scott, Jr. *federal judge*

VIRGINIA

Abingdon
Jones, James Parker *federal judge*

Alexandria
Barry, Lance Leonard *primary examiner*
Bostetter, Martin V. B., Jr. *federal judge*
Brinkema, Leonie Milhomme *federal judge*
Cacheris, James C. *federal judge*
Ellis, Thomas Selby III *federal judge*
Hilton, Claude Meredith *federal judge*
Lee, Gerald Bruce *federal judge*
O'Grady, Liam *federal judge*
Spencer, James R. *federal judge*
Trenga, Anthony John *federal judge*

Arlington
Gelpi, Gustavo Antonio, Jr. *federal judge*
Griswold, Nancy J. *federal judge*

Charlottesville
Crigler, B. Waugh *federal judge*
Wilkinson, J(ames) Harvie III *federal judge*

Chesterfield
Davis, Bonnie Christell *judge*

Lynchburg
Burnette, Ralph Edwin, Jr. *judge*
Moon, Norman K. *federal judge*

Newport News
Adams, David Huntington *federal judge*

Norfolk
Bonney, Hal James, Jr. *federal judge*
Davis, Mark S. *federal judge*
Doumar, Robert George *judge*
Friedman, Jerome B. *federal judge*
Jackson, Raymond A. *federal judge*
Morgan, Henry Coke, Jr. *judge*
Smith, Rebecca Beach *federal judge*
Wright Allen, Arenda L. *federal judge*

Richmond
Agee, G(eorge) Steven *federal judge, former state supreme court justice*
Diaz, Albert *federal judge*
Dohnal, Dennis William *judge*
Floyd, Henry Franklin *federal judge*
Gibney, John Adrian, Jr. *federal judge*
Goodwyn, S. Bernard *state supreme court justice*
Gregory, Roger Lee *federal judge*
Hudson, Henry E. *federal judge*
Keenan, Barbara Milano *federal judge, former state supreme court justice*
Kinser, Cynthia D. *state supreme court chief justice*
Koontz, Lawrence Larkins, Jr. *retired state supreme court justice*
Lacy, Elizabeth Bermingham *state supreme court justice*
Lemons, Donald W. *state supreme court justice*
McClanahan, Elizabeth A. *state supreme court justice*
Millette, LeRoy F., Jr. *state supreme court justice*
Mims, William Cleveland (Bill Mims) *state supreme court justice*
Powell, Cleo E. *state supreme court justice*
Russell, Charles Stevens *retired state supreme court justice*
Tice, Douglas Oscar, Jr. *retired federal judge*
Wynn, James Andrew, Jr. *federal judge*

Roanoke
Conrad, Glen E. *federal judge*
Turk, James Clinton *federal judge*
Urbanski, Michael Francis *federal judge*

Staunton
Cochran, George Moffett *retired judge*

WEST VIRGINIA

Beckley
Berger, Irene Cornelia *federal judge*

Bluefield
Faber, David Alan *federal judge*

Charleston
Benjamin, Brent D. *state supreme court justice, lawyer*
Copenhaver, John Thomas, Jr. *federal judge*
Davis, Robin Jean *state supreme court chief justice*
Goodwin, Joseph Robert *federal judge*
Johnston, Thomas E. *judge*
Ketchum, Menis E., II, *state supreme court justice*
King, Robert Bruce *federal judge*
Loughry, Allen H., II, *state supreme court justice*
Thacker, Stephanie Dawn *federal judge*
Webster, Carrie Lee *judge, former state legislator*
Workman, Margaret Lee *state supreme court justice, lawyer*

Clarksburg
Keeley, Irene Patricia Murphy *federal judge*

Huntington
Chambers, Robert Charles (Chuck Chambers) *federal judge*

Wheeling
Bailey, John Preston *federal judge*
Groh, Gina Marie *federal judge*
Stamp, Frederick Pfarr, Jr. *federal judge*

TERRITORIES OF THE UNITED STATES

PUERTO RICO

Hato Rey
Cerezo, Carmen Consuelo *federal judge*

San Juan
Acosta, Raymond Luis *retired federal judge*
Besosa, Francisco Augusto *federal judge*
Casellas, Salvador E. *federal judge*
Delgado-Colon, Aida M. *federal judge*
Delgado Hernández, Pedro Alberto *federal judge*
Dominguez, Daniel R. *federal judge*
Estrella Martinez, Louis F. *territorial supreme court justice*
Feliberti Cintron, Roberto *territorial supreme court justice*
Fiol Matta, Liana *territorial supreme court justice*
Fusté, José Antonio *federal judge*
Garcia-Gregory, Jay A. *federal judge*
Hernández Denton, Federico *supreme court chief justice*
Kolthoff Caraballo, Erick V. *territorial supreme court justice*
Martinez Torres, Rafael L. *territorial supreme court justice*
Pabon Charneco, Mildred G. *territorial supreme court justice*
Perez-Gimenez, Juan Manuel *federal judge*
Rivera García, Edgardo *territorial supreme court justice*
Rivera Pérez, Efraín E. *former territorial supreme court justice*
Rodriguez, Annabelle *territorial supreme court justice, former attorney general*

VIRGIN ISLANDS

Charlotte Amalie
Barnard, Geoffrey W. *judge*

St Thomas
Cabret, Maria M. *territorial supreme court justice*
Gomez, Curtis V. *federal judge*
Hodge, Rhys S. *territorial supreme court chief justice*
Swan, Ive Arlington *territorial supreme court justice*

ADDRESS UNPUBLISHED

Ablard, Charles David *administrative judge*
Albritton, William Harold III *federal judge*
Anderson, Edward Riley *retired state supreme court justice*
Anthony, Joan Caton *retired administrative judge*
Barker, William M. *retired state supreme court chief justice*
Bertelsman, William Odis *federal judge*
Birch, Adolpho A., Jr. *retired state supreme court justice*
Black, Susan Harrell *federal judge*
Brett, Thomas Rutherford *federal judge*
Campbell, Todd J. *federal judge*
Castagna, William John *federal judge*
Chapman, Robert Foster *federal judge*
Cooper, William S. *retired state supreme court justice*
Couvillion, David Irvin *retired federal judge*
Duncan, Allyson K. *federal judge*
Enoch, Craig Trively *retired judge*
Fay, Peter Thorp *federal judge*
Harwell, David Walker *retired judge*
Herlong, Henry Michael, Jr. *federal judge*
Highsmith, Shelby *federal judge*
Hunter, Jack E. *retired senior district judge*
Johnstone, Douglas Inge *retired state supreme court justice, lawyer*
Kern, John Worth III *retired judge*
Kiser, Jackson L. *federal judge*
Kravitch, Phyllis A. *federal judge*
Lake, I. Beverly, Jr. *retired state supreme court chief justice*
Lambert, Joseph Earl *retired state supreme court chief justice*
Lyons, Champ, Jr. *retired state supreme court justice*
Newbern, William David *retired state supreme court justice*
Prado, Edward Charles *federal judge*
Prather, Lenore Loving *former state supreme court chief justice*
Price, Robert Eben *judge*

Prince, William Taliaferro *retired federal judge*
Schneider, Michael H., Sr. *federal judge*
Shepherd, Bobby E. *federal judge*
Spector, Rose *former state supreme court justice*
Starcher, Larry Victor *retired state supreme court justice*
Stevens, John Paul *retired United States Supreme Court Justice*
Sturgis, Kathy Ann *judge*
Thompson, Ralph Gordon *retired federal judge*
Thurmond, George Murat *judge*
Waller, John Henry, Jr. *retired state supreme court justice*
Watson, Jack Crozier *retired state supreme court justice*
Williams, Karen Johnson *retired federal judge*
Wintersheimer, Donald Carl *retired state supreme court justice*
Wood, James Jerry *judge*
Wroble, Arthur Gerard *retired former judge*

LAW: LAW PRACTICE AND ADMINISTRATION

UNITED STATES

ALABAMA

Anniston
Klinefelter, James Louis *retired lawyer*

Birmingham
Alexander, James Patrick *lawyer, educator*
Balch, Samuel Eason *lawyer*
Buchanan, John D. *lawyer*
Carmody, Richard Patrick *lawyer*
Carruthers, Thomas Neely *lawyer*
Coleman, Brittin Turner *lawyer*
Cooper, N. Lee *lawyer*
Denson, William Frank III *lawyer*
Drew, Mark Livingston *lawyer*
Duke, J. Richard *lawyer*
Friend, Edward Malcolm III *lawyer, educator*
Gale, Fournier Joseph III *lawyer*
Garner, Robert Edward Lee *lawyer*
Gespass, David *lawyer*
Gewin, James W. *lawyer*
Grenier, Beau *lawyer*
Howell, William Ashley III *lawyer*
Irons, William Lee *lawyer*
Jones, D. Paul, Jr. *lawyer, retired bank executive*
Langum, David John *law educator, historian*
Long, Deborah Joyce *lawyer*
Martin, Alice Howze *former prosecutor, executive recruiter*
McWhorter, Hobart Amory, Jr. *lawyer*
Mills, William Hayes *lawyer*
Molen, John Klauminzer *lawyer*
Newton, Alexander Worthy *lawyer*
Piassick, Joel Bernard *lawyer*
Powell, Jerry W. *lawyer*
Rogers, Alan T. *lawyer*
Rogers, Ernest Mabry *lawyer*
Small, Clarence Merilton, Jr. *lawyer*
Smith, Ralph Harrison, II, *lawyer, consultant*
Spransy, Joseph William *corporate lawyer*
Stabler, Lewis Vastine, Jr. *retired lawyer*
Thuston, William Lee *lawyer*
Vance, Joyce White *federal prosecutor*
Vinson, Laurence Duncan, Jr. *lawyer*
Wells, Huey Thomas, Jr. *lawyer*
Whittington, John P. *lawyer*
Wilson, James Charles, Jr. *lawyer*
Woodall, Thomas A. *lawyer, former state supreme court justice*
Wrinkle, John Newton *lawyer*

Gadsden
Hinton, James Forrest, Jr. *lawyer*

Huntsville
Gabig, Jerome S., Jr. *lawyer*

Mobile
Braswell, Louis Erskine *lawyer*
Brown, Kenyen Ray *federal prosecutor*
Harris, Benjamin Harte, Jr. *lawyer*
Holland, Lyman Faith, Jr. *lawyer*
Holmes, Broox Garrett *lawyer*
Murchison, David Roderick *lawyer*
Pierce, Donald Fay *lawyer*
Reeves, W. Boyd *lawyer*
Roedder, William Chapman, Jr. *lawyer*

Montgomery
Beck, George Lamar, Jr. *federal prosecutor*
Byars, Walter Ryland, Jr. *lawyer*
Campbell, Maria Bouchelle *lawyer, consultant*
Hamner, Reginald Turner *lawyer*
McFadden, Frank Hampton *lawyer, former judge*
Neiman, John, Jr. *lawyer*
Segall, Joshua S. *lawyer*
Stevenson, Bryan Allen *legal institute administrator, law educator*
Vance, C. Gibson *lawyer*

Opelika
Samford, Yetta Glenn, Jr. *lawyer, director*

Tuscaloosa
Cook, Camille Wright *retired law educator*
Leonard, James *law librarian, educator*
Spruell, Alyce Manley *lawyer*
Watkins, John Cumming, Jr. *law educator*

Tuskegee
Gray, Fred David *lawyer*

ARKANSAS

Arkadelphia
Turner, Todd *lawyer, former political organization administrator*

El Dorado
Cossé, Steven A. *lawyer, retired oil industry executive*

Fayetteville
Mourton, Kenneth R. *lawyer*
Nance, Cynthia Eleanor (Cyndi Nance) *law educator, former dean*
Pearson, Charles Thomas, Jr. *lawyer, director*

Fort Smith
Eldridge, William Conner, Jr. *federal prosecutor*

Harrison
Sprott, James D. *lawyer*

Helena
Roscopf, Charles Buford *lawyer*

Hot Springs
Drake, Joshua *lawyer*

Hot Springs National Park
Schnipper, Don Martin *lawyer*

Jonesboro
Deacon, John C. *lawyer*

Little Rock
Anderson, Philip Sidney *lawyer*
Boe, Myron Timothy *lawyer*
Brown, Robert Laidlaw *lawyer, former state supreme court justice*
Cross, J. Bruce *lawyer*
Gunter, Russell Allen *lawyer*
Hall, John Wesley, Jr. *lawyer*
Haught, William Dixon *lawyer, writer*
Julian, Jim Lee *lawyer*
May, Ronald Alan *lawyer*
Murphey, Arthur Gage, Jr. *law educator*
Prince, David Cannon *lawyer*
Ramsay, Richard L. *lawyer*
Riordan, Deborah Truby *lawyer*
Sherman, William Farrar *lawyer, former state legislator*
Thyer, Christopher R. *federal prosecutor, former state legislator*
Ursery, Frederick Stanley *lawyer*
Witherspoon, Carolyn Brack *lawyer*

North Little Rock
Patty, Claibourne Watkins, Jr. *lawyer*
Welch, Morgan E. *lawyer*

Pine Bluff
Strode, Joseph Arlin *lawyer*

Prescott
Vasser, Albert Glenn *lawyer*

Rogers
Balfe, Robert Cramer III *lawyer, former prosecutor*

Warren
Claycomb, Hugh Murray *lawyer, writer*

CALIFORNIA

Los Angeles
Tu, Lawrence P. *lawyer, broadcast executive*

COLORADO

Longmont
Freytag, Sharon Nelson *lawyer*

DISTRICT OF COLUMBIA

Washington
Charnovitz, Steve *law educator*
Dellinger, Walter Estes III *lawyer, law educator*
Kovacic, William Evan *law educator, former federal commissioner*
Leo, Leonard A. *legal association administrator, lawyer*
Maiwurm, James John *lawyer*
Norwood, Deborah Anne *law librarian*

FLORIDA

Alachua
Gaines, Weaver Henderson *lawyer*

Boca Raton
Baskies, Jeffrey Alan *lawyer*
Beber, Robert H. *lawyer, diversified financial services company executive*
Buckstein, Mark Aaron *lawyer, mediator, educator*
Garcia, Elisa Dolores *lawyer*
Gracin, Hank *lawyer*
Martin, James Russell *lawyer*
Morris, Stuart R. *lawyer*
Pratt, David *lawyer*
Reinstein, Joel *lawyer*
Roselli, Richard Joseph *lawyer*
Schechterman, Lawrence *lawyer, chef, freelance travel writer, photographer, teacher of English as a foreign language*
Silver, Barry Morris *lawyer*
Wolf, Jerome L. *lawyer*

Bonita Springs
Crutcher, Michael Bayard *lawyer, retired consumer products company executive*
Nevin, Hugh Williamson, Jr. *lawyer*

Cape Coral
Pohl, Michael A. *lawyer*

Clearwater
Vetter, David R. *lawyer*
Zschau, Julius James *lawyer*

Coral Gables
Klock, Joseph Peter, Jr. *lawyer*
Mena, Daniel *lawyer*
Pérez Damera, Myra M. *lawyer*
Rosenn, Keith Samuel *lawyer, educator*
Upshaw, Anthony N. *lawyer*

Davie
Richmond, Gail Levin *law educator*

Daytona Beach
Barker, Robert Osborne (Bob Barker) *mediator, retired educator*
Harris, Christy Franklin *lawyer*
Neitzke, Eric Karl *lawyer*

Delray Beach
Helander, Robert Charles *lawyer, arbitrator, contributing editor*

Fernandina Beach
Johnson, Philip McBride *lawyer*

Fort Lauderdale
Bustamante, Nestor *lawyer*
Cole, James Otis *lawyer*
Dressler, Robert A. *lawyer*
Ferrando, Jonathan P. *lawyer, automotive executive*
Goldberg, Alan Joel *lawyer*
Harbaugh, Joseph Delbert *law educator, former dean*
Hirsch, Jeffrey Allan *lawyer*
Jarvis, Robert Mark *law educator*
Kuehne, Benedict P. *lawyer*
Lyons, Bruce Martin *lawyer*
Morris, Gerald Michael *lawyer, educator*
Moss, Stephen Bruce *lawyer*
Nyce, John Daniel *lawyer*
Picazio, Kim Lowry *lawyer*
Polish, Sheldon S. *lawyer*
Russell, Terrence Joseph *lawyer*
Schlesinger, Sheldon J. *lawyer*
Schneider, Laz Levkoff *lawyer*
Turner, Hugh Joseph, Jr. *lawyer*
Udolf, Bruce Lee *lawyer*

Fort Myers
Medvecky, Robert Stephen *lawyer*
Rothschild, Donald Phillip *retired lawyer, arbitrator*

Fort Pierce
Conklin, Howard Lawrence *lawyer*

Gainesville
Criser, Marshall M. *lawyer, retired academic administrator*
Germain, Claire Madeleine *law librarian, educator*
Hiers, Richard Hyde *lawyer, educator, writer*
Maurer, Virginia Gallaher *law educator*
Price, Mary Kathleen *law librarian, educator*
Smith, David Thornton *lawyer, educator*
Smith, Rod (Rodney Warren Smith) *lawyer, former political organization administrator*

Gulf Stream
Mahon, Arthur J. *lawyer*

Gulfport
Hansen, Kenneth D. *lawyer, ophthalmologist*

Hallandale Beach
Bradford, Barbara Reed *retired lawyer*

Hobe Sound
Pidot, Whitney Dean *retired lawyer*

Jacksonville
Ansbacher, Barry Barnett *lawyer*
Beytagh, Francis X. *law educator*
Boyer, Tyrie Alvis *lawyer*
Bradford, Dana Gibson, II, *lawyer*
Bryan, Joseph Shepard, Jr. *lawyer*
Cavendish, Michael Robert *lawyer*
Coker, Howard Coleman *lawyer*
Commander, Charles Edward *lawyer, real estate consultant*
Corey, Angela B. *prosecutor*
Coxe, Henry M. III *lawyer*
Fitzsimmons, Ellen Marie *lawyer*
Gabel, George DeSaussure, Jr. *lawyer*
Gravelle, Michael L. *lawyer*
Hyde, Kevin E. *lawyer, former councilman*
Israel, Kimberly Held *lawyer*
Moseley, James Francis *lawyer*
Rinaman, James Curtis, Jr. *lawyer*
Sadowski, Peter T. *lawyer*
Weaver, Dianne Jay *lawyer*
Webb, Jack D. *lawyer, former councilman*
Williams, Timothy L. *lawyer*

Jacksonville Beach
McWilliams, John Lawrence III *lawyer*

Jasper
McCormick, John Hoyle *lawyer*

Jupiter
Click, David Forrest *lawyer, investment advisor*
Lamborn, LeRoy Leslie *law educator*

Lake Mary
Silver, Elaine Terry *lawyer*

Lakeland
Attaway, John A., Jr. *lawyer*
Wendel, John Fredric *lawyer, consultant*

Leesburg
Fechtel, Vincent John *legal administrator*

Maitland
Wilder, Charles David *lawyer*

Marco Island
Berenzweig, Jack Charles *lawyer*
Heindl, Phares Matthews *lawyer*
Kerstetter, Wayne Arthur *law educator, artist*

Melbourne
Cacciatore, S. Sammy *lawyer*
Hament, Andrew Stanton *lawyer*
Mikuen, Scott Theodore *lawyer*

Miami
Alonso, Cristina *lawyer*
Alvarez, Cesar L. *lawyer*
Anderson, Terence James *law educator*
Astigarraga, Jose Ignacio *lawyer*
Baker, Thomas Eugene *law educator*
Berman, Bruce Judson *lawyer*
Black, Roy *lawyer*
Blumberg, Edward Robert *lawyer*
Bolton, Joseph D. *lawyer*
Brochin, Robert M. *lawyer*
Bru, Julie O. *lawyer*
Burnett, Henry *retired lawyer*
Calli, Paul Albert *lawyer*
Cantero, Raoul G. III *lawyer, former state supreme court justice*
Cardenas, Alberto R. *lawyer, lobbyist*
Casey, Daniel Arthur *lawyer*
Chasen, Jerry Simon *lawyer*
Coffey, Kendall Brindley *lawyer*
Connor, Terence Gregory *lawyer*
Davis, Jaret L. *lawyer*
Dulin, Amy G. *lawyer*
Eaton, Joel Douglas *lawyer*
Fatovic, Robert Dean *lawyer*
Ferrer, Wifredo A. *federal prosecutor*
Fleming, Joseph Z. *lawyer*
Foreman, Jeffrey Eric *lawyer*
Garrett, Richard G. *lawyer*
Gong, Edmond Joseph *lawyer*
González, Daniel E. *lawyer*
Gragg, Karl Lawrence *lawyer*
Grossman, Robert Louis *lawyer*
Hall, Adam Stuart *lawyer*
Hall, Andrew Clifford *lawyer*
Hartz, Steven Edward Marshall *lawyer, educator*
Hoffman, Larry J. *lawyer*
Jimenez, Marcos Daniel *lawyer, former prosecutor*
Korchin, Judith Miriam *lawyer*
Kreitzer, Michael N. *lawyer*
Lampen, Richard Jay *executive, lawyer, investment banker*
Landy, Burton Aaron *lawyer*
Lauria, Thomas E. *lawyer*
Levine, Robert Jeffrey *lawyer*
Lipoff, Norman Harold *lawyer*
Martinez-Fraga, Pedro J. *lawyer*
Mehta, Eileen Rose *lawyer*
Menéndez Cambó, Patricia *lawyer*
Murphy, Timothy James *lawyer*
Nuernberg, William Richard *lawyer*
Orlin, Karen J. *lawyer*
Osman, Edith Gabriella *lawyer*
Ovelmen, Richard J. *lawyer*
Pasano, Michael S. *lawyer*
Pfenniger, Richard Charles, Jr. *lawyer, healthcare company executive*
Poston, Rebekah Jane *lawyer*
Quentel, Albert Drew *lawyer*
Reid, Benjamine *lawyer*
Rogovin, Lawrence H. *lawyer*
Rubin, Steven D. *lawyer*
Sharpstein, Richard Alan *lawyer*
Smulian, Andrew M. *lawyer*
Sonberg, Steven *lawyer*
Steinberg, Marty *lawyer*
Stokes, Paul Mason *lawyer*
Strafer, G. Richard *lawyer*
Sustana, Mark *lawyer, construction company executive*
Thornburg, Frederick Fletcher *lawyer executive, educator*
Touby, Kathleen Anita *lawyer*
Ullyot, Ted (Theodore Warren Ullyot) *lawyer, former social networking company executive*
Vento, M. Thérèse *lawyer*
Weinstein, Alan Edward *lawyer*
Weinstein, Andrew H. *lawyer*
Wing, James David *lawyer*
Wright, Robert Thomas, Jr. *lawyer*
Zack, Stephen Neal *lawyer*
Zelek, Mark Edward *lawyer*

Miami Gardens
Light, Alfred Robert *law educator*

Naples
Anderson, John Thomas *lawyer*
Bruce, Jackson Martin, Jr. *lawyer*
Crehan, Joseph Edward *lawyer*
Parry, Timothy R. *lawyer*
Rosenberg, Michael *lawyer*
Strauss, Jerome Manfred *lawyer, trust company executive, professional private fiduciary, author*
Westman, Carl Edward *lawyer*

Neptune Beach
Mantle, Raymond Allan *lawyer*

Newberry
Boyes, Patrice Flinchbaugh *lawyer*

Orlando
Ahlers, Glen-Peter, Sr. *law library director, educator, consultant*
Arkin, J. Gordon *lawyer*
Baez, Jose Angel *lawyer*

Brown, C. David, II, *lawyer*
Brumby, Andrew M. *lawyer*
Christiansen, Patrick T. *lawyer*
Clem, Alexander Murphree *lawyer*
deBeaubien, Hugo H. *lawyer*
Doppelt, Ava K. *lawyer*
Downs, Mayanne *lawyer*
Frey, Louis, Jr. *lawyer, federal official*
Fulton, Richard T. *lawyer*
Gerber, Daniel J. *lawyer*
Gray, J. Charles *lawyer, former cattle rancher*
Handley, Leon Hunter *lawyer*
Heaton, Stuart Alan *lawyer*
Hoctor, James Joseph *lawyer*
Langworthy, Robert H. *criminal justice educator*
Leonhardt, Frederick Wayne *lawyer*
Marshall, Byrd F., Jr. *lawyer*
Martinez, Rafael E. (Ralph E. Martinez) *lawyer, former federal commissioner*
Mayhall, Clifford Wesley *lawyer*
Mock, Frank Mackenzie *lawyer*
Nadeau, Robert Bertrand, Jr. *lawyer*
Sebastian, Teresa Mosley *lawyer*
Sims, Roger W. *lawyer*
Skambis, Christopher Charles, Jr. *lawyer*
Snively, Stephen Wayne *lawyer*
Spaulding, Karla Rae *lawyer*
Weiss, Christopher John *lawyer*
Wells, Charles Talley *lawyer, retired state supreme court justice*
Wilson, William Berry *lawyer*
Yates, Leighton Delevan, Jr. *lawyer*

Ormond Beach
Hayes, Larry B. *retired lawyer*
Logan, Sharon Brooks *lawyer*

Osprey
Partoyan, Garo Arakel *lawyer*

Palm Beach
Adler, Frederick Richard *lawyer, corporate financial executive*
Canary, Nancy Halliday *lawyer*

Palm Beach Gardens
Savrann, Richard Allen *lawyer*

Palmetto Bay
Dady, Robert Edward *lawyer*

Pensacola
Bell, Kenneth B. *lawyer, former state supreme court justice*
Bozeman, Frank Carmack *retired lawyer*
Geeker, Nicholas Peter *lawyer, judge*
Papantonio, Mike (James Michael Papantonio) *lawyer, talk radio host*
Windham, John Franklin *lawyer, educator*

Plant City
Buchman, Kenneth William *lawyer*
Sparkman, Steven Leonard *lawyer*

Pompano Beach
Shulmister, M(orris) Ross *lawyer*

Punta Gorda
Bailey, F. Lee (Francis Lee Bailey) *lawyer*

Saint Augustine
Brady, James Joseph *labor arbitrator*
Poland, Richard Clayton *law educator*

Saint Petersburg
Bairstow, Frances Kanevsky *arbitrator, mediator, educator*
Battaglia, Anthony Sylvester *lawyer*
Glass, Roy Leonard *lawyer*
Jacob, Bruce Robert *law educator*
Matecki, Paul L. *lawyer*
Moody, Lizabeth Ann *lawyer, educator*

Sarasota
Ehrlich, Bernard Herbert *lawyer, trade association administrator*
Janney, Oliver James *lawyer*
Lee, Jerome G. *lawyer*
Liner, David B. *lawyer*
Raimi, Burton Louis *lawyer*

South Miami
Keedy, Christian David *lawyer*
Leinoff, Andrew Morris *lawyer*

Stuart
Gary, Willie E. *lawyer*

Tallahassee
Aurell, John Karl *lawyer*
Barnett, Martha Walters *lawyer*
Beaver, Kevin *law educator*
Carson, Leonard Allen *lawyer*
Curtin, Lawrence N. *lawyer*
Dariotis, Terrence Theodore *lawyer*
Ervin, Robert Marvin *lawyer*
Gievers, Karen A. *lawyer*
Johnson, Kelly Overstreet *lawyer*
Kirwin, Thomas F. *prosecutor*
Makar, Scott D. *lawyer*
Marsh, Pamela Cothran *federal prosecutor*
Miller, Gregory R. *retired prosecutor*
Miller, Morris Henry *lawyer*
Phipps, Benjamin Kimball, II, *lawyer*
Reid, Sue Titus *law educator*
Webster, Peter David *lawyer*
Zaiser, Kent Ames *lawyer*

Tampa
Albritton, Brian (A. Brian Albritton) *lawyer, former federal prosecutor*
Barkin, Marvin E. *lawyer*
Barton, Bernard Alan, Jr. *lawyer*
Bedke, Michael A. *lawyer*
Butler, Paul Bascomb, Jr. *lawyer*
Cury, Bruce Paul *lawyer, magistrate, educator*

Diehr, Beverly Hunt *lawyer*
Doliner, Nathaniel Lee *lawyer*
Ellwanger, Thomas John *lawyer*
Gilbert, Leonard Harold *lawyer*
Gonzalez, Joe Manuel *lawyer*
Grammig, Robert James (Bob Grammig) *lawyer*
Gunn, Lee Delton, IV, *lawyer*
Holliday, Ronald Sturgis *lawyer*
Kadow, Joseph J. *lawyer, food service executive*
Koren, Edward Franz, Jr. *lawyer*
Lane, Robin R. *lawyer*
Levine, Jack Anton *lawyer*
Martin, Gary Wayne *lawyer*
McAdams, John Pope *lawyer*
McDevitt, Sheila Marie *retired lawyer, energy executive, business consultant*
O'Neill, Albert Clarence, Jr. *lawyer*
Richter, John Charles *lawyer, former prosecutor*
Robinson, John William, IV, *lawyer*
Schwenke, Roger Dean *lawyer*
Susanin, Timothy Scott *lawyer, health products executive*
Swope, Dale M. *lawyer*
Thomas, Wayne Lee *lawyer*
Wagner, Frederick William (Bill Wagner) *lawyer*
Waller, Edward Martin, Jr. *lawyer*
Weinberg, Morris, Jr., (Sandy Weinberg) *lawyer*
Whatley, Jacqueline Beltram *lawyer*
Yerrid, C. Steven *lawyer*

Tarpon Springs
Hatch, John D. *lawyer*

Vero Beach
Foster, Bill *lawyer, former mayor, St. Petersburg, Florida*
Geiman, J. Robert *lawyer*
Hoynes, Louis LeNoir, Jr. *lawyer*

Village Of Golf
Kempf, Donald G., Jr. *retired lawyer*

Wellington
Bakst, Daren *legal association administrator, think-tank associate*

West Palm Beach
Ackerman, David P. *lawyer*
Aron, Jerry E. *lawyer*
Beall, Kenneth Sutter, Jr. *lawyer*
Beasley, James W., Jr. *lawyer*
Chopin, L. Frank *lawyer*
Kelley, Craig I. *lawyer, educator*
Lamb, Kevin Thomas *lawyer*
Layman, David Michael *lawyer*
Link, Scott J. *lawyer*
Miller, Richard Jackson (Rick Miller) *lawyer*
Moore, George Crawford Jackson *lawyer*
Mrachek, Lorin Louis *lawyer*
Royce, Raymond Watson *lawyer, rancher, investor*
Schneider, Lisa A. *lawyer*
Sklar, William Paul *lawyer, educator*
Tancer, Edward F. *lawyer, utilities executive*
Warner, Tom *lawyer, former state legislator, mediator*

Winter Park
Dempsey, Bernard Hayden, Jr. *lawyer*
Heinle, Richard Alan *lawyer*
Jontz, Jeffry Robert *lawyer*
Kittleson, Henry Marshall *lawyer*
Swann, Richard Rockwell *lawyer, banker*
Troutman, Holmes Russell *lawyer*

GEORGIA

Alpharetta
Hatcher, Barbara A. *lawyer*

Athens
Beaird, James Ralph *lawyer, educator, dean*
Carlson, Ronald Lee *law educator*
Chaffin, Verner Franklin *lawyer, educator*
Cook, J. Vincent *lawyer*
Ellington, Charles Ronald *lawyer, educator*
Hellerstein, Walter *lawyer*
Huszagh, Fredrick Wickett *lawyer, information technology executive, educator*
Kurtz, Paul Michael *retired law educator*
Rutledge, Peter Bowman (Bo Rutledge) *law educator*
Shipley, David Elliott *lawyer, educator*
Tolley, Edward Donald *lawyer*
Watson, Carol A. *law librarian*

Atlanta
Abrams, Harold Eugene *lawyer*
Albert, Ross Alan *lawyer*
Alexander, Miles Jordan *lawyer*
Alford, Carolyn Zander *lawyer*
Altman, Robert *lawyer*
Batson, Richard Neal *lawyer*
Beckham, Walter Hull III *lawyer*
Bell, Griffin Boyette, Jr. *lawyer*
Bennett, Jay D. *lawyer*
Bird, Wendell Raleigh *lawyer*
Blake, Elizabeth K. *lawyer*
Bowden, Henry Lumpkin, Jr. *lawyer*
Bratton, James Henry, Jr. *lawyer*
Brecher, Armin George *lawyer*
Brewster, William Howard *lawyer*
Brown, Jeffrey P. *lawyer*
Butterworth, S. Kendall *lawyer*
Byrne, Granville Bland III *lawyer*
Cadenhead, Alfred Paul *lawyer*
Camp, Damon D., Jr. *law educator*
Campbell, Michael H. *lawyer, air transportation executive*
Cargill, Robert Mason *lawyer*
Carter, Dudley Rochelle *lawyer*
Clarke, Thomas Hal *lawyer*
Cohen, Ezra Harry *lawyer*
Cohen, Lori G. *lawyer*
Cohen, N. Jerold *lawyer*
Coil, James H. III *lawyer*
Cook, Philip Carter *lawyer*
Cooper, Lawrence Allen *lawyer*

Cornwell, David (William David Cornwell Sr.) *lawyer*
Croft, Terrence Lee *lawyer, mediator, arbitrator*
Dalton, John Joseph *lawyer*
Davis, Benjamin Alando *lawyer*
Davis, Frank Tradewell, Jr. *lawyer*
Dawson, Cari K. *lawyer*
Deane, Richard Hunter, Jr., (Rick Deane) *lawyer, former prosecutor*
Denburg, Dorian Sue *lawyer*
Denny, Richard Alden, Jr. *retired lawyer*
Dorris, William E. *lawyer*
Douglas, John Lewis *lawyer*
Dunlevie, Steven S. *lawyer*
Durrett, James Frazer, Jr. *retired lawyer*
Dyson, James David *lawyer*
Edwards, Stephen Allen *lawyer*
Egan, Michael Joseph *retired lawyer, state legislator*
Engsberg, Mark David *law librarian, educator*
Etheridge, Jack Paul *arbitrator, mediator, retired judge*
Farnham, Clayton Henson *lawyer*
Feese, Suzanne *lawyer*
Fellows, Henry David, Jr. *lawyer*
Fleming, Julian Denver, Jr. *lawyer*
Forbes, Theodore McCoy, Jr. *arbitrator, mediator, retired lawyer*
Forry, Robert H. *lawyer*
Forte, Stephen Michael *lawyer*
Fortin, Raymond D. *lawyer, bank executive*
Fortuna, Julian Anthony *lawyer, certified public accountant*
Foulke, Edwin Gerhart, Jr. *lawyer, former federal agency administrator*
Gambrell, David Henry *lawyer*
Garland, Edward T.M. *lawyer*
Genberg, Ira *lawyer*
Glaser, Arthur Henry *lawyer, mediator*
Goepelt, Bernhard *lawyer, beverage products company executive*
Gomes, Matthew Trainor *lawyer*
Grantham, Mark E. *lawyer*
Groton, James Purnell *lawyer, arbitrator*
Grout, Robert W. *lawyer*
Gura, Philip Paul *lawyer*
Haidet, Jeffrey K. *lawyer*
Hampton, Cathy *lawyer*
Harness, William Walter *lawyer*
Harrison, C. Lash *lawyer*
Hasson, James Keith, Jr. *lawyer, educator*
Hatcher, James A. *lawyer, communications executive*
Hawks, Barrett Kingsbury *lawyer*
Hay, Peter Heinrich *law educator*
Hays, Richard R. *lawyer*
Hays, Robert D., Jr. *lawyer*
Hinson, H. Douglas *lawyer*
Hobby, Scott M. *lawyer*
Hoff, Gerhardt Michael *lawyer, insurance company executive*
Hopkins, John David *lawyer*
Howard, Harry Clay *lawyer*
Janney, Donald Wayne *lawyer*
Jeffries, McChesney Hill, Jr. *lawyer*
Jenkins, Albert Felton, Jr. *lawyer*
Johnson, Benjamin Franklin III *retired lawyer*
Johnson, John H. *lawyer*
Jones, Glower Whitehead *lawyer*
Jordak, John A., Jr. *lawyer*
Jordan, Hilary Peter *lawyer*
Katz, Joel Abraham *lawyer*
Kaufman, Mark David *lawyer*
Kaufman, Mark Stuart *lawyer*
Kelly, James Patrick *lawyer*
Kerr, James Yancey, II, *lawyer, utilities executive*
Kessler, Richard Paul, Jr. *lawyer*
Khoury, Kenneth F. *lawyer, air transportation executive*
Kitchens, William H. *lawyer*
Kneisel, Edmund M. *lawyer*
Knowles, Marjorie Fine *retired law educator, dean*
Lamberth, Rebecca McLemore *lawyer*
Landau, Michael B. *law educator*
Leonard, David Morse *lawyer*
Lewis, Stephen E. *lawyer*
Linch, Keth *commercial real estate and partnership lawyer*
Linkous, William Joseph, Jr. *lawyer*
Loveland, L. Joseph, Jr. *lawyer*
Lower, Robert Cassel *lawyer, educator*
Lucas, Lauren Sudeall *lawyer*
Mallory, Sandra Moss *legal administrator*
Marshall, John Treutlen *lawyer, educator*
McAlpin, Kirk Martin *lawyer*
McClure, Teri Plummer *lawyer, delivery service executive*
McNeill, Thomas Ray *lawyer*
Meachum, Daniel Ray *lawyer*
Mixson, Mickey (H. Lamar Mixson) *lawyer*
Moeling, Walter Goos, IV, *lawyer*
Moore, Rodney Gregory *lawyer*
Morgan, Elizabeth Ann *lawyer*
Muhl, Shauna Sullivan *lawyer*
Murray, Patrick Brian *lawyer*
Nelson, Allen W. *lawyer*
Newton, Floyd Childs III *lawyer*
Norman, Albert George, Jr. *lawyer*
O'Day, Stephen Edmund *lawyer*
Owens, Laura Lewis *lawyer*
Partlett, David Frederick *law educator*
Persons, (W.) Ray (W. Ray Persons) *lawyer, legal association administrator*
Petrik, Michael Thomas *lawyer*
Phillips, Barry *lawyer*
Pike, Larry Samuel *lawyer*
Pottle, Steven L. *lawyer*
Prucino, Diane L. *lawyer*
Quillen, Roger K. *lawyer*
Quittmeyer, Peter Charles *lawyer*
Raby, Kenneth Alan *lawyer, retired military officer*
Rafuse, Nancy E. *lawyer, shareholder*
Reed, Glen Alfred *lawyer*
Reinhardt, Daniel Sargent *lawyer*
Remar, Robert Boyle *lawyer*
Rhodes, Thomas Willard *lawyer*
Rogers, C. B. *lawyer*
Rogers, DeWitt Ralph *lawyer*
Roseborough, Teresa Wynn *lawyer*
Rusche, Mark C. *lawyer*
Salo, Ann Sexton Distler *lawyer*

Schroder, Jack Spalding, Jr. *lawyer*
Schulte, Jeffrey Lewis *lawyer*
Sears, Leah Ward *lawyer, retired state supreme court judge*
Shackelford, Richard L. *lawyer*
Shipp, Robbin *prosecutor, former state legislator*
Sibley, James Malcolm *retired lawyer*
Silverstein, Leonard A. *lawyer*
Smith, Edward Kendrick *lawyer*
Smith, Jeffrey Michael *lawyer*
Spalding, William R. (Bill Spalding) *lawyer, former pharmaceutical executive*
Stallings, Ronald Denis *lawyer*
Stephenson, Mason Williams *lawyer*
Stipancich, John K. *lawyer*
Stockton, David A. *lawyer*
Strickland, Frank B. *lawyer*
Tanenbaum, Allan Jay *lawyer*
Taylor, George Kimbrough, Jr. *lawyer*
Thomas, Lizanne *lawyer*
Thompson, Philip C. *lawyer, investment advisor, private equity fund manager, educator, journalist*
Tinsley, Barbara V. *lawyer*
Tran, Dat T. *lawyer, gas industry executive*
Travis, Robert M. *lawyer*
VanderBroek, Mark S. *lawyer*
Varner, Chilton Davis *lawyer*
Volentine, Richard J., Jr. *lawyer*
Walsh, W. Terence *lawyer*
Wasserman, Mark D. *lawyer*
Weathersby, Michael Nelson *lawyer*
Webb, Robert W., Jr. *lawyer*
Wellon, Robert G. *lawyer*
Whitley, Joe Dally (Joe Dally Whitley) *lawyer*
Wilson, Brent Lawrence *lawyer, mediator*
Wood, L. Lin, Jr. *lawyer*
Yates, Sally Quillian *federal prosecutor*
Zealey, Sharon Janine *lawyer*

Cartersville
Tate, Samuel Lester III *lawyer*

Columbus
Brinkley, Jack Thomas *lawyer, former United States Representative, Georgia*
Griffith, G. Sanders III *lawyer*
Hatcher, Samuel F. *lawyer, diversified financial services company executive*
Loudermilk, Joey M. *lawyer, insurance company executive*
McGlamry, Max Reginald *retired lawyer*
Patrick, James Duvall, Jr. *lawyer*
Wooten, Joel Orba, Jr. *lawyer*

Dallas
Richardson, Glenn *lawyer, former state legislator*

Decatur
James, Robert D., Jr. *prosecutor*
Williams, Rita Tucker *lawyer*

Duluth
Daniels, Jennifer M. *lawyer*
Kuper, Debra E. *lawyer, manufacturing executive*

Gainesville
Puryear, W.(illiam) Bradford *lawyer*
Stewart, Jon Douglas *lawyer*

Jasper
Marger, Edwin *lawyer*

Macon
Dantzler, Deryl Daugherty *lawyer, educator, dean*
Floyd, Daisy Hurst *law educator, former dean*
Moore, Michael Jonathan *federal prosecutor*
Robinson, W. Lee *lawyer*
Weston, Charles Hinton *retired law educator*

Madison
DuBose, Charles Wilson *lawyer*

Marietta
Bentley, Fred Douglas, Sr. *lawyer*
Braun, Michael Rene *lawyer*
Lackland, Theodore Howard *lawyer*

Norcross
Koman, Alan James *lawyer, educator*
O'Callaghan, William Lawrence, Jr. *lawyer*
Williams, Jennifer R. *lawyer*

Roswell
Baker, Anita Diane *lawyer*
Birmingham, Richard Gregory *lawyer*

Saint Simons Island
Taylor, Philip Raymond *lawyer*

Sandy Springs
Owen, Robert Hubert *lawyer, real estate broker*

Savannah
Bowman, Catherine McKenzie *lawyer*
Dickey, David Herschel *lawyer, accountant*
Forbes, Morton Gerald *lawyer*
McCracken, Eugene Luke *lawyer*
Stillwell, Walter Brooks III *lawyer*
Tarver, Edward J. *federal prosecutor, former state legislator*

Statesboro
Edenfield, Gerald M. *lawyer*
Franklin, James Burke *lawyer*
Weiss, Lawrence N. *lawyer*

Thomasville
Avera, Stephen R. *lawyer*

Tucker
Taylor, George B., Jr. *lawyer, electric power industry executive*

Valdosta
Dodd, Roger J. *lawyer*

KENTUCKY

Covington
Kerr, Thomas Robert *lawyer, state legislator*
Land, Suzanne Prieur *lawyer*
Schaeffer, Andrew *lawyer*
Smith, Pete A. *lawyer*

Florence
Robinson, William T. III *lawyer*

Frankfort
Hendrix, Laura Hromyak *lawyer*
Palmore, John Stanley, Jr. *retired lawyer*

Lexington
Brickman, Blake (James Blake Brickman) *lawyer, former legislative staff member*
Fryman, Virgil Thomas, Jr. *lawyer*
Harvey, Kerry B. *federal prosecutor*
Larson, Jon S. *lawyer*
Lester, Roy David *lawyer*
Patton, Robert J. *lawyer, electronics executive*
Thro, William Eugene *general counsel*
Varellas, Sandra Motte *lawyer*

London
Jensen, Thomas Lee *lawyer, state legislator*
Keller, John Warren *lawyer*

Louisville
Barr, James Houston III *lawyer*
Campbell, Christian Larsen *lawyer, food service executive*
Chen, James Ming *law educator*
Conner, Stewart Edmund *lawyer*
Crockett, John R. III *lawyer*
Ewald, Robert Charles *lawyer*
Fowler, Michael Ross *political scientist*
Gilman, Sheldon Glenn *lawyer*
Hale, David Jason *federal prosecutor*
Helm, T. Kennedy III *lawyer*
Hollander, William H. *lawyer*
Hopson, Edwin Sharp *lawyer*
Jones, Frances Brooks *lawyer, bank executive*
Keane, Margaret E. *lawyer*
Lay, Norvie Lee *law educator*
Luber, Thomas J(ulian) *lawyer*
Maddox, Victor B. *lawyer*
McClain, Tim S. *lawyer*
McGarvey, John T. *lawyer*
Mellen, Francis Joseph, Jr. *lawyer*
Northern, Richard *lawyer*
Osborn, John Simcoe, Jr. *lawyer*
Pelfrey, D. Patton *lawyer*
Riedman, Mary Suzanne *lawyer*
Runyon, Keith Leslie *lawyer, editor*
Silverthorn, Robert Sterner, Jr. *lawyer*
Skees, William Leonard, Jr. *lawyer*
Todoroff, Christopher M. *lawyer, insurance company executive*
Vish, Donald H. *lawyer, writer, photographer, educator*
Wren, Harold Gwyn *arbitrator, educator*

Newport
Siverd, Robert Joseph *lawyer*

Prospect
Aberson, Leslie Donald *lawyer*
Willenbrink, Rose Ann *retired lawyer*

Somerset
Prather, John Gideon, Jr. *lawyer*

LOUISIANA

Baton Rouge
Aguilar, Rodolfo J., Jr. *lawyer*
Blackman, John Calhoun, IV, *lawyer*
Casey, Robert Reisch *lawyer*
Cazayoux, Don (Donald J. Cazayoux Jr.) *lawyer, former federal prosecutor, former United States Representative from Louisiana*
Costonis, John J. *law educator, former academic administrator*
Donofrio, John *lawyer*
Dugas, David Roy *lawyer, former prosecutor*
Graphia, Gary P. *lawyer, construction executive*
Johnson, Joseph Clayton, Jr. *retired lawyer*
Lamonica, Paul Raymond *law educator, academic administrator*
Moréteau, Olivier *law educator*
Patterson, Michael A. *lawyer*
Pugh, George Willard *law educator*
Richards, Marta Alison *lawyer*
Sloan, Robert D. *law educator, director*
Whittington, Christopher L. *lawyer, former political organization administrator*

Covington
Christian, John Catlett, Jr. *lawyer*
Rice, Winston Edward *lawyer, priest*
Snyder, Charles Aubrey *lawyer*

Franklin
McClelland, James Ray *lawyer*

Hammond
Lane, Kenneth E. *law educator, legal association administrator*

La Place
Cicet, Donald James *lawyer*

Lafayette
Angers, Winston Thomas *lawyer, publishing executive*
Davidson, James Joseph III *lawyer*
Finley, Stephanie A. *federal prosecutor*
Skinner, Michael David *lawyer, lobbyist, consultant*
Washington, Donald W. *lawyer, former prosecutor*

Mandeville
Deano, Edward Joseph, Jr. *lawyer, state legislator*

Marksville
Riddle, Charles Addison III *district attorney, former state legislator*

Metairie
deLaup, Mickey Stephens *lawyer*
Nehrbass, Seth Martin *lawyer*
Rosen, Charles, II, *retired lawyer*
Wax, George Louis *lawyer*

New Orleans
Abaunza, Donald Richard *lawyer*
Acomb, Robert Bailey, Jr. *lawyer, educator*
Adams, Charles P., Jr. *lawyer*
Alsobrook, Henry Bernis, Jr. *lawyer*
Barry, Francis Julian, Jr. *lawyer*
Belleau, Ashley L. *lawyer*
Bieck, Robert Barton, Jr. *lawyer*
Cheatwood, Roy Clifton *lawyer*
Childress, Steven Alan *law educator*
Combe, John Clifford, Jr. *lawyer*
Crusto, Mitchell Ferdinand *lawyer, educator*
Dicharry, Richard N. *lawyer*
Duggan, James Edgar *law librarian, law educator*
Falgoust, Dean Thomas *lawyer, accountant*
Force, Robert *law educator*
Gertler, Meyer H. *lawyer*
Goins, Richard Anthony *lawyer, educator*
Griffin, Stephen M. *law educator, former dean*
Hines, William H. *lawyer*
Hurley, Grady Schell *lawyer*
Jones, Philip Kirkpatrick, Jr. *lawyer*
Lemann, Thomas Berthelot *lawyer*
Lowe, Robert Charles *lawyer*
Marcus, Bernard *lawyer, arbitrator, mediator*
McGlone, Michael Anthony *lawyer*
Mintz, Albert *lawyer*
Neff, Carole Cukell *lawyer*
Osakwe, Christopher *lawyer, educator*
Polite, Kenneth Allen, Jr. *federal prosecutor*
Schnabel, Marta-Ann *lawyer*
Simon, H(uey) Paul *lawyer*
Villarrubia, Todd M. *lawyer*
Worley, Robert Bruce, Jr. *lawyer*

Opelousas
Guillory, Elbert Lee *lawyer, state legislator*

River Ridge
Didriksen, Caleb H. III *lawyer*

Saint Francisville
Mc Clendon, William Hutchinson III *retired lawyer*

Shreveport
Nelson, Ralph Stanley *lawyer*
Payne, Roy Steven *lawyer*

Slidell
Singletary, Alvin D. *lawyer*

MICHIGAN

Harbor Springs
Brennan, Thomas Emmett *lawyer*

MISSISSIPPI

Bay Saint Louis
Bernstein, Joseph *lawyer*

Greenwood
Swayze, Charles J., Jr. *lawyer*

Gulfport
Holland, George Edison, Jr., (Ed) *lawyer, utilities executive*

Jackson
Anderson, Reuben V. *lawyer, board member*
Corlew, John Gordon *lawyer*
Davis, Gregory Keith *federal prosecutor*
Drinkwater, William Wayne *lawyer*
Hafter, Jerome Charles *lawyer*
Hammond, Frank Jefferson III *lawyer*
Houston, Jamie Giles III *lawyer, accountant*
Roberts, Richard Charlton III *lawyer*
Welch, Walter Scott III *lawyer*

Olive Branch
Carnall, George Hursey, II, *lawyer*

Oxford
Adams, Felicia Colette *federal prosecutor*
Alexander, John Marshall *federal prosecutor*
Tollison, Nina Stubblefield *lawyer*

Ridgeland
Clark, Donald, Jr. *lawyer*
Henegan, John C(lark) *lawyer*
Ogletree, Powell G., Jr. *lawyer*
Travis, Jay A. III *lawyer*

Starkville
Yoste, Charles Todd *lawyer*

Tupelo
Franks, Jamie (James R. Franks Jr.) *lawyer, former political organization administrator*

Tylertown
Mord, Irving Conrad, II, *lawyer*

University
Davis, Samuel Marion *law educator, researcher, former dean*

Vicksburg
Bailess, Robert R. *lawyer*

MISSOURI

Springfield
Wilcher, Larry K. *lawyer*

NEW JERSEY

Newark
Blumrosen, Alfred William *law educator, consultant, arbitrator*

NEW YORK

Buffalo
Girth, Marjorie Louisa *lawyer, educator*
Heath, Richard Eddy *lawyer*

New York
Baker, David Remember *lawyer*
Driver, Walter W., Jr. *lawyer, investment company executive*
Nissenbaum, Robert Jay *law librarian, educator*
Shahshahani, Azadeh *legal association administrator*

Purchase
Thompson, Larry Dean *lawyer*

NORTH CAROLINA

Asheville
Bissette, Winston Louis, Jr. *lawyer, mayor*
Davis, Roy Walton, Jr. *lawyer*
Elmore, Bruce Alexander, Jr. *lawyer*
Martin, Harry Corpening *lawyer, retired state supreme court justice*
McDevitt, Larry S. *lawyer*

Burlington
Eberts, F. Samuel III *lawyer, medical products executive*

Cary
Bailey, Robert Short *retired lawyer*
Montgomery, Charles Harvey *lawyer*
Raisig, Paul Jones, Jr. *lawyer*

Chapel Hill
Boger, John Charles (Jack Boger) *law educator, dean*
Brophy, Alfred Laurence III *law educator*
Corrado, Michael Louis *law educator*
Hardin, Paul III *law educator*
Klinefelter, Anne *law librarian, educator*
Loeb, Ben Fohl, Jr. *retired law educator*
Nichol, Gene Ray, Jr. *law educator, former academic administrator*
Wegner, Judith Welch *lawyer, educator, dean*

Charlotte
Ayscue, Edwin Osborne, Jr. *lawyer*
Barber, Martha Gayle *lawyer*
Brackett, Martin Luther, Jr. *lawyer*
Buchan, Jonathan Edward, Jr. *lawyer*
Buckley, Charles Robinson III *lawyer*
Calloway, Mark T. *lawyer, former prosecutor*
Coss, Stephen K. *lawyer*
Cramer, Robert W. *lawyer*
Durham, J(oseph) Porter, Jr. *lawyer, educator*
Farthing, William P., Jr. *lawyer*
Ferguson, James Elliot, II, *lawyer*
Gunson, Douglas Robert *lawyer*
Hanna, George Verner III *lawyer*
Hargrove, Donna L. *lawyer*
Holder, Angela Roddey *retired law educator*
Lewis-Raymond, Jane R. *lawyer, gas industry executive*
Lilly, Kevin L. *lawyer, manufacturing executive*
Linker, Raymond Otho, Jr. *lawyer*
Lynch, Gary G. *lawyer, bank executive*
Marcus, Robert R. *lawyer*
McBryde, Neill Gregory *lawyer*
McCoy, Michael D. *lawyer*
Mehta, Kiran H. *lawyer*
Nedzbala, Michael *lawyer*
Pridgen, Eugene C. *lawyer*
Rawlins, Donald Ray *lawyer*
Reigel, Ernest W. *lawyer*
Snyder, James C., Jr. *lawyer, consumer products company executive*
Thigpen, Richard Elton, Jr. *retired lawyer*
Tompkins, Anne Magee *federal prosecutor*
Trent, B. Keith *lawyer, energy executive*
Van Hoy, Philip Marshall *lawyer*
Vinroot, Richard Allen *lawyer, mayor*

Cherryville
Huffstetler, Palmer Eugene *lawyer*

Durham
Bartlett, Katharine Tiffany *law educator, former dean*
Bayern, Shawn J. *law educator*
Bernard, Pamela Jenks *lawyer*
Carrington, Paul DeWitt *lawyer, educator*
Christie, George Custis *lawyer, educator, writer*
Cox, James D. *law educator*
Cutshaw, Kenneth Andrew *lawyer*
Demott, Deborah Ann *law educator*
Dunshee, Melanie J. *law librarian, educator*
Havighurst, Clark Canfield *law educator*
Marsh, William Andrew III *lawyer*
Maxwell, Richard Callender *retired lawyer, educator*
Rai, Arti K. *law educator*
Robertson, Horace Bascomb, Jr. *retired law educator*
Schroeder, Christopher Henry *law educator, former federal agency administrator*
Schwarcz, Steven Lance *lawyer, educator*

Fayetteville
Townsend, William Jackson *lawyer*

Gastonia
Stott, Grady Bernell *lawyer*

Greensboro
Barnhardt, Zeb Elonzo, Jr. *lawyer*
Bullock, Frank William, Jr. *lawyer, retired federal judge*
Davis, Ferd Leary, Jr. *law educator, consultant*
Davis, Herbert Owen *lawyer*
Friedland, Steven I. *law educator*
Hunter, Bynum Merritt *retired lawyer*
Meagher, Laura Catherine *lawyer, apparel executive*
Melvin, Charles Edward, Jr. *lawyer*
Rand, Ripley Eagles *federal prosecutor*
Swan, George Steven *law educator*

Greenville
Colombo, Michael Allen *lawyer*

Hickory
Johnson, Daniel *lawyer*
Wyatt, Frank B., II, *lawyer*

Lillington
Edwards, Charlene Vernell *lawyer*

Marion
Burgin, Charles Edward *retired lawyer*

Matthews
Mahoney, George R., Jr. *lawyer*

Mc Leansville
Miles, John Benjamin *lawyer*

Mooresville
Keener, Gaither McDonald, Jr. *lawyer, consumer products company executive*

Morganton
Simpson, Daniel Reid *lawyer, mediator*

Murphy
Bata, Rudolph Andrew, Jr. *lawyer*

New Bern
Davis, James Lee *lawyer*
Overholt, Hugh Robert *lawyer, retired military officer*

Pittsboro
Southern, Robert Allen *lawyer*
Tucker, Don Eugene *retired lawyer*

Raleigh
Boyette, Richard T. *lawyer*
Brewer, William E., Jr. *lawyer*
Browning, Christopher *lawyer*
Cain, James Palmer *lawyer, former ambassador*
Carlton, Alfred Pershing, Jr. *lawyer*
Carter, Jean Gordon *lawyer*
Case, Charles Dixon *lawyer*
Cunningham, Michael *lawyer*
Davis, Egbert Lawrence III *lawyer*
Ellis, Richard W. *lawyer*
Joyner, Gary Kelton *lawyer*
Joyner, Walton Kitchin *lawyer*
Kapp, Michael Keith *lawyer*
Lynch, John Christopher *lawyer*
Meek, Jerry (Gerald Francis Meek) *lawyer, former political organization administrator*
Meeker, Charles C. *lawyer, former mayor*
Millberg, John C. *lawyer*
Mitchell, Burley Bayard, Jr. *lawyer*
Patterson, William S. *lawyer*
Philbeck, John Heydt *lawyer*
Roach, Wesley Linville *lawyer, insurance executive*
Simpson, Steven Drexell *lawyer*
Spearman, Robert Worthington *lawyer*
Taylor, Raymond Mason *lawyer, educator, former government official*
Timmons, Sean Abbott *lawyer*
Valois, Robert Arthur *lawyer*
Walker, Thomas Gray *federal prosecutor*

Research Triangle Park
Welborn, Reich Lee *lawyer*
Whichard, Willis Padgett *lawyer, retired educator, judge*

Rocky Mount
Zipf, Robert Eugene, Jr. *medical laboratory director, legal medicine consultant, pathologist*

Statesville
McCanless, Ross William *lawyer, manufacturing executive*

Tarboro
Hopkins, Grover Prevatte *lawyer*

Trinity
Walker, Kenneth Lynn *lawyer*

Willow Spring
Valvo, Barbara-Ann *lawyer, surgeon*

Winston Salem
Barnhill, Henry Grady, Jr. *lawyer*
Blynn, Guy Marc *retired lawyer*
Chilson, John A. *lawyer, retired military officer*
Edwards, Charles Archibald *lawyer*
Graham, William Thomas *lawyer*
Greason, Murray Crossley, Jr. *lawyer*
Gunter, Michael Donwell *lawyer*
Holton, Martin L., III, (Mark Holton) *lawyer, tobacco products manufacturing company executive*
Holton, Walter Clinton, Jr. *lawyer*
Johnson, Robert Jerome, Jr., (Bob Johnson) *lawyer*
Loughridge, John Halsted, Jr. *lawyer*
Moser, Kenneth Allen *lawyer*
Newman, Joel S. *law educator*
Oliver, Patricia *lawyer, executive secretary*
Parker, Marian F. *law librarian, educator*
Quick, Elizabeth L. *lawyer*
Ray, Michael Edwin *lawyer*
Sandridge, William Pendleton, Jr. *lawyer*
Schollander, Wendell Leslie, Jr. *lawyer*

Schollander, Wendell Wes III *lawyer*
Vaughan, Keith W. *lawyer*
Vaughn, Robert Candler, Jr. *lawyer*
Walker, George Kontz *law educator*
Walsh, Robert K. *law educator, former dean*
Womble, William Fletcher *retired lawyer*

OKLAHOMA

Agra
Mather, Stephanie June *lawyer*

Cherokee
Stein, Sam Lee *lawyer*

Chickasha
Cordell, F. Thomas *lawyer*

Claremore
Steidley, Juan Dwayne *lawyer, judge*

Edmond
Angel, Steven Michael *retired lawyer*
Lester, Andrew William *lawyer*

Enid
Jones, Stephen *lawyer*

Eufaula
Reheard, Deborah Ann *lawyer*

Guthrie
Davis, Frank Wayne *lawyer*

Mcalester
Cornish, Richard Pool *lawyer*

Muskogee
Green, Mark Fredrick *federal prosecutor*

Nichols Hills
Ross, William Jarboe *lawyer*

Norman
Coats, Andrew Montgomery *law educator, trial and appellate lawyer, former dean, mayor*
Petersen, Catherine Holland *lawyer*

Oklahoma City
Beveridge, Norwood Pierson *retired law educator*
Christiansen, Mark D. *lawyer*
Coats, Sanford Charles (Sandy Coats) *federal prosecutor*
Court, Leonard *lawyer, educator*
Douglas, Donita Bourns *legal association administrator*
Ford, Michael Raye *lawyer*
Hood, Henry J. *lawyer, energy executive*
Legg, William Jefferson *lawyer*
Lowe, Lyle Justin *lawyer*
McCampbell, Robert Garner *lawyer, former prosecutor*
Moler, Edward Harold *retired lawyer*
Nelon, Robert Dale *lawyer*
Paul, William George *lawyer*
Perry, Steven L. *lawyer*
Rockett, D. Joe *lawyer, director*
Schuster, E. Elaine *lawyer*
Steinhorn, Irwin Harry *lawyer, corporate financial executive, educator*
Taylor, Lyndon Clint *lawyer, energy executive*
Zuhdi, Nabil (Bill) *lawyer, litigator, consultant, producer, film professional boxing and concerts*

Ponca City
Northcutt, Clarence Dewey *lawyer*
Raley, John Wesley, Jr. *lawyer*

Stillwater
Clark, Gary Carl *lawyer*

Tulsa
Arrington, John Leslie, Jr. *lawyer*
Barker, John Roy *lawyer*
Bryant, Hubert Hale *retired lawyer*
Echo-Hawk, Walter R., Jr. *lawyer*
Gaberino, John Anthony, Jr. *lawyer*
Howard, Gene Claude *lawyer, retired state senator*
Luthey, Graydon Dean, Jr. *lawyer, educator*
Mackey, Steven R. *lawyer*
Nemec, Michael Lee *lawyer*
O'Meilia, David E. *lawyer*
Strecker, David Eugene *lawyer*
Sturdivant, James M. *lawyer*
Williams, Danny Chappelle *federal prosecutor*

PENNSYLVANIA

Hershey
Turner, Leslie Marie *lawyer*

RHODE ISLAND

Providence
Traficanti, Joseph J. *lawyer, food products executive*

SOUTH CAROLINA

Aiken
Rudnick, Irene Krugman *lawyer, educator, former state legislator*

Beaufort
Harvey, William Brantley, Jr. *lawyer, retired lieutenant governor*

Bluffton
Edgett, William Maloy *lawyer, arbitrator*

Cayce
Lindsay, Ronald Thomas *lawyer*

Charleston
Cox, Walter Thompson III *lawyer, federal judge, educator*
Fenno, Edward Thorndike *lawyer*
Freer, Robert Elliott, Jr. *lawyer*
Grant, J. Kirkland *lawyer, educator*
Kahn, Ellis Irvin *lawyer*
McCullough, Ralph Clayton, II, *law educator*
Patrick, Charles William, Jr. *lawyer*
Waring, Bradish J. *lawyer*

Clemson
Cox, Headley Morris, Jr. *lawyer, educator*

Columbia
Bailey, George Screven *lawyer*
Blanton, Hoover Clarence *retired lawyer*
Dukes, David E. *lawyer*
Foster, Robert Watson, Sr. *law educator*
Handel, Richard Craig *lawyer*
Harpootlian, Richard Ara (Dick Harpootlian) *lawyer, former political organization administrator*
Hubbard, William C. *lawyer*
Matthews, Steve Allen *lawyer*
Mood, Francis P., Jr. *lawyer, utilities executive*
Nettles, William N. (Bill Nettles) *federal prosecutor*
Nexsen, Julian Jacobs *lawyer*
Pratt, Walter F., Jr. *law educator*
Russell, John R. *lawyer*
Smith, George Murrell, Jr. *lawyer, state legislator*
Solomon, Carl L. *lawyer*
Sowards, John A. *lawyer*
Strom, J. Preston, Jr. *lawyer*
Tate, Harold Simmons, Jr. *lawyer*
Tenenbaum, Inez Moore *lawyer, former federal agency administrator, former school system administrator*

Greenville
Mauldin, John Inglis *public defender*
Micali, James M. *lawyer*
Riley, Richard Wilson *lawyer, former United States Secretary of Education*
Sanders, Harvey Gibert, Jr. *lawyer*
Smoak, Lewis Tyson *lawyer*
Walters, Johnnie McKeiver *lawyer*
White, Daniel Bowman *lawyer*
Wilkins, David Horton *lawyer, former ambassador*
Wyche, Cyril Thomas *lawyer*
Wyche, Madison Baker III *lawyer*

Hilton Head Island
Esposito, John Vincent *lawyer*
Rose, William Shepard, Jr. *lawyer*
Scarminach, Charles Anthony *lawyer*

Mount Pleasant
Schiavo, Mary Fackler *lawyer*

Newberry
Partridge, William Franklin, Jr. *lawyer*

Spartanburg
Anthony, Kenneth C., Jr. *lawyer*

TENNESSEE

Brentwood
Blackstock, James Fielding *lawyer*
Cohen, William Mark *lawyer*
Smith, Andrew (Thomas Andrew Smith) *lawyer*

Chattanooga
Bahner, Thomas Maxfield *lawyer*
Bishop, Liston, II, (Bo Bishop) *lawyer, insurance company executive*
Eason, Marcia Jean (Marcy Eason) *lawyer*
Elliott, Sam *lawyer*
Killian, William Charles (Bill Killian) *federal prosecutor*
Summers, Gerald Howard (Jerry) *lawyer*

Clarksville
Smith, Gregory Dale *lawyer, judge*
Winters, David Douglas *lawyer*

Franklin
Hurley, Rebecca *lawyer*
Rosen, William Warren *lawyer*
Seifert, Rachel A. *lawyer*

Gatlinburg
Catalfo, Alfred, Jr., (Alfio Catalfo) *lawyer*

Goodlettsville
Taylor, Rhonda M. *lawyer*

Knoxville
Bell, James A.H. *lawyer*
Brandow, Peter B. *lawyer*
Gibson, Cynthia L. *lawyer, multimedia company executive*
Rayson, Edwin Hope *lawyer*
Reynolds, Glenn Harlan *law educator, blogger*
Wheeler, John Watson *lawyer*
Worthington, Robert Fletcher, Jr. *lawyer*

Lebanon
Shoaf, Forrest (N.B. Forrest Shoaf, Nathan Bedford Forrest Shoaf) *lawyer*

Mc Ewen
Williams, John Lee *lawyer*

Memphis
Adams, Ben C. *lawyer*
Buckner, Thomas Randolph *lawyer*
Carr, Oscar Clark III *lawyer*
Castle, Darrell *lawyer*
Chambliss, Prince Caesar, Jr. *lawyer*
Crump, Charles Metcalf *lawyer*
Harvey, Albert C. *lawyer*
Heiter, Matthew Stephen *lawyer*
Hermes, Clinton Daniel *lawyer*
Kaput, Jim L. *lawyer*
Kustoff, David F. *lawyer, former prosecutor*
Ledbetter, Paul Mark *lawyer, writer*
Masterson, Kenneth Rhodes *lawyer, board member*
Mc Creary, James Franklin *lawyer, mediator*
McDaniel, A. Stephen *lawyer*
McMullen, Greerson G. *lawyer*
Newman, Charles Forrest *lawyer*
Noel, Randall Deane *lawyer*
Norris, Charles Head *lawyer, manufacturing executive*
Ryan, Sharon R. *lawyer*
Ryder, John L. *lawyer, political organization worker*
Scroggs, Larry Kenneth *lawyer, state legislator*
Stanton, Edward Lesley III *federal prosecutor*
Trammell, Bradley Ellis *lawyer*
Vance, Kim *lawyer*
Weirich, Amy P. *prosecutor*

Nashville
Bass, James Orin, Sr. *lawyer*
Blumstein, James Franklin *lawyer, educator, consultant*
Bostick, Charles Dent *retired lawyer*
Brown, Martin S., Jr. *lawyer*
Cobb, Stephen A. *lawyer*
Conner, Lewis Homer, Jr. *lawyer*
Covington, Robert Newman *retired law educator*
Cowart, Richard G. *lawyer*
Fowler, David *lawyer, state legislator*
Fuchs, Mark *lawyer*
Gillmor, John Edward *lawyer*
Gonzales, Alberto R. *lawyer, law educator, former United States Attorney General*
Hardin, Hal D. *lawyer, former judge, US attorney*
Harwell, Aubrey Biggs *lawyer*
Johnson, Victor S., III, (Torry Johnson) *prosecutor*
Ledyard, Robins Heard *lawyer*
Lowe, Richard C. *lawyer*
Malone, Melvin J. *lawyer*
Martin, Jerry E. (Gerald E. Martin) *lawyer, former federal prosecutor*
Mayden, Barbara Mendel *lawyer*
Peek, Michael S. *lawyer*
Petrovich, Stephen Christopher *lawyer*
Schreiber, Kurt Gilbert *lawyer*
Simmons, Keith B. *lawyer*
Sims, Wilson *lawyer*
Soltman, Ronald P. *lawyer, surgical hospital company executive*
Thomas, Robert Paige *lawyer*
Tishler, John C. *lawyer*
Tuke, Robert Dudley *lawyer, educator*
Viscusi, W(illiam) Gregory Kip *law and economics educator*
Waterman, Robert A. *lawyer*
Yarbrough, Edward Meacham *lawyer, former prosecutor*
Young, Bill *lawyer, former health products executive*
Yuspeh, Alan Ralph *lawyer, hospital executive*

Sevierville
Waters, John B. *lawyer*

Soddy Daisy
Leitner, Paul Revere *lawyer*

Springfield
Wilks, Larry Dean *lawyer*

Trenton
Smith, Jeffrey A. *lawyer*

TEXAS

Addison
Solls, Mark A. *lawyer*

Amarillo
Madden, Wales Hendrix, Jr. *retired lawyer*

Arlington
Goodman, Toby Ray *lawyer*
Harcrow, Edward Earl *lawyer*
Weekley, Frederick Clay, Jr. *lawyer*

Austin
Baker, Mark Bruce *lawyer, educator*
Bayer, Karl *lawyer*
Botsford, David L. *lawyer*
Brister, Scott Andrew *lawyer, former state supreme court justice*
Caldwell, Rodney Kent *lawyer*
Clements, Jerry K. *lawyer*
Cooper, Carl Wade *lawyer*
Crocker, Bill (William R. Crocker) *lawyer*
Davis, Morris *lawyer*
Davis, Robert Larry *lawyer*
Demond, Walter Eugene *lawyer*
Dickie, Martha S. *lawyer*
Drolla, John Casper Dodt, Jr. *lawyer*
Dyer, Cromwell Adair, Jr. *lawyer, legal association administrator*
Gangstad, John Erik *lawyer*
Golemon, Ronald Kinnan *lawyer*
Graglia, Lino Anthony *lawyer, educator*
Gregory, Becky (Rebecca Ann Gregory) *lawyer, former prosecutor*
Greig, Brian Strother *lawyer*
Harrison, Richard Wayne *lawyer*
Helman, Stephen Jody *lawyer*
Henderson, George Ervin *lawyer*
Hull, Robert Joe *lawyer*
Ikard, Frank Neville, Jr. *lawyer*
Jansen, Donald Orville *lawyer*
Keig, Lowell Adams *lawyer*
Keyes, David R. *lawyer*
Lehmberg, Rosemary *prosecutor*
Lochridge, Lloyd Pampell, Jr. *lawyer*
Lochridge, Patton G. *lawyer*
Lorenz, Ted R. *lawyer*
McKetta, John J. III *lawyer*
Mitchell, Jonathan *lawyer, law educator*
Montgomery, Jim *lawyer*
Mullenix, Linda Susan *law educator*
Nevola, Roger *lawyer*
O'Neill, Harriet *lawyer, retired state supreme court justice*
Pena, Richard *lawyer*
Pirkey, Louis Thomas *lawyer*
Prather, Laura Lee *lawyer, educator*
Rider, Brian Clayton *lawyer*
Roan, Forrest Calvin, Jr. *lawyer*
Sager, Lawrence Gene *law educator*
Serafine, Mary Louise *lawyer, educator*
Strauser, Robert Wayne *lawyer*
Sturley, Michael F. *law educator*
Temple, Larry Eugene *lawyer*
Tottenham, Terry Oliver *lawyer*
Volk, William R. *lawyer*
Wainwright, Dale V. *lawyer, former state supreme court justice*
Weddington, Sarah Ragle *lawyer, educator*
Weinberg, Louise *law educator, writer*
Westbrook, Jay Lawrence *law educator*
Whitehurst, William Oscar *lawyer*
Winters, Sam *lawyer*
Wolin, Harry A. *lawyer, electronics company executive*

Beaumont
Bales, John Malcolm *federal prosecutor*
Oxford, Hubert III *lawyer*

Bellaire
Amdur, Arthur R. *lawyer*
Jacobus, Charles Joseph *lawyer, writer*

Brenham
Moorman, Richard Hal, IV, *lawyer*

Brownsville
Rodriguez, Eduardo Roberto *lawyer*
Weisfeld, Sheldon *lawyer*

Brownwood
Bell, William Woodward *lawyer*

Cleburne
MacLean, John Ronald *lawyer*

College Station
Godfrey, Cullen Michael *lawyer, academic administrator*
Martin, Boe Willis *lawyer*

Corpus Christi
Branscomb, Harvie, Jr. *lawyer*
Stukenberg, Michael Wesley *lawyer*

Corsicana
McSpadden, Jody Sodd *lawyer*

Dallas
Acker, Rodney *lawyer*
Adams, Richard Lloyd *lawyer*
Anderson, Barbara McComas *lawyer*
Anderson, E. Karl *lawyer*
Ashby, Danny S. *lawyer*
Askew, Kim Juanita *lawyer*
Attanasio, John Baptist *law educator, former dean*
Baggett, W. Mike *lawyer*
Bangs, Nelson A. (Tony Bangs) *lawyer*
Beane, Jerry Lynn *lawyer*
Beuttenmuller, Rudolf William *lawyer*
Bickel, John W., II, *lawyer*
Bliss, Robert Harms *lawyer*
Bode, Joyce Scruggs *lawyer*
Boyd, Dan Stewart *lawyer*
Brin, Royal Henry, Jr. *lawyer*
Budner, Craig W. *lawyer*
Bumpas, Stuart Maryman *lawyer*
Burke, William Temple, Jr. *lawyer*
Burns, Sandra *lawyer, educator*
Butcher, Daniel L. *lawyer*
Cantrill, Thomas H. *lawyer*
Clancy, Denyse Finn *lawyer*
Coggins, Paul Edward, Jr. *lawyer*
Colson, Randall Elwin *lawyer*
Conner, Terry W. *lawyer*
Copley, Edward Alvin *lawyer*
Cowart, T(homas) David *lawyer*
Cowles, Jim E. *lawyer*
Crichton, Thomas, IV, *lawyer*
Daly, Gail M. *law librarian, educator, dean*
Davis, Clarice McDonald *lawyer*
Davis, Joe A. *lawyer*
Davis, Robert Edwin *lawyer*
Doke, Marshall J., Jr. *lawyer*
Dybala, Kelly Mayo *lawyer*
Dyess, Bobby Dale *lawyer*
Ellis, Alfred Wright (Al Ellis) *lawyer*
Ellis, James A., Jr. *lawyer*
Fankhauser, Mark A. *lawyer*
Fanning, Barry Hedges *lawyer*
Feld, Alan David *lawyer*
Fenner, Suzan Ellen *lawyer*
Figari, Ernest Emil, Jr. *lawyer, educator*
Fijolek, Richard M. *lawyer*
Flanagan, Christie Stephen *lawyer*
Flegle, Jim L. *lawyer*
Flood, Joan Moore *paralegal*
Forshey, Michael S. *lawyer*
Freling, Richard Alan *lawyer*
Frisbie, Curtis Lynn, Jr. *lawyer*
Garner, Bryan Andrew *law educator, writer, consultant, lexicographer*
Gilchrist, Henry *lawyer*
Gilliam, John A. *lawyer*
Glendenning, Don Mark *lawyer*
Gonzalez, Rachel A. *lawyer*
Good, Stephen D. *lawyer*
Goodstein, Barnett Maurice *lawyer*
Goolsby, Bryan L. *lawyer*
Gores, Christopher Merrel *lawyer*
Goyne, Roderick A. *lawyer*
Gregory, Louis P. *lawyer, gas industry executive*
Hale, Earl F., Jr. *mediator, arbitrator*
Hammond, Herbert J. *lawyer, arbitrator, mediator*
Hartnett, Will Ford *lawyer*

Hennessy, Daniel Kraft *lawyer*
Henry, Vic Houston *lawyer*
Hicks, Marion Lawrence, Jr., (Larry Hicks) *lawyer*
Hinshaw, Chester John *lawyer*
Hirschman, Karen L. *lawyer*
Ho, James C. *lawyer*
Howell, John E. *lawyer*
Huffman, Gregory Scott Combest *lawyer*
Humble, Monty Garfield *lawyer*
Hutchison, Kay Bailey (Kathryn Ann Bailey Hutchison) *lawyer, former United States Senator from Texas*
Jayson, Melinda Gayle *lawyer*
Johnston, Kenneth C. *lawyer*
Jolas, Paul M. *lawyer, energy executive*
Jordan, William Davis *lawyer*
Jung, Peter Michael *lawyer*
Kennedy, Marc J. *lawyer*
Kent, David Charles *lawyer*
Kesselman, Marc L. *lawyer*
Kinnebrew, Jackson Metcalfe *lawyer*
Kirk, Ronald *lawyer, former federal official, former mayor*
Kobdish, George Charles *lawyer*
Kober, John A. *lawyer*
Kuhn, Willis Evan, II, *lawyer, mediator*
Lacy, John Ford *retired lawyer*
Lan, Donald Paul, Jr. *lawyer*
Lawson, Gary B. *lawyer*
Levin, Hervey Phillip *lawyer*
Levin, Richard C. *lawyer*
Lowe, John Stanley *law educator*
Mankoff, Ronald Morton *retired lawyer*
Manning, George Taylor *lawyer*
Maris, Stephen S. *lawyer, educator*
Martin, E.X. III *lawyer*
Mason, Thomas P. *lawyer*
McAleenan, Donald Francis *lawyer, construction executive*
McAtee, David Ray *lawyer*
McDowell, John Henry, Jr. *lawyer*
Mc Elhaney, John Hess *lawyer*
McKnight, Joseph Webb *lawyer, educator, historian*
McWatters, Denise C. *lawyer*
McWilliams, Mike C. *lawyer*
Miers, Harriet Ellan *lawyer, former federal official*
Mighell, Kenneth John *lawyer*
Miller, Norman Richard *lawyer*
Miller, R. Terry *lawyer*
Moore, Edward Warren *lawyer*
Moore, Stanley Ray *lawyer*
Mow, Robert Henry, Jr. *lawyer*
Newman, Lawrence Graham *lawyer*
Nihill, Julian Dumontiel *lawyer*
Nivica, Gjon Nelson, Jr. *lawyer*
Nolan, John Michael *lawyer*
Null, Gary G. *lawyer*
Orwig, Matthew Dane *lawyer, former prosecutor*
Perkins, Thomas P., Jr. *lawyer*
Peterson, Edward Adrian *lawyer*
Pew, John Glenn, Jr. *lawyer*
Phelan, Robin Eric *lawyer*
Pingree, Bruce Douglas *lawyer*
Pleasant, James Scott *lawyer*
Portman, Glenn Arthur *lawyer*
Powell, Michael Vance *lawyer*
Purnell, Maurice Eugene, Jr. *lawyer*
Raggio, Thomas Louis *lawyer*
Reid, Rust Endicott *lawyer*
Ringle, Brett Adelbert *lawyer, oil and gas industry executive, trustee*
Rizzieri, L. Stephen *lawyer*
Roberson, Eric N. *lawyer*
Roberts, Harry Morris, Jr. *lawyer*
Robertson, Daryl Bruce *lawyer*
Rodgers, John Hunter *lawyer*
Roper, Richard B. III *lawyer, former prosecutor*
Ruff, Gary Kay *lawyer*
Saldaña, Sarah Ruth *federal prosecutor*
Schieffer, John Thomas (Tom Schieffer) *lawyer, former ambassador*
Schreiber, Howard E. *lawyer*
Schreiber, Sally Ann *lawyer*
Selinger, Jerry Robin *lawyer*
Shaw, Mark R. *lawyer*
Simmons, Terry L. *lawyer*
Stalcup, Joe Alan *retired lawyer, dean*
Steinberg, Lawrence Edward *lawyer*
Stewart, Kenneth L. *lawyer*
Stockard, James Alfred *lawyer*
Sullivan, Kevin A. *lawyer*
Thomson, Basil Henry, Jr. *lawyer*
Tomko, Edwin Joseph *lawyer*
Tompkins, Alan W. *lawyer*
True, Roy Joe *lawyer*
Tubb, James Clarence *lawyer*
Veach, Robert Raymond, Jr. *lawyer*
Walkowiak, Vincent Steven *lawyer*
Watkins, Craig *prosecutor*
Werbner, Mark S. *lawyer*
White, James Richard *lawyer*
Wilbanks, Cody *attorney*
Willingham, Clark Suttles *lawyer*
Wilson, Claude Raymond, Jr. *lawyer*
Wilson, Troy Michael (T. Michael Wilson) *lawyer*
Yang, Emeline *lawyer*
Zlotky, Jeffrey A. *lawyer*

Denton
Gabriel, Eberhard John *lawyer, bank executive*
Lawhon, John III *lawyer, retired county official*

El Paso
Barfield, Lowry *lawyer*
Esparza, Jaime *prosecutor*

Farmers Branch
Blachly, Jack Lee *lawyer*

Fort Worth
Brown, C. Harold *lawyer*
Brown, Richard Lee *lawyer*
Chalk, John Allen, Sr. *lawyer*
Dean, Beale *lawyer*
Elliott, Frank Wallace *lawyer, educator*
Goldberg, David *lawyer*
Hart, John Clifton *lawyer*
Hughes, John W. *lawyer, mediator*
Jones, Paul *lawyer*
Kelly, Raymond Boone III *lawyer*
McConnell, Michael Arthur *lawyer*
Munn, Cecil Edwin *lawyer*
Poole, David P. *lawyer, oil and gas executives*
Tillman, Massie Monroe *mediator, arbitrator, art gallery owner, retired judge*
Watson, Robert Francis *lawyer*

Frisco
Bell, Haney Hardy III *lawyer*

Galveston
Caldwell, Garnett Ernest *lawyer*
Epstein, Jon David *lawyer, educator*

Garland
Irby, Holt *lawyer*

Georgetown
Bryce, William Delf *lawyer*
Darby, Karen Sue *law educator*

Grapevine
Kaufman, Daniel J. *lawyer*

Harker Heights
Miller, Richard Joseph *retired lawyer*

Harlingen
Pope, William L. *lawyer, judge*

Houston
Acosta, Efren Alejandro *lawyer*
Allender, John Roland *lawyer*
Asselin, Heather E. *lawyer*
Atlas, Scott J. *lawyer*
Ayers, Howard T. *lawyer*
Bachmann, Richard H. *lawyer, energy executive*
Baker, C. Mark *lawyer*
Baker, James Addison, III, (Jim Baker) *lawyer, former United States Secretary of State*
Baker, Robert W. *lawyer*
Barnett, Edward William *lawyer*
Beck, David Joseph *lawyer*
Beirne, Martin Douglas *lawyer*
Bellatti, Lawrence Lee *lawyer*
Benkiser, Tina Johns *lawyer, former political organization administrator*
Biery, Evelyn Hudson *lawyer*
Bilger, Bruce R. *lawyer*
Blackshear, A. T., Jr. *lawyer*
Bland, John Lloyd *lawyer*
Block, Nelson Richard *lawyer*
Blodgett, J. Kevin *lawyer, consulting firm executive*
Bluestein, Edwin A., Jr. *lawyer*
Brann, Richard R. *lawyer*
Brinsmade, Lyon Louis *retired lawyer*
Buckley, Vincent H. *lawyer*
Burch, Voris Reagan *retired mediator, arbitrator, lawyer*
Burgert, David Lee *lawyer*
Burman, Darryl Michael *lawyer*
Bux, William John *lawyer*
Caddy, Michael Douglas *lawyer, real estate broker*
Caldwell, Richard H. *lawyer*
Campbell, Bert Louis *lawyer, arbitrator, mediator*
Carabin, Dana A. *lawyer*
Carroll, James Vincent III *lawyer*
Carter, John Loyd *lawyer*
Casarez, Rueben Charles *lawyer*
Caudill, William Howard *lawyer*
Chavez, J. Anthony *lawyer*
Chung, Paul W. *lawyer, energy executive*
Clark, Pat English *lawyer*
Clarke, Robert Logan *lawyer*
Clingman, Rachel Giesber *lawyer*
Clore, Lawrence Hubert *lawyer*
Coghlan, Kelly Jack *lawyer*
Coley, Randolph C. *lawyer*
Collings, Chris D. *lawyer*
Corken, Heather Marie *lawyer*
Cornelison, Albert Otto, Jr., (Bert Cornelison) *lawyer, oil industry executive*
Cunningham, Tom Alan *lawyer*
Cuomo, Paul C. *lawyer*
Dameris, Thad Thano *lawyer*
Davis, Louis J. *lawyer*
DeGuerin, Dick *lawyer*
DeMent, James Alderson, Jr. *lawyer*
Dilg, Joseph Carl *lawyer*
Dillard, Stephen C. *lawyer*
Dinkins, Carol Eggert *lawyer*
Douglas, James Matthew *law educator, dean*
Douglass, John Jay *lawyer, educator*
Duncan, Meredith Johnson *law educator*
Eastland, S. Stacy *lawyer*
Eiland, Gary Wayne *lawyer*
Essmyer, Michael Martin *lawyer*
Eubank, J. Thomas *lawyer*
Farenthold, Frances Tarlton *lawyer*
Farley, Andrew Daniel *lawyer*
Feldman, David M. *lawyer*
Fernandes, Edward F. *lawyer*
Ford, Thomas W., Jr. *lawyer*
Foster, Charles Crawford *lawyer, educator*
Frasier, Curtis R. *lawyer, energy executive*
Frels, Kelly *lawyer*
French, Layne Bryan *lawyer, investor, community volunteer*
Fullenweider, Donn Charles *lawyer*
Gagnon, Stewart Walter *lawyer*
Gates, Stephen Frye *lawyer, director, former oil industry executive, corporate director*
Goodman, Barry Michael *lawyer*
Graham, Michael Paul *lawyer*
Gray, Robert F., Jr. *lawyer*
Gunter, Joseph Clifford III *lawyer*
Hall, Charles Washington *lawyer*
Hamel, Douglas E. *lawyer*
Hardin, Rusty (Russell Hardin Jr.) *lawyer*
Harper, A(lfred) J(ohn), II, *lawyer*
Hasseman, Dean Michael *lawyer*
Hawes, Clay Erik *lawyer*
Haynes, Richard (Racehorse Haynes) *lawyer*
Hedgebeth, Reginald D. *lawyer*
Heeg, Peggy A. *lawyer, former gas industry executive*
Hewitt, Lester L. *lawyer*
Hollyfield, John Scoggins *lawyer*
Holstead, John Burnham *retired lawyer*
Hoyt, Mont Powell *arbitrator*
Hudspeth, Chalmers Mac *lawyer, educator*
Jamail, Joseph Dahr, Jr. *lawyer*
Jewell, Robert V. *lawyer*
Johnson, Arnold Joseph *lawyer, energy executive*
Johnson, Paula Ann *lawyer*
Jones, Frank Griffith *lawyer*
Jordan, Charles Milton *lawyer*
Jordan, W. Carl *lawyer*
Kelly, Hugh Rice *lawyer, retired energy executive*
Kennedy, John Edward *lawyer*
Kerrigan, Sylvia J. *lawyer*
Ketchand, Robert Lee *lawyer*
Koenig, Rodney Curtis *lawyer, rancher*
Kratochvil, L(ouis) Glen *lawyer*
Kruse, Layne E. *lawyer*
LaFuze, William L. *lawyer*
Lake, Kathleen Cooper *lawyer*
Lanier, William Mark (Mark Lanier) *lawyer*
Lannie, Paul Anthony *lawyer*
Lavine, James E. *lawyer*
Lee, William Gentry *lawyer*
Lewis, Kevin Paul *lawyer*
Looser, William Gregory *lawyer*
Lopez, David Tiburcio *lawyer, arbitrator, mediator, educator*
Love, Scott Anthony *lawyer*
Lowenberg, Michael J. *lawyer*
Lykos, Patricia R. *prosecutor, former judge*
Lynch, John F. *lawyer*
Magidson, Kenneth *federal prosecutor*
Mallett, Edward A. *lawyer*
Maloney, James Edward *lawyer*
Maloney, Marilyn C. *lawyer*
Maroney, James Francis III *lawyer, energy executive*
Marston, Edgar Jean III *lawyer*
Massad, Stephen Albert *lawyer*
Masters, Claude Bivin *lawyer*
Mattox, Sharon M. *lawyer*
McClure, Daniel M. *lawyer*
McCreary, Frank E. III *retired lawyer*
McDaniel, Jarrel Dave *retired lawyer*
McLeod, Chanse L. *lawyer*
McMahon, Catherine Driscoll *lawyer*
Medina, David M. *lawyer, former state supreme court justice*
Michel, Arturo G. *lawyer*
Miller, Barry Rixmann *lawyer*
Moehlman, Michael Scott *lawyer*
Moncure, John Lewis *lawyer*
Moore, Charles A. *lawyer*
Moore, Thomas J. *lawyer*
Moore, Tim *lawyer*
Murphy, Ewell Edward, Jr. *lawyer*
Nations, Howard Lynn *lawyer*
Nimmer, Raymond T. *law educator, former dean*
Nolen, Roy Lemuel *retired lawyer*
Norris, John David *lawyer*
Oldham, Darius Dudley *lawyer*
Oshman, Gene Jay *lawyer*
Osterberg, Edward Charles, Jr. *lawyer*
O'Toole, Austin Martin *lawyer, mediator, arbitrator*
Oxford, Patrick C. *lawyer*
Paulsen, James Walter *law educator*
Perich, Thomas J. *lawyer*
Plaeger, Frederick Joseph, II, *lawyer*
Port, P. Allan *lawyer*
Porter, Thomas William III *lawyer*
Ramsey, Michael W. *lawyer*
Ray, Hugh Massey III *lawyer*
Reasoner, Harry Max *lawyer*
Rettig, Dwight William *lawyer*
Rowland, Robert Alexander III *lawyer*
Rozzell, Scott Ellis *lawyer, energy executive*
Rustay, Jennifer Beth *lawyer*
Ryan, Jason Michael *lawyer*
Ryan, Stephen M. *lawyer*
Ryan, Vince *lawyer*
Sales, James Bohus *lawyer*
Schechter, Arthur Louis *lawyer*
Schwartz, Charles Walter *lawyer*
Schwartzel, Charles Boone *lawyer*
Seale, Robert Arthur Pete *lawyer*
Secrest, George McCall, Jr., (Mac Secrest) *lawyer*
Shaddock, Carroll Sidney *lawyer*
Sheinfeld, Myron M. (Mickey Sheinfeld) *lawyer*
Shouse, August Edward *lawyer*
Sing, William Bender *lawyer*
Smith, Alison Leigh *lawyer*
Smith, E. Ashley *lawyer, insurance company executive*
Smith, Walter John *lawyer*
Sonfield, Robert Leon, Jr. *lawyer*
Spalding, Andrew Freeman *lawyer*
Stephenson, Kent R. *lawyer*
Still, Charles Henry, Sr. *lawyer*
Streng, William Paul *lawyer, educator*
Stryker, Steven Charles *lawyer*
Susman, Stephen Daily *lawyer*
Sutton, Neal S. *lawyer, energy executive*
Swan, Michael K. *lawyer*
Swanson, Roy Joel *lawyer*
Swift, Robert J. *lawyer*
Szalkowski, Charles C. *lawyer*
Tartt, Blake *lawyer*
Thompson, Sandra Guerra *lawyer, educator*
Totten, Patricia A. *lawyer*
Varner, David Eugene *lawyer*
Wallace, Barron F. *lawyer*
Walton, Gib (Dan Gibson Walton) *lawyer*
Wayne, Donald Charles *lawyer*
Weber, Fredric Alan *lawyer*
Weiner, Sanford Alan *lawyer*
Wilde, William Key *lawyer*
Williamson, Peter David *lawyer*
Wood, Michael W. *lawyer*
Woods, Ronald G. *lawyer, former prosecutor*
Worthington, William Albert III *lawyer*
Wray, Thomas Jefferson *lawyer*
Yeates, Marie R. *lawyer*
Yetter, R. Paul *lawyer*

Huntsville
Vaughn, Michael S. *law educator*

Irving
Balagia, S. Jack, Jr. *lawyer*
Beach, Charles Addison *lawyer*
Beasley, Mark V. *lawyer*
de Mars, Susan S. *lawyer, health products executive*
Hernandez, Carlos Manuel *lawyer*
Magill, Kent B. *lawyer*
Molay, Hilary S. *lawyer*
Shuff, Ronald F. *lawyer*

Kerrville
Parmley, Robert James *lawyer, consultant*

Kilgore
Rorschach, Richard Gordon *lawyer*

Lakeway
Moss, Bill Ralph *lawyer*

Llano
Wallis, Olney Gray *lawyer*

Longview
Ward, T. John *lawyer, former federal judge*

Lubbock
Beyer, Gerry Wayne *lawyer, educator*
Morton, Harvey Leon *lawyer*
Purdom, Thomas James *lawyer*

Mc Kinney
Hutchison, Larry M. *lawyer, insurance company executive*

Midland
Estes, Andrew Harper *lawyer*

North Richland Hills
Reed, Glenn W. *lawyer*

Plano
Baldwin, James L., Jr. *lawyer, beverage company executive*
Korst, Christopher A. *lawyer, rental company executive*
Markey, James Kevin *lawyer*

Richardson
Conkel, Robert Dale *lawyer, consultant*
Haile, Lawrence Barclay *lawyer*
Olson, Dennis Oliver *lawyer*
Torres, John D. *lawyer, manufacturing executive*

San Angelo
Junell, Robert Alan *lawyer, federal judge*

San Antonio
Aycock, James J. *lawyer*
Bennett, Steven Alan *lawyer, insurance company executive*
Diaz-Dennis, Patricia *lawyer, communications executive*
Emery, Beth (Nancy Beth Emery) *lawyer*
Labenz-Hough, Marlene *administrator*
Lindquist, Judith Dowdle *lawyer*
Parrish, Charles S. *lawyer, oil industry executive*
Pitman, Robert Lee *federal prosecutor, former federal judge*
Reams, Bernard Dinsmore, Jr. *law educator*
Reed, Susan D. *prosecutor*
Schlueter, David Arnold *law educator*
Spears, Sally *lawyer*
Walls, Robert Hamilton, Jr. *lawyer*

Spearman
Jarvis, Billy Britt *lawyer*

The Woodlands
Guest, Floyd Emory, Jr. *lawyer*
Hagerman, John David *lawyer, investment advisor*
Reeves, Robert K. *lawyer, oil industry executive*

Tyler
Patterson, Donald Ross *lawyer, educator*

Waco
Dunnam, James Robert *lawyer, former state legislator*
Quarles, Brandon *law librarian*
Smith, Cullen *lawyer*

Wichita Falls
Briley, Stephen Morris *lawyer*

VIRGINIA

Alexandria
Coffield, Shirley Ann *lawyer, educator*
Cottrell, James Ray *lawyer*
Ellis, Michael *law clerk*
Goolrick, Robert Mason *legal consultant*
Gura, Alan *lawyer*
Mossinghoff, Gerald Joseph *lawyer, educator*
Paturis, E(mmanuel) Michael *lawyer*
Pyle, Howard *lawyer, consultant*
Straub, Peter Thornton *lawyer*
Trigiani, Lucia Anna *lawyer*
Von Drehle, Ramon Arnold *lawyer*
Williams, John Edward *lawyer*
Winzer, P.J. *lawyer*

Arlington
Berliner, Dana *lawyer*
Butler, Henry Nolde *law and business educator*
Delaney, Raighne C. *lawyer*
Ebong, Enoh Titilayo *lawyer*
Gall, Bert *lawyer*
Keene, Deborah M. *law librarian*
Korman, James William *lawyer*
Lauderdale, Katherine Sue *lawyer*
Miller, Brian A. *lawyer, electric power industry executive*
Parker, Jeffrey Scott *law educator*

Schmidt, Paul Wickham *lawyer*
Spencer, George Henry *lawyer*
Tannenwald, Peter *lawyer*
Weinberg, Robert Lester *lawyer, law educator*
Wildhack, William August, Jr. *lawyer*

Charlottesville
Bonnie, Richard Jeffrey *lawyer, educator, consultant*
Cannon, Jonathan Z. *law educator*
Chandler, Lawrence Bradford, Jr. *lawyer*
Dooley, Michael P. *law educator*
Dotson, Donald L. *lawyer*
Fitchett, Taylor *law librarian*
Fox, Charles Dunsmore, IV, *lawyer*
Henderson, Stanley Dale *lawyer, educator, arbitrator*
Henke, Michael John *lawyer, educator*
Howard, Arthur Ellsworth Dick *law educator*
Jeffries, John Calvin, Jr. *law educator, former dean*
Kitch, Edmund Wells *law educator*
Lane, Mark *lawyer, educator, writer*
Laycock, Harold Douglas *law educator, writer*
Martin, David Alan *lawyer, law educator*
Menefee, Samuel Pyeatt *lawyer, academic*
Middleditch, Leigh Benjamin, Jr. *lawyer, educator*
Moore, John Norton *lawyer, educator, diplomat*
Nelson, Caleb Edward *law educator*
O'Brien, David Michael *law educator*
Schauer, Frederick Franklin *law educator*
Slaughter, Edward Ratliff, Jr. *lawyer*
Stroud, Robert Edward *lawyer*
Turner, Robert Foster *law educator, writer, former government official*
Wadlington, Walter James *law educator*
White, George Edward *lawyer, educator*
Whiting, Richard Albert *lawyer*
Wood, R(obert) Craig *lawyer, educator*

Chesapeake
Gorry, James A. III *lawyer*

Daleville
Steele, (Margaret) Anita Martin *law librarian, educator*

Danville
Abreu, Luis Alberto *lawyer*

Fairfax
Arnold, William McCauley *lawyer*
Dowlut, Robert *lawyer*
Folk, Thomas Robert *lawyer*
Greenspun, Peter D. *lawyer*
Rudolph, Lawrence *lawyer*

Falls Church
Benton, Janine Schollnick *lawyer*
Boehm, Kenneth *legal association administrator*
Clegg, Roger Burton *lawyer*
Deckelman, William L., Jr. *lawyer*
Diamond, Robert Michael *lawyer*
Gallopoulos, Gregory Stratis *lawyer*
Mugavero, Thomas Collier *lawyer*
Van Cleve, Ruth Gill *retired lawyer*

Fort Belvoir
Harms, John Kevin *lawyer*

Fredericksburg
Braxton, Herman Harrison, Jr. *lawyer, judge*

Galax
Kapp, John Paul *lawyer, physician, educator*

Great Falls
DiCintio, Michelle S. *lawyer*
Simpson, Carter B. *lawyer*
Wood, John Martin *lawyer*

Hamilton
Head, Elizabeth *lawyer, arbitrator, mediator*

Heathsville
McKerns, Charles Joseph *lawyer*

Henrico
Batzli, Terrence Raymond *lawyer*
Brissette, Martha Blevins *lawyer*

Herndon
DeLeon, Charles *lawyer*

Lancaster
Wright, Wiley Reed, Jr. *lawyer, retired judge, mediator*

Leesburg
Flannery, John Philip *lawyer*

Lexington
Grunewald, Mark Howard *law educator*
Kirgis, Frederic Lee *law educator*
Osborne, Caroline L. *law librarian, educator*
Wiant, Sarah Kirsten *law educator, law librarian, educator*

Lynchburg
Healy, Joseph Francis, Jr. *lawyer, retired air transportation executive*

Manakin Sabot
Bright, Craig Bartley *lawyer*

Mc Lean
Appleby, C. G. *lawyer*
Appler, Thomas L. *lawyer*
Baker, Keith Leon *lawyer*
Becker, Richard K.A. *lawyer*
Brown, Thomas Cartmel, Jr. *lawyer*
Brownlee, John Leslie *lawyer, former prosecutor*
Campbell, Kristin Ann *lawyer*
Church, Randolph Warner, Jr. *lawyer*
Dyke, James Webster, Jr. *lawyer*
Finneran, John G., Jr. *lawyer, diversified financial services company executive*
Horan, Richard T., Jr. *lawyer*
Jackson, William Paul, Jr. *lawyer*
Klinedinst, Duncan Stewart *lawyer*
McClure, Roger John *lawyer*
McDavid, William Henry *lawyer, mortgage company executive*
Mendelsohn, Stuart *lawyer, municipal official*
Miller, David L. *lawyer*
Molineaux, Charles Borromeo *lawyer, arbitrator, columnist, poet*
Morris, James Malachy *lawyer*
Moses, Alfred Henry *lawyer, writer, diplomat*
Murphy, Thomas Patrick *lawyer*
Neidich, George *lawyer*
Osborne, Robert Stephen *lawyer*
Porter, Philip Drew *lawyer*
Price, Ilene Rosenberg *lawyer*
Rath, Manik K. *lawyer*
Raushenbush, Walter Brandeis *retired law educator*
Schultz, Mark D. *lawyer*
Shapiro, Nelson Hirsh *lawyer*
Sirilla, George M. *lawyer*
Stump, John Sutton *retired lawyer*

Midlothian
Crowder, Marjorie Briggs *lawyer*
Hall, Franklin Perkins *lawyer, former state legislator*

Newport News
Hawthorne, Bruce N. *lawyer*
Kamp, Arthur Joseph, Jr. *lawyer*
Segall, James Arnold *lawyer*

Norfolk
Albert, Alan Dale *lawyer, writer*
Baird, Edward Rouzie, Jr. *retired lawyer*
Bishop, Bruce Taylor *lawyer*
Dimino, Joseph C. *lawyer*
Hixon, James A. *lawyer, rail transportation executive*
Martin, Howard W., Jr. *lawyer*
Padgett, John David *lawyer*
Pearson, John Yeardley, Jr. *lawyer*
Poston, Anita Owings *lawyer*
Ryan, John Morgan *lawyer*
Stillman, Gregory N. *lawyer*
Weinberg, Jerrold G. *lawyer*

Oakton
Cohen, Sheldon Irwin *lawyer*

Petersburg
Everitt, Alice Lubin *labor arbitrator*

Prince George
Brown, Del M. Mauhrine *lawyer, educator*

Radford
Turk, James Clinton, Jr. *lawyer*

Reston
Begeman, Gary D. *lawyer*
Bredehoft, Elaine Charlson *lawyer*
Frankel, Kenneth M. *lawyer*
Heleen, Mark L. *lawyer, finance company executive*
Plave, Lee Jonathan *lawyer*
Scharff, Joseph Laurent *lawyer*
Shannon, Stephen C. *lawyer, former state legislator*

Richmond
Addison, David Dunham *lawyer*
Bates, John Wythe III *lawyer*
Belcher, Dennis I. *lawyer*
Betts, James Edward *lawyer*
Blank, Irving Michael *lawyer*
Blue, Robert M. *lawyer, energy executive*
Booker, Lewis Thomas *lawyer*
Brasfield, Evans Booker *lawyer*
Brockenbrough, Henry Watkins *retired lawyer*
Brooks, Robert Franklin, Sr. *lawyer*
Bryson, William Hamilton *law educator*
Burrus, Robert Lewis, Jr. *lawyer*
Cabaniss, Thomas Edward *lawyer*
Cogbill, John Valentine III *lawyer*
Davidson, C. Simon *lawyer, columnist*
Douglass, John G. *law educator*
Dray, Mark Stanley *lawyer*
Fauls, Thomas E. (Ted) *lawyer*
Framme, Lawrence Henry III *lawyer*
Freeman, George Clemon, Jr. *lawyer*
Gary, Richard David *lawyer*
Getchell, E. Duncan *lawyer*
Gluck, Michelle H. *lawyer*
Goodpasture, Philip Henry *lawyer*
Goolsby, Allen Cunningham III *lawyer*
Grey, Robert J., Jr. *lawyer*
Hackney, Virginia Howitz *lawyer*
Hall, Stephen Charles *lawyer*
Hettrick, George Harrison *lawyer*
Horsley, Waller Holladay *retired lawyer*
Howell, George Cook III *lawyer*
Keane, Denise F. *lawyer, food products executive*
Kearfott, Joseph Conrad *lawyer*
Kissam, Luther C., IV, (Luke Kissam) *lawyer, chemicals executive*
LeClair, Gary David *lawyer*
Ledbetter, David Oscar *lawyer*
McClard, Jack Edward *lawyer*
Meath, James V. *lawyer*
Moore, Thurston Roach *lawyer*
Pagan, John Ruston *law educator*
Pearsall, John Wesley *lawyer*
Pinckney, Charles Cotesworth *lawyer*
Pollard, Overton Price *retired lawyer*
Pope, Robert Dean *lawyer*
Powell, Lewis Franklin III *lawyer*
Rainey, Gordon Fryer, Jr. *lawyer*
Redmond, David Dudley *lawyer*
Rhoads, Mark B. *lawyer*
Rigsby, Linda Flory *lawyer, director*
Robertson, Gregory B. *lawyer*
Roday, Leon E. *lawyer, finance company executive*
Rohman, Thomas P. *lawyer*
Rolfe, Robert Martin *lawyer*
Schwarzschild, Jane L. *lawyer*
Sharer, John Daniel *lawyer*
Slater, Thomas Glascock, Jr. *lawyer*
Slaughter, Alexander Hoke *lawyer*
Smith, Julious Perry, Jr. *lawyer*
Smith, R. Gordon *lawyer*
Spahn, Gary Joseph *lawyer*
Starke, Harold Eugene, Jr. *lawyer*
Stone, Jacquelyn Elois *lawyer*
Strickland, William Jesse *lawyer*
Talbott, Frank III *retired lawyer*
Taylor, Ashley L., Jr. *lawyer, former federal commissioner*
Thompson, Paul Michael *lawyer*
Troy, Anthony Francis *lawyer*
Walsh, James Hamilton *lawyer*
Walsh, William Arthur, Jr. *lawyer*
Warthen, Harry Justice III *lawyer*
Webb, Mark O. *lawyer*
Whittemore, Anne Marie *lawyer*
Wigner, Preston Douglas *lawyer, tobacco company executive*
Witt, Walter Francis, Jr. *lawyer*

Roanoke
Cleaveland, William H. (Bill Cleaveland) *lawyer, former state legislator*
Cranwell, C. Richard *lawyer, former political organization administrator*
Dudley, Julia Campbell *prosecutor*
Heaphy, Timothy John *federal prosecutor*
Marshall, Heman Alexander III *lawyer*
Pace, G. Michael, Jr. *lawyer*
Powell, Sarah E. *lawyer, automotive executive*

Springfield
Englert, Roy Theodore *lawyer*

Sterling
Harris, Scott Blake *lawyer*

Tysons Corner
Aucutt, Ronald David *lawyer*
Titus, Bruce Earl *lawyer*

Vienna
Cauley, Michael A. *prosecutor*
Miller, Donald Eugene *lawyer*
Stearns, Frank Warren *lawyer*
Whitaker, Thomas Patrick *lawyer*

Virginia Beach
Baldwin, Stanley Forrest *lawyer, insurance company executive*
Barney, Michael E. *lawyer*
Gregory, Lori-Don M. *lawyer, healthcare company executive*
Haytaian, Peter D. *lawyer, healthcare company executive*
Littel, John E. *lawyer*
Rephan, Jack *lawyer*
Shuttleworth, Thomas B., II, *lawyer*
Spitzli, Donald Hawkes, Jr. *lawyer*
Stredler, Jeffrey L. *lawyer*
Woodward, Lawrence H., Jr. *lawyer*

Ware Neck
McVey, Henry Hanna III *retired lawyer*

Warm Springs
Fields, William Albert *lawyer*

Williamsburg
Church, Dale Walker *lawyer*
Graham, David Browning *lawyer*
Grierson, Kevin William *lawyer*
Haynsworth, Harry Jay, IV, *law educator*
Heller, James Stephen *law librarian, educator*
Marcus, Paul *law educator*

Winchester
Dewey-Balzhiser, Anne Elizabeth Marie *lawyer*

Woodbridge
Sandler, Betty Moore *lawyer*

WEST VIRGINIA

Bridgeport
Nickerson, Gary W. *lawyer*
Steptoe, Robert Mason, Jr. *lawyer*

Charleston
Betts, Rebecca A. *lawyer*
Crandall, Grant *lawyer, labor union administrator*
Goodwin, Robert Booth, II, *federal prosecutor*
McHugh, Thomas Edward *lawyer, former state supreme court justice*
Miller, Charles T. *prosecutor*
Neely, Richard *lawyer*
Rowe, Larry Linwell *lawyer, former state senator*
Southworth, Louis Sweetland, II, *lawyer*
Stuart, Michael B. *lawyer, former political organization administrator*

Keyser
Staggers, Harley Orrin, Jr., (Buckey Staggers) *lawyer, former United States Representative from West Virginia*

Lewisburg
Ford, Richard Edmond *lawyer*

Morgantown
Fisher, John Welton, II, *lawyer, educator, academic administrator*
Fusco, Andrew G. *lawyer*
Garrison, Michael S. *lawyer, educator, former academic administrator*
Hardesty, David Carter, Jr. *lawyer, educator*

Wheeling
Ihlenfeld, William J., II, *federal prosecutor*
Wilmoth, William David *lawyer*

TERRITORIES OF THE UNITED STATES

PUERTO RICO

Guaynabo
Santos de Alvarez, Brunilda *lawyer, retired bank executive*

San Juan
Lasa-Ferrer, Armando *lawyer*
Rodriguez-Velez, Rosa Emilia *federal prosecutor*
Sánchez-Betances, Luis *lawyer, former attorney general*
Wexler, David B. *law educator*

VIRGIN ISLANDS

Charlotte Amalie
Feuerzeig, Henry Louis *lawyer*

Christiansted
Bland, James Theodore, Jr. *lawyer*
Evangelista, Richard T. *lawyer*

St Thomas
Sharpe, Ronald Wesley *federal prosecutor*

ADDRESS UNPUBLISHED

Adams, Daniel Fenton *law educator*
Allday, Martin Lewis, Jr. *retired lawyer*
Allen, William Hayes *lawyer, educator*
Baird, Thomas Bryan, Jr. *retired lawyer*
Benedetto, Anthony R. *religious mediator*
Berkley, Peter Lee *lawyer*
Berrey, Robert Forrest *lawyer*
Best, Laurence Edward *lawyer*
Blackford, Robert Newton *lawyer, director*
Blazzard, Norse Novar *lawyer*
Bonesio, Woodrow Michael *lawyer*
Brister, Bill H. *lawyer, former bankruptcy judge*
Brown, J. E. (J.E. Buster Brown) *lawyer, consultant*
Brown, John Robert *lawyer, librarian*
Builder, J. Lindsay, Jr. *lawyer*
Camilleri, Michael *lawyer, educator*
Chandler, Elizabeth Brannen (Beth Chandler) *lawyer*
Chiles, Stephen Michael *retired lawyer*
Choi, Albert H. *law educator*
Coleman, Robert Winston *lawyer*
Colodny, Edwin Irving *lawyer, retired air transportation executive*
Conant, Allah B., Jr. *lawyer, entrepreneur, small business owner*
Cooper, James Russell *retired law educator*
Coplin, Mark David *lawyer*
Cox, Chapman Beecher *retired lawyer, charitable organization and aerospace executive*
Cramer, Mark Clifton *lawyer*
Crawford, Carol Tallman *law educator*
Cummings, Candace S. *lawyer*
Daniel, Marilyn S. *lawyer*
Darnell, Riley Carlisle *lawyer, former state official*
Davis, Clarence Clinton, Jr. *lawyer*
Davis, William Allison, II, *retired lawyer*
DeGabrielle, Donald J., Jr. *former prosecutor*
Dhillon, Janet L. *lawyer, retail executive*
Donlon, William James *retired lawyer*
Drapkin, Dennis B. *lawyer*
Duncan, Donald William *lawyer*
Dunn, Morris Douglas *lawyer*
Ellis, Lester Neal, Jr. *lawyer*
Elsener, G. Dale *lawyer*
Ennis, Edgar William, Jr. *lawyer*
Esslinger, John Thomas *lawyer*
Everbach, Otto George *lawyer*
Ewen, Pamela Binnings *retired lawyer*
Feldman, H. Larry *lawyer*
Fillmore, Robert M. *lawyer*
Frank, Joe S. *lawyer, retired mayor*
Fuller, Samuel Ashby *retired lawyer, mining executive*
Furman, Howard *arbitrator, lawyer, mediator*
Gary, Stuart Hunter *lawyer*
Gavin, Donald Glenn *lawyer, educator*
Geddy, Vernon Meredith, Jr. *lawyer*
George, Joyce Jackson *lawyer, writer, retired judge, arbitrator, mediator*
Gladden, Joseph Rhea, Jr. *lawyer*
Glancy, Walter John *retired lawyer*
Goetz, Charles John *law and economics educator*
Gold, George Myron *lawyer, editor, writer, consultant*
Grant, Walter Matthews *retired lawyer and corporate executive*
Greene, John Joseph *lawyer*
Greene, Jule Blounte *lawyer*
Groetzinger, Jon, Jr. *lawyer, pharmaceutical, aerospace executive, educator*
Guess, James David *lawyer*
Hamilton, Dagmar Strandberg *lawyer, retired educator*
Hamilton, Robert Woodruff *retired legal association administrator, educator*
Hardy, Ashton Richard *retired attorney*
Harkey, Robert Shelton *retired lawyer*
Hemingway, Richard William *law educator*
Henderson, Thomas Henry, Jr. *lawyer, former legal association executive*
Hendry, Robert Ryon *lawyer*
Herring, Jerone Carson *retired lawyer, bank executive*
Hinchey, John William *lawyer*
Hoffheimer, Michael Harry *law educator*
Horwitz, Kenneth Merrill *lawyer, accountant*
Howell, Donald Lee *lawyer*
Huckaby, Gary Carlton *lawyer*
Jennings, Thomas Parks *lawyer*
Johnson, James Terence *lawyer, writer, minister, educator*
Kay, Joel Phillip *lawyer*
Kelehear, Carole Marchbanks Spann *legal assistant*
Kelley, James Francis *lawyer*

Kelso, Linda Yayoi *retired lawyer*
Killorin, Robert Ware *lawyer*
Klamon, Lawrence Paine *lawyer*
Klein, Linda Ann *lawyer*
Knight, Gary *lawyer, writer, educator*
Kolodey, Fred James *lawyer*
Krebs, Frederick John *retired legal association administrator*
Kumble, Steven Jay *lawyer*
Lamon, Harry Vincent, Jr. *lawyer*
Landon, James Henry *retired lawyer*
Lanigan, Susan S. *retired lawyer*
LaSala, Stephen R. *lawyer*
Lea, Lorenzo Bates *lawyer*
Lilliston, Andrew Wilson, Jr. *lawyer*
Lilly, Thomas Gerald *retired lawyer*
Long, Thad Gladden *lawyer*
Lublinski, Michael *lawyer*
Lutz, Jacob A., III, (Jake Lutz) *lawyer*
Magurno, Richard Peter *lawyer*
Mahoney, George LeFevre *lawyer*
Marinis, Thomas Paul, Jr. *lawyer*
Markoff, Brad Steven *lawyer*
Martineau, Robert John *retired law educator*
Marvin, Charles Arthur *law educator*
Massman, Richard Allan *lawyer*
McConnell, Edward Bosworth *legal association administrator, lawyer*
McCurley, Robert Lee, Jr. *lawyer, educator*
McGuffey, Carroll Wade, Jr. *lawyer*
McQuaid, Janet *lawyer*
Meyers, Tedson Jay *lawyer*
Midkiff, Charles Franklin *lawyer*
Milsten, Robert B. *lawyer*
Mitchell, Billy P. *retired arbitrator*
Nash, Melvin Samuel *lawyer*
Newman, Stephen Michael *lawyer*
Nolen, William Giles *lawyer, accountant*
O'Keefe, Edward Franklin *lawyer*
Otis, Lee (Sarah) Liberman *lawyer, educator*
Panos, Tas *lawyer*
Pfeiffer, Philip John *of counsel, retired lawyer*
Phelan, Marilyn Elizabeth *law educator*
Phillips, Larry Edward *lawyer*
Phillips, Robert James, Jr. *lawyer, corporate financial executive*
Poliakoff, Gary A. *lawyer, educator*
Price, Alfred Lee *lawyer, mining executive*
Puckett, Elizabeth Ann *former law librarian*
Reiss, Jerome *retired lawyer*
Reynolds, William Bradford *lawyer*
Rich, Michael Joseph *lawyer*
Roberts, William B. *lawyer*
Rounsaville, Keith Eugene *retired lawyer*
Rowe, Thomas Dudley, Jr. *law educator*
Rubenfeld, Stanley Irwin *lawyer, director, mediator, arbitrator*
Rudolph, Gilbert Lawrence *lawyer*
Sacher, Steven Jay *lawyer*
Santorum, Rick (Richard John Santorum) *lawyer, former United States Senator from Pennsylvania*
Sapp, John Raymond *lawyer*
Schreiber, Alan Hickman *lawyer*
Sears, Mary Helen *lawyer*
Segal, Robert Martin *lawyer*
Shepherd, Jon Glen *lawyer*
Sinor, Howard Earl, Jr. *lawyer*
Sperling, Sheldon Jay *former federal prosecutor*
Stockburger, Jean Dawson *retired lawyer*
Surles, Richard Hurlbut, Jr. *retired law librarian*
Susman, Morton Lee *lawyer*
Tanner, W(alter) Rhett *lawyer*
Terrell, G. Irvin *lawyer*
Terry, Anne Curtis *lawyer, writer*
Tucker, Laurey Dan *lawyer*
Turnage, Fred Douglas *retired lawyer*
Wagoner, Anna Mills *former prosecutor*
Walmer, Edwin Fitch *retired lawyer*
Weiss, Kenneth Andrew *lawyer, educator*
Williamson, Douglas Franklin, Jr. *lawyer*
Wilson, Rhys Thaddeus *lawyer*
Wolf, Gary Wickert *retired lawyer*
Woodard, Joseph Lamar *law librarian, emeritus professor*
Wright, Frederick Lewis, II, *lawyer*
Wright, Robert Payton *lawyer*
Yokubaitis, Roger T. *lawyer*
Young, Barney Thornton *lawyer*
Zevnik-Sawatzky, Donna Dee *retired litigation coordinator*

MEDICINE *See* HEALTHCARE: MEDICINE

MILITARY

UNITED STATES

ALABAMA

Enterprise
Parker, Ellis D. *retired military officer*

Huntsville
Williamson, Donald Ray *retired military officer*

Perdido Beach
Wilkinson, Edward Anderson, Jr. *retired military officer, manufacturing executive*

COLORADO

Englewood
McNair, Carl Herbert, Jr. *military officer, aeronautical engineer*

FLORIDA

Delray Beach
Evans, Marsha Johnson *retired military officer, former non profit and sports association executive*

Doral
Kelly, John Francis *career military officer*

Eglin AFB
Richardson, Douglas J. *career officer*

Hurlburt Field
Fiel, Eric C. *career military officer*
Travis, Antonio D. (Tony Travis) *career military officer*

Jacksonville
Delaney, Kevin Francis *retired military officer, consultant*

Melbourne
Laposata, Joseph Samuel *army officer*

Miami
Clem, Ralph S. *career officer, educator*
Kernan, Joseph D. *career military officer*

Satellite Beach
Scanlon, Charles Francis *retired military officer, writer, publisher, consultant*

Shalimar
Burke, Kelly Howard *retired military officer, entrepreneur*

Tampa
Austin, Lloyd James III *career military officer*
McRaven, William Harry (Bill McRaven) *career military officer*

West Palm Beach
Chelberg, Robert Douglas *military officer*
Thomashow, Steven Roy *military and intelligence officer, global business leader, counsel, law enforcer*

GEORGIA

Atlanta
Webster, William G., Jr. *career military officer*

Fort Benning
Gittins, Timothy Lee *military officer*

Marietta
Butterworth, Jim B. *military officer, former state legislator*

Warner Robins
Nugteren, Cornelius *air force officer*

LOUISIANA

Barksdale AFB
Kowalski, James M. *career military officer*

New Orleans
Cotton, John G. *career military officer*
Landry, Mary E. *career military officer*

NORTH CAROLINA

Fort Bragg
Helmick, Frank G. *career military officer*

Raleigh
Shelton, Hugh (Henry Hugh Shelton) *former Chairman of the Joint Chiefs of Staff*

Spring Hope
Hildreth, James Robert *retired air force officer*

OKLAHOMA

Oklahoma City
Siewert, Edgar Allen *retired military non-commissioned officer*

Roosevelt
Franks, Tommy Ray *retired military officer*

SOUTH CAROLINA

Beaufort
Miller, Robert *retired military officer*

Bluffton
Pendley, William Tyler *military officer, educator*

Charleston
Watts, Claudius Elmer III *retired military officer*

Columbia
King, Teresa L. *career military officer*
Shuler, Ellie Givan, Jr. *retired military officer, museum administrator*

York
Blackwell, Paul Eugene, Sr. *military officer*

TEXAS

Austin
Inman, Bobby Ray *retired military officer, former dean*

Belton
Shoemaker, Robert Morin *retired military officer, commissioner*

Canyon Lake
Ognibene, Andre John *retired military officer, internist, educator*

Dallas
Bates, Barry D. *career officer*

Fort Sam Houston
Caldwell, William B., IV, (Bill Caldwell) *career military officer*

Houston
Gorie, Dominic L. Pudwill *retired military officer, astronaut*
Johnson, Gregory Harold *career officer, astronaut, experimental test and fighter pilot*

Lubbock
Huffman, Walter B. *retired army officer, dean, law educator*

Randolph AFB
Ellis, Edward R. *career officer*
Looney, William R. III *career military officer*
Rice, Edward A., Jr. *career military officer*

San Antonio
Kline, John William *retired military officer, management consultant*
Sculley, Patrick David *retired army officer, director*
Westermann, Edward Burton *military officer, analyst, educator*

Sheppard AFB
Cook, Sharla J. *career officer*

Universal City
Rubenstein, David Aaron *military officer, healthcare executive*

VIRGINIA

Alexandria
Dunn, Bernard Daniel *former naval officer, consultant*

Arlington
Allen, Thad William *retired military officer*
Barbero, Michael D. *career military officer*
DeFilippi, George *retired air force officer*
Dunie, Deborah B. *military officer*
Gracey, James Steele *retired coast guard officer, management consultant, director*
Grass, Frank Joseph *career military officer*
Hallinan, Patrick K. *civilian military employee*
Jones, Walter F. *civilian military employee, director*
King, James C. *retired military officer*

Fort Monroe
Cone, Robert W. *career military officer*

Fort Myer
Condon, Kathryn A. *civilian military employee*

Great Falls
Cowhill, William Joseph *retired naval officer, consultant*

Haymarket
Seely, James Michael *retired military officer, defense consultant, small business owner*

Herndon
Charlip, Ralph Blair *military officer, health facility administrator*

Langley AFB
Wright, Bruce A. *military officer*

Lynchburg
Snead, George Murrell, Jr. *military officer, research scientist, consultant*

Mc Lean
Jumper, John Phillip *retired military officer, aerospace and defense company executive*
Kimmons, John F. *career military officer, former federal official*
Rogers, Alan Victor *former CEO, air force major general*
Scott, Bruce K. *retired military officer*
Yarborough, William Glenn, Jr. *military officer, forester, international business executive*

Merrifield
Earner, William Anthony, Jr. *naval officer*

Norfolk
Gortney, William Evans (Bill Gortney) *career military officer*

Round Hill
Tice, Raphael Dean *military officer*

Springfield
Ginn, Richard Van Ness *military officer, healthcare executive, author, historian, oral historian*
Roberts, Paul Franklin, II, *financial executive*

Vienna
Chandler, Hubert Thomas *former army officer*

Williamsburg
Jacoby, William Jerome, Jr. *retired military officer, internist*

ADDRESS UNPUBLISHED

Albright, Joseph William *management consultant*
Casey, George William, Jr. *retired military officer*
Conway, James Terry *retired military officer*
DeLuca, Anthony J. *civilian military employee*
Dunwoody, Ann Elizabeth *retired military officer*
Elam, Fred Eldon *retired military officer*
Fallon, William Joseph *retired military officer*
Garner, Jay Montgomery *retired military officer*
Guthrie, Wallace Nessler, Jr. *naval officer*
Haddock, Raymond Earl *retired career officer, major general*
Harper, Henry H. *retired military officer*
Honoré, Russel L. *retired military officer*
Hoover, John Elwood *former military officer, consultant, writer, educator*
Juskowiak, Terry Eugene *career military officer, information technology executive*
Less, Anthony Albert *retired naval officer*
Maples, Michael David *career military officer*
McNabb, Duncan James *retired military officer*
Metz, Thomas Frederic *retired military officer*
Palmer, Dave Richard *retired military officer, academic administrator*
Retz, William Andrew *consultant, retired naval officer*
Robinson, David Brooks *retired naval officer*
Scholes, Edison Earl *military officer*
Smolen, Robert Lee (Bob Smolen) *retired military officer*
Van Antwerp, Robert L., Jr. *retired military officer*
Whitcomb, R. Steven *career officer*
Williams, James Arthur *retired military officer, information technology executive*
Wooley, Michael W. *retired military officer*
Wroth, James Melvin *retired military officer*

REAL ESTATE

UNITED STATES

ALABAMA

Birmingham
Couch, Robert M. *real estate company executive*

ARKANSAS

Hot Springs National Park
Craft, Kay Stark *real estate company executive*

FLORIDA

Bonita Springs
Starkey, Jerry L. *real estate developer*

Cedar Key
Starnes, Earl Maxwell *retired urban and regional planner, architect, educator*

Coral Gables
Peebles, R. Donahue *real estate company executive*

Daytona Beach
McMunn, William H. *real estate company executive*

Deland
Caccamise, Alfred Edward *real estate executive*

Fort Lauderdale
Markos, Chris *retired real estate company executive*
Moraitis, Karen Karl *real estate broker*
Parrish, Lori Nance *property appraiser*

Gainesville
York, Vermelle Cardwell *retired real estate broker and developer*

Jacksonville
Clarkson, Charles Andrew *real estate investment executive*
Pearce, Jennifer Sue *real estate appraiser*
Rood, John Darrell *real estate developer, former ambassador*

Key Biscayne
Margulies, Martin Z. *real estate developer, philanthropist*

Miami
Bluntzer, Elena C. *real estate company executive*
Perez, Jorge M. *real estate developer*
Raffel, Leroy B. *real estate developer*
Reed, Linda L. *real estate company executive*

Naples
Dorio, Martin Matthew, Jr. *real estate company executive, investor*

North Miami Beach
Macken, Jodi *real estate company executive*

Ocala
Booth, Jane Schuele *real estate company officer, broker*

Orlando
Gidel, Robert Hugh *real estate investor*

Palm Beach
Bagby, Martha L. Green *real estate holding company and publishing executive, writer*
Coudert, Dale Hokin *real estate executive, marketing consultant*

Klotsche, Charles Martin *real estate company executive, photographer, writer, financial columnist*

Saint Petersburg Beach
Hurley, Frank Thomas, Jr. *realtor*

Sarasota
McCarthy, Brian Nelson *Real Estate professional*

Sebring
Sherrick, Daniel Noah *real estate broker*

Tampa
Levy, Jonathan A. *real estate company executive*
VanButsel, Michael R. *real estate broker, construction executive*

Vero Beach
Freeman, Donald Wilford *real estate developer, horse breeder*

West Palm Beach
Goddess, Lynn Barbara *real estate investor*

GEORGIA

Athens
Melton, Wayne Charles *real estate executive*

Atlanta
Aka, Ebenezer Osita *urban planner, educator, researcher, consultant*
Bell, Thomas Devereaux, Jr. *real estate company executive*
Charania, Barkat *real estate consultant*
Friedenberg, Karen Rosen *real estate executive*
Hogue, W. Dennis *real estate company executive*
Terwilliger, J. Ronald *real estate company executive*

Columbus
Garrard, Gardiner W., Jr. *real estate development and investment company executive*

Marietta
Cline, Robert Thomas *retired land developer*

Toccoa
Maypole, John Floyd *real estate company executive*

KENTUCKY

Louisville
Brehl, Robert J. *real estate company executive*
Cafaro, Debra A. *real estate company executive*

LOUISIANA

Covington
Maurin, James E. *real estate executive*

Saint Gabriel
Godwin, Ralph Lee, Jr. *real estate executive*

MISSISSIPPI

Clarksdale
Magdovitz, Lawrence Maynard *real estate company executive, lawyer*

NEW YORK

New York
Close, Michael John *property manager, lawyer*
Ross, Stephen Michael *real estate company executive, professional sports team owner*

NORTH CAROLINA

Charlotte
Harris, John W. *real estate company executive*

Greensboro
Perkins, Robbie *real estate company executive, former mayor, Greensboro, North Carolina*

OHIO

Youngstown
DeBartolo, Edward John, Jr. *real estate developer, former professional football team owner*

OKLAHOMA

Oklahoma City
Sullivan, Leonard *realtor, state representative*

Tulsa
Ball, Rex Martin *urban planner, architect*
Henderson, James Ronald *industrial real estate developer*
Matthews, Dane Dikeman *urban planner*

SOUTH CAROLINA

Charleston
Brumley, Frank W. *real estate company executive*

Columbia
Limehouse, Harry Bancroft, Jr. *real estate developer, transportation consultant*

Hilton Head Island
Gruchacz, Robert S. *real estate company officer*

TENNESSEE

Goodlettsville
Aertker, Gayle *real estate company executive*

Memphis
Churchey, Randy L. *real estate company executive*

TEXAS

Austin
Bayless, William C., Jr. *real estate company executive*
Keller, Gary *real estate company executive, writer*

Dallas
Byrne, Tim *real estate company executive*
Dwors, Robert F. *real estate company executive*
Fraker, Jack C. *real estate company executive*
Krasnow, Kenneth *real estate company executive*
Miller, Geraldine (Tincy Miller) *real estate company executive, educational association administrator*
Moss, Robert Williams *real estate developer*

El Paso
Lyle, James Arthur *real estate broker*

Fort Worth
Smith, Tracey *real estate broker*

Galveston
McLeod, E. Douglas *real estate developer, lawyer*

Houston
Daugherty, John A., Jr. *realtor*
Duncan, Robert D. *real estate company executive*
Goldsmith, Billy Joe *real estate broker, rancher*
Heard, Larry *real estate company executive*
Morris, Malcolm Stewart *title company executive, lawyer*
Rigby, Weldon *realtor*
Untermeyer, Charles Graves (Chase Untermeyer) *international business consultant*

Laredo
Stea, David *environmental psychologist urban planner, educator*

Plano
Perot, Ross (H. Ross Perot, Henry Ross Perot) *real estate company, investment company, data processing executive*
Perot, Ross, Jr., (Henry Ross Perot Jr.) *real estate developer, professional sports team executive*

Port Aransas
Turner, Elizabeth Adams Noble (Betty Turner) *real estate company executive, author, architect*

San Antonio
Condos, Barbara Seale *real estate broker, developer, investor*

VIRGINIA

Amissville
Hartke, Anita *real estate broker*

Arlington
Blair, Bryce *real estate company executive*
Noonan, Patrick Francis *conservation executive*

Bristol
Conrad, David Paul *business broker, real estate developer, retired food service executive*

Fairfax
Cockwell, Ian G. *real estate company executive*

Glen Allen
Hill, Melissa A. *real estate company executive*
Sledd, Robert C. *real estate company executive*

Mc Lean
Moran, William A. *real estate company executive*

Newport News
Goldberg, Stanley Irwin *real estate company executive*

Norfolk
Slone, Jordan E. *real estate company executive*

Richmond
Tuck, Grayson Edwin *retired real estate agent, gas industry executive*

Virginia Beach
Pefley, Charles Saunders *real estate broker*

WASHINGTON

Seattle
Kilberg, James Anthony *real estate company executive*

ADDRESS UNPUBLISHED

Aleschus, Justine Lawrence *retired real estate broker*
Aulbach, George Louis *retired real estate company executive*
Bergau, Frank Conrad *real estate, commercial and investment properties executive*

Bowne, Shirlee Pearson *real estate consultant*
Citro, Yolande *real estate agent*
Dasso, Jerome Joseph *real estate educator*
Dysart, Benjamin Clay III *conservationist, engineer, consultant*
Estrin, Richard William *real estate and business broker, retired editor*
Gasper, Ruth Eileen *real estate executive*
Gilbert, Frederick E. *development planner, Africanist, consultant*
Kollaer, Jim C. *real estate executive, architect*
Lamy, M. Rebecca (Mary Rebecca Lamy) *consultant, land developer, government official*
Ledford, Janet Marie Smalley *real estate appraiser, consultant*
Maier, Robert Henry *retired real estate executive*
Mercurio, Renard Michael *real estate company executive*
Simmons, David Jeffrey *real estate executive*
Wilson, James Laurence *real estate development executive, financial services consultant, educator*

RELIGION

UNITED STATES

ALABAMA

Birmingham
Baker, Robert Joseph *bishop*

Florence
Barfield, Kenny Dale *religious organization administrator*

Greensboro
Massey, James Earl *retired clergyman, educator*

Huntsville
Hull, William Edward *theology studies educator*

Mobile
Lipscomb, Oscar Hugh *archbishop emeritus*
Rodi, Thomas John *archbishop*

ARKANSAS

Hot Springs Village
Smith, Preston *retired minister, small business owner*

Little Rock
Taylor, Anthony Basil *bishop*

Russellville
Inch, Morris Alton *theology educator*

DELAWARE

New Castle
Riddle, W. Curtis *publisher*

DISTRICT OF COLUMBIA

Washington
Dunn, James Milton *retired religious organization administrator*

FLORIDA

Ave Maria
Novak, Michael (John) *religion educator, author, editor*

Boynton Beach
Lessard, Raymond William *bishop emeritus*

Fort Lauderdale
Eynon, Steven Scott *pastor*

Jacksonville
Estevez, Felipe de Jesús *bishop*
Galeone, Victor Benito *bishop*
Snyder, John Joseph *bishop emeritus*

Miami
Patterson, Rickey Lee *clergyman*

Miami Shores
Favalora, John Clement *archbishop*
Wenski, Thomas Gerard *archbishop*

Ocala
Massa, Conrad Harry *retired religious studies educator*

Orlando
Johnson, Tim *pastor, retired professional football player*
Noonan, John Gerard *bishop*

Palm Beach Gardens
Barbarito, Gerald Michael *bishop*
Symons, Joseph Keith *bishop emeritus*

Palmetto Bay
Fitzgerald, John Thomas, Jr. *religious studies educator*

Pensacola
Baldwin, Chuck (Charles O. Baldwin) *minister, radio personality*

Mountcastle, William Wallace, Jr. *retired philosophy and religion educator*
Ricard, John Huston *bishop, religious studies educator*
Stokes, Mack Boyd (Marion) *bishop*

Pompano Beach
Nolan, Richard Thomas *clergyman, educator, writer*

Saint Augustine
McCarty, Doran Chester *religious organization administrator*

Saint Petersburg
Lynch, Robert Nugent *bishop*

Sarasota
McFarlin, Diane Hooten *publisher*

Venice
Dewane, Frank Joseph *bishop*
Nevins, John Joseph *bishop emeritus*

GEORGIA

Atlanta
Holifield, E. Brooks *theology educator emeritus*
Keiller, James Bruce *clergyman, dean*
King, Bernice Albertine *minister, advocate*
Runyon, Theodore Hubert, Jr. *religion educator, minister*
Vivian, C.T. (Cordy Tindell Vivian) *retired civil rights organization administrator*
Waters, John W. *minister, educator*

College Park
Dollar, Creflo A. *minister, religious organization administrator*

Flintstone
Ragon, Robert Ronald *clergyman*

Jasper
Walker, Len *minister, former state legislator*

Savannah
Boland, John Kevin *bishop*
Hartmayer, Gregory John *bishop*

Smyrna
Gregory, Wilton Daniel *archbishop*
Zarama, Luis Rafael *bishop*

Woodstock
Collins, David Browning *religious institution administrator*

KENTUCKY

Covington
Foys, Roger Joseph *bishop*

Glasgow
Whittaker, Bill Douglas *minister*

Lexington
Gainer, Ronald William *bishop*
Williams, James Kendrick *bishop emeritus*

Louisville
Boykin, Gladys *retired religious organization administrator*
Kurtz, Joseph Edward *archbishop*

Owensboro
McRaith, John Jeremiah *bishop*
Medley, William Francis *bishop*

LOUISIANA

Alexandria
Herzog, Ronald Paul *bishop*

Baton Rouge
Muench, Robert William *bishop*

Kenner
Carmon, Dominic *bishop emeritus*

Lafayette
Jarrell, Charles Michael *bishop*

Lake Charles
Provost, Glen John *bishop*

Metairie
Sievering, Paul *retired minister, consultant*

New Orleans
Aymond, Gregory Michael *archbishop*
Fabre, Shelton Joseph *bishop*
Hughes, Alfred Clifton *archbishop emeritus*
Schulte, Francis B. *archbishop emeritus*

Schriever
Jacobs, Sam Gallip *bishop*

Shreveport
Duca, Michael Gerard *bishop*

Springhill
Morgan, Larry Ronald *minister*

MISSISSIPPI

Biloxi
Howze, Joseph Lawson Edward *bishop emeritus*
Morin, Roger Paul *bishop*

RELIGION (continued)

Gulfport
McCay, John III *minister*

Jackson
Houck, William Russell *bishop emeritus*
Latino, Joseph Nunzio *bishop*

NORTH CAROLINA

Charlotte
Curlin, William George *bishop emeritus*
Graham, Billy (William Franklin Graham) *evangelist*
Graham, Franklin (William Franklin Graham III) *evangelist, missionary*
Jugis, Peter Joseph *bishop*
Walker, George W. C. *bishop*

Durham
Meyers, Eric Mark *religion educator*

Greenville
Jackson, Bobby Rand *minister*

Hendersonville
Trexler, Edgar Ray *minister, editor*

Lake Junaluska
Goodgame, Gordon Clifton *retired minister*

Monroe
Kyle, John Emery *retired religious organization administrator*

Raleigh
Burbidge, Michael Francis *bishop*

Taylorsville
Ross, David Edmond *church official*

Tobaccoville
Wood, Stephen Wray *minister, educator, legislator, singer, writer*

Weaverville
Edwards, Otis Carl, Jr. *theology studies educator*

Wilmington
Conser, Walter Hurley, Jr. *religion and philosophy educator*

Winston Salem
Rights, Graham Henry *retired minister*

OKLAHOMA

Bethany
Leggett, James Daniel *bishop*
Murrow, Wayne Lee *retired minister, communications educator, dean*

Oklahoma City
Beltran, Eusebius Joseph *archbishop emeritus*
Coakley, Paul Stagg *archbishop*
Ridley, Betty Ann *theology studies educator*

SOUTH CAROLINA

Anderson
Wisler, Darla Lee *pastor*

Charleston
Guglielmone, Robert Eric *bishop*

Irmo
Branham, Mack Carison, Jr. *retired religious organization administrator, minister*

Myrtle Beach
McCaffrey, Edmund F. *abbot emeritus*

Spartanburg
Bullard, John Moore *religious studies educator, church musician*

Taylors
Smith, Morton Howison *religious organization administrator, educator*

White Rock
Aull, James Stroud *retired bishop*

TENNESSEE

Antioch
Worthington, Melvin Leroy *minister, writer*

Cookeville
Adkisson, Randall Lynn *minister*

Knoxville
Stika, Richard F. *bishop*

Memphis
Graves, William H. *minister*
Steib, James Terry *bishop*

Morristown
Starks, Charles Wiley *minister*

Nashville
Bigham, Wanda Durrett *religious organization administrator*
Choby, David Raymond *bishop*
Land, Richard Dale *minister, religious organization administrator*
McKenzie, Vashti Murphy *bishop*
Page, Frank S. *religious organization administrator*
Stooksbury, William Claude *minister*

TeSelle, Eugene Arthur, Jr. *religion educator*

TEXAS

Aledo
Barton, David *religious studies educator, writer, historian, researcher*

Amarillo
Klein, Jerry Lee, Sr. *minister, philosophy and religion professor*
Yanta, John Walter *bishop emeritus*
Zurek, Patrick James *bishop*

Austin
Hitchcock, Joanna *publisher*
McCarthy, John Edward *bishop emeritus*
Vásquez, José Stephen *bishop*

Beaumont
Guillory, Curtis John *bishop*

Brownsville
Flores, Daniel Ernest *bishop*
Pena, Raymundo Joseph *bishop*

Brownwood
Smith, Robert Leonard *pastor, religious studies educator, retired theology studies educator*

Corpus Christi
Carmody, Edmond *bishop*
Gracida, Rene Henry *bishop emeritus*
Mulvey, W(illiam) Michael *bishop*

Dallas
Blue, John Ronald (J. Ronald Blue) *evangelical mission executive*
Crotty, Robert Bell *minister*
Curran, Charles Edward *theology studies educator, priest*
Deshotel, John Douglas *bishop*
Farrell, Kevin Joseph *bishop*
Gross, Harriet P. Marcus *religious studies and writing educator*
Jakes, T.D. (Thomas Dexter Jakes) *bishop, author*
Jones, Ronald E. *pastor, former mayor, Garland, Texas*
Kirby, James Edmund, Jr. *theology educator*
Pinson, William Meredith, Jr. *pastor, writer, administrator, professor*
Seitz, Mark Joseph *bishop*

Flower Mound
Woodring, DeWayne Stanley *religious association executive*

Fort Worth
Vann, Kevin William *bishop*

Houston
Barrett, Michael Joseph *priest*
DiNardo, Daniel Nicholas Cardinal *cardinal, archbishop*
Fiorenza, Joseph Anthony *archbishop emeritus*
Karff, Samuel Egal *rabbi*
Nielsen, Niels Christian, Jr. *retired religious studies educator*
Osteen, Joel *minister*
Rizzotto, Vincent Michael *bishop emeritus*

Humble
Baird, Robert Dahlen *retired theology studies educator*

Jacksonville
Blaylock, James Carl *clergyman, librarian*

Laredo
Tamayo, James Anthony *bishop*

Lubbock
Rodriguez, Placido *bishop*

Plano
Oden, William Bryant *bishop, educator*

River Oaks
Hestand, Joel Dwight *minister, evangelist*

San Angelo
Pfeifer, Michael David *bishop*

San Antonio
Cantú, Oscar *bishop*
Fecher, Vincent John *priest*
Flanagan, Thomas Joseph *bishop emeritus*
Flores, Patrick Fernandez *archbishop emeritus*
Garcia-Siller, Gustavo *archbishop*
Grahmann, Charles Victor *bishop emeritus*
Mc Allister, Gerald Nicholas *retired bishop, minister*

Tyler
Corrada del Rio, Alvaro *bishop*

Victoria
Fellhauer, David Eugene *bishop*

Waco
Hein, Jay Forest *religious studies educator, former federal official*
Talbert, Charles Harold *theologian, educator*

VIRGINIA

Alexandria
Vanderslice, Mara Louise *religious organization executive*

Arlington
Coe, Doug *religious organization administrator*

Kane, Annette Pieslak *religious organization executive*
Loverde, Paul Stephen *bishop*

Falls Church
Benton, Nicholas Frederick *publisher*

Fredericksburg
Edmunds, Jeffrey Garth *Anglican minister*

Front Royal
Andes, Larry Dale *minister*

Great Falls
Sapp, Eric *religious organization executive*

Henrico
DiLorenzo, Francis X. *bishop*

King George
Agnew, Christopher Mack *minister, historian*

Lynchburg
LaHaye, Timothy F. *pastor, writer*

Mechanicsville
Gerrish, Brian Albert *theologian, educator, retired minister*

Mineral
Speer, Jack Atkeson *publisher*

Norfolk
Gallagher, Carol Joy *bishop*

Salem
Hinlicky, Paul Richard *minister*

WEST VIRGINIA

Charleston
Scott, Olof Henderson, Jr. *priest*

Fairmont
Stevens, Earl Patrick *minister*

Huntington
Perkins, Chris (Carl Christopher Perkins) *pastor, former United States Representative from Kentucky*

Wheeling
Bransfield, Michael Joseph *bishop*
Thurston, Bonnie Bowman *religious studies educator, minister, poet*

TERRITORIES OF THE UNITED STATES

PUERTO RICO

San Juan
Fernandez Torres, Daniel *bishop*
González Nieves, Roberto Octavio *archbishop*

VIRGIN ISLANDS

Charlotte Amalie
Thomas, Elliott Griffin *bishop emeritus*

St Thomas
Bevard, Herbert Armstrong *bishop*

ADDRESS UNPUBLISHED

Agler, Richard Dean *rabbi*
Armstrong, (Arthur) James *minister, educator, consultant, writer*
Broadwater, James E. *retired publisher*
Dimond, Robert Edward *publisher, general manager*
Foley, David Edward *bishop emeritus*
Frankson-Kendrick, Sarah Jane *publisher*
Friend, William Benedict *bishop emeritus*
Gemignani, Michael Caesar *clergyman, retired professor and university administrator*
Gralla, Milton *retired publisher*
Hage, Lillian C. *organization administrator, director, dean*
Hultstrand, Donald Maynard *bishop*
Lehrman, Irving *rabbi*
Magrill, Joe Richard, Jr. *religious organization administrator, minister*
McMaster, Belle Miller *religious organization administrator*
Melvin, Billy Alfred *clergyman*
Nunn, Charles Burgess *retired religious organization administrator*
Ochoa, Armando Xavier *bishop*
Popp, Bernard Ferdinand *bishop emeritus*
Shirer, Robert LLoyd *clergyman*
Slattery, Edward James *bishop*
Wantland, William Charles *retired bishop, lawyer*
Westerhoff, John Henry III *priest, theologian, educator*
Wisehart, Mary Ruth *retired religious organization administrator*

Wooten, Cecil Aaron *retired religious organization administrator*

SCIENCE: LIFE SCIENCE

UNITED STATES

ALABAMA

Auburn
Klesius, Phillip Harry *microbiologist, researcher*
Sorokulova, Iryna *microbiologist, educator*

Birmingham
Finley, Sara Crews *medical geneticist, educator*
Korf, Bruce Richard *clinical geneticist, neurologist*
Marchase, Richard Banfield *cell biologist, educator, research administrator*
Page, John Gardner *toxicologist, consultant*
Schafer, James Arthur *physiologist*
Townes, Tim M. *science educator, researcher*

Montgomery
Sass, Neil Leslie *toxicologist*

ARKANSAS

Fayetteville
Brown, Avert Hayden *animal scientist, educator*
Limayem, Moez *science educator, researcher*
Musacchia, X(avier) J(oseph) *physiology and biophysics educator*
Musick, Gerald Joe *retired entomology educator*

Little Rock
Casciano, Daniel Anthony *biologist, educator*
Gealt, Michael A. *environmental microbiologist, educator*
Hinson, Jack Allsbrook *research toxicologist, educator*

DISTRICT OF COLUMBIA

Washington
Bandows Koster, Janet *science association director*
Banks, Richard Charles *ornithologist*
Heinemeier, Dan C. *science association director*

FLORIDA

Boca Raton
Samuels, William Mason *physiology association executive*

Bradenton
Diana, John Nicholas *physiologist*

Coral Gables
Lucà-Moretti, Maurizio *research scientist, nutritionist*

Delray Beach
Chavin, Walter *biological sciences educator, researcher*
Zall, Robert Rouben *food scientist, educator*

Englewood
Dunson, William Albert *biology professor, ecological consultant*

Fort Pierce
Calvert, David Victor *soil science educator*
Rice, Mary Esther *biologist*

Gainesville
Allen, Leon Hartwell *agronomist, educator*
Besch, Emerson Louis *physiologist, educator, retired dean*
Crawford, Patti Cynthai (Cynda) *veterinarian, educator*
Hoy, Marjorie Ann *entomology educator*
Nicoletti, Paul Lee *retired veterinarian, educator*
Purcifull, Dan Elwood *retired plant virologist, educator*
Queensberry, Kenneth Hays *agronomy educator*
Schmidt-Nielsen, Bodil Mimi (Mrs. Roger G. Chagnon) *retired physiologist, educator*
Schuur, Edward Arthur George *ecology professor*
Shabana, Yasser M. *plant pathologist professor, research scientist*
Stall, William M. *weed scientist, educator*
Teixeira, Arthur Alves *food engineer, educator, consultant*
Thompson, Neal Philip *food science and nutrition educator, dean*
Tumlinson, James H. III *agriculturist*
Vierck, Charles John, Jr. *retired neuroscience educator*
Yu, Simon Shyi-Jian *entomologist, educator*

Lake Alfred
Kender, Walter John *horticulturist, educator*

Largo
Briscoe, Anne M. *retired science educator*

Miami
Muench, Karl Hugo *clinical geneticist*

Naples
Goldman, Ralph Frederick *research physiologist, educator*

Charlottesville
Chevalier, Roger Alan *astronomy educator, consultant*
Garrett, Reginald Hooker *biology professor, researcher*
Menaker, Michael *biology professor*
Molhoek, Kerrington Ramsey *research scientist*
Ogle, Roy Clinton *cell biologist, educator*
Tuttle, Jeremy Ballou *neuroscientist*

Fairfax
Fowler, Bruce Andrew *toxicologist, researcher, public health service official*
Kim Joo, Pilju *agronomist*
Schneider, Edwin Kahn *research scientist*

Falls Church
Hart, C(harles) W(illard), Jr. *zoologist, curator*
Simpson, Michael Marcial *science and technology specialist, consultant*

Front Royal
Douglas, J(ocelyn) Fielding *toxicologist, consultant*

Hampton
Jahncke, Michael Lee *professor director*

Keswick
Rafajko, Robert Richard *science administrator*

Lexington
Hickman, Cleveland Pendleton, Jr. *biology professor*
Spencer, Edgar Winston *geology educator*

Mc Lean
DeGiovanni-Donnelly, Rosalie Frances *biologist, educator*
Pyke, Thomas Nicholas, Jr. *science administrator*
Talbot, Lee Merriam *ecologist, educator, administrator*

Norfolk
Oelberg, David George *neonatologist educator, researcher*
Pepe, Gerald J. *physiologist, educator*

Reston
O'Grady, Richard T. *science administrator*

Richmond
Boadle-Biber, Margaret Clare *physiologist, educator*
Holmes, Walter Michael *biology professor*
Skunda, Robert T. *life science organization administrator*

Williamsburg
Guastaferro, Angelo *space science administrator, consultant*

Woodbridge
Thomas, Lindsey Kay, Jr. *research ecology biologist, educator, consultant*

Wytheville
Linzey, Donald Wayne *biologist, educator, researcher*

WEST VIRGINIA

Kearneysville
Biggs, Alan Richard *plant pathologist, educator*

Morgantown
Cochrane, Robert Lowe *biologist*
Wenger, Sharon Louise *cytogeneticist, researcher, educator*

South Charleston
Bhasin, Madan Mohan *research scientist*

TERRITORIES OF THE UNITED STATES

PUERTO RICO

Aguadilla
Gómez-Jiménez, Carlos *science educator, microbiologist, geneticist*

ADDRESS UNPUBLISHED

Ahearne, John Francis *science society director, researcher*
Armstrong, Donald *biochemistry, pathophysiology educator*
Arnott, Howard Joseph *biology professor, dean*
Barkovskii, Andrei L. *microbiologist*
Barnard, Donald Roy *medical and veterinary entomologist*
Barnes, Hoyt Michael *professor, wood scientist, consultant*
Bower, James Mason *neuroscientist, educator, science administrator*
Clark, Eloise Elizabeth *biologist, educator*
Coats, Michael L. *retired science administrator, retired astronaut*
Cohen, Stanley *retired biochemistry educator*
DeBakey, Lois *science administrator, educator*
Farkas, Daniel Frederick *food science and technology educator*
Flemming, David Paul *biologist*
Franks, Allen P. *retired research institute executive, educator*
Goodall, Jane *zoologist*
Hilliard, Sam Bowers *geography educator*
Hillis, William Daniel *biology professor*
Hope, William Duane *retired zoologist, curator*
Howard-Peebles, Patricia N. *clinical cytogeneticist*

Hoye, Robert Earl *systems science educator*
Keller, Nadya Clark *retired biochemistry educator, researcher*
Kessler, Edwin *meteorology educator, consultant*
Krugman, Stanley Liebert *retired science administrator, geneticist*
Kushlan, James Anthony *scientist, science administrator, educator, conservationist, writer*
Layne, James Nathaniel *retired vertebrate biologist*
Lynch, John Thomas *retired science administrator, physicist*
Mattox, Johnny Lynn *biologist, educator*
Maunder, Addison Bruce *agronomic research company executive*
McSwain, Byrdie Engle *laboratory scientist, immunohematologist*
Norman, Thena Monts Durham *microbiologist, researcher, health facility administrator*
Pianka, Eric Rodger *population biologist, educator*
Prentice, Howard Malcolm *research scientist, educator*
Rall, Wilfrid *neuroscientist, researcher, artist*
Robinson, Thomas Christopher *health science educator*
Roeller, Herbert Alfred *biology professor*
Russell, Liane Brauch *retired geneticist*
Saalfeld, Fred Erich *science educator, researcher*
Schultz, Stanley George *physiologist, educator, retired dean*
Shaw, Helen Lester Anderson *nutrition educator, researcher, retired dean*
Spitznagel, John Keith *retired microbiologist, immunologist, physician*
Sullivan, Harry Truman *retired research scientist*
Todhunter, John Anthony *toxicologist, consultant*
Tyler, Brett Merrick *geneticist, researcher*
Unger, Paul Walter *retired soil scientist*
Wang, Taylor Gunjin *science administrator, educator, astronaut*
Watabe, Norimitsu *marine biologist, educator*
Wilkinson, Stanley Ralph *retired agronomist*
Wood, Joseph George *neuroscientist, educator*
Wright, Theodore Robert Fairbank *biologist, educator*

SCIENCE: MATHEMATICS AND COMPUTER SCIENCE *See also* INFORMATION TECHNOLOGY

UNITED STATES

ALABAMA

Auburn
Govil, Narendra Kumar *mathematics professor*

Birmingham
Peeples, William Dewey, Jr. *mathematics professor*

Florence
Johnson, Johnny Ray *retired mathematics professor*

Huntsville
Whigham, Mark Anthony *computer scientist*

Tuscaloosa
Olin, Robert Floyd *mathematician educator, administrator, researcher*

ARKANSAS

Batesville
Carius, Robert Wilhelm *mathematics professor, retired military officer*

CALIFORNIA

Mountain View
Cerf, Vinton Gray *computer scientist, information technology executive*

DISTRICT OF COLUMBIA

Washington
Shaw, William Frederick *statistician*

FLORIDA

Daytona Beach
Seenith, Sivasundaram *mathematician, educator*

Deland
Chung, Wingyan *computer scientist, information scientist, educator*

Delray Beach
Hegstrom, William Jean *retired mathematics professor*

Fort Lauderdale
Littman, Marlyn Kemper *information scientist, educator*

Gainesville
Agresti, Alan *statistics educator*
Dinculeanu, Nicolae *mathematician, educator*
Keesling, James Edgar *mathematics professor*
Khuri, Andre Ilias *statistician, educator*
Mitchell, William John *mathematics educator*

Jacksonville
Reid, William Hill *mathematics professor*

Orlando
Deo, Narsingh *computer scientist, educator*
Marinescu, Dan Cristian *computer sciences educator, consultant*

Pensacola
Ford, Kenneth M. *computer scientist, educator*

Punta Gorda
Smith, Charles Edwin *computer science educator*

Saint Augustine
Jurgens, Julie Graham *retired mathematics professor*

Sarasota
Jacobson, Melvin Joseph *mathematician, educator*

Tallahassee
Kercheval, Alec Norton *mathematician*
Nichols, Eugene Douglas *mathematics professor*

Tampa
Murphy, Robin Roberson *computer scientist, robotics engineer*

Zephyrhills
Wheeling, Robert Franklin *computer consultant*

GEORGIA

Atlanta
Bleicher, Michael Nathaniel *mathematics professor*
DeMillo, Richard Allan *computer scientist, educator, former dean*
Galil, Zvi *computer scientist, mathematician, dean*
Goodman, Seymour Evan *computer science and international studies educator, researcher, consultant*
Kvam, Paul *mathematics professor*
Lim, Sung Kyu *computer scientist, educator*
Mickens, Ronald Elbert *mathematician, physics professor*
Morrison, Gregory Bernard *information scientist*
Nemirovski, Arkadi *mathematics professor*
Oliker, Vladimir *mathematician, educator*
Pan, Yi *computer science educator*
Spruill, Marcus C. *retired mathematics professor*
Thomas, Robin *mathematics professor*
Trotter, William T. *mathematics professor*
Ulmer, Douglas L. *mathematics professor*
Zadeh, Javad Hamadani *mathematics professor*

Statesboro
Peace, Karl E. *biostatistician, scientist, educator, philanthropist*

KENTUCKY

Lexington
Mostert, Paul Stallings *retired mathematician*

LOUISIANA

Baton Rouge
Oxley, James Grieve *mathematics professor*

NORTH CAROLINA

Boone
Johnson, Phillip Eugene *mathematics professor*

Cape Carteret
Mullikin, Thomas Wilson *mathematics professor*

Chapel Hill
Brooks, Frederick Phillips, Jr. *computer scientist, educator*
Lastra, Anselmo A. *computer science educator*

Colerain
Stephens, William A. (Dean Stephens) *computer consultant*

Davidson
Klein, Benjamin Garrett *mathematics professor, consultant*

Durham
Daubechies, Ingrid *mathematics educator*
Tomasi, Carlo *computer science professor*
Warner, Seth L. *mathematician, educator*

Raleigh
Chou, Wushow *retired computer scientist*

Research Triangle Park
Schrager, Mindy Rae *operations management specialist, life coach*

Rocky Mount
Floyd, Nancy Arthur *systems analyst, educator*

Wilmington
Herman, Russell Leland *mathematics, physics professor*

OKLAHOMA

Edmond
Loman, Mary LaVerne *retired mathematics professor*

Norman
Breen, Marilyn *mathematics educator*

Oklahoma City
Decker, Myra Anne *accounting professor*
Tang, Irving Che-hong *mathematician, educator*

SOUTH CAROLINA

Clemson
Brawley, Joel Vincent *mathematician, educator*
Kenelly, John Willis, Jr. *mathematician, educator*

Spartanburg
Shiflet, Angela B. *mathematics professor*
Wilde, Edwin Frederick *retired mathematics professor*

TENNESSEE

Brownsville
Kalin, Robert *retired mathematics professor*

Johnson City
Pleasant, James Carroll *mathematician, computer sciences educator*

Memphis
Franklin, Stanley Phillip *computer scientist, cognitive scientist, retired mathematician*

Nashville
McCowan, Otis Blakely *mathematics professor*
Plummer, Michael David *mathematics professor*
Saff, Edward Barry *mathematics professor*
Williams, Marsha Rhea *computer scientist, educator, researcher, consultant*

Oak Ridge
Raridon, Richard Jay *retired computer scientist*

Sewanee
Cunningham, Joel Luther *mathematics professor, former academic administrator*

TEXAS

Alpine
Morgan, Raymond Victor, Jr. *mathematics professor*

Amarillo
Wetzel, Kathryn C. *mathematics and engineering professor*

Austin
Babuska, Ivo Milan *mathematics professor*
Beckner, William *mathematician*
Caffarelli, Luis Angel *mathematician, educator*
Clark, Charles T(aliferro) *retired statistician*
Emerson, E. Allen *computer science educator*
Martin, Norman Marshall *computer science educator*
Moore, J. Strother *computer scientist, educator*
Novak, Gordon S., Jr. *computer scientist, educator*
Tate, John Torrence *retired mathematics professor, researcher*

Bedford
Dawes, Robert Leo *mathematician, consultant*

College Station
Stroustrup, Bjarne *computer science and engineering professor*
Zheng, Qi *statistician, biomathematician*

Colleyville
Hennessey, Audrey Kathleen *computer researcher, educator*

Dallas
Browne, Richard Harold *statistician, consultant*
Gavish, Bezalel *computer science operations research, information systems educator*

Denton
Renka, Robert Joseph *computer science educator, consultant*
Thompson, Frances McBroom *mathematics professor, writer*

Hewitt
Walbesser, Henry Herman *computer science educator*

Houston
Brown, Dennison Robert *mathematician, educator*
Glowinski, Roland *mathematics professor*
Hassett, Brendan *mathematics professor*
Warren, Joe D. *computer science educator*
Wolf, Michael *mathematics professor*

Prairie View
Haghighi, Aliakbar Montazer *mathematics probability and statistics, queueing theory educator*

Richardson
Wiorkowski, John James *mathematics professor*

San Angelo
Moreland, Ellen D. *mathematics professor*

Valley Mills
Odell, Patrick Lowry *retired mathematics professor*

Waco
Henderson, Johnny *mathematician, educator*
Rolf, Howard Leroy *mathematician, educator*
Sheng, Qin *mathematics professor*

VIRGINIA

Alexandria
Wasserstein, Ronald L. *statistics organization director*

Blacksburg
Arnold, Jesse Charles *retired statistician*
Ryder, Barbara Gershon *computer science professor*

Broyles, Robert Herman *biochemistry and molecular biology educator*

Tulsa
Blais, Roger Nathaniel *physics professor, academic administrator*

SOUTH CAROLINA

Anderson
Stolen, Rogers Hall *optics scientist*

Bluffton
Croft, George T. *physicist*

Clemson
DesMarteau, Darryl Dwayne *chemistry professor*

Columbia
Edge, Ronald Dovaston *physics professor*
Freedom, Barry Mason *physicist, researcher*

Hopkins
Moore, Willard S. *oceanographer, educator*

TENNESSEE

Brentwood
Heiser, Arnold Melvin *astronomer*

Dyersburg
Hoque, Akm Mansurul *chemistry professor*

Knoxville
Gentry, Robert Vance *physicist, researcher, writer*
Hatcher, Robert Dean, Jr. *geologist, educator, research scientist*
McSween, Harry Younger, Jr. *geology educator*
Nazarewicz, Witold *nuclear scientist, educator*
Schweitzer, George Keene *chemistry professor*
Townsend, David W. *physicist, radiology professor*
Williams, Thomas Ffrancon *chemist, educator*

Maryville
Weeks, Robert Andrew *materials science researcher, educator*

Memphis
Desiderio, Dominic Morse, Jr. *chemistry and neurochemistry professor*
Fain, John Nicholas *biochemistry educator*
Franceschetti, Donald Ralph *physicist, educator*
Li, Ying Sing *chemistry professor*

Murfreesboro
Weller, Martha Riherd *physics and astronomy professor, consultant*

Nashville
Cone, Roger D. *biophysics professor*
Fort, Tomlinson *chemist, chemical engineering educator*
Hamilton, Joseph Hants, Jr. *physicist, researcher*
Hercules, David Michael *chemistry professor, consultant*
Inagami, Tadashi *biochemistry professor*
Lukehart, Charles Martin *chemistry professor*

Oak Ridge
Harvey, John Arthur *nuclear physicist*
Krause, Manfred Otto *physicist*
Krstic, Predrag S. *physicist*
Larson, Bennett Charles *solid state physicist, researcher*
Mason, Thomas Edward *physicist, science administrator*
Plasil, Franz *physicist*
Read, Kenneth Francis, Jr. *physics professor, researcher*

Pleasant Hill
Heald, Mark Aiken *physicist, educator*

Signal Mountain
Howe, Lyman Harold III *chemist, researcher*

TEXAS

Arlington
Armstrong, Daniel Wayne *chemist, educator*

Austin
Barbara, Paul Frank *chemistry professor*
Bard, Allen Joseph *chemist, educator*
Bash, Frank Ness *astronomer, educator*
Bengtson, Roger Dean *physicist, department chairman*
Boggs, James Ernest *chemistry professor*
Cowley, Alan Herbert *chemist, educator*
DeWitt-Morette, Cécile *physicist*
Erskine, James Lorenzo *physics professor*
Fisher, William Lawrence *geologist, educator, dean*
Gavenda, John David *physicist*
Gentle, Kenneth William *physicist*
Griffy, Thomas Alan *physics professor*
Groat, Charles George *geologist, former federal agency administrator*
Hazeltine, Richard Deimel *physics professor*
Lambert, David L. *astronomer, educator*
MacDonald, Allan H. *physics professor*
Marcotte, Edward Michael *biochemist, researcher*
Mark, Hans Michael *physicist, former federal agency administrator*
Martin, Stephen F. *chemist, educator, researcher*
McIntyre, John Armin *physics professor*
Mooney, John Bradford, Jr. *oceanographer, engineer, consultant*
Press, William Henry *physicist, computer scientist, educator*
Rossky, Peter Jacob *chemistry professor, chemical engineer, researcher*
Stewart, Kent Kallam *analytical biochemistry educator*
Udagawa, Takeshi *physicist, researcher*
Weinberg, Steven *physicist, educator*
Wilson, Clark R. *geophysicist, educator*
Zheng, Shuang-Cai *physics educator, researcher*

Brownsville
Price, Richard H. *physics professor*

Brownwood
Bryant, Pamela L. *chemistry professor*

Bryan
Eaton, Gordon Pryor *geologist, consultant*

College Station
Arnowitt, Richard Lewis *retired physics professor*
Dessler, Alexander Jack *astrophysicist, educator*
Duce, Robert Arthur *atmospheric chemist, oceanographer, educator*
Hardy, John Christopher *physicist, researcher, educator*
Laane, Jaan *chemistry professor, physics and astronomy professor*
Lee, David Morris *physics professor*
McIntyre, Peter Mastin *physicist, researcher*
Nachman, Ronald James *chemist, researcher*
O'Connor, Rod *chemist, consultant, inventor*
Sun, Yuefeng *research scientist, educator*
Wild, James Robert *biochemistry and genetics professor*

Copper Canyon
Nickon, Alex *chemist, educator*

Dallas
Baxter, Richard Henry Geoffrey *research scientist*
Deisenhofer, Johann *biochemistry professor, researcher*
Garner, Harold Ray *experimental research physicist, biochemist*
Gibbs, James Alanson *geologist*
Goldstein, Joseph Leonard *biochemist, educator, geneticist, educator*

Denton
Saleh, Farida Yousry *chemistry professor*

Fort Worth
Caldwell, Billy Ray *geologist*
Quarles, Carroll Adair, Jr. *physicist, researcher*
Reinecke, Manfred G. *chemistry professor*

Freeport
Stevens, James C. *chemist*

Galveston
Estes, Ernest L. *geologist, educator*
Lee, James Ching *biochemistry researcher, educator*

Houston
Baker, Stephen Denio *physics professor*
Bally, Albert W. *retired geologist, educator*
Bonner, Billy Edward *physics professor*
Burke, Kevin Charles Antony *geologist*
Chu, Paul Ching-Wu *physicist, academic administrator, educator*
Chu, Wei-Kan *physicist, researcher, professor*
Curl, Robert Floyd, Jr. *chemistry professor*
Gibson, Everett Kay, Jr. *space scientist, geochemist*
Hulet, Randall Gardner *physics professor*
Karner, Stephen Leslie *geophysicist*
Kinsey, James Lloyd *chemist, educator*
Kouri, Donald Jack *chemist, educator*
Lane, Neal Francis *physics professor, retired federal agency administrator*
Mackwell, Stephen Joseph *geophysicist, educator*
Meng, Ru-Ling *research scientist*
Reiff, Patricia Hofer *space physicist, educator, entrepreneur*
Reso, Anthony *geologist, educator, earth resources economist*
Si, Qimiao *physics professor*
Stevenson, Paul Michael *physics professor, researcher*
Stoops, James King *biochemistry researcher*
Tour, James M. *chemistry educator, researcher*
Weinstein, Roy *physics professor*
Weisman, R(obert) Bruce *physical chemist, educator, entrepreneur*
Wilson, Thomas Leon *physicist, researcher*
Yang, Chao Yuh *biochemistry professor, medical educator*

Irving
Eaker, Charles William *chemistry professor*

Lubbock
Bartsch, Richard Allen *chemist, educator*
Lodhi, M. A.K. *physicist, educator*

Midland
Berner, Leo De Witte, Jr. *retired oceanographer*

Prairie View
Cudnik, Brian *astronomer, educator*

Richardson
Baughman, Ray Henry *materials scientist*
Hulse, Russell Alan *physicist*
Rutford, Robert Hoxie *geologist, educator*
Salamon, Myron Ben *physicist, educator, dean*

San Antonio
Budalur, Thyagarajan Subbanarayan *chemistry professor*
Goldstein, Jerry *physicist, educator*
Gruber, John Balsbaugh *physics professor*
Schlegel, Eric M. *astrophysicist*
Synek, Miroslav *physicist, chemist, world affairs consultant*
Urbach, Adam Robert *chemistry professor*

San Marcos
Blanda, Michael Thomas *chemist, researcher*

Sugar Land
Clark, Brian *geophysicist, oil industry executive*
Huston, Daniel Cliff *geophysicist*

Uvalde
Graham, Robert Albert *physicist, researcher*

VIRGINIA

Alexandria
Leahy, Pat (P. Patrick Leahy) *geologist, former federal official*
Lipnick, Robert Louis *chemist, toxicologist, consultant*
Masterson, Kleber Sanlin, Jr. *physicist*
Toulmin, Priestley *retired geologist*

Arlington
Erb, Karl Albert *physicist, government official, retired consultant*
Whitcomb, James Hall *geophysicist, foundation administrator*

Ashburn
Rubin, Gerald Mayer *biochemistry researcher, educator*

Blacksburg
Asryan, Levon V. *physicist, electronics engineer, materials scientist*
Graybeal, Jack Daniel *chemist, educator*
McGrath, James Edward *chemistry professor*
Mo, Luke Wei *physicist, researcher*

Chantilly
deMonsabert, Winston Russel *chemist, consultant*

Charlottesville
Andrews, William Lester Self *chemistry educator*
Beasley, Anthony *astrophysicist, observatory administrator*
Bloomfield, Louis Aub *physicist, researcher*
Fredrick, Laurence William *astronomer, educator*
Gallagher, Thomas Francis *physicist*
Gaskin, Felicia *biochemist, educator*
Grimes, Russell Newell *inorganic chemist, educator*
Howard, Alan D. *environmental science professor*
Marshall, James Arthur *chemistry professor*
Sarazin, Craig Leigh *astronomer*
Sundberg, Richard Jay *chemistry professor*
Vanden Bout, Paul Adrian *astronomer, physicist, educator*
Weber, Hans Jürgen *physics professor*
Yates, John Thomas, Jr. *chemistry professor, research scientist*

Fairfax
Duxbury, Thomas Carl *planetary science professor*
Hussam, Abul *chemistry professor*
Morowitz, Harold Joseph *biophysicist, educator*
Trefil, James Stanley *physicist researcher author*

Falls Church
Akkara, Joseph Augustine *chemist, educator, researcher*

Hampton
Tripathi, Ram Kishore *physicist, researcher*

Harrisonburg
Baker, George Harold III *physicist, educator*

Heathsville
Winkel, Raymond Norman *aerospace scientist, consultant, retired military officer*

Newport News
Cardman, Lawrence Santo *physics professor, researcher*

Reston
Naeser, Nancy Dearien *geologist, researcher*

Richmond
Farrell, Nicholas Patrick *chemistry professor, researcher*

Warrenton
Romney, Carl F. *seismologist*

Williamsburg
Starnes, William Herbert, Jr. *chemist, educator*

Winchester
Shropshire, Walter, Jr. *biophysicist, pastor*

WEST VIRGINIA

Charleston
Galya, Thomas Andrew *hydrogeologist*

Montgomery
Carlson, George Theodore *physics professor*

Wheeling
Duffy, Norman Vincent *chemistry professor*

TERRITORIES OF THE UNITED STATES

PUERTO RICO

Arecibo
Kerr, Robert B. *astronomer, atmospheric scientist*

Humacao
Pinto, Nicholas Joaquim *physics professor*

ADDRESS UNPUBLISHED

Ancker-Johnson, Betsy *physicist, engineer, retired automotive executive*
Bajura, Rita A. *retired research scientist*
Bauer, Henry Hermann *chemistry and science educator*
Berlin, Kenneth Darrell *chemistry professor, consultant, researcher*
Bhide, Manohar Gopal *retired nuclear scientist*
Boyes, Stephen Richard *hydrogeologic consultant*
Bradbeer, Clive *biochemistry educator*
Calavia, Jose Emilio *physics professor*
Calvert, Jack George *atmospheric chemist, educator*
Chin, Siu Ah *physicist*
Cooper, Austin Morris *chemist, engineer, researcher, consultant*
Cottam, Gene Larry *retired biochemistry educator*
Debney, George C. *mathematical physicist*
Downs, Hartley H. III *chemist*
Eck, Robert Edwin *retired physicist*
Feldmann, Edward George *pharmaceutical chemist, pharmacologist, medical scientist*
Golden, David Edward *physicist*
Gorenstein, David G. *chemistry and biochemistry professor*
Grady, Lee Timothy *pharmaceutical chemist*
Griffin, Michael Douglas *aerospace scientist, former federal agency administrator*
Heller, Adam *chemist, researcher*
Hornbeck, Larry J. *physicist, researcher*
Huffman, John William *chemist, educator*
Kerr, Donald MacLean, Jr. *physicist, former federal official*
Knowles, Richard Norris *chemist*
Kravitz, Rubin *chemist*
Kribel, Robert Edward *consultant, retired physicist, academic administrator*
Kuhlmann-Wilsdorf, Doris *materials scientist, inventor, retired educator*
Lagow, Richard James *chemistry professor*
Laing, Malcolm Brian *geologist, consultant*
Lin, Ming-Chang *physical chemistry professor, researcher*
Lovinger, Andrew Joseph *polymer scientist*
Lucas, William Ray *aerospace scientist, consultant*
Maddin, Robert *metallurgist, educator*
Mariam, Yitbarek H. *chemistry professor*
Moulton, Grace Charbonnet *retired physicist*
Mueller, Berndt *physics professor*
Ness, Norman Frederick *retired astrophysicist, educator, administrator*
Nevill, William Albert *retired chemistry professor*
Ogliaruso, Michael Anthony *retired chemist, educator, actor*
Orbach, Raymond Lee *physicist, researcher, former federal agency administrator*
O'Shea, Donald C. *physicist, educator, optical engineer*
Plummer, Leonard Niel *retired geochemist*
Roberts, Thomas George *retired physicist*
Rohr, Davis Charles *aerospace consultant, retired military officer*
Salamone, Joseph Charles *polymer chemistry professor*
Schrieffer, John Robert *retired physics professor*
Scully, Marlan Orvil *physics professor*
Singleton, David Michael *chemist, researcher, retired*
Slaugh, Lynn H. *retired chemist*
Squibb, Samuel Dexter *chemistry professor*
Stockbauer, Roger Lewis *retired physicist, researcher*
Stubbs, Gerald *biochemist, educator*
Surowiec, Andrew Julius *biophysicist, researcher*
Theon, John Speridon *meteorologist, researcher*
Uberall, Herbert Michael Stefan *physicist, professor emeritus*
Van Horn, Hugh M. *physicist, astronomer, educator*
Wahl, Floyd Michael *geologist*
Watkins, George Daniels *physics professor*
Watt, William Stewart *retired physical chemist*
Wells, John Calhoun *retired physics professor*
Wood, Joan *retired chemist*
York, James Wesley, Jr. *retired theoretical physicist, educator*
Yu, Robert Kuan-jen *biochemistry professor*
Zucker, Alexander *physicist, researcher*

SOCIAL SCIENCE

UNITED STATES

ALABAMA

Auburn
Clark, Janet Eileen *retired political science professor*
Seroka, James Henry *social studies educator, academic administrator*

Birmingham
Bradley, Laurence Alan *psychologist*
Chew, Stephen Linn *psychology professor*
Nunn, Grady Harrison *retired political science professor*
Taub, Edward *psychology researcher*

Hartselle
Slate, Joe Hutson *psychologist, educator*

Mountain Brook
Passey, George Edward *psychologist, educator*

Tuscaloosa
Baklanoff, Eric Nicholas *economist, educator*
Cramer, Dale Lewis *retired economics professor*

PROFESSIONAL INDEX 999 SOCIAL SCIENCE

ARIZONA

Phoenix
Mossberger, Karen *political science professor, director*

ARKANSAS

Batesville
Lankford, George Emerson III *social sciences educator*

Fayetteville
Costrell, Robert Michael *economist*
Mc Gimsey, Charles Robert III *anthropologist*

Little Rock
Kaza, Greg John *economist, educator*
Ledbetter, Calvin Reville, Jr., (Cal Ledbetter) *political science professor, legislator*

Pine Bluff
Engle, Carole Ruth *aquaculture economics professor*

Siloam Springs
Oliver, Gary J. *psychologist, educator*

CALIFORNIA

Berkeley
DeLong, Brad (James Bradford DeLong) *economics professor*

DISTRICT OF COLUMBIA

Washington
Burtless, Gary Thomas *economist, consultant*
Choi, Woon Gyu *economist*
Cordes, Joseph John *economics professor*
Danziger, Raphael *political scientist, researcher*
Foust, Robert Schmertz *political science professor*
Struelens, Michel Maurice Joseph Georges *political science professor, consultant*

FLORIDA

Amelia Island
Johnson, Edgar McCarthy *psychologist*

Boynton Beach
Stolzberg, Mark Elliott *psychologist*

Cape Coral
Routh, Donald K(ent) *psychologist, historian, educator*

Coral Gables
Frohock, Fred Manuel *political science professor*

Fort Myers
Kaye, Richard William *retired labor economist*

Gainesville
Babb, Florence Evelyn *anthropologist, educator*
Bartoshuk, Linda M. *psychologist, educator*
Brown, William Samuel, Jr. *communication sciences and disorders educator*
Dewsbury, Donald Allen *psychologist*
Harrison, Faye Venetia *anthropologist, educator, writer*
Heesacker, Martin *psychologist, educator*
Teitelbaum, Philip *psychologist*

Jacksonville
Cebula, Richard John *economics professor, writer*
Ejimofor, Cornelius Ogu *political scientist, educator*

Miami
Bruel, Iris Barbara *psychologist*
Estevez, Anne-Marie *psychologist, lawyer*
Jacobson, Leonard I. *psychologist, educator*
Kanet, Roger Edward *political science professor*
Nemeroff, Charles Barnet *neurobiology and psychiatry educator*

Orlando
Gresham, Regina Gina Harwood *psychology professor, researcher*

Panama City
Roberts, Paul Craig III *economics professor, writer, columnist*

Pensacola
Arnold, Barry Raynor *philosophy educator, medical ethicist, counselor*

Pompano Beach
Pigott, Melissa Ann *social psychologist*
Warnath, Maxine Ammer *psychologist, arbitrator*

Ponte Vedra Beach
Wu, Hsiu Kwang *economist, educator*

Port Charlotte
Von Holden, Martin Harvey *psychologist*

Saint Augustine
Sorkin, Robert Daniel *psychologist, industrial engineer, educator*

Saint Petersburg
Howard, Jeffrey A. *psychologist, educator*
Rosenblum, Zina Michelle Zarin *psychology professor, marketing professional, researcher*

Sarasota
Gordon, Sanford Daniel *economics professor*
Masters, John Christopher *psychologist, educator*

Stuart
Grieve, William Roy *psychologist, educator, educational administrator, researcher*

Tallahassee
Brueckheimer, William Rogers *social sciences educator*
Holcombe, Randall Gregory *economics professor*
Hull, Elaine Mangelsdorf *psychology neuroscience professor*
Laird, William Everette, Jr. *economics professor*
Macesich, George *economics professor*
Nam, Charles Benjamin *demographer, sociologist, genealogist, writer*
Quadagno, Jill *sociology professor*

Tampa
Forsythe, Robert Elliott *economics professor*
Kimmel, Ellen Bishop *psychologist, educator*
MacManus, Susan Ann *political science professor, researcher*
Skvoretz, John Vincent *sociologist, educator*
Weiner, Irving Bernard *psychologist*

Venice
Gooding, Charles Thomas *psychologist, educator, retired academic administrator*

West Palm Beach
Dye, Thomas Roy *political science professor*

Weston
Alexander, Cynthia Louise *psychologist, educator*

GEORGIA

Athens
Clute, Robert Eugene *political science professor*
Dunn, Delmer Delano *political science professor*
Garbin, Albeno Patrick *sociology educator*
Johnson, Loch Kingsford *political science educator, researcher*
Kellough, J. Edward *political science professor, department chairman*
Nichols, William Curtis *clinical psychologist, educator, marriage and family therapist, consultant*
O'Toole, Laurence Joseph *public administration and policy educator, researcher*
Walters, Lynda Henley *family and human development professor*

Atlanta
Bahl, Roy Winford *economist, educator, consultant*
Curran, Christopher *economics professor*
Gay, Robert Derril *behavioral health consultant*
Hanson, Victor Arthur *gerontologist, retired surgeon*
King, Preston Theodore *social sciences educator, writer, political philosopher*
Knapp, Charles Boynton *economist, former university president, educator*
Snarey, John Robert *psychologist, educator*
Westen, Drew *psychology professor*

Carrollton
Drummond, Doris Wiggins *psychologist*

Lawrenceville
Rawson, Harve E. *psychologist, writer*

Marietta
Dudley, Gary Edward *psychologist*

Oxford
Cody, William Bermond *political science professor*

Savannah
Martin, Grace Burkett *psychologist*

Statesboro
Henry, Nicholas Llewellyn *retired public administration educator*

Suwanee
Cox, Albert Harrington, Jr. *retired economist*

Young Harris
March, Boyd Lee *dean, political science professor, researcher*

ILLINOIS

Urbana
Gabriel, Michael *psychology professor*

INDIANA

Bloomington
Stryker, Sheldon *sociologist, educator*

KENTUCKY

Bowling Green
Cangemi, Joseph Peter *psychologist, consultant, educator*

Covington
Littleton, Nan Elizabeth Feldkamp *psychologist, mental health educator*

Lexington
Garen, John Edward *economics professor*
Hall, Harry H. *agricultural economics educator*
Hultman, Charles William *economics professor*
Reed, Michael Robert *agricultural economist*
Stilwell, William Earle III *psychology educator, retired military officer*
Stober, William John, II, *economics professor*
Worell, Judith P. *psychologist, educator*
Zentall, Thomas R. *psychologist, educator*

Louisville
Nahata, Babu L. *economics professor, researcher*
Ziegler, Charles Edward *political science professor, university scholar*

Morehead
Hail, Michael Wayne *political science professor*

Paintsville
Hovee, Mark John *psychologist*

Pikeville
Lovel, Gene Artie *economics professor*

LOUISIANA

Baton Rouge
Beard, Thomas Rex *economics professor*
Clark, William A. *political scientist, educator*
Cramer, Gail *economist*

Metairie
Falco, Maria Josephine *political scientist*

New Orleans
Balée, William L. *anthropology educator*
Boudreaux, Kenneth Justin *economist, educator*
Olson, Richard David *psychology professor*

Pineville
Thrasher, Fay C. *clinical psychologist*

Ruston
Gilley, Otis W. *economics professor*

Shreveport
Staats, Thomas Elwyn *neuropsychologist*

NORTH CAROLINA

Asheville
Cutright, Phillips *sociologist, educator*

Belmont
Stamps, Leighton Elderkin *psychology educator*

Biltmore Forest
Sgro, Joseph Anthony *retired psychologist, educator*

Boone
Udogu, E. Ike *social sciences educator, researcher*

Calabash
Strunk, Orlo Christopher, Jr. *psychology professor*

Cary
Wagner, Aureen Pinto *psychologist, educator*

Cashiers
O'Connell, Edward James, Jr. *psychologist, educator, systems administrator, consultant*

Chapel Hill
Baroff, George Stanley *psychologist, educator*
Biglaiser, Gary *economics professor*
Black, Stanley Warren III *retired economics professor*
Brown, Frank *social sciences educator*
Fieleke, Norman Siegfried *economist, educator*
Gray, Virginia Hickman *political science professor*
Kalleberg, Arne Lindeman *sociologist, educator*
Prange, Arthur Jergen, Jr. *psychology and psychiatry professor, neuroscientist*
Richardson, Richard Judson *retired political science professor*
Salemi, Michael Kerry *economist, educator*
Schoultz, Lars *political scientist, educator*
Steponaitis, Vincas Petras *archaeologist, anthropologist, educator*
Wasik, Barbara Hanna *psychologist, educator*

Charlotte
Goolkasian, Paula A. *psychologist, educator*
Neel, Richard Eugene *economist, educator*
Pyle, Gerald Fredric *geographer, educator*
Serra Puche, Jaime Jose *economist*
Webster, Murray Alexander, Jr. *sociologist, educator*

Davidson
Palmer, Edward L. *psychologist, educator, writer*

Durham
Aldrich, John Herbert *political science professor*
Ariely, Dan *behavioral economics educator*
Becker, Charles Maxwell *economics professor*
Burness, John F. *political science professor, former academic administrator*
Caspi, Avshalom *psychology professor, researcher*
Chatterji, Aaron (Ronnie Chatterji) *economics professor*
Cook, Philip Jackson *economist, educator*
Erickson, Robert Porter *psychology professor*
Holsti, Ole Rudolf *political scientist, educator*
Hotz, V. Joseph *economics professor*
Kelley, Allen Charles *economist, educator*
Land, Kenneth Carl *sociologist, educator, demographer*
Lockhead, Gregory Roger *retired psychology professor*
McClain, Paula Denice *political scientist, educator*
Mickiewicz, Ellen Propper *political and social science educator*
Newell, Richard G. *economics professor, educator, former federal agency administrator*
Simons, Elwyn LaVerne *physical anthropologist, primatologist, paleontologist, educator*
Surwit, Richard Samuel *psychology professor*
Swanson, Jeffrey *sociologist, researcher, educator*
Tiryakian, Edward Ashod *sociologist, educator*
Treml, Vladimir Guy *economist, educator*

Greensboro
Eason, Robert Gaston *psychology professor*
Helms-VanStone, Mary Wallace *anthropology educator*

Greenville
Lawler-Row, Kathleen Anne *psychology professor, department chairman*

Hillsborough
Piper, Don Courtney *political scientist, educator*
Talley, Joseph Eugene *psychologist*

Kannapolis
May, Philip Alan *sociologist, educator*

Murphy
Marta, Dawn Reneé *clinical psychologist*

Pittsboro
Murdock, John Carey *economics professor, investor*

Raleigh
Allen, Steven Glen *economics and business professor*
Newman, Slater Edmund *psychologist, educator*

Wilmington
Puente, Antonio E. *psychologist, educator, scientist*

OKLAHOMA

Norman
Henderson, George *educational sociologist, educator*
Kondonassis, Alexander John *economist, educator*
Perkins, Edward Joseph *political science professor, retired ambassador*

Oklahoma City
Adams, Russell Lee *neuropsychologist*
Allbright, Karan Elizabeth *psychologist, consultant*
Craig, George Dennis *economics professor, consultant*
Henderson, J. Neil *medical anthropologist*
Morgan, Catherine Marie *psychologist, writer*
Poole, Richard William *economist*
Schroeder, David J. Dean *retired psychologist*

Stillwater
Darcy, Robert Emmett *political science and statistics professor*

PENNSYLVANIA

Philadelphia
Bailey, Elizabeth Ellery *economics professor, emerita*

SOUTH CAROLINA

Charleston
Carek, Donald J(ohn) *child psychiatry educator*

Clemson
Dougan, William Richmond *alumni distinguished professor*
Dwyer, Gerald Paul, Jr. *economist, bank executive*

Columbia
Kiker, Billy Frazier *economics professor*

Daniel Island
Gillespie, John David *political science educator*

Greer
McAbee, Thomas Allen *psychologist*

Mount Pleasant
Bilas, Richard A. *economist*

TENNESSEE

Chattanooga
Rabin, Alan A. *economics professor*
Wilson, Richard Lee *political science professor*

Germantown
Depperschmidt, Thomas Orlando *retired economist, consultant*

Knoxville
Bass, William Marvin III *anthropology educator*
Harris, Diana Koffman *sociologist, educator*
Simek, Jan F. *anthropology professor, former academic administrator*

Memphis
Pohlmann, Marcus D. *political science professor*

Murfreesboro
Breault, Kevin D. *social studies educator, researcher*
Littlepage, Glenn E. *social psychology educator*

Nashville
Blair, Margaret Mendenhall *economist, consultant, law educator*
Cornfield, Daniel Benjamin *sociology educator*
Driskill, Robert Allen *economics professor*
Gwin, Dorothy Jean Bird *retired psychology professor, dean*
Hargrove, Erwin Charles, Jr. *political science professor*
Havens, Murray Clark *political scientist, educator*
Hetherington, Marc J. *political science professor*
Hinshaw, Carroll Elton *economics professor*
McCarty, Richard Charles *psychology professor, provost*
Morton-Young, Tommie *psychology professor, writer*

Schoggen, Phil H(oward) *psychologist, educator*
Westfield, Fred Meinhard *economics professor*

Oak Ridge
Colston, Freddie Charles *political science professor*

TEXAS

Arlington
Ramsey, Charles Eugene *sociologist, educator*

Austin
Buchanan, Bruce, II, *political science professor*
Burnham, Walter Dean *political science professor*
Cooper, William Wager *economics, accounting and finance professor, dean*
Drake, Stephen Douglas *psychologist, health facility administrator*
Galbraith, James Kenneth *economics professor*
Glade, William Patton, Jr. *economics professor*
Hamermesh, Daniel Selim *economics professor*
Hardin, Dale Wayne *political science professor*
Heinrich, Carolyn J. *political science professor*
Hinich, Melvin J. *economics professor*
Holtzman, Wayne Harold *psychologist, educator*
Kendrick, David Andrew *economist, educator*
Loehlin, John Clinton *psychologist, educator*
Lowry, Alaire Howard *psychologist*
McFadden, Dennis *psychologist, educator*
Norwood, Bernard *economist*
Norwood, Janet Lippe *economist*
Pangle, Thomas Lee *political scientist*
Sasse, Benjamin Eric *public policy educator, former federal agency administrator*
Schmandt, Jurgen A. *public affairs educator*
Schmitt, Karl Michael *retired political scientist*
Springer, David William *social sciences educator*
Stahl, Dale O. *economics professor, department chairman*
Walter, Virginia Lee *psychologist, educator*

Bellaire
Mayo, Clyde Calvin *psychologist, educator*

Bryan
Luepnitz, Roy Robert *psychologist, consultant*

Canyon
Thoman, Roy Edward *political scientist, educator*
Welch, Reed Lynn *political scientist, educator*

College Station
Arnold, J(ames) Barto III *marine archaeologist*
Bass, George Fletcher *retired archaeology educator*
Edwards, George Charles III *political science professor, writer*
Furubotn, Eirik Grundtvig *economics professor*
Meier, Kenneth John *political scientist*
Moroney, John Rodgers *economist, educator*
Phillips, Charles David *gerontologist, health services researcher, public health professional*

Dallas
Bernstein, Ira Harvey *clinical science professor*
Kemper, Robert Van *anthropologist, minister, educator*
Williams, Martha Spring *psychologist*

Denton
Belfiglio, Valentine John *political science professor*
Yang, Philip Q. *sociologist*

El Paso
Himelstein, Philip Nathan *psychology professor*

Fort Worth
Jackson, Donald Wilson *political science professor, lawyer*
Mullendore, Walter Edward *retired economist*

Frisco
McKenzie, Tracey *sociology professor*

Georgetown
Camp, Thomas Harley *economist*
Lopreato, Joseph *evolutionary sociologist, writer*
Purdy, Jesse E. *psychology professor*

Harlingen
Lytle, Michael Allen *forensic criminologist, consultant*

Houston
Allen, Jon G. *psychologist*
Brito, Dagobert Llanos *economics professor*
Bryant, John Bradbury *economics professor, consultant*
Condit, Linda Faulkner *retired economist*
Davidson, F. Chandler *sociologist, educator*
Ebaugh, Helen Rose *sociology educator, researcher*
Gillis, S. Malcolm *economics professor*
Horvitz, Paul Michael *economist*
Jenkins, Sheila Alnita *psychologist*
Lehrer, Kenneth Eugene *economic consulting company executive*
Martin, William C. *social studies educator, writer*
Miller, Janel Howell *psychologist*
Moulin, Hervé *economics professor*
Paul, Gordon Lee *behavioral scientist, psychologist*
Schover, Leslie Ruth *psychologist*
von der Mehden, Fred R. *political science professor*
Yatsenko, Yuri Petrovich *business professor, mathematician*

Prairie View
Prestage, Jewel Limar *political scientist, educational consultant*

Richardson
Berry, Brian Joe Lobley *geographer, urban planner, political economist, educator*
Griffith, Daniel Alva *geography educator*
Sandler, Todd Michael *economist, political scientist, educator*

San Angelo
Butler, Michael Ward *economics professor*

San Antonio
Bellows, Thomas John *political scientist, educator*
Garcia, Sonia R. *political science professor*
Harris, Richard John *social sciences educator*

Victoria
Harrington, Rick *psychology professor*

Waco
Avant, Gayle *political scientist, educator*
Grinols, Earl Leroy III *economist, educator*
Perryman, Marlin Ray *economist, educator*

VIRGINIA

Alexandria
Cahill, Mary Beth *political strategist*
Carville, James, Jr., (Chester James Carville) *political scientist, commentator*
Corrothers, Helen Gladys *criminal justice official*
Jehn, Christopher *economist, think-tank executive, computer company executive, federal official*
Krueger, Gerald Peter *psychologist*
Matalin, Mary Joe *political consultant, editor*
Toal, Gerard *political science professor*
Zakheim, Dov Solomon *economist, former federal agency administrator*

Arlington
Berkowitz, Peter *public policy and government educator*
Boorstein, Laurence *economist, project manager*
Fichtner, Jason J. *political science professor, former federal agency administrator*
Gabarro, John Joseph *organizational behavior and business administration educator*
Hughes Hallett, Andrew *economist, educator*
Martin, Linda Gaye *demographer, economist*
Pfiffner, James Price *university professor*
Tolchin, Susan Jane *political science professor, writer*
Vitz, Paul Clayton *psychologist, educator*

Blacksburg
Crowder, Richard Thomas (Dick Crowder) *economics professor, former ambassador*
Jannuzi, F. Tomasson *economics professor*

Burke
Thomas, Ginni (Virginia Lamp Thomas) *public policy analyst*

Charlottesville
Abraham, Henry Julian *retired political science professor*
Cornell, Dewey Gene *psychologist*
Elzinga, Kenneth Gerald *economics professor*
Handler, Jerome Sidney *anthropology educator*
Harding, Harry *dean, political scientist, educator, consultant*
Henry, Laurin Luther *public affairs educator*
Lanham, Betty Bailey *anthropologist, educator*
Olsen, Edgar Oliver *economics professor*
Pate, Robert Hewitt, Jr. *retired counselor educator*
Reppucci, Nicholas Dickon *psychologist, educator*
Rhoads, Steven Eric *political science professor*
Sabato, Larry Joseph *political science professor, director*
Wagner, Roy *anthropology educator, researcher*
Zelikow, Philip David *public policy educator, professor former federal official*

Claremont
Seward, Troilen Gainey *retired psychologist*

Culpeper
Fish, Mary Martha *economics professor*

Fairfax
Bennett, James Thomas *economics professor*
Cowen, Tyler *economics professor, writer*
Dennis, Rutledge M. *sociologist, educator*
Haines, David W. *social sciences educator*
Joseph, Robert G. *public policy educator, former federal agency administrator*
Kash, Don Eldon *political science professor*
Lindsey, Lawrence Benjamin (Larry Lindsey) *economist, former federal official*
Pruitt, Dean Garner *psychologist, educator*
Steele, Howard Loucks *economic development consultant, author*
Travis, Toni-Michelle C. *political scientist, educator*
Wagner, Richard E. *economist, educator*

Falls Church
Calkins, Susannah Eby *retired economist*
Ershler, William Baldwin *biogerontologist, educator*
Hjort, Howard Warren *economist, consultant*
Weiss, Armand Berl *economist, association management executive*

Farmville
Dorrill, William Franklin *political scientist, educator*
Witschey, Walter Robert Thurmond *anthropologist, educator, former museum director*

Fredericksburg
Crippen, Timothy Alan *sociology educator*
Rampersad, Peggy A. Snellings *sociologist, consultant*

Hampton
Jackson, Alphonso Roy *public policy educator, former United States Secretary of Housing and Urban Development*

Harrisonburg
Grayson, Joann Hess *psychology professor*
Kreider, Leonard Emil *retired economics professor*

Leesburg
Brabender, John *political consultant*

Lexington
Elmes, David Gordon *psychologist, educator*
Jarrard, Leonard Everett *psychologist, educator*
Winfrey, John Crawford *economist, educator*

Manassas
Fulda, Michael *political scientist, educator, space policy researcher*

Mc Lean
Auerbach, Anita L. *clinical psychologist*
Nothaft, Frank Emile *economist*
Schneider, Peter Raymond *retired political scientist*
Stevens, Richard Gordon *political scientist, educator*

Richmond
Eissenberg, Thomas E. *psychology professor*

Sterling
Gillingham, Robert Fenton *economist, consultant*

Sweet Briar
Shea, Brent Mack *social sciences educator*

Virginia Beach
Reinhardt, Uwe Ernst *economist, educator*

Warrenton
Pribram, Karl Harry *neuroscience and psychology educator, brain researcher*

Williamsburg
Haulman, Clyde Austin *economics professor*
Kerns, Virginia B. *anthropologist, writer*
Lange, Carl James *retired psychology professor*
Payne, Roger Lee *geographer*
Peterson, Susan *political science professor, dean*
Smith, Roger Winston *retired political theory educator*

Woodbridge
Jordan, Robert Smith *political science professor, civilian military employee*

Wytheville
Kegley, Charles William, Jr. *political science professor*

WASHINGTON

Seattle
Nelsen, Hart Michael *sociologist, educator*

WEST VIRGINIA

Bethany
Cooey, William Randolph *retired economics professor*

Charleston
Lifton, Walter M. *psychology and education consultant*

Fairmont
Frasure, Carl Maynard *political science professor*

Morgantown
Colyer, Dale Keith *agricultural economics professor*
Kim, Hong Nack *political science professor*

Parkersburg
McClung, Phil Oran *psychology professor*

West Liberty
Wenzel, Loren Alvin *retired accounting professor, dean*

TERRITORIES OF THE UNITED STATES

PUERTO RICO

San Juan
Folch-Serrano, Karen D. *psychologist, consultant*

ADDRESS UNPUBLISHED

Albanese, Jay Samuel *criminologist, educator*
Alexander, Jim R. *social sciences educator*
Andrews, E. Wyllys *archaeologist, educator*
Bernard, H. Russell *anthropologist, educator, editor*
Bernsen, Harold John *political scientist, educator, businessmen, retired military officer*
Bluth, B. J. (Elizabeth Jean Catherine Bluth) *sociologist, aerospace technologist*
Boff, Kenneth Richard *engineering research psychologist*
Bradburn, Norman M. *behavioral science educator*
Bredfeldt, John Creighton *economics educator, writer, retired military officer*
Bricker, Harvey Miller *retired anthropology educator*
Bricker, Victoria Reifler *anthropologist, educator*
Bullock, Mary Brown *history, political science professor, former academic administrator*
Caplow, Theodore *sociologist*
Carvalho, Julie Ann *psychologist*
Christian, James Wayne *economist, writer*
Churchill, Ward LeRoy *social sciences educator, advocate*
Clark, Caleb Morgan *political scientist, educator*
Conway, M. Margaret *political science professor, consultant*
Cotten, Annie Laura *psychologist, educator*
Danielsen, Albert Leroy *economics professor, energy and utilities consultant*
Davidson, John Kenneth, Sr. *sociologist, educator, researcher, writer, consultant*
Engel, Bernard Theodore *psychologist, educator*
Ericson, David Frank *political scientist, educator*
Fisher, Seymour *psychologist, educator*
Foster, Dale Warren *retired political science professor, real estate agent, accountant, management consultant*
Friedman, James Winstein *economist, educator*
Goldman, Bert Arthur *retired professor*
Goldstein, Morris *international economist*
Haywood, H(erbert) Carl(ton) *psychologist, educator*
Hetherington, Eileen Mavis *psychologist, educator*
Hitz, Frederick Porter *public and international affairs educator*
Hughes, Ann Hightower *retired economist*
Jett, Stephen Clinton *geography and textiles educator, researcher, editor*
Johnson, Benjamin F., VI, *economist, consultant*
Johnson, Charles Lavon, Jr. *clinical neuropsychologist, consultant*
Karim, Muhammad Bazlul *political scientist, educator*
Kaslow, Florence Whiteman *psychologist, educator, family business consultant, executive, life transitions and relationship coach*
Keen, Rachel *psychology professor*
Khatena, Joe *psychology professor*
Komechak, Marilyn Gilbert *retired psychologist, writer*
Lanoue, David J. *political science professor, department chairman*
Latané, Bibb *social psychologist*
Laughlin, Louis Gene *economic analyst, consultant*
LeBlanc, Hugh Linus *political science professor, consultant*
Long, Ralph Stewart *clinical psychologist*
MacHovec, Frank J. *psychologist*
Matheny, Adam Pence, Jr. *child psychologist, educator, consultant, researcher*
Miller, Margery *psychologist, educator, consultant, speech pathology/audiology and mental health services professional, university administrator, professor, academic administrator, coach*
Moncarz, Raul *economist, researcher*
Muth, Richard Ferris *economics professor*
Naviaux, LaRee DeVee *retired psychologist, academic, director*
Neilson, William S. *economics professor*
Onunkwo, Emmanuel Nwafor *retired economics professor*
Patterson, Samuel C. *retired political science professor*
Randazzo, Marisa R. *psychologist*
Reese, Hayne Waring *psychologist, educator*
Resnick, Heidi *psychologist, educator*
Robinson, James Arthur *political scientist*
Roussel, Lee Dennison *economist, federal agency administrator*
Rubin, Rose Mohr *economics professor emeritus*
Rubner, Michael *international relations educator, university administrator*
Schmandt-Besserat, Denise *archaeologist, educator*
Silverman, Jerry Mark *political science professor, consultant*
Smith, Vme Edom (Verna Mae Edom Smith) *social sciences educator, freelance photographer, writer*
Sprinthall, Norman Arthur *psychology educator*
Swartz, Jon David *psychologist, educator*
Tasman, Allan *psychiatry educator*
Tideman, T. Nicolaus *economics educator*
Van Riper, Paul Pritchard *retired political science professor*
Warne, William Robert *economist*
Waud, Roger Neil *economist, educator*
Weinstein, Jay A. *social sciences educator, researcher*
Wilkinson, Doris *medical family sociology educator*